DICTIONNAIRE FRANÇAIS ▸ ANGLAIS ANGLAIS ▸ FRANÇAIS

FRENCH ▸ ENGLISH ENGLISH ▸ FRENCH DICTIONARY

COLLINS · ROBERT FRENCH ▸ ENGLISH ENGLISH ▸ FRENCH DICTIONARY

by

Beryl T. Atkins **Alain Duval**
Hélène M. A. Lewis **Rosemary C. Milne**

SECOND EDITION

contributors

Edwin Carpenter **Françoise Morcellet**

based on the

COLLINS–ROBERT
FRENCH–ENGLISH
ENGLISH–FRENCH
DICTIONARY

HarperCollins*Publishers*

Dictionnaires Le Robert
Paris

First published in this format 1993

Latest reprint 1995

Dictionnaires Le Robert
27, rue de la Glacière, 75013 PARIS

ISBN 2 85036 116 X

HarperCollins Publishers
P.O. Box, Glasgow G4 ONB, Great Britain

ISBN 0 00 470311-1 (standard)
ISBN 0 00 470312-X (thumb-indexed)

---

10 East 53rd Street, New York, NY 10022

ISBN 0-06-275513-7

First HarperCollins edition published 1993

Library of Congress Cataloguing-in-Publication Data

Collins-Robert French-English, English-French dictionary / Beryl T. Atkins ... [et al.]. – 2nd ed. / contributors, Edwin Carpenter, Françoise Morcellet.
p. cm.
Title on added t.p. : Dictionnaire français-anglais, anglais-français
ISBN 0-06-275513-7
1. French language–Dictionaries–English. 2. English language–Dictionaries–French. I. Atkins, Beryl T. II. Title: Dictionnaire français-anglais, anglais-français.
PC2640.C688 1993
443'.21–dc20 92-40825
CIP

---

95 96 97 98 99 HCM 10 9 8 7 6 5 4

Trademarks
Words which we have reason to believe constitute registered trademarks are designated as such. However, neither the presence nor the absence of such designation should be regarded as affecting the legal status of any trademark.

Les Marques Déposées
Les termes qui constituent à notre connaissance une marque déposée ont été désignés comme tels. La présence ou l'absence de cette désignation ne peut toutefois être considérée comme ayant valeur juridique.

A catalogue record for this book is available from the British Library

Printed in Great Britain by HarperCollins Manufacturing, Glasgow

TABLE DES MATIÈRES

CONTENTS

PRÉFACE DE LA NOUVELLE ÉDITION

Cette édition du ROBERT & COLLINS JUNIOR a été établie à partir du texte abrégé et remanié de la nouvelle édition du dictionnaire français/anglais et anglais/français ROBERT & COLLINS.

Plus de 10 000 unités de traductions ont été ajoutées à l'ouvrage. Elles rendent compte du profond renouvellement lexical intervenu au cours des dernières années, ainsi que du développement des sciences et des techniques modernes telles que l'informatique.

La part de l'anglais américain a été considérablement augmentée, d'abord en tant que langue source dans la partie anglais/français, mais également au niveau des différentes possibilités de traduction proposées dans la partie français/anglais.

Une attention toute particulière a été accordée au traitement des noms propres, essentiellement d'ordre géographique, qui se trouvent placés dans le corps du dictionnaire. Plusieurs centaines d'éléments (noms de pays et d'habitants, grandes villes, régions, montagnes, fleuves, phénomènes naturels), ont été ajoutés dans chaque partie, afin d'y présenter un vaste panorama. Les abréviations, sigles et acronymes, indispensables à la compréhension de la presse contemporaine, ont été eux aussi revus en détail, et la liste a été considérablement enrichie.

Outre l'ajout de mots nouveaux, cette nouvelle édition s'est attachée à remanier en profondeur de nombreux articles existants pour y apporter les éléments de phraséologie (locutions nouvelles, expressions de langue orale) nécessaires aux besoins de communication actuelle.

Le but du ROBERT & COLLINS JUNIOR est non seulement de donner à l'anglophone et au francophone la possibilité de comprendre la langue étrangère, mais aussi de lui donner les moyens de s'y exprimer avec assurance et précision.

PREFACE TO THE SECOND EDITION

This edition of the COLLINS ROBERT CONCISE dictionary has been compiled from the new edition of the authoritative Collins Robert French-English dictionary.

In excess of 10,000 new references have been added, to take account of the rapidly changing vocabulary of the two languages, and of the continuing advances in science and technology.

The importance of American English has been acknowledged in the increased coverage of this variety of English in both halves of the dictionary.

Particular attention has been paid to the treatment of proper names, especially those denoting geographical areas, which appear in the body of the dictionary text. Several hundred items (names of countries and their inhabitants, towns and cities, regions, mountains, rivers and natural phenomena) have been added to each side of the dictionary. The list of abbreviations and acronyms, indispensable for understanding newspaper articles and contemporary writings, has been carefully revised, and considerably enlarged.

Besides the addition of new entries, many existing entries have been revised and augmented with more examples of usage, both from the written and spoken language, to provide even greater help for the user wishing to express himself in the foreign language.

Thus the COLLINS ROBERT CONCISE dictionary remains, in this edition as in the first, an aid both to comprehension of the foreign language and to self-expression in it.

INTRODUCTION

« Il a été débordé par un diable qui a sauté le mou ! »

Que penseriez-vous du malheureux anglophone vous annonçant cette nouvelle ? Pourtant il voudrait seulement vous dire qu'un camion, en passant au feu rouge, a écrasé quelqu'un ('he was run over by a truck which jumped the lights').

Ne riez pas, vous pourriez affirmer des choses bien plus ridicules en essayant de parler anglais. Tout cela parce que vous utilisez des mots que vous ne connaissez pas. Des mots que vous avez trouvés dans un dictionnaire.

Justement, prenez le verbe **sauter**. Tout le monde vous dira que l'anglais est **to jump**. Mais est-ce toujours vrai ? Ouvrez un dictionnaire et vous aurez le plus souvent une série de mots anglais inconnus, comme **to pop out ; to blow up ; to fuse ; to be cancelled**. Comment choisir celui qui convient ? Il s'agit d'un bouchon de champagne qui saute, il faut utiliser **to pop out** (= partir), pour un pont, ce sera **to blow up** (= exploser), pour un circuit électrique **to fuse** (= fondre), enfin, si c'est un cours qui a sauté, vous devez prendre **to be cancelled** (= être supprimé).

Ce qu'il faut éviter, c'est de dire que le bouchon a fondu, que le cours a explosé ou que le pont est parti.

Vous comprenez donc que vous pouvez dire toutes sortes d'absurdités en anglais en choisissant la première traduction venue du mot français que vous cherchez. Pour trouver le mot juste, vous devez vous laisser guider par des 'panneaux de signalisation', et dans ce dictionnaire ils sont toujours en italique.

Sur la page ci-contre, vous verrez comment cette signalisation fonctionne.

INTRODUCTION

"Attention not to make yourself squash, you've got to walk inside the nails."

You'd probably back away from the poor French-man who said that, leaving him quite mystified, for he'd only been trying to warn you to cross at the pedestrian crossing if you didn't want to get run over. ('Attention de ne pas te faire écraser, tu dois marcher dans les clous.') Don't laugh - if you try to speak French you could find yourself saying even odder things. All because you're not using words that you know, but words that you've found in a dictionary.

Take the word **cut**: most people would say this is **couper** in French - but is it? If you look it up in the dictionary, you're often faced with a row of unknown French words, like **tondre, graver, réduire** or **sécher**. How are you going to decide which is the word you want? Of course it depends what you're going to cut. Cut the grass and you would use **tondre** (= to mow); cut a disc and it would be **graver** (= to engrave) ; if you're cutting expenses you'd need **réduire** (= to reduce), and if you're going to cut classes you'd be looking for **sécher** (= to miss).

What you don't want to say is that you're going to mow the disc, or engrave the lawn and so on.

You'll understand from this that if you look up an English word in the dictionary and take the first French word you come across, you could find yourself talking or writing nonsense. If you want to reach the right French word, you have to read the signposts, and in this dictionary these signposts are in italics.

On the page opposite, you'll see what kind of signposts we've given you...

COMMENT UTILISER LE DICTIONNAIRE

Comment dire en anglais : 'le coucou pousse dans les bois' ? L'article *coucou* vous donne plusieurs mots : cuckoo ; cuckoo clock ; (old) crate ; cowslip. Sans autre indication, vous choisirez au hasard, vous prendrez sans doute la première solution en produisant un effet comique involontaire.

Aussi l'article contient-il autre chose, des mots français en italique placés entre parenthèses devant chaque traduction : *(oiseau)* ; *(pendule)* ; *(péj : avion)* ; *(fleur)*. Voilà vos panneaux de signalisation. Ils correspondent chacun à un sens différent du mot **coucou**. Vous pouvez choisir avec certitude ce que vous voulez, dans notre exemple, bien sûr : *(fleur)* cowslip.

L'exemple est simple, mais prenez le mot **coucher**. Il peut être verbe transitif (coucher quelqu'un ou quelque chose) ou verbe intransitif (coucher dans un lit) ou verbe pronominal (se coucher tard) ; il peut aussi être un nom (l'heure du coucher). Des chiffres vous indiquent ces différentes fonctions pour vous aider dans vos recherches : **1** *vt* (transitif) - **2** *vi* (intransitif) - **3 se** ~ *vpr* (pronominal) - **4** *nm* (nom masculin).

couche [kuʃ] *nf* (**a**) *(gén)* layer; *[peinture]* coat. ~ **sociale** social stratum; *(fig)* **en tenir une** ~ * to be really thick * *ou* dumb *. (**b**) *(Horticulture)* hotbed. (**c**) *[bébé]* nappy, diaper *(US)*. (**d**) *(Méd: accouchement)* ~**s** confinement; **mourir en** ~**s** to die in childbirth. (**e**) *(littér: lit)* bed.

coucher [kuʃe] (1) **1** *vt* (**a**) *(mettre au lit)* to put to bed; *(donner un lit)* to put up. **être/rester couché** to be/stay in bed. (**b**) *blessé* to lay out; *échelle etc* to lay down; *blés* to flatten. **être couché** to be lying. (**c**) *(inscrire)* to inscribe. (**d**) ~ **en joue** *fusil* to aim; *personne* to aim at. **2** *vi (dormir)* to sleep (*avec* with). **cela nous a fait** ~ **très tard** that meant we went to bed very late. **3 se** ~ *vpr* to go to bed; *(s'étendre)* to lie down; *[soleil, lune]* to set, go down; *[bateau]* to keel over. **4** *nm*: **le (moment du)** ~ bedtime; **le** ~ **des enfants** the children's bedtime; **(au)** ~ **du soleil** (at) sunset *ou* sundown *(US)*. ◆ **couchette** *nf [voyageur]* couchette, berth; *[marin]* bunk.

couci-couça * [kusikusa] *adv* so-so *.

coucou [kuku] *nm (oiseau)* cuckoo; *(pendule)* cuckoo clock; *(péj: avion)* (old) crate; *(fleur)* cowslip. ~ **(me voici)!** peek-a-boo!

Vous savez aussi qu'on peut coucher des choses très différentes : un bébé dans son berceau, une échelle sur le sol, des mots sur le papier ; on peut aussi coucher quelqu'un en joue. Pour vous mettre plus rapidement sur la voie, des lettres (**a**) - (**b**) - (**c**) - (**d**) séparent ces grandes zones d'emplois.

Si vous connaissez la traduction dans le premier cas : 'to put to bed', vous devinez qu'elle ne peut s'appliquer ni à l'échelle, ni au blé couché par le vent ; c'est pourquoi ces deux mots en italique (ils sont compléments d'objet du verbe) vous renseignent : *échelle* to lay down ; *blés* to flatten. Mais comment direz-vous, par exemple, 'coucher un meuble sur le côté' ? Comme il n'est pas possible de citer tous les objets que l'on peut coucher, c'est le mot échelle qui est chargé de les représenter, tout comme blés veut dire herbe, avoine, etc. Donc, 'coucher un meuble' se dit 'to lay a piece of furniture down'.

Lorsqu'il s'agit de pourvoir quelqu'un d'un lit, vous pourriez logiquement croire que 'coucher un bébé' et 'coucher un ami pour la nuit' se disent de la même manière, mais de nouveaux panneaux (des synonymes entre parenthèses) vous avertissent que *(mettre au lit)* un bébé se dit 'to put to bed' et que *(donner un lit)* à un ami se dit 'to put up'.

Dans le verbe **se coucher**, de nouveaux panneaux vous aident à trouver votre chemin : *[soleil, lune]* to set, go down ; *[bateau]* to keel over. Ce sont des sujets du verbe et ils sont placés entre crochets pour les distinguer des autres indications dont nous venons de parler.

Regardez maintenant l'article ◆ **couchette**. Comme il ne forme pas un article principal, il est précédé d'un triangle pour le faire ressortir. Il y a d'autres mots entre crochets : *[voyageur]* et *[marin]*. Ce sont des compléments du nom **couchette**. Ils vous indiquent qu'une couchette de *[voyageur]* se dit 'berth' ou 'couchette' alors qu'une couchette de *[marin]* se dit 'bunk'.

Dans l'article **couche**, vous retrouvez un certain nombre d'indications du même type. Il y en a aussi de nouvelles. En voici quelques-unes :

... *(gén)* qui précède le mot anglais 'layer' signifie que cette traduction est la plus générale de **couche**, celle qui est valable dans le plus grand nombre de cas.

... *(US)* qui suit le mot 'diaper' indique que c'est la manière dont on dit 'couche de bébé' en américain.

Il y a aussi un astérisque : * à la fin de l'expression 'en tenir une ~ *', ainsi qu'à la fin de la traduction 'to be really thick *'. Cet astérisque indique que l'une et l'autre sont familières. Si une expression est très familière, elle sera suivie de deux astérisques : ⁑. Si par contre elle est démodée, elle sera suivie d'une croix : †.

Vous remarquerez enfin que le mot **couche** n'est pas repris dans l'article. Il est remplacé par le signe ~ qui évite la répétition.

Dans la partie Anglais-Français du dictionnaire, vous remarquerez que les mots en italique sont en anglais, pour aider le lecteur anglophone. En tant que Français, vous-même n'avez pas besoin de précisions sur le sens des traductions françaises !

aid [eɪd] **1** *n* (**a**) *(help)* aide *f*. **with the ~ of** *sb* avec l'aide de; *sth* à l'aide de; **in ~ of the blind** au profit des aveugles; *(fig)* **what is the meeting in ~ of? *** c'est dans quel but, cette réunion? (**b**) *(helper)* aide *mf*, assistant(e) *m(f)*; *(apparatus)* aide *f*, moyen *m*. **audio-visual ~s** support audio-visuel, moyens audio-visuels; **teaching ~s** outils *mpl* pédagogiques. **2** *vt person* aider (*to do* à faire); *progress, recovery* contribuer à. *(Jur)* **to ~ and abet sb** être complice de qn.

aim [eɪm] **1** *n* (**a**) **to miss one's ~** manquer son coup; **to take ~** viser (*at sb/sth* qn/qch); **his ~ is bad** il vise mal. (**b**) *(purpose)* but *m*. **with the ~ of doing** dans le but de faire; **her ~ is to do** elle a pour but de faire. **2** *vt gun* braquer (*at* sur); *missile* pointer (*at* sur); *stone* lancer (*at* sur); *blow* décocher (*at* à); *remark* diriger (*at* contre). **3** *vi* viser. **to ~ at sth** viser qch; **to ~ at doing** *or* **to do** viser à faire; *(less formally)* avoir l'intention de faire. ◆ **aimless** *adj* sans but. ◆ **aimlessly** *adv wander* sans but; *stand around* sans trop savoir que faire; *chat, kick ball about* pour passer le temps.

alight[1] [ə'laɪt] *vi [person]* descendre (*from* de); *[bird]* se poser (*on* sur).

alight[2] [ə'laɪt] *adj, adv fire* allumé; *building* en feu. **to set sth ~** mettre le feu à qch.

Suppose you want to say in French 'with the aid of a dictionary': you look up **aid** in the dictionary. If you know that in your sentence the word 'aid' is a noun *(n)*, and not a transitive verb *(vt)*, then you will go straight to the section marked **1** *n*. This is in two parts, (**a**) and (**b**). the 'aid' that you're looking for is obviously the one marked (**a**) *(help)*, and not (**b**) *(helper)* or *(apparatus)*. You find the French word 'aide *f*'. Read on and you have the phrase you're looking for; 'a dictionary' is obviously a thing (*sth* means 'something') and not a person (*sb* means 'somebody'), so you can now translate your phrase 'with the aid of a dictionary' - 'à l'aide d'un dictionnaire' ('with the aid of his brother' would be 'avec l'aide de son frère'). You'll see in this particular dictionary the sign ~, which we use to avoid having to keep repeating the headword, in this case **aid**.

You will have noticed that the gender of a French noun is always given, i.e. 'aide *f*'; normally this is done by using *f* for 'feminine' and *m* for 'masculine'. Sometimes the gender is already clear from the adjective which goes with the noun, and there is no need for *m* or *f*; thus, a few lines further on in the **aid** entry, **audio-visual ~s** is translated by 'support audio-visuel, moyens audio-visuels' - the masculine ending of 'audio-visuel' in both cases tells you that it is 'le support' and 'le moyen'.

Suppose however you'd been trying to put into French 'they aimed the searchlights at the plane'. From the entry **aim 2** *vt* (= verb transitive) you have to use the English in italics to help you choose the right French word to translate 'aim' in your sentence. Is 'aiming a *searchlight*' closer to 'aiming a *gun*' or to 'aiming a *stone*' at something? You obviously point a searchlight in the same way as you point a gun, you don't throw it, and so you would choose 'braquer': 'ils ont braqué les projecteurs sur l'avion'.

Further down the page you'll find **aimlessly** (the ◆ sign before it is just to help you find it more easily, since it's not a main headword like **aim**). If you want to talk about someone 'hanging about aimlessly on street corners' you'd pick *stand around* as nearest to 'hang about', and say 'il traînait au coin de la rue sans trop savoir que faire'.

Similarly under **alight**, for passengers who 'alight' from a coach, you would follow the signpost *[person]* and choose 'descendre', rather than 'se poser', which you'd use for a blackbird 'alighting' on a branch.

Lastly, the asterisk (in **aid 1** *n*: **what is the meeting in ~ of? ***) shows that this is something you'd happily say to someone, but not perhaps write in a formal piece of writing like an essay, or an application for a job. If an English or French phrase has two asterisks, this means that it is definitely slangy. The † symbol means that a word or expression is old-fashioned.

In the French-English side of the dictionary you'll notice that the words in italics are in French, to help the French user. As an English speaker you don't need any help with your English!

églantier [eglɑ̃tje] *nm* wild rose(-bush). ◆ **églantine** *nf* wild rose, eglantine.

égout [egu] *nm* sewer. **les ~s** the sewerage system. ◆ **égoutier** *nm* sewer worker.

égoutter [egute] (1) **1** *vt (avec passoire)* to strain; *(en tordant)* to wring out. **2** *vi [vaisselle]* to drain, drip; *[linge, eau]* to drip. **faire ~** *eau* to drain off; *linge* to hang up to drip; **'laisser ~'** 'drip dry'. **3 s'~** *vpr* to drip; to drain. ◆ **égouttoir** *nm (évier)* draining board; *(mobile)* draining rack; *(passoire)* strainer, colander.

égratigner [egʀatiɲe] (1) *vt peau* to scratch, graze; *genou* to graze, scrape; *(fig)* to have a dig at. **le film/l'auteur s'est fait ~ par la critique** the film/the author was given a bit of a rough ride by the critics. ◆ **égratignure** *nf* scratch, graze, scrape; *(fig)* dig. **sans une ~** without a scratch, unscathed.

égrener [egʀəne] (5) *vt pois, blé, épi* to shell; *coton* to gin; *grappe* to pick grapes off. *(fig)* **~ son chapelet** to tell one's beads; **~ les heures** to mark the hours; **les maisons s'égrenaient le long de la route** the houses were dotted along the road.

égrillard, e [egʀijaʀ, aʀd(ə)] *adj* bawdy.

Égypte [eʒipt] *nf* Egypt. ◆ **égyptien, -ienne** *adj,* **É~(ne)** *nm (f)* Egyptian.

eh [e] *excl:* **~ bien** well.

éhonté, e [eɔ̃te] *adj* shameless.

éjecter [eʒɛkte] (1) *vt (Tech)* to eject; (*) to kick out *. **se faire ~ *** to get o.s. kicked out *. ◆ **éjection** *nf (Tech)* ejection; (*) kicking-out *.

élaborer [elabɔʀe] (1) *vt (gén)* to elaborate. ◆ **élaboration** *nf* elaboration.

élaguer [elage] (1) *vt (lit, fig)* to prune. ◆ **élagage** *nm* pruning. ◆ **élagueur** *nm* pruner.

élan[1] [elɑ̃] *nm (Zool)* elk, moose.

élan[2] [elɑ̃] *nm* (**a**) *(début de course)* run up. **saut avec/sans ~** running/standing jump. (**b**) *(vitesse acquise)* momentum. **prendre de l' ~** to gather speed; **emporté par son ~** carried along by his own momentum. (**c**) *[enthousiasme, colère]* surge, burst (*de* of). **~s (d'affection)** rushes of affection; **~s lyriques** lyrical outbursts; **dire qch avec ~** to say sth with fervour *ou* passion. (**d**) *[troupes]* vigour, spirit. **~ patriotique** patriotic fervour. (**e**) *(Écon: dynamisme)* boost. **l' ~ donné à nos exportations** the boost given to our exports.

élancer [elɑ̃se] (3) **1** *vi [blessure]* to give shooting pains. **2 s' ~** *vpr* (**a**) *(se précipiter)* to rush, dash (*vers* towards). **s' ~ d'un bond sur** to leap onto. (**b**) *(se dresser)* to soar (upwards). ◆ **élancé, e** *adj clocher etc* slender. ◆ **élancement** *nm* shooting pain.

élargir [elaʀʒiʀ] (2) **1** *vt* (**a**) *(gén)* to widen; *débat* to broaden. *(Pol)* **majorité élargie** increased majority; **ça lui élargit la taille** that makes his waist look fatter; **~ son horizon** to enlarge *ou* widen one's horizons. (**b**) *(Jur: libérer)* to release, free. **2 s' ~** *vpr [route]* to widen, get wider; *[idées]* to broaden. ◆ **élargissement** *nm* widening; broadening; release.

électeur, -trice [elɛktœʀ, tʀis] *nm, f* (**a**) *(Pol)* voter. *(circonscription)* **~s** constituents. (**b**) *(Hist)* **É~** Elector; **É~trice** Electress. ◆ **électif, -ive** *adj (Pol)* elective.

traductions interchangeables séparées par une virgule

chiffres isolant les fonctions grammaticales différentes

signalisation par sujet du verbe entre crochets

signalisation par complément du verbe

mot souche de l'article (égratigner) ou du sous-article (égratignure) repris par ~

différence minuscule/majuscule signalée

traductions non interchangeables séparées par un point-virgule

chiffres isolant les homographes

éléments non interchangeables à partir d'un tronc commun séparés par une oblique

signalisation par complément de nom entre crochets (= élan d'enthousiasme, de colère etc)

parenthèses isolant les mots que l'on peut omettre sans changer le sens

tables de conjugaison voir p.552

signalisation par nom auquel se rapporte l'adjectif

sens général, valable dans la plupart des cas

traductions non précisées du sous-article séparées par points-virgules. Se reporter à la signalisation de l'article principal

indication du féminin

lettres (a), (b) isolant les sens différents du mot

alternative translations separated by a comma

numbers show different grammatical categories

typical subjects of verb in square brackets

typical objects of headword to show shades of meaning which require different translations

the sign ~ may replace either a main headword (égratigner) or the secondary (égratignure)

French adjectives and nouns of nationality shown

a semi-colon separates shifts in meaning within a category

superior numbers separate homographs

the sign / shows alternatives in a phrase which are reflected exactly in the translation

noun complements shown in square brackets (= élan d'enthousiasme, de colère etc)

brackets round words which can be left out without altering meaning of phrase

French verb tables see p.552

noun complements of adjectives

indicates that the translation works generally or in most cases

translations separated by a semi-colon with no explanations. Refer to the main headword for indications as to shifts in cases

feminine form of French nouns and adjectives

(a), (b) separate distinct meanings of the headword

admiral ['ædm(ə)rəl] *n* amiral *m* (d'escadre). **A~ of the Fleet** ≃ Amiral *m* de France. ◆ **Admiralty Board** *n* (*Brit*) ≃ ministère *m* de la Marine.

admire [əd'maɪəʳ] *vt* admirer. ◆ **admirable** ['ædm(ə)rəbl] *adj* admirable. ◆ **admirably** *adv* admirablement. ◆ **admiration** *n* admiration *f* (*of, for* pour); **to be the admiration of** faire l'admiration de. ◆ **admirer** *n* admirateur *m*, -trice *f*; (†: *suitor*) soupirant† *m*. ◆ **admiring** *adj* admiratif. ◆ **admiringly** *adv* avec admiration.

admissible [əd'mɪsəbl] *adj plan* acceptable; *evidence* recevable.

admission [əd'mɪʃ(ə)n] *n* (**a**) (*entry*) admission *f*, entrée *f* (*to* à). ~ **free** entrée gratuite; **to gain ~ to** *person* trouver accès auprès de; *place* être admis dans. (**b**) (*confession*) aveu *m*. **by one's own ~** de son propre aveu.

admit [əd'mɪt] *vt* (**a**) (*let in*) laisser entrer. **children not ~ted** entrée interdite aux enfants; **this ticket ~s 2** ce billet est valable pour 2 personnes. (**b**) (*acknowledge*) reconnaître, admettre (*that* que); *[criminal]* avouer (*that* que); *crime* reconnaître avoir commis; *one's guilt* reconnaître. **I must ~ that...** je dois avouer *or* admettre que...; **I was wrong I ~** j'ai eu tort, j'en conviens. ◆ **admit of** *vt fus* admettre, permettre. ◆ **admit to** *vt fus crime* reconnaître avoir commis. **to ~ to having done** reconnaître avoir fait; **to ~ to a feeling of** avouer avoir un sentiment de. ◆ **admittance** *n* droit *m* d'entrée, admission *f* (*to sth* à qch); accès *m* (*to sth* à qch; *to sb* auprès de qn); **I gained ~tance** on m'a laissé entrer ; **no ~tance except on business** accès interdit à toute personne étrangère au service. ◆ **admittedly** *adv*: **~tedly this is true** je reconnais *or* il faut reconnaître que c'est vrai.

admonish [əd'mɒnɪʃ] *vt* (*reprove*) réprimander (*for doing* pour avoir fait; *about, for* pour, à propos de); (*warn*) avertir (*against doing* de ne pas faire); (*exhort*) exhorter (*to do* à faire). ◆ **admonition** *n* réprimande *f*; avertissement *m*.

ad nauseam [ˌæd'nɔːsɪæm] *adv* à satiété.

ado [ə'duː] *n*: **much ~ about nothing** beaucoup de bruit pour rien; **without more ~** sans plus de cérémonies.

adolescent [ˌædə(ʊ)lesnt] *adj, n* adolescent(e) *m(f)*. ◆ **adolescence** *n* adolescence *f*.

adopt [ə'dɒpt] *vt child, method, (Pol) motion* adopter; *candidate, career* choisir. ◆ **adopted** *adj child* adopté; *country* d'adoption; *son, family* adoptif. ◆ **adoption** *n* adoption *f*; choix *m*. ◆ **adoptive** *adj parent, child* adoptif; *country* d'adoption.

adore [ə'dɔːʳ] *vt* adorer. ◆ **adorable** *adj* adorable. ◆ **adoration** *n* adoration *f*. ◆ **adoringly** *adv* avec adoration.

adorn [ə'dɔːn] *vt room* orner; *dress* parer (*with* de). **to ~ o.s.** se parer. ◆ **adornment** *n* ornement *m*; parure *f*.

adrenalin(e) [ə'drenəlɪn] *n* adrénaline *f*. (*fig*) **he felt the ~ rising** il a senti son pouls s'emballer.

Adriatic (Sea) [ˌeɪdrɪ'ætɪk('siː)] *n* (mer *f*) Adriatique *f*.

adrift [ə'drɪft] *adv, adj* (*Naut*) à la dérive. **to turn ~** *boat* abandonner à la dérive; (*fig*) *person* laisser se débrouiller tout seul; **to come ~*** *[wire etc]* se détacher; *[plans]* tomber à l'eau.

= Britannique; (US = Américain)	*= British; (US = American)*
équivalent culturel signalé par le signe ≃	*= 'is approximately equivalent to'*
indication du genre: m = masculin; f = féminin	*gender: m = masculine; f = feminine*
emploi vieilli ou archaïque signalé par une croix †	*dagger means old-fashioned or obsolete*
genre indiqué une seule fois dans la catégorie	*gender shown once only per category*
prononciation (notation de l'Association Phonétique Internationale voir p.xviii	*pronunciation in IPA, see p.xviii*
mot souche de l'article repris par ~ (= 'admit')	*the sign ~ replaces main headword 'admit'*
verbes à particule et sous-articles signalés par un losange ◆	*the sign ◆ highlights phrasal verbs and secondary headwords*
même dans les sous-articles ('admittance') le signe ~ remplace le mot souche ('admit')	*even in secondary entries ('admittance') ~ replaces main headword ('admit')*
éléments interchangeables de traduction à partir d'un tronc commun séparés par or	*separates alternative translations of part of a phrase*
précisions grammaticales à la suite de la traduction	*grammatical points given after French translations*
classes grammaticales: *vt = verbe transitif* *adj = adjectif* *n = nom* *adv = adverbe*	*parts of speech:* *vt = verb transitive* *adj = adjective* *n = noun* *adv = adverb*
le genre du nom n'est pas indiqué lorsqu'un adjectif le rend évident	*gender of nouns not specified when clear from accompanying adjective*
parenthèses isolant les mots que l'on peut omettre	*brackets round words which may be left out*
= nautique; liste complète des abréviations voir p.xiv	*= nautical; for full list of such abbreviations see p.xiv*
*emploi familier indiqué par un astérisque * voir p.xvii*	*informal language; see note p.xvii*

ABRÉVIATIONS - ABBREVIATIONS

abréviation	***abbr, abrév***	abbreviated, abbreviation
adjectif	***adj***	adjective
administration	***Admin***	administration
adverbe	***adv***	adverb
agriculture	***Agr***	agriculture
anatomie	***Anat***	anatomy
antiquité	***Antiq***	ancient history
approximativement	***approx***	approximately
archéologie	***Archeol, Archéol***	archaeology
architecture	***Archit***	architecture
argot	***arg***	slang
article	***art***	article
astrologie	***Astrol***	astrology
astronomie	***Astron***	astronomy
automobile	***Aut***	automobiles
auxiliaire	***aux***	auxiliary
aviation	***Aviat***	aviation
biologie	***Bio***	biology
botanique	***Bot***	botany
britannique, Grande-Bretagne	***Brit***	British, Great Britain
canadien, Canada	***Can***	Canadian, Canada
chimie	***Chem, Chim***	chemistry
cinéma	***Cine, Ciné***	cinema
commerce	***Comm***	commerce
comparatif	***comp***	comparative
informatique	***Comput***	computing
conditionnel	***cond***	conditional
conjonction	***conj***	conjunction
construction	***Constr***	building trade
mots composés	***cpd***	compound, in compounds
cuisine	***Culin***	cookery
défini	***def, déf***	definite
démonstratif	***dem, dém***	demonstrative
dialectal, régional	***dial***	dialect
diminutif	***dim***	diminutive
direct	***dir***	direct
écologie	***Ecol***	ecology
économique	***Econ, Écon***	economics
par exemple	***eg***	for example
électricité, électronique	***Elec, Élec***	electricity, electronics
et cetera	***etc***	etcetera
euphémisme	***euph***	euphemism
par exemple	***ex***	for example

ABRÉVIATIONS - ABBREVIATIONS

exclamation	***excl***	exclamation
féminin	***f***	feminine
figuré	***fig***	figuratively
finance	***Fin***	finance
football	***Ftbl***	football
fusionné	***fus***	fused
futur	***fut***	future
en général, généralement	***gen, gén***	in general, generally
géographie	***Geog, Géog***	geography
géologie	***Geol, Géol***	geology
géométrie	***Gem, Géom***	geometry
grammaire	***Gram***	grammar
gymnastique	***Gym***	gymnastics
héraldique	***Her, Hér***	heraldry
histoire	***Hist***	history
humoristique	***hum***	humorous
impératif	***imper, impér***	imperative
impersonnel	***impers***	impersonal
industrie	***Ind***	industry
indéfini	***indef, indéf***	indefinite
indicatif	***indic***	indicative
indirect	***indir***	indirect
infinitif	***infin***	infinitive
inséparable	***insep***	inseparable
interrogatif	***interrog***	interrogative
invariable	***inv***	invariable
irlandais, Irlande	***Ir***	Irish, Ireland
ironique	***iro***	ironic
irrégulier	***irrég***	irregular
droit, juridique	***Jur***	law, legal
linguistique	***Ling***	linguistics
littéral, au sens propre	***lit***	literally
littéraire	***liter***	literary
littérature	***Literat***	literature
littéraire	***littér***	literary
littérature	***Littérat***	literature
masculin	***m***	masculine
mathématiques	***Math***	mathematics
médecine	***Med, Méd***	medicine
météorologie	***Met, Mét***	meteorology
métallurgie	***Metal, Métal***	metallurgy
militaire	***Mil***	military
mines	***Min***	mining
minéralogie	***Miner, Minér***	mineralogy
musique	***Mus***	music
mythologie	***Myth***	mythology

ABRÉVIATIONS - ABBREVIATIONS		
nom	*n*	noun
nautique	*Naut*	nautical, naval
négatif	*neg, nég*	negative
numéral	*num*	numerical
objet	*obj*	object
opposé	*opp*	opposite
optique	*Opt*	optics
informatique	*Ordin*	computing
ornithologie	*Orn*	ornithology
	o.s.	oneself
parlement	*Parl*	parliament
passif	*pass*	passive
péjoratif	*pej, péj*	pejorative
personnel	*pers*	personal
pharmacie	*Pharm*	pharmacy
philatélie	*Philat*	philately
philosophie	*Philos*	philosophy
photographie	*Phot*	photography
	phr vb elem	phrasal verb element
physique	*Phys*	physics
physiologie	*Physiol*	physiology
pluriel	*pl*	plural
politique	*Pol*	politics
possessif	*poss*	possessive
préfixe	*pref, préf*	prefix
préposition	*prep, prép*	preposition
prétérit	*pret, prét*	preterite
pronom	*pron*	pronoun
participe présent	*prp*	present participle
psychiatrie, psychologie	*Psych*	psychiatry, psychology
participe passé	*ptp*	past participle
quelque chose	*qch*	
quelqu'un	*qn*	
radio	*Rad*	radio
relatif	*rel*	relative
religion	*Rel*	religion
	sb	somebody, someone
sciences	*Sci*	science
école	*Scol*	school
écossais, Écosse	*Scot*	Scottish, Scotland
sculpture	*Sculp*	sculpture
séparable	*sep*	separable
singulier	*sg*	singular
argot	*sl*	slang

ABRÉVIATIONS - ABBREVIATIONS		
sociologie	***Soc, Sociol***	sociology, social work
Bourse	***St Ex***	Stock Exchange
	sth	something
subjonctif	***subj***	subjunctive
suffixe	***suf***	suffix
superlatif	***superl***	superlative
chirurgie	***Surg***	surgery
arpentage	***Surv***	surveying
technique	***Tech***	technical
télécom-munications	***Telec, Téléc***	telecom-munications
industrie textile	***Tex***	textiles
théâtre	***Theat, Théât***	theatre
télévision	***TV***	television
typographie	***Typ***	typography
université	***Univ***	university
américain, États-Unis	***US***	American, United States
voir	***V***	see
verbe	***vb***	verb
médecine vétérinaire	***Vet, Vét***	veterinary medicine
verbe intransitif	***vi***	intransitive verb
verbe pronominal	***vpr***	pronominal verb
verbe transitif	***vt***	transitive verb
verbe transitif et intransitif	***vti***	transitive and intransitive verb
verbe transitif indirect	***vt indir***	
zoologie	***Zool***	zoology

SIGNES CONVENTIONNELS		
emploi familier	*	informal language
emploi très familier	**	very informal language
emploi vieilli	†	old-fashioned
marque déposée	®	registered trademark

TRANSCRIPTION PHONÉTIQUE DE L'ANGLAIS

Voyelles et diphtongues	
iː	bead, see
ɑː	bard, calm
ɔː	born, cork
uː	boon, fool
ɜː	burn, fern, work
ɪ	sit, pity
e	set, less
æ	sat, apple
ʌ	fun, come
ɒ	fond, wash
ʊ	full, soot
ə	composer, above
eɪ	bay, fate
aɪ	buy, lie
ɔɪ	boy, voice
əʊ	no, ago
aʊ	now, plough
ɪə	tier, beer
ɛə	tare, fair
ʊə	tour

Consonnes	
p	pat, pope
b	bat, baby
t	tab, strut
d	dab, mended
k	cot, kiss, chord
g	got, agog
f	fine, raffle
v	vine, river
s	pots, sit, rice
z	pods, buzz
θ	thin, maths
ð	this, other
ʃ	ship, sugar
ʒ	measure
tʃ	chance
dʒ	just, edge
l	little, place
r	ran, stirring
m	ram, mummy
n	ran, nut
ŋ	rang, bank
h	hat, reheat
j	yet, million
w	wet, bewail
x	loch

NB : Un caractère entre parenthèses représente un son qui peut ne pas être prononcé ;
ʳ représente un [r] entendu s'il forme une liaison avec la voyelle du mot suivant ;
ˈ accent tonique ; ˌ accent secondaire.

PHONETIC TRANSCRIPTION OF FRENCH

	Vowels
i	**il**, **vi**e, **ly**re
e	**blé**, jou**er**
ɛ	**lait**, jou**et**, m**e**rci
a	**pla**t, **pa**tte
ɑ	**bas**, p**â**te
ɔ	m**o**rt, d**o**nner
o	m**o**t, d**ô**me, **eau**, g**au**che
u	gen**ou**, r**ou**e
y	r**u**e, v**ê**tu
ø	p**eu**, d**eu**x
œ	p**eu**r, m**eu**ble
ə	l**e**, pr**e**mier
ɛ̃	mat**in**, pl**ein**
ɑ̃	s**an**s, v**en**t
ɔ̃	b**on**, **om**bre
œ̃	l**un**di, br**un**

	Semi-consonants
j	**y**eux, pa**ill**e, p**i**ed
w	**ou**i, n**ou**er
ɥ	h**u**ile, l**u**i

	Consonants
p	**p**ère, sou**p**e
t	**t**erre, vi**t**e
k	**c**ou, **qu**i, sa**c**, **k**épi
b	**b**on, ro**b**e
d	**d**ans, ai**d**e
g	**g**are, ba**gu**e
f	**f**eu, neu**f**, **ph**oto
s	**s**ale, **c**elui, **ç**a, de**ss**ous, ta**ss**e, na**t**ion
ʃ	**ch**at, ta**ch**e
v	**v**ous, rê**v**e
z	**z**éro, mai**s**on, ro**s**e
ʒ	**j**e, **g**ilet, **ge**ôle
l	**l**ent, so**l**
ʀ	**r**ue, veni**r**
m	**m**ain, fe**mm**e
n	**n**ous, to**nn**e, a**n**imal
ɲ	a**gn**eau, vi**gn**e
h	**h**op ! (exclamative)
'	**h**aricot (no liaison)
ŋ	words borrowed from English: campi**ng**
x	words borrowed from Spanish or Arabic: **j**ota

VERBES ANGLAIS À PARTICULE
ENGLISH PHRASAL VERBS

vi	verbe intransitif. ex : ◆**blow off** dans 'his hat blew off'.	verb intransitive, e.g. ◆**blow off** in 'his hat blew off'.
vt sep	verbe transitif séparable. ex : ◆**blow off** dans 'the wind blew off his hat' ou 'the wind blew his hat off'. Le complément d'objet du verbe peut se mettre soit après la particule, soit entre les deux éléments du verbe en les séparant. Cette dernière structure est d'ailleurs obligatoire lorsque le complément d'objet est un pronom : 'the wind blew it off'.	verb transitive separable, e.g. ◆**blow off** in 'the wind blew off his hat'. The object of the verb may either come after the second part of the phrasal verb, as in this example, or between the two parts ('the wind blew it off').
vt fus	verbe transitif fusionné. ex : ◆**admit to** dans 'he admitted to the theft'. Le complément d'objet ne peut jamais s'intercaler entre les deux éléments du verbe, même lorsqu'il s'agit d'un pronom : 'he admitted to it'.	verb transitive fused, e.g. ◆**admit to** in 'he admitted to the theft', where the object of the phrasal verb never comes between the two parts (always 'he admitted to it', never 'he admitted it to').

REMARQUE : Pour beaucoup de verbes qui indiquent un mouvement ou une direction, les verbes à particule correspondants n'ont pas été dissociés de l'article principal, car ils peuvent être déduits des illustrations fournies. Ainsi, à partir de **crawl** **2** *vi (gén)* ramper; ... **to** ~ **in/out** *etc* entrer/sortir *etc* en rampant... vous pouvez construire : 'to crawl across' (traverser en rampant), 'to crawl down' (descendre en rampant) etc.

NOTE : For many verbs which involve movement and direction e.g. 'crawl', the related phrasal verbs have not been dealt with separately from the main verb entry, as they may be constructed on the basis of the samples shown. Thus at **crawl** **2** *vi (gén)* ramper; ... **to** ~ **in/out** *etc* entrer/sortir *etc* en rampant...: you can form from that 'to crawl across' (traverser en rampant), 'to crawl down' (descendre en rampant) and so on.

FRANÇAIS - ANGLAIS
FRENCH - ENGLISH

A, a [ɑ] *nm (lettre)* A, a. **de A (jusqu') à Z** from A to Z; **prouver par ~ plus b** to prove conclusively.

à [a] *prép (avec le, les:* **au, aux***)* (**a**) *(déplacement) (vers)* to; *(dans)* into. **aller ~ Paris/au marché** to go to Paris/to (the) market; **aller ~ la pêche** to go fishing; **son voyage ~ Londres** his trip to London; **entrez au salon** go into the lounge; **au lit/au travail les enfants!** time for bed/work children!
(**b**) *(position)* at; *(dans)* in; *(sur)* on. **habiter ~ Paris/au 4e étage** to live in Paris/on the 4th floor; **être ~ l'école/ ~ la maison** to be at school/at home; **c'est ~ 3 km** it's 3 km away; **~ la télévision/radio** on television/the radio; **rester au chaud** to stay in the warm.
(**c**) *(temps)* at; *(date)* on; *(époque)* in; *(jusqu'à)* to, till, until. **~ 6 heures/Noël** at 6 o'clock/Christmas; **le 3 au soir** on the evening of the 3rd; **~ samedi!** see you on Saturday!; **au matin/XIXe siècle** in the morning/the 19th century; **à l'automne** in autumn; **de 2 ~ 4 heures** from 2 to *ou* till 4 (o'clock).
(**d**) *(rapport)* by, per; *(approximation)* to. **faire du 50 ~ l'heure** to do 50 km an *ou* per hour; **faire du 9 litres aux 100** to use 9 litres per 100 km; **être payé au poids/mois** to be paid by weight/the month; **entrer 2 ~ 2** to come in 2 by 2; **4 ~ 5 mètres** 4 to 5 metres; **gagner (par) 2 ~ 1** to win by 2 to 1.
(**e**) *(appartenance)* of, to. **ce sac est ~ moi/Peter** this bag is mine/Peter's, this bag belongs to me/ Peter; **un ami ~ elle** a friend of hers, one of her friends; **ce n'est pas ~ moi de le faire** it's not for me *ou* up to me to do it.
(**f**) *(moyen)* on, by, with. **faire qch ~ la main** to do sth by hand; **aller ~ vélo/~ pied** to go by bike/ on foot; **écrire qch au crayon** to write sth with a pencil *ou* in pencil; **jouer qch au piano** to play sth on the piano; **cuisiné au beurre** cooked in butter; **ils l'ont fait ~ 3** they did it between the 3 of them.
(**g**) *(caractérisation)* with. **robe ~ manches** dress with sleeves; **pompe ~ eau** water pump; **tasse ~ thé** tea cup; **elle est femme ~ le faire** she's the sort of woman to do it.
(**h**) *(destination)* for, to. **maison ~ vendre** house for sale; *(dédicace)* **~ ma sœur** to *ou* for my sister.
(**i**) *(conséquence)* to; *(hypothèse)* from. **~ leur grande surprise** much to their surprise; **~ ce que j'ai compris** from what I understood; **~ le voir si maigre** when I saw he was so thin; **~ bien réfléchir** if you think about it.

abaisser [abese] (1) **1** *vt* (**a**) *(gén) niveau* to lower; *store* to pull down; *température, taux* to bring down; *perpendiculaire* to drop. (**b**) to humiliate; *(Rel)* to humble. **2 s' ~** *vpr* (**a**) *[température, taux]* to fall, drop; *[terrain]* to slope down; *(Théât) [rideau]* to fall (*sur* on). (**b**) *(s'humilier)* to humble o.s. **s' ~ à faire** to stoop to doing. ◆ **abaissant, e** *adj* degrading. ◆ **abaissement** *nm* (**a**) *(action)* lowering; pulling down; dropping; humiliation; humbling. (**b**) *(chute)* fall, drop (*de* in); *[terrain]* downward slope; *[moralité]* decline. (**c**) *(abjection)* degradation.

abandon [abɑ̃dɔ̃] *nm* (**a**) *(délaissement)* desertion, abandonment; *(manque de soin)* neglected state, neglect. **~ de poste** desertion of one's post; **laisser à l' ~** to neglect. (**b**) *[idée, technique etc]* giving up; *[droit]* relinquishment; *[course]* withdrawal (*de* from). **faire ~ de ses biens à qn** to make over one's property to sb; *(fig)* **~ de soi-même** self-abnegation. (**c**) *(relâchement)* lack of constraint. **parler avec ~** to talk freely *ou* without constraint; **moments d' ~** moments of abandon; **l' ~ de son attitude** his relaxed attitude.

abandonner [abɑ̃dɔne] (1) **1** *vt* (**a**) *(délaisser) lieu, personne* to desert, abandon; *technique* to abandon, give up; *(Ordin)* to abort. **son courage l'abandonna** his courage deserted him. (**b**) *(se retirer de) (gén)* to give up; *études, projet* to abandon; *droit* to relinquish; *course* to withdraw from. *(lit, fig)* **~ la lutte** to give up the fight. (**c**) *(donner)* **~ à** *(gén)* to leave to; **~ ses biens à une bonne œuvre** to leave *ou* donate one's wealth to a good cause; **elle lui abandonna sa main** she let him take her hand; **~ à qn le soin de faire qch** to leave it to sb to do sth; **~ au pillage** to leave to be pillaged. **2 s' ~** *vpr* to let o.s. go. **s' ~ à** *(gén)* to give o.s. up to; *désespoir* to give way to; **il s'abandonna au sommeil** he let sleep overcome him. ◆ **abandonné, e** *adj attitude* relaxed; *(avec volupté)* abandoned; *usine* disused.

abasourdir [abazuʀdiʀ] (2) *vt (gén)* to stun.

abat-jour [abaʒuʀ] *nm inv* lampshade.

abats [aba] *nmpl [volaille]* giblets; *[bœuf]* offal.

abattage [abataʒ] *nm [animal]* slaughter; *[arbre]* felling; *(Min)* extracting.

abattant [abatɑ̃] *nm* flap *(of table, desk)*.

abattement [abatmɑ̃] *nm* (**a**) *(dépression)* despondency; *(fatigue)* exhaustion. (**b**) *(rabais)* reduction; *(fiscal)* (tax) allowance.

abattis [abati] *nmpl [volaille]* giblets; *(*: membres)* limbs.

abattoir [abatwaʀ] *nm* slaughterhouse.

abattre [abatʀ(ə)] (41) **1** *vt* (**a**) *arbre* to cut down, fell; *adversaire, quilles, mur* to knock down; *roche* to hew; *avion* to shoot down. **la pluie abat la poussière** the rain settles the dust; **il abattit son bâton sur ma tête** he brought his stick down on my head. (**b**) *(tuer) personne, fauve* to shoot; *chien* to destroy, put down; *bœuf* to slaughter. (**c**) *(physiquement)* to weaken, exhaust; *(moralement)* to demoralize. **abattu par la chaleur** overcome by the heat; **ne te laisse pas ~** don't let things get you down; *(lit, fig)* **~ ses cartes** to lay *ou* put one's cards on the table; **~ du travail** to get through a lot of work. **2 s' ~** *vpr* (**a**) *[personne]* to fall (down); *[cheminée]* to fall *ou* crash down. (**b**) **s' ~ sur** *[pluie]* to beat down on; *[ennemi]* to swoop down on; *[coups, injures]* to rain on. ◆ **abattu, e** *adj (fatigué)* exhausted; *(déprimé)* demoralized, despondent.

abbaye [abei] *nf* abbey. ◆ **abbé** *nm [abbaye]* abbot; *(prêtre)* priest. ◆ **abbesse** *nf* abbess.

abc [abese] *nm (livre)* ABC *ou* alphabet book; *(rudiments)* ABC, fundamentals *(pl)*, rudiments *(pl)*. **l' ~ du métier** the first requirement of the job.

abcès [apsɛ] *nm* abscess. *(fig)* **vider l' ~** to root out the evil.

abdication [abdikɑsjɔ̃] *nf (lit, fig)* abdication. ◆ **abdiquer** *vti [roi]* to abdicate; *(fig)* to give up.

abdomen [abdɔmɛn] *nm* abdomen. ◆ **abdominal, e,** *mpl* **-aux** **1** *adj* abdominal. **2** *nmpl*: ~**aux** stomach muscles.

abeille [abɛj] *nf* bee.

aberrant, e [abɛʀɑ̃, ɑ̃t] *adj conduite, (Bio)* aberrant; *histoire* absurd. ◆ **aberration** *nf (gén)* aberration.

abêtir *vt*, **s'** ~ *vpr* [abetiʀ] **(2)** to turn into a half-wit. ◆ **abêtissant, e** *adj travail* stupefying. ◆ **abêtissement** *nm (état)* stupidity. *(action)* **l'** ~ **des masses par la télévision** the stupefying effect of television on the masses.

abhorrer [abɔʀe] **(1)** *vt (littér)* to abhor, loathe.

abîme [abim] *nm (lit, fig)* gulf, chasm. **au bord de l'** ~ *pays* on the brink *ou* verge of ruin; **au fond de l'** ~ *personne* in the depths of despair; **les ~s de l'enfer** the depths of hell; **dans un ~ de perplexité** utterly perplexed; **c'est un ~ de bêtise** he's abysmally *ou* incredibly stupid.

abîmer [abime] **(1)** **1** *vt* to damage, spoil. **2 s'** ~ *vpr* **(a)** *[objet]* to get spoilt *ou* damaged; *[fruits]* to go bad. **(b)** *(littér) [navire]* to founder. **s'** ~ **dans la réflexion** to be deep *ou* plunged in thought.

abject, e [abʒɛkt] *adj* despicable, abject. ◆ **abjection** *nf* abjectness.

abjuration [abʒyʀɑsjɔ̃] *nf* abjuration, renunciation (*de* of). **faire ~ de** to abjure. ◆ **abjurer** **(1)** *vt* to abjure, renounce.

ablation [ablɑsjɔ̃] *nf (Méd)* removal.

ablutions [ablysjɔ̃] *nfpl (gén)* ablutions.

abnégation [abnegɑsjɔ̃] *nf* (self-)abnegation, self-denial. **avec** ~ selflessly.

aboiement [abwamɑ̃] *nm [chien]* bark; *(péj: cri)* cry. **~s** barking.

abois [abwa] *nmpl*: **aux** ~ at bay.

abolir [abɔliʀ] **(2)** *vt* to abolish. ◆ **abolition** *nf* abolition. ◆ **abolitionnisme** *nm* abolitionism. ◆ **abolitionniste** *adj, nmf* abolitionist.

abominable [abɔminabl(ə)] *adj* abominable; *(sens affaibli)* frightful, terrible. ◆ **abominablement** *adv* abominably; frightfully, terribly. ◆ **abomination** *nf (crime)* abomination; *(parole etc)* abominable remark *etc.* **avoir en** ~ to loathe, abominate; **c'est une ~!** it's abominable! ◆ **abominer** **(1)** *vt* to loathe.

abondant, e [abɔ̃dɑ̃, ɑ̃t] *adj récolte* good; *réserves* plentiful; *végétation* lush; *chevelure* thick; *larmes, conseils, repas* copious. **avec d' ~es photographies** with numerous photographs; **les pêches sont ~es sur le marché** peaches are in plentiful *ou* good supply (on the market); **il lui faut une nourriture ~e** he must have plenty of food. ◆ **abondamment** *adv* abundantly; plentifully; *couler* profusely; *boire* copiously. ◆ **abondance** *nf (profusion)* abundance; *(opulence)* affluence. **des fruits en ~** fruit in plenty; **il y a (une) ~ de** there is an abundance of ; ~ **d'idées** wealth of ideas. ◆ **abonder** **(1)** *vi* **(a)** to abound, be plentiful. ~ **en** to be full of, abound in. **(b) il abonda dans notre sens** he was in complete agreement with us.

abonné, e [abɔne] **1** *adj*: **être ~ à** *journal* to subscribe to; *téléphone, gaz* to have; *(fig)* **il y est ~!** * he's making (quite) a habit of it! **2** *nm, f (Presse, Téléc)* subscriber; *(Élec, Gaz)* consumer; *(Rail, Théât)* season-ticket holder. ◆ **abonnement** *nm (Presse)* subscription; *(Téléc)* rental; *(Rail, Théât)* season ticket. ◆ **abonner** **(1)** **1** *vt*: ~ **qn (à qch)** to take out a subscription (to sth) for sb; to buy sb a season ticket (for sth). **2 s'** ~ *vpr* to subscribe (*à* to); to buy a season ticket (*à* for).

abord [abɔʀ] *nm* **(a)** *(environs)* **~s** surroundings; **aux ~s de** in the area around. **(b)** *(accès)* access, approach; *(accueil)* manner. **d'un ~ difficile** *livre* which is difficult to get into; *personne* unapproachable. **(c) allons d' ~ chez le boucher** let's go to the butcher's first; **il fut (tout) d' ~ poli, puis...** he was polite at first *ou* initially, and then... ; **d'** ~, **il n'a même pas 18 ans** for a start *ou* in the first place, he's not even 18; **dès l'** ~ from the outset; **au premier** ~ at first sight. ◆ **abordable** *adj prix* reasonable; *personne* approachable; *lieu* accessible.

aborder [abɔʀde] **(1)** **1** *vt* **(a)** *lieu* to reach; *personne* to approach, come up to; *sujet* to tackle. **(b)** *(Naut) (attaquer)* to board; *(heurter)* to collide with. **2** *vi (Naut)* to land (*dans, sur* on). ◆ **abordage** *nm (assaut)* attacking; *(accident)* collision. **à l' ~!** away boarders!

aborigène [abɔʀiʒɛn] **1** *adj (gén)* aboriginal; *(australien)* Aboriginal. **2** *nmf* aborigine. ~ **d'Australie** Aboriginal, Australian Aborigine.

aboucher (s') [abuʃe] **(1)** *vpr*: **s'** ~ **avec qn** to get in touch with sb.

aboutir [abutiʀ] **(2)** *vi* **(a)** *(réussir)* to succeed. **faire** ~ to bring to a successful conclusion. **(b)** ~ **à** *ou* **dans** *lieu* to end (up) in; *désordre* to result in, lead to; **j'aboutis à 12 F** I get (it to come to) 12 francs; **il n'aboutira jamais à rien** he'll never get anywhere; **ça n'a abouti à rien** it has come to nothing. ◆ **aboutissement** *nm (résultat)* outcome; *(succès)* success.

aboyer [abwaje] **(8)** *vi* to bark; *(péj: crier)* to shout, yell (*après* at).

abracadabrant, e [abʀakadabʀɑ̃, ɑ̃t] *adj* incredible, preposterous.

abrasif, -ive [abʀazif, iv] *adj, nm* abrasive.

abréger [abʀeʒe] **(3)** *et* **(6)** *vt (gén)* to shorten; *souffrances, visite* to cut short; *texte* to abridge; *mot* to abbreviate. **abrège!** * come *ou* get to the point! ◆ **abrégé** *nm* summary. **faire un ~ de** to summarize; **en** ~ *(en miniature)* in miniature; *(en bref)* in brief.

abreuver [abʀœve] **(1)** **1** *vt animal* to water. *(fig)* ~ **qn de** to overwhelm *ou* shower sb with; **terre abreuvée d'eau** waterlogged ground. **2 s'** ~ *vpr* to drink. ◆ **abreuvoir** *nm (mare)* watering place; *(récipient)* drinking trough.

abréviation [abʀevjɑsjɔ̃] *nf* abbreviation.

abri [abʀi] *nm (cabane)* shelter; *(fig)* refuge (*contre* from). ~ **à vélos** bicycle shed; *(hum)* **tous aux ~s!** take cover!; **mettre à l'** ~ *(des intempéries)* to put under cover; *(du vol, de la curiosité)* to put in a safe place; **se mettre à l'** ~ to shelter (*de* from); *(de regards)* to hide (*de* from); *(de soupçons)* to shield o.s. (*de* from); **c'est à l'** ~ *(de la pluie)* it's under shelter; *(du vol)* it's in a safe place; **à l' ~ du mur** sheltered by the wall; **à l' ~ du besoin** free from financial worries; **je ne suis pas à l' ~ d'une erreur** I'm not beyond making a mistake.

abribus [abʀibys] *nm* bus shelter.

abricot [abʀiko] *nm, adj inv* apricot. ◆ **abricotier** *nm* apricot tree.

abriter [abʀite] **(1)** **1** *vt (pluie, vent)* to shelter (*de* from); *(radiations)* to screen (*de* from). **le bâtiment peut ~ 20 personnes** the building can accommodate 20 people. **2 s'** ~ *vpr* to (take) shelter (*de* from). **s' ~ derrière le règlement** to take cover behind the rules.

abrogation [abʀɔgɑsjɔ̃] *nf* repeal, abrogation. ◆ **abroger** **(3)** *vt* to repeal, abrogate.

abrupt, e [abʀypt, pt(ə)] **1** *adj pente* abrupt, steep; *falaise* sheer; *personne* abrupt. **2** *nm* steep slope. ◆ **abruptement** *adv* steeply; abruptly.

abrutir [abʀytiʀ] **(2)** *vt*: ~ **qn** to make sb stupid; ~ **qn de** to drive sb stupid with; **abruti par l'alcool** stupefied with drink; **abruti de travail** dazed with work. ◆ **abruti, e** ⁑ *nm, f* idiot *, moron ⁑. ◆ **abrutissant, e** *adj bruit* stunning; *travail* mind-destroying. ◆ **abrutissement** *nm (fatigue)* exhaustion; *(abêtissement)* moronic state. **l' ~ des**

masses par la télévision the stupefying effect of television on the masses.

absence [apsɑ̃s] *nf [personne, objet]* absence; *[sentiment]* lack (*de* of). **il constata l' ~ de sa valise** he noticed that his case was missing; ~ **(de mémoire)** mental blank; **en l' ~ de** in the absence of.

absent, e [apsɑ̃, ɑ̃t] **1** *adj* (**a**) *(gén)* away (*de* from); *(malade)* absent (*de* from). **conférence dont la France était ~e** conference from which France was absent. (**b**) *sentiment* lacking; *objet* missing. **toute émotion était ~e** there was no trace of emotion. (**c**) *(distrait) air* vacant. **2** *nm, f (gén)* absent person; *(Scol, Admin)* absentee; *(disparu)* missing person. **le grand ~ de la réunion** the most notable absentee at the meeting. ◆ **absentéisme** *nm* absenteeism. ◆ **absentéiste** *nmf* absentee. *(gén)* **c'est un ~** he is always absent. ◆ **absenter (s')** (1) *vpr (gén)* to go out. **s' ~ de** *pièce* to go out of; *ville* to leave; **elle s'absente souvent de son travail** she is frequently away from work.

abside [apsid] *nf* apse.

absinthe [apsɛ̃t] *nf* absinth(e).

absolu, e [apsɔly] **1** *adj* (**a**) *(gén, Ling, Pol)* absolute. **en cas d' ~e nécessité** if absolutely essential; **règle ~e** hard-and-fast rule. (**b**) *ton* peremptory; *jugement* rigid. **2** *nm*: **l'** ~ the absolute. ◆ **absolument** *adv (gén)* absolutely. **avoir ~ tort** to be quite *ou* absolutely wrong; ~ **pas!** certainly not!

absolution [apsɔlysjɔ̃] *nf (Rel)* absolution (*de* from). **donner l' ~ à qn** to give sb absolution.

absolutisme [apsɔlytism(ə)] *nm* absolutism.

absorber [apsɔʀbe] (1) *vt* (**a**) *aliment* to take; *parti, bruit, dette* to absorb; *firme* to take over; *liquide* to absorb, soak up; *tache* to remove. (**b**) *attention, temps* to occupy, take up. **s' ~/être absorbé dans une lecture** to become/be absorbed in reading. ◆ **absorbant, e** **1** *adj matière* absorbent; *tâche* absorbing; *(Bio)* absorptive. **2** *nm* absorbent. ◆ **absorption** *nf* (**a**) taking; absorption; takeover; removal. (**b**) *(méditation)* absorption.

absoudre [apsudʀ(ə)] (51) *vt* to absolve (*de* from).

abstenir (s') [apstəniʀ] (22) *vpr* (**a**) **s' ~ de qch/de faire** to refrain *ou* abstain from sth/from doing; **je préfère m' ~** I'd rather not. (**b**) *(Pol)* to abstain (*de voter* from voting). ◆ **abstention** *nf* abstention. ◆ **abstentionnisme** *nm* abstaining, nonvoting. ◆ **abstentionniste** *adj, nmf* abstainer, non-voter.

abstinence [apstinɑ̃s] *nf* abstinence. **faire ~** to refrain from eating meat. ◆ **abstinent, e** *adj* abstinent.

abstraction [apstʀaksjɔ̃] *nf* abstraction. **faire ~ de** to leave aside, disregard.

abstraire [apstʀɛʀ] (50) **1** *vt* to abstract (*de* from). **2 s' ~** *vpr* to cut o.s. off (*de* from). ◆ **abstrait, e** *adj* abstract. **dans l' ~** in the abstract; **l'(art) ~** abstract art. ◆ **abstraitement** *adv* abstractly, in the abstract.

absurde [apsyʀd(ə)] *adj* absurd. ◆ **absurdité** *nf* absurdity.

abus [aby] *nm (gén)* abuse. **faire ~ de** *force* to abuse. **l' ~ qu'il fait d'aspirine** his excessive use *ou* overuse of aspirin; **nous avons fait des** *ou* **quelques ~ hier soir** we overdid it last night; **il y a de l' ~!** * that's going a bit too far! *; ~ **de pouvoir** abuse *ou* misuse of power.

abuser [abyze] (1) **1 ~ de** *vt indir* (**a**) *situation, victime* to take advantage of; *autorité, hospitalité* to abuse. **je ne veux pas ~ de votre temps/gentillesse** I don't want to waste your time/to impose on your kindness; **tu abuses!** you're going too far! (**b**) *(user avec excès) médicaments* to overuse; *ses forces* to overtax; *plaisirs* to overindulge in. ~ **de l'alcool** to drink to excess. **2** *vt [escroc]* to deceive; *[ressemblance]* to mislead. **3 s' ~** *vpr (erreur)* to be mistaken; *(illusions)* to delude o.s.

abusif, -ive [abyzif, iv] *adj pratique* improper; *mère* over-possessive; *prix, punition* excessive. **usage ~ de** improper use *ou* misuse of; **c'est ~ de dire** it's putting it a bit strongly to say. ◆ **abusivement** *adv* improperly; excessively.

acabit [akabi] *nm (péj)* sort, type. **être du même ~** to be cast in the same mould.

acacia [akasja] *nm* acacia.

académie [akademi] *nf* (**a**) *(société savante)* learned society; *(Antiq)* academy. *(officielle)* **A~** Academy; *(école)* ~ **de dessin** art school, academy of art. (**b**) *(Univ)* ≃ regional education authority, school district *(US)*. ◆ **académicien, -ienne** *nm, f (gén)* academician; *(Antiq)* academic. ◆ **académique** *adj (gén, péj)* academic; *[Académie française]* of the French Academy; *(Univ)* ≃ of the regional education authority. *(Belgique, Can, Suisse)* **année ~** academic year.

Acadie [akadi] *nf*: **l' ~** the Maritime Provinces.

acajou [akaʒu] *nm, adj inv* mahogany.

acariâtre [akaʀjɑtʀ(ə)] *adj caractère* sour, cantankerous; *femme* shrewish. **d'humeur ~** sour-tempered.

accabler [akɑble] (1) *vt* (**a**) *(gén)* to overwhelm. **accablé sous le nombre** overwhelmed *ou* overpowered by numbers; **sa déposition m'accable** his evidence is overwhelmingly against me. (**b**) ~ **qn de** *critiques* to heap on sb; *impôts, travail* to overburden sb with; *questions, conseils* to overwhelm sb with. ◆ **accablant, e** *adj chaleur, travail* exhausting; *témoignage, responsabilité* overwhelming; *douleur* excruciating. ◆ **accablement** *nm (abattement)* despondency; *(fatigue)* exhaustion.

accalmie [akalmi] *nf (gén)* lull (*de* in); *[fièvre]* respite (*dans* in); *[affaires]* slack period.

accaparer [akapaʀe] (1) *vt pouvoir, conversation, hôte* to monopolize; *temps, attention* to take up. **les enfants l'accaparent** the children take up all her time (and energy). ◆ **accaparant, e** *adj* all-absorbing, demanding. ◆ **accaparement** *nm [pouvoir, production]* monopolizing; *[médecin etc]* involvement (*par* in). ◆ **accapareur, -euse** **1** *adj* monopolistic. **2** *nm, f* monopolizer.

accéder [aksede] (6) **~ à** *vt indir* (**a**) *lieu* to reach, get to; *honneur, indépendance, pouvoir* to attain; *grade* to rise to; *responsabilité* to accede to. (**b**) *prière* to grant; *demande* to accommodate, comply with.

accélérer [akseleʀe] (6) **1** *vt* to speed up. **2** *vi (Aut, fig)* to accelerate, speed up. **accélère!** * get a move on! * **3 s' ~** *vpr [pouls]* to quicken. ◆ **accélérateur** *nm* accelerator. ◆ **accélération** *nf* acceleration, speeding up; quickening.

accent [aksɑ̃] *nm* (**a**) *(prononciation)* accent. (**b**) *(Orthographe)* accent. **e ~ grave/aigu** e grave/acute; ~ **circonflexe** circumflex (accent). (**c**) *(Phonétique)* accent, stress; *(fig)* stress, emphasis. **mettre l' ~ sur** to stress. (**d**) *(inflexion)* tone (of voice). ~ **plaintif** plaintive tone; ~ **de sincérité** note of sincerity; **~s de rage/d'amour** accents of rage/of love; **les ~s de cette musique** the strains of this music.

accentuer [aksɑ̃tɥe] (1) **1** *vt* (**a**) *lettre* to accent; *syllabe* to stress. (**b**) *contraste* to emphasize, accentuate; *goût* to bring out; *effort* to intensify. **2 s' ~** *vpr [tendance, traits]* to become more marked *ou* pronounced; *[inflation]* to become more pronounced *ou* acute. ◆ **accentuation** *nf* accentuation; stressing; emphasizing; intensification. *(Phonétique)* **les règles de l' ~** the rules of stress.

accepter [aksɛpte] (1) *vt (gén, Comm)* to accept; *condition* to agree to, accept. ~ **de faire** to agree to do; **elle accepte tout de sa fille** she puts up with anything from her daughter. ◆ **acceptable** *adj* *travail* satisfactory, fair; *repas* reasonable; *condition* acceptable. ◆ **acceptation** *nf (gén)* acceptance.

acception [aksɛpsjɔ̃] *nf* meaning, sense.

accès [aksɛ] *nm* (**a**) *(action d'entrer)* access; *(porte)* entrance. **interdire l' ~ de qch** to bar entry *ou* prevent access to sth; **~ interdit** no entry, no admittance; **d' ~ facile** *lieu* (easily) accessible; *personne* approachable; *manuel* easily understood; **tous les ~ de la ville** all approaches to the town; **donner/avoir ~ à** to give/have access to. (**b**) *[colère, toux, folie]* fit; *[fièvre]* attack, bout; *[enthousiasme]* burst.

accessible [aksesibl(ə)] *adj lieu* accessible (*à* to); *personne* approachable; *but* attainable. **~ à tous** *(financièrement)* within everyone's pocket; *(intellectuellement)* within the reach of everyone.

accession [aksɛsjɔ̃] *nf*: **~ à** *pouvoir* accession to; *indépendance* attainment of; *rang* rise to; *requête, désir* granting of, compliance with. **mouvement d'~ à la propriété** trend towards home ownership.

accessit [aksesit] *nm (Scol)* ≃ certificate of merit.

accessoire [akseswaʀ] **1** *adj (gén)* secondary, incidental. **2** *nm* (**a**) *(Théât)* prop; *(Aut)* accessory. **~s de toilette** toilet requisites. (**b**) *(Philos)* **l' ~** the unessential. ◆ **accessoirement** *adv* secondarily, incidentally; *(si besoin est)* if need be, if necessary. ◆ **accessoiriste** *nm f* property man (*ou* girl).

accident [aksidɑ̃] *nm* (**a**) *(gén, Philos)* accident; *(Aut, Aviat)* crash; *(Méd)* illness, trouble; *(fig: revers)* setback. *(Admin)* **il n'y a pas eu d' ~ de personnes** there were no casualties, no one was injured; **les ~s de la vie** life's ups and downs, life's trials; *(hasard)* **par ~** by chance, by accident. (**b**) **~ de parcours** chance mishap; **~ de terrain** undulation; **~ de travail** industrial injury. ◆ **accidenté, e** **1** *adj* (**a**) *région* undulating; *terrain* uneven; *vie, carrière* eventful. (**b**) *véhicule* damaged. **2** *nm, f* casualty, injured person. ◆ **accidentel, -elle** *adj (gén)* accidental. ◆ **accidentellement** *adv* (**a**) *(par hasard)* accidentally, by accident *ou* chance. (**b**) *mourir* in an accident. ◆ **accidenter** (1) *vt personne* to injure, hurt; *véhicule* to damage.

acclamer [aklame] (1) *vt* to cheer, acclaim. ◆ **acclamation** *nf*: **~s** cheers; **par ~** by acclamation.

acclimater [aklimate] (1) **1** *vt (Bot, Zool)* to acclimatize. **2 s' ~** *vpr* to become acclimatized (*à* to). ◆ **acclimatation** *nf* acclimatization.

accointances [akwɛ̃tɑ̃s] *nfpl* contacts, links.

accolade [akɔlad] *nf* (**a**) *(protocolaire)* embrace; *(Hist)* accolade. **donner l' ~** to embrace. (**b**) *(Typ)* brace. **mots (mis) en ~** words bracketed together. ◆ **accoler** (1) *vt (gén)* to place side by side; *(Typ)* to bracket together.

accommoder [akɔmɔde] (1) **1** *vt* (**a**) *plat* to prepare (*à* in, with). (**b**) *(combiner)* to combine; *(adapter)* to adapt; *(†: arranger)* to arrange. **2** *vi (Opt)* to focus (*sur* on). **3 s' ~** *vpr*: **s' ~ de** to put up with; **elle s'accommode de tout** she can make do with anything; *(littér)* **s' ~ à qch** to adapt to sth; **s' ~ avec qn** to come to an arrangement with sb (*sur* about). ◆ **accommodant, e** *adj* accommodating. ◆ **accommodation** *nf (Opt)* accommodation; *(adaptation)* adaptation. ◆ **accommodement** *nm* arrangement.

accompagner [akɔ̃paɲe] (1) *vt (gén)* to accompany. **~ un enfant à l'école** to take a child to school; **~ qn chez lui** to see sb home; **il s'était fait ~ de sa mère** he had got his mother to go with him *ou* to accompany him; **tous nos vœux vous accompagnent** all our good wishes go with you; **il s'accompagna à la guitare** he accompanied himself on the guitar; **du chou accompagnait le rôti** cabbage was served with the roast. ◆ **accompagnateur, -trice** *nm, f (Mus)* accompanist; *(guide)* guide; *(Scol)* accompanying adult; *(Tourisme)* courier. ◆ **accompagnement** *nm* (**a**) *(Mus)* accompaniment. **sans ~** unaccompanied. (**b**) *(Culin)* accompanying vegetables.

accomplir [akɔ̃pliʀ] (2) *vt promesse* to fulfil, carry out; *mission, tâche* to perform, carry out, accomplish; *exploit* to perform, achieve; *apprentissage (faire)* to do; *(terminer)* to complete. **la volonté de Dieu s'est accomplie** God's will was done. ◆ **accompli, e** *adj (expérimenté)* accomplished. ◆ **accomplissement** *nm* fulfilment; accomplishment; completion.

accord [akɔʀ] *nm* (**a**) *(gén, Gram)* agreement; *(harmonie)* harmony. **le bon ~ règne** harmony reigns; **~ à l'amiable** informal *ou* amicable agreement; **~ de principe** agreement in principle ; **~ salarial** wage settlement; **en ~ avec le paysage** in harmony *ou* in keeping with the landscape. (**b**) *(Mus) (notes)* chord. **~ parfait** triad; **~ de tierce** third. (**c**) **être d' ~** to agree, be in agreement; **se mettre d' ~ avec qn** to agree *ou* come to an agreement with sb; **mettre 2 personnes d' ~** to make 2 people come to an agreement with each other; **c'est d' ~ (pour demain)** it's agreed *ou* all right *ou* O.K. * (for tomorrow).

accordéon [akɔʀdeɔ̃] *nm* accordion. **en ~** * *voiture* crumpled; *pantalon* wrinkled. ◆ **accordéoniste** *nmf* accordionist.

accorder [akɔʀde] (1) **1** *vt* (**a**) *(gén)* to give, grant; *pension* to award (*à* to). **~ à qn que** to admit (to sb) that; **je vous l'accorde** I'll grant you that; **~ de la valeur à qch** to attach value to sth, value sth. (**b**) *(harmoniser) couleurs* to match; *(Mus)* to tune. *(fig)* **ils ont accordé leurs violons** they agreed on the line to take; *(Gram)* **(faire) ~ un verbe/un adjectif** to make a verb/an adjective agree (*avec* with). **2 s' ~** *vpr* (**a**) *(être d'accord)* to agree. **ils s'accordent pour dire que le film est mauvais** they agree that it's a poor film; **(bien/mal) s' ~ avec qn** to get on (well/badly) with sb. (**b**) *[couleurs]* to match; *[opinions]* to agree; *[caractères]* to be in harmony. **ses actions s'accordent avec ses opinions** his actions are in keeping with his opinions. (**c**) *(Ling)* to agree (*avec* with). ◆ **accordeur** *nm (Mus)* tuner.

accorte [akɔʀt(ə)] *adj f (hum)* winsome.

accoster [akɔste] (1) *vt personne* to accost; *(Naut)* to come alongside; *(emploi absolu)* to berth.

accotement [akɔtmɑ̃] *nm (Aut)* shoulder, verge, berm *(US)*; *(Rail)* shoulder. **~ non stabilisé** soft verge *ou* shoulder *(US)*.

accoter [akɔte] (1) *vt* to lean, rest (*contre* against, *sur* on). **s' ~ à** *ou* **contre** to lean against.

accoucher [akuʃe] (1) **1** *vt*: **~ qn** to deliver sb's baby. **2** *vi* (**a**) *(être en travail)* to be in labour; *(donner naissance)* to give birth. **~ d'un garçon** to give birth to a boy, have a (baby) boy. (**b**) *(fig hum)* **~ de** *roman* to bring forth; **accouche!** ⁑ spit it out! * ◆ **accouchée** *nf* (new) mother. ◆ **accouchement** *nm* delivery. **~ prématuré** premature birth; **~ sans douleur** painless childbirth. ◆ **accoucheur, -euse** **1** *nm, f*: **(médecin) ~** obstetrician. **2** *nf (sage-femme)* midwife.

accouder (s') [akude] (1) *vpr* to lean (on one's elbows) (*sur* on). ◆ **accoudoir** *nm* armrest.

accoupler [akuple] (1) **1** *vt* (**a**) *bœufs* to yoke; *(Tech)* to couple, connect (up) (*à* to); *(fig) mots* to link. (**b**) *(faire copuler)* to mate (*à, avec, et* with). **2 s' ~** *vpr* to mate. ◆ **accouplement** *nm* yoking; coupling; connecting (up); linking; mating.

accourir [akuʀiʀ] (11) *vi (lit)* to rush up, hurry (*à, vers* to).

accoutrement [akutʀəmɑ̃] *nm (péj)* getup *. ◆ **accoutrer** (1) **1** *vt (péj)* to get up * (*de* in). **2 s' ~** *vpr* to get o.s. up * (*de* in).

accoutumer [akutyme] (1) *vt*: ~ **qn à qch/à faire** to accustom sb *ou* get sb used to sth/to doing; **s'** ~ **à faire** to get used *ou* accustomed to doing. ◆ **accoutumance** *nf (habitude)* habituation (*à* to); *(besoin)* addiction (*à* to). ◆ **accoutumé, e** *adj* usual. **comme à l'** ~**e** as usual.

accréditer [akʀedite] (1) **1** *vt rumeur* to substantiate; *personne* to accredit (*auprès de* to). **2 s'** ~ *vpr [rumeur]* to gain ground.

accroc [akʀo] *nm* (**a**) *[tissu]* tear; *[réputation]* blot (*à* on); *[règle]* breach (*à* of). **faire un** ~ **à** *règle* to twist; *tissu* to tear. (**b**) *(anicroche)* hitch. **sans** ~**s** without a hitch, smoothly.

accrochage [akʀɔʃaʒ] *nm (Aut)* collision; *(Mil)* engagement; *(Boxe)* clinch; *(dispute)* clash.

accrocher [akʀɔʃe] (1) **1** *vt* (**a**) *tableau* to hang (up) (*à* on); *wagons* to couple (*à* to). ~ **un ver à l'hameçon** to put a worm on the hook. (**b**) *(accident) jupe* to catch (*à* on); *voiture* to bump into; *piéton* to hit; *assiette* to knock. (**c**) *(*: fig) occasion* to get; *personne* to get hold of; *mots* to catch; *client* to attract. ~ **le regard** to catch the eye. (**d**) *(Mil)* to engage; *(Boxe)* to clinch. **2** *vi* (**a**) *[fermeture éclair]* to jam; *[pourparlers]* to come up against a hitch. **cette planche accroche** this board catches on the cloth. (**b**) *(plaire) [slogan]* to catch on. **3 s'** ~ *vpr* (**a**) *(se cramponner)* to hang on. **s'** ~ **à** *branche, espoir* to cling to. (**b**) (*) *[malade]* to cling on; *[étudiant]* to stick at it; *[importun]* to cling. (**c**) *[voitures]* to bump (each other); *(Boxe)* to get into a clinch; *(Mil)* to engage; *(se disputer)* to have a clash (*avec* with). ◆ **accrocheur, -euse** *adj concurrent* tenacious; *affiche* eye-catching; *slogan* catchy.

accroire [akʀwaʀ] (44) *vt*: **faire** ~ **à qn qch/que** to delude sb into believing sth/that.

accroître *vt*, **s'**~ *vpr* [akʀwatʀ(ə)] (55) to increase. ◆ **accroissement** *nm (gén)* increase (*de* in); *[production]* growth (*de* in).

accroupir (s') [akʀupiʀ] (2) *vpr* to squat *ou* crouch (down). ◆ **accroupi, e** *adj* squatting *ou* crouching (down).

accu * [aky] *nm (Aut etc)* battery. *(fig)* **recharger ses** ~**s** to recharge one's batteries.

accueil [akœj] *nm (gén)* welcome, reception; *[sinistrés, idée]* reception; *(logement)* accommodation. **faire bon** ~ **à** to welcome; **faire mauvais** ~ **à** to receive badly. ◆ **accueillant, e** *adj* welcoming, friendly. ◆ **accueillir** (12) *vt* (**a**) *(aller chercher)* to collect; *(recevoir)* to welcome; *(pouvoir héberger)* to accommodate. **bien/mal** ~ **qn** to give sb a warm/bad reception; ~ **par des huées** to greet with jeers. (**b**) *nouvelle* to receive.

acculer [akyle] (1) *vt*: ~ **qn à** *mur* to drive sb back against; *ruine* to drive sb to the brink of; *choix* to force sb into; ~ **qn dans** *pièce* to corner sb in; *(lit, fig)* **nous sommes acculés** we're cornered.

accumuler [akymyle] (1) **1** *vt (gén)* to accumulate; *marchandises* to stockpile; *énergie* to store. *(Fin)* **les intérêts accumulés pendant un an** the interest accrued over a year. **2 s'** ~ *vpr* to accumulate; *(Fin)* to accrue. ◆ **accumulateur** *nm* accumulator, battery. ◆ **accumulation** *nf* accumulation; stockpiling; storage; *(tas)* accumulation.

accusateur, -trice [akyzatœʀ, tʀis] **1** *adj regard* accusing; *preuves* incriminating. **2** *nm, f* accuser.

accusatif [akyzatif] *nm (Ling)* accusative case.

accusation [akyzɑsjɔ̃] *nf (gén)* accusation; *(Jur)* charge. *(le procureur etc)* **l'** ~ the prosecution; **mettre en** ~ to indict; **mise en** ~ indictment.

accuser [akyze] (1) **1** *vt* (**a**) *(gén)* to accuse (*de* of); *(blâmer)* to blame (*de* for). *(Jur)* ~ **de** to accuse of, charge with; **tout l'accuse** everything points to his guilt; ~ **qn d'incompétence** to blame sb for his incompetence. (**b**) *forme, contraste* to emphasize; *âge, fatigue* to show. *(lit, fig)* ~ **le coup** to stagger under the blow; ~ **réception** to acknowledge receipt (*de* of). **2 s'** ~ *vpr* (**a**) **s'** ~ **de qch/d'avoir fait** *[coupable]* to admit to sth/to having done; *[responsable]* to blame o.s. for sth/for having done. (**b**) *[tendance]* to become more marked. ◆ **accusé, e 1** *adj (marqué)* marked. **2** *nm, f* accused; *[procès]* defendant. ~ **levez-vous!** ≃ the defendant will rise. **3** : ~ **de réception** acknowledgement of receipt.

ace [ɛs] *nm (Tennis)* ace.

acerbe [asɛʀb(ə)] *adj* caustic, acid.

acéré, e [aseʀe] *adj pointe* sharp; *raillerie* scathing, cutting.

acétate [asetat] *nm* acetate.

acétique [asetik] *adj* acetic.

acétone [asetɔn] *nf* acetone.

acétylène [asetilɛn] *nm* acetylene.

achalandé, e [aʃalɑ̃de] *adj*: **bien** ~ *[denrées]* well-stocked; *[clients]* well-patronized.

acharné, e [aʃaʀne] *adj combat, adversaire* fierce; *efforts, poursuivant, travailleur* relentless. ~ **à qch/à faire** bent on sth/on doing; ~ **contre** set against. ◆ **acharnement** *nm [combattant]* fierceness; *[poursuivant]* relentlessness; *[travailleur]* determination. **avec** ~ *poursuivre, travailler* relentlessly; *combattre, résister* fiercely. ◆ **acharner (s')** (1) *vpr*: **s'** ~ **sur** *ou* **contre qn** *[malchance]* to dog sb; *[adversaire]* to set o.s. against sb; **je m'acharne à le leur faire comprendre** I'm desperately trying to explain it to them; **il s'acharne inutilement** he's wasting his efforts.

achat [aʃa] *nm* (**a**) purchase. **faire l'** ~ **de qch** to purchase *ou* buy sth; **faire des** ~**s** to shop, go shopping; **c'est cher à l'** ~ it's expensive to buy; ~ **judicieux** wise buy. (**b**) *(Bourse, Comm)* buying. **la livre vaut 11 F à l'** ~ the buying rate for sterling is 11 francs.

acheminer [aʃmine] (1) **1** *vt colis* to dispatch (*vers* to); *troupes* to convey, transport (*vers* to); *trains* to route (*vers* to). *(fig)* ~ **le pays vers la ruine** to lead the country to ruin. **2 s'** ~ *vpr*: **s'** ~ **vers** *lieu, ruine* to head for; *solution* to move towards. ◆ **acheminement** *nm* dispatch; conveying, transporting; routing. *(Comm)* ~ **de marchandises** carriage of goods.

acheter [aʃte] (5) *vt* (**a**) to buy, purchase (*au vendeur* from the seller; *pour qn* for sb). **je lui ai acheté une robe** I bought her a dress; ~ **qch d'occasion** to buy sth second-hand; ~ **en grosses quantités** to bulk-buy; **(s')** ~ **une conduite** to mend one's ways. (**b**) *(péj) vote* to buy; *juge* to bribe. ◆ **acheteur, -euse** *nm, f* buyer; *(Jur)* vendee; *(profession)* buyer. **il est** ~ he wants to buy it; **la foule des** ~**s** the crowd of shoppers.

achever [aʃve] (5) **1** *vt* (**a**) *discours, repas* to finish, end; *tâche* to complete, finish. ~ **(de parler)** to finish (speaking); **cette remarque acheva de l'exaspérer** this remark really brought his irritation to a head. (**b**) *blessé* to finish off; *cheval* to destroy. **ça m'a achevé!** it was the end of me! **2 s'** ~ *vpr (se terminer)* to end (*par, sur* with); *[jour, vie]* to come to an end, draw to a close. ◆ **achevé, e** *adj canaille* downright, thorough; *artiste* accomplished; *art* perfect. **d'un ridicule** ~ perfectly ridiculous. ◆ **achèvement** *nm [travaux]* completion.

achopper [aʃɔpe] (1) *vi*: ~ **sur** to stumble over.

acide [asid] **1** *adj (lit, fig)* acid, sharp, tart; *(Chim)* acid. **2** *nm* (**a**) acid. (**b**) (*: *LSD*) acid *. ◆ **acidité** *nf (lit, fig)* acidity. ◆ **acidulé, e** *adj goût* slightly acid.

acier [asje] *nm* steel. **d'** ~ *poutre* steel, of steel; *regard* steely. ◆ **aciérie** *nf* steelworks.

acné [akne] *nf* acne. ~ **juvénile** teenage acne.

acolyte [akɔlit] *nm (péj)* confederate, associate.

acompte [akɔ̃t] *nm (arrhes)* deposit; *(sur somme due)* down payment; *(régulier)* instalment; *(sur salaire)* advance.

acoquiner (s') [akɔkine] (1) *vpr (péj)* to team up (*avec* with).

à-côté [akote] *nm [problème]* side issue; *[situation]* side aspect; *(argent)* extra.

à-coup [aku] *nm [moteur]* hiccough; *[machine, économie]* jolt. **par ~s** in fits and starts; **sans ~s** smoothly.

acoustique [akustik] **1** *adj* acoustic. **2** *nf (science)* acoustics *(sg)*; *(sonorité)* acoustics *(pl)*.

acquérir [akeʀiʀ] (21) *vt objet* to acquire, purchase, buy; *célébrité* to win; *habileté, valeur, expérience* to acquire, gain. ~ **la certitude de** to become certain of; **ça s'acquiert facilement** it's easy to pick up; ~ **la preuve de** to gain proof of. ◆ **acquéreur** *nm* buyer, purchaser. **se rendre ~ de qch** to purchase *ou* buy sth.

acquiescer [akjese] (3) *vi (approuver)* to approve, agree; *(de la tête)* to nod (one's approval *ou* agreement); *(consentir)* to acquiesce, assent (*à* to). ◆ **acquiescement** *nm* approval, agreement; acquiescence, assent.

acquis, e [aki, iz] **1** *adj droit, caractères* acquired; *fait* established. **tenir pour ~** *(normal)* to take for granted; *(décidé)* to take as settled; **être ~ à un projet** to be in complete support of a plan. **2** *nm (savoir)* experience. **la connaissance de l'anglais représente un ~ précieux** knowledge of English is a valuable asset. ◆ **acquisition** *nf* acquisition; *(par achat)* purchase.

acquit [aki] *nm (Comm)* receipt. **par ~ de conscience** to set one's mind at rest.

acquitter [akite] (1) **1** *vt* (**a**) *accusé* to acquit. (**b**) *impôt, facture* to pay; *(Comm)* to receipt. ~ **qn de** to release sb from. **2 s'** ~ *vpr*: **s' ~ de** *dette, obligation, devoir* to discharge; *promesse, fonction* to fulfil, carry out; **comment m' ~ (envers vous)?** how can I ever repay you? (*de* for). ◆ **acquittement** *nm* acquittal; payment; discharge; fulfilment.

acre [akʀ(ə)] *nf (Hist)* ≃ acre.

âcre [ɑkʀ(ə)] *adj* acrid, pungent. ◆ **âcreté** *nf* acridity, pungency.

acrimonie [akʀimɔni] *nf* acrimony.

acrobate [akʀɔbat] *nmf (lit, fig)* acrobat. ◆ **acrobatie** *nf (tour)* acrobatic feat; *(art, fig)* acrobatics *(sg)*. ~ **aérienne** aerobatics; *(lit, fig)* **faire des ~s** to perform acrobatics. ◆ **acrobatique** *adj (lit, fig)* acrobatic.

Acropole [akʀɔpɔl] *nf*: **l'** ~ the Acropolis.

acte [akt(ə)] **1** *nm* (**a**) *(action)* act. ~ **réflexe** reflex action; **des ~s!** let's have some action!; **il faut passer aux ~s** we must act *ou* take action; ~ **de bravoure** act of bravery, brave act *ou* action. (**b**) *(Jur) [notaire]* deed; *[état civil]* certificate; *(Théât, fig)* act. *[congrès etc]* **~s** proceedings. (**c**) **donner ~ de qch** to acknowledge sth formally; **faire ~ de citoyen** to act *ou* behave as a citizen; **faire ~ de clémence** to show mercy; **faire ~ de candidature** to apply; **faire ~ de présence** to put in a token appearance; **prendre ~ de** to note, take note of. **2** : ~ **d'accusation** bill of indictment; **les A~s des Apôtres** the Acts of the Apostles; ~ **de foi** act of faith; ~ **gratuit** gratuitous act; ~ **médical** (medical) consultation; ~ **de naissance** birth certificate; ~ **de vente** bill of sale.

acteur [aktœʀ] *nm (Théât, fig)* actor; *V* **actrice**.

actif, -ive [aktif, iv] **1** *adj (gén, Ling)* active; *population* working; *(Bourse) marché* buoyant; *armée* regular. **prendre une part active à qch** to take an active part in sth. **2** *nm* (**a**) *(Ling)* active (voice). (**b**) *(Fin)* assets; *[succession]* credits. **c'est à mettre à son ~** it is a point in his favour; **plusieurs crimes à son ~** several crimes to his name. (**c**) *(qui travaille)* person in active *ou* working life. **3** *nf* regular army.

action [aksjɔ̃] *nf* (**a**) *(acte)* action, act. **bonne ~** good deed; ~ **d'éclat** brilliant feat *ou* deed; **commettre une mauvaise ~** to behave badly. (**b**) *(activité)* action. **passer à l' ~** to take action; *(Mil)* to go into action; **entrer en ~** *[troupes, canon]* to go into action; **mettre en ~** *plan* to put into action; *dispositif* to put into operation. (**c**) *(effet)* action. **sans ~** ineffective; **sous l' ~ de** under the action of. (**d**) *(Théât) (mouvement)* action; *(intrigue)* plot. **film d' ~** action film; **roman d' ~** action-packed novel. (**e**) *(Jur)* action (at law). (**f**) *(Fin)* share. **~s** shares, stocks; **société par ~s** (joint) stock company; ~ **de chasse** hunting rights ; *(fig)* **ses ~s sont en baisse** things are not looking so good for him. (**g**) *(Rel)* ~ **de grâce(s)** thanksgiving.

actionnaire [aksjɔnɛʀ] *nmf* shareholder.

actionner [aksjɔne] (1) *vt mécanisme* to activate; *machine* to drive, work. **actionné par la vapeur** steam-powered. ◆ **actionnement** *nm* activation.

activation [aktivɑsjɔ̃] *nf (Chim, Phys)* activation; *(Bio)* initiation of development.

activement [aktivmɑ̃] *adv* actively.

activer [aktive] (1) **1** *vt travaux* to speed up; *feu* to stoke; *(Chim)* to activate. **2 s'** ~ *vpr (s'affairer)* to bustle about; *(*: se hâter)* to get a move on. **s' ~ à faire** to be busy doing.

activisme [aktivism(ə)] *nm* activism. ◆ **activiste** *adj, nmf* activist.

activité [aktivite] *nf (gén)* activity; *(emploi)* occupation; *[rue]* bustle. **être en ~** *[usine]* to be in operation; *[volcan]* to be active; *[fonctionnaire]* to be in active life; *(Scol)* **~s d'éveil** discovery; *(Scol)* **~s dirigées** class project work.

actrice [aktʀis] *nf (Théât, fig)* actress.

actualiser [aktɥalize] (1) *vt (mettre à jour)* to update, bring up to date. ◆ **actualisation** *nf* updating.

actualité [aktɥalite] *nf [sujet]* topicality. **d' ~** topical; *(événements)* **l' ~** current events; *(nouvelles)* **les ~s** the news *(sg)*. ◆ **actuel, -elle** *adj* (**a**) *(présent)* present. **à l'heure ~le** at the present time; **à l'époque ~le** nowadays; **le monde ~** the world today, the present-day world. (**b**) *(d'actualité)* topical. ◆ **actuellement** *adv* at present.

acuité [akɥite] *nf [son]* shrillness; *[sens, crise]* acuteness.

acupuncteur [akypɔ̃ktœʀ] *nm* acupuncturist. ◆ **acupuncture** *nf* acupuncture.

adage [adaʒ] *nm* adage.

adapter [adapte] (1) **1** *vt (gén)* to adapt (*à* to). *(Tech)* ~ **qch à** to fit sth to; **adapté à la situation** suited to the situation. **2 s'** ~ *vpr (gén)* to adapt (o.s.) (*à* to). *(Tech)* **s' ~ à** to fit. ◆ **adaptable** *adj* adaptable. ◆ **adaptateur, -trice** *nm, f* adapter. ◆ **adaptation** *nf* adaptation. **faire un effort d' ~** to try to adapt.

additionner [adisjɔne] (1) **1** *vt* to add up. ~ **qch à** to add sth to. **2 s'** ~ *vpr* to add up. ◆ **additif** *nm (clause)* rider; *(substance)* additive. **sans ~** additive-free. ◆ **addition** *nf (gén)* addition; *(facture)* bill, check *(US)*. **par ~ de** by adding, by the addition of.

adepte [adɛpt(ə)] *nmf* follower.

adéquat, e [adekwa, at] *adj* appropriate, suitable.

adhérence [adeʀɑ̃s] *nf (gén)* adhesion (*à* to); *[pneus]* grip (*à* on). *[voiture]* ~ **(à la route)** roadholding. ◆ **adhérent, e 1** *adj*: ~ **à** which sticks *ou* adheres to. **2** *nm, f* member, adherent.

adhérer [adeʀe] (6) ~ **à** *vt indir* (**a**) *(coller)* to stick to, adhere to. ~ **à la route** to grip the road. (**b**) *idée* to support. (**c**) *(s'inscrire)* to join; *(être inscrit)* to be a member of.

adhésif, -ive [adezif, iv] *adj, nm* adhesive.

adhésion [adezjɔ̃] *nf* (**a**) *(accord)* support (*à* for) adherence (*à* to). (**b**) *(inscription)* joining; *(fait d'être membre)* membership (*à* of).

adieu, *pl* **~x** [adjø] **1** *nm* farewell, goodbye. *(lit, fig)* **dire ~ à** to say goodbye to; **faire ses ~x (à qn)** to say one's farewells (to sb). **2** *excl* goodbye, cheerio *, farewell (†).

adipeux, -euse [adipø, øz] *adj (Anat)* adipose; *visage* fleshy.

adjacent, e [adʒasɑ̃, ɑ̃t] *adj* adjacent, adjoining. **~ à** adjacent to.

adjectif, -ive [adʒɛktif, iv] **1** *adj* adjectival. **2** *nm* adjective.

adjoindre [adʒwɛ̃dʀ(ə)] (49) *vt (gén)* to add; *mécanisme* to attach, affix (*à* to); *personne* to appoint (as an assistant) (*à* to). ◆ **adjoint, e** *adj, nm, f* assistant. **~ au maire** deputy mayor. ◆ **adjonction** *nf* addition; attaching; affixing; appointment.

adjudant [adʒydɑ̃] *nm* warrant officer.

adjudication [adʒydikɑsjɔ̃] *nf* (**a**) *(vente aux enchères)* sale by auction; *(marché administratif)* invitation to tender. **par (voie d') ~** by auction; by tender. (**b**) *(attribution) [contrat]* awarding (*à* to); *[meuble]* auctioning (*à* to).

adjuger [adʒyʒe] (3) *vt* (**a**) *(enchères)* to auction (*à* to). **adjugé, (vendu)!** going, going, gone!; **ceci fut adjugé pour 30 F** this went for 30 francs. (**b**) *récompense* to award; *(*: donner)* to give. **2 s' ~** *vpr (obtenir)* to win; *(s'approprier)* to take for o.s.

adjurer [adʒyʀe] (1) *vt*: **~ qn de faire** to implore *ou* beg sb to do. ◆ **adjuration** *nf* entreaty, plea.

admettre [admɛtʀ(ə)] (56) *vt* (**a**) *visiteur (faire entrer)* to admit, let in; *(autoriser)* to allow in; *(recevoir)* to receive. **il fut admis dans le salon** he was ushered *ou* shown into the drawing room. (**b**) *(accepter) excuses, attitude* to accept; *nouveau membre* to admit. **je n'admets pas cette conduite** I won't accept *ou* permit such behaviour; **c'est chose admise** it's an accepted *ou* acknowledged fact; **règle qui n'admet pas d'exception** rule which admits of *ou* allows of no exception; **se faire ~ dans un club** to gain admittance to a club. (**c**) *(reconnaître) erreur* to admit, acknowledge. **j'admets que vous avez raison** I admit *ou* acknowledge that you are right. (**d**) *(supposer)* to suppose, assume. **en admettant que** supposing *ou* assuming that. (**e**) *(Scol, Univ) (à un examen)* to pass; *(dans une classe)* to admit, accept. **il a été admis au concours** he passed *ou* got through the exam.

administrateur, -trice [administʀatœʀ, tʀis] *nm, f (gén)* administrator; *[entreprise]* director; *[fondation]* trustee.

administratif, -ive [administʀatif, iv] *adj* administrative. ◆ **administrativement** *adv* administratively.

administré, e [administʀe] *nm, f* ≃ citizen.

administrer [administʀe] (1) *vt* (**a**) *entreprise* to manage, run; *fondation, fortune* to administer; *pays* to run, govern. (**b**) *justice, remède* to administer; *coup* to deal; *preuve* to produce. ◆ **administration** *nf* (**a**) management; running; administration; government. (**b**) *(service public)* (sector of the) public services. **l'A~** ≃ the Civil Service; **l' ~ locale** local government; **être** *ou* **travailler dans l' ~** to work in the public services; **l' ~ des Impôts** the tax department.

admirable [admiʀabl(ə)] *adj* admirable. **être ~ de courage** to show admirable courage. ◆ **admirablement** *adv* admirably. ◆ **admirateur, -trice** *nm, f* admirer. ◆ **admiratif, -ive** *adj* admiring. ◆ **admiration** *nf* admiration. **faire l' ~ de qn** to fill sb with admiration; **en ~ devant qch** filled with admiration for sth. ◆ **admirativement** *adv* admiringly. ◆ **admirer** (1) *vt* to admire.

admis, e [admi, iz] *nm, f (Scol)* successful candidate. ◆ **admissibilité** *nf* eligibility (*à* for). ◆ **admissible 1** *adj conduite* acceptable; *postulant* eligible (*à* for). **2** *nmf* eligible candidate.

admission [admisjɔ̃] *nf* (**a**) *[club]* admission, entry (*à* to); *[école]* acceptance, entrance (*à* to). **demande d' ~** application (*à* to join); **le nombre des ~s au concours** the number of successful candidates in this exam. (**b**) *(Tech: introduction)* intake; *(Aut)* induction.

admonestation [admɔnɛstɑsjɔ̃] *nf* admonition. ◆ **admonester** (1) *vt* to admonish.

adolescence [adɔlesɑ̃s] *nf* adolescence. ◆ **adolescent, e** *nm, f* adolescent, teenager.

adonner (s') [adɔne] (1) *vpr*: **s' ~ à** *études* to devote o.s. to; *vice* to take to; **adonné au jeu** addicted to gambling.

adopter [adɔpte] (1) *vt (gén)* to adopt; *loi* to pass. ◆ **adoptif, -ive** *adj enfant* adopted; *parent* adoptive. ◆ **adoption** *nf* adoption; passing.

adorable [adɔʀabl(ə)] *adj personne* adorable, delightful; *chose* delightful. ◆ **adorablement** *adv* delightfully, adorably. ◆ **adorer** (1) *vt (gén)* to adore; *(Rel)* to worship. ◆ **adorateur, -trice** *nm, f (Rel, fig)* worshipper. ◆ **adoration** *nf* adoration; worship. **être en ~ devant** to worship.

adosser [adose] (1) **1** *vt*: **~ à qch** *meuble* to stand against sth; *bâtiment* to build against sth. **2 s' ~** *vpr:* **s' ~ à** *ou* **contre qch** *[personne]* to lean with one's back against sth.

adoucir [adusiʀ] (2) **1** *vt (gén, Tech)* to soften; *goût* to make milder; *(avec sucre)* to sweeten; *aspérités* to smooth out; *caractère* to mellow; *conditions pénibles* to ease. **pour ~ ses vieux jours** to comfort (him in) his old age; **pour ~ sa solitude** to ease his loneliness; **~ la température** to raise the temperature. **2 s' ~** *vpr [voix, couleur, peau]* to soften; *[caractère]* to mellow; *[température]* to get milder; *[pente]* to become gentler. ◆ **adoucissement** *nm* softening; sweetening; smoothing-out; mellowing; easing. **un ~ de la température** a spell of milder weather. ◆ **adoucisseur** *nm*: **~ (d'eau)** water softener.

adresse¹ [adʀɛs] *nf* (**a**) *(domicile)* address. (**b**) *(message)* address. **à l' ~ de** for the benefit of. (**c**) *(Lexicographie)* headword; *(Ordin)* address.

adresse² [adʀɛs] *nf (habileté)* deftness, skill; *(finesse)* shrewdness, skill; *(tact)* adroitness. **jeu d' ~** game of skill.

adresser [adʀese] (1) **1** *vt lettre (envoyer)* to send; *(écrire l'adresse)* to address (*à* to); *remarque, requête* to address; *reproche, coup* to level, aim (*à* at); *compliment* to pay (*à* to); *sourire* to give. **~ la parole à qn** to speak to *ou* address sb; **il m'adressa un signe de tête** he nodded at me; **~ qn à un spécialiste** to refer sb to a specialist. **2 s' ~** *vpr*: **s' ~ à** *interlocuteur* to speak to, address; *responsable* to go and see; *bureau* to apply to, enquire at; *générosité* to appeal to. **livre qui s'adresse aux femmes** book intended *ou* written for women.

adroit, e [adʀwa, wat] *adj (habile)* skilful, deft; *(subtil)* shrewd; *(plein de tact)* adroit. **~ de ses mains** clever with one's hands. ◆ **adroitement** *adv* skilfully; deftly; shrewdly; adroitly; cleverly.

aduler [adyle] (1) *vt* to adulate. ◆ **adulateur, -trice** *nm, f* adulator. ◆ **adulation** *nf* adulation.

adulte [adylt(ə)] **1** *adj personne* adult; *animal, plante* fully-grown. **2** *nmf* adult, grown-up.

adultère [adyltɛʀ] **1** *adj désir* adulterous. **femme/homme ~** adulteress/adulterer. **2** *nm* adultery.

advenir [advəniʀ] (22) **1** *vb impers* (**a**) *(survenir)* **~ que** to happen that; **~ à** to happen to; **il m'advint de** I happened to; **advienne que pourra** come what may; **quoi qu'il advienne** whatever happens *ou* may happen. (**b**) *(devenir)* ~ **de** to become of; **qu'en adviendra-t-il?** what will come of it? **2** *vi (arriver)* to happen.

adverbe [advɛʀb(ə)] *nm* adverb. ◆ **adverbial, e,** *mpl* **-aux** *adj* adverbial.

adversaire [advɛʀsɛʀ] *nmf (gén)* opponent, adversary. ◆ **adverse** *adj forces* opposing; *sort* adverse. ◆ **adversité** *nf* adversity.

ad vitam æternam * [advitametɛʀnam] *loc adv* till kingdom come.

aérer [aeʀe] (6) **1** *vt pièce* to air; *terre* to aerate; *présentation* to lighten. **2 s'** ~ *vpr [personne]* to get some fresh air. **s'** ~ **les idées** to clear one's mind. ◆ **aérateur** *nm* ventilator. ◆ **aération** *nf* airing; aeration; ventilation. ◆ **aéré, e** *adj pièce* airy; *page* well spaced out.

aérien, -ienne [aeʀjɛ̃, jɛn] *adj* (**a**) *(Aviat, gén)* air; *navigation, photographie* aerial. **base ~ne** air base. (**b**) *silhouette* sylphlike; *démarche* floating; *musique* ethereal. (**c**) *racine* aerial; *câble* overhead; *(Géog) courant* air.

aérium [aeʀjɔm] *nm* sanatorium.

aérobic [aeʀɔbik] *nf* aerobics *(sg)*.

aéro-club [aeʀɔklœb] *nm* flying club.

aérodrome [aeʀɔdʀom] *nm* aerodrome, airfield.

aérodynamique [aeʀɔdinamik] **1** *adj ligne* streamlined, aerodynamic. **2** *nf* aerodynamics *(sg)*.

aérofrein [aeʀɔfʀɛ̃] *nm* air brake.

aérogare [aeʀɔgaʀ] *nf [aéroport]* airport (buildings); *(en ville)* air terminal.

aéroglisseur [aeʀɔglisœʀ] *nm* hovercraft.

aérogramme [aeʀɔgʀam] *nm* airmail letter, aerogramme.

aéronautique [aeʀɔnotik] **1** *adj* aeronautical. **2** *nf* aeronautics *(sg)*.

aéronaval, e, *pl* **~s** [aeʀɔnaval] *adj forces* air and sea. **l'A~e** ≃ the Fleet Air Arm.

aéroplane † [aeʀɔplan] *nm* aeroplane, airplane *(US)*.

aéroport [aeʀɔpɔʀ] *nm* airport.

aéroporté, e [aeʀɔpɔʀte] *adj troupes* airborne; *matériel* air-lifted.

aérosol [aeʀɔsɔl] *nm* aerosol.

aérospatial, e, *mpl* **-aux** [aeʀɔspasjal, o] **1** *adj* aerospace. **2** *nf* aerospace science.

affabilité [afabilite] *nf* affability. ◆ **affable** *adj* affable. ◆ **affablement** *adv* affably.

affabuler [afabyle] (1) *vi* to make up stories.

affaiblir [afebliʀ] (2) **1** *vt (gén)* to weaken. **2 s'** ~ *vpr (gén)* to grow weaker; *[son]* to fade, grow fainter; *[tempête]* to abate, die down. ◆ **affaiblissement** *nm (gén)* weakening.

affaire [afɛʀ] **1** *nf* (**a**) *(gén: histoire)* matter, business; *(Jur)* case. **ce n'est pas une mince** ~ it's no small matter; **il m'a tiré d'** ~ he helped me out; **ce n'est pas ton** ~ it's none of your business; **j'en fais mon** ~ I'll deal with that; **ça fait mon** ~ that's (just) what I want *ou* need; **une grave** ~ **de corruption** a serious corruption case. (**b**) *(transaction)* deal, bargain. **une (bonne)** ~ a good deal, a (good) bargain; **faire** ~ **avec qn** to make a bargain *ou* deal with sb. (**c**) *(firme)* business, concern. (**d**) **~s** *(gén, Pol)* affairs; *(commerce)* business; *(habits)* clothes; *(objets)* things, belongings; **les ~s culturelles** cultural affairs; **venir pour ~s** to come on business; **il est dur en ~s** he's a tough businessman; **mettre de l'ordre dans ses ~s** *(finances)* to put one's affairs in order; *(objets)* to tidy up one's things. (**e**) **avoir** ~ **à** *cas* to be faced with, have to deal with; *personne* to be dealing with; **tu auras** ~ **à moi!** you'll be hearing from me!; **être à son** ~ to be in one's element; **cela ne fait rien à l'** ~ that's got nothing to do with it; **ce n'est pas une** ~! it's nothing to get worked up about!; **c'est toute une** ~ it's quite a business; **(se) faire une** ~ **de qch** to make a fuss about sth; **c'est (une)** ~ **de goût** it's a matter of taste; **c'est l'** ~ **de quelques minutes** it's a matter of a few minutes. **2** : ~ **de cœur** love affair; *(Pol)* ~ **d'État** affair of state; **il en a fait une** ~ **d'état** * he made a great issue of it.

affairer (s') [afeʀe] (1) *vpr* to bustle about (*à faire* doing). **s'** ~ **autour de qn** to fuss around sb. ◆ **affairé, e** *adj* busy. ◆ **affairement** *nm* bustling activity.

affaisser (s') [afese] (1) *vpr* (**a**) *[sol]* to subside; *[corps, poutre]* to sag; *[plancher]* to cave in. (**b**) *(s'écrouler)* to collapse. **affaissé sur le sol** slumped on the ground. ◆ **affaissement** *nm* subsidence; sagging. **~(s) de terrain** subsidence.

affaler (s') [afale] (1) *vpr (tomber)* to collapse; *(se laisser tomber)* to slump.

affamer [afame] (1) *vt* to starve. ◆ **affamé, e** *adj* starving, famished. ~ **de gloire** greedy for fame.

affectation [afɛktɑsjɔ̃] *nf* (**a**) *[immeuble, somme]* allocation, allotment (*à* to, for). (**b**) *(nomination) (à un poste)* appointment; *(à une région)* posting. (**c**) *(simulation)* affectation.

affecter [afɛkte] (1) *vt* (**a**) *(feindre)* to affect. ~ **de faire** to pretend to do; ~ **une forme** to take on *ou* assume a shape. (**b**) *(destiner)* to allocate, allot (*à* to, for). (**c**) *(nommer) (à une fonction)* to appoint; *(à une région)* to post (*à* to). (**d**) *(émouvoir)* to affect, move; *(concerner)* to affect. (**e**) *(Math)* to modify. **affecté du signe** + bearing a plus sign. ◆ **affecté, e** *adj* affected.

affectif, -ive [afɛktif, iv] *adj (gén) vie* emotional; *terme* affective; *(Psych)* affective.

affection [afɛksjɔ̃] *nf* (**a**) *(tendresse)* affection. **avoir de l'** ~ **pour** to be fond of. (**b**) *(Méd)* ailment; *(Psych)* affection.

affectionner [afɛksjɔne] (1) *vt* to be fond of. **votre fils affectionné** your loving *ou* devoted son.

affectivité [afɛktivite] *nf* affectivity.

affectueux, -euse [afɛktɥø, øz] *adj* affectionate. ◆ **affectueusement** *adv* affectionately.

afférent, e [afeʀɑ̃, ɑ̃t] *adj (Admin)* ~ **à** pertaining to; **questions ~es** related questions.

affermir [afɛʀmiʀ] (2) *vt pouvoir, position* to strengthen; *chairs* to tone up; *prise* to make firm *ou* firmer. ~ **sa voix** to steady one's voice. ◆ **affermissement** *nm* strengthening.

affiche [afiʃ] *nf (gén)* poster; *(Théât)* (play)bill. *(officielle)* **par voie d'** ~ by (means of) public notices; *(Théât)* **mettre à l'** ~ to bill; **quitter l'** ~ to come off; **tenir longtemps l'** ~ to have a long run.

afficher [afiʃe] (1) *vt* (**a**) *affiche, résultat* to stick up; *(Théât)* to bill; *(Ordin)* to display. **défense d'** ~ (stick) no bills. (**b**) *(péj) émotion, vice* to display. **s'** ~ **avec sa maîtresse** to show o.s. off with one's mistress. ◆ **affichage** *nm* sticking up; billing; display. **l'** ~ billsticking.

affilée[1] [afile] *nf*: **d'** ~ at a stretch, running; **8 heures d'** ~ 8 hours at a stretch *ou* on end *ou* running; **boire plusieurs verres d'** ~ to drink several glasses in a row *ou* one after the other.

affiler [afile] (1) *vt* to sharpen. ◆ **affilé, e**[2] *adj* sharp.

affiliation [afiljɑsjɔ̃] *nf* affiliation. ◆ **affilié, e** *nm, f* affiliated member. ◆ **affilier** (7) **1** *vt* to affiliate (*à* to). **2 s'** ~ *vpr* to become affiliated (*à* to).

affiner [afine] (1) *vt* (**a**) *métal* to refine; *fromage* to complete the maturing of. (**b**) *esprit, style* to refine; *sens* to sharpen. **son goût s'est affiné** his taste has become more refined. ◆ **affinage** *nm* refining; maturing. ◆ **affinement** *nm* refinement.

affinité [afinite] *nf (gén)* affinity.

affirmatif, -ive [afiʀmatif, iv] **1** *adj réponse, ton* affirmative. **il a été** ~ he was quite positive. **2** *nm (Ling)* affirmative, positive. **à l'** ~ in the affirmative *ou* positive. **3** *nf*: **répondre par l'** ~**ive** to answer yes *ou* in the affirmative; **dans l'** ~**ive** in the event of an affirmative (reply). ◆ **affirmation** *nf (gén, Gram)* assertion. ◆ **affirmativement** *adv* in the affirmative, affirmatively.

affirmer [afiʀme] (1) *vt* (**a**) *(soutenir)* to maintain, assert. **pouvez-vous l'** ~**?** can you swear to it *ou* be positive about it?; ~ **qch sur l'honneur** to maintain sth on one's word of honour; ~ **sa volonté de** to affirm *ou* assert one's wish to. (**b**) *originalité, autorité* to assert. **talent qui s'affirme** talent which is asserting itself.

affleurer [aflœʀe] (1) **1** *vi [récifs, filon]* to show on the surface; *[sentiment]* to come to the surface. **2** *vt (Tech)* to make flush. ◆ **affleurement** *nm (Géol)* outcrop; *(fig)* emergence; *(Tech)* flushing.

affliction [afliksjɔ̃] *nf* affliction.

affliger [afliʒe] (3) *vt* to distress, grieve. **s'** ~ **de qch** to be grieved *ou* distressed about sth; **être affligé de** *(gén)* to be afflicted with; *(hum)* to be cursed with. ◆ **affligeant, e** *adj* distressing; *(iro)* pathetic.

affluence [aflyɑ̃s] *nf [gens]* crowds *(pl)*. **heure d'** ~ peak *ou* rush hour.

affluent [aflyɑ̃] *nm* tributary.

affluer [aflye] (1) *vi [sang]* to rush, flow; *[foule]* to flock (*à, vers* to); *[lettres, argent]* to flood *ou* pour in. ◆ **afflux** *nm [fluide]* inrush, inflow; *[argent, foule]* influx.

affoler [afɔle] (1) **1** *vt (effrayer)* to throw into a panic; *(troubler)* to drive wild. **2 s'** ~ *vpr* to panic, lose one's head. ◆ **affolant, e** *adj* alarming. ◆ **affolé, e** *adj* panic-stricken; driven wild. **je suis** ~ **de voir ça** * I'm appalled at that. ◆ **affolement** *nm* panic, (wild) turmoil. **pas d'** ~**!** * don't panic!

affranchir [afʀɑ̃ʃiʀ] (2) *vt* (**a**) *lettre* to stamp; *(à la machine)* to frank. **non affranchi** unstamped; unfranked. (**b**) *esclave, esprit* to emancipate, free (*de* from); *(Cartes)* to clear. **s'** ~ **des convenances** to free o.s. from convention; (⁑: *prévenir)* ~ **qn** to give sb the low-down ⁑. ◆ **affranchissement** *nm* stamping; franking; emancipation, freeing; *(Poste: prix payé)* postage.

affres [afʀ(ə)] *nfpl*: **les** ~ **de** the pangs *ou* torments of; **les** ~ **de la mort** the throes of death.

affréter [afʀete] (6) *vt* to charter. ◆ **affrètement** *nm* chartering.

affreux, -euse [afʀø, øz] *adj (laid)* hideous, horrible, ghastly; *(abominable)* dreadful, awful. ◆ **affreusement** *adv souffrir* horribly. ~ **laid** hideously ugly; ~ **mauvais** really horrible; ~ **en retard** * dreadfully *ou* awfully late.

affrioler [afʀijɔle] (1) *vt* to tempt, excite.

affront [afʀɔ̃] *nm* affront. **faire (un)** ~ **à** to affront.

affronter [afʀɔ̃te] (1) **1** *vt adversaire, danger* to confront, face; *mort, froid* to brave. **2 s'** ~ *vpr [adversaires]* to confront each other; *[théories]* to clash. ◆ **affrontement** *nm* confrontation.

affubler [afyble] (1) *vt*: ~ **qn de** *vêtement* to rig * sb out in; *nom* to give sb.

affût [afy] *nm* (**a**) ~ **(de canon)** (gun) carriage. (**b**) *(Chasse)* hide. **chasser à l'** ~ to lie in wait for game; **être à l'** ~ **de qch** to be on the look-out for sth.

affûter [afyte] (1) *vt* to sharpen. ◆ **affûtage** *nm* sharpening.

Afghanistan [afganistɑ̃] *nm* Afghanistan. ◆ **afghan, e** *adj*, **A**~**(e)** *nm(f)* Afghan.

afin [afɛ̃] *prép*: ~ **de** to, in order to, so as to; ~ **que** + *subj* so that, in order that.

afrikaans [afʀikɑ̃] *nm, adj inv* Afrikaans.

Afrikaner [afʀikanɛʀ], **Afrikander** [afʀikɑ̃dɛʀ] *nmf* Afrikaner.

Afrique [afʀik] *nf* Africa. **l'** ~ **australe/du Nord/du Sud** Southern/North/South Africa. ◆ **africain, e** *adj*, **A**~**(e)** *nm(f)* African.

afro-asiatique *adj*, **A**~ *nmf* [afʀɔazjatik] Afro-Asian.

agacer [agase] (3) *vt*: ~ **qn** *(énerver)* to get on sb's nerves, irritate sb; *(taquiner)* to pester *ou* tease sb; **agacé par/de** irritated by/at. ◆ **agaçant, e** *adj* irritating. ◆ **agacement** *nm* irritation.

âge [ɑʒ] **1** *nm (gén)* age. **quel** ~ **avez-vous?** how old *ou* what age are you?; **d'un** ~ **avancé** elderly; **d'** ~ **moyen** middle-aged; **sans** ~ ageless; **vieillir avant l'** ~ to get old before one's time; **il a pris de l'** ~ he has aged; **j'ai passé l'** ~ **de le faire** I'm too old to do it; **être en** ~ **de** to be old enough to; **l'** ~ **du bronze** the Bronze Age. **2** : **l'** ~ **adulte** *(gén)* adulthood; *(homme)* manhood; *(femme)* womanhood; **l'** ~ **ingrat** the awkward age; **avoir l'** ~ **(légal)** to be of age; **l'** ~ **mûr** maturity, middle age; **l'** ~ **d'or** the golden age; **l'** ~ **de raison** the age of reason. ◆ **âgé, e** *adj*: **être** ~ to be old; **être** ~ **de 9 ans** to be 9 (years old); **enfant** ~ **de 4 ans** 4 year-old child; **dame** ~**e** elderly lady; **les personnes** ~**es** the elderly, old people.

agence [aʒɑ̃s] *nf (succursale)* branch (office); *(bureaux)* offices; *(organisme)* agency. ~ **immobilière** estate agent's (office); ~ **matrimoniale** marriage bureau; ~ **de placement** employment agency ; ~ **de presse** news *ou* press agency; ~ **de publicité** advertising *ou* publicity agency; ~ **de voyages** travel agency.

agencer [aʒɑ̃se] (3) *vt (disposer)* to arrange; *(équiper)* to equip. ◆ **agencement** *nm* arrangement; equipment.

agenda [aʒɛ̃da] *nm* diary.

agenouiller (s') [aʒnuje] (1) *vpr* to kneel (down); *(fig)* to bow. **être agenouillé** to be kneeling.

agent [aʒɑ̃] **1** *nm* (**a**) ~ **(de police)** policeman; **pardon monsieur l'** ~ excuse me, officer. (**b**) *(Chim, Gram, Sci)* agent. (**c**) *(Comm, Pol)* agent; *(Admin)* officer, official. **les** ~**s du lycée** the ancillary staff of the school.
2 : ~ **d'assurances** insurance agent; ~ **de change** stockbroker; ~ **commercial** (sales) representative; ~ **double** double agent; ~ **du gouvernement** government official; ~ **immobilier** estate agent; *(Mil)* ~ **de liaison** liaison officer; ~ **de maîtrise** supervisor; ~ **de renseignements** intelligence agent; ~ **secret** secret agent.

agglomération [aglɔmeʀɑsjɔ̃] *nf* (**a**) *(ville)* town; *(Aut)* built-up area. **l'** ~ **parisienne** Paris and its suburbs. (**b**) *(Tech)* agglomeration, conglomeration; *(gén)* conglomeration. ◆ **aggloméré** *nm (charbon)* briquette; *(bois)* chipboard; *(pierre)* conglomerate. ◆ **agglomérer** (6) **1** *vt (amonceler)* to pile up; *(Tech) charbon* to briquette; *bois, pierre* to compress. **2 s'** ~ *vpr (Tech)* to agglomerate; *(s'amonceler)* to pile up; *(se rassembler)* to conglomerate.

agglutiner [aglytine] (1) *vt* to stick together; *(Bio)* to agglutinate. *(fig)* **s'** ~ **devant la vitrine** to congregate in front of the shop window. ◆ **agglutination** *nf (Bio, Ling)* agglutination.

aggraver [agʀave] (1) **1** *vt (faire empirer)* to make worse, aggravate; *(renforcer)* to increase. **2 s'** ~ *vpr* to get worse; to increase. ◆ **aggravation** *nf [mal, situation]* worsening, aggravation; *[impôt, chômage]* increase.

agile [aʒil] *adj* agile, nimble. ◆ **agilement** *adv* nimbly, agilely. ◆ **agilité** *nf* agility, nimbleness.

agir [aʒiʀ] (2) **1** *vi (gén)* to act; *(se comporter)* to behave. **il faut** ~ **tout de suite** we must act *ou* take action at once; **il a bien/mal agi envers moi** he

behaved well/badly towards me; ~ **au nom de** to act on behalf of; ~ **sur qch** to act on sth; ~ **auprès de qn** to use one's influence with sb; **il a fait ~ ses amis** he got his friends to act *ou* take action; **le remède agit lentement** the medicine is slow to take effect *ou* acts slowly.
2 s' ~ *vb impers* (**a**) *(il est question de)* **dans ce film il s'agit de 3 bandits** this film is about 3 gangsters; **les livres dont il s'agit** the books in question; **il s'agit de ta santé** your health is at stake; **il s'agirait/il s'agit d'un temple grec** it would appear to be/it is a Greek temple; **de quoi s'agit-il?** what's it (all) about?, what's the matter?; **il ne s'agit pas d'argent** it's not a question of money; **il ne s'agit pas de ça!** that's not it! *ou* the point! (**b**) *(il est nécessaire de faire)* **il s'agit pour lui de réussir** what he has to do is succeed; **il ne s'agit pas de plaisanter** this is no joking matter; **il s'agit de savoir ce qu'il va faire** it's a question of knowing what he's going to do; **s'agissant de telles sommes** when such large amounts are involved.

agissant, e [aʒisɑ̃, ɑ̃t] *adj (actif)* active; *(efficace)* effective. **minorité ~e** active *ou* influential minority.

agissements [aʒismɑ̃] *nmpl (péj)* schemes.

agitateur, -trice [aʒitatœʀ, tʀis] *nm, f (Pol)* agitator.

agitation [aʒitɑsjɔ̃] *nf [personne] (remuant)* restlessness, fidgetiness; *(affairé)* bustle; *(troublé)* agitation; *[rue]* bustle; *(Pol)* unrest.

agité, e [aʒite] *adj* (**a**) *personne (remuant)* restless, fidgety; *(troublé)* agitated. (**b**) *mer* rough, choppy; *vie* hectic; *époque* troubled; *nuit* restless. **avoir le sommeil ~** to toss about in one's sleep.

agiter [aʒite] (1) **1** *vt* (**a**) *bras* to wave; *ailes* to flap; *liquide* to shake; *branches* to sway; *(fig) menace* to brandish. **agité par les vagues** tossed by the waves. (**b**) *(inquiéter)* to trouble, agitate. (**c**) *problème* to discuss, debate. **2 s' ~** *vpr [serveur]* to bustle about; *[malade]* to toss restlessly; *[élève]* to fidget; *[foule, pensées, mer]* to stir.

agneau, *pl* **~x** [aɲo] *nm* lamb; *(fourrure)* lambskin.

agonie [agɔni] *nf (Méd)* death pangs; *(fig)* death throes. **être à l' ~** to be at death's door; **longue ~** slow death. ◆ **agonisant, e** *adj* dying. ◆ **agoniser** (1) *vi* to be dying.

agrafe [agʀaf] *nf [vêtement]* hook; *[papiers]* staple; *(Méd)* clip. ◆ **agrafer** (1) *vt* to hook (up); to staple. ◆ **agrafeuse** *nf* stapler.

agraire [agʀɛʀ] *adj lois* agrarian; *surface* land.

agrandir [agʀɑ̃diʀ] (2) **1** *vt passage* to widen; *écart* to increase; *trou, domaine, photographie* to enlarge; *activités* to expand. **ce miroir agrandit la pièce** this mirror makes the room look bigger; **(faire) ~ sa maison** to extend one's house. **2 s' ~** *vpr [ville, famille, entreprise]* to grow, expand; *[écart]* to widen; *[passage]* to get wider; *[trou]* to get bigger. ◆ **agrandissement** *nm [local]* extension; *[puissance, ville]* expansion; *(Phot)* enlargement. ◆ **agrandisseur** *nm* enlarger.

agréable [agʀeabl(ə)] *adj* pleasant, agreeable, nice. **pour lui être ~** in order to please him; **il me serait ~ de** it would be a pleasure for me to. ◆ **agréablement** *adv* pleasantly, agreeably.

agréer [agʀee] (1) **1** *vt demande* to accept. **veuillez ~ mes sincères salutations** yours sincerely; **fournisseur agréé** authorized *ou* registered dealer. **2 ~ à** *vt indir* to please, suit.

agrégat [agʀega] *nm (gén)* aggregate; *(péj)* medley.

agrégation [agʀegɑsjɔ̃] *nf (Univ)* agrégation *(highest competitive examination for teachers in France)*; *[particules]* aggregation. ◆ **agrégé, e** *nm, f* agrégé.

agréger [agʀeʒe] (3) *et* (6) *vt particules* to aggregate. *(fig)* ~ **qn à un groupe** to incorporate sb into a group.

agrément [agʀemɑ̃] *nm* (**a**) *[personne]* attractiveness, charm; *[conversation, lieu]* pleasantness. **plein d' ~** very enjoyable *ou* pleasant; **sans ~** unattractive; **les ~s de la vie** the pleasant things in life; **voyage d' ~** pleasure trip. (**b**) *(accord)* assent.

agrémenter [agʀemɑ̃te] (1) *vt habit* to embellish; *récit* to accompany (*de* with). **agrémenté de** accompanied by.

agrès [agʀɛ] *nmpl (Naut)* tackle; *(Sport)* (gymnastics) apparatus.

agresser [agʀese] (1) *vt* to attack. ◆ **agresseur** *nm* attacker; *(Pol)* aggressor. ◆ **agressif, -ive** *adj* aggressive. ◆ **agression** *nf* attack; *(Pol)* aggression; *(dans la rue)* mugging. ◆ **agressivement** *adv* aggressively. ◆ **agressivité** *nf* aggressiveness.

agricole [agʀikɔl] *adj (gén)* agricultural; *ouvrier, produits* farm; *population* farming. ◆ **agriculteur** *nm* farmer. ◆ **agriculture** *nf* agriculture, farming.

agripper [agʀipe] (1) *vt* to grab *ou* clutch hold of. **s' ~ à qch** to clutch *ou* grip sth.

agro-alimentaire [agʀoalimɑ̃tɛʀ] **1** *adj industrie* farm-produce. **2** *nm:* **l' ~** the farm-produce industry.

agronome [agʀɔnɔm] *nm* agronomist. **ingénieur ~** agricultural engineer. ◆ **agronomie** *nf* agronomy. ◆ **agronomique** *adj* agronomical.

agrumes [agʀym] *nmpl* citrus fruits.

aguerrir [ageʀiʀ] (2) *vt* to harden (*contre* to *ou* against). **troupes aguerries** *(au combat)* seasoned troops; *(à l'effort)* trained troops; **s' ~** to become hardened.

aguets [agɛ] *nmpl*: **aux ~** on the look-out.

aguicher [agiʃe] (1) *vt* to entice, tantalize.

ah [ɑ] **1** *excl* ah!, oh! ~ **bon?** *(question)* really?; *(résignation)* oh well. **2** *nm:* **pousser un ~ de soulagement** to sigh with relief; **des ~ d'allégresse** oohs and ahs of joy.

ahuri, e [ayʀi] **1** *adj (stupéfait)* stunned, dumbfounded; *(stupide)* stupefied. **2** *nm, f (péj)* blockhead *. ◆ **ahurir** (2) *vt* to dumbfound, stun. ◆ **ahurissant, e** *adj* stupefying, staggering. ◆ **ahurissement** *nm* stupefaction.

aide [ɛd] **1** *nf (assistance)* help, assistance; *(secours financier)* aid. **~ sociale** ≃ social security, welfare; **crier à l' ~** to shout for help; **venir en ~ à qn** to help sb, come to sb's assistance *ou* aid; **à l' ~!** help!; **sans l' ~ de personne** without (any) help, completely unaided; **à l' ~ de** with the help *ou* aid of. **2** *nm, f* assistant. **~-chimiste** assistant chemist; **~ de camp** *nm* aide-de-camp; **~ familiale** home help; **~-maçon** builder's mate; **~ soignante** state enrolled nurse, nurse's aide *(US)*. ◆ **aide-mémoire** *nm inv* crib *(Scol)*, memorandum.

aider [ede] (1) **1** *vt* to help. **~ qn (à faire qch)** to help sb (to do sth); **~ qn de ses conseils** to help *ou* assist sb with one's advice; **je me suis fait ~ par** *ou* **de mon frère** I got my brother to help *ou* assist me; **~ à la clarté de qch** to help *ou* contribute towards the understanding of sth; **aidée de sa canne** with the help *ou* aid of her walking stick; **l'alcool aidant** helped on by the alcohol, with the help of alcohol. **2 s' ~** *vpr*: **s' ~ de** to use, make use of; **en s'aidant d'un escabeau** with the aid of a stool; **aide-toi, le Ciel t'aidera** God helps those who help themselves.

aïe [aj] *excl (douleur)* ouch! **aïe aïe aïe!** dear oh dear!

aïeul [ajœl] *nm* grandfather. **les ~s** the grandparents. ◆ **aïeule** *nf* grandmother. ◆ **aïeux** *nmpl* forefathers.

aigle [ɛgl(ə)] *nm, f* eagle. **~ royal** golden eagle; **regard d' ~** eagle look; **ce n'est pas un ~ *** he's no genius.

aigre [ɛgʀ(ə)] **1** *adj goût, lait* sour; *son* sharp; *vent* bitter, keen; *critique* harsh. **2 : ~-doux, ~-douce,**

mpl ~**s-doux** *adj sauce* sweet and sour; *fruit, propos* bitter-sweet. ◆ **aigrement** *adv dire* sourly.

aigrefin [ɛgʀəfɛ̃] *nm* swindler, crook.

aigrelet, -ette [ɛgʀəlɛ, ɛt] *adj goût* sourish; *voix* shrillish.

aigrette [ɛgʀɛt] *nf (plume)* feather; *(oiseau)* egret.

aigreur [ɛgʀœʀ] *nf [goût]* sourness; *[ton]* harshness, sharpness. ~**s d'estomac** heartburn.

aigrir [egʀiʀ] (2) **1** *vt personne* to embitter; *caractère* to sour. **2 s'** ~ *vpr [aliment]* to turn sour. **il s'est aigri** he has become embittered.

aigu, -uë [egy] **1** *adj* (**a**) *son* high-pitched, shrill; *(Mus)* high. (**b**) *douleur, intelligence* acute, sharp. (**c**) *(pointu)* sharp, pointed. **2** *nm (Mus)* **les** ~**s** the high notes; **l'** ~ high pitch.

aiguillage [egɥijaʒ] *nm (Rail) (instrument)* points, switch *(US)*.

aiguille [egɥij] *nf (gén)* needle; *[horloge]* hand; *[balance, cadran solaire]* pointer; *[clocher]* spire. **travail à l'** ~ needlework; ~ **de glace** icicle ; ~ **de pin** pine needle.

aiguiller [egɥije] (1) *vt* to direct, steer (*vers* towards); *(Rail)* to shunt, switch *(US)*. ◆ **aiguilleur** *nm* pointsman, switchman *(US)*. *(Aviat)* ~ **du ciel** air-traffic controller.

aiguillon [egɥijɔ̃] *nm [insecte]* sting; *[bouvier]* goad; *(fig)* spur. ◆ **aiguillonner** (1) *vt bœuf* to goad; *(fig)* to spur on.

aiguiser [egize] (1) *vt outil, esprit* to sharpen; *appétit* to whet.

ail, *pl* ~**s, aulx** [aj, o] *nm* garlic.

aile [ɛl] *nf (gén)* wing; *[moulin]* sail; *[hélice]* blade; *[nez, voiture]* wing. **l'oiseau disparut d'un coup d'** ~ the bird disappeared with a flap of its wings; **avoir/donner des** ~**s** to have/lend wings; **prendre sous son** ~ to take under one's wing. ◆ **aileron** *nm [poisson]* fin; *[oiseau]* pinion; *(Aviat)* aileron. ◆ **ailette** *nf* fin; blade. ◆ **ailier** *nm (gén)* winger; *(Rugby)* flanker.

ailleurs [ajœʀ] *adv* (**a**) somewhere else, elsewhere. **nulle part/partout** ~ nowhere/everywhere else. (**b**) **par** ~ *(autrement)* otherwise; *(en outre)* moreover, furthermore; **d'** ~ *(de plus)* besides, moreover; *(entre parenthèses)* by the way.

aimable [ɛmabl(ə)] *adj* kind, nice. **c'est très** ~ **à vous** it's most kind of you; **soyez assez** ~ **pour** be so kind as to; ~ **comme une porte de prison** like a bear with a sore head. ◆ **aimablement** *adv* kindly, nicely.

aimant¹ [ɛmɑ̃] *nm* magnet.

aimant², e [ɛmɑ̃, ɑ̃t] *adj* loving, affectionate.

aimanter [ɛmɑ̃te] (1) *vt* to magnetize. **champ aimanté** magnetic field.

aimer [eme] (1) **1** *vt* (**a**) *(amour)* to love, to be in love with; *(amitié, goût)* to like, be fond of. **j'aime une bonne tasse de café** I like *ou* enjoy *ou* love a good cup of coffee; **je n'aime pas beaucoup cet acteur** I don't like that actor very much, I'm not very keen on that actor; **j'aime assez ce livre** I rather *ou* quite like this book; **elle aimerait bien venir** she would like *ou* love to come; **elle n'aime pas qu'il sorte le soir** she doesn't like him going out *ou* him to go out at night; ~ **faire,** ~ **à faire** to like doing *ou* to do. (**b**) *(avec autant, mieux)* **j'aime autant vous dire que** I may as well tell you that; **il aimerait autant ne pas sortir aujourd'hui** he'd just as soon not go out today, he'd be just as happy not going out today; **j'aime autant ça!** * *(menace)* that sounds more like it! *; *(soulagement)* what a relief!; **elle aimerait mieux des livres** she would rather *ou* sooner have books.

2 s' ~ *vpr* to be in love, love each other. **se faire** ~ **de qn** to get sb to fall in love with one, win the love of sb.

aine [ɛn] *nf* groin *(Anat)*.

aîné, e [ene] **1** *adj (entre 2)* elder, older; *(plus de 2)* eldest, oldest. **2** *nm, f* eldest child (*ou* boy *ou* girl). **il est mon** ~ **de 2 ans** he's 2 years older than me, he's 2 years my senior; **respectez vos** ~**s** respect your elders.

ainsi [ɛ̃si] *adv* (**a**) *(de cette façon)* in this way, thus; *(donc, de même)* so. **c'est** ~ **que ça s'est passé** that's the way *ou* how it happened; **s'il en était** ~ if this were the case; ~ **tu vas partir!** so, you're going to leave!; ~ **que je le disais** just as I said; **sa beauté** ~ **que sa candeur** her beauty as well as her innocence. (**b**) **pour** ~ **dire** so to speak, as it were; **et** ~ **de suite** and so on (and so forth); ~ **soit-il** *(gén)* so be it; *(Rel)* amen; ~ **va le monde** that's the way of the world.

air¹ [ɛʀ] **1** *nm* (**a**) *(gaz)* air; *(vent)* (light) breeze; *(courant d'air)* draught, draft *(US)*. **sans** ~ stuffy; **sortir à l'** ~ **libre** to come out into the open air; **mettre la literie à l'** ~ to air the bedclothes; **sortir prendre l'** ~ to go out for a breath of fresh air; **vivre de l'** ~ **du temps** to live on air alone. (**b**) *(espace)* air. **regarde en l'** ~ look up; **jeter qch en l'** ~ to throw sth (up) into the air; **l'avion a pris l'** ~ the plane has taken off. (**c**) *(ambiance)* atmosphere. (**d**) **être dans l'** ~ *[idée]* to be in the air; *[grippe]* to be about; *[orage, dispute]* to be brewing; **flanquer en l'** ~ * *(jeter)* to chuck away *; *(abandonner)* to chuck up ⁑; *(gâcher)* to mess up *; **en l'** ~ *paroles* idle, empty; *parler* rashly; *(en désordre)* upside down.

2 : ~ **comprimé** compressed air; ~ **conditionné** air conditioning; *(Mil)* ~**-sol** *adj inv* air-to-ground.

air² [ɛʀ] *nm* (**a**) *(expression)* look, air; *(manière)* manner, air; *(apparence)* appearance, air. **ils ont un** ~ **de famille** there's a family likeness between them; **prendre un** ~ **entendu** to put on a knowing look. (**b**) **ça m'a l'** ~ **d'un mensonge** it looks to me *ou* sounds to me like a lie; **elle a l'** ~ **intelligente** she looks *ou* seems intelligent; **il a eu l'** ~ **de ne pas comprendre** he looked as if he didn't understand, he didn't seem to understand; **il a l'** ~ **de vouloir neiger** it looks like snow; **cette plante n'a l'** ~ **de rien, pourtant...** this plant doesn't look up to much but...

air³ [ɛʀ] *nm [opéra]* aria; *(mélodie)* tune, air. *(lit, fig)* ~ **connu** familiar tune.

airain [ɛʀɛ̃] *nm (littér)* bronze.

aire [ɛʀ] *nf (gén, Math)* area; *[aigle]* eyrie. ~ **de battage** threshing floor; ~ **de lancement** launching site.

airelle [ɛʀɛl] *nf* bilberry.

aisance [ɛzɑ̃s] *nf (facilité)* ease; *[style]* fluency; *(richesse)* affluence. **vivre dans l'** ~ to be comfortably off; *(Couture)* **redonner de l'** ~ **à qch** to give more fullness to sth.

aise [ɛz] **1** *nf* (**a**) joy, pleasure. **combler d'** ~ to overjoy. (**b**) **être à l'** ~ *ou* **à son** ~ *(situation)* to feel at ease; *(confort)* to feel *ou* be comfortable; *(richesse)* to be comfortably off; **mal à l'** ~ ill at ease; uncomfortable; **mettez-vous à l'** ~ make yourself at home *ou* comfortable; **vous en prenez à votre** ~! you're taking things nice and easy!; **à votre** ~! please yourself!; **aimer ses** ~**s** to be fond of (one's) creature comforts. **2** *adj (littér)* **être bien** ~ **d'avoir fini** to be delighted *ou* most pleased to have finished.

aisé, e [eze] *adj* (**a**) *(facile)* easy. (**b**) *démarche* easy; *style* flowing. (**c**) *(riche)* well-to-do, well-off. ◆ **aisément** *adv* easily.

aisselle [ɛsɛl] *nf (Anat)* armpit.

ajonc [aʒɔ̃] *nm*: ~**(s)** gorse.

ajouré, e [aʒuʀe] *adj mouchoir* hemstitched; *sculpture* which has an openwork design.

ajourner [aʒuʀne] (1) **1** *vt assemblée* to adjourn; *élection, décision* to defer, adjourn; *candidat* to refer. **ajourné d'une semaine/au lundi suivant** adjourned for a week/until the following Monday. **2 s'** ~ *vpr (Pol)* to adjourn. ◆ **ajournement** *nm* adjournment; deferment; referring.

ajouter [aʒute] (1) **1** *vt* to add. **ajoutez à cela qu'il pleuvait** on top of that *ou* in addition to that it was raining; ~ **foi aux dires de qn** to believe sb's statements. **2** ~ **à** *vt indir* to add to, increase. **3 s'** ~ *vpr*: **s'** ~ **à** to add to; **ceci venant s'** ~ **à ses difficultés** this adding further to his difficulties. ◆ **ajout** *nm* addition.

ajuster [aʒyste] (1) **1** *vt* (**a**) *(gén, Tech)* to adjust; *vêtement* to alter; *points de vue* to reconcile. **robe ajustée** close-fitting dress; ~ **qch à** to fit sth to. (**b**) *tir* to aim; *cible* to aim at. (**c**) (†) *tenue* to arrange; *coiffure* to tidy, arrange. **2 s'** ~ *vpr (s'emboîter)* to fit (together). ◆ **ajustage** *nm (Tech)* fitting. ◆ **ajustement** *nm [prix]* adjustment; *(Tech)* fit. ◆ **ajusteur** *nm* metal worker.

alambic [alɑ̃bik] *nm* still *(Chim)*.

alanguir [alɑ̃giʀ] (2) **1** *vt* to make languid *ou* listless. **2 s'** ~ *vpr* to grow languid *ou* weak. ◆ **alangui, e** *adj* languid, listless. ◆ **alanguissement** *nm* languor.

alarme [alaʀm(ə)] *nf (gén)* alarm. **donner l'** ~ to give *ou* sound the alarm; **jeter l'** ~ to cause alarm; **à la première** ~ at the first sign of danger. ◆ **alarmant** *adj* alarming. ◆ **alarmer** (1) **1** *vt* to alarm. **2 s'** ~ *vpr* to become alarmed (*de, pour* about, at). ◆ **alarmiste** *adj, nmf* alarmist.

Alaska [alaska] *nm*: **l'** ~ Alaska.

Albanie [albani] *nf* Albania. ◆ **albanais, e** *adj*, **A~(e)** *nm(f)* Albanian.

albâtre [albɑtʀ(ə)] *nm* alabaster.

albatros [albatʀos] *nm* albatross.

albinos [albinos] *nmf, adj inv* albino.

album [albɔm] *nm* album. ~ **à colorier** colouring book.

albumine [albymin] *nf* albumin.

alcali [alkali] *nm* alkali.

alcalin, e [alkalɛ̃, in] *adj* alkaline.

alchimie [alʃimi] *nf* alchemy. ◆ **alchimiste** *nm* alchemist.

alcool [alkɔl] *nm (gén, Chim)* alcohol; *(type particulier)* spirit. ~ **à brûler/à 90°** methylated/surgical spirit; **boire de l'** ~ *(gén)* to drink alcohol; *(eau de vie)* to drink spirits; ~ **de prune** plum brandy. ◆ **alcoolémie** *nf*: **taux d'** ~ alcohol level (in the blood). ◆ **alcoolique** *adj, nmf* alcoholic. ◆ **alcoolisé, e** *adj* alcoholic. ◆ **alcoolisme** *nm* alcoholism. ◆ **alcoo(l)test** *nm (objet)* Breathalyser ®; *(épreuve)* breath test.

alcôve [alkov] *nf* alcove.

aléa [alea] *nm* hazard, risk. **après bien des ~s** after many ups and downs.

aléatoire [aleatwaʀ] *adj (incertain)* uncertain; *(risqué)* chancy, risky; *(Ordin) nombre* random.

alentour [alɑ̃tuʀ] *adv* around, round about. ◆ **alentours** *nmpl [ville]* surroundings, neighbourhood. **aux ~ de Dijon** in the vicinity *ou* neighbourhood of Dijon; **aux ~ de 8 heures/10 F** round about 8 o'clock/10 francs.

alerte [alɛʀt(ə)] **1** *adj personne* agile; *esprit* alert, agile; *style* brisk. **2** *nf* (**a**) *(signal, durée)* alert, alarm. **donner l'** ~ to give the alert *ou* alarm; **donner l'** ~ **à qn** to alert sb; ~ **aérienne** air raid warning; ~ **à la bombe** bomb scare. (**b**) *(fig) (avertissement)* warning sign; *(inquiétude)* alarm. **3** *excl*: ~! watch out! ◆ **alertement** *adv* agilely; alertly; briskly. ◆ **alerter** (1) *vt (donner l'alarme)* to alert; *(informer)* to inform, notify; *(prévenir)* to warn.

alexandrin [alɛksɑ̃dʀɛ̃] *nm* alexandrine.

alezan, e [alzɑ̃, an] *adj, nm, f* chestnut *(horse)*.

algarade [algaʀad] *nf (gronderie)* angry outburst; *(dispute)* row.

algèbre [alʒɛbʀ(ə)] *nf (Math)* algebra. **par l'** ~ algebraically; **c'est de l'** ~ * it's (all) Greek to me *. ◆ **algébrique** *adj* algebraic.

Alger [alʒe] *n* Algiers.

Algérie [alʒeʀi] *nf* Algeria. ◆ **algérien, -ienne** *adj*, **A~(ne)** *nm(f)* Algerian.

algue [alg(ə)] *nf*: ~**(s)** seaweed.

alias [aljɑs] *adv* alias.

alibi [alibi] *nm* alibi.

aliénation [aljenɑsjɔ̃] *nf (gén)* alienation. *(Méd)* ~ **(mentale)** (mental) derangement.

aliéné, e [aljene] *nm, f* insane person, lunatic.

aliéner [aljene] (6) *vt* (**a**) *(céder) (gén)* to give up; *(Jur)* to alienate. (**b**) *partisans, opinion* to alienate (*à qn* from sb). **s'** ~ **un ami** to alienate a friend.

alignement [aliɲmɑ̃] *nm (action)* aligning, lining up, bringing into alignment; *(rangée)* alignment, line; *(Fin, Pol)* alignment. *(Mil)* **être à l'** ~ to be in line; ~ **monétaire** monetary alignment *ou* adjustment.

aligner [aliɲe] (1) **1** *vt objets* to line up, make lines of; *chiffres* to string together; *arguments* to reel off; *(Mil)* to form into lines. **des peupliers étaient alignés le long de la route** poplars stood in a straight line along the roadside; ~ **sur qch** *[objets, conduite, politique]* to bring into line with sth. **2 s'** ~ *vpr [soldats]* to fall into line, line up. *(Pol)* **s'** ~ **sur** *politique* to conform to the line of; *pays* to align o.s. with.

aliment [alimɑ̃] *nm (nourriture)* food. ~**(s)** food; **comment conserver vos ~s** how to keep (your) food *ou* foodstuffs fresh; **ça a fourni un** ~ **à la conversation** it gave us something to talk about. ◆ **alimentaire** *adj besoins* food. **denrées ~s** foodstuffs.

alimentation [alimɑ̃tɑsjɔ̃] *nf* (**a**) *(gén)* feeding; *[moteur]* supplying. **l'** ~ **en eau des villes** supplying water to *ou* the supply of water to towns. (**b**) *(régime)* diet. (**c**) *(Comm)* food trade; *(enseigne) [magasin]* grocery (store), groceries; *[rayon]* groceries.

alimenter [alimɑ̃te] (1) *vt (gén)* to feed; *conversation* to sustain; *moteur* to supply. ~ **une ville en gaz** to supply a town with gas; **le malade recommence à s'** ~ the patient is starting to eat again.

alinéa [alinea] *nm* paragraph.

aliter (s') [alite] (1) *vpr* to take to one's bed. **rester alité** to remain confined to bed.

alizé [alize] *adj m, nm*: **(vent)** ~ trade wind.

allaiter [alete] (1) *vt [femme]* to (breast-)feed; *[animal]* to suckle. ~ **au biberon** to bottle-feed. ◆ **allaitement** *nm* (breast-)feeding; suckling; bottle-feeding.

allant, e [alɑ̃, ɑ̃t] **1** *adj (alerte)* active; *(entraînant)* lively. **2** *nm (dynamisme)* drive, energy. **avec** ~ energetically.

allécher [aleʃe] (6) *vt [odeur]* to make one's mouth water, tempt; *[proposition]* to entice, tempt. ◆ **alléchant, e** *adj* mouth-watering; enticing; tempting.

allée [ale] *nf* (**a**) *(gén)* path; *[parc]* walk; *(large)* avenue; *(menant à une maison)* drive; *[cinéma, bus]* aisle. *(fig)* **les ~s du pouvoir** the corridors of power. (**b**) **leurs ~s et venues** their comings and goings; **j'ai perdu mon temps en ~s et venues** I've wasted my time going back and forth.

allégation [alegɑsjɔ̃] *nf* allegation.

allégeance [aleʒɑ̃s] *nf* allegiance.

alléger [aleʒe] (6) *et* (3) *vt poids, impôts* to lighten; *bagages* to make lighter; *douleur* to alleviate, soothe; *châtiment* to mitigate. ◆ **allégement** *nm* lightening; alleviation; mitigation.

allégorie [alegɔʀi] *nf* allegory. ◆ **allégorique** *adj* allegorical.

allègre [alɛgʀ(ə)] *adj personne* cheerful, light-hearted; *démarche* lively, jaunty; *musique* lively, merry. ◆ **allégrement** *adv* cheerfully, light-heartedly; jauntily; merrily. ◆ **allégresse** *nf* elation, exhilaration.

alléguer [alege] (6) *vt prétexte* to put forward. **il allégua que...** he argued that...

Allemagne [almaɲ] *nf* Germany. ~ **de l'Ouest/de l'Est** West/East Germany; **l'** ~ **fédérale (RFA)** the Federal Republic of Germany (FRG). ◆ **allemand, e** *adj, nm,* **A~(e)** *nm(f)* German.

aller [ale] (9) **1** *vi* (**a**) *(gén)* to go (*à, vers* to, towards). ~ **et venir** to come and go; ~ **à Paris/au lit/à la pêche** to go to Paris/to bed/fishing; ~ **à la ville à pied/à vélo/en voiture** to go to town on foot/by bike/by car, walk/cycle/drive to town; *(lit, fig)* ~ **loin** to go far; ~ **jusqu'au ministre** to take a matter to the minister; ~ **à la catastrophe** to be heading for disaster; ~ **sur ses 8 ans** to be getting on for 8. (**b**) *(santé, situation)* **comment allez-vous? — ça va *** how are you? — fine *ou* not so bad *; **ça va bien/mal/mieux** I'm well/unwell/feeling better; **ça va (les affaires)? *** how are you getting on?, how's business? *; **ça va mal à la maison** things aren't going too well at home; **ça va mal** ~! there's going to be trouble!; **ta pendule va bien?** is your clock right?; ~ **en empirant** to get worse and worse, go from bad to worse; ~ **en augmentant** to keep increasing, increase more and more. (**c**) *(convenir)* ~ **à qn** *[mesure]* to fit sb; *[plan, genre]* to suit sb; *[climat]* to agree with sb; ~ **(bien) avec** to go (well) with; **la clef ne va pas dans la serrure** the key won't go in *ou* doesn't fit the lock; **ces ciseaux ne vont pas** these scissors won't do *ou* are no good. (**d**) *(excl)* **allons!, allez!** *(stimulation)* go on!; *(incrédulité, consolation)* come on now!; *(résignation)* all right!, O.K.! *; **allez, au revoir!** 'bye then!; **comme tu y vas!** you're going a bit far! (**e**) ~ **de soi** to be self-evident *ou* obvious; **cela va sans dire** it goes without saying; **il en va de même pour les autres** the same applies to the others; **il y va de votre vie** your life is at stake; **il y est allé de sa chanson** he gave us a song.

2 *vb aux (+ infin)* (**a**) *(futur immédiat)* to be going to. **ils allaient commencer** they were going *ou* were about to start. (**b**) ~ **faire qch** to go and do sth; **il est allé me chercher mes lunettes** he went to fetch *ou* get my glasses; **allez donc voir si c'est vrai!** you'll never know if it's true!; **n'allez pas vous imaginer que** don't you go imagining that.

3 s'en ~ *vpr* (**a**) *(partir)* to go (away); *(déménager)* to move, leave; *(mourir)* to die; *(prendre sa retraite)* to retire. **ils s'en vont à Paris** they are going *ou* off to Paris; **je m'en vais leur montrer** I'll show them. (**b**) *[tache]* to come off; *[temps]* to pass, go by. **tout son argent s'en va en disques** all his money goes on records.

4 *nm (trajet)* outward journey; *(billet)* single (ticket), one-way ticket *(US)*. **j'irai vous voir à l'** ~ I'll come and see you on the *ou* my way there; **je ne fais que l'** ~**-retour** I'm just going there and back; **prendre un** ~**-retour** to buy a return (ticket), buy a round-trip ticket *(US)*.

allergie [alɛʀʒi] *nf* allergy. ◆ **allergique** *adj* allergic (*à* to). ◆ **allergologie** *nf* study of allergies. ◆ **allergologiste** *nmf,* **allergologue** *nmf* allergist.

alliage [aljaʒ] *nm* alloy.

alliance [aljɑ̃s] *nf* (**a**) *(Pol)* alliance; *(Bible)* covenant. (**b**) *(mariage)* union, marriage. **oncle par** ~ uncle by marriage. (**c**) *(bague)* (wedding) ring. (**d**) *(fig: mélange)* combination.

allier [alje] (7) **1** *vt efforts* to combine, unite; *couleurs* to match (*à* with). **2 s'** ~ *vpr [efforts]* to combine, unite; *[couleurs]* to match; *(Pol)* to become allies *ou* allied. **s'** ~ **à** to become allied to *ou* with, ally o.s. with. ◆ **allié, e 1** *adj pays* allied. **2** *nm, f (Pol, fig)* ally; *(parent)* relative by marriage.

alligator [aligatɔʀ] *nm* alligator.

allô [alo] *excl (Téléc)* hello!, hullo!

allocation [alɔkɑsjɔ̃] *nf* (**a**) **(V allouer)** allocation; granting; allotment. (**b**) *(somme)* allowance. ~ **de chômage** unemployment benefit; ~**s familiales** *(argent)* family allowance(s), child benefits; *(bureau)* social security office; ~ **de maternité** ≃ maternity allowance *ou* benefit.

allocution [alɔkysjɔ̃] *nf* short speech. ◆ **allocutaire** *nmf* addressee.

allonger [alɔ̃ʒe] (3) **1** *vt* (**a**) *(rendre plus long)* to lengthen, extend (*de* by); *(étendre)* to stretch out. ~ **le pas** to quicken one's step. (**b**) (‡) *somme* to hand out; *coup* to deal. ~ **qn** to knock sb flat. (**c**) *sauce* to thin (down). **2** *vi*: **les jours allongent** the days are growing longer. **3 s'** ~ *vpr* (**a**) *[ombres, jours]* to lengthen; *[enfant]* to grow taller; *[discours]* to drag on. *(fig)* **son visage s'allongea** his face fell; **la route s'allongeait devant eux** the road stretched away before them. (**b**) *(s'étendre)* to lie down, stretch out. ◆ **allongé, e** *adj* (**a**) *(étendu)* **être** ~ to be stretched out, be lying; ~ **sur son lit/sur le dos** lying on one's bed/on one's back. (**b**) *(long)* long; *(étiré)* elongated; *(oblong)* oblong. ◆ **allongement** *nm (gén)* lengthening; *(Métal)* elongation.

allouer [alwe] (1) *vt argent* to allocate; *indemnité* to grant; *(Fin) actions* to allot; *temps* to allot, allow, allocate.

allumage [alymaʒ] *nm [poêle]* lighting; *[électricité]* putting *ou* switching on; *(Aut)* ignition. *(Aut)* **régler l'** ~ to adjust the timing.

allume-cigare [alymsigaʀ] *nm inv* cigar lighter.

allume-gaz [alymgaz] *nm inv* gas lighter *(for cooker)*.

allumer [alyme] (1) **1** *vt* (**a**) *feu* to light. **le feu était allumé** the fire was lit. (**b**) *électricité* to put *ou* switch *ou* turn on; *gaz* to light, turn on. **laisse la lumière allumée** leave the light on; **ça n'allume pas** the light doesn't come on *ou* work; **où est-ce qu'on allume?** where is the switch?; ~ **une pièce** to put the light on in a room; **sa fenêtre était allumée** there was a light on at his window. (**c**) *sentiment* to arouse, stir up; *guerre* to stir up. **2 s'** ~ *vpr [incendie]* to blaze, flare up; *[sentiment]* to be aroused; *[guerre]* to break out. **son regard s'alluma** his face lit up; **sa fenêtre s'alluma** a light came *ou* went on at his window; **où est-ce que ça s'allume?** where do you switch it on?

allumette [alymɛt] *nf* (**a**) match. ~ **de sûreté** safety match. (**b**) *(Culin)* flaky pastry finger.

allumeur [alymœʀ] *nm (Aut)* distributor; *(Tech)* igniter. *(Hist)* ~ **de réverbères** lamplighter.

allure [alyʀ] *nf* (**a**) *(vitesse) [véhicule]* speed; *[piéton]* pace. **à toute** ~ at top *ou* full speed. (**b**) *(démarche)* walk; *(attitude)* air, look, appearance. **avoir fière/piètre** ~ to cut a fine/shabby figure; **d'** ~ **bizarre** odd-looking; **liberté d'** ~**s** free *ou* unconventional behaviour.

allusion [alyzjɔ̃] *nf* allusion (*à* to), hint (*à* at). ~ **malveillante** innuendo; **faire** ~ **à** to allude to, hint at; **par** ~ allusively. ◆ **allusif, -ive** *adj* allusive.

alluvions [alyvjɔ̃] *nfpl* alluvial deposits.

almanach [almana] *nm* almanac.

aloès [alɔɛs] *nm* aloe.

aloi [alwa] *nm*: **de bon ~** *gaieté* wholesome; *individu* worthy; *produit* of genuine quality; **de mauvais ~** unwholesome; of little worth; of doubtful quality.

alors [alɔʀ] *adv (à cette époque)* then, in those days, at that time; *(en conséquence)* then, in that case, so. **~ que** *(simultanéité)* while, when; *(opposition)* whereas; **~ même que** *(même si)* even if, though; *(au moment où)* while, just when; **elle est sortie ~ que le médecin le lui avait interdit** she went out although *ou* even though the doctor had told her not to; **~ tu viens?** well (then), are you coming?; **~ là d'accord** well then all right; **il pleut — et ~?** it's raining — so (what)?

alouette [alwɛt] *nf* lark. **~ des champs** skylark.

alourdir [aluʀdiʀ] (2) **1** *vt (gén)* to make heavy; *impôts* to increase; *véhicule* to weigh down. **le gaz alourdissait l'air** the smell of gas hung heavy on the air, the air was heavy with the smell of gas. **2 s' ~** *vpr* to become *ou* grow heavy. ◆ **alourdissement** *nm [véhicule, objet]* increased weight, heaviness; *[impôts]* increase (*de* in).

aloyau [alwajo] *nm* sirloin.

alpaga [alpaga] *nm (Tex, Zool)* alpaca.

alpaguer ‡ [alpage] (1) *vt* to nab *. **se faire ~** to get nabbed *.

Alpes [alp(ə)] *nfpl*: **les ~** the Alps. ◆ **alpage** *nm* high mountain pasture. ◆ **alpestre** *adj* alpine.

alphabet [alfabɛ] *nm (système)* alphabet; *(livre)* alphabet book. **~ morse** Morse code; **~ phonétique international** International Phonetic Alphabet. ◆ **alphabétique** *adj* alphabetical. ◆ **alphabétiquement** *adv* alphabetically. ◆ **alphabétiser** (1) *vt*: **~ qn** to teach sb how to read and write.

alpin, e [alpɛ̃, in] *adj* alpine.

alpinisme [alpinism(ə)] *nm* mountaineering, climbing. ◆ **alpiniste** *nmf* mountaineer, climber.

Alsace [alzas] *nf*: **l' ~** Alsace.

altérant, e [alteʀɑ̃, ɑ̃t] *adj* thirst-making.

altercation [altɛʀkɑsjɔ̃] *nf* altercation.

altérer [alteʀe] (6) **1** *vt* (**a**) *(assoiffer)* to make thirsty. (**b**) *texte, vérité* to distort, falsify; *aliments* to adulterate. (**c**) *denrées* to spoil; *matière, sentiments* to alter; *visage, voix* to distort; *santé* to impair. (**d**) *(modifier)* to alter, change. **2 s' ~** *vpr [nourriture]* to go off; *[santé, relations]* to deteriorate; *[voix]* to break; *[vin]* to spoil. ◆ **altération** *nf* (**a**) distortion, falsification; alteration; adulteration; impairment; change. **l' ~ de sa santé** the deterioration in his health; **l' ~ de son visage/de sa voix** his distorted features/broken voice. (**b**) *(Mus)* accidental.

alternance [altɛʀnɑ̃s] *nf (gén)* alternation; *(Pol)* changeover of political power between parties. **être en ~** *[émissions]* to alternate; **travailler en ~** to work alternately (*avec* with).

alternateur [altɛʀnatœʀ] *nm* alternator.

alternatif, -ive [altɛʀnatif, iv] **1** *adj* alternate; *(Élec)* alternating. **2** *nf (dilemme)* alternative. **être dans une ~ive** to have to choose between two alternatives. ◆ **alternativement** *adv* alternately, in turn.

alterner [altɛʀne] (1) *vt* to alternate (*avec* with). **ils alternèrent à la présidence** they took turns to be chairman *ou* to chair. ◆ **alterne, alterné, e** *adj* alternate.

altesse [altɛs] *nf (titre)* highness.

altier, -ière [altje, jɛʀ] *adj* haughty.

altitude [altityd] *nf* altitude, height (above sea level). **à 500 mètres d' ~** at a height *ou* an altitude of 500 metres; **en ~** at high altitude, high up; **prendre de l' ~** to gain altitude.

alto [alto] **1** *nm (instrument)* viola. **2** *adj*: **saxo(phone)/flûte ~** alto sax(ophone)/flute.

altruisme [altʀɥism(ə)] *nm* altruism. ◆ **altruiste** **1** *adj* altruistic. **2** *nmf* altruist.

alumine [alymin] *nf* alumina.

aluminium [alyminjɔm] *nm* aluminium.

alun [alœ̃] *nm* alum.

alunir [alyniʀ] (2) *vi* to land on the moon. ◆ **alunissage** *nm* (moon) landing.

alvéole [alveɔl] *nf ou m [ruche, poumon]* cell. **~ dentaire** tooth socket; **~s dentaires** alveolar *ou* teeth ridge.

amabilité [amabilite] *nf* kindness. **ayez l' ~ de** be so kind as to; **faire des ~s à qn** to be polite to sb.

amadou [amadu] *nm* touchwood, tinder.

amadouer [amadwe] (1) *vt (enjôler)* to coax, cajole; *(adoucir)* to mollify.

amaigrir [amegʀiʀ] (2) *vt* to make thin *ou* thinner. ◆ **amaigrissant, e** *adj régime* slimming, reducing *(US)*. ◆ **amaigrissement** *nm (pathologique) [corps]* loss of weight; *[visage, membres]* thinness; *(volontaire)* slimming. **un ~ de 3 kg** a loss in weight of 3 kg.

amalgame [amalgam] *nm (péj)* (strange) combination; *(Métal)* amalgam. ◆ **amalgamer** (1) **1** *vt* to combine; to amalgamate. **2 s' ~** *vpr* to combine.

amande [amɑ̃d] *nf* (**a**) *(fruit)* almond. **en ~** almond-shaped. (**b**) *[noyau]* kernel. ◆ **amandier** *nm* almond (tree).

amant [amɑ̃] *nm* lover. ◆ **amante** † *nf* mistress †.

amarrer [amaʀe] (1) *vt navire* to moor; *paquet* to make fast. ◆ **amarrage** *nm* mooring. ◆ **amarre** *nf* (mooring) rope. **les ~ s** moorings.

amas [amɑ] *nm (lit)* heap, pile; *[idées]* mass; *(Astron)* star cluster; *(Min)* mass.

amasser [amɑse] (1) **1** *vt choses* to pile up, amass; *fortune* to amass; *preuves* to amass, gather (together). **2 s' ~** *vpr [choses, preuves]* to pile up, accumulate; *[foule]* to gather.

amateur [amatœʀ] *nm (non-professionnel)* amateur; *(péj)* dilettante, mere amateur. **équipe ~** amateur team; **faire de la peinture en ~** to do a bit of painting (as a hobby); **photographe ~** amateur photographer, photo hobbyist *(US)*; **~ d'art** art lover; **être ~ de films** to be a keen *ou* avid film-goer; **faire qch en ~** to do sth as a mere amateur; **y a-t-il des ~s?** *(volontaires)* are there any volunteers?; *(acheteurs)* are there any takers? ◆ **amateurisme** *nm (Sport)* amateurism; *(péj)* amateurishness.

Amazone [amazon] *nf* (**a**) *(Géog)* Amazon; *(Myth)* Amazon. (**b**) *(écuyère)* **a~** horsewoman; **monter en a~** to ride sidesaddle.

Amazonie [amazɔni] *nf* Amazonia. ◆ **amazonien, -ienne** *adj* Amazonian.

ambages [ɑ̃bɑʒ] *nfpl*: **sans ~** without beating about the bush, in plain language.

ambassade [ɑ̃basad] *nf (Pol)* embassy; *(mission)* mission. ◆ **ambassadeur** *nm (Pol, fig)* ambassador. **~ extraordinaire** ambassador extraordinary (*auprès de* to). ◆ **ambassadrice** *nf* ambassador; *(épouse)* ambassadress.

ambiance [ɑ̃bjɑ̃s] *nf* atmosphere (*de* in, of).

ambiant, e [ɑ̃bjɑ̃, ɑ̃t] *adj* surrounding; *température* ambient.

ambidextre [ɑ̃bidɛkstʀ(ə)] *adj* ambidextrous.

ambigu, -uë [ɑ̃bigy] *adj* ambiguous. ◆ **ambiguïté** *nf* ambiguity. **sans ~** *(adj)* unambiguous; *(adv)* unambiguously.

ambitieux, -euse [ɑ̃bisjø, øz] *adj* ambitious. **~ de plaire** anxious to please. ◆ **ambitieusement** *adv* ambitiously. ◆ **ambition** *nf* ambition.

◆ **ambitionner** (1) *vt*: **il ambitionne de faire** his ambition is to do.

ambivalence [ɑ̃bivalɑ̃s] *nf* ambivalence. ◆ **ambivalent, e** *adj* ambivalent.

amble [ɑ̃bl(ə)] *nm [cheval]* amble.

amblyope [ɑ̃blijɔp] **1** *adj*: **il est** ~ he has a lazy eye, he is amblyopic. **2** *nmf* person with a lazy eye *ou* amblyopia.

ambre [ɑ̃bʀ(ə)] *nm*: ~ **(jaune)** amber; ~ **gris** ambergris. ◆ **ambré, e** *adj couleur* amber.

ambulance [ɑ̃bylɑ̃s] *nf* ambulance. ◆ **ambulancier, -ière** *nm, f (conducteur)* ambulance driver; *(infirmier)* ambulance man (*ou* woman).

ambulant, e [ɑ̃bylɑ̃, ɑ̃t] *adj musicien* strolling, travelling. **c'est un dictionnaire** ~ * he's a walking dictionary.

âme [ɑm] *nf* (**a**) *(gén)* soul. *(fig)* **avoir l'** ~ **chevillée au corps** to have nine lives; **avoir une** ~ **généreuse** to have great generosity of spirit; **avoir une** ~ **basse** to have an evil heart; **grandeur d'** ~ noble-mindedness; **en mon** ~ **et conscience** in all conscience; **ému jusqu'au fond de l'** ~ profoundly moved; **il est musicien dans l'** ~ he's a musician to the core. (**b**) *(personne)* soul. **on ne voyait** ~ **qui vive** you couldn't see a (living) soul; **bonne** ~ * kind soul; **il erre comme une** ~ **en peine** he is wandering about like a lost soul; **son** ~ **damnée** his henchman; **trouver l'** ~ **sœur** to find a soul mate; **l'** ~ **d'un complot** the moving spirit in a plot. (**c**) *(Tech) [canon]* bore; *[violon]* soundpost.

améliorer *vt*, **s'** ~ *vpr* [ameljɔʀe] (1) *(gén)* to improve. ◆ **amélioration** *nf* improvement. *(Écon)* **une** ~ **de la conjoncture** an economic upturn, an improvement in the state of the economy.

amen [amɛn] *adv (Rel, fig)* amen.

aménager [amenaʒe] (3) *vt* (**a**) *(équiper) local* to fit out; *parc* to lay out; *territoire* to develop. (**b**) *(créer) route* to make, build; *gradins* to fix up; *horaire* to work out. ~ **un bureau dans une chambre** to fit up a study in a bedroom; ~ **une chambre en bureau** to convert a bedroom into a study. ◆ **aménagement** *nm (gén)* development. ~**s** *[local]* fittings; *[quartier]* developments; *[horaire]* adjustments. ◆ **aménageable** *adj horaire* flexible; *grenier* which can be converted (*en* into).

amende [amɑ̃d] *nf* fine. **mettre à l'** ~ to penalize; **donner une** ~ **à** to fine; **faire** ~ **honorable** to make amends.

amender [amɑ̃de] (1) **1** *vt (Pol)* to amend; *(Agr)* to enrich; *conduite* to improve, amend. **2 s'** ~ *vpr* to mend one's ways. ◆ **amendement** *nm (Pol)* amendment; *(Agr) (opération)* enrichment; *(substance)* enriching agent.

amène [amɛn] *adj* affable. **peu** ~ unkind.

amener [amne] (5) **1** *vt* (**a**) *personne, objet* to bring; *catastrophe* to cause, bring about. **qu'est-ce qui vous amène ici?** what brings you here? (**b**) *(inciter)* ~ **qn à faire qch** *[circonstances]* to lead *ou* bring sb to do sth; *[personne]* to get sb to do sth; **je suis amené à croire que** I am led to think that; ~ **qn à ses propres idées** to bring sb round to one's own ideas; ~ **la conversation sur un sujet** to lead the conversation on to a subject; **amené à un haut degré de complexité** brought to a high degree of complexity. (**c**) *transition, conclusion* to present, introduce. **bien amené** well-introduced. (**d**) *poisson* to draw in; *voile, drapeau* to strike. **2 s'** ~ * *vpr (venir)* to come along.

aménité [amenite] *nf* affability. **sans** ~ unkindly.

amenuiser (s') [amənɥize] (1) *vpr [valeur, espoir]* to dwindle; *[chances]* to lessen; *[provisions]* to run low, dwindle. ◆ **amenuisement** *nm* dwindling; lessening.

amer, -ère [amɛʀ] *adj* bitter. ◆ **amèrement** *adv* bitterly.

américain, e [ameʀikɛ̃, ɛn] **1** *adj* American. **2** *nm (Ling)* American (English). **3** *nm(f)*: **A~(e)** American. ◆ **américaniser** (1) *vt* to americanize. ◆ **américanisme** *nm* americanism. ◆ **américaniste** *nmf* Americanist. ◆ **Amérique** *nf* America. ~ **centrale/latine/du Nord/du Sud** Central/Latin/North/South America.

amérindien, -ienne [ameʀɛ̃djɛ̃, jɛn] *adj*, **A~(ne)** *nm(f)* Amerindian, American Indian.

amerrir [ameʀiʀ] (2) *vi (Aviat)* to make a sea-landing; *(Espace)* to splash down. ◆ **amerrissage** *nm* (sea) landing; splashdown.

amertume [amɛʀtym] *nf (lit, fig)* bitterness.

améthyste [ametist(ə)] *nf, adj inv* amethyst.

ameublement [amœbləmɑ̃] *nm (meubles)* furniture. **articles d'** ~ furnishings.

ameublir [amœbliʀ] (2) *vt (Agr)* to loosen.

ameuter [amøte] (1) *vt (attrouper) curieux* to draw a crowd of; *voisins* to bring out; *(soulever)* to rouse, stir up (*contre* against). **des passants s'ameutèrent** a crowd of passers-by gathered (angrily).

ami, e [ami] **1** *nm, f* (**a**) friend. ~ **d'enfance** childhood friend; **elle est avec ses** ~**es** she's with her (girl)friends; **se faire un** ~ **de qn** to make friends with sb; ~**s des bêtes** animal lovers; **club des** ~**s de Balzac** Balzac society; **un professeur de mes** ~**s** a teacher friend of mine; **sans** ~**s** friendless. (**b**) *(amant)* boyfriend; *(maîtresse)* girlfriend, lady-friend. (**c**) **mes chers** ~**s** (ladies and) gentlemen; **mon cher** ~ my dear fellow. **2** *adj* friendly. **être très** ~ **avec qn** to be very friendly *ou* be good friends with sb; **être** ~ **de l'ordre** to be a lover of order.

amiable [amjabl(ə)] *adj*: *(Jur)* **à l'** ~ *vente* private; *accord* amicable; **régler qch à l'** ~ to settle sth out of court.

amiante [amjɑ̃t] *nm* asbestos.

amibe [amib] *nf* amoeba.

amical, e, *mpl* **-aux** [amikal, o] **1** *adj* friendly. **peu** ~ unfriendly. **2** *nf* association, club. ◆ **amicalement** *adv* in a friendly way. *[lettre]* **(bien)** ~ best wishes, yours.

amidon [amidɔ̃] *nm* starch. ◆ **amidonner** (1) *vt* to starch.

amincir [amɛ̃siʀ] (2) **1** *vt couche* to thin (down). **cette robe l'amincit** this dress makes her look slim(mer) *ou* thin(ner). **2 s'** ~ *vpr* to get thinner. ◆ **amincissement** *nm* thinning (down). **cure d'** ~ slimming *ou* reducing *(US)* treatment.

amiral, e, *mpl* **-aux** [amiʀal, o] **1** *adj*: **vaisseau** ~ flagship. **2** *nm* admiral. **3** *nf* admiral's wife. ◆ **amirauté** *nf* admiralty.

amitié [amitje] *nf* (**a**) *(sentiment)* friendship. **prendre qn en** ~ to take a liking to sb; **se lier d'** ~ **avec qn** to make friends with sb; **avoir de l'** ~ **pour qn** to be fond of sb; **faites-moi l'** ~ **de venir** do me the favour of coming. (**b**) *[lettre]* ~**s, Paul** yours, Paul; **elle vous fait toutes ses** ~**s** she sends her regards.

ammoniac [amɔnjak] *nm* ammonia. ◆ **ammoniaque** *nf* liquid ammonia.

amnésie [amnezi] *nf* amnesia. ◆ **amnésique 1** *adj* amnesic. **2** *nmf* amnesiac, amnesic.

amnios [amnjɔs] *nm* amnion. ◆ **amniotique** *adj* amniotic. **cavité/liquide** ~ amniotic cavity/liquid.

amnistie [amnisti] *nf* amnesty. ◆ **amnistier** (7) *vt* to amnesty.

amocher ⁑ [amɔʃe] (1) *vt* to mess up *, make a mess of. **se faire** ~ to get messed up *.

amoindrir [amwɛ̃dʀiʀ] (2) **1** *vt forces* to weaken; *quantité* to diminish, reduce. *(humilier)* ~ **qn** to diminish *ou* belittle sb. **2 s'** ~ *vpr* to grow weaker, weaken; to diminish. ◆ **amoindrissement** *nm* weakening; diminishing; reduction.

amollir [amɔliʀ] (2) **1** *vt chose, esprit* to soften; *forces* to weaken. **2 s'** ~ *vpr [chose]* to go soft; *(fig)* to weaken. ◆ **amollissement** *nm* softening; weakening.

amonceler [amɔ̃sle] (4) **1** *vt choses* to pile *ou* heap up; *difficultés* to accumulate. **2 s'** ~ *vpr* to pile *ou* heap up; to accumulate; *[nuages, neige]* to bank up. ◆ **amoncellement** *nm* (**a**) piling *ou* heaping up; accumulation. (**b**) *(tas)* pile, heap.

amont [amɔ̃] *nm [cours d'eau]* upstream water; *[pente]* uphill slope. **en** ~ upstream; uphill (*de* from); **l'écluse d'** ~ the upstream lock.

amoral, e, *mpl* **-aux** [amɔʀal, o] *adj* amoral.

amorce [amɔʀs(ə)] *nf* (**a**) *(Pêche)* bait; *(de fond)* ground bait. (**b**) *(explosif)* cap. (**c**) *(début)* start, beginning; *[pellicule, film]* trailer. **l'** ~ **d'une réforme** the beginnings of a reform. (**d**) *(Ordin)* **programme d'** ~ bootstrap.

amorcer [amɔʀse] (3) *vt* (**a**) *hameçon* to bait; *(fig) client* to entice. (**b**) *pompe, siphon* to prime. (**c**) *négociations, travaux* to start, begin. **la construction est amorcée depuis 2 mois** work has been in progress *ou* been under way for 2 months; **une descente s'amorce après le virage** after the bend the road starts to go down; **une détente s'amorce** there are signs of a détente. ◆ **amorçage** *nm* baiting; ground baiting; priming.

amorphe [amɔʀf(ə)] *adj* passive.

amortir [amɔʀtiʀ] (2) *vt* (**a**) *coup* to cushion, soften; *bruit* to deaden, muffle; *douleur* to dull. *(Tennis)* **un amorti** a drop shot; *(Ftbl)* **faire un amorti** to trap the ball. (**b**) *(Fin) dette* to pay off; *titre* to redeem; *matériel* to write off. **pour** ~ **la dépense** to recoup the cost. ◆ **amortissable** *adj (Fin)* redeemable. ◆ **amortissement** *nm* cushioning, softening; deadening; muffling; dulling; paying off; redemption. **l'** ~ **de ce matériel se fait en 3 ans** it takes 3 years to recoup *ou* write off the cost of this equipment. ◆ **amortisseur** *nm* shock absorber.

amour [amuʀ] **1** *nm* (**a**) *(sentiment)* love. **roman d'** ~ love story; **faire l'** ~ to make love (*avec* to, with). (**b**) *(personne)* love; *(aventure)* love affair. **mon** ~ my love; **cet enfant est un** ~ that child's a real darling; **tu seras un** ~ there's a darling *ou* a dear; **un** ~ **de bébé/de petite robe** a lovely *ou* sweet little baby/dress. (**c**) **pour l'** ~ **de Dieu/de votre mère** for God's/your mother's sake; **faire qch pour l'** ~ **de l'art** * to do sth for the love of it; **faire qch avec** ~ to do sth with loving care. **2** *nfpl (littér)* ~**s** *(personnes)* loves; *(aventures)* love affairs. **3** : ~**-propre** *nm* self-esteem, pride.

amoureux, -euse [amuʀø, øz] **1** *adj* (**a**) *(épris)* in love (*de* with). **être** ~ **de la nature** to be a nature-lover. (**b**) *aventures* amorous, love; *tempérament* amorous; *regard* loving. **2** *nm, f (gén)* lover; *(†: soupirant)* love, sweetheart. ~ **transi** bashful lover; **partir en vacances en** ~ to go off on holiday like a pair of lovers. ◆ **amoureusement** *adv* lovingly, amorously.

amovible [amɔvibl(ə)] *adj* removable, detachable; *(Jur)* removable.

ampère [ɑ̃pɛʀ] *nm* ampere, amp. ◆ **ampèremètre** *nm* ammeter.

amphibie [ɑ̃fibi] **1** *adj* amphibious. **2** *nm* amphibian.

amphithéâtre [ɑ̃fiteɑtʀ(ə)] *nm (Archit, Géol)* amphitheatre; *(Univ)* lecture hall *ou* theatre; *(Théât)* upper gallery.

amphore [ɑ̃fɔʀ] *nf* amphora.

ample [ɑ̃pl(ə)] *adj jupe* full, ample, roomy; *geste* sweeping, wide; *voix* sonorous; *style* grand; *projet* vast; *sujet* wide-ranging. **faire** ~**(s) provision(s) de** to gather a liberal *ou* plentiful supply of; **donner d'** ~**s détails** to give a wealth of detail *ou* full details; **jusqu'à plus** ~ **informé** until further information is available. ◆ **amplement** *adv mériter* fully, amply. **il a fait** ~ **ce qu'on lui demandait** he has fully accomplished what was asked of him; **ça suffit** ~ that's more than enough, that's ample.

ampleur [ɑ̃plœʀ] *nf [vêtement]* fullness; *[style, geste]* grandeur; *[sujet]* scope, range; *[crise]* scale, extent. **sans grande** ~ of limited scope, small-scale; **prendre de l'** ~ to grow in scale *ou* extent.

amplifier [ɑ̃plifje] (7) **1** *vt (gén)* to expand, develop, increase; *(péj) incident* to magnify; *son* to amplify. **2 s'** ~ *vpr* to grow, increase. ◆ **amplificateur** *nm* amplifier. ◆ **amplification** *nf* expansion, development, increase; magnification; amplification.

amplitude [ɑ̃plityd] *nf (Astron, Phys)* amplitude; *[températures]* range; *[catastrophe]* magnitude.

ampoule [ɑ̃pul] *nf (Élec)* bulb; *(Pharm)* phial, vial; *[main]* blister, ampulla.

amputer [ɑ̃pyte] (1) *vt* (**a**) *(Anat)* to amputate. **il est amputé (d'une jambe)** he has had a leg amputated, he has lost a leg. (**b**) *texte, budget* to cut drastically (*de* by). ◆ **amputation** *nf* amputation; drastic cut (*de* in).

Amsterdam [amstɛʀdam] *n* Amsterdam.

amulette [amylɛt] *nf* amulet.

amusant, e [amyzɑ̃, ɑ̃t] *adj (distrayant)* amusing, entertaining; *(drôle)* amusing, funny.

amuse-gueule [amyzgœl] *nm inv* appetizer.

amusement [amyzmɑ̃] *nm (jeu)* game; *(passe-temps)* diversion, pastime; *(fait de (se) divertir)* amusement.

amuser [amyze] (1) **1** *vt* (**a**) *(divertir)* to amuse, entertain; *(faire rire)* to amuse. **ces remarques ne m'amusent pas** I'm not amused by such remarks; **si vous croyez que ces réunions m'amusent** if you think I enjoy these meetings. (**b**) *(détourner l'attention de)* to distract (the attention of); *(tromper)* to delude.
2 s' ~ *vpr* (**a**) *(jouer) [enfants]* to play. **s'** ~ **avec** *jouet* to play with; *stylo, ficelle* to play *ou* fiddle with; **s'** ~ **à un jeu** to play a game; **s'** ~ **à faire** to amuse o.s. doing; *(fig)* **ne t'amuse pas à recommencer, sinon!** don't do *ou* start that again, or else! (**b**) *(se divertir)* to have fun *ou* a good time, enjoy o.s.; *(rire)* to have a good laugh. **s'** ~ **à faire** to have fun doing, enjoy o.s. doing; **nous nous sommes bien amusés** we had great fun *ou* a great time *; **c'était juste pour s'** ~ it was just for fun *ou* for a laugh; **il ne faut pas qu'on s'amuse** *(se dépêcher)* we mustn't dawdle; *(travailler)* we mustn't idle. (**c**) *(se jouer de)* **s'** ~ **de qn** to make a fool of sb. ◆ **amuseur, -euse** *nm, f* entertainer; *(péj)* clown.

amygdale [amidal] *nf* tonsil.

amylase [amilɑz] *nf* amylase.

an [ɑ̃] *nm* year. **dans 3** ~**s** in 3 years, in 3 years' time; **enfant de six** ~**s** six-year-old (child); **il a 22** ~**s** he is 22 (years old); **il reçoit tant par** ~ he gets so much a year *ou* per annum; **en l'** ~ **de grâce...** in the year of grace...; **je m'en moque comme de l'** ~ **quarante** I couldn't care less; **courbé sous le poids des** ~**s** bowed with age.

anachorète [anakɔʀɛt] *nm* anchorite.

anachronique [anakʀɔnik] *adj* anachronistic. ◆ **anachronisme** *nm* anachronism.

anagramme [anagʀam] *nf* anagram.

analogie [analɔʒi] *nf* analogy. **par** ~ **avec** by analogy with. ◆ **analogique** *adj* analogical. ◆ **analogue 1** *adj* analogous, similar (*à* to). **2** *nm* analogue.

analphabète [analfabɛt] *adj, nmf* illiterate. ◆ **analphabétisme** *nm* illiteracy.

analyse [analiz] *nf (gén)* analysis; *[sang, urine]* test. **ça ne résiste pas à l'** ~ it doesn't stand up to analysis; **avoir l'esprit d'** ~ to have an analytical mind; **se faire faire des ~s** to have some tests done; ~ **grammaticale** parsing; **faire l'** ~ **grammaticale de** to parse; ~ **logique** sentence analysis, diagramming *(US)*; ~ **de marché** market analysis *ou* survey. ◆ **analyser** (1) *vt* to analyse; to test; to parse. ◆ **analyste** *nmf* analyst. ◆ **analytique** *adj* analytical.

anamorphose [anamɔʀfoz] *nf* anamorphosis.

ananas [anana(s)] *nm (fruit, plante)* pineapple.

anarchie [anaʀʃi] *nf (Pol, fig)* anarchy. ◆ **anarchique** *adj* anarchic. ◆ **anarchiquement** *adv* anarchically. ◆ **anarchisme** *nm* anarchism. ◆ **anarchiste 1** *adj* anarchistic. **2** *nmf* anarchist.

anathème [anatɛm] *nm* anathema. *(fig)* **jeter l'** ~ **sur** to anathematize.

anatomie [anatɔmi] *nf (gén)* anatomy; *(analyse)* analysis. ◆ **anatomique** *adj* anatomical.

ancestral, e, *mpl* **-aux** [ɑ̃sɛstʀal, o] *adj* ancestral.

ancêtre [ɑ̃sɛtʀ(ə)] *nmf (aïeul)* ancestor; *(*: vieillard)* old man (*ou* woman); *(fig: précurseur)* ancestor, forerunner.

anchois [ɑ̃ʃwa] *nm* anchovy.

ancien, -ienne [ɑ̃sjɛ̃, jɛn] **1** *adj* **(a)** *(gén)* old; *(ancestral, antique)* ancient; *objet d'art* antique. **dans l'** ~ **temps** in (the) olden days. **(b)** *(précédent)* former, old. **son ~ne femme** his former *ou* previous wife; **mon ~ne école** my old school. **2** *nm (mobilier)* **l'** ~ antiques. **3** *nm, f (par l'âge)* elder, old man (*ou* woman); *(par l'expérience)* senior person. *(Hist)* **les ~s** the Ancients; ~ **combattant** war veteran, ex-serviceman; ~ **élève** former pupil; **l'A~ Régime** the Ancient Régime.

anciennement [ɑ̃sjɛnmɑ̃] *adv* formerly.

ancienneté [ɑ̃sjɛnte] *nf* **(a)** *(durée de service)* (length of) service; *(privilèges obtenus)* seniority. **à l'** ~ by seniority. **(b)** *[maison, famille]* oldness, age; *[objet d'art]* age, antiquity; *[loi, tradition]* ancientness.

ancre [ɑ̃kʀ(ə)] *nf (Naut, Tech)* anchor. **être à l'** ~ to be *ou* lie at anchor; **jeter/lever l'** ~ to cast *ou* drop/weigh anchor. ◆ **ancrage** *nm [grand bateau]* anchorage; *[petit bateau]* moorage.

ancrer [ɑ̃kʀe] (1) **1** *vt (Naut, Tech)* to anchor. **idée bien ancrée** firmly rooted idea. **2 s'** ~ *vpr (Naut)* to anchor. **il s'est ancré dans la tête que...** he got it rooted *ou* fixed in his head that...

Andalousie [ɑ̃daluzi] *nf* Andalusia.

Andes [ɑ̃d] *nfpl:* **les** ~ the Andes.

Andorre [ɑ̃dɔʀ] *nf* Andorra.

andouille [ɑ̃duj] *nf* **(a)** *(Culin)* andouille. **(b)** *(*‡*: imbécile)* clot *, dummy *, fool. **faire l'** ~ to act the fool.

âne [ɑn] *nm (Zool)* donkey, ass; *(fig)* ass, fool.

anéantir [aneɑ̃tiʀ] (2) *vt* **(a)** *(détruire)* to destroy, wipe out. **(b)** *[chaleur, chagrin]* to overwhelm; *[fatigue]* to exhaust. ◆ **anéantissement** *nm (destruction)* destruction, wiping out; *(fatigue)* exhaustion; *(abattement)* dejection.

anecdote [anɛkdɔt] *nf* anecdote. ◆ **anecdotique** *adj* anecdotal.

anémier [anemje] (7) **1** *vt* to make anaemic. **2 s'** ~ *vpr* to become anaemic. ◆ **anémie** *nf* anaemia. ◆ **anémique** *adj* anaemic.

anémone [anemɔn] *nf* anemone. ~ **de mer** sea anemone.

ânerie [ɑnʀi] *nf (caractère)* stupidity; *(parole)* stupid remark; *(gaffe)* blunder. **dire des ~s** to talk rubbish *ou* nonsense.

ânesse [ɑnɛs] *nf* she-ass.

anesthésie [anɛstezi] *nf (technique)* anaesthesia; *(opération)* anaesthetic. **sous** ~ under the anaesthetic, under anaesthesia; **faire une** ~ to give an anaesthetic. ◆ **anesthésier** (7) *vt* to anaesthetize. ◆ **anesthésique** *adj, nm* anaesthetic. ◆ **anesthésiste** *nmf* anaesthetist.

ange [ɑ̃ʒ] *nm (Rel, fig)* angel; *(Zool)* angel fish. **oui mon** ~ yes, darling; **tu seras un** ~ there's an angel *ou* a dear; **avoir une patience d'** ~ to have the patience of a saint; **c'est un** ~ **de bonté** he's the soul of goodness; **un** ~ **passa** there was an awkward pause; **être aux ~s** to be in (the) seventh heaven; ~ **déchu** fallen angel; ~ **gardien** *(Rel, fig)* guardian angel; *(garde du corps)* bodyguard.

angélique [ɑ̃ʒelik] **1** *adj* angelic. **2** *nf* angelica. ◆ **angéliquement** *adv* angelically.

angelot [ɑ̃ʒlo] *nm (Art)* cherub.

angélus [ɑ̃ʒelys] *nm* angelus.

angine [ɑ̃ʒin] *nf* tonsillitis. **avoir une** ~ to have a sore throat; ~ **de poitrine** angina (pectoris).

anglais, e [ɑ̃glɛ, ɛz] **1** *adj* English. **2** *nm* **(a) A~** Englishman; **les A~** *(en général)* English people, the English; *(Britanniques)* British people, the British; *(hommes)* Englishmen. **(b)** *(Ling)* English. ~ **canadien** Canadian English. **3** *nf* **(a) A~e** Englishwoman. **(b)** *(Coiffure)* **~es** ringlets. **(c)** *(Écriture)* ≃ modern English handwriting. **(d) à l' ~e** *légumes* boiled. **4** *adv:* **parler** ~ to speak English.

angle [ɑ̃gl(ə)] *nm [meuble, rue]* corner; *(Math)* angle; *(aspect)* angle, point of view; *(fig) [caractère]* rough edge. **le magasin qui fait l'** ~ the shop on the corner; **faire un** ~ **droit** to be at right angles (*avec* to); **vu sous cet** ~ seen from that angle; ~ **de braquage** lock.

Angleterre [ɑ̃glətɛʀ] *nf* England; *(Grande-Bretagne)* Britain.

anglican, e [ɑ̃glikɑ̃, an] *adj, nm, f* Anglican. ◆ **anglicanisme** *nm* Anglicanism.

angliciste [ɑ̃glisist(ə)] *nmf (étudiant)* student of English; *(spécialiste)* anglicist. ◆ **angliciser** (1) *vt* to anglicize. ◆ **anglicisme** *nm* anglicism.

anglo- [ɑ̃glɔ] *préf* anglo-. ◆ **anglo-américain** *nm (Ling)* American English. ◆ **anglo-canadien** *nm (Ling)* Canadian English. ◆ **anglo-normand, e** *adj, nm* Anglo-Norman. **les îles ~-~es** the Channel Islands. ◆ **anglo-saxon, -onne** *adj, nm, f* Anglo-Saxon.

anglophile [ɑ̃glɔfil] **1** *adj* anglophilic. **2** *nmf* anglophile. ◆ **anglophilie** *nf* anglophilia.

anglophobe [ɑ̃glɔfɔb] **1** *adj* anglophobic. **2** *nmf* anglophobe. ◆ **anglophobie** *nf* anglophobia.

anglophone [ɑ̃glɔfɔn] **1** *adj* English-speaking. **2** *nmf* English speaker.

angoisse [ɑ̃gwas] *nf (gén, Psych)* anguish; *(peur)* fear. **une étrange** ~ **le saisit** a strange feeling of anguish gripped him; **il vivait dans l'** ~ **d'un accident** he lived in fear and dread of an accident. ◆ **angoissant, e** *adj* harrowing, agonizing. **vivre des jours ~s** to suffer days of anguish *ou* agony. ◆ **angoissé, e** *adj voix* anguished; *question* agonized. **cri** ~ cry of anguish; **être** ~ *(inquiet)* to be in anguish; *(oppressé)* to feel suffocated. ◆ **angoisser** (1) *vt* to cause anguish to.

Angola [ɑ̃gɔla] *nm* Angola. ◆ **angolais, e** *adj,* **A~(e)** *nm(f)* Angolan.

anguille [ɑ̃gij] *nf* eel. **filer entre les doigts de qn comme une** ~ to slip right through sb's fingers; **il y a** ~ **sous roche** there's something in the wind.

angulaire [ɑ̃gylɛʀ] *adj* angular.

anguleux, -euse [ɑ̃gylø, øz] *adj* angular, bony.

anicroche * [anikʀɔʃ] *nf* hitch, snag. **sans ~s** smoothly, without a hitch.

ânier, -ière [ɑnje, jɛʀ] *nm, f* donkey-driver.

animal, e, *mpl* **-aux** [animal, o] *adj, nm (Bio, fig)* animal. **quel ~!** * what a lout!

animateur, -trice [animatœʀ, tʀis] *nm, f [spectacle]* compère; *[club]* leader, sponsor *(US)*; *(camp de vacances)* ≃ redcoat *, camp counselor *(US)*; *(Ciné: technicien)* animator. **l' ~ de cette entreprise** the driving force behind this undertaking; **c'est un ~ né** he's a born organizer.

animation [animɑsjɔ̃] *nf* (**a**) *(vie)* life, liveliness; *(affairement)* (hustle and) bustle; *[discussion]* animation, liveliness. **parler avec ~** to speak with great animation; **mettre de l' ~ dans une réunion** to liven up a meeting; **chargé de l' ~ culturelle** in charge of cultural activities. (**b**) *(Ciné)* animation.

animé, e [anime] *adj* (**a**) *(affairé)* busy; *(plein de vie)* lively; *discussion* animated, lively; *(Comm) enchères, marché* brisk. (**b**) *(Ling, Philos)* animate.

animer [anime] (1) **1** *vt* (**a**) *entreprise, groupe* to lead; *réunion* to conduct; *spectacle* to compère; *soirée, conversation* to liven up. **~ une course** to set the pace in a race. (**b**) *[sentiment]* to drive, impel; *[désir, motif]* to prompt. **la joie qui anime son visage** the joy that shines in his face. (**c**) *(mouvoir)* to drive. **animé d'un mouvement régulier** moving in a steady rhythm *ou* swinging steadily. (**d**) *(Philos)* to animate. **2 s' ~** *vpr [personne, rue, objet]* to come to life; *[conversation]* to become animated, liven up; *[yeux]* to light up.

animosité [animozite] *nf* animosity *(contre* towards, against).

anis [ani(s)] *nm (plante)* anise; *(Culin)* aniseed.

ankyloser [ɑ̃kiloze] (1) **1** *vt* to stiffen. **être ankylosé** to be stiff. **2 s' ~** *vpr* to stiffen up.

annales [anal] *nfpl* annals. **ça restera dans les ~** * that'll go down in history.

anneau, *pl* **~x** [ano] *nm (gén)* ring; *[chaîne]* link; *[serpent]* coil. *(Sport)* **les ~x** the rings.

année [ane] *nf* year. **tout au long de l' ~** the whole year round, throughout the whole year; **payé à l' ~** paid annually; **étudiant de deuxième ~** second-year student; *(Fin, Jur)* **~ de référence** relevant year; *(Statistiques)* **l' ~ de référence 1988** the 1988 benchmark; **les ~s 20/30** the 20s/30s ; **d' ~ en ~** from year to year; **~ bissextile/civile** leap/calendar year; **~-lumière** *nf, pl* **~s-~s** light year.

annexe [anɛks(ə)] **1** *adj document* appended; *travail, dépenses* subsidiary; *considérations* related. **les bâtiments ~s** the annexes. **2** *nf (Constr)* annexe; *[document]* annex; *[contrat]* schedule (*de, à* to). ◆ **annexer** (1) *vt territoire* to annex; *document* to append (*à* to). ◆ **annexion** *nf (Pol)* annexation.

annihiler [aniile] (1) *vt efforts* to ruin, destroy; *résistance* to wipe out; *personnalité* to crush. ◆ **annihilation** *nf* ruin; destruction; crushing.

anniversaire [anivɛʀsɛʀ] *nm [naissance]* birthday; *[événement]* anniversary.

annonce [anɔ̃s] *nf* announcement; *(publicité)* (newspaper) advertisement; *(fig: indice)* sign, indication; *(Bridge)* declaration. **petites ~s** small ads, want ads * *(US)*.

annoncer [anɔ̃se] (3) **1** *vt* (**a**) *fait* to announce (*à* to); *(Comm) réclame* to advertise. **je lui ai annoncé la nouvelle** I announced the news to her; *(mauvaise nouvelle)* I broke the news to her; **on annonce un grave incendie** a serious fire is reported to have broken out. (**b**) *(prédire) pluie, chômage* to forecast; *[présage]* to foretell; *[signe avant-coureur]* to herald. **ça n'annonce rien de bon** it bodes no good; **ce radoucissement annonce la pluie** this warmer weather is a sign that rain is on the way *ou* is a sign of rain. (**c**) *(dénoter)* to indicate, point to. (**d**) *personne* to announce. **sans se faire ~** without being announced. (**e**) *(Cartes)* to declare. *(fig)* **~ la couleur** to lay one's cards on the table. **2 s' ~** *vpr [personne]* to announce o.s., say who one is; *[événement]* to approach. **s' ~ bien/mal** to look good/bad; **ça s'annonce difficile** it looks like being difficult.

annonceur [anɔ̃sœʀ] *nm (publicité)* advertiser; *(speaker)* announcer.

annonciateur, -trice [anɔ̃sjatœʀ, tʀis] *adj*: **signe ~ de** portent of.

Annonciation [anɔ̃sjɑsjɔ̃] *nf*: **l' ~** *(événement)* the Annunciation; *(jour)* Annunciation Day, Lady Day.

annoter [anɔte] (1) *vt* to annotate. ◆ **annotation** *nf* annotation.

annuaire [anɥɛʀ] *nm* yearbook, annual; *[téléphone]* (telephone) directory, phone book *.

annuel, -elle [anɥɛl] *adj* annual, yearly. ◆ **annuellement** *adv* annually, yearly. ◆ **annuité** *nf* annual payment.

annulaire [anylɛʀ] *nm* ring *ou* third finger.

annuler [anyle] (1) **1** *vt contrat, élection* to nullify; *mariage* to annul; *commande* to cancel. **2 s' ~** *vpr [poussées]* to nullify each other, cancel each other out. ◆ **annulation** *nf* nullification; cancellation; annulment.

anoblir [anɔbliʀ] (2) *vt* to ennoble. ◆ **anoblissement** *nm* ennoblement.

anode [anɔd] *nf* anode.

anodin, e [anɔdɛ̃, in] *adj personne, détail* insignificant; *blessure* harmless.

anomalie [anɔmali] *nf (gén)* anomaly; *(Bio)* abnormality; *(Tech)* (technical) fault.

ânon [ɑnɔ̃] *nm* ass's foal.

ânonner [ɑnɔne] (1) *vti*: **~ (sa leçon)** to mumble (one's way) through one's lesson.

anonymat [anɔnima] *nm* anonymity. **garder l' ~** to remain anonymous. ◆ **anonyme** *adj (sans nom)* anonymous; *(impersonnel)* impersonal. ◆ **anonymement** *adv* anonymously.

anorak [anɔʀak] *nm* anorak.

anorexie [anɔʀɛksi] *nf* anorexia. ◆ **anorexique** *adj, nmf* anorexic.

anormal, e, *mpl* **-aux** [anɔʀmal, o] *adj (gén)* abnormal. **il est ~ qu'il n'ait pas les mêmes droits** it's abnormal for him not to have the same rights. ◆ **anormalement** *adv* abnormally.

anse [ɑ̃s] *nf [tasse]* handle; *(Géog)* cove.

antagonisme [ɑ̃tagɔnism(ə)] *nm* antagonism. ◆ **antagoniste 1** *adj* antagonistic. **2** *nmf* antagonist.

antan [ɑ̃tɑ̃] *nm*: **d' ~** of yesteryear, of long ago.

antarctique [ɑ̃taʀktik] **1** *adj* antarctic. **2** *nm*: **l'A~** the Antarctic, Antarctica.

antécédent, e [ɑ̃tesedɑ̃, ɑ̃t] **1** *adj* antecedent. **2** *nm (Gram, Philos)* antecedent. **~s** previous history.

antéchrist [ɑ̃tekʀist] *nm* Antichrist.

antédiluvien, -ienne [ɑ̃tedilyvjɛ̃, jɛn] *adj (lit, fig)* antediluvian.

antenne [ɑ̃tɛn] *nf* (**a**) *(Zool)* antenna, feeler; *(Rad)* aerial; *(fig: contact)* contact. *(fig)* **avoir des ~s** to have a sixth sense. (**b**) *(Rad, TV: écoute)* **sur** *ou* **à l' ~** on the air; **gardez l' ~** stay tuned in; **je donne l' ~ à Paris** over to Paris; **hors ~** off the air; **sur notre ~** on our station. (**c**) *(succursale)* sub-branch; *(de renseignements)* information service; *(Mil)* outpost; *(Méd)* (emergency) unit.

antérieur, e [ɑ̃teʀjœʀ] *adj* (**a**) *époque, situation* previous, earlier, former. **c'est ~ à la guerre** it was prior to the war. (**b**) *partie* front. **membre ~** forelimb. ◆ **antérieurement** *adv* earlier. **~ à** prior *ou* previous to. ◆ **antériorité** *nf [événement]* precedence; *(Gram)* anteriority.

anthologie [ɑ̃tɔlɔʒi] *nf* anthology.

anthracite [ɑ̃tʀasit] **1** *nm* anthracite. **2** *adj inv* charcoal grey.

anthropoïde [ɑ̃tʀɔpɔid] *adj, nm* anthropoid.

anthropologie [ɑ̃tʀɔpɔlɔʒi] *nf* anthropology. ◆ **anthropologique** *adj* anthropological. ◆ **anthropologiste** *nmf* anthropologist.

anthropophage [ɑ̃tʀɔpɔfaʒ] *adj, nm* cannibal. ◆ **anthropophagie** *nf* cannibalism.

anti [ɑ̃ti] *préf (gén)* anti-; *(contraire à)* un-. **anticonformisme** nonconformism; **antimatière** antimatter; **antimilitariste** antimilitarist; **antipoétique** unpoetic; **antisémitisme** antisemitism; **sérum antitétanique/antidiphtérique** tetanus/diphtheria serum; **campagne antialcoolique** campaign against alcohol.

antiaérien, -ienne [ɑ̃tiaeʀjɛ̃, jɛn] *adj canon* anti-aircraft; *abri* air-raid.

antiatomique [ɑ̃tiatɔmik] *adj*: **abri** ~ fallout shelter.

antibiotique [ɑ̃tibjɔtik] *adj, nm* antibiotic.

antibrouillard [ɑ̃tibʀujaʀ] *adj, nm (Aut)* **(phare)** ~ fog lamp.

antibuée [ɑ̃tibɥe] *adj inv*: **dispositif** ~ demister; **bombe** ~ anti-mist spray.

antichambre [ɑ̃tiʃɑ̃bʀ(ə)] *nf* antechamber, anteroom. **faire** ~ † to wait (for an audience with sb).

antichoc [ɑ̃tiʃɔk] *adj montre* shockproof.

anticipation [ɑ̃tisipɑsjɔ̃] *nf*: **paiement par** ~ payment in advance; **roman d'** ~ science fiction novel.

anticiper [ɑ̃tisipe] (1) **1** *vi (gén)* to anticipate; *(en imaginant)* to look *ou* think ahead; *(en racontant)* to jump ahead. ~ **sur qch** to anticipate sth; **sans vouloir** ~ **sur ce que je dirai** without wishing to go into what I shall say later. **2** *vt (gén, Fin)* to anticipate. ◆ **anticipé, e** *adj retour* early; *paiement* advance. **avec mes remerciements** ~**s** thanking you in advance.

anticorps [ɑ̃tikɔʀ] *nm* antibody.

anticyclone [ɑ̃tisiklon] *nm* anticyclone.

antidater [ɑ̃tidate] (1) *vt* to backdate.

antidépresseur [ɑ̃tidepʀesœʀ] *adj m, nm* antidepressant.

antidérapant, e [ɑ̃tideʀapɑ̃, ɑ̃t] *adj (Aut)* non-skid; *(Ski)* non-slip.

antidoping [ɑ̃tidɔpiɲ] *adj*, **antidopage** [ɑ̃tidɔpaʒ] *adj loi, test* antidoping; *contrôle* dope.

antidote [ɑ̃tidɔt] *nm (lit, fig)* antidote (*contre, de* for, against).

antiesclavagisme [ɑ̃tiɛsklavaʒism(ə)] *nm* abolitionism.

antigang [ɑ̃tigɑ̃g] *adj inv*: **brigade** ~ police commando squad.

antigel [ɑ̃tiʒɛl] *nm* antifreeze.

antigène [ɑ̃tiʒɛn] *nm* antigen.

antihausse [ɑ̃tios] *adj mesures* aimed at curbing price rises, anti-inflation.

Antilles [ɑ̃tij] *nfpl*: **les** ~ the West Indies. **les Grandes/Petites** ~ the Greater/Lesser Antilles. ◆ **antillais, e** *adj*, **A**~**(e)** *nm(f)* West Indian.

antilope [ɑ̃tilɔp] *nf* antelope.

antimite [ɑ̃timit] *nm* mothballs.

antimoine [ɑ̃timwan] *nm* antimony.

antinomie [ɑ̃tinɔmi] *nf* antinomy. ◆ **antinomique** *adj* antinomic(al).

antiparasite [ɑ̃tipaʀazit] *adj*: **dispositif** ~ suppressor.

antipathie [ɑ̃tipati] *nf* antipathy. **avoir de l'** ~ **pour qn** to dislike sb. ◆ **antipathique** *adj* unpleasant.

antipelliculaire [ɑ̃tipelikylɛʀ] *adj* anti-dandruff.

antipode [ɑ̃tipɔd] *nm (Géog)* **les** ~**s** the antipodes; *(Géog)* **être à l'** ~ *ou* **aux** ~**s** to be on the other side of the world (*de* from, to); *(fig)* **votre théorie est aux** ~**s de la mienne** our theories are poles apart.

antique [ɑ̃tik] *adj (de l'antiquité)* antique, ancient; *(très ancien)* ancient; *(péj)* antiquated, ancient. ◆ **antiquaire** *nmf* antique dealer. ◆ **antiquité** *nf (gén)* antiquity; *(meuble)* antique.

antisèche [ɑ̃tisɛʃ] *nf (Arg Scol)* crib.

antisepsie [ɑ̃tisɛpsi] *nf* antisepsis. ◆ **antiseptique** *adj, nm* antiseptic.

antiterroriste [ɑ̃titɛʀɔʀist(ə)] *adj* antiterrorist.

antithèse [ɑ̃titɛz] *nf (gén)* antithesis. *(fig: le contraire)* **c'est l'** ~ **de** it is the opposite of. ◆ **antithétique** *adj* antithetical.

antivénéneux, -euse [ɑ̃tivenenø, øz] *adj* antidotal.

antivenimeux, -euse [ɑ̃tivənimø, øz] *adj*: **sérum** ~ antivenom.

antivol [ɑ̃tivɔl] *nm, adj inv*: **(dispositif)** ~ anti-theft device.

antonyme [ɑ̃tɔnim] *nm* antonym.

antre [ɑ̃tʀ(ə)] *nm (caverne)* cave; *[animal] (fig)* den, lair.

anus [anys] *nm* anus.

anxieux, -euse [ɑ̃ksjø, øz] **1** *adj personne, regard* anxious, worried; *attente* anxious. ~ **de** anxious to. **2** *nm, f* worrier. ◆ **anxiété** *nf* anxiety. ◆ **anxieusement** *adv* anxiously.

aorte [aɔʀt(ə)] *nf* aorta.

août [u(t)] *nm* August; *pour loc V* **septembre** *et* **quinze**.

apache [apaʃ] *nm* (**a**) *(indien)* **A**~ Apache. (**b**) *(†: voyou)* tough.

apaisant, e [apɛzɑ̃, ɑ̃t] *adj* soothing.

apaisement [apɛzmɑ̃] *nm (calme)* calm, quiet; *(soulagement)* relief; *(pour rassurer)* reassurance. **donner des** ~**s à qn** to reassure sb; **cela lui procura un certain** ~ this brought him some relief.

apaiser [apeze] (1) **1** *vt personne* to calm down, pacify; *(adoucir) (gén)* to assuage; *désir, faim* to appease; *douleur, excitation* to soothe; *conscience* to salve, soothe; *scrupules* to allay. **2 s'** ~ *vpr [personne]* to calm down; *[vacarme, vagues, douleur]* to die down.

apanage [apanaʒ] *nm (privilège)* privilege. **avoir l'** ~ **de qch** to have the sole *ou* exclusive right to sth.

aparté [apaʀte] *nm (entretien)* private conversation; *(Théât)* aside. **en** ~ in an aside.

apartheid [apaʀtɛd] *nm* apartheid.

apathie [apati] *nf* apathy. ◆ **apathique** *adj* apathetic.

apatride [apatʀid] *nmf* stateless person.

apercevoir [apɛʀsəvwaʀ] (28) **1** *vt* (**a**) *(voir)* to see; *(brièvement)* to catch sight of *ou* a glimpse of; *(remarquer)* to notice. (**b**) *danger* to see, perceive; *difficultés* to see, foresee. **2 s'** ~ *vpr*: **s'** ~ **de** *erreur* to notice; *présence* to become aware of; **s'** ~ **que** to notice *ou* realize that.

aperçu [apɛʀsy] *nm (idée générale)* general idea *ou* picture; *(compte-rendu)* general survey. **avoir des** ~**s sur qch** to have some insight into sth.

apéritif [apeʀitif] *nm* aperitif, (pre-dinner *etc)* drink. **venez prendre l'** ~ come for drinks.

apesanteur [apəzɑ̃tœʀ] *nf* weightlessness.

à-peu-près [apøpʀɛ] *nm inv* vague approximation.

apeuré, e [apœʀe] *adj* frightened, scared.

aphone [afɔn] *adj* voiceless.

aphorisme [afɔʀism(ə)] *nm* aphorism.

aphrodisiaque [afʀɔdizjak] *adj, nm* aphrodisiac.

aphte [aft(ə)] *nm* mouth ulcer.

à-pic [apik] *nm* cliff.

apiculteur, -trice [apikyltœʀ, tʀis] *nm, f* beekeeper. ◆ **apiculture** *nf* beekeeping.

apitoyer [apitwaje] (8) **1** *vt* to move to pity. **n'essaie pas de m'** ~ don't try and make me feel sorry for you. **2 s'** ~ *vpr*: **s'** ~ **sur** to feel pity for. ◆ **apitoiement** *nm (pitié)* pity.

aplanir [aplaniʀ] (2) *vt terrain* to level; *difficultés* to smooth away. **les difficultés se sont aplanies** the difficulties smoothed themselves out *ou* were ironed out. ◆ **aplanissement** *nm* levelling ; smoothing away.

aplatir [aplatiʀ] (2) **1** *vt (gén)* to flatten; *couture* to press flat; *pli* to smooth (out). **2 s'** ~ *vpr* (**a**) *[personne]* to flatten o.s. (*contre* against); *(s'étendre)* to lie flat on the ground; *(*: tomber)* to fall flat on one's face; *(s'humilier)* to grovel (*devant* before, to). (**b**) *[choses] (devenir plus plat)* to become flatter; *(s'écraser)* to smash (*contre* against). ◆ **aplati, e** *adj* flat. ◆ **aplatissement** *nm (gén)* flattening; *(humiliation)* grovelling.

aplomb [aplɔ̃] *nm* (**a**) *(assurance)* composure, (self-) assurance; *(péj)* nerve, cheek *. **garder son** ~ to keep one's composure, remain composed; **perdre son** ~ to lose one's composure, get flustered. (**b**) *(équilibre)* balance; *(verticalité)* plumb. **d'** ~ *corps* steady, balanced; *mur* plumb; **se tenir d'** ~ **(sur ses jambes)** to be steady on one's feet; **tu n'as pas l'air d'** ~ * you look out of sorts; *(lit, fig)* **se remettre d'** ~ to get back on one's feet again; **le soleil tombait d'** ~ the sun was beating straight down.

apocalypse [apɔkalips(ə)] *nf (Rel) (livre)* **l'A**~ (the book of) Revelation, the Apocalypse; **vision d'** ~ vision of doom. ◆ **apocalyptique** *adj (Rel)* apocalyptic; *vision* apocalyptic, of doom.

apogée [apɔʒe] *nm (Astron, fig)* apogee.

apolitique [apɔlitik] *adj (indifférent)* apolitical; *(neutre)* non-political.

apologie [apɔlɔʒi] *nf* apology. **faire l'** ~ **de** to praise.

apoplexie [apɔplɛksi] *nf* apoplexy.

a posteriori [apɔsteʀjɔʀi] *loc adv, adj (gén)* after the event.

apostolat [apɔstɔla] *nm (Bible)* apostolate; *(prosélytisme)* proselytism; *(fig)* vocation. ◆ **apostolique** *adj* apostolic.

apostrophe [apɔstʀɔf] *nf (Gram)* apostrophe; *(interpellation)* rude remark. ◆ **apostropher** (1) *vt* to shout at.

apothéose [apɔteoz] *nf* apotheosis; *(Théât, gén: bouquet)* grand finale. **finir dans une** ~ to end in a blaze of glory.

apothicaire † [apɔtikɛʀ] *nm* apothecary †.

apôtre [apotʀ(ə)] *nm* apostle. **faire le bon** ~ to play the saint; **se faire l'** ~ **de** to make o.s. the spokesman *ou* advocate for.

apparaître [apaʀɛtʀ(ə)] (57) *vi (se montrer)* to appear (*à* to); *(sembler)* to seem, appear (*à* to); *[fièvre, boutons]* to break out. **la vérité lui apparut soudain** the truth suddenly dawned on him; **il apparaît que** it appears *ou* turns out that.

apparat [apaʀa] *nm (pompe)* pomp. **d'** ~ ceremonial.

appareil [apaʀɛj] *nm (instrument)* piece of apparatus, device; *(électrique, ménager)* appliance; *(poste)* set; *(Phot)* camera; *(téléphone)* (tele)phone; *(Aviat)* aircraft *(inv)*, craft *(inv)* *(US)*; *(Méd)* appliance; *(dentier)* brace; *(pour fracture)* splint. ~ **digestif** digestive system; **l'** ~ **policier/du parti** the police/party machinery; **qui est à l'** ~**?** who's speaking?; ~ **de mesure** measuring device ; ~**-photo** *nm, pl* ~**s-**~**s** camera; ~ **à sous** *(distributeur)* slot machine; *(jeu)* fruit machine.

appareiller [apaʀeje] (1) **1** *vi (Naut)* to cast off. **2** *vt (assortir)* to match up. ◆ **appareillage** *nm* casting off.

apparemment [apaʀamɑ̃] *adv* apparently.

apparence [apaʀɑ̃s] *nf* (**a**) *(gén)* appearance. ~ **négligée** shabby *ou* uncared-for look *ou* appearance; ~ **souriante** smiling exterior; **fausse** ~ mere façade; **il n'a plus une** ~ **de respect pour** he no longer has the least semblance of respect for. (**b**) **malgré les** ~**s** in spite of appearances; **contre toute** ~ against all expectations; **selon toute** ~ in all probability; **en** ~ *(apparemment)* apparently; *(hypocritement)* outwardly.

apparent, e [apaʀɑ̃, ɑ̃t] *adj* (**a**) *(visible) poutre* visible; *gêne, raison* apparent, obvious. **de façon** ~**e** visibly. (**b**) *(superficiel) solidité, causes* apparent. **ces contradictions ne sont qu'** ~**es** these are only outward *ou* surface discrepancies.

apparenter (s') [apaʀɑ̃te] (1) *vpr*: **s'** ~ **à** *(Pol)* to ally o.s. with; *(par mariage)* to marry into; *(ressembler à)* to be similar to.

appariteur [apaʀitœʀ] *nm (Univ)* ≃ porter, ≃ campus policeman *(US)*.

apparition [apaʀisjɔ̃] *nf* (**a**) *(arrivée) (gén)* appearance; *[boutons, fièvre]* outbreak. **faire son** ~ to appear; to break out. (**b**) *(vision, fantôme)* apparition.

appartement [apaʀtəmɑ̃] *nm* flat, apartment *(US)*; *[hôtel]* suite.

appartenance [apaʀtənɑ̃s] *nf* belonging (*à* to); membership (*à* of).

appartenir [apaʀtəniʀ] (22) **1** ~ **à** *vt indir (possession)* to belong to; *(participation)* to belong to, be a member of; **pour des raisons qui m'appartiennent** for reasons of my own; **un médecin ne s'appartient pas** a doctor's time is not his own. **2** *vb impers*: **il m'appartient de le faire** it is for me *ou* up to me to do it.

appât [apɑ] *nm (gén)* bait. **mordre à l'** ~ to rise to the bait, bite; **l'** ~ **du gain** the lure of gain. ◆ **appâter** (1) *vt gibier, client* to lure, entice; *piège* to bait.

appauvrir [apovʀiʀ] (2) **1** *vt (gén)* to impoverish; *sang* to make thin, weaken. **2 s'** ~ *vpr (gén)* to grow poorer; *[race]* to degenerate. ◆ **appauvrissement** *nm* impoverishment; degeneration.

appel [apɛl] **1** *nm* (**a**) *(cri)* call; *(demande pressante)* appeal. ~ **à l'aide/aux armes** call for help/to arms; **elle a entendu des** ~**s** she heard cries; **à son** ~, **elle se retourna** she turned round when he called; **manifestation à l'** ~ **d'une organisation** demonstration called by an organization; **l'** ~ **du devoir** the call of duty. (**b**) **faire** ~ **à** *générosité* to appeal to; *pompiers* to call on; *souvenirs* to call up; *courage* to summon up; *armée* to call out; **ça fait** ~ **à des connaissances spéciales** it calls for *ou* requires specialist knowledge. (**c**) *(présence)* **faire l'** ~ *(Scol)* to call the register; *(Mil)* to call the roll; *(Mil)* **l'** ~ **d'une classe** the call-up of a class. (**d**) *(Jur)* appeal (*contre* against). **faire** ~ **(d'un jugement)** to appeal (against a judgment); **sans** ~ *(Jur)* without appeal; *(fig)* final. (**e**) *(Cartes)* signal (*à* for). (**f**) *(élan)* take-off. (**g**) *(Ordin)* call. **2** : ~ **d'air** draught; ~ **de fonds** call for capital; *(Comm)* ~ **d'offres** invitation to tender; ~ **téléphonique** phone call; **faire un** ~ **de phares** to flash one's headlights, flash the high beams *(US)*.

appelé [aple] *nm (Mil)* conscript, draftee *(US)*, selectee *(US)*. *(Rel, fig)* **il y a beaucoup d'** ~**s et peu d'élus** many are called but few are chosen.

appeler [aple] (4) **1** *vt* (**a**) *personne, chien* to call; *nom* to call out; *(téléphoner à)* to call, phone. ~

qn par son prénom to call *ou* address sb by his first name; ~ **un chat un chat** to call a spade a spade; ~ **(qn) à l'aide** to call (to sb) for help; ~ **qn (d'un geste) de la main** to beckon to sb. (**b**) *(faire venir: gén)* to summon; *pompiers* to call out; *conscrits* to call up; *médecin* to send for; *(Jur)* to summon. **le patron l'a fait** ~ the boss sent for him. (**c**) *(désigner)* ~ **qn à** *poste* to appoint *ou* assign sb to; **être appelé à un brillant avenir** to be destined for a brilliant future; **la méthode est appelée à se généraliser** the method looks likely *ou* set to become general. (**d**) *(réclamer) [situation, conduite]* to call for. **une lâcheté en appelle une autre** one act of cowardice leads to another; **en** ~ **à** to appeal to; **en** ~ **de** to appeal against.
2 s' ~ *vpr*: **il s'appelle Paul** his name is Paul, he's called Paul; **voilà ce qui s'appelle une gaffe** that's what's called a blunder!

appellation [apelɑsjɔ̃] *nf* designation, appellation; *(mot)* term, name. *(Jur)* ~ **d'origine** label of origin.

appendice [apɛ̃dis] *nm (Anat, gén)* appendix; *(hum: nez)* ~ **nasal** proboscis *(hum)*. ◆ **appendicite** *nf* appendicitis.

appentis [apɑ̃ti] *nm* lean-to.

appesantir [apəzɑ̃tiʀ] (2) **1** *vt membre, objet* to make heavy; *esprit* to dull; *autorité* to strengthen (*sur* over). **2 s'** ~ *vpr [tête, pas]* to grow heavier; *[esprit]* to grow duller; *[autorité]* to grow stronger. **s'** ~ **sur un sujet** to dwell on a subject. ◆ **appesantissement** *nm [démarche]* heaviness; *[esprit]* dullness; *[autorité]* strengthening.

appétit [apeti] *nm (gén, fig)* appetite (*de* for). **avoir de l'** ~ to have a good *ou* hearty appetite; *(lit, fig)* **mettre qn en** ~ to give sb an appetite; **avoir un** ~ **d'oiseau** to eat like a bird; **manger avec** ~ to eat heartily; **l'** ~ **vient en mangeant** *(lit)* eating whets the appetite; *(fig)* the more you have the more you want. ◆ **appétissant, e** *adj* appetizing. **peu** ~ unappetizing.

applaudir [aplodiʀ] (2) **1** *vt (lit)* to applaud, clap; *(fig)* to applaud. **2** *vi* to applaud, clap. ~ **à tout rompre** to bring the house down. **3** ~ **à** *vt indir initiative* to applaud. **4 s'** ~ *vpr* to congratulate o.s., pat o.s. on the back (*d'avoir fait* for having done). ◆ **applaudissement** *nm*: ~**s** applause.

applicable [aplikabl(ə)] *adj* applicable (*à* to).

applicateur [aplikatœʀ] *adj m, nm* applicator.

application [aplikasjɔ̃] *nf* (**a**) **(V appliquer)** application; use; implementation; enforcement. **mettre en** ~ *décision* to implement; *loi* to enforce. (**b**) ~**s** *[théorie, méthode]* applications. (**c**) *(attention)* application (*à qch* to, sth). **travailler avec** ~ to work hard, apply o.s. well.

applique [aplik] *nf* wall lamp.

appliqué, e [aplike] *adj personne* industrious, painstaking; *écriture* careful. **bien** ~ *baiser* firm; *coup* well-aimed; **linguistique** *etc* ~**e** applied linguistics *etc.*

appliquer [aplike] (1) **1** *vt (gén)* to apply (*sur* to); *décision* to implement; *loi* to enforce; *recette* to use; *gifle* to give. ~ **un traitement/son esprit à qch** to apply a treatment/one's mind to sth; ~ **une échelle contre un mur** to put *ou* lean a ladder against a wall; ~ **sa main sur qch** to put one's hand on sth; **faire** ~ **la loi** to enforce the law. **2 s'** ~ *vpr [élève]* to apply o.s. (*à qch* to sth, *à faire qch* to doing sth); **s'** ~ **à qch** *[remarque]* to apply to sth; **s'** ~ **sur qch** *[calque]* to fit over sth.

appoint [apwɛ̃] *nm* (extra) contribution; *(monnaie)* right *ou* exact change. **faire l'** ~ to give the right *ou* exact money *ou* change; **salaire d'** ~ extra income.

appointer [apwɛ̃te] (1) *vt salarié* to pay. ◆ **appointements** *nmpl* salary.

appontement [apɔ̃tmɑ̃] *nm* landing stage.

apport [apɔʀ] *nm [capitaux, culture]* contribution; *[chaleur, eau]* supply. **le tourisme grâce à son** ~ **de devises** tourism, thanks to the currency it brings in; **l'** ~ **en vitamines d'un aliment** the vitamins provided by a food; *(Fin)* ~ **personnel** personal capital contribution.

apporter [apɔʀte] (1) *vt (gén)* to bring (*à* to); *modification* to introduce; *solution* to supply, provide; *soin* to exercise (*à faire* in doing). **apporte-le-lui** take it to him; **apporte-le en montant/en venant/en entrant** bring it up/along/in; **elle y a apporté toute son énergie** she put all her energy into it; **son livre n'apporte rien de nouveau** his book contributes nothing new.

apposer [apoze] (1) *vt (gén)* to affix; *signature* to append.

apposition [apozisjɔ̃] *nf (Gram)* apposition.

apprécier [apʀesje] (7) *vt* (**a**) *distance, importance* to estimate, assess, appraise; *(expertiser) objet* to value. (**b**) *nuance, qualité, repas* to appreciate. **mets très apprécié** much appreciated dish. ◆ **appréciable** *adj* appreciable. ◆ **appréciatif, -ive** *adj (estimatif)* appraising, evaluative; *(admiratif)* appreciative. ◆ **appréciation** *nf* assessment; appraisal; estimation; valuation. **je le laisse à votre** ~ I leave you to judge for yourself; ~**s du professeur sur un élève** teacher's assessment of a pupil; *(sur un livret)* ~ **du professeur** teacher's comments *ou* remarks.

appréhender [apʀeɑ̃de] (1) *vt* (**a**) *(arrêter)* to apprehend. (**b**) *(redouter)* to dread (*de faire* doing). ~ **que** to fear that. ◆ **appréhensif, -ive** *adj* apprehensive, fearful (*de* of). ◆ **appréhension** *nf* apprehension, anxiety. **voir qch avec** ~ to dread sth; **avoir de l'** ~ to be apprehensive.

apprendre [apʀɑ̃dʀ(ə)] (58) *vt* (**a**) *leçon, métier* to learn; *fait* to hear of, learn of. ~ **à connaître** to get to know; **ça s'apprend facilement** it's easy to learn; **apprenez que je ne me laisserai pas faire!** be warned that I won't be trifled with! (**b**) ~ **qch à qn** *nouvelle* to tell sb (of) sth; *science* to teach sb sth; *(iro)* **ça lui apprendra!** that'll teach him!

apprenti, e [apʀɑ̃ti] *nm, f [métier]* apprentice; *(débutant)* novice, beginner. ◆ **apprentissage** *nm (lit)* apprenticeship. **l'** ~ **de la langue** language learning; **l'** ~ **de l'anglais** learning English; **mettre qn en** ~ to apprentice sb (*chez* to); **école d'** ~ training school; **faire l'** ~ **de** *métier* to serve one's apprenticeship in; *douleur* to be initiated into.

apprêter [apʀete] (1) **1** *vt* (**a**) *(préparer)* to get ready. (**b**) *peau* to dress; *(Peinture)* to size. **2 s'** ~ *vpr* (**a**) **s'** ~ **à qch/à faire qch** to get ready for sth/ to do sth. (**b**) *(toilette)* to prepare o.s. ◆ **apprêt** *nm (opération)* dressing; sizing; *(substance)* dressing; size. ◆ **apprêté, e** *adj (affecté)* affected.

apprivoiser [apʀivwaze] (1) *vt* to tame. **s'** ~ to become tame. ◆ **apprivoisable** *adj* tameable. ◆ **apprivoisé, e** *adj* tame. ◆ **apprivoisement** *nm (action)* taming; *(état)* tameness.

approbation [apʀɔbɑsjɔ̃] *nf* approval, approbation. **digne d'** ~ commendable. ◆ **approbateur, -trice** *adj* approving.

approchable [apʀɔʃabl(ə)] *adj (gén)* accessible.

approchant, e [apʀɔʃɑ̃, ɑ̃t] *adj style, genre* similar (*de* to); *résultat* close (*de* to). **rien d'** ~ nothing like that.

approche [apʀɔʃ] *nf (gén)* approach. **à l'** ~ **de l'hiver** at the approach of winter, as winter draws near *ou* approaches; **d'** ~ **difficile** *lieu* inaccessible; *auteur* difficult to understand; **travaux d'** ~ *(Mil)* approaches; *(fig)* manœuvres; **les** ~**s de** *ville, côte* the surrounding area of.

approché, e [apʀɔʃe] *adj* approximate.

approcher [apʀɔʃe] (1) **1** *vt* (**a**) *objet* to move near (*de* to); *(l'un de l'autre)* to bring *ou* move closer together. **approche ta chaise** draw *ou* bring your chair nearer; **il approcha le verre de ses lèvres** he lifted *ou* raised the glass to his lips. (**b**) *personne (lit)* to go near, approach; *(fig)* to approach. **2** *vi [date]* to approach, draw near; *[personne, orage]* to approach, come nearer. **le jour approche où** the day is near when; **approche!** come here!; ~ **de** to approach, near. **3 s'** ~ *vpr (venir)* to come near, approach; *(aller)* to go near, approach. **il s'approcha de moi** he came up to me; **s'** ~ **du micro** *(venir)* to go up to the mike; *(se rapprocher)* to get closer *ou* nearer to the mike; **approche-toi!** come here!

approfondir [apʀɔfɔ̃diʀ] (2) **1** *vt puits* to deepen, make deeper; *étude* to go (deeper) into; *connaissances* to deepen, increase. **2 s'** ~ *vpr [rivière]* to become deeper. ◆ **approfondi, e** *adj* thorough, detailed. ◆ **approfondissement** *nm* deepening.

approprier [apʀɔpʀije] (7) **1** *vt* to suit, adapt (*à* to). **2 s'** ~ *vpr bien, droit* to appropriate. **s'** ~ **à** to suit. ◆ **appropriation** *nf (usurpation)* appropriation; *(adaptation)* suitability, appropriateness. ◆ **approprié, e** *adj* appropriate, suitable.

approuver [apʀuve] (1) *vt (être d'accord avec)* to approve of; *(ratifier)* to approve.

approvisionner [apʀɔvizjɔne] (1) **1** *vt magasin* to supply (*en, de* with); *compte* to pay money into; *fusil* to load. **bien approvisionné en fruits** well stocked with fruit. **2 s'** ~ *vpr* to stock up (*en* with). **s'** ~ **au marché** to shop at the market. ◆ **approvisionnement** *nm (action)* supplying (*en, de* of). *(réserves)* ~**s** supplies, provisions; *(Econ)* ~**s sauvages** panic buying.

approximation [apʀɔksimɑsjɔ̃] *nf* approximation, (rough) estimate. ◆ **approximatif, -ive** *adj calcul, évaluation* rough; *nombre* approximate; *termes* vague. ◆ **approximativement** *adv* roughly; approximately; vaguely.

appui [apɥi] **1** *nm (lit, fig)* support; *(Alpinisme)* press hold. **prendre** ~ **sur** *[personne]* to lean on; *[objet]* to rest on; **il a des** ~**s au ministère** he has connections in the ministry; **avoir l'** ~ **de qn** to have sb's support *ou* backing; **à l'** ~ **de son témoignage** in support of his evidence, to back up his evidence. **2** : **appui(e)-bras** *nm inv* armrest; ~ **de fenêtre** window-sill; **appui(e)-tête** *nm inv* headrest, head restraint.

appuyé, e [apɥije] *adj regard* fixed, intent; *geste* emphatic.

appuyer [apɥije] (8) **1** *vt (presser)* to press (*sur* on); *(soutenir) personne, thèse* to support, back (up); *attaque* to back up. *(poser)* ~ **qch contre qch** to lean *ou* rest sth against sth. **2** *vi:* ~ **sur** *sonnette* to press; *frein* to press on, press down; *levier* to press (down etc); *mot, argument* to stress, emphasize; *(Mus) note* to accentuate. *(Aut)* ~ **sur le champignon** * to step on it * , put one's foot down ; ~ **sur des colonnes** to rest on pillars; ~ **sur la droite** to bear to the right. **3 s'** ~ *vpr* (**a**) **s'** ~ **sur** *mur* to lean on; *preuve* to rely on; *parti* to rely on the support of. (**b**) (*) *importun, corvée* to put up with.

âpre [ɑpʀ(ə)] *adj* (**a**) *goût, hiver, vent* bitter; *temps* raw; *son* harsh. (**b**) *vie* harsh; *combat, discussion, résolution* bitter, grim; *concurrence, critique* fierce. ~ **au gain** grasping, greedy. ◆ **âprement** *adv* bitterly, grimly; fiercely. ◆ **âpreté** *nf* bitterness; rawness; harshness; grimness; fierceness.

après [apʀɛ] **1** *prép* (**a**) *(gén)* after. ~ **coup** after the event, afterwards; ~ **quoi** after which, and afterwards; **page** ~ **page** page after page; ~ **tout** after all; **j'étais** ~ **elle dans la queue** I was behind *ou* after her in the queue; **sa maison est (juste)** ~ **la mairie** his house is (just) past *ou* beyond the town hall; **collé** ~ **le mur** stuck on the wall; **crier** ~ **qn** to shout at sb; **en colère** ~ **qn** angry with sb; ~ **manger** after meals *ou* food; ~ **s'être reposé** after resting, after he had rested; ~ **que vous lui aurez parlé** after you have spoken to him. (**b**) **d'** ~ **lui** according to him, in his opinion; **d'** ~ **ce qu'il a dit** from *ou* according to what he said; **ne jugez pas d'** ~ **les apparences** don't go by appearances; **d'** ~ **les journaux** according to the papers; **d'** ~ **Balzac** adapted from Balzac.
2 *adv (ensuite)* afterwards, after; *(plus tard)* later. **longtemps** ~ long after(wards); **2 jours** ~ 2 days later; ~ **nous avons des articles moins chers** otherwise we have cheaper things; **et (puis)** ~? *(lit)* and then what?; *(fig)* what of it?; ~ **tu iras dire que...** next you'll be saying that...; **le mois d'** ~ the following month, the month after; **il courut** ~ he ran after it.
3 : ~**-demain** *adv* the day after tomorrow ; ~**-guerre** *nm* post-war years; ~**-midi** *nm ou nf inv* afternoon; ~**-rasage** *nm inv* after-shave; ~**-ski** *nm inv* snow boot.

a priori [apʀijɔʀi] *loc adv, adj* a priori.

à-propos [apʀɔpo] *nm [remarque]* aptness. **avoir beaucoup d'** ~ to show great presence of mind.

apte [apt(ə)] *adj*: ~ **à qch** capable of sth; ~ **à faire** capable of doing, able to do; *(Mil)* ~ **(au service)** fit for service; *(Jur)* ~ **à** fit to *ou* for.

aptitude [aptityd] *nf* aptitude (*à faire* for doing); ability (*à faire* to do). **test d'** ~ aptitude test.

aquaculture [akwakyltyʀ] *nf* sea fish farming, aquafarming.

aquaplane [akwaplan] *nm* aquaplane.

aquarelle [akwaʀɛl] *nf (technique)* watercolours; *(tableau)* watercolour.

aquarium [akwaʀjɔm] *nm* aquarium.

aquatique [akwatik] *adj* aquatic.

aqueduc [akdyk] *nm* aqueduct.

aqueux, -euse [akø, øz] *adj* aqueous.

aquilin, e [akilɛ̃, in] *adj* aquiline.

aquilon [akilɔ̃] *nm (Poésie)* north wind.

ara [aʀa] *nm* macaw.

arabe [aʀab] **1** *adj désert* Arabian; *nation* Arab; *art, langue* Arabic, Arab. **(cheval)** ~ Arab (horse). **2** *nm (Ling)* Arabic. **l'** ~ **littéral** written Arabic. **3** *nm*: **A**~ Arab. **un jeune A**~ an Arab boy. **4** *nf:* **A**~ Arab woman (*ou* girl).

arabesque [aʀabɛsk(ə)] *nf* arabesque.

Arabie [aʀabi] *nf* Arabia. ~ **Saoudite,** ~ **Séoudite** Saudi Arabia; **le désert d'** ~ the Arabian desert.

arable [aʀabl(ə)] *adj* arable.

arachide [aʀaʃid] *nf* peanut, groundnut.

araignée [aʀeɲe] *nf* (**a**) *(animal)* spider. ~ **de mer** spider crab. (**b**) *(crochet)* spider.

aratoire [aʀatwaʀ] *adj* ploughing.

arbalète [aʀbalɛt] *nf* crossbow.

arbitraire [aʀbitʀɛʀ] **1** *adj* arbitrary. **2** *nm*: **l'** ~ the arbitrary; **l'** ~ **de qch** the arbitrary nature of sth. ◆ **arbitrairement** *adv* arbitrarily.

arbitre [aʀbitʀ(ə)] *nm* (**a**) *(Boxe, Ftbl, Rugby)* referee; *(Cricket, Hockey, Tennis)* umpire. (**b**) *(conciliateur)* arbiter; *(Jur)* arbitrator. ◆ **arbitrage** *nm* arbitration; refereeing; umpiring. **recourir à l'** ~ to go to arbitration. ◆ **arbitrer** (1) *vt* to arbitrate; to referee; to umpire.

arborer [aʀbɔʀe] (1) *vt (gén)* to display; *vêtement, médaille* to sport; *sourire* to wear; *drapeau* to bear; *gros titre* to carry.

arborétum [aʀbɔʀetɔm] *nm* arboretum.

arboriculture [aʀbɔʀikyltyʀ] *nf* tree cultivation, arboriculture. ◆ **arboriculteur, -trice** *nm, f* tree grower, arboriculturist.

arbre [aʀbʀ(ə)] *nm (Bot, Ling)* tree; *(Tech)* shaft. **les** ~**s vous cachent la forêt** you can't see the wood *ou* forest *(US)* for the trees; ~ **à cames** camshaft; ~ **fruitier** fruit tree; ~ **généalogique** family tree;

~ **de Noël** Christmas tree. ◆ **arbrisseau,** *pl* **~x** *nm* shrub. ◆ **arbuste** *nm* small shrub, bush.

arc [aʀk] *nm (arme)* bow; *(Géom, Élec)* arc; *(Anat, Archit)* arch. **en ~ de cercle** in a semi-circle.

arcade [aʀkad] *nf (Archit, Anat)* arch. **~s** arcade, arches.

arcanes [aʀkan] *nmpl* mysteries.

arc-boutant, *pl* **arcs-boutants** [aʀkbutɑ̃] *nm* flying buttress.

arc-bouter [aʀkbute] (1) **1** *vt* to buttress. **2 s' ~** *vpr* to lean (*contre* against, *sur* on). **il était arc-bouté contre le mur** he was pressing up against the wall.

arceau, *pl* **~x** [aʀso] *nm (Archit)* arch; *(Croquet)* hoop. *(Aut)* **~ de sécurité** roll-over bar; **~ de protection** roll bar.

arc-en-ciel, *pl* **arcs-en-ciel** [aʀkɑ̃sjɛl] *nm* rainbow.

archaïque [aʀkaik] *adj* archaic. ◆ **archaïsme** *nm* archaism.

archange [aʀkɑ̃ʒ] *nm* archangel.

arche [aʀʃ(ə)] *nf (Archit)* arch; *(Rel)* ark. **l' ~ de Noé** Noah's Ark.

archéologie [aʀkeɔlɔʒi] *nf* archaeology. ◆ **archéologique** *adj* archaeological. ◆ **archéologue** *nmf* archaeologist.

archer [aʀʃe] *nm* archer.

archet [aʀʃɛ] *nm (Mus, gén)* bow.

archétype [aʀketip] *nm* archetype.

archevêque [aʀʃəvɛk] *nm* archbishop. ◆ **archevêché** *nm (territoire)* archbishopric; *(palais)* archbishop's palace.

archi... [aʀʃi] *préf* (**a**) *(*: extrêmement)* tremendously, enormously. **~plein** chock-a-block *, full to the gunwales; **~millionnaire** millionaire several times over. (**b**) *(titre)* arch... **~diacre/duc** archdeacon/ archduke.

archipel [aʀʃipɛl] *nm* archipelago.

architecte [aʀʃitɛkt(ə)] *nm (lit, fig)* architect. **~ d'intérieur** interior designer. ◆ **architectural, e,** *mpl* **-aux** *adj* architectural. ◆ **architecture** *nf (lit, Ordin)* architecture; *(fig)* structure.

archives [aʀʃiv] *nfpl* records, archives. **ça restera dans les ~!** * that will go down in history!; **je vais chercher dans mes ~** I'll look through my files *ou* records. ◆ **archiviste** *nmf* archivist.

arçon [aʀsɔ̃] *nm (Equitation)* tree.

arctique [aʀktik] **1** *adj (Géog)* Arctic. **2** *nm*: **l' ~** the Arctic.

ardent, e [aʀdɑ̃, ɑ̃t] *adj* (**a**) *flambeau, chaleur* burning; *feu, soleil* blazing; *yeux* fiery (*de* with). (**b**) *foi, partisan* fervent; *lutte, haine, amant* ardent; *discours* impassioned; *caractère* fiery. ◆ **ardemment** *adv* ardently, fervently. ◆ **ardeur** *nf* fervour; passion; ardour; fieriness. **son ~ au travail** his zeal *ou* enthusiasm for work; **l' ~ du soleil** the heat of the sun.

ardoise [aʀdwaz] **1** *nf (roche)* slate; *(†: dette)* unpaid bill. **2** *adj inv (couleur)* slate-grey.

ardu, e [aʀdy] *adj travail* arduous; *problème* difficult; *pente* steep.

are [aʀ] *nm* are, one hundred square metres.

arène [aʀɛn] *nf (lit, fig) (piste)* arena; *(Géol)* sand.

arête [aʀɛt] *nf* (**a**) *(Zool)* fishbone. **~ centrale** backbone, spine. (**b**) *[cube]* edge; *[montagne]* ridge, crest; *[nez]* bridge.

argent [aʀʒɑ̃] **1** *nm* (**a**) *(métal, couleur)* silver. **en ~** silver. (**b**) *(Fin)* money. **se faire de l' ~** to make money; **~ liquide** ready money, cash; **~ de poche** pocket money; **payer ~ comptant** to pay cash; *(fig)* **prendre qch pour ~ comptant** to take sth at face value; **on en a pour son ~** we get good value for money. **2** *adj inv* silver. ◆ **argenté, e** *adj couleur* silver, silvery; *couverts* silver-plated; **ils ne sont pas très ~s *** they're not very well-off. ◆ **argenter** (1) *vt miroir* to silver; *couverts* to silver-plate. ◆ **argenterie** *nf* silverware; *(de métal argenté)* silver plate. ◆ **argentin, e**[1] *adj son* silvery.

Argentine [aʀʒɑ̃tin] *nf*: **l' ~** Argentina, the Argentine. ◆ **argentin, e**[2] *adj,* **A~(e)** *nm(f)* Argentinian.

argile [aʀʒil] *nf* clay. ◆ **argileux, -euse** *adj* clayey.

argot [aʀgo] *nm* slang. ◆ **argotique** *adj* slangy.

arguer [aʀgɥe] (1) *vt* to deduce. **~ que** to claim that.

argument [aʀgymɑ̃] *nm* argument. **tirer ~ de qch** to use sth as an argument. ◆ **argumentation** *nf* argumentation. ◆ **argumenter** (1) *vi* to argue (*sur* about).

argus [aʀgys] *nm*: guide to secondhand car prices.

aride [aʀid] *adj (lit, fig)* arid; *vent* dry. **un travail ~** a thankless task; **cœur ~** heart of stone. ◆ **aridité** *nf* aridity; dryness; thanklessness. **~ du cœur** stony-heartedness.

aristocrate [aʀistɔkʀat] *nmf* aristocrat. ◆ **aristocratie** *nf* aristocracy. ◆ **aristocratique** *adj* aristocratic.

arithmétique [aʀitmetik] **1** *nf* arithmetic. **2** *adj* arithmetical. ◆ **arithmétiquement** *adv* arithmetically.

arlequin [aʀləkɛ̃] *nm (Théât)* Harlequin.

armateur [aʀmatœʀ] *nm* shipowner.

armature [aʀmatyʀ] *nf (gén)* frame; *(Constr, fig)* framework.

arme [aʀm(ə)] *nf* (**a**) *(gén)* weapon, arm; *(à feu)* gun; *(fig)* weapon. **sans ~(s)** *(lit)* unarmed; *(fig)* defenceless; **se battre à l' ~ blanche** to fight with knives; **~ atomique** atomic weapon; **~ à feu** firearm; **~ à double tranchant** double-edged weapon. (**b**) *(Mil) (section)* arm. *(littér)* **les ~s** the army. (**c**) *(emblème)* **~s** (coat of) arms; **aux ~s de** bearing the arms of. (**d**) **à ~s égales** on equal terms; **déposer les ~s** to lay down (one's) arms; **faire ses premières ~s** to make one's début (*dans* in); **passer qn par les ~s** to shoot sb by firing squad; **partir avec ~s et bagages** to pack up and go; **passer l' ~ à gauche** ⁂ to kick the bucket ⁂; **prendre le pouvoir par les ~s** to take power by force; **prendre les ~s** to take up arms; *(Escrime)* **faire des ~s** to fence; **en ~s** *soldats, peuple* at arms; **aux ~s!** to arms!

armé, e[1] [aʀme] *adj* armed (*de* with). **~ jusqu'aux dents** armed to the teeth; **bien ~ contre le froid** well-armed *ou* well-equipped against the cold.

armée[2] [aʀme] **1** *nf* army. **quelle ~ d'incapables *** what a useless bunch *. **2** : **~ active** regular army; **l' ~ de l'air** the Air Force; **l' ~ de mer** the Navy; **l' ~ de réserve** the reserve; **l' ~ du Salut** the Salvation Army; **l' ~ de terre** the Army.

armement [aʀməmɑ̃] *nm* (**a**) *(action) [pays]* armament; *[personne]* arming; *[fusil]* cocking; *[appareil-photo]* winding-on; *[navire]* fitting-out, equipping. (**b**) *(armes) [soldat]* arms, weapons; *[pays, navire]* arms, armament.

Arménie [aʀmeni] *nf*: **l' ~** Armenia. ◆ **arménien, -ienne** *adj, nm,* **A~(ne)** *nm(f)* Armenian.

armer [aʀme] (1) **1** *vt* (**a**) *personne* to arm (*de* with); *(fig)* to arm, equip (*contre* against). *(Hist)* **~ qn chevalier** to dub sb knight. (**b**) *navire* to fit out, equip; *fusil* to cock; *appareil-photo* to wind on. (**c**) *béton, poutre* to reinforce (*de* with). **2 s' ~** *vpr* to arm o.s. (*de* with, *contre* against).

armistice [aʀmistis] *nm* armistice.

armoire [aʀmwaʀ] *nf (gén)* cupboard; *(penderie)* wardrobe. **~ à pharmacie** medicine cabinet; **~ à glace** *(lit)* wardrobe with a mirror; *(* fig: costaud)* great hulking brute *.

armoiries [aʀmwaʀi] *nfpl* coat of arms.

armure [aʀmyʀ] *nf (Mil, Zool)* armour; *(fig)* defence.

armurier [aʀmyʀje] *nm [fusils]* gunsmith; *[couteaux]* armourer. ◆ **armurerie** *nf* gunsmith's; armourer's.

arnaquer ‡ [aʀnake] (1) *vt* to swindle. ◆ **arnaqueur, -euse** ‡ *nm, f* swindler, hustler *. ◆ **arnaque** ‡ *nm* swindling. **c'est de l'** ~ it's a rip-off *, it's daylight robbery.

arnica [aʀnika] *nf* arnica.

aromate [aʀɔmat] *nm (thym etc)* herb; *(poivre etc)* spice. ~**s** seasoning. ◆ **aromatique** *adj* aromatic. ◆ **aromatiser** (1) *vt* to flavour.

arôme [aʀom] *nm [plat, café]* aroma; *[fleur]* fragrance; *(goût)* flavour.

arpège [aʀpɛʒ] *nm* arpeggio.

arpenter [aʀpɑ̃te] (1) *vt* to pace up and down; *(Tech) terrain* to survey. ◆ **arpentage** *nm* surveying. ◆ **arpenteur** *nm* (land) surveyor.

arqué, e [aʀke] *adj forme, sourcils* arched, curved. **avoir le dos** ~ to be hunchbacked; **il a les jambes** ~**es** he's bow-legged.

arquebuse [aʀkəbyz] *nf* (h)arquebus. ◆ **arquebusier** *nm* (h)arquebusier.

arquer [aʀke] (1) **1** *vt tige* to curve; *dos* to arch. **2** *vi*: **il ne peut plus**~ ‡ he can't walk any more. **3 s'** ~ *vpr* to curve.

arrachage [aʀaʃaʒ] *nm* **(V arracher)** lifting; pulling up; extraction; pulling out.

arraché [aʀaʃe] *nm (Sport)* snatch. *(fig)* **obtenir qch à l'** ~ to snatch sth.

arrachement [aʀaʃmɑ̃] *nm (chagrin)* wrench.

arrache-pied (d') [daʀaʃpje] *adv* relentlessly.

arracher [aʀaʃe] (1) **1** *vt* (**a**) *légume* to lift; *plante* to pull up; *dent* to take out, extract, pull *(US)*; *poil, clou* to pull out; *chemise, affiche* to tear off. **se faire** ~ **une dent** to have a tooth out; *(fig)* **je vais lui** ~ **les yeux** I'll scratch his eyes out; **ça lui arracha le cœur** it broke his heart. (**b**) *(enlever)* ~ **à qn** *arme* to snatch *ou* grab from sb; *larmes, promesse* to wring from sb; *victoire* to wrest from sb. (**c**) *(soustraire)* ~ **qn à** *famille, mort, sort, pays* to snatch sb away from; *vice, soucis* to rescue sb from; *rêve* to snatch sb out of.
2 s' ~ *vpr*: **s'** ~ **(les vêtements)** to tear one's clothes; **s'** ~ **les cheveux** to tear one's hair; **s'** ~ **qn/qch** to fight over sb/sth; **s'** ~ **de** *famille* to tear o.s. away from; *habitude, lit* to force o.s. out of.

arraisonner [aʀɛzɔne] (1) *vt (Naut)* to inspect. ◆ **arraisonnement** *nm* inspection.

arrangeant, e [aʀɑ̃ʒɑ̃, ɑ̃t] *adj* obliging.

arrangement [aʀɑ̃ʒmɑ̃] *nm* (**a**) *(gén, Mil)* arrangement; *[mobilier]* layout; *[mots]* order. **l'** ~ **de sa toilette** the way she is dressed. (**b**) *(accord)* settlement, arrangement.

arranger [aʀɑ̃ʒe] (3) **1** *vt* (**a**) *(disposer) (gén)* to arrange; *coiffure* to tidy up; *tenue* to straighten (up). (**b**) *voyage, rencontre* to arrange, organize. **c'était arrangé à l'avance** it was fixed (in advance). (**c**) *différend* to settle, sort out. **ça n'arrange rien** it doesn't help matters. (**d**) *(contenter)* to suit. **si ça vous arrange** if that suits you, if that's convenient for you. (**e**) *voiture, montre* to fix, put right; *robe (recoudre)* to mend; *(modifier)* to alter; *(Mus)* to arrange. ~ **ses notes** to sort out one's notes. (**f**) *(*: malmener)* to sort out *.
2 s' ~ *vpr* (**a**) *(se mettre d'accord)* to come to an arrangement. **arrangez-vous avec le patron** sort it out with the boss. (**b**) *[querelle]* to be settled; *[situation]* to sort itself out; *[santé, temps, rapports]* to get better. **ça ne s'arrange pas** * things are no better. (**c**) *(se débrouiller)* to manage. **arrangez-vous comme vous voudrez mais...** I don't mind how you do it but...; **je ne sais pas comment tu t'arranges, mais...** I don't know how you manage (it), but...; **arrangez-vous pour venir** arrange it so that you can come. (**d**) **s'** ~ **de qch** to make do with sth, put up with sth. (**e**) *(se rajuster)* to tidy o.s. up. **tu t'es bien arrangé!** * you look a mess!

arrérages [aʀeʀaʒ] *nmpl* arrears.

arrestation [aʀɛstɑsjɔ̃] *nf* arrest. **mettre en état d'** ~ to place *ou* put under arrest.

arrêt [aʀɛ] **1** *nm* (**a**) *(action)* stopping, checking, arrest; *(lieu, pause)* stop. **attendez l'** ~ **complet (du train)** wait until the train has come to a complete stop *ou* standstill; **5 minutes d'** ~ 5 minutes' stop, a 5-minute stop; **véhicule à l'** ~ stationary vehicle; **faire un** ~ *[train]* to make a stop; *(Ftbl)* to make a save; **tomber en** ~ to stop short; **sans** ~ *(sans interruption)* without stopping, non-stop; *(très fréquemment)* continually, constantly; ~ **d'autobus** bus stop. (**b**) *(Mil)* ~**s** arrest; **mettre qn aux** ~**s** to put sb under arrest. (**c**) *(Jur: décision)* ruling, decision. (**d**) *(Tech) [machine]* stop mechanism; *[bouton]* stop button.
2 : ~ **du cœur** cardiac arrest; **l'** ~ **des hostilités** the cessation of hostilities; *(Sport)* ~ **de jeu** stoppage; **jouer les** ~**s de jeu** to play injury time ; ~ **de mort** death sentence; ~ **de travail** *(grève)* stoppage (of work); *(congé)* sick leave; *(certificat)* doctor's certificate.

arrêté, e [aʀete] **1** *adj volonté* firm; *idée* fixed, firm. **c'est une chose** ~**e** the matter is settled. **2** *nm (loi)* order. ~ **municipal** ≃ bye-law; ~ **de compte** *(fermeture)* settlement of account; *(relevé)* statement of account.

arrêter [aʀete] (1) **1** *vt* (**a**) *(gén)* to stop; *moteur* to switch off; *ennemi, progression* to check, halt; *hémorragie, criminel* to arrest. **arrêtez-moi près de la poste** drop me by the post office; **ici, je vous arrête!** I must stop you there!; **on n'arrête pas le progrès** there's no stopping progress; **nous avons été arrêtés par un embouteillage** we were held up by a traffic jam; **seul le prix l'arrête** it's only the price that stops him; *(Police)* **se faire** ~ to get o.s. arrested. (**b**) *études, compétition* to give up; *envois, trafic aérien, représentations* to cancel. ~ **la fabrication d'un produit** to discontinue a product; **on a dû** ~ **les travaux** we had to stop work *ou* call a halt to the work. (**c**) *compte (fermer)* to settle; *(relever)* to make up; *jour, lieu, plan* to decide on; *derniers détails* to finalize; *choix, décision* to make. ~ **ses regards sur** to fix one's gaze on; ~ **un marché** to make a deal; *(Admin)* ~ **que** to rule that; *(Jur)* ~ **les dispositions d'applications** to adopt provisions to implement.
2 *vi* to stop. **arrête de parler!** stop talking!; ~ **de fumer** to give up *ou* stop smoking.
3 s' ~ *vpr* (**a**) *(gén)* to stop; *[train]* to stop, come to a stop *ou* a halt. **nous nous arrêtâmes sur le bas-côté** we pulled up *ou* stopped by the roadside ; **s'** ~ **net** *[personne, bruit]* to stop dead; **s'** ~ **pour manger** to break off *ou* stop to eat; **sans s'** ~ without stopping, without a break. (**b**) **s'** ~ **sur** *[choix, regard]* to fall on; **s'** ~ **à** *détails* to pay too much attention to; *projet* to settle on *ou* fix on.

arrhes [aʀ] *nfpl* deposit.

arrière [aʀjɛʀ] **1** *nm* (**a**) *[voiture]* back; *[bateau]* stern; *[train]* rear; *(Sport)* fullback. *(Naut)* **à l'** ~ aft, at the stern; **à l'** ~ **de** at the stern of, abaft; **se balancer d'avant en** ~ to rock backwards and forwards; *(Mil)* **les** ~**s** the rear; **l'** ~ **(du pays)** the homefront; **assurer** *ou* **protéger ses** ~**s** *(lit)* to protect the rear; *(fig)* to leave o.s. a way out. (**b**) **en** ~ *(derrière)* behind; *(vers l'arrière)* backwards; **rester en** ~ to drop behind; **faire un pas en** ~ to step back(wards); *(Naut)* **en** ~ **toute!** full astern!; **100 ans en** ~ 100 years ago; **revenir en** ~ *(gén)* to go back; *[civilisation]* to regress; *(avec magnétophone)* to rewind; **le chapeau en** ~ his hat tilted

back(wards); **en ~! vous gênez** stand *ou* get back! you're in the way; *(lit, fig)* **en ~ de** behind.
2 *adj inv*: **roue/feu ~** rear wheel/light; **siège ~** back seat.
3 *préf inv (le second élément prend la marque du pluriel et donne le genre)* (**a**) *(famille)* **~-grand-mère** great-grandmother; **~-petit-fils** great-grandson ; **~-petit-cousin** cousin three times removed, distant cousin. (**b**) **~-bouche** back of the mouth ; **~-boutique** back shop; **~-cour** backyard ; **~-cuisine** scullery; **~-garde** rearguard; **~-gorge** back of the throat; *(lit, fig)* **~-goût** aftertaste ; **~-pays** hinterland; **~-pensée** *(raison intéressée)* ulterior motive; *(réserves)* mental reservation ; **~-plan** background; **~-saison** autumn; **~-salle** back room; **~-train** hindquarters.

arriéré, e [aʀjeʀe] **1** *adj* (**a**) *(Comm)* overdue. (**b**) *(Psych)* backward, retarded; *(Scol)* educationally subnormal; *pays* backward; *méthodes, personne* out-of-date. **2** *nm (travail)* backlog; *(paiement)* arrears.

arrimer [aʀime] (1) *vt (Naut) cargaison* to stow; *(gén) colis* to secure. ◆ **arrimage** *nm* stowage.

arrivage [aʀivaʒ] *nm [marchandises]* consignment, delivery, load; *[touristes]* fresh load *ou* influx.

arrivant, e [aʀivɑ̃, ɑ̃t] *nm, f (personne)* newcomer. *(arrivée)* **compter les ~s** to count the new arrivals.

arrivée [aʀive] *nf* (**a**) *[personne, train]* arrival; *[neige]* arrival, coming; *[course]* finish. **à son ~** when he arrived *ou* came in, on his arrival. (**b**) *(Tech)* **~ d'air/de gaz** *(robinet)* air/gas inlet; *(processus)* inflow of air/gas.

arriver [aʀive] (1) **1** *vt* (**a**) *(être au bout)* to arrive; *(approcher)* to come. *(atteindre)* **~ à** *lieu, résultat* to arrive at, get to, reach; *sujet, pouvoir* to come to; **~ chez soi** to arrive *ou* get *ou* reach home; **c'est arrivé jusqu'à lui** *[bruit, nouvelle]* it reached him; **~ le premier** *(course)* to come in first; *(soirée)* to be the first to arrive; **j'arrive!** (I'm) coming!, just coming!; **arrive!** come on!; **pour faire ~ l'eau jusqu'à la maison...** to bring water up to the house...; **je n'ai pas pu ~ jusqu'au chef** I wasn't able to get right to the boss; **l'eau lui arrivait aux genoux** the water came up to his knees, he was knee-deep in water; *(fig)* **il ne t'arrive pas à la cheville** he can't hold a candle to you. (**b**) *(réussir)* to succeed *ou* get on in life. **~ à faire qch** to succeed in doing sth, manage to do sth; **je n'arrive pas à comprendre son attitude** I simply cannot understand his attitude; **~ à ses fins** to get one's way, achieve one's ends; **il n'arrivera jamais à rien** he'll never get anywhere, he'll never achieve anything. (**c**) *(se produire)* to happen. **c'est arrivé hier** it happened yesterday; **il croit que c'est arrivé *** he thinks he's made it *; **faire ~ un accident** to bring about an accident; **tu vas nous faire ~ des ennuis** you'll get us into trouble. (**d**) **on en arrive à se demander si...** we're beginning to wonder whether...; **il faudra bien en ~ là!** it'll have to come to that (eventually).
2 *vb impers* (**a**) **il (lui) est arrivé un malheur** something dreadful has happened (to him); **il est arrivé un télégramme** a telegram has come *ou* arrived; **il lui arrivera des ennuis** he'll get (himself) into trouble; **quoi qu'il arrive** whatever happens; **comme il arrive souvent (dans ces cas-là)** as often happens, as is often the case. (**b**) **il m'arrive d'oublier, il arrive que j'oublie** I sometimes forget; **il peut ~ qu'elle se trompe** she may (occasionally) make mistakes; **s'il lui arrivait de faire une erreur** if she should happen to make a mistake.

arrivisme [aʀivism(ə)] *nm* pushfulness. ◆ **arriviste** *nmf* go-getter *.

arrogance [aʀɔgɑ̃s] *nf* arrogance. ◆ **arrogant, e** *adj* arrogant.

arroger (s') [aʀɔʒe] (3) *vpr pouvoirs, titre* to assume (without right).

arrondir [aʀɔ̃diʀ] (2) **1** *vt* (**a**) *objet* to (make) round; *angle* to round off; *caractère* to smooth the rough edges off. **~ les angles** to smooth things over. (**b**) *fortune* to swell; *domaine* to increase; *salaire* to supplement. (**c**) *(simplifier) somme, nombre* to round off (*à* to). **2 s' ~** *vpr [relief]* to become round(ed); *[taille]* to fill out; *[fortune]* to swell. ◆ **arrondi, e 1** *adj forme* round, rounded; *visage* round. **2** *nm (gén: contour)* roundness; *(Couture)* hemline.

arrondissement [aʀɔ̃dismɑ̃] *nm* ≃ district.

arroser [aʀoze] (1) *vt* (**a**) *(gén)* to water; *rôti* to baste. **~ qch d'essence** to pour petrol over sth; **~ qn de balles** to spray sb with bullets; **se faire ~** to get drenched *ou* soaked; **ville très arrosée** very wet city; **mouchoir arrosé de sang/larmes** blood/tear-soaked handkerchief. (**b**) (*) *succès* to drink to; *repas* to wash down (with wine) *. ◆ **arrosage** *nm* watering. ◆ **arroseuse** *nf* water cart. ◆ **arrosoir** *nm* watering can.

arsenal, *pl* **-aux** [aʀsənal, o] *nm (Mil)* arsenal; *(*: attirail)* gear; *(*: collection)* collection.

arsenic [aʀsənik] *nm* arsenic.

arsouille † [aʀsuj] *nm ou nf (voyou)* ruffian.

art [aʀ] *nm (gén)* art; *(adresse)* skill. **l' ~ de vivre** the art of living; **avec un ~ consommé** with consummate skill; **les ~s et métiers** industrial arts and crafts; **homme de l' ~** expert; **avoir l' ~ de faire qch** to have the art *ou* knack of doing sth.

artère [aʀtɛʀ] *nf (Anat)* artery; *(Aut)* main road. ◆ **artériel, -ielle** *adj* arterial. ◆ **artériole** *nf* arteriole.

arthrite [aʀtʀit] *nf* arthritis. ◆ **arthritique** *adj, nmf* arthritic. ◆ **arthrose** *nf* osteoarthritis.

artichaut [aʀtiʃo] *nm* artichoke.

article [aʀtikl(ə)] **1** *nm* (**a**) *(Comm)* item, article. **~ d'importation** imported product; **faire l' ~ à qn** to give sb the sales patter. (**b**) *[loi, journal]* article; *[dictionnaire]* entry. **sur cet ~** on this point. (**c**) *(Gram)* article. (**d**) *(Ordin)* record, item. (**e**) **à l' ~ de la mort** at the point of death. **2** :**~s de bureau** office accessories; **~ de foi** article of faith; **~ réclame** special offer; **~s de voyage** travel goods.

articuler [aʀtikyle] (1) *vt* (**a**) *(prononcer clairement)* to articulate; *(dire)* to pronounce, utter. **articule!** speak clearly! (**b**) *mécanismes, os* to articulate, joint; *idées* to link. **~ un discours sur deux thèmes principaux** to structure a speech round *ou* on two main themes; **toute sa défense s'articule autour de cet élément** his entire defence hinges *ou* turns on this factor; **ses phrases s'articulent bien** his sentences link *ou* hang * together well. ◆ **articulation** *nf (Anat)* joint; *(Tech, Ling)* articulation; *[doigts]* knuckles; *[discours, raisonnement]* link. ◆ **articulé, e** *adj langage* articulate; *membre, objet* jointed, articulated; *poupée* with moveable joints.

artifice [aʀtifis] *nm* ingenious device, trick; *(péj)* trick. *(Art)* **l' ~** artifice.

artificiel, -ielle [aʀtifisjɛl] *adj (gén)* artificial; *gaieté* forced, unnatural. ◆ **artificiellement** *adv* artificially.

artificier [aʀtifisje] *nm (fabricant)* pyrotechnist; *(désamorçage)* bomb disposal expert.

artificieux, -ieuse [aʀtifisjø, jøz] *adj* guileful.

artillerie [aʀtijʀi] *nf* artillery. **~ de marine** naval guns; **tir d' ~** artillery fire. ◆ **artilleur** *nm* artilleryman, gunner.

artimon [aʀtimɔ̃] *nm* mizzen.

artisan [aʀtizɑ̃] *nm (lit)* craftsman, artisan; *(fig)* architect, author. **~ de la paix** peace maker. ◆ **artisanal, e,** *mpl* **-aux** *adj*: **profession ~e** craft, craft industry; **retraite ~e** pension for self-employed craftsmen; **fabrication ~e** production by craftsmen; **bombe de fabrication ~e** homemade bomb. ◆ **artisanalement** *adv* by craftsmen.

◆ **artisanat** *nm (métier)* craft industry; *(classe sociale)* artisans.

artiste [aRtist(ə)] **1** *nmf* (**a**) *(Art)* artist; *(Spectacle)* artiste; *(chanteur)* singer; *(fantaisiste)* entertainer. ~ **peintre** artist, painter; ~ **dramatique** actor *(ou* actress*)*; **les ~s saluèrent** the performers took a bow. (**b**) *(péj: bohème)* bohemian. **2** *adj personne, style* artistic. ◆ **artistique** *adj* artistic. ◆ **artistiquement** *adv* artistically.

aryen, -yenne [aRjɛ̃, jɛn] *adj,* **A~(ne)** *nm(f)* Aryan.

as [ɑs] *nm* (**a**) *(carte, dé)* ace. *(Hippisme)* **l'** ~ number one. (**b**) *(champion)* ace *. **un ~ de la route** a crack driver; **l' ~ de l'école** the school's star pupil. (**c**) *(Tennis)* ace. **réussir** *ou* **servir un** ~ to serve an ace. (**d**) **être ficelé comme l' ~ de pique** * to be dressed all anyhow *; **être (plein) aux** ~ ⁑ to be loaded *; **c'est passé à l'** ~ ⁑ *(perdu)* it's gone down the drain *; *(inaperçu)* it went unnoticed.

ascendance [asɑ̃dɑ̃s] *nf (généalogique)* ancestry.

ascendant, e [asɑ̃dɑ̃, ɑ̃t] **1** *adj astre, trait* rising; *mouvement* upward; *progression* ascending. **2** *nm* (**a**) *(influence)* ascendancy (*sur* over). (**b**) *(Admin)* **~s** ascendants. (**c**) *(Astron)* rising star; *(Astrol)* ascendant.

ascenseur [asɑ̃sœR] *nm* lift, elevator *(US)*.

ascension [asɑ̃sjɔ̃] *nf* (**a**) *[ballon, fusée]* ascent; *[homme politique]* rise; *(sociale)* rise. *(Rel)* **l'A~** the Ascension; *(jour)* Ascension Day. (**b**) *[montagne]* ascent, climb. **faire l' ~ d'une montagne** to climb a mountain. ◆ **ascensionnel, -elle** *adj force* upward. **vitesse ~le** climbing speed. ◆ **ascensionniste** *nmf* ascensionist.

ascète [asɛt] *nmf* ascetic. ◆ **ascétique** *adj* ascetic. ◆ **ascétisme** *nm* asceticism.

asepsie [asɛpsi] *nf* asepsis. ◆ **aseptique** *adj* aseptic. ◆ **aseptiser** (1) *vt pièce* to fumigate; *pansement* to sterilize; *plaie* to disinfect.

Asie [azi] *nf* Asia. ~ **Mineure** Asia Minor; ~ **centrale** Central Asia. ◆ **asiatique** *adj,* **A~** *nmf* Asian.

asile [azil] *nm (lit, fig)* refuge; *(Pol)* asylum; *(Hist)* sanctuary. ~ **de vieillards** old people's home, retirement home; ~ **de fous** lunatic asylum; ~ **de paix** haven of peace.

asocial, e, *mpl* **-aux** [asɔsjal, o] **1** *adj* antisocial. **2** *nm, f* social misfit, socially maladjusted person.

aspect [aspɛ] *nm (allure)* look, appearance; *(angle)* aspect, side; *(Astrol, Ling)* aspect. **d' ~ sinistre** sinister-looking; **avoir l' ~ de** to look like.

asperge [aspɛRʒ(ə)] *nf* asparagus. *(*: personne)* **(grande)** ~ beanpole *, string bean * *(US)*.

asperger [aspɛRʒe] (3) *vt surface* to spray; *personne* to splash (*de* with).

aspérité [aspeRite] *nf* bump. **~s** *[surface]* bumps, rough patches; *[caractère]* harshness.

asphalte [asfalt(ə)] *nm* asphalt. ◆ **asphalter** (1) *vt* to asphalt.

asphyxier [asfiksje] (7) **1** *vt (lit)* to suffocate, asphyxiate; *(fig)* to stifle. **mourir asphyxié** to die of suffocation *ou* asphyxiation. **2 s'** ~ *vpr (accident)* to suffocate, asphyxiate; *(suicide)* to suffocate o.s.; *(au gaz)* to gas o.s. ◆ **asphyxie** *nf* suffocation, asphyxiation.

aspic [aspik] *nm (Zool)* asp; *(Culin)* meat (*ou* fish *etc*) in aspic.

aspirant, e [aspiRɑ̃, ɑ̃t] **1** *adj* suction. **2** *nm, f (candidat)* candidate (*à* for). **3** *nm (Mil)* officer cadet; *(Naut)* midshipman, middie * *(US)*.

aspirateur [aspiRatœR] *nm* vacuum cleaner, hoover ®. **passer à l'** ~ to vacuum, hoover.

aspirer [aspiRe] (1) **1** *vt air* to inhale, breathe in; *liquide* to suck up; *(Ling)* to aspirate. **2** ~ **à** *vt indir* to aspire to. ◆ **aspiration** *nf* (**a**) *[air]* inhalation; *(Ling)* aspiration; *[liquide]* sucking up. (**b**) *(ambition)* aspiration, longing (*vers, à* for).

aspirine [aspiRin] *nf* aspirin. **(comprimé** *ou* **cachet d')** ~ aspirin; **prenez 2 ~s** take 2 aspirins.

assagir *vt,* **s'** ~ *vpr* [asaʒiR] (2) to quieten down.

assaillir [asajiR] (13) *vt (lit)* to assail, attack; *(fig)* to assail (*de* with). ◆ **assaillant, e** *nm, f* assailant.

assainir [aseniR] (2) *vt quartier, logement* to clean up; *marécage* to drain; *air (lit)* to purify; *finances, monnaie* to stabilize. **la situation s'est assainie** the situation has become healthier; *(fig)* ~ **l'atmosphère** to clear the air. ◆ **assainissement** *nm* cleaning up; stabilization.

assaisonner [asɛzɔne] (1) *vt (gén)* to season; *salade* to dress. ~ **qn** ⁑ *(physiquement)* to knock sb about; *(verbalement)* to tell sb off; *(financièrement)* to clobber sb ⁑. ◆ **assaisonnement** *nm* dressing; seasoning.

assassin, e [asasɛ̃, in] **1** *adj* provocative. **2** *nm (gén)* murderer; *(Pol)* assassin; *(Presse etc)* killer. **à l'** ~! murder! ◆ **assassinat** *nm* murder; assassination. ◆ **assassiner** (1) *vt* to murder; to assassinate.

assaut [aso] *nm (Mil)* assault, attack (*de* on); *(Sport)* bout; *(Alpinisme)* assault. **donner l'** ~ to attack, launch an attack on; **les ~s de l'ennemi** the enemy's attacks *ou* onslaughts; *(lit, fig)* **prendre d'** ~ to storm, take by storm; **faire ~ de politesse** to vie with each other in politeness.

assécher [aseʃe] (6) *vt* to drain; *[évaporation]* to dry. ◆ **assèchement** *nm* drainage; drying.

assembler [asɑ̃ble] (1) **1** *vt (gén)* to assemble; *meuble etc* to put together; *comité* to convene. **2 s'** ~ *vpr* to assemble, gather. ◆ **assemblage** *nm* (**a**) *(action)* assembling, putting together; *(Ordin)* assembly. (**b**) *(jointure)* joint; *(structure)* assembly; *(collection)* collection. ◆ **assemblée** *nf (foule)* gathering; *(convoquée)* meeting; *(Pol)* assembly. *(Rel)* **l' ~ des fidèles** the congregation; **à la grande joie de l'** ~ to the great joy of those present.

asséner [asene] (5) *vt coup* to strike; *argument* to thrust forward. ~ **un coup à qn** to deal sb a blow.

assentiment [asɑ̃timɑ̃] *nm (consentement)* assent, consent; *(approbation)* approval (*à* to).

asseoir [aswaR] (26) **1** *vt* (**a**) ~ **qn** *(personne debout)* to sit sb down; *(personne couchée)* to sit sb up; **faire ~ qn** to ask sb to sit down. (**b**) **être assis** to be sitting *ou* seated; **rester assis** to remain seated; **assis en tailleur** sitting cross-legged; *(fig)* **assis entre deux chaises** in an awkward position. (**c**) *réputation, autorité* to establish. ~ **sa réputation sur qch** to build one's reputation on sth; ~ **une théorie sur des faits** to base a theory on facts. (**d**) *(*: stupéfier)* to stagger, stun.
2 s' ~ *vpr* to sit down; *[personne couchée]* to sit up. **asseyez-vous donc** do sit down *ou* take a seat; **le règlement, je m'assieds dessus!** ⁑ you know what you can do with the rules! ⁑

assermenté, e [asɛRmɑ̃te] *adj témoin, expert* on oath.

assertion [asɛRsjɔ̃] *nf* assertion. ◆ **assertif, -ive** *adj phrase etc* declarative.

asservir [asɛRviR] (2) *vt personne* to enslave; *pays* to subjugate; *nature* to master. ◆ **asservissement** *nm (action)* enslavement; *(lit, fig: état)* slavery, subservience (*à* to).

assesseur [asesœR] *nm* assessor.

assez [ase] *adv* (**a**) enough. **bien ~ grand** quite big enough; **pas ~ souvent** not often enough; **est-ce que 5 F c'est ~? — c'est bien ~** is 5 francs enough? *ou* will 5 francs do? — that will be plenty *ou* quite enough; **avez-vous acheté ~ de pain?** have you bought enough *ou* sufficient bread?; **as-tu trouvé une boîte ~ grande?** have you found a big enough box?; **je n'ai pas ~ d'argent pour m'offrir cette voi-**

ture I can't afford (to buy myself) this car, I haven't enough money to buy myself this car; **il n'est pas ~ sot pour le croire** he is not so stupid as to believe him. (**b**) *(intensif)* **ce serait ~ agréable** it would be rather *ou* quite nice; **il était ~ tard** it was quite *ou* fairly late; **est-ce ~ bête!** how stupid (of me)!; **j'en ai ~ (de toi)!** I've had enough (of you)!, I'm fed up (with you)!; **~ de discours!** enough talk!, enough said!

assidu, e [asidy] *adj (ponctuel)* regular; *(appliqué)* assiduous, painstaking; *(empressé)* assiduous in one's attention (*auprès de* to). ◆ **assiduité** *nf* regularity; assiduity (*à* to). **son ~ aux cours** his regular attendance at classes; *(hum)* **~s** assiduous attentions. ◆ **assidûment** *adv* assiduously.

assiéger [asjeʒe] (3) *et* (6) *vt (Mil)* to besiege; *[tentations]* to beset. **la garnison assiégée** the beleaguered *ou* besieged garrison; **assiégé par l'eau** hemmed in by water. ◆ **assiégeant, e** *nm, f* besieger.

assiette [asjɛt] *nf* (**a**) *(vaisselle)* plate. **~ anglaise** assorted cold roast meats; **~ creuse/plate** soup/ dinner plate. (**b**) *(équilibre) [cavalier]* seat; *[navire]* trim. *(fig)* **il n'est pas dans son ~** he's feeling out of sorts. (**c**) *(Fin)* **~ de l'impôt** tax base; **~ de la TVA** basis upon which VAT is assessed. ◆ **assiettée** *nf (gén)* plateful.

assigner [asiɲe] (1) *vt* (**a**) *place, rôle* to assign, allocate; *valeur* to attach; *cause* to ascribe, attribute; *somme* to allot, allocate; *limite* to set, fix (*à* to). **~ un objectif à qn** to set sb a goal. (**b**) *(Jur)* **~ (à comparaître)** *prévenu* to summons; *témoin* to subpoena, summon; **~ qn à résidence** to put sb under house arrest. ◆ **assignable** *adj* ascribable (*à* to). ◆ **assignation** *nf* allocation; summons.

assimiler [asimile] (1) **1** *vt* (**a**) *(absorber) (gén)* to assimilate; *connaissances* to take in. **notions mal assimilées** ill-digested notions. (**b**) **~ qn/qch à** *(comparer à)* to liken *ou* compare sb/sth to; *(classer comme)* to class sb/sth as; *(faire ressembler à)* to make sb/sth similar to. **2 s' ~** *vpr* to be assimilated. **s' ~ à qn** to liken o.s. to sb. ◆ **assimilable** *adj* easily assimilated. **~ à** comparable to. ◆ **assimilation** *nf* assimilation; comparison (*à* to); classification (*à* as). ◆ **assimilé, e** *adj* comparable. *(Écon)* **produits ~** allied products.

assis, e[1] [asi, iz] *adj* (**a**) *personne* sitting (down), seated; **V asseoir.** (**b**) *situation* stable; *autorité* well-established.

assise[2] [asiz] *nf (Constr)* course; *(Bio, Géol)* stratum; *(fig)* basis.

assises [asiz] *nfpl (Jur)* assizes; *(fig)* meeting.

assistance [asistɑ̃s] *nf* (**a**) *[conférence]* audience; *[messe]* congregation. (**b**) *(aide)* assistance; *(légale, technique)* aid. **donner ~ à qn** to give sb assistance; **~ aux anciens détenus** prisoner after-care; **~ médicale** medical care; **l'A~ publique** ≃ the Health Service; **enfant de l'A~** child in care; **les hôpitaux de l'A~ publique** state- *ou* publicly-owned hospitals; **~ sociale** *(aide)* social aid; *(métier)* social work. (**c**) *(présence)* attendance. ◆ **assistant, e** *nm, f (gén, Scol)* assistant; *(Univ)* assistant lecturer, teaching assistant *(US)*. **~e sociale** social worker; *(spectateurs)* **les ~s** those present.

assister [asiste] (1) **1 ~ à** *vt indir cérémonie, cours* to be (present) at, attend; *spectacle* to be at; *événement* to witness. **2** *vt pauvres* to assist; *mourant* to comfort.

association [asɔsjɑsjɔ̃] *nf* (**a**) *(société)* association; *(Comm, Écon)* partnership. (**b**) *[idées, images]* association; *[couleurs]* combination. (**c**) *(collaboration)* partnership. **son ~ à nos travaux** his joining us in our undertaking. ◆ **associatif, -ive** *adj* associative. **la vie ~ive** community life. ◆ **associé, e** *nm, f (gén)* associate; *(Comm, Fin)* partner.

associer [asɔsje] (7) **1** *vt* (**a**) **~ qn à** *profits* to give sb a share of; *affaire* to make sb a partner in; *triomphe* to include sb in.
(**b**) *idées, mots* to associate; *couleurs, intérêts* to combine (*à* with). **~ qch à** *(relier)* to associate *ou* link sth with; *(mêler)* to combine sth with.
2 s' ~ *vpr* (**a**) *(s'unir)* to join together; *(Comm)* to form a partnership; *[couleurs, qualités]* to be combined (*à* with). **s' ~ qn** to take sb on as a partner; **s' ~ à** to join with; *(Comm)* to go into partnership with. (**b**) **s' ~ à** *projet* to join in; *opinion* associate o.s. with; *douleur* to share in; **je m'associe aux compliments que l'on vous a faits** I should like to join with those who have complimented you.

assoiffer [aswafe] (1) *vt* to make thirsty. **assoiffé de** thirsting for. ◆ **assoiffant, e** *adj* thirst-giving.

assoler [asɔle] (1) *vt champ* to rotate crops on. ◆ **assolement** *nm* rotation of crops.

assombrir [asɔ̃bʀiʀ] (2) **1** *vt (lit)* to darken; *personne* to fill with gloom; *assistance, voyage* to cast a gloom *ou* shadow over. **2 s' ~** *vpr [ciel, pièce]* to darken; *[personne, situation]* to become gloomy; *[visage, regard]* to cloud. ◆ **assombri, e** *adj ciel* darkened; *couleur* sombre; *visage, regard* gloomy, sombre. ◆ **assombrissement** *nm* darkening; gloominess.

assommer [asɔme] (1) *vt (tuer)* to batter sb's skull in; *(étourdir)* to knock out, stun; *(*: ennuyer)* to bore stiff *. **assommé par** *bruit* stunned by; *chaleur* overwhelmed by. ◆ **assommant, e** * *adj* deadly dull *.

Assomption [asɔ̃psjɔ̃] *nf* Assumption; *(jour)* Assumption Day.

assonance [asɔnɑ̃s] *nf* assonance.

assorti, e [asɔʀti] *adj bonbons* assorted. **'fromages ~s'** 'assortment of cheeses'; **bien/mal ~** *magasin* well/poorly-stocked; *couple* well/badly matched; **avec écharpe ~e** with matching scarf; **être ~ de** *conseils* to be accompanied by *ou* with.

assortiment [asɔʀtimɑ̃] *nm* (**a**) *[bonbons]* assortment; *(Comm: lot)* stock. (**b**) *(harmonie)* arrangement, ensemble.

assortir [asɔʀtiʀ] (2) **1** *vt* (**a**) *(accorder)* to match (*à, avec* to, with). (**b**) *(accompagner de)* **~ qch de** to accompany sth by *ou* with. (**c**) *commerçant* to supply; *magasin* to stock (*de* with). **2 s' ~** *vpr* to match (*à* with). **s' ~ de** to be accompanied by.

assoupir [asupiʀ] (2) **1** *vt personne* to make drowsy; *sens, douleur, intérêt* to dull; *passion* to lull. **2 s' ~** *vpr [personne]* to doze off; *(fig)* to be dulled *ou* lulled. **il est assoupi** he is dozing. ◆ **assoupissement** *nm (sommeil)* doze; *(fig)* dulling; lulling.

assouplir [asupliʀ] (2) **1** *vt cuir, membres* to make supple; *règlements* to relax. **~ le caractère de qn** to make sb more amenable. **2 s' ~** *vpr* to become supple; to relax. ◆ **assouplissant, e 1** *adj produit, formule* softening. **2** *nm:* **~ (textile)** (fabric) softener. ◆ **assouplissement** *nm* suppling up; relaxing. **exercices d' ~** limbering up exercises; *(Écon)* **mesures d' ~ du crédit** easing of credit restrictions; **mesures d' ~ des formalités administratives** measures to relax administrative regulations. ◆ **assouplisseur** *nm* (fabric) softener.

assourdir [asuʀdiʀ] (2) *vt personne* to deafen; *bruit* to deaden, muffle. ◆ **assourdissant, e** *adj* deafening.

assouvir [asuviʀ] (2) *vt* to assuage, satisfy, appease. ◆ **assouvissement** *nm* assuaging, satisfaction, appeasement.

assujettir [asyʒetiʀ] (2) **1** *vt peuple* to subjugate. **~ qn à une règle** to subject sb to a rule. **2 s' ~** *vpr*: **s' ~ à qch** to submit to sth. ◆ **assujetti, e** *adj peuple* subjugated. **~ à** *règle, taxe* subject to.

◆ **assujettissant, e** *adj* demanding, exacting. ◆ **assujettissement** *nm (contrainte)* constraint; *(dépendance)* subjection. ~ **à l'impôt** tax liability.

assumer [asyme] (1) *vt* (**a**) *(prendre) (gén)* to assume; *responsabilité, tâche, rôle* to take on; *commandement* to take over; *poste* to take up. ~ **les frais de qch** to meet the cost *ou* expense of sth. (**b**) *(remplir) poste* to hold; *rôle* to fulfil. (**c**) *(accepter) conséquence* to accept.

assurance [asyʀɑ̃s] *nf* (**a**) *(confiance)* self-confidence, (self-)assurance. **avoir de l'** ~ to be self-confident *ou* (self-)assured. (**b**) *(garantie)* assurance. **veuillez agréer l'** ~ **de ma considération distinguée** ≃ yours faithfully. (**c**) *(contrat)* insurance (policy); *(firme)* insurance company. *(métier)* **les ~s** insurance; ~ **au tiers/tous risques** third party/comprehensive insurance; ~ **multirisque** general insurance; ~ **sur la vie** life insurance; **être aux ~s sociales** ≃ to be in the National Insurance scheme.

assuré, e [asyʀe] **1** *adj réussite, situation* certain, assured; *air, voix* assured, confident; *main, pas* steady. **mal** ~ unsteady; **tenir pour** ~ **que** to be confident that; ~ **du succès** sure *ou* assured of success. **2** *nm, f* policyholder. ~ **social** ≃ contributor to the National Insurance scheme.

assurément [asyʀemɑ̃] *adv* assuredly, most certainly.

assurer [asyʀe] (1) **1** *vt* (**a**) ~ **à qn que** to assure sb that; ~ **que** to affirm *ou* contend that; **je vous assure!** I assure you!; ~ **qn de** *amitié etc* to assure sb of. (**b**) *(Fin) maison, personne* to insure (*contre* against). ~ **qn sur la vie** to insure sb's life. (**c**) *surveillance* to ensure, maintain; *service, ravitaillement, soins* to provide; *travaux* to carry out. ~ **la protection de** to protect; ~ **la liaison entre Genève et Aberdeen** to operate between Geneva and Aberdeen; *(Jur)* ~ **sa propre défense** to conduct one's own defence; ~ **la direction d'un service** to head up *ou* be in charge of a department; ~ **le remplacement de pièces défectueuses** to guarantee the replacement of faulty parts. (**d**) *bonheur, succès, paix* to ensure; *fortune, situation* to secure. (**e**) *pas, prise* to steady; *(Alpinisme)* to belay. **2 s'** ~ *vpr* (**a**) **s'** ~ **que/de qch** to make sure that/of sth, check that/sth. (**b**) *(Fin, fig)* to insure o.s. (*contre* against). **s'** ~ **sur la vie** to insure one's life. (**c**) *aide, victoire* to secure, ensure; *revenu* to ensure o.s. (**d**) *(s'affermir)* to steady o.s. (*sur* on); *(Alpinisme)* to belay o.s.

assureur [asyʀœʀ] *nm (agent)* insurance agent; *(société)* insurance company.

astérisque [asteʀisk(ə)] *nm* asterisk.

astéroïde [asteʀɔid] *nm* asteroid.

asthmatique [asmatik] *adj, nmf* asthmatic. ◆ **asthme** *nm* asthma.

asticot [astiko] *nm (gén)* maggot; *(pour la pêche)* gentle; *(*: type)* guy *.

asticoter * [astikɔte] (1) *vt* to needle *.

astiquer [astike] (1) *vt* to polish.

astre [astʀ(ə)] *nm* star. ◆ **astral, e,** *mpl* **-aux** *adj* astral.

astreindre [astʀɛ̃dʀ(ə)] (49) **1** *vt*: ~ **qn à faire** to compel *ou* force sb to do; ~ **qn à un travail** to force a task upon sb. **2 s'** ~ *vpr*: **s'** ~ **à (faire) qch** to force *ou* compel o.s. to do sth. ◆ **astreignant, e** [astʀɛɲɑ̃, ɑ̃t] *adj* exacting, demanding. ◆ **astreinte** *nf* constraint.

astringent, e [astʀɛ̃ʒɑ̃, ɑ̃t] *adj, nm* astringent.

astrologie [astʀɔlɔʒi] *nf* astrology. ◆ **astrologique** *adj* astrological. ◆ **astrologue** *nm* astrologer.

astronaute [astʀɔnot] *nmf* astronaut. ◆ **astronautique** *nf* astronautics *(sg)*.

astronome [astʀɔnɔm] *nm* astronomer. ◆ **astronomie** *nf* astronomy. ◆ **astronomique** *adj (lit, fig)* astronomical.

astuce [astys] *nf (adresse)* shrewdness, astuteness, cleverness; *(truc)* trick; (*) *(jeu de mot)* pun; *(plaisanterie)* wisecrack *. **il a beaucoup d'** ~ he is very shrewd *ou* astute. ◆ **astucieusement** *adv* shrewdly, cleverly, astutely. ◆ **astucieux, -ieuse** *adj* shrewd, astute, clever.

asymétrique [asimetʀik] *adj* asymmetrical.

atavique [atavik] *adj* atavistic. ◆ **atavisme** *nm* atavism.

atelier [atəlje] *nm [artisan]* workshop; *[artiste]* studio; *[couturières]* workroom; *[usine]* workshop. *(Scol)* **les enfants travaillent en ~s** the children work in small groups.

atemporel, -elle [atɑ̃pɔʀɛl] *adj vérité* timeless.

atermoyer [atɛʀmwaje] (8) *vi* to procrastinate. ◆ **atermoiement** *nm*: ~(**s**) procrastination.

athée [ate] **1** *adj* atheistic. **2** *nmf* atheist. ◆ **athéisme** *nm* atheism.

Athènes [atɛn] *n* Athens. ◆ **athénien, -ienne** *adj,* **A~(ne)** *nm(f)* Athenian.

athlète [atlɛt] *nmf* athlete. ◆ **athlétique** *adj* athletic. ◆ **athlétisme** *nm* athletics.

atlantique [atlɑ̃tik] **1** *adj* Atlantic. **2** *nm*: **l'A~** the Atlantic.

atlas [atlɑs] *nm (livre, Anat)* atlas.

atmosphère [atmɔsfɛʀ] *nf (lit, fig)* atmosphere. ◆ **atmosphérique** *adj* atmospheric.

atoll [atɔl] *nm* atoll.

atome [atom] *nm* atom. *(fig)* **avoir des** ~ **crochus avec qn** to have things in common with sb, hit it off with sb *. ◆ **atomique** *adj* atomic. ◆ **atomiste** *nmf* atomic scientist.

atomiseur [atɔmizœʀ] *nm (gén)* spray; *[parfum]* atomizer.

atone [atɔn] *adj être* lifeless; *regard* expressionless; *(Ling)* unstressed.

atours [atuʀ] *nmpl (†, hum)* attire, finery.

atout [atu] *nm* (**a**) *(Cartes)* trump. **on jouait** ~ **cœur** hearts were trumps. (**b**) *(fig) (avantage)* asset; *(carte maîtresse)* trump card. **avoir plus d'un** ~ **dans sa manche** to have more than one ace up one's sleeve.

âtre [ɑtʀ(ə)] *nm* hearth.

atroce [atʀɔs] *adj crime* atrocious, heinous; *douleur* excruciating; *mort, sort* dreadful, terrible; *spectacle, goût, temps* ghastly, atrocious, dreadful. ◆ **atrocement** *adv souffrir* atrociously, horribly; *chanter* dreadfully, terribly. ◆ **atrocité** *nf (caractère)* atrocity, atrociousness; *(acte)* atrocity. **dire des ~s sur qn** to say atrocious things about sb.

atrophie [atʀɔfi] *nf* atrophy. ◆ **atrophier** (7) *vt,* **s'** ~ *vpr* to atrophy.

attabler (s') [atable] (1) *vpr* to sit down at (the) table. **les clients attablés** the seated customers.

attachant, e [ataʃɑ̃, ɑ̃t] *adj* engaging.

attache [ataʃ] *nf [ficelle]* (piece of) string; *[métal]* clip, fastener; *[cuir]* strap. *(Anat)* **~s** wrists and ankles; *(connaissances)* **~s** ties, connections; **être à l'** ~ *[animal]* to be tethered; *(fig) [personne]* to be tied; *[bateau]* to be moored.

attacher [ataʃe] (1) **1** *vt* (**a**) *animal, plante, paquet* to tie up; *(ensemble)* to tie together; *volets* to fasten; *papiers* to attach. ~ **qch/qn à** to tie sth/sb to; **attachés avec une épingle** pinned together; ~ **son nom à une découverte** to put one's name to a discovery; **la ficelle qui attachait le paquet** the string that was round the parcel. (**b**) *robe, ceinture* to do up, fasten; *lacets* to do up, tie; *bouton* to do up. *(Aviat)* **attachez votre ceinture** fasten your seatbelt. (**c**) *(fig) importance, valeur* to attach (*à* to). ~ **son regard sur** to fix one's eyes on; ~ **qn à son**

service to take sb on, engage sb; **ce qui l'attache à elle** what makes him feel attached to her, what keeps him with her; **être attaché à qn/qch** to be attached to sb/sth.
2 s' ~ *vpr [robe]* to do up, fasten (up) (*avec, par* with). **s'** ~ **à son siège** to fasten o.s. in one's seat; **s'** ~ **à qn** to become attached to sb. ◆ **attaché** *nm (Pol, Presse)* attaché; *(Admin)* assistant. ◆ **attachement** *nm* attachment (*à* to).

attaquant, e [atakɑ̃, ɑ̃t] *nm, f (Mil, Sport)* attacker; *(Ftbl)* striker, forward.

attaque [atak] *nf* (**a**) *(Mil, fig)* attack; *(Alpinisme)* start. **passer à l'** ~ to move into the attack; **une** ~ **virulente contre le gouvernement** a virulent attack *ou* onslaught on the government; ~ **à la bombe** bomb attack, bombing; ~ **à main armée** hold-up, armed attack. (**b**) *(Méd) (gén)* attack; *[épilepsie]* fit (*de* of). **avoir une** ~ *(cardiaque)* to have a heart attack, have a stroke. (**c**) (*) **d'** ~ on form; **il n'est pas d'** ~ he's a bit off form; **être assez d'** ~ **pour faire** to feel up to doing.

attaquer [atake] (1) **1** *vt* (**a**) *pays, abus, métal* to attack; *passant* to attack, assault; *jugement, testament* to contest. ~ **(qn) par surprise** to make a surprise attack (on sb); ~ **qn en justice** to bring an action against sb. (**b**) *difficulté, chapitre* to tackle; *discours* to launch upon; *(Mus) morceau* to strike up; *note* to attack; *(Alpinisme)* to start. **il attaqua les hors-d'œuvre** * he tucked into * the hors d'œuvres. **2 s'** ~ *vpr*: **s'** ~ **à** *personne, mal* to attack; *problème* to tackle.

attarder [ataʀde] (1) **1** *vt* to make late. **2 s'** ~ *vpr (gén)* to linger. **s'** ~ **chez des amis** to stay on at friends'; **s'** ~ **derrière les autres** to lag behind the others; **s'** ~ **à des détails** to linger over *ou* dwell on details. ◆ **attardé, e 1** *adj (Psych)* backward; *(en retard)* late; *(démodé)* old-fashioned. **2** *nm, f:* ~ **(mental)** backward *ou* mentally retarded child.

atteindre [atɛ̃dʀ(ə)] (49) **1** *vt* (**a**) *lieu, objectif, objet haut placé* to reach. ~ **son but** *[personne]* to reach one's goal, achieve one's aim; *[mesure]* to be effective; *[missile]* to hit its target, reach its objective; **cette tour atteint 30 mètres** this tower is 30 metres high. (**b**) *(contacter)* to get in touch with, contact. (**c**) *[pierre, tireur]* to hit (*à* in); *[maladie, reproches]* to affect; *[malheur]* to strike. **il a été atteint dans son orgueil** his pride has been hurt. **2** ~ **à** *vt indir perfection* to attain, achieve. ◆ **atteint, e**[1] *adj* (**a**) *(malade)* **être** ~ **de** *(maladie)* to suffer from; **il a été atteint de surdité** he became *ou* went deaf; **gravement** ~ *poumon* badly affected; *malade* seriously ill. (**b**) *(*: fou)* touched *. ◆ **atteinte**[2] *nf* (**a**) *(préjudice)* attack (*à* on). **porter** ~ **à** to undermine. (**b**) *(Méd)* attack (*de* of). **les premières** ~**s du mal** the first effects of the illness.

atteler [atle] (4) *vt cheval, charrette* to hitch up (*à* to); *wagons* to couple. **s'** ~ **à** *tâche* to get down to. ◆ **attelage** *nm [chevaux, bœufs]* team.

attenant, e [atnɑ̃, ɑ̃t] *adj:* ~ **(à)** adjoining.

attendre [atɑ̃dʀ(ə)] (41) **1** *vt* (**a**) *[personne]* to wait for. **nous attendons qu'il vienne** we are waiting for him to come; ~ **la fin/un autre moment** to wait until the end/until another time; ~ **qn au train** to meet sb off the train; ~ **qch/de faire qch avec impatience** to look forward eagerly to sth/to doing sth. (**b**) *[voiture]* to be waiting for; *[maison, dîner]* to be ready for; *[surprise, gloire]* to be in store for, await. (**c**) *(sans objet)* to wait. **attendez voir** * let's see *ou* think; **attendez un peu** wait a second; *(iro)* **tu peux toujours** ~! you've got a hope!; **ces fruits ne peuvent pas** ~ this fruit won't keep. (**d**) **faire** ~ **qn** to keep sb waiting; **se faire** ~ *[personne]* to keep people waiting; *[événement]* to be a long time coming. (**e**) *(escompter)* to expect. ~ **qch de qn** to expect sth from sb; **j'attendais mieux de lui** I expected him to do better *ou* better of him. (**f**) ~ **son tour** to wait one's turn; ~ **un enfant** to be expecting a baby; **il attend son heure!** he's biding his time; **il m'attendait au tournant** * he waited for the chance to catch me out; **en attendant** *(pendant ce temps)* in the meantime; *(en dépit de cela)* all the same; **il a pris froid en attendant** he caught cold while (he was) waiting.
2 ~ **après** * *vt indir* to be waiting for; *(avoir besoin)* to be in a hurry for. **je n'attends pas après lui!** I can get along without him!
3 s' ~ *vpr*: **s'** ~ **à qch** to expect sth (*de* from); **est-ce que tu t'attends à ce qu'il écrive?** do you expect him to write?; **comme il fallait s'y** ~... as one would expect..., predictably enough...

attendrir [atɑ̃dʀiʀ] (2) **1** *vt viande* to tenderize; *personne* to move (to pity); *cœur* to soften. **se laisser** ~ **par** to be moved by. **2 s'** ~ *vpr* to be moved (*sur* by). **s'** ~ **sur qn** to feel sorry for sb. ◆ **attendri, e** *adj* tender. ◆ **attendrissant, e** *adj* moving, touching. ◆ **attendrissement** *nm (tendre)* emotion; *(apitoyé)* pity.

attendu, e [atɑ̃dy] **1** *adj (espéré)* long-awaited; *(prévu)* expected. **2** *prép* given, considering (*que* that).

attentat [atɑ̃ta] *nm* murder attempt; *(Pol)* assassination attempt; *(contre un bâtiment)* attack (*contre* on). ~ **à la bombe** bomb attack, (terrorist) bombing; ~ **aux droits** violation of rights; ~ **aux mœurs** offence against public decency; *(Jur)* ~ **à la pudeur** indecent assault *ou* exposure.

attente [atɑ̃t] *nf* (**a**) wait. **dans l'** ~ **des résultats** while waiting for the results; **dans l'** ~ **de vos nouvelles** looking forward to hearing from you; **le projet est en** ~ the plan is in abeyance *ou* is hanging fire; **laisser un dossier en** ~ to leave a file pending. (**b**) *(espoir)* expectation.

attenter [atɑ̃te] (1) *vi:* ~ **à** *vie* to make an attempt on; *droits* to violate; *sûreté nationale* to conspire against.

attentif, -ive [atɑ̃tif, iv] *adj personne, air* attentive; *travail* careful; *examen* careful, close. **être** ~ **à tout ce qui se passe** to pay attention to all that goes on; ~ **à ses devoirs** heedful of one's duty. ◆ **attentivement** *adv lire* attentively, carefully; *examiner* carefully, closely.

attention [atɑ̃sjɔ̃] *nf* (**a**) *(gén)* attention; *(soin)* care. **avec** ~ *écouter* carefully, attentively; *examiner* carefully, closely; ~! watch!, mind!, careful!; ~ **à la marche** mind the step; ~ **à la peinture** (caution) wet paint; *(sur colis)* ~ **fragile** attention *ou* caution, handle with care; **fais** ~ *(prends garde)* be careful; *(écoute)* listen carefully; *(regarde)* watch carefully; **prêter** ~ **à qch/qn** to pay attention to sth/sb, take notice of sth/sb; **fais** ~ **(à ce) que la porte soit fermée** be sure *ou* make sure *ou* mind the door's shut. (**b**) *(prévenance)* attention. ~**s** attentions, thoughtfulness. ◆ **attentionné, e** *adj* thoughtful, considerate (*pour* towards).

atténuer [atenɥe] (1) **1** *vt douleur* to ease; *propos* to tone down; *faute, punition* to mitigate; *faits* to water down; *(Fin) pertes* to cushion; *couleur, son, coup* to soften; *lumière* to subdue, dim. **2 s'** ~ *vpr [douleur, bruit]* to die down; *[violence]* to subside. ◆ **atténuation** *nf* easing; toning down; watering down; softening; subduing; dimming; *(Jur) [peine]* mitigation; dying down.

atterrer [ateʀe] (1) *vt* to dismay, appal. **son air atterré** his look of utter dismay.

atterrir [ateʀiʀ] (2) *vi* to land, touch down. ~ **sur le ventre** to make a belly landing; ~ **en prison** * to land up * *ou* land * *(US)* in prison. ◆ **atterrissage** *nm* landing. **à l'** ~ at touchdown; ~ **forcé** emergency *ou* forced landing.

attester [atɛste] (1) *vt fait* to testify to. ~ **(de) l'innocence de qn** to testify to *ou* vouch for sb's innocence; *(littér)* **j'atteste les dieux que...** I call the gods to witness that.... ◆ **attestation** *nf* (**a**) *[fait]* attestation. (**b**) *(document)* certificate; *[diplôme]* certificate of accreditation *ou* of attestation.

attiédir [atjediʀ] (2) **1** *vt eau* to make lukewarm; *climat* to make more temperate; *désir* to cool. **2 s'** ~ *vpr* to become lukewarm; to become more temperate; to cool down.

attifer * [atife] (1) **1** *vt (habiller)* to get up *. **2 s'** ~ *vpr* to get o.s. up * (*de* in).

attiger ‡ [atiʒe] (3) *vi* to go a bit far *.

attirail * [atiʀaj] *nm* gear, paraphernalia. ~ **de pêche** fishing tackle; ~ **de bricoleur/de cambrioleur** handyman's/burglar's tools *ou* toolkit.

attirer [atiʀe] (1) *vt* (**a**) *(gén, Phys)* to attract; *(en appâtant)* to lure, entice; *foule* to draw, attract. **il m'attira dans un coin** he drew me into a corner; **être attiré par** to be attracted *ou* drawn to; ~ **l'attention de qn sur qch** to draw sb's attention to sth; **ça attire le regard** it catches the eye; **elle attire les hommes** she appeals to *ou* attracts men. (**b**) *colère* to bring down (*sur* on); *sympathie* to win, gain. **s'** ~ **des ennemis** to make enemies for o.s.; **tu vas t'** ~ **des ennuis** you're going to cause trouble for yourself *ou* bring trouble upon yourself. ◆ **attirance** *nf* attraction (*pour* for). ◆ **attirant, e** *adj* attractive, appealing.

attiser [atize] (1) *vt feu* to poke (up); *(fig)* to stir up.

attitré, e [atitʀe] *adj (habituel)* regular, usual; *(agréé)* accredited.

attitude [atityd] *nf (maintien)* bearing; *(comportement)* attitude; *(affectation)* attitude, façade.

attraction [atʀaksjɔ̃] *nf (gén)* attraction. *(cirque etc)* ~**s** programme of attractions *ou* entertainments.

attrait [atʀɛ] *nm* appeal, attraction. ~**s** attractions; **ses romans ont pour moi beaucoup d'** ~ his novels appeal to me very much; **éprouver de l'** ~ **pour qch** to find sth attractive *ou* appealing.

attraper [atʀape] (1) *vt* (**a**) *(gén)* to catch ; *(* fig)* to get; *(fig: saisir) crayon, mots, accent* to pick up. ~ **qn à faire qch** to catch sb doing sth; **tu vas** ~ **froid** you'll catch cold; **la grippe s'attrape facilement** flu is very catching. (**b**) *(gronder)* to tell off *. **se faire** ~ **(par qn)** to get a telling off (from sb) *. (**c**) *(tromper)* to take in. **tu as été bien attrapé** *(trompé)* you were had all right *; *(surpris)* that startled you! ◆ **attrapade** * *nf* telling off *. ◆ **attrape** *nf (farce)* trick. ◆ **attrape-nigaud** *, *pl* **attrape-nigaud(s)** *nm* con *, con game * *(US)*.

attrayant, e [atʀɛjɑ̃, ɑ̃t] *adj (gén)* attractive; *idée* appealing; *lecture* pleasant. **peu** ~ unattractive, unappealing.

attribuer [atʀibɥe] (1) *vt* (**a**) *prix* to award; *avantages* to grant; *rôle, part* to allocate (*à* to). **s'** ~ **le meilleur rôle** to give o.s. the best role. (**b**) *pensée, échec* to attribute, ascribe (*à* to). (**c**) *invention, mérite* to attribute (*à* to); *intérêt* to find (*à* in); *importance* to attach (*à* to). **s'** ~ **tout le mérite** to claim all the merit for o.s. ◆ **attribuable** *adj* attributable (*à* to). ◆ **attribut** *nm* attribute. **adjectif** ~ predicative adjective; **nom** ~ noun complement. ◆ **attribution** *nf* awarding; allocation; attribution.

attrister [atʀiste] (1) **1** *vt* to sadden. **2 s'** ~ *vpr* to be saddened (*de* by) *ou* be grieved (*de* at, *de voir que* at seeing that).

attrouper (s') [atʀupe] (1) *vpr* to gather (together), form a crowd. ◆ **attroupement** *nm* crowd, mob *(péj)*.

au [o] *V* **à.**

aubade [obad] *nf* dawn serenade.

aubaine [obɛn] *nf* godsend; *(financière)* windfall. **profiter de l'** ~ to make the most of the opportunity.

aube [ob] *nf* (**a**) *(lit)* dawn, daybreak; *(fig)* dawn. (**b**) *(Rel)* alb. (**c**) *[bateau]* paddle; *[moulin, turbine]* vane. **roue à** ~**s** paddle wheel.

aubépine [obepin] *nf* hawthorn.

auberge [obɛʀʒ(ə)] *nf* inn. ~ **de (la) jeunesse** youth hostel. ◆ **aubergiste** *nmf* innkeeper, landlord (*ou* lady).

aubergine [obɛʀʒin] **1** *nf (légume)* aubergine, eggplant. **2** *adj inv* aubergine(-coloured).

aucun, e [okœ̃, yn] **1** *adj (nég)* no, not any; *(positif)* any. **il n'a** ~**e preuve** he has no proof, he hasn't any proof; **sans faire** ~ **bruit** without making a noise *ou* any noise; **il lit plus qu'** ~ **autre enfant** he reads more than any other child. **2** *pron (nég)* none; *(positif)* any (one). **il n'aime** ~ **de ces films** he doesn't like any of these films; ~ **de ses enfants** none of his children; **pensez-vous qu'** ~ **ait compris?** do you think anyone *ou* anybody understood?; **d'** ~**s** some. ◆ **aucunement** *adv* in no way, not in the least.

audace [odas] *nf (témérité)* boldness, audacity; *(originalité)* daring; *(effronterie)* audacity; *(geste osé)* daring gesture; *(innovation)* daring idea. **avoir l'** ~ **de** to have the audacity to, dare to. ◆ **audacieusement** *adv* daringly; boldly; audaciously. ◆ **audacieux, -ieuse** *adj* daring; bold; audacious.

au-deçà, au-dedans *etc V* **deçà, dedans** *etc.*

audible [odibl(ə)] *adj* audible. ◆ **audibilité** *nf* audibility.

audience [odjɑ̃s] *nf (entretien)* audience; *(Jur)* hearing. *(fig)* **ce projet eut beaucoup d'** ~ this project aroused much interest.

audio [odjo] *préf* audio.

audio-visuel, -elle [odjovizɥɛl] **1** *adj* audio-visual. **2** *nm* audio-visual methods.

audit [odit] *nm* audit.

auditeur, -trice [oditœʀ, tʀis] *nm, f (gén, Rad)* listener; *(Fin)* auditor. **les** ~**s** the audience. ◆ **auditif, -ive** *adj* auditory.

audition [odisjɔ̃] *nf* (**a**) *(Mus) (essai)* audition; *(récital)* recital; *[disque]* hearing. (**b**) *(ouïe)* hearing. *(Jur)* **procéder à l'** ~ **d'un témoin** to examine a witness. ◆ **auditionner** (1) *vti* to audition. ◆ **auditoire** *nm* audience. ◆ **auditorium** *nm (Rad)* public studio.

auge [oʒ] *nf* trough.

augmenter [ɔgmɑ̃te] (1) **1** *vt (gén)* to increase, raise; *collection* to enlarge, extend; *revenus* to supplement (*en faisant* by doing). ~ **les prix de 10%** to increase *ou* raise *ou* put up *ou* hike prices by 10%; ~ **qn (de 50 F)** to increase sb's salary (by 50 francs), give sb a (50-franc) rise *ou* raise *(US)*. **2** *vi (gén)* to increase; *[prix]* to rise, go up; *[production, inquiétude]* to grow. ~ **de poids** to increase in weight. ◆ **augmentation** *nf (action)* increasing, raising (*de* of); *(résultat)* increase, rise (*de* in).

augure [ɔgyʀ] *nm* (**a**) *(devin) (Hist)* augur; *(fig hum)* oracle. (**b**) *(présage)* omen; *(Hist)* augury. **de bon/mauvais** ~ of good/ill omen. ◆ **augurer** (1) *vt* to foresee (*de* from). **cela augure bien/mal de la suite** that augurs well/ill for what is to follow.

auguste [ɔgyst(ə)] *adj personnage* august; *geste* noble, majestic.

aujourd'hui [oʒuʀdɥi] *adv* today; *(de nos jours)* nowadays, today. ~ **en huit** a week (from) today; **à dater** *ou* **à partir d'** ~ from today onwards; **je le ferai dès** ~ I'll do it this very day.

au(l)ne [on] *nm* alder.

aumône [ɔmon] *nf* alms. **vivre d'** ~**(s)** to live on charity; **faire l'** ~ to give alms (*à* to); *(fig)* **faire**

l' ~ d'un sourire à qn to favour sb with a smile. ◆ **aumônerie** *nf* chaplaincy. ◆ **aumônier** *nm* chaplain.

auparavant [opaʀavɑ̃] *adv (d'abord)* before, first. *(avant)* **2 mois ~** 2 months before *ou* previously.

auprès [opʀɛ] **1** *prép*: **~ de** *(près de)* next to, close to, by; *(avec) malade, ami* with; *(comparé à)* compared with, in comparison with; *(dans l'opinion de)* in the view *ou* opinion of. **avoir de l'influence ~ de qn** to have a lot of influence on sb; **faire une demande ~ de qn** to apply to sb; **ambassadeur ~ de** ambassador to. **2** *adv* nearby.

auquel [okɛl] *V* **lequel.**

auréole [ɔʀeɔl] *nf (Art, Astron)* halo; *(tache)* ring. **l' ~ du martyre** the crown of martyrdom. ◆ **auréoler** (1) *vt (glorifier)* to glorify. **être auréolé de prestige** to have an aura of prestige.

auriculaire [ɔʀikylɛʀ] **1** *nm* little finger. **2** *adj* auricular.

aurore [ɔʀɔʀ] *nf* dawn, daybreak; *(fig)* dawn. **à l' ~** at dawn; **~ boréale** northern lights.

ausculter [ɔskylte] (1) *vt* to auscultate. ◆ **auscultation** *nf* auscultation.

auspices [ospis] *nmpl (Antiq, fig)* auspices. **sous de mauvais ~** under unfavourable auspices.

aussi [osi] **1** *adv* (**a**) *(également)* too, also. **je suis fatigué et eux ~** I'm tired and so are they *ou* and they are too; **il parle l'italien et ~ l'anglais** he speaks Italian and English too *ou* as well; **faites bon voyage — vous ~** have a good journey — you too *ou* the same to you. (**b**) *(comparaison)* **~ grand** *etc* **que** as tall *etc* as; **pas ~ souvent** *etc* **que** not so *ou* as often *etc* as; **~ vite que possible** as quickly as possible. (**c**) *(si)* so. **je ne te savais pas ~ bête** I didn't think you were so stupid; **comment peut-on laisser passer une ~ bonne occasion?** how can one let slip such a good opportunity?; **~ léger qu'il fût** light though he was. (**d**) *(tout autant)* **ça m'a fait ~ mal** it hurt me just as much; **tu peux ~ bien dire non** you can just as easily *ou* well say no; **~ sec *** on the spot *. **2** *conj (en conséquence)* therefore, consequently.

aussitôt [osito] **1** *adv* straight away, immediately. **~ arrivé** as soon as he arrived; **~ dit, ~ fait** no sooner said than done; **~ après** straight *ou* immediately after; **~ que je le vis** as soon as I saw him. **2** *prép*: **~ mon arrivée** immediately on my arrival, as soon as I arrived.

austère [ɔstɛʀ] *adj personne, vie* austere; *livre* dry; *manteau* severely cut. ◆ **austèrement** *adv* austerely. ◆ **austérité** *nf* austerity; dryness. *(Pol)* **mesures d' ~** austerity measures.

austral, e, *mpl* **~s** [ɔstʀal] *adj* southern.

Australie [ɔstʀali] *nf* Australia. *(Pol)* **l' ~** the commonwealth of Australia; **~-Méridionale/-Occidentale** South/Western Australia. ◆ **australien, -ienne** *adj,* **A~(ne)** *nm(f)* Australian.

autant [otɑ̃] *adv* (**a**) **~ de** *(quantité)* as much (*que* as); *(nombre)* as many (*que* as); **nous sommes ~ qu'eux** there are as many of us as of them; **elle mange deux fois ~ que lui** she eats twice as much as him *ou* as he does; **ils ont ~ de mérite l'un que l'autre** they have equal merit; **ils ont ~ de talents l'un que l'autre** they are both equally talented. (**b**) *(intensité)* as much (*que* as). **il peut crier ~ qu'il veut** he can scream as much as he likes; **courageux ~ que compétent** as courageous as he is competent. (**c**) *(tant)* **~ de** *succès, eau* so much; *personnes, bijoux* so many, such a lot of; **pourquoi travaille-t-il ~?** why does he work so much *ou* so hard? (**d**) *(avec en)* **je ne peux pas en dire/faire ~** I can't say/do as much *ou* the same. (**e**) *(avec de)* **ce sera augmenté d' ~** it will be increased accordingly *ou* in proportion; **c'est d' ~ plus dangereux qu'il n'y a pas de parapet** it's all the more dangerous since *ou* because there is no parapet; **nous le voyons d' ~ moins qu'il habite très loin** we see him even less since *ou* because he lives a long way away. (**f**) **~ il est généreux, ~ elle est avare** he is as generous as she is miserly; **~ que possible** as much *ou* as far as possible; **(pour) ~ que je sache** as far as I know, to the best of my knowledge; **c'est ~ de gagné** at least that's something; **~ dire qu'il est fou** you might as well say that he's mad; **il ne vous remerciera pas pour ~** for all that you won't get any thanks from him; **tous ~ que vous êtes** the whole lot of you; **~ prévenir la police** it would be as well to inform the police.

autarcie [otaʀsi] *nf* autarky.

autel [ɔtɛl] *nm (Rel, lit, fig)* altar. **conduire sa fille à l' ~** to give one's daughter away in marriage; **dresser un ~ à qn** to worship sb.

auteur [otœʀ] *nm (gén)* author; *[opéra]* composer; *[tableau]* painter. **l' ~ de l'accident** the person who caused the accident; **qui est l' ~ de cette affiche?** who designed this poster?; *(Mus)* **~-compositeur** composer-songwriter; *(femme de lettres)* **c'est un ~ connu** she is a well-known author *ou* authoress.

authenticité [ɔtɑ̃tisite] *nf* authenticity. ◆ **authentifier** (7) *vt* to authenticate. ◆ **authentique** *adj* authentic. ◆ **authentiquement** *adv* authentically.

autisme [ɔtism(ə)] *nm* autism. ◆ **autistique** *adj* autistic.

auto [ɔto] **1** *nf (voiture)* car, automobile *(US)*. **~s tamponneuses** dodgems. **2** *adj inv* car. **3** *préf* (**a**) self-. **~discipline/défense/portrait** self-discipline/defence/portrait; **s' ~gérer** to be self-managing; **~-intoxication/suggestion** auto-intoxication/suggestion; **~-allumage** pre-ignition. (**b**) *(automobile)* car. **~(-)radio** car radio.

autoberge [ɔtɔbɛʀʒ(ə)] *nm* riverside *ou* embankment expressway.

autobiographie [ɔtɔbjɔgʀafi] *nf* autobiography. ◆ **autobiographique** *adj* autobiographic(al).

autobus [ɔtɔbys] *nm* bus.

autocar [ɔtɔkaʀ] *nm* coach, bus *(US)*.

autocaravane [ɔtɔkaʀavan] *nf* camping car, motorhome *(US)*, camper *(US)*.

autochtone [ɔtɔktɔn] *adj nmf* native.

autoclave [ɔtɔklav] *nm* autoclave.

autocollant, e [ɔtɔkɔlɑ̃, ɑ̃t] **1** *adj* self-adhesive. **2** *nm* sticker.

autocrate [ɔtɔkʀat] *nm* autocrat. ◆ **autocratie** *nf* autocracy. ◆ **autocratique** *adj* autocratic.

autocritique [ɔtɔkʀitik] *nf* self-criticism. **faire son ~** to criticize o.s.

autocuiseur [ɔtɔkɥizœʀ] *nm* pressure cooker.

autodafé [ɔtɔdafe] *nm* auto-da-fé.

autodidacte [ɔtɔdidakt(ə)] *adj* self-taught.

autodrome [ɔtɔdʀom] *nm* motor-racing track, autodrome.

auto-école [ɔtoekɔl] *nf* driving school.

autofinancer (s') [ɔtɔfinɑ̃se] (1) *vpr [entreprise]* to be ou become self-financing. **programme de recherches autofinancé** self-supporting *ou* self-financed research programme.

autogestion [ɔtɔʒɛstjɔ̃] *nf* joint worker-management control.

autographe [ɔtɔgʀaf] *adj, nm* autograph.

automate [ɔtɔmat] *nm (lit, fig)* automaton.

automation [ɔtɔmɑsjɔ̃] *nf* automation.

automatique [ɔtɔmatik] **1** *adj* automatic. **2** *nm (Téléc)* ≃ subscriber trunk dialling, direct dialing *(US)*; *(revolver)* automatic. ◆ **automatiquement** *adv* automatically. ◆ **automatisation** *nf* automation. ◆ **automatiser** (1) *vt* to automate. ◆ **automatisme** *nm* automatism.

automitrailleuse [ɔtɔmitʀɑjøz] *nf* armoured car.

automne [ɔtɔn] *nm* autumn, fall *(US)*. ◆ **automnal, e,** *mpl* **-aux** *adj* autumnal.

automobile [ɔtɔmɔbil] **1** *adj véhicule, sport* motor; *assurance, industrie* motor, car, automobile *(US)*. **2** *nf* motor car, automobile *(US)*. **l'** ~ the car industry; *(Sport)* **l'** ~ motoring; **termes d'** ~ motoring terms. ◆ **automobiliste** *nmf* motorist.

autonome [ɔtɔnɔm] *adj* autonomous; *territoire* self-governing; *(Ordin)* off-line. **groupuscule** ~ group of political extremists. ◆ **autonomie** *nf* autonomy; self-government; *(Aut, Aviat)* range. ◆ **autonomiste,** *adj, nmf (Pol)* separatist.

autopsie [ɔtɔpsi] *nf* autopsy, post-mortem (examination). ◆ **autopsier** (7) *vt* to carry out an autopsy on.

autorail [ɔtɔʀɑj] *nm* railcar.

autoriser [ɔtɔʀize] (1) **1** *vt manifestation* to give permission for, authorize; *craintes* to justify. ~ **qn** to give sb permission *ou* allow sb (*à faire* to do); **ça autorise à croire que...** that leads one to think that...; **se croire autorisé à dire que...** to feel one is entitled to say that...; **loi qui autorise les abus** law which admits of abuses. **2 s'** ~ *vpr*: **s'** ~ **de qch pour faire** to use sth as an excuse to do. ◆ **autorisation** *nf* permission (*de qch* for sth, *de faire* to do); *(permis)* permit. ◆ **autorisé, e** *adj agent, version* authorized; *opinion* authoritative. **milieux** ~**s** official circles.

autorité [ɔtɔʀite] *nf (pouvoir)* authority (*sur* over); *(expert)* authority. **avoir** ~ **pour faire** to have authority to do; *(Admin)* **l'** ~ **, les** ~**s** the authorities; **agent de l'** ~ representative of authority; **d'** ~ *ton* authoritative; *prendre* unhesitatingly; **de sa propre** ~ on one's own authority; **faire** ~ to be authoritative. ◆ **autoritaire** *adj, nmf* authoritarian. ◆ **autoritairement** *adv* in an authoritarian way. ◆ **autoritarisme** *nm* authoritarianism.

autoroute [ɔtɔʀut] *nf* motorway, highway *(US)*, freeway *(US)*. ~ **à péage** toll motorway, turnpike *(US)*. ◆ **autoroutier, -ière** *adj* motorway.

autosatisfaction [ɔtɔsatisfaksjɔ̃] *nf* self-satisfaction.

auto-stop [ɔtɔstɔp] *nm* hitch-hiking. **faire de l'** ~ to hitch-hike; **prendre qn en** ~ to pick up sb, give a lift to sb. ◆ **auto-stoppeur, -euse** *nm, f* hitch-hiker.

autour [otuʀ] **1** *adv* around, round. **tout** ~ all around; **maison avec un jardin** ~ house with a garden round it.
2 *prép*: ~ **de** around, (round) about; **regarde** ~ **de toi** look around *ou* about you.

autre [otʀ(ə)] **1** *adj indéf* (**a**) *(différent)* other, different. **chercher un** ~ **mode de vie** to try to find an alternative life style; **c'est une** ~ **question** that's another *ou* a different question; **parlons d'** ~ **chose** let's talk about something else *ou* different; **revenez une** ~ **fois** come back some other *ou* another time. (**b**) *(supplémentaire)* other. **elle a 2** ~**s enfants** she has 2 other *ou* 2 more children; **donnez-moi un** ~ **kilo** give me another kilo. (**c**) *(opposé)* other. **de l'** ~ **côté de la rue** on the other *ou* opposite side of the street. (**d**) **et vous** ~**s qu'en pensez-vous?** what do you people think?; **nous** ~ **Français** we Frenchmen; **j'ai d'** ~**s chats à fouetter** I've other fish to fry; ~ **chose, Madame?** anything *ou* something else, madam?; **ce n'est pas** ~ **chose que de la jalousie** that's nothing but jealousy; ~ **part** somewhere else; **d'** ~ **part** *(par contre)* on the other hand; *(de plus)* moreover; **c'est une** ~ **paire de manches** * that's another story; *(Rel)* **l'** ~ **monde** the next world.
2 *pron indéf* (**a**) *(qui est différent)* **un** ~ another (one); **d'** ~**s** others; **personne d'** ~ no one else, nobody else; **prendre une chose pour une** ~ to take sth for sth else; **je n'en veux pas d'** ~ I don't want any other; **à d'** ~**s!** * tell that to the marines! *; **il n'en fait jamais d'** ~**s!** that's just typical of him; **un** ~ **que moi** anyone else but me; **il en a vu d'** ~**s!** he's seen worse!; **les deux** ~**s** the other two, the two others; **XYZ, et** ~**s** XYZ etc. (**b**) *(supplémentaire)* **donnez m'en un** ~ give me another (one) *ou* one more; **qui/rien d'** ~ who/nothing else. (**c**) *(opposition)* **l'** ~ the other (one); **les** ~**s** the others; **d'une minute à l'** ~ *(bientôt)* any minute; *(n'importe quand)* any moment *ou* minute *ou* time; *(soudain)* from one minute *ou* moment to the next.

autrefois [otʀəfwa] *adv* in the past. **d'** ~ of the past, of old, past; ~ **je préférais le vin** in the past I used to prefer wine.

autrement [otʀəmɑ̃] *adv* (**a**) *(différemment)* differently. **il ne peut en être** ~ it can't be any other way; **agir** ~ **que d'habitude** to act differently from usual; **comment aller à Londres** ~ **que par le train?** how can we get to London other than by train?; ~ **appelé** otherwise known as; **faire qch** ~ to do sth another way *ou* differently; **on ne peut pas faire** ~ it's impossible to do otherwise *ou* to do anything else; **il n'a pas pu faire** ~ **que de me voir** he couldn't help seeing me; ~ **dit** *(en d'autres mots)* in other words; *(c'est-à-dire)* that is. (**b**) *(sinon)* otherwise, or else; *(à part cela)* otherwise, apart *ou* aside from that. **cela ne m'a pas** ~ **surpris** that didn't particularly surprise me. (**c**) *(comparatif)* ~ **bon/intelligent** far better/more intelligent (*que* than).

Autriche [otʀiʃ] *nf* Austria. ◆ **autrichien, -ienne** *adj*, **A~(ne)** *nm(f)* Austrian.

autruche [otʀyʃ] *nf* ostrich. *(fig)* **faire l'** ~ to bury one's head in the sand.

autrui [otʀɥi] *pron* others.

auvent [ovɑ̃] *nm* canopy.

aux [o] *V* **à.**

auxiliaire [ɔksiljɛʀ] **1** *adj (Ling, Mil, gén)* auxiliary; *cause* secondary, subsidiary; *(Scol)* assistant. **bureau** ~ sub-office. **2** *nmf (assistant)* assistant. ~ **médical** medical auxiliary. **3** *nm (Gram, Mil)* auxiliary.

auxquels [okɛl] *V* **lequel.**

avachir (s') [avaʃiʀ] (2) *vpr [cuir]* to become limp; *[vêtement]* to become shapeless; *[personne] (physiquement)* to become limp; *(moralement)* to get slack. **avachi sur son pupitre** slumped on his desk. ◆ **avachissement** *nm* loss of shape; limpness; slackness.

aval¹ [aval] *nm [cours d'eau]* downstream water; *[pente]* downhill slope. **en** ~ downstream; downhill (*de* from).

aval², *pl* ~**s** [aval] *nm (fig: soutien)* backing, support; *(Comm, Jur)* guarantee (*de* for).

avalanche [avalɑ̃ʃ] *nf [neige, documents]* avalanche; *[compliments]* flood.

avaler [avale] (1) *vt repas, mensonge, affront* to swallow; *roman* to devour; *(Alpinisme) mou, corde* to take in. *[fumeur]* ~ **la fumée** to inhale; ~ **à petites gorgées** to sip; **il a avalé de travers** sth went down the wrong way; **il n'a rien avalé depuis 2 jours** * he hasn't eaten a thing for 2 days; **ambitieux qui veut tout** ~ ambitious man who thinks he can take on anything; ~ **ses mots** to mumble; **tu as avalé ta langue?** have you lost your tongue?; **on dirait qu'il a avalé son parapluie** he's so stiff and starchy.

avaliser [avalize] (1) *vt plan* to back, support; *(Comm, Jur)* to guarantee.

avance [avɑ̃s] *nf* (**a**) *(marche)* advance. **accélérer/ralentir son** ~ to speed up/slow down one's advance. (**b**) *(sur concurrent etc)* lead. **avoir de l'** ~ **sur qn** to have a lead over sb; **10 minutes d'** ~ a 10 minute lead. (**c**) **avoir de l'** ~ **(sur l'horaire)/dans son travail** to be ahead of schedule/ahead in one's work; **avoir 10 minutes d'** ~ *[train]* to be 10 minutes early *ou* ahead of schedule; *[montre]* to be 10 minutes fast; **le train a perdu son** ~ the train has lost the time it had gained; **ma montre prend de l'** ~ my watch is gaining *ou* gains; **en** ~ *(sur l'heure fixée)* early; *(sur l'horaire etc)* ahead of schedule; *(dans les études)* ahead (*sur qn* of sb); **dépêche-toi, tu n'es pas en** ~! hurry up you're running out of time!; **en** ~ **pour son âge** advanced for his age; **en** ~ **sur son temps** ahead of *ou* in advance of one's time; **à l'** ~ **, d'** ~ in advance, beforehand. (**d**) ~ **(de fonds)** advance; ~ **à l'allumage** ignition advance; ~**s** *(ouvertures)* overtures; *(galantes)* advances.

avancé, e[1] [avɑ̃se] *adj* (**a**) *élève, technique, idée, (Mil) poste* advanced. **la saison était** ~**e** it was late in the season; **à une heure** ~**e de la nuit** late at night; **son roman est déjà assez** ~ he's already quite far ahead with his novel; **les pays les moins** ~**s** the least developed countries; **d'un âge** ~ well on in years; **dans un état** ~ **de...** in an advanced state of...; **il n'en est pas plus** ~ he's no further on than he was; *(iro)* **nous voilà bien** ~**s! *** a long way that's got us! (**b**) *fruit, fromage* overripe. **ce poisson est** ~ this fish is going off *ou* is bad.

avancée[2] [avɑ̃se] *nf* overhang.

avancement [avɑ̃smɑ̃] *nm (promotion)* promotion; *(progrès) [travaux]* progress; *[sciences]* advancement. **possibilités d'** ~ career prospects, prospects *ou* chances of promotion.

avancer [avɑ̃se] (3) **1** *vt* (**a**) *objet* to move *ou* bring forward; *tête* to move forward; *main* to hold out, put out (*vers* to); *pendule* to put forward; *hypothèse* to put forward, advance; *date, départ* to bring forward. (**b**) *(faire progresser) travail* to speed up. **si cela peut vous** ~ if it speeds things up (for you) *ou* helps you; **ça n'avance pas nos affaires** that doesn't improve matters for us; **cela t'avancera à quoi de courir?** what good will it do you to run?; **cela ne t'avancera à rien de crier *** you won't get anywhere by shouting. (**c**) *argent* to advance; *(*: prêter)* to lend.
2 *vi* (**a**) to move forward; *[armée, procession]* to advance (*sur* on). ~ **d'un pas** to move *ou* take a step forward; **faire** ~ **qn** to make sb move on. (**b**) *(fig) [travail]* to make progress; *[nuit]* to be wearing on. **faire** ~ *travail* to speed up; *élève* to bring on; *science* to further; ~ **lentement dans son travail** to make slow progress in one's work; ~ **en grade** to be promoted, get promotion; **tout cela n'avance à rien** that doesn't get us any further *ou* anywhere. (**c**) *[montre]* ~ **de 10 minutes par jour** to gain 10 minutes a day; **j'avance de 10 minutes** I'm 10 minutes fast. (**d**) *[cap, promontoire]* to project, jut out (*dans* into); *[lèvre, menton]* to protrude.
3 s' ~ *vpr* to move forward; *[procession]* to advance; *(fig: s'engager)* to commit o.s. **il s'avança vers nous** he came towards us.

avanie [avani] *nf* snub. **faire des** ~**s à qn** to snub sb.

avant [avɑ̃] **1** *prép* (**a**) *(temps, lieu)* before. ~ **de partir** *ou* **que je (ne) parte** before leaving, before I leave; **pas** ~ **10 heures/une demi-heure** not until *ou* before 10/for another half hour; **j'étais** ~ **lui dans la queue** I was in front of him *ou* before him in the queue; **il me le faut** ~ **demain/un mois** I must have it by *ou* before tomorrow/within a month; ~ **peu** shortly; **X, ce féministe bien** ~ **la lettre** X, a feminist long before the term existed *ou* had been coined. (**b**) *(priorité)* before. ~ **tout** above all; **le travail passe** ~ **tout** work comes before everything; **en classe, elle est** ~ **sa sœur** at school she is ahead of her sister.
2 *adv* (**a**) *(d'abord)* before, beforehand; *(autrefois)* before. **quelques mois** ~ a few months before *ou* previously *ou* earlier; **la semaine d'** ~ the week before, the previous week; **fort** ~ **dans la nuit** far into the night; **réfléchis** ~ think first; **le train d'** ~ **était plein** the previous train was full. (**b**) *(espace)* **aller plus** ~**/trop** ~ *(lit, fig)* to go further (forward)/too far; **être assez** ~ **dans ses recherches** to be quite far ahead in one's research; **en** ~ *(mouvement)* forward; *(position)* in front, ahead (*de* of); **en** ~**, marche!** forward march!; *(Naut)* **en** ~ **toute!** full steam ahead!; *(fig)* **regarder en** ~ to look ahead; *(fig)* **mettre qch en** ~ to put sth forward; *(fig)* **mettre qn en** ~ *(pour se couvrir)* to use sb as a front; *(fig)* **il aime se mettre en** ~ he likes to push himself forward.
3 *nm [voiture, train]* front; *[navire]* bow, stem; *(Sport: joueur) (gén)* forward; *(Volley-ball)* front-line player; *(Mil)* front. **à l'** ~ **(du train)** in the front of the train; *(fig)* **aller de l'** ~ to forge ahead.
4 *adj inv roue* front; *marche* forward. **traction** ~ front-wheel drive; **la partie** ~ the front part.
5 *préf inv (le second élément prend la marque du pluriel et donne le genre)* ~**-bras** forearm; ~**-centre** centre-forward; ~**-coureur** *(nm)* harbinger; *(adj inv)* precursory, premonitory; **signe** ~**-coureur** forerunner; ~**-dernier** *adj* last but one; ~**-garde** *(Mil)* vanguard; *(Art, Pol)* avant-garde; **d'** ~**-garde** avant-garde; ~**-goût** foretaste; ~**-guerre** pre-war years; **d'** ~**-guerre** pre-war; ~**-hier** the day before yesterday; ~**-port** outer harbour; ~**-poste** outpost; ~**-première** preview; ~**-projet** pilot study; ~**-propos** foreword; ~**-scène** *(scène)* apron; *(loge)* box; ~**-train** *[animal]* forequarters; **l'** ~**-veille** two days before *ou* previously; **l'** ~**-veille de** two days before.

avantage [avɑ̃taʒ] *nm* (**a**) *(gén)* advantage. **avoir l'** ~ to have the advantage; **j'ai** ~ **à l'acheter** it's worth my while to buy it; **tirer** ~ **de la situation** to take advantage of the situation, turn the situation to one's advantage; **tu aurais** ~ **à te tenir tranquille *** you'd do well to keep quiet; **ils ont l'** ~ **du nombre** they have the advantage of numbers (*sur* over). (**b**) *(Fin: gain)* benefit. ~**s en nature** fringe benefits, payment in kind; ~**s sociaux** welfare benefits. (**c**) *(plaisir)* pleasure. **que me vaut l'** ~ **de votre visite?** to what do I owe the pleasure of your visit? (**d**) **être à son** ~ *(photo)* to look one's best; *(conversation)* to be at one's best; **se montrer à son** ~ to show o.s. off to advantage; **c'est (tout) à ton** ~ it's (entirely) to your advantage; **changer à son** ~ to change for the better. ◆ **avantager** (3) *vt (donner un avantage à)* to favour, give an advantage to; *(mettre en valeur)* to flatter. *(dans la vie)* **être avantagé dès le départ** to have a head start (*par rapport à* on). ◆ **avantageusement** *adv vendre* at a good price; *décrire* favourably, flatteringly. ◆ **avantageux, -euse** *adj* (**a**) *affaire* worthwhile, profitable; *prix* attractive. (**b**) *(présomptueux)* conceited. (**c**) *portrait* flattering.

avare [avaʀ] **1** *adj* miserly. ~ **de** *paroles, compliments* sparing of. **2** *nmf* miser. ◆ **avarice** *nf* miserliness, avarice. ◆ **avaricieux, -ieuse** *adj* miserly.

avarie [avaʀi] *nf*: ~**(s)** damage.

avarier (s') [avaʀje] (7) *vpr* to go bad, rot. **viande avariée** rotting meat.

avatar [avataʀ] *nm (Rel)* avatar; *(fig)* metamorphosis. *(péripéties)* ~**s *** misadventures.

avec [avɛk] **1** *prép* (**a**) *(gén)* with. **couteau** ~ **(un) manche en bois** knife with a wooden handle, wooden-handled knife; **ragoût fait** ~ **des restes** stew made out of *ou* from (the) left-overs; **c'est fait** ~ **du plomb** it's made of lead; **voyageant** ~ **un passeport qui...** travelling on a passport which...

(**b**) *(relations) combattre* with; *se comporter* with, towards. **doux/gentil** ~ **qn** gentle with/kind to sb; **se marier** ~ **qn** to marry sb; **son mariage** ~ **X** her marriage to X; **ils ont les syndicats** ~ **eux** they've got the unions on their side *ou* behind them. (**c**) *(cause etc)* with. ~ **le temps** in the course of time, with the passing of time; ~ **l'inflation et le prix de l'essence** what with inflation and the price of petrol; ~ **toute ma bonne volonté** with the best will in the world; **ils sont partis** ~ **la pluie** they left in the rain. (**d**) **d'** ~ from; **séparer qch d'** ~ **qch d'autre** to separate sth from sth else. (**e**) *(dans un magasin)* **et** ~ **ça?** is there anything else?; **il conduit mal et** ~ **ça il conduit trop vite** he drives badly and what's more he drives too fast; ~ **cela que tu ne le savais pas!** as if you didn't know!; ~ **tout ça j'ai oublié le pain** in the midst of all this I forgot about the bread.
2 *adv* (*) **tiens mes gants, je ne peux pas conduire** ~ hold my gloves, I can't drive with them on.

aven [avɛn] *nm* swallow hole.

avenant, e [avnɑ̃, ɑ̃t] **1** *adj* pleasant. **2** *nm* (**a**) **à l'** ~ in keeping (*de* with). (**b**) *[police d'assurance]* endorsement; *[contrat]* amendment (*à* to). **faire un** ~ **à** to endorse; to amend.

avènement [avɛnmɑ̃] *nm [roi]* accession (*à* to); *[régime, idée]* advent; *[Messie]* Advent, Coming.

avenir [avniʀ] *nm (gén)* future; *(postérité)* future generations. **dans un proche** ~ in the near future; **à l'** ~ from now on, in future; **il a de l'** ~ **, c'est un homme d'** ~ he's a man with a future *ou* with good prospects.

Avent [avɑ̃] *nm*: **l'** ~ Advent.

aventure [avɑ̃tyʀ] *nf (péripétie)* adventure; *(entreprise)* venture; *(amoureuse)* affair; *(malencontreuse)* experience. **film d'** ~**s** adventure film; **l'** ~ adventure; **marcher à l'** ~ to walk aimlessly; **si, par** ~ *ou* **d'** ~ if by any chance. ◆ **aventuré, e** *adj* risky. ◆ **aventurer** (1) **1** *vt somme, vie* to risk; *remarque* to venture. **2 s'** ~ *vpr* to venture (*dans* into, *sur* onto). **s'** ~ **à faire qch** to venture to do sth. ◆ **aventureusement** *adv (gén)* adventurously; *(dangereusement)* riskily. ◆ **aventureux, -euse** *adj personne, vie* adventurous; *projet* risky. ◆ **aventurier, -ière** *nm, f* adventurer, adventuress.

avenue [avny] *nf* avenue.

avérer (s') [aveʀe] (6) *vpr*: **il s'avère que** it turns out that; **cela s'avéra efficace** it proved (to be) *ou* turned out to be effective; **il est avéré que** it is a known *ou* recognised fact that.

averse [avɛʀs(ə)] *nf (lit, fig)* shower. **forte** ~ heavy shower, downpour.

aversion [avɛʀsjɔ̃] *nf* aversion (*pour* to), loathing (*pour* for). **avoir en** ~ to loathe.

avertir [avɛʀtiʀ] (2) *vt (mettre en garde)* to warn; *(renseigner)* to inform (*de qch* of sth). ◆ **averti, e** *adj public* informed, mature; *expert* well-informed (*de* about). ~ **de** *problèmes etc* aware of. ◆ **avertissement** *nm (gén)* warning. *(Scol)* **recevoir un** ~ to receive a warning, be admonished *(préface)* ~ **(au lecteur)** foreword. ◆ **avertisseur, -euse 1** *adj* warning. **2** *nm (Aut)* horn. ~ **(d'incendie)** (fire) alarm.

aveu, *pl* ~**x** [avø] *nm*: ~**x** confession, admission. **passer aux** ~**x** to make a confession; **de l'** ~ **de qn** according to sb; **sans** ~ *homme* disreputable; **sans l'** ~ **de qn** without sb's consent.

aveugle [avœgl(ə)] **1** *adj (gén)* blind. **devenir** ~ to go blind; ~ **d'un œil** blind in one eye; **son amour le rend** ~ he is blinded by love; **une confiance** ~ an implicit trust; **être** ~ **aux défauts de qn** to be blind to sb's faults. **2** *nmf* blind man (*ou* woman). **les** ~**s** the blind; **faire qch en** ~ to do sth blindly. ◆ **aveuglant, e** *adj* blinding, dazzling. ◆ **aveuglement** *nm* blindness. ◆ **aveuglément** *adv (lit, fig)* blindly. ◆ **aveugler** (1) *vt (lit, fig)* to blind; *(éblouir)* to dazzle, blind. **s'** ~ **sur qn** to be blind to sb's defects. ◆ **aveuglette** *nf*: **à l'** ~ *décider* in the dark, blindly; **avancer à l'** ~ to grope (one's way) along.

aviation [avjɑsjɔ̃] *nf (Mil)* air force. **l'** ~ *(sport, métier)* flying; *(secteur)* aviation; *(transport)* air travel; **d'** ~ *coupe* flying; *usine* aircraft; *base* air; ~ **de chasse** fighter force. ◆ **aviateur, -trice** *nm, f* aviator, pilot.

aviculture [avikyltyʀ] *nf (volailles)* poultry farming. ◆ **avicole** *adj* poultry. ◆ **aviculteur, -trice** *nm, f* poultry farmer.

avide [avid] *adj (cupidité)* greedy; *lecteur* avid, eager (*de qch* for sth). ◆ **avidement** *adv* eagerly; greedily; avidly. ◆ **avidité** *nf* eagerness; greed; avidity (*de* for). **manger avec** ~ to eat greedily.

avilir [aviliʀ] (2) **1** *vt* to degrade. **2 s'** ~ *vpr* to degrade o.s. ◆ **avilissant, e** *adj* degrading. ◆ **avilissement** *nm* degradation.

aviné, e [avine] *adj* inebriated.

avion [avjɔ̃] *nm* aeroplane, plane, airplane *(US)*, aircraft *(pl inv)*. *(sport)* **l'** ~ flying; **aller à Paris en** ~ to go to Paris by air *ou* by plane, fly to Paris; **par** ~ by air(mail); ~**-cargo** (air) freighter, cargo aircraft; ~ **de chasse** fighter (plane); ~**-citerne** air tanker; ~ **de ligne** airliner; ~ **en papier** paper aeroplane; ~ **à réaction** jet (plane); ~**-taxi** taxi-plane.

aviron [aviʀɔ̃] *nm (rame)* oar; *(sport)* rowing. **faire de l'** ~ to row.

avis [avi] *nm* (**a**) *(gén, Admin)* opinion. **donner son** ~ to give one's opinion *ou* view (*sur* on, about); **les** ~ **sont partagés** opinion is divided; **être de l'** ~ **de qn** to be of the same opinion as sb; **à mon** ~ in my opinion, to my mind; **il était d'** ~ **de partir** he thought *ou* was of the opinion that we should leave. (**b**) *(conseil)* advice. **un** ~ **amical** a friendly piece of advice, some friendly advice. (**c**) *(notification)* notice; *(Fin)* advice. ~ **de crédit** credit advice; **(** ~ **d') appel d'offres** invitation to tenter *ou* to bid; **jusqu'à nouvel** ~ until further notice; **sauf** ~ **contraire** unless otherwise informed; *(sur étiquette)* unless otherwise indicated; *(Comm)* ~ **d'expédition** advice of dispatch; ~ **au lecteur** foreword; ~ **au public** notice to the public; ~ **de recherche** *[criminel]* wanted notice; *[disparu]* missing person notice.

aviser [avize] (1) **1** *vt* (**a**) *(avertir)* to advise, inform (*de* of), notify (*de* of, about). (**b**) *(apercevoir)* to catch sight of, notice. **2** *vi* to decide what to do. ~ **au nécessaire** to see to the necessary, do what is necessary. **3 s'** ~ *vpr*: **s'** ~ **de qch** to realize sth suddenly; **s'** ~ **de faire qch** to take it into one's head to do sth. ◆ **avisé, e** *adj* sensible, wise. **bien/mal** ~ well-/ill-advised.

avitaminose [avitaminoz] *nf* vitamin deficiency.

aviver [avive] (1) **1** *vt douleur, appétit* to sharpen; *chagrin* to deepen; *désir* to arouse, excite; *colère* to stir up; *regard, couleur* to brighten; *feu, souvenirs* to revive, stir up. **2 s'** ~ *vpr* to sharpen; to deepen; to be aroused; to be stirred up; to be excited; to brighten; to revive.

avocat, e [avɔka, at] **1** *nm, f (Jur: fonction)* barrister, attorney(-at-law) *(US)*; *(fig)* advocate. **consulter son** ~ to consult one's lawyer; **l'accusé et son** ~ the accused and his counsel; **l'** ~ **de la défense/de la partie civile** the counsel for the defence/the plaintiff; ~ **d'entreprise** company lawyer, corporation lawyer *(US)*; *(Rel, fig)* **l'** ~ **du diable** the devil's advocate; ~ **général** counsel for the prosecution; **se faire l'** ~ **de qch** to advocate sth; **fais toi mon** ~ **auprès de lui** plead with him on my behalf.
2 *nm (fruit)* avocado (pear).

avoine [avwan] *nf* oats.

avoir [avwaʀ] (34) **1** *vt* (**a**) *(gén)* to have; *(recevoir, atteindre)* to get; *(porter) vêtements* to have on, wear. **il n'a pas d'argent** he has no money, he hasn't got any money; **essayez de m' ~ Paris (au téléphone)** could you put me through to Paris; **on les aura!** we'll get them!; **il a les mains qui tremblent** his hands are shaking. (**b**) *âge, formes, couleur* to be. **ils ont le même âge** they are the same age; **~ 3 mètres de haut** to be 3 metres high; **ça a une jolie, forme** it is a nice shape. (**c**) *(éprouver) joie, chagrin* to feel; *intérêt* to show. **~ faim/honte** to be *ou* feel hungry/ashamed; **~ le sentiment que** to have the feeling that; **qu'est-ce qu'il a?** what's the matter with him?; **qu'est-ce qu'il a à pleurer?** what's he crying for? (**d**) *geste, remarque* to make; *rire* to give; *cri* to utter. (**e**) *(*: duper)* to take in, con *. **se faire ~** to be had *, be taken in. (**f**) **en ~ après qn *** to be mad at * *ou* cross with sb; **elle en a toujours après moi** she's always on at me; **qu'est-ce que tu as contre lui?** what have you got against him?; **en ~ pour son argent** to have *ou* get one's money's worth; **j'en ai pour 10 F** it costs me 10 francs; **tu en as pour combien de temps?** how long are you going to be *ou* will it take you?; **en ~ assez * *ou* plein le dos *** to be fed up * (*de qch* with sth); **on en a encore pour 2 km/2 heures** it goes on for another 2 km/2 hours.
2 *vb aux* (**a**) *(avec ptp)* **dis-moi si tu l'as/l'avais vu** tell me if you have/had seen him; **je l'ai vu hier** I saw him yesterday; **il a dû trop manger** he must have eaten too much; **nous aurons terminé demain** we shall have finished tomorrow. (**b**) *(+ infin: devoir)* **~ qch à faire** to have sth to do; **j'ai à travailler** I have to work, I must work; **il n'a pas à se plaindre** he can't complain; **vous n'avez pas à vous en soucier** you needn't worry about it; **vous n'avez qu'à lui écrire** just write to him, you need only write to him; **tu n'avais qu'à ne pas y aller** you shouldn't have gone in the first place; **s'il n'est pas content, il n'a qu'à partir** if he doesn't like it, he can just go. (**c**) **ils ont eu leurs carreaux cassés** they had their windows broken; **vous aurez votre robe nettoyée** your dress will be cleaned.
3 *vb impers* (**a**) **il y a** *(avec sg)* there is; *(avec pl)* there are; **il y avait beaucoup d'eau/de gens** there was a lot of water/were a lot of people; **il n'y avait que moi** I was the only one; **il y avait une fois...** once upon a time, there was...; **il y en a, je vous jure!** * some people, honestly! *; **il n'y a pas de quoi** don't mention it; **qu'y a-t-il?** what's the matter?; **il y a que nous sommes mécontents** * we're annoyed, that's what *; **il n'y a que lui pour faire cela!** only he would do that!; **il n'y a pas à dire *, il est très intelligent** there's no denying he's very intelligent; **il doit y ~ une raison** there must be a reason; **il n'y a qu'à les laisser partir** just let them go; **il n'y en a que pour mon petit frère, à la maison** my little brother gets all the attention at home. (**b**) *(temps écoulé)* **il y a 10 ans que je le connais** I have known him (for) 10 years; **il y a 10 ans, nous étions à Paris** 10 years ago we were in Paris. (**c**) *(distance)* **il y a 10 km d'ici à Paris** it is 10 km from here to Paris; **combien y a-t-il d'ici à Paris?** how far is it from here to Paris?
4 *nm (bien)* resources; *(Comm) (actif)* credit (side); *(billet de crédit)* credit note. *(Fin)* **~ fiscal** tax credit; **~s** holdings, assets; **~s en caisse** *ou* **en numéraire** cash holdings.

avoisiner [avwazine] (1) *vt (lit, fig)* to border on. ◆ **avoisinant, e** *adj pays* neighbouring; *rue* nearby, neighbouring.

avorter [avɔʀte] (1) *vi* (**a**) **(se faire) ~** to have an abortion; **faire ~ qn** *[personne]* to abort sb; *[remède etc]* to make sb abort. (**b**) *(fig)* to fail, come to nothing. **faire ~** to frustrate, wreck; **projet avorté** abortive plan. ◆ **avortement** *nm (Méd)* abortion; *(fig)* failure. **campagne contre l' ~** antiabortion campaign. ◆ **avorteur, -euse** *nm, f* abortionist. ◆ **avorton** *nm (péj: personne)* little runt *(péj)*; *(arbre, animal)* puny specimen.

avouer [avwe] (1) **1** *vt amour* to confess; *fait* to admit; *faiblesse, crime* to admit to, confess to. **~ que** to admit *ou* confess that; **elle est douée, je l'avoue** she is gifted, I must admit. **2** *vi [coupable]* to confess, own up. *(fig)* **tu avoueras!** you must admit *ou* confess! **3 s' ~** *vpr*: **s' ~ coupable** to admit *ou* confess one's guilt; **s' ~ vaincu** to admit defeat; **s' ~ déçu** to admit to being disappointed. ◆ **avouable** *adj* respectable. **peu ~** disreputable. ◆ **avoué, e 1** *adj* avowed. **2** *nm* ≃ solicitor, attorney-at-law *(US)*.

avril [avʀil] *nm* April. **en ~ ne te découvre pas d'un fil** ≃ never cast a clout till May is out; *V* **septembre.**

axe [aks(ə)] *nm (Tech)* axle; *(Sci, Math)* axis; *(route)* trunk *ou* main road, main highway *(US)*; *(fig) [politique]* main line. **cette rue est dans l' ~ de l'église** this street is directly in line with the church; **mets-toi dans l' ~ de la cible** get directly in line with the target. ◆ **axer** (1) *vt*: **~ qch sur/autour de** to centre sth on/round. ◆ **axial, e,** *mpl* **-iaux** *adj* axial.

axiome [aksjom] *nm* axiom. ◆ **axiomatique 1** *adj* axiomatic. **2** *nf* axiomatics *(sg)*.

axis [aksis] *nm* axis (vertebra).

ayant droit, *pl* **ayants droit** [ɛjɑ̃dʀwa] *nm (Jur)* assignee; *[prestation]* eligible party.

ayatollah [ajatɔla] *nm* ayatollah.

azalée [azale] *nf* azalea.

azimut [azimyt] *nm* azimuth. **dans tous les ~s *** all over the place; *(fig)* **offensive tous ~s contre les fraudeurs du fisc** all-out attack on tax-evaders.

azote [azɔt] *nf* nitrogen. ◆ **azoté, e** *adj* nitrogenous.

aztèque [aztɛk] *adj,* **A~** *nmf* Aztec.

azur [azyʀ] *nm (couleur)* azure; *(ciel)* sky. ◆ **azuré, e** *adj* azure. ◆ **azurer** (1) *vt* to tinge with blue.

azyme [azim] *adj* unleavened.

had:
j'eus nous eûmes
tu eus vous eûtes
il eut ils eurent

B

B, b [be] *nm (lettre)* B, b.

baba [baba] **1** *nm (Culin)* baba. ~ **au rhum** rum baba. **2** *adj inv:* **en être** ~ * to be flabbergasted * *ou* dumbfounded.

babiller [babije] (1) *vi [personne]* to prattle, chatter; *[bébé]* to babble; *[oiseau]* to twitter. ◆ **babillage** *nm* babble; prattle; twitter; chatter.

babines [babin] *nfpl (lit, fig)* chops.

babiole [babjɔl] *nf (bibelot)* trinket; *(fig: vétille)* triviality; *(petit cadeau)* token gift.

bâbord [babɔʀ] *nm* port side.

babouche [babuʃ] *nf* babouche, Turkish slipper.

babouin [babwɛ̃] *nm* baboon.

baby-foot [babifut] *nm* table football.

bac [bak] *nm* (**a**) *abrév de* **baccalauréat.** (**b**) *(bateau)* ferry, ferryboat. ~ **à voitures** car-ferry. (**c**) *(récipient)* tub; *(abreuvoir)* trough; *(Ind)* tank, vat; *(Peinture, Phot)* tray; *[évier]* sink. ~ **à glace** ice-tray; ~ **à légumes** vegetable compartment *ou* tray.

baccalauréat [bakalɔʀea] *nm secondary school examination giving university entrance qualification,* ≃ G.C.E. A-levels, ≃ high school diploma *(US).* ~ **en droit** ≃ diploma in law.

bacchantes * [bakɑ̃t] *nfpl* moustache, whiskers *.

bâche [bɑʃ] *nf* canvas cover. ~ **goudronnée** tarpaulin. ◆ **bâcher** (1) *vt* to cover (with a canvas sheet *ou* a tarpaulin). **camion bâché** covered lorry *ou* truck.

bachelier, -ière [baʃəlje, jɛʀ] *nm, f person who has passed the baccalauréat.*

bachot * [baʃo] *nm* = **baccalauréat.**

bachoter [baʃɔte] (1) *vi (Scol)* to cram (for an exam). ◆ **bachotage** *nm* cramming.

bacille [basil] *nm* germ.

bâcler [bɑkle] (1) *vt devoir* to scamp; *ouvrage* to throw together; *cérémonie* to skip through. **c'est du travail bâclé** it's slapdash work.

bacon [bekɔn] *nm (lard)* bacon; *(jambon fumé)* smoked loin of pork.

bactérie [bakteʀi] *nf* bacterium. ◆ **bactérien, -ienne** *adj* bacterial. ◆ **bactériologie** *nf* bacteriology. ◆ **bactériologique** *adj* bacteriological. ◆ **bactériologiste** *nmf* bacteriologist.

badaud, e [bado, od] *nm, f (curieux)* curious onlooker; *(promeneur)* stroller.

baderne [badɛʀn(ə)] *nf (péj)* (**vieille**) ~ old fogey *.

badge [badʒ(ə)] *nm* badge.

badigeonner [badiʒɔne] (1) *vt intérieur* to distemper; *extérieur* to whitewash; *(en couleur)* to colourwash; *(péj)* to smear, cover, daub (*de* with); *gorge, plaie* to paint (*à, avec* with). ◆ **badigeon** *nm* distemper; whitewash; colourwash.

badine [badin] *nf* switch.

badiner [badine] (1) *vi (†: plaisanter)* to jest †. **c'est qn qui ne badine pas** he's a man who really means what he says; **il ne badine pas sur la discipline** he's a stickler for discipline; **et je ne badine pas!** I'm not joking! ◆ **badinage** *nm:* ~**(s)** banter, jesting talk.

baffe * [baf] *nf* slap, clout *.

bafouer [bafwe] (1) *vt* to hold up to ridicule.

bafouiller [bafuje] (1) **1** *vi (bredouiller)* to splutter, stammer. **2** *vt* to splutter (out), stammer (out). **qu'est-ce qu'il bafouille?** what's he babbling on about? * ◆ **bafouilleur, -euse** *nm, f* splutterer, stammerer.

bâfrer ⁑ [bɑfʀe] (1) **1** *vi* to guzzle *, gobble. **2** *vt* to guzzle (down) *, gobble (down).

bagage [bagaʒ] *nm* (**a**) *(valise)* bag, piece of luggage; *(Mil)* kit. ~**s** luggage, baggage; **faire/défaire ses** ~**s** to pack/unpack (one's luggage); ~**s accompagnés** registered luggage; ~**s à main** hand luggage. (**b**) *(diplômes)* qualifications. **son** ~ **intellectuel** his stock *ou* store of general knowledge. ◆ **bagagiste** *nm* porter, luggage *ou* baggage handler.

bagarre [bagaʀ] *nf (rixe)* fight, scuffle, brawl; *(dispute)* set-to. **aimer la** ~ to love fighting *ou* a fight; ~ **générale** free-for-all. ◆ **bagarrer** * (1) **1** *vi (lutter)* to fight; *(se disputer)* to argue. **2 se** ~ *vpr (se battre)* to fight; *(se disputer)* to have a set-to. **ça s'est bagarré (dur)** there was (heavy *ou* violent) rioting. ◆ **bagarreur, -euse** * **1** *adj caractère* aggressive. **2** *nm, f* fighter.

bagatelle [bagatɛl] *nf (objet)* trinket; *(petite somme)* small *ou* paltry sum; *(fig: vétille)* trifle. **perdre son temps à des** ~**s** to fritter away one's time.

Bagdad [bagdad] *n* Baghdad.

bagne [baɲ] *nm (Hist) (prison)* penal colony; *(peine)* hard labour. *(fig)* **quel** ~! * it's a hard grind!, it's sheer slavery! ◆ **bagnard** *nm* convict.

bagnole * [baɲɔl] *nf* car, buggy ⁑. **vieille** ~ jalopy *.

bagou(t) * [bagu] *nm* volubility. **avoir du** ~ to have the gift of the gab.

bague [bag] *nf (bijou)* ring; *[cigare]* band; *[oiseau]* ring; *(Tech)* collar.

baguenauder (se) * [bagnode] (1) *vpr (faire un tour)* to go for a stroll, go for a jaunt; *(traîner)* to mooch about *, trail around.

baguette [bagɛt] **1** *nf* (**a**) switch, stick. *(pour manger)* ~**s** chopsticks; ~ **de chef d'orchestre** conductor's baton; **sous la** ~ **de X** conducted by X; *(fig)* **mener qn à la** ~ to rule sb with an iron hand. (**b**) *(pain)* stick of French bread. **2** : ~ **magique** magic wand; ~ **de sourcier** divining rod; ~ **de tambour** drumstick.

bah [ba] *excl (indifférence)* pooh!; *(doute)* really!

Bahamas [baamas] *nfpl:* **les (îles)** ~ the Bahamas.

Bahrein [baʀɛn] *nm* Bahrain.

bahut [bay] *nm* (**a**) *(coffre)* chest; *(buffet)* sideboard. (**b**) *(arg Scol)* school.

bai, e[1] [bɛ] *adj cheval* bay.

baie[2] [bɛ] *nf* (**a**) *(Géog)* bay. (**b**) ~ (**vitrée**) picture window. (**c**) *(Bot)* berry.

baignade [bɛɲad] *nf (action)* bathing; *(bain)* bathe; *(lieu)* bathing place. ~ **interdite** no bathing *ou* swimming.

baigner [beɲe] (1) **1** *vt* (**a**) *bébé* to bath; *pieds, visage* to bathe. **visage baigné de larmes** face bathed in tears; **chemise baignée de sueur** shirt soaked with sweat, sweat-soaked shirt. (**b**) *[mer, rivière]* to wash, bathe; *[lumière]* to bathe. **2** *vi [linge, fruits]* to soak (*dans* in). ~ **dans son sang/la graisse** to lie in a pool of blood/fat; ~ **dans la brume/le mys-**

tère to be shrouded *ou* wrapped in mist/mystery; *(fig)* **tout baigne dans l'huile** * everything's looking great *; **il baigne dans la joie** he is bursting with joy. **3 se** ~ *vpr (mer)* to go bathing *ou* swimming; *(piscine)* to go swimming; *(baignoire)* to have a bath. ◆ **baigneur, -euse 1** *nm, f* bather, swimmer. **2** *nm (jouet)* baby doll.

baignoire [bɛɲwaʀ] *nf* (**a**) bath(tub). ~ **sabot** ≃ hip-bath. (**b**) *(Théât)* ground floor box.

bail [baj], *pl* **baux** [bo] *nm (Jur)* lease. **prendre à** ~ to lease; **donner à** ~ to lease (out); *(fig)* **ça fait un** ~**!** * it's ages (*que* since).

bâiller [bɑje] (1) *vi [personne]* to yawn (*de* with); *[col, couture, soulier]* to gape; *[porte]* to be half-open. ~ **à s'en décrocher la mâchoire** to yawn one's head off. ◆ **bâillement** *nm* yawn.

bailleur, bailleresse [bajœʀ, bajʀɛs] *nm, f* lessor. ~ **de fonds** backer, sponsor.

bâillon [bɑjɔ̃] *nm (lit, fig)* gag. ◆ **bâillonner** (1) *vt* to gag.

bain [bɛ̃] **1** *nm* (**a**) *[baignoire]* bath; *[piscine]* swim; *[mer]* bathe. ~ **de boue/sang** mud/blood bath; **prendre un** ~ to have a bath; to have a swim. (**b**) *(liquide)* bath(water); *(Chim, Phot)* bath. (**c**) *(récipient) (baignoire)* bath(tub); *[teinturier]* vat. (**d**) *(piscine)* **petit/grand** ~ shallow/deep end; *(lieu)* ~**s publics** public baths. (**e**) (*) **en avouant, il nous a tous mis dans le** ~ by owning up he has involved us all (in it); **nous sommes tous dans le même** ~ we're all in the same boat; **tu seras vite dans le** ~ you'll soon get the hang of it *.

2 : **prendre un** ~ **de foule** to mingle with the crowd, go on a walkabout; **j'ai pris un** ~ **de jouvence** it made me feel years younger; **faire chauffer au** ~**-marie** *sauce* to heat in a double boiler; *boîte de conserve* to immerse in boiling water; ~**s de mer** sea bathing; ~ **moussant** *ou* **de mousse** bubble bath; ~ **de pieds** *(récipient)* foot-bath; *(baignade)* paddle; ~ **de siège** hipbath; **prendre un** ~ **de soleil** to sunbathe; ~**s de soleil** sunbathing ; ~ **turc** Turkish bath; ~ **de vapeur** steam bath.

baïonnette [bajɔnɛt] *nf (Élec, Mil)* bayonet. ~ **au canon** with fixed bayonets.

baisemain [bɛzmɛ̃] *nm*: **il lui fit le** ~ he kissed her hand.

baiser [beze] **1** *nm* kiss. *(fin de lettre)* **bons** ~**s** love (and kisses). **2** (1) *vt* (**a**) *main, visage* to kiss. (**b**) (‡*: avoir, l'emporter sur)* to outdo.

baisse [bɛs] *nf (gén)* fall, drop (*de* in). **être en** ~ to be falling *ou* dropping; ~ **de l'activité économique** downturn *ou* downswing in the economy; ~ **sur le beurre** butter down in price *ou* reduced.

baisser [bese] (1) **1** *vt* (**a**) *main, bras, objet* to lower; *tête* to lower, bend; *(de chagrin, honte)* to hang (*de* in). **baisse la branche pour que je puisse l'attraper** pull the branch down so that I can reach it; ~ **les yeux** to look down, lower one's eyes; ~ **le nez dans son assiette** * to bend over one's plate; *(fig)* ~ **les bras** to give up; ~ **pavillon** *(Naut)* to lower the flag; *(fig)* to show the white flag. (**b**) *chauffage, lampe, radio* to turn down; *voix* to lower. *(Aut)* ~ **ses phares** to dip one's headlights; **baisse un peu le ton!** * pipe down! * (**c**) *prix* to bring down, reduce.

2 *vi* (**a**) *(gén)* to fall, drop; *[marée]* to go out, ebb; *[eaux]* to subside, go down; *[réserves, provisions]* to run *ou* get low; *[soleil]* to go down, sink. **il a baissé dans mon estime** he has sunk *ou* gone down in my estimation. (**b**) *[vue, mémoire, forces]* to fail; *[talent]* to decline. **le jour baisse** the light is failing; **il a beaucoup baissé ces derniers temps** *(physiquement)* he has got a lot weaker recently; *(mentalement)* his mind has got a lot weaker recently.

3 se ~ *vpr (pour ramasser)* to bend down, stoop; *(pour éviter)* to duck. **il n'y a qu'à se** ~ **pour les ramasser** * they are lying thick on the ground.

bajoues [baʒu] *nfpl [animal]* chops; *[personne]* heavy cheeks, jowls.

bal, *pl* ~**s** [bal] *nm (réunion)* dance; *(habillé)* ball; *(lieu)* dance hall. **aller au** ~ to go dancing; ~ **costumé/masqué** fancy dress/masked ball; ~ **musette** popular dance *(to the accordion)*.

balader * [balade] (1) **1** *vt (traîner)* to trail round; *(promener)* to take for a walk. **2 se** ~ *vpr (à pied)* to go for a walk *ou* stroll; *(en auto)* to go for a drive *ou* run; *(traîner)* to traipse round. **aller se** ~ **en Afrique** to go touring round Africa. ◆ **balade** * *nf* walk, stroll; run. **être en** ~ to be out for a stroll (*ou* a run).

baladin † [baladɛ̃] *nm* wandering entertainer.

balafre [balafʀ(ə)] *nf (blessure)* gash; *(cicatrice)* scar. ◆ **balafrer** (1) *vt* to gash; to scar.

balai [balɛ] *nm (gén)* broom, brush; *(Élec)* brush; *(Aut) [essuie-glace]* blade. **passer le** ~ to give the floor a sweep; **donner un coup de** ~ *(lit)* to give the floor a (quick) sweep; *(fig)* to make a clean sweep; ~**-brosse** (long-handled) scrubbing brush; ~ **mécanique** carpet sweeper.

balance [balɑ̃s] *nf* (**a**) *(gén)* pair of scales, scales; *(à bascule)* weighing machine; *(Chim, Phys)* balance. (**b**) **tenir la** ~ **égale entre** to hold the scales even between; **être en** ~ *[proposition]* to hang in the balance; *[candidat]* to be under consideration; **mettre dans la** ~ **le pour et le contre** to weigh up the pros and cons; **il a mis toute son autorité dans la** ~ he used his authority to tip the scales; **si on met dans la** ~ **son ancienneté** if you take his seniority into account. (**c**) *(Écon, Pol)* balance. ~ **commerciale/des comptes/des forces** balance of trade/of payments/of power. (**d**) *(Astron)* **la B**~ Libra. (**e**) *(Pêche)* drop-net.

balancer [balɑ̃se] (3) **1** *vt* (**a**) *chose, jambe* to swing; *branches, bateau, bébé* to rock; *(sur balançoire)* to swing. (**b**) (‡*: lancer)* to fling, chuck *. (**c**) (‡*: se débarrasser de) objet, employé* to chuck out *; *métier* to chuck up ‡. (**d**) *(équilibrer) compte, phrases, paquets* to balance. **tout bien balancé** everything considered. (**e**) *(arg crime: dénoncer)* to finger *(arg)*.

2 *vi* (**a**) (†*: hésiter)* to waver. (**b**) *(osciller)* to swing.

3 se ~ *vpr [bras, jambes]* to swing; *[bateau]* to rock; *[branches]* to sway; *(sur balançoire)* to swing; *(sur bascule)* to seesaw. **se** ~ **sur ses jambes** to sway from side to side; **ne te balance pas sur ta chaise!** don't tip back on your chair!; **je m'en balance** ‡ I couldn't give a darn * (about it), I couldn't care less (about it). ◆ **balancé, e** *adj*: **bien** ~ *phrase* nicely balanced; (*) *personne* well-built. ◆ **balancement** *nm [corps]* sway; *[bras]* swinging; *[bateau]* rocking; *[hanches, branches]* swaying; *(Littérat, Mus)* balance. ◆ **balancier** *nm [pendule]* pendulum; *[montre]* balance wheel; *[équilibriste]* (balancing) pole. ◆ **balançoire** *nf (suspendue)* swing; *(sur pivot)* seesaw. **faire de la** ~ to have a go on a swing (*ou* a seesaw).

balayer [baleje] (8) *vt* (**a**) *poussière* to sweep up; *pièce, trottoir* to sweep. **le vent balaie la plaine** the wind sweeps across the plain. (**b**) *(chasser) feuilles* to sweep away; *soucis, ennemi, objection* to sweep aside. **le gouvernement a été balayé** the government was swept out of office. (**c**) *[phares, tir]* to sweep (across); *[radar]* to scan. ◆ **balayage** *nm* sweeping; scanning. ◆ **balayette** *nf* small (hand)brush. ◆ **balayeur, -euse** *nm, f* roadsweeper.

balbutiement [balbysimɑ̃] *nm*: ~**(s)** *(paroles confuses)* stammering, mumbling; *[bébé]* babbling; *(fig: débuts)* ~**s** beginnings. ◆ **balbutier** (7) **1** *vi* to stammer, mumble. **2** *vt* to stammer *ou* falter out.

balcon [balkɔ̃] *nm* balcony. *(Théât)* **premier/deuxième** ~ dress/upper circle.

baldaquin [baldakɛ̃] *nm* canopy.

Baléares [baleaʀ] *nfpl*: **les** ~ the Balearic Islands.

baleine [balɛn] *nf* (**a**) whale. (**b**) *[corset]* stay; *[parapluie]* rib. ◆ **baleinier, -ière 1** *adj* whaling. **2** *nm (pêcheur, bateau)* whaler. **3** *nf* whaling boat.

balèze ‡ [balɛz] *adj (musclé)* hefty *; *(doué)* great * (*en* at).

balise [baliz] *nf (Naut, Aviat)* beacon; *(Aut)* (road) sign; *[piste de ski]* marker. ◆ **balisage** *nm* (**a**) *(action)* beaconing; marking-out. (**b**) *(signaux)* beacons; (road)signs; markers. ◆ **baliser** (1) *vt* to mark out with beacons; to signpost; to mark out.

balivernes [balivɛʀn] *nfpl* nonsense. **dire des ~s** to talk nonsense; **s'amuser à des ~s** to fool around.

Balkans [balkɑ̃] *nmpl*: **les** ~ the Balkans.

ballade [balad] *nf* ballade.

ballant, e [balɑ̃, ɑ̃t] **1** *adj bras, jambes* dangling. **2** *nm (mou) [câble]* slack; *[chargement]* sway, roll. **avoir du** ~ to be slack.

ballast [balast] *nm (Rail)* ballast, roadbed *(US)*; *(Naut)* ballast tank.

balle[1] [bal] *nf* (**a**) *(projectile)* bullet. **criblé de ~s** riddled with bullets; ~ **perdue** stray bullet. (**b**) *(Sport)* ball. **jouer à la** ~ to play (with a) ball; **c'est une belle** ~ that's a good shot; **faire des ~s** to have a knock-up; *(Tennis)* ~ **de set** set point; *(fig)* **saisir la ~ au bond** to jump at the opportunity. (**c**) **~s** * francs.

balle[2] [bal] *nf (Agr, Bot)* husk, chaff; *[coton, laine]* bale; *(visage)* chubby face.

baller [bale] (1) *vi [bras, jambes]* to dangle, hang loosely; *[tête]* to hang; *[chargement]* to be slack *ou* loose.

ballerine [balʀin] *nf (danseuse)* ballerina, ballet dancer; *(soulier)* ballet shoe.

ballet [balɛ] *nm (danse, spectacle, compagnie)* ballet; *(musique)* ballet music.

ballon [balɔ̃] *nm* (**a**) *(Sport)* ball. ~ **de football** football, soccer ball *(US)*; *(fig)* **le ~ rond** soccer; **le ~ ovale** rugger; football *(US)*. (**b**) ~ **(en baudruche)** (child's toy) balloon. (**c**) *(Aviat)* balloon. ~ **dirigeable** airship. (**d**) *(verre)* wineglass; *(contenu)* glass (of wine). (**e**) *[eau chaude]* tank; *[oxygène]* bottle. (**f**) *(fig)* ~ **d'essai** feeler; **lancer un ~ d'essai** to fly a kite.

ballonner [balɔne] (1) *vt ventre* to distend. **je suis ballonné** I feel bloated. ◆ **ballonnement** *nm*: ~**(s)** flatulence.

ballot [balo] *nm* (**a**) *(paquet)* bundle. (**b**) *(*: nigaud)* nitwit ‡. **c'est** ~ it's a bit daft *.

ballottage [balɔtaʒ] *nm*: **il y a** ~ there will have to be a second ballot.

ballotter [balɔte] (1) **1** *vi [objet]* to roll around, bang about; *[tête, membres]* to loll; *[poitrine]* to bounce; *[bateau]* to toss. **2** *vt personne* to shake about, jolt; *bateau* to toss. **ballotté entre 2 sentiments** torn between 2 feelings; **cet enfant a été ballotté entre plusieurs écoles** this child has been shifted around from school to school. ◆ **ballottement** *nm* banging about; rolling; lolling ; bouncing; tossing, shaking.

balluchon [balyʃɔ̃] *nm* (†) bundle (of clothes). **faire son** ~ * to pack up one's traps.

balnéaire [balneɛʀ] *adj* bathing, swimming.

balourd, e * [baluʀ, uʀd(ə)] *nm, f* dolt, oaf. ◆ **balourdise** *nf* (**a**) *(manuelle)* clumsiness; *(manque de finesse)* doltishness. (**b**) *(gaffe)* blunder.

balte [balt] *adj pays, peuple* Baltic. **les pays ~s** the Baltic States.

balustrade [balystʀad] *nf (Archit)* balustrade; *(garde-fou)* railing.

bambin [bɑ̃bɛ̃] *nm* small child, little lad * *ou* guy * *(US)*.

bambocher * [bɑ̃bɔʃe] (1) *vi* to live it up *, have a wild time. ◆ **bambocheur, -euse** * **1** *adj* revelling. **2** *nm, f* reveller.

bambou [bɑ̃bu] *nm* bamboo.

bamboula * [bɑ̃bula] *nf*: **faire la** ~ to live it up *, have a wild time.

ban [bɑ̃] *nm* (**a**) *[mariage]* **~s** banns. (**b**) *[applaudissements]* round of applause. **un ~ pour X!** three cheers for X! (**c**) *(Hist)* proclamation. (**d**) **être au ~ de la société** to be outlawed from society; **le ~ et l'arrière-~ de** every last one of.

banal, e, *mpl* **~s** [banal] *adj (gén)* banal; *idée* trite; *vie* humdrum; *personne* ordinary; *incident (courant)* commonplace; *(insignifiant)* trivial. **grippe ~e** common or garden case of flu; **peu** ~ unusual. ◆ **banalement** *adv* tritely; in a humdrum way. **tout** ~ simply. ◆ **banalité** *nf* (**a**) *(caractère)* banality; triteness; ordinariness; triviality. (**b**) *(propos)* truism, trite remark.

banaliser [banalize] (1) *vt* (**a**) *expression* to make trite; *vie* to rob of its originality. (**b**) *campus* to open to the police. **voiture banalisée** unmarked police car. ◆ **banalisation** *nf [campus]* opening to the police; **la ~ de la violence** the way in which violence has become an everyday fact *ou* feature of life.

banane [banan] *nf* banana. ◆ **bananeraie** *nf* banana plantation. ◆ **bananier** *nm (arbre)* banana tree; *(bateau)* banana boat.

banc [bɑ̃] **1** *nm* (**a**) *(siège)* seat, bench. ~ **(d'école)** (desk) seat. (**b**) *(Géol) (couche)* layer; *[coraux]* reef. ~ **de sable/vase** sand/mudbank. (**c**) *[poissons]* shoal, school *(US)*. (**d**) *(Tech)* (work)bench. (**e**) *(Mét)* bank, patch. **2** : ~ **des accusés** dock; ~ **des avocats** bar; ~ **d'église** pew; ~ **d'essai** *(Tech)* test bed; *(fig)* testing ground; *(Parl)* ~ **des ministres** ≃ government front bench.

bancaire [bɑ̃kɛʀ] *adj système etc* banking. **chèque** ~ (bank) cheque *ou* check *(US)*.

bancal, e, *mpl* **~s** [bɑ̃kal] *adj* (**a**) *(boiteux)* lame; *(jambes arquées)* bandy-legged. (**b**) *chaise* wobbly, rickety. (**c**) *idée* shaky.

bandage [bɑ̃daʒ] *nm* (**a**) *(objet)* bandage. ~ **herniaire** surgical appliance, truss. (**b**) *(action)* bandaging.

bande[1] [bɑ̃d] **1** *nf* (**a**) *(de tissu, métal)* band, strip; *(de terre, papier)* strip; *(Ciné)* film; *[magnétophone, ordinateur]* tape; *(Presse)* wrapper; *(Méd)* bandage; *(Phys, Rad)* band. *(Mil)* ~ **(de mitrailleuse)** (ammunition) belt. (**b**) *(dessin, motif)* stripe; *[chaussée]* line. (**c**) *(Billard)* cushion. *(fig)* **par la** ~ in a roundabout way. (**d**) *(Naut)* list. **donner de la** ~ to list. **2** : *(Ciné)* **~-annonce** trailer; ~ **dessinée** comic strip, strip cartoon; ~ **magnétique** magnetic tape; ~ **molletière** puttee; ~ **sonore** sound track; ~ **Velpeau** crêpe bandage, Ace ® bandage *(US)*.

bande[2] [bɑ̃d] *nf [gens]* band, group; *[oiseaux]* flock; *[animaux]* pack. **ils sont partis en** ~ they set off in a group; **toute une ~ d'amis** a whole crowd *ou* group of friends; *(Pol)* **la ~ des Quatre** the Gang of Four; **faire ~ à part** *[groupe]* to make a separate group; *[personne]* to keep o.s. to o.s; *(fig: faire exception)* to be an exception; **venez avec nous, ne faites pas ~ à part** come with us, don't stay on your own; ~ **d'imbéciles!** bunch *ou* pack of idiots! *

bandeau, *pl* **~x** [bɑ̃do] *nm (ruban)* headband; *(pansement)* head bandage; *(pour les yeux)* blindfold. **avoir un ~ sur l'œil** to wear an eye patch; *(fig)* **avoir un ~ sur les yeux** to be blind *(fig)*.

bandelette [bɑ̃dlɛt] *nf [momie]* wrapping, bandage.

bander [bɑ̃de] (1) *vt* (**a**) *plaie* to bandage. ~ **les yeux à qn** to blindfold sb; **les yeux bandés** blindfold(ed). (**b**) *(tendre)* to tense; *arc* to bend.

banderole [bɑ̃dʀɔl] *nf (drapeau)* banderole. ~ **publicitaire** advertising streamer.

bandit [bɑ̃di] *nm (voleur)* gangster; *(brigand)* bandit; *(fig: escroc)* crook, shark *; *(*: enfant)* rascal. ~ **armé** gunman, armed gangster, hitman * ; ~ **de grand chemin** highwayman. ◆ **banditisme** *nm* crime. **le grand** ~ organized crime.

bandoulière [bɑ̃duljɛʀ] *nf* shoulder strap. **en** ~ slung across the shoulder.

bang [bɑ̃ŋ] *nm inv, excl* bang. **le big** ~ the Big Bang.

Bangladesh [bɑ̃gladɛʃ] *nm:* **le** ~ Bangladesh.

banjo [bɑ̃ʒo] *nm* banjo.

banlieue [bɑ̃ljø] *nf* suburbs. **proche/grande** ~ inner/outer suburbs; **de** ~ *maison* suburban; *train* commuter. ◆ **banlieusard, e** *nm, f* suburbanite, (suburban) commuter.

bannière [banjɛʀ] *nf* banner; *[chemise]* shirt-tail.

bannir [baniʀ] (2) *vt* to banish (*de* from); *usage* to prohibit. ◆ **banni, e** *nm, f* exile. ◆ **bannissement** *nm* banishment.

banque [bɑ̃k] *nf* (**a**) *(établissement)* bank. **en** ~ in the bank; **la grande** ~ the big banks; ~ **d'affaires/d'organes/du sang/de sperme** commercial/organ/blood/sperm bank. (**b**) *(activité)* banking. (**c**) *(Jeux)* bank. **tenir la** ~ to be (the) banker. ◆ **banquier** *nm (Fin, Jeux)* banker.

banqueroute [bɑ̃kʀut] *nf (Fin, Pol)* bankruptcy; *(fig)* failure. **faire** ~ to go bankrupt.

banquet [bɑ̃kɛ] *nm* dinner; *(d'apparat)* banquet. ◆ **banqueter** (4) *vi* to banquet.

banquette [bɑ̃kɛt] *nf [train]* seat; *[auto, café]* (bench) seat.

banquise [bɑ̃kiz] *nf* ice field; *(flottante)* ice floe.

baptême [batɛm] **1** *nm* (**a**) *(sacrement)* baptism; *(cérémonie)* christening, baptism. **recevoir le** ~ to be baptized *ou* christened. (**b**) *[cloche]* blessing; *[navire]* christening. **2** : ~ **de l'air** first flight ; ~ **du feu** baptism of fire.

baptiser [batize] (1) *vt* (**a**) *(Rel)* to baptize, christen. (**b**) *cloche* to bless; *navire* to christen. (**c**) *(appeler)* to call, christen, name; *(*: surnommer)* to dub. ◆ **baptismal, e,** *mpl* **-aux** *adj* baptismal. ◆ **baptisme** *nm* baptism. ◆ **baptiste** *nmf, adj* Baptist.

baquet [bakɛ] *nm* tub.

bar [baʀ] *nm (lieu)* bar; *(poisson)* bass.

baragouiner * [baʀagwine] (1) *vt paroles* to gabble. **il baragouine un peu l'espagnol** he can speak a bit of Spanish *ou* say a few words of Spanish; *(péj)* **qu'est-ce qu'il baragouine?** what's he gabbling on about? * ◆ **baragouin** * *nm* gibberish, double Dutch.

baraque [baʀak] *nf (abri)* shed; *(boutique)* stall; *(*: maison)* place *; *(péj: entreprise)* dump *.

baraqué, e * [baʀake] *adj*: **bien** ~ well-built.

baraquement [baʀakmɑ̃] *nm*: ~**(s)** group of huts; *(Mil)* camp.

baratin * [baʀatɛ̃] *nm (boniment)* sweet talk; *(verbiage)* chatter, hot air; *(Comm)* patter, sales talk, pitch *(US)*. **assez de** ~! cut the chat! * ◆ **baratiner** * (1) **1** *vt* ~ **qn** to sweet-talk sb; ~ **le client** to give a customer the patter. **2** *vi (bavarder)* to natter *, chatter. ◆ **baratineur, -euse** * *nm, f (beau parleur)* smooth talker; *(bavard)* gasbag ‡.

baratte [baʀat] *nf [beurre]* churn.

barbant, e * [baʀbɑ̃, ɑ̃t] *adj* boring, deadly dull.

barbare [baʀbaʀ] **1** *adj invasion* barbarian; *crime* barbarous. **2** *nm (Hist, fig)* barbarian. ◆ **barbarement** *adv* barbarously. ◆ **barbarie** *nf* barbarism; *(cruauté)* barbarity. ◆ **barbarisme** *nm (Gram)* barbarism.

barbe [baʀb(ə)] **1** *nf* (**a**) *(Anat)* beard. **il a une** ~ **de 3 jours** he has 3 days' growth of beard; **sans** ~ beardless. (**b**) *(aspérités)* ~**s** *[papier]* ragged edge; *[métal]* jagged edge. (**c**) **à la** ~ **de qn** under sb's nose; **rire dans sa** ~ to laugh up one's sleeve; **la** ~! * damn (it)! ‡; **quelle** ~! * what a drag! *; **oh toi, la** ~! * oh shut up, you! * **2** : **B**~ **bleue** *nm* Bluebeard; ~ **à papa** candy-floss.

barbecue [baʀbəkju] *nm (repas, cuisine)* barbecue; *(matériel)* barbecue set.

barbelé, e [baʀbəle] *adj, nm:* **(fil de fer)** ~ barbed wire; **les** ~**s** the barbed wire (fence).

barber * [baʀbe] (1) *vt* to bore stiff *. **se** ~ to be bored stiff * (*à faire* doing).

barbichette * [baʀbiʃɛt] *nf* goatee beard.

barbier † [baʀbje] *nm* barber.

barbiturique [baʀbityʀik] **1** *adj* barbituric. **2** *nm* barbiturate.

barbon [baʀbɔ̃] *nm († ou péj)* **(vieux)** ~ old fogey *.

barboter [baʀbɔte] (1) **1** *vt (*: voler)* to pinch *, steal (*à* from). **2** *vi [canard, enfant]* to dabble, splash about; *[gaz]* to bubble.

barbouiller [baʀbuje] (1) *vt* (**a**) *(salir)* to smear (*de* with); *(péj: peindre)* to daub *ou* slap paint on. **il barbouille des toiles en amateur** he does a bit of painting as a hobby; ~ **une feuille de dessins** to scribble drawings on a piece of paper. (**b**) (*) ~ **l'estomac** to upset the stomach; **être barbouillé** to feel queasy. ◆ **barbouillage** *nm (peint)* daub; *(écrit)* scribble, scrawl. ◆ **barbouille** * *nf (péj)* painting. *(hum)* **il fait de la** ~ he does a bit of painting. ◆ **barbouilleur, -euse** *nm, f (péj)* dauber; *(en bâtiment)* slapdash painter.

barbouze * [baʀbuz] *nf* (**a**) beard. (**b**) *(policier)* secret police agent; *(garde du corps)* bodyguard.

barbu, e [baʀby] *adj* bearded. **un** ~ a man with a beard.

Barcelone [baʀsəlɔn] *n* Barcelona.

barda * [baʀda] *nm* gear; *(Mil)* kit.

barde [baʀd(ə)] **1** *nm (poète)* bard. **2** *nf (Culin)* bard.

barder [baʀde] (1) **1** *vt* (**a**) *(Culin)* to bard. (**b**) **bardé de fer** *cheval* barded; *soldat* armour-clad; *porte* with iron bars; **poitrine bardée de décorations** chest covered with medals; **être bardé (contre)** to be immune (to). **2** *vb impers* (*) **ça va** ~ sparks are going to fly!

barème [baʀɛm] *nm (table)* table, list; *(tarif)* price list; *(Rail)* fare schedule; *[échelle]* scale. *(Scol)* ~ **de correction** scale of marking *ou* grading *(US)*.

baril [baʀi(l)] *nm (gén)* barrel; *[poudre]* keg; *[lessive]* drum.

barillet [baʀijɛ] *nm [revolver]* cylinder.

bariolé, e [baʀjɔle] *adj* gaily-coloured. ◆ **bariolure** *nf* gay colours.

baromètre [baʀɔmɛtʀ(ə)] *nm* barometer. **le** ~ **est au beau fixe/à la pluie** the barometer is set at fair/is pointing to rain. ◆ **barométrique** *adj* barometrical.

baron, -onne [baʀɔ̃, ɔn] *nm, f* baron; baroness.

baroque [baʀɔk] *adj idée* weird, wild; *(Art)* baroque.

baroud [baʀud] *nm*: ~ **d'honneur** gallant last stand.

barque [baʀk(ə)] *nf* small boat.

barrage [baʀaʒ] *nm* (**a**) *[rivière]* dam; *(à fleur d'eau)* weir. (**b**) *(barrière)* barrier; *(d'artillerie, de questions)* barrage. ~ **de police** (police) roadblock; **faire** ~ **à** to stand in the way of.

barre [baʀ] **1** *nf* (**a**) *(gén)* bar; *(de fer, bois)* rod, bar; *(de savon)* cake, bar; *(Danse)* barre. *(Ftbl, Rugby)* ~ **(transversale)** crossbar. (**b**) *(Naut)* helm; *(petite)* tiller. *(lit, fig)* **être à la** ~ to be at the helm. (**c**) *(Jur)* ~ **du tribunal** bar; ~ **(des témoins)** witness box; **comparaître à la** ~ to appear as a witness. (**d**) *(houle)* *(gén)* race; *(à l'estuaire)* bore; *(banc de* *sable)* (sand) bar. (**e**) *(trait)* line; *(du t, f)* stroke. **mets une** ~ **à ton t** cross your t; *(Math)* ~ **de fraction** fraction line. (**f**) *(niveau)* mark. **dépasser la** ~ **des 10%** to pass the 10% mark; *(Scol)* **placer la** ~ **à 10** to set the pass mark at 10. **2** : ~ **d'appui** (window) rail; ~**s asymétriques** asymetric bars; ~ **fixe** horizontal bar; *(Mus)* ~ **de mesure** bar line; *(Tech)* ~ **à mine** crowbar; ~**s parallèles** parallel bars.

barreau, *pl* ~**x** [baʀo] *nm* (**a**) *[échelle]* rung; *[cage]* bar. (**b**) *(Jur)* bar. **entrer au** ~ to be called to the bar.

barrer [baʀe] (1) **1** *vt* (**a**) *porte* to bar; *fenêtre* to bar up; *route (par accident)* to block; *(pour travaux, par la police)* to close (off), shut off; *(par barricades)* to barricade. *(lit, fig)* ~ **la route à qn** to bar *ou* block sb's way. (**b**) *mot* to cross *ou* score out; *feuille* to cross. **chèque barré/non barré** crossed/open *ou* uncrossed cheque. (**c**) *(Naut)* to steer. **quatre barré** coxed four. **2 se** ~ ‡ *vpr* to clear off *.

barrette [baʀɛt] *nf [cheveux]* (hair) slide, barrette *(US)*; *(Rel)* biretta.

barreur [baʀœʀ] *nm (gén)* helmsman; *(Aviron)* cox. **avec/sans** ~ coxed/coxless.

barricader [baʀikade] (1) **1** *vt* to barricade. **2 se** ~ *vpr*: **se** ~ **dans/derrière** to barricade o.s. in/behind; *(fig)* **se** ~ **chez soi** to lock o.s. in. ◆ **barricade** *nf* barricade.

barrière [baʀjɛʀ] *nf (clôture)* fence; *(porte)* gate; *(obstacle)* barrier. ~ **douanière** trade *ou* tariff barrier; ~ **(de passage à niveau)** level crossing gate.

barrique [baʀik] *nf* barrel, cask.

barrir [baʀiʀ] (2) *vi* to trumpet. ◆ **barrissement** *nm*: ~**(s)** trumpeting.

baryton [baʀitɔ̃] *adj, nm* baritone. ~**-basse** bass-baritone.

bas¹, basse [bɑ, bɑs] **1** *adj* (**a**) *(gén)* low; *maison* low-roofed. **pièce basse de plafond** room with a low ceiling; **les basses branches** the lower *ou* bottom branches; ~ **sur pattes** short-legged; **la Basse Seine** the lower Seine; **je l'ai eu à** ~ **prix** I got it cheap; **c'est la basse mer** the tide is out, it's low tide. (**b**) *(humble)* low, lowly; *(subalterne)* menial; *(abject)* base, mean. (**c**) **être au plus** ~ *[personne]* to be very low; *[prix]* to be at their lowest; **au** ~ **mot** at the very least; **en ce** ~ **monde** here below; **de** ~ **étage** *(humble)* lowborn; *(médiocre)* poor, second-rate; **en** ~ **âge** young.
2 *adv* (**a**) *parler* softly, in a low voice. **très/trop** *etc* ~ very/too *etc* low; **mettez vos livres plus** ~ put your books lower down; **voir plus** ~ see below; **mettez la radio plus** ~ turn the radio down. (**b**) **traiter qn plus** ~ **que terre** to treat sb like dirt; *(dans l'abjection)* **tomber bien** ~ to sink really low; **mettre** ~ to give birth; **mettre** ~ **les armes** *(Mil)* to lay down one's arms; *(fig)* to throw in the sponge; ~ **les pattes!** (‡) paws off! ‡; *(à un chien)* down!; **à** ~ **le fascisme!** down with fascism!
3 *nm [page]* foot, bottom; *[visage]* lower part; *[pantalon]* bottom. **dans le** ~ at the bottom; **le tiroir du** ~ the bottom drawer; **les appartements du** ~ the downstairs flats; **lire de** ~ **en haut** to read from the bottom up; **il habite en** ~ he lives downstairs *ou* down below.
4 *nf (Mus)* bass.
5 : ~**-côté** *nm, pl* ~**-**~**s** *[route]* verge; *[église]* side aisle; **basse-cour** *nf, pl* **basses-cours** *(lieu)* farmyard; *(volaille)* poultry; *(Naut)* ~**-fond** *nm, pl* ~**-**~**s** shallow, shoal; **les** ~**-**~**s de la société** the dregs of society; **les** ~**-**~**s de la ville** the seediest parts of the town; *(Boucherie)* **les** ~ **morceaux** the cheap cuts; ~**-relief** *nm, pl* ~**-**~**s** bas relief, low relief; ~**-ventre** *nm, pl* ~**-**~**s** stomach, guts.

bas² [bɑ] *nm* stocking; *(de footballeur)* sock; *(de bandit masqué)* stocking mask. ~ **à varices** support stockings; *(fig)* ~ **de laine** savings.

basalte [bazalt(ə)] *nm* basalt. ◆ **basaltique** *adj* basalt(ic).

basané, e [bazane] *adj* tanned; *indigène* swarthy.

basculer [baskyle] (1) *vi [personne, objet]* to fall *ou* topple over; *[benne]* to tip up. **il bascula dans le vide** he toppled over the edge; *(Pol)* ~ **dans l'opposition** to swing over to the opposition; **faire** ~ *benne* to tip up; *contenu* to tip out; *personne* to topple over. ◆ **bascule** *nf (balançoire)* seesaw; *(balance)* weighing machine. *[personne]* ~ **(automatique)** scales; **fauteuil à** ~ rocking chair.

base [bɑz] **1** *nf* (**a**) *(lit, Chim, Mil)* base; *(Ling: racine)* root. *(Pol)* **la** ~ the rank and file, the grass roots. (**b**) *(principe fondamental)* basis. **des** ~**s solides en anglais** a sound basic knowledge of English. (**c**) **produit à** ~ **de soude** soda-based product; **être à la** ~ **de** to be at the root of; **sur la** ~ **de ces renseignements** on the basis of this information; **de** ~ *prix, modèle, règles* basic; *(Ling)* **forme de** ~ base form; **camp de** ~ base camp. **2** *(fig)* ~ **de départ** starting point *(fig)*; ~ **de données** database; ~ **d'imposition** taxable amount; ~ **de lancement** launching site; ~ **de maquillage** make-up base. ◆ **baser** (1) *vt opinion, théorie* to base (*sur* on). *(Mil)* **être basé à** to be based at; **sur quoi vous basez-vous?** what basis *ou* grounds have you? (*pour dire* for saying); **économie basée sur le pétrole** oil-based economy.

base-ball [bɛzbol] *nm* baseball.

Basic [bazik] *nm* BASIC.

basilique [bazilik] *nf* basilica.

basket-ball [baskɛtbol] *nm* basketball. ◆ **basket** * *nm* basketball. ~**s** sneakers, trainers, tennis shoes *(US)*. ◆ **basketteur, -euse** *nm, f* basketball player.

basque¹ [bask(ə)] **1** *adj* Basque. **le Pays** ~ the Basque Country. **2** *nm* **B**~ *nmf* Basque.

basque² [bask(ə)] *nf [habit]* skirt(s); *[robe]* basque.

basse [bɑs] *V* **bas¹**.

bassesse [bɑsɛs] *nf* (**a**) *(servilité)* servility; *(mesquinerie)* baseness; *(vulgarité)* vileness. (**b**) *(acte)* servile *ou* base act. **faire des** ~**s à qn pour obtenir** to grovel to sb in order to get. ◆ **bassement** *adv* basely, meanly.

basset [bɑsɛ] *nm* basset hound.

bassin [basɛ̃] *nm (pièce d'eau)* pond; *[piscine]* pool; *[fontaine]* basin; *(cuvette)* bowl; *(Méd)* bedpan; *(Géol)* basin; *(Anat)* pelvis; *(Naut)* dock. ~ **de radoub** dry dock; ~ **houiller** coalfield. ◆ **bassine** *nf* bowl; *(contenu)* bowlful.

bassiner [basine] (1) *vt* (**a**) *plaie* to bathe; *(Agr)* to spray (water on). (**b**) *lit* to warm (with a warming pan). (**c**) (*: *ennuyer)* to bore.

bassiste [bɑsist(ə)] *nmf* double bass player.

basson [bɑsɔ̃] *nm (instrument)* bassoon; *(musicien)* bassoonist.

bastingage [bastɛ̃gaʒ] *nm (Naut)* (ship's) rail; *(Hist)* bulwark.

bastion [bastjɔ̃] *nm* bastion.

bât [bɑ] *nm* packsaddle. *(fig)* **c'est là où le** ~ **blesse** that's where the shoe pinches. ◆ **bâter** (1) *vt* to put a packsaddle on.

bataclan * [bataklɑ̃] *nm* junk *. **et tout le** ~ and what have you, the whole caboodle *.

bataille [bataj] *nf* (**a**) *(Mil)* battle; *(rixe, fig)* fight. ~ **de rue** street fight *ou* battle; ~ **rangée** pitched battle. (**b**) *(Cartes)* beggar-my-neighbour. (**c**) **il a les cheveux en** ~ his hair's all tousled; **le chapeau en** ~ with one's hat on askew. ◆ **batailler** (1) *vi* to fight, battle. ◆ **batailleur, -euse 1** *adj* aggressive. **2** *nm, f* fighter *(fig)*. ◆ **bataillon** *nm (Mil)* battalion; *(fig)* crowd.

bâtard, e [bɑtaʀ, aʀd(ə)] **1** *adj enfant* illegitimate, bastard † *(péj)*; *(fig) œuvre* hybrid. **2** *nm, f (personne)* illegitimate child, bastard † *(péj)*; *(chien)* mongrel. **3** *nm* ≃ Vienna roll. ◆ **bâtardise** *nf* bastardy † *(péj)*, illegitimacy.

bateau, *pl* **~x** [bato] **1** *nm* (**a**) *(gén)* boat; *(grand)* ship. **faire du** ~ *(à voiles)* to go sailing; *(à rames etc)* to go boating. (**b**) *[trottoir]* driveway entrance *(depression in kerb)*. **2** *adj inv (*: banal)* hackneyed. **3** : ~ **amiral** flagship; **~-citerne** *nm, pl* **~x-~s** tanker; ~ **de commerce** merchant ship; ~ **de guerre** warship, battleship; **~-lavoir** *nm, pl* **~x-~s** wash-shed; ~ **de sauvetage** lifeboat; ~ **à vapeur** steamer, steamship.

bateleur, -euse † [batlœʀ, øz] *nm, f* tumbler.

batelier [batəlje] *nm* boatman; *[bac]* ferryman.

batellerie [batɛlʀi] *nf* canal transport.

bâti, e [bɑti] **1** *adj* (**a**) **bien/mal** ~ *[personne]* well-built/of clumsy build; *[dissertation]* well/badly constructed. (**b**) **terrain ~/non** ~ developed/undeveloped site. **2** *nm* (**a**) *(Couture)* tacking. (**b**) *[porte, machine]* frame.

batifoler [batifɔle] (1) *vi (†, hum)* (**a**) *(folâtrer)* to lark about. (**b**) *(flirter)* to dally †, flirt (*avec* with).

bâtiment [bɑtimɑ̃] *nm* (**a**) *(édifice)* building. **~s d'habitation** living quarters. (**b**) *(industrie)* **le** ~ the building industry *ou* trade. (**c**) *(Naut)* ship.

bâtir [bɑtiʀ] (2) *vt* (**a**) *(Constr)* to build. **(se) faire ~ une maison** to have a house built; **terrain à** ~ building land. (**b**) *fortune, réputation, hypothèse* to build; *phrase* to construct. (**c**) *(Couture)* to tack, baste. ◆ **bâtisse** *nf* building. ◆ **bâtisseur, -euse** *nm, f* builder.

bâton [bɑtɔ̃] *nm* (**a**) *(canne)* stick; *(Rel)* staff; *(trique)* cudgel; *(Mil, Police)* baton. (**b**) *[craie etc]* stick. ~ **de rouge (à lèvres)** lipstick. (**c**) *(trait)* vertical stroke. (**d**) **il m'a mis des ~s dans les roues** he put a spoke in my wheel; **parler à ~s rompus** to talk casually about this and that.

batracien [batʀasjɛ̃] *nm* batrachian.

battage [bataʒ] *nm* (**a**) *[tapis]* beating; *[céréales]* threshing. (**b**) *(*: publicité)* publicity campaign. **faire du ~ autour de qch/de qn** to give sth/sb a plug *.

battant [batɑ̃] *nm* (**a**) *[cloche]* tongue; *[porte]* flap, door; *[fenêtre]* window. **porte à double** ~ double door. (**b**) *(personne)* fighter *(fig)*.

batte [bat] *nf* bat.

battement [batmɑ̃] *nm* (**a**) **~(s)** *[porte]* banging; *[pluie]* beating; *[voile, ailes]* flapping; *[paupières]* blinking; *[cœur]* beating. **~s de jambes** leg movements; **avoir des ~s de cœur** to have palpitations. (**b**) *(intervalle)* interval. **2 minutes de** ~ *(pause)* a 2-minute break; *(attente)* 2 minutes' wait; *(temps libre)* 2 minutes to spare.

batterie [batʀi] *nf* (**a**) *(Mil)* battery. **mettre en** ~ to unlimber; *(fig)* **dévoiler ses ~s** to unmask one's guns. (**b**) *(Tech: série)* battery; *(Aut, Élec)* battery. *(Jazz)* **la** ~ the drums; ~ **de cuisine** pots and pans.

batteur [batœʀ] *nm (Culin)* whisk; *(Mus)* drummer; *(Agr)* thresher; *(Cricket)* batsman; *(Baseball)* batter. ◆ **batteuse** *nf* threshing machine.

battoir [batwaʀ] *nm [linge]* beetle; *[tapis]* beater. **~s** * great paws *.

battre [batʀ(ə)] (41) **1** *vt* (**a**) *personne* to beat, strike, hit. ~ **qn à mort** to batter *ou* beat sb to death.

(**b**) *adversaire* to beat, defeat; *record* to beat. **se faire** ~ to be beaten; ~ **qn à plate(s) couture(s)** to beat sb hollow, beat sb hands down.

(**c**) *tapis, fer* to beat; *blé* to thresh. ~ **le fer pendant qu'il est chaud** to strike while the iron is hot; **il battit l'air des bras** his arms thrashed the air; **son manteau lui bat les talons** his coat is flapping round his ankles.

(**d**) *blanc d'œuf* to beat (up), whisk; *crème* to whip; *cartes* to shuffle. **œufs battus en neige** stiff egg whites.

(**e**) *(parcourir) région* to scour, comb. *(Chasse)* ~ **les buissons** to beat the bushes; **hors des sentiers battus** off the beaten track; *(fig)* ~ **la campagne** to wander in one's mind.

(**f**) *(heurter) [pluie]* to beat against. **battu par les tempêtes** storm-lashed.

(**g**) ~ **la mesure/le tambour** to beat time/the drum; ~ **le rappel** to call to arms; ~ **le rappel de ses amis** to rally one's friends; ~ **la retraite** to sound the retreat.

(**h**) ~ **en brèche une théorie** to demolish a theory; ~ **froid à qn** to give sb the cold shoulder; ~ **son plein** *[saison, fête]* to be at its height; ~ **pavillon britannique** to fly the British flag; ~ **monnaie** to strike *ou* mint coins.

2 *vi* (**a**) *[cœur]* to beat; *[pluie]* to beat, lash (*contre* against); *[porte]* to bang; *[drapeau]* to flap; *[tambour]* to beat. (**b**) ~ **en retraite** to beat a retreat, fall back.

3 ~ **de** *vt indir:* ~ **des mains** to clap one's hands; *(fig)* to dance for joy; ~ **de l'aile** *(lit)* to flap its wings; *(fig)* to be in a shaky state.

4 se ~ *vpr (combat)* to fight (*avec* with, *contre* against); *(fig)* to fight, battle (*contre* against). **se ~ comme des chiffonniers** to fight like cat and dog; **se ~ la poitrine** to beat one's breast; *(fig)* **se ~ les flancs** to strain every nerve, rack one's brains. ◆ **battue** *nf (Chasse)* beat.

baudet [bodɛ] *nm (Zool)* donkey, ass.

baudrier [bodʀije] *nm [épée]* baldric; *[drapeau]* shoulder-belt; *(Alpinisme)* harness; *(pour matériel)* gear sling.

baume [bom] *nm (lit, fig)* balm.

baux [bo] *nmpl de* **bail.**

bauxite [boksit] *nf* bauxite.

bavarder [bavaʀde] (1) *vi (gén: parler)* to chat, talk; *(jacasser)* to chatter; *(commérer)* to gossip; *(divulguer)* to talk. *(Scol)* **arrêtez de** ~ stop talking *ou* chattering. ◆ **bavard, e 1** *adj* talkative. **2** *nm, f* chatterbox *; *(péj)* gossip. ◆ **bavardage** *nm* chatting, talking; chattering; gossiping. **j'entendais leur** ~ *ou* **leurs ~s** I could hear their talking *ou* chattering.

baver [bave] (1) *vi* (**a**) *[personne]* to dribble; *[animal]* to slaver; *[chien enragé]* to foam at the mouth; *[stylo]* to leak; *[pinceau]* to drip; *[liquide]* to run. (**b**) **en ~ d'admiration** * to gasp in admiration; **en** ~ ⁑ to have a rough time of it. ◆ **bave** *nf* dribble; slaver; foam; *[escargot]* slime; *[crapaud]* spittle. ◆ **baveux, -euse** *adj personne* dribbling; *omelette* runny. ◆ **bavoir** *nm* bib. ◆ **bavure** *nf (tache)* smudge; *(Tech)* burr; *(euph)* mistake. **sans** ~ *(adj)* flawless; *(adv)* flawlessly.

Bavière [bavjɛʀ] *nf:* **la** ~ Bavaria.

bayer [baje] (1) *vi:* ~ **aux corneilles** to stand gaping.

bazar [bazaʀ] *nm* (**a**) *(magasin)* general store; *(oriental)* bazaar. (**b**) (*) *(affaires)* gear; *(désordre)* clutter, jumble. **quel ~!** what a shambles! *; **et tout le** ~ the whole caboodle *. ◆ **bazarder** * (1) *vt (jeter)* to chuck out *; *(vendre)* to flog ⁑, sell off.

bazooka [bazuka] *nm* bazooka.

béant, e [beɑ̃, ɑ̃t] *adj* gaping.

béat, e [bea, at] *adj (hum) personne* blissfully happy; *(péj)* smug; *sourire* beatific; *admiration* blind, dumb. ◆ **béatement** *adv* smugly; beatifically. ◆ **béatification** *nf* beatification. ◆ **béatifier** (7) *vt* to beatify. ◆ **béatitude** *nf (Rel)* beatitude; *(bonheur)* bliss.

beatnik [bitnik] *nmf* beatnik. **la génération ~ *ou* des ~s** the beat generation.

beau [bo], **bel** *devant voyelle ou h muet,* **belle** *f, mpl* **beaux 1** *adj* (**a**) *objet, paysage, femme* beautiful, lovely; *homme* handsome, good-looking. **les beaux quartiers** the smart districts; **mettre ses beaux habits** to put on one's best clothes.
(**b**) *discours, match, roman* fine. **belle mort** fine death; **~ geste** noble *ou* fine gesture.
(**c**) *(agréable) temps* fine, beautiful; *voyage* lovely; *mer* calm. **aux beaux jours** in (the) summertime; *(fig)* **il y a encore de beaux jours pour les escrocs** there are good times ahead *ou* there's a bright future for crooks; **il fait (très) ~ (temps)** the weather's very good, it's very fine; **c'est le bel âge** those are the best years of life; **c'est la belle vie!** this is the (good) life!
(**d**) *(*: intensif) revenu, profit* handsome, tidy *; *résultat, occasion* excellent, fine. **il en reste un ~ morceau** there's still a good bit (of it) left; **95 ans, c'est un bel âge** it's a good age, 95; **un ~ jour** one (fine) day.
(**e**) *(iro: déplaisant) désordre* fine; *gifle* good; *brûlure, peur* nasty; *vacarme* terrible. **c'est un bel escroc** he's a thorough crook; **la belle affaire!** so what? *; **en faire de belles** to get up to mischief; **en dire de belles sur qn** * to say some nice things about sb *(iro)*; **être dans un ~ pétrin** to be in a fine old mess.
(**f**) *(locutions)* **ce n'est pas ~ de mentir** it isn't nice to tell lies; **ça me fait une belle jambe!** * a fat lot of good it does me! *; *(iro)* **c'est du ~ travail!** well done! *(iro)*; **de plus belle** more than ever, even more; **crier de plus belle** to shout louder than ever *ou* even louder; **à la belle étoile** out in the open; **il y a belle lurette que** it is ages since; **faire qch pour les beaux yeux de qn** to do sth just to please sb; **le plus ~ de l'histoire, c'est que...** the best part about it is that...; **c'est trop ~ pour être vrai** it's too good to be true; **se faire ~** to get dressed up; **on a ~ faire/~ protester, personne n'écoute** whatever you do/however much you protest no one listens; **on a ~ dire, il n'est pas bête** say what you like, he is not stupid; **bel et bien** well and truly.
(**g**) *(famille)* **~-père,** *pl* **~x-~s** father-in-law; *(remariage)* step-father; **belle-fille,** *pl* **~s-~s** daughter-in-law; *(remariage)* step-daughter; **mes beaux-parents** my husband's *(ou* wife's*)* parents, my in-laws *.
2 *nm* (**a**) **le ~** the beautiful, beauty; **elle n'achète que le ~** she only buys the best quality. (**b**) **faire le ~** *[chien]* to sit up and beg; *[temps]* **être au ~** to be set fair; **être au ~ (fixe)** *[baromètre]* to be set fair, be settled; *(fig) [relations, atmosphère]* to be looking rosy; **c'est du ~!** that's a fine thing to do!
3 *nf* (**a**) beauty, belle; *(compagne)* lady friend. **ma belle!** * my girl!; **la Belle au bois dormant** Sleeping Beauty; **la Belle et la Bête** Beauty and the Beast. (**b**) *(Jeux)* deciding match.
4 : **les beaux-arts** *nmpl (Art)* fine art; *(école)* the Art School; **~ parleur** smooth talker; **le ~ sexe** the fair sex.

beaucoup [boku] *adv* (**a**) a lot, (very) much, a great deal. **elle ne lit pas ~** she doesn't read much *ou* a great deal; **il s'intéresse ~ à la peinture** he is very interested in painting.
(**b**) **~ de** *(quantité)* a great deal of, a lot of, much; *(nombre)* a lot of, a good many; **~ de monde** a lot of people, a great *ou* good many people; **avec ~ de soin** with great care; **il ne reste pas ~ de pain** there isn't a lot of *ou* isn't (very) much bread left; **j'ai ~ (de choses) à faire** I have a lot (of things) to do; **il a eu ~ de chance** he's been very lucky.
(**c**) *(employé seul: personnes)* many. **~ croient que** many *ou* a lot of people think that.
(**d**) *(avec trop, plus etc)* **~ plus rapide** much *ou* a good deal *ou* a lot quicker; **~ trop lentement** much *ou* far too slowly; **~ moins de gens** a lot *ou* far fewer people.
(**e**) **de ~** by far; **il est de ~ ton aîné** he is very much *ou* is a great deal older than you; **de ~ supérieur** greatly *ou* far superior; **il préférerait de ~ s'en aller** he'd much *ou* far rather go.
(**f**) *(locutions)* **c'est déjà ~ de l'avoir fait** it was quite something to have done it at all; **à ~ près** far from it; **c'est ~ dire** that's saying a lot; **être pour ~ dans une décision** to be largely responsible for a decision.

beauf ⁑ [bof] *nm* brother-in-law.

beaupré [bopʀe] *nm* bowsprit.

beauté [bote] *nf* (**a**) *(gén)* beauty; *[femme]* beauty, loveliness; *[homme]* handsomeness. **de toute ~** very beautiful; **se (re)faire une ~** to powder one's nose; **finir qch en ~** to finish sth with a flourish. (**b**) *(femme)* beauty. (**c**) **les ~s de Rome** the beauties *ou* sights of Rome.

bébé [bebe] **1** *nm (gén)* baby; *(poupée)* dolly. **2** *adj* babyish.

bébête * [bebɛt] **1** *adj* silly. **2** *nf:* **une petite ~** a little insect, a creepy crawly *.

bec [bɛk] **1** *nm* (**a**) *(Orn)* beak, bill. **(nez en) ~ d'aigle** aquiline *ou* hook nose. (**b**) *[plume]* nib; *[carafe]* lip; *[théière]* spout. (**c**) *(*: bouche)* mouth. (**d**) **tomber sur un ~** * to come unstuck *; **rester le ~ dans l'eau** * to be left in the lurch. **2** : **~ Bunsen** Bunsen burner; **~-de-cane** *nm, pl* **~s-~-~** doorhandle; **~ fin** * gourmet ; **~ de gaz** lamp post, gaslamp; *(Méd)* **~-de-lièvre** *nm, pl* **~s-~-~** harelip; **~ verseur** pouring lip.

bécane * [bekan] *nf (vélo)* bike; *(machine)* machine.

bécarre [bekaʀ] *nm (Mus)* natural.

bécasse [bekas] *nf (Zool)* woodcock; *(*: sotte)* (silly) goose *.

bêche [bɛʃ] *nf* spade. ◆ **bêcher** (1) *vt* to dig.

bécoter * [bekɔte] (1) **1** *vt* to kiss. **2 se ~** * *vpr* to smooch *. ◆ **bécot** * *nm* kiss.

becquée [beke] *nf* beakful. **donner la ~ à** to feed. ◆ **becqueter** (4) *vt (Orn)* to peck (at); (⁑) to eat.

bedaine * [bədɛn] *nf* paunch, potbelly *.

bedeau, *pl* **~x** [bədo] *nm* verger, beadle †.

bedonnant, e * [bədɔnɑ̃, ɑ̃t] *adj* potbellied *, portly.

bédouin, e [bedwɛ̃, in] *adj,* **B~(e)** *nm(f)* Bedouin.

bée [be] *adj*: **être bouche ~** *(lit)* to stand open-mouthed *ou* gaping; *(d'admiration)* to be lost in wonder; *(de surprise)* to be flabbergasted * *(devant* at).

beffroi [befʀwa] *nm* belfry.

bégayer [begeje] (8) **1** *vi* to stammer, stutter. **2** *vt* to stammer (out), falter (out). ◆ **bégaiement** *nm* stammering, stuttering. ◆ **bègue** *nmf* stammerer, stutterer.

bégonia [begɔnja] *nm* begonia.

béguin * [begɛ̃] *nm*: **avoir le ~ pour qn/qch** to fancy sb/sth.

beige [bɛʒ] *adj, nm* beige.

beignet [bɛɲɛ] *nm [fruits]* fritter; *(pâte frite)* doughnut. **~ aux pommes** apple doughnut *ou* fritter.

bel [bɛl] *adj V* **beau.**

bêler [bele] (1) *vi (Zool, fig)* to bleat. ◆ **bêlement** *nm* bleating.

belette [bəlɛt] *nf* weasel.

belge [bɛlʒ(ə)] *adj,* **B~** *nmf* Belgian. ◆ **Belgique** *nf* Belgium.

Belgrade [bɛlgʀad] *n* Belgrade.

bélier [belje] *nm (Zool, Tech)* ram. *(Astron)* **le B~** Aries, the Ram.

belladone [beladɔn] *nf (Bot)* deadly nightshade; *(Méd)* belladonna.

belle [bɛl] *V* **beau.**

belligérance [beliʒeʀɑ̃s] *nf* belligerence. ◆ **belligérant, e** *adj, nm, f* belligerent.

belliqueux, -euse [belikø, øz] *adj humeur* quarrelsome; *politique, peuple* warlike.

belvédère [bɛlvedɛʀ] *nm (édifice)* belvedere; *(vue)* (panoramic) viewpoint.

bémol [bemɔl] *nm (Mus)* flat.

bénédicité [benedisite] *nm* grace, blessing. **dire le ~** to say grace *ou* the blessing.

bénédiction [benediksjɔ̃] *nf (gén)* blessing ; *(*: aubaine)* blessing, godsend.

bénéfice [benefis] *nm* (**a**) *(Comm)* profit. **faire du ~** to make *ou* turn a profit. (**b**) *(avantage)* advantage, benefit. **concert donné au ~ de** concert given to raise funds for *ou* in aid of; **le ~ du doute** the benefit of the doubt; **au ~ de l'âge** by prerogative of age. (**c**) *(Rel)* benefice, living. ◆ **bénéficiaire** *nmf (gén)* beneficiary. **être le ~ de** to benefit by. ◆ **bénéficier de** (7) *vt indir (jouir de)* to have, enjoy; *(obtenir)* to get, have; *(tirer profit de)* to benefit by *ou* from. **~ de circonstances atténuantes** to be granted extenuating circumstances; **faire ~ qn d'une remise** to give *ou* allow sb a discount. ◆ **bénéfique** *adj* beneficial.

Bénélux [benelyks] *nm*: **le ~** the Benelux countries.

benêt [bənɛ] **1** *nm* simpleton. **2** *adj m* silly.

bénévole [benevɔl] **1** *adj* voluntary, unpaid. **2** *nmf* volunteer, voluntary helper *ou* worker. ◆ **bénévolement** *adv* voluntarily. ◆ **bénévolat** *nm* voluntary help.

Bengale [bɛ̃gal] *nm*: **le ~** Bengal.

Bénin [benɛ̃] *nm*: **le ~** Benin.

bénin, -igne [benɛ̃, iɲ] *adj accident* slight, minor; *maladie, remède* mild; *tumeur* benign.

bénir [beniʀ] (2) *vt* (**a**) *(Rel)* to bless. (**b**) *occasion* to thank God for. *personne* **soyez béni!** bless you!; *(iro)* **ah, toi, je te bénis!** oh curse you! ◆ **bénit, e** *adj* consecrated; *eau* holy. ◆ **bénitier** *nm (Rel)* stoup.

benjamin, ine [bɛ̃ʒamɛ̃, in] *nm, f* youngest child (*ou* son, *ou* daughter).

benjoin [bɛ̃ʒwɛ̃] *nm* benzoin.

benne [bɛn] *nf* (**a**) *(Min)* skip, truck. (**b**) *[camion] (basculante)* tipper; *(amovible)* skip; *[grue]* scoop; *[téléphérique]* (cable-)car.

benzène [bɛ̃zɛn] *nm* benzene.

béquille [bekij] *nf [infirme]* crutch; *[moto]* stand.

berbère [bɛʀbɛʀ] *adj*, **B~** *nmf* Berber.

berceau, *pl* **~x** [bɛʀso] *nm (lit)* cradle, crib; *(lieu d'origine)* birthplace; *(charmille)* arbour.

bercer [bɛʀse] (3) *vt (gén)* to rock; *douleur* to lull, soothe. *(tromper)* **~ de** to delude with; **se ~ d'illusions** to delude o.s. ◆ **bercement** *nm* rocking movement. ◆ **berceur, -euse 1** *adj rythme* soothing. **2** *nf (chanson)* lullaby.

béret [beʀɛ] *nm* beret.

berge [bɛʀʒ(ə)] *nf [rivière]* bank. **il a 50 ~s** ⁑ he's 50 (years old).

berger [bɛʀʒe] *nm (lit, Rel)* shepherd. **(chien de) ~** sheepdog; **~ allemand** alsatian, German sheepdog *ou* shepherd. ◆ **bergère** *nf* (**a**) shepherdess. (**b**) *(fauteuil)* wing chair. ◆ **bergerie** *nf* sheepfold.

bergeronnette [bɛʀʒəʀɔnɛt] *nf* wagtail.

berk * [bɛʀk] *excl* yuk ⁑.

Berlin [bɛʀlɛ̃] *n* Berlin. **~-Est/-Ouest** East/West Berlin.

berline [bɛʀlin] *nf (Aut)* saloon (car), sedan *(US)*; *(†: à chevaux)* berlin; *(Min)* truck.

berlingot [bɛʀlɛ̃go] *nm (bonbon)* boiled sweet; *(emballage)* (pyramid-shaped) carton; *(pour shampooing)* sachet.

berlue [bɛʀly] *nf*: **j'ai la ~** I must be seeing things.

bermuda(s) [bɛʀmyda] *nm* bermuda shorts.

Bermudes [bɛʀmyd] *nfpl* Bermuda.

bernard-l'(h)ermite [bɛʀnaʀlɛʀmit] *nm inv* hermit crab.

berne [bɛʀn(ə)] *nf*: **en ~** ≃ at half-mast; **mettre en ~** ≃ to half-mast.

Berne [bɛʀn] *n* Bern.

berner [bɛʀne] (1) *vt (tromper)* to fool, hoax.

bernique [bɛʀnik] **1** *nf* limpet. **2** *excl* (*) nothing doing! *

besace [bəzas] *nf* beggar's bag.

besicles [bezikl(ə)] *nfpl (Hist)* spectacles.

besogne [bəzɔɲ] *nf (travail)* work, job.

besoin [bəzwɛ̃] *nm* (**a**) *(exigence)* need (*de* for, *de faire* to do). **~s essentiels** basic needs; **il a de grands/petits ~s** his needs are great/small. (**b**) *(pauvreté)* **le ~** need, want; **famille dans le ~** needy family; **ceux qui sont dans le ~** the needy. (**c**) *(euph)* **~s naturels** nature's needs; **faire ses ~s** *[personne]* to relieve o.s.; *[animal domestique]* to do its business. (**d**) **avoir ~ de qch/de faire qch** to need sth/to do sth; **il n'a pas ~ de venir** he doesn't need *ou* have to come, there's no need for him to come; **il a ~ que vous l'aidiez** he needs your help *ou* you to help him; **pas ~ de dire que** it goes without saying that; *(iro)* **il avait bien ~ de ça!** that's just what he needed! *(iro)*; **est-ce que tu avais ~ d'y aller?** * did you really have to go? (**e**) **au ~ , si ~ est** if necessary, if need be; **pour les ~s de la cause** for the purpose in hand.

bestial, e, *mpl* **-aux** [bɛstjal, o] *adj* bestial, brutish. ◆ **bestialement** *adv* bestially, brutishly. ◆ **bestialité** *nf* bestiality, brutishness.

bestiaux [bɛstjo] *nmpl (gén)* livestock; *(bovins)* cattle.

bestiole [bɛstjɔl] *nf* (tiny) creature, creepy crawly *.

bêta, -asse * [bɛta, ɑs] *adj, nm, f* silly.

bétail [betaj] *nm (gén)* livestock; *(bovins, fig)* cattle. ◆ **bétaillère** *nf* livestock truck.

bête [bɛt] **1** *nf* (**a**) *(animal)* animal; *(insecte)* bug, creature. **~ sauvage** wild beast *ou* creature; **pauvre petite ~** poor little thing *ou* creature; **ces sales ~s** those wretched creatures. (**b**) *(personne) (bestial)* beast; *(†: stupide)* fool. *(hum)* **c'est une bonne ~!** he is a good-natured sort; *(terme d'affection)* **grosse ~!** * you big silly! *

2 *adj* (**a**) *(stupide)* stupid, silly, foolish. **ce qu'il peut être ~!** what a fool he is!; **être ~ comme ses pieds** ⁑ to be as thick as a brick; **je ne suis pas si ~** I'm not that silly; **c'est ~ j'ai oublié** it's silly *ou* stupid, I forgot; **ce n'est pas ~** that's not a bad idea. (**b**) *(*: très simple)* **c'est tout ~** it's quite *ou* dead * simple.

3 : **~ à bon dieu** ladybird; **~ à cornes** horned animal; *(iro)* **~ curieuse** strange animal; **~ fauve** big cat; **c'est ma ~ noire** *[chose]* that's my pet hate; *[personne]* I just can't stand him; **~ de somme** beast of burden.

◆ **bêtement** *adv* stupidly, foolishly. **tout ~** quite simply.

bêtise [betiz] *nf* (**a**) *(stupidité)* stupidity, folly. **j'ai eu la ~ de** I was foolish enough to. (**b**) *(action stupide)* silly *ou* stupid action; *(erreur)* blunder. **dire des ~s** to talk nonsense; **ne faites pas de ~s** don't do anything silly *ou* stupid. (**c**) *(bagatelle)* trifle. **dépenser son argent en ~s** to spend one's money on rubbish *ou* trash *(US)*. (**d**) **~ de Cambrai** ≃ mint humbug, hard mint candy *(US)*.

béton [betɔ̃] *nm* concrete. ~ **armé** reinforced concrete; *(fig)* **accord en ~ armé** ironclad agreement. ◆ **bétonner** (1) *vt (Constr)* to concrete. ◆ **bétonnière** *nf* cement mixer.

betterave [bɛtʀav] *nf*: ~ **fourragère** mangel-wurzel, beet; ~ **(rouge)** beetroot; ~ **sucrière** sugar beet.

beugler [bøgle] (1) **1** *vi* (**a**) *[vache]* to moo; *[taureau]* to bellow. (**b**) (*) *[personne]* to bellow; *[radio]* to blare. **faire ~ sa télé** to have one's TV on full blast *. **2** *vt* (*) to bellow out. ◆ **beuglement** *nm* mooing; bellowing; blaring.

beurre [bœʀ] **1** *nm* (**a**) butter. ~ **fondu** melted butter, drawn butter *(US)*; ~ **noir** brown (butter) sauce; ~ **d'anchois** anchovy paste; ~ **de cacahuètes** peanut butter. (**b**) (*) **entrer comme dans du ~** to go *ou* get in with the greatest (of) ease; **ça va mettre du ~ dans les épinards** that will add a little to the kitty; **faire son ~** to make a packet *. **2** : **~-frais** *adj inv* buttercup yellow. ◆ **beurrer** (1) *vt* to butter. ◆ **beurrier** *nm* butter dish.

beuverie [bœvʀi] *nf* drinking bout.

bévue [bevy] *nf* blunder.

Beyrouth [beʀut] *n* Beirut.

Bhoutan [butɑ̃] *nm*: **le ~** Bhutan.

bi... [bi] *préf* bi... **bilatéral/bivalent** bilateral/bivalent; **bicolore** two-coloured; **biréacteur** twin-engined jet; **biquotidien** twice-daily.

Biafra [bjafʀa] *nm* Biafra. ◆ **biafrais, e** *adj*, **B~(e)** *nm, f* Biafran.

biais [bjɛ] *nm* (**a**) *(artifice)* device, means. **par le ~ de** by means of; *(aspect)* **abordons le problème par ce ~** let's tackle the problem from this angle. (**b**) *(Tex)* bias; *(ligne oblique)* slant. **en ~** *poser* slantwise; *couper* diagonally; **regarder qn de ~** to give sb a sidelong glance; **prendre une question de ~** to tackle a question in a roundabout way. ◆ **biaiser** (1) *vi (louvoyer)* to sidestep the issue, prevaricate; *(obliquer)* to change direction.

bibelot [biblo] *nm (sans valeur)* trinket; *(de valeur)* curio.

biberon [bibʀɔ̃] *nm* baby's bottle. **l'heure du ~** (baby's) feeding time; **nourrir au ~** to bottle-feed.

bibine * [bibin] *nf* weak beer.

bible [bibl(ə)] *nf (livre, fig)* bible. ◆ **biblique** *adj* biblical.

bibliographie [biblijɔgʀafi] *nf* bibliography. ◆ **bibliographique** *adj* bibliographic(al).

bibliophile [biblijɔfil] *nmf* booklover.

bibliothèque [biblijɔtɛk] *nf (édifice, collection)* library; *(meuble)* bookcase. ~ **de gare** station bookstall. ◆ **bibliothécaire** *nmf* librarian.

bicarbonate [bikaʀbɔnat] *nm* bicarbonate. ~ **de soude** sodium bicarbonate.

bicentenaire [bisɑ̃tnɛʀ] *nm* bicentenary, bicentennial.

bicéphale [bisefal] *adj* two headed.

biceps [bisɛps] *nm* biceps. **avoir des ~** * to have a strong pair of arms.

biche [biʃ] *nf* doe. *(fig)* **ma ~** darling.

bicher * [biʃe] (1) *vi* to be pleased with o.s. **ça biche?** how's things? *

bichonner [biʃɔne] (1) **1** *vt (pomponner)* to titivate; *(prendre soin de)* to fuss over. **2 se ~** *vpr* to titivate.

bicoque [bikɔk] *nf (péj)* shack *.

bicorne [bikɔʀn(ə)] *nm* cocked hat.

bicyclette [bisiklɛt] *nf* bicycle, bike; *(sport)* cycling. **faire de la ~** *(promenade)* to go for a cycle ride; *(transport)* to go by bike.

bide [bid] *nm* (‡: *ventre)* belly *; *(arg Théât)* flop.

bidet [bidɛ] *nm* (**a**) bidet. (**b**) *(cheval)* nag.

bidirectionnel, -elle [bidiʀɛksjɔnɛl] *adj* bi-directional.

bidon [bidɔ̃] **1** *nm* (**a**) *(gén)* can, tin; *[lait]* churn; *[campeur, soldat]* flask. (**b**) (‡) *(ventre)* belly *; *(bluff)* hot air. **2** *adj inv* (‡) *attentat* mock. **société ~** ghost company. ◆ **bidonville** *nm* shanty town.

bidule * [bidyl] *nm* thingumabob *.

bielle [bjɛl] *nf (locomotive)* connecting rod; *(voiture)* track rod.

bien [bjɛ̃] **1** *adv* (**a**) *(gén)* well; *fonctionner* properly, well. **être ~ portant** to be well, be in good health; **il parle ~ l'anglais** he speaks good English, he speaks English well; **il a ~ pris ce que je lui ai dit** he took what I had to say in good part; **il s'y est ~ pris (pour le faire)** he went about it the right way; **si je me rappelle ~** if I remember right *ou* correctly; **vous avez ~ fait** you did the right thing; **faire ~ les choses** to do things properly *ou* in style; **vous feriez ~ de** you'd do well *ou* you'd be well advised to; **on comprend ~ pourquoi** you can quite easily see why; **il peut très ~ le faire** he can quite easily do it.
(**b**) *(très)* very; *(beaucoup)* very much; *(trop)* rather. ~ **mieux** much better; ~ **souvent** quite often; ~ **content** very glad; ~ **plus heureux/cher** far *ou* much happier/more expensive; **nous avons ~ ri** we had a good laugh; **tout cela est ~ joli mais** that's all very well but; **c'est ~ long** it's rather long *ou* a bit on the long side.
(**c**) *(effectivement)* indeed, definitely. **j'avais ~ dit que** I DID say *ou* I certainly did say that; **c'est ~ une erreur** it's definitely *ou* certainly a mistake; **c'est ~ à ton frère que je pensais** it was indeed your brother I was thinking of; **est-ce ~ mon manteau?** is it really my coat?; **il s'agit ~ de cela!** as if that's the point!; **voilà ~ les femmes!** that's just like women!, that's women all over!; **c'est ~ ma veine!** * it's just my luck!; **c'était ~ la peine!** after all that trouble!; **où peut-il ~ être?** where on earth can he be?
(**d**) *(complètement)* **ferme ~ la porte** shut the door properly; **écoute-moi ~** listen to me carefully; **mets-toi ~ en face** stand right *ou* straight opposite; **ça m'est ~ égal** it's all the same to me; **c'est ~ compris?** is that clearly *ou* quite understood?
(**e**) *(hypothèse, fatalité)* **j'espère ~!** I should hope so!; **on verra ~** we'll see, time will tell; **il se pourrait ~ qu'il pleuve** it could well rain; **il fallait ~ que ça arrive** it was bound to happen; **il faut ~ le supporter** one just has to put up with it; **j'irais ~ mais...** I'd willingly *ou* gladly go but...; **je voudrais ~ t'y voir!** I'd like to see you try!
(**f**) *(au moins)* at least. **il y a ~ 3 jours que je ne l'ai vu** I haven't seen him for at least 3 days.
(**g**) ~ **de**: ~ **des gens** a good many *ou* quite a few (people); **ils ont eu ~ de la chance** they were really very lucky; **elle a eu ~ du mal à faire** she had a great deal of difficulty in doing.
(**h**) ~ **que** although, though.
(**i**) **ah ~ (ça) alors!** well really!; ~ **sûr** of course; **ni ~ ni mal** so-so *; **c'est ~ fait (pour lui)** it serves him right.
2 *adj inv* (**a**) *(de qualité)* good; *(en bonne santé)* well; *(beau) personne* good-looking; *chose* nice. **donnez-lui quelque chose de ~** give him something really good; *(approbation)* ~! good!, fine!; *(exaspération)* **c'est ~!** all right!, all right! (**b**) *(à l'aise)* **il est ~ partout** he feels at home anywhere; **on est ~ à l'ombre** it's pleasant *ou* nice in the shade; **je suis ~ dans ce fauteuil** I'm very comfortable in this chair; **elle se trouve ~ dans son nouveau poste** she's very happy in her new job; **il est ~ où il est!** he's quite all right where he is; *(iro)* **vous voilà ~!** now you've done it!; **être/se mettre ~ avec qn** to be/get on good terms with sb.(**c**) *(moralement)* nice. **ce n'est pas ~ de** it's not nice to;

c'est ~ à vous de les aider it's good *ou* nice of you to help them.
3 *nm* (**a**) good. **faire le ~** to do good; **ça m'a fait du ~** it did me good; **c'est pour ton ~!** it's for your own good!; **ça a été un ~** it was a good thing; **changer en ~** to change for the better; **dire du ~ de** to speak highly of; **vouloir du ~ à qn** to wish sb well; **grand ~ vous fasse!** much good may it do you! (**b**) *(gén: possession)* possession; *(argent)* fortune; *(terres)* estate. **~ mal acquis ne profite jamais** ill-gotten gains seldom prosper.
4 : **~ -aimé(e)** *adj, nm(f)* beloved; **~s de consommation** consumer goods; **~s durables** consumer durables; **~-être** *nm (physique)* well-being; *(matériel)* comfort; **~-fondé** *nm [opinion]* validity; *[plainte]* cogency; **~ pensant** *adj (Rel)* God-fearing; *(Pol, gén)* right-thinking.

bienfaisance [bjɛ̃fəzɑ̃s] *nf* charity. **œuvres de ~** charities, charitable organisations. ◆ **bienfaisant, e** *adj (remède)* beneficial; *personne* beneficent, kind.

bienfait [bjɛ̃fɛ] *nm* kindness. **c'est un ~ du ciel!** it's a godsend! *ou* blessing!; **les ~s de** *science* the benefits of; *cure* the beneficial effects of. ◆ **bienfaiteur, -trice** *nm, f* benefactor, benefactress.

bienheureux, -euse [bjɛ̃nœʀø, øz] *adj (Rel)* blessed.

biennale [bjenal] *nf* biennial event.

bienséance [bjɛ̃seɑ̃s] *nf* propriety. ◆ **bienséant, e** *adj* proper, becoming.

bientôt [bjɛ̃to] *adv* soon. **à ~!** see you soon!; **on est ~ arrivé** we'll soon be there, we'll be there shortly; **c'est pour ~?** is it due soon?; **il est ~ minuit** it's nearly midnight; **il eut ~ fait de finir son travail** † he lost no time in finishing his work.

bienveillance [bjɛ̃vɛjɑ̃s] *nf* benevolence, kindness (*envers* to). **examiner avec ~** to give favourable consideration to. ◆ **bienveillant, e** *adj* benevolent, kindly.

bienvenu, e [bjɛ̃vny] **1** *adj remarque* apposite, well-chosen. **2** *nm, f*: **être le ~** *(ou* **la ~e***)* to be most welcome. **3** *nf* welcome. **souhaiter la ~e à qn** to welcome sb.

bière[1] [bjɛʀ] *nf* beer. **~ blonde** lager; **~ brune** brown ale; **~ pression** draught beer.

bière[2] [bjɛʀ] *nf* coffin, casket *(US)*.

biffer [bife] (1) *vt* to cross out.

bifteck [biftɛk] *nm* steak. **~ dans le filet** fillet steak; **deux ~s** two steaks, two pieces of steak.

bifurquer [bifyʀke] (1) *vi [route]* to fork, branch off; *[véhicule]* to turn off (*vers, sur* for, towards). **~ sur la droite** to bear *ou* turn right. ◆ **bifurcation** *nf* fork.

bigame [bigam] **1** *adj* bigamous. **2** *nmf* bigamist. ◆ **bigamie** *nf* bigamy.

bigarré, e [bigaʀe] *adj vêtement, groupe* gaily-coloured; *(fig) foule* motley; *peuple* mixed. ◆ **bigarrure** *nf* coloured pattern.

bigorneau, *pl* **~x** [bigɔʀno] *nm* winkle.

bigot, e [bigo, ɔt] *(péj)* **1** *adj* over-devout. **2** *nm, f* (religious) bigot. ◆ **bigoterie** *nf* (religious) bigotry.

bigoudi [bigudi] *nm* (hair-)curler *ou* roller.

bigre [bigʀ(ə)] *excl (hum)* gosh! * ◆ **bigrement** *adv bon* darn *, dead *; *changer* a heck of a lot *.

bijou, *pl* **~x** [biʒu] *nm* jewel; *(fig)* gem, marvel. **mon ~** my love. ◆ **bijouterie** *nf (boutique)* jeweller's (shop); *(commerce)* jewellery business. ◆ **bijoutier, -ière** *nm, f* jeweller.

bikini [bikini] *nm* bikini.

bilan [bilɑ̃] *nm* (**a**) *(évaluation)* assessment; *(résultats)* results; *(conséquences)* consequences. **faire le ~ de** to take stock of, assess; **~ de santé** (medical) checkup. (**b**) *(Fin)* balance sheet.

bilboquet [bilbɔkɛ] *nm* ≃ cup-and-ball game.

bile [bil] *nf* bile. **se faire de la ~ (pour)** * to get worried (about). ◆ **bileux, -euse** * **1** *adj* easily worried. **2** *nm, f* worrier, fretter *.

bilingue [bilɛ̃g] *adj* bilingual. ◆ **bilinguisme** *nm* bilingualism.

billard [bijaʀ] *nm* (**a**) *(jeu)* billiards *(sg)*; *(table)* billiard table. **boule de ~** billiard ball; **faire un ~** to play a game of billiards; **~ électrique** pinball machine. (**b**) (*) **passer sur le ~** to have an operation; **c'est du ~** it's quite *ou* dead * easy.

bille [bij] *nf* (**a**) *[enfant]* marble; *[billard]* (billiard) ball. **jouer aux ~s** to play marbles; **déodorant à ~** roll-on deodorant. (**b**) **~ de bois** block of wood. (**c**) *(*: visage)* face, mug ‡.

billet [bijɛ] **1** *nm* (**a**) ticket. **~ aller/aller-retour** single *ou* one-way *(US)*/return *ou* round-trip *(US)* ticket. (**b**) *(argent)* note, bill *(US)*. (**c**) *(†: lettre)* note, short letter. **je te fiche** *ou* **flanque mon ~ que** * I bet you my bottom dollar that *. **2**: **~ de banque** banknote; **~ de commerce** promissory note ; **~ doux** love letter; **~ de faveur** complimentary ticket; *(Mil)* **~ de logement** billet; *(Scol)* **~ de retard** late slip, tardy slip *(US)*. ◆ **billetterie** *nf (Banque)* cash dispenser.

billion [biljɔ̃] *nm* billion, trillion *(US)*.

billot [bijo] *nm* block.

binaire [binɛʀ] *adj* binary.

biner [bine] (1) *vt* to hoe, harrow. ◆ **binette** *nf* (**a**) *(Agr)* hoe. (**b**) *(*: visage)* face.

bing [biŋ] *excl* smack!, thwack!

biniou [binju] *nm (Mus)* Breton bagpipes.

binôme [binom] *nm* binomial.

biochimie [bjɔʃimi] *nf* biochemistry. ◆ **biochimique** *adj* biochemical. ◆ **biochimiste** *nmf* biochemist.

biodégradable [bjɔdegʀadabl(ə)] *adj* biodegradable.

biographe [bjɔgʀaf] *nmf* biographer. ◆ **biographie** *nf* biography. ◆ **biographique** *adj* biographical.

biologie [bjɔlɔʒi] *nf* biology. ◆ **biologique** *adj* biological. ◆ **biologiste** *nmf* biologist.

bipartite [bipaʀtit] *adj* bipartite.

bipède [bipɛd] *adj, nm* biped.

biplan [biplɑ̃] *nm* biplane.

bique [bik] *nf* nanny-goat. *(péj)* **vieille ~** old hag *. ◆ **biquet, -ette** *nm, f (Zool)* kid.

Birmanie [biʀmani] *nf* Burma. ◆ **birman, e** *adj*, **B~(e)** *nm(f)* Burmese.

bis[1] [bis] *adv (sur partition)* repeat. **~!** encore!; *(numéro)* **12 ~** 12a.

bis[2]**, e** [bi, biz] *adj* greyish-brown.

bisaïeul [bizajœl] *nm* great-grandfather.

bisaïeule [bizajœl] *nf* great-grandmother.

biscornu, e [biskɔʀny] *adj forme* crooked; *idée, esprit* tortuous, cranky. **chapeau ~** shapeless hat.

biscoteaux * [biskɔto] *nmpl* biceps.

biscotte [biskɔt] *nf* rusk, melba toast *(US)*.

biscuit [biskɥi] *nm (mou)* sponge cake; *(sec)* biscuit, cookie *(US)*. **~ à la cuiller** sponge finger, lady finger *(US)*; **~ salé** cheese biscuit, cracker *(US)*. ◆ **biscuiterie** *nf (usine)* biscuit *ou* cookie *(US)* factory.

bise [biz] *nf* (**a**) North wind. (**b**) kiss.

biseau, *pl* **~x** [bizo] *nm [glace]* bevel; *(Menuiserie)* chamfer; *(outil)* bevel. **en ~** bevelled; chamfered. ◆ **biseauter** (1) *vt* to bevel; to chamfer; *cartes* to mark.

bismuth [bismyt] *nm* bismuth.

bison [bizɔ̃] *nm* bison, American buffalo.

bisquer * [biske] (1) *vi* to be riled *. **faire ~** to rile *.

bissecteur, -trice [bisɛktœʀ, tʀis] **1** *adj* bisecting. **2** *nf* bisector.

bisser [bise] (1) *vt acteur* to encore.

bistouri [bistuʀi] *nm* lancet.

bistre [bistʀ(ə)] *adj, nm* bistre. ◆ **bistré, e** *adj teint* swarthy.

bistro(t) [bistʀo] *nm* café, bar.

bit [bit] *nm (Ordin)* bit.

bitume [bitym] *nm (Chim, Min)* bitumen; *(revêtement)* asphalt, tarmac ®. ◆ **bitum(in)er** (1) *vt* to asphalt, tarmac. ◆ **bitum(in)eux, -euse** *adj* bituminous.

bivouac [bivwak] *nm* bivouac. ◆ **bivouaquer** (1) *vi* to bivouac.

bizarre [bizaʀ] *adj* strange, odd, peculiar. **le ~ dans tout cela...** the strange *ou* odd part about it all... ◆ **bizarrement** *adv* strangely, oddly, peculiarly. ◆ **bizarrerie** *nf* strangeness, oddness. **~s** peculiarities, oddities. ◆ **bizarroïde** *adj* odd.

bizut(h) [bizy] *nm (arg Scol)* fresher *(arg)*, freshman, first-year student. ◆ **bizuter** (1) *vt (arg Scol)* to rag, haze *(US)*.

blablabla * [blablabla] *nm* claptrap *.

blackbouler [blakbule] (1) *vt (élection)* to blackball; *(examen)* to fail.

black-out [blakawt] *nm (Élec, Mil)* blackout.

blafard, e [blafaʀ, aʀd(ə)] *adj* wan, pale.

blague [blag] *nf* (**a**) (*) *(histoire)* joke; *(farce)* hoax. **faire une ~ à qn** to play a trick on sb; **sans ~?** you're kidding! ‡; **~ à part** seriously, joking apart, kidding aside * *(US)*; **pas de ~s!** no messing about! * (**b**) *(*: erreur)* blunder. (**c**) **~ (à tabac)** tobacco pouch. ◆ **blaguer** * (1) **1** *vi* to be joking *ou* kidding ‡. **2** *vt* to tease, kid ‡. ◆ **blagueur, -euse 1** *adj* teasing. **2** *nm, f* joker.

blaireau, *pl* **~x** [blɛʀo] *nm (Zool)* badger; *(pour barbe)* shaving brush.

blairer ‡ [bleʀe] (1) *vt*: **je ne peux pas le ~** I can't stand him, he gives me the creeps ‡.

blâme [blɑm] *nm (désapprobation)* blame; *(réprimande)* reprimand, rebuke; *(punition)* reprimand. **donner un ~ à qn** to reprimand sb. ◆ **blâmable** *adj* blameful. ◆ **blâmer** (1) *vt* to blame; to reprimand; to rebuke.

blanc, blanche [blɑ̃, blɑ̃ʃ] **1** *adj* (**a**) *(gén)* white (*de* with); *(pas bronzé)* pale. **il était ~ à 30 ans** he had white hair at 30; **~ comme un linge** as white as a sheet; *(fig)* **~ comme neige** as pure as the driven snow. (**b**) *page, copie* blank; *papier non quadrillé* unlined, plain.

2 *nm* (**a**) *(couleur)* white; *(poudre)* white powder; *(vin)* white wine. *(lavage)* **le ~ et la couleur** white and coloureds; *(tissu)* **vente de ~** white sale, sale of household linen. (**b**) *(espace)* blank. **'laisser en ~'** 'leave (this space) blank'. (**c**) *(Culin)* **~ (d'œuf)** (egg) white; **~ (de poulet)** breast (of chicken). (**d**) *(homme)* **B~** White, white man. (**e**) **à ~** *charger* with blanks; **tirer à ~** to fire blanks; **cartouche à ~** blank (cartridge).

3 *nf* (**a**) *(femme)* **Blanche** white woman. (**b**) *(Mus)* minim, half-note *(US)*.

4 : **~ bec** * greenhorn; **~ cassé** off-white; **~ d'Espagne** whitening; **Blanche-Neige (et les sept nains)** Snow White (and the Seven Dwarfs). ◆ **blanchâtre** *adj* whitish, off-white. ◆ **blancheur** *nf* whiteness.

blanchir [blɑ̃ʃiʀ] (2) **1** *vt* (**a**) *(gén)* to whiten, lighten; *cheveux* to turn grey *ou* white; *toile* to bleach. **~ à la chaux** to whitewash. (**b**) *linge, (fig) argent* to launder. **il est blanchi** his laundry is done for him. (**c**) *(disculper)* to clear. (**d**) **(faire) ~** *(Culin, Agr)* to blanch. **2** *vi [cheveux]* to go grey *ou* white; *[couleur]* to become lighter. **3 se ~** *vpr* to clear one's name. ◆ **blanchissage** *nm* laundering. **note de ~** laundry bill. ◆ **blanchissement** *nm* whitening. ◆ **blanchisserie** *nf* laundry. ◆ **blanchisseur, euse** *nm, f* launderer, launderess.

blanquette [blɑ̃kɛt] *nf*: **~ de veau** blanquette of veal.

blaser [blaze] (1) *vt* to make blasé. **être blasé de** to be bored with. ◆ **blasé, e** *adj* blasé.

blason [blazɔ̃] *nm* coat of arms.

blasphémateur, -trice [blasfematœʀ, tʀis] *nm, f* blasphemer. ◆ **blasphématoire** *adj* blasphemous. ◆ **blasphème** *nm* blasphemy. ◆ **blasphémer** (6) *vti* to blaspheme.

blatte [blat] *nf* cockroach.

blé [ble] *nm* wheat; *(‡: argent)* dough ‡, lolly ‡. **~ dur** hard wheat; **~ noir** buckwheat.

bled * [blɛd] *nm* village. **un ~ perdu** a hole *, dump ‡.

blême [blɛm] *adj* pale, wan. **~ de rage** livid with rage. ◆ **blêmir** (2) *vi* to turn pale (*de* with).

blesser [blese] (1) *vt* (**a**) *(gén)* to hurt, injure; *(Mil)* to wound. **être blessé au bras** to have an arm injury *ou* wound; **il s'est blessé en tombant** he fell and injured himself; **ses souliers lui blessent le talon** his shoes hurt his heel; **couleurs qui blessent la vue** colours which offend *ou* shock the eye. (**b**) *(offenser) personne* to hurt (the feelings of), wound; *convenances* to offend against. **paroles qui blessent** wounding *ou* cutting remarks; **il se blesse pour un rien** he's easily hurt *ou* offended. ◆ **blessant, e** *adj* cutting. ◆ **blessé, e** *nm, f* wounded *ou* injured man (*ou* woman). **l'accident a fait 10 ~s** 10 people were injured *ou* hurt in the accident; **~ grave** seriously injured person; **les ~s de guerre** the war wounded; **~s de la route** road casualties. ◆ **blessure** *nf* injury; wound. **c'est une ~ d'amour-propre** his pride is hurt.

blet, blette [blɛ, blɛt] *adj* overripe.

bleu, e [blø] **1** *adj couleur* blue; *steak* very rare. **2** *nm* (**a**) *(couleur)* blue. *(fig)* **il n'y a vu que du ~** * he didn't smell a rat; **le ~ de ce ciel** the blueness of that sky; **~ marine/nuit/roi** navy/midnight/royal blue; **~-noir** blue-black. (**b**) **~ (de lessive)** (dolly) blue. (**c**) *(sur la peau)* bruise. (**d**) *(vêtement)* **~(s) (de travail)** dungarees, overalls. (**e**) *(arg Mil: recrue)* rookie *(arg)*, raw recruit; *(gén: débutant)* beginner, greenhorn. (**f**) *(fromage)* blue(-veined) cheese. (**g**) *(Culin)* **truite au ~** trout au bleu. ◆ **bleuâtre** *adj* bluish. ◆ **bleuet** *nm* cornflower. ◆ **bleuir** (2) *vti* to turn blue. ◆ **bleuté, e** *adj reflet* bluish; *verre* blue-tinted.

blinder [blɛ̃de] (1) *vt* (**a**) *(Mil)* to armour; *porte* to reinforce. (**b**) *(*: endurcir)* to harden, make immune (*contre* to). ◆ **blindage** *nm* armour plating; reinforcing. ◆ **blindé** *nm (Mil)* armoured car, tank. **les ~s** the armour.

blizzard [blizaʀ] *nm* blizzard.

bloc [blɔk] **1** *nm* (**a**) *[marbre, bois]* block. **fait d'un seul ~** made from a single piece. (**b**) *(papeterie)* pad. (**c**) *(système d'éléments)* unit; *(Ordin)* block; *(groupe)* group; *(Pol)* bloc. (**d**) *(‡: prison)* **mettre qn au ~** to clap sb in clink ‡; **faire ~ avec/contre qn** to unite with/against sb; **visser qch à ~** to screw sth up tight; **vendre qch en ~** to sell sth as a whole; **il refuse en ~ tous mes arguments** he rejects all my arguments wholesale; **se retourner tout d'un ~** to swivel round. **2 ~-calendrier** *nm, pl* **~s-~s** tear-off calendar; **~-cuisine** *nm, pl* **~s-~s** kitchen unit; *(Sport)* **~ de départ** starting-block; **~-évier** *nm, pl* **~s-~s** sink unit; *(Aut)* **~-moteur** *nm, pl* **~s-~s** engine block; **~-notes** *nm, pl* **~s-~** *(cahier)* desk-pad, scratch pad; *(avec pince)* clipboard; *(Méd)* **~ opératoire** operating theatre suite; *(Aut)* **~ optique** headlamp assembly.

blocage [blɔkaʒ] *nm* (**a**) *[prix]* freeze; *[compte]* freezing. (**b**) *(Psych)* block. (**c**) *[frein, roues]* locking; *[écrou]* overtightening.

blockhaus [blɔkos] *nm (Mil)* blockhouse.

blocus [blɔkys] *nm* blockade.

blond, e [blɔ̃, ɔ̃d] **1** *adj cheveux* fair, blond; *personne* fair, fair-haired; *blé, sable* golden. ~ **cendré** ash-blond. **2** *nm (couleur)* blond, light gold; *(homme)* fair-haired man. **3** *nf (bière)* lager, ≃ light ale; *(cigarette)* Virginia cigarette; *(femme)* blonde. ◆ **blondinet, -ette** *nm, f* fair-haired child. ◆ **blondir** (2) *vi [cheveux]* to go fairer.

bloquer [blɔke] (1) **1** *vt* (**a**) *(grouper)* to lump *ou* group together. *(Scol)* **des cours bloqués sur six semaines** a six-week modular course. (**b**) *porte, machine* to jam; *écrou* to overtighten; *roue (accidentellement)* to lock; *(exprès)* to chock; *ballon* to block. ~ **les freins** to jam on the brakes; ~ **qn contre un mur** to pin sb against a wall; **bloqué par un accident** held up by an accident; **je suis bloqué chez moi** I'm stuck at home. (**c**) *(obstruer)* to block (up). **route bloquée par la glace/la neige** icebound/snowbound road. (**d**) *marchandises* to stop, hold up; *salaires, compte* to freeze; *négociations* to block, hold up. **être bloqué** *[situation]* to be at a standstill. **2 se** ~ *vpr [porte, frein, machine]* to jam; *[roue]* to lock.

blottir (se) [blɔtiʀ] (2) *vpr* to curl up, snuggle up. **blotti parmi les arbres** nestling among the trees.

blouse [bluz] *nf (tablier)* overall; *[médecin]* white coat; *[paysan]* smock; *(Billard)* pocket.

blouson [bluzɔ̃] *nm* windjammer, blouson-style jacket. ~ **de laine** lumber jacket; ~ **d'aviateur** bomber *ou* pilot jacket; ~ **noir** ≃ teddy-boy, hell's angel *(US)*.

blue-jean, *pl* **blue-jeans** [bludʒin] *nm* jeans, denims.

blues [bluz] *nm inv (Mus)* blues.

bluff * [blœf] *nm* bluff. **c'est du** ~! he's just bluffing! ◆ **bluffer** * (1) **1** *vi* to bluff. **2** *vt* to fool; *(Cartes)* to bluff. ◆ **bluffeur, -euse** * *nm, f* bluffer.

boa [bɔa] *nm (Habillement, Zool)* boa.

boat-people [botpipɔl] *nmpl* boat people.

bobard * [bɔbaʀ] *nm* lie, fib *.

bobine [bɔbin] *nf* (**a**) *[fil]* reel, bobbin; *(sur machine)* spool; *(Photo)* reel; *(Aut, Élec)* coil. *(Phot)* ~ **de pellicule** roll of film. (**b**) *(*: visage)* face.

bobo * [bobo] *nm (plaie)* sore; *(coupure)* cut. **avoir** ~ to have a pain; **ça (te) fait** ~? does it hurt?

bob(sleigh) [bɔb(slɛg)] *nm* bobsleigh.

bocage [bɔkaʒ] *nm (Géog)* bocage; *(bois)* grove. ◆ **bocager, -ère** *adj (boisé)* wooded; *(Géog)* bocage.

bocal, *pl* **-aux** [bɔkal, o] *nm* jar. **mettre en** ~**aux** to preserve, bottle.

bock [bɔk] *nm* glass of beer; *(verre)* beer glass.

bœuf [bœf], *pl* ~**s** [bø] **1** *nm (bête) [labour]* ox; *[boucherie]* bullock; *(viande)* beef. ~**s de boucherie** beef cattle. **2** *adj inv*: **effet** ~ * fantastic effect *.

bof! [bɔf] *excl* so what!

Bogota [bɔgɔta] *n* Bogota.

bohème [bɔɛm] **1** *adj* bohemian. **2** *nmf* bohemian.

bohémien, -ienne [bɔemjɛ̃, jɛn] *nm, f (gitan)* gipsy.

boire [bwaʀ] (53) **1** *vt* (**a**) to drink. ~ **un verre** to have a drink; ~ **qch à longs traits** to take great gulps of sth; **donner à** ~ **à qn** to give sb sth to drink *ou* a drink; ~ **à la santé/au succès de qn** to drink sb's health/to sb's success; **ça se boit bien** it is very drinkable; **faire** ~ *personne* to give sth to drink to; *cheval* to water; ~ **comme un trou** * to drink like a fish; **il boit (sec)** he's a (heavy) drinker. (**b**) *[plante, buvard]* to soak up. (**c**) ~ **les paroles de qn** to drink in sb's words; ~ **le calice jusqu'à la lie** to drain one's cup to the last bitter drop; ~ **un bouillon** * *(fortune)* to make a big loss; *(bain)* to swallow a mouthful; ~ **du (petit) lait** to lap it up *; **il y a à** ~ **et à manger** you have to pick and choose what to believe.
2 *nm*: **le** ~ **et le manger** food and drink.

bois [bwa] **1** *nm* (**a**) *(gén)* wood. **en** ~ made of wood, wooden; **chaise de** *ou* **en** ~ wooden chair; **rester de** ~ to remain impassive *ou* unmoved; *(fig)* **chèque en** ~ cheque that bounces, rubber check * *(US)*. **il va voir de quel** ~ **je me chauffe!** I'll show him (what I'm made of)! (**b**) *(Zool)* antler. *(Mus)* **les** ~ the woodwind instruments. **2** ~ **blanc** whitewood, deal; ~ **de charpente** timber; ~ **de chauffage** firewood; ~ **de lit** bedstead. ◆ **boisé, e** *adj* wooded. ◆ **boiserie** *nf*: ~**(s)** panelling.

boisson [bwasɔ̃] *nf* drink. **usé par la** ~ ravaged by drink; **pris de** ~ under the influence of drink.

boîte [bwat] **1** *nf* (**a**) *(gén)* box; *(en métal)* tin; *[conserves]* can. **mettre en** ~ to can; *(fig)* **mettre qn en** ~ * to pull sb's leg *. (**b**) (*) *(cabaret)* night club; *(firme)* firm; *(bureau)* office; *(école)* school. **quelle (sale)** ~! what a dump! ‡
2 : ~ **d'allumettes** box of matches; ~ **crânienne** cranium; ~ **à gants** glove compartment; ~ **à** *ou* **aux lettres** letterbox; ~ **à musique** musical box; ~ **à ordures** dustbin, trash can *(US)*; ~ **à outils** toolbox; ~ **à ouvrage** workbox; ~ **de Pandore** Pandora's box; ~ **postale 150** P.O. Box 150 ; ~ **de vitesses** gearbox.

boiter [bwate] (1) *vi* to limp. ~ **bas** to limp badly. ◆ **boitement** *nm* limping. ◆ **boiteux, -euse 1** *adj personne, explication* lame; *meuble* wobbly; *paix, raisonnement* shaky; *vers, phrase* faulty, clumsy. **2** *nm, f* lame person.

boîtier [bwatje] *nm* case; *(pour appareil photo)* body. ~ **électrique** electric torch.

boitiller [bwatije] (1) *vi* to limp slightly, hobble.

bol [bɔl] *nm* bowl. ~ **d'air** breath of fresh air; **avoir du** ~ ‡ to be lucky.

boléro [bɔleʀo] *nm (gén)* bolero.

bolide [bɔlid] *nm (Astron)* meteor; *(voiture)* racing car. **comme un** ~ at top speed, like a rocket.

Bolivie [bɔlivi] *nf* Bolivia. ◆ **bolivien, -ienne** *adj,* **B~(ne)** *nm(f)* Bolivian.

Bologne [bɔlɔɲ] *n* Bologna.

bombance * † [bɔ̃bɑ̃s] *nf* revel. **faire** ~ to revel.

bombarder [bɔ̃baʀde] (1) *vt (gén, Phys)* to bombard; *(bombes)* to bomb; *(obus)* to shell. *(fig)* ~ **de** *cailloux* to pelt with; *questions, lettres* to bombard with; **on l'a bombardé directeur** * he was suddenly pitchforked into the position of manager. ◆ **bombardement** *nm* bombardment; bombing; shelling; pelting. ~ **aérien** air raid; ~ **atomique** atom-bomb attack, atomic attack. ◆ **bombardier** *nm (avion)* bomber.

bombe [bɔ̃b] **1** *nf* (**a**) *(Mil)* bomb. **attentat à la** ~ bombing, bomb *ou* bombing attack; **éclater comme une** ~ to come as a bombshell, be like a bolt out of the blue. (**b**) *(atomiseur)* ~ **(insecticide)** *etc* (fly) *etc* spray. (**c**) *(Équitation)* riding hat. (**d**) **faire la** ~ * to go on a binge *. **2** *(Aut)* ~ **antigel** de-icing spray; ~ **anti-crevaison** instant puncture sealant; ~ **atomique** atom(ic) bomb; **la** ~ **atomique** the Bomb; ~ **au cobalt** telecobalt machine; ~ **glacée** ice pudding.

bombé, e [bɔ̃be] *adj (gén)* rounded; *front* domed; *mur* bulging; *dos* humped; *route* steeply cambered.

bomber [bɔ̃be] (1) *vt* (**a**) ~ **le torse** *(lit)* to throw out one's chest; *(fig)* to swagger about. (**b**) *(Peinture)* to spray(-paint).

bon[1]**, bonne**[1] [bɔ̃, bɔn] **1** *adj* (**a**) *(gén)* good; *outil, produit* good (quality); *odeur, ambiance* good, nice, pleasant; *placement, entreprise* sound. **être ~ en anglais** to be good at English; **une personne de ~ conseil** a man of sound judg(e)ment; **tout lui est ~ pour me discréditer** he'll stop at nothing to discredit me; **il a la bonne vie** he's got it easy *; **c'était le ~ temps!** those were the days!; **dans la bonne société** in polite society.

(**b**) *(charitable) personne, action* good, kind, kindly. **~ mouvement** nice gesture; **elle est bonne fille** she's a good-hearted girl; **mon ~ monsieur** my good man.

(**c**) *(utilisable) billet, passeport* valid. **médicament ~ jusqu'au 5 mai** medicine to be consumed *ou* used before 5th May; **est-ce que ce vernis est encore ~?** is this varnish still usable?; **est-ce que cette eau est bonne?** is this water safe to drink?

(**d**) *(recommandé)* **est-ce bien ~ de fumer tant?** is it a good thing *ou* very wise to smoke so much?; **il est ~ de louer de bonne heure** it's as well *ou* it's advisable to book early; **croire ~ de faire** to think *ou* see fit to do; **comme ~ vous semble** as you think best.

(**e**) *(apte)* **~ pour le service** fit for service; **le voilà ~ pour recommencer** now he'll have to start all over again; **c'est ~ pour ceux qui n'ont rien à faire** it's all right *ou* fine for people who have nothing to do; **cet enfant n'est ~ à rien** this child is no good *ou* use at anything; **c'est ~ à jeter** it's fit for the dustbin; **c'est ~ à nous créer des ennuis** it will only create problems for us; **c'est ~ à savoir** it's useful to know that, that's worth knowing.

(**f**) *(correct) méthode, calcul* right; *fonctionnement* efficient, proper. **au ~ moment** at the right *ou* proper time; **le ~ usage** correct usage (of language); **il est de ~ ton de** it is good manners to; **si ma mémoire est bonne** if my memory serves me well, if I remember correctly.

(**g**) *(intensif)* good. **une bonne heure** a good hour; **bonne raclée *** thorough *ou* sound hiding; **une bonne averse** a heavy shower; **après un ~ moment** after quite some time; **faire ~ poids** to give good weight; **je te le dis une bonne fois** I'm telling you once and for all; **(un) ~ nombre de** a good many; **arriver ~ dernier** to come in a long way *ou* well behind the others; **une bonne moitié** fully half.

(**h**) *(souhaits)* **~ anniversaire!** happy birthday!; **~ appétit!** enjoy your meal!; **~ courage!** good luck!; **~ retour!** safe journey back!, safe return!; **bonne santé!** I hope you keep well!; **bonnes vacances!** have a good holiday! *ou* vacation! *(US)*.

(**i**) *(locutions)* **c'est ~!** (all) right!, OK! *; **~ sang!** damn it! *; **~s baisers** much love; **~ débarras!** good riddance!; **~ gré mal gré** willy-nilly; **(à) ~ marché** cheap; **de ~ cœur** *manger, rire* heartily; *accepter* willingly, readily; **à ~ compte** *s'en sortir* lightly; *acheter* cheap; **de bonne heure** early; **à la bonne heure!** that's fine!; **être ~ enfant** to be good-natured; **cette fois-ci, on est ~! *** this time we've had it! *; **c'est de bonne guerre** that's fair enough; *(iro)* **elle est bien bonne celle-là! *** that's a good one!; **tenir le ~ bout *** to be past the worst; **garder qch pour la bonne bouche** to save sth till the end; **voilà une bonne chose de faite** that's one good job done.

2 *adv*: **il fait ~ ici** it's nice *ou* pleasant here; **il ne ferait pas ~ le contredire** it would be unwise to contradict him.

3 *nm (personne)* good *ou* upright person. *(morceau)* **mange le ~ et laisse le mauvais** eat what's good and leave what's bad; **cette solution a du ~** this solution has its good points; *V aussi* **bon²**.

4 *nf*: **en voilà une bonne!** that's a good one!; *(iro)* **tu en as de bonnes, toi! *** you must be joking! *; **avoir qn à la bonne *** to like sb, be in (solid) with sb *(US)*; *V aussi* **bonne²**.

5 : **bonne amie †** sweetheart; **le B~ Dieu** the good Lord; **bonne étoile** lucky star; *(péj)* **bonne femme** woman; **~ mot** witty, remark; **bonnes œuvres** charity; *(Rel)* **la bonne parole** the word of God; *(Scol)* **~ point** star; *(fig)* **un ~ point pour vous!** that's a point in your favour!; **~ à rien, bonne à rien** *(nm, f)* good-for-nothing; **~ sens** common sense; **bonne sœur *** nun; **~ vivant** *(adj)* jovial; *(nm)* jovial fellow.

bon² [bɔ̃] *nm (formulaire)* slip, form; *(coupon d'échange)* coupon, voucher; *(Fin)* bond. **~ de caisse** cash voucher; **~ de commande** order form; **~ d'épargne** savings bond; **~ de garantie** guarantee slip; **~ du Trésor** (Government) Treasury bond.

bonbon [bɔ̃bɔ̃] *nm* sweet, candy *(US)*. **~ acidulé** acid drop; **~ à la menthe** mint, humbug.

bonbonne [bɔ̃bɔn] *nf* demijohn; *(Ind)* carboy.

bonbonnière [bɔ̃bɔnjɛʀ] *nf (boîte)* sweet *ou* candy *(US)* box; *(fig: appartement)* bijou residence.

bond [bɔ̃] *nm* leap, bound; *[balle]* bounce. **faire des ~s** to leap about; **faire un ~ d'indignation** to leap up indignantly; **faire un ~ de surprise** to start with surprise; **se lever d'un ~** to leap *ou* spring up; **l'économie a fait un ~** there has been a boom *ou* surge in the economy; **les prix ont fait un ~** prices have shot up *ou* soared.

bonde [bɔ̃d] *nf [tonneau]* bung; *[évier]* plug; *[étang]* sluice gate; *(trou)* bung-hole; plughole.

bondé, e [bɔ̃de] *adj* packed, cram-full.

bondir [bɔ̃diʀ] (**2**) *vi (gén)* to leap *ou* spring up; *[balle]* to bounce; *(gambader)* to leap about; *(sursauter)* to start (*de* with). **~ de joie** to jump for joy; *(fig)* **cela me fait ~ *** it makes me hopping mad *; **~ vers** to rush to; **~ sur sa proie** to pounce on one's prey. ◆ **bondissement** *nm* bound, leap.

bonheur [bɔnœʀ] *nm* (**a**) *(félicité)* **le ~** happiness; **avoir le ~ de voir son fils réussir** to have the joy of seeing one's son succeed; **faire le ~ de qn** to make sb happy; **quel ~!** what bliss!, what a delight! (**b**) *(chance)* (good) luck, good fortune. **il ne connaît pas son ~!** he doesn't know how lucky he is!; **par ~** fortunately, luckily; **au petit ~ (la chance) *** haphazardly.

bonhomme [bɔnɔm], *pl* **bonshommes** [bɔ̃zɔm] **1** *nm* (*) *(homme)* man, chap *, fellow; *(mari)* old man ⁑; *(enfant)* lad. **aller son petit ~ de chemin** to carry on in one's own sweet way; **~ de neige** snowman. **2** *adj inv* good-natured. ◆ **bonhomie** *nf* good-naturedness.

bonification [bɔnifikɑsjɔ̃] *nf [terre, vins]* improvement; *(Fin, Sport)* bonus. ◆ **bonifier** *vt,* **se ~** *vpr* (**7**) to improve.

boniment [bɔnimɑ̃] *nm (baratin)* sales talk, patter; *(*: mensonge)* fib *. **faire le ~ à qn** to give sb the sales talk; **raconter des ~s *** to spin yarns *ou* tall stories. ◆ **bonimenteur** *nm* smooth talker.

bonjour [bɔ̃ʒuʀ] *nm (gén)* hello; *(matin)* good morning; *(après-midi)* good afternoon. **donnez-lui le ~ de ma part** give him my regards.

bonne² [bɔn] *nf* maid. **~ d'enfants** nanny; **~ à tout faire** general help, skivvy; *(hum)* maid of all work; *V aussi* **bon¹**.

bonnement [bɔnmɑ̃] *adv*: **tout ~** quite simply.

bonnet [bɔnɛ] *nm* bonnet. **prendre qch sous son ~** to make sth one's concern; **c'est ~ blanc et blanc ~** it's six of one and half a dozen of the other, it amounts to the same thing; **~ d'âne/de bain** dunce's/bathing cap; **~ de nuit** nightcap; *(* fig)* wet blanket; **~ à poils** bearskin. ◆ **bonneterie** *nf (objets)* hosiery; *(magasin)* hosier's shop; *(commerce)* hosiery trade. ◆ **bonnetier, -ière** *nm, f* hosier.

bonsoir [bɔ̃swaʀ] *nm* good evening; *(en se couchant)* good night. **~! *** *(rien à faire)* nothing doing! *

bonté [bɔ̃te] *nf (vertu)* kindness, goodness; *(acte)* (act of) kindness. **ayez la ~ de faire** would you be so kind *ou* good as to do?; **~ divine!** good heavens!

bonus [bɔnys] *nm (Assurances)* no-claims bonus.

bonze [bɔ̃z] *nm (Rel)* bonze; *(*: chef)* bigwig *. **vieux ~*** old fossil *.

boomerang [bumʀɑ̃g] *nm (lit, fig)* boomerang.

boots [buts] *nmpl* boots.

boqueteau, *pl* **~x** [bɔkto] *nm* copse.

bord [bɔʀ] *nm* (**a**) *(gén)* edge; *[route, lac]* side; *[précipice]* brink; *[verre]* brim, rim. **le ~ de la mer** the seashore; **~ du trottoir** kerb, curb *(US)*; **au ~ de la rivière** *marcher* along the river bank; *s'asseoir* by the river; **passer ses vacances au ~ de la mer** to spend one's holidays at the seaside *ou* by the sea; **rempli à ras ~** full to the brim *ou* to overflowing; **chapeau à large(s) ~(s)** broad-brimmed hat.
(**b**) *(Naut)* side. **les hommes du ~** the crew; *(Aviat, Naut)* **à ~** on board, aboard; **jeter par-dessus ~** to throw overboard; **M X, à ~ d'une voiture bleue** Mr X, driving *ou* in a blue car.
(**c**) *(bordée)* tack. **tirer des ~s** to tack.
(**d**) **au ~ de la ruine** on the verge *ou* brink of ruin; **au ~ des larmes** on the verge of tears; **nous sommes du même ~** we are on the same side; **un peu fantaisiste sur les ~s *** a bit of an eccentric.

bordeaux [bɔʀdo] **1** *nm (vin)* Bordeaux (wine). **~ rouge** claret. **2** *adj inv* maroon, burgundy.

bordée [bɔʀde] *nf (salve)* broadside; *(quart)* watch; *(parcours)* tack. **tirer des ~s** to tack; *(fig)* **~ d'injures** torrent *ou* volley of abuse.

bordel ‡ [bɔʀdɛl] *nm (hôtel)* brothel; *(chaos)* mess, shambles *(sg)*. **quel ~!** what a shambles! *; **mettre le ~** to create havoc (*dans* in). ◆ **bordélique** ‡ *adj* shambolic *.

border [bɔʀde] (1) *vt* (**a**) *(Couture)* to edge (*de* with); *(ourler)* to hem. (**b**) *[arbres, maisons]* to line; *[sentier]* to run alongside. **bordé de fleurs** bordered with flowers. (**c**) *personne, couverture* to tuck in.

bordereau, *pl* **~x** [bɔʀdəʀo] *nm* note, slip; *(facture)* invoice.

bordure [bɔʀdyʀ] *nf (gén)* edge; *(cadre)* frame; *(de fleurs)* border; *(d'arbres)* line; *(Couture)* border. **en ~ de** *(le long de)* alongside, along the edge of; *(à côté de)* next to, by.

boréal, e, *mpl* **-aux** [bɔʀeal, o] *adj* boreal.

borgne [bɔʀɲ(ə)] *adj personne* one-eyed, blind in one eye; *(fig) hôtel* shady.

borne [bɔʀn(ə)] *nf* (**a**) *[route]* kilometre-marker, ≃ milestone; *[terrain]* boundary marker; *[monument]* stone post; *(Élec)* terminal. **3 ~s *** 3 kilometres. (**b**) *(fig)* **~s** limit(s), bounds; **dépasser les ~s** to go too far; **sans ~s** limitless, boundless; **mettre des ~s à** to limit. ◆ **borné, e** *adj personne* narrow-minded; *esprit, vie* narrow; *intelligence* limited. ◆ **borner** (1) *vt besoins, enquête, vue* to limit, restrict (*à faire* to doing, *à qch* to sth); *terrain* to mark out *ou* off. **arbres qui bornent un champ** trees which border a field; **se ~ à faire/à qch** *[personne]* to restrict *ou* limit o.s. to doing/to sth; **je me borne à vous faire remarquer que** I would just *ou* merely like to point out to you that.

Bornéo [bɔʀneo] *n* Borneo.

bosquet [bɔskɛ] *nm* copse, grove.

bosse [bɔs] *nf [chameau, bossu]* hump; *(coup, monticule)* bump. **route pleine de ~s** bumpy road; **avoir la ~ du théâtre** to be a born actor.

bosseler [bɔsle] (4) *vt (déformer)* to dent; *(marteler)* to emboss.

bosser * [bɔse] (1) **1** *vi* to work; *(travailler dur)* to slog away *. **2** *vt examen* to swot for, slog away for *. ◆ **bosseur, -euse** * *nm, f* slogger *.

bossu, e [bɔsy] **1** *adj personne* hunchbacked. **dos ~** hunched back. **2** *nm, f* hunchback.

bot [bo] *adj*: **pied ~** club-foot.

botanique [bɔtanik] **1** *adj* botanical. **2** *nf* botany. ◆ **botaniste** *nmf* botanist.

Botswana [bɔtswana] *nm* Botswana.

botte [bɔt] *nf* (**a**) (high) boot; *[cavalier]* riding boot; *[égoutier]* wader. **~ de caoutchouc** wellington (boot), gumboot; **sous la ~ de l'ennemi** under the enemy's heel. (**b**) *[légumes]* bunch; *[foin]* sheaf; *(au carré)* bale. (**c**) *(Escrime)* thrust.

botter [bɔte] (1) *vt* (**a**) to put boots on. **se ~** to put one's boots on; **botté de cuir** with leather boots on, wearing leather boots; **ça me botte** ‡ I like *ou* dig * that. (**b**) *(Ftbl)* to kick. **~ les fesses de qn** ‡ to give sb a kick in the pants ‡. ◆ **bottier** *nm* bootmaker. ◆ **bottillon** *nm* ankle boot. ◆ **bottine** *nf* (ankle) boot.

Bottin [bɔtɛ̃] *nm* ® directory, phonebook.

bouc [buk] *nm (Zool)* (billy) goat; *(barbe)* goatee (beard). **~ émissaire** scapegoat.

boucan * [bukɑ̃] *nm* din, racket. **faire du ~** *(bruit)* to kick up * a din *ou* a racket; *(protestation)* to kick up * a fuss.

bouche [buʃ] **1** *nf* (**a**) *(gén)* mouth. **j'ai la ~ pâteuse** my tongue feels coated. (**b**) *(fig)* **fermer la ~ à qn** to shut sb up; **dans sa ~ , ce mot choque** when he says *ou* uses it, that word sounds offensive; **il a toujours l'injure à la ~** he's always ready with an insult; **il n'a que ce mot-là à la ~** that word is never off his lips; **de ~ à oreille** by word of mouth; **~ cousue! *** mum's the word! *; **passer de ~ en ~** to be rumoured about; **il en a plein la ~** he can talk of nothing else; **faire la fine ~** to turn one's nose up; **avoir la ~ en cœur** to simper.
2 : **~ d'aération** air vent; **~ à ~** *(nm inv)* kiss of life, mouth-to-mouth resuscitation *ou* respiration *(US)*; **faire du ~ à ~ à qn** to give sb the kiss of life *ou* mouth-to-mouth resuscitation ; **~ d'égout** manhole; **~ d'incendie** fire hydrant ; **~ de métro** metro entrance.

bouchée[1] [buʃe] *nf* (**a**) mouthful. **pour une ~ de pain** for a song; **mettre les ~s doubles** to put on a spurt; **ne faire qu'une ~ de** to make short work of. (**b**) **une ~ (au chocolat)** a chocolate; **~ à la reine** savoury vol-au-vent.

boucher[1] [buʃe] (1) **1** *vt* (**a**) *bouteille* to cork, put the *ou* a cork in; *trou* to fill up; *fuite* to plug, stop; *fenêtre, nez, lavabo* to block (up); *vue* to block. **~ le passage** to be in the way. (**b**) **ça lui en a bouché un coin** ‡ it floored * *ou* threw * him. **2 se ~** *vpr [évier]* to get blocked up; *[temps]* to become overcast. **se ~ le nez** to hold one's nose; **se ~ les oreilles** to put one's fingers in one's ears. ◆ **bouché, e[2]** *adj temps* overcast; (‡) *personne* thick ‡. **les maths sont ~es** there's no future in maths. ◆ **bouche-trou,** *pl* **bouche-trous** *nm* stopgap.

boucher[2] [buʃe] *nm (lit, fig)* butcher. ◆ **bouchère** *nf* (woman) butcher; *(épouse)* butcher's wife. ◆ **boucherie** *nf (magasin)* butcher's (shop); *(métier)* butchery (trade); *(fig)* slaughter.

bouchon [buʃɔ̃] *nm* (**a**) *(en liège)* cork; *(en verre, plastique)* stopper; *(en chiffon)* plug; *[bidon]* cap; *[tube]* top; *[évier]* plug. *(Phot)* **~ d'objectif** lens cap; **~ anti-vol** locking petrol cap. (**b**) *(Pêche)* float. (**c**) *(Aut: embouteillage)* holdup, traffic jam.

boucle [bukl(ə)] *nf [ceinture]* buckle; *[cheveux]* curl, lock; *[lacet]* bow; *[rivière]* loop; *(Sport)* lap; *(Aviat, Écriture, Ordin)* loop. **B~s d'or** Goldilocks; **~ d'oreille** earring.

boucler [bukle] (1) **1** *vt* (**a**) *ceinture* to buckle, fasten (up); (*) *porte* to shut. *(lit, fig)* **~ sa valise** to pack one's bags; **tu vas la ~!** ‡ will you belt up! ‡ (**b**) *(fig) affaire* to finish off; *circuit* to complete; *budget* to balance. **arriver à ~ ses fins de mois** to manage to stay in the black at the end of the month. (**c**) *(*: enfermer)* to lock up. **être bouclé chez soi** to be cooped up *ou* stuck at home. (**d**) *(Mil: encercler)* to seal off, cordon off. **2** *vi* to curl, be curly. ◆**bouclage** *nm* locking up; sealing off. ◆**bouclé, e** *adj* curly.

bouclier [buklije] *nm (gén)* shield; *(Police)* riot shield.

Bouddha [buda] *nm* Buddha. ◆**bouddhique** *nm* Buddhistic. ◆**bouddhisme** *adj* Buddhism. ◆**bouddhiste** *adj, nmf* Buddhist.

bouder [bude] (1) **1** *vi* to sulk. **2** *vt* to refuse to have anything to do with. ~ **la nourriture** to have no appetite; **spectacle boudé par le public** show that is ignored by the public; **il se boudent** they're not on speaking terms. ◆**bouderie** *nf (état)* sulkiness; *(action)* sulk. ◆**boudeur, -euse** *adj* sulky.

boudin [budɛ̃] *nm* (**a**) ~ **noir/blanc** ≃ black/white pudding. (**b**) *(bourrelet)* roll.

boudiné, e [budine] *adj* (**a**) *doigt* podgy. (**b**) *(serré)* ~ **dans** squeezed into, bulging out of.

boudoir [budwaʀ] *nm (salon)* boudoir; *(biscuit)* sponge finger.

boue [bu] *nf (gén, fig)* mud; *[canal]* sludge.

bouée [bwe] *nf* buoy; *[baigneur]* rubber ring. ~ **de sauvetage** lifebuoy.

boueux, -euse [bwø, øz] **1** *adj* muddy. **2** *nm* dustman, garbage collector *(US)*.

bouffée [bufe] *nf [parfum]* whiff; *[pipe]* puff; *[colère]* outburst; *[orgueil]* fit; *[vent]* puff, gust. *(Méd)* ~ **de chaleur** hot flush *ou* flash *(US)*.

bouffer[1] [bufe] (1) *vi [manche]* to puff out; *[cheveux]* to be bouffant. ◆**bouffant, e** *adj* puffed-out; bouffant. **pantalon** ~ baggy breeches.

bouffer[2] * [bufe] (1) **1** *vt* to eat, gobble up *. **se ~ le nez** to scratch each other's eyes out; ~ **du curé** to be violently anti-church. **2** *vi* to eat, nosh ‡. **on a bien bouffé** the grub was great ‡. ◆**bouffe** ‡ *nf* grub ‡.

bouffir [bufiʀ] (2) *vt* to puff up. ◆**bouffi, e** *adj visage, (fig)* puffed up; *yeux* swollen. ◆**bouffissure** *nf* puffiness.

bouffon, -onne [bufɔ̃, ɔn] **1** *adj* farcical, comical. **2** *nm (pitre)* buffoon, clown; *(Hist)* jester. ◆**bouffonnerie** *nf* (**a**) *[situation]* drollery. (**b**) ~**s** *(comportement)* antics; *(paroles)* jesting; **faire des ~s** to clown about.

bougeoir [buʒwaʀ] *nm (bas)* candle-holder; *(haut)* candlestick.

bouger [buʒe] (3) **1** *vi* to move, stir; *(protester)* to stir. **ne bouge pas** keep still, don't move; **il n'a pas bougé (de chez lui)** he stayed in *ou* at home; **ne pas ~** *[idées, prix]* to stay the same; **ce tissu ne bouge pas** this cloth wears well; *(dimension)* this cloth is shrink-resistant; *(couleur)* this cloth will not fade. **2** *vt* (*) *objet* to move, shift. **il n'a pas bougé le petit doigt** he didn't lift a finger (to help). **3 se ~** ‡ *vpr* to move. **bouge-toi de là!** shift over! *, shift out of the way! *, scoot over! * *(US)*; **il faut se ~ pour obtenir satisfaction** you have to put yourself out to get satisfaction. ◆**bougeotte** * *nf*: **avoir la ~** *(remuer)* to have the fidgets; *(voyager)* to be always on the move.

bougie [buʒi] *nf* (**a**) candle; *(Aut)* spark plug; *(Élec)* watt. (**b**) *(*: visage)* face.

bougon, -onne [bugɔ̃, ɔn] **1** *adj* grumpy, grouchy. **2** *nm, f* grumbler. ◆**bougonnement** *nm* grumbling, grouching. ◆**bougonner** (1) *vi* to grouch, grumble.

bougre * [bugʀ(ə)] *nm* guy *, chap *, fellow *. **pauvre ~** poor devil *; ~ **d'idiot!** stupid idiot! *; **il le savait, le ~!** the so-and-so knew it! ◆**bougrement** * *adv* damned *.

bouillant, e [bujɑ̃, ɑ̃t] *adj (brûlant)* boiling (hot); *(qui bout)* boiling; *tempérament* fiery.

bouillasse * [bujas] *nf (gadoue)* muck.

bouille * [buj] *nf (visage)* face.

bouillie [buji] *nf [bébé]* baby cereal; *[vieillard]* porridge. **mettre en ~** to reduce to a pulp.

bouillir [bujiʀ] (15) *vi* (**a**) *(lit)* to boil, be boiling. **faire ~** *eau* to boil, bring to the boil; *linge* to boil; *biberon* to sterilize. (**b**) *(fig)* to boil. **faire ~ qn** to make sb's blood boil; ~ **d'impatience** to seethe with impatience. ◆**bouilloire** *nf* kettle.

bouillon [bujɔ̃] **1** *nm* (**a**) *(soupe)* stock. **prendre un ~** * *(en nageant)* to swallow a mouthful; *(Fin)* to take a tumble *, come a cropper *. (**b**) *(bouillonnement)* bubble (in boiling liquid). **couler à gros ~s** to gush out. **2** : ~ **cube** stock cube; *(Bio)* ~ **de culture** (culture) medium.

bouillonner [bujɔne] (1) *vi [liquide chaud]* to bubble; *[torrent]* to foam; *[idées]* to bubble up; *[esprit]* to seethe. **il bouillonne d'idées** his mind is teeming with ideas, he's bubbling with ideas. ◆**bouillonnement** *nm* bubbling; seething; foaming.

bouillotte [bujɔt] *nf* hot-water bottle.

boulanger [bulɑ̃ʒe] *nm* baker. ◆**boulangère** *nf* (woman) baker; *(épouse)* baker's wife. ◆**boulangerie** *nf (magasin)* baker's (shop), bakery; *(commerce)* bakery trade.

boule [bul] **1** *nf* (**a**) *(Billard)* ball; *(Boules)* bowl; *(Casino)* boule. **roulé en ~** rolled up in a ball. (**b**) **avoir une ~ dans la gorge** to have a lump in one's throat; **perdre la ~** * to go nuts *; **être/se mettre en ~** * to be/get mad *. **2** : ~ **de cristal** crystal ball; ~ **de gomme** fruit pastille, gumdrop; ~ **de neige** snowball; *(fig)* **faire ~ de neige** to snowball; ® ~ **Quiès** earplug, ear stopper.

bouleau, *pl* ~**x** [bulo] *nm* silver birch.

bouledogue [buldɔg] *nm* bulldog.

boulet [bulɛ] *nm* (**a**) *[forçat]* ball and chain. ~ **(de canon)** cannonball; *(fig)* **traîner un ~** to have a millstone round one's neck. (**b**) *[charbon]* (coal) nut.

boulette [bulɛt] *nf* (**a**) *[papier]* pellet; *(Culin)* meatball; *(empoisonnée)* poison ball. (**b**) *(* fig)* blunder, bloomer *.

boulevard [bulvaʀ] *nm* boulevard. **pièce de ~** light comedy.

bouleverser [bulvɛʀse] (1) *vt* (**a**) *objets* to turn upside down; *plans* to disrupt. (**b**) *(émouvoir)* to distress deeply, overwhelm, shatter. **bouleversé par la peur** distraught with fear. ◆**bouleversant, e** *adj récit* deeply moving; *nouvelle* shattering. ◆**bouleversement** *nm* upheaval, disruption. **le ~ de son visage** the utter distress on his face.

boulier [bulje] *nm (calcul)* abacus.

boulimie [bulimi] *nf* bulimia. **il fait de la ~** * he is a compulsive eater.

boulodrome [bulɔdʀom] *nm* bowling pitch.

boulon [bulɔ̃] *nm* bolt. ◆**boulonner** (1) **1** *vt* to bolt (down *ou* on *etc*). **2** *vi* (*) to work. ~ **dur** to slog *ou* slave away *.

boulot[1], **-otte** [bulo, ɔt] *adj* plump, tubby *.

boulot[2] * [bulo] *nm (gén)* work; *(emploi)* job. **quel ~!** what a job!; **allons, au ~!** let's get cracking! *

boulotter * [bulɔte] (1) **1** *vi* to eat, nosh ‡. **on a bien boulotté** we had a good meal *ou* nosh ‡. **2** *vt* to eat.

boum [bum] **1** *excl* bang!, wallop! ~ **par terre!** whoops a daisy! **2** *nm (explosion)* bang. **être en plein ~** ‡ to be in full swing. **3** *nf (*: fête)* party.

bouquet [bukɛ] *nm* (**a**) *[fleurs]* bunch of flowers; *(soigneusement composé)* bouquet; *[thym etc]* bunch. ~ **d'arbres** clump of trees. (**b**) *[feu d'artifice]* crowning piece. *(fig)* **c'est le ~!** * that takes the cake! * (**c**) *[vin]* bouquet. (**d**) *(crevette)* prawn.

bouquin * [bukɛ̃] *nm* book. ◆ **bouquiner** * (1) *vti* to read.

bourbier [buʀbje] *nm* quagmire; *(fig)* mess.

bourde * [buʀd(ə)] *nf* blunder, bloomer *.

bourdon [buʀdɔ̃] *nm (Zool)* bumblebee; *(cloche)* great bell. **avoir le ~** * to have the blues *.

bourdonnement [buʀdɔnmɑ̃] *nm [voix, insecte]* buzz; *[moteur]* drone. **avoir des ~s d'oreilles** to have a buzzing noise in one's ears. ◆ **bourdonner** (1) *vi* to buzz; to drone.

bourg [buʀ] *nm* market town; *(petit)* village. ◆ **bourgade** *nf* village, (small) town.

bourgeois, e [buʀʒwa, waz] **1** *adj (gén)* middle-class; *(Pol, péj)* bourgeois. **2** *nm, f* (**a**) bourgeois, middle-class person. **grand ~** upper middle-class person. (**b**) *(Hist) (citoyen)* burgess; *(riche roturier)* bourgeois. **3** *nf (*hum: épouse)* **ma ~e** the wife *. ◆ **bourgeoisement** *adv penser* conventionally; *vivre* comfortably. ◆ **bourgeoisie** *nf* middle classes, bourgeoisie. **petite ~** lower middle class.

bourgeon [buʀʒɔ̃] *nm* bud. ◆ **bourgeonner** (1) *vi* to (come into) bud.

bourgmestre [buʀgmɛstʀ(ə)] *nm* burgomaster.

bourgogne [buʀgɔɲ] *nm (vin)* burgundy.

Bourkina [buʀkina] *nm:* **le ~** Burkina Faso.

bourlinguer [buʀlɛ̃ge] (1) *vi (naviguer)* to sail; *(*: voyager)* to knock about a lot *.

bourrade [buʀad] *nf (du poing)* thump; *(du coude)* poke.

bourrage [buʀaʒ] *nm:* **~ de crâne** * brainwashing; *(Scol)* cramming.

bourrasque [buʀask(ə)] *nf* gust of wind, squall. **~ de neige** flurry of snow.

bourratif, -ive [buʀatif, iv] *adj* filling, stodgy.

bourre [buʀ] *nf [coussin]* stuffing; *[fusil]* wad. **à la ~** ⁑ *(gén)* late; **être à la ~ dans son travail** ⁑ to be behind with one's work.

bourré, e [buʀe] *adj* (**a**) *(plein)* packed, crammed (*de* with). (**b**) *(⁑: ivre)* tight *, plastered ⁑.

bourreau, *pl* **~x** [buʀo] **1** *nm (tortionnaire)* torturer; *(Hist)* executioner; *[pendaison]* hangman. **2** : **~ des cœurs** ladykiller; **~ d'enfants** child *ou* baby batterer; **~ de travail** glutton for work *.

bourrelet [buʀlɛ] *nm (gén)* roll; *[porte]* draught excluder. **~ (de chair)** roll of flesh, spare tyre *.

bourrer [buʀe] (1) *vt* (**a**) *coussin* to stuff; *pipe* to fill; *valise* to cram full. **~ un sac de papiers** to cram papers into a bag; **~ qn de nourriture** to stuff sb with food; **les frites, ça bourre!** chips are very filling! (**b**) **~ le crâne à qn** * *(endoctriner)* to brainwash sb; *(tromper)* to feed sb a lot of eyewash *; *(Scol)* to cram sb; **~ qn de coups** to pummel sb.

bourrique [buʀik] *nf* (**a**) *(âne)* donkey, ass; *(ânesse)* she-ass. (**b**) *(* fig) (imbécile)* ass; *(têtu)* mule. **faire tourner qn en ~** to drive sb mad *.

bourru, e [buʀy] *adj* surly.

bourse [buʀs(ə)] **1** *nf* (**a**) *(porte-monnaie)* purse. **la ~ ou la vie!** your money or your life!; **sans ~ délier** without spending a penny; **ils font ~ commune** they pool their resources; **ils font ~ à part** they keep their finances separate. (**b**) **la B~** *(activité)* ≃ the Stock Exchange *ou* Market; *(bâtiment) [Paris]* the Bourse; *[Londres]* the (London) Stock Exchange; *[New York]* Wall Street; **la B~ monte/descend** the market is going up/down. (**c**) *(Univ)* **~ (d'études)** (student) grant; *(obtenue par concours)* scholarship. **2** : **B~ du commerce** commodity market; **B~ du travail** ≃ trade union centre. ◆ **boursier, -ière** **1** *adj* Stock Market. **2** *nm, f (Univ)* grant-holder, fellow *(US)* ; scholarship-holder.

boursoufler [buʀsufle] (1) **1** *vt* to puff up, bloat. **2 se ~** *vpr [peinture]* to blister. ◆ **boursouflé, e** *adj* puffy, bloated; blistered; *style* bombastic. ◆ **boursouflure** *nf* puffiness; pomposity; *(cloque)* blister.

bousculer [buskyle] (1) **1** *vt (pousser)* to jostle; *(heurter)* to bump into; *(presser)* to rush. *(fig)* **être très bousculé** to be rushed off one's feet. **2 se ~** *vpr* to jostle each other. *(bégayer)* **ça se bouscule au portillon** * he can't get his words out fast enough; *(s'enthousiasmer)* **les gens ne se bousculent pas au portillon** * people aren't exactly queuing up *. ◆ **bousculade** *nf (remous)* jostle, crush; *(hâte)* rush, scramble.

bouse [buz] *nf* cow pat. **de la ~** (cattle) dung.

bousiller * [buzije] (1) *vt travail* to botch; *appareil, voiture* to smash up; *personne* to bump off ⁑.

boussole [busɔl] *nf* compass. *(fig)* **perdre la ~** * to go off one's head.

bout [bu] *nm* (**a**) *(extrémité) (gén)* end; *[nez, canne, oreille etc]* tip. **du ~ du pied** with one's toe; **à ~ de bras** at arm's length; *(fig)* **du ~ des lèvres** reluctantly, half-heartedly; **sur le ~ de la langue** on the tip of one's tongue; **jusqu'au ~ des ongles** to one's fingertips; **savoir qch sur le ~ du doigt** to have sth at one's fingertips.
(**b**) *[espace, durée]* end. **à l'autre ~ de la pièce** at the far *ou* other end of the room; **au ~ d'un mois** at the end of a month; **on n'en voit pas le ~** there doesn't seem to be any end to it; **d'un ~ à l'autre de ses œuvres/du voyage** throughout his works/ the journey; *(fig)* **ce n'est pas le ~ du monde!** it's not the end of the world!
(**c**) *(morceau) [ficelle, pain]* piece, bit. **il m'a fait un ~ de conduite** he went part of the way with me; **cela fait un ~ (de chemin)** it's some distance *ou* quite a long way away; **il est resté un (bon) ~ de temps** he stayed a while *ou* quite some time; **un ~ de terrain/ciel** a patch of land/sky; **un petit ~ de chou** * a little kid *.
(**d**) **être à ~** *(fatigué)* to be all in *; *(en colère)* to have had enough; **à ~ de souffle** out of breath; **être à ~ de ressources** to have no money left; **être à ~ de nerfs** to be at the end of one's tether; **pousser qn à ~** to push sb to the limit (of his patience).
(**e**) *(locutions)* **au ~ du compte** in the end; **être au ~ de son rouleau** * *(idées)* to have run out of ideas; *(ressources)* to be running short of money; *(forces)* to be at the end of one's tether; **il n'est pas au ~ de ses peines** he's not out of the wood yet; **jusqu'au ~** right to the end; **~ à ~** end to end; **de ~ en ~** right through, from start to finish; **à ~ portant** at point-blank range.

boutade [butad] *nf* sally.

boute-en-train [butɑ̃tʀɛ̃] *nm inv* live wire *. **le ~ de la soirée** the life and soul of the party.

bouteille [butɛj] *nf (gén)* bottle; *[gaz]* cylinder. ® **~ Thermos** Thermos ® flask *ou* bottle *(US)*; **~ de vin** *(récipient)* wine bottle; *(contenu)* bottle of wine; **mettre en ~s** to bottle; **prendre de la ~** * to be getting on in years; *(dans son métier)* **il a de la ~** * he's been around a long time; **c'est la ~ à l'encre** the whole business is about as clear as mud.

boutique [butik] *nf* shop, store. **~ de gestion** business consultancy; **~ de droit** law centre; **quelle sale ~!** what a dump! * ◆ **boutiquier, -ière** *nm, f* shopkeeper, storekeeper *(US)*.

bouton [butɔ̃] **1** *nm (Couture)* button; *(Élec)* switch; *[porte, radio]* knob; *[sonnette]* (push-)button; *(Méd)* spot, pimple; *(Bot)* bud. **en ~** in bud; **~ de rose** rosebud. **2** : **~ de col** collar stud; **~ de manchette** cufflink; **~-d'or** *nm, pl* **~s-~** buttercup;, **~-pression** *nm, pl* **~s-~** press-stud. ◆ **boutonner** (1) **1** *vt* to button (up). **2 se ~** *vpr [vêtement]* to button (up); *[personne]* to button (up) one's coat *etc*.

◆**boutonneux, -euse** *adj* pimply, spotty. ◆**boutonnière** *nf* buttonhole.

bouture [butyʀ] *nf* cutting. **faire des ~s** to take cuttings. ◆**bouturer** (1) *vt* to take a cutting from.

bouvier [buvje] *nm (personne)* herdsman; *(chien)* sheepdog.

bouvreuil [buvʀœj] *nm* bullfinch.

bovin, e [bɔvɛ̃, in] **1** *adj (lit, fig)* bovine. **2** *nmpl*: **~s** cattle.

bowling [buliŋ] *nm (jeu)* (tenpin) bowling; *(salle)* bowling alley.

box, *pl* **boxes** [bɔks] *nm [dortoir]* cubicle; *[écurie]* loose-box; *(garage)* lock-up (garage). **~ des accusés** dock.

boxe [bɔks(ə)] *nf* boxing. ◆**boxer**[1] [bɔkse] (1) **1** *vi* to box, be a boxer. **2** *vt* to box against, fight; *(‡: frapper)* to thump. ◆**boxeur** *nm* boxer.

boxer[2] [bɔksɛʀ] *nm* boxer (dog).

boxer[3] [bɔksœʀ] ou **boxer-short** [bɔksœʀʃɔʀt] *nm* boxer shorts.

boyau, *pl* **~x** [bwajo] *nm* (**a**) *(intestins)* **~x** guts; **~ (de chat)** (cat)gut. (**b**) *(passage)* (narrow) passageway. (**c**) *[bicyclette]* racing tyre. (**d**) *(pour saucisse)* casing.

boycotter [bɔjkɔte] (1) *vt* to boycott. ◆**boycott(age)** *nm* boycott.

bracelet [bʀaslɛ] *nm [poignet]* bracelet; *[bras, cheville]* bangle; *[montre]* strap. **~-montre** *nm, pl* **~s-~s** wrist watch.

braconnage [bʀakɔnaʒ] *nm* poaching. ◆**braconner** (1) *vi* to poach. ◆**braconnier** *nm* poacher.

brader [bʀade] (1) *vt (vendre à prix réduit)* to sell cut-price *ou* cut-rate *(US)*; *(vendre en solde)* to have a clearance sale of; *(lit, fig: se débarrasser de)* to sell off. ◆**braderie** *nf (magasin)* discount centre; *(sur un marché)* stall selling cut-price *ou* cut-rate *(US)* goods.

braguette [bʀagɛt] *nf* fly, flies *(of trousers)*.

brailler [bʀɑje] (1) **1** *vi* to bawl. **2** *vt chanson* to bawl out. ◆**braillard, e 1** *adj* bawling. **2** *nm, f* bawler. ◆**braillement** *nm* bawling.

brain trust [bʀɛntʀəst] *nm* brain(s) trust.

braire [bʀɛʀ] (50) *vi (lit, fig)* to bray. **faire ~ qn** ‡ to get on sb's wick ‡.

braise [bʀɛz] *nf*: **~(s)** embers; **de ~** *yeux* fiery.

braiser [bʀeze] (1) *vt* to braise.

bramer [bʀɑme] (1) *vi [cerf]* to bell; *(* fig)* to wail.

brancard [bʀɑ̃kaʀ] *nm (bras)* shaft; *(civière)* stretcher. ◆**brancardier, -ière** *nm, f* stretcherbearer.

branche [bʀɑ̃ʃ] *nf* (**a**) *(Bot)* branch, bough. **asperges en ~s** asparagus spears; **céleri en ~s** sticks of celery. (**b**) *[nerfs, famille, rivière]* branch; *[lunettes]* side-piece; *[compas]* leg; *[ciseaux]* blade. **la ~ maternelle** the maternal branch *ou* the mother's side of the family. (**c**) *(secteur)* branch. **s'orienter vers une ~ technique** to go in for the technical side. ◆**branchage** *nm* branches, boughs. **~s** fallen branches.

brancher [bʀɑ̃ʃe] (1) *vt prise* to plug in; *tuyau, téléphone* to connect up. **~ qch sur** to plug sth into; to connect sth up with; *(fig)* **~ qn sur un sujet** to start sb off *ou* launch sb on a subject; **ce qui me branche** * what grabs * me *ou* gives me a buzz *. ◆**branché, e** * *adj (dans le vent)* switched-on *. **il est ~** he's a swinger *, he's switched-on *. ◆**branchement** *nm (action)* plugging-in; connecting-up; *(conduite)* connection; *(Ordin)* branch; *(Gram)* branching.

branchies [bʀɑ̃ʃi] *nfpl* gills.

brandir [bʀɑ̃diʀ] (2) *vt* to brandish, flourish.

branlant, e [bʀɑ̃lɑ̃, ɑ̃t] *adj (gén)* shaky; *dent* loose.

branle [bʀɑ̃l] *nm [cloche]* swing. **mettre en ~** *cloche* to swing, set swinging; *(fig) forces* to set in motion, set off; **se mettre en ~** to get going *ou* moving.

branle-bas [bʀɑ̃lbɑ] *nm inv* bustle, commotion. **être en ~** to be in a state of commotion; **~ de combat!** 'action stations!'

branler [bʀɑ̃le] (1) **1** *vt*: **~ la tête** to shake one's head. **2** *vi (gén, fig)* to be shaky; *[dent]* to be loose. *(fig)* **ça branle dans le manche** the situation is very unsettled.

braquage [bʀakaʒ] *nm (Aut)* (steering) lock.

braquer [bʀake] (1) **1** *vt* (**a**) **~ une arme** *etc* **sur** to point *ou* aim a weapon *etc* at; **~ les yeux sur qch** to fix one's eyes on sth; **~ (son arme sur) qn** to pull one's gun on sb *. (**b**) *(Aut)* to swing. (**c**) *(‡: attaquer) banque* to hold up. (**d**) *(fig: buter)* **~ qn** to antagonize sb; **~ qn contre qch** to turn sb against sth. **2** *vi (Aut)* to turn the steering wheel. *[voiture]* **~ bien/mal** to have a good/bad lock. **3 se ~** *vpr* to dig one's heels in. **se ~ contre** to set one's face against. ◆**braqueur** ‡ *nm (gangster)* hold-up man *.

braquet [bʀakɛ] *nm* gear ratio.

bras [bʀa] *nm* (**a**) *(lit, fig)* arm. **donner le ~ à qn** to give sb one's arm; **être au ~ de qn** to be on sb's arm; **se donner le ~** to link arms; **~ dessus, ~ dessous** arm in arm; *(lit)* **les ~ croisés** with one's arms folded; *(fig)* **rester les ~ croisés** to sit idly by; *(fig)* **~ droit** right-hand man. (**b**) *(travailleur)* hand, worker. **manquer de ~** to be short-handed. (**c**) *[outil]* handle; *[fauteuil, électrophone]* arm; *[grue]* jib; *[croix]* limb; *[brancard]* shaft. (**d**) *[fleuve]* branch. (**e**) **en ~ de chemise** in one's shirt sleeves; **saisir qn à ~ le corps** to seize sb bodily; **avoir le ~ long** to have a long arm; *(lit, fig)* **à ~ ouverts** with open arms; **tomber sur qn à ~ raccourcis** * to set on sb; **lever les ~ au ciel** to throw up one's arms; **les ~ m'en tombent** I'm stunned; **avoir qch/qn** *ou* **se retrouver avec qch/qn sur les ~** * to have sth/sb on one's hands, be stuck * with sth/sb; **dans les ~ de Morphée** in the arms of Morpheus; **faire un ~ d'honneur à qn** ≃ to put two fingers up at sb *, give sb the V-sign; **faire une partie de ~ de fer avec qn** to arm-wrestle with sb; *(fig)* **la partie de ~ de fer entre patronat et syndicats** the wrestling match between the bosses and the unions.

brasier [bʀɑzje] *nm* inferno.

brassage [bʀasaʒ] *nm* (**a**) *[bière]* brewing. (**b**) *(mélange)* mixing. **~ de races** intermixing of races.

brassard [bʀasaʀ] *nm* armband.

brasse [bʀas] *nf* (**a**) *(Sport)* breast-stroke. **~ papillon** butterfly(-stroke). (**b**) *(Naut)* fathom.

brassée [bʀase] *nf* armful.

brasser [bʀase] (1) *vt* (**a**) *(remuer)* to stir (up); *(mélanger)* to mix; *salade* to toss; *cartes* to shuffle; *argent* to handle a lot of. **~ des affaires** to be in big business; *(fig)* **~ du vent** to blow hot air *. (**b**) *bière* to brew. ◆**brasserie** *nf (café)* ≃ pub, bar, brasserie; *(usine)* brewery. ◆**brasseur, -euse** *nm, f [bière]* brewer. **~ d'affaires** big businessman.

brassière [bʀasjɛʀ] *nf [bébé]* vest.

bravade [bʀavad] *nf* act of bravado. **par ~** out of bravado.

brave [bʀav] **1** *adj* (**a**) *(courageux)* brave. **faire le ~** to put on a bold front. (**b**) *(bon)* nice; *(honnête)* decent, honest. **de ~s gens** good *ou* decent people; **mon ~ (homme)** my good man. **2** *nm (gén)* brave man; *(indien)* brave. ◆**bravement** *adv* bravely.

braver [bʀave] (1) *vt autorité* to defy; *danger* to brave. **~ l'opinion** to fly in the face of (public) opinion.

bravo [bʀavo] **1** *excl (félicitation)* well done!, bravo!; *(approbation)* hear! hear! **2** *nm* cheer. **un grand ~ pour...!** a big cheer for...!, let's hear it for...! *(US)*.

bravoure [bʀavuʀ] *nf* bravery.

break [bʀɛk] *nm (Aut)* estate (car), station wagon *(US)*.

brebis [bʀəbi] *nf (Zool)* ewe; *(Rel: pl)* flock. **~ égarée/galeuse** stray/black sheep.

brèche [bʀɛʃ] *nf (gén)* breach. **faire une ~ à sa fortune** to make a hole in one's fortune; *(fig)* **il est toujours sur la ~** he's still beavering away *ou* hard at it *.

bredouille [bʀəduj] *adj (gén)* empty-handed.

bredouiller [bʀəduje] (1) **1** *vi* to stammer, mumble. **2** *vt* to mumble, stammer (out). ◆ **bredouillement** *nm* mumbling, stammering.

bref, brève [bʀɛf, ɛv] **1** *adj (gén)* brief, short; *voyelle, syllabe* short. **soyez ~** be brief; **à ~ délai** shortly. **2** *adv (pour résumer)* in short, in brief; *(passons)* anyway. **en ~** in short, in brief.

brelan [bʀəlɑ̃] *nm (Cartes)* three of a kind. **~ d'as** three aces.

breloque [bʀəlɔk] *nf* bracelet charm.

Brésil [bʀezil] *nm* Brazil. ◆ **brésilien, -ienne** *adj*, **B~(ne)** *nm(f)* Brazilian.

Bretagne [bʀətaɲ] *nf* Brittany.

bretelle [bʀətɛl] *nf* (**a**) *(gén)* strap; *[fusil]* sling. *[pantalon]* **~s** braces, suspenders *(US)*. (**b**) *(Rail)* crossover; *(Aut)* link road. **~ de raccordement** access road; **~ de contournement** bypass.

breton, -onne [bʀətɔ̃, ɔn] *adj*, **B~ (ne)** *nm(f)* Breton.

breuvage [bʀœvaʒ] *nm* drink, beverage.

brève [bʀɛv] *V* **bref.**

brevet [bʀəvɛ] *nm (diplôme)* diploma, certificate; *(Scol)* ≃ (G.C.E.) 'O' level; *[pilote]* licence; *(fig: garantie)* guarantee. *(Naut)* **~ de capitaine** master's ticket; **~ (d'invention)** patent; **~ de technicien** vocational training certificate taken at age 16; **~ de technicien supérieur** vocational training certificate taken at age 18. ◆ **brevetable** *adj* patentable. ◆ **breveté, e** *adj invention* patented; *technicien* qualified. ◆ **breveter** (4) *vt* to patent. **faire ~ qch** to take out a patent for sth.

bréviaire [bʀevjɛʀ] *nm (Rel)* breviary; *(fig)* bible.

bribe [bʀib] *nf* bit. **~s de** *conversation* snatches of; *nourriture* scraps of; *fortune* remnants of; **par ~s** in snatches.

bric-à-brac [bʀikabʀak] *nm inv (objets, fig)* bric-a-brac; *(magasin)* junk shop.

bric et de broc [bʀikedbʀɔk] *loc adv*: **de ~** any old how *; *meublé* with bits and pieces.

brick [bʀik] *nm (Naut)* brig.

bricole * [bʀikɔl] *nf (babiole)* trifle; *(cadeau)* token; *(travail)* easy job. **il ne reste que des ~s** there are only a few bits and pieces left; **10 F et des ~s** 10 francs odd *.

bricoler [bʀikɔle] (1) **1** *vi* to do odd jobs; *(passe-temps)* to tinker about. **2** *vt (réparer)* to fix up, mend; *(fabriquer)* to knock up. ◆ **bricolage** *nm* odd jobs; tinkering about; *(réparation)* makeshift repair. **rayon ~** do-it-yourself department. ◆ **bricoleur, -euse** *nm, f* handyman (*ou* woman).

bride [bʀid] *nf* (**a**) *(Équitation)* bridle. **tenir en ~** *cheval, passions* to curb; **laisser la ~ sur le cou** *ou* **col à un cheval** to give a horse his head; **laisser la ~ sur le cou à qn** to leave sb a free hand ; **à ~ abattue** hell for leather. (**b**) *[bonnet]* string; *(en cuir)* strap. ◆ **brider** (1) *vt (lit)* to bridle; *(fig)* to keep in check. **il est bridé dans son costume** his suit is too tight for him; **avoir les yeux bridés** to have slit eyes.

bridge [bʀidʒ(ə)] *nm (jeu, dents)* bridge; *(partie)* game of bridge. ◆ **bridger** (3) *vi* to play bridge. ◆ **bridgeur, -euse** *nm, f* bridge player.

brièvement [bʀijɛvmɑ̃] *adv* briefly. ◆ **brièveté** *nf* brevity.

brigade [bʀigad] *nf (Mil)* brigade; *(Police)* squad; *(équipe)* team. ◆ **brigadier** *nm (Police)* ≃ sergeant; *(Mil)* corporal.

brigand [bʀigɑ̃] *nm* (†) brigand; *(filou)* crook; *(hum: enfant)* rascal. ◆ **brigandage** *nm* brigandage. **(actes de) ~** robbery; *(fig)* **c'est du ~!** it's daylight robbery!

briguer [bʀige] (1) *vt emploi, faveur* to covet; *amitié, suffrages* to solicit.

brillant, e [bʀijɑ̃, ɑ̃t] **1** *adj* (**a**) *(luisant)* shiny; *(étincelant)* sparkling; *couleur* bright. **yeux ~s de fièvre/colère** eyes bright with fever/glittering with anger. (**b**) *personne, idées etc* brilliant. **ce n'est pas ~** it's not outstanding *ou* up to much. **2** *nm* (**a**) *(étincelant)* sparkle; *(luisant)* shine; *[couleur]* brightness; *[étoffe]* sheen; *(par usure)* shine; *(fig) [esprit]* brilliance. **donner du ~ à** to polish up. (**b**) *(diamant)* brilliant. ◆ **brillamment** *adv* brilliantly.

briller [bʀije] (1) *vi* (**a**) *(gén)* to shine; *[diamant]* to sparkle; *[étoile]* to twinkle; *[éclair]* to flash; *[surface humide]* to glisten. **faire ~** *meuble etc* to polish; *(fig) avantages* to paint a glowing picture of; **ses yeux brillaient de joie** his eyes shone *ou* sparkled with joy. (**b**) *[personne]* to shine. **~ par son talent** to be outstandingly talented; **il ne brille pas par le courage** courage is not his strong point; **~ par son absence** to be conspicuous by one's absence.

brimer [bʀime] (1) *vt* to bully; *(Mil, Scol)* to rag, haze *(US)*. **je suis brimé *** I'm being got at *. ◆ **brimade** *nf* vexation. **~(s)** ragging, hazing *(US)*.

brin [bʀɛ̃] *nm* (**a**) *[herbe]* blade; *[muguet]* sprig; *[osier]* twig; *[paille]* wisp. *(fig)* **un beau ~ de fille** a fine-looking girl. (**b**) *[corde]* strand. (**c**) **un ~ de** a touch *ou* grain of; **faire un ~ de causette** to have a bit of a chat *, have a little chat; **faire un ~ de toilette** to have a quick wash; **il n'y a pas un ~ de vent** there isn't a breath of wind; **un ~ embêté */plus grand** a shade worried/bigger. ◆ **brindille** *nf* twig.

bringue * [bʀɛ̃g] *nf* (**a**) binge *. **faire la ~** to go on a binge *. (**b**) *(femme)* **grande ~** beanpole *.

bringuebaler * [bʀɛ̃gbale] (1) **1** *vi [tête, voiture]* to shake about, joggle; *(avec bruit)* to rattle. **2** *vt* to cart about. ◆ **bringuebalant, e** * *adj auto* ramshackle. ◆ **bringuebalement** * *nm* shaking (about); rattle.

brio [bʀijo] *nm* brilliance; *(Mus)* brio. **avec ~** brilliantly.

brioche [bʀijɔʃ] *nf* brioche, bun; *(*: ventre)* paunch. **jambon en ~** ham in a pastry case.

brique [bʀik] **1** *nf (Constr)* brick; (*) a million (old) francs. **2** *adj inv* brick red.

briquer * [bʀike] (1) *vt* to polish up.

briquet [bʀikɛ] *nm* (cigarette) lighter.

bris [bʀi] *nm* breaking. **~ de clôture** breaking-in; **~ de glaces** broken windows.

brisant [bʀizɑ̃] *nm (vague)* breaker; *(écueil)* reef.

brise [bʀiz] *nf* breeze.

briser [bʀize] (1) **1** *vt* (**a**) *(gén)* to break. **~ en mille morceaux** to smash to smithereens; *(lit, fig)* **~ la glace** to break the ice. (**b**) *(fig) cœur, traité etc* to break; *carrière* to ruin, wreck; *volonté, espoir, rebelle* to crush. **d'une voix brisée par l'émotion** in a voice choked with emotion; **ça l'a brisé** it has left him a broken man; **brisé (de fatigue)** worn out, exhausted; **brisé (de chagrin)** broken-hearted. **2** *vi* to break (*avec* with, *contre* against).

3 se ~ *vpr [verre]* to break, smash; *[vagues]* to break (*contre* against); *[résistance]* to break down; *[assaut]* to break up; *[espoir]* to be dashed; *[cœur, voix]* to break.
◆ **brise-** *préf*: ~**fer** *nm inv (enfant)* wrecker ; ~**glace** *nm inv* icebreaker; ~**lames** *nm inv* breakwater; ~**mottes** *nm inv* harrow. ◆ **briseur, -euse** *nm, f*: ~ **de grève** blackleg, strikebreaker. ◆ **brisure** *nf* break.

britannique [bRitanik] **1** *adj* British. **2** *nmf*: **B~** British citizen *ou* person; **les B~s** the British.

broc [bRo] *nm* pitcher.

brocante [bRɔkɑ̃t] *nf* secondhand goods (trade). ◆ **brocanteur, -euse** *nm, f* secondhand (furniture) dealer.

broche [bRɔʃ] *nf (bijou)* brooch; *(Culin)* spit; *(Tech, Méd)* pin. *(Culin)* **faire cuire à la** ~ to spit-roast.

brocher [bRɔʃe] (1) *vt* to bind *(with paper)*. **livre broché** softback, softcover, paperback.

brochet [bRɔʃɛ] *nm (Zool)* pike.

brochette [bRɔʃɛt] *nf (ustensile)* skewer; *(plat)* kebab. *(fig)* ~ **de** *décorations etc* row *ou* string of.

brochure [bRɔʃyR] *nf* (**a**) *(magazine)* brochure, pamphlet. (**b**) *(reliure)* (paper) binding.

brodequin [bRɔdkɛ̃] *nm* (laced) boot.

broder [bRɔde] (1) *vti (lit, fig)* to embroider (*de* with). ~ **sur un sujet** to elaborate on a subject. ◆ **broderie** *nf (art)* embroidery; *(objet)* piece of embroidery. ◆ **brodeur, -euse** *nm, f* embroiderer, embroideress.

brome [bRom] *nm* bromine. ◆ **bromure** *nm* bromide.

bronche [bRɔ̃ʃ] *nf*: ~**s** bronchial tubes; **il est faible des** ~**s** he has a weak chest.

broncher [bRɔ̃ʃe] (1) *vi [cheval]* to stumble. **personne n'osait** ~ * no one dared move a muscle *ou* make a move; **sans** ~ *(sans peur)* without flinching; *(sans protester)* uncomplainingly; *(sans se tromper)* without faltering.

bronchite [bRɔ̃ʃit] *nf*: **la** ~ bronchitis; **une** ~ a bout of bronchitis. ◆ **broncho-pneumonie,** *pl* ~**-**~**s** *nf* broncho-pneumonia.

bronze [bRɔ̃z] *nm (métal, objet)* bronze.

bronzer [bRɔ̃ze] (1) **1** *vt* to tan. **2** *vi* to get a tan. **3 se** ~ *vpr* to sunbathe. ◆ **bronzage** *nm* suntan. ◆ **bronzé, e** *adj* (sun)tanned, sunburnt. ◆ **bronzette** * *nf*: **faire de la** ~ to do a bit of sunbathing.

brosse [bRɔs] *nf* (**a**) *(gén)* brush; *(en chiendent)* scrubbing-brush. ~ **à dents/à habits** *etc* tooth/clothes-brush *etc*; ~ **métallique** wire brush; **donne un coup de** ~ **à ta veste** give your jacket a brush. (**b**) *(Coiffure)* **avoir les cheveux en** ~ to have a crew cut. ◆ **brossage** *nm* brushing. ◆ **brosser** (1) **1** *vt* (**a**) to brush; to scrub. ~ **qn** to brush sb's clothes. (**b**) *(Art, fig)* to paint. **2 se** ~ *vpr* to brush one's clothes. **se** ~ **les dents** to brush one's teeth; **tu peux te** ~! ⁑ you can whistle for it! *

brouette [bRuɛt] *nf* wheelbarrow.

brouhaha [bRuaa] *nm* hubbub.

brouillage [bRujaʒ] *nm (Rad) (intentionnel)* jamming; *(accidentel)* interference.

brouillard [bRujaR] *nm* fog; *(léger)* mist; *(avec fumée)* smog; *(très dense)* peasouper *. ~ **de chaleur** heat haze; ~ **givrant** freezing fog; **il fait du** ~ it's foggy; *(fig)* **être dans le** ~ to be lost.

brouillasser [bRujase] (1) *vi* to drizzle.

brouiller [bRuje] (1) **1** *vt* (**a**) *contour, vue* to blur; *papiers, idées* to muddle up; *message* to scramble. *(fig)* ~ **les pistes** *ou* **cartes** to confuse *ou* cloud the issue. (**b**) *(fâcher)* to set at odds, put on bad terms (*avec* with). **être brouillé avec qn** to have fallen out with sb; **être brouillé avec les dates** to be hopeless at dates. (**c**) *(Rad) (exprès)* to jam; *(par accident)* to cause interference to. **2 se** ~ *vpr* (**a**) to become blurred; to get muddled up. **tout se brouilla dans sa tête** everything became confused in his mind. (**b**) *(se fâcher)* **se** ~ **avec qn** to fall out with sb. (**c**) *[ciel]* to cloud over. **le temps se brouille** the weather is breaking. ◆ **brouille** *nf* quarrel; *(légère)* tiff.

brouillon, -onne [bRujɔ̃, ɔn] **1** *adj (soin)* untidy; *(organisation)* muddle-headed. **élève** ~ careless pupil. **2** *nm, f* muddler. **3** *nm [devoir]* rough copy; *(ébauche)* (rough) draft; *(notes etc)* rough work. **(papier)** ~ rough paper; **prendre qch au** ~ to make a rough copy of sth.

broussaille [bRusaj] *nf*: ~**s** undergrowth, scrub; **en** ~ *cheveux* unkempt, tousled. ◆ **broussailleux, -euse** *adj* bushy, scrubby; *barbe* bushy.

brousse [bRus] *nf*: **la** ~ the bush; *(fig)* **en pleine** ~ * in the middle of nowhere.

brouter [bRute] (1) **1** *vti [ruminant]* to graze; *[lapin]* to nibble. **2** *vi [embrayage]* to judder.

broutille [bRutij] *nf* trifle. **c'est de la** ~ * *(mauvaise qualité)* it's cheap rubbish; *(sans importance)* it's not worth mentioning, it's nothing of any consequence.

broyer [bRwaje] (8) *vt* to grind; *main* to crush. *(fig)* ~ **du noir** to be down in the dumps *. ◆ **broyage** *nm* grinding. ◆ **broyeur, -euse 1** *adj* grinding. **2** *nm* grinder.

bru [bRy] *nf* daughter-in-law.

brugnon [bRyɲɔ̃] *nm* nectarine.

bruine [bRɥin] *nf* drizzle. ◆ **bruiner** (1) *vi* to drizzle.

bruire [bRɥiR] (2) *vi [tissu, vent]* to rustle; *[ruisseau]* to murmur; *[insectes]* to hum. ◆ **bruissement** *nm* rustle; murmur; humming.

bruit [bRɥi] *nm* (**a**) *(gén)* noise; *(sourd)* thud; *(strident)* screech; *[train]* rumble; *[coup de feu]* crack, bang; *[voix, moteur]* sound; *[vaisselle]* clatter. **des** ~**s de pas** footsteps; ~ **de fond** background noise; **on n'entend aucun** ~ you can't hear a sound; **dans un** ~ **de tonnerre** with a thunderous roar; **faire du** ~ to make a noise; **travailler dans le** ~ to work against noise; **sans** ~ noiselessly. (**b**) *(fig)* **beaucoup de** ~ **pour rien** much ado about nothing; **faire grand** ~ **autour de** to make a great to-do about; **il fait plus de** ~ **que de mal** his bark is worse than his bite. (**c**) *(nouvelle)* rumour. **le** ~ **court que** rumour has it that; **faux** ~**s** false rumours. ◆ **bruitage** *nm* sound effects. ◆ **bruiteur** *nm* sound-effects engineer.

brûler [bRyle] (1) **1** *vt* (**a**) *(gén) [acide, flamme]* to burn; *[eau bouillante]* to scald; *[fer à repasser]* to scorch; *[gel]* to nip. **brûlé par le soleil** *(bronzage)* sunburnt, tanned; *(lésion)* burnt by the sun; *herbe* sun-scorched; ~ **ses dernières cartouches** to shoot one's bolt; ~ **ses vaisseaux** to burn one's boats; **brûlé vif** *(accident)* burnt alive *ou* to death; *(supplice)* burnt at the stake; **grand brûlé** badly burnt person. (**b**) *café* to roast. (**c**) *électricité* to burn, use. **ils ont brûlé tout leur bois** they've burnt up all their wood; ~ **la chandelle par les deux bouts** to burn the candle at both ends. (**d**) *(Aut)* ~ **un stop** to ignore a stop sign; ~ **un feu rouge** to go through a red light, run a red light *(US)*; ~ **une étape** to cut out a stop; *(fig)* ~ **les étapes** *(réussite)* to shoot ahead; *(précipitation)* to take short cuts. (**e**) *(sensation)* to burn. **les yeux me brûlent** my eyes are smarting; **j'ai la figure qui (me) brûle** my face is burning; **l'argent lui brûle les doigts** money burns a hole in his pocket; **le désir de l'aventure le brûlait** he was burning for adventure.
2 *vi* (**a**) *[lumière, feu]* to burn; *[maison]* to be on fire; *(Culin)* to burn. **ça sent le brûlé** *(lit)* there's a smell of burning; *(fig)* trouble's brewing; **goût de brûlé** burnt taste. (**b**) *[front, objet]* to be burning (hot); *[liquide]* to be scalding. **ça brûle** you'll burn yourself, you'll get burnt; *(jeu)* **tu brûles!** you're

getting hot! (**c**) ~ **(d'envie) de faire qch** to be burning to do sth; ~ **d'impatience** to seethe with impatience; ~ **(d'amour) pour qn** to be madly in love with sb.
3 se ~ *vpr* to burn o.s.; *(s'ébouillanter)* to scald o.s. **se** ~ **la cervelle** to blow one's brains out. ◆ **brûlant, e** *adj objet* burning (hot); *plat, liquide* piping hot; *soleil* scorching; *regard, pages* fiery; *sujet* ticklish. ~ **(de fièvre)** burning (with fever); **c'est d'une actualité** ~**e** it's the burning question of the hour. ◆ **brûle-parfum** *nm inv* perfume burner. ◆ **brûle-pourpoint** *adv*: **à** ~ point-blank. ◆ **brûleur** *nm* burner. ◆ **brûlure** *nf (lésion)* burn; *(sensation)* burning sensation. ~ **(d'eau bouillante)** scald; ~**s d'estomac** heartburn.

brume [bʀym] *nf (gén)* mist; *(dense)* fog; *(légère)* haze. ◆ **brumeux, -euse** *adj* misty; foggy; *(fig)* obscure, hazy.

brumisateur [bʀymizatœʀ] *nm* spray, atomiser.

brun, e [bʀœ̃, yn] **1** *adj (gén)* brown; *cheveux, tabac* dark; *peau* swarthy; *(bronzé)* tanned, brown. **il est** ~ he's dark-haired; ~ **roux** (dark) auburn. **2** *nm (couleur)* brown; *(homme)* dark-haired man. **3** *nf (bière)* brown ale; *(femme)* brunette. ◆ **brunâtre** *adj* brownish. ◆ **brunette** *nf* brunette. ◆ **brunir** (2) **1** *vi [personne]* to get sunburnt; *[cheveux]* to go darker. **2** *vt peau* to tan; *cheveux* to darken.

brushing [bʀœʃiŋ] *nm* blow-dry. **faire un** ~ **à qn** to blow-dry sb's hair.

brusque [bʀysk(ə)] *adj (sec)* abrupt, blunt; *(soudain)* abrupt, sudden; *virage* sharp. ◆ **brusquement** *adv* abruptly; bluntly; suddenly; sharply. ◆ **brusquer** (1) *vt (gén)* to rush. **attaque brusquée** sudden attack. ◆ **brusquerie** *nf* abruptness, bluntness.

brut, e[1] [bʀyt] **1** *adj* (**a**) *diamant* rough; *pétrole* crude; *sucre* unrefined; *soie, métal* raw; *champagne* brut; *fait, idée* crude, raw. **à l'état** ~ in the rough. (**b**) *(Comm)* gross. **ça fait 100 F/kg** ~ that makes 100 francs/kg gross. **2** *nm* crude oil. ~ **lourd** heavy crude.

brutal, e, *mpl* **-aux** [bʀytal, o] *adj* (**a**) *caractère* rough, brutal; *instinct* savage; *jeu* rough. **force** ~**e** brute force. (**b**) *réponse, franchise* blunt; *vérité* plain; *réalité* stark. (**c**) *mort* sudden; *coup* brutal. ◆ **brutalement** *adv* roughly; brutally; bluntly; plainly; suddenly. ◆ **brutaliser** (1) *vt personne* to bully, manhandle; *machine* to ill-treat. ◆ **brutalité** *nf* brutality; roughness; suddenness; *(acte)* brutality. ~**s** *(Sport)* rough play; ~**s policières** police brutality. ◆ **brute**[2] *nf (brutal)* brute, animal; *(grossier)* boor, lout. **taper sur qch comme une** ~ * to bash away at sth *; ~ **épaisse** * brutish lout; **grosse** ~**!** * big bully!

Bruxelles [bʀysɛl] *n* Brussels.

bruyant, e [bʀɥijɑ̃, ɑ̃t] *adj* noisy. ◆ **bruyamment** *adv* noisily.

bruyère [bʀyjɛʀ] *nf (plante)* heather; *(terrain)* heath(land). **pipe en (racine de)** ~ briar pipe.

bu, e [by] *ptp de* **boire.**

buanderie [bɥɑ̃dʀi] *nf* wash house, laundry.

Bucarest [bykaʀɛst] *n* Bucharest.

bûche [byʃ] *nf* (**a**) log. ~ **de Noël** Yule log. (**b**) (*) *(lourdaud)* blockhead *; *(chute)* fall. **ramasser une** ~ to come a cropper *.

bûcher[1] [byʃe] *nm* (**a**) *(remise)* woodshed. (**b**) *(funéraire)* (funeral) pyre; *(supplice)* stake.

bûcher[2] * [byʃe] (1) **1** *vt* to swot up *. **2** *vi* to swot *.

bûcheron [byʃʀɔ̃] *nm* woodcutter, lumberjack.

bûcheur, -euse * [byʃœʀ, øz] **1** *adj* hard-working. **2** *nm, f* slogger *, grind * *(US)*.

bucolique [bykɔlik] *adj, nf* bucolic.

Budapest [bydapɛst] *n* Budapest.

budget [bydʒɛ] *nm* budget. **vacances pour petits** ~**s** *ou* ~**s modestes** low-cost *ou* budget holidays. ◆ **budgétaire** *adj (gén)* budgetary. **année** ~ financial year.

buée [bɥe] *nf* mist, steam, condensation. **couvert de** ~ misted up, steamed up; **faire de la** ~ to make steam.

Buenos Aires [bwenɔzɛʀ] *n* Buenos Aires.

buffet [byfɛ] *nm* (**a**) *(meuble)* sideboard. ~ **de cuisine** kitchen dresser. (**b**) *[réception]* buffet. ~ **(de gare)** station buffet. (**c**) (*: *ventre)* belly *.

buffle [byfl(ə)] *nm* buffalo.

buggy [bygi] *nm (Aut)* buggy.

buis [bɥi] *nm (arbre)* box tree; *(bois)* box(wood).

buisson [bɥisɔ̃] *nm* bush.

bulbe [bylb(ə)] *nm (Bot)* bulb; *(Archit)* onion-shaped dome. *(Anat)* ~ **pileux** hair bulb; ~ **rachidien** medulla. ◆ **bulbeux, -euse** *adj* bulbous.

Bulgarie [bylgaʀi] *nf* Bulgaria. ◆ **bulgare** *adj, nm,* **B**~ *nmf* Bulgarian.

bulldozer [buldozœʀ] *nm* bulldozer.

bulle [byl] *nf* (**a**) bubble; *[bande dessinée]* balloon. **faire des** ~**s** to blow bubbles. (**b**) *(Rel)* bull.

bulletin [byltɛ̃] **1** *nm (communiqué, magazine)* bulletin; *(formulaire)* form; *(certificat)* certificate; *(billet)* ticket; *(Scol)* report; *(Pol)* ballot paper. **2** : ~ **météorologique** weather forecast; ~**-réponse** *nm, pl* ~**s-**~**s** *(dans un concours)* entry form; ~ **de salaire** pay-slip; ~ **de vote par correspondance** postal vote, absentee ballot *(US)*.

bungalow [bœ̃galo] *nm (Inde)* bungalow; *[motel]* (holiday) chalet.

buraliste [byʀalist(ə)] *nmf [tabac]* tobacconist, tobacco dealer *(US)*; *[poste]* clerk.

bureau, *pl* ~**x** [byʀo] **1** *nm* (**a**) *(meuble)* desk; *(chambre)* study; *[firme]* office. **heures de** ~ office hours; **nos** ~**x seront fermés** the office will be closed. (**b**) *(section)* department; *(comité)* committee; *(exécutif)* board. **2** : ~ **de change** bureau de change; ~ **d'études** research unit; *(indépendant)* research consultancy; ~ **de location** booking *ou* box office; ~ **des objets trouvés** lost property *ou* lost and found *(US)* office; ~ **de placement** employment agency; ~ **de poste** post office; ~ **de renseignements** information service; ~ **de tabac** tobacconist's (shop), tobacco *ou* smoke shop *(US)*; ~ **de vote** polling station. ◆ **bureautique** *nf* office automation.

bureaucrate [byʀokʀat] *nmf* bureaucrat. ◆ **bureaucratie** *nf (péj) (gén)* bureaucracy; *(employés)* officialdom. **toute cette** ~ **m'agace** all this red tape gets on my nerves. ◆ **bureaucratique** *adj* bureaucratic.

burette [byʀɛt] *nf (Culin, Rel)* cruet; *[mécanicien]* oilcan.

burin [byʀɛ̃] *nm (Art)* burin; *(Tech)* (cold) chisel. ◆ **buriné, e** *adj visage* seamed, craggy.

burlesque [byʀlɛsk(ə)] *adj (Théât)* burlesque; *(comique)* comical; *(ridicule)* ludicrous.

Burundi [buʀundi] *nm* Burundi.

bus [bys] *nm (Aut, Ordin)* bus.

buse[1] [byz] *nf (Orn)* buzzard.

buse[2] [byz] *nf (tuyau) (gén)* pipe; *(Tech)* duct.

busqué, e [byske] *adj*: **nez** ~ hooked nose.

buste [byst(ə)] *nm (torse)* chest; *(seins, sculpture)* bust.

but [by] *nm* (**a**) *(destination, objectif)* goal. **errer sans** ~ to wander aimlessly about; **il a pour** ~ **de faire** he is aiming to do; **aller droit au** ~ to go straight to the point; **nous touchons au** ~ the end *ou* our goal is in sight; **nous sommes encore loin du** ~ we still have a long way to go; **à** ~ **lucratif** profit-making, profit-seeking. (**b**) *(intention)* aim, purpose, object; *(raison)* reason. **dans le** ~ **de faire**

with the aim of doing; **le ~ de l'opération** the object *ou* point of the operation. (**c**) *(Ftbl)* goal; *(Tir)* target, mark. (**d**) **de ~ en blanc** *demander* point-blank; *répondre* off the cuff.

butane [bytan] *nm (Chim)* butane; *(en bouteille)* calor gas ®.

buter [byte] (1) **1** *vi* (**a**) to stumble, trip. ~ **contre** *(trébucher)* to stumble over; *(cogner)* to bump into; *(s'appuyer)* to rest against; *(fig) difficulté* to come up against; **nous butons sur ce problème** we are stuck over this problem. (**b**) *(Ftbl)* to score a goal. **2** *vt (irriter)* to antagonize; (*: *tuer)* to bump off *. **3 se** ~ *vpr* to dig one's heels in. ◆ **buté, e**[1] *adj* stubborn, obstinate. ◆ **butée**[2] *nf (Archit)* abutment; *(Tech)* stop. ◆ **buteur** *nm (Ftbl)* striker ; (*: *tueur)* killer.

butin [bytɛ̃] *nm [armée]* spoils; *[voleur]* loot; *(fig)* booty.

butiner [bytine] (1) *vi* to gather nectar.

butoir [bytwaʀ] *nm (Tech)* stop.

butor [bytɔʀ] *nm (péj)* boor, lout.

butte [byt] *nf* mound, hillock. ~ **de tir** butts ; ~-**témoin** outlier; *(fig)* **être en ~ à** to be exposed to.

buvable [byvabl(ə)] *adj* drinkable; *(Méd)* to be taken orally.

buvard [byvaʀ] *nm (papier)* blotting paper; *(sous-main)* blotter.

buvette [byvɛt] *nf (café)* refreshment room; *(en plein air)* refreshment stall.

buveur, -euse [byvœʀ, øz] *nm, f (ivrogne)* drinker; *[café]* customer. ~ **de bière** beer drinker.

Byzance [bizɑ̃s] *n* Byzantium.

C

C, c [se] *nm (lettre)* C, c.
c' [s] *abrév de* **ce.**
ça [sa] *pron dém* = **cela** *(dans la langue courante).*
çà [sa] *adv*: ~ **et là** here and there.
cabale [kabal] *nf* cabal. ◆ **cabalistique** *adj* cabalistic.
caban [kabɑ̃] *nm* reefer jacket.
cabane [kaban] *nf (hutte)* cabin; *(remise)* shed; *(péj)* shack. *(*: prison)* **en** ~ in (the) clink ⁑; ~ **à lapins** *(lit)* rabbit hutch; *(fig)* box. ◆ **cabanon** *nm (maison)* cottage, cabin; *(remise)* shed.
cabaret [kabaʀɛ] *nm* night club, cabaret; *(Hist: café)* inn. ◆ **cabaretier, -ière** *nm, f* innkeeper.
cabas [kabɑ] *nm* shopping bag.
cabestan [kabɛstɑ̃] *nm* capstan.
cabillaud [kabijo] *nm* (fresh) cod *(pl inv).*
cabine [kabin] *nf (Espace, Naut)* cabin; *[avion]* cockpit; *[grue]* cab; *[piscine]* cubicle; *(Audio-visuel)* booth. ~ **d'ascenseur** lift (cage), (elevator) car *(US)*; ~ **de bain** bathing hut; ~ **d'essayage/de projection** fitting/projection room; ~ **de téléphérique** cablecar; ~ **téléphonique** phone box *ou* booth.
cabinet [kabinɛ] **1** *nm* (**a**) *(toilettes)* ~**s** toilet. (**b**) *[médecin]* surgery, consulting-room; *[notaire]* office; *[immobilier]* agency; *(clientèle)* practice. (**c**) *(gouvernement)* cabinet; *[ministre]* advisers. (**d**) *[exposition]* exhibition room. (**e**) *(meuble)* cabinet. **2** : ~ **d'affaires** business consultancy; ~ **d'aisances** † water closet †, lavatory ; ~**-conseil** consulting firm; ~ **particulier** private dining room; ~ **de toilette** bathroom; ~ **de travail** study.
câble [kɑbl(ə)] *nm (gén)* cable. ~ **d'amarrage** mooring line. ◆ **câblage** *nm* cabling. ◆ **câbler** (1) *vt* to cable. *(TV)* ~ **un pays** to put cable television into a country.
caboche * [kabɔʃ] *nf* head, nut ⁑. ◆ **cabochard, e** * *adj* pigheaded *.
cabosser [kabɔse] (1) *vt* to dent.
cabot [kabo] *nm (péj: chien)* dog, cur *(péj)*, mutt.
cabotage [kabɔtaʒ] *nm* coastal navigation. **faire du** ~ to ply along the coast. ◆ **caboteur** *nm* tramp, coaster.
cabotin, e [kabɔtɛ̃, in] **1** *adj (péj)* theatrical. **2** *nm, f (péj)* show-off; *(acteur)* ham (actor). ◆ **cabotinage** *nm* showing off; ham acting. ◆ **cabotiner** (1) *vi* to show off.
cabrer [kɑbʀe] (1) **1** *vt cheval* to make rear up; *avion* to nose up. ~ **qn** to put sb's back up ; ~ **qn contre** to turn sb against. **2 se** ~ *vpr* to rear up; to nose up; *[personne]* to rebel (*contre* against).
cabri [kabʀi] *nm (Zool)* kid.
cabriole [kabʀijɔl] *nf [enfant, chevreau]* caper; *[gymnaste]* somersault. ◆ **cabrioler** (1) *vi* to caper about.
cabriolet [kabʀijɔlɛ] *nm (Hist)* cabriolet; *(décapotable)* convertible.
caca * [kaka] *nm*: **faire** ~ to do a job *; **marcher dans du** ~ to step in some muck; *(couleur)* ~ **d'oie** greenish-yellow.
cacah(o)uète [kakawɛt] *nf* peanut.
cacao [kakao] *nm* cocoa.
cacatoès [kakatɔɛs] *nm* cockatoo.
cachalot [kaʃalo] *nm* sperm whale.
cache [kaʃ] **1** *nm (gén)* card; *(Phot)* mask. **2** *nf* hiding place; *(pour butin)* cache.
cachemire [kaʃmiʀ] *nm (laine)* cashmere; *(dessin)* paisley pattern.
cacher [kaʃe] (1) **1** *vt (gén)* to hide, conceal. ~ **son jeu** *(lit)* to keep one's cards up; *(fig)* to hide one's game; **tu me caches la lumière** you're in my light; ~ **son âge** to keep one's age a secret; **il n'a pas caché que** he made no secret (of the fact) that. **2 se** ~ *vpr (gén)* to hide; *[évadé]* to be in hiding; *[maison, défaut]* to be concealed. **va te** ~! get out of my sight!; **faire qch sans se** ~ to do sth openly, do sth without hiding *ou* concealing the fact. ◆ **caché, e** *adj (gén)* hidden; *(à l'écart)* secluded; *(secret)* secret. ◆ **cache-cache** *nm inv (lit, fig)* hide-and-seek. ◆ **cache-col** *nm inv ou* ◆ **cache-nez** *nm inv* scarf, muffler. ◆ **cache-pot** *nm inv* flowerpot holder. ◆ **cache-prise** *nm inv* socket cover. ◆ **cache-radiateur** *nm inv* radiator cover. ◆ **cache-tampon** *nm inv* hunt-the-thimble.
cachet [kaʃɛ] *nm* (**a**) *(Pharm)* tablet. (**b**) *(timbre)* stamp; *(sceau)* seal. ~ **(de la poste)** postmark. (**c**) *(fig: caractère)* style, character. **robe qui a du** ~ stylish dress; **un** ~ **d'originalité** the stamp *ou* mark of originality. (**d**) *(rétribution)* fee. ◆ **cacheter** (4) *vt* to seal.
cachette [kaʃɛt] *nf* hiding-place. **en** ~ secretly; **en** ~ **de qn** unknown to sb.
cachot [kaʃo] *nm (cellule)* dungeon; *(punition)* solitary confinement.
cachotterie [kaʃɔtʀi] *nf* mystery. **faire des** ~**s** to be secretive, make mysteries about things. ◆ **cachottier, -ière** *adj* secretive.
cacophonie [kakɔfɔni] *nf* cacophony.
cactus [kaktys] *nm inv* cactus.
cadastre [kadastʀ(ə)] *nm (registre)* cadastre; *(service)* cadastral survey. ◆ **cadastral, e,** *mpl* **-aux** *adj* cadastral.
cadavre [kadɑvʀ(ə)] *nm* corpse, (dead) body ; *(*: bouteille)* empty (bottle). ◆ **cadavérique** *adj* deathly pale.
caddie [kadi] *nm (Golf)* caddie; ® *(chariot)* (supermarket) trolley.
cadeau, *pl* ~**x** [kado] *nm* present, gift (*de qn* from sb). ~ **de Noël** Christmas present; ~ **publicitaire** free gift, give away * *(US)*; **faire** ~ **de qch à qn** *(offrir)* to give sb sth as a present; *(laisser)* to let sb keep sth, give sth away (to sb); *(fig)* **ils ne font pas de** ~**x** they don't let you off lightly.
cadenas [kadnɑ] *nm* padlock. ◆ **cadenasser** (1) *vt* to padlock.
cadence [kadɑ̃s] *nf [vers, chant]* rhythm; *[tir, production]* rate; *[marche]* pace. **en** ~ *(régulièrement)* rhythmically; *(en mesure)* in time. ◆ **cadencé, e** *adj* rhythmic(al). ◆ **cadencer** (3) *vt* to give rhythm to.
cadet, -ette [kadɛ, ɛt] **1** *adj (entre 2)* younger; *(plus de 2)* youngest. **2** *nm, f* (**a**) youngest child (*ou* boy *ou* girl). **mon (frère/fils)** ~ my younger brother/son; **il est mon** ~ **de 2 ans** he's 2 years younger than me, he's 2 years my junior; **c'est le** ~ **de**

mes soucis it's the least of my worries. (**b**) *(Sport)* 15-17 year-old players. **3** *nm (Hist Mil)* cadet.

cadrage [kadʀaʒ] *nm (Phot)* centring (of image).

cadran [kadʀɑ̃] *nm (gén)* dial; *[baromètre]* face. ~ **solaire** sundial.

cadre [kɑdʀ(ə)] *nm* (**a**) *(chassis)* frame; *(caisse)* crate; *[radio]* frame antenna; *(sur formulaire)* space, box. (**b**) *(décor)* setting; *(entourage)* surroundings. **le ~ étroit de** the strait jacket *ou* the narrow confines of; ~ **de vie** (living) environment. (**c**) *(limites)* scope; *(contexte)* framework. **dans le ~ de** *fonctions* within the scope *ou* limits of; *festival* within the context *ou* framework of; **respecter le ~ de la légalité** to remain within (the bounds of) the law. (**d**) *(chef)* executive, manager; *(Mil)* officer. **les ~s** the managerial staff ; ~ **supérieur/moyen** senior/middle manager *ou* executive; **les ~s moyens** middle management, middle-grade managers *(US)*. (**e**) *(personnel)* **figurer sur les ~s** to be (placed) on the books; **rayé des ~s** *(licencié)* dismissed; *(libéré)* discharged.

cadrer [kɑdʀe] (1) **1** *vi* to tally (*avec* with), conform (*avec* to, with). **2** *vt (Phot)* to centre.

caduc, caduque [kadyk] *adj (Bot)* deciduous; *(Jur)* null and void; *(périmé)* outmoded, obsolete.

cafard[1] [kafaʀ] *nm* (**a**) *(insecte)* cockroach. (**b**) (*) **accès de** ~ fit of the blues *; **avoir le** ~ to have the blues *, be feeling blue *; **ça lui donne le** ~ that gets him down *. ◆ **cafardeux, -euse** *adj personne* feeling blue *; *tempérament* gloomy.

cafard[2], **e** [kafaʀ, aʀd(ə)] *nm, f (péj)* sneak. ◆ **cafardage** *nm* sneaking. ◆ **cafarder** (1) *vi* to sneak.

café [kafe] *nm (produit, moment)* coffee; *(lieu)* café. ~ **au lait** *(nm)* white coffee, coffee with milk ; *(adj inv)* coffee-coloured; ~ **liégeois** coffee ice cream *(with whipped cream topping)*; ~ **soluble** instant coffee. ◆ **caféier** *nm* coffee tree. ◆ **cafetier, -ière** **1** *nm, f* café-owner. **2** *nf (pot)* coffeepot ; *(percolateur)* coffee-maker; (⁑: *tête)* nut ⁑.

cafouiller * [kafuje] (1) *vi [organisation, discussion]* to be in a shambles; *[équipe]* to go to pieces; *[candidat]* to flounder; *[moteur]* to work in fits and starts. ~ **(avec) le ballon** to fumble the ball. ◆ **cafouillage** * *nm* muddle, shambles *(sg)*. ◆ **cafouilleur, -euse** * **1** *adj* shambolic *. **2** *nm, f* muddler.

cage [kaʒ] *nf (gén, Anat, Min)* cage; *(Tech)* casing; *(Sport: buts)* goal. ~ **d'ascenseur** lift *ou* elevator *(US)* shaft; ~ **d'escalier** stairwell; ~ **à lapins** *(lit)* (rabbit) hutch; *(péj)* box.

cageot [kaʒo] *nm [légumes, fruits]* crate.

cagibi [kaʒibi] *nm* box room.

cagneux, -euse [kaɲø, øz] *adj* knock-kneed. **genoux** ~ knock knees.

cagnotte [kaɲɔt] *nf (caisse commune)* kitty; (*: *économies)* nest egg.

cagoule [kagul] *nf [moine]* cowl; *[pénitent, bandit]* hood; *[enfant]* balaclava.

cahier [kaje] *nm (Scol)* notebook, exercise book; *(revue)* journal. ~ **de brouillon** roughbook, notebook (for rough drafts) *(US)*; ~ **de textes** homework notebook; ~ **de travaux pratiques** lab book.

cahin-caha * [kaɛ̃kaa] *adv*: **aller** ~ *[vie, marcheur]* to jog along; *[santé]* to be so-so *.

cahot [kao] *nm* jolt, bump. ◆ **cahotant, e** *adj route* bumpy, rough; *véhicule* bumpy, jolting. ◆ **cahoter** (1) **1** *vt* to jolt. **cahoté par la guerre** buffeted about by the war. **2** *vi* to jog *ou* trundle along.

cahute [kayt] *nf* shack.

caïd [kaid] *nm (meneur)* big chief *; (*: *as)* ace (*en* at). **le ~ de l'équipe** * the star of the team.

caillasse [kajas] *nf* loose stones.

caille [kɑj] *nf* quail.

caillebotis [kɑjbɔti] *nm* duckboard.

cailler [kɑje] (1) **1** *vt*: **(faire)** ~ to curdle. **2** *vi*, **se** ~ *vpr* (**a**) *[lait]* to curdle; *[sang]* to clot. (**b**) (⁑: *avoir froid)* to be cold. **ça caille** it's freezing. ◆ **caillot** *nm* (blood) clot.

caillou, *pl* ~**x** [kaju] *nm (gén)* stone; *(petit galet)* pebble; *(grosse pierre)* boulder; (*: *tête)* head, nut ⁑; (*: *diamant)* stone. **il a un ~ à la place du cœur** he has a heart of stone; **il n'a pas un poil sur le ~ *** he's as bald as a coot *ou* an egg. ◆ **caillouteux, -euse** *adj* stony; pebbly. ◆ **cailloutis** *nm (gén)* gravel; *[route]* (road) metal.

caïman [kaimɑ̃] *nm* cayman, caiman.

Caire [kɛʀ] *n*: **le** ~ Cairo.

caisse [kɛs] **1** *nf* (**a**) *(boîte)* box; *(cageot)* crate; *[horloge]* casing; *[véhicule]* bodywork. (**b**) *(machine)* cash register, till; *(portable)* cashbox. **avoir de l'argent en** ~ to have ready cash; **faire la** ~ to do the till; **les ~s de l'État** the coffers of the state; **voler la** ~ to steal the contents of the till, steal the takings. (**c**) *[boutique]* cashdesk; *[banque]* cashier's desk; *[supermarché]* check-out. **passer à la** ~ *(lit)* to go to the cashdesk; *(payé)* to collect one's money; *(licencié)* to get paid off. (**d**) *(bureau)* office; *(organisme)* fund. (**e**) *(Mus)* drum. **2** : ~ **d'emballage** packing case; ~ **enregistreuse** cash register; ~ **d'épargne** savings bank; ~ **noire** secret funds; ~ **à outils** toolbox; ~ **de résonance** resonance chamber; ~ **de retraite** superannuation *ou* pension fund; *(Scol)* ~ **de solidarité** school fund. ◆ **caissette** *nf* (small) box. ◆ **caissier, -ière** *nm, f (gén)* cashier; *[banque]* teller; *[supermarché]* check-out assistant *ou* clerk *(US)*; *[cinéma]* box-office assistant.

caisson [kɛsɔ̃] *nm (Archit, Mil, Tech)* caisson. **le mal des ~s** caisson disease, the bends *.

cajoler [kaʒɔle] (1) *vt* to cuddle, make a fuss of. ◆ **cajolerie** *nf* cuddle. **faire des ~s à qn** to cuddle sb, make a fuss of sb.

cake [kɛk] *nm* fruit cake.

calage [kalaʒ] *nm [meuble]* wedging; *[roue]* chocking.

calamité [kalamite] *nf (malheur)* calamity. **quelle ~!** * what a calamity *ou* disaster! ◆ **calamiteux, -euse** *adj* calamitous.

calandre [kalɑ̃dʀ(ə)] *nf [automobile]* radiator grill; *(machine)* calender.

calcaire [kalkɛʀ] **1** *adj (gén)* chalky; *eau* hard; *(Géol)* limestone. **2** *nm (Géol)* limestone; *[bouilloire]* fur, sediment *(US)*.

calciner [kalsine] (1) *vt (Tech)* to calcine; *rôti* to burn to a cinder. ◆ **calciné, e** *adj débris* charred, burned to ashes. ~ **par le soleil** scorched by the sun.

calcium [kalsjɔm] *nm* calcium.

calcul [kalkyl] *nm* (**a**) *(gén, fig)* calculation; *(exercice scolaire)* sum. **erreur de** ~ miscalculation; **d'après mes ~s** by my reckoning, according to my calculations; **par** ~ with an ulterior motive, out of (calculated) self-interest. (**b**) *(discipline)* **le** ~ arithmetic; ~ **des probabilités** probability theory; **le ~ intégral** integral calculus. (**c**) *(Méd)* stone, calculus. ◆ **calculateur, -trice** **1** *adj (intéressé)* calculating. **2** *nm* computer. ~ **numérique/analogique** digital/analog computer. **3** *nf* calculator. ~ **de poche** hand-held *ou* pocket calculator, minicalculator. **4** *nm, f (personne)* calculator. ◆ **calculer** (1) **1** *vt prix, quantité, conséquences* to calculate, work out; *geste, effets* to plan, calculate. ~ **son élan** to judge one's run-up; ~ **son coup** to plan one's move (carefully); **ils avaient calculé leur coup** they had it all figured out *; **avec une gentillesse calculée** with calculated kindness; **tout bien calculé** everything *ou* all things considered. **2** *vi (Math)* to calculate; *(économiser)* to count the pennies. ◆**calculette** *nf* hand-held *ou* pocket calculator, minicalculator.

cale [kal] *nf* (**a**) *(soute)* hold; *(plan incliné)* slipway. ~ **de radoub/sèche** graving/dry dock. (**b**) *[meuble]* wedge; *(Golf)* wedge; *[roue]* chock, wedge.

calé, e * [kale] *adj personne* bright; *problème* tough.

calebasse [kalbɑs] *nf* calabash.

calèche [kalɛʃ] *nf* barouche.

caleçon [kalsɔ̃] *nm* underpants, shorts *(US)*. ~**(s) de bain** bathing trunks.

calembour [kalɑ̃buʀ] *nm* pun.

calendes [kalɑ̃d] *nfpl (Antiq)* calends.

calendrier [kalɑ̃dʀije] *nm (jours et mois)* calendar; *(programme)* timetable.

cale-pied [kalpje] *nm inv [vélo]* toe clip.

calepin [kalpɛ̃] *nm* notebook.

caler [kale] (1) **1** *vt* (**a**) *meuble* to wedge; *roue* to chock, wedge; *malade, pile de livres* to prop up. **ça vous cale l'estomac** * it fills you up; **se ~ dans un fauteuil** to settle o.s. comfortably in an armchair. (**b**) *moteur* to stall. **2** *vi* (**a**) *[véhicule]* to stall. (**b**) *(*: abandonner)* to give up.

calfeutrer [kalføtʀe] (1) **1** *vt* to (make) draughtproof. **2 se ~** *vpr* to make o.s. snug. ◆**calfeutrage** *nm* draughtproofing.

calibre [kalibʀ(ə)] *nm* (**a**) *[fusil]* calibre, bore; *[tuyau, instrument de musique]* bore; *[obus]* calibre; *[câble]* diameter; *[œufs, fruits]* grade; *[boule]* size. (**b**) *(instrument)* gauge; *(fig: envergure)* calibre. ◆**calibrer** (1) *vt œufs* to grade; *(Tech)* to gauge.

calice [kalis] *nm (Rel)* chalice; *(Bot)* calyx.

calicot [kaliko] *nm (tissu)* calico; *(banderole)* banner.

calife [kalif] *nm* caliph.

califourchon [kalifuʀʃɔ̃] *nm*: **à ~** astride.

câlin, e [kɑlɛ̃, in] **1** *adj enfant, chat* cuddly; *mère, ton* tender, loving. **2** *nm* cuddle. ◆**câliner** (1) *vt* to fondle, cuddle. ◆**câlinerie** *nf* tenderness. ~**s** caresses.

calleux, -euse [kalø, øz] *adj peau* horny, callous.

calligramme [kaligʀam] *nm (poème)* calligramme.

calligraphier [kaligʀafje] (7) *vt* to write artistically.

callosité [kalozite] *nf* callosity.

calmant, e [kalmɑ̃, ɑ̃t] **1** *adj (pour les nerfs)* tranquillizing; *(contre la douleur)* painkilling; *paroles* soothing. **2** *nm* tranquillizer; painkiller.

calmar [kalmaʀ] *nm* squid.

calme [kalm(ə)] **1** *adj (gén)* quiet, calm; *(paisible)* peaceful; *nuit, air* still. **rester ~** to remain calm *ou* cool. **2** *nm* quietness, peacefulness; stillness; calm, calmness; *(sang-froid)* sangfroid. *(tranquillité)* **le ~** quietness, peace (and quiet); **du ~!** *(restez tranquille)* quieten down!; *(pas de panique)* keep cool! *ou* calm!; **ramener le ~** *(arranger les choses)* to calm things down; *(rétablir l'ordre)* to restore order; *(Naut)* ~ **plat** dead calm; *(fig)* **c'est le ~ plat** things are at a standstill. ◆**calmement** *adv agir* calmly; *se dérouler* quietly.

calmer [kalme] (1) **1** *vt personne* to calm (down); *querelle* to quieten down; *révolte, flots* to calm; *douleur, nerfs, crainte, fièvre* to soothe; *impatience, désir* to curb; *faim* to appease; *soif* to quench. **2 se ~** *vpr [personne, mer]* to calm down; *[discussion]* to quieten down; *[douleur, faim, inquiétude]* to ease; *[fièvre, colère, ardeur]* to subside.

calomnier [kalɔmnje] (7) *vt* to slander; *(par écrit)* to libel. ◆**calomniateur, -trice** *nm, f* slanderer; libeller. ◆**calomnie** *nf* slander; libel. **dire des ~s** to make slanderous remarks. ◆**calomnieux, -euse** *adj* slanderous; libellous.

calorie [kalɔʀi] *nf* calorie. ◆**calorifique** *adj* calorific.

calorifuger [kalɔʀifyʒe] (3) *vt* to lag, insulate. ◆**calorifuge** **1** *adj* (heat-)insulating. **2** *nm* insulating material. ◆**calorifugeage** *nm* lagging, insulation.

calot [kalo] *nm* forage cap, overseas cap *(US)*.

calotte [kalɔt] *nf (bonnet)* skullcap; *(partie supérieure)* crown; *(*: gifle)* slap. **la ~ des cieux** the vault of heaven; ~ **glaciaire** icecap.

calque [kalk(ə)] *nm (dessin)* tracing; *(papier)* tracing paper; *(fig)* exact copy; *(Ling)* calque, loan translation. ◆**calquer** (1) *vt* to trace; to copy exactly.

calumet [kalymɛ] *nm* calumet. **le ~ de la paix** the pipe of peace.

calvaire [kalvɛʀ] *nm (croix, peinture)* Calvary; *(épreuve)* suffering, martyrdom. *(Rel)* **Le C~** Calvary.

calvinisme [kalvinism(ə)] *nm* Calvinism. ◆**calviniste** *adj, nmf* Calvinist.

calvitie [kalvisi] *nf* baldness.

camaïeu [kamajø] *nm* monochrome.

camarade [kamaʀad] *nmf* companion, friend, mate *; *(Pol)* comrade. ~ **d'atelier/d'école** workmate/schoolmate. ◆**camaraderie** *nf* good-companionship.

Camargue [kamaʀg] *nf*: **la ~** the Camargue.

Cambodge [kɑ̃bɔdʒ] *nm* Kampuchea, Cambodia †. ◆**cambodgien, -ienne** *adj*, **C~(ne)** *nm(f)* Kampuchean, Cambodian †.

cambouis [kɑ̃bwi] *nm* dirty oil *ou* grease.

cambrer [kɑ̃bʀe] (1) **1** *vt pied, dos* to arch; *bois* to bend; *métal* to curve. **2 se ~** *vpr* to arch one's back. ◆**cambré, e** *adj reins* arched; *pied, chaussures* with a high instep.

cambrioler [kɑ̃bʀijɔle] (1) *vt* to burgle, burglarize *(US)*. ◆**cambriolage** *nm* burglary. ◆**cambrioleur** *nm* burglar.

cambrousse ‡ [kɑ̃bʀus] *nf* country. **en pleine ~** in the middle of nowhere, out in the sticks *.

cambrure [kɑ̃bʀyʀ] *nf* (**a**) *[poutre, reins]* curve; *[pied]* arch; *[route]* camber. (**b**) *(partie)* ~ **du pied** instep; ~ **des reins** small of the back.

cambuse [kɑ̃byz] *nf* (**a**) *(‡) (pièce)* pad ‡; *(maison)* shack *, place; *(taudis)* hovel. (**b**) *(Naut)* storeroom.

came [kam] *nf (Tech)* cam; *(arg Drogue) (gén)* junk *(arg)*; *(cocaïne)* snow *(arg)*; *(‡: marchandise)* stuff *; *(*: pacotille)* junk *. ◆**camé, e**[1] *nm, f (arg)* junkie *(arg)*, druggy ‡.

camée[2] [kame] *nm* cameo.

caméléon [kameleɔ̃] *nm* chameleon.

camélia [kamelja] *nm* camellia.

camelot [kamlo] *nm* street pedlar.

camelote * [kamlɔt] *nf* (**a**) *(pacotille)* **c'est de la ~** it's junk * *ou* trash * *ou* rubbish * *ou* shlock ‡ *(US)*. (**b**) *(marchandise)* stuff *. **il vend de la belle ~** he sells nice stuff.

camer (se) [kame] *vpr (arg Drogue)* to be on drugs.

caméra [kameʀa] *nf (Ciné, TV)* camera; *[amateur]* cine-camera, movie camera *(US)*. ◆**cameraman,** *pl* **cameramen** *nm* cameraman.

Cameroun [kamʀun] *nm* Cameroon. ◆**camerounais, e** *adj*, **C~(e)** *nm(f)* Cameroonian.

caméscope [kameskɔp] *nm* camcorder.

camion [kamjɔ̃] *nm (ouvert)* lorry, truck *(US)*; *(fermé)* van, truck *(US)*. ~**-citerne** *nm, pl* ~**s-~s** tanker (lorry), tank truck *(US)*; ~ **de déménagement** removal *ou* moving *(US)* van. ◆**camionnage** *nm* haulage. ◆**camionnette** *nf* (small) van; *(ouverte)* pick-up (truck). ◆**camionneur** *nm* lorry *ou* truck *(US)* driver; *(entrepreneur)* road haulier.

camisole [kamizɔl] *nf*: ~ **de force** strait jacket.

camomille [kamɔmij] *nf* camomile.

camoufler [kamufle] (1) *vt (Mil)* to camouflage; *(cacher)* to conceal; *(déguiser)* to disguise. ◆ **camouflage** *nm (Mil) (action)* camouflaging; *(résultat)* camouflage.

camp [kɑ̃] *nm (gén, Mil: emplacement)* camp; *(parti, Sport)* side; *(Pol)* camp. ~ **de concentration** concentration camp; ~ **d'extermination** death camp; ~ **de toile** campsite.

campagne [kɑ̃paɲ] *nf* (**a**) *(gén)* country; *(paysage)* countryside. **en pleine** ~ right in the middle of the country(side); **auberge de** ~ country inn. (**b**) *(Mil, Pol, Presse)* campaign. **faire** ~ to fight a campaign; **en** ~ on campaign; **canon de** ~ field gun; **mener une** ~ **pour/contre** to campaign for/against; **tout le monde se mit en** ~ everybody set to work *ou* got busy (*pour faire* to do). ◆ **campagnard, e 1** *adj* country. **2** *nm* countryman. ~**s** countryfolk. **3** *nf* countrywoman.

campanile [kɑ̃panil] *nm* campanile.

campanule [kɑ̃panyl] *nf* bellflower, campanula.

camper [kɑ̃pe] (1) **1** *vi* to camp. **2** *vt* (**a**) *troupes* to camp out. (**b**) *personnage* to portray; *portrait* to fashion, shape. (**c**) *lunettes etc* to plant (*sur* on). **se** ~ **devant** to plant o.s. in front of. ◆ **campement** *nm* camp, encampment. ◆ **campeur, -euse** *nm, f* camper. ◆ **camping** *nm* (**a**) *(activité)* **le** ~ camping; **faire du** ~ to go camping. (**b**) *(lieu)* campsite. (**c**) *(voiture)* ~**-car** camper, camping-van; motorhome *(US)*.

camphre [kɑ̃fʀ(ə)] *nm* camphor.

campus [kɑ̃pys] *nm* campus.

camus, e [kamy, yz] *adj personne* pug-nosed.

Canada [kanada] *nm* Canada. ◆ **canadianisme** *nm* Canadianism. ◆ **canadien, -ienne 1** *adj* Canadian. **2** *nm(f)*: **C~(ne)** Canadian. **3** *nf (veste)* fur-lined jacket.

canadair [kanadɛʀ] *nm* ® fire-fighting aircraft, tanker plane *(US)*.

canaille [kanɑj] **1** *adj* low, coarse. **2** *nf (salaud)* bastard ‡; *(escroc)* crook, shyster *(US)*, chiseler *(US)*; *(hum: enfant)* rascal. *(populace)* **la** ~ the rabble *(péj)*. ◆ **canaillerie** *nf [manières]* lowness, coarseness; *[procédés]* crookedness; *(action malhonnête)* dirty *ou* low trick.

canal, *pl* **-aux** [kanal, o] *nm (artificiel)* canal; *(détroit)* channel; *(tuyau, fossé)* conduit, duct; *(Anat)* canal, duct; *(TV, Ordin)* channel. **le C~ de Panama/Suez** the Panama/Suez Canal; **par le** ~ **d'un collègue** through a colleague. ◆ **canalisation** *nf (tuyau)* (main) pipe; *(Élec)* cable. ◆ **canaliser** (1) *vt foule, demandes* to channel, funnel; *fleuve* to canalize; *plaine* to provide with a network of canals.

canapé [kanape] *nm (meuble)* settee, couch; *(Culin)* canapé.

canard [kanaʀ] *nm (gén)* duck; *(mâle)* drake; *(*: journal)* rag *. *(Mus)* **faire un** ~ to hit a false note; **mon (petit)** ~ * pet *; ~ **de Barbarie** Muscovy *ou* musk duck; ~ **sauvage** wild duck.

canarder * [kanaʀde] (1) *vt (fusil)* to snipe at; *(pierres)* to pelt (*avec* with).

canari [kanaʀi] *nm* canary.

Canaries [kanaʀi] *nfpl*: **les (îles)** ~ the Canary Islands, the Canaries.

cancans [kɑ̃kɑ̃] *nmpl* gossip. ◆ **cancaner** (1) *vi* to gossip, tittle-tattle. ◆ **cancanier, -ière** *adj* gossipy, tittle-tattling.

cancer [kɑ̃sɛʀ] *nm* cancer. **être (du) C~** to be Cancer *ou* a Cancerian. ◆ **cancéreux, -euse** *adj tumeur* cancerous; *personne* with cancer. ◆ **cancérigène** *adj* carcinogenic. ◆ **cancérologie** *nf* cancerology. ◆ **cancérologue** *nmf* cancerologist.

cancre [kɑ̃kʀ(ə)] *nm (péj: élève)* dunce.

cancrelat [kɑ̃kʀəla] *nm* cockroach.

candélabre [kɑ̃delɑbʀ(ə)] *nm* candelabra.

candeur [kɑ̃dœʀ] *nf* naïvety.

candidat, e [kɑ̃dida, at] *nm, f (gén)* candidate (*à* at); *[poste]* applicant (*à* for). ~ **sortant** present *ou* outgoing incumbent; *(Pol)* **être** ~ **à la présidence** to stand *ou* run for president, run for the presidency. ◆ **candidature** *nf* candidature, candidacy *(US)*; application (*à* for). **poser sa** ~ **à** *poste* to apply for.

candide [kɑ̃did] *adj* naïve. ◆ **candidement** *adv* naïvely.

cane [kan] *nf* (female) duck. ◆ **caneton** *nm*, **canette**[1] *nf* duckling.

canette[2] [kanɛt] *nf (bouteille)* bottle (of beer).

canevas [kanva] *nm* (**a**) *[livre]* framework. (**b**) *(toile)* canvas; *(ouvrage)* tapestry (work).

caniche [kaniʃ] *nm* poodle.

canicule [kanikyl] *nf (chaleur)* scorching heat; *(période)* heatwave. *(juillet-août)* **la** ~ the dog days. ◆ **caniculaire** *adj* scorching.

canif [kanif] *nm* penknife, pocket knife.

canin, e [kanɛ̃, in] **1** *adj espèce* canine; *exposition* dog. **2** *nf (dent)* canine (tooth).

canisses [kanis] *nfpl* (type of) wattle fence.

caniveau, *pl* ~**x** [kanivo] *nm* (roadside) gutter.

canna [kana] *nm (fleur)* canna.

cannabis [kanabis] *nm* cannabis.

cannage [kanaʒ] *nm (partie cannée)* canework; *(opération)* caning.

canne [kan] *nf* walking stick. ~ **à pêche** fishing rod; ~ **à sucre** sugar cane.

canneler [kanle] (4) *vt* to flute. ◆ **cannelure** *nf [colonne]* flute.

cannelle [kanɛl] *nf* cinnamon.

canner [kane] (1) *vt* to cane. **chaise cannée** cane chair. ◆ **canneur, -euse** *nm, f* cane worker.

cannibale [kanibal] **1** *adj* cannibal. **2** *nmf* cannibal, man-eater. ◆ **cannibalisme** *nm* cannibalism.

canoë [kanɔe] *nm* canoe. **faire du** ~ to canoe. ◆ **canoéiste** *nmf* canoeist.

canon [kanɔ̃] *nm* (**a**) *(arme)* gun; *(Hist)* cannon; *[fusil, clé]* barrel. **fusil à** ~ **scié** sawn-off *ou* sawed-off *(US)* shotgun; ~ **à eau** water cannon; ~ **à neige** snow blower. (**b**) *(Rel, Mus)* canon. *(code)* ~**s** canons.

cañon [kaɲɔ̃] *nm* canyon.

canonique [kanɔnik] *adj (Rel)* canonical; *âge* venerable. ◆ **canonisation** *nf* canonization. ◆ **canoniser** (1) *vt* to canonize.

canonner [kanɔne] (1) *vt* to bombard, shell. ◆ **canonnade** *nf* cannonade. ◆ **canonnier** *nm* gunner. ◆ **canonnière** *nf* gunboat.

canot [kano] *nm* boat, ding(h)y. ~ **automobile** motorboat; ~ **pneumatique** rubber *ou* inflatable ding(h)y; ~ **de sauvetage** lifeboat. ◆ **canotage** *nm* boating, rowing. **faire du** ~ to go boating *ou* rowing. ◆ **canotier** *nm (chapeau)* boater.

cantate [kɑ̃tat] *nf* cantata.

cantatrice [kɑ̃tatʀis] *nf* (opera) singer.

cantine [kɑ̃tin] *nf* (**a**) *[usine]* canteen; *[école]* dining hall, cafeteria; *(service)* school meals. (**b**) *(malle)* tin trunk. ◆ **cantinière** *nf (Hist Mil)* canteen woman.

cantique [kɑ̃tik] *nm* hymn.

canton [kɑ̃tɔ̃] *nm (gén)* district; *(Admin)* canton. ◆ **cantonal, e,** *mpl* **-aux** *adj* district; cantonal.

cantonade [kɑ̃tɔnad] *nf*: **dire qch à la** ~ to say sth to no one in particular *ou* to everyone in general; **ce n'est pas la peine de le crier à la** ~ you don't need to tell the whole world *ou* to shout it from the housetops.

cantonner [kɑ̃tɔne] (1) *vt (Mil)* to station; *(chez l'habitant etc)* to quarter, billet (*chez, dans* on). *(fig)* ~ **qn dans un travail** to confine sb to a job; **se**

~ **dans** to confine o.s. to. ◆ **cantonnement** *nm (action)* stationing; billeting, quartering; *(lieu)* quarters, billet; *(camp)* camp.

cantonnier [kɑ̃tɔnje] *nm* roadman.

canular [kanylaʀ] *nm* hoax.

caoutchouc [kautʃu] *nm (matière)* rubber; *(élastique)* rubber *ou* elastic band; *(plante verte)* rubber plant. ® ~ **mousse** foam *ou* sponge rubber. ◆ **caoutchouter** (1) *vt* to rubberize. ◆ **caoutchouteux, -euse** *adj* rubbery.

cap [kap] *nm* (**a**) *(Géog)* cape; *(promontoire)* point, headland. **le ~ Canaveral** Cape Canaveral; **le ~ Horn** Cape Horn; **le ~ de Bonne Espérance** the Cape of Good Hope; **les îles du C~ Vert** the Cape Verde Islands; **doubler un ~** to round a cape; **passer le ~ de l'examen** to get over the hurdle of the exam; **franchir le ~ des 40 ans** to turn 40; **franchir le ~ des 50 millions** to pass the 50-million mark. (**b**) *(lit, fig)* **changer de ~** to change course; *(Aut, Naut)* **mettre le ~ sur** to head for. (**c**) *(ville)* **Le C~** Cape Town.

capable [kapabl(ə)] *adj* able, capable. ~ **de faire/de qch** capable of doing/of sth; **te sens-tu ~ de tout manger?** do you feel you can eat it all?, do you feel up to eating it all?; **il est ~ de l'avoir perdu** he's quite likely to have lost it, he may well have lost it.

capacité [kapasite] *nf (contenance)* capacity; *(aptitude)* ability (*à faire* to do); *(civile, légale)* capacity. ~**s intellectuelles** intellectual abilities *ou* capacities; *(Tourisme)* **la ~ d'accueil d'une ville** the total amount of tourist accommodation in a town; **avoir ~ pour** to be (legally) entitled to.

caparaçonner [kapaʀasɔne] (1) *vt cheval* to caparison. *(fig)* **caparaçonné de cuir** all clad in leather.

cape [kap] *nf (courte)* cape; *(longue)* cloak.

capharnaüm * [kafaʀnaɔm] *nm* clutter, muddle.

capillaire [kapilɛʀ] **1** *adj (Sci)* capillary; *lotion* hair. **2** *nm (Anat)* capillary.

capilotade [kapilɔtad] *nf*: **mettre en ~** *fruits* to squash to a pulp; *adversaire* to beat to a pulp; **il avait les reins en ~** his back was aching like hell ‡.

capitaine [kapitɛn] *nm (Mil, Naut, Sport)* captain; *(armée de l'air)* flight lieutenant, captain *(US)*; *(littér: chef)* (military) leader. ~ **d'industrie** captain of industry; ~ **au long cours** master mariner ; ~ **des pompiers** fire chief, marshall *(US)*.

capital, e, *mpl* **-aux** [kapital, o] **1** *adj (gén)* major, main; *erreur* chief, major; *importance* cardinal, capital; *peine* capital. **il est ~ d'y aller** it is vital *ou* absolutely essential that we go. **2** *nm (Fin, Pol)* capital. ~**aux** money, capital; ~ **initial** *ou* **de lancement** seed *ou* start-up money; ~**-risques** venture capital; *(fig)* ~ **de connaissances** stock *ou* fund of knowledge; **cela constitue un ~ appréciable** it is a major asset; **le ~ artistique du pays** the artistic wealth *ou* resources of the country. **3** *nf* (**a**) **(lettre)** ~**e** capital (letter); **en ~es d'imprimerie** in block capitals. (**b**) *(métropole)* capital (city).

capitaliser [kapitalize] (1) **1** *vt* (**a**) *somme* to amass; *(fig) expériences* to build up, accumulate. **l'intérêt capitalisé pendant un an** interest accrued *ou* accumulated in a year. (**b**) *(Fin: ajouter au capital) intérêts* to capitalize. **2** *vi* to save. ◆ **capitalisation** *nf* capitalization. ◆ **capitalisme** *nm* capitalism. ◆ **capitaliste** *adj, nmf* capitalist.

capiteux, -euse [kapitø, øz] *adj vin* heady; *beauté* intoxicating.

Capitole [kapitɔl] *nm:* **le ~** the Capitole.

capitonner [kapitɔne] (1) *vt* to pad (*de* with). ◆ **capitonnage** *nm* padding.

capituler [kapityle] (1) *vi* to capitulate, surrender. ◆ **capitulation** *nf* capitulation, surrender. ~ **sans conditions** unconditional surrender.

caporal, *pl* **-aux** [kapɔʀal, o] *nm* corporal.

capot [kapo] *nm* bonnet, hood *(US)*.

capote [kapɔt] *nf [voiture]* hood, top *(US)*; *(manteau)* greatcoat.

capoter [kapɔte] (1) *vi* to overturn. **faire ~** *véhicule* to overturn; *négociations* to scupper *, put paid to.

câpre [kɑpʀ(ə)] *nf (Culin)* caper.

caprice [kapʀis] *nm* whim, caprice. **faire un ~** to throw a tantrum; **cet enfant fait des ~s** this child is being awkward *ou* temperamental; ~ **de la nature** freak of nature; ~**s** *[chemin]* windings; *[mode]* vagaries, whims; *[sort]* quirks. ◆ **capricieusement** *adv* capriciously, whimsically. ◆ **capricieux, -ieuse** *adj* capricious, whimsical; *(péj)* temperamental; awkward.

Capricorne [kapʀikɔʀn(ə)] *nm*: **le ~** Capricorn; **être du ~** to be (a) Capricorn.

capsule [kapsyl] *nf (Espace, Sci)* capsule; *[bouteille]* capsule, cap; *[arme]* cap. ◆ **capsuler** (1) *vt* to put a capsule *ou* cap on.

capter [kapte] (1) *vt suffrages, confiance* to win; *émission* to pick up; *source* to harness; *courant* to tap. ◆ **capteur** *nm:* ~ **solaire** solar panel.

captif, -ive [kaptif, iv] *adj, nm, f* captive. ◆ **captiver** (1) *vt* to captivate. ◆ **captivité** *nf* captivity.

captivant, e [kaptivɑ̃, ɑ̃t] *adj film, lecture* enthralling, captivating; *personne* fascinating, captivating.

capturer [kaptyʀe] (1) *vt* to catch, capture. ◆ **capture** *nf (action)* capture, catching; *(animal)* catch; *(personne)* capture.

capuche [kapyʃ] *nf* hood. ◆ **capuchon** *nm* hood; *(Rel)* cowl; *(pèlerine)* hooded raincoat; *[stylo]* top, cap.

capucine [kapysin] *nf (Bot)* nasturtium.

caquet [kakɛ] *nm* (*) *[personne]* prattle; *[poule]* cackle. **rabattre le ~ à qn** * to bring sb down a peg or two. ◆ **caqueter** (4) *vi* to prattle; to cackle.

car[1] [kaʀ] *nm* coach, bus *(US)*. ~ **de police** police van; ~ **(de ramassage) scolaire** school bus.

car[2] [kaʀ] *conj* because, for.

carabine [kaʀabin] *nf* rifle.

carabiné, e * [kaʀabine] *adj fièvre* raging, violent; *facture* stiff.

carabinier [kaʀabinje] *nm (Espagne)* carabinero; *(Italie)* carabiniere.

Caracas [kaʀakas] *n* Caracas.

caracoler [kaʀakɔle] (1) *vi* to caracole.

caractère [kaʀaktɛʀ] *nm* (**a**) *(gén)* character, nature. **avoir bon/mauvais ~** to be good-/ill-natured, be good-/bad-tempered; *[personne, maison]* **avoir du ~** to have character; **la situation n'a aucun ~ de gravité** the situation shows no sign *ou* evidence of seriousness. (**b**) *(gén pl: caractéristique)* characteristic, feature. (**c**) *(Typ)* character, letter. ~**s gras** bold type; ~**s d'imprimerie** block capitals. ◆ **caractériel, -elle 1** *adj* (**a**) *enfant* emotionally disturbed, maladjusted. (**b**) **traits ~s** traits of character; **troubles ~s** emotional disturbance *ou* problems. **2** *nmf* problem *ou* maladjusted child. ◆ **caractériser** (1) *vt (être typique de)* to characterize, be characteristic of; *(décrire)* to characterize. **se ~ par** to be characterized by; **erreur caractérisée** blatant mistake. ◆ **caractéristique 1** *adj* characteristic (*de* of). **2** *nf* characteristic, (typical) feature. *(Admin)* ~**s signalétiques** particulars, personal details; ~**s techniques** design features.

carafe [kaʀaf] *nf (gén)* carafe; *(en cristal)* decanter.

caraïbe [kaʀaib] *adj* Caribbean. **les C~s** the Caribbean.

carambolage [kaʀɑ̃bɔlaʒ] *nm* pile-up. ◆ **se caramboler** (1) *vpr* to collide.

caramel [kaʀamɛl] *nm (Culin)* caramel; *(mou)* fudge, chewy toffee; *(dur)* toffee, butterscotch. ◆ **caraméliser** (1) *vt sucre* to caramelize; *moule* to coat with caramel; *boisson* to flavour with caramel.

carapace [kaʀapas] *nf (lit, fig)* shell.

carat [kaʀa] *nm* carat.

caravane [kaʀavan] *nf (convoi)* caravan; *(fig)* stream; *(véhicule)* caravan, trailer *(US)*. **une ~ de voitures/de touristes** a stream of cars/of tourists; **la ~ du Tour de France** the whole retinue of the Tour de France. ◆ **caravanier, -ière 1** *adj* caravan. **2** *nm* caravanner. ◆ **caravaning** *nm* caravanning. ◆ **caravansérail** *nm (lit, fig)* caravanserai.

caravelle [kaʀavɛl] *nf* caravel.

carbone [kaʀbɔn] *nm* carbon. **le ~ 14** carbon-14. ◆ **carbonate** *nm* carbonate. ◆ **carbonique** *adj* carbonic.

carboniser [kaʀbɔnize] (1) *vt bois* to carbonize; *maison* to burn to the ground; *rôti* to burn to a cinder. ◆ **carbonisé, e** *adj restes* charred. **mort ~** burned to death.

carburant [kaʀbyʀɑ̃] *nm* fuel. ◆ **carburateur** *nm* carburettor. ◆ **carburation** *nf [essence]* carburation. ◆ **carbure** *nm* carbide. ◆ **carburer** (1) *vi*: **~ bien/mal** *[moteur]* to be well/badly tuned; (*‡: fig*) to be going well/badly; **~ à plein rendement** to be working at full capacity.

carcan [kaʀkɑ̃] *nm (Hist)* iron collar; *(contrainte)* yoke; *(fig:col)* vice *(fig)*.

carcasse [kaʀkas] *nf [corps]* carcass; *[abat-jour]* frame; *[bateau]* skeleton; *[immeuble]* shell, skeleton.

carcéral, e, *mpl* **-aux** [kaʀseʀal, o] *adj* prison. **régime ~** prison regime.

cardan [kaʀdɑ̃] *nm* universal joint.

carder [kaʀde] (1) *vt* to card.

cardiaque [kaʀdjak] **1** *adj* cardiac. **être ~** to have a heart condition. **2** *nmf* heart patient.

cardinal, e, *mpl* **-aux** [kaʀdinal, o] **1** *adj* cardinal. **2** *nm (Rel)* cardinal; *(nombre)* cardinal number.

cardiologie [kaʀdjɔlɔʒi] *nf* cardiology. ◆ **cardiologue** *nmf* cardiologist, heart specialist. ◆ **cardio-vasculaire** *adj* cardiovascular.

carême [kaʀɛm] *nm (jeûne)* fast. *(Rel: période)* **le C~** Lent.

carence [kaʀɑ̃s] *nf (incompétence)* incompetence; *(manque)* shortage (*en* of); *(Méd)* deficiency. **les ~s de** the shortcomings of.

carène [kaʀɛn] *nf (Naut)* hull. ◆ **caréner** (6) *vt (Naut)* to careen; *véhicule* to streamline.

caresser [kaʀese] (1) *vt* (**a**) to caress, stroke. **~ qn du regard** to give sb a caressing look. (**b**) *projet* to entertain, toy with. ◆ **caressant, e** *adj enfant* affectionate; *voix, brise* caressing.

cargaison [kaʀgɛzɔ̃] *nf* cargo, freight; *(fig)* load, stock. **des ~s de** *lettres, demandes* heaps *ou* piles of; *touristes* busloads *ou* shiploads of. ◆ **cargo** *nm* cargo boat, freighter.

carguer [kaʀge] (1) *vt voiles* to furl.

caricature [kaʀikatyʀ] *nf* (**a**) caricature; *(politique)* (satirical) cartoon. **une ~ de procès** a mockery of a trial; **une ~ de la vérité** a caricature *ou* gross distortion of the truth. (**b**) *(*: personne)* fright *. ◆ **caricatural, e,** *mpl* **-aux** *adj (ridicule)* ridiculous, grotesque; *(exagéré)* caricatured. ◆ **caricaturer** (1) *vt* to caricature. ◆ **caricaturiste** *nmf* caricaturist; (satirical) cartoonist.

carie [kaʀi] *nf*: **la ~ dentaire** tooth decay, (dental) caries; **j'ai une ~** I've got a bad tooth *ou* a hole in my tooth. ◆ **carier** (7) *vt,* **se ~** *vpr* to decay. **dent cariée** bad *ou* decayed tooth.

carillon [kaʀijɔ̃] *nm (cloches)* peal of bells; *(horloge)* chiming clock; *(sonnette)* (door) chime; *(air)* chimes. ◆ **carillonner** (1) **1** *vi [cloches]* to ring, chime; *(à la porte)* to ring very loudly. **2** *vt heure* to chime, ring; *(fig) nouvelle* to broadcast.

cariste [kaʀist(ə)] *nm* fork-lift truck operator.

carlingue [kaʀlɛ̃g] *nf (Aviat)* cabin.

carmin [kaʀmɛ̃] *nm, adj inv* carmine.

carnage [kaʀnaʒ] *nm (lit, fig)* carnage, slaughter. **quel ~!** what a slaughter *ou* massacre; *(fig)* **je vais faire un ~** I'm going to massacre someone.

carnassier, -ière [kaʀnasje, jɛʀ] **1** *adj animal* carnivorous, flesh-eating. **2** *nm* carnivore.

carnaval, *pl* **~s** [kaʀnaval] *nm* carnival. ◆ **carnavalesque** *adj* carnivalesque.

carne [kaʀn(ə)] *nf (péj)* tough *ou* leathery meat.

carnet [kaʀnɛ] *nm (calepin)* notebook; *[timbres etc]* book. **~ de chèques** cheque book; **~ de notes** school report, report card; **~ de santé** health record.

carnivore [kaʀnivɔʀ] **1** *adj animal* carnivorous, flesh-eating. *[personne]* **il est ~** he's a meat-lover. **2** *nm* carnivore.

carotide [kaʀɔtid] *adj, nf* carotid.

carotte [kaʀɔt] **1** *nf* carrot; *(Tech)* core; *[tabac]* plug. **les ~s sont cuites!** * they've (*ou* we've *etc*) had it! *. **2** *adj inv* carroty.

carotter ‡ [kaʀɔte] (1) *vt objet* to swipe ‡, pinch * (*à* from); *client* to do * (*de* out, of).

carpe [kaʀp(ə)] **1** *nf* carp. **2** *nm (Anat)* carpus.

carpette [kaʀpɛt] *nf (tapis)* rug; *(fig, péj)* doormat *(fig)*.

carquois [kaʀkwa] *nm* quiver.

carre [kaʀ] *nf [ski]* edge.

carré, e [kaʀe] **1** *adj* (**a**) *(Math, forme)* square. **mètre ~** square metre. (**b**) *(franc) personne* forthright, straightforward; *réponse* straight(forward). **2** *nm (gén, Math, écharpe)* square; *(Naut: mess)* wardroom. **~ de terre** patch *ou* plot (of land); **3 au ~** 3 squared; **mettre un nombre au ~** to square a number; *(Cartes)* **un ~ d'as** four aces. **3** *nf* (*‡: chambre*) pad ‡.

carreau, *pl* **~x** [kaʀo] *nm* (**a**) *(par terre)* (floor) tile; *(au mur)* (wall) tile; *(sol)* (tiled) floor; *[mine]* bank. (**b**) *(vitre)* (window) pane. *(*: lunettes)* **~x** specs *. (**c**) *(sur un tissu)* check; *(sur du papier)* square. **à ~x** *papier* squared; *mouchoir* checked; **à petits ~x** with a small check. (**d**) *(Cartes)* diamond. (**e**) *(flèche)* bolt. (**f**) (‡) **il est resté sur le ~** *(bagarre)* he was laid out cold *; *(examen)* he didn't make the grade; **se tenir à ~** to keep one's nose clean *.

carrefour [kaʀfuʀ] *nm (gén)* crossroads. **au ~ de plusieurs sciences** at the junction *ou* meeting point of many different sciences; **~ d'idées** forum for ideas.

carreler [kaʀle] (4) *vt* to tile. ◆ **carrelage** *nm (action)* tiling; *(sol)* tiled floor. ◆ **carreleur** *nm* tiler.

carrelet [kaʀlɛ] *nm (poisson)* plaice; *(filet)* square fishing net.

carrément [kaʀemɑ̃] *adv (crûment)* bluntly, straight out; *(directement)* straight. **vas-y ~** go right ahead; **il est ~ timbré** * he's definitely cracked *.

carrer (se) [kaʀe] (1) *vpr* **se ~ dans** to settle (o.s.) comfortably in.

carrière [kaʀjɛʀ] *nf* (**a**) *[sable]* (sand)pit; *[roches etc]* quarry. (**b**) *(profession)* career. **faire ~ dans la banque** *(gén)* to make banking one's career; *(réussir)* to make a good career for o.s. in banking. (**c**) *(littér)* **le jour achève sa ~** the day has run its course; **donner (libre) ~ à** to give free rein to.

◆ **carriériste** *nmf (péj)* careerist. ◆ **carriérisme** *nm* careerism.

carriole [kaʀjɔl] *nf (péj)* (ramshackle) cart.

carrossable [kaʀɔsabl(ə)] *adj* suitable for (motor) vehicles.

carrosse [kaʀɔs] *nm* (horse-drawn) coach.

carrosserie [kaʀɔsʀi] *nf* body, coachwork; *(métier)* coachbuilding. ◆ **carrossier** *nm* coachbuilder.

carrousel [kaʀuzɛl] *nm (Équitation)* carrousel; *(fig)* whirligig.

carrure [kaʀyʀ] *nf [personne]* build; *[vêtement]* breadth across the shoulders; *(fig)* calibre, stature. **de forte** ~ well-built, burly.

cartable [kaʀtabl(ə)] *nm* (school)bag; *(à bretelles)* satchel.

carte [kaʀt(ə)] *nf* (**a**) *(gén)* card; *(Rail)* season ticket. ~ **de crédit/de vœux** credit/New Year card; ~ **d'électeur** elector's card; *(Banque)* **C~ Bleue** ® Visa Card ®; ~ **grise** logbook; ~ **d'identité** identity card; ~ **de lecteur** library ticket; ~ **à mémoire** intelligent credit card, smart card *(US)*; *(pour téléphone)* phone card; ~ **postale** postcard; ~ **de visite** visiting card; **avoir** ~ **blanche** to have carte blanche *ou* a free hand. (**b**) *(Jeux)* ~ **(à jouer)** (playing) card; **faire les ~s à qn** to read sb's cards; ~ **maîtresse** *(lit)* master (card); *(fig)* trump card; *(lit, fig)* **~s sur table** cards on the table; **jouer la** ~ **de la concurrence** to play the competition card. (**c**) *(Géog)* map; *(Astron, Mét, Naut)* chart. ~ **routière** roadmap; ~ **d'état-major** ≃ Ordnance Survey map. (**d**) *(au restaurant)* menu. **repas à la** ~ à la carte meal; ~ **des vins** wine list; *(fig)* **programme à la** ~ free-choice curriculum; *(fig)* **avoir un horaire à la** ~ to have flexible working hours.

cartel [kaʀtɛl] *nm (Pol, Écon)* cartel; *(pendule)* wall clock.

carter [kaʀtɛʀ] *nm [bicyclette]* chain guard; *[moteur]* crankcase.

cartilage [kaʀtilaʒ] *nm (Anat)* cartilage; *[viande]* gristle. ◆ **cartilagineux, -euse** *adj* cartilaginous; gristly.

cartographe [kaʀtɔgʀaf] *nmf* cartographer. ◆ **cartographie** *nf* cartography. ◆ **cartographique** *adj* cartographic(al).

cartomancie [kaʀtɔmɑ̃si] *nf* fortune-telling *(with cards)*. ◆ **cartomancien, -ienne** *nm, f* fortune-teller.

carton [kaʀtɔ̃] **1** *nm* (**a**) *(matière)* cardboard; *(morceau)* piece of cardboard; *(boîte)* (cardboard) box, carton; *(contenu)* boxful; *(cartable)* (school)bag; *(dossier)* file; *(carte)* card. ~ **d'invitation** invitation card. (**b**) *(cible)* target. **faire un** ~ *(à la fête)* to have a go at the rifle range; *(*: sur l'ennemi)* to take a potshot * *(sur* at); **faire un bon** ~ to make a good score. (**c**) *(Peinture)* sketch. **2** : ~ **à chapeau** hatbox; ~ **à dessin** portfolio; ~ **pâte** pasteboard; **de** ~ **pâte** cardboard. ◆ **cartonnage** *nm (emballage)* cardboard (packing); *(couverture)* binding.

cartouche [kaʀtuʃ] **1** *nf (gén)* cartridge; *[cigarettes]* carton. **2** *nm (Archéol, Archit)* cartouche. ◆ **cartoucherie** *nf (fabrique)* cartridge factory; *(dépôt)* cartridge depot. ◆ **cartouchière** *nf (ceinture)* cartridge belt; *(sac)* cartridge pouch.

cas [kɑ] *nm (gén)* case; *(situation)* case, situation; *(événement)* occurrence; *(exemple)* case, instance. **comme c'est son** ~ as is the case with him; **il s'est mis dans un mauvais** ~ he's got himself into a tricky situation *ou* position; *(hum)* **c'est un** ~ **pendable** he deserves to be shot *(hum)*; ~ **social** person with social problems, social misfit; **faire (grand)** ~ **de/peu de** ~ **de** to set great/little store by; **il ne fait jamais aucun** ~ **de nos observations** he never pays any attention to *ou* takes any notice of our comments; **c'est bien le** ~ **de le dire!** you've said it!; **c'est le** ~ **ou jamais** it's now or never; **au** ~ **où il pleuvrait** in case it rains; **en ce** ~ in that case; **le** ~ **échéant** if such is the case, if need be; **en** ~ **d'absence** in case of *ou* in the event of absence; **en** ~ **de besoin** if need be; **en** ~ **d'urgence** in an emergency; **en aucun** ~ on no account, under no circumstances; **en tout** ~ anyway, in any case, at any rate; **selon les** ~ as the case may be; **il a un** ~ **de conscience** he's in a moral dilemma.

casanier, -ière [kazanje, jɛʀ] *adj nm, f* stay-at-home.

casaque [kazak] *nf [jockey]* blouse; *[mousquetaire]* tabard.

cascade [kaskad] *nf (lit)* waterfall, cascade; *[mots etc]* stream, torrent; *[rires]* peal. *(fig)* **des démissions en** ~ a spate of resignations. ◆ **cascader** (1) *vi* to cascade. ◆ **cascadeur, -euse** *nm, f* stuntman; stuntgirl.

case [kɑz] *nf* (**a**) *(carré)* square. *(Jeux)* **la** ~ **départ** the start; *(fig)* **nous voilà revenus à la** ~ **départ** we're back to square one. (**b**) *[courrier]* pigeonhole; *[tiroir]* compartment. *(Ordin)* ~ **de réception** card stacker; **il a une** ~ **vide** * he has a screw loose *. (**c**) *(hutte)* hut. **la C~ de l'Oncle Tom** Uncle Tom's Cabin.

casemate [kazmat] *nf* blockhouse.

caser * [kaze] (1) **1** *vt (placer) objets* to shove *, stuff; *(loger)* to put up; *(marier)* to find a husband (*ou* wife) for; *(dans un métier)* to find a job for. **il est casé** *(mariage)* he's married; *(emploi)* he's fixed up. **2 se** ~ *vpr (mariage)* to settle down; *(emploi)* to find a (steady) job; *(logement)* to find a place (to live).

caserne [kazɛʀn(ə)] *nf (Mil, fig)* barracks *(gén sg)*. ~ **de pompiers** fire station. ◆ **casernement** *nm (action)* quartering in barracks; *(bâtiments)* barrack buildings. ◆ **caserner** (1) *vt* to barrack.

cash * [kaʃ] *adv*: **payer** ~ to pay cash down.

casier [kɑzje] *nm (gén)* compartment; *(tiroir)* drawer; *(fermant à clef)* locker; *[courrier]* pigeonhole; *(meuble)* cabinet; *(Pêche)* (lobster *etc*) pot. ~ **à bouteilles** bottle rack; ~ **judiciaire** police *ou* criminal record; ~ **de consigne automatique** luggage locker.

casino [kazino] *nm* casino.

casque [kask(ə)] *nm (gén)* helmet; *[motocycliste etc]* crash helmet; *(sèche-cheveux)* (hair-)drier. ~ **(à écouteurs)** headphones, headset, earphones; **les C~s bleus** the U.N. peace-keeping troops. ◆ **casqué, e** *adj* wearing a helmet. ◆ **casquette** *nf* cap.

casquer * [kaske] (1) *vi (payer)* to fork out *.

cassable [kɑsabl(ə)] *adj* breakable.

cassant, e [kɑsɑ̃, ɑ̃t] *adj substance* brittle; *bois* easily broken; *ton, manières* brusque, abrupt. **ce n'est pas** ~ * it's not exactly back-breaking *ou* tiring work.

cassation [kɑsɑsjɔ̃] *nf (Jur)* cassation; *(Mil)* reduction to the ranks.

casse [kɑs] **1** *nf (action)* breaking, breakage; *(objets cassés)* damage, breakages. **il va y avoir de la** ~ * there's going to be (some) rough stuff *; **mettre à la** ~ to scrap; **bon pour la** ~ ready for the scrap heap. **2** *nm (arg Crime)* break-in. **3** *préf V* **casser.**

cassé, e [kɑse] *adj voix* broken; *vieillard* bent.

cassement [kɑsmɑ̃] *nm*: ~ **de tête** * headache *(fig)*, worry.

casser [kɑse] (1) **1** *vt* (**a**) *(gén)* to break; *noix* to crack; *branche* to snap; *vin* to spoil the flavour of; (*) *appareil* to bust *. ~ **un bras à qn** to break sb's arm; ~ **les prix** to slash prices. (**b**) *(dégrader) (Mil)* to reduce to the ranks, break; *(Admin)* to demote. (**c**) *jugement* to quash; *mariage, arrêt* to annul. (**d**) ~ **la croûte** * to have a bite to eat; ~ **la figure à qn** * to smash sb's face in ⁂; ~ **les pieds à qn** * *(fatiguer)* to bore sb stiff; *(irriter)* to get on

sb's nerves; ~ **sa pipe** * to snuff it ‡, kick the bucket ‡; **ça ne casse rien** * it's nothing special, it's no great shakes *; ~ **du sucre sur le dos de qn** to gossip *ou* talk about sb behind his back; **il nous casse la tête avec sa trompette** he deafens us with his trumpet; **à tout** ~ * *(extraordinaire) film, repas* fantastic *; *succès* runaway; *(tout au plus)* at the outside, at the most.
2 *vi* to break; to snap. *[pantalon]* ~ **sur la chaussure** to rest on the shoe.
3 se ~ *vpr [objet]* to break. *[personne]* **se** ~ **une jambe** to break a leg; **se** ~ **la figure** * *(faire faillite, tomber)* to come a cropper *; *(d'une certaine hauteur)* to crash down; *(se tuer)* to smash o.s. up *; **se** ~ **le nez** to find no one in; **il ne s'est pas cassé (la tête)** * he didn't overtax himself; **se** ~ **la tête sur un problème** * to rack one's brains over a problem.
4 : **casse-cou** * *nmf inv* daredevil, reckless person; **casse-croûte** *nm inv* snack, lunch *(US)*; **casse-noisettes** *nm inv*, **casse-noix** *nm inv* (pair of) nutcrackers; **casse-pieds** * *nmf inv (importun)* nuisance, pain in the neck *; *(ennuyeux)* bore; *(Mil)* **aller au casse-pipes** to go to the front; **casse-tête** *nm inv (problème)* headache; *(jeu)* puzzle, brain teaser; *(massue)* club.

casserole [kasʀɔl] *nf (Culin)* saucepan; *(péj: piano)* tinny piano. **passer à la** ~ ‡ *(tuer)* to bump off ‡.

cassette [kasɛt] *nf (coffret)* casket; *[roi]* privy purse; *[magnétophone, ordinateur]* cassette.

casseur [kɑsœʀ] *nm (*: bravache)* tough guy ‡; *(ferrailleur)* scrap dealer; *(manifestant)* rioter, demonstrator; *(arg Crime: cambrioleur)* burglar.

cassis [kasis] *nm (fruit)* blackcurrant; *(‡: tête)* nut ‡; *[route]* bump, ridge.

cassure [kɑsyʀ] *nf* (**a**) *(lit, fig)* break; *[col]* fold. (**b**) *(Géol) (gén)* break; *(fissure)* crack; *(faille)* fault.

castagnettes [kastaɲɛt] *nfpl* castanets. **il avait les dents qui jouaient des** ~ * he could feel his teeth chattering *ou* rattling.

caste [kast(ə)] *nf (lit, péj)* caste.

Castille [kastij] *nf* Castile.

castor [kastɔʀ] *nm* beaver.

castrer [kastʀe] (1) *vt (gén)* to castrate; *cheval* to geld; *chat, chien* to neuter. ◆ **castration** *nf* castration; gelding; neutering. ◆ **castrateur, -trice** *adj (Psych)* castrating.

cataclysme [kataklism(ə)] *nm* cataclysm.

catacombes [katakɔ̃b(ə)] *nfpl* catacombs.

catafalque [katafalk(ə)] *nm* catafalque.

catalepsie [katalɛpsi] *nf* catalepsy. **tomber en** ~ to have a cataleptic fit. ◆ **cataleptique** *adj, nmf* cataleptic.

Catalogne [katalɔɲ] *nf* Catalonia. ◆ **catalan, e** *adj, nm*, **C~(e)** *nm(f)* Catalan.

catalogue [katalɔg] *nm (gén)* catalogue; *(Ordin)* directory. **prix de** ~ list price. ◆ **cataloguer** (1) *vt objets* to catalogue, list; (*) *personne* to categorize, label (*comme* as).

catalyse [kataliz] *nf* catalysis. ◆ **catalyseur** *nm (Chim, fig)* catalyst. ◆ **catalytique** *adj* catalytic.

catamaran [katamaʀɑ̃] *nm (voilier)* catamaran; *[hydravion]* floats.

cataplasme [kataplasm(ə)] *nm (Méd)* poultice, cataplasm; *(fig)* lead weight.

catapulte [katapylt(ə)] *nf* catapult. ◆ **catapulter** (1) *vt* to catapult. **il a été catapulté à ce poste** he was pitchforked into this job.

cataracte [kataʀakt(ə)] *nf (gén, Méd)* cataract. *(fig)* **des ~s de pluie** torrents of rain.

catarrhe [kataʀ] *nm* catarrh.

catastrophe [katastʀɔf] *nf* disaster, catastrophe. ~ **aérienne** air crash *ou* disaster; **en** ~ *partir* in a mad rush; **atterrir en** ~ to make an emergency landing. ◆ **catastropher** * (1) *vt* to shatter *, stun. ◆ **catastrophique** *adj* disastrous, catastrophic.

catch [katʃ] *nm* wrestling. ◆ **catcheur, -euse** *nm, f* (all-in) wrestler. ◆ **catcher** (1) *vi* to wrestle.

catéchisme [kateʃism(ə)] *nm (gén)* catechism. ◆ **catéchiser** (1) *vt* to catechize. ◆ **catéchiste** *nmf* catechist.

catégorie [kategɔʀi] *nf (gén, Philos)* category; *(Boxe, Hôtellerie)* class; *[personnel]* grade. ◆ **catégorique** *adj (gén)* categorical; *refus* flat. ◆ **catégoriquement** *adv* categorically; flatly. ◆ **catégorisation** *nf* categorization. ◆ **catégoriser** (1) *vt* to categorize.

caténaire [katenɛʀ] *adj, nf (Rail)* catenary.

cathédrale [katedʀal] *nf* cathedral.

cathode [katɔd] *nf* cathode. ◆ **cathodique** *adj* cathodic.

catholique [katɔlik] **1** *adj (Rel)* (Roman) Catholic. **pas (très)** ~ * fishy *, shady. **2** *nmf* (Roman) Catholic. ◆ **catholicisme** *nm* (Roman) Catholicism.

catimini [katimini] *adv*: **en** ~ on the sly; **sortir en** ~ to steal *ou* sneak out; **il me l'a dit en** ~ he whispered it in my ear.

catin [katɛ̃] *nf (prostituée)* trollop.

cation [katjɔ̃] *nm* cation.

Caucase [kɔkɑz] *nm*: **le** ~ the Caucasus.

cauchemar [kɔʃmaʀ] *nm (lit, fig)* nightmare. ◆ **cauchemardesque** *adj* nightmarish.

causalité [kozalite] *nf* causality.

causant, e [kozɑ̃, ɑ̃t] *adj* talkative, chatty.

cause [koz] *nf* (**a**) *(raison)* cause (*de* of). **la chaleur en est la** ~ it is caused by the heat; **la** ~ **en demeure inconnue** the cause remains unknown, the reason for it remains unknown; **les ~s qui l'ont poussé à agir** the reasons that caused him to act. (**b**) *(Jur)* case; *(à plaider)* brief. *(fig)* **la** ~ **est entendue** there's no doubt in our minds; **plaider sa** ~ to plead one's case; **avocat sans** ~ briefless barrister. (**c**) *(parti)* cause. **faire** ~ **commune avec qn** to make common cause with sb, take sides with sb. (**d**) **à** ~ **de** *(en raison de)* because of, owing to, on account of; *(par égard pour)* because of, for the sake of; **être en** ~ *[personne, intérêts etc]* to be involved; **son honnêteté n'est pas en** ~ his honesty is not in question; **mettre en** ~ *projet* to call into question; *personne* to implicate; **ça remet tout en** ~ it re-opens the whole question, we're back to square one *; **mettre qn hors de** ~ to clear *ou* exonerate sb; **c'est hors de** ~ it is out of the question; **pour** ~ **de** on account of; **et pour** ~! and for (a very) good reason!; **non sans** ~! not without (good) cause *ou* reason!

causer[1] [koze] (1) *vt (provoquer)* to cause; *(entraîner)* to bring about. ~ **des ennuis à qn** to get sb into trouble, bring trouble to sb; ~ **de la peine à qn** to hurt sb.

causer[2] [koze] (1) *vti (s'entretenir)* to chat, talk (*de* about); *(*: discourir)* to speak, talk; *(jaser)* to talk, gossip (*sur qn* about sb); *(‡: avouer)* to talk. ~ **politique** to talk politics; ~ **à qn** * to talk *ou* speak to sb. ◆ **causerie** *nf (conférence)* talk; *(conversation)* chat. ◆ **causette** *nf*: **faire la** ~ to have a chat *ou* natter * (*avec* with). ◆ **causeur, -euse** **1** *adj* talkative, chatty. **2** *nm, f* talker.

causticité [kostisite] *nf (lit, fig)* causticity. ◆ **caustique** *adj, nmf* caustic.

cautère [kotɛʀ] *nm* cautery. ◆ **cautérisation** *nf* cauterization. ◆ **cautériser** (1) *vt* to cauterize.

caution [kosjɔ̃] *nf (Fin)* guarantee, security; *(Jur)* bail (bond); *(morale)* guarantee; *(appui)* backing, support. **libéré sous** ~ released on bail; **payer la**

~ **de qn** to stand bail for sb, bail sb out. ◆ **cautionnement** *nm (somme)* guaranty, guarantee, security; *[politique]* backing. ◆ **cautionner** (1) *vt (Fin, fig)* to guarantee; *politique* to support, back.

cavalcade [kavalkad] *nf (désordonnée)* stampede; *(défilé)* cavalcade.

cavaler ⁑ [kavale] (1) **1** *vi (courir)* to run. **2** *vt (ennuyer)* to bore, annoy. **3 se** ~ *vpr (se sauver)* to clear off ⁑.

cavalerie [kavalʀi] *nf (Mil)* cavalry; *[cirque]* horses. *(Mil)* ~ **légère** light cavalry *ou* horse ; *(*: Comm)* **c'est de la grosse** ~ it's uninspiring stuff.

cavalier, -ière [kavalje, jɛʀ] **1** *adj* (**a**) *(impertinent)* casual, cavalier, offhand. (**b**) **allée/piste ~ière** riding/bridle path. **2** *nm, f (Équitation)* rider; *(partenaire)* partner. *(fig)* **faire ~ seul** to go it alone. **3** *nm* (**a**) *(Mil)* trooper, cavalryman. **troupe de 20 ~s** troop of 20 horses. (**b**) *(accompagnateur)* escort. (**c**) *(Échecs)* knight. ◆ **cavalièrement** *adv* casually, in cavalier fashion, offhandedly.

cave [kav] **1** *nf (gén)* cellar. **2** *adj joues* hollow, sunken. ◆ **caveau,** *pl* **~x** *nm (sépulture)* vault, tomb; *(cave)* (small) cellar.

caverne [kavɛʀn(ə)] *nf* cave, cavern. ◆ **caverneux, -euse** *adj (gén)* cavernous.

caviar [kavjaʀ] *nm (Culin)* caviar(e). ~ **rouge** salmon roe.

caviste [kavist(ə)] *nm* cellarman.

cavité [kavite] *nf* cavity.

Cayenne [kajɛn] *n* Cayenne.

C.B. [sibi] *nf (abrév de* **citizen's band***)* **la** ~ CB radio.

ce [sə], **cet** [sɛt] *devant voyelle ou h muet au masculin,* **cette** [sɛt] *f,* **ces** [se] *pl* **1** *adj dém* (**a**) *(proximité)* this; *(pl)* these; *(non-proximité)* that; *(pl)* those. **ce chapeau(-ci)/(-là)** this/that hat; **et ce rhume? *** and how's the cold (doing)? *; **cette nuit** *(qui vient)* tonight; *(passée)* last night; **en ces temps troublés** *(de nos jours)* in these troubled days; *(dans le passé)* in those troubled days; **un de ces jours** one of these days; **ces messieurs sont en réunion** the gentlemen are in a meeting; **cet ami chez qui elle habite** the friend she's living with; **c'est un de ces livres que l'on lit en vacances** it's one of those books *ou* the sort of book you read on holiday. (**b**) *(intensif)* **aurait-il vraiment ce courage?** would he really have that sort of *ou* that much courage?; **cette idée!** what an idea!; **cette générosité me semble suspecte** such *ou* this generosity strikes me as suspicious.

2 *pron dém* (**a**) **qui est-ce? — c'est un médecin** *(en désignant)* who's he? *ou* who's that? — he is a doctor; *(au téléphone)* who is it? — it's a doctor; **c'était le bon temps!** those were the days!; **qui est-ce qui a crié? — c'est lui** who shouted? — HE did *ou* it was him; **c'est eux *** *ou* **ce sont eux qui mentaient** they (are the ones who) *ou* it's they who were lying; **c'est toi qui le dis!** that's what YOU say!; **c'est à se demander si** you really wonder *ou* it makes you wonder if.

(**b**) **ce qui, ce que** what; *(reprenant une proposition)* which; **tout ce que je sais** all (that) I know; **elle fait ce qu'on/tout ce qu'on lui dit** she does what *ou* as she is told/all that she is told; **il ne comprenait pas ce à quoi on faisait allusion/ce dont on l'accusait** he didn't understand what they were hinting at/what he was being accused of; **il faut être diplômé, ce qu'il n'est pas** you have to have qualifications, which *ou* and he hasn't; **ce que ce film est lent!** how slow this film is!, what a slow film this is!; **voilà ce que c'est que de conduire trop vite** that's what comes of driving too fast.

(**c**) **c'est (vous) dire s'il a eu peur** that shows (you) how frightened he was; **à ce qu'on dit** from *ou* according to what they say; **ce faisant** in so doing; **ce disant** so saying; **pour ce faire** to this end, with this end in view; **il a refusé, et ce, après toutes nos prières** he refused, (and this) after all our entreaties.

ceci [səsi] *pron dém* this. **ce cas a ~ de surprenant que...** this case is surprising in that...; **à ~ près que** except that; ~ **compense cela** one thing makes up for another.

cécité [sesite] *nf* blindness.

céder [sede] (6) **1** *vt* (**a**) *part, tour* to give up. ~ **qch à qn** to let sb have sth; **je cède l'antenne à Paris** over to Paris; *(Jur)* ~ **ses biens** to make over one's property. (**b**) ~ **le pas à qn/qch** to give precedence to sb/sth; ~ **du terrain** *(Mil)* to lose *ou* yield ground; *(fig)* to make concessions; *[épidémie]* to recede; *(fig)* **la livre a cédé du terrain** the pound went into retreat *ou* lost ground (*par rapport à* against); **son courage ne le cède en rien à son intelligence** he's as brave as he is intelligent. **2** *vi [personne]* to give in; *[branche]* to give way; *[colère]* to subside. ~ **à** *(succomber)* to give way to, yield to; *(consentir)* to give in to.

cédille [sedij] *nf* cedilla.

cèdre [sɛdʀ(ə)] *nm* cedar.

ceindre [sɛ̃dʀ(ə)] (52) *vt (littér) écharpe* to put on; *épée* to gird. **la tête ceinte d'un diadème** wearing a diadem; **ville ceinte de murs** town surrounded *ou* encircled by walls.

ceinture [sɛ̃tyʀ] *nf* (**a**) *[pantalon]* belt; *[pyjamas]* cord; *(écharpe)* sash; *(gaine)* girdle. **se mettre la ~ *** to tighten one's belt *(fig)*; *(Judo)* ~ **noire** *etc* black *etc* belt; ~ **de flanelle** flannel binder; ~ **de natation** swimmer's float belt; ~ **de sauvetage** life belt; ~ **de sécurité (à enrouleur)** (inertia reel) seat *ou* safety belt; *(Boxe, fig)* **au-dessous de la ~** below the belt. (**b**) *(taille) (Couture)* waistband; *(Anat)* waist. **l'eau lui arrivait à la ~** he was waist-deep in *ou* up to his waist in water. (**c**) *[murailles]* ring; *[arbres]* belt; *(métro, bus)* circle line. ◆ **ceinturer** (1) *vt personne* to seize round the waist; *ville* to surround, encircle. ◆ **ceinturon** *nm* belt.

cela [s(ə)la] *pron dém* (**a**) that; *(sujet apparent)* it. **qu'est-ce que ~ veut dire?** what does that *ou* this mean?; ~ **vaut la peine qu'il essaie** it's worth his trying; **faire des études, ~ ne le tentait guère** studying did not really appeal to him. (**b**) *(pour renforcer)* ~ **fait 10 jours qu'il est parti** it is 10 days since he left, he left 10 days ago; **j'ai vu X — qui ~?/quand ~?/où ~?** I've seen X — who do you mean? *ou* who is that?/when was that?/where was that?; **voyez-vous ~!** did you ever hear of such a thing!; **à ~ près que** except that; **il y a ~ de bien que** the (one) good thing is that.

célébrer [selebʀe] (6) *vt mariage, messe, fête* to celebrate; *cérémonie* to hold. ~ **les louanges de qn** to sing sb's praises. ◆ **célébrant** *nm* celebrant. ◆ **célébration** *nf* celebration. ◆ **célèbre** *adj* famous, celebrated (*par* for). ◆ **célébrité** *nf (renommée)* fame, celebrity; *(personne)* celebrity.

céleri [sɛlʀi] *nm*: ~ **en branche(s)** celery; **~(-rave)** celeriac.

célérité [seleʀite] *nf* promptness, swiftness.

céleste [selɛst(ə)] *adj (Rel)* celestial, heavenly; *(fig)* heavenly.

célibat [seliba] *nm [homme]* bachelorhood; *[femme]* spinsterhood; *[prêtre]* celibacy. ◆ **célibataire 1** *adj (gén)* single, unmarried; *prêtre* celibate; *(Admin)* single. **père (*ou* mère)** ~ single parent. **2** *nm* bachelor; *(Admin)* single man. **la vie de ~** (the) single life; **club pour ~s** singles club. **3** *nf* single *ou* unmarried woman; *(moins jeune)* spinster.

celle [sɛl] *pron dém* **V celui.**

cellier [selje] *nm* storeroom *(for wine and food).*

cellophane [selɔfan] *nf* ® cellophane ®.

cellule [selyl] *nf (gén)* cell; *[électrophone]* cartridge. *(Sociol)* ~ **familiale** family unit; **réunir une ~ de crise** to convene an emergency committee ; ~ **photo-électrique** electric eye. ◆ **cellulaire** *adj (Bio)* cellular. **fourgon ~** prison van.

cellulite [selylit] *nf (graisse)* cellulite; *(inflammation)* cellulitis.

celluloïd [selylɔid] *nm* celluloid.

cellulose [selyloz] *nf* cellulose. ◆ **cellulosique** *adj* cellulose.

celte [sɛlt(ə)] **1** *adj* Celtic. **2** *nmf*: **C~** Celt. ◆ **celtique** *adj, nm* Celtic.

celui [səlɥi], **celle** [sɛl], *mpl* **ceux** [sø], *fpl* **celles** [sɛl] *pron dém* (**a**) **celui-ci, celle-ci** this one; **ceux-ci, celles-ci** these (ones); **celui-là, celle-là** that one; **ceux-là, celles-là** those (ones).
(**b**) *(avec antécédent)* **j'ai vu mon frère et mon oncle, celui-ci était malade** I saw my brother and my uncle and the latter was ill; **elle écrivit à son frère , celui-ci ne répondit pas** she wrote to her brother, but he did not answer; **ceux-là, ils auront de mes nouvelles** as for them, I'll give them a piece of my mind; **il a vraiment de la chance, celui-là!** that fellow certainly has a lot of luck!; **elle est bien bonne, celle-là!** that's a bit much!
(**c**) (+ *de, que*) **je n'aime pas cette pièce, celle de X est meilleure** I don't like this play, X's is better; **il n'a qu'un désir, celui de devenir ministre** he only wants one thing and that's to become a minister; **s'il cherche un local, celui d'en dessous est libre** if he's looking for a place, the one below is free; **pour ceux d'entre vous qui...** for those of *ou* among you who...; **ses romans sont ceux qui se vendent le mieux** his novels are the ones that sell best; **celui dont je t'ai parlé** the one I told you about; **cette marque est celle recommandée par X** this is the brand recommended by X.

cénacle [senakl(ə)] *nm* (literary) coterie; *(Rel)* cenacle.

cendre [sɑ̃dʀ(ə)] *nf (gén)* ash. **~(s)** *[charbon]* ash, ashes, cinders; *(braises)* embers; *[mort]* **~s** ashes; **couleur de ~** ashen, ash-coloured; *(Rel)* **les C~s** Ash Wednesday; *(Géol)* **~s volcaniques** volcanic ash. ◆ **cendré, e 1** *adj (couleur)* ashen. **gris/blond ~** ash grey/blond. **2** *nf (piste)* cinder track. ◆ **cendreux, -euse** *adj* ashy; *teint* ashen. ◆ **cendrier** *nm [fumeur]* ashtray; *[poêle]* ash pan.

Cendrillon [sɑ̃dʀijɔ̃] *nf (lit, fig)* Cinderella.

Cène [sɛn] *nf*: **la ~** the Last Supper.

cénotaphe [senɔtaf] *nm* cenotaph.

cens [sɑ̃s] *nm*: ~ **électoral** ≃ poll tax.

censé, e [sɑ̃se] *adj*: **être ~ faire qch** to be supposed to do sth. ◆ **censément** *adv (en principe)* supposedly; *(pratiquement)* virtually.

censeur [sɑ̃sœʀ] *nm (Hist, Presse)* censor; *(fig)* critic; *(Scol)* ≃ deputy *ou* assistant head; ≃ assistant *ou* vice-principal *(US)*. **Madame le ~** the deputy headmistress, the assistant principal *(US)*.

censurer [sɑ̃syʀe] (1) *vt (Ciné, Presse)* to censor; *(fig, Pol, Rel)* to censure. ◆ **censure** *nf (Ciné, Presse) (examen)* censorship; *(censeurs)* (board of) censors; *(Psych)* censor. **les ~s de** the censure of.

cent [sɑ̃] **1** *adj* (**a**) one hundred, a hundred. **quatre ~ treize** four hundred and thirteen; **deux ~s chaises** two hundred chairs; *(ordinal: inv)* **page quatre ~** page four hundred. (**b**) **il a ~ fois raison** he's absolutely right; ~ **fois mieux** a hundred times better; **je préférerais ~ fois faire votre travail** I'd far rather do your job; **il est aux ~ coups** he is frantic; **faire les ~ pas** to pace up and down; **quatre ~s mètres haies** 400 metres hurdles; **tu ne vas pas attendre ~ sept ans *** you can't wait for ever; **je vous le donne en ~** you'll never guess. **2** *nm* (**a**) a hundred. **il y a ~ contre un à parier que** it's a hundred to one that; **~ pour ~** a hundred per cent; *pour autres locutions V* **six.** (**b**) *(US, Can: monnaie)* cent.

centaine [sɑ̃tɛn] *nf* hundred. *(environ cent)* **une ~ de** about a hundred, a hundred or so; **plusieurs ~s (de)** several hundred; **des ~s de** hundreds of; **10 F la ~** 10 francs a hundred; *V* **soixantaine.**

centaure [sɑ̃tɔʀ] *nm* centaur.

centenaire [sɑ̃tnɛʀ] **1** *adj*: **cet arbre est ~** this tree is a hundred years old, this is a hundred-year-old tree. **2** *nmf (personne)* centenarian. **3** *nm (anniversaire)* centenary.

centième [sɑ̃tjɛm] **1** *adj, nmf* hundredth; *pour loc V* **sixième. 2** *nf (Théât)* hundredth performance.

centigrade [sɑ̃tigʀad] *adj* centigrade. ◆ **centigramme** *nm* centigramme. ◆ **centilitre** *nm* centilitre. ◆ **centime** *nm* centime. *(fig)* **je n'ai pas un ~** I haven't got a penny *ou* a cent *(US)*. ◆ **centimètre** *nm* centimetre; *(ruban)* tape measure.

centrafricain, e [sɑ̃tʀafʀikɛ̃, ɛn] *adj* of the Central African Republic. **République ~e** Central African Republic.

centrage [sɑ̃tʀaʒ] *nm* centring.

central, e, *mpl* **-aux** [sɑ̃tʀal, o] **1** *adj (gén)* central; *partie* centre; *bureau* main. **2** *nm (Téléc)* **~ (téléphonique)** (telephone) exchange. **3** *nf (prison)* prison, ≃ county jail *(US)* , ≃ (state) penitentiary *(US)*. **~e (électrique)** power station *ou* plant *(US)*; **~e syndicale** trade union.

centralien, -ienne [sɑ̃tʀaljɛ̃, jɛn] *nm, f* student *ou* former student of the École centrale.

centraliser [sɑ̃tʀalize] (1) *vt* to centralize. ◆ **centralisateur, -trice** *adj* centralizing. ◆ **centralisation** *nf* centralization. ◆ **centralisme** *nm* centralism.

centre [sɑ̃tʀ(ə)] **1** *nm (gén)* centre. **le C~ (de la France)** central France; **~-ville** town *ou* city centre; **il se croit le ~ du monde** he thinks the universe revolves around him; **les grands ~s universitaires** the great academic centres; *(Pol)* **~ gauche** centre left. **2** : **~ commercial** shopping centre *ou* arcade, shopping mall *(US)*; **~ culturel** arts centre; **~ de détention préventive** remand prison; **~ de documentation** resource centre, reference library; **~ d'éducation surveillée** community home with education, reformatory *(US)* ; **~ hospitalier** hospital complex; *(Poste)* **~ de tri** sorting office; *(lit, fig)* **~s vitaux** vital organs.

centrer [sɑ̃tʀe] (1) *vt (Sport, Tech)* to centre. **~ une discussion sur** to centre *ou* focus a discussion on.

centrifuge [sɑ̃tʀifyʒ] *adj* centrifugal. ◆ **centrifuger** (3) *vt* to centrifuge. ◆ **centrifugeuse** *nf* centrifuge.

centripète [sɑ̃tʀipɛt] *adj* centripetal.

centuple [sɑ̃typl(ə)] **1** *adj* a hundred times as large (*de* as). **2** *nm*: **le ~ de 10** a hundred times 10; **au ~** a hundredfold. ◆ **centupler** (1) *vti* to increase a hundred times *ou* a hundredfold.

centurion [sɑ̃tyʀjɔ̃] *nm* centurion.

cep [sɛp] *nm*: **~ (de vigne)** vine stock. ◆ **cépage** *nm* (type of) vine.

cèpe [sɛp] *nm (Culin)* cepe; *(Bot)* boletus.

cependant [s(ə)pɑ̃dɑ̃] *conj* (**a**) *(pourtant)* nevertheless, however, yet. **et ~ c'est vrai** yet *ou* but nevertheless it is true. (**b**) *(pendant ce temps)* meanwhile. **~ que** while.

céramique [seʀamik] *nf* ceramic. *(art)* **la ~** ceramics; **vase en ~** ceramic vase.

cerceau, *pl* **~x** [sɛʀso] *nm* hoop.

cercle [sɛʀkl(ə)] *nm* (**a**) *(lit)* circle, ring; *(Géom)* circle. **faire ~ (autour de qn/qch)** to make a circle *ou* ring (round sb/sth); **~ vicieux** vicious circle. (**b**) *[famille, amis]* circle; *[connaissances]* scope, range; *(club)* club. **~ littéraire** literary circle *ou* society. (**c**) *[tonneau]* hoop, band; *[roue]* metal rim. ◆ **cercler** (1) *vt* to ring; to hoop; to rim (*de* with). **lunettes cerclées d'écaille** horn-rimmed spectacles.

cercueil [sɛʀkœj] *nm* coffin, casket *(US)*.

céréale [seʀeal] *nf* cereal. ~**s vivrières** *ou* **alimentaires** food grains.

cérébral, e, *mpl* **-aux** [seʀebʀal, o] *adj (Méd)* cerebral; *travail* mental.

cérémonie [seʀemɔni] *nf* ceremony. **sans** ~ *manger* informally; *réception* informal; **faire des** ~**s** to stand on ceremony; **habit(s) de** ~ formal dress. ◆ **cérémonial,** *pl* ~**s** *nm* ceremonial. ◆ **cérémonieusement** *adv* ceremoniously, formally. ◆ **cérémonieux, -euse** *adj* ceremonious, formal.

cerf [sɛʀ] *nm* stag. ◆ **cerf-volant,** *pl* ~**s-**~**s** *nm* kite. **jouer au** ~ to fly a kite.

cerfeuil [sɛʀfœj] *nm* chervil.

cerise [s(ə)ʀiz] **1** *nf* cherry. **2** *adj inv* cherry(-red). ◆ **cerisier** *nm* cherry tree.

cerner [sɛʀne] (1) *vt ennemi* to encircle, surround; *problème* to delimit, define, zero in on. **avoir les yeux cernés** to have dark rings under one's eyes. ◆ **cerne** *nm (gén)* ring.

certain, e [sɛʀtɛ̃, ɛn] **1** *adj* (**a**) *(après n: incontestable) (gén)* certain; *preuve* positive, sure, definite; *cause* undoubted, sure. **c'est la raison** ~**e de son départ** it's undoubtedly the reason for his going; **c'est** ~ there's no doubt about it, that's quite certain. (**b**) *(convaincu)* sure, certain (*de qch* of sth, *de faire* of doing).
2 *adj indéf (avant n)* (**a**) *(mal défini)* certain. **elle a un** ~ **charme** she's got a certain charm; **dans un** ~ **village où** in a certain *ou* some village where; **un** ~ **M. X** a (certain) *ou* one Mr. X; **dans un** ~ **sens** in a way, in a certain sense, in some senses; **dans une** ~**e mesure** to some extent; **dans** ~**s cas** in some *ou* certain cases. (**b**) *(intensif)* some. **c'est à une** ~**e distance d'ici** it's quite a *ou* some distance from here; **d'un** ~ **âge** elderly.
3 *pron indéf pl:* ~**s** *(personnes)* some (people); *(choses)* some.
◆ **certainement** *adv* certainly. ◆ **certes** *adv (concession)* certainly, admittedly; *(affirmation)* indeed, most certainly; *(bien sûr)* of course.

certificat [sɛʀtifika] *nm (attestation)* certificate, attestation; *(diplôme)* certificate, diploma; *(recommandation) [domestique]* testimonial; *(fig)* guarantee. ~ **médical** doctor's certificate; ~ **de scolarité** attestation of attendance at school *ou* university; ~ **de travail** attestation of employment.

certifier [sɛʀtifje] (7) *vt document* to certify; *signature* to attest, witness. ~ **qch à qn** to assure sb of sth, guarantee sth to sb; **copie certifiée conforme à l'original** certified copy of the original. ◆ **certification** *nf* attestation, witnessing.

certitude [sɛʀtityd] *nf* certainty. **j'ai la** ~ **d'être le plus fort** I am certain *ou* (quite) sure of being the strongest.

cerveau, *pl* ~**x** [sɛʀvo] *nm* brain; *(personne, intelligence)* brain, mind; *(fig: centre de direction)* brain(s). **avoir le** ~ **dérangé** to be deranged *ou* (a bit) cracked *; **c'est le** ~ **de la bande** he's the brain(s) of the gang, he masterminds the gang; **la fuite des** ~**x** the braindrain.

cervelas [sɛʀvəla] *nm* saveloy.

cervelet [sɛʀvəlɛ] *nm* cerebellum.

cervelle [sɛʀvɛl] *nf (Anat)* brain; *(Culin)* brains; *(tête)* head. **se brûler la** ~ to blow one's brains out; **avoir une** ~ **d'oiseau** to be feather-brained *ou* bird-brained.

cervical, e, *mpl* **-aux** [sɛʀvikal, o] *adj* cervical.

ces [se] *adj dém V* **ce.**

césarienne [sezaʀjɛn] *nf* Caesarean (section).

cessation [sɛsɑsjɔ̃] *nf* cessation; *[paiements]* suspension.

cesse [sɛs] *nf* (**a**) **sans** ~ *(tout le temps)* continually, incessantly; *(sans interruption)* continuously, without ceasing. (**b**) **il n'a de** ~ **que** he will not rest until.

cesser [sese] (1) **1** *vt (gén)* to stop; *relations* to (bring to an) end, break off; *fabrication* to discontinue; *(Admin) fonctions* to relinquish, give up. *(Comm)* ~ **tout commerce** to cease trading; ~ **le combat** to stop (the) fighting. **2** ~ **de** *vt indir:* ~ **de faire qch** *(gén)* to stop doing sth; *(renoncer)* to give up doing sth; **ça a cessé d'exister** it has ceased to exist; **son effet n'a pas cessé de se faire sentir** its effect is still making itself felt; **il ne cesse de dire que** he is constantly *ou* he keeps on saying that. **3** *vi (gén)* to stop; *[bruit, activités]* to stop, cease; *[fonctions]* to come to an end; *[fièvre]* to pass, die down. **faire** ~ *bruit* to put a stop to, stop; *scandale* to put an end *ou* a stop to. ◆ **cessez-le-feu** *nm inv* ceasefire.

cession [sɛsjɔ̃] *nf* transfer. **faire** ~ **de** to transfer.

c'est-à-dire [setadiʀ] *conj* that is (to say). ~ **que** *(conséquence)* which means that; *(excuse)* the thing is that.

cet [sɛt] *adj dém V* **ce.**

ceux [sø] *adj dém V* **celui.**

Ceylan [selɑ̃] *nm* Ceylon.

chacal, *pl* ~**s** [ʃakal] *nm* jackal.

chacun, e [ʃakœ̃, yn] *pron indéf* (**a**) *(isolément)* each (one). ~ **de** each (one) *ou* every one of ; ~ **à notre/leur tour** each (of us/of them) in turn. (**b**) *(tous)* everyone, everybody. ~ **son tour!** everyone in turn!, each in turn!; ~ **son goût/pour soi** every man to his (own) taste/for himself.

chagrin, e [ʃagʀɛ̃, in] **1** *adj (triste)* woeful, dejected; *(bougon)* ill-humoured, morose. **2** *nm* grief, sorrow. ~ **d'amour** unhappy love affair; **faire du** ~ **à qn** to grieve *ou* distress sb; **avoir du** ~ to be sorry *ou* upset. ◆ **chagrinant, e** *adj* distressing. ◆ **chagriner** (1) *vt (désoler)* to grieve, distress, upset; *(tracasser)* to worry, bother.

chah [ʃa] *nm* = **shah.**

chahut [ʃay] *nm* uproar. ◆ **chahuter** (1) **1** *vi (faire du bruit)* to make an uproar; *(faire les fous)* to scrap, romp. **2** *vt professeur* to play up, rag; *(*: cahoter) objet* to knock about. ◆ **chahuteur, -euse 1** *adj* rowdy, unruly. **2** *nm, f* rowdy.

chai [ʃɛ] *nm* wine and spirits store(house).

chaîne [ʃɛn] *nf (gén)* chain; *[montagnes]* range, chain; *[magasins]* string, chain; *(Tex)* warp; *(TV, Rad)* channel. *(fig: esclavage)* ~**s** chains, bonds; ~ **d'arpenteur** chain measure; ~ **compacte** music centre; ~ **hi-fi** hi-fi system; ~ **de fabrication/de montage** production/assembly line; *(Aut)* ~ **à neige** snow chain; ~ **de sûreté** safety chain; **produire à la** ~ to massproduce. ◆ **chaînette** *nf* (small) chain. ◆ **chaînon** *nm (lit, fig)* link; *(Géog)* secondary range. *(Ordin)* ~ **de données** data link.

chair [ʃɛʀ] *nf* flesh. **entrer dans les** ~**s** to penetrate the flesh; **en** ~ **et en os** in the flesh; **(couleur)** ~ flesh-coloured; **donner la** ~ **de poule** to give goose-flesh *ou* goosebumps *(US)*; ~ **à saucisse** sausage meat; *(fig)* **je vais en faire de la** ~ **à pâté** I'm going to make mincemeat of him; **bien en** ~ well-padded *(hum)*, plump; **sa propre** ~ his own flesh and blood.

chaire [ʃɛʀ] *nf [prédicateur]* pulpit; *[pape]* throne; *[professeur] (estrade)* rostrum; *(poste)* chair.

chaise [ʃɛz] *nf* chair. ~ **de bébé** highchair ; ~ **électrique** electric chair; ~ **longue** deckchair ; ~ **(à porteurs)** sedan(-chair). ◆ **chaisière** *nf* (female) chair attendant.

chaland [ʃalɑ̃] *nm (Naut)* barge.

châle [ʃɑl] *nm* shawl.

chalet [ʃalɛ] *nm* chalet.

chaleur [ʃalœʀ] *nf* (**a**) *(gén, Phys)* heat; *(agréable)* warmth. **les grandes ~s (de l'été)** the hot (summer) days *ou* weather; **'craint la ~'** 'to be kept in a cool place'. (**b**) *[discussion]* heat; *[accueil]* warmth; *[convictions]* fervour. **défendre avec ~** to defend hotly *ou* heatedly. (**c**) *(Zool)* **être en ~** to be on *ou* in heat; *(Méd)* **avoir des ~s** to have hot flushes *ou* flashes *(US)*. ◆ **chaleureusement** *adv* warmly. ◆ **chaleureux, -euse** *adj* warm.

challenge [ʃalɑ̃ʒ] *nm (épreuve)* contest, tournament; *(trophée)* trophy.

chaloupe [ʃalup] *nf* launch. **~ de sauvetage** lifeboat.

chaloupé, e [ʃalupe] *adj danse* swaying; *démarche* rolling.

chalumeau, *pl* **~x** [ʃalymo] *nm (Tech)* blowlamp, blowtorch *(US)*.

chalut [ʃaly] *nm* trawl (net). **pêcher au ~** to trawl. ◆ **chalutier** *nm (bateau)* trawler; *(pêcheur)* trawlerman.

chamailler (se) * [ʃamɑje] (1) *vpr* to squabble, bicker. ◆ **chamaillerie** * *nf* squabble. ◆ **chamailleur, -euse** * **1** *adj* quarrelsome. **2** *nm, f* squabbler.

chaman [ʃaman] *nm* Shaman. ◆ **chamanisme** *nm* shamanism.

chamarré, e [ʃamaʀe] *adj* richly coloured. **~ d'or** bedecked with gold.

chambard * [ʃɑ̃baʀ] *nm (vacarme)* row, rumpus *; *(bagarre)* scuffle, brawl; *(désordre)* shambles * *(sg)*, mess; *(bouleversement)* upheaval. ◆ **chambardement** * *nm* upheaval. ◆ **chambarder** * (1) *vt (bouleverser)* to turn upside down; *(se débarrasser de)* to chuck out ‡.

chambellan [ʃɑ̃belɑ̃] *nm* chamberlain.

chamboulement * [ʃɑ̃bulmɑ̃] *nm (désordre)* chaos; *(bouleversement)* upheaval. ◆ **chambouler** * (1) *vt objets* to turn upside down; *projets* to mess up *, make a mess of.

chambranle [ʃɑ̃bʀɑ̃l] *nm [porte]* frame; *[cheminée]* mantelpiece.

chambre [ʃɑ̃bʀ(ə)] **1** *nf* (**a**) bedroom; *(littér: pièce)* chamber *(littér)*. **~ à un lit/à deux lits** single-/twin-bedded room; **~ pour deux personnes** double room; **faire ~ à part** to sleep in separate rooms; **travailler en ~** to work at home. (**b**) *(Pol)* House, Chamber; *(Jur: section)* division ; *(tribunal)* court; *(Admin, groupement)* chamber. (**c**) *(Anat, Tech)* chamber. **2** : **~ à air** inner tube ; **~ d'amis** spare *ou* guest room; **~ de bonne** maid's room; **~ de commerce** Chamber of Commerce; **la C~ des communes** the House of Commons ; **~ à coucher** *(pièce)* bedroom; *(mobilier)* bedroom suite; **la C~ des députés** the Chamber of Deputies; **~ forte** strongroom; **~ froide** cold room ; **~ à gaz** gas chamber; **la C~ des lords** the House of Lords; *(Phot)* **~ noire** dark room. ◆ **chambrée** *nf* room; *[soldats]* barrack-room. ◆ **chambrer** (1) *vt vin* to bring to room temperature.

chameau, *pl* **~x** [ʃamo] *nm (Zool)* camel; *(* péj)* beast *. ◆ **chamelier** *nm* camel driver. ◆ **chamelle** *nf* she-camel.

chamois [ʃamwa] *nm* chamois.

chamoisine [ʃamwazin] *nf* shammy leather.

champ [ʃɑ̃] **1** *nm* (**a**) *(Agr, Sci)* field; *(fig: domaine)* field, area. *(campagne)* **les ~s** the country(side); **fleurs des ~s** wild flowers; *(Phot)* **être dans le/sortir du ~** to be in/go out of shot; **pas assez de ~** not enough depth of focus. (**b**) **avoir du ~** to have elbowroom, have room to move; **laisser le ~ libre à qn** to leave sb a clear field; **prendre du ~** *(lit, fig)* to draw back. **2** : **~ d'action** sphere of activity; **~ d'aviation** airfield; **~ de bataille** battlefield; **~ de courses** racecourse; **~ de foire** fairground; **mort au ~ d'honneur** killed in action; **~ de tir** *(terrain)* rifle range; *(visée)* field of fire. ◆ **champêtre** *adj (gén)* rural; *vie* country.

champagne [ʃɑ̃paɲ] **1** *nm* champagne. **2** *nf:* **la C~** Champagne, the Champagne region.

champignon [ʃɑ̃piɲɔ̃] *nm (gén)* mushroom; *(vénéneux)* toadstool; *(Méd, terme de botanique)* fungus; *(Aut *)* accelerator. **~ atomique** mushroom cloud.

champion, -onne [ʃɑ̃pjɔ̃, ɔn] **1** *adj* (*) first-rate. **2** *nm, f (gén)* champion. **se faire le ~ d'une cause** to champion a cause. ◆ **championnat** *nm* championship.

chance [ʃɑ̃s] *nf* (**a**) *(bonne fortune)* (good) luck. **il a la ~ d'y aller** he's lucky *ou* fortunate enough to be going, he has the good luck *ou* good fortune to be going; **par ~** luckily, fortunately; **pas de ~!** hard *ou* bad luck!; *(iro)* **c'est bien ma ~** (that's) just my luck! (**b**) *(hasard)* luck, chance. **tenter sa ~** to try one's luck; **mettre toutes les ~s de son côté** to take no chances; **mauvaise ~** ill-luck. (**c**) *(possibilité)* chance. **quelles sont ses ~s?** what are his chances *ou* what chance has he got?; **les ~s d'un accord...** the chances of a settlement...; **il y a toutes les ~s que** the chances are that.

chanceler [ʃɑ̃sle] (4) *vi [personne]* to totter, stagger; *[objet]* to wobble, totter; *[autorité]* to totter, falter; *[résolution]* to waver, falter. ◆ **chancelant, e** *adj pas* unsteady, faltering; *objet* wobbly; *mémoire, santé, autorité* shaky.

chancelier [ʃɑ̃səlje] *nm (Pol)* chancellor; *[ambassade]* secretary. **le C~ de l'Échiquier** the Chancellor of the Exchequer. ◆ **chancellerie** *nf* chancellery.

chanceux, -euse [ʃɑ̃sø, øz] *adj* lucky, fortunate.

chancre [ʃɑ̃kʀ(ə)] *nm* canker.

chandail [ʃɑ̃daj] *nm* (thick) jersey *ou* sweater.

Chandeleur [ʃɑ̃dlœʀ] *nf*: **la ~** Candlemas.

chandelier [ʃɑ̃dəlje] *nm* candlestick; *(à plusieurs branches)* candelabra.

chandelle [ʃɑ̃dɛl] *nf (bougie)* (tallow) candle; *(Aviat)* chandelle; *(Rugby, Ftbl)* up-and-under; *(Tennis)* lob; *(Gym)* shoulder stand. **dîner aux ~s** dinner by candlelight; *(loc) (hum)* **tenir la ~** to play gooseberry; *(Golf)* **lancer en ~** to loft; **~ romaine** roman candle.

change [ʃɑ̃ʒ] *nm (Fin) [devises]* exchange; *(taux)* exchange rate. *(Banque)* **faire le ~** to exchange money; **au cours actuel du ~** at the current rate of exchange; *(fig)* **gagner/perdre au ~** to gain/lose on the exchange *ou* deal; **donner le ~ à qn** to put sb off the scent *ou* off the track.

changeant, e [ʃɑ̃ʒɑ̃, ɑ̃t] *adj personne, fortune* changeable, fickle, changing; *paysage* changing; *temps* changeable, unsettled.

changement [ʃɑ̃ʒmɑ̃] *nm (gén)* change (*de* in); *(transformation)* alteration; *(Admin: mutation)* transfer. **le ~ de la roue** changing the wheel, the wheel change; **la situation reste sans ~** the situation remains unchanged *ou* unaltered; **~ en bien** change for the better; **~ de programme** *(projet)* change of plan; *(spectacle etc)* change in the programme; **~ de direction** *(sens)* change of direction; *(dirigeants)* change of management; **~ de vitesse** *(dispositif)* gears, gear stick *ou* lever; *(action)* change of gears; *[bicyclette]* gear(s).

changer [ʃɑ̃ʒe] (3) **1** *vt* (**a**) *(modifier)* to change, alter. **ce chapeau la change** this hat makes her look different; **cela change tout!** that makes all the difference!, that changes everything!; **une promenade lui changera les idées** a walk will take his mind off things; **cela ne change rien au fait que** it doesn't change *ou* alter the fact that; **~ qch/qn en** to change *ou* turn sth/sb into; **cela les changera de leur routine** it will be *ou* make a change for them from their routine. (**b**) *(rem-*

placer) (gén) to change; *décor* to change, shift; *marchandise, argent* to exchange (*contre* for). **j'ai changé ma place contre la sienne** I changed *ou* swapped * places with him, I exchanged my place for his; ~ **un malade** to change a patient. (**c**) *(déplacer)* to move. ~ **qn/qch de place** to move sb/sth to a different place, shift sb/sth; *(fig)* ~ **son fusil d'épaule** to change *ou* alter one's stand.
2 ~ **de** *vt indir (gén)* to change; *(modifier)* to alter; *(échanger)* to exchange. ~ **de nom** to change one's name; ~ **de domicile** to move house; ~ **d'avis** to change one's mind; **elle a changé de visage** *(d'émotion)* her expression changed *ou* altered; **change de disque!** ‡ put another record on! * ; ~ **de train** to change trains; ~ **de camp** to change sides; ~ **de position** to alter *ou* change one's position; ~ **de côté** *(dans la rue)* to cross over (to the other side); ~ **de propriétaire** *ou* **de mains** to change hands; **changeons de sujet** let's change the subject; *(Naut)* ~ **de cap** to change *ou* alter course; ~ **de place avec qn** to change *ou* swap * places with sb.
3 *vi (se transformer)* to change, alter; *(Rail)* to change. ~ **en bien/en mal** to change for the better/the worse; **pour (ne pas)** ~ **!** (just) for *ou* by way of a change!; **ça change (de la routine)** it makes a change (from the routine).
4 se ~ *vpr* to change (one's clothes). **se** ~ **en** to change *ou* turn into.

changeur [ʃɑ̃ʒœʀ] *nm* moneychanger. ~ **(de disques)** record changer; ~ **de monnaie** change machine.

chanoine [ʃanwan] *nm (personne)* canon.

chanson [ʃɑ̃sɔ̃] *nf* song. **c'est toujours la même** ~ it's always the same old story; ~ **folklorique** folksong; ~ **de geste** chanson de geste. ◆ **chansonnette** *nf* ditty.

chant [ʃɑ̃] *nm (action, art)* singing; *(chanson)* song; *(Poésie: chapitre)* canto. **le** ~ **de l'oiseau** *(musique)* the warbling *ou* singing of the bird; *(mélodie)* the song of the bird; **au** ~ **du coq** at cockcrow; *(lit, fig)* ~ **du cygne** swan song; ~ **de Noël** (Christmas) carol; ~ **religieux** hymn; **cours de** ~ singing lessons; ~ **grégorien** Gregorian chant.

chantage [ʃɑ̃taʒ] *nm* blackmail. **faire du** ~ **à qn** to blackmail sb.

chanter [ʃɑ̃te] (1) **1** *vt (gén)* to sing; *exploits* to sing (of). **qu'est-ce qu'il nous chante là?** * what's this he's telling us?; ~ **qch sur tous les tons** to harp on *ou* go on about sth. **2** *vi (gén)* to sing; *[oiseau]* to sing, warble; *[coq]* to crow; *[poule]* to cackle; *[insecte]* to chirp; *[ruisseau]* to babble. **c'est comme si on chantait** * it's like talking to a deaf man, it's a waste of breath; *(par chantage)* **faire** ~ **qn** to blackmail sb; **vas-y si le programme te chante** * go if the programme appeals to you *ou* if you fancy the programme. ◆ **chantant, e** *adj voix* singsong, lilting; *musique* tuneful. ◆ **chanteur, -euse** *nm, f* singer.

chantier [ʃɑ̃tje] *nm (Constr)* (building) site; *(entrepôt)* depot, yard. *(sur une route) (écriteau)* **'fin de** ~**'** 'road clear', 'end of roadworks'; **quel** ~ **dans ta chambre!** * what a shambles * *ou* mess in your room!; **avoir/mettre un ouvrage en** ~ to have/put a piece of work in hand *ou* on the go; **nous sommes en** ~ **depuis 2 mois** we've had workmen in *ou* alterations going on for 2 months; ~ **de démolition** demolition site; ~ **naval** shipyard.

chantonner [ʃɑ̃tɔne] (1) *vti* to sing softly, hum, croon.

chantre [ʃɑ̃tʀ(ə)] *nm (Rel)* cantor; *(poète)* bard; *(laudateur)* exalter.

chanvre [ʃɑ̃vʀ(ə)] *nm (Bot, Tex)* hemp.

chaos [kao] *nm (lit, fig)* chaos. ◆ **chaotique** *adj* chaotic.

chaparder * [ʃapaʀde] (1) *vti* to pinch *, pilfer (*à* from). ◆ **chapardage** * *nm* petty theft. ◆ **chapardeur, -euse** * **1** *adj* light-fingered. **2** *nm, f* pilferer.

chapeau, *pl* ~**x** [ʃapo] *nm (gén)* hat; *(Bot, Tech)* cap. **tirer son** ~ **à qn** * to take off one's hat to sb; ~**!** * well done, jolly good *; *(Aut)* ~ **de roue** hub cap; **sur les** ~**x de roues** * at top speed; ~ **haut-de-forme** top hat; ~ **melon** bowler (hat); ~ **mou** trilby (hat), fedora *(US)*. ◆ **chapeauter** (1) *vt (Admin etc)* to head (up), oversee.

chapelain [ʃaplɛ̃] *nm* chaplain.

chapelet [ʃaplɛ] *nm (Rel)* rosary. **dévider son** ~ * to recite one's grievances; ~ **de** *oignons, injures* string of; *bombes* stick of.

chapelier, -ière [ʃapəlje, jɛʀ] **1** *adj* hat. **2** *nm, f* hatter.

chapelle [ʃapɛl] *nf* chapel; *(coterie)* coterie, clique. ~ **ardente** *(dans une église)* chapel of rest; **l'école a été transformée en** ~ **ardente** the school was turned into a temporary morgue.

chapelure [ʃaplyʀ] *nf* (dried) bread-crumbs.

chaperon [ʃapʀɔ̃] *nm (personne)* chaperon. **le petit** ~ **rouge** Little Red Riding Hood. ◆ **chaperonner** (1) *vt* to chaperon.

chapiteau, *pl* ~**x** [ʃapito] *nm [colonne]* capital; *[cirque]* big top.

chapitre [ʃapitʀ(ə)] *nm [livre]* chapter; *[budget]* section, item; *(Rel)* chapter. **sur ce** ~ on that subject *ou* score. ◆ **chapitrer** (1) *vt (réprimande)* to admonish, reprimand; *(recommandation)* to lecture (*sur* on, about).

chaque [ʃak] *adj (défini)* every, each; *(indéfini)* every. ~ **élève** every *ou* each pupil; **10 F** ~ 10 francs each *ou* apiece; ~ **homme naît libre** every man is born free; **à** ~ **instant** every other second.

char [ʃaʀ] *nm (Mil)* tank; *[carnaval]* (carnival) float; *(charrette)* waggon, cart; *(Antiq)* chariot. *(fig)* **le** ~ **de l'État** the ship of state; ~ **à voile** sand yacht, land yacht; **faire du** ~ **à voile** to go sand-yachting.

charabia * [ʃaʀabja] *nm* gibberish, gobbledygook *.

charade [ʃaʀad] *nf (parlée)* riddle; *(mimée)* charade.

charbon [ʃaʀbɔ̃] *nm* coal; *(Méd)* anthrax; *(crayon)* piece of charcoal; *[arc électrique]* carbon. ~ **actif** active carbon; ~ **de bois** charcoal; **être sur des** ~**s ardents** to be like a cat on hot bricks *ou* on a hot tin roof *(US)*. ◆ **charbonnages** *nmpl (houillères)* collieries, coalmines; *(ministère)* Coal Board. ◆ **charbonnier** *nm (personne)* coalman; *(navire)* collier.

charcutier, -ière [ʃaʀkytje, jɛʀ] *nm, f* pork butcher; *(traiteur)* delicatessen dealer; *(* fig)* butcher * *(fig)*. ◆ **charcuter** * (1) *vt* to butcher *. ◆ **charcuterie** *nf (magasin)* pork butcher's shop and delicatessen; *(produits)* cooked pork meats; *(commerce)* pork meat trade; delicatessen trade.

chardon [ʃaʀdɔ̃] *nm* thistle.

chardonneret [ʃaʀdɔnʀɛ] *nm* goldfinch.

charge [ʃaʀʒ(ə)] *nf* (**a**) *(lit, fig: fardeau)* burden; *[véhicule, voûte]* load; *[navire]* freight, cargo. *[camion]* ~ **maximale** maximum load. (**b**) *(responsabilité)* responsibility; *(poste)* office. (**c**) *(dépenses)* ~**s** expenses, costs, outgoings; *[locataire]* maintenance charges; ~**s sociales** social security contributions; **les** ~**s de l'État** government expenditure. (**d**) *(Mil, Jur)* charge; *(caricature)* caricature. *(Sport)* ~ **irrégulière** illegal tackle. (**e**) *[fusil] (action)* loading, charging; *(explosifs)* charge; *(Élec) (action)* charging; *(quantité)* charge. **mettre une batterie en** ~ to put a battery on charge. (**f**) **être à la** ~ **de qn** *[frais]* to be chargeable to sb, be payable by sb; *[personne]* to be dependent upon sb, be supported by sb; ~**s de famille** dependents; **enfants à** ~ dependent children; **les enfants confiés à sa**

~ the children in his care; **avoir la ~ de qn/de faire qch** to be responsible for sb/for doing sth; **à ~ pour lui de payer** on condition that he meets the costs; **prendre en ~** *personne* to take charge of; *frais* to take care of; *passager* to pick up, take on; **prendre un enfant en ~** *[Assistance publique]* to take a child into care; *(fig)* **l'adolescent doit se prendre en ~** the adolescent must look after himself *ou* take charge of himself; **prise en ~** *[taxi]* minimum (standard) charge; *[Sécurité sociale]* acceptance (of financial liability).

chargé, e [ʃarʒe] **1** *adj (gén)* loaded; *estomac* overloaded; *programme* full, busy; *conscience* troubled. ~ **de** *honneurs* laden with; *sens, menaces* full of; *nuages, parfums* heavy with; *tâche, enfant* in charge of; **homme au passé ~** man with a past; **avoir la langue ~e** to have a coated *ou* furred tongue. **2** : ~ **d'affaires** *nm* chargé d'affaires; ~ **de famille** *adj* with family responsibilities; ~ **de mission** *nm* official representative.

chargement [ʃaʀʒəmɑ̃] *nm (action)* loading; *(marchandises)* load; *[navire]* freight, cargo.

charger [ʃaʀʒe] (3) **1** *vt* (**a**) *(gén)* to load; *(à l'excès)* to overload. **table chargée de mets** table laden *ou* loaded with dishes; ~ **qn de** *paquets* to load sb up *ou* weigh sb down with; *impôts* to burden sb with, weigh sb down with; *[taxi]* ~ **un client** to pick up a passenger. (**b**) *fusil, caméra* to load; *(Élec)* to charge; *chaudière* to stoke. (**c**) *(responsabilité)* ~ **qn de qch** to put sb in charge of sth; ~ **qn de faire** to give sb the responsibility *ou* job of doing, ask sb to do; **être chargé de faire** to be put in charge of doing, be made responsible for doing; **on l'a chargé d'une mission importante** he was given *ou* assigned an important mission; **on m'a chargé d'appliquer le règlement** I've been instructed to apply the rule; **il m'a chargé de ses amitiés pour vous** he asked me to give you his regards. (**d**) *(accuser)* to bring all possible evidence against. ~ **qn de** *crime* to charge sb with. (**e**) *(attaquer) (Mil)* to charge (at); *(Sport)* to charge, tackle. (**f**) *(caricaturer) portrait* to make a caricature of; *description* to overdo, exaggerate; *rôle* to overact.

2 se ~ *vpr*: **se ~ de** to see to, take care of, attend to; **se ~ de faire** to undertake to do; **je me charge de lui** leave it to me to look after him; **je me charge de le faire venir** I'll make sure *ou* I'll see to it that he comes.

chargeur [ʃaʀʒœʀ] *nm* (**a**) *(personne) (gén, Mil)* loader; *(Naut: négociant)* shipper. (**b**) *(Phot)* cartridge; *[arme]* magazine; *(balles)* clip. ~ **de batterie** (battery) charger.

chariot [ʃaʀjo] *nm (charrette)* waggon; *(petit)* cart; *(à roulettes)* trolley; *(de manutention)* truck; *[machine à écrire]* carriage.

charitable [ʃaʀitabl(ə)] *adj (gén)* charitable; *(gentil)* kind (*envers* towards); *(iro) conseil* friendly, kindly. ◆ **charitablement** *adv* charitably; kindly.

charité [ʃaʀite] *nf* (**a**) *(gén, Rel)* charity; *(gentillesse)* kindness. **ayez la ~ de** have the kindness to, be kind enough to. (**b**) *(aumône)* charity. **demander la ~** *(lit)* to beg for charity; *(fig)* to come begging; **faire la ~ à** to give (something) to; **la ~ publique** (public) charity; ~ **bien ordonnée commence par soi-même** charity begins at home; **vente de ~** sale of work.

charivari * [ʃaʀivaʀi] *nm* hullabaloo *.

charlatan [ʃaʀlatɑ̃] *nm (péj) (gén)* charlatan; *(médecin)* quack; *(vendeur)* mountebank. ◆ **charlatanesque** *adj (de guérisseur)* quack; *(d'escroc)* phoney, bogus. ◆ **charlatanisme** *nm* charlatanism.

charme [ʃaʀm(ə)] *nm* (**a**) *(attrait)* charm, appeal; *(envoûtement)* spell. **le ~ de la nouveauté** the attraction(s) of novelty; **ça offre peu de ~ pour moi** it does not really appeal to me, it holds few attractions for me; *(hum)* ~**s** charms *(hum)*; **exercer un ~ sur qn** to have sb under one's spell; **tenir qn sous le ~ (de)** to captivate sb (with), hold sb spellbound (with); **faire du ~ à qn** to make eyes at sb; **se porter comme un ~** to be *ou* feel as fit as a fiddle. (**b**) *(Bot)* hornbeam. ◆ **charmant, e** *adj (gén)* charming, delightful; *soirée* delightful, lovely. *(iro)* **c'est ~!** charming! *(iro)*. ◆ **charmer** (1) *vt* to charm, delight; *serpents* to charm. **être charmé de faire** to be delighted to do. ◆ **charmeur, -euse** **1** *adj* winning, engaging. **2** *nm, f* charmer. ~ **de serpent** snake charmer.

charnel, -elle [ʃaʀnɛl] *adj instincts* carnal; *créature* earthly. ◆ **charnellement** *adv désirer* sexually.

charnier [ʃaʀnje] *nm* mass grave.

charnière [ʃaʀnjɛʀ] *nf (lit)* hinge; *(fig)* turning point; *(Mil)* pivot. **discipline-~** interlinking field of study; **époque-~** transition period.

charnu, e [ʃaʀny] *adj* fleshy.

charogne [ʃaʀɔɲ] *nf (cadavre)* carrion; *(*‡*: salaud)* swine ‡ *(inv)*. ◆ **charognard** *nm (lit, fig)* vulture.

charpente [ʃaʀpɑ̃t] *nf (gén)* framework; *(carrure)* build, frame. ◆ **charpenté, e** *adj*: **bien ~** well built. ◆ **charpentier** *nm* carpenter; *(Naut)* shipwright.

charpie [ʃaʀpi] *nf (pansement)* shredded linen. *(lit, fig)* **être/mettre en ~** to be/tear in shreds.

charrette [ʃaʀɛt] *nf* cart. ~ **à bras** handcart, barrow. ◆ **charretée** *nf* cartload (*de* of). *(* fig)* **des ~s de** loads * *ou* stacks * of. ◆ **charretier** *nm* carter. **de ~** *langage* coarse.

charrier [ʃaʀje] (7) **1** *vt* (**a**) *(avec brouette)* to cart (along), wheel (along); *(sur le dos)* to heave (along); *[camion]* to carry, cart; *[fleuve]* to carry (along), sweep (along). (**b**) (‡*: se moquer de)* ~ **qn** to take sb for a ride *, kid sb on *. **2** *vi* (‡) *(abuser)* to go too far. *(plaisanter)* **tu charries** you must be kidding * *ou* joking.

charron [ʃaʀɔ̃] *nm* cartwright, wheelwright.

charrue [ʃaʀy] *nf* plough, plow *(US)*. **mettre la ~ avant les bœufs** to put the cart before the horse.

charte [ʃaʀt(ə)] *nf* charter; *(Hist: titre)* title, deed.

charter [ʃaʀtɛʀ] **1** *nm (vol)* charter flight; *(avion)* chartered plane. **2** *adj inv billet* charter; *avion* chartered.

chas [ʃa] *nm* eye *(of needle)*.

chasse [ʃas] **1** *nf* (**a**) *(gén)* hunting; *(au fusil)* shooting. **aller à la ~ aux papillons** to go butterfly-hunting; **habits de ~** hunting clothes. (**b**) *(période)* hunting *ou* shooting season; *(gibier)* game; *(terrain)* hunting ground. **faire (une) bonne ~** to get a good bag; ~ **gardée** *(lit)* private hunting (ground); *(fig)* private ground. (**c**) **la ~** *(chasseurs)* the hunt; *(Aviat)* the fighters. (**d**) *(poursuite)* chase. **faire la ~ à** *moustiques, abus* to hunt down; **faire la ~ aux appartements** to be *ou* go flat- *ou* apartment- *(US)* hunting; **donner la ~** to give chase (*à* to); **se mettre en ~ pour trouver qch** to go hunting for sth.

2 : ~ **à l'affût** hunting (from a hide); ~ **à courre** hunting; ~ **d'eau** toilet flush; **tirer la ~ (d'eau)** to flush the toilet; ~ **à l'homme** manhunt; ~ **sous-marine** harpoon fishing.

◆ **chasse-clou,** *pl* ~-~**s** *nm* nail punch. ◆ **chassé-croisé** *nm (Danse)* chassé-croisé; *(erreur)* mix-up. **avec tous ces ~s-~s** with all these to-ings and fro-ings *ou* mix-ups. ◆ **chasse-neige** *nm inv* snowplough.

châsse [ʃɑs] *nf (reliquaire)* reliquary, shrine.

chasser [ʃase] (1) **1** *vt* (**a**) *(gén)* to hunt; *(au fusil)* to shoot, hunt. ~ **à l'affût** to hunt from a hide; ~ **le faisan** to go pheasant-shooting. (**b**) *importun, ennemi* to drive *ou* chase away; *domestique, manifestant* to turn out; *immigrant* to drive out, expel. **chassant de la main les insectes** brushing away *ou* driving off the insects with his hand; **chassez le naturel, il revient au galop** what's bred in the bone comes out in the flesh *(Prov)*. (**c**) *odeur, doute* to dispel, drive away; *idée* to dismiss, chase away. **le vent a chassé le brouillard** the wind dispelled *ou* blew away the fog. (**d**) *clou* to drive in. **2** *vi* (**a**) *(gén)* to go hunting; *(au fusil)* to go shooting. (**b**) *[véhicule]* to skid; *[ancre]* to drag.

chasseur [ʃasœʀ] **1** *nm* (**a**) hunter, huntsman. **c'est un grand ~ de perdrix** he's a great one for partridge-shooting. (**b**) *(Mil) (soldat)* chasseur; *(avion)* fighter. *(régiment)* **le 3ᵉ ~** the 3rd chasseurs. (**c**) *[hôtel]* page (boy), messenger (boy). **2** : **~ alpin** mountain infantryman; **~-bombardier** *nm, pl* **~s-~s** fighter-bomber; **~ d'images** roving photographic enthusiast; *(lit, fig)* **~ de têtes** headhunter.

chassis [ʃɑsi] *nm [véhicule]* chassis, subframe; *(Agr)* cold frame.

chaste [ʃast(ə)] *adj* chaste; *oreilles* innocent. ◆ **chastement** *adv* chastely. ◆ **chasteté** *nf* chastity.

chasuble [ʃazybl(ə)] *nf* chasuble.

chat [ʃa] **1** *nm (gén)* cat; *(mâle)* tomcat. **petit ~** kitten; **mon petit ~** * pet *, love; **jouer à ~** to play tig *ou* tag; **(c'est toi le) ~!** you're it! *ou* he!; **il n'y avait pas un ~ dehors** there wasn't a soul outside; **avoir un ~ dans la gorge** to have a frog in one's throat; **~ échaudé craint l'eau froide** once bitten, twice shy; **quand le ~ n'est pas là, les souris dansent** when the cat's away, the mice will play. **2** : **le C~ Botté** Puss in Boots; **~ de gouttière** alley cat; *(jeu)* **~ perché** 'off-ground' tag *ou* tig; **~ sauvage** wild cat.

châtaigne [ʃɑtɛɲ] *nf (fruit)* (sweet) chestnut; *(*: coup)* clout, biff *; *(*: décharge électrique)* (electric) shock. ◆ **châtaignier** *nm* (sweet) chestnut tree.

châtain [ʃɑtɛ̃] *adj inv cheveux* chestnut (brown); *personne* brown-haired.

château, *pl* **~x** [ʃɑto] *nm (forteresse)* castle; *(palais)* palace, castle; *(manoir)* mansion; *(en France)* château. **bâtir des ~x en Espagne** to build castles in the air *ou* in Spain; **~ de cartes** house of cards; **~ d'eau** water tower; **~ fort** stronghold, fortified castle.

châtelain [ʃɑtlɛ̃] *nm (Hist)* (feudal) lord; *(propriétaire)* squire; *(nouveau riche)* manor-owner. ◆ **châtelaine** *nf* manor-owner; *(épouse)* lady of the manor.

châtier [ʃɑtje] (7) *vt coupable, faute* to punish; *style, langage* to refine. ◆ **châtiment** *nm* punishment.

chatoiement [ʃatwamɑ̃] *nm* glistening, shimmer(ing), sparkle.

chaton [ʃatɔ̃] *nm* (**a**) *(Zool)* kitten; *(Bot)* catkin. **~s** *[saule]* pussy willows; *[poussière]* balls of fluff. (**b**) *(monture)* setting; *(pierre)* stone.

chatouiller [ʃatuje] (1) *vt (lit)* to tickle; *(fig)* to titillate. ◆ **chatouille** * *nf* tickle. **craindre les ~s** to be ticklish. ◆ **chatouillement** *nm*: **~(s)** *(gén)* tickling; *[nez, gorge]* tickle. ◆ **chatouilleux, -euse** *adj (lit)* ticklish; *(susceptible)* touchy, (over-) sensitive (*sur* on, about).

chatoyer [ʃatwaje] (8) *vi* to glisten, shimmer, sparkle.

châtrer [ʃɑtʀe] (1) *vt (gén)* to castrate; *cheval* to geld; *chat* to neuter.

chatte [ʃat] *nf (Zool)* (she-)cat. **ma (petite) ~** * (my) pet *, love.

chattemite [ʃatmit] *nf*: **faire la ~** to be a bit of a coaxer.

chatterie [ʃatʀi] *nf* (**a**) **~s** *(caresses)* playful caresses; *(minauderies)* kittenish ways. (**b**) *(friandise)* titbit.

chatterton [ʃatɛʀtɔn] *nm* insulating tape.

chaud, e [ʃo, od] **1** *adj* (**a**) *(agréable)* warm; *(brûlant)* hot. **cela sort tout ~ du four** it's (piping) hot from the oven. (**b**) *félicitations* warm, hearty; *partisan* keen, ardent; *discussion* heated; *nouvelle, tempérament* hot; *voix, couleur* warm; *bataille* fierce. **il n'est pas très ~ pour le faire** * he is not very keen on doing it, he is not enthusiastic about doing it; **l'alerte a été ~e** it was a near *ou* close thing; **points ~s** hot spots.
2 *nm*: **le ~** (the) heat, the warmth; *(Méd)* **~ et froid** chill; **elle souffre du ~** she suffers from the heat; **restez au ~** stay in the warmth; **garder qch au ~** to keep sth warm *ou* hot; **il a été opéré à ~** he had an emergency operation; **reportage à ~** on-the-spot report.
3 *adv*: **avoir ~** to be *ou* feel warm; *(trop)* to be *ou* feel hot; **j'ai eu ~!** * I got a real fright; **ça ne me fait ni ~ ni froid** it makes no odds to me, I couldn't care less, it cuts no ice with me; **'servir ~'** 'serve hot'; **tenir ~ à qn** to keep sb warm; *(tenir trop chaud)* to make sb too hot. ◆ **chaudement** *adv s'habiller* warmly; *féliciter* warmly, heartily; *défendre* heatedly, hotly.

chaudière [ʃodjɛʀ] *nf* boiler.

chaudron [ʃodʀɔ̃] *nm* cauldron. ◆ **chaudronnerie** *nf (métier)* boilermaking; *(boutique)* coppersmith's workshop; *(usine)* boilerworks. ◆ **chaudronnier** *nm (artisan)* coppersmith; *(ouvrier)* boilermaker.

chauffage [ʃofaʒ] *nm (action)* heating; *(appareils)* heating (system). **~ central** central heating; **mets le ~** *(maison)* put on the heating; *(voiture)* put on the heater.

chauffagiste [ʃofaʒist(ə)] *nm* heating engineer *ou* specialist.

chauffard [ʃofaʀ] *nm (péj)* reckless driver. **~!** * roadhog!

chauffer [ʃofe] (1) **1** *vt* (**a**) **(faire) ~** *soupe* to warm up, heat up; *assiette* to warm, heat. (**b**) *(gén, Tech)* to heat; *[soleil]* to warm; *[soleil brûlant]* to heat. **~ qch à blanc** to make sth white-hot; *(fig)* **~ qn à blanc** to galvanize sb into action. (**c**) (*) *candidat* to cram; *commando* to train up. **2** *vi [aliment, eau, assiette]* to be heating (up), be warming (up); *[moteur]* to warm up; *[four]* to heat up; *(trop chaud)* to overheat; *(donner de la chaleur) [soleil]* to be hot; *[poêle]* to give out a good heat. **le mazout chauffe bien** oil gives out a good heat; **ça va ~!** * sparks will fly!; **le but chauffe** they're on the brink of a goal; *(cache-tampon)* **tu chauffes!** you're getting warm(er)! **3 se ~** *vpr* to warm o.s. **se ~ au bois/gaz** to use wood/gas for heating. ◆ **chauffe-eau** *nm inv* immersion heater. ◆ **chauffe-plats** *nm inv* plate-warmer, hotplate.

chaufferie [ʃofʀi] *nf [usine]* boiler room; *[navire]* stokehold.

chauffeur [ʃofœʀ] *nm* (**a**) driver; *(privé)* chauffeur. **voiture sans ~** self-drive car. (**b**) *[chaudière]* fireman, stoker.

chaume [ʃom] *nm [champ]* stubble; *[toit]* thatch. ◆ **chaumière** *nf* (little) cottage; *(de chaume)* thatched cottage.

chaussée [ʃose] *nf (route)* road, roadway; *(surélevée)* causeway. **~ bombée** cambered road ; **' ~ déformée'** 'uneven road surface'.

chausser [ʃose] (1) *vt souliers, lunettes* to put on. **~ du 40** to take size 40 in shoes; **chausse les enfants** put the children's shoes on (for them), help the children on with their shoes; **se ~** to put one's shoes on; **chaussé de bottes** wearing boots; **se (faire) ~ chez** to buy *ou* get one's shoes at; **ces chaussures chaussent large/bien** these are wide-fitting/well-fitting shoes. ◆ **chausse-pied,** *pl* **~-~s** *nm* shoehorn. ◆ **chaussetrappe,** *pl* **~-~s** *nf* trap. ◆ **chaussette** *nf* sock. ◆ **chausseur** *nm* shoemaker.

chausson [ʃosɔ̃] *nm* slipper; *[bébé]* bootee; *[danseur]* ballet shoe; *(Culin)* turnover.

chaussure [ʃosyʀ] *nf (basse)* shoe; *(montante)* boot. **la ~** *(industrie)* the shoe industry; *(commerce)* the shoe trade; **rayon ~s** shoe *ou* footwear department.

chauve [ʃov] *adj personne* bald(-headed); *crâne* bald; *colline* bare. **~ comme un œuf** * as bald as a coot. ◆ **chauve-souris,** *pl* **~s-~** *nf* bat.

chauvin, e [ʃovɛ̃, in] **1** *adj* chauvinistic, jingoistic. **2** *nm, f* chauvinist, jingoist. ◆ **chauvinisme** *nm* chauvinism, jingoism.

chaux [ʃo] *nf* lime. **blanchi à la ~** whitewashed.

chavirer [ʃaviʀe] (1) **1** *vi (lit)* to capsize, keel over, overturn; *[paysage, esprit]* to reel. **2** *vt* (**a**) **(faire)** ~ *bateau* to capsize, overturn. (**b**) *(bouleverser)* to bowl over.

chef [ʃɛf] **1** *nm [usine]* head, boss *; *[tribu]* chief(tain), headman; *[mouvement]* leader; *(Culin)* chef; *(littér: tête)* head. **tu es un ~** * you're the greatest *; **commandant en ~** commander-in-chief; **rédacteur en ~** chief editor; **de son propre ~** on his own initiative; **au premier ~** greatly; **de ce ~** accordingly.
2 *adj inv*: **gardien ~** chief warden.
3 : **~ d'accusation** charge; **~ d'atelier** (shop) foreman; **~ de bataillon** major; **~ de bureau** head clerk; **~ de chantier** (works *ou* site) foreman ; **~ de classe** class prefect *ou* monitor, class president *(US)*; **~ comptable** chief accountant; **~ d'entreprise** company manager; **~ d'État** head of state ; **~ d'état-major** chief of staff; **~ de famille** head of the family *ou* household; **~ de file** leader; **~ de gare** station master; **~-lieu** *nm, pl* **~-~x** ≃ county town; **~ d'œuvre** *nm, pl* **~s-~** masterpiece, chef d'œuvre; **~ d'orchestre** conductor, leader *(US)*; *(Admin)* **~ de projet** project manager; **~ de service** section *ou* departmental head ; *(Méd)* ≃ consultant; **~ de train** guard.

cheftaine [ʃɛftɛn] *nf [louveteaux]* cubmistress; *[éclaireuses]* (guide) captain.

cheik [ʃɛk] *nm* sheik.

chelem [ʃlɛm] *nm*: **petit/grand ~** small/grand slam.

chemin [ʃ(ə)mɛ̃] **1** *nm* (**a**) *(gén)* path; *(route)* lane; *[piste]* track. **le ~ de la ruine** the road *ou* path to ruin. (**b**) *(trajet, direction)* way (*de, pour* to). **il y a une heure de ~** it takes an hour to get there; **quel ~ a-t-elle pris?** which way did she go?; **ils ont fait tout le ~ à pied** they walked all the way; **se mettre en ~** to set out *ou* off; **poursuivre son ~** to carry on one's way; **nous avons pris le ~ des écoliers** we came the long way round. (**c**) *(fig)* **il a encore du ~ à faire** he's still got a long way to go; **se mettre en travers du ~** to stand in the way *ou* path; **faire du ~** *[véhicule, chercheur]* to come a long way; *[idée]* to gain ground; *[ambitieux]* to make one's way; *(concession)* **faire la moitié du ~** to go halfway (to meet sb); **cela n'en prend pas le ~** it doesn't look likely; **il ne doit pas s'arrêter en si beau ~** he mustn't stop (now) when he's doing so well; **être sur le bon ~** to be on the right track *ou* lines; *(Rel)* **le ~ de Damas** the road to Damascus; *(fig)* **trouver son ~ de Damas** to see the light *(fig)*.
2 : **~ charretier** cart track; **~ creux** sunken lane; *(Ordin)* **~ critique** critical path; **le ~ de croix** the Way of the Cross; **~ de fer** railway, railroad *(US)*; **par ~ de fer** by rail; **~ de halage** tow-path.

cheminée [ʃ(ə)mine] *nf (extérieure)* chimney (stack); *(Naut, Rail)* funnel; *(intérieure)* fireplace; *(encadrement)* mantelpiece; *[volcan, lampe]* chimney. **~ d'aération** ventilation shaft.

cheminement [ʃ(ə)minmɑ̃] *nm [marcheurs]* progress, advance; *[sentier]* course, way; *[pensée]* development, progression. ◆ **cheminer** (1) *vi [personne]* to walk (along); *[ruisseau etc]* to follow its course (*dans* along).

cheminot [ʃ(ə)mino] *nm* railwayman, railroad man *(US)*.

chemise [ʃ(ə)miz] *nf [homme]* shirt; *[femme, bébé]* vest; *[dossier]* folder. **être en bras de ~** to be in one's shirt sleeves; **il s'en moque comme de sa première ~** he doesn't care a fig *; **~ de nuit** *[femme]* nightdress; *[homme]* nightshirt. ◆ **chemiserie** *nf (magasin)* man's shop; *(commerce)* shirt(-making) trade. ◆ **chemisette** *nf* short-sleeved shirt. ◆ **chemisier** *nm (marchand)* shirtmaker; *(vêtement)* blouse.

chenal, *pl* **-aux** [ʃənal, o] *nm (canal)* channel, fairway; *(rigole)* channel; *[moulin]* millrace; *[usine]* flume.

chenapan [ʃ(ə)napɑ̃] *nm* rascal.

chêne [ʃɛn] *nm* oak. **~-liège** *nm, pl* **~s-~s** cork-oak; **~ vert** holm oak.

chenet [ʃ(ə)nɛ] *nm* fire-dog, andiron.

chènevis [ʃɛnvi] *nm* hempseed.

chenil [ʃ(ə)ni(l)] *nm* kennels. **mettre son chien dans un ~** to put one's dog in kennels.

chenille [ʃ(ə)nij] *nf (Aut, Zool)* caterpillar. ◆ **chenillette** *nf* tracked vehicle.

cheptel [ʃɛptɛl] *nm* livestock.

chèque [ʃɛk] *nm* cheque, check *(US)*; *(bon)* voucher. **~ de 100 F** cheque for 100 francs *ou* in the amount of 100 francs *(US)*; **~-repas** *ou* **-restaurant** luncheon voucher; **~-cadeau** gift token; *(lit, fig)* **~ en blanc** blank cheque; **~ en bois** * dud * chèque; **~ postal** ≃ (Post Office) Girocheque ; **~ sans provision** bad *ou* dud * cheque; **~ de voyage** traveller's cheque . ◆ **chéquier** *nm* cheque *ou* check *(US)* book.

cher, chère[1] [ʃɛʀ] **1** *adj* (**a**) *(aimé)* dear (*à* to). **les êtres ~s** the loved ones; **c'est mon vœu le plus ~** it's my fondest *ou* dearest wish; **son bien le plus ~** his most precious possession; **ce ~ (vieux) Louis!** * dear old Louis!; **ses ~s parents** his beloved parents; *(sur lettre)* **~ tous** dear all. (**b**) *(coûteux)* expensive, dear. **pas ~** cheap, inexpensive; **la vie est chère** the cost of living is high; **c'est trop ~ pour ce que c'est** it's overpriced. **2** *nm, f*: **mon ~, ma chère** my dear. **3** *adv coûter, payer* a lot *ou* a great deal (of money). **vendre ~** to charge high prices; **je ne l'ai pas acheté ~** I bought it very cheaply, I didn't pay much for it; **ça vaut ~** it's expensive, it costs a lot; *(fig)* **il ne vaut pas ~** he's a bad lot; *(fig)* **ça lui a coûté ~** it cost him dear *ou* a great deal, he paid dearly *ou* heavily for it.

chercher [ʃɛʀʃe] (1) *vt* (**a**) *(gén)* to look for, search for, try to find; *ombre, moyen* to look for, seek; *gloire, alliance* to seek; *danger* to court; *(sur un livre)* to look up; *(dans sa mémoire)* to try to think of. **~ qn des yeux** to look (around) for sb; **il n'a pas bien cherché** he didn't look *ou* search very hard; **~ ses mots** to search for words; *(à un chien)* **cherche! cherche!** find it, boy!; **il ne cherche que son intérêt** he is concerned only with his own interest; **~ la difficulté** to look for difficulties ; **~ la bagarre** to be looking for a fight; **tu l'auras cherché!** you've been asking for it!; **~ à faire** to try *ou* attempt to do.
(**b**) **aller ~ qch/qn** to go for sth/sb, go and fetch *ou* get sth/sb; **va me ~ mon sac** go and fetch *ou* get me my bag; **aller ~ qch dans un tiroir** to go and get sth out of a drawer; **il est venu le ~ à la gare** he came to meet *ou* collect him at the station; **envoyer (qn) ~ le médecin** to send (sb) for the doctor; **où va-t-il ~ tout cela!** where does he get all that from!; **ça va ~ dans les 30 F** it'll add up to something like 30 francs; **ça va ~ dans les 5 ans de prison** it will mean something like

5 years in prison; *(amende)* **ça peut aller ~ loin** it could mean a heavy fine.
(**c**) *(fig)* ~ **fortune** to seek one's fortune; ~ **des histoires à qn** to try to make trouble for sb ; ~ **midi à quatorze heures** to look for complications; ~ **noise à qn** to pick a quarrel with sb; ~ **la petite bête** to split hairs; ~ **une aiguille dans une meule de foin** to look for a needle in a haystack; ~ **son salut dans la fuite** to seek *ou* take refuge in flight; **artiste qui se cherche** artist who is searching for an identity.

chercheur, -euse [ʃɛʀʃœʀ, øz] **1** *adj esprit* inquiring. **2** *nm, f* researcher, research worker. ~ **de** *(gén)* seeker of; ~ **d'or** gold digger; ~ **de trésors** treasure hunter.

chère² [ʃɛʀ] *nf (littér)* food, fare. **faire bonne** ~ to eat well.

chèrement [ʃɛʀmɑ̃] *adv aimer* dearly, fondly; *conserver* lovingly; *vendre* at a high price. ~ **payé** *victoire* dearly bought *ou* won; **vendre** ~ **sa vie** to sell one's life dearly.

chérir [ʃeʀiʀ] (2) *vt* to cherish. ◆ **chéri, e** **1** *adj* beloved. **maman** ~**e** mother dear *ou* darling. **2** *nm, f* darling.

cherté [ʃɛʀte] *nf* high price, dearness. **la** ~ **de la vie** the high cost of living.

chérubin [ʃeʀybɛ̃] *nm (lit, fig)* cherub.

chétif, -ive [ʃetif, iv] *adj enfant* puny; *plante* puny, weedy, stunted; *récolte* meagre; *repas* meagre, scanty; *raisonnement* paltry. ◆ **chétivement** *adv* punily.

cheval, *pl* **-aux** [ʃ(ə)val, o] **1** *nm (animal)* horse; *(Drogue, arg)* horse *(arg)*, big H *(arg)*. *(Aut)* ~ *ou* ~**aux (vapeur)** horsepower; **ce n'est pas le mauvais** ~ * he's not a bad sort; **au travail, c'est un vrai** ~ he works like a Trojan; **à** ~ on horseback; **à** ~ **sur une chaise** (sitting) astride a chair; **à** ~ **sur deux mois** overlapping two (different) months; **être (très) à** ~ **sur le règlement** to be a (real) stickler for the rules; **de** ~ * *remède* drastic; *fièvre* raging. **2** : ~ **d'arçons** pommel horse; ~ **à bascule** rocking horse; *(fig)* ~ **de bataille** hobby horse; ~**aux de bois** roundabout, merry-go-round, carousel *(US)*; ~ **de course** racehorse; ~**aux de frise** chevaux-de-frise; ~ **de labour** carthorse, plough horse; **(vieux)** ~ **de retour** old lag; ~ **de trait** draught horse, draft horse *(US)*; *(lit, fig)* **le** ~ **de Troie** the Trojan horse, the Wooden Horse of Troy.

chevalet [ʃ(ə)valɛ] *nm [peintre]* easel; *(Menuiserie)* trestle; *[violon etc]* bridge.

chevalier [ʃ(ə)valje] *nm (Hist)* knight; *[légion d'honneur]* chevalier. **faire qn** ~ to knight sb, dub sb knight; ~ **errant** knight-errant; ~ **servant** (attentive) escort; ~ **de la Table Ronde** Knight of the Round Table. ◆ **chevaleresque** *adj* chivalrous, gentlemanly; *honneur* knightly. ◆ **chevalerie** *nf (institution)* chivalry; *(chevaliers)* knighthood.

chevalière [ʃ(ə)valjɛʀ] *nf* signet ring.

chevalin, e [ʃ(ə)valɛ̃, in] *adj race* equine; *visage* horsy.

chevaucher [ʃ(ə)voʃe] (1) **1** *vt* to be *ou* sit astride; *[pont]* to span; *[tuiles]* to overlap. **2 se** ~ *vpr* to overlap. **3** *vi* to ride (on horseback). ◆ **chevauchée** *nf (course)* ride; *(cavaliers)* cavalcade. ◆ **chevauchement** *nm (gén)* overlapping.

chevet [ʃ(ə)vɛ] *nm* (**a**) *[lit]* bed(head). **au** ~ **de qn** at sb's bedside. (**b**) *(Archit)* chevet.

cheveu, *pl* ~**x** [ʃ(ə)vø] *nm* (**a**) *(poil)* hair. *(chevelure)* ~**x** hair; **aux** ~**x blonds** fair-haired; **2** ~**x blancs** 2 white hairs; **épingle à** ~**x** hairpin. (**b**) **leur vie n'a tenu qu'à un** ~ their life hung by a thread; **il s'en est fallu d'un** ~ **qu'ils ne se tuent** they escaped death by a hair's breadth, they were within an ace of being killed; **avoir un** ~ * **(sur la langue)** to have a lisp; **se faire des** ~**x** * **(blancs)** to worry o.s. grey *ou* stiff *, worry o.s. to death; **arriver comme un** ~ **sur la soupe** * *[visiteur]* to come at the most awkward moment; *[remarque]* to be completely irrelevant; **tiré par les** ~**x** far-fetched; **il y a un** ~ * there's a hitch *ou* snag. ◆ **chevelu, e** *adj* long-haired. ◆ **chevelure** *nf (cheveux)* hair; *[comète]* tail. **elle avait une** ~ **abondante** she had thick hair *ou* a thick head of hair.

cheville [ʃ(ə)vij] *nf (Anat)* ankle; *(pour joindre)* peg, pin; *(pour clou)* rawlplug; *[poème]* cheville. *(Aut, fig)* ~ **ouvrière** kingpin; **il n'arrive pas à la** ~ **de son frère** he can't hold a candle to his brother; **être en** ~ **avec qn pour faire qch** to have an arrangement with sb to do sth. ◆ **cheviller** (1) *vt (Menuiserie)* to peg.

chèvre [ʃɛvʀ(ə)] **1** *nf* (she-)goat, (nanny-)goat. **rendre qn** ~ * to drive sb up the wall *. **2** *nm* goat('s milk) cheese. ◆ **chevreau,** *pl* ~**x** *nm* kid.

chèvrefeuille [ʃɛvʀəfœj] *nm* honeysuckle.

chevreuil [ʃəvʀœj] *nm (Zool)* roe deer; *(mâle)* roebuck; *(Culin)* venison.

chevron [ʃəvʀɔ̃] *nm (poutre)* rafter; *(galon)* stripe, chevron. *(motif)* ~**s** herring bone (pattern); *(grands)* chevron pattern.

chevronné, e [ʃəvʀɔne] *adj* practised, seasoned.

chevroter [ʃəvʀɔte] (1) *vi* to quaver. ◆ **chevrotement** *nm* quavering.

chevrotine [ʃəvʀɔtin] *nf*: ~**(s)** buckshot.

chez [ʃe] *prép*: **rentrer** ~ **soi** to go (back) home; **faites comme** ~ **vous** make yourself at home; ~ **nous** *(gén)* at home; *(maison)* at our place *ou* house; *(famille)* in our family; *(pays)* in our country; **il est** ~ **sa tante** he's at his aunt's (place *ou* house); **c'est petit** ~ **lui** his place *ou* house is small; **être/aller** ~ **le boucher** to be at/go to the butcher's; *(adresse)* ~ **M X** c/o Mr. X; **c'est une coutume bien de** ~ **nous** it's one of our typical local customs; ~ **les Romains** among the Romans; **on trouve cela** ~ **les animaux/Balzac** you find this in animals/Balzac; **c'est une habitude** ~ **lui** it's a habit with him.

chiader ⁑ [ʃjade] (1) **1** *vt examen* to swot for *. **2** *vi* to swot *. ◆ **chiadé, e** ⁑ *adj (difficile)* tough *, stiff *; *(approfondi)* brainy *; *(perfectionné)* clever. ◆ **chiadeur, -euse** * *nm, f* swot *.

chialer ⁑ [ʃjale] (1) *vi* to blubber *.

chiard ⁑ [ʃjaʀ] *nm* brat.

chiasse ⁑ [ʃjas] *nf*: **avoir la** ~ *(colique)* to have the runs *; *(peur)* to be in a funk ⁑.

chic [ʃik] **1** *nm [toilette]* stylishness; *[personne]* style. **avoir du** ~ to have style; **habillé avec** ~ stylishly dressed; **avoir le** ~ **pour faire qch** to have the knack of doing sth; **de** ~ *peindre* without a model, from memory; *écrire* off the cuff. **2** *adj inv (élégant)* stylish, smart; *(riche)* smart, posh *; *(*: gentil)* decent, nice (*avec* to). **3** *excl*: ~ terrific! *, great! *

chicane [ʃikan] *nf* (**a**) *[route]* in and out. (**b**) *(querelle)* squabble. ◆ **chicaner** (1) **1** *vt*: ~ **qn** to quibble *ou* squabble with sb (*sur qch* over sth). **2** *vi* to quibble (*sur* about). ◆ **chicanier, -ière** **1** *adj* quibbling. **2** *nm, f* quibbler.

Chicano [ʃikano] *nm, f* Chicano.

chiche¹ [ʃiʃ] *adj*: **pois** ~ chick pea.

chiche² [ʃiʃ] *adj* (**a**) *personne, rétribution* niggardly, mean; *repas* scanty, meagre. **être** ~ **de paroles** to be sparing with one's words. (**b**) (*) **es-tu** ~ **de le faire?** are you game to do it?; ~ **que je le fais!** I bet you I do it! * ◆ **chichement** *adv* meanly, meagrely.

chichis * [ʃiʃi] *nmpl* fuss. **faire des** ~ to make a fuss; **sans** ~ informally.

chicorée [ʃikɔʀe] *nf (salade)* endive; *(à café)* chicory. ~ **frisée** curly endive (lettuce).

chicot [ʃiko] *nm (dent)* stump.

chien [ʃjɛ̃] **1** *nm (animal)* dog; *[fusil]* hammer. **petit ~** *(jeune)* puppy; **en ~ de fusil** curled up; **vie de ~** dog's life; **de ~** *temps, métier* rotten *; **comme un ~** like a dog; **elle a du ~ *** she has a certain something *; **entre ~ et loup** in the twilight *ou* dusk; **être comme ~ et chat** to fight like cat and dog; **recevoir qn comme un ~ dans un jeu de quilles** to give sb a cold reception; *(Prov)* **les ~s aboient, la caravane passe** let the world say what it will. **2** *adj inv (avare)* mean, stingy *; *(méchant)* rotten *. **3** : **~ d'arrêt** pointer; **~ d'aveugle** guide dog; **~ de berger** sheepdog; **~ de chasse** retriever; **~ couchant** setter; **faire le ~ couchant** to toady (*auprès de* to); **~ courant** hound; **~ de garde** watchdog; **~-loup** *nm, pl* **~s-~s** wolfhound; **~ policier** police dog; **~ savant** *(lit)* performing dog; **~ de traîneau** husky.

chiendent [ʃjɛ̃dɑ̃] *nm* couch grass.

chienne [ʃjɛn] *nf* bitch.

chier ⁑ [ʃje] (7) *vi* to shit ⁑. **faire ~ qn** *(ennuyer)* to bore the pants off sb ⁑; *(tracasser)* to bug sb ⁑.

chiffe [ʃif] *nf (péj)* spineless individual, wet *. **je suis comme une ~** *(fatigué)* I feel like a wet rag.

chiffon [ʃifɔ̃] *nm* (piece of) rag. **mettre en ~** to crumple; **parler ~s *** to talk (about) clothes ; **~ à chaussures** shoe cloth; **~ de papier** scrap of paper; **~ à poussière** duster, dustcloth *(US)*. ◆ **chiffonner** (1) **1** *vt* (**a**) *papier* to crumple; *habits* to crease, crumple. (**b**) *(*: contrarier)* **ça me chiffonne** it bothers me. **2 se ~** *vpr* to crease *ou* crumple easily. ◆ **chiffonnier** *nm (personne)* ragman; *(meuble)* chiffonier. **se battre comme des ~s** to fight like cat and dog.

chiffre [ʃifʀ(ə)] *nm* (**a**) *(caractère)* figure, numeral. **~ arabe** Arab numeral; **nombre de 7 ~s** 7-figure number; **inflation à deux/trois ~s** two/three figure *ou* double/triple digit inflation; **science des ~s** science of numbers. (**b**) *(somme)* sum; *(total)* total. **ça atteint des ~s astronomiques** it reaches an astronomical figure *ou* sum; **le ~ des chômeurs** the unemployment figures *ou* total; **~ (d'affaires)** turnover. (**c**) *[message]* code; *[coffre-fort]* combination. **écrire une lettre en ~s** to write a letter in code. (**d**) *(initiales)* initials, monogram; *(Mus: indice)* figure.

chiffrer [ʃifʀe] (1) **1** *vt (coder)* to encode; *(évaluer)* to put a figure on, assess (the amount of); *(numéroter)* to number; *linge* to mark (with one's initials); *(Mus)* to figure. **2** *vi*, **se ~** *vpr*: **(se) ~ à** to add up to, amount to; **ça finit par ~ *** it adds up to *ou* amounts to quite a lot in the end. ◆ **chiffrage** *nm* encoding; assessing; numbering; marking; figuring.

chignole [ʃiɲɔl] *nf* drill.

chignon [ʃiɲɔ̃] *nm* bun, chignon.

Chi'ite [ʃiit] *adj, nm, f* Shiite.

Chili [ʃili] *nm* Chile. ◆ **chilien, -ienne** *adj*, **C~(ne)** *nm(f)* Chilean.

chimère [ʃimɛʀ] *nf (utopie)* chimera; *(irréalisable)* pipe dream, (idle) fancy; *(Myth)* Chim(a)era. ◆ **chimérique** *adj* (**a**) *esprit, projet* fanciful; *rêve* idle. (**b**) *(imaginaire)* imaginary, chimerical.

chimie [ʃimi] *nf* chemistry. ◆ **chimique** *adj* chemical. ◆ **chimiquement** *adv* chemically. ◆ **chimiste** *nmf* chemist *(scientist)*.

chimiothérapie [ʃimjoteʀapi] *nf* chemotherapy.

chimpanzé [ʃɛ̃pɑ̃ze] *nm* chimpanzee.

Chine [ʃin] *nf* China. **~ populaire** communist China.

chiné, e [ʃine] *adj (Tex)* chiné.

chiner * [ʃine] (1) *vt* to tease, rag.

chinois, e [ʃinwa, waz] **1** *adj* (**a**) *(de Chine)* Chinese. (**b**) *(péj) personne* fussy; *règlement* hair-splitting. **2** *nm* (**a**) *(Ling)* Chinese. *(péj)* **c'est du ~ *** it's all Greek to me *. (**b**) **C~** Chinese(man); **les C~** the Chinese. (**c**) *(* péj: maniaque)* hair-splitter. **3** *nf*: **C~e** Chinese woman. ◆ **chinoiseries** *nfpl* unnecessary fuss. **les ~ de l'administration** red tape. ◆ **chinoiser** (1) *vi* to split hairs. **~ sur** to quibble over.

chiot [ʃjo] *nm* pup(py).

chiper * [ʃipe] (1) *vt objet* to pinch *, filch *, make off with; *rhume* to catch.

chipie [ʃipi] *nf* minx.

chipoter * [ʃipɔte] (1) *vi (manger)* to be a fussy eater; *(ergoter)* to quibble (*sur* over); *(marchander)* to haggle (*sur* over). ◆ **chipoteur, -euse** * **1** *adj* haggling; quibbling; *(en mangeant)* fussy. **2** *nm, f* haggler; quibbler; fussy eater.

chips [ʃip(s)] *nfpl (Culin)* crisps.

chique [ʃik] *nf (tabac)* quid; *(*: enflure)* lump (on the cheek).

chiqué * [ʃike] *nm*: **le ~** *(pour impressionner)* bluffing; *(factice)* sham; *(maniéré)* airs and graces; **il a fait ça au ~** he bluffed it out; **c'est du ~** it's all put on *; **c'est pas du ~**, that's for real *; **faire du ~** to put on airs (and graces).

chiquement * [ʃikmɑ̃] *adv s'habiller* smartly, stylishly; *traiter* kindly, decently.

chiquenaude [ʃiknod] *nf* flick.

chiquer [ʃike] (1) **1** *vt* to chew. **2** *vi* to chew tobacco.

chiromancie [kiʀɔmɑ̃si] *nf* palmistry. ◆ **chiromancien, -ienne** *nm, f* palmist.

chiropracteur [kiʀɔpʀaktœʀ] *nm* chiropractor. ◆ **chiropraxie** *nf* chiropractic.

chirurgie [ʃiʀyʀʒi] *nf* surgery *(science)*. ◆ **chirurgical, e**, *mpl* **-aux** *adj* surgical. ◆ **chirurgien** *nm* surgeon. **~-dentiste** dental surgeon.

chlore [klɔʀ] *nm* chlorine. ◆ **chlorer** (1) *vt* to chlorinate. ◆ **chlorhydrique** *adj* hydrochloric. ◆ **chlorure** *nm* chloride.

chloroforme [klɔʀɔfɔʀm(ə)] *nm* chloroform. ◆ **chloroformer** (1) *vt* to chloroform.

chlorophylle [klɔʀɔfil] *nf* chlorophyll. ◆ **chlorophyllien, -ienne** *adj* chlorophyllous.

choc [ʃɔk] *nm* (**a**) *(heurt) [objets]* impact, shock; *[vagues, véhicules]* crash; *[troupes, intérêts]* clash; *(sur la tête etc)* blow, bump. **cela se brise au moindre ~** it breaks at the slightest bump; **ça s'est déformé sous le ~** it twisted under the impact; **résister au ~** *[instrument]* to be shock resistant; *[armée]* to stand up to the onslaught; **~ opératoire** post-operative shock. (**b**) *(bruit) (violent)* crash; *(sourd)* thud; *(métallique)* clang; *(cristallin)* clink. (**c**) *(émotion)* shock. **ça m'a fait un drôle de ~** it gave me a nasty shock. (**d**) **de ~** *troupe, traitement* shock; *patron* dynamic, high-powered; **argument/photo(-) ~** shock argument/photo; **prix-~** special price. (**e**) *:* **~ culturel** cultural shock; *(Écon)* **~ pétrolier** oil crisis; **~ en retour** *(Élec)* return shock; *(fig)* backlash.

chocolat [ʃɔkɔla] **1** *nm (gén)* chocolate. **mousse au ~** chocolate mousse; **~ en poudre/à croquer** drinking/plain chocolate. **2** *adj inv* chocolate(-coloured). ◆ **chocolaté, e** *adj* chocolate-flavoured. ◆ **chocolaterie** *nf* chocolate factory. ◆ **chocolatier, -ière 1** *adj* chocolate. **2** *nm, f* chocolate maker.

chocottes ⁑ [ʃɔkɔt] *nfpl*: **avoir les ~** to have the jitters * *ou* the willies *.

chœur [kœʀ] *nm (gén, fig)* chorus; *(Rel: chanteurs)* choir; *(nef)* choir, chancel. **en ~** in chorus; **tous en ~!** all together now!

choir [ʃwaʀ] *vi (littér)* to fall. **faire ~** to cause to fall; **laisser ~** *objet* to drop; *amis* to let down; **se laisser ~ dans un fauteuil** to sink into an armchair.

choisir [ʃwaziʀ] (2) *vt (gén)* to choose; *candidat, produit* to select. **il faut savoir ~ ses amis** you must know how to pick *ou* choose your friends; **se ~ un mari** to choose a husband; **~ de faire qch** to choose to do sth. ◆ **choisi, e** *adj passages* selected; *langage* carefully chosen; *clientèle* select.

choix [ʃwa] *nm* (**a**) *(décision)* choice; *(échantillonnage)* choice, selection. **je n'avais pas d'autre ~** I had no choice, I had no other option; **un aménagement de son ~** alterations of one's (own) choosing; **le ~ d'un cadeau** choosing a gift, the choice of a gift; **il y a du ~** there is a choice *ou* a wide selection; **vous avez, au ~, fruits ou fromages** you have a choice between *ou* of fruit or cheese; **faire son ~** to make one's choice; **je n'avais pas le ~** I had no option *ou* choice; **laisser le ~ à qn (de faire)** to leave sb (free) to choose (to do), give sb the choice (of doing); **porter son ~ sur qch** to settle on sth. (**b**) *(qualité)* **de ~** choice, selected; **de premier ~** *fruits, viande* top grade, highest quality; **de ~ courant** standard quality; **de second ~** grade two, market grade *(US)*; **articles de second ~** seconds.

choléra [kɔleʀa] *nm* cholera. ◆ **cholérique 1** *adj* choleraic. **2** *nmf* cholera patient.

cholestérol [kɔlɛsteʀɔl] *nm* cholesterol.

chômage [ʃomaʒ] *nm* unemployment. **(être) au ~** (to be) unemployed *ou* out of work; **s'inscrire au ~** to apply for unemployment benefit; **mettre qn au ~** to make sb redundant, put sb out of work; **~ partiel** short-time working; **~ technique** lay-offs; **mettre en ~ technique** to lay off. ◆ **chômer** (1) *vi* (**a**) *(gén)* to be idle; *[travailleur]* to be unemployed; *[usine]* to be at a standstill. (**b**) *(en congé)* to have a holiday. **jour chômé** public holiday. ◆ **chômeur, -euse** *nm, f (gén)* unemployed person; *(mis au chômage)* redundant worker. **les ~s** the unemployed, people out of work.

chope [ʃɔp] *nf* tankard; *(contenu)* pint.

choper ⁑ [ʃɔpe] (1) *vt (voler)* to pinch *; *(attraper)* to catch; **se faire ~ par la police** to get nabbed * by the police. *.

chopine * [ʃɔpin] *nf* bottle (of wine).

choquer [ʃɔke] (1) **1** *vt* (**a**) *(scandaliser)* to shock, appal. **ce roman risque de ~** people may find this novel offensive *ou* shocking; **j'ai été choqué par son indifférence** I was shocked *ou* appalled by his indifference. (**b**) *délicatesse, raison* to offend (against); *vue, oreilles* to offend. (**c**) *[chute]* to shake (up); *[accident]* to shake (up), shock; *[deuil]* to shake. *(Méd)* **être choqué** to be in shock. (**d**) *objet* to knock (against); *verres* to clink. **2 se ~** *vpr (s'offusquer)* to be shocked. ◆ **choquant, e** *adj* shocking; appalling; offensive.

choral, e, *mpl* **~s** [kɔʀal] **1** *adj* choral. **2** *nm* choral(e). **3** *nf* choral society, choir.

chorégraphe [kɔʀegʀaf] *nmf* choreographer. ◆ **chorégraphie** *nf* choreography. ◆ **chorégraphique** *adj* choreographic.

choriste [kɔʀist(ə)] *nmf (Rel)* choir member, chorister; *(Théât)* member of the chorus. **les ~s** the choir; the chorus.

chorus [kɔʀys] *nm*: **faire ~ (avec qn)** to voice one's agreement (with sb).

chose [ʃoz] **1** *nf* (**a**) *(gén)* thing. **~ étrange, il a accepté** the strange thing is that he accepted, strangely enough he accepted; **c'est une ~ admise que** it's an accepted fact that; **c'est ~ faite** it's done; **peu de ~** nothing much; **avant toute ~** above all else; **de 2 ~s l'une** it's got to be one thing or the other; **faire bien les ~s** to do things in style; **dites-lui bien des ~s de ma part** give him my regards; **nous avons parlé de ~s et d'autres** we talked about this and that *ou* about one thing and another. (**b**) *(question)* matter. **la ~ en question** the matter in hand; **la ~ dont je parle** the thing I'm talking about; **c'est tout autre ~** it's another matter; **dans l'état actuel des ~s** as things *ou* matters stand at present.
(**c**) *(situation)* it, things. **il va vous expliquer la ~** he'll tell you about it; **il a bien pris la ~** he took it very well; **les ~s se sont passées ainsi** it *ou* things happened like this; **en mettant les ~s au mieux/pire** at best/worst.
2 *nm* (*) *(truc)* thing, contraption; *(personne)* what's-his-name *, thingumajig *. **eh! C~** hey you.
3 *adj inv*: **être tout ~** *(bizarre)* to feel a bit peculiar; *(malade)* to be out of sorts; **ça l'a rendu tout ~** it made him go all funny *.

chou[1], *pl* **~x** [ʃu] *nm (Bot)* cabbage; *(ruban)* rosette; *(gâteau)* puff. **notre projet est/il est dans les ~x** * our plan has/he has had it *; **faire ~ blanc** * to draw a blank; **~ de Bruxelles** Brussels sprout; **~-fleur** *nm, pl* **~x-~s** cauliflower; **~ rouge** red cabbage. ◆ **chou**[2], **-te** *, *mpl* **~x 1** *nm, f (amour)* darling. **2** *adj inv (ravissant)* delightful. ◆ **chouchou, -te** * *nm, f* pet. ◆ **chouchouter** * (1) *vt* to pamper, pet. ◆ **choucroute** *nf* sauerkraut.

choucas [ʃukɑ] *nm* jackdaw.

chouette[1] * [ʃwɛt] *adj (beau)* smashing *, great *; *(gentil)* nice. **sois ~** be a dear *ou* sport *; **~ (alors)!** smashing! *, great! * ◆ **chouettement** * *adv* nicely.

chouette[2] [ʃwɛt] *nf* owl. **~-effraie** barn owl, screech owl; **~ hulotte** tawny owl; *(péj)* **vieille ~** old harpy.

choyer [ʃwaje] (8) *vt* to pamper, spoil.

chrétien, -ienne [kʀetjɛ̃, jɛn] *adj*, **C~(ne)** *nm(f)* Christian. ◆ **chrétiennement** *adv* as a Christian; **être enseveli ~** to have a Christian burial. ◆ **chrétienté** *nf* Christendom.

christ [kʀist] *nm* (**a**) **le C~** Christ. (**b**) *(objet)* figure of Christ. ◆ **christique** *adj* Christlike. ◆ **christianisation** *nf* conversion to Christianity. ◆ **christianiser** (1) *vt* to convert to Christianity. ◆ **christianisme** *nm* Christianity.

chromatique [kʀɔmatik] *adj (Mus, Peinture)* chromatic; *(Bio)* chromosomal.

chrome [kʀom] *nm (Chim)* chromium. *(Aut)* **faire les ~s** * to polish the chrome. ◆ **chromer** (1) *vt* to chromium-plate.

chromo [kʀomo] *nm* chromo.

chromosome [kʀɔmozom] *nm* chromosome. ◆ **chromosomique** *adj* chromosomal.

chronique [kʀɔnik] **1** *adj* chronic. **2** *nf (Littérat)* chronicle; *(Presse)* column, page. *(Bible)* **le livre des C~s** the Book of Chronicles. ◆ **chroniquement** *adv* chronically. ◆ **chroniqueur** *nm (Littérat)* chronicler; *(Presse, gén)* columnist. **~ sportif** sports editor; **~ dramatique** drama critic.

chrono * [kʀono] *nm* stopwatch. *(Aut)* **faire du 80 (km/h) (au) ~** to be timed at 80; **faire un bon ~** to do a good time.

chronologie [kʀɔnɔlɔʒi] *nf* chronology. ◆ **chronologique** *adj* chronological. ◆ **chronologiquement** *adv* chronologically.

chronomètre [kʀɔnɔmɛtʀ(ə)] *nm* chronometer; *(Sport)* stopwatch. ◆ **chronométrage** *nm* timing. ◆ **chronométrer** (6) *vt* to time. ◆ **chronométreur** *nm (Sport)* timekeeper. ◆ **chronométrique** *adj* chronometric.

chrysalide [kʀizalid] *nf* chrysalis.

chrysanthème [kʀisɑ̃tɛm] *nm* chrysanthemum.

chuchoter [ʃyʃɔte] (1) *vti (gén, fig)* to whisper; *[ruisseau]* to murmur. ◆ **chuchotement** *nm* whisper; murmur.

chuinter [ʃɥɛ̃te] (1) *vi* to hiss softly. ◆ **chuintement** *nm* soft hiss.

chut [ʃyt] *excl* sh!

chute [ʃyt] *nf* (**a**) *(gén)* fall; *[cheveux]* loss; *[empire, commerce]* collapse; *[régime]* downfall (*de* of); *[monnaie, température]* drop (*de* in); *(Théât) [pièce]* failure (*de* of). **faire une ~ de 3 mètres** to fall 3 metres; **faire une ~ de cheval** to fall off a horse; **loi de la ~ des corps** law of gravity; **~ libre** free fall; **faire du parachutisme en ~ libre** to skydive, do skydiving; **économie en ~ libre** plummeting economy; *[ventes]* **être en ~ libre** to take a nose dive; **attention, ~ de pierres** danger, falling rocks. (**b**) *(Géog)* **~ d'eau** waterfall; **les ~s du Niagara/Zambèze** the Niagara/Victoria Falls; **fortes ~s de pluie/neige** heavy rainfalls/snowfalls. (**c**) *(déchet) [tissu]* clipping, scrap; *[bois]* off-cut. (**d**) **la ~ des reins** the small of the back; **~ du jour** nightfall.

chuter [ʃyte] (1) *vi* to fall; *(échouer)* to come a cropper *, fall on one's face; *(Théât)* to flop. *(lit, fig)* **faire ~ qn** to bring sb down.

Chypre [ʃipʀ(ə)] *n* Cyprus; **à ~** in Cyprus. ◆ **chypriote** *adj*, **C~** *nmf* = **cypriote.**

ci [si] **1** *adv*: **celui-~ , celle-~** this one; **ceux-~** these (ones); **ce livre-~** this book; **à cette heure-~** *(indue)* at this hour of the day; *(actuelle)* by now; **ces jours-~** *(avenir)* in the next few days; *(passé)* these past few days; *(présent)* these days; **de-~ de-là** here and there. **2** : **~-après** *(gén)* below; **~-contre** opposite; **~-dessous** below; **~-dessus** above; **~-gît** here lies; **~-inclus une enveloppe** envelope enclosed; **les papiers ~-joints** the enclosed papers.

cibiste [sibist(ə)] *nm, f* CB enthusiast.

cible [sibl(ə)] *nf (lit, fig)* target. **~ mouvante** moving target. ◆ **cibler** (1) *vt* to target (*sur* at).

ciboire [sibwaʀ] *nm (Rel)* ciborium *(vessel)*.

ciboule [sibul] *nf*, **ciboulette** [sibulɛt] *nf* chives.

cicatrice [sikatʀis] *nf (lit, fig)* scar. ◆ **cicatrisation** *nf* healing. ◆ **cicatriser** *vt*, **se ~** *vpr* (1) to heal (over).

cidre [sidʀ(ə)] *nm* cider.

ciel [sjɛl] **1** *nm* (**a**) *(espace: pl littér* **cieux***)* sky, heavens *(pl, littér)*. **sous des cieux plus cléments** *(climat)* beneath more clement skies; *(hum: moins dangereux)* in healthier climes. (**b**) *(Peinture: pl* **ciels***)* sky. (**c**) *(Rel)* **le ~, les cieux** heaven; **juste ~!** good heavens!; **c'est le ~ qui vous envoie!** you're heaven-sent! (**d**) **à ~ ouvert** *égout* open; *piscine* open-air; *mine* opencast, open cut *(US)*. **2** : **~ de lit** canopy.

cierge [sjɛʀʒ(ə)] *nm (Rel)* candle.

cigale [sigal] *nf* cicada.

cigare [sigaʀ] *nm* cigar; *(*: tête)* head, nut ⁑. ◆ **cigarette** *nf* cigarette. **~ (à) bout filtre** (filter-)tipped cigarette.

cigogne [sigɔɲ] *nf (Orn)* stork.

ciguë [sigy] *nf* hemlock.

cil [sil] *nm (Anat)* eyelash. **~s vibratiles** cilia. ◆ **ciller** [sije] (1) *vi*: **~ (des yeux)** to blink (one's eyes).

cime [sim] *nf [montagne]* summit; *[arbre]* top; *[gloire]* peak, height.

ciment [simɑ̃] *nm* cement. **~ armé** reinforced concrete; **~ (à prise) rapide** quick-setting cement. ◆ **cimenter** (1) *vt* to cement. ◆ **cimenterie** *nf* cement works.

cimetière [simtjɛʀ] *nm [ville]* cemetery; *[église]* graveyard, churchyard. **~ de voitures** scrapyard.

cinéma [sinema] *nm (gén)* cinema; *(salle)* cinema, movie theater *(US)*. **~ muet/parlant** silent/talking films; **faire du ~** to be a film actor (*ou* actress); **de ~** *producteur, studio* film; *écran* cinema; **être dans le ~** to be in the film *ou* movie business; **aller au ~** to go to the pictures *ou* movies; **quel ~!** *(frime)* what a performance, what an act; *(complication)* what a to-do *ou* fuss. ◆ **ciné** * *nm abrév de* **cinéma.** ◆ **cinéaste** *nmf* filmmaker, moviemaker *(US)*. ◆ **ciné-club,** *pl* **~-~s** *nm* film society. ◆ **cinémascope** *nm* ® Cinemascope ®. ◆ **cinémathèque** *nf* film library; *(salle)* film theatre, movie theatre *(US)*. ◆ **cinématographique** *adj* film, cinema. ◆ **cinéphile** *nmf* film enthusiast. ◆ **cinoche** * *nm* flicks * *pl*, movies * *pl (US)*.

cingler [sɛ̃gle] (1) **1** *vt (gén, fig)* to lash. **le visage cinglé par le vent** with his face stung *ou* whipped by the wind. **2** *vi (Naut)* **~ vers** to make for. ◆ **cinglant, e** *adj vent* biting, bitter; *pluie* lashing; *propos* scathing, cutting. ◆ **cinglé, e** * **1** *adj* nutty ⁑, cracked *, loony *. **2** *nm, f* crackpot *, nut ⁑.

cinq [sɛ̃k] *adj, nm* five. **en ~ sec** ⁑ in a flash, in two ticks *; *V* **six.**

cinquante [sɛ̃kɑ̃t] *adj, nm* fifty. ◆ **cinquantaine** *nf* about fifty. ◆ **cinquantenaire** *nm* fiftieth anniversary, golden jubilee. ◆ **cinquantième** *adj, nmf* fiftieth; *V* **six, soixantaine, sixième.**

cinquième [sɛ̃kjɛm] **1** *adj, nmf* fifth. **être la ~ roue du carrosse** * to count for nothing; *V* **sixième.** **2** *nf (Scol)* second year, seventh grade *(US)*. ◆ **cinquièmement** *adv* in the fifth place.

cintre [sɛ̃tʀ(ə)] *nm (Archit)* arch; *[manteau]* coat hanger. *(Théât)* **les ~s** the flies. ◆ **cintré, e** *adj porte* arched; *veste* waisted; *chemise* slim-fitting.

cirage [siʀaʒ] *nm (produit)* (shoe) polish; *(action)* polishing. **être dans le ~** * *(malaise)* to be dazed; *(ignorance)* to be all at sea *; **quand il est sorti du ~** * when he came to *ou* round.

circoncire [siʀkɔ̃siʀ] (37) *vt* to circumcize. ◆ **circoncision** *nf* circumcision.

circonférence [siʀkɔ̃feʀɑ̃s] *nf* circumference.

circonflexe [siʀkɔ̃flɛks(ə)] *adj*: **accent ~** circumflex.

circonlocution [siʀkɔ̃lɔkysjɔ̃] *nf* circumlocution.

circonscription [siʀkɔ̃skʀipsjɔ̃] *nf* district, area. **~ (électorale)** constituency, district *(US)*.

circonscrire [siʀkɔ̃skʀiʀ] (39) *vt feu, épidémie* to contain, confine; *territoire* to mark out; *sujet* to define. **se ~** *ou* **être circonscrit à qch** to be limited *ou* confined *ou* restricted to sth.

circonspection [siʀkɔ̃spɛksjɔ̃] *nf* caution, wariness, circumspection. ◆ **circonspect, e** *adj* circumspect, cautious, wary.

circonstance [siʀkɔ̃stɑ̃s] *nf (occasion)* occasion; *[accident]* circumstance. *(situation)* **~s** circumstances; **en la ~** on this occasion; **dans ces ~s** in these circumstances; **~s atténuantes** mitigating circumstances; **~ aggravante** aggravating circumstance; **de ~** *mine* appropriate; *poésie* occasional. ◆ **circonstancié, e** *adj* detailed. ◆ **circonstanciel, -ielle** *adj* adverbial.

circonvenir [siʀkɔ̃vniʀ] (22) *vt* to circumvent.

circonvolution [siʀkɔ̃vɔlysjɔ̃] *nf (Anat)* convolution; *[itinéraire]* twist.

circuit [siʀkɥi] *nm (touristique)* tour, (round) trip; *(compliqué)* roundabout *ou* circuitous route; *(Sport, Élec)* circuit; *(Écon)* circulation. **mettre qch en ~** to connect sth up; *[machine]* **tous les ~s ont grillé** all the fuses have blown, there's been a burnout; **être dans le ~** * to be around; **~ de distribution** distribution network; **~ fermé** *(Élec, fig)* closed circuit; *(Aut)* **~ hydraulique** hydraulic circuit; **~ intégré/imprimé** integrated/printed circuit; **~ de refroidissement** cooling system.

circulaire [siʀkylɛʀ] *adj, nf (gén)* circular.

circulation [siʀkylɑsjɔ̃] *nf [air, sang, argent]* circulation; *[marchandises, travailleurs]* movement; *[trains]* running; *(Aut, Aviat)* traffic. **mettre en ~** *argent* to put into circulation; *livre, voiture* to put on the market, bring out; **mise en ~** circulation; marketing; *(fig)* **disparaître de la ~** to drop out of sight, disappear from the scene. ◆ **circulatoire** *adj* circulatory.

circuler [sirkyle] (1) *vi* (**a**) *(Anat, Écon)* to circulate; *[rumeur]* to circulate, go round. **faire** ~ *(lit)* to circulate; *bruits* to spread, circulate *(sur* about*)*. (**b**) *[voiture]* to go; *[passant]* to walk; *[foule]*, to move (along); *[plat]* to be handed round. **circulez!** move along!; **faire** ~ *voitures* to move on; *plat* to hand round.

cire [sir] *nf (gén)* wax; *[meubles]* polish; *[oreille]* (ear)wax. ~ **d'abeille** beeswax; ~ **à cacheter** sealing wax. ◆ **ciré** *nm* oilskin. ◆ **cirer** (1) *vt* to polish. ◆ **cireur, -euse 1** *nm, f [souliers]* shoe-shiner, bootblack (†). **2** *nf* floor polisher. ◆ **cireux, -euse** *adj matière* waxy; *teint* waxen.

cirque [sirk(ə)] *nm (spectacle)* circus; *(Antiq: arène)* amphitheatre; *(Géog)* cirque. **quel** ~! * *(tracas)* what a carry-on *!; *(désordre)* what absolute chaos!

cirrhose [siroz] *nf* cirrhosis.

cisailles [sizɑj] *nfpl [métal, arbre]* shears; *[fil de fer]* wire cutters. ◆ **cisailler** (1) *vt métal* to cut; *arbuste* to clip; *(par l'usure)* to shear off; *(*: maladroitement)* to hack; (*) *personne* to cripple the career of.

ciseau, *pl* ~**x** [sizo] *nm* (**a**) **(paire de)** ~**x** *(gén)* (pair of) scissors; *[métal, laine]* shears. (**b**) *(Sculp, Tech)* chisel. ~ **à froid** cold chisel. (**c**) *(Sport: prise)* scissors (hold); *(Ski)* **montée en** ~**x** herringbone climb; *(Catch)* ~ **de jambes** leg scissors.

ciseler [sizle] (5) *vt pierre* to chisel, engrave; *métal* to chase, engrave. ◆ **ciselure** *nf* chased pattern, engraving.

Cisjordanie [sisʒɔrdani] *nf:* **la** ~ the West Bank (of Jordan).

citadelle [sitadɛl] *nf (lit, fig)* citadel.

citadin, e [sitadɛ̃, in] **1** *adj* urban, town, city. **2** *nm, f* city dweller, urbanite *(US)*.

citation [sitɑsjɔ̃] *nf [auteur]* quotation. ~ **à comparaître** *(à accusé)* summons to appear; *(à témoin)* subpoena; ~ **à l'ordre de l'armée** mention in dispatches.

cité [site] *nf* city; *(petite)* town; **la C**~ **du Vatican** the Vatican City; ~**-dortoir** *nf, pl* ~**s**-~**s** dormitory town; ~**-jardin** *nf, pl* ~**s**-~**s** garden city; ~ **ouvrière** ≃ (workers') housing estate; ~ **universitaire** (student) halls of residence.

citer [site] (1) *vt* to quote, cite. ~ **qn (en exemple)** to cite sb *ou* hold sb up as an example; ~ **un soldat à l'ordre du jour** to mention a soldier in dispatches; ~ **(à comparaître)** *accusé* to summon to appear; *témoin* to subpoena.

citerne [sitɛrn(ə)] *nf* tank.

citoyen, -enne [sitwajɛ̃, ɛn] **1** *nm, f* citizen. **2** *nm (*: type)* fellow, guy *. ◆ **citoyenneté** *nf* citizenship.

citron [sitrɔ̃] **1** *nm (fruit)* lemon; *(‡: tête)* head, nut ‡. **2** *adj inv* lemon (-coloured). ◆ **citronnade** *nf* lemon squash, lemonade *(US)*. ◆ **citronnier** *nm* lemon tree.

citrouille [sitruj] *nf* pumpkin; *(‡: tête)* head, nut ‡.

civet [sivɛ] *nm* stew; **un** ~ **de lièvre** ≃ jugged hare.

civière [sivjɛr] *nf* stretcher.

civil, e [sivil] **1** *adj guerre, mariage* civil; *(non militaire)* civilian; *(poli)* civil, courteous. **2** *nm* civilian. **en** ~ *soldat* in civilian clothes; *policier* in plain clothes; **dans le** ~ in civilian life. ◆ **civilement** *adv* (**a**) **être** ~ **responsable** to be legally responsible; **se marier** ~ to have a civil wedding. (**b**) *(poliment)* civilly.

civilisation [sivilizɑsjɔ̃] *nf* civilization. ◆ **civiliser** (1) **1** *vt* to civilize. **2 se** ~ *vpr* to become civilized.

civilité [sivilite] *nf* civility. ~**s** civilities, compliments.

civique [sivik] *adj* civic. ◆ **civisme** *nm* public-spiritedness.

clac [klak] *excl [porte]* slam!; *[élastique]* snap!; *[fouet]* crack!

clair, e [klɛr] **1** *adj* (**a**) *pièce* bright, light; *couleur (vive)* bright; *(pâle)* light; *robe* light-coloured. **bleu** ~ light blue. (**b**) *soupe, tissu usé* thin. (**c**) *(lit, fig: limpide)* clear. **par temps** ~ on a clear day; **avoir un esprit** ~ to be a clear thinker; **il est** ~ **qu'il se trompe** it is clear *ou* plain that he's mistaken; ~ **comme le jour** as clear as daylight, crystal-clear. **2** *adv parler, voir* clearly. **il fait** ~ it is daylight; **il ne fait guère** ~ it's not very light. **3** *nm*: **tirer qch au** ~ to clear sth up; **en** ~ *(c'est-à-dire)* to put it plainly; *(non codé)* in clear; **gaspiller le plus** ~ **de son temps/argent** to waste most of one's time/the better part of one's money; **au** ~ **de lune** in the moonlight. ◆ **clairement** *adv* clearly. ◆ **claire-voie,** *pl* ~**s**-~**s** *nf* openwork fence. **à** ~-~ openwork.

clairière [klɛrjɛr] *nf* clearing, glade.

clairon [klɛrɔ̃] *nm* bugle; *(joueur)* bugler. ◆ **claironnant, e** *adj voix* resonant. ◆ **claironner** (1) *vt nouvelle* to trumpet.

clairsemé, e [klɛrsəme] *adj maisons, auditoire* scattered; *gazon, cheveux* thin, sparse.

clairvoyance [klɛrvwajɑ̃s] *nf* clear-sightedness, perceptiveness. ◆ **clairvoyant, e** *adj* clear-sighted, perceptive.

clamecer ‡ [klamse] (3) *vi* to kick the bucket ‡.

clamer [klame] (1) *vt (gén)* to shout out; *innocence* to proclaim. ◆ **clameur** *nf (cris)* clamour. ~**s** protests.

clamser ‡ [klamse] = **clamecer.**

clan [klɑ̃] *nm (lit, fig)* clan.

clandestin, e [klɑ̃dɛstɛ̃, in] *adj réunion* secret, clandestine; *mouvement* underground; *commerce* clandestine, illicit. **(passager)** ~ stowaway. ◆ **clandestinement** *adv* secretly; clandestinely; illicitly. ◆ **clandestinité** *nf [activité]* secret nature. **dans la** ~ *travailler* in secret, clandestinely; *vivre* underground.

clapet [klapɛ] *nm (Tech)* valve. **ferme ton** ~ * hold your tongue *, shut up *.

clapier [klapje] *nm (lit)* hutch; *(péj)* dump ‡, hole *.

clapoter [klapɔte] (1) *vi* to lap. ◆ **clapotement** *nm ou* ◆ **clapotis** *nm* lap(ping).

clapper [klape] (1) *vi:* ~ **de la langue** to click one's tongue.

claquage [klakaʒ] *nm (blessure)* strained muscle.

claquant, e * [klakɑ̃, ɑ̃t] *adj (fatigant)* killing *, exhausting.

claque [klak] **1** *nf (gifle)* slap; *(Théât)* claque. **2** *adj, nm*: **(chapeau)** ~ opera hat.

claquemurer [klakmyre] (1) **1** *vt* to coop up. **2 se** ~ *vpr* to shut o.s. away *ou* up.

claquer [klake] (1) **1** *vi* (**a**) *[volet]* to bang; *[drapeau]* to flap; *[fouet]* to crack; *[coup de feu]* to ring out. **faire** ~ *porte* to bang, slam; *fouet* to crack; *doigts* to snap; *langue* to click; ~ **dans ses mains** to clap (one's hands); ~ **des talons** to click one's heels; **il claquait des dents** his teeth were chattering. (**b**) *(‡: mourir) [personne]* to kick the bucket ‡; *[lampe]* to conk out ‡, pack in ‡; *[élastique]* to snap. ~ **dans les mains de qn** *[malade]* to die on sb *; *[affaire]* to go bust on sb ‡. **2** *vt (gifler)* to slap; *(fermer)* to snap shut; *(*: fatiguer)* to exhaust, tire out; *(*: casser)* to bust; *(‡: dépenser)* to blow ‡, blue ‡. *(lit, fig)* ~ **la porte** to slam the door *(de* on); **se** ~ **un muscle** to strain a muscle. ◆ **claquement** *nm* bang; slam; crack; click; snap. *(répété)* **le** ~ *ou* **les** ~**s de** the banging (*ou* flapping *ou* cracking *etc*) of.

claquette [klakɛt] *nf (Danse)* ~**s** tap-dancing.

clarifier *vt*, **se** ~ *vpr* [klaʀifje] (7) *(lit, fig)* to clarify. ◆ **clarification** *nf* clarification.

clarinette [klaʀinɛt] *nf* clarinet. ◆ **clarinettiste** *nmf* clarinettist.

clarté [klaʀte] *nf (gén: lumière)* light; *[flamme, pièce, ciel]* brightness; *[eau, son]* clearness; *[explication, pensée]* clarity. *(fig: précisions)* **~s** knowledge (*sur* about); **à la ~ de la lampe/lune** in the lamplight/moonlight; **~ d'esprit** clear thinking.

classe [klɑs] *nf* (**a**) *(catégorie) (gén)* class; *(grade)* grade; *[utilisateurs]* category. **les ~s moyennes** the middle classes; **la ~ ouvrière** the working class; **la ~ politique** the political community; **société sans ~s** classless society; **de première ~** *employé* top *ou* first grade; *hôtel, billet* 1st class; **établissement de ~** high-class establishment; **de ~ internationale** of international standing; *(Aviat)* **~ touriste** economy class; **~ d'âge** age group. (**b**) *(gén, Sport: valeur)* class. **de (grande) ~** of great distinction; **de ~ internationale** of international class; **elle a de la ~** she's got class. (**c**) *(Scol) (élèves, cours)* class; *(année)* year, grade *(US)*; *(salle)* classroom. **la ~** *(l'école)* school; **il est (le) premier/(le) dernier de la ~** he is top/bottom of the class; **aller en ~** to go to school; **après la ~** after school (hours); **c'est M. X qui leur fait la ~** Mr X is their teacher; **turbulent en ~** disruptive in class *ou* in the classroom; **partir en ~ de neige/de mer** ≃ to go skiing/to the seaside with the school. (**d**) *(Mil)* **soldat de 1re** *(ou* **2e***)* **~** ≃ private; **la ~ 1972** the class of '72; **faire ses ~s** to do one's training.

classer [klɑse] (1) **1** *vt* (**a**) *papiers* to file; *livres, plantes* to classify. (**b**) *(hiérarchiser)* to grade. **X, que l'on classe parmi** X, who ranks among. (**c**) *(clore) affaire* to close. (**d**) *(péj: cataloguer) personne* to size up, categorize. **2 se ~** *vpr*: **se ~ parmi les premiers** to be *ou* come *ou* come in *(US)* among the first; **se ~ parmi les meilleurs** to rank among the best; **être bien classé** to be well placed. ◆ **classé, e** *adj monument* listed; *vins* classified; *joueur* graded. ◆ **classement** *nm* (**a**) *(action)* filing; classification; grading; closing. **j'ai fait du ~ toute la journée** I've spent all day filing. (**b**) *(rang) [élève]* place *ou* rank *(US)*; *[coureur]* placing; *(liste) [élèves]* class list; *[coureurs]* finishing list; *[équipes]* league table. **avoir un bon/mauvais ~** *[élève]* to get a high/low place in class, be ranked high/low in class *(US)*; *[coureur]* to be well/poorly placed; **je vais vous lire le ~** I'm going to read you your placings; **~ général** overall placings. ◆ **classeur** *nm (meuble)* filing cabinet; *(dossier)* (loose-leaf) file.

classifier [klasifje] (7) *vt* to classify. ◆ **classification** *nf* classification.

classique [klasik] **1** *adj auteur, musique, études* classical; *vêtement, ameublement* classic(al); *argument* standard, classic; *conséquence* usual. **c'est ~!** it's the usual *ou* classic situation!; **grâce à une opération maintenant ~** thanks to an operation which is now quite usual *ou* standard; *(Scol)* **il est en section ~** he's in the classics stream. **2** *nm (auteur) (Antiq)* classical author; *(XVIIe siècle)* classic, classicist; *(écrivain, œuvre célèbre)* classic. **le ~** *(musique)* classical music; *(mobilier)* the classic(al) style. ◆ **classicisme** *nm (Art)* classicism; *(conformisme)* conventionality. ◆ **classiquement** *adv* classically.

claudiquer [klodike] (1) *vi* to limp. ◆ **claudication** *nf* limp.

clause [kloz] *nf (gén)* clause.

claustrophobie [klostʀɔfɔbi] *nf* claustrophobia. ◆ **claustrophobe** *adj, nmf* claustrophobic.

clavecin [klavsɛ̃] *nm* harpsichord.

clavicule [klavikyl] *nf* collarbone.

clavier [klavje] *nm (lit)* keyboard; *[orgue]* manual; *(fig)* range.

claviste [klavist(ə)] *nmf* keyboard operator.

clé *ou* **clef** [kle] **1** *nf (gén, fig)* key (*de* to); *(Tech)* spanner, wrench; *[violon]* peg; *[gamme]* clef. **altération à la ~** change in the key signature; **avec une récompense à la ~** with a reward into the bargain; **prix ~s en main** *[voiture]* price on the road, on-the-road price, sticker price *(US)*; *[appartement]* price with immediate entry *ou* possession *ou* occupation; **mettre sous ~** to put under lock and key; **mettre la ~ sous la porte** *(faire faillite)* to shut up shop; *(s'enfuir)* to clear out; **prendre la ~ des champs** to run away. **2** *adj inv* key. **position-/ poste-~** key position/job. **3** : **~ anglaise, ~ à molette** adjustable wrench *ou* spanner, monkey wrench; **~ en croix** wheel brace; **~ dynamométrique** torque wrench; *(lit, fig)* **~ de voûte** keystone.

clématite [klematit] *nf* clematis.

clémence [klemɑ̃s] *nf [temps]* mildness; *[juge]* clemency, leniency. ◆ **clément, e** *adj* mild; lenient.

clémentine [klemɑ̃tin] *nf* clementine.

clenche [klɑ̃ʃ] *nf* latch.

cleptomane [klɛptɔman] *nmf* = **kleptomane.**

clerc [klɛʀ] *nm [notaire etc]* clerk; *(Rel)* cleric; *(Hist)* (learned) scholar. **être (grand) ~ en la matière** to be an expert on the subject.

clergé [klɛʀʒe] *nm* clergy. ◆ **clérical, e,** *mpl* **-aux** *adj, nmf (Rel)* clerical.

clic [klik] *nm* click. **le ~-clac de** the clickety-clack of.

cliché [kliʃe] *nm (banal)* cliché; *(Phot)* negative; *(Typ)* plate.

client, e [klijɑ̃, ɑ̃t] *nm, f (gén)* customer; *[avocat]* client; *[hôtel]* guest, patron; *[médecin]* patient; *[taxi]* fare; *(* péj: individu)* fellow, guy *; *(Antiq: protégé)* client. **être ~ d'un magasin** to patronize a shop, be a regular customer at a shop. ◆ **clientèle** *nf [magasin]* customers, clientèle; *[avocat, médecin]* practice; *[parti]* supporters. **accorder sa ~ à qn** to give sb one's custom *ou* business, patronize sb.

cligner [kliɲe] (1) *vt, vt indir:* **~ les** *ou* **des yeux** to blink; *(à moitié)* to screw up one's eyes; **~ de l'œil** to wink (*en direction de* at). ◆ **clignement** *nm*: **~(s)** blinking; **un ~ d'œil** a wink.

clignoter [kliɲɔte] (1) *vi [yeux]* to blink; *[étoile]* to twinkle; *[lampe]* to flicker; *(pour signal)* to flash, wink. ◆ **clignotant** *nm (Aut)* indicator. ◆ **clignotement** *nm*: **~(s)** blinking; twinkling; flickering; flashing, winking.

climat [klima] *nm (lit, fig)* climate; *(littér: contrée)* clime *(littér)*. ◆ **climatique** *adj* climatic. ◆ **climatisation** *nf* air conditioning. ◆ **climatiser** (1) *vt* to air-condition. ◆ **climatiseur** *nm* air conditioner.

clin [klɛ̃] *nm*: **~ d'œil** wink; **faire un ~ d'œil** to wink (*à* at); **en un ~ d'œil** in the twinkling of an eye.

clinicien, -ienne [klinisjɛ̃, jɛn] *nmf* clinician.

clinique [klinik] **1** *adj* clinical. **2** *nf (établissement)* nursing home; *(section)* clinic. **~ d'accouchement** maternity home.

clinquant, e [klɛ̃kɑ̃, ɑ̃t] **1** *adj* flashy. **2** *nm (lit)* tinsel; *(bijoux)* tawdry jewellery; *[style]* flashiness.

clip [klip] *nm* brooch.

clique [klik] *nf (Mus)* band; *(péj)* clique, set. **prendre ses ~s et ses claques *** to pack up (and go).

cliqueter [klikte] (4) *vi (gén)* to clink; *[vaisselle]* to clatter; *[chaînes, ferraille]* to jangle; *[armes]* to clash. ◆ **cliquetis** *nm* clink; clatter; jangle; clash.

clivage [klivaʒ] *nm (action)* cleaving; *(résultat)* cleavage; *(fig)* split (*de* in).

cloaque [klɔak] *nm* cesspool, cesspit.

clochard, e * [klɔʃaʀ, aʀd(ə)] *nm, f* down-and-out, tramp.

cloche [klɔʃ] **1** *nf (gén)* bell; *[plat]* lid; *[plantes]* cloche; *(*: imbécile)* idiot *. ~ **à fromage** cheese cover; ~ **à plongeur** diving bell. **2** *adj* (**a**) *jupe* bell-shaped. **chapeau** ~ cloche hat. (**b**) *(*: idiot)* idiotic. ◆ **cloche-pied** *adv*: **à** ~ *sauter* to hop. ◆ **clochette** *nf* small bell; *(fleur)* bellflower.

clocher[1] [klɔʃe] *nm (en pointe)* steeple; *(quadrangulaire)* church tower; *(fig: village)* village. **de** ~ *mentalité* parochial. ◆ **clocheton** *nm (Archit)* pinnacle.

clocher *[2] [klɔʃe] (1) *vi*: **il y a qch qui cloche** there's sth up * *ou* wrong (*dans* with).

cloison [klwazɔ̃] *nf (gén)* partition; *(Naut)* bulkhead; *(fig)* barrier. ◆ **cloisonnement** *nm* compartmentalization. ◆ **cloisonner** (1) *vt activités etc* to compartmentalize.

cloître [klwatʀ(ə)] *nm* cloister. ◆ **cloîtrer** (1) **1** *vt* to shut away (*dans* in); *(Rel)* to cloister. **religieux cloîtré** enclosed monk. **2 se** ~ *vpr* to shut o.s. up *ou* away (*dans* in). **vivre cloîtré** to live a cloistered life.

clone [klon] *nm* clone. ◆ **cloner** (1) *vt* to clone. ◆ **clonage** *nm* cloning.

clopiner [klɔpine] (1) *vi* to hobble *ou* limp along. ◆ **clopin-clopant** *adv*: **aller** ~ *[marcheur]* to hobble along; *[affaires]* to be so-so *.

clopinettes *[klɔpinɛt] *nfpl*: **gagner des** ~ to earn peanuts *, earn next to nothing; *(rien à faire)* **des** ~! nothing doing!

cloporte [klɔpɔʀt(ə)] *nm (Zool)* woodlouse; *(fig péj)* creep *.

cloque [klɔk] *nf* blister. ◆ **cloquer** (1) *vi* to blister.

clore [klɔʀ] (45) *vt (terminer)* to close, end, conclude; *(entourer)* to enclose (*de* with); *(fermer) porte* to close, shut; *lettre* to seal. ~ **le bec à qn** * to shut sb up *. ◆ **clos, e 1** *adj système, yeux* closed; *espace* enclosed. **2** *nm (pré)* (enclosed) field; *(vignoble)* vineyard.

clôture [klotyʀ] *nf* (**a**) *(planches)* fence; *(fil de fer)* (wire) fence; *(haies)* hedge; *(ciment)* wall. **mur de** ~ outer wall. (**b**) *[débat, liste, compte]* closing, closure; *[bureaux]* closing. *(Théât)* ~ **annuelle** annual closure; **avant la** ~ before it closes; **date** *etc* **de** ~ closing date *etc*; **combien valait le dollar en** ~? what did the dollar close at?; **débat de** ~ adjournment debate. ◆ **clôturer** (1) *vt champ* to enclose; *liste* to close.

clou [klu] *nm* (**a**) *(gén)* nail; *(décoratif, pour chaussée)* stud; *[tapissier]* tack. **traverser dans les** ~**s** to cross at the pedestrian crossing *ou* at the crosswalk *(US)*. (**b**) *(Méd)* boil. (**c**) *(fig) [spectacle]* star attraction *ou* turn. **mettre sa montre au** ~ * to pawn one's watch, put one's watch in hock *; **(vieux)** ~ * *(gén)* ancient machine; *(voiture)* old banger; **des** ~**s!** ⁑ nothing doing! *; ~ **de girofle** clove. ◆ **clouer** (1) *vt (lit)* to nail down; *ennemi* to pin down. ~ **qn sur place** to nail *ou* root sb to the spot; ~ **qn au lit** to keep sb confined to bed; ~ **le bec à qn** * to shut sb up *. ◆ **clouté, e** *adj ceinture* studded; *souliers* hob-nailed.

clown [klun] *nm* clown. **faire le** ~ to clown (about), play the fool. ◆ **clownerie** *nf* silly trick. ~**s** clowning.

club [klœb] *nm (gén)* club.

co [kɔ] *préf* co-, joint. **coaccusé** codefendant, co-accused; **coacquéreur** joint purchaser; **codétenu** fellow prisoner; **coéquipier** team mate.

coaguler *vti*, **se** ~ *vpr* [kɔagyle] (1) to coagulate; *[sang]* to clot, congeal; *[lait]* to curdle. ◆ **coagulant, e 1** *adj* coagulative. **2** *nm* coagulant. ◆ **coagulation** *nf* coagulation.

coaliser *vt*, **se** ~ *vpr* [kɔalize] (1) to unite (in a coalition). ◆ **coalition** *nf* coalition.

coaltar [kɔltaʀ] *nm (lit)* coal tar. *(fig)* **être dans le** ~ ⁑ to be in a daze *ou* stupor.

coasser [kɔase] (1) *vi* to croak. ◆ **coassement** *nm*: ~**(s)** croaking.

cobalt [kɔbalt] *nm* cobalt.

cobaye [kɔbaj] *nm (lit, fig)* guinea-pig.

cobra [kɔbʀa] *nm* cobra.

cocaïne [kɔkain] *nf* cocaine.

cocarde [kɔkaʀd(ə)] *nf* rosette; *(Hist)* cockade; *[avion]* roundel; *(sur voiture)* sticker.

cocasse [kɔkas] *adj* comical, funny. ◆ **cocasserie** *nf* comicalness, funniness.

coccinelle [kɔksinɛl] *nf* ladybird.

coccyx [kɔksis] *nm* coccyx.

cocher[1] [kɔʃe] (1) *vt (crayon)* to tick (off), check off; *(entaille)* to notch.

cocher[2] [kɔʃe] *nm* coachman; *[fiacre]* cabman.

cochon[1] [kɔʃɔ̃] *nm (animal)* pig; *(*: viande)* pork. ~ **d'Inde** guinea-pig; ~ **de lait** sucking-pig; **un** ~ **n'y retrouverait pas ses petits** it's like a pigsty in there. ◆ **cochon**[2]**, -onne 1** *adj (⁑: obscène)* dirty, smutty. **2** *nm, f (⁑ péj: personne) (sale, vicieux)* dirty pig ⁑ *ou* beast ⁑; *(méchant)* swine ⁑. **quel temps de** ~! what lousy weather! * ◆ **cochonner** * (1) *vt* to mess up *. ◆ **cochonnerie** * *nf (histoire)* dirty joke; *(tour)* dirty trick. **de la** ~ *(nourriture)* disgusting food; *(marchandise)* rubbish; *(saleté)* filth; **faire des** ~**s** to make a mess. ◆ **cochonnet** *nm (Zool)* piglet; *(Boules)* jack.

cocker [kɔkɛʀ] *nm* cocker spaniel.

cocktail [kɔktɛl] *nm (réunion)* cocktail party; *(boisson)* cocktail; *(fig)* mixture. ~ **Molotov** Molotov cocktail, petrol bomb.

coco [koko] *nm (*: œuf)* eggie *; *(réglisse)* liquorice powder. **oui mon** ~ yes, darling; *(*: péj)* **drôle de** ~ odd guy *, oddbod * , oddball * *(US)*.

cocon [kɔkɔ̃] *nm* cocoon; *(fig)* shell.

cocorico [kɔkɔʀiko] *nm, excl* cock-a-doodle-do.

cocotier [kɔkɔtje] *nm* coconut palm.

cocotte [kɔkɔt] *nf (*: poule)* hen; *(marmite)* casserole; *(* péj: femme)* tart *. **hue** ~! gee up!; **oui ma** ~ yes darling; ~ **minute** ® pressure cooker.

cocu, e ⁑ [kɔky] *adj, nm, f* cuckold. **faire qn** ~ to be unfaithful to sb.

code [kɔd] *nm (gén)* code. **C**~ **de la route** highway code; **écrire qch en** ~ to write sth in code, (en)code sth; **(phares)** ~ dipped headlights, low beams *(US)*; **se mettre en** ~ to dip one's headlights. ◆ **codage** *nm* (en)coding. ◆ **coder** (1) *vt* to code.

codifier [kɔdifje] (7) *vt* to codify. ◆ **codification** *nf* codification.

coefficient [kɔefisjɑ̃] *nm (Math, Phys)* coefficient. ~ **d'erreur** margin of error; *(Scol)* **cette matière est affectée d'un** ~ **trois** marks in this subject are weighted by a factor of three.

cœlioscopie [seljɔskɔpi] *nf* coelioscopy.

coercition [kɔɛʀsisjɔ̃] *nf* coercion.

cœur [kœʀ] *nm* (**a**) *(Anat, Cartes, forme)* heart. **en (forme de)** ~ heart-shaped; **on l'a opéré à** ~ **ouvert** he had an open-heart operation.

(**b**) *(fig: estomac)* **avoir mal au** ~ to feel sick; **il faut avoir le** ~ **bien accroché** you need guts * *ou* a strong stomach; **odeur qui soulève le** ~ nauseating *ou* sickening smell.

(**c**) *(âme)* heart. **c'est un** ~ **pur** he is a candid soul; **avoir le** ~ **sensible** to be tender-hearted; **elle lui a donné son** ~ she has lost her heart to him; **spectacle à vous fendre le** ~ heartrending *ou* heart-breaking sight; **avoir le** ~ **gros** to have a heavy heart; **il avait la rage au** ~ he was inwardly seething with anger; **ce geste lui est allé (droit) au** ~ this gesture went straight to his heart; **connaître le fond du** ~ **de qn** to know sb's inner-

most feelings; **des paroles venues (du fond) du ~** heartfelt words; **au fond de son ~** in his heart of hearts; **il m'a parlé à ~ ouvert** he had a heart-to-heart talk with me.
(**d**) *(bonté, générosité)* **avoir bon ~** to be kind-hearted; **avoir le ~ sur la main** to be open-handed; **sans ~** heartless; **c'est un ~ de pierre/ d'or** he has a heart of stone/gold; **femme de ~** noble-hearted woman.
(**e**) *(humeur)* **avoir le ~ gai** to feel happy; **je n'ai pas le ~ à rire** I do not feel like laughing, I am not in the mood for laughing; **si le ~ vous en dit** if you feel like it.
(**f**) *(courage)* heart, courage. **le ~ lui manqua** his heart *ou* courage failed him; **mettre tout son ~ dans qch/à faire qch** to put all one's heart into sth/into doing sth; **comment peut-on avoir le ~ de refuser?** how can one have the heart to refuse?; **donner du ~ au ventre à qn** * to buck sb up *; **avoir du ~ au ventre** * to have guts *.
(**g**) *[chou]* heart; *[arbre]* heart, core; *[fruit]* core; *[problème, ville]* heart. **au ~ de** in the heart of; **~ de palmier** heart of palm; **~ d'artichaut** artichoke heart.
(**h**) **par ~** by heart; **ça m'est resté sur le ~** I still feel sore about it; **je vais lui dire ce que j'ai sur le ~** I'm going to tell him what's on my mind; **à ~ joie** to one's heart's content; **je suis de tout ~ avec vous** I DO sympathize with you; **ne pas porter qn dans son ~** to have no great liking for sb; **je veux en avoir le ~ net** I want to be clear in my own mind (about it); **avoir à ~ de faire** to make a point of doing; **prendre les choses à ~** to take things to heart; **ce voyage me tient à ~** I have set my heart on this journey; **ce sujet me tient à ~** this subject is close to my heart.

coexister [kɔɛgziste] (1) *vi* to coexist. ◆ **coexistence** *nf* coexistence.

coffre [kɔfʀ(ə)] *nm (meuble)* chest; *(Aut)* boot, trunk *(US)*; *(coffrage)* case; *(Banque, hôtel)* safe; *(Hist, fig: cassette)* coffer; *(*: poitrine)* chest. **~-fort** *nm, pl* **~s-~s** safe; *(Banque)* **la salle des ~s** the strong room; **~ à jouets** toybox. ◆ **coffrage** *nm [bois]* case; *[béton]* form. ◆ **coffrer** * (1) *vt* to throw *ou* put inside *. **se faire ~** * to get put inside *. ◆ **coffret** *nm* casket. **~ à bijoux** jewel box; **~ de luxe, ~-cadeau** presentation box.

cogiter [kɔʒite] (1) **1** *vi (hum)* to cogitate. **2** *vt:* **qu'est-ce qu'il cogite?** what's he thinking up? ◆ **cogitation** *nf (hum)* cogitation.

cognac [kɔɲak] *nm* cognac, French brandy.

cogner [kɔɲe] (1) **1** *vt objet* to knock; *(*: battre)* to beat up. **2** *vt indir:* **~ sur** *clou* to hammer; *mur* to knock on; *(fort)* to bang on; **~ du poing sur la table** to thump one's fist on the table; **~ à** *porte* to knock at; *(fort)* to bang at; **~ contre** to hit, strike. **3** *vi [volet]* to bang (*contre* against); (*) *[boxeur]* to hit out (hard); *[soleil]* to beat down; *[moteur]* to knock. **ça va ~** * there's going to be some rough stuff *. **4 se ~** *vpr*: **se ~/se ~ le genou contre** to bang o.s/one's knee against; *(fig)* **c'est à se ~ la tête contre les murs** it's enough to drive you up the wall. ◆ **cognée** *nf* felling axe. ◆ **cognement** *nm*: **~(s)** banging; knocking. ◆ **cogneur** * *nm* bruiser *.

cohabiter [kɔabite] (1) *vi* to live together, cohabit. **~ avec** to live with. ◆ **cohabitation** *nf* living together, cohabitation.

cohérent, e [kɔeʀɑ̃, ɑ̃t] *adj* coherent, consistent. ◆ **cohérence** *nf* coherence, consistency.

cohésion [kɔezjɔ̃] *nf* cohesion.

cohorte [kɔɔʀt(ə)] *nf (groupe)* troop; *(Hist Mil)* cohort.

cohue [kɔy] *nf (foule)* crowd; *(bousculade)* crush.

coi, coite [kwa, kwat] *adj* silent.

coiffe [kwaf] *nf* headdress.

coiffer [kwafe] (1) *vt* (**a**) **~ qn** to do sb's hair; **se faire ~** to have one's hair done; **se ~** to do one's hair. (**b**) *(mettre) chapeau* to put on. **se ~ d'une casquette** to put on a cap; **~ qn** to put a hat on sb's head; **ça te coiffe bien** it suits you; **coiffé d'un chapeau** wearing a hat; **pic coiffé de neige** snow-capped peak. (**c**) *(fig) organismes* to head up, have overall responsibility for; (*) *concurrent* to get the better of, beat. ◆ **coiffé, e** *adj*: **il est toujours mal/ bien ~** his hair always looks untidy/nice; **être ~ en brosse** to have a crew cut; **il était ~ en arrière** he had his hair brushed back. ◆ **coiffeur, euse 1** *nm, f* hairdresser. **2** *nf (meuble)* dressing table. ◆ **coiffure** *nf* hair style, hairdo *; *(chapeau)* hat. *(métier)* **la ~** hairdressing.

coin [kwɛ̃] *nm* (**a**) *(angle)* corner. **au ~ du feu** by the fireside; **le magasin qui fait le ~** the corner shop, the shop at the corner; **à tous les ~s de rue** on every street corner; **sourire en ~** half smile; **regard en ~** side glance; **surveiller qn du ~ de l'œil** to watch sb out of the corner of one's eye. (**b**) *(région)* area; *(village)* place; *(endroit) [plage, mémoire]* corner. **le ~ du bricoleur** the handyman's corner; **un ~ de terre/ciel** a patch of land/sky; **je l'ai mis dans un ~** I put it somewhere; **dans tous les ~s (et recoins)** in every nook and cranny; **~-repas** dining area; **l'épicier du ~** the local grocer; **un ~ perdu** a place miles from anywhere; **un petit ~ pas cher** somewhere nice and cheap, a nice inexpensive spot. (**c**) *(cale)* wedge; *(poinçon)* hallmark; *(pour graver)* die; *(pour sous-main)* corner-piece.

coincer [kwɛ̃se] (3) **1** *vt* (**a**) *(intentionnellement)* to wedge; *(accidentellement)* to jam. **le tiroir est coincé** the drawer is stuck *ou* jammed; **il se trouva coincé contre un mur** he was pinned against a wall; **il m'a coincé pour me dire** he cornered me to tell me. (**b**) (*) *voleur* to nab *; *fraudeur* to catch up with; *candidat* to catch out. **coincé entre son désir et la peur** caught between his desire and fear; **nous sommes coincés** we are stuck *ou* cornered. **2** *vi [porte]* to stick. *(fig)* **ça coince au niveau de la direction** there are problems at management level. **3 se ~** *vpr* to jam, stick, get jammed *ou* stuck.

coïncidence [kɔɛ̃sidɑ̃s] *nf (gén)* coincidence. ◆ **coïncident, e** *adj* coincident. ◆ **coïncider** (1) *vi* to coincide (*avec* with). **faire ~ les dates** to get the dates to coincide.

coing [kwɛ̃] *nm* quince.

coke [kɔk] *nm* coke.

col [kɔl] *nm* (**a**) *[chemise]* collar. **~ roulé** polo-neck sweater; **~ bleu** *(ouvrier)* blue-collar worker; *(marin)* blue jacket. (**b**) *(Géog)* pass; *(Anat, fig)* neck.

colchique [kɔlʃik] *nm* autumn crocus.

coléoptère [kɔleɔptɛʀ] *nm* beetle.

colère [kɔlɛʀ] **1** *nf (gén)* anger; *(littér)* wrath; *(accès)* (fit of) rage. **être/se mettre/mettre qn en ~** to be/ get/make sb angry (*contre* with); **faire une ~** to throw a tantrum. **2** *adj inv*: **être ~** * to be cross *ou* angry. ◆ **coléreux, -euse** *ou* ◆ **colérique** *adj* quick-tempered.

colibacille [kɔlibasil] *nm* colon bacillus.

colibri [kɔlibʀi] *nm* hummingbird.

colifichet [kɔlifiʃɛ] *nm* trinket.

colimaçon [kɔlimasɔ̃] *nm* snail. **escalier en ~** spiral staircase.

colin [kɔlɛ̃] *nm (merlu)* hake; *(lieu noir)* saithe, coal-fish, coley.

colin-maillard [kɔlɛ̃majaʀ] *nm* blind man's buff.

colique [kɔlik] *nf (diarrhée)* diarrhoea. *(douleurs)* **~s** stomach pains, colic; **~s néphrétiques** renal colic.

colis [kɔli] *nm* parcel. **par ~ postal** by parcel post; **~ piégé** parcel bomb, mailbomb.

collaborateur, -trice [kɔlabɔʀatœʀ, tʀis] *nm, f (gén)* colleague; *[journal]* contributor; *[livre]* collaborator; *(Pol)* collaborationist. ◆ **collaboration** *nf* collaboration (*à* on); contribution (*à* to). **en ~ avec** in collaboration with. ◆ **collaborer** (1) *vi* to collaborate (*à* on); to contribute (*à* to).

collage [kɔlaʒ] *nm* (**a**) *(à la colle forte)* sticking, gluing; *(à la colle blanche)* pasting. ~ **de papiers peints** paperhanging; ~ **d'affiches** billposting. (**b**) *(Art)* collage.

collant, e [kɔlɑ̃, ɑ̃t] **1** *adj (ajusté)* tight-fitting, clinging; *(poisseux)* sticky. *(importun)* **être ~** * to cling. **2** *nm* (**a**) *(maillot) [femme]* body stocking; *[danseur]* leotard. (**b**) *(bas) (gén)* tights, *pl* pantyhose *(US)*; *[danseuse]* tights *pl.*

collation [kɔlɑsjɔ̃] *nf* snack.

colle [kɔl] *nf* (**a**) *(gén)* glue; *(à papier)* paste. (**b**) *(*: question)* poser *. (**c**) *(examen blanc)* mock oral exam; *(retenue)* detention.

collecteur, -trice [kɔlɛktœʀ, tʀis] **1** *nm, f* collector. **2** *nm*: **(égout)** ~ main sewer. ◆ **collecte** *nf* collection. ◆ **collecter** (1) *vt* to collect.

collectif, -ive [kɔlɛktif, iv] **1** *adj (gén)* collective; *billet* group; *hystérie, licenciements* mass; *installations* public. **immeuble ~** block of flats. **2** *nm (Gram)* collective noun. *(Fin)* ~ **budgétaire** minibudget. ◆ **collectivement** *adv (gén)* collectively. ◆ **collectiviser** (1) *vt* to collectivize.

collection [kɔlɛksjɔ̃] *nf (gén)* collection; *(Comm) [échantillons]* line. ◆ **collectionner** (1) *vt* to collect. ◆ **collectionneur, -euse** *nm, f* collector.

collectivité [kɔlɛktivite] *nf* (**a**) *(groupe)* group; *(organisation)* body, organisation. **la ~** the community; **vivre en ~** to live in the community. (**b**) *(possession commune)* collective ownership.

collège [kɔlɛʒ] *nm* (**a**) *(école)* school; *(privé)* private school. ~ **(d'enseignement secondaire)** middle school, secondary school, junior high school *(US)*; ~ **expérimental/technique** experimental/technical school. (**b**) *(Pol, Rel)* college. ~ **électoral** electoral college. ◆ **collégial, e,** *mpl* **-iaux** *adj* collegiate. ◆ **collégien, -ienne** *nm, f* schoolboy; schoolgirl; *(fig)* novice.

collègue [kɔlɛg] *nmf* colleague.

coller [kɔle] (1) **1** *vt* (**a**) *(à la colle forte)* to stick, glue; *(à la colle blanche)* to paste; *timbre* to stick; *affiche* to stick up (*à, sur* on); *enveloppe* to stick down; *papier peint* to hang; *film* to splice. ~ **2 morceaux (ensemble)** to stick *ou* glue 2 pieces together; ~ **son oreille à la porte** to press one's ear to the door; **il colla l'armoire contre le mur** he stood the wardrobe right against the wall; **il m'a collé (après) toute la journée** * he clung to me all day. (**b**) (*) *(mettre)* to stick, shove *; *(donner)* to give; *(écrire)* to write. **colle tes valises dans un coin** stick *ou* shove * *ou* dump * your bags in a corner; **il se colla devant moi** he plonked * *ou* planted himself in front of me; **ils l'ont collé ministre** they've gone and made him a minister *; **on lui a collé la responsabilité** he's got stuck * *ou* landed * with the responsibility. (**c**) *(arg Scol) (consigner)* to give a detention to, keep in; *(poser une question)* to catch out; *(recaler)* to fail. **se faire ~** to be given a detention; to be failed.

2 *vi* (**a**) *(être poisseux)* to be sticky; *(adhérer)* to stick (*à* to). ~ **au peloton** to stick to the pack; **robe qui colle au corps** tight-fitting *ou* clinging dress; ~ **au sujet** to stick to the subject. (**b**) *(*: bien marcher)* **ça colle?** O.K.? *; **ça ne colle pas** it doesn't work, there's something wrong.

3 se ~ *vpr* (**a**) (*) *tâche, personne* to get stuck *ou* landed with *. **se ~ à (faire) qch** to get down to (doing) sth. (**b**) **se ~ à qn** *[danseur, importun]* to cling to sb; **se ~ devant la télé** * to be glued to the telly *; **ils sont toujours collés ensemble** ‡ they are always together.

collet [kɔlɛ] *nm (piège)* noose; *[dent]* neck; *(Tech)* collar, flange. **prendre qn au ~** to seize sb by the collar; **elle est très ~ monté** she's very strait-laced *ou* stuffy. ◆ **colleter** (4) *vt* to collar. *(lit, fig)* **se ~ avec** * to wrestle *ou* grapple with.

colleur, -euse [kɔlœʀ, øz] **1** *nm, f*: ~ **d'affiches** billsticker; ~ **de papiers peints** wallpaperer. **2** *nf (Ciné)* splicer; *(Phot)* mounting press.

collier [kɔlje] *nm [femme]* necklace; *[maire]* chain; *[animal]* collar; *(Tech)* collar. ~ **de fleurs** garland of flowers; **reprendre le ~** * to get back into harness; ~ **(de barbe)** beard (along the line of the jaw).

collimateur [kɔlimatœʀ] *nm* collimator. *(lit, fig)* **avoir qn dans son ~** to have sb in one's sights.

colline [kɔlin] *nf* hill.

collision [kɔlizjɔ̃] *nf [véhicules]* collision; *(fig)* clash. **entrer en ~** to collide (*avec* with); *(Aut)* ~ **en chaîne** pileup.

colloque [kɔlɔk] *nm* colloquium.

collusion [kɔlyzjɔ̃] *nf* collusion.

collyre [kɔliʀ] *nm* eye lotion.

colmater [kɔlmate] (1) *vt fuite* to seal (off); *fissure* to fill in, plug. *(fig, Mil)* ~ **une brèche** to seal a gap.

Cologne [kɔlɔɲ] *n* Cologne; *V* **eau.**

colombage [kɔlɔ̃baʒ] *nm* half-timbering. **maison à ~** half-timbered house.

colombe [kɔlɔ̃b] *nf* dove. ◆ **colombier** *nm* dovecote.

Colombie [kɔlɔ̃bi] *nf* Colombia. ~ **britannique** British Columbia. ◆ **colombien, -ienne** *adj,* **C~(ne)** *nm(f)* Colombian.

colon [kɔlɔ̃] *nm (pionnier)* settler, colonist; *(enfant)* child, boarder; *(arg Mil)* colonel.

côlon [kolɔ̃] *nm (Anat)* colon.

colonel [kɔlɔnɛl] *nm (armée de terre)* colonel; *(armée de l'air)* group captain, colonel *(US)*.

colonie [kɔlɔni] *nf (gén)* colony. ~ **de vacances** (children's) holiday camp, summer camp *(US)*. ◆ **colonial, e,** *mpl* **-aux 1** *adj* colonial. **2** *nm (habitant)* colonial. ◆ **colonialisme** *nm* colonialism. ◆ **colonialiste** *adj, nmf* colonialist.

coloniser [kɔlɔnize] (1) *vt* to colonize. **les colonisés** the colonized peoples. ◆ **colonisateur, -trice 1** *adj* colonizing. **2** *nm, f* colonizer. ◆ **colonisation** *nf* colonization.

colonne [kɔlɔn] *nf (gén)* column. ~ **d'air** airstream; ~ **blindée** armoured column; ~ **montante** rising main; ~ **de secours** rescue party; ~ **vertébrale** spine, spinal column. ◆ **colonnade** *nf* colonnade. ◆ **colonnette** *nf* small column.

colorer [kɔlɔʀe] (1) **1** *vt substance* to colour; *tissu* to dye; *bois* to stain; *récit* to colour (*de* with). ~ **qch en bleu** to colour sth blue. **2 se ~** *vpr [tomate, visage]* to turn red. **le ciel se colore de rose** the sky takes on a rosy tinge; *(fig)* **se ~ de** to be coloured *ou* tinged with. ◆ **colorant, e** *adj, nm* colouring. ◆ **coloration** *nf* (**a**) *(action)* colouring; dyeing; staining. (**b**) *(couleur)* colouring, colour; *[peau]* colouring; *[voix]* coloration. ◆ **coloré, e** *adj teint* ruddy; *objet* coloured; *foule, récit* colourful.

colorier [kɔlɔʀje] (7) *vt* to colour (in). ◆ **coloriage** *nm (action)* colouring; *(dessin)* coloured drawing. ◆ **coloris** *nm (gén)* colour, shade; *[peau]* colouring.

colosse [kɔlɔs] *nm (personne)* giant; *(institution)* colossus, giant. ◆ **colossal, e,** *mpl* **-aux** *adj* colossal, huge.

colporter [kɔlpɔʀte] (1) *vt* to hawk, peddle. ◆ **colportage** *nm* hawking, peddling. ◆ **colporteur, -euse** *nm, f* hawker, pedlar. ~ **de fausses nouvelles** newsmonger.

colt [kɔlt] *nm (revolver)* gun, Colt.

coltiner [kɔltine] (1) **1** *vt colis* to carry *ou* lug * around. **2 se** ~ * *vpr colis* to lug around *, carry; (*) *travail, personne* to get stuck *ou* landed with *.

columbarium [kɔlɔ̃baʀjɔm] *nm (cimetière)* columbarium.

colza [kɔlza] *nm* rape(seed).

coma [kɔma] *nm (Méd)* coma. **dans le** ~ in a coma; **dans un** ~ **dépassé** brain-dead. ◆ **comateux, -euse** *adj*: **état** ~ comatose state.

combat [kɔ̃ba] *nm (gén)* fight; *(Mil)* battle; *(fig)* fight, struggle; *(Sport)* match. **tué au** ~ killed in action; **aller au** ~ to go into battle; **les ~s continuent** the fighting goes on; ~ **de rues** street fighting, street battle; ~ **singulier** single combat. ◆ **combatif, -ive** *adj troupes* ready to fight; *personne* of a fighting spirit; *humeur* fighting. ◆ **combativité** *nf [troupe]* readiness to fight; *[personne]* fighting spirit. ◆ **combattant, e 1** *adj* fighting, combatant. **2** *nm, f [guerre]* combatant; *[bagarre]* brawler. ◆ **combattre** (41) **1** *vt* to fight; *(fig) théorie, vice* to combat, fight (against). **2** *vi* to fight.

combien [kɔ̃bjɛ̃] **1** *adv*: ~ **de** *(quantité)* how much; *(nombre)* how many; ~ **y en a-t-il (en moins)?** *(quantité)* how much (less) is there (of it)?; *(nombre)* how many (fewer) are there (of them)?; **(depuis)** ~ **de temps?** how long?; ~ **vous avez raison!** how right you are!; ~ **d'ennui je vous cause** what a lot of trouble I'm causing you ; ~ **mesure-t-il?** how big is it?; **ça va faire une différence de** ~? what will the difference be? ; ~ **y a-t-il d'ici à la ville?** how far is it from here to the town? **2** *nm* (*) *(rang)* **le** ~ **êtes-vous?** where were you placed?; *(date)* **le** ~ **sommes-nous?** what date is it?; *(fréquence) [trains]* **il y en a tous les** ~? how often do they come?

combinaison [kɔ̃binɛzɔ̃] *nf* (**a**) *(gén, Math)* combination. ~ **(ministérielle)** government. (**b**) *(vêtement) [femme]* slip; *[aviateur]* flying suit; *[mécanicien]* boiler suit; *(Ski)* ski-suit. (**c**) *(astuce)* device; *(manigance)* scheme. ◆ **combinard, e** * *adj, nm, f (péj)* **il est** ~ he's a schemer. ◆ **combine** * *nf (astuce)* trick (*pour faire* to do) *(péj)* scheme. **il est dans la** ~ he's in on it *; **ça sent la** ~ I smell a rat, it's a fix; **toutes leurs ~s** all their little schemes, all their fiddles *. ◆ **combiné** *nm (Chim)* compound; *[téléphone]* receiver; *(Sport)* combination. ◆ **combiner** (1) **1** *vt (grouper)* to combine (*avec* with); *(élaborer)* to devise, work out. **2 se** ~ *vpr* to combine (*avec* with).

comble [kɔ̃bl(ə)] **1** *adj* packed. **2** *nm* (**a**) **le** ~ **de** the height of; **au** ~ **du désespoir** in the depths of despair; **pour** ~ **(de malheur) il...** to cap *ou* crown it all he...; **c'est le** *ou* **un** ~! that's the last straw! (**b**) *(charpente)* roof timbers. *(pièce)* **les ~s** the attic.

comblement [kɔ̃bləmɑ̃] *nm [cavité]* filling(-in).

combler [kɔ̃ble] (1) *vt* (**a**) *trou* to fill in; *déficit* to make good; *lacune* to fill. ~ **son retard** to make up lost time. (**b**) *désir, besoin* to fulfil; *personne* to gratify. **c'est une femme comblée** she has all that she could wish for; ~ **qn de** *cadeaux* to shower sb with; *joie* to fill sb with; **comblé d'honneurs** laden with honours; **vraiment, vous nous comblez!** really, you're too good to us!

combustible [kɔ̃bystibl(ə)] **1** *adj* combustible. **2** *nm* fuel. ◆ **combustion** *nf* combustion.

comédie [kɔmedi] *nf (Théât)* comedy. ~ **musicale** musical; **de** ~ *(Théât)* comedy; *(fig)* comic; *(fig)* **jouer la** ~ to put on an act; **faire la** ~ to make a fuss *ou* a scene. ◆ **comédien, -ienne** *nm, f* (comedy) actor *ou* actress; *(hypocrite)* sham; *(pitre)* show-off.

comestible [kɔmɛstibl(ə)] **1** *adj* edible. **2** *nmpl*: **~s** (fine) foods, delicatessen.

comète [kɔmɛt] *nf* comet.

comique [kɔmik] **1** *adj (Théât)* comic; *(fig)* comical. **2** *nm* (**a**) *[situation]* comic aspect; *[habillement]* comic look *ou* appearance. **d'un** ~ **irrésistible** hilariously funny; **le** ~ **de la chose, c'est que...** the funny thing about it is that... (**b**) *(Littérat)* **le** ~ comedy; ~ **de caractère** character comedy; **avoir le sens du** ~ to have a sense of the comic. (**c**) *(artiste)* comic, comedian; *(dramaturge)* comedy writer. ◆ **comiquement** *adv* comically.

comité [kɔmite] *nm (gén)* committee. *(fig)* **se réunir en petit** ~ *(petite réception)* to have a small get-together; ~ **consultatif/exécutif** advisory/executive committee; ~ **directeur** board of management.

commandant [kɔmɑ̃dɑ̃] *nm* (**a**) *(gén)* commander, commandant; *(armée de terre)* major; *(armée de l'air)* squadron leader, major *(US)*. (**b**) *(Aviat, Naut)* captain. ~ **en second** second in command.

commande [kɔmɑ̃d] *nf* (**a**) *(Comm)* order. **passer une** ~ to put in an order (*de* for); **en** ~ on order; **fait sur** ~ made to order. (**b**) *(Tech) (action)* control, controlling. *(dispositif)* **~(s)** controls; ~ **à distance** remote control; **être/se mettre aux ~s** to be in/take control. (**c**) **de** ~ *sourire* forced, artificial; *(Art) œuvre* commissioned; **agir sur** ~ to act on orders; **s'amuser sur** ~ to enjoy o.s. to order; **ouvrage écrit/composé sur** ~ commissioned work/ composition.

commandement [kɔmɑ̃dmɑ̃] *nm (direction, ordre, état-major)* command; *(Rel)* commandment. **prendre le** ~ **de** to take command of; **ton de** ~ commanding tone; **à mon** ~ on my command.

commander [kɔmɑ̃de] (1) **1** *vt* (**a**) *obéissance* to order, command. **il me commanda le silence** he ordered *ou* commanded me to keep quiet; ~ **l'admiration** to compel admiration; **la prudence commande que...** prudence demands that... (**b**) *marchandise, repas* to order; *(Art) œuvre* to commission. (**c**) *armée* to command; *(emploi absolu)* to be in command *ou* in charge. **je n'aime pas qu'on me commande** I don't like to be ordered about; **ce bouton commande la sirène** this switch controls the siren. **2** ~ **à** *vt indir passions, muscles* to have command *ou* control over. **3 se** ~ *vpr [pièces]* to lead into one another; *[personne]* to control o.s. **ces choses-là ne se commandent pas** you can't help these things. ◆ **commandeur** *nm* commander *(of an Order)*. ◆ **commanditaire** *nm* sleeping partner. **les ~s d'un meurtre** the people behind a murder. ◆ **commanditer** (1) *vt (Comm: financer)* to finance.

commando [kɔmɑ̃do] *nm (groupe, homme)* commando.

comme [kɔm] **1** *conj* (**a**) *(temps)* as; *(cause)* as, since. **(juste)** ~ **le rideau se levait** (just) as the curtain was rising; ~ **il pleut** seeing that it's raining, since it's raining. (**b**) *(comparaison)* as, like (*devant n et pron*). **il pense** ~ **nous** he thinks as we do *ou* like us; **c'est un homme** ~ **lui qu'il nous faut** we need a man like him *ou* such as him; **en ville** ~ **à la campagne** in town and *ou* as well as in the country; **il écrit** ~ **il parle** he writes as *ou* the way he speaks; **dur** ~ **du fer** (as) hard as iron; **il y eut** ~ **une lueur** there was a sort *ou* kind of light. (**c**) *(en tant que)* as. ~ **étudiant** as a student. (**d**) ~ **si** as if, as though; ~ **pour faire** as if to do; ~ **si nous ne savions pas!** as if we didn't know!; ~ **quoi il ne fallait pas l'écouter** which goes to show that you shouldn't have listened to him; **il était** ~ **fasciné** it was as though *ou* as if he were fascinated. (**e**) ~ **cela** like that; ~ **ci** ~ **ça** so-so, (fair to) middling; **alors,** ~ **ça, vous nous quittez?** so you're leaving us?; ~ **il vous plaira** as you wish; ~ **de juste** naturally; ~ **par hasard, il était absent** he just HAPPENED to be away; ~ **il faut** *manger*

properly; *personne* decent; **c'était amusant** ~ **tout** it was terribly funny.
2 *adv*: ~ **ces enfants sont bruyants!** how noisy these children are!; ~ **il fait beau!** what a lovely day!, what lovely weather!

commémorer [kɔmemɔʀe] (1) *vt* to commemorate. ◆ **commémoratif, -ive** *adj* commemorative, memorial. ◆ **commémoration** *nf* commemoration. **en** ~ **de** in commemoration of.

commencer [kɔmɑ̃se] (3) **1** *vt* to begin, start, commence. ~ **un élève (en maths)** to start a pupil (off) (in maths). **2** *vi* to begin, start, commence. **le concert va** ~ the concert is about to begin *ou* start; **ça commence bien!** that's a good start!; **pour** ~ to begin *ou* start with; ~ **à** *(ou* **de***)* **faire** to begin *ou* start to do *ou* doing; **ça commence à bien faire** * it's getting a bit much *; ~ **par qch/par faire qch** to start *ou* begin with sth/by doing sth. ◆ **commençant, e** **1** *adj* beginning. **2** *nm, f* beginner. ◆ **commencement** *nm (début)* beginning; *(départ)* start. **au/dès le** ~ in/from the beginning, at/from the outset *ou* start; **du** ~ **à la fin** from beginning to end, from start to finish; ~**s** *[science, métier]* beginnings.

comment [kɔmɑ̃] **1** *adv* (**a**) how. ~ **appelles-tu cela?** what do you call that?; ~ **allez-vous?** how are you?; ~ **faire?** how shall we do it?; ~ **se fait-il que...?** how is it that...? (**b**) *(excl)* ~**?** pardon?, sorry?, what? *; ~ **cela?** what do you mean?; ~**, il est mort?** what! is he dead?; **et** ~**!** * not half! *, and how! *; ~ **donc!** by all means!, of course! **2** *nm*: **le** ~ the how.

commentaire [kɔmɑ̃tɛʀ] *nm (remarque)* comment; *(gén, Littérat: exposé)* commentary (*sur, de* on); *(Radio, TV)* commentary. ~**s de presse** press comments; **et pas de** ~**s!** and no arguments *ou* and that's final!; **ça se passe de** ~**s** it speaks for itself. ◆ **commentateur, -trice** *nm, f (gén)* commentator. ◆ **commenter** (1) *vt poème, match* to give a commentary on; *conduite, événement* to comment on.

commérage [kɔmeʀaʒ] *nm*: ~**(s)** gossip.

commerçant, e [kɔmɛʀsɑ̃, ɑ̃t] **1** *adj nation* trading; *ville* commercial; *rue* shopping. **il est très** ~ he's got good business sense. **2** *nm* shopkeeper, tradesman, merchant *(US)* , storekeeper *(US)*. **3** *nf* shopkeeper, storekeeper *(US)*.

commerce [kɔmɛʀs(ə)] *nm* (**a**) **le** ~ trade, commerce; *(affaires)* business. *(commerçants)* **le petit** ~ small shopkeepers; **opération de** ~ commercial operation; ~ **de gros/détail** wholesale/retail trade; **faire du** ~ **avec** to trade with; **dans le** ~ *objet* in the shops *ou* stores *(US)*; **vendu hors-**~ sold direct to the public. (**b**) *(boutique)* business. (**c**) *(littér) (compagnie)* company; *(rapport)* dealings. ◆ **commercer** (3) *vi* to trade *(avec* with). ◆ **commercial, e,** *mpl* **-iaux** **1** *adj* commercial. **accord** ~ trade *ou* trading agreement. **2** *nm* marketing man. **l'un de nos** ~**iaux** one of our marketing people. **3** *nf (véhicule)* (light) van. ◆ **commercialisable** *adj* marketable, tradable. ◆ **commercialisation** *nf* marketing. ◆ **commercialiser** (1) *vt* to market.

commère [kɔmɛʀ] *nf (péj: bavarde)* gossip.

commettre [kɔmɛtʀ(ə)] (56) **1** *vt* (**a**) *crime* to commit; *erreur* to make. (**b**) *(†: confier)* ~ **qch à qn** to commit *ou* entrust sth to sb. (**c**) *(nommer)* to appoint, nominate (*à* to). **2 se** ~ *vpr (péj)* to lower o.s. **se** ~ **avec** to associate with.

commis [kɔmi] *nm* (shop) assistant. ~ **de bureau** office clerk; ~ **voyageur** commercial traveller.

commisération [kɔmizeʀɑsjɔ̃] *nf* commiseration.

commissaire [kɔmisɛʀ] *nm (police)* ≃ *(police)* superintendent, (police) captain *(US)*; *(Sport etc)* steward; *(envoyé)* representative; *[commission]* commissioner. *(Naut)* ~ **du bord** purser; ~**-priseur** *nm, pl* ~**s-**~**s** auctioneer. ◆ **commissariat** *nm* (**a**) *(poste)* ~ **(de police)** police station. (**b**) *(organisme officiel)* board.

commission [kɔmisjɔ̃] *nf* (**a**) *(nommée)* commission; *(comité)* committee. **travail en** ~ work in committee. (**b**) *(message)* message. (**c**) *(course)* errand; *(Comm, Jur: mandat)* commission. *(emplettes)* ~**s** shopping; **faire les** ~**s** to do the *ou* go shopping. (**d**) *(pourcentage)* commission (*sur* on). ◆ **commissionnaire** *nm (livreur)* delivery man; *(messager)* messenger; *(Comm: intermédiaire)* agent, broker. ◆ **commissionner** (1) *vt* to commission.

commissure [kɔmisyʀ] *nf [bouche]* corner.

commode [kɔmɔd] **1** *adj* (**a**) *(gén)* convenient; *outil* handy (*pour faire* for doing). (**b**) *(facile)* easy. ~ **à vivre** easy to get on with; **il n'est pas** ~ he's an awkward customer. **2** *nf (meuble)* chest of drawers. ◆ **commodément** *adv porter* conveniently; *s'asseoir* comfortably; *transporter* easily. ◆ **commodité** *nf* convenience.

commotion [kɔmosjɔ̃] *nf (secousse)* shock; *(révolution)* upheaval. ~ **cérébrale** concussion. ◆ **commotionner** (1) *vt*: ~ **qn** to give sb a shock, shake sb.

commuer [kɔmɥe] (1) *vt peine* to commute (*en* to).

commun, e[1] [kɔmœ̃, yn] **1** *adj* (**a**) *(gén, Math)* common; *effort, démarche* joint; *ami* mutual; *pièce* shared. **d'un** ~ **accord** of one accord; **il y a une cuisine** ~**e** there is a communal *ou* shared kitchen; **être** ~ **à** to be shared by; **la vie** ~**e** *[couple]* conjugal life; *[communauté]* communal life; **ils n'ont rien de** ~ they have nothing in common (*avec* with); **il n'y a pas de** ~**e mesure entre eux** there's no possible comparison between them. (**b**) **avoir qch en** ~ to have sth in common; **faire la cuisine en** ~ to share (in) the cooking; **vivre en** ~ to live communally; **mettre ses ressources en** ~ to share *ou* pool one's resources. (**c**) *accident, métal, (péj) manières* common; *opinion* commonly held, widespread. **peu** ~ uncommon, unusual. **2** *nm* (**a**) **le** ~ **des mortels** the common run of people. (**b**) *(bâtiments)* **les** ~**s** the outbuildings. ◆ **communément** *adv* commonly.

communauté [kɔmynote] *nf* (**a**) *[idées]* identity; *[culture]* community. (**b**) *(Pol, Rel etc)* community. ~ **urbaine** urban community; **vivre en** ~ to live communally; **mettre qch en** ~ to pool sth; **la C**~ **Économique Européenne** the European Economic Community. (**c**) *(entre époux)* shared estate. ◆ **communautaire** *adj* community; *(Pol)* Community.

commune[2] [kɔmyn] *nf* (**a**) *(ville)* town; *(village)* village; *(territoire)* district; *(autorités)* town (*ou* district) council. (**b**) *(Brit Pol)* **les C**~**s** the (House of) Commons. ◆ **communal, e,** *mpl* **-aux** *adj (Admin)* district; *(local)* local.

communicatif, -ive [kɔmynikatif, iv] *adj rire* infectious; *personne* communicative.

communication [kɔmynikɑsjɔ̃] *nf* (**a**) *(gén, fig: liaison)* communication. **les** ~**s sont coupées** communications are cut (off); **porte de** ~ communicating door; **être en** ~ **avec** to be in communication *ou* contact with; **mettre qn en** ~ **avec qn** to put sb in touch *ou* contact with sb. (**b**) *[fait]* communication; *[dossier]* transmission. **avoir** ~ **d'un fait** to be informed of a fact; **demander** ~ **d'un dossier** to ask for a file. (**c**) *(message)* message, communication; *(Univ: exposé)* paper. (**d**) ~ **(téléphonique)** (phone) call; **mettre qn en** ~ **(avec)** to put sb through (to), connect sb (with); ~ **en PCV** reverse charge call, collect call *(US)*; **je n'ai pas pu avoir la** ~ I couldn't get through.

communier [kɔmynje] (7) *vi (Rel)* to receive communion. ~ **dans** *sentiment* to be united in.

◆ **communiant, e** *nm, f* communicant. **premier** ~ child making his first communion. ◆ **communion** *nf (Rel, fig)* communion. **faire sa (première)** ~ to make one's first communion; *(fig)* **être en** ~ **avec** *personne* to be in communion with; *sentiments* to be in sympathy with.

communiquer [kɔmynike] (1) **1** *vt nouvelle, mouvement, peur* to communicate; *dossier (donner)* to give; *(envoyer)* to send; *maladie* to pass on, give; *lumière, chaleur* to transmit (*à* to). **2** *vi [personnes, pièces]* to communicate (*avec* with). **3 se** ~ *vpr [feu etc]* **se** ~ **à** to spread to. ◆ **communiqué** *nm* communiqué. ~ **de presse** press release.

communisme [kɔmynism(ə)] *nm* communism. ◆ **communisant, e 1** *adj* communistic. **2** *nm, f* communist sympathizer, fellow traveller. ◆ **communiste** *adj, nmf* communist.

commuter [kɔmyte] (1) *vt* to commute. ◆ **commutateur** *nm (Élec)* switch. ◆ **commutation** *nf* commutation. *(Ordin)* ~ **des messages** message switching.

Comores [kɔmɔʀ] *nfpl:* **les (îles)** ~ the Comoro Islands, the Comoros.

compact, e [kɔ̃pakt, akt(ə)] *adj* dense; *véhicule, appareil* compact; *majorité* solid.

compagnie [kɔ̃paɲi] *nf* (**a**) *(présence)* company. **en** ~ **de** in company with; **en bonne/mauvaise** ~ in good/bad company; **tenir** ~ **à qn** to keep sb company; **bonsoir la** ~! goodnight all! (**b**) *(Comm, Mil, Théât)* company; *[perdreaux]* covey. **la banque X et** ~ the bank of X and company; **tout ça, c'est voleurs et** ~ * they're all a bunch * *ou* lot of thieves. ◆ **compagne** *nf* companion; *(maîtresse)* ladyfriend; *[animal]* mate. ~ **de classe** classmate. ◆ **compagnon** *nm* (**a**) *(gén)* companion. ~ **de travail** fellow worker, workmate; ~ **d'armes** companion- *ou* comrade-in-arms; ~ **de bord** shipmate; ~ **de voyage** travelling companion; ~ **de misère** companion in suffering. (**b**) *(ouvrier)* craftsman, journeyman †.

comparaison [kɔ̃paʀɛzɔ̃] *nf* (**a**) *(gén)* comparison (*à* to, *avec* with). **mettre qch en** ~ **avec** to compare sth with; **il n'y a pas de** ~ **(entre)** there is no comparison (between); **en** ~ **(de)** in comparison (with); **il est sans** ~ **le meilleur** he is far and away the best. (**b**) *(Gram)* comparison; *(Littérat)* simile, comparison. ◆ **comparable** *adj* comparable (*à* to, *avec* with).

comparaître [kɔ̃paʀɛtʀ(ə)] (57) *vi (Jur)* to appear.

comparer [kɔ̃paʀe] (1) *vt (confronter)* to compare (*à, avec* with); *(identifier)* to compare, liken (*à* to). **il ose se comparer à Picasso** he dares to compare himself to Picasso; **ça ne se compare pas** there's no comparison. ◆ **comparatif, -ive** *adj, nm* comparative. ◆ **comparativement** *adv* comparatively. ~ **à** by comparison with. ◆ **comparé, e** *adj* comparative.

comparse [kɔ̃paʀs(ə)] *nmf (Théât)* walker-on; *(péj)* stooge. *(péj, fig)* **rôle de** ~ minor part.

compartiment [kɔ̃paʀtimɑ̃] *nm* compartment. ◆ **compartimentage** *nm [armoire]* partitioning; *[administration]* compartmentalization. ◆ **compartimenter** (1) *vt* to partition; to compartmentalize.

comparution [kɔ̃paʀysjɔ̃] *nf (Jur)* appearance.

compas [kɔ̃pa] *nm (Géom)* (pair of) compasses; *(Naut)* compass. *(fig)* **avoir le** ~ **dans l'œil** to have an accurate eye.

compassion [kɔ̃pɑsjɔ̃] *nf* compassion.

compatible [kɔ̃patibl(ə)] *adj* compatible. ◆ **compatibilité** *nf* compatibility.

compatir [kɔ̃patiʀ] (2) *vi* to sympathize. ~ **à la douleur de qn** to sympathize *ou* commiserate with sb in his grief. ◆ **compatissant, e** *adj* compassionate, sympathetic.

compatriote [kɔ̃patʀijɔt] *nmf* compatriot, fellow countryman (*ou* woman).

compenser [kɔ̃pɑ̃se] (1) **1** *vt perte* to make good, compensate for, offset; *infirmité* to compensate (for). ~ **qch par** to make up for sth with; **pour** ~ to compensate, to make up for it. **2 se** ~ *vpr [forces]* to compensate each other; *[gains et pertes]* to cancel each other out. ◆ **compensation** *nf (gén, Phys, Psych)* compensation; *(équilibrage)* balancing. **en** ~ **(des dégâts)** in compensation (for the damage). ◆ **compensatoire** *adj* compensatory. *(Fin)* **droits** ~**s** countervailing duties. ◆ **compensé, e** *adj:* **chaussures à semelles** ~**es** platform shoes, shoes with platform soles.

compère [kɔ̃pɛʀ] *nm* (**a**) *(complice)* accomplice; *(aux enchères)* puffer. (**b**) *(†: ami)* comrade.

compétence [kɔ̃petɑ̃s] *nf (gén, Jur)* competence. ~**s** abilities; **ce n'est pas de ma** ~ that's not (in) my sphere. ◆ **compétent, e** *adj* competent, capable; *(Jur)* competent. ~ **en** competent in; **l'autorité** ~**e** the authority concerned.

compétition [kɔ̃petisjɔ̃] *nf* (**a**) *(épreuve)* event. *(activité)* **faire de la** ~ to go in for competitive sport; **la** ~ **automobile** motor racing. (**b**) *(concurrence)* competition. **être en** ~ to be competing *ou* in competition (*avec* with). ◆ **compétitif, -ive** *adj* competitive. ◆ **compétitivité** *nf* competitiveness.

compiler [kɔ̃pile] (1) *vt* to compile. ◆ **compilateur, -trice** *nm, f* compiler. ◆ **compilation** *nf* compilation.

complainte [kɔ̃plɛ̃t] *nf* lament.

complaire [kɔ̃plɛʀ] (54) **1** ~ **à** *vt indir* to (try to) please. **2 se** ~ *vpr*: **se** ~ **dans qch/à faire qch** to delight *ou* revel in sth/in doing sth.

complaisance [kɔ̃plɛzɑ̃s] *nf (obligeance)* kindness (*envers* to, towards); *(indulgence)* indulgence; *(connivence)* connivance; *(fatuité)* smugness, complacency. ◆ **complaisamment** *adv* obligingly, kindly; smugly, complacently. ◆ **complaisant, e** *adj* kind; indulgent; conniving; smug; complacent. **prêter une oreille** ~**e à qn/qch** to lend a willing ear to sb/sth.

complément [kɔ̃plemɑ̃] *nm* (**a**) *(gén, Bio, Math)* complement; *(reste)* rest, remainder. ~ **d'information** further *ou* additional information. (**b**) *(Gram) (gén)* complement. ~ **circonstanciel de lieu** adverbial phrase of place; ~ **(d'objet) direct/indirect** direct/indirect object; ~ **d'agent** agent; ~ **de nom** possessive phrase. ◆ **complémentaire** *adj (gén, Math)* complementary; *(additionnel)* supplementary; *renseignement* further, additional.

complet, -ète [kɔ̃plɛ, ɛt] **1** *adj* (**a**) *(exhaustif) (gén)* complete, full; *rapport* comprehensive; *examen* thorough. **le dossier est-il** ~? is the file complete?; **pain** ~ ≃ granary *ou* wholemeal bread. (**b**) *échec, obscurité* complete, utter. (**c**) *(après n) acteur* complete. **athlète** ~ all-round *ou* complete athlete. (**d**) *train* full. *(écriteau)* **'** ~ **'** *[hôtel]* 'no vacancies'; *[parking]* 'full (up)'; **eh bien! c'est** ~**!** * well, that's the limit! **2** *nm* (**a**) **nous sommes au** ~ we are all here; **la famille au grand** ~ the whole *ou* entire family. (**b**) ~**(-veston)** suit. ◆ **complètement** *adv démonter* completely; *lire* right through; *étudier* fully, thoroughly; *citer* in full; *faux* completely, utterly. ~ **nu** stark naked.

compléter [kɔ̃plete] (6) **1** *vt* (**a**) *(terminer) somme, effectifs* to make up; *collection, dossier* to complete; *études, repas* to round off. **et pour** ~ **le tableau** and to crown it all *ou* as a finishing touch. (**b**) *(augmenter) formation* to complement, supplement; *garde-robe* to add to. **2 se** ~ *vpr [caractères, fonctions]* to complement one another.

complexe [kɔ̃plɛks(ə)] *adj, nm* complex. ~ **d'Œdipe** Oedipus complex; **être bourré de** ~**s** * to have loads of hang-ups *. ◆ **complexer** (1) *vt*: **ça le**

complexe it gives him a complex; **être très complexé** to be full of complexes *ou* hang-ups *, be very hung-up * (*par* about). ◆ **complexité** *nf* complexity.

complication [kɔ̃plikɑsjɔ̃] *nf (complexité)* complexity; *(ennui)* complication. *(Méd)* **~s** complications; **faire des ~s** to make life difficult *ou* complicated.

complice [kɔ̃plis] **1** *adj regard* knowing; *attitude* conniving. **être ~ de qch** to be (a) party to sth. **2** *nmf (criminel)* accomplice; *(amant)* lover; *(maîtresse)* mistress. ◆ **complicité** *nf (Jur, fig)* complicity.

compliment [kɔ̃plimɑ̃] *nm (louange)* compliment. **~s** *(félicitations)* congratulations; *(hommages)* compliments; **faire des ~s à qn (pour)** to compliment *ou* congratulate sb (on); **avec les ~s de la direction** with the compliments of the management. ◆ **complimenter** (1) *vt* to congratulate, compliment (*pour, sur, de* on).

compliquer [kɔ̃plike] (1) **1** *vt* to complicate. **2 se ~** *vpr* to become *ou* get complicated. **se ~ l'existence** to make life difficult *ou* complicated for o.s. ◆ **compliqué, e** *adj (gén)* complicated; *esprit* tortuous; *(Méd) fracture* compound. **ce n'est pas ~, moi je pars** that simplifies the problem — I'm leaving.

complot [kɔ̃plo] *nm* plot. ◆ **comploter** (1) *vti* to plot (*de faire* to do, *contre* against). ◆ **comploteur, -euse** *nm, f* plotter.

comporter [kɔ̃pɔʀte] (1) **1** *vt (consister en)* to be composed of, consist of, comprise; *(être muni de) dispositif* to have, be equipped with; *exceptions* to have, include; *(impliquer) risques* to entail, involve. **2 se ~** *vpr [personne]* to behave (*en* like); *[voiture]* to perform. **notre équipe s'est très bien comportée** our team played very well *ou* acquitted itself *ou* put up a good performance. ◆ **comportement** *nm (gén)* behaviour (*envers* towards); *[pneus]* performance. ◆ **comportementalisme** *nm* behaviourism. ◆ **comportementaliste** *adj, nmf* behaviourist.

composer [kɔ̃poze] (1) **1** *vt* (**a**) *(confectionner) plat* to concoct, make (up); *équipe* to select; *assemblée* to form, set up; *lettre* to write, compose; *symphonie* to compose; *tableau* to paint; *numéro de téléphone* to dial; *programme* to work out, draw up; *bouquet* to arrange, make up; *étalage* to lay out, set up; *(Typ)* to set. (**b**) *(constituer) ensemble, produit* to make up, form. (**c**) *(littér)* **~ son visage** to assume an affected expression. **2** *vi* (**a**) *(Scol)* to do a test. **~ en anglais** to take an English test. (**b**) *(traiter)* to compromise (*avec* with). **3 se ~** *vpr*: **se ~ de** *ou* **être composé de** to be composed of, consist of, comprise. ◆ **composant, e** *adj, nm, f* component. *(Pol)* **les diverses ~es du parti** the various elements in the party. ◆ **composé, e 1** *adj* compound; *(guindé)* studied. **2** *nm (Chim, Gram)* compound; *(fig)* combination, mixture.

composite [kɔ̃pozit] *adj éléments* heterogeneous; *foule* motley; *(Archit)* composite.

compositeur, -trice [kɔ̃pozitœʀ, tʀis] *nm, f (Mus)* composer; *(Typ)* typesetter.

composition [kɔ̃pozisjɔ̃] *nf* (**a**) *(action: V* **composer**) concocting, making(-up); formation, setting-up; selection; writing; composition; painting; drawing up; arranging; laying out; (type)setting. **une œuvre de ma ~** a work of my own composition. (**b**) *(résultat, œuvre)* composition; *(structure)* structure. **quelle est la ~ du gâteau?** what is the cake made of?; **la nouvelle ~ du parlement européen** the new line-up in the European Parliament. (**c**) *(Scol: examen)* test, exam. **~ de français** *(en classe)* French test *ou* exam; *(à l'examen)* French paper; *(rédaction)* **~ française** French essay. (**d**) **venir à ~** to come to terms; **amener qn à ~** to get sb to come to terms; **être de bonne ~** to have a nice nature.

compost [kɔ̃pɔst] *nm* compost.

composter [kɔ̃pɔste] (1) *vt (dater)* to (date) stamp; *(poinçonner)* to punch.

compote [kɔ̃pɔt] *nf (Culin)* stewed fruit, compote. **~ de pommes** stewed apples, compote of apples; **en ~ *** *jambes* like jelly * *ou* cotton wool; *visage* black and blue. ◆ **compotier** *nm* fruit dish.

comprendre [kɔ̃pʀɑ̃dʀ(ə)] (58) *vt* (**a**) *(être composé de)* to be composed of, consist of, comprise. **le loyer ne comprend pas le chauffage** the rent doesn't include *ou* cover (the) heating.
(**b**) *problème, langue, personne* to understand. **vous m'avez mal compris** you've misunderstood me; **il ne comprend pas la plaisanterie** he can't take a joke; **c'est à n'y rien ~** it's completely baffling *ou* puzzling; it's beyond me, I can't understand it; **se faire ~** to make o.s. understood; **il est difficile de bien se faire ~** it's difficult to get one's ideas across (*de qn* to sb); **j'espère que je me suis bien fait ~** I hope I've made myself quite clear; **tu comprends, ce que je veux c'est...** you see, what I want is...; **dois-je ~ que...?** am I to take it *ou* understand that...?
(**c**) *(concevoir) (gén)* to understand; *point de vue* to see; *difficultés* to appreciate; *gravité* to realize. **c'est comme ça que je le comprends** that's how I see *ou* understand it; **ça se comprend** it's quite understandable; **il m'a fait ~ que je devais faire attention** he made me realize that I should be careful.
◆ **compréhensible** *adj (clair)* comprehensible; *(concevable)* understandable. ◆ **compréhensif, -ive** *adj (tolérant)* understanding; *(Logique)* comprehensive. ◆ **compréhension** *nf* understanding; *(Logique)* comprehension.

compression [kɔ̃pʀesjɔ̃] *nf (gén, Aut, Phys)* compression; *(Écon)* reduction, cutback (*de* in). **~s budgétaires** cutbacks in spending, budget restrictions *ou* cuts; **~ des coûts** cost-cutting. ◆ **compresse** *nf* compress. ◆ **compresseur** *nm* compressor. ◆ **compressible** *adj (Phys)* compressible; *dépenses* reducible.

comprimer [kɔ̃pʀime] (1) *vt* (**a**) *air, artère* to compress; *(pour emballer)* to press *ou* pack tightly together. **ça lui comprimait l'estomac** it was pressing into his stomach; **comprimés dans la voiture** packed tightly together in the car. (**b**) *dépenses, personnel* to cut down, reduce; *larmes, colère* to hold back. ◆ **comprimé** *nm (Pharm)* tablet.

compris, e [kɔ̃pʀi, iz] *adj* (**a**) *(inclus)* **emballage (y)/non ~** including/excluding packaging, packaging included/not included. (**b**) *(situé)* **être ~ entre** to be contained between *ou* by; **les chapitres ~ entre les pages 12 et 145** the chapters contained *ou* included in pages 12 to 145. (**c**) *(d'accord)* **(c'est) ~** ! (it's) agreed!; **pars tout de suite, ~!** go immediately, understand? *ou* is that understood?

compromettre [kɔ̃pʀɔmɛtʀ(ə)] (56) **1** *vt réputation, chances* to compromise, jeopardize. **2 se ~** *vpr* to compromise o.s. ◆ **compromettant, e** *adj lettres* compromising. **ce n'est pas très ~** you won't commit yourself to much, there's no great commitment involved. ◆ **compromis** *nm* compromise. ◆ **compromission** *nf* shady deal.

comptabiliser [kɔ̃tabilize] (1) *vt (Fin)* to post. ◆ **comptabilité** *nf (science)* accountancy, book-keeping; *(comptes)* accounts, books; *(service)* accounts department; *(profession)* accountancy. **s'occuper de la ~** to keep the books. ◆ **comptable 1** *adj (Fin) règles, etc* accounting, book, book-keeping. **il manque une pièce ~** one of the accounts is missing; *(Ling)* **nom ~** countable *ou* count noun. **2** *nmf* accountant. ~

du Trésor *local official of the Treasury;* **chèque adressé au ~ du Trésor** cheque addressed to the Treasury.

comptant [kɔ̃tɑ̃] **1** *adv payer* (in) cash; *acheter* for cash. **verser 10 F ~** to pay 10 francs down. **2** *nm (argent)* cash. **vente au ~** cash sale.

compte [kɔ̃t] **1** *nm* (**a**) *(calcul)* count. **faire le ~ de** *prisonniers* to count (up), make a count of; *dépenses* to calculate, work out.
(**b**) *(nombre)* number. **le ~ y est** *(paiement)* that's the right amount; *(inventaire)* that's the right number; **~ rond** round number *ou* figure; **nous sommes loin du ~** we are a long way short of the target.
(**c**) *(Banque, comptabilité)* account; *(facture)* account, bill. **~ (en banque** *ou* **bancaire)** (bank) account; **faire/tenir ses ~s** to do/keep one's accounts *ou* books; **être en ~ avec qn** to have an *ou* be in account with sb; **donner son ~ à un employé** *(payer)* to settle up with an employee; *(renvoyer)* to give an employee his cards *; **il avait son ~ *** *(mort)* he'd had it *; *(soûl)* he'd had more than he could hold; **son ~ est bon** his number's up *, he's had it *; **devoir/rendre des ~s à qn** to owe/give sb an explanation; **cela fait mon ~** that suits me.
(**d**) *(responsabilité)* **prendre qch à son ~** *dépense* to pay for sth; *maxime* to make sth one's motto; **s'installer à son ~** to set up one's own business; **mettre qch sur le ~ de** to put sth down to, attribute sth to; **dire qch sur le ~ de qn** to say sth about sb; **pour le ~ de** on behalf of; **pour mon ~** *(opinion)* personally; *(usage)* for my own use; *(au restaurant)* **mettez-le sur mon ~** put it on *ou* charge it to my account.
(**e**) *(locutions) (Boxe)* **aller au tapis pour le ~** to go down for the count; **tenir ~ de qch/qn** to take sth/sb into account; **ne pas tenir ~ de qch** to disregard *ou* ignore sth; **~ tenu de** considering, in view of; **à ce ~-là** *(dans ce cas)* in this case; *(à ce train-là)* at this rate; **tout ~ fait** all things considered, when all is said and done.
2 : **~ chèque postal** ≃ Giro account; **~ à rebours** countdown; **~ rendu** *(gén)* account, report; *[film]* review; *(sur travaux en cours)* progress report; **~ rendu d'audience** court record.

compte- [kɔ̃t] *préf*: **~-gouttes** *nm inv (pipette)* dropper; **au ~-gouttes** *(fig)* sparingly; **~-tours** *nm inv* revolution counter.

compter [kɔ̃te] (1) **1** *vt* (**a**) *(calculer)* to count. **combien en avez-vous compté?** how many did you count?, how many did you make it?; **il a 50 ans bien comptés** he's a good 50 (years old); **ses gaffes ne se comptent plus** we can't keep count of his blunders. (**b**) *(prévoir)* to allow, reckon. **j'ai compté qu'il nous en fallait 10** I reckoned we'd need 10; **il faut (bien) ~ 10 jours** you must allow (a good) 10 days, you must reckon on it taking (a good) 10 days. (**c**) *(tenir compte de)* to take into account; *(inclure)* to include. **t'es-tu compté?** did you count *ou* include yourself?; **sans ~** *(sans inclure)* not counting; *(sans parler de)* not to mention, to say nothing of. (**d**) *(facturer)* to charge for; *(payer)* to pay. **combien vous ont-ils compté le café?** how much did they charge you for the coffee? (**e**) *(avoir)* to have. **il ne compte pas d'ennemis** he has no enemies. (**f**) *(classer, ranger)* to consider. **il le compte au nombre de ses amis** he considers him one of his friends, he numbers him among his friends. (**g**) *(parcimonie) argent* to count; *permissions* to ration. **il ne compte pas sa peine** he spares no trouble; **ses jours sont comptés** his days are numbered. (**h**) *(avoir l'intention de)* to intend, plan, mean (*faire* to do); *(s'attendre à)* to expect. **je ne compte pas qu'il vienne aujourd'hui** I am not expecting him to come today.
2 *vi* (**a**) *(calculer)* to count. **comment est-ce que tu as compté?** how did you work it out?; **tu as mal compté** you counted wrong, you miscounted; **à ~ de** (starting *ou* as) from. (**b**) *(être économe)* to economize. **sans ~** *(lit)* regardless of expense; **se dépenser sans ~** to spare no effort. (**c**) *(avoir de l'importance)* to count, matter. **35 ans de mariage, ça compte!** 35 years of marriage, that's quite something!; **~ double** to count double; **ça compte pour beaucoup dans sa décision** it has a lot to do with his decision, it is a big factor in his decision. (**d**) *(tenir compte de)* **~ avec qch** to reckon with sth, take account of sth, allow for sth. (**e**) *(figurer)* **~ parmi** to be *ou* rank among. (**f**) *(se fier à)* **~ sur** to count on, rely on; **nous comptons sur vous (pour) demain** we're relying on you for tomorrow; **j'y compte bien!** I should hope so!; **vous pouvez ~ là-dessus** you can depend upon it; **ne comptez pas sur moi** (you can) count me out.

compteur [kɔ̃tœʀ] *nm* meter. **~ Geiger** Geiger counter; **~ (kilométrique)** milometer; **~ (de vitesse)** speedometer.

comptine [kɔ̃tin] *nf (gén: chanson)* nursery rhyme.

comptoir [kɔ̃twaʀ] *nm* (**a**) *[magasin]* counter; *[bar]* bar. (**b**) *(colonial)* trading post. (**c**) *(agence)* branch.

compulser [kɔ̃pylse] (1) *vt* to consult.

comte [kɔ̃t] *nm* count; *(Brit)* earl. ◆ **comté** *nm (Hist)* earldom; *(Admin)* county. ◆ **comtesse** *nf* countess.

con ‡ [kɔ̃] **1** *adj* damned ‡ stupid. **2** *nm* damned ‡ fool, stupid idiot ‡. **faire le ~** to ass about ‡; **idée à la ~** lousy ‡ *ou* crummy ‡ idea.

concasser [kɔ̃kɑse] (1) *vt* to crush; *poivre* to grind. ◆ **concassage** *nm* crushing; grinding. ◆ **concasseur** *nm* crusher.

concave [kɔ̃kav] *adj* concave. ◆ **concavité** *nf (Opt)* concavity; *(cavité)* cavity.

concéder [kɔ̃sede] (6) *vt droit, point* to grant, concede; *but* to concede, give away. **je vous concède que** I'll grant you that.

concentrer *vt*, **se ~** *vpr* [kɔ̃sɑ̃tʀe] (1) *(gén)* to concentrate; *attention, regards* to fix, focus (*sur* on). ◆ **concentration** *nf (gén)* concentration. **~ urbaine** conurbation; *(Écon)* **~ horizontale** horizontal integration; **~ d'esprit** concentration. ◆ **concentré, e 1** *adj acide* concentrated; *lait* condensed; *candidat* in a state of concentration. **2** *nm (chimique)* concentrated solution; *(bouillon)* concentrate, extract. **~ de tomates** tomato purée.

concentrique [kɔ̃sɑ̃tʀik] *adj cercle* concentric.

conception [kɔ̃sɛpsjɔ̃] *nf* (**a**) *(Bio)* conception. (**b**) *(action) [idée]* conception. **d'une ~ géniale** brilliantly conceived; **voilà quelle est ma ~ de la chose** this is how I see it; **~ assistée par ordinateur** computer-aided design. (**c**) *(idée)* notion, idea; *(réalisation)* creation. ◆ **concept** *nm* concept. ◆ **concepteur** *nm* ideas man. ◆ **conceptualiser** (1) *vt* to conceptualize.

concerner [kɔ̃sɛʀne] (1) *vt* to affect, concern. **des mesures concernant ce problème** steps concerning *ou* regarding this matter; **en ce qui concerne cette question** with regard to this question, as far as this question is concerned; **en ce qui me concerne** as far as I'm concerned; **il ne se sent pas concerné** *(directement impliqué)* he is not affected (*par* by); *(moralement)* he is not concerned (*par* about).

concert [kɔ̃sɛʀ] *nm (Mus)* concert; *(accord)* entente, agreement. *(fig)* **~ de louanges/ d'avertisseurs** chorus of praise/horns; **de ~** *(ensemble)* together, in unison; *(d'accord)* in concert; **de ~ avec** *(accord)* in conjunction with; *(ensemble)* together with. ◆ **concertiste** *nmf* concert artiste. ◆ **concerto** *nm* concerto.

concertation [kɔ̃sɛʀtɑsjɔ̃] *nf (dialogue)* dialogue; *(rencontre)* meeting. **sans ~ préalable** without preliminary consultations. ◆ **concerté, e** *adj* concerted. ◆ **concerter** (1) **1** *vt* to devise. **2 se ~** *vpr* to consult (each other).

concession [kɔ̃sesjɔ̃] *nf (gén)* concession (*à* to); *[cimetière]* plot. ◆ **concessionnaire** *nmf (Comm)* agent, dealer.

concevoir [kɔ̃s(ə)vwaʀ] (28) *vt* (**a**) *idée* to conceive of; *solution, projet* to conceive, devise, think up; *déception* to understand. ~ **que** to conceive *ou* imagine that; **leur maison est bien/mal conçue** their house is well/badly designed; **voilà comment je conçois la chose** that's how I see it *ou* view it; **cela se conçoit facilement** it's quite understandable; **lettre ainsi conçue** letter expressed *ou* couched in these terms. (**b**) *(littér: éprouver) doutes* have, feel; *jalousie* to feel. (**c**) *(engendrer)* to conceive. ◆ **concevable** *adj* conceivable.

concierge [kɔ̃sjɛʀʒ(ə)] *nmf [immeuble]* caretaker; manager (of an apartment building) *(US)*; *[hôtel]* porter.

concile [kɔ̃sil] *nm (Rel)* council.

conciliabule [kɔ̃siljabyl] *nm* consultation.

concilier [kɔ̃silje] (7) *vt* (**a**) *exigences* to reconcile (*avec* with). (**b**) *partisans, amitié* to win, gain. **se ~ (les bonnes grâces de) qn** to win *ou* gain sb's favour. ◆ **conciliable** *adj* reconcilable. ◆ **conciliant, e** *adj* conciliatory. ◆ **conciliateur, -trice** *nm, f* conciliator. ◆ **conciliation** *nf (apaisement)* conciliation; *(compatibilité)* reconciliation.

concis, e [kɔ̃si, iz] *adj* concise. ◆ **concision** *nf* concision, conciseness.

concitoyen, -yenne [kɔ̃sitwajɛ̃, jɛn] *nm, f* fellow citizen.

conclave [kɔ̃klav] *nm (Rel)* conclave.

conclure [kɔ̃klyʀ] (35) **1** *vt* (**a**) *accord* to conclude; *marché* to conclude, clinch. **marché conclu!** it's a deal! (**b**) *(gén), texte* to conclude, end (*par* with); *discours* to wind up, bring to a close. **et pour ~** and to conclude; *(Jur)* ~ **sa plaidoirie** to rest one's case. (**c**) *(déduire)* to conclude (*qch de qch* sth from sth). **2** *vi* ~ **à: ils ont conclu au suicide** they concluded that it was suicide. ◆ **concluant, e** *adj* conclusive. ◆ **conclusion** *nf (gén)* conclusion; *[discours]* close. **~s** *(Jur) [demandeur]* submissions; *[avocat]* summing-up; *[jury]* findings; **déposer des ~s auprès d'un tribunal** to file submissions with a court; **en ~** in conclusion.

concocter * [kɔ̃kɔkte] (1) *vt breuvage* to concoct; *discours* to elaborate.

concombre [kɔ̃kɔ̃bʀ(ə)] *nm* cucumber.

concorder [kɔ̃kɔʀde] (1) *vi [faits, dates, résultats]* to agree, tally; *[idées, caractères]* to match. **ses actes concordent-ils avec ses idées?** is his behaviour in accordance with his ideas? ◆ **concordance** *nf [témoignages]* agreement (*de* of); *[résultats]* similarity (*de* of *ou* between). *(Gram)* ~ **des temps** sequence of tenses. ◆ **concordant, e** *adj résultats* similar; **témoignages ~s** testimonies which agree *ou* tally. ◆ **concordat** *nm (Rel)* concordat. ◆ **concorde** *nf* concord.

concourir [kɔ̃kuʀiʀ] (11) **1** *vi* (**a**) *[concurrent]* to compete (*pour* for). (**b**) *(converger)* to converge (*vers* towards, on). **2** ~ **à** *vt indir*: ~ **à qch/à faire qch** to work towards sth/towards doing sth. ◆ **concours** *nm* (**a**) *(gén: jeu)* competition; *(examen)* competitive examination. ~ **agricole** agricultural show; ~ **hippique** *(Sport)* show-jumping; *(épreuve)* horse show; ~ **de beauté** beauty contest; ~ **de recrutement** competitive entry examination. (**b**) *(participation)* aid, help. **prêter son ~ à qch** to lend one's support to sth; ~ **de circonstances** combination of circumstances.

concret, -ète [kɔ̃kʀɛ, ɛt] *adj (gén)* concrete; *avantages* positive. ◆ **concrètement** *adv* in concrete terms. ◆ **concrétiser** (1) **1** *vt* to give concrete expression to. **2 se ~** *vpr* to materialize. ◆ **concrétisation** *nf [promesses, etc]* realization.

concubinage [kɔ̃kybinaʒ] *nm* cohabitation.

concupiscence [kɔ̃kypisɑ̃s] *nf* concupiscence. ◆ **concupiscent, e** *adj* concupiscent.

concurremment [kɔ̃kyʀamɑ̃] *adv (conjointement)* conjointly.

concurrence [kɔ̃kyʀɑ̃s] *nf (gén, Comm)* competition. **prix défiant toute ~** absolutely unbeatable price; **faire ~ à qn** to compete with sb; **jusqu'à ~ de...** up to..., to a limit of... ◆ **concurrencer** (3) *vt* to compete with. ◆ **concurrent, e** *nm, f (Comm, Sport)* competitor; *[concours]* candidate. ◆ **concurrentiel, -elle** *adj (Écon)* competitive.

condamner [kɔ̃dɑne] (1) *vt* (**a**) *coupable* to sentence (*à* to, *pour* for); *livre, délit, expression* to condemn. ~ **à mort** to sentence to death; ~ **qn à une amende** to fine sb, impose a fine on sb; **X, plusieurs fois condamné pour vol...** X, several times convicted of theft...; **il ne faut pas le ~ d'avoir fait cela** you mustn't condemn *ou* blame him for doing that; **sa rougeur le condamne** his blushes condemn him; **je suis condamné à me lever tôt** I'm doomed to get up early. (**b**) *(Méd) malade* to give up hope for. **il était condamné** *[malade, projet]* he (*ou* it) was doomed *ou* done for; **c'est condamné à sombrer dans l'oubli** it's doomed to sink into oblivion. (**c**) *porte* to fill in, block up; *pièce* to lock up; *portière de voiture* to lock. *(fig)* ~ **sa porte à qn** to bar one's door to sb. ◆ **condamnable** *adj* reprehensible, blameworthy. ◆ **condamnation** *nf* (**a**) *[coupable] (action)* sentencing (*à* to, *pour* for); *(peine)* sentence. **il a 3 ~s à son actif** he (already) has 3 convictions; ~ **à mort** death sentence, capital sentence; ~ **à une amende** imposition of a fine. (**b**) *[livre, délit, conduite]* condemnation. (**c**) *(fig: échec)* end. (**d**) *(Aut) (action)* locking; *(système)* locking device. ◆ **condamné, e** *nm, f* sentenced person, convict. ~ **(à mort)** condemned man; **les malades ~s** the terminally ill.

condé [kɔ̃de] *nm (arg Police: policier)* cop ‡.

condenser *vt*, **se ~** *vpr* [kɔ̃dɑ̃se] (1) to condense. ◆ **condensateur** *nm* condenser. ◆ **condensation** *nf* condensation. ◆ **condensé** *nm (Presse)* digest.

condescendance [kɔ̃desɑ̃dɑ̃s] *nf* condescension. ◆ **condescendant, e** *adj* condescending. ◆ **condescendre** (41) *vi:* ~ **à (faire)** to condescend to (do).

condiment [kɔ̃dimɑ̃] *nm* condiment.

condisciple [kɔ̃disipl(ə)] *nm (Scol)* schoolfellow; *(Univ)* fellow student.

condition [kɔ̃disjɔ̃] *nf* (**a**) *(circonstances)* **~s** conditions; **dans ces ~s** under these conditions; **améliorer la ~ des travailleurs immigrés** to improve the lot of foreign workers. (**b**) *(stipulation)* condition; *(exigence)* condition, requirement. ~ **préalable** prerequisite; **poser ses ~s** to lay down one's conditions; **remplir les ~s requises** to fulfil the requirements; **sans ~(s)** *(adj)* unconditional; *(adv)* unconditionally; **à une ~** on one condition; **à ~ d'être** *ou* **que tu sois sage** provided *ou* on condition that you're good; **sous ~** *libérer* conditionally. (**c**) *(Comm)* **~s** terms; **faire ses ~s** to make one's terms. (**d**) *(état)* **en bonne ~** *envoi* in good condition; *athlète* in condition, fit; **(se) mettre en ~** to get into condition, get fit; **la mise en ~ des téléspectateurs** the conditioning of viewers. (**e**) *(socialement) (métier)* profession, trade; *(rang)* station, condition. **étudiant de ~ modeste** student from a modest home *ou* background; **la ~ ouvrière** the position of the workers; **la ~ d'artisan/d'intellectuel** the situation of the craftsman/intellectual. ◆ **conditionnel, -elle** *adj, nm* conditional. ◆ **conditionnellement** *adv* conditionally.

◆ **conditionner** (1) *vt (emballer)* to package, pre-pack; *(influencer)* to condition. ◆ **conditionnement** *nm* packaging; conditioning.

condoléances [kɔ̃dɔleɑ̃s] *nfpl* condolences. **faire ses ~ à qn** to offer sb one's sympathy *ou* condolences.

conducteur, -trice [kɔ̃dyktœʀ, tʀis] **1** *adj (Élec)* conductive, conducting. **2** *nm, f (Aut, Rail)* driver; *[machine]* operator. **~ d'engins** heavy plant driver; **~ d'hommes** leader. **3** *nm (Élec)* conductor. ◆ **conductibilité** *nf* conductivity. ◆ **conductible** *adj* conductive. ◆ **conduction** *nf (Méd, Phys)* conduction.

conduire [kɔ̃dɥiʀ] (38) **1** *vt* (**a**) **~ qn quelque part** *[personne, véhicule]* to take sb somewhere; *[guide, route, études]* to lead sb somewhere; **~ qn à la gare** *(en voiture)* to take *ou* drive sb to the station; *(à pied)* to walk sb to the station; **~ les hommes à l'assaut** to lead the men into the attack; **cela nous conduit à penser que** that leads us to think that; **ça l'a conduit en prison** it landed him in prison. (**b**) *véhicule* to drive; *embarcation* to steer; *avion* to pilot; *cheval [cavalier]* to ride; *[cocher]* to drive. **il conduit bien** he is a good driver, he drives well. (**c**) *affaires, pays* to run; *travaux* to supervise; *négociations, enquête* to conduct; *orchestre [chef]* to conduct; *[violon]* to lead. (**d**) *électricité* to conduct; *eau* to carry. **2 se ~** *vpr* to behave (*comme* as). **il s'est mal conduit** he behaved badly. ◆ **conduit** *nm (Tech)* conduit, pipe; *(Anat)* duct, canal; *[fumée]* flue. **~ de ventilation** ventilation shaft; **~ d'aération** air duct. ◆ **conduite** *nf* (**a**) (*V* **conduire b**) driving; steering ; piloting. **voiture avec ~ à gauche** left-hand drive car; **faire un brin de ~ à qn** * to walk along with sb for a bit. (**b**) (*V* **conduire c**) running; supervision; conducting. **sous la ~ de** *guide* under the leadership of. (**c**) *(comportement)* behaviour; *(Scol)* conduct. (**d**) *(tuyau)* pipe; *[eau, gaz]* main.

cône [kon] *nm (gén)* cone.

confectionner [kɔ̃fɛksjɔne] (1) *vt mets* to prepare, make; *vêtement* to make. ◆ **confection** *nf* making; preparation. **être dans la ~** to be in the ready-made clothes business.

confédéral, e, *mpl* **-aux** [kɔ̃fedeʀal, o] *adj* confederal. ◆ **confédération** *nf* confederation, confederacy. ◆ **confédéré, e** *adj, nm, f* confederate.

conférence [kɔ̃feʀɑ̃s] *nf (exposé)* lecture; *(réunion)* conference, meeting; *(poire)* conference pear. **faire une ~ sur qch** to lecture on sth, give a lecture on sth; **être en ~** to be in *ou* at a meeting; **~ de presse** press conference. ◆ **conférencier, -ière** *nm, f* speaker, lecturer.

conférer [kɔ̃feʀe] (6) **1** *vt (gén)* to give (*à* to); *prestige, dignité* to confer (*à* on); *autorité* to impart (*à* to). **2** *vi* to confer (*sur* on, about).

confesser [kɔ̃fese] (1) **1** *vt péchés* to confess. **~ qn** to hear sb's confession, confess sb. **2 se ~** *vpr (Rel)* to go to confession. **se ~ à** to confess to; **se ~ de** *(littér)* to confess. ◆ **confesse** *nf*: **aller à ~** to go to confession. ◆ **confesseur** *nm* confessor. ◆ **confession** *nf (aveu)* confession; *(religion)* denomination. ◆ **confessional,** *pl* **-aux** *nm* confessional. ◆ **confessionnel, -elle** *adj* denominational. **école ~le** denominational *ou* sectarian school; **non ~** nondenominational, nonsectarian.

confetti [kɔ̃feti] *nm*: **~(s)** confetti.

confiance [kɔ̃fjɑ̃s] *nf (en l'honnêteté)* confidence, trust; *(en la valeur)* confidence, faith (*en* in). **avoir ~ en, faire ~ à** to have confidence in; **c'est quelqu'un en qui on peut avoir ~** he's (*ou* she's) a person you can rely on; *(Pol)* **voter la ~** to pass a vote of confidence; **mettre qn en ~** to win sb's trust; **avec ~** *se confier* trustingly; *espérer* confidently; **de ~** *acheter* with confidence; *homme, maison* trustworthy, reliable; **un poste de ~** a position of trust; **~ en soi** self-confidence. ◆ **confiant, e** *adj (assuré)* confident; *(sans défiance)* confiding.

confidence [kɔ̃fidɑ̃s] *nf* confidence. **faire une ~ à qn** to confide sth to sb; **en ~** in confidence; **mettre qn dans la ~** to let sb into the secret. ◆ **confident, e** *nm, f* confidant; confidante. ◆ **confidentiel, -ielle** *adj* confidential; *(sur enveloppe)* private. ◆ **confidentiellement** *adv* confidentially. ◆ **confidentialité** *nf* confidentiality.

confier [kɔ̃fje] (7) **1** *vt secret, projet, espoir* to confide (*à* to). **je vous confie le soin de le faire** I entrust you with the task of doing it. **2 se ~** *vpr*: **se ~ à qn** *(secret)* to confide in sb; *(protection)* to place o.s. in sb's hands.

configuration [kɔ̃figyʀɑsjɔ̃] *nf* (general) shape, configuration; *[lieux]* layout.

confiner [kɔ̃fine] (1) **1** *vt*: **~ qn dans** to confine sb in. **2 ~ à** *vt indir* to border on. **3 se ~** *vpr* to confine o.s. (*à* to). **se ~ chez soi** to shut o.s. up at home. ◆ **confiné, e** *adj* close, stuffy. ◆ **confinement** *nm* confining.

confins [kɔ̃fɛ̃] *nmpl* borders; *(limite extrême)* furthermost bounds.

confire [kɔ̃fiʀ] (37) *vt* to preserve; *(vinaigre)* to pickle. ◆ **confit, e 1** *adj fruit* crystallized, candied; *cornichon etc* pickled. **2** *nm*: **~ d'oie** conserve of goose. ◆ **confiture** *nf* jam. **~ d'oranges/de citrons** (orange)/lemon marmalade; *(fig)* **donner de la ~ aux cochons** to cast pearls before swine.

confirmer [kɔ̃fiʀme] (1) *vt (gén, Rel)* to confirm. **la nouvelle se confirme** the news has been confirmed, there is some confirmation of the news. ◆ **confirmation** *nf* confirmation. **en ~ de** in confirmation of; **c'est la ~ de** it is confirmation of.

confiserie [kɔ̃fizʀi] *nf (magasin)* confectioner's (shop); *(métier, marchandise)* confectionery. **manger une ~** to eat a sweet. ◆ **confiseur, -euse** *nm, f* confectioner.

confisquer [kɔ̃fiske] (1) *vt (gén, Jur)* to confiscate, seize. ◆ **confiscation** *nf* confiscation, seizure.

conflictuel, -elle [kɔ̃fliktɥɛl] *adj pulsions, intérêts* conflicting. **situation ~le** situation of conflict; **avoir des rapports ~s avec qn** to have a relationship of conflict with sb.

conflit [kɔ̃fli] *nm (gén, Mil)* conflict, clash; *(Ind: grève)* dispute. **entrer en ~ avec qn** to clash with sb; **~ social** industrial dispute; **~s internes** infighting; **le ~ israélo-arabe** the Arab-Israeli wars.

confluent [kɔ̃flyɑ̃] *nm (endroit)* confluence.

confondre [kɔ̃fɔ̃dʀ(ə)] (41) **1** *vt* (**a**) *choses, dates* to mix up, confuse. **~ qch avec qch d'autre** to mistake sth for sth else; **j'ai dû ~** I must have made a mistake. (**b**) *(déconcerter)* to astound (*par* with). **confondu de reconnaissance** overcome with gratitude. (**c**) *menteur* to confound. (**d**) *(fusionner)* to join. **2 se ~** *vpr* (**a**) *[couleurs, silhouettes]* to merge; *[souvenirs]* to become confused; *[fleuves]* to join. **nos intérêts se confondent** our interests are one and the same. (**b**) **se ~ en excuses/remerciements** to apologize (to sb)/thank sb profusely.

conforme [kɔ̃fɔʀm(ə)] *adj* true. **~ à** *modèle* true to; *plan, règle* in accordance *ou* conformity with; *moyens, opinions* in keeping with; **c'est peu ~ à ce que j'ai dit** it bears little resemblance to what I said; **ce n'est pas ~ à** *accord, commande, normes* it does not comply with; **ce n'est pas ~ à l'original** it does not match the original.

conformer [kɔ̃fɔʀme] (1) **1** *vt*: **~ qch à** to model sth on. **2 se ~** *vpr*: **se ~ à** to conform to. ◆ **conformation** *nf* conformation. ◆ **conformé, e** *adj*: **bien/mal ~** well/ill-formed. ◆ **conformément** *adv*: **~ à** in accordance with.

conformisme [kɔ̃fɔʀmism(ə)] *nm (gén)* conformity. ◆ **conformiste** *adj, nmf (gén)* conformist.

conformité [kɔ̃fɔʀmite] *nf (identité)* similarity; *(fidélité)* faithfulness (*à* to). **en ~ avec** *plan, ordres* in accordance with; *idées* in keeping *ou* in conformity with.

confort [kɔ̃fɔʀ] *nm* comfort. **appartement tout ~** flat with all mod cons *ou* modern conveniences. ◆ **confortable** *adj (gén, fig)* comfortable. **peu ~** rather uncomfortable. ◆ **confortablement** *adv* comfortably. **vivre ~** *(confort)* to live in comfort; *(richesse)* to live very comfortably.

conforter [kɔ̃fɔʀte] (1) *vt* to reinforce, confirm.

confrère [kɔ̃fʀɛʀ] *nm [profession]* colleague; *[association]* fellow member; *(journal)* (fellow) newspaper. ◆ **confrérie** *nf* brotherhood.

confronter [kɔ̃fʀɔ̃te] (1) *vt opinions* to confront; *textes* to compare. ◆ **confrontation** *nf* confrontation; comparison.

confus, e [kɔ̃fy, yz] *adj* (**a**) *(gén)* confused; *esprit, style* muddled; *idée* hazy. (**b**) *(honteux)* ashamed, embarrassed (*de qch* of sth, *d'avoir fait* at having done). ◆ **confusément** *adv distinguer, ressentir* vaguely; *parler* confusedly. ◆ **confusion** *nf (honte)* embarrassment; *(trouble, désordre)* confusion; *(erreur)* confusion (*de* in). **vous avez fait une ~** you've made a mistake; **mettre la ~ dans les esprits** to throw people into disarray *ou* confusion.

congé [kɔ̃ʒe] *nm* (**a**) *(vacances)* holiday, vacation *(US)*; *(Mil)* leave. **3 jours de ~ pour** *ou* **à Noël** 3 days' holiday *ou* 3 days off at Christmas; **en ~** on holiday; **quand avez-vous ~?** when are you off?, when do you get a holiday?; **avoir ~ le mercredi** to have Wednesdays off; **~s payés/scolaires** paid/school holidays. (**b**) *(arrêt)* **prendre/donner du ~** to take/give time off *ou* some leave; **~ sans solde/de maladie** unpaid/sick leave; **~ de longue maladie** prolonged *ou* extended sick leave; **~ de conversion** retraining period. (**c**) *(départ)* notice. **donner son ~** *[employé]* to give in one's notice; *[employeur, locataire]* to give notice (*à* to); **il a demandé son ~** he's asked to leave. (**d**) *(adieu)* **prendre ~ (de qn)** to take one's leave (of sb). (**e**) *(Admin: autorisation)* clearance certificate; *[alcool]* release. ◆ **congédier** (7) *vt* to dismiss.

congeler [kɔ̃ʒle] (5) **1** *vt* to freeze. **produits congelés** (deep-)frozen *ou* deep-freeze foods. **2 se ~** *vpr* to freeze. ◆ **congélateur** *nm (meuble)* freezer, deep-freeze; *(compartiment)* freezer compartment. ◆ **congélation** *nf* freezing. **sac de ~** freezer bag.

congénère [kɔ̃ʒenɛʀ] *nmf* fellow creature. ◆ **congénital, e,** *mpl* **-aux** *adj* congenital.

congère [kɔ̃ʒɛʀ] *nf* snowdrift.

congestionner [kɔ̃ʒɛstjɔne] (1) *vt rue* to congest; *personne* to flush, make flushed. **être congestionné** to be flushed. ◆ **congestion** *nf* congestion. **~ (cérébrale)** stroke.

conglomérat [kɔ̃glɔmeʀa] *nm (gén)* conglomeration; *(Écon, Géol)* conglomerate.

Congo [kɔ̃go] *nm*: **le ~** the Congo. ◆ **congolais, e 1** *adj*, **C~(e)** *nm(f)* Congolese. **2** *nm (gâteau)* coconut cake.

congratuler [kɔ̃gʀatyle] (1) *vt* to congratulate. ◆ **congratulations** *nfpl* congratulations.

congre [kɔ̃gʀ(ə)] *nm* conger eel.

congrégation [kɔ̃gʀegɑsjɔ̃] *nf (Rel)* congregation.

congrès [kɔ̃gʀɛ] *nm* congress. ◆ **congressiste** *nmf* participant at a congress.

conifère [kɔnifɛʀ] *nm* conifer.

conique [kɔnik] *adj* cone-shaped.

conjecture [kɔ̃ʒɛktyʀ] *nf* conjecture. ◆ **conjecturer** (1) *vt* to conjecture.

conjoint, e [kɔ̃ʒwɛ̃, wɛ̃t] **1** *adj action* joint. **2** *nm, f (époux)* spouse. **les ~s** the couple, the husband and wife. ◆ **conjointement** *adv* jointly. **~ avec** together with; *(Jur)* **~ et solidairement** jointly and severally.

conjonction [kɔ̃ʒɔ̃ksjɔ̃] *nf* conjunction. ◆ **conjonctif, -ive** *adj (Gram)* conjunctive.

conjoncture [kɔ̃ʒɔ̃ktyʀ] *nf* situation, circumstances. **crise de ~** economic crisis.

conjugaison [kɔ̃ʒygɛzɔ̃] *nf (Bio, Gram)* conjugation; *(union)* union.

conjugal, e, *mpl* **-aux** [kɔ̃ʒygal, o] *adj amour* conjugal; *vie* married, conjugal. ◆ **conjugalement** *adv vivre* as a married couple.

conjuguer [kɔ̃ʒyge] (1) **1** *vt (Gram)* to conjugate; *(combiner)* to combine. **action conjuguée** joint *ou* combined action. **2 se ~** *vpr [efforts]* to combine. *[verbe]* **se ~ (avec)** to be conjugated (with).

conjurer [kɔ̃ʒyʀe] (1) **1** *vt* (**a**) *échec* to avert; *diable, sort* to ward off. (**b**) **~ qn de faire qch** to beseech *ou* entreat sb to do sth. **2 se ~** *vpr* to conspire (*contre* against). ◆ **conjuration** *nf* conspiracy. ◆ **conjuré, e** *nm, f* conspirator.

connaissance [kɔnɛsɑ̃s] *nf* (**a**) *(savoir)* knowledge. **une profonde ~ du cœur humain** a deep understanding of *ou* insight into the human heart; **faire étalage de ses ~s** to display one's knowledge *ou* learning; **c'est un garçon qui a des ~s** he's a knowledgeable fellow; **il a de bonnes ~s en anglais** he has a good command of English. (**b**) *(personne)* acquaintance. (**c**) *(conscience)* consciousness. **sans ~** unconscious; **reprendre ~** to regain consciousness, come round, come to. (**d**) **(pas) à ma ~** (not) to my knowledge, (not) as far as I know; **venir à la ~ de qn** to come to sb's knowledge; **donner ~ de qch à qn** to inform sb of sth; **en ~ de cause** with full knowledge of the facts; **en pays de ~** *(gens)* among familiar faces; *(sujet)* on familiar ground; **qn de sa ~** someone he knew; **faire ~ avec qn** to meet sb; **prendre ~ de qch** to read sth; **je leur ai fait faire ~** I introduced them (to each other). ◆ **connaisseur, -euse 1** *adj* expert. **2** *nm, f* connoisseur.

connaître [kɔnɛtʀ(ə)] (57) **1** *vt* (**a**) *(gén)* to know; *fait, personne* to be acquainted with; *texte, coutume* to be familiar with; *restaurant* to know of. **connaît-il la nouvelle?** has he heard the news?; **~ qn de vue** to know sb by sight; **apprendre à ~ qn** to get to know sb; **il l'a connu à l'université** he met *ou* knew him at university; **tu connais les oiseaux/la mécanique?** do you know anything about birds/engineering?; **~ la vie** to know about life; **il connaît son affaire** he knows what he's talking about; **elle n'y connaît rien** she doesn't know a thing about it, she hasn't a clue about it *; *(fig)* **je connais la chanson** I've heard it all before. (**b**) *succès* to enjoy, have; *privations* to know, experience. **nous connaissons de tristes heures** we are going through sad times. (**c**) **faire ~ (qn/qch)** to make (sb/sth) known; **faire ~** *décision* to announce, make public; **il m'a fait ~ son frère/la pêche** he introduced me to his brother/fishing; **se faire ~** *(gén)* to make o.s. known ; *[artiste]* to make a name for o.s.

2 se ~ *vpr* (**a**) **se ~ (soi-même)** to know o.s.; *(rage)* **il ne se connaît plus** he's beside himself with anger. (**b**) *(se rencontrer)* to meet. (**c**) **s'y ~ en qch** to know a lot about sth, be an expert on sth. ◆ **connu, e** *adj terre, animal* known; *idée, auteur* well-known. **mal ~** little known; **il est ~ comme le loup blanc** everybody knows him; *(Statistiques etc)* **chiffres non encore ~s** figures not yet available.

conne ‡ [kɔn] **1** *adj* damned ‡ stupid. **2** *nf* damned ‡ fool, stupid idiot ‡.

connecter [kɔnɛkte] (1) *vt* to connect. ◆ **connexion** *nf* connection.

connétable [kɔnetabl(ə)] *nm (Hist)* constable.

connivence [kɔnivɑ̃s] *nf* connivance. **de ~ avec** in connivance with; **sourire de ~** smile of complicity; **ils sont de ~** they're in league with each other.

conquérir [kɔ̃keʀiʀ] (21) *vt (gén)* to conquer; *galons* to win; *estime* to win, gain; *personnage influent* to win over. **conquis à une doctrine** won over *ou* converted to a doctrine; **ils ont conquis une grande partie de ce marché** they have captured a large part of that market. ◆ **conquérant, e 1** *adj peuple* conquering; *ardeur* masterful; *regard* swaggering. **2** *nm, f* conqueror. ◆ **conquête** *nf* conquest. **faire la ~ de** to conquer; to win over.

consacrer [kɔ̃sakʀe] (1) *vt* (**a**) **~ à** *(dédier à)* to devote to, dedicate to, consecrate to; *(affecter à)* to devote to, give to; **pouvez-vous me ~ un instant?** can you spare me a moment?; **se ~ à Dieu** to dedicate *ou* give o.s. to God. (**b**) *(Rel)* to consecrate; *coutume, droit* to establish; *abus* to sanction. ◆ **consacré, e** *adj (habituel, accepté)* accepted; *itinéraire* traditional; *écrivain* established, recognized. **c'est l'expression consacrée** it's the accepted way of saying it.

conscience [kɔ̃sjɑ̃s] *nf* (**a**) *(psychologique)* **la ~ de qch** the awareness *ou* consciousness of sth; *(Philos, Psych)* **la ~** consciousness; **avoir ~ que** to be aware *ou* conscious that; **prendre ~ de qch** to become aware of sth, realize sth; **perdre/reprendre ~** to lose/regain consciousness. (**b**) *(morale)* conscience. **avoir qch sur la ~** to have sth on one's conscience; **avoir bonne/mauvaise ~** to have a good *ou* clear/bad *ou* guilty conscience; **en (toute) ~** in all conscience *ou* honesty. (**c**) **~ (professionnelle)** conscientiousness. ◆ **consciemment** *adv* consciously. ◆ **consciencieusement** *adv* conscientiously. ◆ **consciencieux, -ieuse** *adj* conscientious. ◆ **conscient, e** *adj (non évanoui)* conscious; *(lucide)* lucid; *décision* conscious. **~ de** conscious *ou* aware of.

conscrit [kɔ̃skʀi] *nm* conscript, draftee *(US)*. ◆ **conscription** *nf* conscription, draft *(US)*.

consécration [kɔ̃sekʀɑsjɔ̃] *nf (Rel)* consecration; *[coutume, droit]* establishment; *[abus]* sanctioning; *[artiste]* consecration.

consécutif, -ive [kɔ̃sekytif, iv] *adj* consecutive. **sa blessure est ~ive à un accident** his (*ou* her) injury is the result of an accident. ◆ **consécutivement** *adv* consecutively. **~ à** following upon.

conseil [kɔ̃sɛj] **1** *nm* (**a**) **~(s)** advice; **un ~** some advice, a piece of advice; **prendre ~ de qn** to take advice from sb; **un petit ~** a word of advice; **~ d'ami** friendly piece of advice; **~s à la ménagère** hints *ou* tips for the housewife. (**b**) *(personne)* consultant, adviser (*en* in). **ingénieur-~** consulting engineer; **avocat-~** legal consultant. (**c**) *(groupe) [entreprise]* board; *[organisme]* council, committee; *(séance)* meeting. **tenir ~** *(se réunir)* to hold a meeting; *(délibérer)* to deliberate.
2 : **~ d'administration** *[société]* board of directors; *[hôpital]* board of governors; **~ de classe** staff meeting; **~ de discipline** disciplinary committee; *(Scol)* **~ d'établissement** ≃ governing board, ≃ board of education *(US)*; **~ de guerre** *(réunion)* council of war; *(tribunal)* court-martial; **le C~ des ministres** the Cabinet; **~ municipal** town council; **~ de révision** recruiting board; **C~ de Sécurité** Security Council.

conseiller[1] [kɔ̃seje] (1) *vt* (**a**) *prudence, méthode* to recommend (*à qn* to sb). **~ à qn de faire qch** to advise sb to do sth; **la peur lui conseilla de...** fear prompted him to...; **il est conseillé de** it is advisable to; **il est conseillé aux parents de...** parents are advised to... (**b**) *(guider)* to advise, give advice to. **bien/mal conseillé** well/badly advised.

conseiller[2], **-ère** [kɔ̃seje, jɛʀ] *nm, f (expert)* adviser; *(Admin, Pol)* council member, councillor. **~ municipal** town councillor, city council man *(US)*; **~ d'orientation** careers adviser, (school) counselor *(US)*; **~ pédagogique** educational adviser; **~ d'éducation** year head, dean *(US)*.

consentir [kɔ̃sɑ̃tiʀ] (16) **1** *vi* to agree, consent (*à* to). **~ (à ce) que qn fasse qch** to consent *ou* agree to sb's doing sth. **2** *vt délai, prêt* to grant (*à* to). **~ une dérogation** to grant *ou* accord exemption (*à* to). ◆ **consentant, e** *adj* willing; *(Jur)* consenting. **êtes-vous ~?** do you consent to it?, does it have your consent? ◆ **consentement** *nm* consent.

conséquence [kɔ̃sekɑ̃s] *nf* (**a**) *(gén)* consequence; *(conclusion)* conclusion. **cela a eu pour ~ de** the result *ou* consequence of this was that; **avoir d'heureuses ~s** to have a happy outcome *ou* happy results; **tirer les ~s** to draw conclusions *ou* inferences (*de* from). (**b**) **de ~** of (some) consequence; **en ~** *(donc)* consequently; *agir* accordingly; **en ~ de** *(par suite de)* in consequence of; **sans ~** *(fâcheuse)* without repercussions; *(sans importance)* of no consequence; **cela ne tire pas à ~** it's of no consequence. ◆ **conséquent, e** *adj (logique)* consistent; *(*: important)* sizeable; *(Géol)* consequent. **par ~** consequently.

conservateur, -trice [kɔ̃sɛʀvatœʀ, tʀis] **1** *adj (gén)* conservative. **2** *nm, f [musée]* curator; *[bibliothèque]* librarian; *(Pol)* conservative. **3** *nm (produit chimique)* preservative. ◆ **conservatisme** *nm* conservatism.

conservatoire [kɔ̃sɛʀvatwaʀ] *nm* school, academy (of music, drama). **le C~** the (Paris) Conservatoire.

conserver [kɔ̃sɛʀve] (1) **1** *vt* (**a**) *(gén)* to keep; *denrée* to store; *vitesse* to maintain; *habitude* to keep up; *espoir, sens* to retain; *qualité, droits, vie* to conserve. **il a conservé sa tête** *(lucidité)* he still has his wits about him. (**b**) *(en bon état)* to preserve. **bien conservé** *personne* well-preserved. (**c**) *(Culin)* to preserve, can; *(au vinaigre)* to pickle; *(en bocal)* to bottle. **2 se ~** *vpr [aliments]* to keep. ◆ **conservation** *nf [archives]* keeping; *[aliments, monuments]* preservation. **en bon état de ~** well-preserved. ◆ **conserve 1** *nf*: **les ~s** tinned (*ou* canned *ou* bottled) food(s); **~s en bocaux** bottled preserves; **l'industrie de la ~** the canning industry; **mettre en ~** *(boîte)* to can; *(bocal)* to bottle; *(fig)* **tu ne vas pas en faire des ~s! *** you're not going to hoard it away for ever! **2** *adv*: **de ~** *naviguer* in convoy; *agir* in concert. ◆ **conserverie** *nf (usine)* canning factory.

considérable [kɔ̃sideʀabl(ə)] *adj (gén)* considerable; *rôle* significant; *dégâts* extensive; *(littér) personnage* eminent. ◆ **considérablement** *adv* considerably; significantly; extensively.

considération [kɔ̃sideʀɑsjɔ̃] *nf* (**a**) *(examen)* consideration. **ceci mérite ~** this is worth considering *ou* consideration; **prendre qch en ~** to take sth into consideration *ou* account, make allowances for sth; **en ~ de** *(en raison de)* because of; *(par rapport à)* considering; **sans ~ de** *dangers* regardless of; *personne* without taking into consideration. (**b**) *(motif)* consideration. (**c**) *(remarques)* **~s** reflections. (**d**) *(respect)* esteem, respect. **'veuillez agréer l'assurance de ma ~ distinguée'** 'yours faithfully', 'yours truly' *(US)*. ◆ **considérer** (6) *vt* (**a**) *(gén)* to consider. **~ qch avec inquiétude** to view sth with anxiety; **tout bien considéré** all things considered; **je le considère comme mon fils** I look upon him as my son; **il se considère comme un génie** he considers himself a genius; **considérant que** *(gén)* considering that; *(Jur)* whereas. (**b**) *(respecter)* to respect, have a high regard for.

consigner [kɔ̃siɲe] (1) *vt* (**a**) *fait* to record. ~ **qch par écrit** to put sth down in writing *ou* on paper. (**b**) *soldat* to confine to barracks; *élève* to keep in (after school); *salle* to bar entrance to. (**c**) *bagages* to put in the left-luggage office. (**d**) *bouteille* to put a deposit on. ◆ **consigne** *nf (instructions)* orders; *(punition) (Mil)* confinement to barracks; *(Scol)* detention; *[bagages]* left-luggage (office); *[bouteille]* deposit. ~ **automatique** (left-luggage) lockers. ◆ **consigné, e** *adj emballage* returnable. **non** ~ non-returnable.

consistance [kɔ̃sistɑ̃s] *nf* consistency. **donner de la** ~ **à** *pâte* to give body to; *rumeur* to give strength to; **prendre** ~ *[liquide]* to thicken; **sans** ~ *substance* lacking in consistency; *caractère* spineless; *rumeur* ill-founded, groundless. ◆ **consistant, e** *adj repas* substantial; *nourriture, argument* solid; *sirop* thick.

consister [kɔ̃siste] (1) *vi (se composer de)* ~ **en** to consist of, be made up of; *(résider dans)* ~ **dans** to consist in; ~ **à faire** to consist in doing.

consoler [kɔ̃sɔle] (1) **1** *vt personne* to console; *chagrin* to soothe. **si ça peut te** ~... if it is of any consolation *ou* comfort to you... **2 se** ~ *vpr* to console o.s., find consolation. **se** ~ **d'une perte** to be consoled for *ou* get over a loss. ◆ **consolant, e** *adj* consoling, comforting. ◆ **consolation** *nf (action)* consolation. *(réconfort)* ~**(s)** consolation, comfort; **c'est une** ~ that's one consolation.

consolider [kɔ̃sɔlide] (1) **1** *vt (gén)* to strengthen; *accord, fortune* to consolidate. **2 se** ~ *vpr [régime]* to strengthen *ou* consolidate its position. ◆ **consolidation** *nf* strengthening; consolidation.

consommer [kɔ̃sɔme] (1) *vt* (**a**) *(gén)* to consume; *nourriture* to eat; *boissons* to drink; *carburant* to use. **il se consomme beaucoup de vin** a lot of wine is consumed *ou* drunk; **je désirerais** ~ I would like a drink; *(Aut)* **elle consomme beaucoup d'essence** it's heavy on petrol, it uses a lot of petrol. (**b**) *acte sexuel* to consummate; *crime* to perpetrate, commit; *ruine* to confirm. **ce qui a consommé la rupture...** what put the seal on the break-up... ◆ **consommateur, -trice** *nm, f (acheteur)* consumer; *[café]* customer. ◆ **consommation** *nf* (**a**) consumption; consummation; perpetration; confirmation. **il fait une grande** ~ **de papier** he goes through * *ou* uses a lot of paper; **de** ~ *biens, société* consumer; **produit de** ~ consumable. (**b**) *(boisson)* drink. **prendre les** ~**s** to take the orders. ◆ **consommé, e 1** *adj habileté* consummate; *écrivain* accomplished. **2** *nm* consommé.

consonne [kɔ̃sɔn] *nf* consonant.

consortium [kɔ̃sɔʀsjɔm] *nm* consortium.

conspirer [kɔ̃spiʀe] (1) *vi* to conspire, plot (*contre* against). ~ **à faire** to conspire to do. ◆ **conspirateur, -trice 1** *adj* conspiratorial. **2** *nm, f* conspirer, plotter. ◆ **conspiration** *nf* conspiracy.

conspuer [kɔ̃spɥe] (1) *vt* to boo.

constant, e [kɔ̃stɑ̃, ɑ̃t] **1** *adj (gén)* constant; *effort* steadfast. **2** *nf (Math)* constant; *(fig)* permanent feature. ◆ **constamment** *adv* constantly. ◆ **constance** *nf* constancy, steadfastness.

Constantinople [kɔ̃stɑ̃tinɔpl(ə)] *n* Constantinople.

constater [kɔ̃state] (1) *vt* (**a**) *(remarquer)* to note, notice, see. **je constatai sa disparition** I noticed *ou* saw that it had disappeared; **je ne fais que** ~ I'm merely stating a fact, I'm merely making an observation; **constatez par vous-même** see for yourself. (**b**) *(consigner) effraction* to record; *décès* to certify. ◆ **constat** *nm*: ~ **(d'huissier)** certified report ; ~ **(d'accident)** (accident) report. ◆ **constatation** *nf* (**a**) *(action)* noting; noticing; seeing; recording; certifying. (**b**) *(remarque)* observation. ~**s** *[enquête]* findings.

constellation [kɔ̃stelɑsjɔ̃] *nf (gén)* constellation. ◆ **constellé, e** *adj*: ~ **de** *astres, lumières* spangled *ou* studded with; *taches* spotted *ou* dotted with.

consternation [kɔ̃stɛʀnɑsjɔ̃] *nf* consternation, dismay. ◆ **consterner** (1) *vt* to dismay, fill with consternation. **air consterné** air of consternation *ou* dismay.

constiper [kɔ̃stipe] (1) *vt* to constipate. ◆ **constipation** *nf* constipation. ◆ **constipé, e** *adj (péj: guindé)* stiff; *(Méd)* constipated.

constituer [kɔ̃stitɥe] (1) **1** *vt* (**a**) *(fonder) comité, gouvernement* to set up, form; *bibliothèque* to build up; *dossier* to make up, put together. (**b**) *(composer) [éléments]* to make up, constitute. **constitué de plusieurs morceaux** made up *ou* composed of several pieces. (**c**) *délit, motif* to constitute. (**d**) *(Jur) rente* to settle (*à* on); *avocat* to retain. ~ **qn son héritier** to appoint sb one's heir. **2 se** ~ *vpr*: **se** ~ **prisonnier** to give o.s. up. ◆ **constituant, e** *adj (gén, Pol)* constituent. ◆ **constitué, e** *adj*: **bien/mal** ~ of sound/unsound constitution. ◆ **constitutif, -ive** *adj* constituent, component. ◆ **constitution** *nf* (**a**) setting-up, formation; building-up; putting together; making-up; settlement; retaining. (**b**) *(composition)* composition, make-up. (**c**) *(Méd, Pol)* constitution. ◆ **constitutionnel, -elle** *adj* constitutional.

construire [kɔ̃stʀɥiʀ] (38) *vt (gén)* to build, construct; *(Géom)* to construct; *théorie, phrase* to construct, put together, build up. **ça s'est beaucoup construit ici** there's a lot of building here; **ça se construit avec le subjonctif** it takes the subjunctive. ◆ **constructeur, -trice** *nm, f (fabricant)* maker, manufacturer; *(bâtisseur)* builder, constructor. ~ **de navires** shipbuilder. ◆ **constructif, -ive** *adj* constructive. ◆ **construction** *nf* (**a**) *(action)* building; construction. **de** ~ **française/robuste** French/ solidly built; **matériaux de** ~ building materials; **en** ~ under construction. (**b**) *(industrie)* **la** ~ the building trade; **les** ~**s navales** shipbuilding; **les** ~**s aéronautiques** the aircraft industry. (**c**) *(édifice)* building.

consul [kɔ̃syl] *nm* consul. ~ **général** consul general. ◆ **consulaire** *adj* consular. ◆ **consulat** *nm* (**a**) *(bureaux, charge)* consulate. (**b**) *(Hist française)* **le C**~ the Consulate.

consulter [kɔ̃sylte] (1) **1** *vt (gén)* to consult. **ne** ~ **que sa raison** to be guided only by one's reason. **2** *vi [médecin]* to hold surgery, be in (the office) *(US)*. **3 se** ~ *vpr* to confer, consult each other. **se** ~ **du regard** to look questioningly at one another. ◆ **consultatif, -ive** *adj* consultative, advisory. ◆ **consultation** *nf* (**a**) *(action)* consultation. **après** ~ **de son agenda** (after) having consulted his diary; **d'une** ~ **difficile** difficult to consult. (**b**) *[médecin, expert]* consultation. **aller à la** ~ to go to the surgery, pay a visit to the doctor; **les heures de** ~ surgery *ou* consulting hours; **service (hospitalier) de** ~ **externe** outpatients' clinic. (**c**) *(échange de vues)* consultation. **en** ~ **avec** in consultation with.

consumer [kɔ̃syme] (1) **1** *vt [incendie]* to consume, burn; *[fièvre, ambition]* to consume, devour; *forces* to expend; *fortune* to squander, fritter away. **débris consumés** charred debris. **2 se** ~ *vpr [bois]* to burn; *(littér: dépérir)* to waste away.

contact [kɔ̃takt] *nm (gén)* contact; *(toucher)* touch. *(Aut)* **mettre le** ~ to switch on the ignition; **prendre** ~ *(Rad)* to make contact; *(affaires)* to get in touch *ou* contact (*avec* with); **mettre en** ~ *objets* to bring into contact; *(affaires)* to put in touch; *(Rad)* to put in contact; **prise de** ~ *(entrevue)* first meeting; **au** ~ **de l'air** in contact with (the) air. ◆ **contacter** (1) *vt* to contact, get in touch with.

contagion [kɔ̃taʒjɔ̃] *nf (Méd)* contagion; *(fig: épidémie)* epidemic. **la ~ de la violence** the infectiousness of violence. ◆**contagieux, -euse** *adj maladie (gén)* infectious; *(par le contact)* contagious; *peur, rire* infectious, contagious.

contaminer [kɔ̃tamine] (1) *vt personne* to infect, contaminate; *cours d'eau* to contaminate. ◆**contamination** *nf* infection; contamination.

conte [kɔ̃t] *nm* tale, story. *(lit, fig)* **~ de fée** fairy tale *ou* story.

contempler [kɔ̃tɑ̃ple] (1) *vt* to contemplate, gaze at. ◆**contemplatif, -ive** *adj (gén)* contemplative. ◆**contemplation** *nf* contemplation.

contemporain, e [kɔ̃tɑ̃pɔʀɛ̃, ɛn] **1** *adj* contemporary (*de* with). **2** *nm* contemporary.

contenir [kɔ̃tniʀ] (22) **1** *vt* (**a**) *(en capacité) [récipient]* to hold, take; *[cinéma, avion]* to seat, hold. (**b**) *(en contenu) [récipient, livre, minerai]* to contain. (**c**) *(maîtriser) (gén)* to contain; *larmes* to hold back; *foule, ennemi* to hold in check. **2 se ~** *vpr* to contain o.s. ◆**contenance** *nf* (**a**) *(capacité)* capacity. (**b**) *(attitude)* attitude. **pour se donner une ~** to give an impression of composure; **faire bonne ~ (devant)** to put on a bold front (in the face of); **perdre ~** to lose one's composure. ◆**contenant** *nm*: **le ~** the container. ◆**conteneur** *nm* container.

content, e [kɔ̃tɑ̃, ɑ̃t] **1** *adj* pleased, glad, happy. **~ de** *élève, voiture* pleased *ou* happy with; *changement* pleased *ou* glad at *ou* about; **être ~ de soi** to be pleased with o.s.; **non ~ d'être/d'avoir fait...** not content with being/with having done... **2** *nm*: **avoir (tout) son ~ de qch** to have had one's fill of sth. ◆**contentement** *nm* contentment, satisfaction. **~ de soi** self-satisfaction. ◆**contenter** (1) **1** *vt besoin, curiosité* to satisfy; *personne* to satisfy, please. **cette explication l'a contenté** he was satisfied *ou* happy with this explanation. **2 se ~** *vpr*: **se ~ de qch/de faire qch** to content o.s. *ou* make do with sth/with doing sth.

contentieux, -euse [kɔ̃tɑ̃sjø, øz] **1** *adj (Jur)* contentious. **2** *nm (litige)* dispute, disagreement; *(Comm)* litigation; *(service)* legal department.

contenu, e [kɔ̃tny] **1** *adj colère* restrained, suppressed. **2** *nm [récipient]* contents; *[texte]* content; *(Ling)* content.

conter [kɔ̃te] (1) *vt (littér) histoire* to recount, relate. **~ qch à qn** to tell sth to sb; **il lui en a conté de belles!** he told him some incredible stories!; **elle ne s'en laisse pas ~** she's not easily taken in; **~ fleurette à qn** to murmur sweet nothings to sb.

contester [kɔ̃tɛste] (1) **1** *vt* to question, dispute, contest. **roman/écrivain très contesté** very controversial novel/author. **2** *vi* to protest. **il ne conteste jamais** he never takes issue over anything. ◆**contestable** *adj* questionable, disputable. ◆**contestataire 1** *adj* anti-establishment, antiauthority. **2** *nmf* protester. ◆**contestation** *nf* (**a**) *(action)* contesting; questioning; disputing. (**b**) *(discussion)* dispute; *(objection)* objection. (**c**) *(Pol)* **la ~** anti-establishment *ou* antiauthority activity; **faire de la ~** to protest (against the establishment). ◆**conteste** *nf*: **sans ~** unquestionably, indisputably.

conteur, -euse [kɔ̃tœʀ, øz] *nm, f (écrivain)* storywriter; *(narrateur)* storyteller.

contexte [kɔ̃tɛkst(ə)] *nm* context.

contigu, -uë [kɔ̃tigy] *adj choses* adjoining, adjacent; *sujets* closely related. **être ~ à qch** to be adjacent *ou* next to sth. ◆**contiguïté** *nf [choses]* proximity; *[sujets]* relatedness.

continence [kɔ̃tinɑ̃s] *nf* continence. ◆**continent[1], e** *adj* continent.

continent[2] [kɔ̃tinɑ̃] *nm* continent. *(terre ferme)* **le ~** the mainland. ◆**continental, e,** *mpl* **-aux** *adj* continental.

contingence [kɔ̃tɛ̃ʒɑ̃s] *nf (gén)* contingency. ◆**contingent, e 1** *adj* contingent. **2** *nm* (**a**) *(Mil: groupe)* contingent. *(en France)* **le ~** soldiers on national service, the draft *(US)*. (**b**) *(quota)* quota; *(part)* share. ◆**contingenter** (1) *vt (Comm)* to place *ou* fix a quota on.

continu, e [kɔ̃tiny] *adj (gén)* continuous; *ligne, silence* unbroken. ◆**continuateur, -trice** *nm, f* continuator. ◆**continuation** *nf* continuation. ◆**continuel, -elle** *adj (continu)* continuous; *(qui se répète)* continual. ◆**continuellement** *adv* continuously; continually.

continuer [kɔ̃tinɥe] (1) **1** *vt effort* to continue (with), carry on with; *droite, route* to continue. **~ son chemin** to go on, continue on one's way. **2** *vi [bruit, spectacle]* to continue, go on. **~ de** *ou* **à manger** *etc* to go on *ou* keep on *ou* continue eating *etc*; **s'il continue...** if he goes on *ou* keeps on *ou* continues... **3 se ~** *vpr* to go on, continue *(jusqu'à* as far as). ◆**continuité** *nf [politique]* continuation; *[action]* continuity. ◆**continûment** *adv* continuously. ◆**continuum** *nm* continuum.

contondant, e [kɔ̃tɔ̃dɑ̃, ɑ̃t] *adj* blunt.

contorsion [kɔ̃tɔʀsjɔ̃] *nf* contortion. ◆**contorsionner (se)** (1) *vpr* to contort o.s. ◆**contorsionniste** *nmf* contortionist.

contour [kɔ̃tuʀ] *nm* outline, contour. ◆**contourner** (1) *vt (gén)* to go (*ou* walk *ou* drive *etc*) round; *ville* to bypass; *difficulté* to get round.

contraception [kɔ̃tʀasɛpsjɔ̃] *nf* contraception. ◆**contraceptif, -ive** *adj, nm* contraceptive.

contracter [kɔ̃tʀakte] (1) **1** *vt* (**a**) *(raidir) muscle, visage* to tense; *(fig) personne* to make tense. **la peur lui contracta la gorge** fear gripped his throat. (**b**) *(Phys: réduire)* **~ un corps** to make a body contract. (**c**) *dette, alliance, maladie* to contract; *assurance* to take out. **2 se ~** *vpr [muscle, visage]* to tense; *[gorge]* to tighten; *(fig) [personne]* to become tense; *(Phys) [corps]* to contract. ◆**contracté, e** *adj (Ling)* contracted; *personne* tense. ◆**contraction** *nf (action)* tensing, contraction; *(état)* tenseness; *(spasme)* contraction. *(Scol)* **~ de texte** summary, précis.

contractuel, -elle [kɔ̃tʀaktɥɛl] **1** *adj* contractual. **2** *nm (Police)* ≃ traffic warden; *(Admin)* contract employee. **3** *nf [parking]* ≃ traffic warden, ≃ meter maid *(US)*.

contradiction [kɔ̃tʀadiksjɔ̃] *nf* contradiction. **être en ~ avec** to contradict. ◆**contradictoire** *adj* contradictory, conflicting. **débat ~** debate; **~ à** in contradiction to, in conflict with.

contraindre [kɔ̃tʀɛ̃dʀ(ə)] (52) *vt*: **~ qn à faire qch** to force *ou* compel *ou* constrain sb to do sth; **se ~ avec peine** to restrain o.s. with difficulty. ◆**contraignant, e** *adj* restricting, constraining. ◆**contraint, e[1]** *adj air* constrained, forced. **être ~ et forcé de faire** to be forced to do. ◆**contrainte[2]** *nf* (**a**) *(violence)* constraint. **sous la ~** under constraint *ou* duress. (**b**) *(gêne)* constraint, restraint. **sans ~** unrestrainedly, unconstrainedly, without restraint *ou* constraint.

contraire [kɔ̃tʀɛʀ] **1** *adj (gén)* opposite; *vent, action* contrary; *intérêts* conflicting; *destin* adverse. **l'alcool m'est ~** alcohol doesn't agree with me; **le sort lui fut ~** fate was against him; **~ à la santé** bad for the health. **2** *nm [mot, concept]* opposite. **c'est tout le ~** it's just the reverse *ou* opposite; **je ne vous dis pas le ~** I'm not saying anything to the contrary, I'm not disputing it; **tout au ~** on the contrary; **au ~ des autres** unlike the others. ◆**contrairement** *adv*: **~ à** contrary to; **~ aux autres...** unlike the others...

contralto [kɔ̃tʀalto] *nm* contralto.

contrarier [kɔ̃tʀaʀje] (7) *vt (irriter)* to annoy; *(gêner) projets* to frustrate, thwart; *mouvement* to impede. **forces qui se contrarient** forces which act against each other. ◆ **contrariant, e** *adj* annoying. ◆ **contrariété** *nf* annoyance.

contraste [kɔ̃tʀast(ə)] *nm (gén)* contrast. **par** ~ by contrast; **en** ~ **avec** in contrast to; **mettre en** ~ to contrast. ◆ **contrasté, e** *adj couleurs* contrasting. *(Phot)* **trop** ~ with too much contrast. ◆ **contraster** (1) **1** *vt éléments* to contrast; *photo* to give contrast to. **2** *vi* to contrast (*avec* with).

contrat [kɔ̃tʀa] *nm (gén)* contract; *(fig: accord)* agreement. *[équipe]* **remplir son** ~ to fulfil one's pledges.

contravention [kɔ̃tʀavɑ̃sjɔ̃] *nf* (**a**) *(Aut) (gén)* fine; *(papillon)* parking ticket. **dresser** ~ **(à qn)** to book * *ou* fine sb. (**b**) *(Jur: infraction)* ~ **à** contravention of.

contre [kɔ̃tʀ(ə)] **1** *prép et adv* (**a**) *(contact)* against. **appuyez-vous** ~ lean against *ou* on it; **son bateau est amarré** ~ **le mien** his boat is moored alongside mine; **serrer qn** ~ **son cœur** to clasp sb to one's breast; **son garage est juste** ~ **notre maison** his garage is built onto our house; **joue** ~ **joue** cheek to cheek. (**b**) *(hostilité)* against. *(Sport)* **Poitiers** ~ **Lyon** Poitiers versus *ou* against Lyons; **en colère** ~ **qn** angry with sb; **je n'ai rien** ~ **(cela)** I have nothing against it. (**c**) *(protection)* **s'abriter** ~ **le vent** to take shelter from the wind; **des comprimés** ~ **la grippe** flu tablets, tablets for flu; **s'assurer** ~ **les accidents** to insure (o.s.) against *ou* for accidents. (**d**) *(échange) argent* (in exchange) for; *promesse* in return for. **envoi** ~ **remboursement** cash on delivery. (**e**) *(rapport)* **1 bon** ~ **3 mauvais** 1 good one for 3 bad ones; **9 voix** ~ **4** 9 votes to 4. (**f**) *(locutions)* ~ **toute attente** contrary to (all) expectations; ~ **toute apparence** despite (all) appearances to the contrary; **par** ~ on the other hand.
2 *nm (riposte)* retort; *(Cartes)* double. *(Rugby)* **faire un** ~ to charge down a kick.
3 *préf (le second élément donne le genre et prend seul la marque du pl)* **~-attaque/-révolution/-espionnage** counter-attack/revolution/espionage; **~-expertise/-visite** *etc* second assessment/(medical) opinion *etc*; **~-allée** *(ville)* service road; *(parc)* side path; **~-amiral** rear admiral; **~-braquer** to steer into the skid; **~-courant** counter-current; **à ~-courant** against the current; **~-exemple** counter-example; **en ~-haut (de)** above; **~-indication** contra-indication; **~-indiqué, e** *(Méd)* contra-indicated; *(déconseillé)* unadvisable; **~-interrogatoire** cross-examination; **faire subir un ~-interrogatoire à qn** to cross-examine sb; **~-jour** *(éclairage)* back-lighting; *(photographie)* backlit shot; **à ~-jour** *se profiler* against the sunlight; *photographier* into the light; *lire* with one's back to the light; ~ **la montre** against the clock; **épreuve** ~ **la montre** time-trial; **~-offensive** counter-offensive; **~-performance** substandard performance; **prendre le ~-pied de ce que dit qn** to say exactly the opposite of sb else; *(Sport)* **à ~-pied** on the wrong foot; **~-plaqué** plywood; **~-publicité** adverse publicity; **~-ut** top *ou* high C; **~-valeur** exchange value; **~-vérité** untruth, falsehood.

contrebalancer [kɔ̃tʀəbalɑ̃se] (3) *vt [poids]* to counterbalance; *[influence]* to offset.

contrebande [kɔ̃tʀəbɑ̃d] *nf (activité)* contraband, smuggling. **faire de la** ~ to do some smuggling; **produits de** ~ contraband, smuggled goods. ◆ **contrebandier, -ière** *nm, f* smuggler.

contrebas [kɔ̃tʀəbɑ] *nm*: **en** ~ (down) below; **en** ~ **de** below.

contrebasse [kɔ̃tʀəbɑs] *nf (instrument)* (double) bass; *(musicien)* (double) bass player.

contrebasson [kɔ̃tʀəbɑsɔ̃] *nm* contrabassoon.

contrecarrer [kɔ̃tʀəkaʀe] (1) *vt* to thwart.

contrecœur [kɔ̃tʀəkœʀ] *adv*: **à** ~ reluctantly.

contrecoup [kɔ̃tʀəku] *nm* repercussions.

contredire [kɔ̃tʀədiʀ] (37) **1** *vt [personne]* to contradict; *[faits]* to be at variance with. **2 se** ~ *vpr [personne]* to contradict o.s.; *[témoins, témoignages]* to contradict each other. ◆ **contredit** *nm*: **sans** ~ unquestionably.

contrée [kɔ̃tʀe] *nf (littér) (pays)* land; *(région)* region.

contrefaire [kɔ̃tʀəfɛʀ] (60) *vt (imiter)* to imitate; *(déguiser)* to disguise; *(falsifier)* to counterfeit, forge; *brevet* to infringe; *(†: feindre)* to feign. ◆ **contrefaçon** *nf (action)* counterfeiting; forgery, forging; infringement; *(produit)* imitation; *(billets, signature)* forgery, counterfeit.

contrefort [kɔ̃tʀəfɔʀ] *nm* (**a**) *(Archit)* buttress. (**b**) *[soulier]* stiffener. (**c**) *(Géog) [arête]* spur. *[chaîne]* **~s** foothills.

contremaître, -maîtresse [kɔ̃tʀəmɛtʀ(ə), mɛtʀɛs] *nm, f* foreman; forewoman.

contrepartie [kɔ̃tʀəpaʀti] *nf* compensation. **en** ~ *(en échange)* in return; *(en revanche)* in compensation (*de* for); **obtenir de l'argent en** ~ to get money in compensation; **en** ~ **je vous donne ce livre** to make up for it I'll give you this book.

contrepoids [kɔ̃tʀəpwa] *nm (lit)* counterweight, counterbalance; *[acrobate]* balancing-pole. **faire** ~ to act as a counterbalance.

contrepoint [kɔ̃tʀəpwɛ̃] *nm* counterpoint. *(Mus, fig)* **en** ~ *(adj)* contrapuntal; *(adv)* contrapuntally.

contrepoison [kɔ̃tʀəpwazɔ̃] *nm* antidote.

contrer [kɔ̃tʀe] (1) **1** *vt (gén)* to counter; *(Cartes)* to double. *(Rugby)* ~ **un coup de pied** to charge down a kick. **2** *vi (Cartes)* to double.

contresens [kɔ̃tʀəsɑ̃s] *nm* misinterpretation; *(traduction)* mistranslation. **à** ~ *(Aut)* the wrong way; *(Couture)* against the grain; **à** ~ **de** against.

contresigner [kɔ̃tʀəsiɲe] (1) *vt* to countersign.

contretemps [kɔ̃tʀətɑ̃] *nm (retard)* hitch. **à** ~ *(Mus)* off the beat; *(fig)* at an inopportune moment.

contrevenir [kɔ̃tʀəvniʀ] (22) ~ **à** *vt indir* to contravene. ◆ **contrevenant, e** *nm, f* offender.

contrevent [kɔ̃tʀəvɑ̃] *nm (volet)* shutter.

contribuer [kɔ̃tʀibɥe] (1) ~ **à** *vt indir* to contribute to(wards). ◆ **contribuable** *nmf* taxpayer. ◆ **contribution** *nf* (**a**) *(participation)* contribution. **mettre qn à** ~ to make use of sb. (**b**) *(impôts)* **~s** *[commune]* rates, (local) taxes *(US)*; *[État]* taxes; *(administration)* tax office; **~s directes** direct taxation.

contrit, e [kɔ̃tʀi, it] *adj* contrite. ◆ **contrition** *nf* contrition.

contrôler [kɔ̃tʀole] (1) **1** *vt* (**a**) *(vérifier) (gén)* to check; *billets* to inspect; *qualité* to control. (**b**) *(surveiller) opérations, employés* to supervise; *prix* to control. (**c**) *(maîtriser) colère, (Écon, Sport)* to control; *(Mil)* to be in control of. **2 se** ~ *vpr* to control o.s. ◆ **contrôle** *nm* (**a**) *(action)* checking; inspecting; controlling; supervising. (**b**) *(opération)* check; inspection; control; supervision. **exercer un** ~ **sur** to maintain control over; *firme etc* **sous** ~ **étranger** foreign-owned; ~ **d'identité** identity check; *(Scol)* ~ **continu** continuous assessment; **(exercice de)** ~ (written) test; ~ **de soi-même** self-control; **garder le** ~ **de sa voiture** to remain in control of one's vehicle. (**c**) *(Théât: bureau)* (advance) booking office. *(Mil: registres)* **~s** lists. ◆ **contrôleur, -euse** *nm, f (gén)* inspector.

contrordre [kɔ̃tʀɔʀdʀ(ə)] *nm* counter-order.

controverse [kɔ̃tʀɔvɛʀs(ə)] *nf* controversy. ◆ **controversé, e** *adj* much debated.

contumace [kɔ̃tymas] *nf (Jur)* **par** ~ in his (*ou* her *etc*) absence.

contusion [kɔ̃tyzjɔ̃] *nf* bruise. ◆ **contusionner** (1) *vt* to bruise.

conurbation [kɔnyʀbɑsjɔ̃] *nf* conurbation.

convaincre [kɔ̃vɛ̃kʀ(ə)] (42) *vt* to convince (*de qch* of sth). ~ **qn de faire qch** to persuade sb to do sth, talk sb into doing sth; ~ **qn de meurtre** to prove sb guilty of *ou* convict sb of murder. ◆ **convaincant, e** *adj* convincing. ◆ **convaincu, e** *adj* convinced. **d'un ton** ~ with conviction.

convalescence [kɔ̃valesɑ̃s] *nf* convalescence. **être en** ~ to be convalescing; **maison de** ~ convalescent home. ◆ **convalescent, e** *adj, nm, f* convalescent.

convection [kɔ̃vɛksjɔ̃] *nf* convection.

convenable [kɔ̃vnabl(ə)] *adj* (**a**) *(approprié)* fitting, suitable. (**b**) *(décent)* decent, respectable. **peu** ~ improper. (**c**) *(acceptable) devoir, salaire* acceptable, adequate. **à peine** ~ scarcely acceptable *ou* adequate. ◆ **convenablement** *adv placé* suitably; *payé, logé* adequately; *manger, se tenir, s'exprimer* properly. **s'habiller** ~ *(décemment)* to dress respectably *ou* properly; *(en fonction du temps)* to dress appropriately.

convenance [kɔ̃vnɑ̃s] *nf (préférence)* convenience; *[caractères]* affinity; *[équipement]* suitability. **est-ce à votre** ~? is it to your liking?; **les** ~**s** *(préférences)* preferences; *(sociales)* the proprieties.

convenir [kɔ̃vniʀ] (22) **1** ~ **à** *vt indir*: ~ **à qn** *[offre]* to suit sb; *[lecture]* to be suitable for sb; *[climat]* to agree with sb; *[date]* to be convenient for sb. **2** ~ **de** *vt indir* (**a**) *erreur* to admit, recognize. ~ **d'avoir fait** to admit (to) having done. (**b**) *date, lieu* to agree upon. **comme convenu** as agreed. **3** *vt*: ~ **que** *(avouer)* to admit that; *(s'accorder sur)* to agree that. **4** *vb impers*: **il convient de faire** *(il vaut mieux)* it's advisable to do; *(il est bienséant de)* it is polite *ou* proper to do; **il convient de faire remarquer** we should point out.

convention [kɔ̃vɑ̃sjɔ̃] *nf (gén)* agreement; *(tacite)* understanding; *(Art, Pol, bienséance)* convention. ◆ **conventionnel, -elle** *adj (gén)* conventional. ◆ **conventionné, e** *adj établissement, médecin* ≃ National Health, linked to the State health scheme. **prix** ~ government-regulated price.

converger [kɔ̃vɛʀʒe] (3) *vi (gén)* to converge; *[regards]* to focus (*sur* on). ◆ **convergence** *nf* convergence. ◆ **convergent, e** *adj* convergent.

conversation [kɔ̃vɛʀsɑsjɔ̃] *nf (gén)* conversation; *(Pol)* talk. **en (grande)** ~ **avec** (deep) in conversation with; **faire la** ~ **à** to make conversation with, speak to; **avoir de la** ~ to be a good conversationalist; **dans la** ~ **courante** in informal *ou* conversational speech. ◆ **converser** (1) *vi* to converse (*avec* with).

convertir [kɔ̃vɛʀtiʀ] (2) **1** *vt* to convert (*à* to, *en* into). **2 se** ~ *vpr* to be converted (*à* to). ◆ **conversion** *nf* conversion (*à* to, *en* into). ◆ **converti, e 1** *adj* converted. **2** *nm, f* convert. ◆ **convertible 1** *adj* convertible (*en* into). **2** *nm (canapé)* bed-settee, sofa bed. ◆ **convertisseur** *nm* converter. *(Ordin)* ~ **numérique** digitizer.

convexe [kɔ̃vɛks(ə)] *adj* convex. ◆ **convexité** *nf* convexity.

conviction [kɔ̃viksjɔ̃] *nf (gén)* conviction.

convier [kɔ̃vje] (7) *vt*: ~ **à** *soirée etc* to invite to. ◆ **convive** *nmf* guest.

convivialité [kɔ̃vivjalite] *nf (rapports)* social interaction; *(jovialité)* conviviality; *(Ordin)* user-friendliness. ◆ **convivial, e,** *mpl* **-aux** *adj* convivial ; user-friendly.

convoiter [kɔ̃vwate] (1) *vt* to covet. ◆ **convoitise** *nf*: **la** ~ covetousness; **la** ~ **de qch** the lust for sth; **l'objet de sa** ~ *ou* **de ses** ~**s** the object of his desire; **regard de** ~ covetous look.

convoler [kɔ̃vɔle] (1) *vi († ou hum)* ~ **(en justes noces)** to be wed.

convoquer [kɔ̃vɔke] (1) *vt assemblée* to convene; *membre de club etc* to invite (*à* to); *candidat* to ask to attend; *prévenu, subordonné* to summon. ~ **qn (pour une entrevue)** to call *ou* invite sb for an interview; **le chef m'a convoqué** I was summoned by *ou* called before the boss. ◆ **convocation** *nf* (**a**) *(action)* convening; inviting; summoning. (**b**) *(gén, Jur: avis)* summons; *(lettre)* (written) notification to attend.

convoyer [kɔ̃vwaje] (8) *vt (gén)* to escort; *(Mil, Naut)* to escort, convoy. ◆ **convoi** *nm (funèbre)* funeral procession; *(train)* train; *(véhicules)* convoy. ◆ **convoyeur** *nm (navire)* convoy, escort ship; *(personne)* escort. ~ **de fonds** (mobile) security guard.

convulser [kɔ̃vylse] (1) *vt* to convulse, distort. ◆ **convulsif, -ive** *adj* convulsive. ◆ **convulsion** *nf (gén)* convulsion. ◆ **convulsionner** (1) *vt* to convulse. ◆ **convulsivement** *adv* convulsively.

cool * [kul] *adj* cool *.

coopérer [kɔɔpeʀe] (6) *vi* to cooperate (*à* in). ◆ **coopérant** *nm* person serving in the coopération. ◆ **coopératif, -ive** *adj, nf* cooperative. ~ **scolaire** school fund. ◆ **coopération** *nf (gén)* cooperation; *(Pol) scheme of aid to developing countries* ≃ Voluntary Service Overseas *(Brit)*, Peace Corps *(US)*.

coopter [kɔɔpte] (1) *vt* to coopt. ◆ **cooptation** *nf* coopting.

coordonner [kɔɔʀdɔne] (1) *vt* to coordinate. ◆ **coordination** *nf* coordination. ◆ **coordonnant** *nm (Ling)* coordinating conjunction. ◆ **coordonnateur, -trice 1** *adj* coordinating. **2** *nm, f* coordinator. ◆ **coordonné, e 1** *adj (gén)* coordinated; *proposition* coordinate. **papiers peints** ~**s** matching *ou* coordinated wallpapers. **2** ~**es** *nfpl (Math)* coordinates ; *(adresse)* whereabouts.

copain *, **copine** * [kɔpɛ̃, in] **1** *nm, f* pal *, chum *, buddy * *(US)*. **2** *adj*: **très** ~ **avec** (very) pally ‡ with.

copeau, *pl* ~**x** [kɔpo] *nm [bois]* shaving; *[métal]* turning.

Copenhague [kɔpənag] *n* Copenhagen.

copier [kɔpje] (7) **1** *vt (gén)* to copy; *(Scol)* to crib (*sur* from). ~ **qch au propre** to make a fair copy of sth; **vous me la copierez** * well, I won't forget that in a hurry! * **2** *vi (Scol)* to crib (*sur* from). ◆ **copie** *nf* (**a**) *(action)* copying; *(exemplaire, Presse, Typ)* copy. *(Admin)* ~ **certifiée conforme** certified copy; *(Ciné)* ~ **étalon** master print; *(Ciné)* ~ **d'exploitation** release print; *(Ordin)* ~ **papier** hard copy; **prendre** ~ **de** to make a copy of; **pâle** ~ pale imitation; **c'est la** ~ **de sa mère** she's the (spitting) image of her mother. (**b**) *(Scol) (feuille)* sheet (of paper); *(devoir)* exercise; *(examen)* paper. ◆ **copieur, -euse 1** *nm, f (Scol)* cribber. **2** *nm (machine)* copier.

copieux, -euse [kɔpjø, øz] *adj (gén)* copious; *repas* hearty; *portion* generous. ◆ **copieusement** *adv* copiously, heartily; generously. **on s'est fait** ~ **arroser** we got thoroughly soaked.

copilote [kɔpilɔt] *nmf* co-pilot; *(Aut)* navigator.

copiner * [kɔpine] (1) *vi* to be pally ‡ (*avec* with). ◆ **copine** *nf V* **copain.**

copiste [kɔpist(ə)] *nmf* copyist.

coprésidence [kɔpʀezidɑ̃s] *nf* co-presidency, co-chairmanship. ◆ **coprésident** *nm* co-president, co-chairman.

coproduction [kɔpʀɔdyksjɔ̃] *nf (Ciné, TV)* co-production, joint production.

copuler [kɔpyle] (1) *vi* to copulate. ◆ **copulation** *nf* copulation.

coq[1] [kɔk] *nm* cock. *(Boxe)* **poids ~** bantam-weight; **être comme un ~ en pâte** to be in clover, live the life of Riley; **mollets de ~** wiry legs; **sauter du ~ à l'âne** to jump from one subject to another; **le ~ gaulois** the French cockerel; *(fig)* **~ du village** the local swell * *ou* lady killer; *(Culin)* **~ au vin** coq au vin. ◆ **coquelet** *nm (Culin)* cockerel.

coq[2] [kɔk] *nm (Naut)* (ship's) cook.

coque [kɔk] *nf* (**a**) *[bateau]* hull; *[avion]* fuselage; *[auto]* body; *[œuf]* shell. *(embarcation légère)* **~ de noix** skiff; *(Culin)* **à la ~** (soft-)boiled. (**b**) *(mollusque)* cockle. ◆ **coquetier** *nm* egg cup.

coquelicot [kɔkliko] *nm* poppy.

coqueluche [kɔklyʃ] *nf (Méd)* whooping cough. *(fig)* **être la ~ de** to be the idol of.

coquerie [kɔkʀi] *nf (Naut)* (ship's) galley.

coquet, -ette [kɔkɛ, ɛt] **1** *adj* (**a**) *ville* pretty, charming; *logement, vêtement* smart, stylish; *personne (dans sa tenue)* smart; *(par tempérament)* clothes-conscious. (**b**) (*) *revenu* tidy *. (**c**) (†) flirtatious, coquettish. **2** *nf* (†) coquette, flirt. ◆ **coquettement** *adv* smartly, stylishly; prettily; coquettishly. ◆ **coquetterie** *nf* (**a**) *(élégance)* smartness, stylishness; *(caractère)* consciousness of one's appearance. (**b**) *(amoureuse)* coquetry, flirtatiousness. **~s** coquetries; *(amour propre)* **il mettait sa ~ à marcher sans canne** he prided himself on walking without a stick.

coquillage [kɔkijaʒ] *nm (coquille)* shell. *(mollusque)* **~(s)** shellfish.

coquille [kɔkij] **1** *nf (gén)* shell; *(récipient)* scallop; *(Typ)* misprint; *(Méd: plâtre)* spinal bed. **2** : **~ de beurre** whorl of butter; *(Naut)* **~ de noix** * cockleshell; **~ Saint-Jacques** *(animal)* scallop; *(carapace)* scallop shell. ◆ **coquillettes** *nfpl* pasta shells.

coquin, e [kɔkɛ̃, in] **1** *adj (malicieux)* mischievous; *(grivois)* naughty. **~ de sort!** * the devil! * **2** *nm, f (enfant)* rascal, mischief. **tu es un petit ~!** you're a little monkey! *ou* rascal! **3** *nm (†: gredin)* rogue. **4** *nf* (†) strumpet †. ◆ **coquinerie** *nf* (**a**) *(caractère)* mischievousness, roguishness; *[gredin]* roguery. (**b**) *(acte)* mischievous trick; rascally trick.

cor [kɔʀ] *nm* (**a**) *(Mus)* horn. **~ anglais** cor anglais; **~ de chasse** hunting horn; **~ d'harmonie** French horn; **demander qch à ~ et à cri** to clamour for sth. (**b**) **~ (au pied)** corn.

corail, *pl* **-aux** [kɔʀaj, o] *nm, adj inv* coral.

coran [kɔʀɑ̃] *nm* Koran.

corbeau, *pl* **~x** [kɔʀbo] *nm (gén)* crow. **(grand) ~** raven.

corbeille [kɔʀbɛj] *nf* (**a**) *(panier)* basket. **~ de mariage** wedding presents; **~ à papiers** waste paper basket. (**b**) *(Théât)* (dress) circle.

corbillard [kɔʀbijaʀ] *nm* hearse.

corde [kɔʀd(ə)] **1** *nf* (**a**) *(câble)* rope. *(Boxe)* **~s** ropes; *(fig)* **mériter la ~** to deserve to be hanged; **de ~** *tapis* whipcord; **sandales à semelle de ~** rope-soled sandals; **monter à la ~** to shin up *ou* climb a rope. (**b**) *[violon, arc, raquette]* string. **les (instruments à) ~s** the stringed instruments, the strings; **quatuor à ~s** string quartet. (**c**) *[tissu]* thread; *(Math)* chord. (**d**) **se mettre la ~ au cou** to put one's head in the noose; **avoir plusieurs ~s à son arc** to have more than one string to one's bow; **c'est dans ses ~s** it's in his line; *(Courses)* **tenir la ~** to be on the inside (lane); **prendre un virage à la ~** to hug the bend; **tirer sur la ~** to go too far; **il pleut des ~s** * it's bucketing (down) *.
2 : **~ à linge** clothes line; **~ à nœuds** knotted climbing rope; **~ à piano** pianowire; **~ raide** tightrope; **~ à sauter** skipping rope; **~s vocales** vocal cords. ◆ **cordage** *nm* rope. *[voilure]* **~s** rigging. ◆ **cordeau,** *pl* **~x** *nm* (**a**) *[jardinier]* line. *(fig)* **tiré au ~** as straight as a die. (**b**) *(mèche)* fuse. ◆ **cordée** *nf* roped party. ◆ **cordelette** *nf* cord.

cordial, e, *mpl* **-iaux** [kɔʀdjal, jo] **1** *adj* warm, cordial. **2** *nm* cordial. ◆ **cordialement** *adv* warmly, cordially. **~ (vôtre)** kind regards. ◆ **cordialité** *nf* warmth, cordiality.

cordillère [kɔʀdijɛʀ] *nf*: **la ~ des Andes** the Andes cordillera; **la ~ australienne** the Great Dividing Range.

cordon [kɔʀdɔ̃] **1** *nm [rideau]* cord; *[tablier]* tie; *[sac]* string; *[souliers]* lace; *[soldats]* cordon; *(décoration)* ribbon. **~ de sonnette** bell-pull; *(fig)* **tenir les ~s de la bourse** to hold the purse strings. **2** : **~-bleu** * *nm, pl* **~s-~s** cordon-bleu cook; **~ littoral** offshore bar; **~ ombilical** umbilical cord; *(Méd, Pol)* **~ sanitaire** quarantine line.

cordonnerie [kɔʀdɔnʀi] *nf (boutique)* shoemender's (shop); *(métier)* shoemending. ◆ **cordonnier, -ière** *nm, f (réparateur)* shoemender, cobbler.

Corée [kɔʀe] *nf* Korea. **la ~ du Sud/du Nord** South/North Korea. ◆ **coréen, -enne** *adj,* **C~(ne)** *nm(f)* Korean.

Corfou [kɔʀfu] *n* Corfu.

coriace [kɔʀjas] *adj (lit, fig)* tough.

Corinthe [kɔʀɛ̃t] *n* Corinth.

cormoran [kɔʀmɔʀɑ̃] *nm* cormorant.

corne [kɔʀn(ə)] **1** *nf (gén, instrument)* horn; *[cerf]* antler; *[page]* dog-ear. **à ~s** horned; **donner un coup de ~ à qn** to butt sb; **blesser qn d'un coup de ~** to gore sb; *(fig)* **faire les ~s à qn** to make a face at sb; *(peau)* **avoir de la ~** to have patches of hard skin, have calluses. **2** : **~ d'abondance** horn of plenty; **~ de brume** foghorn; **~ à chaussures** shoehorn.

cornée [kɔʀne] *nf* cornea.

corneille [kɔʀnɛj] *nf* crow.

cornemuse [kɔʀnəmyz] *nf* bagpipes. **joueur de ~** bagpiper.

corner[1] [kɔʀne] (1) **1** *vt* (**a**) *livre* to make dog-eared; *page* to turn down the corner of. (**b**) *nouvelle* to shout out. **2** *vi (Aut)* to sound one's horn.

corner[2] [kɔʀnɛʀ] *nm (Ftbl)* corner (kick).

cornet [kɔʀnɛ] *nm (récipient)* cornet; *[orgue]* cornet stop. **~ acoustique** ear trumpet; **~ à dés** dice cup; *(Mus)* **~ (à pistons)** cornet.

corniaud [kɔʀnjo] *nm (chien)* mongrel; (‡: *imbécile)* nitwit *.

corniche [kɔʀniʃ] *nf (Archit)* cornice; *(Géog)* ledge. **(route en) ~** cliff road.

cornichon [kɔʀniʃɔ̃] *nm (lit)* gherkin; *(*: fig)* nitwit *.

Cornouailles [kɔʀnwaj] *nf* Cornwall.

cornue [kɔʀny] *nf (Tech)* retort.

corollaire [kɔʀɔlɛʀ] *nm* corollary.

corolle [kɔʀɔl] *nf* corolla.

coronaire [kɔʀɔnɛʀ] *adj* coronary.

corossol [kɔʀɔsɔl] *nm* soursop.

corporatif, -ive [kɔʀpɔʀatif, iv] *adj système* corporative; *esprit* corporate. ◆ **corporation** *nf* professional body; *(Hist)* guild. **dans notre ~** in our profession. ◆ **corporatiste** *adj* corporatist.

corporel, -elle [kɔʀpɔʀɛl] *adj châtiment* corporal; *besoin* bodily.

corps [kɔʀ] **1** *nm (gén, Chim, fig)* body; *(cadavre)* corpse, (dead) body. **trembler de tout son ~** to tremble all over; **je n'ai rien dans le ~** I have eaten nothing; **se donner ~ et âme à qch** to give o.s. heart and soul to sth; **perdu ~ et biens** lost with all hands; *(fig)* **à ~ perdu** headlong; **donner ~ à qch** to give substance to sth; **faire ~** *[idées]* to form one body (*avec* with); *[choses concrètes]* to be joined (*avec* to); **prendre ~** to take shape; **à son ~**

défendant against one's will; **mais qu'est-ce qu'il a dans le ~?** whatever's got into him?
2 : ~ **d'armée** army corps; ~ **de ballet** corps de ballet; ~ **de bâtiment** building; ~ **à** ~ *(adv)* hand-to-hand; *(nm)* hand-to-hand fight; ~ **diplomatique** diplomatic corps; ~ **électoral** electorate; **le** ~ **enseignant** *(gén)* the teaching profession, teachers; *[lycée, collège]* the teaching staff; ~ **expéditionnaire** task force; ~ **franc** irregular force; ~ **de garde** *(local)* guardroom; ~ **gras** greasy substance; **le** ~ **médical** the medical profession; ~ **de métier** trade association; ~ **de sapeurs-pompiers** fire-brigade; ~ **de troupe** unit (of troops).

corpulence [kɔʀpylɑ̃s] *nf* stoutness, corpulence. **de moyenne** ~ of medium build. ◆ **corpulent, e** *adj* stout, corpulent.

corpus [kɔʀpys] *nm* corpus. ◆ **corpuscule** *nm (Anat, Phys)* corpuscle.

correct, e [kɔʀɛkt, ɛkt(ə)] *adj (gén)* correct; *réponse* right; *fonctionnement, tenue* proper; *(*: acceptable) repas, hôtel, salaire* reasonable, decent. ~ **en affaires** correct in business matters. ◆ **correctement** *adv* correctly; properly; reasonably, decently. ◆ **correcteur, -trice 1** *adj* corrective. **2** *nm, f [examen]* marker; *(Typ)* proofreader. **3** *nm (Tech)* corrector. ◆ **correctif, -ive 1** *adj* corrective. **2** *nm (mise au point)* qualifying statement.

correction [kɔʀɛksjɔ̃] *nf* (**a**) *(action) (gén)* correction; *(Typ)* proofreading; *[examen]* marking, grading *(US)*; *(Ordin) [programme]* patching; *[mise au point]* debugging. (**b**) *(résultat)* correction; *(châtiment)* thrashing. (**c**) *(exactitude)* correctness; propriety. ◆ **correctionnel, -elle** *adj, nf*: **le tribunal** ~, **la ~le** * the criminal court.

corrélation [kɔʀelɑsjɔ̃] *nf* correlation. **mettre en** ~ to correlate.

correspondance [kɔʀɛspɔ̃dɑ̃s] *nf* (**a**) *(conformité)* correspondence. (**b**) *(Math)* relation; *(fig: rapport)* relation, connection. (**c**) *(échange de lettres)* correspondence; *(courrier)* mail. **être en** ~ to be in correspondence; **apprendre qch par** ~ to learn sth by a correspondence course. (**d**) *(transports)* connection. **assurer la** ~ **avec** to connect with. ◆ **correspondant, e 1** *adj* corresponding. **2** *nm, f (gén, Presse)* correspondent; *(Scol)* penfriend.

correspondre [kɔʀɛspɔ̃dʀ(ə)] (41) **1** ~ **à** *vt indir goûts* to suit; *capacités, description* to fit; *dimension, système* to correspond to. **ça ne correspond pas à la réalité** it doesn't tally with *ou* fit the facts. **2** *vi (écrire)* to correspond; *[chambres]* to communicate (*avec* with). *(Transport)* ~ **avec** to connect with. **3 se** ~ *vpr* to communicate.

corrida [kɔʀida] *nf* bullfight; *(*fig)* to-do *.

corridor [kɔʀidɔʀ] *nm* corridor.

corriger [kɔʀiʒe] (3) **1** *vt* (**a**) *(gén)* to correct; *(Typ)* to proofread; *examen* to mark; *abus* to remedy. ~ **le tir** *(Mil)* to adjust the firing; *(fig)* to straighten things up; **corrigé des variations saisonnières** seasonally adjusted. (**b**) ~ **qn de** *défaut* to cure sb of. (**c**) *(punir)* to thrash. **2 se** ~ *vpr (devenir raisonnable)* to mend one's ways. **se** ~ **de** *défaut* to cure *ou* rid o.s. of. ◆ **corrigé** *nm [exercice]* correct version; *[traduction]* fair copy. **recueil de ~s** key to exercises.

corroborer [kɔʀɔbɔʀe] (1) *vt* to corroborate.

corroder [kɔʀɔde] (1) *vt* to corrode.

corrompre [kɔʀɔ̃pʀ(ə)] (41) *vt témoin* to bribe, corrupt; *mœurs, texte* to corrupt; *langage* to debase; *aliments* to taint. ◆ **corrompu, e** *adj* corrupt.

corrosion [kɔʀozjɔ̃] *nf* corrosion. ◆ **corrosif, -ive** *adj* corrosive; *(fig)* caustic, scathing.

corruption [kɔʀypsjɔ̃] *nf* corruption. ◆ **corrupteur, -trice 1** *adj* corrupting. **2** *nm, f* briber; *(littér: dépravateur)* corrupter. ◆ **corruptible** *adj* corruptible.

corsage [kɔʀsaʒ] *nm (chemisier)* blouse; *[robe]* bodice.

corsaire [kɔʀsɛʀ] *nm (Hist)* privateer.

Corse [kɔʀs(ə)] *nf* Corsica. ◆ **corse** *adj*, **C~** *nmf* Corsican.

corser [kɔʀse] (1) *vt repas* to make spicier; *boisson* to spike; *difficulté* to intensify, aggravate; *récit* to liven up. **ça se corse** things are hotting up. ◆ **corsé, e** *adj vin* full-bodied; *café* strong (and flavourful); *mets, histoire* spicy; *problème* stiff.

corset [kɔʀsɛ] *nm* corset.

corso [kɔʀso] *nm*: ~ **(fleuri)** procession of floral floats.

cortège [kɔʀtɛʒ] *nm [prince]* retinue. *(littér)* ~ **de** *malheurs* trail of; *souvenirs* succession of.

corvée [kɔʀve] *nf (Mil)* fatigue duty; *(gén)* chore. **être de** ~ to be on fatigue duty; ~ **de ravitaillement** supply duty; **quelle** ~! what a chore!

corvette [kɔʀvɛt] *nf* corvette.

cosaque [kɔzak] *nm* cossack.

cosmétique [kɔsmetik] *nm* hair oil.

cosmos [kɔsmos] *nm (univers)* cosmos; *(Espace)* outer space. ◆ **cosmique** *adj* cosmic. ◆ **cosmonaute** *nmf* cosmonaut. ◆ **cosmopolite** *adj* cosmopolitan.

cosse [kɔs] *nf [pois]* pod; *(Élec)* terminal spade tag. *(Aut)* ~ **de batterie** battery lead connection; **avoir la** ~ * to be in a lazy mood.

cossu, e [kɔsy] *adj personne* well-off; *maison* grand.

Costa Rica [kɔstaʀika] *nm* Costa Rica. ◆ **costaricien, -ienne** *adj*, **C~(ne)** *nm, f*: Costa Rican.

costaud, e * [kɔsto, od] **1** *adj* strong, sturdy. **2** *nm*: **c'est du** ~ *[alcool, tissu]* it's strong stuff; *[maison]* it's strongly built.

costume [kɔstym] *nm (régional)* costume, dress; *(Théât)* costume; *(complet)* suit. ~ **de bain** bathing costume. ◆ **costumer** (1) **1** *vt*: ~ **qn en** to dress sb up as. **2 se** ~ *vpr [acteur]* to get into costume; **se** ~ **en** to dress up as; **être costumé** to wear fancy dress.

cotation [kɔtɑsjɔ̃] *nf (Bourse)* quotation; *[voiture]* valuation; *[devoir]* marking, grading *(US)*.

cote [kɔt] *nf* (**a**) *(Bourse) (cours)* quotation; *(liste)* share index; *[timbre]* quoted value; *[devoir]* mark; *[cheval]* odds (*de* on); *[film]* rating; *(Impôts)* assessment. (**b**) *(popularité)* rating. **avoir la** ~ * to be very popular (*auprès de* with) *ou* highly rated (*auprès de* by); **sa** ~ **est en baisse** his popularity is on the decline. (**c**) *[carte]* spot height; *[croquis]* dimensions; *[bibliothèque]* classification mark. *(Mil)* **la** ~ **215** hill 215; ~ **d'alerte** *[rivière, prix]* danger mark; *[situation]* crisis point; ~ **mal taillée** rough-and-ready settlement.

côte [kot] *nf* (**a**) *(Anat, Bot)* rib. **se tenir les ~s (de rire)** to split one's sides (with laughter); ~ **à** ~ side by side. (**b**) *[bœuf]* rib; *[veau, agneau]* cutlet; *[mouton, porc]* chop. ~ **première** loin chop. (**c**) *[colline]* slope; *(Aut) [route]* hill. (**d**) *(littoral)* coast. **les ~s de France** the coasts of France; **la** ~ **d'Azur** the Riviera; **la** ~ **d'Émeraude** the northern coast of Brittany; **la C~-d'Ivoire** the Ivory Coast.

côté [kote] **1** *nm* (**a**) side. **l'épée au** ~ (with) his sword by his side; **à son** ~ at *ou* by his side, beside him; **salon** ~ **rue** room overlooking the street; **se mettre du** ~ **du plus fort** to side *ou* take sides with the strongest. (**b**) *(aspect)* side. **les bons ~s de qch** the good sides *ou* points of sth; **prendre qch du bon/mauvais** ~ to take sth well/badly; **prendre qn par son** ~ **faible** to attack sb's weak spot; **par certains ~s** in some respects *ou* ways; **d'un** ~ ... **d'un autre** ~ ... *(alternative)* on (the) one hand... on the other hand...; *(hésitation)* in one respect... in another respect...; **(du)** ~ **santé** * healthwise *, as far as his *etc* health is concerned.

(**c**) *(précédé de 'de': direction)* way, direction. **de ce ~-ci** this way; **de l'autre ~** the other way, in the other direction; **aller/venir du ~ de la mer** to go towards/come from the sea; **de tous ~s** everywhere; *(fig)* **je l'ai entendu dire de divers ~s** I've heard it from several quarters *ou* sources ; *(fig)* **de mon ~** for my part.
2 à ~ *adv* (**a**) *(proximité)* nearby. **les gens (d')à ~** the people next door, our next-door neighbours; **à ~ de** next to, beside; **(tout) à ~** close by. (**b**) **viser à ~ (du but)** to miss (the goal); **à ~ de la cible** wide of the target; **à ~ de la question** off the point; **on passe à ~ de beaucoup de choses en ne voyageant pas** you miss a lot by not travelling; **mettre à ~ de la plaque ‡** to misjudge things, be wide of the mark. (**c**) *(comparaison)* by comparison. **à ~ de** compared to; *(par contre)* **à ~ de ça** but on the other hand.
3 de ~ *adv se tourner* sideways; *sauter, laisser* aside, to one side. **mettre qch de ~** to put sth aside; **regard de ~** sidelong look.

coteau, *pl* **~x** [kɔto] *nm (colline)* hill; *(versant)* hillside.

côtelette [kotlɛt] *nf [mouton, porc]* chop; *[veau, agneau]* cutlet.

coter [kɔte] (1) *vt* (**a**) to quote; *timbre* to quote the market price of; *devoir* to mark; *film* to rate. **bien/mal coté** highly/not highly thought of; **coté à l'Argus** listed in the secondhand car book *ou* in the Blue Book *(US)*. (**b**) *carte* to put spot heights on; *croquis* to mark in the dimensions on; *(en bibliothèque)* to put a classification mark on.

coterie [kɔtʀi] *nf (gén péj)* set. **~ littéraire** literary coterie *ou* clique *ou* set.

côtier, -ière [kotje, jɛʀ] *adj pêche* inshore; *navigation, région* coastal.

cotisation [kɔtizɑsjɔ̃] *nf [club]* subscription; *[sécurité sociale, syndicat]* contributions. ◆ **cotisant, e** *nm, f* subscriber; contributor. ◆ **cotiser** (1) **1** *vi* to subscribe, pay one's subscription; to pay one's contributions (*à* to). **2 se ~** *vpr* to club together.

côtoiement [kotwamɑ̃] *nm (fréquentation)* association; *(coudoiement)* mixing (*de* with).

coton [kɔtɔ̃] **1** *nm (gén)* cotton; *(tampon)* (cotton-wool *ou (US)* cotton) swab. **~ à repriser** darning thread; **~ hydrophile** cotton wool; **avoir du ~ dans les oreilles** * to be deaf, have cloth ears *; **j'ai les jambes en ~** my legs feel like cotton wool. **2** *adj (*: ardu)* stiff *. ◆ **cotonnade** *nf* cotton fabric. ◆ **cotonneux, -euse** *adj brouillard* wispy; *nuage* fluffy. ◆ **cotonnier, -ière 1** *adj* cotton. **2** *nm (Bot)* cotton plant.

côtoyer [kotwaje] (8) **1** *vt* (**a**) *(longer)* to drive (*ou* walk *etc*) alongside; *[rivière, route]* to run alongside. (**b**) *(être à côté de)* to be next to; *(fréquenter)* to rub shoulders with. **~ la malhonnêteté** to be bordering *ou* verging on dishonesty. **2 se ~** *vpr [individus]* to rub shoulders; *[genres]* to meet.

cotte [kɔt] *nf* (**a**) *(Hist)* **~ de mailles** coat of mail; **~ d'armes** coat of arms *(surcoat)*. (**b**) *(salopette)* dungarees, overalls.

cou [ku] **1** *nm* neck. **jusqu'au ~** *enlisé, endetté* up to one's neck; **sauter au ~ de qn** to throw one's arms around sb's neck. **2** : **~-de-pied** *nm, pl* **~s-~-~** instep.

couac [kwak] *nm* false note.

couard, e [kwaʀ, aʀd(ə)] **1** *adj* cowardly. **2** *nm, f* coward.

couchage [kuʃaʒ] *nm (installation)* sleeping arrangements. **matériel de ~** sleeping equipment, bedding.

couchant [kuʃɑ̃] **1** *adj*: **soleil ~** setting sun. **2** *nm (ouest)* west; *(ciel du soir)* sunset.

couche [kuʃ] *nf* (**a**) *(gén)* layer; *[peinture]* coat. **~ sociale** social stratum; *(fig)* **en tenir une ~** * to be really thick * *ou* dumb *. (**b**) *(Horticulture)* hotbed. (**c**) *[bébé]* nappy, diaper *(US)*. (**d**) *(Méd: accouchement)* **~s** confinement; **mourir en ~s** to die in childbirth. (**e**) *(littér: lit)* bed.

coucher [kuʃe] (1) **1** *vt* (**a**) *(mettre au lit)* to put to bed; *(donner un lit)* to put up. **être/rester couché** to be/stay in bed. (**b**) *blessé* to lay out; *échelle etc* to lay down; *blés* to flatten. **être couché** to be lying. (**c**) *(inscrire)* to inscribe. (**d**) **~ en joue** *fusil* to aim; *personne* to aim at. **2** *vi (dormir)* to sleep (*avec* with). **cela nous a fait ~ très tard** that meant we went to bed very late. **3 se ~** *vpr* to go to bed; *(s'étendre)* to lie down; *[soleil, lune]* to set, go down; *[bateau]* to keel over. **4** *nm*: **le (moment du) ~** bedtime; **le ~ des enfants** the children's bedtime; **(au) ~ du soleil** (at) sunset *ou* sundown *(US)*. ◆ **couchette** *nf [voyageur]* couchette, berth; *[marin]* bunk.

couci-couça * [kusikusa] *adv* so-so *.

coucou [kuku] *nm (oiseau)* cuckoo; *(pendule)* cuckoo clock; *(péj: avion)* (old) crate; *(fleur)* cowslip. **~ (me voici)!** peek-a-boo!

coude [kud] *nm (Anat)* elbow; *[route, tuyau]* bend. *(fig)* **se serrer les ~s** to stick together; **~ à ~** shoulder to shoulder. ◆ **coudée** *nf*: **avoir les ~s franches** to have elbow room; *(fig)* **dépasser qn de cent ~s** † to stand head and shoulders above sb.

coudoyer [kudwaje] (8) *vt (fréquenter)* to rub shoulders with; *(être à côté de)* to be next to. ◆ **coudoiement** *nm* mixing.

coudre [kudʀ(ə)] (48) *vt* to sew; *bouton* to sew on; *vêtement, plaie* to sew up; *(Reliure)* to stitch.

coudrier [kudʀije] *nm* hazel tree.

couenne [kwan] *nf [lard]* rind; *(‡: peau)* hide *.

couiner [kwine] (1) *vi* to squeal.

couler [kule] (1) **1** *vi* (**a**) *[liquide, paroles]* to flow; *[larmes, sueur]* to run down; *[fromage, bougie]* to run. *[vin]* **~ à flots** to flow freely; **le sang a coulé** blood has been shed; **faire ~** *eau, bain* to run; **faire ~ le sang** to shed blood; *(fig)* **ça a fait ~ beaucoup d'encre** it caused much ink to flow; **~ de source** *(être clair)* to be obvious; *(s'enchaîner)* to follow naturally. (**b**) *[robinet, nez]* to run; *(fuir)* to leak. (**c**) *[vie, temps]* to slip by. (**d**) *[bateau, personne]* to sink; *[firme]* to go bankrupt. **~ à pic** to sink straight to the bottom. **2** *vt* (**a**) *ciment* to pour; *métal, statue* to cast. (**b**) *bateau* to sink; (*) *personne* to discredit; *candidat* to bring down; *entrepreneur, firme* to wreck, ruin. (**c**) *regard* to steal. **~ des jours heureux** to enjoy happy days. **3 se ~** *vpr*: **se ~ dans/à travers** to slip into/through; **se la ~ douce** * to have an easy time of it. ◆ **coulant, e 1** *adj pâte* runny; *style* flowing; *(*: indulgent)* easy-going. **2** *nm [ceinture]* sliding loop. ◆ **coulée** *nf [métal]* casting. **~ de lave** lava flow; **~ de boue** mud slide.

couleur [kulœʀ] *nf* (**a**) *(gén, fig)* colour; *(nuance)* shade, tint; *(peinture)* paint; *(Cartes)* suit. **de ~ claire** light-coloured; **(de) ~ chair/paille** flesh/straw-coloured; **film en ~s** colour film; **de ~** *personne* coloured; *vêtements* colourful; **les ~s** *(linge)* coloureds; *(emblème)* the colours; **boîte de ~s** paintbox; **reprendre des ~s** to get back one's colour; **sans ~** colourless; **~ locale** local colour. (**b**) *(locutions)* **sous ~ de qch** under the guise of sth; **sous ~ de faire** while pretending to do; **sous de fausses ~s** in a false light; **peindre qch sous les plus sombres ~s** to paint sth in the darkest colours; **elle n'a jamais vu la ~ de son argent** * she's never seen the colour of his money *.

couleuvre [kulœvʀ(ə)] *nf* grass snake.

coulisse [kulis] *nf* (**a**) *(Théât: gén pl)* wings. **en ~** *(Théât)* in the wings; *(fig)* behind the scenes. (**b**) *[porte]* runner. **porte à ~** sliding door; *(fig)* **regard en ~** sidelong look. ◆**coulisser** (1) *vi [porte]* to slide.

couloir [kulwaʀ] *nm* corridor, passage; *[wagon]* corridor; *(bande de circulation)* lane; *(ravin)* gully. **~ d'avalanches** avalanche corridor; *(Pol)* **bruits de ~(s)** rumours; *(Pol)* **intrigues de ~(s)** backstage manœuvring.

coup [ku] **1** *nm* (**a**) *(choc)* knock; *(affectif)* blow. **se donner un ~ à la tête** to hit *ou* bang one's head; **donner des ~s dans la porte** to bang at the door.
(**b**) *(hostile)* blow. **~ de pied** kick; **~ de poing** punch; **donner un ~** to hit; **recevoir un ~ de bâton** to be struck with a stick; **il a reçu un ~ de griffe/de couteau** he was clawed/knifed; **tuer qn à ~s de pierres** to stone sb to death; **donner un ~ de dents/de bec** to take a bite, peck (*dans* at); **~ de feu** shot; **tuer qn d'un ~ de fusil** to shoot sb dead (with a rifle).
(**c**) *(avec le corps)* **~ d'œil** *(regard)* glance; *(spectacle)* view; **jeter un ~ d'œil à** to glance at; **ça vaut le ~ d'œil** it's worth seeing; **~ de coude** nudge; **~ d'ongle** scratch; **l'oiseau donna un ~ d'aile** the bird flapped its wings *ou* gave a flap of its wings; **d'un ~ de tête/de genou** with a nudge *ou* thrust of his head/knee; **donner un ~ de tête contre qch** to bang one's head against sth.
(**d**) *(habileté)* **avoir le ~ *** to have the knack; **avoir le ~ d'œil** to have a good eye.
(**e**) *(avec instrument)* **~ de crayon** stroke of a pencil; **~ de marteau** blow of a hammer; **passer un ~ de chiffon/balai à qch** to give sth a wipe/sweep sth; **donner un ~ de peinture à un mur** to give a wall a coat of paint; **~ de téléphone** phone call; **donner un ~ de frein** to brake.
(**f**) *(Golf, Tennis)* stroke; *(Boxe)* punch; *(Échecs)* move. *(Boxe, fig)* **~ bas** punch below the belt; *(Tennis)* **~ droit** drive; *(Ftbl, Rugby)* **~ d'envoi** kick-off; **~ franc** *(Ftbl, Rugby)* free kick; *(Basketball)* free throw shot.
(**g**) *(bruit)* **~ de tonnerre** *(lit)* thunderclap; *(fig)* bombshell; **~ de sonnette** ring; **arrêtez au ~ de sifflet** stop when the whistle blows; **les douze ~s de midi** the twelve strokes of noon.
(**h**) *(produit par les éléments)* **~ de vent** gust of wind; **passer en ~ de vent** to rush past like a whirlwind; *(visite)* to pay a flying visit; **~(s) de soleil** sunburn; **prendre un ~ de soleil** to get sunburnt *ou* sunburned *(US)*; **prendre un ~ de froid** to catch a chill.
(**i**) *(événement fortuit)* **~ du sort** blow dealt by fate; **~ de chance** stroke of luck; **~ dur** hard blow; **c'est un sale ~ *** it's a dreadful blow.
(**j**) *(entreprise) [cambrioleurs]* job. **tenter le ~ *** to have a go *; **réussir un beau ~** to pull it off; **être dans le ~/hors du ~** to be/not to be in on it.
(**k**) *(*: contre qn)* trick. **faire un sale ~ à qn** to play a dirty trick on sb; **il nous fait le ~ chaque fois** he never fails to do that; **tu ne vas pas nous faire le ~ d'être malade** you're not going to go and be ill on us *; **un ~ en traître** a stab in the back.
(**l**) *(*: verre)* **boire un ~** to have a drink; **il a bu un ~ de trop** he's had one too many *.
(**m**) *(*: fois)* time. **à tous (les) ~s** every time; **du premier ~** first time, right off the bat * *(US)*; **pour un ~** for once; **rire un bon ~** to have a good laugh.
(**n**) *(effet)* **sous le ~ de** *surprise* in the grip of, affected by; *(Admin)* **tomber sous le ~ de la loi** to be a statutory offence.
(**o**) *(locutions)* **à ~ sûr** definitely; **après ~** after the event; **~ sur ~** in quick succession; **du ~** as a result; **c'est pour le ~ qu'il se fâcherait** then he'd really get angry; **sur le ~** *(gén)* outright; *tué* instantly; **sur le ~ je n'ai pas compris** at the time I didn't understand; **d'un seul ~** at one go; **tout à ~** all of a sudden; **tenir le ~** to hold out.
2 : *(fig)* **~ d'arrêt** sharp check; *(Jur)* **~s et blessures** assault and grievous bodily harm; **~ de boutoir** thrust; *(lit, fig)* **~ de dés** toss of the dice; **~ d'éclat** glorious feat; **~ d'essai** first attempt; **~ d'État** coup (d'état); *(fig)* **~ de filet** haul; **~ de force** armed takeover; *(fig)* **~ de foudre** love at first sight; *(lit, fig)* **~ de grâce** finishing blow; **~ de grisou** firedamp explosion; **~ de Jarnac** stab in the back; **~ de main** *(aide)* helping hand; *(raid)* raid; **donne-moi un ~ de main** give me a hand; **~ de maître** master stroke; **~ monté** set-up *; **~ de pouce** *(pour aider qn)* push in the right direction; **~ de sang** stroke; **~ de tête** sudden impulse; **~ de théâtre** *(Théât)* coup de théâtre; *(gén)* dramatic turn of events; **~ de Trafalgar** underhand trick.

coupable [kupabl(ə)] **1** *adj personne* guilty (*de* of); *désirs* guilty; *négligence* culpable. **2** *nmf* culprit.

coupage [kupaʒ] *nm (action)* blending; *(avec de l'eau)* dilution; *(résultat)* blend. **~s** blended wines.

coupant, e [kupɑ̃, ɑ̃t] *adj lame, ton* sharp.

coupe¹ [kup] *nf* (**a**) *(à fruits)* dish; *(contenu)* dishful; *(à boire)* goblet. (**b**) *(Sport)* cup. **la ~ de France de football** the French football cup.

coupe² [kup] *nf* (**a**) *(action) (gén)* cutting; *[tissu]* cutting-out; *[arbre]* cutting-down. (**b**) *(résultat)* cut. **~ de cheveux** haircut. (**c**) *(section)* section. (**d**) **être sous la ~ de qn** to be under sb's control; **faire des ~s sombres dans** to make drastic cuts in; **mettre en ~ réglée** to bleed systematically *(fig)*; *V aussi* **couper 5.**

coupé [kupe] *nm (Aut, Danse)* coupé.

couper [kupe] (1) **1** *vt* (**a**) *(gén)* to cut; *bois* to chop; *arbre* to cut down; *rôti* to carve; *(Couture) vêtement* to cut out; *gâteau* to slice; *(fig) [vent]* to sting. **~ la gorge à qn** to slit sb's throat; **~ la tête à qn** to chop sb's head off; **se faire ~ les cheveux** to get one's hair cut. (**b**) *(raccourcir, retrancher)* to cut; *(séparer)* to cut off; *(entailler)* to slit. (**c**) *route, relations, vivres* to cut off; *fièvre* to bring down; *appétit* to take away; *eau, gaz* to cut off; *(au compteur)* to turn off. *(Aut)* **~ le contact** to switch off the ignition; **~ le vent** to cut out the wind; **~ la route à qn** to cut in front of sb; **~ qn de** to cut sb off from; **~ les ponts avec qn** to break off communications with sb. (**d**) *voyage* to break; *journée* to break up. (**e**) *[ligne]* to cut; *[route]* to cut across. *(fig)* **l'électorat était coupé en deux** the voters were split down the middle. (**f**) *(Cartes) jeu* to cut; *(avec l'atout)* to trump. (**g**) *[vin]* to blend; *(avec de l'eau)* to dilute. (**h**) *(locutions)* **~ les bras à qn** *[travail]* to wear sb out; *[nouvelle]* to knock sb for six; **j'en ai les jambes coupées** I'm stunned by it; **~ la poire en deux** to meet halfway; **~ les cheveux en quatre** to split hairs; **~ ses effets à qn** to steal sb's thunder; **~ l'herbe sous le pied à qn** to cut the ground from under sb's feet; **~ la parole à qn** *[personne]* to cut sb short; *[émotion]* to leave *ou* render sb speechless; **~ le sifflet * à qn** to shut sb up *; **~ le souffle à qn** *(lit)* to wind sb; *(fig)* to take sb's breath away; **c'est à vous ~ le souffle** it's breathtaking; **brouillard/accent à ~ au couteau** fog/accent you could cut with a knife.
2 ~ à *vt indir* (**a**) *corvée* to get out of. **tu n'y couperas pas** you won't get out of it. (**b**) **~ court à** to cut short.
3 *vi (gén)* to cut; *(jouer atout)* to trump. **~ à travers champs** to cut across country; **~ au plus court** to take the quickest way.
4 se ~ *vpr* (**a**) to cut o.s. **se ~ à la jambe/les ongles** to cut one's leg/one's nails. (**b**) (*) to give o.s. away.
5 : **coupe-circuit** *nm inv* cutout; **coupe-coupe** *nm inv* machete; **coupe-faim** *nm inv* appetite suppressant; **coupe-feu** *nm inv* firebreak; **coupe-gorge** *nm inv* death-trap; **coupe-papier** *nm inv* paper knife; **coupe-vent** *nm inv (haie)* windbreak; *(vêtement)* windcheater, windbreaker *(US)*.

couperet [kupʀɛ] *nm [boucher]* cleaver, chopper; *[guillotine]* blade.

couple [kupl(ə)] *nm (gén)* couple; *(patineurs, animaux)* pair; *(moteur, de torsion)* torque. ◆ **coupler** (1) *vt* to couple together; *(Ordin)* to interface (*avec* with).

couplet [kuplɛ] *nm [chanson]* verse.

coupole [kupɔl] *nf* dome; *(petite)* cupola.

coupon [kupɔ̃] *nm* (**a**) *(Couture) (reste)* remnant; *(rouleau)* roll. (**b**) *(Fin: ticket)* coupon. **~-réponse** reply coupon.

coupure [kupyʀ] *nf (gén)* cut; *(fig: fossé)* break; *(billet de banque)* note. ~ **(de presse)** (newspaper) cutting; ~ **(de courant)** power cut.

cour [kuʀ] *nf* (**a**) *(gén)* (court)yard; *[gare]* forecourt; *[caserne]* square. **être sur (la)** ~ to look onto the (court)yard; ~ **d'école** schoolyard, playground; ~ **de ferme** farmyard; ~ **de récréation** playground. (**b**) *(Jur)* court. ~ **d'appel/de cassation** Court of Appeal/of Cassation; *(Mil)* ~ **martiale** court martial. (**c**) *[roi]* court; *[écrivain, femme]* following. **faire sa** ~ **à** *roi* to pay court to; *supérieur* to pay one's respects to; **être bien/mal en** ~ to be in/out of favour (*auprès de qn* with sb); **faire la** ~ **à une femme** to court a woman.

courage [kuʀaʒ] *nm (bravoure)* courage, bravery; *(ardeur)* will, spirit. **vous n'aurez pas le** ~ **de** you won't have the heart to; **entreprendre qch avec** ~ to undertake sth with a will; **je ne m'en sens pas le** ~ I don't feel up to it; **ça vous donnera du** ~ it'll buck you up *; ~! cheer up!, take heart!; **perdre** ~ to lose heart; **reprendre** ~ to take fresh heart. ◆ **courageusement** *adv* bravely, courageously; *entreprendre* with a will. ◆ **courageux, -euse** *adj* brave, courageous. **il n'est pas très** ~ **pour l'étude** he hasn't got much will for studying.

couramment [kuʀamɑ̃] *adv* (**a**) *(aisément)* fluently. (**b**) *(souvent)* commonly. **ce mot s'emploie** ~ this word is in current usage; **cela se fait** ~ it's quite common practice.

courant, e [kuʀɑ̃, ɑ̃t] **1** *adj* (**a**) *dépenses, usage* everyday, standard; *(Comm) modèle* standard; *incident* common. **il n'est pas** ~ **de voir** it is quite uncommon to see. (**b**) *(en cours) année* current. *(Comm)* **votre lettre du 5** ~ your letter of the 5th inst. *ou* instant *ou* of the 5th of this month. **2** *nm* (**a**) *[cours d'eau]* current; *[populations, commerce]* movement; *[opinions]* trend. ~ **(atmosphérique)** airstream, current; **un** ~ **de sympathie** a wave of sympathy; *(Littérat)* **le** ~ **surréaliste** the surrealist movement. (**b**) *(Élec)* current. **couper le** ~ to cut off the power. (**c**) **dans le** ~ **du mois** in the course of the month; **dans le** ~ **de la conversation** in the course of the conversation *ou* as the conversation was (*ou* is) going on; **être au** ~ **de** *nouvelle* to know about; *science* to be well-informed about; *méthodes* to be up to date on; **mettre qn au** ~ **de** *faits* to tell sb (about); *théories* to bring sb up to date on; **tenez-moi au** ~ keep me informed ; **il se tient au** ~ he keeps himself up to date *ou* informed.

courbature [kuʀbatyʀ] *nf* ache. ◆ **courbaturé, e** *adj* aching (all over).

courber [kuʀbe] (1) **1** *vt* to bend. **l'âge l'avait courbé** he was bowed *ou* bent with age; ~ **la tête** *(lit)* to bow *ou* bend one's head; *(fig)* to submit. **2** *vi* to bend. **3 se** ~ *vpr [branche]* to bend; *(lit, fig) [personne]* to bend down. ◆ **courbe 1** *adj* curved. **2** *nf* curve. ~ **de niveau** contour line; ~ **de température** temperature curve. ◆ **courbette** *nf* low bow. *(fig)* **faire des ~s à** *ou* **devant qn** to kowtow to sb, bow and scrape to sb. ◆ **courbure** *nf* curve.

courette [kuʀɛt] *nf* small courtyard.

coureur, -euse [kuʀœʀ, øz] **1** *nm, f (Athlétisme)* runner. ~ **de fond** long-distance runner; ~ **automobile** racing(-car) driver; ~ **cycliste** racing cyclist; ~ **de dot** fortune hunter. **2** *nm*: **c'est un** ~ **de cafés** he hangs round *ou* around cafés ; ~ **(de filles)** womanizer. **3** *nf (péj)* manhunter.

courge [kuʀʒ(ə)] *nf (plante)* gourd; *(Culin)* marrow, squash *(US)*. ◆ **courgette** *nf* courgette.

courir [kuʀiʀ] (11) **1** *vi* (**a**) *(gén)* to run; *(Aut, Cyclisme)* to race. **entrer/sortir en courant** to run in/out; ~ **à toutes jambes** to run like the wind; ~ **ventre à terre** to run flat out; **faire** ~ **un cheval** to race a horse. (**b**) *(se précipiter)* to rush. ~ **chercher le docteur** to rush *ou* run for the doctor; **je cours l'appeler** I'll run and call him; **faire qch en courant** to do sth in a rush; **tu peux toujours** ~! * you can whistle for it! * (**c**) *(avec à, après, sur)* ~ **à l'échec** to be heading *ou* headed for failure; ~ **à sa perte** *ou* **ruine** to be on the road to ruin; ~ **après qch** to chase after sth; *(lit, fig)* ~ **après qn** to run after sb; ~ **sur ses 20 ans** to be approaching 20. (**d**) *[nuages, ombres, reflets]* to speed, race; *[eau]* to rush; *[chemin]* to run. **un frisson lui courut par tout le corps** a shiver ran through his body. (**e**) **faire** ~ **un bruit** to spread a rumour; **le bruit court que...** there is a rumour going round that... (**f**) *(se passer)* **le mois qui court** the current month; **par les temps qui courent** nowadays; **laisser** ~ * to let things alone. (**g**) *(Fin) [intérêt]* to accrue. **2** *vt* (**a**) *(Sport) épreuve* to compete in. ~ **un 100 mètres** to run (in) *ou* compete in a 100 metres race; ~ **le Grand Prix** to race in the Grand Prix. (**b**) *(Chasse)* ~ **le cerf** to go staghunting; *(fig)* ~ **deux lièvres à la fois** to have one's finger in more than one pie. (**c**) *(rechercher) honneurs, aventure* to seek; *risque* to run. **il court de graves dangers** he's running a great risk; ~ **sa chance** to try one's luck. (**d**) *le monde, les bois* to roam; *les magasins* to go round. ~ **les rues** *(lit)* to roam the streets; *(fig)* to be run-of-the-mill; **ça ne court pas les rues** it is hard to find; ~ **les théâtres** to do the rounds of the theatres; ~ **les filles** to chase the girls.

couronne [kuʀɔn] *nf* (**a**) *[fleurs]* wreath. ~ **mortuaire/de lauriers** funeral/laurel wreath; ~ **d'épines** crown of thorns. (**b**) *[roi, pape]* crown; *[noble]* coronet. (**c**) *(objet) [dent]* crown; *(Astron)* corona. **la grande** ~ the outer suburbs (of Paris). ◆ **couronnement** *nm [roi]* coronation, crowning; *[édifice]* top, crown; *[carrière]* crowning achievement. ◆ **couronner** (1) **1** *vt (gén, Méd, fig)* to crown; *ouvrage, auteur* to award a prize to. **front couronné de fleurs** head crowned with flowers; *(iro)* **et pour** ~ **le tout** and to crown it all; **couronné de succès** crowned with success. **2 se** ~ *vpr*: **se** ~ **le genou** to graze its (*ou* one's) knee.

courrier [kuʀje] *nm* (**a**) *(reçu)* mail, letters; *(à écrire)* letters. *(Ordin)* ~ **électronique** electronic mail. (**b**) (†) *(avion, bateau)* mail; *(Mil: estafette)* courier. (**c**) *(Presse) (rubrique)* column, page. ~ **du cœur** broken hearts' column; ~ **des lecteurs** letters to the Editor.

courroie [kuʀwa] *nf* strap; *(Tech)* belt.

courroucer [kuʀuse] (3) *vt (littér)* to incense. ◆ **courroux** *nm* wrath.

cours [kuʀ] *nm* (**a**) *(déroulement, Astron, gén)* course; *[guerre, maladie]* progress; *[rivière] (cheminement)* course; *(écoulement)* flow. **descendre le** ~ **de la Seine** to go down the Seine; ~ **d'eau** river, stream. (**b**) *(Fin) [monnaie]* currency; *[titre, objet]* price; *[devises]* rate. ~ **légal** legal tender. (**c**) *(leçon) (Scol)* class; *(Univ)* lecture; *(série de leçons)* course; *(manuel)* coursebook, textbook. **faire un** ~ **sur** to give a class on; ~ **du soir** *(pl)* evening classes; ~ **par correspondance** correspondence course; ~ **de vacances** holiday course, summer school *(US)*; ~ **intensif** crash course (*de, en* in). (**d**) *(Scol) (établissement)* school. *(année)* ~ **élémentaire** *etc* primary *etc* class *ou* year; ~ **privé** private school. (**e**) *(avenue)* walk. (**f**) *(locutions)* **avoir** ~ *[monnaie]* to be legal tender; *(fig)* to be current; **en** ~ *année* current; *affaires* in hand; *essais* in progress; **en** ~ **de réparation** in the process of being repaired; *(Jur)* **brevet en** ~ **d'agrément** patent pending; **en** ~ **de route** on the way; **au** ~ **de** in the course of; **donner libre** ~ **à** to give free expression to.

course [kuʀs(ə)] *nf* (**a**) *(action)* running. **prendre sa** ~ to start running. (**b**) *(épreuve)* race; *(discipline) (Athlétisme)* running; *(Aut, Courses, Cyclisme)* racing. **faire de la** ~ to go running; **faire de la** ~ **de haies** to hurdle; ~ **de haies** hurdling; ~ **de fond** *(spécialité)* long-distance running; *(épreuve)* long-distance race; *(fig)* **la** ~ **aux armements** the arms race; **faire la** ~ **avec qn** to race with sb; *(Courses)* **parier aux** ~**s** to bet on the races; ~ **de taureaux** bullfight; ~ **de trot** trotting race; ~ **de trot attelé** harness race; ~ **de vitesse** sprint. (**c**) *(fig) [projectile]* flight; *[navire]* course; *[nuages, temps]* swift passage. (**d**) *(excursion) (à pied)* hike; *(ascension)* climb; *(voyage)* journey. *(taxi)* **payer la** ~ to pay the fare. (**e**) *(commission)* errand. **faire une** *ou* **des** ~**s** *[ménagère]* to do some shopping; *[coursier]* to run an errand *ou* errands. (**f**) *(Tech)* movement; *[piston]* stroke. (**g**) **être à bout de** ~ to be worn out; **il n'est plus dans la** ~ * he's out of things now.

courser * [kuʀse] (1) *vt* to chase *ou* hare * after.

coursier, -ière [kuʀsje, jɛʀ] **1** *nm, f* messenger. **2** *nm (littér, cheval)* steed, horse.

court[1], e [kuʀ, kuʀt(ə)] **1** *adj* (**a**) *(gén)* short. **il a été très** ~ he was very brief; **de** ~**e durée** *joie* short-lived; **c'est plus** ~ **par le bois** it's quicker *ou* shorter through the wood; **avoir le souffle** ~ to be short-winded. (**b**) *(insuffisant)* **c'est un peu** ~ it's a bit on the short side. (**c**) **tirer à la** ~**e paille** to draw straws; **à sa** ~**e honte** to his great shame; **être à** ~ **d'argent** to be short of money; **prendre au plus** ~ to go the shortest way; **prendre qn de** ~ to catch sb unawares *ou* unprepared. **2** *adv* short. **s'arrêter** ~ to stop short. **3** : ~**-bouillon** *nm, pl* ~**s-**~**s** court-bouillon; *(Élec)* ~**-circuit** *nm, pl* ~**s-**~**s** short(-circuit); ~**-circuiter** (1) *vt (lit, fig)* to short-circuit; **faire la** ~**e échelle à qn** to give sb a leg up *ou* a boost *(US)*; ~ **métrage** short film.

court[2] [kuʀ] *nm* tennis court. ~ **central** centre court.

courtaud, e [kuʀto, od] *adj* dumpy, squat.

courtier, -ière [kuʀtje, jɛʀ] *nm, f* broker.

courtiser [kuʀtize] (1) *vt* to pay court to. ◆ **courtisan** *nm (Hist)* courtier; *(fig)* sycophant. ◆ **courtisane** *nf (Hist)* courtesan.

courtoisie [kuʀtwazi] *nf* courtesy. ◆ **courtois, e** *adj* courteous; *(Littérat)* courtly. ◆ **courtoisement** *adv* courteously.

couru, e [kuʀy] *adj restaurant* popular. **c'est** ~ * **(d'avance)** it's a sure thing, it's a foregone conclusion.

cousin, e [kuzɛ̃, in] **1** *nm, f* cousin. ~ **germain** first cousin. **2** *nm* mosquito.

coussin [kusɛ̃] *nm* cushion.

cousu, e [kuzy] *adj* sewn, stitched. *(fig)* **c'est** ~ **de fil blanc** it doesn't hold *ou* hang together; ~ **main** *(lit)* handsewn; *(*fig)* **c'est du** ~ **main** it's top quality stuff.

coût [ku] *nm (lit, fig)* cost. **le** ~ **de la vie** the cost of living; **à des** ~**s majorés** on a cost-plus basis; ~**s de base** baseline costs; ~ **du crédit** credit charges; ~ **d'utilisation** cost-in-use. ◆ **coûtant** *adj m*: **prix** ~ cost price.

couteau, *pl* ~**x** [kuto] *nm* (**a**) *(pour couper)* knife; *[balance]* knife edge; *(coquillage)* razor-shell, razor clam *(US)*. ~ **à poisson** fish knife; ~ **à cran d'arrêt** flick-knife; ~ **à découper** carving knife. (**b**) **vous me mettez le** ~ **sous la gorge** you're holding a gun at my head; **être à** ~**x tirés** to be at daggers drawn (*avec* with); **remuer le** ~ **dans la plaie** to twist the knife in the wound.

coutellerie [kutɛlʀi] *nf (industrie)* cutlery industry; *(magasin)* cutler's (shop); *(produits)* cutlery.

coûter [kute] (1) *vti* to cost. **les vacances, ça coûte!** holidays are expensive *ou* cost a lot!; **ça coûte une fortune** it costs a fortune *ou* an arm and a leg; *(fig)* **ça va lui** ~ **cher** he'll pay for that, it will cost him dear; **ça ne coûte rien d'essayer** it costs nothing to try; **cet aveu m'a coûté** this confession cost me; **cette démarche me coûte** it costs me a great effort to take this step; **ça lui a coûté la vie** it cost him his life; **coûte que coûte** at all costs. ◆ **coûteusement** *adv* expensively. ◆ **coûteux, -euse** *adj* costly, expensive.

coutume [kutym] *nf (gén, Jur)* custom. **avoir** ~ **de** to be in the habit of; **plus que de** ~ more than usual; **comme de** ~ as usual; **selon sa** ~ following his usual custom. ◆ **coutumier, -ière** *adj* customary, usual. *(gén péj)* **il est** ~ **du fait** that is what he usually does.

couture [kutyʀ] *nf* (**a**) *(action, ouvrage)* sewing. **la** ~ *(métier)* dressmaking; *(industrie)* the fashion industry; **faire de la** ~ to sew. (**b**) *(suite de points)* seam; *(cicatrice)* scar; *(suture)* stitches. **sans** ~**(s)** seamless; **sous toutes les** ~**s** from every angle. ◆ **couturier** *nm* couturier, fashion designer. ◆ **couturière** *nf* dressmaker.

couvent [kuvɑ̃] *nm [sœurs]* convent; *[moines]* monastery; *(internat)* convent school.

couver [kuve] (1) **1** *vi* (**a**) *[feu, incendie, haine]* to smoulder; *[émeute]* to be brewing; *[complot]* to be hatching. (**b**) *[poule]* to sit on its eggs. **2** *vt* (**a**) *œufs [poule]* to sit on; *[appareil]* to hatch. (**b**) *(fig) enfant* to be overcareful with, cocoon; *maladie* to be sickening for; *vengeance* to brew, plot. ~ **qch des yeux** *(tendresse)* to look lovingly at sth; *(convoitise)* to look covetously *ou* longingly at sth. ◆ **couvée** *nf [poussins, enfants]* brood, clutch; *[œufs]* clutch.

couvercle [kuvɛʀkl(ə)] *nm (gén)* lid; *[aérosol]* cap, top.

couvert, e [kuvɛʀ, ɛʀt(ə)] **1** *adj* (**a**) *(habillé)* covered (up). **trop** ~ too wrapped up; *(chapeau)* **il est resté** ~ he kept his hat on. (**b**) ~ **de** covered in *ou* with; ~ **de chaume** thatched. (**c**) *ciel* overcast. (**d**) *rue* covered. (**e**) *(fig: protégé)* covered. **2** *nm* (**a**) *(ustensiles)* place setting. **les** ~**s en argent** the silver cutlery; **mettre 4** ~**s** to lay *ou* set 4 places, lay *ou* set the table for 4; **le gîte et le** ~ board and lodging, bed *ou* room and board. (**b**) *(au restaurant)* cover charge. (**c**) *(abri)* shelter. **à** ~ **de** sheltered from; *(Mil)* **être/se mettre à** ~ to be/get under *ou* take cover; **se mettre à** ~ **(contre des réclamations)** to cover o.s. (against claims); **sous (le)** ~ **de** *prétexte* under cover of; **sous (le)** ~ **de la plaisanterie** while trying to appear to be joking, under the guise of a joke; **Monsieur le Ministre sous** ~ **de Monsieur le Recteur** the Minister through the person of the Director of Education.

couverture [kuvɛʀtyʀ] *nf* (**a**) *(literie)* blanket. ~ **de voyage** travelling rug; *(fig)* **tirer la** ~ **à soi** to take all the credit. (**b**) *(toiture)* roofing; *[cahier]* cover; *(jaquette)* dust cover; *(Mil, Fin, fig)* cover. ~ **sociale** Social Security cover.

couveuse [kuvøz] *nf (poule)* broody hen. ~ **(artificielle)** incubator.

couvre- [kuvʀ(ə)] *préf V* **couvrir.**

couvreur [kuvʀœʀ] *nm* roofer.

couvrir [kuvʀiʀ] (18) **1** *vt* (**a**) *(gén)* to cover (*de, avec* with). ~ **un toit de chaume/de tuiles** to thatch/tile a roof; **couvre bien les enfants** wrap the children up well; **un châle lui couvrait les épaules** her shoulders were covered with *ou* by a shawl; **couvert de bleus** bruised all over, covered in bruises; ~ **qn d'injures/de cadeaux** to shower insults/gifts on sb; **ça l'a couvert de ridicule** it covered him with ridicule. (**b**) *voix* to drown; *énigme, sentiments* to conceal; *(lit, fig) personne* to cover, shield. ~ **qch du nom de charité** to pass sth off as charity. (**c**) *distance, frais* to cover.
2 se ~ *vpr [personne]* to wrap (o.s.) up; *(chapeau)* to put one's hat on; *[ciel]* to become overcast; *(Boxe, Escrime)* to cover. **se** ~ **de** *taches* to get o.s. covered in; *boutons* to become covered in *ou* with; *gloire, honte* to cover o.s. with.
3 : *(hum)* **couvre-chef** *nm, pl* ~-~**s** hat; **couvre-feu** *nm, pl* ~-~**x** curfew; **couvre-lit** *nm, pl* ~-~**s** bedspread; **couvre-pied(s)** *nm, pl*~-~**s** quilt; **couvre-plat** *nm, pl* ~-~**s** dish cover.

coyote [kɔjɔt] *nm* coyote, prairie wolf.

crabe [kʀɑb] *nm (Zool)* crab. **marcher en** ~ to walk crab-wise.

crac [kʀak] *excl [bois, glace etc]* crack; *[étoffe]* rip; *(fig)* bang.

cracher [kʀaʃe] (1) **1** *vi* (**a**) to spit (*sur* at). **il ne crache pas sur le caviar** * he doesn't turn his nose up at caviar; **il ne faut pas** ~ **sur cette offre** * this offer is not to be sneezed at; **il ne faut pas** ~ **dans la soupe** * you shouldn't turn your nose up at it; **c'est comme si je crachais en l'air** * it's like banging my head against a brick wall. (**b**) *[stylo, plume]* to sputter; *[micro]* to crackle. **2** *vt* (**a**) *sang etc* to spit; *bouchée, injures* to spit out; (‡) *argent* to cough up *, stump up *. (**b**) *[canon]* to spit out; *[cheminée]* to belch out. ◆ **crachat** *nm*: ~**(s)** spit, spittle. ◆ **craché, e** * *adj*: **c'est son père tout** ~ he's the spitting image of his father; **c'est lui tout** ~ that's just like him. ◆ **crachement** *nm [vapeur]* burst; *[étincelles]* shower. ~**(s)** *[salive etc]* spitting; *[radio]* crackle.

crachin [kʀaʃɛ̃] *nm* drizzle.

crack [kʀak] *nm (poulain)* star horse; *(*: as)* ace. **un** ~ **en informatique** an ace *ou* a wizard * at computing.

Cracovie [kʀakɔvi] *n* Cracow.

craie [kʀɛ] *nf* chalk.

craindre [kʀɛ̃dʀ(ə)] (52) *vt* (**a**) *[personne]* to fear, be afraid *ou* scared of. **craignant de manquer le train** afraid of missing *ou* afraid he might miss the train; **elle craignait qu'il ne se blesse** she was afraid that he would *ou* might hurt himself. (**b**) ~ **pour** *vie, réputation, personne* to fear for. (**c**) *[aliment]* ~ **le froid** to be easily damaged by the cold; **'craint l'humidité'** 'keep *ou* store in a dry place'; **c'est un vêtement qui ne craint pas** it's a hard-wearing garment; **il craint la chaleur** he can't stand the heat.

crainte [kʀɛ̃t] *nf* fear. **avoir la** ~ **de qch** to fear *ou* be afraid of sth; **soyez sans** ~ have no fear; **j'ai des** ~**s à son sujet** I'm worried about him; **sans** ~ *(adj)* fearless; *(adv)* fearlessly; **avec** ~ fearfully; **par** ~ **de** for fear of; **de** ~ **que** for fear that, fearing that. ◆ **craintif, -ive** *adj personne* timorous, timid; *ton* timid. ◆ **craintivement** *adv* timorously, timidly.

cramoisi, e [kʀamwazi] *adj* crimson.

crampe [kʀɑ̃p] *nf*: ~**(s)** cramp.

crampon [kʀɑ̃pɔ̃] *nm (Tech)* cramp, clamp; *[chaussure]* stud; *[chaussures de course]* spike; *(*: personne)* clinging bore. ~ **(à glace)** crampon. ◆ **cramponner** (1) **1** *vt (* fig)* to cling to. **2 se** ~ *vpr* to hold on. **se** ~ **à** *branche* to cling to. ◆ **cramponnage** *nm (Alp)* crampon technique, cramponing.

cran [kʀɑ̃] *nm* (**a**) *[crémaillère]* notch; *[arme]* catch; *[ceinture]* hole; *(Couture, Typ)* nick; *[cheveux]* wave. (**b**) **avoir du** ~ * to have guts *; **monter/descendre d'un** ~ to go up/down a notch *ou* peg (*dans* in); **être à** ~ to be very edgy; **ne le mets pas à** ~ don't make him mad *. ◆ **cranté, e** *adj* notched.

crâne [kʀɑn] **1** *nm (Anat)* skull; *(fig)* head. **2** *adj* (†) gallant. ◆ **crânien, -ienne** *adj* cranial.

crâner * [kʀɑne] (1) *vi* to show off. ◆ **crâneur, -euse** * *nm, f* show-off.

crapahuter [kʀapayte] (1) *vi (arg Mil)* to trudge over difficult ground.

crapaud [kʀapo] *nm (Zool)* toad; *[diamant]* flaw.

crapule [kʀapyl] *nf* scoundrel. ◆ **crapulerie** *nf* villainy. ◆ **crapuleux, -euse** *adj action* villainous.

craqueler *vt*, **se** ~ *vpr* [kʀakle] (4) to crack. ◆ **craquelure** *nf* crack.

craquer [kʀake] (1) **1** *vi* (**a**) *(bruit) [parquet]* to creak; *[feuilles]* to crackle; *[neige, biscuit]* to crunch; *[chaussures]* to squeak. (**b**) *(céder) [bas]* to rip; *[glace etc]* to crack; *[branche]* to snap; *[entreprise, athlète]* to collapse; *[accusé, malade]* to break down, collapse. (**c**) *(‡: être enthousiasmé)* to go wild *, flip *, freak out ‡. **2** *vt pantalon, bas* to rip; *allumette* to strike. ◆ **craquement** *nm*: ~**(s)** creak; squeak; crackle; crunch; **casser avec un** ~ to break with a crack *ou* a snap.

crasse [kʀas] **1** *nf (saleté)* grime, filth; *(*: sale tour)* dirty trick *. **2** *adj bêtise* crass. **être d'une ignorance** ~ to be abysmally ignorant *ou* pig ignorant *. ◆ **crasseux, -euse** *adj* grimy, filthy.

cratère [kʀatɛʀ] *nm* crater.

cravache [kʀavaʃ] *nf* riding crop. *(fig)* **mener qn à la** ~ to drive sb ruthlessly. ◆ **cravacher** (1) **1** *vt cheval* to use the crop on. **2** *vi* (*) *(foncer)* to belt along *; *(travailler)* to work like mad *.

cravate [kʀavat] *nf* tie; *(décoration)* ribbon; *(Lutte)* headlock. ◆ **cravater** (1) *vt* (**a**) to put a tie on. **cravaté** wearing a tie; **se** ~ to put one's tie on. (**b**) *(prendre au collet) (gén)* to grab round the neck; *(Lutte)* to put in a headlock; *(*: arrêter)* to collar. **se faire** ~ **par un journaliste** to be collared *ou* buttonholed by a journalist.

crayeux, -euse [kʀɛjø, øz] *adj* chalky.

crayon [kʀɛjɔ̃] *nm (gén)* pencil; *(dessin)* pencil drawing. **notes au** ~ pencilled notes; ~ **à bille** ballpoint pen; ~ **de couleur** crayon, coloured pencil; ~**-feutre** felt-tip pen; ~ **noir** *ou* **à papier** lead pencil; ~ **optique** light pen; ~ **pour les yeux** eyeliner pencil. ◆ **crayonner** (1) *vt notes* to scribble; *dessin* to sketch.

créance [kʀeɑ̃s] *nf* (**a**) *[créancier]* financial claim; *(titre)* letter of credit. *(Fin)* ~**s** accounts receivable. (**b**) *(†: foi)* credence. **donner** ~ **à qch** *(rendre croyable)* to lend credibility to sth; *(ajouter foi à)* to give credence to sth. ◆ **créancier, -ière** *nm, f* creditor.

créateur, -trice [kʀeatœʀ, tʀis] **1** *adj* creative. **2** *nm, f (gén, Rel)* creator. ◆ **créatif, -ive 1** *adj* creative, inventive. **2** *nm* designer. ◆ **création** *nf (gén)* creation; *(Théât: représentation)* first production; *(Comm: produit)* product. *(Scol, Ind etc)* **il y a deux** ~**s de poste** two new posts have been created. ◆ **créativité** *nf* creativity.

créature [kʀeatyʀ] *nf (gén)* creature.

crécelle [kʀesɛl] *nf* rattle.

crèche [kʀɛʃ] *nf* (**a**) *(Rel: de Noël)* crib. (**b**) *(établissement)* crèche, day nursery.

crédibilité [kʀedibilite] *nf* credibility. ◆ **crédible** *adj* credible.

crédit [kʀedi] *nm* (**a**) *(Fin)* credit. **faire** ~ **à qn** to give sb credit; **acheter/vendre qch à** ~ to buy/sell sth on credit; **porter une somme au ~ de qn** to credit a sum to sb; ~ **hypothécaire** mortgage; ~ **d'appoint** standby credit; ~ **bail** leasing; ~**s budgétaires** budget allocation; ~ **à la consommation** consumer credit; *(Scol, Admin)* ~**s d'enseignement** government grant (to each school); ~**s extraordinaires** extraordinary funds. (**b**) *(prestige, confiance)* credit. **donner du ~ à qch** to give credit to sth; **avoir du ~** *[firme]* to be creditworthy; *[théorie]* to be widely accepted (*auprès de* by); **faire ~ à** to trust *ou* have faith in; **trouver/perdre ~ auprès de qn** to win/lose sb's confidence. ◆ **créditer** (1) *vt (Fin, Sport)* ~ **qn de** to credit sb with. ◆ **créditeur, -trice 1** *adj* in credit. **solde ~** credit balance. **2** *nm, f* customer in credit.

credo [kʀedo] *nm (Rel, fig)* creed.

crédule [kʀedyl] *adj* credulous, gullible. ◆ **crédulité** *nf* credulity, gullibility.

créer [kʀee] (1) *vt* (**a**) *(gén)* to create. **la joie de ~** the joy of creation; **se ~ une clientèle** to build up a clientèle; ~ **des ennuis à qn** to create problems for sb. (**b**) *(Théât) rôle* to create; *pièce* to produce for the first time.

crémaillère [kʀemajɛʀ] *nf* (**a**) *[cheminée]* trammel. *(fig)* **pendre la ~** to have a house-warming party. (**b**) *(Rail, Tech)* rack.

crémation [kʀemɑsjɔ̃] *nf* cremation. ◆ **crématoire 1** *adj* crematory. **2** *nm* crematorium.

crème [kʀɛm] **1** *nf (gén)* cream; *(peau du lait)* skin; *(entremets)* cream dessert. *(liqueur)* ~ **de bananes** crème de bananes; **gâteau à la ~** cream cake; *(fig: les meilleurs)* **la ~** the cream; **la ~ des pères** the best of fathers. **2** *adj inv* cream-coloured. **3** *nm (café)* white coffee. **un grand/petit ~** a large/small cup of white coffee. **4** : ~ **anglaise** egg custard; ~ **de beauté** beauty cream; ~ **Chantilly** *ou* **fouettée** whipped cream; ~ **fraîche** ≃ fresh cream; ~ **fraîche épaisse** ≃ double cream; ~ **glacée** ice cream; ~ **pâtissière** confectioner's custard; ~ **à raser** shaving cream. ◆ **crémerie** *nf (magasin)* dairy. ◆ **crémeux, -euse** *adj* creamy. ◆ **crémier, -ière** *nm, f* dairyman (*ou* woman).

crémone [kʀemɔn] *nf* espagnolette bolt.

créneau, *pl* ~**x** [kʀeno] *nm* (**a**) *[rempart]* crenel. **les ~x** the battlements. (**b**) *(Aut)* **faire un ~** to park *(between two cars)*. (**c**) *[horaire etc]* gap; *(Rad)* slot. ~ **porteur** promising gap in the market. ◆ **crénelé, e** *adj mur* crenellated.

créole [kʀeɔl] **1** *adj* creole. **2** *nmf* Creole.

crêpe [kʀɛp] **1** *nf (Culin)* pancake. **2** *nm (matière)* crepe; *(ruban de deuil)* black ribbon; *(au bras)* black armband.

crêper [kʀepe] (1) *vt cheveux* to backcomb. **se ~ le chignon** * to have a set-to *.

crêperie [kʀɛpʀi] *nf* pancake shop.

crépir [kʀepiʀ] (2) *vt* to roughcast. ◆ **crépi, e** *adj, nm* roughcast. ◆ **crépissage** *nm* roughcasting.

crépiter [kʀepite] (1) *vi [feu]* to crackle; *[friture]* to splutter; *[mitrailleuse]* to rattle out; *[grésil]* to rattle, patter; *[applaudissements]* to break out. ◆ **crépitement** *nm*: ~**(s)** crackling; spluttering; rattle, patter.

crépu, e [kʀepy] *adj cheveux* frizzy.

crépuscule [kʀepyskyl] *nm (lit, fig)* twilight. ◆ **crépusculaire** *adj*: **lumière ~** twilight glow.

crescendo [kʀeʃɛndo] *adv, nm (Mus)* crescendo. *(fig)* **aller ~** to rise in a crescendo, grow louder and louder.

cresson [kʀesɔ̃] *nm*: ~ **(de fontaine)** watercress.

crête [kʀɛt] *nf* (**a**) *[oiseau]* crest. ~ **de coq** cockscomb. (**b**) *[mur]* top; *[toit, montagne]* ridge ; *[vague]* crest; *[graphique]* peak.

Crète [kʀɛt] *nf* Crete. ◆ **crétois, e** *adj, nm,* **C~(e)** *nm(f)* Cretan.

crétin, e [kʀetɛ̃, in] **1** *adj (péj)* cretinous *. **2** *nm, f (péj)* cretin *; *(Méd)* cretin. ◆ **crétinerie** *nf* idiocy.

creuser [kʀøze] (1) **1** *vt* (**a**) *(gén)* to dig; *puits* to sink, bore; *sillon* to plough, plow *(US)*; *(fig) abîme* to create; *problème, idée* to go into deeply, look into closely. (**b**) *(évider) bois* to hollow out; *sol* to dig out, dig a hole in. (**c**) *(locutions)* **la fatigue lui creusait les joues** his face looked gaunt with tiredness; **visage creusé de rides** face furrowed with wrinkles; ~ **les reins** to draw o.s. up; **ça creuse (l'estomac)** * it gives you a real appetite; **se ~ (la cervelle)** * to rack one's brains; **il ne s'est pas beaucoup creusé!** * he didn't overtax himself!; *(lit, fig)* ~ **l'écart** to establish a convincing lead (*par rapport à* over). **2** *vi* to dig (*dans* into). ◆ **creusement** *nm* digging.

creuset [kʀøzɛ] *nm* crucible; *(fig: lieu de brassage)* melting pot.

creux, -euse [kʀø, øz] **1** *adj objet, son* hollow; *estomac* empty; *paroles* empty, hollow; *idées* barren, futile; *raisonnement* weak, flimsy. **les heures ~euses** *(gén)* slack periods; *(pour électricité etc)* off-peak periods. **2** *nm* (**a**) *(gén)* hollow; *(trou)* hole. **le ~ des reins** the small of the back; **le ~ de la main** the hollow of one's hand; **manger dans le ~ de la main** to eat out of one's hand; **le ~ de l'estomac** the pit of the stomach; **avoir un ~ (dans l'estomac)** to feel empty. (**b**) *(Écon: période)* slack period. (**c**) *(Naut) [voile]* belly; *[vague]* trough. **des ~ de 2 mètres** 2-metre high waves; *(fig)* **il est dans le ~ de la vague** his fortunes are at their lowest ebb.

crevaison [kʀəvɛzɔ̃] *nf (Aut)* puncture, flat.

crevant, e ⁑ [kʀəvɑ̃, ɑ̃t] *adj (gén)* killing *.

crevasse [kʀəvas] *nf (gén)* crack; *[mur]* crevice; *[glacier]* crevasse. ◆ **crevasser** *vt,* **se ~** *vpr* (1) to crack.

crever [kʀəve] (5) **1** *vt* (**a**) *(gén)* to burst; *pneu* to puncture. ~ **les yeux à qn** to blind sb; **j'ai un pneu (de) crevé** I've got a flat *ou* a puncture; *(fig)* ~ **le cœur à qn** to break sb's heart; *(fig)* **cela crève les yeux** it stares you in the face!; **cet acteur crève l'écran** this actor has tremendous presence on the screen. (**b**) *(*: exténuer)* ~ **qn** *[personne]* to work sb to death; *[tâche]* to kill sb *; **se ~ (au travail)** to work o.s. to death. (**c**) (⁑) ~ **la faim** to be starving * *ou* famished *.
2 *vi* (**a**) *[pneu]* to puncture. ~ **de jalousie** to be bursting with jealousy. (**b**) *(mourir) [animal, plante]* to die (off); (⁑) *[personne]* to die, snuff it ⁑. **chien crevé** dead dog; ~ **de faim/froid** ⁑ to starve/freeze to death; ~ **de soif** ⁑ to die of thirst; **on crève de chaud ici** * it's boiling in here *; **faire ~ qn** ⁑ to kill sb. (**c**) *(Aut)* to have a puncture, have a flat tyre. ◆ **crevé, e** ⁑ *adj (mort)* dead; *(las)* dead-beat *. ◆ **crève-cœur** *nm inv* heartbreak. ◆ **crève-la-faim** *nmf inv* down-and-out.

crevette [kʀəvɛt] *nf*: ~ **(rose)** prawn; ~ **grise** shrimp.

cri [kʀi] *nm* (**a**) *(gén)* shout, cry; *(hurlement)* yell, howl; *(aigu)* squeal; *[peur]* scream, shriek; *(appel)* call; *(exclamation)* cry. ~ **du cœur** cry from the heart; ~ **de guerre** war cry; ~ **primal** primal scream; **elle jeta un ~ de douleur** she cried out in pain, she gave a cry of pain. (**b**) *[animal] (appel)* call; *(douleur)* squeal. *(générique)* **quel est le ~ du chien?** what noise does a dog make? (**c**) *(littér: crissement)* screech.

criailler [kʀiɑje] (1) *vi (rouspéter)* to grouse *, grumble. ~ **après qn** to nag at sb. ◆ **criailleries** *nfpl* grousing *, grumbling; nagging.

criant, e [kʀijɑ̃, ɑ̃t] *adj (gén)* glaring; *vérité* striking. **portrait ~ de vérité** portrait strikingly true to life.

criard, e [kʀijaʀ, aʀd(ə)] *adj (péj) enfant* squalling; *femme* scolding; *oiseau* squawking; *son* piercing; *couleurs, vêtement* loud, garish.

cribler [kʀible] (1) *vt graines* to sift; *charbon* to riddle, screen. ~ **qn de** *balles* to riddle sb with; *questions* to bombard sb with. ◆ **criblage** *nm* sifting; riddling; screening. ◆ **crible** *nm (à main)* riddle; *(Ind)* screen. **passer au** ~ *(lit)* to riddle; *(fig)* to examine closely. ◆ **criblé, e** *adj*: ~ **de** *taches* covered in; *dettes* crippled with.

cric [kʀik] *nm* (car) jack.

cricket [kʀikɛt] *nm (Sport)* cricket.

criée [kʀije] *nf (salle)* auction room. **(vente à la)** ~ (sale by) auction.

crier [kʀije] (7) **1** *vi* (**a**) *(gén)* to shout, cry out; *(hurler)* to yell, howl; *(aigu)* to squeal; *(de peur)* to scream, shriek (*de* with); *[appel]* to call out. ~ **de douleur** to cry *ou* scream out in pain; ~ **contre qn** to nag at *ou* go on at sb; **tes parents vont** ~ your parents are going to make a fuss; ~ **contre qch** to shout about sth; ~ **au scandale** to call it a scandal; ~ **au loup** to cry wolf. (**b**) *[animal] (appel)* to call; *(douleur)* to squeal; *[plancher]* to creak; *[frein]* to screech.
2 *vt ordre, injures* to shout out, yell out; *mépris, innocence* to proclaim; *marchandise* to shout, cry. ~ **à qn de se taire** to shout at sb to be quiet; ~ **qch sur les toits** to cry sth from the rooftops; ~ **casse-cou** to warn of a danger; **sans** ~ **gare** without a warning; ~ **grâce** to beg for mercy; ~ **famine** to cry famine; ~ **vengeance** to cry out for vengeance. ◆ **crieur, -euse** *nm, f*: ~ **de journaux** newspaper seller; *(Hist)* ~ **public** town crier.

crime [kʀim] *nm (gén)* crime; *(meurtre)* murder. ~**s de guerre** war crimes; **le** ~ **ne paie pas** crime doesn't pay; **ce n'est pas un** ~! it's not a crime! ◆ **criminalité** *nf* criminality. **grande/petite** ~ serious/petty crime. ◆ **criminalisation** *nf* criminalization. ◆ **criminel, -elle 1** *adj (gén, Jur)* criminal. **2** *nm, f* murderer (*ou* murderess); criminal. *(hum)* **voilà le** ~ there's the culprit *ou* the guilty party. ◆ **criminellement** *adv agir* criminally. ◆ **criminologie** *nf* criminology.

Crimée [kʀime] *nf*: **la** ~ the Crimea, the Crimean peninsula; **la guerre de** ~ the Crimean War.

crin [kʀɛ̃] *nm* horsehair. *(fig)* **à tout** ~ diehard. ◆ **crinière** *nf [animal]* mane; *[personne]* mop of hair.

crique [kʀik] *nf* creek, inlet.

criquet [kʀikɛ] *nm* locust.

crise [kʀiz] *nf* (**a**) *(Méd)* attack; *[épilepsie]* fit; *(fig: accès)* outburst, fit; *(lubie)* mood. ~ **cardiaque/de foie** heart/liverish attack; ~ **de nerfs** fit of hysterics; ~ **de toux** fit *ou* bout of coughing; **piquer une** ~ * to throw a tantrum. (**b**) *(moral, Pol, Écon)* crisis. **en état de** ~ in a state of crisis. ~ **de la quarantaine** midlife crisis. (**c**) *(pénurie)* shortage. ~ **du logement** housing shortage.

crisper [kʀispe] (1) **1** *vt* (**a**) *(contracter) muscles* to tense; *poings* to clench. (**b**) *(*: agacer)* ~ **qn** to get on sb's nerves *. **2 se** ~ *vpr [visage]* to tense; *[sourire]* to become strained; *[poing]* to clench; *[personne]* to get tense. **ses mains se crispèrent sur le volant** his hands tightened *ou* tensed on the wheel. ◆ **crispant, e** *adj (énervant)* irritating. ◆ **crispation** *nf* (**a**) *[traits, visage]* tensing; *[muscles]* contraction. (**b**) *(spasme)* twitch. **des** ~**s nerveuses** nervous twitches. (**c**) *(nervosité)* state of tension. ◆ **crispé, e** *adj* tense.

crisser [kʀise] (1) *vi [gravier]* to crunch; *[pneus]* to screech; *[soie]* to rustle. ◆ **crissement** *nm*: ~**(s)** crunch; screech; rustle.

cristal, *pl* **-aux** [kʀistal, o] *nm* crystal; *(objet)* piece of crystal. ~ **de roche** rock crystal; ~**aux de soude** washing soda; ~**aux de givre** ice crystals; **affichage à** ~**aux liquides** liquid crystal display. ◆ **cristallerie** *nf* crystal glassworks. ◆ **cristallin, e 1** *adj (Min)* crystalline; *son* crystal-clear. **2** *nm (Anat)* crystalline lens. ◆ **cristallisation** *nf (gén)* crystallization. ◆ **cristalliser** *vti,* **se** ~ *vpr* (1) to crystallize.

critère [kʀitɛʀ] *nm* criterion.

critérium [kʀiteʀjɔm] *nm (Cyclisme)* rally; *(Natation)* gala.

critique [kʀitik] **1** *adj (gén, Sci)* critical. **avoir l'esprit** ~ to have a critical mind; **il s'est montré très** ~ **(au sujet de...)** he was very critical (of...). **2** *nf* (**a**) *(blâme)* criticism. **la** ~ **est aisée** it's easy to criticize. (**b**) *[œuvre]* appreciation, critique; *[livre, spectacle]* review. **la** ~ *(métier)* criticism; *(personnes)* the critics; **faire la** ~ **de** *film* to review; *poème* to write an appreciation *ou* a critique of. **3** *nmf* critic. ~ **d'art** art critic. ◆ **critiquable** *adj* open to criticism. ◆ **critiquer** (1) *vt (blâmer)* to criticize, find fault with; *(juger) œuvre* to write a critique of.

croasser [kʀɔase] (1) *vi* to caw. ◆ **croassement** *nm* caw.

croc [kʀo] *nm (dent)* fang; *(crochet)* hook. *(lit, fig)* **montrer les** ~**s** to bare its (*ou* one's) teeth. ◆ **croc-en-jambe,** *pl* **crocs-en-jambe** *nm (lit, fig)* **faire un** ~ **à qn** to trip sb up.

croche [kʀɔʃ] *nf (Mus)* quaver.

croche-pied, *pl* **croche-pieds** [kʀɔʃpje] *nm* = **croc-en-jambe.**

crochet [kʀɔʃɛ] **1** *nm* (**a**) *(gén, Boxe)* hook; *[vêtement]* fastener; *[serpent]* fang; *[cambrioleur]* picklock. *(Typ)* **entre** ~**s** in square brackets; **vivre aux** ~**s de qn** to live off sb. (**b**) *(aiguille)* crochet hook; *(technique)* crochet. **faire qch au** ~ to crochet sth. (**c**) *[véhicule]* sudden swerve; *[route]* sudden turn; *[voyage]* detour. **faire un** ~ *(pour éviter)* to swerve; *(par une ville)* to make a detour (*par* through). **2** : ~ **radiophonique** talent show. ◆ **crocheter** (5) *vt serrure* to pick; *porte* to pick the lock on. ◆ **crochu, e** *adj nez* hooked; *doigts* claw-like.

crocodile [kʀɔkɔdil] *nm* crocodile.

crocus [kʀɔkys] *nm* crocus.

croire [kʀwaʀ] (44) **1** *vt* (**a**) to believe. **auriez-vous cru cela de lui?** would you have believed it of him?; **je te crois sur parole** I'll take your word for it; **le croira qui voudra, mais...** believe it or not (but)... (**b**) *(penser)* to believe, think. **elle croyait avoir perdu son sac** she thought she had lost her bag; **il a cru bien faire** he meant well; **je crois que oui** I think so; **on les croyait morts/en France** they were believed dead/to be in France; **il n'a pas cru utile de me prévenir** he didn't think it necessary to warn me. (**c**) **en** ~: **à l'en** ~ if you were to listen to what he says; **s'il faut en** ~ **les journaux** if we are to believe the papers; **vous pouvez m'en** ~ you can take it from me; **si vous m'en croyez** if you want my opinion; **il n'en croyait pas ses yeux** he couldn't believe his eyes. (**d**) *(locutions)* **c'est à** ~ **qu'il est sourd** you'd think he was deaf; **c'est à n'y pas** ~! it's unbelievable!; **il est à** ~ **que, il faut** ~ **que** it would seem that; **il ne croyait pas si bien dire!** he didn't know how right he was!; **on croirait une hirondelle** it looks like a swallow; **on croirait une clarinette** it sounds like a clarinet; **on croirait qu'elle ne comprend pas** she doesn't seem to understand; **tu ne peux pas** ~ **combien il nous manque** you cannot imagine how much we miss him; **je vous crois!** * you bet! *, rather!; **on croit rêver!** * the mind boggles! * **2** *vi (Rel)* to be a believer. **3** ~ **à,** ~ **en** *vt indir* to believe in; *(avec confiance)* to have faith *ou* confidence in. **on a cru d'abord à un accident** at first they took it for an accident; **veuillez** ~ **à mes sentiments dévoués** yours sincerely; **il croit trop en lui-même** he is too self-confident. **4 se** ~ *vpr* to have an inflated opinion of o.s. **il se croit malin** he thinks he's clever.

croisade [kʀwazad] *nf (Hist, fig)* crusade.

croisé, e [kʀwaze] **1** *adj veste* double-breasted; *rimes* alternate. **2** *nm (Hist)* crusader. **3** *nf (littér: fenêtre)* casement *(littér)*. *(lit, fig)* **à la ~ des chemins** at the crossroads, at the parting of the ways.

croisement [kʀwazmɑ̃] *nm* (**a**) *[fils]* crossing; *[véhicules]* passing. (**b**) *(Bio, Zool) (action)* crossing (*avec* with); *(résultat)* cross. (**c**) *(carrefour)* crossroads, junction. **au ~ des deux routes** where the two roads cross.

croiser [kʀwaze] (1) **1** *vt* (**a**) *(gén)* to cross; *bras* to fold; *[route, ligne]* to cut across. **elle croisa son châle sur sa poitrine** she folded her shawl across her chest; **les jambes croisées** cross-legged; *(lit, fig)* **~ le fer** to cross swords (*avec* with). (**b**) *véhicule, passant* to pass. **son regard croisa le mien** his eyes met mine. (**c**) *animaux, plantes* to cross (*avec* with). **2** *vi (Habillement)* to overlap; *(Naut)* to cruise. **3 se ~** *vpr [chemins, lignes, lettres]* to cross; *[regards]* to meet; *[personnes, véhicules]* to pass each other. *(fig)* **se ~ les bras** to sit around idly.

croiseur [kʀwazœʀ] *nm* cruiser *(warship)*.

croisière [kʀwazjɛʀ] *nf* cruise. **faire une ~** to go on a cruise.

croissance [kʀwasɑ̃s] *nf* growth, development.

croissant [kʀwasɑ̃] *nm (forme)* crescent; *(Culin)* croissant. **en ~** crescent-shaped.

croître [kʀwatʀ(ə)] (55) *vi [enfant, plante]* to grow; *[sentiment, bruit, quantité]* to grow, increase; *[jours]* to get longer; *[chaleur]* to get more and more intense, keep on rising; *[lune]* to wax.

croix [kʀwa] *nf (gén)* cross. **C~-Rouge/de guerre** *etc* Red/Military *etc* Cross; **~ gammée** swastika; **disposé en ~** arranged crosswise; **mettre en ~** to crucify; **mise en ~** crucifixion; **les bras en ~** with one's arms out-spread; **pour le faire sortir, c'est la ~ et la bannière** * it's the devil's own job to get him to go out *; **les noms marqués d'une ~** the names with a cross against *ou* by *(US)* them; **tu peux faire une ~ dessus** * you might as well forget it! *, you can kiss that goodbye *.

croquant, e [kʀɔkɑ̃, ɑ̃t] *adj* crisp, crunchy.

croquer [kʀɔke] (1) **1** *vt* (**a**) *bonbons* to crunch; *fruits* to munch. **~ de l'argent** to squander money. (**b**) *(dessiner)* to sketch. **joli à ~** as pretty as a picture; **tu es à ~ avec ce chapeau** you look good enough to eat in this hat. **2** *vi [fruit]* to be crunchy, be crisp; *[salade]* to be crisp. **~ dans une pomme** to bite into an apple. ◆ **croque-mitaine,** *pl* **croque-mitaines** *nm* bog(e)y man, ogre. ◆ **croque-monsieur** *nm inv toasted cheese sandwich with ham.* ◆ **croque-mort,** *pl* **croque-morts** *nm* undertaker's *ou* mortician's *(US)* assistant.

croquet [kʀɔkɛ] *nm* croquet.

croquette [kʀɔkɛt] *nf* croquette.

croquis [kʀɔki] *nm* sketch.

cross(-country) [kʀɔs(kuntʀi)] *nm (course)* cross-country race *ou* run; *(Sport)* cross-country racing *ou* running. **faire du ~** to do cross-country running.

crosse [kʀɔs] *nf* (**a**) *[fusil]* butt; *[revolver]* grip; *[violon]* head. (**b**) *(bâton) (Rel)* crook, crosier. *(Sport)* **~ de golf** golf club; **~ de hockey** hockey stick. (**c**) **chercher des ~s à qn** * to pick a quarrel with sb.

crotale [kʀɔtal] *nm* rattlesnake, rattler * *(US)*.

crotte [kʀɔt] *nf*: **de la ~** *(excrément)* manure, dung; *(boue)* mud; **~s** *[lapin]* droppings; **des ~s** *ou* **une ~ de chien** some dog's dirt; **~ de chocolat** chocolate. ◆ **crotter** (1) *vt* to muddy. **souliers tout crottés** muddy shoes. ◆ **crottin** *nm* (**a**) dung, manure. (**b**) *(fromage)* (small) cheese *(usually made of goat's milk)*.

crouler [kʀule] (1) *vi (lit, fig: s'écrouler)* to collapse; *[toit]* to cave in; *[civilisation]* to totter; *[empire, mur]* to crumble. **la salle croulait sous les applaudissements** the room shook with the applause. ◆ **croulant, e** *adj mur* crumbling, tumbledown; *autorité, empire* crumbling.

croup [kʀup] *nm (Méd)* croup.

croupe [kʀup] *nf [cheval]* rump, hindquarters; (*) *[personne]* rump; *[colline]* top. **monter en ~** to ride pillion.

croupier [kʀupje] *nm* croupier.

croupir [kʀupiʀ] (2) *vi [eau]* to stagnate. **feuilles qui croupissent dans la mare** leaves which rot in the pond; *(fig)* **~ dans le vice** to wallow in vice; **~ dans un bled isolé** * to stay in a godforsaken hole *. ◆ **croupi, e** *adj eau* stagnant. ◆ **croupissant, e** *adj eau* stagnant. *(fig)* **une vie ~e** a dead-end life.

croustiller [kʀustije] (1) *vi [pâte]* to be crusty; *[chips]* to be crisp.

croûte [kʀut] *nf* (**a**) *[pain]* crust; *[fromage]* rind; *[vol-au-vent]* case; *[terre, glace]* layer; *[plaie]* scab. **la ~ terrestre** the earth's crust; **à la ~!** * *(allons manger)* let's go and eat! (**b**) *(cuir)* hide. (**c**) *(péj: tableau)* daub.

croûton [kʀutɔ̃] *nm (bout du pain)* crust; *(Culin)* crouton; *(péj: personne)* old fossil *.

croyance [kʀwajɑ̃s] *nf* belief (*à, en* in). **la ~ populaire** folk *ou* conventional wisdom. ◆ **croyable** *adj* credible, believable. **pas ~** unbelievable, incredible. ◆ **croyant, e** *nm, f* believer.

cru[1], e[1] [kʀy] *adj* (**a**) *(Culin, Tech)* raw; *fruits* uncooked, raw. **lait ~** milk straight from the cow. (**b**) *lumière, couleur* harsh; *(réaliste) mot* forthright, blunt; *description* raw, blunt; *(grossier)* crude, coarse.

cru[2] [kʀy] *nm (vignoble)* vineyard; *(vin)* wine. *(lit, fig)* **du ~** local; **grand ~** great wine *ou* vintage; **de son (propre) ~** of his own invention.

cruauté [kʀyote] *nf* cruelty (*envers* to); *[animal]* ferocity.

cruche [kʀyʃ] *nf* (**a**) *(récipient)* pitcher, jug. (**b**) *(*: imbécile)* ass *, twit ⁑.

crucial, e, *mpl* **-aux** [kʀysjal, o] *adj* crucial.

crucifier [kʀysifje] (7) *vt (lit, fig)* to crucify. ◆ **crucifix** *nm* crucifix. ◆ **crucifixion** *nf* crucifixion.

cruciforme [kʀysifɔʀm(ə)] *adj* cruciform. **tournevis ~** Phillips screwdriver; **vis ~** Phillips screw.

crudité [kʀydite] *nf* (**a**) *[langage]* crudeness, coarseness; *[description]* bluntness; *[couleur, lumière]* harshness. (**b**) *(Culin)* **~s** ≃ mixed salad.

crue[2] [kʀy] *nf (montée des eaux)* rise in the water level; *(inondation)* flood. **en ~** in spate.

cruel, -elle [kʀyɛl] *adj (gén)* cruel; *animal* ferocious; *sort* harsh; *froid, nécessité* bitter. ◆ **cruellement** *adv* cruelly; ferociously; harshly; bitterly. **~ éprouvé** sorely distressed; **c'est ~ vrai** it's sadly true.

cruiser [kʀuzœʀ] *nm (bateau de plaisance)* cruiser.

crûment [kʀymɑ̃] *adv (nettement)* bluntly, forthrightly; *(grossièrement)* crudely, coarsely. **éclairer ~** to cast a harsh *ou* garish light over.

crustacé [kʀystase] *nm (Zool)* shellfish. *(Culin)* **~s** seafood, shellfish.

cryobiologie [kʀjɔbjɔlɔʒi] *nf* cryobiology.

cryochirurgie [kʀjɔʃiʀyʀʒi] *nf* cryosurgery.

crypte [kʀipt(ə)] *nf* crypt.

Cuba [kyba] *nf* Cuba. **à ~** in Cuba. ◆ **cubain, e** *adj*, **C~(e)** *nm(f)* Cuban.

cube [kyb] **1** *nm (gén)* cube; *[jeu]* wooden brick. **élever au ~** to cube. **2** *adj*: **mètre ~** cubic metre. ◆ **cubage** *nm* cubage. **~ d'air** air space. ◆ **cuber** (1) **1** *vt* to cube. **2** *vi (*: augmenter)* to mount up. ◆ **cubique** *adj* cubic. ◆ **cubisme** *nm* cubism. ◆ **cubiste** *adj, nmf* cubist.

cubitus [kybitys] *nm* ulna.

cucul *[kyky] *adj:* ~ **(la praline)** silly, goofy *.

cueillir [kœjiʀ] (12) *vt fleurs, fruits* to pick, gather; *(isolément)* to pick, pluck; *ballon* to catch; *baiser* to snatch; (*) *voleur* to catch, nab *. *(fig)* **il m'a cueilli à froid** he caught me off guard. ◆ **cueillette** *nf (action)* picking; gathering; *(récolte)* harvest *ou* crop of fruit.

cui-cui [kyikyi] *excl, nm* tweet-tweet. **faire** ~ to go tweet-tweet.

cuiller, cuillère [kɥijɛʀ] *nf* spoon; *(contenu)* spoonful; *(Pêche)* spoon, spoon-bait. **serrer la** ~ **à qn** ⁑ to shake sb's paw *; *(gén, Rugby)* ~ **de bois** wooden spoon; ~ **à café** coffee spoon, ≃ teaspoon; ~ **à soupe** soupspoon, ≃ tablespoon. ◆ **cuillerée** *nf* spoonful.

cuir [kɥiʀ] *nm* leather; *(avant tannage)* hide. ~ **brut** rawhide; ~ **chevelu** scalp.

cuirasse [kɥiʀas] *nf [chevalier]* breastplate; *(Zool)* cuirass; *(Naut)* armour(-plate *ou* -plating); *(fig)* armour. ◆ **cuirassé** *nm* battleship. ◆ **cuirasser** (1) *vt chevalier* to put a breastplate on; *navire* to armour-plate; *(fig: endurcir)* to harden *(contre* against). **se** ~ **contre** to harden o.s. against. ◆ **cuirassier** *nm (Hist)* cuirassier. *(régiment)* **le 3e** ~ the 3rd armoured cavalry.

cuire [kɥiʀ] (38) **1** *vt* (**a**) *(aussi* **faire** ~*)* to cook. ~ **à petit feu** to simmer *ou* cook gently; ~ **au bain-marie** ≃ to heat in a double boiler; ~ **à la broche** to roast on the spit; ~ **au four** *gâteau* to bake; *viande* to roast; ~ **à la vapeur/au gril/à la poêle/à l'eau** to steam/grill/fry/boil; **faire trop** ~ **qch** to overcook sth; **ne pas faire assez** ~ **qch** to undercook sth. (**b**) *pain* to bake; *briques* to fire. (**c**) **à** ~ *chocolat, pommes* cooking; *poires* stewing. **2** *vi* (**a**) *[aliment]* to cook. ~ **à gros bouillon(s)** to boil hard. (**b**) *[personne]* ~ **au soleil** to roast in the sun; **on cuit ici!** * it's boiling in here! * (**c**) **les mains/yeux me cuisaient** my hands/eyes were smarting; **mon dos me cuit** my back is burning. (**d**) **il vous en cuira** you'll rue the day you did it.

cuisant, e [kɥizɑ̃, ɑ̃t] *adj douleur* smarting, burning; *froid, échec, regret* bitter; *remarque* stinging.

cuisine [kɥizin] *nf* (**a**) *(pièce)* kitchen; *(art)* cookery, cooking; *(nourriture)* cooking, food. **elle fait la** ~ *(en général)* she does the cooking *ou* is the cook; *(en ce moment)* she's cooking the meal. (**b**) *(péj)* shady schemings. ◆ **cuisiner** (1) *vt plat* to cook; (⁑ *fig) personne* to grill *. ◆ **cuisinier, -ière** **1** *nm, f (personne)* cook. **2** *nf* cooker, stove; *(vieux modèle)* kitchen range.

cuissardes [kɥisaʀd(ə)] *nfpl [pêcheur]* waders; *(mode féminine)* thigh boots.

cuisse [kɥis] *nf (Anat)* thigh. ~ **de poulet** chicken leg; *(fig)* **se croire sorti de la** ~ **de Jupiter** * to think a lot of o.s.

cuisson [kɥisɔ̃] *nf [aliments]* cooking; *[pain]* baking; *[gigot]* roasting; *[briques]* firing. *(Culin)* **temps de** ~ cooking time.

cuistance ⁑ [kɥistɑ̃s] *nf (nourriture)* grub ⁑.

cuistot * [kɥisto] *nm* cook.

cuit, e [kɥi, kɥit] **1** *adj* (**a**) *plat* cooked; *pain, viande* ready, done. **bien** ~ well cooked *ou* done; **trop** ~ overdone; **pas assez** ~ underdone; ~ **à point** *(parfaitement)* done to a turn; *(peu saignant)* medium-cooked. (**b**) **c'est du tout** ~ * it's a cinch * *ou* a walkover *; **il est** ~ * he's had it *. **2** *nf:* **prendre une** ~ ⁑ to get plastered ⁑.

cuivre [kɥivʀ(ə)] *nm:* ~ **(rouge)** copper; ~ **jaune** brass; **faire les** ~**s** to do the brass *(ou* the copper); *(Mus)* **les** ~**s** the brass. ◆ **cuivré, e** *adj reflets* coppery; *teint* bronzed; *voix* resonant, sonorous.

cul [ky] **1** *nm (Anat:* ⁑*)* backside *; *[bouteille]* bottom. **faire** ~ **sec** to down one's drink in one go *; **en tomber** *ou* **en rester sur le** ~ * to be taken aback, be flabbergasted; **être comme** ~ **et chemise** * to be as thick as thieves *(avec* with). **2** : ~**-de-jatte** *nm, pl* ~**s-**~**-**~ legless cripple; ~**-de-sac** *nm, pl* ~**s**~**-**~ *(rue)* cul-de-sac, dead end; *(fig)* blind alley. **3** *adj inv* (⁑*: stupide)* silly, clottish *.

culasse [kylas] *nf [moteur]* cylinder head; *[fusil]* breech.

culbute [kylbyt] *nf (cabriole)* somersault; *(chute)* tumble, fall; *(*: ruine)* collapse. **faire la** ~ *(ruine)* to collapse; *(profit)* to double one's money.

culbuter [kylbyte] (1) **1** *vi [personne]* to tumble; *[chose]* to topple over; *[voiture]* to overturn. **2** *vt chaise etc* to knock over; *ennemi* to overwhelm; *ministère etc* to bring down, topple.

culinaire [kylinɛʀ] *adj* culinary.

culminer [kylmine] (1) *vi* (**a**) *[sommet]* to tower *(au-dessus de* above). ~ **à** to reach its highest point at. (**b**) *(fig) [colère]* to reach a peak.

culot [kylo] *nm* (**a**) *(*: effronterie)* cheek *. (**b**) *[ampoule]* cap; *[obus]* base.

culotte [kylɔt] *nf* (**a**) *(pantalon)* trousers; *(Hist)* breeches; *(short)* shorts; *(slip) [femme]* panties, knickers; *[homme]* underpants. ~**(s) courte(s)/longue(s)** short/long trousers; ~ **de cheval** riding breeches; ~ **de golf** plus-fours; *(fig)* **c'est elle qui porte la** ~ she wears the trousers. (**b**) *(Boucherie)* rump.

culotté, e [kylɔte] *adj* (**a**) (*) cheeky *. (**b**) *pipe* seasoned.

culpabilité [kylpabilite] *nf* guilt, culpability. ◆ **culpabiliser** (1) *vt:* ~ **qn** to make sb feel guilty.

culte [kylt(ə)] *nm (vénération)* cult, worship; *(pratiques)* cult; *(religion)* religion; *(office)* church service. **le** ~ **de Dieu** the worship of God; **avoir le** ~ **de** to worship; **les objets du** ~ liturgical objects.

cultiver [kyltive] (1) **1** *vt champ, art, personne, don,* to cultivate; *légumes* to grow, cultivate. ~ **la terre** to cultivate the soil, farm the land. **2 se** ~ *vpr* to cultivate one's mind. ◆ **cultivable** *adj terrain* cultivable. ◆ **cultivateur, -trice** *nm, f* farmer. ◆ **cultivé, e** *adj (instruit)* cultured.

culture [kyltyʀ] *nf* (**a**) *[champ]* cultivation; *[légumes]* growing, cultivation. **méthodes de** ~ farming methods; ~ **intensive/fruitière** intensive/fruit farming; ~ **de rapport** cash crop; ~ **vivrière** food crop; *(terres)* ~**s** land under cultivation. (**b**) *[esprit]* cultivation. **la** ~ culture; ~ **générale** general knowledge *ou* education; **faire de la** ~ **physique** to do physical training. (**c**) *(Bio)* culture. ◆ **culturel, -elle** *adj* cultural. ◆ **culturisme** *nm* body-building. ◆ **culturiste** *nmf* body-builder.

cumin [kymɛ̃] *nm (Culin)* caraway, cumin.

cumuler [kymyle] (1) *vt fonctions* to hold concurrently *ou* simultaneously. ~ **2 traitements** to draw 2 separate salaries; *(Fin)* **calcul des intérêts cumulés** calculation of the interests accrued. ◆ **cumul** *nm [fonctions]* plurality; *[avantages]* amassing; *[traitements]* concurrent drawing.

cupide [kypid] *adj* greedy. ◆ **cupidement** *adv* greedily. ◆ **cupidité** *nf* greed.

curare [kyʀaʀ] *nm* curare.

cure [kyʀ] *nf* (**a**) *(traitement)* course of treatment. ~ **d'amaigrissement** slimming course, reducing treatment *(US)*; ~ **de sommeil** sleep therapy; ~ **de fruits/de repos** fruit/rest cure. (**b**) *(Rel) (fonction, paroisse)* cure; *(maison)* presbytery. (**c**) *(littér)* **je n'en ai** ~! I care not a whit! ◆ **curable** *adj* curable. ◆ **curatif, -ive** *adj* curative.

curé [kyʀe] *nm* parish priest. *(péj)* **les** ~**s** clerics.

curée [kyʀe] *nf (Chasse)* quarry; *(fig: ruée)* scramble.

curer [kyʀe] (1) **1** *vt* to clean out. **se** ~ **les dents** to pick one's teeth; **se** ~ **les ongles** to clean one's nails. **2** : **cure-dent** *nm, pl* ~**-**~**s** toothpick; **cure-**

pipe *nm, pl* ~-~**s** pipe cleaner. ◆ **curage** *nm* cleaning-out.

curieux, -euse [kyʀjø, øz] **1** *adj* (**a**) *(intéressé) esprit* inquiring. ~ **de qch** interested in *ou* keen on sth; ~ **de savoir** interested *ou* curious to know. (**b**) *(indiscret)* curious, inquisitive. (**c**) *(bizarre)* curious, funny. **2** *nm*: **le** ~ **dans cette affaire** the funny *ou* curious thing about this business. **3** *nm, f (indiscret)* busybody, nosey-parker *; *(badaud)* onlooker, bystander. **venir en** ~ to come just for a look. ◆ **curieusement** *adv* strangely, curiously. ◆ **curiosité** *nf* (**a**) *(intérêt)* curiosity; *(indiscrétion)* curiosity, inquisitiveness. ~**s malsaines** unhealthy curiosity. (**b**) *(site)* curious *ou* unusual sight *ou* feature; *(bibelot)* curio.

curiste [kyʀist(ə)] *nmf* person taking the waters at a spa.

curriculum vitæ [kyʀikylɔmvite] *nm inv* curriculum vitae.

cursus [kyʀsys] *nm* degree course.

cutané, e [kytane] *adj* skin.

cuti(-réaction) [kyti(ʀeaksjɔ̃)] *nf* skin test.

cuve [kyv] *nf [vin, teinture]* vat; *[mazout, eau, photo]* tank. ◆ **cuvée** *nf (contenu)* vatful; *(produit, année)* vintage. ◆ **cuver** (1) **1** *vt*: ~ **son vin** to sleep it off *. **2** *vi [vin]* to ferment.

cuvette [kyvɛt] *nf (gén)* bowl; *[évier]* basin ; *[W.-C.]* pan; *(Géog)* basin.

cyanose [sjanoz] *nf (Méd)* cyanosis. ◆ **cyanosé, e** *adj* cyanotic. **avoir le visage** ~ to be blue in the face.

cyanure [sjanyʀ] *nm* cyanide.

cybernétique [sibɛʀnetik] *nf* cybernetics *(sg).*

cyclamen [siklamɛn] *nm* cyclamen.

cycle [sikl(ə)] *nm (gén)* cycle; *(vélo)* bicycle, cycle. ~ **élémentaire** ≃ first five years of primary school, ≃ grades one through five *(US)*; **premier/ deuxième** ~ *(Scol)* middle/upper school; *(Univ)* first and second/final year. ◆ **cyclique** *adj* cyclical. ◆ **cyclisme** *nm* cycling. ◆ **cycliste 1** *adj course* cycle; *coureur* racing. **2** *nmf* cyclist. ◆ **cyclomoteur** *nm* moped, motorized bike *ou* bicycle. ◆ **cyclomotoriste** *nmf* moped rider. ◆ **cyclo-tourisme** *nm* bicycle touring. **pour les vacances nous allons faire du** ~ we're going on a cycling holiday.

cyclone [siklon] *nm (Mét)* cyclone; *(fig)* whirlwind.

Cyclope [siklɔp] *nm (Myth)* Cyclops.

cyclothymie [siklɔtimi] *nf* manic-depression, cyclothymia. ◆ **cyclothymique** *adj, nm, f* manic-depressive, cyclothymic.

cygne [siɲ] *nm* swan; *(jeune)* cygnet; *(mâle)* cob.

cylindre [silɛ̃dʀ(ə)] *nm (Aut, Typ, Géom)* cylinder; *(rouleau)* roller. ◆ **cylindrée** *nf* capacity. **les petites** ~**s** small-engined cars. ◆ **cylindrique** *adj* cylindrical.

cymbale [sɛ̃bal] *nf* cymbal.

cynique [sinik] **1** *adj* cynical. **2** *nm* cynic. ◆ **cyniquement** *adv* cynically. ◆ **cynisme** *nm* cynicism.

cyprès [sipʀɛ] *nm* cypress.

cypriote [sipʀijɔt] *adj,* **C**~ *nmf* Cypriot.

cytise [sitiz] *nm* laburnum.

cytologie [sitɔlɔʒi] *nf* cytology.

cytoplasme [sitɔplasm(ə)] *nm* cytoplasm.

D

D, d [de] *nm (lettre)* D, d. ◆**d'** *V* **de.**

dactylo [daktilo] *nf* typist. ◆**dactylo(graphie)** *nf* typing, typewriting. ◆**dactylographier** (7) *vt* to type (out).

dada [dada] *nm (*: cheval)* horsy *; *(fig: marotte)* hobby-horse, pet subject.

dadais [dadɛ] *nm*: **grand** ~ awkward lump.

dague [dag] *nf* dagger.

dahlia [dalja] *nm* dahlia.

Dahomey [daɔme] *nm* Dahomey.

daigner [deɲe] (1) *vt* to deign, condescend. **daignez nous excuser** be so good as to excuse us.

daim [dɛ̃] *nm* fallow deer; *(mâle)* buck; *(peau)* buckskin, doeskin; *(cuir)* suede. ◆**daine** *nf* doe.

dais [dɛ] *nm* canopy.

dalaï-lama [dalajlama] *nm* Dalaï-Lama.

dalle [dal] *nf* paving stone, flag(stone). ~ **funéraire** tombstone, gravestone; **je n'y vois que** ~ ‡ I can't see a damn ‡ thing. ◆**dallage** *nm (gén)* paving. ◆**daller** (1) *vt* to pave.

daltonien, -ienne [daltɔnjɛ̃, jɛn] *adj* colour-blind.

dam [dɑ̃] *nm*: **au (grand)** ~ **de** *(détriment)* to the detriment of; *(déplaisir)* to the displeasure of.

Damas [dama] *n* Damascus.

dame [dam] **1** *nf* (**a**) *(gén)* lady; *(*: épouse)* wife. **pour** ~**s** *coiffeur* ladies'; **de** ~ *sac* lady's. (**b**) *(Cartes, Échecs)* queen; *(Dames)* crown. **le jeu de** ~**s** draughts, checkers *(US)*; **aller à** ~ *(Dames)* to make a crown; *(Échecs)* to make a queen. **2** *excl* (†) ~ **oui/non!** why yes/no! **3** : ~ **de charité** benefactress; ~ **de compagnie** lady's companion; ~ **d'honneur** lady-in-waiting; ~ **patronnesse** patroness.

damer [dame] (1) *vt terre, neige* to pack down. *(fig)* ~ **le pion à qn** to get the better of sb.

damier [damje] *nm (Dames)* draughtboard, checkerboard *(US)*. *(dessin)* **à** ~ chequered.

damnation [dɑnɑsjɔ̃] *nf* damnation. ◆**damné, e** **1** *adj (*: maudit)* cursed *. **2** *nm, f* damned person. **les** ~**s** the damned. ◆**damner** (1) *vt* to damn. **faire** ~ **qn** * to drive sb mad *.

dancing [dɑ̃siŋ] *nm* dance hall.

dandiner (se) [dɑ̃dine] (1) *vpr* to waddle. ◆**dandinement** *nm* waddle.

Danemark [danmaʀk] *nm* Denmark.

danger [dɑ̃ʒe] *nm* danger. **hors de/en** ~ out of/in danger; **mettre en** ~ to endanger; **il est en** ~ **de mort** he is in danger *ou* peril of his life; **courir un** ~ to run a risk; **en cas de** ~ in case of emergency; ~ **public** public menace; **les** ~**s de la route** road hazards; **sans** ~ *(adj)* safe; *(adv)* safely; **pas de** ~ **qu'il vienne!** * there's no fear *ou* danger that he'll come. ◆**dangereusement** *adv* dangerously. ◆**dangereux, -euse** *adj (gén)* dangerous (*pour* to); *entreprise* hazardous, risky. **zone** ~**euse** danger zone.

danois, e [danwa, waz] **1** *adj* Danish. **2** *nm (Ling)* Danish; *(chien)* Great Dane. **3 D**~**(e)** *nm(f)* Dane.

dans [dɑ̃] *prép* (**a**) *(lieu)* in; *(mouvement)* into; *(but)* to; *(parcours)* through; *(intérieur)* inside; *(limites)* within. **être/pénétrer** ~ **la forêt** to be in/go into the forest; **il a plu** ~ **toute la France** it rained throughout France *ou* in all parts of France; **ils sont partis** ~ **la montagne** they have gone off to the mountains; **elle erra** ~ **la ville** she wandered round *ou* about *ou* through the town; ~ **un rayon restreint** within a restricted radius; **ils ont voyagé** ~ **le même train** they travelled on the same train; **cherche** ~ **la boîte** look inside *ou* in the box; **jeter l'eau sale** ~ **l'évier** to pour the dirty water down the sink; ~ **le fond de l'armoire** at the back of the wardrobe; **boire** ~ **une tasse** to drink out of *ou* from a cup. (**b**) *(temps)* in; *(limites)* within, inside. **il est** ~ **sa 6e année** he's in his 6th year; ~ **le temps** in the past, at one time; **cela pourrait se faire** ~ **le mois** it could be done within the month; **je l'attends** ~ **la nuit** I'm expecting him some time tonight. (**c**) *(état etc)* in. **être** ~ **les affaires** to be in business; ~ **la plus grande confusion** in a state of great confusion; **il est** ~ **le secret** he's in on the secret; **il l'a fait** ~ **ce but** he did it with this aim in view. (**d**) *(approximation)* about. **cela coûte** ~ **les 50 F** it costs in the region of 50 francs *ou* about 50 francs; **il vous faut** ~ **les 3 mètres de tissu** you'll need about *ou* something like 3 metres of fabric; **la pièce fait** ~ **les 8 m²** the room is about 8 m².

dansant, e [dɑ̃sɑ̃, ɑ̃t] *adj mouvement* dancing; *musique* lively. **soirée** ~**e** dance.

danse [dɑ̃s] *nf (valse etc)* dance. **la** ~ *(Art)* dancing; ~ **de guerre** war dance; **la** ~ **classique** ballet dancing; **avoir la** ~ **de Saint Guy** *(Méd)* to have St Vitus's dance; *(fig)* to have the fidgets; **de** ~ *professeur* dancing; *musique* dance; **si le gouvernement entre dans la** ~... if the government decides to get involved *ou* to join in... ◆**danser** (1) *vti (gén)* to dance. **faire** ~ **qn** to dance with sb; ~ **de joie** to dance for joy. ◆**danseur, -euse** *nm, f (gén)* dancer; *(partenaire)* partner; *[ballet]* ballet dancer.

Danube [danyb] *nm*: **le** ~ the Danube.

dard [daʀ] *nm [animal]* sting.

darder [daʀde] (1) *vt* (**a**) *(lancer) flèche, regard* to shoot (*sur* at). **le soleil dardait ses rayons** the sun's rays beat down (*sur* on). (**b**) *(dresser) piquants* to point.

dare-dare * [daʀdaʀ] *loc adv* double-quick.

datation [datɑsjɔ̃] *nf* dating. ~ **au carbone 14** carbon dating.

date [dat] *nf* date. ~ **de naissance** date of birth; ~ **de clôture** closing date; ~ **limite de vente** sell-by date; ~ **limite de fraîcheur** best-before date; **à quelle** ~**?** on what date?; **à cette** ~**-là** by that time, by then; **lettre en** ~ **du 23 mai** letter dated May 23rd; ~ **limite** deadline; **à cette** ~ **il ne le savait pas encore** at that time he did not yet know about it; **prendre** ~ **avec qn** to set *ou* fix a date with sb; **faire** ~ *[événement]* to stand out (*dans* in); **le premier/dernier en** ~ the first/latest *ou* most recent; **sans** ~ undated; **de longue** ~ *(adj)* long-standing; **de fraîche** ~ *(adj)* recent; **connaître qn de longue/fraîche** ~ to have known sb for a long/short time.

dater [date] (1) **1** *vt* to date. **daté du 6/de Paris** dated from the 6th/from Paris; **non daté** undated. **2** *vi* (**a**) ~ **de** to date back to, date from; **ça ne date pas d'hier** *[maladie]* it has been going on a long time; *[amitié, situation]* it goes back a long way, it has a long history; *[objet]* it's as old as the hills; **à ~ de demain** as from tomorrow, from tomorrow onwards; **de quand date votre dernière rencontre?** when did you last meet? (**b**) *(faire date)* *[événement]* to stand out (*dans* in); *(être démodé)* to be dated.

datif, -ive [datif, iv] *adj, nm* dative.

datte [dat] *nf* date. ◆ **dattier** *nm* date palm.

daube [dob] *nf* stew, casserole. **bœuf en ~** casserole of beef, beef stew.

dauphin [dofɛ̃] *nm* (**a**) *(Zool)* dolphin. (**b**) *(Hist)* **le D~** the Dauphin. (**c**) *(fig: successeur)* heir apparent.

Dauphine [dofin] *nf* Dauphine.

daurade [dɔʀad] *nf* sea bream.

davantage [davɑ̃taʒ] *adv* (**a**) *(plus)* more; *(négatif)* any more; *(interrogatif)* (any) more (*que* than). **bien/encore ~** much/still more. (**b**) *(plus longtemps)* longer; *(négatif, interrogatif)* any longer (*que* than). (**c**) *(de plus en plus)* more and more. **chaque jour ~** more and more every day. (**d**) **~ de** (some) more; *(négatif)* any more.

de [d(ə)] *(devant voyelle et h muet:* **d'**; *contraction avec* **le, les: du, des***)* **1** *prép* (**a**) *(provenance)* out of, from; *(localisation)* in, on. **sortir ~ la maison** to come out of the house; **arriver du Japon** to arrive from Japan; **l'avion ~ Londres** *(provenance)* the plane from London; *(destination)* the plane for London, the London plane; **les magasins ~ Paris** the Paris shops, the shops in Paris; **les voisins du 2ᵉ** the neighbours on the 2nd floor; **le meilleur ~ la classe/du monde** the best in the class/in the world; **né ~ parents pauvres** born of poor parents; **~ 6 qu'ils étaient au départ** (out) of the original 6. (**b**) *(appartenance)* of. **la maison ~ mon ami** the house of my friend, my friend's house; **un roman ~ Wells** a novel by Wells, a novel of Wells'; **le pied ~ la table** the leg of the table, the table leg; **ses collègues ~ bureau** his colleagues at work.
(**c**) *(caractérisation)* of. **regard ~ haine** look of hatred; **le professeur d'anglais** the English teacher, the teacher of English; **objet ~ cristal/métal** crystal/metal object; **il est d'une bêtise!** he's so stupid!; **c'est bien ~ lui!** it's just like him *ou* typical of him!; **2 verres ~ cassés** 2 broken glasses, 2 glasses broken.
(**d**) *(contenu)* of. **une tasse ~ thé** a cup of tea.
(**e**) *(temps)* **une heure d'attente** an hour's wait, a wait of one hour; **~ nos jours** nowadays; **~ jour** by day, during the day; **travailler ~ nuit** to work at night; **~ 6 à 8** from 6 to 8; **3 heures du matin** 3 (o'clock) in the morning; **il n'a rien fait ~ l'année** he hasn't done a thing all year; **d'une minute à l'autre** *(incessamment)* any minute now; *(progressivement)* from one minute to the next; **3 jours ~ libre** 3 days free.
(**f**) *(mesure)* **pièce ~ 6 m²** room measuring 6 m²; **enfant ~ 5 ans** 5-year-old child; **promenade ~ 3 heures/km** 3-hour/3-km walk; **ce poteau a 5 mètres ~ haut** this post is 5 metres high; **plus grand ~ 5 cm** 5 cm taller; **il gagne 90 F ~ l'heure** he earns 90 francs an hour *ou* per hour; **un chèque ~ 100 dollars** a cheque to the value of $100, a check in the amount of $100 *(US)*.
(**g**) *(moyen, manière, cause)* **frapper ~ la main** to strike with one's hand; **se nourrir ~ racines** to live on roots; **il vit ~ sa peinture** he lives by his painting; **faire qch ~ rien** to make sth out of nothing; **parler d'une voix ferme** to speak in a firm voice; **mourir ~ vieillesse** to die of old age; **rougir ~ honte** to blush with shame; **~ colère, il la gifla** he slapped her in anger; **étonné ~ voir** astonished at seeing *ou* to see.
(**h**) *(copule)* **décider ~ faire** to decide to do; **empêcher qn ~ faire** to prevent sb from doing; **content ~ qch** pleased with sth; **le mois ~ juin** the month of June; **le prénom ~ Paul** the name Paul; **ton idiot ~ fils** that stupid son of yours; **ce cochon ~ temps** this rotten weather; **et elle ~ se moquer ~ nous!** and she poked fun at us!
2 *art partitif (affirmation)* some *(souvent omis)*; *(interrogation)* any, some; *(négation)* any, no. **boire ~ l'eau au robinet** to drink (some) water from the tap; **voulez-vous du pain?** do you want any bread?; **il n'y a plus d'espoir** there is no hope left; **c'est du vol!** that's robbery!; **faire du bruit** to make a noise; **avoir ~ l'humour** to have a sense of humour; **il y a ~ la lumière** there's a light on.
3 des, de *art indéf pl* some *(souvent omis)*; *(négation)* any, no. **des enfants ont cassé les carreaux** some children have broken the window panes; **je n'ai pas de voisins** I haven't any neighbours, I have no neighbours; **j'ai attendu des heures (et des heures)** I waited for hours (and hours).

dé [de] *nm* (**a**) **~ (à coudre)** thimble; *(petit verre)* tiny glass. (**b**) *(Jeux)* die, dice. **~s** dice; **les ~s sont jetés** the die is cast; *(Culin)* **couper en ~s** to dice.

déambuler [deɑ̃byle] (1) *vi* to stroll (about).

débâcle [debɑkl(ə)] *nf [armée]* rout; *[régime, économie, monnaie]* collapse; *[glaces]* breaking up. **c'est une vraie ~!** it's a complete disaster!

déballer [debale] (1) *vt affaires* to unpack; *marchandises* to display; (*) *sentiments* to pour out. ◆ **déballage** *nm (action)* unpacking; *(marchandises)* display *(of loose goods)*.

débandade [debɑ̃dad] *nf (déroute)* headlong flight; *(dispersion)* scattering. *(fig: fuite)* **c'est la ~ générale** it's a general exodus; **en ~** in disorder.

débander [debɑ̃de] (1) **1** *vt (Méd)* to unbandage. **~ les yeux de qn** to remove the blindfold from sb's eyes. **2 se ~** *vpr [armée]* to scatter.

débaptiser [debatize] (1) *vt* to rename.

débarbouiller *vt,* **se ~** *vpr* [debaʀbuje] (1) to wash.

débarcadère [debaʀkadɛʀ] *nm* landing stage.

débardeur [debaʀdœʀ] *nm (ouvrier)* docker; *(vêtement)* slipover.

débarquer [debaʀke] (1) **1** *vt (gén, Mil)* to land; *marchandises* to unload. **2** *vi* to disembark, land. **il a débarqué chez moi** * he turned up at my place; **tu débarques!** * where have you been?; **je n'en sais rien, je débarque** * I don't know, that's the first I've heard of it. ◆ **débarquement** *nm* landing; unloading. **l'anniversaire du ~** the anniversary of the Normandy landing.

débarras [debaʀa] *nm (pièce)* lumber room; *(placard)* cupboard. **bon ~!** good riddance!

débarrasser [debaʀase] (1) **1** *vt* (**a**) *local* to clear (*de* of). **~ (la table)** to clear the table; **débarrasse le plancher!** * clear off! *, make yourself scarce! *. (**b**) **~ qn de** *fardeau* to relieve sb of; *ennemi, mal* to rid sb of; *liens* to release sb from. **2 se ~** *vpr*: **se ~ de** *(gén)* to get rid of, rid o.s. of; *vêtement* to take off, remove.

débat [deba] *nm* discussion, debate. *(Jur, Pol)* **~s** debates; *(Parl)* **~ de clôture** ≃ adjournment debate.

débattre [debatʀ(ə)] (41) **1** *vt* to discuss, debate. **2 se ~** *vpr* to struggle, wrestle (*contre* with).

débauchage [deboʃaʒ] *nm (Écon)* laying off.

débauche [deboʃ] *nf* (**a**) *(vice)* debauchery. **partie de ~** orgy. (**b**) *(abondance)* **~ de** profusion of; **~ de couleurs** riot of colour.

débaucher [deboʃe] (1) **1** *vt* (†: *corrompre)* to debauch; *(licencier)* to lay off. **2** *vi (pointer à la sortie)* to clock out. **3 se ~** *vpr* to become debauched. ◆ **débauché, e 1** *adj* debauched. **2** *nm, f* debauched person. **une vie de ~** a debauched life.

débile [debil] *adj corps, esprit* feeble; *(péj)* moronic, stupid. **c'est un ~ mental** *(lit)* he is mentally deficient; *(péj)* he's a moron. ◆ **débilité** *nf (péj) [pro-*

pos, attitude] stupidity. ~ **(mentale)** mental deficiency.

débiliter [debilite] (1) *vt [climat]* to debilitate, enervate; *[propos]* to demoralize.

débiner * [debine] (1) **1** *vt* to run down. **2 se** ~ *vpr* to clear off *.

débit [debi] **1** *nm* (**a**) *(Fin)* debit. **mettre 10 F au** ~ **de qn** to debit sb with 10 francs. (**b**) *(Comm: vente)* turnover. **cette boutique a du** ~ this shop has a quick turnover. (**c**) *[fleuve, pompe]* flow; *[tuyau]* discharge; *[machine, gaz]* output. (**d**) *(élocution)* delivery. **elle a un sacré** ~ * she has a long tongue, she's a great talker. **2** : ~ **de boissons** *(Admin)* drinking establishment; ~ **de tabac** tobacconist's (shop), tobacco *ou* smoke shop *(US)*.

débitant, e [debitɑ̃, ɑ̃t] *nm, f*: ~ **(de boissons)** ≃ licensed grocer; ~ **(de tabac)** tobacconist, tobacco dealer *(US)*.

débiter [debite] (1) *vt compte* to debit; *marchandises* to retail, sell; *[usine]* to produce; *(péj: dire)* to pour out; *(tailler)* to cut up.

débiteur, -trice [debitœʀ, tʀis] **1** *adj solde* debit. **mon compte est** ~ **de 50 F** my account has a debit balance of 50 francs. **2** *nm, f (Fin, fig)* debtor.

déblayer [debleje] (8) *vt décombres* to clear away; *chemin* to clear; *pièce* to clear up; *travail* to prepare. ◆ **déblaiement** *nm* clearing. ◆ **déblais** *nmpl (gravats)* rubble; *(terre)* earth.

débloquer [deblɔke] (1) **1** *vt* (**a**) *compte, prix* to free; *stocks, crédits* to release. **pour** ~ **la situation** in order to get things moving again. (**b**) *machine* to unjam; *écrou, freins* to release; *route* to unblock. **2** *vi* (⁑) *(dire des bêtises)* to talk twaddle *; *(être fou)* to be off one's rocker ⁑. ◆ **déblocage** *nm* freeing; releasing; unjamming; unblocking.

déboires [debwaʀ] *nmpl (déceptions)* disappointments; *(échecs)* setbacks; *(ennuis)* difficulties.

déboiser [debwaze] (1) *vt montagne* to deforest; *forêt* to clear of trees. ◆ **déboisement** *nm* deforestation; clearing.

déboîter [debwate] (1) **1** *vt membre* to dislocate; *tuyaux* to disconnect; *objet* to dislodge. **se** ~ **l'épaule** to dislocate one's shoulder. **2** *vi (Aut)* to pull out. ◆ **déboîtement** *nm* dislocation; pulling out.

débonnaire [debɔnɛʀ] *adj personne* good-natured; *air* kindly.

débordant, e [debɔʀdɑ̃, ɑ̃t] *adj activité* exuberant; *joie* overflowing. *(Mil)* **mouvement** ~ outflanking manoeuvre.

débordement [debɔʀdəmɑ̃] *nm* (**a**) ~**(s)** *[liquide]* overflowing; *(par ébullition)* boiling over; *(Mil, Sport)* outflanking; *(manifestation)* **afin d'éviter les** ~**s** to prevent demonstrators from getting out of hand. (**b**) *[joie]* outburst; *[paroles]* torrent; *[activité]* explosion. *(débauches)* ~**s** excesses.

déborder [debɔʀde] (1) **1** *vi* (**a**) *[liquide] (gén)* to overflow; *(en bouillant)* to boil over. **plein à** ~ full to the brim *ou* to overflowing (*de* with) ; ~ **de la casserole** to overflow (*ou* boil over) the saucepan; *(fig)* **cela a fait** ~ **le vase, c'est la goutte qui a fait** ~ **le vase** that was the last straw (that broke the camel's back); ~ **de santé** *etc* to be bursting with health *etc*. (**b**) *(d'un alignement)* to stick out; *(en dessinant)* to go over the edge. **2** *vt* (**a**) *(dépasser) (gén)* to extend beyond; *(Mil, Sport)* to outflank; *(d'un alignement)* to stick *ou* jut out beyond. **être débordé de travail** to be snowed under with work *. (**b**) *lit* to untuck.

déboucher [debuʃe] (1) **1** *vt tuyau* to unblock; *bouteille* to uncork; *tube* to uncap. **2** *vi*: ~ **de** to emerge from, come out of; ~ **sur qch** *[rue]* to run *ou* open into sth; *[voiture]* to come out *ou* emerge into sth; *[discussion]* to lead up to sth; *[études]* to lead on to sth; **ça n'a débouché sur rien** it ended inconclusively. **3 se** ~ *vpr [tuyau]* to come unblocked. ◆ **débouchage** *nm* unblocking; uncorking. ◆ **débouché** *nm [pays, économie]* outlet; *[vallée, carrière]* opening.

déboucler [debukle] (1) *vt ceinture* to unbuckle, undo.

débouler [debule] (1) **1** *vi [lapin]* to bolt; *(dégringoler)* to tumble down. *(arriver)* ~ **chez qn** * to land on sb. **2** *vt* (*: *dévaler)* to belt down *.

débourser [debuʀse] (1) *vt* to pay out, lay out. ◆ **débours** *nm* outlay.

déboussoler * [debusɔle] (1) *vt* to disorientate. **il est complètement déboussolé** he is completely at sea, he is completely lost *ou* disorientated.

debout [dəbu] *adv, adj inv* (**a**) *personne* standing; *(levé)* up. **être** ~ to stand; *(levé)* to be up; *(guéri)* to be up and about; **se mettre** ~ to stand up, get up; **rester** ~ to remain standing; *(veiller)* to stay up; **il l'aida à se remettre** ~ he helped him back up *ou* back to his feet; ~! get up!, on your feet! (**b**) *objet* standing upright. **mettre qch** ~ to stand sth upright; **tenir** ~ *[objet]* to stand up; *[édifice]* to be standing; *[théorie]* to stand, hold; **ça ne tient pas** ~ **ce que tu dis** what you say doesn't stand up *ou* doesn't hold water.

déboutonner [debutɔne] (1) **1** *vt* to unbutton, undo. **2 se** ~ *vpr [personne]* to unbutton *ou* undo o.s.; *[habit]* to come unbuttoned *ou* undone.

débraillé, e [debʀɑje] **1** *adj tenue* untidy; *manières* slovenly; *style* sloppy. **2** *nm* slovenliness; sloppiness.

débrancher [debʀɑ̃ʃe] (1) *vt (gén)* to disconnect.

débrayer [debʀeje] (8) *vi (Aut)* to disengage the clutch; *(faire grève)* to stop work. ◆ **débrayage** *nm* clutch; stoppage.

débridé, e [debʀide] *adj* unbridled.

débris [debʀi] *nm (gén)* fragment. **les** ~ *(décombres)* the debris *(sg)*; *(détritus)* the rubbish; *[repas]* the leftovers *ou* scraps; *[armée, fortune]* the remains.

débrouiller [debʀuje] (1) **1** *vt fils* to disentangle; *papiers, problème* to sort out; *mystère* to unravel. ~ **qn** * to teach sb the basics (*en* in). **2 se** ~ *vpr* to manage. **il m'a laissé me** ~ **tout seul** he left me to cope alone *ou* sort things out myself; **elle se débrouille en allemand** she has a working knowledge of German, she can get by in German. ◆ **débrouillard, e** * *adj* smart *, resourceful. ◆ **débrouillardise** * *nf* smartness *, resourcefulness.

débroussailler [debʀusɑje] (1) *vt terrain* to clear; *problème* to do the spadework on.

débusquer [debyske] (1) *vt* to drive out.

début [deby] *nm* (**a**) *(gén)* beginning, start. **du** ~ **à la fin** from beginning to end, from start to finish; **salaire de** ~ starting salary; **dès le** ~ from the outset *ou* start *ou* beginning; **au** ~ at first, in *ou* at the beginning; ~ **février** in early February; **au** ~ **du mois prochain** early next month. (**b**) ~**s** start; **à ses** ~**s** *projet* in its early stages; **faire ses** ~**s** *(gén)* to start; *(Théât)* to make one's début.

débutant, e [debytɑ̃, ɑ̃t] **1** *adj* novice. **2** *nm, f (gén)* beginner, novice; *(Théât)* debutant actor (*ou* actress). **grand/faux** ~ **en anglais** absolute/virtual beginner in English.

débuter [debyte] (1) **1** *vi* to start, begin (*par, sur* with); *[acteur]* to make one's début (*dans* in). **2** *vt* (*) to start, begin.

déca [deka] *préf* deca.

deçà [dəsa] *adv* (**a**) **en** ~ **de** *fleuve* on this side of; **en** ~ **de ses moyens** within his means; **c'est très en** ~ **de la vérité** it is far short of the truth. (**b**) *(littér)* ~, **delà** here and there.

décacheter [dekaʃte] (4) *vt lettre* to unseal, open. ◆ **décachetage** *nm* unsealing, opening.

décade [dekad] *nf (décennie)* decade; *(dix jours)* period of ten days.

décadence [dekadɑ̃s] *nf (processus)* decline; *(état)* decadence. **tomber en ~** to fall into decline. ◆ **décadent, e 1** *adj* decadent, declining. **2** *nm, f* decadent.

décaféiner [dekafeine] (1) *vt* to decaffeinate.

décalage [dekalaʒ] *nm (entre concepts)* gap; *(entre cause et effet)* interval, time-lag (*entre* between). **~ horaire** time difference; *(en avion)* **mal supporter le ~ horaire** to suffer from jet lag.

décalaminer [dekalamine] (1) *vt* to decarbonize.

décalcifier *vt,* **se décalcifier** *vpr* [dekalsifje] (7) to decalcify. ◆ **décalcification** *nf* decalcification.

décalcomanie [dekalkɔmani] *nf (image)* transfer. **faire de la ~** to do transfers.

décaler [dekale] (1) *vt* (**a**) *(avancer)* to move forward; *(reculer)* to move back. **se ~ d'un rang** to move forward (*ou* back) a row; **décalé par rapport aux autres** out of line with *ou* sticking out beyond the others; **décalé d'une heure** *(avancé)* brought forward an hour; *(retardé)* put back an hour. (**b**) *(déséquilibrer)* to unwedge.

décalquer [dekalke] (1) *vt* to trace; *(par pression)* to transfer. ◆ **décalque** *nm* tracing; transfer.

décamper * [dekɑ̃pe] (1) *vi* to clear off *. **faire ~ qn** to chase sb out (*de* from).

décanter [dekɑ̃te] (1) **1** *vt* to allow to settle. **2 se ~** *vpr [vin]* to settle; *[idées]* to become clear. **laisser les choses se ~** to let things clarify themselves, allow the dust to settle; **attendre que la situation se décante** to wait until the situation becomes clearer. ◆ **décantation** *nf* settling; clarification.

décaper [dekape] (1) *vt (gén)* to clean; *(à l'abrasif)* to scour; *(à l'acide)* to pickle; *(à la brosse)* to scrub; *(au papier de verre)* to sand.

décapiter [dekapite] (1) *vt personne* to behead; *(accidentellement)* to decapitate. **le parti s'est trouvé décapité** the party was left without a leader *ou* leaderless. ◆ **décapitation** *nf* beheading.

décapotable [dekapɔtabl(ə)] *adj, nf:* **(voiture) ~** convertible.

décapsuler [dekapsyle] (1) *vt* to take the cap *ou* top off. ◆ **décapsuleur** *nm* bottle-opener.

décarcasser (se) * [dekaʀkase] (1) *vpr* to go to a lot of trouble (*pour faire* to do; *pour qn* for sb).

décati, e [dekati] *adj (péj) vieillard* decrepit; *visage* aged; *beauté* faded; *immeuble* shabby-looking.

décéder [desede] (6) *vi* to die. **les biens des personnes décédées** the property of deceased persons *ou* of those who have died.

déceler [desle] (5) *vt (trouver)* to detect; *(montrer)* to indicate. ◆ **décelable** *adj* detectable.

décélération [deseleʀɑsjɔ̃] *nf* deceleration.

décembre [desɑ̃bʀ(ə)] *nm* December; *V* **septembre.**

décence [desɑ̃s] *nf (bienséance)* decency. ◆ **décemment** *adv* decently. ◆ **décent, e** *adj* decent.

décennie [deseni] *nf* decade.

décentraliser [desɑ̃tʀalize] (1) **1** *vt* to decentralize. **2 se ~** *vpr [usine]* to be decentralized. ◆ **décentralisation** *nf* decentralization.

déception [desɛpsjɔ̃] *nf* disappointment.

décerner [desɛʀne] (1) *vt* to award.

décès [desɛ] *nm* death.

décevoir [desvwaʀ] (28) *vt* to disappoint. ◆ **décevant, e** *adj* disappointing.

déchaîner [deʃene] (1) **1** *vt violence* to unleash; *enthousiasme* to arouse; *opinion publique* to rouse; *campagne (organiser)* to set up; *(avoir comme résultat)* to trigger off. **~ les huées/les rires** to raise a storm of booing/laughter. **2 se ~** *vpr [fureur]* to burst out; *[rires, tempête]* to break out; *[personne]* to loose one's anger (*contre* upon). ◆ **déchaîné, e** *adj passions, flots* raging; *enthousiasme, personne* wild; *opinion publique* furious. **il est ~ contre moi** he is furious with me. ◆ **déchaînement** *nm* bursting out; breaking out; *[passions etc]* fury. **un ~ d'injures** a torrent of abuse.

déchanter [deʃɑ̃te] (1) *vi* to become disillusioned.

décharge [deʃaʀʒ(ə)] *nf* (**a**) *(salve)* volley of shots. **~ (électrique)** electrical discharge. (**b**) *(Jur)* discharge; *(Comm: reçu)* receipt. *(Scol)* **~ (de service)** reduction in teaching load; *(fig)* **il faut dire à sa ~ que...** it must be said in his defence that... (**c**) *(dépôt)* **~ (publique)** rubbish *ou* garbage *(US)* dump.

décharger [deʃaʀʒe] (3) *vt véhicule, bagages* to unload (*de* from); *conscience* to unburden (*auprès de* to); *accusé, arme* to discharge. **~ sa colère** to vent one's anger (*sur qn* on sb); **~ qn de** *tâche* to relieve sb of; **se ~ de ses responsabilités** to pass off *ou* off-load one's responsibilities (*sur qn* onto sb); *(Élec)* **se ~** to go flat, lose its charge. ◆ **déchargement** *nm* unloading.

décharné, e [deʃaʀne] *adj corps* emaciated; *doigts* bony; *visage* gaunt; *paysage* bare.

déchausser [deʃose] (1) **1** *vt:* **~ un enfant** to take a child's shoes off. **2 se ~** *vpr [personne]* to take one's shoes off; *[dents]* to come loose. ◆ **déchaussé, e** *adj personne* barefooted.

déchéance [deʃeɑ̃s] *nf (morale)* decay; *(physique)* degeneration; *(Rel)* fall; *(Pol) [souverain]* deposition.

déchet [deʃɛ] *nm [viande, tissu]* scrap; *(perte)* waste. **~s domestiques/industriels** kitchen/industrial waste *ou* wastes *(US)*; **~s nucléaires/ radio-actifs** nuclear/radioactive waste; **jeter les ~s à la poubelle** to throw the rubbish out; **il y a du ~** there is some wastage; *(péj)* **~ (humain)** human wreck.

déchiffrer [deʃifʀe] (1) *vt message* to decipher; *code* to decode; *(Mus)* to sight-read; *énigme* to unravel. ◆ **déchiffrable** *adj* decipherable; decodable. ◆ **déchiffrage** *nm* deciphering; decoding; sight-reading; unravelling.

déchiqueter [deʃikte] (4) *vt (lit, fig)* to tear to pieces. **déchiqueté par l'explosion** blown to pieces by the explosion; **déchiqueté par un lion** mauled *ou* savaged by a lion. ◆ **déchiqueté, e** *adj relief* jagged; *corps* mutilated.

déchirer [deʃiʀe] (1) **1** *vt* (**a**) *(lacérer)* to tear up; *(faire un accroc)* to tear, rip; *(arracher)* to tear out (*de* from); *(ouvrir)* to tear open. **~ en deux** to tear in two. (**b**) *[querelle, remords]* to tear apart. **cris qui déchirent l'air/les oreilles** cries which rend the air/split one's ears; **spectacle qui déchire le cœur** heartrending *ou* harrowing sight. **2 se ~** *vpr [vêtement]* to tear, rip; *[sac]* to burst; *[cœur]* to break; *[couple]* to tear each other apart. **attention, tu vas te ~** be careful, you'll tear your coat *(ou dress etc)*; **se ~ un muscle** to tear a muscle; **se ~ les mains** to graze one's hands. ◆ **déchirant, e** *adj* heartbreaking. ◆ **déchirement** *nm (douleur)* wrench, heartbreak. *(Pol: divisions)* **~s** rifts. ◆ **déchirure** *nf [tissu]* tear, rip; *[ciel]* break in the clouds. **se faire une ~ musculaire** to tear a muscle.

déchoir [deʃwaʀ] (25) *vi [personne]* to demean o.s.; *[réputation, influence]* to wane. ◆ **déchu, e** *adj roi* deposed; *(Rel)* fallen. *(Jur)* **être ~ de ses droits** to be deprived of one's rights.

déci [desi] *préf* deci.

décidé, e [deside] *adj air, ton* determined, decided; *personne* determined (*à faire* to do); *question* settled, decided. **bon, c'est ~** right, that's settled then.

décidément [desidemɑ̃] *adv (certainement)* certainly, undoubtedly, indeed; *(vraiment)* really. **~, il est fou** he's really mad.

décider [deside] (1) **1** *vt* (**a**) *(établir)* **~ qch** to decide on sth; **~ que** to decide that; **~ de faire qch/de ne pas faire qch** to decide to do sth/against doing sth; **c'est à lui de ~** it's up to him to decide. (**b**) *(persuader) [personne]* to persuade; *[conseil, événement]* to decide. **~ qn à faire** to persuade sb to do. (**c**) *[chose] (provoquer)* to cause, bring about. **2 ~ de** *vt indir*: **~ de qch** *[personne]* to decide on sth; *[événements]* to decide *ou* determine sth; **le sort en a décidé autrement** fate has decided *ou* ordained otherwise. **3 se ~** *vpr* (**a**) *[personne]* to come to *ou* make a decision, make up one's mind. **se ~ à** *ou* **pour qch** to decide on sth; **je ne peux pas me ~ à lui mentir** I cannot bring myself *ou* I cannot make up my mind to lie to him. (**b**) *[problème]* to be decided *ou* settled. **est-ce qu'il va se ~ à faire beau? *** do you think it'll turn out fine after all? ◆ **décideur** *nm* decision-maker. **avoir un rôle de ~** to have a decision-making role.

décimal, e, *mpl* **-aux** [desimal, o] *adj, nf* decimal.

décimer [desime] (1) *vt* to decimate. ◆ **décimation** *nf* decimation.

décisif, -ive [desizif, iv] *adj (gén)* decisive; *argument* conclusive; *coup, facteur* deciding. *(fig)* **tournant ~** watershed *(fig)*; **porter un coup ~ au terrorisme** to deal terrorism a decisive blow.

décision [desizjɔ̃] *nf (choix, verdict)* decision; *(fermeté)* decisiveness. **soumettre qch à la ~ de qn** to submit sth to sb for his decision; **nommé à un poste de ~** appointed to a decision-making job. ◆ **décisionnel, -elle** *adj rôle, responsabilité* decision-making.

déclamer [deklame] (1) **1** *vt* to declaim; *(péj)* to spout. **2** *vi (péj)* to rant. *(littér)* **~ contre** to inveigh against. ◆ **déclamation** *nf (Art)* declamation. *(péj)* **~(s)** ranting. ◆ **déclamatoire** *adj (gén)* declamatory; *(péj) ton* ranting.

déclarable [deklaʀabl(ə)] *adj* declarable.

déclaration [deklaʀɑsjɔ̃] **1** *nf (proclamation)* declaration; *(discours, commentaire)* statement; *(aveu)* admission; *(révélation)* revelation; *[décès]* registration; *[vol]* notification. **faire une ~ d'accident** *(à l'assurance)* to file an accident claim; *(à la police)* to report an accident. **2** : **~ (d'amour)** declaration of love; **~ de guerre** declaration of war; **~ d'impôts** statement of income; *(formulaire)* tax return; **~ sous serment** statement under oath.

déclaré, e [deklaʀe] *adj opinion* professed; *athée, ennemi* avowed; *intention* avowed, declared. **revenus non ~s** undeclared income.

déclarer [deklaʀe] (1) **1** *vt (gén)* to declare; *(annoncer)* to announce; *(avouer)* to admit; *décès* to register; *vol* to notify. **~ la guerre** to declare war (*à* on); **~ qn coupable** to find sb guilty ; **~ que...** to declare that...; **je vous déclare que** I tell you that. **2 se ~** *vpr* (**a**) **se ~ en faveur de** to declare o.s. *ou* come out in favour of; **se ~ satisfait** to declare o.s. satisfied; **il s'est déclaré offensé** he said he was offended. (**b**) *[incendie, épidémie]* to break out. (**c**) *[amoureux]* to declare one's love.

déclasser [deklɑse] (1) *vt coureur* to relegate; *fiches* to get out of order. ◆ **déclassement** *nm* relegation.

déclencher [deklɑ̃ʃe] (1) **1** *vt mécanisme* to release; *sonnerie* to set off; *ouverture* to activate; *attaque, grève* to launch; *catastrophe, commentaires* to trigger off; *violence* to loose; *(Mil) tir* to open. **2 se ~** *vpr [mécanisme]* to release itself; *[sonnerie]* to go off; *[attaque, grève]* to start; *[crise]* to be triggered off. ◆ **déclenchement** *nm* release; setting off; triggering off; activating; launching; starting; opening. ◆ **déclencheur** *nm (Tech)* release mechanism. *(Phot)* **~ souple** cable release.

déclic [deklik] *nm (bruit)* click; *(mécanisme)* trigger mechanism. *(mentalement)* **ça a été le ~** it triggered something in my (*ou* her *etc*) mind.

décliner [dekline] (1) **1** *vt* (**a**) *nom, identité* to state, give; *offre* to decline, turn down, refuse. **~ toute responsabilité** to decline *ou* refuse to accept any responsibility. (**b**) *(Ling)* to decline. **2** *vi* (**a**) *(s'affaiblir) (gén)* to decline; *[santé]* to deteriorate; *[forces, beauté]* to wane, fade. (**b**) *(baisser) [jour]* to draw to a close; *[soleil]* to go down; *[lune]* to wane; *[astre]* to set. ◆ **déclin** *nm* decline; deterioration; waning; fading (*de* in). **le ~ du jour/de la vie** the close of day/of life; **être à son ~** *[soleil]* to be setting; *[lune]* to be waning; **être en ~** to be on the decline. ◆ **déclinable** *adj* declinable. ◆ **déclinaison** *nf (Ling)* declension; *(Astron, Phys)* declination.

déclivité [deklivite] *nf* incline.

décloisonner [deklwazɔne] (1) *vt* to decompartmentalize. ◆ **décloisonnement** *nm* decompartmentalization.

décocher [dekɔʃe] (1) *vt flèche, regard* to shoot; *coup* to throw; *ruade, remarque* to let fly.

décoder [dekɔde] (1) *vt code* to decode; *(TV, Ordin)* to decode; *message* to decipher. ◆ **décodage** *nm* decoding; deciphering.

décoiffer [dekwafe] (1) *vt*: **~ qn** *(cheveux)* to disarrange sb's hair; *(chapeau)* to take sb's hat off; **je suis toute décoiffée** my hair is in a mess; **se ~** to take one's hat off.

décoincer [dekwɛ̃se] (3) *vt (gén)* to unjam.

décolérer [dekɔleʀe] (6) *vi*: **il ne décolère pas depuis hier** he hasn't calmed down *ou* cooled off * since yesterday.

décoller [dekɔle] (1) **1** *vt (gén)* to unstick; (*) *poursuivants* to shake off. **2** *vi (Aviat, fig)* to take off; *[fusée]* to lift off (*de* from); (*) *[gêneur]* to budge. **3 se ~** *vpr [timbre]* to come unstuck. ◆ **décollage** *nm* (**a**) *[Avion]* takeoff; *[fusée]* lift-off. **au ~** at takeoff; at lift-off. (**b**) *[timbre]* unsticking.

décolleté, e [dekɔlte] **1** *adj robe* low-cut. **~ dans le dos** cut low at the back. **2** *nm* low neckline.

décoloniser [dekɔlɔnize] (1) *vt* to decolonize. ◆ **décolonisateur, -trice 1** *adj* decolonizing. **2** *nm, f* decolonizer. ◆ **décolonisation** *nf* decolonization.

décolorer [dekɔlɔʀe] (1) **1** *vt liquide* to decolour; *cheveux* to bleach; *tissu* to fade. **lèvres décolorées** colourless lips. **2 se ~** *vpr (gén)* to lose its colour; *[tissu]* to fade. ◆ **décoloration** *nf (gén)* decoloration. **se faire faire une ~** to have one's hair bleached.

décombres [dekɔ̃bʀ(ə)] *nmpl* rubble, debris *(sg)*.

décommander [dekɔmɑ̃de] (1) **1** *vt marchandise, invitation* to cancel; *invités* to put off. **2 se ~** *vpr* to cancel an appointment.

décomplexer [dekɔ̃plɛkse] (1) *vt* to rid of complexes.

décomposer [dekɔ̃poze] (1) **1** *vt* (**a**) *mouvement, lumière* to break up; *problème, phrase* to break down; *(Chim)* to decompose. (**b**) *(altérer) visage* to contort; *viande* to cause to decompose. **2 se ~** *vpr [viande]* to decompose; *[visage]* to change dramatically. ◆ **décomposition** *nf* decomposition; breaking up; breaking down; contortion. **en ~** *cadavre* in a state of decomposition; *société* in decay.

décompte [dekɔ̃t] *nm (compte)* detailed account; *(déduction)* deduction. **faire le ~ des points** to count up the points. ◆ **décompter** (1) *vt* to deduct (*de* from).

déconcentrer [dekɔ̃sɑ̃tʀe] (1) **1** *vt (Admin)* to devolve, decentralize; *(Ind)* to disperse. **2 se ~** *vpr [athlète]* to lose concentration.

déconcerter [dekɔ̃sɛʀte] (1) *vt* to disconcert.

déconfit, e [dekɔ̃fi, it] *adj* crestfallen, downcast.

déconfiture * [dekɔ̃fityʀ] *nf* defeat; *(financière)* (financial) collapse.

décongeler [dekɔ̃ʒle] **(5)** *vt* to defrost, unfreeze.

décongestionner [dekɔ̃ʒɛstjɔne] **(1)** *vt (Méd), rue* to relieve congestion in; *administration* to relieve the pressure on.

déconnecter [dekɔnɛkte] **(1)** *vt* to disconnect.

déconseiller [dekɔ̃seje] **(1)** *vt*: ~ **qch à qn** to advise sb against sth; **c'est déconseillé** it's inadvisable.

déconsidérer [dekɔ̃sideʀe] **(6)** *vt* to discredit.

décontaminer [dekɔ̃tamine] **(1)** *vt* to decontaminate. ◆ **décontamination** *nf* decontamination.

décontenancer [dekɔ̃tnɑ̃se] **(3)** *vt* to disconcert.

décontracter *vt,* **se** ~ *vpr* [dekɔ̃tʀakte] **(1)** to relax. ◆ **décontraction** *nf* relaxation.

déconvenue [dekɔ̃vny] *nf* disappointment.

décor [dekɔʀ] *nm* (**a**) *(Théât)* **le** ~, **les** ~**s** the scenery, the décor; ~ **de cinéma/théâtre** film/ stage set; **quel beau** ~! what a lovely set!; *[véhicule]* **entrer dans le** ~ * to run off the road; **envoyer qn dans le** ~ * to force sb off the road. (**b**) *(paysage)* scenery; *(milieu)* setting. ◆ **décorateur, -trice** *nm, f* (**a**) *(d'intérieurs)* (interior) decorator. (**b**) *(Théât)* set designer. ◆ **décoratif, -ive** *adj* decorative. ◆ **décoration** *nf* decoration. ◆ **décorer** **(1)** *vt (gén)* to decorate; *robe* to trim.

décortiquer [dekɔʀtike] **(1)** *vt crevettes* to shell; *riz* to hull; *texte* to dissect.

décorum [dekɔʀɔm] *nm*: **le** ~ decorum.

découcher [dekuʃe] **(1)** *vi* to stay out all night.

découdre [dekudʀ(ə)] **(48)** **1** *vt* (**a**) *vêtement* to unpick; *bouton* to take off. (**b**) *(littér)* **en** ~ to fight. **2 se** ~ *vpr [robe]* to come unstitched; *[bouton]* to come off.

découler [dekule] **(1)** *vi* to ensue, follow (*de* from).

découpage [dekupaʒ] *nm* (**a**) *[papier, gâteau]* cutting up; *[viande]* carving; *[image, métal]* cutting out; *(Ciné)* cutting. ~ **électoral** division into constituencies, ≃ apportionment *(US)*. (**b**) *(image)* cutout (figure).

découpé, e [dekupe] *adj relief, côte* jagged, indented; *feuille* jagged.

découper [dekupe] **(1)** **1** *vt viande* to carve; *gâteau, papier, tissu* to cut up; *images, métal* to cut out. **indentations qui découpent la côte** indentations which cut into the coastline. **2 se** ~ *vpr [silhouette]* to stand out (*sur* against).

découpure [dekupyʀ] *nf* (**a**) *(contour)* jagged *ou* indented outline. ~**s** *[côte]* indentations. (**b**) *(morceau)* piece cut out.

décourager [dekuʀaʒe] **(3)** **1** *vt (démoraliser)* to discourage, dishearten; *(dissuader)* to discourage, put off. ~ **qn d'une entreprise** to discourage sb from an undertaking, put sb off an undertaking. **2 se** ~ *vpr* to lose heart, become discouraged. ◆ **décourageant, e** *adj* disheartening, discouraging. ◆ **découragement** *nm* discouragement, despondency.

décousu, e [dekuzy] *adj (Couture)* unstitched; *(fig)* disjointed.

découvert, e [dekuvɛʀ, ɛʀt(ə)] **1** *adj tête* bare, uncovered; *lieu* open, exposed. **être à** ~ to be exposed; **agir à** ~ to act openly. **2** *nm [compte]* overdraft; *[caisse]* deficit. ~ **bancaire** bank overdraft; ~ **budgétaire** budget deficit; ~ **de trésorerie** cash deficit; **tirer de l'argent à** ~ to overdraw one's account. **3** *nf* discovery. **aller à la** ~**e de** to go in search of.

découvrir [dekuvʀiʀ] **(18)** **1** *vt* (**a**) *(trouver)* to discover; *cause, vérité* to discover, find out, unearth. ~ **que/comment** to find out *ou* discover that/how; **elle s'est découvert un cousin en Amérique** she found out *ou* discovered she had a cousin in America; **quand ils découvriront le pot aux roses *** when they find out what's been going on. (**b**) *casserole* to take the lid off; *statue* to unveil; *corps, ruines* to uncover; *membres* to bare, uncover. **il resta découvert devant elle** he kept his hat off in her presence; **robe qui découvre le dos** dress which reveals the back. (**c**) *panorama* to see, have a view of. (**d**) *(révéler, dévoiler) projets* to reveal, disclose (*à qn* to sb). **se** ~ **à qn** to confide in sb. **2 se** ~ *vpr* (**a**) *[personne] (chapeau)* to take off one's hat; *(habits)* to take off one's clothes; *(couvertures)* to uncover o.s. **il ne faut pas se** ~ you must keep covered up. (**b**) *(Boxe, Escrime)* to leave o.s. open to attack. (**c**) *[ciel, temps]* to clear.

décrasser [dekʀase] **(1)** *vt (gén)* to clean; *chaudière* to clean out. **se** ~ to give o.s. a good clean-up. ◆ **décrassage** *nm* cleaning; cleaning-out; clean-up.

décrêper [dekʀepe] **(1)** *vt cheveux* to straighten.

décrépitude [dekʀepityd] *nf [personne]* decrepitude; *[nation]* decay. **tomber en** ~ to become decrepit; to decay. ◆ **décrépit, e** *adj* decrepit.

décréter [dekʀete] **(6)** *vt mobilisation, nomination* to order; *état d'urgence* to declare; *mesure (hum: décider)* to decree. ◆ **décret** *nm (gén)* decree.

décrier [dekʀije] **(7)** *vt (gén)* to disparage.

décrire [dekʀiʀ] **(39)** *vt (dépeindre)* to describe; *(parcourir)* to follow, describe. **l'avion décrivait des cercles** the plane flew in circles.

décrisper [dekʀispe] **(1)** *vt situation* to defuse, de-escalate. **pour** ~ **les relations** to make relations less strained, to take the heat out of relations.

décrocher [dekʀɔʃe] **(1)** **1** *vt* (**a**) *rideau* to take down, unhook; *fermoir* to undo; *wagon* to uncouple; *(Sport) concurrents* to leave behind; *téléphone (pour répondre)* to pick up, lift; *(pour l'empêcher de sonner)* to take off the hook; *objet coincé* to free. **le rideau s'est décroché** the curtain came unhooked. (**b**) (*: *obtenir)* to get, land *. *(lit, fig)* ~ **le gros lot** to hit the jackpot. **2** *vi* (**a**) *(Téléc)* to pick up *ou* lift the receiver. (**b**) *(Mil)* to break off the action; *[coureur]* to fall behind. (**c**) (*) *(ne pas comprendre)* to fail to keep up; *(se désintéresser)* to drop out; *(cesser d'écouter)* to switch off *. ◆ **décroché** *nm (Constr)* recess.

décroiser [dekʀwaze] **(1)** *vt* to uncross.

décroître [dekʀwatʀ(ə)] **(55)** *vi (gén)* to decrease; *[fièvre, crue]* to go down; *[lune]* to wane; *[jours]* to get shorter; *[lumière]* to fade. ◆ **décroissance** *nf (gén)* decrease, decline (*de* in). ◆ **décrue** *nf [rivière]* fall in the level (*de* of).

décrotter [dekʀɔte] **(1)** *vt chaussures* to get the mud off.

déçu, e [desy] *adj* disappointed.

décupler [dekyple] **(1)** *vti* to increase tenfold; *(fig)* to double.

dédaigner [dedeɲe] **(1)** *vt (mépriser)* to scorn, disdain; *(négliger) offre, adversaire* to spurn; *menaces* to disregard. **ce n'est pas à** ~ *(offre)* it's not to be sniffed at *ou* despised; *(danger)* it can't just be shrugged off; *(littér)* **il dédaigna d'y aller** he did not deign to go; **il ne dédaigne pas la plaisanterie** *ou* **de plaisanter** he's not averse to a good joke. ◆ **dédaigneusement** *adv* disdainfully. ◆ **dédaigneux, -euse** *adj* disdainful (*de* of). ◆ **dédain** *nm* disdain (*de* for).

dédale [dedal] *nm [rues, idées]* maze.

dedans [d(ə)dɑ̃] **1** *adv* inside. **nous sommes restés (au-)**~ **toute la journée** we stayed indoors all day; **elle cherche son sac, tout son argent est** ~ she is looking for her bag — all her money is in it; **du** ~ from inside; **en** *ou* **au** ~ **(de lui)** deep down; **au** ~ **(de)** inside; **il est rentré** ~ * *(accident)* he ran *ou* crashed straight into it; *(bagarre)* he laid into him *; **il s'est fichu ~ *** he got it all wrong. **2** *nm* inside.

dédicacer [dedikase] (3) *vt* to autograph (*à qn* for sb), inscribe (*à qn* to sb). ◆ **dédicace** *nf* dedication; *(manuscrite)* inscription (*à* to).

dédier [dedje] (7) *vt*: ~ **à** *(gén, Rel)* to dedicate to; *efforts* to devote to.

dédire (se) [dediʀ] (37) *vpr (engagements)* to go back on one's word; *(affirmation)* to withdraw. ◆ **dédit** *nm (caution)* forfeit, penalty; *(non-paiement)* default. **en cas de** ~ if you fail to keep your word; in case of default.

dédommager [dedɔmaʒe] (3) *vt*: ~ **qn** to compensate sb (*de* for); **comment vous ~ du dérangement?** how can I ever make up for the trouble? ◆ **dédommagement** *nm* compensation. **en** ~ in compensation (*de* for).

dédouaner [dedwane] (1) *vt (Comm)* to clear through customs; (*) *personne* to clear. **marchandises dédouanées** duty-paid goods. ◆ **dédouanement** *nm* customs clearance.

dédoubler [deduble] (1) *vt classe* to divide in two. ~ **un train** to put on a relief train; **je ne peux pas me ~ *** I can't be in two places at once. ◆ **dédoublement** *nm (Psych)* **souffrir d'un ~ de la personnalité** to suffer from a split *ou* dual personality.

dédramatiser [dedʀamatize] (1) *vt examen, opération* to make less alarming *ou* awesome. ~ **la mort** to take the drama out of dying.

déduction [dedyksjɔ̃] *nf* (**a**) *(Comm)* deduction. ~ **faite de** after deduction of. (**b**) *(raisonnement)* deduction, inference; *(conclusion)* conclusion. ◆ **déductible** *adj* deductible (*de* from). ◆ **déductif, -ive** *adj* deductive.

déduire [dedɥiʀ] (38) *vt (Comm)* to deduct (*de* from); *(conclure)* to deduce, infer (*de* from).

déesse [deɛs] *nf* goddess.

défaillance [defajɑ̃s] *nf (évanouissement)* blackout; *(lit, fig: faiblesse)* weakness; *(panne)* fault, failure, breakdown (*de* in); *(Jur)* default. **avoir une** ~ *(évanouissement)* to faint, have a blackout; *(faiblesse)* to feel faint; **élève qui a des ~s** pupil who has certain shortcomings *ou* weak points (*en* in); **mémoire sans** ~ faultless memory; ~ **cardiaque** heart failure; ~ **de mémoire** lapse of memory. ◆ **défaillant, e** *adj forces, mémoire* failing; *courage* weakening; *voix, pas* unsteady; *personne* weak, faint (*de* with). **candidat** ~ candidate who fails to appear. ◆ **défaillir** (13) *vi [personne]* to faint; *[forces, courage]* to weaken. **sans** ~ without flinching.

défaire [defɛʀ] (60) **1** *vt* (**a**) *installation* to take down, dismantle; *nœud, fermeture, robe* to undo; *valise* to unpack. ~ **le lit** *(changer les draps)* to strip the bed; *(se coucher)* to pull back the sheets; *(désordre)* to unmake the bed. (**b**) *contrat* to break. **elle se plaît à ~ tout ce que je fais** she takes pleasure in undoing everything I do. (**c**) *(littér) ennemi, armée* to defeat. (**d**) ~ **qn de** *liens, gêneur* to rid sb of; *habitude* to break sb of. **2 se** ~ *vpr* (**a**) *[ficelle]* to come undone. (**b**) **se ~ de** *gêneur* to get rid of; *idée* to put out of one's mind; *habitude* to break o.s. of; *souvenir* to part with. ◆ **défait, e**[1] *adj visage* haggard; *cheveux* tousled; *lit* rumpled; *armée* defeated. ◆ **défaite**[2] *nf (Mil, fig)* defeat. ~ **électorale** defeat at the polls *ou* at the election. ◆ **défaitisme** *nm* defeatism. ◆ **défaitiste** *adj, nmf* defeatist.

défalquer [defalke] (1) *vt* to deduct. ◆ **défalcation** *nf* deduction.

défaut [defo] *nm* (**a**) *[diamant, verre]* flaw; *[étoffe, machine]* fault; *[roman, système]* flaw, defect; *(Ordin)* bug; *[personne]* fault, failing. ~ **de prononciation** speech defect; **c'est un vilain** ~ it's a bad fault; **sans** ~ flawless, faultless. (**b**) *(désavantage)* drawback. **le ~ avec cette voiture, c'est que...** the snag *ou* drawback with this car is that... (**c**) *(manque)* ~ **de** *raisonnement* lack of; *main-d'œuvre* shortage of. (**d**) **faire** ~ *[argent]* to be lacking; **le temps lui fait** ~ he lacks time; **mes amis m'ont fait** ~ my friends let me down; **à ~ de** for lack *ou* want of; **à ~ prenez du vinaigre** failing that use some vinegar; **être en** ~ to be at fault; **prendre qn en** ~ to catch sb out; **si ma mémoire ne me fait pas** ~ if my memory serves me right; **juger qn par** ~ to judge sb in his absence; **calculer qch par** ~ to calculate sth to the nearest decimal point; *(lit, fig)* **le ~ de la cuirasse** the chink in the armour.

défaveur [defavœʀ] *nf* disfavour (*auprès de* with). ◆ **défavorable** *adj* unfavourable (*à* to). ◆ **défavorablement** *adv* unfavourably.

défavoriser [defavɔʀize] (1) *vt [décision]* to penalize; *[timidité]* to put at a disadvantage. **j'ai été défavorisé par rapport aux autres** I was put at an unfair disadvantage compared with the others; **les couches défavorisées de la population** the underprivileged *ou* disadvantaged sections of the population.

défectif, -ive [defɛktif, iv] *adj verbe* defective.

défection [defɛksjɔ̃] *nf [amis]* desertion; *[troupes]* failure to assist; *[candidats, invités]* failure to appear. **faire** ~ *[partisans]* to fail to lend support.

défectueux, -euse [defɛktɥø, øz] *adj* defective. ◆ **défectuosité** *nf (état)* defectiveness; *(défaut)* defect, fault (*de* in).

défendable [defɑ̃dabl(ə)] *adj* defensible.

défendeur, -deresse [defɑ̃dœʀ, dʀɛs] *nm, f (Jur)* defendant.

défendre [defɑ̃dʀ(ə)] (41) **1** *vt* (**a**) *(protéger) (gén)* to defend; *opinion* to stand up for; *cause* to champion (*contre* against); *(du froid)* to protect (*de* from). (**b**) *(interdire)* ~ **qch à qn** to forbid sb sth; ~ **à qn de faire** to forbid sb to do; **il est défendu de fumer** smoking is prohibited *ou* not allowed. **2 se** ~ *vpr* (**a**) *(se protéger)* to defend o.s. (*contre* against). **se ~ de la pluie** to protect o.s. from the rain; **il se défend bien/mal en affaires** he does quite well/he doesn't do very well in business. (**b**) *(se justifier)* **se ~ d'avoir fait qch** to deny doing sth; **sa position se défend** his position is quite defensible; **ce qu'il dit se défend** he has a point. (**c**) *(s'empêcher de)* **se ~ de faire** to refrain from doing.

défense [defɑ̃s] *nf* (**a**) *(gén, Jur, Mil, sport)* defence. *(fortifications etc)* **~s** defences; **une entreprise travaillant pour la ~ nationale** a firm working for the Ministry of Defence; **un contrat concernant la ~ nationale** a defence contract; **prendre la ~ de qn** to stand up for sb, defend sb; **sans** ~ defenceless; **la parole est à la** ~ the defence may speak. (**b**) *(interdiction)* ~ **d'entrer** no admittance; **danger: ~ d'entrer** danger — keep out; ~ **de fumer** no smoking, smoking prohibited; **j'ai oublié la ~ qu'il m'a faite** I forgot that he forbade me to do that ; ~ **d'en parler à quiconque** it is forbidden to speak of it to anyone. (**c**) *[éléphant]* tusk.

défenseur [defɑ̃sœʀ] *nm (gén, Mil)* defender; *[cause]* champion; *[doctrine]* advocate; *(Jur)* counsel for the defence.

défensif, -ive [defɑ̃sif, iv] **1** *adj* defensive. **2** *nf*: **sur la ~ive** on the defensive.

déférence [defeʀɑ̃s] *nf* deference. **par ~ pour** in deference to. ◆ **déférent, e** *adj* deferential.

déférer [defeʀe] (6) *vt* (**a**) *(Jur) affaire* to refer to the court. ~ **qn à la justice** to hand sb over to the law. (**b**) *(céder)* to defer (*à* to).

déferler [defɛʀle] (1) *vi [vagues]* to break. ~ **sur le pays** *[violence]* to sweep through the country; *[touristes]* to pour into the country. ◆ **déferle-**

ment *nm [vagues]* breaking; *[violence]* spread; *[véhicules, touristes]* flood; *[enthousiasme]* wave.

défi [defi] *nm* challenge. **lancer un ~ à qn** to challenge sb; **mettre qn au ~** to defy sb (*de faire* to do); **c'est un ~ au bon sens** it defies common sense; **d'un air de ~** defiantly.

défiance [defjɑ̃s] *nf* mistrust. **sans ~** *(adj)* unsuspecting; *(adv)* unsuspectingly. ◆ **défiant, e** *adj* mistrustful.

déficience [defisjɑ̃s] *nf (Méd, fig)* deficiency. **~ immunologique** immunodeficiency; **~ mentale** *ou* **intellectuelle** mental deficiency *ou* retardation ; **~ de mémoire** lapse of memory. ◆ **déficient, e** *adj (gén)* deficient; *raisonnement* weak.

déficit [defisit] *nm* deficit. **~ budgétaire/de la balance des paiements** budget/balance of payments deficit. ◆ **déficitaire** *adj (Fin)* in deficit; *année* poor (*en* in), bad (*en* for). **être ~** to be in deficit ; **~ en main-d'œuvre** deficient in *ou* short of manpower.

défier [defje] (7) **1** *vt adversaire* to challenge (*à* to); *adversité* to defy. **à des prix qui défient toute concurrence** at absolutely unbeatable prices; **~ qn de faire qch** to defy sb to do sth. **2 se ~** *vpr*: **se ~ de** to mistrust; (†) **défie-toi de lui!** beware of him!

défigurer [defigyʀe] (1) *vt visage [blessure]* to disfigure; *[bouton]* to spoil; *pensée, réalité* to distort; *texte, tableau* to mutilate, deface; *paysage* to disfigure, mar.

défilé [defile] *nm* (**a**) *(cortège)* procession; *(manifestation)* march; *(Mil)* march-past, parade. **~ de mode** fashion parade. (**b**) *[voitures, impressions]* stream. (**c**) *(Géog)* narrow pass.

défiler [defile] (1) **1** *vi (Mil)* to march past, parade; *[manifestants]* to march (*devant* past); *[paysage, souvenirs]* to pass (*dans* through, *devant* before). *(Ordin)* **faire ~ un programme** to scroll a program. **2 se ~** *vpr (s'éclipser)* to slip away. *(refuser)* **il s'est défilé** he wriggled out of it. ◆ **défilement** *nm (Ordin)* scrolling.

définir [definiʀ] (2) *vt* to define. **notre politique se définit comme...** our policies can be defined as... ◆ **défini, e** *adj (gén, Gram)* definite. ◆ **définissable** *adj* definable.

définitif, -ive [definitif, iv] **1** *adj (gén)* final; *victoire, fermeture, édition* definitive; *refus* definite. **2** *nf*: **en ~ive** *(à la fin)* eventually; *(somme toute)* when all is said and done. ◆ **définitivement** *adv partir* for good; *résoudre* conclusively, definitively; *refuser* definitely; *nommer* permanently.

définition [definisjɔ̃] *nf* definition; *[mots croisés]* clue.

déflagration [deflagʀɑsjɔ̃] *nf (gén)* explosion.

déflation [deflɑsjɔ̃] *nf* deflation.

défolier [defɔlje] (7) *vti* to defoliate. ◆ **défoliant** *nm* defoliant. ◆ **défoliation** *nf* defoliation.

défoncer [defɔ̃se] (3) **1** *vt caisse, porte* to stave in; *sommier* to break the springs of; *route* to break up. **fauteuil défoncé** sunken armchair. **2 se ~** *vpr (*: travailler dur)* to work like a dog * *(pour qn* for sb; *pour faire qch* to do sth*)*; *(‡: s'amuser)* to have a wild time; *(arg Drogue)* to get high *(arg)*.

déformer [defɔʀme] (1) **1** *vt objet* to put out of shape; *corps* to deform; *visage, image, vision, vérité* to distort; *esprit, goût* to warp. **déformé par son métier** conditioned by one's job; **chaussée déformée** uneven road surface; **mes propos ont été déformés** *(involontairement)* I've been misquoted; *(volontairement)* my words have been twisted. **2 se ~** *vpr* to lose its shape. ◆ **déformant, e** *adj miroir* distorting. ◆ **déformation** *nf (action)* putting out of shape; deformation; distortion; warping; *(résultat)* loss of shape; *(Méd)* deformation. **c'est de la ~ professionnelle** it's force of habit (because of his job).

défouler (se) [defule] (1) *vpr* to release one's pent-up feelings, unwind (*en faisant* by doing). ◆ **défoulement** *nm* release.

défraîchir (se) [defʀeʃiʀ] (2) *vpr (passer)* to fade; *(s'user)* to become worn. **articles défraîchis** shop-soiled items.

défrayer [defʀeje] (8) *vt*: **~ qn** to pay sb's expenses; **~ la chronique** to be widely talked about.

défricher [defʀiʃe] (1) *vt terrain* to clear *(for cultivation)*; *sujet* to do the spadework on. *(fig)* **~ le terrain** to clear the way. ◆ **défrichage** *nm* clearing *(for cultivation)*. *(fig)* **~ d'un sujet** spadework done on a subject.

défriper [defʀipe] (1) *vt* to smooth out.

défriser [defʀize] (1) *vt cheveux* to uncurl; *(*: contrarier)* to annoy. **ce qui me défrise** * what gets me *.

défroisser [defʀwase] (1) *vt* to smooth out.

défunt, e [defœ̃, œ̃t] **1** *adj personne* late; *espoir, année* which is dead and gone; *projet* defunct. **son ~ père** his late father. **2** *nm, f* deceased.

dégagé, e [degaʒe] *adj route, ciel* clear; *vue* wide, open; *front* bare; *ton, manières* casual.

dégagement [degaʒmɑ̃] *nm* (**a**) *(action: V* **dégager***)* freeing; relief; clearing; release; redemption. *(Aut)* **voie de ~** slip road; *(Aut)* **itinéraire de ~** alternative route. (**b**) *(émanation)* emission. (**c**) *(Ftbl)* clearance. (**d**) *(espace libre) [forêt]* clearing; *[appartement]* passage.

dégager [degaʒe] (3) **1** *vt* (**a**) *personne, objet* to free; *(Mil)* to relieve; *ballon* to clear; *crédits* to release; *objet en gage* to redeem. **cela devrait se ~ facilement** it should come free easily; **~ qn de sa promesse** to free sb from his promise; **~ sa responsabilité d'une affaire** to disclaim responsibility in a matter; **être dégagé de ses obligations militaires** to have been discharged from the army, have done one's military service; **robe qui dégage le cou** dress which leaves the neck bare. (**b**) *passage, nez* to clear (*de* of). **allons, dégagez!** * move along! (**c**) *odeur, chaleur* to give off, emit. (**d**) *conclusion* to draw; *sens* to bring out; *impressions* to single out. **~ la vérité de l'erreur** to separate truth from untruth.

2 se ~ *vpr* (**a**) *[personne]* to free *ou* extricate o.s.; *[armée]* to extricate itself (*de* from). **se ~ de** *obligation* to free o.s. from; *affaire* to back out of; *promesse* to go back on. (**b**) *[ciel, rue, nez]* to clear. (**c**) *[odeur, chaleur]* to be given off; *[enthousiasme]* to radiate; *[rumeur]* to rise (*de* from). (**d**) *[conclusion]* to be drawn; *[impression]* to emerge (*de* from).

dégainer [degene] (1) *vt épée, pistolet* to draw.

dégarnir [degaʀniʀ] (2) **1** *vt maison* to empty, clear; *compte* to drain; *(Mil)* to withdraw troops from. **2 se ~** *vpr [salle]* to empty; *[tête]* to go bald; *[arbre]* to lose its leaves; *[rayons, stock]* to be cleaned out. ◆ **dégarni, e** *adj front, salle, rayon* bare; *compte* low; *portefeuille* empty; *magasin* low in stock; *tête* balding.

dégât [degɑ] *nm*: **du ~, des ~s** damage.

dégeler [deʒle] (5) **1** *vt lac, invité, réunion* to thaw; *atmosphère, crédits* to unfreeze. **2** *vi* to thaw. *(Culin)* **faire ~** to thaw, leave to thaw. **3** *vb impers:* **ça dégèle** it's thawing. **4 se ~** *vpr [personne] (lit)* to warm up; *(fig)* to thaw. ◆ **dégel** *nm (lit, fig)* thaw.

dégénérer [deʒeneʀe] (6) *vi (gén)* to degenerate (*en* into). *[manifestation]* **ça a rapidement dégénéré** it soon got out of hand. ◆ **dégénéré, e** *adj, nm, f* degenerate. ◆ **dégénérescence** *nf* degeneracy.

dégingandé, e * [deʒɛ̃gɑ̃de] *adj* gangling, gawky.

dégivrer [deʒivʀe] (1) *vt* to defrost; *(Aviat)* to de-ice. ◆ **dégivrage** *nm* defrosting; de-icing.

déglinguer * [deglɛ̃ge] (1) **1** *vt objet, appareil* to bust *. **2 se** ~ *vpr* to fall apart. **fauteuil déglingué** armchair which is falling apart.

dégobiller * [degɔbije] (1) *vt* to vomit, throw up ‡, puke ‡.

dégonfler [degɔ̃fle] (1) **1** *vt pneu, ballon* to deflate; *enflure* to reduce. **2 se** ~ *vpr (lit)* to go down; *(*: avoir peur)* to chicken out *, back out. ◆ **dégonflé, e** *adj* (**a**) *pneu* flat. (**b**) *(‡: lâche)* yellow ‡, cowardly. **c'est un** ~ he's a yellow-belly ‡. ◆ **dégonflement** *nm* deflation; reduction.

dégorger [degɔʀʒe] (3) **1** *vt (déboucher)* to clear out; *(lit, fig: déverser)* to pour out (*dans* into). **2** *vi [étoffe, viande]* to soak; *[concombres]* to sweat. **faire** ~ to soak; to (leave to) sweat.

dégot(t)er * [degɔte] (1) *vt* to dig up *, unearth.

dégouliner [deguline] (1) *vi [filet]* to trickle; *[goutte]* to drip. ◆ **dégoulinade** *nf*, **dégoulinure** *nf* trickle.

dégourdir [deguʀdiʀ] (2) **1** *vt membres* to bring the circulation back to. **le service militaire le dégourdira** military service will teach him a thing or two. **2 se** ~ *vpr [provincial]* to get a bit livelier. **se** ~ **(les jambes)** to stretch one's legs a bit. ◆ **dégourdi, e** * *adj (malin)* smart, bright.

dégoût [degu] *nm*: **le** ~ disgust, distaste (*pour, de* for); ~ **de la vie** world-weariness. ◆ **dégoûtant, e** *adj* disgusting. ◆ **dégoûté, e** *adj*: **je suis** ~! I am fed up! *; **être** ~ **de** to be sick of. ◆ **dégoûter** (1) *vt* to disgust. **ce plat me dégoûte** I find this dish disgusting; ~ **qn de qch** to put sb off sth; **se** ~ **de qn/qch** to get sick of sb/sth.

dégoutter [degute] (1) *vi* to drip.

dégrader [degʀade] (1) **1** *vt* (**a**) *personne* to degrade; *qualité* to debase. (**b**) *[pluie]* to erode; *[vandales]* to deface, damage. (**c**) *(Art) couleurs* to shade off. **2 se** ~ *vpr (moralement)* to degrade o.s.; *[situation, santé, bâtiment]* to deteriorate; *[temps]* to break. ◆ **dégradant, e** *adj* degrading. ◆ **dégradation** *nf* degradation; debasement; erosion; damaging, defacing; deterioration. **subir des** ~**s** to suffer damage; *(Ordin)* **la** ~ **des données** the corruption of the data. ◆ **dégradé** *nm [couleurs]* gradation.

dégrafer [degʀafe] (1) **1** *vt* to unfasten, undo. **2 se** ~ *vpr (par accident)* to come undone *ou* unfastened.

dégraisser [degʀese] (1) *vt vêtement* to take the grease marks out of; *bouillon* to skim; *viande* to remove the fat from; *(Econ) personnel* to cut back, slim down. ◆ **dégraissage** *nm [personnel]* cutback (*de* in).

degré [dəgʀe] *nm* (**a**) *(gén: niveau)* degree. **à un** ~ **avancé de** at an advanced stage of; **au plus haut** ~ in the extreme, to a degree; **jusqu'à un certain** ~ to some extent *ou* degree; **par** ~**(s)** by degrees. (**b**) *(Gram, Mus, Sci)* degree. **équation du 1er/2e** ~ equation of the 1st/2nd degree; ~ **en alcool d'un liquide** percentage of alcohol in a liquid; **alcool à 90** ~**s** 90% proof alcohol; **vin de 11** ~**s** 11° ~ wine; ~ **centigrade/Fahrenheit** degree centigrade/Fahrenheit. (**c**) *(Méd)* **brûlure du premier/deuxième** ~ first/second degree burn; *(Scol)* **enseignement du premier/second** ~ primary/secondary education; ~ **de parenté** degree of family relationship; **cousins au premier/au second** ~ first/second cousins; **parents au premier/deuxième** ~ relatives of the first/second degree. (**d**) *(littér: marche)* step.

dégressif, -ive [degʀesif, iv] *adj* : **appliquer un tarif** ~ to use a sliding scale of charges. ◆ **dégressivité** *nf [impôts]* degression.

dégrever [degʀəve] (5) *vt produit* to reduce the tax(es) on; *contribuable* to grant tax relief to. ◆ **dégrèvement** *nm [produit]* reduction of tax (*de* on). **bénéficier de** ~**s fiscaux** to be granted tax relief *ou* tax exemption.

dégriffé, e [degʀife] *adj*: **robe** ~**e** unlabelled designer dress; **ils vendent du** ~ they sell designer seconds.

dégringoler [degʀɛ̃gɔle] (1) *vi (lit)* to tumble down; *[monnaie]* to collapse. **elle a fait** ~ **toute la pile** she toppled the whole pile over. **2** *vt pente* to rush *ou* leap down. ◆ **dégringolade** *nf* tumble; collapse.

dégriser *vt*, **se** ~ *vpr* [degʀize] (1) *(lit, fig)* to sober up.

dégrossir [degʀosiʀ] (2) *vt bois* to trim; *marbre* to rough-hew; *travail* to rough out, do the spadework on; (*) *personne* to knock the rough edges off. **il est mal dégrossi** he is unrefined.

dégrouiller (se) * [degʀuje] (1) *vpr* to hurry up, get a move on *. **se** ~ **de** *ou* **pour faire qch** to hurry to do sth.

déguenillé, e [degnije] *adj* ragged, tattered.

déguerpir * [degɛʀpiʀ] (2) *vi* to clear off *. **faire** ~ to drive off.

dégueulasse ‡ [degœlas] *adj (mauvais, injuste)* lousy ‡ , rotten ‡; *(sale)* filthy.

dégueuler ‡ [degœle] (1) *vt* to throw up ‡, puke ‡.

déguiser [degize] (1) **1** *vt voix, pensée* to disguise; *étonnement* to conceal; *enfant* to dress up (*en* as). **non déguisé** undisguised. **2 se** ~ *vpr (pour tromper)* to disguise o.s.; *(pour s'amuser)* to dress up. **se** ~ **en courant d'air** * to make o.s. scarce *. ◆ **déguisement** *nm (pour tromper)* disguise; *(pour s'amuser)* fancy dress.

déguster [degyste] (1) **1** *vt vins* to taste; *fromages* to sample; *repas, spectacle* to enjoy, savour. **2** *vi (*: souffrir)* to have a rough time of it *, be in agony *. ◆ **dégustateur** *nm* wine taster. ◆ **dégustation** *nf* sampling. ~ **de vin(s)** wine-tasting session.

dehors [dəɔʀ] **1** *adv* (**a**) outside. **passer la journée (au)** ~ to spend the day out of doors *ou* outside; **de** ~ from (the) outside; **passez par** ~ go round the outside; **dîner** ~ to eat *ou* dine out; **mettre qn** ~ * *(gén)* to throw *ou* kick * sb out; *[patron]* to sack * *ou* fire * sb. (**b**) *(locutions)* **en** ~ **de** *maison, fenêtre* outside; *sujet* outside, irrelevant to; **en** ~ **de cela** apart from that; **il a voulu rester en** ~ he wanted to stay uninvolved; **au** ~**, elle paraît calme** outwardly she looks relaxed. **2** *nm* (**a**) *(extérieur)* outside. **les bruits du** ~ the noise from outside. (**b**) *(apparences: pl)* appearances. **sous des** ~ **aimables** under a friendly exterior.

déifier [deifje] (7) *vt* to deify. ◆ **déification** *nf* deification.

déisme [deism(ə)] *nm* deism. ◆ **déiste** *adj, nmf* deist.

déjà [deʒa] *adv* (**a**) already. **est-il** ~ **rentré?** has he come home yet?; **j'aurais** ~ **fini si** I would have finished by now *ou* already if; **je suis sûr de l'avoir** ~ **rencontré** I'm sure I've met him before *ou* I've already met him; **c'est du** ~**-vu** we've seen it all before, it's old hat *. (**b**) *(intensif)* **c'est** ~ **pas mal** * that's not bad at all; **c'est** ~ **un gros camion** that's quite a big truck, that's a fair-sized truck; **il est** ~ **assez paresseux** he's lazy enough as it is; **c'est** ~ **quelque chose!** it's better than nothing! (**c**) *(*: interrogatif)* **c'est combien,** ~? how much is it again?

déjeuner [deʒœne] (1) **1** *vi* to have lunch; *(le matin)* to have breakfast. **inviter qn à** ~ to invite sb to lunch; **nous avons déjeuné sur l'herbe** we had a picnic lunch. **2** *nm* lunch, luncheon; *(du matin)* breakfast; *(tasse et soucoupe)* breakfast cup and saucer. ~ **d'affaires/sur l'herbe** business/picnic lunch; **prendre son** ~ to have lunch; **à** ~ for lunch; **ça a été un vrai** ~ **de soleil** it didn't last long.

déjouer [deʒwe] (1) *vt complot* to foil, thwart; *ruse* to outsmart; *surveillance* to elude.

déjuger (se) [deʒyʒe] (3) *vpr* to go back on one's decision.

delà [dəla] **1** *adv*: **au-~, par-~** beyond (that); **ça coûte bien au-~** it costs much more (than that). **2** *prép*: **au** ~ **de** beyond; *somme* over, above; *(littér)* **au** ~ **des mers, par** ~ **les mers** overseas, beyond *ou* over the seas; **par** ~ **les apparences** beneath appearances; **par** ~ **les siècles** across the centuries. **3** *nm*: **l'au-~** the beyond.

délabrer [delɑbʀe] (1) **1** *vt* to ruin. **2 se** ~ *vpr [mur]* to become dilapidated, fall into decay; *[santé]* to break down. ◆ **délabré, e** *adj maison* dilapidated; *santé* broken; *affaires* in a poor state ; *fortune* depleted. ◆ **délabrement** *nm [maison]* dilapidation; *[santé, affaires]* poor state; *[fortune]* depletion. **état de** ~ dilapidated state.

délacer [delase] (3) **1** *vt chaussures* to undo; *corset* to unlace. **2 se** ~ *vpr (par accident)* to come unlaced *ou* undone.

délai [delɛ] **1** *nm* (**a**) *(limite)* time limit. **c'est un** ~ **trop court pour...** it's too short a time for...; ~ **impératif** *ou* **de rigueur, dernier** ~ absolute deadline; **dans un** ~ **de 6 jours** within a period of 6 days. (**b**) *(période d'attente)* waiting period. **il faut compter un** ~ **de huit jours** you'll have to allow a week. (**c**) *(sursis)* extension (of time). **il va demander un** ~ he's going to ask for more time. (**d**) **dans le(s) plus bref(s)** ~**(s)** as soon *ou* as quickly as possible; **dans les** ~**s** within the time limit; **à bref** ~ *(vite)* at short notice; *(bientôt)* shortly, very soon; **sans** ~ without delay. **2** *(pour un travail)* ~ **d'exécution** turnaround time; *(Jur, Fin)* ~ **de grâce** grace period; **avant le 30 juin** ~ **de rigueur** before the final deadline of June 30th; ~ **de livraison** delivery time; ~ **de paiement** term of payment, time for payment.

délaisser [delese] (1) *vt travail, enfant (abandonner)* to abandon; *(négliger)* to neglect. **épouse délaissée** deserted wife. ◆ **délaissement** *nm (action)* abandonment, desertion; *(état)* state of neglect.

délasser [delɑse] (1) **1** *vt (reposer)* to refresh, relax; *(divertir)* to entertain. **2 se** ~ *vpr* to relax (*en faisant qch* by doing sth). ◆ **délassement** *nm* relaxation.

délation [delɑsjɔ̃] *nf* informing. ◆ **délateur, -trice** *nm, f* informer.

délavé, e [delave] *adj tissu* faded; *inscription* washed-out; *terre* waterlogged.

délayer [deleje] (8) *vt farine, poudre* to mix (*dans* with); *(péj) idée* to spin out; *texte* to pad out. ◆ **délayage** *nm (Culin)* mixing. *(péj)* **du** ~ padding.

delco [dɛlko] *nm* ® distributor.

délecter (se) [delɛkte] (1) *vpr*: **se** ~ **de qch/à faire** to delight *ou* revel in sth/in doing. ◆ **délectable** *adj* delectable. ◆ **délectation** *nf* delight.

délégation [delegɑsjɔ̃] *nf (groupe, mandat)* delegation. **venir en** ~ to come as a delegation; **agir par** ~ to act on sb's authority; ~ **de pouvoirs** delegation of powers. ◆ **délégué, e 1** *adj*: **membre** ~ delegate. **2** *nm, f* delegate. ~ **de classe** class representative. ◆ **déléguer** (6) *vt* to delegate (*à* to).

délester [delɛste] (1) **1** *vt ballon* to unballast; *(Élec)* to cut off power from. ~ **qn de qch** to relieve sb of sth. **2 se** ~ *vpr*: **se** ~ **de** *lest* to jettison; *colis* to unload. ◆ **délestage** *nm (Élec)* power cut. *(Aut)* **établir un itinéraire de** ~ to set up a relief route.

délétère [deletɛʀ] *adj* deleterious.

Delhi [dɛli] *n* Delhi.

déliasser [deljase] (1) *vt (Ordin)* to decollate. ◆ **déliassage** *nm* decollation.

délibération [delibeʀɑsjɔ̃] *nf* deliberation. ~**s** *(discussion)* deliberations; *(décision)* resolutions; **après** ~ **du jury** after the jury's deliberation.

délibéré, e [delibeʀe] *adj (intentionnel)* deliberate; *(assuré)* resolute. ◆ **délibérément** *adv* deliberately; resolutely.

délibérer [delibeʀe] (6) *vi (gén)* to deliberate. **après avoir mûrement délibéré** after duly considering the matter; ~ **sur qch** to deliberate upon sth; ~ **de qch** to deliberate sth; ~ **de faire qch** to resolve to do sth.

délicat, e [delika, at] *adj* (**a**) *(gén)* delicate; *voile, travail* fine; *mets* dainty; *nuance* subtle; *oreille* sensitive; *toucher, mouvement* gentle; *prévenance* thoughtful. **avoir le palais** ~ to have a discerning palate. (**b**) *(difficile) problème* delicate, tricky *(épineux) sujet* sensitive. (**c**) *(scrupuleux)* scrupulous; *(plein de tact)* tactful (*envers* to, towards). **peu** ~ unscrupulous, dishonest. (**d**) *(exigeant)* particular. **faire le** ~ *(nourriture)* to be particular; *(spectacle)* to be squeamish; *(propos)* to be easily shocked. ◆ **délicatement** *adv* delicately; finely; daintily; subtly; gently; thoughtfully; tactfully. ◆ **délicatesse** *nf* delicacy; daintiness; fineness; subtlety; sensitivity; gentleness; thoughtfulness; scrupulousness; tact.

délice [delis] *nm* delight. **c'est un vrai** ~ it is quite delightful *ou* delicious; **les** ~**s de l'étude** the delights of study; **faire ses** ~**s de qch** to take delight in sth; **ça ferait les** ~**s de mon père** it would delight my father. ◆ **délicieusement** *adv (gén)* delightfully; *beau* exquisitely; *parfumé* deliciously; *(avec délice)* with delight. ◆ **délicieux, -ieuse** *adj fruit* delicious; *lieu, sensation* delightful.

délié, e [delje] **1** *adj* (**a**) *doigts* nimble; *esprit* astute. **avoir la langue** ~**e** to have a ready tongue. (**b**) *taille* slender; *fil, écriture* fine. **2** *nm [lettre]* upstroke.

délier [delje] (7) *vt* to untie. ~ **la langue de qn** to loosen sb's tongue; ~ **qn de** to free sb from.

délimiter [delimite] (1) *vt (gén)* to delimit. ◆ **délimitation** *nf* delimitation.

délinquance [delɛ̃kɑ̃s] *nf* delinquency. ~ **juvénile** juvenile delinquency. ◆ **délinquant, e 1** *adj* delinquent. **2** *nm, f* delinquent, offender.

déliquescence [delikesɑ̃s] *nf (Chim)* deliquescence; *(fig)* decay. ◆ **déliquescent, e** *adj* deliquescent; decaying.

délire [deliʀ] *nm (Méd)* delirium; *(frénésie)* frenzy. **avoir le** ~ to be delirious; **c'est du** ~! * it's sheer madness!; **foule en** ~ frenzied crowd; **quand l'acteur parut, ce fut le** ~ * when the actor appeared there was a frenzy of excitement; ~ **de persécution** persecution mania. ◆ **délirant, e** *adj idée, architecture* extraordinary, wild. ◆ **délirer** (1) *vi* to be delirious (*de* with). **il délire!** * he's raving! *

délit [deli] *nm* offence. **être poursuivi pour** ~ **d'opinion** to be prosecuted for one's beliefs *ou* convictions.

délivrer [delivʀe] (1) **1** *vt* (**a**) *prisonnier* to set free. ~ **qn de** to relieve sb of. (**b**) *reçu* to issue, give. **2 se** ~ *vpr* to free o.s. (*de* from); *(fig)* to get relief (*de* from). ◆ **délivrance** *nf* (**a**) *[prisonniers]* release; *[pays]* deliverance. (**b**) *(fig: soulagement)* relief. (**c**) *[reçu]* issue. *(Jur)* ~ **d'un brevet** issue of a patent.

déloger [delɔʒe] (3) **1** *vt locataire* to turn out; *fugitif* to flush out; *ennemi* to dislodge (*de* from). **2** *vi* to move out.

déloyal, e, *mpl* **-aux** [delwajal, o] *adj ami* unfaithful, disloyal (*envers* towards); *adversaire* underhand; *procédé* unfair. ◆ **déloyalement** *adv* disloyally. ◆ **déloyauté** *nf* disloyalty; unfairness; *(acte)* disloyal act.

Delphes [dɛlf] *n* Delphi.

delta [dɛlta] *nm (Géog, Ling)* delta.

deltaplane [dɛltaplan] *nm (appareil)* hang-glider; *(sport)* hang gliding. **faire du** ~ to hang glide, go hang gliding.

déluge [delyʒ] *nm (pluie)* downpour; *[larmes, paroles]* flood; *[coups]* shower. *(Bible)* **le** ~ the Flood; **ça remonte au** ~ it's ancient history.

déluré, e [delyʀe] *adj (débrouillard)* smart; *(impertinent)* forward, pert.

démagogie [demagɔʒi] *nf* demagogy. ◆ **démagogique** *adj* demagogic. ◆ **démagogue** *nm* demagogue.

démailler (se) [demɑje] (1) *vpr [bas]* to ladder, run.

demain [d(ə)mɛ̃] *adv* tomorrow. ~ **matin** tomorrow morning; ~ **il fera jour** tomorrow is another day; **ce n'est pas** ~ **la veille** * it's not just around the corner; **à** ~! see you tomorrow!; **le monde de** ~ tomorrow's world.

demande [d(ə)mɑ̃d] *nf (requête)* request (*de qch* for sth); *(revendication)* claim, demand (*de* for); *(question)* question; *[emploi, naturalisation]* application (*de* for); *[remboursement]* claim (*de* for); *[renseignement]* enquiry; *(Écon: opposé à offre)* demand. *(formulaire)* **remplir une** ~ to fill in a claim form (*de* for); **adressez votre** ~ **au ministère** apply to the ministry; *(Écon)* **pour répondre à la** ~ to meet the demand; ~ **(en mariage)** proposal (of marriage); **faire sa** ~ **(en mariage)** to propose; ~ **de divorce** divorce petition; ~ **de rançon** ransom demand; **à** *ou* **sur la** ~ **de qn** at sb's request; **sur** ~ on request; *(Admin)* on application.

demandé, e [d(ə)mɑ̃de] *adj (Comm etc)* in demand. **il est très** ~ he is (very) much in demand *ou* sought after.

demander [d(ə)mɑ̃de] (1) **1** *vt* (**a**) *conseil, entrevue* to ask for, request; *emploi, divorce* to apply for; *indemnité* to claim; *réunion, volontaire* to call for. ~ **qch à qn** to ask sb for sth; ~ **un service à qn** to ask sb a favour; ~ **la permission de faire** to ask permission to do; ~ **à voir qn** to ask to see sb; ~ **à qn de faire** *ou* **qu'il fasse qch** to ask sb to do sth; **vous n'avez qu'à** ~ you only have to ask.
(**b**) *médecin, plombier* to send for; *personne, numéro* to ask for. *(au téléphone)* **demandez-moi M. X** get me Mr X; **le patron vous demande** the boss wants to see you.
(**c**) *(désirer)* to be asking for, want. **il demande qu'on le laisse partir** he wants us *ou* is asking us to let him go; **il ne demandera pas mieux que de vous aider** he'll be only too pleased to help you; **'on demande une vendeuse'** 'shop assistant required *ou* wanted'.
(**d**) *heure, nom, chemin* to ask. ~ **qch à qn** to ask sb sth; ~ **l'heure à qn** to ask sb the time; ~ **un renseignement à qn** to ask sb for some information; ~ **des nouvelles de qn,** ~ **après qn** * to enquire *ou* ask after sb; **je ne te demande rien** I'm not asking you.
(**e**) *(nécessiter) [travail, décision etc]* to require, need. **ce travail va (lui)** ~ **6 heures** this job will require 6 hours, he'll need 6 hours to do this job; **ça demande toute votre attention** it calls for *ou* requires your full attention.
(**f**) *(exiger)* ~ **qch de qn** to ask sth of sb; **il ne faut pas trop lui en** ~! you mustn't ask too much of him!
(**g**) *(locutions)* ~ **la paix** to sue for peace; ~ **l'impossible** to ask the impossible; ~ **la lune** to ask for the moon; ~ **pardon à qn** to apologize to sb (*de qch* for sth); ~ **la parole** to ask to be allowed to speak; **il l'a demandée en mariage** he asked if he could marry her; ~ **la main de qn** to ask for sb's hand in marriage; **il est parti sans** ~ **son reste** he left wihout a murmur.
2 se ~ *vpr* to wonder. **il se demanda: suis-je vraiment aussi bête?** he asked himself *ou* wondered: am I really so stupid?

demandeur[1], -deresse [d(ə)mɑ̃dœʀ, dʀɛs] *nm, f (Jur)* plaintiff, complainant.

demandeur[2], -euse [d(ə)mɑ̃dœʀ, øz] *nm, f*: ~ **d'emploi** person looking for work, job-seeker; **ils sont très** ~**s (de nos produits)** they are eager buyers (of our goods).

démanger [demɑ̃ʒe] (3) *vt*: **ça (me** *etc***) démange** it itches, it's itching; *(fig)* **ça me démange de faire...** I'm dying *ou* itching * to do... ◆ **démangeaison** *nf* itching sensation. **avoir des** ~**s** to be itching; **j'ai une** ~ I've got an itch; *(fig)* ~ **de faire** itch *ou* urge to do.

démanteler [demɑ̃tle] (5) *vt (Mil)* to demolish; *gang* to break up; *empire* to bring down; *réseau d'espionnage* to crack; *compagnie, service* to dismantle. ◆ **démantèlement** *nm* demolition; breaking up; bringing down; cracking; dismantling.

démantibuler * [demɑ̃tibyle] (1) **1** *vt* to demolish. **2 se** ~ *vpr* to fall apart. **se** ~ **le bras** to dislocate one's arm.

démaquiller [demakije] (1) **1** *vt* to remove the make-up from. **2 se** ~ *vpr* to remove one's make-up. ◆ **démaquillage** *nm* removal of make-up. ◆ **démaquillant, e 1** *adj* make-up removing. **2** *nm* make-up remover.

démarcation [demaʀkɑsjɔ̃] *nf* demarcation (*de, entre* between).

démarche [demaʀʃ(ə)] *nf* (**a**) *[personne]* gait, walk; *[pensée]* processes. (**b**) *(intervention)* step. **faire des** ~**s** to take steps; **faire une** ~ **auprès de qn (pour obtenir qch)** to approach sb (to obtain sth).

démarcheur, -euse [demaʀʃœʀ, øz] *nm, f* door-to-door *ou* doorstep salesman (*ou* woman).

démarquer [demaʀke] (1) **1** *vt (Comm) article* to mark down; *œuvre, auteur* to plagiarize. **2 se** ~ *vpr*: **se** ~ **de** to distinguish *ou* differentiate o.s. from. ◆ **démarqué, e** *adj joueur* unmarked. **robe** ~**e** unlabelled designer dress.

démarrage [demaʀaʒ] *nm* (**a**) *[véhicule] (départ)* moving off; *(mise en marche)* starting. **à chaque** ~ **du bus** every time the bus moved off; ~ **en côte** hill start. (**b**) *[affaire, élève] (action)* starting; *(résultat)* start. **le** ~ **d'une campagne** getting a campaign going. (**c**) *(Sport)* **placer plusieurs** ~**s** to pull ahead several times.

démarrer [demaʀe] (1) **1** *vi [moteur, conducteur]* to start up; *[véhicule]* to move off; *[coureur]* to pull away; *[campagne]* to get moving; *[débutant]* to start off. **l'affaire a bien démarré** the affair got off to a good *ou* fast start *ou* started off well; ~ **en trombe** to shoot off; **il ne veut pas** ~ **de son idée** he just won't let go of his idea. **2** *vt (plus courant:* **faire** ~ *) véhicule* to start, get started; *affaire, travail* to get going on. ~ **qn en anglais** to get sb started at English. ◆ **démarreur** *nm (Aut)* starter.

démasquer [demaske] (1) **1** *vt (gén)* to unmask; *plan* to unveil. **2 se** ~ *vpr [imposteur]* to drop one's mask.

démêlé [demele] *nm* dispute, quarrel. ~**s** problems.

démêler [demele] (1) **1** *vt ficelle* to disentangle; *cheveux* to untangle; *problème, situation* to sort out. ~ **qch d'avec** *ou* **de** to distinguish *ou* tell sth from; ~ **le vrai du faux** to sort the truth out from the lies *ou* falsehood. **2 se** ~ *vpr*: **se** ~ **de** *embarras* to extricate o.s. from.

démembrer [demɑ̃bʀe] (1) *vt domaine* to carve up.

déménager [demenaʒe] (3) **1** *vt affaires* to move, remove; *maison* to move the furniture out of. **2** *vi* (**a**) to move (house). ~ **à la cloche de bois** to shoot the moon. (**b**) (‡) *(partir)* to clear off ‡; *(être fou)* to be off one's rocker ‡. ◆ **déménagement** *nm [meubles]* removal; *(changement de domicile)* move. **le** ~ **du bureau** moving the furniture out of the office. ◆ **déménageur** *nm (entrepreneur)* furniture remover; *(ouvrier)* removal man.

démence [demɑ̃s] *nf* madness, insanity. ◆ **dément, e** **1** *adj (fou)* mad, insane; *(*: fantastique)* terrific *, fantastic *. **c'est** ~! *(incroyable)* it's incredible! **2** *nm, f (Méd)* lunatic. ◆ **démentiel, -ielle** *adj* insane.

démener (se) [dɛmne] (5) *vpr (se débattre)* to thrash about, struggle; *(se dépenser)* to exert o.s.

démentir [demɑ̃tiʀ] (16) **1** *vt* (**a**) *[personne] nouvelle* to deny; *personne* to contradict. (**b**) *[faits] témoignage* to refute; *apparences* to belie; *espoirs* to disappoint. **ses actes démentent ses paroles** his actions belie his words. **2 se** ~ *vpr:* **ça ne s'est jamais démenti** it has never failed. ◆ **démenti** *nm* denial; refutation.

démériter [demeʀite] (1) **1** ~ **de** *vt indir* to show o.s. unworthy of. **2** *vi* to do badly. ◆ **démérite** *nm (littér)* demerit.

démesure [deməzyʀ] *nf [personnage]* immoderation; *[propos]* outrageousness. ◆ **démesuré, e** *adj orgueil* immoderate; *taille* disproportionate; *territoire, membres* enormous. ◆ **démesurément** *adv* immoderately; disproportionately; enormously.

démettre [demɛtʀ(ə)] (56) *vt* (**a**) *articulation* to dislocate. **se** ~ **le poignet** to dislocate one's wrist. (**b**) *fonctionnaire* to dismiss (*de* from). **se** ~ **de ses fonctions** to resign (from) one's duties, hand in one's resignation.

demeure [dəmœʀ] *nf* residence. **à** ~ *installations* permanent; *domestique* live-in, resident; *s'installer* permanently; **mettre qn en** ~ **de faire qch** to order sb to do sth; *(Jur)* **mettre qn en** ~ **de payer** to give sb notice to pay.

demeurer [dəmœʀe] (1) *vi* (**a**) *(avec avoir) (habiter)* to live. **il demeure au 12 rue d'Ulm** he lives at number 12 in the rue d'Ulm. (**b**) *(avec être) (rester)* to remain, stay. ~ **fidèle** to remain faithful; **l'odeur demeurait dans la pièce** the smell lingered in the room; **la conversation en est demeurée là** the conversation was taken no further *ou* was left at that; **la maison leur est demeurée** the house was left to them; **au demeurant** for all that. ◆ **demeuré, e** **1** *adj* half-witted. **2** *nm, f* half-wit.

demi, e [d(ə)mi] **1** *adv*: **(à)** ~ **plein** *etc* half-full *etc*; **il ne te croit qu'à** ~ he only half believes you; **il a fait le travail à** ~ he has only done half the work; **je ne fais pas les choses à** ~ I don't do things by halves. **2** *adj (après n)* **une livre et** ~**e** one and a half pounds, a pound and a half; **à six heures et** ~**e** at half past six; **2 fois et** ~**e plus grand** 2 and a half times greater. **3** *nm, f* (**a**) half. **une bouteille? — non une** ~**e** one bottle? — no, a half *ou* half a bottle *ou* a half-bottle; **deux** ~**s** two halves. **4** *nf (à l'horloge)* **la** ~**e a sonné** the half-hour has struck; **c'est déjà la** ~**e** it's already half past. **5** *nm* (**a**) *(bière)* glass of beer, ≃ half-pint, half *. (**b**) *(Sport)* half-back. ~ **de mêlée/ d'ouverture** scrum/stand-off half. **6** *préf inv (le 2ᵉ élément donne le genre et porte la marque du pluriel)* half. *(Ordin)* ~**-additionneur** half-adder; **une** ~**-douzaine d'œufs** half a dozen *ou* a half-dozen eggs; **dans une** ~**-heure** in half an hour; **la première** ~**-heure** the first half-hour; ~**-litre/-journée/-sommeil/ -teinte** *etc* half-litre/-day/-sleep/-tone *etc*; ~**-cercle** semicircle; **en** ~**-cercle** semicircular ; ~**-dieu** demigod; ~**-finale** semifinal; ~**-fond** *(discipline)* medium-distance *ou* middle-distance running; ~**-frère** half-brother; *(Comm)* ~**-gros** wholesale trade; ~**-mal: ce n'est que** ~**-mal** it could have been worse; ~**-mot: se faire comprendre à** ~**-mot** to make o.s. understood without having to spell it out; ~**-pension** half-board; ~**-pensionnaire** pupil who takes school lunches; ~**-saison: manteau de** ~**-saison** light coat; ~**-sel** *(adj inv) beurre* slightly salted; ~**-sœur** half-sister; ~**-tarif: billet** *etc* **(à)** ~**-tarif** half-price ticket *etc*; **voyager à** ~**-tarif** to travel at half-fare; ~**-tour** *(sur soi-même)* about-turn; *(Aut)* U-turn; *(de clé)* half-turn; *(repartir)* **faire** ~**-tour** to make an about-turn, do a U-turn; *[radiation]* ~**-vie** half-life.

démilitarisation [demilitaʀizɑsjɔ̃] *nf* demilitarization. ◆ **démilitariser** (1) *vt* to demilitarize.

déminéraliser [demineʀalize] (1) **1** *vt (Tech)* to demineralize; *(Méd)* to make deficient in essential minerals. **eau déminéralisée** distilled *ou* demineralized water. **2 se** ~ *vpr (Méd)* to become deficient in essential minerals. ◆ **déminéralisation** *nf* demineralization.

démission [demisjɔ̃] *nf (lit)* resignation; *(fig)* abdication. **donner sa** ~ to hand in *ou* tender one's resignation. ◆ **démissionner** (1) *vi* to resign; *(fig) [parents]* to give up.

démobilisation [demɔbilizɑsjɔ̃] *nf* demobilization. ◆ **démobilisateur, trice** *adj* demobilizing. ◆ **démobiliser** (1) *vt* to demobilize. **se** ~ to become demobilized *ou* apathetic.

démocrate [demɔkʀat] **1** *adj* democratic. **2** *nmf* democrat. ◆ **démocratie** *nf* democracy. ~ **populaire** people's democracy. ◆ **démocratique** *adj* democratic. **la République** ~ **de...** the Democratic Republic of... ◆ **démocratiquement** *adv* democratically. ◆ **démocratisation** *nf* democratization. ◆ **démocratiser** *vt*, **se** ~ *vpr* (1) to democratize.

démodé, e [demɔde] *adj* old-fashioned, out-of-date. ◆ **démoder (se)** (1) *vpr* to become old-fashioned, go out of fashion.

démographie [demɔgʀafi] *nf* demography. ◆ **démographique** *adj* demographic. **poussée** ~ population increase.

demoiselle [d(ə)mwazɛl] *nf (jeune)* young lady; *(âgée)* single lady. **la** ~ **du téléphone** the telephone lady; ~ **d'honneur** *[mariage]* bridesmaid; *[reine]* maid of honour.

démolir [demɔliʀ] (2) *vt maison, objet, doctrine* to demolish; *santé* to ruin; *autorité* to overthrow, shatter; *personne (*: épuiser)* to do for *; *(‡: battre)* to beat up; *(*: critiquer)* to tear to pieces. ◆ **démolisseur** *nm* demolition worker; *(entrepreneur)* demolition contractor. ◆ **démolition** *nf* demolition. **en** ~ in the course of being demolished.

démon [demɔ̃] *nm (Rel)* demon, fiend; *(Myth)* genius; *(fig) (harpie)* harpy; *(enfant)* demon. **le** ~ the Devil; **le** ~ **du jeu** a passion for gambling; **le** ~ **de la curiosité** the demon curiosity; **mauvais** ~ evil spirit. ◆ **démoniaque** *adj* diabolical, fiendish.

démonstration [demɔ̃stʀɑsjɔ̃] *nf [vérité]* demonstration; *[théorème]* proof; *(Comm)* demonstration. **faire une** ~ to give a demonstration; **appareil de** ~ demonstration model; ~**s de** *joie, force* show of. ◆ **démonstrateur, -trice** *nm, f (gén)* demonstrator *(of commercial products)*. ◆ **démonstratif, -ive** *adj* demonstrative. **peu** ~ undemonstrative.

démonter [demɔ̃te] (1) **1** *vt* (**a**) *(gén)* to dismantle; *étagères* to take down; *appareil* to take to pieces, take apart; *pneu, porte* to take off. (**b**) *(déconcerter)* to disconcert. **il ne se laisse jamais** ~ he never gets flustered. (**c**) *cavalier* to throw. **2 se** ~ *vpr [assemblage] (accidentellement)* to come apart; *[personne]* to become flustered. ◆ **démontable** *adj* *(gén)* that can be dismantled. ◆ **démontage** *nm* dismantling; taking down; taking to pieces; taking apart; taking off. ~ **difficile** difficult dismantling operation. ◆ **démonté, e** *adj mer* raging. ◆ **démonte-pneu**, *pl* **démonte-pneus** *nm* tyre lever.

démontrer [demɔ̃tʀe] (1) *vt vérité, fonctionnement* to demonstrate; *théorème* to prove; *nécessité* to show, demonstrate. ~ **qch (à qn) par A plus B** to prove sth conclusively (to sb); **ça démontrait son inquiétude** that clearly indicated his anxiety. ◆ **démontrable** *adj* demonstrable.

démoraliser [demɔʀalize] (1) **1** *vt* to demoralize. **2 se** ~ *vpr* to become demoralized. ◆ **démoralisant, e** *adj* demoralizing. ◆ **démoralisation** *nf* demoralization.

démordre [demɔʀdʀ(ə)] (41) *vi*: **il ne démord pas de sa décision** he is sticking to his decision; **il ne veut pas en** ~ he won't budge an inch, he is sticking to his guns.

démouler [demule] (1) *vt statue* to remove from the mould; *gâteau* to turn out. ◆ **démoulage** *nm* removal from the mould; turning out.

démultiplier [demyltiplije] (7) *vt* to reduce, gear down. ◆ **démultiplication** *nf (procédé)* reduction; *(rapport)* reduction ratio.

démunir [demyniʀ] (2) **1** *vt*: ~ **qn de** to deprive sb of; ~ **qch de** to divest sth of. **2 se** ~ *vpr (financièrement)* to part with one's money. **se** ~ **de** to part with. ◆ **démuni, e** *adj (sans ressources)* destitute. **nous sommes** ~**s** *(sans argent)* we are destitute; *(sans défense)* we are powerless (*devant* in the face of); ~ **de** without; ~ **de protection** unprotected; ~ **d'intérêt** devoid of *ou* without interest; ~ **de tout** destitute.

démystifier [demistifje] (7) *vt* to enlighten, demystify. ◆ **démystification** *nf* enlightenment, demystification.

dénatalité [denatalite] *nf* fall in the birth rate.

dénaturer [denatyʀe] (1) *vt faits* to distort, misrepresent; *(Tech)* to denature; *goût* to alter completely. ◆ **dénaturé, e** *adj mœurs, parents* unnatural.

dénégation [denegɑsjɔ̃] *nf (gén, Jur)* denial.

déni [deni] *nm* denial. *(Jur)* ~ **de justice** denial of justice.

déniaiser [denjeze] (1) *vt*: ~ **qn** to teach sb a thing or two.

dénicher [deniʃe] (1) *vt* (**a**) (*) *objet* to unearth; *bistro* to discover; *personne* to track down. (**b**) *(débusquer) fugitif, animal* to drive out of hiding.

denier [dənje] *nm (à Rome)* denarius; *(en France, Tex)* denier. **pas un** ~ † not a farthing *ou* a cent *(US)*; **de mes propres** ~**s** out of my own pocket; **le** ~ **du culte** the contribution to parish costs; **les** ~**s publics** public monies.

dénier [denje] (7) *vt responsabilité* to deny, disclaim; *faute* to deny. ~ **qch à qn** to deny sb sth.

dénigrer [denigʀe] (1) *vt* to denigrate. ◆ **dénigrement** *nm* denigration.

dénivellation [denivɛlɑsjɔ̃] *nf (pente)* slope. ~ **entre deux points** difference in height *ou* level between two points.

dénombrer [denɔ̃bʀe] (1) *vt (compter)* to count; *(énumérer)* to enumerate. ◆ **dénombrable** *adj* countable. *(Ling)* **nom** ~ countable *ou* count noun. ◆ **dénombrement** *nm* counting.

dénominateur [denɔminatœʀ] *nm* denominator.

dénommer [denɔme] (1) *vt* to name. **le dénommé X** the man called X. ◆ **dénomination** *nf* designation.

dénoncer [denɔ̃se] (3) **1** *vt* (**a**) *(révéler) coupable, injustice, traité* to denounce; *forfait* to expose. **sa hâte le dénonça** his haste betrayed him; ~ **qn à la police** to inform against sb. (**b**) *(littér: dénoter)* to indicate. **2 se** ~ *vpr (gén)* to come forward; *[criminel]* to give o.s. up. **se** ~ **à la police** to give o.s. up to the police. ◆ **dénonciateur, -trice** **1** *adj* denunciatory. **2** *nm, f* denouncer, informer; exposer. ◆ **dénonciation** *nf* denunciation; exposure.

dénoter [denɔte] (1) *vt* to denote.

dénouement [denumɑ̃] *nm (Théât)* dénouement; *[aventure]* outcome.

dénouer [denwe] (1) **1** *vt lien* to untie, undo; *situation* to untangle, resolve. **2 se** ~ *vpr* to come untied *ou* undone; to be resolved.

dénoyauter [denwajote] (1) *vt fruit* to stone, pit. ◆ **dénoyauteur** *nm* stoner, pitter.

denrée [dɑ̃ʀe] *nf (aliment)* foodstuff; *(fig)* commodity. ~**s coloniales** colonial produce.

densité [dɑ̃site] *nf (Phys)* density; *[brouillard]* denseness, thickness; *[foule]* denseness. **à forte/faible** ~ **de population** densely/sparsely populated; *(Ordin)* ~ **d'implantation** packing density. ◆ **dense** *adj* dense, thick; *style* condensed.

dent [dɑ̃] *nf* (**a**) *[homme, scie, peigne]* tooth; *[fourche]* prong; *[engrenage]* cog. ~ **de lait/de sagesse** milk *ou* baby/wisdom tooth; **en** ~**s de scie** *couteau* serrated; *montagne* jagged; **carrière en** ~**s de scie** switchback career. (**b**) *(locutions)* **avoir la** ~ * to be hungry; **avoir la** ~ **dure** to be scathing in one's comments (*envers* about); **avoir/garder une** ~ **contre qn** to have/hold a grudge against sb; **avoir les** ~**s longues** *(ambitieux)* to have one's sights fixed high; **être sur les** ~**s** *(épuisé)* to be worn out; *(très occupé)* to be working flat out *; **faire** *ou* **percer ses** ~**s** to teethe; **croquer qch à belles** ~**s** to bite into sth with gusto; **manger du bout des** ~**s** to eat half-heartedly; **ils n'ont rien à se mettre sous la** ~ they have nothing to eat. ◆ **dentaire** *adj* dental. ◆ **denté, e** *adj (Tech)* toothed; *(Bot)* dentate.

dentelé, e [dɑ̃tle] *adj arête, côte* jagged; *timbre* perforated; *bord* serrated.

dentelle [dɑ̃tɛl] *nf* lace. ◆ **dentellière** *nf* lacemaker; *(machine)* lacemaking machine.

dentelure [dɑ̃tlyʀ] *nf [timbre]* perforations; *[feuille]* serration; *[côte, arête]* jagged outline.

dentiste [dɑ̃tist(ə)] *nmf* dentist. ◆ **dentier** *nm* denture. ◆ **dentifrice** *nm* toothpaste, dentifrice. ◆ **dentition** *nf* dentition. ◆ **denture** *nf* teeth *(pl)*.

dénuder [denyde] (1) **1** *vt* to bare, strip. **2 se** ~ *vpr [personne]* to strip; *[colline]* to become bare. ◆ **dénudé, e** *adj (gén)* bare; *crâne* bald.

dénué, e [denɥe] *adj*: ~ **de** *bon sens* devoid of; *talent* lacking in, without; ~ **de tout** destitute; ~ **de tout fondement** completely unfounded *ou* groundless. ◆ **dénuement** *nm* destitution.

déodorant [deɔdɔʀɑ̃] *adj m, nm*: **(produit)** ~ deodorant.

dépanner [depane] (1) *vt véhicule* to fix, repair; *automobiliste* to fix the car of; (*: *tirer d'embarras)* to help out. ◆ **dépannage** *nm* fixing; repairing; helping out. **service de** ~ breakdown service; **ils ont fait 3** ~**s** they've fixed 3 breakdowns; **partir pour un** ~ to go out on a repair *ou* breakdown job. ◆ **dépanneur** *nm (Aut)* breakdown mechanic; *(TV)* television repairman. ◆ **dépanneuse** *nf* breakdown lorry, tow truck *(US)*.

déparasiter [depaʀazite] (1) *vt poste de radio* to fit a suppressor to.

dépareillé, e [depaʀeje] *adj collection* incomplete; *objet* odd. *(Comm)* **articles** ~**s** oddments.

déparer [depaʀe] (1) *vt* to spoil, mar.

départ [depaʀ] *nm* (**a**) *[voyageur, train]* departure. **observer le** ~ **du train** to watch the train leave *ou* depart; **mon** ~ **de l'hôtel** my departure from *ou* my leaving the hotel; **le** ~ **du courrier se fait**

à 9 heures the mail leaves town at 9 o'clock. (**b**) *(Sport)* start. *(lit, fig)* **faux** ~ false start; **donner le ~ aux coureurs** to give the runners the starting signal; ~ **décalé** staggered start. (**c**) *[employé]* departure. **le ~ du ministre a fait l'effet d'une bombe** the minister's leaving *ou* departure was something of a bombshell. (**d**) *[processus]* start. **la substance de ~** the original substance. (**e**) **être sur le ~** to be about to leave *ou* go; **excursions au ~ de Chamonix** excursions (leaving *ou* departing) from Chamonix; *(fig)* **au ~** at the start *ou* outset. (**f**) *(littér: distinction)* distinction.

départager [depaʀtaʒe] (3) *vt* to decide between. ~ **l'assemblée** to settle the voting in the assembly.

département [depaʀtəmɑ̃] *nm (gén)* department. ~ **ministériel** ministry department; *(aux USA)* **le ~ d'État** the State Department. ◆ **départemental, e,** *mpl* **-aux** *adj* departmental, ministerial. **route ~e** secondary road.

départir (se) [depaʀtiʀ] (16) *vpr (gén nég)* **se ~ de** to abandon.

dépassé, e [depɑse] *adj (périmé)* out-moded, old-fashioned, out of date.

dépassement [depɑsmɑ̃] *nm* (**a**) *(Aut)* overtaking, passing. **après plusieurs ~s...** after overtaking several vehicles... (**b**) *[limite, prix] (action)* exceeding; *(excès)* excess. (**c**) ~ **(de soi-même)** surpassing of oneself.

dépasser [depɑse] (1) **1** *vt* (**a**) *endroit* to pass, go past; *véhicule, piéton* to overtake, pass. (**b**) *alignement (horizontalement)* to jut *ou* stick out beyond; *(verticalement)* to jut out above. **son succès a dépassé les frontières** his success has reached beyond national boundaries. (**c**) *limite, quantité* to exceed. ~ **qch en hauteur/largeur** to be higher/wider than sth, exceed sth in height/width; ~ **en nombre** to outnumber; **tout colis qui dépasse 20 kg** all parcels exceeding *ou* over 20 kg; ~ **le nombre prévu** to be more than expected; **la réunion ne devrait pas ~ 3 heures** the meeting shouldn't last longer than 3 hours; **il ne veut pas ~ 100 F** he won't go above 100 francs; **elle a dépassé la quarantaine** she is over forty. (**d**) *valeur, prévisions* to exceed; *rival* to outstrip. ~ **qn (en intelligence** *etc***)** to surpass sb (in intelligence *etc*); **pour la paresse il dépasse tout le monde** he beats everybody for laziness; **il dépasse tous ses camarades** he surpasses all his friends; **sa bêtise dépasse tout ce qu'on peut imaginer** his stupidity goes beyond all imagining; **l'homme doit se ~** man must try to surpass himself. (**e**) *instructions, attributions* to go beyond, overstep; *crédits* to exceed. **cela dépasse les bornes** that's going too far; **cela a dépassé le stade de la plaisanterie** it has gone beyond a joke; **cela dépasse mes forces/ma compétence** it's beyond my strength/capabilities; **il a dépassé ses forces** he has overtaxed himself. (**f**) *(*: dérouter)* **cela me dépasse!** it is beyond me!; **être dépassé par les événements** to be overtaken by events; **il est complètement dépassé!** he is completely out of his depth!

2 *vi* (**a**) *(Aut)* to overtake, pass. (**b**) *[tour, balcon, clou]* to stick out (*de* of); *[jupon]* to show (*de* below).

dépassionner [depasjɔne] (1) *vt débat* to take the heat out of.

dépaysement [depeizmɑ̃] *nm (désorientation)* disorientation; *(agréable)* change of surroundings. ◆ **dépaysé, e** *adj*: **être ~** to be completely disoriented. ◆ **dépayser** (1) *vt* to disorientate; to give a change of surroundings to.

dépecer [depəse] (5) *vt [boucher]* to joint, cut up; *[lion]* to dismember; *territoire* to carve up. ◆ **dépeçage** *nm* jointing, cutting up; dismembering ; carving up.

dépêche [depɛʃ] *nf* dispatch. ~ **télégraphique** telegram, wire.

dépêcher [depeʃe] (1) **1** *vt* to dispatch, send (*auprès de* to). **2 se ~** *vpr* to hurry. **dépêche-toi!** hurry up!; **se ~ de faire qch** to hurry to do sth.

dépeigner [depeɲe] (1) *vt*: ~ **qn** to make sb's hair untidy; **dépeigné** with dishevelled hair.

dépeindre [depɛ̃dʀ(ə)] (52) *vt* to depict.

dépenaillé, e [depənɑje] *adj (en haillons)* tattered.

dépendance [depɑ̃dɑ̃s] *nf* (**a**) *(interdépendance)* dependence, dependency. **~s** dependencies. (**b**) *(asservissement)* subordination. **sous la ~ de qn** subordinate to sb. (**c**) *(bâtiment)* outbuilding; *(territoire)* dependency. (**d**) *(Drogue)* dependence, dependency.

dépendre [depɑ̃dʀ(ə)] (41) **1** ~ **de** *vt indir (gén)* to depend on, be dependent on; *[employé]* to be answerable to. **ce terrain dépend de leur domaine** this piece of land is part of their property; **ne ~ que de soi-même** to be answerable only to oneself; **— ça dépend —** it (all) depends; **il ne dépend que de vous que...** it depends entirely on you whether..., it's entirely up to you whether... **2** *vt lustre* to take down.

dépens [depɑ̃] *nmpl* (**a**) *(Jur)* costs. **condamné aux ~** ordered to pay costs. (**b**) **aux ~ de** at the expense of; **je l'ai appris à mes ~** I learnt this to my cost.

dépense [depɑ̃s] *nf* (**a**) *(argent dépensé)* expense; *(sortie)* outlay, expenditure. **contrôler les ~s de qn** to control sb's expenditure *ou* spending; **c'est une grosse ~** it's a large outlay, it's a lot to lay out; **~s publiques** public *ou* government expenditure *ou* spending; ~ **d'investissement** *ou* **d'équipement** capital expenditure; **pousser qn à la ~** to make sb spend money; **faire la ~ de qch** to spend money on sth; **regarder à la ~** to watch one's spending. (**b**) *[électricité, essence]* consumption; *[imagination]* expenditure. ~ **physique** (physical) exercise; ~ **de temps** spending of time.

dépenser [depɑ̃se] (1) **1** *vt argent, temps* to spend; *électricité* to use; *énergie, jeunesse* to use up. ~ **inutilement qch** to waste sth. **2 se ~** *vpr* to exert o.s. **il faut que les enfants se dépensent** children have to let off steam. ◆ **dépensier, -ière 1** *adj* extravagant. **2** *nm, f* spendthrift.

déperdition [depɛʀdisjɔ̃] *nf (Sci, gén)* loss.

dépérir [depeʀiʀ] (2) *vi [personne]* to waste away; *[forces]* to fail; *[plante]* to wither; *[affaire]* to go downhill. ◆ **dépérissement** *nm* wasting away ; failing; withering.

dépêtrer [depetʀe] (1) **1** *vt*: ~ **qn de** to extricate sb from. **2 se ~** *vpr* to extricate o.s. (*de* from).

dépeupler [depœple] (1) **1** *vt ville* to depopulate; *rivière* to empty of fish; *région* to empty of wildlife; *forêt* to clear (of trees *etc*). **2 se ~** *vpr* to be depopulated; to be emptied of fish (*ou* wildlife); to be cleared (of trees *etc*). ◆ **dépeuplement** *nm* depopulation; emptying of fish (*ou* wildlife); clearing (of trees *etc*); *(résultat)* disappearance of fish (*ou* wildlife *ou* trees *etc*).

déphasé, e [defaze] *adj (lit, fig)* out of phase.

dépilatoire [depilatwaʀ] **1** *adj* depilatory. **2** *nm* depilatory *ou* hair-removing cream.

dépister [depiste] (1) *vt gibier, criminel* to track down; *maladie* to detect; *cause* to unearth, detect. ◆ **dépistage** *nm* tracking down; detection; unearthing.

dépit [depi] *nm* pique, vexation. **causer du ~ à qn** to vex sb greatly; **il l'a fait par ~** he did it out of pique *ou* in a fit of pique; **en ~ de** in spite of, despite; **faire qch en ~ du bon sens** to do sth any old how. ◆ **dépité, e** *adj* piqued. ◆ **dépiter** (1) *vt (littér)* to vex greatly.

déplacer [deplase] (3) **1** *vt meuble, élève* to move, shift; *usine, fonctionnaire* to transfer, move; *(fig) problème* to shift the emphasis of; *(Naut)* to displace. **se ~ une articulation** to displace a joint. **2 se ~** *vpr (gén)* to move; *(voyager)* to travel; *[air]* to move, be displaced. ◆ **déplacé, e** *adj propos* uncalled-for, out of place. ◆ **déplacement** *nm (action)* moving; shifting; transfer; displacement; *(mouvement)* movement; displacement; *(voyage)* trip; *(Naut)* displacement. **ça vaut le ~** it's worth the journey; **frais de ~** travelling expenses.

déplafonner [deplafɔne] (1) *vt crédit* to derestrict; *cotisations* to remove the ceiling on. ◆ **déplafonnement** *nm* derestriction; removal of the ceiling (*de* from).

déplaire [deplɛʀ] (54) *vt*: **~ à qn** *(être antipathique)* to be disliked by sb; *(irriter)* to displease sb; **ça me déplaît** I dislike *ou* don't like it; **il cherche à ~** he is trying to be disagreeable; **n'en déplaise à son mari** whether her husband likes it or not *ou* agrees or not; **elle se déplaît ici** she dislikes it *ou* doesn't like it here. ◆ **déplaisant, e** *adj* disagreeable, unpleasant. ◆ **déplaisir** *nm* displeasure.

déplâtrer [deplɑtʀe] (1) *vt (Méd)* to take out of plaster.

déplier [deplije] (7) *vt serviette, carte* to unfold; *jambes* to stretch out. ◆ **dépliant, e** **1** *adj* extendible. **2** *nm* leaflet, folder.

déplorer [deplɔʀe] (1) *vt incident* to deplore; *(littér) mort* to lament. ◆ **déplorable** *adj* deplorable. ◆ **déplorablement** *adv* deplorably.

déployer [deplwaje] (8) **1** *vt carte* to spread out; *voile* to unfurl; *ailes* to spread; *troupes* to deploy; *échantillons* to spread out, lay out; *richesses, talents, forces* to display; *efforts* to expend. **~ en éventail** *troupes* to fan out; **~ beaucoup d'efforts** to expend a lot of effort. **2 se ~** *vpr [drapeau]* to unfurl; *[ailes]* to spread; *[troupes]* to deploy; *[cortège]* to spread out. ◆ **déploiement** *nm* unfurling; spreading; deployment; display. **~ de force** deployment of troops (*ou* police).

déplumer (se) [deplyme] (1) *vpr [oiseau]* to moult; (*) *[personne]* to go bald.

dépoétiser [depɔetize] (1) *vt* to make prosaic.

dépolitiser [depɔlitize] (1) *vt* to depoliticize.

dépolluer [depɔlye] (1) *vt* to clean up, rid *ou* clear of pollution. ◆ **dépollution** *nf*: **la ~ des plages souillées par le mazout** the cleaning (up) of oil-polluted beaches.

dépopulation [depɔpylɑsjɔ̃] *nf* depopulation.

déporter [depɔʀte] (1) *vt* (**a**) *(exiler)* to deport; *(interner)* to send to a concentration camp. (**b**) *[vent]* to carry off course. **se ~ vers la gauche** to swerve to the left. ◆ **déportation** *nf* deportation; imprisonment (in a concentration camp). ◆ **déporté, e** *nm, f* deportee; prisoner (in a concentration camp).

déposer [depoze] (1) **1** *vt* (**a**) *gerbe, armes* to lay down; *ordures* to dump; *colis* to leave; *passager* to drop; *(Fin)* to deposit (*sur un compte* in an account). **est-ce que je peux vous ~ quelque part?** can I give you a lift anywhere?, can I drop you anywhere? (**b**) *plainte* to lodge; *réclamation* to file; *marque de fabrique* to register; *projet de loi* to bring in; *rapport* to send in. **~ son bilan** to go into voluntary liquidation. (**c**) *(destituer) souverain* to depose. (**d**) *tenture* to take down; *tapis* to take up; *moteur* to take out. **2** *vi* (**a**) *[liquide]* to leave some sediment. **laisser ~** to leave to settle. (**b**) *(Jur)* to give evidence, testify. **3 se ~** *vpr [poussière, lie]* to settle. ◆ **déposant, e** *nm, f (Fin)* depositor; *(Jur)* deponent. ◆ **dépositaire** *nmf [objet confié]* depository; *[secret, vérité]* possessor; *(Comm)* agent (*de* for). ◆ **déposition** *nf (gén)* deposition; *(à un procès)* evidence; *(écrite)* (sworn) statement.

déposséder [depɔsede] (6) *vt*: **~ qn de** *terres* to dispossess sb of; *place, charge* to deprive sb of. ◆ **dépossession** *nf* dispossession; deprivation.

dépôt [depo] *nm* (**a**) *(action)* **procéder au ~ d'une gerbe** to lay a wreath; **le ~ des manteaux au vestiaire est obligatoire** coats must be left *ou* deposited in the cloakroom; **~ de bilan** (voluntary) liquidation. (**b**) *(garde)* **avoir qch en ~** to hold sth in trust; **confier qch en ~ à qn** to entrust sth to sb; **~ sacré** sacred trust. (**c**) *(Comm) [marque]* registration. (**d**) *(garantie)* deposit. (**e**) **du ~, un ~** *[liquide]* sediment, deposit; *[tartre]* fur. (**f**) *(entrepôt)* warehouse; *[autobus, trains]*, *(Mil)* depot. **il y a un ~ de pain à l'épicerie** the grocer supplies *ou* sells bread; **~ de munitions** ammunition dump; **~ d'ordures** rubbish dump. (**g**) *(prison)* jail, prison.

dépotoir [depɔtwaʀ] *nm (lit, fig)* dumping ground.

dépouille [depuj] *nf (peau)* skin, hide. *(cadavre)* **~ (mortelle)** (mortal) remains; *(butin)* **~s** plunder, spoils.

dépouillé, e [depuje] *adj décor* bare; *style* bald. **~ de** *poésie* lacking in; *ornements* stripped of.

dépouiller [depuje] (1) **1** *vt* (**a**) *comptes, courrier* to go through, peruse; *scrutin* to count. (**b**) *animal* to skin; *arbre* to strip; *voyageur* to strip of his possessions; *héritier* to deprive of his inheritance. **~ de qch** *(gén)* to strip of sth; *droits* to divest *ou* deprive of sth; *(fig)* **~ Pierre pour habiller Paul** to rob Peter to pay Paul; **~ le pays** to plunder the country, lay the country bare. (**c**) *(se défaire de)* to shed.
2 se ~ *vpr*: **se ~ de** *vêtements* to shed; *possessions* to divest o.s. of; *arrogance* to cast aside; **les arbres se dépouillent** the trees are shedding their leaves; **la campagne se dépouille** the countryside is beginning to look bare. ◆ **dépouillement** *nm* (**a**) perusal; counting. *(Pol)* **après le ~** after the count. (**b**) *(sobriété)* lack of ornamentation. (**c**) *(de biens, droits)* deprivation, stripping.

dépourvu, e [depuʀvy] **1** *adj*: **~ de** *(gén)* lacking in, without; *bons sens* devoid of; **~ d'ornements** unornamented, bare of ornaments; **~ d'argent** penniless; **des gens ~s (de tout)** destitute people. **2** *nm*: **prendre qn au ~** to catch sb unprepared *ou* unawares.

dépravation [depʀavɑsjɔ̃] *nf (état)* depravity. ◆ **dépravé, e** **1** *adj* depraved. **2** *nm, f* degenerate. ◆ **dépraver** (1) *vt* to deprave.

déprécier *vt*, **se ~** *vpr* [depʀesje] (7) to depreciate. ◆ **dépréciatif, -ive** *adj* disparaging, derogatory. ◆ **dépréciation** *nf* depreciation.

déprédations [depʀedɑsjɔ̃] *nfpl (dégâts)* damage. **commettre des ~** to cause damage.

dépression [depʀɛsjɔ̃] *nf*: **~ (de terrain)** depression; **~ atmosphérique** atmospheric depression, trough of low pressure; **une ~ (nerveuse)** a (nervous) breakdown; **elle fait de la ~** she is having a bad fit of depression; **~ (économique)** (economic) depression *ou* slump. ◆ **dépressif, -ive** *adj* depressive.

dépressuriser [depʀesyʀize] (1) *vt (Aviat, Astron)* to depressurize. ◆ **dépressurisation** *nf* depressurization. **en cas de ~ de la cabine** should the pressure drop in the cabin.

déprimer [depʀime] (1) *vt (moralement)* to depress; *(physiquement)* to debilitate. ◆ **déprimant, e** *adj (moralement)* depressing; *(physiquement)* debilitating. ◆ **déprimé, e** *adj (moralement)* depressed; *(physiquement)* low; *terrain* low-lying.

depuis [dəpɥi] **1** *prép* (**a**) *(point de départ dans le temps)* since, ever since *(intensif)*. **il attend/attendait ~ hier** he has/had been waiting since yesterday;

~ **son plus jeune âge** since *ou* from early childhood; ~ **cette affaire il est très méfiant** (ever) since that affair he has been very suspicious; ~ **quand le connaissez-vous?** how long have you known him?; ~ **quelle date êtes-vous ici?** since when have you been here?; ~ **cela,** ~ **lors** since then *ou* that time, ever since; ~ **le matin jusqu'au soir** from morning till night.

(**b**) *(durée)* for. **il est malade** ~ **une semaine** he has been ill for a week (now); ~ **ces derniers mois il a bien changé** he has changed a great deal in *ou* over the last *ou* past few months; **tu le connais** ~ **longtemps? —** ~ **toujours** have you known him long? *ou* for a long time? — I've known him all my life; **je la connaissais** ~ **peu quand elle est partie** I had known her only a short time when she left; ~ **peu elle a recommencé à sortir** lately *ou* recently she has started going out again.

(**c**) *(lieu)* since, from. ~ **Nice il a fait le plein 3 fois** he's filled up 3 times since Nice; **le concert est retransmis** ~ **Paris** the concert is broadcast from Paris.

(**d**) *(rang, quantité)* from. ~ **le premier jusqu'au dernier** from the first to the last; **toutes les tailles** ~ **le 36** all sizes from 36 upwards.

(**e**) ~ **que,** ~ **le temps que:** ~ **qu'il est ministre** since he became a minister; ~ **le temps qu'il apprend le français** considering how long he's been learning French; ~ **le temps que je voulais voir ce film!** I had been waiting to see that film for ages!

2 *adv* ever since, since (then). **je ne l'ai pas revu** ~ I haven't seen him since (then).

député [depyte] *nm (gén, Pol)* deputy; *(en Grande-Bretagne)* member of Parliament; *(aux USA)* representative. ~ **au parlement européen** member of the European Parliament; **le** ~**-maire** the deputy and mayor. ◆ **députation** *nf (groupe)* deputation, delegation. **candidat à la** ~ parliamentary candidate. ◆ **députer** (1) *vt:* ~ **qn pour faire** to delegate sb to do; ~ **qn auprès de** to send sb as representative to.

déqualifier [dekalifje] (7) *vt personnel, emploi* to deskill. ◆ **déqualification** *nf* deskilling.

déraciner [deʀasine] (1) *vt arbre, personne* to uproot; *erreur* to eradicate. ◆ **déracinement** *nm* uprooting; eradication.

dérailler [deʀɑje] (1) *vi [train]* to be derailed; *(*: divaguer)* to rave, be off one's head *; *(*: mal fonctionner)* to be on the blink *. **faire** ~ **un train** to derail a train; **tu déràilles!** * *(être fou)* you're nuts *; *(se tromper)* you're talking through your hat *. ◆ **déraillement** *nm* derailment. ◆ **dérailleur** *nm [bicyclette]* dérailleur gears.

déraisonner [deʀɛzɔne] (1) *vi* to rave. ◆ **déraisonnable** *adj* unreasonable.

déranger [deʀɑ̃ʒe] (3) **1** *vt papiers, personne* to disturb; *coiffure* to ruffle; *projets, routine* to disrupt, upset; *machine* to put out of order; *temps* to unsettle. ~ **qn inutilement** to bother *ou* trouble sb unnecessarily; **ça vous dérange si je fume?** do you mind if I smoke?; **il a le cerveau dérangé** his mind is deranged *ou* unhinged; **il a l'estomac dérangé** his stomach is upset. **2 se** ~ *vpr* (**a**) *[médecin]* to come out; *(pour une démarche)* to go along, come along. **sans vous** ~ without leaving your home; **surtout, ne vous dérangez pas pour moi** please don't put yourself out on my account. (**b**) *(changer de place)* to move. ◆ **dérangement** *nm (gêne)* trouble, inconvenience; *(déplacement)* trip; *(bouleversement)* disorder (*de* in). **en** ~ *machine* out of order.

déraper [deʀape] (1) *vi [véhicule]* to skid; *[personne, échelle]* to slip; *[prix, salaires]* to get out of hand, soar. ◆ **dérapage** *nm* skid; *(Ski)* side-slipping. ~ **de l'indice des prix** unexpected increase in the price index.

dérégler [deʀegle] (6) **1** *vt (gén)* to upset; *temps* to unsettle; *mécanisme* to disturb. **2 se** ~ *vpr [appareil]* to go wrong; *[pouls, estomac, temps]* to be upset. ◆ **déréglé, e** *adj* out of order; upset; unsettled; *mœurs* dissolute. ◆ **dérèglement** *nm* upset; disturbance. *[mœurs]* ~**(s)** dissoluteness.

dérider *vt,* **se** ~ *vpr* [deʀide] (1) *personne* to brighten up; *front* to uncrease.

dérision [deʀizjɔ̃] *nf* derision, mockery. **par** ~ derisively, mockingly; **tourner en** ~ to mock, ridicule. ◆ **dérisoire** *adj* derisory, pathetic. **pour une somme** ~ for a nominal *ou* derisory sum. ◆ **dérisoirement** *adv* pathetically.

dérivatif, -ive [deʀivatif, iv] **1** *adj* derivative. **2** *nm* distraction.

dérivation [deʀivɑsjɔ̃] *nf [rivière]* diversion; *(Ling, Math)* derivation; *(Élec)* shunt; *(Aviat, Naut)* deviation.

dérive [deʀiv] *nf* (**a**) *(déviation)* drift. ~ **des continents** continental drift; *(lit)* **à la** ~ adrift; *(fig)* **tout va à la** ~ everything is going to the dogs *ou* is going downhill. (**b**) *(dispositif) (Aviat)* fin; *(Naut)* centre-board.

dériver [deʀive] (1) **1** *vt rivière* to divert; *(Chim, Ling, Math)* to derive; *(Élec)* to shunt. **2** ~ **de** *vt indir* to derive from. **3** *vi (Aviat, Naut)* to drift; *[orateur]* to drift off the subject. ◆ **dérivé, e 1** *adj* derived. **2** *nm (Chim, Ling, Math)* derivative; *(produit)* by-product. **3** *nf (Math)* derivative.

dermatologie [dɛʀmatɔlɔʒi] *nf* dermatology. ◆ **dermatologue** *nmf* dermatologist.

dernier, -ière [dɛʀnje, jɛʀ] **1** *adj* (**a**) *(espace) (gén)* last; *étage* top; *rang* back; *branche* highest. **arriver** ~ to come in last; **la** ~**ière marche** *(en bas)* the bottom step; *(en haut)* the top step; *(Presse)* **en** ~**ière page** on the back page; **les 100** ~**ières pages** the last 100 pages.

(**b**) *(temps) (gén)* last; *(plus récent)* latest; *(final)* final; *(précédent)* previous. **durant les** ~**s jours du mois** in the last few days of the month; **voici les** ~**ières nouvelles** here is the latest news; **l'artiste dans ses** ~**ières œuvres** the artist in his final *ou* last works; **les** ~**s propriétaires étaient belges** the previous *ou* last owners were Belgians; **il faut payer avant le 15,** ~ **délai** it must be paid by the 15th at the latest, the 15th is the final date for payment; **le mois** ~ last month; **ces** ~**s temps** lately, of late; **c'est le** ~ **cri** it's the very latest thing *ou* fashion; **un ordinateur** ~ **cri** a state-of-the-art computer.

(**c**) *(en mérite) élève* bottom, last; *qualité* lowest, poorest. **de** ~ **ordre** very inferior; **il est toujours** ~ **(en classe)** he's always bottom (of the class), he's always last (in the class).

(**d**) *(extrême)* **grossier au** ~ **point** *ou* **degré** extremely rude, rude in the extreme; **il a protesté avec la** ~**ière énergie** he protested most vigorously *ou* with the utmost vigour; **c'est du** ~ **chic** it's the last word in elegance; **c'est de la** ~**ière importance** it is of the utmost importance.

(**e**) *(ultime) grade* top, highest; *regard, effort* last, final. **quel est votre** ~ **prix?** *(pour vendre)* what's the lowest you'll go?; *(pour acheter)* what's your final offer?; **en** ~**ière analyse** in the final *ou* last analysis; **en** ~ **lieu** finally; **mettre la** ~**ière main à qch** to put the finishing touches to sth; **avoir le** ~ **mot** to have the last word; **en** ~ **ressort** *ou* **recours** as a last resort; **rendre le** ~ **soupir** to breathe one's last; **accompagner qn à sa** ~**ière demeure** to accompany sb to his final resting place.

2 *nm, f* last (one); *(enfant)* youngest (child). **sortir le** ~ to leave last; **les** ~**s arrivés** the last ones to arrive; **il est le** ~ **de sa classe** he's at the bottom of the class; **il est le** ~ **à pouvoir faire cela** he's the last person to be able to do that; **c'est le** ~

de mes soucis it's the least of my worries; *(péj)* **le ~ des imbéciles** a complete and utter fool; *(péj)* **c'est le ~ des ~s!** he's the lowest of the low; **ce ~, cette ~ière** *(de deux)* the latter; *(de plusieurs)* this last, the last-mentioned; **~-né** youngest (child). **3** *nm (étage)* top floor. **acheter qch en ~** to buy sth last.
4 *nf (Théât)* last performance. **vous connaissez la ~ière?** * have you heard the latest?

dernièrement [dɛʀnjɛʀmɑ̃] *adv* recently.

dérober [deʀɔbe] (1) **1** *vt* (**a**) *(voler)* to steal (*à qn* from, sb). (**b**) *(cacher)* to hide, conceal (*à qn* from sb). **~ qn à la justice** to shield sb from justice. **2 se ~** *vpr* (**a**) *(refuser d'assumer)* to shy away. **je lui ai posé la question mais il s'est dérobé** I put the question to him but he evaded it. (**b**) *(se cacher de)* to hide, conceal o.s. (*à* from). (**c**) *(se libérer)* to slip away. **se ~ à l'étreinte de qn** to slip out of sb's arms. (**d**) *[sol, genoux]* to give way. (**e**) *(Équitation)* to refuse. ◆ **dérobade** *nf* evasion; *(Équitation)* refusal. ◆ **dérobé, e 1** *adj porte* secret, hidden. **2** *nf*: **à la ~e** secretly, surreptitiously; **regarder qn à la ~e** to give sb a surreptitious *ou* stealthy glance.

dérogation [deʀɔgɑsjɔ̃] *nf* (special) dispensation. ◆ **dérogatoire** *adj* dispensatory. **à titre ~** by special dispensation.

déroger [deʀɔʒe] (3) *vi* (**a**) *(déchoir) (gén)* to lower o.s.; *(Hist)* to lose rank and title. (**b**) *(enfreindre)* **~ à qch** to go against sth; **~ aux règles** to depart from the rules.

dérouler [deʀule] (1) **1** *vt fil* to unwind; *cordage* to uncoil; *nappe* to unroll. **~ qch dans son esprit** to go over sth in one's mind. **2 se ~** *vpr* (**a**) *[fil]* to unwind; *[cordage]* to uncoil; *[carte]* to unroll; *[paysage]* to unfold. (**b**) *(se produire, se situer)* to take place; *(accidentellement)* to happen, occur. **c'est là que toute ma vie s'est déroulée** it was there that my whole life was spent. (**c**) *(se développer) [histoire]* to develop, unfold. **la manifestation s'est déroulée dans le calme** the demonstration went off peacefully; **à mesure que l'histoire se déroulait** as the story unfolded *ou* developed. ◆ **déroulement** *nm* (**a**) *[cérémonie]* progress; *[action]* development. **pendant le ~ des opérations** during the course of the operations, while the operations were in progress. (**b**) unwinding; uncoiling; unrolling. ◆ **dérouleur** *nm (Ordin)* **~ de bande magnétique** magnetic tape drive.

déroute [deʀut] *nf* rout. **en ~** routed; **mettre en ~** to rout.

dérouter [deʀute] (1) *vt avion* to reroute; *candidat* to disconcert; *poursuivants* to throw off the scent. ◆ **déroutant, e** *adj* disconcerting.

derrick [dɛʀik] *nm* derrick.

derrière [dɛʀjɛʀ] **1** *prép* (**a**) *(gén, fig)* behind. **passe (par) ~ la maison** go round the back of *ou* round behind the house; **faire qch ~ (le dos de) qn** to do sth behind sb's back; *(fig)* **je suis ~ vous** I'll back you up, I'm on your side; **il faut toujours être ~ son dos** you've always got to keep an eye on him; **vin de ~ les fagots** extra-special wine. (**b**) *(Naut) (dans le bateau)* abaft; *(sur la mer)* astern of.
2 *adv* (**a**) behind. **assis 3 rangs ~** sitting 3 rows back *ou* behind; *(Aut)* **monter ~** to sit in the back; **regarde ~** *(tourne-toi)* look behind *ou* back; *(au fond de la voiture)* look in the back; *(derrière un objet)* look behind it; **par-~** *entrer* by the back; *attaquer* from behind, from the rear; *s'attacher* at the back; *médire* behind sb's back. (**b**) *(Naut) (dans le bateau)* abaft; *(sur la mer)* astern.
3 *nm [personne]* bottom, behind *; *[animal]* hindquarters, rump; *[objet]* back; *[maison]* back, rear. **habiter sur le ~** to live at the back (of the house); **porte de ~** back *ou* rear door.

derviche [dɛʀviʃ] *nm* dervish. **~ tourneur** dancing dervish.

des [de] *V* **de.**

dès [dɛ] *prép* (**a**) *(temps)* from. **il a commencé à pleuvoir ~ le matin** it rained from the morning onwards; **~ le début** from the start; **~ qu'il aura fini il viendra** as soon as he's finished he'll come; **~ son retour il fera le nécessaire** as soon as he's back he'll do what's necessary; **~ l'époque romaine** as early as *ou* as far back as Roman times; **~ son enfance** from (his) childhood, ever since he was a child; **on peut dire ~ maintenant** one can say (right) here and now. (**b**) *(espace etc)* **~ Lyon il a plu sans arrêt** it never stopped raining from Lyons onwards *ou* after Lyons; **~ l'entrée je sentis qu'il se passait qch** as soon as I walked in at the door I sensed that sth was going on; **~ le premier verre il roula sous la table** after the first glass he collapsed under the table. (**c**) **~ lors** from that moment; **~ lors que** *(puisque)* since, as.

désabusé, e [dezabyze] *adj* disenchanted, disillusioned.

désaccord [dezakɔʀ] *nm* (**a**) *(mésentente)* discord. **être en ~ avec sa famille** to be at odds with one's family. (**b**) *(divergence) (entre points de vue)* disagreement; *(entre intérêts)* conflict. **leurs intérêts sont en ~ avec les nôtres** their interests conflict with ours. (**c**) *(contradiction)* discrepancy. **ce qu'il dit est en ~ avec ce qu'il fait** there is a discrepancy between what he says and what he does.

désaccordé, e [dezakɔʀde] *adj piano* out of tune.

désaccoutumer [dezakutyme] (1) *vt*: **~ qn de qch/de faire** to get sb out of the habit of sth/of doing; **se ~ de qch/de faire** to lose the habit of sth/of doing.

désaffecter [dezafɛkte] (1) *vt* to close down. ◆ **désaffectation** *nf* closing down. ◆ **désaffecté, e** *adj* disused.

désaffection [dezafɛksjɔ̃] *nf* loss of affection (*pour* for).

désagréable [dezagʀeabl(ə)] *adj* disagreeable. ◆ **désagréablement** *adv* disagreeably.

désagréger *vt*, **se ~** *vpr* [dezagʀeʒe] (3) *et* (6) to disintegrate, break up. ◆ **désagrégation** *nf* disintegration, breaking up.

désagrément [dezagʀemɑ̃] *nm (déboire)* annoyance; *(déplaisir)* displeasure. **malgré tous les ~s que cela entraîne** despite all the annoyances *ou* trouble it involves.

désaltérer [dezalteʀe] (6) **1** *vt* to quench the thirst of. **2 se ~** *vpr* to quench one's thirst. ◆ **désaltérant, e** *adj* thirst-quenching.

désamorcer [dezamɔʀse] (3) *vt fusée* to remove the primer from; *pompe* to drain; *(fig) situation, crise* to defuse.

désappointer [dezapwɛ̃te] (1) *vt* to disappoint. ◆ **désappointement** *nm* disappointment.

désapprouver [dezapʀuve] (1) *vt* to disapprove of. **elle désapprouve qu'il vienne** she disapproves of his coming. ◆ **désapprobateur, -trice** *adj* disapproving. ◆ **désapprobation** *nf* disapproval.

désarçonner [dezaʀsɔne] (1) *vt (lit)* to unseat; *(fig) [réponse]* to nonplus.

désargenté, e * [dezaʀʒɑ̃te] *adj (sans un sou)* broke *, penniless. **je suis ~ en ce moment** I'm a bit short of cash *ou* a bit tight for cash * at the moment.

désarmer [dezaʀme] (1) **1** *vt (Mil, fig)* to disarm; *(Naut)* to lay up. **2** *vi [pays]* to disarm; *(fig) [haine]* to abate. **il ne désarme pas contre son fils** he is unrelenting in his attitude towards his son. ◆ **désarmant, e** *adj* disarming. ◆ **désarmé, e** *adj (lit)* unarmed; *(fig)* helpless. ◆ **désarmement**

nm [forteresse] disarming; *[pays]* disarmament; *[navire]* laying up.

désarroi [dezaʀwa] *nm [personne]* helplessness; *[armée, équipe]* confusion. **être en plein** ~ to feel quite helpless; to be in utter confusion.

désarticuler (se) [dezaʀtikyle] (1) *vpr [acrobate]* to contort o.s. **se** ~ **l'épaule** to dislocate one's shoulder.

désastre [dezastʀ(ə)] *nm (lit, fig)* disaster. **les** ~**s causés par la tempête** the damage caused by the storm. ◆ **désastreux, -euse** *adj (gén)* disastrous; *conditions, temps* terrible, appalling.

désavantage [dezavɑ̃taʒ] *nm (gén)* disadvantage; *(handicap)* handicap; *(inconvénient)* drawback. **avoir un** ~ **sur qn** to be at a disadvantage *ou* be handicapped in comparison with sb; **se montrer à son** ~ to show o.s. to one's disadvantage *ou* in an unfavourable light.

désavantager [dezavɑ̃taʒe] (3) *vt* to disadvantage, put at a disadvantage (*par rapport à* by comparison with). **cela désavantage surtout les plus pauvres** this puts the very poor at the greatest disadvantage, this penalizes the very poor in particular; **les couches sociales les plus désavantagées** the most under-privileged *ou* disadvantaged sectors of society. ◆ **désavantageusement** *adv* unfavourably, disadvantageously. ◆ **désavantageux, -euse** *adj* unfavourable, disadvantageous.

désavouer [dezavwe] (1) **1** *vt (renier)* to disclaim, disavow; *(blâmer)* to disown. **2 se** ~ *vpr* to retract. ◆ **désaveu** *nm* disavowal; disowning.

désaxer [dezakse] (1) *vt esprit* to unhinge. ◆ **désaxée, e** *nmf* lunatic, maniac.

desceller [desele] (1) **1** *vt pierre* to pull free. **2 se** ~ *vpr [objet]* to come loose.

descendance [desɑ̃dɑ̃s] *nf (enfants)* descendants; *(origine)* descent.

descendant, e [desɑ̃dɑ̃, ɑ̃t] **1** *adj direction* downward, descending; *gamme* falling, descending; *(Rail) voie, train* down. **marée** ~**e** ebb tide; **à marée** ~**e** when the tide is going out *ou* on the ebb. **2** *nm, f* descendant (*de* of).

descendre [desɑ̃dʀ(ə)] (41) **1** *vi (avec aux être)* (**a**) *(aller)* to go down; *(venir)* to come down (*à, vers* to, *dans* into); *[avion]* to come down, descend. **descends me voir** come down and see me; ~ **à pied/en parachute** to walk/parachute down; ~ **en train** to go down by train; **nous sommes descendus en 10 minutes** we got down in 10 minutes; ~ **à Marseille** to go down to Marseilles; ~ **en ville** to go into town; **la rue descend en pente douce** the street slopes gently down; **cheveux qui descendent sur les épaules** shoulder-length hair.
(**b**) ~ **de** *arbre* to climb *ou* come down from; *voiture* to get out of; **fais** ~ **le chien du fauteuil** get the dog (down) off the armchair; ~ **à terre** to go ashore; ~ **de cheval** to dismount; ~ **de bicyclette** to get off one's bicycle.
(**c**) *[obscurité, neige]* to fall; *[soleil]* to go down (*sur* on); *[brouillard]* to come down (*sur* over); *[prix, température]* to fall, drop; *[marée]* to go out.
(**d**) *(s'abaisser)* ~ **dans l'estime de qn** to go down in sb's estimation; **il est descendu jusqu'à mendier** he has stooped to begging.
(**e**) *(lieu)* ~ **à l'hôtel** to put up *ou* stay at a hotel; **la police est descendue dans cette boîte de nuit** the police have raided the night club.
2 ~ **de** *vt indir (avec aux être) ancêtre* to be descended from.
3 *vt (avec aux avoir)* (**a**) *escalier, rivière, gamme* to go down. ~ **la rue en courant** to run down the street.
(**b**) *(apporter) valise* to take *ou* bring down. **faire** ~ **ses bagages** to have one's luggage brought *ou* taken down; **descends-moi mes lunettes** bring *ou* fetch me my glasses down; **je te descends en ville** I'll take you into town, I'll give you a lift into town.
(**c**) *(baisser) store, étagère, rayon* to lower.
(**d**) *(*: abattre) avion* to shoot down; *personne* to bump off ‡; *bouteille* to down. **se faire** ~ to get o.s. bumped off ‡; ~ **qn en flammes** to shoot sb down in flames.

descente [desɑ̃t] **1** *nf* (**a**) *(gén, Aviat, alpinisme)* descent. **la** ~ **dans le puits est dangereuse** going down the well is dangerous; **la** ~ **des bagages prend du temps** it takes time to bring down the luggage; **le téléphérique est tombé en panne dans la** ~ the cable car broke down on the way down; ~ **en parachute** parachute drop; *(Ski)* **(épreuve de)** ~ downhill race; ~ **en slalom** slalom descent; **accueillir qn à la** ~ **du train** to meet sb off the train; **à ma** ~ **de voiture** as I got out of the car. (**b**) *(raid)* raid. **faire une** ~ **sur** *ou* **dans** to raid, make a raid on. (**c**) *(partie descendante)* downward slope, incline. **freiner dans les** ~**s** to brake going downhill; **la** ~ **de la cave** the stairs *ou* steps down to the cellar; **la** ~ **du garage** the slope down to the garage. **2** : ~ **de croix** Deposition; ~ **aux enfers** descent into Hell; ~ **de lit** bedside rug.

description [dɛskʀipsjɔ̃] *nf* description. **faire la** ~ **de** to describe. ◆ **descriptif, -ive** *adj* descriptive.

désembuer [dezɑ̃bye] (1) *vt vitre* to demist.

désemparé, e [dezɑ̃paʀe] *adj* helpless, distraught; *navire* crippled.

désemparer [dezɑ̃paʀe] (1) *vi*: **sans** ~ without stopping.

désemplir [dezɑ̃pliʀ] (2) *vi*: **le magasin ne désemplit jamais** the shop is never empty *ou* is always full.

désenchantement [dezɑ̃ʃɑ̃tmɑ̃] *nm* disenchantment, disillusion. ◆ **désenchanté, e** *adj* disenchanted, disillusioned.

désenclaver [dezɑ̃klave] (1) *vt* to open up. ◆ **désenclavement** *nm* opening up.

désenfler [dezɑ̃fle] (1) *vi* to go down, become less swollen.

désennuyer [dezɑ̃nɥije] (8) *vt*: ~ **qn** to relieve sb's boredom.

désensibiliser [desɑ̃sibilize] (1) *vt* to desensitize. ◆ **désensibilisation** *nf* desensitization.

désépaissir [dezepesiʀ] (2) *vt cheveux* to thin (out).

déséquilibre [dezekilibʀ(ə)] *nm (entre quantités)* imbalance (*entre* between); *(mental)* unbalance; *[objet]* unsteadiness. **en** ~ *armoire* unsteady; *budget* unbalanced. ◆ **déséquilibré, e 1** *adj budget* unbalanced; *esprit* disordered, unhinged. **2** *nm, f* unbalanced person. ◆ **déséquilibrer** (1) *vt (lit)* to throw off balance; *esprit* to unbalance; *budget* to create an imbalance in.

désert, e [dezɛʀ, ɛʀt(ə)] **1** *adj* deserted. **2** *nm* desert. ◆ **désertique** *adj* desert.

déserter [dezɛʀte] (1) *vti* to desert. ◆ **déserteur** *nm* deserter. ◆ **désertion** *nf* desertion.

désespérer [dezɛspeʀe] (6) **1** *vt* to drive to despair. **2** *vi* to despair. **3** ~ **de** *vt indir*: ~ **de qn/de faire** to despair of sb/of doing; **je ne désespère pas de réussir** I haven't lost hope *ou* given up hope of succeeding. **4 se** ~ *vpr* to despair. ◆ **désespérant, e** *adj lenteur, nouvelle* appalling; *enfant* hopeless; *temps* maddening, sickening. **d'une naïveté** ~**e** hopelessly naïve. ◆ **désespéré, e 1** *adj (gén) cas* hopeless. **appel** ~ cry of despair. **2** *nm, f (suicidé)* suicide *(person)*. ◆ **désespérément** *adv tenter* desperately. ~ **vide** hopelessly empty.

désespoir [dezɛspwaʀ] *nm* despair. **faire le** ~ **de qn** to be the despair of sb, drive sb to despair; **être au** ~ to be in despair; **je suis au** ~ **de ne**

pouvoir venir I'm desperately sorry not to be able to come; **en** ~ **de cause** in desperation.

déshabiller [dezabije] (1) **1** *vt* to undress. **2 se** ~ *vpr* to undress; *(manteau etc)* to take off one's coat *ou* things. ◆ **déshabillé** *nm* négligée.

déshabituer [dezabitɥe] (1) **1** *vt*: ~ **qn de (faire) qch** to break sb of the habit of (doing) sth. **2 se** ~ *vpr*: **se** ~ **de qch/de faire qch** to get out of the habit of sth/of doing sth.

désherber [dezɛʀbe] (1) *vt* to weed. ◆ **désherbage** *nm* weeding. ◆ **désherbant** *nm* weed-killer.

déshériter [dezeʀite] (1) *vt héritier* to disinherit; *(désavantager)* to deprive. **déshérité par la nature** ill-favoured by nature; **les déshérités** the deprived.

déshonorer [dezɔnɔʀe] (1) **1** *vt profession* to disgrace, dishonour; *personne* to dishonour, bring disgrace *ou* dishonour upon. **2 se** ~ *vpr* to bring disgrace *ou* dishonour on o.s. ◆ **déshonneur** *nm* disgrace, dishonour. ◆ **déshonorant, e** *adj* dishonourable, degrading.

déshumaniser [dezymanize] (1) *vt* to dehumanize.

déshydrater *vt*, **se** ~ *vpr* [dezidʀate] (1) to dehydrate. ◆ **déshydratation** *nf* dehydration.

désigner [deziɲe] (1) *vt* (**a**) *(du doigt)* to point out; *(d'un mot)* to refer to. **tout le désigne comme coupable** everything points to his guilt. (**b**) *(nommer)* to appoint, designate (*à un poste* to a post). **que des volontaires se désignent!** volunteers step forward!; **successeur désigné** successor elect *ou* designate. (**c**) *(qualifier)* to mark out. **sa hardiesse le désigne pour cette tentative** his boldness marks him out for this attempt; **c'était la victime désignée** he was the classic victim; **être tout désigné pour faire qch** to be cut out to do sth. ◆ **désignation** *nf* designation.

désillusionner [dezilyzjɔne] (1) *vt* to disillusion. ◆ **désillusion** *nf* disillusion. ◆ **désillusionnement** *nm* disillusionment.

désinence [dezinɑ̃s] *nf (Ling)* ending, inflexion.

désinfecter [dezɛ̃fɛkte] (1) *vt* to disinfect. ◆ **désinfectant, e** *adj, nm* disinfectant. ◆ **désinfection** *nf* disinfection.

désinformation [dezɛ̃fɔʀmasjɔ̃] *nf* disinformation.

désintégrer [dezɛ̃tegʀe] (6) **1** *vt (Phys)* to split; *(fig)* to split up, break up. **2 se** ~ *vpr (gén)* to disintegrate; *(Phys)* to split; *[fusée]* to selfdestruct. ◆ **désintégration** *nf* splitting; splitting-up ; breaking-up; disintegration.

désintéresser [dezɛ̃teʀese] (1) **1** *vt créancier* to pay off. **2 se** ~ *vpr*: **se** ~ **de** to lose interest in. ◆ **désintéressé, e** *adj* disinterested. ◆ **désintéressement** *nm (gén)* disinterestedness; *[créancier]* paying off. ◆ **désintérêt** *nm* disinterest.

désintoxiquer [dezɛ̃tɔksike] (1) *vt* to treat for alcoholism (*ou* drug addiction), detoxify. **se faire** ~ *[alcoolique]* to dry out; *[drogué]* to come off drugs. ◆ **désintoxication** *nf* treatment for alcoholism (*ou* drug addiction), detoxification.

désinvolte [dezɛ̃vɔlt(ə)] *adj* casual, offhand, airy. ◆ **désinvolture** *nf* casualness.

désir [deziʀ] *nm (souhait)* wish, desire; *(convoitise)* desire (*de qch* for sth, *de faire* to do). **vos ~s sont des ordres** your wish is my command; **prendre ses ~s pour des réalités** to indulge in wishful thinking. ◆ **désirable** *adj* desirable. **peu** ~ undesirable.

désirer [deziʀe] (1) *vt (vouloir)* to want; *(convoiter)* to desire. ~ **faire qch** to want *ou* wish to do sth; **que désirez-vous?** *(au café)* what would you like?; *(dans un bureau)* what can I do for you?; **il désire que tu viennes tout de suite** he wants you to come at once; **ça laisse beaucoup à** ~ it leaves a lot to be desired. ◆ **désireux, -euse** *adj*: ~ **de qch** avid for sth, desirous of sth; ~ **de faire** anxious to do, desirous of doing.

désister (se) [deziste] (1) *vpr* to withdraw. ◆ **désistement** *nm* withdrawal.

désobéir [dezɔbeiʀ] (2) *vi* to be disobedient. ~ **à qn/à un ordre** to disobey sb/an order. ◆ **désobéissance** *nf* disobedience (*à* to). ◆ **désobéissant, e** *adj* disobedient.

désobliger [dezɔbliʒe] (3) *vt* to offend. ◆ **désobligeant, e** *adj* disagreeable.

désodoriser [dezɔdɔʀize] (1) *vt* to deodorize. ◆ **désodorisant, e** *adj, nm* deodorant.

désœuvré, e [dezœvʀe] *adj* idle. **rester** ~ **pendant des heures** to do nothing *ou* remain idle for hours on end. ◆ **désœuvrement** *nm* idleness. **par** ~ for want of anything better to do.

désoler [dezɔle] (1) **1** *vt* to distress, upset; *(dévaster)* to desolate. **2 se** ~ *vpr* to be upset. ◆ **désolant, e** *adj nouvelle, situation* distressing; *enfant, temps* disappointing. **il est** ~ **que** it's a terrible shame *ou* such a pity that. ◆ **désolation** *nf (consternation)* distress, grief; *(dévastation)* desolation. ◆ **désolé, e** *adj* (**a**) *endroit* desolate. (**b**) *(affligé)* distressed; *(contrit)* sorry. **(je suis)** ~ **de vous avoir dérangé** (I'm) sorry to have disturbed you.

désolidariser (se) [desɔlidaʀize] (1) *vpr*: **se** ~ **de** to dissociate o.s. from.

désopilant, e [dezɔpilɑ̃, ɑ̃t] *adj* hilarious, killing *.

désordre [dezɔʀdʀ(ə)] *nm* (**a**) *[pièce, vêtements]* untidiness, disorderliness; *[service public]* disorder; *[esprits]* confusion; *(Méd)* disorder; *[vie]* dissoluteness. **mettre/être en** ~ to make/be untidy; **quel** ~! what a muddle! *ou* mess! (**b**) *(agitation)* disorder. **faire du** ~ *[élève]* to cause a commotion *ou* a disturbance; *[agitateur]* to spread unrest; *(émeute)* **de graves ~s** serious disturbances, serious outbreaks of violence. ◆ **désordonné, e** *adj personne* untidy, disorderly; *mouvements* uncoordinated; *fuite, vie* disorderly; *esprit* muddled. ~ **dans son travail** disorganized in one's work.

désorganiser [dezɔʀganize] (1) *vt (gén)* to disorganize. ◆ **désorganisation** *nf* disorganization.

désorienter [dezɔʀjɑ̃te] (1) *vt (lit)* to disorientate; *(fig)* to bewilder, confuse.

désormais [dezɔʀmɛ] *adv* in future, henceforth.

désosser [dezɔse] (1) *vt viande* to bone.

desperado [dɛspeʀado] *nm* desperado.

despote [dɛspɔt] **1** *adj* despotic. **2** *nm (lit, fig)* despot, tyrant. ◆ **despotique** *adj* despotic, tyrannical. ◆ **despotisme** *nm (lit, fig)* despotism, tyranny.

desquels, desquelles [dekɛl] *V* **lequel.**

dessaisir [deseziʀ] (2) **1** *vt*: ~ **un tribunal d'une affaire** to remove a case from a court. **2 se** ~ *vpr*: **se** ~ **de** to part with.

dessaler [desale] (1) *vt* (**a**) *(aussi* **faire** ~ *ou* **mettre à** ~ *) viande* to soak. (**b**) *(*: délurer)* ~ **qn** to teach sb a thing or two *.

dessécher [deseʃe] (6) **1** *vt terre* to dry out; *plante* to wither; *(fig) cœur* to harden. **2 se** ~ *vpr (gén)* to dry out; *[terre, bouche]* to become parched; *[plante]* to wither; *[aliments]* to go dry. ◆ **dessèchement** *nm* dryness.

dessein [desɛ̃] *nm (gén)* design; *(intention)* intention; *(projet)* plan. **il a le** ~ **de faire** he intends *ou* means to do; **avoir des ~s sur qn** to have designs on sb; **dans le** ~ **de faire** with the intention of doing; **faire qch à** ~ to do sth intentionally *ou* on purpose.

desseller [desele] (1) *vt* to unsaddle.

desserrer [deseʀe] (1) **1** *vt (gén)* to loosen; *nœud* to slacken; *étreinte* to relax; *poing, dents* to unclench; *écrou* to unscrew; *frein, étau* to release; *mots* to space out. ~ **sa ceinture de 2 crans** to loosen *ou* slacken one's belt 2 notches; *(fig)* **il n'a pas desserré les dents** he hasn't opened his mouth *ou* lips. **2 se** ~ *vpr [nœud, écrou]* to come loose *ou* undone; *[frein]* to release itself; *[étreinte]* to relax, loosen. ◆ **desserré, e** *adj* loose; *nœud* slack.

dessert [desɛʀ] *nm* dessert.

desserte [desɛʀt(ə)] *nf* (**a**) *(meuble)* sideboard. (**b**) *(transport)* service. **la** ~ **de la ville est assurée par un car** there is a bus service to the town.

desservir[1] [desɛʀviʀ] (14) *vt* (**a**) *plat, table* to clear away. (**b**) *(nuire à) personne* to go against; *intérêts* to harm. **il m'a desservi auprès de mes amis** he did me a disservice with my friends.

desservir[2] [desɛʀviʀ] (14) *vt* (**a**) *(Transport)* to serve. **le village est desservi par 3 lignes d'autobus** the village is served by *ou* has 3 bus services. (**b**) *[couloir]* to lead into.

dessin [desɛ̃] *nm* (**a**) *(gén)* drawing. ~ **animé** cartoon film; ~ **humoristique** cartoon; **il faut lui faire un** ~! * you'll have to spell it out for him. (**b**) *(art)* **le** ~ drawing; **école de** ~ *(d'art)* art school; *(industriel)* technical college (for draughtsmen); **professeur de** ~ art teacher; ~ **de mode** fashion design; ~ **industriel** draughtsmanship; **planche à** ~ drawing board; ~ **assisté par ordinateur** computer-aided design. (**c**) *(motif)* pattern, design. **tissu avec des ~s jaunes** material with a yellow pattern on it. (**d**) *(contour)* outline, line. ◆ **dessinateur, -trice** *nm, f (artiste)* drawer. ~ **industriel** draughtsman; ~ **humoristique** cartoonist ; ~ **de mode** fashion designer.

dessiner [desine] (1) **1** *vt* (**a**) *(gén)* to draw; *véhicule* to design; *jardin* to lay out, landscape. ~ **au crayon** to draw in pencil; **bouche bien dessinée** finely delineated mouth. (**b**) *[chose]* **les champs dessinent un damier** the fields from *ou* are laid out like a checkerboard; **vêtement qui dessine bien la taille** garment that shows off the waist well. **2 se** ~ *vpr [contour]* to stand out; *[tendance]* to become apparent; *[projet]* to take shape. **un sourire se dessina sur ses lèvres** a smile formed on his lips.

dessoûler * [desule] (1) *vti* to sober up. **il n'a pas dessoûlé de la semaine** he's been drunk non-stop all week.

dessous [d(ə)su] **1** *adv* (**a**) *(sous)* under, underneath, beneath; *(plus bas)* below. **mettez votre valise** ~ put your suitcase underneath (it) *ou* under it; **retirer qch de** ~ **le lit** to get sth from under *ou* from beneath the bed. (**b**) **en** ~ **, au-** ~ *(sous)* under, underneath; *(plus bas)* below; **en** ~ **de, au-**~ **de** below; **les enfants au-**~ **de 7 ans** children under 7; **20° au-**~ **de zéro** 20° below zero; **être au-**~ **de tout** to be quite hopeless; **les locataires d'en** ~ the people who rent the flat below, the tenants downstairs *ou* underneath; **regarder qn en** ~ to give sb a shifty look; **faire qch en** ~ to do sth in an underhand manner.

2 *nm* (**a**) *[objet]* bottom, underside; *[pied]* sole; *[voiture, animal]* underside. **drap du** ~ bottom sheet; **les gens du** ~ the people downstairs; **le** ~ **de la table est poussiéreux** the table is dusty underneath; **les fruits du** ~ the fruit at the bottom, the fruit underneath; **avoir le** ~ to get the worst of it, come off worst. (**b**) *(côté secret)* **les** ~ **de la politique** the hidden side of politics; **connaître le** ~ **des cartes** to have inside information. (**c**) *(Habillement)* **les** ~ underwear.

3 : ~ **de bouteille** bottle mat; ~ **de plat** table mat; ~ **de robe** slip, petticoat; ~ **de table** under the counter payment; ~ **de verre** coaster.

dessus [d(ə)sy] **1** *adv* (**a**) *placé* on top (of it); *collé, écrit* on it; *lancer* over (it); *(plus haut)* above. **montez** ~ *(échelle)* get up on it; **passez (par)** ~ go over it; **ôter qch de** ~ **la table** to take sth off the table; **il lui a tapé/tiré** ~ he hit him/shot at him. (**b**) **au-** ~ above; *(étage)* upstairs; *(posé sur)* on top; *(plus cher etc)* over, above; **au-**~ **de** *(plus haut que)* above; *(sur)* on top of; *prix, limite* over, above; *possibilités* beyond; **les enfants au-**~ **de 7 ans** children over 7; **20° au-**~ **de zéro** 20° above zero; *(prix)* **c'est au-**~ **de ce que je peux mettre** it's beyond my means, it's more than I can afford; **c'est au-**~ **de mes forces** it's too much for me; **être au-**~ **de tout soupçon/reproche** to be above suspicion/ beyond reproach.

2 *nm* top. **drap du** ~ top sheet; **les gens du** ~ the people upstairs; *(fig)* **le** ~ **du panier** the pick of the bunch; *(élite sociale)* the upper crust; **avoir/ prendre le** ~ to have/get the upper hand; **reprendre le** ~ to get over it.

3 : ~ **de cheminée** mantelpiece; ~ **de lit** bedspread; ~ **de table** table runner.

destabiliser [destabilize] (1) *vt (Pol) régime* to destabilize.

destin [dɛstɛ̃] *nm (sort)* fate; *(avenir, vocation)* destiny.

destinataire [dɛstinatɛʀ] *nmf [lettre]* addressee; *[marchandise]* consignee; *[mandat]* payee.

destination [dɛstinɑsjɔ̃] *nf (direction)* destination; *(usage)* purpose. **à** ~ **de** *avion, train* to; *bateau* bound for; *voyageur* travelling to; **arriver à** ~ to reach one's destination.

destiner [dɛstine] (1) *vt* (**a**) *(attribuer)* ~ **qch à qn** *(gén)* to intend *ou* mean sth for sb; *ballon* to aim sth at sb; **livre destiné aux enfants** book (intended *ou* meant) for children; **il vous destine ce poste** he intends *ou* means you to have this post; **le sort qui lui était destiné** the fate that was in store for him. (**b**) *(affecter)* ~ **une somme à l'achat de qch** to intend to use a sum *ou* earmark a sum to buy sth; **les fonds seront destinés à la recherche** the money will be devoted to *ou* used for research. (**c**) *(vouer)* ~ **qn à une fonction/à être médecin** to destine sb for a post/to be a doctor; **destiné à mourir jeune** destined *ou* fated to die young; **il se destine à l'enseignement** he intends to go into teaching. ◆ **destinée** *nf (sort)* fate; *(avenir, vocation)* destiny.

destituer [dɛstitɥe] (1) *vt ministre* to dismiss; *roi* to depose; *officier* to discharge; *fonctionnaire* to dismiss from office. ◆ **destitution** *nf* dismissal; deposition; discharge.

destruction [dɛstʀyksjɔ̃] *nf*: ~**(s)** *(gén)* destruction; *[rats]* extermination. ◆ **destructeur, -trice 1** *adj* destructive. **2** *nm, f* destroyer. ◆ **destructible** *adj* destructible. ◆ **destructif, -ive** *adj* destructive.

désuet, -ète [desɥɛ, ɛt] *adj (gén)* outdated; *charme* old-fashioned. ◆ **désuétude** *nf* disuse. **tomber en** ~ *[loi]* to fall into abeyance; *[coutume]* to become obsolete, fall into disuse.

désunir [dezyniʀ] (2) *vt famille* to divide, disunite. ◆ **désunion** *nf* disunity.

détacher [detaʃe] (1) **1** *vt* (**a**) *prisonnier, paquet* to untie; *wagon* to take off, detach (*de* from). (**b**) *(dénouer) (gén)* to undo; *nœud* to untie; *soulier, ceinture* to unfasten. (**c**) *(ôter) (gén)* to remove, take off; *papier collé* to unstick; *rideau* to take down (*de* from); *reçu* to tear out (*de* of), detach (*de* from). **il ne pouvait** ~ **son regard du spectacle** he could not take his eyes off the sight; **'** ~ **suivant le pointillé'** 'tear off along the dotted line'. (**d**) *(envoyer) personne* to send, dispatch; *(Admin: affecter)* to second. **être détaché** to be on secondment. (**e**) *(mettre en relief) mots* to separate; *contour* to bring out; *(Mus) notes* to detach. (**f**) *(éloigner)* ~

qn de qch/qn to turn sb away from sth/sb. (**g**) *(nettoyer)* to clean.
2 se ~ *vpr* (**a**) *[prisonnier]* to free o.s., get loose (*de* from); *[paquet, nœud]* to come undone *ou* untied. (**b**) *[écorce, papier collé]* to come off; *[page, épingle]* to come out; *[rideau]* to come down. (**c**) *[coureur etc]* to pull *ou* break away (*de* from). (**d**) *(ressortir)* to stand out (*sur* against). (**e**) **se** ~ **de** *(renoncer à)* to renounce; *(se désintéresser de)* to grow away from.
◆ **détachable** *adj* detachable. ◆ **détachage** *nm (nettoyage)* stain removal. ◆ **détachant** *nm* stain remover. ◆ **détaché, e** *adj air* detached. ◆ **détachement** *nm (indifférence)* detachment; *(Mil)* detachment; *[fonctionnaire]* secondment.

détail [detaj] *nm* (**a**) *(particularité)* detail. **entrer dans les ~s** to go into details *ou* particulars. (**b**) *[facture, compte]* breakdown. **faire le** ~ **de qch** to give a breakdown of sth; **il nous a fait le** ~ **de ses aventures** he gave us a detailed account of his adventures; **en** *ou* **dans le** ~ in detail. (**c**) *(Comm)* retail. **vendre au** ~ *vin* to (sell) retail; *articles* to sell separately; **marchand de** ~ retailer, retail dealer. ◆ **détaillant, e** *nm, f* retailer, retail dealer. ◆ **détaillé, e** *adj* detailed. ◆ **détailler** (1) *vt* (**a**) *(Comm) articles* to sell separately; *marchandise* to sell retail. (**b**) *plan, raison* to detail, explain in detail. **il m'a détaillé de la tête aux pieds** he examined me from head to foot.

détaler [detale] (1) *vi [lapin]* to bolt; (*) *[personne]* to scarper *. **il a détalé comme un lapin** he made a bolt for it *, he skedaddled *.

détartrer [detaʀtʀe] (1) *vt dents* to scale; *chaudière etc* to descale. ◆ **détartrage** *nm* scaling; descaling. **se faire faire un** ~ to have one's teeth scaled.

détaxer [detakse] (1) *vt (réduire)* to reduce the tax on; *(supprimer)* to remove the tax on. **produits détaxés** tax-free goods. ◆ **détaxe** *nf* reduction in tax; removal of tax (*de* from); *(remboursement)* tax refund.

détecter [detɛkte] (1) *vt* to detect. ◆ **détecteur, -trice 1** *adj* detecting, detector. **2** *nm* detector. ~ **de mensonges** polygraph, lie detector. ◆ **détection** *nf* detection.

détective [detɛktiv] *nm*: ~ **(privé)** private detective *ou* investigator, private eye *.

déteindre [detɛ̃dʀ(ə)] (52) **1** *vt* to take the colour out of. **2** *vi (gén)* to lose its colour; *(au lavage)* to run; *(au soleil)* to fade. ~ **sur** *[couleur]* to run into; *[caractère]* to rub off on; **elle a déteint sur sa fille** she had an influence on her daughter.

dételer [detle] (4) **1** *vt chevaux etc* to unharness; *voiture* to unhitch. **2** *vi* (*) to leave off working *. **sans** ~ without a break.

détendre [detɑ̃dʀ(ə)] (41) **1** *vt ressort* to release; *corde* to slacken, loosen; *corps, esprit* to relax; *atmosphère* to relieve, ease; *nerfs* to calm, soothe. **2 se** ~ *vpr [ressort]* to lose its tension; *[corde]* to become slack, slacken; *[atmosphère, esprit, corps]* to relax; *[nerfs]* to calm down. **détendez-vous!** relax!, let yourself unwind! *; **se** ~ **les jambes** to unbend one's legs. ◆ **détendu, e** *adj personne, atmosphère* relaxed; *câble* slack; *ressort* unextended.

détenir [detniʀ] (22) *vt titre* to hold; *secret, objets volés* to hold, be in possession of; *moyen* to have (in one's possession); *prisonnier* to detain. ~ **le pouvoir** to be in power; **il détient la clef de l'énigme** he holds the key to the enigma; **il a été détenu dans un camp** he was held prisoner in a camp.

détente [detɑ̃t] *nf* (**a**) *(délassement)* relaxation; *(dans les relations)* easing (*dans* of). *(Pol)* **la** ~ détente. (**b**) *(élan) [sauteur]* spring; *[lanceur]* thrust. **d'une** ~ **rapide** with a swift bound. (**c**) *(lit, fig: gâchette)* trigger.

détention [detɑ̃sjɔ̃] *nf* (**a**) *[armes]* possession; *[titres]* holding. (**b**) *(captivité)* detention. ~ **préventive** custody; **mettre en** ~ **préventive** to remand in custody, put on remand. ◆ **détenteur, -trice** *nm, f* possessor; holder. ◆ **détenu, e** *nm, f* prisoner. ~ **de droit commun** ordinary prisoner.

détergent, e [detɛʀʒɑ̃, ɑ̃t] *adj, nm* detergent.

détériorer [deteʀjɔʀe] (1) **1** *vt* to damage, spoil. **2 se** ~ *vpr* to deteriorate. ◆ **détérioration** *nf* damaging (*de* of), damage (*de* to); deterioration (*de* in). **~s** damage.

déterminer [detɛʀmine] (1) *vt (gén)* to determine; *(par calcul)* to calculate, work out; *(motiver) retard* to cause, bring about. ◆ **déterminant, e** *adj* determining. **ça a été** ~ that was the deciding *ou* determining factor (*dans* in). ◆ **détermination** *nf (précision)* determining; *(résolution)* decision, resolution; *(fermeté)* determination. ◆ **déterminé, e** *adj air* determined; *but* definite, well-defined. **quantité ~e** given quantity.

déterrer [deteʀe] (1) *vt (gén)* to dig up; *(lit, fig) objet* to unearth; *mort* to disinter. *(péj)* **avoir une tête de déterré** to look deathly pale.

détersif, -ive [detɛʀsif, iv] *adj, nm* detergent.

détester [detɛste] (1) *vt* to hate, detest. **elle déteste attendre** she hates *ou* can't bear having to wait; **il ne déteste pas le chocolat** he is rather fond of *ou* is not averse to chocolate. ◆ **détestable** *adj* foul, dreadful, appalling. ◆ **détestablement** *adv* appallingly, dreadfully.

détoner [detɔne] (1) *vi*: **(faire)** ~ to detonate, explode. ◆ **détonant, e** *adj*: **mélange** ~ explosive mixture. ◆ **détonateur** *nm* detonator. ◆ **détonation** *nf [obus]* detonation, explosion; *[fusil]* bang.

détonner [detɔne] (1) *vi [couleurs]* to clash; *[conduite]* to be out of place.

détour [detuʀ] *nm* (**a**) *(sinuosité)* bend, curve. **faire des ~s** to wind about; **au** ~ **du chemin** at the bend of the path. (**b**) *(déviation)* detour. (**c**) *(subterfuge)* roundabout means; *(circonlocution)* circumlocution. **sans ~s** plainly, without beating about the bush.

détourner [detuʀne] (1) **1** *vt* (**a**) *route, convoi* to divert; *avion [pirate de l'air]* to hijack, skyjack *; *soupçon, conversation* to divert (*sur* on to); *coup, colère* to ward off. ~ **les yeux** to look away; ~ **la tête** to turn one's head away; ~ **qn de** *chemin, devoir, soucis* to divert sb from; *projet* to dissuade sb from; *sa famille* to turn sb away from; ~ **qn du droit chemin** to lead sb astray. (**b**) *(voler)* to misappropriate. **2 se** ~ *vpr* to turn away. **se** ~ **de sa route** *(pour aller ailleurs)* to make a detour; *(par erreur)* to go off the right road. ◆ **détourné, e** *adj chemin, moyen* roundabout. **de façon ~e** in a roundabout way. ◆ **détournement** *nm [rivière]* diversion. ~ **d'avion** hijacking, skyjacking *; ~ **de fonds** misappropriation of funds; ~ **de mineur** *(perversion)* corruption of a minor.

détraquer [detʀake] (1) **1** *vt machine* to put out of order; *personne (physiquement)* to put out of sorts; *(nerveusement)* to upset; *(mentalement)* to unhinge. **ces orages ont détraqué le temps** these storms have unsettled the weather; **c'est un détraqué** * he's a headcase ⁑, he's cracked *. **2 se** ~ *vpr [machine]* to go wrong; *[estomac]* to be upset; *[temps]* to break. ◆ **détraquement** *nm [machine]* breakdown; *[santé, nerfs]* upset, breakdown.

détremper [detʀɑ̃pe] (1) *vt* to soak. **chemins détrempés** sodden paths; **chemise détrempée** soaking (wet) shirt.

détresse [detʀɛs] *nf* distress. **en** ~ *personne, bateau* in distress; *entreprise* in difficulties; *cœur* anguished; **appel de** ~ distress call.

détriment [detʀimɑ̃] *nm*: **au** ~ **de** to the detriment of.

détritus [detRitys] *nmpl* rubbish, refuse, garbage.

détroit [detRwa] *nm (Géog)* strait. **le ~ de Bering** *ou* **Behring** the Bering Strait; **le ~ du Bosphore** the strait of the Bosphorus; **le ~ de Gibraltar** the Strait of Gibraltar; **le ~ de Magellan** the Magellan Strait, the Strait of Magellan.

détromper [detRɔ̃pe] (1) **1** *vt personne* to disabuse (*de* of). **2 se ~** *vpr:* **détrompez-vous, il n'est pas venu** you're quite mistaken, he didn't come.

détrôner [detRone] (1) *vt (lit, fig)* to dethrone.

détrousser [detRuse] (1) *vt († ou hum)* to rob.

détruire [detRɥiR] (38) *vt (gén)* to destroy; *population* to wipe out; *insectes* to exterminate; *santé, espoir, projet* to ruin, wreck. **les effets se détruisent** the effects cancel each other out.

dette [dɛt] *nf (Fin, fig)* debt. **faire des ~s** to get into debt; **~ de jeu** gambling *ou* gaming debt; **avoir 1000 F de ~s** to be 1,000 francs in debt; **la ~ publique** the national debt; *(fig)* **je suis en ~ envers vous** I am indebted to you.

deuil [dœj] *nm* (**a**) *(perte)* bereavement. **plusieurs ~s dans sa famille** several deaths in his family. (**b**) *(affliction)* grief. **plonger qn dans le ~** to plunge sb into mourning *ou* grief. (**c**) *(vêtements)* mourning (clothes). **en grand ~** in deep mourning; **être/se mettre en ~** to be in/go into mourning. (**d**) *(durée)* mourning. **jour de ~** day of mourning; **~ national** national mourning. (**e**) **faire son ~ de qch** * to say goodbye to sth *.

deux [dø] **1** *adj* (**a**) two. **~ fois** twice; **je les ai vus tous (les) ~** I saw them both, I saw both of them, I saw the two of them; *(lit, fig)* **à ~ tranchants** double-edged; **inflation à ~ chiffres** double-figure *ou* two-figure inflation; **des ~ côtés de la rue** on both sides *ou* on either side of the street; **tous les ~ jours** every other *ou* every second day, every two days; *(en épelant)* **~ t/l** double t/l. (**b**) *(quelques)* a couple, a few. **c'est à ~ minutes d'ici** it's just a few minutes *ou* only a couple of minutes from here; **vous y serez en ~ secondes** you'll be there in no time (at all); **j'ai ~ mots à vous dire** I want to have a word with you. (**c**) *(deuxième)* second. (**d**) *(locutions)* **essayer et réussir, cela fait ~** to try and to succeed are two entirely different things; **pris entre ~ feux** caught in the crossfire; **il ne faut plus qu'il y ait ~ poids (et) ~ mesures** we must no longer have two different standards *ou* two sets of rules; *(fig)* **être assis entre ~ chaises** to be in a difficult predicament; **~ précautions valent mieux qu'une** better safe than sorry; **en ~ temps, trois mouvements** in two ticks *.

2 *nm* two. **couper en ~ /en ~ morceaux** to cut in two *ou* in half/into two pieces; **marcher ~ par ~** to walk two by two *ou* in pairs; **à nous ~** *(à un interlocuteur)* I'm with you now; *(à un ennemi)* now let's fight it out!; *V* **six.**

3 : **~-pièces** *nm inv (ensemble)* two-piece suit; *(maillot)* two-piece (swimsuit); *(appartement)* two-room flat; **~-points** *nm inv* colon; **~-roues** *nm inv* two-wheeled vehicle.

◆ **deuxième** *adj, nmf* second. *(Mil)* **~ classe** private; *V* **sixième.** ◆ **deuxièmement** *adv* second(ly).

dévaler [devale] (1) **1** *vt* to tear down, hurtle down. **2** *vi [rochers]* to hurtle down; *[lave]* to rush down; *[terrain]* to fall away sharply. *[personne]* **~ dans les escaliers** to tumble down the stairs.

dévaliser [devalize] (1) *vt maison* to burgle, burglarize *(US)*. *banque, personne* to rob. *(fig) [clients]* **~ un magasin** to buy up a shop; **~ le réfrigérateur** to raid the fridge.

dévaloriser *vt*, **se ~** *vpr* [devalɔRize] (1) to depreciate. ◆ **dévalorisation** *nf* depreciation.

dévaluer *vt*, **se ~** *vpr* [devalɥe] (1) to devalue. ◆ **dévaluation** *nf* devaluation.

devancer [dəvɑ̃se] (3) *vt (distancer)* to get ahead of; *(précéder)* to arrive ahead of; *objection, désir* to anticipate. *(Mil)* **~ l'appel** to enlist before call-up; **il m'a devancé de 3 minutes/3 points** he beat me by 3 minutes/3 points, he was 3 minutes/3 points ahead of me. ◆ **devancier, -ière** *nm, f* precursor.

devant [d(ə)vɑ̃] **1** *prép* (**a**) *(position)* in front of; *(distance)* ahead of; *(dépassement)* past. **il est passé ~ moi sans me voir** he walked past me without seeing me; **assis ~ la fenêtre** sitting at *ou* by the window; **va-t-en de ~ la vitrine** move away from (in front of) the window; **il marchait ~ moi** he was walking in front of *ou* ahead of me; **il est ~ moi en classe** *(banc)* he sits in front of me at school; *(résultats)* he is ahead of me at school; **fuir ~ qn** to flee before *ou* from sb; **avoir du temps/de l'argent ~ soi** to have time/money to spare; *(lit, fig)* **aller droit ~ soi** to go straight on. (**b**) *(en présence de)* before. **s'incliner ~ qn** to bow before sb; **imperturbable ~ le malheur d'autrui** unmoved by other people's misfortune; *(fig)* **reculer ~ ses responsabilités** to shrink from one's responsibilities; **par-~ notaire** in the presence of a notary; **~ la situation** *(étant donné)* in view of *ou* considering the situation; *(face à)* faced *ou* confronted with the situation; **rester ferme ~ le danger** to stand fast in the face of danger.

2 *adv*: **vous êtes juste ~** you are right in front of it; **corsage qui se boutonne (par-)~** blouse which buttons up at the front; **il est loin ~** he's a long way ahead; **je suis passé ~** *boutique* I went past *ou* by it; *coureur* I went ahead of *ou* in front of him; **fais passer le plateau ~** pass the tray forward; **il a pris des places ~** he has got seats at the front; *(Aut)* **monter ~** to sit in the front; **marchez ~, les enfants** walk in front, children.

3 *nm* (**a**) *(gén)* front; *[bateau]* fore, bows. **habiter sur le ~** to live at the front; **roue de ~** front wheel. (**b**) **prendre les ~s** to make the first move, take the initiative; **je suis allé au-~(de lui)** I went to meet him; **aller au-~ des désirs de qn** to anticipate sb's wishes; **courir au-~ du danger** to court danger; **aller au-~ des ennuis** to be asking for trouble.

devanture [d(ə)vɑ̃tyR] *nf (étalage)* display; *(vitrine)* (shop) window; *(façade)* (shop) front.

dévaster [devaste] (1) *vt* to devastate. ◆ **dévastateur, -trice** *adj orage* devastating; *passion* destructive. ◆ **dévastation** *nf*: **~(s)** devastation.

déveine * [devɛn] *nf* rotten luck *.

développer [devlɔpe] (1) **1** *vt (gén, Phot)* to develop; *commerce* to expand; *argument* to enlarge (up)on; *paquet* to unwrap; *parchemin* to unroll; *coupon de tissu* to unfold; *troupes* to deploy. **poitrine bien/peu développée** well-developed/ underdeveloped bust. **2 se ~** *vpr [personne, plante]* to develop; *[affaire]* to expand, develop; *[armée]* to spread out; *[habitude]* to spread. ◆ **développement** *nm* development; expansion. **en plein ~** fast-expanding, fast-developing; **pays en voie de ~** developing country; **appareil/photographie à ~ instantané** instant camera/photograph.

devenir [dəvniR] (22) **1** *vi* (**a**) to become. **~ médecin** to become a doctor; **que veux-tu ~ dans la vie?** what do you want to do *ou* be in life?; **cet enfant est devenu un homme solide** that child has turned into *ou* has become a strong man; **il est devenu tout rouge** he turned *ou* went quite red; **~ vieux** to grow *ou* get old; **c'est à ~ fou!** it's enough to drive you mad! (**b**) *(advenir de)* **bonjour, que devenez-vous?** * hullo, how are you getting on? *ou* doing? *; **que sont devenues mes lunettes?** where have my glasses got to?; **qu'allons-nous ~?** what will become of us? **2** *nm* evolution.

dévergonder (se) [devɛʀgɔ̃de] (1) *vpr* to run wild. ◆ **dévergondé, e** *adj* shameless.

déverser [devɛʀse] (1) **1** *vt ordures* to tip (out), dump; *bombes* to unload; *voyageurs* to disgorge; *colère* to pour out. **2 se** ~ *vpr* to pour out (*dans* into).

dévêtir *vt*, **se** ~ *vpr* [devetiʀ] (20) to undress.

déviance [devjɑ̃s] *nf (Psych)* deviancy, deviance. ◆ **déviant, e** *adj, nm, f* deviant.

déviation [devjɑsjɔ̃] *nf (lit, fig: écart)* deviation; *(Aut)* diversion; *[colonne vertébrale]* curvature.

dévider [devide] (1) *vt bobine* to unwind; *reproches* to reel off. ◆ **dévidoir** *nm* reel.

dévier [devje] (7) **1** *vi* (**a**) *[aiguille]* to deviate; *[bateau, projectile]* to veer off course. **le poteau a fait ~ le ballon** the post deflected the ball. (**b**) *[doctrine]* to alter. **la conversation déviait dangereusement** the conversation was taking a dangerous turn; ~ **par rapport au projet initial** to move away *ou* diverge from the original plan; ~ **de sa ligne politique** to deviate *ou* depart from one's political line; **il fit ~ la conversation** he turned *ou* diverted the conversation (*sur* onto). **2** *vt circulation* to divert; *coup* to deflect.

deviner [d(ə)vine] (1) *vt (gén)* to guess; *énigme* to solve. ~ **l'avenir** to foretell the future; **devine pourquoi** guess why. ◆ **devin, devineresse** *nm, f* soothsayer. **je ne suis pas ~** * I haven't got second sight. ◆ **devinette** *nf* riddle.

devis [d(ə)vi] *nm* estimate, quotation.

dévisager [devizaʒe] (3) *vt* to stare at, look hard at.

devise [d(ə)viz] *nf* motto; *(Comm)* slogan; *(Fin)* currency. ~ **forte** hard *ou* strong currency; ~ **faible** soft *ou* weak currency; ~**s** (foreign) currency.

dévisser [devise] (1) *vt* to unscrew.

dévoiler [devwale] (1) *vt statue, secret* to unveil; *nom, date* to reveal, disclose.

devoir [d(ə)vwaʀ] (28) **1** *vt argent, respect etc* to owe. **il réclame ce qui lui est dû** he is asking for what is owing *ou* due to him; **il ne veut rien ~ à personne** he doesn't want to be indebted to anyone *ou* to owe anyone anything; **je dois à mes parents d'avoir réussi** I have my parents to thank for my success, I owe my success to my parents; **il lui doit bien cela!** it's the least he can do for him!; **avec les honneurs dûs à son rang** with honours due to *ou* befitting his rank.

2 *vb aux* (**a**) *(obligation)* to have to. **il aurait dû la prévenir** he should have *ou* ought to have warned her; **dois-je lui écrire tout de suite?** must I *ou* do I have to *ou* have I got to write to him immediately?; **vous ne devez pas entrer sans frapper** you are not to *ou* you must not come in without knocking; **non, tu ne dois pas le rembourser** no, you need not *ou* don't have to pay it back. (**b**) *(fatalité)* **cela devait arriver** it was bound to happen; **elle ne devait pas apprendre la nouvelle avant le lendemain** she was not to hear the news until the next day; **même s'il devait être condamné, il refuserait** even if he were (to be) found guilty he would refuse; **les choses semblent ~ s'arranger** things seem to be sorting themselves out. (**c**) *(prévision)* **il doit arriver ce soir** he is due to arrive tonight, he is to arrive tonight; **vous deviez le lui cacher** you were (supposed) to hide it from him. (**d**) *(probabilité)* **vous devez vous tromper** you must be mistaken; **elle ne doit pas être bête** she can't be stupid; **cela devrait pouvoir s'arranger** it should be *ou* ought to be possible to put that right.

3 se ~ *vpr*: **se ~ à qn/qch** to have to devote o.s. to sb/sth; **nous nous devons de le lui dire** it is our duty to tell him; **comme il se doit** *(comme il faut)* as is proper *ou* right; *(comme prévu)* as expected.

4 *nm* (**a**) *(obligation)* duty. **agir par ~** to act from a sense of duty; **se faire un ~ de faire** to make it one's duty to do; **~s religieux** religious duties; **se mettre en ~ de faire** to set about doing; **présenter ses ~s à qn** to pay one's respects to sb. (**b**) *(Scol) (à la maison)* homework; *(en classe)* exercise. **faire ses ~s** to do one's homework; ~ **sur table** written) test.

dévolu, e [devɔly] *adj*: **être ~ à qn** *[droits]* to be devolved upon sb; *[charge]* to be handed down to sb; **budget ~ à la recherche** funds allotted to research; **le sort qui lui sera ~** the fate that is in store for him.

dévorer [devɔʀe] (1) *vt* (**a**) *aliment, livre* to devour; *fortune* to consume; *larmes* to choke back. **cet enfant dévore!** this child has a huge appetite!; **dévoré par les moustiques** eaten alive by mosquitoes; ~ **qch à belles dents** to wolf sth down; ~ **qn du regard** to eye sb greedily. (**b**) *[jalousie, feu]* to consume, devour. **la soif le dévore** he has a burning thirst; **voiture qui dévore les kilomètres** car which eats up the miles; **c'est une tâche qui dévore tous mes loisirs** it's a task which swallows up all my free time. ◆ **dévorant, e** *adj faim* raging; *curiosité, soif* burning; *passion* devouring, consuming.

dévot, e [devo, ɔt] **1** *adj (gén)* devout, pious; *(péj)* churchy *, over-pious. **2** *nm, f* deeply religious person; *(péj)* excessively pious person. ◆ **dévotement** *adv* devoutly, piously. ◆ **dévotion** *nf (piété)* devoutness; *(culte)* devotion. **avoir une ~ pour qn** to worship sb.

dévouer (se) [devwe] (1) *vpr (se sacrifier)* to sacrifice o.s. (*pour* for). *(se consacrer à)* **se ~ à qn/qch** to devote *ou* dedicate o.s. to sb/sth. ◆ **dévoué, e** *adj* devoted, dedicated (*à* to). ◆ **dévouement** *nm* devotion, dedication. **avec ~** devotedly.

dévoyer [devwaje] (8) **1** *vt* to lead astray. **2 se** ~ *vpr* to go astray. ◆ **dévoyé, e** *adj, nm, f* delinquent.

dextérité [dɛksteʀite] *nf* skill, dexterity.

diabète [djabɛt] *nm* diabetes *(sg)*. ◆ **diabétique** *adj, nmf* diabetic.

diable [djɑbl(ə)] *nm* (**a**) devil. **il a le ~ au corps** he is the very devil; **il est très ~** he is a real little devil; **tirer le ~ par la queue** to live from hand to mouth; **habiter au ~ vauvert** to live miles from anywhere; **il faisait un vent du ~** there was the devil of a wind; **il est menteur en ~** he is the devil of a liar; **ce ~ de temps** this wretched weather. (**b**) *(excl)* **D~!** well!; **qu'il aille au ~!** the devil take him!; **du courage que ~!** cheer up, dash it!; **pourquoi/quand ~ l'as-tu jeté?** why/when the devil did you throw it out?; **c'est bien le ~ si** it would be most unusual *ou* surprising if; **ce n'est pas le ~!** it's not that bad! (**c**) *(enfant)* devil, rogue. *(personne)* **pauvre ~** poor devil; **grand ~** tall fellow; **ce n'est pas un mauvais ~** he's not a bad fellow. (**d**) *(chariot)* hand truck. *(jouet)* ~ **(à ressort)** jack-in-the-box. ◆ **diablement** * *adv* dashed *. ◆ **diabolique** *adj* diabolical, devilish. ◆ **diaboliquement** *adv* diabolically.

diabolo [djabɔlo] *nm (jouet)* diabolo. *(boisson)* ~ **menthe** mint and lemonade.

diacre [djakʀ(ə)] *nm* deacon.

diadème [djadɛm] *nm (lit, fig)* diadem; *(bijou)* tiara.

diagnostiquer [djagnɔstike] (1) *vt (lit, fig)* to diagnose. ◆ **diagnostic** *nm* diagnosis.

diagonal, e, *mpl* **-aux** [djagɔnal, o] *adj, nf* diagonal. **en ~e** diagonally; **lire en ~e** to skim through.

diagramme [djagʀam] *nm (schéma)* diagram; *(graphique)* chart, graph.

dialecte [djalɛkt(ə)] *nm* dialect. ◆ **dialectal, e,** *mpl* **-aux** *adj* dialectal.

dialectique [djalɛktik] *adj, nf* dialectic.

dialogue [djalɔg] *nm (gén)* dialogue; *(conversation)* conversation. **c'est un ~ de sourds** it's a dialogue of the deaf. ◆ **dialoguer** (1) *vi [amis]* to have a conversation; *[syndicats]* to have a dialogue. **~ avec un ordinateur** to interact with a computer.

diamant [djamɑ̃] *nm (gén)* diamond. ◆ **diamantaire** *nm (tailleur)* diamond-cutter; *(vendeur)* diamond merchant.

diamètre [djamɛtʀ(ə)] *nm* diameter. ◆ **diamétralement** *adv* diametrically.

diantre [djɑ̃tʀ(ə)] *excl (†, hum)* by Jove! *(†, hum)*. **qui ~...?** who the devil...? †. ◆ **diantrement** *adv (†, hum)* devilish †.

diapason [djapazɔ̃] *nm (gén)* diapason. **se mettre au ~ de qn** to get in tune with sb.

diaphane [djafan] *adj* diaphanous.

diaphragme [djafʀagm(ə)] *nm (gén)* diaphragm; *(Phot)* aperture. *(Phot)* **ouvrir de 2 ~s** to open 2 stops.

diapositive [djapozitiv] *nf (Phot)* slide.

diarrhée [djaʀe] *nf* diarrhœa.

diaspora [djaspɔʀa] *nf (gén)* diaspora. **la ~ (juive)** the (Jewish) Diaspora.

diatribe [djatʀib] *nf* diatribe.

dichotomie [dikɔtɔmi] *nf* dichotomy.

dictateur [diktatœʀ] *nm* dictator. ◆ **dictatorial, e,** *mpl* **-aux** *adj* dictatorial. ◆ **dictature** *nf* dictatorship. *(fig)* **c'est de la ~!** this is tyranny!

dicter [dikte] (1) *vt lettre, condition* to dictate (*à* to); *volonté* to impose (*à* upon). **je n'aime pas qu'on me dicte ce que je dois faire!** I won't be dictated to! ◆ **dictée** *nf* dictation. **écrire sous la ~ de qn** to take down sb's dictation.

diction [diksjɔ̃] *nf (débit)* diction, delivery; *(art)* speech production.

dictionnaire [diksjɔnɛʀ] *nm* dictionary. *(Ordin)* **~ de données** data directory *ou* dictionary; **c'est un vrai ~** he's a walking encyclopaedia.

dicton [diktɔ̃] *nm* saying, dictum.

didacticiel [didaktisjɛl] *nm (Ordin)* educational software program. **il fait des ~s** he writes educational software.

dièse [djɛz] *adj, nm (Mus)* sharp. **fa ~** F sharp.

diesel [djezɛl] *nm* diesel.

diète [djɛt] *nf* (**a**) *(Méd) (jeûne)* starvation diet; *(régime)* diet. **mettre qn à la ~** to put sb on a starvation diet. (**b**) *(Hist)* diet. ◆ **diététicien, -ienne** *nm, f* dietician. ◆ **diététique 1** *adj* dietary. **restaurant ~** health-food *ou* organic *(US)* restaurant; **magasin** *ou* **centre ~** health-food shop. **2** *nf* dietetics *(sg)*.

dieu, *pl* **~x** [djø] *nm* (**a**) *(Myth, fig)* god. (**b**) **D~** God; **D~ le père** God the Father; **société sans D~** godless society; **le bon D~** the good Lord; **on lui donnerait le bon D~ sans confession** he looks as if butter wouldn't melt in his mouth. (**c**) *(locutions)* **mon D~!** my goodness!, goodness me!; **mon D~ oui** well yes; **D~ vous bénisse!** God bless you!; **à D~ ne plaise!, D~ m'en garde!** God forbid!; **D~ vous entende!** may God hear you!; **D~ seul le sait** God only *ou* alone knows; **D~ sait s'il est généreux!** God knows he is generous!; **D~ soit loué!** praise God! *ou* the Lord!; **D~ merci, il n'a pas plu** it didn't rain, thank goodness ; **à-D~-vat!** *(entreprise risquée)* well, it's in God's hands; *(départ)* God be with you; **tu vas te taire bon D~!** ‡ for Christ's sake ‡ *ou* sakes ‡ *(US)* will you be quiet!

diffamer [difame] (1) *vt (en paroles)* to slander; *(par écrit)* to libel. ◆ **diffamateur, -trice** *nm, f* slanderer. ◆ **diffamation** *nf*: **~(s)** slander; libel ; **campagne de ~** smear campaign. ◆ **diffamatoire** *adj* slanderous; libellous.

différé, e [difeʀe] *adj (TV)* (pre-)recorded.

différemment [difeʀamɑ̃] *adv* differently.

différence [difeʀɑ̃s] *nf (gén)* difference. **~ d'âge** difference in age, age difference; **quelle ~ avec les autres!** what a difference from the others!; **ne pas faire de ~** to make no distinction (*entre* between); **à la ~ de** unlike; **à cette ~ que** with this difference that.

différencier [difeʀɑ̃sje] (7) **1** *vt* to differentiate. **2 se ~** *vpr (être différent de)* to differ (*de* from); *(devenir différent)* to become differentiated (*de* from); *(se rendre différent)* to differentiate o.s. (*de* from). ◆ **différenciation** *nf* differentiation.

différend [difeʀɑ̃] *nm* difference of opinion, disagreement; *(Jur, Fin)* controversy.

différent, e [difeʀɑ̃, ɑ̃t] *adj* (**a**) *(dissemblable)* different (*de* from). (**b**) *(pl: divers)* different, various. **à ~es heures de la journée** at different times of day; **pour ~es raisons** for various reasons.

différentiel, -elle [difeʀɑ̃sjɛl] *adj, nm, nf (gén)* differential.

différer [difeʀe] (6) **1** *vi* (**a**) *(être dissemblable)* to differ, be different (*de* from, *en, par* in). (**b**) *(diverger)* to differ. **2** *vt (gén)* to postpone, put off; *jugement* to defer.

difficile [difisil] *adj* (**a**) *travail, problème* difficult; *situation* difficult, awkward, tricky *. **il a eu un moment ~** he went through a difficult *ou* hard *ou* trying time; **il a trouvé l'expédition ~** he found the expedition hard going *ou* heavy going; **~ à faire** difficult *ou* hard to do; **ils ont des fins de mois ~s** they have a hard time making ends meet. (**b**) *personne (contrariant)* difficult, trying; *(exigeant)* fussy. **être ~ sur la nourriture** to be difficult *ou* fussy about one's food; **faire le ~** to be hard to please. ◆ **difficilement** *adv marcher, s'exprimer* with difficulty. **c'est ~ visible** it's difficult *ou* hard to see; **il gagne ~ sa vie** he finds it difficult *ou* hard to earn a living. ◆ **difficulté** *nf (gén)* difficulty. **avoir de la ~ à faire qch** to have difficulty (in) doing sth, find it difficult *ou* hard to do sth; **avoir des ~s financières** to be in financial difficulties; **faire des ~s pour accepter** to make *ou* raise difficulties about accepting; **être en ~** to be in difficulties *ou* in trouble; **avion/navire en ~** aircraft/ship in distress; **mettre qn en ~** to put sb in a difficult position; *(Scol, Psych)* **enfant en ~** problem child; **~s d'apprentissage** learning disabilities *ou* difficulties.

difforme [difɔʀm(ə)] *adj corps* deformed, misshapen; *visage, arbre* twisted. ◆ **difformité** *nf* deformity, misshapenness; twistedness. *(Méd)* **~s** deformities.

diffus, e [dify, yz] *adj (gén)* diffuse.

diffuser [difyze] (1) *vt lumière, chaleur* to diffuse; *livres* to distribute; *(Jur) document* to circulate; *émission* to broadcast. **programme diffusé en direct** live broadcast *ou* programme. ◆ **diffuseur** *nm (Presse: distributeur)* distributor. ◆ **diffusion** *nf* diffusion; distribution; circulation; broadcasting.

digérer [diʒeʀe] (6) *vt aliment, connaissance* to digest; *insulte* to stomach *, put up with. **~ bien/mal** to have a good/bad digestion. ◆ **digeste** *adj aliment* easily digested, digestible. ◆ **digestif, -ive 1** *adj* digestive. **2** *nm (liqueur)* liqueur. ◆ **digestion** *nf* digestion.

digital, e, *mpl* **-aux** [diʒital, o] **1** *adj (gén)* digital. **2** *nf* digitalis.

digne [diɲ] *adj (auguste)* dignified; *(à la hauteur)* worthy. **son ~ fils** his worthy son; **~ de** worthy of; **~ d'éloges** praiseworthy, deserving of praise; **~ de foi** trustworthy; **~ de pitié** pitiable; **~ d'envie** enviable; **il n'est pas ~ de vivre** he's not fit to live;

(lit, péj) **tu es le ~ fils de ton père!** you're fit to be your father's son!; **avec une attitude peu ~ d'un juge** with an attitude ill-befitting a judge. ◆ **dignement** *adv se conduire* with dignity; *récompenser* fittingly, justly. ◆ **dignitaire** *nm* dignitary. ◆ **dignité** *nf (gén)* dignity. **la ~ de la personne humaine** human dignity.

digression [digʀesjɔ̃] *nf* digression.

digue [dig] *nf (gén)* dyke; *(pour protéger la côte)* sea wall; *(fig)* barrier.

dilapider [dilapide] (1) *vt* to squander, waste. ◆ **dilapidation** *nf* squandering, wasting.

dilater [dilate] (1) **1** *vt (gén)* to dilate; *métal, gaz* to cause to expand. **2 se ~** *vpr* to dilate; to expand. **se ~ la rate *** to split one's sides (laughing) *. ◆ **dilatation** *nf* dilation; expansion.

dilemme [dilɛm] *nm* dilemma. **sortir du ~** to resolve the dilemma.

dilettante [diletɑ̃t] *nmf (en art)* dilettante; *(péj: amateur)* amateur. ◆ **dilettantisme** *nm* amateurishness.

diligence [diliʒɑ̃s] *nf* (**a**) *(empressement)* haste. **faire ~** to make haste. (**b**) *(soin)* diligence. (**c**) *(Hist: voiture)* stagecoach. ◆ **diligent, e** *adj (rapide)* speedy, prompt; *(assidu)* diligent.

diluer [dilɥe] (1) *vt liquide* to dilute; *peinture* to thin down; *(fig) discours* to pad out. ◆ **dilution** *nf* dilution; thinning down; padding out.

diluvienne [dilyvjɛn] *adj f pluie* torrential.

dimanche [dimɑ̃ʃ] *nm* Sunday. **le ~ de Pâques** Easter Sunday; **ses habits du ~** one's Sunday clothes, one's Sunday best; **peintre du ~** spare-time painter; **chauffeur du ~** Sunday driver; *V* **samedi.**

dîme [dim] *nf (Hist)* tithe.

dimension [dimɑ̃sjɔ̃] *nf* (**a**) *(taille)* size. **avoir la même ~** to be the same size; **de grande/petite ~** large/small-sized; **une tâche à la ~ de son talent** a task equal to *ou* commensurate with one's talent. (**b**) *(mesures)* **~s** dimensions; **quelles sont les ~s de la pièce?** what are the dimensions *ou* measurements of the room?; **dans la plus grande ~** at the widest (*ou* longest) point; **à 2/3 ~s** 2/3 dimensional. (**c**) *(Philos)* dimension.

diminuer [diminɥe] (1) **1** *vt* (**a**) *(gén)* to reduce, decrease; *prix* to bring down; *son* to lower, turn down; *plaisir, intérêt* to lessen, diminish. **~ les effectifs** to cut back on numbers, reduce *ou* cut back the numbers; **ça l'a beaucoup diminué** this has greatly undermined his health; **c'est un homme très diminué** he has really gone downhill, he is not at all the man he was; **très ~ physiquement** physically very run-down; **très ~ mentalement** mentally much less alert; **~ un employé** to cut *ou* reduce the salary of an employee. (**b**) *(dénigrer)* to belittle.
2 *vi* (**a**) *[violence, intensité]* to diminish; *[circulation]* to die down; *[pluie]* to let up; *[orage, bruit]* to die down *ou* away. **~ d'intensité** to die down, decrease in intensity, subside. (**b**) *[nombre, valeur, pression]* to decrease, diminish, go down, fall; *[jours]* to grow shorter. **ça a diminué de volume** it has been reduced in volume. ◆ **diminutif, -ive** *adj, nm* diminutive. ◆ **diminution** *nf* (**a**) *(réduction)* reduction. **consentir une ~ à** to allow a reduction to. (**b**) *(décroissance)* diminishing; decrease. **une ~ du nombre des accidents** a decrease in the number of accidents.

dinde [dɛ̃d] *nf* turkey(hen). ◆ **dindon** *nm* turkey(cock). **être le ~ (de la farce)** to be cheated. ◆ **dindonneau,** *pl* **~x** *nm* turkey poult.

dîner [dine] (1) **1** *vi* to have dinner. **~ d'une tranche de pain** to have a slice of bread for dinner; **avoir qn à ~** to have sb for *ou* to dinner. **2** *nm* dinner; *(réception)* dinner party. ◆ **dînette** *nf (jeu)* doll's tea party. *(repas)* **on fera la ~ *** we'll have a snack. ◆ **dîneur, -euse** *nm, f* diner.

ding [diŋ] *excl* ding. **~ dong!** ding dong!

dingue * [dɛ̃g] **1** *adj personne* nuts *, crazy * (*de* about); *bruit, prix* fantastic, incredible, stupendous. **tu verrais les prix, c'est ~!** you should see the prices, they're crazy *ou* incredible!; **un film ~** a really way out * film; **un vent ~** a hell of * a wind. **2** *nmf* nutcase *, loony ‡. **c'est un ~ de la voiture** he's crazy * *ou* nuts * about cars.

dinosaure [dinozɔʀ] *nm* dinosaur.

diocèse [djɔsɛz] *nm* diocese.

diphtérie [difteʀi] *nf* diphtheria. ◆ **diphtérique** *adj* diphtherial.

diphtongue [diftɔ̃g] *nf* diphthong.

diplomate [diplɔmat] **1** *adj* diplomatic. **2** *nmf (Pol)* diplomat; *(fig)* diplomatist. **3** *nm (Culin)* ≃ trifle. ◆ **diplomatie** *nf (Pol, fig)* diplomacy. ◆ **diplomatique** *adj* diplomatic. **c'est une maladie ~** it's a sort of 'diplomatic' *ou* face-saving illness.

diplôme [diplom] *nm (titre) (gén)* diploma; *(licence)* degree. **avoir des ~s** to have qualifications. ◆ **diplômé, e** **1** *adj* qualified. **2** *nm, f* holder of a diploma.

dire [diʀ] (37) **1** *vt* (**a**) *paroles* to say. **'j'ai froid' dit-il** 'I'm cold' he said; **~ bonjour à qn** to say hullo to sb; **comme disent les Anglais** as the English put it *ou* say; **~ ce qu'on pense** to speak one's mind; **il n'a pas dit un mot** he hasn't said *ou* spoken *ou* uttered a single word; **qu'est-ce que les gens vont ~!** whatever will people say!; **il ne croyait pas si bien ~** he didn't know how right he was, he never spoke a truer word; **ce n'est pas une chose à ~** it is better left unsaid; **que dis-je!** what am I saying?
(**b**) **~ que** to say that; **doit-il venir? — elle dit que oui** is he coming? — she says he is *ou* she says so; **la loi dit clairement que** the law says clearly that *ou* clearly states that; **l'espoir fait vivre, dit-on** you can live on hope, as the saying goes; **on le dit malade** he's rumoured to be ill; **il sait ce qu'il dit** he knows what he's talking about.
(**c**) **~ à qn que** to tell sb that, say to sb that; **~ qch à qn** to tell sb sth; **j'ai qch à vous ~** there's sth I want to tell you *ou* say to you; **~ la bonne aventure à qn** to tell sb's fortune; **il nous a dit sa joie** he told us of his joy, he told us how happy he was; **ce nom me dit qch** this name rings a bell; **dites-lui de partir/qu'il parte ce soir** tell him to go/that he must leave tonight; **fais ce qu'on te dit!** do as you are told!; **'méfie-toi' me dit-il** he told me *ou* he said to me, 'be cautious'.
(**d**) *(objecter)* to say (*à, contre* against). **tu n'as rien à ~, tu es bien servi** you can't complain, you've done all right.
(**e**) *poèmes, messe, prière* to say; *rôle* to speak; *mensonge, renseignement* to tell. **~ des bêtises** to talk nonsense.
(**f**) *(plaire)* **cela vous dit de sortir?** do you feel like going out?; **rien ne me dit en ce moment** I am not in the mood for anything just now; **cela ne me dit rien qui vaille** I don't like the look of that.
(**g**) *[chose] (indiquer)* to say, show. **son silence en dit long** his silence speaks for itself.
(**h**) *(penser)* to think. **qu'est-ce que tu dis de ma robe?** what do you think of *ou* how do you like my dress?; **qu'est-ce que vous dites de la question?** what do you think about the matter?; **qu'est-ce que vous diriez d'une promenade?** what would you say to a walk?, how about a walk?; **on dirait qu'il n'aime pas cette ville** he doesn't seem to like this town; **on dirait qu'il le fait exprès!** you'd almost think he does it on purpose!; **on dirait qu'il va pleuvoir** it looks like rain; **on dirait du poulet** it tastes like chicken; **on dirait du Brahms** it sounds like Brahms; **on dirait du parfum** it smells like

perfume; **on dirait de la soie** it feels like silk; **qui l'eût dit!** who would have thought it!
(**i**) *(décider)* **venez bientôt, disons demain** come soon, let's make it tomorrow *ou* let's say tomorrow; **il est dit que je ne gagnerai jamais** I'm destined *ou* fated never to win; **bon, voilà qui est dit** right, it's settled; **à l'heure dite** at the appointed time.
(**j**) *(admettre)* to say, admit. **il faut bien ~ que** I must say *ou* admit that; **disons-le, il nous ennuie** let's be frank, he bores us.
(**k**) *(locutions)* **X, dit le Chacal** X, known as the Jackal; **qui dit argent dit problèmes** money means problems; **tu l'as dit!** quite true!, you've said it!; **ceci dit** having said this; **pour ainsi ~** so to speak, as it were; **comme qui dirait *** as you might say; **ou pour mieux ~...** or, to put it another way...; **dis donc!** *(à propos)* by the way; *(holà)* hey!; **comme dit l'autre *** as they say, so to speak; **pour tout ~** in fact; **je vous l'avais bien dit!** I told you so!; **que tu dis! ‡** sez you! ‡; **à qui le dites-vous!** you're telling ME! *; **cela va sans ~** it goes without saying; **il va sans dire que c'était faux** needless to say it was wrong; **à vrai ~** actually, to tell (you) the truth; **il n'y a pas à ~** there's no doubt about it; **je ne vous dis que cela!** just let me tell you!; **on a beau ~** say what you like; **comment dirais-je...** how shall I put it?; **c'est ~ s'il est content** that just shows you how pleased he is; **c'est beaucoup ~** that's saying a lot; **c'est peu ~** that's an understatement; **c'est (tout) ~** that (just) shows you; **c'est moi qui vous le dis** you take my word for it; **ce n'est pas pour ~, mais...** *(se vanter)* I don't wish to boast but...; *(se plaindre)* I don't wish to complain but...; **c'est-à-~** that is to say; **c'est-à-~ que je ne le savais pas** well actually I didn't know; **entre nous soit dit** between the two of us *ou* you and me; **soit dit en passant** by the way, incidentally.
(**l**) *(avec faire, laisser, vouloir)* **faire ~ qch à qn** to send word of sth to sb; **faire ~ à qn de venir** to send for sb; **il ne se l'est pas fait ~ deux fois** he did not need to be told twice; **je ne lui ai pas fait ~** I didn't make him say it; **je ne vous le fais pas ~!** I'm not putting words into your mouth; **laisser ~** to let people talk; **je me suis laissé ~ que** I heard that, I was told that; **vouloir ~** to mean; **cette phrase ne veut rien ~** this sentence does not mean a thing.
2 se ~ *vpr* (**a**) **il se dit qu'il était tard** he said to himself that it was late; **il se dit malade** he claims to be ill; **elles se dirent au revoir** they said goodbye (to each other). (**b**) *(sens passif)* **cela ne se dit pas** it's not the sort of thing one says; **cela ne se dit plus** this expression is no longer used; **comment se dit... en français?** what is the French for...?
3 *nm (déclaration)* statement. **d'après ses ~s** according to him *ou* what he says.

direct, e [diʀɛkt, ɛkt(ə)] **1** *adj (gén)* direct. **il m'a parlé de manière très ~e** he spoke to me in a very direct *ou* straightforward way; **ses chefs ~s** his immediate superiors; **être en rapport ~ avec** to deal directly *ou* be in direct contact with; **il a pris une part très ~e à cette affaire** he was directly involved in this business; **ce train est ~ jusqu'à Lyon** this is a fast *ou* non-stop train to Lyons. **2** *nm (Rail)* express (train), fast train; *(Boxe)* jab. **~ du gauche** straight left; *(Rad, TV)* **c'est du ~** it's live; **en ~ de New York** live from New York; **ce sont les risques du ~** those are the risks of live broadcasting *ou* of broadcasting live.

directement [diʀɛktəmɑ̃] *adv (immédiatement)* straight, directly; *(personnellement)* directly; *(sans intermédiaire)* direct, straight; *(tout à fait)* completely. **il est ~ allé se coucher** he went straight *ou* directly to bed, he went to bed straight *ou* right away; **tout ceci ne me concerne pas ~ mais...** none of this concerns me directly but...; **adressez-vous ~ au patron** apply to the boss direct *ou* in person; **~ contraire** completely contrary.

directeur, -trice [diʀɛktœʀ, tʀis] **1** *adj (dirigeant)* directing; *idée* leading, main; *principe* guiding. **2** *nm [banque, usine] (responsable, gérant)* manager; *(administrateur)* director; *(Admin)* head; *(Police)* ≃ chief constable; *(Ciné, TV)* director. **~ (d'école)** headmaster, principal *(US)*; *(Pol)* **~ de cabinet (d'un ministre)** principal private secretary; **~ général** general manager, chief executive officer *(US)*; **~ général adjoint** assistant general manager; **~ de journal** newspaper editor. **3** *nf [entreprise]* manageress; *(propriétaire)* director; *(Admin)* head. **~trice d'école** headmistress, principal *(US)*.

direction [diʀɛksjɔ̃] *nf* (**a**) *(lit, fig: sens)* direction. **dans quelle ~ est-il parti?** which way did he go?; **prendre la ~ de Paris** to go towards *ou* in the direction of Paris; **train en ~ de...** train for *ou* going to... (**b**) *(gén)* running; *[firme]* management; *[journal]* editorship; *[parti]* leadership; *[opérations]* directing; *[recherches]* supervision. **on lui a confié la ~ des travaux** he has been put in charge of the work; **prendre la ~ de** *entreprise* to take over the running of; *opérations* to take charge *ou* control of. (**c**) *(fonction) [entreprise]* post of manager; *[école]* headship, post of head *ou* principal; *[journal]* editorship, post of editor; *(Admin)* post of chief executive. *(personnel dirigeant)* **la ~** the management. (**d**) *(bureau)* director's *ou* manager's *ou* headmaster's *ou* editor's office. (**e**) *(service)* department. **la ~ du personnel** the personnel department; **la D~ de la surveillance du territoire** the counter-espionage services, ≃ MI5, ≃ CIA *(US)*. (**f**) *(Aut: mécanisme)* steering. **~ assistée** power assisted steering. ◆ **directorial, e,** *mpl* **-iaux** *adj (Comm, Ind)* managerial. **bureau ~** manager's *ou* director's *ou* headmaster's *ou* principal's *(US) etc* office.

directive [diʀɛktiv] *nf* directive.

directrice [diʀɛktʀis] *V* **directeur.**

dirigeable [diʀiʒabl(ə)] *nm* airship.

dirigeant, e [diʀiʒɑ̃, ɑ̃t] **1** *adj classe* ruling. **cadre ~** senior manager *ou* executive. **2** *nm, f, [parti, pays]* leader. **~ d'entreprise** company director; *(salarié)* company manager.

diriger [diʀiʒe] (3) **1** *vt* (**a**) *(gén)* to run; *entreprise* to manage; *journal* to edit; *pays, parti* to lead; *opération* to direct; *recherches* to supervise, oversee; *enquête, débat* to lead; *orchestre* to conduct. *(Mil)* **~ le tir** to direct the firing; **cette idée dirige toute notre politique** this idea guides *ou* determines our whole policy. (**b**) *voiture, bateau* to steer; *avion* to pilot, fly. *(fig)* **bien ~ sa barque** to run one's affairs well. (**c**) *(acheminer) marchandises* to send; *personnes* to direct, send (*sur, vers* to). (**d**) *arme* to point, aim (*sur* at); *critique* to aim, direct (*contre* at); *lampe* to shine (*sur* on). **~ son attention sur qch** to turn one's attention to sth; **~ son regard sur qch** to look towards sth; **la flèche est dirigée vers la gauche** the arrow is pointing left *ou* to the left; **~ ses pas vers un lieu** to make one's way towards a place; **on devrait ~ ce garçon vers les sciences** we should guide this boy towards the sciences; **cet élève a été mal dirigé** this pupil has been badly advised *ou* guided.
2 se ~ *vpr* (**a**) **se ~ vers** *lieu* to make one's way towards; *carrière* to turn towards; **l'avion se dirigea vers le nord** the plane flew *ou* headed northwards; **se ~ droit sur qch** to make a beeline *ou* make straight for sth; *(fig)* **nous nous dirigeons vers une solution** we seem to be heading towards a solution. (**b**) *(se guider)* to find one's way. **se ~ au radar** to navigate by radar; *(fig, Scol)* **se ~ vers les sciences** to specialise in sciences; **se ~ vers les**

carrières juridiques to opt for *ou* be headed for a career in law.

discerner [disɛʀne] (1) *vt* (**a**) *(distinguer) forme* to discern, make out; *bruit* to detect. (**b**) *(différencier)* to distinguish, discriminate (*entre* between). ~ **le vrai du faux** to distinguish *ou* tell truth from falsehood. ◆ **discernable** *adj* discernible. ◆ **discernement** *nm (sagesse)* discernment; *(action)* distinguishing, discriminating. **sans** ~ *(réflexion)* without proper judgment; *(distinction)* without distinction.

disciple [disipl(ə)] *nm* disciple.

discipliner [disipline] (1) *vt élèves* to discipline; *cheveux* to control. **se** ~ to discipline oneself. ◆ **disciplinable** *adj* disciplinable. ◆ **disciplinaire** *adj* disciplinary. ◆ **disciplinairement** *adv* in a disciplinary way. ◆ **discipline** *nf (règle)* discipline; *(matière)* discipline, subject. ~ **de base** core *ou* basic subject. ◆ **discipliné, e** *adj* well-disciplined.

disc-jockey [diskʒɔkɛ] *nm* disc jokey, DJ.

disco [disko] **1** *adj musique* disco. **2** *nm*: **le** ~ disco music.

discontinu, e [diskɔ̃tiny] *adj (gén)* discontinuous; *bruit* intermittent. *(Aut)* **bande jaune** ~**e** dotted yellow line. ◆ **discontinuer** (1) *vi*: **sans** ~ without stopping, without a break. ◆ **discontinuité** *nf* discontinuity.

disconvenir [diskɔ̃vniʀ] (22) *vi*: **je n'en disconviens pas** I don't deny it.

discorder [diskɔʀde] (1) *vi [sons]* to be discordant; *[couleurs]* to clash; *[témoignages]* to conflict. ◆ **discordance** *nf [caractères]* conflict; *[sons]* discordance; *[couleurs]* clash. *[témoignages]* **présenter des** ~**s** to show discrepancies, conflict. ◆ **discordant, e** *adj (gén)* discordant; *caractères, opinions* conflicting; *bruits* harsh; *couleurs* clashing. ◆ **discorde** *nf* discord, dissension. **mettre la** ~ to cause dissension.

discothèque [diskɔtɛk] *nf (collection)* record collection; *(meuble)* record cabinet; *(bâtiment)* record library; *(club)* disco.

discount [diskunt] **1** *nm rabais* **faire du** ~ to give a discount. **2** *adj inv*: **magasin** ~ discount store *ou* shop; **à des prix** ~ at discount prices.

discours [diskuʀ] *nm* (**a**) *(allocution)* speech. *(péj)* **tous ces beaux** ~ all this fine talk; **suis-moi sans faire de** ~! follow me and no arguing; **perdre son temps en** ~ to waste one's time talking. (**b**) *(Ling)* **(au)** ~ **direct/indirect** (in) direct/indirect speech. (**c**) *(Philos: traité)* discourse. ◆ **discourir** (11) *vi (faire un discours)* to discourse; *(péj)* to hold forth (*sur, de* upon); *(bavarder)* to chat.

discourtois, e [diskuʀtwa, waz] *adj* discourteous.

discréditer [diskʀedite] (1) **1** *vt (gén)* to discredit. **2 se** ~ *vpr [personne]* to discredit o.s. ◆ **discrédit** *nm* discredit, disrepute. **tomber dans le** ~ to fall into disrepute.

discret, -ète [diskʀɛ, ɛt] *adj* (**a**) *(réservé, silencieux)* discreet. (**b**) *(timide, neutre) personne* unassuming; *maquillage, regard* discreet; *vêtement* sober, plain; *couleur, endroit* quiet; *lumière* subdued. **'envoi** ~**'** 'sent under plain cover'. ◆ **discrètement** *adv* discreetly; soberly; quietly. **il a** ~ **fait allusion à** he made a discreet allusion to. ◆ **discrétion** *nf* discretion; sobriety; plainness; *(discernement)* discretion. **vin** *etc* **à** ~ unlimited wine *etc.*

discrimination [diskʀiminɑsjɔ̃] *nf* discrimination. ◆ **discriminatoire** *adj mesures* discriminatory. ◆ **discriminer** (1) *vt* to discriminate.

disculper [diskylpe] (1) **1** *vt* to exonerate (*de* from). **2 se** ~ *vpr* to exonerate o.s. (*auprès de qn* in sb's eyes). ◆ **disculpation** *nf* exoneration.

discuter [diskyte] (1) **1** *vt* (**a**) *(gén)* to discuss; *projet de loi* to debate; *prix* to argue about. (**b**) *(contester) ordre* to question, dispute. **théorie très discutée** very controversial theory; **ça se discute** that's debatable. (**c**) ~ **le coup** * *(parler)* to have a chat; *(parlementer)* to argue away. **2** *vi (conférer)* to confer; *(parler)* to talk; *(parlementer, protester)* to argue (*avec* with). ~ **de qch** to discuss sth; **j'en ai discuté avec lui** I have discussed the matter *ou* talked the matter over with him. ◆ **discussion** *nf (gén)* discussion; *(débat)* debate; *(pourparlers)* discussion, talks; *(conversation)* talk; *(querelle)* argument. **sans** ~ **possible** indisputably, undoubtedly; **suis-moi et pas de** ~**s** follow me and no argument. ◆ **discutable** *adj* debatable, questionable.

disette [dizɛt] *nf (manque)* scarcity, shortage; *(famine)* food shortage.

diseuse [dizøz] *nf*: ~ **de bonne aventure** fortune-teller.

disgrâce [disgʀɑs] *nf* disgrace. **tomber en** ~ to fall into disgrace. ◆ **disgracier** (7) *vt* to disgrace.

disgracieux, -ieuse [disgʀasjø, jøz] *adj démarche* awkward, ungainly; *visage* ill-favoured; *forme* unsightly.

disjoindre [disʒwɛ̃dʀ(ə)] (49) **1** *vt planches* to take apart; *problèmes* to separate. **2 se** ~ *vpr* to come apart *ou* loose.

disjoncteur [disʒɔ̃ktœʀ] *nm (Élec)* circuit breaker.

disloquer [dislɔke] (1) **1** *vt* (**a**) *bras* to dislocate. (**b**) *machine, cortège, empire* to break up. **2 se** ~ *vpr* (**a**) **se** ~ **le bras** to dislocate one's arm. (**b**) *[meuble]* to come apart; *[cortège]* to disperse, break up. ◆ **dislocation** *nf* dislocation; breaking up; dispersal.

disparaître [disparɛtʀ(ə)] (57) *vi* (**a**) *(gén)* to disappear, vanish. **le fuyard disparut dans la foule** the fugitive disappeared *ou* vanished into the crowd; ~ **discrètement** to slip away quietly; ~ **furtivement** to sneak away *ou* out; **il a disparu de son domicile** he has gone missing *ou* has disappeared from home. (**b**) *(mourir) [race, coutume]* to die out; *[personne]* to die; *[navire]* to sink, be lost. ~ **en mer** to be lost at sea; *(Naut)* ~ **corps et biens** to go down with all hands. (**c**) **faire** ~ *tache, obstacle* to remove; *personne* to get rid of; *crainte* to dispel; **cela a fait** ~ **la douleur/la rougeur** it made the pain/red mark go away, it got rid of the pain/all trace of the red mark; **faire** ~ **un objet** *[prestidigitateur]* to make an object vanish; *[voleur]* to conceal an object; *(enlever)* to remove an object; *(jeter)* to dispose of *ou* get rid of an object.

disparate [disparat] *adj éléments* disparate; *couple* ill-assorted. ◆ **disparité** *nf* disparity (*de* in); ill-assortedness.

disparition [disparisjɔ̃] *nf (gén)* disappearance; *[soleil]* setting; *[tache, obstacle]* removal; *[objet, bateau]* loss; *(mort)* death. **espèce en voie de** ~ endangered species.

disparu, e [dispary] **1** *adj époque* bygone, vanished; *bonheur* lost, departed; *(mort) personne* dead; *coutume* vanished. **il a été porté** ~ he has been reported missing; **marin** ~ **en mer** sailor lost at sea. **2** *nm, f (mort)* dead person; *(manquant)* missing person. **le cher** ~ the dear departed.

dispendieux, -ieuse [dispɑ̃djø, jøz] *adj* extravagant.

dispensaire [dispɑ̃sɛʀ] *nm* community *ou* free *(US)* clinic.

dispenser [dispɑ̃se] (1) **1** *vt* (**a**) *(exempter)* to exempt (*de faire* from doing, *de qch* from sth). **dispensez-moi de sa vue** spare me the sight of him; **se faire** ~ to get exempted. (**b**) *bienfaits, lumière* to dispense. ~ **à qn son dévouement** to lavish one's devotion on sb; *(Méd)* ~ **des soins à un malade** to give medical care to a patient. **2 se** ~ *vpr*: **se** ~ **de** *corvée* to avoid, get out of;

remarque to refrain from making; **se ~ de faire qch** to get out of doing sth; **il peut se ~ de travailler** he doesn't need to work. ◆ **dispense** *nf (exemption)* exemption (*de* from); *(permission)* special permission; *(Rel)* dispensation (*de* from).

disperser [dispɛʀse] (1) **1** *vt papiers* to scatter, spread about; *brouillard* to disperse; *collection* to break up; *foule, ennemi* to scatter, disperse; *ses efforts* to dissipate. **tous nos amis sont maintenant dispersés** all our friends are scattered now. **2 se ~** *vpr [foule]* to scatter, disperse; *[élève]* to dissipate one's efforts. ◆ **dispersé, e** *adj habitat* scattered; *esprit* unselective; *travail* disorganized, fragmented. ◆ **dispersion** *nf* scattering; dispersal; breaking up; dissipation; *(Chim, Phys)* dispersion. **évitez la ~ dans votre travail** don't attempt to do too many things at once.

disponible [dispɔnibl(ə)] *adj* (**a**) *livre, place* available. **je ne suis pas ~ ce soir** I'm not free tonight. (**b**) *auditoire* receptive. ◆ **disponibilité** *nf* availability; receptiveness. *(Fin)* **~s** liquid assets; *(Admin)* **mettre en ~** *fonctionnaire* to grant leave of absence to.

dispos, e [dispo, oz] *adj personne* refreshed. **avoir l'esprit ~** to have a fresh mind.

disposer [dispoze] (1) **1** *vt* (**a**) *(mettre)* to place, set, lay; *(arranger)* to arrange. (**b**) **~ qn à faire/à qch** *(engager à)* to dispose *ou* incline sb to do/towards sth; *(préparer à)* to prepare sb to do/for sth. **2** *vi (partir)* to leave. **vous pouvez ~** you may leave. **3 ~ de** *vt indir argent, moyens* to have (available *ou* at one's disposal). **il disposait de quelques heures** he had a few hours to spare; **vous pouvez en ~** you can use it; **il dispose de ses amis de manière abusive** he takes advantage of his friends; **droit des peuples à ~ d'eux-mêmes** right of nations to self-determination. **4 se ~** *vpr*: **se ~ à faire** *(se préparer à)* to prepare to do, be about to do. ◆ **disposé, e** *adj* (**a**) **être ~ à faire** to be disposed *ou* prepared to do; **bien/mal ~** in a good/bad mood; **bien/mal ~ à l'égard de** *ou* **pour** *ou* **envers qn** well-/ill-disposed towards sb. (**b**) *terrain* situated. **bien/mal ~** *pièces, vitrine* well-/badly-laid-out.

dispositif [dispozitif] *nm* (**a**) *(mécanisme)* device. (**b**) *(moyens)* plan of action. **~ de défense** defence system; **un important ~ (policier) a été mis en place** a large police operation was set up *ou* a large contingent of police was brought in. (**c**) *(Jur) [jugement]* pronouncement; *[loi]* purview.

disposition [dispozisjɔ̃] *nf* (**a**) *[meubles]* arrangement; *[invités]* placing; *[terrain]* situation; *[pièces]* layout. (**b**) *(usage)* disposal. **mettre qch/être à la ~ de qn** to put sth/be at sb's disposal; **mis à la ~ de la justice** handed over to the law. (**c**) *(mesures)* **~s** *(préparatifs)* arrangements; *(précautions)* measures, steps; **prendre des** *ou* **ses ~s** to make arrangements. (**d**) *(humeur)* mood, frame of mind. **être dans de bonnes ~s pour faire qch** to be in the right mood to do sth; **être dans de bonnes ~s à l'égard de qn** to feel well-disposed towards sb; **est-il toujours dans les mêmes ~s à l'égard de ce projet?** does he still feel the same way about this plan? (**e**) *(aptitude)* **~s** aptitude, natural ability; **avoir des ~s pour les langues** to have a special aptitude for *ou* a gift for languages. (**f**) *(tendance)* tendency (*à* to). (**g**) *(Jur)* clause. **~s testamentaires** provisions of a will.

disproportion [dispʀɔpɔʀsjɔ̃] *nf* disproportion (*de* in). ◆ **disproportionné, e** *adj objet* disproportionately large. **~ à** disproportionate to, out of all proportion with.

disputer [dispyte] (1) **1** *vt* (**a**) **~ qch/qn à qn** to fight with sb for *ou* over sth/sb; **elle essaya de lui ~ la gloire de son invention** she tried to rob him of the glory of his invention; **le ~ en beauté à qn** to rival sb in beauty. (**b**) *combat* to fight; *match* to play. (**c**) *(*: gronder)* to tell off *. **se faire ~** to get a telling-off * (*par* from). **2 se ~** *vpr* (**a**) *(se quereller)* to quarrel, have an argument (*avec* with). (**b**) *objet* to fight over; *poste* to contest. ◆ **dispute** *nf* argument, quarrel. ◆ **disputé, e** *adj match* close, closely fought; *siège de député* hotly contested.

disquaire [diskɛʀ] *nm* record-dealer.

disqualifier [diskalifje] (7) *vt (Sport)* to disqualify; *(fig: discréditer)* to bring discredit on. ◆ **disqualification** *nf* disqualification.

disque [disk(ə)] *nm (gén, Méd)* disc; *(Sport)* discus; *(Mus)* record; *(Ordin)* disc, disk. **~ dur/souple** hard/floppy disc *ou* disk.

disquette [diskɛt] *nf (Ordin)* floppy (disc *ou* disk), diskette *(US)*.

dissection [disɛksjɔ̃] *nf* dissection.

dissemblable [disɑ̃blabl(ə)] *adj* dissimilar (*de* to). ◆ **dissemblance** *nf* dissimilarity (*de* in).

disséminer *vt*, **se ~** *vpr* [disemine] (1) to scatter, spread (out). ◆ **dissémination** *nf (action)* scattering, spreading; *(état) [maisons, points de vente]* scattered lay out *ou* distribution.

dissension [disɑ̃sjɔ̃] *nf* dissension.

dissentiment [disɑ̃timɑ̃] *nm* disagreement.

disséquer [diseke] (6) *vt (lit, fig)* to dissect.

disserter [disɛʀte] (1) *vi*: **~ sur** *(parler)* to speak on; *(écrire)* to write an essay on; *(péj)* to hold forth about. ◆ **dissertation** *nf (Scol, hum)* essay.

dissidence [disidɑ̃s] *nf (Pol)* dissidence; *(Rel)* dissent; *(divergence)* disagreement, dissidence. ◆ **dissident, e 1** *adj (Pol)* dissident; *(Rel)* dissenting. **2** *nm, f (Pol)* dissident; *(Rel)* dissenter.

dissimilitude [disimilityd] *nf* dissimilarity.

dissimuler [disimyle] (1) **1** *vt* to conceal, hide (*à qn* from sb). **je ne vous dissimulerai pas que** I won't disguise *ou* conceal the fact that; **savoir ~** to be good at pretending. **2 se ~** *vpr* to conceal *ou* hide o.s. ◆ **dissimulateur, -trice 1** *adj* dissembling. **2** *nm, f* dissembler. ◆ **dissimulation** *nf (duplicité)* dissimulation; *(action de cacher)* concealment. ◆ **dissimulé, e** *adj caractère, enfant* secretive.

dissiper [disipe] (1) **1** *vt* (**a**) *fumée* to dispel; *nuage* to disperse; *soupçon, crainte* to dispel; *malentendu* to clear up. (**b**) *fortune* to dissipate, squander; *jeunesse* to waste. (**c**) **~ qn** *(corrompre)* to lead sb astray; *(distraire)* to distract sb. **2 se ~** *vpr* (**a**) *[fumée]* to drift away; *[nuages]* to disperse; *[brouillard]* to clear, lift; *[inquiétude]* to vanish; *[malaise]* to disappear, wear off. (**b**) *[élève]* to misbehave. ◆ **dissipé, e** *adj élève* undisciplined; *vie* dissolute, dissipated. ◆ **dissipation** *nf* (**a**) *(indiscipline)* misbehaviour; *(débauche)* dissipation. (**b**) *[fortune]* squandering, dissipation. (**c**) *[fumée, nuage]* dispersal; *[brouillard]* clearing, lifting; *[craintes]* dispelling. **après ~ des brouillards matinaux** after the early morning fog has lifted *ou* cleared.

dissocier [disɔsje] (7) **1** *vt* to dissociate. **2 se ~** *vpr [éléments]* to break up, split up. *(fig)* **se ~ de qn** to dissociate o.s. from sb. ◆ **dissociable** *adj molécules* dissociable; *problèmes* separable. ◆ **dissociation** *nf* dissociation.

dissolu, e [disɔly] *adj* dissolute.

dissolution [disɔlysjɔ̃] *nf (Jur)* dissolution; *[groupe]* breaking-up; *[empire, unité]* crumbling. **prononcer la ~ de** to dissolve; *[sucre etc]* **tourner jusqu'à ~ complète** stir until it has completely dissolved.

dissolvant, e [disɔlvɑ̃, ɑ̃t] **1** *adj* solvent. **2** *nm* solvent; *(pour ongles)* nail varnish remover.

dissonance [disɔnɑ̃s] *nf*: **~(s)** dissonance. ◆ **dissonant, e** *adj sons* dissonant; *couleurs* clashing.

dissoudre [disudʀ(ə)] (51) **1** *vt* (**a**) *(aussi* **faire** ~ *) sel* to dissolve. (**b**) *(Jur, Pol)* to dissolve; *parti* to break up. **2 se** ~ *vpr* (**a**) *[sel]* to dissolve. (**b**) *[association]* to break up.

dissuader [disɥade] (1) *vt* to dissuade (*de qch* from sth, *de faire* from doing). ◆ **dissuasion** *nf* dissuasion. ◆ **dissuasif, -ive** *adj* dissuasive. **avoir un effet** ~ **sur** to have a dissuasive *ou* deterrent effect upon; **à un prix trop** ~ at too high a price.

dissymétrie [disimetʀi] *nf* dissymmetry. ◆ **dissymétrique** *adj* dissymmetrical.

distance [distɑ̃s] *nf* (**a**) *(lit)* distance. **à quelle** ~ **est la gare?** how far away is the station?, what's the distance to the station?; **habiter à une grande** ~**/à quelques kilomètres de** ~ to live a long way away/a few kilometres away (*de* from); **à 2 ans de** ~ **je m'en souviens encore** 2 years later I can still remember it; **nés à quelques années de** ~ born within a few years of one another. (**b**) *(fig: écart)* gap. (**c**) *(locutions)* **garder ses** ~**s** to keep one's distance (*vis à vis de* from); **les syndicats ont pris leurs** ~**s envers le gouvernement** the unions have distanced themselves from the government; **tenir qn à** ~ to keep sb at a distance *ou* at arm's length; **se tenir à** ~ to keep one's distance; **faire qch à** ~ to do sth at *ou* from a distance; **mettre en marche à** ~ *appareil* to start up by remote control; ~ **focale** focal length. ◆ **distancer** (3) *vt voiture* to outdistance, leave behind; *concurrent* to outstrip, leave behind. **se laisser** *ou* **se faire** ~ to be left behind. ◆ **distant, e** *adj lieu, événement* distant, far-off; *attitude* distant, aloof. **une ville** ~**e de 10 km** a town 10 km away.

distancier (se) [distɑ̃sje] (7) *vpr* to distance o.s. (*de* from). ◆ **distanciation** *nf* distance.

distendre [distɑ̃dʀ(ə)] (41) **1** *vt peau* to distend; *muscle, (fig) lien* to strain. **2 se** ~ *vpr [lien]* to slacken; *[peau]* to distend. ◆ **distendu, e** *adj* distended ; slack. ◆ **distension** *nf* distension; slackening.

distiller [distile] (1) *vt (lit)* to distil; *(fig)* to exude. ◆ **distillateur** *nm* distiller. ◆ **distillation** *nf* distillation, distilling. ◆ **distillerie** *nf (usine)* distillery; *(industrie)* distilling.

distinct, e [distɛ̃(kt), distɛ̃kt(ə)] *adj (gén)* distinct (*de* from). ◆ **distinctement** *adv* distinctly. ◆ **distinctif, -ive** *adj* distinctive. ◆ **distinction** *nf (gén)* distinction. **faire la** ~ **entre** to make a distinction between.

distinguer [distɛ̃ge] (1) **1** *vt* (**a**) *objet, bruit* to make out, distinguish. ~ **qn dans la foule** to pick out *ou* spot sb in the crowd; **il distingue mal sans lunettes** he can't see very well without his glasses. (**b**) *(différencier)* to distinguish. ~ **une chose d'avec une autre** to distinguish *ou* tell one thing from another. (**c**) *(rendre différent)* to distinguish, set apart (*de* from). (**d**) *(choisir)* to single out; *(honorer)* to honour. **2 se** ~ *vpr* (**a**) *(différer)* to be distinguished (*de* from). **ces objets se distinguent par leur couleur** these objects can be distinguished by their colour; **il se distingue par son accent** his accent makes him stand out. (**b**) *(réussir)* to distinguish o.s. **il se distingue par son absence** he is conspicuous by his absence. ◆ **distinguable** *adj* distinguishable. ◆ **distingué, e** *adj* distinguished. **veuillez agréer l'expression de ma considération** ~**e** yours faithfully. ◆ **distinguo** *nm (nuance)* distinction.

distordre *vt,* **se** ~ *vpr* [distɔʀdʀ(ə)] (41) to twist.

distorsion [distɔʀsjɔ̃] *nf (gén)* distortion; *(déséquilibre)* imbalance; *(Jur)* bias.

distraction [distʀaksjɔ̃] *nf* (**a**) *(inattention)* absentmindedness. **j'ai eu une** ~ my concentration lapsed. (**b**) *(passe-temps)* entertainment, amusement. (**c**) *(Jur: vol)* abstraction.

distraire [distʀɛʀ] (50) **1** *vt (divertir)* to entertain, amuse; *(déranger)* to distract, divert; *(voler)* to abstract (*de* from). ~ **qn de son chagrin** to take sb's mind off his grief. **2 se** ~ *vpr* to amuse o.s., enjoy o.s. ◆ **distrait, e** *adj personne* absent-minded; *attitude* inattentive, abstracted. ◆ **distraitement** *adv* absent-mindedly, abstractedly. ◆ **distrayant, e** *adj* entertaining.

distribuer [distʀibɥe] (1) *vt* (**a**) *(donner) (gén)* to distribute; *gâteau* to share out; *courrier* to deliver; *travail, rôle* to allocate, assign; *cartes* to deal (out); *ordres* to hand out; *saluts, enseignement* to dispense (*à* to). (**b**) *(disposer) (gén)* to distribute; *emploi du temps* to arrange; *plan de maison* to lay out. **savoir** ~ **son temps** to know how to divide up one's time. (**c**) *(gén, Comm: acheminer)* to distribute; *eau* to supply. ◆ **distributeur, -trice 1** *nm, f* distributor. **2** *nm (appareil)* machine; *(Aut)* distributor. ~ **automatique** slot machine; *(Banque)* ~ **automatique de billets** cash dispenser. ◆ **distribution** *nf* (**a**) distribution; sharing out; delivery; allocation; deal; arrangement; layout; supply. ~ **gratuite** free gifts; ~ **des prix** prize giving; *(fig)* **ce résultat a conduit à une nouvelle** ~ **des cartes** this result has shifted *ou* altered the balance of power *ou* has given a new look to the situation. (**b**) *(Ciné, Théât: acteurs)* cast. (**c**) *(Comm, Aut, Tech)* distribution.

district [distʀik(t)] *nm* district.

dithyrambique [ditiʀɑ̃bik] *adj éloges* extravagant.

diurétique [djyʀetik] *adj, nm* diuretic.

diurne [djyʀn(ə)] *adj* diurnal.

divaguer [divage] (1) *vi (délirer)* to ramble; (*)to rave. ◆ **divagation** *nf* rambling; (*) raving.

divan [divɑ̃] *nm* divan.

diverger [divɛʀʒe] (3) *vi* to diverge. ◆ **divergence** *nf* divergence. ◆ **divergent, e** *adj* divergent.

divers, e [divɛʀ, ɛʀs(ə)] *adj* (**a**) *(pl) (varié)* diverse, varied; *(différent)* different, various; *(plusieurs)* various, several. **frais** ~ miscellaneous expenses. (**b**) *(changeant)* varied. ◆ **diversement** *adv* in various ways.

diversifier [divɛʀsifje] (7) **1** *vt exercices* to vary; *production* to diversify. **2 se** ~ *vpr* to diversify. ◆ **diversification** *nf* diversification.

diversion [divɛʀsjɔ̃] *nf* diversion. **faire** ~ to create a diversion.

diversité [divɛʀsite] *nf (variété)* variety, diversity; *(divergence)* diversity.

divertir [divɛʀtiʀ] (2) **1** *vt (amuser)* to amuse, entertain, divert; *(voler)* to divert; *(†: détourner)* to distract (*de* from). **2 se** ~ *vpr* to amuse o.s., enjoy o.s. **se** ~ **l'esprit** to occupy one's mind; **se** ~ **de qn** to laugh at sb. ◆ **divertissant, e** *adj* amusing, entertaining. ◆ **divertissement** *nm (passe-temps)* distraction, entertainment, amusement; *(Mus)* divertissement; *(Jur: vol)* misappropriation; *(Philos)* distraction. **le** ~ recreation.

dividende [dividɑ̃d] *nm (Fin, Math)* dividend.

divin, e [divɛ̃, in] *adj (gén)* divine; *(*: excellent)* divine *, heavenly. **notre** ~ **Sauveur** our Holy Saviour. ◆ **divinement** *adv* divinely. ◆ **divinité** *nf* divinity.

diviniser [divinize] (1) *vt* to deify. ◆ **divinisation** *nf* deification.

diviser [divize] (1) **1** *vt (gén, Math)* to divide; *tâche, ressources* to share out; *gâteau* to divide up. ~ **en 3/en 3 parties** to divide *ou* split in 3/into 3 parts; ~ **pour régner** divide and rule; **une famille divisée** a broken family; **les historiens sont divisés à ce sujet** historians are divided on this subject. **2 se** ~ *vpr (se scinder)* to split up, divide (*en* into); *(se ramifier)* to fork, divide. **se** ~ **en 3 chapitres** to be divided into 3 chapters. ◆ **diviseur** *nm*

(Math) divisor; *(personne)* divisive influence. ◆ **divisibilité** *nf* divisibility. ◆ **divisible** *adj* divisible. ◆ **division** *nf (gén)* division; *(dans un parti)* split, rift. ~ **du travail** division of labour; **semer la** ~ to sow discord (*entre* among); *(Math)* **faire une** ~ to do a division (sum).

divorcer [divɔʀse] (3) *vi* (**a**) *(Jur)* to get divorced. ~ **d'avec sa femme** to divorce one's wife. (**b**) *(fig)* to break (*d'avec* with). ◆ **divorce** *nm (lit, fig)* divorce (*d'avec* from). **obtenir le** ~ to get a divorce; ~ **par consentement mutuel** divorce by consent, no-fault divorce *(US)*. ◆ **divorcé, e 1** *adj (lit, fig)* divorced (*de* from). **2** *nm, f* divorcee.

divulguer [divylge] (1) *vt* to divulge, disclose. ◆ **divulgation** *nf* disclosure.

dix [dis] **1** *adj inv, nm* ten. **elle a eu un** ~ **sur** ~ she got ten out of ten, she got full marks; **avoir** ~ **dixièmes à chaque œil** to have twenty-twenty vision. **2** : ~**-huit** *adj inv, nm* eighteen; ~**-huitième** *adj, nmf* eighteenth; ~**-neuf** *adj inv, nm* nineteen; ~**-neuvième** *adj, nmf* nineteenth; ~**-sept** *adj inv, nm* seventeen; ~**-septième** *adj, nmf* seventeenth. ◆ **dixième** *adj, nmf* tenth; *(de la Loterie)* tenth share in a ticket. ◆ **dixièmement** *adv* tenthly. ◆ **dizaine** *nf (dix)* ten; *(environ dix)* about ten; *V* **soixantaine.**

Djibouti [dʒibuti] *n* Djibouti.

do [do] *nm inv (note)* C; *(chanté)* doh.

doberman [dɔbɛʀman] *nm* Doberman pinscher.

docile [dɔsil] *adj* docile; *cheveux* manageable. ◆ **docilement** *adv* docilely. ◆ **docilité** *nf* docility.

dock [dɔk] *nm (bassin)* dock; *(bâtiment)* warehouse. ◆ **docker** [dɔkɛʀ] *nm* docker.

docteur [dɔktœʀ] *nm (gén, Univ)* doctor (*ès, en* of). **le** ~ **Lebrun** Dr Lebrun. ◆ **doctorat** *nm* doctorate (*ès, en* in). ~ **de 3ᵉ cycle, d'État** doctorate, ≃ Ph.D. ◆ **doctoresse** *nf* lady doctor.

doctrine [dɔktʀin] *nf* doctrine. ◆ **doctrinaire 1** *adj (dogmatique)* doctrinaire; *(sentencieux)* sententious. **2** *nmf* doctrinarian. ◆ **doctrinal, e,** *mpl* **-aux** *adj* doctrinal.

document [dɔkymɑ̃] *nm* document. ~ **de référence** *ou* **d'information** background paper. ◆ **documentaire 1** *adj intérêt* documentary. **2** *nm (film)* documentary (film). ◆ **documentaliste** *nmf (Presse, TV)* researcher; *(Scol)* (assistant) librarian. ◆ **documentation** *nf* documentation, literature. ◆ **documenté, e** *adj personne* well-informed; *livre* well-documented. ◆ **se documenter** (1) *vpr* to gather information *ou* material (*sur* on, about).

dodeliner [dɔdline] (1) *vi*: **il dodelinait de la tête** his head kept nodding gently.

dodo * [dɔdo] *nm* beddy-bye *, sleep. **aller au** ~ to go to beddy-bye *; **il fait** ~ he's asleep.

dodu, e [dɔdy] *adj (gén)* plump; *enfant, joue* chubby.

doge [dɔʒ] *nm* doge.

dogme [dɔgm(ə)] *nm (lit, fig)* dogma. ◆ **dogmatique** *adj* dogmatic.

dogue [dɔg] *nm (Zool)* mastiff.

doigt [dwa] *nm* (**a**) *[main, gant]* finger; *[animal]* digit. ~ **de pied** toe; **se mettre les** ~**s dans le nez** to pick one's nose. (**b**) *(mesure)* inch. **un** ~ **de vin** a drop of wine; **il a été à deux** ~**s de se tuer** he was within an ace *ou* an inch *ou* a hair's-breadth of being killed. (**c**) *(locutions)* **avoir des** ~**s de fée** *[ménagère]* to have nimble fingers; *[infirmière]* to have gentle hands; **il ne sait rien faire de ses dix** ~**s** he's a good-for-nothing; **faire marcher qn au** ~ **et à l'œil** to have sb at one's beck and call; **se mettre le** ~ **dans l'œil** * to be kidding o.s. *; **il n'a pas levé le petit** ~ **pour nous aider** he didn't lift a finger to help us; **son petit** ~ **le lui a dit** a little bird told him; **mettre le** ~ **sur le problème** to put one's finger on the problem; **mettre le** ~ **dans l'engrenage** to get involved in something; **je le ferais les** ~**s dans le nez** * I could do it standing on my head. ◆ **doigté** *nm [chirurgien]* touch; *(fig: tact)* tact. ◆ **doigtier** *nm* fingerstall.

doléances [dɔleɑ̃s] *nfpl (plaintes)* complaints; *(réclamations)* grievances.

dolent, e [dɔlɑ̃, ɑ̃t] *adj* doleful.

dollar [dɔlaʀ] *nm* dollar.

domaine [dɔmɛn] *nm (propriété)* estate, domain, property; *(sphère)* domain, sphere. **dans le** ~ **public** in the public domain, in public ownership.

dôme [dom] *nm* dome. *(fig)* ~ **de verdure** canopy of foliage.

domestique [dɔmɛstik] **1** *nmf* servant. **2** *adj travaux* domestic, household; *soucis* domestic, family; *(Zool)* domestic, domesticated. ◆ **domesticité** *nf (personnel)* domestic staff, household. ◆ **domestiquer** (1) *vt animal* to domesticate; *marée* to harness.

domicile [dɔmisil] *nm* home, domicile *(Admin)*; *(adresse)* address. **le** ~ **conjugal** the marital home; **dernier** ~ **connu** last known address; **travailler à** ~ to work at home; **'livraisons à** ~**'** 'deliveries'. ◆ **domiciliation** *nf* payment by banker's order. ◆ **domicilier** (7) *vt facture* to pay by banker's order. **être domicilié** to be domiciled *(Admin)*, have one's home (*à* in).

dominant, e [dɔminɑ̃, ɑ̃t] **1** *adj (gén)* dominant; *opinion, vent* prevailing; *idée, préoccupation* main, chief; *position* dominating. **2** *nf (caractéristique)* dominant characteristic; *(couleur)* dominant colour; *(Mus)* dominant.

dominateur, -trice [dɔminatœʀ, tʀis] *adj caractère* domineering; *geste* imperious; *pays* dominating; *passion* ruling.

domination [dɔminɑsjɔ̃] *nf* domination. **les pays sous la** ~ **britannique** countries under British rule *ou* dominion; **exercer sa** ~ **sur qn** to exert one's influence on sb; ~ **de soi-même** self-control, self-possession.

dominer [dɔmine] (1) **1** *vt (gén)* to dominate; *concurrent* to outclass, surpass; *sentiment, situation* to master; *(par la taille)* to tower above. ~ **le monde** to rule the world; ~ **ses élèves** to keep control over one's pupils; **parler fort pour** ~ **le bruit de la rue** to speak loudly to overcome the noise from the street; **ce problème domine tous les autres** this problem overshadows all others; *(Comm)* ~ **un marché** to control a market; **se** ~ to control o.s., keep o.s. under control; **la préoccupation qui domine toute son œuvre** the preoccupation which dominates his whole work; **rocher qui domine la mer** rock which overlooks *ou* dominates the sea. **2** *vi* (**a**) *[orateur, concurrent]* to be in the dominant position; *[équipe]* to be on top. *(fig)* ~ **de la tête et des épaules** to be head and shoulders above the others. (**b**) *(prédominer) (gén)* to dominate; *[idée, théorie]* to prevail. **c'est le jaune qui domine** it is yellow which stands out *ou* which is the dominant colour.

dominion [dɔminjɔn] *nm (Brit: état)* dominion.

Dominique [dɔminik] *nf*: **la** ~ Dominica.

domino [dɔmino] *nm (gén)* domino. *(jeu)* **les** ~**s** dominoes *(sg)*.

dommage [dɔmaʒ] **1** *nm (préjudice)* harm, injury. *(dégât)* ~**(s)** damage; **causer un** ~ **à qn** to do sb harm; **c'est** ~**!, quel** ~**!** what a pity! *ou* shame! **2** : ~**(s) corporel(s)** physical injury; ~**s de guerre** war damages; ~**s et intérêts** damages. ◆ **dommageable** *adj* harmful, injurious (*à* to).

dompter [dɔ̃te] (1) *vt fauve, nature* to tame; *cheval* to break in; *rebelles* to subdue; *passions* to master, control. ◆ **domptage** *nm* taming. ◆ **dompteur,**

-euse *nm, f (gén)* tamer, trainer. ~ **(de lions)** lion-tamer; ~ **de chevaux** horsebreaker.

don [dɔ̃] *nm* (**a**) *(aptitude)* gift, talent (*pour* for). **elle a le** ~ **de m'énerver** she has a knack of getting on my nerves; **ça n'a pas eu le** ~ **de lui plaire** it didn't happen to please him. (**b**) *(cadeau)* gift; *(offrande)* donation. *(Méd)* ~ **d'organes** donation of organs; **faire** ~ **de** *fortune* to donate; *livre* to give (as a present); **le** ~ **de soi** self-sacrifice; **faire (le)** ~ **de sa vie pour sauver qn** to give one's life to save sb. ◆ **donataire** *nmf* donee. ◆ **donateur, -trice** *nm, f* donor. ◆ **donation** *nf (Jur)* ≃ settlement. **faire une** ~ **à qn** to make a settlement on sb.

donc [dɔ̃k] *conj* (**a**) *(par conséquent)* therefore, thus, so; *(après digression, marquant la surprise)* so, then. **c'était** ~ **un espion?** he was a spy then?, so he was a spy? (**b**) *(de renforcement)* **allons** ~! come on!; **tais-toi** ~! do be quiet!; **regardez** ~ **ça** just look at that; **dis** ~ *(question)* tell me, I say; *(menace)* look here.

donjon [dɔ̃ʒɔ̃] *nm* keep.

don Juan [dɔ̃ʒɥɑ̃] *nm* Don Juan.

donnant, e [dɔnɑ̃, ɑ̃t] *adj* (†) generous. **avec lui, c'est** ~, ~ he always wants something in return for a service.

donne [dɔn] *nf (Cartes)* deal. **mauvaise** ~ misdeal.

donné, e [dɔne] **1** *adj lieu, date* given, fixed. **étant** ~ **la situation** in view of *ou* given *ou* considering the situation. **2** *nf (Math, Sci)* datum; *(gén)* fact. ~**es** data; facts. *(Écon)* **en** ~**es corrigées des variations saisonnières** figures adjusted for seasonal variation(s); **modifier les** ~**es du problème** to refine the problem.

donner [dɔne] (1) **1** *vt* (**a**) *(gén)* to give (*à* to); *lettre* to hand; *copie d'examen* to hand *ou* give in; *parts de gâteau* to hand *ou* give out; *vieux habits* to give away; *cartes* to deal (out); *sa vie, sa place* to give up; *permission* to grant; *décoration* to award. ~ **à manger à qn** to give sb sth to eat; ~ **son corps à la science** to donate one's body to research; **pouvez-vous me** ~ **l'heure?** could you tell me the time?; **ça lui donne un air triste** it makes him look sad; **donne-toi un coup de peigne** give your hair a quick comb; ~ **une gifle à qn** to slap sb's face, box sb's ears; ~ **un ordre à qn** to give sb an order, order sb to do sth; **il n'est pas donné à tout le monde d'être riche** it is not given to everybody to be rich; **c'est donné** * it's dirt cheap, it's a giveaway *; *(fig)* ~ **le ton** to set the tone; **je vous le donne en mille** you'll never guess; **on lui donnerait le bon Dieu sans confession** he looks as if butter wouldn't melt in his mouth. (**b**) *(causer) plaisir, courage* to give (*à* to); *mal* to cause, give (*à* to). ~ **de l'appétit à qn** to give sb an appetite; **cela donne soif** this makes you (feel) thirsty. (**c**) *(avec à + infin: faire)* **il m'a donné à penser que** he made me think that; **ça nous a donné à réfléchir** it has given us food for thought; ~ **à rire** to give cause for laughter; ~ **ses chaussures à ressemeler** to take one's shoes (in) to be resoled *ou* to the cobbler's. (**d**) *(organiser) réception* to give, hold (*à* for); *film* to show; *pièce* to perform, put on. **ça se donne encore?** *[film]* is it still on *ou* showing? (**e**) *(attribuer)* **quel âge lui donnez-vous?** how old do you take him to be *ou* would you say he was?; ~ **un fait pour certain** to present a fact as a certainty; **on le donne pour un homme habile** he is said to be a clever man. (**f**) *(produire) récolte* to yield; *résultat* to produce. **les pommiers ont bien donné** the apple trees have produced a good crop *ou* given a good yield; **elle lui a donné un fils** she bore him a son; **cette méthode ne donne rien** this method is unrewarding *ou* is producing nothing. (**g**) (‡: *dénoncer) complice* to shop ‡, give away.

2 *vi* (**a**) *(frapper)* **aller** ~ **sur** to strike; ~ **de la tête contre** to knock one's head against; **le soleil donne en plein sur la voiture** the sun is beating down on the car; **ne savoir où** ~ **de la tête** * not to know which way to turn. (**b**) ~ **dans** *piège* to fall into; *défaut* to lapse into; ~ **dans le snobisme** to be rather snobbish. (**c**) ~ **sur** *[pièce, porte]* to give onto, open onto; **la maison donne sur la mer** the house faces *ou* looks onto the sea front.

3 se ~ *vpr* (**a**) **se** ~ **à** *cause* to devote o.s. to; **se** ~ **à fond** to give one's all. (**b**) **se** ~ **à un maître** to choose o.s. a master; **se** ~ **de la peine** to take (great) trouble; **se** ~ **du bon temps** to have a good time; **se** ~ **un air sévère** to put on a strict air; **se** ~ **pour généreux** to profess *ou* make o.s. out to be generous.

donneur, -euse [dɔnœʀ, øz] *nm, f (gén)* giver; *(Cartes)* dealer; (‡: *dénonciateur)* squealer ‡, informer; *(Méd)* donor.

dont [dɔ̃] *pron rel* (**a**) *(reprenant complément de nom) (chose)* whose, of which; *(personne)* whose. **la maison** ~ **on voit le toit** the house the roof of which *ou* whose roof you can see. (**b**) *(partie d'un tout)* **ils ont 3 filles** ~ **2 sont mariées** they have 3 daughters, 2 of whom are married; **il a écrit 2 romans** ~ **un est autobiographique** he has written 2 novels one of which is autobiographical. (**c**) (*reprenant* **de**) **la façon** ~ **elle s'habille** the way (in which) she dresses, her way of dressing; **la maladie** ~ **elle souffre** the illness she suffers from *ou* from which she suffers.

doper [dɔpe] (1) **1** *vt* to dope. **2 se** ~ *vpr* to dope o.s. ◆ **doping** *nm (action)* doping. *(excitant)* ~**(s)** dope.

dorénavant [dɔʀenavɑ̃] *adv* from now on.

dorer [dɔʀe] (1) **1** *vt objet* to gild; *rôti* to brown; *peau* to bronze, tan. **faire** ~ **un cadre** to have a frame gilded; ~ **la pilule à qn** * to sugar the pill for sb; **se** ~ **au soleil** to lie and get brown in the sun, sunbathe. **2** *vi [rôti]* to brown. **faire** ~ **au four** to put in the oven to brown. ◆ **doré, e 1** *adj objet* gilt, gilded; *peau* bronzed, tanned; *blé, cheveux, rêves* golden; *rôti* browned. **2** *nm (matière)* gilt.

dorique [dɔʀik] *adj, nm* Doric.

dorloter [dɔʀlɔte] (1) *vt* to pamper, cosset. **trop dorloté** mollycoddled.

dormir [dɔʀmiʀ] (16) *vi* (**a**) to sleep; *(être endormi)* to be asleep, be, sleeping. **avoir envie de** ~ to feel sleepy; **ça m'empêche de** ~ *[café]* it keeps me awake; *[soucis]* I'm losing sleep over it; **parler en dormant** to talk in one's sleep. (**b**) *[eau, nature]* to be still; *[argent]* to lie idle. **tout dormait dans la ville** everything was quiet *ou* still in the town; **ce n'est pas le moment de** ~! this is no time for slacking *ou* idling! (**c**) *(locutions)* **je dors debout** I'm asleep on my feet; **histoire à** ~ **debout** cock-and-bull story; ~ **comme un loir** to sleep like a log; **ne** ~ **que d'un œil** to sleep with one eye open; **il dort à poings fermés** he is sound *ou* fast asleep, he's dead to the world; *(fig)* ~ **tranquille** *(sans soucis)* to rest easy. ◆ **dormant, e 1** *adj eau* still; *châssis* fixed. *(Jur, Fin)* **compte** ~ dead account. **2** *nm [porte]* frame. ◆ **dormeur, -euse** *nm, f* sleeper.

dorsal, e, *mpl* **-aux** [dɔʀsal, o] *adj (gén)* dorsal.

dortoir [dɔʀtwaʀ] *nm* dormitory. **cité-**~ dormitory town.

dorure [dɔʀyʀ] *nf (couche d'or)* gilt, gilding; *(action)* gilding.

dos [do] *nm* (**a**) *(gén)* back; *[livre]* spine; *[langue]* back; *[lame]* blunt edge. **avoir le** ~ **rond** to be round-shouldered; **au** ~ **de la lettre** on the back of the letter; **robe décolletée dans le** ~ low-backed dress; **'voir au** ~**'** 'see over *ou* overleaf'; **aller à** ~ **d'âne** to ride on a donkey; **(vu) de** ~ (seen) from behind *ou* from the back. (**b**) **être ~ à ~** to be back to back; **le train a bon ~ *** (that's right) blame the train; **il s'est mis tout le monde à ~** he has turned everybody against him; *(fig)* **j'ai toujours mon patron sur le ~** my boss is always breathing down my neck *ou* is always standing over me; **on l'a dans le ~!** ‡ we've had it! *; **mettre qch sur le ~ de qn** *(responsabilité)* to saddle sb with sth; *(accusation)* to pin sth on sb; **il s'est mis une sale affaire sur le ~** he has got himself mixed up in a nasty bit of business; **faire des affaires sur le ~ de qn** to do a bit of business at sb's expense; **il n'a rien à se mettre sur le ~** he hasn't got a thing to wear; **tomber sur le ~ de qn** *(arriver)* to drop in on sb; *(attaquer)* to go for sb; **faire qch derrière le ~ de qn** to do sth behind sb's back; *(fig)* **faire un enfant dans le ~ * à qn** to play a dirty trick on sb *; **il n'y va pas avec le ~ de la cuiller *,** he certainly doesn't go in for half-measures; **(pont en) ~ d'âne** humpback bridge.

dose [doz] *nf (Pharm)* dose; *(gén: proportion)* amount, quantity. **en avoir sa ~ *** to have had more than one's share of it; **forcer la ~** to overdo it, overstep the mark; **~ d'ironie** touch of irony; **à petites ~s** in small doses. ◆ **dosage** *nm (action)* measuring out; correct proportioning; *(mélange)* mixture; *(équilibre)* balance. ◆ **doser** (1) *vt (Chim, gén)* to measure out; *mélange* to proportion correctly; *(fig: équilibrer)* to strike a balance between; *(mesurer) exercices, difficultés* to grade. **savoir ~ ses efforts** to know how much effort to expend. ◆ **doseur** *nm* measure.

dossier [dosje] *nm [siège]* back; *(documents)* file, dossier; *(Jur: affaire)* case; *(classeur)* file.

doter [dɔte] (1) *vt épouse* to provide with a dowry; *institution* to endow; *(Admin) université, organisme* to grant money to, give a grant to. **~ de** *matériels* to equip with; *qualités* to endow with. ◆ **dot** [dɔt] *nf* dowry. **apporter qch en ~** to bring a dowry of sth. ◆ **dotation** *nf* endowment, grant.

douairière [dwɛʀjɛʀ] *nf* dowager.

douane [dwan] *nf (service)* **les ~s** the Customs; *(poste)* **la ~** the customs; **marchandises en ~** goods in bond; **passer (à) la ~** to go through customs. ◆ **douanier, -ière 1** *adj* customs. **2** *nm, f* customs officer.

doublage [dublaʒ] *nm (gén)* doubling; *[film]* dubbing. **le ~ d'un acteur** dubbing an actor.

double [dubl(ə)] **1** *adj* double; *avantage* double, twofold. **le prix est ~ de ce qu'il était** the price is double *ou* twice what it was; **faire qch en ~ exemplaire** to make two copies of sth; **ustensile à ~ usage** dual-purpose utensil; **faire ~ emploi** to be redundant; **fermer à ~ tour** to double-lock; *(lit, fig)* **à ~ tranchant** double-edged; **valise à ~ fond** case with a false bottom; **jouer un ~ jeu** to play a double game; **phrase à ~ sens** sentence with a double meaning; **avoir le don de ~ vue** to have the gift of second sight; **personnage à personnalité ~** person with a dual personality *ou* a Jekyll-and-Hyde personality. **2** *nm* (**a**) **manger le ~ (de qn)** to eat twice as much (as sb) *ou* double the amount (that sb does); **4 est le ~ de 2** 4 is two times *ou* twice 2; **c'est le ~ du prix normal** it is twice *ou* double the normal price; **plier qch en ~** to fold sth in half *ou* two. (**b**) *(copie)* copy; *(sosie)* double. **avoir qch en ~** *(document)* to have a copy of sth; *(timbre)* to have two *ou* a duplicate of sth; **se faire faire un ~ de clef** to have a second key cut. (**c**) *(Tennis)* doubles. **faire un ~** to play a doubles match. **3** *adv* double. **4** : **~ commande** *nf* dual controls; **~ croche** *nf* semiquaver, sixteenth note *(US)*; **~-décimètre** *nm* (20-cm) ruler; **~s rideaux** *nmpl* double curtains.

doubler [duble] (1) **1** *vt (augmenter)* to double; *ficelle* to use double; *(Scol) classe* to repeat; *film, acteur* to dub; *(Couture)* to line (*de* with); *(dépasser) véhicule* to overtake, pass; *(Naut) cap* to round. **~ le cap des 50 ans** to turn 50; **~ le pas** to quicken one's pace, speed up; *(*: tromper)* **~ qn** to pull a fast one on sb *; **veste non doublée** unlined jacket. **2** *vi (augmenter)* to double, increase twofold; *(Aut)* to overtake, pass. **~ de poids** to double in weight. **3 se ~** *vpr*: **se ~ de** to be coupled with; **c'est un savant doublé d'un pédagogue** he is a teacher as well as a scholar. ◆ **doublé** *nm (victoire)* double. ◆ **doublement 1** *adv (pour deux raisons)* for a double reason; *(à un degré double)* doubly. **2** *nm* doubling; *(Aut)* overtaking, passing. ◆ **doublure** *nf* (**a**) *(étoffe)* lining. (**b**) *(Théât)* understudy; *(Ciné)* stand-in; *(cascadeur)* stuntman (*ou* stuntwoman).

douce [dus] *V* **doux.**

douceur [dusœʀ] *nf* (**a**) *[peau]* softness; *[temps]* mildness; *[personne]* gentleness. **prendre qn par la ~** to deal gently with sb; **les ~s de l'amitié** the pleasures of friendship. (**b**) *(sucrerie)* sweet. (**c**) **en ~** *démarrage* smooth; *démarrer* smoothly; *commencer* gently. ◆ **douceâtre** *adj saveur* sickly sweet, cloying; *air* mawkish. ◆ **doucement** *adv (sans violence)* gently, softly; *(gentiment)* gently; *(sans bruit)* quietly; *(prudemment)* carefully; *rouler* slowly; *démarrer* smoothly. **comment allez-vous? — (tout) ~** how are you? — so-so *; **allez-y ~!** * easy *ou* gently does it! ◆ **doucereux, -euse** *adj goût* sickly sweet; *ton* sugary; *manières* smooth.

douche [duʃ] *nf (jet, système)* shower; *(*: averse)* soaking, drenching. *(salle)* **~s** shower room; **~ (froide)** *(déception)* let-down; **pratiquer la politique de la ~ écossaise** to blow hot and cold. ◆ **doucher** (1) **1** *vt*: **~ qn** to give sb a shower; *[orage]* to soak *ou* drench sb. **2 se ~** *vpr* to have *ou* take a shower.

doué, e [dwe] *adj (talentueux)* gifted, talented (*en* in). **être ~ pour** to have a gift for; **~ sur le plan scolaire** academically able; *(pourvu de)* **~ de** *vie, raison* endowed with.

douille [duj] *nf [cartouche]* (cartridge) case; *(Élec)* socket.

douillet, -ette [dujɛ, ɛt] *adj* (**a**) *(péj) personne* soft. (**b**) *atmosphère, lit* cosy. ◆ **douillettement** *adv* cosily. *(péj)* **élever ~** to mollycoddle.

douleur [dulœʀ] *nf (physique)* pain; *(morale)* distress. **'nous avons la ~ d'apprendre que...'** 'it is with great sorrow that we learn that...' ◆ **douloureusement** *adv* painfully; grievously. ◆ **douloureux, -euse** *adj* painful; distressing; *regard* sorrowful.

doute [dut] *nm* doubt. **être dans le ~** to be doubtful *ou* uncertain (*sur* about); **laisser qn dans le ~** to leave sb in (a state of) uncertainty; **le ~ n'est plus permis** there is no more room for doubt; **il a émis des ~s à propos de...** he expressed (his) doubts *ou* misgivings about...; **dans le ~, abstiens-toi** when in doubt, don't!; **sans ~** doubtless, no doubt; **sans aucun ~** without a doubt; **ceci ne fait aucun ~** there is no doubt *ou* question about it; **mettre en ~** to question, challenge, cast doubt on.

douter [dute] (1) **1 ~ de** *vt indir (gén)* to doubt, have (one's) doubts as to; *réussite* to be doubtful of; *authenticité* to question. **j'en doute** I have my doubts, I doubt it; **n'en doutez pas** there's no doubt about that; **je doute d'avoir jamais fait cela** I doubt that I ever did that; **je doute qu'il vienne** I doubt if *ou* whether he'll come; **à n'en pas ~** undoubtedly; **il ne doute de rien!** * he's got some nerve!; **il doute de lui (-même)** he has doubts about himself. **2 se ~** *vpr*: **se ~ de qch** to suspect sth; **se ~ que** to suspect that, have an idea that; **je m'en doute** I can well imagine that.

douteux, -euse [dutø, øz] *adj* (**a**) *(incertain) (gén)* doubtful; *fait* questionable; *résultat* uncertain. **il est ~ que** it is doubtful *ou* questionable that *ou* whether; **il n'est pas ~ que** there is no doubt that. (**b**) *(péj) qualité, goût* dubious, questionable; *aliment, individu* dubious-looking; *mœurs* doubtful.

douve [duv] *nf [château]* moat.

Douvres [duvʀ(ə)] *n* Dover.

doux, douce [du, dus] **1** *adj (au toucher)* soft; *temps* mild; *brise, chaleur* gentle; *(sucré, agréable)* sweet; *moutarde* mild; *son* sweet, gentle; *lumière, couleur* soft; *pente* gentle; *démarrage* smooth; *caractère, manières* mild, gentle. **~ comme un agneau** as meek *ou* gentle as a lamb; **cuire à feu ~** to simmer gently (over a low flame); **se faire une douce violence** to inflict a pleasant burden upon o.s.; **cette pensée lui était douce** this thought gave him great pleasure; **en douce** * on the quiet; **préférer le ~ à l'amer** to prefer sweet tastes *ou* things to sour. **2** *adv*: **ça va tout ~** * things are going so-so *; *(† ou hum)* **tout ~!** gently (now)!

douze [duz] *adj, nm inv* twelve; *V* **six.** ◆ **douzaine** *nf (douze)* dozen. *(environ douze)* **une ~** about twelve, a dozen or so. ◆ **douzième** *adj, nmf* twelfth; *V* **sixième.** ◆ **douzièmement** *adv* in twelfth place, twelfthly.

doyen, -enne [dwajɛ̃, ɛn] *nm, f (Rel, Univ †)* ≃ dean; *[groupe]* most senior member; *[assemblée]* doyen. **la ~ne des Français** France's oldest citizen.

draconien, -ienne [dʀakɔnjɛ̃, jɛn] *adj* draconian.

dragée [dʀaʒe] *nf* sugared almond. **tenir la ~ haute à qn** to be a fair *ou* good match for sb. ◆ **dragéifié** *adj* sugared.

dragon [dʀagɔ̃] *nm (Myth, fig)* dragon; *(Hist Mil)* dragoon.

draguer [dʀage] (1) *vt* (**a**) *(Pêche)* to fish with a dragnet; *(pour nettoyer, trouver)* to dredge; *mines* to sweep. *[ancre]* **~ (le fond)** to drag. (**b**) *(*: baratiner)* to chat up *. ◆ **drague** *nf (Pêche)* dragnet; *(machine)* dredge; *(navire)* dredger. ◆ **dragueur** *nm (bateau)* dredger. **~ de mines** minesweeper.

drainer [dʀene] (1) *vt (gén)* to drain. ◆ **drain** *nm* drain. ◆ **drainage** *nm* drainage.

drame [dʀam] *nm* (**a**) *(Théât)* drama. (**b**) *(événement tragique)* drama, tragedy. **n'en faites pas un ~** don't make such a fuss about it. ◆ **dramatique** **1** *adj (Théât)* dramatic; *(tragique)* tragic; *(spectaculaire)* dramatic. **2** *nf (TV)* (television) play *ou* drama. ◆ **dramatiquement** *adv* tragically. ◆ **dramatisation** *nf* dramatization. ◆ **dramatiser** (1) *vt* to dramatize. ◆ **dramaturge** *nmf* dramatist, playwright.

drap [dʀa] *nm* (**a**) *(tissu)* woollen cloth. (**b**) **~ (de lit)** sheet; **~-housse** fitted sheet; **~ de bain** bath sheet; *(fig)* **mettre qn dans de beaux ~s** to land sb in a fine mess.

drapeau, *pl* **~x** [dʀapo] *nm (gén)* flag. **le ~ tricolore** the tricolour; **être sous les ~x** to do one's national service.

draper [dʀape] (1) **1** *vt* to drape. **2 se ~** *vpr*: **se ~ dans** to drape o.s. in; *(fig péj)* **se ~ dans sa dignité** to stand on one's dignity. ◆ **draperie** *nf* drapery. ◆ **drapier** *nm* draper.

dresser [dʀese] (1) **1** *vt* (**a**) *liste, acte* to draw up. **~ (une) contravention à qn** to report sb, book sb *; **~ le bilan de qch** to give a review of sth. (**b**) *(ériger) (gén)* to put up, erect; *échelle* to set up; *tente* to pitch; *mât* to raise. **~ un buffet** to set *ou* lay out a buffet; **~ la table** to lay *ou* set the table. (**c**) *(inciter)* **~ qn contre** to set sb against. (**d**) *tête* to raise, lift. *(fig)* **~ l'oreille** to prick up one's ears; **faire ~ les cheveux sur la tête à qn** to make sb's hair stand on end. (**e**) *lion* to tame; *cheval* to break in; *chien* to train. *(Cirque)* **animaux dressés** performing animals; **ça le dressera!** * that'll teach him a lesson; **~ un enfant** * to teach a child his place. **2 se ~** *vpr (gén)* to stand; *[tour, sommet]* to tower; *[personne] (debout)* to stand up; *[cheveux]* to stand on end. **se ~ de toute sa taille** to draw o.s. up to one's full height; **se ~ contre qn** to rise up against sb; **se ~ en justicier** to set o.s. up as a dispenser of justice. ◆ **dressage** *nm (domptage)* taming; breaking in; training. ◆ **dresseur, -euse** *nm, f* trainer, tamer. **~ de lions** liontamer; **~ de chevaux** horsebreaker.

dressing [dʀɛsiŋ] *nm* dressing room.

dressoir [dʀɛswaʀ] *nm* dresser.

drille [dʀij] *nm* (†) **joyeux ~** cheerful character.

drogue [dʀɔg] *nf* drug. **la ~** drugs. ◆ **drogué, e** *nm, f* drug addict. ◆ **droguer** (1) *vt malade (péj)* to dose up; *victime* to drug. **il se drogue** he's on drugs, he's taking drugs.

droguiste [dʀɔgist(ə)] *nmf* hardware merchant. ◆ **droguerie** *nf (commerce)* hardware trade; *(magasin)* hardware shop.

droit[1], e[1] [dʀwa, dʀwat] **1** *adj bras* right; *poche* right(-hand). **du côté ~** on the right-hand side. **2** *nm (Boxe)* right. **3** *nf* (**a**) **la ~e** *(gén, Aut, Pol)* the right; *(côté)* the right-hand side; **à ~e** *rue, rouler* on the right; *tourner* to the right; **chemin de ~e** right-hand path; **à ~e de la fenêtre** to the right of the window; **de ~e à gauche** from right to left; *(fig)* **de ~e et de gauche** everywhere; **garder sa ~e** to keep to the right; **idées de ~e** right-wing ideas. (**b**) *(Boxe)* right. ◆ **droitier, -ière** *adj* right-handed.

droit[2], e[2] [dʀwa, dʀwat] **1** *adj* (**a**) *ligne, route* straight. **4 km en ligne ~e** 4 km as the crow flies; *(fig)* **cela vient en ~e ligne de...** that comes straight *ou* direct from...; *(fig)* **cette décision s'inscrit dans le ~ fil d'une politique** this decision is totally in keeping with *ou* in line with a policy; *(Rel)* **le ~ chemin** the straight and narrow way. (**b**) *arbre, mur* upright, straight. **tiens ta tasse ~e** hold your cup straight *ou* level; **tiens-toi ~** *(debout)* stand up straight; *(assis)* sit up straight. (**c**) *(loyal) personne* upright, straight. (**d**) *(judicieux) jugement* sound, sane. **2** *nf*: **(ligne) ~e** straight line. **3** *adv couper* straight. **c'est ~ devant vous** it's straight ahead of you *ou* right in front of you; *(fig)* **aller ~ au but** to go straight to the point. ◆ **droiture** *nf* uprightness.

droit[3] [dʀwa] **1** *nm* (**a**) *(prérogative)* right. **c'est bien votre ~** you've every right to do so, you're perfectly within your rights; **de quel ~ est-il entré?** what right had he to come in?; **avoir ~ de regard sur** to have the right to examine; **avoir le ~ de faire** *(permission)* to be allowed to do; *(Admin, Jur)* to have the right to do; **avoir ~ à** to be entitled to; *(hum)* **il a eu ~ à une bonne raclée** * he earned himself a good hiding; **être dans son (bon) ~** to be quite within one's rights; **c'est à lui de (plein) ~** it's his by right; **membre de (plein) ~** ex officio member; **le ~ du plus fort** the law of the jungle; **faire ~ à** *requête* to grant; **monarque de ~ divin** monarch by divine right; **le ~ des peuples à disposer d'eux-mêmes** the right of peoples to self-determination. (**b**) *(Jur)* **le ~** law; *(Univ)* **faire son ~** to study law; **délit de ~ commun** common law crime. (**c**) *(gén pl) (taxe)* duty, tax; *(d'inscription etc)* fee, fees. **~ d'entrée** entrance fee; **~s de douane/de succession** customs/death duties. **2** : **~ d'aînesse** birthright; **~ d'asile** right of asylum; **~s d'auteur** royalties; **avoir ~ de cité dans** to be established in; **~ de grâce** right of reprieve; **le ~ de grève** the right to strike; **le ~ de vote** the right to vote, the vote, the franchise.

drôle [dʀol] *adj (amusant)* funny, comical, amusing; *(bizarre)* funny, peculiar, strange; *(*: intensif)* fantastic. **ça me fait (tout) ~ (de le voir)** * it gives me a funny *ou* an odd feeling (to see him); **c'est un**

~ **de numéro** he's a bit of a character; **faire une** ~ **de tête** to pull a wry face, look disgruntled; **de** ~**s de progrès** fantastic *ou* terrific progress *. ◆ **drôlement** *adv* funnily; comically; amusingly; peculiarly; strangely. **il fait** ~ **froid** * it's terribly *ou* awfully cold; **il a** ~ **changé** * he really has changed, he's changed an awful lot. ◆ **drôlerie** *nf* funny remark *etc*. **la** ~ funniness.

dromadaire [dʀɔmadɛʀ] *nm* dromedary.

dru, e [dʀy] **1** *adj herbe* thick; *barbe* bushy; *pluie* heavy. **2** *adv* thickly; heavily; *[coups]* thick and fast.

druide [dʀɥid] *nm* druid.

du [dy] *V* **de.**

dû, due [dy] **1** *adj (à restituer)* owing, owed; *(à échéance)* due. **la somme qui lui est due** the sum owing to him; **troubles** ~**s à...** troubles due to...; **en (bonne et) due forme** in due form. **2** *nm* due; *(argent)* dues. ◆ **dûment** *adv* duly.

dualité [dɥalite] *nf* duality.

Dublin [dyblɛ̃] *n* Dublin.

duc [dyk] *nm* duke. ◆ **ducal, e,** *mpl* **-aux** *adj* ducal. ◆ **duché** *nm* dukedom. ◆ **duchesse** *nf* duchess.

duel [dɥɛl] *nm* duel. **se battre en** ~ to fight a duel (*avec* with); ~ **d'artillerie** artillery battle. ◆ **duelliste** *nm* duellist.

dulcinée [dylsine] *nf* († *ou hum)* lady-love.

dune [dyn] *nf* dune. ~ **de sable** sand dune.

Dunkerque [dœ̃kɛʀk] *n* Dunkirk.

duo [dɥo] *nm (Mus)* duet; *(Théât, fig)* duo.

duodénum [dyɔdenɔm] *nm* duodenum.

dupe [dyp] *nf* dupe. **être (la)** ~ **de qn** to be taken in *ou* fooled by sb; **je ne suis pas** ~ I'm not taken in by it. ◆ **duper** (1) *vt* to dupe, deceive, fool. **se** ~ **(soi-même)** to deceive o.s. ◆ **duperie** *nf* deception. **la** ~ dupery.

duplex [dyplɛks] *nm (appartement)* maisonette, duplex; *(Télec)* link-up.

duplicata [dyplikata] *nm inv* duplicate. ◆ **duplicateur** *nm* duplicator.

duplicité [dyplisite] *nf* duplicity.

dur, e [dyʀ] **1** *adj* (**a**) *(résistant) (gén)* hard; *carton, serrure, brosse* stiff; *viande* tough. **être** ~ **d'oreille** to be hard of hearing. (**b**) *(difficile) (gén)* hard, stiff, tough; *enfant* difficult. ~ **à croire** hard to believe. (**c**) *(pénible, sévère) (gén)* harsh, hard; *vin* bitter. **les temps sont** ~**s** times are hard; **être** ~ **avec qn** to be tough with sb, be hard on sb; **il a le cœur** ~ he's a hard-hearted man. (**d**) *(endurant)* **être** ~ **à la douleur** to be inured to suffering, be stoical about pain; **être** ~ **à l'ouvrage** to be a tireless worker. **2** *adv* (*) *(gén)* hard. **le soleil tape** ~ the sun is beating down; **croire à qch** ~ **comme fer** to have a blind belief in sth. **3** *nm, f (*: gén)* tough one *ou* nut *; *(Pol: intransigeant)* hard-liner. **un** ~ **à cuire** * a hard nut to crack *; **jouer les** ~**s** to act the tough guy *, act tough; **construction en** ~ permanent structure; **élevé à la** ~**e** brought up the hard way; **coucher sur la** ~**e** to sleep rough; **en voir de** ~**es** * to have a hard *ou* tough time of it. ◆ **durement** *adv* harshly; fiercely; heartedly. ~ **éprouvé** sorely tried; **élever qn** ~ to bring sb up the hard way.

durable [dyʀabl(ə)] *adj (gén)* lasting; *étoffe* durable, long-lasting. ◆ **durablement** *adv s'installer* on a long-term basis. **bâti** ~ built to last.

durant [dyʀɑ̃] *prép (gén: pendant)* for; *(au cours de)* during, in the course of. **il a plu** ~ **la nuit** it rained in (the course of) *ou* during the night; **2 heures** ~ for (a whole) 2 hours; **sa vie** ~ throughout his life; ~ **le spectacle** during the show.

durcir *vt*, **se** ~ *vpr* [dyʀsiʀ] (2) *(lit, fig)* to harden. ◆ **durcissement** *nm* hardening.

durée [dyʀe] *nf (gén)* duration, length; *[bail]* term; *[matériau, ampoule]* life. **pendant une** ~ **d'un mois** for a period of one month; **pendant la** ~ **des réparations** for the duration of repairs, while repairs are being carried out; **de courte** ~ *séjour* short; *bonheur* short-lived; **de longue** ~ long-lasting; **croire en la** ~ **de qch** to believe in the continuance of sth, believe that sth will last.

durer [dyʀe] (1) *vi (gén)* to last. **la fête a duré toute la nuit** the party went on *ou* lasted all night; **sa maladie dure depuis 2 mois** he has been ill for 2 months (now); **ça ne peut plus** ~! this can't go on any longer!; *(iro)* **faire** ~ **le plaisir** to prolong the agony; **le temps me dure** time hangs heavy on my hands; **cette somme doit te** ~ **un mois** this sum will have to last you a month.

dureté [dyʀte] *nf (gén)* hardness; *[brosse]* stiffness; *[viande]* toughness; *[traitement]* harshness. ~ **de cœur** hard-heartedness.

durillon [dyʀijɔ̃] *nm* callus.

duvet [dyvɛ] *nm (gén)* down; *(sac de couchage)* sleeping bag. ◆ **duveteux, -euse** *adj* downy.

dynamique [dinamik] **1** *adj (gén)* dynamic. **2** *nf (Phys)* dynamics *(sg)*. ◆ **dynamiquement** *adv* dynamically. ◆ **dynamisme** *nm* dynamism.

dynamite [dinamit] *nf (lit, fig)* dynamite. ◆ **dynamiter** (1) *vt* to dynamite.

dynamo [dinamo] *nf* dynamo.

dynastie [dinasti] *nf* dynasty. ◆ **dynastique** *adj* dynastic.

dysenterie [disɑ̃tʀi] *nf* dysentery. ◆ **dysentérique** *adj* dysenteric.

E

E, e [ə] *nm (lettre)* E, e. ~ **dans l'o** e and o joined together.

eau, *pl* ~**x** [o] **1** *nf* (**a**) *(gén, Bijouterie)* water; *(pluie)* rain. **sans** ~ *vin* neat; **cuire à l'** ~ to boil. (**b**) *(locutions)* **tout cela apporte de l'** ~ **à son moulin** all that is grist to his mill; *(Méd)* **prendre les** ~**x** to take the waters; **j'en avais l'** ~ **à la bouche** it made my mouth water; **être en** ~ to be bathed in perspiration *ou* sweat; **faire** ~ **(de toutes parts)** to leak (like a sieve); *(Naut)* **mettre à l'** ~ to launch; **mettre de l'** ~ **dans son vin** *(lit)* to water down one's wine; *(fig)* to climb down; *[chaussures]* **prendre l'** ~ to leak, let in water; **il passera beaucoup d'** ~ **sous les ponts** much water will have flowed under the bridge; **il y a de l'** ~ **dans le gaz** * things aren't running too smoothly. **2** : ~ **bénite** holy water; ~ **de Cologne** eau de Cologne; ~ **courante** running water; ~ **douce** fresh water; ~ **forte** *(Art)* etching; *(Chim)* aqua fortis; ~ **gazeuse** soda water; ~ **de javel** bleach; ~ **minérale** mineral water; ~ **oxygénée** hydrogen peroxide; ~ **plate** plain water; **roman à l'** ~ **de rose** sentimental novel; ~ **salée** salt water; ~ **de toilette** toilet water; ~**x usées** liquid waste; ~ **de vie (de prune** *etc*) (plum *etc*) brandy.

ébahir [ebaiʀ] (2) *vt* to astound. ◆ **ébahi, e** *adj* astounded. ◆ **ébahissement** *nm* astonishment.

ébattre (s') [ebatʀ(ə)] (41) *vpr* to frolic, gambol about. ◆ **ébats** *nmpl* frolics.

ébaucher [eboʃe] (1) **1** *vt livre, tableau* to sketch out; *plan* to outline; *amitié, conversation* to start up. ~ **un sourire** to give a faint smile; ~ **un geste** to give a hint of a movement. **2 s'** ~ *vpr [plan, solution, livre]* to take shape; *[amitié]* to form; *[conversation]* to start up. ◆ **ébauche** *nf* (**a**) *(action)* sketching out; outlining; starting up. (**b**) *(résultat) [livre, projet]* rough outline; *[amitié]* beginnings. **une** ~ **de sourire** the ghost of a smile; **l'** ~ **d'un geste** the hint of a gesture; **première** ~ rough draft; **à l'état d'** ~ in the early stages.

ébène [ebɛn] *nf* ebony. **cheveux d'** ~ ebony hair. ◆ **ébéniste** *nm* cabinetmaker. ◆ **ébénisterie** *nf* *(métier)* cabinetmaking; *(façon)* cabinetwork.

éberluer [ebɛʀlɥe] (1) *vt* to astound.

éblouir [ebluiʀ] (2) *vt (lit, fig)* to dazzle. ◆ **éblouissement** *nm* (**a**) *[lampe]* dazzle. (**b**) *(émerveillement)* bedazzlement; *(spectacle)* dazzling sight. (**c**) *(Méd)* **avoir un** ~ to have a dizzy turn.

ébonite [ebɔnit] *nf* ebonite.

éborgner [ebɔʀɲe] (1) *vt*: ~ **qn** to blind sb in one eye, poke sb's eye out.

éboueur [ebwœʀ] *nm* dustman, garbage collector *(US)*.

ébouillanter [ebujɑ̃te] (1) **1** *vt (gén)* to scald. **2 s'** ~ *vpr* to scald o.s.

ébouler [ebule] (1) **1** *vt* (*aussi* **faire** ~) to cause to collapse *ou* crumble. **2 s'** ~ *vpr (progressivement)* to crumble; *(soudainement)* to collapse; *[sable]* to fall. ◆ **éboulement** *nm* (**a**) *(action)* crumbling; collapse; fall. (**b**) *(amas)* heap of rocks, earth *etc*. ◆ **éboulis** *nm* heap of fallen rocks, earth *etc*. **pente couverte d'** ~ scree-covered slope.

ébouriffer [ebuʀife] (1) *vt* (**a**) *(gén)* to ruffle. ~ **qn** to tousle *ou* ruffle sb's hair. (**b**) *(*: surprendre)* to astound. ◆ **ébouriffant, e** * *adj vitesse, prix* hair-raising.

ébranler [ebʀɑ̃le] (1) **1** *vt (gén)* to shake; *(affaiblir)* to weaken; *esprit* to disturb. **ébranlé par cette nouvelle** shaken *ou* shattered by the news; **se laisser** ~ **par des prières** to allow o.s. to be swayed by pleas. **2 s'** ~ *vpr [cortège]* to move off. ◆ **ébranlement** *nm (action)* shaking; weakening; disturbance; *(résultat)* shock.

ébrécher [ebʀeʃe] (6) *vt assiette* to chip; *lame* to nick; *fortune* to break into. ◆ **ébréchure** *nf* chip; nick.

ébriété [ebʀijete] *nf* intoxication.

ébrouer (s') [ebʀue] (1) *vpr [cheval]* to snort; *[personne, chien]* to shake o.s.

ébruiter [ebʀɥite] (1) **1** *vt* to spread about. **2 s'** ~ *vpr* to leak out. ◆ **ébruitement** *nm* spreading.

ébullition [ebylisjɔ̃] *nf [eau]* boiling; *(fig: agitation)* turmoil. **porter à (l')** ~ to bring to the boil; **avant l'** ~ before boiling point is reached; **être en** ~ *[liquide]* to be boiling; *[maison]* to be in an uproar; *[pays]* to be seething with unrest.

écaille [ekɑj] *nf [poisson, reptile]* scale; *[huître]* shell; *[peinture]* flake. **lunettes d'** ~ horn-rimmed spectacles; **peigne en** ~ tortoiseshell comb. ◆ **écailler** (1) **1** *vt poisson* to scale; *peinture etc* to chip. **2 s'** ~ *vpr [peinture]* to flake off.

écarlate [ekaʀlat] *adj, nf* scarlet. *(fig)* **devenir** ~ to turn scarlet *ou* crimson.

écarquiller [ekaʀkije] (1) *vt*: ~ **les yeux** to stare wide-eyed (*devant* at).

écart [ekaʀ] **1** *nm* (**a**) *[objets, dates]* gap; *[chiffres, températures, opinions]* difference (*entre* between). ~ **par rapport à la règle** departure from the rule; ~ **important de prix** big difference in price; *(lit, fig)* **réduire l'** ~ **entre** to narrow the gap between. (**b**) **faire un** ~ *[cheval]* to shy; *[voiture]* to swerve; *[piéton]* to leap aside; *(Danse)* **faire le grand** ~ to do the splits. (**c**) **être à l'** ~ *[hameau]* to be isolated; **tirer qn à l'** ~ to take sb aside; **tenir qn à l'** ~ *(fig)* to keep sb in the background; *(lit)* to hold sb back; **rester à l'** ~ *(s'isoler)* to hold o.s. aloof; *(ne pas approcher)* to stay in the background; *(ne pas participer)* to keep out of things; **à l'** ~ **de la route** (well) off the road, off the beaten track; **tenir qn à l'** ~ **d'un lieu** to keep sb well away from a place; **tenir qn à l'** ~ **d'une affaire** to keep sb out of a deal. **2** : ~ **de conduite** misdemeanour; ~ **de langage** bad language; ~ **de régime** lapse in one's diet.

écarteler [ekaʀtəle] (5) *vt (Hist)* to quarter. *(fig)* **écartelé entre 2 choses** torn between 2 things. ◆ **écartèlement** *nm* quartering.

écartement [ekaʀtəmɑ̃] *nm* space, gap (*de, entre* between). *(Rail)* ~ **(des rails)** gauge.

écarter [ekaʀte] (1) **1** *vt* (**a**) *objets* to move apart; *doigts* to spread; *rideaux* to draw (back). **il écarta la foule pour passer** he pushed his way through the crowd; **les jambes écartées** with his legs wide apart; **les bras écartés** with his arms outspread. (**b**) *objection, idée* to dismiss; *candidature* to turn down; *personne* to remove (*de* from). (**c**) *(éloigner) meuble* to move away; *personne* to push back; *(fig: de l'étude)* to distract (*de* from). **tout danger est**

maintenant écarté there is no further risk of danger; **ça nous écarte de notre propos** this is leading us off the subject. **2 s'** ~ *vpr (se séparer)* to draw aside, part; *(s'éloigner)* to withdraw, move away; *(reculer)* to step back (*de* from). **s'** ~ **de** *route, sujet* to stray *ou* wander off; *norme* to deviate *ou* depart from. **les deux routes s'écartent l'une de l'autre** the two roads diverge. ◆ **écarté, e** *adj lieu* remote, isolated. **chemin** ~ lonely road.

ecchymose [ekimoz] *nf* bruise.

ecclésiastique [eklezjastik] **1** *adj* ecclesiastical. **2** *nm* ecclesiastic, clergyman.

écervelé, e [esɛʀvəle] **1** *adj* scatterbrained. **2** *nm, f* scatterbrain.

échafaud [eʃafo] *nm* scaffold. **il risque l'** ~ he's risking his neck.

échafauder [eʃafode] (1) *vt* (**a**) *fortune* to build up; *théorie* to construct. (**b**) *(empiler)* to pile up. ◆ **échafaudage** *nm* (**a**) *(Constr)* ~**(s)** scaffolding; **dresser un** ~ to put up some scaffolding. (**b**) *[objets]* heap, pile. (**c**) building up, construction.

échalote [eʃalɔt] *nf* shallot.

échancré, e [eʃɑ̃kʀe] *adj robe* with a plunging neckline; *côte* indented; *feuille* serrated. ◆ **échancrure** *nf* plunging neckline; indentation; serration.

échange [eʃɑ̃ʒ] *nm (gén)* exchange; *(troc)* swap. ~**s commerciaux** trade; ~ **de vues** exchange of views; *(dans un débat)* **vifs** ~**s** heated exchanges; **en** ~ *(par contre)* on the other hand; *(troc)* in exchange (*de* for); *(pour compenser)* to make up for it; **faire (l')** ~ **de qch** to swap *ou* exchange sth; *(Comm)* **nous faisons l'** ~ **standard** we give a straight exchange. ◆ **échanger** (3) *vt (gén)* to exchange, swap (*contre* for); *injures* to bandy. ◆ **échangeur** *nm (Aut)* interchange.

échantillon [eʃɑ̃tijɔ̃] *nm* sample. ◆ **échantillonnage** *nm (action)* sampling; *(collection)* range.

échapper [eʃape] (1) **1** *vi* (**a**) ~ **à** *(gén)* to escape; *(en fuyant)* to escape (from), get away from; *(par ruse)* to evade; ~ **à la règle** to be an exception to the rule; **il échappe à tout contrôle** he is beyond control; **tu ne m'échapperas pas!** I'll get you yet!; **son nom m'échappe** his name escapes me *ou* has slipped my mind; **ce qu'il a dit m'a échappé** *(entendre)* I did not catch what he said; *(comprendre)* I did not grasp what he said; **ce mot malheureux m'a échappé** this unfortunate remark just slipped out; **l'opportunité d'une telle mesure m'échappe** I fail to see the point of such a measure; **rien ne lui échappe** he doesn't miss a thing. (**b**) ~ **des mains de qn** to slip out of sb's hands. (**c**) **laisser** ~ *parole, occasion, objet* to let slip; *détail* to overlook; **laisser** ~ **un prisonnier** to let a prisoner escape; **il l'a échappé belle** he had a narrow escape.

2 s' ~ *vpr* (**a**) *[prisonnier]* to escape (*de* from), break out (*de* of); *[oiseau]* to fly away; *[coureur]* to pull away; *[cri]* to escape, burst (*de* from). **la voiture réussit à s'** ~ the car got away; *(fig)* **je m'échappe un instant** I'll slip away for a moment. (**b**) *[gaz]* to escape, leak; *[odeur, lumière]* to come (*de* from). **des flammes s'échappaient du toit** flames were coming out of the roof. ◆ **échappatoire** *nf* way out. ◆ **échappé, e** **1** *nm, f (Sport)* **les** ~**s** the breakaway group. **2** *nf* (**a**) *(Sport)* breakaway. (**b**) *(vue)* vista; *(soleil)* gleam. ◆ **échappement** *nm (Aut)* exhaust; *(Tech)* escapement. ~ **libre** cutout.

écharde [eʃaʀd(ə)] *nf* splinter *ou* sliver (of wood).

écharpe [eʃaʀp(ə)] *nf [femme]* scarf; *[maire]* sash; *(bandage)* sling. **bras en** ~ arm in a sling.

écharper [eʃaʀpe] (1) *vt (lit, fig)* to tear to pieces.

échasse [eʃɑs] *nf (gén)* stilt. ◆ **échassier** *nm* wader *(bird)*.

échauder [eʃode] (1) *vt* (**a**) *(ébouillanter)* to scald. (**b**) *(faire réfléchir)* ~ **qn** to teach sb a lesson; **se faire** ~ to get one's fingers burnt.

échauffer [eʃofe] (1) **1** *vt moteur* to overheat; *imagination* to fire. **échauffé par la course** hot after the race; **les esprits étaient très échauffés** people were getting very heated *ou* worked up. **2 s'** ~ *vpr (Sport)* to warm up; *[débat]* to become heated. ◆ **échauffement** *nm (Sport)* warm-up; *[moteur]* overheating.

échauffourée [eʃofuʀe] *nf (Police)* clash; *(Mil)* skirmish.

échéance [eʃeɑ̃s] *nf* (**a**) *[délai]* expiry *ou* expiration *(US)* date; *[bon]* maturity date; *[traite]* redemption date; *[loyer]* date of payment; *[facture, dette]* settlement date. *(Fin)* **venir à** ~ to fall due. (**b**) *(règlements)* **l'** ~ **de fin de mois** the end-of-month payments; **faire face à ses** ~**s** to meet one's financial obligations *ou* commitments. (**c**) *(laps de temps)* term. *(Fin)* **à longue/courte** ~ long-/short-term; *(fig)* **à longue** ~ in the long run; *(fig)* **à courte** ~ before long.

échec [eʃɛk] *nm* (**a**) *(insuccès)* failure; *(défaite)* defeat; *(revers)* setback. **voué à l'** ~ bound to fail, doomed to failure; **tenir qn en** ~ to hold sb in check; **faire** ~ **à qn** to foil sb *ou* sb's plans. (**b**) *(Jeux)* **les** ~**s** chess; **jeu d'** ~**s** *(échiquier)* chessboard; *(pièces)* chessmen; **être/mettre en** ~ to be/put in check; **faire** ~ **au roi** to check the king; **faire** ~ **et mat** to checkmate.

échelle [eʃɛl] *nf* (**a**) *(objet)* ladder. *(fig)* **il n'y a plus qu'à tirer l'** ~ we may as well give it up. (**b**) *[croquis, salaires etc]* scale; *[hiérarchie]* ladder. **à grande** ~ large-scale; **à l'** ~ **mondiale** on a world scale; ~ **sociale** social scale. (**c**) *[bas]* ladder, run. ◆ **échelon** *nm [échelle]* rung; *[hiérarchie]* grade; *(Admin: niveau)* level. **grimper rapidement les** ~**s** to get quick promotion; **à l'** ~ **national** at the national level.

échelonner [eʃlɔne] (1) *vt objets, paiements* to space out; *congés* to stagger; *difficultés (en complexité)* to grade; *(dans le temps)* to introduce gradually (*sur* over). **service d'ordre échelonné sur le parcours** police positioned *ou* stationed at intervals along the route; **s'** ~ **sur 3 km** to stretch over *ou* be spaced out over a distance of 3 km. ◆ **échelonnement** *nm* spacing out; staggering; grading; gradual introduction.

écheveau, *pl* ~**x** [eʃvo] *nm* skein, hank; *(fig)* tangle.

échevelé, e [eʃəvle] *adj personne* tousled; *rythme* frenzied.

échevin [ɛʃvɛ̃] *nm (Hist)* alderman; *(Belgique)* deputy burgomaster.

échine [eʃin] *nf* backbone, spine; *(Culin)* loin. **courber l'** ~ to submit. ◆ **s'échiner** (1) *vpr (fig)* to work o.s. to death (*à faire qch* doing sth).

échiquier [eʃikje] *nm* chessboard. **l'** ~ **mondial** the scene of world affairs.

écho [eko] *nm* (**a**) *(lit)* echo; *(rumeur)* rumour, echo; *(témoignage)* account, report; *(réponse)* response. **se faire l'** ~ **de** to echo, repeat; **sa proposition est restée sans** ~ his suggestion wasn't taken up; **l'** ~ **donné à cette nouvelle** the coverage *ou* publicity given to this news item. (**b**) *(Presse: nouvelle)* item of gossip. *(rubrique)* ~**s** gossip column.

échographie [ekogʀafi] *nf (technique)* ultrasound. **passer une** ~ to have a scan.

échoir [eʃwaʀ] *vi* (**a**) **il vous échoit de faire** it falls to you to do. (**b**) *[loyer]* to fall due; *[délai]* to expire.

échoppe † [eʃɔp] *nf* workshop.

échouer [eʃwe] (1) **1** *vi* (**a**) *[personne]* to fail; *[plan]* to fail, fall through; *[négociations]* to break down. ~ **à un examen/dans une tentative** to fail an exam/

in an attempt; **faire** ~ *complot* to foil; *projet* to wreck; **faire** ~ **les plans de qn** to foil sb's plans. (**b**) *(aboutir)* to end up (*dans* in). (**c**) *(Naut: aussi* **s'** *~) [bateau]* to run aground; *[débris]* to be washed up. **le bateau s'est échoué** *ou* **a échoué sur un écueil** the boat ran onto a reef. **2** *vt (Naut) (accidentellement)* to ground; *(volontairement)* to beach.

éclabousser [eklabuse] (1) *vt* to splash, spatter (*de* with). **ils ont été éclaboussés par le scandale** their good name has been smeared by the scandal ; ~ **qn de son luxe** *(éblouir)* to show off one's wealth to sb. ◆ **éclaboussure** *nf [boue]* splash; *[sang]* spatter; *[eau]* spot; *(fig)* smear, blot.

éclair [eklɛʀ] **1** *nm* (**a**) *(Mét)* flash of lightning; *(Phot)* flash. **~s de chaleur** summer lightning ; ~ **de** *génie etc* flash *ou* spark of; **passer comme un** ~ to flash past *ou* by; **en un** ~ in a flash ; **un** ~ **dans sa vie** a ray of sunshine in his life. (**b**) *(Culin)* éclair. **2** *adj inv visite* lightning. **raid** ~ hit-and-run raid; **voyage** ~ flying visit.

éclairage [eklɛʀaʒ] *nm (intérieur)* lighting; *(luminosité)* light (level). *(lit, fig)* **sous cet** ~ in this light. ◆ **éclairagiste** *nm (Théât)* electrician; *(Ciné)* lighting engineer.

éclairant, e [eklɛʀɑ̃, ɑ̃t] *adj (fig)* illuminating, enlightening; *(lit) propriétés* lighting.

éclaircir [eklɛʀsiʀ] (2) **1** *vt* (**a**) *teinte* to lighten. (**b**) *soupe* to make thinner; *plantes, cheveux* to thin. (**c**) *mystère* to clear up; *pensée, situation* to clarify. **pouvez-vous nous** ~ **sur ce point?** can you enlighten us on this point? **2 s'** ~ *vpr* (**a**) *[ciel]* to clear; *[temps]* to clear up. **s'** ~ **la voix** to clear one's throat. (**b**) *[arbres, foule]* to thin out; *[cheveux]* to get thin *ou* thinner. (**c**) *[idées, situation]* to become clearer; *[mystère]* to be cleared up. ◆ **éclaircie** *nf (de soleil)* bright interval, sunny spell; *(dans nuages)* break; *(fig: dans la vie)* ray of sunshine. ◆ **éclaircissement** *nm [mystère]* clearing up; *[texte obscur]* clarification. **j'exige des ~s** I demand an explanation.

éclairer [ekleʀe] (1) **1** *vt* (**a**) *[lampe]* to light (up); *[soleil]* to shine (down) on; *[fenêtre]* to give light to. **une seule fenêtre était éclairée** only one window was lit up; **un sourire éclaira son visage** his face lit up in a smile; **bien/mal éclairé** well-/badly-lit. (**b**) *situation, texte* to throw light on. (**c**) ~ **qn** *(lit)* to light the way for sb; *(fig: renseigner)* to enlighten sb (*sur* about). (**d**) *(Mil)* ~ **le terrain** to scout out the ground. **2** *vi*: ~ **bien/mal** to give a good/poor light. **3 s'** ~ *vpr [rue]* to be lit; *[visage]* to light up, brighten; *[situation]* to get clearer. **tout s'éclaire!** everything's becoming clear!; **s'** ~ **à la bougie** to use candlelight. ◆ **éclairé, e** *adj minorité* enlightened.

éclaireur [eklɛʀœʀ] *nm* (**a**) *(Mil)* scout. *(lit, fig)* **partir en** ~ to go off and scout around. (**b**) *(Scoutisme)* (boy) scout. ◆ **éclaireuse** *nf* (girl) guide.

éclat [ekla] *nm* (**a**) *[os, bois]* splinter; *[grenade, pierre]* fragment. ~ **d'obus** piece of shrapnel. (**b**) *[lumière, diamant, couleur]* brilliance; *[braise]* glow; *[vernis]* shine; *[satin, perle]* sheen; *[phares]* glare; *[yeux]* sparkle; *[teint, jeunesse]* radiance. (**c**) *[nom]* fame; *[cérémonie, époque]* brilliance; *[personnage]* glamour. **réception donnée avec** ~ dazzling reception. (**d**) *(scandale)* fuss. **faire un** ~ to make a fuss. (**e**) **~s de voix** shouts; ~ **de colère** angry outburst; ~ **de rire** roar *ou* burst of laughter. ◆ **éclatant, e** *adj* (**a**) *lumière, couleur* bright; *soleil* blazing; *blancheur* dazzling; *teint* radiant. (**b**) *succès* dazzling; *revanche* shattering; *gloire* shining; *vérité* manifest; *exemple* striking; *mensonge* blatant. **il a des dons ~s** he is brilliantly gifted; ~ **de santé** radiant with health. (**c**) *rire, bruit* loud; *voix* ringing.

éclater [eklate] (1) *vi* (**a**) *[bombe]* to explode, blow up; *[bourgeon]* to burst open; *[pneu, chaudière]* to burst; *[verre]* to shatter; *[parti]* to break up. (**b**) *[fléau, applaudissement]* to break out; *[scandale, orage]* to break. **la nouvelle a éclaté comme un coup de tonnerre** the news came like a thunderbolt, the news burst like a bombshell; **des cris ont éclaté** shouts were raised; **un coup de tonnerre éclata** there was a peal of thunder. (**c**) *[vérité]* to shine out. **la joie éclate dans ses yeux** joy shines in his eyes, his eyes are shining with joy. (**d**) ~ **de rire** to burst out laughing; ~ **(de rage)** to explode (with rage); ~ **en sanglots** to burst into tears; ~ **en applaudissements** to burst into applause. (**e**) **faire** ~ *mine* to detonate, blow up; *bombe* to explode; *pétard* to let *ou* set off; *ballon, tuyau* to burst; *verre* to shatter; **faire** *ou* **laisser** ~ **sa joie/colère** to give free rein to one's joy/anger. ◆ **éclatement** *nm* explosion; bursting (*de* of); break-up (*de* in).

éclectique [eklɛktik] *adj* eclectic.

éclipse [eklips(ə)] *nf (Astron, fig)* eclipse. ◆ **éclipser** (1) **1** *vt (Astron)* to eclipse; *[gloire]* to eclipse, overshadow. **2 s'** ~ * *vpr* to slip away.

éclopé, e [eklɔpe] **1** *adj* lame. **2** *nm, f (hum)* (slightly) injured person.

éclore [eklɔʀ] (45) *vi [œuf]* to hatch, be hatched; *[poussin]* to hatch (out); *[fleur]* to open out; *[amour, jour]* to dawn. **faire** ~ *œuf* to hatch; *sentiment* to kindle. ◆ **éclosion** *nf* hatching; opening; dawn.

écluse [eklyz] *nf (Naut)* lock. ◆ **éclusier, -ière** *nm, f* lock keeper.

écœurer [ekœʀe] (1) *vt*: ~ **qn** *[gâteau]* to make sb feel sick; *[conduite]* to disgust sb, make sb sick; *[échec]* to sicken sb. ◆ **écœurant, e** *adj (gén)* disgusting; *conduite* sickening; *gâteau* sickly. ◆ **écœurement** *nm (lit)* nausea; *(fig)* disgust; *(lassitude)* discouragement.

école [ekɔl] *nf* school. *(éducation)* **l'** ~ education; **navire-~** training ship; **être à bonne** ~ to be in good hands; **il a été à dure** ~ he learned about life the hard way; **faire l'** ~ to teach; **faire l'** ~ **buissonnière** to play truant *ou* hooky; **faire** ~ *[personne]* to collect a following; *[théorie]* to gain widespread acceptance; ~ **de conduite** driving school; ~ **hôtelière** catering school; ~ **maternelle** nursery school; ~ **normale** ≃ teachers' training college; ~ **de police** police academy; ~ **primaire** primary *ou* elementary school, grade school *(US)*; ~ **de secrétariat** secretarial college. ◆ **écolier** *nm* schoolboy; *(fig: novice)* novice. ◆ **écolière** *nf* schoolgirl.

écologie [ekɔlɔʒi] *nf* ecology. ◆ **écologique** *adj* ecological. **mouvement** ~ ecomovement. ◆ **écologiste** *nmf* ecologist, environmentalist.

éconduire [ekɔ̃dɥiʀ] (38) *vt visiteur* to dismiss; *soupirant* to reject; *solliciteur* to put off.

économat [ekɔnɔma] *nm (fonction)* bursarship; *(bureau)* bursar's office; *(magasin)* staff cooperative.

économe [ekɔnɔm] **1** *adj* thrifty. **être** ~ **de son temps** *etc* to be sparing of one's time *etc*. **2** *nmf (Admin)* bursar.

économie [ekɔnɔmi] *nf* (**a**) *(science)* economics *(sg)*; *(Pol: système)* economy. (**b**) *(épargne)* economy, thrift. (**c**) *(gain)* saving. **faire une** ~ **de temps** to save time; **~s** savings; **faire des ~s** to save up, save money; **faire des ~s de chauffage** to economize on heating; **les ~s d'énergie sont nécessaires** energy conservation is essential; **réaliser d'importantes ~s d'énergie** to make significant energy savings; **il n'y a pas de petites ~s** every little helps; *(fig péj)* **faire des ~s de bouts de chandelle** to make footling economies. ◆ **économique** *adj (Écon)* economic; *(bon marché)* economical; *(Aut)* fuel-efficient. ◆ **économiquement** *adv* economically. **les** ~ **faibles** the lower-income groups. ◆ **économiser** (1) *vt électricité* to economize on, save on; *temps, forces* to save; *argent* to save up. ~ **sur** to economize on, cut down on; ~ **l'énergie** to conserve *ou* save energy. ◆ **économiste** *nmf* economist.

écoper [ekɔpe] (1) *vti (Naut)* to bale (out). ~ **(d')une punition** * to catch it *. ◆ **écope** *nf (Naut)* baler.

écorce [ekɔʀs(ə)] *nf [arbre]* bark; *[orange]* peel, skin. **l'~ terrestre** the earth's crust.

écorcher [ekɔʀʃe] (1) *vt* (**a**) *(dépecer) animal* to skin; *criminel* to flay. (**b**) *(égratigner)* to graze, scratch; *(par frottement)* to chafe, rub. (**c**) *(fig) mot* to mispronounce. **il écorche l'allemand** he speaks broken German. (**d**) (*) ~ **le client** to fleece one's customers; ~ **les oreilles de qn** *[bruit]* to grate on sb's ears; *[personne]* to hurt sb's ears. ◆ **écorché** *nm (Anat)* écorché. *(fig)* **c'est un ~ vif** he is a tormented soul. ◆ **écorchure** *nf* graze, scratch.

écorner [ekɔʀne] (1) *vt meuble* to chip the corner of; *fortune* to make a hole in. **livre écorné** dog-eared book.

écossais, e [ekɔsɛ, ɛz] **1** *adj temps, caractère* Scottish; *whisky* Scotch; *tissu* tartan. **2** *nm* (**a**) **É~** Scot, Scotsman; **les É~** the Scots. (**b**) *(Ling)* **l'~** Scots. **3** *nf*: **É~e** Scot, Scotswoman. ◆ **Écosse** *nf* Scotland.

écosser [ekɔse] (1) *vt* to shell, pod.

écot [eko] *nm* share (of a bill).

écouler [ekule] (1) **1** *vt (Comm)* to sell; *faux billets* to get rid of. **2 s'~** *vpr* (**a**) *(suinter)* to seep out; *(fuir)* to leak out; *(couler)* to flow out. (**b**) *[temps]* to pass, go by; *[argent]* to melt away; *[foule]* to drift away; *(Comm)* to sell. **sa vie écoulée** his past life. ◆ **écoulement** *nm [eau, voitures]* flow; *[pus]* discharge; *[foule]* dispersal; *[temps]* passage, passing; *(Comm)* selling.

écourter [ekuʀte] (1) *vt (gén)* to shorten; *visite, attente* to cut short; *texte* to cut down.

écouter [ekute] (1) **1** *vt disque, confidence, conseil* to listen to; *discours, (Jur) témoin* to hear. ~ **qn jusqu'au bout** to hear sb out; ~ **qn parler** to hear sb speak; ~ **aux portes** to eavesdrop; **faire ~ un disque à qn** to play a record to sb; **ses conseils sont très écoutés** his advice is greatly valued *ou* greatly sought after; ~ **ses parents** to listen to one's parents; **faire ~ qn** to get sb to listen *ou* obey; **n'écoutant que son courage** letting courage be his only guide. **2 s' ~** *vpr [malade]* **elle s'écoute trop** she coddles herself; **si je m'écoutais je n'irais pas** I've a good mind not to go; **s' ~ parler** to savour one's words. ◆ **écoute** *nf (Rad)* listening (*de* to). **nous restons à l' ~** we are staying tuned in; **reprendre l'** ~ to retune; *(TV)* **heures de grande ~** peak viewing hours; **avoir une grande** ~ to have a large audience; **l'indice d' ~ d'une émission** the ratings (of a programme); **être aux ~s** to be listening (*de* to); *(Police)* **les ~s téléphoniques** phone-tapping; **ils sont sur ~** their phone is tapped. ◆ **écouteur, -euse 1** *nm, f (attentif)* listener; *(indiscret)* eavesdropper. **2** *nm [téléphone]* receiver. *(Rad)* **~s** earphones, headphones.

écrabouiller * [ekʀabuje] (1) *vt* to crush. **se faire ~ par une voiture** to get crushed by a car.

écran [ekʀɑ̃] *nm (gén)* screen. *(Ordin)* ~ **à fenêtres** split screen; **porter un roman à l'** ~ to adapt a novel for the screen; **faire ~ à qn** *(abriter)* to screen *ou* shelter sb; *(gêner)* to get in the way of sb; *(éclipser)* to put sb in the shade.

écraser [ekʀɑze] (1) **1** *vt* (**a**) *(gén)* to crush; *mouche* to swat; *mégot* to stub out; *(en purée)* to mash; *(en poudre)* to grind (*en* to); *(pour le jus)* to squeeze; *(en aplatissant)* to flatten (out); *(en piétinant)* to trample down. ~ **sous la dent** *biscuit* to crunch; **vous m'écrasez les pieds** you're treading on my feet. (**b**) *(tuer) [voiture]* ~ **qn** to run sb over; **il s'est fait** ~ he was run over. (**c**) *(fig: accabler)* to crush. **être écrasé de** *impôts* to be crushed by; *chaleur, sommeil* to be overcome by; *travail* to be snowed under with. (**d**) *(vaincre) ennemi* to crush. **notre équipe s'est fait** ~ our team was beaten hollow *ou* was hammered *; **il écrase tout le monde** he outdoes everyone (*en* at). **2** *vi*: **en** ~ ‡ to sleep like a log *. **3 s'** ~ *vpr* (**a**) *[avion]* to crash; *[objet, corps]* to be dashed (*contre* on, against); *(dans le métro)* to get crushed (*dans* in). (**b**) *(‡: se taire)* to pipe down *. ◆ **écrasant, e** *adj (gén)* crushing; *travail* back-breaking; *victoire, chaleur, responsabilité, nombre, supériorité* overwhelming. *(Pol)* **majorité/victoire ~e** landslide *ou* crushing majority/victory. ◆ **écrasé, e** *adj nez* flat; *relief* dwarfed. ◆ **écrasement** *nm* crushing.

écrémer [ekʀeme] (6) *vt lait* to skim.

écrevisse [ekʀəvis] *nf* (freshwater) crayfish.

écrier (s') [ekʀije] (7) *vpr* to exclaim, cry out.

écrin [ekʀɛ̃] *nm* (jewellery) case.

écrire [ekʀiʀ] (39) *vt (gén)* to write; *(orthographier)* to spell; *(inscrire)* to write down. ~ **gros** to have large handwriting; ~ **à la machine** to type; **comment est-ce que ça s'écrit?** how do you spell it *ou* write it?; **ça s'écrit comme ça se prononce** it's spelt how it sounds, you write it the same way as you pronounce it; **c'est écrit en noir sur blanc** *ou* **en toutes lettres** it's written in black and white; **c'était écrit** it was bound to happen; **il est écrit que je ne pourrai jamais y arriver!** I'm doomed never to succeed! ◆ **écrit** *nm (ouvrage)* piece of writing; *(examen)* written paper; *(Jur)* document. **par** ~ in writing. ◆ **écriteau,** *pl* **~x** *nm* notice, sign. ◆ **écriture** *nf* (**a**) *(à la main)* (hand)writing; *(alphabet)* writing, script; *(style)* style. (**b**) *(Fin, Comm)* **~s** accounts, books; **tenir les ~s** to do the book-keeping. (**c**) *(Rel)* **l'É~ (Sainte)** the Scriptures. ◆ **écrivain** *nm (homme)* writer. **(femme-)~** woman writer.

écrou [ekʀu] *nm (Tech)* nut.

écrouer [ekʀue] (1) *vt* to imprison.

écrouler (s') [ekʀule] (1) *vpr (gén)* to collapse; *[empire, espoir]* to crumble; *[personne] (tomber)* to collapse; *(*: s'endormir)* to fall fast asleep; *[accusé]* to break down. **s' ~ de fatigue** to be overcome with weariness. ◆ **écroulé, e** *adj*: **à moitié ~** *maison* half-ruined, tumbledown, dilapidated; **être ~** *(par le malheur)* to be prostrate with grief; *(de rire)* to be doubled up with laughter. ◆ **écroulement** *nm* collapse.

écru, e [ekʀy] *adj tissu* raw; *couleur* natural-coloured. **toile ~e** unbleached linen.

écu [eky] *nm (monnaie ancienne)* crown; *(monnaie de la CEE)* Ecu; *(arme)* shield.

écueil [ekœj] *nm (lit)* reef; *(problème)* stumbling block; *(piège)* pitfall.

écuelle [ekɥɛl] *nf* bowl.

éculé, e [ekyle] *adj soulier* down-at-heel; *plaisanterie* hackneyed, worn.

écumer [ekyme] (1) **1** *vt* (**a**) *bouillon* to skim. (**b**) *(piller)* to plunder; *(chercher)* to scour. ~ **les mers** to scour the seas. **2** *vi (gén)* to foam; *[cheval]* to lather. *(fig)* ~ **(de rage)** to foam with rage. ◆ **écume** *nf (gén)* foam; *[cheval]* lather. **pipe en ~ de mer** meerschaum pipe; *(fig)* **l' ~ de la société** the dregs of society. ◆ **écumeux, -euse** *adj* foamy. ◆ **écumoire** *nf* skimmer.

écureuil [ekyʀœj] *nm* squirrel.

écurie [ekyʀi] *nf* stable; *(fig: sale)* pigsty. **mettre à l'** ~ to stable; ~ **de course** racing stable.

écusson [ekysɔ̃] *nm* badge.

écuyer [ekɥije] *nm (cavalier)* rider, horseman; *(d'un chevalier)* squire; *(à la cour)* equerry. ◆ **écuyère** *nf* rider, horsewoman.

eczéma [ɛgzema] *nm* eczema.

Éden [edɛn] *nm*: **l'** ~ (the garden of) Eden.

édicter [edikte] (1) *vt* to decree.

édifier [edifje] (7) *vt maison* to build, erect; *fortune, empire* to build (up); *(moralement)* to edify. ◆ **édification** *nf* erection; *[esprit]* edification. ◆ **édifice** *nm* edifice, building. ~ **public** public building ; **l'** ~ **social** the social structure *ou* fabric.

Édimbourg [edɛ̃buʀ] *n* Edinburgh.

édit [edi] *nm (Hist)* edict.

éditer [edite] (1) *vt (publier)* to publish; *(annoter)* to edit. ◆ **éditeur, -trice** *nm, f* publisher; editor. *(Ordin)* ~ **de texte** text editor. ◆ **édition** *nf (action)* publishing; editing; *(livre, journal)* edition. **l'** ~ the publishing business; ~ **spéciale** *(journal)* special edition; *(magazine)* special issue.

éditorial, *pl* **-iaux** [editɔʀjal, jo] *nm* leader, editorial. ◆ **éditorialiste** *nmf* leader writer.

édredon [edʀədɔ̃] *nm* eiderdown.

éducation [edykɑsjɔ̃] *nf (Scol, gén)* education; *(familiale)* upbringing; *[goût]* training. **j'ai fait mon** ~ **à Paris** I was educated *ou* went to school in Paris; ~ **physique** physical training *ou* education; **sans** ~ *(instruction)* ill-educated; *(bonnes manières)* ill-mannered, ill-bred. ◆ **éducateur, -trice 1** *adj* educational. **2** *nm, f (gén)* teacher; *(prison)* tutor, instructor; *(théoricien)* educationalist. ◆ **éducatif, -ive** *adj* educational.

édulcorer [edylkɔʀe] (1) *vt (Pharm)* to sweeten; *(fig)* to tone down.

éduquer [edyke] (1) *vt (à l'école)* to educate; *(à la maison)* to bring up; *peuple* to educate; *goût* to train. **bien éduqué** well-mannered, well-bred; **mal éduqué** ill-mannered, ill-bred, badly brought up.

effacer [efase] (3) **1** *vt (gén)* to efface, erase; *écran d'ordinateur* to clear; *tableau noir* to clean, wipe; *(à la gomme)* to rub out; *(au chiffon)* to wipe off; *(au grattoir)* to scratch out; *souvenir* to efface; *faute* to erase; *craintes* to dispel; *concurrent* to outshine. ~ **son passé** to blot out one's past; **le temps efface tout** everything fades with time; **on efface tout et on recommence** *(oublier le passé)* we'll let bygones be bygones; *(reprendre à zéro)* let's go back to square one, let's make a fresh start; ~ **le corps** to draw o.s. in. **2 s'** ~ *vpr* (**a**) *(gén)* to fade; *[inscription]* to wear off. **ça s'efface bien** *[crayon]* it rubs out *ou* erases easily; *[tableau]* it's easy to clean. (**b**) *(lit: s'écarter)* to move *ou* step aside; *(fig: se tenir en arrière)* to keep in the background; *(se retirer)* to withdraw. ◆ **effacé, e** *adj teinte (passé)* faded; *(sans éclat)* subdued; *personne, vie* retiring; *rôle* unobtrusive. ◆ **effacement** *nm* (**a**) erasing; effacing; dispelling; fading. (**b**) *(modestie)* retiring *ou* self-effacing manner; *(retrait)* withdrawal; *(éclipse)* eclipse.

effarer [efaʀe] (1) *vt* to alarm. **cette bêtise m'effare** I am aghast at *ou* appalled by such stupidity. ◆ **effarant, e** *adj (gén)* alarming. ◆ **effarement** *nm* alarm.

effaroucher [efaʀuʃe] (1) **1** *vt (gén)* to frighten *ou* scare away; *(choquer)* to shock, upset. **2 s'** ~ *vpr (timidité)* to take fright (*de* at); *(pudeur)* to be shocked *ou* upset (*de* by).

effectif, -ive [efɛktif, iv] **1** *adj aide, travail* effective, actual. **être** ~ **à partir de** to take effect *ou* become effective as from. **2** *nm [lycée]* size; *[parti]* size, strength. *(Mil, Pol)* ~**s** numbers; *(Mil)* **l'** ~ **est au complet** we are at full strength. ◆ **effectivement** *adv aider* effectively; *se produire* actually, really. **c'est** ~ **plus rapide** it's actually faster; **oui,** ~! yes, indeed!

effectuer [efɛktɥe] (1) **1** *vt (gén)* to make; *opération, expérience* to carry out, perform; *geste* to execute; *paiement* to effect; *trajet* to complete. **le franc/le coureur a effectué une remontée spectaculaire** the franc/the runner made *ou* staged a spectacular recovery. **2 s'** ~ *vpr* to be made. **le voyage s'est effectué sans incident** the journey went off without a hitch.

efféminé, e [efemine] *adj* effeminate.

effervescence [efɛʀvesɑ̃s] *nf (lit)* effervescence; *(fig)* agitation. **être en** ~ to be in a turmoil. ◆ **effervescent, e** *adj* effervescent.

effet [efɛ] *nm* (**a**) *(résultat)* effect. **c'est l'** ~ **du hasard** it is quite by chance; **être sans** ~ to be ineffective, have no effect; ~ **de surprise** effect of surprise; **avoir pour** ~ **de faire** to have the effect of doing; **ce médicament (me) fait de l'** ~**/a fait son** ~ this medicine is effective *ou* works (on me)/has taken effect *ou* has worked. (**b**) *(impression)* impression (*sur* on). **il a fait son petit** ~ he managed to cause a bit of a stir; **c'est tout l'** ~ **que ça te fait?** is that all it means to you?; **faire bon/mauvais** ~ **sur qn** to make a good/bad impression on sb; **il me fait l'** ~ **d'(être) une belle crapule** he seems like a real crook to me; **cette déclaration a fait l'** ~ **d'une bombe** this statement came as a bombshell. (**c**) *(procédé)* effect. ~ **de style/de perspective** stylistic/visual effect; *(Ciné)* ~**s spéciaux** special effects; **elle lui a coupé ses** ~**s** she stole his thunder; **manquer son** ~ *[personne]* to spoil one's effect; *[plaisanterie]* to fall flat. (**d**) *(Sport) [balle]* spin. **donner de l'** ~ **à** to spin. (**e**) **avec** ~ **rétroactif au 1er janvier** backdated to January 1st; **prendre** ~ **à la date de** to take effect from. (**f**) *(Comm: valeur)* ~ **(de commerce)** bill (of exchange). (**g**) *(vêtements)* ~**s** things, clothes. (**h**) **en** ~ *(parce que)* because; **oui, en** ~ yes indeed; **c'est en** ~ **plus rapide** it's actually faster. (**i**) *(locutions)* **mettre à** ~ to put into effect; **à cet** ~ to that effect *ou* end; **sous l'** ~ **de** *alcool* under the effect *ou* influence of; **il était encore sous l'** ~ **de la colère** he was still angry.

efficace [efikas] *adj mesure* effective; *remède* efficacious; *personne, machine* efficient. ◆ **efficacement** *adv* effectively; efficaciously; efficiently. ◆ **efficacité** *nf* effectiveness; efficacy; efficiency.

effigie [efiʒi] *nf* effigy. **à l'** ~ **de** bearing the effigy of.

effiler [efile] (1) **1** *vt étoffe* to fray. **2 s'** ~ *vpr [objet]* to taper; *[étoffe]* to fray. ◆ **effilé, e** *adj* slender, tapering.

effilocher *vt,* **s'** ~ *vpr* [efilɔʃe] (1) to fray.

efflanqué, e [eflɑ̃ke] *adj animal* raw-boned.

effleurer [eflœʀe] (1) *vt (frôler)* to touch lightly, brush (against); *(érafler)* to graze; *(fig) sujet* to touch (lightly) upon, skim over. ~ **l'esprit de qn** to cross sb's mind. ◆ **effleurement** *nm* light touch.

effluve [eflyv] *nm*: ~**s** exhalations.

effondrer (s') [efɔ̃dʀe] (1) *vpr (gén)* to collapse; *[empire, espoir]* to crumble; *[accusé]* to break down. ◆ **effondré, e** *adj (abattu)* shattered, crushed (*de* by). ~ **de douleur** prostrate with grief; **les parents** ~**s** the grief-stricken parents. ◆ **effondrement** *nm* (**a**) collapse; break-down. (**b**) *(abattement)* utter dejection.

efforcer (s') [efɔʀse] (3) *vpr*: **s'** ~ **de faire** to try hard to do, do one's best to do, endeavour to do.

effort [efɔʀ] *nm* (**a**) effort. **après bien des** ~**s** after much effort; **nécessiter un** ~ **financier** to require a financial outlay; ~ **de volonté** effort of will; **faire un** ~ **de mémoire** to make an effort to remember; **faire de gros** ~**s pour réussir** to make a great effort *ou* great efforts to succeed, try very hard to succeed; **faire tous ses** ~**s** to do one's utmost, make every effort; **faire l'** ~ **de** to make the effort to; **encore un** ~ just one more go, just a little more effort; **sans** ~ effortlessly. (**b**) *(Tech)* stress, strain.

effraction [efʀaksjɔ̃] *nf (action)* breaking-in. **plusieurs ~s** several break-ins; **entrer par ~** to break in; **~ informatique** (computer) hacking.

effranger *vt,* **s' ~** *vpr* [efʀɑ̃ʒe] (3) to fray.

effrayer [efʀeje] (8) **1** *vt* to frighten. **2 s' ~** *vpr* to be frightened (*de* by), take fright (*de* at), be afraid (*de* of). ◆ **effrayant, e** *adj* frightening, fearsome; *(sens affaibli)* frightful.

effréné, e [efʀene] *adj course* frantic; *passion, luxe* unbridled.

effriter [efʀite] (1) **1** *vt biscuit* to crumble; *roche* to cause to crumble. **2 s' ~** *vpr (lit, fig)* to crumble (away). ◆ **effritement** *nm* crumbling(-away).

effroi [efʀwɑ] *nm* terror, dread.

effronté, e [efʀɔ̃te] *adj* insolent, cheeky; *mensonge, menteur* brazen, shameless. ◆ **effrontément** *adv* insolently, cheekily; brazenly, shamelessly. ◆ **effronterie** *nf* insolence, cheek; shamelessness.

effroyable [efʀwajabl(ə)] *adj* horrifying, appalling. ◆ **effroyablement** *adv* appallingly, horrifyingly.

effusion [efyzjɔ̃] *nf* effusion. **avec ~** effusively; **~ de sang** bloodshed.

égal, e, *mpl* **-aux** [egal, o] **1** *adj* (**a**) *(valeur)* equal (*en* in, *à* to). **de poids ~** of equal weight; **à poids ~** weight for weight; **à ~e distance de** equidistant from. (**b**) *justice, pas* even, unvarying; *climat, caractère* equable; *terrain* even, level; *bruit, vent* steady. (**c**) **ça m'est ~** I don't mind; *(je m'en fiche)* I don't care; **c'est ~, il aurait pu écrire** all the same he might have written; **la partie n'est pas ~e (entre eux)** they are not evenly matched; **ça n'a d' ~ que** it is matched *ou* equalled only by; **rester ~ à soi-même** to remain true to form. **2** *nm, f (personne)* equal. **discuter d' ~ à ~** to talk as equals; **être à l' ~ de** *(égal à)* to be equalled *ou* matched by; *(comme)* to be just like; **sans ~** matchless, unequalled. ◆ **égalable** *adj*: **difficilement ~** difficult to equal *ou* match. ◆ **également** *adv (gén)* equally. *(aussi)* **elle lui a ~ parlé** she spoke to him too *ou* as well. ◆ **égaler** (1) **1** *vt* to equal (*en* in). **2 plus 2 égalent 4** 2 plus 2 equals 4; **~ qn à** to rank sb with; **~ qn en qch** to equal sb in sth, match sb for sth. **2 s' ~** *vpr*: **s' ~ à** to equal, be equal to; *(comparaison)* to liken o.s. to.

égaliser [egalize] (1) **1** *vt chances* to equalize; *sol, revenus* to level (out). **2** *vi (Sport)* to equalize, tie *(US)*. ◆ **égalisateur, -trice** *adj* equalizing. ◆ **égalisation** *nf* equalization; levelling.

égalité [egalite] *nf [chances, hommes]* equality; *(Math)* identity; *[climat]* equableness; *[pouls]* regularity; *[surface]* evenness, levelness; *(Tennis)* deuce. **~ d'humeur** equanimity; **~ des chances** equality of opportunity; **être à ~** *(gén)* to be equal; *(match nul)* to draw, tie *(US)*; *(Tennis: à 40/40)* to be at deuce. ◆ **égalitariste** *adj, nmf* egalitarian.

égard [egaʀ] *nm* (**a**) *(respect)* **~s** consideration; **montrer beaucoup d' ~s pour** to show great consideration for, be very considerate towards. (**b**) **à l' ~ de** *(envers)* towards; *(contre)* concerning, with regard to; **par ~ pour** out of consideration for; **sans ~ pour** without regard for; **à tous ~s** in all respects; **à cet ~** in this respect.

égarer [egaʀe] (1) **1** *vt voyageur* to lead out of his way; *enquêteurs* to mislead; *objet* to mislay; *(moralement)* to lead astray. **égaré par la douleur** distraught with grief. **2 s' ~** *vpr [voyageur, lettre]* to get lost; *[discussion]* to wander from the point. *(fig, Rel)* **s' ~ hors du droit chemin** to wander from the straight and narrow; **mon esprit s'égare** I feel distraught. ◆ **égaré, e** *adj voyageur* lost; *animal, obus* stray; *village* remote; *air* distraught. ◆ **égarement** *nm (trouble)* distraction. **dans un moment d' ~** in a moment of madness; *(inconduite)* **~s** aberrations.

égayer [egeje] (8) **1** *vt (gén)* to brighten up; *(divertir)* to amuse, cheer up. **2 s' ~** *vpr* to amuse o.s. **s' ~ aux dépens de qn** to amuse o.s. at sb's expense.

Égée [eʒe] *adj*: **la mer ~** the Aegean (sea).

égide [eʒid] *nf*: **sous l' ~ de** under the aegis of.

églantier [eglɑ̃tje] *nm* wild rose(-bush). ◆ **églantine** *nf* wild rose, eglantine.

église [egliz] *nf (gén)* church.

ego [ego] *nm (Philo, Psych)* ego.

égoïsme [egɔism(ə)] *nm* selfishness, egoism. ◆ **égoïste** **1** *adj* selfish, egoistic. **2** *nmf* egoist. ◆ **égoïstement** *adv* selfishly, egoistically.

égorger [egɔʀʒe] (3) *vt (lit)* to slit *ou* cut the throat of; (*) *client* to bleed white.

égout [egu] *nm* sewer. **les ~s** the sewerage system. ◆ **égoutier** *nm* sewer worker.

égoutter [egute] (1) **1** *vt (avec passoire)* to strain; *(en tordant)* to wring out. **2** *vi [vaisselle]* to drain, drip; *[linge, eau]* to drip. **faire ~** *eau* to drain off; *linge* to hang up to drip; **'laisser ~ '** 'drip dry'. **3 s' ~** *vpr* to drip; to drain. ◆ **égouttoir** *nm (évier)* draining board; *(mobile)* draining rack; *(passoire)* strainer, colander.

égratigner [egʀatiɲe] (1) *vt peau* to scratch, graze; *genou* to graze, scrape; *(fig)* to have a dig at. **le film/l'auteur s'est fait ~ par la critique** the film/the author was given a bit of a rough ride by the critics. ◆ **égratignure** *nf* scratch, graze, scrape; *(fig)* dig. **sans une ~** without a scratch, unscathed.

égrener [egʀəne] (5) *vt pois, blé, épi* to shell; *coton* to gin; *grappe* to pick grapes off. *(fig)* **~ son chapelet** to tell one's beads; **~ les heures** to mark the hours; **les maisons s'égrenaient le long de la route** the houses were dotted along the road.

égrillard, e [egʀijaʀ, aʀd(ə)] *adj* bawdy.

Égypte [eʒipt] *nf* Egypt. ◆ **égyptien, -ienne** *adj,* **É~(ne)** *nm (f)* Egyptian.

eh [e] *excl*: **~ bien** well.

éhonté, e [eɔ̃te] *adj* shameless.

éjecter [eʒɛkte] (1) *vt (Tech)* to eject; (‡) to kick out *. **se faire ~ ‡** to get o.s. kicked out *. ◆ **éjection** *nf (Tech)* ejection; (‡) kicking-out *.

élaborer [elabɔʀe] (1) *vt (gén)* to elaborate. ◆ **élaboration** *nf* elaboration.

élaguer [elage] (1) *vt (lit, fig)* to prune. ◆ **élagage** *nm* pruning. ◆ **élagueur** *nm* pruner.

élan¹ [elɑ̃] *nm (Zool)* elk, moose.

élan² [elɑ̃] *nm* (**a**) *(début de course)* run up. **saut avec/sans ~** running/standing jump. (**b**) *(vitesse acquise)* momentum. **prendre de l' ~** to gather speed; **emporté par son ~** carried along by his own momentum. (**c**) *[enthousiasme, colère]* surge, burst (*de* of). **~s (d'affection)** rushes of affection; **~s lyriques** lyrical outbursts; **dire qch avec ~** to say sth with fervour *ou* passion. (**d**) *[troupes]* vigour, spirit. **~ patriotique** patriotic fervour. (**e**) *(Écon: dynamisme)* boost. **l' ~ donné à nos exportations** the boost given to our exports.

élancer [elɑ̃se] (3) **1** *vi [blessure]* to give shooting pains. **2 s' ~** *vpr* (**a**) *(se précipiter)* to rush, dash (*vers* towards). **s' ~ d'un bond sur** to leap onto. (**b**) *(se dresser)* to soar (upwards). ◆ **élancé, e** *adj clocher etc* slender. ◆ **élancement** *nm* shooting pain.

élargir [elaʀʒiʀ] (2) **1** *vt* (**a**) *(gén)* to widen; *débat* to broaden. *(Pol)* **majorité élargie** increased majority; **ça lui élargit la taille** that makes his waist look fatter; **~ son horizon** to enlarge *ou* widen one's horizons. (**b**) *(Jur: libérer)* to release, free. **2 s' ~** *vpr [route]* to widen, get wider; *[idées]* to broaden. ◆ **élargissement** *nm* widening; broadening; release.

élastique [elastik] **1** *adj objet* elastic; *démarche* springy; *sens, esprit* flexible; *(péj) conscience* accommodating; *(Écon)* elastic. **2** *nm (de bureau)* elastic *ou* rubber band; *(Couture)* elastic. **en ~** elasticated. ◆ **élasticité** *nf* elasticity; spring; flexibility; accommodating nature.

élastomère [elastɔmɛʀ] *nm* elastomer.

Elbe [ɛlb] *nf:* **l'île d' ~** (the isle of) Elba; *(fleuve)*: **l' ~** the Elbe.

électeur, -trice [elɛktœʀ, tʀis] *nm, f* (**a**) *(Pol)* voter. *(circonscription)* **~s** constituents. (**b**) *(Hist)* **É~** Elector; **É~trice** Electress. ◆ **électif, -ive** *adj (Pol)* elective. ◆ **élection** *nf* (**a**) *(Pol, gén)* election. **jour des ~s** polling *ou* election day; **l' ~ présidentielle** the presidential election; **~ partielle** ≃ by-election; **~s législatives** ≃ general election. (**b**) *(choix)* **patrie d' ~** chosen country. ◆ **électoral, e,** *mpl* **-aux** *adj* election. ◆ **électorat** *nm* (**a**) *(électeurs)* electorate; *(dans une circonscription)* constituency; *(d'un parti)* voters. (**b**) *(Hist)* electorate.

électricité [elɛktʀisite] *nf* electricity. *(fig)* **il y a de l' ~ dans l'air *** the atmosphere is electric. ◆ **électricien** *nm* electrician. ◆ **électrification** *nf* electrification. ◆ **électrifier** (7) *vt* to electrify. ◆ **électrique** *adj* electrical. ◆ **électriquement** *adv* electrically. ◆ **électriser** (1) *vt (lit, fig)* to electrify.

électro [elɛktʀɔ] *préf* electro. **~-aimant** electromagnet; **~cardiogramme** electrocardiogram ; **~choc(s)** electric shock treatment.

électrocuter [elɛktʀɔkyte] (1) *vt* to electrocute. ◆ **électrocution** *nf* electrocution.

électrode [elɛktʀɔd] *nf* electrode.

électroménager [elɛktʀɔmenaʒe] *adj appareil* (domestic) electrical.

électron [elɛktʀɔ̃] *nm* electron.

électronique [elɛktʀɔnik] **1** *adj (gén)* electronic; *optique* electron. **2** *nf* electronics *(sg)*. ◆ **électronicien, -ienne** *nm, f* electronics engineer.

électrophone [elɛktʀɔfɔn] *nm* record player.

élégant, e [elegɑ̃, ɑ̃t] *adj (gén)* elegant, smart, stylish; *conduite* generous. ◆ **élégamment** *adv* elegantly. ◆ **élégance** *nf* elegance, smartness, stylishness; generosity.

élégie [eleʒi] *nf* elegy.

élément [elemɑ̃] *nm (gén, Chim)* element; *[machine]* part, component; *[pile]* cell; *(Mil)* unit; *(fait)* fact. *(rudiments)* **~s** rudiments, elements; **~s préfabriqués de cuisine** ready-made kitchen units; **~s de rangement** storage units; **aucun ~ nouveau n'est survenu** there have been no new developments, no new facts have come to light; **nous manquons d' ~s** we lack information *ou* facts; **c'est le meilleur ~ de ma classe** he's the best pupil in my class; **les ~s (naturels)** the elements; **être dans son ~ *** to be in one's element. ◆ **élémentaire** *adj* elementary; rudimentary; *(Chim)* elemental.

éléphant [elefɑ̃] *nm* elephant. **comme un ~ dans un magasin de porcelaine** like a bull in a china shop.

élevage [ɛlvaʒ] *nm* (**a**) *(gén)* breeding. **l' ~ (du bétail)** cattle breeding *ou* rearing; **l' ~ des abeilles** beekeeping; **faire l' ~ de** to breed; **pays d' ~** cattle-breeding area; **truite/saumon d' ~** farmed trout/salmon. (**b**) *(ferme)* cattle farm. **~ de poulets/de truites** poultry/trout farm.

élévation [elevɑsjɔ̃] *nf (action d'élever)* raising; *(action de s'élever)* rise (*de* in); *(tertre)* elevation, rise (in the ground); *(coupe, plan)* elevation; *[pensée, style]* loftiness; *[âme]* elevation. *(Rel)* **l' ~** the Elevation.

élève [elɛv] *nmf* pupil, student. **~ infirmière** student nurse.

élevé, e [ɛlve] *adj (gén)* high; *pertes* heavy; *cime* lofty. **peu ~** low; *pertes* slight; *(Jur)* **dommages-intérêts ~s** substantial damages; **bien ~** well-mannered; **mal ~** *(rustre)* ill-mannered; *(impoli)* rude; **c'est mal ~ de** it's bad manners *ou* it's rude to.

élever [ɛlve] (5) **1** *vt* (**a**) *enfant* to bring up, raise; *bétail* to rear, breed; *abeilles* to keep; *plantes* to grow; *vin* to produce. (**b**) *mur (dresser)* to put up. *(hausser)* **~ (d'un étage)** to raise (by one storey), make (one storey) higher. (**c**) *objection* to raise; *critique* to make. (**d**) *poids, regard* to lift, raise; *niveau, prix, voix* to raise. (**e**) *(promouvoir)* to raise, elevate (*au rang de* to the rank of). (**f**) *(gén, Math)* to raise. **~ un nombre au carré** to square a number.
2 s' ~ *vpr* (**a**) *[niveau, prix]* to rise, go up. *[somme]* **s' ~ à** to add up to, amount to. (**b**) *[immeuble] (se dresser)* to rise; *(se bâtir)* to go up. **un mur s'élevait entre** a wall stood between. (**c**) *[avion]* to go up; *[oiseau]* to fly up; *(dans la société)* to rise. **s' ~ jusqu'au sommet de l'échelle** to climb to the top of the ladder. (**d**) *[discussions]* to arise; *[objections, doutes]* to be raised, arise; *[voix]* to rise. **s' ~ contre** to rise up against.

éleveur, -euse [ɛlvœʀ, øz] *nm, f* stockbreeder.

elfe [ɛlf(ə)] *nm* elf.

éligible [eliʒibl(ə)] *adj (Pol)* eligible. ◆ **éligibilité** *nf* eligibility.

élimer *vt*, **s' ~** *vpr* [elime] (1) to fray.

éliminer [elimine] (1) *vt (gén, Math, Méd)* to eliminate; *données secondaires* to discard. ◆ **élimination** *nf* elimination. ◆ **éliminatoire 1** *adj épreuve* eliminatory; *note* disqualifying. **2** *nf (Sport)* heat.

élire [eliʀ] (43) *vt* to elect. **il a été élu président** he was elected president, he was voted in as president.

élite [elit] *nf* élite. **l' ~** the cream *ou* élite; **d' ~** *élève* first-class; *âme* noble; *(Mil)* **corps d' ~** crack corps. ◆ **élitisme** *nm* élitism.

élixir [eliksiʀ] *nm* elixir.

elle [ɛl] *pron pers f* (**a**) *(sujet) (personne, nation)* she; *(chose)* it; *(animal, bébé)* she, it. **~s** they; **~, ~ n'aurait jamais fait ça** SHE would never have done that; **~ renoncer?** HER give up? (**b**) *(objet) (personne, nation)* her; *(animal)* her, it; *(chose)* it. **~s** them; **c'est ~ qui me l'a dit** she told me herself, it's she who told me; *(iro)* **c'est ~s qui le disent** that's what THEY say!; **c'est ~ que j'avais invitée** it's her I had invited. (**c**) (*avec prép*) *(personne)* her; *(animal)* her, it; *(chose)* it. **ce livre est à ~** this book belongs to her *ou* is hers; **ces disques sont à ~s** these records belong to them *ou* are theirs; **elle ne pense qu'à ~** she only thinks of herself; **elle a une maison à ~** she has a house of her own; **ses enfants à ~** HER children. (**d**) *(comparaison) (sujet)* she; *(objet)* her. **il est plus grand qu' ~s** he is taller than they are *ou* than them. (**e**) *(interrog, emphatique)* **sa lettre est-~ arrivée?** has his (*ou* her) letter come?; **ta tante, ~ n'est pas très aimable!** your aunt isn't very nice!

ellipse [elips(ə)] *nf (Géom)* ellipse; *(Ling)* ellipsis.

élocution [elɔkysjɔ̃] *nf (débit)* delivery; *(clarté)* diction. **défaut d' ~** speech impediment.

éloge [elɔʒ] *nm* (**a**) *(louange)* **~(s)** praise; **faire des ~s à qn** to praise sb; **faire l' ~ de** to praise; **faire son propre ~** to sing one's own praises. (**b**) *(panégyrique)* eulogy. **~ funèbre** funeral oration. ◆ **élogieusement** *adv parler* very highly. ◆ **élogieux, -ieuse** *adj* laudatory.

éloigné, e [elwaɲe] *adj (dans l'espace)* distant, remote, far-off; *événement* distant, remote (*de* from); *parent* distant; *ancêtre* remote. **est-ce très**

~ de la gare? — oui, c'est très ~ is it very far *ou* a long way from the station? — yes, it's a long way; **~ de 3 km** 3 km away; **dans un avenir peu ~** in the not-too-distant future; **sentiment pas très ~ de la haine** emotion not far removed from hatred; **rien n'est plus ~ de mes pensées** nothing is farther from my thoughts; **tenir ~ de** to keep away from; **se tenir ~ des querelles** to steer clear of quarrels.

éloignement [elwaɲmɑ̃] *nm (gén)* removal; *(report)* postponement; *(désaffection)* estrangement; *(banissement)* banishment; *(distance)* distance. **avec l' ~** *(temps, espace)* from a distance.

éloigner [elwaɲe] (1) **1** *vt* (**a**) *objet* to move *ou* take away; *personne* to take away; *(fig: exiler)* to send away (*de* from). *(fig)* **~ qn de** *être aimé* to estrange sb from; *tentations* to remove sb from. (**b**) *(fig: dissiper) (gén)* to remove; *idée, crainte* to dismiss; *danger* to ward off; *soupçons* to avert (*de* from). (**c**) *visite (reporter)* to put off, postpone; *(espacer)* to space out. **2 s' ~** *vpr (gén)* to go away (*de* from); *[souvenir]* to grow more distant *ou* remote. **s' ~ en courant** to run away *ou* off; **éloignez-vous, les enfants** move *ou* stand back, children; **s' ~ de** *être aimé* to grow away from; *sujet* to wander from; *position prise* to move away from; *devoir, vérité* to stray from; **s' ~ du droit chemin** to stray from the straight and narrow.

élongation [elɔ̃gɑsjɔ̃] *nf*: **se faire une ~** to strain a muscle.

éloquent, e [elɔkɑ̃, ɑ̃t] *adj* eloquent. **ces chiffres sont ~s** these figures speak for themselves; **un silence ~** a silence that speaks volumes, a meaningful *ou* an eloquent silence. ◆ **éloquemment** *adv* eloquently. ◆ **éloquence** *nf* eloquence.

élu, e [ely] **1** *adj (Rel)* chosen; *(Pol)* elected. **2** *nm, f (député)* elected member; *(conseiller)* councillor. **les ~s locaux** the local *ou* town councillors. *(hum)* **l'heureux ~** the lucky man; *(Rel)* **les É~s** the Chosen ones, the Elect.

élucider [elyside] (1) *vt* to elucidate. ◆ **élucidation** *nf* elucidation.

élucubrations [elykybʀɑsjɔ̃] *nfpl (péj)* wild imaginings.

éluder [elyde] (1) *vt* to evade, elude.

Élysée [elize] *nm:* **(le palais de) l' ~** the Élysée palace; **les Champs-~s** the Champs-Élysées.

émacié, e [emasje] *adj* emaciated.

émailler [emaje] (1) *vt (lit)* to enamel; *[étoiles]* to spangle; *[fautes]* to pepper. **voyage émaillé d'incidents** journey punctuated by incidents. ◆ **émail,** *pl* **-aux** *nm* enamel. **en ~** enamel(led); *(Art)* **~aux** pieces of enamel work. ◆ **émaillage** *nm* enamelling.

émanation [emanɑsjɔ̃] *nf* (**a**) *(odeurs)* **~s** smells, emanations; **~s toxiques** toxic fumes. (**b**) *(fig)* product.

émanciper [emɑ̃sipe] (1) **1** *vt (Jur)* to emancipate; *esprit* to liberate. **2 s' ~** *vpr* to become liberated. ◆ **émancipation** *nf* emancipation; liberation.

émaner [emane] (1) **~ de** *vt indir [pouvoir, ordres]* to come from; *[chaleur, odeur]* to emanate *ou* come from; *[charme]* to emanate from.

émarger [emaʀʒe] (3) **1** *vt* to sign. **2** *vi* to be paid. ◆ **émargement** *nm* signing. **feuille d' ~** *(paye)* paysheet; *(présence)* attendance sheet.

emballer [ɑ̃bale] (1) **1** *vt* (**a**) *(empaqueter)* to pack (up); *(dans du papier)* to wrap up. (**b**) (⁑*: emprisonner)* to run in ⁑. (**c**) *moteur* to race. (**d**) *(*: enthousiasmer)* to thrill. **2 s' ~** *vpr* (**a**) (*) *(enthousiasme)* to get carried away; *(colère)* to fly off the handle *. (**b**) *[moteur]* to race; *[cheval]* to bolt. **cheval emballé** bolting horse. ◆ **emballage** *nm* packing; wrapping-up; *(boîte etc)* package. ◆ **emballement** *nm* (**a**) (*) *(enthousiasme)* craze; *(colère)* angry outburst, flash of anger. (**b**) *[moteur]* racing; *[cheval]* bolting.

embarcadère [ɑ̃baʀkadɛʀ] *nm* landing stage.

embarcation [ɑ̃baʀkɑsjɔ̃] *nf* (small) boat *ou* craft *(inv)*.

embardée [ɑ̃baʀde] *nf (Aut)* swerve. **faire une ~** to swerve.

embargo [ɑ̃baʀgo] *nm* embargo. **mettre l' ~ sur qch** to put an embargo on sth.

embarquer [ɑ̃baʀke] (1) **1** *vt passagers* to embark; *cargaison* to load; (⁑) *(emporter, emprisonner)* to cart off *; *(voler)* to pinch *. **se faire ~ par la police** to get picked up by the police *; **~ qn dans une histoire** to get sb mixed up in * *ou* involved in an affair. **2** *vi (aussi* **s' ~** *) (en bateau)* to embark, board, go aboard; *(en train, avion)* to board. **~ pour la France** to sail for France. **3 s' ~** *vpr* (**a**) = **2.** (**b**) **s' ~ dans** *aventure* to embark on. ◆ **embarquement** *nm* loading; embarkation; boarding.

embarras [ɑ̃baʀa] *nm (ennui)* trouble; *(gêne)* confusion, embarrassment; *(situation délicate)* predicament, awkward position. **être dans l' ~** to be in a predicament *ou* an awkward position; *(dans un dilemme)* to be in a quandary *ou* in a dilemma; *(sans argent)* to be in financial difficulties; **~ gastrique** stomach upset; **~ de circulation** (road) congestion; **faire des ~** *(chichis)* to make a fuss; *(ennuis)* to make trouble (*à qn* for sb); **je ne veux pas être un ~ pour vous** I don't want to bother you, I don't want to be a nuisance *ou* trouble to you *ou* to be in your way; **ne vous mettez pas dans l' ~ pour moi** don't put yourself out for me; **elle a l' ~ du choix** her only problem is that she has too great a choice.

embarrasser [ɑ̃baʀase] (1) **1** *vt* (**a**) *[paquets]* to clutter; *[vêtements]* to hinder, hamper. **ça m'embarrasse** it's in my way; **~ l'estomac** to lie heavy on the stomach. (**b**) *(désorienter)* **~ qn** to put sb in a predicament *ou* an awkward position; **~ qn par des questions indiscrètes** to embarrass sb with indiscreet questions; **ça m'embarrasse de te le dire mais...** I don't like to tell you this but...; **il y a qch qui m'embarrasse là-dedans** there's sth about it that bothers me. **2 s' ~** *vpr*: **s' ~ de** *paquets, scrupules* to burden o.s. with; *détails* to trouble o.s. *ou* worry about; **s' ~ dans** *vêtements* to get tangled up in; *explications* to get in a muddle with, get mixed up in. ◆ **embarrassant, e** *adj* (**a**) *situation* embarrassing; *problème* awkward. (**b**) *paquets* cumbersome. **cet enfant est ~!** this child is always in the way! ◆ **embarrassé, e** *adj (gêné)* embarrassed; *(peu clair)* muddled, confused; *(encombré)* cluttered. **avoir l'estomac ~** to have an upset stomach; **j'ai les mains ~es** my hands are full.

embaucher [ɑ̃boʃe] (1) *vt* to take on, hire. ◆ **embauche** *nf* hiring. **est-ce qu'il y a de l' ~?** are there any vacancies?; **bureau d' ~** labour *ou* employment office.

embaumer [ɑ̃bome] (1) **1** *vt cadavre* to embalm. **l'air embaumait le lilas** the air was fragrant with the scent of lilac. **2** *vi* to be fragrant. ◆ **embaumé, e** *adj air* balmy, fragrant. ◆ **embaumement** *nm* embalming.

embellir [ɑ̃beliʀ] (2) **1** *vt (gén)* to beautify, make (more) attractive; *récit* to embellish. **2** *vi* to grow more attractive. ◆ **embellissement** *nm* improvement; *[récit]* embellishment.

embêter * [ɑ̃bete] (1) **1** *vt (gén)* to bother, worry; *(importuner)* to pester; *(irriter)* to annoy; *(lasser)* to bore. **2 s' ~** *vpr* to be bored. ◆ **embêtant, e** * *adj* worrying, annoying; *situation* awkward, tricky. ◆ **embêtement** * *nm* problem, trouble. **causer des ~s à qn** to make trouble for sb.

emblée [ɑ̃ble] *adv*: **d'** ~ straightaway, right away. **détester qn d'** ~ to detest sb on sight, take an instant dislike to sb.

emblème [ɑ̃blɛm] *nm* emblem.

emboîter [ɑ̃bwate] (1) **1** *vt* to fit together. ~ **qch dans** to fit sth into; ~ **le pas à qn** *(lit)* to follow close on sb's heels; *(fig: imiter)* to follow suit. **2 s'** ~ *vpr* to fit together.

embonpoint [ɑ̃bɔ̃pwɛ̃] *nm* stoutness. **avoir/prendre de l'** ~ to be/get stout.

embouchure [ɑ̃buʃyʀ] *nf [fleuve]* mouth; *(Mus)* mouthpiece.

embourber *vt*, **s'** ~ *vpr* [ɑ̃buʀbe] (1) *voiture* to get stuck in the mud.

embourgeoiser (s') [ɑ̃buʀʒwaze] (1) *vpr* to become middle-class.

embout [ɑ̃bu] *nm [canne]* tip; *[tuyau]* nozzle.

embouteiller [ɑ̃buteje] (1) *vt (Aut)* to jam, block; *(Téléc) lignes* to block. **les routes sont très embouteillées** the roads are very congested. ◆ **embouteillage** *nm (Aut)* traffic jam, holdup.

emboutir [ɑ̃butiʀ] (2) *vt métal* to stamp; *(Aut: percuter)* to crash *ou* run into. **avoir une aile emboutie** to have a dented *ou* damaged wing; **il s'est fait** ~ **par un camion** he was hit by a lorry, his car was dented by a lorry.

embranchement [ɑ̃bʀɑ̃ʃmɑ̃] *nm (jonction)* junction; *(route)* side road; *(voie)* branch line; *(rivière)* embranchment; *(Bot, Zool: catégorie)* branch. **à l'** ~ **des 2 routes** at the fork in the roads, where the roads fork.

embraser [ɑ̃bʀɑze] (1) **1** *vt forêt etc* to set ablaze; *cœur* to fire. **2 s'** ~ *vpr* to blaze up; to be fired (*de* with); *[pays en révolte]* to rise up in arms. ◆ **embrasement** *nm (action)* blazing-up; *(résultat)* blaze.

embrasser [ɑ̃bʀase] (1) **1** *vt* to kiss; *(étreindre)* to embrace; *cause, aspects* to embrace; *carrière* to take up. ~ **qch du regard** to take sth in at a glance. **2 s'** ~ *vpr* to kiss (each other). ◆ **embrassade** *nf* embrace.

embrasure [ɑ̃bʀɑzyʀ] *nf* embrasure. **dans l'** ~ **de la porte** in the doorway.

embrayer [ɑ̃bʀeje] (8) **1** *vt (Aut, Tech)* to put into gear. **2** *vi (Aut)* to let in *ou* engage the clutch. ◆ **embrayage** *nm (mécanisme)* clutch; *(action)* engaging the clutch.

embrigader [ɑ̃bʀigade] (1) *vt* to dragoon (*dans* into).

embrocher [ɑ̃bʀɔʃe] (1) *vt (Culin) (broche)* to spit; *(brochette)* to skewer. *(fig)* ~ **qn** to run sb through.

embrouille * [ɑ̃bʀuj] *nf*: **il y a de l'** ~ **là-dessous** there's some hanky-panky * *ou* something funny at the bottom of this; **toutes ces** ~**s** all this carry-on *.

embrouiller [ɑ̃bʀuje] (1) **1** *vt (gén)* to muddle up; *ficelle* to tangle (up). **2 s'** ~ *vpr [idées, situation]* to become muddled *ou* confused; *[personne]* to get in a muddle, become confused. **s'** ~ **dans** to get in a muddle with. ◆ **embrouillement** *nm (action)* tangling; muddling up; confusion; *(état)* tangle; muddle; confusion.

embroussaillé, e [ɑ̃bʀusɑje] *adj chemin* overgrown; *barbe* bushy, shaggy.

embrumer [ɑ̃bʀyme] (1) *vt* to mist over, cloud over (*de* with). **il avait l'esprit embrumé par l'alcool** his mind was fuddled *ou* clouded with drink.

embruns [ɑ̃bʀœ̃] *nmpl* spindrift, sea spray.

embryon [ɑ̃bʀijɔ̃] *nm* embryo. ◆ **embryonnaire** *adj* embryonic.

embûche [ɑ̃byʃ] *nf* pitfall, trap.

embuer [ɑ̃bɥe] (1) *vt* to mist up *ou* over.

embuscade [ɑ̃byskad] *nf* ambush. **être en** ~ to lie in ambush. ◆ **s'embusquer** (1) *vpr* to lie in ambush.

éméché, e [emeʃe] *adj* tipsy, merry.

émeraude [ɛmʀod] *nf, adj inv* emerald.

émerger [emɛʀʒe] (3) *vi* to emerge; *(faire saillie)* to stand out. ~ **du brouillard** to rise out of the fog. ◆ **émergence** *nf* emergence.

émeri [ɛmʀi] *nm* emery. **toile** ~ emery paper.

émerveiller [emɛʀveje] (1) **1** *vt* to fill with wonder. **2 s'** ~ *vpr* to be filled with wonder. **s'** ~ **de** to marvel at. ◆ **émerveillement** *nm (sentiment)* wonder; *(vision)* marvel.

émettre [emɛtʀ(ə)] (56) *vt (gén)* to emit; *lumière* to give out; *son* to send out; *odeur* to give off; *(Rad, TV)* to transmit; *monnaie, emprunt* to issue; *chèque* to draw; *hypothèse* to put forward; *vœux* to express. ~ **sur ondes courtes** to broadcast *ou* transmit on short wave. ◆ **émetteur, -trice 1** *adj (Rad)* transmitting; *(Fin)* issuing. **2** *nm* transmitter. ~**-récepteur** transmitter-receiver.

émeute [emøt] *nf* riot. ~**s** riots, rioting. ◆ **émeutier, -ière** *nm, f* rioter.

émietter *vt*, **s'** ~ *vpr* [emjete] (1) *pain, terre* to crumble; *pouvoir* to disperse; *énergie* to dissipate. ◆ **émiettement** *nm* crumbling; dispersion; dissipation.

émigrer [emigʀe] (1) *vi* to emigrate. ◆ **émigrant, e** *nm, f* emigrant. ◆ **émigration** *nf* emigration. ◆ **émigré, e** *nm, f (Hist)* émigré; *(Pol)* expatriate. *(Écon)* **(travailleur)** ~ migrant worker.

émincer [emɛ̃se] (3) *vt* to slice thinly.

éminence [eminɑ̃s] *nf [terrain]* hill, rise; *[qualité]* distinction, eminence; *(cardinal)* Eminence. *(fig)* ~ **grise** éminence grise. ◆ **éminemment** *adv* eminently. ◆ **éminent, e** *adj* distinguished, eminent.

émir [emiʀ] *nm* emir. ◆ **émirat** *nm* emirate. **les É~s arabes unis** the United Arab Emirates.

émissaire [emisɛʀ] *nm (gén)* emissary.

émission [emisjɔ̃] *nf* (**a**) *(V* **émettre***)* emission; transmission; broadcast; issue; *actions* flotation; drawing. (**b**) *(Rad, TV: spectacle)* programme, broadcast. ~ **(de télévision) par câble** cablecast.

emmagasiner [ɑ̃magazine] (1) *vt (gén: amasser)* to accumulate; *chaleur* to store; *(Comm)* to store. ◆ **emmagasinage** *nm* accumulation; storage.

emmailloter [ɑ̃majɔte] (1) *vt* to wrap up.

emmêler [ɑ̃mele] (1) **1** *vt fil* to tangle (up); *(fig) affaire* to confuse, muddle. *(fig)* **tu emmêles tout** you're getting everything muddled (up) *ou* confused. **2 s'** ~ *vpr (lit)* to get in a tangle; *(fig)* to get in a muddle (*dans* with). **s'** ~ **les pieds dans le tapis** to catch one's feet in the carpet. ◆ **emmêlement** *nm (action)* tangling; *(état)* tangle; muddle.

emménager [ɑ̃menaʒe] (3) *vi* to move in. ~ **dans** to move into. ◆ **emménagement** *nm (action)* moving in. **il y a eu plusieurs** ~**s** there have been several moves.

emmener [ɑ̃mne] (5) *vt (gén)* to take; *otage* to take away. ~ **qn au cinéma** to take sb to the cinema; ~ **promener qn** to take sb for a walk.

emmitoufler [ɑ̃mitufle] (1) *vt* to wrap *ou* muffle up. **s'** ~ to wrap *ou* muffle o.s. up.

emmurer [ɑ̃myʀe] (1) *vt* to wall up, immure.

émoi [emwa] *nm (trouble)* agitation, emotion; *(de joie)* excitement; *(tumulte)* commotion. **en** ~ *cœur* in a flutter; *sens* agitated, excited; *rue* in turmoil, in a commotion.

émoluments [emɔlymɑ̃] *nmpl (Admin)* emolument, fee.

émotion [emosjɔ̃] *nf* emotion; *(peur)* fright. **donner des** ~**s à qn** * to give sb a nasty turn * *ou* fright. ◆ **émotif, -ive** *adj* emotional. ◆ **émotionnel,**

-elle *adj* emotional. ◆ **émotionner** * (1) **1** *vt* to upset. **2 s'** ~ *vpr* to get upset (*de* about). ◆ **émotivité** *nf* emotionalism.

émoulu, e [emuly] *adj*: **frais** ~ **(de l'école)** fresh from school, just out of school.

émoussé, e [emuse] *adj couteau* blunt; *goût* blunted, dulled.

émoustiller * [emustije] (1) *vt* to tantalize.

émouvoir [emuvwaʀ] (27) **1** *vt [beauté]* to rouse, stir; *[misère]* to touch, move; *[menace]* to disturb, worry, upset. ~ **qn jusqu'aux larmes** to move sb to tears; **se laisser** ~ **par des prières** to be moved by entreaties; ~ **la pitié de qn** to move sb to pity, rouse sb's pity. **2 s'** ~ *vpr* to be roused *ou* stirred *ou* touched *ou* moved *ou* disturbed *ou* worried *ou* upset (*de* by). **il ne s'émeut de rien** nothing upsets *ou* disturbs him. ◆ **émouvant, e** *adj* moving, touching.

empailler [ɑ̃pɑje] (1) *vt animal* to stuff. ◆ **empailleur, -euse** *nm, f* taxidermist.

empaqueter [ɑ̃pakte] (4) *vt marchandises* to pack; *colis* to wrap up.

emparer (s') [ɑ̃paʀe] (1) *vpr* (**a**) *[personne]* **s'** ~ **de** *(gén)* to seize; *objet* to grab (hold of), snatch up; *conversation* to take over; *prétexte* to seize on; *(fig)* **les journaux se sont emparés de l'affaire** the papers picked up the story. (**b**) *[sentiment]* **s'** ~ **de** to take *ou* seize hold of; **le remords s'empara d'elle** she was seized with remorse.

empâter [ɑ̃pɑte] (1) **1** *vt bouche* to coat, fur (up); *traits* to thicken, coarsen. **2 s'** ~ *vpr [silhouette]* to thicken out.

empêcher [ɑ̃peʃe] (1) **1** *vt* to prevent, stop. ~ **que qch (ne) se produise** to prevent sth from happening, stop sth happening; ~ **qn de faire** to prevent sb from doing, stop sb (from) doing; *(fig)* **ça ne m'empêche pas de dormir** I don't lose any sleep over it; **ça n'empêche rien** * it makes no odds * *ou* no difference; **(il) n'empêche qu'il a tort** nevertheless *ou* all the same he's wrong. **2 s'** ~ *vpr*: **s'** ~ **de faire** to stop o.s. (from) doing, refrain from doing; **il n'a pas pu s'** ~ **de rire** he couldn't help laughing, he couldn't stop himself (from) laughing. ◆ **empêché, e** *adj (retenu)* detained, held up. **il a été** ~ **par ses obligations** his commitments prevented him from coming; **tu es bien** ~ **de me le dire** you seem at a loss to know what to tell me. ◆ **empêchement** *nm* (unexpected) difficulty, hitch. **il a eu un** ~ sth prevented him from coming.

empereur [ɑ̃pʀœʀ] *nm* emperor.

empeser [ɑ̃pəze] (5) *vt* to starch. ◆ **empesé, e** *adj col* starched; *(fig)* stiff, starchy.

empester [ɑ̃pɛste] (1) *vt odeur* to stink of, reek of; *pièce* to stink out (*de* with). **ça empeste ici** it stinks in here, it smells foul in here.

empêtrer (s') [ɑ̃petʀe] (1) *vpr*: **s'** ~ **dans** *habits, explications* to get tangled up in; *affaire* to get (o.s.) mixed up in.

emphase [ɑ̃fɑz] *nf* pomposity. **sans** ~ simply. ◆ **emphatique** *adj* pompous; *(Ling)* emphatic.

empiéter [ɑ̃pjete] (6) *vi*: ~ **sur** *(lit, fig)* to encroach (up)on; *[terrain]* to overlap into; *attributions* to trespass on. ◆ **empiètement** *nm* encroachment (*sur* upon).

empiffrer (s') ‡ [ɑ̃pifʀe] (1) *vpr* to stuff o.s. * (*de* with), gorge o.s. (*de* on).

empiler [ɑ̃pile] (1) **1** *vt* to pile, stack. **2 s'** ~ *vpr* to be piled up (*sur* on). **s'** ~ **dans** *véhicule* to squeeze into. ◆ **empilement** *nm (action)* piling, stacking; *(pile)* pile, stack.

empire [ɑ̃piʀ] *nm* (**a**) *(Pol)* empire. **pas pour un** ~! not for all the world! (**b**) *(emprise)* influence, authority. **sous l'** ~ **de** *colère* in the grip of; *boisson* under the influence of; ~ **sur soi-même** self-control, self-command.

empirer [ɑ̃piʀe] (1) **1** *vi* to get worse, deteriorate. **2** *vt* to make worse.

empirique [ɑ̃piʀik] *adj* empirical. ◆ **empirisme** *nm* empiricism.

emplacement [ɑ̃plasmɑ̃] *nm (gén: endroit)* place; *(site)* site, location. **sur l'** ~ **de** on the site of.

emplâtre [ɑ̃plɑtʀ(ə)] *nm (Méd)* plaster; *(Aut)* patch.

emplette † [ɑ̃plɛt] *nf* purchase. **faire l'** ~ **de** to purchase; **faire des** ~**s** to do some shopping.

emplir [ɑ̃pliʀ] (2) **1** *vt verre, pièce* to fill (*de* with). **2 s'** ~ *vpr*: **s'** ~ **de** to fill with.

employer [ɑ̃plwaje] (8) *vt (gén)* to use; *moyen, ouvrier* to employ; *temps* to spend (*à qch* on sth, *à faire qch* doing sth). ~ **toute son énergie à faire qch** to apply *ou* devote all one's energies to doing sth; **mal** ~ to misuse; **s'** ~ **à faire qch/à qch** to apply *ou* devote o.s. to doing sth/to sth. ◆ **emploi** *nm* (**a**) *(gén)* use; *[mot]* usage. **je n'en ai pas l'** ~ I have no use for it; ~ **du temps** timetable, schedule. (**b**) *(poste)* job. **l'** ~ employment; **sans** ~ unemployed, jobless. ◆ **employé, e** *nm, f* employee. ~ **de bureau** office worker, clerk; ~ **des postes** postal worker; **l'** ~ **du gaz** the gas man; ~ **de maison** domestic employee; **les** ~**s de cette firme** the staff *ou* employees of this firm. ◆ **employeur, -euse** *nm, f* employer.

empocher * [ɑ̃pɔʃe] (1) *vt* to pocket.

empoigner [ɑ̃pwaɲe] (1) *vt* to grasp, grab hold of. **2 s'** ~ * *vpr* to have a row. ◆ **empoignade** *nf* row.

empoisonner [ɑ̃pwazɔne] (1) **1** *vt* (**a**) ~ **qn** *[assassin]* to poison sb; *[aliments]* to give sb food poisoning; *(fig:*) [contretemps]* to annoy sb; *[gêneur, travail]* to drive sb mad *. (**b**) *air* to make foul; *relations* to poison. **2 s'** ~ *vpr (lit)* to poison o.s.; *(intoxication)* to get food poisoning. *(fig:*)* to get bored. **s'** ~ **à faire qch** to go to the trouble of doing sth. ◆ **empoisonnant, e** * *adj* annoying. ◆ **empoisonné, e** *adj flèche* poisoned; *paroles* poisonous. *[personne]* **être bien** ~ to be in a real mess *. ◆ **empoisonnement** *nm* poisoning. *(*: ennui)* ~**(s)** bother. ◆ **empoisonneur, -euse** *nm, f (lit)* poisoner; *(fig:*)* bore.

emporté, e [ɑ̃pɔʀte] *adj* quick-tempered.

emportement [ɑ̃pɔʀtəmɑ̃] *nm* fit of anger, rage. **avec** ~ angrily.

emporte-pièce [ɑ̃pɔʀtəpjɛs] *nm inv (Tech)* punch. *(fig)* **à l'** ~ incisive.

emporter [ɑ̃pɔʀte] (1) **1** *vt* (**a**) *(comme bagage)* to take; *(enlever)* to take away. **si vous gagnez, vous pouvez l'** ~ **(avec vous)** if you win, you can take it away (with you); **plats chauds à** ~ take-away hot meals; **il ne l'emportera pas en paradis!** he'll soon be smiling on the other side of his face! (**b**) *[vent, train]* to carry along; *[colère, imagination]* to carry away. **emporté par son élan** carried along by his own momentum. (**c**) *(arracher) bras* to take off; *cheminée* to blow off; *pont* to wash away; *(euph: tuer) [maladie]* to carry off. **la vague a emporté 3 passagers** the wave swept 3 passengers overboard; *(fig)* **plat qui emporte la bouche** dish that takes the roof off your mouth *. (**d**) *prix* to carry off; *(Mil) position* to take, win. ~ **la décision** to carry *ou* win the day; **l'** ~ **(sur)** *[personne]* to get the upper hand (of); *[méthode]* to prevail (over); **l'** ~ **sur son adversaire** to get the better of one's opponent; **l'** ~ **sur qn en adresse** to outmatch sb in skill. **2 s'** ~ *vpr* (**a**) *(de colère)* to lose one's temper (*contre* with). (**b**) *[cheval]* to bolt.

empoté, e * [ɑ̃pɔte] **1** *adj* awkward. **2** *nm, f (péj)* awkward lump *.

empourprer *vt,* **s'** ~ *vpr* [ɑ̃puʀpʀe] (1) to turn crimson.

empreindre [ɑ̃pʀɛ̃dʀ(ə)] (52) *vt (littér)* to imprint. **empreint de** *regret* tinged with; *bonté* stamped with; *menaces* fraught with.

empreinte [ɑ̃pʀɛ̃t] *nf* (**a**) *(gén)* imprint, impression; *[animal]* track. ~ **de pas** footprint; ~**s digitales** fingerprints. (**b**) *(fig)* stamp.

empresser (s') [ɑ̃pʀese] (1) *vpr* (**a**) *(s'affairer)* to bustle about; *(péj)* to fuss about. **s'** ~ **auprès** *ou* **autour de qn** to surround sb with attentions, fuss around sb. (**b**) *(se hâter)* **s'** ~ **de faire** to hasten to do. ◆ **empressé, e** *adj serveur* attentive; *aide* willing; *admirateur* assiduous; *subordonné* overzealous. **faire l'** ~ **(auprès d'une femme)** to fuss around (a woman). ◆ **empressement** *nm* (**a**) *(zèle)* attentiveness; willingness; assiduity; overzealousness. (**b**) *(hâte)* eagerness. **il montrait peu d'** ~ **à...** he showed little desire to...

emprise [ɑ̃pʀiz] *nf* hold, ascendancy (*sur* over). **sous l'** ~ **de la colère** in the grip of anger, gripped by anger.

emprisonner [ɑ̃pʀizɔne] (1) *vt (prison)* to imprison; *(chambre)* to shut up; *[vêtement]* to confine; *[doctrine, routine]* to trap. ◆ **emprisonnement** *nm* imprisonment. **10 ans d'** ~ 10 years in prison.

emprunter [ɑ̃pʀœ̃te] (1) *vt argent, idée* to borrow (*à* from); *chaleur* to derive (*à* from); *nom, autorité* to assume, take on; *style* to use, adopt; *route* to take; *itinéraire* to follow. ◆ **emprunt** *nm (action)* borrowing; *(somme)* loan; *(Ling: mot)* borrowing. *(Fin)* **faire un** ~ to raise a loan; **faire un** ~ **pour payer sa voiture** to borrow money *ou* take out a loan to pay for one's car; **d'** ~ *nom, autorité* assumed; *matériel* borrowed. ◆ **emprunté, e** *adj air, personne* ill-at-ease, awkward; *gloire, éclat* sham, feigned. ◆ **emprunteur, -euse** *nm, f* borrower.

empuantir [ɑ̃pɥɑ̃tiʀ] (2) *vt* to stink out (*de* with).

ému, e [emy] *adj (compassion, gratitude)* moved, touched; *(joie)* excited; *(timidité, peur)* nervous, agitated; *air* filled with emotion; *voix* emotional; *souvenirs* tender. **encore tout** ~**, il la remercia** still quite overcome he thanked her.

émulateur [emylatœʀ] *nm (Ordin)* emulator.

émulation [emylɑsjɔ̃] *nf* emulation. ◆ **émule** *nmf (littér)* emulator; *(égal)* equal.

émulsion [emylsjɔ̃] *nf* emulsion.

en¹ [ɑ̃] *prép* (**a**) *(lieu)* in; *(direction)* to. **vivre** ~ **France** to live in France; **aller** ~ **Angleterre** to go to England; **de ville** ~ **ville** from town to town; **il voyage** ~ **Grèce** he's travelling around Greece; **être** ~ **ville** to be in town; **aller** ~ **ville** to go (in)to town. (**b**) *(date)* in. ~ **semaine** in *ou* during the week; **de jour** ~ **jour** from day to day, daily. (**c**) *(moyen de transport)* by. ~ **taxi** by taxi; **aller à Londres** ~ **avion** to fly to London; **ils y sont allés** ~ **voiture** they went by car *ou* in a car, they drove there. (**d**) *(état, manière)* in, on. ~ **sang** covered in *ou* with blood; **être** ~ **sueur** to be bathed in sweat; **partir** ~ **vacances** to go on holiday; ~ **flammes** on fire, in flames; **être** ~ **noir** to be dressed in black, be wearing black; **elle était** ~ **bigoudis** she was in her rollers; **être** ~ **guerre** to be at war; **carte** ~ **couleur** coloured postcard; ~ **groupe/cercle** in a group/circle. (**e**) *(transformation) traduire, changer etc* into. **se déguiser** ~ to dress up as; **casser** ~ **deux/en deux morceaux** to cut in two/into two pieces. (**f**) *(variante)* in. **la même valise** ~ **plus grand** the same suitcase in a bigger size. (**g**) *(conformité)* as. ~ **tant qu'ami** as a friend; **agir** ~ **tyran** to act like a tyrant; ~ **bon commerçant (qu'il est)** good tradesman that he is; **donné** ~ **cadeau** given as a present. (**h**) *(composition)* made of; *(présentation)* in. **c'est** ~ **or** it is made of gold; **une bague** ~ **or** a gold ring; **c'est** ~ **quoi?** * what's it made of?; ~ **6 volumes** in 6 volumes; **écrit** ~ **prose** written in prose. (**i**) *(matière)* in, at, of. ~ **musique** in music; **bon** ~ **géographie** good at geography; **docteur** ~ **droit** doctor of law. (**j**) *(mesure)* in. **compter** ~ **francs** to count in francs; ~ **long** lengthwise; ~ **hauteur** in height. (**k**) *(avec gérondif)* **monter/entrer** ~ **courant** to run up/in; **elle est arrivée** ~ **chantant** she arrived singing, she was singing when she arrived; **endormir un enfant** ~ **le berçant** to rock a child to sleep; **faire obéir qn** ~ **le punissant** to make sb obey by punishing him; **se couper** ~ **ouvrant qch** to cut o.s. opening sth; **il a fait une folie** ~ **achetant cette bague** it was very extravagant of him to buy this ring; **aller jusqu'à la poste** ~ **se promenant** to go for a walk as far as the post office; ~ **apprenant la nouvelle** when he heard the news, on hearing the news; **il a buté** ~ **montant dans l'autobus** he tripped getting into *ou* as he got into the bus; **il s'est endormi** ~ **lisant le journal** he fell asleep while reading the newspaper; **fermez la porte** ~ **sortant** shut the door as you go out; **il est sorti** ~ **haussant les épaules** he left with a shrug of his shoulders.

en² [ɑ̃] *pron* (**a**) *(lieu)* **il** ~ **revient** he's just come back (from there); **le bénéfice qu'il** ~ **a tiré** the profit he got out of it *ou* from it; **où** ~ **sommes-nous?** where are we now? (**b**) *(agent etc)* **il saisit sa canne et l'** ~ **frappa** he seized his stick and struck him with it; ~ **mourir** *(maladie)* to die of it; *(blessure)* to die because of it *ou* as a result of it; **elle** ~ **est aimée** she is loved by him. (**c**) *(complément de vb, d'adj, de n)* **qu'est-ce que tu** ~ **feras?** what will you do with it (*ou* them)?; **je t'** ~ **donne/offre 10 F** I'll give/offer you 10 francs for it. (**d**) *(quantitatif, indéf)* of it, of them *(souvent omis)*. **si vous aimez les pommes, prenez-**~ **plusieurs** if you like apples, take several; **il n'y** ~ **a pas beaucoup** there isn't much (of it); **si j'** ~ **avais** if I had any; **il n'y** ~ **a plus** *(pain)* there isn't any left, there's none left; *(pommes)* there aren't any left, there are none left; **j'** ~ **ai assez** I've had enough (of it); **il** ~ **aime une autre** he loves somebody else. (**e**) *(renforcement) non traduit.* **il s'** ~ **souviendra de cette réception** he'll certainly remember that party. (**f**) *(locutions verbales) non traduit.* **il** ~ **est à penser que** he has come to think that; **ne vous** ~ **faites pas** don't worry, never mind; **il** ~ **va de même pour** the same goes for.

encadrer [ɑ̃kɑdʀe] (1) *vt tableau* to frame; *visage, plaine* to frame, surround; *étudiants, recrues* to train; *prisonnier* to surround; *(par 2 personnes)* to flank. **je ne peux pas l'** ~ ⁑ I can't stand him *. ◆ **encadrement** *nm* (**a**) framing; training. **personnel d'** ~ *(Admin)* executive *ou* managerial staff. (**b**) *(embrasure, cadre)* frame. **dans l'** ~ **de la porte** in the doorway. (**c**) *(Écon)* ~ **du crédit** credit squeeze *ou* restriction.

encaisser [ɑ̃kese] (1) *vt* (**a**) *argent* to collect, receive; *chèque* to cash. (**b**) (*) *coups, défaite* to take. **qu'est-ce qu'il a encaissé!** what a hammering he got! * (**c**) (⁑) **je ne peux pas l'** ~ *personne* I can't stand him *; *décision* I can't take it *. ◆ **encaissé, e** *adj vallée* deep; *route* hemmed in by steep hills. ◆ **encaissement** *nm (Fin)* collection; receipt; cashing; *[vallée]* depth. ◆ **encaisseur** *nm* collector (of debts *etc*).

encart [ɑ̃kaʀ] *nm* insert, inset. ~ **publicitaire** publicity *ou* advertising insert.

en-cas [ɑ̃kɑ] *nm (nourriture)* snack.

encastrer [ɑ̃kastʀe] (1) **1** *vt (dans mur)* to embed (*dans* in); *(dans boîtier)* to fit (*dans* into). **four encastré** built-in oven. **2 s'** ~ *vpr [pièces]* to fit (*dans* into).

encaustique [ɑ̃kɔstik] *nf* polish. ◆ **encaustiquer** (1) *vt* to polish.

enceindre [ɑ̃sɛ̃dʀ(ə)] (52) *vt* to encircle, surround.

enceinte¹ [ɑ̃sɛ̃t] *adj f* pregnant (*de qn* by sb). ~ **de 5 mois** 5 months pregnant.

enceinte[2] [ɑ̃sɛ̃t] *nf* (**a**) *(mur)* wall; *(palissade)* enclosure, fence. **mur d'** ~ surrounding wall. (**b**) *(espace clos)* enclosure; *[couvent]* precinct. **dans l'** ~ **de la ville** inside the town; ~ **militaire** military area *ou* zone. (**c**) ~ **(acoustique)** loudspeaker.

encens [ɑ̃sɑ̃] *nm* incense. ◆ **encenser** (1) *vt* to incense; *(fig)* to heap praise upon. ◆ **encensoir** *nm* censer.

encercler [ɑ̃sɛʀkle] (1) *vt* to surround. ◆ **encerclement** *nm* surrounding.

enchaîner [ɑ̃ʃene] (1) **1** *vt* (**a**) *prisonnier* to chain up (*à* to); *(fig) peuple* to enslave; *presse* to muzzle; *[secret, sentiment]* to bind. (**b**) *faits, épisodes* to link together, connect. **2** *vi* to go on, continue; *(Ciné, Théât)* to move on. **3 s'** ~ *vpr* to be linked (together). ◆ **enchaînement** *nm (liaison)* linking; *(Danse)* enchaînement. *(série)* ~ **de** *circonstances* series *ou* string *ou* sequence of.

enchanter [ɑ̃ʃɑ̃te] (1) *vt (ensorceler)* to enchant, bewitch; *(ravir)* to enchant, delight. ◆ **enchanté, e** *adj* (**a**) *(ravi)* enchanted (*de* by), delighted (*de* with). ~ **(de vous connaître)** pleased to meet you. (**b**) *(magique)* enchanted. ◆ **enchantement** *nm (magie)* enchantment; *(ravissement)* delight, enchantment. **comme par** ~ as if by magic. ◆ **enchanteur, -teresse 1** *adj* enchanting. **2** *nm (sorcier)* enchanter; *(fig)* charmer. **3** *nf* enchantress.

enchère [ɑ̃ʃɛʀ] *nf* (**a**) *(Comm, Cartes: offre)* bid. **les** ~**s** the bidding. (**b**) *(vente)* **mettre aux** ~**s** to put up for auction; **vendu aux** ~**s** sold by auction.

enchérir [ɑ̃ʃeʀiʀ] (2) *vi (Comm)* to make a higher bid. *(fig)* ~ **sur** to go further than.

enchevêtrer [ɑ̃ʃ(ə)vetʀe] (1) **1** *vt ficelle* to tangle (up); *idées, intrigue* to confuse, muddle. **2 s'** ~ *vpr [ficelles]* to become entangled; *[situations]* to become confused *ou* muddled. **s'** ~ **dans** *explications* to get tangled up in. ◆ **enchevêtrement** *nm [ficelles] (action)* entanglement; *(résultat)* tangle; *[idées, situation]* confusion, muddle.

enclave [ɑ̃klav] *nf (lit, fig)* enclave. ◆ **enclavement** *nm (action)* enclosing; *(résultat)* enclosed situation. ◆ **enclaver** (1) *vt* to enclose.

enclencher [ɑ̃klɑ̃ʃe] (1) *vt mécanisme* to engage; *affaire* to set in motion, get under way.

enclin, e [ɑ̃klɛ̃, in] *adj*: ~ **à qch/à faire qch** inclined *ou* prone to sth/to do sth.

enclore [ɑ̃klɔʀ] (45) *vt* to enclose, shut in. ◆ **enclos** *nm (gén)* enclosure; *[chevaux]* paddock; *[moutons]* fold.

enclume [ɑ̃klym] *nf* anvil. *(fig)* **entre l'** ~ **et le marteau** between the devil and the deep blue sea.

encoche [ɑ̃kɔʃ] *nf* notch (*à* in).

encoder [ɑ̃kɔde] (1) *vt* to encode. ◆ **encodage** *nm* encoding. ◆ **encodeur** *nm* encoder.

encoignure [ɑ̃kɔɲyʀ] *nf* corner.

encoller [ɑ̃kɔle] (1) *vt papier* to paste; *(colle forte)* to glue.

encolure [ɑ̃kɔlyʀ] *nf (cou)* neck; *(mesure)* collar size.

encombrer [ɑ̃kɔ̃bʀe] (1) **1** *vt pièce, mémoire* to clutter (up); *couloir* to obstruct; *profession* to saturate; *(Téléc) lignes* to block; *(Comm) marché* to glut. **ces boîtes m'encombrent** *(je les porte)* I'm loaded down with these boxes; *(elles gênent)* these boxes are in my way. **2 s'** ~ *vpr*: **s'** ~ **de** *paquets* to load o.s. with; *enfants* to burden o.s. with; **il ne s'encombre pas de scrupules** he's not overburdened with scruples. ◆ **encombrant, e** *adj paquet* cumbersome, bulky; *présence* burdensome. ◆ **encombre** *nm*: **sans** ~ without mishap *ou* incident. ◆ **encombrement** *nm* (**a**) *(gén)* congestion; *(Aut)* traffic jam. **être pris dans un** ~ to be stuck in a traffic jam. **à cause de l'** ~ **des lignes téléphoniques** because of the telephone lines being blocked. (**b**) *(volume)* bulk; *(taille)* size. **objet de faible** ~ small object.

encontre [ɑ̃kɔ̃tʀ(ə)] *prép*: **à l'** ~ **de** *(contre)* against; *(au contraire de)* contrary to; **aller à l'** ~ **de** *[décision]* to go against; **cela va à l'** ~ **du but recherché** it's counterproductive, it defeats the purpose.

encore [ɑ̃kɔʀ] *adv* (**a**) *(toujours)* still. **il n'est** ~ **que caporal** he's only a corporal as yet, he's still only a corporal; **le malfaiteur court** ~ the criminal is still at large. (**b**) **pas** ~ not yet; **il n'est pas** ~ **prêt** he's not ready yet; **ça ne s'était** ~ **jamais vu** that had never been seen before. (**c**) *(pas plus tard que)* only. **ce matin** ~ only this morning. (**d**) *(de nouveau)* again. ~ **une fois** (once) again, once more, one more time; **ça s'est** ~ **défait** it has come undone (yet) again *ou* once more; ~ **vous!** (not) you again! (**e**) *(de plus)* more. ~ **un rhume** (yet) another cold; ~ **un peu de thé?** a little more tea?, more tea?; **j'en veux** ~ I want some more; **que te faut-il** ~? what else *ou* more do you want?; **pendant** ~ **2 jours** for another 2 days, for 2 more days; **mais** ~? is that all?, what else? (**f**) (*avec comp*) even, still. **il fait** ~ **plus froid qu'hier** it's even *ou* still colder than yesterday; ~ **pire** even *ou* still worse; ~ **autant** as much again (*que* as). (**g**) *(aussi)* too, also, as well. (**h**) *(restriction)* ~ **ne sait-il pas tout** even then he doesn't know everything; ~ **faut-il le faire** you still have to do it; ~ **heureux qu'il ne se soit pas plaint** (still) at least he didn't complain; **c'est passable, et** ~! it'll do, but only just!; **si** ~ if only. (**i**) *(littér)* ~ **que** even though.

encourager [ɑ̃kuʀaʒe] (3) *vt (gén)* to encourage; *équipe* to cheer. ~ **qn à l'effort** to encourage sb to make an effort. ◆ **encourageant, e** *adj* encouraging. ◆ **encouragement** *nm* encouragement.

encourir [ɑ̃kuʀiʀ] (11) *vt frais* to incur; *punition* to bring upon o.s., incur.

encrasser (s') [ɑ̃kʀase] (1) *vpr [arme]* to foul up; *[cheminée, bougie]* to soot up; *[poêle, piston]* to clog up. ◆ **encrassement** *nm* fouling up; sooting up; clogging up.

encre [ɑ̃kʀ(ə)] *nf* ink. **écrire à l'** ~ to write in ink; ~ **de Chine** Indian ink. ◆ **encrier** *nm* inkwell.

encroûter (s') * [ɑ̃kʀute] (1) *vpr [personne]* to stagnate, get into a rut. **s'** ~ **dans** *préjugés* to become entrenched in.

encyclique [ɑ̃siklik] *adj, nf*: **(lettre)** ~ encyclical.

encyclopédie [ɑ̃siklɔpedi] *nf* encyclopaedia. ◆ **encyclopédique** *adj* encyclopaedic.

endémique [ɑ̃demik] *adj (Méd, fig)* endemic.

endetter *vt*, **s'** ~ *vpr* [ɑ̃dete] (1) to get into debt. ◆ **endetté, e** *adj (lit)* in debt. *(fig)* ~ **envers qn** indebted to sb. ◆ **endettement** *nm* debt. **notre** ~ **extérieur** our foreign debt; **causer l'** ~ **de l'entreprise** to put the company in debt.

endeuiller [ɑ̃dœje] (1) *vt* to plunge into mourning; *épreuve sportive* to cast a tragic shadow over.

endiablé, e [ɑ̃djɑble] *adj* furious, wild.

endiguer [ɑ̃dige] (1) *vt fleuve* to dyke up; *révolte, invasion* to hold back, contain; *progrès* to check, hold back; *inflation, chômage* to curb.

endimanché, e [ɑ̃dimɑ̃ʃe] *adj* in one's Sunday best.

endive [ɑ̃div] *nf*: ~**(s)** chicory.

endoctriner [ɑ̃dɔktʀine] (1) *vt* to indoctrinate. ◆ **endoctrinement** *nm* indoctrination.

endolori, e [ɑ̃dɔlɔʀi] *adj* painful, aching, sore.

endommager [ɑ̃dɔmaʒe] (3) *vt* to damage. ◆ **endommagement** *nm* damaging.

endormir [ɑ̃dɔʀmiʀ] (16) **1** *vt* (**a**) *(lit, fig) personne* to send to sleep. (**b**) *douleur* to deaden; *soupçons* to allay, lull. (**c**) *(tromper)* to beguile. **se laisser** ~ **par des promesses** to let o.s. be beguiled by promises. **2 s'** ~ *vpr* (**a**) to go to sleep, fall asleep;

(euph: mourir) to pass away. *(fig)* **ce n'est pas le moment de nous** ~ now is not the time to slow up *ou* slacken off; **s'** ~ **sur ses lauriers** to rest on one's laurels. (**b**) *[ville]* to fall asleep; *[douleur]* to die down; *[facultés]* to go to sleep. ◆ **endormant, e** *adj* deadly boring. ◆ **endormi, e** *adj (lit)* sleeping, asleep; *(*: apathique)* sluggish; *(engourdi)* numb; *passion* dormant; *facultés* dulled; *ville, rue* sleepy, drowsy. **à moitié** ~ half asleep; **quel** ~ * what a sleepyhead.

endosser [ɑ̃dose] (1) *vt vêtement* to put on; *responsabilité* to take, shoulder (*de* for); *(Comm, Fin)* to endorse. ◆ **endossement** *nm* endorsement.

endroit [ɑ̃dʀwa] *nm* (**a**) *(gén)* place; *[récit]* passage, part. **un** ~ **idéal pour le pique-nique** an ideal spot *ou* place for a picnic; **les gens de l'** ~ the local people; **il arrêta sa lecture à cet** ~ he stopped reading at that point; **à quel** ~? whereabouts?, where exactly?; **par** ~**s** in places; **à l'** ~ **de** *(à l'égard de)* regarding, with regard to. (**b**) *(bon côté)* right side. **à l'** ~ *vêtement* the right way out; *objet posé* the right way round; **remets tes chaussettes à l'** ~ turn your socks right side out; **une maille à l'** ~**, une maille à l'envers** knit one, purl one.

enduire [ɑ̃dɥiʀ] (38) *vt* to coat (*de* with). ◆ **enduit** *nm* coating.

endurance [ɑ̃dyʀɑ̃s] *nf* endurance. *[coureur]* **avoir beaucoup d'** ~ to have a lot of staying power *ou* a lot of stamina. ◆ **endurant, e** *adj (fort)* tough, hardy; *(patient)* patient.

endurcir [ɑ̃dyʀsiʀ] (2) **1** *vt corps* to toughen; *âme* to harden. **2 s'** ~ *vpr* to become tough; to become hardened. ◆ **endurci, e** *adj criminel* hardened; *célibataire* confirmed. ◆ **endurcissement** *nm (action)* toughening; hardening; *(état)* toughness; hardness. ~ **à la douleur** being hardened to pain.

endurer [ɑ̃dyʀe] (1) *vt* to endure, bear. ~ **de faire** to bear to do; **il fait froid, on endure un pull** it's cold, one needs a jersey.

énergétique [enɛʀʒetik] *adj ressources* energy; *aliment* energy-giving. *(Physiol)* **dépense** ~ energy expenditure; *(Écon)* **nos dépenses** ~**s** the nation's fuel *ou* energy bill.

énergie [enɛʀʒi] *nf* (**a**) *(physique)* energy; *(morale)* spirit, vigour. **avec toute son** ~ with all one's energy; **être sans** ~ to feel unenergetic, be lacking in energy. (**b**) *(Phys)* energy; *(Tech)* power. **réaction qui libère de l'** ~ reaction that releases energy; **consommation d'** ~ power consumption. ◆ **énergique** *adj personne* energetic; *résistance, ton, refus* forceful, vigorous; *remède* powerful; *mesures* drastic; *punition* severe. ◆ **énergiquement** *adv* energetically; forcefully; vigorously; powerfully; drastically; severely.

énergumène [enɛʀgymɛn] *nmf* rowdy character.

énerver [enɛʀve] (1) **1** *vt*: ~ **qn** *(agiter)* to overstimulate *ou* overexcite sb; *(agacer)* to irritate sb, annoy sb, get on sb's nerves. **2 s'** ~ *vpr* to get worked up. **ne t'énerve pas!** take it easy! ◆ **énervant, e** *adj* irritating, annoying. ◆ **énervé, e** *adj (agacé)* irritated, annoyed; *(agité)* nervous. ◆ **énervement** *nm* irritation, annoyance; nervousness.

enfant [ɑ̃fɑ̃] **1** *nmf (gén)* child; *(garçon)* (little) boy; *(fille)* (little) girl. **quand il était** ~ when he was a child; **c'est un grand** ~ he's such a child; **il est resté très** ~ he has remained very childlike; **faire l'** ~ to behave childishly; **sans** ~ childless; *(fig)* **ce livre est son** ~ this book is his baby; **c'est un** ~ **du pays** he's a native of these parts; *(*: personnes)* **les** ~**s!** folks! * **2** : ~ **de chœur** altar boy; *(ingénu)* innocent; **ce n'est pas un** ~ **de chœur!** * he's no angel; ~ **prodige** child prodigy ; ~ **prodigue** prodigal son; ~ **trouvé** foundling; **il est** ~ **unique** he is an only child. ◆ **enfance** *nf (jeunesse)* childhood; *[garçon]* boyhood; *[fille]* girlhood; *(petite enfance)* infancy; *(fig: début)* infancy. **c'est l'** ~ **de l'art** it's child's play; *(enfants)* ~ **déshéritée** deprived children.

enfanter [ɑ̃fɑ̃te] (1) **1** *vt* (†, *Bible)* to bring forth †. **2** *vi* to give birth. ◆ **enfantement** *nm* (†, *Bible)* childbirth; *[œuvre]* giving birth (*de* to).

enfantillage [ɑ̃fɑ̃tijaʒ] *nm* childishness. **se livrer à des** ~**s** to behave childishly.

enfantin, e [ɑ̃fɑ̃tɛ̃, in] *adj* childlike; *(puéril)* childish. *(facile)* **c'est** ~ it's simple, it's child's play; **rire/jeu** ~ child's laugh/game.

enfer [ɑ̃fɛʀ] *nm (lit, fig)* hell. *(Myth)* **les** ~**s** Hell, the Underworld; **l'** ~ **est pavé de bonnes intentions** the road to hell is paved with good intentions; **l'** ~ **de la guerre** the purgatory of war; **vivre un véritable** ~ to live a life of hell; **bruit/vision d'** ~ hellish *ou* infernal noise/vision; **feu d'** ~ raging fire; **rouler à un train d'** ~ to tear along at breakneck speed.

enfermer [ɑ̃fɛʀme] (1) **1** *vt (gén)* to shut up; *(à clef)* to lock up (*dans* in); *(dans conventions)* to imprison, confine (*dans* within); *(dans un dilemme)* to trap (*dans* in). **il est bon à** ~ **(à l'asile)** * he ought to be locked up; **ne reste pas enfermé par ce beau temps** don't stay indoors *ou* inside in this lovely weather; *(littér)* **les collines qui enfermaient le vallon** the hills that enclosed the valley. **2 s'** ~ *vpr (lit)* to shut o.s. up *ou* in. **s'** ~ **à clef** to lock o.s. away *ou* in; **s'** ~ **dans** *mutisme* to retreat into; *rôle* to stick to.

enferrer (s') [ɑ̃feʀe] (1) *vpr* to tie o.s. in knots. **s'** ~ **dans** *contradictions* to get embroiled in, get tangled up in; **il s'enferre de plus en plus** he's getting himself in more and more of a mess *ou* into deeper and deeper water.

enfiévrer [ɑ̃fjevʀe] (6) *vt imagination* to fire; *esprits* to rouse. ◆ **enfiévré, e** *adj* feverish.

enfilade [ɑ̃filad] *nf*: **une** ~ **de** *maisons* a row *ou* string of; **prendre en** ~ *(Mil)* to rake, enfilade.

enfiler [ɑ̃file] (1) **1** *vt aiguille, perles* to thread; *rue* to take; (*) *vêtement* to slip on. ~ **qch sur une tringle** to slip sth onto a rod; *(*: fourrer)* ~ **un objet dans** to stick * an object into. **2 s'** ~ *vpr* (**a**) **s'** ~ **dans** *couloir* to disappear into. (**b**) (**) *nourriture* to down; *corvée* to get landed with *.

enfin [ɑ̃fɛ̃] *adv* (**a**) *(à la fin)* at last, finally. **il y est** ~ **arrivé** he has at last *ou* finally succeeded; ~ **seuls!** alone at last! (**b**) *(en dernier lieu)* lastly, finally. ~ **et surtout** and last but not least. (**c**) *(en conclusion)* ~ **(bref)** in short, in a word. (**d**) *(restrictif)* well. ~**, dans un sens, oui** well — in a way, yes; **mais** ~ but; **car** ~ because. (**e**) *(somme toute)* after all. **c'est un élève qui,** ~ **, n'est pas bête** this pupil is not stupid, after all. (**f**) *(toutefois)* still. ~**, si ça vous plaît, prenez-le** still, if you like it take it; **moi je veux bien,** ~...! I don't mind, but... *ou* still...! (**g**) *(exclamatif)* ~! **que veux-tu y faire!** still, what can you do!; ~ **, tu aurais pu le faire!** all the same *ou* even so, you could have done it!; **(mais)** ~! **je viens de te le dire!** but I've just TOLD you!; ~! **un grand garçon comme toi!** come now, a big boy like you!

enflammer [ɑ̃flame] (1) **1** *vt bois* to set on fire, set fire to; *allumette* to strike; *ciel* to set ablaze; *colère, désir* to inflame; *imagination* to fire. **2 s'** ~ *vpr [bois]* to catch fire; *[visage]* to blaze; *[désir]* to flare up; *[imagination]* to be fired; *[orateur]* to become impassioned. **s'** ~ **(de colère)** to flare up (in anger). ◆ **enflammé, e** *adj allumette, torche, paille* burning, blazing; *ciel* blazing; *caractère, paroles* fiery, passionate; *déclaration* impassioned; *plaie* inflamed.

enfler [ɑ̃fle] (1) **1** *vt membre, fleuve* to cause to swell; *(littér) voiles* to swell. **se faire** ~ **de 10 F** * to be done out of 10 francs *. **2** *vi [membre]* to become swollen, swell (up); *(grossir)* to fill out. **3 s'** ~ *vpr [voix]* to rise; *[son, fleuve, voiles]* to swell. ◆ **enflé, e** *nm, f* (*: *imbécile)* twit *, clot *. ◆ **enflure** *nf (Méd)* swelling; (*: *imbécile)* twit *, clot *.

enfoncer [ɑ̃fɔ̃se] (3) **1** *vt* (**a**) *pieu* to drive in; *punaise* to stick in, push in. ~ **un couteau dans** to plunge a knife into; ~ **qch à coups de marteau** to hammer sth in. (**b**) *(mettre)* ~ **les mains dans ses poches** to thrust one's hands into one's pockets; ~ **son chapeau jusqu'aux yeux** to pull one's hat down over one's eyes; **qui a bien pu lui** ~ **ça dans le crâne?** who on earth put that into his head?; ~ **qn dans la misère** to plunge sb into poverty. (**c**) *porte* to break down; *véhicule* to smash in; *(fig) ennemi* to break through. *(fig)* ~ **une porte ouverte** to labour an obvious point. (**d**) (*) *(battre)* to beat hollow *; *(surpasser)* to lick *; *(causer la perte de)* **elle a cherché à** ~ **son complice** she tried to put all the blame on her accomplice; **l'examinateur a voulu** ~ **le candidat** the examiner tried to destroy the candidate. **2** *vi (pénétrer)* to sink in; *(céder)* to yield. **3 s'** ~ *vpr* (**a**) *(gén)* to sink (*dans* in, into). **s'** ~ **dans** *forêt* to disappear into; *vice* to plunge into; **s'** ~ **sous les couvertures** * to snuggle down under the covers; **il s'est enfoncé jusqu'au cou dans une sale histoire** he's up to his neck in a nasty bit of business; **à mentir, tu ne fais que t'** ~ **davantage** by lying, you're just getting yourself into deeper and deeper water. (**b**) *(céder)* to give way. (**c**) **s'** ~ **une arête dans la gorge** to get a bone stuck in one's throat; **s'** ~ **une aiguille dans la main** to stick a needle into one's hand; **enfoncez-vous bien ça dans le crâne** * now get this firmly into your head *. ◆ **enfoncé, e** *adj yeux* deep-set; *côtes* broken; *recoin* deep. **la tête** ~**e dans les épaules** with his head sunk between his shoulders. ◆ **enfoncement** *nm* (**a**) *(action)* driving in; breaking down; breaking through; giving way; sinking. **avoir un** ~ **de la cage thoracique** to have broken ribs. (**b**) *(recoin)* recess, nook.

enfouir [ɑ̃fwiʀ] (2) **1** *vt* to bury (*dans* in). **2 s'** ~ *vpr*: **s'** ~ **dans/sous** to bury o.s. in/under. ◆ **enfouissement** *nm* burying.

enfourcher [ɑ̃fuʀʃe] (1) *vt* to mount. *(fig)* ~ **son dada** to get on one's hobby-horse.

enfourner [ɑ̃fuʀne] (1) *vt* to put in the oven; *(*: avaler)* to guzzle down. *(*: enfoncer)* ~ **qch dans** to stuff * sth into.

enfreindre [ɑ̃fʀɛ̃dʀ(ə)] (52) *vt* to infringe.

enfuir (s') [ɑ̃fɥiʀ] (17) *vpr* to run away (*chez, dans* to); *(s'échapper)* to run away, escape (*de* from); *(littér) [temps]* to fly.

enfumer [ɑ̃fyme] (1) *vt pièce* to fill with smoke; *ruche* to smoke out. **pièce enfumée** smoky room.

engagé, e [ɑ̃gaʒe] **1** *adj écrivain* committed. *(Pol)* **non** ~ uncommitted. **2** *nm (soldat)* enlisted man; *(coureur)* entrant, competitor; *(cheval)* runner. ~ **volontaire** volunteer.

engageant, e [ɑ̃gaʒɑ̃, ɑ̃t] *adj proposition* attractive, appealing; *air, sourire* engaging, winning; *gâteau* inviting.

engagement [ɑ̃gaʒmɑ̃] *nm* (**a**) *(promesse)* agreement, promise. **sans** ~ **de votre part** without obligation *ou* commitment on your part; **prendre l'** ~ **de** to undertake to; **manquer à ses** ~**s** to fail to keep one's promises; **faire face à ses** ~**s** to fulfil one's promises *ou* commitments. (**b**) *(Théât: contrat)* engagement. (**c**) *(embauche)* taking on, engaging. (**d**) *[capitaux]* investing; *[dépenses]* incurring. ~**s financiers** financial commitments *ou* liabilities. (**e**) *[débat, négociations]* start. (**f**) *(Sport) (inscription)* entry; *(coup d'envoi)* kick-off; *(Boxe)* attack; *(Escrime)* engagement. (**g**) *(Mil) [recrues]* enlistment; *[combat, troupes fraîches]* engaging. **tué dans un** ~ killed in an engagement. (**h**) *(Littérat, Pol)* commitment. **politique de non** ~ policy of non-commitment. (**i**) *(mise en gage)* pawning. (**j**) *(encouragement)* encouragement.

engager [ɑ̃gaʒe] (3) **1** *vt* (**a**) *[promesse]* to bind. **ça n'engage à rien** it doesn't commit you to anything; ~ **sa parole** to give one's word. (**b**) *ouvrier* to take on, hire; *artiste* to engage. (**c**) *(entraîner)* to involve (*dans* in). (**d**) *(encourager)* ~ **qn à faire qch** to urge sb to do sth. (**e**) *(introduire)* to insert (*dans* in, into). ~ **sa voiture dans une ruelle** to drive (one's car) into a lane. (**f**) *discussion* to start (up); *négociations* to enter into; *(Jur) poursuites* to institute (*contre* against). **l'affaire semble bien/mal engagée** things seem to have got off to a good/bad start. (**g**) *(mettre en gage)* to pawn; *(investir)* to invest. (**h**) *(Sport) concurrents* to enter; *match* to begin. **la partie est bien engagée** the match is well under way. (**i**) *(Mil) recrues* to enlist; *troupes fraîches* to throw in, engage. ~ **le combat contre l'ennemi** to engage the enemy.
2 s' ~ *vpr* (**a**) *(promettre)* to commit o.s. **s'** ~ **à faire** to undertake to do. (**b**) *(s'embaucher)* to take a job (*chez* with). (**c**) **s'** ~ **dans** *frais* to incur; *discussion* to enter into; *affaire* to become involved in; **le pays s'engage dans une politique dangereuse** the country is embarking on a dangerous policy *ou* is steering a dangerous course. (**d**) **s'** ~ **dans** *[mécanisme]* to fit into; *[véhicule]* to turn into; **s'** ~ **sur la chaussée** to step (out) onto the road. (**e**) *[pourparlers]* to start, get under way. (**f**) *(Sport)* to enter (*dans* for). (**g**) *(Mil) [recrues]* to enlist. **s'** ~ **dans l'armée de l'air** to join the air force; **le combat s'engagea** the fight began.

engazonner [ɑ̃gazɔne] (1) *vt terrain* to turf.

engelure [ɑ̃ʒlyʀ] *nf* chilblain.

engendrer [ɑ̃ʒɑ̃dʀe] (1) *vt (littér) enfant* to father; *(Ling, Math, Phys)* to generate; *malheurs* to breed.

engin [ɑ̃ʒɛ̃] *nm (machine)* machine; *(outil)* instrument; *(Aut)* heavy vehicle; *(Aviat)* aircraft; *(*: truc)* contraption, gadget. ~ **balistique** ballistic missile; ~ **explosif** explosive device; ~ **de terrassement** earth-mover.

englober [ɑ̃glɔbe] (1) *vt* to include, encompass (*dans* in).

engloutir [ɑ̃glutiʀ] (2) **1** *vt nourriture* to gobble up, gulp down; *navire* to engulf; *fortune* to devour. **2 s'** ~ *vpr [navire]* to be engulfed. ◆ **engloutissement** *nm* gobbling up; engulfing; devouring.

engoncer [ɑ̃gɔ̃se] (3) *vt (gén ptp)* to cramp.

engorger [ɑ̃gɔʀʒe] (3) **1** *vt tuyau* to block; *(Comm)* to glut. **2 s'** ~ *vpr [tuyau]* to become blocked. ◆ **engorgement** *nm* blocking (*de* of); glut (*de* in).

engouer (s') [ɑ̃gwe] (1) *vpr*: **s'** ~ **de qch** to develop a craze for sth; **s'** ~ **de qn** to become infatuated with sb. ◆ **engouement** *nm* infatuation; craze (*pour* for). ~ **passager** *(pour qn)* passing fancy; *(pour qch)* brief craze.

engouffrer [ɑ̃gufʀe] (1) **1** *vt charbon* to shovel (*dans* into); (*) *fortune* to devour; (*) *nourriture* to gobble up; *navire* to swallow up, engulf. **2 s'** ~ *vpr (gén)* to rush.

engourdir [ɑ̃guʀdiʀ] (2) **1** *vt membres* to numb; *esprit, douleur* to dull; *[chaleur]* to make sleepy *ou* drowsy. **2 s'** ~ *vpr* to go numb; to grow dull. ◆ **engourdi, e** *adj membre* numb; *esprit* dull, dulled. ◆ **engourdissement** *nm* (**a**) *(état)* numbness; sleepiness, drowsiness; dullness. (**b**) *(action)* numbing; dulling.

engrais [ɑ̃gʀɛ] *nm (chimique)* fertilizer; *(animal)* manure. **mettre à l'** ~ to fatten up.

engraisser [ɑ̃gʀese] (1) **1** *vt volailles* to cram; *bétail* to fatten (up); *terre* to manure, fertilize; (*) *per-*

sonne to fatten up. **2** *vi* (*) to put on weight. ◆ **engraissement** *nm* fattening up; cramming.

engrenage [ɑ̃gʀənaʒ] *nm* gearing; *(fig)* chain. **être pris dans l'** ~ to get caught up in the system; **l'** ~ **de la violence** the spiral of violence.

engueuler ‡ [ɑ̃gœle] (1) **1** *vt*: ~ **qn** to bawl sb out *; **se faire** ~ to get bawled out *. **2 s'** ~ *vpr* to have a row (*avec* with). ◆ **engueulade** ‡ *nf (dispute)* row; *(réprimande)* bawling out *.

enguirlander * [ɑ̃giʀlɑ̃de] (1) *vt*: ~ **qn** to give sb a telling-off *ou* ticking-off.

enhardir [ɑ̃aʀdiʀ] (2) **1** *vt* to make bolder. **2 s'** ~ *vpr* to get bolder.

énigme [enigm(ə)] *nf (mystère)* enigma, riddle; *(jeu)* riddle, puzzle. ◆ **énigmatique** *adj* enigmatic. ◆ **énigmatiquement** *adv* enigmatically.

enivrer [ɑ̃nivʀe] (1) **1** *vt* to intoxicate. **2 s'** ~ *vpr* to get drunk (*de* on), become intoxicated (*de* with). ◆ **enivrant, e** *adj* intoxicating. ◆ **enivrement** *nm* (†: *ivresse)* intoxication; *(fig: exaltation)* elation, exhilaration.

enjamber [ɑ̃ʒɑ̃be] (1) *vt obstacle* to stride *ou* step over; *fossé* to step *ou* stride across; *[pont]* to span, stretch across. *(s'asseoir)* ~ **qch** to sit down astride sth. ◆ **enjambée** *nf* stride.

enjeu, *pl* ~**x** [ɑ̃ʒø] *nm [pari, guerre]* stake, stakes (*de* in). **quel est l'** ~**?** what is at stake?

enjoindre [ɑ̃ʒwɛ̃dʀ(ə)] (49) *vt*: ~ **à qn de faire** to enjoin sb to do.

enjôler [ɑ̃ʒole] (1) *vt (ensorceler)* to bewitch. *(amadouer)* ~ **qn** to get round sb; ~ **qn pour obtenir qch** to coax *ou* wheedle sb into giving sth. ◆ **enjôleur, -euse 1** *adj* coaxing, wheedling. **2** *nm, f (charmeur)* coaxer, wheedler.

enjoliver [ɑ̃ʒɔlive] (1) *vt objet* to embellish; *réalité, récit* to embroider, embellish. ◆ **enjoliveur** *nm (Aut)* hub cap.

enjoué, e [ɑ̃ʒwe] *adj* cheerful. ◆ **enjouement** *nm* cheerfulness.

enlacer [ɑ̃lase] (3) **1** *vt (étreindre)* to clasp, hug; *(enchevêtrer)* to intertwine; *(s'enrouler autour)* to wind round, entwine. **2 s'** ~ *vpr* to hug *ou* clasp each other; to intertwine. **s'** ~ **autour de** to twine *ou* wind round. ◆ **enlacement** *nm (étreinte)* embrace; *(enchevêtrement)* intertwining.

enlaidir [ɑ̃lediʀ] (2) **1** *vt* to make ugly. **2** *vi* to become ugly. ◆ **enlaidissement** *nm:* **l'** ~ **du paysage par les usines** the ruining *ou* defacing of the countryside by factories.

enlever [ɑ̃lve] (5) **1** *vt* (**a**) *(gén)* to remove; *étiquette, vêtement* to take off; *tache* to take out; *(en brossant ou lavant etc)* to brush *ou* wash *etc* off; *lustre* to take down. ~ **le couvert** to clear the table; **enlève tes coudes de la table** take your elbows off the table. (**b**) *craintes, scrupules* to allay; *doutes* to dispel. ~ **à qn** *courage* to rob sb of; *espoir* to deprive sb of, rob sb of; *commandement* to relieve sb of; **on lui a enlevé la garde de l'enfant** the child was taken *ou* removed from his care; **ça lui enlèvera le goût de recommencer** that'll cure him of trying that again, perhaps that'll make him think twice before he does it again; **ça n'enlève rien à son mérite** that doesn't in any way detract from his worth. (**c**) *(emporter) objet* to take away, remove; *ordures* to collect. **faire** ~ **qch** to have sth taken away; **enlevé par un mal foudroyant** borne off by a sudden illness; **la mort nous l'a enlevé** death has taken him from us. (**d**) *(kidnapper)* to kidnap, abduct. **se faire** ~ **par son amant** to elope with one's lover. (**e**) *victoire* to win; *(Mil) position* to capture, take. ~ **la décision** to carry the day; ~ **une affaire** *(tractation)* to pull off a deal; *(commande)* to get *ou* secure an order; *(marchandise)* to carry off a bargain; **ça a été vite enlevé** *(marchandise)* it sold quickly; *(*: travail)* it was done in no time. **2 s'** ~ *vpr [tache]* to come off; *[peinture, écorce]* to peel off, come off. **enlève-toi de là** * mind out of the way!; **ça s'enlève comme des petits pains** * it's selling like hot cakes *; **comment est-ce que ça s'enlève?** *[étiquette]* how does one remove it *ou* take it off?; *[vêtement]* how does one get out of it *ou* take it off?
◆ **enlevé, e** *adj récit* spirited; *musique* executed with spirit. ◆ **enlèvement** *nm [personne]* kidnapping, abduction; *[objet]* taking away; *[ordures, bagages]* collection; *(Mil) [position]* capture; *[organe]* removal.

enliser [ɑ̃lize] (1) **1** *vt*: ~ **sa voiture** to get one's car stuck in the mud *(ou* sand *etc)*. **2 s'** ~ *vpr* to sink (*dans* into); *(dans les détails)* to get bogged down (*dans* in). ◆ **enlisement** *nm*: **causer l'** ~ **d'un bateau** to cause a ship to get stuck in the mud *(ou* sand *etc)*.

enneigé, e [ɑ̃neʒe] *adj montagne* snow-covered; *sommet* snow-capped; *route* blocked by snow, snowed up. ◆ **enneigement** *nm* snow coverage. **bulletin d'** ~ snow report; **les conditions d'** ~ the snow conditions.

ennemi, e [ɛnmi] **1** *adj (Mil)* enemy; *(hostile)* hostile. **2** *nm, f* enemy. **se faire un** ~ **de qn** to make an enemy of sb; **être** ~ **de qch** to be opposed to sth, be against sth.

ennui [ɑ̃nɥi] *nm (désœuvrement)* boredom; *(monotonie)* tedium, tediousness; *(tracas)* trouble, worry. **avoir des** ~**s** to have problems *ou* troubles; **avoir des** ~**s d'argent** to have money worries; **avoir des** ~**s avec la police** to be in trouble with the police; **faire des** ~**s à qn** to make trouble for sb; **j'ai eu un** ~ **avec ma montre** I had some trouble *ou* bother with my watch; **si ça vous cause le moindre** ~ if it's any bother to you; **l'** ~**, c'est que...** the trouble *ou* the hitch is that...

ennuyer [ɑ̃nɥije] (8) **1** *vt (lasser)* to bore; *(préoccuper)* to worry; *(importuner)* to bother. *(irriter)* ~ **qn** to annoy sb, get on sb's nerves; **il y a qch qui m'ennuie** there's sth that worries *ou* bothers me; **ça m'ennuierait beaucoup de te voir fâché** I'd really hate to see you cross; **ça m'ennuie de te le dire, mais...** I'm sorry to have to tell you but..., I hate to say it but...; **ça m'ennuierait beaucoup d'y aller** it would really annoy me to go; **si cela ne vous ennuie pas trop** if you wouldn't mind, if it isn't too much bother; **je ne voudrais pas vous** ~ I don't want to put you to any trouble, I don't want to bother you. **2 s'** ~ *vpr* to be bored (*de, à* with). **s'** ~ **à mourir** to be bored to tears, be bored stiff; **s'** ~ **de qn** to miss sb. ◆ **ennuyé, e** *adj (préoccupé)* worried, bothered (*de* about); *(contrarié)* annoyed (*de* at, about). ◆ **ennuyeux, -euse** *adj (lassant)* boring, tedious; *(qui importune)* annoying, tiresome; *(préoccupant)* worrying.

énoncer [enɔ̃se] (3) *vt idée* to express; *conditions* to state. ◆ **énoncé** *nm (Scol) [sujet]* exposition; *[problème]* terms; *(Jur) [loi]* wording; *(Ling)* utterance; *[faits, décision]* statement. *(Scol)* **pendant l'**~ **du sujet** while the subject is being read out.

enorgueillir (s') [ɑ̃nɔʀgœjiʀ] (2) *vpr*: **s'** ~ **de** *(être fier de)* to pride o.s. on, boast about; *(avoir)* to boast.

énorme [enɔʀm(ə)] *adj* enormous, tremendous, huge. **ça lui a fait un bien** ~ it's done him a great deal of good; **il a accepté, c'est déjà** ~ he has accepted and that's quite something. ◆ **énormément** *adv* (**a**) enormously, tremendously, hugely. **ça m'a** ~ **déçu** it greatly disappointed me. (**b**) ~ **d'argent** a tremendous *ou* an enormous *ou* a huge amount of money; ~ **de gens** a tremendous *ou* an enormous *ou* a huge number of people, a great many people. ◆ **énormité** *nf [poids, somme]* hugeness; *[demande]* enormity;

(propos inconvenant) outrageous remark; *(erreur)* big blunder, howler *.

enquérir (s') [ɑ̃keʀiʀ] (21) *vpr* to inquire, ask (*de* about).

enquête [ɑ̃kɛt] *nf (gén, Jur)* inquiry; *(après décès)* inquest; *(Police)* investigation; *(sondage)* survey, (opinion) poll. ◆ **enquêter** (1) *vi* to hold an inquiry (*sur* on); to investigate; to conduct a survey (*sur* on). ~ **sur qch** to investigate sth, carry out an investigation into sth. ◆ **enquêteur, -euse** *nm, f (Police)* officer; *[sondage]* pollster. **les ~s poursuivent leurs recherches** the police are continuing their investigations.

enquiquiner * [ɑ̃kikine] (1) **1** *vt (importuner)* to bother; *(préoccuper)* to worry; *(lasser)* to bore. **2 s' ~** *vpr* to be bored. ◆ **enquiquinement** * *nm*: **quel ~!** what a flipping *ou* darned * nuisance! *; **avoir des ~s** to have trouble (*avec* with). ◆ **enquiquineur, -euse** * *nm, f* pest *.

enraciner [ɑ̃ʀasine] (1) **1** *vt* to root. **solidement enraciné** *préjugé* deep-rooted; *famille* firmly rooted. **2 s' ~** *vpr [arbre, préjugé]* to take root.

enrager [ɑ̃ʀaʒe] (3) *vi* (**a**) **faire ~ qn** * *(taquiner)* to tease sb; *(importuner)* to pester sb. (**b**) to be furious (*de faire* at doing). ◆ **enragé, e** *adj* (**a**) *chasseur, joueur* keen (*de* on). **c'est un ~ de la voiture** he's mad about cars *, he's a car fanatic. (**b**) *(en colère)* furious; *(Vét)* rabid.

enrayer [ɑ̃ʀeje] (8) **1** *vt maladie* to check, stop; *chômage, inflation* to check, curb; *arme* to jam. **2 s' ~** *vpr* to jam.

enrégimenter [ɑ̃ʀeʒimɑ̃te] (1) *vt (péj)* to enrol.

enregistrer [ɑ̃ʀʒistʀe] (1) *vt voix* to record; *(sur bande)* to tape(-record); *(sur magnétoscope)* to video(-tape); *(Jur) acte* to register; *(Comm) commande* to enter; *constatation* to note; *(mentalement)* to retain, register. **d'accord, j'enregistre** * all right, I'll bear it in mind; **(faire) ~ ses bagages** to register one's luggage; *(Aviat)* to check in one's luggage; *(Téléc)* **vous écoutez un message enregistré** this is a recorded message; **nous avons enregistré de bonnes ventes** we've rung up good sales; **la plus forte hausse/température enregistrée** the greatest rise/highest temperature recorded. ◆ **enregistrement** *nm* registration; check-in. ~ **magnétique** tape recording; ~ **magnétoscopique** video recording. ◆ **enregistreur, -euse 1** *adj* recording. **2** *nm* recorder, recording machine.

enrhumer [ɑ̃ʀyme] (1) **1** *vt* to give a cold to. **être enrhumé** to have a cold. **2 s' ~** *vpr* to catch a cold.

enrichir [ɑ̃ʀiʃiʀ] (2) **1** *vt esprit, collection* to enrich; *[argent]* to make rich. **2 s' ~** *vpr [commerçant]* to grow rich; *[esprit]* to grow richer (*de* in); *[collection]* to be enriched (*de* with). ◆ **enrichi, e** *adj (Tech)* enriched. **shampooing formule ~e** enriched formula shampoo. ◆ **enrichissant, e** *adj* enriching. ◆ **enrichissement** *nm* enrichment.

enrober [ɑ̃ʀɔbe] (1) *vt bonbon* to coat (*de* with); *paroles* to wrap up (*de* in). ◆ **enrobage** *nm* coating.

enrôler *vt,* **s' ~** *vpr* [ɑ̃ʀole] (1) to enlist. ◆ **enrôlé** *nm* recruit. ◆ **enrôlement** *nm* enlistment.

enrouer [ɑ̃ʀwe] (1) **1** *vt* to make hoarse. **2 s' ~** *vpr (froid)* to go hoarse; *(cri)* to make o.s. hoarse. ◆ **enroué, e** *adj* hoarse. ◆ **enrouement** *nm* hoarseness.

enrouler [ɑ̃ʀule] (1) **1** *vt (gén)* to roll up; *cheveux* to coil up; *fil* to wind (*autour de* round). **2 s' ~** *vpr [serpent]* to coil up; *[fil]* to wind. **s' ~ dans une couverture** to wrap *ou* roll o.s. up in a blanket.

ensabler *vt,* **s' ~** *vpr* [ɑ̃sɑble] (1) *port* to silt up; *voiture* to get stuck in the sand.

ensanglanter [ɑ̃sɑ̃glɑ̃te] (1) *vt visage* to cover with blood; *vêtement* to soak with blood. **un accident a ensanglanté la course** an accident cast a tragic shadow over the race.

enseignant, e [ɑ̃sɛɲɑ̃, ɑ̃t] **1** *adj* teaching. **2** *nm, f* teacher. **~-chercheur** teacher-cum-researcher; **poste d' ~** teaching position *ou* post *ou* job.

enseigne [ɑ̃sɛɲ] **1** *nf (Comm)* (shop) sign; *(drapeau)* ensign. ~ **lumineuse** neon sign; *(littér)* **à telle(s) ~(s) que** so much so that. **2** *nm (Hist)* ensign. ~ **de vaisseau** lieutenant.

enseignement [ɑ̃sɛɲmɑ̃] *nm* (**a**) *(Admin)* education. ~ **ménager** home economics *(sg)*; ~ **par correspondance** postal tuition; ~ **secondaire/technique** secondary/technical education; ~ **professionnel** vocational training; ~ **programmé** programmed learning; ~ **spécialisé** special education *ou* schooling; ~ **assisté par ordinateur** computer-aided learning. (**b**) *(art d'enseigner)* teaching. ~ **moderne** modern teaching methods. (**c**) *(carrière)* teaching profession. **être dans l' ~** to be a teacher. (**d**) *(leçon)* lesson. ◆ **enseigner** (1) *vt* to teach. ~ **qch à qn** to teach sb sth; ~ **à qn à faire qch** to teach sb (how) to do sth.

ensemble [ɑ̃sɑ̃bl(ə)] **1** *adv* together. **tous ~** all together; **ils ont répondu ~** *(deux)* they both answered together; *(plusieurs)* they all answered together; **ils vont bien ~** they go together well; **l'armoire et la table vont mal ~** the wardrobe and the table don't go (very well) together; *[personnes]* **être bien/mal ~** to be on good/bad terms. **2** *nm* (**a**) *(unité)* unity. **avec un parfait ~** simultaneously, with one accord. (**b**) *(totalité)* whole. **l' ~ du personnel** the entire *ou* whole staff, all the members of staff; **dans l' ~** on the whole, by and large; **dans l' ~ nous sommes d'accord** basically we agree; **les spectateurs dans leur ~** the audience as a whole; **d' ~** *vue etc* overall, general. (**c**) *[personnes]* group; *[objets]* set; *[lois]* body; *(Mus)* ensemble; *[immeubles]* housing scheme *ou* development; housing project *(US)*; *(Math)* set; *(Couture)* outfit, suit.

ensemencer [ɑ̃smɑ̃se] (3) *vt (Agr)* to sow. ◆ **ensemencement** *nm* sowing.

ensevelir [ɑ̃səvliʀ] (2) *vt (gén)* to bury; *(d'un linceul)* to shroud (*de* in). ◆ **ensevelissement** *nm* burying; shrouding.

ensoleiller [ɑ̃sɔleje] (1) *vt (lit)* to fill with sunshine; *(fig)* to brighten, light up. ◆ **ensoleillé, e** *adj* sunny. ◆ **ensoleillement** *nm* hours of sunshine.

ensommeillé, e [ɑ̃sɔmeje] *adj* sleepy, drowsy.

ensorceler [ɑ̃sɔʀsəle] (4) *vt (lit, fig)* to bewitch.

ensuite [ɑ̃sɥit] *adv (puis)* then, next; *(par la suite)* afterwards, later. ~ **de quoi** after which.

ensuivre (s') [ɑ̃sɥivʀ(ə)] (40) *vpr* to follow. **et tout ce qui s'ensuit** and all the rest; **torturé jusqu'à ce que mort s'ensuive** tortured to death.

entaille [ɑ̃tɑj] *nf (gén)* cut; *(profonde)* gash; *(sur objet)* notch; *(allongée)* groove. ◆ **entailler** (1) *vt* to cut; to gash; to notch.

entamer [ɑ̃tame] (1) *vt* (**a**) *pain* to start (upon); *bouteille* to start, open; *patrimoine* to dip into; *journée, livre* to start; *travail* to start on; *discussion* to start, open; *poursuites* to institute. **la journée est déjà bien entamée** we are already well into the day, the day is already quite far advanced; *(Cartes)* ~ **la partie** to open the game. (**b**) *résistance* to wear down, break down; *conviction* to shake, weaken; *optimisme, moral* to wear down; *réputation* to damage, harm. (**c**) *(inciser)* to cut (into). ◆ **entame** *nf* first slice.

entartrer *vt,* **s' ~** *vpr* [ɑ̃taʀtʀe] (1) to scale. ◆ **entartrage** *nm* scaling.

entasser *vt,* **s' ~** *vpr* [ɑ̃tɑse] (1) to pile up (*sur* onto). **s' ~ dans** to cram *ou* pack into. ◆ **entas-**

sement *nm* (**a**) *(action)* piling up; cramming in, packing together. (**b**) *(tas)* pile, heap.

entendre [ɑ̃tɑ̃dʀ(ə)] (41) **1** *vt* (**a**) *voix, témoin, messe* to hear; *conseil, discours* to listen to. **j'entendais quelqu'un parler** I heard *ou* could hear somebody speaking; *(fig)* **il ne l'entend pas de cette oreille** he's not prepared to accept that; **à l'** ~ to hear him talk, to listen to him; ~ **raison** to listen to *ou* see reason. (**b**) *(comprendre)* to understand; *(vouloir)* to intend, mean; *(vouloir dire)* to mean. **entendez-vous par là que...** are you trying to say that..., do you mean that...; **laisser** ~ **à qn que** *(faire comprendre)* to give sb to understand that; *(donner l'impression)* to give sb the impression that; **faites comme vous l'entendez** do as you see fit *ou* think best; **j'entends être obéi** I intend *ou* mean to be obeyed, I WILL be obeyed. (**c**) *(locutions)* ~ **parler de** to hear of *ou* about; *(fig)* **il ne veut pas en** ~ **parler** he won't hear of it; **d'après ce que j'ai entendu dire** from what I have heard; **on entend dire que** it is said *ou* rumoured that; **sa voix se fit** ~ his voice was heard.
2 s' ~ *vpr* (**a**) *(être d'accord)* to agree (*sur* on). **ils s'entendent bien/ne s'entendent pas** they get on *ou* along well (together)/don't get on *ou* along (together). (**b**) *(s'y connaître)* **il s'y entend pour le faire** he's very good at it, he knows how to do it. (**c**) *(se comprendre)* **quand je dis énorme je m'entends, disons grand** when I say huge what I really mean is big; *(bien sûr)* **(cela) s'entend** of course; **entendons-nous bien!** let's be quite clear about this; **ça s'entend de 2 manières** that can be taken 2 ways *ou* to mean 2 different things. (**d**) *(être entendu)* **on ne s'entend plus ici** you can't hear yourself think in here.
◆ **entendement** *nm (Philos)* understanding. ◆ **entendeur** *nm*: **à bon** ~, **salut** a word to the wise is enough. ◆ **entendu, e** *adj* (**a**) *(convenu)* agreed. *(évidemment)* **bien** ~! of course!; *(concessif)* **c'est** ~ all right. (**b**) *sourire, air* knowing. ◆ **entente** *nf (amitié, compréhension)* understanding; *(accord)* agreement. **vivre en bonne** ~ to live in harmony; **vivre en bonne** ~ **avec les voisins** to be on good terms with the neighbours.

entériner [ɑ̃teʀine] (1) *vt* to ratify, confirm.

entérite [ɑ̃teʀit] *nf* enteritis.

enterrer [ɑ̃teʀe] (1) *vt (gén)* to bury; *projet* to drop. **tu nous enterreras tous!** you'll outlive us all!; **enterrons cette querelle** (let's) let bygones be bygones; **il a enterré son passé** he put his past behind him. ◆ **enterrement** *nm [mort]* burial; *[espoir]* end, death; *(cérémonie)* funeral; *(convoi)* funeral procession. **faire une tête d'** ~ * to look gloomy.

en-tête, *pl* **en-têtes** [ɑ̃tɛt] *nm* heading; *(Ordin)* header-block.

entêter [ɑ̃tete] (1) **1** *vt [parfum]* to go to the head of. **2 s'** ~ *vpr* to persist (*dans qch* in sth, *à faire qch* in doing sth). ◆ **entêtant, e** *adj vin* heady. ◆ **entêté, e 1** *adj* stubborn. **2** *nm, f* mule, stubborn individual. **quel** ~ **tu fais!** what a stubborn thing you are! ◆ **entêtement** *nm* stubbornness.

enthousiasme [ɑ̃tuzjasm(ə)] *nm* enthusiasm. ◆ **enthousiasmant, e** *adj* exciting, exhilarating. ◆ **enthousiasmer** (1) **1** *vt* to fill with enthusiasm. **2 s'** ~ *vpr* to be enthusiastic (*pour* about, over). ◆ **enthousiaste** *adj* enthusiastic (*de* about, over).

enticher (s') [ɑ̃tiʃe] (1) *vpr (péj)* **s'** ~ **de** *femme* to become infatuated with; *choses* to have a passion for.

entier, -ière [ɑ̃tje, jɛʀ] **1** *adj* (**a**) *quantité* whole, full; *surface* whole, entire. **payer place ~ière** to pay the full price; **une heure ~ière** a whole hour; **dans la France ~ière** throughout France, in the whole of France; **tout** ~ entirely, completely. (**b**) *(intact)* intact; *(absolu)* absolute, complete. **la question reste ~ière** the matter still remains unresolved. (**c**) *personne, caractère* unyielding, unbending. (**d**) **pain** ~ wholemeal *ou* wholewheat bread; **lait** ~ full-cream milk, whole milk *(US)*. **2** *nm* (**a**) *(Math)* whole; *(Ordin)* integer. (**b**) **en** ~ entirely; **boire une bouteille en** ~ to drink a whole bottle; **lire qch en** ~ to read the whole of sth, read sth right through; **la nation dans son** ~ the nation as a whole, the entire nation. ◆ **entièrement** *adv* entirely, completely, wholly, fully.

entité [ɑ̃tite] *nf* entity.

entonner [ɑ̃tɔne] (1) *vt chanson* to strike up.

entonnoir [ɑ̃tɔnwaʀ] *nm (Culin)* funnel. *forme, conduit* **en** ~ funnel-shaped.

entorse [ɑ̃tɔʀs(ə)] *nf (Méd)* sprain; *[loi]* infringement (*à* of). **se faire une** ~ **au poignet** to sprain one's wrist; **faire une** ~ **à** *vérité* to twist; *habitudes* to break; *règlement* to bend.

entortiller [ɑ̃tɔʀtije] (1) *vt* (**a**) *ficelle* to twist, wind; *objet* to wrap (up). (**b**) *(duper)* to hoodwink. *(enjôler)* ~ **qn** to get round sb.

entourer [ɑ̃tuʀe] (1) **1** *vt* (**a**) *(mettre autour)* ~ **qch de** *(gén)* to surround sth with; *couverture* to wrap sth in; ~ **qn de ses bras** to put one's arms round sb. (**b**) *(être autour) (gén)* to surround; *[écharpe]* to be round; *(fig) personne souffrante* to rally round. **le monde qui nous entoure** the world about us. **2 s'** ~ *vpr*: **s'** ~ **de** to surround o.s. with; **s'** ~ **de précautions** to take elaborate precautions; **s'** ~ **de toutes les garanties** to avail o.s. of all possible guarantees. ◆ **entourage** *nm (famille)* family circle; *(compagnie)* set, circle; *[président]* entourage; *[fenêtre etc]* surround. **les gens de son** ~ **disent que...** people round about him say that... ◆ **entouré, e** *adj (admiré)* popular.

entracte [ɑ̃tʀakt(ə)] *nm [spectacle]*, *(Ciné)* interval; *(fig)* interlude.

entraide [ɑ̃tʀɛd] *nf* mutual aid. *(Admin)* **service d'** ~ support service. ◆ **entraider (s')** (1) *vpr* to help one another.

entrailles [ɑ̃tʀɑj] *nfpl (gén)*, *(littér)* entrails; *[mère]* womb; *(fig) [terre]* bowels. **sans** ~ heartless; **spectacle qui vous prend aux** ~ sight that shakes your very soul *ou* shakes you to the core.

entrain [ɑ̃tʀɛ̃] *nm* spirit, drive, liveliness. **avec** ~ *répondre, manger* with gusto; *travailler* spiritedly; **faire qch sans** ~ to do sth half-heartedly; **être sans** ~ to feel dispirited, have no energy. ◆ **entraînant, e** *adj paroles* stirring, rousing; *rythme* brisk, lively.

entraîner [ɑ̃tʀene] (1) **1** *vt* (**a**) *objets arrachés* to carry *ou* drag along; *(Tech) machine* to drive; *(tirer) wagons* to pull. **il entraîna son camarade dans sa chute** he pulled *ou* dragged his friend down in his fall; **il m'entraîna vers la sortie** he dragged *ou* took me off towards the exit. (**b**) *(fig: influencer)* to lead. ~ **qn à voler qch** to get sb to steal sth; ~ **ses camarades à boire** to encourage one's friends to drink. (**c**) *dépenses, chutes (impliquer)* to entail, mean; *(causer)* to bring about, lead to. ~ **qn à une dépense** to lead sb into some expense. (**d**) *[rythme]* to carry along; *[enthousiasme]* to carry away. **se laisser** ~ **par ses passions** to (let o.s.) get *ou* be carried away by one's passions. (**e**) *(préparer) athlète* to train, coach; *cheval* to train (*à* for). **2 s'** ~ *vpr (gén)* to train o.s.; *(Sport)* to train (*à, pour* for). **s'** ~ **à faire un mouvement** to practise a movement; **il s'entraîne à parler en public** he is training himself to speak in public. ◆ **entraînement** *nm [roue]* driving; *[athlète]* training. **se blesser à l'** ~ to hurt o.s. at training *ou* during a training session. **manquer d'** ~ to be out of training. ◆ **entraîneur** *nm [cheval]* trainer; *[coureur]* coach, trainer.

entraver [ɑ̃tʀave] (1) *vt circulation* to hold up; *action* to hinder, hamper; *animal* to fetter; *prisonnier* to chain up. ◆**entrave** *nf* hindrance (*à* to). *[prisonnier]* **~s** chains; *liberté, bonheur* **sans ~** unbridled; *(fig)* **les ~s de** the fetters of.

entre [ɑ̃tʀ(ə)] *prép* (**a**) *(gén)* between. **la vérité est ~ les deux** the truth is somewhere between the two.
(**b**) *(parmi) (gén)* among, amongst; *choisir* between. **lui, ~ autres, n'est pas d'accord** he, for one, doesn't agree; **~ autres (choses)** among other things; **l'un d' ~ eux** one of them; **cette heure ~ toutes** this (hour) of all hours; **difficile ~ tous** exceptionally difficult.
(**c**) *(dans)* in, into. **prendre ~ ses bras** to take in one's arms; **~ parenthèses** in brackets.
(**d**) *(à travers)* through. *(lit, fig)* **passer ~ les mailles du filet** to slip through the net.
(**e**) *(relation) (deux choses)* between; *(plus de deux)* among. **~ nous** between you and me, between ourselves; **~ eux 4** among the 4 of them; **il n'y a rien de commun ~ eux** they have nothing in common; **ils préfèrent rester ~ eux** they prefer to be on their own; **entendez-vous ~ vous** sort it out among yourselves; **ils se sont disputés ~ eux** they have quarrelled with each other *ou* with one another; **on ne va pas se battre ~ nous** we're not going to fight among ourselves.
(**f**) *(locutions)* **~ chien et loup** when the shadows are falling, at dusk; **~ deux âges** middle-aged; *(fig)* **~ deux portes** briefly; **~ deux eaux** just below the surface; **pris ~ deux feux** caught in the crossfire; **parler ~ ses dents** to mumble.

entrebâiller [ɑ̃tʀəbɑje] (1) *vt* to half-open. ◆**entrebâillé, e** *adj*: **être ~** to be ajar *ou* half-open. ◆**entrebâillement** *nm*: **dans l' ~ de la porte** in the half-open door.

entrechoquer [ɑ̃tʀəʃɔke] (1) **1** *vt (gén)* to knock together; *verres* to clink. **2 s' ~** *vpr (gén)* to knock together; *[verres]* to clink; *[dents]* to chatter; *[épées]* to clash together; *[idées, mots]* to jostle together.

entrecôte [ɑ̃tʀəkot] *nf* entrecôte *ou* rib steak.

entrecouper [ɑ̃tʀəkupe] (1) **1** *vt*: **~ de** *(gén)* to interrupt with; *citations* to intersperse *ou* pepper with; **voix entrecoupée** broken voice. **2 s' ~** *vpr [lignes]* to intersect, cut across each other.

entrecroiser *vt,* **s' ~** *vpr* [ɑ̃tʀəkʀwaze] (1) *fils* to intertwine; *lignes* to intersect.

entrée [ɑ̃tʀe] *nf* (**a**) *(arrivée) [personne]* entry, entrance; *[véhicule, marchandise]* entry. *(Théât)* **~ (en scène)** entrance; **à son ~** as he came *ou* walked in *ou* entered; **faire une ~ discrète** to make a discreet entry *ou* entrance, enter discreetly; **faire son ~ dans le monde** *[bébé]* to come into the world; *[jeune fille]* to make one's début (in society); *(Admin)* **à son ~ en fonctions** when he took up office. (**b**) *(accès)* admission (*de, dans* to); *(sur pancarte)* 'way in'. **' ~ libre'** *(dans boutique)* 'come in and look round'; *(dans musée)* 'admission free'; **' ~ interdite'** 'no admittance', 'no entry'; **on lui a refusé l' ~ de la salle** he was refused admission *ou* entrance to the hall; **~ à l'université** university entrance; **depuis son ~ à l'université/dans le club** since he went to university/joined the club; **avoir ses ~s auprès de qn** to have easy access to sb. (**c**) *(Tech) [pièce]* insertion. **~ d'air** air inlet. (**d**) *(billet)* ticket. **billet d' ~** entrance ticket; **les ~s couvriront tous les frais** the takings will cover all expenses; **ils ont fait 10 000 ~s** they sold 10,000 tickets. (**e**) *(porte)* entrance; *[trou]* mouth. *(Théât)* **~ des artistes** stage door; **~ de service** service entrance. (**f**) *(vestibule)* entrance (hall). (**g**) *(début)* **à l' ~ de l'hiver** at the onset *ou* beginning of winter; **à l' ~ de la vie** at life's outset; **d' ~ (de jeu)** from the outset; **~ en matière** introduction. (**h**) *(Culin)* entrée. (**i**) *(Comm, Statistique)* entry; *(Fin) [capital]* inflow; *(Lexicographie)* headword. (**j**) *(Ordin)* input.

entrefaites [ɑ̃tʀəfɛt] *nfpl*: **sur ces ~** at that moment.

entre-jambes [ɑ̃tʀəʒɑ̃b] *nm inv (Couture)* crotch.

entrelacer *vt,* **s' ~** *vpr* [ɑ̃tʀəlase*]* (3) to intertwine, interlace. ◆**entrelacement** *nm*: **un ~ de branches** a network *ou* crisscross of branches.

entremêler [ɑ̃tʀəmele] (1) **1** *vt choses* to intermingle, intermix. **~ un récit de** to intersperse a tale with. **2 s' ~** *vpr* to intermingle.

entremets [ɑ̃tʀəmɛ] *nm* (cream) sweet *ou* dessert.

entremettre (s') [ɑ̃tʀəmɛtʀ(ə)] (56) *vpr* to intervene (*dans* in). ◆**entremetteur, -euse** *nm, f (péj)* go-between. ◆**entremise** *nf* intervention. **par l' ~ de** through.

entreposer [ɑ̃tʀəpoze] (1) *vt* to store, put into storage. ◆**entrepôt** *nm (gén)* warehouse; *(port)* entrepot.

entreprendre [ɑ̃tʀəpʀɑ̃dʀ(ə)] (58) *vt (gén)* to begin *ou* start on, embark upon. **~ qn** *(pour bavarder)* to buttonhole sb; *(sur un problème)* to tackle sb; **~ de faire qch** to undertake to do sth. ◆**entreprenant, e** *adj (gén)* enterprising; *(avec les femmes)* forward.

entrepreneur, -euse [ɑ̃tʀəpʀənœʀ, øz] *nm, f* contractor. **~ (en bâtiment)** building contractor; **~ de pompes funèbres** undertaker, funeral director, mortician *(US)*.

entreprise [ɑ̃tʀəpʀiz] *nf (firme)* firm; *(dessein)* undertaking, venture.

entrer [ɑ̃tʀe] (1) **1** *vi* (**a**) *(aller)* to go in, get in, enter; *(venir)* to come in; *(à pied)* to walk in; *(en voiture)* to drive in. **~ dans** to go *ou* come into, enter; **~ en coup de vent** to burst in, come bursting in; **entrez!** come in!; **les gens entraient et sortaient** people were going in and out; **~ par la fenêtre** to get in by the window; **je suis entré chez eux** I called in *ou* dropped in at their house.
(**b**) *[marchandises, devises]* to enter; *[objet]* to go in; *(s'adapter)* to fit in. **ça n'entre pas** it won't go *ou* fit in; **son coude m'entrait dans les côtes** his elbow was digging into my ribs; **l'eau entre par le toit** water comes in through the roof; **l'air entre dans la pièce** air comes into *ou* enters the room; **la rage est entrée dans son cœur** his heart was filled with rage; **à force d'explications ça finira par ~ *** explain it for long enough and it'll sink in *; **alors ces maths, ça entre? *** are you getting the hang of maths then? *; **c'est entré comme dans du beurre *** it went (in) like a hot knife through butter.
(**c**) **laisser ~** to let in; **laisser ~ qn dans** to let sb into.
(**d**) **faire ~** *visiteur* to show in; *objet* to fit in; *marchandises* to take *ou* bring in; *(en fraude)* to smuggle in; *accusé, témoin* to bring in, call; **il m'a fait ~ dans leur club** *(persuadé)* he got me to join their club; *(aidé)* he got me into their club, he helped me join their club; *(contraint)* he made me join their club; *(comme employé)* he got me a job in their club; **il me fit ~ dans la cellule** he showed me into the cell.
(**e**) *(commencer)* **~ en convalescence** to begin convalescence; **~ en ébullition** to reach boiling point, begin to boil.
(**f**) **~ dans** *club, parti* to join; *groupe, métier* to go into; *profession libérale* to enter; **~ dans les affaires** to go into business; **~ en religion** to enter the religious life; **~ dans les ordres** to take orders; **~ à l'université** to go to *ou* enter university *ou* college; **~ au service de qn** to enter sb's service; **~ dans l'histoire** to go down in history; **~ dans la légende** to become a legend.
(**g**) **~ dans** *arbre* to hit, go into; *(Aut)* **on lui est entré dedans *** sb banged into him.

(**h**) ~ **dans** *vues, peines de qn* to share.
(**i**) ~ **dans** *catégorie* to fall into, come into; *mélange* to go into; **c'est entré pour beaucoup dans sa décision** it counted for a good deal in his decision; **il n'entre pas dans mes intentions de le faire** I don't have any intention of doing so; **faire ~ qch dans une catégorie** to put sth into a category.
(**j**) ~ **dans** *période, discussion* to enter into; *rêverie, considérations, colère* to go into; ~ **dans la vie active** to enter active life; ~ **dans la cinquantaine** to turn fifty; ~ **dans le vif du sujet** to get to the heart of the matter.
2 *vt*: ~ **les bras dans les manches** to put one's arms into the sleeves; **ne m'entre pas ta canne dans les côtes** don't dig your stick into my ribs; *(Ordin)* ~ **des données** to key data in.

entresol [ɑ̃tʀəsɔl] *nm* mezzanine.

entre-temps [ɑ̃tʀətɑ̃] *adv* meanwhile, (in the) meantime.

entretenir [ɑ̃tʀətniʀ] (22) **1** *vt* (**a**) *propriété* to maintain, look after; *route, machine* to maintain; *famille* to support, keep; *souvenir, espoir* to keep alive; *craintes* to have; *correspondance* to keep up. **ça entretient de l'humidité** *(qualité)* it keeps up *ou* maintains the humidity; *(défaut)* it holds the damp; ~ **le feu** to keep the fire going *ou* burning; **il m'a entretenu dans l'erreur** he didn't disabuse me (of it); ~ **sa forme, s' ~ (en bonne forme)** to keep (o.s.) fit. (**b**) *(converser)* ~ **qn** to speak to sb (*de* about). **2 s' ~** *vpr* (**a**) *(converser)* **s' ~ avec qn** to speak to sb (*de* about). (**b**) *(pourvoir à ses besoins)* to be self-supporting. ◆ **entretenu, e** *adj femme* kept. **jardin bien/mal** ~ well-/badly-kept garden. ◆ **entretien** *nm* (**a**) *[maison]* upkeep; *[route, machine]* maintenance; *[famille]* keep, support. (**b**) *(conversation)* conversation; *(entrevue)* interview; *(débat)* discussion. *(Pol)* ~**(s)** talks, discussions; ~ **télévisé** televised interview.

entre-tuer (s') [ɑ̃tʀətɥe] (1) *vpr* to kill one another.

entrevoir [ɑ̃tʀəvwaʀ] (30) *vt (indistinctement)* to make out; *(brièvement)* to catch sight of; *(fig: pressentir) objections* to foresee, anticipate; *amélioration* to glimpse.

entrevue [ɑ̃tʀəvy] *nf (discussion)* meeting; *(audience)* interview; *(Pol)* talks, discussions. **venir se présenter à** *ou* **pour une** ~ to come for *ou* to an interview.

entrouvrir *vt*, **s' ~** *vpr* [ɑ̃tʀuvʀiʀ] (18) to half-open. ◆ **entrouvert, e** *adj (gén)* half-open; *porte* ajar.

envahir [ɑ̃vaiʀ] (2) *vt [ennemi, herbes]* to invade, overrun; *[douleur, sommeil]* to overcome. **la foule envahit la place** the crowd swarmed into the square; *(déranger)* ~ **qn** to invade sb's privacy. ◆ **envahissant, e** *adj personne* intrusive; *passion* invading; *odeur, goût* strong, pervasive. ◆ **envahisseur 1** *adj m* invading. **2** *nm* invader.

envaser [ɑ̃vɑze] (1) **1** *vt port* to silt up. **2 s' ~** *vpr [port]* to silt up; *[bateau]* to stick in the mud. ◆ **envasement** *nm* silting up.

enveloppe [ɑ̃vlɔp] *nf* (**a**) *(pli postal)* envelope. ~ **à fenêtre** window envelope; ~ **auto-collante** self-seal envelope; **sous** ~ *envoyer* under cover; **mettre sous** ~ to put in an envelope. (**b**) *(emballage) (gén)* covering; *(en papier, toile)* wrapping; *(en métal)* casing; *[graine]* husk; *[pneu]* cover. (**c**) *(apparence)* exterior. (**d**) *(fig: somme d'argent)* sum of money; *(crédits)* budget; *[départ en retraite]* golden handshake. ~ **budgétaire** budget; **l'** ~ **de la recherche** the research budget.

envelopper [ɑ̃vlɔpe] (1) *vt* (**a**) *objet, enfant* to wrap up. **il s'enveloppa dans une cape** he wrapped himself in a cape; *(fig)* ~ **qn de son affection** to surround sb with one's affection; ~ **sa pensée** to veil one's thoughts. (**b**) *[brume]* to envelop, shroud. **le silence enveloppe la ville** the town is wrapped *ou* shrouded in silence; **enveloppé de mystère** shrouded *ou* veiled in mystery; ~ **qn du regard** to envelop sb with one's gaze; ~ **dans sa réprobation** † to include in one's disapproval.

envenimer [ɑ̃vnime] (1) **1** *vt plaie* to make septic; *querelle, situation* to inflame. **2 s' ~** *vpr [plaie]* to go septic; *[querelle, situation]* to grow more bitter.

envergure [ɑ̃vɛʀgyʀ] *nf [oiseau, avion]* wingspan; *[voile]* breadth; *[personne]* calibre; *[entreprise]* scale, scope; *[intelligence]* scope, range. **de grande** ~ large-scale.

envers[1] [ɑ̃vɛʀ] *prép* towards, to. ~ **et contre tous** despite all opposition.

envers[2] [ɑ̃vɛʀ] *nm* (**a**) *[étoffe]* wrong side; *[papier]* back; *[médaille]* reverse (side). **l' ~ et l'endroit** the wrong (side) and the right side; *(fig)* **l' ~ du décor** *ou* **du tableau** the other side of the picture. (**b**) **à l'** ~ *vêtement* inside out; *objet (vertical)* upside down; *(horizontal)* the wrong way round, back to front; **tout va à l'** ~ everything is upside down; **faire qch à l'** ~ *(à rebours)* to do sth the wrong way round; *(mal)* to do sth all wrong; **elle avait la tête à l'** ~ her mind was in a whirl.

envie [ɑ̃vi] *nf* (**a**) ~ **de qch/de faire** *(désir)* desire for sth/to do; *(grand désir)* longing for sth/to do; *(besoin)* need for sth/to do; **avoir ~ de** to want; **j'ai ~ d'y aller** I feel like going, I would like to go; **elle a ~ de cette voiture, cette voiture lui fait** ~ she would like this car; **avoir bien/presque ~ de faire qch** to have a good mind/half a mind to do sth; **j'ai ~ qu'il s'en aille** I would like him to go away, I wish he would go away; **avoir ~ de rire** to feel like laughing; **cela lui a donné (l') ~ de rire** it made him want to laugh; **avoir ~ *** *(d'aller aux toilettes)* to need the loo * *ou* the toilet. (**b**) *(convoitise)* envy. **mon bonheur lui fait** ~ he envies my happiness. (**c**) *(Anat) [peau]* birthmark; *[ongles]* hangnail. ◆ **enviable** *adj* enviable. ◆ **envier** (7) *vt* to envy, be envious of. **je vous envie votre maison** I wish I had your house, I envy you your house; **il n'a rien à m' ~** *(comme avantage)* he has no cause to be jealous of me; *(comme désavantage)* he's just as badly off as I am. ◆ **envieusement** *adv* enviously. ◆ **envieux, -euse** *adj* envious. **faire des** ~ to arouse envy.

environ [ɑ̃viʀɔ̃] **1** *adv* about. **c'est à 100 km ~ d'ici** it's about 100 km from here, it's 100 km or so from here. **2** *nmpl*: **les ~s** the surroundings; **aux ~s de 10 F** round about 10 francs, 10 francs or thereabouts; **dans les ~s du château** in the vicinity of the castle; **qu'y a-t-il à voir dans les ~s?** what is there to see round about here? ◆ **environnant, e** *adj* surrounding. ◆ **environnement** *nm* environment. **le Ministère de l' ~** ≃ the Department of the Environment, the Environmental Protection Agency *(US)*. ◆ **environner** (1) *vt* to surround, encircle. **s' ~ de** to surround o.s. with.

envisager [ɑ̃vizaʒe] (3) *vt* to envisage, contemplate (*de faire* doing). ◆ **envisageable** *adj* conceivable.

envoi [ɑ̃vwa] *nm* (**a**) *(V* **envoyer***)* sending; sending off; dispatching; shipment. ~ **contre remboursement** cash on delivery. (**b**) *(colis)* parcel. ~ **en nombre** mass mailing.

envoler (s') [ɑ̃vɔle] (1) *vpr [oiseau]* to fly away; *[avion]* to take off; *[chapeau]* to blow off; *[feuille, papiers]* to blow away; *[temps]* to fly (past); *[espoirs, objet volé]* to vanish. ◆ **envol** *nm [oiseau]* taking flight; *[avion]* takeoff; *[pensée]* flight. **prendre son** ~ *[oiseau]* to take flight. ◆ **envolée** *nf*: ~ **(poétique)** flight of poetry; **l' ~ des prix** the explosion in prices; **l' ~ du dollar** the soaring rise in *ou* of the dollar.

envoûter [ɑ̃vute] (1) *vt* to bewitch, cast a spell on. **être envoûté par qn** to be under sb's spell. ◆ **envoûtant, e** *adj* bewitching, spellbinding. ◆ **envoûtement** *nm* bewitchment.

envoyer [ɑ̃vwaje] (8) **1** *vt* (**a**) *(gén)* to send; *marchandises* to dispatch, send off; *(par bateau)* to ship; *(en vacances)* to send off; *(en mission)* to send out (*chez* to); *candidature* to send in. **envoie-moi un mot** drop me a line. (**b**) *pierre* to throw; *(avec force)* to hurl; *obus* to fire; *signaux* to send out; *ballon* to send. ~ **des baisers à qn** to blow sb kisses; ~ **des sourires à qn** to smile at sb; ~ **des coups de poing à qn** to punch sb; **ne m'envoie pas ta fumée dans les yeux** don't blow smoke in my eyes; ~ **qn à terre** to knock sb down; *(Naut)* ~ **par le fond** to send down *ou* to the bottom; *(Mil)* ~ **les couleurs** to run up the colours. (**c**) ~ **chercher qn/qch** to send for sb/sth; ~ **promener qn** * to send sb packing *; ~ **valser qch** * to send sth flying; **il a tout envoyé promener** * he has chucked (up) everything ⁑; **il ne le lui a pas envoyé dire** * he told him straight to his face. **2 s'** ~ ⁑ *vpr corvée* to get stuck with; *nourriture* to down. **je m'enverrais des gifles** * I could kick myself *. ◆ **envoyé, e 1** *adj réponse* well-aimed, sharp. **2** *nm, f (gén)* messenger; *(Pol)* envoy; *(Presse)* correspondent. **un ~ du Ministère** a government official. ◆ **envoyeur, -euse** *nm, f* sender.

épagneul, e [epaɲœl] *nm, f* spaniel.

épais, -aisse [epɛ, ɛs] **1** *adj* (**a**) *(gén)* thick; *neige, silence* deep; *barbe* bushy; *corps* thickset; *nuit* pitch-black. ~ **de 5 cm** 5 cm thick. (**b**) *(péj) esprit* dull; *personne* dense, thickheaded; *plaisanterie* clumsy. **2** *adv semer* thick, thickly. **il n'y en a pas** ~! * there's not much of it! ◆ **épaisseur** *nf* thickness; depth; dullness. **la neige a un mètre d'** ~ the snow is a metre deep; **plusieurs ~s de peinture** several layers of paint. ◆ **épaissir** (2) **1** *vt (lit)* to thicken. **l'air était épaissi par les fumées** the air was thick with smoke. **2** *vi (gén)* to get thicker, thicken; *[personne]* to thicken out. **3 s'** ~ *vpr (lit)* to thicken, get thicker; *[ténèbres, mystère]* to deepen. ◆ **épaississement** *nm* thickening.

épancher [epɑ̃ʃe] (1) **1** *vt sentiments* to pour forth. **2 s'** ~ *vpr [personne]* to pour out one's feelings (*auprès de* to); *[sang]* to pour out. ◆ **épanchement** *nm [sang]* effusion; *[sentiments]* outpouring.

épanouir (s') [epanwiʀ] (2) *vpr [fleur]* to bloom, open out; *[visage]* to light up; *[personne]* to blossom. ◆ **épanoui, e** *adj fleur* in full bloom; *visage, sourire* radiant. ◆ **épanouissement** *nm* opening out; blossoming. **en plein** ~ in full bloom.

épargner [epaʀɲe] (1) *vt* (**a**) *(économiser)* to save. **je n'épargnerai rien pour le faire** I'll spare nothing to get it done. (**b**) *(éviter)* ~ **qch à qn** to spare sb sth; **pour t'** ~ **des explications** to save giving you *ou* to spare you explanations; **pour m'** ~ **la peine de venir** to save *ou* spare myself the bother of coming. (**c**) *(ménager) ennemi etc* to spare. ◆ **épargnant, e** *nm, f* saver. ◆ **épargne** *nf (somme)* savings. *(vertu)* **l'** ~ saving; ~ **forcée** forced savings.

éparpiller [epaʀpije] (1) **1** *vt (gén)* to scatter; *efforts* to dissipate. **2 s'** ~ *vpr* to scatter; to dissipate one's efforts. ◆ **éparpillement** *nm* scattering; dissipation. ◆ **épars, e** *adj* scattered.

épatant, e * [epatɑ̃, ɑ̃t] *adj* splendid, great *.

épaté, e [epate] *adj nez* flat.

épater * [epate] (1) *vt (étonner)* to amaze, stagger; *(impressionner)* to impress.

épaulard [epolaʀ] *nm* killer whale.

épaule [epol] *nf (Anat, Culin)* shoulder.

épauler [epole] (1) *vt* (**a**) *personne* to back up, support. (**b**) *fusil* to raise. **il épaula** he took aim, he raised his rifle.

épaulette [epolɛt] *nf (Mil)* epaulette.

épave [epav] *nf (lit, fig)* wreck; *(débris)* piece of wreckage.

épée [epe] *nf* sword.

épeler [eple] (4) *ou* (5) *vt mot* to spell; *texte* to spell out.

éperdu, e [epɛʀdy] *adj* (**a**) *personne* distraught, overcome (*de* with). (**b**) *gratitude* boundless; *regard* wild, distraught; *amour* passionate; *fuite* headlong; *désir* frantic. ◆ **éperdument** *adv* frantically; *aimer* passionately. **je m'en moque** ~ I couldn't care less.

éperonner [epʀɔne] (1) *vt cheval* to spur on; *navire* to ram. ◆ **éperon** *nm (gén)* spur.

épervier [epɛʀvje] *nm (Orn)* sparrowhawk; *(filet)* casting net.

éphémère [efemɛʀ] *adj* fleeting, short-lived.

épi [epi] *nm [blé]* ear; *[fleur]* spike; *[cheveux]* tuft. **être garé en** ~ to be parked at an angle to the kerb.

épice [epis] *nf* spice. ◆ **épicé, e** *adj (gén)* spicy. ◆ **épicer** (3) *vt* to spice.

épicerie [episʀi] *nf (magasin)* grocer's (shop); *(nourriture)* groceries; *(métier)* grocery trade. *(supermarché)* **rayon** ~ grocery stand *ou* counter; **aller à l'** ~ to go to the grocer's; ~ **fine** ≃ delicatessen. ◆ **épicier, -ière** *nm, f (gén)* grocer; *(fruits et légumes)* greengrocer.

épidémie [epidemi] *nf* epidemic. ◆ **épidémique** *adj (lit)* epidemic; *(fig)* contagious.

épiderme [epidɛʀm(ə)] *nm* skin. ◆ **épidermique** *adj (Anat)* skin. *(fig)* **réaction** ~ automatic reaction, gut reaction.

épier [epje] (7) *vt personne* to spy on; *geste* to watch closely; *bruit* to listen out for; *occasion* to watch out for.

épilepsie [epilɛpsi] *nf* epilepsy. **crise d'** ~ epileptic fit. ◆ **épileptique** *adj, nmf* epileptic.

épiler [epile] (1) *vt jambes* to remove the hair from; *sourcils* to pluck.

épilogue [epilɔg] *nm (littér)* epilogue; *(fig)* conclusion.

épinard [epinaʀ] *nm*: ~**(s)** spinach.

épine [epin] *nf* (**a**) *[buisson]* thorn; *[hérisson, oursin]* spine, prickle; *[porc-épic]* quill. ~ **dorsale** backbone; **vous m'enlevez une belle ~ du pied** you have got me out of a spot *. (**b**) *(arbre)* thorn bush. ~ **blanche** hawthorn. ◆ **épineux, -euse** *adj plante* thorny, prickly; *problème* thorny, tricky.

épingle [epɛ̃gl(ə)] *nf* pin. **virage en ~ à cheveux** hairpin bend *ou* turn *(US)*; ~ **à linge** clothes peg *ou* pin *(US)*; ~ **de nourrice** safety pin; **tirer son ~ du jeu** *(bien manœuvrer)* to play one's game well; *(s'en sortir à temps)* to manage to extricate o.s. ◆ **épingler** (1) *vt (attacher)* to pin (on) (*à, sur* to); (⁑: *arrêter*) to nick ⁑, nab *.

Épiphanie [epifani] *nf*: **l'** ~ Epiphany, Twelfth Night.

épique [epik] *adj (lit, fig)* epic.

épiscopat [episkɔpa] *nm (siège)* bishopric; *(corps)* episcopacy. ◆ **épiscopal, e,** *mpl* **-aux** *adj* episcopal.

épiscope [episkɔp] *nm* episcope, opaque projector *(US)*.

épisode [epizɔd] *nm* episode. **film à ~s** serial. ◆ **épisodique** *adj (occasionnel)* occasional; *(secondaire)* minor, secondary. ◆ **épisodiquement** *adv* occasionally.

épitaphe [epitaf] *nf* epitaph.

épithète [epitɛt] *nf* (**a**) *(Gram)* attribute. **adjectif** ~ attributive adjective. (**b**) *(qualificatif)* epithet.

épître [epitʀ(ə)] *nf* epistle.

éploré, e [eplɔʀe] *adj (littér) visage* bathed in tears; *personne, voix* tearful.

éplucher [eplyʃe] (1) *vt (gén)* to peel; *salade* to clean; *bonbon* to unwrap; *comptes* to dissect. ◆ **épluchage** *nm* cleaning; peeling; unwrapping; dissection. ◆ **épluchure** *nf* piece of peeling.

éponge [epɔ̃ʒ] *nf* sponge. **passons l'** ~! let's forget all about it!; ~ **métallique** scouring pad. ◆ **éponger** (3) *vt liquide* to mop *ou* sponge up; *visage* to mop; *dette* to absorb. **s'** ~ **le front** to mop one's brow.

épopée [epɔpe] *nf (lit, fig)* epic.

époque [epɔk] *nf (gén)* time; *(Hist)* age, era, epoch; *(Géol)* period; *(Art: style)* period. **à l'** ~ at the time; **être de son** ~ to be in tune with one's time; **quelle** ~! what times these are!; **à l'** ~ **où nous sommes** in this day and age; **meuble d'** ~ genuine antique, piece of period furniture.

époumoner (s') [epumɔne] (1) *vpr* to shout *etc* o.s. hoarse.

épouser [epuze] (1) *vt* (**a**) *personne* to marry; *idée* to embrace, take up. (**b**) *[robe]* to fit; *[route, tracé]* to follow. ◆ **épouse** *nf* wife.

épousseter [epuste] (4) *vt* to dust.

époustoufler * [epustufle] (1) *vt* to stagger, flabbergast.

épouvanter [epuvɑ̃te] (1) *vt (gén)* to appal, frighten. **s'** ~ **de qch** to get frightened at sth. ◆ **épouvantable** *adj* appalling, dreadful. ◆ **épouvantablement** *adv* appallingly, dreadfully. ◆ **épouvantail** *nm (à oiseaux)* scarecrow; *(menace) (personne)* bogey; *(chose)* bugbear. ◆ **épouvante** *nf* terror. **saisi d'** ~ terror-stricken; **avec** ~ with dread; **film d'** ~ horror film.

époux [epu] *nm* husband. **les** ~ the husband and wife.

éprendre (s') [epʀɑ̃dʀ(ə)] (58) *vpr (littér)* **s'** ~ **de** to fall in love with.

épreuve [epʀœv] *nf* (**a**) *(essai)* test. *(fig)* ~ **de force** showdown, confrontation; ~ **de vérité** litmus test; **mettre à l'** ~ to put to the test; **à l'** ~ **des balles/du feu** bulletproof/fireproof; *(fig)* **à toute** ~ *amitié, foi* staunch; *mur* solid as a rock; **courage à toute** ~ unfailing courage. (**b**) *(initiatique)* ordeal; *(malheur)* ordeal, trial. **subir de rudes** ~**s** to undergo great trials *ou* ordeals. (**c**) *(Scol)* test; *(Sport)* event. ~ **de sélection** heat; ~ **contre la montre** time-trial. (**d**) *(Typ)* proof; *(Phot)* print.

épris, e [epʀi, iz] *adj (littér)* in love (*de* with).

éprouver [epʀuve] (1) *vt* (**a**) *sensation* to feel, experience; *perte* to suffer; *difficultés* to experience. (**b**) *(tester)* to test. (**c**) *[maladie]* to afflict; *[nouvelle]* to distress. ◆ **éprouvant, e** *adj* testing. ◆ **éprouvé, e** *adj remède* well-tried, proven; *spécialiste* well-proven.

éprouvette [epʀuvɛt] *nf* test-tube.

épuiser [epɥize] (1) **1** *vt (gén)* to exhaust; *personne* to tire out, wear out. **2 s'** ~ *vpr [réserves]* to run out; *[source]* to dry up; *[forces]* to fail; *[personne]* to exhaust o.s., wear *ou* tire o.s. out (*à faire qch* doing sth). ◆ **épuisant, e** *adj* exhausting. ◆ **épuisé, e** *adj (gén)* exhausted; *(Comm) article* sold out; *livre* out of print. ~ **de fatigue** tired out, worn out. ◆ **épuisement** *nm (gén)* exhaustion. **devant l'** ~ **de ses finances** seeing that his money was exhausted *ou* had run out.

épuisette [epɥizɛt] *nf* landing net; *(à crevettes)* shrimping net.

épurer [epyʀe] (1) *vt (lit)* to purify; *(Pol)* to purge. ◆ **épuration** *nf* purification; purge.

équateur [ekwatœʀ] *nm* equator. *(pays)* **république de l'É**~ Ecuador. ◆ **équatorial, e,** *mpl* **-aux** *adj* equatorial. ◆ **équatorien, -ienne** *adj,* **É~(ne)** *nm(f)* Ecuadorian.

équation [ekwasjɔ̃] *nf* equation.

équerre [ekɛʀ] *nf (pour tracer)* set square; *(de soutien)* brace. **en** ~ at right angles; **être d'** ~ to be straight *ou* level.

équestre [ekɛstʀ(ə)] *adj* equestrian.

équidistant, e [ekɥidistɑ̃, ɑ̃t] *adj* equidistant (*de* between).

équilatéral, e, *mpl* **-aux** [ekɥilateʀal, o] *adj* equilateral.

équilibre [ekilibʀ(ə)] *nm (gén)* balance, equilibrium; *(harmonie)* harmony. **perdre l'** ~ to lose one's balance; **être en** ~ **sur** *[personne]* to balance on; *[objet]* to be balanced on; **mettre qch en** ~ to balance sth (*sur* on); ~ **(mental)** (mental) equilibrium *ou* stability; ~ **budgétaire** balance in the budget; **budget en** ~ balanced budget; **l'** ~ **du monde** the world balance of power. ◆ **équilibrage** *nm (Aut)* balancing. ◆ **équilibré, e** *adj personne* stable, well-balanced; *vie* well-regulated. **mal** ~ unbalanced. ◆ **équilibrer** (1) **1** *vt (gén)* to balance; *(contrebalancer)* to counterbalance. **2 s'** ~ *vpr [forces etc]* to counterbalance each other, cancel each other out. ◆ **équilibriste** *nmf* tightrope walker; *(fig)* juggler.

équinoxe [ekinɔks(ə)] *nm* equinox.

équipage [ekipaʒ] *nm (Aviat)* (air)crew; *(Naut)* crew; (†) *[seigneur, chevaux]* equipage †.

équipe [ekip] *nf (Sport) (gén)* team; *[rameurs]* crew; *[ouvriers]* gang; *(par roulement)* shift; *(*: péj, fig)* bunch *, crew *. ~ **de secours** rescue party; ~ **de nuit** night shift; **faire** ~ **avec** to team up with. ◆ **équipier, -ière** *nm, f (Sport)* team member.

équipée [ekipe] *nf [prisonnier]* escape; *[aventurier]* undertaking, venture; *[promeneur]* jaunt.

équiper [ekipe] (1) *vt (gén)* to equip; *local* to fit out; *sportif* to kit out (*de* with). ~ **une machine de** to fit a machine out with; **s'** ~ *[sportif]* to equip o.s., kit o.s. out. ◆ **équipement** *nm (action)* equipping; fitting out; kitting out (*de* with); *(matériel)* equipment, kit. **l'** ~ **hôtelier d'une région** the hotel resources of a region; ~**s sportifs** sports equipment; *(Jur)* ~**s collectifs** public amenities.

équitable [ekitabl(ə)] *adj jugement* equitable, fair; *personne* fair. ◆ **équitablement** *adv* equitably, fairly.

équitation [ekitasjɔ̃] *nf* (horse-)riding. **faire de l'** ~ to go horse-riding.

équité [ekite] *nf* equity.

équivalence [ekivalɑ̃s] *nf* equivalence. ◆ **équivalent, e 1** *adj* equivalent (*à* to). **à prix** ~ for the same *ou* equivalent price. **2** *nm* equivalent (*de* of). ◆ **équivaloir** (29) *vi* to be equivalent (*à* to). **ça équivaut à dire que...** it amounts to *ou* it is equivalent to saying that...

équivoque [ekivɔk] **1** *adj (ambigu)* equivocal, ambiguous; *(louche)* dubious. **2** *nf (ambiguïté)* ambiguity; *(incertitude)* doubt; *(malentendu)* misunderstanding. **sans** ~ *conduite* unequivocal, **pour lever l'** ~ to remove any doubt.

érable [eʀabl(ə)] *nm* maple.

érafler [eʀɑfle] (1) *vt* to scratch, graze. ◆ **éraflure** *nf* scratch, graze.

éraillé, e [eʀɑje] *adj voix* rasping, hoarse.

ère [ɛʀ] *nf* era. **avant notre** ~ B.C.; **de notre** ~ A.D.

érection [eʀɛksjɔ̃] *nf (lit)* erection; *[société etc]* setting-up.

éreinter [eʀɛ̃te] (1) *vt (épuiser)* to exhaust, wear out; *(critiquer)* to pull to pieces. ◆ **éreintant, e** * *adj* exhausting, backbreaking. ◆ **éreinté, e** * *adj* worn out, shattered *.

ergonomie [ɛʀgɔnɔmi] *nf* ergonomics *(sg)*. ◆ **ergonomique** *adj* ergonomic(al).

ergot [ɛʀgo] *nm [coq]* spur.

ergoter [ɛʀgɔte] (1) *vi* to quibble (*sur* about). ◆ **ergotage** *nm*: ~**(s)** quibbling. ◆ **ergoteur, -euse** *nm, f* quibbler.

ériger [eʀiʒe] (3) *vt bâtiment* to erect; *société etc* to set up. ~ **ses habitudes en doctrine** to give one's habits the status of a doctrine; **il s'érige en maître** he sets himself up as a master.

ermite [ɛʀmit] *nm* hermit. ◆ **ermitage** *nm* hermitage; *(fig)* retreat.

éroder [eʀɔde] (1) *vt* to erode. ◆ **érosion** *nf* erosion.

érotisme [eʀɔtism(ə)] *nm* eroticism. ◆ **érotique** *adj* erotic.

errata [eʀata] *nm inv* errata.

erratum [eʀatɔm] *nm sg* erratum.

errer [ɛʀe] (1) *vi (littér)* (**a**) *[voyageur, regard]* to wander, roam (*sur* over); *[sourire]* to hover. (**b**) *(se tromper)* to err. ◆ **errant, e** *adj (gén)* wandering. **chien** ~ stray dog.

erreur [ɛʀœʀ] *nf* (**a**) *(gén)* mistake, error. ~ **de calcul** miscalculation; ~ **typographique** misprint, typographical error; ~ **de sens** wrong meaning; ~ **de traduction** mistranslation; ~ **judiciaire** miscarriage of justice; **sauf** ~ unless I'm (very much) mistaken; **par** ~ by mistake; **faire une** ~ to make a mistake (*sur* about); **faire** ~ to be wrong *ou* mistaken; **l'** ~ **est humaine** to err is human. (**b**) *(dérèglements)* ~**s** errors; ~**s de jeunesse** mistakes of youth. ◆ **erroné, e** *adj* erroneous.

ersatz [ɛʀzats] *nm (lit, fig)* ersatz.

érudit, e [eʀydi, it] **1** *adj* erudite, scholarly. **2** *nm, f* scholar. ◆ **érudition** *nf* erudition, scholarship.

éruption [eʀypsjɔ̃] *nf* eruption. **entrer en** ~ to erupt.

ès [ɛs] *prép*: **licencié** ~ **lettres** ≃ Bachelor of Arts.

escabeau, *pl* ~**x** [ɛskabo] *nm (tabouret)* stool; *(échelle)* stepladder.

escadre [ɛskadʀ(ə)] *nf (Naut)* squadron; *(Aviat)* wing. ◆ **escadrille** *nf (Aviat)* flight. ◆ **escadron** *nm (Mil)* squadron; *(fig: bande)* crowd. ~ **de gendarmerie** platoon of gendarmes.

escalader [ɛskalade] (1) *vt* to climb; *forteresse* to scale. ◆ **escalade** *nf (action)* climbing; scaling; *(Pol etc)* escalation. *(Sport)* **l'** ~ (rock) climbing; **une belle** ~ a beautiful climb; **l'** ~ **de la violence** an escalation of violence; **pour éviter l'** ~ to avoid an escalation.

escalator [ɛskalatɔʀ] *nm* escalator.

escale [ɛskal] *nf* (**a**) *(endroit) (Naut)* port of call; *(Aviat)* stop. **faire** ~ **à** *(Naut)* to call at; *(Aviat)* to stop over at. (**b**) *(temps d'arrêt) (Naut)* call; *(Aviat)* stop. **vol sans** ~ non-stop flight; *(Aviat)* ~ **technique** refuelling stop.

escalier [ɛskalje] *nm (marches)* stairs; *(cage)* staircase. **dans l'** ~ on the stairs; ~ **de service** backstairs; ~ **roulant** escalator; ~ **de secours** fire escape; *(Ski)* **montée en** ~ side-stepping.

escalope [ɛskalɔp] *nf* escalope.

escamoter [ɛskamɔte] (1) *vt cartes etc* to conjure away; *difficulté, question* to evade; *mot* to skip; *(*: voler)* to pinch *; *(Aviat)* to retract. ◆ **escamotable** *adj (gén)* retractable; *lit* collapsible, foldaway. ◆ **escamotage** *nm [train d'atterrissage]* retraction. ◆ **escamoteur, -euse** *nm, f* conjurer.

escapade [ɛskapad] *nf (promenade)* jaunt. *[écolier]* **faire une** ~ to run away.

escargot [ɛskaʀgo] *nm* snail. *(manifestation)* **opération** ~ lorry drivers' go-slow.

escarmouche [ɛskaʀmuʃ] *nf (lit, fig)* skirmish.

escarpé, e [ɛskaʀpe] *adj* steep. ◆ **escarpement** *nm (côte)* steep slope.

escarpin [ɛskaʀpɛ̃] *nm* flat shoe.

escarre, eschare [ɛskaʀ] *nf* bedsore.

escient [esjɑ̃] *nm*: **à bon** ~ advisedly; **à mauvais** ~ ill-advisedly.

esclaffer (s') [ɛsklafe] (1) *vpr* to burst out laughing.

esclandre [ɛsklɑ̃dʀ(ə)] *nm (scandale)* scene.

esclave [ɛsklav] *nm* slave (*de qn/qch* to sb/sth). ◆ **esclavage** *nm* slavery. **réduire en** ~ to enslave; **c'est de l'** ~ it's sheer slavery. ◆ **esclavagisme** *nm* proslavery.

escompte [ɛskɔ̃t] *nm (Banque)* discount. ◆ **escompter** (1) *vt (Banque)* to discount; *(fig)* to expect. ~ **faire qch** to expect to do sth, count on doing sth.

escorte [ɛskɔʀt(ə)] *nf (gén)* escort. **sous bonne** ~ under escort. ◆ **escorter** (1) *vt* to escort.

escouade [ɛskwad] *nf (gén, Mil)* squad.

escrime [ɛskʀim] *nf* fencing. **faire de l'** ~ to fence. ◆ **escrimer (s')** * (1) *vpr*: **s'** ~ **à faire qch** to wear o.s. out doing sth. ◆ **escrimeur, -euse** *nm, f* fencer.

escroc [ɛskʀo] *nm* swindler. ◆ **escroquer** (1) *vt* to swindle. ~ **qch à qn** to swindle sb out of sth. ◆ **escroquerie** *nf (gén)* swindle; *(Jur)* fraud. **être victime d'une** ~ to be a victim of fraud; **c'est de l'**~ it's a swindle *ou* a rip-off ‡.

ésotérique [ezɔteʀik] *adj* esoteric.

espace [ɛspas] *nm (gén)* space. *(Phys)* ~**-temps** space-time; ~ **de temps** space of time, interval; **manquer d'** ~ to be short of space *ou* room; **laisser un** ~ **entre** to leave a space *ou* gap between; **en l'** ~ **de 3 minutes** within the space of 3 minutes; ~ **parcouru** distance covered; ~**s verts** green spaces; ~ **vital** living space; **dans l'** ~ **intersidéral** in deep space. ◆ **espacement** *nm (action)* spacing out; *(résultat)* spacing. ◆ **espacer** (3) **1** *vt* to space out. **2 s'** ~ *vpr* to become less frequent.

espadon [ɛspadɔ̃] *nm* swordfish.

espadrille [ɛspadʀij] *nf* rope-soled sandal.

Espagne [ɛspaɲ] *nf* Spain. ◆ **espagnol, e** **1** *adj* Spanish. **2** *nm (Ling)* Spanish. **3** *nm(f)*: **E**~**(e)** Spaniard.

espèce [ɛspɛs] *nf* (**a**) *(Bio, Philos, Rel)* species. ~ **humaine** human race. (**b**) *(sorte)* sort, kind, type. **ça n'a aucune** ~ **d'importance** that is of absolutely no importance; **de la pire** ~ of the worst kind *ou* sort; **une** *ou* **un** ~ **d'excentrique** an eccentric sort of person; ~ **de maladroit!** you clumsy clot! * (**c**) *(Fin)* ~**s** cash; **en** ~**s** in cash.

espérance [ɛspeʀɑ̃s] *nf* hope. **dans l'** ~ **de faire** hoping to do, in the hope of doing; **contre toute** ~ against all expectations *ou* hope; **donner de grandes** ~**s** to show great promise; **avoir de grandes** ~**s (d'avenir)** to have great prospects; **garder l'** ~ **de pouvoir...** to remain hopeful of being able to...; ~ **de vie** life expectancy, expectation of life.

espérer [ɛspeʀe] (6) **1** *vt succès etc* to hope for. ~ **réussir** to hope to succeed; — **je l'espère (bien)** — I hope so; **ceci nous laisse** ~ **un succès rapide** this gives us hope *ou* makes us hopeful of quick success; **j'espère bien n'avoir rien oublié** I hope I haven't forgotten anything. **2** *vi (avoir confiance)* to have faith. **il faut** ~ you must have faith; ~ **en** *Dieu etc* to have faith in, trust in.

espiègle [ɛspjɛgl(ə)] **1** *adj enfant* mischievous; *air* roguish. **2** *nmf* imp. ◆ **espièglerie** *nf* mischievousness; roguishness; *(tour)* prank.

espion, -onne [ɛspjɔ̃, ɔn] *nm, f* spy. ◆ **espionnage** *nm* espionage, spying. **film d'** ~ spy film; ~ **industriel** industrial espionage. ◆ **espion(n)ite** *nf* spy mania. ◆ **espionner** (1) *vt* to spy on.

esplanade [ɛsplanad] *nf* esplanade.

espoir [ɛspwaʀ] *nm (gén)* hope. **dans l'** ~ **de vous voir** hoping to see you soon, in the hope of seeing you; **avoir l' ~ que** to be hopeful that; **avoir bon ~ de faire/que** to be confident of doing/that; **sans** ~ *situation* hopeless; *aimer* without hope.

esprit [ɛspʀi] **1** *nm* (**a**) *(gén: pensée)* mind. **avoir l' ~ large/étroit** to be broad-/narrow-minded; **à l' ~ lent** slow-witted; **avoir l' ~ clair** to have a clear head *ou* mind; **où ai-je l' ~?** what am I thinking of?; **je n'ai pas l' ~ à rire** I'm not in the mood for laughing; **il m'est venu à l' ~ que** it crossed my mind that, it occurred to me that. (**b**) *(humour)* wit. **faire de l' ~** to try to be witty *ou* funny. (**c**) *(être humain)* person; *(savant)* mind; *(fantôme)* spirit. **c'est un ~ subtil** he is a shrewd man, he has a shrewd mind. (**d**) *[loi, époque, texte]* spirit. (**e**) *(aptitude)* **avoir l' ~ d'analyse** to have an analytical mind; **avoir l' ~ des affaires** to have a good head for business; **avoir l' ~ critique** to have a critical eye; **avoir l' ~ de critique** to be a fault-finder. (**f**) *(attitude)* spirit. **l' ~ de cette classe** the attitude of this class; **faire preuve de mauvais ~** to be a disruptive influence. **2** : **~ de clan** clannishness; **~ de compétition** competitive spirit; **~ de contradiction** argumentativeness; **~ d'équipe** team spirit; **~ de famille** family feeling; *(péj)* clannishness; **~ frappeur** spirit-rapper; **l' ~ malin** the Evil spirit; *(Rel)* **l'E~ Saint** the Holy Ghost; **~ de suite** consistency of thought.

esquimau, -aude, *mpl* **~x** [ɛskimo, od] **1** *adj* Eskimo. **2** *nm (Ling)* Eskimo; *(glace)* choc-ice, Eskimo *(US)*; *(chien)* husky. **3** *nm(f)*: **E~(de)** Eskimo.

esquinter * [ɛskɛ̃te] (1) **1** *vt objet* to mess up; *santé* to ruin; *adversaire* to bash up *; *voiture* to smash up; *(critiquer)* to pull to pieces. **2 s' ~** *vpr* to tire o.s. out (*à faire* doing).

esquisse [ɛskis] *nf (Peinture)* sketch; *[projet]* outline; *[geste]* suggestion. ◆ **esquisser** (1) *vt* to sketch (out); to outline. **~ un geste** to half-make a gesture; **un progrès commence à s' ~** one can begin to detect some progress.

esquiver [ɛskive] (1) **1** *vt coup, question, personne* to dodge, evade. **2 s' ~** *vpr* to slip *ou* sneak away. ◆ **esquive** *nf* dodge; evasion.

essai [esɛ] *nm* (**a**) *(test) (action)* trying out, testing; *(épreuve)* test. **~s** *(Aut, Aviat: tests techniques)* trials; *(Course automobile)* practice; **prendre qn à l' ~** to take sb on for a trial period; **il a été pris à l' ~** he's been taken on for a trial period; **mettre à l' ~** to test (out), put to the test; *(première utilisation)* **faire l' ~ d'un produit** to try out a product. (**b**) *(tentative)* attempt, try; *(Sport)* attempt. **premier ~** first try *ou* attempt *ou* go. (**c**) *(Rugby)* try. (**d**) *(Littérat)* essay.

essaim [esɛ̃] *nm (lit, fig)* swarm. ◆ **essaimage** *nm* swarming; scattering; spreading. ◆ **essaimer** [eseme] (1) *vi (lit)* to swarm; *[famille]* to scatter; *[firme]* to spread.

essayer [eseje] (8) **1** *vt* (**a**) *(tester)* to test (out), try (out); *(pour la première fois)* to try (out); *vêtement* to try on. (**b**) *(tenter)* to try. **~ de faire** to try *ou* attempt to do; **essaie de le faire** try to do it, try and do it; **je vais ~** I'll try, I'll have a go *ou* a try. **2 s' ~** *vpr*: **s' ~ à qch/à faire** to try one's hand at sth/at doing, have a go at sth/at doing. ◆ **essayage** *nm (Couture)* fitting.

essence [esɑ̃s] *nf* (**a**) *(carburant)* petrol, gas(oline) *(US)*; *(solvant)* spirit. **~ minérale** mineral oil; **~ ordinaire** two-star petrol, regular gas *(US)*; **~ sans plomb** lead-free petrol, unleaded gas *(US)*. (**b**) *(extrait) [plantes etc]* oil, essence. **~ de rose** rose oil. (**c**) *[question, doctrine]* gist, essence; *(Philos)* essence. **par ~** in essence, essentially. (**d**) *(espèce)* species.

essentiel, -elle [esɑ̃sjɛl] **1** *adj (indispensable)* essential (*à* to, *pour* for); *(de base)* essential, basic. **2** *nm*: **l' ~** *(objets nécessaires)* the basic essentials; *(points principaux)* the essentials, the essential *ou* basic points; *(l'important)* the main thing; **l' ~ de** the main part of; **l' ~ de ce qu'il dit** most of what he says. ◆ **essentiellement** *adv* essentially; basically.

essieu, *pl* **~x** [esjø] *nm* axle(-tree).

essor [esɔʀ] *nm [oiseau, imagination]* flight; *[pays]* expansion; *[art]* blossoming. **prendre son ~** *[oiseau]* to fly off; *[société]* to expand rapidly.

essorer [esɔʀe] (1) *vt (manuellement)* to wring (out); *(à la machine)* to spin-dry. ◆ **essorage** *nm* wringing; spin-drying. ◆ **essoreuse** *nf* spin-dryer.

essouffler [esufle] (1) **1** *vt* to make breathless. **être essoufflé** to be out of breath. **2 s' ~** *vpr [coureur]* to get out of breath; *[travail]* to fall off; *[romancier]* to exhaust o.s. ◆ **essoufflement** *nm* breathlessness.

essuyer [esɥije] (8) **1** *vt* (**a**) *(gén)* to wipe; *tableau noir* to clean, wipe; *poussière* to dust; *eau* to wipe up, mop up. **s' ~ les mains** to wipe one's hands (dry), dry one's hands; **~ la vaisselle** to wipe *ou* dry up; **nous avons essuyé les plâtres** * we had all the initial problems to put up with. (**b**) *pertes, reproches* to suffer; *refus* to meet with; *tempête* to weather. **~ le feu de l'ennemi** to come under enemy fire; **~ un coup de feu** to be shot at. **2 s' ~** *vpr [baigneur]* to dry o.s. **3** : **essuie-glace** *nm inv* windscreen *ou* windshield *(US)* wiper; **essuie-mains** *nm inv* hand towel; **essuie-tout** *nm inv* kitchen paper.

est¹ [ɛ] *V* **être.**

est² [ɛst] **1** *nm* east. **vent d' ~** east wind; **à l' ~** *(situation)* in the east; *(direction)* to the east, east(wards); **à l' ~ de** east of, to the east of; *(Pol)* **les pays de l'E~** the eastern countries; **le bloc de l'E~** the Eastern bloc; **l'Europe de l'E~** Eastern Europe; **l'Allemagne de l'E~** East Germany. **2** *adj inv région* eastern; *côté* east; *direction* eastward, easterly.

estafette [ɛstafɛt] *nf (Mil)* Courier.

estafilade [ɛstafilad] *nf* slash.

estaminet † [ɛstaminɛ] *nm* tavern †.

estampe [ɛstɑ̃p] *nf (image)* engraving, print; *(outil)* stamp.

estamper [ɛstɑ̃pe] (1) *vt* (*: *voler)* to swindle, diddle * (*de qch* out of sth); *(Tech)* to stamp.

estampille [ɛstɑ̃pij] *nf* stamp.

esthétique [ɛstetik] **1** *adj jugement* aesthetic; *carrosserie* attractive. **2** *nf* attractiveness. *(discipline)* **l' ~** aesthetics *(sg)*; **l' ~ industrielle** industrial design. ◆ **esthète** *nmf* aesthete. ◆ **esthéticien, -ienne** *nm, f (maquillage)* beautician. ◆ **esthétiquement** *adv* aesthetically. ◆ **esthétisme** *nm* aestheticism.

estimer [ɛstime] (1) *vt* (**a**) *objet* to appraise, value; *distance, dégâts, prix* to assess, estimate. (**b**) *(respecter) personne* to esteem. **estimé de tous** respected *ou* esteemed by everyone. (**c**) *qualité* to value greatly, prize. **~ qch à sa juste valeur** to recognize the true worth *ou* value of sth; **savoir ~ un service rendu** to know how to appreciate a favour; **c'est un plat très estimé** this dish is considered a great delicacy. (**d**) *(considérer)* **~ que...** to consider that...; **nous estimons nécessaire de dire** we consider it necessary to say; **~ inutile de faire** to see no point in doing, consider it pointless to do; **s' ~ heureux d'un résultat** to consider o.s. fortunate with a result. ◆ **estimable** *adj (respectable)* estimable; *(assez bon)* honest, sound; *(déterminable)* assessable. ◆ **estimation** *nf* appraisal, valuation; assessment, estimation; *(chiffre)* estimate. **~ approximative** guesstimate; **~ des coûts** cost estimate; *(sondage d'opinion, vote)* **~s** projections. ◆ **estime** *nf* (**a**) *(considération)* esteem, respect. (**b**) *(Naut)* **à l'** ~ by dead reckoning.

estival, e, *mpl* **-aux** [ɛstival, o] *adj* summer. ◆ **estivant, e** *nm, f* holiday-maker, vacationer *(US)*.

estomac [ɛstɔma] *nm* (**a**) stomach. **partir l'** ~ **creux** to set off on an empty stomach; **avoir l'** ~ **creux/bien rempli** to feel empty/full (up). (**b**) (‡) **avoir de l'** ~ *(du culot)* to have a nerve; *(du courage)* to have guts *; **il lui a fait ça à l'** ~ he hoodwinked him.

estomaquer * [ɛstɔmake] (1) *vt* to stagger.

estomper [ɛstɔ̃pe] (1) **1** *vt dessin* to shade off; *contours, souvenir* to blur. **2 s'** ~ *vpr* to become blurred.

estourbir ‡ [ɛstuʀbiʀ] (2) *vt (assommer)* to stun; *(tuer)* to do in ‡.

estrade [ɛstʀad] *nf* platform, rostrum.

estragon [ɛstʀagɔ̃] *nm* tarragon.

estropier [ɛstʀɔpje] (7) *vt personne* to cripple, disable; *citation* to twist, distort; *langue étrangère, musique* to murder. ◆ **estropié, e** *nm, f* cripple.

estuaire [ɛstɥɛʀ] *nm* estuary; *(en Écosse)* firth.

estudiantin, e [ɛstydjɑ̃tɛ̃, in] *adj* student.

esturgeon [ɛstyʀʒɔ̃] *nm* sturgeon.

et [e] *conj* and. ~ **lui** ~ **vous** both he and you; **j'aime beaucoup ça,** ~ **vous?** I'm very fond of that, aren't you? *ou* what about you?; ~ **moi alors?** what about me then?; ~ **puis** and then; *(qu'importe)* so what? *; ~ **moi, je peux venir?** can I come too?; **vingt/trente** *etc* ~ **un** twenty-/thirty- *etc* one; **à midi** ~ **quart** at a quarter past twelve; **le vingt** ~ **unième** the twenty-first.

étable [etabl(ə)] *nf* cowshed.

établi [etabli] *nm* workbench.

établir [etabliʀ] (2) **1** *vt* (**a**) *(gén)* to establish; *usine, record, communications* to set up; *règlement* to lay down, institute. ~ **son camp/Q.G. dans** to pitch one's camp/set up one's H.Q. in; ~ **son fils médecin** to set one's son up *ou* establish one's son in medical practice; ~ **son pouvoir sur le pays** to establish control over the country; **il est établi que** it's an established fact that. (**b**) *empire, fortune* to build up; *démonstration* to base (*sur* on). (**c**) *liste* to draw up, make out; *programme* to arrange; *chèque* to make out; *plans* to draw up; *prix* to fix. **2 s'** ~ *vpr [commerçant, colon]* to establish o.s; *[usage]* to become customary; *[pouvoir]* to become established; *[amitié, contacts]* to develop. **une nouvelle usine s'est établie** a new factory has been set up; **l'ennemi s'est établi sur la colline** the enemy has taken up position on the hill; **s'** ~ **boulanger** to set o.s. up as a baker; **un grand silence s'établit** a great silence fell. ◆ **établissement** *nm* (**a**) *(action)* establishing; setting-up; institution; laying-down; building up; basing; drawing-up; making-out; arranging; fixing; development. (**b**) *(bâtiment)* establishment; *(colonie)* settlement. ~ **d'enseignement secondaire** secondary school, high school *(US)*; ~ **privé** independent *ou* private school; ~ **hospitalier** hospital; ~ **religieux** religious institution; ~ **industriel** factory; **avec les compliments des** ~**s X** with the compliments of X and Co.

étage [etaʒ] *nm [bâtiment]* floor, storey; *[fusée]* stage; *[mine, jardin]* level; *[gâteau]* tier. **au premier** ~ on the first floor; **maison à deux** ~**s** three-storeyed house; **il grimpa 3** ~**s** he went up *ou* walked up 3 floors *ou* flights. ◆ **étagement** *nm* terracing. ◆ **étager** (3) **1** *vt* to lay out in tiers. **2 s'** ~ *vpr* to rise in tiers *ou* terraces. ◆ **étagère** *nf (tablette)* shelf; *(meuble)* shelves.

étai [etɛ] *nm (gén, Naut)* stay.

étain [etɛ̃] *nm (Min)* tin; *(Orfèvrerie) (matière)* pewter; *(objet)* piece of pewterware.

étal, *pl* ~**s** [etal] *nm* stall.

étalage [etalaʒ] *nm* (**a**) *(Comm) (action)* displaying; *(devanture)* shop window; *(tréteaux)* stand; *(articles)* display. **disposer l'** ~ to dress the window, do the window display; **chemise qui a fait l'** ~ shop-soiled shirt. (**b**) *[luxe, connaissances]* display, show. **faire** ~ **de** to show off; ~ **de force** show of strength. ◆ **étalagiste** *nmf* window dresser.

étale [etal] *adj mer, situation* slack.

étaler [etale] (1) **1** *vt* (**a**) *objets* to spread (*sur* over); *journal* to spread out (*sur* on); *marchandise* to display, lay out (*sur* on). ~ **ses cartes** to display one's cards. (**b**) *beurre* to spread (*sur* on); *peinture, crème solaire* to apply. (**c**) *paiements* to spread; *vacances* to stagger (*sur* over). **étalez vos envois** space out your consignments. (**d**) *luxe, savoir* to flaunt; *malheurs* to make a show of. **2 s'** ~ *vpr [plaine, cultures]* to stretch out; *[vacances]* to be staggered (*sur* over); *[vaniteux]* to flaunt o.s.; *[titre de journal]* **s'~ sur** to be splashed on *ou* across. **son ignominie s'étale au grand jour** his ignominy is plain for all to see; **s'** ~ **sur un divan** to sprawl on a divan; **étalé sur le tapis** sprawling on *ou* stretched out on the carpet; **s'** ~ **(par terre)** * to fall flat on one's face *. ◆ **étalement** *nm* spreading; spreading-out; displaying; laying-out; application; staggering.

étalon [etalɔ̃] *nm (mesure)* standard; *(fig)* yardstick; *(cheval)* stallion. ~**-or** gold standard.

étamine [etamin] *nf (Bot)* stamen.

étanche [etɑ̃ʃ] *adj vêtements, montre* waterproof; *compartiment, (fig)* watertight. ~ **à l'air** airtight; **enduit** ~ sealant; **rendre qch** ~ to make sth waterproof. ◆ **étanchéité** *nf* waterproofness; watertightness; airtightness.

étancher [etɑ̃ʃe] (1) *vt sang* to stem; *soif* to quench, slake.

étang [etɑ̃] *nm* pond.

étape [etap] *nf (gén)* stage; *(but) (gén)* stop; *(Sport)* stopover point. **faire** ~ **à** to stop off at; **par petites** ~**s** in easy stages; ~ **de ravitaillement** staging post.

état [eta] *nm* (**a**) *[personne]* state. ~ **(de santé)** health; ~ **de veille** waking state; ~ **d'âme** mood; ~ **d'esprit** frame *ou* state of mind; **il n'est pas en** ~ **de le faire** he's in no condition *ou* (fit) state to do it; **être dans un triste** ~ to be in a sad *ou* sorry state; **être en** ~ **de choc** to be in (a state of) shock; **il était dans tous ses** ~**s** he was all worked up * *ou* in a terrible state; **il n'était pas dans son** ~ **normal** he wasn't his normal self. (**b**) *[connaissances, corps chimique]* state. *(situation)* ~ **d'alerte/de guerre/de siège/d'urgence** state of alert/of war/of siege/of emergency; ~ **de choses** situation; **quel est l'** ~ **de la question?** where *ou* how do things stand in the matter?, what stage have things reached? (**c**) *[objet]* condition, state. **en bon/mauvais** ~ in good/poor *ou* bad condition; *(Naut)* **en** ~ **de naviguer** sea-worthy; **en** ~ **de marche** in working order; **remettre en** ~ to repair, do up; **sucre à l'** ~ **brut** sugar in its raw *ou* unrefined state; **à l'** ~ **(de) neuf** as good as new. (**d**) *(nation)* **É**~ state. (**e**) (†: *métier)* profession, trade; *(statut social)* station. **tailleur de son** ~ tailor by trade; ~ **civil** civil, status. (**f**) *(comptes)* statement, account; *(inventaire)* inventory. ~**s de service** service record. (**g**) **faire** ~ **de** *ses services etc* to instance; **mettre en** ~ **d'arrestation** to put under arrest; **en tout** ~ **de cause** in any case; **(bureau de) l'** ~ **civil** registry office; **c'est un** ~ **de fait** it is an established fact; **en** ~ **d'ivresse** in a drunken state, under the influence (of drink); **mettre qn hors d'** ~ **de nuire** to make sb harmless. ◆ **étatisé, e** *adj* state-controlled. ◆ **étatiser** (1) *vt* to establish state control over. ◆ **état-major,** *pl* ~**s-**~**s** *nm (officiers)* staff; *(bureaux)* staff headquarters; *[parti politique]* administrative staff; *[entre-*

prise] top management. ◆ **États-Unis** *nmpl*: **les** ~ **(d'Amérique)** the United States (of America).

étau, *pl* ~**x** [eto] *nm (Tech)* vice. *(fig)* **l'** ~ **se resserre** the noose is tightening; **se trouver pris comme dans un** ~ to find o.s. caught in a stranglehold.

étayer [eteje] (8) *vt mur* to prop up; *(fig) théorie* to support. ◆ **étayage** *nm* propping-up.

et cetera [ɛtseteʀa] *locution* et cetera, etc, and so on (and so forth).

été [ete] *nm* summer. ~ **de la Saint-Martin** Indian summer; **en** ~ in (the) summer *ou* summertime.

éteindre [etɛ̃dʀ(ə)] (52) **1** *vt* (**a**) *flamme* to put out, extinguish; *bougie* to blow out; *gaz, lampe, radio* to turn off, switch off; *pièce* to put out *ou* turn off the lights in. **laisse** ~ **le feu** let the fire go out; **tous feux éteints** without lights. (**b**) *colère* to subdue; *envie* to kill; *soif* to quench. **2 s'** ~ *vpr [agonisant]* to pass away, die; *[colère]* to abate; *[amour]* to die; *[feu, gaz etc]* to go out; *[dette]* to be nullified; *[famille]* to die out. ◆ **éteint, e** *adj couleur* faded; *race, volcan* extinct; *regard* dull; *voix* faint. **c'est un homme** ~ he's a broken man.

étendard [etɑ̃daʀ] *nm (lit, fig)* standard.

étendre [etɑ̃dʀ(ə)] (41) **1** *vt* (**a**) *journal* to spread out; *beurre, ailes* to spread; *bras, blessé* to stretch out. ~ **du linge** *(sur un fil)* to hang out *ou* hang up the washing; **étendu sur le sol** stretched (out) *ou* lying on the ground. (**b**) (*) *adversaire* to floor; *candidat* to fail. **se faire** ~ to be flattened *. (**c**) *(agrandir) (gén)* to extend (*sur* over); *domaine* to expand; *fortune* to increase; *vocabulaire* to widen. (**d**) *vin, sauce* to let down (*de* with).
2 s' ~ *vpr* (**a**) *(s'allonger)* to stretch out; *(se reposer)* to lie down; *(fig: en expliquant)* to elaborate (*sur* on). (**b**) *[forêt, travaux]* to stretch, extend (*sur* over). **la plaine s'étendait à perte de vue** the plain stretched away as far as the eye could see. (**c**) *[brouillard, épidémie]* to spread; *[pouvoirs, parti, fortune]* to expand; *[connaissances, vocabulaire]* to widen. (**d**) *(s'appliquer) [loi, avis]* to apply (*à* to). **cette mesure s'étend à tous** this measure applies to everyone. (**e**) *(s'étaler) [substance]* to spread. **cette peinture s'étend facilement** this paint goes on *ou* spreads easily.
◆ **étendu, e**[1] *adj (gén)* wide; *vocabulaire, pouvoirs* extensive, wide. ◆ **étendue**[2] *nf* (**a**) *(surface)* area; *(durée)* duration, length. **sur une** ~ **de** over an area of; over a period of; **grande** ~ **de sable** large stretch *ou* expanse of sand; **l'** ~ **du territoire** the size *ou* extent of the territory. (**b**) *(importance)* extent; *[connaissances]* range, scope. **devant l'** ~ **du désastre** faced with the scale of the disaster. (**c**) *(Mus) [voix]* range; *(Philos)* extent.

éternel, -elle [etɛʀnɛl] **1** *adj (Philos, Rel)* eternal; *(sans fin)* eternal, everlasting; *(perpétuel)* perpetual. **soucis** ~**s** never-ending worries; **son** ~ **chapeau sur la tête** * the inevitable hat on his head. **2** *nm (Rel)* **l'É**~ the Eternal, the Everlasting; *(hum)* **grand joueur devant l'É**~ inveterate gambler. ◆ **éternellement** *adv* eternally; everlastingly; perpetually.

éterniser [etɛʀnize] (1) **1** *vt débats* to drag *ou* draw out. **2 s'** ~ *vpr [attente]* to drag on; *[visiteur]* to linger too long, linger on. **on ne peut pas s'** ~ **ici** we can't stay here for ever.

éternité [etɛʀnite] *nf* eternity. **il y a des** ~**s que tu m'as promis cela** you promised me that ages ago; **ça a duré une** ~ it lasted for ages; **de toute** ~ from time immemorial; **pour l'** ~ to all eternity.

éternuer [etɛʀnɥe] (1) *vi* to sneeze. ◆ **éternuement** *nm* sneeze.

éther [etɛʀ] *nm (Chim, Poésie)* ether.

Éthiopie [etjɔpi] *nf* Ethiopia. ◆ **éthiopien, -ienne** *adj*, **É**~**(ne)** *nm (f)* Ethiopian.

éthique [etik] **1** *adj* ethical. **2** *nf (Philos)* ethics *(sg)*; *(code moral)* moral code.

ethnie [ɛtni] *nf* ethnic group. ◆ **ethnique** *adj* ethnic. **minorité** ~ ethnic minority.

ethnologie [ɛtnɔlɔʒi] *nf* ethnology. ◆ **ethnologique** *adj* ethnological. ◆ **ethnologue** *nmf* ethnologist.

étinceler [etɛ̃sle] (4) *vi [lame]* to sparkle, glitter; *[étoile, diamant]* to twinkle; *[esprit, beauté]* to sparkle. *[yeux]* ~ **de colère** to glitter *ou* flash with anger; ~ **de joie** to sparkle *ou* shine with joy. ◆ **étincelle** *nf* (**a**) *(incandescente)* spark. **jeter des** ~**s** to throw out sparks; *(fig)* **faire des** ~**s** * *[élève]* to shine; *[dispute]* to make the sparks fly. (**b**) *[lame, regard]* flash, glitter; *[raison]* gleam, glimmer. ~ **de génie** spark *ou* flash of genius. ◆ **étincellement** *nm* sparkle; glitter; twinkling; flash; shining.

étioler [etjɔle] (1) **1** *vt plante* to blanch; *personne* to weaken. **2 s'** ~ *vpr [plante]* to wilt; *[personne]* to wither away. ◆ **étiolement** *nm* blanching; weakening; wilting; withering away.

étiquette [etikɛt] *nf* label. *(protocole)* **l'** ~ etiquette. ◆ **étiquetage** [etiktaʒ] *nm* labelling. ◆ **étiqueter** [etikte] (4) *vt* to label.

étirer [etiʀe] (1) **1** *vt* to stretch; *métal* to draw out. **2 s'** ~ *vpr [personne]* to stretch; *[convoi, route]* to stretch out.

étoffe [etɔf] *nf* material, fabric. *(fig)* **avoir l'** ~ **de** to have the makings of; **avoir de l'** ~ to have a strong personality.

étoffer [etɔfe] (1) **1** *vt style* to enrich; *discours* to fill out. **2 s'** ~ *vpr [personne]* to fill out.

étoile [etwal] *nf* star. ~ **filante** shooting star; ~ **polaire** pole *ou* north star; ~ **du berger** evening star; ~ **de mer** starfish; **sans** ~ starless; **à la clarté des** ~**s** by starlight; **dormir à la belle** ~ to sleep out in the open; **(hôtel) trois** ~**s** three-star hotel; ~ **de la danse** dancing star; **avoir foi en son** ~ to trust one's lucky star; **né sous une bonne/mauvaise** ~ born under a lucky/an unlucky star; **son** ~ **a pâli** his star has set. ◆ **étoilé, e** *adj nuit* starry, starlit; *ciel* starry; *pare-brise* crazed.

étole [etɔl] *nf (Rel, gén)* stole.

étonner [etɔne] (1) **1** *vt* to surprise, amaze, astonish. **2 s'** ~ *vpr* to be amazed, wonder, marvel (*de qch* at sth, *de voir* at seeing, *que + subj* that). ◆ **étonnamment** *adv* surprisingly, amazingly, astonishingly. ◆ **étonnant, e** *adj (surprenant)* surprising, amazing, astonishing; *(remarquable) personne* amazing, incredible. **l'** ~ **est que** the astonishing *ou* amazing thing is that; **rien d'** ~ **à cela** no wonder, there's nothing (so) surprising about that; **vous êtes** ~ you're incredible *ou* amazing. ◆ **étonnement** *nm* surprise, amazement, astonishment.

étouffer [etufe] (1) , **1** *vt* (**a**) *[assassin]* to smother; *[chaleur]* to suffocate; *[sanglots, aliment]* to choke. **les scrupules ne l'étouffent pas** he isn't hampered *ou* overburdened by scruples. (**b**) *bruit* to muffle; *bâillement, cris* to smother, suppress, stifle. (**c**) *scandale* to hush up; *rumeurs, sentiments* to stifle; *révolte* to put down, quell. (**d**) *flammes* to smother, extinguish; *feu* to put out, smother. **2** *vi (mourir)* to die of suffocation; *(fig)* to suffocate. ~ **de colère** to choke with anger; ~ **de chaleur** to be overcome with the heat. **3 s'** ~ *vpr (mourir)* to suffocate; *(en mangeant)* to choke. ◆ **étouffant, e** *adj* stifling. ◆ **étouffe-chrétien** * *nm inv*: **c'est de l'** ~ it's stodgy (food). ◆ **étouffé, e**[1] *adj rire* suppressed; *voix* subdued; *rumeur* muffled. ◆ **étouffée**[2] *nf*: **cuire à l'** ~ *poisson, légumes* to steam; *viande* to braise. ◆ **étouffement** *nm* (**a**) *(mort)* suffocation. *(Méd)* **sensation d'** ~ feeling of suffocation. (**b**) *(action)* hushing-up; stifling; suppression.

étoupe [etup] *nf [lin]* tow; *[cordes]* oakum.

étourdir [etuʀdiʀ] (2) *vt [coup]* to stun, daze; *[bruit]* to deafen. ~ **qn** *[altitude, vin]* to make sb dizzy; *[succès]* to go to sb's head; **s'** ~ **de paroles** to get drunk on words. ◆ **étourderie** *nf (caractère)* absent-mindedness; *(faute)* careless mistake. ◆ **étourdi, e 1** *adj* absent-minded. **2** *nm, f* scatterbrain. ◆ **étourdiment** *adv* carelessly. ◆ **étourdissant, e** *adj bruit* deafening; *succès, beauté* stunning. **à un rythme** ~ at a tremendous pace. ◆ **étourdissement** *nm (syncope)* blackout; *(vertige)* dizzy spell; *(littér: griserie)* intoxication. **ça me donne des ~s** it makes me feel dizzy.

étourneau, *pl* **~x** [etuʀno] *nm (Orn)* starling ; *(*: distrait)* scatterbrain, birdbrain *(US)*.

étrange [etʀɑ̃ʒ] *adj* strange, odd, queer, peculiar, weird, funny. **et chose** ~ strangely enough. ◆ **étrangement** *adv* strangely, oddly; *(étonnamment)* surprisingly, amazingly.

étranger, -ère [etʀɑ̃ʒe, ɛʀ] **1** *adj* (**a**) *(autre pays)* foreign. **être** ~ to be a foreigner, come from abroad. (**b**) *(autre groupe)* strange (*à* to). **être** ~ **à un groupe** not to belong to a group, be an outsider; **entrée interdite à toute personne ~ère** no entry for unauthorized persons. (**c**) *(inconnu)* strange, unfamiliar (*à* to). **son nom ne m'est pas** ~ his name is not unknown *ou* not unfamiliar to me. (**d**) *donnée, fait* extraneous (*à* to). ~ **au sujet** irrelevant to the subject; **être** ~ **à un complot** to have nothing to do with a plot. (**e**) *(Méd, fig)* **corps** ~ foreign body. **2** *nm, f (autre pays)* foreigner; *(péj, Admin)* alien; *(inconnu)* stranger. **3** *nm (pays)* **l'** ~ foreign parts; **vivre à l'** ~ to live abroad *ou* in a foreign country.

étrangeté [etʀɑ̃ʒte] *nf* strangeness, oddness, queerness; *(événement)* odd *ou* strange event.

étrangler [etʀɑ̃gle] (1) **1** *vt* (**a**) *(tuer)* to strangle, choke, throttle. (**b**) *[rage etc]* to choke. **voix étranglée par l'émotion** voice choking with emotion. (**c**) *presse* to strangle, stifle. *(financièrement)* ~ **qn** to bleed sb white. (**d**) *(resserrer)* to squeeze. **taille étranglée** tightly constricted waist. **2 s'** ~ *vpr* (**a**) **s'** ~ **de rire/en mangeant** to choke with laughter/whilst eating. (**b**) *[voix]* to catch in one's throat. (**c**) *[rue]* to narrow. ◆ **étranglement** *nm [victime]* strangulation; *[presse]* stifling; *[vallée]* neck; *[rue]* bottleneck; *[taille, tuyau]* constriction; *[voix]* strain. ◆ **étrangleur, -euse** *nm, f* strangler.

être [ɛtʀ(ə)] (61) **1** *vb copule* (**a**) *(gén)* to be. **elle veut** ~ **médecin** she wants to be a doctor; **soyez sages!** be good!; **si j'étais vous** if I were you; **nous sommes 10 à vouloir partir** there are 10 of us wanting *ou* who want to go. (**b**) *(date)* **nous sommes le 12 janvier** it is January 12th. (**c**) *(appartenance)* **à qui est ce livre? — il est à moi** whose book is this? — it's mine *ou* it belongs to me; **je suis à vous** I'll be with you; **c'était à elle de protester** it was up to her to protest; ~ **de l'expédition** to take part in the expedition; **je ne pourrai pas** ~ **des vôtres jeudi** I shan't *ou* won't be able to join you on Thursday. (**d**) *(état, fait etc)* to be. **il n'est pas à son travail** his mind is not on his work; **il est au travail** he is working; **elle n'y est pour rien** it has nothing to do with her; **je suis pour dormir ici** I am for sleeping here *, I am in favour of sleeping here.
2 *vb aux* (**a**) *(temps composés actifs)* **est-il venu?** has he come?; **il est passé hier** he came yesterday. (**b**) *(passif)* ~ **fabriqué par...** to be made by...; **il a été blessé** he was injured. (**c**) *(avec à + infin)* **le poisson est à manger tout de suite** the fish is to be eaten *ou* must be eaten at once; **il est à travailler** he is busy working; **elle est toujours à le taquiner** she's forever teasing him.
3 *vi* (**a**) *(exister)* to be. **que la lumière soit** let there be light; **un menteur s'il en est** a liar if ever there was one. (**b**) *(habiter)* **il est maintenant à Lille** he now lives *ou* he is now in Lille; **elle n'y est pour personne** she is not at home *ou* available to anyone. (**c**) *(*: être allé)* **il n'avait jamais été à Londres** he'd never been to London; **j'ai été en Italie l'an dernier** I went to Italy last year.
4 *vb impers* (**a**) *(avoir atteint)* **en** ~ **à la page 9** to be at page 9, have reached page 9; **où en est-il dans ses études?** how far has he got with his studies?, what point has he reached in his studies?; **l'affaire en est là** that's how the matter stands. (**b**) *(se voir réduit à)* **j'en suis à me demander si** I'm beginning to wonder if, I've come to wonder if; **il en est à mendier** he has been reduced to begging. (**c**) *(locutions)* **il était une fois** once upon a time; **il n'en est rien** it's nothing of the sort; **tu y es?** * *(tu es prêt)* are you ready?; *(comprends-tu)* do you get it? * (**d**) *(pour mettre en relief gén non traduit)* **c'est lui qui me l'a dit** he (is the one who) told me; **c'est à qui dira son mot** they all want to have their say; **est-ce que vous saviez?** did you know?; **il fait beau, n'est-ce pas?** it's a lovely day, isn't it?; **vous viendrez, n'est-ce pas?** you will come, won't you? (**e**) *(supposition)* **si ce n'était** were it not for; **ne serait-ce que pour nous ennuyer** if only to annoy us; **comme si de rien n'était** as if nothing had happened; *(Math)* **soit une droite XY** let XY be a straight line.
5 *nm (gén, Sci)* being. ~ **humain** human being; **un** ~ **cher** a loved one; **un** ~ **merveilleux** a wonderful person; **de tout son** ~ with all his heart; **au plus profond de notre** ~ deep down in our souls.

étreindre [etʀɛ̃dʀ(ə)] (52) *vt ami* to embrace, hug, clasp in one's arms; *ennemi* to seize, grasp; *(avec les mains)* to clutch, grip; *[douleur]* to grip. ◆ **étreinte** *nf* embrace, hug; grip; clutch; grasp.

étrenner [etʀene] (1) **1** *vt* to use for the first time. **2** *vi (*: écoper)* to catch it *, get it *.

étrennes [etʀɛn] *nfpl [enfant]* New Year's gift; *[facteur etc]* ≃ Christmas box. **que veux-tu pour tes ~s?** what would you like for Christmas?

étrier [etʀije] *nm* stirrup.

étriqué, e [etʀike] *adj habit* skimpy, tight; *esprit, vie* narrow. **il fait tout** ~ **dans son manteau** he looks cramped in his coat.

étroit, e [etʀwa, wat] *adj* (**a**) *(lit) (gén)* narrow; *espace* cramped, confined; *vêtement, étreinte* tight. **être à l'** ~ *(logé)* to live in cramped conditions; *(habillé)* to be cramped in one's clothes. (**b**) *(borné)* narrow, limited. **à l'esprit** ~ narrow-minded. (**c**) *amitié, surveillance, liens* close; *subordination* strict. **en collaboration ~e avec** in close collaboration with. (**d**) *(Ling) acception* narrow, strict. ◆ **étroitement** *adv lier* closely; *obéir* strictly; *tenir* tightly. **être** ~ **logé** to live in cramped conditions. ◆ **étroitesse** *nf* narrowness; crampedness; tightness; closeness. ~ **(d'esprit)** narrow-mindedness.

étrusque [etʀysk] *adj, nm,* **É~** *nmf* Etruscan.

étude [etyd] *nf* (**a**) *(action) (gén)* study. **mettre un projet à l'** ~ to investigate *ou* study a project; **avoir le goût de l'** ~ to like study *ou* studying; **une** ~ **gratuite de vos besoins** a free assessment of your needs; **voyage/frais d'** ~ study trip/costs; **~(s) de marché** market research; ~ **de cas** case study. (**b**) *(Scol, Univ)* **~s** studies; **payer ses ~s** to pay for one's education; **faire des ~s (de droit)** to study (law); **~s secondaires/supérieures** secondary/higher education. (**c**) *(ouvrage)* study. **~s de fleurs** studies of flowers. (**d**) *(Scol)* **(salle d')** ~ study *ou* prep room; **l'** ~ **(du soir)** preparation; ~ **surveillée** (supervised) study period, study hall *(US)*; **mettre des élèves en** ~ to leave pupils to study on their own. (**e**) *(Jur) (bureau)* office; *(clientèle)* practice.

étudiant, e [etydjɑ̃, ɑ̃t] *adj, nm, f* student.

étudier [etydje] (7) *vt* (**a**) *(gén)* to study; *leçon* to learn. **les deux adversaires s'étudiaient de près** the two opponents observed each other closely. (**b**) *(concevoir) procédé* to devise; *machine* to design. (**c**) *gestes, ton* to study. ◆ **étudié, e** *adj geste* studied; *conception* carefully designed; *prix* competitive, keen.

étui [etɥi] *nm (gén)* case; *[revolver]* holster.

étuve [etyv] *nf (bains)* steamroom; *(de désinfection)* sterilizer; *(fig)* oven.

étymologie [etimɔlɔʒi] *nf* etymology. ◆ **étymologique** *adj* etymological.

eucalyptus [økaliptys] *nm* eucalyptus.

Eucharistie [økaʀisti] *nf*: **l'** ~ the Eucharist, the Lord's Supper.

euh [ø] *excl* er!...

eunuque [ønyk] *nm* eunuch.

euphémisme [øfemism(ə)] *nm* euphemism. ◆ **euphémique** *adj* euphemistic.

euphorie [øfɔʀi] *nf* euphoria. ◆ **euphorique** *adj* euphoric.

eurasien, -ienne [øʀazjɛ̃,jɛn] *adj,* **E~(ne)** *nm(f)* Eurasian.

Europe [øʀɔp] *nf* Europe. ~ **Centrale** Central Europe; **l'** ~ **des douze** the Twelve (Common Market countries); **l'** ~ **politique** Europe as a single political entity; **l'** ~ **de l'espace** the joint European space venture; **l'** ~ **verte** European *ou* Community agriculture. ◆ **eurodevises** *nfpl* Eurocurrency. ◆ **euromissile** *nm* European missile. ◆ **euro-obligations** *nfpl* Euro-bonds. ◆ **eurodollar** *nm* Eurodollar. ◆ **européaniser** (1) *vt* to europeanize. ◆ **européen, -éenne** *adj,* **E~(ne)** *nm(f)* European. ◆ **Eurovision** *nf* Eurovision.

euthanasie [øtanazi] *nf* euthanasia.

eux [ø] *pron pers (sujet)* they; *(objet)* them. **nous y allons,** ~ **non** we are going but they aren't *ou* but not them; ~ **mentir?** them tell a lie?; **ce sont** ~ **qui répondront** they are the ones who will reply, they'll reply; **cette maison est-elle à** ~**?** does this house belong to them?, is this house theirs?; **ils ne pensent qu'à** ~ they only think of themselves.

évacuer [evakɥe] (1) *vt (gén)* to evacuate. ◆ **évacuation** *nf* evacuation. ◆ **évacué, e** *nm, f* evacuee.

évader (s') [evade] (1) *vpr (lit, fig)* to escape (*de* from). **faire s'** ~ **qn** to help sb escape. ◆ **évadé, e** *nm, f* escaped prisoner.

évaluer [evalɥe] (1) *vt bijou* to appraise, value; *dégâts, prix* to assess, evaluate; *(approximativement)* to estimate (*à* at). **faire** ~ **qch par un expert** to have sth valued by an expert. ◆ **évaluable** *adj* assessable. ◆ **évaluation** *nf* appraisal; valuation; assessment; estimation.

évangile [evɑ̃ʒil] *nm (Rel, fig)* gospel. **ce n'est pas parole d'** ~ it's not gospel. ◆ **évangélique** *adj* evangelical. ◆ **évangéliser** (1) *vt* to evangelize. ◆ **évangéliste** *nm* evangelist.

évanouir (s') [evanwiʀ] (2) *vpr* to faint (*de* from); *[rêves, craintes]* to vanish, disappear, fade. ◆ **évanoui, e** *adj* unconscious. **tomber** ~ to faint. ◆ **évanouissement** *nm (syncope)* fainting fit; *(fig)* disappearance, fading.

évaporer [evapɔʀe] (1) **1** *vt (gén* **faire** ~*)* to evaporate. **2 s'** ~ *vpr (lit)* to evaporate; *(*: disparaître)* to vanish into thin air. ◆ **évaporation** *nf* evaporation. ◆ **évaporé, e 1** *adj (péj) personne* scatterbrained. **2** *nm, f* scatterbrain, birdbrain *(US)*.

évaser *vt,* **s'** ~ *vpr* [evɑze] (1) *tuyau* to open out; *jupe* to flare. **à bords évasés** with a curving rim. ◆ **évasement** *nm* opening-out; flare.

évasion [evazjɔ̃] *nf (lit, fig: fuite)* escape. **besoin d'** ~ need to escape; ~ **des capitaux** flight of capital; ~ **fiscale** tax evasion. ◆ **évasif, -ive** *adj* evasive; *réponse* noncommittal. ◆ **évasivement** *adv* evasively.

évêché [eveʃe] *nm (région)* bishopric; *(palais)* bishop's palace; *(ville)* cathedral town.

éveiller [eveje] (1) **1** *vt* (**a**) *(littér: réveiller)* to awaken. **tenir éveillé** to keep awake. (**b**) *curiosité, sentiment* to arouse, awaken; *passion* to kindle; *intelligence* to stimulate. **2 s'** ~ *vpr (lit)* to wake up, awaken; *[ville, nature]* to wake (up); *[sentiment, curiosité]* to be aroused; *[intelligence]* to develop. **s'** ~ **à** *amour* to awaken to. ◆ **éveil** *nm* awakening; arousing. **être en** ~ *[personne]* to be on the alert; *[sens]* to be alert *ou* aroused; **donner l'** ~ to raise the alarm *ou* alert; *(Scol)* **activités d'** ~ early-learning games *etc.* ◆ **éveillé, e** *adj (alerte)* alert, sharp, bright; *(réveillé)* (wide-)awake.

événement [evɛnmɑ̃] *nm* event. **semaine chargée en ~s** eventful week; **l'** ~ **de la semaine** the main story *ou* news of the week.

éventail [evɑ̃taj] *nm (instrument)* fan; *(fig: gamme)* range. **en** ~ fan-shaped; *(Mil)* **se déployer en** ~ to fan out; ~ **des salaires** salary *ou* wage range ; **l'~ politique** the political spectrum.

éventaire [evɑ̃tɛʀ] *nm (corbeille)* tray; *(étalage)* stand.

éventer [evɑ̃te] (1) **1** *vt* (**a**) *(avec éventail)* to fan. (**b**) *secret* to discover. **2 s'** ~ *vpr [bière]* to go flat; *[parfum]* to go stale.

éventrer [evɑ̃tʀe] (1) *vt* (**a**) *(couteau)* to disembowel; *(corne)* to gore. (**b**) *sac* to tear open; *coffre* to smash open; *matelas* to rip open. ◆ **éventration** *nf (Méd)* rupture.

éventualité [evɑ̃tɥalite] *nf* possibility. **dans cette** ~ in that case. ◆ **éventuel, -elle** *adj* possible. **les profits ~s seraient réinvestis** any profits which might be made would be reinvested. ◆ **éventuellement** *adv* possibly.

évêque [evɛk] *nm* bishop.

évertuer (s') [evɛʀtɥe] (1) *vpr*: **s'** ~ **à faire** to do one's utmost *ou* struggle hard to do; **je m'évertue à t'expliquer** I'm doing my best *ou* my utmost to explain to you.

éviction [eviksjɔ̃] *nf (Jur)* eviction; *[rival]* ousting.

évidence [evidɑ̃s] *nf (caractère)* obviousness, evidence; *(fait)* obvious fact. **se rendre à l'** ~ to yield to the facts *ou* the evidence; **nier l'** ~ to deny the obvious *ou* the facts; **c'est une** ~ **que de dire** it's a statement of the obvious to say; **(être) en** ~ (to be) conspicuous *ou* in evidence; **mettre en** ~ *personne, fait* to bring to the fore; *objet* to put in a conspicuous position; **se mettre en** ~ to make o.s. conspicuous; **de toute** ~ quite obviously *ou* evidently. ◆ **évidemment** *adv (gén)* obviously; *(bien sûr)* of course. ◆ **évident, e** *adj* obvious, evident.

évider [evide] (1) *vt* to hollow out.

évier [evje] *nm* sink. ~ **(à) un bac/deux bacs** single/double sink.

évincer [evɛ̃se] (3) *vt* to oust, supplant. ◆ **évincement** *nm* ousting, supplanting.

éviter [evite] (1) *vt (gén)* to avoid; *coup* to dodge; *regard* to evade. ~ **qu'une situation n'empire** to avoid *ou* prevent the worsening of a situation; ~ **de faire qch** to avoid doing sth; ~ **le sel** to avoid *ou* keep off salt; **ça lui a évité d'avoir à se déplacer** that saved him the bother of going. ◆ **évitable** *adj* avoidable.

évocation [evɔkɑsjɔ̃] *nf* evocation. ◆ **évocateur, -trice** *adj* evocative (*de* of).

évoluer [evɔlɥe] (1) *vi* (**a**) *(changer) (gén)* to evolve; *[maladie]* to develop. **ses parents ont évolué** his parents have moved with the times. (**b**) *[danseur]* to move about; *[avion]* to circle; *[troupes]* to manoeuvre. ◆ **évolué, e** *adj peuple* (highly) developed, advanced; *personne (compréhensif)* broad-minded; *(indépendant)* independent; *procédé* advanced. ◆ **évolution** *nf* evolution; development; advancement; movement.

évoquer [evoke] (1) *vt (gén)* to evoke; *souvenir* to recall; *scène* to conjure up; *problème* to touch on.

exacerber [ɛgzasɛʀbe] (1) *vt* to exacerbate. **sensibilité exacerbée** exaggerated sensitivity.

exact, e [ɛgza, akt(ə)] *adj* (**a**) *reproduction, compte rendu* exact, accurate; *réponse, calcul* correct, right; *(précis) dimension* exact, precise; *pendule* accurate. **est-il ~ que?** is it right *ou* correct that?; **c'est l'~e vérité** that's the exact truth; **l'heure ~e** the exact time. (**b**) *(ponctuel)* punctual, on time; *(littér: strict)* strict. ◆ **exactement** *adv* exactly; accurately; correctly; precisely; strictly. ◆ **exactitude** *nf* exactness; accuracy; correctness; precision; punctuality; *(littér: minutie)* exactitude.

exaction [ɛgzaksjɔ̃] *nf* exaction.

ex æquo [ɛgzeko] **1** *adj inv* equally placed, place equal. **2** *adv classer* equal.

exagérer [ɛgzaʒeʀe] (6) **1** *vt (gén)* to exaggerate. **sans ~** without any exaggeration; **il exagère** he goes too far. **2 s'~** *vpr difficultés* to exaggerate; *avantages* to overrate. ◆ **exagération** *nf (gén)* exaggeration. ◆ **exagéré, e** *adj (amplifié)* exaggerated; *(excessif)* excessive. **c'est un peu ~** it's a bit much *; **il n'est pas ~ de dire** it is not an exaggeration to say. ◆ **exagérément** *adv* excessively, exaggeratedly.

exalter [ɛgzalte] (1) *vt* (**a**) *esprit, courage* to fire, excite. **exalté par** *(excité)* excited by; *(euphorique)* elated by; **il s'exalte facilement** he is easily carried away. (**b**) *(glorifier)* to exalt, praise. ◆ **exaltant, e** *adj* exalting, elating. ◆ **exaltation** *nf* (**a**) *(nerveuse)* intense excitement; *(joyeuse)* elation; *(mystique)* exaltation. (**b**) *(glorification)* praising, exalting. ◆ **exalté, e 1** *adj sentiments* elated; *imagination* wild; *esprit* excited. **2** *nm, f (impétueux)* hothead; *(fanatique)* fanatic.

examiner [ɛgzamine] (1) *vt* (**a**) *(analyser) (gén)* to examine; *demande* to consider; *comptes* to go through. **~ en détail** to scrutinize. (**b**) *objet, visage* to examine, study; *ciel* to scan; *appartement* to have a look round. **s'~ devant la glace** to examine o.s. in the mirror. (**c**) *(Méd, Scol)* to examine. **se faire ~** to be examined. ◆ **examen** *nm* (**a**) *(action)* examination; consideration. **~ détaillé** scrutiny; **la question est à l'~** the matter is under consideration. (**b**) *(Méd)* medical examination. **se faire faire des ~s** to have some tests done. (**c**) *(Scol)* exam, examination. **~ blanc/de passage** mock/end-of-the-year exam. ◆ **examinateur, -trice** *nm, f* examiner.

exaspérer [ɛgzaspeʀe] (6) *vt (irriter)* to exasperate; *(littér: aviver)* to exacerbate, aggravate. ◆ **exaspération** *nf* exasperation.

exaucer [ɛgzose] (3) *vt vœu, prière* to grant. **~ qn** to grant sb's wish. ◆ **exaucement** *nm* fulfilment.

excavation [ɛkskavɑsjɔ̃] *nf* excavation.

excédent [ɛksedɑ̃] *nm* surplus (*sur* over). **un ~ de poids** some excess weight; **~ de la balance des paiements** balance of payments surplus; **budget en ~** surplus budget; **~ budgétaire** budget surplus. ◆ **excédentaire** *adj production* excess, surplus. **budget ~** surplus budget; **la production est ~** production is over target.

excéder [ɛksede] (6) *vt* (**a**) *longueur, prix* to exceed. **les avantages excèdent les inconvénients** the advantages outweigh the disadvantages. (**b**) *pouvoir* to overstep, exceed; *forces* to overtax. (**c**) *(accabler: gén passif)* to exhaust. **excédé de fatigue** exhausted, tired out; **excédé de travail** overworked. (**d**) *(agacer: gén passif)* to exasperate.

excellence [ɛksɛlɑ̃s] *nf* (**a**) excellence. **par ~** *héros* par excellence; *aimer* above all else. (**b**) **Son E~** His (*ou* Her) Excellency. ◆ **excellemment** *adv* excellently. ◆ **excellent, e** *adj* excellent. ◆ **exceller** (1) *vi* to excel (*dans ou* en at *ou* in, *à faire* in doing).

excentrique [ɛksɑ̃tʀik] **1** *adj personne, (Math)* eccentric; *quartier* outlying. **2** *nmf* eccentric. ◆ **excentricité** *nf* eccentricity.

excepter [ɛksɛpte] (1) *vt* to except (*de* from). **sans ~ personne** without excluding anyone. ◆ **excepté, e 1** *adj*: **sa mère ~e** apart from *ou* aside from *(US) ou* except his mother. **2** *prép* except, apart from, aside from *(US)*. **~ quand/que** except when/that. ◆ **exception** *nf* exception. **d'~** *mesure* special, exceptional; **faire une ~ à** *règle* to make an exception to; **faire ~ (à la règle)** to be an exception (to the rule); **faire ~ de** to make an exception of; **à l'~ de** except for. ◆ **exceptionnel, -elle** *adj* exceptional. ◆ **exceptionnellement** *adv (à titre d'exception)* in this particular instance; *(très)* exceptionally.

excès [ɛksɛ] *nm* (**a**) *(surplus) [argent]* excess, surplus; *[marchandises]* glut, surplus. **il y a un ~ d'acide** there is too much acid; **~ de précautions** excessive care; **~ de zèle** overzealousness. (**b**) *(abus)* excess. **des ~ de langage** immoderate language; **tomber dans l'~ inverse** to go to the opposite extreme; **faire un ~ de vitesse** to exceed the speed limit; **faire des ~ de table** to overindulge; **jusqu'à l'~, avec ~** to excess, excessively. ◆ **excessif, -ive** *adj* excessive. **elle est ~ive en tout** she's a woman of extremes, she takes everything to extremes; **c'est ~!** that's far too much!, that's excessive! ◆ **excessivement** *adv* excessively.

exciter [ɛksite] (1) **1** *vt* (**a**) *désir* to arouse, excite; *rire* to cause; *pitié* to rouse; *imagination* to fire, stir; *appétit* to whet; *ardeur* to increase. **cela ne fit qu'~ sa colère** that only made him even more angry. (**b**) *(enthousiasmer)* to thrill, excite. **excitant pour l'esprit** mentally stimulating. (**c**) *(rendre nerveux) personne* to arouse; *chien* to excite. **le café excite** coffee acts as a stimulant. (**d**) *(*: irriter)* to irritate. **il commence à m'~** he's getting on my nerves. (**e**) *(encourager)* to urge on. **~ qn contre qn** to set sb against sb; **~ qn à faire qch** to urge sb to do sth. (**f**) *(Méd, Élec)* to excite. **2 s'~** *vpr (enthousiaste)* to get excited (*sur* about, over); *(nerveux)* to get worked up *; *(*: fâché)* to get angry, fly off the handle *. ◆ **excitable** *adj* excitable. ◆ **excitant, e 1** *adj (gén)* exciting. **2** *nm* stimulant. ◆ **excitation** *nf (gén)* excitement; *(Méd, Élec)* excitation. *(incitation)* **~ à** incitement to. ◆ **excité, e** *nm, f (impétueux)* hothead; *(fanatique)* fanatic.

exclamer (s') [ɛksklame] (1) *vpr* to exclaim. **s'~ de colère** to exclaim *ou* cry out in anger. ◆ **exclamation** *nf* exclamation.

exclure [ɛksklyʀ] (35) *vt* (**a**) *(d'une salle)* to turn out; *(d'un parti, d'une école)* to expel; *(temporairement)* to suspend, exclude. **se faire ~ de** to get o.s. expelled from. (**b**) *solution, hypothèse* to exclude. **~ qch de son régime** to cut sth out of one's diet; **je tiens à être exclu de cette affaire** count me out of this business; **c'est tout à fait exclu** it's quite out of the question. ◆ **exclusif, -ive** *adj* exclusive. *(Comm)* **droits ~s** sole *ou* exclusive rights. ◆ **exclusion** *nf* exclusion; expulsion (*de* from). **à l'~ de** *(en écartant)* to the exclusion of; *(sauf)* with the exclusion of. ◆ **exclusivement** *adv (seulement)* exclusively, solely. **~ réservé au personnel** reserved for staff only; *(non inclus)* **du 10 au 15 ~** from the 10th to the 15th exclusive. ◆ **exclusivité** *nf (Comm)* exclusive rights; *[sentiments]* exclusiveness. **ce film passe en ~ à** this film is showing exclusively at; **il n'en a pas l'~ *** he's not the only one to have it, he hasn't a monopoly on it *; **avoir l' ~ d'un reportage** to have (the) exclusive coverage of an event.

excommunier [ɛkskɔmynje] (7) *vt* to excommunicate. ◆ **excommunication** *nf* excommunication.

excrément [ɛkskʀemɑ̃] *nm*: ~**(s)** excrement.

excrétion [ɛkskʀesjɔ̃] *nf* excretion.

excroissance [ɛkskʀwasɑ̃s] *nf* outgrowth.

excursion [ɛkskyʀsjɔ̃] *nf (en car etc)* excursion, trip; *(à pied)* walk, hike. ◆ **excursionniste** *nmf* (day) tripper, traveler *(US)*; hiker, walker.

excuser [ɛkskyze] (1) **1** *vt* (**a**) *(pardonner)* to excuse, forgive. **excusez-moi** excuse me, I'm sorry; **excusez-moi de ne pas venir** excuse my not coming, I'm sorry I can't come. (**b**) *(justifier, dispenser)* to excuse. **se faire** ~ to ask to be excused; « **M. Dupont: (absent) excusé** » 'Mr Dupont has sent an apology'. **2 s'** ~ *vpr*: **s'** ~ **de qch** to apologize for sth *(auprès de* to). ◆ **excusable** *adj* excusable, forgivable. ◆ **excuse** *nf* (**a**) *(prétexte)* excuse. **mauvaise** ~ poor excuse; **sans** ~ inexcusable; **prendre qch pour** ~ to use sth as an excuse. (**b**) *(regret)* ~**s** apology; **faire des** ~**s** to apologize; **je vous dois des** ~**s** I owe you an apology.

exécrer [ɛgzekʀe] (6) *vt* to loathe, execrate. ◆ **exécrable** *adj* atrocious, execrable. ◆ **exécrablement** *adv* atrociously, execrably. ◆ **exécration** *nf* execration, loathing.

exécuter [ɛgzekyte] (1) **1** *vt* (**a**) *(accomplir) (gén)* to carry out; *travail, mouvements* to execute; *promesse* to fulfil; *tâche* to perform. **il a fait** ~ **des travaux** he had some work done. (**b**) *objet* to produce, make; *tableau* to paint; *commande* to fulfil, carry out; *ordonnance* to make up; *(Mus) morceau* to perform, execute. (**c**) *(tuer)* to execute, put to death. (**d**) *décret* to enforce; *contrat* to perform. (**e**) *(Ordin) programme* to run. **2 s'** ~ *vpr (obéir)* to comply; *(payer)* to pay up. ◆ **exécutant, e** *nm, f (Mus)* performer; *(fig péj: agent)* underling. ◆ **exécuteur** *nm (Jur)* ~ **(testamentaire)** *(homme)* executor; *(femme)* executrix. ◆ **exécutif, -ive** *adj, nm* executive. ◆ **exécution** *nf* execution; carrying out; fulfilment; performance; production; making; painting; making up; enforcement. **mettre à** ~ *projet, idées, menaces* to carry out; **en** ~ **de la loi** in compliance with the law ; ~ **capitale** capital execution.

exemplaire [ɛgzɑ̃plɛʀ] **1** *adj* exemplary. **2** *nm [livre]* copy; *(échantillon)* example.

exemple [ɛgzɑ̃pl(ə)] *nm (modèle)* example; *(spécimen)* example, instance. **citer qn en** ~ to quote sb as an example; **donner l'** ~ to set an example *(de* of); **prendre** ~ **sur qn** to take sb as an example; **à l'** ~ **de son père** just like his father; **faire un** ~ **de qn** to make an example of sb; **le seul** ~ **que je connaisse** the only example *ou* instance I know of; **par** ~ *(explicatif)* for example *ou* instance; *(*: par contre)* on the other hand; **(ça) par** ~! *(surprise)* my word!; *(indignation)* oh really!

exempt, e [ɛgzɑ̃, ɑ̃t] *adj*: ~ **de** *corvée* exempt from; *dangers* free from; ~ **de taxes** duty-free; ~ **de TVA** zero-rated for VAT. ◆ **exempter** (1) *vt* to exempt *(de* from). ◆ **exemption** *nf* exemption.

exercer [ɛgzɛʀse] (3) **1** *vt* (**a**) *profession* to practise; *fonction* to fulfil; *talents, droit, charité* to exercise; *contrôle, influence* to exert *(sur* over); *représailles* to take *(sur* on); *poussée* to exert *(sur* on). **quel métier exercez-vous?** what job do you do?; *(Jur)* ~ **des poursuites contre qn** to bring an action against sb.(**b**) *(aguerrir) corps, esprit* to train, exercise, *(à* to, for); *facultés* to exercise. (**c**) *(éprouver) patience* to tax. **2 s'** ~ *vpr [pianiste, sportif]* to practise. **s'** ~ **à** *technique* to practise; **s'** ~ **à faire qch** to train o.s. to do sth. ◆ **exercé, e** *adj oreille* keen, trained.

exercice [ɛgzɛʀsis] *nm* (**a**) *[métier]* practice; *[droit]* exercising; *[facultés]* exercise. **l'** ~ **du culte ne se fait plus dans ce bâtiment** religious services are no longer conducted in this building; **dans l'** ~ **de ses fonctions** in the execution of his duties; **être en** ~ *[médecin]* to be in practice; *[fonctionnaire]* to hold office; **juge en** ~ sitting judge; **président en** ~ serving chairman. (**b**) *(entraînement, devoir)* exercise. **faire de l'** ~ to take some exercise; *(Gym)* ~**s au sol** floor exercises; *(Incendie)* ~ **d'évacuation** fire drill; *(Mil)* **l'** ~ drill; *(Ling)* ~**s structuraux** structure drills. (**c**) *(Fin)* ~ **financier** financial year.

exhaler [ɛgzale] (1) *vt (littér) odeur* to exhale; *soupir* to breathe; *plainte* to utter. **s'** ~ **de** to rise from. ◆ **exhalaison** *nf* exhalation.

exhaustif, -ive [ɛgzostif, iv] *adj* exhaustive. ◆ **exhaustivement** *adv* exhaustively. ◆ **exhaustivité** *nf* exhaustiveness.

exhiber [ɛgzibe] (1) **1** *vt (péj) savoir, richesse* to flaunt; *chiens savants, passeport* to show. **2 s'** ~ *vpr (péj)* to show o.s. off; *(indécemment)* to expose o.s. ◆ **exhibition** *nf* flaunting; showing. *(péj)* ~**(s)** showing off. ◆ **exhibitionnisme** *nm* exhibitionism. ◆ **exhibitionniste** *nmf* exhibitionist.

exhorter [ɛgzɔʀte] (1) *vt* to exhort *(à faire* to do, *à qch* to sth). ◆ **exhortation** *nf* exhortation.

exhumer [ɛgzyme] (1) *vt corps* to exhume; *ruines* to excavate; *faits, vieux livres* to unearth; *souvenirs* to recollect. ◆ **exhumation** *nf* exhumation; excavation; unearthing; recollection.

exiger [ɛgziʒe] (3) *vt* to demand, require *(qch de qn* sth of *ou* from sb). **j'exige que vous le fassiez** I insist on your doing it, I demand that you do it; **des titres universitaires sont exigés** university degrees are required; **trop** ~ **de ses forces** to overtask o.s.; **cette plante exige beaucoup d'eau** this plant needs *ou* requires a lot of water. ◆ **exigeant, e** *adj client* demanding, hard to please; *travail* demanding, exacting. ◆ **exigence** *nf* (**a**) *[client]* particularity; *[maître]* strictness. (**b**) *(revendication, besoin)* demand, requirement.

exigible [ɛgziʒibl(ə)] *adj dette* payable. ◆ **exigibilité** *nf [dette]* payability.

exigu, -uë [ɛgzigy] *adj lieu* cramped; *ressources* scanty; *délais* short. ◆ **exiguïté** *nf* crampedness; scantiness; shortness.

exil [ɛgzil] *nm* exile. ◆ **exilé, e** *nm, f* exile. ◆ **exiler** (1) **1** *vt (Pol)* to exile; *(fig)* to banish. **2 s'** ~ *vpr (Pol)* to go into exile. *(fig)* **s'** ~ **loin du monde** to cut o.s. off from the world.

exister [ɛgziste] (1) *vi* to exist. **la vie existe-t-elle sur Mars?** is there life on Mars?; *(il y a)* **il existe** there is, there are; **il en existe en plusieurs couleurs** they come *ou* are found in several colours. ◆ **existant, e** *adj* existing. ◆ **existence** *nf (gén)* existence. **dans l'** ~ in life.

exocet [ɛgzɔsɛt] *nm (poisson)* flying fish; ® *(missile)* exocet ®.

exode [ɛgzɔd] *nm (lit, fig)* exodus. ~ **rural** drift from the land.

exonérer [ɛgzɔneʀe] (6) *vt (Fin)* to exempt *(de* from). ◆ **exonération** *nf* exemption.

exorbitant, e [ɛgzɔʀbitɑ̃, ɑ̃t] *adj* exorbitant.

exorciser [ɛgzɔʀsize] (1) *vt* to exorcise. ◆ **exorcisme** *nm* exorcism. ◆ **exorciste** *nm* exorcist.

exotique [ɛgzɔtik] *adj* exotic. ◆ **exotisme** *nm* exoticism.

expansion [ɛkspɑ̃sjɔ̃] *nf* (**a**) *(extension)* expansion. **en** ~ *économie* booming, fast-expanding; *univers* expanding. (**b**) *(effusion)* expansiveness. **avec de grandes** ~**s** expansively. ◆ **expansif, -ive** *adj* expansive. **peu** ~ not very forthcoming. ◆ **expansivité** *nf* expansiveness.

expatrier [ɛkspatʀije] (7) **1** *vt* to expatriate. **2 s'** ~ *vpr* to expatriate o.s. ◆ **expatriation** *nf* expatriation. ◆ **expatrié, e** *nm, f* expatriate.

expectative [ɛkspɛktativ] *nf (incertitude)* state of uncertainty. **être dans l'** ~ to be still waiting (to see *etc*).

expectorer [ɛkspɛktɔʀe] (1) *vti* to expectorate. ◆ **expectoration** *nf* expectoration.

expédient, e [ɛkspedjɑ̃, ɑ̃t] *adj, nm* expedient.

expédier [ɛkspedje] (7) *vt* (**a**) *lettre* to send, dispatch. ~ **par la poste** to send through the post *ou* mail; ~ **par le train** to send by rail; ~ **par bateau** *lettres* to send surface mail; *produits* to ship. (**b**) (*) *client, affaire* to dispose of, deal with; *déjeuner* to polish off. ◆ **expéditeur, -trice 1** *adj* dispatching. **2** *nm, f* sender. ◆ **expéditif, -ive** *adj* expeditious. ◆ **expédition** *nf (action)* dispatch; shipping; *(paquet)* consignment; *(par bateau)* shipment; *(Mil, Sci)* expedition. ◆ **expéditionnaire 1** *adj (Mil)* expeditionary. **2** *nmf (Comm)* forwarding clerk. ◆ **expéditivement** *adv* expeditiously.

expérience [ɛkspeʀjɑ̃s] *nf* (**a**) *(gén)* experience. **sans** ~ inexperienced; **savoir par** ~ to know by *ou* from experience; **il a une longue** ~ **de l'enseignement** he has a lot of teaching experience; **tente l'** ~ try it; **faire l'** ~ **de qch** to experience sth. (**b**) *(scientifique)* experiment. **vérité d'** ~ experimental truth; **faire une** ~ **sur** to do an experiment on.

expérimenter [ɛkspeʀimɑ̃te] (1) *vt appareil* to test; *remède* to experiment with; *méthode* to test out. ◆ **expérimental, e,** *mpl* **-aux** *adj* experimental. ◆ **expérimentalement** *adv* experimentally. ◆ **expérimentateur, -trice** *nm, f (gén)* experimenter; *(Sci)* bench scientist. ◆ **expérimentation** *nf* experimentation. ◆ **expérimenté, e** *adj* experienced.

expert, e [ɛkspɛʀ, ɛʀt(ə)] **1** *adj* expert, skilled (*en* in, *à* at). **2** *nm* expert (*en* in, at); *(d'assurances)* valuer. ~**-comptable** independent auditor, ≃ chartered accountant. ◆ **expertement** *adv* expertly.

expertiser [ɛkspɛʀtize] (1) *vt bijou* to value, appraise; *dégâts* to assess, evaluate. **faire** ~ **qch** to have sth valued. ◆ **expertise** *nf (évaluation)* valuation; *(rapport)* expert's report.

expier [ɛkspje] (7) *vt* to expiate, atone for. ◆ **expiation** *nf* expiation (*de* of), atonement (*de* for).

expirer [ɛkspiʀe] (1) **1** *vt air* to breathe out. **2** *vi (mourir, prendre fin)* to expire. ◆ **expiration** *nf (terme)* expiration; *(respiration)* expiration. **venir à** ~ to expire; **à l'** ~ **de** at the expiry of.

explication [ɛksplikɑsjɔ̃] *nf* explanation (*de* for); *(discussion)* discussion; *(dispute)* argument; *(bagarre)* fight; *(Scol)* analysis (*de* of). **j'exige des** ~**s** I demand an explanation. ◆ **explicable** *adj* explicable.

expliciter [ɛksplisite] (1) *vt* to make explicit. ◆ **explicite** *adj* explicit. ◆ **explicitement** *adv* explicitly.

expliquer [ɛksplike] (1) **1** *vt (faire comprendre)* to explain (*à qn* to sb); *(rendre compte de)* to account for, explain; *(Scol) texte* to analyse. **2 s'** ~ *vpr* (**a**) *(préciser)* to explain o.s., make o.s. clear. **s'** ~ **sur ses projets** to explain one's plans. (**b**) *(comprendre)* to understand. (**c**) *(être compréhensible)* **ça s'explique par le mauvais temps** it is explained by the bad weather; **tout s'explique!** it's all clear now! (**d**) *(discuter)* **s'** ~ **avec qn** to explain o.s. to sb; **après s'être longuement expliqués** after having discussed the matter for a long time; **ils sont allés s'** ~ **dehors** * they went off to sort it out outside; **s'** ~ **à coups de fusil** to shoot it out.

exploit [ɛksplwa] *nm* exploit, feat. **quel** ~! what a feat! *ou* achievement!

exploiter [ɛksplwate] (1) *vt mine* to work; *entreprise* to run; *ressources, idée, personne* to exploit. **pouvoir** ~ **un avantage** to be able to capitalize on an advantage *ou* exploit an advantage; **nous sommes des exploités** we are exploited. ◆ **exploitable** *adj (gén)* exploitable. ◆ **exploitant, e** *nm, f* farmer. ◆ **exploitation** *nf* (**a**) *(action)* working; exploitation; running. **mettre en** ~ to exploit; **frais d'**~ running costs; *(Ciné)* **copie d'** ~ release print. (**b**) *(entreprise)* concern. ~ **agricole** farm; ~ **minière** mining development. ◆ **exploiteur, -euse** *nm, f* exploiter.

explorer [ɛksplɔʀe] (1) *vt* to explore. ◆ **explorateur, -trice** *nm, f* explorer. ◆ **exploration** *nf* exploration.

exploser [ɛksploze] (1) *vi (lit, fig)* to explode; *[joie]* to burst out; *[bombe]* to blow up. ~ **(de colère)** to explode with anger; **faire** ~ *bombe* to explode; *bâtiment* to blow up; **cette remarque le fit** ~ he blew up at that remark. ◆ **explosif, -ive** *adj, nm* explosive. ◆ **explosion** *nf* explosion. **faire** ~ to explode; to blow up; ~ **de colère** angry outburst *ou* explosion of anger; ~ **de joie** outburst *ou* explosion of joy.

exporter [ɛkspɔʀte] (1) *vt* to export. ◆ **exportable** *adj* exportable. ◆ **exportateur, -trice 1** *adj* exporting. **2** *nm, f* exporter. ~ **de pétrole** oil exporter. ◆ **exportation** *nf (gén)* export. **faire de l'** ~ to export, be in the export business.

exposer [ɛkspoze] (1) **1** *vt* (**a**) *marchandises* to display; *tableaux* to show. **c'est resté exposé pendant 3 mois** it has been on display for 3 months. (**b**) *(expliquer) (gén)* to explain; *faits, théorie* to expound, set out. (**c**) *(mettre en danger) personne, objet* to expose (*à* to); *vie, réputation* to risk. **sa conduite l'expose à des reproches** his behaviour lays him open to blame; **c'est exposé à être découvert** it is liable to be discovered. (**d**) *(gén, Phot: orienter)* to expose. **exposé au sud** facing (due) south; **maison bien exposée** well-situated house; **endroit très exposé** very exposed place. **2 s'** ~ *vpr* to expose o.s. **s'** ~ **à** to expose o.s. to, lay o.s. open to; **s'** ~ **au soleil** to stay out in the sun. ◆ **exposant, e 1** *nm, f [foire]* exhibitor. **2** *nm (Math)* exponent. ◆ **exposé** *nm (action)* account, statement; *(conférence: gén, Scol)* talk (*sur* on). **faire un** ~ **de la situation** to give an account *ou* overview of the situation. ◆ **exposition** *nf* (**a**) *[marchandises]* display; *[raisons]* exposition; *(au danger)* exposure (*à* to). (**b**) *(foire)* exhibition. **l'E**~ **Universelle** the World Fair. (**c**) *(Phot)* exposure. (**d**) *(Littérat, Mus)* exposition. **scène d'** ~ introductory scene. (**e**) *(orientation) [maison]* aspect.

exprès[1] [ɛkspʀɛ] *adv (spécialement)* specially; *(intentionnellement)* on purpose.

exprès[2], **-esse** [ɛkspʀɛs] *adj* (**a**) *interdiction* formal. (**b**) *(inv)* **(lettre)** ~ express *ou* special delivery *(US)* letter; **envoyer qch en** ~ to send sth express.

express [ɛkspʀɛs] *adj, nm inv*: **(train)** ~ fast train; **(café)** ~ espresso coffee.

expressément [ɛkspʀesemɑ̃] *adv (formellement)* expressly; *(spécialement)* specially.

expression [ɛkspʀɛsjɔ̃] *nf (gén)* expression. **au-delà de toute** ~ inexpressible; **visage sans** ~ expressionless face; ~ **corporelle** self-expression through movement; *(locution)* ~ **figée** set expression *ou* phrase. ◆ **expressif, -ive** *adj* expressive. ◆ **expressivement** *adv* expressively. ◆ **expressivité** *nf* expressiveness.

exprimer [ɛkspʀime] (1) **1** *vt* (**a**) *(gén)* to express. **le signe + exprime l'addition** the sign + stands for addition. (**b**) *jus* to press out. **2 s'** ~ *vpr [personne]* to express o.s.; *[sentiment]* to be expressed.

si je peux m' ~ ainsi if I may put it like that. ◆ **exprimable** *adj* expressible.

exproprier [ɛkspʀɔpʀije] (7) *vt* to expropriate, place a compulsory purchase order on.

expulser [ɛkspylse] (1) *vt (gén) élève* to expel; *étranger* to deport, expel; *locataire* to evict; *manifestant* to eject (*de* from); *joueur* to send off; *(Anat)* to evacuate. ◆ **expulsion** *nf* expulsion; deportation; eviction; ejection; sending off; evacuation.

expurger [ɛkspyʀʒe] (3) *vt* to expurgate.

exquis, -ise [ɛkski, iz] *adj (lit)* exquisite; *personne, temps* delightful.

extase [ɛkstɑz] *nf (Rel, fig)* ecstasy. **être en ~ devant** to be in ecstasies over. ◆ **extasier (s')** (7) *vpr* to go into ecstasies (*sur* over). ◆ **extatique** *adj* ecstatic.

extension [ɛkstɑ̃sjɔ̃] *nf [membre, ressort]* stretching; *[épidémie]* extension, spreading; *[commerce, domaine]* expansion; *[loi, sens]* extension (*à* to). **par ~ (de sens)** by extension; **prendre de l' ~** *[épidémie]* to spread; *[entreprise]* to expand. ◆ **extensible** *adj matière* extensible; *définition* extendable. ◆ **extensif, -ive** *adj* extensive.

exténuer [ɛkstenɥe] (1) **1** *vt* to exhaust. **2 s' ~** *vpr* to exhaust o.s. (*à faire* doing).

extérieur, e [ɛksteʀjœʀ] **1** *adj* (**a**) *(gén)* outside; *cour* outer; *bruit, réalité* external; *décoration* exterior; *[personne] apparence* outward; *amabilité* superficial. **signes ~s de richesse** outward signs of wealth; **être ~ à un sujet** to be external to *ou* outside a subject; **interdit à toute personne ~e au chantier** site workers only, no entry for unauthorized. (**b**) *commerce, politique* foreign. **2** *nm [objet, maison]* outside, exterior; *[personne]* exterior, outward appearance. **c'est à l' ~ (de la ville)** it's outside (the town); *(Ciné)* **~s** location shots; *(pays)* **l' ~** foreign countries; **vendre à l' ~** to sell abroad. ◆ **extérieurement** *adv (du dehors)* on the outside, externally; *(en apparence)* outwardly. ◆ **extérioriser** (1) *vt joie etc* to show.

exterminer [ɛkstɛʀmine] (1) *vt (lit, fig)* to exterminate. ◆ **extermination** *nf* extermination.

externe [ɛkstɛʀn(ə)] **1** *adj surface etc* external, outer; *angle* exterior. **à usage ~** for external use only. **2** *nmf (Scol)* day pupil. *(Méd)* **~ (des hôpitaux)** non-resident student. ◆ **externat** *nm (Scol)* day school.

extincteur [ɛkstɛ̃ktœʀ] *nm* fire extinguisher.

extinction [ɛkstɛ̃ksjɔ̃] *nf [incendie]* extinguishing; *[peuple]* extinction; *[droit]* extinguishment. **~ de voix** loss of voice; **espèce en voie d' ~** endangered species.

extirper [ɛkstiʀpe] (1) *vt* to eradicate. **impossible de lui ~ une parole!** * it's impossible to drag a word out of him!; **s' ~ de son manteau** to extricate o.s. from one's coat. ◆ **extirpation** *nf* eradication.

extorquer [ɛkstɔʀke] (1) *vt* to extort (*à qn* from sb). ◆ **extorqueur, -euse** *nm, f* extortioner. ◆ **extorsion** *nf* extortion. **~ de fonds** extortion of money.

extra [ɛkstʀa] **1** *nm inv (domestique)* extra servant *ou* help; *(gâterie)* special treat. **2** *adj inv fromage, vin* first-rate; *tissu* top-quality; (*) *film, personne* terrific *, great *. **de qualité ~** of the finest quality. **3** *préf* extra. **~-fin** superfine, extra fine; **(voyante) ~-lucide** clairvoyant.

extraction [ɛkstʀaksjɔ̃] *nf* (*V* **extraire**) extraction; mining; quarrying; *(†: origine)* extraction.

extrader [ɛkstʀade] (1) *vt* to extradite. ◆ **extradition** *nf* extradition.

extraire [ɛkstʀɛʀ] (50) *vt (gén, Méd, Math)* to extract; *charbon* to mine; *marbre* to quarry. **~ de** *poche* to take *ou* bring out of; *prison* to get out of; **passage extrait d'un livre** extract from a book, passage taken from a book; **s' ~ de son manteau** * to extricate o.s. from one's coat. ◆ **extrait** *nm (gén)* extract; *[livre]* extract, excerpt. **~ de naissance** *etc* birth *etc* certificate; *(Fin)* **~ de compte** abstract of accounts.

extraordinaire [ɛkstʀaɔʀdinɛʀ] *adj (étrange)* extraordinary; *(exceptionnel)* exceptional, extraordinary; *(Pol)* special. **acteur ~** extraordinary *ou* remarkable actor; **ce n'est pas ~** it isn't up to much *; **si par ~** if by some unlikely chance; **quand par ~** on those rare occasions when. ◆ **extraordinairement** *adv* extraordinarily; exceptionally.

extraterrestre [ɛkstʀatɛʀɛstʀ] *adj, n* extraterrestrial.

extravagance [ɛkstʀavagɑ̃s] *nf (caractère)* eccentricity, extravagance. *(acte)* **~(s)** eccentric *ou* extravagant behaviour. ◆ **extravagant, e** *adj idée, prix* extravagant; *conduite* eccentric.

extrême [ɛkstʀɛm] **1** *adj (gén)* extreme; *point* furthest; *mesures* drastic. **à l' ~ opposé (de)** at the opposite extreme (of). **2** *nm (gén)* extreme. **jusqu'à l' ~** in the extreme, to a degree. **3 : ~ droite/gauche** extreme right/left (wing); **~-onction** Extreme Unction; **E~-Orient** Far East; **E~-Oriental, e,** *mpl* **E~-Orientaux** *adj* Far Eastern, Oriental. ◆ **extrêmement** *adv* extremely. ◆ **extrémisme** *nm* extremism. ◆ **extrémiste** *adj, nmf* extremist.

extrémité [ɛkstʀemite] *nf* (**a**) *(bout) (gén)* end; *[aiguille]* point; *[objet mince]* tip; *[village, île]* extremity, limit. *(Anat)* **~s** extremities. (**b**) **à la dernière ~** *(misère)* in the most dire plight; *(mort)* on the point of death; **se porter à des ~s** to go to extremes.

exubérance [ɛgzybeʀɑ̃s] *nf (caractère)* exuberance. *(action)* **~(s)** exuberant behaviour. ◆ **exubérant, e** *adj (gén)* exuberant.

exulter [ɛgzylte] (1) *vi* to exult. ◆ **exultation** *nf* exultation.

exutoire [ɛgzytwaʀ] *nm* outlet, release.

ex-voto [ɛksvoto] *nm inv* monumental tablet.

F, f [ɛf] *nm ou nf (lettre)* F, f. *(abrév de* **franc***)* **F** fr; *(appartement)* **un F2** a 2-roomed flat *ou* apartment *(US)*.

fa [fɑ] *nm inv (Mus)* F; *(en chantant)* fa.

fable [fɑbl(ə)] *nf (gén)* fable; *(mensonge)* tale. **être la ~ de toute la ville** to be the laughing stock of the whole town.

fabriquer [fabʀike] (1) *vt (gén)* to make; *(industriellement)* to manufacture; *histoire* to fabricate, make up; *fausse monnaie* to forge. **~ en série** to mass-produce; **il s'est fabriqué une cabane** he built *ou* made himself a shed; **qu'est-ce qu'il fabrique? *** what on earth is he up to? * ◆ **fabricant, e** *nm, f* manufacturer. ◆ **fabrication** *nf* making; manufacturing; forging; fabricating. **~ en série** mass production; **de ~ française** made in France, of French make; **de bonne ~** well-made; **une robe de sa ~** a dress of her own making. ◆ **fabrique** *nf (établissement)* factory. **~ de papier** paper mill.

fabuler [fabyle] (1) *vi* to fantasize.

fabuleux, -euse [fabylø, øz] *adj (gén)* fabulous. ◆ **fabuleusement** *adv* fabulously.

fac [fak] *nf (arg Univ) abrév de* **faculté.**

façade [fasad] *nf* (**a**) *[maison]* façade, front; *(latérale)* side; *[magasin]* front. **la ~ arrière de la maison** the back of the house. (**b**) *(fig) (apparence)* façade, appearance; *(couverture)* cover. **de ~** *luxe* sham.

face [fas] *nf* (**a**) *(visage)* face. **les blessés de la ~** people with facial injuries; **sauver/perdre la ~** to save/lose face. (**b**) *[objet]* side; *[médaille]* front; *(Alpinisme)* face, wall; *(lit, fig) [monde]* face. **question à double ~** two-sided question; **sous** *ou* **sur toutes ses ~s** from all sides; **la pièce est tombée sur ~** the coin fell face up; *(jeu de pile ou face)* **~!** heads!; **la ~ des choses** the face of things. (**c**) **faire ~** to face up to things; **faire ~ à** *lieu, difficulté* to face; *épreuve* to face up to, face; *engagement* to meet; **se faire ~** *[maisons]* to be facing each other; *[adversaires]* to be face to face. (**d**) **en ~** opposite; **la dame d'en ~** the lady from across the street, the lady opposite; **regarder qn en ~** to look sb in the face; **il lui a dit en ~ que** he told him to his face that; **il faut voir les choses en ~** one must face facts. (**e**) **~ à, en ~ de** *maison* opposite, facing; *examinateur* in front of; *danger* confronted *ou* faced with; **être ~ à ~** to be facing each other, be face to face; *(TV)* **un ~ à ~** a face to face discussion; **les deux ennemis étaient maintenant l'un en ~ de l'autre** the two enemies now stood facing each other *ou* face to face. (**f**) **de ~** *portrait* fullface; *attaque* frontal; *(Théât) place* facing the stage; **voir qn de ~** to see sb face on; **avoir une vue de ~ sur qch** to have a front view of sth.

facétie [fasesi] *nf (drôlerie)* joke; *(farce)* prank. ◆ **facétieux, -euse** *adj* facetious.

facette [fasɛt] *nf (lit, fig)* facet.

fâcher [fɑʃe] (1) **1** *vt (mettre en colère)* to anger, make angry; *(contrarier)* to distress. **2 se ~** *vpr (se mettre en colère)* to get angry (*contre* with); *(se brouiller)* to quarrel, fall out (*avec* with). ◆ **fâché, e** *adj (en colère)* angry, cross (*contre* with); *(contrarié)* sorry (*de qch* about sth). **je suis ~ de ne pas venir** I am sorry that I cannot come; *(hum)* **il est ~ avec l'orthographe** he can't spell to save himself; *(hum)* **je ne serais pas ~ de m'asseoir** I wouldn't mind a seat. ◆ **fâcherie** *nf (brouille)* quarrel.

fâcheux, -euse [fɑʃø, øz] *adj exemple* unfortunate; *situation* unfortunate, awkward. **il est ~ que** it's unfortunate *ou* a pity that. ◆ **fâcheusement** *adv* unfortunately, awkwardly. **~ surpris** unpleasantly surprised.

facho [faʃo] *nmf (abrév de* **fasciste***) (péj)* fascist. **il est un peu ~** he's a bit of a fascist.

facile [fasil] **1** *adj* (**a**) *(aisé)* easy (*à faire* to do). **plus ~ à dire qu'à faire** easier said than done; **~ comme bonjour *** easy as pie *, dead easy *; **avoir la larme ~** to be easily moved to tears; **il a le couteau ~** he's very ready with his knife. (**b**) *(péj)* **effet/ironie ~** facile effect/irony. (**c**) *caractère* easy-going. **il est ~ à vivre** he's easy to get on with; **c'est un bébé très ~** he's a very easy baby; *(péj)* **fille ~** woman of easy virtue. **2** *adv* (⁂) **elle a 50 ans ~** she's easily 50. ◆ **facilement** *adv (gén)* easily. **~ toléré par l'organisme** easily *ou* readily tolerated by the body.

facilité [fasilite] *nf* (**a**) *[problème]* easiness; *[succès]* ease; *[style]* fluency. **il travaille avec ~** he works with ease. (**b**) *(aptitude)* ability, aptitude; *(tendance)* tendency. **il a beaucoup de ~ pour les langues** he has a great aptitude for languages. (**c**) *(gén pl:* **possibilité***)* facility. **avoir toutes ~s de faire qch** to have every opportunity to do sth; **~s de transport** transport facilities; *(Comm)* **~s de paiement** easy terms. ◆ **faciliter** (1) *vt* to make easier, facilitate. **ça ne va pas ~ les choses** that's not going to make matters any easier.

façon [fasɔ̃] *nf* (**a**) *(manière)* way. **de quelle ~ est-ce arrivé?** how did it happen?; **je le ferai à ma ~** I shall do it my own way; **à la ~ d'un enfant** like a child, as a child would do; **(c'est une) ~ de parler** it's a way of putting it; **d'une certaine ~** in a way, in some ways; **d'une ~ générale** generally speaking; **de toute(s) ~(s)** in any case, at any rate; **de cette ~** (in) this way; **d'une ~ ou d'une autre** one way or another; **en aucune ~** in no way; **un plat de ma ~** a dish of my own making; **de ~ à ne pas le déranger** so as not to disturb him; **de ~ à ce qu'il puisse regarder** so that he can see. (**b**) **sans ~** *accepter* without fuss; *repas* unpretentious; *personne* unaffected; **merci, sans ~** no thanks honestly; **et sans plus de ~s** and without further ado. (**c**) **~s** manners, behaviour; **en voilà des ~s!** that's no way to behave!; **faire des ~s** *(minauderies)* to be affected; *(chichis)* to make a fuss. (**d**) *(Couture) [robe]* cut, making-up. **payer la ~** to pay for the tailoring *ou* making-up. (**e**) *(imitation)* **veste ~ daim** jacket in imitation suede. (**f**) *(†: genre)* **une ~ de roman** a novel of sorts.

façonner [fasɔne] (1) *vt (gén)* to make; *(industriellement)* to manufacture; *argile* to shape, fashion; *personne* to mould, form.

fac-similé, *pl* **fac-similés** [faksimile] *nm* facsimile.

facteur [faktœʀ] *nm (Poste)* postman, mailman *(US)*; *(élément, Math)* factor. *(Math)* **mettre en ~s** to factorize; *(fabricant)* **~ de pianos** piano maker.

factice [faktis] *adj marbre, beauté* artificial; *bijou* imitation; *barbe* false; *bouteille en vitrine* dummy; *enthousiasme* feigned.

factieux, -euse [faksjø, øz] **1** *adj* factious. **2** *nm, f* seditionary.

faction [faksjɔ̃] *nf* (**a**) *(groupe)* faction. (**b**) *[soldat]* guard; *(fig)* long watch. **être de** *ou* **en** ~ to be on *ou* stand guard; *(fig)* to keep watch. ◆**factionnaire** *nm* guard.

factrice [faktʀis] *nf* postwoman, mailwoman *(US)*.

factuel, -elle [faktɥɛl] *adj* factual.

facture [faktyʀ] *nf (gén)* bill; *(Comm)* invoice. *(Écon)* **notre ~ pétrolière** the nation's oil bill. ◆**facturer** (1) *vt (établir une facture)* to invoice. *(compter)* ~ **qch 20 F (à qn)** to charge (sb) 20 francs for sth.

facultatif, -ive [fakyltatif, iv] *adj* optional. **arrêt** ~ request stop; **matière ~ive** optional subject, elective (subject) *(US)*.

faculté [fakylte] *nf* (**a**) *(Univ)* faculty. **quand j'étais en** ~ when I was at university. (**b**) *(don)* faculty; *(pouvoir)* power; *(propriété)* property. **avoir une grande ~ de mémoire** to have great powers of memory; **avoir la ~ de marcher** to have the ability to walk *ou* the power of walking; *(aptitudes)* **~s** faculties. (**c**) *(droit)* right; *(possibilité)* freedom. **je te laisse la ~ de choisir** I'll give you the freedom to choose.

fadaise [fadɛz] *nf (littér)* **dire des ~(s)** to mouth insipid, empty phrases.

fade [fad] *adj plat* tasteless, insipid, bland; *teinte* dull; *plaisanterie* tame; *décor, individu, conversation* dull, insipid. ◆**fadeur** *nf* tastelessness; insipidness; blandness; dullness. *(platitudes)* **~s** sweet nothings.

fagot [fago] *nm* bundle of sticks.

fagoter * [fagɔte] (1) **1** *vt (péj)* to rig out *. **2 se** ~ *vpr* to rig o.s. out * (*en* as a).

Fahrenheit [faʀɛnajt] *adj, nm* Fahrenheit. **32 degrés** ~ 32 degrees Fahrenheit.

faible [fɛbl(ə)] **1** *adj (gén)* weak. *monnaie* weak, soft; *somme, intensité* low; *quantité, différence* small, slight; *espoir, bruit, odeur* slight, faint; *lumière* dim; *voix, pouls* faint, feeble; *vent* light; *rendement, devoir, raisonnement* poor. **avoir la vue** ~ to have weak *ou* poor eyesight; **il est trop ~ avec elle** he is too soft with her; **à une ~ profondeur** at a slight depth below the surface; *(Pol)* **une ~ majorité** a narrow *ou* slight majority; **~ en alcool** low in alcohol; **~ en français** poor at French. **2** *nm* (**a**) *(sans volonté)* weakling. *(sans défense)* **les ~s** the weak; **un ~ d'esprit** a feeble-minded person. (**b**) *(déficience)* weak point; *(penchant)* weakness, partiality. **il a un ~ pour sa fille** he has a soft spot for his daughter.
◆**faiblement** *adv* weakly; slightly; faintly; dimly; lightly. ◆**faiblesse** *nf* (**a**) weakness; softness; smallness; slightness; faintness; feebleness; dimness; lightness. **la ~ de la demande** the low *ou* poor demand; **~ d'esprit** feeble-mindedness; **avoir la ~ d'accepter** to be weak enough to accept. (**b**) *(syncope)* sudden weakness. (**c**) *(défaut)* weakness. **chacun a ses petites ~s** we all have our little foibles *ou* weaknesses. ◆**faiblir** (2) *vi* to get weaker *(ou* slighter *ou* smaller *etc)*; *[résolution, résistance]* to weaken; *[forces, courage, vue]* to fail; *[vent]* to slacken; *[rendement]* to slacken off. **l'écart faiblit entre eux** the gap is narrowing between them.

faïence [fajɑ̃s] *nf* (**a**) **la** ~ *(substance)* earthenware; *(objets)* crockery, earthenware. (**b**) *(objet)* piece of earthenware.

faille [faj] *nf (Géol)* fault; *[raisonnement]* flaw; *[amitié]* rift.

faillir [fajiʀ] *vi* (**a**) *(manquer)* **j'ai failli tomber** I almost *ou* very nearly fell. (**b**) ~ **à** *devoir* to fail in; *promesse* to fail to keep; **sans** ~ unfailingly. (**c**) *(†: fauter)* to lapse.

faillite [fajit] *nf (Comm)* bankruptcy; *[espoir, méthode, gouvernement]* collapse. **la ~ du gouvernement en matière économique** the government's failure on the economic front; **faire** ~ *(Comm)* to go bankrupt; *(fig)* to collapse; **mettre qn en** ~ to make sb bankrupt.

faim [fɛ̃] *nf* hunger. **donner/avoir** ~ to make sb/be hungry; **manger à sa** ~ to eat one's fill; **avoir ~ de** *honneur etc* to hunger for; **sa ~ de richesses** his yearning for wealth; **j'ai une ~ de loup** I'm ravenous *ou* famished.

fainéant, e [feneɑ̃, ɑ̃t] **1** *adj* lazy, idle. **2** *nm, f* idler. ◆**fainéanter** (1) *vi* to idle about. ◆**fainéantise** *nf* laziness, idleness.

faire [fɛʀ] (60) **1** *vt* (**a**) *(fabrication) (gén)* to make; *maison* to build; *pain* to bake; *repas* to cook; *liste* to draw up; *chèque* to make out; *cours* to give; *livre* to write; *tableau* to paint; *dessin* to draw; *farce* to play; *faute, promesse* to make. **~ du thé** to make (some) tea; **qu'avez-vous fait de votre sac?** what have you done with your bag?, where have you left *ou* put your bag? (**b**) *(activité) (gén)* to do; *piano, tennis, match* to play; *rêve, chute* to have; *geste, projet* to make. **que faites-vous?** *(dans la vie)* what do you do?, what is your job?; *(en ce moment)* what are you doing?; **~ du français** to do *ou* study French; **elle fait du tricot/un peu de tricot** she knits/does a bit of knitting. (**c**) *(fonction) (Théât) rôle* to play, be. **~ le malade** to pretend to be ill; **~ l'innocent** to play *ou* act the innocent; **il fait le jardinier pendant les vacances** he is acting as gardener during the holidays; **quel idiot je fais!** what a fool I am! *ou* I look!; **il en a fait un avocat/son héritier** he's made a lawyer of him/made him his heir; **on le fait plus riche qu'il n'est** people make him out to be richer than he is; **ils ont fait de cette pièce une cuisine** they made *ou* turned the room into a kitchen; **la cuisine fait salle à manger** the kitchen serves as *ou* is used as a dining room; **cet hôtel fait aussi restaurant** this hotel is also run as a restaurant. (**d**) *(parcours)* to do. **~ un voyage/une promenade** to go on a journey/go for *ou* take a walk; **~ du 100 km/h** to do 100 km/h; **~ les magasins** to go round the shops. (**e**) *(Comm) l'épicerie* to sell, deal in; *blé* to grow, produce. **nous ne faisons pas cette marque** we don't stock *ou* keep that make. (**f**) *(nettoyage) pièce* to clean, do; *lit* to make; *chaussures* to clean. **~ le ménage** to do the housework, clean the house; **~ la vaisselle** to do the washing-up *ou* the dishes. (**g**) *(Méd) diabète etc* to have, suffer from. **~ de la fièvre** to have *ou* run a temperature; **~ ses besoins** to go to the toilet. (**h**) *(mesure)* to be. **2 et 2 font 4** 2 and 2 are *ou* make 4; **ça fait 3 mètres de long** it is 3 metres long; **ça fait 3 kg** it weighs 3 kg; **il fait 23 degrés** it is 23 degrees; **combien fait cette chaise?** how much is this chair? *ou* does this chair cost?; **je vous la fais 100 F** I'll let you have it *ou* I'll give it to you for 100 F. (**i**) *(effet) piqûres etc* to give. **~ du bien/du mal à...** to do good/harm to...; **~ du chagrin à qn** to cause unhappiness to sb, make sb unhappy; **~ le bonheur de qn** to make sb happy; **qu'est-ce que cela peut bien te ~?** what does it matter to you?; **la mort de son père ne lui a rien fait** his father's death didn't affect him; **cela ne vous ferait rien de sortir?** would you mind going out?; **qu'est-ce qu'on t'a donc fait!** whatever have they done to you!; **ça ne fait rien** it doesn't matter; **l'épidémie a fait 10 victimes** the epidemic has claimed 10 victims *ou* lives. (**j**) *(locutions)* **pour ce qu'on en fait!** for all that we do with it!; **n'en faites rien** do nothing of the sort; **n'avoir que ~ de** to have no need of; **ne ~ que de protester** to keep on and on protesting, be constantly protesting; **je ne fais que d'arriver** I've only just arrived.

2 *vi* (**a**) *(agir)* to do. **~ vite** to act quickly, be quick; **il a bien fait** he did the right thing; **~ de son mieux** to do one's best; **on ferait bien de le prévenir** it would be a good idea to warn him; **je ferais mieux de partir** I'd better go; **faites comme vous voulez** do as you please; **faites comme chez vous** make yourself at home; **il n'y a rien à ~** it's no use. (**b**) *(dire)* to say. **vraiment? fit-il** really? he said; **il fit un 'ah' de surprise** he gave a surprised 'ah'. (**c**) *(durer)* **ce chapeau (me) fera encore un hiver** this hat will last *ou* do me another winter. (**d**) *(paraître)* to look. **ce vase fait bien sur la table** the vase looks nice on the table; **~ vieux/ jeune** to look old/ young (for one's age). (**e**) *(devenir)* to make, be. **cet enfant fera un bon musicien** this child will make a good musician; **il veut ~ médecin** he wants to be a doctor.

3 *vb impers*: **il fait jour** it is daylight; **il fait du soleil** the sun is shining, it is sunny; **il fait lourd** it *ou* the weather is close *ou* thundery; **cela fait 2 ans que je ne l'ai pas vu** it is 2 years since I last saw him, I haven't seen him for 2 years; **ça fait 2 ans qu'il est parti** he left 2 years ago, it's 2 years since he left; **il fait bon se promener** it is nice to go for a walk; **il ne fait pas bon le contredire** it is better not to contradict him; **il fait bon vivre** life is good; **cela fait que nous devons partir** the result is that we must leave.

4 *vb substitut* to do. **il travaille mieux que je ne fais** he works better than I do; **— faites, je vous en prie —** (yes) please do, (yes) by all means.

5 se ~ *vpr* (**a**) *robe, amis* to make o.s. **il se fait sa cuisine** he does his own cooking; **il se fait 8000 F par mois** he earns *ou* makes 8,000 francs a month; **s'en ~** to worry. (**b**) *[fromage, vin]* to mature. *(fig)* **il s'est fait tout seul** he is a self-made man. (**c**) *(devenir) prêtre etc* to become. **se ~ vieux** to be getting old; **il se faisait tard** it was getting late; **ça ne se fera pas** it won't happen; **se ~ beau** to make o.s. beautiful. (**d**) **se ~ à** to get used to; **il ne peut pas se ~ au climat** he can't get used to the climate. (**e**) **cela ne se fait pas** it's not done; **une chose qui se fait** a done thing; **ça ne se fera pas** it won't take place. (**f**) *(impers)* **il peut/il pourrait se ~ qu'il pleuve** it may/it might rain; **comment se fait-il qu'il soit absent?** how is it that he is absent? (**g**) **se ~** + *infin*: **se ~ vomir** to make o.s. vomit; **il s'est fait remettre le document** he had the document handed over to him; **il s'est fait ouvrir par le voisin** he got the neighbour to let him in.

6 *vb aux* + *infin*: **j'ai fait démarrer la voiture** I made the car start, I got the car started; **~ traverser la rue à un aveugle** to help a blind man across the road; **~ entrer** *visiteur* to show *ou* ask in; *livreur* to let in; **(se) ~ faire une robe** to have a dress made; **~ faire la vaisselle à qn** to get sb to do the dishes; **il lui a fait ouvrir le coffre-fort** he made him open *ou* forced him to open the safe.

7 : **~-part** *nm inv* announcement (of a birth *ou* death *etc*); **~-part de mariage** wedding announcement, ≃ wedding invitation.

faisable [fəzabl(ə)] *adj* feasible. **est-ce ~ en 2 jours?** can it be done in 2 days? ◆**faisabilité** *nf* feasibility.

faisan [fəzɑ̃] *nm* pheasant. ◆**faisandé, e** *adj goût* high; *(péj)* corrupt.

faisceau, *pl* **~x** [fɛso] *nm (fagot)* bundle; *(Élec, Phys)* beam. **~ de preuves** body of proof.

fait¹ [fɛ] *nm* (**a**) *(événement)* event, occurrence; *(donnée, acte)* fact; *(phénomène)* phenomenon. **~ nouveau** new development; **il me faut des ~s concrets** I must have concrete facts *ou* evidence; *(Jur)* **les ~s qui lui sont reprochés** the charges against him; **il s'est produit un ~ curieux** a strange thing has happened; **le ~ de bouger** the fact of moving; **~ d'armes** feat of arms; **~ divers** (short) news item; *(rubrique)* **~s divers** news in brief; **~s et gestes** actions. (**b**) *(cause)* **c'est le ~ du hasard** it's the work of fate; **c'est le ~ de son inexpérience** it's because of *ou* owing to his inexperience. (**c**) **au ~** *(à propos)* by the way; **en venir au ~** to get to the point; **est-il au ~?** does he know?, is he informed?; **mettre qn au ~ (d'une affaire)** to inform sb of *ou* acquaint sb with a matter; **de ~** *(de facto)* de facto; *(en fait)* in fact; **il est de ~ que** it is a fact that; **de ce ~** therefore; **du ~ de qch** on account of sth; **en ~** in fact; **en ~ de** *(en guise de)* by way of a; *(en matière de)* as regards, in the way of; **le ~ est là** it's a fact; **être le ~ de** *(être typique de)* to be typical of; **par ce ~** by this very fact; **dire son ~ à qn** to talk straight to sb; **prendre ~ et cause pour qn** to side with sb; **comme par un ~ exprès** almost as if on purpose; **mettre qn devant le ~ accompli** to present sb with a fait accompli.

fait², e [fɛ, fɛt] *adj* (**a**) **être ~ pour** to be made *ou* meant for; **ceci n'est pas ~ pour lui plaire** this is not likely to please him; **il est ~ pour être médecin** he's cut out to be a doctor. (**b**) *(fini)* **c'en est ~ de notre vie calme** that's the end of our quiet life; **c'est toujours ça de ~** that's one job done. (**c**) *(mûr) personne* mature; *fromage* ripe. **fromage ~ à cœur** fully ripened cheese. (**d**) *(maquillé)* made-up. **avoir les ongles ~s** to have painted nails. (**e**) **tout ~** ready-made; **acheter des vêtements tout ~s** to buy ready-made *ou* ready-to-wear clothes. (**f**) *(constitué)* **une femme bien ~e** a good-looking woman; **avoir la jambe bien ~e** to have nice legs; **comment est-il ~?** what is he like?, what does he look like?; **le monde est ainsi ~** that's the way of the world; **les gens sont ainsi ~s que** people are such that. (**g**) *(locutions)* **il est ~ (comme un rat) *** he's cornered!; **c'est bien ~!** it serves them (*ou* him *etc*) right!

faîte [fɛt] *nm [montagne]* summit; *[arbre]* top. **~ du toit** rooftop; **~ de la gloire** height of glory.

faitout *nm* [fɛtu] stewpot.

fakir [fakiʀ] *nm (Rel)* fakir; *(Music-Hall)* wizard.

falaise [falɛz] *nf* cliff.

fallacieux, -euse [falasjø, øz] *adj* fallacious. ◆**fallacieusement** *adv* fallaciously.

falloir [falwaʀ] (29) **1** *vb impers* (**a**) *(besoin)* **il me le faut à tout prix** I must have it at all costs; **il lui faut qn pour l'aider** he needs sb to help him; **il vous faut tourner à gauche** you have to *ou* need to turn left; *(au magasin)* **qu'est-ce qu'il vous faut?** what are you looking for?; **il n'en faut pas beaucoup pour qu'il se mette à pleurer** it doesn't take much to make him cry; **il faut du courage pour le faire!** it takes some courage to do it; **s'il le faut** if need be. (**b**) *(obligation)* **il va ~ y aller** we'll have to go; **il faut que tu y ailles** you must go; **il faudrait qu'il parte** he ought to *ou* should go; **que faut-il leur dire?** what shall I (*ou* we *etc*) tell them?; **il ne faut pas être en retard** we mustn't be *ou* we can't afford to be late; **il va ~ qu'il parte** he'll have to go. (**c**) *(intensif)* **il fallait me le dire** you should have told me; **il faut voir ce spectacle** this show is a must, you must see this show; **il ne faudrait pas qu'il essaie!** he'd better not try!; **(il) faut dire qu'il est culotté *** you've got to admit he's got a nerve; **il a fallu qu'elle le perde!** she HAD to go and lose it! (**d**) *(probabilité)* **il faut que tu te sois trompé** you must have made a mistake; **faut-il donc être bête!** some people are so stupid; **faut-il qu'il soit bête!** he must be so *ou* really stupid; **il ne faut pas être intelligent pour dire ça** it's not very clever to say sth like that; **il faut toujours que ça tombe sur moi!** it always has to happen to me. (**e**) *(locutions)* **(il) faut le faire!** *(admiratif)* that takes some doing!; **il faut de tout pour faire un monde** it takes all sorts to make a world; **il ne faut jamais remettre au lendemain ce qu'on peut faire le jour même** procrastination is the thief of time; **ce qu'il faut entendre!** the things you hear!

2 s'en ~ *vpr*: **il ne s'en fallait que de 100 F pour qu'il ait la somme** he was only *ou* just 100 francs short of the full amount; **il s'en faut de beaucoup** not by a long way *ou* chalk, far from it; **il s'en faut de beaucoup qu'il soit heureux** he is far from happy; **il s'en est fallu d'un cheveu qu'il ne soit pris** he was within a hair's breadth *ou* an ace of being caught; **peu s'en est fallu (pour) qu'il pleure** he almost *ou* very nearly wept.

falot[1] [falo] *nm* lantern.

falot[2]**, e** [falo, ɔt] *adj personne* colourless; *lumière* wan, pale.

falsifier [falsifje] (7) *vt* to falsify, alter, tamper with.

famélique [famelik] *adj* scrawny, scraggy, raw-boned.

fameux, -euse [famø, øz] *adj* (**a**) (*: *bon) mets, voiture* first-rate; *idée* bright, great *. **pas** ~ *mets, roman* not too good, not up to much *; **il n'est pas** ~ **en maths** he's not too hot at maths *. (**b**) (*: *avant n: intensif)* **c'est un** ~ **problème** it's a real *ou* it's quite a problem; **c'est une ~euse assiettée** that's a huge *ou* great plateful; **c'est un** ~ **gaillard** *(bien bâti)* he's a strapping fellow. (**c**) (*: *référence)* **quel est le nom de cette ~euse rue?** what's the name of that (famous) street? (**d**) *(célèbre)* famous (*pour* for). ◆**fameusement** *adv* remarkably, really.

familial, e, *mpl* **-aux** [familjal, o] **1** *adj* family. **2** *nf* family estate car, station wagon *(US)*.

familiariser [familjaʀize] (1) **1** *vt*: ~ **qn avec** to familiarize sb with. **2 se** ~ *vpr*: **se** ~ **avec** *lieu, personne, méthode* to familiarize o.s. with, get to know, become acquainted with; *bruit, danger* to get used *ou* accustomed to; **être (peu) familiarisé avec** to be (un)familiar with.

familier, -ière [familje, jɛʀ] **1** *adj* (**a**) *(bien connu)* familiar. **ça m'est** ~ I'm familiar with it; **cette attitude lui est ~ière** this is a familiar *ou* customary attitude of his; **le mensonge lui était devenu** ~ he had become quite used to lying. (**b**) *(amical)* informal, friendly; *(désinvolte) personne, surnom* (over)familiar; *attitude* offhand, casual; *(non recherché) expression, style* familiar, colloquial. **expression ~ière** colloquialism. **2** *nm [club, théâtre]* regular visitor (*de* to); *[famille]* friend (*de* of). ◆**familiarité** *nf* familiarity. *(privautés)* **~s** familiarities; ~ **avec** *langue, méthode* familiarity with. ◆**familièrement** *adv* informally; familiarly; colloquially.

famille [famij] *nf (gén)* family. **on a prévenu la** ~ the relatives *ou* the next of kin have been informed; **dîner de** ~ family dinner; **ça tient de** ~ it runs in the family; **passer ses vacances en** ~ to spend one's holidays with the family; **ils sont de la même** ~ **politique** they're of the same political persuasion.

famine [famin] *nf (épidémie)* famine. **nous allons à la** ~ we are heading for starvation.

fan * [fan] *nm (admirateur)* fan.

fanal, *pl* **-aux** [fanal, o] *nm (gén)* lantern; *[train]* headlight; *(phare)* beacon.

fanatique [fanatik] **1** *adj* fanatical (*de* about). **2** *nmf (gén, Sport)* fanatic. ◆**fanatiquement** *adv* fanatically. ◆**fanatiser** (1) *vt* to rouse to fanaticism. ◆**fanatisme** *nm* fanaticism.

fane [fan] *nf [radis etc]* top.

faner [fane] (1) **1** *vi* to make hay. **2** *vt* (**a**) *herbe* to toss. (**b**) *fleur, beauté* to fade. **3 se** ~ *vpr [plante, teint]* to fade; *[peau]* to wither.

fanfare [fɑ̃faʀ] *nf (orchestre)* brass band; *(musique)* fanfare. **en** ~ *réveil* clamorous, tumultuous; *partir* noisily, with great commotion; **annoncer en** ~ *réforme etc* to blazon *ou* trumpet forth.

fanfaron, -onne [fɑ̃faʀɔ̃, ɔn] **1** *adj* boastful. **2** *nm, f* braggart. **faire le** ~ to brag, boast. ◆**fanfaronnade** *nf*: ~**(s)** bragging, boasting. **arrête tes ~s** stop boasting. ◆**fanfaronner** (1) *vi* to brag, boast.

fanfreluche [fɑ̃fʀəlyʃ] *nf* trimming.

fange [fɑ̃ʒ] *nf (littér)* mire.

fanion [fanjɔ̃] *nm* pennant.

fantaisie [fɑ̃tezi] *nf* (**a**) *(caprice)* whim; *(extravagance)* extravagance. **je me suis payé une petite** ~ I bought myself a little present; **il veut vivre à sa** ~ he wants to live as he pleases; **il lui a pris la** ~ **de faire** he took it into his head to do; **à votre** ~ as it may please you. (**b**) *(imagination)* fancy, imagination. **manquer de** ~ *[vie]* to be monotonous; *[personne]* to be lacking in imagination. (**c**) **rideaux/boutons** *etc* ~ fancy curtains/buttons *etc*. (**d**) *(œuvre) (Littérat)* fantasy; *(Mus)* fantasia. ◆**fantaisiste 1** *adj (faux)* fanciful; *(bizarre)* eccentric; *(farceur)* whimsical. **2** *nmf (Théât)* variety artist; *(original)* eccentric; *(péj: fumiste)* phoney *.

fantasme [fɑ̃tasm(ə)] *nm* fantasy. **il vit dans ses ~s** he lives in a fantasy world. ◆**fantasmer** (1) *vi* to fantasize (*sur* about).

fantasque [fɑ̃task(ə)] *adj humeur* whimsical; *chose* weird, fantastic.

fantassin [fɑ̃tasɛ̃] *nm* foot soldier, infantryman.

fantastique [fɑ̃tastik] *adj* (**a**) *(étrange)* uncanny, weird, fantastic. **le cinéma** ~ the cinema of the fantastic. (**b**) (*: *excellent, énorme, incroyable)* fantastic *. ◆**fantastiquement** *adv* fantastically.

fantoche [fɑ̃tɔʃ] *nm, adj* puppet. **gouvernement** ~ puppet government.

fantôme [fɑ̃tom] **1** *nm (spectre)* ghost. **2** *adj firme* bogus. **bateau** ~ ghost *ou* phantom ship. ◆**fantomatique** *adj* ghostly.

faon [fɑ̃] *nm (Zool)* fawn.

faramineux, -euse * [faʀaminø, øz] *adj bêtise etc* staggering; *prix* astronomical; *idée* brilliant.

farandole [faʀɑ̃dɔl] *nf (danse)* farandole.

farce [faʀs(ə)] *nf* (**a**) *(tour)* practical joke, hoax. **faire une** ~ **à qn** to play a joke on sb; **magasin de ~s-attrapes** joke shop. (**b**) *(Théât, fig)* farce. **grosse** ~ slapstick comedy. (**c**) *(Culin)* stuffing. ◆**farceur, -euse** *nm, f (blagueur)* joker; *(péj: fumiste)* phoney *.

farcir [faʀsiʀ] (2) **1** *vt (Culin)* to stuff. **farci de fautes** crammed *ou* packed with mistakes. **2 se** ~ *vpr* (‡) *travail, personne* to get landed with *; *bouteille* to knock back *. **il faut se le ~!** *(bavard)* he's a bit of a pain in the neck *.

fard [faʀ] *nm* make-up; (†: *poudre)* rouge; *[acteur]* greasepaint. **sans** ~ *parler* openly.

fardeau, *pl* **~x** [faʀdo] *nm (lit)* load; *(fig)* burden. **sous le** ~ **de** under the weight *ou* burden of.

farder [faʀde] (1) **1** *vt acteur* to make up; *visage* to rouge; *vérité* to disguise. **2 se** ~ *vpr* to make o.s. up; to paint one's face.

farfelu, e * [faʀfəly] **1** *adj* cranky, scatty *. **2** *nm, f* eccentric.

farfouiller * [faʀfuje] (1) *vi* to rummage about (*dans* in).

farine [faʀin] *nf [blé]* flour. ~ **d'avoine** oatmeal; ~ **complète** wholemeal *ou* wholewheat flour; ~ **de froment** wheat flour. ◆**fariner** (1) *vt* to flour. ◆**farineux, -euse 1** *adj aspect, goût* floury, chalky. **2** *nm*: **(aliment)** ~ starchy food.

farouche [faʀuʃ] *adj* (**a**) *(timide)* shy, timid; *(peu sociable)* unsociable. (**b**) *(hostile)* fierce. **ennemi** ~ bitter enemy. (**c**) *(opiniâtre) volonté, résistance* unshakeable; *énergie* irrepressible. (**d**) *(indompté)* savage, wild. ◆**farouchement** *adv* fiercely. **nier** ~ **qch** to deny sth fiercely *ou* heatedly.

fart [faʀ(t)] *nm* (ski) wax. ◆**farter** (1) *vt* to wax.

Far-West [farwɛst] *nm:* **le** ~ the Wild West.

fascicule [fasikyl] *nm [livre]* instalment.

fasciner [fasine] (1) *vt (gén)* to fascinate; *[charme]* to bewitch. ◆ **fascination** *nf* fascination (*sur* on, over).

fascisme [faʃism(ə)] *nm* fascism. ◆ **fasciste** *adj, nmf* fascist.

faste¹ [fast(ə)] *nm* splendour.

faste² [fast(ə)] *adj (littér)* lucky.

fast food [fastfud] *nm* fastfood restaurant.

fastidieux, -euse [fastidjø, øz] *adj* tedious, boring. ◆ **fastidieusement** *adv* tediously, boringly.

fastueux, -euse [fastɥø, øz] *adj décor* sumptuous; *repas, réception* lavish. ◆ **fastueusement** *adv* sumptuously; lavishly.

fatal, e, *mpl* **~s** [fatal] *adj accident* fatal; *coup* fatal, deadly; *ton, instant* fateful. **erreur ~e!** grievous *ou* fatal error!; **être ~ à qn** to be *ou* prove fatal to *ou* for sb; **c'était ~!** it was inevitable, it was bound to happen. ◆ **fatalement** *adv* inevitably. ◆ **fatalisme** *nm* fatalism. ◆ **fataliste 1** *adj* fatalistic. **2** *nmf* fatalist. ◆ **fatalité** *nf (destin)* fate; *(coïncidence)* fateful coincidence; *(inévitabilité)* inevitability.

fatidique [fatidik] *adj* fateful.

fatigant, e [fatigɑ̃, ɑ̃t] *adj (épuisant)* tiring; *(agaçant)* tiresome, tedious. **c'est ~ pour le cœur** it's a strain on the heart; **tu es vraiment ~** you really are tiresome *ou* a nuisance.

fatigue [fatig] *nf (gén)* tiredness; *(Méd, Tech)* fatigue. **tomber de ~** to be dead tired; **il a voulu nous épargner cette ~** he wanted to spare us the strain; **les ~s du voyage** the strain *ou* the tiring effects of the journey.

fatiguer [fatige] (1) **1** *vt* (**a**) *personne* to tire; *moteur* to strain; *poutre* to put a strain on; *terre* to exhaust, impoverish. *[patron]* **~ qn/qch** to overwork sb/sth; **ça vous fatigue** it tires *ou* wears you out; **ça fatigue le cœur** it puts a strain on the heart. (**b**) *(fig: agacer)* to annoy; *(lasser)* to wear out. **2** *vi [moteur]* to labour, strain; *[poutre]* to become strained; *[personne]* to tire. **3 se ~** *vpr* to get tired; *(se surmener)* to overwork o.s. **se ~ à faire qch** to tire o.s. out doing sth; **se ~ les yeux** to strain one's eyes; *(se lasser de)* **se ~ de qch/de faire** to get tired of sth/of doing; **pas la peine de te ~** * there's no need to wear yourself out *ou* no point wearing yourself out. ◆ **fatigué, e** *adj personne, voix, traits* tired, weary; *yeux, cœur* strained; *estomac* upset; *poutre, joint, habit* worn. **~ de** tired of.

fatras [fatra] *nm* jumble.

fatuité [fatɥite] *nf* self-complacency.

faubourg [fobur] *nm* (inner) suburb. ◆ **faubourien, -ienne** *adj accent* Paris working-class.

fauchaison [foʃɛzɔ̃] *nf (époque, action)* mowing, reaping.

faucher [foʃe] (1) *vt* (**a**) *blé* to reap; *champs* to mow; *herbe* to mow, cut; *(avec une faux)* to scythe. (**b**) *(fig) [véhicule, tir]* to mow down. **la mort l'a fauché** death cut him down; **avoir une jambe fauchée par le train** to have a leg cut off by the train. (**c**) (‡: *voler)* to pinch *, swipe *. ◆ **fauche** ‡ *nf (vol)* pinching *, swiping *. **il y a beaucoup de ~** there's a lot of thieving. ◆ **fauché, e** * *adj (sans argent)* stony-broke *. ◆ **faucheur, -euse** *nm, f* mower, reaper.

faucille [fosij] *nf* sickle.

faucon [fokɔ̃] *nm* falcon, hawk.

faufiler (se) [fofile] (1) *vpr:* **se ~ parmi la foule** to worm *ou* inch one's way through the crowd; **se ~ entre les voitures** to thread one's way through the traffic; **se ~ à l'intérieur/au dehors** to slip *ou* sneak in/out.

faune¹ [fon] *nm (Myth)* faun.

faune² [fon] *nf (Zool)* wildlife; *(péj)* set.

faussaire [fosɛr] *nmf* forger.

faussement [fosmɑ̃] *adv accuser* wrongly; *croire* wrongly, falsely. **~ modeste** falsely modest; **d'un ton ~ indifférent** in a tone of feigned indifference.

fausser [fose] (1) *vt calcul, réalité, sens* to distort; *esprit* to disturb; *clef* to bend; *serrure* to break; *charnière* to buckle; *hélice* to warp. **~ compagnie à qn** to give sb the slip.

fausseté [foste] *nf* (**a**) *[accusation, dogme]* falseness, falsity; *[caractère, personne]* duplicity. (**b**) (†: *mensonge)* falsehood.

faute [fot] *nf (erreur)* mistake, error; *(mauvaise action)* misdeed; *(Jur)* offence; *(péché)* sin; *(Ftbl etc)* offence; *(Tennis)* fault; *(responsabilité)* fault. **~ de frappe** typing error; **~ d'impression** misprint; **~ d'inattention** careless mistake; **~ d'orthographe** spelling mistake; **faire une ~** to make a mistake (*de* in); **candidat qui a fait un sans ~** * candidate who hasn't put a foot wrong; **renvoyé pour faute professionnelle** dismissed for professional misconduct; **c'est de la ~ de Richard** it's Richard's fault, it's because of Richard; **à qui la ~?** whose fault is it?, who's to blame?; **être/se sentir en ~** to be/feel at fault *ou* in the wrong; **prendre qn en ~** to catch sb out; **il ne se fait pas ~ de faire** he doesn't fail to do; **~ d'argent** for want of money; **~ de mieux** failing anything better; **~ de quoi** failing which; **relâché ~ de preuves** released for *ou* through lack of evidence.

fauteuil [fotœj] *nm (gén)* armchair, easy chair; *[président]* chair; *[théâtre, académicien]* seat. *(fig)* **il est arrivé dans un ~** * he romped home; **~ à bascule** rocking chair; **~ roulant** wheelchair.

fauteur [fotœr] *nm:* **~ de troubles** troublemaker; **~ de guerre** warmonger.

fautif, -ive [fotif, iv] **1** *adj* (**a**) *élève* naughty, guilty. **être ~** to be at fault *ou* in the wrong. (**b**) *liste, calcul* faulty. **2** *nm, f:* **c'est moi le ~** I'm the one to blame *ou* the culprit. ◆ **fautivement** *adv* by mistake.

fauve [fov] **1** *adj couleur* tawny, fawn. **2** *nm* big cat.

faux¹ [fo] *nf* scythe.

faux², fausse [fo, fos] **1** *adj* (**a**) *argent, documents* forged, fake; *marbre* imitation; *tableau* fake; *(fig) savant* bogus; *dent, nez* false. **~ papiers** forged identity papers. (**b**) *bonhomie, colère* feigned; *attitude, promesse* false; *situation* awkward. **fausse dévotion** false piety. (**c**) *(inexact) (gén)* wrong; *affirmation* untrue; *balance, raisonnement* inaccurate, faulty; *piano, voix* out of tune; *rumeur, soupçons* false. **c'est ~** that's wrong; **faire fausse route** *(lit)* to go the wrong way; *(fig)* to be on the wrong track; **faire un ~ pas** *(lit)* to stumble; *(fig)* to make a foolish mistake; **avoir de fausses craintes** to have groundless fears.

2 *nm* (**a**) *(mensonge, Philos)* **le ~** falsehood. (**b**) *(contrefaçon)* forgery; *(tableau, document)* fake, forgery. **faire un ~** to commit a forgery.

3 *adv chanter* out of tune. **sonner ~** *[rire]* to have a false ring.

4 : **fausse alerte** false alarm; **~ ami** *(traître)* false friend; *(Ling)* faux ami, deceptive cognate; **faire ~ bond à qn** to let sb down; **fausse clef** skeleton key; **~ col** detachable collar; **fausses côtes** floating ribs; **fausse couche** miscarriage; *(lit, fig)* **~ départ** false start; **fausse fenêtre** blind window; **~-filet** sirloin; **~ frais** *(pl)* incidental expenses; **~-fuyant** evasion, equivocation; **user de ~-fuyants** to equivocate; **~ jeton** * devious character; **fausse joie** vain joy; **~ jour** *(lit)* deceptive light; *(fig)* **sous**

un ~ jour in a false light; **fausse manœuvre** wrong move; **~-monnayeur** forger; **~ mouvement** awkward movement; **~ nom** false name; **fausse note** *(Mus)* wrong note; *(fig)* sour note; *(lit, fig)* **fausse piste** wrong track; **~ pli** crease; **fausse porte** false door; **~ problème** non-problem; **~ semblant** sham, pretence; **~ sens** mistranslation; **~ témoignage** false evidence; *(délit)* perjury; **~ témoin** lying witness.

faveur [favœʀ] *nf* (**a**) favour. **faites-moi la ~ de...** would you be so kind as to...; **gagner/perdre la ~ du public** to win/lose public favour; **être en ~** to be in favour (*auprès de qn* with sb); **de ~** *billet* complimentary; *régime* preferential; **en ~ de** *(à cause de)* on account of; *(au profit de)* in favour of; *(but charitable)* in aid of; **être en ~ de qch** to be in favour of sth; **à la ~ de** thanks to; **à la ~ de la nuit** under cover of darkness. (**b**) *(ruban)* favour. ◆ **favorable** *adj* favourable. **sous un jour ~** in a favourable light; **prêter une oreille ~ à** to lend a sympathetic ear to; **d'un œil ~** with a favourable eye; **être ~ à** to be favourable to. ◆ **favorablement** *adv* favourably. ◆ **favori, -ite** *adj, nm, f* favourite. ◆ **favoris** *nmpl* side whiskers. ◆ **favoriser** (1) *vt (gén)* to favour. ◆ **favoritisme** *nm* favouritism.

fébrile [febʀil] *adj (lit, fig)* feverish. ◆ **fébrilement** *adv* feverishly. ◆ **fébrilité** *nf* feverishness.

fécond, e [fekɔ̃, ɔ̃d] *adj femelle (non stérile)* fertile; *(prolifique)* prolific; *sujet, idée, terre* fruitful; *esprit* fertile. **~ en** rich in *ou* abounding in. ◆ **féconder** (1) *vt femme* to make pregnant; *animal, fleur* to fertilize. ◆ **fécondation** *nf* impregnation; fertilization. ◆ **fécondité** *nf* fertility, fruitfulness.

fécule [fekyl] *nf* starch. ◆ **féculent, e** **1** *adj* starchy. **2** *nm* starchy food.

fédéral, e, *mpl* **-aux** [fedeʀal, o] *adj* federal. ◆ **fédéraliser** (1) *vt* to federalize. ◆ **fédéralisme** *nm* federalism. ◆ **fédéraliste** *adj, nmf* federalist.

fédération [fedeʀɑsjɔ̃] *nf* federation.

fée [fe] *nf* fairy.

féerie [fe(e)ʀi] *nf (Ciné, Théât)* extravaganza; *(vision)* enchantment. ◆ **féerique** *adj* magical.

feindre [fɛ̃dʀ(ə)] (52) **1** *vt enthousiasme, ignorance* to feign. **~ d'être/de faire** to pretend to be/do. **2** *vi* to dissemble. ◆ **feint, e**[1] *adj* feigned.

feinter [fɛ̃te] (1) **1** *vt (Ftbl)* to dummy; *(Boxe)* to feint at; (‡: *rouler)* to trick, take in. **2** *vi (Escrime)* to feint. ◆ **feinte**[2] *nf (manœuvre)* dummy move; *(Boxe)* feint; *(ruse)* ruse. **parler sans ~** to speak without dissimulation.

fêler *vt,* **se ~** *vpr* [fele] (1) to crack. **voix fêlée** cracked *ou* hoarse voice.

félicité [felisite] *nf (Rel)* bliss.

féliciter [felisite] (1) **1** *vt* to congratulate (*qn de ou sur qch* sb on sth). **2 se ~** *vpr* to congratulate o.s. (*de* on). **je n'y suis pas allé et je m'en félicite** I didn't go and I'm glad *ou* very pleased I didn't. ◆ **félicitations** *nfpl* congratulations (*pour* on).

félin, e [felɛ̃, in] **1** *adj race* feline; *allure* feline, catlike. **2** *nm* feline.

félon, -onne [felɔ̃, ɔn] **1** *adj* perfidious. **2** *nm* traitor. **3** *nf* traitress. ◆ **félonie** *nf* perfidy.

fêlure [felyʀ] *nf (lit, fig)* crack.

femelle [fəmɛl] **1** *adj (gén)* female; *souris etc* she-; *oiseau* hen-; *baleine, éléphant* cow-. **2** *nf (Zool, péj)* female.

féminin, e [feminɛ̃, in] **1** *adj (gén, Ling)* feminine; *sexe* female; *mode, équipe* women's. **2** *nm (Ling)* feminine. **au ~** in the feminine. ◆ **féminisme** *nm* feminism. ◆ **féministe** *adj, nmf* feminist. ◆ **féminité** *nf* femininity.

femme [fam] **1** *nf (individu)* woman; *(épouse)* wife. **la ~** woman; **~ médecin/professeur** (lady *ou* woman) doctor/teacher. **2** *adj inv*: **être ~** *(nubile)* to have reached womanhood; **être très ~** to be very womanly. **3** : **~ d'affaires** businesswoman; **~ auteur** authoress; **~ de chambre** chambermaid; **~ au foyer** housewife, woman who stays at home; **~ d'intérieur** (conscientious) housewife; **~ de lettres** woman of letters; **~ de ménage** domestic help, cleaning lady; **~ du monde** society woman; **~-objet** woman as a sex object; **~ de service** *(nettoyage)* cleaner; *(cantine)* dinner lady; **~ soldat** woman soldier.

fémur [femyʀ] *nm* thighbone, femur.

fenaison [fənɛzɔ̃] *nf* haymaking.

fendiller *vt,* **se ~** *vpr* [fɑ̃dije] (1) *vernis* to craze; *bois* to spring; *peau* to chap.

fendre [fɑ̃dʀ(ə)] (41) **1** *vt (gén)* to split; *rochers* to cleave; *plâtre* to crack. **~ du bois** to chop wood; **il lui fendit le crâne** he split his skull open; **~ la foule** to cut *ou* push one's way through the crowd; **récit qui fend le cœur** story which breaks one's heart, heartbreaking story. **2 se ~** *vpr* (**a**) *(se fissurer)* to crack. **se ~ la lèvre** to cut one's lip; **se ~ la pipe** ‡ to laugh one's head off. (**b**) *(Escrime)* to lunge. (**c**) (‡) **se ~ de** *somme* to shell out *; *cadeau* to lash out on *. ◆ **fendu, e** *adj manche* slashed; *veste* with a vent; *jupe* slit. **la bouche ~e jusqu'aux oreilles** with a grin stretching from ear to ear.

fenêtre [f(ə)nɛtʀ(ə)] *nf (gén)* window. *(train)* **coin ~** window seat; **~ à guillotine** sash window ; **~ à battants** casement window.

fente [fɑ̃t] *nf* (**a**) *(fissure)* crack; *[rocher]* cleft. (**b**) *[volet]* slit; *[boîte à lettres]* slot; *[veston]* vent.

féodal, e, *mpl* **-aux** [feɔdal, o] **1** *adj* feudal. **2** *nm* feudal lord. ◆ **féodalité** *nf* feudalism.

fer [fɛʀ] **1** *nm* (**a**) *(métal)* iron. **volonté de ~** iron will. (**b**) *(poutre)* (iron) girder; *(épée)* sword; *[cheval]* shoe; *[soulier]* steel tip; *[flèche, lance]* head point; *[rabot]* blade. (**c**) **~s** (*†: chaînes)* chains, irons; *(Méd †)* forceps. **2** : **~-blanc** tinplate; **~ à cheval** horseshoe; **~ forgé** wrought iron; **~ à friser** curling tongs; *(fig)* **~ de lance** spearhead; **~ à repasser** iron; **~ à souder** soldering iron; **~ à vapeur** steam iron.

férié, e [feʀje] *adj*: **jour ~** public holiday; **le lundi est ~** the Monday is a holiday.

ferme[1] [fɛʀm(ə)] **1** *adj (gén)* firm; *viande* tough; *écriture* steady; *trait* confident; *résolution, acheteur* definite. **~ sur ses jambes** steady on one's legs; **d'un pas ~** with a firm step; **rester ~ dans l'adversité** to remain steadfast in adversity; **prix ~s et définitifs** firm prices. **2** *adv travailler* hard; *discuter* vigorously; *(Comm) acheter* definitely.

ferme[2] [fɛʀm(ə)] *nf (domaine)* farm; *(habitation)* farmhouse.

fermé, e [fɛʀme] *adj* (**a**) *porte etc* shut, closed; *(à clef)* locked; *espace* closed-in; *angle* narrow; *ensemble* closed; *robinet* off. (**b**) *milieu, club* exclusive. **cette carrière lui est ~e** this career is closed to him; **économie ~e** closed economy. (**c**) *visage* impassive; *personne* uncommunicative. (**d**) **être ~ à** *sentiment* to be impervious to; *art* to have no feeling for.

fermement [fɛʀməmɑ̃] *adv (lit, fig)* firmly.

ferment [fɛʀmɑ̃] *nm (lit, fig)* ferment. ◆ **fermentation** *nf* fermentation. **en ~** *(lit)* fermenting; *(fig)* in a ferment. ◆ **fermenter** (1) *vi* to ferment.

fermer [fɛʀme] (1) **1** *vt* (**a**) *(lit)* to close, shut; *lettre, poing, (fig) compte, liste* to close; *manteau* to do up, fasten; *gaz* to turn *ou* switch off; *robinet* to turn off. **~ à clef** to lock; **~ au verrou** to bolt; **~ la porte au nez de qn** to shut *ou* slam the door in sb's face; *(fig)* **toutes les portes lui sont fermées** all doors are closed to him; **ferme-la!** ‡ shut *ou* belt up! ‡; **je n'ai pas fermé l'œil de la nuit** I didn't sleep a wink all night; *(fig)* ~ **les yeux** to turn a blind eye, look the other way; ~ **les yeux sur** *misère* to close one's eyes to; *abus* to turn a blind eye to. (**b**) *chemin* to block, bar; *accès* to shut off; *frontière, col* to close; *aéroport* to close *ou* shut down. **champ fermé par une haie** field enclosed by a hedge; ~ **la marche** to bring up the rear. (**c**) *(cesser d'exploiter) magasin, école* to close *ou* shut down. ~ **boutique** to close down; **obliger qn à** ~ **(boutique)** to put sb out of business. **2** *vi (gén)* to close, shut; *[vêtement]* to do up, fasten. **cette porte ferme mal** this door doesn't close *ou* shut properly; **ce robinet ferme mal** this tap doesn't turn off properly; **ça ferme à 7 heures** closing time is 7 o'clock. **3 se** ~ *vpr* to close, shut; *[fleur, blessure]* to close up; *[vêtement]* to do up, fasten. **pays qui se ferme aux produits étrangers** country which closes its markets to foreign produce; **se** ~ **à la pitié** to close one's heart to pity.

fermeté [fɛʀməte] *nf (V* **ferme**[1]*)* firmness; steadiness; confidence; steadfastness.

fermette [fɛʀmɛt] *nf* country cottage.

fermeture [fɛʀmətyʀ] *nf* (**a**) *(action) (gén)* closing; shutting; *(à clef)* locking; *(au verrou)* bolting; *(Comm: définitive)* closing down. ~ **annuelle** annual closure; **à (l'heure de) la** ~ at closing time. (**b**) *(mécanisme) [coffre-fort]* catch; *[vêtement]* fastener. ~ **éclair** ® zip (fastener), zipper.

fermier, -ière [fɛʀmje, jɛʀ] **1** *adj* farm. **beurre** ~ dairy butter. **2** *nm (cultivateur)* farmer. **3** *nf* farmer's wife; *(indépendante)* (woman) farmer.

fermoir [fɛʀmwaʀ] *nm [collier]* clasp.

féroce [feʀɔs] *adj (lit)* ferocious; *envie, joie* savage; *appétit* ravenous. ◆ **férocement** *adv* ferociously; savagely. ◆ **férocité** *nf* ferocity; savagery.

ferraille [fɛʀɑj] *nf (déchets)* scrap iron; *(*: monnaie)* small change. **bruit de** ~ clanking noise; **mettre à la** ~ to scrap. ◆ **ferrailleur** *nm* scrap merchant.

ferrer [fɛʀe] (1) *vt* (**a**) *cheval* to shoe; *soulier* to nail. (**b**) *poisson* to strike. ◆ **ferré, e** *adj* (**a**) *canne* steel-tipped; *soulier* hobnailed; *cheval* shod; *roue* steel-rimmed. (**b**) *(*: calé)* **être** ~ **sur un sujet** to be well up * in a subject.

ferreux [fɛʀø] *adj m* ferrous.

ferronnerie [fɛʀɔnʀi] *nf (atelier)* ironworks; *(métier)* ironwork; *(objets)* ironware. **grille en** ~ wrought iron gate. ◆ **ferronnier** *nm (artisan)* craftsman in wrought iron; *(commerçant)* ironware merchant.

ferroviaire [fɛʀɔvjɛʀ] *adj* railway, railroad *(US)*, rail.

ferry-boat, *pl* **ferry-boats** [fɛʀibot] *nm [voitures]* (car) ferry; *[trains]* (train) ferry.

fertile [fɛʀtil] *adj (gén)* fertile, fruitful. **journée** ~ **en événements** eventful day. ◆ **fertilisation** *nf* fertilization. ◆ **fertiliser** (1) *vt* to fertilize. ◆ **fertilité** *nf (lit, fig)* fertility.

fervent, e [fɛʀvɑ̃, ɑ̃t] **1** *adj* fervent. **2** *nm, f* devotee. ~ **de musique** music lover. ◆ **ferveur** *nf* fervour.

fesse [fɛs] *nf (Anat)* buttock. **les ~s** the buttocks, the bottom, the backside *; **le bébé a les ~s rouges** the baby's got a bit of nappy *ou* diaper *(US)* rash, the baby's got a sore bottom. ◆ **fessée** *nf* spanking. ◆ **fesser** (1) *vt* to spank.

festin [fɛstɛ̃] *nm* feast.

festival, *pl* **~s** [fɛstival] *nm* festival.

festivités [fɛstivite] *nfpl (gén)* festivities.

festoyer [fɛstwaje] (8) *vi* to feast.

fêtard, e * [fɛtaʀ, aʀd(ə)] *nm, f (péj)* roisterer.

fête [fɛt] **1** *nf* (**a**) *(religieuse)* feast; *(civile)* holiday. **Noël est la** ~ **des enfants** Christmas is the children's festival. (**b**) *(prénom)* saint's *ou* name day. **la** ~ **de la Saint-Jean** Saint John's day; **souhaiter sa** ~ **à qn** to wish sb a happy saint's day. (**c**) *(congé)* holiday. **3 jours de** ~ 3 days off, 3 days' holiday; **les ~s (de fin d'année)** the (Christmas and New Year) celebrations *ou* holidays. (**d**) *(foire)* fair; *(kermesse)* fête, fair; *(exposition)* festival, show. ~ **de la bière/de la moisson** beer/harvest festival; **la** ~ **de la ville** the town festival; **la foule en** ~ the festive crowd; **air de** ~ festive air. (**e**) *(réception)* party. **les ~s** the celebrations (*en l'honneur de* in honour of). (**f**) *(locutions)* **être à la** ~ to have a great time; **je n'étais pas à la** ~ it was no picnic for me *; **être de la** ~ to be one of the party; **faire sa** ~ **à qn** ‡ to bash sb up ‡; **faire la** ~ * to live it up *; **faire** ~ **à qn** to give sb a warm reception; *[chien]* to fawn on sb; **elle se faisait une** ~ **d'y aller** she was really looking forward to going.
2 : ~ **de charité** charity fair; ~ **de famille** family celebration; ~ **foraine** fun fair; ~ **légale** public holiday; **la** ~ **des Mères** Mother's Day; ~ **nationale** national holiday; **la** ~ **des Pères** Father's Day; **la** ~ **des Rois** Twelfth Night; **la** ~ **du travail** Labour Day, First of May; ~ **de village** village fête. ◆ **fêter** (1) *vt anniversaire* to celebrate; *personne* to have a celebration for.

fétiche [fetiʃ] *nm (lit)* fetish; *(mascotte)* mascot. ◆ **fétichisme** *nm* fetishism. ◆ **fétichiste** *adj, nmf* fetishist.

fétide [fetid] *adj* fetid.

fétu [fety] *nm*: ~ **(de paille)** wisp of straw.

feu[1], *pl* **~x** [fø] **1** *nm* (**a**) *(source de chaleur)* fire. **faire du** ~ to have *ou* make a fire; *(cigarette)* **avez-vous du ~?** do you have a light?; **prendre** ~ to catch fire; **mettre le** ~ **à qch** to set fire to sth; **en** ~ on fire; **il y a le** ~ there's a fire; *(fig)* **il n'y a pas le ~!** * there's no panic! *; *(fig)* **j'ai la gorge en** ~ my throat is burning. (**b**) *(lumineux)* light. **le** ~ **était (au) rouge** the lights were at red; **être sous le** ~ **des projecteurs** *(lit)* to be in the glare of the spotlights; *(fig)* to be in the limelight; **mettre pleins ~x sur** to put the spotlight on; **les ~x de la rampe** the footlights; **les ~x de l'actualité sont dirigés sur eux** the spotlight is on them, the full glare of the media is on them. (**c**) *(Culin) (brûleur)* burner. **mettre qch/être sur le** ~ to put sth/be on the stove; **plat qui va au** ~ fireproof dish; **faire cuire à** ~ **vif** to cook over a brisk heat; **faire cuire à petit** ~ to cook gently. (**d**) *(Mil) (combat)* action; *(tir)* fire. **faire** ~ to fire; *(lit, fig)* ~ **roulant** running fire; **des ~x croisés** crossfire. (**e**) *(ardeur)* fire. **dans le** ~ **de la discussion** in the heat of the discussion; **tempérament de** ~ fiery temperament. (**f**) *[diamant]* **~x** fire; **jeter mille ~x** to flash *ou* sparkle brilliantly. (**g**) **avoir le** ~ **sacré** to be dedicated; **mettre le** ~ **aux poudres** to touch off a crisis; **mettre une ville à** ~ **et à sang** to put a town to fire and the sword; **mettre à** ~ **une fusée** to fire off a rocket; **au moment de la mise à** ~ at the moment of blast-off; **être tout** ~ **tout flamme** to be wildly enthusiastic.
2 *adj inv*: **rouge** ~ flame red.
3 : ~ **d'artifice** firework display, fireworks; ~ **de Bengale** Bengal light; **~x anti-brouillard** fog lights; **~x clignotants** flashing lights; **~x de détresse** hazard warning lights; ~ **follet** will-o'-the-wisp; ~ **de joie** bonfire; *(fig)* ~ **de paille** flash in the pan; ~ **de position** sidelight; ~ **rouge** set of traffic lights; ~ **de stop** stop *ou* brake light; *(lit, fig)* ~ **vert** green light.

feu[2] [fø] *adj*: ~ **ma tante, ma ~e tante** my late aunt.

feuille [fœj] **1** *nf [plante]* leaf; *[papier, acier]* sheet; *(bulletin)* slip; *(formulaire)* form; *(journal)* paper. *(Ordin)* ~ **de programmation** work *ou* coding sheet; *(Scol)* ~ **d'appel** daily register (sheet), attendance sheet *(US)*. **2** : ~ **de chou** *(péj: journal)* rag; ~ **d'impôt** tax form; ~ **de paye** pay slip; ~ **de présence** attendance sheet; ~ **de route** travel warrant; ~ **de température** temperature chart; ~

volante loose sheet. ◆**feuillage** *nm*: ~**(s)** foliage. ◆**feuillet** *nm* leaf, page.

feuilleter [fœjte] (4) *vt* (**a**) *livre* to leaf through. (**b**) *(Culin)* **pâte feuilletée** puff pastry. ◆**feuilleté** *nm* pastry.

feuilleton [fœjtɔ̃] *nm (à suivre)* serial; *(histoire complète)* series *(sg)*.

feuillu, e [fœjy] **1** *adj* leafy. **2** *nm* broad-leaved tree.

feutre [føtʀ(ə)] *nm (Tex)* felt; *(chapeau)* felt hat; *(stylo)* felt(-tip) pen. ◆**feutré, e** *adj étoffe* felt-like; *atmosphère, bruit* muffled.

fève [fɛv] *nf (Bot)* broad bean; *[gâteau]* charm.

février [fevʀije] *nm* February; *V* **septembre**.

fi [fi] *excl (hum)* pooh! **faire** ~ **de** to snap one's fingers at.

fiable [fjabl(ə)] *adj* reliable, dependable. ◆**fiabilité** *nf* reliability, dependability.

fiacre [fjakʀ(ə)] *nm* hackney cab.

fiancer [fjɑ̃se] (3) **1** *vt* to betroth *(avec, à* to). **2** **se** ~ *vpr* to become engaged *(avec, à* to). ◆**fiançailles** *nfpl* engagement. ◆**fiancé, e** **1** *adj* engaged. **2** *nm* fiancé. *(couple)* **les** ~**s** the engaged couple. **3** *nf* fiancée.

fiasco [fjasko] *nm* fiasco. **faire** ~ to be a fiasco.

fibre [fibʀ(ə)] *nf* (**a**) *(lit: gén)* fibre. ~ **nerveuses** nerve fibres; ~ **de verre** fibre-glass, Fiberglas ® *(US)*; ~ **de carbone** carbon fibre; **la** ~ **optique** fibre optics; **dans le sens des** ~**s** with the grain. (**b**) *(fig: âme)* **elle a la** ~ **maternelle** she has a strong maternal streak in her. ◆**fibreux, -euse** *adj texture* fibrous; *viande* stringy.

ficelle [fisɛl] *nf (matière)* string; *(morceau)* piece of string; *(pain)* stick of French bread. **tirer les** ~**s** to pull the strings; **connaître les** ~**s du métier** to know the tricks of the trade. ◆**ficeler** (4) *vt* (*: *habiller)* to rig out *.

fichage [fiʃaʒ] *nm:* **le** ~ **de la population** filing *ou* recording information on the population.

fiche [fiʃ] *nf* (**a**) *(carte)* index card; *(feuille)* sheet, slip; *(formulaire)* form. ~ **d'état civil** record of civil status, ≃ birth and marriage certificate; ~ **perforée** perforated card; ~ **de paye** pay slip; **mettre en** ~ to index. (**b**) *(cheville)* pin; *(Élec) (broche)* pin; *(prise)* plug.

ficher¹ [fiʃe] (1) *vt* (**a**) *renseignements* to file; *suspects* to put on file. (**b**) ~ **qch en terre** to drive sth into the ground; **se** ~ **une épine dans le doigt** to get a thorn stuck in one's finger.

ficher² * [fiʃe] (1) **1** *vt* (**a**) *(faire)* to do. **qu'est-ce qu'il fiche?** what on earth is he doing?; **je n'en ai rien à fiche** I couldn't care less *(de* about). (**b**) *(donner)* to give. **ce truc me fiche la migraine** this thing gives me a headache; **fiche-moi la paix!** leave me in peace!; **ça va nous** ~ **la poisse** that'll bring us bad luck; **je vous fiche mon billet que...** I bet you my bottom dollar that *... (**c**) *(mettre)* to put. **fiche-le dans le tiroir** stick it in the drawer *; ~ **qn à la porte** to chuck sb out *; ~ **qch en l'air** *(gâcher)* to mess sth up; *(jeter)* to chuck sth up *; ~ **le camp** to clear off *. **2** **se** ~ *vpr* (**a**) *(se mettre)* **tu vas te** ~ **ce truc dans l'œil** you're going to stick that thing in your eye; **se** ~ **qch dans le crâne** to get sth into one's head; **se** ~ **par terre** to fall flat on one's face. (**b**) *(se gausser)* **se** ~ **de qn** to pull sb's leg; **se** ~ **de qch** to make fun of sth; *(être indifférent)* **il s'en fiche** he couldn't care less about it; **ce garagiste se fiche du monde!** that garage man has got a darned nerve! *; **là, ils ne se sont vraiment pas fichus de nous** they really did us proud!; **va te faire fiche!** ‡ get lost! *, take a running jump! ‡

fichier [fiʃje] *nm* file; *[bibliothèque]* catalogue. ~ **(informatisé)** data file; *(Ordin)* ~ **de travail** scratch *ou* work file.

fichu¹ [fiʃy] *nm* (head)scarf.

fichu², e * [fiʃy] *adj* (**a**) *(avant n) temps, métier* wretched, rotten *, lousy *. **il y a une** ~**e différence** there's one heck of a *ou* a heck of a difference *. (**b**) *(après n:* **perdu***) malade, vêtement* done for. **le pique-nique est** ~ the picnic has had it *. (**c**) *(habillé)* rigged out *. (**d**) *(conçu)* **ce livre est bien/mal** ~ this is a clever/hopeless book; **comment c'est** ~ **ce truc?** how does this thing work? (**e**) *[malade]* **être mal** ~ to feel rotten * *ou* out of sorts *. (**f**) *(capable)* **il est** ~ **d'y aller** he's quite likely *ou* liable to go; **il n'est (même) pas** ~ **de réparer ça** he can't even mend the darned thing *.

fictif, -ive [fiktif, iv] *adj (imaginaire)* imaginary; *(faux)* fictitious. ◆**fiction** *nf (imagination)* fiction; *(fait)* invention. ◆**fictivement** *adv* in fiction.

fidèle [fidɛl] **1** *adj (gén)* faithful (à to); *lecteur, client* regular; *récit, appareil* accurate. **rester** ~ **à une promesse** to remain faithful *ou* true to a promise; **être** ~ **à un produit/une marque** to remain loyal to a product/a brand; ~ **serviteur** trusty *ou* loyal servant; ~ **à lui-même** *ou* **à son habitude** true to form, true to character. **2** *nmf (Rel)* believer; *(client)* regular customer; *(lecteur)* regular reader; *[doctrine]* follower. **les** ~**s** *(croyants)* the faithful; *(assemblée)* the congregation. ◆**fidèlement** *adv* faithfully, loyally; regularly; accurately. ◆**fidélité** *nf* faithfulness; loyalty; accuracy; *(à un produit, sa femme)* fidelity. ◆**fidéliser** (1) *vt:* ~ **sa clientèle** to establish *ou* develop customer loyalty.

Fidji [fidʒi] *nmpl:* **les (îles)** ~ the Fiji Islands.

fief [fjɛf] *nm (Hist)* fief; *[firme]* preserve; *[parti]* stronghold; *(hum: domaine)* kingdom.

fiel [fjɛl] *nm (lit, fig)* gall, venom.

fier¹, fière [fjɛʀ] *adj* (**a**) proud. ~ **comme Artaban** as proud as a peacock; **faire le** ~ *(méprisant)* to be aloof; *(brave)* to be full of o.s.; **c'est qn de pas** ~ * he's not stuck-up *; **avoir fière allure** to cut a fine figure; **il n'y a pas de quoi être** ~ there's nothing to be proud of *ou* to boast about. (**b**) *(avant n) imbécile* first-class, prize; *canaille* downright; *toupet* incredible. **je te dois une fière chandelle** I'm terribly indebted to you. ◆**fièrement** *adv* proudly. ◆**fierté** *nf (gén)* pride. **tirer** ~ **de** to get a sense of pride from.

fier² (se) [fje] (7) *vpr*: **se** ~ **à** *(gén)* to trust; *appareil, mémoire* to rely on; **ne vous fiez pas aux apparences** don't go by *ou* trust appearances.

fiesta * [fjɛsta] *nf* rave-up *. **faire la** ~ to have a rave-up *.

fièvre [fjɛvʀ(ə)] *nf* (**a**) *(température)* fever, temperature. **avoir beaucoup de** ~ to have *ou* run a high temperature; **avoir 39 de** ~ to have a temperature of 104(°F) *ou* 39(°C); **une** ~ **de cheval** a raging fever. (**b**) *(maladie)* fever. ~ **jaune** yellow fever; ~ **aphteuse** foot-and-mouth disease. (**c**) *(fig: agitation)* fever, excitement. **avec** ~ excitedly; **la** ~ **des élections** election fever; **pris d'une** ~ **d'écrire** seized with a feverish urge to write. ◆**fiévreusement** *adv* feverishly, excitedly. ◆**fiévreux, -euse** *adj* feverish.

fifre [fifʀ(ə)] *nm* fife; *(joueur)* fife player.

figer *vti*, **se** ~ *vpr* [fiʒe] (3) *huile* to congeal; *sang* to clot, coagulate; *attitude* to freeze. **histoire à vous** ~ **le sang** bloodcurdling story; *(fig)* **son sang se figea dans ses veines** his blood froze in his veins. ◆**figé, e** *adj style, manières* stiff; *mœurs* rigid; *sourire* fixed. **expression** ~**e** set expression; ~ **par la peur** terror-stricken; ~ **par la mort** rigid in death.

fignoler * [fiɲɔle] (1) *vt* to put the finishing touches to. **du travail fignolé** a really neat job *. ◆**fignoleur, -euse** *nm, f* meticulous worker.

figue [fig] *nf (Bot)* fig. ~ **de Barbarie** prickly pear. ◆**figuier** *nm* fig tree. ~ **de Barbarie** prickly pear.

figurant, e [figyRɑ̃, ɑ̃t] *nm, f (Ciné)* extra; *(Théât)* walker-on; *(fig) (pantin)* puppet; *(complice)* stooge.

figuratif, -ive [figyRatif, iv] *adj (Art)* representational.

figuration [figyRɑsjɔ̃] *nf*: **faire de la** ~ *(Théât)* to do walk-on parts; *(Ciné)* to work as an extra.

figure [figyR] *nf (visage)* face; *(personnage)* figure; *(Cartes)* face card; *(image)* illustration; *(Danse, Math)* figure. **faire** ~ **de favori** to be looked on as the favourite; **faire bonne** ~ to put up a good show; **faire triste** ~ to look a sorry sight; ~ **de style** stylistic device.

figurer [figyRe] (1) **1** *vt* to represent. **2** *vi* to appear. **mon frère figure parmi les gagnants** my brother is listed among the winners *ou* is in the list of the winners. **3 se** ~ *vpr* to imagine. **figurez-vous que** would you believe that. ◆ **figuré, e** *adj* figurative. **mot employé au** ~ word used figuratively *ou* in the figurative sense.

figurine [figyRin] *nf* figurine.

fil [fil] **1** *nm* (**a**) *(brin) [coton, araignée]* thread; *[laine]* yarn; *[cuivre]* wire; *[haricots, marionnette]* string; *[rasoir électrique]* cord. *(téléphone)* **j'ai ta mère au bout du** ~ I have your mother on the line *ou* phone; **téléphone sans fil** cordless phone; **haricots pleins de ~s/sans ~s** stringy/stringless beans. (**b**) *(Tex: matière)* linen. (**c**) *[bois, viande]* grain. **dans le sens du** ~ with the grain. (**d**) *(tranchant)* edge. **passer au** ~ **de l'épée** to put to the sword. (**e**) *[discours, pensée]* thread. **au** ~ **des jours** with the passing days, as the days go (*ou* went) by; **le** ~ **de l'eau** the current. (**f**) *(locutions)* **donner du** ~ **à retordre à qn** to make life difficult for sb; **ne tenir qu'à un** ~ to hang by a thread; **de** ~ **en aiguille** one thing leading to another. **2** : ~ **conducteur** *[enquête]* vital lead; *[récit]* main theme; ~ **de fer** wire; ~ **(à linge)** washing *ou* clothes line; ~ **(à pêche)** fishing line; ~ **à plomb** plumbline.

filament [filamɑ̃] *nm (Bio, Élec)* filament; *[bave]* thread.

filandreux, -euse [filɑ̃dRø, øz] *adj viande* stringy; *discours* long-winded.

filasse [filas] **1** *nf* tow. **2** *adj inv* tow-coloured.

filature [filatyR] *nf* (**a**) *(Tex) (action)* spinning; *(usine)* mill. (**b**) *(surveillance)* shadowing.

file [fil] *nf* line; *(Aut: couloir)* lane. ~ **(d'attente)** queue, line *(US)*; **se garer en double** ~ to double-park; **se mettre en** ~ to line up; **prendre la** ~ to join the queue *ou* the line *(US)*; **marcher en** ~ to walk in line; **entrer à la** ~ to file in; **en** ~ **indienne** in single file; **à la** ~ *(à la suite)* in succession, one after the other.

filer [file] (1) **1** *vt* (**a**) *(gén)* to spin; *comparaison, note* to draw out. ~ **un mauvais coton** * to be in a bad way. (**b**) *(Police etc: suivre)* to shadow. (**c**) *(*: donner) argent, objet* to slip; *coup* to land, deal. (**d**) *bas* to ladder. (**e**) **navire qui file 20 nœuds** ship which does 20 knots. **2** *vi* (**a**) *[liquide]* to run, trickle; *[lampe]* to smoke. ~ **qch entre ses doigts** to run *ou* trickle sth through one's fingers. (**b**) (*) *(courir)* to fly by; *(s'en aller)* to slip off *ou* away. **il fila comme une flèche** he darted away; ~ **voir qn** to dash to see sb; **il faut que je file** I must dash *ou* fly *; **allez, file!** off with you! ; ~ **à l'anglaise** to take French leave; ~ **entre les doigts de qn** to slip between sb's fingers; ~ **doux** to behave o.s. (**c**) *[maille]* to run; *[collant]* to ladder.

filet [filɛ] *nm* (**a**) *[eau]* trickle; *[fumée]* wisp; *[lumière]* streak; *[vinaigre]* drop, dash; *(trait)* thread. (**b**) *[poisson, viande]* fillet. (**c**) *(Pêche, Sport)* net; *(piège)* snare. ~ **(à provisions)** string bag; ~ **(à bagages)** luggage rack; ~ **à cheveux/de pêche** hair/fishing net; **travailler sans** ~ to work without a safety net.

filial, e, *mpl* **-aux** [filjal, o] **1** *adj* filial. **2** *nf (Comm)* subsidiary company.

filière [filjɛR] *nf [carrière]* path; *[administration]* channels; *[drogue]* network. *(métier)* **la** ~ **électronique** careers in electronics; *(Univ)* **les nouvelles ~s** new subjects.

filiforme [filifɔRm(ə)] *adj antenne* threadlike; (*) *corps* spindly.

filigrane [filigRan] *nm [billet]* watermark; *[objet]* filigree. **mais on devinait, en** ~**, sa colère** but his anger was showing through.

filin [filɛ̃] *nm* rope.

fille [fij] *nf (opp de* **fils***)* daughter; *(opp de* **garçon***)* girl; *(† péj: prostituée)* whore. **brave** ~ nice girl, good sort; **rester** ~ † to remain unmarried; **vieille** ~ old maid; ~ **de ferme** farm girl; ~ **d'auberge** serving maid; ~ **d'honneur** maid of honour; *(péj)* **~-mère** unmarried mother. ◆ **fillette** *nf* (little) girl. **rayon ~s** girls' department.

filleul, -eule [fijœl] *nm, f* godchild, godson (*ou* goddaughter).

film [film] *nm* (**a**) *(pellicule)* film; *(œuvre)* film, picture, movie *(US)*. ~ **d'animation** cartoon film; ~ **muet/parlant** silent/talking film; ~ **à succès** blockbuster * , box-office success; *(fig)* **le** ~ **des événements** the pattern of events. (**b**) *(couche)* film. ◆ **filmer** (1) *vt personne* to film; *scène* to film, shoot.

Filofax [filofaks] *nm* ® Filofax ®.

filon [filɔ̃] *nm (Minér)* vein; *(sujet)* theme, line; *(*: combine)* cushy number *. *(fig)* **trouver le** ~ to strike it lucky *ou* rich.

filou * [filu] *nm* rogue. ◆ **filouter** * (1) *vti* to cheat (*de* out of).

fils [fis] *nm* son. **M. Martin** ~ young Mr Martin; *(Comm)* Mr Martin junior; **le** ~ **Martin** the Martin boy; ~ **de famille** young man of means; *(péj)* ~ **à papa** daddy's boy.

filtre [filtR(ə)] *nm (gén)* filter; *[cigarette]* filter tip. **(café-)**~ (filter) coffee. ◆ **filtrer** (1) **1** *vt (lit)* to filter; *nouvelles, spectateurs* to screen. **2** *vi* to filter (*à travers* through). ◆ **filtrage** *nm* filtering; screening. ◆ **filtrant, e** *adj substance* filtering; *pouvoir* of filtration; *verre* filter.

fin[1], fine[1] [fɛ̃, fin] **1** *adj* (**a**) *(en épaisseur)* thin; *(en grosseur)* fine; *lame* sharp; *taille, jambe* slender, slim. (**b**) *(de qualité)* fine. **perles fines** real pearls; **fines herbes** (sweet) herbs; **petits pois ~s** (graded) garden peas; **la fine fleur de** the flower of; **le** ~ **du** ~ the last word (*de* in). (**c**) *vue, ouïe* sharp; *goût, odorat* fine. (**d**) *personne, esprit* shrewd; *remarque* subtle. **fine mouche** sharp customer; ~ **limier** (keen) sleuth; **il n'est pas très** ~ he's not very bright; *(iro)* **c'est** ~ **ce que tu as fait!** that was clever of you! *(iro)*; **tu as l'air** ~**!** you look a fool!; **jouer au plus** ~ **avec qn** to try to outsmart sb. (**e**) *(avant n: connaisseur)* expert. ~ **connaisseur** connoisseur; ~ **tireur** crack shot. (**f**) *(avant n: intensif)* **au** ~ **fond de la campagne** right in the heart of the country, in the depths of the country; **au** ~ **fond du tiroir** right at the back of the drawer; **savoir le** ~ **mot de l'histoire** to know the real story behind it all. **2** *adv moudre* finely. **écrire** ~ to write small; ~ **prêt** quite *ou* all ready.

fin[2] [fɛ̃] *nf* (**a**) *(gén)* end. ~ **juin** at the end of June; **jusqu'à la** ~ **des temps** until the end of time; **à la** ~ eventually, in the end, finally; **ça suffit à la** ~**!** * that's enough now!; **en** ~ **de compte** in the end; **sans** ~ *(adj)* endless; *(adv)* endlessly; **prendre** ~ to come to an end; **tirer à sa** ~ to be coming to an end, be drawing to a close; **mettre** ~ **à** to put an end to, end; **mener qch à bonne** ~ to bring sth to a successful conclusion; **faire une** ~ to settle down; **c'est la** ~ **des haricots** * it's all up! *; **avoir une** ~ **tragique** to die a tragic death; *(Comm)* ~

de série oddment. (**b**) *(but)* end, aim, purpose; *(Philos)* end. **la ~ justifie les moyens** the end justifies the means; **à seule ~ de faire** for the sole purpose of doing; **à toutes ~s utiles** for your information.

final, e, *mpl* **~s** [final] **1** *adj* final. **2** *nm (Mus)* finale. **3** *nf (Sport)* final. **quart de ~e** quarter final. ◆ **finalement** *adv* in the end, finally. ◆ **finaliste** *adj, nmf* finalist. ◆ **finalité** *nf (but)* end, aim; *(fonction)* purpose, function.

finance [finɑ̃s] *nf*: **~s** finances; *(administration)* **les F~s** ≃ the Treasury; **la haute ~** *(activité)* high finance; *(personne)* top financiers. ◆ **financement** *nm* financing. **plan de ~** financial plan. ◆ **financer** (3) *vt* to finance. ◆ **financier, -ière** **1** *adj* financial. **2** *nm* financier. ◆ **financièrement** *adv* financially.

fine² [fin] *nf* (**a**) *(alcool)* liqueur brandy. (**b**) *(huître)* **~ de claire** oyster.

finement [finmɑ̃] *adv ciselé* finely, delicately; *faire remarquer* subtly; *agir* cleverly, shrewdly.

finesse [finɛs] *nf* (**a**) *(V* **fin¹***)* thinness; fineness; sharpness; slimness; shrewdness; subtlety. (**b**) **~s** *[langue]* niceties; *[affaire]* ins and outs; **il connaît toutes les ~s** he knows all the tricks.

fini, e [fini] **1** *adj* (**a**) *(gén, Ind)* finished. **tout est ~** it's all over. (**b**) *(péj) menteur, escroc* utter, out-and-out. (**c**) *(Math, Philos)* finite. **2** *nm [ouvrage]* finish.

finir [finiʀ] (2) **1** *vt* (**a**) *travail, parcours* to finish, complete; *discours, affaire* to end. **il a fini ses jours à Paris** he ended his days in Paris; **~ son verre** to finish one's glass, drink up; **finis ton pain!** eat up *ou* finish your bread! (**b**) *(arrêter)* to stop (*de faire* doing). (**c**) *(parachever)* to put the finishing touches to. **2** *vi* (**a**) *(gén)* to finish, end; *[réunion]* to draw to a close. **les vacances finissent demain** the holidays end *ou* are over tomorrow; **il a fini directeur** he ended up as (a) director; **il finira en prison** he will end up in prison; **il a fini dans un accident de voiture** he died in a car accident; **ça finit en pointe** it ends in a point; **il a fini par se décider** he finally *ou* eventually made up his mind, he made up his mind in the end; **tu finis par m'ennuyer** you're beginning to annoy me. (**b**) **en ~ avec une situation** to put an end to a situation; **nous en aurons bientôt fini** we'll soon be finished with it; **quand en auras-tu fini avec tes jérémiades?** when will you ever stop moaning?; **pour vous en ~** to cut the story short; **qui n'en finit pas** never-ending, endless; **elle n'en finit pas de se préparer** she takes an age to get ready; **on n'en aurait jamais fini de raconter ses bêtises** you could go on for ever recounting the stupid things he has done.

finish [finiʃ] *nm (Sport)* finish.

finition [finisjɔ̃] *nf (action)* finishing; *(résultat)* finish.

Finlande [fɛ̃lɑ̃d] *nf* Finland. ◆ **finlandais, e** *ou* ◆ **finnois, e** **1** *adj, nm* Finnish. **2** *nm(f)*: **F~(e)** Finn.

fiole [fjɔl] *nf* phial; *(*: tête)* face.

fioriture [fjɔʀityʀ] *nf* flourish.

firmament [fiʀmamɑ̃] *nm* firmament. *(fig)* **au ~ de** at the height of.

firme [fiʀm(ə)] *nf* firm.

fisc [fisk] *nm* tax department, ≃ Inland Revenue *(Brit)*, ≃ Internal Revenue *(US)*. ◆ **fiscal, e,** *mpl* **-aux** *adj* fiscal, tax. **année ~e** tax year. ◆ **fiscalité** *nf (système)* tax system; *(impôts)* taxation.

fission [fisjɔ̃] *nf* fission. **~ de l'atome** atomic fission.

fissurer *vt*, **se ~** *vpr* [fisyʀe] (1) to crack, fissure. ◆ **fissure** *nf* crack, fissure.

fiston * [fistɔ̃] *nm* son, lad.

fixateur [fiksatœʀ] *nm (Art)* fixative spray; *(Phot)* fixer.

fixation [fiksasjɔ̃] *nf* (**a**) *(Chim, Psych, Zool)* fixation; *(Phot)* fixing. (**b**) *(attache)* fastening. *(Ski)* **~ (de sécurité)** (safety) binding.

fixe [fiks(ə)] **1** *adj (gén)* fixed; *personnel* permanent; *emploi* permanent, steady. **à heure ~** at a set time. **2** *nm (paye)* fixed salary.

fixer [fikse] (1) **1** *vt* (**a**) *(attacher)* to fix, fasten (*à, sur* to); *regard* to fix, fasten (*sur* on). **il le fixa longuement** he stared at him; **~ qch dans sa mémoire** to fix sth firmly in one's memory. (**b**) *prix, date* to fix, set; *règle* to lay down. *(fig)* **~ son choix sur qch** to decide *ou* settle on sth; *(fig)* **je ne suis pas encore fixé** I haven't made up my mind yet; **à l'heure fixée** at the agreed time; **~ ses idées sur le papier** to set one's ideas down on paper; **mot fixé par l'usage** word fixed by usage. (**c**) *(renseigner)* **~ qn sur qch** * to put sb in the picture about sth *; **être fixé sur le compte de qn** to have sb sized up *; **alors, es-tu fixé maintenant?** * have you got the picture now? * (**d**) *(Phot)* to fix. **2 se ~** *vpr (s'installer)* to settle; *[usage]* to become fixed.

fixité [fiksite] *nf [opinions]* fixedness; *[regard]* fixedness, steadiness.

fjord [fjɔʀ(d)] *nm* fiord, fjord.

flac [flak] *excl* splash!

flacon [flakɔ̃] *nm* bottle; *(Chim)* flask.

flagada * [flagada] *adj inv*: **être ~** to be dog-tired * *ou* washed-out.

flageller [flaʒele] (1) *vt* to flog, scourge.

flageoler [flaʒɔle] (1) *vi*: **~ sur ses jambes** *(de faiblesse)* to be sagging at the knees; *(de peur)* to quake at the knees.

flagrant, e [flagʀɑ̃, ɑ̃t] *adj erreur, injustice* blatant, glaring. **prendre qn en ~ délit** to catch sb red-handed.

flair [flɛʀ] *nm [chien]* nose; *(fig)* sixth sense, intuition. **avoir du ~** to have a good nose; to have intuition. ◆ **flairer** (1) *vt* to sniff (at); *(Chasse)* to scent; *(fig)* to scent, sense. **~ quelque chose de louche** to smell a rat; **~ le vent** to see which way the wind's blowing, read the wind *(US)*.

flamand, e [flamɑ̃, ɑ̃d] **1** *adj, nm* Flemish. **2** *nm(f)*: **F~(e)** Flemish man (*ou* woman).

flamant [flamɑ̃] *nm*: **~ (rose)** (pink) flamingo.

flambant [flɑ̃bɑ̃] *adv*: **~ neuf** brand new.

flambeau, *pl* **~x** [flɑ̃bo] *nm (lit, fig)* torch; *(chandelier)* candlestick.

flamber [flɑ̃be] (1) **1** *vi [bois]* to burn; *[feu]* to blaze. **2** *vt crêpe* to flambé; *volaille, cheveux* to singe; *(Méd) aiguille* to sterilize. ◆ **flambé, e¹** ** *adj* finished. ◆ **flambée²** *nf* (**a**) *(feu)* quick blaze. (**b**) *[violence]* outburst. **la ~ des prix** the explosion in prices.

flambeur * [flɑ̃bœʀ] *nm* big-time gambler.

flamboyer [flɑ̃bwaje] (8) *vi [flamme]* to blaze; *[yeux]* to flash; *[ciel]* to blaze; *[épée]* to gleam, flash. ◆ **flamboiement** *nm* blaze; flash; gleam. ◆ **flamboyant, e** *adj (Archit)* flamboyant.

flamme [flam] *nf* (**a**) *(lit)* flame. **en ~s** on fire; *(Aviat, fig)* **descendre en ~s** to shoot down in flames. (**b**) *(fig: ardeur, éclat)* fire; *(littér: amour)* ardour, love. **plein de ~** passionate, fiery. (**c**) *(drapeau)* pennant, pennon.

flan [flɑ̃] *nm (Culin)* custard tart.

flanc [flɑ̃] *nm* side; *[animal, armée]* flank; *[montagne]* slope. **tirer au ~** * to swing the lead *; **être sur le ~** *(malade)* to be laid up; *(fatigué)* to be all in *; *[maladie]* **mettre qn sur le ~** * to knock sb out; **à ~ de coteau** on the hillside; **prendre de ~** *(Naut, fig)* to catch broadside on; *(Mil)* to attack on the flank.

flancher * [flɑ̃ʃe] (1) *vi [cœur]* to give out, pack up *; *[troupes]* to quit; *[accusé]* to lose one's nerve.

sa mémoire a flanché his memory failed him; ~ **en math** to come down in maths.

Flandre [flɑ̃dʀ(ə)] *nf*: **la ~ , les ~s** Flanders.

flanelle [flanɛl] *nf (Tex)* flannel.

flâner [flɑne] (1) *vi* to stroll, saunter; *(péj)* to hang about. ◆ **flânerie** *nf* stroll, saunter. *(péj)* **perdre son temps en ~(s)** to waste one's time lounging about. ◆ **flâneur, -euse 1** *adj* idle. **2** *nm, f* stroller; *(péj)* idler, lounger.

flanquer [flɑ̃ke] (1) *vt* (**a**) to flank. **flanqué de** flanked by. (**b**) *(*: jeter)* ~ **qch par terre** *(lit)* to fling sth to the ground; *(fig)* to put paid to sth; ~ **qn à la porte** to chuck sb out ‡; *(licencier)* to sack *ou* fire sb; ~ **tout en l'air** to chuck it all up ‡; **se ~ par terre** to fall flat on one's face. (**c**) *(*: donner)* to give. ~ **2 ans de prison à qn** to put sb behind bars for 2 years.

flaque [flak] *nf*: ~ **de sang** *etc* pool of blood *etc*; ~ **d'eau** puddle.

flash [flaʃ] *nm* (**a**) *(Phot)* flash. **au ~** by flash. (**b**) *(Rad, TV)* newsflash. *(Rad)* ~ **publicitaire** commercial.

flash-back [flaʃbak] *nm* flashback.

flasque [flask(ə)] *adj peau* flabby; *(fig)* limp.

flatter [flate] (1) **1** *vt* (**a**) *personne, goût* to flatter; *vice* to pander to, encourage; *regard* to delight, charm. ~ **servilement qn** to fawn upon sb. (**b**) *(caresser)* to stroke, pat. **2 se ~** *vpr (se leurrer)* to delude o.s. **il se flatte de le faire** he flatters himself he can do it; **se ~ de qch** to pride o.s. on sth; **et je m'en flatte!** and I'm proud of it! ◆ **flatterie** *nf* flattery. ◆ **flatteur, -euse 1** *adj* flattering. **2** *nm, f* flatterer.

fléau, *pl* **~x** [fleo] *nm* (**a**) *(calamité)* scourge, curse. (**b**) *[balance]* beam; *(Agr)* flail.

flèche [flɛʃ] *nf* (**a**) *(arme)* arrow; *(de direction)* arrow, pointer; *(critique)* shaft. ~ **en caoutchouc** rubber-tipped dart; **monter en ~** *(lit)* to rise like an arrow; *(fig)* to soar, rocket; **partir comme une ~** to set off like a shot; **la ~ du Parthe** the Parthian shot; **il fait ~ de tout bois** he'll use any means he can. (**b**) *[église]* spire; *[grue]* jib; *[attelage, mât]* pole. ◆ **flécher** (1) *vt* to arrow, mark with arrows. ◆ **fléchette** *nf* dart.

fléchir [fleʃiʀ] (2) **1** *vt* (**a**) *(plier)* to bend; *articulation* to flex. ~ **le genou devant qn** to bend the knee to sb. (**b**) *(apaiser) personne* to sway; *colère* to soothe. **2** *vi* (**a**) *(gén)* to bend; *[planches, genoux]* to sag; *[armée]* to yield; *[volonté]* to weaken; *[attention]* to flag; *[nombre]* to fall off; *[prix]* to drop. **la courbe de l'inflation fléchit** there is a downturn in inflation. (**b**) *(s'apaiser)* to yield. **se laisser ~** to allow o.s. to be swayed. ◆ **fléchissement** *nm (gén)* bending; *[prix]* drop.

flegme [flɛgm(ə)] *nm* composure, phlegm. ◆ **flegmatique** *adj* phlegmatic. ◆ **flegmatiquement** *adv* phlegmatically.

flemme * [flɛm] *nf* laziness. **j'ai la ~ de le faire** I can't be bothered doing it. ◆ **flemmard, e * 1** *adj* bone-idle *. **2** *nm, f* lazybones *, slacker.

flétrir [fletʀiʀ] (2) **1** *vt (faner)* to wither, fade; *(stigmatiser)* to condemn. **2 se ~** *vpr* to wither.

fleur [flœʀ] *nf* (**a**) *(lit, fig)* flower; *[arbre]* blossom. **en ~(s)** in blossom; in flower; ~ **d'oranger** orange blossom; **assiette à ~s** flower-patterned *ou* flowery plate; **chapeau à ~s** flowery hat; *(fig)* **couvrir qn de ~s** to shower praise on sb. (**b**) **dans la ~ de l'âge** in the prime of life; **à ~ de terre/d'eau** just above the ground/the water; **j'ai les nerfs à ~ de peau** my nerves are all on edge; **faire une ~ à qn *** to do sb a good turn; **ils s'envoient des ~s** they pat each other on the back.

fleurer [flœʀe] (1) *vt*: **ça fleure bon la lavande** *etc* there's a lovely smell of lavender *etc*.

fleuret [flœʀɛ] *nm (épée)* foil.

fleurir [flœʀiʀ] (2) **1** *vi* (**a**) *[arbre]* to blossom, flower; *[fleur]* to flower, bloom; *[sentiment]* to blossom. (**b**) (*imparfait* **florissait,** *ptp* **florissant)** *[commerce, arts]* to flourish. **2** *vt salon* to decorate with flowers. ~ **une tombe** to put flowers on a grave. ◆ **fleuri, e** *adj fleur* in bloom; *branche* in blossom; *jardin* in flower *ou* bloom; *tissu* flowery; *style* flowery, florid. ◆ **fleuriste** *nmf (personne)* florist; *(boutique)* florist's (shop).

fleuron [flœʀɔ̃] *nm [couronne]* floweret; *[bâtiment]* finial; *(fig)* jewel.

fleuve [flœv] **1** *nm* river. **2** *adj inv discours* interminable.

flexible [flɛksibl(ə)] **1** *adj (lit)* flexible, pliable; *caractère (compréhensif)* flexible, adaptable; *(faible)* pliable. **2** *nm (tuyau)* flexible tubing. ◆ **flexibilité** *nf* flexibility. **la ~ de l'emploi** flexibility in employment.

flexion [flɛksjɔ̃] *nf (courbure)* flexion, bending; *(Ling)* inflection.

flibustier [flibystje] *nm* freebooter.

flic * [flik] *nm* cop *.

flic flac [flikflak] *excl* splash! **faire ~** to go splash splash.

flingue ‡ [flɛ̃g] *nm* gun, rifle. ◆ **flinguer** ‡ (1) *vt* to gun down.

flipper [flipœʀ] *nm (électrique)* pin-ball machine.

flirt [flœʀt] *nm (amourette)* brief romance; *(amoureux)* boyfriend (*ou* girlfriend). *(action)* **le ~** flirting. ◆ **flirter** (1) *vi* to flirt. *(fig)* ~ **avec** *idée* to flirt with; *personne* to go about with.

floc [flɔk] *nm, excl* plop.

flocon [flɔkɔ̃] *nm [écume]* fleck; *[laine]* flock. ~ **de neige** snowflake; **purée en ~ s** dehydrated potato flakes.

floraison [flɔʀɛzɔ̃] *nf [fleurs, talents]* flowering, blossoming; *[affiches]* rash; *(époque)* flowering time.

floral, e, *mpl* **-aux** [flɔʀal, o] *adj* floral; *exposition* flower. **parc ~** floral garden.

floralies [flɔʀali] *nfpl* flower show.

flore [flɔʀ] *nf* flora.

Florence [flɔʀɑ̃s] *n (ville)* Florence. ◆ **florentin, e** *adj,* **F~(e)** *nm(f)* Florentine.

florilège [flɔʀilɛʒ] *nm* anthology.

florin [flɔʀɛ̃] *nm* florin.

florissant, e [flɔʀisɑ̃, ɑ̃t] *adj pays* flourishing; *santé, teint* blooming.

flot [flo] *nm [véhicules, insultes]* flood, stream. *(marée)* **le ~** the floodtide; **les ~s** the waves; **à (grands) ~s** in streams; **la lumière entre à ~s** light is streaming in *ou* flooding in; **être à ~** *[bateau]* to be afloat; *[personne, entreprise]* to be on an even keel; **remettre à ~** *bateau* to refloat; *entreprise* to bring back onto an even keel; *(lit, fig)* **mettre à ~** to launch.

flottaison [flɔtɛzɔ̃] *nf*: **ligne de ~** waterline.

flottant [flɔtɑ̃] *nm (short)* shorts.

flotte [flɔt] *nf* (**a**) *(Aviat, Naut)* fleet. ~ **aérienne/de guerre/de commerce** air/naval/merchant navy fleet. (**b**) (*) *(pluie)* rain; *(eau)* water. (**c**) *(flotteur)* float.

flottement [flɔtmɑ̃] *nm [foule]* wavering, hesitation; *[électeurs]* indecision; *[soldats]* sway; *[copie]* vagueness; *[travail]* unevenness (*dans* in).

flotter [flɔte] (1) **1** *vi [bateau, monnaie]* to float; *[brume, parfum]* to hang; *[pensée]* to wander; *(en hésitant)* to waver; *[cheveux]* to stream out; *[drapeau]* to flap, flutter (*au vent* in the wind). **il flotte dans ses vêtements** his clothes are too big for him; **faire ~** to float. **2** *vb impers (*: pleuvoir)* to rain. **3** *vt bois* to float.

flotteur [flɔtœʀ] *nm (gén)* float; *[chasse d'eau]* ballcock, floater *(US)*.

flottille [flɔtij] *nf [bateaux]* flotilla; *[avions]* squadron.

flou, e [flu] **1** *adj contour, photo* blurred; *image* hazy; *robe* loose(-fitting); *coiffure* soft; *théorie* woolly, vague. **2** *nm* blurredness; looseness; vagueness, woolliness.

flouse ‡, flouze ‡ [fluz] *nm (argent)* bread ‡, dough ‡, lolly ‡.

fluctuer [flyktɥe] (1) *vi* to fluctuate. ◆**fluctuation** *nf* fluctuation (*de* in).

fluet, -ette [flyɛ, ɛt] *adj corps* slight, slender; *taille* slender, slim; *voix* thin.

fluide [flyid] **1** *adj (lit, fig)* fluid; *main-d'œuvre* flexible. **la circulation est ~** traffic flows freely. **2** *nm* fluid; *(fig: pouvoir)* mysterious power. ◆**fluidité** *nf* fluidity; flexibility; free flow.

fluor [flyɔʀ] *nm* fluorine.

fluorescent, e [flyɔʀesɑ̃, ɑ̃t] *adj* fluorescent.

flûte [flyt] **1** *nf* flute; *(verre)* flute glass; *(pain)* long French loaf. **petite ~** piccolo; **~ à bec** recorder; **~ de Pan** Pan's pipes. **2** *excl* (*) drat it! *, dash it! * ◆**flûtiste** *nmf* flautist, flutist.

fluvial, e, *mpl* **-aux** [flyvjal, o] *adj eaux* river; *érosion* fluvial.

flux [fly] *nm [argent etc]* flood; *(Phys)* flux. *(marée)* **le ~** the floodtide; **le ~ et le reflux** the ebb and flow; *(Écon)* **~ de capitaux** capital flow.

fluxion [flyksjɔ̃] *nf* swelling; *(dentaire)* gumboil. **~ de poitrine** pneumonia.

foc [fɔk] *nm* jib.

focal, e, *mpl* **-aux** [fɔkal, o] **1** *adj* focal. **2** *nf* focal distance.

fœtus [fetys] *nm* foetus.

foi [fwa] *nf* (**a**) *(croyance)* faith. **avoir la ~** to have faith; **il faut avoir la ~!** * you've got to be really dedicated!; **sans ~ ni loi** fearing neither God nor man. (**b**) *(confiance)* faith, trust. **avoir ~ en** to have faith *ou* trust in; **digne de ~** reliable, trustworthy. (**c**) *(assurance)* word. **~ d'honnête homme!** on my word as a gentleman!; **cette lettre en fait ~** this letter proves it; **sous la ~ du serment** under *ou* on oath; **sur la ~ de** on the strength of; **de bonne/mauvaise ~** in good/bad faith; **faire qch en toute bonne ~** to do sth in all good faith; **en toute bonne ~ je l'ignore** honestly I don't know; **ma ~...** well...

foie [fwa] *nm* liver. **~ gras** foie gras.

foin [fwɛ̃] *nm* hay. **faire les ~s** to make hay; *(saison)* **les ~s** the haymaking season; **faire du ~** * to kick up a fuss *.

foire [fwaʀ] *nf (marché)* fair; *(fête)* fun fair. **faire la ~** * to go on a spree; **c'est la ~ ici!** * it's bedlam in here!; **c'est une ~ d'empoigne** it's a free-for-all.

foirer [fwaʀe] (1) *vi* (*) *[vis]* to slip; *[obus]* to hang fire; (‡) *[projet]* to fall through.

fois [fwa] *nf* (**a**) time. **une ~** once; **deux ~** twice; **trois ~** three times; *(aux enchères)* **une ~, deux ~, trois ~ adjugé** going, going, gone!; **quand je l'ai vu pour la première/dernière ~** when I first/ last saw him; **c'est bon pour cette ~** I'll let you off this time; **peu de ~** on few occasions; **y regarder à deux ~ avant d'acheter qch** to think twice before buying sth; **s'y prendre à plusieurs ~ pour faire qch** to take several attempts to do sth; **payer en plusieurs ~** to pay in several instalments. (**b**) *(calcul)* **une ~ tous les deux jours** once every two days, once every other day; **3 ~ par an** 3 times a year; **9 ~ sur 10** 9 times out of 10; **4 ~ plus d'eau/de voitures** 4 times as much water/as many cars; **6 ~ moins d'argent/de gens** 6 times less money/fewer people; **il avait deux ~ rien** *(argent)* he had absolutely nothing; *(blessure)* he had the merest scratch. (**c**) **une ~** once; **il était une ~** once upon a time there was; **une ~ n'est pas coutume** once in a while does no harm; **pour une ~!** for once!; **une (bonne) ~ pour toutes** once and for all; **une ~ (qu'il sera) parti** once he has left. (**d**) (*) **des ~** *(parfois)* sometimes; **si des ~ vous le rencontrez** if you should happen to meet him; **non mais, des ~!** *(scandalisé)* do you mind!; **non mais des ~ pour qui te prends-tu?** look here, who do you think you are?; **attendons, des ~ qu'il viendrait** let's wait in case he comes. (**e**) **à la ~** *répondre* at once, at the same time; **il était à la ~ grand et gros** he was both tall and fat.

foison [fwazɔ̃] *nf*: **il y a des légumes à ~** there is an abundance of vegetables, there are vegetables galore. ◆**foisonnement** *nm* profusion, abundance. ◆**foisonner** (1) *vi* to abound. **foisonnant d'idées** teeming with ideas.

folâtrer [fɔlɑtʀe] (1) *vi* to frolic. **au lieu de ~** instead of fooling around. ◆**folâtre** *adj* playful.

folichon, -onne * [fɔliʃɔ̃, ɔn] *adj*: **ce n'est pas très ~** it's not much fun.

folie [fɔli] *nf* (**a**) **la ~** madness, lunacy; **~ furieuse** *(Méd)* raving madness; *(fig)* sheer lunacy; **avoir la ~ des grandeurs** to have delusions of grandeur; **il a la ~ des timbres-poste** he is mad about stamps; **aimer qn à la ~** to be madly in love with sb; **il a eu la ~ de refuser** he was mad enough *ou* crazy enough to refuse. (**b**) *(erreur)* extravagance. **~s de jeunesse** youthful follies; **vous avez fait des ~s en achetant ce cadeau** you have been far too extravagant in buying this present; **il ferait des ~s pour elle** he would do anything for her; **il ferait des ~s pour la revoir** he would give anything to see her again.

folklore [fɔlklɔʀ] *nm* folklore. ◆**folklorique** *adj costume* folk; *(*: excentrique)* outlandish. ◆**folk song** *nm* folk music.

folle [fɔl] *V* **fou.**

follement [fɔlmɑ̃] *adv* madly, wildly. **on s'est ~ amusé** we had a fantastic time; **il désire ~ lui parler** he is longing to speak to her.

fomenter [fɔmɑ̃te] (1) *vt (lit, fig)* to foment, stir up.

foncer[1] * [fɔ̃se] (3) *vi* to tear along *. **~ sur** to charge at, make a rush at; **~ dans la foule** to charge into the crowd; **~ (tête baissée) dans le piège** to walk straight into the trap; *(fig)* **~ dans le brouillard** to forge ahead in the dark. ◆**fonceur, -euse** * *nm, f* fighter *(fig)*.

foncer[2] [fɔ̃se] (3) **1** *vt couleur* to make darker. **2** *vi* to turn *ou* go darker. ◆**foncé, e** *adj* dark.

foncier, -ière [fɔ̃sje, jɛʀ] *adj* (**a**) *impôt* land; *propriété* landed. (**b**) *(fondamental)* fundamental, basic. ◆**foncièrement** *adv* fundamentally, basically.

fonction [fɔ̃ksjɔ̃] *nf* (**a**) *(métier)* post, office. *(tâches)* **~s** duties; **entrer en ~s** to take up one's post; **ça n'entre pas dans mes ~s** it's not part of my duties; **être en ~** to be in office; **la ~ publique** the public service. (**b**) *(gén, Gram: rôle)* function. **faire ~ de directeur** to act as a manager; **il n'y a pas de porte, ce rideau en fait ~** there is no door but this curtain does instead *ou* does duty for it. (**c**) *(Math)* function. *(fig)* **sa réussite est ~ de son travail** his success depends on how well he works; **en ~ de** according to.

fonctionnaire [fɔ̃ksjɔnɛʀ] *nmf (gén)* state employee; *[ministère]* gouvernment official, ≃ civil servant; *[municipalité]* local government officer *ou* official. **les ~s de l'enseignement** state-employed teacher; **~ de (la) police** police officer, officer of the law.

fonctionnel, -elle [fɔ̃ksjɔnɛl] *adj* functional.

fonctionner [fɔ̃ksjɔne] (1) *vi (gén)* to work, operate; *[entreprise]* to function, run. **faire ~** *machine* to operate. ◆**fonctionnement** *nm* working, operating; functioning, running. **en état de bon ~** in good working order; **mauvais ~ du carburateur** fault in the carburettor; **pendant le ~ de l'appareil** while the machine is in operation; **frais de** ~ running *ou* upkeep costs.

fond [fɔ̃] **1** *nm* (**a**) *[récipient, vallée etc]* bottom; *[gorge]* back; *[pièce]* far end, back; *[chapeau]* crown; *[chaise]* seat. *(Min)* **le** ~ the coal face; **être/tomber au** ~ **de l'eau** to be at/fall to the bottom of the water; *(Naut)* **envoyer par le** ~ to send to the bottom; **y a-t-il beaucoup de** ~**?** is it very deep?; **l'épave repose par 10 mètres de** ~ the wreck is lying 10 metres down; **au** ~ **du couloir** at the far end of the corridor; **au** ~ **de la province** in the depths *ou* heart of the country; *(lit, fig)* **sans** ~ bottomless. (**b**) *(fig: tréfonds)* **merci du** ~ **du cœur** I thank you from the bottom of my heart; **au** ~ **de son cœur** deep down, in his heart of hearts; **je vais vous dire le** ~ **de ma pensée** I shall tell you what I really think; **regarder qn au** ~ **des yeux** to look deep into sb's eyes; **il a un bon** ~ he's a good person at heart; **il y a chez lui un** ~ **d'honnêteté** he's fundamentally honest; ~ **de vérité** element of truth; **toucher le** ~ **de la douleur** to plumb the depths of sorrow. (**c**) *(Littérat, gén: contenu)* content; *(Jur)* substance; *(arrière-plan)* background; *[question]* heart; *[discours]* basis. **il faut aller jusqu'au** ~ **de cette histoire** we must get to the root of this business; **ouvrage de** ~ basic work; **article de** ~ feature *ou* in-depth article; **avec** ~ **sonore** *ou* **musical** with background music. (**d**) *(lie)* sediment. *(petite quantité)* **juste un** ~ **(de verre)** just a drop; **ils ont vidé les** ~**s de bouteilles** they emptied what was left in the bottles; ~ **de magasin** old stock; **racler les** ~**s de tiroirs** to scrape around for pennies. (**e**) *(Sport)* **de** ~ long-distance. (**f**) *(locutions)* **le** ~ **de l'air est frais** * it's a bit chilly; **au** ~, **dans le** ~ in fact; **à** ~ *étudier* thoroughly, in depth; *soutenir* to the hilt; *visser* right home; **respirer à** ~ to breathe deeply; **à** ~ **de train** hell for leather *, full tilt; **de** ~ **en comble** *fouiller* from top to bottom; *détruire* completely, utterly; *modifier* completely. **2** : ~ **d'artichaut** artichoke heart; **les** ~**s marins** the sea-bed; ~ **de robe** (full-length) slip *ou* petticoat; ~ **de tarte** *(pâte)* pastry base; *(crème)* custard base; ~ **de teint** (make-up) foundation.

fondamental, e, *mpl* **-aux** [fɔ̃damɑ̃tal, o] *adj* fundamental, basic. *(Scol)* **matière** ~**e** basic subject, core subject. ◆**fondamentalement** *adv* fundamentally, basically.

fonder [fɔ̃de] (1) **1** *vt* (**a**) *(créer)* to found; *famille* to start. *(Comm)* **'maison fondée en 1850'** 'Established 1850'. (**b**) *(baser) (gén)* to base, found; *richesse* to build; *espoirs* to place (*sur* on). **2 se** ~ *vpr*: **se** ~ **sur** *[personne]* to go on; *[théorie]* to be based on; **sur quoi vous fondez-vous pour l'affirmer?** what grounds do you have for saying this? ◆**fondateur, -trice** *nm, f* founder. ◆**fondation** *nf (action)* foundation. *(Constr)* ~**s** foundations. ◆**fondé, e 1** *adj* well-founded, justified. **mal** ~ ill-founded; ~ **sur des ouï-dire** based on hearsay; **être** ~ **à dire** to have good reason to say. **2** *nm*: ~ **(de pouvoir)** *(Jur)* authorized representative; *(Banque)* senior executive. ◆**fondement** *nm* foundation. **sans** ~ without foundation, unfounded.

fondre [fɔ̃dʀ(ə)] (41) **1** *vt* (**a**) *(aussi* **faire** ~ *) (lit, fig)* to melt; *minerai* to smelt. (**b**) *statue* to cast, found; *couleurs* to blend; *idées* to fuse together (*en* into). **2** *vi* (**a**) *(à la chaleur)* to melt; *(dans l'eau)* to dissolve. (**b**) *(fig) [colère]* to melt away; *[réserves]* to vanish. **j'ai fondu de 5 kg** I've lost 5 kg; ~ **en larmes** to dissolve into tears. (**c**) ~ **sur qn** *[ennemi]* to swoop down on sb; *[malheurs]* to sweep down on sb. **3 se** ~ *vpr* to merge (*dans* into). ◆**fonderie** *nf (usine)* smelting works; *(de moulage)* foundry.

fondrière [fɔ̃dʀijɛʀ] *nf* pothole, rut.

fonds [fɔ̃] *nm* (**a**) ~ **de commerce** business. (**b**) *[musée]* collection; *[œuvre d'entraide]* fund. **le F~ Monétaire International** the International Monetary Fund; *(fig)* ~ **folklorique** folk heritage. (**c**) *(Fin: pl) (argent)* money; *(capital)* capital; *(pour un achat)* funds. ~ **d'État** government securities; ~ **publics/secrets** public/secret funds; **mise de** ~ **initiale** initial (capital) outlay; **ne pas être/être en** ~ to be out of/be in funds; **prêter de l'argent à** ~ **perdus** to lend money for an indefinite period; ~ **de roulement** working capital.

fondu, e [fɔ̃dy] **1** *adj beurre* melted; *métal* molten; *contours* blurred, hazy; *couleurs* blending. **neige** ~**e** slush. **2** *nf (Culin)* (cheese) fondue. ~ **e bourguignonne** meat fondue. **3** *nm (Ciné)* ~ **(enchaîné)** dissolve, fade-in-fade-out.

fontaine [fɔ̃tɛn] *nf (ornementale)* fountain; *(naturelle)* spring. *(fig)* ~ **de** fountain of.

fonte [fɔ̃t] *nf* (**a**) *(action) (gén)* melting; *[minerai]* smelting; *[cloche]* casting, founding. **à la** ~ **des neiges** when the snow melts. (**b**) *(métal)* cast iron. ~ **brute** pig-iron; **en** ~ *tuyau* cast-iron.

fonts [fɔ̃] *nmpl*: ~ **baptismaux** font.

football [futbol] *nm* football, soccer. **jouer au** ~ to play football. ◆**foot** * *nm abrév de* **football.** ◆**footballeur, -euse** *nm, f* footballer.

footing [futiŋ] *nm*: **faire du** ~ to go jogging; **faire un** ~ to go for a jog.

forage [fɔʀaʒ] *nm [roche]* drilling, boring; *[puits]* sinking, boring. **se livrer à des** ~**s d'essai** to test-drill.

forain, e [fɔʀɛ̃, ɛn] **1** *adj* fairground. **2** *nm (acteur)* fairground entertainer. **(marchand)** ~ stallholder.

forban [fɔʀbɑ̃] *nm (Hist)* pirate; *(fig)* shark, crook.

forçat [fɔʀsa] *nm (bagnard)* convict; *(galérien, fig)* galley slave.

force [fɔʀs(ə)] **1** *nf* (**a**) *[personne]* **la** ~, **les** ~**s** strength; **avoir de la** ~ **dans les bras** to be strong in the arm; **à la** ~ **du poignet** *(lit)* by the strength of one's arms; *(fig)* by the sweat of one's brow; **c'est une** ~ **de la nature** he's a mighty figure; **dans la** ~ **de l'âge** in the prime of life; **de toutes ses** ~**s** *frapper* with all one's might; *désirer* with all one's heart. (**b**) *[personne] (violence)* force. **la** ~ **brutale** brute force. (**c**) *(de la nature)* force; *[argument, alcool etc]* strength. **vent de** ~ **4** force 4 wind; **dans toute la** ~ **du terme** in the strongest sense of the word; **la** ~ **de l'habitude** force of habit; **par la** ~ **des choses** by force of circumstances; **avoir** ~ **de loi** to have force of law. (**d**) *(Mil)* strength. ~**s** forces; **d'importantes** ~**s de police** large contingents *ou* numbers of police; **dans une position de** ~ in a position of strength. (**e**) *(valeur)* **de la même** ~ *joueurs* evenly matched; *cartes* of the same value; **il est de première** ~ **au bridge** he's a first-class bridge player; **il est de** ~ **à le faire** he's equal to it; **tu n'es pas de** ~ **à lutter avec lui** you're no match for him; **à** ~**s égales** on equal terms. (**f**) *(Phys)* force. *(Élec)* **la** ~ ≃ 30-amp circuit; ~ **de gravité** force of gravity. (**g**) **en** ~ *attaquer* in force; *venir* in strength; **de** ~, **par** ~ by force; **faire entrer qn de** ~ *ou* **par la** ~ to force sb to enter; **entrer de** ~ **chez qn** to force one's way into sb's house; **avec** ~ firmly; **vouloir à toute** ~ to want at all costs; **à** ~ **d'essayer/de gentillesse** by dint of trying/kindness; **à** ~, **tu vas le casser** * you'll end up breaking it; ~ **lui est d'accepter** he has no choice but to accept, he is forced to accept. **2** *adv (hum)* many. **3** : ~ **d'âme** fortitude; **la** ~ **armée** the army; **les** ~**s armées** the armed forces; ~ **de caractère** strength of character; ~ **de dissuasion** deterrent power; ~ **de frappe** strike force; ~**s de maintien de la paix** peace-keeping force(s); **les** ~**s de l'ordre** the police; **faire intervenir la** ~ **publique** to call in the police.

forcé, e [fɔʀse] *adj (gén)* forced; *bain* unintended; *conséquence* inevitable; *amabilité* affected. **atterrissage** ~ forced *ou* emergency landing; **c'est** ~**!** it's inevitable!

forcément [fɔʀsemɑ̃] *adv (inévitablement)* inevitably; *(évidemment)* of course. **ça devait ~ arriver** it was bound to happen; **pas ~** not necessarily.

forcené, e [fɔʀsəne] **1** *adj (fou)* deranged; *ardeur, travailleur* frenzied; *partisan* fanatical. **2** *nm, f (fou)* maniac; *(fanatique)* fanatic. **travailler comme un ~** to work like a maniac *.

forceps [fɔʀsɛps] *nm* forceps.

forcer [fɔʀse] (3) **1** *vt* (**a**) *(contraindre)* to force, compel (*à faire* to do). **ils m'ont forcé la main** they forced my hand; **~ qn au silence** to force sb to keep silent. (**b**) *serrure, porte* to force open; *blocus* to run; *barrage* to force; *ville* to take by force. **~ le passage** to force one's way through; **sa conduite force le respect** his behaviour commands respect; *(Sport)* **~ la décision** to settle the outcome. (**c**) *cerf* to hunt down; *ennemi* to track down. (**d**) *(pousser) cheval* to override; *plantes* to force; *talent, voix* to strain; *allure* to increase; *destin* to tempt. **~ le sens d'un texte** to stretch the meaning of a text; *(fig)* **~ la dose** * *ou* **la note** * to overdo it. **2** *vi (exagérer)* to overdo it; *(en tirant)* to force it; *(être coincé)* to jam. **sans ~** * easily; **il force sur l'alcool** * he overdoes the drink a bit *. **3 se ~** *vpr* to force o.s. (*pour faire* to do).

forcing [fɔʀsiŋ] *nm* pressure. **faire du ~** to pile on the pressure.

forcir [fɔʀsiʀ] (2) *vi* to fill out.

forer [fɔʀe] (1) *vt roche* to drill, bore; *puits* to drill, sink, bore. ◆ **foret** *nm* drill.

forêt [fɔʀɛ] *nf (lit, fig)* forest. **~ vierge** virgin forest; **~ tropicale** rainforest; **~ domaniale** national *ou* state-owned forest; **la Forêt-Noire** the Black Forest. ◆ **forestier, -ière 1** *adj région* forest. **exploitation ~ière** *(activité)* forestry; *(lieu)* forestry site. **2** *nm* forester.

forfait [fɔʀfɛ] *nm* (**a**) *(à payer)* fixed *ou* set price; *(à percevoir)* lump sum. **~-vacances** package holiday; **~-skieur(s)** ski-pass; *[impôts]* **être au (régime du) ~** to be taxed on estimated income. (**b**) *(abandon)* withdrawal. **gagner par ~** to win by default; **déclarer ~** to withdraw. (**c**) *(crime)* infamy. ◆ **forfaitaire** *adj* standard, uniform. ◆ **forfaitairement** *adv* uniformly.

forger [fɔʀʒe] (3) *vt métal* to forge; *(fig) caractère* to form, mould; *mot* to coin; *prétexte* to make up. **c'est forgé de toutes pièces** it's a complete fabrication; **se ~** *illusions* to build up; *réputation* to earn o.s.; *idéal* to create for o.s. ◆ **forge** *nf (atelier)* forge, smithy; *(fourneau)* forge. *(fonderie)* **~s** ironworks. ◆ **forgeron** *nm* blacksmith.

formaliser [fɔʀmalize] (1) **1** *vt* to formalize. **2 se ~** *vpr* to take offence (*de* at). ◆ **formalisation** *nf* formalization.

formalisme [fɔʀmalism(ə)] *nm (péj)* formality; *(Art, Philos)* formalism. ◆ **formaliste 1** *adj (péj)* formalistic; *(Art, Philos)* formalist. **2** *nmf* formalist.

formalité [fɔʀmalite] *nf* formality. *(fig)* **sans autre ~** without any further ado.

format [fɔʀma] *nm* format.

formater [fɔʀmate] (1) *vt* to format. ◆ **formatage** *nm* formatting.

formation [fɔʀmɑsjɔ̃] *nf* (**a**) *(développement)* formation, forming. **en cours de ~** in the process of formation. (**b**) *(apprentissage)* training; *(éducation)* education. **~ professionnelle** professional *ou* vocational training; **~ permanente** continuing education; **~ continue au sein de l'entreprise** (staff) in-service training. (**c**) *(groupement) (gén)* formation. **~ musicale** music group; **~ politique** political grouping *ou* formation. ◆ **formateur, -trice** *adj* formative.

forme [fɔʀm(ə)] *nf* (**a**) *(contour)* form, shape; *(silhouette)* figure. **en ~ de cloche** bell-shaped; **sans ~** *chapeau* shapeless; *pensée* formless; **prendre la ~ d'un entretien** to take the form of a talk; **prendre ~** *[statue, projet]* to take shape; **sous ~ de comprimés** in tablet form; **sous toutes ses ~s** in all its forms. (**b**) *(genre)* **~ de vie** form of life; *(coutumes)* way of life; **~ de pensée** way of thinking. (**c**) *(Art, Jur)* form. **de pure ~** purely formal; **pour la ~** as a matter of form, for form's sake; **en bonne (et due) ~** in due form; *(fig)* **sans autre ~ de procès** without further ado. (**d**) *(convenances)* **~s** proprieties; **refuser en y mettant des ~s** to decline as tactfully as possible. (**e**) *(Ling)* form. **mettre à la ~ passive** to put in the passive. (**f**) *(moule)* mould; *(Typ)* form; *[cordonnier]* last; *[modiste]* (dress) form. (**g**) *(physique)* form. **être en ~** to be on form; **hors de ~** off form.

formel, -elle [fɔʀmɛl] *adj (catégorique)* definite, positive; *(Art, Philos)* formal; *politesse* formal. ◆ **formellement** *adv* positively; formally.

former [fɔʀme] (1) **1** *vt* (**a**) *(gén)* to form; *train, phrase* to make up. **formé de 3 éléments** made up of 3 elements; **~ l'idée de faire** to form *ou* have the idea of doing; **ça forme un rond** it makes *ou* forms a circle. (**b**) *ingénieurs* to train; *intelligence, caractère* to form, develop. **2 se ~** *vpr (gén)* to form; *[autodidacte]* to teach *ou* train o.s.

formidable [fɔʀmidabl(ə)] *adj (très important)* tremendous; *(*: très bien)* fantastic *, great *, tremendous *; *(*: incroyable)* incredible; *(effrayant)* fearsome. ◆ **formidablement** *adv* tremendously *; fantastically *.

formol [fɔʀmɔl] *nm* formalin.

Formose [fɔʀmoz] *n* Formosa.

formulaire [fɔʀmylɛʀ] *nm* form.

formule [fɔʀmyl] *nf* (**a**) *(Chim, Math)* formula. (**b**) *(expression)* phrase, expression; *(magique, consacrée)* formula. **~ de politesse** *(en fin de lettre)* letter ending; **~ publicitaire** advertising slogan. (**c**) *(méthode)* system, way. **~ de paiement** method of payment; **~ de vacances** holiday schedule. (**d**) *(formulaire)* form. (**e**) *(Aut)* **la ~ un** Formula One; **voiture de ~ un** Formula-One car.

formuler [fɔʀmyle] (1) *vt plainte* to formulate, set out, word; *sentiment* to formulate, express. ◆ **formulation** *nf* formulation; expression.

fornication [fɔʀnikɑsjɔ̃] *nf* fornication.

fort, e [fɔʀ, fɔʀt(ə)] **1** *adj* (**a**) *(gén)* strong; *(euph: gros)* large; *bruit* loud; *pluie, rhume* heavy; *fièvre, augmentation* high; *chaleur, sentiment* great; *différence, somme* great, large, big; *secousse* hard; *pente* steep. **~ comme un bœuf** as strong as an ox; **armée ~e de 20 000 hommes** army 20,000 strong; **la dame est plus ~e que le valet** the queen is higher than the jack; **avoir affaire à ~e partie** to have a strong *ou* tough opponent; **user de la manière ~e** to use strong-arm methods; **rayon (pour) femmes ~es** outsize department; **il avait une ~e envie de rire** he very much wanted to laugh; **il y a de ~es chances pour qu'il vienne** there's a strong *ou* good chance he'll come, he's very likely to come; **faire payer le prix ~** to charge the full price; **être ~ dans l'adversité** to be strong in adversity; **âme ~e** steadfast soul; **~e tête** rebel. (**b**) *(doué)* good (*en, à* at). **il a trouvé plus ~ que lui** he has met (more than) his match; **ce n'est pas très ~ de sa part** * that's not very bright of him. (**c**) **~ de cette garantie** fortified by this guarantee; **être ~ de son bon droit** to be confident of one's rights; **il se fait ~ de le faire** he's quite sure *ou* confident he can do it; **au sens ~ du terme** in the strongest sense of the term; **à plus ~e raison, tu aurais dû venir** all the more reason for you to have come; **c'est plus ~ que moi** I can't help it; **c'est plus ~ que de jouer au bouchon!** it's a real puzzle!; **c'est trop ~!** that's too much!; **c'est trop ~ pour moi** it's above *ou* beyond me; **elle est ~e celle-là!** * that takes the biscuit! *; **et le plus ~ c'est que...** and the best part of it is that...

2 *adv* (**a**) *crier* loudly, loud; *lancer, frapper* hard. **parlez plus** ~ speak up *ou* louder; **respirez bien** ~ take a deep breath; **tu y vas un peu** ~ * you're going a bit far. (**b**) *détester* greatly; *mécontent* most, highly. **j'en doute** ~ I very much doubt it; **j'ai** ~ **à faire avec lui** I have a hard job with him; **il y avait** ~ **peu de monde** there were very few people; **tu le sais** ~ **bien** you know very well.
3 *nm* (**a**) *(forteresse)* fort. (**b**) *(personne)* **le** ~ **et le faible** the strong and the weak; ~ **des Halles** market porter. (**c**) *(spécialité)* strong point. (**d**) *(milieu)* **au** ~ **de** *été* at the height of; *hiver* in the depths of; *combat* in the thick of.

fortement [fɔʀtəmɑ̃] *adv conseiller* strongly; *tenir* fast; *frapper* hard; *serrer* hard, tight. ~ **marqué** strongly marked; **il en est** ~ **question** it is being seriously considered; **j'espère** ~ **que** I very much hope that; ~ **intéressé par** most interested in.

forteresse [fɔʀtəʀɛs] *nf* fortress, stronghold.

fortiche * [fɔʀtiʃ] *adj* clever, smart.

fortifier [fɔʀtifje] (7) *vt* to strengthen, fortify. ◆**fortifiant, e 1** *adj médicament* fortifying; *air* invigorating, bracing. **2** *nm* tonic. ◆**fortification** *nf* fortification.

fortuit, e [fɔʀtɥi, ɥit] *adj* fortuitous, chance. ◆**fortuitement** *adv* fortuitously, by chance.

fortune [fɔʀtyn] *nf* (**a**) *(richesse)* fortune. **situation de** ~ financial situation; **avoir de la** ~ to have private means; **faire** ~ to make one's fortune; **le mot a fait** ~ the word has become really popular. (**b**) *(chance)* luck, fortune; *(destinée)* fortune. **chercher** ~ to seek one's fortune; **connaître des** ~**s diverses** to have varying luck; **il a eu la (bonne)** ~ **de le rencontrer** he was fortunate enough to meet him, he had the good fortune to meet him; **mauvaise** ~ misfortune; **venez dîner à la** ~ **du pot** come to dinner and take pot luck with us. (**c**) **de** ~ *installation* makeshift, rough-and-ready. ◆**fortuné, e** *adj (riche)* wealthy; *(heureux)* fortunate.

forum [fɔʀɔm] *nm* forum.

fosse [fos] *nf (trou)* pit; *(tombe)* grave; *(pour le saut)* sandpit. ~ **d'aisances** cesspool; ~ **commune** communal grave; *(lit, fig)* ~ **aux lions** lions' den; ~ **d'orchestre** orchestra pit; ~ **septique** septic tank.

fossé [fose] *nm (gén)* ditch; *(fig)* gulf, gap. ~ **culturel** culture gap.

fossette [fosɛt] *nf* dimple.

fossile [fosil] *nm, adj (lit, fig)* fossil. ◆**fossiliser** *vt*, **se** ~ *vpr* (1) to fossilize.

fossoyeur [foswajœʀ] *nm* gravedigger.

fou [fu], **fol** *devant n commençant par une voyelle ou h muet,* **folle** [fɔl] *f* **1** *adj* (**a**) *personne, idée etc* mad, crazy, insane; *imagination, gestes, course* wild. **devenir/rendre** ~ to go/drive mad *ou* crazy; ~ **à lier** raving mad; ~ **de colère** beside o.s. with anger; ~ **d'amour** madly *ou* wildly in love (*pour* with); **elle est folle de lui** she's mad * *ou* crazy * about him; **pas folle, la guêpe** * he's (*ou* she's) not stupid *ou* daft * you know!; **avoir le** ~ **rire** to have the giggles. (**b**) (*) *courage, vitesse, succès* fantastic *, terrific, tremendous; *prix* enormous, huge. **j'ai eu un mal** ~ **pour venir** I had a terrific *ou* terrible job to get here; **tu as mis un temps** ~ you've taken absolutely ages *; **dépenser un argent** ~ to spend loads *ou* pots of money *; **il y a un monde** ~ there are masses of people; **c'est** ~ **ce qu'il a changé** it's incredible *ou* unbelievable how he has changed. (**c**) *boussole* erratic; *camion, cheval* runaway; *cheveux* unruly. **avoir une patte folle** * to have a limp *ou* a dicky leg *. **2** *nm, f (insensé)* madman (*ou* madwoman), lunatic; *(bête)* fool. **faire le** ~ to play *ou* act the fool. **3** *nm (Échecs)* bishop; *(Hist: bouffon)* jester, fool.

foudre [fudʀ(ə)] *nf* lightning; *(Myth)* thunderbolt. **frappé par la** ~ struck by lightning; **s'attirer les** ~**s de qn** to bring down sb's wrath upon o.s.

foudroyer [fudʀwaje] (8) *vt [foudre]* to strike; *[maladie etc]* to strike down. ~ **qn du regard** to look daggers at sb. ◆**foudroyant, e** *adj vitesse* lightning; *poison, maladie* violent; *mort* instant; *succès* stunning. **nouvelle** ~**e** devastating piece of news.

fouetter [fwete] (1) *vt (gén, fig)* to whip; *(punition)* to flog; *(Culin)* to whisk; *imagination* to fire; *désir* to whip up. **la pluie fouette les vitres** the rain lashes *ou* whips the window panes; **il n'y a pas de quoi** ~ **un chat** it's nothing to make a fuss about. ◆**fouet** *nm* whip; whisk.

fougère [fuʒɛʀ] *nf* fern. **couvert de** ~**(s)** overgrown with bracken.

fougue [fug] *nf* ardour, spirit. **plein de** ~ fiery. ◆**fougueusement** *adv* with spirit, ardently. ◆**fougueux, -euse** *adj* fiery, ardent; *jeunesse* hotheaded; *cheval* mettlesome; *attaque* spirited.

fouiller [fuje] (1) **1** *vt (gén)* to search; *personne* to frisk; *région* to scour; *ciel* to scan; *question* to go (deeply) into; *sol* to dig. **il fouilla l'obscurité des yeux** he peered into the darkness; **très fouillé** very detailed. **2** *vi*: ~ **dans** *armoire* to rummage in; *bagages* to go through; *mémoire* to search; *archives* to ransack; *passé de quelqu'un* to delve into. **3 se** ~ *vpr* to search one's pockets. ◆**fouille** *nf* search; (‡: poche) pocket. *(gagner de l'argent)* **s'en mettre plein les** ~**s** to line one's pockets, make a packet *; *(Archéol)* ~**s** excavation(s); **faire des** ~**s** to carry out excavations; ~ **corporelle** body search.

fouillis [fuji] *nm [objets]* jumble; *[branchages]* tangle. **faire du** ~ to make a mess; **être en** ~ to be in a mess.

fouine [fwin] *nf (Zool)* stone marten; *(péj)* snooper *. **visage de** ~ weasel face. ◆**fouiner** (1) *vi (péj)* to nose around *ou* about. ◆**fouineur, -euse** *(péj)* **1** *adj* prying, nosey *. **2** *nm, f* snooper *.

fouir [fwiʀ] (2) *vi* to dig.

foulant, e * [fulɑ̃, ɑ̃t] *adj* killing, back-breaking.

foulard [fulaʀ] *nm (écharpe) (long)* scarf; *(carré)* headscarf, headsquare; *(tissu)* foulard.

foule [ful] *nf (gén)* crowd; *(péj)* mob. *(le peuple)* **la** ~ the masses; **il n'y avait pas** ~! there was hardly anyone there!; **une** ~ **de** *gens* a crowd of; *objets, questions* masses *ou* heaps * of; **ils vinrent en** ~ **à l'exposition** they came in crowds *ou* they flocked to the exhibition.

fouler [fule] (1) **1** *vt raisins* to press; *sol* to walk *ou* tread upon. *(fig)* ~ **aux pieds** to trample underfoot. **2 se** ~ *vpr* (**a**) **se** ~ **la cheville** to sprain one's ankle. (**b**) (*: *travailler)* to flog o.s. to death *, strain o.s. ◆**foulée** *nf [cheval, coureur]* stride. **être dans la** ~ **de qn** to follow (close) on sb's heels; *(fig)* **il l'a fait dans la** ~ he did it while he was at it *ou* while he was in his stride. ◆**foulure** *nf* sprain.

four [fuʀ] *nm* (**a**) *(Culin)* oven; *[potier]* kiln; *(Ind)* furnace. **cuire au** ~ *gâteau* to bake; *viande* to roast; **plat allant au** ~ ovenproof dish; **poisson cuit au** ~ fish baked in the oven; ~ **à micro-ondes** micro-wave oven; ~ **crématoire** crematorium furnace. (**b**) *(arg Théât)* flop, fiasco. **faire un** ~ to be a flop. (**c**) **(petit)** ~ fancy cake.

fourbe [fuʀb(ə)] *adj* deceitful, treacherous. ◆**fourberie** *nf (acte)* deceit. **la** ~ deceitfulness, treachery.

fourbi * [fuʀbi] *nm (attirail)* gear *; *(fouillis)* mess. **et tout le** ~ and the whole caboodle *.

fourbu, e [fuʀby] *adj* exhausted.

fourche [fuʀʃ(ə)] *nf (gén)* fork; *(à foin)* pitchfork. *[route]* **faire une** ~ to fork. ◆**fourcher** (1) *vi*: **ma langue a fourché** it was a slip of the tongue. ◆**fourchette** *nf (lit)* fork; *(Statistique)* margin. **il a une**

bonne ~ he has a hearty appetite. ◆ **fourchu, e** *adj arbre* forked. **pied** ~ cloven hoof; **elle a les cheveux fourchus** she's got split ends.

fourgon [fuʀgɔ̃] *nm (wagon)* waggon; *(camion)* (large) van; *(diligence)* coach. ~ **mortuaire** hearse. ◆ **fourgonnette** *nf* small van.

fourgonner [fuʀgɔne] (1) *vi* to poke about, rake about (*dans* in).

fourguer * [fuʀge] (1) *vt* to unload * (*à* onto).

fourmi [fuʀmi] *nf* ant. **avoir des ~s dans les jambes** to have pins and needles in one's legs; **elle s'affaire comme une** ~ she bustles about as busy as a bee. ◆ **fourmilière** *nf (monticule)* ant-hill; *(intérieur)* ants' nest; *(fig)* hive of activity.

fourmiller [fuʀmije] (1) *vi* to swarm. ~ **de** to be swarming *ou* teeming with. ◆ **fourmillement** *nm* swarming. **un** ~ **d'idées** a welter of ideas; *(picotement)* ~**s** pins and needles (*dans* in).

fournaise [fuʀnɛz] *nf* blaze; *(fig)* furnace, oven.

fourneau, *pl* ~**x** [fuʀno] *nm* (**a**) *(poêle)* stove. (**b**) *[forge]* furnace; *[pipe]* bowl.

fournée [fuʀne] *nf (lit, fig)* batch.

fourni, e [fuʀni] *adj herbe, barbe* thick. **peu** ~ sparse, thin; **bien** ~ *(en marchandises)* well-stocked.

fourniment * [fuʀnimɑ̃] *nm* gear *.

fournir [fuʀniʀ] (2) **1** *vt* (**a**) *(approvisionner)* to supply. ~ **qn en** to supply sb with. (**b**) *(procurer) (gén)* to supply, provide; *pièce d'identité* to produce; *prestation, exemple* to give; *effort* to put in. ~ **qch à qn** to supply *ou* provide sb with sth; *(Cartes)* ~ **à cœur** to follow suit in hearts. **2** ~ **à** *vt indir besoins* to provide for. **3 se** ~ *vpr* to provide o.s. (*de* with). **je me fournis chez cet épicier** I shop at this grocer's. ◆ **fournisseur** *nm (commerçant)* tradesman, merchant; *(détaillant)* stockist, retailer; *(Comm, Ind)* supplier. ◆ **fourniture** *nf* supply. ~**s de bureau** office supplies.

fourrage [fuʀaʒ] *nm* fodder. ~ **vert** silage.

fourrager [fuʀaʒe] (3) *vi*: ~ **dans** to rummage through.

fourré[1] [fuʀe] *nm* thicket. **les ~s** the bushes.

fourreau, *pl* ~**x** [fuʀo] *nm [épée]* sheath; *[parapluie]* cover. **robe** ~ sheath dress; **jupe** ~ tight skirt.

fourrer [fuʀe] (1) **1** *vt* (**a**) (*: *mettre)* to stick *. ~ **qch dans un sac** to stick * *ou* shove * sth into a bag; ~ **son nez partout** to poke *ou* stick * one's nose into everything; ~ **qn dans le pétrin** to land sb in the soup *. (**b**) *volaille* to stuff; *gâteau* to fill; *manteau* to line (with fur). **2 se** ~ * *vpr*: **il s'est fourré dans la tête que...** he has got it into his head that...; **se** ~ **dans un coin** to get in a corner; **où a-t-il encore été se** ~? where has he got to now?; **il ne savait plus où se** ~ he didn't know where to put himself. ◆ **fourré**[2]**, e** *adj bonbon* filled; *gants* fur-lined. **chocolats ~s** chocolate creams; ~ **à la crème** cream(-filled). ◆ **fourre-tout** *nm inv (placard)* junk cupboard, glory-hole; *(sac)* holdall.

fourreur [fuʀœʀ] *nm* furrier.

fourrière [fuʀjɛʀ] *nf (gén, Aut)* pound; *[chiens]* dog pound. **emmener une voiture à la** ~ to tow away a car, impound a car.

fourrure [fuʀyʀ] *nf (pelage)* coat; *(manteau etc)* fur.

fourvoyer [fuʀvwaje] (8) **1** *vt*: ~ **qn** *[guide]* to mislead sb; *[mauvais exemple]* to lead sb astray. **2 se** ~ *vpr (lit, fig)* to go astray. **se** ~ **dans** *lieu* to stray into; *aventure* to get involved in.

foutaise ‡ [futɛz] *nf*: **de la** ~ **, des ~s** rubbish *, bullshit ‡.

foutre ‡ [futʀ(ə)] **1** *vt (faire)* to do; *(donner)* to give; *(mettre)* to stick *, shove *. **qu'est-ce qu'il fout** what the hell ‡ is he doing *ou* up to; ~ **qn à la porte** to give sb the boot *, kick sb out *; **tout** ~ **en l'air** *(métier)* to chuck it all up ‡; *(objet)* to chuck it all away ‡; **ça la fout mal** it looks pretty bad *; **fous-moi le camp!** clear off! **2 se** ~ *vpr*: **se** ~ **dedans** to boob *; **se** ~ **par terre** to go sprawling; **se** ~ **dans une sale affaire** to get mixed up in a messy business; **se** ~ **de qn** to get a laugh at sb *, take the mickey out of sb ‡; **je m'en fous** I couldn't give a damn ‡. ◆ **foutu, e** ‡ *adj*: **être** ~ *[malade]* to be done for; *[appareil]* to be bust *; **être bien/mal**~ *[appareil]* to be damned clever/hopeless ‡; *(habillé)* to be well/badly got up *; **se sentir mal** ~ to feel lousy ‡; **il n'est pas** ~ **de le faire** he's damn well incapable of doing it ‡; **ce** ~ **temps** this damned weather ‡.

fox(-terrier), *pl* **fox(-terriers)** [fɔks(tɛʀje)] *nm* fox terrier.

foyer [fwaje] *nm* (**a**) *(maison)* home; *(famille)* family. (**b**) *[chaudière]* firebox; *(âtre)* hearth, fireplace. (**c**) *[vieillards, soldats]* home; *[étudiants]* hostel; *(club)* club; *(Théât)* foyer. ~ **des artistes** greenroom. (**d**) *(Opt, Phys)* focus. **verres à double** ~ bifocal lenses. (**e**) ~ **de** *incendie, infection* seat of; *lumière, infection* source of; *agitation, extrémistes* centre of.

fracas [fʀaka] *nm (gén)* crash; *[train, tonnerre]* roar; *[bataille]* din. ◆ **fracassant, e** *adj bruit* deafening; *déclaration* shattering, sensational. ◆ **fracasser** (1) **1** *vt* to smash, shatter. **2 se** ~ *vpr*: **se** ~ **contre** *ou* **sur** to crash against.

fraction [fʀaksjɔ̃] *nf (Math)* fraction; *(gén: partie)* part. **une** ~ **de seconde** a split second; **par** ~ **de** in fractions of. ◆ **fractionnement** *nm* splitting up, division. ◆ **fractionner** *vt*, **se** ~ *vpr* (1) to divide (up), split up.

fracture [fʀaktyʀ] *nf (Géol, Méd)* fracture. ◆ **fracturer** (1) *vt (Géol, Méd)* to fracture; *serrure* to break.

fragile [fʀaʒil] *adj (lit, fig: gén)* fragile; *peau* delicate; *verre* brittle; *équilibre* shaky; *bonheur, argument* frail, flimsy. *(sur étiquette)* **'attention** ~**'** 'fragile, (handle) with care'; **avoir l'estomac** ~ **, être** ~ **de l'estomac** to have a weak stomach. ◆ **fragiliser** (1) *vt* to weaken. ◆ **fragilité** *nf* fragility; delicacy; brittleness; flimsiness, frailty.

fragment [fʀagmɑ̃] *nm* fragment, bit; *[conversation, chanson]* snatch; *[lettre]* part; *(extrait)* passage, extract. ◆ **fragmentaire** *adj* sketchy, fragmentary.

fragmenter [fʀagmɑ̃te] (1) **1** *vt état, terrain* to fragment, split up; *travail, somme* to split up (*en* into). **2 se** ~ *vpr [roches]* to fragment. ◆ **fragmentation** *nf* fragmentation; splitting up.

frais[1]**, fraîche** [fʀɛ, fʀɛʃ] **1** *adj* (**a**) *vent, accueil* cool. **il fait** ~ it's rather cool. (**b**) *couleur, joues, parfum* fresh; *voix* clear; *joie, âme* pure. (**c**) *plaie, traces, nouvelles* fresh; *peinture* wet; *aliment, vêtement, troupes* fresh. **un peu d'air** ~ a breath of fresh air; ~ **et dispos,** ~ **comme une rose** as fresh as a daisy; ~ **comme la rosée** bright-eyed and bushy-tailed; ~ **comme un gardon** bright as a button; *(Comm)* **argent** ~ *(disponible)* ready cash; *(à investir)* fresh money; **nous voilà** ~**!** * we're in a fix! * **2** *adv* (**a**) **il fait** ~ it's cool; **en été, il faut boire** ~ in summer you need cool drinks. (**b**) *(récemment)* newly. ~ **débarqué de sa province** fresh *ou* newly up from the country; **habillé de** ~ freshly changed. **3** *nm*: **prendre le** ~ to take a breath of cool air; **mettre (qch) au** ~ to put (sth) in a cool place. ◆ **fraîchement** *adv (récemment)* freshly, newly; *accueillir* coolly. **comment ça va? — ~!** * how are you? — a bit chilly! ◆ **fraîcheur** *nf* coolness; freshness; chilliness; purity. **la** ~ **du soir** the cool of the evening.

frais[2] [fʀɛ] *nmpl* (**a**) *(gén)* expenses; *(charges)* costs; *(Admin: droits)* charges, fees. ~ **de déplacement** travelling expenses *ou* costs; ~ **d'entretien** *[machine]* maintenance costs; ~ **de timbre** stamp charges; ~ **de port et d'emballage** postage and packing; ~ **d'enregistrement** registration fees; ~ **généraux** overheads; ~ **de gestion,** *ou* **d'exploitation** running costs; ~ **bancaires** banking charges; ~ **divers** miscellaneous expenses; ~ **de scolarité** school fees;

séjour tous ~ compris all-in holiday; **avoir de gros ~** to have heavy outgoings. (**b**) *(lit)* **se mettre en ~** to go to great expense; **se mettre en ~ pour qn** to put o.s. out for sb; **faire les ~ de la conversation** *(parler)* to keep the conversation going; *(en être le sujet)* to be the main topic of conversation; **faire les ~ d'une erreur** to bear the brunt of a mistake; **j'en ai été pour mes ~** I was wasting my time; **à ses ~** at one's own expense; **aux ~ de la princesse *** at the firm's (*ou* the taxpayer's *etc*) expense; **à peu de ~** *acheter* cheaply; *s'en tirer* lightly.

fraise [fʀɛz] *nf* (**a**) *(fruit)* strawberry. **~ des bois** wild strawberry. (**b**) *[métallurgiste]* milling-cutter; *[dentiste]* drill. ◆**fraiser** (1) *vt trou* to counter-sink; *pièce* to mill. ◆**fraisier** *nm* straw-berry plant.

framboise [fʀɑ̃bwaz] *nf (fruit)* raspberry. ◆**framboisier** *nm* raspberry bush.

franc[1], franche [fʀɑ̃, fʀɑ̃ʃ] **1** *adj* (**a**) *personne, regard* frank, candid; *gaieté* open. **~ comme l'or** perfectly frank. (**b**) *situation, différence* clear-cut; *cassure* clean; *répugnance* clear, definite; *couleur* clear, pure. **5 jours ~s** 5 clear days. (**c**) *(péj: total) imbécile, ingratitude* downright. (**d**) *zone, ville* free. *(Comm)* **~ de port** postage paid. **2** *adv*: **à vous parler ~** to be frank with you. **3** : **~-maçon** *nm, pl* **~s-~s** freemason; **~-maçonnerie** *nf* freemasonry ; **~-parler** *nm* outspokenness; **~-tireur** *nm, pl* **~s -~s** *(Mil)* irregular; *(fig)* freelance; **agir en ~-tireur** to act independently.

franc[2] [fʀɑ̃] *nm (monnaie)* franc. **~ CFA** CFA franc *(unit of currency used in certain African states)*.

français, e [fʀɑ̃sɛ, ɛz] **1** *adj* French. **2** *nm* (**a**) **F~** Frenchman; **les F~** *(gens)* the French, French people; *(hommes)* Frenchmen. (**b**) *(Ling)* **le ~** French. **3** *nf*: **F~e** Frenchwoman. ◆**France** *nf* France.

Francfort [fʀɑ̃kfɔʀ] *n* Frankfurt. **~-sur-le-Main** Frankfurt-am-Main.

franchement [fʀɑ̃ʃmɑ̃] *adv* (**a**) *(honnêtement) parler* frankly, candidly; *agir* openly. **~ , qu'en pensestu?** what do you honestly think?; **il y a des gens, ~!** really! *ou* honestly! some people!; **~ non** frankly no. (**b**) *(sans hésiter) frapper* boldly; *demander* clearly, straight out. **allez-y ~** *(explication)* go straight to the point; *(manœuvre etc)* go right ahead; **c'est ~ plus lourd** it's distinctly heavier. (**c**) *(tout à fait) mauvais, laid* downright, really; *bon* really. **on s'est ~ bien amusé** we really *ou* thoroughly enjoyed ourselves; **c'est ~ trop cher** it's much *ou* far too expensive.

franchir [fʀɑ̃ʃiʀ] (2) *vt obstacle* to clear, jump over; *rue, seuil* to cross; *porte* to go through; *distance* to cover; *mur du son* to break (through); *difficulté* to surmount; *limite* to overstep. **il lui reste 10 mètres à ~** he still has 10 metres to go; **~ le cap de la soixantaine** to turn sixty; *[chiffre, vote]* **ne pas réussir à ~ la barre de...** to be *ou* fall short of... ◆**franchissement** *nm* clearing; crossing; overstepping.

franchise [fʀɑ̃ʃiz] *nf* (**a**) *[personne, réponse]* frankness; *[regard]* candour. (**b**) *(exemption)* exemption; *(Hist) [ville]* franchise. **~ fiscale** tax exemption; **'~ postale'** ≃ 'official paid'; **~ de bagages** baggage allowance. (**c**) *(Assurance)* excess. (**d**) *(Comm)* franchise.

franco [fʀɑ̃ko] *adv (Comm)* **~ (de port)** postage-paid; **~ de port et d'emballage** free of charge; **y aller ~ *** *(explication)* to go straight to the point; *(manœuvre)* to, go right ahead.

franco- [fʀɑ̃ko] *préf* franco-. ◆**franco-canadien** *nm (Ling)* French Canadian. ◆**francophile** *adj, nmf* francophile. ◆**francophilie** *nf* francomania. ◆**francophobe** *adj, nmf* francophobe. ◆**francophobie** *nf* francophobia. ◆**francophone 1** *adj* French-speaking. **2** *nmf* (native) French speaker. ◆**francophonie** *nf* French-speaking communities. ◆**franco-québécois** *nm (Ling)* Quebec French.

frange [fʀɑ̃ʒ] *nf (lit)* fringe; *[conscience]* threshold. ◆**franger** (3) *vt* to fringe (*de* with).

frangin * [fʀɑ̃ʒɛ̃] *nm* brother. ◆**frangine *** *nf* sister.

franquette * [fʀɑ̃kɛt] *nf*: **à la bonne ~** simply, without any fuss.

frappant, e [fʀapɑ̃, ɑ̃t] *adj* striking.

frappe [fʀap] *nf* (**a**) *[médaille] (action)* striking; *(empreinte)* stamp. (**b**) *[dactylo] (souplesse)* touch; *(impression)* typeface. **la lettre est à la ~** the letter is being typed; **la première ~** the top copy.

frapper [fʀape] (1) **1** *vt* (**a**) *(lit, fig)* to strike; *[projectile, mesure]* to hit; *[couteau]* to stab. **~ le sol du pied** to stamp one's foot on the ground; **~ le regard/l'imagination** to catch the eye/the imagination; **la pluie/la lumière frappait le mur** the rain lashed against/the light fell on the wall; **frappé à mort** fatally wounded; **frappé de paralysie/par le malheur** stricken with paralysis/by misfortune; **frappé de stupeur** thunderstruck; **frappé de panique** panic-stricken; **il a frappé tout le monde par son énergie** he amazed everybody by his energy; **j'ai été frappé d'entendre que...** I was amazed to hear that...; **~ qn d'une amende/d'un impôt** to impose a fine/a tax upon sb; **la loi doit ~ les coupables** the law must punish the guilty. (**b**) *monnaie, médaille* to strike. (**c**) *(glacer) vin* to put on ice, chill; *café* to ice. **à boire frappé** serve chilled. **2** *vi* to strike (*sur* on, *contre* against). **~ sur la table** to bang on the table (*avec* with); **~ dans ses mains** to clap one's hands; **entrez sans ~** come in without knocking, come straight in; *(fig)* **~ à toutes les portes** to try every door; *(fig)* **~ à la bonne/mauvaise porte** to go to the right/wrong person *ou* place. **3 se ~** *vpr* (**a**) **se ~ la poitrine** to beat one's breast; **se ~ le front** to tap one's forehead. (**b**) (*: *se tracasser)* to get (o.s.) worked up.

frasque [fʀask(ə)] *nf* escapade. **~s de jeunesse** youthful indiscretions.

fraternel, -elle [fʀatɛʀnɛl] *adj* brotherly, fraternal. ◆**fraternisation** *nf* fraternization. ◆**fraterniser** (1) *vi* to fraternize (*avec* with). ◆**fraternité** *nf* fraternity.

fraude [fʀod] *nf*: **la ~** fraud; *(à un examen)* cheating; **en ~** *vendre* fraudulently; *lire* secretly; **passer qch en ~** to smuggle sth in; **~ électorale** electoral fraud; **~ fiscale** tax evasion. ◆**frauder** (1) **1** *vt* to cheat. **~ le fisc** to evade taxation. **2** *vi (gén)* to cheat (*sur* over). ◆**fraudeur, -euse** *nm, f (gén)* person guilty of fraud; *(à la douane)* smuggler; *(envers le fisc)* tax evader. ◆**frauduleusement** *adv* fraudulently. ◆**frauduleux, -euse** *adj* fraudulent.

frayer [fʀeje] (8) **1** *vt chemin* to open up, clear. *(fig)* **~ la voie** to pave the way. **2 se ~** *vpr*: **se ~ un passage (dans la foule)** to force one's way through (the crowd).

frayeur [fʀɛjœʀ] *nf* fright. **cri de ~** cry of fear; **se remettre de ses ~s** to recover from one's fright.

fredaine [fʀədɛn] *nf* escapade, prank.

fredonner [fʀədɔne] (1) *vt* to hum.

freezer [fʀizœʀ] *nm* ice-box, freezer *(of refrigerator)*.

frégate [fʀegat] *nf* frigate.

frein [fʀɛ̃] *nm (lit, fig)* brake; *[cheval]* bit. **mets le ~** put the brake on; **mettre un ~ à** to curb, check; **sans ~** unbridled, unchecked; **~ à main** handbrake; **~ moteur** engine braking. ◆**freinage** *nm* braking. ◆**freiner** (1) **1** *vt véhicule* to pull up, slow down; *progression* to hold up; *joie, évolution* to check. **il faut que je me freine** I have to cut down *(dans* on*)*. **2** *vi (Aut)* to brake; *(à ski etc)* to slow down.

frelaté, e [fʀəlate] *adj aliment* adulterated; *milieu* dubious.

frêle [fʀɛl] *adj (lit, fig)* frail.

frelon [fʀəlɔ̃] *nm* hornet.

frémir [fʀemiʀ] (2) *vi* (**a**) *(de peur)* to shiver, shudder; *(de fièvre, froid)* to shiver, tremble; *(de colère)* to shake; *(d'espoir)* to tremble (*de* with). **toute la salle frémissait** the whole audience trembled. (**b**) *[lèvres, feuillage]* to tremble, quiver; *[eau chaude]* to simmer. ◆ **frémissement** *nm* shudder; shiver; quiver. **un ~ de plaisir** a thrill *ou* quiver of pleasure; **le ~** *ou* **les ~s de** *lèvres* the trembling *ou* quivering of; *eau* the simmering of.

frêne [fʀɛn] *nm* ash (tree).

frénésie [fʀenezi] *nf* frenzy. ◆ **frénétique** *adj* frenzied, frenetic. ◆ **frénétiquement** *adv* frenetically, furiously.

fréquent, e [fʀekɑ̃, ɑ̃t] *adj* frequent. ◆ **fréquemment** *adv* frequently. ◆ **fréquence** *nf* frequency.

fréquenter [fʀekɑ̃te] (1) *vt lieu* to frequent; *voisins* to see frequently; *jeune fille* to go around with. **~ la bonne société** to move in fashionable circles. ◆ **fréquentable** *adj*: **sont-ils ~s?** are they the sort of people one can associate with? ◆ **fréquentation** *nf* (**a**) *[établissement]* frequenting. **la ~ de ces gens** frequent contact with these people. (**b**) *(relations)* **~s** company. ◆ **fréquenté, e** *adj lieu* busy. *(fig)* **bien/mal ~** of good/ill repute.

frère [fʀɛʀ] *nm (gén)* brother. **partager en ~s** to share like brothers; **~s d'armes** brothers in arms; **peuples ~s** sister countries; *(Rel)* **mes ~s** brethren; **~ lai** lay brother; **~ Antoine** Brother Antoine, Friar Antoine; **mettre qn chez les ~s** to send sb to a Catholic boarding school.

fresque [fʀɛsk(ə)] *nf (Art)* fresco; *(Littérat)* portrait.

fret [fʀɛ] *nm (prix) (Aviat, Naut)* freightage; *(Aut)* carriage; *(cargaison) (Aviat, Naut)* freight, cargo; *(Aut)* load. ◆ **fréter** (6) *vt (prendre à fret)* to charter; *(donner à fret)* to freight.

frétiller [fʀetije] (1) *vi [poisson, personne]* to wriggle; *[chien]* to wag its tail. **~ de joie** to quiver with joy. ◆ **frétillement** *nm [poisson]* ~(s) wriggling; **~ d'impatience** quiver of impatience.

freux [fʀø] *nm (Orn)* rook.

friable [fʀijabl(ə)] *adj* crumbly, flaky.

friand, e [fʀijɑ̃, ɑ̃d] **1** *adj*: **~ de** fond of. **2** *nm (pâté)* (minced) meat pie. ◆ **friandise** *nf* titbit, delicacy.

fric ⁑ [fʀik] *nm (argent)* bread ⁑, dough ⁑, cash *, lolly ⁑.

fric-frac *, *pl* **fric-frac(s)** [fʀikfʀak] *nm* break-in.

friche [fʀiʃ] *nf* fallow land. *(lit, fig)* **être/laisser en ~** to lie/let lie fallow.

friction [fʀiksjɔ̃] *nf (Phys, Tech, fig)* friction; *(massage)* rub-down; *(chez le coiffeur)* scalp massage. ◆ **frictionner** (1) *vt* to rub.

frigidaire [fʀiʒidɛʀ] *nm* ®, **frigo** * [fʀigo] *nm* refrigerator, fridge. ◆ **frigorifier** (7) *vt (lit)* to refrigerate. **être frigorifié** * to be frozen stiff. ◆ **frigorifique** *adj camion* refrigerator.

frileux, -euse [fʀilø, øz] *adj personne* sensitive to the cold; *geste* shivery. ◆ **frileusement** *adv* shiveringly.

frime * [fʀim] *nf*: **c'est de la ~** that's a lot of eyewash *; **c'est pour la ~** it's all *ou* just for show. ◆ **frimer** (1) *vi* to put on an act *.

frimousse [fʀimus] *nf* (sweet) little face.

fringale * [fʀɛ̃gal] *nf* raging hunger.

fringant, e [fʀɛ̃gɑ̃, ɑ̃t] *adj cheval* frisky; *personne* dashing.

fringuer (se) * [fʀɛ̃ge] (1) *vpr* to get dressed. ◆ **fringues** * *nfpl* gear * , togs *, threads ⁑ *(US)*. **elle a toujours de belles ~** she always has smashing gear *.

friper *vt*, **se ~** *vpr* [fʀipe] (1) to crumple.

fripier, -ière [fʀipje, jɛʀ] *nm, f* secondhand clothes dealer. ◆ **fripes** * *nfpl* togs *. **vendre des ~** to sell second-hand clothes.

fripon, -onne [fʀipɔ̃, ɔn] **1** *adj* roguish. **2** *nm, f* rogue. ◆ **friponnerie** *nf (acte)* piece of mischief, prank, escapade.

fripouille [fʀipuj] *nf (péj)* rogue.

frire [fʀiʀ] *vti*: **~ , faire ~** to fry.

frisbee [fʀizbi] *nm* frisbee.

frise [fʀiz] *nf (Archit, Art)* frieze.

friser [fʀize] (1) **1** *vt* (**a**) *cheveux* to curl; *moustache* to twirl. **~ qn** to curl sb's hair. (**b**) *surface* to graze, skim; *mort* to come within a hair's breadth of; *insolence* to border on. **~ la soixantaine** to be nearly sixty. **2** *vi [cheveux]* to curl; *[personne]* to have curly hair. **se faire ~** to have one's hair curled. ◆ **frisé, e 1** *adj cheveux* curly; *personne* curly-haired. **2** *nf (chicorée)* curly endive. ◆ **frisette** *nf* little curl.

frisquet * [fʀiskɛ] *adj m* chilly.

frissonner [fʀisɔne] (1) *vi* (**a**) *(de peur)* to shiver, shudder; *(de fièvre, froid)* to shiver, tremble; *(de désir)* to quiver, tremble; *(de colère)* to shake (*de* with). (**b**) *[feuillage]* to quiver, tremble; *[lac]* to ripple. ◆ **frisson** *nm* shiver; shudder; quiver. **~ de désir** quiver of desire; **ça me donne le ~** it gives me the shivers *. ◆ **frissonnement** *nm* shiver, shudder. **le ~ du feuillage** the quivering of the leaves.

frit, e [fʀi, fʀit] **1** *adj* fried. **2** *nf* chip. **~es** chips, French fries *(US)*; *(fig)* **avoir la ~** ⁑ to be feeling cheery, be full of beans *. ◆ **friteuse** *nf* chip pan, deep fryer. **~ électrique** electric fryer. ◆ **friture** *nf* (**a**) *(Culin) (méthode)* frying; *(graisse)* deep fat; *(mets)* fried fish. (**b**) *(Rad *)* crackle.

frivole [fʀivɔl] *adj* frivolous. ◆ **frivolement** *adv* frivolously. ◆ **frivolité** *nf* frivolity.

froc [fʀɔk] *nm (Rel)* frock, habit; *(⁑: pantalon)* trousers, bags *.

froid, e [fʀwa, fʀwad] **1** *adj (gén)* cold; *accueil* cold, cool; *calcul* cool. **ça me laisse ~** it leaves me cold; **garder la tête ~e** to keep cool, keep a cool head; **souder à ~** to cold-weld; **démarrer à ~** to start (from) cold; **cueillir qn à ~** * to catch sb unawares *ou* off guard. **2** *nm* (**a**) **le ~** *(gén)* the cold; *(industrie)* refrigeration; **j'ai ~** I am cold; **j'ai ~ aux pieds** my feet are cold; **il fait un ~ de canard** * it's freezing cold *ou* perishing *; **ça me fait ~ dans le dos** *(lit)* it makes my back cold; *(fig)* it sends shivers down my spine; **prendre (un coup de) ~** to catch cold *ou* a chill; **vague de ~** cold spell; **n'avoir pas ~ aux yeux** to be adventurous. (**b**) *(brouille)* coolness. **être en ~ avec qn** to be on bad terms with sb. ◆ **froidement** *adv accueillir* coldly; *calculer* coolly; *tuer* in cold blood. ◆ **froideur** *nf* coldness. **recevoir qn avec ~** to greet sb coldly.

froisser [fʀwase] (1) **1** *vt habit* to crumple, crease; *personne* to hurt, offend. **2 se ~** *vpr [tissu]* to crease, crumple; *[personne]* to take offence (*de* at). **se ~ un muscle** to strain a muscle. ◆ **froissement** *nm [tissu]* crumpling, creasing; *(bruit)* rustle.

frôler [fʀole] (1) *vt (lit) (toucher)* to brush against; *(passer près de)* to skim. **~ la mort** to come within a hair's breadth of death. ◆ **frôlement** *nm (contact)* light touch *ou* contact; *(bruit)* rustle.

fromage [fʀɔmaʒ] *nm* cheese. **plat au ~** cheese dish; **trouver un (bon) ~** * to find a cushy job *, get on the gravy train * *(US)*; **~ blanc** soft white cheese; **~ de chèvre** goat's milk cheese; **~ de tête** pork brawn. ◆ **fromager, -ère 1** *adj* cheese. **2** *nm (marchand)* cheesemonger, cheese merchant. ◆ **fromagerie** *nf* cheese dairy.

froment [fʀɔmɑ̃] *nm* wheat.

froncer [fʀɔ̃se] (3) *vt (Couture)* to gather. ~ **les sourcils** to frown, knit one's brows. ◆ **fronce** *nf* gather. **à** ~**s** gathered. ◆ **froncement** *nm*: ~ **de sourcils** frown.

fronde [fʀɔ̃d] *nf (arme)* sling; *(jouet)* catapult, slingshot *(US)*; *(fig)* revolt. ◆ **frondeur, -euse** *adj* rebellious.

front [fʀɔ̃] *nm (Anat)* forehead, brow; *[bâtiment]* façade, front; *(Mét, Mil, Pol)* front. **marcher le** ~ **haut** to hold one's head up high; **la honte sur son** ~ the shame on his face; ~ **de mer** sea front; **tué au** ~ killed in action; **de** ~ *attaque* frontal; *choc, heurter* head-on; **marcher à trois de** ~ to walk three abreast; **mener plusieurs tâches de** ~ to have several tasks on the go at one time; **aborder de** ~ **un problème** to tackle a problem head-on; **faire** ~ to face up to things; **faire** ~ **à l'ennemi** to face up *ou* stand up to the enemy; **faire** ~ **commun contre** to join forces against; **avoir le** ~ **de faire** to have the effrontery *ou* front to do. ◆ **frontal, e,** *mpl* **-aux** *adj collision* head-on; *attaque, (Anat, Géom)* frontal.

frontière [fʀɔ̃tjɛʀ] *nf (Géog, Pol)* frontier, border. **à l'intérieur et au-delà de nos** ~**s** at home and abroad; ~ **naturelle** natural boundary; **les** ~**s du savoir** the frontiers of knowledge; *(fig)* **à la** ~ **du rêve et de la réalité** on the borderline between dream and reality; **ville** ~ frontier *ou* border town. ◆ **frontalier, -ière 1** *adj* border, frontier. **2** *nm, f* inhabitant of the frontier zone.

fronton [fʀɔ̃tɔ̃] *nm* pediment.

frotter [fʀɔte] (1) **1** *vt (gén)* to rub; *allumette* to strike; *meubles, chaussures* to rub up, shine; *plancher* to scrub; *(pour enlever la terre)* to scrape. ~ **les oreilles à qn** to box sb's ears. **2** *vi* to rub, scrape. **3 se** ~ *vpr* to rub o.s. *(lit, fig)* **se** ~ **les mains** to rub one's hands; **se** ~ **à qn** to cross swords with sb. ◆ **frottement** *nm (action)* rubbing; *(lit, fig: friction)* friction.

frottis [fʀɔti] *nm (Méd)* smear; *(Art)* scumble.

frousse * [fʀus] *nf* fright. **avoir la** ~ to be scared stiff *. ◆ **froussard, e** * *nm, f (péj)* coward.

fructifier [fʀyktifje] (7) *vi [investissement]* to yield a profit. **faire** ~ to increase.

fructueux, -euse [fʀyktɥø, øz] *adj* fruitful, profitable. ◆ **fructueusement** *adv* fruitfully, profitably.

frugal, e, *mpl* **-aux** [fʀygal, o] *adj* frugal. ◆ **frugalement** *adv* frugally. ◆ **frugalité** *nf* frugality.

fruit [fʀɥi] *nm* fruit. **il y a des** ~**s** there is some fruit; **3** ~**s** 3 pieces of fruit; *(espèce)* 3 fruits; **les** ~**s de son travail** the fruits of one's work; **porter ses** ~**s** to bear fruit; **avec** ~ fruitfully; **sans** ~ fruitlessly; ~**s confits** candied fruits; ~**s de mer** seafood. ◆ **fruité, e** *adj* fruity. ◆ **fruitier, -ière 1** *adj* fruit. **2** *nm, f* fruiterer, greengrocer. ◆ **fruiticulteur** *nm* fruit farmer.

frusques [fʀysk(ə)] *nfpl (péj)* gear * , togs *. **vieilles** ~ rags.

fruste [fʀyst(ə)] *adj* coarse, unrefined.

frustrer [fʀystʀe] (1) *vt* to frustrate. ~ **qn de** *satisfaction* to deprive sb of; *biens* to defraud sb of. ◆ **frustration** *nf* frustration.

fuel(-oil) [fjul(ɔjl)] *nm* fuel oil. ~ **(domestique)** domestic *ou* heating oil.

fugitif, -ive [fyʒitif, iv] **1** *adj personne* runaway; *impression etc* fleeting. **2** *nm, f* fugitive.

fugue [fyg] *nf* (**a**) **faire une** ~ to run away, abscond *(Admin)*. (**b**) *(Mus)* fugue. ◆ **fuguer** * (1) *vi* to run away *ou* off.

fuir [fɥiʀ] (17) **1** *vt personne, danger* to shun, avoid; *obligation* to evade, shirk; *patrie, bourreaux* to flee from, run away from. **2** *vi* (**a**) *[prisonnier]* to run away, escape; *[troupes]* to take flight, flee. **faire** ~ *(Mil)* to put to flight; *(fig)* to chase off *ou* away; ~ **devant** to run away from; **il a fui chez ses parents** he has fled to his parents. (**b**) *[bateau]* to glide swiftly along; *[temps]* to fly by, slip by; *[paysage]* to recede. (**c**) *[liquide, récipient]* to leak. ◆ **fuite** *nf* (**a**) *[fugitif]* flight, escape. **la** ~ **des capitaux/des galaxies** the flight of capital/of the galaxies; **chercher la** ~ **dans le sommeil** to seek escape *ou* flight in sleep; **prendre la** ~ to take flight; **mettre qn en** ~ to put sb to flight; **les prisonniers sont en** ~ the prisoners are on the run; **les voleurs en** ~ the runaway thieves. (**b**) *[temps, bateau]* swift passage. (**c**) *[liquide, nouvelle, récipient]* leak. **avaries dues à des** ~**s** damage caused by leakage.

fulgurant, e [fylgyʀɑ̃, ɑ̃t] *adj vitesse, réplique* lightning; *regard* blazing; *douleur* searing.

fulminer [fylmine] (1) *vi* to be enraged. ~ **contre** to fulminate against.

fumer [fyme] (1) **1** *vi [feu]* to smoke; *[liquide]* to steam; *[produit chimique]* to fume; *(*: être en colère)* to be fuming * (*de* with). ~ **comme un pompier** to smoke like a chimney. **2** *vt tabac* to smoke; *(Culin)* to smoke; *(Agr)* to manure. ◆ **fumé, e**[1] *adj* smoked. ◆ **fume-cigarette** *nm inv* cigarette holder. ◆ **fumée**[2] *nf* smoke; steam. *(Chim)* ~**s** fumes; **la** ~ **ne vous gêne pas?** do you mind my smoking?; **sans** ~ smokeless; **partir en** ~ to go up in smoke; **il n'y a pas de** ~ **sans feu** there's no smoke without fire.

fumet [fymɛ] *nm* aroma.

fumeur, -euse[1] [fymœʀ, øz] *nm, f* smoker. **je suis non-**~ I'm a non-smoker; **compartiment non-**~**s** non-smoking compartment *ou* car *(US)* , non-smoker.

fumeux, -euse[2] [fymø, øz] *adj* (**a**) *(confus)* woolly. (**b**) *flamme* smoky; *horizon* misty.

fumier [fymje] *nm (engrais)* dung, manure; *(‡: salaud)* bastard ‡.

fumiste [fymist(ə)] **1** *nm (réparateur)* heating mechanic; *(ramoneur)* chimney sweep. **2** *nmf (péj) (employé)* shirker; *(philosophe)* phoney *. ◆ **fumisterie** *nf (péj)* **c'est une** ~ it's a fraud *ou* a con ‡.

fumure [fymyʀ] *nf (engrais)* manure.

funambule [fynɑ̃byl] *nmf* tightrope walker.

funèbre [fynɛbʀ(ə)] *adj (gén)* funeral; *ton* mournful, funereal; *atmosphère* gloomy, dismal. **veillée** ~ deathbed vigil.

funérailles [fyneʀɑj] *nfpl* funeral.

funéraire [fyneʀɛʀ] *adj* funeral. **pierre** ~ gravestone.

funeste [fynɛst(ə)] *adj* (**a**) *(désastreux) (gén)* disastrous; *erreur* grievous; *conseil, influence* harmful. **jour** ~ fateful *ou* ill-fated day. (**b**) *(de mort) vision* of death. (**c**) *accident* fatal; *coup* fatal, lethal, deadly; *projet* lethal, deadly.

funiculaire [fynikylɛʀ] *nm* funicular railway.

funky * [fœ̃ki] *adj* funky *.

fur [fyʀ] *nm*: **au** ~ **et à mesure** *(gén)* little by little; **dépenser au** ~ **et à mesure** to spend as fast *ou* as soon as one earns; **passe-moi les assiettes au** ~ **et à mesure** pass the plates to me as you go along; **au** ~ **et à mesure que vous les recevez** as (soon as) you receive them; **au** ~ **et à mesure de vos besoins** as and when you need it.

furax ‡ [fyʀaks] *adj inv* hopping mad *.

furet [fyʀɛ] *nm (animal)* ferret.

fureter [fyʀte] (5) *vi* to nose *ou* ferret *ou* pry about. ◆ **fureteur, -euse** *adj* prying, inquisitive.

fureur [fyʀœʀ] *nf (gén)* fury. **crise de** ~ fit of rage; **être en** ~ to be infuriated *ou* enraged; **mettre en** ~ to infuriate, enrage; **la** ~ **du jeu** a passion for gambling; **avec** ~ *dire* with rage, furiously; *aimer* madly, passionately; **faire** ~ to be all the rage. ◆ **furibond, e** *adj* furious. ◆ **furie** *nf (péj: mégère)* shrew; *(Myth)* Fury; *(colère, violence)* fury. **la ~ du jeu** a passion for gambling; **en ~** *personne* infuriated, enraged; *mer* raging. ◆**furieusement** *adv* furiously; tremendously. ◆**furieux, -euse** *adj (gén)* furious (*contre* with, at); *(hum: fort) envie, coup* tremendous. **elle est ~euse d'avoir refusé** she is furious at having refused.

furoncle [fyʀɔ̃kl(ə)] *nm* boil.

furtif, -ive [fyʀtif, iv] *adj* furtive, stealthy. ◆**furtivement** *adv* furtively, stealthily.

fusain [fyzɛ̃] *nm (crayon)* charcoal crayon; *(croquis)* charcoal drawing; *(arbre)* spindle-tree.

fuseau, *pl* **~x** [fyzo] *nm [fileuse]* spindle; *[dentellière]* bobbin. **(pantalon) ~ , ~x** stretch ski pants; **en (forme de) ~** *colonne* swelled; *jambes* slender; **~ horaire** time zone.

fusée [fyze] *nf (gén)* rocket; *[obus, mine]* fuse. **~ air-air/sol-air** air-to-air/ground-to-air missile; **~ éclairante** flare; **~ de lancement** launch vehicle; **~ spatiale** space rocket; **partir comme une ~** to shoot *ou* whizz off like a rocket.

fuselage [fyzlaʒ] *nm* fuselage.

fuselé, e [fyzle] *adj colonne* swelled; *jambes* slender.

fuséologie [fyzeɔlɔʒi] *nf* rocket technology.

fuser [fyze] (1) *vi [cris]* to burst forth; *[liquide]* to gush *ou* spurt out; *[étincelles]* to fly; *[lumière]* to stream out.

fusible [fyzibl(ə)] *nm* fuse.

fusil [fyzi] *nm* (**a**) *(arme)* rifle, gun; *(de chasse)* shotgun. *(fig)* **c'est un bon ~** he's a good shot; **changer son ~ d'épaule** to change one's plans; **~ à harpon** harpoon gun; **~ mitrailleur** machine gun; **~ sous-marin** (underwater) speargun. (**b**) *(allume-gaz)* gas lighter; *(à aiguiser)* steel. ◆**fusilier** *nm (Hist)* fusilier. **~ marin** marine. ◆**fusillade** *nf (bruit)* gunfire, shooting; *(combat)* shoot-out, shooting battle. ◆**fusiller** (1) *vt (lit)* to shoot; *(*: casser)* to bust *. **~ qn du regard** to look daggers at sb.

fusion [fyzjɔ̃] *nf* (**a**) *(gén, Phys)* fusion; *[métal, glace]* melting; *[idées]* merging, blending. (**b**) *(Comm)* merger, amalgamation. ◆**fusionner** (1) *vti (Comm)* to merge, amalgamate; *(Pol)* to merge; *(Ordin)* to merge.

fustiger [fystiʒe] (3) *vt adversaire* to flay; *pratiques* to censure, denounce.

fût [fy] *nm* (**a**) *[arbre]* trunk; *[colonne]* shaft. (**b**) *(tonneau)* barrel.

futaie [fytɛ] *nf* forest.

futé, e [fyte] *adj* crafty, sly.

futile [fytil] *adj (gén)* futile; *personne* frivolous. ◆**futilité** *nf* futility; frivolousness. **~s** trivialities.

futur, e [fytyʀ] **1** *adj* future. **~e maman** mother-to-be; **~ champion** budding *ou* future champion. **2** *nm (Ling, avenir)* **le ~** the future; **le ~ proche** the immediate future; **le ~ antérieur** *ou* **du passé** the future perfect. **3** *nm, f* fiancé(e), husband-(*ou* wife-)to-be.

futurologie [fytyʀɔlɔʒi] *nf* futurology. ◆**futurologue** *nmf* futurist, futurologist.

fuyant, e [fɥijɑ̃, ɑ̃t] *adj regard, personne* evasive; *front* receding; *lignes, vision* fleeting.

fuyard, e [fɥijaʀ, aʀd(ə)] *nm, f* runaway.

G

G, g [ʒe] *nm (lettre)* G, g.

gabardine [gabaʀdin] *nf (tissu)* gabardine; *(manteau)* gaberdine (raincoat).

gabarit [gabaʀi] *nm (dimension)* size; *(fig: valeur)* calibre; *(maquette)* template. *[personne]* **du même ~** of the same build.

Gabon [gabɔ̃] *nm*: **le ~** the Gabon. ◆ **gabonais, e** *adj*, **G~(e)** *nm(f)* Gabonese.

gâcher [gɑʃe] (1) *vt* (**a**) *plâtre* to temper; *mortier* to mix. (**b**) *(gaspiller)* to waste; *(bâcler)* to botch; *(gâter)* to spoil. **une vie gâchée** a wasted *ou* misspent life; **~ sa vie** to fritter away *ou* waste one's life; **il nous a gâché notre plaisir** he spoiled our pleasure. ◆ **gâcheur, -euse 1** *adj* wasteful. **2** *nm, f* wasteful person; *(d'argent)* spendthrift. ◆ **gâchis** *nm (désordre)* mess; *(gaspillage)* waste.

gâchette [gɑʃɛt] *nf [arme]* trigger. **il a la ~ facile** he's trigger-happy, he's quick on the draw.

gadget [gadʒɛt] *nm (gén: machin)* thingummy *; *(ustensile)* gadget; *(trouvaille)* gimmick.

gadoue [gadu] *nf (boue)* mud, sludge; *(neige)* slush.

gaélique [gaelik] *adj, nm (Ling)* Gaelic.

gaffe [gaf] *nf* (**a**) *(bévue)* blunder, boob *. (**b**) *(Naut)* boat hook; *(Pêche)* gaff. (**c**) (*) **faire ~** to be careful (*à* of). ◆ **gaffer** (1) **1** *vi* to blunder, boob *. **2** *vt* to hook; to gaff. ◆ **gaffeur, -euse** *nm, f* blunderer.

gag [gag] *nm (gén, Ciné, Théât)* gag.

gaga * [gaga] *adj* gaga *, senile.

gage [gaʒ] *nm* (**a**) *(à créancier)* security; *(à prêteur)* pledge. **mettre qch en ~** to pawn sth; **laisser qch en ~** to leave sth as (a) security; **~ de sincérité** proof *ou* evidence of one's sincerity; **~ d'amour** token of one's love; **en ~ de notre amitié** as a token *ou* in token of our friendship. (**b**) *(Jeux)* forfeit. (**c**) *(salaire)* **~s** wages; **tueur à ~s** hired killer; **être aux ~s de qn** *(gén)* to be employed by sb; *(péj)* to be in the pay of sb.

gager [gaʒe] (3) *vt* (**a**) *(parier)* **~ que** to wager that, bet that. (**b**) *emprunt* to guarantee.

gageure [gaʒyʀ] *nf (pari)* wager. **c'est une véritable ~ que de vouloir le faire** it's attempting the impossible to try to do it.

gagner [gaɲe] (1) **1** *vt* (**a**) *(par le travail, l'effort)* to earn. **~ sa vie/sa croûte** * to earn one's living/one's bread and butter; **~ de l'argent** *(dans une affaire)* to make money. (**b**) *(par le hasard, la lutte)* to win. *(lit, fig)* **~ le gros lot** to hit *ou* win the jackpot; **~ qn de vitesse** to beat sb to it *. (**c**) *(obtenir)* to gain. **vous n'y gagnerez rien** you'll gain nothing by it; **~ du temps** *(temporiser)* to gain time; *(économiser)* to save time; **c'est toujours ça de gagné!** that's always something!; **vous y gagnerez un bon rhume** you'll get nothing but a bad cold. (**d**) *gardiens, témoins* to win over; *confiance* to win, gain. **se laisser ~ par les prières de qn** to be won over by sb's prayers. (**e**) *lieu, refuge* to reach. **~ qn** *[sommeil, peur]* to overcome sb, creep over sb; **le feu gagna le toit** the fire spread to the roof; **l'eau/l'ennemi gagne du terrain** the water/the enemy is gaining ground.
2 *vi* (**a**) *(être vainqueur)* to win. **~ aux courses** to win on the horses *ou* at the races; **il gagne sur tous les tableaux** he's winning all the way; **tu as gagné!** * you got what you asked for! (**b**) *(trouver un avantage)* **vous y gagnez** it's in your interest, it's to your advantage; **qu'est-ce que j'y gagne?** what do I get out of it? *ou* gain from it?; **vous gagneriez à partir en groupe** you'd be better off going in a group; **~ au change** to make (something) on the deal. (**c**) *(s'améliorer)* **~ en hauteur** to increase in height; **il gagne à être connu** he improves on acquaintance; **ce roman gagne à être relu** this novel gains by a second reading. (**d**) *[incendie, épidémie]* to spread, gain ground. ◆ **gagnable** *adj* winnable. ◆ **gagnant, e 1** *adj* winning. **on le donne ~** he is the favourite to win; **il joue ~ dans cette affaire** he's bound to win *ou* come out on top in this deal; *(Jur)* **la partie ~e** the prevailing party. **2** *nm, f* winner. ◆ **gagneur, -euse** *nm, f* winner. **il a un tempérament de ~** he has the determination to succeed. ◆ **gagne-pain** * *nm inv* job. ◆ **gagne-petit** *nm inv* low wage earner.

gai, e [ge] *adj* (**a**) *personne, voix* cheerful, happy; *caractère* cheerful, merry. **~ luron** cheery fellow; **~ comme un pinson** happy as a lark. (**b**) *(euph: ivre)* merry, tipsy. (**c**) *couleur, robe* bright, gay; *pièce* bright, cheerful. (**d**) *(iro: amusant)* **c'est ~!** that's great *; **ça va être ~, les vacances avec lui!** the holidays are going to be great fun with him around! (**e**) *(homosexuel)* gay. ◆ **gaiement** *adv* cheerfully; happily; cheerily; merrily. *(iro)* **allons-y ~!** let's get on with it! ◆ **gaieté** *nf [personne, roman]* cheerfulness, gaiety; *[couleur]* brightness, gaiety. **de ~ de cœur** lightheartedly; *(joies)* **les ~s de** the delights *ou* joys of.

gaillard, e [gajaʀ, aʀd(ə)] **1** *adj* (**a**) *personne* strong; *allure* lively, sprightly. (**b**) *(grivois)* bawdy. **2** *nm (costaud)* strapping *ou* robust fellow; (*: *type)* fellow, guy *. **toi, mon ~, je t'ai à l'œil!** I've got my eye on you, mate! * **3** *nf* (*) strapping woman *. **4** : **~ (d'avant)** forecastle, fo'c'sle; *(Hist)* **~ d'arrière** quarter-deck. ◆ **gaillardement** *adv* stoutly, vigorously.

gain [gɛ̃] *nm* (**a**) *(salaire)* earnings, wages. (**b**) *(lucre)* **le ~** gain. (**c**) *(bénéfices)* **~s** *[société]* profits; *(au jeu)* winnings. (**d**) *(avantage)* gains; *(spirituel)* benefit. **tirer un ~ de qch** to draw benefit from sth. (**e**) *(économie)* saving. **ça nous permet un ~ de temps** it saves us time. (**f**) *(obtention) [bataille]* winning; *[voix d'électeurs]* gaining. **obtenir ~ de cause** *(lit)* to win the case; *(fig)* to win the day; **donner ~ de cause à qn** *(Jur)* to decide the case in favour of sb; *(fig)* to pronounce sb right.

gaine [gɛn] *nf (Habillement)* girdle; *(Bot, fourreau)* sheath. **~ d'aération** ventilation shaft.

gala [gala] *nm* official reception; *(pour collecter des fonds)* fund-raising reception. **de ~** *soirée, représentation* gala.

galant, e [galɑ̃, ɑ̃t] **1** *adj* (**a**) *(courtois)* gallant, courteous, gentlemanly. (**b**) *propos* flirtatious, gallant; *rendez-vous* romantic. **en ~e compagnie** with a lady (*ou* gentleman) friend. **2** *nm* suitor. ◆ **galamment** *adv* courteously, gallantly. ◆ **galanterie** *nf* gallantry; *(propos)* gallant remark.

galaxie [galaksi] *nf* galaxy.

galbe [galb(ə)] *nm* curve. ◆ **galbé, e** *adj* curved.

gale [gal] *nf (Méd)* scabies, itch; *(Vét) [chien, chat]* mange; *[mouton]* scab. **je n'ai pas la ~!** ‡ I'm not infectious!; **il est méchant comme la ~** he's a nasty piece of work *.

galère [galɛʀ] *nf (Hist)* galley. **qu'est-il allé faire dans cette ~?** why did he have to get involved in this business?

galerie [galʀi] *nf* (**a**) *(couloir)* gallery. **~ marchande** shopping arcade. (**b**) *(Art) (magasin)* gallery; *(salle de musée)* room, gallery. (**c**) *(Théât)* circle. **premières/deuxièmes ~s** dress/upper circle. (**d**) *(public)* gallery, audience. **pour amuser la ~** to amuse the audience. (**e**) *(Aut)* roof rack.

galérien [galeʀjɛ̃] *nm* galley slave.

galet [galɛ] *nm* pebble. **~s** shingle.

galette [galɛt] *nf (gâteau)* round, flat cake; *(crêpe)* pancake; *(‡: argent)* dough ‡, lolly ‡, bread ‡. **il a de la ~** he's loaded ‡.

galeux, -euse [galø, øz] *adj personne* affected with scabies; *chien* mangy; *mouton* scabby. **traiter comme un chien ~** to treat like dirt.

galimatias [galimatja] *nm* gibberish.

galipette * [galipɛt] *nf* somersault. **faire la ~** to somersault.

Galles [gal] *nfpl*: **le pays de ~** Wales. ◆ **gallois, e 1** *adj* Welsh. **2** *nm* (**a**) **G~** Welshman; **les G~** the Welsh. (**b**) *(Ling)* Welsh. **3** *nf*: **G~e** Welshwoman.

gallicisme [galisism(ə)] *nm* gallicism.

gallon [galɔ̃] *nm* gallon.

gallup [galœp] *nm*: **(sondage) ~** Gallup poll.

galoche [galɔʃ] *nf* clog.

galon [galɔ̃] *nm (Couture)* (piece of) braid; *(Mil)* stripe. *(fig)* **prendre du ~** to get promotion.

galop [galo] *nm* gallop. **petit ~** canter; **~ d'essai** *(lit)* trial gallop; *(fig)* trial run; **cheval au ~** galloping horse; **se mettre au ~** to break into a gallop; **partir au ~** *[cheval]* to set off at a gallop; *[personne]* to rush off *ou* away; **va chercher tes affaires au ~!** go and get your things, at *ou* on *(US)* the double! ◆ **galopade** *nf* stampede. ◆ **galopant, e** *adj inflation* galloping, runaway. ◆ **galoper** (1) *vi [cheval]* to gallop; *[imagination]* to run wild, run riot; *[enfant]* to run.

galopin * [galɔpɛ̃] *nm* rascal.

galvaniser [galvanize] (1) *vt (Tech)* to galvanize; *(fig)* to galvanize into action. ◆ **galvanisation** *nf* galvanization.

galvauder [galvode] (1) **1** *vt réputation* to tarnish; *talent* to prostitute; *expression* to debase. **2** *vi (vagabonder)* to idle around.

gambade [gɑ̃bad] *nf* leap, caper. ◆ **gambader** (1) *vi* to gambol, leap (about), caper (about). **~ de joie** to jump for joy.

gambas [gɑ̃mbas] *nfpl* Mediterranean prawns, gambas.

Gambie [gɑ̃bi] *nf* Gambia.

gamelle [gamɛl] *nf [soldat]* mess tin, kit *(US)*; *[ouvrier]* billy-can. **prendre une ~** * to come a cropper *, fall flat on one's face.

gamin, e [gamɛ̃, in] **1** *adj (espiègle)* mischievous, playful; *(puéril)* childish. **2** *nm, f* (*) kid *. ◆ **gaminerie** *nf* playfulness; childishness. **faire des ~s** to get up to mischief; to be childish.

gamme [gam] *nf* (**a**) *(Mus)* scale; *(fig)* range. **faire des ~s** to practise scales. (**b**) *(série) [couleurs, articles]* range; *[sentiments]* gamut, range. **~ de produits** range of products; **haut/bas de ~** up/down market.

Gand [gɑ̃] *n* Ghent.

gang [gɑ̃g] *nm* gang (of crooks).

Gange [gɑ̃ʒ] *nm*: **le ~** the Ganges.

ganglion [gɑ̃glijɔ̃] *nm* ganglion.

gangrène [gɑ̃gʀɛn] *nf (Méd)* gangrene; *(fig)* corruption.

gangster [gɑ̃gstɛʀ] *nm* gangster, mobster *(US)*; *(fig)* shark, crook. ◆ **gangstérisme** *nm* gangsterism.

gant [gɑ̃] *nm* glove. **~s de boxe** boxing gloves; **~ de crin** massage glove; **~ de cuisine** oven glove; **~ de toilette** face flannel, wash glove; **ça me va comme un ~** *[robe]* it fits me like a glove; *[idée]* it suits me down to the ground; **tu ferais mieux de prendre des ~s avec lui** you'd better handle him with kid gloves; **il va falloir prendre des ~s pour lui annoncer la nouvelle** we'll have to break the news to him gently; *(lit, fig)* **jeter/relever le ~** to throw down/take up the gauntlet. ◆ **se ganter** (1) *vpr* to put on one's gloves. **ganté de cuir** wearing leather gloves.

garage [gaʀaʒ] *nm (Aut)* garage. **~ d'autobus** bus depot; **~ d'avions** hangar; **~ de bicyclettes** bicycle shed; **~ de canots** boathouse. ◆ **garagiste** *nm (propriétaire)* garage owner; *(mécanicien)* garage mechanic.

garantir [gaʀɑ̃tiʀ] (2) *vt* (**a**) *(gén: assurer)* to guarantee; *emprunt* to guarantee, secure. **~ que** to assure *ou* guarantee that; **je te garantis que ça ne se passera pas comme ça!** * I can assure you things won't turn out like that! (**b**) *(protéger)* **~ qch de** to protect sth from; **se ~ du soleil** to protect o.s. from the sun. ◆ **garant, e** *nm, f (personne, état)* guarantor (*de* for); *(chose)* guarantee (*de* of). **servir de ~ à qn** to stand surety for sb; **se porter ~ de qch** to vouch for sth, guarantee sth. ◆ **garanti, e**[1] *adj*: **~ étanche/3 ans** guaranteed waterproof/for 3 years; **c'est ~ pour cinq ans** it carries a five-year guarantee, it is guaranteed for five years; **c'est ~ sur facture** * it's as sure as anything, it's a cert *. ◆ **garantie**[2] *nf (gén, Comm)* guarantee; *(gage)* security, surety; *(protection)* safeguard. *[police d'assurance]* **~s** cover; **si on a la ~ qu'ils se conduiront bien...** if we have a firm undertaking *ou* a guarantee that they'll behave...; **servir de ~** to be used as a security; **sous ~** under guarantee; **c'est une ~ de succès** it's a guarantee of success; **c'est une ~ contre le chômage** it's a safeguard against unemployment; *(caution)* **donner sa ~ à** to guarantee, stand security *ou* surety for; **je vous dis ça, mais c'est sans ~** I can't guarantee that what I'm telling you is right.

garçon [gaʀsɔ̃] **1** *nm* (**a**) boy. **traiter qn comme un petit ~** to treat sb like a child *ou* a little boy; **~ manqué** tomboy; **c'est un brave ~** he's a good sort *ou* a nice fellow *ou* a nice young man. (**b**) *(commis)* shop assistant; *(serveur)* waiter. **~ boucher** butcher's assistant. (**c**) *(célibataire)* bachelor. **rester ~** to remain a bachelor. **2** : **~ de bureau** office assistant; **~ de café** waiter; **~ de courses** messenger; **~ d'écurie** stable lad *ou* boy; **~ d'étage** bellboy; **~ de ferme** farm hand; **~ d'honneur** best man. ◆ **garçonnet** *nm* small boy. **taille/rayon ~** boy's size/department. ◆ **garçonnière** *nf* bachelor flat.

garde[1] [gaʀd(ə)] *nf* (**a**) *(surveillance)* **se charger de la ~ de qch** to undertake to look after *ou* to guard *ou* to keep an eye on sth; **prendre en ~** to take into one's care; **laisser qch en ~ à qn** to leave sth in sb's care; **sous la ~ de la police** under police guard; **être/mettre qn sous bonne ~** to be/put sb under guard; **~ à vue** police custody; **être mis** *ou* **placé en ~ à vue** ≃ to be kept in police custody, be held for questioning; **l'enfant a été laissé à la ~ de la mère** the child was left in the custody of the mother. (**b**) *(service) [soldat]* guard duty; *[infirmière etc]* ward duty. **être de ~** *[infirmière, sentinelle]* to be on duty; *[médecin]* to be on call *ou* on duty; **pharmacie de ~** chemist *ou* pharmacist *(US)* on (weekend or night) duty. (**c**) *(escorte)* guard. (**d**) *(infirmière)* nurse. **~ d'enfant** *(personne)* childminder; *(activité)* child minding. (**e**) *(Boxe, Escrime)* guard. **en ~!** on guard!; **se mettre en ~** to take one's guard. (**f**) *[épée]* hilt. *(lit, fig)* **jusqu'à la ~** (up) to the hilt. (**g**) **mettre qn en ~** to put sb on his guard (*contre* against); **mise en ~** warning; **faire bonne ~** to keep a close watch; **prenez ~ de ne pas tomber** mind you don't fall, be careful not to fall; **prends ~!** *(exhortation)* watch out!; *(menace)* watch it! *; **prends ~ aux voitures** watch out for *ou* mind the cars; **sans prendre ~ au danger** without considering the danger; **sans y prendre ~** without realizing it; **être sur ses ~s** to be on one's guard.

garde² [gaRd(ə)] *nm [prisonnier]* guard; *[château]* warden; *[jardin public]* keeper; *(soldat)* guardsman; *(sentinelle)* guard. **~ champêtre** rural policeman; **~ du corps** body-guard; **~ forestier** forest warden, (park) ranger *(US)*; **~ des Sceaux** French Minister of Justice ≃ Lord Chancellor.

garde- [gaRd(ə)] *préf*: **garde-barrière** *nmf, pl* **~s-~(s)** level-crossing keeper; **garde-boue** *nm inv* mudguard; **garde-chasse** *nm, pl* **~s-~(s)** gamekeeper; **garde-chiourme** *nm, pl* **~(s)-~(s)** martinet; **garde-côte** *nm, pl* **~-~(s)** *(Mil)* coastguard ship; *(garde-pêche)* fisheries protection ship; **garde-fou** *nm, pl* **~-~s** *(en fer)* railing; *(en pierre)* parapet; **garde-malade** *nmf, pl* **~s-~s** home nurse; **garde-manger** *nm inv (armoire)* meat safe, cooler *(US)*; *(pièce)* pantry, larder; **garde-meuble** *nm, pl* **~-~(s)** furniture store; **garde-pêche** *nm inv (personne)* water bailiff, fish (and game) warden *(US)*; *(frégate)* fisheries protection ship; **garde-robe** *nf, pl* **~-~s** *(habits)* wardrobe; *(Mil)* **garde-à-vous (fixe)!** attention!; **se mettre au garde-à-vous** to stand to attention.

garder [gaRde] (1) **1** *vt* (**a**) *(surveiller)* to look after, guard; *(défendre)* to guard. **~ qn à vue** ≃ to keep sb in custody; **~ des enfants (à domicile)** to baby-sit, child mind; **garde ma valise** look after *ou* keep an eye on my suitcase; **on n'a pas gardé les cochons ensemble!** * you've a nerve to take liberties like that! *; **ça vous gardera du froid** it'll protect you from the cold; **Dieu vous garde** God be with you; **le musée qui garde ces trésors** the museum which houses these treasures; **passage à niveau gardé/non gardé** manned/unmanned level-crossing. (**b**) *(conserver) (gén)* to keep; *jeunesse* to retain; *habitude* to keep up; *vêtement* to keep on; *[police]* to detain. **~ la chambre/le lit** to stay in one's room/in bed; **~ qn à déjeuner** to have sb stay for lunch; **~ en retenue** to keep in detention; **je lui ai gardé une côtelette pour ce soir** I've kept *ou* saved a chop for him for tonight; **je lui garde un chien de ma chienne** * he's got it coming to him (from me *); **~ une poire pour la soif** to keep sth for a rainy day; **gardez cela pour vous** keep this to yourself; **il a gardé toutes ses facultés** *ou* **toute sa tête** he still has all his faculties; **~ son calme/le silence** to keep calm/silent; **~ la tête froide** to keep a cool head; **~ les idées claires** to keep a clear head; **~ l'anonymat** to remain anonymous; **~ la ligne** to keep one's figure; **~ rancune à qn** to bear sb a grudge; **toutes proportions gardées** relatively speaking. **2 se ~** *vpr* (**a**) *[denrées]* to keep. (**b**) **se ~ de qch** *(se défier de)* to be wary of sth; *(se protéger de)* to protect o.s. from sth, guard against sth; **gardez-vous de vos amis** be wary of your own friends; **se ~ de faire qch** to be careful not to do sth; **je m'en garderai bien!** that's the last thing I'd do!

garderie [gaRdəRi] *nf*: **~ (d'enfants)** *(jeunes enfants)* day nursery, day-care center *(US)*; *(Scol)* ≃ after-school club, ≃ after-school center *(US)*.

gardien, -ienne [gaRdjɛ̃, jɛn] *nm, f (gén)* guard; *[château]* warden, keeper *(US)*; *[musée, hôtel]* attendant; *[jardin public, phare, zoo]* keeper; *(fig: défenseur)* guardian. **~ de but** goalkeeper; **~ne d'enfants** child minder; **~ d'immeuble** caretaker; **~ de nuit** night watchman; **~ de la paix** policeman, *(police)* constable, patrolman *(US)*; **~ de prison** prison warder *ou* officer *ou* guard.

gare¹ [gaR] *nf* station. **~ de marchandises** goods station; **~ maritime** harbour station; **~ routière** *(camions)* haulage depot; *(autocars)* coach *ou* bus station; **~ de triage** marshalling yard.

gare² * [gaR] *excl*: **~ à toi!** just watch it! *; **~ au premier qui bouge!** the first one to move will be for it! *; **sinon ~!** or else! *; **~ à ta tête** mind your head; **~ aux conséquences** beware of the consequences.

garer [gaRe] (1) **1** *vt véhicule* to park; *embarcation* to dock. **2 se ~** *vpr* to park; *[véhicule]* to draw into the side, pull over; *[piéton]* to get out of the way.

gargariser (se) [gaRgaRize] (1) *vpr* to gargle. *(fig péj)* **se ~ de grands mots** to revel in big words. ◆ **gargarisme** *nm* gargle.

gargote [gaRgɔt] *nf (péj)* cheap restaurant.

gargouille [gaRguj] *nf (Archit)* gargoyle. ◆ **gargouiller** (1) *vi [eau]* to gurgle; *[intestin]* to rumble. ◆ **gargouillement** *nm ou* ◆ **gargouillis** *nm* gurgling; rumbling.

garnement [gaRnəmɑ̃] *nm (gamin)* rascal; *(adolescent)* tearaway, hellion *(US)*.

garnir [gaRniR] (2) **1** *vt* (**a**) *(équiper) caisse* to fill; *réfrigérateur, bibliothèque* to stock; *chaudière* to stoke; *hameçon* to bait (*de* with). **~ qch de pneus** *etc* to put tyres *etc* on sth, fit sth out with tyres *etc*; **~ une muraille de canons** to range guns along a wall; **~ une boîte de tissu** to line a box with material. (**b**) *(remplir)* to fill; *(couvrir)* to cover. **la foule garnissait les rues** the crowd packed the streets; **boîte garnie de chocolats** box full of *ou* filled with chocolates; **les canons qui garnissent la muraille** the guns which line the wall *ou* which are ranged along the wall. (**c**) *(décorer) robe* to trim; *aliment* to garnish (*de* with). **~ de fleurs** to decorate with flowers. **2 se ~** *vpr [salle]* to fill up (*de* with). ◆ **garni, e 1** *adj plat (décoré)* garnished; *(accompagné)* served with vegetables. **bien ~** *portefeuille* well-lined; *réfrigérateur, bibliothèque* well-stocked; *estomac, boîte* full. **2** *nm* furnished rooms *ou* accommodation.

garnison [gaRnizɔ̃] *nf* garrison. **(ville de) ~** garrison town; **être en ~ à** to be stationed *ou* garrisoned at.

garniture [gaRnityR] *nf [chaudière]* lagging; *[coffret, freins]* lining; *[aliment] (décoration)* garnish; *(légumes)* garnish, fixings *(US)*. *(Culin)* **servi avec ~** served with vegetables, vegetables included; *[robe]* **~(s)** trimming; *(Aut)* **~ intérieure** upholstery, interior trim; **~ de cheminée** mantelpiece ornaments; **~ de toilette** toilet set; **~ périodique** sanitary towel *ou* napkin *(US)*; **avec ~ en cuir** with leather fittings.

garrot [gaRo] *nm [cheval]* withers; *(Méd)* tourniquet; *(supplice)* garrotte. ◆ **garrotter** (1) *vt* to tie up.

gars * [gɑ] *nm (enfant)* lad; *(type)* fellow, guy *. **au revoir les ~!** cheerio boys! * *ou* fellows! *

Gascogne [gaskɔɲ] *nf* Gascony.

gas-oil [gɑzɔjl] *nm* diesel oil.

gaspiller [gaspije] (1) *vt (gén)* to waste; *fortune* to squander. ◆ **gaspillage** *nm* wasting; squandering. *(résultat)* **quel ~!** what a waste! ◆ **gaspilleur, -euse 1** *adj* wasteful. **2** *nm, f* waster; squanderer.

gastrique [gastRik] *adj* gastric. ◆ **gastrite** *nf* gastritis.

gastronome [gastRɔnɔm] *nmf* gourmet, gastronome. ◆ **gastronomie** *nf* gastronomy. ◆ **gastronomique** *adj* gastronomic.

gâteau, *pl* **~x** [gɑto] *nm* cake; *(au restaurant)* gateau. **~x à apéritif** (small) savoury biscuits, appetizers;

~ **de riz** rice pudding; ~ **sec** biscuit; ~ **de miel** honeycomb; **se partager le** ~ * to share out the loot *; **c'est du** ~ * it's a piece of cake *, it's a walkover *, it's a snap * *(US)*.

gâter [gɑte] (1) **1** *vt (gén)* to ruin, spoil; *enfant* to spoil; *jugement* to have a harmful effect on. ~ **des fruits** to make fruit go bad; **avoir les dents gâtées** to have bad teeth; **et, ce qui ne gâte rien** and, which is an added bonus *ou* is even better; **nous avons été gâtés cette année** we've been really lucky this year. **2 se** ~ *vpr [viande]* to go bad, go off; *[relations]* to go sour. **le temps va se** ~ the weather's going to break; **ça commence à se** ~ **(entre eux)** things are beginning to go wrong (between them); **ça va se** ~! there's going to be trouble!, things are going to turn nasty! ◆ **gâterie** *nf* little treat. **se payer une** ~ to treat o.s. to sth.

gâteux, -euse * [gɑtø, øz] **1** *adj* senile, gaga *. **2** *nm, f*: **(vieux)** ~ doddering old man. ◆ **gâtisme** *nm* senility. ◆ **gâtifier** * (1) *vi* to go soft in the head *.

gauche [goʃ] **1** *adj* (**a**) *bras* left; *poche* left-hand. **du côté** ~ on the left-hand side. (**b**) *(maladroit)* clumsy, awkward; *(tordu)* warped. **2** *nm (Boxe)* left. **3** *nf* (**a**) **la** ~ *(gén, Aut, Pol)* the left; *(côté)* the left-hand side; **à** ~ *rue, rouler* on the left; *tourner* to the left; **tiroir de** ~ left-hand drawer; **à** ~ **de la porte** to the left of the door; **garder sa** ~ to keep to the left; **idées de** ~ left-wing ideas; **mettre de l'argent à** ~ * to put money aside. (**b**) *(coup)* left. ◆ **gauchement** *adv* clumsily, awkwardly. ◆ **gaucher, -ère** *adj* left-handed. ◆ **gaucherie** *nf* awkwardness, clumsiness. ◆ **gauchir** (2) **1** *vt (lit)* to warp; *fait* to distort. **2 se** ~ *vpr* to warp. ◆ **gauchisme** *nm* leftism. ◆ **gauchissement** *nm* warping; distortion. ◆ **gauchiste** *adj, nmf* leftist.

gaudriole * [godʀijɔl] *nf (propos)* broad joke.

gaufre [gofʀ(ə)] *nf* waffle. ◆ **gaufré, e** *adj papier* embossed; *tissu* goffered. ◆ **gaufrette** *nf* wafer. ◆ **gaufrier** *nm* waffle iron.

Gaule [gol] *nf* Gaul.

gaule [gol] *nf* pole; *(Pêche)* fishing rod. ◆ **gauler** (1) *vt arbre* to beat; *fruits* to bring down, shake down.

gaullisme [golism(ə)] *nm* Gaullism. ◆ **gaulliste** *adj, nmf* Gaullist.

gaulois, e [golwa, waz] **1** *adj* (**a**) *(de Gaule)* Gallic. (**b**) *(grivois)* bawdy. **2** *nm(f)*: **G~(e)** Gaul. **3** *nf* (®: *cigarette)* Gauloise. ◆ **gauloiserie** *nf (propos)* bawdy story. **la** ~ bawdiness.

gausser (se) [gose] (1) *vpr (littér) (rire)* to laugh; *(se moquer)* to be joking. **se** ~ **de** to poke fun at.

gaver [gave] (1) **1** *vt animal* to force-feed; *personne* to fill up (*de* with). **je suis gavé!** I'm full (up)! **2 se** ~ *vpr*: **se** ~ **de** *nourriture* to stuff o.s. with; *romans* to devour.

gavroche [gavʀɔʃ] *nm* street urchin *(in Paris)*.

gay * [gɛ] *adj, nm* gay.

gaz [gɑz] **1** *nm inv (Chim)* gas. *(Mil)* **les** ~ gas; **l'employé du** ~ the gasman; **se chauffer au** ~ to have gas(-fired) heating; **cuisinière** *etc* **à** ~ gas cooker *etc*; **vous avez le** ~? are you on gas?; **il s'est suicidé au** ~ he gassed himself; *(Aut)* **mettre les** ~ * to step on the gas *; *(euph)* **avoir des** ~ to have wind. **2** : ~ **asphyxiant** poison gas; ~ **carbonique** carbon dioxide; ~ **d'échappement** exhaust gas; ~ **lacrymogène** teargas; ~ **neurotoxique** nerve gas; ~ **de ville** town gas. ◆ **gazoduc** *nm* gas pipeline. ◆ **gazogène** *nm* gas producer *(plant)*. ◆ **gazole** *nm* diesel oil. ◆ **gazomètre** *nm* gasometer.

Gaza [gaza] *n*: **la bande** *ou* **le Territoire de** ~ the Gaza Strip.

gaze [gɑz] *nf* gauze.

gazelle [gazɛl] *nf* gazelle.

gazer [gɑze] (1) **1** *vi* (*) **ça gaze?** how's things? *, how goes it? *; **ça a gazé?** did it go O.K.? *; **ça ne gaze pas fort** things aren't too good *ou* too hot *; **il y a qch qui ne gaze pas** there's sth wrong somewhere. **2** *vt (Mil)* to gas. ◆ **gazage** *nm (Mil)* gassing.

gazette [gazɛt] *nf (hum)* newspaper.

gazeux, -euse [gɑzø, øz] *adj (Chim)* gaseous; *boisson* fizzy.

gazinière [gazinjɛʀ] *nf* gas cooker.

gazon [gɑzɔ̃] *nm (pelouse)* lawn. *(herbe)* **le** ~ turf, grass; **une motte de** ~ a turf, a sod.

gazouiller [gazuje] (1) *vi [oiseau]* to chirp, warble; *[ruisseau, bébé]* to babble. ◆ **gazouillement** *nm ou* ◆ **gazouillis** *nm* chirping, warbling; babbling.

geai [ʒɛ] *nm* jay.

géant, e [ʒeɑ̃, ɑ̃t] **1** *adj* gigantic; *paquet* giant-sized, giant. **2** *nm (lit, fig)* giant; *(Écon, Pol)* giant power. **3** *nf* giantess.

geindre [ʒɛ̃dʀ(ə)] (52) *vi (gémir)* to groan, moan (*de* with); *(péj)* to moan. ◆ **geignard, e** * *nm, f* moaner. ◆ **geignement** *nm*: ~**(s)** moaning.

gel [ʒɛl] *nm* (**a**) *(froid)* frost. **'craint le** ~**'** 'keep away from extreme cold'. (**b**) *[crédits]* freezing. (**c**) *(pâte)* gel; ~ **coiffant** hair gel.

gélatine [ʒelatin] *nf* gelatine. ◆ **gélatineux, -euse** *adj* gelatinous.

geler [ʒ(ə)le] (5) **1** *vt* (**a**) *eau, sol* to freeze; *membre* to cause frostbite to. **mourir gelé** to freeze to death; **j'ai les mains gelées** *(froides)* my hands are frozen (stiff); *(blessées)* my hands are frost-bitten; **tu nous gèles** * you're making us freeze. (**b**) *(Fin)* to freeze. **2 se** ~ * *vpr* to freeze. **3** *vi* (**a**) *[eau]* to freeze (over), ice over; *[sol, plante]* to freeze; *[récoltes]* to be blighted *ou* nipped by frost; *[membre]* to be frostbitten. (**b**) *(avoir froid)* to freeze. **4** *vb impers:* **il gèle** it's freezing; **il a gelé à pierre fendre** it froze hard. ◆ **gelé, e**[1] *adj public* cold, unresponsive; (*: *soûl)* tight *. ◆ **gelée**[2] *nf* (**a**) *(gel)* frost. ~ **blanche** hoarfrost. (**b**) *(Culin)* jelly.

gélifier [ʒelifje] (7) **1** *vt* to make gel. **2 se** ~ *vpr* to gel.

gélule [ʒelyl] *nf (Méd)* capsule.

gelure [ʒ(ə)lyʀ] *nf (Méd)* ~**(s)** frostbite.

Gémeaux [ʒemo] *nmpl (Astron)* Gemini.

gémir [ʒemiʀ] (2) *vi [blessé]* to groan, moan (*de* with); *[plancher]* to creak; *[vent]* to moan, whine. ◆ **gémissement** *nm*: ~**(s)** groaning; moaning; creaking; whining.

gênant, e [ʒɛnɑ̃, ɑ̃t] *adj situation, témoin* awkward, embarrassing; *révélations* embarrassing. *(irritant)* **c'est** ~ it's a nuisance.

gencive [ʒɑ̃siv] *nf* gum.

gendarme [ʒɑ̃daʀm(ə)] *nm* gendarme, policeman. **jouer aux** ~**s et aux voleurs** to play cops and robbers; ~ **mobile** member of the anti-riot police. ◆ **gendarmer (se)** (1) *vpr*: **se** ~ **pour obtenir qch** to have to take a strong line to get sth. ◆ **gendarmerie** *nf (corps)* Gendarmerie, police force; *(bureaux)* police station; *(caserne)* police barracks. ~ **mobile** anti-riot police; ~ **maritime** coastguard.

gendre [ʒɑ̃dʀ(ə)] *nm* son-in-law.

gène [ʒɛn] *nm* gene.

gêne [ʒɛn] *nf (physique)* discomfort; *(dérangement)* trouble, bother; *(manque d'argent)* financial difficulties; *(embarras)* embarrassment. **il ressentait une certaine** ~ **à respirer** he experienced some difficulty in breathing; **je ne voudrais vous causer aucune** ~ I wouldn't like to put you to any trouble *ou* bother, I wouldn't want to be a nuisance.

généalogie [ʒenealɔʒi] *nf* genealogy. ◆ **généalogique** *adj* genealogical.

gêner [ʒene] (1) **1** *vt* (**a**) *[fumée]* to bother; *[bruit]* to bother, disturb; *[vêtement étroit, obstacle]* to hamper. ~ **le passage** to be in the way; **ça me gêne pour respirer** it hampers my breathing. (**b**) *(déranger) personne* to bother; *projet* to hamper, hinder. **j'espère que ça ne vous gêne pas d'y aller** I hope it won't inconvenience you to go; **cela vous gênerait de ne pas fumer?** would you mind not smoking?; **et alors, ça te gêne?** * so what? * (**c**) *(financièrement)* to put in financial difficulties. (**d**) *(embarrasser)* ~ **qn** to make sb feel ill-at-ease *ou* uncomfortable; **ça me gêne de vous dire ça mais...** I hate to tell you but... **2 se** ~ *vpr* (**a**) *(se contraindre)* **ne vous gênez pas pour moi** don't mind me, don't put yourself out for me; **il ne faut pas vous** ~ **avec moi** don't stand on ceremony with me; **il ne s'est pas gêné pour le lui dire** he didn't mind telling him. (**b**) *(économiser)* to tighten one's belt. ◆ **gêné, e** *adj personne, air* embarrassed, self-conscious; *silence* uncomfortable, embarrassed, awkward. *(financièrement)* **être** ~ **(aux entournures)** to be short of money *ou* hard up *.

général, e, *mpl* **-aux** [ʒeneʀal, o] **1** *adj* general. **un tableau** ~ **de la situation** a general *ou* an overall picture of the situation; **dans l'intérêt** ~ in the general interest; **à la surprise ~e** to the surprise of most *ou* many people; **en ~, de façon ~e** generally, in general; **secrétaire** ~ *(gén)* general secretary; *[organisation internationale]* secretary-general. **2** *nm* general. ~ **d'armée** general; *(Aviat)* air chief marshal, general *(US)*; ~ **de brigade** brigadier; ~ **en chef** general-in-chief. **3** *nf* (**a**) *(épouse)* general's wife. (**b**) *(Théât)* **(répétition) ~e** (final) dress rehearsal. ◆ **généralement** *adv* generally, usually. ~ **parlant** generally speaking; **coutume assez** ~ **répandue** fairly widespread custom.

généraliser [ʒeneʀalize] (1) **1** *vt (gén)* to generalize; *méthode* to put *ou* bring into general use. **cancer généralisé** general cancer; *(Méd)* **infection généralisée** systemic infection. **2 se** ~ *vpr* to become widespread. ◆ **généralisable** *adj* which can be applied generally. ◆ **généralisation** *nf* generalization.

généraliste [ʒeneʀalist(ə)] *nm*: **médecin** ~ G.P., general *ou* family practitioner.

généralité [ʒeneʀalite] *nf* (**a**) *(majorité)* majority. (**b**) **~s** *(introduction)* general points; *(péj: banalités)* generalities.

générateur, -trice [ʒeneʀatœʀ, tʀis] **1** *adj* generative, generating. ~ **de désordres** which causes trouble. **2** *nf (Élec)* generator.

générer [ʒeneʀe] (6) *vt* to generate. ◆ **génération** *nf* generation.

généreux, -euse [ʒeneʀø, øz] *adj* generous. ◆ **généreusement** *adv* generously. ◆ **générosité** *nf* generosity. *(largesses)* **~s** kindnesses.

générique [ʒeneʀik] **1** *adj* generic. **2** *nm (Ciné)* credit titles, credits, cast (and credits) *(US)*.

genèse [ʒənɛz] *nf (élaboration)* genesis. *(Bible)* **(le livre de) la G~** (the Book of) Genesis.

genêt [ʒ(ə)nɛ] *nm (Bot)* broom.

génétique [ʒenetik] **1** *adj* genetic. **2** *nf* genetics *(sg)*. ◆ **généticien, -ienne** *nm, f* geneticist.

gêneur, -euse [ʒɛnœʀ, øz] *nm, f (importun)* intruder. **supprimer un** ~ to do away with a person who stands in one's way.

Genève [ʒ(ə)nɛv] *n* Geneva.

génial, e, *mpl* **-aux** [ʒenjal, o] *adj écrivain, invention* of genius; *idée* inspired; *(*: formidable)* fantastic *, tremendous *, great *. **ce n'est pas ~!** *[idée]* that's not very clever!; *[film]* it's not brilliant! *. ◆ **génialement** *adv* with genius, brilliantly.

génie [ʒeni] *nm* **1** (**a**) *(savant, talent)* genius. **avoir du** ~ to have genius; **avoir le** ~ **des affaires** to have a genius for business; **avoir le** ~ **du mal** to have an evil bent. (**b**) *(allégorie)* spirit. *[histoires arabes]* **le** ~ **de la lampe** the genie of the lamp; **le bon/mauvais** ~ **de qn** sb's good/evil genius. (**c**) *(Mil)* **le** ~ ≃ the Engineers; **soldat du** ~ engineer. **2** ~ **atomique/chimique** atomic/chemical engineering; ~ **civil** *(branche)* civil engineering; *(corps)* civil engineers; ~ **électronique** electronic engineering; ~ **génétique** genetic engineering.

genièvre [ʒənjɛvʀ(ə)] *nm (boisson)* Hollands *ou* geneva gin; *(arbre)* juniper; *(fruit)* juniper berry.

génisse [ʒenis] *nf* heifer.

génital, e, *mpl* **-aux** [ʒenital, o] *adj* genital.

génitif [ʒenitif] *nm* genitive (case).

génocide [ʒenɔsid] *nm* genocide.

genou, *pl* **~x** [ʒ(ə)nu] *nm* knee. **il était à ~x** he was kneeling, he was on his knees; **se mettre à ~x** to kneel down; *(fig)* **se mettre à ~x devant qn** to go down on one's knees to sb; **c'est à se mettre à ~x!** * it's out of this world! *; **j'en suis tombé à ~x!** * I just about dropped! *; **demander qch à (deux) ~x** to ask for sth on bended knee; **prendre qn sur ses ~x** to take sb on one's knee; **faire du** ~ **à qn** * to play footsie with sb *; **plier le** ~ **devant qn** to bend the knee to sb; **être sur les ~x** * to be ready to drop, be on one's last legs, be on one's knees *.

genre [ʒɑ̃ʀ] *nm* (**a**) *(espèce)* kind, type, sort. ~ **de vie** lifestyle, way of life; **cette maison n'est pas mauvaise en son** ~ that house isn't bad of *ou* for *(US)* its type; **ce qui se fait de mieux dans le** ~ the best of its kind; **chaussures en tout** ~ *ou* **en tous ~s** all kinds *ou* sorts of shoes; **qch du même** ~ sth of the kind; **il a écrit un** ~ **de roman** he wrote a novel of sorts. (**b**) *(allure)* manner. **avoir bon** ~ to look a nice sort; **avoir mauvais** ~ to be coarse-looking; **il a un drôle de** ~ he's a bit weird; **avoir le** ~ **artiste** to be an arty type; **faire du** ~ to stand on ceremony; **il aime se donner un** ~ he likes to stand out *ou* to be a bit different; **ce n'est pas son** ~ **de ne pas répondre** it's not like him not to answer. (**c**) *(Art)* genre; *(Gram)* gender; *(Philos, Sci)* genus. **le** ~ **humain** mankind, the human race.

gens [ʒɑ̃] *nmpl (accord féminin de l'adjectif antéposé)* people, folk; *(serviteurs)* servants. **les** ~ **de la ville** townspeople, townsfolk; **les** ~ **du pays** *ou* **du coin** * the local people, the locals; **de braves** ~ good people *ou* folk; **les** ~ **d'Église** the clergy; ~ **de lettres** men of letters; **les** ~ **de loi** † the legal profession; ~ **de maison** people in service.

gentil, -ille [ʒɑ̃ti, ij] *adj* (**a**) *(aimable)* kind, nice *(avec, pour* to). **c'est** ~ **à toi de...** it's very kind *ou* nice *ou* good of you to...; **tout ça, c'est bien** ~ **mais...** that's all very nice but...; **sois ~, va me le chercher** be a dear and go, and get it for me, would you mind going to get it for me. (**b**) *(sage)* good. **il n'a pas été** ~ he hasn't been a good boy. (**c**) *visage, endroit* nice, pleasant; *somme* tidy, fair. **c'est** ~ **comme tout chez vous** you've got a lovely little place. ◆ **gentillesse** *nf (gén)* kindness. **une** ~ **en vaut une autre** one good turn deserves another. ◆ **gentiment** *adv* kindly, nicely.

gentilhomme [ʒɑ̃tijɔm], *pl* **gentilshommes** [ʒɑ̃tizɔm] *nm* gentleman. ~ **campagnard** country squire. ◆ **gentilhommière** *nf* manor house.

génuflexion [ʒenyflɛksjɔ̃] *nf* genuflexion.

géochimie [ʒeɔʃimi] *nf* geochemistry.

géode [ʒeɔd] *nf* geode.

géodésie [ʒeɔdezi] *nf* geodesy. ◆ **géodésique** *adj* geodesic.

géographie [ʒeɔgʀafi] *nf* geography. ◆ **géographe** *nmf* geographer. ◆ **géographique** *adj* geographical.

geôle [ʒol] *nf* gaol, jail. ◆ **geôlier, -ière** *nm, f* gaoler, jailer.

géologie [ʒeɔlɔʒi] *nf* geology. ◆ **géologique** *adj* geological. ◆ **géologue** *nmf* geologist.

géométrie [ʒeɔmetʀi] *nf* geometry. ~ **dans l'espace** solid geometry; **à** ~ **variable** swing-wing. ◆ **géomètre** *nm (arpenteur)* surveyor; *(mathématicien)* geometer. ◆ **géométrique** *adj* geometrical. ◆ **géométriquement** *adv* geometrically.

géophysique [ʒeɔfizik] **1** *adj* geophysical. **2** *nf* geophisics *(sg)*. ◆ **géophysicien, -ienne** *nm, f* geophysicist.

géopolitique [ʒeɔpɔlitik] **1** *adj* geopolitical. **2** *nf* geopolitics *(sg)*.

géostationnaire [ʒeɔstasjɔnɛʀ] *adj* geostationary.

géothermique [ʒeɔtɛʀmik] *adj* geothermal.

gérance [ʒeʀɑ̃s] *nf* management. **prendre qch en** ~ to take over the management of sth; **mettre qch en** ~ to appoint a manager for sth. ◆ **gérant** *nm* manager; *[immeuble]* managing agent. ◆ **gérante** *nf* manageress.

géranium [ʒeʀanjɔm] *nm* geranium. ~**-lierre** ivy leaf geranium.

gerbe [ʒɛʀb(ə)] *nf [blé]* sheaf; *[osier]* bundle; *[preuves]* collection. ~ **de fleurs** spray of flowers; ~ **d'eau** spray *ou* shower of water; *(fusée)* **retomber en** ~ to fall in a shower *ou* burst of sparks.

gerber [ʒɛʀbe] (1) **1** *vt (Agr)* to sheave, bind into sheaves. **2** *vi* (⁑: *vomir)* to throw up ⁑, puke (up) ⁑.

gercer *vt*, **se** ~ *vpr* [ʒɛʀse] (3) *peau* to chap; *sol* to crack. ◆ **gerçure** *nf* crack.

gérer [ʒeʀe] (6) *vt* to manage. **mal** ~ to mismanage.

gerfaut [ʒɛʀfo] *nm (Orn)* gyrfalcon.

gériatrie [ʒeʀjatʀi] *nf* geriatrics *(sg)*. ◆ **gériatrique** *adj* geriatric.

germain, e [ʒɛʀmɛ̃, ɛn] *adj*: **cousin** ~ first cousin.

germe [ʒɛʀm(ə)] *nm [embryon, idée]* germ; *[pomme de terre]* eye; *[erreur, vie]* seed; *(microbe)* germ. **avoir en** ~ to contain in embryo, contain the seeds of; **cette idée est en** ~ the idea is beginning to take root. ◆ **germer** (1) *vi* to germinate. **pomme de terre germée** sprouting potato. ◆ **germination** *nf* germination.

gérondif [ʒeʀɔ̃dif] *nm* gerund.

gérontologie [ʒeʀɔ̃tɔlɔʒi] *nf* gerontology. ◆ **gérontologique** *adj* gerontological. ◆ **gérontologiste** *ou* ◆ **gérontologue** *nmf* gerontologist.

gésier [ʒezje] *nm* gizzard.

gésir [ʒeziʀ] *vi*: **il gît/gisait sur le sol** he is lying/was lying *ou* lay on the ground.

gestation [ʒɛstɑsjɔ̃] *nf* gestation. **en** ~ in gestation.

geste [ʒɛst(ə)] *nm* (**a**) *(mouvement)* gesture. **pas un** ~ **ou je tire!** one move and I'll shoot!; **faire un** ~ **de la tête** *(affirmatif)* to nod (one's head); *(négatif)* to shake one's head; **il le fit entrer d'un** ~ he motioned *ou* gestured *ou* waved to him to come in; **s'exprimer par** ~**s** to use one's hands to express o.s.; **il ne fit pas un** ~ **pour l'aider** he didn't lift a finger *ou* make a move to help him. (**b**) *(action)* act, deed; *(généreux)* gesture. **faites un** ~ make a gesture.

gesticuler [ʒɛstikyle] (1) *vi* to gesticulate. ◆ **gesticulation** *nf* gesticulation.

gestion [ʒɛstjɔ̃] *nf* management. **mauvaise** ~ mismanagement, bad management; ~ **de l'économie** economic management; ~ **des stocks** inventory control. ◆ **gestionnaire** **1** *adj* administrative, management. **2** *nmf* administrator.

gestuel, -elle [ʒɛstyɛl] **1** *adj* gestural. **2** *nf* hand movements.

geyser [ʒɛzɛʀ] *nm* geyser.

Ghana [gana] *nm* Ghana.

ghetto [gɛto] *nm* ghetto.

G I [dʒiaj] *nm (soldat américain)* G I.

gibecière [ʒibsjɛʀ] *nf (gén)* shoulder bag; *[chasseur]* gamebag; *[écolier]* satchel.

gibet [ʒibɛ] *nm* gallows.

gibier [ʒibje] *nm (lit)* game; *(fig)* prey. ~ **d'eau** waterfowl; ~ **à poil** game animals; ~ **à plume** game birds; ~ **de potence** gallows bird; *(lit, fig)* **le gros** ~ big game.

giboulée [ʒibule] *nf* (sudden) shower. ~ **de mars** April shower.

giboyeux, -euse [ʒibwajø, øz] *adj* well-stocked with game.

Gibraltar [ʒibʀaltaʀ] *nm* Gibraltar.

gicler [ʒikle] (1) *vi* to spurt. **faire** ~ **de l'eau** *(d'un robinet)* to squirt water; *[véhicule]* to send up a spray of water. ◆ **giclée** *nf* spurt. ◆ **gicleur** *nm (Aut)* jet.

gifler [ʒifle] (1) *vt*: ~ **qn** to smack sb's face, slap sb in the face. ◆ **gifle** *nf* slap in the face, box on the ear.

gigantesque [ʒigɑ̃tɛsk(ə)] *adj* gigantic, immense.

gigolo [ʒigɔlo] *nm* gigolo.

gigot [ʒigo] *nm* joint. ~ **de mouton** leg of mutton; ~ **de chevreuil** haunch of venison.

gigoter * [ʒigɔte] (1) *vi* to wriggle (about).

gilet [ʒilɛ] *nm (de complet)* waistcoat, vest *(US)*; *(cardigan)* cardigan. ~ **(de corps)** vest, undershirt *(US)*; ~ **pare-balles** bulletproof jacket, flak jacket *; ~ **de sauvetage** life jacket, life preserver *(US)*.

gin [dʒin] *nm* gin.

gingembre [ʒɛ̃ʒɑ̃bʀ(ə)] *nm* ginger.

ginseng [ʒinsɑ̃g] *nm* ginseng.

girafe [ʒiʀaf] *nf (Zool)* giraffe; *(péj: personne)* beanpole *. ◆ **girafeau** *nm* baby giraffe.

giration [ʒiʀɑsjɔ̃] *nf* gyration. ◆ **giratoire** *adj* gyrating.

girofle [ʒiʀɔfl(ə)] *nm*: **clou de** ~ clove.

giroflée [ʒiʀɔfle] *nf* wallflower.

girolle [ʒiʀɔl] *nf* chanterelle.

giron [ʒiʀɔ̃] *nm (genoux)* lap; *(fig: sein)* bosom. **enfant élevé dans le** ~ **maternel** child reared in the bosom of his family.

Gironde [ʒiʀɔ̃d] *nf*: **la** ~ the Gironde.

girouette [ʒiʀwɛt] *nf* weather cock. *(fig)* **c'est une vraie** ~ he changes (his mind) with the weather.

gisement [ʒizmɑ̃] *nm (Minér)* deposit.

gisent [ʒiz], **gît** *[ʒi] V* **gésir.**

gitan, e [ʒitɑ̃, an] **1** *adj*, **G~(e)** *nm(f)* gipsy. **2** *nf* (®: *cigarette)* Gitane.

gîte [ʒit] *nm (abri)* shelter; *(maison)* home; *[lièvre]* form; *[minerai]* deposit. **le** ~ **et le couvert** room and board, board and lodging; ~ **(à la noix)** topside.

givre [ʒivʀ(ə)] *nm* hoarfrost. ◆ **givré, e** *adj* (**a**) *arbre* covered in frost; *fenêtre, hélice* frosted-up, iced-up; *verre* frosted. (**b**) (*) *(ivre)* tight *; *(fou)* cracked ⁑, nuts ⁑. **devenir complètement** ~ * to go completely off one's head *ou* rocker ⁑. ◆ **givrer** *vt*, **se** ~ *vpr* (1) to frost up, ice up.

glaçage [glasaʒ] *nm [papier, aliment]* glazing; *(au sucre)* icing.

glace [glas] *nf* (**a**) *(eau)* ice. *(lit, fig)* **briser la** ~ to break the ice; *(Géog)* ~**s** ice sheets *ou* fields; ~**s flottantes** ice floes; **bloqué par les** ~**s** *canal* blocked with ice; *bateau* icebound. (**b**) *(Culin)* ice cream. ~ **à l'eau** water ice, sherbet *(US)*; ~ **à la crème**

dairy ice cream, iced-milk ice cream *(US)*; ~ **à l'italienne** soft ice cream. (**c**) *(miroir)* mirror. (**d**) *(plaque de verre)* sheet of plate glass; *[vitrine]* glass; *[véhicule]* window.

glacer [glase] (3) **1** *vt* (**a**) *liquide (geler)* to freeze; *(rafraîchir)* to chill, ice. **mettre à** ~ to put to chill; **ce vent glace les oreilles** this wind is freezing to the ears *ou* freezes your ears. (**b**) ~ **qn** *(lit, fig: réfrigérer)* to turn sb cold; *(paralyser)* to make sb's blood run cold; **glacé d'horreur** frozen with horror. (**c**) *papier, aliment* to glaze; *(au sucre)* to ice. **2 se** ~ *vpr (lit, fig)* to freeze. ◆ **glacé, e** *adj lac* frozen; *vent, chambre* icy, freezing; *boisson* iced, ice-cold; *papier* glazed; *fruit* glacé; *accueil* icy, frosty. **je suis** ~ I'm frozen (stiff); **j'ai les mains ~es** my hands are 2 frozen *ou* freezing; **à servir** ~ serve iced *ou* ice-cold; **café** ~ iced coffee.

glaciaire [glasjɛʀ] *adj période, calotte* ice; *relief* glacial.

glacial, e, *mpl* ~**s** *ou* **-aux** [glasjal, o] *adj* icy, freezing; *(fig)* icy, frosty.

glaciation [glasjɑsjɔ̃] *nf* glaciation.

glacier [glasje] *nm* (**a**) *(Géog)* glacier. (**b**) *(fabricant)* ice-cream maker; *(vendeur)* ice-cream man.

glacière [glasjɛʀ] *nf (lit, fig)* icebox.

glaciologie [glasjɔlɔʒi] *nf* glaciology. ◆ **glaciologique** *adj* glaciological. ◆ **glaciologue** *nmf* glaciologist.

glaçon [glasɔ̃] *nm [rivière]* block of ice; *[toit]* icicle; *[boisson]* ice cube; *(péj: personne)* iceberg. **un whisky avec des** ~**s** a whisky on the rocks.

gladiateur [gladjatœʀ] *nm* gladiator.

glaïeul [glajœl] *nm* gladiolus.

glaire [glɛʀ] *nf [œuf]* white; *(Méd)* phlegm.

glaise [glɛz] *nf* clay. ◆ **glaiseux, -euse** *adj* clayey.

gland [glɑ̃] *nm (Bot)* acorn; *(ornement)* tassel. (‡: *imbécile)* **quel** ~! what a prick! ‡

glande [glɑ̃d] *nf* gland. ◆ **glandulaire** *adj* glandular.

glaner [glane] (1) *vt (lit, fig)* to glean. ◆ **glaneur, -euse** *nm, f* gleaner.

glapir [glapiʀ] (2) *vi (lit, fig)* to yelp. ◆ **glapissement** *nm*: ~**(s)** yelping.

glas [glɑ] *nm* knell. **on sonne le** ~ they are tolling the knell.

glauque [glok] *adj yeux, eau* dull blue-green.

glissade [glisad] *nf (par jeu)* slide; *(chute)* slip; *(dérapage)* skid; *(Danse)* glissade.

glissant, e [glisɑ̃, ɑ̃t] *adj* slippery.

glisse [glis] *nf (Ski)* glide.

glissement [glismɑ̃] *nm*: ~ **électoral** electoral swing; ~ **de sens** shift in meaning; ~ **de terrain** landslide, landslip.

glisser [glise] (1) **1** *vi* (**a**) *(gén)* to slide; *[voilier, nuages]* to glide along. **il fit** ~ **le fauteuil sur le sol** he slid the armchair along the floor; **il se laissa** ~ **le long du mur** he slid down the wall; **une larme glissa le long de sa joue** a tear trickled *ou* slid down his cheek; **le pays glisse vers l'anarchie/la droite** the country is slipping *ou* sliding towards anarchy/is moving *ou* swinging towards the right. (**b**) *(déraper) [personne]* to slip; *[véhicule]* to skid; *[parquet]* to be slippery. **il m'a fait** ~ he made me slip. (**c**) *(échapper de)* ~ **de la table/des mains** to slip *ou* slide off the table/out of one's hands; **le voleur leur a glissé entre les mains** the thief slipped (right) through their fingers. (**d**) *(effleurer)* **ses doigts glissaient sur les touches** his fingers slipped over the keys; **les reproches glissent sur lui** reproaches roll off him; ~ **sur un sujet** to skate over a subject; **la balle glissa sur le blindage** the bullet glanced off the armour plating. **2** *vt (introduire)* ~ **qch sous/dans qch** to slip *ou* slide sth under/into sth; **il me glissa un regard en coulisse** he gave me a sidelong glance; **il me glissa que...** he whispered to me that... **3 se** ~ *vpr*: **se** ~ **dans** *[personne]* to slip into; *[soupçon, erreur]* to creep into; **se** ~ **dans les draps** to slip *ou* slide between the sheets; **le voleur se glissa dans la maison** the thief slipped *ou* sneaked into the house; **se** ~ **jusqu'au premier rang** to edge *ou* worm one's way to the front.

glissière [glisjɛʀ] *nf* groove; *(Aut) [siège]* runner. **porte à** ~ sliding door; ~ **de sécurité** crash barrier.

global, e, *mpl* **-aux** [glɔbal, o] *adj (gén)* overall; *somme* global, total, aggregate; *vue* global, comprehensive. **méthode** ~**e** word recognition method *(of teaching reading)*. ◆ **globalement** *adv (en bloc)* globally; *(dans son ensemble)* taken as a whole. ~ **nous sommes tous d'accord** overall *ou* in the main we are in agreement.

globe [glɔb] *nm* globe. ~ **oculaire** eyeball; **le** ~ **terrestre** the globe; *(fig)* **mettre qn/qch sous** ~ to keep sb/sth in cotton wool, keep sb/sth in a glass case.

globine [glɔbin] *nf* globin.

globule [glɔbyl] *nm (gén, Chim)* globule. ~**s rouges/blancs** red/white corpuscles. ◆ **globulaire** *adj* global; corpuscular. ◆ **globuleux, -euse** *adj forme* globular; *œil* protruding.

globuline [glɔbylin] *nf* globulin.

gloire [glwaʀ] *nf* (**a**) *(renommée)* glory, fame; *(Rel: éclat)* glory. **en pleine** ~ at the height of one's fame; **couvert de** ~ covered in glory; **elle a eu son heure de** ~ she has had her hour of glory; **pour la** ~ for the glory of it. (**b**) *(distinction)* **sa plus grande** ~ **a été de faire** his greatest distinction *ou* his greatest claim to fame was to do; **s'attribuer toute la** ~ **de qch** to give o.s. all the credit for sth; **tirer** ~ **de qch** to vaunt sth; **il s'en fait** ~! he's proud of it! (**c**) *(louange)* glory, praise. ~ **à Dieu** glory to God, praise be to God; **à la** ~ **de** in praise of; **célébrer la** ~ **de** to sing the praises of. (**d**) *(personne: célébrité)* celebrity. ◆ **glorieusement** *adv* gloriously. ◆ **glorieux, -euse** *adj* glorious; *(fier)* proud.

glorifier [glɔʀifje] (7) **1** *vt* to glorify. **2 se** ~ *vpr*: **se** ~ **de** to glory in, take great pride in. ◆ **glorification** *nf* glorification.

gloriole [glɔʀjɔl] *nf* vainglory.

glossaire [glɔsɛʀ] *nm* glossary.

glotte [glɔt] *nf* glottis. **coup de** ~ glottal stop.

glouglou [gluglu] *nm [eau]* gurgling; *[dindon]* gobble-gobble. **faire** ~ to gurgle; to gobble.

glousser [gluse] (1) *vi [personne]* to chuckle; *[poule]* to cluck. ◆ **gloussement** *nm* chuckle; cluck.

glouton, -onne [glutɔ̃, ɔn] **1** *adj personne* gluttonous; *appétit* voracious. **2** *nm, f* glutton. ◆ **gloutonnement** *adv* gluttonously; voraciously. ◆ **gloutonnerie** *nf* gluttony.

glu [gly] *nf (pour oiseaux)* birdlime. **on dirait de la** ~ it's like glue; *(fig: personne)* **quelle** ~ **ce type!** * what a leech the guy is! *. ◆ **gluant, e** *adj (substance)* sticky, gummy; *(fig: répugnant) personne* slimy.

glucose [glykoz] *nm* glucose.

glycérine [gliseʀin] *nf*, **glycérol** [gliseʀɔl] *nm* glycerine, glycerol.

glycéropthalique [gliseʀɔftalik] *adj*: **peinture** ~ oil-based paint.

glycine [glisin] *nf (plante)* wisteria.

gnangnan * [ɲɑ̃ɲɑ̃] *nmf* moan *, drip *.

gnognote * [ɲɔɲɔt] *nf*: **c'est de la** ~! it's rubbish!

gnôle * [ɲol] *nf* hooch *. **un petit verre de** ~ a snifter ‡, a dram *.

gnome [gnom] *nm* gnome.

gnon * [ɲɔ̃] *nm* blow, bash *. **prendre un** ~ *ou* **des** ~**s** to get bashed *.

go [go] **1** *nm (jeu)* go. **2** *loc adv*: **tout de ~** *dire* straight out; *aller* straightaway.

goal [gol] *nm* goalkeeper, goalie *.

gobelet [gɔblɛ] *nm [enfant]* beaker; *[étain]* tumbler; *[dés]* cup. ~ **en papier** paper cup.

gober [gɔbe] (1) *vt œuf, mensonge* to swallow. **je ne peux pas le ~** * I can't stand him; **ne reste pas là à ~ les mouches** don't just stand there gawping.

godasse * [gɔdas] *nf* shoe.

godet [gɔdɛ] *nm (gén)* pot; *(*: verre)* glass.

godiche [gɔdiʃ] *adj (péj)* lumpish, oafish.

godille [gɔdij] *nf (Sport)* scull. *(*: péj)* **à la ~** *système* ropey *, crappy * *(US)*.

godillot * [gɔdijo] *nm* boot.

goéland [gɔelɑ̃] *nm* seagull, gull.

goélette [gɔelɛt] *nf* schooner.

goémon [gɔemɔ̃] *nm* wrack.

gogo * [gɔgo] **1** *nm* sucker *, mug ⁑. **c'est bon pour les ~s** it's a mug's game ⁑. **2** *adv*: **du vin** *etc* **à ~** wine *etc* galore.

goguenard, e [gɔgnaʀ, aʀd(ə)] *adj* mocking.

goguette * [gɔgɛt] *nf*: **être en ~** to be on the binge *, be on a spree.

goinfre * [gwɛ̃fʀ(ə)] *(glouton)* **1** *adj* piggish *. **2** *nm* pig *. ◆ **se goinfrer** * (1) *vpr* to make a pig of o.s. *. **se ~ de** to guzzle. ◆ **goinfrerie** * *nf* piggishness *.

goitre [gwatʀ(ə)] *nm* goitre.

golden [gɔldɛn] *nf inv* Golden Delicious.

golf [gɔlf] *nm (Sport)* golf; *(terrain)* golf course *ou* links. ~ **miniature** miniature golf.

golfe [gɔlf(ə)] *nm* gulf; *(petit)* bay. **le ~ Arabique** the Arabian Gulf; **le ~ de Gascogne** the Bay of Biscay; **le ~ du Lion** the Gulf of Lions; **le ~ du Mexique** the Gulf of Mexico; **le ~ Persique** the Persian Gulf; **les États du G~** the Gulf States.

gomme [gɔm] *nf (substance)* gum; *(pour effacer)* rubber, eraser *(US)*. **mettre toute la ~** * to step on the gas, put one's foot right down *; **à la ~** * useless, hopeless. ◆ **gommer** (1) *vt mot* to rub out, erase; *(fig)* to erase. **papier gommé** gummed paper. ◆ **gommage** *nm* rubbing-out; erasing.

gond [gɔ̃] *nm* hinge.

gondole [gɔ̃dɔl] *nf* gondola. ◆ **gondolier, -ière** *nm, f* gondolier.

gondoler [gɔ̃dɔle] (1) **1** *vi [papier]* to crinkle; *[planche]* to warp; *[tôle]* to buckle. **2 se ~** *vpr* to crinkle; to warp; to buckle; *(*: rire)* to split one's sides laughing *. ◆ **gondolant, e** * *adj* side-splitting *, hilarious.

gonflant, e [gɔ̃flɑ̃, ɑ̃t] **1** *adj coiffure* bouffant. **2** *nm*: **donner du ~ à ses cheveux** to give body to one's hair.

gonfler [gɔ̃fle] (1) **1** *vt* (**a**) *ballon etc (gén)* to inflate; *(avec pompe)* to pump up; *(en soufflant)* to blow up; *joues, narines* to puff out; *poumons* to fill (*de* with). (**b**) *rivière, voiles* to swell. **un paquet gonflait sa poche** his pocket was bulging with a package; **gonflé d'eau** swollen with water; **ça me gonfle l'estomac** it makes me feel bloated; **gonflé d'orgueil** *personne* puffed up (with pride); *cœur* swollen with pride; **cœur gonflé de joie** heart bursting with joy; **il nous les gonfle!** ⁑ he gets on our wick! ⁑, he's a pain in the butt! ⁑ (**c**) *prix, résultat* to inflate; *effectif (augmenter)* to swell; *(exagérer)* to exaggerate. **chiffres gonflés** inflated *ou* exaggerated figures. **2** *vi [cheville, bois]* to swell; *[pâte]* to rise. **faire ~ le riz** to leave the rice to swell. **3 se ~** *vpr* to swell. **son cœur se gonfle (de tristesse)** his heart is heavy (with sorrow). ◆ **gonflable** *adj* inflatable. ◆ **gonflage** *nm* inflation. ◆ **gonflé, e** *adj* (**a**) *yeux, visage* puffy, swollen. **joues bien ~es** chubby cheeks; **je me sens ~** I feel bloated. (**b**) *(* fig)* **il est ~!** *(courageux)* he's got some nerve! *; *(impertinent)* he's got a nerve! * *ou* some cheek! *; **être ~ à bloc** to be raring to go *. ◆ **gonflement** *nm* inflation; swelling; exaggeration. ◆ **gonfleur** *nm* air pump.

gong [gɔ̃(g)] *nm (Mus)* gong; *(Boxe)* bell.

gorge [gɔʀʒ(ə)] *nf* (**a**) *(gosier)* throat; *(poitrine)* breast. **avoir la ~ sèche** to have a dry throat; **avoir la ~ serrée** *ou* **nouée** to have a lump in one's throat; **à ~ déployée** *rire* heartily; *chanter* at the top of one's voice; **prendre qn à la ~** *[créancier]* to put a gun to sb's head *(fig)*; *[agresseur]* to grab sb by the throat; *[fumée]* to get in sb's throat; *[peur]* to grip sb by the throat; *(fig)* **ça lui est resté en travers de la ~** he found it hard to take, he couldn't swallow it. (**b**) *(vallée, défilé)* gorge. (**c**) *(rainure) [poulie]* groove; *[serrure]* tumbler.

gorgée [gɔʀʒe] *nf* mouthful. **boire son vin à grandes/petites ~s** to gulp down/sip one's wine; **d'une seule ~** in one gulp.

gorger [gɔʀʒe] (3) **1** *vt* to fill, stuff (*de* with). **gorgé d'eau** saturated with *ou* full of water; **gorgé de soleil** bursting with sunshine. **2 se ~** *vpr* to gorge o.s., stuff o.s. * (*de* with).

gorille [gɔʀij] *nm* gorilla; *(*: garde)* bodyguard.

gosier [gozje] *nm* throat.

gospel [gɔspɛl] *nm* gospel (music).

gosse * [gɔs] *nmf* kid *. **sale ~** little brat *.

gothique [gɔtik] *adj* Gothic. **écriture ~** Gothic script.

gouache [gwaʃ] *nf* gouache.

goudron [gudʀɔ̃] *nm* tar. ◆ **goudronner** (1) *vt route* to tar.

gouffre [gufʀ(ə)] *nm (Géog)* abyss, gulf. **le ~ de l'oubli** the depths of oblivion; **c'est un ~ d'ignorance** he's abysmally ignorant; **au bord du ~** on the brink of the abyss.

goujat [guʒa] *nm* boor. ◆ **goujaterie** *nf* boorishness.

goulag [gulag] *nm* Gulag. **(Archipel du) ~** Gulag Archipelago.

goulée [gule] *nf* gulp. ~ **d'air frais** gulp *ou* lungful of fresh air.

goulet [gulɛ] *nm (Naut)* narrows; *(Géog)* gully. ~ **d'étranglement** bottleneck.

goulot [gulo] *nm [bouteille]* neck. **boire au ~** to drink straight from the bottle; *(fig)* ~ **d'étranglement** bottleneck.

goulu, e [guly] **1** *adj* greedy, gluttonous. **2** *nm, f* glutton. ◆ **goulûment** *adv* greedily, gluttonously.

goupille [gupij] *nf (Tech)* pin.

goupiller [gupije] (1) **1** *vt* (**a**) *(*: combiner)* to fix *. **bien/mal goupillé** *machine* well/badly thought out. (**b**) *(Tech)* to pin. **2 se ~** * *vpr* to work. **comment est-ce que ça se goupille pour demain?** what's the setup * for tomorrow?

goupillon [gupijɔ̃] *nm (Rel)* sprinkler; *(à bouteille)* bottle brush.

gourd, e[1] [guʀ, guʀd(ə)] *adj* numb (with cold).

gourde[2] [guʀd(ə)] **1** *nf (Bot)* gourd; *(à eau)* flask; *(*: empoté)* clot *. **2** *adj* (*) thick *, thick-headed * *(US)*.

gourdin [guʀdɛ̃] *nm* club, bludgeon.

gourer (se) ⁑ [guʀe] (1) *vpr* to boob ⁑, slip up. **se ~ de numéro** to boob ⁑ over the number; **se ~ dans** to boob in ⁑.

gourmand, e [guʀmɑ̃, ɑ̃d] **1** *adj (lit, fig)* greedy (*de* for). **2** *nm, f* gourmand. **3** *nm (Agr)* sucker. ◆ **gourmandise** *nf* (**a**) greed, greediness. (**b**) *(gâterie)* delicacy, titbit.

gourmet [guʀmɛ] *nm* gourmet.

gourmette [guʀmɛt] *nf [poignet]* chain bracelet.

gousse [gus] *nf [vanille etc]* pod. ~ **d'ail** clove of garlic.

gousset [gusɛ] *nm [gilet]* fob; *[slip]* gusset.

goût [gu] *nm* (**a**) *(sens)* taste. **ça a mauvais** ~ it has a bad taste, it tastes nasty; **ça a un** ~ **de fraise** it tastes like strawberry, it has a strawberry taste *ou* flavour; **la soupe a un** ~ the soup has a funny taste; **sans** ~ tasteless, flavourless. (**b**) *(jugement)* taste. **sans/avec** ~ tastelessly/tastefully; **elle s'habille avec beaucoup de** ~ she has very good taste in dress, she has very good dress sense; **à mon/son** ~ for my/his liking *ou* my/his taste; **de bon** ~ tasteful, in good taste; **de mauvais** ~ tasteless, in bad *ou* poor taste; *(iro)* **il serait de bon** ~ **d'y aller** it would be as well to go. (**c**) *(penchant)* taste, liking (*de, pour* for). **il n'a aucun** ~ **pour les sciences** the sciences don't appeal to him, he has no taste for *ou* he is not keen on the sciences; **prendre** ~ **à qch** to get a taste for sth, get to like sth; **il n'avait** ~ **à rien** he didn't feel like (doing) anything; **il la trouve à son** ~ she suits his taste; **avoir des** ~**s modestes** to have simple tastes; **tous les** ~**s sont dans la nature** it takes all sorts to make a world. (**d**) *(style)* style. **dans le** ~ **classique** in the classical style; **ou qch dans ce** ~**-là** * or sth of that sort; **se mettre au** ~ **du jour** to bring o.s. into line with current tastes.

goûter [gute] (1) **1** *vt aliment* to taste; *repos, spectacle* to enjoy; *plaisanterie* to appreciate. **2** ~**à** *vt indir aliment, plaisir* to taste, sample. **il y a à peine goûté** he's hardly touched it. **3** ~ **de** *vt indir* to have a taste of. **4** *vi (manger)* to have tea, have an afterschool snack *(US)*. **5** *nm* (afterschool) snack. **donner un** ~ to give a tea party, invite children for a snack *(US)*.

goûteur, -euse [gutœʀ, øz] *nm, f*: ~ **d'eau** *etc* water *etc* taster.

goutte [gut] *nf* (**a**) *(lit, fig)* drop. ~ **de rosée** dewdrop; ~ **de sueur** bead of sweat; **pleuvoir à grosses** ~**s** to rain heavily; **il est tombé quelques** ~**s** a few spots *ou* drops of rain have fallen; **tomber** ~ **à** ~ to drip. (**b**) *(*: eau-de-vie)* **prendre la** ~ to have a nip *. (**c**) *(Méd)* gout. (**d**) **avoir la** ~ **au nez** to have a running nose; **c'est une** ~ **d'eau dans la mer** it's a drop in the ocean *ou* bucket; **c'est la** ~ **(d'eau) qui fait déborder le vase** it's the last straw (that breaks the camel's back). ◆ **goutte-à-goutte** *nm inv* drip, IV *(US)*. **faire du** ~**-à-**~ **à qn** to put sb on the drip. ◆ **gouttelette** *nf* droplet. ◆ **goutter** (1) *vi* to drip (*de* from).

gouttière [gutjɛʀ] *nf (horizontale)* gutter; *(verticale)* drainpipe; *(Méd)* (plaster) cast.

gouvernable [guvɛʀnabl(ə)] *adj* governable. **difficilement** ~ difficult to govern.

gouvernail [guvɛʀnaj] *nm (pale)* rudder; *(barre)* helm, tiller. *(fig)* **tenir le** ~ to be at the helm.

gouvernante [guvɛʀnɑ̃t] *nf (institutrice)* governess; *(intendante)* housekeeper.

gouvernants [guvɛʀnɑ̃] *nmpl (Pol)* **les** ~ the government.

gouverne [guvɛʀn(ə)] *nf*: **pour ta** ~ for your guidance.

gouvernement [guvɛʀnəmɑ̃] *nm (régime)* government; *(cabinet)* Cabinet, Government. **sous un** ~ **socialiste** under socialist rule *ou* government. ◆ **gouvernemental, e,** *mpl* **-aux** *adj député* of the governing party; *politique* government, governmental; *journal* pro-government; *troupes* government. **le parti** ~ the party in office.

gouverner [guvɛʀne] (1) **1** *vt* (**a**) *(Pol)* to govern, rule; *(fig: contrôler)* to control. **le parti qui gouverne** the party in power *ou* in office; **l'intérêt gouverne le monde** self-interest rules the world. (**b**) *(Naut)* to steer. (**c**) *(Gram)* to govern, take. **2 se** ~ *vpr [peuple]* to govern it's own affairs; *[personne]* to control o.s.

gouverneur [guvɛʀnœʀ] *nm* governor.

goyave [gɔjav] *nf (fruit)* guava. ◆ **goyavier** *nm (arbres)* guava.

Graal [gʀɑl] *nm* Grail.

grabat [gʀaba] *nm* pallet. ◆ **grabataire** *adj* bedridden.

grabuge * [gʀabyʒ] *nm*: **il va y avoir du** ~ there'll be a rumpus * *ou* a ruckus * *(US)*; **faire du** ~ to create havoc *ou* mayhem.

grâce [gʀɑs] *nf* (**a**) *(charme) [personne]* grace; *[paysage]* charm. **plein de** ~ graceful; **faire des** ~**s** to put on airs and graces. (**b**) *(faveur)* favour. **il nous a fait la** ~ **d'accepter** he did us the honour of accepting; **être dans les bonnes** ~**s de qn** to be in sb's good books; **rentrer en** ~ to come back into favour, come in from the cold; **gagner les bonnes** ~**s de qn** to gain sb's favour; **donner à qn une semaine de** ~ to give sb a week's grace; ~ **à qn/qch** thanks to sb/sth; ~ **à Dieu!** thank God, thank goodness! (**c**) **de** *ou* **avec bonne/mauvaise** ~ with (a) good/bad grace; **il a eu la bonne** ~ **de** he had the grace to; **il aurait mauvaise** ~ **à refuser** it would be in bad taste for him to refuse. (**d**) *(miséricorde)* mercy; *(Jur)* pardon. **crier** ~ to beg *ou* cry for mercy; ~! (have) mercy!; **de** ~ for pity's sake, for goodness' sake; **je vous fais** ~ **des détails** I'll spare you the details. (**e**) *(Rel)* grace; *(fig: don)* gift. *(fig)* **c'est la** ~ **que nous lui souhaitons** that is what we wish for him; **à la** ~ **de Dieu!** it's in God's hands!; **nous réussirons par la** ~ **de Dieu** with God's blessing we shall succeed. (**f**) *(déesse)* **les trois G**~**s** the three Graces. (**g**) *(titre)* **Sa G**~... *(homme)* His Grace...; *(femme)* Her Grace...

gracier [gʀasje] (7) *vt* to pardon.

gracieux, -ieuse [gʀasjø, jøz] *adj (élégant)* graceful; *(aimable)* kindly; *(gratuit)* gratuitous. **notre** ~**euse souveraine** our gracious sovereign. ◆ **gracieusement** *adv* gracefully; kindly; *(gratuitement)* free of charge. ◆ **gracieuseté** *nf (amabilité)* kindliness; *(geste élégant)* graceful gesture; *(cadeau)* free gift.

gracile [gʀasil] *adj* slender.

gradation [gʀadɑsjɔ̃] *nf* gradation.

grade [gʀad] *nm (Admin, Mil)* rank; *(diplôme)* degree; *(Mil, Tech)* grade. **monter en** ~ to be promoted; **en prendre pour son** ~ * to get a proper dressing-down *. ◆ **gradé** *nm (gén)* officer.

gradin [gʀadɛ̃] *nm (Théât)* tier; *[stade]* step (of the terracing); *(Agr)* terrace. **en** ~**s** terraced.

graduer [gʀadɥe] (1) *vt difficultés* to increase gradually; *thermomètre* to graduate. ◆ **graduation** *nf* graduation. ◆ **gradué, e** *adj exercices* graded; *règle* graduated. ◆ **graduel, -elle** *adj progression* gradual; *difficultés* progressive. ◆ **graduellement** *adv* gradually.

graffiti [gʀafiti] *nmpl* graffiti. **un** ~ a piece of graffiti, a (scribbled) slogan.

grain [gʀɛ̃] *nm* (**a**) *[blé, sable]* grain; *[café]* bean; *[poussière]* speck; *[chapelet]* bead. *(fig)* ~ **de vérité** *etc* grain of truth *etc*; **alcool de** ~**(s)** grain alcohol; *(Rel)* **le bon** ~ the good seed; ~ **de raisin** grape; ~ **de poivre** peppercorn; ~ **de groseille/ cassis** red currant/blackcurrant (berry); ~ **de beauté** mole, beauty spot; **mettre son** ~ **de sel** * to put one's oar in *; **un** ~ **de fantaisie** a touch of fantasy; **un** ~ **de bon sens** a grain *ou* an ounce of common sense; **il n'y a pas un** ~ **de vérité dans ce qu'il dit** there's not a grain *ou* scrap of truth in what he says; **il a un (petit)** ~ he's a bit touched *. (**b**) *(texture)* grain. **à gros** ~**s** coarsegrained. (**c**) *(averse)* heavy shower; *(bourrasque)* squall.

graine [gʀɛn] *nf (Agr)* seed. **prends-en de la** ~ * take a leaf out of his (*ou* her) book *. ◆ **graineterie**

nf (commerce) seed trade; *(magasin)* seed shop. ◆ **grainetier, -ière** *nm, f* seed merchant.

graisse [gʀɛs] *nf (gén)* fat; *(lubrifiant)* grease. ◆ **graissage** *nm* greasing. *(Aut)* **faire faire un ~** to have a lubricating job done. ◆ **graisser** (1) *vt (gén)* to grease; *(salir)* to get grease on. *(fig)* **~ la patte à qn *** to grease sb's palm. ◆ **graisseux, -euse** *adj objet* greasy; *tumeur* fatty.

grammaire [gʀamɛʀ] *nf* grammar. **règle de ~** grammatical rule; **livre de ~** grammar book. ◆ **grammairien, -ienne** *nm, f* grammarian. ◆ **grammatical, e,** *mpl* **-aux** *adj* grammatical. ◆ **grammaticalité** *nf* grammaticality. ◆ **grammaticalement** *adv* grammatically.

gramme [gʀam] *nm* gramme. **il n'a pas un ~ de jugeote** he hasn't an ounce of commonsense.

grand, e [gʀɑ̃, gʀɑ̃d] **1** *adj* (**a**) *(gén)* big; *(haut)* tall; *(important, remarquable)* great; *distance* long; *quantité* large; *(lit, fig) marge* wide; *bruit* loud; *vent* strong, high; *chaleur* intense; *soupir* deep; *dégâts* extensive. **plus ~ que nature** larger than life; **ouvrir la fenêtre toute ~e** to open the window wide; **la ~e majorité des gens** the great *ou* vast majority of people; **le ~ capital** big investors; **les ~s esprits se rencontrent** great minds think alike. (**b**) *(plus âgé)* **son ~ frère** his big *ou* older *ou* elder brother; **ils ont 2 ~s enfants** they have 2 grown-up children; **il est assez ~ pour savoir** he's big *ou* old enough to know; **les ~es classes** the senior forms. (**c**) *(principal)* main. **c'est la ~e question** *(problème)* it's the main *ou* major issue *ou* question; *(interrogation)* it's the big question. (**d**) *(intensif) travailleur* hard; *collectionneur, ami, menteur* great; *buveur* heavy; *mangeur* big. **~e jeunesse** extreme youth; **~ âge** great age, old age; **un ~ mois** a good month; **un ~ panier de champignons** a full basket of mushrooms; **les ~s malades** the seriously ill; **un ~ invalide** a seriously disabled person; **de ~s mots** high-sounding words; **prendre de ~s airs** to put on airs, give o.s. airs. (**e**) *(de gala) dîner* grand. **en ~e pompe** with great pomp; **en ~e tenue** in full dress. (**f**) *(noble) âme* noble, great. **se montrer ~ (et généreux)** to be big-hearted *ou* magnanimous. (**g**) *(locutions)* **~-chose**: **cela ne vaut pas ~-chose** it's not worth much, it's not up to much *; **il n'y a pas ~-chose à dire** there's nothing much to say; **à ma ~e surprise** much to my surprise, to my great surprise; **de ~e classe** *produit* high-class; *œuvre* admirable; **de ~ cœur** wholeheartedly; **le groupe au ~ complet** the whole group; **à ~s cris** vociferously; **de ~e envergure** *opération* large-scale; *auteur* of great stature; *réforme* far-reaching; **à ~s frais** at great expense; **au ~ jour** *(lit)* in broad daylight; *(fig)* in the open; **de ~ matin** very early in the morning; **en ~e partie** largely; **à ~-peine** with great difficulty; **à ~ renfort de** *publicité* with the help of much; *arguments* with the help of many; **à ~ spectacle** *revue* spectacular; **boire qch à ~s traits** to take big gulps of sth. (**h**) *(beaucoup de)* **avoir ~e allure** to look very impressive; **cela te fera (le plus) ~ bien** that'll do you the world of good; **~ bien vous fasse!** much good may it do you!; **faire ~ bruit** to cause quite a stir; **faire ~ cas de** to attach great importance to, set great store by; **il n'y a pas ~ monde** there aren't very many (people) here; **avoir ~-peine à faire qch** to have great difficulty in doing sth. (**i**) *(bien, très)* **avoir ~ avantage à** to be well advised to; **il a ~ besoin d'un bain** he is in great need of a bath, he badly needs a bath; **elle avait ~e envie de faire** she very much wanted to do, she was longing to do; **avoir ~ faim** to be very hungry; **il fait ~ jour** it's broad daylight; **avoir ~ peur** to be very much afraid; **il est ~ temps de faire ceci** it's high time this was done.

2 *adv*: **voir ~** to think big *; **il a vu trop ~** he was over-ambitious; **ces souliers chaussent ~** these shoes are big-fitting *ou* run large *(US)*; **faire qch en ~** to do sth on a large scale *ou* in a big way; **ouvrir (tout) ~ la fenêtre** to open the window wide.

3 *nm* (**a**) *(Scol)* older *ou* bigger *ou* senior boy. **pour petits et ~s** for old and young alike, for the young and the not-so-young; **aller à l'école tout seul comme un ~** to go to school on one's own like a big boy. (**b**) *(terme d'affection)* **mon ~** son, my lad. (**c**) **les ~s de ce monde** those in high places; *(Pol)* **les quatre G~s** the Big Four. (**d**) **Pierre** *etc* **le G~** Peter *etc* the Great.

4 *nf* older *ou* bigger *ou* senior girl. *(terme d'affection)* **ma ~e** (my) dear.

5 : **le ~ air** the open air; *(Phot)* **~ angle** wide-angle lens; *(Aut)* **~s axes** (main) trunk roads, main highways *(US)*; **la ~e banlieue** the outer suburbs; **la G~e Barrière (de Corail)** the Great Barrier Reef; **la G~e-Bretagne** Great Britain; **~ chef** big boss; *(Scol)* **les ~es classes** the senior forms, the high school grades *(US)*; **~-duc** *nm, pl* **~s-~s** *(prince)* grand duke; *(Orn)* eagle owl; **les ~es eaux de Versailles** the fountains of Versailles; **le ~ écart** the splits; **la ~e échelle (des pompiers)** the (firemen's) big (turntable) ladder; *(Univ)* **~e école** grande école, *school of university level with competitive entrance examination; (Scol)* **être à la ~e école *** to be at primary school; **~ électeur** *(en France) elector who votes in the elections for the French Senate; (aux USA)* presidential elector; *(Ciné)* **le ~ écran** the big screen; **~ ensemble** housing scheme; **le ~ film *** the main film; **les G~s Lacs** the Great Lakes; **le ~ large** the high seas; **~ magasin** department store; **~ manitou *** big boss *; **~ mât** mainmast; **~-mère** *nf, pl* **~s-~s** grandmother; *(*: vieille dame)* granny *; **~-messe** *nf, pl* **~-~s** high mass; **le ~ monde** high society; **la G~e Muraille de Chine** the Great Wall of China; **le G~ Nord** the far North; **~-oncle** *nm, pl* **~s-~s** great-uncle; **~s-parents** *nmpl* grandparents; **~-père** *nm, pl* **~s-~s** grandfather; *(*: vieux monsieur)* old man; **~e personne** grown-up; **les G~es Plaines** the Great Plains; **~ prêtre** high priest; **le ~ public** the general public; *(Pol)* **~e puissance** major power, superpower; G~ **Quartier Général** General Headquarters; **la ~-rue** the high *ou* main street; **~e surface** hypermarket; **~-tante** *nf, pl* **~s-~s** great-aunt; **~ teint** *adj inv* colourfast; **les ~es vacances** the summer holidays *ou* vacation *(US)*; *(Univ)* the long vacation; **~-voile** *nf, pl* **~s-~s** mainsail.

grandement [gʀɑ̃dmɑ̃] *adv*: **se tromper ~** to be greatly mistaken; **avoir ~ tort** to be absolutely wrong; **il a ~ le temps** he has plenty of time; **nous ne sommes pas ~ logés** we haven't (very) much room; **il est ~ temps de partir** it's high time we went.

grandeur [gʀɑ̃dœʀ] *nf* (**a**) *[objet]* size; *[sacrifice]* greatness. **~ nature** life-size; *(fig)* **de première ~** of the first order. (**b**) *(gloire, dignité)*, greatness; *(magnanimité)* magnanimity. **~ d'âme** nobility of soul; **~ et décadence de** rise and fall of; **politique de ~** politics of grandeur.

grandiloquent, e [gʀɑ̃dilɔkɑ̃, ɑ̃t] *adj* grandiloquent, bombastic.

grandiose [gʀɑ̃djoz] *adj* grandiose.

grandir [gʀɑ̃diʀ] (2) **1** *vi (en taille)* to grow; *(en importance)* to grow, increase; *[bruit]* to grow louder; *[ombre]* to grow bigger. **~ de 10 cm** to grow 10 cm; **~ dans l'estime de qn** to grow *ou* go up in sb's estimation *ou* esteem; **en grandissant tu verras que** as you grow up you'll see that. **2** *vt [microscope]* to magnify. **~ les dangers** to exaggerate the dangers; **ça le grandit** *(en taille)* it makes him look taller; *(en prestige)* it increases his stature.

grange [gʀɑ̃ʒ] *nf* barn.

granit(e) [gʀanit] *nm* granite.

granulé [gRanyle] *nm* granule.

granuleux, -euse [gRanylø, øz] *adj (gén)* granular; *peau* grainy.

graphique [gRafik] **1** *adj* graphic. **2** *nm (courbe)* graph. ◆ **graphiste** *nmf* graphic designer.

graphite [gRafit] *nm* graphite.

graphologie [gRafɔlɔʒi] *nf* graphology.

grappe [gRap] *nf* cluster. ~ **de raisin** bunch of grapes; **en ~s** in clusters.

grappiller [gRapije] (1) *vt argent, connaissances etc* to pick up.

grappin [gRapɛ̃] *nm* grapnel. **mettre le ~ sur** to grab.

gras, grasse [gRɑ, gRɑs] **1** *adj* (**a**) *bouillon* fatty. **fromage ~** full fat cheese. (**b**) *(gros) personne* fat; *volaille* plump. (**c**) *(graisseux) mains, cheveux* greasy; *sol* slimy. (**d**) *(épais) trait* thick. (**e**) *toux* loose, phlegmy; *voix, rire* throaty. (**f**) *(vulgaire)* coarse, crude. (**g**) *(abondant) pâturage* rich; *récompense* fat *. **la paye n'est pas grasse** it's not much of a salary. (**h**) **faire la grasse matinée** to have a long lie *ou* a sleep in *(US)*. **2** *nm (Culin)* fat; *(sale)* grease. **~-double** tripe; **le ~ de la jambe** the fleshy part of the leg; *(Typ)* **c'est imprimé en ~** it's printed in bold (type). ◆ **grassement** *adv rétribuer* generously; *rire* coarsely. ~ **payé** highly paid, well paid. ◆ **grassouillet, -ette** * *adj* podgy, pudgy *(US)*, plump.

gratification [gRatifikɑsjɔ̃] *nf (Admin)* bonus.

gratifier [gRatifje] (7) *vt*: ~ **qn de** *récompense, amende* to present sb with; *sourire* to favour sb with; *punition* to reward sb with.

gratin [gRatɛ̃] *nm (Culin) (plat)* cheese(-topped) dish; *(croûte)* cheese topping. (*: *haute société)* **le ~** the upper crust; **au ~** au gratin. ◆ **gratiné, e 1** *adj* (**a**) *(Culin)* au gratin. (**b**) (*) *épreuve* stiff *; *plaisanterie* wild *. **c'est un type ~** he's absolutely incredible. **2** *nf* onion soup au gratin. ◆ **gratiner** (1) *vi [sauce]* to stick.

gratis [gRatis] **1** *adj* free. **2** *adv* free, for nothing.

gratitude [gRatityd] *nf* gratitude.

gratouiller * [gRatuje] (1) *vt* (**a**) *(démanger)* ~ **qn** to make sb itch. (**b**) ~ **sa guitare** to strum on one's guitar.

gratter [gRate] (1) **1** *vt* (**a**) *surface* to scratch; *(avec un outil)* to scrape; *tache* to scratch off; *inscription* to scratch out; *boue* to scrape off. (**b**) *(irriter)* **ce drap me gratte** this sheet is making me itch; **ça (me) gratte** I've got an itch; **vin qui gratte la gorge** wine which catches in one's throat. (**c**) (*) ~ **quelques francs** to make a few francs *, pick up a bit extra on the side *(US)*; ~ **les fonds de tiroir** to raid the piggy bank. **2** *vi* (**a**) *[plume]* to scratch. (**b**) *[drap] (irriter)* to be scratchy; *(démanger)* to be itchy. (**c**) (*) *(économiser)* to save; *(travailler)* to slog away *, slave away *; *(écrire)* to scribble. **3 se ~** *vpr* to scratch (o.s.). ◆ **gratte-ciel** *nm inv* skyscraper. ◆ **gratte-papier** *nm inv (péj)* penpusher. ◆ **gratte-pieds** *nm inv* shoe-scraper. ◆ **grattoir** *nm* scraper.

gratuit, e [gRatɥi, ɥit] *adj* (**a**) *(sans payer)* free. (**b**) *affirmation* unwarranted; *cruauté, geste* gratuitous. ◆ **gratuité** *nf* (**a**) **la ~ de l'éducation** *etc* free education *etc*. (**b**) unwarranted nature; gratuitousness. ◆ **gratuitement** *adv* (**a**) free of charge. (**b**) gratuitously.

gravats [gRavɑ] *nmpl (Constr)* rubble.

grave [gRav] **1** *adj (solennel)* grave, solemn; *(important, alarmant)* serious, grave; *(Ling) accent* grave; *note* low; *son, voix* deep. **blessé ~** seriously injured man; **ce n'est pas ~** there's no harm done, it's not serious. **2** *nm (Rad)* **' ~-aigu'** 'bass-treble'; **les ~ s** *(Rad)* the bass tones; *(Mus)* the low notes. ◆ **gravement** *adv* gravely, solemnly; seriously.

graver [gRave] (1) *vt (gén)* to engrave; *(sur bois)* to carve *(dans* on); *disque* to cut. ~ **à l'eau-forte** to etch; **faire ~ des cartes de visite** to get some visiting cards printed; **c'est gravé sur son front** it's written all over his face. ◆ **graveur** *nm* engraver; *(sur bois)* woodcutter. ~ **à l'eau-forte** etcher.

gravier [gRavje] *nm (caillou)* bit of gravel. **le ~** gravel; **allée de ~** gravel path.

gravillon [gRavijɔ̃] *nm (caillou)* bit of grit *ou* gravel. **du ~, des ~s** loose chippings, gravel.

gravir [gRaviR] (2) *vt (lit, fig)* to climb. ~ **péniblement une côte** to struggle up a slope.

gravité [gRavite] *nf* (**a**) *[ton, assemblée]* gravity, solemnity; *[situation, faute]* seriousness. **c'est un accident sans ~** it was a minor accident, it wasn't a serious accident. (**b**) *(Phys)* gravity.

graviter [gRavite] (1) *vi (lit, fig)* to revolve (*autour de* round). **il gravite dans les milieux diplomatiques** he moves in diplomatic circles.

gravure [gRavyR] *nf* (**a**) *(gén)* engraving; *(sur bois)* carving; *[disque]* cutting. (**b**) *(dans une revue)* plate; *(au mur)* print. ~ **sur bois** *(technique)* woodcutting; *(dessin)* woodcut; ~ **sur cuivre** copperplate engraving; ~ **à l'eau-forte** etching; ~ **de mode** fashion plate.

gré [gRe] *nm* (**a**) *[personnes]* **à mon/votre ~** *(goût)* to my/your liking *ou* taste; *(désir, choix)* as I/you like *ou* please; **contre le ~ de qn** against sb's will; **de ~ à ~** by mutual agreement; **il le fera de ~ ou de force** he'll do it whether he likes it or not; **de son plein ~** of one's own free will, of one's own accord; **de bon ~** willingly; **de mauvais ~** grudgingly. (**b**) *[choses]* **flottant au ~ de l'eau** drifting on *ou* with the current; **volant au ~ du vent** flying in the wind; **agir au ~ des événements** to act according to events; **au ~ de sa fantaisie** as the fancy took him (*ou* her).

Grèce [gRɛs] *nf* Greece. ◆ **grec, grecque 1** *adj (gén)* Greek; *vase, beauté* Grecian. **2** *nm (Ling)* Greek. **3** *nm(f)*: **G~(que)** Greek. **4** *nf*: *(Culin)* **champignons** *etc* **à la ~** mushrooms *etc* à la grecque.

gredin [gRədɛ̃] *nm* rascal.

gréer [gRee] (1) *vt (Naut)* to rig. ◆ **gréement** *nm* rigging.

greffe[1] [gRɛf] *nf [organe]* transplant; *[tissu, branche]* graft. **une ~ du cœur** a heart transplant; *(action)* **la ~ de qch** the transplanting (*ou* grafting) of sth. ◆ **greffer** (1) *vt* to transplant; to graft. **On lui a greffé un rein** he's been given a kidney transplant; *[problème]* **se ~ sur qch** to come on top of *ou* in addition to sth. ◆ **greffon** *nm* transplant; graft.

greffe[2] [gRɛf] *nm* Clerk's Office *(of courts)*. ◆ **greffier** *nm* clerk of the court.

grégaire [gRegɛR] *adj* gregarious.

grêle[1] [gRɛl] *adj jambes* spindly; *personne* lanky; *son* shrill.

grêle[2] [gRɛl] *nf* hail. **averse de ~** hail storm; ~ **de** *coups etc* hail *ou* shower of. ◆ **grêlé, e** *adj peau* pockmarked. ◆ **grêler** (1) *vb impers*: **il grêle** it is hailing. ◆ **grêlon** *nm* hailstone.

grelot [gRəlo] *nm* bell.

grelotter [gRəlɔte] (1) *vi (trembler)* to shiver (*de* with).

grenade [gRənad] *nf (Bot)* pomegranate; *(explosif)* grenade. ~ **lacrymogène** teargas grenade; ~ **sous-marine** depth charge. ◆ **grenadine** *nf* grenadine.

Grenade [gRənad] **1** *n (ville)* Granada. **2** *(état)* Grenada.

grenat [gRəna] **1** *nm* garnet. **2** *adj inv* dark red.

grenier [gRənje] *nm* attic, garret; *(pour grain etc)* loft. ~ **à blé** *(lit)* corn loft, wheat loft *(US)*; *(fig)* granary; ~ **à foin** hayloft.

grenouille [gʀənuj] *nf* frog. *(péj)* ~ **de bénitier** Holy Joe *, churchy old man (*ou* woman).

grenouillère [gʀənujɛʀ] *nf (pyjama)* sleepsuit; *(manteau)* snowsuit.

grès [gʀɛ] *nm (Géol)* sandstone; *(Poterie)* stoneware. **pot de** ~ stoneware pot.

grésil [gʀezi(l)] *nm (Mét)* (fine) hail.

grésiller [gʀezije] (1) *vi [huile]* to sizzle; *[radio]* to crackle. ◆ **grésillement** *nm*: ~**(s)** sizzling ; crackling.

grève [gʀɛv] *nf* (**a**) *(arrêt de travail)* strike. **se mettre en** ~ to strike, go on strike, take industrial action; **être en** ~**, faire** ~ to be on strike; **usine en** ~ striking factory; ~ **de la faim** hunger strike; ~ **patronale** lockout; ~ **sauvage** wildcat strike; ~ **de solidarité** sympathy strike; ~ **sur le tas** sit-down strike; ~ **totale** all-out strike; ~ **tournante** strike by rota, staggered strike *(US)*; ~ **du zèle** ≃ work-to-rule. (**b**) *[mer]* shore; *[rivière]* bank.

grever [gʀəve] (5) *vt budget* to put a strain on; *pays* to burden. **grevé d'impôts** weighed down with *ou* crippled by taxes.

gréviste [gʀevist(ə)] *nmf* striker.

gribouiller [gʀibuje] (1) **1** *vt (écrire)* to scribble, scrawl; *(dessiner)* to scrawl. **2** *vi (dessiner)* to doodle. ◆ **gribouillage** *nm ou* ◆ **gribouillis** *nm* scribble; doodle. ◆ **gribouilleur, -euse** *nm, f* scribbler.

grief [gʀijɛf] *nm* grievance. **faire** ~ **à qn de qch** to hold sth against sb.

grièvement [gʀijɛvmɑ̃] *adv*: ~ **blessé** (very) seriously injured.

griffe [gʀif] *nf* (**a**) *(Zool)* claw. **le chat fait ses** ~**s** the cat is sharpening its claws; *(lit, fig)* **sortir** *ou* **montrer/rentrer ses** ~**s** to show/draw in one's claws; **arracher qn des** ~**s d'un ennemi** to snatch sb from the clutches of an enemy. (**b**) *[couturier]* maker's label; *[fonctionnaire]* signature stamp; *(fig: empreinte)* stamp. ◆ **griffer** (1) *vt* to scratch; *(avec force)* to claw.

griffon [gʀifɔ̃] *nm (chien)* griffon; *(vautour)* griffon vulture; *(Myth)* griffin.

griffonner [gʀifɔne] (1) **1** *vt (écrire)* to scribble, scrawl; *(dessiner)* to scrawl. **2** *vi (dessiner)* to doodle. ◆ **griffonnage** *nm* scribble; doodle.

grignoter [gʀiɲɔte] (1) **1** *vt* (**a**) *[personne, souris]* to nibble (at). (**b**) *libertés* to eat away at, whittle away; *avantage* to win gradually. ~ **du terrain** to gain ground gradually. **2** *vi* to nibble (at one's food). ◆ **grignotement** *nm*: ~**(s)** nibbling.

gril [gʀi(l)] *nm (Culin)* steak pan, grill pan. *(supplice)* **Saint Laurent a subi le supplice du** ~ Saint Laurence was roasted alive; *(fig)* **être sur le** ~ * to be on tenterhooks; **faire cuire au** ~ to grill. ◆ **grillade** *nf (viande)* grill.

grillage [gʀijaʒ] *nm* wire netting; *[clôture]* wire fencing. ◆ **grillager** (3) *vt* to put wire netting (*ou* wire fencing) on.

grille [gʀij] *nf* (**a**) *(clôture)* railings; *(portail)* (metal) gate. (**b**) *[cellule]* bars; *[parloir]* grille; *[égout]* (metal) grate *ou* grating; *[poêle à charbon]* grate. (**c**) *[salaires, tarifs]* scale; *[horaires]* schedule; *(codage)* (code) grid. ~ **de mots croisés** crossword puzzle (grid).

griller [gʀije] (1) **1** *vt* (**a**) *(Culin) pain, amandes* to toast; *viande* to grill; *café, châtaignes* to roast. (**b**) *corps* to burn; *végétation* to scorch. **se** ~ **au soleil** to roast in the sun. (**c**) *lampe* to blow; *moteur* to burn out. (**d**) (*) ~ **une cigarette** to have a smoke; ~ **un feu rouge** to jump the lights, run a stoplight *(US)*; ~ **une étape** to cut out a stop; ~ **qn à l'arrivée** to pip sb at the post *, beat sb (out) by a nose *(US)*. **2** *vi*: ~ **(d'envie) de faire** to be burning *ou* itching to do; **on grille ici!** * we're *ou* it's roasting in here! * ◆ **grille-pain** *nm inv* toaster.

grillon [gʀijɔ̃] *nm* cricket.

grill-room [gʀilʀum] *nm* ≃ steakhouse.

grimace [gʀimas] *nf (gén)* grimace; *(sourire)* grin. **s'amuser à faire des** ~**s** to play at making *ou* pulling (funny) faces; **il fit une** ~ he pulled a wry face, he grimaced; **il fit la** ~ **quand il connut la décision** he pulled a face when he learned of the decision. ◆ **grimacer** (3) *vi (sourire)* to grin. ~ **(de douleur)** to grimace with pain; ~ **(sous l'effort)** to grimace *ou* screw one's face up (with the effort); **il grimaça de dégoût** he grimaced *ou* his face twisted with disgust.

grimer *vt*, **se** ~ *vpr* [gʀime] (1) *(Théât)* to make up.

grimoire [gʀimwaʀ] *nm (littér)* book.

grimper [gʀɛ̃pe] (1) **1** *vi* to climb; *(avec difficulté)* to clamber up; *[fièvre, prix]* to soar. ~ **aux arbres** to climb trees; ~ **à l'échelle** to climb (up) the ladder; **ça grimpe dur!** it's a stiff *ou* steep climb! **2** *vt* to climb, go up. **3** *nm (Athlétisme)* **le** ~ (rope)climbing. ◆ **grimpant, e** *adj* climbing. ◆ **grimpette** * *nf* (steep little) climb.

grincer [gʀɛ̃se] (3) *vi [métal]* to grate; *[plancher]* to creak; *[plume]* to scratch. ~ **des dents (de colère)** to grind one's teeth (in anger); **ce bruit vous fait** ~ **des dents** this noise sets your teeth on edge. ◆ **grinçant, e** *adj (lit, fig)* grating. ◆ **grincement** *nm*: ~**(s)** grating; creaking; scratching.

grincheux, -euse [gʀɛ̃ʃø, øz] *adj* grumpy.

gringalet [gʀɛ̃galɛ] *adj m (péj: chétif)* puny.

grippe [gʀip] *nf*: **la** ~ (the) flu; **une petite** ~ a slight touch of flu; ~ **intestinale** gastric flu; **prendre qn/qch en** ~ to take a sudden dislike to sb/sth. ◆ **grippé, e** *adj*: **il est** ~ he's got (the) flu.

gripper [gʀipe] (1) *vti (Tech)* to jam. **le moteur a grippé** the engine has seized up *ou* jammed.

gris, e [gʀi, gʀiz] **1** *adj (lit)* grey, gray *(US)*; *(morne)* dull; *(soûl)* tipsy. ~ **perle/-bleu** pearl/blue-grey; **il fait** ~ it's a grey *ou* dull day; **faire** ~**e mine à qn** to give sb a cool reception; **faire** ~**e mine** to look put out. **2** *nm* grey, gray *(US)*. ◆ **grisaille** *nf* greyness; dullness. ◆ **grisâtre** *adj* greyish.

griser [gʀize] (1) **1** *vt*: ~ **qn** to intoxicate sb, go to sb's head; **se laisser** ~ **par l'ambition** to be carried away by ambition. **2 se** ~ *vpr*: **se** ~ **de** *vitesse* to get drunk on; *paroles* to be intoxicated by *ou* carried away by. ◆ **griserie** *nf (lit, fig)* intoxication. ◆ **grisant, e** *adj (stimulant)* exhilarating; *(enivrant)* intoxicating.

grisonner [gʀizɔne] (1) *vi* to be going grey.

grisou [gʀizu] *nm* firedamp. ◆ **grisoumètre** *nm* firedamp detector.

grive [gʀiv] *nf (Orn)* thrush.

grivois, e [gʀivwa, waz] *adj* saucy. ◆ **grivoiserie** *nf (attitude)* sauciness; *(histoire)* saucy story.

Groenland [gʀɔɛnlɑ̃d] *nm* Greenland. ◆ **groenlandais, e** **1** *adj* of *ou* from Greenland. **2** *nm, f*: **G** ~**(e)** Greenlander.

grog [gʀɔg] *nm* grog.

grogne * [gʀɔɲ] *nf*: **la** ~ **des étudiants/patrons** the rumbling *ou* simmering discontent of students/employers.

grogner [gʀɔɲe] (1) *vi [personne]* to grumble, growl; *[cochon]* to grunt; *[sanglier]* to snort; *[ours, chien]* to growl. ◆ **grognement** *nm* growl; grunt; snort. ◆ **grognon** **1** *adj* grumpy, surly. **2** *nmf* grumbler.

groin [gʀwɛ̃] *nm [animal]* snout.

grommeler [gʀɔmle] (4) **1** *vi* to mutter, grumble to o.s. **2** *vt insultes* to mutter. ◆ **grommellement** *nm*: ~**(s)** muttering, grumbling.

gronder [gʀɔ̃de] (1) **1** *vt enfant* to scold, tell off *. **2** *vi [canon, orage]* to rumble; *[chien]* to growl;

[foule] to mutter (angrily); *[colère, émeute]* to be brewing. ◆ **grondement** *nm*: ~(**s**) rumbling; growling; (angry) muttering. ◆ **gronderie** *nf* scolding. ◆ **grondeur, -euse** *adj* grumbling.

groom [gʀum] *nm* bellboy.

gros, grosse [gʀo, gʀos] **1** *adj* (**a**) *(gén)* big, large; *(épais)* thick; *(gras)* fat; *(lourd)* heavy. **de grosses pluies** heavy rainfalls; **c'est ~ comme une tête d'épingle** it's the size of *ou* it's no bigger than a pinhead; **un mensonge ~ comme une maison** * a gigantic lie; **je l'ai vu venir ~ comme une maison** * I could see it coming a mile off *. (**b**) *(fig) travail* big; *somme, firme* large; *progrès* great; *dégâts* extensive, serious; *mer, averse* heavy; *rhume* heavy, bad; *fièvre* high; *soupir* deep. **les grosses chaleurs** the height of summer, the hot season; *(fig)* **c'est un ~ morceau** * *(travail)* it's a big job; *(obstacle)* it's a big hurdle; **la grosse industrie** heavy industry; **acheter par** *ou* **en grosses quantités** to bulk-buy, buy in bulk; ~ **rire** guffaw; **un ~ banquier/mangeur** a big banker/ eater; **un ~ buveur** a heavy drinker; ~ **nigaud** * big *ou* great silly *. (**c**) *drap* coarse; *traits du visage* thick, heavy. **le ~ travail** the heavy work; **grosse plaisanterie** obvious *ou* unsubtle joke; **c'est vraiment un peu ~** it's a bit thick * *ou* a bit much *. (**d**) **avoir les yeux ~ de larmes** to have eyes filled with tears; **cœur ~ de chagrin** heart heavy with sorrow; **femme grosse de 6 mois** woman 6 months pregnant; **jouer ~ jeu** to play for high stakes; **avoir le cœur ~** to have a heavy heart, be sad at heart; **le chat fait le ~ dos** the cat is arching its back; **faire les ~ yeux (à un enfant)** to glower (at a child). **2** *nm* (**a**) *(personne) (corpulent)* fat man; *(riche)* rich man. **mon ~** * old man *. (**b**) *(principal)* **le ~ du travail** the bulk of *ou* the main part of the work; **le ~ de l'armée** the main body of the army; **le ~ de l'orage** the worst of the storm; **dites-moi, en ~, ce qui s'est passé** tell me roughly what happened. (**c**) *(milieu)* **au ~ de l'hiver** in the depth of winter; **au ~ de l'été** at the height of summer. (**d**) *(Comm)* **le (commerce de)** ~ the wholesale business; **prix de ~** wholesale price; **papetier en ~** wholesale stationer; **vendre en ~** to sell wholesale; **commande en ~** bulk order.
3 *nf (personne)* fat woman.
4 *adv*: **écrire ~** to write big, write in large letters; **il risque ~** he's risking a great deal; **il y a ~ à parier que...** it's a safe bet that...; **en avoir ~ sur le cœur** to be upset.
5 : ~ **bétail** cattle; ~ **bonnet** * bigwig *, big shot *; *(Mus)* **grosse caisse** (bass) drum; **(fusil de) ~ calibre** large-bore shotgun; **grosse cavalerie** * heavy stuff *; ~ **gibier** big game; ~ **intestin** large intestine; **grosse légume** * = ~ **bonnet** *; *(lit, fig)* ~ **lot** jackpot; ~ **mot** coarse word; ~ **orteil** big toe; ~ **plan** close-up; ~ **rouge** * (red) plonk *, rough (red) wine; ~ **sel** cooking salt; **par ~ temps** in rough weather; ~ **titre** headline.

groseille [gʀozɛj] **1** *nf*: ~ **(rouge)** red currant; ~ **(blanche)** white currant; ~ **à maquereau** gooseberry. **2** *adj inv* (cherry-)red. ◆ **groseillier** *nm* currant bush. ~ **à maquereau** gooseberry bush.

grossesse [gʀosɛs] *nf* pregnancy.

grosseur [gʀosœʀ] *nf* (**a**) *[objet]* size; *[fil, bâton]* thickness; *[personne]* weight, fatness. (**b**) *(tumeur)* lump.

grossier, -ière [gʀosje, jɛʀ] *adj* (**a**) *(sans finesse) matière, traits* coarse; *esprit* unrefined; *imitation, instrument, ruse* crude; *plaisanterie* unsubtle; *plaisirs* base; *travail* roughly done; *dessin, réparation, estimation* rough. (**b**) *erreur* stupid, gross; *ignorance* crass. (**c**) *(insolent)* rude (*envers* to); *(vulgaire)* coarse. ◆ **grossièrement** *adv* roughly; crudely; coarsely; rudely. **se tromper ~** to make a gross error. ◆ **grossièreté** *nf* rudeness; crudeness; coarseness. **dire des ~s** to use coarse language; **la ~ de ses manières** his crude manners.

grossir [gʀosiʀ] (2) **1** *vi* (**a**) *[personne]* to put on weight. (**b**) *(en quantité etc)* to grow; *(en taille)* to get bigger; *[bruit]* to get louder. **2** *vt* (**a**) *[lunettes]* to enlarge, magnify; *(exagérer)* to exaggerate. **ils ont grossi l'affaire à des fins politiques** they've blown up the issue for political reasons; *[vêtement]* ~ **qn** to make sb look fatter. (**b**) *foule, cours d'eau* to swell; *voix* to raise; *somme* to increase, add to. ~ **les rangs de** to add to *ou* swell the ranks of. ◆ **grossissement** *nm [tumeur]* swelling; *[objet, dangers etc]* magnification.

grossiste [gʀosist(ə)] *nmf* wholesaler.

grosso modo [gʀosomɔdo] *adv (en gros)* roughly; *(tant bien que mal)* after a fashion.

grotesque [gʀɔtɛsk(ə)] *adj (risible)* ludicrous; *(difforme)* grotesque.

grotte [gʀɔt] *nf (naturelle)* cave; *(artificielle)* grotto.

grouiller [gʀuje] (1) **1** *vi [foule]* to mill about; *[rue]* to be swarming with people. **2 se ~** *vpr* (*) to get a move on *, shake a leg * *(US)*. ◆ **grouillement** *nm* milling; swarming.

groupe [gʀup] *nm* group. **le ~ de la majorité** the M.P.s *ou* Congressmen *(US)* of the majority party; **des ~s de gens** groups *ou* knots of people; **un ~ de touristes** a group *ou* party of tourists; **par ~s de 3** in groups of 3, in threes; **marcher en ~** to walk in a group; ~ **d'arbres** clump of trees; *(Ling)* ~ **nominal/verbal** nominal/verbal group; ~ **de combat** fighter group; ~ **électrogène** generating set, generator; ~ **hospitalier/scolaire** hospital/school complex; ~ **d'intervention de la Gendarmerie nationale** anti-terrorist squad; ~ **de pression** pressure group; ~ **sanguin** blood group. ◆ **groupement** *nm (action)* grouping; *(groupe)* group. ~ **d'achats** (commercial) bulk-buying organisation. ◆ **grouper** (1) **1** *vt* to group; *(Comm) colis* to bulk; *efforts, ressources* to pool; *idées* to order. **2 se ~** *vpr [foule]* to gather; *(en association)* to band together. **se ~ autour d'un chef** to rally round a leader. ◆ **groupuscule** *nm (Pol péj)* small group.

gruau [gʀyo] *nm*: **farine de ~** fine wheat flour.

grue [gʀy] *nf (Tech, Orn)* crane; (‡ *péj: prostituée)* tart ‡ *(péj)*, hooker ‡ *(US péj)*.

gruger [gʀyʒe] (3) *vt (littér: duper)* to dupe. **se faire ~** to be duped, be had *.

grumeau, *pl* ~**x** [gʀymo] *nm [sauce]* lump.

gruyère [gʀyjɛʀ] *nm* gruyère (cheese), Swiss cheese *(US)*.

Guadeloupe [gwadlup] *nf* Guadeloupe. ◆ **guadeloupéen, -éenne** **1** *adj* Guadelupian. **2** *nm, f*: **G~(ne)** inhabitant *ou* native of Guadeloupe.

Guatémala [gwatemala] *nm* Guatemala. ◆ **guatémaltèque** *adj*, **G~** *nmf* Guatemalan.

gué [ge] *nm* ford. **passer (une rivière) à ~** to ford a river.

guenille [gənij] *nf* rag. ~**s** (old) rags; **en ~s** in rags (and tatters).

guenon [gənɔ̃] *nf (Zool)* female monkey.

guépard [gepaʀ] *nm* cheetah.

guêpe [gɛp] *nf* wasp. ◆ **guêpier** *nm (piège)* trap; *(nid)* wasp's nest.

guère [gɛʀ] *adv* hardly, scarcely. **il n'y a ~ de monde** there's hardly *ou* scarcely anybody there; **il n'y a ~ que lui qui...** he's about the only one who...; **ça ne fera ~ moins de 100F** that won't be (very) much less than 100 francs; **je n'aime ~ qu'on me questionne** I don't much like being questioned; **cela ne durera ~** that won't last (for) very long.

guéridon [geʀidɔ̃] *nm* pedestal table.

guérilla [geʀija] *nf* guerrilla war *ou* warfare. ◆ **guérillero** *nm* guerrilla.

guérir [geʀiʀ] (2) **1** *vt malade, maladie* to cure; *membre, blessure* to heal. **2** *vi [malade]* to get better, be cured (*de* of); *[blessure, chagrin]* to heal. **3 se** ~ *vpr* to get better, be cured. **se** ~ **d'une habitude** to cure *ou* break o.s. of a habit. ◆ **guérison** *nf [malade]* recovery; *[maladie]* curing; *[membre, plaie]* healing. ◆ **guérissable** *adj* curable. ◆ **guérisseur, -euse** *nm, f* healer; *(péj)* quack (doctor).

guérite [geʀit] *nf (Mil)* sentry box; *(sur chantier)* workman's hut; *(servant de bureau)* site office.

Guernesey [gɛʀn(ə)zɛ] *nf* Guernsey.

guerre [gɛʀ] *nf* (**a**) *(conflit)* war; *(technique)* warfare. **correspondant** *etc* **de** ~ war correspondent *etc*; ~ **atomique** atomic war; ~ **froide/mondiale** cold/world war; **la** ~ **de Sécession** the American Civil War; **la** ~ **de quatorze** the 1914-18 war; **la** ~ **d'embuscade** guerrilla warfare. (**b**) **entre eux c'est la** ~ **ouverte** there's open war between them; *(lit, fig)* **en** ~ at war (*avec, contre* with, against); **faire la** ~ **à** *pays, abus* to wage war on; **soldat qui a fait la** ~ soldier who was in the war; **ton chapeau a fait la** ~ * your hat has been in the wars *; **faire la** ~ **à qn pour obtenir qch** to battle with sb to get sth; **de** ~ **lasse elle accepta** she gave up the struggle and accepted; **à la** ~ **comme à la** ~ we'll just have to make the best of things, you must take things as you find them *ou* as they come. ◆ **guerrier, -ière 1** *adj nation, air* warlike; *danse, exploits* war. **2** *nm, f* warrior.

guet [gɛ] *nm* (**a**) **faire le** ~ to be on the watch *ou* look-out; **avoir l'œil au** ~ to keep one's eyes open. (**b**) *(Hist)* watch. ◆ **guet-apens,** *pl* **guets-apens** *nm (lit, fig)* ambush.

guêtre [gɛtʀ(ə)] *nf* gaiter.

guetter [gete] (1) *vt (épier)* to watch (intently); *(attendre)* to watch out for, be on the look-out for; *(hostilement)* to lie in wait for. ~ **le passage de qn** to watch out for sb (to pass by); *(fig)* ~ **l'occasion** to watch out for the opportunity; *(fig)* **la crise cardiaque le guette** there's a heart attack lying in wait for him. ◆ **guetteur** *nm (Mil)* look-out; *(Hist)* watch.

gueule [gœl] *nf* (**a**) (‡: *bouche)* mouth; (*: *figure)* face; *(aspect)* look. **ferme ta** ~! shut your trap! ‡ *ou* face! ‡; **faire la** ~ to look sulky; **il a fait une sale** ~ he pulled a face; **ça a une drôle de** ~ it looks really weird. (**b**) *[animal, four]* mouth; *[canon]* muzzle. *(fig)* **se jeter dans la** ~ **du loup** to throw o.s. into the lion's jaws. ◆ **gueule-de-loup,** *pl* **gueules-de-loup** *nf* snapdragon. ◆ **gueulement** ‡ *nm (cri)* bawl; *(de douleur)* yell. ◆ **gueuler** ‡ (1) **1** *vi* (**a**) to bawl; *(de douleur)* to yell (*de* with); *(protester)* to shout, bellyache ‡ (*contre* about). **ça va** ~ there'll be one hell of a row ‡. (**b**) *[poste]* to blast out, blare out. **faire** ~ **sa télé** to turn one's TV up full blast *. **2** *vt ordres* to bawl out.

gueuleton * [gœltɔ̃] *nm* blow-out *.

gueux [gø] *nm (mendiant)* beggar; *(coquin)* rogue.

gui [gi] *nm* (**a**) *(Bot)* mistletoe. (**b**) *(Naut)* boom.

guibol(l)e * [gibɔl] *nf (jambe)* leg.

guichet [giʃɛ] *nm* (**a**) *(comptoir individuel)* window; *[banque]* counter; *[théâtre]* box office; *[gare]* ticket office. **adressez-vous au** ~ **d'à côté** inquire at the next window; *(à la poste)* **'** ~ **fermé'** 'position closed'. (**b**) *[mur]* hatch; *(grillage)* grille. ◆ **guichetier, -ière** *nm, f* counter clerk.

guide [gid] **1** *nm (gén)* guide; *(livre)* guide(book). **2** *nfpl (rênes)* ~**s** reins. ◆ **guidage** *nm (Aviat)* guidance. ◆ **guider** (1) *vt (gén)* to guide. **organisme qui guide les étudiants** organization that provides guidance for students; **se laissant** ~ **par son instinct** letting himself be guided by his instinct; **se guidant sur les étoiles** using the stars as a guide.

guidon [gidɔ̃] *nm [vélo]* handlebars.

guigne * [giɲ(ə)] *nf* rotten luck *. **avoir la** ~ to be jinxed *.

guigner [giɲe] (1) *vt* to eye.

guignol [giɲɔl] *nm (marionnette)* puppet *(name of popular French glove puppet)*; *(péj)* clown; *(spectacle)* puppet show *(≃ Punch and Judy show)*. **c'est du** ~! it's a real farce!

guillemet [gijmɛ] *nm* inverted comma, quotation mark. **ouvrez les** ~**s** open (the) inverted commas; **mettre un mot entre** ~**s** to put a word in quotation marks *ou* inverted commas.

guilleret, -ette [gijʀɛ, ɛt] *adj* (**a**) *(enjoué)* perky. **être tout** ~ to be full of beans *. (**b**) *(grivois)* saucy.

guillotine [gijɔtin] *nf* guillotine. ◆ **guillotiner** (1) *vt* to guillotine.

guimauve [gimov] *nf (Bot)* marsh mallow; *(Culin)* marshmallow. *(fig péj)* **c'est de la** ~ *(mou)* it's jelly; *(sentimental)* it's mush *, it's schmaltzy *.

guimbarde * [gɛ̃baʀd(ə)] *nf*: **(vieille)** ~ old banger *, old rattletrap * *(US)*, clunker * *(US)*.

guindé, e [gɛ̃de] *adj personne* stiff, starchy; *style* stilted. **il est** ~ **dans ses vêtements** his clothes make him look stiff.

Guinée [gine] *nf* Guinea. ~ **équatoriale** Equatorial Guinea; ~**-Bissau** Guinea-Bissau. ◆ **guinéen, -éenne 1** *adj* Guinean. **2** *nm, f* **G**~**(ne)** native of Guinea, Guinean.

guingois * [gɛ̃gwa] *adv*: **de** ~ askew, skew-whiff *.

guinguette [gɛ̃gɛt] *nf open-air café or dance hall.*

guirlande [giʀlɑ̃d] *nf* garland. ~ **de Noël** tinsel garland; ~ **de papier** paper chain.

guise [giz] *nf*: **n'en faire qu'à sa** ~ to do as one pleases *ou* likes; **à ta** ~! as you wish! *ou* please! *ou* like!; **en** ~ **de** by way of.

guitare [gitaʀ] *nf* guitar. ◆ **guitariste** *nmf* guitarist.

guitoune * [gitun] *nf* tent.

gus * [gys] *nm (type)* guy *.

guttural, e, *mpl* **-aux** [gytyʀal, o] *adj* guttural.

Guyane [gɥijan] *nf* Guiana. ◆ **guyanais, e** *adj,* **G**~**(e)** *nm(f)* Guyanese.

gym [ʒim] *nf* gym, P.E.

gymkhana [ʒimkana] *nm* rally. ~ **motocycliste** motorcycle scramble.

gymnastique [ʒimnastik] *nf* gymnastics *(sg)*. **professeur de** ~ physical education *ou* P.E. teacher; ~ **corrective** remedial gymnastics; ~ **rythmique** eurhythmics; ~ **respiratoire** breathing exercices; **faire de la** ~ *(Sport)* to do gymnastics; *(au réveil)* to do exercises; ~ **intellectuelle** mental gymnastics; **quelle** ~ **pour aller d'une banlieue à une autre** * what a palaver * to get from one suburb to another. ◆ **gymnase** *nm* gymnasium, gym. ◆ **gymnaste** *nmf* gymnast.

gynécologie [ʒinekɔlɔʒi] *nf* gynaecology. ◆ **gynécologique** *adj* gynaecological. ◆ **gynécologiste** *nmf ou* ◆ **gynécologue** *nmf* gynaecologist.

gypse [ʒips(ə)] *nm* gypsum.

gyrophare [ʒiʀɔfaʀ] *nm* revolving *ou* flashing light *(on vehicle)*.

gyroscope [ʒiʀɔskɔp] *nm* gyroscope.

H, h [aʃ] *nm* ou *nf (lettre)* H, h. **H aspiré/muet** aspirate/silent *ou* mute h.

ha ['ɑ, hɑ] *excl [surprise, colère etc]* oh! ho!; *[rire]* ha-ha!

habile [abil] *adj mains, ouvrier* skilful, skilled; *diplomate, tactique* skilful, clever. **être ~ à (faire) qch** to be clever *ou* skilful at (doing) sth. ◆ **habilement** *adv* skilfully; cleverly. ◆ **habileté** *nf* skill, skilfulness; cleverness.

habiller [abije] (1) **1** *vt* (**a**) *(vêtir)* to dress (*de* in); *(déguiser)* to dress up (*en* as). **cette robe vous habille bien** that dress really suits you; **un rien l'habille** she can wear anything. (**b**) *miséreux* to clothe; *recrues* to provide with uniforms. *(Couture)* **c'est X qui l'habille** X makes all her clothes. (**c**) *mur, fauteuil* to cover (*de* with). **2 s' ~** *vpr* to dress (o.s.), get dressed; *(se déguiser)* to dress up (*en* as). **elle s'habille long** she wears long skirts; **elle ne sait pas s' ~** she has no dress sense; **faut-il s' ~ pour la réception?** must we dress (up) for the reception?; *(Couture)* **s' ~ chez un tailleur** to buy *ou* get one's clothes from a tailor. ◆ **habillé, e** *adj* (**a**) *robe, soirée* dressy. (**b**) *personne* **bien/mal ~** well/badly dressed; **être ~ de noir** to be dressed in *ou* wearing black; **tout ~** fully dressed, with all one's clothes on. ◆ **habillement** *nm (action)* clothing; *(costume)* clothes; *(profession)* clothing trade.

habit [abi] *nm* (**a**) **~s** clothes; **~s de travail/du dimanche** working/Sunday clothes. (**b**) *(costume)* suit; *(Théât)* costume; *(de cérémonie)* tails. *(tenue)* **son ~** his dress; **l' ~ ne fait pas le moine** do not judge by appearances; **en ~ (de soirée)** wearing tails; **l' ~ ecclésiastique** clerical dress; **~ de gala** formal dress; **~ religieux** (monk's) habit.

habitable [abitabl(ə)] *adj* (in)habitable.

habitacle [abitakl(ə)] *nm (Naut)* binnacle; *(Aviat)* cockpit.

habitant, e [abitɑ̃, ɑ̃t] *nm, f [maison]* occupant; *[ville, pays]* inhabitant. **loger chez l' ~** *[touristes]* to stay with local people in their own homes; *[soldats]* to be billeted on the locals *ou* local people.

habitat [abita] *nm (Bot, Zool)* habitat; *(conditions de logement)* housing *ou* living conditions. *(Géog)* **~ rural** rural settlement.

habitation [abitɑsjɔ̃] *nf (maison)* house; *(domicile)* place of residence. **conditions d' ~** housing *ou* living conditions; **~ à loyer modéré** *(appartement)* ≃ council flat, public housing unit *(US)*; *(immeuble)* ≃ (block of) council flats, public sector housing.

habiter [abite] (1) **1** *vt maison* to live in; *région* to inhabit; *(fig) [idée]* to dwell in. **la maison n'a pas l'air habitée** the house doesn't look lived-in *ou* occupied. **2** *vi* to live (*en, dans* in).

habitude [abityd] *nf* (**a**) *(accoutumance)* habit. **avoir l' ~ de faire** to be used to doing, be in the habit of doing; **mauvaises ~s** bad habits; **perdre une ~** to get out of a habit; **faire perdre une ~ à qn** to break sb of a habit; **avoir une longue ~ de** to have long experience of; **j'ai l' ~!** I'm used to it; **il a ses petites ~s** he has his (pet) ways *ou* habits; **d' ~** usually; **par ~** out of habit; **comme d' ~** as usual; **comme à son ~** as he usually does. (**b**) *(coutume)* **~s** customs.

habituer [abitɥe] (1) **1** *vt*: **~ qn à qch/à faire** *(endurcir)* to accustom sb to sth/to doing, get sb used to sth/to doing; *(apprendre)* to teach sb sth/to do. **2 s' ~** *vpr*: **s' ~ à qch/à faire** to get used *ou* accustomed to sth/to doing. ◆ **habitué, e** *nm, f [maison]* regular visitor; *[café]* regular customer. ◆ **habituel, -elle** *adj* usual, customary, habitual. ◆ **habituellement** *adv* usually, generally, as a rule.

hacher ['aʃe] (1) *vt (au couteau)* to chop; *(avec un appareil)* to mince, grind *(US)*; *(fig) discours* to break up; *récolte* to slash to pieces. **~ menu** to mince, chop finely; **il se ferait ~ pour vous** he'd go through fire for you. ◆ **hache** *nf* axe. **~ de guerre** hatchet; *(fig)* **déterrer la ~ de guerre** to take up the hatchet. ◆ **haché, e 1** *adj viande* minced, ground *(US)*; *style* jerky. **2** *nm* mince, ground beef *(US)*. ◆ **hache-légumes** *nm inv* vegetable-chopper. ◆ **hachette** *nf* hatchet. ◆ **hache-viande** *nm inv* (meat-)mincer, grinder *(US)*. ◆ **hachis** *nm [légumes]* chopped vegetables; *[viande]* mince. **~ Parmentier** ≃ shepherd's pie. ◆ **hachoir** *nm (couteau)* chopper; *(appareil)* (meat-)mincer, grinder *(US)*.

hachisch ['aʃiʃ] *nm* hashish.

haddock ['adɔk] *nm* smoked haddock.

hagard, e ['agaʀ, aʀd(ə)] *adj yeux* wild; *visage, air* frantic, distraught, wild.

haie ['ɛ] *nf* (**a**) *(clôture)* hedge. **~ vive** quickset hedge. (**b**) *[coureur]* hurdle; *[chevaux]* fence. **course de ~s** *[coureur]* hurdles (race); *[chevaux]* steeplechase; **110 mètres ~s** 110 metres hurdles. (**c**) *[spectateurs]* line, row. **faire une ~ d'honneur** to form a guard of honour.

haillon ['ɑjɔ̃] *nm* rag. **en ~s** in rags, in tatters.

haine ['ɛn] *nf* hatred, hate (*de, pour* of, for). **prendre qn en ~** to take a violent dislike to sb; **avoir de la ~ pour** to be filled with hate *ou* hatred for; **par ~ de** out of *ou* through hatred of. ◆ **haineusement** *adv* with hatred. ◆ **haineux, -euse** *adj parole* full of hatred *ou* hate; *joie* malevolent.

haïr ['aiʀ] (10) *vt* to detest, hate. ◆ **haïssable** *adj* detestable, hateful.

Haïti [aiti] *nf* Haiti. ◆ **haïtien, -ienne** *adj,* **H~(ne)** *nm(f)* Haitian.

halage ['alaʒ] *nm* towing. **chemin de ~** towpath.

hâle ['ɑl] *nm* tan, sunburn. ◆ **hâlé, e** *adj* tanned, sunburnt.

haleine [alɛn] *nf (souffle)* breath; *(respiration)* breathing. **hors d' ~** out of breath, breathless; **perdre ~** to lose one's breath, get out of breath; **d'une seule ~** *dire* in one breath; **avoir mauvaise ~** to have bad breath; **tenir qn en ~** *(attention)* to hold sb spellbound; *(incertitude)* to keep sb in suspense; **travail de longue ~** long-term job; **à perdre ~** until one is out of breath.

haler ['ale] (1) *vt ancre* to haul in; *bateau* to tow.

haleter ['alte] (5) *vi* (**a**) *(manquer d'air)* to pant, gasp for breath, puff; *(de soif, d'émotion)* to pant (*de* with); *[chien]* to pant. (**b**) *[poitrine]* to heave; *[moteur]* to puff. ◆ **haletant, e** *adj* panting; puffing; heaving; *voix* breathless. **être ~** to be out of breath. ◆ **halètement** *nm*: **~(s)** panting ; puffing; heaving.

hall ['ol] *nm [hôtel, immeuble]* hall, foyer; *[gare]* arrival (*ou* departure) hall.

halle ['al] *nf (marché)* (covered) market. **les H~s (de Paris)** *formerly the central food market of Paris.*

hallucination [alysinɑsjɔ̃] *nf* hallucination. **tu as des ~s!** * you must be seeing things! ◆ **hallucinant, e** *adj* staggering * , incredible.

halo ['alo] *nm (Astron, Tech)* halo. ~ **de gloire** cloud of glory.

halogène [alɔʒɛn] **1** *adj (gén)* halogenous; *lampe* halogen. **2** *nm* halogen.

halte ['alt(ə)] *nf (pause)* stop, break; *(fig)* pause; *(endroit)* stopping place; *(Rail)* halt. **faire ~** to (make a) stop; **~(-là)!** *(gén)* stop!; *(Mil)* halt!; *(fig)* hold on!; ~ **aux essais nucléaires!** an end to *ou* no more nuclear tests!

haltère [altɛʀ] *nm (à boules)* dumbbell; *(à disques)* barbell. **faire des ~s** to do weight lifting. ◆ **haltérophile** *nmf* weight lifter. ◆ **haltérophilie** *nf* weight lifting.

hamac ['amak] *nm* hammock.

Hamburg ['ɑ̃buʀ] *n* Hamburg.

hamburger ['ɑ̃buʀgœʀ] *nm* hamburger, beefburger.

hameau, *pl* **~x** ['amo] *nm* hamlet.

hameçon [amsɔ̃] *nm* fish hook.

hampe ['ɑ̃p] *nf [drapeau]* pole; *[lance]* shaft; *[cerf]* breast; *[bœuf]* flank.

hamster ['amstɛʀ] *nm* hamster.

hanche ['ɑ̃ʃ] *nf [personne]* hip; *[cheval]* haunch.

hand-ball ['ɑ̃dbal] *nm* handball.

handicap ['ɑ̃dikap] *nm (lit, fig)* handicap. ◆ **handicapé, e** **1** *adj* handicapped. **2** *nm, f* handicapped person. ~ **moteur** spastic. ◆ **handicaper** (1) *vt* to handicap.

hangar ['ɑ̃gaʀ] *nm (gén)* shed; *[marchandises]* warehouse; *[avions]* hangar.

hanneton ['antɔ̃] *nm* maybug.

hanter ['ɑ̃te] (1) *vt* to haunt.

hantise ['ɑ̃tiz] *nf* obsessive fear.

happer ['ape] (1) *vt (avec la gueule)* to snap up; *(avec la main)* to snatch up. **se faire ~ par une voiture** to be hit by a car.

happy end ['apiɛnd] *nm* happy ending.

harangue ['aʀɑ̃g] *nf* harangue. ◆ **haranguer** (1) *vt* to harangue.

haras ['aʀɑ] *nm* stud farm.

harassement ['aʀasmɑ̃] *nm* exhaustion. ◆ **harasser** (1) *vt* to exhaust. **harassé de travail** overwhelmed with work.

harceler ['aʀsəle] (5) *vt* to harass (*de* with); *gibier* to hunt down. ◆ **harcèlement** *nm* harassing.

hardes ['aʀd(ə)] *nfpl (péj: vieux habits)* old clothes, rags.

hardi, e ['aʀdi] *adj (gén)* bold, daring. ~ **les gars!** come on lads! ◆ **hardiesse** *nf* boldness, daring. **~s** *[livre]* bold statements; *[domestique]* liberties; **~s de langage** bold language. ◆ **hardiment** *adv* boldly, daringly.

hardware ['aʀdwɛʀ] *nm* hardware.

harem ['aʀɛm] *nm* harem.

hareng ['aʀɑ̃] *nm* herring. ~ **saur** smoked herring, kipper.

hargne ['aʀɲ(ə)] *nf* spite, resentment. ◆ **hargneusement** *adv* aggressively. ◆ **hargneux, -euse** *adj* aggressive.

haricot ['aʀiko] *nm* bean. **des ~s!** ⁑ nothing doing! *; ~ **blanc** haricot bean; ~ **grimpant** *ou* **à rame** runner bean; ~ **rouge** kidney bean; ~ **vert** French bean; ~ **de mouton** mutton stew.

harmonica [aʀmɔnika] *nm* harmonica, mouth organ.

harmonie [aʀmɔni] *nf (gén)* harmony; *(fanfare)* wind band. **être en ~ avec** to be in harmony *ou* in keeping with; **vivre en bonne ~** to get on well together (*avec* with). ◆ **harmonieusement** *adv* harmoniously. ◆ **harmonieux, -euse** *adj (gén)* harmonious; *couleurs* well-matched.

harmoniser *vt,* **s'** ~ *vpr* [aʀmɔnize] (1) to harmonize. ◆ **harmonisation** *nf* harmonization.

harmonium [aʀmɔnjɔm] *nm* harmonium.

harnacher ['aʀnaʃe] (1) *vt cheval* to harness; *(péj: habiller)* to rig out *. ◆ **harnachement** *nm [cheval] (action)* harnessing; *(objet)* harness; *[personne]* rig-out *.

harnais ['aʀnɛ] *nm* harness.

harpe ['aʀp(ə)] *nf (Mus)* harp. ◆ **harpiste** *nmf* harpist.

harpie ['aʀpi] *nf (Myth, péj)* harpy.

harpon ['aʀpɔ̃] *nm* harpoon. ◆ **harponner** (1) *vt baleine* to harpoon; (⁑) *malfaiteur* to collar *; (⁑) *passant* to waylay.

hasard ['azaʀ] *nm* (**a**) *(coïncidence)* coincidence. **un ~ heureux/malheureux** a stroke *ou* piece of luck/bad luck; **par le plus grand des ~s** quite by chance *ou* coincidence; **les ~s de la vie** the fortunes of life. (**b**) *(destin)* chance, fate, luck; *(Statistique)* chance. **les caprices du ~** the whims of fate; **il ne laisse jamais rien au ~** he never leaves anything to chance; **le ~ a voulu qu'il soit absent** as luck would have it he was not there; **c'est un fait du ~** it's a matter of chance. (**c**) *(risques)* **~s** hazards. (**d**) **au ~** *aller* aimlessly; *agir* haphazardly; *tirer, citer* at random; **il a acheté ces livres au ~ de ses voyages** he bought these books as he came across them by chance on his trips; **à tout ~** *(en cas de besoin)* just in case; **je suis entré à tout ~** I looked in on the off chance; **par ~** by chance, by accident; **tu n'aurais pas par ~ 100 F?** you wouldn't by any chance have *ou* you wouldn't happen to have 100 francs on you?; **comme par ~!** what a coincidence! ◆ **hasarder** (1) **1** *vt vie* to risk; *hypothèse* to hazard, venture. **2 se ~** *vpr*: **se ~ dans** to venture into; **se ~ à faire** to risk doing, venture to do. ◆ **hasardeux, -euse** *adj entreprise* hazardous, risky; *hypothèse* dangerous, rash.

hâte ['ɑt] *nf (empressement)* haste; *(impatience)* impatience. **à la ~** hurriedly, hastily, in a hurry; **en toute ~** posthaste; **avoir ~ de faire** to be eager *ou* anxious to do; **sans ~** unhurriedly. ◆ **hâter** (1) **1** *vt (gén)* to hasten. ~ **le pas** to quicken one's pace. **2 se ~** *vpr* to hurry, hasten (*de faire* to do). **hâtez-vous** hurry up; **je me hâte de dire que** I hasten to say that; **hâte-toi lentement** more haste, less speed. ◆ **hâtif, -ive** *adj développement* precocious; *fruit* early; *travail* hurried; *décision* hasty. ◆ **hâtivement** *adv* hurriedly, hastily.

hausse ['os] *nf* rise, increase (*de* in). ~ **de salaire** (pay) rise *ou* raise *(US)*; **être en ~** to be going up (in price); *(Bourse)* **marché à la ~** rising market; **tendance à la ~** rising *ou* upward trend; *(fig)* **ses actions sont en ~** things are looking up for him.

hausser ['ose] (1) **1** *vt (gén)* to raise; *(surélever)* to heighten. ~ **les épaules** to shrug one's shoulders. **2 se ~** *vpr*: **se ~ sur la pointe des pieds** to stand up on tiptoe; **se ~ au niveau de qn** to raise o.s. up to sb's level. ◆ **haussement** *nm*: ~ **d'épaules** shrug.

haut, e ['o, 'ot] **1** *adj* (**a**) *(gén)* high; *(en taille)* tall. **un mur ~ de 3 mètres** a wall 3 metres high; **les plus ~es branches de l'arbre** the topmost branches of the tree; *(lit, fig)* **marcher la tête ~e** to walk with one's head held high; **la mer est ~e** it is high tide, the tide is in; **en ~e mer** on the open sea; **pousser les ~s cris** to exclaim in horror; **à voix ~e** aloud, out loud; **le prix de l'or est au plus ~** the price of gold has reached a peak. (**b**) *(supé-*

H
O

rieur) qualité, rang high; *âme, pensée* lofty, noble. **du plus ~ comique** highly amusing; **~ en couleur** *(pittoresque)* colourful; **avoir la ~e main sur qch** to have supreme control of sth; **discussions au plus ~ niveau** top-level discussions; **de ~e naissance** of noble *ou* high birth; **~e cuisine** *etc* haute cuisine *etc*; **~ fonctionnaire** high-ranking civil servant; *(lit, fig)* **de ~e voltige** acrobatic. **la ~e bourgeoisie** the upper middle classes. (**c**) *(ancien)* **dans la plus ~e antiquité** in earliest antiquity; **le ~ moyen âge** the Early Middle Ages. (**d**) *(Géog)* **la H~e Normandie** Upper Normandy; **la H~e Volta** Upper Volta.

2 *nm* (**a**) top. **le mur a 3 mètres de ~** the wall is 3 metres high; **en ~ de l'arbre** at the top of the tree; **le ~ du visage** the top part of the face; **les pièces du ~** the upstairs rooms; **l'étagère du ~** the top shelf; **des ~s et des bas** ups and downs; **du ~ d'un arbre** from the top of a tree; **parler du ~ d'une tribune** to speak from a platform. (**b**) **voir les choses de ~** to take a detached view of things; **tomber de ~** *(lit)* to fall from a height; *(fig)* to have one's hopes dashed; **prendre qch de ~** to take sth in a high and mighty way; **traiter qn de ~** to look down on sb; **regarder qn de ~ en bas** to look sb up and down; **frapper de ~ en bas** to strike downwards; **d'en ~** from above.

3 *nf*: **(les gens de) la ~e** ‡ the upper crust *, the swells † *.

4 *adv* high; *(sur colis)* 'this side up'. **mettez vos livres plus ~** put your books higher up; **lire tout ~** to read aloud *ou* out loud; **des gens ~ placés** people in high places; **aussi ~ qu'on peut remonter** as far back as we can go; **'voir plus ~'** 'see above'; **~ les mains!** hands up!, stick 'em up! ‡; **gagner ~ la main** to win hands down.

5 : **~-le-cœur** *nm inv* retch; **avoir un ~-le-cœur** to retch; **~ commissaire** high commissioner (*à* of); **~-le-corps** *nm inv* sudden start, jump; **avoir un ~-le-corps** to start, jump; **~e fidélité** hi-fi, high fidelity; **~-fond** *nm, pl* **~s-~s** shallow, shoal ; **~-de-forme** *nm, pl* **~s-~-~** top hat; **~-fourneau** *nm, pl* **~s-~x** blast *ou* smelting furnace; **le ~ lieu de la culture** the Mecca of culture; **en ~ lieu** in high places; **~-parleur** *nm, pl* **~-~s** loudspeaker; **~e trahison** high treason; **de ~ vol, de ~e volée** *personne* high-flying; *projet* far-reaching.

hautain, e ['otɛ̃, ɛn] *adj* haughty.

hautbois ['obwɑ] *nm* oboe.

hautement ['otmɑ̃] *adv (extrêmement)* highly; *(ouvertement)* openly.

hauteur ['otœʀ] *nf* (**a**) *[tour, personne]* height; *[son]* pitch. *(Aut)* **~ maximum 3 mètres** headroom 3 metres; **tomber de toute sa ~** *[personne]* to fall headlong *ou* flat; *[armoire]* to come crashing down; **prendre de la ~** to climb, gain height; **à ~ des yeux** at eye level; **arriver à la ~ de qn** to draw level with sb; *(fig)* **être à la ~ de la situation** to be equal to the situation; **il n'est pas à la ~ *** he's not up to it. (**b**) *(Géom)* perpendicular height; *(ligne)* perpendicular; *(Astron)* altitude. (**c**) *(colline)* height, hill. (**d**) *(noblesse)* loftiness, nobility; *(arrogance)* haughtiness.

Havane ['avan] *nf*: **la ~** Havana.

hâve ['ɑv] *adj* gaunt, haggard.

havre ['ɑvʀ(ə)] *nm (lit, fig)* haven. **~ de paix** haven of peace.

Hawaï *ou* **Hawaii** [awai] *n* Hawaii. **les îles ~** the Hawaiian Islands. ◆ **hawaïen, ïenne** *adj, nm,* **H~(ne)** *nm(f)* Hawaiian.

Haye ['ɛ] *nf*: **La ~** the Hague.

hé ['e, he] *excl (pour appeler)* hey!; *(pour renforcer)* well.

hebdomadaire [ɛbdɔmadɛʀ] *adj, nm* weekly.

héberger [ebɛʀʒe] (**3**) *vt (gén)* to accommodate; *(provisoirement)* to put up; *réfugiés* to take in. ◆ **hébergement** *nm* accommodation; putting up; taking in.

hébéter [ebete] (**6**) *vt [alcool]* to stupefy; *[lecture, télévision]* to daze; *[fatigue]* to numb. ◆ **hébétement** *nm* stupor.

hébraïque [ebʀaik] *adj* Hebrew, Hebraic.

hébreu, *pl* **~x** [ebʀø] *adj m, nm* Hebrew. **pour moi, c'est de l' ~ *** it's all Greek to me!

Hébrides [ebʀid] *nfpl*: **les ~** the Hebrides.

hécatombe [ekatɔ̃b] *nf* slaughter.

hectare [ɛktaʀ] *nm* hectare.

hecto... [ɛkto] *préf* hecto... **~litre/mètre** hectolitre/metre.

hégémonie [eʒemɔni] *nf* hegemony.

hein * ['ɛ̃, hɛ̃] *excl* eh *?, what?

hélas ['elɑs] *excl* alas! **~ non!** I'm afraid not!, unfortunately not.

héler ['ele] (**6**) *vt* to hail.

hélice [elis] *nf* propeller, screw.

hélicoptère [elikɔptɛʀ] *nm* helicopter. ◆ **héligare** *nf* heliport. ◆ **héliport** *nm* heliport. ◆ **héliporté, e** *adj* transported by helicopter.

hélium [eljɔm] *nm* helium.

hellénique [elenik] *adj* Hellenic.

Helvétie [ɛlvesi] *nf* Helvetia. ◆ **helvète** *adj,* **H~** *nmf* Helvetian.

helvétique [ɛlvetik] *adj* Swiss.

hématie [emati] *nf* red (blood) corpuscle.

hématome [ematom] *nm* bruise.

hémicycle [emisikl(ə)] *nm* semicircle, hemicycle. *(Pol)* **l' ~** the benches *(of the Assemblée Nationale)*.

hémiplégie [emipleʒi] *nf* paralysis of one side, hemiplegia.

hémisphère [emisfɛʀ] *nm (gén)* hemisphere. **~ sud/nord** southern/northern hemisphere. ◆ **hémisphérique** *adj* hemispherical.

hémistiche [emistiʃ] *nm* hemistich.

hémoglobine [emɔglɔbin] *nf* haemoglobin.

hémophile [emɔfil] **1** *adj* haemophilic. **2** *nmf* haemophiliac. ◆ **hémophilie** *nf* haemophilia.

hémorragie [emɔʀaʒi] *nf* bleeding, haemorrhage.

hémorroïde [emɔʀɔid] *nf (gén pl)* haemorrhoid, pile.

hémostatique [emɔstatik] *adj, nm* haemostatic.

henné ['ene] *nm* henna.

hennir ['eniʀ] (**2**) *vi* to neigh, whinny. ◆ **hennissement** *nm* neigh, whinny.

hep ['ɛp, hɛp] *excl* hey!

hépatique [epatik] **1** *adj* hepatic. **2** *nmf* person who suffers from a liver complaint. ◆ **hépatite** *nf* hepatitis.

héraldique [eʀaldik] **1** *adj* heraldic. **2** *nf* heraldry.

héraut ['eʀo] *nm (Hist, fig)* herald.

herbage [ɛʀbaʒ] *nm* pasture.

herbe [ɛʀb(ə)] *nf*: **l' ~** grass; **une ~** *(espèce)* a grass; *(brin)* a blade of grass; *(Culin, Méd)* a herb; **mauvaise ~** weed; **~s folles** wild grasses; **~s potagères** pot herbs; **en ~** *blé* green, unripe; *avocat* budding; **couper l' ~ sous les pieds de qn** to cut the ground from under sb's feet. ◆ **herbeux, -euse** *adj* grassy. ◆ **herbicide 1** *adj* herbicidal. **2** *nm* weedkiller. ◆ **herbier** *nm* herbarium. ◆ **herbivore 1** *adj* herbivorous. **2** *nm* herbivore.

herboriste [ɛʀbɔʀist(ə)] *nmf* herbalist. ◆ **herboristerie** *nf (commerce)* herb trade; *(magasin)* herbalist's shop.

Hercule [ɛʀkyl] *nm (Myth)* Hercules. *(fig)* **c'est un h~** he's a real Hercules. ◆ **herculéen, -éenne** *adj* Herculean.

héréditaire [eʀeditɛʀ] *adj* hereditary. ◆ **hérédité** *nf (Bio)* heredity; *(droit)* right of inheritance; *(caractère)* hereditary nature.

hérésie [eʀezi] *nf (Rel)* heresy. *(fig)* **c'est une ~!** it's sacrilege! ◆ **hérétique 1** *adj* heretical. **2** *nmf* heretic.

hérisser ['eʀise] (1) **1** *vt* (**a**) **le chat hérisse ses poils** the cat makes its coat bristle; **l'oiseau hérisse ses plumes** the bird ruffles its feathers; **le vent hérisse mes cheveux** the wind makes my hair stand on end. (**b**) *(armer)* **~ une planche de clous** to spike a plank with nails; **de nombreuses difficultés hérissent le texte** numerous difficulties are scattered through the text. (**c**) *(mettre en colère)* **~ qn** to put sb's back up *. **2 se ~** *vpr* (**a**) *[poils]* to stand on end, bristle; *[animal]* to bristle. (**b**) *(se fâcher)* to bristle, get one's back up *. ◆ **hérissé, e** *adj cheveux* standing on end, bristling. **~ de** *poils, obstacles* bristling with; *épines* spiked with.

hérisson ['eʀisɔ̃] *nm* hedgehog.

héritage [eʀitaʒ] *nm* inheritance; *(culturel)* heritage, legacy. **faire un ~** to come into an inheritance; **laisser qch en ~ à qn** to leave sth to sb, bequeath sth to sb; **tante à ~** wealthy *ou* rich aunt. ◆ **hériter** (1) *vti* to inherit. **~ (de) qch de qn** to inherit sth from sb; **~ de son oncle** to inherit one's uncle's property; **il a hérité d'un rhume *** he's picked up a cold. ◆ **héritier** *nm* heir. ◆ **héritière** heiress.

hermétique [ɛʀmetik] *adj joint* airtight, watertight, hermetic; *barrage, secret, visage* impenetrable; *écrivain, livre (obscur)* abstruse, obscure; *(Littérat)* hermetic. ◆ **hermétiquement** *adv* tightly, hermetically; abstrusely, obscurely. **secret ~ gardé** closely guarded secret. ◆ **hermétisme** *nm (obscurité)* abstruseness, obscurity; *(Alchimie, Littérat)* hermetism.

hermine [ɛʀmin] *nf (fourrure)* ermine; *(animal)* ermine, stoat.

hernie ['ɛʀni] *nf (Méd)* hernia, rupture; *[pneu]* bulge. **~ discale** slipped disc. ◆ **herniaire** *adj* hernial.

héroïne [eʀɔin] *nf (femme)* heroine; *(drogue)* heroin.

héroïque [eʀɔik] *adj* heroic. **l'époque ~** the pioneering days. ◆ **héroïquement** *adv* heroically. ◆ **héroïsme** *nm* heroism.

héron ['eʀɔ̃] *nm* heron.

héros ['eʀo] *nm* hero.

herse ['ɛʀs(ə)] *nf (Agr)* harrow; *[château]* portcullis.

hertz [ɛʀts] *nm* hertz. ◆ **hertzien, -ienne** *adj* Hertzian.

hésiter [ezite] (1) *vi (gén)* to hesitate. **il n'y a pas à ~** there are no two ways about it; **il hésitait sur la route à suivre** he hesitated over which road to take; **~ entre plusieurs possibilités** to waver between several possibilities; **~ en récitant sa leçon** to falter in reciting one's lesson. ◆ **hésitant, e** *adj (gén)* hesitant; *caractère* wavering; *voix, pas* faltering. ◆ **hésitation** *nf* hesitation. **sans ~** without hesitation, unhesitatingly; **après bien des ~s** after much hesitation.

hétéroclite [eteʀɔklit] *adj ensemble* heterogeneous; *objets* assorted.

hétérogène [eteʀɔʒɛn] *adj* heterogeneous. **c'est un groupe ~** it's a very mixed group. ◆ **hétérogénéité** *nf* heterogeneousness.

hêtre ['ɛtʀ(ə)] *nm (arbre)* beech (tree); *(bois)* beech (wood).

heure [œʀ] *nf* (**a**) *(mesure)* hour; *(Scol)* period, class. **pendant les ~s de bureau** during office hours; **gagner 10 F de l'~** to earn 10 francs an hour *ou* per hour; **1 ~/3 ~s de travail** 1 hour's/3 hours' work; **il y a 2 ~s de route** it's a 2-hour drive, it takes 2 hours by car (to get there); **faire des/10 ~s supplémentaires** to work *ou* do overtime/10 hours' overtime.

(**b**) *(de la journée)* **avez-vous l'~?** have you got the time?; **quelle ~ est-il?** what time is it?; **il est 6 ~s/6 ~s 10/6 ~s moins 10/6 ~s et demie** it is 6 (o'clock)/10 past 6/10 to 6/half past 6; **10 ~s du matin/du soir** 10 (o'clock) in the morning/at night, 10 a.m./p.m.; **il est 8 ~s passées** it's gone 8; **à 4 ~s juste(s)** at 4 sharp; **à une ~ avancée (de la nuit)** at a late hour (of the night).

(**c**) *(fixée)* time. **c'est l'~** it's time; **avant l'~** before time, ahead of time, early; **à l'~** on time; **après l'~** late; **~ d'été** daylight saving time; **mettre sa montre à l'~** to set *ou* put one's watch right; **l'~ c'est l'~** on time is on time.

(**d**) *(moment)* time. **l'~ du déjeuner** lunchtime; **aux ~s des repas** at mealtimes; **~ de pointe** *(trains)* rush hour, peak hour; *(magasin)* peak shopping period; *(téléphone)* peak period; **les ~s creuses** *(gén)* the slack periods; *(pour électricité)* off-peak periods; **les problèmes de l'~** the problems of the moment; **à l'~ H** at zero hour; **l'~ est grave** it is a grave moment; **l'~ de vérité** the hour of truth.

(**e**) (*avec adj poss*) **il est poète à ses ~s** he writes poetry when the fancy takes him; **elle a eu son ~ de gloire** she has had her hour of glory; **il attend son ~** he is biding his time; **son ~ viendra** his time will come.

(**f**) *(locutions)* **à l'~ qu'il est il doit être arrivé** he must have arrived by now; **repas chaud à toute ~** hot meals all day; **24 ~s sur 24** round the clock, 24 hours a day; **d'~ en ~** hourly, hour by hour; **d'une ~ à l'autre** *varier* from one hour to the next; *attendre* any time now; **'Paris à l'~ écossaise'** 'Paris goes Scottish'; **la France à l'~ de l'ordinateur** France in the computer age; **tout à l'~** *(passé)* a short while ago; *(futur)* in a little while, shortly.

heureusement [œʀøzmɑ̃] *adv (par bonheur)* fortunately, luckily; *(judicieusement)* happily. **il est parti, ~!** he has gone, thank goodness!; **mot ~ choisi** well *ou* happily chosen word.

heureux, -euse [œʀø, øz] *adj* (**a**) *(content, comblé)* happy. **vivre ~** to live happily; **~ comme un poisson dans l'eau** happy as a sandboy *ou* clam *(US)*; **ces jouets vont faire des ~** these toys will make some children very happy; **c'est une ~euse nature** he has a happy *ou* cheerful nature; **je suis très ~ d'apprendre la nouvelle** I am very glad *ou* happy *ou* pleased to hear the news; **je suis ~ du résultat** I am pleased *ou* happy with the result. (**b**) *(chanceux) effet, résultat* happy; *choix* fortunate, happy; *personne* fortunate, lucky. **~ en amour** lucky in love; *(iro)* **c'est encore ~!** it's just as well!; **par un ~ hasard** by a fortunate coincidence; **attendre un ~ événement** to be expecting a happy event.

heurt ['œʀ] *nm (lit: choc)* collision; *(fig: conflit)* clash. **sans ~s** *(adj)* smooth; *(adv)* smoothly.

heurter ['œʀte] (1) **1** *vt* (**a**) *objet* to strike, hit; *personne* to collide with; *(bousculer)* to jostle; *(entrechoquer) verres* to knock together. (**b**) *(fig: choquer) personne* to offend; *bon sens, tradition* to go against; *opinions* to conflict *ou* clash with. **~ qn de front** to clash head-on with sb. **2** *vt indir*: **~ à la porte** to knock at the door; **~ contre qch** *[personne]* to stumble against sth; *[objet]* to knock *ou* bang against sth. **3 se ~** *vpr* to collide (with each other); *(fig)* to clash (with each other). **se ~ à un problème/refus** to come up against a problem/refusal. ◆ **heurté, e** *adj couleurs* clashing; *style, rythme* jerky.

hexagone [ɛgzagɔn] *nm (Géom)* hexagon. *(fig)* **l'~ (national)** France. ◆ **hexagonal, e,** *mpl* **-aux** *adj* hexagonal.

hiatus [jatys] *nm (Ling)* hiatus; *(fig)* break, hiatus.

hiberner [ibɛʀne] (1) *vi* to hibernate. ◆ **hibernation** *nf* hibernation.

hibou, *pl* **~x** ['ibu] *nm* owl.

hic * ['ik] *nm*: **c'est là le ~** that's the snag *ou* the trouble.

hideux, -euse ['idø, øz] *adj* hideous. ◆ **hideusement** *adv* hideously.

hier [jɛʀ] *adv* yesterday. ~ **(au) soir** yesterday evening, last night; **toute la journée d'** ~ all day yesterday; **je ne suis pas né d'** ~ I wasn't born yesterday.

hiérarchie ['jeʀaʀʃi] *nf* hierarchy. ◆ **hiérarchique** *adj* hierarchical. **chef** ~ senior in rank. ◆ **hiérarchiquement** *adv* hierarchically.

hiéroglyphe ['jeʀɔglif] *nm* hieroglyphic.

hi-fi ['ifi] *adj, nf* hi-fi.

hilarité [ilaʀite] *nf* hilarity, mirth. ◆ **hilarant** *adj aventure* hilarious, side - splitting. ◆ **hilare** *adj personne, visage* beaming, smiling.

Himalaya [imalaja] *nm:* **l'** ~ the Himalayas. ◆ **himalayen, -enne** *adj* Himalayan.

hindou, e [ɛ̃du] *adj*, **H~(e)** *nm(f) (citoyen)* Indian; *(croyant)* Hindu. ◆ **hindouisme** *nm* Hinduism.

hippie ['ipi] *adj, nmf* hippy.

hippique [ipik] *adj*: **concours** ~ horse show; **le sport** ~ equestrian sport.

hippocampe [ipɔkɑ̃p] *nm* sea horse.

hippodrome [ipɔdʀom] *nm* racecourse.

hippopotame [ipɔpɔtam] *nm* hippopotamus, hippo *.

hirondelle [iʀɔ̃dɛl] *nf* swallow.

hirsute [iʀsyt] *adj tête* tousled; *personne* shaggy-haired; *barbe* shaggy.

hispanique [ispanik] *adj* Hispanic.

hispano-américain(e) [ispanɔameʀikɛ̃,ɛn] *adj*, **Hispano-Américain(e)** *nm(f)* Spanish-American.

hispano-arabe [ispanɔaʀab] *adj* Hispano-Moresque.

hisser ['ise] (1) *vt (Naut, fig)* to hoist; *objet* to hoist, haul up. **se** ~ **sur un toit** to haul o.s. up onto a roof.

histoire [istwaʀ] *nf* (**a**) *(science)* **l'** ~ history; **l'** ~ **jugera** posterity will be the judge; **l'H~ sainte** Biblical *ou* sacred history; **la petite** ~ the footnotes of history; **pour la petite** ~ for the record; **c'est de l'** ~ **ancienne** * all that's ancient history *. (**b**) *(récit)* story; *(historique)* history; *(*: mensonge)* story *, fib *. ~ **drôle** funny story, joke; ~ **de fous** shaggy-dog story; **c'est une** ~ **à dormir debout** it's a cock-and-bull story; **qu'est-ce que c'est que cette** ~? what on earth is all this about?; ~ **de prendre l'air** * just for a breath of fresh air; ~ **de rire** just for a laugh *, just for fun; **tu me racontes des** ~**s** you're pulling my leg. (**c**) *(*: affaire)* business. **c'est une drôle d'** ~ it's a funny business; **il vient de lui arriver une drôle d'** ~ something funny has just happened to him; **c'est toujours la même** ~! it's always the same old story. **c'est une toute autre** ~ it's a whole new ball game *. (**d**) (*) ~**s** *(ennuis)* trouble; *(complications)* fuss; **faire des** ~**s à qn** to make trouble for sb; **quelle** ~ **pour si peu!** what a to-do *ou* fuss over so little. ◆ **historien, -ienne** *nm, f* historian. ◆ **historique 1** *adj étude* historical; *événement* historic. **2** *nm*: **faire l'** ~ **de** *problème* to review; *institution* to examine the history of. ◆ **historiquement** *adv* historically.

hit-parade, *pl* **hit-parades** ['itpaʀad] *nm (Mus)* **le** ~ the charts; **premier au** ~ number one in the charts.

hiver [ivɛʀ] *nm* winter. **il fait un temps d'** ~ it's like winter, it's wintry weather; **sports d'** ~ winter sports. ◆ **hivernal, e,** *mpl* **-aux** *adj (lit)* winter; *(fig: glacial) temps* wintry.

ho ['o,ho] *excl (appel)* hey (there)!; *(surprise, indignation)* oh!

hocher ['ɔʃe] (1) *vt*: ~ **la tête** *(affirmativement)* to nod (one's head); *(négativement)* to shake one's head. ◆ **hochement** *nm*: ~ **de tête** nod (of the head); shake of the head. ◆ **hochet** *nm [bébé]* rattle; *(fig)* toy.

hockey ['ɔkɛ] *nm* hockey. ~ **sur glace** ice hockey; ~ **sur gazon** field hockey.

holà ['ɔla, hɔla] **1** *excl* hold! **2** *nm*: **mettre le** ~ **à qch** to put a stop *ou* an end to sth.

holding ['ɔldiŋ] *nm* holding company.

hold-up ['ɔldœp] *nm inv* hold-up.

Hollande ['ɔlɑ̃d] **1** *nf* Holland. **2** *nm*: **h~** *(fromage)* Dutch cheese. ◆ **hollandais, e 1** *adj* Dutch. **2** *nm* (**a**) **H~** Dutchman. (**b**) *(Ling)* Dutch. **3** *nf*: **H~e** Dutchwoman.

holocauste [ɔlɔkost(ə)] *nm (Rel, fig)* sacrifice; *(Rel juive)* holocaust.

homard ['ɔmaʀ] *nm* lobster.

homélie [ɔmeli] *nf* homily.

homéopathe [ɔmeɔpat] *nmf* homoeopath. ◆ **homéopathie** *nf* homoeopathy. ◆ **homéopathique** *adj* homoeopathic.

homérique [ɔmeʀik] *adj* Homeric.

homicide [ɔmisid] *nm* murder, homicide *(US)*. ~ **involontaire,** ~ **par imprudence** manslaughter.

hommage [ɔmaʒ] *nm* (**a**) *(marque d'estime)* tribute. **rendre** ~ **à qn** to pay homage *ou* tribute to sb. (**b**) *(civilités)* ~**s** respects; **présenter ses** ~**s à une dame** to pay one's respects to a lady. (**c**) *(don)* **en** ~ **de ma gratitude** as a mark *ou* token of my gratitude; **faire** ~ **d'un livre** to give a presentation copy of a book; ~ **de l'éditeur** with the publisher's compliments. (**d**) *(Hist)* homage.

homme [ɔm] **1** *nm* man. *(espèce)* **l'** ~ man, mankind; **des vêtements d'** ~ men's clothes; **parler d'** ~ **à** ~ to have a man-to-man talk; **il n'est pas** ~ **à mentir** he's not one to lie *ou* a man to lie; **comme un seul** ~ as one man; **un** ~ **averti en vaut deux** forewarned is forearmed; *(Naut)* **un** ~ **à la mer!** man overboard! **2** : ~ **d'action** man of action; ~ **d'affaires** businessman; ~ **des cavernes** cave man; ~ **de confiance** right-hand man; ~ **d'équipage** member of a ship's crew; **navire avec 30** ~**s d'équipage** ship with a crew of 30 (men); ~ **d'esprit** man of wit; ~ **d'État** statesman; ~ **fort du régime** muscleman of the regime; ~**-grenouille** *nm, pl* ~**s-**~**s** frogman; **l'** ~ **de la rue** the man in the street; ~ **de lettres** man of letters; ~ **de loi** man of law; ~ **de main** hired man; ~ **du monde** man about town, socialite; ~**-orchestre** *nm, pl* ~**s-**~**s** one-man band; ~ **de paille** man of straw; ~ **de peine** workhand; ~ **de science** man of science; ~ **à tout faire** odd-job man; ~ **de troupe** private.

homogène [ɔmɔʒɛn] *adj* homogeneous. ◆ **homogénéisation** *nf* homogenization. ◆ **homogénéiser** (1) *vt* to homogenize. ◆ **homogénéité** *nf* homogeneity.

homologue [ɔmɔlɔg] **1** *adj* homologous (*de* to). **2** *nm (personne)* counterpart, opposite number.

homologuer [ɔmɔlɔge] (1) *vt (Sport)* to ratify; *(Jur)* to approve, sanction. ◆ **homologation** *nf* ratification; approval, sanction.

homonyme [ɔmɔnim] **1** *adj* homonymous. **2** *nm (Ling)* homonym; *(personne)* namesake. ◆ **homonymie** *nf* homonymy.

homosexualité [ɔmɔsɛksɥalite] *nf* homosexuality. ◆ **homosexuel, -elle** *adj, nm, f* homosexual.

Honduras ['ɔ̃dyʀas] *nm:* **le** ~ Honduras.

Hong-Kong ['ɔ̃gkɔ̃g] *n* Hong Kong.

Hongrie ['ɔ̃gʀi] *nf* Hungary. ◆ **hongrois, e** *adj, nm,* **H~(e)** *nm(f)* Hungarian.

honnête [ɔnɛt] *adj (intègre)* honest; *(satisfaisant)* reasonable, fair; *(hum: poli)* courteous. **d'** ~**s gens** decent people; ~ **homme** gentleman. ◆ **honnêtement** *adv* honestly; decently; fairly; reasonably; courteously. ~ **, vous le saviez bien!**

come now, you knew! ◆ **honnêteté** *nf* honesty; decency; fairness; courtesy.

honneur [ɔnœʀ] *nm* (**a**) *(réputation)* honour. **mettre son (point d') ~ à faire qch** to make it a point of honour to do sth; **jurer sur l' ~** to swear on one's honour. (**b**) *(mérite)* credit. **avec ~** creditably; **c'est tout à son ~** it is much to his credit; **faire ~ à sa famille** to be a credit *ou* an honour to one's family. (**c**) *(faveur)* honour. **avoir l' ~ de** to have the honour of; *(Admin)* **j'ai l' ~ de solliciter...** I am writing to ask...; **invité d' ~** guest of honour; **membre d' ~** honorary member; **couvert d' ~s** covered in honours; **avoir les ~s de la première page** to get a mention on the first page. (**d**) *(Cartes)* honour. (**e**) *(titre)* **votre H~** Your Honour. (**f**) **~ aux dames** ladies first; **à vous l'~** after you; *[mode]* **être en ~** to be in favour; **en l' ~ de nos hôtes** in honour of our guests; **en l' ~ de cet événement** in honour of this event; **à qui ai-je l' ~?** to whom do I have the honour of speaking?; **faire les ~s de la maison** to do the honours of one's house; **faire ~ à un repas** to do justice to a meal.

honorable [ɔnɔʀabl(ə)] *adj personne, buts* honourable; *sentiments* creditable; *résultats* decent. ◆ **honorabilité** *nf* worthiness. ◆ **honorablement** *adv* honourably; creditably; decently.

honoraire [ɔnɔʀɛʀ] **1** *adj* honorary. **professeur ~** professor emeritus. **2** *nmpl*: **~s** fee, fees.

honorer [ɔnɔʀe] (1) **1** *vt (vénérer)* to honour; *(estimer)* to hold in high regard *ou* esteem; *(faire honneur à) pays* to be a credit to; *signature* to honour. **~ qn de qch** to honour sb with sth; **je suis très honoré** I am highly *ou* greatly honoured; **cette franchise l'honore** this frankness does him credit. **2 s' ~** *vpr*: **s' ~ de** to pride o.s. upon.

honorifique [ɔnɔʀifik] *adj* honorary.

honte ['ɔ̃t] *nf* (**a**) *(déshonneur)* disgrace, shame. **couvrir qn de ~** to bring disgrace *ou* shame on sb, disgrace sb; **c'est une ~!** that's disgraceful! *ou* a disgrace! (**b**) *(gêne)* shame. **à ma grande ~** to my great shame; **sans ~** shamelessly; **avoir ~ (de qch/ de faire)** to be *ou* feel ashamed (of sth/of doing); **faire ~ à qn** to make sb feel ashamed. ◆ **honteusement** *adv* shamefully; disgracefully. ◆ **honteux, -euse** *adj (déshonorant)* shameful; *(confus)* ashamed (*de* of). **c'est ~!** it's a disgrace!, it's disgraceful!

hôpital, *pl* **-aux** [ɔpital, o] *nm* hospital. **c'est l'~ qui se moque de la charité!** ≃ it's the pot calling the kettle black.

hoquet ['ɔkɛ] *nm* hiccough. **avoir le ~** to have (the) hiccoughs. ◆ **hoqueter** (4) *vi* to hiccough.

horaire [ɔʀɛʀ] **1** *adj* hourly. **débit ~** rate per hour. **2** *nm* timetable, schedule.

horde ['ɔʀd(ə)] *nf* horde.

horizon [ɔʀizɔ̃] *nm* (**a**) horizon. **la ligne d' ~** the horizon; **à l' ~** *voir* on the horizon; *disparaître* below the horizon. (**b**) *(paysage)* landscape, view; *(fig: perspective)* horizon. **changer d' ~** to have a change of scene; **l' ~ politique** the political scene. ◆ **horizontal, e,** *mpl* **-aux** **1** *adj* horizontal. **2** *nf* horizontal. **à l' ~e** in a horizontal position. ◆ **horizontalement** *adv* horizontally. ◆ **horizontalité** *nf* horizontality.

horloge [ɔʀlɔʒ] *nf* clock. **il a la régularité d'une ~** he's as regular as clockwork; **il est 2 heures à l' ~** it's 2 o'clock by *ou* according to the clock; **l' ~ parlante** the speaking clock; **~ normande** grandfather clock. ◆ **horloger, -ère** **1** *adj* watchmaking. **2** *nm, f* watchmaker. **~ bijoutier** watchmaker and jeweller. ◆ **horlogerie** *nf (métier)* watch-making; *(magasin)* watchmaker's (shop). **~ bijouterie** watchmaker's and jeweller's shop.

hormis ['ɔʀmi] *prép* save.

hormone [ɔʀmɔn] *nf* hormone. **~ de croissance/ sexuelle** growth/sex hormone. ◆ **hormonal, e,** *mpl* **-aux** *adj* hormonal, hormone.

horodateur [ɔʀɔdatœʀ] *nm [parking etc]* ticket machine.

horoscope [ɔʀɔskɔp] *nm* horoscope.

horreur [ɔʀœʀ] *nf (gén)* horror; *(répugnance)* loathing. **frappé d' ~** horror-stricken; **vision d' ~** horrific *ou* horrifying sight; **l'esclavage dans toute son ~** slavery in all its horror; **les ~s de la guerre** the horrors of war; **c'est une ~** * *[film]* it is terrible *ou* dreadful; *[chapeau]* it is a fright, it is hideous; *[enfant]* **c'est une petite ~!** he (*ou* she) is a little horror!; **quelle ~!** how dreadful! *ou* awful!; **débiter des ~s sur qn** to say dreadful *ou* terrible things about sb; **avoir ~ de qch/de faire qch** to loathe *ou* detest sth/doing sth; **le mensonge me fait ~** I loathe *ou* detest lying, I have a horror of lying; **prendre qch/qn en ~** to come to loathe *ou* detest sth/sb.

horrible [ɔʀibl(ə)] *adj (effrayant)* horrible; *(laid)* hideous; *(mauvais)* terrible, dreadful. ◆ **horriblement** *adv* horribly; hideously; terribly, dreadfully. ◆ **horrifier** (7) *vt* to horrify.

horripiler [ɔʀipile] (1) *vt* to exasperate.

hors ['ɔʀ] **1** *prép* (**a**) *(excepté)* except (for), apart from. (**b**) *(espace, temps)* **~ de** out of; **vivre ~ de la ville** to live out of town *ou* outside the town; **habiter ~ du centre** to live away from *ou* outside the centre; **~ d'ici!** get out of here! (**c**) *(fig)* **il est ~ d'affaire** he's over the worst; **~ d'atteinte** *(lit)* out of reach (*de* of); *(fig)* beyond reach; **mettre ~ de combat** to put out of the fight; **être ~ de danger** to be out of danger; **il est ~ de doute que** it is beyond doubt that; **mettre ~ d'état de nuire** to render harmless; **~ d'haleine** out of breath; **~ de prix** exorbitant, outrageous; **~ de propos** untimely; **c'est ~ de question** it is out of the question; **être ~ de soi** to be beside o.s. (with anger); **mettre ~ d'usage** to put out of action. (**d**) *(dans loc)* **mettre qn ~ de ses gonds** to make sb wild with rage; **être présenté ~-concours** to be shown outside the competition *because of outstanding merit;* **être mis ~-concours** to be declared ineligible to compete, be disqualified; *(fig)* **il est ~-concours** he's in a class of his own. **2** : **~-bord** *nm inv* speedboat; **~-d'œuvre** *nm inv* hors d'œuvre; **~-jeu** *adj inv joueur* offside; *ballon* out of play ; **~-jeu** *nm inv* offside; **~-la-loi** *nm inv* outlaw; **~ ligne, ~ pair** *adj inv* outstanding, matchless; *(Ski)* **~-piste** *adj, adv* off-piste; **~-taxe** *adj inv, adv* duty-free; **~-texte** *nm inv* plate; **~ tout** *adj longueur* overall.

hortensia [ɔʀtɑ̃sja] *nm* hydrangea.

horticole [ɔʀtikɔl] *adj* horticultural. ◆ **horticulteur, -trice** *nm, f* horticulturist. ◆ **horticulture** *nf* horticulture.

hospice [ɔspis] *nm* (**a**) *(hôpital)* home. **~ de vieillards** old people's home. (**b**) *[monastère]* hospice.

hospitalier, -ière [ɔspitalje, jɛʀ] *adj (Méd)* hospital; *(accueillant)* hospitable.

hospitaliser [ɔspitalize] (1) *vt* to hospitalize. **malade hospitalisé** in-patient. ◆ **hospitalisation** *nf* hospitalization. **~ à domicile** home (medical) care.

hospitalité [ɔspitalite] *nf* hospitality.

hospitalo-universitaire [ɔspitalɔynivɛʀsitɛʀ] *adj*: **centre ~** teaching hospital.

hostie [ɔsti] *nf (Rel)* host.

hostile [ɔstil] *adj* hostile (*à* to). ◆ **hostilité** *nf* hostility. *(Mil)* **les ~s** hostilities.

hôte [ot] **1** *nm (maître de maison)* host; *(aubergiste)* landlord. **2** *nmf (invité)* guest. **~ payant** paying guest.

hôtel [otɛl] *nm* hotel. **~ des impôts** tax office ; **~-meublé** *nm, pl* **~s-~s** lodging house; **~ particulier**

(private) mansion; ~ **des ventes** saleroom; ~ **de ville** town hall, city hall *(US)*. ◆ **hôtelier, -ière 1** *adj* hotel. **2** *nm, f* hotelier. ◆ **hôtellerie** *nf (auberge)* inn; *(profession)* hotel business.

hôtesse [otɛs] *nf* hostess; *(aubergiste)* landlady. ~ **de l'air** air hostess, stewardess; ~ **d'accueil** *[hôtel, bureau]* receptionist; *[exposition, colloque]* hostess.

hotte ['ɔt] *nf (panier)* basket; *[cheminée]* hood. ~ **aspirante** cooker *ou* range *(US)* hood; **la ~ du Père Noël** Father Christmas's sack.

hou ['u, hu] *excl [peur]* boo!; *[honte]* tut-tut!

houblon ['ublɔ̃] *nm (plante)* hop; *(dans la bière)* hops. ◆ **houblonnière** *nf* hopfield.

houe ['u] *nf* hoe.

houille ['uj] *nf* coal. ~ **blanche** hydroelectric power. ◆ **houiller, -ère 1** *adj* coal. **2** *nf* coalmine.

houle ['ul] *nf* swell. ◆ **houleux, -euse** *adj mer* heavy, stormy; *séance* stormy; *foule* turbulent.

houppe ['up] *nf [cheveux]* tuft; *[fils]* tassel. ◆ **houppette** *nf* powder puff.

hourra ['uʀa] *excl* hurrah!

houspiller ['uspije] (1) *vt* to scold, tell off.

housse ['us] *nf* dust cover; *(pour recouvrir à neuf)* loose cover; *(élastique)* stretch cover.

houx ['u] *nm* holly.

hovercraft [ɔvœʀkʀaft] *nm* hovercraft.

hublot ['yblo] *nm [bateau]* porthole; *[avion, machine à laver]* window.

huche ['yʃ] *nf (coffre)* chest. ~ **à pain** bread bin.

hue ['y, hy] *excl* gee up! *(fig)* **ils tirent tous à ~ et à dia** they are all pulling in opposite directions.

huer ['ɥe] (1) *vt* to boo. ◆ **huées** *nfpl* boos.

huile [ɥil] *nf* (**a**) *(liquide)* oil. ~ **de table** salad oil; ~ **d'arachide** groundnut *ou* peanut *(US)* oil; ~ **de foie de morue** cod-liver oil; ~ **de lin** linseed oil; ~ **de tournesol** sunflower oil; **jeter de l' ~ sur le feu** to add fuel to the flames; **une mer d' ~** a glassy sea. (**b**) *(*: notabilité)* bigwig *, big shot *. (**c**) *(Peinture)* oil painting. **fait à l' ~** done in oils. ◆ **huiler** (1) *vt machine* to oil, lubricate. ◆ **huileux, -euse** *adj* oily.

huis [ɥi] *nm (littér)* door. *(Jur)* **à ~ clos** in camera; *(fig)* **les négociations se poursuivrent à ~ clos** the talks are continuing behind closed doors.

huisserie [ɥisʀi] *nf [porte]* doorframe; *[fenêtre]* window frame.

huissier [ɥisje] *nm* (**a**) *(appariteur)* usher. (**b**) ~ **(de justice)** ≃ bailiff.

huit ['ɥi(t)] *adj, nm inv* eight. **lundi en ~** a week on *ou* from *(US)* Monday; **dans ~ jours** in a week; **donner ses ~ jours à un domestique** to give a servant a week's notice; *V* **six.** ◆ **huitaine** *nf* eight or so, about eight. **dans une ~ (de jours)** in a week or so. ◆ **huitante** *adj inv (Suisse)* eighty. ◆ **huitième** *adj, nmf* eighth. **la ~ merveille du monde** the eighth wonder of the world; *V* **sixième.** ◆ **huitièmement** *adv* eighthly.

huître [ɥitʀ(ə)] *nf* oyster. ◆ **huîtrier, -ière 1** *nm (oiseau)* oyster catcher. **2** *adj industrie* oyster.

hululer [ylyle] (1) *vi* to hoot. ◆ **hululement** *nm*: ~**(s)** hooting.

hum ['œm, hœm] *excl* hem!, h'm!

humain, e [ymɛ̃, ɛn] **1** *adj (gén)* human; *(compatissant)* humane. **se montrer ~** to show humanity, act humanely (*envers* towards); **c'est ~!** it's only human! **2** *nm* human (being). ◆ **humainement** *adv (avec bonté)* humanely; *(par l'homme)* humanly. ◆ **humaniser** (1) *vt* to humanize. ◆ **humanisme** *nm* humanism. ◆ **humaniste 1** *adj* humanist, humanistic. **2** *nmf* humanist. ◆ **humanitaire** *adj* humanitarian.

humanité [ymanite] *nf (gén)* humanity. *(humaine)* **l' ~** humanity, mankind.

humble [œ̃bl(ə)] *adj* humble. ◆ **humblement** *adv* humbly.

humecter [ymɛkte] (1) *vt linge* to dampen; *front* to moisten.

humer ['yme] (1) *vt plat* to smell; *air* to breathe in.

humérus [ymeʀys] *nm* humerus.

humeur [ymœʀ] *nf* (**a**) *(momentanée)* mood, humour. **de bonne ~** in a good mood *ou* humour, in good spirits; **de mauvaise ~** in a bad mood; **se sentir d' ~ à travailler** to feel in the mood for work; **plein de bonne ~** good-humoured, full of good humour. (**b**) *(tempérament)* temper, temperament. **il est d' ~ inégale/égale** he is moody/even-tempered. (**c**) *(irritation)* bad temper, ill humour. **geste d' ~** bad-tempered gesture; **dire qch avec ~** to say sth ill-humouredly. (**d**) *(Méd)* secretion.

humide [ymid] *adj (gén)* damp; *mains* moist; *climat (chaud)* humid; *(froid)* damp; *cave* dank, damp; *saison* wet. ◆ **humidificateur** *nm* humidifier. ◆ **humidification** *nf* humidification. ◆ **humidifier** (7) *vt* to humidify. ◆ **humidité** *nf* dampness; humidity; dankness. **traces d' ~** traces of moisture *ou* of damp; **'craint l' ~ ', 'à protéger de l' ~ '** 'keep in a dry place'.

humilier [ymilje] (7) *vt* to humiliate. **s' ~ devant** to humble o.s. before. ◆ **humiliation** *nf* humiliation.

humilité [ymilite] *nf* humility.

humoriste [ymɔʀist(ə)] *nmf* humorist. ◆ **humoristique** *adj* humorous.

humour [ymuʀ] *nm* humour. ~ **noir** sick humour; **avoir beaucoup d' ~** to have a good sense of humour; **faire de l' ~** to make jokes.

humus [ymys] *nm* humus.

hune ['yn] *nf (Naut)* top.

huppé, e * ['ype] *adj (riche)* posh *, classy *.

hurler ['yʀle] (1) **1** *vi (gén)* to howl; *[foule]* to roar, yell (*de* with); *[sirène]* to wail; *[radio]* to blare; *[couleurs]* to clash. ~ **comme une bête qu'on égorge** to howl like a wounded animal; **chien qui hurle à la lune** *ou* **à la mort** dog baying at the moon; ~ **avec les loups** to follow the pack *ou* crowd *(fig)*; **faire ~ sa télé** to have one's TV going full blast *. **2** *vt* to roar, bellow out. ◆ **hurlement** *nm* howl; roar; yell; wail.

hurluberlu [yʀlybɛʀly] *nm* crank.

hutte ['yt] *nf* hut.

hybride [ibrid] *adj, nm* hybrid. ◆ **hybridation** *nf* hybridization. ◆ **hybrider** (7) *vt* to hybridize. ◆ **hybridité** *nf* hybridism.

hydrate [idʀat] *nm* hydrate. ~ **de carbone** carbohydrate. ◆ **hydratant, e** *adj* moisturizing. ◆ **hydratation** *nf* moisturizing, hydration. ◆ **hydrater** (1) *vt* to moisturize, hydrate.

hydraulique [idʀolik] **1** *adj* hydraulic. **2** *nf* hydraulics *(sg)*.

hydravion [idʀavjɔ̃] *nm* seaplane, hydroplane.

hydre [idʀ(ə)] *nf* hydra.

hydrocarbure [idʀɔkaʀbyʀ] *nm* hydrocarbon.

hydrocution [idʀɔkysjɔ̃] *nf* immersion syncope.

hydroélectricité [idʀɔelɛktʀisite] *nf* hydroelectricity. ◆ **hydro-électrique** *adj* hydroelectric.

hydrofoil [idʀɔfɔjl] *nm* hydrofoil *(boat)*.

hydrogène [idʀɔʒɛn] *nm* hydrogen. ~ **lourd** heavy hydrogen.

hydroglisseur [idʀɔglisœʀ] *nm* hydroplane, jetfoil.

hydrolyse [idʀɔliz] *nf* hydrolysis.

hydromel [idʀɔmɛl] *nm* mead.

hydropisie [idʀɔpizi] *nf* dropsy.

hydroxyde [idʀɔksid] *nm* hydroxide.

hyène [jɛn] *nf* hyena.

hygiaphone [iʒjafɔn] *nf* ® *speaking grill at counter in stations, banks etc.* **veuillez parler devant l'** ~ please speak at the open section of the window.

hygiène [iʒjɛn] *nf* hygiene. ~ **alimentaire** food hygiene; ~ **du travail** industrial hygiene. ◆ **hygiénique** *adj* hygienic.

hymne [imn(ə)] *nm (Littérat, Rel)* hymn. ~ **national** national anthem.

hyper... [ipɛʀ] *préf* hyper...

hyperbole [ipɛʀbɔl] *nf (Math)* hyperbola; *(Littérat)* hyperbole.

hyperémotivité [ipɛʀemɔtivite] *nf* excess emotionality.

hypermarché [ipɛʀmaʀʃe] *nm* hypermarket.

hypermétrope [ipɛʀmetʀɔp] *adj* long-sighted. ◆ **hypermétropie** *nf* long-sightedness.

hypernerveux, -euse [ipɛʀnɛʀvø, øz] *adj* over-excitable. ◆ **hypernervosité** *nf* over-excitability.

hyperréalisme [ipɛʀʀealism(ə)] *nm* hyperrealism.

hypersensibilité [ipɛʀsɑ̃sibilite] *nf* hypersensitivity. ◆ **hypersensible** *adj* hypersensitive.

hypertension [ipɛʀtɑ̃sjɔ̃] *nf* high blood pressure, hypertension. ◆ **hypertendu, e** *adj* suffering from high blood pressure.

hypertrophie [ipɛʀtʀɔfi] *nf* hypertrophy. ◆ **hypertrophier** *vt*, **s'** ~ *vpr* (7) to hypertrophy.

hypervitaminose [ipɛʀvitaminoz] *nf* hypervitaminosis.

hypnose [ipnoz] *nf* hypnosis. ◆ **hypnotique** *adj* hypnotic. ◆ **hypnotiser** (1) *vt* to hypnotize. **s'** ~ **sur un problème** to be hypnotized by a problem. ◆ **hypnotiseur** *nm* hypnotist. ◆ **hypnotisme** *nm* hypnotism.

hypo... [ipɔ] *préf* hypo...

hypocalorique [ipɔkalɔʀik] *adj aliments* low-calory.

hypocrisie [ipɔkʀizi] *nf* hypocrisy. ◆ **hypocrite** **1** *adj* hypocritical. **2** *nmf* hypocrite. ◆ **hypocritement** *adv* hypocritically.

hypodermique [ipɔdɛʀmik] *adj* hypodermic.

hypotension [ipɔtɑ̃sjɔ̃] *nf* low blood pressure. ◆ **hypotendu, e** *adj* suffering from low blood-pressure.

hypoténuse [ipɔtenyz] *nf* hypotenuse.

hypothèque [ipɔtɛk] *nf* mortgage. ◆ **hypothécaire** *adj* hypothecary. **garantie** ~ mortgage security. ◆ **hypothéquer** (6) *vt maison* to mortgage; *créance* to secure (by mortgage).

hypothèse [ipɔtɛz] *nf* hypothesis, surmise, assumption. **émettre l'** ~ **que...** to theorize that..., make the assumption that...; **dans la meilleure des** ~**s** at an optimistic estimate; ~ **de travail** working hypothesis. ◆ **hypothétique** *adj* hypothetical. *(Jur)* **cas** ~ moot case.

hypovitaminose [ipɔvitaminoz] *nf* hypovitaminosis.

hystérie [isteʀi] *nf* hysteria. ~ **collective** mass hysteria. ◆ **hystérique** **1** *adj* hysterical. **2** *nmf (Méd)* hysteric; *(péj)* hysterical sort.

I

I, i [i] *nm (lettre)* I, i.

ibérique [ibeʀik] *adj* Iberian. **la péninsule I~** the Iberian Peninsula.

ibis [ibis] *nm* ibis.

iceberg [isbɛʀg] *nm* iceberg.

ici [isi] *adv* (**a**) here. **d' ~ à Paris** from here to Paris; **passez par ~** come this way; **~ même** on this very spot, in this very place; **c'est ~ que** this is the place where, it is (*ou* was *etc*) here that; **le bus vient jusqu' ~** the bus comes as far as this. (**b**) *(temporel)* **d' ~ demain** by tomorrow; **d' ~ peu** before long, shortly; **d' ~ là** in the meantime; **jusqu' ~** (up) until now; **d' ~ à ce qu'il accepte, ça risque de faire long** it might be (quite) some time before he says yes; **d' ~ à 1992** by 1992. (**c**) **les gens d' ~** the local people; **je vois ça d' ~!** * I can just see that!; **vous êtes ~ chez vous** please make yourself (quite) at home; **~ présent** here present; **' ~ X'** *(au téléphone)* 'X speaking'; *(à la radio)* 'this is X'; **~ et là** here and there; *(Rel, hum)* **~-bas** here below; **par ~ la sortie** this way out; **par ~** *(dans le coin)* around here.

icône [ikon] *nf* icon.

idéal, e, *mpl* **als** *ou* **-aux** [ideal, o] *adj, nm* ideal. **l' ~ serait d'y aller** the ideal thing would be for us to go. ◆ **idéalement** *adv* ideally. ◆ **idéalisation** *nf* idealization. ◆ **idéaliser** (1) *vt* to idealize. ◆ **idéalisme** *nm* idealism. ◆ **idéaliste 1** *adj* idealistic. **2** *nmf* idealist.

idée [ide] **1** *nf* (**a**) *(gén)* idea. **il a eu l' ~ de faire** he had the idea *ou* hit upon the idea of doing; **ça m'a donné l' ~ qu'il ne viendrait pas** that made me think that he wouldn't come; **à l' ~ de faire qch** at the idea *ou* thought of doing sth; **avoir une ~ derrière la tête** to have something at the back of one's mind; **tu te fais des ~s** you're imagining things; **je n'en ai pas la moindre ~** I haven't the faintest *ou* slightest idea; **vous n'avez pas ~ de sa bêtise** you have no idea how stupid he is; **j'ai ~ que** I have an idea *ou* a feeling that; **on n'a pas ~!** * it's incredible!; **de nouvelles ~s-vacances** some new holiday tips *ou* hints. (**b**) *(opinion)* **~s** ideas, views; **ce n'est pas dans ses ~s** he doesn't hold with these views; **avoir les ~s larges/étroites** to be broad-minded/narrow-minded; **avoir des ~s avancées** to have progressive ideas. (**c**) *(goût)* **agir selon** *ou* **à son ~** to act as one sees fit; **il n'en fait qu'à son ~** he does just as he likes; **il faut un peu d' ~** you have to have some imagination *ou* a few ideas; **il y a de l' ~ *** there's sth in it, it's an idea. (**d**) *(esprit)* **avoir dans l' ~ que** to have it in one's mind that; **il a dans l' ~ de partir au Mexique** he's thinking of going to Mexico; **il s'est mis dans l' ~ de faire** he took it into his head to do. **2** : **~ fixe** idée fixe, obsession; **~ de génie** brainwave; **~ noire** black thought; **~ reçue** generally accepted idea.

identique [idɑ̃tik] *adj* identical (*à* to). ◆ **identifiable** *adj* identifiable. ◆ **identificateur** *nm (Ling, Ordin)* identifier. ◆ **identification** *nf* identification. **~ génétique** genetic fingerprinting. ◆ **identifier** *vt*, **s' ~** *vpr* (7) to identify (*à* with). ◆ **identiquement** *adv* identically. ◆ **identité** *nf (gén)* identity. **une ~ de goûts** *etc* similar *ou* shared tastes *etc*.

idéologie [ideɔlɔʒi] *nf* ideology. ◆ **idéologique** *adj* ideological.

idiome [idjom] *nm* idiom *(language)*. ◆ **idiomatique** *adj* idiomatic. **expression ~** idiom.

idiot, e [idjo, idjɔt] **1** *adj* idiotic, stupid; *(Méd)* idiotic. **2** *nm, f* idiot. **ne fais pas l' ~ *** *(n'agis pas bêtement)* don't be an idiot *ou* a fool; *(ne simule pas la bêtise)* stop acting stupid *. ◆ **idiotement** *adv* idiotically, stupidly. ◆ **idiotie** *nf* idiocy, stupidity. **c'est une ~** *(gén)* it's an idiotic thing to do (*ou* say); *(film)* it's rubbish *ou* trash; **ne fais pas d' ~s** don't do anything stupid.

idiotisme [idjɔtism(ə)] *nm* idiom, idiomatic phrase.

idole [idɔl] *nf (Rel, fig)* idol. ◆ **idolâtre** *adj* idolatrous (*de* of). ◆ **idolâtrer** (1) *vt* to idolize. ◆ **idolâtrie** *nf* idolatry.

idylle [idil] *nf (gén)* idyll. ◆ **idyllique** *adj* idyllic.

if [if] *nm* yew (tree).

igloo, iglou [iglu] *nm* igloo.

ignare [iɲaʀ] *(péj)* **1** *adj* ignorant. **2** *nmf* ignoramus.

ignifuger [ignifyʒe] (3) *vt* to fireproof. ◆ **ignifuge 1** *adj produit* fireproofing. **2** *nm* fireproofing material. ◆ **ignifugeant, e 1** *adj* fireproof. **2** *nm* fireproofing material *ou* substance.

ignoble [iɲɔbl(ə)] *adj* vile, base; *(sens affaibli)* revolting.

ignominie [iɲɔmini] *nf (caractère)* ignominy; *(acte)* ignominious *ou* disgraceful act. ◆ **ignominieux, -euse** *adj* ignominious.

ignorance [iɲɔʀɑ̃s] *nf* ignorance. **être dans l' ~ de qch** to be in ignorance of *ou* in the dark about sth; **dans l' ~ des résultats** ignorant of the results; **d'une ~ crasse *** pig ignorant ‡; **il a de graves ~s en anglais** there are serious gaps in his knowledge of English. ◆ **ignorant, e 1** *adj* ignorant (*en* about). **~ des usages** ignorant *ou* unaware of the customs. **2** *nm, f* ignoramus. **quel ~ tu fais!** what an ignoramus you are!; **ne fais pas l' ~** stop pretending you don't know what I mean.

ignorer [iɲɔʀe] (1) *vt* (**a**) *(ne pas connaître)* not to know. **vous n'ignorez pas que** you know *ou* are aware that; **j'ignore tout de cette affaire** I don't know anything about this business; **j'ignore avoir dit cela** I am not aware of having said that; **~ la misère** to have had no experience of poverty; **c'est un poète qui s'ignore** he's an unconscious poet. (**b**) *(bouder) personne* to ignore. ◆ **ignoré, e** *adj* unknown. **~ de tous** *(inconnu)* unknown to anybody; *(boudé)* ignored by all.

iguane [igwan] *nm* iguana.

il [il] *pron pers m* (**a**) *(personne)* he; *(bébé, animal)* it, he; *(chose)* it; *(bateau, nation)* she, it. **~s** they; **~ était journaliste** he was a journalist. (**b**) *(impers)* it. **~ fait beau** it's a fine day; **~ y a 3 enfants** there are 3 children; **~ est vrai que** it is true that. (**c**) *(non traduit)* **Paul est-~ rentré?** is Paul back?; **~ est si beau cet arbre** this tree is so beautiful.

île [il] *nf* island. **les ~s anglo-normandes** the Channel Islands; **les ~s Britanniques** the British Isles; *(Culin)* **~ flottante** floating island; **l'~ Maurice**

Mauritius; **les ~s du Vent/sous le Vent** the Windward/Leeward Islands.

iléon [ileɔ̃] *nm* ileum.

illégal, e, *mpl* **-aux** [ilegal, o] *adj* illegal, unlawful *(Admin)*; *organisation, société* illegal, outlawed. **c'est ~** it's illegal, it's against the law. ◆ **illégalement** *adv* illegally, unlawfully. ◆ **illégalité** *nf* illegality.

illégitime [ileʒitim] *adj* illegitimate. ◆ **illégitimité** *nf* illegitimacy.

illettré, e [iletʀe] *adj, nm, f* illiterate. ◆ **illettrisme** *nm* illiteracy. **campagne contre l' ~** literacy campaign.

illicite [ilisit] *adj* illicit. ◆ **illicitement** *adv* illicitly.

illico * [iliko] *adv* at once, pronto *.

illimité, e [ilimite] *adj (gén)* unlimited; *confiance* boundless.

illisibilité [ilizibilite] *nf* illegibility. ◆ **illisible** *adj (indéchiffrable)* illegible; *(mauvais)* unreadable.

illogique [ilɔʒik] *adj* illogical. ◆ **illogiquement** *adv* illogically. ◆ **illogisme** *nm* illogicality.

illuminer [ilymine] (1) **1** *vt (lit, fig)* to light up, illuminate; *[projecteurs]* to floodlight. **2 s' ~** *vpr [visage, ciel]* to light up (*de* with); *[rue]* to be lit up. ◆ **illumination** *nf* (**a**) lighting; illumination; floodlighting. *(lumières)* **~s** illuminations, lights. (**b**) *(inspiration)* flash of inspiration. ◆ **illuminé, e** *nm, f (péj: visionnaire)* crank *(péj)*.

illusion [ilyzjɔ̃] *nf* illusion. **~ d'optique** optical illusion; **tu te fais des ~s** you're deluding yourself; **ça ne fera pas ~ longtemps** it won't delude *ou* fool people for long. ◆ **s'illusionner** (1) *vpr* to delude o.s. (*sur* about). ◆ **illusionniste** *nmf* conjurer. ◆ **illusoire** *adj* illusory.

illustrer [ilystʀe] (1) **1** *vt* to illustrate (*de* with). **2 s' ~** *vpr* to win fame, become famous (*par, dans* through). ◆ **illustrateur, -trice** *nm, f* illustrator. ◆ **illustration** *nf (gén)* illustration. ◆ **illustre** *adj* illustrious, renowned. ◆ **illustré, e** **1** *adj* illustrated. **2** *nm (journal)* comic.

îlot [ilo] *nm (île)* small island; *(maisons)* block; *(fig: zone)* island. **~ de résistance** pocket of resistance.

îlotage [ilɔtaʒ] *nm* community policing. ◆ **îlotier** *nm* ≃ community policeman.

image [imaʒ] *nf (dessin, représentation)* picture; *(métaphore, ressemblance, Phys)* image; *(reflet)* reflexion. **les ~s d'un film** the frames of a film; **popularisé par l' ~** popularized by the camera; **Dieu créa l'homme à son ~** God created man in his own image; **~ de marque** *[produit]* brand image; *[parti, firme]* public image. ◆ **imagé, e** *adj* full of imagery.

imaginer [imaʒine] (1) **1** *vt* (**a**) *(supposer)* to imagine. **je l'imaginais plus vieux** I imagined him to be older; **qu'allez-vous ~ là?** what on earth are you thinking of? (**b**) *(inventer)* to devise, dream up. **qu'est-il encore allé ~?** * now what has he dreamed up? **2 s' ~** *vpr* (**a**) *(se figurer)* to imagine. **s' ~ que** to imagine *ou* think that. (**b**) *(se voir)* to imagine o.s., picture o.s. ◆ **imaginable** *adj* conceivable, imaginable. ◆ **imaginaire** *adj* imaginary; *monde* make-believe. ◆ **imaginatif, -ive** *adj* imaginative. ◆ **imagination** *nf (faculté)* imagination. **ce sont de pures ~s** that's sheer imagination, those are pure fancies; **avoir de l' ~** to be imaginative, have a good imagination; **avoir trop d' ~** to be over-imaginative; **une ~ débordante** a lively *ou* wild imagination.

imbattable [ɛ̃batabl(ə)] *adj* unbeatable.

imbécile [ɛ̃besil] **1** *adj* stupid, idiotic; *(Méd)* imbecilic, idiotic. **2** *nmf* idiot, imbecile. **ne fais pas l'~** * *(n'agis pas bêtement)* don't be an idiot * *ou* a fool; *(ne simule pas la bêtise)* stop acting stupid *; **c'est un ~ heureux** he's living in a fool's paradise. ◆ **imbécillité** *nf* idiocy, imbecility. **c'est une ~** *(gén)* it's an idiotic thing to do (*ou* say); *(film)* it's rubbish *ou* trash; **tu racontes des ~s** you're talking rot * *ou* rubbish.

imberbe [ɛ̃bɛʀb(ə)] *adj* beardless.

imbiber [ɛ̃bibe] (1) **1** *vt*: **~ un tampon de** to soak *ou* moisten a pad with; **imbibé d'eau** *étoffe* saturated (with water), soaked; *terre* waterlogged. **2 s' ~** *vpr*: **s' ~ de** to become saturated *ou* soaked with.

imbriquer (s') [ɛ̃bʀike] (1) *vpr [problèmes]* to be linked *ou* interwoven; *[plaques]* to overlap; *[cubes]* to fit into each other. ◆ **imbrication** *nf* interweaving; overlapping.

imbroglio [ɛ̃bʀɔljo] *nm* imbroglio.

imbu, e [ɛ̃by] *adj*: **~ de** full of; **~ de lui-même** *ou* **de sa personne** pompous, full of himself *ou* of self-importance.

imbuvable [ɛ̃byvabl(ə)] *adj (lit)* undrinkable; (*) *personne* unbearable, insufferable.

imiter [imite] (1) *vt* (**a**) *(gén)* to imitate; *personnage* to impersonate; *geste* to mimic; *signature* to forge. **il se leva et tout le monde l'imita** he got up and everybody did likewise *ou* followed suit. (**b**) *[matière]* to look like. ◆ **imitateur, -trice** **1** *adj* imitative. **2** *nm, f (gén)* imitator; *(Théât) [personnage]* impersonator. ◆ **imitatif, -ive** *adj* imitative. ◆ **imitation** *nf* imitation; impersonation; mimicry; forgery. **à l' ~ de** in imitation of; **c'est en ~ cuir** it's imitation leather.

immaculé, e [imakyle] *adj* spotless, immaculate. **d'un blanc ~** spotlessly white.

immangeable [ɛ̃mɑ̃ʒabl(ə)] *adj* uneatable, inedible.

immanquable [ɛ̃mɑ̃kabl(ə)] *adj cible* impossible to miss. **c'était ~!** it was inevitable! ◆ **immanquablement** *adv* inevitably, without fail.

immatriculer [imatʀikyle] (1) *vt* to register. **faire ~, se faire ~** to register. ◆ **immatriculation** *nf* registration. **numéro d' ~** registration *ou* license *(US)* number.

immature [imatyʀ] *adj* immature.

immédiat, e [imedja, at] **1** *adj (gén)* immediate. **2** *nm*: **dans l' ~** for the time being. ◆ **immédiatement** *adv* immediately.

immémorial, e, *mpl* **-aux** [imemɔʀjal, o] *adj* age-old. **de temps ~** from time immemorial.

immense [imɑ̃s] *adj (gén)* immense; *espace* boundless; *foule* huge; *avantage, succès* tremendous. *(fig)* **un ~ acteur** a stupendous actor. ◆ **immensément** *adv* immensely, hugely, tremendously. ◆ **immensité** *nf* immensity, hugeness.

immerger [imɛʀʒe] (3) *vt objet* to immerse, submerge; *déchets* to dump at sea; *câble* to lay under water; *corps* to bury at sea. ◆ **immergé, e** *adj terres* submerged. **~ par 100 mètres de fond** lying 100 metres down. ◆ **immersion** *nf* immersion; submersion; dumping at sea; underwater laying; burying at sea.

immérité, e [imeʀite] *adj* undeserved, unmerited.

immettable [ɛ̃mɛtabl(ə)] *adj vêtement* unwearable.

immeuble [imœbl(ə)] *nm (bâtiment)* building; *(d'habitation)* block of flats, apartment building *(US)*. **~ de bureaux** office block *ou* building *(US)*.

immigrer [imigʀe] (1) *vi* to immigrate (*à, dans* into). ◆ **immigrant, e** *adj, nm, f* immigrant. ◆ **immigration** *nf* immigration. **(les services de) l' ~** the immigration department.

imminence [iminɑ̃s] *nf* imminence. ◆ **imminent, e** *adj* imminent, impending.

immiscer (s') [imise] (3) *vpr*: **s' ~ dans** to interfere in. ◆ **immixtion** *nf*: **~ dans** interference in.

immobile [imɔbil] *adj* motionless. **rester ~** to keep still.

immobilier, -ière [imɔbilje, jɛʀ] **1** *adj vente* property; *biens* in real estate. **2** *nm*: **l'** ~ the property *ou* real-estate business.

immobiliser [imɔbilize] (1) **1** *vt (gén)* to immobilize; *véhicule* to stop, bring to a standstill. **ça l'immobilise à son domicile** it keeps him housebound; **immobilisé par la peur** paralyzed with fear. **2 s'** ~ *vpr [personne]* to stop, stand still; *[véhicule]* to come to a standstill. ◆ **immobilisation** *nf* immobilization. **attendez l'** ~ **totale de l'avion** wait until the aircraft has come to a complete standstill *ou* halt. ◆ **immobilité** *nf* stillness, motionlessness. **le médecin lui a ordonné l'** ~ **complète** the doctor ordered him not to move (at all); ~ **forcée** forced immobility; ~ **politique** political inertia.

immodéré, e [imɔdeʀe] *adj* immoderate, inordinate.

immoler [imɔle] (1) *vt (gén)* to sacrifice (*à* to). ◆ **immolation** *nf* sacrifice.

immonde [imɔ̃d] *adj taudis* squalid, foul; *personne* base, vile. ◆ **immondices** *nfpl (ordures)* refuse.

immoral, e, *mpl* **-aux** [imɔʀal, o] *adj* immoral. ◆ **immoralité** *nf* immorality.

immortaliser [imɔʀtalize] (1) **1** *vt* to immortalize. **2 s'** ~ *vpr* to win immortality. ◆ **immortalité** *nf* immortality. ◆ **immortel, -elle 1** *adj* immortal. **2** *nf (fleur)* everlasting flower.

immotivé, e [imɔtive] *adj action* unmotivated; *crainte* groundless.

immuable [imɥabl(ə)] *adj (gén)* unchanging; *loi* immutable. **son chapeau** ~ his eternal hat. ◆ **immuablement** *adv* immutably.

immuniser [imynize] (1) *vt (Méd)* to immunize. *(fig)* **être immunisé contre les tentations** to be immune to temptation. ◆ **immunisation** *nf* immunization. ◆ **immunité** *nf (Bio, Jur)* immunity. ~ **parlementaire** ≃ parliamentary privilege. ◆ **immunitaire** *adj* immune. **réactions** ~**s** immune reactions.

immuno-dépresseur [imynɔdepʀesœʀ] *adj, nm* immunodepressant.

immunoglobuline [imynɔglɔbylin] *nf* immunoglobulin.

immunologie [imynɔlɔʒi] *nf* immunology. ◆ **immunologique** *adj* immunological. ◆ **immunologiste** *nmf* immunologist.

impact [ɛ̃pakt] *nm (lit, fig)* impact.

impair, e [ɛ̃pɛʀ] **1** *adj* odd. **2** *nm (gaffe)* blunder. *(Casino)* **l'** ~ the odd numbers.

impalpable [ɛ̃palpabl(ə)] *adj* impalpable.

imparable [ɛ̃paʀabl(ə)] *adj* unstoppable.

impardonnable [ɛ̃paʀdɔnabl(ə)] *adj* unforgivable, unpardonable.

imparfait, e [ɛ̃paʀfɛ, ɛt] **1** *adj (gén)* imperfect. **2** *nm (Ling)* **l'** ~ the imperfect (tense). ◆ **imparfaitement** *adv* imperfectly.

impartial, e, *mpl* **-aux** [ɛ̃paʀsjal, o] *adj* impartial, unbiased. ◆ **impartialement** *adv* impartially. ◆ **impartialité** *nf* impartiality.

impasse [ɛ̃pas] *nf* (**a**) *(cul-de-sac)* dead end; *(sur panneau)* 'no through road'. (**b**) *(fig)* impasse. **être dans l'** ~ *[négociations]* to be at deadlock; ~ **budgétaire** budget deficit. (**c**) *(Cartes)* finesse. *(Scol)* **j'ai fait 3** ~**s** I missed out *ou* skipped over 3 topics.

impassibilité [ɛ̃pasibilite] *nf* impassiveness. ◆ **impassible** *adj* impassive. ◆ **impassiblement** *adv* impassively.

impatience [ɛ̃pasjɑ̃s] *nf* impatience. **il était dans l'** ~ **de la revoir** he was impatient to see her again. ◆ **impatiemment** *adv* impatiently. ◆ **impatient, e** *adj* impatient. ~ **de faire** eager to do. ◆ **impatienter** (1) **1** *vt* to irritate, annoy. **2 s'** ~ *vpr* to get impatient (*contre* with, at).

impayable * [ɛ̃pɛjabl(ə)] *adj (drôle)* priceless *.

impayé, e [ɛ̃peje] *adj* unpaid.

impeccable [ɛ̃pekabl(ə)] *adj (gén)* impeccable. ◆ **impeccablement** *adv* impeccably.

impédance [ɛ̃pedɑ̃s] *nf (Élec)* impedance.

impénétrable [ɛ̃penetʀabl(ə)] *adj (gén)* impenetrable (*à* to, by); *visage* inscrutable.

impénitent, e [ɛ̃penitɑ̃, ɑ̃t] *adj* unrepentant.

impensable [ɛ̃pɑ̃sabl(ə)] *adj événement hypothétique* unthinkable; *événement arrivé* unbelievable.

imper * [ɛ̃pɛʀ] *nm (abrév de* **imperméable***)* raincoat, mac *.

impératif, -ive [ɛ̃peʀatif, iv] **1** *adj (obligatoire)* imperative; *(impérieux) ton* commanding. **2** *nm* (**a**) *(Ling)* **l'** ~ the imperative (mood). (**b**) *[fonction]* requirement; *[mode, horaire]* demand; *[situation]* necessity; *(Mil)* imperative. ◆ **impérativement** *adv* imperatively.

impératrice [ɛ̃peʀatʀis] *nf* empress.

imperceptible [ɛ̃pɛʀsɛptibl(ə)] *adj* imperceptible (*à* to). ◆ **imperceptiblement** *adv* imperceptibly.

imperfection [ɛ̃pɛʀfɛksjɔ̃] *nf (gén)* imperfection.

impérial, e, *mpl* **-aux** [ɛ̃peʀjal, o] **1** *adj* imperial. **2** *nf [autobus]* top deck. **autobus à** ~**e** ≃ double-decker (bus). ◆ **impérialisme** *nm* imperialism. ◆ **impérialiste** *adj, nmf* imperialist.

impérieux, -euse [ɛ̃peʀjø, øz] *adj (autoritaire)* imperious; *(pressant)* urgent, pressing. ◆ **impérieusement** *adv* imperiously; urgently.

impérissable [ɛ̃peʀisabl(ə)] *adj œuvre* imperishable; *souvenir* undying.

imperméable [ɛ̃pɛʀmeabl(ə)] **1** *adj roches* impermeable; *tissu* waterproof. ~ **à l'eau** waterproof; ~ **à l'air** airtight; *(fig: insensible)* ~ **à** impervious to. **2** *nm (manteau)* raincoat. ◆ **imperméabiliser** (1) *vt* to waterproof. ◆ **imperméabilité** *nf* impermeability.

impersonnel, -elle [ɛ̃pɛʀsɔnɛl] *adj* impersonal.

impertinence [ɛ̃pɛʀtinɑ̃s] *nf* impertinence. **arrête tes** ~**s!** that's enough impertinence!, that's enough of your impertinent remarks! ◆ **impertinent, e** *adj* impertinent.

imperturbable [ɛ̃pɛʀtyʀbabl(ə)] *adj* imperturbable. **rester** ~ to remain unruffled. ◆ **imperturbablement** *adv* imperturbably.

impétueux, -euse [ɛ̃petɥø, øz] *adj (gén)* impetuous; *torrent* raging. ◆ **impétueusement** *adv* impetuously. ◆ **impétuosité** *nf* impetuosity.

impie [ɛ̃pi] *adj* impious, ungodly. ◆ **impiété** *nf* impiety, ungodliness.

impitoyable [ɛ̃pitwajabl(ə)] *adj* merciless, pitiless. ◆ **impitoyablement** *adv* mercilessly, pitilessly.

implacable [ɛ̃plakabl(ə)] *adj* implacable. ◆ **implacablement** *adv* implacably.

implanter [ɛ̃plɑ̃te] (1) **1** *vt usage* to introduce; *race* to introduce, settle; *usine* to set up, establish; *idée, (Méd)* to implant. **2 s'** ~ *vpr [usines]* to be set up *ou* established; *[race]* to settle. **il semble s'** ~ **chez eux** he seems to be making himself quite at home with them; **des traditions solidement implantées** deeply-rooted *ou* deeply-entrenched traditions. ◆ **implant** *nm (Méd)* implant. ◆ **implantation** *nf* introduction; settlement; establishment; implantation.

implication [ɛ̃plikɑsjɔ̃] *nf (gén)* implication.

implicite [ɛ̃plisit] *adj* implicit. *(Ling)* **connaissance** ~ tacit knowledge. ◆ **implicitement** *adv* implicitly.

impliquer [ɛ̃plike] (1) *vt* (**a**) *(supposer)* to imply (*que* that). (**b**) ~ **qn dans** to implicate sb in. ◆ **s'**~ *vpr:* **il s'implique dans son travail** he gives his work all he's got.

implorer [ɛ̃plɔʀe] (1) *vt* to implore. ~ **qn de faire** to implore *ou* beseech sb to do. ◆ **imploration** *nf* entreaty.

imploser [ɛ̃ploze] (1) *vi* to implode. ◆ **implosion** *nf* implosion.

impoli, e [ɛ̃pɔli] *adj* impolite, rude (*envers* to). ◆ **impoliment** *adv* impolitely, rudely. ◆ **impolitesse** *nf (attitude)* impoliteness, rudeness; *(remarque)* impolite *ou* rude remark; *(acte)* impolite action. **c'est une** ~ **que de faire** it is impolite *ou* rude to do.

impondérable [ɛ̃pɔ̃deʀabl(ə)] *adj, nm* imponderable.

impopulaire [ɛ̃pɔpylɛʀ] *adj* unpopular. ◆ **impopularité** *nf* unpopularity.

import [ɛ̃pɔʀ] *nm (abrév de* **importation***)* import. **faire de l'** ~**-export** to be in the import-export business.

importance [ɛ̃pɔʀtɑ̃s] *nf (gén)* importance; *[fait]* significance; *[somme]* size; *[dégâts]* extent. **avoir de l'** ~ to be important; **sans** ~ unimportant, insignificant; **ça n'a pas d'** ~ it doesn't matter; **de la plus haute** ~**, de la première** ~ of paramount *ou* of the highest importance; **d'une certaine** ~ *firme* sizeable; *dégâts* considerable, extensive; **prendre de l'** ~ *(gén)* to become more important; *[firme]* to increase in size; *(péj)* **se donner de l'**~ to put on self-important airs. ◆ **important, e** *adj* important; significant; sizeable; extensive; *(péj) airs* self-important. **peu** ~ of little importance *ou* significance; **l'** ~ **est de** the important thing is to.

importer[1] [ɛ̃pɔʀte] (1) *vt* to import (*de* from). ◆ **importateur, -trice 1** *adj* importing. **2** *nm, f* importer. ◆ **importation** *nf (action)* importation; *(produit)* import. **articles d'** ~ imported articles.

importer[2] [ɛ̃pɔʀte] (1) *vi (être important)* to matter. **que lui importe!** what does he care about it!, what does it matter to him!; **il importe de faire/que** it is important to do/that; **peu m'importe** *(pas de préférence)* I don't mind; *(je m'en moque)* I don't care; **n'importe** it doesn't matter, I don't mind; **n'importe qui** anybody, anyone; **n'importe quoi** anything; **n'importe comment** anyhow; **n'importe où** anywhere; **n'importe quand** anytime; **venez à n'importe quelle heure** come any time; **il fait/dit n'importe quoi!** * he's no idea what he's doing/saying!

importun, e [ɛ̃pɔʀtœ̃, yn] **1** *adj présence* troublesome; *visite* inopportune; *personne* importunate. **2** *nm, f (gêneur)* irksome individual; *(visiteur)* intruder. ◆ **importunément** *adv* importunately, inopportunely. ◆ **importuner** (1) *vt* to importune, bother. **je ne veux pas vous** ~ I don't wish to bother you *ou* to disturb you *ou* to intrude. ◆ **importunité** *nf* importunity.

imposer [ɛ̃poze] (1) **1** *vt (gén)* to impose; *tâche* to set; *conditions* to lay down; *(Fin: taxer)* to tax; *(Typ)* to impose. ~ **sa présence à qn** to impose *ou* force one's company on sb; ~ **un régime à qn** to put sb on a diet; ~ **son nom** *[artiste]* to make o.s. known; *[firme]* to establish itself; **sa conduite impose le respect** his behaviour compels respect; *(Rel)* ~ **les mains** to lay on hands; **en** ~ **à qn** to impress sb. **2 s'** ~ *vpr* (**a**) *(être nécessaire)* to be essential *ou* vital *ou* imperative. **une visite au Louvre s'impose** a visit to the Louvre is a must. (**b**) **s'** ~ **une tâche** to set o.s. a task; **s'** ~ **de faire** to make it a rule to do. (**c**) *[artiste]* to make o.s. known; *[firme]* to become firmly established; *[sportif]* to emerge as the best. (**d**) *(importuner)* **s'** ~ **à qn** to impose (o.s.) upon sb; **je ne voudrais pas m'** ~ I do not want to impose. ◆ **imposable** *adj* taxable. ◆ **imposant, e** *adj stature* imposing; *allure* stately; *(considérable)* imposing, impressive. ◆ **imposition** *nf (Fin)* taxation; *(Typ)* imposition. *(Rel)* **l'** ~ **des mains** the laying on of hands.

impossibilité [ɛ̃pɔsibilite] *nf* impossibility. **être dans l'** ~ **de faire qch** to find it impossible to do sth; **se heurter à des** ~**s** to come up against insuperable obstacles. ◆ **impossible 1** *adj (gén)* impossible. **il m'est** ~ **de le faire** it's impossible for me to do it, I can't possibly do it; *(Prov)* ~ **n'est pas français** there's no such word as 'can't'. **2** *nm*: **je ferai l'** ~ **(pour venir)** I'll do my utmost (to come); **par** ~ by some miracle.

imposteur [ɛ̃pɔstœʀ] *nm* impostor. ◆ **imposture** *nf* imposture.

impôt [ɛ̃po] *nm (taxe)* tax; *(taxation)* taxation. **payer des** ~**s** to pay tax; ~ **sur les bénéfices** tax on profits, ≃ corporation tax; ~ **sur le chiffre d'affaires** tax on turnover; ~ **direct/indirect** direct/indirect tax; ~ **foncier** ≃ land tax; ~ **(de solidarité) sur la fortune** wealth tax; ~**s locaux** rates; ~ **sur les plus-values** ≃ capital gains tax; ~ **sur le revenu** income tax.

impotent, e [ɛ̃pɔtɑ̃, ɑ̃t] **1** *adj* disabled, crippled. **2** *nm, f* cripple. ◆ **impotence** *nf* disability.

impraticable [ɛ̃pʀatikabl(ə)] *adj idée* impracticable, unworkable; *(Sport) terrain* unfit for play, unplayable; *route* impassable.

imprécation [ɛ̃pʀekɑsjɔ̃] *nf* imprecation, curse.

imprécis, e [ɛ̃pʀesi, iz] *adj (gén)* imprecise; *tir* inaccurate. ◆ **imprécision** *nf* imprecision; inaccuracy.

imprégner [ɛ̃pʀeɲe] (6) *vt tissu* to impregnate, soak (*de* with); *air* to permeate, fill (*de* with); *esprit* to imbue (*de* with). **imprégné de lumière** flooded with light; **s'** ~ **d'eau** to become soaked with water; **s'** ~ **d'une langue** to immerse o.s. in a language. ◆ **imprégnation** *nf (gén)* impregnation; permeation; immersion.

imprenable [ɛ̃pʀənabl(ə)] *adj forteresse* impregnable. **vue** ~ unimpeded *ou* unrestricted outlook.

imprésario [ɛ̃pʀesaʀjo] *nm* impresario.

impression [ɛ̃pʀesjɔ̃] *nf* (**a**) *(sensation)* impression. **faire bonne/mauvaise** ~ to create a good/bad impression; **avoir l'** ~ **que** to have a feeling *ou* the impression that; **faire** ~ to make an impression. (**b**) *[livre] (action)* printing; *(tirage)* impression. (**c**) *(motif)* pattern. (**d**) *(Phot)* exposure. (**e**) *(Peinture)* undercoat.

impressionner [ɛ̃pʀesjɔne] (1) *vt* (**a**) *(frapper)* to impress; *(bouleverser)* to upset. (**b**) *(Opt, Phot) [image]* to show up on; *[photographe]* to expose. ◆ **impressionnable** *adj* impressionable. ◆ **impressionnant, e** *adj* impressive; upsetting.

imprévisibilité [ɛ̃pʀevizibilite] *nf* unpredictability. ◆ **imprévisible** *adj* unpredictable.

imprévoyance [ɛ̃pʀevwajɑ̃s] *nf* lack of foresight; *(d'argent)* improvidence. ◆ **imprévoyant, e** *adj* lacking (in) foresight; improvident.

imprévu, e [ɛ̃pʀevy] **1** *adj événement* unforeseen, unexpected; *geste* unexpected; *dépense* unforeseen. **2** *nm*: **l'** ~ the unexpected, the unforeseen; **plein d'** ~ full of surprises; **en cas d'** ~ if anything unexpected *ou* unforeseen crops up; **tous ces** ~**s** all these unexpected *ou* unforeseen events.

imprimante [ɛ̃pʀimɑ̃t] *nf* printer. ~ **matricielle/ligne par ligne/à jet d'encre/à marguerite/laser** dot-matrix/line/ink-jet/daisy-wheel/laser printer.

imprimer [ɛ̃pʀime] (1) *vt livre* to print; *cachet* to stamp; *rides, marque* to imprint (*dans* in, on); *(publier)* to publish. ~ **un mouvement à** to transmit a movement to. ◆ **imprimé, e 1** *adj* printed. **2** *nm (formulaire)* printed form. *(Poste)* ~**(s)** printed matter; *(tissu)* **l'** ~ printed material. ◆ **imprimerie** *nf (firme)* printing works; *(atelier)* printing house; *(section)* printery. *(technique)* **l'** ~ printing ;

l'I~ nationale ≃ the Government Printing Office. ◆ **imprimeur** *nm* printer.

improbabilité [ɛ̃pʀɔbabilite] *nf* unlikelihood, improbability. ◆ **improbable** *adj* unlikely, improbable.

improductif, -ive [ɛ̃pʀɔdyktif, iv] *adj* unproductive.

impromptu, e [ɛ̃pʀɔ̃pty] **1** *adj départ* sudden; *visite* surprise; *repas, exposé* impromptu. **2** *nm (Littérat, Mus)* impromptu. **3** *adv* impromptu.

imprononçable [ɛ̃pʀɔnɔ̃sabl(ə)] *adj* unpronounceable.

impropre [ɛ̃pʀɔpʀ(ə)] *adj terme* inappropriate. ~ **à** unsuitable for; ~ **à la consommation** unfit for (human) consumption. ◆ **improprement** *adv nommer* incorrectly, improperly. ◆ **impropriété** *nf [forme]* incorrectness. ~ **(de langage)** (language) error, mistake.

improviser [ɛ̃pʀɔvize] (1) **1** *vt* to improvise. **2 s'** ~ *vpr*: **s'** ~ **cuisinier** to act as cook; **on ne s'improvise pas menuisier** you don't become a carpenter just like that. ◆ **improvisation** *nf* improvisation. ◆ **improvisé, e** *adj (de fortune)* improvised, makeshift; *(impromptu)* improvised.

improviste [ɛ̃pʀɔvist(ə)] *nm*: **à l'** ~ unexpectedly, without warning; **prendre qn à l'** ~ to catch sb unawares.

imprudent, e [ɛ̃pʀydɑ̃, ɑ̃t] **1** *adj (gén)* careless, imprudent, foolish; *remarque* unwise. **il est** ~ **de** it's unwise to. **2** *nm, f* imprudent *ou* careless person. ◆ **imprudemment** *adv* carelessly, imprudently, foolishly; unwisely. ◆ **imprudence** *nf (caractère)* carelessness, imprudence, foolishness. *(action)* **commettre une** ~ to do something foolish *ou* imprudent.

impudence [ɛ̃pydɑ̃s] *nf (caractère)* impudence; *(acte)* impudent action. ◆ **impudent, e** *adj* impudent.

impudeur [ɛ̃pydœʀ] *nf* immodesty. ◆ **impudique** *adj* immodest.

impuissance [ɛ̃pɥisɑ̃s] *nf [personne]* powerlessness, helplessness; *(sexuelle)* impotence; *[efforts]* ineffectiveness. ◆ **impuissant, e** *adj* powerless, helpless; impotent; ineffectual.

impulsion [ɛ̃pylsjɔ̃] *nf (Phys, Psych)* impulse; *(fig: élan)* impetus. **l'** ~ **donnée à l'économie** the boost *ou* impetus given to the economy. ◆ **impulsif, -ive** *adj* impulsive.

impunément [ɛ̃pynemɑ̃] *adv* with impunity. ◆ **impuni, e** *adj* unpunished. ◆ **impunité** *nf* impunity.

impur, e [ɛ̃pyʀ] *adj* impure. ◆ **impureté** *nf (gén)* impurity.

imputer [ɛ̃pyte] (1) *vt*: ~ **à** to impute to, attribute to, ascribe to; *(Fin)* to charge to. ◆ **imputable** *adj*: ~ **à** ascribable to, attributable to; chargeable to. ◆ **imputation** *nf (accusation)* imputation. *(Fin)* ~ **à** charging to.

in * [in] *adj* in *, trendy *, with-it *. **les bottes sont** ~ **cette année** boots are in * *ou* big * this year.

inabordable [inabɔʀdabl(ə)] *adj personne* unapproachable; *lieu* inaccessible; *prix* prohibitive.

inaccentué, e [inaksɑ̃tɥe] *adj* unstressed.

inacceptable [inaksɛptabl(ə)] *adj* unacceptable.

inaccessible [inaksesibl(ə)] *adj* inaccessible. ~ **à** *(insensible à)* impervious to.

inaccoutumé, e [inakutyme] *adj* unusual. ~ **à** unaccustomed to, unused to.

inachevé, e [inaʃve] *adj* unfinished, uncompleted. ◆ **inachèvement** *nm* incompletion.

inactif, -ive [inaktif, iv] **1** *adj* (**a**) *(oisif)* idle, inactive; *population* non-working. (**b**) *(inefficace)* ineffective. **2** *nmpl*: **les** ~**s** the non-working population, those not in active employment. ◆ **inaction** *nf* inactivity, idleness. ◆ **inactivité** *nf* inactivity.

inadapté, e [inadapte] *adj personne* maladjusted; *outil, moyens* unsuitable (*à* for). ~ **à** not adapted *ou* adjusted to. ◆ **inadaptation** *nf* maladjustment. **l'** ~ **d'un enfant à la vie scolaire** a child's inability to cope with school life.

inadéquat, e [inadekwa, at] *adj* inadequate.

inadmissible [inadmisibl(ə)] *adj (gén)* inadmissible.

inadvertance [inadvɛʀtɑ̃s] *nf*: **par** ~ inadvertently, by mistake.

inaliénable [inaljenabl(ə)] *adj* inalienable.

inaltérable [inalteʀabl(ə)] *adj substance* stable; *encre* permanent; *principes etc* steadfast, unshakeable. ~ **à l'air** unaffected by air.

inamical, e, *mpl* **-aux** [inamikal, o] *adj* unfriendly.

inamovible [inamɔvibl(ə)] *adj fonctionnaire* irremovable; *panneau* fixed; *(hum) casquette etc* eternal.

inanimé, e [inanime] *adj matière* inanimate; *(évanoui)* unconscious; *(mort)* lifeless; *(Ling)* inanimate.

inanité [inanite] *nf [conversation]* inanity; *[efforts]* futility.

inanition [inanisjɔ̃] *nf*: **tomber d'** ~ to faint with hunger.

inaperçu, e [inapɛʀsy] *adj* unnoticed. **passer** ~ to pass unnoticed.

inapplicable [inaplikabl(ə)] *adj* inapplicable (*à* to), which cannot be applied (*à* to).

inapplication [inaplikɑsjɔ̃] *nf [élève]* lack of application. ◆ **inappliqué, e** *adj* lacking in application.

inappréciable [inapʀesjabl(ə)] *adj aide* invaluable; *bonheur* inestimable; *nuance* imperceptible.

inapte [inapt(ə)] *adj* incapable (*à faire* of doing). ~ **aux affaires** unsuited to business; *(Mil)* ~ **(au service)** unfit (for military service). ◆ **inaptitude** *nf (mentale)* inaptitude, incapacity; *(physique)* unfitness (*à* for).

inarticulé, e [inaʀtikyle] *adj* inarticulate.

inassouvi, e [inasuvi] *adj* unappeased.

inattaquable [inatakabl(ə)] *adj position* unassailable; *preuve* irrefutable; *conduite* irreproachable; *métal* corrosion-proof, rustproof.

inattendu, e [inatɑ̃dy] **1** *adj* unexpected, unforeseen. **2** *nm*: **l'** ~ the unexpected, the unforeseen; **l'** ~ **d'une remarque** the unexpectedness of a remark.

inattention [inatɑ̃sjɔ̃] *nf* (**a**) *(distraction)* lack of attention, inattention. **(faute d')** ~ careless mistake. (**b**) ~ **à** *détails* lack of concern for. ◆ **inattentif, -ive** *adj* inattentive (*à* to); unconcerned (*à* by).

inaudible [inodibl(ə)] *adj* inaudible.

inaugurer [inɔgyʀe] (1) *vt (gén, fig)* to inaugurate; *monument* to unveil; *exposition* to open; *(hum) chapeau* to christen. ◆ **inaugural, e,** *mpl* **-aux** *adj (gén)* inaugural. **voyage** ~ maiden voyage. ◆ **inauguration** *nf* inauguration; unveiling; opening. **(cérémonie d')** ~ inaugural ceremony.

inavouable [inavwabl(ə)] *adj* shameful. ◆ **inavoué, e** *adj* unconfessed.

incalculable [ɛ̃kalkylabl(ə)] *adj (gén)* incalculable.

incandescence [ɛ̃kɑ̃desɑ̃s] *nf* incandescence. **en** ~ white-hot, incandescent. ◆ **incandescent, e** *adj* incandescent, white-hot.

incantation [ɛ̃kɑ̃tɑsjɔ̃] *nf* incantation. ◆ **incantatoire** *adj* incantatory.

incapable [ɛ̃kapabl(ə)] **1** *adj (gén)* incapable (*de faire* of doing). ~ **de bouger** unable to move, incapable of movement *ou* of moving. **2** *nmf*: **c'est un** ~ he's useless *, he's an incompetent. ◆ **inca-**

pacité *nf (incompétence)* incapability; *(invalidité)* disablement; *(Jur)* incapacity. *(impossibilité)* ~ **de faire** incapability *ou* inability to do; **être dans l'** ~ **de faire** to be unable to do, be incapable of doing; ~ **de travail** industrial disablement *ou* disability.

incarcérer [ɛ̃kaʀseʀe] (6) *vt* to incarcerate. ◆ **incarcération** *nf* incarceration.

incarner [ɛ̃kaʀne] (1) **1** *vt* to embody; *(Théât)* to play; *(Rel)* to incarnate. **2 s'** ~ *vpr*: **s'** ~ **dans** to be embodied in; *(Rel)* to be incarnate in. ◆ **incarnation** *nf* incarnation; embodiment. ◆ **incarné, e** *adj* (**a**) incarnate. **c'est la méchanceté** ~**e** he is wickedness incarnate *ou* personified. (**b**) *ongle* ingrown.

incartade [ɛ̃kaʀtad] *nf* prank.

incassable [ɛ̃kɑsabl(ə)] *adj* unbreakable.

incendier [ɛ̃sɑ̃dje] (7) *vt* (**a**) *(mettre le feu à)* to set fire to; *(brûler complètement)* to burn down. (**b**) *désir, imagination* to fire; *gorge* to burn. (**c**) *(*: réprimander)* ~ **qn** to give sb a stiff telling-off *; **elle l'a incendié du regard** she looked daggers at him, she shot him a baleful look. ◆ **incendiaire 1** *nmf* arsonist. **2** *adj balle, discours* incendiary ; *œillade* passionate. ◆ **incendie** *nm* fire. ~ **criminel** case of arson; ~ **de forêt** forest fire.

incertain, e [ɛ̃sɛʀtɛ̃, ɛn] *adj* (**a**) *personne* uncertain, unsure *(de, sur* about). (**b**) *démarche, temps* uncertain; *contour* indistinct, blurred; *lumière* dim. (**c**) *succès, fait, origine* uncertain, doubtful. ◆ **incertitude** *nf (gén)* uncertainty. **être dans l'** ~ to be in a state of uncertainty; **être dans l'** ~ **sur ce qu'on doit faire** to be uncertain as to the best course to follow.

incessamment [ɛ̃sɛsamɑ̃] *adv* (very) shortly.

incessant, e [ɛ̃sɛsɑ̃, ɑ̃t] *adj (gén)* incessant, unceasing; *efforts* ceaseless, unremitting.

inceste [ɛ̃sɛst(ə)] *nm* incest. ◆ **incestueux, -euse** *adj* incestuous.

inchangé, e [ɛ̃ʃɑ̃ʒe] *adj* unchanged, unaltered. ◆ **inchangeable** *adj* unchangeable.

incidemment [ɛ̃sidamɑ̃] *adv* incidentally, in passing.

incidence [ɛ̃sidɑ̃s] *nf (conséquence)* effect; *(Écon, Phys)* incidence. **avoir une** ~ **sur** to affect, have an effect (up)on.

incident [ɛ̃sidɑ̃] *nm (gén)* incident. ~ **imprévu** unexpected incident; ~ **de parcours** *(gén)* (slight) setback; *(lit, fig)* ~ **technique** technical hitch ; **l'**~ **est clos** that's an end of the matter.

incinérer [ɛ̃sineʀe] (6) *vt* to incinerate; *(au crématorium)* to cremate. **se faire** ~ to be cremated. ◆ **incinérateur** *nm* incinerator. ◆ **incinération** *nf* incineration; cremation.

inciser [ɛ̃size] (1) *vt* to incise. ◆ **incisif, -ive 1** *adj ton* cutting, incisive; *regard* piercing. **2** *nf (dent)* incisor. ◆ **incision** *nf* incision.

inciter [ɛ̃site] (1) *vt*: ~ **qn à faire** to incite *ou* urge sb to do; **ça n'incite pas au travail** it's no incentive to work. ◆ **incitation** *nf (au meurtre, à la révolte)* incitement; *(à l'effort, au travail)* incentive (*à* to, *à faire* to do).

incivilité [ɛ̃sivilite] *nf* incivility, rudeness; *(propos)* uncivil *ou* rude remark.

inclassable [ɛ̃klɑsabl(ə)] *adj* unclassifiable.

incliner [ɛ̃kline] (1) **1** *vt* (**a**) *(pencher)* to tilt; *(courber)* to bend. ~ **la tête** to bow *ou* incline one's head; ~ **le buste** *(saluer)* to bow; *(pencher)* to lean *ou* bend forward. (**b**) ~ **qn à** to encourage sb to; **ceci m'incline à penser que** that leads me to believe that. **2** *vi* (**a**) ~ **à** to be inclined to. (**b**) *(bifurquer)* ~ **vers** to veer towards *ou* to. **3 s'** ~ *vpr* (**a**) *(se courber)* to bow; *(s'avouer battu)* to admit defeat. *(lit, fig)* **s'** ~ **devant qn** to bow before *ou* to sb; **s'** ~ **devant un ordre** to accept an order; **Marseille s'est incliné devant Saint-Étienne** Marseilles went down to *ou* lost to Saint-Étienne. (**b**) *[arbre]* to bend over; *[mur]* to lean; *[chemin]* to slope. ◆ **inclinable** *adj dossier de siège* reclining; *lampe* adjustable. ◆ **inclinaison** *nf [route]* gradient; *[toit]* slope, pitch; *[mur]* lean; *[chapeau, tête]* tilt; *[navire]* list; *(Géom) [droite]* angle. ◆ **inclination** *nf* (**a**) *(penchant)* inclination. **avoir de l'** ~ **pour** to have a strong liking *ou* a penchant for. (**b**) ~ **de (la) tête** *(acquiescement)* nod; *(salut)* inclination of the head; ~ **(du buste)** bow. ◆ **incliné, e** *adj* (**a**) *pente* steep; *mur* leaning; *récipient* tilted. (**b**) **être** ~ **à penser que...** to be inclined to think that...; **être** ~ **au mal** to have a tendency towards what is bad.

inclure [ɛ̃klyʀ] (35) *vt* to include; *(dans une enveloppe)* to enclose (*dans* in). **jusqu'au 10 mars inclus** until March 10th inclusive, up to and including March 10th. ◆ **inclusion** *nf* inclusion. ◆ **inclusivement** *adv*: **jusqu'au 1er janvier** ~ until January 1st inclusive, up to and including January 1st.

incognito [ɛ̃kɔɲito] **1** *adv* incognito. **2** *nm*: **garder l'** ~ to remain incognito.

incohérent, e [ɛ̃kɔeʀɑ̃, ɑ̃t] *adj (confus)* incoherent; *(illogique)* inconsistent. ◆ **incohérence** *nf* incoherence; inconsistency. ~**s dans un texte** inconsistencies *ou* discrepancies in a text.

incollable [ɛ̃kɔlabl(ə)] *adj* (**a**) *(qui ne colle pas)* **riz** ~ non-stick rice. (**b**) *(*: imbattable)* unbeatable. **il est** ~ **(en histoire)** you can't catch him out * (on history).

incolore [ɛ̃kɔlɔʀ] *adj* colourless; *vernis* clear.

incomber [ɛ̃kɔ̃be] (1) ~ **à** *vt indir [responsabilité]* to be incumbent (up)on; *[frais]* to be sb's responsibility. **il nous incombe de** it falls to us to.

incombustible [ɛ̃kɔ̃bystibl(ə)] *adj* incombustible.

incommode [ɛ̃kɔmɔd] *adj heure* awkward, inconvenient; *outil* impractical; *siège* uncomfortable; *position* awkward, uncomfortable. ◆ **incommodément** *adv* inconveniently; awkwardly, uncomfortably. ◆ **incommodité** *nf* inconvenience; awkwardness; impracticality; lack of comfort.

incommoder [ɛ̃kɔmɔde] (1) *vt*: ~ **qn** to disturb *ou* bother sb. ◆ **incommodant, e** *adj odeur* unpleasant, offensive; *bruit* annoying; *chaleur* uncomfortable. ◆ **incommodé, e** *adj* indisposed, unwell. **elle est** ~**e par la fumée** the smoke makes her uncomfortable, she is bothered by the smoke.

incommunicabilité [ɛ̃kɔmynikabilite] *nf* incommunicability.

incomparable [ɛ̃kɔ̃paʀabl(ə)] *adj (sans pareil)* incomparable, matchless; *(dissemblable)* not comparable. ◆ **incomparablement** *adv* incomparably.

incompatibilité [ɛ̃kɔ̃patibilite] *nf* incompatibility. ~ **d'humeur** (mutual) incompatibility; ~ **de groupes sanguins** incompatibility of blood groups. ◆ **incompatible** *adj* incompatible (*avec* with).

incompétence [ɛ̃kɔ̃petɑ̃s] *nf (incapacité)* incompetence; *(ignorance)* lack of knowledge. ◆ **incompétent, e** *adj* incompetent; ignorant.

incomplet, -ète [ɛ̃kɔ̃plɛ, ɛt] *adj* incomplete. ◆ **incomplètement** *adv renseigné* incompletely; *guéri* not completely.

incompréhension [ɛ̃kɔ̃pʀeɑ̃sjɔ̃] *nf (par ignorance)* lack of understanding; *(par hostilité)* lack of sympathy. ◆ **incompréhensible** *adj (gén)* incomprehensible. ◆ **incompréhensif, -ive** *adj* unsympathetic. ◆ **incompris, e** *adj* misunderstood.

inconcevable [ɛ̃kɔ̃svabl(ə)] *adj (gén)* inconceivable.

inconciliable [ɛ̃kɔ̃siljabl(ə)] *adj* irreconcilable.

inconditionnel, -elle [ɛ̃kɔ̃disjɔnɛl] **1** *adj* unconditional; *partisan* unquestioning. **2** *nm, f [doctrine]* unquestioning supporter (*de* of); *[écrivain]* ardent admirer (*de* of). **les ~s des sports d'hiver** winter sports enthusiasts *ou* fanatics. ◆ **inconditionnalité** *nf* unreservedness, wholeheartedness.

inconduite [ɛ̃kɔ̃dɥit] *nf* wild *ou* loose behaviour.

inconfort [ɛ̃kɔ̃fɔʀ] *nm [logement]* lack of comfort, discomfort. **vivre dans l'** ~ to live in uncomfortable surroundings. ◆ **inconfortable** *adj maison* uncomfortable; *(lit, fig) position* uncomfortable, awkward.

incongelable [ɛ̃kɔ̃ʒlabl(ə)] *adj* non-freezable, unsuitable for freezing.

incongru, e [ɛ̃kɔ̃gʀy] *adj attitude* unseemly; *remarque* incongruous, ill-placed. ◆ **incongruité** *nf* incongruity, unseemliness. **une** ~ an unseemly remark (*ou* action).

inconnu, e [ɛ̃kɔny] **1** *adj* unknown. **son visage m'était** ~ his face was new *ou* unknown to me; **une joie ~e** a strange joy; ~ **à cette adresse** not known at this address; *(fig)* **il est ~ au bataillon** no one's ever heard of him. **2** *nm, f* stranger, unknown person. **3** *nm*: **l'** ~ the unknown. **4** *nf (Math, fig)* unknown quantity.

inconscient, e [ɛ̃kɔ̃sjɑ̃, ɑ̃t] **1** *adj (évanoui, machinal)* unconscious; *(irréfléchi)* thoughtless, reckless; (*: *fou)* mad *, crazy. ~ **de** unaware of. **2** *nm (Psych)* **l'** ~ the unconscious. **3** *nm, f* (*) nutcase ‡. ◆ **inconsciemment** *adv* unconsciously; thoughtlessly; recklessly. ◆ **inconscience** *nf* unconsciousness; thoughtlessness; recklessness. **c'est de l'** ~ that's sheer madness.

inconséquent, e [ɛ̃kɔ̃sekɑ̃, ɑ̃t] *adj (illogique)* inconsistent, inconsequent; *(irréfléchi)* thoughtless. ◆ **inconséquence** *nf* inconsistency; thoughtlessness.

inconsidéré, e [ɛ̃kɔ̃sideʀe] *adj* thoughtless, rash. ◆ **inconsidérément** *adv* thoughtlessly, rashly.

inconsistant, e [ɛ̃kɔ̃sistɑ̃, ɑ̃t] *adj preuve* flimsy; *caractère* weak; *crème* runny. ◆ **inconsistance** *nf* flimsiness; weakness; runniness.

inconsolable [ɛ̃kɔ̃sɔlabl(ə)] *adj* inconsolable.

inconstance [ɛ̃kɔ̃stɑ̃s] *nf [temps, sort]* fickleness; *[amour]* inconstancy; *[comportement]* inconsistency. ◆ **inconstant, e** *adj* fickle; inconstant; inconsistent.

incontestable [ɛ̃kɔ̃tɛstabl(ə)] *adj* incontestable, indisputable. ◆ **incontestablement** *adv* incontestably, indisputably. ◆ **incontesté, e** *adj* uncontested, undisputed.

incontinence [ɛ̃kɔ̃tinɑ̃s] *nf* incontinence. ◆ **incontinent, e** *adj* incontinent.

incontrôlable [ɛ̃kɔ̃tʀolabl(ə)] *adj (non vérifiable)* unverifiable; *(irrépressible)* uncontrollable. ◆ **incontrôlé, e** *adj* unverified; uncontrolled. **un groupe ~ de manifestants** an uncontrolled *ou* undisciplined group of demonstrators.

inconvenant, e [ɛ̃kɔ̃vnɑ̃, ɑ̃t] *adj comportement* improper, unseemly; *question* improper; *personne* ill-mannered. ◆ **inconvenance** *nf* (**a**) *(caractère)* impropriety, unseemliness. (**b**) *(acte, remarque)* impropriety.

inconvénient [ɛ̃kɔ̃venjɑ̃] *nm (désavantage)* disadvantage, drawback, inconvenience; *(risque)* risk. **nous ne voulons pas en supporter les ~s** we don't want to have to suffer the consequences; **peut-on en boire sans ~?** can one safely drink it?, is there any risk in drinking it?; **l'** ~ **c'est que** the snag is that, the annoying thing is that, the one drawback is that; **si vous n'y voyez pas d'** ~... if you have no objections...

incorporer [ɛ̃kɔʀpɔʀe] (1) *vt (gén)* to incorporate; *(Mil)* to enlist (*dans* into); *substance* to mix (*à, avec* with). **se faire ~ dans l'infanterie** to enlist in the infantry. ◆ **incorporation** *nf* incorporation; mixing; enlistment.

incorrect, e [ɛ̃kɔʀɛkt, ɛkt(ə)] *adj* (**a**) *réglage* faulty; *solution* incorrect, wrong. (**b**) *langage* improper; *tenue* indecent; *personne* discourteous, impolite. (**c**) *(déloyal) personne, procédé* underhand. ◆ **incorrectement** *adv* faultily; incorrectly; wrongly; improperly; indecently; discourteously, impolitely; in an underhand way. ◆ **incorrection** *nf* (**a**) **l'** ~ impropriety, incorrectness. (**b**) *(terme)* impropriety; *(action)* impolite action.

incorrigible [ɛ̃kɔʀiʒibl(ə)] *adj* incorrigible.

incorruptible [ɛ̃kɔʀyptibl(ə)] *adj* incorruptible.

incrédule [ɛ̃kʀedyl] **1** *adj (sceptique)* incredulous; *(Rel)* unbelieving. **2** *nmf (Rel)* non-believer. ◆ **incrédulité** *nf* incredulity; unbelief.

incrémenter [ɛ̃kʀemɑ̃te] (1) *vt (Ordin)* to increment. ◆ **incrément** *nm (Ordin)* increment. ◆ **incrémentation** *nf (Ordin)* incrementation. ◆ **incrémentiel, -elle** *adj (Ordin)* incremental.

increvable [ɛ̃kʀəvabl(ə)] *adj pneu* puncture-proof; (‡: *infatigable)* tireless.

incriminer [ɛ̃kʀimine] (1) *vt personne* to incriminate, accuse; *conduite* to bring under attack; *honnêteté* to call into question.

incrochetable [ɛ̃kʀɔʃtabl(ə)] *adj serrure* burglar-proof.

incroyable [ɛ̃kʀwajabl(ə)] *adj* incredible, unbelievable. ~ **mais vrai** incredible *ou* unbelievable but true. ◆ **incroyablement** *adv* incredibly, unbelievably.

incroyance [ɛ̃kʀwajɑ̃s] *nf (Rel)* unbelief. ◆ **incroyant, e** **1** *adj* unbelieving. **2** *nm, f* non-believer.

incruster [ɛ̃kʀyste] (1) **1** *vt (Art)* to inlay. **2 s'** ~ *vpr* (**a**) *[caillou]* **s'** ~ **dans** to become embedded in. (**b**) *(fig) [invité]* to take root. (**c**) *[radiateur]* to become incrusted (*de* with). ◆ **incrustation** *nf (Art) (technique)* inlaying; *(ornement)* inlay; *(sur roche)* incrustation.

incuber [ɛ̃kybe] (1) *vt* to incubate. ◆ **incubateur** *nm* incubator. ◆ **incubation** *nf* incubation.

inculper [ɛ̃kylpe] (1) *vt* to charge (*de* with), accuse (*de* of). ◆ **inculpation** *nf* charging. **sous l'** ~ **de** on a charge of; **notifier à qn son** ~ to inform sb of the charge against him. ◆ **inculpé, e** *nm, f*: **l'** ~ ≃ the accused.

inculquer [ɛ̃kylke] (1) *vt*: ~ **à qn** to inculcate in sb.

inculte [ɛ̃kylt(ə)] *adj terre* uncultivated; *barbe* unkempt; *personne* uneducated. ◆ **inculture** *nf [personne]* lack of education; *[terre]* lack of cultivation.

incurable [ɛ̃kyʀabl(ə)] *adj, nmf* incurable. **les malades ~s** the incurably ill.

incursion [ɛ̃kyʀsjɔ̃] *nf (lit, fig)* incursion, foray (*en, dans* into).

incurver *vt*, **s'** ~ *vpr* [ɛ̃kyʀve] (1) to curve.

Inde [ɛ̃d] *nf* India. **les ~s** the Indies.

indécent, e [ɛ̃desɑ̃, ɑ̃t] *adj* indecent; *(fig) chance* disgusting. ◆ **indécemment** *adv* indecently. ◆ **indécence** *nf* indecency.

indéchiffrable [ɛ̃deʃifʀabl(ə)] *adj (illisible)* indecipherable; *(incompréhensible)* incomprehensible; *regard* inscrutable.

indéchirable [ɛ̃deʃiʀabl(ə)] *adj* tear-proof.

indécis, e [ɛ̃desi, iz] **1** *adj personne (par nature)* indecisive; *(temporairement)* undecided (*sur* about); *résultat* undecided; *temps, paix* unsettled; *réponse* vague; *forme* indistinct. **2** *nm, f (gén)* indecisive person; *(Sondages)* 'don't know'; *(dans une élection)* floating voter. ◆ **indécision** *nf* indecisiveness; *(temporaire)* indecision (*sur* about).

indécrottable * [ɛ̃dekʀɔtabl(ə)] *adj (borné)* hopelessly thick *, dumb *.

indéfectible [ɛ̃defɛktibl(ə)] *adj foi, confiance* indestructible, unshakeable; *soutien, attachement* unfailing.

indéfendable [ɛ̃defɑ̃dabl(ə)] *adj (lit, fig)* indefensible.

indéfini, e [ɛ̃defini] *adj (vague)* undefined; *(indéterminé)* indefinite. ◆ **indéfiniment** *adv* indefinitely. ◆ **indéfinissable** *adj* indefinable.

indélébile [ɛ̃delebil] *adj (lit, fig)* indelible.

indélicat, e [ɛ̃delika, at] *adj (mufle)* indelicate; *(malhonnête)* dishonest. ◆ **indélicatement** *adv* indelicately; dishonestly. ◆ **indélicatesse** *nf* indelicacy; dishonesty.

indémaillable [ɛ̃demɑjabl(ə)] *adj* run-resistant.

indemne [ɛ̃dɛmn(ə)] *adj* unharmed, unhurt, unscathed. **il est sorti** ~ **de l'accident** he came out of the accident unharmed *ou* unscathed.

indemniser [ɛ̃dɛmnize] (1) *vt (gén)* to indemnify (*de* for); *(d'une perte)* to compensate (*de* for). **se faire** ~ to get indemnification *ou* compensation; ~ **qn de ses frais** to reimburse sb for his expenses. ◆ **indemnisation** *nf (action)* indemnification; *(somme)* indemnity, compensation. **900 F d'** ~ 900 francs compensation. ◆ **indemnité** *nf [perte]* indemnity; *[frais]* allowance. ~ **de licenciement** redundancy payment *ou* money; ~ **de transport** travel allowance; ~ **parlementaire** M.P.'s salary; *(Jur)* ~ **pour charges de famille** dependency allowance.

indéniable [ɛ̃denjabl(ə)] *adj* undeniable. ◆ **indéniablement** *adv* undeniably.

indentation [ɛ̃dɑ̃tɑsjɔ̃] *nf* indentation.

indépendance [ɛ̃depɑ̃dɑ̃s] *nf (gén)* independence. ◆ **indépendamment** *adv (seul)* independently. ~ **de cela** apart from that. ◆ **indépendant, e** *adj (gén)* independent (*de* of). **pour des causes** ~**es de notre volonté** for reasons beyond our control; **'à louer: chambre** ~**e'** to let: self-contained bedsitter; **maison** ~**e** detached house; **travailler en** ~ to work freelance, be self-employed; **travailleur** ~ freelance *ou* self-employed worker.

indépendantiste [ɛ̃depɑ̃dɑ̃tist(ə)] **1** *adj*: **mouvement** ~ independence movement. **2** *nmf* member of an independence movement, freedom fighter.

indescriptible [ɛ̃dɛskʀiptibl(ə)] *adj* indescribable.

indésirable [ɛ̃deziʀabl(ə)] *adj, nmf* undesirable.

indestructible [ɛ̃dɛstʀyktibl(ə)] *adj* indestructible.

indéterminé, e [ɛ̃detɛʀmine] *adj date, cause* unspecified; *quantité* indeterminate; *impression, contours* vague. **pour des raisons** ~**es** for reasons which were not specified; **je suis encore** ~ **sur** I'm still undecided *ou* uncertain about. ◆ **indétermination** *nf (imprécision)* vagueness; *(irrésolution)* indecision.

index [ɛ̃dɛks] *nm (doigt)* forefinger; *(repère)* pointer; *(liste, indice)* index. *(fig)* **mettre qn/qch à l'I~** to blacklist sb/sth. ◆ **indexation** *nf* indexing, indexation. ◆ **indexer** (1) *vt* to index (*sur* to).

indication [ɛ̃dikɑsjɔ̃] *nf (gén)* indication (*de* of); *(directive)* instruction, direction; *(renseignement)* piece of information. **quelle** ~ **porte la pancarte?** what does the notice say?; **sauf** ~ **contraire** unless otherwise stated *ou* indicated. ◆ **indicateur, -trice 1** *nm, f*: ~ **(de police)** (police) informer. **2** *nm (guide)* guide; *(horaire)* timetable; *(Tech)* gauge, indicator. ~ **immobilier** property gazette; ~ **des rues** street directory; ~ **de vitesse** *(Aut)* speedometer; *(Aviat)* airspeed indicator. ◆ **indicatif, -ive 1** *adj* indicative (*de* of). **2** *nm* (**a**) *(Rad) (mélodie)* signature tune; *[Télex]* answer-back code. *[poste émetteur]* ~ **(d'appel)** call sign; ~ **téléphonique** (dialling) code; *(Télec)* ~ **départemental** area code; (**b**) *(Ling)* **l'** ~ the indicative.

indice [ɛ̃dis] *nm* (**a**) *(signe)* indication, sign; *(élément d'enquête)* clue; *(Jur: preuve)* piece of evidence. (**b**) *(Math)* suffix; *(Admin: grade)* grading. *(TV, radio)* ~ **d'écoute** audience rating; **l'** ~ **de l'INSEE** ≃ the retail price index; ~ **des prix** price index.

indicible [ɛ̃disibl(ə)] *adj* inexpressible.

indien, -ienne [ɛ̃djɛ̃, jɛn] **1** *adj* Indian. **2** *nm(f)*: **I~(ne)** *[Inde]* Indian; *[Amérique]* (Red *ou* American) Indian.

indifférence [ɛ̃difeʀɑ̃s] *nf (gén)* indifference (*envers* to, towards). ◆ **indifféremment** *adv*: **supporter** ~ **le froid et le chaud** to stand cold and heat equally well, stand either cold or heat; **manger de tout** ~ to eat anything. ◆ **indifférent, e** *adj* indifferent (*à* to). **cela m'est** ~ it is immaterial to me, it doesn't matter to me; **son sort m'est** ~ his fate is of no interest to me *ou* is a matter of indifference to me; **parler de choses** ~**es** to talk of this and that; **ça le laisse** ~ it doesn't touch him in the least, he is quite unconcerned about it. ◆ **indifférer** (6) *vt*: **ceci l'indiffère** he's indifferent to this, he couldn't care less about this.

indigence [ɛ̃diʒɑ̃s] *nf (misère)* poverty, destitution; *(fig)* poverty. ◆ **indigent, e 1** *adj* destitute, poor. **2** *nm, f* pauper. **les** ~**s** the destitute, the poor.

indigène [ɛ̃diʒɛn] **1** *adj (du pays)* local; *(aux colonies)* native; *(Bot, Zool)* indigenous. **2** *nmf* local; native.

indigestion [ɛ̃diʒɛstjɔ̃] *nf* indigestion. **avoir une** ~ to get indigestion *ou* an attack of indigestion; *(fig)* **avoir une** ~ **de qch** to be sick of sth. ◆ **indigeste** *adj (lit, fig)* indigestible.

indigne [ɛ̃diɲ] *adj acte* shameful; *personne* unworthy. ~ **de** *amitié* unworthy of; **il est** ~ **de vivre** he doesn't deserve to live, he's not fit to live. ◆ **indignement** *adv* shamefully. ◆ **indignité** *nf* (**a**) *(caractère) [personne]* unworthiness; *[conduite]* shamefulness. (**b**) *(acte)* shameful act.

indigner [ɛ̃diɲe] (1) **1** *vt*: ~ **qn** to make sb indignant. **2 s'** ~ *vpr* to get indignant (*de* about, at, *contre* with). ◆ **indignation** *nf* indignation. **avec** ~ indignantly. ◆ **indigné, e** *adj* indignant (*par* at).

indigo [ɛ̃digo] *nm, adj inv* indigo.

indiqué, e [ɛ̃dike] *adj (conseillé)* advisable; *(adéquat)* appropriate, suitable. **c'est tout** ~ it's just what we need, it's just the thing.

indiquer [ɛ̃dike] (1) *vt* (**a**) *(montrer)* to show, indicate. ~ **qch du doigt** to point sth out (*à qn* to sb), point to sth; *[montre]* ~ **l'heure** to show *ou* tell the time; ~ **la réception à qn** to direct sb to *ou* show sb the way to reception; **qu'indique la pancarte?** what does the sign say?; **cela indique de la négligence** it points to *ou* indicates negligence. (**b**) *(dire) solution* to tell; *dangers* to point out. ~ **un hôtel à qn** to tell sb of a hotel, suggest a hotel to sb. (**c**) *(fixer) date* to give, name. **à l'heure indiquée** at the agreed *ou* appointed time. (**d**) *[étiquette]* to show; *[facture]* to give, mention. ~ **qch sur un plan** to mark *ou* draw sth on a plan.

indirect, e [ɛ̃diʀɛkt, ɛkt(ə)] *adj (gén)* indirect. ◆ **indirectement** *adv* indirectly; *apprendre qch* in a roundabout way.

indiscipline [ɛ̃disiplin] *nf* lack of discipline. ◆ **indiscipliné, e** *adj* undisciplined, unruly.

indiscret, -ète [ɛ̃diskʀɛ, ɛt] *adj (gén)* indiscreet; *(curieux)* inquisitive. **à l'abri des regards** ~**s** away from prying *ou* inquisitive eyes. ◆ **indiscrétion** *nf* (**a**) indiscretion; inquisitiveness. **il pousse l'** ~ **jusqu'à lire mon courrier** his inquisitiveness is such that he even reads my mail; **sans** ~ without being indiscreet. (**b**) *(parole)* indiscreet word, indiscretion.

indiscutable [ɛ̃diskytabl(ə)] *adj* indisputable, unquestionable. ◆ **indiscutablement** *adv* indisputably, unquestionably. ◆ **indiscuté, e** *adj* undisputed.

indispensable [ɛ̃dispɑ̃sabl(ə)] **1** *adj (vital)* essential, vital; *(nécessaire)* necessary. **se rendre** ~ to make o.s. indispensable; **ça m'est** ~ it's indispensable to me, I can't do without it. **2** *nm*: **faire l'** ~ to do what is essential *ou* absolutely necessary.

indisponible [ɛ̃dispɔnibl(ə)] *adj* unavailable.

indisposer [ɛ̃dispoze] (1) *vt (rendre malade)* to upset, indispose; *(mécontenter)* to antagonize, alienate. ◆ **indisposé, e** *adj (malade)* indisposed, unwell. ◆ **indisposition** *nf* (slight) indisposition, upset.

indissociable [ɛ̃disɔsjabl(ə)] *adj problèmes* indissociable.

indissoluble [ɛ̃disɔlybl(ə)] *adj* indissoluble.

indistinct, e [ɛ̃distɛ̃(kt), ɛ̃kt(ə)] *adj (gén)* indistinct; *murmure* confused; *couleurs* vague. ◆ **indistinctement** *adv* (**a**) indistinctly; vaguely; confusedly. (**b**) *(indifféremment)* **ça marche ~ au gaz ou à l'électricité** it runs equally well on gas or on electricity; **tuant ~ femmes et enfants** killing women and children indiscriminately.

individu [ɛ̃dividy] *nm (gén)* individual; *(corps)* body; *(péj: homme)* fellow. **un drôle d'** ~ an odd-looking character *ou* individual.

individualiser [ɛ̃dividɥalize] (1) **1** *vt (caractériser)* to individualize; *(personnaliser)* to personalize; *horaire* to tailor to individual requirements. **2 s'** ~ *vpr* to acquire an identity of one's own. ◆ **individualisé, e** *adj caractères, groupe* distinctive. ◆ **individualisme** *nm* individualism. ◆ **individualiste 1** *adj* individualistic. **2** *nmf* individualist. ◆ **individualité** *nf (gén)* individuality; *(personnalité)* personality. ◆ **individuel, -elle** *adj (gén)* individual; *liberté* personal; *caractères* distinctive. ◆ **individuellement** *adv* individually.

indivisibilité [ɛ̃divizibilite] *nf* indivisibility. ◆ **indivisible** *adj* indivisible.

Indochine [ɛ̃dɔʃin] *nf* Indochina. ◆ **indochinois, e** *adj*, **I~(e)** *nm(f)* Indochinese.

indo-européen, -enne [ɛ̃doøʀɔpeɛ̃, ɛn] *adj, nm*, **Indo-Européen(ne)** *nm(f)* Indo-European.

indolence [ɛ̃dɔlɑ̃s] *nf (gén)* indolence; *[pouvoirs publics]* apathy, lethargy. ◆ **indolent, e** *adj* indolent; apathetic, lethargic.

indolore [ɛ̃dɔlɔʀ] *adj* painless.

indomptable [ɛ̃dɔ̃tabl(ə)] *adj (gén)* untameable; *enfant* unmanageable; *volonté* indomitable. ◆ **indompté, e** *adj* untamed, wild.

Indonésie [ɛ̃dɔnezi] *nf* Indonesia. ◆ **indonésien, -enne** *adj*, **I~(ne)** *nm(f)* Indonesian.

indu, e [ɛ̃dy] *adj joie* unseemly; *dépenses* unwarranted, unjustified. **sans optimisme** ~ without undue optimism.

indubitable [ɛ̃dybitabl(ə)] *adj* indubitable. **il est ~ qu'il a tort** he is undoubtedly wrong, there's no doubt (that) he's wrong. ◆ **indubitablement** *adv* indubitably.

induction [ɛ̃dyksjɔ̃] *nf (gén)* induction.

induire [ɛ̃dɥiʀ] (38) *vt* (**a**) ~ **qn en erreur** to mislead sb, lead sb astray. (**b**) *(inférer)* to infer, induce (*de* from). (**c**) *(Élec)* to induce.

indulgent, e [ɛ̃dylʒɑ̃, ɑ̃t] *adj (gén)* indulgent (*avec* with); *juge, examinateur* lenient (*envers* towards). ◆ **indulgence** *nf* indulgence; leniency. **critique sans** ~ harsh criticism.

indûment [ɛ̃dymɑ̃] *adv protester* unduly; *détenir* wrongfully.

industrie [ɛ̃dystʀi] *nf* (**a**) *(activité)* industry. **doter un pays d'une ~** to provide a country with an industrial infrastructure; **Ministère de l'I~** ≃ Department of Industry; ~ **alimentaire** food (processing) industry; ~ **légère/lourde** light/heavy industry; **l'** ~ **du spectacle** show business. (**b**) *(entreprise)* industry, industrial concern. (**c**) *(ingéniosité)* ingenuity. ◆ **industrialisation** *nf* industrialization. ◆ **industrialiser** (1) **1** *vt* to industrialize. **2 s'** ~ *vpr* to become industrialized. ◆ **industriel, -elle 1** *adj* industrial. **pain ~** factory-baked bread; **équipement à usage ~** heavy-duty equipment. **2** *nm* industrialist, manufacturer. ◆ **industriellement** *adv* industrially.

industrieux, -euse [ɛ̃dystʀijø, øz] *adj* industrious.

inébranlable [inebʀɑ̃labl(ə)] *adj (résolu)* unshakeable, steadfast, unwavering; *(inamovible)* immovable.

inédit, e [inedi, it] *adj texte* unpublished; *trouvaille* new, original.

ineffable [inefabl(ə)] *adj* ineffable.

inefficace [inefikas] *adj mesure* ineffective; *machine* inefficient. ◆ **inefficacité** *nf* ineffectiveness; inefficiency.

inégal, e, *mpl* **-aux** [inegal, o] *adj (irrégulier)* uneven; *(disproportionné)* unequal. ◆ **inégalable** *adj* incomparable, matchless. ◆ **inégalé, e** *adj* unequalled, unmatched. ◆ **inégalement** *adv* unequally; unevenly. ◆ **inégalité** *nf (différence)* difference (*de* between); *(injustice)* inequality; *(irrégularité)* unevenness. **l'** ~ **sociale** social inequality; **~s d'humeur** unevenness of temper ; **~s de terrain** unevenness of the ground, bumps in the ground.

inélégant, e [inelegɑ̃, ɑ̃t] *adj toilette* inelegant; *procédés* discourteous.

inéligibilité [ineliʒibilite] *nf (Pol)* ineligibility. ◆ **inéligible** *adj* ineligible.

inéluctable [inelyktabl(ə)] *adj, nm* inescapable. ◆ **inéluctabilité** *nf* inescapability. ◆ **inéluctablement** *adv* inescapably.

inénarrable [inenaʀabl(ə)] *adj (désopilant)* priceless *; *(incroyable)* incredible.

inenvisageable [inɑ̃vizaʒabl(ə)] *adj* which cannot be considered, unthinkable.

inepte [inɛpt(ə)] *adj* inept. ◆ **ineptie** *nf (gén)* ineptitude. **dire des ~s** to talk nonsense.

inépuisable [inepɥizabl(ə)] *adj* inexhaustible.

inerte [inɛʀt(ə)] *adj (gén)* inert; *corps* lifeless; *personne* passive, apathetic. ◆ **inertie** *nf* inertia; passivity, apathy.

inescompté, e [inɛskɔ̃te] *adj* unexpected, unhoped-for.

inespéré, e [inɛspere] *adj* unexpected, unhoped-for.

inestimable [inɛstimabl(ə)] *adj aide* inestimable, invaluable; *valeur* priceless, incalculable.

inévitable [inevitabl(ə)] *adj obstacle, accident* unavoidable; *résultat* inevitable, inescapable. **c'était ~!** it was inevitable!, it was bound to happen!; **l'** ~ the inevitable. ◆ **inévitablement** *adv* inevitably.

inexact, e [inɛgza(kt), akt(ə)] *adj (faux)* inaccurate, inexact; *(sans ponctualité)* unpunctual. ◆ **inexactitude** *nf* inaccuracy; unpunctuality.

inexcusable [inɛkskyzabl(ə)] *adj* inexcusable, unforgivable.

inexistant, e [inɛgzistɑ̃, ɑ̃t] *adj* non-existent.

inexorable [inɛgzɔʀabl(ə)] *adj destin* inexorable; *juge* inflexible. ◆ **inexorabilité** *nf* inexorability; inflexibility. ◆ **inexorablement** *adv* inexorably.

inexpérience [inɛkspeʀjɑ̃s] *nf* inexperience. ◆ **inexpérimenté, e** *adj personne* inexperienced; *gestes* inexpert.

inexplicable [inɛksplikabl(ə)] *adj* inexplicable. ◆ **inexplicablement** *adv* inexplicably. ◆ **inexpliqué, e** *adj* unexplained.

inexploitable [inɛksplwatabl(ə)] *adj* unexploitable. ◆ **inexploité, e** *adj* unexploited; *(Fin) ressources* untapped.

inexploré, e [inɛksplɔʀe] *adj* unexplored.

inexpressif, -ive [inɛkspʀesif, iv] *adj visage* expressionless, inexpressive.

inexprimable [inɛkspʀimabl(ə)] *adj, nm* inexpressible.

inexprimé, e [inɛkspʀime] *adj sentiment* unexpressed; *reproches, doutes* unspoken.

inextinguible [inɛkstɛ̃gibl(ə)] *adj (littér) passion* inextinguishable; *soif* unquenchable; *rire* uncontrollable.

in extremis [inɛkstʀemis] **1** *loc adv arriver* at the last minute. **2** *loc adj sauvetage* last-minute.

inextricable [inɛkstʀikabl(ə)] *adj* inextricable. ◆ **inextricablement** *adv* inextricably.

infaillible [ɛ̃fajibl(ə)] *adj* infallible. ◆ **infaillibilité** *nf* infallibility. ◆ **infailliblement** *adv (à coup sûr)* inevitably; *(sans erreur)* infallibly.

infaisable [ɛ̃fəzabl(ə)] *adj* impossible, impracticable.

infâme [ɛ̃fɑm] *adj (gén)* vile, loathsome; *action* unspeakable; *traître* infamous; *taudis* revolting, disgusting. ◆ **infamant, e** *adj acte* infamous; *propos* defamatory. ◆ **infamie** *nf* (**a**) infamy. (**b**) *(insulte)* scandalous remark; *(action)* infamous *ou* vile *ou* loathsome action.

infanterie [ɛ̃fɑ̃tʀi] *nf* infantry.

infantile [ɛ̃fɑ̃til] *adj maladie* infantile; *médecine* child; *(puéril)* infantile, childish. ◆ **infantilisme** *nm (Méd, Psych)* infantilism. **c'est de l'** ~! how childish!

infarctus [ɛ̃faʀktys] *nm*: ~ **(du myocarde)** coronary thrombosis; **il a fait trois** ~ he has had three coronaries.

infatigable [ɛ̃fatigabl(ə)] *adj* indefatigable, tireless. ◆ **infatigablement** *adv* indefatigably, tirelessly.

infatuer (s') [ɛ̃fatɥe] (1) *vpr*: **s'** ~ **de** to become infatuated with. ◆ **infatuation** *nf* self-conceit. ◆ **infatué, e** *adj air* conceited. ~ **de lui-même** full of self-conceit.

infect, e [ɛ̃fɛkt, ɛkt(ə)] *adj (gén)* vile, revolting; *temps* filthy, foul.

infecter [ɛ̃fɛkte] (1) **1** *vt atmosphère* to contaminate; *(Méd, fig)* to poison, infect. **2 s'** ~ *vpr [plaie]* to become infected, turn septic. ◆ **infectieux, -euse** *adj* infectious. ◆ **infection** *nf (Méd)* infection; *(puanteur)* stench.

inférer [ɛ̃feʀe] (6) *vt* to infer, gather (*de* from).

inférieur, e [ɛ̃feʀjœʀ] **1** *adj partie, rang, vitesse* lower; *quantité, nombre* smaller; *qualité, intelligence* inferior. **descendez à l'étage** ~ go to the next floor down; ~ **à** *nombre* less *ou* smaller than, below; ~ **à la moyenne** below average; **roman** ~ **à un autre** novel inferior to another. **2** *nm, f* inferior. ◆ **infériorité** *nf* inferiority. ~ **en nombre** inferiority in numbers; **en état d'** ~ in an inferior position.

infernal, e, *mpl* **-aux** [ɛ̃fɛʀnal, o] *adj (gén)* infernal; *douleur, enfant* diabolical.

infertile [ɛ̃fɛʀtil] *adj (lit, fig)* infertile.

infester [ɛ̃fɛste] (1) *vt (gén)* to infest. **infesté de souris** infested with *ou* overrun with mice.

infidèle [ɛ̃fidɛl] **1** *adj ami, récit* unfaithful (*à* to); *mémoire* unreliable; *(Rel)* infidel. **2** *nmf (Rel)* infidel. ◆ **infidélité** *nf* (**a**) unfaithfulness; unreliability. (**b**) *(acte déloyal)* infidelity. **faire une** ~ **à qn** to be unfaithful to sb.

infiltrer (s') [ɛ̃filtʀe] (1) *vpr (gén)* to infiltrate; *[liquide]* to percolate (through); *[lumière]* to filter through. **s'** ~ **dans** to infiltrate; to percolate (through); to filter into. ◆ **infiltration** *nf* infiltration; percolation. **il y a une** ~ *ou* **des** ~**s dans la cave** there are leaks in the cellar, water is leaking into the cellar; *(Méd)* **se faire faire des** ~**s** to have injections.

infime [ɛ̃fim] *adj* tiny, minute.

infini, e [ɛ̃fini] **1** *adj (gén)* infinite; *patience* unlimited; *douleur* immense; *propos* interminable, never-ending. **avec d'** ~**es précautions** with infinite *ou* endless precautions. **2** *nm*: **l'** ~ *(Philos)* the infinite; *(Math, Phot)* infinity; **à l'** ~ endlessly. ◆ **infiniment** *adv (gén)* infinitely. **avec** ~ **de soin** with infinite care; **je regrette** ~ I'm extremely sorry; **l'** ~ **grand** the infinitely great; **l'** ~ **petit** the infinitesimal. ◆ **infinité** *nf* infinity. **une** ~ **de** an infinite number of. ◆ **infinitésimal, e,** *mpl* **-aux** *adj* infinitesimal.

infinitif, -ive [ɛ̃finitif, iv] *adj, nm* infinitive.

infirme [ɛ̃fiʀm(ə)] **1** *adj* crippled, disabled; *(avec l'âge)* infirm. **être** ~ **de naissance** to be disabled from birth, be born disabled. **2** *nmf* cripple. ~ **mental/moteur** mentally/physically handicapped *ou* disabled person; ~ **du travail** industrially disabled person; ~ **de guerre** war cripple. ◆ **infirmerie** *nf (gén)* infirmary; *[école, navire]* sick bay. ◆ **infirmier** *nm* male nurse. ◆ **infirmière** *nf* nurse. ~ **en chef** sister, charge nurse, head nurse *(US)*; ~ **diplômée d'État** state registered nurse. ◆ **infirmité** *nf* disability. **les** ~**s de la vieillesse** the infirmities of old age.

infirmer [ɛ̃fiʀme] (1) *vt* to invalidate.

inflammable [ɛ̃flamabl(ə)] *adj* inflammable, flammable.

inflammation [ɛ̃flamɑsjɔ̃] *nf* inflammation. ◆ **inflammatoire** *adj* inflammatory.

inflation [ɛ̃flɑsjɔ̃] *nf* inflation. ◆ **inflationniste** *adj danger* inflationary; *politique* inflationist.

infléchir [ɛ̃fleʃiʀ] (2) **1** *vt (lit, fig)* to bend; *rayons* to inflect. **2 s'** ~ *vpr [route]* to bend; *[poutre]* to sag; *[politique]* to shift.

inflexible [ɛ̃flɛksibl(ə)] *adj (gén)* inflexible; *caractère* unyielding; *règle* rigid. ◆ **inflexibilité** *nf* inflexibility; rigidity.

inflexion [ɛ̃flɛksjɔ̃] *nf [direction]* bend; *[voix]* inflexion; *[politique]* shift (*de* in). **d'une** ~ **de la tête/du corps** with a nod/bow.

infliger [ɛ̃fliʒe] (3) *vt (gén)* to inflict; *amende* to impose (*à* on). *(Scol)* ~ **un avertissement** *ou* **un blâme à qn** to give sb an order mark *ou* a bad mark *ou* a demerit point *(US)*.

influence [ɛ̃flyɑ̃s] *nf* influence (*sur* on). **il a de l'** ~ he's an influential person; **avoir une** ~ **néfaste sur** to have a harmful effect on; **sous l'** ~ **de** under the influence of. ◆ **influençable** *adj* easily influenced. ◆ **influencer** (3) *vt (gén)* to influence; *(agir sur)* to act upon. ◆ **influent, e** *adj* influential. ◆ **influer** (1) *vi*: ~ **sur** to influence, have an influence on.

influx [ɛ̃fly] *nm*: ~ **nerveux** (nerve) impulse.

infographie [ɛ̃fɔgʀafi] *nf* computer graphics.

informateur, -trice [ɛ̃fɔʀmatœʀ, tʀis] *nm, f (gén)* informant; *(Police)* informer.

informaticien, -ienne [ɛ̃fɔʀmatisjɛ̃, jɛn] *nm, f* computer scientist, computerist *(US)*.

information [ɛ̃fɔʀmɑsjɔ̃] *nf* (**a**) *(renseignement)* piece of information; *(nouvelle)* piece of news. **voici nos** ~**s** here is the news; **écouter/regarder les** ~**s** to listen to/watch the news (bulletins); **une** ~ **de dernière minute** some last-minute news. (**b**) *(diffusion)* information. **pour l'** ~ **des voyageurs** for the information of travellers; **mettre la main sur l'** ~ to get hold of the information network. (**c**) *(connaissances)* information. (**d**) *(Ordin, Sci)* **l'** ~ information; **traitement de l'** ~ data processing. (**e**) *(Jur)* ~ **officielle** (judicial) inquiry.

informatique [ɛ̃fɔʀmatik] **1** *nf (science)* computer science, computing; *(techniques)* data processing. **l'ère de l'** ~ the age of the computer. **2** *adj* computer. ◆ **informatiquement** *adv*: **traiter qch** ~ to use a computer to solve sth, process sth on a computer. ◆ **informatiser** (1) *vt* to computerize.

informe [ɛ̃fɔʀm(ə)] *adj masse* shapeless, formless; *visage* misshapen.

informer [ɛ̃fɔʀme] (1) **1** *vt* to inform, tell (*de* of, about). **informez-vous s'il est arrivé** find out *ou* ascertain whether he has arrived; **on vous a mal informé** you've been misinformed; **milieux bien informés** well-informed circles. **2 s'** ~ *vpr (d'un fait)* to inquire, find out, ask (*de* about); *(dans une matière)* to inform o.s. (*sur* about).

infortune [ɛ̃fɔʀtyn] *nf* misfortune. ◆ **infortuné, e** **1** *adj* ill-fated, wretched. **2** *nm, f* (poor) wretch.

infra [ɛ̃fʀa] *adv*: **voir** ~ see below.

infraction [ɛ̃fʀaksjɔ̃] *nf (délit)* offence. *(Aut)* **être en** ~ to be committing an offence, be in breach of the law; ~ **au code de la route** offence against the Highway Code.

infranchissable [ɛ̃fʀɑ̃ʃisabl(ə)] *adj (lit)* impassable; *(fig)* insurmountable, insuperable.

infrarouge [ɛ̃fʀaʀuʒ] *adj, nm* infrared. **missile guidé par** ~ heat-seeking missile.

infrastructure [ɛ̃fʀastʀyktyʀ] *nf (Constr)* substructure; *(Écon, fig)* infrastructure.

infroissable [ɛ̃fʀwasabl(ə)] *adj* uncrushable, crease-resistant.

infructueux, -euse [ɛ̃fʀyktɥø, øz] *adj* fruitless, unfruitful.

infuser [ɛ̃fyze] (1) *vt* (**a**) *(plus gén* **faire** ~ *) tisane* to infuse. **laisser** ~ **le thé** to leave the tea to brew *ou* infuse. (**b**) *(fig)* to infuse (*à* into). ◆ **infusion** *nf (action)* infusion; *(tisane)* infusion, herb tea. ~ **de tilleul** lime tea.

ingénier (s') [ɛ̃ʒenje] (7) *vpr*: **s'** ~ **à faire** to try hard to do.

ingénieur [ɛ̃ʒenjœʀ] *nm* engineer. ~ **chimiste** chemical engineer; ~**-conseil** engineering consultant; ~ **du son** sound engineer; ~ **des travaux publics** construction *ou* civil engineer. ◆ **ingénierie** *nf* engineering.

ingénieux, -euse [ɛ̃ʒenjø, øz] *adj* ingenious. ◆ **ingénieusement** *adv* ingeniously. ◆ **ingéniosité** *nf* ingenuity.

ingénu, e [ɛ̃ʒeny] *adj* naïve, artless. ◆ **ingénuité** *nf* naïvety, artlessness. ◆ **ingénument** *adv* naïvely, artlessly.

ingérer [ɛ̃ʒeʀe] (6) **1** *vt* to ingest. **2 s'** ~ *vpr*: **s'** ~ **dans** to interfere in. ◆ **ingérence** *nf* interference (*dans* in). ◆ **ingestion** *nf* ingestion.

ingouvernable [ɛ̃guvɛʀnabl(ə)] *adj (Pol)* ungovernable.

ingrat, e [ɛ̃gʀa, at] *adj personne* ungrateful (*envers* to); *métier, sujet* thankless; *sol* sterile; *visage* unattractive. ◆ **ingratitude** *nf* ingratitude, ungratefulness (*envers* towards). **avec** ~ ungratefully.

ingrédient [ɛ̃gʀedjɑ̃] *nm* ingredient.

inguérissable [ɛ̃geʀisabl(ə)] *adj (gén)* incurable; *chagrin* inconsolable.

ingurgiter [ɛ̃gyʀʒite] (1) *vt nourriture* to swallow, ingurgitate; *(fig)* to ingest, ingurgitate. **faire** ~ **des connaissances à qn** to force *ou* stuff knowledge into sb.

inhabile [inabil] *adj (manuellement)* clumsy; *(tactiquement)* inept. ◆ **inhabilité** *nf* clumsiness; ineptitude.

inhabitable [inabitabl(ə)] *adj* uninhabitable. ◆ **inhabité, e** *adj* uninhabited.

inhabituel, -elle [inabitɥɛl] *adj* unusual, unaccustomed.

inhaler [inale] (1) *vt* to inhale, breathe in. ◆ **inhalation** *nf* inhalation. **prendre une** ~ to use an inhalation bath.

inhérent, e [ineʀɑ̃, ɑ̃t] *adj* inherent (*à* in).

inhiber [inibe] (1) *vt* to inhibit. ◆ **inhibition** *nf* inhibition.

inhospitalier, -ière [inɔspitalje, jɛʀ] *adj* inhospitable.

inhumain, e [inymɛ̃, ɛn] *adj* inhuman.

inhumer [inyme] (1) *vt* to inter. ◆ **inhumation** *nf* interment.

inimaginable [inimaʒinabl(ə)] *adj* unimaginable, unbelievable.

inimitable [inimitabl(ə)] *adj* inimitable.

inimité, e [inimite] *adj*: **artiste qui est resté** ~ artist who has never been imitated.

inimitié [inimitje] *nf* enmity.

ininflammable [inɛ̃flamabl(ə)] *adj* nonflammable.

inintelligent, e [inɛ̃teliʒɑ̃, ɑ̃t] *adj* unintelligent.

inintelligible [inɛ̃teliʒibl(ə)] *adj* unintelligible. ◆ **inintelligibilité** *nf* unintelligibility.

inintéressant, e [inɛ̃teʀɛsɑ̃, ɑ̃t] *adj* uninteresting.

ininterrompu, e [inɛ̃tɛʀɔ̃py] *adj ligne* unbroken; *flot* steady, uninterrupted.

inique [inik] *adj* iniquitous. ◆ **iniquité** *nf* iniquity.

initial, e, *mpl* **-aux** [inisjal, o] *adj, nf* initial. ◆ **initialement** *adv* initially.

initialiser [inisjalize] (1) *vt (Ordin)* to initialize. ◆ **initialisation** *nf (Ordin)* initialization.

initiative [inisjativ] *nf (gén)* initiative. **prendre l'** ~ **d'une action/de faire** to take the initiative for an action/in doing; **avoir de l'** ~ to have *ou* show initiative; **conférence à l'** ~ **des USA** conference initiated by the USA; **à l'** ~ **de la France...** following France's initiative...

initier [inisje] (7) **1** *vt (gén)* to initiate (*à* into); *(à un sport)* to introduce (*à* to). **2 s'** ~ *vpr* to become initiated. ◆ **initiateur, -trice** *nm, f (gén)* initiator; *[mode]* innovator. ◆ **initiation** *nf* initiation (*à* into). *(titre)* ~ **à la philosophie** introduction to philosophy. ◆ **initié, e** **1** *adj* initiated. **2** *nm, f* initiated person. **les non** ~**s** the uninitiated.

injecter [ɛ̃ʒɛkte] (1) *vt (Méd, Tech)* to inject. ~ **des fonds dans une entreprise** to pump money into a project; **yeux injectés de sang** bloodshot eyes. ◆ **injectable** *adj* injectable. ◆ **injection** *nf* injection.

injonction [ɛ̃ʒɔ̃ksjɔ̃] *nf* injunction, command.

injure [ɛ̃ʒyʀ] *nf* insult. **bordée d'** ~**s** string of abuse *ou* insults; **il m'a fait l'** ~ **de ne pas venir** he insulted *ou* affronted me by not coming. ◆ **injurier** (7) *vt* to abuse, insult. ◆ **injurieusement** *adv* abusively, insultingly. ◆ **injurieux, -euse** *adj* abusive, insulting (*pour* to).

injuste [ɛ̃ʒyst(ə)] *adj (gén)* unjust; *(partial)* unfair (*avec* to). ◆ **injustement** *adv* unjustly; unfairly. ◆ **injustice** *nf* (**a**) *(caractère)* injustice; unfairness. (**b**) *(acte)* injustice.

injustifiable [ɛ̃ʒystifjabl(ə)] *adj* unjustifiable. ◆ **injustifié, e** *adj* unjustified, unwarranted.

inlassable [ɛ̃lɑsabl(ə)] *adj* tireless, unflagging. ◆ **inlassablement** *adv* tirelessly, unflaggingly.

inné, e [ine] *adj* innate, inborn.

innerver [inɛʀve] (1) *vt* to innervate. ◆ **innervation** *nf* innervation.

innocent, e [inɔsɑ̃, ɑ̃t] **1** *adj (gén)* innocent (*de* of); *farce* harmless. **2** *nm, f* innocent. **l'** ~ **du village** the village simpleton *ou* idiot. ◆ **innocemment** *adv* innocently. ◆ **innocence** *nf* innocence; harmlessness. ◆ **innocenter** (1) *vt* to clear, prove innocent (*de* of).

innombrable [inɔ̃bʀabl(ə)] *adj détails* innumerable, countless; *foule* vast.

innommable [inɔmabl(ə)] *adj conduite* unspeakable, loathsome; *nourriture, ordures* foul, vile.

innover [inɔve] (1) **1** *vi* to innovate. **ce peintre innove** this painter is breaking new ground. **2** *vt* to create, invent. ◆ **innovateur, -trice 1** *adj* innovatory. **2** *nm, f* innovator. ◆ **innovation** *nf* innovation.

inoccupé, e [inɔkype] *adj (gén)* unoccupied.

inoculer [inɔkyle] (1) *vt*: **~ un virus à qn** *(volontairement)* to inoculate sb with a virus; *(accidentellement)* to infect sb with a virus; **~ une passion** *etc* **à qn** to infect sb with a passion *etc*. ◆ **inoculation** *nf* inoculation; infection.

inodore [inɔdɔʀ] *adj gaz* odourless; *fleur* scentless.

inoffensif, -ive [inɔfɑ̃sif, iv] *adj* harmless, innocuous.

inonder [inɔ̃de] (1) *vt* to flood; *(fig: de produits)* to flood, swamp, inundate (*de* with). **inondé de soleil/de sueur** bathed in sunlight/in sweat; **inondé de larmes** *joues* streaming with tears; *yeux* full of tears; **se faire ~ (par la pluie)** to get soaked *ou* drenched (by the rain). ◆ **inondation** *nf (action)* flooding; swamping; inundation; *(résultat)* flood.

inopérable [inɔpeʀabl(ə)] *adj* inoperable.

inopiné, e [inɔpine] *adj (gén)* unexpected; *mort* sudden. ◆ **inopinément** *adv* unexpectedly.

inopportun, e [inɔpɔʀtœ̃, yn] *adj* ill-timed, inopportune, untimely. ◆ **inopportunément** *adv* inopportunely.

inorganisé, e [inɔʀganize] *adj* unorganized.

inoubliable [inublijabl(ə)] *adj* unforgettable.

inouï, e [inwi] *adj événement* unprecedented, unheard-of; *nouvelle, vitesse* incredible. **il est ~! *** he's incredible!

inox [inɔks] *ou* **inoxydable** [inɔksidabl(ə)] **1** *adj acier* stainless; *couteau* stainless steel. **2** *nm* stainless steel.

inqualifiable [ɛ̃kalifjabl(ə)] *adj* unspeakable.

inquiet, -ète [ɛ̃kjɛ, ɛt] **1** *adj (momentanément)* worried; *(par nature)* anxious; *gestes, attente* uneasy. **je suis ~ de ne pas le voir** I'm worried *ou* anxious at not seeing him. **2** *nm, f* worrier. ◆ **inquiétant, e** *adj* disturbing, worrying. ◆ **inquiéter** (6) **1** *vt (gén)* to worry, disturb; *(Mil)* to harass. **être inquiété (par la police)** to be troubled *ou* bothered by the police. **2 s' ~** *vpr* to worry. **s' ~ de** *(s'enquérir)* to inquire about; *(se soucier)* to worry about, trouble (o.s.) about, bother about. ◆ **inquiétude** *nf* anxiety. **donner des ~s à qn** to give sb cause for worry *ou* anxiety; **soyez sans ~** have no fear.

inquisiteur, -trice [ɛ̃kizitœʀ, tʀis] **1** *adj* inquisitive. **2** *nm* inquisitor. ◆ **inquisition** *nf* inquisition.

insaisissable [ɛ̃sezisabl(ə)] *adj fugitif* elusive; *nuance* imperceptible.

insalubre [ɛ̃salybʀ(ə)] *adj climat* insalubrious. ◆ **insalubrité** *nf* insalubrity.

insanité [ɛ̃sanite] *nf (folie)* insanity, madness; *(acte)* insane act. *(propos)* **~(s)** insane talk.

insatiable [ɛ̃sasjabl(ə)] *adj* insatiable. ◆ **insatiablement** *adv* insatiably.

insatisfait, e [ɛ̃satisfɛ, ɛt] *adj (non comblé)* unsatisfied; *(mécontent)* dissatisfied. **c'est un éternel ~** he's never satisfied, he's perpetually dissatisfied. ◆ **insatisfaction** *nf* dissatisfaction.

inscription [ɛ̃skʀipsjɔ̃] *nf* (**a**) *(écrite)* inscription. **l' ~ d'une question à l'ordre du jour** putting a question on the agenda. (**b**) *(immatriculation)* enrolment, registration, admission; *(à l'université)* matriculation, registration (*à* at); *(à un concours)* enrolment (*à* in). **l' ~ à un club** joining a club; **il y a déjà 20 ~s pour jeudi** 20 people have already signed on *ou* enrolled for Thursday; **votre ~ sur la liste dépend de...** the inclusion of your name on the list depends on...; **les ~s sont en baisse de 5%** the intake is down by 5%.

inscrire [ɛ̃skʀiʀ] (39) **1** *vt* (**a**) *nom, date* to note down, write down; *(Ftbl) but* to score, notch up; *(dans la pierre)* to inscribe, engrave. **~ une question à l'ordre du jour** to put a question on the agenda; **il est inscrit sur la liste** his name is (written) on the list. (**b**) *étudiant* to register, enrol; *(pour rendez-vous)* to put down. **(faire) ~ un enfant à l'école** to put a child's name down for school, enrol *ou* register a child for school. **2 s' ~** *vpr* (**a**) *(s'enrôler) (gén)* to join; *(sur une liste)* to put one's name down (*sur* on); *(à l'université)* to register, enrol (*à* at). **s' ~ à un parti/un club** to join a party/a club. (**b**) *(s'insérer) (Math)* to be inscribed. *(fig)* **s' ~ dans le cadre de qch** to lie *ou* come within the framework of sth, fit into sth. (**c**) **s' ~ en faux contre qch** to deny sth strongly. ◆ **inscrit, e** *nm, f* registered member (*ou* student *ou* candidate).

insecte [ɛ̃sɛkt(ə)] *nm* insect. ◆ **insecticide** *adj, nm* insecticide.

insécurité [ɛ̃sekyʀite] *nf* insecurity.

inséminer [ɛ̃semine] (1) *vt* to inseminate. ◆ **insémination** *nf* insemination. **~ artificielle** artificial insemination. ◆ **inséminateur** *nm* inseminator.

insensé, e [ɛ̃sɑ̃se] *adj* insane. **c'est un ~!** he's demented! *ou* insane!

insensible [ɛ̃sɑ̃sibl(ə)] *adj* (**a**) insensible, insensitive (*à* to). (**b**) *(imperceptible)* imperceptible. ◆ **insensibiliser** (1) *vt* to anaesthetize. ◆ **insensibilité** *nf* insensitivity, insensibility. ◆ **insensiblement** *adv* imperceptibly.

inséparable [ɛ̃sepaʀabl(ə)] *adj* inseparable (*de* from).

insérer [ɛ̃seʀe] (6) **1** *vt* to insert (*dans* into). **2 s' ~** *vpr* (**a**) *(faire partie de)* **s' ~ dans** to fit into. (**b**) *(s'introduire dans)* **s' ~ dans** to filter into. (**c**) *(s'attacher)* to be inserted *ou* attached. ◆ **insertion** *nf* insertion. **~ sociale** social integration.

insidieux, -euse [ɛ̃sidjø, øz] *adj* insidious. ◆ **insidieusement** *adv* insidiously.

insigne[1] [ɛ̃siɲ] *adj honneur* distinguished; *faveur* notable; *maladresse* remarkable.

insigne[2] [ɛ̃siɲ] *nm (cocarde)* badge. *(emblème)* **l' ~ de, les ~s de** the insignia of.

insignifiant, e [ɛ̃siɲifjɑ̃, ɑ̃t] *adj (gén)* insignificant; *somme* trifling. ◆ **insignifiance** *nf* insignificance.

insinuer [ɛ̃sinɥe] (1) **1** *vt* to insinuate, imply. **2 s' ~** *vpr*: **s' ~ dans** *[personne]* to worm one's way into, insinuate o.s. into; *[eau]* to seep *ou* creep into. ◆ **insinuation** *nf* insinuation, innuendo.

insipide [ɛ̃sipid] *adj (gén)* insipid.

insister [ɛ̃siste] (1) *vi* (**a**) **~ sur** *sujet* to stress; *syllabe* to emphasize, stress; **n'insistons pas!** let us not dwell on it; **j'ai compris, inutile d' ~!** I understand, no need to dwell on it! (**b**) *(s'obstiner)* to be insistent (*auprès de* with), insist. **sonnez encore, insistez, elle est un peu sourde** ring again and keep (on) trying because she's a little deaf; **je n'insiste pas, je m'en vais *** I won't insist — I'll go. ◆ **insistance** *nf* insistence (*sur qch* on sth, *à faire* on doing). **avec ~** insistently. ◆ **insistant, e** *adj* insistent.

insolation [ɛ̃sɔlɑsjɔ̃] *nf* (**a**) *(malaise)* sunstroke. **une ~** a touch of sunstroke. (**b**) *(ensoleillement)* (period of) sunshine. (**c**) *(exposition au soleil)* exposure.

insolent, e [ɛ̃sɔlɑ̃, ɑ̃t] *adj personne, attitude* insolent; *luxe, joie* unashamed. **il a une chance ~e!** he has the luck of the devil! ◆ **insolemment** *adv* insolently; unashamedly. ◆ **insolence** *nf* insolence; *(remarque)* insolent remark.

insolite [ɛ̃sɔlit] *adj* unusual, strange.

insoluble [ɛ̃sɔlybl(ə)] *adj problème* insoluble, insolvable. ~ **(dans l'eau)** insoluble (in water).

insolvable [ɛ̃sɔlvabl(ə)] *adj* insolvent. ◆ **insolvabilité** *nf* insolvency.

insomnie [ɛ̃sɔmni] *nf* insomnia. **nuits d'** ~ sleepless nights; **ses** ~**s** his (periods of) insomnia. ◆ **insomniaque** *nmf* insomniac.

insondable [ɛ̃sɔ̃dabl(ə)] *adj* unfathomable.

insonore [ɛ̃sɔnɔʀ] *adj* soundproof. ◆ **insonorisation** *nf* soundproofing. ◆ **insonoriser** (1) *vt* to soundproof. **immeuble mal insonorisé** badly soundproofed building.

insouciant, e [ɛ̃susjɑ̃, ɑ̃t] *adj personne* carefree, happy-go-lucky; *paroles* carefree. ~ **de** careless *ou* heedless of. ◆ **insouciance** *nf* heedless *ou* happy-go-lucky attitude. **vivre dans l'** ~ to live a carefree life. ◆ **insoucieux, -euse** *adj* carefree. ~ **du lendemain** unconcerned about the future, not caring about what tomorrow may bring.

insoumis, e [ɛ̃sumi, iz] **1** *adj enfant* rebellious; *tribu* unsubdued; *soldat* absent without leave. **2** *nm (Mil)* absentee. ◆ **insoumission** *nf* rebelliousness; *(Mil)* absence without leave.

insoupçonnable [ɛ̃supsɔnabl(ə)] *adj* above suspicion. ◆ **insoupçonné, e** *adj* unsuspected (*de* by).

insoutenable [ɛ̃sutnabl(ə)] *adj douleur* unbearable; *théorie* untenable.

inspecter [ɛ̃spɛkte] (1) *vt* to inspect. ◆ **inspecteur, -trice** *nm, f (gén)* inspector. ~ **des finances** ≃ tax inspector; ~ **de police** police inspector, lieutenant *(US)*; ~ **du travail** factory inspector; ~ **des travaux finis** * skiver * , layabout * *(who returns to work when there is nothing left to do)*. ◆ **inspection** *nf* (**a**) *(examen)* inspection. **faire l'** ~ **de** to inspect; **soumettre qch à une** ~ **en règle** to give sth a good *ou* thorough inspection *ou* going-over *. (**b**) *(inspecteurs)* inspectorate. *(Pol)* **l'I** ~ **générale des services** the police monitoring service, ≃ the Police Complaints Board.

inspirer [ɛ̃spiʀe] (1) **1** *vt (gén)* to inspire. **cette idée ne m'inspire pas beaucoup** * I'm not all that keen on this idea; **sa santé m'inspire des inquiétudes** his health gives me cause for concern; **il ne m'inspire pas confiance** he doesn't inspire me with confidence; ~ **de l'horreur à qn** to fill sb with horror; **être bien/mal inspiré de faire qch** to be truly inspired/ill-inspired to do sth; **il serait bien inspiré de partir** he'd be well advised *ou* he'd well to leave. **2** *vi (respirer)* to breathe in. **3 s'** ~ *vpr*: **s'** ~ **d'un modèle** to be inspired by a model. ◆ **inspirateur, -trice** *nm, f (animateur)* inspirer; *(instigateur)* instigator. ◆ **inspiration** *nf* (**a**) *(poétique etc)* inspiration. **avoir de l'** ~ to have inspiration; **selon l'**~ **du moment** according to the mood of the moment; **j'eus la bonne** ~ **de refuser** I had the bright idea of refusing. (**b**) *(instigation)* instigation. **sous l'** ~ **de qn** at sb's instigation, prompted by sb. (**c**) *(respiration)* inspiration.

instable [ɛ̃stabl(ə)] *adj (gén)* unstable; *temps* unsettled; *échafaudage* unsteady. ◆ **instabilité** *nf* instability; unsteadiness. **l'**~ **du temps** the unsettled weather.

installateur [ɛ̃stalatœʀ] *nm* fitter.

installation [ɛ̃stalɑsjɔ̃] *nf* (**a**) *[téléphone]* installation, putting in; *[rideaux]* putting up; *[local]* fitting out. (**b**) *[locataire]* settling in; *[artisan]* setting up. **il voulait fêter son** ~ he wanted to celebrate moving in. (**c**) *(appareils etc: gén pl)* fittings, installations. **l'** ~ **électrique est défectueuse** the wiring is faulty; **les** ~**s industrielles d'une région** the industrial plant of a region. (**d**) *(ameublement etc)* **ils ont une** ~ **provisoire** they have temporary living arrangements.

installer [ɛ̃stale] (1) **1** *vt* (**a**) *électricité, meuble* to install, put in; *étagère, tente* to put up; *appartement* to fit out. **cuisine bien installée** well equipped *ou* fitted kitchen; **ils ont installé leur bureau dans le grenier** they've turned the attic into a study. (**b**) *malade, jeune couple* to get settled, settle; *invité, fonctionnaire* to install. **il a installé son fils dentiste** he set his son up as a dentist. **2 s'** ~ *vpr* (**a**) *[commerçant]* to set o.s. up (*comme* as), set up shop (*comme* as). **s'** ~ **à son compte** to set up on one's own. (**b**) *(se loger)* to settle, set up house; *(emménager)* to settle in. **il s'est installé chez des amis** he has moved in *ou* he is living with friends; **ils sont bien installés** they have made themselves a very comfortable home. (**c**) *(à un emplacement)* to settle down. **installe-toi comme il faut** *(confortablement)* make yourself comfortable; *(tiens-toi bien)* sit properly. (**d**) *[grève, maladie]* to take a firm hold, become firmly established. **s'** ~ **dans la guerre** to settle into war.

instamment [ɛ̃stamɑ̃] *adv* insistently, earnestly.

instance [ɛ̃stɑ̃s] *nf* (**a**) *(autorité)* authority. **les** ~**s internationales** the international authorities; **les** ~**s communautaires** the E.E.C. authorities. (**b**) *(Jur)* **introduire une** ~ to institute (legal) proceedings; **en seconde** ~ on appeal; **tribunal de première** ~ court of first instance; **tribunal d'** ~ ≃ magistrates' court; **tribunal de grande** ~ ≃ County court. (**c**) *(prière)* **demander qch avec** ~ to ask earnestly for sth; ~**s** entreaties. (**d**) *(en cours)* **l'affaire est en** ~ the matter is pending; **être en** ~ **de divorce** to be waiting for a divorce; **en** ~ **de départ** on the point of departure; **courrier en** ~ mail ready for posting *ou* due to be dispatched.

instant[1] [ɛ̃stɑ̃] *nm* moment, instant. **vivre dans l'** ~ to live in the present (moment); **il faut le faire à l'** ~ we must do it this instant *ou* minute; **à l'** ~ **où je vous parle** as I'm speaking to you now; **à chaque** ~, **à tout** ~ *(d'un moment à l'autre)* at any moment *ou* minute; *(tout le temps)* all the time, every minute; **dans un** ~ in a moment *ou* minute; **en un** ~ in an instant; **de tous les** ~**s** constant; **par** ~**s** at times; **pour l'** ~ for the moment, for the time being; **dès l'** ~ **où vous êtes d'accord** *(puisque)* since you agree; **dès l'** ~ **où je l'ai vu** *(dès que)* as soon as I saw him, from the moment I saw him.

instant[2]**, e** [ɛ̃stɑ̃, ɑ̃t] *adj (pressant)* insistent.

instantané, e [ɛ̃stɑ̃tane] **1** *adj* instantaneous; *café* instant. **2** *nm (Phot)* snapshot. ◆ **instantanément** *adv* instantaneously; *dissoudre* instantly.

instar [ɛ̃staʀ] *nm*: **à l'** ~ **de** following the example of, after the fashion of.

instaurer [ɛ̃stɔʀe] (1) *vt* to institute. **la révolution a instauré la république** the revolution established the republic; **le doute s'est instauré dans les esprits** doubts began to creep into people's minds. ◆ **instauration** *nf* institution.

instigation [ɛ̃stigɑsjɔ̃] *nf* instigation. ◆ **instigateur, -trice** *nm, f* instigator.

instinct [ɛ̃stɛ̃] *nm (gén)* instinct. **d'** ~ instinctively. ◆ **instinctif, -ive** *adj* instinctive. ◆ **instinctivement** *adv* instinctively.

instituer [ɛ̃stitɥe] (1) *vt (gén)* to institute.

institut [ɛ̃stity] *nm* institute. ~ **de beauté** beauty salon; **I**~ **Universitaire de Technologie** ≃ Polytechnic, technical school *ou* institute *(US)*; ~ **médico-légal** mortuary.

instituteur, -trice [ɛ̃stitytœʀ, tʀis] *nm, f* (primary school) teacher.

institution [ɛ̃stitysjɔ̃] *nf (gén)* institution; *(école)* private school.

institutionnel, -elle [ɛ̃stitysjɔnɛl] *adj* institutional.

instructeur [ɛ̃stʀyktœʀ] *nm* instructor.

instructif, -ive [ɛ̃stʀyktif, iv] *adj* instructive.

instruction [ɛ̃stʀyksjɔ̃] *nf* (**a**) education. **niveau d'** ~ academic standard; ~ **civique** civics *(sg)*; ~ **militaire** army training; ~ **religieuse** religious instruction; **avoir de l'** ~ to be well educated. (**b**) *(Jur) pretrial investigation of a case.* **ouvrir une** ~ to initiate an investigation into a crime. (**c**) *(Admin: circulaire)* directive. (**d**) ~**s** *(ordres)* instructions; *(mode d'emploi)* instructions, directions. *(étiquette)* ~**s de lavage** care label, washing instructions.

instruire [ɛ̃stʀɥiʀ] (38) **1** *vt* (**a**) *(gén)* to teach, educate; *recrue* to train. **instruit par son exemple** having learnt from his example. (**b**) ~ **qn de qch** to inform *ou* advise sb of sth. (**c**) *(Jur) affaire* to conduct the investigation for. **2 s'** ~ *vpr* to educate o.s. **s'** ~ **de qch** to obtain information about sth, find out about sth. ◆ **instruit, e** *adj* educated.

instrument [ɛ̃stʀymɑ̃] *nm (lit, fig)* instrument. ~ **de musique** musical instrument; ~**s de travail** tools; *(Aviat)* **les** ~**s de bord** the controls; *(fig)* **être l'** ~ **de qn** to be sb's tool; **elle a été l'** ~ **de sa réussite** she was instrumental in his success. ◆ **instrumental, e,** *mpl* **-aux** *adj (Ling, Mus)* instrumental. ◆ **instrumentation** *nf* instrumentation, orchestration. ◆ **instrumenter** (1) *vt (Mus)* to orchestrate. ◆ **instrumentiste** *nmf* instrumentalist.

insu [ɛ̃sy] *nm* (**a**) *(en cachette de)* **à l'** ~ **de qn** without sb's knowledge, without sb's knowing. (**b**) *(inconsciemment)* **à mon** ~ without my *ou* me knowing it.

insubmersible [ɛ̃sybmɛʀsibl(ə)] *adj* unsinkable.

insubordination [ɛ̃sybɔʀdinɑsjɔ̃] *nf* insubordination. ◆ **insubordonné, e** *adj (gén)* insubordinate.

insuccès [ɛ̃syksɛ] *nm* failure.

insuffisant, e [ɛ̃syfizɑ̃, ɑ̃t] *adj (en quantité)* insufficient; *(en qualité)* inadequate; *(Scol) (sur une copie)* poor. **c'est** ~ it's not enough; **il est** ~ **en math** he's not up to standard in maths; **en nombre** ~ insufficient in number. ◆ **insuffisamment** *adv* insufficiently; inadequately. ◆ **insuffisance** *nf* insufficiency; inadequacy. **une** ~ **de personnel** a shortage of staff; ~**s** *(faiblesses)* inadequacies; *(Méd)* insufficiency.

insuffler [ɛ̃syfle] (1) *vt (lit, fig)* to blow (*à, dans* into).

insulaire [ɛ̃sylɛʀ] **1** *adj population* island; *attitude* insular. **2** *nmf* islander.

insuline [ɛ̃sylin] *nf* insulin.

insulte [ɛ̃sylt(ə)] *nf* insult. **hurler des** ~**s** to shout insults *ou* abuse. ◆ **insultant, e** *adj* insulting (*pour* to). ◆ **insulter** (1) *vt* to insult.

insupportable [ɛ̃sypɔʀtabl(ə)] *adj* unbearable, insufferable. ◆ **insupporter** (1) *vt (hum)* **cela m'insupporte/l'insupporte** I/he can't stand this.

insurger (s') [ɛ̃syʀʒe] (3) *vpr (lit, fig)* to rebel, revolt (*contre* against). ◆ **insurgé, e** *adj, nm, f* rebel, insurgent.

insurmontable [ɛ̃syʀmɔ̃tabl(ə)] *adj obstacle* insurmountable, insuperable; *dégoût* unconquerable.

insurrection [ɛ̃syʀɛksjɔ̃] *nf* insurrection, revolt. ◆ **insurrectionnel, -elle** *adj* insurrectionary.

intact, e [ɛ̃takt, akt(ə)] *adj* intact.

intangible [ɛ̃tɑ̃ʒibl(ə)] *adj* inviolable. ◆ **intangibilité** *nf* inviolability.

intarissable [ɛ̃taʀisabl(ə)] *adj (lit, fig)* inexhaustible. **il est** ~ he could talk for ever (*sur* about). ◆ **intarissablement** *adv* inexhaustibly.

intégral, e, *mpl* **-aux** [ɛ̃tegʀal, o] **1** *adj* complete. **le remboursement** ~ **de qch** the repayment in full of sth; *(Ciné)* **version** ~**e** uncut version; *(Presse)* **texte** ~ unabridged version. **2** *nf (Math)* integral; *(œuvre)* complete works. ◆ **intégralement** *adv* in full, fully. ◆ **intégralité** *nf* whole. **l'** ~ **de la somme** the whole of the sum, the whole *ou* full sum; **dans son** ~ in its entirety, in full.

intégrer [ɛ̃tegʀe] (6) **1** *vt* to integrate (*à, dans* into). **2** *vi (arg Univ)* ~ **à** to get into. **3 s'** ~ *vpr* to become integrated (*à, dans* into). **cette maison s'intègre mal dans le paysage** this house doesn't really fit into the surrounding countryside. ◆ **intégration** *nf* integration (*à, dans* into). *(arg Univ)* **après son** ~ after getting into the college; *(Ordin)* ~ **à très grande échelle** very large-scale integration.

intégrisme [ɛ̃tegʀism(ə)] *nm* Muslim fundamentalism. ◆ **intégriste** *adj, nmf* Muslim fundamentalist.

intégrité [ɛ̃tegʀite] *nf (totalité)* integrity; *(honnêteté)* integrity, honesty, uprightness. ◆ **intègre** *adj* upright, honest.

intellect [ɛ̃telɛkt] *nm* intellect. ◆ **intellectuel, -elle** **1** *adj (gén)* intellectual; *fatigue* mental; *(péj)* highbrow. **2** *nm, f* intellectual; *(péj)* highbrow. ◆ **intellectuellement** *adv* mentally; intellectually.

intelligence [ɛ̃teliʒɑ̃s] *nf* (**a**) *(aptitude)* intelligence. **avoir l'** ~ **vive** to have a sharp *ou* quick mind; **les grandes** ~**s** great minds *ou* intellects; ~ **artificielle** artificial intelligence. (**b**) *(compréhension)* ~ **de** understanding of; **avoir l'** ~ **des affaires** to have a good grasp *ou* understanding of business matters, have a good head for business. (**c**) *(complicité)* secret agreement. **agir d'** ~ **avec qn** to act in (secret) agreement with sb; **signe d'** ~ sign of complicity; **vivre en bonne/mauvaise** ~ **avec qn** to be on good/bad terms with sb; **avoir des** ~**s dans la place** to have secret contacts in the place. ◆ **intelligent, e** *adj (gén)* intelligent; *(à l'esprit vif)* clever, bright. ◆ **intelligemment** *adv* intelligently; cleverly.

intelligentsia [ɛ̃teligɛntsja] *nf:* **l'** ~ the intelligentsia.

intelligible [ɛ̃teliʒibl(ə)] *adj* intelligible. **à haute et** ~ **voix** loudly and clearly. ◆ **intelligibilité** *nf* intelligibility. ◆ **intelligiblement** *adv* intelligibly.

intempérant, e [ɛ̃tɑ̃peʀɑ̃, ɑ̃t] *adj* intemperate. ◆ **intempérance** *nf* intemperance. ~**s** excesses; **une telle** ~ **de langage** such excessive language.

intempéries [ɛ̃tɑ̃peʀi] *nfpl* bad weather.

intempestif, -ive [ɛ̃tɑ̃pɛstif, iv] *adj (gén)* untimely; *zèle* excessive, misplaced. ◆ **intempestivement** *adv* at an untimely moment.

intemporel, -elle [ɛ̃tɑ̃pɔʀɛl] *adj (sans durée)* timeless; *(immatériel)* immaterial.

intenable [ɛ̃tnabl(ə)] *adj situation* intolerable, unbearable; *personne* unruly; *théorie* untenable.

intendance [ɛ̃tɑ̃dɑ̃s] *nf (Mil) (service)* Supply Corps; *(bureau)* Supplies office; *(Scol) (métier)* school management; *(bureau)* bursar's office. **les problèmes d'** ~ the problems of supply. ◆ **intendant** *nm (Mil)* quartermaster; *(Scol)* bursar; *(régisseur)* steward. ◆ **intendante** *nf (Scol)* bursar; *(régisseur)* steward.

intense [ɛ̃tɑ̃s] *adj (gén)* intense; *circulation* dense, heavy. ◆ **intensément** *adv* intensely. ◆ **intensif, -ive** *adj* intensive. ◆ **intensification** *nf* intensification. ◆ **intensifier** *vt*, **s'** ~ *vpr* (7) to intensify. ◆ **intensité** *nf* intensity; density, heaviness. *(Ling)* **accent d'** ~ stress accent. ◆ **intensivement** *adv* intensively.

intenter [ɛ̃tɑ̃te] (1) *vt:* ~ **un procès contre** *ou* **à qn** to start *ou* institute proceedings against sb.

intention [ɛ̃tɑ̃sjɔ̃] *nf* (**a**) intention. **agir dans une bonne** ~ to act with good intentions; **c'est l'** ~ **qui compte** it's the thought that counts; **à cette** ~ with this intention, to this end; **avoir l'** ~ **de faire** to intend *ou* mean to do, have the intention of doing. (**b**) **à l'** ~ **de qn** *collecte* in aid of sb;

cadeau, messe for sb; **livre à l' ~ des enfants** book aimed at children. ◆ **intentionné, e** *adj*: **bien ~** well-meaning, well-intentioned; **mal ~** illintentioned. ◆ **intentionnel, -elle** *adj* intentional. ◆ **intentionnellement** *adv* intentionally.

inter [ɛ̃tɛʀ] **1** *nm (Téléc)* = **interurbain**; *(Sport)* **~ gauche/droit** inside-left/-right. **2** *préf* inter... **~continental/ministériel/syndical** *etc* intercontinental/departmental/union *etc*; **~allié** interAllied; **opération ~armes** combined arms operation; **tournoi ~scolaire** inter-schools tournament.

interaction [ɛ̃tɛʀaksjɔ̃] *nf* interaction.

intercaler [ɛ̃tɛʀkale] (1) **1** *vt mot* to insert; *feuillet* to inset, insert. **~ quelques jours de repos dans un mois de stage** to fit a few days' break into a month of training. **2 s' ~** *vpr*: **s' ~ entre** to come in between. ◆ **intercalaire** *adj*: **feuillet ~** inset, insert.

intercéder [ɛ̃tɛʀsede] (6) *vi* to intercede (*auprès de* with).

intercepter [ɛ̃tɛʀsɛpte] (1) *vt* to intercept. ◆ **interception** *nf* interception.

interchangeable [ɛ̃tɛʀʃɑ̃ʒabl(ə)] *adj* interchangeable.

interclasse [ɛ̃tɛʀklɑs] *nm (Scol)* break *(between classes)*.

interclubs [ɛ̃tɛʀklœb] *adj inv tournoi, rencontre* interclub.

interdépendance [ɛ̃tɛʀdepɑ̃dɑ̃s] *nf* interdependence. ◆ **interdépendant, e** *adj* interdependent.

interdire [ɛ̃tɛʀdiʀ] (37) **1** *vt* (**a**) *(prohiber)* to forbid; *(Admin) stationnement etc* to prohibit, ban; *journal* to ban. **on a interdit les camions dans la ville** lorries have been banned from *ou* prohibited in the town. (**b**) *[difficulté]* to preclude, prevent; *[obstacle]* to block. **son état de santé lui interdit tout travail** his state of health does not allow *ou* permit him to do any work; **la gravité de la crise interdit tout espoir** the gravity of the crisis precludes all hope; **une porte interdisait le passage** a door blocked *ou* barred the way. **2 s' ~** *vpr*: **s' ~ toute remarque** to refrain *ou* abstain from making any remark; **s' ~ la boisson** to abstain from drink *ou* drinking; **il s'interdit d'y penser** he doesn't allow himself to think about it. ◆ **interdiction** *nf (gén)* ban (*de* on). **' ~ absolue de fumer'** 'smoking strictly prohibited'; **' ~ de tourner à droite'** 'no right turn'; **~ de parler à quiconque** it is (strictly) forbidden to talk to anyone; **écriteau portant une ~** notice prohibiting *ou* forbidding sth. ◆ **interdit, e 1** *adj* (**a**) *livre* banned. **film ~ aux moins de 18/13 ans** ≃ X/A film (†), ≃ 18/PG film; **stationnement ~** no parking; **il est strictement ~ de faire** it is strictly forbidden *ou* prohibited to do; **être ~ de chéquier** to have chequebook facilities withdrawn. (**b**) *(surpris)* dumbfounded, taken aback, disconcerted. **2** *nm (interdiction) (Rel)* interdict; *(social)* prohibition. *(fig)* **jeter l' ~ sur** *ou* **contre qn** to bar sb.

interdisciplinaire [ɛ̃tɛʀdisiplinɛʀ] *adj* interdisciplinary.

intéresser [ɛ̃teʀese] (1) **1** *vt (captiver)* to interest; *(concerner)* to affect, concern. **~ qn à** *problème* to interest sb in; *bénéfices* to give sb a share *ou* an interest in; **ça pourrait vous ~** this might interest you *ou* be of interest to you; *(Fin)* **être intéressé dans une affaire** to have a stake *ou* a financial interest in a business. **2 s' ~** *vpr*: **s' ~ à qch/qn** to be interested in sth/sb, take an interest in sth/sb. ◆ **intéressant, e** *adj (captivant)* interesting; *(avantageux)* attractive, worthwhile. *(péj)* **un personnage peu ~** a worthless individual; **c'est une personne ~e à connaître** he *ou* she is someone worth knowing; **faire son ~** to show off. ◆ **intéressé, e** *adj* (**a**) *(en cause)* concerned, involved. **c'est lui le principal ~** he is the person *ou* party principally involved *ou* concerned. (**b**) *(égoïste) personne* self-interested; *motif* interested. **une visite ~e** a visit motivated by self-interest. ◆ **intéressement** *nm*: **l' ~ des travailleurs aux bénéfices** the workers' sharing of the profits.

intérêt [ɛ̃teʀɛ] *nm* (**a**) *(attention)* interest. **porter de l' ~ à qn** to take an interest in sb. (**b**) *(valeur) [livre]* interest; *[recherches, découverte]* significance, relevance. **dénué d' ~** devoid of interest; **considérations sans ~** unimportant *ou* minor considerations; **c'est sans ~ pour la suite de l'histoire** it's of no relevance *ou* importance for the rest of the story; **être déclaré d' ~ public** to be officially recognized as of benefit to the country, be officially declared a national asset. (**c**) *(avantage)* interest. **dans l' ~ général** in the general interest; **il y trouve son ~** he finds it worth his while; **il sait où est son ~** he knows which side his bread is buttered; **il a ~ à accepter** it's in his interest to accept, he'd be well advised to accept; **y a-t-il un ~ quelconque à se réunir?** is there any point at all in getting together?; **dépêche-toi, il y a ~ *** you'd better hurry up. (**d**) *(Fin, Écon)* interest. **7% d' ~** 7% interest; **prêter à ~** to lend at *ou* with interest; *(péj)* **agir par ~** to act out of self-interest; **il a des ~s dans l'affaire** he has a stake *ou* a financial interest in the deal.

interface [ɛ̃tɛʀfas] *nf* interface. **~ utilisateur** user interface. ◆ **interfacer** *vt*, **s' ~** *vpr* (3) to interface (*avec* with).

interférence [ɛ̃tɛʀfeʀɑ̃s] *nf (gén)* interference (*dans* in). **l' ~ de ces problèmes** *(fusion)* the conjunction of these problems; *(immixtion)* the intrusion of these problems (*dans* into). ◆ **interférer** (6) *vi* to interfere (*avec* with, *dans* in).

intérieur, e [ɛ̃teʀjœʀ] **1** *adj (gén)* inner; *poche* inside; *paroi, angle* interior; *navigation, mer* inland; *marché* home; *politique, (Aviat) vol* domestic, internal. **2** *nm* (**a**) *[tiroir]* inside; *[maison]* inside, interior. **à l' ~** *(de la ville)* inside (the town); **à l' ~ de lui-même** inwardly, within himself; **rester à l' ~** *(gén)* to stay inside; *(de la maison)* to stay indoors; **veste d' ~** indoor jacket; **chaussures d' ~** indoor *ou* house shoes. (**b**) *[pays]* interior. **les villes de l' ~** the inland cities, the cities of the interior; **l' ~ est sauvage** the hinterland is wild; **à l' ~ de nos frontières** within *ou* inside our frontiers. (**c**) *(mobilier)* interior. (**d**) *(Ftbl)* **~ gauche/droit** inside-left/-right. ◆ **intérieurement** *adv* inwardly. **rire ~** to laugh inwardly *ou* to o.s. ◆ **intérioriser** (1) *vt* to internalize, interiorize.

intérim [ɛ̃teʀim] *nm* (**a**) *(période)* interim period. **il assure l' ~ en l'absence du directeur** he deputizes for the manager in his absence *ou* in the interim; **ministre par ~** acting *ou* interim minister. (**b**) *(travail à temps partiel)* temporary work, temping. **société d' ~** temping agency, temporary employment office *(US)*; **faire de l' ~** to temp. ◆ **intérimaire 1** *adj directeur* acting, interim; *secrétaire* temporary; *mesure* interim; *gouvernement* caretaker. **2** *nmf (secrétaire)* temporary secretary, temp, Kelly girl *(US)*; *(fonctionnaire)* deputy; *(médecin, prêtre)* locum (tenens). **travailler comme ~** to temp.

interjection [ɛ̃tɛʀʒɛksjɔ̃] *nf* interjection.

interligne [ɛ̃tɛʀliɲ] *nm* space between the lines. **double ~** double spacing.

interlocuteur, -trice [ɛ̃tɛʀlɔkytœʀ, tʀis] *nm, f* speaker. **mon ~** the person I was speaking to; *(Pol)* **~ valable** authorized negotiator; **ce sont nos ~s privilégiés** they have a privileged relationship with us.

interlope [ɛ̃tɛʀlɔp] *adj (équivoque)* shady; *(illégal)* illicit, unlawful.

interloquer [ɛ̃tɛʀlɔke] (1) *vt* to take aback.

interlude [ɛ̃tɛʀlyd] *nm (Mus, TV)* interlude.

intermède [ɛ̃tɛʀmɛd] *nm (Théât, gén)* interlude.

intermédiaire [ɛ̃tɛʀmedjɛʀ] **1** *adj* intermediate, middle, intermediary. **une couleur ~ entre** a colour halfway between. **2** *nm*: **sans ~** *vendre* directly; **par l' ~ de** *personne* through (the intermediary of); *presse* through the medium of. **3** *nmf* intermediary, go-between; *(Comm, Écon)* middleman.

interminable [ɛ̃tɛʀminabl(ə)] *adj* endless, interminable, never-ending. ◆ **interminablement** *adv* endlessly, interminably.

intermittent, e [ɛ̃tɛʀmitɑ̃, ɑ̃t] *adj* sporadic, intermittent. ◆ **intermittence** *nf*: **par ~** sporadically, intermittently.

international, e, *mpl* **-aux** [ɛ̃tɛʀnasjɔnal, o] **1** *adj* international. **2** *nm, f (Ftbl, Tennis etc)* international player.

interne [ɛ̃tɛʀn(ə)] **1** *adj (gén)* internal; *oreille* inner; *angle* interior. **médecine ~** internal medicine. **2** *nmf (Scol)* boarder. **être ~** to be at boarding school; *(Univ, Méd)* **~ (des hôpitaux)** houseman, intern *(US)*; **~ en médecine/en chirurgie** house physician/surgeon. ◆ **internat** *nm (Scol)* boarding school; *(Univ Méd) (concours)* entrance examination (for hospital work); *(stage)* ≃ period as a houseman *ou* an intern *(US)*.

interner [ɛ̃tɛʀne] (1) *vt (Pol)* to intern; *(Méd)* to confine to a mental hospital, institutionalize *(US)*. **on devrait l' ~ *** he ought to be locked up *ou* certified *. ◆ **interné, e** *nm, f* internee; inmate (of a mental hospital). ◆ **internement** *nm* internment; confinement (to a mental hospital).

interpeller [ɛ̃tɛʀpele] (1) *vt (appeler)* to call out to, shout out to; *(apostropher)* to shout at; *orateur, malfaiteur* to question. ◆ **interpellation** *nf*: **il y a eu une dizaine d' ~s** about ten people were detained *ou* taken in for questioning.

interphone [ɛ̃tɛʀfɔn] *nm* intercom, interphone; *[immeuble]* entry phone.

Interpol [ɛ̃tɛʀpɔl] *nm* Interpol.

interpoler [ɛ̃tɛʀpɔle] (1) *vt* to interpolate.

interposer [ɛ̃tɛʀpoze] (1) **1** *vt (lit, fig)* to interpose (*entre* between). **2 s' ~** *vpr* to intervene (*dans* in).

interpréter [ɛ̃tɛʀpʀete] (6) *vt* (**a**) *(Mus, Théât, gén)* to perform, interpret; *personnage, sonate* to play; *chanson* to sing. (**b**) *(comprendre)* to interpret. **mal ~** to misinterpret. ◆ **interprétariat** *nm* interpreting. **école d' ~** interpreting school. ◆ **interprétation** *nf* interpretation. ◆ **interprète** *nmf* (**a**) *(Mus, Théât)* performer, interpreter; singer. (**b**) *(traducteur)* interpreter. *(porte-parole)* **servir d' ~ à qn/aux idées de qn** to act *ou* serve as a spokesman for sb/for sb's ideas.

interroger [ɛ̃teʀɔʒe] (3) **1** *vt (gén)* to question, ask; *(Police)* to interview, question; *(minutieusement)* to interrogate (*sur* about); *ciel* to examine; *mémoire* to search; *(sondage)* to poll; *(Ordin) données* to interrogate; *élève* to test, examine (orally). **~ qn du regard** to give sb a questioning *ou* an inquiring look; *(sondage)* **personne interrogée** respondent. **2 s' ~** *vpr* to question o.s., wonder (*sur* about). **s' ~ sur la conduite à tenir** to wonder what course to follow. ◆ **interrogateur, -trice** **1** *adj air* questioning, inquiring. **2** *nm, f* (oral) examiner. ◆ **interrogatif, -ive** *adj, nm air, (Ling)* interrogative. ◆ **interrogation** *nf* (**a**) *(V* **interroger***)* questioning; interrogation; examination; testing. (**b**) *(question)* question. *(Scol)* **~ (écrite)** (written) test; **~ (orale)** oral (test); *(Gram)* **~ directe/indirecte** direct/indirect question; *(réflexions)* **ses ~s** his questioning. ◆ **interrogatoire** *nm (Police)* questioning; *(au tribunal)* cross-examination; *(fig)* interrogation. **subir un ~ en règle** to undergo a thorough *ou* detailed interrogation.

interrompre [ɛ̃tɛʀɔ̃pʀ(ə)] (41) **1** *vt voyage, études* to break off, interrupt; *grossesse* to terminate. **il a interrompu la conversation pour dire** he broke *ou* cut into the conversation to say; **~ qn** to interrupt sb; **je ne veux pas ~ mais...** I don't want to cut in *ou* interrupt but... **2 s' ~** *vpr [personne, conversation]* to break off. ◆ **interrupteur** *nm (Élec)* switch. ◆ **interruption** *nf (action)* interruption; *(état)* break, interruption. **~ (volontaire) de grossesse** termination (of pregnancy); **~ de courant** power cut; **après l' ~ des hostilités** after hostilities had ceased; **sans ~** without a break; **un moment d' ~** a moment's break.

intersection [ɛ̃tɛʀsɛksjɔ̃] *nf* intersection.

intersidéral, e, *mpl* **-aux** [ɛ̃tɛʀsideʀal,o] *adj* intersidereal.

interstice [ɛ̃tɛʀstis] *nm* crack, chink, interstice.

interurbain, e [ɛ̃tɛʀyʀbɛ̃, ɛn] **1** *adj communication* long-distance. **2** *nm*: **l' ~** the long-distance telephone service.

intervalle [ɛ̃tɛʀval] *nm (espace)* space; *(temps)* interval; *(Mus)* interval. **c'est arrivé à 2 jours d' ~** it happened after an interval of 2 days; **dans l'~** *(temporel)* in the meantime, meanwhile; *(spatial)* in between.

intervenant, e [ɛ̃tɛʀvənɑ̃, ɑ̃t] *nm, f (Jur)* intervener; *(conférencier)* contributor. **inviter un ~ extérieur** to invite an outside contributor.

intervenir [ɛ̃tɛʀvəniʀ] (22) *vi* (**a**) *(entrer en action)* to intervene. **on a dû faire ~ l'armée** the army had to be brought in. (**b**) *(Méd)* to operate. (**c**) *[événement]* to take place, occur; *[accord]* to be reached; *[décision]* to be taken; *[élément nouveau]* to arise, come up. ◆ **intervention** *nf (gén, Jur)* intervention; *(Méd)* operation; *(discours)* speech. **prix d' ~** intervention price; **beurre d' ~** (EEC) subsidized butter; **cela a nécessité l' ~ de la police** the police had to be brought in.

intervertir [ɛ̃tɛʀvɛʀtiʀ] (2) *vt* to invert (the order of).

interview [ɛ̃tɛʀvju] *nf (Presse, TV)* interview. ◆ **interviewé, e** [ɛ̃tɛʀvjuve] *nm, f* interviewee. ◆ **interviewer**[1] [ɛ̃tɛʀvjuve] (1) *vt* to interview. ◆ **interviewer**[2] [ɛ̃tɛʀvjuvœʀ] *nm* interviewer.

intestin [ɛ̃tɛstɛ̃] *nm* intestine. **~s** intestines, bowels. ◆ **intestinal, e,** *mpl* **-aux** *adj* intestinal.

intime [ɛ̃tim] **1** *adj* (**a**) *vie* private; *confidences, hygiène* intimate; *cérémonie* quiet; *atmosphère* intimate, cosy. **journal ~** private diary; **être ~ avec qn** to be close to sb; **avoir des relations** *ou* **rapports ~s avec qn** to be on intimate terms with sb, have close relations with sb. (**b**) *mélange, conviction* intimate. **2** *nmf* close friend. ◆ **intimement** *adv* intimately. **~ persuadé** deeply *ou* firmly convinced.

intimer [ɛ̃time] (1) *vt* (**a**) **~ à qn l'ordre de faire** to order sb to do. (**b**) *(Jur) (assigner)* to summon; *(signifier)* to notify.

intimider [ɛ̃timide] (1) *vt* to intimidate. ◆ **intimidable** *adj* easily intimidated. ◆ **intimidant, e** *adj* intimidating. ◆ **intimidateur, -trice** *adj* intimidating. ◆ **intimidation** *nf* intimidation.

intimité [ɛ̃timite] *nf* (**a**) *(vie privée)* privacy. **nous serons dans l' ~** there will only be a few of us; **se marier dans l' ~** to have a quiet wedding; **dans la plus stricte ~** in the strictest privacy; **pénétrer dans l' ~ de qn** to be admitted into sb's private life; **vivre dans l' ~ de qn** to share sb's private life. (**b**) *(familiarité)* intimacy. **dans l' ~ conjugale** in the intimacy of one's married life. (**c**) *(confort)* cosiness, intimacy.

intituler [ɛ̃tityle] (1) **1** *vt* to entitle, call. **2 s' ~** *vpr [livre]* to be entitled *ou* called; *[personne]* to call o.s. ◆ **intitulé** *nm* title.

intolérable [ɛ̃tɔleʀabl(ə)] *adj* intolerable. ◆ **intolérablement** *adv* intolerably.

intolérance [ɛ̃tɔleʀɑ̃s] *nf* intolerance. ~ **à un médicament** inability to tolerate a drug. ◆ **intolérant, e** *adj* intolerant.

intonation [ɛ̃tɔnɑsjɔ̃] *nf (Ling, Mus)* intonation. **voix aux ~s douces** soft-toned voice.

intouchable [ɛ̃tuʃabl(ə)] *adj, nmf* untouchable.

intoxiquer [ɛ̃tɔksike] (1) **1** *vt (lit)* to poison; *(Pol)* to brainwash. **2 s'** ~ *vpr* to poison o.s. ◆ **intoxication** *nf* poisoning; brainwashing. ~ **alimentaire** food poisoning. ◆ **intoxiqué, e** *nm, f (drogue)* drug addict; *(alcool)* alcoholic.

intradermique [ɛ̃tʀadɛʀmik] *adj* intradermal, intradermic, intracutaneous. ◆ **intradermo (-réaction)** *nf* skin test.

intraduisible [ɛ̃tʀadɥizibl(ə)] *adj texte* untranslatable; *idée* inexpressible.

intraitable [ɛ̃tʀɛtabl(ə)] *adj* uncompromising, inflexible.

intra-muros [ɛ̃tʀamyʀos] *adv:* **habiter** ~ to live inside the town (*ou* city *etc*); **Paris ~ comprend plusieurs millions d'habitants** the inner-city area of Paris has several million inhabitants.

intramusculaire [ɛ̃tʀamyskylɛʀ] *adj* intramuscular.

intransigeant, e [ɛ̃tʀɑ̃ziʒɑ̃, ɑ̃t] *adj personne* uncompromising, intransigent, hard-nosed *; *morale* uncompromising. **se montrer** ~ *ou* **adopter une ligne (de conduite) ~e envers qn** to take a hard line with sb; **les ~s** the intransigents. ◆ **intransigeance** *nf* intransigence.

intransitif, -ive [ɛ̃tʀɑ̃zitif, iv] *adj, nm* intransitive.

intransportable [ɛ̃tʀɑ̃spɔʀtabl(ə)] *adj objet* untransportable; *malade* unfit to travel.

intraveineux, -euse [ɛ̃tʀavɛnø, øz] **1** *adj* intravenous. **2** *nf* intravenous injection.

intrépide [ɛ̃tʀepid] *adj (courageux)* intrepid, dauntless; *menteur* barefaced, unashamed. ◆ **intrépidité** *nf* intrepidity, dauntlessness.

intriguer [ɛ̃tʀige] (1) **1** *vt* to intrigue, puzzle. **2** *vi* to scheme, intrigue. ◆ **intrigant, e 1** *adj* scheming. **2** *nm, f* schemer, intriguer. ◆ **intrigue** *nf (manœuvre)* intrigue, scheme; *(liaison)* (love) affair, intrigue; *(Théât)* plot.

intrinsèque [ɛ̃tʀɛ̃sɛk] *adj* intrinsic. ◆ **intrinsèquement** *adv* intrinsically.

introduire [ɛ̃tʀɔdɥiʀ] (38) **1** *vt (gén)* to introduce (*dans* into, *auprès de* to); *visiteur* to show in; *idées nouvelles* to bring in. **il introduisit sa clef dans la serrure** he placed his key in the lock, he inserted his key into the lock; **on m'introduisit dans le salon** I was shown into *ou* ushered into the lounge; ~ **des marchandises en contrebande** to smuggle in goods; *(Rugby)* ~ **la balle en mêlée** to put the ball into the scrum. **2 s'** ~ *vpr* (**a**) *(pénétrer)* to get in. **s'** ~ **dans un groupe** to work one's way into a group; **s'** ~ **chez qn par effraction** to break into sb's home; **s'** ~ **dans une pièce** to get into *ou* enter a room. (**b**) *[usage]* to be introduced (*dans* into). ◆ **introduction** *nf* introduction; *(Rugby)* put-in. **chapitre d'** ~ introductory chapter; **lettre d'** ~ letter of introduction. ◆ **introducteur, -trice** *nm, f (initiateur)* initiator.

introuvable [ɛ̃tʀuvabl(ə)] *adj* which (*ou* who) cannot be found. **l'accord ~ entre les deux pays** the unattainable agreement between the two countries.

intrus, e [ɛ̃tʀy, yz] *nm, f* intruder. *(jeu)* **cherchez l'** ~ find the odd one out. ◆ **intrusion** *nf (gén)* intrusion (*dans* in).

intuition [ɛ̃tɥisjɔ̃] *nf* intuition. ◆ **intuitif, -ive** *adj* intuitive. ◆ **intuitivement** *adv* intuitively.

inusable [inyzabl(ə)] *adj vêtement* hard-wearing.

inusité, e [inyzite] *adj* uncommon.

inutile [inytil] *adj (qui ne sert pas)* useless; *(superflu)* needless, unnecessary. **c'est ~ d'insister!** it's no use *ou* no good insisting!, there's no point insisting!; ~ **de vous dire que** I hardly need say that. ◆ **inutilement** *adv* needlessly, unnecessarily. ◆ **inutilité** *nf* uselessness; needlessness.

inutilisable [inytilizabl(ə)] *adj* unusable.

inutilisé, e [inytilize] *adj* unused.

invaincu, e [ɛ̃vɛ̃ky] *adj* unconquered; *(Sport)* unbeaten.

invalide [ɛ̃valid] **1** *nmf* disabled person. ~ **de guerre** disabled ex-serviceman; ~ **du travail** industrially disabled person. **2** *adj (Méd)* disabled. ◆ **invalidité** *nf* disablement. ◆ **invalidant, e** *adj maladie* incapacitating, disabling.

invalider [ɛ̃valide] (1) *vt (Jur)* to invalidate; *député* to remove from office. ◆ **invalidation** *nf* invalidation; removal (from office).

invariable [ɛ̃vaʀjabl(ə)] *adj (gén, Ling)* invariable. ◆ **invariablement** *adv* invariably. ◆ **invariant, e** *adj, nm* invariant.

invasion [ɛ̃vɑzjɔ̃] *nf* invasion.

invective [ɛ̃vɛktiv] *nf* invective. **~s** abuse, invectives. ◆ **invectiver** (1) **1** *vt* to hurl *ou* shout abuse at. **s'** ~ to hurl *ou* shout abuse at each other. **2** *vi* to inveigh, rail (*contre* against).

invendable [ɛ̃vɑ̃dabl(ə)] *adj (gén)* unsaleable; *(Comm)* unmarketable.

invendu, e [ɛ̃vɑ̃dy] **1** *adj* unsold. **2** *nm* unsold article.

inventaire [ɛ̃vɑ̃tɛʀ] *nm (gén, Jur)* inventory; *(Comm) (liste)* stocklist; *(opération)* stocktaking; *(fig: recensement)* survey. *(fig)* **faire l'** ~ **de** to assess, take stock of.

inventer [ɛ̃vɑ̃te] (1) *vt (gén)* to invent; *moyen* to devise; *mot* to coin; *jeu* to make *ou* think up. **il n'a pas inventé la poudre** he'll never set the Thames on fire; **je n'invente rien** I'm not making anything up, I'm not inventing a thing. ◆ **inventeur, -trice** *nm, f* inventor. ◆ **inventif, -ive** *adj* resourceful, inventive. ◆ **inventivité** *nf* inventiveness ; resourcefulness. ◆ **invention** *nf (gén)* invention. **esprit d'** ~ inventiveness; **c'est une pure** ~ it is a pure invention *ou* fabrication; **un cocktail de mon** ~ a cocktail of my own creation.

invérifiable [ɛ̃veʀifjabl(ə)] *adj* unverifiable.

inverse [ɛ̃vɛʀs(ə)] **1** *adj (gén)* opposite. **arriver en sens** ~ to arrive from the opposite direction; **dans l'ordre** ~ in the reverse order; **dans le sens ~ des aiguilles d'une montre** anticlockwise, counterclockwise. **2** *nm:* **l'** ~ *(gén)* the opposite, the reverse; **t'a-t-il attaqué ou l' ~?** did he attack you or was it the other way round?; **à l'** ~ conversely. ◆ **inversé, e** *adj image* reversed; *relief* inverted. ◆ **inversement** *adv (gén)* conversely; *(Math)* inversely. **...et/ou** ~ ...and/or vice versa. ◆ **inverser** (1) *vt ordre* to reverse, invert; *(Élec)* to reverse. ◆ **inversion** *nf (gén)* inversion; *(Élec)* reversal.

invertébré, e [ɛ̃vɛʀtebʀe] *adj, nm* invertebrate.

investigation [ɛ̃vɛstigɑsjɔ̃] *nf* investigation. **après de minutieuses ~s** after a detailed investigation *ou* inspection.

investir [ɛ̃vɛstiʀ] (2) *vt (Fin, Mil)* to invest; *fonctionnaire* to induct; *évêque* to invest. ~ **qn de pouvoirs** to invest *ou* vest sb with powers; ~ **qn de sa confiance** to place one's trust in sb. ◆ **investissement** *nm (Écon, Méd, Psych)* investment; *(Mil)* investing. ◆ **investiture** *nf [candidat]* nomination, appointment; *[évêché]* investiture.

invétéré, e [ɛ̃veteʀe] *adj* inveterate.

invincible [ɛ̃vɛ̃sibl(ə)] *adj (gén)* invincible; *difficultés* insurmountable. ◆ **invincibilité** *nf* invincibility.

inviolable [ɛ̃vjɔlabl(ə)] *adj droit* inviolable; *serrure* impregnable; *diplomate* immune.

invisible [ɛ̃vizibl(ə)] **1** *adj (impossible à voir)* invisible; *(minuscule)* barely visible (*à* to); *(Écon)* invisible. **danger ~** unseen *ou* hidden danger; **M. X est ~** *(occupé)* Mr X cannot be seen; *(disparu)* Mr X isn't to be found. **2** *nm*: **l' ~** the invisible. ◆ **invisibilité** *nf* invisibility.

inviter [ɛ̃vite] (1) *vt (gén)* to invite (*à* to). **~ qn à dîner** to invite *ou* ask sb to *ou* for dinner; **il s'est invité** he invited himself; **il m'invita à avancer** he motioned (to) me to come forward; **ceci invite à croire que...** this leads us to believe that..., this suggests that...; **la chaleur invitait au repos** the heat tempted one to rest. ◆ **invitation** *nf* invitation (*à* to). **à** *ou* **sur son ~** at his invitation. ◆ **invité, e** *nm, f* guest.

in vitro [invitʀo] *adj, adv* in vitro.

invivable [ɛ̃vivabl(ə)] *adj* unbearable.

in vivo [invivo] *adj, adv* in vivo.

invocation [ɛ̃vɔkɑsjɔ̃] *nf* invocation (*à* to).

involontaire [ɛ̃vɔlɔ̃tɛʀ] *adj mouvement* involuntary; *peine* unintentional, unwitting; *complice* unwitting. ◆ **involontairement** *adv* involuntarily; unintentionally; unwittingly.

invoquer [ɛ̃vɔke] (1) *vt* (**a**) *argument* to put forward; *témoignage* to call upon; *excuse, ignorance* to plead; *loi* to cite, refer to. *(Jur)* **les arguments de fait et de droit invoqués** the points of fact and law relied on. (**b**) *Dieu* to invoke, call upon.

invraisemblable [ɛ̃vʀɛsɑ̃blabl(ə)] *adj nouvelle* unlikely, improbable; *argument* implausible; *insolence, habit* incredible. ◆ **invraisemblance** *nf* unlikelihood, improbability; implausibility. **plein d' ~s** full of improbabilities *ou* implausibilities.

invulnérable [ɛ̃vylneʀabl(ə)] *adj* invulnerable (*à* to). ◆ **invulnérabilité** *nf* invulnerability.

iode [jɔd] *nm* iodine.

ion [jɔ̃] *nm* ion. ◆ **ionisation** *nf* ionization. ◆ **ioniser** (1) *vt* to ionize.

ipso facto [ipsofakto] *adv* ipso facto.

Irak [iʀak] *nm* Iraq. ◆ **irakien, -ienne** *adj, nm,* **I~(ne)** *nm(f)* Iraqi.

Iran [iʀɑ̃] *nm* Iran. ◆ **iranien, -ienne** *adj, nm,* **I~(ne)** *nm (f)* Iranian.

irascible [iʀasibl(ə)] *adj* irascible. ◆ **irascibilité** *nf* irascibility.

iris [iʀis] *nm (gén)* iris.

Irlande [iʀlɑ̃d] *nf*: **l' ~** *(pays)* Ireland; *(État)* the Irish Republic, Eire; **l' ~ du Nord** Northern Ireland, Ulster. ◆ **irlandais, e** **1** *adj* Irish. **2** *nm* (**a**) *(Ling)* Irish. (**b**) **I~** Irishman; **les I~** the Irish; **les I~ du Nord** the Northern Irish. **3** *nf*: **I~e** Irishwoman.

ironie [iʀɔni] *nf* irony. ◆ **ironique** *adj* ironic(al). ◆ **ironiquement** *adv* ironically. ◆ **ironiser** (1) *vi* to be ironic(al) (*sur* about).

irradier [iʀadje] (7) **1** *vt* to irradiate. **2** *vi* to radiate.

irraisonné, e [iʀɛzɔne] *adj* irrational.

irrationnel, -elle [iʀasjɔnɛl] *adj (gén, Math)* irrational. ◆ **irrationalité** *nf* irrationality.

irratrapable [iʀatʀapabl(ə)] *adj bévue* irretrievable.

irréalisable [iʀealizabl(ə)] *adj but* unrealizable, unachievable; *projet* unworkable.

irréaliste [iʀealist(ə)] *adj* unrealistic.

irrecevable [iʀəsvabl(ə)] *adj (Jur)* inadmissible. **témoignage ~** inadmissible evidence.

irréconciliable [iʀekɔ̃siljabl(ə)] *adj* irreconcilable.

irrécupérable [iʀekypeʀabl(ə)] *adj argent* irretrievable; *ferraille* unreclaimable; *voiture* beyond repair; *personne* irredeemable.

irrécusable [iʀekyzabl(ə)] *adj témoin* unimpeachable; *preuve* indisputable.

irréductible [iʀedyktibl(ə)] *adj (gén, Sci)* irreducible; *obstacle* insurmountable; *volonté* indomitable, invincible; *ennemi* implacable. ◆ **irréductiblement** *adv* implacably.

irréel, -elle [iʀeɛl] *adj* unreal.

irréfléchi, e [iʀefleʃi] *adj action* thoughtless, unconsidered; *personne* unthinking. ◆ **irréflexion** *nf* thoughtlessness.

irréfutable [iʀefytabl(ə)] *adj* irrefutable. ◆ **irréfutabilité** *nf* irrefutability.

irrégulier, -ière [iʀegylje, jɛʀ] *adj (gén)* irregular; *terrain, travail* uneven; *vent* fitful; *élève, athlète* erratic; *homme d'affaires* dubious. *(Jur)* **absence ~** unauthorized absence. ◆ **irrégularité** *nf* irregularity. ◆ **irrégulièrement** *adv* irregularly; unevenly; fitfully; erratically; dubiously.

irrémédiable [iʀemedjabl(ə)] *adj perte* irreparable; *mal* incurable, irremediable. **essayer d'éviter l' ~** to try to avoid reaching the point of no return. ◆ **irrémédiablement** *adv* irreparably; incurably, irremediably.

irremplaçable [iʀɑ̃plasabl(ə)] *adj* irreplaceable.

irréparable [iʀepaʀabl(ə)] *adj (lit, fig)* irreparable. **la voiture est ~** the car is beyond repair *ou* is a write-off.

irrépressible [iʀepʀesibl(ə)] *adj* irrepressible.

irréprochable [iʀepʀɔʃabl(ə)] *adj conduite* irreproachable; *tenue* impeccable.

irrésistible [iʀezistibl(ə)] *adj (gén)* irresistible. **il est ~!** *(amusant)* he's hilarious! ◆ **irrésistiblement** *adv* irresistibly.

irrésolu, e [iʀezɔly] *adj personne* irresolute, indecisive. ◆ **irrésolution** *nf* irresoluteness, indecisiveness.

irrespectueux, -euse [iʀɛspɛktɥø, øz] *adj* disrespectful (*envers* to, towards).

irrespirable [iʀɛspiʀabl(ə)] *adj (lit)* unbreathable; *(étouffant)* oppressive, stifling; *(dangereux)* unsafe, unhealthy.

irresponsable [iʀɛspɔ̃sabl(ə)] *adj* irresponsible. ◆ **irresponsabilité** *nf* irresponsibility.

irrévérencieux, -euse [iʀeveʀɑ̃sjø, øz] *adj* irreverent. ◆ **irrévérence** *nf (caractère)* irreverence; *(propos)* irreverent word.

irréversible [iʀevɛʀsibl(ə)] *adj* irreversible.

irrévocable [iʀevɔkabl(ə)] *adj (gén)* irrevocable. ◆ **irrévocablement** *adv* irrevocably.

irriguer [iʀige] (1) *vt (Agr, Méd)* to irrigate. ◆ **irrigation** *nf* irrigation.

irriter [iʀite] (1) **1** *vt* (**a**) *(agacer)* to irritate, annoy. (**b**) *peau* to irritate. **2 s' ~** *vpr*: **s' ~ de qch/contre qn** to feel irritated *ou* annoyed at sth/with sb. ◆ **irritabilité** *nf* irritability. ◆ **irritable** *adj* irritable. ◆ **irritant, e** **1** *adj* irritating, annoying; *(Méd)* irritant. **2** *nm* irritant. ◆ **irritation** *nf (colère)* irritation, annoyance; *(Méd)* irritation.

irruption [iʀypsjɔ̃] *nf* irruption. **faire ~ (chez qn)** to burst in (on sb).

Islam [islam] *nm*: **l' ~** Islam. ◆ **islamique** *adj* Islamic. **la République ~ de...** the Islamic Republic of...

Islande [islɑ̃d] *nf* Iceland. ◆ **islandais, e** **1** *adj, nm* Icelandic. **2** *nm(f)*: **I~(e)** Icelander.

isocèle [izɔsɛl] *adj* isoceles.

isoler [izɔle] (1) **1** *vt (gén)* to isolate; *(Élec)* to insulate; *(contre le bruit)* to soundproof. **ville isolée du reste du monde** town cut off from the rest of the world. **2 s' ~** *vpr (gén)* to isolate o.s. **ils s'isolèrent quelques instants** they stood aside for a few seconds. ◆ **isolant, e** **1** *adj (gén)* insulating; *(insonorisant)* soundproofing. **2** *nm* insulator. **~ thermique/électrique** heat/electrical insulator. ◆ **isolation** *nf* insulation. **~ phonique** soundproofing. ◆ **isolationnisme** *nm* isolationism. ◆ **isolation-**

niste *adj, nmf* isolationist. ◆ **isolé, e 1** *adj (gén)* isolated; *lieu* lonely, remote. **tireur** ~ lone sniper. **2** *nm, f (théoricien)* loner; *(personne délaissée)* lonely person. ◆ **isolement** *nm (gén)* isolation; *[personne délaissée, maison]* loneliness; *(Élec)* insulation. ◆ **isolément** *adv* in isolation, individually, separately. ◆ **isoloir** *nm* polling booth.

isomère [izɔmɛʀ] **1** *adj* isomeric. **2** *nm* isomer.

isorel [izɔʀɛl] *nm* ® hardboard.

isotherme [izɔtɛʀm(ə)] *adj* isothermal. **camion** ~ refrigerated lorry *ou* truck *(US)*.

isotope [izɔtɔp] **1** *adj* isotopic. **2** *nm* isotope.

Israël [isʀaɛl] *nm* Israel. **l'État d'** ~ the state of Israel. ◆ **israélien, -ienne** *adj*, **I~(ne)** *nm(f)* Israeli. ◆ **israélite 1** *adj* Jewish. **2** *nm*: **I~** *(gén)* Jew ; *(Hist)* Israelite. **3** *nf*: **I~** Jewess; Israelite.

issu, e[1] [isy] *adj*: **être ~ de** *(résulter de)* to stem from; *(être né de)* to be descended from.

issue[2] [isy] *nf* (**a**) *(sortie)* exit; *[vapeur]* outlet. **voie sans** ~ *(lit, fig)* dead end; *(panneau)* 'no through road'; ~ **de secours** emergency exit; *(fig)* **se ménager une** ~ to leave o.s. a way out. (**b**) *(solution)* way out. **la situation est sans** ~ there is no way out of *ou* no solution to the situation; **un avenir sans** ~ a future without prospects. (**c**) *(fin)* outcome. ~ **fatale** fatal outcome; **à l'** ~ **de** at the conclusion *ou* close of

Istamboul *ou* **Istanbul** [istɑ̃bul] *n* Istambul.

isthme [ism(ə)] *nm (Anat, Géog)* isthmus.

Italie [itali] *nf* Italy. ◆ **italien, -ienne** *adj, nm*, **I~(ne)** *nm(f)* Italian.

italique [italik] *nm (Typ)* italics. **mettre un mot en ~(s)** to put a word in italics, italicize a word.

itinéraire [itineʀɛʀ] *nm (chemin)* route, itinerary; *(Alpinisme)* route. *(fig)* **son** ~ **philosophique** his philosophical path.

itinérant, e [itineʀɑ̃, ɑ̃t] *adj* itinerant. **ambassadeur** ~ roving ambassador.

itou * † [itu] *adv* likewise. **et moi** ~! (and) me too! *

ivoire [ivwaʀ] *nm* ivory.

ivoirien, -ienne [ivwaʀjɛ̃, jɛn] **1** *adj* of *ou* from the Ivory Coast. **2** *nm, f*: **I~(ne)** inhabitant *ou* native of the Ivory Coast.

ivre [ivʀ(ə)] *adj (lit)* drunk. ~ **de colère/de joie** wild *ou* beside o.s. with anger/joy; ~ **mort** dead *ou* blind drunk. ◆ **ivresse** *nf* drunkenness. **l'** ~ **de la victoire** the exhilaration of victory; **l'** ~ **du plaisir** the (wild) ecstasy of pleasure; **avec** ~ rapturously, ecstatically. ◆ **ivrogne** *nmf* drunkard. ◆ **ivrognerie** *nf* drunkenness.

J

J, j [ʒi] *nm (lettre)* J, j.

j' [ʒ(ə)] *V* **je.**

jabot [ʒabo] *nm [oiseau]* crop; *(Habillement)* jabot.

jacasser [ʒakase] (1) *vi (gén)* to chatter. ◆ **jacassement** *nm*: ~**(s)** chatter.

jachère [ʒaʃɛʀ] *nf*: **mettre une terre en** ~ to leave a piece of land fallow; **rester en** ~ to lie fallow.

jacinthe [ʒasɛ̃t] *nf* hyacinth. ~ **des bois** bluebell.

Jacques [ʒak] *nm*: **faire le** ~ * to play *ou* act the fool.

jacquet [ʒakɛ] *nm* backgammon.

jacter ⁑ [ʒakte] (1) *vi* to jabber, gas *; *(arg Police)* to talk, come clean ⁑.

jade [ʒad] *nm (pierre)* jade; *(objet)* jade object.

jadis [ʒadis] **1** *adv* formerly, long ago. **mes amis de** ~ my friends of long ago. **2** *adj*: **dans le temps** ~ in days of old.

jaguar [ʒagwaʀ] **1** *nm (animal)* jaguar. **2** *nf (voiture:* ®*)* **J**~ Jaguar ®.

jaillir [ʒajiʀ] (2) *vi [liquide]* to spurt out, gush forth; *[larmes]* to flow; *[flammes]* to shoot up; *[étincelles]* to fly out; *[lumière]* to flash; *[cris]* to burst out; *[idée, vérité]* to spring (*de* from). **il jaillit dans la pièce** he burst into the room. ◆ **jaillissement** *nm [liquide]* spurt, gush.

jais [ʒɛ] *nm (Minér)* jet; *(couleur)* jet black.

jalon [ʒalɔ̃] *nm (lit)* ranging-pole; *(fig)* step. *(fig)* **poser les premiers** ~**s de qch** to prepare the ground for sth. ◆ **jalonner** (1) *vt (pour construire)* to mark out *ou* off; *(border, s'espacer sur)* to line. **carrière jalonnée de succès** career punctuated with successes.

jaloux, -ouse [ʒalu, uz] *adj (gén)* jealous. **faire des** ~ to make people jealous. ◆ **jalousement** *adv* jealously. ◆ **jalouser** (1) *vt* to be jealous of. ◆ **jalousie** *nf* (**a**) *(sentiment)* jealousy. **être malade de** ~ to be green with envy. (**b**) *(persienne)* slatted blind, jalousie.

Jamaïque [ʒamaik] *nf* Jamaica. ◆ **jamaïquain, e** *adj*, **J**~**(e)** *nm(f)* Jamaican.

jamais [ʒamɛ] *adv* (**a**) *(négatif)* never. **il ne lui a** ~ **plus écrit** he never wrote to her again, he has never written to her since; **il partit pour ne** ~ **plus revenir** he departed never to return; **nous sommes restés 2 ans sans** ~ **recevoir de nouvelles** we went for 2 years without ever hearing any news; **ça ne fait** ~ **que 2 heures qu'il est parti** it's no more than 2 hours since he left; **ce n'est** ~ **qu'un enfant** he is only *ou* but a child (after all); ~**, au grand** ~**!,** ~ **de la vie!** never!; ~ **plus!** never again!; **presque** ~ hardly ever, practically never; **c'est le moment ou** ~ it's now or never; ~ **deux sans trois!** there's always a third time! (**b**) *(temps indéfini)* ever. **si** ~ **j'avais un poste pour vous je vous préviendrais** if I ever had a job for you I'd let you know; **si** ~ **tu rates le train, reviens** if by any chance you miss *ou* if you should happen to miss the train come back; **les œufs sont plus chers que** ~ eggs are more expensive than ever; **à tout** ~ for ever (and ever).

jambe [ʒɑ̃b] *nf* leg. ~ **de pantalon** trouser leg; ~ **de bois** wooden leg; *(Constr)* ~ **de force** strut; **avoir les** ~**s comme du coton** *ou* **en coton** to have legs like jelly *ou* cotton wool; *(fig)* **n'avoir plus de** ~**s** to be worn out; **traîner la** ~ *(par fatigue)* to drag one's steps; *(boîter)* to limp along; **elle ne peut plus se tenir sur ses** ~**s** she can hardly stand; **prendre ses** ~**s à son cou** to take to one's heels; **faire qch par dessous** *ou* **par dessus la** ~ * to do sth in a slipshod way; **il m'a tenu la** ~ **pendant des heures** * he kept me hanging about talking for hours *; **elle est toujours dans mes** ~**s** * she's always getting in my way.

jambon [ʒɑ̃bɔ̃] *nm* ham. ~ **fumé** smoked ham, gammon; ~ **blanc** *ou* **de Paris** boiled ham. ◆ **jambonneau,** *pl* ~**x** *nm* knuckle of ham.

jante [ʒɑ̃t] *nf [charrette]* felly; *[voiture, vélo]* rim. *(Aut)* ~**s alu** alloy wheels.

janvier [ʒɑ̃vje] *nm* January; *V* **septembre.**

Japon [ʒapɔ̃] *nm* Japan. ◆ **japonais, e** *adj, nm,* **J**~**(e)** *nm(f)* Japanese.

japper [ʒape] (1) *vi* to yap, yelp. ◆ **jappement** *nm* yap, yelp.

jaquette [ʒakɛt] *nf [homme]* morning coat; *[livre]* (dust) jacket.

jardin [ʒaʀdɛ̃] *nm* garden, yard *(US)*. **siège de** ~ garden seat; ~ **d'agrément** pleasure garden; ~ **botanique** botanical garden(s); ~ **d'enfants** kindergarten, ≃ playschool; ~ **potager** vegetable *ou* kitchen garden; ~ **public** (public) park, public gardens. ◆ **jardinage** *nm* gardening. ◆ **jardiner** (1) *vi* to garden, do some gardening. ◆ **jardinier, -ière** **1** *adj* garden. **2** *nm, f* gardener. **3** *nf* (**a**) *(caisse à fleurs)* window box. (**b**) ~**ière (de légumes)** mixed vegetables, jardiniere. (**c**) ~**ière d'enfants** kindergarten teacher, ≃ playschool supervisor.

jargon [ʒaʀgɔ̃] *nm (baragouin)* gibberish, double Dutch *; *(professionnel)* jargon. ~ **administratif** officialese, official jargon; ~ **informatique** computerese *; ~ **de métier** trade jargon *ou* slang.

jarret [ʒaʀɛ] *nm [homme]* back of the knee, ham; *[animal]* hock. *(Culin)* ~ **de veau** knuckle of veal.

jarretelle [ʒaʀtɛl] *nf* suspender, garter *(US)*.

jarretière [ʒaʀtjɛʀ] *nf* garter.

jars [ʒaʀ] *nm (animal)* gander.

jaser [ʒaze] (1) *vi [enfant]* to chatter, prattle; *[oiseau]* to twitter; *[ruisseau]* to babble; *(arg Police)* to talk; *[personne] (parler)* to chat; *(médire)* to gossip. **cela va faire** ~ **les gens** that'll set tongues wagging.

jasmin [ʒasmɛ̃] *nm* jasmine.

jatte [ʒat] *nf* (shallow) bowl, basin.

jauge [ʒoʒ] *nf* (**a**) *(compteur)* gauge; *(règle graduée)* dipstick. (**b**) *(capacité) [réservoir]* capacity; *[navire]* tonnage, burden. ◆ **jauger** (3) **1** *vt réservoir* to gauge the capacity of; *navire* to measure the tonnage of; *personne* to size up. **il le jaugea du regard** he gave him an appraising look. **2** *vi* to have a capacity of. **navire qui jauge 500 tonneaux** ship of 500 tonnes *ou* tons burden.

jaune [ʒon] **1** *adj* yellow. ~ **d'or** golden yellow; ~ **citron** lemon, lemon yellow; ~ **paille** straw-coloured; ~ **serin** *ou* **canari** canary yellow. **2** *nm* (**a**) **J**~ Asian; **les J**~**s** the yellow races. (**b**) *(couleur)* yellow. (**c**) ~ **(d'œuf)** (egg) yolk. (**d**) *(péj: non gréviste)* blackleg, scab ⁑. **3** *nf* (**a**) **J**~ Asian woman. (**b**) *(péj)* blackleg, scab ⁑. ◆ **jaunâtre** *adj* yellowish. ◆ **jaunir** (2) *vti* to turn yellow. **doigts jaunis par la nicotine** fingers yellowed *ou* discoloured with nicotine. ◆ **jaunisse** *nf (Méd)* jaundice. **en faire une** ~ * *(de dépit)* to be pretty miffed *; *(de jalousie)* to be *ou* turn green with envy.

Java [ʒava] *nf* Java. ◆ **javanais, e** *adj, nm,* **J~(e)** *nm(f)* Javanese.

java [ʒava] *nf (danse)* popular waltz. *(fig)* **faire la** ~ ‡ to live it up *, have a rave-up ‡; **ils ont fait une de ces ~s** they had a really wild time * *ou* a real rave-up ‡.

javelliser [ʒavelize] (1) *vt* to chlorinate.

javelot [ʒavlo] *nm (Mil, Sport)* javelin.

jazz [dʒaz] *nm* jazz. ◆ **jazzman,** *pl* **jazzmen** *nm* jazzman, jazz player.

je, j' [ʒ(ə)] *pron pers* I. **elle a un je ne sais quoi qui attire** there's (a certain) something about her that is very attractive; **son je-m'en-fichisme** * his (I-) couldn't-care-less attitude *.

jean [dʒin] *nm* (pair of) jeans.

jeanfoutre [ʒɑ̃futʀ(ə)] *nm inv (péj)* jackcass *(péj)*.

jeep [ʒip] *nf* jeep.

jérémiades * [ʒeʀemjad] *nfpl* moaning, whining.

jerrycan [ʒeʀikan] *nm* jerry can.

jersey [ʒɛʀzɛ] **1** *nm (tissu)* jersey (cloth). **point de** ~ stocking stitch. **2** : **J~** *nf* Jersey.

Jerusalem [ʒeʀyzalɛm] *n* Jerusalem.

jésuite [ʒezɥit] *nm, adj* Jesuit.

jésus [ʒezy] *nm* (**a**) **J~** Jesus; **J~-Christ** Jesus Christ; **en 300 avant/après J~-Christ** in 300 B.C./A.D. (**b**) *(statue)* statue of the infant Jesus. *(terme d'affection)* **mon** ~ (my) darling. (**c**) *(saucisson) kind of pork sausage.*

jet¹ [ʒɛ] *nm* (**a**) *[eau etc]* jet; *[sang]* spurt; *[salive]* stream; *[lumière]* beam. (**b**) *[pierre] (action)* throwing; *(résultat)* throw. **à un ~ de pierre** at a stone's throw. (**c**) **premier** ~ first sketch; **écrire d'un (seul)** ~ to write in one go; **à ~ continu** in a continuous *ou* an endless stream; ~ **d'eau** *(fontaine)* fountain; *(gerbe)* spray.

jet² [dʒɛt] *nm (Aviat)* jet.

jetée [ʒ(ə)te] *nf* jetty; *(grande)* pier.

jeter [ʒ(ə)te] (4) **1** *vt* (**a**) *(lancer)* to throw; *(avec force)* to fling, hurl; *(au rebut)* to throw away *ou* out. *(*: mettre rapidement)* ~ **une veste sur ses épaules** to slip a jacket over one's shoulders; ~ **une idée sur le papier** to jot down an idea; ~ **qch à qn** *(pour qu'il l'attrape)* to throw sth to sb; *(agressivement)* to throw sth at sb; ~ **qch par terre/par la fenêtre** to throw sth on the ground/out of the window; **il s'est fait** ~ ‡ he got thrown out; ~ **qch à la poubelle** to throw sth in the dustbin; **jette l'eau sale dans l'évier** pour the dirty water down the sink; ~ **dehors** *visiteur* to throw out; *employé* to fire, sack. (**b**) *(construire) pont* to throw (*sur* over); *fondations* to lay. (**c**) *lueur* to give, give out, cast, shed; *cri* to give, utter, let out; *regard* to cast. ~ **un coup d'œil sur qch** *(rapidement)* to glance at sth; *(pour surveiller)* to take a look at sth; **le diamant jette mille feux** the diamond sparkles brilliantly; **elle en jette, cette voiture!** that's a really smart car!, that's some car! * (**d**) *(dans le désespoir)* to plunge; *(dans l'embarras)* to throw (*dans* into). **ça me jette hors de moi** it drives me frantic *ou* wild. (**e**) *discrédit, sort* to cast. ~ **le trouble chez qn** to disturb *ou* trouble sb; **sa remarque a jeté un froid** his remark cast a chill. (**f**) *(dire)* to say (*à* to); *insultes* to hurl (*à* at). **il me jeta en passant que c'était commencé** he said to me as he went by that it had begun; ~ **un cri** to let out *ou* give a cry; ~ **des cris** to cry out, scream. (**g**) *(locutions)* ~ **son dévolu sur qch/qn** to set one's heart on sth/sb; ~ **la première pierre** to cast the first stone; **je ne veux pas lui ~ la pierre** I don't want to be too hard on him; ~ **du lest** *(lit)* to dump ballast; *(fig)* to sacrifice sth, make concessions; **on va s'en ~ un derrière la cravate** ‡ we'll have a quick one *; ~ **l'argent par les fenêtres** to spend money like water; ~ **sa gourme** to sow one's wild oats; ~ **le manche après la cognée** to throw in one's hand; ~ **de la poudre aux yeux de qn** to impress sb; *(Boxe)* ~ **l'éponge** to throw in the sponge *ou* towel.
2 se ~ *vpr* (**a**) **se ~ par la fenêtre/à genoux** to throw o.s. out of the window/down on one's knees; **se ~ du douzième étage** to throw o.s. off the twelfth floor; **se ~ sur qn** to launch o.s. at sb, rush at sb; **se ~ sur sa proie** to pounce on one's prey; **sa voiture s'est jetée contre un arbre** his car crashed into a tree; **se ~ à l'eau** *(lit)* to plunge into the water; *(fig)* to take the plunge; **se ~ à corps perdu dans une entreprise** to throw o.s. wholeheartedly into an enterprise. (**b**) *[rivière]* to flow (*dans* into).

jeton [ʒ(ə)tɔ̃] *nm* (**a**) *(pièce) (gén)* token; *(Jeu)* counter; *(Roulette)* chip. ~ **de téléphone** telephone token; ~ **(de présence)** *(argent)* director's fees. (**b**) (‡) *(coup)* biff *. **avoir les ~s** to have the jitters *.

jeu, *pl* **~x** [ʒø] **1** *nm* (**a**) *(gén avec règles)* game. ~ **d'adresse/de hasard** game of skill/chance; ~ **de société** parlour game; **~-concours** competition; ~ **radiophonique** radio game; ~ **télévisé** *(avec questions)* television quiz; ~ **de patience** jigsaw puzzle; ~ **vidéo** video game. (**b**) *(Sport) (partie)* game. *(Tennis)* **mener par 5 ~x à 2** to lead by 5 games to 2; **' ~, set et match'** 'game, set and match'; **hors** ~ *(Tennis)* out (of play); *(Ftbl, Rugby)* offside; *(Ftbl, Rugby)* **mettre qn hors** ~ to put sb offside; **remettre en** ~ to throw in; **remise en** ~ throw-in. (**c**) *(série) [pions, clefs]* set. ~ **de construction** building set; ~ **de 52 cartes** pack of 52 cards. (**d**) *(lieu)* ~ **de boules** bowling ground; ~ **de quilles** skittle alley. (**e**) *(Cartes: main)* hand. **avoir du** ~ to have a good hand; *(fig)* **cacher son** ~ to conceal one's hand. (**f**) *(façon de jouer) (Sport)* game; *(Théât)* acting. **il a un ~ rapide** *(Sport)* he plays a swift game; *(Mus)* he plays quickly; **j'observais son petit** ~ I watched his little game. (**g**) **le** ~ *(amusement)* play; *(Casino)* gambling; **le ~ est nécessaire à l'homme** play is necessary to man, man needs to play. (**h**) *(fonctionnement) [institutions]* working, interplay; *(Tech)* play. **donner du ~ à qch** to give a bit of play to sth, loosen sth up a bit; **il y a du** ~ it's a bit loose, there's a bit of play. (**i**) *(locutions)* **le ~ n'en vaut pas la chandelle** the game is not worth the candle; **il a beau ~ de protester maintenant** it's easy for him to complain now; **les forces en** ~ the forces at work; **ce qui est en** ~ what is at stake; **mettre/entrer en** ~ to bring/come into play; **entrer dans le ~ de qn** to play sb's game, join in sb's game; **faire le ~ de qn** to play into sb's hands; **faire ~ égal avec qn** to be evenly matched (against sb); **c'est un ~ d'enfant** it's child's play, it's a snap * *(US)*; **ce n'est qu'un** ~ it's just a game; **par** ~ for fun; **être pris à son propre** ~ to be caught out at one's own game; **~x de main, ~x de vilain!** stop fooling around or it will end in tears!; **les ~x sont faits** *(Casino)* 'les jeux sont faits'; *(fig)* the die is cast.
2 : *(Comm)* ~ **d'écritures** dummy entry; *(Ordin)* ~ **d'essai** benchmark; ~ **de massacre** *(à la foire)* Aunt Sally; *(fig)* wholesale slaughter; ~ **de mots** play on words, pun; ~ **de l'oie** ≃ snakes and ladders; **J~x olympiques** Olympic games; **J~x olympiques d'hiver** Winter Olympics; **J~x olympiques pour handicapés** wheelchair Olympics.

jeudi [ʒødi] *nm* Thursday. **le ~ de l'Ascension** Ascension Day; **le ~ saint** Maundy Thursday; *V* **samedi.**

jeun [ʒœ̃] *adv*: **être à** ~ to have eaten (*ou* drunk) nothing; *(pas ivre)* to be sober; *(Méd)* **à prendre à** ~ to be taken on an empty stomach.

jeune [ʒœn] **1** *adj* (**a**) *(gén)* young; *apparence* youthful; *industrie* new. **dans mon ~ âge** in my younger days, in my youth; **il n'est plus tout ~** he's not as young as he was; **il est plus ~ que moi de 5 ans** he's 5 years younger than me, he's 5 years my junior; **s'habiller ~** to dress young for one's age; **être ~ d'allure** to be young-looking, be youthful in appearance; **être ~ de caractère** *(puéril)* to be childish; *(dynamique)* to have a youthful outlook. (**b**) *(inexpérimenté)* inexperienced, green *. **être ~ dans le métier** to be new *ou* a newcomer to the trade. (**c**) *(cadet)* junior. **mon ~ frère** my younger brother; **mon plus ~ frère** my youngest brother; **Durand ~** Durand junior. (**d**) *(*: insuffisant)* short, skimpy. **c'est un peu ~** *[temps]* it's cutting it a bit short *ou* fine; *[argent]* it's a bit on the short side, it's pretty tight *.
2 *nm* youth, young man. **les ~s** young people; **club de ~s** youth club.
3 *nf* girl.
4 : **~ chien** puppy; **~ femme** young woman; **~ fille** girl; **la ~ génération** the younger generation; **~s gens** young people; **~ homme** young man; **~ marié** bridegroom; **~ mariée** bride; **les ~s mariés** the newly-weds; *(Théât)* **~ premier** leading man; **~ première** leading lady.

jeûne [ʒøn] *nm* fast. ◆**jeûner** (1) *vi (gén)* to go without food; *(Rel)* to fast.

jeunesse [ʒœnɛs] *nf* (**a**) *(gén)* youth; *[apparence, esprit]* youthfulness; *[vin]* youngness. **dans ma ~** in my youth, in my younger days; **erreur de ~** youthful mistake; **il faut que ~ se passe** youth must have its fling; **la ~ de son visage** his youthful face. (**b**) *(personnes)* **la ~** young people; **la ~ dorée** the young jet set; **la ~ des écoles** young people at school; **les ~s communistes** the Communist Youth Movement.

jiu-jitsu [ʒ(j)yʒitsy] *nm* jujitsu.

joaillerie [ʒɔɑjʀi] *nf (commerce)* jeweller's trade; *(marchandise)* jewellery; *(magasin)* jeweller's (shop). ◆**joaillier, -ière** *nm, f* jeweller.

job * [dʒɔb] *nm (travail)* (temporary) job.

jobard, e * [ʒɔbaʀ, aʀd(ə)] **1** *adj* gullible. **2** *nm, f (dupe)* sucker *, mug *; wally ⁑.

jockey [ʒɔkɛ] *nm* jockey.

jogging [dʒɔgiŋ] *nm* jogging. **faire du ~** to go jogging.

joie [ʒwa] *nf* joy. **à ma grande ~** to my great joy *ou* delight; **être au comble de la ~** to be overjoyed; **quand aurons-nous la ~ de vous revoir?** when shall we have the pleasure of seeing you again?; **les ~s du mariage** the joys of marriage; **être plein de ~ de vivre** to be full of the joys of life; **faire la ~ de qn** to delight sb, give great pleasure to sb; **le clown tomba pour la plus grande ~ des enfants** the clown fell over to the (great) delight of the children; **il se faisait une telle ~ d'y aller** he was so looking forward to going; **je me ferai une ~ de le faire** I shall be delighted *ou* only too pleased to do it.

joindre [ʒwɛ̃dʀ(ə)] (49) **1** *vt* (**a**) *(gén)* to join (*à* to); *objets* to put together; *villes* to link (*à* with); *efforts* to combine. **les talons joints** with one's heels together; **~ l'utile à l'agréable** to combine work with pleasure; **~ le geste à la parole** to suit the action to the word; *(fig)* **~ les deux bouts *** to make (both) ends meet. (**b**) *(inclure) timbre, chèque etc* to enclose (*à* with). **les avantages joints à ce poste** the advantages attached to this post; **carte jointe à un cadeau** card attached to a gift. (**c**) *(communiquer avec) personne* to get in touch with, contact. **2** *vi [fenêtre, porte]* to shut, close; *[planches etc]* to join. **3 se ~** *vpr* (**a**) *(s'unir à)* **se ~ à** *groupe* to join; **se ~ à la foule** to mingle *ou* mix with the crowd; **se ~ à la discussion** to join in the discussion. (**b**) *[mains]* to join.

◆**joint** *nm* (**a**) *(articulation)* joint; *(ligne de jonction)* join; *(en ciment, mastic)* pointing. **~ de robinet** washer; **~ de cardan** cardan joint; **~ de culasse** cylinder head gasket; **~ d'étanchéité** seal. (**b**) *(arg Drogue)* joint *(arg)*. (**c**) **faire le ~ *** *[provisions]* to last *ou* hold out; *[argent]* to bridge the gap (*jusqu'à* until); **trouver le ~ *** to come up with the solution. ◆**jointure** *nf* joint; join. **faire craquer ses ~s** to crack one's knuckles.

joker [ʒɔkɛʀ] *nm (Cartes)* joker.

joli, e [ʒɔli] *adj* (**a**) *(gén)* nice; *femme* pretty; *vue* attractive. **~ comme un cœur** pretty as a picture; **il est ~ garçon** he is (quite) good-looking. (**b**) (*) *profit, résultat* nice, good. **ça fait une ~e somme** it's a tidy *ou* handsome sum of money. (**c**) *(iro: déplaisant)* fine *(iro)*, nice *(iro)*. **un ~ gâchis** a fine mess; **un ~ monsieur** a nasty character. (**d**) *(locutions)* **tout ça c'est bien ~ mais** that's all very well but; **le plus ~ (de l'histoire) c'est que** the best bit of it all is that; **vous avez fait du ~!** you've made a fine mess of things!; **tu as encore menti, c'est du ~!** you've lied again — that's great! * *ou* that's a great help!; **faire le ~ cœur** to play the lady-killer; **ce n'est pas ~ de mentir** it's not nice to tell lies; **elle est ~e, votre idée!** that's a nice *ou* great * idea!; *(iro)* **c'est ~ de dire du mal des gens!** that's nice spreading nasty gossip about people! ◆**joliment** *adv* nicely; attractively; prettily. **il était ~ en retard *** he was pretty * late.

jonc [ʒɔ̃] *nm (plante)* bulrush; *(canne)* cane, rattan. *(bijou)* **~ d'or** (plain gold) bangle *ou* ring.

joncher [ʒɔ̃ʃe] (1) *vt*: **~ qch de** to strew sth with.

jonction [ʒɔ̃ksjɔ̃] *nf* junction. **point de ~** junction, meeting point.

jongler [ʒɔ̃gle] (1) *vi (lit, fig)* to juggle (*avec* with). ◆**jonglerie** *nf* jugglery, juggling. ◆**jongleur, -euse** *nm, f* juggler; *(Hist)* jongleur.

jonque [ʒɔ̃k] *nf (Naut)* junk.

jonquille [ʒɔ̃kij] *nf* daffodil, jonquil.

Jordanie [ʒɔʀdani] *nf* Jordan. ◆**jordanien, -ienne** *adj*, **J~(ne)** *nm(f)* Jordanian.

joue [ʒu] *nf* (**a**) *(Anat)* cheek. **~ contre ~** cheek to cheek. (**b**) *(Mil)* **en ~!** take aim!; **mettre en ~** *cible* to aim at; *fusil* to aim.

jouer [ʒwe] (1) **1** *vi* (**a**) to play (*avec* with). **~ à la poupée/aux soldats/aux cartes/à courir** to play with one's dolls/(at) soldiers/cards/at running; **~ aux cowboys et aux Indiens** to play (at) cowboys and Indians; *(fig)* **~ avec** *son crayon, une idée* to toy with; *sa santé* to gamble with; *(fig)* **on ne joue pas avec ces choses-là** matters like these are not to be treated lightly; **~ au chat et à la souris avec qn** to play cat and mouse with sb; **~ avec *ou* contre X aux échecs** to play X at chess; **~ au héros** to play the hero. (**b**) *(Mus)* to play. **~ du piano** to play the piano. (**c**) *(Casino)* to gamble. **~ à la Bourse** to speculate *ou* gamble on the Stock Exchange; **~ à la roulette** to play roulette; **~ aux courses** to bet on the horses; **ils ont joué sur la surprise** they were banking *ou* relying on the element of surprise. (**d**) *(Théât)* to act. **elle joue bien** she is a good actress, she acts well; **on joue à guichets fermés** the performance is fully booked *ou* is booked out. (**e**) *(fonctionner)* to work. **faire ~ un ressort** to activate *ou* trigger a spring. (**f**) *(joindre mal)* to fit loosely, be loose; *[bois] (travailler)* to warp. (**g**) *(intervenir, s'appliquer)* to apply (*pour* to); *[facteur]* to matter, count. **cet argument joue à plein** this argument is entirely applicable; **cette mesure joue pour tout le monde** this measure applies to everybody; **ça a joué en ma faveur** it worked in my favour; **il a fait ~ ses appuis politiques** he made use of his political connections; **le temps joue contre lui** time is against him *ou* is not on his side. (**h**) *(locutions)* **~ sur les mots** to play with words; **faire qch pour ~** to do sth for

fun; ~ **serré** to play a close game; ~ **perdant/gagnant** to play a losing/winning game; ~ **au plus fin** to try to outsmart sb; ~ **de malheur** to be dogged by ill luck; *(lit, fig)* **à vous de** ~! your go! *ou* turn!; *(Échecs)* your move!; **bien joué!** well done! ; ~ **avec le feu** to play with fire.
2 *vt* (**a**) *(Théât) rôle* to play, act; *(représenter) film* to put on, show. **on joue 'Macbeth' ce soir** 'Macbeth' is on this evening; *(fig)* ~ **un rôle** to play a part; *(fig)* ~ **la comédie** to put on an act; *(fig)* **le drame s'est joué très rapidement** the tragedy happened very quickly. (**b**) *(simuler)* ~ **les victimes** to play the victim; ~ **la surprise** to affect *ou* feign surprise. (**c**) *(Mus, Sport)* to play; *pion* to play, move. ~ **atout** to play trumps. (**d**) *argent (Casino)* to stake, wager; *(Courses)* to bet, stake (*sur* on); *cheval* to back, bet on; *réputation* to wager. ~ **les consommations** to play for drinks; *(fig: décidé)* **rien n'est encore joué** nothing is settled *ou* decided yet. (**e**) *(littér: tromper) personne* to deceive. (**f**) *(locutions)* **il faut** ~ **le jeu** you've got to play the game; ~ **franc jeu** to play fair; ~ **un double jeu** to play a double game; ~ **son va-tout** to stake one's all; ~ **un tour à qn** to play a trick on sb; **cela te jouera un mauvais** *ou* **vilain tour** you'll get your comeuppance *, you'll be sorry for it; ~ **sa dernière carte** to play one's last card.
3 ~ **de** *vt indir couteau, influence* to use, make use of. ~ **des jambes** * to run away, take to one's heels; ~ **des coudes pour entrer** to elbow one's way in; **il joue de sa maladie pour ne rien faire** he plays on his illness to get out of doing anything.
4 se ~ *vpr: (littér)* **se** ~ **de qn** to deceive sb; **se** ~ **des difficultés** to make light of the difficulties; **il a réussi cet examen comme en se jouant** that exam was a walkover for him *.
◆ **jouet** *nm* toy, plaything. **être le** ~ **d'une illusion** to be the victim of an illusion; **être/devenir le** ~ **du hasard** to be/become a hostage to fortune. ◆ **joueur, -euse** *nm, f* player; *(Casino)* gambler. ~ **de golf** golfer; **être beau/mauvais** ~ to be a good/bad loser; *[enfant]* **il est très** ~ he's very playful.

joufflu, e [ʒufly] *adj personne* chubby-cheeked; *visage* chubby.

joug [ʒu] *nm* (**a**) *(Agr, fig)* yoke. **sous le** ~ under the yoke. (**b**) *[balance]* beam.

jouir [ʒwiʀ] (2) **1** ~ **de** *vt indir (gén, Jur)* to enjoy. ~ **de toutes ses facultés** to be in full possession of one's faculties; **le Midi jouit d'un bon climat** the South of France has a good climate. **2** *vi* (⁑) *(plaisir sexuel)* to come⁑, have an orgasm. ◆ **jouissance** *nf* (**a**) *(volupté)* pleasure. (**b**) *(Jur: usage)* use, enjoyment.

joujou *, *pl* ~**x** [ʒuʒu] *nm* toy; *(*: revolver)* gun. **faire** ~ to play (*avec* with).

jour [ʒuʀ] **1** *nm* (**a**) *(lumière)* day(light); *(période)* day(-time). **il fait** ~ it is daylight; **je fais ça le** ~ I do it during the day *ou* in the daytime; **voyager de** ~ to travel by day; **se lever avant le** ~ to get up before dawn *ou* daybreak; **le** ~ **tombe** it's getting dark; **avoir le** ~ **dans les yeux** to have the light in one's eyes; **c'est le** ~ **et la nuit!** there's absolutely no comparison! (**b**) *(espace de temps)* day. **d'un** ~ *célébrité, joie* short-lived, fleeting; **c'est à 2** ~**s de marche de...** it is a 2 days' walk from... ; **dans 2** ~**s** in 2 days' time, in 2 days; **un de ces** ~**s** one of these days; **à un de ces** ~**s!** see you again sometime!, be seeing you! *; **le** ~ **d'avant** the day before, the previous day; **le** ~ **d'après** the day after, the next day, the following day; **le** ~ **de Pâques** Easter Day; **il m'a téléphoné l'autre jour** he phoned me the other day; *(iro)* **c'est mon** ~! it's just not my day today!; **ce n'est vraiment pas le** ~! you (*ou* we *etc*) have picked the wrong day!; **le goût du** ~ the style of the day; **un œuf du** ~ a new-laid egg, a freshly-laid egg. (**c**) *(indéterminé)* **la fuite des** ~**s** the swift passage of time; **mettre fin à ses** ~**s** to put an end to one's life; **nous gardons cela pour nos vieux** ~**s/pour les mauvais** ~**s** we're keeping that for our old age/for a rainy day *ou* for hard times. (**d**) *(éclairage: lit, fig)* light. **jeter un** ~ **nouveau sur** to throw (a) new light on; **se présenter sous un** ~ **favorable** *[projet]* to look promising; *[personne]* to show o.s. in a favourable light; **nous le voyons sous son véritable** ~ we see him in his true colours. (**e**) *(ouverture) [mur, haie]* gap. *(Couture)* ~**s** hemstitching. (**f**) *(locutions)* **donner le** ~ **à** to give birth to; **voir le** ~ to be born; **mettre au** ~ *(révéler)* to bring to light; **se faire** ~ to become clear; **vivre au** ~ **le** ~ to live from day to day; **être/mettre à** ~ to be/bring up to date; **mise à** ~ *(action)* updating; *(résultat)* update; **un** ~ **ou l'autre** sooner or later; **du** ~ **au lendemain** overnight; **être dans un bon/mauvais** ~ to be in a good/bad mood; **chose de tous les** ~**s** everyday *ou* ordinary thing; **de nos** ~**s** these days, nowadays; **3 fois par** ~ 3 times a day; **il y a 2 ans** ~ **pour** ~ 2 years ago to the day.
2 : **le** ~ **de l'An** New Year's day; ~ **de congé** day off, holiday; ~ **de deuil** day of mourning; ~ **férié** public holiday; ~ **de fête** feastday, holiday; **le** ~ **du Grand Pardon** the Day of Atonement; **le** ~ **J** D-day; **le** ~ **des Morts** All Souls' Day; ~ **ouvrable** weekday, working day; **le** ~ **des Rois** Epiphany, Twelfth Night; **le** ~ **du Seigneur** Sunday; ~ **de sortie** day off; ~ **de travail** working day.

journal, *pl* **-aux** [ʒuʀnal, o] *nm* (**a**) *(Presse)* (news)paper; *(magazine)* magazine; *(bulletin)* journal. (**b**) *(intime)* diary, journal; *(Rad)* news. ~ **de bord** ship's log; ~ **pour enfants** children's comic *ou* paper; *(TV)* ~ **télévisé** television news.

journalier, -ière [ʒuʀnalje, jɛʀ] *adj (de chaque jour)* daily; *(banal)* everyday, humdrum. **c'est** ~ it happens every day.

journalisme [ʒuʀnalism(ə)] *nm* journalism. ◆ **journaliste** *nmf* journalist. ~ **sportif** sports correspondent; ~ **de radio/de télévision** radio/television reporter. ◆ **journalistique** *adj* journalistic.

journée [ʒuʀne] *nf* (**a**) day. **pendant la** ~ during the day, in the daytime; **dans la** ~ **d'hier** yesterday, in the course of yesterday. (**b**) *[ouvrier]* ~ **(de travail)** day's work; ~ **(de salaire)** day's wages *ou* pay; **faire de dures** ~**s** to put in a heavy day's work; **être payé à la** ~ to be paid by the day; **faire la** ~ **continue** to work over lunch; **la** ~ **de 8 heures** the 8-hour day; ~ **de repos** day off.

journellement [ʒuʀnɛlmɑ̃] *adv (quotidiennement)* daily; *(souvent)* every day.

joute [ʒut] *nf (Hist, fig)* joust. ~**s nautiques** water tournament. ◆ **jouter** (1) *vi (Hist, fig)* to joust (*contre* against).

jouvenceau, *pl* ~**x** [ʒuvɑ̃so] *nm* (†, *hum)* stripling †. ◆ **jouvencelle** *nf* (†, *hum)* damsel (†).

jouxter [ʒukste] (1) *vt* to adjoin, be next to.

jovial, e, *mpl* **-aux** *ou* ~**s** [ʒɔvjal, o] *adj* jovial, jolly. ◆ **jovialement** *adv* jovially. ◆ **jovialité** *nf* joviality, jollity.

joyau, *pl* ~**x** [ʒwajo] *nm (lit, fig)* gem, jewel.

joyeux, -euse [ʒwajø, øz] *adj (gén)* joyful; *groupe* merry; *repas* cheerful. **un** ~ **luron** a jolly fellow; **il était tout** ~ **à l'idée de partir** he was overjoyed at the idea of going; ~ **Noël!** merry *ou* happy Christmas!; ~**euse fête!** many happy returns! ◆ **joyeusement** *adv* joyfully; merrily; cheerfully.

jubilé [ʒybile] *nm* jubilee.

jubiler * [ʒybile] (1) *vi* to be jubilant. ◆ **jubilation** *nf* jubilation.

jucher *vt,* **se** ~ *vpr* [ʒyʃe] (1) to perch (*sur* on).

judaïque [ʒydaik] *adj loi* Judaic; *religion* Jewish. ◆**judaïsme** *nm* Judaism. ◆**judéo-** *préf* Judeo-. ◆**judéo-allemand, e** *adj, nm* Yiddish.

Judée [ʒyde] *nf* Judaea, Judea.

judiciaire [ʒydisjɛʀ] *adj* judicial. **poursuites ~s** judicial *ou* legal proceedings.

judicieux, -euse [ʒydisjø, øz] *adj* judicious. ◆**judicieusement** *adv* judiciously.

judo [ʒydo] *nm* judo. ◆**judoka** *nmf* judoka.

juge [ʒyʒ] **1** *nm (gén)* judge. **oui, Monsieur le J~** yes, your Honour; **(madame)/(monsieur) le ~ X** Mrs/Mr Justice X; **être à la fois ~ et partie** to be both judge and judged; **je vous fais ~** I'll let you be the judge; **il est seul ~ en la matière** he is the only one who can judge; **aller devant le ~** to go before the judge. **2** : **~-arbitre** referee; **~ des enfants** children's judge, ≃ juvenile magistrate ; **~ d'instruction** examining judge *ou* magistrate, committing magistrate *(US)*; **~ de paix** justice of the peace, magistrate; **~ de touche** linesman.

jugé [ʒyʒe] *nm*: **au ~** by guesswork; **tirer au ~** to fire blind.

jugement [ʒyʒmɑ̃] *nm* (**a**) *(Jur) [criminel]* sentence; *[civil]* decision, award. **rendre un ~** to pass sentence; **passer en ~** to stand trial; **faire passer qn en ~** to put sb on trial; **poursuivre qn en ~** to sue sb, take legal proceedings against sb; **~ par défaut** judgment by default. (**b**) *(opinion)* judgment, opinion. **porter un ~ sur** to pass judgment on; **~ préconçu** prejudgment. (**c**) *(discernement)* judgment. **manquer de ~** to lack judgment. (**d**) *(Rel)* judgment.

jugeote * [ʒyʒɔt] *nf* commonsense, gumption *.

juger [ʒyʒe] (3) **1** *vt* (**a**) *affaire* to judge, try; *accusé* to try (*pour* for); *différend* to arbitrate in. **le jury a jugé qu'il n'était pas coupable** the jury found him not guilty; **l'affaire doit se ~ à l'automne** the case is to be heard in the autumn. (**b**) *(décider)* to judge. **à vous de ~** it's up to you to decide *ou* to judge. (**c**) *(apprécier)* to judge. **il ne faut pas ~ d'après les apparences** you must not judge *ou* go by appearances; **jugez combien j'étais surpris** imagine how surprised I was. (**d**) *(estimer)* **~ qch/qn ridicule** to consider *ou* find sth/sb ridiculous; **~ que** to think *ou* consider that; **~ mal qn** to think badly of sb; **~ bon de faire** to consider it a good thing *ou* advisable to do; **il se juge capable de le faire** he thinks *ou* reckons he can do it. **2 ~ de** *vt indir* to appreciate, judge. **si j'en juge par mon expérience** judging by my experience; **à en ~ par ce résultat, il...** if this result is any indication, he...; **autant que je puisse en ~** as far as I can judge. **3** *nm* = **jugé**.

juguler [ʒygyle] (1) *vt maladie* to arrest; *envie* to suppress; *inflation* to curb; *révolte* to put down.

juif, juive [ʒɥif, ʒɥiv] **1** *adj* Jewish. **2** *nm*: **J~** Jew. **3** *nf*: **Juive** Jewess.

juillet [ʒɥijɛ] *nm* July; *V* **septembre**.

juin [ʒɥɛ̃] *nm* June; *V* **septembre**.

jumeau, -elle, *mpl* **~x** [ʒymo, ɛl] **1** *adj (gén)* twin. **mon frère ~** my twin brother; **maisons ~elles** semidetached houses. **2** *nm, f (personne)* twin; *(sosie)* double. **j'aimerais trouver le ~ de ce vase ancien** I'd like to find the partner to this antique vase. **3** *nf*: **~elle(s)** binoculars; **~elles de théâtre** opera glasses. ◆**jumelage** *nm* twinning. ◆**jumelé, e** *adj colonnes, villes* twin; *roues, billets* double. ◆**jumeler** (4) *vt villes* to twin; *efforts* to join.

jument [ʒymɑ̃] *nf* mare.

jumping [dʒœmpiŋ] *nm (gén)* jumping.

jungle [ʒɔ̃gl(ə)] *nf (lit, fig)* jungle. **la ~ des affaires** the jungle of the business world, the rat race of business.

junior [ʒynjɔʀ] *adj, nmf* junior. **mode ~** young *ou* junior fashion.

junte [ʒœ̃t] *nf* junta.

jupe [ʒyp] *nf* skirt. *(fig)* **être toujours dans les ~s de sa mère** to cling to one's mother's apron strings; **il est toujours dans mes ~s** he's always under my feet. ◆**jupon** *nm* waist petticoat *ou* slip, underskirt. **courir le ~** to chase anything in a skirt.

Jura [ʒyʀa] *nm*: **le ~** the Jura (Mountains).

jurer [ʒyʀe] (1) **1** *vt* to swear. **~ fidélité à qn** to swear *ou* pledge loyalty to sb; **~ la perte de qn** to swear to ruin sb; **faire ~ à qn de garder le secret** to swear *ou* pledge sb to secrecy; **'levez la main droite et dites je le jure'** 'raise your right hand and say I swear'; **il jurait ses grands dieux qu'il n'avait rien fait** he swore blind * *ou* to heaven that he hadn't done anything; **je vous jure que ce n'est pas facile** I can tell you *ou* assure you that it isn't easy; **ah! je vous jure!** honestly!; **on ne jure plus que par lui** everyone swears by him. **2 ~ de** *vt indir* to swear to. **j'en jurerais** I'd swear to it; **il ne faut ~ de rien** you never can tell. **3** *vi* (**a**) *(pester)* to swear, curse. (**b**) *[couleurs]* to clash, jar; *[propos]* to jar. **4 se ~** *vpr*: **se ~ qch** *(à soi-même)* to vow sth (to o.s.); *(l'un à l'autre)* to pledge *ou* swear *ou* vow sth to each other. ◆**juré, e 1** *adj* sworn. **2** *nm, f* juror, juryman (*ou* woman). **les ~s** the members of the jury; **être convoqué comme ~** to have to report for jury duty.

juridiction [ʒyʀidiksjɔ̃] *nf (compétence)* jurisdiction; *(tribunal)* court(s) of law.

juridique [ʒyʀidik] *adj* legal. ◆**juridiquement** *adv* legally.

juriste [ʒyʀist(ə)] *nm [compagnie]* lawyer; *(auteur)* jurist.

juron [ʒyʀɔ̃] *nm* oath, swearword. **dire des ~s** to swear, curse.

jury [ʒyʀi] *nm (Jur)* jury; *(Art, Sport)* panel of judges; *(Scol)* board of examiners. *(Univ)* **un ~ de thèse** Ph. D. examining board.

jus [ʒy] *nm* (**a**) *(liquide)* juice. **~ de fruit** fruit juice; **~ de viande** juice(s) from the meat, ≃ gravy. (**b**) (*) *(café)* coffee; *(courant)* juice *; *(eau)* water. **au ~!** coffee's ready!; **tomber dans le ~** to fall into the water.

jusant [ʒyzɑ̃] *nm* ebb tide.

jusque [ʒysk(ə)] **1** *prép* (**a**) *(lieu)* **jusqu'à la, jusqu'au** to; **j'ai couru jusqu'à la maison** I ran all the *ou* right the way home; **j'ai marché jusqu'au village** I walked to *ou* as far as the village; **jusqu'où?** how far?; **il avait de la neige jusqu'aux genoux** he was knee-deep in snow; **la nouvelle est venue jusqu'à moi** the news has reached me; **en avoir ~-là *** to be fed up *; **s'en mettre ~-là *** to stuff o.s. *; **j'en ai ~-là!** I'm sick and tired of it!, I've had about as much as I can take! (**b**) *(temps)* **jusqu'à, jusqu'en** until, till, up to; **jusqu'à quand?** until when?, how long?; **jusqu'à présent** until now, so far; **jusqu'au bout** to the end; **du matin jusqu'au soir** from morning till night; **jusqu'à 5 ans** until *ou* up to the age of 5. (**c**) *(limite)* up to. **jusqu'à 20 kg** up to 20 kg, not exceeding 20 kg; **pousser l'indulgence jusqu'à la faiblesse** to carry indulgence to the point of weakness; **aller jusqu'à dire/faire** to go so far as to say/do; **tu vois jusqu'à quel point tu t'es trompé** you see how wrong you were. (**d**) *(y compris)* even. **ils ont regardé ~ sous le lit** they even looked under the bed; **tous jusqu'au dernier** every single *ou* last one of them. **2** *adv*: **~s et y compris** up to and including; **jusqu'à** *(même)* even; **tout jusqu'au paysage avait changé** even the landscape had changed. **3** *conj*: **jusqu'à ce que** until.

juste [ʒyst(ə)] **1** *adj* (**a**) *(légitime)* just; *(équitable)* just, fair; *colère* righteous, justifiable. **pour être ~ envers lui** in fairness to him, to be fair to him; **à ~ titre** justly, rightly; ~ **ciel!** † heavens above! (**b**) *calcul, réponse* right; *raisonnement* sound; *remarque* apt; *appareil* accurate; *oreille* good; *note de musique, voix* true; *piano* well-tuned. **à l'heure ~** right on time; **à 6 heures ~s** on the stroke of 6; **apprécier qch à son ~ prix** to appreciate the true worth of sth; **le ~ milieu** the happy medium; **très ~!** quite right!; **c'est ~** that's right, that's a fair point. (**c**) *(trop court) vêtement* tight; *(longueur)* on the short side. *(quantité)* **1 kg pour 6, c'est un peu ~** 1 kg for 6 people — it's barely enough *ou* it's a bit on the short side; **elle n'a pas raté son train mais c'était ~** she didn't miss her train but it was a close thing.
2 *adv* (**a**) *compter, viser* accurately; *raisonner* soundly; *deviner* rightly, correctly; *chanter* in tune. **tomber ~** *(deviner)* to hit the nail on the head; **division qui tombe ~** division which works out exactly; **la pendule va ~** the clock is keeping good time. (**b**) *(exactement)* just, exactly. ~ **au-dessus** just above; **3 kg ~** 3 kg exactly. (**c**) *(seulement)* only, just. **il est parti il y a ~ un moment** he left just *ou* only a moment ago. (**d**) **(un peu) ~** *prévoir* not quite enough, too little; **il a mesuré trop ~** he cut it a bit too fine. (**e**) *(locutions)* **que veut-il au ~?** what exactly does he want?; **au plus ~ prix** at the minimum price; **comme de ~** of course; **tout ~** *(seulement)* only just; *(à peine)* hardly, barely; *(exactement)* exactly. **3** *nm (Rel)* just man. **les ~s** the just.

justement [ʒystəmɑ̃] *adv* (**a**) *(précisément)* just, precisely. **on parlait ~ de vous** we were just talking about you. (**b**) *remarquer* rightly, justly, soundly. ~ **puni** justly punished; ~ **fier** justifiably proud.

justesse [ʒystɛs] *nf (gén)* accuracy; *[raisonnement]* soundness; *[remarque]* aptness. **de ~** *gagner* by a narrow margin, narrowly; *s'en tirer* by the skin of one's teeth, narrowly; **j'ai évité l'accident de ~** I avoided the accident by a hair's breadth, I had a narrow escape.

justice [ʒystis] *nf* (**a**) *(gén)* justice. **rendre la ~** to dispense justice; **rendre ~ à qn** to do sb justice; **traiter qn avec ~** to treat sb justly *ou* fairly; **rendre ~ au talent de qn** to give fair recognition to sb's talent; **on doit lui rendre cette ~ que** it must be said in fairness to him that; **ce n'est que ~** it's only fair; **se faire ~** *(se venger)* to take the law into one's own hands; *(se suicider)* to take one's life. (**b**) *(tribunal)* court; *(autorités)* law. *(loi)* **la ~** the law; **la ~ le recherche** he is wanted by the law; **il a eu des démêlés avec la ~** he's had a brush *ou* he's had dealings with the law; **passer en ~** to stand trial; **aller en ~** to take the case to court. ◆ **justiciable 1** *adj*: ~ **de** subject to. **2** *nmf (Jur) person subject to trial.* ◆ **justicier, -ière** *nm, f (gén)* upholder of the law.

justifier [ʒystifje] (7) **1** *vt (gén)* to justify. ~ **qn d'une erreur** to clear sb of having made a mistake; **ça justifie mon point de vue** it bears out *ou* vindicates my opinion; **cette quittance justifie du paiement** this invoice is evidence *ou* proof of payment. **2 ~ de** *vt indir* to prove. **3 se ~** *vpr* to justify o.s. **se ~ d'une accusation** to clear o.s. of an accusation. ◆ **justifiable** *adj* justifiable. ◆ **justificatif, -ive** *adj* justificatory. **pièce ~ive** written proof *ou* evidence. ◆ **justification** *nf (explication)* justification; *(preuve)* proof.

jute [ʒyt] *nm* jute.

juteux, -euse [ʒytø, øz] *adj fruit* juicy; (*) *affaire* lucrative.

juvénile [ʒyvenil] *adj allure* youthful.

juxtaposer [ʒykstapoze] (1) *vt* to juxtapose. ◆ **juxtaposition** *nf* juxtaposition.

K, k [ka] *nm (lettre)* K, k; *(Ordin)* K.

Kabylie [kabili] *nf* Kabylia. ◆ **kabyle** *adj, nm,* **K~** *nmf* Kabyle.

kaki [kaki] **1** *adj* khaki. **2** *nm* (**a**) *(couleur)* khaki. (**b**) *(Agr)* persimmon.

kaléidoscope [kaleidɔskɔp] *nm* kaleidoscope.

kamikaze [kamikaze] *nm* kamikaze.

kangourou [kɑ̃guʀu] *nm* kangaroo.

kaolin [kaɔlɛ̃] *nm* kaolin.

kapok [kapɔk] *nm* kapok.

karaté [kaʀate] *nm* karate. ◆ **karateka** *nm* karate expert.

kart [kaʀt] *nm* go-cart, kart. ◆ **karting** *nm* go-carting, karting. **faire du** ~ to go-cart, go karting.

kascher [kaʃɛr] *adj* kasher, kosher.

kayak [kajak] *nm (eskimo)* kayak; *(Sport)* canoe, kayak. **faire du** ~ to go canoeing.

Kenya [kenja] *nm* Kenya. ◆ **kényen, -yenne** *adj,* **K~(ne)** *nm(f)* Kenyan.

képi [kepi] *nm* kepi.

kératine [keʀatin] *nf* keratin.

kermesse [kɛʀmɛs] *nf* fair; *(de charité)* bazaar, fête. *(fig)* **c'est une vraie** ~ **là-dedans** * it's absolute bedlam in there.

kérosène [keʀozɛn] *nm [avion]* aviation fuel, kerosene *(US)*; *[jet]* jet fuel; *[fusée]* rocket fuel.

khôl [kol] *nm* khol, kajal.

kibboutz [kibuts] *nm inv* kibbutz.

kidnapper [kidnape] (1) *vt* to kidnap. ◆ **kidnappeur, -euse** *nm, f* kidnapper.

kif [kif] *nm* (**a**) *(Drogue)* kef, kif. (**b**) (*) **c'est du** ~, **c'est** ~-~ it's all the same, it makes no odds *.

kilo [kilo] **1** *nm* kilo. **2** *préf* kilo... ◆ **kilocalorie** *nf* kilocalory. ◆ **kilogramme** *nm* kilogramme. ◆ **kilométrage** *nm [voiture]* ≃ mileage. ◆ **kilomètre** *nm* kilometre. ◆ **kilo-octet** *nm* kilobyte. ◆ **kilotonne** *nf* kiloton. ◆ **kilowatt** *nm* kilowatt. ~**-heure** *nm* kilowatt-hour.

kilt [kilt] *nm* kilt; *(pour femme)* pleated *ou* kilted skirt.

kimono [kimɔno] *nm* kimono.

kinésithérapeute [kineziteʀapøt] *nmf* physiotherapist. ◆ **kinésithérapie** *nf* physiotherapy.

kiosque [kjɔsk(ə)] *nm [fleurs etc]* kiosk, stall; *[jardin]* pavilion. ~ **à musique** bandstand; ~ **à journaux** newsstand, newspaper kiosk.

kirsch [kiʀʃ] *nm* kirsch.

kit [kit] *nm* kit. **en** ~ in kit form.

kitsch [kitʃ] *adj inv* kitsch.

kiwi [kiwi] *nm* (**a**) *(oiseau)* kiwi. (**b**) *(arbre)* kiwi tree; *(fruit)* kiwi (fruit), Chinese gooseberry.

klaxon [klaksɔn] *nm* ® *(Aut)* horn. ◆ **klaxonner** (1) *vi* to hoot (one's horn), sound one's horn.

kleenex [klinɛks] *nm* ® tissue, paper hanky, Kleenex ®.

kleptomane [klɛptɔman] *adj, nmf* kleptomaniac. ◆ **kleptomanie** *nf* kleptomania.

knock-out [nɔkawt] *(Boxe,* ⁎*)* **1** *adj* knocked out. **mettre qn** ~ to knock sb out. **2** *nm* knock-out.

koala [kɔala] *nm* koala (bear).

kolkhoze [kɔlkoz] *nm* kolkhoz, Russian collective farm.

kouglof [kuglɔf] *nm* kugelhopf *(kind of bun)*.

Koweit *ou* **Kuweit** [kɔwɛt] *nm* Kuwait.

krach [kʀak] *nm (Bourse)* crash.

kraft [kʀaft] *nm:* **papier** ~ strong wrapping paper.

Kremlin [kʀɛmlɛ̃] *nm:* **le** ~ the Kremlin.

kumquat [kumkwat] *nm* kumquat.

Kurdistan [kuʀdistɑ̃] *nm* Kurdistan. ◆ **kurde** **1** *adj, nm* Kurdish. **2** *nmf:* **K~** Kurd.

kyrielle [kiʀjɛl] *nf [réclamations, personnes]* stream; *[objets]* pile.

kyste [kist(ə)] *nm* cyst.

L

L, l [ɛl] *nm ou nf (lettre)* L, l.

l' [l(ə)] *V* **le¹, le²**.

la¹ [la] *V* **le¹, le²**.

la² [la] *nm inv (note)* A; *(chanté)* lah. **donner le ~** *(lit)* to give an A; *(fig)* to set the tone.

là [la] **1** *adv* (**a**) *(espace)* there. **c'est ~ où** *ou* **que je suis né** that's where I was born; **c'est à 3 km de ~** it's 3 km away (from there); **quelque part par ~** somewhere around there; **passez par ~** go that way; **M. X n'est pas ~** Mr X isn't there *ou* in; **qu'est-ce que tu fais ~?** *(lit)* what are you doing here?; *(fig: manigancer)* what are you up to? (**b**) *(temps)* then. **c'est ~ qu'il comprit** that was when he realized, it was then that he realized; **à partir de ~** from then on, after that; **à quelques jours de ~** a few days later. (**c**) *(situation)* that. **il faut en rester ~** we'll have to leave it at that; **la situation en est ~** that's how the situation stands at the moment; **ils en sont ~** that's the stage they've reached; **~ est la difficulté** that's where the difficulty lies. (**d**) *(intensif)* that. **ce jour-~** that day; **en ce temps-~** in those days; **ce qu'il dit ~ n'est pas bête** what he has just said isn't a bad idea; **de ~ son désespoir** hence his despair; **de ~ vient que nous ne le voyons plus** that's why we no longer see him; **de ~ à prétendre qu'il a tout fait seul, il y a loin** there's a big difference between saying that and claiming that he did it all himself; **il n'a pas travaillé, de ~ son échec** he didn't work, hence his failure *ou* which explains his failure; **loin de ~** far from it; **tout est ~** that's the whole question; **comme menteur, il est** *ou* **se pose ~** he isn't half a liar *; **alors ~, ça ne me surprend pas** (oh) now, that doesn't surprise me; **hé ~!** *(appel)* hey!; *(surprise)* good grief!; **~, ~ du calme** now, now *ou* there, there, calm down; **oh ~ ~ (~ ~)** dear! dear!

2 : **~-bas** (over) there; **~-bas dans le nord** up (there) in the north; **~-dedans** *(lit)* inside; **je ne comprends rien ~-dedans** I don't understand a thing about it; **il n'a rien à voir ~-dedans** it's nothing to do with him; **quand il s'est embarqué ~-dedans** when he got involved in that *ou* in it; **~-dessous** underneath; *(fig)* **il y a qch ~-dessous** there's sth odd about it *ou* that; **~-dessus** on that; *(sur ces mots)* at that point; *(à ce sujet)* about that; **~-haut** up there; *(dessus)* up on top; *(à l'étage)* upstairs; *(fig: au ciel)* in heaven above.

label [labɛl] *nm (Comm)* stamp, seal. **~ politique** political label.

labeur [labœʀ] *nm (littér)* labour. **c'est un dur ~** it's hard work.

laboratoire [labɔʀatwaʀ] *nm* laboratory. ◆ **labo** * *nm* lab *. ◆ **laborantin, e** *nm, f* laboratory *ou* lab * assistant.

laborieux, -euse [labɔʀjø, øz] *adj* (**a**) *(pénible) (gén)* laborious; *récit* laboured; *digestion* heavy. **ça a été ~!** * it has been heavy going. (**b**) *(travailleur)* hard-working, industrious. **les classes ~euses** the working *ou* labouring classes; **une vie ~euse** a life of hard work. ◆ **laborieusement** *adv* laboriously, with much effort.

labourer [labuʀe] (1) *vt* (**a**) *(avec charrue)* to plough, plow *(US)*; *(avec bêche)* to dig (over). **terre qui se laboure bien** land which ploughs well. (**b**) *visage, corps* to gash. **labouré de rides** lined *ou* furrowed with wrinkles; **ça me laboure les côtes** it is digging into my sides. ◆ **labour** *nm (action)* ploughing, plowing *(US)*; digging; *(champ)* ploughed field. ◆ **labourage** *nm* ploughing, plowing *(US)*; digging. ◆ **laboureur** *nm* ploughman, plowman *(US)*.

Labrador [labʀadɔʀ] *nm (Géog, chien)* Labrador.

labyrinthe [labiʀɛ̃t] *nm (lit, fig)* maze, labyrinth.

lac [lak] *nm* lake. **le ~ Léman** *ou* **de Genève** Lake Geneva; **le ~ Majeur** Lake Maggiore; **c'est dans le ~** * it has fallen through.

lacer [lɑse] (3) *vt chaussure* to tie (up); *corset* to lace up. **ça se lace (par) devant** it laces up at the front.

lacérer [laseʀe] (6) *vt vêtement* to tear *ou* rip up; *corps* to lacerate; *papiers* to tear up, shred. ◆ **lacération** *nf* ripping up, tearing up; laceration; shredding.

lacet [lɑsɛ] *nm* (**a**) *[chaussure]* (shoe) lace; *[corset]* lace. **chaussures à ~s** lace-up shoes. (**b**) *[route]* sharp bend, twist. **en ~** winding, twisty. (**c**) *(piège)* snare. **prendre des lièvres au ~** to trap *ou* snare hares.

lâche [lɑʃ] **1** *adj* (**a**) *corde* slack; *nœud, style, règlement* loose; *discipline* lax. (**b**) *(couard)* cowardly. **se montrer ~** to show o.s. a coward. (**c**) *(bas, vil) attentat* vile, despicable; *procédés* low. **2** *nmf* coward. ◆ **lâchement** *adv* loosely; in a cowardly way.

lâcher [lɑʃe] (1) **1** *vt* (**a**) *ceinture* to loosen, let out, slacken. (**b**) *main, proie* to let go of; *bombes* to drop, release; *pigeon, frein* to release. **lâche-moi!** let *ou* leave go (of me)!; **attention! tu vas ~ le verre** careful, you're going to drop the glass; **~ un chien sur qn** to set a dog on sb; **il va falloir qu'il les lâche** * *ou* **qu'il lâche ses sous** * he'll have to part with the cash *; **il les lâche difficilement** * he hates to part with his money. (**c**) *bêtise, juron* to come out with. (**d**) *(*: abandonner) personne* to throw over *; *métier* to give up, throw up *. *(Sport)* **~ le peloton** to leave the rest of the field behind; **il ne m'a pas lâché** *[poursuivant]* he stuck to me; *[importun, représentant]* he didn't leave me alone; *[mal de tête]* it didn't leave me; **il nous a lâché en plein milieu du travail** he walked out on us right in the middle of the work; **une bonne occasion, ça ne se lâche pas** you don't miss *ou* pass up * an opportunity like that. (**e**) *(locutions)* **~ prise** *(lit)* to let go; *(fig)* to loosen one's grip; **~ pied** to fall back; **~ du lest** *(Naut)* to throw out ballast; *(* fig)* to climb down; **~ la bride à un cheval/à qn** to give a horse/sb his head. **2** *vi [corde]* to break, give way; *[frein]* to fail. **ses nerfs ont lâché** he broke down. **3** *nm*: **~ de ballons/de pigeons** release of balloons/of pigeons.

lâcheté [lɑʃte] *nf* cowardice, cowardliness; *(acte)* cowardly act, act of cowardice.

lâcheur, -euse * [lɑʃœʀ, øz] *nm, f* unreliable so-and-so *.

lacis [lɑsi] *nm [ruelles]* maze; *[veines]* network; *[scie]* web.

laconique [lakɔnik] *adj* laconic, terse. ◆ **laconiquement** *adv* laconically, tersely. ◆ **laconisme** *nm* terseness.

lacté, e [lakte] *adj sécrétion* milky; *régime, farine* milk.

lacune [lakyn] *nf (Anat, Bot)* lacuna; *[connaissances, texte]* gap, deficiency.

ladite [ladit] *adj V* **ledit.**

Lagos [lagɔs] *n* Lagos.

lagon [lagɔ̃] *nm* lagoon. ◆ **lagune** *nf* lagoon.

lai, e [lɛ] *adj (Rel)* lay. **frère** ~ lay brother.

laïciser [laisize] (1) *vt* to secularize. ◆ **laïcité** *nf (caractère)* secularity. **préserver la ~ de l'enseignement** to maintain the non-religious nature of the education system, keep religion out of education.

laid, e [lɛ, lɛd] *adj* (**a**) *(gén)* ugly; *région* unattractive; *bâtiment* unsightly. ~ **comme un pou** ugly as sin; **il est ~ de visage** he's got an ugly face. (**b**) *action* despicable, disgusting, low, mean. **c'est ~ de montrer du doigt** it's rude *ou* not nice to point. ◆ **laideron** *nm* ugly girl *ou* woman. ◆ **laideur** *nf* ugliness; unattractiveness; unsightliness; lowness, meanness. **la guerre dans toute sa ~** the full horror of war; **les ~s de la vie** the ugly things in life.

laine [lɛn] *nf (matière)* wool. **de** ~ *vêtement* wool, woollen; *(vêtement)* **il faut mettre une petite ~** you'll need a woolly * *ou* a cardigan; ~ **peignée** *[veston]* worsted wool; *[pull]* combed wool; ~ **de verre** glass wool; ~ **vierge** new wool. ◆ **lainage** *nm (vêtement)* woollen (garment); *(étoffe)* woollen material. ◆ **laineux, -euse** *adj* woolly. ◆ **lainier, -ière** *adj industrie* woollen; *région* wool-producing.

laïque [laik] **1** *adj tribunal* lay, civil; *vie* secular; *habit* ordinary; *collège* non-religious. **l'enseignement ~** state education *(in France)*. **2** *nm* layman. **les ~s** laymen, the laity. **3** *nf* laywoman.

laisse [lɛs] *nf* leash, lead. **tenir en ~** to keep on a leash *ou* lead.

laisser [lese] (1) **1** *vt* (**a**) *(abandonner) (gén)* to leave. **laisse-moi ta clé** leave me your key, leave your key with me; **laisse-lui du gâteau** leave *ou* save him some cake; **il m'a laissé ce vase pour 10 F** he let me have this vase for 10 francs; **laisse-moi le soin de le lui dire** leave it to me to tell him; **laisse-moi le temps d'y réfléchir** give me time to think about it; **laisse-moi devant la banque** drop *ou* leave me at the bank; **il a laissé un bras dans l'accident** he lost an arm in the accident; **il y a laissé sa vie** it cost him his life; ~ **qn indifférent** to leave sb unmoved; ~ **qn debout** to keep sb standing (up); **on lui a laissé ses illusions** we didn't disillusion him; **elle m'a laissé une bonne impression** she left *ou* made a good impression on me; **vous laissez le village sur votre droite** you go past the village on your right; ~ **la vie à qn** to spare sb's life; ~ **qn en liberté** to allow sb to stay free; **cette opération ne doit pas laisser de séquelles** this operation should leave *ou* have no aftereffects. (**b**) *(locutions) (lit, fig)* ~ **la porte ouverte** to leave the door open; **il ne laisse jamais rien au hasard** he never leaves anything to chance; **c'était à prendre ou à ~** it was a case of take it or leave it; **avec lui il faut en prendre et en ~** you must take what he tells you with a pinch of salt; **on l'a laissé pour mort** he was left for dead; **il laisse tout le monde derrière en math** he is head and shoulders above *ou* streets * *ou* miles ahead of the others in maths; ~ **le meilleur pour la fin** to leave the best till last; *(littér)* **cela n'a pas laissé de me surprendre** I couldn't fail to be surprised by *ou* at that; *(littér)* **ça ne laisse pas d'être vrai** it is true nonetheless; **je te laisse à penser combien il était content** you can imagine *ou* I don't need to tell you how pleased he was.
2 *vb aux:* ~ **(qn) faire qch** to let sb do sth; **le gouvernement laisse faire!** the government does nothing!; **laissez-moi rire** don't make me laugh; ~ **voir ses sentiments** to let one's feelings show; **il faut ~ faire le temps** we must let things take their course.
3 se ~ *vpr:* **se ~ exploiter** to let o.s. be exploited; **se ~ attendrir** to be moved; **je me suis laissé surprendre par la pluie** I got caught in the rain; **il se laisse mener par le bout du nez** he lets himself be led by the nose *ou* be pushed around; **se ~ aller** to let o.s. go; **je me suis laissé faire *** I let myself be persuaded; **je n'ai pas l'intention de me ~ faire** I'm not going to let myself be pushed around; **laisse-toi faire!** *(à qn qu'on soigne)* let me do it!
◆ **laisser-aller** *nm inv (gén)* casualness, carelessness. ◆ **laisser-faire** *nm (Écon)* laissez-faire policy. ◆ **laissez-passer** *nm inv* pass. ◆ **laissé-pour-compte,** *f* **~e-~-~**, *pl* **~s-~-~** **1** *adj (lit, fig)* rejected. **2** *nm (Comm) (refusé)* reject; *(invendu)* unsold article. *(fig)* **les ~s-~-~ de la société** society's rejects; **ce sont les ~s-~-~ du progrès** these people are the casualties of progress.

lait [lɛ] **1** *nm* milk. ~ **de vache** cow's milk; **petit** ~ whey; *(fig)* **boire du (petit) ~** to lap it up; **cela se boit comme du petit ~** you don't notice you're drinking it; **frère de ~** foster brother; **chocolat au ~** milk chocolate. **2** : ~ **de beauté** beauty lotion; ~ **caillé** curds; ~ **de chaux** lime water; ~ **de coco** coconut milk; ~ **cru** milk straight from the cow; ~ **démaquillant** cleansing milk; ~ **entier** unskimmed milk; ~ **maternel** mother's milk, breast milk; ~ **en poudre** dried *ou* powdered milk; *(Cul)* ~ **de poule** eggflip. ◆ **laitage** *nm* milk *ou* milk-based product. ◆ **laitance** *nf* soft roe. ◆ **laiterie** *nf (magasin)* dairy; *(industrie)* dairy industry. ◆ **laiteux, -euse** *adj* milky. ◆ **laitier, -ière** **1** *adj* dairy. **2** *nm* (**a**) *(livreur)* milkman; *(vendeur)* dairyman. (**b**) *(Ind)* slag. **3** *nf (vendeuse)* dairywoman. *(vache)* **une (bonne) ~ière** a (good) milker.

laiton [lɛtɔ̃] *nm* brass.

laitue [lety] *nf* lettuce.

laïus * [lajys] *nm inv (discours)* long-winded speech; *(verbiage)* verbiage, padding.

lama [lama] *nm (Zool)* llama; *(Rel)* lama.

lambda [lɑ̃bda] *nm* lambda. **le citoyen ~** the uninformed citizen.

lambeau, *pl* **~x** [lɑ̃bo] *nm* scrap. **en ~x** *vêtements* in tatters *ou* rags; *affiche* in tatters; **mettre en ~x** to tear to shreds; **tomber en ~x** to fall to pieces.

lambin, e * [lɑ̃bɛ̃, in] **1** *adj* slow. **2** *nm, f* slowcoach *, slowpoke * *(US)*. ◆ **lambiner** * (1) *vi* to dawdle.

lambris [lɑ̃bʀi] *nm* panelling.

lame [lam] **1** *nf* (**a**) *[métal, verre]* strip; *[ressort]* leaf; *(pour microscope)* slide. (**b**) *[poignard, tondeuse]* blade. **visage en ~ de couteau** hatchet face. (**c**) *(épée)* sword; *(escrimeur)* swordsman. (**d**) *(vague)* wave. **2** : **~s de fond** ground swell; ~ **de parquet** floorboard; ~ **de rasoir** razor blade. ◆ **lamé, e** *adj, nm* lamé. ◆ **lamelle** *nf (gén)* (small) strip; *[persiennes]* slat; *[champignon]* gill; *(pour microscope)* coverglass. **couper en ~s** *légumes* to cut into thin strips *ou* slices.

lamentable [lamɑ̃tabl(ə)] *adj (gén)* appalling, awful; *état* lamentable; *spectacle* pitiful. ◆ **lamentablement** *adv échouer* lamentably.

lamenter (se) [lamɑ̃te] (1) *vpr* to moan, lament. **se ~ sur qch** to moan over sth, bemoan sth; **arrête de te ~ sur ton propre sort** stop feeling sorry for yourself. ◆ **lamentation** *nf* lamentation. *(péj)* **~(s)** moaning; *(Bible)* **le livre des L~s** (the Book of) Lamentations.

laminer [lamine] (1) *vt métal* to laminate. *(fig)* **les petites formations politiques ont été laminées aux dernières élections** the small political groupings were wiped out *ou* obliterated at the last election.

◆**laminage** *nm* lamination. ◆**laminoir** *nm* rolling mill.

lampadaire [lɑ̃padɛʀ] *nm [intérieur]* standard lamp; *[rue]* street lamp. **(pied de)** ~ *[intérieur]* lamp standard; *[rue]* lamp-post.

lampe [lɑ̃p(ə)] *nf* lamp; *(ampoule)* bulb; *(Rad)* valve. ~ **d'architecte** Anglepoise lamp ®; ~ **de bureau** desk light; ~ **de chevet** bedside light; ~ **électrique** torch, flashlight; ~ **halogène** *ou* **à iode** halogen lamp; ~ **au néon** neon light; ~ **à pétrole** oil lamp; ~ **de poche** torch, flashlight *(US)*; ~ **à souder** blowlamp; ~**-tempête** storm lantern, hurricane lamp. ◆**lampion** *nm* Chinese lantern.

lance [lɑ̃s] *nf* (**a**) *(arme)* spear; *[tournoi]* lance. (**b**) *(tuyau)* hose. ~ **d'incendie** fire hose.

lancer [lɑ̃se] (3) **1** *vt* (**a**) *(gén)* to throw; *(violemment)* to hurl, fling; *bombes* to drop; *(Sport) poids* to put. ~ **qch à qn** to throw sth to sb; *(hostilement)* to throw *ou* hurl sth at sb; ~ **une balle en l'air** to throw *ou* toss a ball up in the air; ~ **les jambes en avant** to fling one's legs forward; ~ **un coup de poing** to lash out with one's fist; ~ **son poing dans la figure de qn** to punch sb in the face; *(Sport)* ~ **le poids** to put the shot. (**b**) *fumée* to send up *ou* out; *flammes, lave* to throw out. *[yeux, bijoux]* ~ **des éclairs** to flash (fire). (**c**) *menaces* to hurl, fling; *proclamation* to issue; *S.O.S.* to send out; *fausse nouvelle* to put out; *hurlement* to give out. ~ **un cri** to cry out; **elle lui lança un coup d'œil furieux** she flashed *ou* darted a furious glance at him; **'je refuse' lança-t-il** 'I refuse' he said. (**d**) *navire, idée, produit* to launch; *entreprise* to start up; *emprunt* to issue, float. **ne le lancez pas sur son sujet favori** don't set him off on *ou* don't let him get launched on his pet subject; ~ **ses hommes à l'assaut** to launch one's men into the attack; ~ **une nouvelle mode** to launch *ou* start a new fashion; ~ **qn dans la politique** to launch sb into politics; **ce chanteur est lancé** this singer has made a name for himself. (**e**) *moteur* to open up; *voiture* to get up to full speed; *balançoire* to set going. ~ **un cheval** to give a horse its head.

2 se ~ *vpr (prendre de l'élan)* to build up *ou* get up momentum *ou* speed; *(sauter)* to leap, jump; *(se précipiter)* to dash, rush (*contre* at). **se** ~ **à l'assaut** to leap to the attack; **se** ~ **dans la bagarre** to pitch into the fight; **n'hésite pas, lance-toi** don't hesitate, off you go *ou* let yourself go; **se** ~ **dans** *discussion etc* to launch into, embark on; **acteur qui cherche à se** ~ actor who's trying to make a name for himself.

3 *nm* (**a**) *(Sport)* **un** ~ a throw; *(Alpinisme)* ~ **de corde** lassoing, lasso; **le** ~ **du poids** *etc V* **lancement.** (**b**) *(Pêche) (attirail)* rod and reel; *(genre de pêche)* rod and reel fishing.

◆**lance-flammes** *nm inv* flamethrower. ◆**lance-grenades** *nm inv* grenade launcher. ◆**lance-missiles** *nm inv* missile launcher. ◆**lance-pierre(s)** *nm inv* catapult. ◆**lance-torpilles** *nm inv* torpedo tube. ◆**lancée** *nf*: **être sur sa** ~ to be *ou* have got under way; **continuer sur sa** ~ to keep going; **je peux encore courir 2 km sur ma** ~ now I'm in my stride I can run another 2 km. ◆**lancement** *nm [navire, campagne etc]* launching; *[emprunt]* issuing, floating; *(en Bourse)* flotation. **le** ~ **du disque** throwing the discus; **le** ~ **du poids** putting the shot, shot put. ◆**lanceur, -euse 1** *nm, f* (**a**) *[javelot etc]* thrower; *(Baseball)* pitcher. (**b**) *[entreprise]* promoter. **2** *nm (Espace)* launcher. ~ **de satellites** satellite launcher.

lanciner [lɑ̃sine] (1) **1** *vi* to throb. **2** *vt [pensée]* to haunt; (*) *[enfant]* to torment. ◆**lancinant, e** *adj douleur* shooting, throbbing, piercing; *souvenir* haunting; *musique* insistent. **ce que tu peux être** ~ * you get on my nerves.

landau [lɑ̃do] *nm (d'enfant)* pram, baby carriage *(US)*; *(carrosse)* landau.

lande [lɑ̃d] *nf* moor. **les L~s** *(Géog)* the Landes (region) *(south-west France)*.

langage [lɑ̃gaʒ] *nm* language. **changer de** ~ to change one's tune; ~ **argotique** slang speech; ~ **chiffré** cipher, code (language); ~ **populaire** popular speech.

lange [lɑ̃ʒ] *nm* baby's flannel blanket. *(Hist)* **~s** swaddling clothes. ◆**langer** (3) *vt bébé* to change (the nappy *ou* diaper *(US)* of). **table à** ~ changing table.

langoureux, -euse [lɑ̃guʀø, øz] *adj* languorous. ◆**langoureusement** *adv* languorously.

langouste [lɑ̃gust(ə)] *nf* crayfish, spiny lobster *(US)*. ◆**langoustine** *nf* Dublin bay prawn. *(Culin)* ~**s** scampi.

langue [lɑ̃g] *nf* (**a**) *(Anat)* tongue. **tirer la** ~ to stick out *ou* put out one's tongue; *(*: être dans le besoin)* to have a rough time of it *; *(*: avoir soif)* **il tirait la** ~ his tongue was hanging out, he was dying of thirst *. (**b**) *(organe de la parole)* tongue. **avoir la** ~ **déliée** *ou* **bien pendue** to have a ready tongue; **il a la** ~ **trop longue** he talks too much; **il ne sait pas tenir sa** ~ he can't hold his tongue; **il n'a pas la** ~ **dans sa poche** he's never at a loss for words; **perdre/retrouver sa** ~ to lose/find one's tongue; **donner sa** ~ **au chat** to give in *ou* up; **j'ai le mot sur (le bout de) la** ~ the word is on the tip of my tongue. (**c**) *(personne)* **mauvaise** ~**,** ~ **de vipère** spiteful gossip. (**d**) *(Ling)* language. **la** ~ **française** the French language; **les gens de** ~ **anglaise** English-speaking people; ~ **maternelle** mother tongue; ~ **populaire** *(idiome)* popular language; *(usage)* popular speech; *(péj)* ~ **de bois** set language, stereotyped formal language; *(lit, fig)* **nous ne parlons pas la même** ~ we don't speak the same language. (**e**) ~ **de terre** spit of land. ◆**languette** *nf [bois, cuir]* tongue.

Languedoc [lɑ̃gdɔk] *nm:* **le** ~ (the) Languedoc.

langueur [lɑ̃gœʀ] *nf* languidness, languor. ◆**languide** *adj (littér)* languid, languishing. ◆**languir** (2) *vi* (**a**) *[personne]* to languish; *[conversation etc]* to flag. ~ **après qn/qch** to languish for *ou* pine for sb/sth. (**b**) *(*: attendre)* to wait, hang around *. **faire** ~ **qn** to keep sb waiting. ◆**languissant, e** *adj personne* languid; *regard* languishing; *récit* dull; *affaires* slack.

lanière [lanjɛʀ] *nf [cuir]* strap; *[étoffe]* strip; *[fouet]* lash.

lanterne [lɑ̃tɛʀn(ə)] *nf* lantern; *(électrique)* lamp, light. *(Aut)* **se mettre en** ~**s** to switch on one's (side)lights; **éclairer la** ~ **de qn** to enlighten sb; **éclairer sa propre** ~ to make o.s. clear; *(Aut)* ~ **arrière** rear light; ~ **magique** magic lantern; ~ **rouge** *(fig: dernier)* tail-ender; ~ **vénitienne** Chinese lantern.

Laos [laɔs] *nm* Laos. ◆**laotien, -ienne** *adj, nm,* **L~(ne)** *nm(f)* Laotian.

lapalissade [lapalisad] *nf* statement of the obvious.

La Paz [lapaz] *n* La Paz.

laper [lape] (1) **1** *vt* to lap up. **2** *vi* to lap.

lapider [lapide] (1) *vt* to stone.

lapin [lapɛ̃] *nm (animal)* (buck) rabbit; *(fourrure)* rabbitskin. ~ **de garenne** wild rabbit; **mon petit** ~ my lamb; **poser un** ~ **à qn** * to stand sb up *. ◆**lapine** *nf* (doe) rabbit.

Laponie [lapɔni] *nf* Lapland. ◆**lapon, e 1** *adj, nm* Lapp. Lappish. **2** *nm, f:* **L~(e)** Lapp, Laplander.

laps [laps] *nm*: ~ **de temps** lapse of time.

lapsus [lapsys] *nm* slip of the tongue.

laquais [lakɛ] *nm* lackey, footman; *(péj)* flunkey.

laque [lak] *nf (produit brut)* shellac; *(peinture)* lacquer; *(pour cheveux)* hair lacquer *ou* spray. *(peinture)* ~ **brillante** gloss paint.

laquelle [lakɛl] *V* **lequel.**

laquer [lake] (1) *vt* to lacquer. **meuble (en) laqué blanc** piece of furniture with a white gloss finish; **murs laqués blanc** walls painted in white gloss; *(Culin)* **canard laqué** Peking duck.

larbin ‡ [laʀbɛ̃] *nm (péj)* flunkey.

larcin [laʀsɛ̃] *nm (vol)* theft; *(butin)* spoils, booty.

lard [laʀ] *nm (gras)* fat (of pig); *(viande)* bacon. ~ **(maigre)** ≃ streaky bacon; *(péj)* **un gros** ~ ‡ a fat lump ‡, a clod ‡ *(US)*; **on ne sait jamais avec lui si c'est du** ~ **ou du cochon** * you never know where you are with him * *ou* whether or not he's being serious. ◆ **larder** (1) *vt (Culin)* to lard. ~ **qn de coups de couteau** to hack at sb with a knife. ◆ **lardon** *nm* lardon.

large [laʀʒ(ə)] **1** *adj* (**a**) *surface* wide, broad; *concessions, pouvoirs* wide. **trop** ~ **de 3 mètres** 3 metres too wide; **chapeau à** ~**s bords** broadbrimmed *ou* wide-brimmed hat; **ouvrir une** ~ **bouche** to open one's mouth wide; **d'un geste** ~ with a broad *ou* sweeping gesture; **pantalon** ~ baggy trousers *ou* pants *(US)*; **être** ~ **d'épaules** *[personne]* to be broad-shouldered; *[vêtements]* to be wide *ou* broad at the shoulders; **faire une** ~ **part à qch** to give great weight to sth; **dans une** ~ **mesure** to a great *ou* large extent. (**b**) *(généreux) personne* generous. **1 kg de viande pour 4, c'est** ~ 1 kg of meat for 4 is ample *ou* plenty; **une vie** ~ a life of ease. (**c**) *sens, esprit* broad; *conscience* accommodating. ~**s vues** liberal views; ~ **d'idées** broad-minded. **2** *adv*: **prévoir** ~ to allow a bit extra; **cette marque taille** ~ the sizes in this brand tend to be on the large side. **3** *nm* (**a**) *(largeur)* width. **avenue de 8 mètres de** ~ avenue 8 metres wide *ou* 8 metres in width; **être au** ~ *(place)* to have plenty of room; *(argent)* to be well-provided for, have plenty of money; **cela se fait en 2 mètres de** ~ that comes in 2-metre widths. (**b**) *(Naut)* **le** ~ the open sea; **l'appel du** ~ the call of the sea; **au** ~ **de Calais** off Calais; *(fig)* **prendre le** ~ * to clear off *, hop it *, make o.s. scarce.

largement [laʀʒəmɑ̃] *adv* (**a**) *(gén)* widely. **fenêtre** ~ **ouverte** wide open window; **idée** ~ **répandue** widely held *ou* widespread view. (**b**) *(de loin)* considerably, greatly. **déborder** ~ **le sujet** to go well beyond the limits of the subject; **elle vaut** ~ **son frère** she's every bit as good (*ou* as bad) as *ou* at least as good (*ou* as bad) as her brother. (**c**) *(amplement)* **vous avez** ~ **le temps** you have ample time *ou* plenty of time; **c'est** ~ **suffisant** that's plenty, that's more than enough; **il est** ~ **temps de commencer** it's high time we started; **j'ai été** ~ **récompensé** I have been amply rewarded; **ça vaut** ~ **la peine** it's well worth the trouble. (**d**) *(généreusement)* generously. **vivre** ~ to live handsomely. (**e**) *(au moins)* easily, at least. **il est** ~ **2 heures** it's well past 2 o'clock.

largesse [laʀʒɛs] *nf (caractère)* generosity; *(cadeau)* generous gift.

largeur [laʀʒœʀ] *nf (lit)* width, breadth; *[idées]* broadness. **sur toute la** ~ all the way across; **dans le sens de la** ~ widthways, widthwise; ~ **d'esprit** broad-mindedness.

larguer [laʀge] (1) *vt amarres* to cast off, slip; *parachutiste* to drop; (*) *objet, ami, emploi* to chuck ‡; *collaborateur* to drop, get rid of, dump *. **être largué** * to be all at sea *.

larme [laʀm(ə)] *nf (lit)* tear; (*: *goutte)* drop. **en** ~**s** in tears; **au bord des** ~**s** on the verge of tears; **verser toutes les** ~**s de son corps** to cry one's eyes out; ~**s de crocodile** crocodile tears. ◆ **larmoyant, e** *adj voix* tearful; *récit* maudlin. ◆ **larmoyer** (8) *vi* (**a**) *[yeux]* to water, run. (**b**) *(pleurnicher)* to whimper, snivel.

larron [laʀɔ̃] *nm* (†, *Bible)* thief. **s'entendre comme** ~**s en foire** to be as thick as thieves.

larve [laʀv(ə)] *nf (Zool)* larva; *(asticot)* grub; *(péj)* worm. ◆ **larvé, e** *adj guerre* latent. **inflation** ~**e** creeping inflation.

larynx [laʀɛ̃ks] *nm* larynx. ◆ **laryngite** *nf* laryngitis. ◆ **laryngologiste** *nmf* throat specialist, laryngologist.

las, lasse [lɑ, lɑs] *adj* weary, tired (*de* of).

lascar * [laskaʀ] *nm (louche)* character; *(malin)* rogue.

lascif, -ive [lasif, iv] *adj* lascivious, lustful. ◆ **lascivité** *nf* lasciviousness, lustfulness.

laser [lazɛʀ] *nm* laser.

lasser [lɑse] (1) **1** *vt* to weary, tire. **2 se** ~ *vpr*: **se** ~ **de qch/de faire qch** to grow weary of sth/of doing sth; **sans se** ~ without tiring. ◆ **lassant, e** *adj* wearisome, tiresome. ◆ **lassitude** *nf* weariness, lassitude.

lasso [laso] *nm* lasso. **prendre au** ~ to lasso.

latent, e [latɑ̃, ɑ̃t] *adj (gén)* latent. ◆ **latence** *nf* latency.

latéral, e, *mpl* **-aux** [lateʀal, o] *adj* side, lateral. ◆ **latéralement** *adv (gén)* laterally; *être situé* on the side.

latex [latɛks] *nm inv* latex.

latin, e [latɛ̃, in] *adj, nm,* **L~(e)** *nm (f)* Latin. ~ **de cuisine** dog Latin; **j'y perds mon** ~ I can't make head nor tail of it. ◆ **latino-américain, e 1** *adj* Latin-American, Hispanic. **2** *nm, f*: **L~(e)** Latin-American, Hispanic.

latitude [latityd] *nf (gén, fig)* latitude. **Paris est à 48° de** ~ **Nord** Paris is situated at latitude 48° north; **avoir toute** ~ **de faire qch** to be quite free *ou* have full scope to do sth.

latte [lat] *nf (gén)* lath; *[plancher]* board. *(Ski)* ~**s** * boards *.

lauréat, e [lɔʀea, at] **1** *adj* prize-winning. **2** *nm, f* prize winner, award-winner.

laurier [lɔʀje] *nm* bay-tree, (sweet) bay. **feuille de** ~ bay leaf; *(fig)* ~**s** laurels; **être couvert de** ~**s** to be showered with praise. ◆ **laurier-rose,** *pl* **lauriers-roses** *nm* oleander.

lavande [lavɑ̃d] *nf* lavender.

lavandière [lavɑ̃djɛʀ] *nf* washerwoman; *(oiseau)* wagtail.

lave [lav] *nf*: ~**(s)** lava.

laver [lave] (1) **1** *vt* (**a**) *(gén)* to wash; *plaie* to bathe; *tache* to wash out *ou* off; *(Méd) intestin* to wash out; *(à la brosse)* to scrub (down); *(à l'éponge)* to wash with a sponge. ~ **à grande eau** to swill down; ~ **la vaisselle** to wash the dishes, do the washing up. (**b**) *(emploi absolu) [personne]* to do the washing. **ce savon lave bien** this soap washes well. (**c**) *affront* to avenge; *honte* to wash away. ~ **qn de qch** to clear sb of sth.

2 se ~ *vpr* to wash, have a wash. **se** ~ **la figure** to wash one's face; **se** ~ **les dents** to clean *ou* brush one's teeth; **ce tissu se lave bien** this material washes well; **ça ne se lave pas** it isn't washable *ou* won't wash; **se** ~ **de** *accusation* to clear o.s. of; **je m'en lave les mains** I wash my hands of the matter.

◆ **lave-glace,** *pl* **lave-glaces** *nm* windscreen *ou* windshield *(US)* washer. ◆ **lave-linge** *nm inv* washing machine. ◆ **lave-mains** *nm inv* wash-stand. ◆ **lave-vaisselle** *nm inv* dishwasher. ◆ **lavable** *adj* washable. ◆ **lavabo** *nm* washbasin. *(euph)* ~**s** toilets. ◆ **lavage** *nm (gén)* washing; *(lessive)* wash; *[plaie]* bathing. **pour un meilleur** ~**, utilisez...** for a better wash, use...; **on a dû faire 3** ~**s** it had to be washed 3 times; ~ **d'intestin** intestinal wash; **on lui a fait un** ~ **d'estomac** he had his stomach pumped out; ~ **de cerveau** brainwashing; **on lui a fait subir un** ~ **de cerveau** he was brainwashed. ◆ **lavasse** * *nf* dishwater *. ◆ **lavement** *nm* enema. ◆ **laverie** *nf* laundry. ~ **automatique** launderette. ◆ **lavette** *nf (chiffon)* dish cloth; *(péj)* wimp *, drip *. ◆ **laveur** *nm* washer. ~ **de carreaux** *ou* **de vitres** window cleaner. ◆ **laveuse** *nf* washerwoman. ◆ **lavoir** *nm (dehors)* washing-place; *(édifice)* wash house ; *(bac)* washtub.

laxatif, -ive [laksatif, iv] *adj, nm* laxative.

laxisme [laksism(ə)] *nm* latitudinarianism. ◆ **laxiste** *adj, nmf* latitudinarian.

layette [lɛjɛt] *nf* baby clothes, layette. **rayon** ~ babywear department.

le[1] [l(ə)], **la** [la], **les** [le] *art déf (avec à, de* **au, aux, du, des***)* (**a**) *(détermination)* the. **les enfants sont en retard** the children are late; **il n'a pas** ~ **droit de le faire** he has no right to do it; **la femme de l'épicier** the grocer's wife; **l'Italie de Mussolini** Mussolini's Italy. (**b**) *(temps)* the *(souvent omis)*. **venez** ~ **dimanche de Pâques** come on Easter Sunday; **l'hiver dernier** last winter; **il ne travaille pas** ~ **samedi** he doesn't work on Saturdays *ou* on a Saturday; ~ **matin** in the morning; **vers les 5 heures** at about 5 o'clock; **il est parti** ~ **5 mai** he left on the 5th of May *ou* on May the 5th *(style parlé)*; he left on May 5th *(style écrit)*. (**c**) *(distribution)* a, an. **5 F** ~ **mètre/la pièce** 5 francs a metre/each *ou* apiece; **60 km à l'heure** 60 km an *ou* per hour; **j'en ai fait la moitié/** ~ **dixième** I have done half/a tenth of it. (**d**) *(généralisation, abstraction) gén non traduit*. ~ **hibou vole surtout la nuit** owls fly *ou* the owl flies mainly at night; **l'homme est un roseau pensant** man is a thinking reed; **l'enfant n'aime pas** *ou* **les enfants n'aiment pas l'obscurité** children don't like the dark; **la tuberculose** tuberculosis; **la jeunesse** youth; ~ **café est cher** coffee is expensive; **j'aime la musique** I like music; ~ **beau** the beautiful; **les riches** the rich. (**e**) *(possession)* **elle ouvrit les yeux** she opened her eyes; **j'ai mal au pied** I've a pain in my foot; **il a la jambe cassée** he has got a broken leg; **avoir mal à la tête** to have a headache; **il a les cheveux noirs** he has black hair. (**f**) *(valeur démonstrative)* **faites attention, les enfants!** be careful children!; **oh** ~ **beau chien!** what a lovely dog!, (just) look at that lovely dog!

le[2] [l(ə)], **la** [la], **les** [le] *pron m, f, pl* (**a**) *(homme)* him; *(femme, nation, bateau)* her; *(animal, bébé)* it, him, her; *(chose)* it. **les** them; **regarde-~/-la/-les** look at him *ou* it/her *ou* it/them. (**b**) *(emphatique)* **cette femme-là, je la déteste** I can't bear that woman; **vous l'êtes, beau** you really do look smart. (**c**) *(neutre: souvent non traduit)* **je l'ai entendu dire** I have heard it said, so I have heard; **demande-~-lui** ask him; **je** ~ **savais bien** I thought so.

lécher [leʃe] (6) *vt* (**a**) *(gén)* to lick; *assiette* to lick clean; *[vagues]* to wash *ou* lap against. **se** ~ **les doigts** to lick one's fingers; *(fig)* **s'en** ~ **les doigts** to lick one's lips over it; ~ **les bottes de qn** * to suck up to sb ‡, lick sb's boots *. (**b**) *(*: fignoler)* to polish up. ◆ **lèche** ‡ *nf* bootlicking *. **faire de la** ~ to be a bootlicker *. ◆ **lèche-bottes** * *nmf inv* bootlicker *. ◆ **lèche-vitrines** * *nm*: **faire du** ~ to go window-shopping. ◆ **lécheur, -euse** * *nm, f* bootlicker *.

leçon [l(ə)sɔ̃] *nf (gén)* lesson. ~**s particulières** private lessons *ou* tuition; *(fig)* **il peut vous donner des ~s** he could teach you a thing or two; **faire la** ~ **à qn** *(endoctriner)* to give sb instructions; *(réprimander)* to give sb a lecture; **que cela te serve de** ~ let that be a lesson to you; **cela lui donnera une** ~ that'll teach him a lesson.

lecteur, -trice [lɛktœʀ, tʀis] *nm, f* (**a**) *(gén)* reader. **le nombre de ~s de ce journal** the readership of this paper. (**b**) *(Univ)* university assistant, lector, (foreign language) assistant, (foreign) teaching assistant *(US)*. (**c**) *(Ordin)* ~ **de cartes perforées** card reader; ~ **de cassettes** cassette player. *(Ordin)* ~ **de disquettes** disk drive; *(Ordin)* ~ **de document** document reader; *(Ordin)* ~ **optique** optical character reader.

lecture [lɛktyʀ] *nf (gén)* reading. **d'une** ~ **facile** easy to read, very readable; ~ **à haute voix** reading aloud; **faire la** ~ **à qn** to read to sb; **donner** ~ **de qch** to read sth out *(à qn* to sb); **méthode de** ~ method of teaching reading; ~ **rapide** speed reading; **apportez-moi de la** ~ bring me something to read; ~**s pour la jeunesse** books for children; *(interprétation)* **il y a plusieurs ~s possibles de ce texte** there are several possible readings *ou* interpretations of this text; *(Ordin)* **procédé de ~-écriture** read-write cycle.

ledit [lədi], **ladite** [ladit], *m(f)pl* **lesdit(e)s** [ledi(t)] *adj* the aforementioned, the aforesaid.

légal, e, *mpl* **-aux** [legal, o] *adj (gén)* legal; *adresse* official. ◆ **légalement** *adv* legally. ◆ **légalisation** *nf* legalization. ◆ **légaliser** (1) *vt* to legalize. ◆ **légalité** *nf [acte]* legality. **rester dans la** ~ to keep within the law.

légat [lega] *nm*: ~ **(du Pape)** (papal) legate.

légataire [legatɛʀ] *nmf* legatee, devisee. ~ **universel** sole legatee.

légation [legɑsjɔ̃] *nf (Diplomatie)* legation.

légende [leʒɑ̃d] *nf* (**a**) *(mythe)* legend. **entrer dans la** ~ to go down in legend. (**b**) *[médaille]* legend; *[dessin]* caption; *[carte]* key. (**c**) *(péj: mensonge)* fairy tale. ◆ **légendaire** *adj (gén)* legendary.

léger, -ère [leʒe, ɛʀ] *adj* (**a**) *poids, parfum* light. **construction ~ère** light *ou* flimsy *(péj)* building; **cuisine ~ère** light cooking; **faire qch d'un cœur** ~ to do sth with a light heart. (**b**) *allure* light, nimble; *taille* light, slender. **d'un pas** ~ with a light *ou* springy step. (**c**) *bruit, surprise* slight, faint; *thé* weak; *vin, coup* light; *maladie, châtiment* mild, slight. **une ~ère pointe d'ironie** a light touch of irony; **un blessé** ~ a slightly injured person; **il a été condamné à une peine ~ère** he was given a mild *ou* light (prison) sentence. (**d**) *(superficiel) personne, propos* thoughtless; *argument* lightweight, flimsy. **agir à la ~ère** to act thoughtlessly; **il prend toujours tout à la ~ère** he never takes anything seriously. (**e**) *(frivole) personne* fickle; *plaisanterie* ribald, broad. **femme ~ère** loose woman, woman of easy virtue. ◆ **légèrement** *adv* lightly; nimbly; slightly; faintly; thoughtlessly. ~ **plus grand** slightly bigger. ◆ **légèreté** *nf* lightness; flimsiness; nimbleness; mildness; thoughtlessness; fickleness; ribaldry.

légion [leʒjɔ̃] *nf* legion. **ils sont** ~ they are legion. ◆ **légionnaire** *nm (Hist)* legionary; *[Légion étrangère]* legionnaire.

législation [leʒislɑsjɔ̃] *nf* legislation. ◆ **législateur, -trice** *nm, f* legislator. ◆ **législatif, -ive 1** *adj* legislative. **élections ~ives** ≃ general election. **2** *nm*: **le** ~ the legislature. ◆ **législature** *nf (Parl) (durée)* term (of office); *(corps)* legislature. ◆ **légiste** *nm* legist, jurist.

légitime [leʒitim] *adj (gén)* legitimate; *femme* lawful; *colère* justifiable, justified; *revendication* rightful. **j'étais en état de** ~ **défense** I was acting in self-defence. ◆ **légitimement** *adv (gén)* rightfully; *(Jur)* legitimately. ◆ **légitimer** (1) *vt* to legitimate. ◆ **légitimité** *nf (gén)* legitimacy.

legs [lɛg] *nm (Jur, fig)* legacy. **faire un** ~ **à qn** to leave sb a legacy; ~ **(de biens immobiliers)** devise; ~ **(de biens mobiliers)** legacy. ◆ **léguer** (6) *vt (Jur)* to bequeath; *tradition, tare* to hand down, pass on.

légume [legym] **1** *nm* vegetable. ~**s secs/verts** dry/green vegetables. **2** *nf*: **une grosse** ~ * a bigwig *. ◆ **légumier** *nm* vegetable dish. ◆ **légumineuse** *nf* leguminous plant.

leitmotiv [lajtmɔtif] *nm (lit, fig)* leitmotiv, leitmotif.

lémurien [lemyʀjɛ̃] *nm* lemur.

lendemain [lɑ̃dmɛ̃] *nm* (**a**) *(jour suivant)* **le ~** the next *ou* following day, the day after; **le ~ de son arrivée** the day after he arrived, the day following his arrival; **le ~ soir** the next *ou* following evening; **il ne faut jamais remettre au ~ ce qu'on peut faire le jour même** never put off till tomorrow what you can do today; **au ~ de la défaite** soon after *ou* in the days following the defeat. (**b**) *(avenir)* **le ~** tomorrow, the future; **succès sans ~** short-lived success. (**c**) **~s** *(conséquences)* consequences; *(perspectives)* prospects.

lénifiant, e [lenifjɑ̃,ɑ̃t] *adj médicament, propos* soothing. ◆ **lénifier** (7) *vt* to soothe.

lent, e[1] [lɑ̃, lɑ̃t] *adj (gén)* slow; *poison* slow-acting; *(Fin) croissance* sluggish, slow. **à l'esprit ~** slow-witted. ◆ **lentement** *adv* slowly. ◆ **lenteur** *nf* slowness. **~ d'esprit** slow-wittedness; **la ~ de la construction** the slow progress of the building.

lente[2] [lɑ̃t] *nf (Zool)* nit.

lentille [lɑ̃tij] *nf (Bot, Culin)* lentil; *(Opt)* lens. **~s cornéennes** contact lenses; **~s (cornéennes) dures/souples** hard/soft contact lenses.

léonin, e [leɔnɛ̃,in] *adj mœurs, aspect* leonine; *(fig) contrat, partage* one-sided.

léopard [leɔpaʀ] *nm* leopard; *(fourrure)* leopard-skin.

lèpre [lɛpʀ(ə)] *nf (Méd)* leprosy; *(fig: mal)* plague. ◆ **lépreux, -euse 1** *adj (lit)* leprous; *mur* flaking, peeling. **2** *nm, f (lit, fig)* leper. ◆ **léproserie** *nf* leper-house.

lequel [ləkɛl], **laquelle** [lakɛl], *m(f)pl* **lesquel(le)s** [lekɛl] *(avec à, de* **auquel, auxquels, auxquelles, duquel, desquels, desquelles**) **1** *pron* (**a**) *(relatif) (personne: sujet)* who; *(personne: objet)* whom; *(chose)* which. **j'ai écrit au directeur, ~ n'a jamais répondu** I wrote to the manager, who has never answered; **le règlement d'après ~** the ruling whereby...; **la femme à laquelle j'ai acheté mon chien** the woman from whom I bought my dog; **le pont sur ~ vous êtes passé** the bridge you came over *ou* over which you came. (**b**) *(interrogatif)* which. **~ des 2 acteurs préférez-vous?** which of the 2 actors do you prefer?; **va voir ma sœur — laquelle?** go and see my sister — which one? **2** *adj*: **son état pourrait empirer, auquel cas je reviendrais** his condition could worsen, in which case I would come back.

les [le] *V* **le**[1], **le**[2].

lesbienne [lɛsbjɛn] *nf* lesbian. ◆ **lesbianisme** *nm* lesbianism.

lèse-majesté [lɛzmaʒɛste] *nf* lese-majesty.

léser [leze] (6) *vt* (**a**) *personne* to wrong; *droits* to infringe on; *intérêts* to damage. (**b**) *(Méd)* to injure.

lésiner [lezine] (1) *vi* to skimp (*sur qch* on sth). ◆ **lésinerie** *nf* stinginess.

lésion [lezjɔ̃] *nf (Jur, Méd)* lesion. *(Méd)* **~s internes** internal injuries.

lessiver [lesive] (1) *vt* (**a**) *(lit)* to wash. (**b**) *(*: battre) (au jeu)* to clean out *; *adversaire* to lick *. (**c**) *(*: fatiguer)* to tire out, exhaust. **être lessivé** to be dead-beat * *ou* all-in * *ou* tired out. ◆ **lessivable** *adj papier peint* washable. ◆ **lessivage** *nm* washing. ◆ **lessive** *nf (produit)* washing powder; *(linge)* washing; *(lavage)* washing, wash. **faire la ~** to do the washing; **faire 4 ~s par semaine** to do 4 washes a week. ◆ **lessiveuse** *nf* (laundry) boiler. ◆ **lessiviel** *adj m*: **produit ~** detergent product.

lest [lɛst] *nm* ballast. ◆ **lester** (1) *vt (lit)* to ballast; *(*: remplir) poches* to fill.

leste [lɛst(ə)] *adj* (**a**) *(agile)* nimble, agile, sprightly. (**b**) *plaisanterie* risqué. ◆ **lestement** *adv* nimbly, agilely. **mener ~ une affaire** to conduct a piece of business briskly.

let [lɛt] *nm (Tennis)* let. **jouer un ~** to play a let.

léthargie [letaʀʒi] *nf* lethargy. **tomber en ~** to fall into a state of lethargy. ◆ **léthargique** *adj* lethargic.

lettre [lɛtʀ(ə)] **1** *nf* (**a**) *(caractère)* letter. **c'est écrit en toutes ~s** it's there *ou* it's written in black and white; **écrire en (toutes) ~s** *nom, somme* to write in full. (**b**) *(missive)* letter. **~s** *(courrier)* letters, mail; **mettre une ~ à la boîte** to post a letter; **écris-lui une petite ~** write him a note. (**c**) **les (belles) ~s** literature; **homme de ~s** man of letters; **avoir des ~s** to be well-read. (**d**) *(Scol)* **fort en ~s** good at arts subjects; **professeur de ~s** teacher of French *(in France)*; **~s modernes** French language and literature; **~s classiques** classics *(sg)*. (**e**) *(locutions)* **rester ~ morte** *[protestation]* to go unheeded; **devenir ~ morte** *[loi]* to become a dead letter; **c'est passé comme une ~ à la poste *** it went off smoothly *ou* without a hitch; **prendre qch au pied de la ~** to take sth literally; **exécuter qch à la ~** to carry out sth to the letter.

2 : **~ de change** bill of exchange; **~s de créance** credentials; *(lit)* **~s de noblesse** letters patent of nobility; *(fig)* **gagner ses ~s de noblesse** to win acclaim, establish one's pedigree; **~ recommandée** *(attestant sa remise)* recorded delivery letter; *(assurant sa valeur)* registered letter. ◆ **lettré, e** *adj* well-read.

leucémie [løsemi] *nf* leukaemia. ◆ **leucémique 1** *adj* leukaemic. **2** *nmf* person suffering from leukaemia.

leucotomie [løkɔtɔmi] leucotomy.

leur [lœʀ] **1** *pron pers mf* them. **il ~ est facile de le faire** it is easy for them to do it. **2** *adj poss* (**a**) their. **ils ont ~s petites manies** they have their little fads. (**b**) *(littér)* theirs, their own. **ils ont fait ~s ces idées** they made these ideas their own. **3** *pron poss*: **le ~, la ~, les ~s** theirs; **ces sacs sont les ~s** these bags are theirs. **4** *nm* (**a**) **ils ont mis du ~** they pulled their weight. (**b**) **les ~s** *(famille)* their family; *(partisans)* their own people; **ils ont encore fait des ~s *** they've (gone and) done it again *; **nous étions des ~s** we were with them.

leurre [lœʀ] *nm (illusion)* delusion; *(duperie)* deception; *(piège)* trap, snare; *(Pêche, Chasse)* lure. ◆ **leurrer** (1) **1** *vt* to delude. **2 se ~** *vpr* to delude o.s.

levage [ləvaʒ] *nm (Tech)* lifting.

levain [ləvɛ̃] *nm* leaven. **sans ~** unleavened; **pain au ~** leavened bread.

levant [ləvɑ̃] **1** *adj*: **soleil ~** rising sun; **au soleil ~** at sunrise. **2** *nm*: **le ~** the East; *(pays)* **le L~** the Levant; **les chambres sont au ~** the bedrooms are on the east side.

lever [l(ə)ve] (5) **1** *vt* (**a**) *(lit) (gén)* to raise; *objet* to lift; *yeux, tête* to lift up; *main (en classe)* to put up. **~ le visage vers qn** to look up at sb. (**b**) *blocus* to raise; *séance* to close; *difficulté, scrupules* to remove; *interdiction* to lift. **on lève la séance? *** shall we break up?, shall we call it a day? (**c**) *impôts, armée* to levy. (**d**) *plan, carte* to draw. (**e**) *enfant, malade* to get up. **faire ~ qn** *(d'une chaise)* to make sb stand up; *(du lit)* to get sb up; *(lit, fig)* **~ un lièvre** to uncover sth by chance. (**f**) *(locutions)* **~ l'ancre** *(Naut)* to weigh anchor; *(fig)* to make tracks *; **~ le camp** *(lit)* to break camp; *(fig: partir)* to clear off *; **~ le siège** *(lit)* to raise the siege; *(fig: partir)* to clear off *; **il n'a pas levé le petit doigt pour m'aider** he didn't lift a finger to help me; *[chien]* **~ la patte** to cock its leg; **~ le pied** *(disparaître)* to vanish; *(Aut: ralentir)* to slow down; **~ la main sur qn** to raise one's hand to sb; **~ le voile** to reveal the truth (*sur* about); **~ son verre à la santé de qn** to drink to sb's health.

2 *vi* (**a**) *[plante]* to come up. (**b**) *(Culin)* to rise. **faire ~ la pâte** to make the dough rise, leave the dough to rise.
3 se ~ *vpr* (**a**) *[rideau, main]* to go up. (**b**) *[personne]* to get up. **se ~ de table** to get up from the table; **faire se ~ qn** *(du lit)* to get sb up; *(d'une chaise)* to make sb stand up; *(fig)* **il s'est levé du pied gauche** he got out of bed on the wrong side; **se ~ sur son séant** to sit up. (**c**) *[soleil, lune]* to rise; *[jour]* to break. (**d**) *[vent, orage]* to get up, rise; *[brume]* to lift, clear. **le temps se lève** the weather is clearing.
4 *nm* (**a**) **~ de soleil** sunrise; **~ du jour** daybreak, dawn. (**b**) *(au réveil)* **prenez 3 comprimés au ~** take 3 tablets when you get up *ou* on rising; **le ~ du roi** the levee of the king. (**c**) *(Théât)* **le ~ du rideau** *(commencement)* the curtain; *(action)* the raising of the curtain; *(pièce)* **un ~ de rideau** a curtain raiser. ◆ **levé**[1] *nm (plan)* survey. ◆ **levé**[2]**, e**[1] *adj*: **être ~** to be up. ◆ **levée**[2] **1** *nf* (**a**) *[siège]* raising; *[séance]* closing; *[interdiction]* lifting. (**b**) *(Poste)* collection. (**c**) *(Cartes)* trick. **faire une ~** to take a trick. (**d**) *[impôts, armée]* levying. (**e**) *(remblai)* levee. **2** : **~ de boucliers** general outcry; **la ~ du corps aura lieu à 10 heures** the funeral will start from the house at 10 o'clock; **~ d'écrou** release (from prison). ◆ **lève-glace** *nm inv*, **lève-vitre** *nm inv* (window) winder. ◆ **lève-tard** *nm inv* late riser. ◆ **lève-tôt** *nm inv* early riser.

levier [ləvje] *nm* lever. **~ de frein** handbrake (lever); **faire ~ sur qch** to lever sth up; *(fig)* **être aux ~s de commande** to be in control *ou* command.

lévitation [levitasjɔ̃] *nf* levitation.

lèvre [lɛvʀ(ə)] *nf (gén)* lip; *(Géog) [faille]* side.

lévrier [levʀije] *nm* greyhound.

levure [l(ə)vyʀ] *nf (ferment)* yeast.

lexique [lɛksik] *nm* vocabulary, lexis; *(glossaire)* lexicon. ◆ **lexicographie** *nf* lexicography.

lézard [lezaʀ] *nm (animal)* lizard; *(peau)* lizardskin. **faire le ~ (au soleil)** * to bask in the sun.

lézarde [lezaʀd(ə)] *nf (fissure)* crack. ◆ **se lézarder** (1) *vpr* to crack.

liaison [ljɛzɔ̃] *nf* (**a**) *(fréquentation)* **~ (amoureuse)** (love) affair; **~ (d'affaires)** business relationship *ou* connection. (**b**) *(contact)* **entrer en ~ avec qn** to get in contact with sb; **travailler en ~ étroite avec qn** to work in close collaboration with sb; **~ radio** radio contact; **les ~s téléphoniques avec le Japon** telephone links with Japan; **officier de ~** liaison officer. (**c**) *(entre événements, idées)* connection. (**d**) *(Phonétique)* liaison. *(Gram)* **mot de ~** linkword. (**e**) *(Transport)* link. (**f**) *(Culin)* liaison. (**g**) *(Ordin)* **~ de transmission** data link. (**h**) *(Mus)* tie.

liane [ljan] *nf* creeper, liana.

liant, e [ljɑ̃, ɑ̃t] *adj* sociable.

liasse [ljas] *nf* bundle, wad.

Liban [libɑ̃] *nm*: **le ~** (the) Lebanon. ◆ **libanais, e** *adj*, **L~(e)** *nm (f)* Lebanese.

libations [libɑsjɔ̃] *nfpl* libations.

libeller [libele] (1) *vt acte* to draw up; *chèque* to make out (*au nom de* to); *lettre* to word. ◆ **libellé** *nm* wording.

libellule [libelyl] *nf* dragonfly.

libéral, e, *mpl* **-aux** [libeʀal, o] *adj, nm, f (gén)* liberal. ◆ **libéralement** *adv* liberally. ◆ **libéralisation** *nf* liberalization. ◆ **libéraliser** (1) *vt* to liberalize. ◆ **libéralisme** *nm* liberalism. **être partisan du ~ économique** to be a supporter of economic liberalism *ou* of free enterprise. ◆ **libéralité** *nf* liberality; *(don)* generous *ou* liberal gift, liberality.

libérer [libeʀe] (6) **1** *vt* (**a**) *prisonnier* to release; *soldat* to discharge (*de* from). **libéré sous caution/sur parole** released on bail/on parole. (**b**) *pays, peuple* to free, liberate; *(d'une promesse)* to release (*de* from). (**c**) *énergie, gaz, cran d'arrêt* to release; *échanges commerciaux* to ease restrictions on; *prix* to decontrol. **~ le passage** to free *ou* unblock the way. (**d**) *conscience* to unburden; *instincts* to give free rein to. **2 se ~** *vpr (de ses liens)* to free o.s. (*de* from); *(d'une promesse)* to release o.s. (*de* from); *(d'une dette)* to clear o.s. (*de* of). **jeudi je ne peux pas me ~** I can't be free on Thursday. ◆ **libérateur, -trice 1** *adj (Psych)* liberating. **guerre ~trice** war of liberation. **2** *nm, f* liberator. ◆ **libération** *nf* release; discharge; freeing; liberation; decontrolling. **~ anticipée** early release; **~ conditionnelle** release on parole; **~ de la femme** Women's Liberation; *(Hist)* **la L~** the Liberation. ◆ **libéré, e** *adj* liberated.

Libéria [libeʀja] *nm* Liberia.

liberté [libɛʀte] *nf* (**a**) *(gén, Jur)* freedom, liberty. **mettre en ~** to free, release, set free; **être mis en ~ surveillée** to be put on probation; **mise en ~** *[prisonnier]* release; **être en ~** to be free; **animaux en ~** animals in freedom; **le voleur est encore en ~** the thief is still at large; *[épouse]* **elle a repris sa ~** she has regained her freedom *ou* her independence; **avoir toute ~ pour agir** to have full liberty *ou* freedom to act; **~, égalité, fraternité** liberty, equality, fraternity. (**b**) *(loisir)* **moments de ~** free moments, spare *ou* free time; **jour de ~** free day, day off. (**c**) *(absence de contrainte)* liberty. **~ de mœurs** freedom of morals; **prendre la ~ de faire** to take the liberty of doing; **prendre des ~s avec** *texte* to take liberties with. (**d**) *(droit)* right. **les ~s syndicales** union rights.

libertin, e [libɛʀtɛ̃, in] *adj, nm, f* libertine.

libraire [libʀɛʀ] *nmf* bookseller. ◆ **librairie** *nf (magasin)* bookshop. **~-papeterie** bookseller's and stationer's; **la ~** *(activité)* bookselling.

libre [libʀ(ə)] *adj* (**a**) *(sans contrainte)* free. **en vente ~** on open *ou* unrestricted sale; **garder l'esprit ~** to keep one's mind free, keep a clear mind; **être ~ comme l'air** to be as free as a bird; **rester ~** *(non marié)* to remain unattached; **~ de tout préjugé** free from all prejudice; **vous êtes ~ de refuser** you're free *ou* at liberty to refuse; **le sujet de la dissertation est ~** the subject of this essay is left open; **un partisan de la ~ entreprise** *ou* **concurrence** a supporter of the free-market economy *ou* of free enterprise; *(Pol)* **le monde ~** the free world. (**b**) *(non occupé) (gén)* free; *passage* clear; *taxi* empty. *(Téléc)* **la ligne n'est pas ~** the line *ou* number is engaged *ou* busy; **est-ce que cette place est ~?** is this seat free? *ou* vacant?; **avoir du temps ~** to have some spare *ou* free time; *(non payant)* **'entrée ~'** 'entrance free'; *(Univ)* **auditeur ~** non-registered student. (**c**) *(Scol) enseignement* private and Roman Catholic. (**d**) *(sans retenue) personne* free *ou* open in one's behaviour; *plaisanteries* broad; *propos* blunt. **être très ~ avec qn** to be very free with sb; **donner ~ cours à sa colère** to give free rein *ou* give vent to one's anger. ◆ **libre arbitre** *nm* free will. ◆ **libre-échange** *nm* free trade. ◆ **libre penseur** *nm* freethinker. ◆ **libre-service,** *pl* **libres-services** *nm (restaurant)* self-service restaurant; *(magasin)* self-service store. ◆ **librement** *adv* freely.

Libye [libi] *nf* Libya. ◆ **libyen, -enne** *adj*, **L~(ne)** *nm (f)* Libyan.

licence [lisɑ̃s] *nf* (**a**) *(Univ)* degree, ≃ bachelor's degree. **~ ès lettres** Arts degree, ≃ B.A.; **~ ès sciences** Science degree, ≃ B.Sc.; **faire une ~ d'anglais** to do a degree course in English. (**b**) *(autorisation, Sport)* permit; *(Comm, Jur)* licence. **produit sous ~** licensed product. (**c**) **~ (des mœurs)** licentiousness; **~ poétique** poetic licence. ◆ **licencié, e** *nm, f* (**a**) **~ ès lettres/ès sciences/en**

droit Bachelor of Arts/of Science/of Law, arts/science/law graduate. (**b**) *(Sport)* permit-holder. (**c**) *(Jur)* licensee.

licencier [lisɑ̃sje] (7) *vt (débaucher)* to make redundant; *(renvoyer)* to dismiss. ◆ **licenciement** *nm (action)* dismissal. *(résultat)* **plusieurs ~s** several redundancies; **~ (pour raison) économique** lay-off, redundancy; **lettre de ~** letter of dismissal, pink slip *(US)*.

licencieux, -euse [lisɑ̃sjø, øz] *adj* licentious.

lichen [likɛn] *nm* lichen.

lichette * [liʃɛt] *nf*: **~ de pain** *etc* nibble of bread *etc*.

licite [lisit] *adj* lawful, licit.

licorne [likɔʀn(ə)] *nf* unicorn.

lie [li] **1** *nf [vin]* dregs, sediment. **la ~ de la société** the dregs of society. **2** : **~ de vin** *adj* wine(-coloured).

Liechtenstein [liʃtɛnʃtajn] *nm* Liechtenstein.

liège [ljɛʒ] *nm* cork.

lien [ljɛ̃] *nm* (**a**) *(lit, fig: attache)* bond, tie. **~s de parenté** family ties; **~s d'amitié** bonds of friendship. (**b**) *(corrélation)* link, connection. **idées sans ~** unconnected *ou* unrelated ideas.

lier [lje] (7) **1** *vt* (**a**) *(attacher)* to bind, tie up. **~ qn à un arbre** to tie sb to a tree. (**b**) *(relier)* to link up. **tous ces événements sont étroitement liés** all these events are closely linked *ou* connected. (**c**) *(unir) personnes* to bind, unite. (**d**) *(Culin) sauce* to thicken. (**e**) **~ amitié/conversation** to strike up a friendship/conversation. **2 se ~** *vpr* to make friends *(avec qn* with sb); *(par un serment)* to bind o.s. **ils sont très liés** they are very close friends.

lierre [ljɛʀ] *nm* ivy.

liesse [ljɛs] *nf (littér: joie)* jubilation. **en ~** jubilant.

lieu[1], *pl* **~x** [ljø] **1** *nm* (**a**) *(gén: endroit)* place; *[événement]* scene. **en quelque ~ qu'il soit** wherever he is; **en tous ~x** everywhere; **en ~ sûr** in a safe place; **être sur les ~x de l'accident** to be on the scene of the accident. (**b**) *(locaux)* **les ~x** the premises; **quitter les ~x** *(gén)* to get out, leave; *(Admin)* to vacate the premises. (**c**) *(temps)* **en premier ~** in the first place; **en dernier ~** lastly; **en son ~** in due course. (**d**) **au ~ de qch** instead of sth; **en ~ et place de qn** on behalf of sb; **avoir ~** *(se produire)* to take place; **avoir ~ d'être inquiet** to have (good) grounds for being worried, have (good) reason to be worried; **s'il y a ~** if necessary; **donner ~ à des critiques** to give rise to criticism; **tenir ~ de qch** to take the place of sth, serve as sth.

2 : **~x d'aisances** † lavatory; **~ commun** commonplace; **~-dit**, *pl* **~x-~s** locality; **~ de naissance** *(gén)* birthplace; *(Admin)* place of birth; **~ de passage** *(entre régions)* crossing point; *(dans un bâtiment)* place where people are constantly coming and going; **~ de perdition** den of iniquity; **~ de vacances** *(ville)* holiday resort.

lieu[2] [ljø] *nm: (poisson)* **~ jaune** pollack, pollock; **~ noir** saithe, coley, coalfish.

lieue [ljø] *nf* league. **j'étais à cent ~s de supposer cela** that never occurred to me.

lieuse [ljøz] *nf (Agr)* binder.

lieutenant [ljøtnɑ̃] *nm (Mil, fig)* lieutenant; *(marine marchande)* mate. **~-colonel** lieutenant colonel.

lièvre [ljɛvʀ(ə)] *nm* hare.

lifting [liftiŋ] *nm* face lift. **se faire faire un ~** to have a face lift.

ligament [ligamɑ̃] *nm* ligament.

ligature [ligatyʀ] *nf* ligature. ◆ **ligaturer** (1) *vt* to ligature.

ligne [liɲ] **1** *nf* (**a**) *(trait, limite)* line. **~ brisée** broken *ou* dotted line; **~ de départ/d'arrivée** starting/finishing line; **la ~ des x/des y** the X/Y axis; **courir en ~ droite** to run in a straight line; *(Aut)* **~ droite** stretch of straight road; *(lit, fig)* **la dernière ~ droite avant l'arrivée** the final *ou* home straight. (**b**) *[meuble, voiture]* line(s); *[femme]* figure. **garder la ~** to keep one's figure; **la ~ lancée par la mode** the look launched by the collections. (**c**) *(règle)* line. **~ de conduite** line of conduct; **les grandes ~s d'un programme** the broad lines of a programme. (**d**) *(rangée)* line, row. **mettre des personnes en ~** to line people up; **se mettre en ~** to line up, get into line; *(Ordin)* **en ~** on line. (**e**) *(Rail)* line. **~ d'autobus** *(service)* bus service; *(parcours)* bus route; **~ d'aviation** *(compagnie)* air line; *(trajet)* (air) route; **~ de métro** underground *ou* subway line; **quelle ~ faut-il prendre?** which train (*ou* bus) should I take? (**f**) *(Élec) (gén)* line; *(câbles)* wires. **être en ~** to be connected. (**g**) *[texte]* line. *(dictée)* **'à la ~'** 'new paragraph'; **lire entre les ~s** to read between the lines. (**h**) *(Pêche)* fishing line. (**i**) *(locutions)* **mettre sur la même ~** to put on the same level; **faire entrer en ~ de compte** to take into account *ou* consideration; **sur toute la ~** from start to finish.

2 : *(Aut)* **~ blanche** white line *(in the centre of the road)*; **~ blanche continue/discontinue** solid/broken *ou* dotted white line; **~ de but** goal line; **~ de démarcation** *(gén)* boundary; *(Mil)* line of demarcation, demarcation line; **~ directrice** *(Géom)* directrix; *(fig)* guiding line; **~ de feu** line of fire; **~ de flottaison** water line; *(Pêche)* **~ de fond** ledger line; **~ à haute tension** high-tension line; **~ d'horizon** skyline; *(Sport)* **~ médiane** halfway line; **~ de mire** line of sight; **~ de partage des eaux** watershed; **~ de touche** *(Ftbl, Rugby etc)* touchline; *(Basketball)* boundary line.

◆ **lignée** *nf (postérité)* descendants; *(race)* line; *(tradition)* tradition.

ligoter [ligɔte] (1) *vt personne* to bind hand and foot. **~ à un arbre** to tie to a tree.

ligue [lig] *nf* league. ◆ **liguer** (1) **1** *vt* to unite (*contre* against). **être ligué avec** to be in league with. **2 se ~** *vpr* to form a league, be in league (*contre* against).

lilas [lilɑ] *nm, adj inv* lilac.

Lima [lima] *n* Lima.

limace [limas] *nf (Zool)* slug; *(‡: chemise)* shirt; *(*: personne)* slowcoach, slowpoke *(US)*.

limande [limɑ̃d] *nf (poisson)* dab. **~-sole** lemon sole.

lime [lim] *nf* file. **~ à ongles** nail file. ◆ **limer** (1) *vt* to file; *aspérité* to file off.

limier [limje] *nm (Zool)* bloodhound; *(fig)* sleuth, detective.

limite [limit] **1** *nf (gén)* limit; *[jardin]* boundary. **~ de rupture** breaking point; **~ d'âge** age limit; **~ des arbres** tree line; **~ des neiges** snow line; **sans ~** boundless, limitless; **la bêtise a des ~s!** foolishness has its limits!; **il dépasse les ~s!** he's going a bit too far!; **à la ~ on croirait qu'il le fait exprès** you'd almost think he is doing it on purpose; **à la ~ tout roman est réaliste** ultimately *ou* at a pinch you could say any novel is realistic; **dans une certaine ~** up to a point, to a certain extent; **dans les ~s de mes moyens** *(aptitude)* within (the limits of) my capabilities; *(argent)* within my means; **jusqu'à la dernière ~** to the (bitter) end; **jusqu'à la ~ de ses forces** to the point of exhaustion; *(Boxe)* **tenir jusqu'à la ~** to go the distance. **2** *adj*: **cas ~** borderline case; **vitesse/âge ~** maximum speed/age; **date ~** deadline.

◆ **limitatif, -ive** *adj* restrictive. **liste ~ive/non-~ive** open/closed list. ◆ **limitation** *nf (gén)* limitation. **~ des prix/des naissances** price/birth control; **sans ~ de temps** with no time limit; **~ de vitesse** speed limit. ◆ **limiter** (1) **1** *vt* (**a**) *(restreindre)* to limit, restrict. **~ les dégâts** * to stop things getting any worse; *(financièrement)* to cut one's losses. (**b**) *[frontière, montagnes]* to border. **2 se** ~ *vpr [personne]* **se** ~ **(à qch/à faire)** to limit *ou* confine o.s. (to sth/to doing); *[chose]* **se** ~ **à** to be limited to.

limitrophe [limitʀɔf] *adj département* border.

limoger [limɔʒe] (3) *vt* to dismiss, fire.

limon [limɔ̃] *nm (Géog)* silt; *[attelage]* shaft.

limonade [limɔnad] *nf* lemonade.

limpide [lɛ̃pid] *adj (gén)* limpid; *explication* lucid. ◆ **limpidité** *nf [eau, ciel]* clearness; *[regard]* limpidity; *[explication]* clarity, lucidity.

lin [lɛ̃] *nm (plante)* flax; *(tissu)* linen.

linceul [lɛ̃sœl] *nm (lit, fig)* shroud.

linéaire [lineɛʀ] *adj* linear.

linge [lɛ̃ʒ] *nm* (**a**) **le** ~, **du** ~ linen; **le gros/petit** ~ the main/small items of linen; ~ **de corps/de table** body/table linen; ~ **de toilette** bathroom linen. (**b**) *(lessive)* **le** ~ the washing. (**c**) *(morceau)* cloth. **blanc comme un** ~ as white as a sheet. ◆ **lingerie** *nf (local)* linen room; *(sous-vêtements)* lingerie, underwear.

lingot [lɛ̃go] *nm* ingot.

linguiste [lɛ̃gɥist(ə)] *nmf* linguist. ◆ **linguistique** **1** *nf* linguistics *(sg)*. **2** *adj* linguistic. **communauté** ~ speech community.

linoléum [linɔleɔm] *nm* linoleum.

lion [ljɔ̃] *nm* lion. *(Astron)* **le L**~ Leo, the Lion; **être (du) L**~ to be Leo. ◆ **lionceau,** *pl* ~**x** *nm* lion cub. ◆ **lionne** *nf* lioness.

lippu, e [lipy] *adj* thick-lipped.

liquéfier *vt*, **se** ~ *vpr* [likefje] (7) to liquefy. ◆ **liquéfaction** *nf* liquefaction.

liqueur [likœʀ] *nf (boisson)* liqueur; *(Chim)* solution.

liquide [likid] **1** *adj* liquid. **sauce trop** ~ sauce which is too runny *ou* too thin. **2** *nm* (**a**) *(substance)* liquid. (**b**) *(argent)* **du** ~ ready money, ready cash.

liquider [likide] (1) *vt* (**a**) *société, biens* to liquidate; *(lit, fig) compte* to settle; *retraite* to pay. (**b**) *(vendre)* to sell (off). (**c**) (‡) *(tuer)* to liquidate; *(se débarrasser de)* to get rid of; *(finir)* to finish off. **c'est liquidé maintenant** it is all finished *ou* over now. ◆ **liquidation** *nf* liquidation; settlement; payment; sale. **mettre en** ~ *compagnie* to liquidate. ◆ **liquidateur, -trice** *nm, f (Jur)* ≃ liquidator, receiver. ◆ **liquidatif, -ive** *adj:* **valeur** ~**ive** market price *ou* value.

liquidité [likidite] *nf (Chim, Jur)* liquidity. ~**s** liquid assets.

liquoreux, -euse [likɔʀø, øz] *adj vin* syrupy.

lire[1] [liʀ] (43) *vt (gén)* to read; *discours* to read out. **il l'a lu dans le journal** he read (about) it in the paper; **ça se lit très vite** it makes quick reading; ~ **entre les lignes** to read between the lines; **lu et approuvé** read and approved; ~ **dans le cœur de qn** to see into sb's heart; **elle m'a lu les lignes de la main** she read my hand; ~ **dans le jeu de qn** to see sb's game; **nous espérons vous** ~ **bientôt** we hope to hear from you soon.

lire[2] [liʀ] *nf* lira.

lis [lis] *nm* lily.

Lisbonne [lizbɔn] *n* Lisbon.

liseré [lizʀe] *nm,* **liséré** [lizeʀe] *nm (bordure)* border, edging. **un** ~ **de ciel bleu** a strip of blue sky.

liseron [lizʀɔ̃] *nm* bindweed, convolvulus.

liseur, -euse [lizœʀ, øz] **1** *nm, f* reader. **2** *nf (vêtement)* bed jacket.

lisible [lizibl(ə)] *adj écriture* legible; *livre* readable. ◆ **lisibilité** *nf* legibility; readability. ◆ **lisiblement** *adv* legibly.

lisière [lizjɛʀ] *nf [bois, village]* edge.

lisse [lis] *adj (gén)* smooth; *cheveux* sleek. ◆ **lisser** (1) *vt cheveux* to smooth (down); *papier froissé* to smooth out. **l'oiseau se lisse les plumes** the bird is preening its feathers. ◆ **lissage** *nm* smoothing.

listage [listaʒ] *nm (action)* listing; *(liste)* list; *(Ordin)* listing.

liste [list(ə)] *nf* list. **faire la** ~ **de** to make out a list of, list; ~ **nominative des élèves** class roll *ou* list; ~ **électorale** electoral roll; ~ **noire** blacklist; *(pour élimination)* hit list; *(Téléc)* **demander à être sur la** ~ **rouge** (to ask) to go ex-directory *ou* unlisted *(US)*.

lister [liste] (1) *vt* to list.

lit [li] **1** *nm* bed. ~ **d'une personne/de deux personnes** single/double bed; ~ **de fer** iron bedstead; **se mettre au** ~ to go to bed; **faire le** ~ to make the bed; **faire** ~ **à part** to sleep in separate beds; **au** ~ **les enfants!** bedtime *ou* off to bed children!; **enfants du premier** ~ children of the first marriage. **2** : ~ **de camp** campbed; ~ **d'enfant** cot; ~ **gigogne** bunk bed; ~**s jumeaux** twin beds; ~ **de mort** deathbed; ~ **en portefeuille** apple pie bed; ~**s superposés** bunk beds; *(Naut)* **le** ~ **du vent** the set of the wind.

litanie [litani] *nf (Rel, péj)* litany.

litchi [litʃi] *nm* litchi.

literie [litʀi] *nf* bedding.

lithographie [litɔgʀafi] *nf (technique)* lithography; *(image)* lithograph.

litière [litjɛʀ] *nf* litter. ~ **pour chats** cat litter, kitty litter *(US)*.

litige [litiʒ] *nm (gén)* dispute; *(Jur)* lawsuit. *(Jur)* **les parties en** ~ the litigant, the disputants *(US)*; **objet de** ~ object of contention. ◆ **litigieux, -ieuse** *adj* litigious, contentious.

litote [litɔt] *nf (Littérat)* litotes, understatement.

litre [litʀ(ə)] *nm (mesure)* litre; *(récipient)* litre bottle.

littéral, e, *mpl* **-aux** [liteʀal, o] *adj* literal. ◆ **littéralement** *adv (lit, fig)* literally.

littérature [liteʀatyʀ] *nf* literature; *(profession)* writing. ◆ **littéraire** *adj (gén)* literary.

littoral, e, *mpl* **-aux** [litɔʀal, o] **1** *adj* coastal. **2** *nm* coast.

liturgie [lityʀʒi] *nf* liturgy. ◆ **liturgique** *adj* liturgical.

livide [livid] *adj (pâle)* pallid; *(bleuâtre)* livid.

livraison [livʀɛzɔ̃] *nf* delivery. *(avis)* '~ **à domicile**' 'we deliver'.

livre[1] [livʀ(ə)] *nm* book. *(commerce)* **le** ~ the book trade *ou* industry; *(Scol)* ~ **du maître/de l'élève** teacher's/pupil's text book; ~ **blanc** report *(on disasters, atrocities etc published by independent organization)*; ~ **de bord** logbook; ~ **de caisse** cashbook; ~ **de classe** schoolbook; ~ **de comptes** account(s) book; ~ **de cuisine** cookery book, cookbook; ~ **de messe** mass book, missel, prayer book; ~ **d'or** visitors' book; ~ **de poche** paperback.

livre[2] [livʀ(ə)] *nf* (**a**) *(poids)* ≃ pound, half a kilo. (**b**) *(monnaie)* pound; *(Hist française)* livre. ~ **sterling** pound sterling; ~ **égyptienne** Egyptian pound.

livrée [livʀe] *nf (uniforme)* livery.

livrer [livʀe] (1) **1** *vt* (**a**) *(Comm)* to deliver. (**b**) *(à l'ennemi)* to hand over (*à* to). ~ **qn à la mort** to send sb to his death; **être livré au pillage** to be given over to pillage; ~ **son âme au diable** to give one's soul to the devil; **être livré à soi-même** to be left to o.s. *ou* to one's own devices. (**c**) *confidence* to give away, reveal. (**d**) ~ **bataille** to join *ou* do battle (*à* with); ~ **passage à qn** to let sb pass. **2 se** ~ *vpr* (**a**) **se** ~ **à** *destin* to abandon o.s. to; *excès, douleur* to give o.s. over to; *boisson* to indulge in; *sport* to practise; *occupation* to be engaged in; *recherches* to do, carry out; *enquête* to hold; **se** ~ **à l'étude** to devote o.s. to study.

(**b**) *(à la police)* to give o.s. up; *(à un confident)* to open up (*à* to). ◆ **livreur, -euse** *nm, f* delivery boy (*ou* girl).

livret [livʀɛ] *nm* (**a**) *(Mus)* libretto. (**b**) ~ **de caisse d'épargne** (savings) bankbook; ~ **de famille** (official) family record book; ~ **scolaire** (school) report (book).

lob [lɔb] *nm (Tennis)* lob. ~ **lifté** top spin lob.

lobe [lɔb] *nm (Anat, Bot)* lobe.

lobotomie [lɔbɔtɔmi] *nf* lobotomy.

local, e, *mpl* **-aux** [lɔkal, o] **1** *adj* local. **2** *nm (salle)* room. *(bureaux)* ~**aux** offices, premises; **dans les ~aux de la police** on police premises. ◆ **localement** *adv (ici)* locally; *(par endroits)* in places. ◆ **localisation** *nf* localization. ◆ **localiser** (1) *vt* (**a**) *(circonscrire) (gén)* to localize; *épidémie* to confine. (**b**) *(repérer)* to locate. ◆ **localité** *nf (ville)* town; *(village)* village.

location [lɔkɑsjɔ̃] *nf* (**a**) *(par locataire) [maison]* renting; *[voiture]* hiring, renting *(US)*. **prendre en ~** *maison* to rent; *bateau* to hire, rent *(US)*. (**b**) *(par propriétaire) [maison]* renting (out), letting; *[voiture]* hiring (out), renting *(US)*. **donner en ~** *maison* to rent out, let; *véhicule* to hire out, rent *(US)*; ~ **de voitures** *(écriteau)* 'cars for hire', 'car rental' *(US)*. (**c**) *(bail)* **(contrat de)** ~ lease; ~**-vente** hire purchase. (**d**) *(maison)* **il a une** ~ *[locataire]* he is renting a house; *[propriétaire]* he has property for letting; **habiter en** ~ to live in rented accommodation. (**e**) *(réservation)* booking. **bureau de** ~ (advance) booking office. ◆ **locataire** *nmf (gén)* leaseholder, tenant; *(habitant avec le propriétaire)* lodger, roomer *(US)*.

locomotion [lɔkɔmosjɔ̃] *nf* locomotion.

locomotive [lɔkɔmɔtiv] *nf* locomotive, engine.

locution [lɔkysjɔ̃] *nf* phrase, locution, idiom. ~ **figée** set phrase.

loden [lɔdɛn] *nm (tissu)* loden. *(manteau)* **il avait mis son** ~ he was wearing his loden coat.

logarithme [lɔgaʀitm(ə)] *nm* logarithm.

loge [lɔʒ] *nf [concierge, francs-maçons]* lodge; *[bûcheron]* hut; *[artiste]* dressing room; *(spectateur)* box. *(fig)* **être aux premières ~s** to have a ringside seat.

loger [lɔʒe] (3) **1** *vi* to live (*dans* in, *chez* with, at). ~ **rue X** to live in X street; *(Mil)* ~ **chez l'habitant** to be billeted on the local inhabitants. **2** *vt* (**a**) *amis* to put up; *clients* to accommodate; *objet* to put; *soldats (chez l'habitant)* to billet. (**b**) *(contenir)* to accommodate. **salle qui loge beaucoup de monde** room which can hold *ou* accommodate a lot of people. (**c**) *(envoyer)* ~ **une balle dans** to lodge a bullet in. **3 se** ~ *vpr* (**a**) *[jeunes mariés]* to find somewhere to live; *[touristes]* to find accommodation; *[étudiant]* to find lodgings *ou* accommodation. *(fig)* **la haine se logea dans son cœur** hatred filled his heart. (**b**) *(tenir)* **se ~ dans qch** to fit into sth. (**c**) *(se coincer dans)* **se ~ dans/entre** to lodge itself in/between. ◆ **logé, e** *adj*: **être ~ et nourri** to have board and lodging; **être bien/mal** ~ to have good/poor lodgings *ou* accommodation; **être ~ à la même enseigne** to be in the same boat. ◆ **logeable** *adj (habitable)* habitable; *(spacieux)* roomy. ◆ **logement** *nm* (**a**) *(hébergement)* housing. (**b**) *(appartement)* flat, apartment *(US)*. **trouver un** ~ to find lodgings *ou* accommodation *ou* a flat. (**c**) *(Mil) (à la caserne)* quartering; *(chez l'habitant)* billeting. ~**s** quarters; billet. ◆ **logeur, -euse** *nm, f* landlord (*ou* landlady). ◆ **logis** *nm (littér)* dwelling. **le ~ paternel** the paternal home.

loggia [lɔdʒja] *nf* loggia.

logiciel [lɔʒisjɛl] *nm* software, application program *ou* package. ~ **intégré** integrated software. ◆ **logithèque** *nf* software library.

logique [lɔʒik] **1** *nf* logic. **cela est dans la ~ des choses** it's in the nature of things. **2** *adj* logical. ◆ **logiquement** *adv* logically.

logistique [lɔʒistik] **1** *adj* logistic. **2** *nf* logistics *(sg)*.

logo [lɔgo] *nm* logo.

loi [lwa] *nf*: **la** ~ the law; **la ~ du plus fort** the law of the strongest; **c'est la ~ de la jungle** it's the law of the jungle; **se faire une ~ de faire** to make it a rule to do; **il n'a pas la ~ chez lui! *** he's not the boss in his own house! *; **ce qu'il dit fait** ~ his word is law; **les ~s de la mode** the dictates of fashion; **les ~s de l'honneur** the code of honour; **les ~s de l'hospitalité** the laws of hospitality; **les ~s de l'étiquette** the rules of etiquette; **voter une** ~ to pass a law *ou* an act; ~**-cadre** *nf, pl* ~**s-**~**s** outline *ou* blueprint law; ~ **martiale** martial law; *(fig)* **appliquer la ~ du talion** to demand an eye for an eye.

loin [lwɛ̃] *adv* (**a**) *(distance)* far, a long way. **est-ce ~?** is it far?; **ce n'est pas très** ~ it's not very far; **c'est assez ~ d'ici** it's quite a long way from here; **plus** ~ further, farther; **moins** ~ not so far (*de* from); **il est ~ derrière** he's far *ou* a long way behind; **au** ~ in the distance, far off; **de** ~ from a distance; **de ~ en** ~ at distant intervals, here and there; **ça ne doit pas faire ~ de 5 km** it can't be far off *ou* far short of 5 km. (**b**) *(temps)* **il n'est pas ~ de minuit** it isn't far off midnight; **de ~ en** ~ every now and then; **il n'y a pas ~ de 5 ans qu'il est parti** it's not far off 5 years since he left; **c'est ~ tout cela!** *(passé)* that was a long time ago!; *(futur)* that's a long way off!; ~ **dans le passé** in the remote past, in far-off times; **voir** ~ to see a long way *ou* far ahead; **d'aussi ~ que je me rappelle** for as long as I can remember. (**c**) *(fig)* far. **j'irais même plus** ~ I would go even further; **il est de (très) ~ le meilleur** he is by far the best; **d'ici à l'accuser de vol il n'y a pas** ~ it's tantamount to *ou* practically an accusation of theft; **il ne leur doit pas ~ de 1000 F** he owes them little short of *ou* nor far off 1.000 francs. (**d**) *(fig)* ~ **de là** far from it; **on est encore ~ de la vérité/d'un accord** we're still a long way from the truth/from reaching an agreement; *(fig)* **on est ~ du compte** it falls far short of the target *ou* of what is needed; **être très ~ du sujet** to be way off the subject; ~ **de moi la pensée de vous blâmer!** far be it from me to blame you! (**e**) *(Prov)* ~ **des yeux,** ~ **du cœur** out of sight, out of mind *(Prov)*.

lointain, e [lwɛ̃tɛ̃, ɛn] **1** *adj (lit, fig)* distant, remote; *regard* faraway. **2** *nm*: **dans le** ~ in the distance.

loir [lwaʀ] *nm* dormouse.

Loire [lwaʀ] *nf*: **la** ~ *(fleuve, département)* the Loire.

loisir [lwaziʀ] *nm* (**a**) ~**s** *(temps libre)* leisure (time), spare *ou* free time; *(activités)* leisure *ou* spare-time activities. (**b**) *(littér)* **avoir le ~ de faire** to have leisure *ou* time to do; **donner à qn le ~ de faire** to allow sb (the opportunity) to do. ◆ **loisible** *adj (littér)* **il vous est ~ de faire** you are at liberty to do.

Lombardie [lɔ̃baʀdi] *nf* Lombardy.

Londres [lɔ̃dʀ(ə)] *n* London. ◆ **londonien, -ienne** **1** *adj* London. **2** *nm(f)*: **L~(ne)** Londoner.

long, longue [lɔ̃, lɔ̃g] **1** *adj* (**a**) *(gén)* long; *voyage* lengthy; *amitié* long-standing. **un pont ~ de 30 mètres** a bridge 30 metres long; **ce travail est ~ à faire** this work takes a long time; **il a été ~ à s'habiller** he took a long time to get dressed; **il était ~ à venir** he was a long time coming. (**b**) *(locutions)* **ils se connaissent de longue date** they have known each other for a very long time; **à ~ terme** *prévoir* in the long term *ou* run; *projet* long-term; **à plus ou moins longue échéance** sooner or later; **ça n'a pas fait ~ feu** it didn't last long; **de longue haleine** *travail* long-term; **préparé**

de longue main prepared well beforehand; **les chômeurs de longue durée** the long-term unemployed; **à longue portée** *canon* long-range. **2** *adv*: **s'habiller** ~ to wear long clothes; **en savoir ~/trop ~/plus** ~ to know a lot/too much/more (*sur* about); *[attitude etc]* **en dire** ~to speak volumes. **3** *nm* (**a**) **un bateau de 7 mètres de** ~ a boat 7 metres long; **en** ~ lengthways, lengthwise. (**b**) **tomber de tout son** ~ to measure one's length; **étendu de tout son** ~ spread out at full length; **(tout) le** ~ **du fleuve** (all) along the river; **tout au** ~ **de son récit** throughout his story; **l'eau coule le** ~ **de la gouttière** the water flows down *ou* along the gutter; **grimper le** ~ **d'un mât** to climb up a mast; **tirer un trait tout du** ~ **(de la page)** to draw a line right along the page; **tout du** ~ throughout the whole time, all along; **tout au** ~ **du parcours** all along the route, the whole way along the route; **de** ~ **en large** back and forth, to and fro, up and down; **en** ~ **et en large** at great length. **4** *nf*: **à la longue** in the end.
◆ **long-courrier,** *pl* **long-courriers** *nm* (*Naut*) ocean liner; (*Aviat*) long-haul *ou* long-distance aircraft. ◆ **long métrage** *nm* full-length film. ◆ **longue-vue**, *pl* **longues-vues** *nf* telescope. ◆ **longuement** *adv* (*longtemps*) for a long time; (*en détail*) at length. ◆ **longuet, -ette** * *adj* a bit long.

longer [lɔ̃ʒe] (3) *vt [mur, sentier]* to border; *[personne, train]* to go along *ou* alongside. ~ **la côte** *[bateau, route]* to hug the coast; *[voiture]* to drive along *ou* keep to the coast.

longévité [lɔ̃ʒevite] *nf* longevity.

longiligne [lɔ̃ʒiliɲ] *adj forme, silhouette* rangy.

longitude [lɔ̃ʒityd] *nf* longitude. **à** *ou* **par 50° de** ~ **est** at 50° longitude east. ◆ **longitudinal, e,** *mpl* **-aux** *adj* longitudinal.

longtemps [lɔ̃tɑ̃] *adv* (for) a long time; (*dans phrase nég ou interrog*) (for) long. **pendant** ~ (for) a long time; (for) long; **pas avant** ~ not for a long time; ~ **avant/après** long before/after; **il n'en a plus pour** ~ (*finir*) he hasn't much longer to go; (*mourir*) he can't last much longer now; **je n'en ai pas pour** ~ I won't be long, it won't take me long; **il habite ici depuis** ~**, il y a** ~ **qu'il habite ici** he has been living here (for) a long time; **c'était il y a ~/il n'y a pas** ~ that was a long time ago/not long ago.

longue [lɔ̃g] *V* **long.**

longueur [lɔ̃gœʀ] *nf* (*gén*) length. **la plage s'étend sur une** ~ **de 7 km** the beach stretches for 7 km; **dans le sens de la** ~ lengthways, lengthwise; (*lit, fig*) ~ **d'onde** wavelength; **à** ~ **de journée** all day long; **à** ~ **de temps** all the time; **traîner en** ~ to drag on; **prendre 2 ~s d'avance** to go into a 2-length lead; (*dans un film*) **~s** boringly long moments.

look * [luk] *nm* (*style, allure*) look, image. **soigner son** ~ to pay great attention to one's look *ou* one's image.

lopin [lɔpɛ̃] *nm*: ~ **(de terre)** patch of land, plot (of land).

loquace [lɔkas] *adj* talkative.

loque [lɔk] *nf*: **~s** rags; **tomber en ~s** to be in tatters; (*fig péj*) **une** ~ **(humaine)** a (human) wreck.

loquet [lɔkɛ] *nm* latch.

lorgner * [lɔʀɲe] (1) *vt objet* to eye; *héritage* to have one's eye on. ◆ **lorgnette** *nf* spyglass. ◆ **lorgnon** *nm* pince-nez.

lors [lɔʀ] *adv*: ~ **de** at the time of; ~ **même que** even though *ou* if.

lorsque [lɔʀsk(ə)] *conj* when.

losange [lɔzɑ̃ʒ] *nm* diamond, lozenge.

lot [lo] *nm* (**a**) (*Loterie*) prize. **le gros** ~ the first prize, the jackpot. (**b**) (*portion*) share. ~ **(de terre)** plot (of land). (**c**) (*assortiment*) batch; *[draps, vaisselle]* set; (*aux enchères*) lot. (**d**) (*littér: destin*) lot, fate.

loterie [lɔtʀi] *nf* (*lit, fig*) lottery. **gagner à la** ~ to win on the lottery; **la vie est une** ~ life is a game of chance, life is a lottery.

lotion [losjɔ̃] *nf* lotion.

lotir [lɔtiʀ] (2) *vt* (*diviser*) to divide up. ~ **qn de qch** to allot sth to sb, provide sb with sth; **être bien/mal loti** to be well-/badly off. ◆ **lotissement** *nm* (**a**) (*ensemble*) housing estate; (*parcelle*) plot, lot. (**b**) (*action*) division.

loto [lɔto] *nm* (*jeu*) lotto; (*matériel*) lotto set. ~ **(national)** national bingo game; **le** ~ **sportif** ≃ the pools.

lotus [lɔtys] *nm* lotus.

louable [lwabl(ə)] *adj* praiseworthy, laudable. ◆ **louange** *nf* praise. **à la** ~ **de qn** in praise of sb. ◆ **louangeur, -euse** *adj* laudatory.

loubar(d) [lubaʀ] *nm* hooligan, thug.

louche[1] [luʃ] *adj* shady, fishy *, suspicious. **c'est** ~ that's funny *ou* odd.

louche[2] [luʃ] *nf* ladle.

loucher [luʃe] (1) *vi* to squint, have a squint.

louer[1] [lwe] (1) **1** *vt* to praise. ~ **qn de** *ou* **pour qch** to praise sb for sth; (*fig*) **Dieu soit loué!** thank God! **2 se** ~ *vpr*: **se** ~ **de** *employé, appareil* to be very pleased with; **se** ~ **d'avoir fait qch** to congratulate o.s. on having done sth.

louer[2] [lwe] (1) *vt* (**a**) *[propriétaire] maison* to let (out), rent out; *voiture* to hire out, rent (out). (**b**) *[locataire] maison* to rent; *voiture* to hire, rent; *place* to book. **à** ~ *chambre etc* to let, to rent (*US*); *voiture etc* for hire, for rent (*US*). ◆ **loueur, -euse** *nm, f* (*propriétaire*) hirer out, renter out.

loufoque * [lufɔk] *adj* crazy, barmy *.

loukoum [lukum] *nm* Turkish delight. **manger 3 ~s** to eat 3 pieces of Turkish delight.

loup [lu] **1** *nm* (**a**) (*carnassier*) wolf; (*poisson*) bass; (*masque*) (eye) mask. **mon petit** ~ * (my) pet * *ou* love; **mettre le** ~ **dans la bergerie** to set the fox to mind the geese. (**b**) (*malfaçon*) flaw. **2** : **~-garou** *nm, pl* **~s-~s** werewolf; (*hum*) **le ~-garou** Mr Bogeyman; ~ **de mer** (**: marin*) old salt *; (*vêtement*) (short-sleeved) jersey.

loupe [lup] *nf* magnifying glass.

louper * [lupe] (1) **1** *vt train* to miss; *travail* to mess up *, spoil; *examen* to flunk *. **il a loupé son coup** he bungled *ou* botched * it; (*iro*) **il n'en loupe pas une!** he's forever putting his big foot in it! * **2** *vi*: **je t'ai dit qu'il ferait une erreur; ça n'a pas loupé!** I told you that he'd make a mistake and sure enough he did!; **ça va tout faire** ~ that'll muck everything up *. ◆ **loupé** * (*ptp de* **louper**) *nm* (*échec*) failure; (*défaut*) defect, flaw.

lourd, e [luʀ, luʀd(ə)] *adj* (*lit, fig*) heavy; *temps, chaleur* sultry, close; *faute* serious; *plaisanterie* heavy-handed. **yeux ~s de sommeil** eyes heavy with sleep; **avoir l'estomac** ~ to feel bloated; **j'ai la tête ~e** my head feels fuzzy, I feel a bit headachy; **avoir l'esprit** ~ to be slow-witted; ~ **de menaces** heavy with threat; ~ **de conséquences** fraught with consequences; **il n'y a pas** ~ **de pain** * there isn't much bread; **il n'en sait pas** ~ he doesn't know much. ◆ **lourdaud, e 1** *adj* oafish. **2** *nm, f* oaf. ◆ **lourdement** *adv* (*gén*) heavily. **se tromper** ~ to make a big mistake; **insister** ~ **sur qch** to insist strenuously on sth. ◆ **lourdeur** *nf* (*gén*) heaviness. ~ **d'esprit** slow-wittedness; **avoir des ~s d'estomac** to feel bloated.

lourder ‡ [luʀde] (1) *vt* to kick out *, boot out ‡. **se faire** ~ to get kicked out * *ou* booted out ‡.

loustic * [lustik] *nm* (*enfant*) kid *; (*taquin*) villain * (*hum*); (*type*) (funny) guy *.

loutre [lutʀ(ə)] *nf (animal)* otter; *(fourrure)* otter-skin.

louve [luv] *nf* she-wolf. ◆ **louveteau,** *pl* ~**x** *nm (Zool)* (wolf) cub; *(scout)* cub scout.

louvoyer [luvwaje] (8) *vi (Naut)* to tack; *(fig)* to hedge, evade the issue.

loyal, e, *mpl* **-aux** [lwajal, o] *adj (fidèle)* loyal, faithful, trusty; *(honnête)* fair, honest. ◆ **loyalement** *adv* loyally, faithfully; fairly, honestly. ◆ **loyauté** *nf* loyalty, faithfulness; fairness, honesty.

loyer [lwaje] *nm* rent.

lubie [lybi] *nf* whim, craze, fad. **il lui a pris la ~ de faire** he has taken it into his head to do; **c'est sa dernière ~** it's his latest craze.

lubrifier [lybʀifje] (7) *vt* to lubricate. ◆ **lubrifiant, e 1** *adj* lubricating. **2** *nm* lubricant. ◆ **lubrification** *nf* lubrication.

lubrique [lybʀik] *adj* lewd.

lucarne [lykaʀn(ə)] *nf [toit]* skylight; *(en saillie)* dormer window.

lucide [lysid] *adj vieillard* lucid; *accidenté* conscious; *observateur* clear-headed; *raisonnement* lucid, clear. ◆ **lucidement** *adv* lucidly, clearly. ◆ **lucidité** *nf* lucidity; consciousness; clearheadedness; clearness.

lucratif, -ive [lykʀatif, iv] *adj* lucrative. **association à but non ~** non-profit-making organization. ◆ **lucrativement** *adv* lucratively.

ludiciel [lydisjɛl] *nm* computer game. ~**s** computer games, game software.

ludique [lydik] *adj (Psych)* play. **activité ~** play activity.

lueur [lɥœʀ] *nf*: ~**(s)** *(lit)* (faint) light; *[braises, soleil couchant]* glow; *[flamme, raison, espoir]* glimmer; *[désir, colère]* gleam; **à la ~ d'une bougie** by candlelight; **les premières ~s de l'aube** the first light of dawn.

luge [lyʒ] *nf* sledge, sled *(US)*. **faire de la ~** to sledge, sled *(US)*.

lugubre [lygybʀ(ə)] *adj* gloomy, dismal.

lui [lɥi] **1** *pron pers mf (objet indirect) (homme)* him; *(femme)* her; *(bateau, nation)* her, it; *(animal, bébé)* it, him, her; *(chose)* it. **je ne le ~ ai jamais caché** I have never kept it from him *ou* her; **il ~ est facile de le faire** it's easy for him *ou* her to do it. **2** *pron m* (**a**) *(fonction objet) (personne)* him; *(pays, bateau)* her; *(animal)* him, her, it; *(chose)* it. **c'est ~, je le reconnais** it's him, I recognize him. (**b**) *(sujet, gén emphatique) (personne)* he, him; *(chose)* it; *(animal)* it, she, he. **le Japon, ~, serait d'accord** Japan, for its *ou* her part, would agree; **elle est venue mais pas ~** she came but not him *ou* but he didn't; **c'est ~ qui me l'a dit** he told me himself, it's he who told me; **chasse ce chien, c'est ~ qui m'a mordu** chase that dog away — it's the one that bit me. (**c**) *(avec prép) (personne)* him; *(chose)* it. **ce livre est à ~** this book belongs to him *ou* is his; **il a un appartement à ~** he has a flat of his own; **un ami à ~** a friend of his, one of his friends; **il ne pense qu'à ~** he only thinks of himself; **elle veut une photo de ~** she wants a photo of him. (**d**) *(dans comparaisons) (sujet)* he, him *; *(objet)* him. **j'ai mangé plus que ~** I ate more than he did *ou* than him *; **ne fais pas comme ~** don't do as he did.

luire [lɥiʀ] (38) *vi (gén)* to shine; *(reflet humide)* to glisten; *(reflet moiré)* to shimmer, glimmer; *(éclat bref)* to glint; *(rougeoiement)* to glow. **rendu luisant par l'usure** shiny with wear; **yeux luisants de fièvre** eyes bright with fever. ◆ **luisant** *nm [étoffe]* sheen; *[pelage]* gloss.

lumbago [lɔ̃bago] *nm* lumbago.

lumière [lymjɛʀ] *nf (gén)* light. **la ~ du jour** daylight; **la ~ du soleil l'éblouit** he was dazzled by the sunlight; **donne-nous de la ~** switch *ou* put the light on, will you?; **il y a de la ~ dans sa chambre** there's a light on in his room; **à la ~ des récents événements** in the light of recent events; **faire (toute) la ~ sur qch** to get right to the bottom of sth; **entrevoir la ~ au bout du tunnel** to see the light at the end of the tunnel; **le pauvre garçon n'est pas une ~** the poor boy, he's no bright spark *; **avoir des ~s sur une question** to have some knowledge of a question; **~ stroboscopique** strobe lightning. ◆ **luminaire** *nm* light, lamp. **magasin de ~s** lighting shop, shop selling lighting fitments. ◆ **lumineux, -euse** *adj (gén)* luminous; *fontaine, enseigne* illuminated; *rayon* of light; *(iro) exposé* limpid, brilliant. **source ~euse** light source; **c'est ~!** it's as clear as daylight! *ou* it's crystal clear. ◆ **luminosité** *nf* luminosity. **il y a beaucoup de ~** the light is very bright.

lump [lœ̃p] *nm* lumpfish, lumpsucker. **œufs de ~** lumpfish roe.

lunapark [lynapaʀk] *nm* (fun) fair.

lunch [lœntʃ] *nm* buffet.

lundi [lœ̃di] *nm* Monday; *V* **samedi.**

lune [lyn] *nf* moon. **pleine/nouvelle ~** full/new moon; **nuit sans ~** moonless night; **~ de miel** honeymoon; **être dans la ~** to be in a dream; **demander la ~** to ask *ou* cry for the moon. ◆ **lunaire** *adj paysage* lunar. ◆ **lunatique** *adj* quirky, temperamental. ◆ **luné, e** * *adj*: **être bien/mal ~** to be in a good/bad mood.

lunette [lynɛt] *nf* (**a**) ~**s** glasses, specs *; *(de protection)* goggles, glasses; **~s de soleil** sunglasses, shades *. (**b**) *(télescope)* telescope; *[fusil]* sight(s). **~ d'approche** telescope; *(Aut)* **~ arrière** rear window.

luron * [lyʀɔ̃] *nm* lad *. **gai ~** gay dog.

lustre [lystʀ(ə)] *nm* (**a**) *[peau, vernis]* lustre, shine; *[cérémonie]* lustre. (**b**) *(luminaire)* centre light *(with several bulbs)*. (**c**) **depuis des ~s** for ages.

lustrer [lystʀe] (1) *vt (Tech) étoffe* to lustre; *(gén: faire briller)* to shine; *(par l'usure)* to make shiny. ◆ **lustré, e** *adj poil* glossy; *manche usée* shiny.

luth [lyt] *nm* lute.

lutin [lytɛ̃] *nm (lit, fig)* imp.

lutte [lyt] *nf* (**a**) *(bataille)* struggle, fight (*contre* against). *(action)* **la ~** fighting; **~ armée** armed struggle; **~ des classes** class-struggle *ou* war; **~ contre le crime** crime prevention; **~ anti-drogue/antipollution** fight against drugs/against pollution; **~ d'intérêts** clash of interests; **être en ~ contre qn** to be in conflict with sb; **le pays en ~** the country at war. (**b**) *(Sport)* wrestling. **~ libre** all-in wrestling. ◆ **lutter** (1) *vi* to struggle, fight. **~ contre** *adversaire* to struggle *ou* fight against; *incendie* to fight; *sommeil, mort* to battle against; **ils luttaient de vitesse** they were racing each other. ◆ **lutteur, -euse** *nm, f (Sport)* wrestler; *(fig)* fighter.

luxe [lyks(ə)] *nm (richesse)* luxury; *[maison, objet]* luxuriousness. **de ~** *voiture* luxury; *(Comm) produits* de luxe; *(Aut)* **modèle (de) grand ~** de luxe model; **je ne peux pas me payer le ~ d'être malade** I can't afford the luxury of being ill; **un ~ de détails** a host *ou* wealth of details. ◆ **luxueusement** *adv* luxuriously. ◆ **luxueux, -euse** *adj* luxurious.

Luxembourg [lyksɑ̃buʀ] *nm* Luxembourg. ◆ **luxembourgeois, e 1** *adj* of Luxembourg. **2** *nm(f)*: **L~(e)** native of Luxembourg.

luxer [lykse] (1) *vt* to dislocate. **se ~ un membre** to dislocate a limb. ◆ **luxation** *nf* dislocation.

luxure [lyksyʀ] *nf* lust.

luxuriance [lyksyʀjɑ̃s] *nf* luxuriance. ◆ **luxuriant, e** *adj* luxuriant.

luzerne [lyzɛʀn(ə)] *nf* lucerne, alfalfa.

lycée [lise] *nm* lycée, ≃ secondary school, high school *(US)*. **~ technique, ~ professionnel** tech nical school. ◆ **lycéen, -enne** *nm, f* secondary school *ou* high-school *(US)* pupil (*ou* boy *ou* girl).

lymphe [lɛ̃f] *nf* lymph. ◆ **lymphatique** *adj (Bio)* lymphatic; *(fig)* sluggish.

lyncher [lɛ̃ʃe] (1) *vt* to lynch.

lynx [lɛ̃ks] *nm* lynx.

Lyon [ljɔ̃] *n* Lyons. ◆ **lyonnais, e** **1** *adj* of *ou* from Lyons. **2** *nm, f* **L~(e)** inhabitant *ou* native of Lyons.

lyophiliser [ljɔfilize] (1) *vt* to freeze-dry, lyophilize. **café lyophilisé** freeze-dried coffee.

lyre [liʀ] *nf* lyre. ◆ **lyrique** *adj* (**a**) *(Mus, Poésie)* lyric. **artiste** ~ opera singer. (**b**) *(enthousiaste)* lyrical. ◆ **lyrisme** *nm* lyricism.

lys [lis] *nm* = **lis.**

M

M, m [ɛm] *nm ou nf (lettre)* M, m.

m' [m(ə)] *V* **me.**

ma [ma] *adj poss V* **mon.**

mac ‡ [mak] *nm (souteneur)* pimp, ponce ‡.

macabre [makɑbʀ(ə)] *adj* macabre, gruesome.

macadam [makadam] *nm [pierres]* macadam; *[goudron]* Tarmac(adam) ®; *(fig: rue)* road. ◆ **macadamiser** (1) *vt* to macadamize; to tarmac.

macaque [makak] *nm (Zool)* macaque. ~ **rhésus** rhesus monkey.

macaron [makaʀɔ̃] *nm (Culin)* macaroon; *(insigne)* (round) badge; *(autocollant)* (round) sticker.

macaroni [makaʀɔni] *nm* piece of macaroni. **manger des ~s** to eat macaroni.

macchabée ‡ [makabe] *nm* stiff ‡ *(corpse)*.

macédoine [masedwan] *nf*: ~ **de légumes** mixed vegetables; ~ **de fruits** *(gén)* fruit salad; *(en boîte)* fruit cocktail.

macérer [maseʀe] (6) **1** *vt* (*aussi* **faire** *ou* **laisser ~**) to macerate. **2** *vi (faire attendre)* **laisser ~ qn (dans son jus)** * to keep sb hanging about *, keep sb waiting. ◆ **macération** *nf* maceration.

Mach [mak] *nm* mach. **voler à ~ 2** to fly at mach 2.

mâche [mɑʃ] *nf* corn salad, lambs' lettuce.

mâchefer [mɑʃfɛʀ] *nm* clinker, cinders.

mâcher [mɑʃe] (1) *vt [personne]* to chew; *(avec bruit)* to munch; *[animal]* to chomp. **il faut lui ~ tout le travail** you have to do half his work for him; **il ne mâche pas ses mots** he doesn't mince his words.

machiavélique [makjavelik] *adj* Machiavellian.

machin, e[1] * [maʃɛ̃, in] **1** *nm, f* thing; *(dont le nom échappe)* thingummyjig *, thingamajig *(US)*, what-d'you-call-it *. **2** *nm (personne)* **M~ (chouette)** what's-his-name *, what d'you-call-him *; **hé! M ~!** hey there you!; **le père M~** Mr what's-his-name *. **3 M~e** *nf (personne)* what's-her-name *.

machine[2] [maʃin] **1** *nf (gén, fig)* machine; *(locomotive)* engine, locomotive; *(Naut: moteur)* engine; *(avion)* plane; *(*: moto)* bike. **la ~ administrative** the bureaucratic machinery; **fait à la ~** machine-made; **faire ~ arrière** *(Naut)* to go astern; *(fig)* to back-pedal, draw back, retreat; **le gouvernement a dû faire ~ arrière** the government was forced to retreat. **2** : ~ **à affranchir/à calculer** franking/calculating machine; ~ **à coudre** sewing machine; ~ **à écrire** typewriter; ~ **à laver** washing machine; ~ **à laver la vaisselle** dishwasher; **~-outil** *nf, pl* **~s-~s** machine tool; ~ **à sous** *(Casino)* one-armed bandit, fruit machine; *(distributeur)* slot machine; ~ **à traitement de texte (dédiée)** word processor; ~ **à vapeur** steam engine. ◆ **machinal, e,** *mpl* **-aux** *adj* mechanical. ◆ **machinalement** *adv* mechanically. ◆ **machinisme** *nm* mechanization. ◆ **machiniste** *nm (Théât)* stagehand; *(Transport)* driver.

machiner [maʃine] (1) *vt trahison etc* to plot, engineer. **il a tout machiné** he engineered the whole thing. ◆ **machination** *nf (complot)* plot, machination. **odieuses ~s** foul machinations *ou* schemings.

machisme [matʃism(ə)] *nm* (**a**) *(phallocratie)* male chauvinism. (**b**) *(virilité)* machismo. ◆ **machiste** *adj* (male) chauvinist. ◆ **macho** * *nm* (**a**) *(phallocrate)* male chauvinist (pig) *. (**b**) *(viril)* macho.

mâchoire [mɑʃwaʀ] *nf* jaw.

mâchonner * [mɑʃɔne] (1) *vt*, **mâchouiller** * [mɑʃuje] (1) *vt* to chew at *ou* on.

maçon [masɔ̃] *nm (gén)* builder; *[pierre]* (stone)mason; *[briques]* bricklayer. ◆ **maçonnerie** *nf* (**a**) *[pierres]* masonry, stonework; *[briques]* brickwork. (**b**) *(travail)* building; bricklaying. **entreprise de ~** building firm.

macro... [makʀɔ] *préf* macro...

macrobiotique [makʀɔbjɔtik] **1** *adj* macrobiotic. **2** *nf* macrobiotics.

macromolécule [makʀɔmɔlekyl] *nf* macromolecule.

maculer [makyle] (1) *vt* to stain (*de* with). **une chemise maculée de boue** a shirt spattered *ou* covered with mud.

Madagascar [madagaskaʀ] *nf* Madagascar.

Madame [madam], *pl* **Mesdames** [medam] *nf* (**a**) *(s'adressant à qn)* **bonjour ~** *(courant)* good morning; *(nom connu)* good morning, Mrs X; *(avec déférence)* good morning, Madam; *(devant un auditoire)* **Mesdames(, Messieurs)** ladies (and gentlemen); ~ **la Présidente** Madam Chairman; **oui ~ la Marquise** yes Madam; *(Scol)* ~! please Mrs X!, please Miss! (**b**) *(parlant de qn)* ~ **X est malade** Mrs X is ill; **je vais le dire à ~** I will inform Mrs X; ~ **dit que c'est à elle** the lady says it belongs to her; ~ **la Présidente** the chairperson, the chairman. (**c**) *(sur une enveloppe)* ~ **X** Mrs X; **Mesdames X** the Mrs X; **Mesdames X et Y** Mrs X and Mrs Y; **Monsieur X et ~** Mr and Mrs X; ~ **la Maréchale X** Mrs X; ~ **la Marquise de X** the Marchioness of X. (**d**) *(en-tête de lettre)* Dear Madam. **Chère ~** Dear Mrs X; **~, Mademoiselle, Monsieur** Dear Sir or Madam; ~ **la Maréchale** Dear Madam. (**e**) *(sans majuscule, pl* **~s**: * *ou péj)* lady.

Mademoiselle [madmwazɛl], *pl* **Mesdemoiselles** [medmwazɛl] *nf* (**a**) *(s'adressant à qn)* **bonjour ~** *(courant)* good morning; *(nom connu)* good morning, Miss X; **bonjour Mesdemoiselles** good morning ladies; *(au restaurant)* **et pour vous ~?** and for the young lady?, and for you, miss? (**b**) *(parlant de qn)* ~ **X est malade** Miss X is ill; ~ **est sortie** Miss X is out; **je vais le dire à ~** I shall tell Miss X. (**c**) *(sur une enveloppe)* ~ **X** Miss X; **Mesdemoiselles X** the Misses X; **Mesdemoiselles X et Y** Miss X and Miss Y. (**d**) *(en-tête de lettre)* Dear Madam. **Chère ~** Dear Miss X.

Madère [madɛʀ] **1** *nf* Madeira. **2** *nm*: **m~** Madeira (wine).

madone [madɔn] *nf* madonna.

Madrid [madʀid] *n* Madrid. ◆ **madrilène** **1** *adj* of *ou* from Madrid. **2** *nmf*: **M~** inhabitant *ou* native of Madrid.

maf(f)ia [mafja] *nf* (**a**) **la M~** the Maf(f)ia. (**b**) *[trafiquants]* gang, ring. ~ **d'anciens élèves** old boys' network. ◆ **maf(f)ioso,** *pl* **maf(f)iosi** *nm* maf(f)ioso.

magasin [magazɛ̃] *nm* (**a**) *(boutique)* shop, store; *(entrepôt)* warehouse. ~ **à grande surface** hypermarket, supermarket; ~ **à succursales multiples** chain store; *(Mil)* ~ **de vivres** quartermaster's stores; **faire les ~s** to go shopping; **nous ne l'avons pas en** ~ we haven't got it in stock. (**b**) *(Tech) [fusil, appareil-photo]* magazine. ◆ **magasinier** *nm [usine]* storeman; *[entrepôt]* warehouseman.

magazine [magazin] *nm (Presse)* magazine. *(Rad, TV)* ~ **féminin** woman's hour; ~ **d'actualités** news magazine.

mage [maʒ] *nm* magus.

Maghreb [magʀɛb] *nm*: **le** ~ the Maghreb, NW Africa. ◆ **maghrébin, e 1** *adj* of *ou* from the Maghreb *ou* North Africa. **2** *nm, f*: **M~(e)** North African.

magie [maʒi] *nf* magic. **comme par** ~ like magic, as if by magic; *[prestidigitateur]* **faire de la** ~ to perform *ou* do magic tricks. ◆ **magicien, -ienne** *nm, f* magician. ◆ **magique** *adj (lit)* magic; *(fig: enchanteur)* magical. ◆ **magiquement** *adv* magically.

magistral, e, *mpl* **-aux** [maʒistʀal, o] *adj (éminent)* masterly; *(hum: gigantesque)* thorough, colossal; *(doctoral) ton* authoritative, masterful. *(Univ)* **cours** ~ lecture. ◆ **magistralement** *adv* in a masterly manner.

magistrat [maʒistʀa] *nm* magistrate. ◆ **magistrature** *nf (Jur)* magistracy; *(Admin, Pol)* public office. **la** ~ **suprême** the supreme *ou* highest office.

magma [magma] *nm (Sci)* magma; *(fig)* jumble.

magnanime [maɲanim] *adj* magnanimous. ◆ **magnanimité** *nf* magnanimity.

magnat [magna] *nm* tycoon, magnate. ~ **de la presse** press baron *ou* lord *ou* tycoon; ~ **du pétrole** oil tycoon.

magner (se) ‡ [maɲe] (1) *vpr* to get a move on *, hurry up.

magnésium [maɲezjɔm] *nm* magnesium.

magnétiser [maɲetize] (1) *vt (Phys, fig)* to magnetize; *(hypnotiser)* to hypnotize. ◆ **magnétique** *adj (Phys, fig)* magnetic. ◆ **magnétisation** *nf* magnetization; hypnotization. ◆ **magnétiseur, -euse** *nm, f* hypnotizer. ◆ **magnétisme** *nm* magnetism; hypnotism.

magnéto [maɲeto] **1** *nf (Élec)* magneto. **2** *préf* magneto. **3** *nm* (*) tape recorder. ◆ **magnétophone** *nm* tape recorder. ~ **à cassettes** cassette recorder. ◆ **magnétoscope** *nm (appareil)* video (tape *ou* cassette) recorder; *(bande)* video-tape. **enregistrer au** ~ to video, video-tape, take a video (recording) of.

magnificence [maɲifisɑ̃s] *nf (faste)* magnificence.

magnifique [maɲifik] *adj (gén)* magnificent; *fleur, temps* gorgeous, superb; *projet* marvellous. ~! * fantastic! *, great! * ◆ **magnifiquement** *adv* magnificently; gorgeously, superbly; marvellously.

magnolia [maɲɔlija] *nm,* **magnolier** [maɲɔlije] *nm* magnolia.

magot [mago] *nm* (**a**) *(Zool)* Barbary ape. (**b**) *(Sculp)* magot. (**c**) (*) *(somme d'argent)* pile (of money) *, packet *; *(économies)* savings, nest egg.

magouiller * [maguje] (1) *vi (péj)* to scheme *(péj)*. ◆ **magouillage** * *nm,* **magouille** * *nf (péj)* scheming *(péj)*. **c'est le roi de la** ~ he's a born schemer; ~ **électoral** pre-election scheming; **sombre** ~ dirty bit of business.

magret [magʀɛ] *nm*: ~ **(de canard)** steaklet of duck, duck cutlet.

mahara(d)jah [maaʀa(d)ʒa] *nm* Maharajah.

mahatma [mahatma] *nm* mahatma.

mai [mɛ] *nm* May; *V* **septembre**.

maigre [mɛgʀ(ə)] **1** *adj* (**a**) *personne* thin, skinny *(péj)*; *visage* thin, lean. ~ **comme un clou** * as thin as a rake. (**b**) *bouillon* clear; *viande* lean; *fromage* low-fat. (**c**) *(Rel)* **faire** ~ *(gén)* to abstain from meat; *(manger du poisson)* to eat fish; **le vendredi est un jour** ~ people don't eat meat on Fridays. (**d**) *profit* meagre, small, slim, scanty; *ration, résultat, salaire* meagre, poor; *exposé* sketchy, skimpy; *espoir* slim, slight. **c'est un peu** ~ it's a bit skimpy, it's a bit on the short side. (**e**) *végétation* thin, sparse; *récolte, terre* poor. **un** ~ **filet d'eau** a thin trickle of water. **2** *nmf* thin person. **3** *nm (viande)* lean meat; *(jus)* thin gravy.
◆ **maigrement** *adv* poorly, meagrely. ◆ **maigreur** *nf* thinness; leanness; smallness, scantiness; meagreness; sketchiness; sparseness; poverty. **il est d'une** ~! he's so thin! ◆ **maigrir** (2) **1** *vi* to get thinner, lose weight. **il a maigri de 5 kg** he has lost 5 kg; **se faire** ~ to slim, diet (to lose weight). **2** *vt*: ~ **qn** *[vêtement]* to make sb look slim (*ou* slimmer); *[maladie]* to make sb lose weight.

mailing [mɛliŋ] *nm* mailing. **faire un** ~ to do a mailing *ou* a mailshot.

maille [maj] *nf* (**a**) *(Couture)* stitch. *[bas]* ~ **filée** ladder, run; **une** ~ **à l'endroit, une** ~ **à l'envers** knit one, purl one; **tissu à fines ~s** fine-knit material. (**b**) *[filet]* mesh. *(lit, fig)* **passer à travers les ~s (du filet)** to slip through the net; **filet à larges/fines ~s** wide/fine mesh net. (**c**) *[armure, grillage]* link. (**d**) **avoir** ~ **à partir avec qn** to get into trouble with sb.

maillet [majɛ] *nm* mallet.

mailloche [majɔʃ] *nf (Tech)* beetle.

maillon [mɑjɔ̃] *nm (lit, fig)* link.

maillot [majo] *nm (gén)* vest; *(Danse)* leotard; *(Sport)* jersey; *[bébé]* baby's wrap. ~ **de bain** *[homme]* swimming trunks; *[femme]* swimming costume, swimsuit; ~ **de bain une pièce/deux pièces** one-piece/two-piece swimsuit; ~ **de corps** vest, undershirt *(US)*.

main [mɛ̃] **1** *nf* (**a**) hand. **serrer la** ~ **à** *ou* **de qn** to shake hands with sb; **donner la** ~ **à qn** to hold sb's hand; **il me salua de la** ~ he waved to me; **être adroit de ses ~s** to be clever with one's hands; **des deux ~s** with both hands; **la** ~ **dans la** ~ *[promeneurs]* hand in hand; *[escrocs]* hand in glove; **les ~s en l'air!** hands up!, stick 'em up! *; **trouver une** ~ **secourable** to find a helping hand; *(aider)* **donner la** ~ **à qn** to give sb a hand; *(s'aider)* **se donner la** ~ to give one another a helping hand; **tomber aux ~s de l'ennemi** to fall into the hands of the enemy; **accorder la** ~ **de sa fille à qn** to give sb one's daughter's hand in marriage. (**b**) *(locutions)* **à** ~ **droite/gauche** on the right-hand/left-hand side; **de** ~ **de maître** with a master's hand; **en ~s sûres** in(to) safe hands; **avoir une voiture bien en** ~ to have the feel of a car; **avoir la situation bien en** ~ to have the situation well in hand *ou* well under control; **de la** ~ **à la** ~ directly *(without receipt)*; **préparé de longue** ~ prepared long beforehand; **de première/seconde** ~ firsthand/secondhand; **fait (à la)** ~ handmade, done *ou* made by hand; **cousu (à la)** ~ hand-sewn; **vol à** ~ **armée** armed robbery; **(pris) la** ~ **dans le sac** caught red-handed, caught in the act; **en sous** ~ *agir* secretly; **les ~s vides** empty-handed; **avoir tout sous la** ~ to have everything at hand; **à** ~ **levée** *vote* by a show of hands; *dessin* freehand. (**c**) *(locutions verbales)* **avoir la** ~ **heureuse** to be lucky; **avoir la** ~ **lourde** to be heavy-handed; *(gifler)* **avoir la** ~ **leste** to be free with one's hands; **je ne suis pas à ma** ~ I can't get a proper hold *ou* grip; **perdre la** ~ to lose one's touch; **se faire la** ~ to get one's hand in; **faire** ~ **basse sur qch** * to run off *ou* make off with sth; **laisser les ~s libres à qn** to give sb a free hand *ou* rein; **mettre la** ~ **au collet de qn** to arrest sb; **en venir aux ~s** to come to blows; **mettre la** ~ **sur** *objet, livre* to lay hands on; **mettre la** ~ **à la pâte** to lend a hand;

mettre la dernière ~ **à** to put the finishing touches to; **passer la** ~ to stand down, make way for someone else; **si tu en veux, tu n'as qu'à te prendre par la** ~ if you want some, you just have to go and get it; **prendre qch/qn en** ~ to take sth/sb in hand; **remettre qch en ~s propres à qn** to hand sth to sb personally; **il n'y va pas de** ~ **morte** *(exagérer)* he doesn't do things by halves; *(frapper)* he doesn't pull his punches; **j'en mettrais ma** ~ **au feu** *ou* **à couper** I'd stake my life on it; **prêter ~-forte à qn** to come to sb's assistance.

2 : ~ **courante** handrail; **~-d'œuvre** *nf* labour, manpower, labour force, work force.

mainmise [mɛ̃miz] *nf (Jur, Pol)* seizure. **la** ~ **de l'État sur cette entreprise** the seizure of this company by the state.

maint, e [mɛ̃, ɛ̃t] *adj (littér)* many. ~ **étranger** many a foreigner; **~s étrangers** many foreigners.

maintenance [mɛ̃tnɑ̃s] *nf* maintenance, servicing.

maintenant [mɛ̃tnɑ̃] *adv* now. **il doit être arrivé** ~ he must have arrived by now; **les jeunes de** ~ young people nowadays *ou* today.

maintenir [mɛ̃tniʀ] (22) **1** *vt (gén)* to keep; *édifice* to hold *ou* keep up, support; *tradition* to maintain, uphold; *décision* to stand by; *affirmation* to maintain. ~ **qch en équilibre** to keep *ou* hold sth balanced; ~ **la tête hors de l'eau** to keep one's head above water; ~ **l'ordre** to keep *ou* maintain law and order. **2 se** ~ *vpr [temps]* to stay fair; *[amélioration, préjugé]* to persist; *[malade]* to hold one's own; *[prix]* to hold steady. *(Scol)* **se** ~ **dans la moyenne** to keep up with the middle of the class; **se** ~ **en équilibre sur un pied/sur une poutre** to balance on one foot/on a beam. ◆ **maintien** *nm* (**a**) *(sauvegarde) (gén)* maintenance; *[tradition]* upholding. (**b**) *(posture)* bearing, deportment. **professeur de** ~ teacher of deportment.

maire [mɛʀ] *nm* mayor. ◆ **mairie** *nf (bâtiment)* town hall; *(administration)* town council.

mais [mɛ] **1** *conj* but. **tu me crois? — ~ oui** do you believe me? — (but) of course *ou* of course I do; ~ **si je veux bien!** but of course I agree!, sure, I agree!; ~ **ne te fais pas de soucis!** don't you worry!; ~ **dites-moi, c'est intéressant!** well now that's interesting!; ~ **j'y pense,...** by the way I've just thought,...; **ah ~!, non ~ (des fois)!** look here! **2** *nm*: **je ne veux pas de** ~ I don't want any buts; **il y a un** ~ there's one snag.

maïs [mais] *nm* maize, corn *(US)*.

maison [mɛzɔ̃] **1** *nf* (**a**) *(bâtiment)* house; *(immeuble)* building; *(locatif)* block of flats, apartment building *(US)*. ~ **individuelle** (detached) house; *(secteur)* **la** ~ **individuelle** private housing. (**b**) *(foyer)* home. **être/rester à la** ~ to be/stay at home; **rentrer à la** ~ to go (back) home; **les dépenses de la** ~ household expenses; **fait à la** ~ home-made. (**c**) *(famille)* family. **il n'est pas heureux à la** ~ he doesn't have a happy home *ou* family life. (**d**) *(entreprise)* firm, company; *(magasin) (grand)* store; *(petit)* shop. (**e**) *(famille royale)* House. (**f**) *(domesticité)* household. **la** ~ **du Roi** the Royal Household; **employés de** ~ domestic staff.

2 *adj inv* (**a**) *gâteau* home-made; *ingénieur* trained by the firm. **pâté** ~ pâté maison, chef's own pâté. (**b**) *(*: très réussi)* first-rate. **une bagarre** ~ an almighty * *ou* a stand-up row.

3 : ~ **d'arrêt** prison; **la M~ Blanche** the White House; ~ **de campagne** *(grande)* house in the country; *(petite)* (country) cottage; ~ **close** *ou* **de passe** brothel; ~ **de jeu** gambling club; ~ **des jeunes et de la culture** ≃ youth club and arts centre; ~ **jumelle** semi-detached (house), duplex *(US)*; *(Comm)* ~ **mère** parent company; ~ **de poupée** doll's house; ~ **de repos** convalescent home; ~ **de retraite** old people's home; ~ **de santé** *(clinique)* nursing home; *(asile)* mental home. ◆ **maisonnée** *nf* house-hold, family. ◆ **maisonnette** *nf* small house.

maître, maîtresse [mɛtʀ(ə), mɛtʀɛs] **1** *adj* (**a**) *(gén)* main; *œuvre* major; *qualité* chief, major; *(Cartes) atout* master. **position maîtresse** major *ou* key position; **idée maîtresse** principal *ou* governing idea. (**b**) *(intensif)* **un** ~ **filou** an arrant *ou* out-and-out rascal; **une maîtresse femme** a managing woman.

2 *nm* (**a**) *(gén)* master; *(Pol: dirigeant)* ruler. **agir en** ~ to act authoritatively; **d'un ton de** ~ in an authoritative *ou* a masterful tone; **le** ~ **de céans** the master of the house; ~ **(d'école)** teacher, (school)master; ~ **charpentier** master carpenter. (**b**) *(titre) (pour artistes etc)* **M~** Sir; *(dans la marine)* petty officer; **mon cher M~** Dear Mr X; *(Jur)* **M** ~ **X** Mr X. (**c**) *(locutions)* **être** ~ **chez soi** to be master in one's own home; **être son propre** ~ to be one's own master; **être** ~ **de faire** to be free to do; **rester** ~ **de soi** to keep one's self-control; **être** ~ **de soi** to have control of o.s.; **être** ~ **de la situation** to be in control of the situation; **être** ~ **de sa destinée** to be the master of one's fate; **se rendre** ~ **de** *pays* to gain control of; *incendie* to bring *ou* get under control; **il est passé** ~ **dans l'art de mentir** he's a past master in the art of lying.

3 *nf* (**a**) *(gén)* mistress. (**b**) *(Scol)* **maîtresse (d'école)** teacher, (school)mistress; **maîtresse!** Miss!

4 : ~ **d'armes** fencing master; ~ **de cérémonie** master of ceremonies; *(Crime)* ~ **chanteur** blackmailer; **~-chien** dog handler; ~ **de conférences** ≃ senior lecturer, assistant professor *(US)*; ~ **d'équipage** boatswain; ~ **d'hôtel** *[maison]* butler; *[restaurant]* head waiter; ~ **de maison** host; **maîtresse de maison** *(ménagère)* housewife; *(hôtesse)* hostess; ~ **nageur** swimming teacher *ou* instructor; *(Constr)* ~ **d'œuvre** projet manager; **la mairie est** ~ **d'œuvre de ce projet** the town council is in charge of the project.

maîtrise [metʀiz] *nf* (**a**) *(sang-froid)* ~ **(de soi)** self-control, self-possession. (**b**) *(contrôle)* mastery, control. *(Mil)* **avoir la** ~ **de** to have control of, control. (**c**) *(habileté)* skill, expertise. (**d**) *(Ind)* supervisory staff. (**e**) *(Rel) (école)* choir school; *(groupe)* choir. (**f**) *(Univ) research degree,* ≃ master's degree. ~ **de conférence** ≃ senior lectureship. ◆ **maîtriser** (1) **1** *vt forcené* to control; *adversaire* to overcome, overpower; *émeute , révolte* to suppress, bring under control; *difficulté, langue* to master; *inflation* to curb; *larmes, rire* to force back, restrain. **2 se** ~ *vpr* to control o.s. ◆ **maîtrisable** *adj* controllable.

majesté [maʒɛste] *nf (gén)* majesty. **Votre M~** Your Majesty; **Sa M~** *(roi)* His Majesty; *(reine)* Her Majesty. ◆ **majestueusement** *adv* majestically. ◆ **majestueux, -euse** *adj (gén)* majestic; *taille* imposing.

majeur, e [maʒœʀ] **1** *adj* (**a**) *(principal)* major. **sa préoccupation ~e** his major *ou* main concern; **en ~e partie** for the most part; **la ~e partie des gens** most people, the majority (of people). (**b**) *(Jur)* **être** ~ to be of age; **il sera** ~ **en 1995** he will come of age in 1995. (**c**) *(Mus)* major. **2** *nm, f (Jur)* major. **3** *nm* middle finger.

major [maʒɔʀ] *nm (Mil)* ≃ adjutant. *(Mil)* **(médecin)** ~ medical officer; *(Univ etc)* **être** ~ **de promotion** ≃ to be *ou* come first in one's year.

majorer [maʒɔʀe] (1) *vt impôt, prix* to increase, raise (*de* by). ◆ **majoration** *nf (hausse)* rise, increase (*de* in); *(supplément)* surcharge.

majorité [maʒɔʀite] *nf (gén)* majority; *(parti majoritaire)* government, party in power. **élu à une** ~ **de** elected by a majority of; **être en** ~ to be in the majority; **groupe composé en** ~ **de** group mainly composed of; *(Jur)* **atteindre sa** ~ to come of age, reach one's majority. ◆ **majoritaire** **1** *adj* majority. **vote** ~ majority vote. **2** *nmf (Pol)* member of the majority party. **ils sont ~s à l'assemblée** they are the majority party *ou* in the majority in Parliament.

Majorque [maʒɔʀk(ə)] *nf* Majorca.

majuscule [maʒyskyl] **1** *adj* capital. **2** *nf* capital letter; *(Typ)* upper case letter. **en ~s d'imprimerie** in block *ou* capital letters; **écrivez votre nom en ~s (d'imprimerie)** please print your name in block letters.

mal [mal] **1** *adv* (**a**) *(de façon défectueuse)* badly, not properly. **cette porte ferme** ~ this door shuts badly *ou* doesn't shut properly; **nous sommes ~ nourris** the food we're given is poor *ou* bad; **il a ~ pris ce que je lui ai dit** he took exception to what I said to him; **il s'y est ~ pris** he set about it *ou* he went about it the wrong way; **de ~ en pis** from bad to worse. (**b**) ~ **choisi** *etc* ill-chosen *etc*; ~ **à l'aise** *(gêné)* ill-at-ease; *(malade)* unwell; ~ **famé** of ill fame, disreputable; ~ **en point** in a bad *ou* sorry state; ~ **à propos** at the wrong moment; **avoir l'esprit ~ tourné** to have a low mind; **il est ~ venu de se plaindre** he is scarcely in a position to complain. (**c**) ~ **comprendre** to misunderstand; ~ **interpréter** to misinterpret; ~ **renseigner** to misinform. (**d**) *(avec difficulté)* with difficulty. **on comprend ~ pourquoi** it is not easy *ou* it is difficult to understand why. (**e**) *(de façon répréhensible)* badly, wrongly. **trouves-tu ~ qu'il y soit allé?** do you think it was wrong of him to go? (**f**) *(malade)* **se sentir** ~ to feel ill; **être ~ portant** to be in poor health; **se trouver** ~ to faint. (**g**) **il n'a pas ~ travaillé ce trimestre** he's worked quite well this term; **vous (ne) feriez pas ~ de le surveiller** you would be well-advised to keep *ou* it wouldn't be a bad thing if you kept an eye on him. (**h**) *(beaucoup)* **pas ~ (de)** * quite a lot (of); **on a pas ~ travaillé aujourd'hui** we've worked pretty hard today *; **je m'en fiche pas ~!** I couldn't care less!, I don't give a damn! ⁑

2 *adj inv* (**a**) *(contraire à la morale)* wrong, bad. **c'est ~ à lui de dire cela** it's bad *ou* wrong of him to say this. (**b**) *(malade)* ill. **il est au plus** ~ he is very close to death, he's on the point of death. (**c**) *(mal à l'aise)* uncomfortable. **il est ~ dans sa peau** he's at odds with himself; **on n'est pas ~ (assis) dans ces fauteuils** these armchairs are quite comfortable. (**d**) **être ~ avec qn** to be on bad terms with sb; **se mettre ~ avec qn** to get on the wrong side of sb. (**e**) **pas** ~ * *(bien)* not bad *, quite *ou* rather good; *(beau)* quite attractive; *(compétent)* quite competent.

3 *nm, pl* **maux** [mo] (**a**) *(ce qui est mauvais)* evil, ill. **le** ~ evil; ~ **nécessaire** necessary evil; **penser/dire du ~ de qn** to think/speak ill of sb. (**b**) *(qui cause un dommage)* harm. **faire du ~ à** to harm, hurt; **il n'y a pas de ~ à cela** there's no harm in that; ~ **m'en a pris de sortir** going out was a grave mistake (on my part). (**c**) *(douleur)* pain; *(maladie)* illness, disease; *(tristesse)* sorrow, pain. **avoir ~ partout** to be aching all over; **se faire (du)** ~ to hurt o.s.; **ça fait ~, j'ai** ~ it hurts; **j'ai ~ dans le dos** I've got a pain in my back, my back hurts; **avoir un ~ de tête** to have a headache; **avoir ~ à la gorge** to have a sore throat; **avoir ~ aux dents** to have toothache; **avoir ~ au pied** to have a sore foot; **des maux d'estomac** stomach pains, an upset stomach; **un ~ blanc** a whitlow; **avoir le ~ de mer** to be seasick; **contre le ~ de mer** against seasickness; ~ **du pays** homesickness; **être en ~ de tendresse** to yearn for a little tenderness; **en ~ d'argent** short of money. (**d**) *(effort)* difficulty, trouble. **se donner du ~ à faire qch** to take trouble *ou* pains over sth; **avoir du ~ à faire qch** to have trouble *ou* difficulty doing sth; **ne vous donnez pas le ~ de faire ça** don't bother to do that; **on n'a rien sans** ~ you get nothing without (some) effort.

malabar * [malabaʀ] *nm* muscle man *.

malade [malad] **1** *adj homme* ill, sick, unwell; *organe, plante* diseased; *dent, jambe* bad. **être ~ du cœur, avoir le coeur** ~ to have heart trouble *ou* a bad heart *ou* a heart condition; **tomber** ~ to fall ill *ou* sick; **ça me rend** ~ it makes me sick (*de* with); *(fou)* **tu n'es pas ~?** * are you mad *ou* out of your mind?; **l'entreprise est bien** ~ the business is in a shaky state. **2** *nmf (gén)* invalid, sick person; *(d'un médecin)* patient. ~ **mental** mentally sick person; **les ~s** the sick. ◆ **maladie** *nf* (**a**) *(Méd)* illness, disease; *[plante, vin]* disease. ~ **de cœur/foie** heart/liver complaint *ou* disease; **il en a fait une** ~ * he was in a terrible state about it. (**b**) *(*: obsession)* mania. **avoir la ~ de la vitesse** to be a speed maniac. ◆ **maladif, -ive** *adj (lit)* sickly; *obsession* pathological.

maladroit, e [maladʀwa, wat] **1** *adj (gén)* clumsy, awkward. ~ **de ses mains** useless with one's hands; **ce serait ~ de lui en parler** it would be a mistake to mention it to him. **2** *nm, f (inhabile)* clumsy clot; *(qui fait tout tomber)* butterfingers; *(indélicat)* tactless person *ou* blunderer *. ◆ **maladresse** *nf* (**a**) clumsiness, awkwardness; tactlessness. (**b**) *(gaffe)* blunder, gaffe. ◆ **maladroitement** *adv* clumsily, awkwardly; tactlessly.

malais, e[1] [malɛɛz] **1** *adj*, **M~(e)** *nm(f)* Malay(an). **2** *nm (Ling)* Malay.

malaise[2] [malɛz] *nm* (**a**) *(Méd)* dizzy turn. **avoir un** ~ to feel faint *ou* dizzy. (**b**) *(fig: trouble)* uneasiness, disquiet. **le ~ étudiant** student discontent *ou* unrest.

malaisé, e [maleze] *adj* difficult. ◆ **malaisément** *adv* with difficulty.

Malaisie [malɛzi] *nf* Malaya, Malaysia. ◆ **malaisien, -ienne** *adj*, **M~(e)** *nm(f)* Malaysian.

malappris, e [malapʀi, iz] **1** *adj* boorish. **2** *nm, f* lout, boor.

malavisé, e [malavize] *adj* ill-advised, unwise.

malaxer [malakse] (1) *vt (triturer)* to knead; *muscle* to massage; *(mélanger)* to mix.

malchance [malʃɑ̃s] *nf (déveine)* bad luck, misfortune; *(mésaventure)* misfortune. **par** ~ unfortunately. ◆ **malchanceux, -euse** *adj* unlucky.

malcommode [malkɔmɔd] *adj* inconvenient.

Maldives [maldiv] *nfpl*: **les** ~ the Maldives.

maldonne [maldɔn] *nf (Cartes)* misdeal. **il y a** ~ *(lit)* there's been a misdeal; *(fig)* there's been a mis understanding *ou* a mistake somewhere.

mâle [mɑl] **1** *adj (Bio, Tech)* male; *(viril)* manly. **2** *nm* male. **(éléphant)** ~ bull (elephant); **(lapin)** ~ buck (rabbit); **(moineau)** ~ cock (sparrow); **(ours)** ~ he-bear; **souris** ~ male mouse.

malédiction [malediksjɔ̃] *nf* curse.

maléfice [malefis] *nm* evil spell. ◆ **maléfique** *adj* evil.

malencontreux, -euse [malɑ̃kɔ̃tʀø, øz] *adj* unfortunate. ◆ **malencontreusement** *adv arriver* at the wrong moment; *faire tomber* inadvertently.

malentendant [malɑ̃tɑ̃dɑ̃] *nm*: **les ~s** the hard of hearing.

malentendu [malɑ̃tɑ̃dy] *nm* misunderstanding.

malfaçon [malfasɔ̃] *nf* fault, defect.

malfaisant, e [malfəzɑ̃, ɑ̃t] *adj* evil, harmful.

malfaiteur [malfɛtœʀ] *nm (gén)* criminal; *(gangster)* gangster; *(voleur)* burglar, thief. **dangereux** ~ dangerous criminal.

malformation [malfɔʀmɑsjɔ̃] *nf* malformation.

malfrat [malfʀa] *nm (escroc)* crook; *(bandit)* thug, gangster.

malgache [malgaʃ] **1** *nm (Ling)* Malagasy. **2** *adj*, **M~** *nmf* Malagasy, Madagascan.

malgré [malgʀe] *prép* in spite of, despite. ~ **son intelligence** in spite of *ou* for all his intelligence; **j'ai signé ~ moi** *(en hésitant)* I signed reluctantly *ou* against my better judgment; *(contraint et forcé)* I signed against my will; ~ **tout, c'est dangereux** all the same *ou* after all it's dangerous.

malhabile [malabil] *adj* clumsy, awkward. ◆ **malhabilement** *adv* clumsily, awkwardly.

malheur [malœʀ] *nm* (**a**) misfortune; *(accident)* accident. **un ~ ne vient jamais seul** it never rains but it pours; **grand ~** great tragedy. (**b**) **le ~** *(adversité)* adversity; *(malchance)* bad luck, misfortune; **famille dans le ~** family in misfortune *ou* faced with adversity; **le ~ a voulu qu'un agent le voie** as bad luck would have it a policeman saw him. (**c**) *(maudit)* **de ~** * wretched. (**d**) **par ~** unfortunately; **le ~ c'est que...** the trouble *ou* snag is that...; **faire le ~ de ses parents** to bring sorrow to one's parents; **faire un ~** * *[artiste]* to make a great hit; *(par colère)* to do sth violent, go wild; **quel ~ qu'il ne soit pas venu** what a shame *ou* pity he didn't come. ◆ **malheureusement** *adv* unfortunately. ◆ **malheureux, -euse 1** *adj* (**a**) *victime, geste, parole* unfortunate; *enfant, vie* unhappy, miserable; *air* distressed; *candidat* unsuccessful, unlucky. **c'est bien ~** it's a great pity *ou* shame; **il est ~ de ne pas venir** he's distressed *ou* upset at not coming; **rendre qn ~** to make sb unhappy. (**b**) *(*: insignifiant)* wretched, miserable. **il y avait 2 ou 3 ~ spectateurs** there was a miserable handful of spectators. **2** *nm, f (infortuné)* poor wretch; *(indigent)* needy person. **le ~!** the poor man!; **ne fais pas cela, petit ~!** don't do that, you so-and-so! *

malhonnête [malɔnɛt] *adj (déloyal)* dishonest, crooked; *(impoli)* rude. ◆ **malhonnêtement** *adv* dishonestly, crookedly; rudely. ◆ **malhonnêteté** *nf* dishonesty, crookedness; rudeness. **une ~** *(action)* a crooked deal; *(parole)* a rude remark.

Mali [mali] *nm* Mali. ◆ **malien, -ienne 1** *adj* Malian, of *ou* from Mali. **2** *nm, f*: **M~(ne)** Malian, inhabitant *ou* native of Mali.

malice [malis] *nf (espièglerie)* mischief, mischievousness; *(méchanceté)* malice, spite. **il n'y entend pas ~** he means no harm by it; **boîte à ~** box of tricks. ◆ **malicieusement** *adv* mischievously. ◆ **malicieux, -euse** *adj* mischievous.

malin, -igne [malɛ̃, iɲ] *ou* **-ine** * [in] **1** *adj* (**a**) *(intelligent)* smart, clever. **il est ~ comme un singe** he is as artful as a cartload of monkeys; *(iro)* **c'est ~!** that's clever *ou* bright, isn't it? (**b**) *(*: difficile)* **ce n'est pourtant pas bien ~** but it isn't difficult *ou* tricky. (**c**) *(mauvais) influence* malignant, malicious; *(Méd)* malignant. **2** *nm, f*: **c'est un (petit) ~** he's a crafty one, he knows a thing or two; **le M~** the Devil.

malingre [malɛ̃gʀ(ə)] *adj* puny.

malinois [malinwa] *nm* police dog, ≃ Alsatian, German shepherd.

malintentionné, e [malɛ̃tɑ̃sjɔne] *adj* ill-intentioned (*envers* towards).

malle [mal] *nf (valise)* trunk; *(Aut)* boot, trunk *(US)*. **ils ont fait la ~** ⁑ they've hightailed it * , they've scarpered ⁑. ◆ **mallette** *nf (valise)* (small) suitcase; *(porte-documents)* briefcase, attaché case.

malléable [maleabl(ə)] *adj* malleable. ◆ **malléabilité** *nf* malleability.

malmener [malməne] (5) *vt* to manhandle, handle roughly.

malnutrition [malnytʀisjɔ̃] *nf* malnutrition.

malodorant, e [malɔdɔʀɑ̃, ɑ̃t] *adj* foul- *ou* ill-smelling.

malotru, e [malɔtʀy] *nm, f* lout, boor.

Malouines [malwin] *nfpl*: **les ~** the Falkland Islands.

malpoli, e [malpɔli] *adj* impolite, discourteous.

malpropre [malpʀɔpʀ(ə)] *adj objet* dirty; *travail* shoddy; *histoire* smutty; *action* dishonest, despicable. ◆ **malproprement** *adv* in a dirty way. ◆ **malpropreté** *nf* dirtiness.

malsain, e [malsɛ̃, ɛn] *adj* unhealthy.

malséant, e [malseɑ̃, ɑ̃t] *adj* unseemly, unbecoming.

malt [malt] *nm* malt. **whisky pur ~** malt (whisky).

Malte [malt] *nf* Malta. ◆ **maltais, e** *adj, nm*, **M~(e)** *nm(f)* Maltese.

malthusien, -ienne [maltyzjɛ̃, jɛn] *adj* Malthusian. ◆ **malthusianisme** *nm* Malthusianism.

maltraiter [maltʀete] (1) *vt personne* to manhandle, handle roughly, ill-treat; *grammaire* to misuse.

malus [malys] *nm* car insurance surcharge.

malveillance [malvɛjɑ̃s] *nf* spite, malevolence. **avec ~** malevolently; *(Jur)* **avoir agi sans ~** to have acted without malicious intent. ◆ **malveillant, e** *adj* malevolent.

malvoyant [malvwajɑ̃] *nm*: **les ~s** the partially sighted.

maman [mamɑ̃] *nf* mummy, mother.

mamelle [mamɛl] *nf (Zool)* teat; *(pis)* udder, dug; *[femme]* breast. ◆ **mamelon** *nm (Anat)* nipple; *(Géog)* knoll, hillock.

mamie [mami] *nf (grand-mère)* granny *, gran *.

mammifère [mamifɛʀ] *nm* mammal.

mammographie [mamɔgʀafi] *nf* mammography.

mammouth [mamut] *nm* mammoth.

manche[1] [mɑ̃ʃ] *nf* (**a**) *(Habillement)* sleeve. **à ~s longues** long-sleeved; **sans ~s** sleeveless; *(fig)* **avoir qn dans sa ~** to have sb in one's pocket. (**b**) *(partie) (gén, Pol, Sport)* round; *(Cartes)* game; *(Tennis)* set. (**c**) *(Géog)* **la M~** the English Channel. (**d**) **~ à air** *(Aviat)* wind sock; *(Naut)* airshaft.

manche[2] [mɑ̃ʃ] *nm* (**a**) *(gén)* handle; *(long)* shaft. **~ à balai** *(gén)* broomstick; *(Aviat)* joystick. (**b**) *(*: incapable)* clumsy fool.

manchette [mɑ̃ʃɛt] *nf* (**a**) *[chemise]* cuff; *(protectrice)* over-sleeve. (**b**) *(Presse)* headline. (**c**) *(Lutte)* forearm blow.

manchon [mɑ̃ʃɔ̃] *nm* muff.

manchot, -ote [mɑ̃ʃo, ɔt] **1** *adj (d'un bras)* one-armed; *(des deux bras)* armless; *(d'une main)* one-handed; *(des deux mains)* with no hands, handless. *(adroit)* **il n'est pas ~!** * he's clever with his hands! **2** *nm (Orn)* penguin.

mandale ⁑ [mɑ̃dal] *nf* biff *, clout, cuff.

mandarin [mɑ̃daʀɛ̃] *nm (Hist, péj)* mandarin.

mandarine [mɑ̃daʀin] *nf* mandarin (orange), tangerine.

mandat [mɑ̃da] *nm* (**a**) *(gén, Pol)* mandate. **donner à qn ~ de faire** to give sb a mandate to do. (**b**) *(Poste)* postal order, money order. (**c**) *(Jur: procuration)* power of attorney, proxy; *(Police etc)* warrant. **~ d'amener** ≃ summons; **~ d'arrêt** ≃ warrant for arrest; **placer qn sous ~ de dépôt** ≃ to place sb under a committal order; **~ d'expulsion** eviction order; *(Fin)* **~ international** international money order; **~ de perquisition** search warrant. ◆ **mandataire** *nmf (Jur)* proxy, attorney; *(représentant)* representative; *(aux Halles)* (sales) agent. ◆ **mandatement** *nm [somme]* payment (by money order). ◆ **mandater** (1) *vt* (**a**) *personne* to commission. (**b**) *somme* to make over.

Mandchourie [mɑ̃tʃuʀi] *nf* Manchuria.

mandoline [mɑ̃dɔlin] *nf* mandolin(e).

manège [manɛʒ] *nm* (**a**) **~ (de chevaux de bois)** roundabout, merry-go-round, carousel *(US)*. (**b**) *(Équitation) (école)* riding school; *(piste)* ring, school. (**c**) *(fig: agissements)* game, ploy.

manette [manɛt] *nf* lever, tap.

mange-disques [mɑ̃ʒdisk] *nm inv slot-in record player.*

manger [mɑ̃ʒe] (3) **1** *vt* (**a**) to eat. **il ne mange pas en ce moment** he's off his food at present; **vous mangerez bien un morceau avec nous?** * won't you have a bite to eat with us?; **cela se mange?** can you eat it?; **ça se mange chaud** it should be eaten hot; **donner à ~ à qn, faire ~ qn** to feed sb; **faire ~ qch à qn** to give sb sth to eat; **mange!** eat up!; **on mange bien/mal à cet hôtel** the food is good/bad at this hotel. (**b**) *(faire un repas)* **~ au restaurant** to eat out, have a meal out; **c'est l'heure de ~** *(midi)* it's lunchtime; *(soir)* it's dinnertime; **inviter qn à ~** to invite sb for a meal; **boire en mangeant** to drink with a meal; **~ sur le pouce** to have a (quick) snack. (**c**) *[soleil]* to fade; *[rouille]* to eat away. **mangé aux mites** moth-eaten. (**d**) *électricité, économies* to go through; *temps* to take up; *mots* to swallow. **les grosses entreprises mangent les petites** the big firms swallow up the smaller ones; **l'entreprise mange de l'argent** the business is wasting money. (**e**) *(locutions)* **~ la consigne** to forget one's errand; **~ comme quatre** to eat like a horse; **~ à sa faim** to have enough to eat; **~ du bout des dents** to pick *ou* nibble at one's food; *(fig)* **~ le morceau** ⁑ to spill the beans ⁑; **je ne mange pas de ce pain-là!** I'm having nothing to do with that!; **~ à tous les rateliers** * to cash in * on all sides; **~ qn des yeux** to devour sb with one's eyes.
2 *nm (nourriture)* food; *(repas)* meal.
◆ **mangeotter** * (1) *vt* to nibble. ◆ **mangeable** *adj* edible, eatable. ◆ **mangeaille** *nf (péj)* food. ◆ **mangeoire** *nf* trough, manger. ◆ **mangeur, -euse** *nm, f* eater.

mangoustan [mɑ̃gustɑ̃] *nm* mangosteen.

mangouste [mɑ̃gust(ə)] *nf (animal)* mongoose; *(fruit)* mangosteen.

mangue [mɑ̃g] *nf* mango *(fruit)*.

maniaque [manjak] **1** *adj* finicky, fussy. **2** *nmf (fou)* maniac, lunatic; *(fanatique)* fanatic; *(méticuleux)* fusspot *. ◆ **maniaco-dépressif, -ive** *adj* manic-depressive.

manichéen, -enne [manikeɛ̃, ɛn] *adj, nm, f* Manich(a)ean. ◆ **manichéisme** *nm (Philos)* Maniche(an)ism. **faire du ~** to see things in black and white.

manie [mani] *nf (habitude)* odd *ou* queer habit; *(obsession)* mania. **une de ses ~s** one of his (*ou* her) funny habits.

manier [manje] (7) *vt* to handle. ◆ **maniabilité** *nf* handiness, manageability; *[voiture]* driveability; *[avion]* manoeuvrability. ◆ **maniable** *adj* handy, manageable, easy to handle *ou* drive *ou* manœuvre. ◆ **maniement** *nm* handling. **d'un ~ difficile** difficult to handle; **~ d'armes** arms drill, manual of arms *(US)*.

manière [manjɛʀ] *nf* (**a**) *(façon)* way; *(Art: style)* style. **sa ~ de parler** his way of speaking, the way he speaks; **il le fera à sa ~** he'll do it his own way; **~ de vivre** way of life; **de quelle ~ as-tu fait cela?** how did you do that?; **à la ~ d'un singe** like a monkey; **c'est une ~ de pastiche** it's a kind of pastiche. (**b**) *(locutions)* **employer la ~ forte** to use strong-arm measures *ou* tactics; **en ~ d'excuse** by way of (an) excuse; **d'une certaine ~** in a way, in some ways; **d'une ~ générale** generally speaking; **de toute(s) ~(s)** in any case, anyway; **de telle ~ que** in such a way that; **d'une ~ ou d'une autre** somehow or other; **en aucune ~** in no way, under no circumstances; **de ~ à faire** so as to do; **de ~ (à ce) que nous arrivions à l'heure, de ~ à arriver à l'heure** so that we get there on time. (**c**) **~s**: **avoir de bonnes/mauvaises ~s** to have good/bad manners; **ce ne sont pas des ~s!** that's no way to behave!; **faire des ~s** *(minauderies)* to put on airs; *(chichis)* to make a fuss. ◆ **maniéré, e** *adj (péj: affecté)* affected; *(Art)* genre mannered.

manifester [manifɛste] (1) **1** *vt (gén)* to show; *sentiment* to express; *courage* to demonstrate. **~ le désir de faire** to indicate one's wish to do. **2** *vi (Pol)* to demonstrate. **3 se ~** *vpr* (**a**) *[émotion]* to show itself, express itself; *[difficultés]* to emerge, arise. **une certaine détente se manifesta** there was evidence of a certain thaw in the atmosphere. (**b**) *[candidat, témoin]* to come forward; *[personne] (se présenter)* to appear, turn up; *(se faire remarquer)* to make o.s. known, attract attention; *(dans un débat)* to make o.s. heard. **Dieu s'est manifesté aux hommes** God revealed himself to mankind. ◆ **manifestant, e** *nm, f* demonstrator, protestor. ◆ **manifestation** *nf* (**a**) *(Pol)* demonstration. (**b**) *[opinion, sentiment]* expression; *[maladie] (apparition)* appearance; *(symptômes)* outward sign. **~ de mauvaise humeur** show of bad temper. (**c**) *[Dieu, vérité]* revelation. (**d**) *(réunion, fête)* event. ◆ **manifeste 1** *adj* obvious, evident, manifest. **erreur ~** glaring error. **2** *nm (Littérat, Pol)* manifesto. ◆ **manifestement** *adv* obviously, evidently, manifestly.

manigancer [manigɑ̃se] (3) *vt* to plot, devise. **qu'est-ce qu'il manigance maintenant?** what's he up to now? ◆ **manigance** *nf* trick, scheme, ploy.

Manille [manij] *n* Manila.

manioc [manjɔk] *nm* manioc, cassava.

manipuler [manipyle] (1) *vt objet* to handle; *(péj) électeurs* to manipulate; *comptes* to rig, fiddle *. ◆ **manipulateur, -trice** *nmf (technicien)* technician. ◆ **manipulation** *nf (maniement)* handling; *(Scol: Chim, Phys)* experiment. *(Méd, péj)* **~s** manipulation; **les ~s génétiques posent des problèmes éthiques** genetic engineering poses ethical problems.

manitou [manitu] *nm* (**a**) **grand ~** * big shot *. (**b**) *(Rel)* manitou.

manivelle [manivɛl] *nf* crank.

manne [man] *nf (aubaine)* godsend. *(Rel)* **la ~** manna.

mannequin [mankɛ̃] *nm (personne)* model; *(objet)* dummy; *(fig: pantin)* stuffed dummy.

manœuvrer [manœvʀe] (1) **1** *vt véhicule* to manœuvre; *machine* to operate, work; *(fig: manipuler) personne* to manipulate. **2** *vi (gén)* to manœuvre. *(fig)* **il a manœuvré habilement** he moved *ou* manœuvred skilfully. ◆ **manœuvre 1** *nf (gén)* manœuvre. **la ~ d'un bateau est difficile** manœuvring a boat is difficult; *(Rail)* **faire la ~** to shunt; **~ d'encerclement** encircling movement; **~ d'obstruction** obstructive move; **~s frauduleuses** fraudulent schemes *ou* devices; **terrain de ~s** parade ground; **grandes ~s** army manœuvres *ou* exercises. **2** *nm (gén)* labourer; *(en usine)* unskilled worker. **~ agricole** farm labourer.

manoir [manwaʀ] *nm* manor house.

manomètre [manɔmɛtʀ(ə)] *nm* gauge, manometer.

manouche [manuʃ] *nmf (péj)* gipsy.

manquer [mɑ̃ke] (1) **1** *vt* (**a**) *photo, gâteau* to spoil, make a mess of; *examen* to fail; *but, train, personne* to miss. **je l'ai manqué de peu/de 5 minutes** I missed him by a fraction/by 5 minutes; **c'est à ne pas ~** it's a must *; *(iro)* **il n'en manque jamais une!** * he puts his foot in it every time! *; **~ sa vie** to waste one's life; **ils ont manqué leur coup** their attempt failed. (**b**) *(être absent de)* to be absent from, miss.
2 *vi* (**a**) *(faire défaut) (gén)* to be lacking. **l'argent vint à ~** money ran out *ou* ran short; **ce qui me manque c'est le temps** what I need *ou* lack is time; **les mots me manquent pour exprimer** I can't find (the) words to express; **le temps me manque pour dire** there's no time for me to say; **ce n'est pas**

l'envie *ou* **le désir qui me manque d'y aller** it's not that I don't want to go, it's not that I am unwilling to go; **le pied lui manqua** his foot slipped, he missed his footing. (**b**) *(être absent)* to be absent; *(avoir disparu)* to be missing. (**c**) *(échouer)* to fail.

3 ~ **à** *vt indir*: ~ **à son honneur** to fail in one's honour; ~ **à tous ses devoirs** to neglect all one's duties; ~ **à ses promesses** to renege on one's promises, fail to keep one's word; ~ **à l'appel** *(lit)* to be absent from roll call; *(fig)* to be missing; **il nous manque, sa présence nous manque** we miss him.

4 ~ **de** *vt indir* (**a**) *intelligence* to lack; *argent, main d'œuvre* to be short of, lack. **le pays ne manque pas d'un certain charme** the country is not without a certain charm; **on manque d'air ici** there's no air in here; **il ne manque pas d'audace!** he's got a nerve! (**b**) *(faillir)* **il a manqué mourir** he nearly *ou* almost died. (**c**) *(formules nég)* **ne manquez pas de le remercier** don't forget to thank him; **il n'a pas manqué de le lui dire** he made sure he told him; **nous ne manquerons pas de vous informer** we shall inform you without fail; **on ne peut** ~ **d'être frappé par** one cannot fail to marvel at, one cannot help but be struck by; **ça ne va pas** ~ **(d'arriver)** * it's bound to happen.

5 *vb impers*: **il (nous) manque 2 chaises** *(elles ont disparu)* there are 2 chairs missing; *(on en a besoin)* we are 2 chairs short, we are short of 2 chairs; **il ne manquera pas de gens pour dire** there'll be no shortage of people to say; **il ne manquait plus que ça** that's all we needed, that's the last straw.

6 se ~ *vpr (suicide)* to fail.

◆ **manquant, e** *adj* missing. ◆ **manque** *nm* (**a**) ~ **de** *(faiblesse)* lack of, want of; *(pénurie)* shortage of; **quel** ~ **de chance!** what bad *ou* hard luck!; ~ **à gagner** loss of profit. (**b**) ~**s** *[roman]* faults; *[personne]* failings, shortcomings; *[connaissances]* gaps. (**c**) *(vide)* gap, emptiness; *(Drogue)* withdrawal. (**d**) **à la** ~ ‡ *chanteur, idée* crummy ‡. ◆ **manqué, e** *adj essai* failed, abortive; *rendez-vous* missed; *photo* spoilt; *(Tech) pièce* faulty; *occasion* lost, wasted. **c'est un écrivain** ~ *(mauvais écrivain)* he is a failure as a writer; *(il aurait dû être écrivain)* he should have been a writer. ◆ **manquement** *nm*: ~ **à** *règle* breach of; **au moindre** ~ at the slightest lapse.

mansarde [mɑ̃saʀd(ə)] *nf* attic. ◆ **mansardé, e** *adj*: **chambre** ~**e** attic room.

mansuétude [mɑ̃sɥetyd] *nf* leniency, indulgence.

manteau, *pl* ~**x** [mɑ̃to] *nm* coat. ~ **trois-quarts** three-quarter length coat; **sous le** ~ clandestinely, on the sly; ~ **de cheminée** mantelpiece.

mantille [mɑ̃tij] *nf* mantilla.

manucure [manykyʀ] *nmf* manicurist. ◆ **manucurer** (1) *vt* to manicure.

manuel, -elle [manɥɛl] **1** *adj* manual. **2** *nm (livre)* manual, handbook. ~ **de lecture** reader; ~ **scolaire** textbook. ◆ **manuellement** *adv* manually.

manufacture [manyfaktyʀ] *nf (usine)* factory; *(fabrication)* manufacture. ◆ **manufacturer** (1) *vt* to manufacture.

manuscrit, e [manyskʀi, it] **1** *adj* handwritten. **pages** ~**es** manuscript pages. **2** *nm* manuscript; *(dactylographié)* typescript.

manutention [manytɑ̃sjɔ̃] *nf (opération)* handling; *(local)* storehouse. *(Com)* **frais de** ~ handling charges. ◆ **manutentionnaire** *nmf* packer.

mappemonde [mapmɔ̃d] *nf (carte)* map of the world; *(sphère)* globe.

maquereau, *pl* ~**x** [makʀo] *nm (poisson)* mackerel; (‡) *(proxénète)* pimp, ponce ‡.

maquette [makɛt] *nf* (scale) model.

maquiller [makije] (1) **1** *vt visage* to make up; *vérité, faits* to fake, doctor; *chiffres* to fiddle *; *voiture* to do over *, disguise. **meurtre maquillé en accident** murder faked up to look like an accident. **2 se** ~ *vpr* to make up. ◆ **maquillage** *nm* make-up. **le** ~ **des faits** faking the facts.

maquis [maki] *nm (Géog)* scrub, bush; *(labyrinthe)* maze; *(Hist)* maquis. **prendre le** ~ to go underground. ◆ **maquisard, e** *nm, f* maquis.

maraîcher, -ère [maʀeʃe, maʀɛʃɛʀ] **1** *nm, f* market gardener, truck farmer *(US)*. **2** *adj*: **produits** ~**s** market garden produce, truck *(US)*.

marais [maʀɛ] *nm* marsh, swamp. ~ **salant** saltern.

marasme [maʀasm(ə)] *nm* (**a**) *(Écon, Pol)* stagnation, slump. (**b**) *(accablement)* dejection, depression.

marathon [maʀatɔ̃] *nm (Sport, fig)* marathon. ◆ **marathonien** *nm* marathon runner.

marâtre [maʀɑtʀ(ə)] *nf* cruel mother.

marauder [maʀode] (1) *vi* to thieve, pilfer. ◆ **maraude** *nf* thieving, pilfering. **taxi en** ~ cruising *ou* prowling taxi. ◆ **maraudeur, -euse** *nm, f* *(voleur)* prowler; *(soldat)* marauder.

marbre [maʀbʀ(ə)] *nm (Géol)* marble; *(surface)* marble top; *(Typ)* stone, bed. **rester de** ~ to be stony-faced; **avoir un cœur de** ~ to have a heart of stone; *(Aut)* **passer une voiture au** ~ to check a car for structural damage. ◆ **marbrer** (1) *vt papier, cuir* to marble; *peau, bois* to mottle. **(gâteau) marbré** marble cake. ◆ **marbrier** *nm (funéraire)* monumental mason. ◆ **marbrure** *nf*: ~**(s)** marbling; mottling.

marc [maʀ] *nm (raisin)* marc; *(alcool)* brandy. ~ **(de café)** (coffee) grounds *ou* dregs.

marcassin [maʀkasɛ̃] *nm* young wild boar.

marchand, e [maʀʃɑ̃, ɑ̃d] **1** *adj valeur* market. **2** *nm, f* shopkeeper; *(sur un marché)* stallholder; *[vins, fruits, charbon, grains]* merchant; *[meubles, bestiaux]* dealer. ~ **au détail** retailer; ~ **en gros** wholesaler; **la** ~**e de chaussures** the woman in the shoeshop. **3** : ~ **ambulant** hawker, pedlar; ~ **de biens** ≃ estate agent, realtor *(US)*; ~ **de couleurs** ironmonger, hardware dealer; ~ **de journaux** newsagent; ~ **de légumes** greengrocer, produce dealer *(US)*; ~ **de quatre saisons** costermonger; ~ **de sable** sandman; ~ **de tapis** carpet dealer; **des discussions de** ~ **de tapis** fierce bargaining, endless haggling.

marchander [maʀʃɑ̃de] (1) *vt objet* to haggle over, bargain over; *(emploi absolu)* to haggle, bargain. **il n'a pas marchandé ses compliments** he wasn't sparing of his compliments. ◆ **marchandage** *nm* bargaining, haggling. ◆ **marchandisage** *nm* marketing. ◆ **marchandise** *nf (article)* commodity. ~**s** goods, merchandise; *(stock)* **la** ~ the goods *ou* merchandise; **gare de** ~ goods station; **il a de la bonne** ~ he sells good stuff; **vanter la** ~ * to show o.s. off to advantage.

marche[1] [maʀʃ(ə)] *nf* (**a**) *(action, Sport)* walking. **poursuivre sa** ~ to walk on; **chaussures de** ~ walking shoes. (**b**) *(démarche)* walk, step; *(rythme)* pace, step. (**c**) *(trajet)* walk. **c'est à 2 heures de** ~ it's a 2-hour walk from here. (**d**) *(Mus, Mil, Pol)* march. **chanson de** ~ marching song; **fermer la** ~ to bring up the rear; **ouvrir la** ~ to lead the way; **faire** ~ **sur** to march upon; **en avant,** ~! forward march! (**e**) *[véhicule]* running; *[machine, usine]* running, working; *[navire]* sailing; *[étoile]* course; *[horloge]* working. **dans le sens de la** ~ facing the engine; **dans le sens contraire de la** ~ with one's back to the engine; **véhicule en** ~ moving vehicle; **en état de** ~ in working order; *(Tech)* ~ — **arrêt** on — off; ~ **arrière** reverse; **faire** ~ **arrière** *(Aut)* to reverse; *(fig)* to back-pedal, backtrack; ~ **à suivre** (correct) procedure; *(mode d'emploi)* directions (for use). (**f**) *[maladie]* progress; *[événements]* course; *[temps, progrès]* march. (**g**) **être en ~** *[personnes]* to be on the move; *[moteur etc]* to be running; **se mettre en ~** *[personne]* to get moving; *[machine]* to start; **mettre en ~** *voiture* to start (up); *machine* to set going.

marche² [maʀʃ(ə)] *nf [escalier]* step. **sur les ~s** on the stairs; *(escalier extérieur, escabeau)* on the steps.

marché [maʀʃe] **1** *nm* (**a**) *(lieu)* market; *(ville)* trading centre. **faire son ~** to go to the market; *(plus gén)* to go shopping. (**b**) *(Écon, Fin)* market. **lancer qch sur le ~** to launch sth on the market; **le ~ du travail** the labour market; **le ~ des valeurs** the stockmarket. (**c**) *(transaction)* bargain, deal. **passer un ~ avec qn** to make a deal with sb; **~ conclu!** it's a deal!; **mettre le ~ en main à qn** to force sb to accept or refuse. **2** : **le M~ commun** the Common Market, the E.E.C; **~ noir** black market; **~ aux puces** flea market.

marchepied [maʀʃəpje] *nm (Rail)* step; *(Aut)* running board; *(fig)* stepping stone.

marcher [maʀʃe] (1) *vi* (**a**) to walk; *[soldats]* to march. **~ à grands pas** to stride (along); **on va ~ un peu** let's have a walk, let's go for a walk; **faire ~ un bébé** to help a baby walk; **son père saura le faire ~ droit** his father will soon have him toeing the line; **~ dans une flaque d'eau** to step in a puddle; **défense de ~ sur les pelouses** keep off the grass; *(lit, fig)* **~ sur les pieds de qn** to tread on sb's toes; **~ sur les pas de qn** to follow in sb's footsteps; **il marche à côté de ses pompes *** he doesn't know what he's doing; **~ sur une ville** to advance on a town. (**b**) (*) *(consentir)* to agree; *(être dupé)* to be taken in. **il n'a pas voulu ~ dans la combine** he did not want to get mixed up in the business; **faire ~ qn** *(taquiner)* to pull sb's leg; *(tromper)* to take sb for a ride *. (**c**) *(avec véhicule)* **le train a bien marché jusqu'à Lyon** the train made good time as far as Lyons; **nous marchions à 100 à l'heure** we were doing a hundred. (**d**) *[appareil, usine]* to work; *[ruse]* to come off; *[affaires, études]* to go (well). **faire ~** *appareil* to work, operate; *entreprise* to run; **ça fait ~ les affaires** it's good for business; **est-ce que le métro marche?** is the underground running?; **ces deux opérations marchent ensemble** these two procedures go *ou* work together; **les études, ça marche? *** how's the work going? ◆ **marcheur, -euse** *nm, f (gén)* walker; *(Pol etc)* marcher.

mardi [maʀdi] *nm* Tuesday. **M~ gras** Shrove Tuesday; *V* **samedi**.

mare [maʀ] *nf (étang)* pond; *(flaque)* pool. **~ de sang** pool of blood.

marécage [maʀekaʒ] *nm* marsh, swamp, bog. ◆ **marécageux, -euse** *adj* marshy, swampy, boggy.

maréchal, *pl* **-aux** [maʀeʃal, o] *nm (Mil)* marshal. **~-ferrant** blacksmith; **~ des logis** sergeant.

marée [maʀe] *nf* (**a**) tide. **~ montante/descendante** flood *ou* rising/ebb tide; **à ~ basse/haute** at low/high tide *ou* water; **~ noire** oil slick, black tide. (**b**) *(fig)* flood. (**c**) *(poissons)* **la ~** fresh (sea) fish.

marelle [maʀɛl] *nf* hopscotch.

margarine [maʀgaʀin] *nf* margarine, marge *.

marge [maʀʒ(ə)] **1** *nf (gén)* margin. **j'ai encore de la ~** I still have time (*ou* money *etc*) to spare; **en ~ de la société** on the fringe of society; **vivre en ~ du monde** to live cut off from the world. **2** : **~ bénéficiaire** profit margin, mark-up; **~ d'erreur** margin of error; **~ de manœuvre** room to manœuvre; **~ de sécurité** safety margin. ◆ **marginal, e,** *mpl* **-aux** **1** *adj (gén, Écon)* marginal; *coût* incremental. **2** *nm (artiste, homme politique)* independent; *(déshérité)* dropout. *(contestataires)* **les ~aux** the dissident minority *ou* fringe.

marguerite [maʀgəʀit] *nf (Bot)* marguerite, (oxeye) daisy; *(Typ)* daisy wheel. **imprimante à ~** daisy wheel printer.

mari [maʀi] *nm* husband.

mariage [maʀjaʒ] *nm* (**a**) *(union)* marriage. **50 ans de ~** 50 years of married life *ou* of marriage; **on parle de ~ entre eux** there is talk of their getting married; **donner qn en ~ à** to give sb in marriage to; **~ d'amour** love match; **faire un ~ d'argent** to marry for money. (**b**) *(cérémonie)* wedding. **cadeau de ~** wedding present. (**c**) *[couleurs, parfums]* marriage, blend. ◆ **marié, e** **1** *adj* married. **non ~** unmarried, single. **2** *nm* (bride)groom. **les ~s** *(jour du mariage)* the bride and (bride)groom; *(après le mariage)* the newly-weds. **3** *nf* bride. **trouver que la ~e est trop belle** to object that everything's too good to be true; **robe de ~e** wedding dress. ◆ **marier** (7) **1** *vt personne* to marry; *couleurs, goûts* to blend, harmonize. **il a encore 2 filles à ~** he still has 2 daughters to marry off; *(fig)* **on n'est pas mariés avec lui!** * we don't have to suit him all the time!, we're not obliged to do as he says! **2 se ~** *vpr [personne]* to get married; *[couleurs, goûts]* to blend, harmonize. **se ~ à** *ou* **avec qn** to marry sb, get married to sb.

marijuana [maʀiʒɥana] *nf* marijuana, pot *(arg)*.

marin, e¹ [maʀɛ̃, in] **1** *adj air* sea; *faune* marine, sea. **missile ~** sea-based missile; **costume ~** sailor suit. **2** *nm* sailor; *(grade)* ordinary seaman. **~ d'eau douce** landlubber.

marine² [maʀin] **1** *nf* (**a**) navy. **terme de ~** nautical term; **~ (de guerre)** navy; **~ marchande** merchant navy. (**b**) *(tableau)* seascape. **2** *nm (soldat)* marine.

mariner [maʀine] (1) *vti* to marinade. **harengs marinés** soused *ou* pickled herrings.

marionnette [maʀjɔnɛt] *nf (lit, fig)* puppet. *(spectacle)* **~s** puppet show; **~ à fils** marionette; **~ à gaine** glove puppet. ◆ **marionnettiste** *nmf* puppeteer.

marital, e, *mpl* **-aux** [maʀital, o] *adj: (Jur)* **autorisation ~e** husband's permission *ou* authorization. ◆ **maritalement** *adv*: **vivre ~** to live as husband and wife.

maritime [maʀitim] *adj (gén)* maritime; *province* seaboard, coastal; *commerce, droit* shipping.

marmaille * [maʀmɑj] *nf* gang of kids * *ou* brats * *(péj)*.

marmelade [maʀməlad] *nf* stewed fruit, compote. *(lit, fig)* **réduire en ~** to reduce to a pulp.

marmite [maʀmit] *nf* (cooking-)pot.

marmonner [maʀmɔne] (1) *vti* to mumble, mutter. **~ dans sa barbe** to mutter into one's beard, mutter to o.s. ◆ **marmonnement** *nm*: **~(s)** mumbling, muttering.

marmot * [maʀmo] *nm* kid *, brat * *(péj)*.

marmotte [maʀmɔt] *nf (Zool)* marmot; *(fig)* dormouse.

marmotter [maʀmɔte] (1) *vti* to mumble, mutter.

Maroc [maʀɔk] *nm* Morocco. ◆ **marocain, e** *adj*, **M~(e)** *nm (f)* Moroccan.

maroquin [maʀɔkɛ̃] *nm (cuir)* morocco (leather); *(fig: portefeuille)* (minister's) portfolio. ◆ **maroquinerie** *nf (boutique)* shop selling fine leather goods; *(métier)* fine leather trade. **(articles de) ~** fine leather goods. ◆ **maroquinier** *nm* dealer in fine leather goods.

marotte [maʀɔt] *nf* hobby, craze.

marquer [maʀke] (1) **1** *vt* (**a**) *(par une trace) (gén, fig)* to mark; *animal, criminel* to brand; *arbre* to blaze; *marchandise* to label, stamp. **j'ai marqué nos places avec nos valises** I've reserved our seats with our cases; **pour ~ cette journée** to mark this day; **la souffrance l'a marqué** suffering has left its mark on him; *(influencer)* **~ son époque** to put

one's mark *ou* stamp on one's time. (**b**) *(indiquer, montrer) (gén)* to show; *[balance]* to register. **la pendule marque 6 heures** the clock points to *ou* shows 6 o'clock; **robe qui marque la taille** dress which shows off *ou* emphasizes the waistline; **cela marque bien que le pays veut la paix** that definitely indicates that the country wants peace; **la déception se marquait sur son visage** disappointment showed in his face *ou* was written all over his face. (**c**) *(écrire)* to note down, make a note of. **on l'a marqué absent** he was marked absent; **qu'y a-t-il de marqué?** what does it say?, what's written on it? (**d**) *(Sport) joueur* to mark; *but* to score. ~ **qn de très près** to mark sb very closely *ou* tightly. (**e**) *(locutions)* ~ **le coup** * to mark the occasion; ~ **un point sur qn** to be one up on sb; ~ **la mesure** to keep the beat; *(lit, fig)* ~ **le pas** to mark time; ~ **un temps d'arrêt** to mark a pause.
2 *vi* (**a**) *[événement, personnalité]* to stand out; *[coup]* to reach home, tell. (**b**) *[crayon]* to write; *[tampon]* to stamp. **ne pose pas le verre là, ça marque** don't put the glass down there, it will leave a mark. ◆ **marquant, e** *adj personnage, événement* outstanding; *souvenir* vivid. **le fait le plus** ~ the most significant *ou* striking fact. ◆ **marque** *nf* (**a**) *(repère, trace) (lit, fig)* mark; *[linge personnel]* name tab; *[viande, œufs]* stamp. ~**s de doigts** fingermarks, fingerprints; ~**s de pas** footmarks, footprints; *(Sport)* **à vos** ~**s! prêts! partez!** on your marks!, get set!, go!, ready, steady, go!; ~ **de confiance** sign *ou* mark of confidence; **la** ~ **du génie** the hallmark of genius. (**b**) *(Comm) [nourriture]* brand; *[produits manufacturés]* make. ~ **de fabrique** trademark, trade name; ~ **déposée** registered trademark *ou* trade name; **produits de** ~ high-class products; **visiteur de** ~ important *ou* distinguished visitor, V.I.P. (**c**) *(Sport, Cartes: décompte)* **la** ~ the score. ◆ **marqué, e** *adj (accentué)* marked, pronounced; *(Ling)* marked. **le prix** ~ the marked price, the price on the label; *(fig)* **c'est un homme** ~ he's a marked man; **il est** ~ **par la vie** life has left its mark on him. ◆ **marqueur** *nm (stylo effaçable)* felt-tip pen; *(stylo indélébile)* marker pen.

marquis [maʀki] *nm* marquess.

marquise [maʀkiz] *nf* (**a**) *(noble)* marchioness. (**b**) *(auvent)* glass canopy. (**c**) *(Culin)* ~ **au chocolat** *type of chocolate ice-cream.*

marraine [maʀɛn] *nf [enfant]* godmother; *[navire]* christener, namer.

marre ‡ [maʀ] *adv*: **en avoir** ~ to be fed up * (*de* with), be sick * (*de* of).

marrer (se) ‡ [maʀe] (1) *vpr* to laugh. ◆ **marrant, e** * *adj (amusant)* funny, killing *; *(étrange)* funny, odd.

marron [maʀɔ̃] **1** *nm* (**a**) chestnut. ~ **d'Inde** horse chestnut; ~**s chauds** roast chestnuts; ~ **glacé** marron glacé; **tirer les** ~**s du feu** *(profiter)* to steal a march; *(être victime)* to be a cat's paw. (**b**) *(couleur)* brown. (**c**) (‡: *coup)* thump, clout. **2** *adj inv* (**a**) *(couleur)* brown. (**b**) (‡: *être trompé)* **être** ~ to be had *. ◆ **marronnier** *nm* chestnut tree. ~ **(d'Inde)** horse chestnut tree.

Mars [maʀs] **1** *nm (Myth)* Mars. **2** *nf (planète)* Mars.

mars [maʀs] *nm (mois)* March; *V* **septembre**.

Marseille [maʀsɛj] *n* Marseilles. ◆ **marseillais, e** **1** *adj* of *ou* from Marseilles. **2** *nm, f:* **M~(e)** inhabitant *ou* native of Marseilles. **3** *nf:* **la M~e** the Marseillaise *(French National anthem).*

marsouin [maʀswɛ̃] *nm (Zool)* porpoise.

marteau, *pl* ~**x** [maʀto] **1** *nm* hammer; *[horloge]* striker; *[porte]* knocker. **entre le** ~ **et l'enclume** between the devil and the deep blue sea; **être** ~ * to be nuts * *ou* cracked *. **2** : ~**-pilon** *nm, pl* ~**x-**~**s** power hammer; ~**-piqueur** *nm, pl* ~**x-**~**s** pneumatic drill. ◆ **martèlement** *nm*: ~**(s)** hammering, pounding. ◆ **marteler** (5) *vt* to hammer, pound; *mots* to hammer out; *objet d'art* to planish, beat. **cuivre martelé** planished *ou* beaten copper; *(Mus)* **notes martelées** martelé notes.

martial, e, *mpl* **-aux** [maʀsjal, o] *adj* martial.

martien, -ienne [maʀsjɛ̃, jɛn] *adj, nm, f* Martian.

martinet [maʀtinɛ] *nm* (**a**) small whip. (**b**) *(Orn)* swift.

Martinique [maʀtinik] *nf* Martinique. ◆ **martiniquais, e** **1** *adj* of *ou* from Martinique. **2** *nm, f:* **M~(e)** inhabitant *ou* native of Martinique.

martin-pêcheur, *pl* **martins-pêcheurs** [maʀtɛ̃ pɛʃœʀ] *nm* kingfisher.

martre [maʀtʀ(ə)] *nf* marten. ~ **zibeline** sable.

martyr, e[1] [maʀtiʀ] **1** *adj peuple* martyred. **mère** ~**e** stricken mother; **enfant** ~ battered child. **2** *nm, f* martyr. ◆ **martyre**[2] *nm (Rel, fig)* martyrdom. **mettre au** ~ to martyrize; **souffrir le** ~ to suffer agonies. ◆ **martyriser** (1) *vt personne, animal* to martyrize; *élève* to bully; *enfant* to batter; *(Rel)* to martyr.

marxisme [maʀksism(ə)] *nm* Marxism. ◆ **marxiste** *adj, nmf* Marxist. ~**-léniniste** *adj, nmf* MarxistLeninist.

mascara [maskaʀa] *nm* mascara.

mascarade [maskaʀad] *nf* masquerade. **ce procès est une** ~ this trial is a farce.

mascotte [maskɔt] *nf* mascot.

masculin, e [maskylɛ̃, in] **1** *adj (gén)* male; *(viril)* manly; *(péj: hommasse)* mannish; *(Gram)* masculine. **2** *nm (Gram)* masculine.

masochisme [mazɔʃism(ə)] *nm* masochism. ◆ **masochiste** **1** *adj* masochistic. **2** *nmf* masochist.

masque [mask(ə)] *nm (gén, fig)* mask. **jeter le** ~ to unmask o.s.; ~ **antirides** face pack; ~ **à gaz/de plongée** gas/diving mask. ◆ **masqué, e** *adj bandit* masked; *enfant* wearing a mask. *(Aut)* **sortie** ~**e** concealed exit. ◆ **masquer** (1) **1** *vt (gén)* to mask, conceal (*à qn* from sb); *lumière* to screen, shade. ~ **la vue** to block (out) the view; ~ **l'essentiel** to mask *ou* obscure the essential point. **2 se** ~ *vpr* (**a**) *(mettre un masque)* to put on a mask. (**b**) *(se cacher) [sentiment]* to be hidden; *[personne]* to hide, conceal o.s. (*derrière* behind). ◆ **masquage** *nm* masking.

massacre [masakʀ(ə)] *nm* slaughter, massacre. *[gibier]* **c'est du** ~ it is sheer butchery; *(sabotage)* **c'est un vrai** ~! * it's a real mess! ◆ **massacrer** (1) *vt* (**a**) *(tuer)* to slaughter, massacre; *animaux* to slaughter. **se** ~ to massacre *ou* slaughter one another. (**b**) (*) *opéra* to murder; *travail* to make a mess *ou* hash * of; *adversaire* to make mincemeat * of. ◆ **massacreur, -euse** * *nm, f (saboteur)* bungler.

masse [mas] *nf* (**a**) *(volume, Phys)* mass; *(forme)* massive shape. ~ **de nuages** bank of clouds; ~ **monétaire** amount of money in circulation; **taillé dans la** ~ carved from the block; **tomber comme une** ~ to fall in a heap. (**b**) *(foule)* **la** ~, **les** ~**s** the masses; **la** ~ **des lecteurs** the majority of readers; **manifestation de** ~ mass demonstration; **une** ~ **de** *, **des** ~**s de** * *objets* masses of, loads of *; *touristes* crowds of; **il n'y en a pas des** ~**s** * *[objets]* there aren't very many; *[argent]* there isn't very much. (**c**) *(Élec)* earth, ground *(US).* **faire** ~ to act as an earth *ou* a ground *(US).* (**d**) *(maillet)* sledgehammer; *[huissier]* mace. ~ **d'armes** mace. (**e**) **exécutions en** ~ mass executions; **fabriquer en** ~ to mass-produce; **venir en** ~ to come in a body *ou* en masse.

massepain [maspɛ̃] *nm* marzipan.

masser[1] *vt,* **se** ~ *vpr* [mase] (1) to mass.

masser[2] [mase] (1) *vt personne* to massage. **se faire** ~ to have a massage. ◆ **massage** *nm* massage.

◆ **masseur, -euse** *nm, f* masseur, masseuse. ~ **kinésithérapeute** physiotherapist.

massif, -ive [masif, iv] **1** *adj* (**a**) *meuble, bâtiment* massive, solid; *personne* sturdily built. (**b**) *(pur)* **or/chêne** ~ solid gold/oak. (**c**) *dose* massive, heavy. **départs ~s** mass exodus *(sg)*. **2** *nm (Géog)* massif; *[fleurs, arbres]* clump. ◆ **massivement** *adv répondre* en masse; *injecter* in massive doses. **ils ont ~ approuvé le projet** the overwhelming *ou* massive majority was in favour of the project.

mass(-)media [masmedja] *nmpl* mass media.

massue [masy] *nf* club, bludgeon.

mastiquer [mastike] (1) *vt* (**a**) *(Bio)* to chew, masticate. (**b**) *vitre* to putty; *fissure* to fill. ◆ **mastic 1** *nm [vitrier]* putty; *[menuisier]* filler, mastic. **2** *adj* putty-coloured, off-white.

mastodonte [mastɔdɔ̃t] *nm (Zool)* mastodon; *(fig hum)* great hulk.

masure [mazyʀ] *nf* hovel.

mat[1] [mat] *(Échecs)* **1** *adj inv*: **être** ~ to be checkmate; **faire** ~ to checkmate. **2** *nm* checkmate.

mat[2]**, e** [mat] *adj métal, couleur* mat(t), dull; *peinture, teint* mat(t). **bruit** ~ dull noise, thud.

mât [mɑ] *nm (Naut)* mast; *(pylône)* pole, post; *(hampe)* flagpole; *(Sport)* climbing pole. ~ **d'artimon** mizzenmast; ~ **de charge** derrick; ~ **de cocagne** greasy pole; ~ **de misaine** foremast.

matador [matadɔʀ] *nm* matador, bullfighter.

mataf [mataf] *nm (arg Marine)* sailor.

matamore [matamɔʀ] *nm (fanfaron)* bully boy. **faire le** ~ to throw one's weight around.

match [matʃ] *nm (Sport)* match, game *(US)*. ~ **aller/retour** first/second leg; ~ **nul** draw, tie *(US)*; **faire ~ nul** to draw, tie *(US)*.

matelas [matla] *nm* mattress. ~ **pneumatique** air mattress *ou* bed, Lilo ®. ◆ **matelasser** (1) *vt meuble* to pad; *tissu* to quilt. **veste matelassée** quilted *ou* padded jacket. ◆ **matelassier, -ière** *nm, f* mattress maker.

matelot [matlo] *nm (gén: marin)* sailor, seaman; *(dans la Marine de guerre)* ordinary rating, seaman recruit *(US)*.

mater [mate] (1) *vt* (**a**) *rebelles, enfant* to subdue; *terroristes* to bring *ou* get under control; *révolution* to put down, quell; *incendie* to bring under control. (**b**) *(Échecs)* to checkmate, mate. (**c**) *(marteler)* to burr.

matérialiser [mateʀjalize] (1) **1** *vt (concrétiser)* to make materialize; *(symboliser)* to embody. **2 se** ~ *vpr* to materialize. ◆ **matérialisation** *nf* materialization.

matérialisme [mateʀjalism(ə)] *nm* materialism. ◆ **matérialiste 1** *adj* materialistic. **2** *nmf* materialist.

matériau [mateʀjo] *nm inv (Constr)* material. ◆ **matériaux** *nmpl (Constr)* materials; *(documents)* material.

matériel, -elle [mateʀjɛl] **1** *adj (gén)* material; *(financier)* financial; *(pratique) organisation* practical. **je n'ai pas le temps ~ de le faire** I simply have not the time to do it. **2** *nm (équipement)* equipment, materials; *(attirail)* gear; *(fig: corpus)* material. *(Ordin)* **le** ~ the hardware; ~ **de bureau** *(meubles)* office equipment; *(fournitures)* office materials ; ~ **d'exploitation** plant; ~ **de guerre** weaponry ; ~ **roulant** rolling stock. ◆ **matériellement** *adv* materially; financially; practically.

maternel, -elle [matɛʀnɛl] *adj* (**a**) *(gén)* maternal; *geste, amour* motherly. **il avait gardé les habitudes ~les** he had retained his mother's habits. (**b**) **(école) ~le** (state) nursery school. ◆ **maternellement** *adv* maternally, like a mother. ◆ **maternité** *nf* (**a**) *(bâtiment)* maternity hospital *ou* home. (**b**) *(accouchement)* pregnancy. (**c**) *(état de mère)* motherhood, maternity. ◆ **materner** (1) *vt* to mother, baby *, cosset; *(mâcher le travail)* to spoon-feed. **se faire** ~ to be babied *; to be spoonfed. ◆ **maternage** *nm* mothering, babying *, cosseting; spoon-feeding.

mathématique [matematik] **1** *adj* mathematical. **c'est ~!** * it's bound to happen, it's logical! **2** *nfpl*: **les ~s** mathematics. ◆ **math(s)** * *nfpl* maths *, math * *(US)*. ◆ **mathématicien, -ienne** *nm, f* mathematician. ◆ **mathématiquement** *adv* mathematically. ◆ **matheux, -euse** * *nm, f (Scol)* maths *ou* math *(US)* specialist; *(hum)* maths expert.

matière [matjɛʀ] **1** *nf (produit)* material, substance; *(sujet, Scol)* subject. **la** ~ matter; **fournir la ~ d'un discours** to provide the material *ou* subject matter for a speech; **ignorant en la** ~ ignorant on the matter *ou* subject; **en ~ poétique** as far as poetry is concerned, as regards poetry; **donner ~ à plaisanter** to give cause for laughter; **ça lui a donné ~ à réflexion** it gave him food for thought; **il n'y a pas là ~ à se réjouir** this is no matter for rejoicing. **2** : **~(s) grasse(s)** fat content, fat; **~s fécales** faeces; *(lit, fig)* ~ **grise** grey matter; ~ **plastique** plastic; ~ **première** raw material.

matin [matɛ̃] *nm* morning. **le 10 au** ~ on the morning of the 10th; **2h du** ~ 2 a.m., 2 in the morning; **du ~ au soir** from morning till night; **de bon** ~ early in the morning. ◆ **matinal, e,** *mpl* **-aux** *adj tâches* morning; *heure* early. **être** ~ to be an early riser, get up early. ◆ **matinée** *nf* (**a**) *(matin)* morning. **en fin de** ~ at the end of the morning. (**b**) *(Ciné, Théât)* matinée, afternoon performance. ~ **dansante** afternoon dance; ~ **enfantine** children's matinée.

matois, e [matwa, waz] *adj* wily, sly, crafty.

maton [matɔ̃] *nm (arg Prison)* screw.

matou [matu] *nm* tomcat.

matraque [matʀak] *nf [police]* truncheon, billy *(US)*, night stick *(US)*; *[malfaiteur]* cosh, club. ◆ **matraquer** (1) *vt* (**a**) *[police]* to beat up; *[malfaiteur]* to cosh, club. *(* fig)* ~ **le client** to soak ‡ *ou* overcharge customers. (**b**) *(Rad) publicité* to plug, hype *; *public* to bombard (*de* with). ◆ **matraquage** *nm* beating up; plugging; bombarding. **le ~ publicitaire** media hype * *ou* overkill.

matrice [matʀis] *nf (utérus)* womb; *(Tech)* mould, die; *(Typ, Ling, Math)* matrix.

matricule [matʀikyl] *nm (Mil)* regimental number; *(Admin)* reference number.

matrimonial, e, *mpl* **-aux** [matʀimɔnjal, o] *adj* matrimonial.

matrone [matʀɔn] *nf (péj) (mère de famille)* matronly woman; *(femme forte)* stout woman.

mâture [mɑtyʀ] *nf* masts. **dans la** ~ aloft.

maturité [matyʀite] *nf* maturity. **venir à** ~ to come to maturity; **manquer de** ~ to be immature. ◆ **mature** *adj (mûr)* mature.

maudire [modiʀ] (2) *vt* to curse. ◆ **maudit, e 1** *adj* (**a**) *(*: sacré)* blasted *, confounded *. (**b**) *(littér)* **poète** ~ accursed poet; **~e soit la guerre!** cursed be the war! **2** *nm, f* damned soul. **les ~s** the damned. **3** *nm*: **le M~** the Devil.

maugréer [mogʀee] (1) *vi* to grouse, grumble (*contre* about, at).

Maurice [mɔʀis] *nf*: **(l'île)** ~ Mauritius. ◆ **mauricien, -ienne** *adj*, **M~(ne)** *nm(f)* Mauritian.

Mauritanie [mɔʀitani] *nf* Mauritania. ◆ **mauritanien, -ienne** *adj*, **M~(ne)** *nm(f)* Mauritanian.

mausolée [mozɔle] *nm* mausoleum.

maussade [mosad] *adj (gén)* gloomy, sullen.

mauvais, e [mɔvɛ, ɛz] **1** *adj* (**a**) *(en qualité) (gén)* bad; *appareil* faulty; *santé, film, élève* poor. **~e excuse** poor *ou* lame excuse; *(Élec)* **~ contact** faulty contact; **~ en géographie** bad *ou* weak at geography. (**b**) *(erroné)* wrong. **le ~ numéro** the wrong number; **c'est un ~ calcul de sa part** he's badly misjudged it; **il ne serait pas ~ de se renseigner** it wouldn't be a bad idea if we found out more about this. (**c**) *(inapproprié) jour, heure* awkward, bad, inconvenient. **il a choisi un ~ moment** he picked an awkward *ou* a bad time. (**d**) *(nuisible) (gén)* bad; *blessure* nasty; *temps, goût, odeur* unpleasant; *sourire, joie, personne* malicious, spiteful. *(Scol)* **~e note** bad mark; **la mer est ~e** the sea is rough; **être en ~e posture** to be in a tricky *ou* nasty position; **la soupe a un ~ goût** the soup tastes nasty; **il a passé un ~ quart d'heure** he had a nasty time of it; **ce n'est pas un ~ garçon** he's not a bad boy; **aujourd'hui il fait ~** today the weather is bad; **prendre qch en ~e part** to take sth in bad part, take sth amiss; **faire contre ~e fortune bon cœur** to put a brave face on things; **se faire du ~ sang** to worry, get in a state.
2 *nm*: **enlève le ~ et mange le reste** cut out the bad part and eat the rest; *(personnes)* **les ~** the wicked.
3 : **~ coucheur** awkward customer; **recevoir un ~ coup** to get a nasty blow; **faire un ~ coup** to commit a crime; **~ esprit** troublemaker; **faire du ~ esprit** to make snide remarks; **~ garçon** tough; **c'est de la ~e graine** he's (*ou* she's) a bad lot; **~e herbe** weed; **~e langue** gossip, scandalmonger; **~ lieu** place of ill repute; **le ~ œil** the evil eye; **tirer qn d'un ~ pas** to get sb out of a tight spot *ou* corner; **~e passe** difficult situation; **~ plaisant** hoaxer; **faire la ~e tête** to sulk; **~ traitement** ill treatment; **~ traitements à enfants** child abuse, child battering; **faire subir de ~ traitements à** to ill-treat.

mauve [mov] **1** *adj, nm (couleur)* mauve. **2** *nf (Bot)* mallow.

mauviette [movjɛt] *nf (péj)* weakling.

maxi... [maksi] *préf*: maxi...

maxillaire [maksilɛʀ] **1** *adj* maxillary. **2** *nm* jawbone.

maxime [maksim] *nf* maxim.

maximum [maksimɔm], *f* **~** *ou* **maxima** [maksima], *pl* **~s** *ou* **maxima** *adj, nm* maximum. **la température ~** the maximum *ou* highest temperature; **au** *(grand)* **~** at the (very) maximum, at the (very) most; **il faut rester au** *ou* **le ~ à l'ombre** one must stay as much as possible in the shade. ◆ **maximal, e,** *mpl* **-aux** *adj* maximal. ◆ **maximiser** (1) *vt* to maximize.

mayonnaise [majɔnɛz] *nf* mayonnaise.

mazout [mazut] *nm* heating oil. **poêle à ~** oil-fired stove.

me, m' [m(ə)] *pron pers* me; *(réfléchi)* myself. **il m'en a parlé** he spoke to me about it; **je ne ~ vois pas dans ce rôle-là** I can't see myself in that part.

méandre [meɑ̃dʀ(ə)] *nm (Art, Géog)* meander; *(fig)* twists and turns.

mec ⁑ [mɛk] *nm* guy.

mécanique [mekanik] **1** *adj (gén)* mechanical; *jouet* clockwork. **les industries ~s** mechanical engineering industries; *(Aut, Aviat)* **avoir des ennuis ~s** to have engine trouble. **2** *nf (gén)* mechanics *(sg)*; *(science)* (mechanical) engineering; *(mécanisme)* mechanism. ◆ **mécanicien, -ienne** *nm, f (Aut)* (garage *ou* motor) mechanic; *(Naut)* engineer; *(Rail)* engine driver, engineer *(US)*. ◆ **mécaniquement** *adv* mechanically. ◆ **mécanisation** *nf* mechanization. ◆ **mécaniser** (1) *vt* to mechanize. ◆ **mécanisme** *nm* mechanism. ◆ **mécanographie** *nf (procédé)* (mechanical) data processing; *(service)* comptometer department.

mécène [mesɛn] *nm (Art)* patron. ◆ **mécénat** *nm (Art)* patronage.

méchant, e [meʃɑ̃, ɑ̃t] **1** *adj* (**a**) nasty, wicked; *(sens affaibli) enfant* naughty. **ce n'est pas un ~ homme** he's not such a bad fellow; **ce n'est pas bien ~** * *[blessure]* it's not too serious; *[examen]* it's not too difficult *ou* stiff *. (**b**) *(insignifiant)* **un ~ morceau de fromage** one miserable bit of cheese; **que de bruit pour une ~e clef perdue** what a fuss over one wretched lost key. (**c**) (⁑: *sensationnel)* **il a une ~e moto** he's got a fantastic * *ou* terrific * bike; **une ~e cicatrice** a hell of a scar ⁑. **2** *nm, f (enfant)* naughty child; *(personne)* wicked person. **les~s** *(dans un western)* the baddies *, the bad guys * *(US)*; **faire le ~** * to be difficult, be nasty. ◆ **méchamment** *adv (cruellement)* nastily, wickedly; *(*: très) bon* fantastically *, terrifically *; *abîmé* badly. ◆ **méchanceté** *nf* (**a**) nastiness, wickedness; naughtiness. **par ~** out of spite. (**b**) *(action, parole)* nasty *ou* wicked action *ou* remark. **dire des ~s à qn** to say spiteful things to sb.

mèche [mɛʃ] *nf [lampe]* wick; *[bombe]* fuse; *[cheveux]* lock of hair; *[chignole]* bit. **~ postiche** hairpiece; **être de ~ avec qn** * to be hand in glove with sb *, be in league with sb.

mécompte [mekɔ̃t] *nm (désillusion)* disappointment; *(erreur de calcul)* miscalculation, miscount.

méconnaître [mekɔnɛtʀ(ə)] (57) *vt faits* to be unaware of, not to know; *gravité d'un problème* to misjudge; *mérites, personne* to underrate, underestimate; *devoirs* to ignore. ◆ **méconnaissable** *adj* unrecognizable; *(presque)* hardly recognizable. ◆ **méconnaissance** *nf (ignorance)* lack of knowledge (*de* about), ignorance (*de* of). ◆ **méconnu, e** *adj (gén)* unrecognized; *inventeur* misunderstood.

mécontentement [mekɔ̃tɑ̃tmɑ̃] *nm (Pol)* discontent; *(déplaisir)* dissatisfaction, displeasure; *(irritation)* annoyance. ◆ **mécontent, e** **1** *adj* displeased, dissatisfied; annoyed (*de* with). **2** *nm, f* grumbler; *(Pol)* malcontent. ◆ **mécontenter** (1) *vt* to displease, annoy.

Mecque [mɛk] *nf*: **la ~** *(lit)* Mecca; *(fig)* the Mecca.

médaille [medaj] *nf* (**a**) *(décoration)* medal ; (* *fig: tache)* stain, mark. (**b**) *(insigne) [employé]* badge; *[chien]* name tag; *[volaille]* guarantee tag. ◆ **médaillé, e** *nm, f* medal-holder. **il est** *ou* **c'est un ~ olympique** he is an Olympic medallist, he is the holder of an Olympic medal. ◆ **médailler** (1) *vt* to award a medal to. *(se tacher)* **se ~** * to get a stain *ou* mark on one's clothing. ◆ **médaillon** *nm (Art, Culin)* medallion; *(bijou)* locket.

médecin [mɛdsɛ̃] *nm* doctor. **~ de famille** family practitioner *ou* doctor; **~ d'hôpital** ≃ consultant; **~ légiste** forensic surgeon; **~ généraliste** general practitioner, G.P.; **~ militaire** army medical officer; **~ scolaire** school doctor, schools medical officer *(Brit Admin)*. ◆ **médecine** *nf* medicine. **~ générale** general medicine; **~ préventive** preventive medicine; **~ du travail** occupational *ou* industrial medicine.

media [medja] *nm*: **les ~s** the media; **dans les ~s** in the media. ◆ **médiatique** *adj* media.

médiation [medjɑsjɔ̃] *nf (gén, Pol)* mediation; *(Ind)* arbitration. **offrir sa ~ dans un conflit** *(Pol)* to offer to mediate in a conflict; *(Ind)* to offer to arbitrate *ou* intervene in a dispute. ◆ **médiateur, -trice** **1** *nm, f* mediator; arbitrator. **2** *nf (Géom)* median.

médical, e, *mpl* **-aux** [medikal, o] *adj* medical. ◆ **médicalement** *adv* medically. ◆ **médicaliser** (1) *vt*: **~ la maternité** to medicalize childbirth; **~ la population rurale** to provide the rural population with medical care. ◆ **médicalisation** *nf* medicalization; bringing medical care to.

◆ **médicament** *nm* medicine, drug. ◆ **médicinal, e,** *mpl* **-aux** *adj* medicinal.

médiéval, e, *mpl* **-aux** [medjeval, o] *adj* medieval.

médiocre [medjɔkʀ(ə)] **1** *adj (gén)* mediocre; *qualité, salaire, copie d'élève* poor; *personne, emploi* second-rate. **il a montré un intérêt ~ pour ce projet** he showed little interest in the project. **2** *nmf* nonentity, second-rater *. ◆ **médiocrement** *adv intelligent* not particularly; *satisfait* barely; *travailler* indifferently. **gagner ~ sa vie** to earn a poor living. ◆ **médiocrité** *nf* mediocrity; poorness. **cet homme est une ~** this man is a complete mediocrity *ou* second-rater.

médire [mediʀ] (37) *vi*: **~ de qn** to speak ill of sb; *(à tort)* to malign *ou* slander sb. ◆ **médisance** *nf (propos)* piece of scandal. **la ~** scandalmongering; **dire des ~s** to spread scandal *ou* malicious gossip. ◆ **médisant, e 1** *adj paroles* slanderous. **être ~** to spread scandal. **2** *nm, f* scandalmonger, slanderer.

méditer [medite] (1) **1** *vt pensée* to meditate on, ponder (over); *projet* to meditate. **~ de faire qch** to contemplate doing sth, plan to do sth. **2** *vi* to meditate. **~ sur qch** to ponder over sth. ◆ **méditatif, -ive** *adj* meditative, thoughtful. ◆ **méditation** *nf* meditation. **après de longues ~s** after much *ou* deep thought, after lengthy meditation.

Méditerranée [mediteʀane] *nf*: **la (mer) ~** the Mediterranean (Sea). ◆ **méditerranéen, -enne** *adj* Mediterranean.

méduse [medyz] *nf* jellyfish. *(Myth)* **M~** Medusa.

méduser [medyze] (1) *vt (gén pass)* to dumbfound.

meeting [mitiŋ] *nm (Pol, Sport)* meeting. **~ d'aviation** air show.

méfait [mefɛ] *nm* wrongdoing; *(hum)* misdeed. **les ~s de** *temps, épidémie, alcoolisme* the ravages of.

méfiance [mefjɑ̃s] *nf* distrust, mistrust, suspicion. **éveiller la ~ de qn** to arouse sb's suspicion(s); **venir sans ~** to come unsuspectingly. ◆ **méfiant, e** *adj* distrustful, mistrustful, suspicious. ◆ **méfier (se)** (7) *vpr*: **se ~ de** *personne, conseil* to distrust, mistrust; *ses impulsions* to be wary of; **méfiez-vous de lui** don't trust him; **il faut vous ~** you must be careful; **méfie-toi de cette marche** mind *ou* watch the step.

méga [mega] **1** *préf* mega... **~hertz** *nm* megahertz; **~lopole** *nf* megalopolis; **~octet** *nm* megabyte; **~tonne** megaton. **2** *adj inv* (‡) enormous. **~dissertation** hell of a long essay ‡.

mégalomanie [megalɔmani] *nf* megalomania. ◆ **mégalomane** *adj, nmf* megalomaniac.

mégarde [megaʀd(ə)] *nf*: **par ~** *(accidentellement)* accidentally, by accident; *(par erreur)* by mistake, inadvertently.

mégère [meʒɛʀ] *nf (péj: femme)* shrew. *(Théât)* **la M~ apprivoisée** the Taming of the Shrew.

mégot * [mego] *nm* cigarette butt *ou* end.

mégoter * [megɔte] (1) *vi* to skimp (*sur* over). ◆ **mégotage** * *nm* cheeseparing *ou* miserly attitude.

meilleur, e [mɛjœʀ] **1** *adj* better (*que* than). **le ~ des deux** the better of the two; **le ~ de tous** the best of the lot; **ce gâteau est ~ avec du rhum** this cake tastes *ou* is better with rum; **~ marché** cheaper; **le ~ marché** the cheapest; *(Comm)* **acheter au ~ prix** to buy at the lowest price; **~s vœux** best wishes; **il n'y a rien de ~** there's nothing better, there's nothing to beat it. **2** *adv sentir* better, nicer. **3** *nm, f*: **le ~, la ~e** the best one; **les ~s** the best (people); **tu connais la ~e? il n'est même pas venu!** haven't you heard the best (bit) though? he didn't even come! **4** *nm*: **le ~** the best; **pour le ~ et pour le pire** for better or for worse; **donner le ~ de soi-même** to give of one's best; **le ~ de son temps** the best part of one's time; **prendre le ~ sur qn** to get the better of sb.

mélancolie [melɑ̃kɔli] *nf* melancholy. ◆ **mélancolique** *adj* melancholy. ◆ **mélancoliquement** *adv* melancholically.

mélanger [melɑ̃ʒe] (3) **1** *vt (gén)* to mix; *couleurs, vins, tabacs* to blend; *dates, documents* to mix up, muddle up. **public très mélangé** very varied *ou* mixed public. **2 se ~** *vpr* to mix; to blend. **tout se mélange dans ma tête** I'm getting all mixed up. ◆ **mélange** *nm* (**a**) *(opération)* mixing; blending. (**b**) *(résultat)* mixture; blend. **~ détonant** explosive mixture; **joie sans ~** unalloyed joy; *(Littérat)* **~s** miscellanies.

mélasse [melas] *nf (Culin)* treacle, molasses *(US)*; *(boue)* muck. **être dans la ~** * *(ennuis)* to be in the soup *; *(misère)* to be down and out, be on one's beam ends *.

mêler [mele] (1) **1** *vt* (**a**) *(unir)* to mingle; *races* to mix; *(Vét)* to cross; *(Culin)* to mix, blend; *traits de caractère* to combine. **~ la douceur à la fermeté** to combine gentleness with firmness. (**b**) *papiers* to muddle up, mix up; *(battre) cartes* to shuffle. **~ la réalité et le rêve** to confuse reality and dream. (**c**) **~ qn à** *affaire* to involve sb in, get sb mixed up in; *conversation* to bring *ou* draw sb into. **2 se ~** *vpr* (**a**) to mix; to mingle; to combine. (**b**) **se ~ à** *querelle* to get involved in; *conversation* to join in; *groupe* to join, mix with; *[cris, sentiments]* to mingle with. (**c**) **se ~ de qch** to meddle with sth; **mêle-toi de tes affaires!** mind your own business!; **se ~ de faire qch** to take it upon o.s. to do sth.
◆ **mêlé, e 1** *adj sentiments* mixed, mingled; *monde* mixed. **2** *nf (bataille)* mêlée; *(Rugby)* pack, scrum. **~e générale** free-for-all; **rester au-dessus de la ~e** to keep clear of the fray.

mélèze [melɛz] *nm* larch.

méli-mélo * [melimelo] *nm [situation]* muddle; *[objets]* jumble.

mélo * [melo] **1** *adj (abrév de* **mélodramatique***) film, roman* soppy *, sentimental. **feuilleton ~** *(gén)* sentimental serial; *(TV)* soap (opera). **2** *nm abrév de* **mélodrame.**

mélodie [melɔdi] *nf (gén)* tune. *(genre)* **les ~s de Debussy** Debussy's melodies. ◆ **mélodieusement** *adv* melodiously, tunefully. ◆ **mélodieux, -euse** *adj* melodious, tuneful. ◆ **mélodique** *adj* melodic.

mélodrame [melɔdʀam] *nm (Littérat, péj)* melodrama. ◆ **mélodramatique** *adj* melodramatic.

mélomane [melɔman] *adj, nmf*: **être ~** to be a music lover.

melon [m(ə)lɔ̃] *nm (Bot)* melon. **(chapeau) ~** bowler hat.

membrane [mɑ̃bʀan] *nf* membrane.

membre [mɑ̃bʀ(ə)] *nm* (**a**) *(Anat)* limb. (**b**) *(personne)* member. **être ~ de** to be a member of; **ce club a 300 ~s** this club has a membership of 300 *ou* has 300 members; **pays ~** member country. (**c**) *(Math, Ling)* member.

même [mɛm] **1** *adj* (**a**) *(identique)* same. **ils ont la ~ taille, ils sont de ~ taille** they are the same size; **ils ont la ~ voiture que nous** they have the same car as we have *ou* as us; **c'est toujours la ~ chose!** it's always the same (old story)!; **arriver en ~ temps (que)** to arrive at the same time (as). (**b**) *(réel)* very. **ce sont ses paroles ~s** those are his very *ou* actual words; **il est la générosité ~** he is generosity itself *ou* the soul of generosity. (**c**) **moi-~** myself; **toi-~** yourself; **lui-~** himself; **elle-~** herself; **nous-~s** ourselves; **vous-~** yourself; **vous-~s** yourselves; **eux-** *ou* **elles-~s** themselves; **on est soi-~ conscient de ses propres erreurs** one is aware (oneself) of one's own mistakes; **au plus**

profond d'eux-~s in their heart of hearts; **elle fait ses robes elle-~** she makes her own dresses, she makes her dresses herself; **elle se disait en elle-~ que...** she thought to herself that...; **faire qch de soi-~** to do sth on one's own initiative ; **faire qch (par) soi-~** to do sth (by) oneself.
2 *pron indéf*: **le** *ou* **la** ~ the same one; *(fig)* **ce sont toujours les ~s** it's always the same ones.
3 *adv* (**a**) even. **il n'a ~ pas de quoi écrire** he hasn't even got anything to write with; **personne ne sait, ~ pas lui** nobody knows, not even him; ~ **si** even if, even though. (**b**) *(précisément)* **ici** ~ in this very place; **c'est celui-là ~ qui** he's the very one who; **c'est cela** ~ that's just *ou* exactly it. (**c**) **boire à ~ la bouteille** to drink straight from the bottle; **coucher à ~ le sol** to lie on the bare ground; **à ~ la peau** next to the skin; **être à ~ de faire** to be able *ou* in a position to do; **il fera de** ~ he'll do the same *ou* likewise; **vous le détestez? moi de** ~ you hate him? so do I *ou* I do too; **de ~ qu'il nous a dit que...** just as he told us that...; **il en est de ~ pour moi** it's the same for me, same here *; **quand ~, tout de** ~ all the same, even so.

mémé * [meme] *nf*, **mémère** * [memɛʀ] *nf* granny *. **elle fait ~ avec ce chapeau** she looks ancient in that hat *.

mémoire[1] [memwaʀ] *nf* (**a**) *(gén)* memory. **citer de** ~ to quote from memory; **pour** ~ as a matter of interest; **avoir la ~ des noms** to have a good memory for names; **si j'ai bonne** ~ if I remember rightly, if my memory serves me right; **avoir la ~ courte** to have a short memory; **j'ai gardé la ~ de cette conversation** I remember this conversation; **ça me revient en** ~ it comes back to me; **il me l'a remis en** ~ he reminded me of it; **de glorieuse** ~ of blessed memory; **à la ~ de** in memory of, to the memory of; **salir la ~ de qn** to sully the memory of sb. (**b**) *(Ordin)* memory, store, storage. ~ **vive** RAM, random access memory; ~ **morte** ROM, read only memory; **capacité de** ~ storage capacity, memory size.

mémoire[2] [memwaʀ] *nm* *(requête)* memorandum; *(rapport)* report; *(exposé)* paper; *(facture)* bill. *(souvenirs)* **~s** memoirs.

mémorable [memɔʀabl(ə)] *adj* memorable.

mémorandum [memɔʀɑ̃dɔm] *nm* memorandum.

mémorial, *pl* **-aux** [memɔʀjal, o] *nm* *(Archit)* memorial.

mémoriser [memɔʀize] (1) *vt* to memorize; *(Ordin)* to store.

menace [mənas] *nf* threat. **paroles de** ~ threatening words; **sous la** ~ under threat; ~ **d'épidémie** impending epidemic, threat of an epidemic. ◆ **menaçant, e** *adj* threatening, menacing. ◆ **menacer** (3) *vt* to threaten. ~ **qn de mort/d'un revolver** to threaten sb with death/with a gun ; **espèces menacées** threatened *ou* endangered species; **la paix est menacée** peace is endangered ; **la pluie menace** it looks like rain; **chaise qui menace de se casser** chair which is about to break *ou* which looks like breaking; **ça menace de durer** it threatens *ou* looks set to last some time.

ménage [menaʒ] *nm* (**a**) *(entretien)* housekeeping; *(nettoyage)* housework. **tenir son** ~ to look after one's house; **faire le** ~ *(lit: nettoyer)* to do the housework; *(fig: Pol)* to get rid of the lame ducks *etc* in a party; *(fig: Sport)* to sort out the opposition; **faire des ~s** to go out charring, work as a cleaning woman. (**b**) *(couple)* couple. **être heureux en** ~ to have a happy married life; **se mettre en ~ avec qn** to set up house with sb; **scènes de** ~ domestic rows; **faire bon/mauvais ~ avec qn** to get on well/badly with sb. (**c**) *(†: ordinaire)* **de** ~ *chocolat* for ordinary *ou* everyday consumption; *pain* homemade.

ménager[1], **-ère** [menaʒe, ɛʀ] **1** *adj* (**a**) *ustensiles* household, domestic. **travaux ~s** housework. (**b**) *(économe)* ~ **de** *forces, efforts* sparing of. **2** *nf* *(femme)* housewife; *(couverts)* canteen of cutlery.

ménager[2] [menaʒe] (3) *vt* (**a**) *adversaire* to handle carefully; *susceptibilité* to spare; *temps, argent* to use carefully *ou* sparingly; *forces* to conserve; *santé* to take care of; *paroles* to moderate, tone down. **il faut vous** ~ you should take things easy; **il n'a pas ménagé ses efforts** he spared no effort; **elle est très sensible, il faut la** ~ she is very sensitive, you must treat her gently; ~ **les deux partis** to humour both parties; ~ **la chèvre et le chou** *(rester neutre)* to sit on the fence; *(être conciliant)* to keep both parties sweet *. (**b**) *rencontre* to arrange, organize; *transition* to bring about. ~ **l'avenir** to prepare for the future; **il nous ménage une surprise** he has a surprise in store for us. (**c**) *porte* to put in; *chemin* to cut. ~ **une place pour** to make room for; **se ~ une porte de sortie** to leave o.s. a way out. ◆ **ménagement** *nm* care. **traiter avec** ~ *interlocuteur* to treat considerately; *malade* to treat gently; **traiter sans** ~ to handle roughly; **annoncer qch sans ~ à qn** to tell sb sth bluntly; **elle a besoin de** ~ she needs care and attention; *(égards)* **~s** (respectful) consideration *ou* attention.

ménagerie [menaʒʀi] *nf* *(lit, fig)* menagerie.

mendier [mɑ̃dje] (7) **1** *vt* to beg (for). ~ **qch à qn** to beg sb for sth, beg sth from sb. **2** *vi* to beg (for alms). ◆ **mendiant, e** *nm, f* beggar. ◆ **mendicité** *nf* begging.

mener [məne] (5) *vt* (**a**) *(conduire)* *(gén)* to lead; *(vers un lieu)* to take; *(en voiture)* to drive (*à* to, *dans* into). ~ **un enfant à l'école** to take a child to school; **mène ton ami à sa chambre** show *ou* take your friend to his room; *(fig)* ~ **qn en bateau** * to take sb for a ride *, have sb on *; **chemin qui mène à la mer** path (leading) to the sea; **où tout cela va-t-il nous ~?** where's all this going to get *ou* lead us?; **ces études mènent au journalisme** this training prepares one for journalism; **de telles infractions pourraient le ~ loin** offences such as these could get him into trouble; ~ **qn à faire** to lead sb to do.
(**b**) *(commander)* *(gén)* to lead; *pays* to run, rule; *entreprise* to manage, run; *enquête* to carry out, conduct. ~ **les choses rondement** to manage things efficiently; ~ **qch à bien** to carry sth through to a successful conclusion; ~ **qn par le bout du nez** to lead sb by the nose; ~ **qn à la baguette** to rule sb with an iron hand; **l'argent mène le monde** money rules the world, money makes the world go round; ~ **les débats** to chair the discussion.
(**c**) *(Sport)* to lead. **la France mène (l'Écosse par 2 buts à 1)** France is in the lead (by 2 goals to 1 against Scotland), France is leading (Scotland by 2 goals to 1).
(**d**) ~ **la vie dure à qn** to rule sb with an iron hand; **il n'en menait pas large** his heart was in his boots; ~ **grand bruit autour d'une affaire** to give an affair a lot of publicity.
◆ **menées** *nfpl* intrigues, machinations. ~ **subversives** subversive activities. ◆ **meneur, -euse** *nm, f* *(chef)* ringleader; *(agitateur)* agitator. ~ **d'hommes** born leader; ~ **de jeu** *(spectacle)* compère; *(jeu)* quiz-master; *(Music-hall)* **~euse de revue** cabaret star.

ménestrel [menɛstʀɛl] *nm* minstrel.

menhir [meniʀ] *nm* menhir, standing stone.

méninge [menɛ̃ʒ] *nf* *(Méd)* meninx. **~s** meninges; **se creuser les ~s** to rack one's brains. ◆ **méningite** *nf* meningitis. **faire une** ~ to have meningitis.

ménopause [menɔpoz] *nf* menopause.

menotte [mənɔt] *nf* (**a**) ~**s** handcuffs; **mettre les ~s à qn** to handcuff sb. (**b**) *(*: main)* hand, handy *.

mensonge [mɑ̃sɔ̃ʒ] *nm* lie, fib *, untruth. **pieux ~** white lie; *(acte)* **le ~** lying, untruthfulness. ◆ **mensonger, -ère** *adj* untrue, false.

menstruation [mɑ̃stʀyɑsjɔ̃] *nf* menstruation.

mensuel, -elle [mɑ̃sɥɛl] **1** *adj* monthly. **2** *nm, f* employee paid by the month. **3** *nm (Presse)* monthly (magazine). ◆ **mensualiser** (1) *vt* to pay on a monthly basis. ◆ **mensualité** *nf (traite)* monthly payment; *(salaire)* monthly salary. ◆ **mensuellement** *adv* monthly, every month.

mensuration [mɑ̃syʀɑsjɔ̃] *nf (calcul)* mensuration. *(mesures)* ~**s** measurements.

mental, e, *mpl* **-aux** [mɑ̃tal, o] *adj* mental. ◆ **mentalement** *adv* mentally. ◆ **mentalité** *nf* mentality.

menteur, -euse [mɑ̃tœʀ, øz] **1** *adj proverbe* false; *enfant* untruthful, lying. **il est très ~** he is a great liar. **2** *nm, f* liar, fibber *.

menthe [mɑ̃t] *nf (Bot)* mint; *(boisson)* peppermint cordial. **~ poivrée** peppermint; **~ verte** spearmint; **de ~, à la ~** mint.

mention [mɑ̃sjɔ̃] *nf* (**a**) *(action)* mention. **faire ~ de** to mention, make mention of. (**b**) *(annotation)* note, comment. *(Admin)* **'rayer la ~ inutile'** 'delete as appropriate'. (**c**) *(Scol)* **~ passable/assez bien/ bien/très bien** *(examen)* ≃ grade D/C/B/A pass; *(Univ: licence)* IIIrd class/lower IInd class/upper IInd class/Ist class Honours; **être reçu avec ~** to pass with distinction. ◆ **mentionner** (1) *vt* to mention.

mentir [mɑ̃tiʀ] (**16**) *vi* to lie (*à qn* to sb, *sur* about). **sans ~** (quite) honestly; **il ment comme il respire** he's a compulsive liar; **faire ~ le proverbe** to give the lie to the proverb; **~ à sa réputation** to belie one's reputation; **se ~ à soi-même** to fool o.s.

menton [mɑ̃tɔ̃] *nm* chin.

menu[1] [məny] *nm* (**a**) *(repas)* meal; *(carte)* menu; *(régime)* diet. **~ (à prix fixe)** set menu; **~ du jour** today's menu; **~ touristique** standard menu; **~ gastronomique** gourmet's menu. (**b**) *(Ordin)* menu.

menu[2]**, e** [məny] **1** *adj tige, taille* slim, slender; *personne* slim, slight; *herbe* fine; *écriture, pas* small, tiny; *voix* thin; *incidents* minor, trifling. **en ~s morceaux** in tiny pieces; **dans les ~s détails, par le ~** in minute detail; *(lit, fig)* **~ fretin** small fry; **~e monnaie** small *ou* loose change. **2** *adv hacher* fine. **écrire ~** to write small.

menuisier [mənɥizje] *nm [meubles]* joiner; *[bâtiment]* carpenter. **~ d'art** cabinetmaker. ◆ **menuiserie** *nf* (**a**) *(métier)* joinery; carpentry. **~ d'art** cabinet work; *(passe-temps)* **faire de la ~** to do woodwork *ou* carpentry *ou* joinery. (**b**) *(atelier)* joiner's workshop. (**c**) *(ouvrage)* piece of woodwork *ou* joinery.

méprendre (se) [mepʀɑ̃dʀ(ə)] (**58**) *vpr (littér)* to make a mistake, be mistaken (*sur* about).

mépris [mepʀi] *nm* contempt, scorn. **avec ~** contemptuously, scornfully; **avoir le ~ des convenances** to have no regard for conventions; **au ~ du danger** regardless *ou* in defiance of danger. ◆ **mépriser** (1) *vt (gén)* to scorn, despise; *personne* to look down on; *conseil* to spurn. ◆ **méprisable** *adj* contemptible, despicable. ◆ **méprisant, e** *adj* contemptuous, scornful.

méprise [mepʀiz] *nf (erreur)* mistake, error; *(malentendu)* misunderstanding.

mer [mɛʀ] **1** *nf* (**a**) sea. **~ fermée** inland sea; **~ de sable** sea of sand; **~ d'huile** glassy sea; **vent de ~** sea breeze; **gens de ~** sailors. (**b**) *(marée)* tide. **la ~ est haute/basse** the tide is high *ou* in/ low *ou* out; **c'est la haute/basse ~** it is high/low tide. (**c**) **en ~** at sea; **en haute** *ou* **pleine ~** on the open sea; **prendre la ~** to put out to sea; **mettre (une embarcation) à la ~** to bring *ou* get out a boat; *(fig)* **ce n'est pas la ~ à boire!** it's not asking the impossible! **2** : **la ~ des Antilles** *ou* **des Caraïbes** the Caribbean (Sea); **la ~ Baltique** the Baltic Sea; **la ~ Caspienne** the Caspian Sea; **la ~ Égée** the Aegean Sea; **la ~ d'Irlande** the Irish Sea; **la ~ Morte** the Dead Sea; **la ~ du Nord** the North Sea; **la ~ Rouge** the Red Sea; **la ~ des Sargasses** the Sargasso Sea.

mercantile [mɛʀkɑ̃til] *adj* mercenary, venal. ◆ **mercantilisme** *nm (péj)* mercenary *ou* venal attitude; *(Écon, Hist)* mercantile system, mercantilism.

mercenaire [mɛʀsənɛʀ] *adj, nm* mercenary.

mercerie [mɛʀsəʀi] *nf (boutique)* haberdasher's shop, notions store *(US)*; *(articles)* haberdashery, notions *(US)*. ◆ **mercier, -ière** *nm, f* haberdasher, notions dealer *(US)*.

merci [mɛʀsi] **1** *excl* thank you (*de, pour* for); *(pour refuser)* no, thank you. **~ bien** *ou* **beaucoup** thank you very much, many thanks; **~ d'avoir répondu** thank you for replying; **dire ~ à qn** to thank sb, say thank you to sb. **2** *nm* thank-you. **je n'ai pas eu un ~** I didn't get a word of thanks; **mille ~s** (very) many thanks. **3** *nf* mercy. **crier ~** to cry for mercy; **sans ~** *combat etc* merciless, ruthless; **à la ~ de** at the mercy of; **tout le monde est à la ~ d'une erreur** anyone can make a mistake.

mercredi [mɛʀkʀədi] *nm* Wednesday. **~ des Cendres** Ash Wednesday; *V* **samedi.**

mercure [mɛʀkyʀ] *nm* mercury. ◆ **mercurochrome** *nm* mercurochrome.

merde ‡ [mɛʀd(ə)] **1** *nf* shit ‡; *(livre, film)* crap ‡; *(fig: ennuis)* mess. **2** *excl* hell! ‡ ◆ **merdique** ‡ *adj film, discours, idée* pathetic, moronic, crappy ‡. **c'était ~, cette soirée** that party was bloody awful ‡.

mère [mɛʀ] *nf* (**a**) mother. **~ de famille** mother, housewife; **~ porteuse** surrogate mother; **M~ Supérieure** Mother Superior; *(péj)* **la ~ X *** old Mrs X. (**b**) **cellule/maison ~** parent cell/company; *(Ordin)* **disquette ~** master disk.

méridien, -enne [meʀidjɛ̃, ɛn] *adj, nm* meridian.

méridional, e, *mpl* **-aux** [meʀidjɔnal, o] **1** *adj* southern. **2** *nm (f)*: **M~(e)** Southerner.

meringue [məʀɛ̃g] *nf* meringue.

mériter [meʀite] (1) *vt louange, châtiment* to deserve, merit. **il mérite la prison** he deserves to go to prison; **repos bien mérité** well-deserved rest; **ça mérite d'être noté** it is worth noting; **ceci mérite réflexion** *(exiger)* this calls for *ou* requires careful thought; *(valoir)* this merits *ou* deserves careful thought; **ça lui a mérité le respect de tous** this earned him everyone's respect. ◆ **méritant, e** *adj* deserving. ◆ **mérite** *nm (gén)* merit. **il n'y a aucun ~ à cela** there's no merit in that, one deserves no credit for that; **de grand ~** of great worth *ou* merit; **si nombreux que soient ses ~s** however many qualities he may have; **ça a le ~ d'être simple** it has the merit of being simple. ◆ **méritoire** *adj* meritorious, commendable.

merlan [mɛʀlɑ̃] *nm* whiting.

merle [mɛʀl(ə)] *nm* blackbird. ◆ **merlette** *nf* female blackbird, she-blackbird.

merlu [mɛʀly] *nm* hake.

merveille [mɛʀvɛj] *nf* marvel, wonder. **à ~** *fonctionner* perfectly; **se porter à ~** to be in excellent health; **ça tombe à ~** this comes just at the right time; **faire ~** to work wonders; **c'est ~ que** it's a wonder *ou* a marvel that; **on en dit ~** it's praised to the skies. ◆ **merveilleusement** *adv* marvellously, wonderfully. ◆ **merveilleux, -euse 1** *adj* *(magnifique)* marvellous, wonderful; *(après n: surnaturel)* magic. **2** *nm*: **le ~** the supernatural.

mes [me] *adj poss V* **mon.**

mésalliance [mezaljɑ̃s] *nf* misalliance.

mésange [mezɑ̃ʒ] *nf* tit(mouse).

mésaventure [mezavɑ̃tyʀ] *nf* misadventure, misfortune.

Mesdames [medam] *nfpl V* **Madame.**

Mesdemoiselles [medmwazɛl] *nfpl V* **Mademoiselle.**

mésentente [mezɑ̃tɑ̃t] *nf* dissension, disagreement.

mésestimer [mezɛstime] (1) *vt difficulté* to underestimate, underrate; *personne* to have little regard for.

Mésopotamie [mezɔpɔtami] *nf* Mesopotamia.

mesquin, e [mɛskɛ̃, in] *adj (avare)* mean, stingy; *(vil)* mean, petty. ◆ **mesquinement** *adv agir* meanly, stingily; pettily. ◆ **mesquinerie** *nf* meanness, stinginess; pettiness. **une ~** a mean *ou* petty trick.

mess [mɛs] *nm (Mil)* mess.

message [mesaʒ] *nm* message. **~ publicitaire** advertisement. ◆ **messager, -ère** *nm, f* messenger. ◆ **messageries** *nfpl* freight company.

messe [mɛs] *nf* mass. **aller à la ~** to go to mass; **~ basse** low mass; **finissez vos ~s basses** stop muttering together.

messie [mesi] *nm* messiah. **le M~** the Messiah.

Messieurs [mesjø] *nmpl V* **Monsieur.**

mesure [m(ə)zyʀ] *nf* (**a**) *(évaluation, dimension)* measurement. **prendre les ~s de qch** to take the measurements of sth. (**b**) *(étalon, quantité)* measure. **~ de longueur** measure of length; **faire bonne ~** to give good measure; **la bonne ~** the happy medium; **la ~ est comble** that's the limit; **dépasser la ~** to overstep the mark; **boire outre ~** to drink to excess. (**c**) *(fig) [forces, sentiments]* measure. **monde à la ~ de l'homme** world on a human scale; **il est à ma ~** *[travail]* it is within my capabilities; *[adversaire]* he's a good match for me; **donner toute sa ~** to show one's worth. (**d**) *(modération)* moderation. **avec ~** in moderation; **il a beaucoup de ~** he's very moderate; **sans ~** *orgueil* immoderate, measureless; **se dépenser sans ~** *(se dévouer)* to give one's all. (**e**) *(moyen)* measure, step. **prendre des ~s d'urgence** to take emergency action *ou* measures; **des ~s de rétorsion** reprisals, retaliatory measures; **j'ai pris mes ~s pour qu'il vienne** I have made arrangements for him to come. (**f**) *(Mus) (cadence)* time, tempo; *(division)* bar. **être/ne pas être en ~** to be in/out of time; **jouer quelques ~s** to play a few bars. (**g**) *(Habillement)* **prendre les ~s de qn** to take sb's measurements; **est-ce que ce costume est bien à ma ~?** is this suit my size?, will this suit fit me?; **s'habiller sur ~** to have one's clothes made to measure; **j'ai un patron sur ~** my boss suits me down to the ground. (**h**) *(locutions)* **dans la ~ du possible/de mes moyens** as far as possible/as I am able; **dans la ~ où** inasmuch as, insofar as; **dans une certaine/large ~** to some/to a large extent; **être en ~ de faire qch** to be in a position to do sth; **(au fur et) à ~ que** as; **donne-les moi (au fur et) à ~** hand them to me one by one *ou* as you go along. ◆ **mesurable** *adj* measurable.

mesurer [məzyʀe] (1) **1** *vt* (**a**) *chose* to measure; *personne* to take the measurements of, measure (up); *(par calcul)* to calculate. **il me mesura 3 mètres de tissu** he measured me off *ou* out 3 metres of fabric. (**b**) *dégâts, valeur* to assess; *conséquences* to consider, weigh up. (**c**) *(hostilement)* **~ ses forces avec qn** to pit o.s. against sb; **~ qn du regard** to look sb up and down; **se ~ des yeux** to weigh *ou* size each other up. (**d**) *(avoir pour mesure)* to measure. **cette pièce mesure 3 mètres sur 10** this room measures 3 metres by 10; **il mesure 1 mètre 80** it (*ou* he) measures 1 metre 80. (**e**) *(avec parcimonie)* to limit. **le temps nous est mesuré** our time is limited. (**f**) *(avec modération)* **~ ses paroles** *(savoir rester poli)* to moderate one's language; *(être prudent)* to weigh one's words. (**g**) *(proportionner)* to match (*à, sur* to). **2 se ~** *vpr*: **se ~ avec** *personne* to pit o.s. against; *difficulté* to confront, tackle. ◆ **mesuré, e** *adj ton, pas* measured; *personne* moderate (*dans* in).

métabolisme [metabɔlism(ə)] *nm* metabolism.

métal, *pl* **-aux** [metal, o] *nm* metal. *(Fin)* **le ~ jaune** gold. ◆ **métallique** *adj (gén, fig)* metallic; *objet (en métal)* metal; *(qui ressemble au métal)* metallic. **bruit ~** jangle, clank. ◆ **métallisé, e** *adj peinture* metallic. ◆ **métallurgie** *nf (industrie)* metallurgical industry; *(technique)* metallurgy. ◆ **métallurgique** *adj* metallurgic. ◆ **métallurgiste** *nm (ouvrier)* steel *ou* metal-worker; *(industriel)* metallurgist.

métamorphose [metamɔʀfoz] *nf* metamorphosis. ◆ **métamorphoser** (1) **1** *vt* to transform, metamorphose (*en* into). **2 se ~** *vpr* to be metamorphosed *ou* transformed (*en* into).

métaphore [metafɔʀ] *nf* metaphor. ◆ **métaphorique** *adj* metaphorical. ◆ **métaphoriquement** *adv* metaphorically.

métastase [metastɑz] *nf* metastasis. **il y a des ~s** there are metastases.

météore [meteɔʀ] *nm* meteor. ◆ **météorique** *adj* meteoric. ◆ **météorite** *nm ou f* meteorite.

météorologie [meteɔʀɔlɔʒi] *nf (Sci)* meteorology; *(services)* Meteorological Office, Met Office *. ◆ **météo** *nf (bulletin)* weather forecast, weather report. **la ~ est bonne/mauvaise** the weather forecast is good/bad. ◆ **météorologique** *adj phénomène, observation* meteorological; *carte, station* weather. ◆ **météorologiste** *nmf ou* ◆ **météorologue** *nmf* meteorologist.

métèque [metɛk] *nmf (péj)* wog ‡ *(péj)*, wop ‡ *(péj)*.

méthane [metan] *nm* methane.

méthanol [metanɔl] *nm* methanol.

méthode [metɔd] *nf* (**a**) method. **avoir sa ~ pour faire qch** to have one's own way *ou* method for *ou* of doing sth; **il a beaucoup de ~** he's very methodical; **faire qch avec/sans ~** to do sth methodically/unmethodically. (**b**) *(livre)* manual, tutor. **~ de latin** latin primer. ◆ **méthodique** *adj* methodical. ◆ **méthodiquement** *adv* methodically.

méticuleux, -euse [metikylø, øz] *adj* meticulous. ◆ **méticuleusement** *adv* meticulously.

métier [metje] *nm* (**a**) *(gén: travail)* job; *(Admin)* occupation; *(commercial)* trade; *(artisanal)* craft; *(intellectuel)* profession. **les ~s manuels** (the) manual occupations; **il est plombier de son ~** he is a plumber by *ou* to trade; **il est du ~** he is in the trade *ou* profession *ou* business; **il connaît son ~** he knows his job. (**b**) *(expérience)* (acquired) skill *ou* technique, experience. **avoir du ~** to have practical experience; **avoir 2 ans de ~** to have been 2 years in the job (*ou* trade *ou* profession); **homme de ~** expert, professional, specialist. (**c**) **~ à tisser** (weaving) loom.

métis, -isse [metis] **1** *adj personne* half-caste, half-breed; *animal* crossbreed, mongrel; *plante* hybrid. **2** *nm, f (personne)* half-caste, half-breed; *(animal, plante)* mongrel. **3** *nm (Tex)* **(toile de) ~** fabric made of cotton and linen mixture. ◆ **métisser** (1) *vt* to crossbreed, cross.

métonymie [metɔnimi] *nf* metonymy.

mètre [mɛtʀ(ə)] *nm (gén)* metre; *(instrument)* (metre) rule. **~ carré/cube** square/cubic metre; **~ pliant** folding rule; **~ à ruban** tape measure, measuring tape; **vendre qch au ~ linéaire** to sell sth by the metre; *(Sport)* **un 100 ~s** a 100-metre race. ◆ **métrage** *nm (Couture)* length, yardage; *(mesure)* measurement. ◆ **métrer** (6) *vt* to measure (in metres); *[vérificateur]* to survey. ◆ **métreur, -euse** *nm, f*: ~ **(vérificateur)** quantity surveyor. ◆ **métrique** *adj* metric.

métro [metʀo] *nm* underground, subway *(US)*. **le ~ de Londres** the tube.

métronome [metʀɔnɔm] *nm* metronome. *(fig)* **avec la régularité d'un ~** with clockwork regularity, like clockwork.

métropole [metʀɔpɔl] *nf (ville)* metropolis; *(état)* home country. **en ~ comme à l'étranger** at home and abroad. ◆ **métropolitain, e** *adj* metropolitan.

mets [mɛ] *nm (Culin)* dish.

mettable [mɛtabl(ə)] *adj* wearable, decent.

metteur [mɛtœʀ] *nm*: ~ **en ondes** producer; ~ **en scène** *(Théât)* producer; *(Ciné)* director.

mettre [mɛtʀ(ə)] (56) **1** *vt* (**a**) *(placer)* to put (*dans* in, into, *sur* on). **elle lui mit la main sur l'épaule** she put *ou* laid her hand on his shoulder; **elle met son travail avant sa famille** she puts her work before her family; **je mets Molière parmi les plus grands écrivains** I rank *ou* rate Molière among the greatest writers; ~ **qch à plat** to lay sth down flat; ~ **qch droit** to put *ou* set sth straight; **ne mets pas d'encre sur la nappe** don't get ink on the tablecloth; ~ **un enfant à l'école** to send a child to school; *(combat)* **qu'est-ce qu'ils nous ont mis!** * what a hiding they gave us! *; ~ **qch à cuire** to put sth on to cook. (**b**) *vêtements, lunettes* to put on. **je ne mets plus mon gilet** I've stopped wearing my cardigan; **mets-lui son chapeau** put his hat on (for him); **il avait mis un manteau** he was wearing a coat, he had a coat on; **elle avait mis du bleu** she was wearing blue, she was dressed in blue. (**c**) *(consacrer)* **j'ai mis 2 heures à le faire** I took 2 hours to do it, I spent 2 hours on *ou* over it; ~ **beaucoup de soin à faire** to take great care in doing; **il y a mis le temps!** he's taken his time (about it)! (**d**) *radio, chauffage* to put *ou* switch *ou* turn on. ~ **le réveil (à 7 heures)** to set the alarm (for 7 o'clock); ~ **le réveil à l'heure** to put the alarm clock right; ~ **le verrou** to bolt *ou* lock the door. (**e**) *(installer) placards* to put in; *eau* to lay on; *étagères* to put up *ou* in; *moquette* to fit, lay; *rideaux* to put up. ~ **du papier peint** to hang some wallpaper; ~ **de la peinture** to put on a coat of paint. (**f**) *(écrire)* ~ **en anglais/au pluriel** to put into English/the plural; ~ **un mot à qn** * to drop a line to sb *; **mettez bien clairement que** put (down) quite clearly that; **il met qu'il est bien arrivé** he says in his letter *ou* writes that he arrived safely. (**g**) *argent (gén)* to put. ~ **de l'argent sur un cheval** to put money on a horse; **je suis prêt à ~ 500 F** I'm willing to give 500 francs; **il faut y ~ le prix** you have to pay for it. (**h**) *(supposer)* **mettons que je me sois trompé** let's say *ou* (just) suppose I've got it wrong.

2 se ~ *vpr* (**a**) *[personne]* to put o.s.; *[objet]* to go. **mets-toi là** *(debout)* (go and) stand there; *(assis)* (go and) sit there; **se ~ dans un fauteuil** to sit down in an armchair; *(fig)* **elle ne savait plus où se ~** she didn't know where to hide herself; **se ~ autour (de)** to gather round; **ces verres se mettent dans le placard** these glasses go in the cupboard; **se ~ une idée dans la tête/de l'encre sur les doigts** to get an idea into one's head/ink on one's fingers; **il s'en est mis partout** * he's covered in it, he's got it all over him. (**b**) *[temps]* **se ~ au froid** to turn cold; **ça se met à la pluie** it looks like rain. (**c**) *(s'habiller)* **se ~ en robe** to put on a dress; **se ~ en bras de chemise** to take off one's jacket; **je n'ai rien à me ~** I've got nothing to wear. (**d**) **se ~ à rire** to start laughing, start *ou* begin to laugh; **se ~ au régime** to go on a diet; **se ~ au travail** to set to work, get down to work; **se ~ à boire** to take to drink; **il s'est bien mis à l'anglais** he's really taken to English. (**e**) *(se grouper)* **ils se sont mis à plusieurs/2 pour pousser la voiture** several of them/the 2 of them joined forces to push the car; **se ~ avec qn** *(faire équipe)* to team up with sb; *(prendre parti)* to side with sb; **se ~ d'un parti** to join a party. (**f**) **qu'est-ce qu'ils se sont mis!** * *(manger)* they had a real blowout! ⁑; *(combat)* they didn't half lay into each other! ⁑

meuble [mœbl(ə)] **1** *nm (objet)* piece of furniture. **les ~s** the furniture; *(ameublement)* **le ~** furniture; ~ **de rangement** cupboard, storage unit; **être dans ses ~s** to be settled in one's own home. **2** *adj* (**a**) *terre* loose; *roche* soft. (**b**) *(Jur)* **biens ~s** movables. ◆ **meublé, e 1** *adj* furnished. **non ~** unfurnished. **2** *nm (appartement)* furnished flat *ou* rooms. ◆ **meubler** (1) **1** *vt pièce* to furnish; *loisirs* to fill (*de* with). ~ **la conversation** to keep the conversation going. **2 se ~** *vpr* to buy *ou* get (some) furniture.

meugler [møgle] (1) *vi* to moo. ◆ **meuglement** *nm*: ~**(s)** mooing.

meule [møl] *nf (à moudre)* millstone; *(à polir)* buff wheel; *(de paille)* stack. ~ **(à aiguiser)** grindstone; ~ **(de gruyère)** round of gruyère; ~ **de foin** haystack.

meunier, -ière [mønje, jɛʀ] **1** *adj (Tech)* milling. **sole ~ière** sole meunière. **2** *nm* miller. **3** *nf* miller's wife.

meurtre [mœʀtʀ(ə)] *nm* murder. **au ~!** murder! ◆ **meurtrier, -ière 1** *adj intention* murderous; *arme, combat* deadly; *épidémie* fatal. **cette route est ~ière** this road is lethal *ou* a deathtrap. **2** *nm* murderer. **3** *nf* (**a**) murderess. (**b**) *(Archit)* loophole.

meurtrir [mœʀtʀiʀ] (2) *vt* to bruise. **être tout meurtri** to be covered in bruises, be black and blue all over. ◆ **meurtrissure** *nf* bruise.

Meuse [møz] *nf*: **la ~** the Meuse, the Maas.

meute [møt] *nf (Chasse, fig)* pack.

mévente [mevɑ̃t] *nf* slump in sales.

Mexique [mɛksik] *nm* Mexico. ◆ **mexicain, e** *adj*, **M~(e)** *nm (f)* Mexican. ◆ **Mexico** *n* Mexico City.

mi [mi] *nm (Mus)* E; *(en chantant)* mi, me.

mi- [mi] *préf* half, mid-. **la mi-janvier** the middle of January, mid-January; **la mi-carême** the third Thursday in Lent; **les yeux mi-clos** with half-closed eyes; **mi-long, mi-longue** *adj bas* knee-length; *manteau, jupe* calf-length; **manche mi-longue** elbow-length sleeve; **mi-pleurant** half-crying; **mi-figue mi-raisin** *sourire, remarque* wry; *accueil* mixed; **je l'ai rencontré à mi-chemin** I met him halfway there; *(lit, fig)* **à mi-chemin entre** halfway *ou* midway between; **à mi-côte** halfway up *ou* down the hill; **il a de l'eau à mi-cuisses** he is thigh-deep in water, water comes up to his thighs; **à mi-corps/mi-jambes** up (*ou* down) to the waist/knees; **à mi-vitesse** at half-speed; **à mi-voix** in a low voice; *V* **mi-temps**.

miam-miam * [mjamjam] *excl* yum-yum *.

miaou [mjau] *nm* miaow. **faire ~** to miaow.

miauler [mjole] (1) *vi* to mew; *(fortement)* to caterwaul. ◆ **miaulement** *nm*: ~**(s)** mewing; caterwauling.

mica [mika] *nm (roche)* mica.

miche [miʃ] *nf* round loaf, cob loaf.

micheline [miʃlin] *nf* railcar.

micmac * [mikmak] *nm (péj) (intrigue)* (little) game *; *(complications)* fuss, carry-on *.

micro [mikʀo] **1** *nm* (**a**) *(abrév de* **microphone***)* microphone, mike *. *(Rad, TV)* **dites-le au** ~ *ou* **devant le** ~ say it in front of the mike *; ~**-cravate** *nm* lapel microphone, lapel mike *. (**b**) = **micro-ordinateur. 2** *nf* = **micro-informatique.**

micro... [mikʀo] *préf* micro...

microbe [mikʀɔb] *nm* germ, microbe; *(*: enfant)* tich *; *(péj: nabot)* little runt *. ◆ **microbien, -ienne** *adj culture* microbial; *infection* bacterial. **maladie** ~**ienne** bacterial disease.

microbiologie [mikʀobjɔlɔʒi] *nf* microbiology.

microchirurgie [mikʀoʃiʀyʀʒi] *nf* microsurgery.

microclimat [mikʀoklima] *nm* microclimate.

microcosme [mikʀokɔsm(ə)] *nm* microcosm.

microculture [mikʀokyltyʀ] *nf (Bio)* microculture.

micro-économie [mikʀoekɔnɔmi] *nf* microeconomics *(sg)*.

microfiche [mikʀofiʃ] *nf* microfiche.

microfilm [mikʀofilm] *nm* microfilm.

micro-informatique [mikʀoɛ̃fɔʀmatik] *nf* microcomputing.

micron [mikʀɔ̃] *nm* micron.

micro-onde [mikʀoɔ̃d] *nf* microwave. **(four à)** ~ microwave oven.

micro-ordinateur [mikʀoɔʀdinatœʀ] *nm* microcomputer.

microphone [mikʀofɔn] *nm* microphone.

microplaquette [mikʀoplakɛt] *nf (Ordin)* microchip.

microprocesseur [mikʀopʀosɛsœʀ] *nm* microprocessor.

microscope [mikʀoskɔp] *nm* microscope. **au** ~ under a microscope. ◆ **microscopique** *adj* microscopic.

microsillon [mikʀosijɔ̃] *nm (sillon)* microgroove. **(disque)** ~ long-playing record, L.P.

midi [midi] *nm* (**a**) *(heure)* 12 (o'clock). ~ **10** 10 past 12; **de** ~ **à 2 heures** from 12 *ou* (12) noon to 2; **à** ~ at 12 o'clock, at noon, at midday. (**b**) *(déjeuner)* lunchtime. **à** ~ at lunchtime; **qu'est-ce que tu as eu à** ~**?** what did you have for lunch? (**c**) *(période)* **ça s'est passé en plein** ~ it happened right in the middle of the day. (**d**) *(Géog: sud)* south. **le M**~ **(de la France)** the South of France, the Midi.

mie [mi] *nf* crumb (of the loaf).

miel [mjɛl] *nm* honey. **bonbon au** ~ honey sweet *ou* candy *(US)*; *[personne]* **être tout** ~ to be unctuous *ou* syrupy. ◆ **mielleusement** *adv (péj)* unctuously. ◆ **mielleux, -euse** *adj (péj) personne* unctuous; *paroles* honeyed; *sourire* sugary; *saveur* sickly sweet.

mien, mienne [mjɛ̃, mjɛn] **1** *pron poss*: **le** ~**, la mienne, les** ~**s, les miennes** mine, my own. **2** *nm*: **les** ~**s** my family; *V* **sien. 3** *adj poss*: **un** ~ **cousin** a cousin of mine.

miette [mjɛt] *nf [pain]* crumb; *[conversation]* scrap. **en** ~**s** *verre* in bits *ou* pieces; *gâteau* in crumbs; *casser* to bits, to smithereens; **les** ~**s de sa fortune** the remnants of his fortune; **je n'en prendrai qu'une** ~ I'll just have a tiny bit; **il n'en a pas laissé une** ~ he didn't leave a scrap.

mieux [mjø] *(comp, superl de* **bien***)* **1** *adv* (**a**) better. **aller** ~ to be better; **elle joue** ~ **que lui** she plays better than he does; **espérer** ~ to hope for better (things). (**b**) **le** ~**, la** ~**, les** ~ (the) best; *(de deux)* (the) better; **c'est ici qu'il dort le** ~ this is where he sleeps best; **tout va le** ~ **du monde** everything's going beautifully; **un dîner des** ~ **réussis** a most *ou* highly successful dinner; **j'ai fait le** ~ *ou* **du** ~ **que j'ai pu** I did my best *ou* the best I could; **elle est la** ~ **habillée** *(de deux)* she is the better dressed; *(de toutes)* she is the best dressed. (**c**) ~ **que jamais** better than ever; ~ **vaut tard que jamais** better late than never; ~ **vaut prévenir que guérir** prevention is better than cure; **il va de** ~ **en** ~ he's getting better and better; **il nous a écrit,** ~ **il est venu nous voir** he wrote to us, and better still he came to see us; **ils criaient à qui** ~ ~ each tried to outdo the other in shouting; **c'est on ne peut** ~ it's (just) perfect.

2 *adj inv* (**a**) *(gén)* better; *(plus beau)* better-looking, more attractive. **le** ~ **serait de** the best thing would be to; **être le** ~ **du monde** to be in perfect health *ou* excellent form; **c'est à l'ombre qu'elle sera le** ~ she'll be best *ou* most comfortable in the shade; **son aînée est la** ~ *(de 2)* his elder daughter is the better-looking; *(de toutes)* his eldest daughter is the best-looking. (**b**) **au** ~ *(gén)* at best; **faites pour le** ~ do what you think best; **être le** ~ **du monde avec qn** to be on the best of terms with sb; **tu n'as rien de** ~ **à faire?** haven't you got anything better to do?; **qui** ~ **est** even better, better still.

3 *nm* (**a**) best. **aider qn de son** ~ to do one's best to help sb, help sb the best one can. (**b**) *(progrès)* improvement.

mièvre [mjɛvʀ(ə)] *adj (gén)* vapid; *(sentimental)* mawkish. ◆ **mièvrerie** *nf* vapidity; mawkishness. ~**(s)** *(comportement)* childish *ou* silly behaviour; *(propos)* vapid *ou* silly talk.

mignard, e [miɲaʀ, aʀd(ə)] *adj style* mannered.

mignon, -onne [miɲɔ̃, ɔn] **1** *adj* pretty, nice, sweet. **donne-le-moi, tu seras** ~**ne** * give it to me there's a dear *. **2** *nm, f* (little) darling.

migraine [migʀɛn] *nf* headache; *(Méd)* migraine.

migration [migʀɑsjɔ̃] *nf (gén)* migration. ◆ **migrateur** *nm* migrant, migratory bird. ◆ **migratoire** *adj* migratory. ◆ **migrer** (1) *vi* to migrate (*vers* to).

mijaurée [miʒɔʀe] *nf* affected woman *ou* girl.

mijoter [miʒɔte] (1) **1** *vt* (**a**) *(Culin)* **(faire)** ~ *(lentement)* to simmer; *(avec soin)* to cook lovingly. (**b**) (*) *tour* to plot, cook up *; *complot* to hatch. **qu'est-ce qu'il peut bien** ~**?** what's he up to? *; **laisser qn** ~ **dans son jus** to leave sb to stew *. **2** *vi [plat]* to simmer.

mil [mil] *nm (dans une date)* a *ou* one thousand.

Milan [milɑ̃] *n* Milan. ◆ **milanais, e** *adj,* **M**~**(e)** *nm(f)* Milanese.

mile [mil] *nm* mile *(1609 mètres)*.

milice [milis] *nf* militia. ◆ **milicien** *nm* militiaman. ◆ **milicienne** *nf* woman serving in the militia.

milieu, *pl* ~**x** [miljø] *nm* (**a**) *(centre)* middle. **la porte du** ~ the middle *ou* centre door; **celui du** ~ the one in the middle, the middle one; *(Ftbl)* ~ **de terrain** midfield player; *(Ftbl)* **le** ~ **du terrain** the midfield; **vers le** ~ **de l'après-midi** towards the middle of the afternoon, about mid-afternoon; **au** ~ **de** *(au centre de)* in the middle of; *(parmi)* among, in the midst of; **au beau** ~ **(de)** right in the middle (of), in the very middle (of); **au** ~ **de son affolement** in the middle *ou* midst of his panic; **au** ~ **de la nuit** in the middle of the night, at dead of night; **comment travailler au** ~ **de ce vacarme?** how can anyone work in *ou* surrounded by this din?; **au** ~ **de la descente** halfway down; **au** ~ **de l'hiver** in mid-winter.

(**b**) *(état intermédiaire)* middle course *ou* way. **il n'y a pas de** ~ **(entre)** there is no middle course *ou* way (between); **le juste** ~ the happy medium, the golden mean; **il est innocent ou coupable, il n'y a pas de** ~ he is either innocent or guilty, he can't be both.

(**c**) *(Bio, Géog)* environment. *(Phys)* ~ **réfringent** refractive medium.

(**d**) *(entourage)* milieu, environment; *(groupe)* set, circle; *(provenance)* background. **le** ~ **familial** the family circle; *(Sociol)* the family background, the home environment; **elle est dans son** ~ **chez nous** she feels (quite) at home with us; **de quel ~ sort-il?** what is his (social) background?; **~x bien informés** well-informed circles; **~ très fermé** exclusive set; *(Crime)* **le ~, les gens du ~** (people of) the underworld; *(Crime)* **membre du ~** gangster, mobster.

militaire [militɛʀ] **1** *adj* military, army. **2** *nm* serviceman. **~ de carrière** regular (soldier). ◆ **militairement** *adv saluer* in military fashion. **occupé ~** occupied by the army. ◆ **militarisation** *nf* militarization. ◆ **militariser** (1) *vt* to militarize.

militer [milite] (1) *vi [personne]* to be a militant. **~ pour les droits de l'homme** to campaign for human rights; *[arguments]* **~ pour** to militate in favour of, argue for; **~ contre** to militate *ou* tell against. ◆ **militant, e** *adj, nm, f* militant. ◆ **militantisme** *nm* militancy.

mille[1] [mil] **1** *adj inv* a *ou* one thousand. **~ un** a *ou* one thousand and one; **trois ~** three thousand; **deux ~ neuf cents** two thousand nine hundred; **~ regrets** I'm terribly *ou* extremely sorry; **c'est ~ fois trop grand** it's far too big; **les contes des ~ et une nuits** tales from the Arabian Nights. **2** *nm inv* (**a**) *(Comm, Math)* a *ou* one thousand. **2 ~ de boulons** 2 thousand bolts. (**b**) *[cible]* bull's-eye. *(lit, fig)* **mettre dans le ~** to hit the bull's-eye. ◆ **mille-pattes** *nm inv* centipede.

mille[2] [mil] *nm* (**a**) **~ (marin)** nautical mile. (**b**) *(Can)* mile *(1609 mètres)*.

millénaire [milenɛʀ] **1** *nm* millennium. **2** *adj (lit)* millennial; *(fig: très vieux)* ancient.

millésime [milezim] *nm (date)* year, date; *[vin]* year, vintage. ◆ **millésimé, e** *adj*: **bordeaux ~** vintage Bordeaux; **bouteille ~e** bottle of vintage wine.

millet [mijɛ] *nm (Agr)* millet.

milli... [mili] *préf* milli... **~gramme** *etc* milligram(me) *etc*.

milliard [miljaʀ] *nm* thousand million, milliard, billion *(US)*. **10 ~s de francs** 10 thousand million francs, 10 billion francs *(US)*. ◆ **milliardaire** *nmf* millionaire, billionaire *(US)*. ◆ **milliardième** *adj, nmf* thousand millionth, billionth *(US)*.

millième [miljɛm] *adj, nmf* thousandth.

millier [milje] *nm* thousand. **un ~ de gens** a thousand (or so) people, (about) a thousand people; **il y en a des ~s** there are thousands (of them).

million [miljɔ̃] *nm* million. **2 ~s de francs** 2 million francs; **être riche à ~s** to be a millionaire. ◆ **millionième** *adj, nmf* millionth. ◆ **millionnaire** *nmf* millionaire.

mime [mim] *nm* (**a**) *(personne)* mimic; *(professionnel)* mime. (**b**) *(art, pièce)* mime. ◆ **mimer** (1) *vt (Théât)* to mime; *(singer)* to mimic, imitate; *(pour ridiculiser)* to take off. ◆ **mimétisme** *nm (Bio)* (protective) mimicry; *(fig)* unconscious mimicry, mimetism. ◆ **mimique** *nf (expression)* comical expression, funny face; *(geste)* expressive gesture.

mimosa [mimoza] *nm* mimosa.

minable [minabl(ə)] **1** *adj (décrépit)* shabbylooking, seedy-looking; *(médiocre)* hopeless *, pathetic *; *salaire, vie* miserable, wretched. **2** *nmf (péj)* dead loss *, second-rater *, washout *. **c'est un ~** he's a dead loss, he's (just) hopeless * *ou* pathetic *.

minauder [minode] (1) *vi* to mince about. ◆ **minauderies** *nfpl* mincing ways.

mince [mɛ̃s] **1** *adj* (**a**) *(peu épais)* thin; *(svelte)* slim, slender. (**b**) *profit, preuve, chances* slender; *salaire* meagre, small; *prétexte, connaissances, rôle* slight. **l'intérêt du film est bien ~** the film is decidedly lacking in interest; **ce n'est pas une ~ affaire** it's no easy task; **c'est un peu ~ comme réponse** that's not much of an answer. **2** *adv couper* thinly, in thin slices. **3** *excl* (*) **~ (alors)!** drat (it)! * ◆ **minceur** *nf* slenderness. ◆ **mincir** (2) *vi* to get slimmer *ou* thinner.

mine[1] [min] *nf* (**a**) *(physionomie)* expression, look; *(allure)* appearance. **ne fais pas cette ~-là** stop pulling that face; *(péj)* **faire des ~s** to put on simpering airs; **tu as la ~ de qn qui n'a rien compris** you look as if you haven't understood a single thing; **faire triste ~** to look a sorry sight; **votre poulet a bonne ~** your chicken looks good *ou* inviting; *(iro)* **tu as bonne ~ maintenant!** now you look an utter idiot! (**b**) *(teint)* **avoir bonne ~** to look well; **il a mauvaise ~** he doesn't look well; **il a meilleure ~** he looks better. (**c**) **faire ~ de faire** to make a show *ou* pretence of doing; **j'ai fait ~ de lui donner une gifle** I made as if to slap him; **il est venu pour voir ~ de rien** * he came all casual like * to have a look.

mine[2] [min] *nf (gén, Mil, fig)* mine. *(lit, fig)* **~ d'or** gold mine; **la nationalisation des ~s** the nationalization of the mining industry; **~ de charbon** *(gén)* coalmine; *(puits)* pit, mine; *(entreprise)* colliery; **ingénieur des M~s** (state qualified) mining engineer; **~ de renseignements** mine of information; **~ (de crayon)** lead (of pencil).

miner [mine] (1) *vt falaise, société, énergie* to undermine; *(avec explosifs)* to mine. **miné par le chagrin** worn down by grief; **miné par la jalousie** consumed by jealousy.

minerai [minʀɛ] *nm* ore.

minéral, e, *mpl* **-aux** [mineʀal, o] **1** *adj huile, sel* mineral; *(Chim)* inorganic. **2** *nm* mineral. ◆ **minéralogie** *nf* mineralogy. ◆ **minéralogiste** *nmf* mineralogist.

minéralogique [mineʀalɔʒik] *adj (Géol)* mineralogical. *(Aut)* **numéro ~** registration *ou* license *(US)* number; **plaque ~** number *ou* license *(US)* plate.

minet, -ette * [minɛ, ɛt] *nm, f (chat)* puss *, pussy (-cat).

mineur, e [minœʀ] **1** *adj (gén, Jur)* minor. **en do ~** in C minor; **être ~** to be under age. **2** *nm, f (Jur)* minor. **établissement interdit aux ~s** no person under 18 allowed on the premises. **3** *nm* (**a**) *(Mus)* minor. **en ~** in a minor key. (**b**) *(Ind)* miner; *[houille]* (coal)miner. **~ de fond** pitface worker; **village de ~s** mining village.

mini... [mini] **1** *préf* mini... **on va faire un ~-repas** we'll have a snack lunch. **2** *adj inv*: **la mode ~** the mini-length fashion; **~ budget** tiny budget. **3** *nf* = **mini-informatique. 4** *nm inv* (**a**) *(Mode)* **elle s'habille (en) ~** she wears minis. (**b**) = **mini-ordinateur.**

miniature [minjatyʀ] **1** *nf (gén)* miniature; *(*: nabot)* (little) shrimp *. **en ~** in miniature. **2** *adj* miniature. ◆ **miniaturisation** *nf* miniaturization. ◆ **miniaturiser** (1) *vt* to miniaturize.

minibus [minibys] *nm* minibus.

minier, -ière [minje, jɛʀ] *adj* mining.

mini-informatique [miniɛ̃fɔʀmatik] *nf* minicomputing.

mini-jupe [miniʒyp] *nf* miniskirt.

minimum [minimɔm], *f* **~** *ou* **minima** [minima], *pl* **~s** *ou* **minima 1** *adj* minimum. **2** *nm (gén, Math)* minimum; *(Jur)* minimum sentence. **dans le ~ de temps** in the shortest time possible; **un ~ de temps** a minimum amount of time; **travailler un ~** to do a minimum (amount) of work; **la production a atteint son ~** production has sunk to its lowest level (yet) *ou* an all-time low; **au (grand) ~** at the very least; **il faut rester le ~ au soleil** you must stay in the sun as little as possible. ◆ **minimal, e,** *mpl* **-aux** *adj* minimum. ◆ **minime** *adj dégât, rôle, différence* minor, minimal; *fait* trivial; *salaire* paltry. ◆ **minimiser** (1) *vt* to minimize. ◆ **minimisation** *nf* minimization.

mini-ordinateur [miniɔʀdinatœʀ] *nm* minicomputer.

ministère [ministɛʀ] **1** *nm* (**a**) *(département)* ministry, department *(surtout US)*. **employé de ~** government employee; **~ de la Culture/de l'Éducation (nationale)** *etc* ministry *(Brit) ou* department *(surtout US)* of Arts/Education *etc; V aussi* **2.** (**b**) *(cabinet)* government. **~ de coalition** coalition government. (**c**) *(Jur)* **le ~ public** *(partie)* the Prosecution; *(service)* the public prosecutor's office. (**d**) *(Rel)* ministry. **exercer son ~ à la campagne** to have a country parish. (**e**) *(littér: entremise)* agency. **2** : **~ des Affaires étrangères** Ministry of Foreign Affairs, Foreign Office *(Brit)*, Department of State *(US)*; **~ de la Défense nationale** Ministry of Defence *(Brit)*, Department of Defense *(US)*; **~ de l'Économie et des Finances** Ministry of Finance, Treasury *(Brit)*, Treasury Department *(US)*; **~ de l'Intérieur** Ministry of the Interior, Home Office *(Brit)*; **~ du Travail** Ministry of Employment *(Brit)*, Department of Labor *(US)*. ◆ **ministériel, -elle** *adj (gén)* ministerial; *remaniement* cabinet.

ministre [ministʀ(ə)] *nm* **1** (**a**) *[gouvernement]* minister, secretary *(surtout US)*. **~ de la Culture/de l'Éducation (nationale)** *etc* minister *(Brit) ou* secretary *(surtout US)* of Arts/Education *etc*; **~ délégué** minister of state (*auprès de* to); **~ sans portefeuille** minister without portfolio; *V aussi* **2.** (**b**) *[ambassade]* envoy. **~ plénipotentiaire** minister plenipotentiary. (**c**) *(Rel)* **~ (du culte)** minister (of religion). (**d**) *(littér: représentant)* agent. **2** : **~ des Affaires étrangères** Minister of Foreign Affairs, Foreign Secretary *(Brit)*, Secretary of State *(US)*; **~ de la Défense nationale** Defence Minister *(Brit)*, Defense Secretary *(US)*; **~ de l'Économie et des Finances** Finance Minister *ou* Secretary, Chancellor of the Exchequer *(Brit)*, Secretary of the Treasury *(US)*; **~ de l'Intérieur** Minister of the Interior, Home Secretary *(Brit)*; **~ du Travail** Minister of Employment *(Brit)*, Labor Secretary *(US)*.

minitel [minitɛl] *nm* ® *home terminal of the French telecommunications system.* **obtenir un renseignement par le ~** to get information on minitel ®.

minium [minjɔm] *nm* red lead paint.

minois [minwa] *nm* (pretty) little face.

minorer [minɔʀe] (1) *vt* to cut, reduce. ◆ **minoration** *nf* cut, reduction (*de* in).

minorité [minɔʀite] *nf (gén)* minority; *(groupe)* minority (group). *(Jur)* **pendant sa ~** while he is under age, during his minority; **être en ~** to be in the minority; **le gouvernement a été mis en ~** the government was defeated (*sur* on). ◆ **minoritaire** *adj groupe* minority. **être ~** to be a minority *ou* in the minority.

Minorque [minɔʀk] *nf* Minorca.

minoterie [minɔtʀi] *nf (industrie)* flour-milling (industry); *(usine)* (flour-)mill. ◆ **minotier** *nm* miller.

minou * [minu] *nm* pussy(-cat) *, puss *.

minuit [minɥi] *nm* midnight, twelve (o'clock) (at night).

minuscule [minyskyl] **1** *adj* minute, tiny, minuscule. **2** *nf*: **(lettre) ~** small letter; *(Typ)* lower case letter. ◆ **minus** *nmf (péj)* dead loss *, second-rater *, washout *.

minute [minyt] *nf* (**a**) minute; *(moment)* minute, moment. **une ~ d'inattention a suffi** a moment's inattention was enough; **~ papillon!** * hey, just a minute!; **la ~ de vérité** the moment of truth; **steak ~** minute steak; **talons ~** heels repaired while you wait, heel-bar; **on me l'a apporté à la ~** it has just this instant *ou* moment been brought to me; **il faut toujours tout faire à la ~** you always have to do things there and then. (**b**) *(Jur)* minute. ◆ **minutage** *nm* timing. ◆ **minuter** (1) *vt (organiser)* to time (carefully); *(limiter)* to time. **emploi du temps minuté** strict schedule.

minuterie [minytʀi] *nf [lumière]* time switch.

minutie [minysi] *nf* (**a**) *[personne, travail]* meticulousness; *[inspection]* detail. **ça demande beaucoup de ~** it requires a great deal of precision. (**b**) *(détails: péj)* **~s** trifling details, minutiae. ◆ **minutieusement** *adv (avec soin)* meticulously; *(dans le détail)* in minute detail. ◆ **minutieux, -euse** *adj personne, soin* meticulous; *inspection* minute. **il s'agit d'un travail ~** it's a job that demands great care.

mioche [mjɔʃ] *nmf (*: gosse)* kid *, nipper *; *(péj)* brat *.

mirabelle [miʀabɛl] *nf* cherry plum.

miracle [miʀɑkl(ə)] *nm* miracle. **cela tient du ~** it's a miracle; *(lit, fig)* **faire des ~s** to work miracles; **par ~** miraculously; **le remède ~** the miracle cure. ◆ **miraculé, e** *adj, nm, f: (malade)* **~** (person) who has been miraculously cured. ◆ **miraculeusement** *adv* miraculously. ◆ **miraculeux, -euse** *adj* miraculous. **ça n'a rien de ~** there's nothing so miraculous *ou* extraordinary about that.

mirador [miʀadɔʀ] *nm (Mil)* watchtower.

mirage [miʀaʒ] *nm (lit, fig)* mirage.

miraud, e ⁑ [miʀo, od] *adj (myope)* short-sighted. **tu es ~!** you need glasses!

mire [miʀ] *nf (TV)* test card. *(viser)* **prendre sa ~** to take aim.

mirobolant, e * [miʀɔbɔlɑ̃, ɑ̃t] *adj* fabulous *, fantastic.

miroir [miʀwaʀ] *nm* mirror. **est-ce le ~ de la réalité?** is it a reflexion of reality?, does it mirror *ou* reflect reality?; *(lit, fig)* **~ aux alouettes** lure. ◆ **se mirer** (1) *vpr* to gaze at o.s.; *[chose]* to be mirrored *ou* reflected *(in the water etc)*.

miroiter [miʀwate] (1) *vi (étinceler)* to sparkle, gleam; *(chatoyer)* to shimmer. *(fig)* **il lui fit ~ les avantages** he painted in glowing colours the advantages, he painted an enticing picture of the advantages. ◆ **miroitement** *nm*: **~(s)** sparkling, gleaming; shimmering.

miroiterie [miʀwatʀi] *nf* (**a**) *(Comm)* mirror trade; *(Ind)* mirror industry. (**b**) *(usine)* mirror factory. ◆ **miroitier, -ière** *nm, f (vendeur)* mirror dealer; *(fabricant)* mirror manufacturer.

mis, e[1] [mi, miz] *adj*: **bien ~** well-dressed.

misaine [mizɛn] *nf*: **(voile de) ~** foresail.

misanthrope [mizɑ̃tʀɔp] **1** *nmf* misanthropist. **2** *adj* misanthropic. ◆ **misanthropie** *nf* misanthropy.

mise[2] [miz] **1** *nf* (**a**) *(action de mettre)* putting, setting. **~ en service** putting into service; **~ en bouteilles** bottling; **~ en marche** starting; **~ à jour** updating. (**b**) *(enjeu)* stake; *(Comm)* outlay. **récupérer sa mise** to recoup one's outlay. (**c**) *(habillement)* clothing. (**d**) **être de ~** *[remarque]* to be in place; **ces propos ne sont pas de ~** those remarks are out of place. **2** : **~ en accusation** indictment; *(lit)* **~ en boîte** canning; *(fig)* **il ne supporte pas la ~ en boîte** * he can't stand having his leg pulled; *(Fin)* **~ de fonds** capital outlay; *(Fin)* **~ de fonds initiale** seed money, venture capital; **~ à mort** kill; *(Coiffure)* **~ en plis** set; **~ au point** *(Aut)* tuning; *(Phot)* focusing; *(Tech)* adjustment; *(Ordin)* debugging; *[affaire]* finalizing, settling; *[procédé technique]* perfecting; *(explication)* clarification; **~ à prix** *(enchères)* reserve price, upset price *(US)*; **~ en scène** production; *(fig)* performance; **~ en valeur** *[terre]* development; *[maison]* improvement; *[tableau]* setting-off.

miser [mize] (1) *vt argent* to stake, bet (*sur* on). *(fig)* **il a misé sur le mauvais cheval** he backed the wrong horse *(fig)*; *(*: compter sur)* ~ **sur** to bank on, count on.

misère [mizɛʀ] *nf* (**a**) *(pauvreté)* poverty, destitution. **être dans la** ~ to be destitute *ou* poverty-stricken; **vivre dans la** ~ to live in poverty; **salaire de** ~ starvation wage. (**b**) *(malheur)* ~**s** woes, miseries; *(*: ennuis)* **petites** ~**s** little troubles; **faire des** ~**s à qn** * to be nasty to sb; **quelle** ~! what a wretched shame! (**c**) *(somme)* **il l'a eu pour une** ~ he got it for a song *ou* for next to nothing. (**d**) *(plante)* wandering sailor. ◆ **misérable** **1** *adj* (**a**) *(pauvre) personne* destitute; *région* impoverished, poverty-stricken; *logement* seedy, mean; *vêtements* shabby. (**b**) *(pitoyable) existence, conditions* miserable, wretched, pitiful; *personne* pitiful, wretched. (**c**) *(sans valeur) somme d'argent* paltry, miserable. **tout ça pour un** ~ **billet de 20 F** all this because of a paltry *ou* measly * 20-franc note. **2** *nmf (méchant)* wretch; *(pauvre)* poor wretch. **petit** ~! you (little) wretch! ◆ **misérablement** *adv (pitoyablement)* miserably, wretchedly; *(pauvrement)* in wretched poverty. ◆ **miséreux, -euse** **1** *adj* poverty-stricken. **2** *nm, f* down-and-out.

miséricorde [mizeʀikɔʀd(ə)] *nf* mercy. ◆ **miséricordieux, -ieuse** *adj* merciful.

misogyne [mizɔʒin] **1** *adj* misogynous. **2** *nmf* misogynist. ◆ **misogynie** *nf* misogyny.

miss [mis] *nf* (**a**) beauty queen. **M~ France** Miss France. (**b**) *(gouvernante)* governess.

missel [misɛl] *nm* missal.

missile [misil] *nm* missile.

mission [misjɔ̃] *nf (gén)* mission; *(Pol)* assignment. ~ **lui fut donnée de** he was commissioned to; **il s'est donné pour** ~ **de faire** he set himself the task of doing. ◆ **missionnaire** *adj, nmf* missionary.

missive [misiv] *nf (littér)* missive.

mite [mit] *nf* clothes moth. ◆ **se miter** (1) *vpr* to be *ou* become moth-eaten. ◆ **miteux, -euse** *adj lieu* seedy, dingy; *vêtement, personne* shabby.

mi-temps [mitɑ̃] *nf inv* (**a**) *(Sport) (période)* half; *(repos)* half-time. **à la** ~ at half-time. (**b**) **travailler à** ~ to work part-time.

mitigé, e [mitiʒe] *adj ardeur* mitigated; *convictions* lukewarm; *sentiments* mixed.

mitonner [mitɔne] (1) **1** *vt (à feu doux)* to simmer; *(avec soin)* to cook with loving care. **2** *vi* to simmer.

mitoyen, -enne [mitwajɛ̃, ɛn] *adj*: **mur** ~ party wall; **maisons** ~**nes** *(deux)* semi-detached houses, duplex houses *(US)*; *(plus de deux)* terraced houses, town houses *(US)*; **notre jardin est** ~ **avec le leur** our garden adjoins theirs.

mitrailler [mitʀɑje] (1) *vt (Mil)* to machine gun. ~ **au sol** to strafe; ~ **qn avec des élastiques** * to pelt sb with rubber bands; ~ **qn de questions** to bombard sb with questions; *(Phot)* ~ **un monument** to snap away at a monument. ◆ **mitraille** *nf (projectiles)* grapeshot; *(décharge)* hail of bullets; *(monnaie)* loose *ou* small change. ◆ **mitraillette** *nf* submachine gun. ◆ **mitrailleuse** *nf* machine gun.

mitre [mitʀ(ə)] *nf (Rel)* mitre.

mitron [mitʀɔ̃] *nm* baker's boy.

mixage [miksaʒ] *nm (Ciné, Rad)* (sound) mixing.

mixer, mixeur [miksœʀ] *nm* liquidizer, mixer.

mixte [mikst(ə)] *adj* (**a**) *(deux sexes) (gén)* mixed; *école* coeducational. (**b**) *(hétérogène) (gén)* mixed; *équipe* combined; *commission* joint; *rôle* dual. **lycée** ~ ≃ comprehensive school; **outil à usage** ~ dual-purpose tool; **cargo** ~ cargo-passenger ship; **cuisinière** ~ combined gas and electric cooker *ou* stove. ◆ **mixité** *nf* coeducation.

mixture [mikstyʀ] *nf (lit)* mixture; *(péj, fig)* concoction.

mobile [mɔbil] **1** *adj pièce de moteur* moving; *casier, panneau* movable; *feuillets* loose; *main-d'œuvre, population, troupes* mobile; *reflet* changing; *traits, regard* mobile. **avec la voiture on est très** ~ having a car makes you very mobile. **2** *nm* (**a**) *(impulsion)* motive (*de* for). **chercher le** ~ **du crime** to look for the motive for the crime. (**b**) *(Art)* mobile. (**c**) *(Phys)* moving object *ou* body.

mobilier, -ière [mɔbilje, jɛʀ] **1** *adj bien* movable, personal; *valeurs* transferable. **2** *nm (ameublement)* furniture; *(Jur)* personal *ou* movable property.

mobiliser [mɔbilize] (1) *vt (gén)* to mobilize. ~ **les esprits** to rouse people's interest. ◆ **mobilisation** *nf* mobilization.

mobilité [mɔbilite] *nf (gén)* mobility.

mobylette [mɔbilɛt] *nf* ® moped.

mocassin [mɔkasɛ̃] *nm* mocassin.

moche * [mɔʃ] *adj (laid)* ugly, awful, ghastly *; *(mauvais)* rotten *. **il a la grippe, c'est** ~ **pour lui** he's got the flu, that's hard on him *ou* that's rotten for him *. ◆ **mocheté** * *nf* (**a**) *(laideur)* ugliness. (**b**) *(femme)* fright; *(objet)* eyesore.

mode[1] [mɔd] *nf (gén)* fashion; *(péj: engouement)* craze. **suivre la** ~ to keep in fashion; **à la** ~ *personne, vêtement* fashionable; *(dans le vent)* trendy *; **c'est la** ~ **des boucles d'oreilles** earrings are in fashion *ou* are in *; **habillé à la** ~ fashionably *ou* trendily * dressed; **travailler dans la** ~ to work in the fashion industry *ou* business; **journal de** ~ fashion magazine; **coloris** ~ fashion colours; **selon la** ~ **de l'époque** according to the custom of the day; **à la** ~ **du 18ᵉ siècle** in the style of the 18th century.

mode[2] [mɔd] *nm* (**a**) *(méthode)* method; *(genre)* way. ~ **de vie** way of life; ~ **de paiement** method *ou* mode of payment; ~ **d'emploi** directions for use. (**b**) *(Gram, Ling)* mood; *(Ordin, Mus, Philos)* mode. *(Ordin)* ~ **synchrone/asynchrone/interactif** synchronous/asynchronous/interactive mode. ◆ **modal, e,** *mpl* **-aux** **1** *adj* modal. **2** *nm (verbe)* modal (verb). ◆ **modalité** *nf* (**a**) *(forme)* mode. ~ **d'application de la loi** mode of enforcement of the law; ~**s de paiement** methods *ou* modes of payment; *(Scol)* ~**s de contrôle** methods of assessment. (**b**) *(Ling, Mus, Philos)* modality. (**c**) *(Jur: condition)* clause.

modèle [mɔdɛl] **1** *nm (gén, Écon)* model; *(Tech)* pattern; *(type)* type; *(exemple)* example, model; *(Ling)* model, pattern; *(Scol: corrigé)* fair copy. ~ **réduit/de série** small-scale/production model; ~ **déposé** registered design; **petit/grand** ~ small/large version *ou* model; *(boîte)* **voulez-vous le petit ou le grand** ~? do you want the small or the big size (box)?; *(voiture)* **il a le** ~ **5 portes** he has the 5-door hatchback model *ou* version; *(Mode)* **X présente ses** ~**s d'automne** X presents his autumn models *ou* styles; **X est le** ~ **du bon élève** X is a model pupil, X is the epitome of the good pupil; **prendre qn pour** ~ to model o.s. upon sb. **2** *adj conduite, ouvrier, ferme* model.

modeler [mɔdle] (5) *vt statue* to model, mould; *caractère* to shape, mould. **cuisse bien modelée** shapely thigh; ~ **ses attitudes sur** to model one's attitudes on; **se** ~ **sur qn/qch** to model o.s. on sb/sth. ◆ **modelage** *nm (activité)* modelling; *(statue)* piece of sculpture. ◆ **modelé** *nm [corps]* contours; *(Géog)* relief.

modem [mɔdɛm] *nm* modem.

modérer [mɔdeʀe] (6) **1** *vt (gén)* to curb, moderate; *vitesse* to reduce. **modérez vos expressions!** moderate *ou* mind your language! **2 se** ~ *vpr (s'apaiser)* to calm down, control o.s.; *(montrer de la mesure)* to restrain o.s. ◆ **modérateur, -trice**

1 *adj* moderating, restraining. **2** *nm (Tech)* regulator; *(atomique)* moderator. ◆ **modération** *nf (retenue)* moderation, restraint; *(diminution)* reduction. ◆ **modéré, e** *adj (gén)* moderate. ◆ **modérément** *adv manger* in moderation. **être ~ satisfait** to be moderately satisfied.

moderne [mɔdɛʀn(ə)] **1** *adj (gén)* modern; *équipement* up-to-date. **la jeune fille ~** the young woman of today. **2** *nm (style)* modern style; *(meubles)* modern furniture. ◆ **modernisateur, -trice 1** *adj* modernizing. **2** *nm, f* modernizer. ◆ **modernisation** *nf* modernization. ◆ **moderniser** (1) *vt* to modernize, bring up to date. ◆ **modernisme** *nm* modernism. ◆ **moderniste 1** *nmf* modernist. **2** *adj* modernistic.

modeste [mɔdɛst(ə)] *adj (gén)* modest. **c'est un cadeau bien ~** it's a very modest gift; **je ne suis qu'un ~ ouvrier** I'm only a simple *ou* modest working man; **d'origine ~** from a modest *ou* humble background; **faire le ~** to make a show of modesty; **avoir le triomphe ~** to be modest about one's successes. ◆ **modestement** *adv* modestly. ◆ **modestie** *nf* modesty. **fausse ~** false modesty.

modifier [mɔdifje] (7) **1** *vt* to modify, alter. **2 se ~** *vpr* to alter, be modified. ◆ **modification** *nf* modification, alteration. *(Psych)* **~ du comportement** behaviour modification.

modique [mɔdik] *adj (gén)* modest, low; *salaire* meagre. ◆ **modicité** *nf* lowness.

modiste [mɔdist(ə)] *nf* milliner.

module [mɔdyl] *nm (Espace)* module; *(Math, Phys)* modulus; *(éléments d'un ensemble)* unit. **~ lunaire** lunar module, mooncraft; **acheter une cuisine par ~s** to buy a kitchen in separate units.

moduler [mɔdyle] (1) *vti* to modulate. **~ les peines en fonction des délits** to adjust the punishment to fit the crime. ◆ **modulation** *nf* modulation. **poste à ~ de fréquence** VHF *ou* FM radio.

moelle [mwal] *nf (Anat)* marrow; *(Bot)* pith. **~ épinière** spinal cord; *(lit, fig)* **pourri jusqu'à la ~** rotten to the core.

moelleux, -euse [mwalø, øz] **1** *adj tapis, couleur* soft; *aliment* creamy, smooth; *son, vin* mellow. **2** *nm* softness; creaminess, smoothness; mellowness. ◆ **moelleusement** *adv s'étendre* luxuriously.

mœurs [mœʀ(s)] *nfpl* (**a**) *(morale)* morals. **avoir des ~ sévères** to have strict moral standards; **contraire aux bonnes ~** contrary to accepted standards of behaviour; **femme de ~ légères** woman of easy virtue; *(Jur, Presse)* **affaire de ~** sex case; **la police des ~** ≃ the vice squad. (**b**) *(coutumes)* customs, habits. **c'est entré dans les ~** it's become normal practice; **les ~ politiques** the political practices *ou* usages; **avoir des ~ simples** to have simple tastes. (**c**) *(manières)* manners, ways. **quelles ~!** what a way to behave!, what manners!; **comédie de ~** comedy of manners.

moi [mwa] **1** *pron pers* (**a**) *(objet)* me. **il nous a regardés ma femme et ~** he looked at my wife and me; **écoute-~ ça! *** just listen to that!; **il n'obéit qu'à ~** he only obeys me, I'm the only one he obeys; **~ elle me déteste** she hates me. (**b**) *(sujet)* I, me *. **qui a fait cela? — (ce n'est) pas ~** who did this? — I didn't *ou* not me *; **~, le saluer?, jamais!** me, greet him?, never!; **mon mari et ~ refusons** my husband and I refuse; **~ parti, que ferez-vous?** when I'm gone what will you do?, what will you do with me away?; **et ~ de rire de plus belle!** and so I (just) laughed all the more!; **je ne l'ai pas vu, ~** I (myself) didn't see him. (**c**) *(avec qui, que)* **~ qui vous parle, je l'ai vu** I myself *ou* personally saw him; **c'est ~ qu'elle veut voir** it's me she wants to see; **et ~ qui avais espéré gagner!** and to think that I had hoped to win! (**d**) *(avec prép)* **venez chez ~** come to my place; **le poème n'est pas de ~** the poem isn't one I wrote *ou* isn't one of mine; **un élève à ~** a pupil of mine; **j'ai un appartement à ~** I have a flat of my own; **ce livre est à ~** this book belongs to me *ou* is mine; **il veut une photo de ~** he wants a photo of me. (**e**) *(dans comparaisons)* I, me. **il mange plus que ~** he eats more than I (do) *ou* than me; **fais comme ~** do as I do, do like me *; *V* **même. 2** *nm*: **le ~** the self, the ego; **notre vrai ~** our true self.

moignon [mwaɲɔ̃] *nm* stump.

moindre [mwɛ̃dʀ(ə)] *adj* (**a**) *(moins grand)* less, lesser; *(inférieur)* lower, poorer. **les dégâts sont bien ~s** the damage is much less; **à un ~ degré** to a lesser degree; **à ~ prix** at a lower price; **c'est un inconvénient ~** it's less of a drawback, it's a lesser drawback. (**b**) **le ~, la ~, les ~s** the least, the slightest; *(de deux)* the lesser; **la ~ idée** the slightest *ou* remotest idea; **le ~ de deux maux** the lesser of two evils; **c'est la ~ de mes difficultés** that's the least of my difficulties; **merci — c'est la ~ des choses!** thank you — it's a pleasure!, it's the least I could do!; **certains spécialistes et non des ~s disent que** some specialists and important ones at that say that. ◆ **moindrement** *adv*: **il n'était pas le ~ surpris** he was not in the least *ou* slightest surprised.

moine [mwan] *nm* monk, friar.

moineau, *pl* **~x** [mwano] *nm* sparrow.

moins [mwɛ̃] **1** *adv emploi comparatif* (**a**) (*avec adj ou adv*) less. **3 fois ~** 3 times less; **il est ~ grand que son frère/que je ne pensais** he is not as *ou* so tall as his brother/as I thought, he is less tall than his brother/than I thought; **rien n'est ~ sûr** nothing is less certain; **c'est tellement ~ cher** it's so much cheaper *ou* so much less expensive; **c'est le même genre, en ~ bien** it's the same kind, only (it's) not so good. (**b**) (*avec vb*) less. **donner ~** to give less; **vous ne l'obtiendrez pas à ~** you won't get it for less; **cela coûtait trois fois ~** it was one-third as expensive; **il a fait encore ~ beau qu'en juillet** the weather was even worse than in July. (**c**) **~ de** *(quantité)* less, not so much; *(nombre)* fewer, not so many; *(heure)* before, not yet; *(durée, âge, distance)* less than, under; **mange ~ de bonbons et de chocolat** eat fewer sweets and less chocolate; **les enfants de ~ de 4 ans** children under 4 *ou* of less than 4 years of age; **il est ~ de minuit** it is not yet midnight; **il était un peu ~ de 6 heures** it was a little before 6 o'clock; **vous ne pouvez pas lui donner ~ de 100 F** you can't give him less than 100 francs; **il a eu ~ de mal que nous** he had less trouble than we had; **nous l'avons fait en ~ de 5 minutes** we did it in less than *ou* in under 5 minutes; **en ~ de deux *** in a flash; **il y aura ~ de monde demain** there will be fewer people tomorrow. (**d**) **de ~, en~: il gagne 500 F de ~ qu'elle** he earns 500 francs less than she does; **vous avez 5 ans de ~ qu'elle** you are 5 years younger than she is; **il y a 3 verres en ~** *(qui manquent)* there are 3 glasses missing; *(trop peu)* we are 3 glasses short; **c'est le même climat, le brouillard en ~** it's the same climate except for the fog *ou* minus the fog. (**e**) **~... ~** the less... the less; **~... plus** the less... the more; **~ je mange, ~ j'ai d'appétit** the less I eat, the less hungry I feel; **~ je fume, plus je mange** the less I smoke, the more I eat. (**f**) *(locutions)* **à ~ qu'il ne vienne** unless he comes; **à ~ d'un accident, ça devrait marcher** accidents apart it should work; **c'est de ~ en ~ bon** it is less and less good.

2 *adv emploi superlatif* (**a**) (*avec adj ou adv*) **le ~, la ~** *(de plusieurs)* the least; *(de deux)* the less; **c'est la ~ douée de mes élèves** she is the least gifted of my pupils; **c'est le ~ doué des deux** he's the less gifted of the two; **la température la ~ haute de l'été** the lowest temperature of the summer. (**b**) (*avec vb*) **le ~** (the) least; **c'est celui que j'aime**

le ~ it's the one I like (the) least. (**c**) *(locutions)* **c'est bien le** ~ **que l'on puisse faire** it's the least one can do; **si vous êtes le** ~ **du monde soucieux** if you are in the slightest bit *ou* in the least (bit) worried; **au** ~ at least; **600 au** ~ at least 600, fully 600; **la moitié au** ~ at least half, fully half; **pour le** ~ to say the least, at the very least; **du** ~ **je le pense** I think so at least; **laissez-le sortir, si du** ~ **il ne fait pas froid** let him go out, that is (only) if it is not cold.
3 *prép* (**a**) *(soustraction)* **6** ~ **2 font 4** 6 minus 2 equals 4, 2 from 6 makes 4; **j'ai retrouvé mon sac,** ~ **le portefeuille** I found my bag, minus the wallet. (**b**) *(heure)* to. **il est 4 heures** ~ **5 (minutes)** it is 5 (minutes) to 4; **il n'est que** ~ **10** * it's only 10 to *; *(fig)* **il s'en est tiré, mais il était** ~ **cinq** * *ou* ~ **une** * he got out of it but it was a close shave * *ou* a near thing *. (**c**) *(température)* below. **il fait** ~ **5°** it is 5° below freezing *ou* minus 5°.
4 *nm (Math)* **(le signe)** ~ the minus sign.
5 : **moins que rien** * *nmf (péj: minable)* dead loss *, second-rater *, washout *; *(Comm)* **moins-value** *nf* depreciation.

moire [mwaʀ] *nf* moiré. ◆ **moiré, e** *adj, nm* moiré.

mois [mwa] *nm* (**a**) *(période)* month. **dans un** ~ in a month('s time); **être payé au** ~ to be paid monthly; **louer au** ~ to rent by the month; **30F par** ~ 30 francs a *ou* per month; **un bébé de 6** ~ a 6-month(-old) baby; **devoir 3** ~ **de loyer** to owe 3 months' rent. (**b**) *(salaire)* monthly pay *ou* salary. ~ **double** extra month's pay *(as end-of-year bonus)*.

moisir [mwaziʀ] (2) **1** *vt* to make mouldy. **2** *vi* (**a**) to go mouldy. (**b**) *(en province)* to stagnate; *(dans un cachot)* to rot. **on ne va pas** ~ **ici jusqu'à la nuit!** * we're not going to hang around here till night-time! * ◆ **moisi, e 1** *adj* mouldy, mildewed. **2** *nm* mould, mildew. **odeur de** ~ musty smell; **ça sent le** ~ it smells musty. ◆ **moisissure** *nf (gén)* mould; *(par l'humidité)* mildew. **enlever les** ~**s sur un fromage** to scrape the mould off a piece of cheese.

moisson [mwasɔ̃] *nf* harvest. **faire la** ~ to harvest; ~ **de renseignements** wealth *ou* crop of information. ◆ **moissonner** (1) *vt céréale* to harvest, gather in; *champ* to reap; *renseignements, souvenirs* to gather, collect. ◆ **moissonneur, -euse 1** *nm, f* harvester. **2** *nf (machine)* harvester. **3** : ~**euse-batteuse (-lieuse)** *nf, pl* ~**s-**~**s (-**~**s)** combine harvester.

moite [mwat] *adj (gén)* sticky; *mains* sweaty; *atmosphère* muggy. ◆ **moiteur** *nf* stickiness; sweatiness; mugginess.

moitié [mwatje] *nf* (**a**) *(partie)* half. **partager qch en deux** ~**s** to halve sth, divide sth in half *ou* into two halves; **donne-m'en la** ~ give me half (of it); **faire la** ~ **du chemin** to go halfway *ou* half of the way; **la** ~ **du temps** half the time; **il en faut** ~ **plus/moins** you need half as much again/half (of) that. (**b**) *(milieu)* halfway mark, half. **à la** ~ **du chemin** having reached halfway *ou* the half-way mark; **arrivé à la** ~ **du travail** having done half the work *ou* got halfway through the work. (**c**) *(hum: épouse)* **ma** ~ my better half *, my wife. (**d**) **il a fait le travail à** ~ he has (only) half done the work; **il ne fait jamais rien à** ~ he never does things by halves; **à** ~ **plein** half-full; **à** ~ **chemin** (at) halfway, at the halfway mark; **à** ~ **prix** (at) half-price; **réduire de** ~ to cut by half, halve; **plus grand de** ~ half as big again, bigger by half; **diviser qch par** ~ to divide sth in two *ou* in half; **on a partagé le pain** ~ ~ we shared the bread half-and-half *ou* fifty-fifty *.

moka [mɔka] *nm (gâteau à la crème)* cream gâteau; *(gâteau au café)* mocha *ou* coffee gâteau; *(café)* mocha coffee.

molaire [mɔlɛʀ] *nf (dent)* molar.

môle [mol] *nm (digue)* breakwater, jetty; *(quai)* pier, jetty.

molécule [mɔlekyl] *nf* molecule. ◆ **moléculaire** *adj* molecular.

molester [mɔlɛste] (1) *vt* to manhandle, maul.

molette [mɔlɛt] *nf* toothed wheel; *[briquet]* knurl. ◆ **moleté, e** *adj* knurled.

mollesse [mɔlɛs] *nf [substance, contours]* softness; *[relief]* gentleness; *[traits du visage]* flabbiness; *[geste]* lifelessness; *[protestations]* weakness, feebleness; *[personne] (indolence)* sluggishness; *(manque d'autorité)* spinelessness; *(grande indulgence)* laxness. ◆ **mollasse** * *adj (péj) (apathique)* sluggish; *(flasque)* flabby, flaccid. ◆ **molle** *adj f V* **mou.** ◆ **mollement** *adv tomber* softly; *couler* gently; *travailler* half-heartedly; *protester* feebly, weakly.

mollet [mɔlɛ] *nm (Anat)* calf.

molletonner [mɔltɔne] (1) *vt* to line warmly. **anorak molletonné** quilted anorak, anorak with a warm lining.

mollir [mɔliʀ] (2) *vi* (**a**) *[sol, ennemi]* to yield, give way; *[père]* to come round, relent; *[courage]* to flag. (**b**) *[substance]* to soften, go soft. (**c**) *[vent]* to die down.

mollusque [mɔlysk(ə)] *nm (Zool)* mollusc; *(* péj)* lazy lump *, lazybones.

molosse [mɔlɔs] *nm* big dog *ou* hound.

môme [mom] *nmf (*: enfant)* kid *; *(péj)* brat *; *(‡: fille)* bird ‡, chick ‡ *(US)*.

moment [mɔmɑ̃] *nm* (**a**) *(instant)* while, moment. **je ne l'ai pas vu depuis un (bon)** ~ I haven't seen him for a (good) while *ou* for quite a time *ou* while; **ça va prendre un** ~ it will take some time *ou* a good while; **il réfléchit (pendant) un** ~ he thought for a moment; **c'est l'affaire d'un** ~ it won't take a minute *ou* moment; **dans un** ~ in a little while, in a moment; **un** ~! just a moment *ou* a minute! (**b**) *(période)* time. **à quel** ~ **est-ce arrivé?** at what point *ou* when exactly did this occur?; **ce n'est pas le** ~ this is not the time *ou* the moment (*de* to); **passer de bons** ~**s** to spend (some) happy times; **arriver au bon** ~ to come at the right time; **passer un mauvais** ~ to have a rough *ou* difficult time; **il est dans un de ses mauvais** ~**s** it's one of his off * *ou* bad spells; **à ses** ~**s perdus** in his spare time; **les grands** ~**s de l'histoire** the great moments of history; **le succès du** ~ the success of the moment *ou* day; **profiter du** ~ to take advantage of the opportunity (*de* to); **c'était le** ~ **de réagir** it was time to react, a reaction was called for. (**c**) *(Tech)* moment; *(Phys)* momentum. (**d**) *(locutions)* **en ce** ~ at the moment, at present, just now; **au** ~ **de l'accident** at the time of the accident, when the accident happened; **au** ~ **de partir** just as I *(ou he etc)* was about to leave; **au** ~ **où elle entrait** when *ou* as she was going in; **à un** ~ **donné** at a certain point; **le** ~ **venu** when the time comes (*ou* came); **il peut arriver à tout** ~ *ou* **d'un** ~ **à l'autre** he may arrive (at) any time (now) *ou* any moment (now); **à ce** ~**-là** *(temps)* at that time; *(circonstance)* in that case; **le bruit grandissait de** ~ **en** ~ the noise grew louder every moment; **du** ~ **où** *ou* **que** since, seeing that; **dès le** ~ **que** *ou* **où** as soon as; **par** ~**s** now and then, at times; **pour le** ~ for the time being; **sur le** ~ at the time. ◆ **momentané, e** *adj* momentary. ◆ **momentanément** *adv (en ce moment)* at the moment, at present; *(un court instant)* momentarily.

momie [mɔmi] *nf* mummy.

mon [mɔ̃], **ma** [ma], **mes** [me] *adj poss* my. **j'ai** ~ **idée là-dessus** I have my own ideas *ou* views about that; **j'ai** ~ **samedi cette année** * I've got

Saturday(s) off this year; ~ **vieux** * my dear fellow, old chap * *ou* fellow *; *(Rel)* **oui** ~ **Père** yes Father; ~ **Dieu** *(Rel)* dear Lord; *(excl)* good heavens!; **oui** ~ **général** yes sir *ou* general; *V* **son.**

Monaco [mɔnako] *nm:* **(la principauté de)** ~ (the principality of) Monaco.

monarchie [mɔnaʀʃi] *nf* monarchy. ◆ **monarchique** *adj* monarchistic. ◆ **monarchiste** *adj, nmf* monarchist. ◆ **monarque** *nm* monarch. ~ **absolu** absolute monarch; ~ **de droit divin** monarch *ou* king by divine right.

monastère [mɔnastɛʀ] *nm* monastery. ◆ **monastique** *adj* monastic.

monceau, *pl* ~**x** [mɔ̃so] *nm* heap.

mondain, e [mɔ̃dɛ̃, ɛn] **1** *adj* (**a**) *réunion, chronique* society; *obligations* social; *public* fashionable. **plaisirs** ~**s** pleasures of society; **vie** ~**e** social *ou* society life; **soirée** ~**e** evening reception *(with people from high society)*. (**b**) *politesse, ton* refined. **il a été très** ~ **avec moi** he treated me with studied politeness *ou* courtesy. (**c**) *(Philos)* mundane; *(Rel)* worldly, earthly. (**d**) **la (police)** ~**e** ≃ the vice squad. **2** *nm, f* society man (*ou* woman), socialite. ◆ **mondanités** *nfpl (divertissements)* society life; *(propos)* society small talk.

monde [mɔ̃d] *nm* (**a**) world. **dans le** ~ **entier** all over the world, the world over, throughout the world; **le** ~ **entier s'indigna** the whole world was outraged; **il se moque** *ou* **se fiche** * **du** ~ he's got a nerve *ou* cheek *; **mettre/venir au** ~ to bring/come into the world; **si je suis encore de ce** ~ if I'm still here *ou* in the land of the living *ou* of this world; **dans ce bas** ~ here below; **l'Ancien/le Nouveau M**~ the Old/New World; **le Tiers-/Quart-**~ the Third/Fourth World; **le** ~ **de la folie** the world *ou* realm of madness.
(**b**) *(intensif)* **le meilleur du** ~ the best in the world; **c'est le meilleur homme du** ~ he's the finest man alive; **tout s'est passé le mieux du** ~ everything went (off) perfectly *ou* like a dream *; **il n'était pas le moins du** ~ **anxieux** he was not the least bit worried; **pour rien au** ~ not for all the world; **nul au** ~ **ne peut...** nobody in the world can...; **j'en pense tout le bien du** ~ I have the highest opinion of him (*ou* her *ou* it).
(**c**) *(locutions)* **c'est le** ~ **à l'envers** it's a topsy-turvy *ou* crazy world; **comme le** ~ **est petit!** it's a small world!; **se faire tout un** ~ **de qch** to make a fuss about sth; **c'est un** ~**!** * if that doesn't beat all! *; **il y a un** ~ **entre ces deux concepts** there is a world of difference between these two concepts.
(**d**) *(gens)* **j'entends du** ~ **à côté** I can hear people in the next room; **est-ce qu'il y a du** ~**?** *(qn est-il présent)* is there anybody there?; *(y a-t-il foule)* are there a lot of people there?; **il y a du** ~ *(ce n'est pas vide)* there are some people there; *(il y a foule)* there's quite a crowd; **il y a beaucoup de** ~ there's a real crowd; **ils reçoivent beaucoup de** ~ they entertain a lot; **ce week-end nous avons du** ~ we have people coming *ou* visitors this weekend; **tout ce petit** ~ **s'est bien amusé?** and did everyone have a nice time?, did we all enjoy ourselves?; **il connaît son** ~ he knows the people he deals with.
(**e**) *(milieu social)* set, circle. **le** *(grand)* ~ (high) society; **il n'est pas de notre** ~ he's not one of our set *ou* crowd *; **homme/femme/gens du** ~ society man/woman/people.
◆ **mondial, e,** *mpl* **-aux** *adj guerre, population* world; *crise* world-wide. **à l'échelle** ~**e** on a world-wide scale. ◆ **mondialement** *adv* throughout the world, the (whole) world over. ~ **connu** world-famous. ◆ **mond(i)ovision** *nf* television broadcast by satellite.

monégasque [mɔnegask(ə)] *adj,* **M**~ *nmf* Monegasque, Monacan.

mongol, e [mɔ̃gɔl] **1** *adj* Mongol, Mongolian. **2** *nm (Ling)* Mongolian. **3** *nm, f:* **M~(e)** *(gén)* Mongol, Mongoloid; *(habitant ou originaire de la Mongolie)* Mongolian. ◆ **Mongolie** *nf* Mongolia. **République populaire de** ~ People's Republic of Mongolia.

mongolien, -ienne [mɔ̃gɔljɛ̃, jɛn] *adj, nm, f (Méd)* mongol. ◆ **mongolisme** *nm* mongolism, Down's syndrome.

moniteur, -trice [mɔnitœʀ, tʀis] **1** *nm, f (Sport)* instructor, instructress; *[colonie de vacances]* supervisor, (camp) counsellor *(US)*; *(Univ)* graduate assistant. ~ **de ski** skiing instructor; ~ **d'auto-école** driving instructor. **2** *nm (Tech, Ordin: appareil)* monitor. ~ **cardiaque** heart-rate monitor. ◆ **monitorat** *nm (formation)* training to be an instructor; *(fonction)* instructorship.

monnaie [mɔnɛ] *nf* (**a**) *(devises)* currency. (**b**) *(pièce, médaille)* coin. (**c**) *(appoint)* change. **petite** *ou* **menue** ~ small change; **auriez-vous de la** ~**?** could you give me some change?; **faire la** ~ **de 100 F** to get change for 100 francs. (**d**) *(bâtiment)* **la M**~, **l'hôtel des** ~**s** the Mint. (**e**) **c'est** ~ **courante** *[faits]* it's a common occurrence; *[pratiques]* it's common practice; *(fig)* **rendre à qn la** ~ **de sa pièce** to pay sb back in his own coin; **servir de** ~ **d'échange** to be used as money *ou* as a currency; *(fig)* to be used as bargaining counters; **payer qn en** ~ **de singe** to fob sb off with empty promises. ◆ **monétaire** *adj (gén)* monetary. **la circulation** ~ the circulation of currency. ◆ **monétarisme** *nm* monetarism. ◆ **monétariste** *adj, nmf* monetarist. ◆ **monnayer** (8) *vt terres, titres* to convert into cash; *talent* to make money *ou* earn a living from.

mono... [mɔnɔ] *préf* mono...

monochrome [mɔnɔkʀom] *adj* monochrome, monochromatic.

monocle [mɔnɔkl(ə)] *nm* monocle, eyeglass.

monocoque [mɔnɔkɔk] **1** *adj voiture, avion* monocoque. **voilier** ~ monohull *ou* single-hull sailing dinghy. **2** *nm (voilier)* monohull.

monocorde [mɔnɔkɔʀd(ə)] *adj voix, discours* monotonous.

monoculture [mɔnɔkyltyʀ] *nf* single-crop farming, monoculture.

monocycle [mɔnɔsikl(ə)] *nm* unicycle.

monogramme [mɔnɔgʀam] *nm* monogram.

monographie [mɔnɔgʀafi] *nf* monograph.

monokini [mɔnɔkini] *nm* topless swimsuit, monokini.

monolingue [mɔnɔlɛ̃g] *adj* monolingual.

monolithique [mɔnɔlitik] *adj (lit, fig)* monolithic.

monologue [mɔnɔlɔg] *nm* monologue, soliloquy. ◆ **monologuer** (1) *vi* to soliloquize.

monôme [mɔnom] *nm (Math)* monomial; *(arg Scol)* ≃ students' rag.

monomoteur, -trice [mɔnɔmɔtœʀ, tʀis] **1** *adj* single-engined. **2** *nm* single-engined aircraft.

monoparental, -e, *mpl* **-aux** [mɔnɔpaʀɑ̃tal, o] *adj:* **familles** ~**es** single-parent *ou* one-parent families.

monophonie [mɔnɔfɔni] *nf* monophony. ◆ **monophonique** *adj* monophonic.

monoplace [mɔnɔplas] *nmf* single-seater.

monopole [mɔnɔpɔl] *nm (Écon, fig)* monopoly. ◆ **monopolisateur, -trice** *nm, f* monopolizer. ◆ **monopolisation** *nf* monopolization. ◆ **monopoliser** (1) *vt (lit, fig)* to monopolize.

monoprix [mɔnɔpʀi] *nm* ® department store *(for inexpensive goods)*, ≃ five and ten *(US)*, ≃ Woolworth's ® *(Brit)*.

monosyllabe [mɔnɔsilab] *nm (lit, fig)* monosyllable. ◆ **monosyllabique** *adj* monosyllabic.

monothéisme [mɔnɔteism(ə)] *nm* monotheism. ◆ **monothéiste 1** *adj* monotheistic. **2** *nmf* monotheist.

monotone [mɔnɔtɔn] *adj (gén)* monotonous; *spectacle* dull, dreary; *vie* humdrum. ◆ **monotonie** *nf* monotony; dullness, dreariness.

monseigneur [mɔ̃sɛɲœʀ], *pl* **messeigneurs** [mesɛɲœʀ] *nm* (**a**) *(formule d'adresse) (à archevêque, duc)* Your Grace; *(à cardinal)* Your Eminence; *(à prince)* Your Highness. (**b**) *(à la troisième personne)* His Grace; His Eminence; His Highness.

Monsieur [məsjø], *pl* **Messieurs** [mesjø] *nm* (**a**) *(s'adressant à qn)* **bonjour** ~ *(courant)* good morning; *(nom connu)* good morning Mr X; *(avec déférence)* good morning sir; *(au restaurant)* **et pour (vous)~/Messieurs?** and for you, sir/gentlemen?; ~ **le Président** Mr President; **oui,** ~ **le Juge** ≃ yes, Your Honour *ou* Your Worship; ~ **le curé** Father; ~ **le ministre** Minister; ~ **le duc** Your Grace, your Lordship; ~ **le comte** *etc* Your Lordship, my Lord; **mon bon** *ou* **pauvre** ~ * my dear sir. (**b**) *(parlant de qn)* ~ **est sorti** Mr X is not at home; ~ **dit que c'est à lui** the gentleman says it's his; ~ **le Président** the President; ~ **le juge X** ≃ (His Honour) Judge X; ~ **le duc de X** (His Grace) the Duke of X; ~ **l'abbé (X)** Father X; ~ **tout le monde** the average man. (**c**) *(sur une enveloppe)* ~ **John X** Mr John X; *(à un enfant)* Master John *etc* X; **Messieurs X et Y** Messrs X and Y. (**d**) *(en-tête de lettre) (gén)* Dear Sir; *(personne connue)* Dear Mr X; ~ **le Président** Dear Mr President. (**e**) *(sans majuscule)* gentleman. **c'est un grand m~** he is a great man.

monstre [mɔ̃stʀ(ə)] **1** *nm (gén)* monster. **c'est un** ~ **de laideur** he is monstrously ugly; **quel** ~ **d'égoïsme/d'orgueil!** what fiendish *ou* monstrous egoism/pride!; *(Ciné, Théât)* ~ **sacré** superstar, public idol. **2** *adj* (*) *rabais etc* monstrous, colossal, mammoth. **succès** ~ runaway *ou* raving * success; **j'ai un travail** ~ I've got loads * of work to do. ◆ **monstrueusement** *adv laid* monstrously; *intelligent* stupendously. ◆ **monstrueux, -euse** *adj* monstrous. ◆ **monstruosité** *nf (gén)* monstrosity; *(Méd)* deformity. **dire des ~s** to say monstrous things.

mont [mɔ̃] *nm* mountain. *(avec nom propre)* **le** ~ **Everest** *etc* Mount Everest *etc*; **être toujours par ~s et par vaux** * to be always on the move. ◆ **mont-de-piété**, *pl* **~s-~-~** *nm* (state-owned) pawnshop *ou* pawnbroker's; **mettre qch au** ~ to pawn sth.

montage [mɔ̃taʒ] *nm [appareil]* assembly; *[bijou]* setting; *(Ciné)* editing; *(Typ)* page make-up; **le** ~ **d'une opération publicitaire** the mounting *ou* organization of an advertising campaign; *(Élec)* ~ **en parallèle** connection in parallel; ~ **de photographies** photomontage.

montagne [mɔ̃taɲ] **1** *nf (sommet)* mountain. *(région)* **la** ~ the mountains; **moyenne** ~ medium mountains; **plantes des ~s** mountain plants; *(fig)* **une** ~ **de** mountains of; **il se fait une** ~ **de cet examen** he's making a great song and dance *ou* a great fuss over this exam. **2** : **les ~s Rocheuses** the Rocky Mountains, the Rockies; **~s russes** big dipper, roller coaster. ◆ **montagnard, e 1** *adj* mountain. **2** *nm, f* mountain dweller. ◆ **montagneux, -euse** *adj (gén, Géog)* mountainous; *(accidenté)* hilly.

montant, e [mɔ̃tɑ̃, ɑ̃t] **1** *adj mouvement* upward, rising; *col* high; *robe* high-necked; *chemin* uphill. **chaussures ~es** boots; **train** ~ up train. **2** *nm* (**a**) *[échelle, fenêtre]* upright; *[lit]* post. (**b**) *(somme)* sum total, total amount. *(Marché Commun)* ~ **compensatoire** subsidy; *(Fin, Jur)* ~ **dû/forfaitaire** outstanding/flatorate amount.

montée [mɔ̃te] *nf* (**a**) *(escalade)* climb, climbing. **c'est une** ~ **difficile** it's a difficult climb; **on a fait la** ~ **à pied** we walked up, we went up on foot. (**b**) *[ballon, avion]* ascent. **pendant la** ~ **de l'ascenseur** while the lift is going up. (**c**) *[eaux, sève, homme politique, colère, prix]* rise. (**d**) *(côte)* hill, uphill slope.

monter[1] [mɔ̃te] (1) **1** *vi (avec auxiliaire être)* (**a**) *(gén)* to go up (*à* to, *dans* into); *[oiseau]* to fly up; *[avion]* to climb. ~ **à pied/à vélo** to walk/cycle up; ~ **par l'ascenseur** to go up in the lift; ~ **en courant dans sa chambre** to run up(stairs) to one's room; **monte me voir** come up and see me. (**b**) ~ **sur** *table, toit* to climb (up) on; *colline, échelle* to climb up; **il était monté sur une chaise** he was standing on a chair; **monté sur un cheval** riding *ou* on a horse. (**c**) *(moyen de transport)* ~ **dans un train** to get on *ou* into a train, board a train; ~ **à bord d'un navire** to go on board *ou* aboard a ship; ~ **à cheval** *(se mettre en selle)* to get on *ou* mount a horse; *(faire du cheval)* to ride, go riding. (**d**) *[vedette]* to be on the way up; *[réputation]* to rise, go up. ~ **en grade** to be promoted; **les générations montantes** the rising generations. (**e**) *[eau, vêtements]* ~ **à** to come up to; **robe qui monte jusqu'au cou** high-necked dress. (**f**) *[colline, route]* to go up, rise; *[soleil, flamme]* to rise. ~ **en pente douce** to slope gently upwards, rise gently; **un bruit montait de la cave** a noise was coming from down in the cellar. (**g**) *[mer]* to come in; *[fleuve, colère]* to rise; *[prix, température]* to rise, go up; *(Mus) [voix, note]* to go up. **les prix montent en flèche** prices are rocketing *ou* soaring; **ça a fait** ~ **les prix** it put prices up; *(Culin)* **les blancs montent/n'arrivent pas à** ~ the egg whites are whipping up/won't whip up *ou* are going stiff/won't go stiff. (**h**) *(émotions)* **le sang lui monta au visage** the blood rushed to his face; **les larmes lui montent aux yeux** tears come into his eyes; **le vin lui monte à la tête** wine goes to his head; **un cri lui monta à la gorge** a cry rose in his throat. (**i**) *[plante]* ~ **(en graine)** to bolt, go to seed. (**j**) *(locutions)* ~ **à l'assaut** to go into the attack; ~ **à l'assaut de** to launch an attack on; ~ **au créneau pour défendre sa politique** to come to the defence of one's policies; ~ **sur ses ergots** to get one's hackles up; ~ **sur ses grands chevaux** to get on one's high horse; ~ **sur le trône** to come to *ou* ascend the throne.
2 *vt (avec auxiliaire avoir)* (**a**) to go up. ~ **l'escalier** to go upstairs; ~ **la gamme** to go up the scale. (**b**) *valise* to take *ou* carry up. **faire** ~ **ses valises** to have one's luggage brought up. (**c**) ~ **un cheval** to ride a horse. (**d**) ~ **qn contre qn** to set sb against sb; **on lui a monté la tête** sb has got him all worked up. (**e**) *(organiser) opération, campagne publicitaire* to mount, organize, set up. **c'est lui qui a tout monté** he organized *ou* set up the whole thing. (**f**) *(Mil)* ~ **la garde** to mount guard. (**g**) *(Culin)* **(faire)** ~ **les blancs en neige** to whip *ou* beat *ou* whisk (up) egg whites (until they are stiff).
3 se ~ *vpr [prix, frais]* **se** ~ **à** to come to, add up to; **se** ~ **la tête** to get worked up.
◆ **monte-charge** *nm inv* service elevator. ◆ **monte-plats** *nm inv* dumbwaiter.

monter[2] [mɔ̃te] (1) *vt (avec auxiliaire avoir)* (**a**) *machine, robe* to assemble; *tente* to pitch; *film* to edit; *diamant* to set; *pneu* to put on. *(Élec)* ~ **en série** to connect in series. (**b**) *pièce de théâtre* to put on, produce; *affaire* to set up; *farce* to play; *complot* to hatch. ~ **un coup** to plan a job; ~ **le coup à qn** ⁑ to take sb for a ride ⁑; **coup monté** put-up job *, frame-up *. (**c**) *(équiper)* to equip. **être bien/mal monté en qch** to be well-/ill-equipped with sth; **tu es bien montée, avec deux garnements pareils!** * you're well set up with that pair of rascals! * ◆ **monteur, -euse** *nm, f (Tech)* fitter; *(Ciné)* (film) editor; *(Typ)* paste-up artist.

monticule [mɔ̃tikyl] *nm (colline)* hillock; *(tas)* mound.

montre¹ [mɔ̃tʀ(ə)] *nf* watch. **~-bracelet** wrist watch; **~ de plongée** diver's watch; **~ à quartz** quartz watch; **il est 2 heures à ma ~** it is 2 o'clock by my watch; **j'ai mis 2 heures ~ en main** it took me exactly *ou* precisely 2 hours.

montre² [mɔ̃tʀ(ə)] *nf*: **faire ~ de** *courage* to show.

Montréal [mɔ̃ʀeal] *n* Montreal.

montrer [mɔ̃tʀe] (1) **1** *vt* (**a**) *(gén)* to show; *(par un geste)* to point to; *détail* to point out; *surprise, courage* to display; *(ostensiblement) richesse* to show off, display (*à* to). **je vais vous ~ le jardin** I'll show you (round) the garden; **l'avenir montrera qui avait raison** the future will show *ou* prove who was right; **...ce qui montre bien que j'avais raison** ...which just goes to show that I was right; **~ à qn à faire qch** to show sb how *ou* the way to do sth. (**b**) *(locutions)* **c'est l'avocat qui montre le bout de l'oreille** it's the lawyer in him showing through; **je lui montrerai de quel bois je me chauffe** I'll show him what I'm made of; *(lit, fig)* **~ les dents** to bare one's teeth; **~ le bon exemple** to set a good example; *(lit, fig)* **~ le chemin** to show the way; **~ le bout du nez** to show one's face; **~ patte blanche** to show one's pass. **2 se ~** *vpr* to appear, show o.s.; *(se faire respecter)* to assert o.s. **se ~ ferme** to appear firm, show firmness; **se ~ désagréable** to be unpleasant, behave unpleasantly; **se ~ lâche** to show cowardice; **se ~ efficace** to prove effective.

monture [mɔ̃tyʀ] *nf* (**a**) *(cheval)* mount. (**b**) *(Tech)* mounting; *[lunettes]* frame; *[bijou]* setting.

monument [mɔnymɑ̃] *nm (gén, fig)* monument; *(commémoratif)* memorial. **~ (funéraire)** monument; **~ aux morts** war memorial; **~ historique** ancient monument; **visiter les ~s de Paris** to go sight-seeing in Paris; **c'est un ~ de bêtise!** * what monumental stupidity! ◆ **monumental, e,** *mpl* **-aux** *adj* monumental.

moquer (se) [mɔke] (1) *vpr*: **se ~ de** to make fun of, laugh at, poke fun at; **on va se ~ de toi** people will laugh at you, you'll make yourself a laughing stock; **vous vous moquez du monde!** you've got an absolute nerve!; **je m'en moque (pas mal)** * I couldn't care less *; **elle se moque du qu'en-dira-t-on** she doesn't care what people say (about her). ◆ **moquerie** *nf*: **~(s)** mockery. ◆ **moqueur, -euse** *adj* mocking. ◆ **moqueusement** *adv* mockingly.

moquette [mɔkɛt] *nf* fitted carpet. **faire poser une** *ou* **de la ~** to have a fitted *ou* a wall-to-wall *(US)* carpet laid. ◆ **moquetter** (1) *vt* to carpet (with a fitted carpet).

moral, e, *mpl* **-aux** [mɔʀal, o] **1** *adj (gén)* moral. **2** *nm* (**a**) **au ~ comme au physique** mentally as well as physically. (**b**) *(état d'esprit)* morale. **avoir un ~ d'acier** to be in fighting form; **avoir bon/mauvais ~** to be in good/low spirits; **les troupes ont bon/mauvais ~** the morale of the troops is high/low. **3** *nf* (**a**) *(doctrine)* moral code; *(mœurs)* morals; *(valeurs traditionnelles)* moral standards. *(Philos)* **la ~e** moral philosophy; **action conforme à la ~e** act in keeping with morality *ou* moral standards; **faire la ~e à qn** to lecture sb. (**b**) *[fable]* moral. ◆ **moralement** *adv* morally. ◆ **moralisateur, -trice 1** *adj ton* moralizing; *histoire* edifying. **2** *nm, f* moralizer. ◆ **moraliser** (1) **1** *vi* to moralize. **2** *vt*: **~ qn** to lecture sb. ◆ **moraliste 1** *adj* moralistic. **2** *nmf* moralist. ◆ **moralité** *nf* (**a**) *(mœurs)* morals, morality, moral standards. **d'une haute ~** *personne* of high moral standards; *discours* of a high moral tone; **la ~ publique** public morality. (**b**) *(valeur) [attitude, action]* morality. (**c**) *[fable]* moral. **~, j'ai eu une indigestion** * the result was (that) I had indigestion.

morbide [mɔʀbid] *adj* morbid. ◆ **morbidité** *nf* morbidity.

morceau, *pl* **~x** [mɔʀso] *nm (gén)* piece; *(bout)* bit; *(Littérat, Mus: passage)* passage; *[sucre]* lump; *[terre]* patch, plot; *(chez le boucher)* cut. **~ de choix** choice cut *ou* piece; **manger un ~** to have a bite to eat *ou* a snack; **lâcher le ~** ‡ to spill the beans *, talk *; **couper en ~x** to cut into pieces; **mettre qch en ~x** to pull sth to pieces; **~x choisis** selected extracts *ou* passages; **~ de bravoure** purple passage; **c'est un sacré ~** * he (*ou* it *etc*) is a hell of a size *. ◆ **morceler** (4) *vt (gén)* to divide up, split up. ◆ **morcellement** *nm* division.

mordoré, e [mɔʀdɔʀe] *adj, nm* (lustrous) bronze.

mordre [mɔʀdʀ(ə)] (41) **1** *vt* (**a**) to bite. **~ qn à la jambe** to bite sb's leg, bite sb on the leg; **~ une pomme** to bite into an apple; **~ la poussière** to bite the dust. (**b**) *[lime, vis]* to bite into; *[acide]* to eat into; *[froid]* to bite, nip. **la jalousie lui mordait le cœur** jealousy was gnawing at his heart. (**c**) *(empiéter sur)* **la balle a mordu la ligne** the ball (just) touched the line. **2 ~ sur** *vt indir (empiéter sur)* to cut into, go over into, overlap into; *(corroder)* to bite into. **3** *vi* (**a**) **~ dans une pomme** to bite into an apple. (**b**) *(Pêche, fig)* to bite; *(lit, fig)* **~ à l'hameçon** to bite, rise to the bait; **il a mordu aux maths** * he's taken to maths; **l'engrenage ne mord plus** the gear won't mesh any more. **4 se ~** *vpr*: **se ~ la langue** *(lit, se repentir)* to bite one's tongue; *(se retenir)* to hold one's tongue; **maintenant il s'en mord les doigts** he could kick himself now *; **tu t'en mordras les doigts** you'll live to regret it, you'll rue the day. ◆ **mordant, e 1** *adj ton* cutting, scathing; *polémiste* scathing; *froid* biting. **2** *nm [personne]* spirit, drive; *[style]* bite, punch; *[scie]* bite. ◆ **mordiller** (1) *vt* to nibble at. ◆ **mordu, e** * **1** *adj*: **être ~ de** to be mad * *ou* crazy * about. **2** *nm, f (*: fanatique)* enthusiast, buff *, fan. **un ~ de la musique** a great music lover; **un ~ de l'ordinateur** a computer buff * *ou* freak *; **c'est un ~ du football** he is a great football fan *ou* buff.

morfondre (se) [mɔʀfɔ̃dʀ(ə)] (42) *vpr* to languish.

morgue [mɔʀg(ə)] *nf* (**a**) pride, haughtiness. (**b**) *(Police)* morgue; *[hôpital]* mortuary.

moribond, e [mɔʀibɔ̃, ɔ̃d] **1** *adj (lit, fig)* dying, moribund. **2** *nm, f*: **un ~** a dying man.

morille [mɔʀij] *nf* morel.

morne [mɔʀn(ə)] *adj visage* doleful, glum; *ton, temps* gloomy, dismal; *vie, paysage* dreary.

morose [mɔʀoz] *adj* sullen, morose. ◆ **morosité** *nf* sullenness, moroseness. **climat de ~ économique/sociale** gloomy *ou* depressed economic/social climate.

morphine [mɔʀfin] *nf* morphine.

morphologie [mɔʀfɔlɔʒi] *nf* morphology. ◆ **morphologique** *adj* morphological.

mors [mɔʀ] *nm (Équitation)* bit; *(Tech)* jaw. **prendre le ~ aux dents** *[cheval]* to take the bit between its teeth; *(fig) (agir)* to take action; *(s'emporter)* to fly off the handle * , blow one's top * *ou* stack * *(US)*.

morse [mɔʀs(ə)] *nm* (**a**) *(Zool)* walrus. (**b**) *(code)* Morse (code).

morsure [mɔʀsyʀ] *nf* bite.

mort¹ [mɔʀ] *nf* (**a**) death. **donner la ~ à qn** to kill sb; **se donner la ~** to take one's own life, kill o.s.; **en danger de ~** in danger of dying *ou* of one's life; **mourir dans son sommeil, c'est une belle ~** dying in one's sleep is a good way to go; **à la ~ de sa mère** on the death of his mother, when his mother died; **il n'y a pas eu ~ d'homme** no one was killed, there was no loss of life; **le supermarché sera la ~ du petit commerce** supermarkets will mean the end of *ou* the death of small businesses; ~ **au tyran!, à ~ le tyran!** death to the tyrant! (**b**) **silence de** ~ deathly hush; **engin de** ~ deadly weapon; **peine de** ~ death penalty; *(fig)* **il avait signé son arrêt de** ~ he had signed his own death warrant; **menaces de** ~ threats of death. (**c**) **lutte à** ~ fight to the death; **blessé à** ~ *(combat)* mortally wounded; *(accident)* fatally injured; **condamnation à** ~ death sentence; **frapper qn à** ~ to strike sb dead; **mettre qn à** ~ to put sb to death; **nous sommes fâchés à** ~ we're at daggers drawn; **en vouloir à qn à** ~ to be bitterly resentful of sb; **freiner à** ~ * to jam on the brakes; **visser qch à** ~ * to screw sth right home, screw sth tight. (**d**) *(douleur)* **souffrir mille ~s** to suffer agonies; **il avait la ~ dans l'âme** his heart ached.

mort², e [mɔʀ, mɔʀt(ə)] **1** *adj (lit, fig)* dead. **il est ~ depuis 2 ans** he's been dead (for) 2 years, he died 2 years ago; **laissé pour** ~ left for dead; ~ **et enterré** dead and buried; ~ **ou vif** dead or alive; ~ **au champ d'honneur** killed in action; ~ **(de fatigue)** dead tired, dead beat *; ~ **de peur** frightened to death, scared stiff *. **2** *nm* (**a**) dead man. **les ~s** the dead; **il y a eu un** ~ one man was killed; **prière des ~s** prayer for the dead; **cet homme est un ~ vivant** this man is more dead than alive; **faire le** ~ *(lit)* to pretend to be dead; *(fig: ne pas se manifester)* to lie low; *(Aut)* **la place du** ~ the (front) seat next to the driver. (**b**) *(Cartes)* dummy. **être le** ~ to be dummy. **3** *nf* dead woman. ◆ **mort-né, e,** *pl* **~-~(e)s** *adj* stillborn. ◆ **mort-aux-rats** *nf* rat poison. ◆ **morte-saison** *nf* slack *ou* off season.

mortadelle [mɔʀtadɛl] *nf* mortadella.

mortalité [mɔʀtalite] *nf* mortality, death rate. ~ **infantile** infant mortality.

mortel, -elle [mɔʀtɛl] **1** *adj (gén)* mortal; *blessure* fatal; *poison* deadly, lethal; *froid, attente* deadly; *pâleur, silence* deathly; *livre, soirée* deadly boring *ou* dull. **cette révélation lui serait ~elle** such a discovery would kill him; **il est** ~ * he's a deadly * bore. **2** *nm, f (littér, hum)* mortal. **heureux ~!** * lucky chap! * ◆ **mortellement** *adv blesser* fatally; *vexer* mortally. ~ **pâle** deathly pale; ~ **ennuyeux** deadly boring *ou* dull.

mortier [mɔʀtje] *nm (gén)* mortar.

mortifier [mɔʀtifje] (7) *vt* to mortify. ◆ **mortification** *nf* mortification.

mortuaire [mɔʀtɥɛʀ] *adj chapelle, rites* mortuary. **chambre** ~ death chamber; **la maison** ~ the house of the deceased.

morue [mɔʀy] *nf (Zool)* cod.

mosaïque [mozaik] *nf (Art, Bot)* mosaic; *[idées, peuples]* medley.

Moscou [mɔsku] *n* Moscow. ◆ **moscovite** **1** *adj* of *ou* from Moscow, Muscovite. **2** *nmf:* **M~** Muscovite.

mosquée [mɔske] *nf* mosque.

mot [mo] **1** *nm* (**a**) *(gén)* word. **c'est bien le ~!** that's the right word for it!; **à/sur ces ~s** at/with these words; **à ~s couverts** in veiled terms; **en un** ~ in brief, in a word; ~ **à** ~ word for word; ~ **pour** ~ word for word, verbatim. (**b**) *(message)* word; *(courte lettre)* note. ~ **d'excuse** excuse note; **en toucher un ~ à qn** to have a word with sb about it; **se donner le** ~ to pass the word round *ou* on. (**c**) *(locutions)* **avoir des ~s avec qn** to have words with sb; **avoir toujours le ~ pour rire** to be a born joker; **tenir le ~ de l'énigme** to hold the key to the mystery; **avoir le ~ de la fin** to have the last word; **j'estime avoir mon ~ à dire dans cette affaire** I think I'm entitled to have my say in this matter; **je vais lui dire deux ~s** I'll give him a piece of my mind; **prendre qn au** ~ to take sb at his word. **2** : **~-clé** *nm, pl* **~s-~s** keyword; **~s croisés** crossword (puzzle); ~ **d'enfant** child's (funny) remark *ou* saying; ~ **d'esprit, bon** ~ witticism, witty remark; ~ **d'ordre** watchword; ~ **de passe** password; **~-valise** portmanteau word.

motard [mɔtaʀ] *nm* motorcyclist; *(Police)* motorcycle policeman.

motel [mɔtɛl] *nm* motel.

moteur¹ [mɔtœʀ] *nm (gén)* engine; *(électrique)* motor. ~ **électrique** electric motor; ~ **turbo** turbo(-charged) engine; ~ **à 2/4 temps** 2-/4-stroke engine; **à** ~ power-driven, motor; *(fig)* **être le ~ de qch** to be the driving force behind sth.

moteur², -trice¹ [mɔtœʀ, tʀis] *adj muscle, nerf, troubles* motor; *(Tech), (lit, fig) force* driving.

motif [mɔtif] *nm* (**a**) *(gén)* reason, grounds; *(Jur)* motive (*de* for). (**b**) *[tissu, papier]* pattern; *(Peinture, Mus)* motif.

motion [mosjɔ̃] *nf* motion. **déposer une ~ de censure** to take a censure motion *ou* a motion of censure; **voter la ~ de censure** to pass a vote of no confidence *ou* of censure.

motiver [mɔtive] (1) *vt (justifier) action, attitude* to justify, account for; *(fournir un motif à) refus, jugement* to motivate; *(intéresser) personne* to motivate. ◆ **motivant, e** *adj* rewarding. ◆ **motivation** *nf* motivation. **quelles sont ses ~s?** what are his motives? (*pour* for). ◆ **motivé, e** *adj* justified, well-founded, motivated; *personne* (well-) motivated. *(Scol)* **absence ~e** legitimate *ou* genuine absence.

moto * [moto] *nf* (motor)bike *. ◆ **moto-cross** *nm inv* motocross. ◆ **motoculteur** *nm* (motorized) cultivator. ◆ **motocyclette** *nf* motorcycle. ◆ **motocycliste** *nmf* motorcyclist. ◆ **motonautisme** *nm* speedboat racing. ◆ **motopompe** *nf* motor-pump.

motoriser [mɔtɔʀize] (1) *vt (Mil, Tech)* to motorize. **être motorisé** * to have a car. ◆ **motorisation** *nf* motorization.

motrice² [mɔtʀis] *nf* power unit; *V* **moteur²**.

motte [mɔt] *nf:* ~ **(de terre)** lump of earth, clod (of earth); ~ **de gazon** turf, sod; ~ **de beurre** lump *ou* block of butter.

motus * [mɔtys] *excl* don't breathe a word!

mou, molle [mu, mɔl] *(masc.* **mol** [mɔl] *devant voyelle ou h muet)* **1** *adj substance* soft; *tige, geste* limp; *chair* flabby; *relief* soft, gentle; *traits du visage* weak; *protestations, opposition* weak, feeble; *style, (Mus) exécution* dull. **personne molle** *(sans énergie)* lethargic *ou* sluggish person; *(sans autorité)* spineless character; *(trop indulgent)* lax *ou* soft person; **bruit** ~ muffled noise. **2** *nm* (**a**) *[corde]* **avoir du** ~ to be slack; **donner du** ~ *(à qch)* to slacken (sth). (**b**) *(Boucherie)* lights.

mouchard [muʃaʀ] *nm* (**a**) (*) *(Scol)* sneak *; *(arg Police)* grass *(arg)*, fink *(US arg)*, informer. (**b**) *[veilleur de nuit]* control clock; *(Mil)* spy plane. ◆ **moucharder** * (1) *vt (Scol)* to sneak on *; *(arg Police)* to grass on *(arg)*, inform on.

mouche [muʃ] *nf* fly; *(en taffetas)* patch. ~ **bleue,** ~ **à vers** bluebottle, blowfly; **quelle ~ t'a piqué?** what has bitten you? *; **tomber comme des ~s** to fall like flies; **prendre la** ~ to take the huff *; **faire** ~ *(Tir)* to score a bull's-eye; *(fig)* to hit home.

moucher [muʃe] (1) **1** *vt* (**a**) ~ **(le nez de) qn** to blow sb's nose. (**b**) *(* fig)* ~ **qn** to put sb in his place. **2 se** ~ *vpr* to blow one's nose.

moucheron [muʃʀɔ̃] *nm* midge; *(*: enfant)* kid *.

moucheté, e [muʃte] *adj œuf* speckled; *poisson* spotted; *laine* flecked; *fleuret* buttoned.

mouchoir [muʃwaʀ] *nm* handkerchief. ~ **en papier** tissue, paper hanky; **jardin grand comme un ~ de poche** garden as big as *ou* no bigger than a pocket handkerchief; **ils sont arrivés dans un** ~ it was a close finish.

moudre [mudʀ(ə)] (47) *vt (gén)* to grind.

moue [mu] *nf* pout. **faire la** ~ *(tiquer)* to pull a face; *[enfant gâté]* to pout.

mouette [mwɛt] *nf* seagull.

moufle [mufl(ə)] *nf* mitten.

mouiller [muje] (1) **1** *vt* (**a**) *(gén)* to wet. **se faire** ~ to get wet *ou* drenched *ou* soaked. (**b**) *vin, lait* to water (down). (**c**) *(Naut) mine* to lay; *sonde* to heave. ~ **l'ancre** to cast *ou* drop anchor. (**d**) *(Ling)* to palatalize. **2** *vi (Naut)* to lie at anchor. **3 se** ~ *vpr* (**a**) to get o.s. wet. **se** ~ **les pieds** to get one's feet wet. (**b**) *[yeux]* to fill with tears. (**c**) (‡: *risquer)* to get one's feet wet, commit o.s. ◆ **mouillage** *nm (rade)* anchorage, moorage. ◆ **mouillé, e** *adj* wet. **tout** ~ soaked through; **ne marche pas dans le** ~ don't walk in the wet.

moulage [mulaʒ] *nm [briques]* moulding; *[statue]* casting; *(objet)* cast.

moule[1] [mul] *nm (lit, fig)* mould; *(Typ)* matrix. ~ **à gâteaux** cake tin, cake pan *(US)*; ~ **à gaufre** waffle-iron; ~ **à tarte** pie plate, flan case.

moule[2] [mul] *nf* (**a**) *(Zool)* mussel. ~**s marinières** moules marinières *(mussels cooked in their own juice with onions)*. (**b**) (*: *idiot)* idiot, twit *.

mouler [mule] (1) *vt* (**a**) *briques* to mould; *caractères d'imprimerie, statue* to cast; *lettre* to form with care. ~ **son style sur** to model one's style on. (**b**) *(coller à) cuisses, hanches* to hug, fit closely round. **robe qui moule** close-fitting *ou* tight-fitting dress.

moulin [mulɛ̃] *nm* mill; (*: *moteur)* engine. ~ **à eau** water mill; ~ **à vent** windmill. ◆ **mouliner** (1) *vt (Culin)* to put through a vegetable mill; *(Pêche)* to reel in. ◆ **moulinet** *nm (Pêche)* reel; *(Escrime)* flourish. **faire des** ~**s avec une canne** to twirl *ou* whirl a stick. ◆ **moulinette** *nf* ® vegetable mill.

moulu, e [muly] *adj*: ~ **(de fatigue)** * dead-beat *, worn-out; **ils l'ont** ~ **de coups** they thrashed him black and blue.

moulure [mulyʀ] *nf* moulding.

mourir [muʀiʀ] (19) *vi* (**a**) to die. ~ **de sa belle mort** to die a natural death; ~ **avant l'âge** to die before one's time; ~ **assassiné** to be murdered; ~ **en héros** to die a hero's death; **faire** ~ **qn** to kill sb; *(fig)* **cet enfant me fera** ~ this child will be the death of me; *(hum)* **tu n'en mourras pas!** * it won't kill you! (**b**) *[feu, coutume]* to die out; *[bruit, vague]* to die away; *[jour]* to fade, die; *[flamme]* to die down. (**c**) ~ **de qch**: ~ **d'inquiétude** to be worried to death; **il meurt d'envie de le faire** he's dying to do it; ~ **d'ennui** to be bored to death *ou* to tears; ~ **de faim** *(lit)* to starve to death; *(fig)* to be famished *ou* starving; **je meurs de soif** I am parched; **faire** ~ **qn à petit feu** *(lit)* to kill sb slowly; *(fig)* to torment the life out of sb; **c'est à** ~ **de rire** it would make you die laughing *. ◆ **mourant, e 1** *adj* dying; *voix* faint; (*) *rythme* deadly (dull). **2** *nm, f*: **un** ~ a dying man; **les** ~**s** the dying.

mousquetaire [muskətɛʀ] *nm* musketeer.

mousse[1] [mus] *nf (Bot)* moss; *[bière, eau]* froth, foam; *[savon]* lather; *[champagne]* bubbles; *(Culin)* mousse. ~ **au chocolat** chocolate mousse; **balle (en)** ~ rubber ball; **collant** ~ stretch tights; ~ **de caoutchouc** foam rubber; **se faire de la** ~ * to worry o.s. sick *.

mousse[2] [mus] *nm* ship's boy.

mousseline [muslin] *nf (coton)* muslin; *(soie, tergal)* chiffon.

mousser [muse] (1) *vi* (**a**) *[bière, eau]* to froth, foam; *[champagne]* to bubble, sparkle; *[savon]* to lather. (**b**) **faire** ~ **qn** ‡ *(vanter)* to lay off about sb ‡ , boost sb *; *(mettre en colère)* to make sb mad * *ou* wild *; **se faire** ~ ‡ to give o.s. a boost * (*auprès de* with). ◆ **mousseux, -euse 1** *adj* sparkling; frothy. **eau** ~**euse** soapy water. **2** *nm* sparkling wine.

mousson [musɔ̃] *nf* monsoon.

moustache [mustaʃ] *nf [homme]* moustache. *[animal]* ~**s** whiskers.

moustique [mustik] *nm (Zool)* mosquito; (*: *enfant)* tich *, (little) kid *. ◆ **moustiquaire** *nf (rideau)* mosquito net; *[fenêtre]* screen.

moutarde [mutaʀd(ə)] *nf* mustard. ~ **forte** English mustard; ~ **à l'estragon** *ou* **aux aromates** French mustard; *(fig)* **la** ~ **me monta au nez** I flared up, I lost my temper.

mouton [mutɔ̃] *nm* (**a**) *(animal, fig)* sheep; *(viande)* mutton. **doublé de** ~ lined with sheepskin; **se conduire en** ~**s de Panurge** to behave like a lot of sheep. (**b**) ~**s** *(sur la mer)* white horses, caps *(US)*; *(sur le plancher)* (bits of) fluff; *(dans le ciel)* fluffy *ou* fleecy clouds. ◆ **moutonneux, -euse** *adj mer* flecked with white horses *ou* with caps *(US)*; *ciel* flecked with fleecy *ou* fluffy clouds.

mouvement [muvmɑ̃] *nm* (**a**) *(geste)* movement. ~**s de gymnastique** (physical) exercises; **il approuva d'un** ~ **de tête** he gave a nod of approval; **elle refusa d'un** ~ **de tête** she refused with a shake of her head; **elle eut un** ~ **de recul** she started back. (**b**) *(impulsion)* impulse, reaction. **avoir un bon** ~ to make a kind gesture; ~ **de colère** burst *ou* upsurge of anger; ~**s dans l'auditoire** a stir in the audience; **discours accueilli avec des** ~**s divers** speech which got a mixed reception; **agir de son propre** ~ to act of one's own accord. (**c**) *(activité)* activity, bustle. **rue pleine de** ~ busy *ou* lively street. (**d**) *(déplacement)* movement; *(Mil: manœuvre)* move. **être sans cesse en** ~ to be constantly on the move *ou* on the go; **mettre qch en** ~ to set sth in motion, set sth going; **se mettre en** ~ to start *ou* set off; **suivre le** ~ to follow the general movement; **le** ~ **perpétuel** perpetual motion; ~ **de foule** sway in the crowd; ~**s de population** shifts in population; ~**s de troupes** troop movements; ~ **de fonds** movement of capital; ~ **de personnel** changes in staff. (**e**) *(évolution)* **le** ~ **des idées** the evolution of ideas; **être dans le** ~ to keep up-to-date; ~ **d'opinion** trend of opinion; **le** ~ **des prix** the trend of prices; ~ **de baisse/ de hausse** downward/upward trend. (**f**) *[phrase]* rhythm; *[tragédie]* action; *[draperie]* drape; *[collines]* undulations. (**g**) *(groupe)* movement. ~ **politique** political movement; **M**~ **de libération de la femme** Women's Liberation Movement, Women's Lib *. (**h**) *[symphonie]* movement. (**i**) *(Tech: mécanisme)* movement. **par un** ~ **d'horlogerie** by clockwork.

◆ **mouvant, e** *adj situation* unsettled, fluid; *ombre, flamme* moving, changing; *terrain* shifting. ◆ **mouvementé, e** *adj vie, poursuite, récit* eventful; *séance* turbulent, stormy. ◆ **mouvoir** (27) **1** *vt* (**a**) *machine* to drive; *bras, levier* to move. **comme mû par un ressort** as if propelled by a spring. (**b**) *[sentiment]* to drive, prompt. **2 se** ~ *vpr* to move.

moyen, -enne [mwajɛ̃, ɛn] **1** *adj (gén)* average. **être** ~ **en maths** to be average at maths; **résultats très** ~**s** mediocre *ou* poor results; **de taille** ~**enne** *personne* of medium *ou* average height; *entreprise, bâtiment* medium-sized; **avoir un temps** ~ to have mixed weather; **une solution** ~**enne** a middle-of-the-road solution.

2 *nm* (**a**) *(possibilité, manière)* means, way. ~**s de défense/production** *etc* means of defence/production *etc*; ~**s audio-visuels** audio-visual aids; **trouver un** ~ **terme** to find a middle course; *(péj)* **par tous les** ~**s** by fair means or foul, by hook or by crook; **c'est l'unique** ~ **de s'en sortir** it's the only way out; **employer les grands** ~**s** to have to resort to drastic means *ou* measures; **se débrouiller avec les** ~**s du bord** *ou* **avec des** ~**s de fortune** to make do and mend, use makeshift devices; **au** ~ **de** by means of. (**b**) **est-ce qu'il y a** ~ **de lui parler?** is it possible to speak to him?; **il n'y a**

pas ~ de sortir par ce temps you can't go out in this weather; **le ~ de dire autre chose!** what else could I say! (**c**) *(physiques)* **~s** abilities; **être en possession de tous ses ~s** to be at one's peak; **par ses propres ~s** all by himself. (**d**) *(financiers)* **~s** means; **c'est au-dessus de ses ~s** he can't afford it, it's beyond his means; **avoir de gros/petits ~s** to have a large/small income.
3 *nf* (**a**) *(gén)* average. **la ~enne d'âge** the average age; **la ~ enne des gens** most people; **faire du 100 de ~enne** to average 100 km/h; **~enne arithmétique** arithmetic mean; **en ~enne** on average. (**b**) *(Scol)* **avoir la ~enne** *(devoir)* to get half marks; *(examen)* to get a pass; **~enne générale (de l'année)** average (for the year); **cet élève est dans la ~enne/la bonne ~enne** this pupil is about/above average. ◆ **moyen âge** *nm*: **le ~** the Middle Ages. ◆ **moyenâgeux, -euse** *adj ville* medieval; *(péj)* antiquated. ◆ **moyen-courrier,** *pl* **~s-~s** *nm* medium-haul (aeroplane). ◆ **Moyen-Orient** *nm*: **le ~** the Middle East. ◆ **moyennant** *prép argent* for; *service* in return for; *travail, effort* with. **~ finance** for a fee *ou* a consideration; **~ quoi** in return for which. ◆ **moyennement** *adv content* fairly, moderately ; *travailler* fairly *ou* moderately well.

moyeu, *pl* **~x** [mwajø] *nm [roue]* hub.

Mozambique [mɔzɑ̃bik] *nm* Mozambique.

muer [mɥe] (1) **1** *vi (gén)* to moult; *[serpent]* to slough. **sa voix mue** his voice is breaking *ou* changing *(US)*. **2** *vt*, **se ~** *vpr* to change *ou* turn (*en* into). ◆ **mue** *nf* moulting; sloughing; *(époque)* moulting *ou* sloughing season; *(peau, plumes)* slough; moulted hair, feathers *etc*. *[voix]* **au moment de la ~** when the voice breaks *ou* changes *(US)*.

müesli [myɛsli] *nm* muesli.

muet, -ette [mɥɛ, ɛt] **1** *adj (infirme)* dumb; *(lit, fig: silencieux)* silent; *(Ling)* mute, silent; *(Géog) carte* blank. **en rester ~** to stand speechless (*de* with); **il est resté ~ comme une carpe** he never opened his mouth. **2** *nm, f* mute, dumb man (*ou* woman). **3** *nm*: **le ~** the silent cinema.

muezzin [mɥɛdzin] *nm* muezzin.

mufle [myfl(ə)] *nm* (**a**) *[chien etc]* muzzle. (**b**) (*‡: goujat)* boor, lout. ◆ **muflerie** *nf* boorishness, loutishness. **une ~** a boorish remark (*ou* thing to do).

mugir [myʒiʀ] (2) *vi [vache]* to moo; *[bœuf]* to bellow; *[vent, sirène]* to howl. ◆ **mugissement** *nm*: **~(s)** mooing; bellowing; howling.

muguet [mygɛ] *nm (Bot)* lily of the valley.

mulâtre, -esse [mylɑtʀ(ə), ɛs] *nm, f* mulatto.

mule [myl] *nf (Zool)* (she-)mule; *(pantoufle)* mule. ◆ **mulet** *nm (âne)* (he-)mule; *(poisson)* mullet. ◆ **muletier, -ière** **1** *adj*: **sentier ~** mule track. **2** *nm, f* mule-driver.

mulot [mylo] *nm* field mouse.

multi... [mylti] *préf* multi...

multicolore [myltikɔlɔʀ] *adj* multicoloured.

multicoque [myltikɔk] *adj, nm:* **(voilier) ~** multihull.

multiforme [myltifɔʀm(ə)] *adj apparence* multiform; *problème* many-sided.

multimillionnaire [myltimiljɔnɛʀ] *nmf* multimillionaire.

multinational, e, *mpl* **-aux** [myltinasjɔnal, o] **1** *adj* multinational. **2 multinationale** *nf* multinational (company).

multipartisme [myltipaʀtizm(ə)] *nm (Pol)* multiparty system.

multiple [myltipl(ə)] **1** *adj occasions, raisons* numerous, multiple; *fracture* multiple; *aspects* multifarious, manifold; *problème* many-sided. **outil à usages ~s** multi-purpose tool; **choix ~** multiple choice; **100 est ~ de 10** 100 is a multiple of 10. **2** *nm* multiple. ◆ **multiplication** *nf (prolifération)* increase in the number of; *(Bot, Math)* multiplication. ◆ **multiplicité** *nf* multiplicity. ◆ **multiplier** (7) **1** *vt (gén)* to multiply (*par* by). **2 se ~** *vpr (gén)* to multiply; *[infirmier]* to do one's utmost.

multiplex [myltiplɛks] *adj, nm (Téléc)* multiplex. ◆ **multiplexage** *nm (Téléc)* multiplexing. ◆ **multiplexeur** *nm (Téléc)* multiplexer.

multiprogrammation [myltipʀɔgʀamɑsjɔ̃] *nf (Ordin)* multiprogramming.

multipropriété [myltipʀɔpʀijete] *nf* time sharing.

multirisque [myltiʀisk(ə)] *adj* multiple-risk.

multisalles [myltisal] *adj:* **(cinéma) ~** film centre, cinema complex.

multistandard [myltistɑ̃daʀ] *adj:* **(téléviseur) ~** multichannel television.

multitraitement [myltitʀɛtmɑ̃] *nm (Ordin)* multiprocessing.

multitude [myltityd] *nf* (**a**) **une ~ de** a multitude of, a vast number of; **la ~ de** the mass of; **la ~ des gens** the (vast) majority of people. (**b**) *(littér: foule)* multitude, throng.

Munich [mynik] *n* Munich.

municipal, e, *mpl* **-aux** [mynisipal, o] *adj élection, stade* municipal; *conseil* local, town. **arrêté ~** local by-law; **piscine ~e** public swimming pool. ◆ **municipalité** *nf (ville)* town; *(conseil)* town council.

munir [myniʀ] (2) **1** *vt personne, objet* to provide, equip (*de* with). **muni de ces conseils** armed with this advice. **2 se ~** *vpr*: **se ~ de** to provide o.s. with; **se ~ de patience** to arm o.s. with patience.

munitions [mynisjɔ̃] *nfpl* (**a**) ammunition, munitions. **dépôt de ~** munitions *ou* ammunition dump. (**b**) *(†: ressources)* supplies.

muqueuse [mykøz] *nf* mucous membrane.

mur [myʀ] *nm (gén)* wall. **~ d'enceinte** outer wall *ou* walls; **une maison aux ~s de brique** a brick house; **faire le ~ *** to jump the wall; **l'ennemi est dans nos ~s** the enemy is within our gates; **M. X est dans nos ~s aujourd'hui** we have Mr X with us today; **avoir le dos au ~** to have one's back to the wall; **on parle à un ~** it's like talking to a brick wall; **franchir le ~ du son** to break the sound barrier. ◆ **muraille** *nf* (high) wall. **couleur (de) ~** stone grey. ◆ **mural, e,** *mpl* **-aux** *adj* wall; *(Art)* mural. ◆ **murer** (1) **1** *vt ouverture* to wall up, brick up. **2 se ~** *vpr (chez soi)* to shut o.s. away. **se ~ dans son silence** to immure o.s. in silence.

mûr, e[1] [myʀ] *adj* (**a**) *fruit, projet* ripe; *tissu* worn. **fruit pas ~/trop ~** unripe/overripe fruit. (**b**) *personne (sensé)* mature; *(âgé)* middle-aged. **il est ~ pour le mariage** he is ready for marriage; **une femme assez ~e** a woman of mature years. (**c**) (*‡: ivre)* tight *, plastered ‡. (**d**) **après ~e réflexion** after mature reflection. ◆ **mûrement** *adv*: **ayant ~ réfléchi** after much thought, after mature reflection *ou* lengthy deliberation. ◆ **mûrir** (2) **1** *vi [fruit]* to ripen; *[idée, personne]* to mature; *[abcès]* to come to a head. **2** *vt fruit* to ripen; *projet* to nurture; *personne* to make mature.

mûre[2] [myʀ] *nf [ronce]* blackberry, bramble; *[mûrier]* mulberry. ◆ **mûrier** *nm* mulberry bush.

murmurer [myʀmyʀe] (1) **1** *vt* to murmur. **on murmure que...** it's whispered that..., rumour has it that... **2** *vi (chuchoter)* to murmur; *(protester)* to mutter, grumble (*contre* about). ◆ **murmure** *nm* murmur. **obéir sans ~** to obey without a murmur; **~s** *(protestations)* murmurings, grumblings; *(objections)* objections.

muscade [myskad] *nf* nutmeg.

muscat [myska] *nm (raisin)* muscat grape; *(vin)* muscatel (wine).

muscle [myskl(ə)] *nm* muscle. ◆ **musclé, e** *adj corps* muscular; *homme* brawny; *régime* strong-arm. ◆ **musculaire** *adj force* muscular. **fibre** ~ muscle fibre. ◆ **musculature** *nf* muscle structure.

muse [myz] *nf (Littérat, Myth)* Muse.

museau, *pl* ~**x** [myzo] *nm [chien, bovin]* muzzle; *[porc]* snout; *(Culin)* brawn, headcheese *(US)*; *(*: visage)* face. ◆ **museler** (4) *vt (lit, fig)* to muzzle. ◆ **muselière** *nf* muzzle.

musée [myze] *nm [tableaux, sculptures]* art gallery; *(technique)* museum. *(lit, fig)* **pièce de** ~ museum piece. ◆ **muséum** *nm* museum.

musique [myzik] *nf (art)* music; *(orchestre)* band. ~ **sacrée/d'ambiance/de chambre** sacred/background/chamber music; **elle fait de la** ~ she plays an instrument; **mettre un poème en** ~ to set a poem to music; **c'est toujours la même** ~ * it's always the same old refrain. ◆ **musical, e,** *mpl* **-aux** *adj* musical. ◆ **musicalement** *adv* musically. ◆ **musicalité** *nf* musicality, musical quality. ◆ **music-hall,** *pl* ~**-**~**s** *nm (salle)* variety theatre, music hall. **faire du** ~ to be in variety; **numéro de** ~ variety turn. ◆ **musicien, -ienne** **1** *adj* musical. **2** *nm, f* musician.

musulman, e [myzylmɑ̃, an] *adj, nm, f* Moslem, Muslim.

muter [myte] (1) *vt (Admin)* to transfer. ◆ **mutant, e** *adj, nm, f* mutant. ◆ **mutation** *nf (gén)* transformation; *(Bio)* mutation; *(Admin, Jur)* transfer. **société en** ~ changing society.

mutiler [mytile] (1) *vt (gén)* to mutilate; *personne* to maim; *statue, arbre* to deface. **être mutilé des deux jambes** to have lost both legs; **se** ~ to maim *ou* injure o.s. ◆ **mutilation** *nf* mutilation. ◆ **mutilé, e** **1** *adj*: **être** ~ to be disabled. **2** *nm, f* cripple, disabled person. ~ **de la face** disfigured person; ~ **de guerre** disabled ex-serviceman.

mutiner (se) [mytine] (1) *vpr (Mil, Naut)* to mutiny; *(gén)* to rebel, revolt. ◆ **mutin, e** **1** *adj (espiègle)* mischievous. **2** *nm* mutineer; rebel. ◆ **mutiné, e** **1** *adj* mutinous. **2** *nm* mutineer; rebel. ◆ **mutinerie** *nf* mutiny; rebellion, revolt.

mutisme [mytism(ə)] *nm (gén)* silence; *(Méd)* muteness.

mutuel, -elle [mytɥɛl] **1** *adj* mutual. **2** *nf* mutual benefit society. ◆ **mutuellement** *adv s'aider* one another, each other. ~ **ressenti** mutually felt.

myope [mjɔp] *adj* short-sighted, near-sighted, myopic. ~ **comme une taupe** * (as) blind as a bat. ◆ **myopie** *nf* short-sightedness, near-sightedness, myopia.

myosotis [mjɔzɔtis] *nm* forget-me-not.

myriade [miʀjad] *nf* myriad.

myrtille [miʀtij] *nf* bilberry, blueberry *(US)*.

mystère [mistɛʀ] *nm* mystery. ◆ **mystérieusement** *adv* mysteriously. ◆ **mystérieux, -euse** *adj* mysterious.

mystifier [mistifje] (7) *vt* to fool, take in. ◆ **mystification** *nf (farce)* hoax; *(péj: mythe)* myth. ◆ **mystificateur, -trice** *nm, f* hoaxer.

mystique [mistik] **1** *adj* mystical. **2** *nmf (personne)* mystic. **3** *nf (science)* mysticism; *(péj: vénération)* blind belief (*de* in). ◆ **mysticisme** *nm* mysticism. ◆ **mystiquement** *adv* mystically.

mythe [mit] *nm (gén)* myth. ◆ **mythique** *adj* mythical. ◆ **mythologie** *nf* mythology. ◆ **mythologique** *adj* mythological. ◆ **mythomane** *adj, nmf* mythomaniac.

myxomatose [miksɔmatoz] *nf* myxomatosis.

N

N, n [ɛn] *nm (lettre)* N, n.

n' [n] *V* **ne.**

nacre [nakʀ(ə)] *nf* mother-of-pearl. ◆ **nacré, e** *adj* pearly.

nager [naʒe] (3) **1** *vi [personne]* to swim; *[objet]* to float. **ça nage dans la graisse** it is swimming in fat; ~ **dans l'opulence** to be rolling in money *; **il nage dans ses vêtements** he is lost in his clothes; **en allemand, je nage complètement** * I'm completely at sea * in German. **2** *vt* to swim. ~ **la brasse** to swim breast-stroke. ◆ **nage** *nf* (**a**) swimming; *(manière)* stroke, style of swimming. ~ **sur le dos** backstroke; ~ **indienne** sidestroke; ~ **libre** freestyle; **gagner la rive à la** ~ to swim to the bank. (**b**) **être en** ~ to be bathed in sweat; **cela m'a mis en** ~ that made me sweat. ◆ **nageoire** *nf [poisson]* fin; *[phoque etc]* flipper. ◆ **nageur, -euse** *nm, f* swimmer.

naguère [nagɛʀ] *adv (récemment)* not long ago; *(autrefois)* formerly.

naïf, naïve [naif, naiv] **1** *adj* naïve. **2** *nm, f* gullible fool, innocent. ◆ **naïvement** *adv* naïvely. ◆ **naïveté** *nf* naïvety.

nain, e [nɛ̃, nɛn] **1** *adj* dwarfish. **chêne** ~ dwarf oak. **2** *nm, f* dwarf. *(Cartes)* **le** ~ **jaune** pope Joan.

Nairobi [naiʀɔbi] *n* Nairobi.

naissance [nɛsɑ̃s] *nf (gén)* birth; *[rivière]* source; *[cheveux, ongles]* root; *[cou]* base. **à la** ~ at birth; **de** ~ *aveugle* from birth; *français* by birth; **prendre** ~ to take form; **donner** ~ **à** *enfant* to give birth to; *rumeurs* to give rise to.

naître [nɛtʀ(ə)] (59) **1** *vi* (**a**) to be born. **il vient de** ~ he has just been born; **X est né le 4 mars** X was born on March 4; **l'homme naît libre** man is born free; **il est né poète** he is a born poet; **l'enfant qui va** ~ the unborn child; **l'enfant qui vient de** ~ the newborn child; **en naissant** at birth; **Mme Durand, née Dupont** Mme Durand, née Dupont; **être né de parents français** to be born of French parents; **être né coiffé** to be born lucky; **il n'est pas né d'hier** he wasn't born yesterday. (**b**) *[idée]* to be born; *[ville]* to spring up; *[jour]* to break; *[sentiment, difficultés]* to arise; *[plante]* to burst forth; *[rivière]* to rise. **un sourire naquit sur son visage** a smile crept over his face; **faire** ~ *industrie* to create; *soupçons, désir* to arouse. (**c**) ~ **de: la haine née de ces querelles** the hatred which sprang from these quarrels. (**d**) *(littér: s'éveiller à)* ~ **à l'amour** to awaken to love. **2** *vb impers:* **il naît plus de filles que de garçons** there are more girls born than boys.

nana * [nana] *nf (femme)* bird ‡, chick ‡.

nantir [nɑ̃tiʀ] (2) *vt* to provide (*de* with). **se** ~ **de** to provide o.s. with. ◆ **nanti, e** *adj* affluent, well-to-do.

napalm [napalm] *nm* napalm.

naphtaline [naftalin] *nf* mothballs.

Naples [napl(ə)] *n* Naples. ◆ **napolitain, e** *adj,* **N~(e)** *nm(f)* Neapolitan.

nappe [nap] *nf* tablecloth; *[gaz, pétrole]* layer; *[brouillard]* blanket; *[eau, feu]* sheet. ~ **de mazout** oil slick. ◆ **napper** (1) *vt (Culin)* to coat (*de* with). ◆ **napperon** *nm* doily; *(pour vase, lampe etc)* mat.

narcisse [naʀsis] *nm (Bot)* narcissus; *(péj: égocentrique)* narcissistic individual. *(Myth)* **N~** Narcissus.

narcotique [naʀkɔtik] *adj, nm* narcotic.

narguer [naʀge] (1) *vt danger* to flout; *personne* to scoff at.

narine [naʀin] *nf* nostril.

narquois, e [naʀkwa, waz] *adj* mocking, derisive. ◆ **narquoisement** *adv* mockingly, derisively.

narrer [naʀe] (1) *vt* to narrate. ◆ **narrateur, -trice** *nm, f* narrator. ◆ **narratif, -ive** *adj* narrative. ◆ **narration** *nf (action)* narration; *(récit)* narrative, account; *(Scol: rédaction)* essay.

nasal, e, *mpl* **-aux** [nazal, o] *adj* nasal.

nase ‡ [naz] *adj* bust *, kaput. **ma télé est** ~ my TV has gone bust *.

naseau, *pl* **~x** [nazo] *nm [cheval]* nostril.

nasiller [nazije] (1) *vi [personne]* to have a (nasal) twang; *[micro]* to whine. ◆ **nasillard, e** *adj* nasal; whiny. ◆ **nasillement** *nm* (nasal) twang; whine.

nasse [nas] *nf* hoop net.

natal, e, *mpl* **~s** [natal] *adj* native. ◆ **natalité** *nf* birth rate.

natation [natɑsjɔ̃] *nf* swimming.

natif, -ive [natif, iv] *adj, nm, f (gén)* native.

nation [nɑsjɔ̃] *nf* nation. **les N ~s Unies** the United Nations. ◆ **national, e,** *mpl* **-aux** *adj (gén)* national; *économie, monnaie* domestic; *obsèques, éducation* state. **au plan** ~ **et international** at home and abroad; *(Écon)* **entreprise** ~**e** state-owned company; **grève** ~**e** nation-wide *ou* national strike; **(route)** ~**e** ≃ 'A' *ou* trunk road, state highway *(US)*. ◆ **nationalisable** *adj* targeted for nationalization. ◆ **nationalisation** *nf* nationalization. ◆ **nationaliser** (1) *vt* to nationalize. ◆ **nationalisme** *nm* nationalism. ◆ **nationaliste** *adj, nmf* nationalist. ◆ **nationalité** *nf* nationality.

natte [nat] *nf (tresse)* pigtail, plait; *(paillasse)* mat.

naturaliser [natyʀalize] (1) *vt* to naturalize. **se faire** ~ **français** to become a naturalized Frenchman. ◆ **naturalisation** *nf* naturalization.

nature [natyʀ] **1** *nf* (**a**) *(caractère)* nature. **la** ~ **humaine** human nature; **c'est/ce n'est pas de** ~ **à arranger les choses** it's liable to/not likely to make things easier; **il n'est pas de** ~ **à accepter** he's not the sort of person who would agree. (**b**) *(monde)* **la** ~ nature; **vivre (perdu) dans la** ~ to live (out) in the country *ou* at the back of beyond; **disparaître dans la** ~ * to vanish into thin air. (**c**) *(sorte)* nature, kind. **de toute(s)** ~**(s)** of all kinds, of every kind. (**d**) *(Art)* **peindre d'après** ~ to paint from life; **plus grand que** ~ more than life-size, larger than life; ~ **morte** still life. (**e**) *(Fin)* **en** ~ in kind. **2** *adj inv eau, thé etc* plain. **café** ~ black coffee; **boire le whisky** ~ to drink whisky neat *ou* straight.

naturel, -elle [natyʀɛl] **1** *adj (gén)* natural; *besoins* bodily. **avec sa voix** ~**elle** in his (*ou* her) normal voice; **c'est** ~ **chez lui** it's natural for him, it comes naturally to him; **ne me remerciez pas, c'est tout** ~ please don't mention it. **2** *nm* (**a**) *(caractère)* nature, disposition. (**b**) *(absence d'affectation)* naturalness. (**c**) *(indigène)* native. (**d**) **au** ~ *(Culin)* water-packed; **elle est mieux en photo qu'au** ~

she's better in photos than in real life. ◆ **naturellement** *adv (gén)* naturally; *(bien sûr)* naturally, of course.

naufrage [nofRaʒ] *nm [bateau]* wreck; *(fig)* ruin. **un** ~ a shipwreck; **faire** ~ *[bateau]* to be wrecked; *[marin]* to be shipwrecked. ◆ **naufragé, e 1** *adj* shipwrecked. **2** *nm, f* shipwrecked person; *(sur une île)* castaway.

nausée [noze] *nf (sensation)* nausea. **avoir la** ~ to feel sick; **avoir des** ~**s** to have bouts of nausea; *(lit, fig)* **ça me donne la** ~ it makes me (feel) sick. ◆ **nauséabond, e** *adj (lit)* putrid, evil-smelling, foul-smelling, nauseating, sickening; *(fig)* nauseating, sickening.

nautique [notik] *adj science* nautical. **sports** ~**s** water sports; **fête** ~ water festival.

naval, e, *mpl* ~**s** [naval] *adj (gén)* naval; *industrie* ship-building.

navet [navɛ] *nm* (**a**) *(légume)* turnip. (**b**) *(péj)* third-rate film *(ou* novel).

navette [navɛt] *nf* (**a**) *(Tex)* shuttle. (**b**) *(transport)* shuttle (service). **faire la** ~ **entre** *[banlieusard]* to commute between; *[véhicule]* to operate a shuttle service between; *[bateau]* to ply between. (**c**) *(Espace)* ~ **spatiale** space shuttle.

naviguer [navige] (1) *vi* (**a**) *(voyager) [bateau, marin]* to sail; *[avion, pilote]* to fly. **ce type a beaucoup navigué** * this guy has been around a lot *; **bateau en état de** ~ seaworthy ship. (**b**) *(piloter) [marin]* to navigate, sail; *[aviateur]* to navigate, fly. *(fig)* **il sait** ~ * he knows the ropes. ◆ **navigabilité** *nf [rivière]* navigability; *[bateau]* seaworthiness; *[avion]* airworthiness. ◆ **navigable** *adj rivière* navigable. ◆ **navigant, e** *adj: (Aviat)* **personnel** ~ flying personnel. ◆ **navigateur** *nm (gén)* navigator. ~ **solitaire** single-handed sailor. ◆ **navigation** *nf* (**a**) *(Naut)* sailing, navigation; *(trafic)* (sea) traffic. **ouvert à la** ~ open to shipping *ou* ships; **terme de** ~ nautical term. (**b**) *(Aviat) (trafic)* air traffic; *(pilotage)* navigation, flying.

navire [naviR] *nm* ship; *(Jur)* vessel. ~ **amiral** flagship; ~ **de guerre** warship.

navrer [navRe] (1) *vt [conduite, nouvelle]* to distress, upset; *[contretemps]* to annoy. ◆ **navré, e** *adj* sorry *(de* to). **ton** ~ *(excuse)* apologetic tone; *(compassion)* sympathetic tone; *(émotion)* distressed *ou* upset voice.

nazi, e [nazi] *adj, nm, f* Nazi. ◆ **nazisme** *nm* Nazism.

ne [n(ə)] *adv nég,* **n'** *devant voyelles et h muet* (**a**) not. **il n'a rien dit** he did not *ou* didn't say anything, he said nothing; **nul n'a compris** nobody *ou* no one understood; **je n'ai pas d'argent** I have no money, I haven't (got) any money; ~ **me dérangez pas** don't *ou* do not disturb me; **il** ~ **sait pas parler** he can't *ou* cannot speak; **pas un seul** ~ **savait** not a single one knew; **il n'a que faire de vos conseils** he has no use for your advice, he's not interested in your advice; **que n'a-t-il songé à me prévenir** if only he had thought to warn me; **n'était la situation internationale, il serait parti** had it not been for *ou* were it not for the international situation he would have left; **cela fait des années que je n'ai été au cinéma** it's years since I (last) went to the cinema. (**b**) ~...**que** only; **elle n'a confiance qu'en nous** she trusts only us; **il n'a que trop d'assurance** he is only too self-assured; **il n'y a pas que vous** you're not the only one; **et il n'y a pas que ça!** and that's not all! (**c**) *(sans valeur nég)* **j'ai peur qu'il** ~ **vienne** I am afraid (that) he will come; **mangez avant que la viande** ~ **refroidisse** do eat before the meat gets cold; **il est plus malin qu'on** ~ **pense** he is more cunning than you think.

né, e [ne] *adj, nm, f* born. **son premier/dernier** ~ her first-/last-born.

néanmoins [neɑ̃mwɛ̃] *adv* nevertheless, yet. **c'est incroyable mais** ~ **vrai** it's incredible but nonetheless true *ou* but it's true nevertheless.

néant [neɑ̃] *nm*: **le** ~ nothingness; **le** ~ **de la vie** the emptiness of life; **signes particuliers:** ~ special peculiarities: none.

nébuleux, -euse [nebylø, øz] **1** *adj ciel* cloudy; *discours* nebulous. **2** *nf (Astron)* nebula.

nécessaire [nesesɛR] **1** *adj (gén)* necessary; *personne* indispensable *(à* to). **il est** ~ **qu'on le fasse** we need to do it, we have (got) to do it, we must do it, it's necessary *ou* essential for us to do it; ~ **à la vie/aux hommes** necessary for life/to man; **un bon repos vous est** ~ you need a good rest; **avoir le temps** ~ **(pour qch/pour faire)** to have the necessary time *ou* the time required (for sth/to do). **2** *nm*: **je n'ai pas le** ~ **pour le faire** I haven't got what's needed *ou* necessary to do it; **le strict** ~ the bare necessities *ou* essentials; **je vais faire le** ~ I'll see to it, I'll make the necessary arrangements. **3** : ~ **à couture** sewing box; ~ **à ongles** manicure set; ~ **de toilette** toilet bag; ~ **de voyage** overnight bag, grip. ◆ **nécessairement** *adv faux etc* necessarily. **dois-je** ~ **m'en aller?** is it necessary for me to go?, must I go?, do I have to go?; **il va** ~ **échouer** he's bound to fail, he'll inevitably fail. ◆ **nécessité** *nf* (**a**) necessity. **je ne vois pas la** ~ **de le faire** I don't see the necessity of doing that *ou* the need for doing that; **être dans la** ~ **de faire qch** to have no choice *ou* alternative but to do sth. (**b**) **les** ~**s de la vie** the necessities *ou* essentials of life; **les** ~**s du service** the demands *ou* requirements of the job. (**c**) *(†: pauvreté)* destitution. ◆ **nécessiter** (1) *vt* to require, necessitate. ◆ **nécessiteux, -euse** *adj* needy.

nécrologie [nekRɔlɔʒi] *nf (liste)* obituary column; *(biographie)* obituary. ◆ **nécrologique** *adj* obituary.

nécropole [nekRɔpɔl] *nf* necropolis.

nécrose [nekRoz] *nf* necrosis. ◆ **nécroser** *vt,* **se** ~ *vpr* (1) to necrose.

nectar [nɛktaR] *nm (Bot, Myth, fig)* nectar.

nectarine [nɛktaRin] *nf* nectarine.

néerlandais, e [neɛRlɑ̃dɛ, ɛz] **1** *adj* Dutch. **2** *nm* (**a**) **N**~ Dutchman; **les N**~ the Dutch. (**b**) *(Ling)* Dutch. **3** *nf*: **N**~**e** Dutchwoman.

nef [nɛf] *nf* nave. ~ **latérale** side aisle.

néfaste [nefast(ə)] *adj (nuisible)* harmful *(à* to); *(funeste)* ill-fated, unlucky.

négatif, -ive [negatif, iv] **1** *adj* negative. **2** *nm (Phot, Ling)* negative. **au** ~ in the negative. **3** *nf*: **dans la** ~**ive** in the negative. ◆ **négation** *nf* negation. ◆ **négativement** *adv* negatively.

négliger [negliʒe] (3) **1** *vt (gén)* to neglect; *tenue* to be careless about; *conseil* to disregard; *occasion* to miss. **ce n'est pas à** ~ *(offre)* it's not to be sneezed at; *(difficulté)* it mustn't be overlooked; **ne rien** ~ **pour réussir** to leave no stone unturned in an effort to succeed; **il a négligé de le faire** he did not bother *ou* he neglected to do it. **2 se** ~ *vpr (santé)* to neglect o.s.; *(tenue)* to neglect one's appearance. ◆ **négligé, e 1** *adj épouse* neglected; *tenue* slovenly; *travail, style* slipshod. **2** *nm (laisser-aller)* slovenliness; *(vêtement)* négligée. ◆ **négligeable** *adj (gén)* negligible; *détail* trivial; *adversaire* insignificant. **non** ~ not inconsiderable. ◆ **négligemment** *adv (sans soin)* carelessly, negligently; *(nonchalamment)* casually. ◆ **négligence** *nf* negligence, slovenliness; *(erreur)* omission. **il est d'une (telle)** ~! he's so careless!; **c'est une** ~ **de ma part** it's an oversight *ou* a careless mistake on my part; **par** ~ out of carelessness. ◆ **négligent, e** *adj (sans soin)* negligent, careless; *(nonchalant)* casual.

négocier [negɔsje] (7) *vti (gén)* to negotiate. ◆ **négoce** *nm* (†: *commerce)* business. **faire du** ~ to be in business; **faire du** ~ **avec un pays** to trade with a country. ◆ **négociable** *adj* negotiable. ◆ **négociant, e** *nm, f* merchant. ~ **en gros** wholesaler. ◆ **négociateur, -trice** *nm, f* negotiator. ◆ **négociation** *nf* negotiation. ~**s commerciales** trade talks.

nègre [nɛgʀ(ə)] **1** *nm (péj) (indigène)* Negro, nigger *(péj)*; *(écrivain)* ghost writer. **travailler comme un** ~ to work like a slave. **2** *adj* Negro. ◆ **négresse** *nf* Negress.

neige [nɛʒ] *nf (gén, arg)* snow. **aller à la** ~ * to go to the ski resorts; ~ **carbonique** dry ice; ~ **fondue** *(pluie)* sleet. ◆ **neiger** (3) *vb impers* to snow, be snowing. ◆ **neigeux, -euse** *adj sommet* snow-covered, snow-clad; *aspect* snowy.

nénuphar [nenyfaʀ] *nm* water lily.

néo- [neɔ] *préf* neo-.

néolithique [neɔlitik] *adj, nm* neolithic.

néologisme [neɔlɔʒism(ə)] *nm* neologism.

néon [neɔ̃] *nm (gaz)* neon; *(éclairage)* neon lighting.

néophyte [neɔfit] *nmf (gén)* beginner; *(Rel)* neophyte.

néo-zélandais, e [neɔzelɑ̃dɛ, ɛz] **1** *adj* New Zealand. **2** *nm(f):* **N~(e)** New Zealander.

Népal [nepal] *nm* Nepal. ◆ **népalais, e** *adj, nm,* **N~(e)** *nm(f)* Nepalese, Nepali.

nerf [nɛʀ] *nm* nerve. **avoir les** ~**s malades** to suffer from nerves; **avoir les** ~**s à vif** to be very nervy *ou* edgy, be on edge; **avoir ses** ~**s** to have a fit of nerves; **être sur les** ~**s** to be all keyed up; **taper * sur les** ~**s de qn** to get on sb's nerves; **ses** ~**s ont lâché** * his nerves have gone to pieces, he has cracked up *; **allons du** ~! come on, buck up! *; **ça manque de** ~ it has got no go about it; **l'argent est le** ~ **de la guerre** money is the sinews of war. ◆ **nerveusement** *adv (excité)* nervously, tensely; *(agacé)* touchily, nervily. **ébranlé** ~ shaken. ◆ **nerveux, -euse** *adj* (**a**) *tension, système* nervous; *cellule* nerve. (**b**) *(agité)* nervous, tense; *(irritable)* touchy, nervy. **c'est un grand** ~ he's very highly strung. (**c**) *(vigoureux) corps, style* energetic, vigorous; *moteur* responsive. (**d**) *(sec) personne, main* wiry; *viande* stringy. ◆ **nervosité** *nf* (**a**) *(agitation) (permanente)* nervousness; *(passagère)* agitation, tension. (**b**) *(irritabilité)* irritability, nerviness. (**c**) *[moteur]* responsiveness. **manque de** ~ sluggishness.

nervure [nɛʀvyʀ] *nf (Bot)* nervure; *(Archit)* rib.

n'est-ce pas [nɛspɑ] *adv*: **il est fort,** ~? he is strong, isn't he?; **il l'ignore,** ~? he doesn't know, does he?

net, nette [nɛt] **1** *adj* (**a**) *surface* clean; *intérieur, travail* clean, neat, tidy; *conscience* clear. **mettre au** ~ *rapport, devoir* to make a fair copy of sth; *plan, travail* to tidy up. (**b**) *prix, poids* net. ~ **de** free of; **revenu** ~ disposable income. (**c**) *idée, explication, voix* clear; *réponse* straight, plain; *refus* flat; *situation* clear-cut. *(bizarre)* **ce type n'est pas très** ~ * this guy is slightly odd *ou* strange *. (**d**) *différence, amélioration etc* marked, distinct, sharp. **il est très** ~ **qu'il le savait** it is quite clear *ou* obvious that he knew. (**e**) *dessin, écriture, souvenir* clear; *contour, (Phot) image* sharp; *cassure* clean. **2** *adv* (**a**) *s'arrêter* dead; *tué* outright. **se casser** ~ to break clean through. (**b**) *parler* frankly, bluntly; *refuser* flatly. **pour vous parler** ~ to be blunt *ou* frank with you. (**c**) *(Comm)* net. **2 kg** ~ 2 kg net. ◆ **nettement** *adv (gén)* clearly; *refuser* flatly; *dire* bluntly, frankly; *apparaître* distinctly, sharply; *s'améliorer* markedly. ◆ **netteté** *nf [tenue, travail]* neatness; *[explication, souvenir, voix]* clearness, clarity; *[contour, image]* sharpness; *[cassure]* cleanness.

nettoyer [nɛtwaje] (8) *vt* (**a**) *(gén) objet* to clean; *jardin* to clear. ~ **au chiffon** to dust; ~ **avec du savon** to wash with soap; ~ **à la brosse** to brush; ~ **à sec** to dry-clean. (**b**) (*) *(tuer)* to finish off *; *(ruiner)* to clean out; *(vider)* to clean out, empty. (**c**) *(Mil, Police)* to clean up. ◆ **nettoiement** *nm* cleaning. ◆ **nettoyage** *nm (gén)* cleaning; *(Mil, Police)* cleaning up. ~ **de printemps** spring-cleaning; ~ **à sec** dry cleaning.

neuf[1] [nœf] *adj inv, nm inv* nine; *V* **six.**

neuf[2]**, neuve** [nœf, nœv] **1** *adj (gén)* new; *pensée* fresh; *pays* young. **à l'état** ~ as good as new. **2** *nm*: **il y a du** ~ there has been a new development; **quoi de/rien de** ~? what's/nothing new?; **vêtu de** ~ dressed in new clothes; **remettre à** ~ to do up like new; **on ne peut pas faire du** ~ **avec du vieux** you can't make new things out of old.

neurasthénie [nøʀasteni] *nf (gén)* depression. **faire de la** ~ to be depressed. ◆ **neurasthénique** *adj* depressed.

neuro... [nøʀɔ] *préf* neuro...

neurochirurgie [nøʀɔʃiʀyʀʒi] *nf* neurosurgery.

neurologie [nøʀɔlɔʒi] *nf* neurology. ◆ **neurologue** *nmf* neurologist.

neurophysiologie [nøʀɔfisjɔlɔʒi] *nf* neurophysiology.

neuropsychiatrie [nøʀɔpsikjatʀi] *nf* neuropsychiatry. ◆ **neuropsychiatre** *nmf* neuropsychiatrist.

neuropsychologie [nøʀɔpsikɔlɔʒi] *nf* neuropsychology.

neutre [nøtʀ(ə)] **1** *adj (gén)* neutral; *(Ling, Zool)* neuter; *(sans excès)* middle-of-the-road. **2** *nm (Ling)* neuter; *(Élec)* neutral; *(Pol)* neutral country. ◆ **neutralisation** *nf* neutralization. ◆ **neutraliser** (1) *vt* to neutralize. ◆ **neutralité** *nf* neutrality. ◆ **neutron** *nm* neutron.

neuvième [nœvjɛm] *adj, nmf* ninth; *V* **sixième.** ◆ **neuvièmement** *adv* ninthly; *V* **sixièmement.**

neveu, *pl* ~**x** [n(ə)vø] *nm* nephew.

névralgie [nevʀalʒi] *nf* neuralgia. **avoir des** ~**s** to suffer from neuralgia. ◆ **névralgique** *adj* neuralgic. *(Méd, fig)* **point** ~ nerve centre.

névrose [nevʀoz] *nf* neurosis. ◆ **névrosé, e** *adj, nm, f* neurotic. ◆ **névropathe** *adj, nmf* neurotic. ◆ **névrotique** *adj* neurotic.

new-look * [njuluk] *adj, nm inv* new look.

New York [njujɔʀk] **1** *n (ville)* New York. **2** *nm:* **l'État de** ~ New York State. ◆ **new yorkais, e 1** *adj* of *ou* from New York. **2** *nm, f:* **N~ Y~(e)** New Yorker.

nez [ne] *nm* (**a**) *(gén)* nose. **parler du** ~ to talk through one's nose; **comme le** ~ **au milieu du visage** as plain as the nose on your face *ou* as a pikestaff; **cela sent le brûlé à plein** ~ there's a strong smell of burning; **tu as le** ~ **dessus!** it's right under your nose! (**b**) *(visage)* **baisser/lever le** ~ to bow/raise one's head, look down/up; **mettre le** ~ **à la fenêtre** to show one's face at the window; **fermer la porte au** ~ **de qn** to shut the door in sb's face; ~ **à** ~ face to face (*avec* with); **faire un drôle de** ~ to pull a funny face. (**c**) *(flair)* **avoir du** ~ to have flair; **j'ai eu le** ~ **creux de m'en aller** * I was quite right to leave. (**d**) **au** ~ **et à la barbe de qn** under sb's very nose; **il m'a dans le** ~ * he can't stand me *, he has got sth against me; **se bouffer le** ~ ‡ to be at each others' throats; **mettre son** ~ **dans qch** to poke one's nose into sth; **l'affaire lui est passée sous le** ~ * the bargain slipped through his fingers.

ni [ni] *conj* nor, or. **ni... ni...** neither... nor...; **il ne pouvait (**~**) parler** ~ **entendre** he could neither speak nor hear, he couldn't speak or hear; **je ne veux** ~ **ne peux accepter** I neither wish to nor can accept; ~ **plus** ~ **moins** no more no less; ~

l'un ~ l'autre neither one nor the other, neither of them; **~ vu ~ connu** * no one'll know; **cela ne me fait ~ chaud ~ froid** it makes no odds to me.

Niagara [njagaʀa] *nm* Niagara.

niais, e [njɛ, ɛz] **1** *adj (gén)* silly, simple; *rire* inane. **2** *nm, f* simpleton. ◆ **niaisement,** *adv* inanely. ◆ **niaiserie** *nf* silliness, simpleness; inanity. **~s** foolish remarks *etc.*

Nicaragua [nikaʀagwa] *nm* Nicaragua. ◆ **nicaraguayen, -enne** *adj,* **N~(ne)** *nm(f)* Nicaraguan.

niche [niʃ] *nf* (**a**) *(alcôve)* niche, recess; *[chien]* kennel. (**b**) *(farce)* trick, hoax.

nichée [niʃe] *nf [oiseaux, enfants]* brood; *[chiens]* litter.

nicher [niʃe] (1) **1** *vi [oiseau]* to nest; (*) *[personne]* to hang out *. **2 se ~** *vpr [oiseau]* to nest; *[village etc]* to nestle (*dans* in); (*) *[personne]* to stick * *ou* put o.s.; *[objet]* to lodge itself.

nickel [nikɛl] **1** *nm* nickel. **2** *adj (*: impeccable)* spick and span. ◆ **nickeler** (4) *vt* to nickel-plate.

Nicosie [nikɔsi] *n* Nicosia.

nicotine [nikɔtin] *nf* nicotine.

nid [ni] *nm (Zool)* nest; *(foyer)* cosy little nest; *(repaire)* den. **surprendre qn au ~** to find sb at home *ou* in; **~ de mitrailleuses** nest of machine guns; **~ de poule** pothole; **~ à poussière** dust trap; **~ de résistance** pocket of resistance. ◆ **nidification** *nf* nesting.

nièce [njɛs] *nf* niece.

nier [nje] (7) *vt* to deny (*avoir fait* having done). **~ l'évidence** to deny the obvious; **l'accusé nia** the accused denied the charges.

nigaud, e [nigo, od] **1** *adj* silly, simple. **2** *nm, f* simpleton. **gros ~!** big silly *ou* ninny! *

Niger [niʒɛʀ] *nm:* **le ~** the Niger. ◆ **nigérien, -ienne 1** *adj* of *ou* from Niger. **2** *nm, f:* **N~(ne)** inhabitant *ou* native of Niger.

Nigéria [niʒeʀja] *nm ou f* Nigeria. ◆ **nigérian, e** *adj,* **N~(e)** *nm(f)* Nigerian.

night-club, *pl* **~s** [najtklœb] *nm* nightclub.

Nil [nil] *nm:* **le ~** the Nile.

nipper * [nipe] (1) **1** *vt* to tog out *. **2 se ~** *vpr* to get togged up *. ◆ **nippes** † * *nfpl* togs *.

nippon, e *ou* **-onne** [nipɔ̃, ɔn] *adj,* **N~(e)** *nm (f)* Japanese, Nipponese.

nitrate [nitʀat] *nm* nitrate. ◆ **nitrique** *adj* nitric. ◆ **nitroglycérine** *nf* nitroglycerine.

niveau, *pl* **~x** [nivo] *nm* (**a**) *[huile, eau]* level. **au ~ du sol** at ground level; **la neige m'arrivait au ~ des genoux** the snow came up to my knees *ou* was knee-deep; **serré au ~ de la taille** tight at the waist; **au ~ du village, il s'arrêta** once level with the village he stopped; **de ~ avec, au même ~ que** level with; **mettre/être de** *ou* **à ~** to make/be level. (**b**) *[études]* standard; *[intelligence, qualité]* level. **~ de langue** register; **~ social** social standing; **~ de vie** standard of living; **le ~ d'instruction baisse** educational standards are falling; **atteindre son ~ le plus bas** to reach its lowest ebb *ou* level; *(Scol)* **au ~** up to standard; **au ~ européen** at the European level; **négociations au plus haut ~** top-level negotiations. (**c**) *(objet) (Constr)* level; *(Aut: jauge)* gauge. ◆ **niveler** (4) *vt (gén)* to level; *[érosion]* to wear down *ou* away. **~ par le bas** to level down. ◆ **nivelage** *nm ou* ◆ **nivellement** *nm* levelling. **~ par le bas** levelling down. ◆ **niveleuse** *nf (Constr)* grader.

noble [nɔbl(ə)] **1** *adj* noble. **2** *nmf* nobleman; noblewoman. **les ~s** the nobility. ◆ **noblement** *adv* nobly. ◆ **noblesse** *nf (gén)* nobility. **~ oblige** noblesse oblige; **la petite ~** the (landed) gentry.

noce [nɔs] *nf (cérémonie)* wedding; *(cortège)* wedding party. **~s** wedding; **être de ~** to be invited to a wedding; **repas de ~(s)** wedding banquet; **~s d'or** golden wedding; **il l'avait épousée en premières ~s** she was his first wife; **faire la ~** * to live it up *, have a wild time; **je n'étais pas à la ~** I was having a pretty uncomfortable time. ◆ **noceur, -euse** * *nm, f* reveller.

nocif, -ive [nɔsif, iv] *adj* noxious, harmful. ◆ **nocivité** *nf* noxiousness, harmfulness.

noctambule [nɔktɑ̃byl] *nmf (noceur)* night reveller; *(qui veille la nuit)* night bird, night owl.

nocturne [nɔktyʀn(ə)] **1** *adj* nocturnal, night. **2** *nm (oiseau)* night hunter; *(Mus)* nocturne; *(Sport)* evening fixture.

Noël [nɔɛl] *nm (fête)* Christmas; *(chant)* (Christmas) carol; *(cadeau)* Christmas present. **joyeux ~!** merry *ou* happy Christmas!; **~ au balcon, Pâques au tison** a warm Christmas means a cold Easter.

nœud [nø] **1** *nm (gén)* knot; *(ruban)* bow; *(Phys)* node. **faire son ~ de cravate** to knot *ou* tie one's tie; **avoir un ~ dans la gorge** to have a lump in one's throat; **il y a un ~!** * there's a hitch *ou* snag!; **le ~ de** *problème, (Théât) intrigue* the knot of; *(littér: lien)* **les ~s de l'amitié** the bonds *ou* ties of friendship. **2** : **~ coulant** slipknot; *(ville)* **~ ferroviaire** rail junction; **~ gordien** Gordian knot; **~ papillon** bow tie; **~ de vipères** nest of vipers.

noir, e [nwaʀ] **1** *adj* (**a**) *(couleur)* black; *peau (par le soleil)* tanned; *(par les coups etc)* black and blue; *yeux, cheveux* dark. **je l'ai vu ~ sur blanc** I saw it in black and white; **~ de saleté** black with dirt. (**b**) *race* black, coloured. **l'Afrique ~e** black Africa; **le problème ~** the colour problem. (**c**) *(obscur)* dark. **il faisait ~ comme dans un four** * it was as black as pitch; **il faisait nuit ~e** it was pitch-dark; **rue ~e de monde** street teeming with people. (**d**) *désespoir, humeur, avenir, colère* black; *misère* utter; *idée* gloomy; *(macabre) film* macabre. (**e**) *(hostile)* black. **être dans la misère ~e** to be in utter *ou* abject poverty; **regarder qn d'un œil ~** to give sb a black look. (**f**) *(*: ivre)* drunk, tight.

2 *nm* (**a**) *(couleur)* black; *(pour les yeux)* mascara. **elle avait du ~ sur le menton** she had a black mark on her chin; **elle est en ~** she is in black; *(en deuil)* she is in mourning; **voir les choses en ~** to look on the black side. (**b**) *(obscurité)* dark, darkness. (**c**) **vendre au ~** to sell on the black market; **travailler au ~** to work on the side, moonlight *; **le travail au ~** moonlighting *. (**d**) *(personne)* **N~** black.

3 *nf* (**a**) *(personne)* **N~e** black, black woman. (**b**) *(Mus)* crotchet, quarter note *(US)*.

◆ **noirâtre** *adj* blackish. ◆ **noirceur** *nf* blackness; darkness; *(acte perfide)* black deed. ◆ **noircir** (2) **1** *vt (gén, fig)* to blacken; *[charbon]* to dirty; *(à la cire)* to darken. *(fig)* **~ du papier** to write page after page; **le soleil l'a noirci** the sun has tanned him; **~ la situation** to paint a black picture of the situation. **2** *vi [peau]* to tan; *[ciel, couleur]* to darken. **3 se ~** *vpr [ciel, couleur]* to darken; *[temps]* to turn stormy. ◆ **noircissement** *nm* blackening; dirtying; darkening. ◆ **noircissure** *nf* black mark.

noise [nwaz] *nf:* **chercher ~ à qn** to try to pick a quarrel with sb.

noisette [nwazɛt] **1** *adj inv* hazel. **2** *nf (fruit)* hazelnut. **~ de beurre** knob of butter. ◆ **noisetier** *nm* hazel tree.

noix [nwa] *nf (fruit)* walnut; *[côtelette]* eye. **à la ~** * rubbishy; **~ de beurre** knob of butter; **~ de cajou** cashew nut; **~ de coco** coconut; **~ de muscade** nutmeg; **~ de veau** cushion of veal.

noliser [nɔlize] (1) *vt* to charter. **avion nolisé** charter plane.

nom [nɔ̃] **1** *nm (gén)* name. **petit ~** Christian *ou* first name; **il appelle les choses par leur ~** he's not afraid to call a spade a spade *ou* to call things by their proper name; **le beau ~ de liberté** the great name of liberty; **il n'est spécialiste que de** ~ he is a specialist in name only; **un crime sans** ~ *ou* **qui n'a pas de** ~ an unspeakable crime; **se faire un** ~ to make a name for o.s.; **parler au** ~ **de qn** to speak for *ou* on behalf of sb; **au** ~ **de la loi, ouvrez** open up in the name of the law; **au** ~ **de quoi vous permettez-vous...?** whatever gives you the right to...?; **au** ~ **du ciel!** in heaven's name!; **au** ~ **de ce que vous avez de plus cher** in the name of everything you hold most dear; ~ **de** ~ * *ou* **d'un chien!** * damn ‡ *ou* dash * it!; **traiter qn de tous les** ~**s** to call sb names, call sb everything under the sun. **2** : ~ **de baptême** Christian name, given name *(US)*; ~ **commun** common noun; ~ **déposé** (registered) tradename; ~ **d'emprunt** *(gén)* alias, assumed name; *[écrivain]* pen name; nom de plume; ~ **de famille** surname; ~ **de femme mariée** married name; ~ **de guerre** nom de guerre; ~ **de jeune fille** maiden name; ~ **propre** proper noun; ~ **de théâtre** stage name.

nomade [nɔmad] **1** *adj* nomadic. **2** *nmf* nomad.

nombre [nɔ̃bʀ(ə)] *nm* (**a**) *(gén)* number. **depuis** ~ **d'années** for many years, for a number of years; **les gagnants sont au** ~ **de 3** there are 3 winners; **supérieur en** ~ superior in numbers; **ils sont en** ~ **égal** their numbers are equal *ou* even, they are equal in numbers; **des ennemis sans** ~ innumerable *ou* countless enemies. (**b**) *(masse)* numbers. **être en** ~ to be in large numbers; **faire** ~ to make up the numbers; **submergé par le** ~ overcome by sheer weight of numbers; **le plus grand** ~ the great majority of people. (**c**) *(parmi)* **je le compte au** ~ **de mes amis** I number him among my friends; **est-il du** ~ **des reçus?** is he among those who passed?; **il y en avait dans le** ~ **qui riaient** some among them were laughing.

nombreux, -euse [nɔ̃bʀø, øz] *adj* (**a**) numerous, many. **les** ~**euses personnalités** the numerous *ou* many personalities; **de** ~ **accidents** many *ou* numerous accidents; **être** ~ to be numerous; **les gens étaient venus** ~ people had come in great numbers; **peu** ~ few; **le public était moins/plus** ~ **hier** there were fewer/more spectators yesterday. (**b**) *foule, collection* large.

nombril [nɔ̃bʀi] *nm* navel, belly button *. **il se prend pour le** ~ **du monde** * he thinks he is the cat's whiskers * *ou* God's gift to mankind. ◆ **nombrilisme** * *nm: (péj)* **faire du** ~ to be self-centred, be wrapped up in o.s. *ou* one's own concerns.

nomenclature [nɔmɑ̃klatyʀ] *nf (gén: liste)* list; *(Ling, Sci)* nomenclature; *[dictionnaire]* word list.

nominal, e, *mpl* **-aux** [nɔminal, o] *adj (gén)* nominal; *(Ling)* noun. **liste** ~**e** list of names; **syntagme** ~ noun phrase; *(Fin)* **valeur** ~**e** face value. ◆ **nominalement** *adv (gén, Ling)* nominally. ◆ **nominatif, -ive** **1** *adj (Fin)* registered. **liste** ~**ive** list of names. **2** *nm (Ling)* nominative. ◆ **nominativement** *adv* by name.

nommer [nɔme] (1) **1** *vt* (**a**) *fonctionnaire* to appoint; *candidat* to nominate (*à* to). (**b**) *(citer)* to name; *(appeler) personne* to call, name. **ce que nous nommons le bonheur** what we name *ou* call happiness; **qn que je ne nommerai pas** sb who shall remain nameless. **2** **se** ~ *vpr (s'appeler)* to be called; *(se présenter)* to introduce o.s. ◆ **nomination** *nf (promotion)* appointment, nomination (*à* to); *(document)* appointment *ou* nomination papers. ◆ **nominé, e** *adj film, acteur* nominated. **être** ~ **à qch** to be nominated *ou* shortlisted for sth. ◆ **nommément** *adv* (**a**) *(par son nom)* by name. (**b**) *(spécialement)* particularly.

non [nɔ̃] **1** *adv* (**a**) no. **le connaissez-vous? —** ~ do you know him? — no (I don't); **est-elle chez elle? —** ~ is she at home? — no (she isn't); **je ne dis pas** ~ *(ce n'est pas de refus)* I wouldn't say no; *(je n'en disconviens pas)* I don't disagree; **certes** ~**!** most certainly *ou* definitely not!; **bien sûr que** ~**!** of course not!, I should think not!; **répondre (par)** ~ to answer no; **faire** ~ **de la tête** to shake one's head. (**b**) *(remplaçant une proposition)* not. **je pense que** ~ I don't think so; **je crains que** ~ I am afraid not; **elle veut mais lui** ~ she wants to but he doesn't; **ah** ~**?** really?, no?; **partez-vous ou** ~**?** are you going or not?; **erreur ou** ~ mistake or no mistake. (**c**) *(littér: pas)* not. **c'est mon avis** ~ **(pas) le vôtre** it's my opinion not yours; ~ **(pas) que...** not that... (**d**) *(impatience, indignation)* **tu vas cesser de pleurer** ~**?** will you stop crying?; ~ **par exemple!** good gracious! (**e**) *(doute)* no? **il me l'a dit lui-même —** ~**?** he told me so himself — no?; **c'est bon** ~**?** it's good isn't it? (**f**) **nous ne l'avons pas vu — nous** ~ **plus** we didn't see him — neither did we *ou* we didn't either; **il parle** ~ **plus en médecin mais en ami** he is talking now not as a doctor but as a friend. (**g**) (*modifiant adv*) not. ~ **loin de là il y a...** not far from there there's...; **c'est** ~ **moins intéressant** it's no less interesting; ~ **sans raison/** ~ **sans peine** not without reason/difficulty; ~ **seulement il est impoli mais...** not only is he impolite but... (**h**) (*modifiant adj, participe*) **toutes les places** ~ **réservées** all the unreserved seats, all seats not reserved.

2 *nm inv* no. **il y a eu 30** ~ there were 30 votes against *ou* 30 noes.

3 *préf* non-, un-. ~**-ferreux** non-ferrous; ~**-vérifié** unverified.

4 : **non-agression** non-aggression; **non-aligné, e** nonaligned; **les pays non-alignés** the nonaligned countries; **non-alignement** nonalignment; **non-assistance à personne en danger** failure to render assistance to a person in danger; **non-combattant** noncombatant; **non-conformisme** nonconformism; **non-croyant** non-believer; **non-existant** non-existent; **non-fumeur** *(adj)* no-smoking; *(nm)* non-smoker; **non-ingérence** noninterference; **noninitié, e** lay person; **non-intervention** nonintervention; **non-lieu**: **bénéficier d'un non-lieu** to be discharged *ou* have one's case dismissed for lack of evidence; **non-paiement** nonpayment; **non-parution** failure to appear *ou* be published; **non-retour** no return; **non-sens** *(absurdité)* (piece of) nonsense; *(en traduction)* meaningless word; **non-stop** nonstop.

nonante [nɔnɑ̃t] *adj (Belgique, Suisse)* ninety.

nonchalance [nɔ̃ʃalɑ̃s] *nf* nonchalance. ◆ **nonchalant, e** *adj* nonchalant. ◆ **nonchalamment** *adv* nonchalantly.

nord [nɔʀ] **1** *nm* north. **le vent du** ~ the north wind; **un vent du** ~ a northerly *ou* north wind; **le vent est au** ~ the wind is blowing from the north; **au** ~ *(situation)* in the north; *(direction)* to the north, northwards; **au** ~ **de** north of; **l'Europe du** ~ Northern Europe; **l'Amérique du N**~ North America. **2** *adj inv région* northern; *entrée, pôle* north; *direction* northward; *(Mét)* northerly. **3** : ~**-africain** *etc* North African *etc*; ~**-est/-ouest** north-east/-west. ◆ **nordique** **1** *adj* Nordic. **2** *nmf*: **N**~ Scandinavian. ◆ **nordiste** *(Hist USA)* **1** *adj* Northern, Yankee. **2** *nmf*: **N**~ Northerner, Yankee.

normal, e, *mpl* **-aux** [nɔʀmal, o] **1** *adj (gén)* normal; *(courant)* normal, usual. **de dimension** ~**e** normal-sized, standard-sized; **il n'est pas** ~ there's sth wrong with him; **c'est** ~**!** it's (quite) natural! **2** *nf*: **s'écarter de la** ~**e** to diverge from the norm; **revenir à la** ~**e** to return to normality, get back to normal; **au-dessus de la** ~**e** above average; **température voisine des** ~**s saisonnières** temperature close to the seasonal average. ◆ **normalement** *adv* normally, usually. ◆ **normaliser** (1) *vt situation* to normalize; *produit* to standardize. ◆ **normalisation** *nf* normalization; standardization.

Normandie [nɔʀmɑ̃di] *nf* Normandy. ◆ **normand, e** *adj*, **N~(e)** *nm (f)* Norman.

norme [nɔʀm(ə)] *nf (gén)* norm; *(Tech)* standard. **rester dans la** ~ to keep within limits.

Norvège [nɔʀvɛʒ] *nf* Norway. ◆ **norvégien, -ienne** *adj, nm,* **N~(ne)** *nm (f)* Norwegian.

nos [no] *adj poss V* **notre.**

nostalgie [nɔstalʒi] *nf* nostalgia. ◆ **nostalgique 1** *adj* nostalgic. **2** *nmf*: **les ~s du nazisme** those who long for the return of the Nazis.

notable [nɔtabl(ə)] *adj, nm* notable. ◆ **notabilité** *nf* notability. ◆ **notablement** *adv* notably.

notaire [nɔtɛʀ] *nm* ≃ lawyer, solicitor.

notamment [nɔtamɑ̃] *adv* notably.

note [nɔt] *nf* (**a**) *(écrite)* note. **prendre des ~s** to take notes; **prendre bonne ~ de qch** to take good note of sth; **prendre qch en ~** to make a note of sth, write sth down; **~ en bas de page** footnote; **~ de la rédaction** editor's note; **~ de service** memorandum. (**b**) *(chiffrée)* mark, grade. **bonne/ mauvaise ~** good/bad mark. (**c**) *(facture)* bill, check *(US)*. **~ de frais** *(bulletin)* claim form (for expenses); *(argent dépensé)* expenses; **~ d'honoraires** (doctor's *ou* lawyer's) account. (**d**) *(Mus, fig)* note. **ses paroles étaient dans la ~** his words struck the right note; **~ de tristesse** note *ou* touch of sadness.
◆ **notation** *nf [signes]* notation; *[devoir, employé]* marking, grading. *(remarque)* **une ~ intéressante** an interesting touch. ◆ **noter** (1) *vt* (**a**) *adresse etc* to write down, note down. **notez-le** make a note of it; **notez que nous serons absents** note that we'll be away. (**b**) *(remarquer) faute, progrès* to notice. **notez (bien) que je n'ai rien dit** I didn't say anything, mark you; **il faut ~ qu'il a des excuses** he has an excuse mind *ou* mark you. (**c**) *(cocher)* to mark. **~ d'une croix** to mark with a cross, put a cross against, check off. (**d**) *devoir* to mark, grade; *élève, employé* to give a mark to, grade. ◆ **notice** *nf (gén)* note; *(mode d'emploi)* directions, instructions.

notifier [nɔtifje] (7) *vt* to notify. ◆ **notification** *nf* notification.

notion [nosjɔ̃] *nf* notion. **perdre la ~ du temps** to lose all notion of time; **avoir quelques ~s de grammaire** to have some notion of grammar.

notoire [nɔtwaʀ] *adj criminel* notorious; *fait* well-known. **il est ~ que** it is common knowledge that. ◆ **notoirement** *adv* notoriously. **~ reconnu** well known. ◆ **notoriété** *nf [fait]* notoriety; *(renommée)* fame. **c'est de ~ publique** that's common knowledge.

notre [nɔtʀ(ə)], *pl* **nos** [no] *adj poss* our; *(emphatique)* our own. **~ homme a filé** the chap *ou* fellow has run off; **~ esprit** our minds; **N~ Seigneur** Our Lord.

nôtre [notʀ(ə)] **1** *pron poss:* **le ~, la ~, les ~s** ours, our own. **2** *nm* (**a**) **nous y mettrons du ~** we'll do our bit. (**b**) **les ~s** *(famille)* our family; *(partisans)* our own people; **il sera des ~s** he will join us. **3** *adj poss (littér)* ours, our own. **ces principes, nous les avons faits ~s** we have made these principles our own; *V* **sien.**

nouba ‡ [nuba] *nf*: **faire la ~** to live it up *.

nouer [nwe] (1) **1** *vt ficelle* to tie, knot, fasten; *paquet* to tie up, do up; *alliance, amitié* to form; *(Littérat) action* to build up. **avoir la gorge nouée** to have a lump in one's throat; **~ conversation avec qn** to start *ou* strike up a conversation with sb. **2 se ~** *vpr [mains]* to join together; *[amitié]* to be formed; *[conversation]* to start. *(pièce de théâtre)* **c'est là où l'intrigue se noue** it's at that point that the plot takes shape. ◆ **noueux, -euse** *adj* gnarled.

nougat [nuga] *nm (Culin)* nougat. *(pieds)* **~s** ‡ feet; **c'est du ~** * it's dead easy *.

nouille [nuj] *nf* (**a**) *(Culin)* piece *ou* bit of pasta. **~s** pasta, noodles. (**b**) (*) *(imbécile)* noodle *, idiot; *(mollasson)* big lump *.

nounou * [nunu] *nf* nanny.

nounours [nunuʀs] *nm* teddy (bear).

nourrice [nuʀis] *nf* (**a**) *(gardienne)* child-minder; *(qui allaite)* wet nurse. **~ sèche** dry nurse; **mettre un enfant en ~** to foster a child. (**b**) *(bidon)* jerry can, can *(US)*.

nourrir [nuʀiʀ] (2) **1** *vt (lit)* to feed; *feu* to stoke; *projet* to nurse; *espoir, haine* to nourish. **~ au sein** to breast-feed; **bien/mal nourri** well-/poorly-fed; **cette entreprise nourrit 10 000 ouvriers** this firm provides work for 10,000 workers; **ça ne nourrit pas son homme** it doesn't earn a man his bread *ou* doesn't give a man a living wage. **2** *vi* to be nourishing. **3 se ~** *vpr* to eat. **se ~ de** *viande* to feed (o.s.) on, eat; *illusions* to feed on, live on. ◆ **nourri, e** *adj fusillade* heavy; *conversation* lively. ◆ **nourrissant, e** *adj* nourishing, nutritious. ◆ **nourrisson** *nm* infant. ◆ **nourriture** *nf (aliments, fig)* food. *(alimentation)* **une ~ saine** a healthy diet; **la lecture est une bonne ~ pour l'esprit** reading is good nourishment for the mind.

nous [nu] *pron pers* (**a**) *(sujet)* we. **~ vous écrirons** we'll write to you; **~, accepter?, jamais!** us accept that?, never!; **c'est ~ qui sommes fautifs** we are the ones to blame. (**b**) *(objet)* us. **écoutez-~** listen to us; **~, elle ~ déteste** she hates us; **c'est ~ qu'elle veut voir** it's us she wants to see. (**c**) *(avec prép)* us. **à ~ cinq** between the 5 of us; **cette maison est à ~** this house belongs to us *ou* is ours; **un élève à ~** one of our pupils. (**d**) *(comparaison)* we, us. **il est aussi fort que ~** he is as strong as we are *ou* as us *; **faites comme ~** do as we do, do the same as us *. (**e**) *(avec vpr)* **~ ~ sommes bien amusés** we thoroughly enjoyed ourselves; **~ ~ détestons** we hate each other; **asseyons-~ donc** let's sit down.

nouveau, nouvelle[1] [nuvo, nuvɛl] (**nouvel** [nuvɛl] *devant nm commençant par voyelle ou h muet*), *mpl* **nouveaux** [nuvo] **1** *adj* (**a**) *(gén)* new. **carottes nouvelles** spring carrots; **c'est tout ~** this is brand-new; **ce travail est ~ pour lui** he's new to this job; **le ~ président** the new *ou* newly-elected president; **les ~x parents** today's parents, the parents of today. (**b**) *(original) idée* novel, new; *méthode* new, up-to-date. (**c**) *(qui s'ajoute)* new, fresh. **avez-vous lu son ~ livre?** have you read his new *ou* latest book?; **un ~ Napoléon** a second Napoleon; **il y a eu un ~ tremblement de terre** there has been a further *ou* a fresh earthquake. **2** *nm, f* new man (*ou* woman); *(Scol)* new boy (*ou* girl).
3 *nm*: **y a-t-il du ~ à ce sujet?** is there anything new on this?; **il y a du ~ dans cette affaire** there has been a fresh *ou* a new *ou* further development in this business; **faire qch de** *ou* **à ~** to do sth again; **nous examinerons la question à ~** we'll examine the question anew.
4: **Nouvel An** New Year; **Nouvelle-Angleterre** New England; **Nouvelle-Calédonie** New Caledonia; **Nouvelle-Galles du Sud** New South Wales; **Nouvelle-Guinée** New Guinea; **Nouvelles-Hébrides** New Hebrides; **nouvelle lune** new moon; **nouveaux mariés** newly-weds; **N~ Mexique** New Mexico; **N~ Monde** New World; **~-né,** *mpl* **~-nés** *(adj)* newborn; *(nm)* newborn child; **~ riche** nouveau riche; **~ venu, nouvelle venue** newcomer; **Nouvelle-Zélande** New Zealand.

nouveauté [nuvote] *nf (actualité, originalité)* novelty; *(chose)* new thing; *(objet)* new thing *ou* article. **il n'aime pas la ~** he hates anything new; **c'est une ~!** that's new!; *(Habillement)* **~s de printemps** new spring fashions; *(disque)* **les ~s du mois** the month's new releases; *(machine, voiture)* **les ~s du salon 89** the new models of the 1989 show.

nouvelle[2] [nuvɛl] *nf* (**a**) *(écho)* **une** ~ a piece of news; **vous connaissez la ~?** have you heard the news?; **aller aux ~s** to go and find out what is happening; **avez-vous de ses ~s?** have you heard from him?, have you had any news from him?; **j'irai prendre de ses ~s** I'll go and see how he's getting on; **pas de ~ s, bonnes ~s** no news is good news; **il aura de mes ~s! *** I'll give him a piece of my mind! *, I'll give him what for! *; **(goûtez mon vin) vous m'en direz des ~s** (taste my wine) I'm sure you'll like it; *(Presse)* **voici les ~s** here is the news. (**b**) *(court récit)* short story.

nouvellement [nuvɛlmɑ̃] *adv* recently, newly.

novembre [nɔvɑ̃bʀ(ə)] *nm* November; *V* **septembre.**

novice [nɔvis] **1** *adj* inexperienced (*dans* in), green * (*dans* at). **2** *nmf* novice, beginner; *(Rel)* novice, probationer.

noyau, *pl* **~x** [nwajo] *nm [fruit]* stone, pit; *(Astron, Bio, Phys)* nucleus; *(Géol)* core; *(Ling)* kernel, nucleus; *(Ordin)* kernel; *(groupe de fidèles)* circle; *(manifestants)* small group. ~ **de résistance** centre of resistance.

noyer[1] [nwaje] *nm (arbre)* walnut (tree); *(bois)* walnut.

noyer[2] [nwaje] (8) **1** *vt* (**a**) *(gén)* to drown; *moteur, rives* to flood. **les yeux noyés de larmes** with his eyes full of *ou* brimming with tears; ~ **le poisson *** to duck *ou* sidestep the question, introduce a red herring into the discussion; ~ **qn sous un déluge d'explications** to swamp sb with explanations; **noyé dans l'obscurité** shrouded in darkness; **noyé dans la foule** lost in the crowd; **noyé dans la masse** put together with the rest. (**b**) *(Tech) pilier* to embed. **2 se** ~ *vpr (accidentellement)* to drown; *(volontairement)* to drown o.s. **se ~ dans les détails** to get bogged down in details; **se ~ dans un verre d'eau** to make a mountain out of a molehill. ◆ **noyade** *nf* drowning. **de nombreuses ~s** many drowning accidents, many deaths by drowning. ◆ **noyé, e 1** *adj (fig: perdu)* **être** ~ to be out of one's depth, be all at sea (*en* in). **2** *nm, f* drowned person.

nu, e [ny] **1** *adj* (**a**) *personne* naked, bare. **~-pieds** barefoot, with bare feet; **(la) tête ~e** bareheaded; **~ jusqu'à la ceinture** stripped to the waist; **à moitié** ~ half-naked; **tout** ~ stark naked; **se mettre** ~ to strip (off), take one's clothes off; **se montrer ~ à l'écran** to appear in the nude on the screen. (**b**) *mur, arbre, plaine* bare; *vérité* plain, naked. (**c**) **mettre à** ~ *fil électrique* to strip; **mettre son cœur à** ~ to lay bare one's heart. **2** *nm (Peinture, Phot)* nude. ◆ **nu-pieds** *nmpl (sandales)* beach sandals, flip-flops. ◆ **nu-propriétaire, ~e-propriétaire** *nm, f* owner without usufruct.

nuage [nɥaʒ] *nm* cloud. **le ciel se couvre de ~s** the sky is clouding over; **juste un ~ de lait** just a drop of milk; *(fig)* **il est dans les ~s** his head is in the clouds; **sans ~s** *ciel* cloudless; *bonheur* unmarred, unclouded. ◆ **nuageux, -euse** *adj temps* cloudy ; *ciel* cloudy, overcast; **zone ~euse** cloud zone.

nuance [nɥɑ̃s] *nf [couleur]* shade, hue; *(Littérat)* nuance; *(différence)* slight difference; *(touche)* touch, note. ~ **de sens** shade of meaning, nuance; ~ **de style** nuance of style; ~ **politique** shade of political opinion; **tout en ~s** *discours* subtle; **sans** ~ unsubtle. ◆ **nuancer** (3) *vt opinion* to qualify.

nucléaire [nykleɛʀ] **1** *adj* nuclear. **2** *nm:* **le** ~ *(énergie)* nuclear energy; *(technologie)* nuclear technology.

nudité [nydite] *nf [personne]* nakedness, nudity; *[mur]* bareness. ◆ **nudisme** *nm* nudism. ◆ **nudiste** *adj, nmf* nudist.

nuée [nɥe] *nf (littér: nuage)* cloud; *[insectes, flèches]* cloud; *[ennemis]* horde, host.

nues [ny] *nfpl:* **porter qn aux ~s** to praise sb to the skies; **tomber des ~s** to be completely taken aback.

nuire [nɥiʀ] (38) **1** ~ **à** *vt indir* to harm, injure. **sa laideur lui nuit beaucoup** his ugliness is very much against him *ou* is a great disadvantage to him. **2 se** ~ *vpr (à soi-même)* to do o.s. a lot of harm; *(l'un l'autre)* to work against each other's interests, harm each other. ◆ **nuisible** *adj* harmful, injurious (*à* to). **animaux ~s** pests.

nuit [nɥi] *nf* (**a**) *(obscurité)* darkness, night. **il fait ~ noire** it's pitch-dark; **la ~ tombe** it's getting dark, night is falling; **à la ~ tombante** at nightfall, at dusk; **rentrer avant la** ~ to come home before dark; **la ~ polaire** the polar night *ou* darkness. (**b**) *(temps)* night. **cette** ~ *(passée)* last night; *(qui vient)* tonight; **dans la ~ de jeudi** during Thursday night; **~ blanche** sleepless night; **ouvert la** ~ open at night; **rouler la** ~ *ou* **de** ~ to drive at night; **de** ~ *service etc* night; **ça se perd dans la ~ des temps** it is lost in the mists of time; **ça remonte à la ~ des temps** that goes back to the dawn of time, that's as old as the hills; **la ~ de Noël** Christmas Eve.

nul, nulle [nyl] **1** *adj indéf* (**a**) *(aucun)* no. **il n'avait ~ besoin de sortir** he had no need to go out; **~ autre** no one else; **il ne l'a trouvé nulle part** he couldn't find it anywhere, he could find it nowhere; **sans ~ doute** without any doubt. (**b**) *résultat, risque* nil; *testament, élection* null and void; *récolte etc* non-existent. **le score est** ~ *(zéro à zéro)* the result is a nil draw; *(2 à 2 etc)* the result is a draw; **~ et non avenu** invalid, null and void; **rendre** ~ to annul, nullify; **nombre ~/non-~** zero/non-zero number. (**c**) *personne, travail* worthless, useless. **~ en géographie** hopeless *ou* useless at geography; **ce devoir est** ~ this piece of work is worth nothing *ou* doesn't deserve any marks. **2** *pron indéf* no one. **~ d'entre vous** none of you. ◆ **nullement** *adv* not at all, not in the least. ◆ **nullité** *nf* (**a**) *(Jur)* nullity; *[personne]* uselessness; *[objection]* invalidity. (**b**) *(personne)* nonentity, wash-out *.

numéraire [nymeʀɛʀ] *nm* cash.

numéro [nymeʀo] *nm* (**a**) *(gén, Aut, Phys)* number. **j'habite au ~ 6** I live at number 6; **~ minéralogique** registration *ou* license *(US)* number, car number; **composer un** ~ to dial a number; **~ vert** *(Brit)* freephone, *(US)* tollfree number. (**b**) *(Presse)* issue, number. **vieux** ~ back number, back issue. (**c**) *[chant, danse]* number; *[cirque, music-hall]* act, turn. **il nous a fait son petit** ~ he put on his usual act for us. (**d**) *(personne)* **c'est un drôle de ~!** * what a character! ◆ **numéral, e,** *mpl* **-aux** *adj, nm* numeral. ◆ **numérique** *adj* numerical. ◆ **numériquement** *adv* numerically. ◆ **numérotation** *nf* numbering, numeration. **~ téléphonique** telephone number system. ◆ **numéroter** (1) *vt* to number.

numerus clausus [nymeʀysklozys] *nm* restricted intake.

nuptial, e, *mpl* **-aux** [nypsjal, o] *adj bénédiction* nuptial; *cérémonie* wedding.

nuque [nyk] *nf* nape of the neck.

nurse [nœʀs(ə)] *nf* nanny, (children's) nurse.

nutrition [nytʀisjɔ̃] *nf* nutrition. ◆ **nutritif, -ive** *adj (nourrissant)* nourishing, nutritious; *(Méd)* nutritive. **valeur ~ive** food *ou* nutritional value.

nylon [nilɔ̃] *nm* ® nylon.

nymphe [nɛ̃f] *nf (Myth, fig)* nymph.
nymphéa [nɛ̃fea] *nm* white water lily.
nymphomane [nɛ̃fɔman] *adj, nf* nymphomaniac.
◆ **nymphomanie** *nf* nymphomania.

O, o [o] *nm (lettre)* O, o.

oasis [ɔazis] *nf (lit)* oasis; *(fig)* oasis, haven. ~ **de paix** haven of peace.

obéir [ɔbeiʀ] (2) ~ **à** *vt indir* (**a**) *(gén)* to obey. **il sait se faire** ~ he knows how to make people obey him *ou* how to enforce obedience; ~ **à une impulsion** to act on an impulse. (**b**) *[voilier, moteur, monture]* to respond to. ◆ **obéissance** *nf [animal, personne]* obedience (*à* to). ◆ **obéissant, e** *adj* obedient (*à* to).

obélisque [ɔbelisk(ə)] *nm (monument)* obelisk.

obèse [ɔbɛz] *adj* obese. ◆ **obésité** *nf* obesity.

objecter [ɔbʒɛkte] (1) *vt* (**a**) *(à une suggestion)* ~ **une raison à un argument** to put forward a reason against an argument; **il m'objecta que...** he objected to me that...; **je n'ai rien à** ~ I have no objection (to make). (**b**) *(à une demande)* **il objecta la fatigue** he pleaded tiredness; **il m'objecta mon manque d'expérience** he objected that I lacked experience. ◆ **objecteur** *nm*: ~ **de conscience** conscientious objector. ◆ **objection** *nf* objection. **faire une** ~ to raise *ou* make an objection, object.

objectif, -ive [ɔbʒɛktif, iv] **1** *adj (gén)* objective. **2** *nm (gén)* objective; *[caméra]* lens, objective. **braquer son** ~ **sur** to train one's camera on. ◆ **objectivement** *adv* objectively. ◆ **objectivité** *nf* objectivity.

objet [ɔbʒɛ] *nm* (**a**) *(article)* object, thing. ~**s de première nécessité** basic essentials, essential items *ou* things; ~**s de toilette** toilet requisites *ou* articles; **les** ~**s trouvés** the lost property office, lost and found *(US)*. (**b**) *[rêve, désir]* object; *[discussion, litige, science]* subject. **il était l'** ~ **de la curiosité des autres** he was an object of curiosity to the others; **faire** *ou* **être l'** ~ **de** *discussion, recherches* to be the subject of; *enquête* to be subjected to; *soins* to be given *ou* shown. (**c**) *[visite, démarche]* object, purpose. **craintes sans** ~ unfounded *ou* groundless fears; **votre plainte est sans** ~ your complaint is not applicable. (**d**) *(Ling, Philos)* object.

obligation [ɔbligɑsjɔ̃] *nf* (**a**) *(gén)* obligation. **avoir l'** ~ **de faire** to be under an obligation to do; **sans** ~ **d'achat** with no obligation to buy; ~**s** *militaires, scolaires etc* obligations, duties; *(Pol)* **remplir ses** ~**s vis à vis d'un autre pays** to discharge one's commitments towards another country. (**b**) *(Fin: titre)* bond, debenture. ~ **d'État** government bond. ◆ **obligatoire** *adj* compulsory, obligatory. **c'était** ~! * it was inevitable!, it was bound to happen! ◆ **obligatoirement** *adv* (**a**) **devoir** ~ **faire** to be strictly obliged to do. (**b**) *(*: sans doute)* inevitably.

obliger [ɔbliʒe] (3) *vt* (**a**) *(forcer)* ~ **qn à faire** *[règlement]* to require sb to do; *[circonstances]* to force *ou* oblige *ou* compel sb to do; **mes principes m'y obligent** I'm bound by my principles (to do it); **je suis obligé de vous laisser** I have to *ou* I must leave you, I'm obliged to leave you; **il est bien obligé** he has no choice *ou* alternative. (**b**) *(rendre service à)* to oblige. **je vous serais très obligé de bien vouloir** I should be greatly obliged if you would kindly; **entre voisins, il faut bien s'** ~ neighbours have to help each other. ◆ **obligé, e 1** *adj* (**a**) *(redevable)* **être** ~ **à qn** to be obliged *ou* indebted to sb (*de qch* for sth). (**b**) *(*: inévitable)* **c'était** ~! it had to happen!, it was bound to happen! **2** *nm, f* (**a**) *(Jur)* debtor. (**b**) **être l'** ~ **de qn** to be under an obligation to sb. ◆ **obligeamment** *adv* obligingly. ◆ **obligeance** *nf*: **il a eu l'** ~ **de me reconduire** he was obliging *ou* kind enough to take me back. ◆ **obligeant, e** *adj personne* obliging, kind, helpful; *offre* kind.

oblique [ɔblik] **1** *adj (gén)* oblique. **regard** ~ sidelong glance. **2** *nf (Math)* oblique line. ◆ **obliquement** *adv* obliquely. ◆ **obliquer** (1) *vi*: **obliquez avant l'église** turn off before the church.

oblitérer [ɔbliteʀe] (6) *vt timbre* to cancel. ◆ **oblitération** *nf* cancelling, cancellation.

oblong, -ongue [ɔblɔ̃, ɔ̃g] *adj* oblong.

obnubiler [ɔbnybile] (1) *vt* to obsess.

obole [ɔbɔl] *nf (contribution)* offering. **verser** *ou* **apporter son** ~ **à qch** to make one's small (financial) contribution to sth.

obscène [ɔpsɛn] *adj* obscene. ◆ **obscénité** *nf* obscenity. **dire des** ~**s** to make obscene remarks.

obscur, e [ɔpskyʀ] *adj (lit)* dark; *(fig)* obscure; *pressentiment* vague, dim. **de naissance** ~**e** of obscure *ou* humble birth. ◆ **obscurcir** (2) **1** *vt* to darken; *(fig)* to obscure. **2 s'** ~ *vpr [ciel]* to darken, grow dark; *[jour]* to grow dark; *[style]* to become obscure; *[vue]* to grow dim; *[mystère]* to deepen. ◆ **obscurcissement** *nm* darkening; obscuring; dimming. ◆ **obscurément** *adv* obscurely. ◆ **obscurité** *nf (lit)* darkness; *(fig)* obscurity. **dans l'** ~ in the dark, in darkness; *(fig)* **laisser qch dans l'** ~ to throw no light on sth.

obséder [ɔpsede] (6) *vt* to haunt, obsess. **être obsédé par** to be haunted *ou* obsessed by. ◆ **obsédant, e** *adj* haunting, obsessive. ◆ **obsédé, e** *nm, f*: ~ **(sexuel)** sex maniac; *(hum)* **un** ~ **du tennis** a tennis fanatic.

obsèques [ɔpsɛk] *nfpl* funeral.

obséquieux, -euse [ɔpsekjø, øz] *adj* obsequious. ◆ **obséquiosité** *nf* obsequiousness.

observer [ɔpsɛʀve] (1) **1** *vt* (**a**) *(regarder)* to observe; *adversaire* to watch; *(au microscope)* to examine. (**b**) *(contrôler)* ~ **ses gestes** to watch one's gestures. (**c**) *(remarquer)* to notice, observe. **faire** ~ **que** to point out *ou* remark *ou* observe that; **faire** ~ **un détail à qn** to point out a detail to sb. (**d**) *(respecter) (gén)* to observe; *jeûne* to keep; *attitude, maintien* to keep (up), maintain. ~ **une minute de silence** to observe a minute's silence. **2 s'** ~ *vpr (surveiller sa tenue)* to keep a check on o.s., be careful of one's behaviour. ◆ **observance** *nf* observance. ◆ **observateur, -trice 1** *adj* observant. **2** *nm, f* observer. ◆ **observation** *nf* (**a**) *(obéissance)* observance. (**b**) *(expérience, surveillance)* observation. *(Méd)* **être en** ~ to be under observation. (**c**) *(remarque)* observation, remark; *(objection)* objection; *(reproche)* reproof. **je lui en fis l'** ~ I pointed it out to him; **ce film appelle quelques** ~**s** this film calls for some comment; **faire une** ~ **à qn** to reprove sb. ◆ **observatoire** *nm (Astron)* observatory; *(gén: lieu)* observation *ou* look-out post.

obsession [ɔpsesjɔ̃] *nf* obsession. **il avait l' ~ de la mort** he had an obsession with death. ◆ **obsessionnel, -elle** *adj* obsessional.

obstacle [ɔpstakl(ə)] *nm (lit, fig)* obstacle; *(Équitation)* jump, fence. **faire ~ à** *la lumière* to block, obstruct; *un projet* to hinder.

obstétrique [ɔpstetʀik] *nf* obstetrics *(sg)*. ◆ **obstétricien, -ienne** *nm, f* obstetrician.

obstination [ɔpstinɑsjɔ̃] *nf* obstinacy, stubbornness. **~ à faire** obstinate *ou* stubborn determination to do. ◆ **obstiné, e** *adj personne* obstinate, stubborn; *efforts, demandes* persistent, obstinate. ◆ **obstinément** *adv* obstinately, stubbornly; persistently. ◆ **s'obstiner** (1) *vpr* to insist, dig one's heels in. **s' ~ à faire** to persist obstinately *ou* stubbornly in doing; **s' ~ au silence** to remain obstinately silent.

obstruer [ɔpstʀye] (1) *vt* to obstruct, block. ◆ **obstruction** *nf* obstruction, blockage; *(tactique)* obstruction. **faire de l' ~** to be obstructive; **faire de l' ~ parlementaire** to filibuster.

obtempérer [ɔptɑ̃peʀe] (6) **~ à** *vt indir* to obey.

obtenir [ɔptəniʀ] (22) *vt* (**a**) *permission, diplôme* to obtain, get. **il m'a fait ~ de l'avancement** he got me promoted; **il obtint de lui parler** he was (finally) allowed to speak to him; **elle a obtenu qu'il paie** she got him to pay, she managed to make him pay. (**b**) *résultat* to achieve, obtain; *total* to reach, arrive at. **cette couleur s'obtient par un mélange** this colour is obtained by blending. ◆ **obtention** *nf* obtaining, achievement. **pour l' ~ du visa** to obtain the visa.

obturer [ɔptyʀe] (1) *vt (gén)* to seal; *dent* to fill. ◆ **obturateur** *nm (Phot)* shutter; *(Tech)* obturator. ◆ **obturation** *nf* sealing; filling. *(Phot)* **vitesse d' ~** shutter speed.

obtus, e [ɔpty, yz] *adj (lit, fig)* obtuse.

obus [ɔby] *nm* shell.

occasion [ɔkɑzjɔ̃] *nf* (**a**) *(circonstance)* occasion; *(conjoncture favorable)* opportunity, chance. **avoir l' ~ de faire** to have the chance *ou* opportunity of doing; **à l' ~ de** on the occasion of; **la robe des grandes ~s** the dress kept for special *ou* great occasions; **à l' ~ venez dîner** come and have dinner some time; **à la première ~** at the first opportunity. (**b**) *(Comm)* secondhand buy; *(*: avantageuse)* bargain. **d' ~** *(adj, adv)* secondhand. ◆ **occasionnel, -elle** *adj (gén)* occasional; *client* casual; *(fortuit)* chance. ◆ **occasionnellement** *adv* occasionally. ◆ **occasionner** (1) *vt frais, dérangement* to occasion, cause; *accident* to cause, bring about. **~ du dérangement à qn** to put sb to *ou* cause sb a lot of trouble.

occident [ɔksidɑ̃] *nm* west. ◆ **occidental, e,** *mpl* **-aux 1** *adj* western. **2** *nm (f)*: **O~(e)** Westerner.

occulte [ɔkylt(ə)] *adj* occult.

occuper [ɔkype] (1) **1** *vt (gén)* to occupy; *logement* to live in; *surface, temps* to take up; *poste* to hold; *main d'œuvre* to employ. **leurs bureaux occupent tout l'étage** their offices take up *ou* occupy the whole floor; **ça occupe une trop petite part de mon temps** it takes up *ou* fills *ou* occupies far too little of my time; **comment ~ ses loisirs?** how should one occupy *ou* employ one's free time?; **mon travail m'occupe beaucoup** my work keeps me very busy; **le sujet qui nous occupe aujourd'hui** the matter which concerns us today, the matter we are dealing with today; **ils ont occupé tout le pays** they took over *ou* occupied the whole country. **2 s' ~** *vpr* (**a**) **s' ~ de** *(s'attaquer à)* to deal with, take care of; *(être chargé de)* to be in charge of; *(s'intéresser à)* to take an interest in; *enfant, malade* to look after; *client* to attend to. **je m'occupe de tout** I'll see to everything, I'll take care of everything; **occupe-toi de tes affaires *** mind your own business; **est-ce qu'on s'occupe de vous Madame?** are you being attended to? *ou* served? (**b**) **s' ~ à faire qch/à qch** to busy o.s. doing sth/with sth; **il y a de quoi s' ~** there is plenty to do *ou* to keep one busy *ou* occupied. ◆ **occupant, e 1** *adj (Mil)* occupying. **2** *nm, f [maison]* occupant, occupier; *[place, voiture]* occupant. **3** *nm*: **l' ~** the occupying forces. ◆ **occupation** *nf (Mil)* occupation; *(logement)* occupancy, occupation; *(passe-temps)* occupation; *(emploi)* occupation, job. **grève avec ~ des locaux** sit-in, sit-down strike; **vaquer à ses ~s** to go about one's business. ◆ **occupé, e** *adj personne* busy; *toilettes, téléphone* engaged; *places* taken, occupied; *zone, usine* occupied.

occurrence [ɔkyʀɑ̃s] *nf* (**a**) instance, case. **en l' ~** in this case. (**b**) *(Ling)* occurrence, token.

océan [ɔseɑ̃] *nm (lit)* ocean. **~ de verdure** sea of greenery. ◆ **Océanie** *nf*: **l' ~** Oceania, the South Sea Islands. ◆ **océanien, -ienne 1** *adj* Oceanian, Oceanic. **2** *nm, f* Oceanian, South Sea Islander. ◆ **océanique** *adj* oceanic.

ocre [ɔkʀ(ə)] *nf, adj inv* ochre.

octane [ɔktan] *nm* octane.

octante [ɔktɑ̃t] *adj inv (dialectal)* eighty.

octave [ɔktav] *nf (Mus)* octave.

octet [ɔktɛ] *nm* byte.

octobre [ɔktɔbʀ(ə)] *nm* October; *V* **septembre.**

octogénaire [ɔktɔʒenɛʀ] *adj, nmf* octogenarian.

octogone [ɔktɔgɔn] *nm* octagon. ◆ **octogonal, e,** *mpl* **-aux** *adj* octagonal, eight-sided.

octroyer [ɔktʀwaje] (8) **1** *vt* to grant (*à* to). **2 s' ~** *vpr* to accord *ou* grant o.s. ◆ **octroi** *nm* (**a**) granting. (**b**) *(Hist)* city toll.

oculaire [ɔkylɛʀ] *adj (Anat)* ocular. ◆ **oculiste** *nmf* eye specialist, oculist, eye doctor *(US)*.

ode [ɔd] *nf* ode.

odeur [ɔdœʀ] *nf (gén)* smell, odour; *(de fleurs etc)* fragrance, scent. **sans ~** odourless; **mauvaise ~** bad *ou* unpleasant smell *ou* odour; **~ de brûlé** smell of burning; **avoir une bonne/une mauvaise ~** to smell nice/bad; **être/ne pas être en ~ de sainteté** to be in favour/out of favour (*auprès de* with). ◆ **odorant, e** *adj* sweet-smelling. ◆ **odorat** *nm* sense of smell.

odieux, -euse [ɔdjø, øz] *adj (gén)* odious; *élève* unbearable; *tâche, conduite* obnoxious; *crime* heinous. **ça m'est ~** I can't bear it. ◆ **odieusement** *adv* odiously; obnoxiously.

odyssée [ɔdise] *nf* odyssey. *(littér)* **l'O~** the Odyssey.

œdème [edɛm] *nm* oedema.

œil [œj], *pl* **yeux** [jø] *nm* (**a**) *(Anat)* eye. **aux yeux bleus** blue-eyed; **avoir les yeux faits** to have make-up on one's eyes; **avoir de bons/mauvais yeux** to have good/bad eyes *ou* eyesight; **visible à l' ~ nu** visible to the naked eye; **avoir un ~ au beurre noir** to have a black eye. (**b**) *(expression)* look. **il a un ~ malin** there's a mischievous look in his eye; **d'un ~ d'envie** with an envious look. (**c**) *(jugement)* **voir qch d'un bon/mauvais ~** to view sth favourably/unfavourably; **d'un ~ critique** with a critical eye; **il ne voit pas cela du même ~ qu'elle** he doesn't see *ou* view that in the same light as she does. (**d**) *(coup d'œil)* **avoir l' ~ du spécialiste** to have a trained eye; **il a l' ~** he has sharp eyes; **risquer un ~ au dehors** to take a quick look outside. (**e**) *(regard)* **sous l' ~ de** under the eye *ou* gaze of; **faire qch aux yeux de tous** to do sth in full view of everyone; **chercher qn des yeux** to glance *ou* look (a)round for sb; **n'avoir d'yeux que pour qch/qn** to have eyes only for sth/sb. (**f**) *[aiguille, pomme de terre, cyclone]* eye; *[porte d'entrée]* spyglass; *(bourgeon)* bud. **les yeux du bouillon** the globules of fat in the stock. (**g**) *(locutions avec œil)*

à l' ~ * *(gratuitement)* for nothing, for free *; **mon ~! *** *(je n'y crois pas)* my eye! *, my foot! *; *(je ne le donnerai pas)* nothing doing! *, no way! *; **avoir qn à l'** ~ to keep a watch *ou* an eye on sb; **faire de l'** ~ **à qn** to make eyes at sb, give sb the eye *. (**h**) *(locutions avec* **yeux***)* **à ses yeux** in his eyes; **ouvrir de grands yeux** to look surprised; **coûter les yeux de la tête** to cost the earth; *(lit, fig)* **les yeux fermés** with one's eyes shut; **faire les yeux doux à qn** to make sheep's eyes at sb; **faire des yeux ronds** to stare round-eyed; **avoir les yeux battus** to have rings under one's eyes.
◆ **oeillade** *nf* wink. **faire des ~s à qn** to make eyes at sb. ◆ **oeillères** *nfpl (lit, fig)* blinkers. ◆ **oeilleton** *nm [télescope]* eyepiece.

oeillet [œjɛ] *nm* carnation. ~ **d'Inde** French marigold; ~ **(mignardise)** pink.

oesophage [ezɔfaʒ] *nm* œsophagus.

oeuf [œf], *pl* **~s** [∅] *nm* (**a**) egg. ~ **frais** new-laid *ou* fresh egg; **~s brouillés** scrambled eggs; ~ **à la coque** (soft-)boiled egg; ~ **dur** hard-boiled egg ; ~ **mimosa** eggs mimosa *(hors d'œuvre made with chopped egg yolks)*; ~ **sur le plat** fried egg; **détruire qch dans l'** ~ to nip sth in the bud; **mettre tous ses ~s dans le même panier** to put all one's eggs in one basket. (**b**) *(idiot)* blockhead *.

oeuvre [œvʀ(ə)] **1** *nf* (**a**) *(livre etc)* work; *(production globale)* works. **~s complètes/choisies** complete/selected works. (**b**) *(travail) (à faire)* undertaking, task; *(achevé)* work. **ce beau gâchis est l'** ~ **des enfants** this fine mess is the children's doing *ou* work; **être/se mettre à l'** ~ to be at/get down to work; **voir qn à l'** ~ to see sb at work; **mettre en** ~ *moyens* to implement; **mise en** ~ implementation; **il avait tout mis en** ~ **pour les aider** he had done everything possible to help them. (**c**) *(acte)* deed, work. **(bonnes) ~s** good *ou* charitable works; **ce sera une bonne** ~ that will be a kind act; **faire** ~ **utile** to do valuable work; **faire** ~ **de pionnier** to act as a pioneer; **le feu avait fait son** ~ the fire had wrought its havoc *ou* had done its work. (**d**) *(organisation)* ~ **(de bienfaisance)** charitable organization, charity. **2** *nm (littér)* **l'** ~ **gravé de Picasso** the etchings of Picasso.

off [ɔf] *adj inv (Ciné) voix, son* off; *concert, festival* fringe, alternative. **dire qch en voix** ~ to say sth in a voice off.

offenser [ɔfɑ̃se] (1) **1** *vt personne, souvenir, bon goût* to offend; *règles* to offend against. **2 s'** ~ *vpr* to take offence (*de qch* at sth). ◆ **offensant, e** *adj* offensive, insulting. ◆ **offense** *nf (affront)* insult; *(Rel: péché)* trespass, offence. ~ **envers** *chef d'État* libel against; *Dieu* offence against.

offensif, -ive [ɔfɑ̃sif, iv] **1** *adj (Mil, Pol)* offensive. **2** *nf* offensive. **passer à l' ~ive** to go into the offensive; *(fig)* **l' ~ive de l'hiver** the onslaught of winter.

office [ɔfis] **1** *nm* (**a**) *(métier)* office; *(fonction)* function. **l'** ~ **de directeur** the office of manager; **faire** ~ **de** to act *ou* serve as; **remplir son** ~ *[objet]* to fulfil its function; *[fonctionnaire]* to perform one's duties. (**b**) *(bureau)* office, bureau, agency. ~ **de publicité** advertising agency; ~ **du tourisme** tourist bureau. (**c**) *(messe)* (church) service; *(prières)* prayers. **l'** ~ **(divin)** the (divine) office. (**d**) **être nommé d'** ~ to be appointed automatically. (**e**) *(littér: service)* office. *(Pol)* **bons ~s** good offices; **Monsieur bons ~s *** mediator. **2** *nm ou f (cuisine)* pantry.

officiel, -elle [ɔfisjɛl] **1** *adj (gén)* official. **2** *nm, f* official. ◆ **officialiser** (1) *vt* to make official. ◆ **officiellement** *adv* officially.

officier[1] [ɔfisje] *nm* officer. ~ **de marine** naval officer; ~ **d'ordonnance** aide-de-camp; ~ **de police** senior police officer; ~ **ministériel** member of the legal profession; ~ **de l'état civil** ≃ registrar.

officier[2] [ɔfisje] (7) *vi (Rel, hum)* to officiate.

officieux, -euse [ɔfisj∅, ∅z] *adj* unofficial. ◆ **officieusement** *adv* unofficially.

offrir [ɔfʀiʀ] (18) **1** *vt* (**a**) *(donner)* to give (*à* to); *(acheter)* to buy (*à* for). **c'est pour** ~? is it for a present?; **la joie d'** ~ the joy of giving. (**b**) *aide, marchandise, choix* to offer; *démission* to tender. **puis-je vous** ~ **à boire?** can I offer you a drink?; ~ **de faire** to offer to do; ~ **sa vie à la patrie** to offer up one's life to the homeland. (**c**) *spectacle, avantage* to present, offer; *exemple, explication* to provide; *analogie* to offer, have. **cela n'offre rien de particulier** there is nothing special about that; ~ **de la résistance** to offer resistance. **2 s'** ~ *vpr* (**a**) *[femme]* to offer o.s. (*à* to). **s'** ~ **aux regards** *[personne]* to expose o.s. to the public gaze; *[spectacle]* to present itself to the gaze; **s'** ~ **comme guide** to volunteer to act as a guide. (**b**) *repas, vacances* to treat o.s. to; *disque* to buy o.s. (**c**) **s'** ~ **à faire qch** to offer *ou* volunteer to do sth.
◆ **offrande** *nf* offering. ◆ **offrant** *nm (Jur, Fin)* offerer, bidder. **au plus** ~ to the highest bidder.
◆ **offre** *nf (gén)* offer; *(aux enchères)* bid. *(Écon)* **l'** ~ **et la demande** supply and demand; *(Écon)* **théorie de l'** ~ supply-side economics; *(Presse)* **~s d'emploi** situations vacant column, job ads *; **il y avait plusieurs ~s d'emploi** there were several jobs advertised; ~ **publique d'achat** takeover bid, tender offer *(US)*; **~s de service** offers of service; **~s de paix** peace overtures.

offusquer [ɔfyske] (1) **1** *vt* to offend. **2 s'** ~ *vpr* to take offence (*de* at).

oflag [ɔflag] *nm* oflag.

ogive [ɔʒiv] *nf* (**a**) *(Archit)* rib. **voûte en** ~ rib vault. (**b**) *[fusée etc]* nose cone. ~ **nucléaire** nuclear warhead.

ogre, ogresse [ɔgʀ(ə), ɔgʀɛs] *nm, f* ogre, ogress. **manger comme un** ~ to eat like a horse.

oie [wa] *nf (Zool)* goose; *(péj)* silly goose.

oignon [ɔɲɔ̃] *nm (légume)* onion; *[tulipe etc]* bulb; *(Méd)* bunion. **petits ~s** pickling onions; **être soigné aux petits ~s** to be looked after really well, be given first-rate attention; **ce n'est pas mes ~s** ⁑ it's no business of mine.

oiseau, *pl* **~x** [wazo] *nm* bird. ~ **de mauvais augure** bird of ill omen; **~-mouche** *nm, pl* **~x-~s** hummingbird; ~ **de paradis** bird of paradise; ~ **de proie** bird of prey; **trouver l'** ~ **rare** to find the man (*ou* woman) in a million; **drôle d'** ~ * queer fish * *ou* customer *. ◆ **oiseleur** *nm* bird-catcher.
◆ **oiselier, -ière** *nm, f* bird-seller. ◆ **oisellerie** *nf (magasin)* birdshop; *(commerce)* bird-selling.

oiseux, -euse [waz∅, ∅z] *adj propos* pointless; *question* trivial, trifling.

oisif, -ive [wazif, iv] **1** *adj* idle. **2** *nm, f* man (*ou* woman) of leisure. ◆ **oisiveté** *nf* idleness. ~ **forcée** forced idleness *ou* inactivity.

oléagineux, -euse [ɔleaʒin∅, ∅z] **1** *adj* oleaginous. **2** *nm* oleaginous plant.

oléoduc [ɔleɔdyk] *nm* oil pipeline.

olfaction [ɔlfaksjɔ̃] *nf* olfaction. ◆ **olfactif, -ive** *adj* olfactory.

olive [ɔliv] **1** *nf* olive. **2** *adj inv* olive(-green).
◆ **olivâtre** *adj (gén)* olive-greenish; *teint* sallow.
◆ **oliveraie** *nf* olive grove. ◆ **olivier** *nm (arbre)* olive tree; *(bois)* olive(-wood).

olivette [ɔlivɛt] *nf* plum tomato.

olympique [ɔlɛ̃pik] *adj* Olympic. ◆ **olympiade** *nf* Olympiad.

ombrage [ɔ̃bʀaʒ] *nm* (**a**) *(ombre)* shade. (**b**) **prendre** ~ **de qch** to take umbrage *ou* offence at sth.
◆ **ombragé, e** *adj* shaded, shady. ◆ **ombrager** (3) *vt* to shade. ◆ **ombrageux, -euse** *adj personne* touchy, easily offended; *cheval* skittish, nervous.

ombre [ɔ̃bʀ(ə)] *nf* (**a**) shade; *(ombre portée)* shadow; *(obscurité)* darkness. **25° à l'** ~ 25° in the shade; **tu me fais de l'** ~ you're in my light; **places sans ~/pleines d'** ~ shadeless/shady squares. (**b**) *(forme vague)* shadow, shadowy figure; *(fantôme)* shade. (**c**) *(fig) (anonymat)* obscurity; *(secret, incertitude)* dark. **laisser dans l'** ~ to leave in the dark; **travailler dans l'** ~ to work behind the scenes; **rester dans l'** ~ *[artiste]* to remain in obscurity; *[meneur]* to keep in the background; *[détail]* to be still obscure, remain unclear. (**d**) *(soupçon)* **une ~ de moustache** a hint *ou* suspicion of a moustache; **il n'y a pas l'** ~ **d'un doute** there's not the shadow of a doubt; **pas l'** ~ **d'une chance** not the ghost of a chance. (**e**) *(locutions)* **jeter une ~ sur qch** to cast a gloom over sth; **mettre qn à l'** ~ * to put sb behind bars, lock sb up; **il y a une ~ au tableau** there's a fly in the ointment; **n'être plus que l'** ~ **de soi-même** to be the mere shadow of one's former self; **~s chinoises** *(improvisées)* shadowgraph; *(spectacle)* shadow show; ~ **à paupières** eye shadow. ◆ **ombrelle** *nf* parasol, sunshade. ◆ **ombreux, -euse** *adj* shady.

omelette [ɔmlɛt] *nf* omelette. ~ **baveuse** runny omelette; ~ **norvégienne** baked Alaska.

omettre [ɔmɛtʀ(ə)] (**56**) *vt* to leave out, miss out, omit. ~ **de faire qch** to fail *ou* omit to do sth. ◆ **omission** *nf (action)* omission; *(chose oubliée)* omission, oversight.

omnibus [ɔmnibys] *nm* slow *ou* local train; *(Hist: bus)* omnibus.

omnipotence [ɔmnipɔtɑ̃s] *nf* omnipotence. ◆ **omnipotent, e** *adj* omnipotent.

omniprésent, e [ɔmnipʀezɑ̃, ɑ̃t] *adj* omnipresent.

omniscient, e [ɔmnisjɑ̃, ɑ̃t] *adj* omniscient.

omnisports [ɔmnispɔʀ] *adj inv salle* multipurpose; *terrain* general-purpose.

omnivore [ɔmnivɔʀ] *adj* omnivorous.

omoplate [ɔmɔplat] *nf* shoulder blade.

on [ɔ̃] *pron* (**a**) *(indétermination)* ~ **l'interrogea** he was questioned; ~ **va encore augmenter l'essence** petrol is going up again; ~ **prétend que** they say that, it is said that; ~ **se précipita sur les places vides** there was a rush for the empty seats. (**b**) *(quelqu'un)* someone. ~ **frappa à la porte** there was a knock at the door; **est-ce qu'** ~ **est venu réparer la porte?** has anyone *ou* someone been to repair the door?; ~ **peut très bien aimer la pluie** some people may well like the rain. (**c**) *(celui qui parle)* you, one, we. ~ **aimerait être sûr que...** one *ou* we would like to be sure that...; ~ **a trop chaud ici** it's too hot here; ~ **ne pense jamais à tout** one *ou* you can't think of everything. (**d**) *(éloignement)* they, people. **en Chine ~ mange avec des baguettes** in China they eat with chopsticks. (**e**) *(*: nous)* we. ~ **a décidé tous les trois de partir** the three of us decided to leave; ~ **a amené notre chien** we've brought along the dog; *(hum)* ~ **ne dit plus bonjour?** don't we say hello any more?; **alors,** ~ **est content?** well, are you pleased? (**f**) *(intensif)* **c'est ~ ne peut plus beau** it couldn't be lovelier.

once [ɔ̃s] *nf* ounce.

oncle [ɔ̃kl(ə)] *nm* uncle.

onctueux, -euse [ɔ̃ktɥø, øz] *adj (lit)* creamy; *(fig)* unctuous, smooth. ◆ **onctueusement** *adv* unctuously. ◆ **onctuosité** *nf* unctuousness, smoothness; creaminess.

onde [ɔ̃d] *nf* (**a**) *(gén, Phys)* wave. **petites ~s, ~s moyennes** medium waves; **~s courtes** short waves; **grandes ~s** long waves; **sur les ~s et dans la presse** on the radio and in the press; **il passe sur les ~s demain** he's on the air tomorrow; **mettre en ~s** to produce for the radio. (**b**) *(littér: lac, mer)* **l'** ~ the waters.

ondée [ɔ̃de] *nf* shower *(of rain)*.

on-dit [ɔ̃di] *nm inv* rumour. **ce ne sont que des** ~ it's only hearsay.

onduler [ɔ̃dyle] (**1**) *vi (gén)* to undulate; *[drapeau]* to ripple, wave; *[route]* to snake up and down; *[cheveux]* to be wavy. ◆ **ondulation** *nf* undulation. *[cheveux]* **~s** waves. ◆ **onduleux, -euse** *adj ligne* wavy; *plaine* undulating; *démarche* swaying, supple.

onéreux, -euse [ɔneʀø, øz] *adj* expensive, costly.

ongle [ɔ̃gl(ə)] *nm [personne]* (finger)nail; *[animal]* claw. ~ **de pied** toenail; **se faire les ~s** to cut (*ou* file) one's nails; **avoir les ~s faits** to have painted nails.

onomatopée [ɔnɔmatɔpe] *nf* onomatopoeia.

Ontario [ɔ̃taʀjo] *nm* Ontario. **le lac** ~ Lake Ontario. ◆ **ontarien, -ienne** *adj*, **O ~(ne)** *nm(f)* Ontarian.

onyx [ɔniks] *nm* onyx.

onze [ɔ̃z] *adj, nm inv* eleven. **le ~ novembre** Armistice Day; **le ~ de France** the French eleven *ou* team; *V* **six**. ◆ **onzième** *adj, nmf* eleventh. ◆ **onzièmement** *adv* in the eleventh place.

opale [ɔpal] *nf* opal.

opaque [ɔpak] *adj verre, corps* opaque (*à* to); *brouillard, nuit* impenetrable. ◆ **opacité** *nf* opaqueness; impenetrableness.

opéra [ɔpeʀa] *nm (œuvre)* opera; *(édifice)* opera house. ~ **bouffe** opera bouffe, comic opera ; **~-comique** light opera, opéra comique. ◆ **opérette** *nf* operetta, light opera.

opercule [ɔpɛʀkyl] *nm* protective cap.

opérer [ɔpeʀe] (**6**) **1** *vt* (**a**) *malade, organe* to operate on (*de* for); *tumeur* to remove. **se faire** ~ to have an operation, have surgery; **se faire ~ des amygdales** to have one's tonsils removed *ou* out *. (**b**) *transformation, réforme* to carry out, implement; *choix, redressement* to make. ~ **des miracles** to work wonders; **ça a opéré un changement** it brought about a change; **un changement s'était opéré** a change had taken place *ou* had occurred. **2** *vi [remède]* to work, take effect; *[technicien etc]* to proceed. **comment faut-il ~?** what's the procedure? (*pour* for). ◆ **opérable** *adj* operable. ◆ **opérateur, -trice** *nm, f (sur machine)* operator; *(Ciné)* cameraman. ~ **de saisie** computer operator. ◆ **opération** *nf* (**a**) *(gén, Math, Méd, Mil)* operation. **salle d'** ~ operating theatre. (**b**) *(Comm)* deal. ~ **financière** financial deal; **~s de bourse** stock exchange dealings. (**c**) *(Tech, gén)* process, operation. *(iro)* **par l'** ~ **du Saint-Esprit** by magic. ◆ **opérationnel, -elle** *adj* operational. ◆ **opératoire** *adj (Méd)* operating. ◆ **opéré, e** *nm, f (Méd)* patient.

ophtalmologie [ɔftalmɔlɔʒi] *nf* ophthalmology. ◆ **ophtalmologique** *adj* ophthalmological. ◆ **ophtalmologiste** *nmf* ophthalmologist.

opiner [ɔpine] (**1**) *vi*: ~ **de la tête** to nod one's agreement, nod assent.

opiniâtre [ɔpinjɑtʀ(ə)] *adj personne* stubborn, obstinate; *efforts, haine* unrelenting. ◆ **opiniâtrement** *adv* stubbornly, obstinately; unrelentingly. ◆ **opiniâtreté** *nf* stubbornness, obstinacy; unrelentingness.

opinion [ɔpinjɔ̃] *nf (gén)* opinion (*sur* on, about). **se faire une** ~ to form an opinion (*sur* on), make up one's mind (*sur* about); **j'ai la même** ~ I am of *ou* I hold the same opinion *ou* view; **~s toutes faites** cut-and-dried opinions, uncritical opinions; **l'** ~ **française** French public opinion; **sans opinion** *nmpl* don't know.

opium [ɔpjɔm] *nm* opium.

opportun, e [ɔpɔʀtœ̃, yn] *adj* timely, opportune. **il serait ~ de faire** it would be appropriate *ou* advisable to do; **en temps** ~ at the appropriate *ou* right time. ◆ **opportunément** *adv* opportunely. ◆ **opportunisme** *nm* opportunism. ◆ **opportuniste** *adj, nmf* opportunist. ◆ **opportunité** *nf* timeliness, opportuneness; appropriateness.

opposer [ɔpoze] (1) **1** *vt* (**a**) *équipes* to bring together; *rivaux* to bring into conflict (*à* with); *idées, couleurs* to contrast (*à* with). **ce qui nous oppose** what divides us. (**b**) *arguments* to put forward; *résistance* to put up. ~ **son refus/des protestations** to refuse/protest; ~ **une armée à qn** to set an army against sb; **il nous opposa que cela coûtait cher** he objected that it was expensive. **2 s'** ~ *vpr* (**a**) *[équipes]* to confront each other, meet; *[rivaux]* to clash; *[théories]* to conflict; *[styles]* to contrast (*à* with). **haut s'oppose à bas** high is the opposite of low. (**b**) **s'** ~ **à** *parents* to rebel against; *mesure, progrès* to oppose; **rien ne s'oppose à leur bonheur** nothing stands in the way of their happiness; **je m'oppose à ce que vous y alliez** I am opposed to *ou* I am against your going there; **ma conscience s'y oppose** it goes against my conscience. ◆ **opposant, e** *nm, f* opponent (*à* of). ◆ **opposé, e 1** *adj* (**a**) *rive, direction* opposite; *équipe* opposing. **la maison ~e à la nôtre** the house opposite *ou* facing ours; **l'équipe ~e à la nôtre** the team playing against ours. (**b**) *intérêts, opinions* conflicting; *caractères* opposite; *forces* opposing; *couleurs, styles* contrasting. **ils sont d'un avis** ~ *(au nôtre)* they are of the opposite opinion; *(l'un à l'autre)* they are of conflicting opinions; ~ **à** opposed to, against. **2** *nm* (**a**) *(contraire)* **l'** ~ the opposite, the reverse (*de* of); **à l'** ~ **de Paul, je pense que...** contrary to *ou* unlike Paul, I think that... (**b**) **à l'** ~ *(dans l'autre direction)* the other *ou* opposite way (*de* from); *(de l'autre côté)* on the other *ou* opposite side (*de* from). ◆ **opposition** *nf* (**a**) *(résistance)* opposition (*à* to). *(Pol)* **l'O**~ the Opposition; **l'** ~ **parlementaire** the parliamentary opposition, the opposition in parliament. (**b**) *(conflit) (gén)* opposition; *[idées, intérêts]* conflict; *[styles, caractères]* contrast. **mettre en** ~ to oppose, contrast; **ceci est en** ~ **avec les faits** this conflicts with the facts; **mettre** ~ **à** *décision* to oppose; *chèque* to stop; **par** ~ **à** as opposed to, in contrast with.

oppresser [ɔpʀese] (1) *vt (gén)* to oppress; *[vêtement serré]* to suffocate; *[remords]* to weigh down. **avoir une respiration oppressée** to have difficulty with one's breathing; **se sentir oppressé** to feel breathless. ◆ **oppressant, e** *adj* oppressive. ◆ **oppresseur** *nm* oppressor. ◆ **oppressif, -ive** *adj* oppressive. ◆ **oppression** *nf (asservissement)* oppression; *(gêne)* feeling of suffocation *ou* oppression.

opprimer [ɔpʀime] (1) *vt* (**a**) *peuple* to oppress; *opinion* to suppress, stifle. (**b**) *[chaleur etc]* to suffocate, oppress.

opprobre [ɔpʀɔbʀ(ə)] *nm (littér)* opprobrium, shame.

opter [ɔpte] (1) *vi:* ~ **pour** to opt for, decide upon; ~ **entre** to choose *ou* decide between.

opticien, -ienne [ɔptisjɛ̃, jɛn] *nm, f* optician.

optimisme [ɔptimism(ə)] *nm* optimism. ◆ **optimiste 1** *adj* optimistic. **2** *nmf* optimist.

optimum, *pl* **~s** *ou* **optima** [ɔptimɔm, a] **1** *nm* optimum. **2** *adj* optimum, optimal. ◆ **optimal, e,** *mpl* **-aux** *adj* optimal, optimum.

option [ɔpsjɔ̃] *nf (gén)* option; *(accessoire auto)* optional extra. **matière à** ~ optional subject *(Brit)*, option, elective *(US)*. ◆ **optionnel, -elle** *adj* optional.

optique [ɔptik] **1** *adj verre* optical; *nerf* optic. **2** *nf* (**a**) *(science, appareils)* optics *(sg)*. **instrument d'** ~ optical instrument. (**b**) *(perspective)* perspective. **voir qch avec une certaine** ~ to look at sth from a certain angle *ou* viewpoint.

opulent, e [ɔpylɑ̃, ɑ̃t] *adj pays, prairie* rich; *personne* wealthy, rich; *luxe, vie* opulent. ◆ **opulence** *nf* richness; wealthiness; opulence. **vivre dans l'** ~ to live an opulent life.

opuscule [ɔpyskyl] *nm* opuscule.

or[1] [ɔʀ] *nm* (**a**) *(métal)* gold. ~ **massif** solid gold; ~ **noir** oil, black gold; **blés/cheveux d'** ~ golden cornfields/hair; **en lettres d'** ~ in gilt *ou* gold lettering; **étalon** ~ gold standard. (**b**) **en** ~ *objet* gold; *occasion* golden; *mari, sujet* marvellous, wonderful; **c'est une affaire en** ~ *(achat)* it's a real bargain; *(commerce, magasin)* it's a gold mine; **pour tout l'** ~ **du monde** for all the money in the world; **faire des affaires d'** ~ to run a gold mine.

or[2] [ɔʀ] *conj (transition)* now; *(pourtant)* but, yet.

oracle [ɔʀɑkl(ə)] *nm (gén)* oracle.

orage [ɔʀaʒ] *nm (tempête)* (thunder)storm; *(dispute)* row, upset. **pluie d'** ~ thundery *ou* stormy shower; **les ~s de la vie** the turmoils of life; *(lit, fig)* **il y a de l'** ~ **dans l'air** there is a storm brewing. ◆ **orageux, -euse** *adj ciel, vie, séance* stormy; *pluie, temps* thundery.

oraison [ɔʀɛzɔ̃] *nf* orison, prayer. ~ **funèbre** funeral oration.

oral, e, *mpl* **-aux** [ɔʀal, o] *adj, nm (gén, Scol)* oral. ◆ **oralement** *adv* orally.

orange [ɔʀɑ̃ʒ] **1** *adj inv, nm (couleur)* orange. **2** *nf (fruit)* orange. ~ **sanguine** blood orange. ◆ **orangé, e** *adj* orangey. ◆ **orangeade** *nf* orangeade. ◆ **oranger** *nm* orange tree. ◆ **orangeraie** *nf* orange grove. ◆ **orangerie** *nf (serre)* orangery.

orang-outan(g), *pl* **orangs-outan(g)s** [ɔʀɑ̃utɑ̃] *nm* orang-outang.

orateur, -trice [ɔʀatœʀ, tʀis] *nm, f (gén)* speaker. **être bon** ~ to be a good speaker *ou* orator. ◆ **oratoire 1** *adj* oratorical. **2** *nm (chapelle)* oratory.

oratorio [ɔʀatɔʀjo] *nm* oratorio.

orbite [ɔʀbit] *nf (Anat)* (eye-)socket; *(Astron, Phys)* orbit; *(zone d'influence)* sphere of influence. **mettre sur** ~ *satellite* to put into orbit· *projet* to launch; **être sur** ~ to be in orbit. ◆ **orbital, e,** *mpl* **-aux** *adj* orbital.

Orcades [ɔʀkad] *nfpl:* **les** ~ Orkney, the Orkneys, the Orkney Islands.

orchestre [ɔʀkɛstʀ(ə)] *nm* (**a**) *(musiciens)* orchestra; *[jazz, danse]* band. (**b**) *(Ciné, Théât: emplacement)* stalls, orchestra *(US)*. ◆ **orchestral, e,** *mpl* **-aux** *adj* orchestral. ◆ **orchestrateur, -trice** *nm, f* orchestrator. ◆ **orchestration** *nf* orchestration; organization. ◆ **orchestrer** (1) *vt (Mus)* to orchestrate; *propagande* to organize.

orchidée [ɔʀkide] *nf* orchid.

ordinaire [ɔʀdinɛʀ] **1** *adj* (**a**) *(habituel)* ordinary, usual; *session* ordinary. **peu** ~ *fait* unusual; **(*)** *audace* incredible. (**b**) *vin* ordinary; *service de table* everyday; *qualité* standard; *essence* two-star, 2-star, regular *(US)*; *(péj: commun)* common. **2** *nm:* **l'** ~ *(banalité)* the ordinary; *(nourriture)* the food; **qui sort de l'** ~ which is out of the ordinary; **comme à l'** ~ as usual; **d'** ~ ordinarily, usually, as a rule; **plus que d'** ~ more than usual. ◆ **ordinairement** *adv* ordinarily, usually, as a rule.

ordinal, e, *mpl* **-aux** [ɔʀdinal, o] **1** *adj* ordinal. **2** *nm* ordinal number.

ordinateur [ɔʀdinatœʀ] *nm* computer. **mettre sur** ~ to computerize; **mise sur** ~ computerization.

ordonnance [ɔʀdɔnɑ̃s] *nf* (**a**) *(Méd)* prescription. (**b**) *(Jur: arrêté)* order. (**c**) *[phrase, tableau]* organization, layout; *[bâtiment]* plan, layout; *[cérémonie]* organization; *[repas]* order. (**d**) *(Mil: domestique)* batman.

ordonner [ɔʀdɔne] (1) **1** *vt* (**a**) *idées, éléments, discours* to organize. (**b**) *traitement* to prescribe; *huis-*

clos to order. ~ **que** to order that; **il nous ordonna le silence** he ordered us to be quiet. (**c**) *(Rel) prêtre* to ordain. **être ordonné prêtre** to be ordained priest. **2 s'** ~ *vpr [idées, faits]* to organize themselves. ◆ **ordonné, e 1** *adj maison, enfant* tidy, orderly; *employé* methodical; *vie* well-ordered. **2** *nf (Math)* ordinate.

ordre [ɔʀdʀ(ə)] *nm* (**a**) *(succession)* order. **par** ~ **alphabétique** in alphabetical order; *(Mil)* **en** ~ **de marche** in marching order. (**b**) *(Archit, Bio: catégorie)* order. (**c**) *(nature)* **dans le même** ~ **d'idées** similarly; **dans un autre** ~ **d'idées** in a different connection; **motifs d'** ~ **personnel** reasons of a personal nature; **c'est dans l'** ~ **des choses** it's in the nature of things; **du même** ~ of the same nature *ou* order; **un chiffre de l'** ~ **de 2 millions** a figure of the order of 2 million; *(prix)* **donnez-nous un** ~ **de grandeur** give us a rough estimate *ou* a rough idea; **de premier** ~ first-rate; **de dernier** ~ third-rate. (**d**) *(légalité)* **l'** ~ order; **l'** ~ **public** law and order; **rentrer dans l'** ~ to be back in order; **un partisan de l'** ~ a supporter of law and order. (**e**) *[personne, chambre]* tidiness, orderliness. **sans** ~ untidy, disorderly; **avoir de l'** ~ *(rangements)* to be tidy *ou* orderly; *(travail)* to be methodical; **en** ~ *maison* tidy, orderly; *comptes* in order; **(re)mettre en** ~ to tidy up; **mettre bon** ~ **à qch** to put sth to rights, sort out sth. (**f**) *(état)* **en** ~ **de marche** in working order. (**g**) *(association)* order; *[profession libérale]* ≃ professional association. *(Rel)* **entrer dans les** ~**s** to take (holy) orders ; **l'** ~ **des médecins** ≃ the Medical Association ; **l'** ~ **des avocats** ≃ the Bar. (**h**) *(commandement) (gén, Fin)* order; *(Mil)* order, command. ~ **de mission** orders *(for a mission)*; *(Mil)* ~ **de route** marching orders; **par** ~ **du ministre** by order of the minister; **j'ai reçu des** ~**s formels** I have formal instructions; **être aux** ~**s de qn** to be at sb's disposal; *(formule de politesse)* **je suis à vos** ~**s** I am at your service; *(Mil)* **à vos** ~**s!** yes sir!; **combattre sous les** ~**s de qn** to fight under sb's command; **payable à l'** ~ **de** payable to the order of. (**i**) **l'** ~ **du jour** *(Mil)* the order of the day; *(programme)* the agenda; **cité à l'** ~ **du jour** mentioned in dispatches; **être à l'** ~ **du jour** *(lit)* to be on the agenda; *(d'actualité)* to be topical.

ordure [ɔʀdyʀ] *nf (saleté) (lit)* dirt, filth; *(fig)* filth; *(péj: personne)* swine ⁑. ~**s** *(saleté)* dirt; *(grossièretés)* obscenities, filth; *(détritus)* rubbish, refuse, garbage *(US)*; **jeter qch aux** ~**s** to throw sth into the dustbin *ou* garbage can *(US)*; **écrire des** ~**s** to write filth. ◆ **ordurier, -ière** *adj* lewd, filthy.

orée [ɔʀe] *nf [bois]* edge.

oreille [ɔʀɛj] *nf* (**a**) *(Anat)* ear. **les** ~**s ont dû lui tinter** his ears must have been burning; **écouter de toutes ses** ~**s** to be all ears; **venir aux** ~**s de qn** to come to sb's attention; **dire qch à qn dans le creux de l'** ~ to have a word in sb's ear about sth; **n'écouter que d'une** ~ to listen with only one ear; **avoir les** ~**s rebattues de qch** to have heard enough of sth, be sick of hearing sth; **tirer les** ~**s à qn** *(lit)* to tweak sb's ears; *(fig)* to tell sb off *; **se faire tirer l'** ~ to need a lot of persuading; **ouvre tes** ~**s** listen to what you are told; **l'** ~ **basse** crestfallen. (**b**) *(ouïe)* hearing, ear. **avoir l'** ~ **fine** to be sharp of hearing, have a sharp ear; **avoir de l'** ~ to have a good ear (for music). ◆ **oreiller** *nm* pillow. ◆ **oreillons** *nmpl*: **les** ~ (the) mumps.

orfèvre [ɔʀfɛvʀ(ə)] *nm* silversmith, goldsmith. **être** ~ **en la matière** to be an expert on the subject. ◆ **orfèvrerie** *nf (commerce)* silversmith's (*ou* goldsmith's) trade; *(magasin)* silversmith's (*ou* goldsmith's) shop; *(ouvrage)* (silver) plate, (gold) plate.

organe [ɔʀgan] *nm (gén, Anat)* organ; *(porte-parole)* spokesman; *(littér: voix)* voice. ~**s de commande** controls; ~**s de transmission** transmission system.

organigramme [ɔʀganigʀam] *nm (hiérarchie)* organization chart; *(procédure, Ordin)* flow chart.

organique [ɔʀganik] *adj (Chim, Jur, Méd)* organic.

organiser [ɔʀganize] (1) **1** *vt (gén)* to organize, arrange. **2 s'** ~ *vpr* to organize o.s. (*ou* itself), get (o.s. *ou* itself) organized. ◆ **organisateur, -trice 1** *adj* organizing. **2** *nm, f* organizer. ◆ **organisation** *nf* (**a**) *(action)* organization, arranging; *(résultat)* organization, arrangement. (**b**) *(parti, syndicat)* organization. **O**~ **mondiale de la santé** World Health Organization; **O**~ **des Nations Unies** United Nations Organization.

organisme [ɔʀganism(ə)] *nm (organes, bureaux)* body, organism; *(Zool: individu)* organism.

organiste [ɔʀganist(ə)] *nmf* organist.

orgasme [ɔʀgasm(ə)] *nm* orgasm, climax.

orge [ɔʀʒ(ə)] *nf* barley.

orgie [ɔʀʒi] *nf* orgy. **une** ~ **de** a profusion of.

orgue [ɔʀg(ə)] *nm* organ. ~ **de Barbarie** barrel organ, hurdy-gurdy.

orgueil [ɔʀgœj] *nm* pride. **tirer** ~ **de qch** to take pride in sth, pride o.s. on sth; **mettre son** ~ **à faire qch** to take a pride in doing sth. ◆ **orgueilleusement** *adv* proudly. ◆ **orgueilleux, -euse** *adj* proud.

orgues [ɔʀg(ə)] *nfpl* organ. **les grandes** ~ the great organs.

orient [ɔʀjɑ̃] *nm (littér: est)* orient. **l'O**~ the East, the Orient *(littér)*. ◆ **oriental, e,** *mpl* **-aux 1** *adj région* eastern; *langue, produits* oriental. **2** *nm*: **O**~ Oriental. **3** *nf*: **O**~**e** Oriental woman.

orienter [ɔʀjɑ̃te] (1) **1** *vt* (**a**) *objet* to position, adjust. ~ **une maison vers le sud** to build a house facing south; ~ **une antenne vers le nord** to turn *ou* direct an aerial towards the north; **maison bien orientée** well-positioned house, house with a good aspect. (**b**) *voyageurs, recherches* to direct (*vers* towards). ~ **un élève** to advise a pupil on what courses to follow *ou* what subjects to specialize in; ~ **la conversation vers un sujet** to turn the conversation onto a subject. (**c**) *(marquer) carte* to orientate; *(Math) droite* to orient. **2 s'** ~ *vpr [voyageur]* to find one's bearings. **s'** ~ **vers** *(lit, fig)* to turn towards; *[société]* to move towards; *[étudiant]* **s'** ~ **vers les sciences** to specialize in science, turn to science. ◆ **orientable** *adj antenne* adjustable. ◆ **orientation** *nf* (**a**) *(action)* positioning, adjustment; directing; orientation. **l'** ~ **professionnelle** careers advising; **l'** ~ **scolaire** advice on courses to be followed; **conseiller d'** ~ careers adviser. (**b**) *(position) [maison]* aspect; *[antenne]* direction. **l'** ~ **du jardin au sud** the garden's southern aspect. (**c**) *(tendance) [recherches]* direction, orientation; *[science]* trends; *[magazine]* leanings, (political) tendencies. **quelle** ~ **va-t-il choisir?** *[parti]* which line will they move towards?; *[élève]* which direction will he take? ◆ **orienté, e** *adj (partial) article* slanted, biased.

orifice [ɔʀifis] *nm (gén)* opening; *[tuyau]* mouth; *[organe]* orifice.

originaire [ɔʀiʒinɛʀ] *adj* (**a**) ~ **de** *plante, mets* native to; **il est** ~ **de** he is a native of, he was born in. (**b**) *propriétaire* original; *vice* innate. ◆ **originairement** *adv* originally, at first.

original, e, *mpl* **-aux** [ɔʀiʒinal, o] **1** *adj* original; *(péj: bizarre)* eccentric, odd. **édition** ~**e** original *ou* first edition. **2** *nm, f* eccentric. **3** *nm (tableau)* original; *(document)* original (copy); *(texte dactylographié)* top copy, original *(US)*. ◆ **originalement** *adv* originally. ◆ **originalité** *nf* (**a**) originality; eccentricity, oddness. (**b**) *(caractéristique)* original aspect *ou* feature. *(conduite)* ~**(s)** eccentric behaviour.

origine [ɔʀiʒin] *nf (gén)* origin. **avoir son** ~ **dans** to have one's origins in, originate in; **d'** ~ *pays* of origin; *pneus* original; **d' ~ française** of French origin *ou* extraction; **être d' ~ paysanne/ouvrière** to come of farming/working-class stock; **coutume d' ~ ancienne** long-standing custom, custom of long standing; **à l' ~** originally, to begin with; **dès l' ~** at *ou* from the outset *ou* the very beginning; **à l' ~ de** at the origin of. ◆ **originel, -elle** *adj* original. ◆ **originellement** *adv (primitivement)* originally; *(dès le début)* from the outset.

oripeaux [ɔripo] *nmpl* rags.

orme [ɔrm(ə)] *nm* elm.

orner [ɔrne] (1) *vt* (**a**) *chambre, vêtement* to decorate; *discours* to embellish (*de* with). **robe ornée d'un galon** dress trimmed with braid; **livre orné de dessins** book illustrated with drawings. (**b**) *[statue, bibelot]* to adorn, decorate. ◆ **orné, e** *adj style* ornate, florid. ◆ **ornement** *nm (gén)* ornament; *(Archit, Art)* embellishment, adornment. **sans ~(s)** *toilette, style* plain, unadorned; **d' ~** *arbre, jardin* ornamental. ◆ **ornemental, e,** *mpl* **-aux** *adj plante* ornamental; *motif* decorative. ◆ **ornementation** *nf* ornamentation.

ornière [ɔrnjɛr] *nf (lit)* rut. *(fig)* **il est sorti de l' ~ maintenant** he's out of the wood now.

ornithologie [ɔrnitɔlɔʒi] *nf* ornithology. ◆ **ornithologique** *adj* ornithological. ◆ **ornithologiste** *nmf ou* ◆ **ornithologue** *nmf* ornithologist.

orphelin, e [ɔrfəlɛ̃, in] **1** *adj* orphan(ed). **2** *nm, f* orphan. **être ~ de père** to be fatherless, have lost one's father. ◆ **orphelinat** *nm (lieu)* orphanage; *(orphelins)* children of the orphanage.

orque [ɔrk] *nm* killer whale.

orteil [ɔrtɛj] *nm* toe. **gros ~** big toe.

orthodoxe [ɔrtɔdɔks(ə)] **1** *adj (Rel, gén)* orthodox. **2** *nmf* orthodox. ◆ **orthodoxie** *nf* orthodoxy.

orthogénie [ɔrtɔʒeni] *nf* family planning. **centre d' ~** family planning *ou* birth control centre.

orthographe [ɔrtɔgraf] *nf (gén)* spelling; *(système)* spelling (system). ◆ **orthographier** (7) *vt* to spell *(in writing)*. ◆ **orthographique** *adj* spelling, orthographical.

orthopédie [ɔrtɔpedi] *nf* orthopaedics *(sg)*. ◆ **orthopédique** *adj* orthopaedic. ◆ **orthopédiste** *nmf* orthopaedist.

ortie [ɔrti] *nf* (stinging) nettle. **~ blanche** white dead-nettle.

os [ɔs] *nm* bone. **~ de seiche** cuttle-bone; **viande sans ~** boned meat; **à manche en ~** bone-handled; **trempé jusqu'aux ~** soaked to the skin, wet through; **il y a un ~** * there's a snag *ou* hitch; **tomber sur un ~** * to come across *ou* hit * a snag.

oscar [ɔskar] *nm (Ciné)* Oscar; *(gén)* prize, award (*de* for).

osciller [ɔsile] (1) *vi (Sci)* to oscillate; *[pendule]* to swing; *[tête, navire]* to rock. **le vent fit ~ la flamme** the wind made the flame flicker; *(fig)* **~ entre** *[personne]* to waver between; *[prix]* to fluctuate between. ◆ **oscillation** *nf* oscillation; fluctuation. ◆ **oscillatoire** *adj* oscillatory.

oseille [ozɛj] *nf (Bot)* sorrel; *(‡: argent)* dough ‡.

oser [oze] (1) *vt* to dare. **il faut ~** one must take risks; **il n'osait (pas) bouger** he did not dare (to) move; **je n'ose pas** I dare not; **ose le répéter!** I dare you to repeat it!; **si j'ose dire** if I may say so; **j'ose l'espérer** I like to hope so. ◆ **osé, e** *adj tentative, toilette* bold, daring; *sujet* risqué, daring.

osier [ozje] *nm (Bot)* willow; *(fibres)* wicker. **corbeille en ~** wicker(work) basket.

osmose [ɔsmoz] *nf (lit, fig)* osmosis.

ossature [ɔsatyr] *nf [corps]* frame, bone structure; *[machine, discours]* framework. ◆ **osselets** *nmpl* knucklebones. ◆ **ossements** *nmpl (squelettes)* bones. ◆ **osseux, -euse** *adj (Anat, Méd)* bone ; *(maigre)* bony.

Ostende [ɔstɑ̃d] *n* Ostend.

ostensible [ɔstɑ̃sibl(ə)] *adj* conspicuous. ◆ **ostensiblement** *adv* conspicuously.

ostentation [ɔstɑ̃tɑsjɔ̃] *nf* ostentation. **avec ~** ostentatiously; **faire qch sans ~** to do sth unostentatiously. ◆ **ostentatoire** *adj* ostentatious.

ostraciser [ɔstrasize] (1) *vt* to ostracize. ◆ **ostracisme** *nm* ostracism.

otage [ɔtaʒ] *nm* hostage. **prendre qn en** *ou* **comme ~** to take sb hostage.

otarie [ɔtari] *nf* sea-lion.

ôter [ote] (1) **1** *vt* (**a**) *(gén)* to remove (*de* from); *ornement, scrupules, somme* to take away; *vêtement* to take off; *arêtes, tache* to take out (*de* of). **ôte les assiettes** clear the dishes; **ôte tes mains de la porte!** take your hands off the door! (**b**) *(prendre)* **~ qch à qn** *(lit)* to take sth (away) from sb ; **~ à qn ses forces** to deprive sb of his strength ; **~ à qn toute envie de faire** to rid sb of any desire to do; **on ne m'ôtera pas de l'idée que...** I can't get it out of my mind *ou* head that... **2 s' ~** *vpr*: **ôtez-vous de là!** move yourself!, get out of there!

otite [ɔtit] *nf* ear infection.

oto-rhino(-laryngologie) [ɔtɔrinɔlarɛ̃gɔlɔʒi] *nf* otorhinolaryngology. ◆ **oto-rhino(-laryngologiste)** *nmf* ear, nose and throat specialist.

ou [u] *conj* or. **aujourd'hui ~ demain** (either) today or tomorrow; **avec ~ sans sucre?** with or without sugar?; **que vous le vouliez ~ non** whether you like it or not; **~ pour mieux dire** or rather; **~ il est malade ~ (bien) il est fou** he's either sick or mad, either he's sick or (else) he's mad.

où [u] **1** *pron* (**a**) *(lit)* where. **la ville ~ j'habite** the town I live in *ou* where I live; **le mur ~ il est appuyé** the wall he's leaning against; **le livre ~ il a copié ceci** the book from which he copied this; **le village par ~ il est passé** the village he went through. (**b**) *(abstrait)* **la famille d' ~ il sort** the family he comes from; **dans l'état ~ il est** in the state he is in; **la mélancolie ~ il se complaît** the melancholy in which he wallows; **au prix ~ c'est** at the price it is; **voilà ~ nous en sommes** that's the position to date *ou* so far, that's where we're at *. (**c**) *(temporel)* when. **le jour ~ je l'ai rencontré** the day (when *ou* on which) I met him; **à l'instant ~ il est arrivé** the moment he arrived. **2** *adv rel* where. **s'établir ~ l'on veut** to settle where one likes; **~ que l'on aille** wherever one goes; **savoir ~ s'arrêter** to know where *ou* when to stop ; **d' ~ l'on peut conclure que...** from which one may conclude that...; **d' ~ son silence** hence his silence. **3** *adv interrog* where. **~ es-tu?** where are you?; **par ~ y aller?** which way should we go?; **~ ça?** * where's that?; **d' ~ vient cette attitude?** what's the reason for this attitude?; **~ voulez-vous en venir?** what are you getting at?

ouailles [wɑj] *nfpl (Rel, hum)* flock.

ouate [wat] *nf (pour pansement)* cotton wool, cotton *(US)*; *(pour rembourrage)* padding. ◆ **ouaté, e** *adj vêtement* quilted; *bruit* muffled; *ambiance* cocoon-like.

oublier [ublije] (7) **1** *vt (gén)* to forget; *soucis, client* to forget (about); *fautes d'orthographe* to miss; *phrase* to leave out. **~ de faire/pourquoi** to forget to do/why; **oublions le passé** let's forget about the past, let's let bygones be bygones; **il essaie de se faire ~** he's trying to keep out of the limelight; **on l'a oublié sur la liste** he's been left off the list. **2 s' ~** *vpr [personne]* to forget o.s. **ça s'oublie facilement** it's easily forgotten. ◆ **oubli** *nm* (**a**) forgetting. **l' ~ de cet objet** forgetting this thing ; **l' ~ de soi(-même)** self-effacement. (**b**) *(trou de mémoire)* lapse of memory; *(omission)* omission; *(négligence)* oversight. **cet ~ lui coûta la vie** this omission *ou* oversight cost him his life;

il y a des ~s dans ce récit there are gaps *ou* things missed out in this account. (**c**) **l'** ~ oblivion, forgetfulness. ◆ **oubliettes** *nfpl* oubliettes. ◆ **oublieux, -euse** *adj* forgetful (*de* of).

ouest [wɛst] **1** *nm* west. **le vent d'** ~ the west wind; **un vent d'** ~ a west(erly) wind; **à l'** ~ *(situation)* in the west; *(direction)* to the west, westwards; **à l'** ~ **de** west of; **l'Europe de l'** ~ Western Europe; **Allemagne de l'** ~ West Germany; *(Pol)* **l'O**~ the West. **2** *adj inv région* western; *entrée* west; *direction* westward, westerly. ~**-allemand** West German.

ouf [uf] *excl* phew!, whew! **sans avoir le temps de dire** ~ * before they had time to catch their breath.

Ouganda [ugɑ̃da] *nm* Uganda. ◆ **ougandais, e** *adj*, **O~(e)** *nm(f)* Ugandan.

oui [wi] **1** *adv* (**a**) yes. **le connaissez-vous? —** ~ do you know him? — yes (I do); **est-elle chez elle? —** ~ is she at home? — yes (she is); **ah, ça** ~! I should say so!, yes indeed!; **vous en voulez? —** ~**, bien sûr** do you want some? — of course (I do) *ou* I most certainly do; **répondre (par)** ~ to answer yes; **faire** ~ **de la tête** to nod (one's head). (**b**) *(remplaçant une proposition)* **je pense que** ~ (yes) I think so; **j'espère que** ~ I hope so; **j'ai demandé si elle était venue, lui dit que** ~ I asked if she had been and he says she has. (**c**) *(intensif)* **il va accepter,** ~ **ou non?** is he or isn't he going to accept?; **tu te presses,** ~ **ou non?** will you please hurry up. **2** *nm inv* yes. **il y a eu 30** ~ there were 30 votes for, there were 30 ayes; **pleurer pour un** ~ **ou pour un non** to cry at the drop of a hat.

ouïe [wi] *nf* hearing. ◆ **ouï-dire** *nm inv*: **par** ~ by hearsay. ◆ **ouïr** (**10**) *vt (littér, Jur)* to hear. **j'ai ouï dire que** I've heard it said that.

ouïes [wi] *nfpl (Zool)* gills; *(Mus)* sound holes.

ouille [uj] *excl* ouch!

ouragan [uʀagɑ̃] *nm (lit)* hurricane. *(fig)* **déchaîner un** ~ to create a storm; **arriver comme un** ~ to arrive like a whirlwind *ou* tornado.

Oural [uʀal] *nm: (fleuve)* **l'** ~ the Ural; **l'** ~**, les monts** ~ the Urals, the Ural Mountains.

ourler [uʀle] (**1**) *vt* to hem. ◆ **ourlet** *nm* hem.

ours [uʀs] *nm (Zool)* bear; *(péj: misanthrope)* (old) bear. *(jouet)* ~ **(en peluche)** teddy bear; ~ **blanc** polar bear; ~ **brun** brown bear; ~ **mal léché** * lout. ◆ **ourse** *nf* she-bear. ◆ **ourson** *nm* bear cub.

oursin [uʀsɛ̃] *nm* sea urchin.

oust(e) * [ust(ə)] *excl* beat it! *, off with you!

outil [uti] *nm (lit, fig)* tool; *(agricole)* implement. ~ **de travail** tool; ~ **pédagogique** teaching aid; *(Ordin)* ~ **de programmation** programming tool. ◆ **outillage** *nm [bricoleur]* set of tools; *[jardinier]* implements; *[usine]* equipment. ◆ **outiller** (**1**) *vt (gén)* to equip; *ouvrier* to supply with tools, kit out, outfit *(US)*; *atelier* to fit out. **bien/mal outillé** well-/badly-equipped.

outrage [utʀaʒ] *nm* insult (*à* to). **faire** ~ **à** *mémoire* to insult, offend; *pudeur* to outrage; ~ **à agent** insulting a police officer; ~ **à magistrat** contempt of court; ~ **à la pudeur** indecent behaviour. ◆ **outragé, e** *adj* gravely offended. ◆ **outrageant, e** *adj* offensive. ◆ **outrager** (**3**) *vt (littér) personne* to offend gravely; *mœurs* to outrage; *raison* to insult.

outrageux, -euse [utʀaʒø, øz] *adj* outrageous, excessive. ◆ **outrageusement** *adv* outrageously, excessively.

outrance [utʀɑ̃s] *nf (caractère)* extravagance; *(excès)* excess. **méticuleux à** ~ meticulous in the extreme. ◆ **outrancier, -ière** *adj* extreme.

outre [utʀ(ə)] **1** *prép* besides. ~ **son salaire** on top of *ou* in addition to his salary; ~ **le fait que** as well as *ou* besides the fact that; **en** ~ moreover, besides; **en** ~ **de** on top of; ~ **mesure** to excess; **passer** ~ to carry on regardless; **passer** ~ **à un ordre** to disregard an order; ~ **qu'il a le temps, il sait le faire** apart from having the time he knows how to do it. **2** : ~**-Atlantique** across the Atlantic; ~**-Manche** across the Channel; ~**-mer** overseas; **les territoires d'** ~**-mer** overseas territories; **voix d'** ~**-tombe** lugubrious voice.

outrepasser [utʀəpɑse] (**1**) *vt droits, pouvoir, ordres* to exceed; *limites* to go beyond, overstep.

outrer [utʀe] (**1**) *vt (exagérer)* to exaggerate; *(indigner)* to outrage. ◆ **outré, e** *adj* (**a**) *éloges* excessive, exaggerated; *description* exaggerated, extravagant. (**b**) *(indigné)* outraged (*de, par* at, by).

outsider [awtsajdœʀ] *nm (Sport, fig)* possible winner.

ouvert, e [uvɛʀ, ɛʀt] *etc V* **ouvrir.**

ouvrage [uvʀaʒ] *nm* (**a**) *(travail)* work. **se mettre à l'** ~ to set to *ou* start work. (**b**) *(objet)* piece of work; *(Couture, Constr)* work; *(livre) (œuvre)* work; *(volume)* book. ~ **d'art** structure *(bridge or tunnel etc)*. ◆ **ouvragé, e** *adj meuble* finely carved; *napperon* finely embroidered; *bijou* finely worked.

ouvrier, -ière [uvʀije, ijɛʀ] **1** *adj quartier* working-class; *conflit, agitation, législation* industrial, labour. **2** *nm (gén, Pol, Sociol)* worker; *(membre du personnel)* workman. ~ **d'usine** factory worker *ou* hand; ~ **agricole** farm labourer, farm hand; ~ **qualifié/spécialisé** skilled/unskilled worker. **3** *nf* female worker. ~**ière (d'usine)** female factory worker *ou* factory hand.

ouvrir [uvʀiʀ] (**18**) **1** *vt* (**a**) *(gén)* to open; *porte fermée à clef* to unlock; *ailes* to spread; *manteau* to undo, unfasten. ~ **par effraction** to break open; **il a ouvert brusquement la porte** he threw *ou* flung the door open; ~ **la porte aux abus** to throw the door open to abuses; **on a frappé: va** ~! there was a knock: go and open *ou* answer the door!; **ouvrez, au nom de la loi!** open up, in the name of the law!; **fais-toi** ~ **par la concierge** ask *ou* get the caretaker to let you in; ~ **l'œil** to keep one's eyes open *(fig)*; **ça m'a ouvert les yeux** it opened my eyes, it was an eye-opener (to me); ~ **les oreilles** to pin back one's ears *; **ça m'a ouvert l'appétit** that whetted my appetite; ~ **sa bourse (à qn)** to put one's hand in one's pocket (to help sb). (**b**) *(percer) mur* to open up; *membre, ventre* to open up, cut open; *autoroute* to build; *perspectives* to open up. **ils lui ont ouvert un passage dans la foule** they made a passage for him through the crowd; *(fig)* ~ **la voie (à qn)** to lead the way (for sb). (**c**) *(commencer) théâtre, magasin* to open (up); *compte, enquête, bal* to open. ~ **les hostilités** to start up *ou* begin hostilities; ~ **le feu** to open fire; ~ **le jeu** *(Sport)* to open up the game; *(Cartes)* to open play. (**d**) *(être au début de) liste* to head; *procession* to lead. ~ **la marche** to take the lead; ~ **la danse** to lead off the dance. (**e**) *gaz, radio* to turn on, switch on, put on; *eau, robinet* to turn on; *vanne* to open.

2 *vi* to open (*sur* on, *par* with).

3 s' ~ *vpr* (**a**) *(gén)* to open; *[fleur]* to open out. **robe qui s'ouvre par devant** dress that undoes *ou* unfastens at the front; **la foule s'ouvrit pour le laisser passer** the crowd parted to let him through; **s'** ~ **un passage dans la foule** to cut one's way through the crowd; **la porte a dû s'** ~ the door must have come open; **la vie qui s'ouvre devant elle** the life which is opening in front of *ou* before her. (**b**) **s'** ~ **à** *amour, problèmes* to become aware of; *confident* to open one's heart to (*de qch* about sth). (**c**) **s'** ~ **les veines** to cut *ou* slash one's wrists; **s'** ~ **la jambe** to cut open *ou* gash one's leg.

◆ **ouvre-boîte(s)** *nm inv* tin opener. ◆ **ouvre-bouteille(s)** *nm inv* bottle-opener. ◆ **ouvert, e** *adj (gén, fig)* open; *angle* wide; *ensemble* open-ended; *robinet* on, running; *col* undone. **la bouche ~e** open-mouthed, with open mouth; **entrez, c'est ~!** come in, the door isn't locked! *ou* the door's open!; ~ **au public** open to the public; **à l'esprit** ~ open-minded. ◆ **ouvertement** *adv dire* openly; *agir* openly, overtly. ◆ **ouverture** *nf* (**a**) *(action: V* **ouvrir***)* opening; unlocking; opening up; opening-out. **heures d'** ~ opening hours; **'** ~ **de 10 h à 15 h'** 'open from 10 to 3'; **à l'** ~ at opening time; **l'** ~ **de la porte est automatique** the door opens automatically. (**b**) *(trou)* opening; *(Phot)* aperture; *(Mus)* overture; *(Cartes)* opening. ~ **d'esprit** open-mindedness. (**c**) *(avances)* **~s** overtures; **faire des ~s de paix** to make peace overtures (*à qn* to sb). ◆ **ouvrable** *adj*: **jour** ~ weekday, working day; **heures ~s** business hours. ◆ **ouvreuse** *nf* usherette.

ovaire [ɔvɛʀ] *nm* ovary.

ovale [ɔval] *adj, nm* oval.

ovation [ɔvɑsjɔ̃] *nf* ovation. **faire une** ~ **à qn** to give sb an ovation.

overdose [ɔvɛʀdoz] *nf* overdose.

ovin, e [ɔvɛ̃, in] **1** *adj* ovine. **2** *nm*: **les ~s** the ovine race.

ovule [ɔvyl] *nm (Physiol)* ovum. ◆ **ovuler** (1) *vi* to ovulate. ◆ **ovulation** *nf* ovulation.

oxyder [ɔkside] (1) **1** *vt* to oxidize. **2 s'** ~ *vpr* to become oxidized. ◆ **oxydant, e 1** *adj* oxidizing. **2** *nm* oxidizer. ◆ **oxydation** *nf* oxidization, oxidation. ◆ **oxyde** *nm* oxide. ~ **de carbone** carbon monoxide.

oxygène [ɔksiʒɛn] *nm* oxygen. ◆ **oxygénation** *nf* oxygenation. ◆ **oxygéner** (6) **1** *vt (Chim)* to oxygenate. **2 s'** ~ *vpr* (*) to get some fresh air.

oxymore [ɔksimɔʀ] *nm,* **oxymoron** [ɔksimɔʀɔ̃] *nm* oxymoron.

ozone [ozon] *nm* ozone.

P

P, p [pe] *nm (lettre)* P, p.

pacage [pakaʒ] *nm* pasture *ou* grazing (land). ◆**pacager** (3) **1** *vt* to pasture, graze. **2** *vi* to graze.

pacha [paʃa] *nm* pasha. **mener une vie de** ~ to live like a lord.

pachyderme [paʃidɛʀm(ə)] *nm (éléphant)* elephant.

pacifique [pasifik] **1** *adj* (**a**) *coexistence, manifestation* peaceful; *humeur* peaceable; *intention* pacific. **utilisé à des fins** ~**s** used for peaceful purposes. (**b**) *(Géog)* Pacific. **2** *nm (Géog)* **le P~** the Pacific. ◆**pacificateur, -trice 1** *adj* pacificatory. **2** *nm, f (personne)* peacemaker; *(chose)* pacifier. ◆**pacification** *nf* pacification. ◆**pacifier** (7) *vt* to pacify. ◆**pacifiquement** *adv* peacefully; peaceably; pacifically. ◆**pacifisme** *nm* pacifism. ◆**pacifiste** *nmf, adj* pacifist. **manifestation** ~ *(en faveur de la paix)* peace march *ou* demonstration.

pacotille [pakɔtij] *nf* poor-quality stuff, cheap and nasty goods; *(clinquant)* showy stuff. **c'est de la** ~ it's cheap rubbish; **meubles de** ~ cheap(-jack) furniture.

pacte [pakt(ə)] *nm* pact. ◆**pactiser** (1) *vt (péj) (se liguer)* to take sides (*avec* with); *(transiger)* to come to terms (*avec* with).

pactole [paktɔl] *nm* gold mine.

paella [paela] *nf* paella.

pagaie [pagɛ] *nf* paddle.

pagaïe, pagaille [pagaj] *nf (objets)* mess, shambles; *(désorganisation)* chaos. **mettre la** ~ **dans qch** to mess sth up; **il y en a en** ~ * there are loads * *ou* masses of them.

paganisme [paganism(ə)] *nm* paganism, heathenism.

pagayer [pageje] (8) *vi* to paddle. ◆**pagayeur, -euse** *nm, f* paddler.

page¹ [paʒ] *nf* (**a**) page. ~ **de garde** flyleaf; **une** ~ **d'écriture** a page of writing; **les plus belles** ~**s de Corneille** the finest passages of Corneille; **une** ~ **glorieuse de notre histoire** a glorious page *ou* chapter in our history; **mettre en** ~ to make up (into pages). (**b**) **être à la** ~ *(mode)* to be up-to-date *ou* with it *; *(actualité)* to keep in touch *ou* up-to-date; **ne plus être à la** ~ to be out of touch *ou* behind the times.

page² [paʒ] *nm (Hist)* page (boy).

pagne [paɲ] *nm (en tissu)* loincloth; *(en paille etc)* grass skirt.

pagode [pagɔd] *nf* pagoda.

paie [pɛ] *nf (gén)* pay; *[ouvrier]* wages. **feuille de** ~ paysheet; **jour de** ~ pay day; **ça fait une** ~ **que nous ne nous sommes pas vus** * it's ages since we last saw each other. ◆**paiement** *nm* payment (*de* for). ~ **comptant** payment in full; ~ **en liquide** cash payment.

païen, -ïenne [pajɛ̃, jɛn] *adj, nm, f* pagan, heathen.

paille [pɑj] **1** *nf* straw; *(pour boire)* (drinking) straw; *(Tech: défaut)* flaw. ~ **de fer** steel wool; ~ **de riz** straw; **chapeau de** ~ straw hat; **être sur la** ~ to be penniless; **mettre sur la** ~ to reduce to poverty; **2 millions de francs? une** ~**!** * 2 million francs? peanuts! * **2** *adj inv* straw-coloured. ◆**paillasse** *nf* (**a**) *(matelas)* straw mattress. (**b**) *[évier]* draining board. ◆**paillasson** *nm (lit, péj)* doormat. ◆**paillé, e** *adj* straw-bottomed.

paillette [pajɛt] *nf* (**a**) *(Habillement)* sequin, spangle. (**b**) *[or]* speck; *[mica, lessive]* flake. ◆**pailleté, e** *adj robe* sequined. ◆**pailleter** (4) *vt (gén)* to spangle; *robe* to sew sequins on.

pain [pɛ̃] **1** *nm (gén)* bread; *(miche)* loaf; *[cire]* bar; *[savon]* bar, cake; *[plastic]* stick. *(Culin)* ~ **de poisson** *etc* fish *etc* loaf; **avoir du** ~ **sur la planche** * to have a lot to do, have a lot on one's plate *(Brit)*; **notre** ~ **quotidien** our daily bread. **2** : ~ **brioché** brioche loaf; ~ **de campagne** farmhouse bread; ~ **complet** wholemeal bread; ~ **d'épice(s)** ≃ gingerbread; ~ **de Gênes** sponge cake; ~ **grillé** toast; ~ **de gruau** *ou* **viennois** Vienna bread; ~ **de mie** sandwich loaf; ~ **aux raisins** currant bun; ~ **de seigle** rye bread; **petit** ~ **(au lait)** ≃ plain bun; **se vendre comme des petits** ~**s** to sell like hot cakes.

pair¹ [pɛʀ] *nm (personne)* peer; *(Fin)* par. **remboursé au** ~ repayable at par; **travailler au** ~ to work in exchange for board and lodging; **jeune fille au** ~ au pair girl; **ça va de** ~ it goes hand in hand (*avec* with). ◆**pairesse** *nf* peeress. ◆**pairie** *nf* peerage.

pair², e¹ [pɛʀ] *adj nombre* even. **le côté** ~ **de la rue** the even-numbers side of the street; **jours** ~**s** even dates.

paire² [pɛʀ] *nf (gén)* pair; *[bœufs]* yoke; *[pigeons]* brace. **donner une** ~ **de gifles à qn** to box sb's ears; *(hum)* **les deux font la** ~ they're two of a kind; **c'est une autre** ~ **de manches** * that's another story.

paisible [pezibl(ə)] *adj* peaceful, quiet; *(sans agressivité)* peaceable. ◆**paisiblement** *adv* peacefully, quietly; peaceably.

paître [pɛtʀ(ə)] (57) **1** *vi* to graze. **envoyer** ~ **qn** ‡ to send sb packing *. **2** *vt*: ~ **l'herbe d'un pré** to graze in a meadow.

paix [pɛ] *nf* (**a**) *(gén, Mil)* peace. **signer la** ~ to sign a peace treaty; **en temps de** ~ in peacetime; **Mouvement pour la** ~ Peace Movement; **faire la** ~ **avec qn** to make one's peace with sb, make it up with sb; **ramener la** ~ **entre** to make peace between. (**b**) *(tranquillité)* peace, quiet; *(silence)* stillness, peacefulness. **avoir la** ~ to have a bit of peace and quiet; ~ **à sa mémoire** God rest his soul; **avoir la conscience en** ~ to have a clear conscience, be at peace with one's conscience; **qu'il repose en** ~ may he rest in peace; **fiche-moi** * **la** ~**!** leave me alone!; **la** ~**!** * shut up! *

Pakistan [pakistɑ̃] *nm* Pakistan. ◆**pakistanais, e** *adj*, **P~(e)** *nm (f)* Pakistani.

palace [palas] *nm* luxury hotel.

palais [palɛ] *nm (édifice)* palace; *(Anat)* palate. ~ **des expositions** exhibition centre; **le P~ de Justice** the Law Courts; **le P~ du Luxembourg** *the seat of the French Senate;* ~ **des sports** sports stadium.

palan [palɑ̃] *nm* hoist.

pale [pal] *nf [hélice]* blade; *[roue]* paddle.

pâle [pɑl] *adj* pale; *(maladif)* pallid; *style* weak; *imitation* poor; *sourire* faint, wan. ~ **comme un linge** as white as a sheet; ~ **de peur** white with fear.

palefrenier [palfʀənje] *nm [auberge]* ostler; *[château]* groom.

Palerme [palɛʀm(ə)] *n* Palermo.

Palestine [palɛstin] *nf* Palestine. ◆**palestinien, -ienne** *adj,* **P~(ne)** *nm (f)* Palestinian.

paletot [palto] *nm* knitted jacket. **il m'est tombé sur le ~** ‡ he jumped on me.

palette [palɛt] *nf (Peinture)* palette; *(Boucherie)* shoulder; *[roue]* paddle.

pâleur [pɑlœʀ] *nf* paleness; *(maladive)* pallor.

palier [palje] *nm [escalier]* landing; *[route]* level; *(Tech)* bearing; *(fig: étape)* stage. **habiter sur le même ~** to live on the same floor; **les prix ont atteint un nouveau ~** prices have risen to a new level.

pâlir [pɑliʀ] (2) **1** *vi [personne]* to turn *ou* go pale (*de* with); *[étoiles]* to grow dim; *[ciel]* to grow pale; *[couleur]* to fade; *[souvenir]* to fade (away), dim. **faire ~ qn d'envie** to make sb green with envy. **2** *vt* to turn pale. ◆**pâlissant, e** *adj teinte, lumière* wan, fading.

palissade [palisad] *nf [pieux]* fence; *[planches]* boarding.

pallier [palje] (7) *vt difficulté* to overcome, get round; *manque* to offset, compensate for, make up for. ◆**palliatif** *nm (mesure)* palliative, stopgap measure; *(réparation)* makeshift repair.

palmarès [palmaʀɛs] *nm (Scol)* prize list; *(Sport)* (list of) medal winners; *[athlète etc]* record (of achievements). **il a de nombreux exploits à son ~** he has a number of exploits to his credit.

palme [palm(ə)] *nf (Bot)* palm leaf; *(symbole)* palm (*de* of); *[nageur]* flipper. **vin de ~** palm wine; *(lit, fig)* **la ~ revient à...** the prize goes to...; **disputer la ~ à qn** to compete with sb; **elle a remporté la ~** she was the winner; *(Ciné)* **la P ~ d'or** the Palme d'or. ◆**palmé, e** *adj patte* webbed; *oiseau* web-footed. ◆**palmeraie** *nf* palm grove. ◆**palmier** *nm (Bot)* palm tree; *(gâteau)* palmier.

palombe [palɔ̃b] *nf* woodpigeon.

pâlot, -otte * [pɑlo, ɔt] *adj* pale, peaky *.

palourde [paluʀd(ə)] *nf* clam.

palper [palpe] (1) *vt objet* to feel, finger; *(Méd)* to palpate; (‡) *argent* to get, make. ◆**palpable** *adj (lit, fig)* palpable.

palpiter [palpite] (1) *vi [cœur]* to beat; *(violemment)* to pound; *[paupières]* to flutter; *[narines, flamme]* to quiver. ◆**palpitant, e** *adj livre* thrilling, exciting. **être ~ d'émotion** to be quivering with emotion. ◆**palpitation** *nf*: **~(s)** *[cœur]* pounding; *[flamme]* quivering; *(Méd)* **avoir des ~s** to have palpitations.

paluche ‡ [palyʃ] *nf (main)* hand, paw *. **serrer la ~ à qn** to shake hands with sb.

paludisme [palydism(ə)] *nm* malaria.

pampa [pɑ̃pa] *nf* pampas *(pl).*

pamphlet [pɑ̃flɛ] *nm* satirical tract, lampoon.

pamplemousse [pɑ̃pləmus] *nm* grapefruit.

pan[1] [pɑ̃] *nm (morceau)* piece; *(basque)* tail; *(côté)* side, face. **~ de ciel** patch of sky; **~ de mur** (section of) wall; **il est en ~ de chemise** he has just his shirt on.

pan[2] [pɑ̃] *excl [coup de feu]* bang!; *[gifle]* slap!, whack!

pan[3] [pɑ̃], *devant voyelle* [pan] *préf* Pan-. **panaméricain** *etc* Pan-American *etc.*

panacée [panase] *nf* panacea.

panache [panaʃ] *nm (plumet)* plume; *(héroïsme)* gallantry. **~ de fumée** plume of smoke.

panaché, e [panaʃe] **1** *adj fleur* many-coloured; *foule, assortiment* motley; *glace* mixed-flavour. **2** *nm (boisson)* shandy.

Panama [panama] *nm* Panama. ◆**panaméen, -enne** *adj,* **P~(ne)** *nm(f)* Panamanian.

panard ‡ [panaʀ] *nm* foot, hoof ‡.

panaris [panaʀi] *nm* whitlow.

pancarte [pɑ̃kaʀt(ə)] *nf (gén)* sign, notice; *(Aut)* (road)sign; *[manifestant]* placard.

pancréas [pɑ̃kʀeɑs] *nm* pancreas.

panda [pɑ̃da] *nm* panda.

panel [panɛl] *nm (jury)* panel; *(échantillon)* sample group.

paner [pane] (1) *vt* to coat with breadcrumbs.

panier [panje] **1** *nm* **(a)** *(gén, Sport)* basket; *(contenu)* basket(ful). *(fig)* **ils sont tous à mettre dans le même ~** they are all much of a muchness; **jeter au ~** to throw out. **(b)** *(Phot: pour diapositives)* magazine. **~ circulaire** rotary magazine. **(c)** *(vêtement)* pannier. **2** : **~ à bouteilles** bottlecarrier; **c'est un ~ de crabes** they fight to get ahead of each other; **~ percé** spendthrift; **~ à salade** *(Culin)* salad shaker *ou* basket; *(* fig)* police van, Black Maria *. ◆**panière** *nf* large basket.

panique [panik] *adj, nf* panic. **pris de ~** panic-stricken; **c'est la ~!** * everything's in a state of panic *ou* chaos!; **pas de ~!** * no need to panic!; **peur ~** pathological fear. ◆**paniquer** * (1) **1** *vt:* **~ qn** to put the wind up sb *, give sb a scare. **2** *vi,* **se ~** * *vpr* to panic, get the wind up *.

panne [pan] *nf (incident)* breakdown. **je suis tombé en ~** my car has broken down; **je suis tombé en ~ sèche** I have run out of petrol *ou* gas *(US)*; **~ de courant** power failure; **~ de moteur** engine failure; **rester en ~ devant une difficulté** to be stuck over a difficulty; **laisser qn en ~** to let sb down.

panneau, *pl* **~x** [pano] *nm [porte etc]* panel; *(écriteau)* sign, notice. **~ d'affichage** *(pour résultats)* notice board, bulletin board *(US)*; *(pour publicité)* hoarding, billboard *(US)*; **~ indicateur** signpost; **~ de signalisation** road-sign; **~ de stop** halt sign; **~ vitré** glass panel; **tomber dans le ~** * to fall *ou* walk (right) into the trap, fall for it *. ◆**panonceau,** *pl* **~x** *nm (plaque)* plaque; *(publicitaire)* sign.

panoplie [panɔpli] *nf (jouet)* outfit; *[moyens etc]* range. **~ d'armes** *(collection)* display of weapons; *(équipement)* armoury.

panorama [panɔʀama] *nm (lit, fig)* panorama. ◆**panoramique** *adj* panoramic.

panse [pɑ̃s] *nf* paunch; *(*: ventre)* belly ‡. **se remplir la ~** * to eat one's fill.

panser [pɑ̃se] (1) *vt* **(a)** *plaie* to dress; *bras* to put a dressing on; *blessé* to dress the wounds of. **(b)** *cheval* to groom. ◆**pansage** *nm* grooming. ◆**pansement** *nm* dressing; *(bandage)* bandage. **faire un ~** to dress a wound; **couvert de ~s** all bandaged up; **~ (adhésif)** (sticking) plaster, Band Aid ® *(US)*.

pantalon [pɑ̃talɔ̃] *nm* (pair of) trousers *ou* pants *(US)*. **10 ~s** 10 pairs of trousers.

pantelant, e [pɑ̃tlɑ̃, ɑ̃t] *adj personne* panting (*de* with); *gorge, chair* heaving.

panthéon [pɑ̃teɔ̃] *nm* pantheon.

panthère [pɑ̃tɛʀ] *nf* panther; *(fig: mégère)* hellcat *.

pantin [pɑ̃tɛ̃] *nm (jouet)* jumping jack; *(péj: personne)* puppet.

pantomime [pɑ̃tɔmim] *nf (art)* mime; *(spectacle)* mime show; *(fig)* pantomime, scene, fuss.

pantoufle [pɑ̃tufl(ə)] *nf* slipper. ◆**pantouflard, e** * *adj caractère* stay-at-home; *vie* quiet.

paon [pɑ̃] *nm* peacock.

papa [papa] *nm* dad, daddy. **la musique de ~** * old-fashioned music; **conduire à la ~** * to potter along in one's car; **c'est un ~ gâteau** he spoils his (grand)children.

pape [pap] *nm* pope. ◆**papal, e,** *mpl* **-aux** *adj* papal. ◆**papauté** *nf* papacy.

papelard * [paplaʀ] *nm* paper.

paperasse [papʀas] *nf (péj)* ~**(s)** papers; *(à remplir)* forms. ◆ **paperasserie** *nf (péj)* papers; *(à remplir)* forms; *(routine)* red tape. **il y a trop de ~ à faire dans ce travail** there's too much paperwork in this job.

papeterie [papetʀi] *nf (magasin)* stationer's (shop); *(fourniture)* stationery; *(fabrique)* paper mill; *(fabrication)* papermaking industry; *(commerce)* stationery trade. ◆ **papetier, -ière** *nm, f (vendeur)* stationer; *(fabricant)* paper-maker.

papier [papje] **1** *nm* (**a**) *(matière)* paper. **sac en ~** paper bag; **mettre qch sur ~** to write sth down; **sur ~ libre** on plain paper; **sur le ~** *(théoriquement)* on paper. (**b**) *(feuille écrite)* paper; *(feuille blanche)* sheet *ou* piece of paper; *(Presse: article)* article. **un ~ à signer** a form to be signed; **~s (d'identité)/militaires** *etc* (identity)/army *etc* papers; *(Aut)* **vos ~s, s'il vous plaît!** may I see your driving licence *ou* driver's license *(US)*, please?; **rayez cela de vos ~s!** you can forget about that!; **être dans les petits ~s de qn** to be in sb's good books.
2 : **~ aluminium** aluminium *ou* aluminum *(US)* foil, tinfoil; **~ d'argent** silver foil *ou* paper, tinfoil; **~ brouillon** scrap paper; **~ buvard** blotting paper; **~ calque** tracing paper; **~ carbone** carbon paper; **~ à cigarettes** cigarette paper; **~ collant** gummed paper; *(Ordin)* **~ en continu** continuous stationery; **~ crépon** crêpe paper; **~ à dessin** drawing paper; **~ d'emballage** wrapping paper; **~ filtre** filter paper; *(ordures)* **~s gras** litter, rubbish; **~ hygiénique** toilet paper; **~ journal** newspaper; **~ kraft** ® brown wrapping paper; **~ à lettres** writing paper, notepaper; **~ mâché** papier-mâché; *(fig)* **mine de ~ mâché** pasty complexion; **~ machine** typing paper; **~ monnaie** paper money; **~ peint** wallpaper; **~ de soie** tissue paper; **~ timbré** stamped paper; **~ de verre** glass-paper, sandpaper.

papillon [papijɔ̃] *nm (insecte)* butterfly; *(écrou)* wing *ou* butterfly nut; *(contravention)* (parking) ticket; *(autocollant)* sticker. **~ de nuit** moth.

papillote [papijɔt] *nf [cheveux]* curlpaper; *[bonbon]* (sweet *ou* candy *(US)*) paper; *[gigot]* frill; *(papier aluminium)* tinfoil. **poisson en ~** fish cooked in tinfoil.

papilloter [papijɔte] (1) *vi [lumière]* to twinkle; *[paupières]* to flutter, flicker; *[yeux]* to blink. ◆ **papillotement** *nm*: ~**(s)** twinkling; fluttering, flickering; blinking.

papoter [papɔte] (1) *vi* to chatter. ◆ **papotage** *nm (action)* chattering. *(propos)* ~**(s)** (idle) chatter.

papou, e [papu] *adj, nm,* **P~(e)** *nm(f)* Papuan.

Papouasie-Nouvelle-Guinée [papwazinuvɛl gine] *nf* Papua New Guinea.

paquebot [pakbo] *nm* liner, (steam)ship.

pâquerette [pɑkʀɛt] *nf* daisy.

Pâques [pɑk] **1** *nm* Easter. *(fig)* **à ~ ou à la Trinité** never in a month of Sundays. **2** *nfpl*: **joyeuses ~** Happy Easter; **faire ses ~** to go to Easter mass (and take communion).

paquet [pakɛ] *nm* (**a**) *[café]* bag; *[cigarettes]* packet, pack *(US)*; *[cartes]* pack; *[linge]* bundle. **~-cadeau** gift-wrapped parcel. (**b**) *(colis)* parcel. **faire un ~** to make up a parcel. (**c**) **~ de** *neige* pile *ou* mass of; *boue* lump of; *billets* wad of; **il a touché un bon ~ *** he got a fat sum *. (**d**) *(Rugby)* **~ (d'avants)** pack (of forwards). (**e**) *(Naut)* **~ de mer** heavy sea, big wave. (**f**) **faire ses ~s** to pack one's bags; **il y a mis le ~ *** *(argent)* he spared no expense; *(efforts)* he put everything into it. ◆ **paquetage** *nm (Mil)* pack, kit.

par [paʀ] *prép* (**a**) *(agent, cause)* by. **cassé ~ l'orage** broken by the storm; **accablé ~ le désespoir** overwhelmed with despair; **il a appris la nouvelle ~ un ami** he learned the news from *ou* through a friend; **elle veut tout faire ~ elle-même** she wants to do everything (for) herself; **la décision ~ le patron de...** the boss's decision to...
(**b**) *(manière, moyen)* by. **obtenir qch ~ la force/la persuasion/la ruse** to obtain sth by force/with persuasion/by *ou* through cunning; **la porte ferme ~ un verrou** the gate is locked with a bolt *ou* by means of a bolt; **payer ~ chèque** to pay by cheque; **~ le train** by rail *ou* train; **~ bien des côtés** in many ways; **honnête ~ nature** honest by nature.
(**c**) *(motif etc)* out of, from, for. **étonnant ~ son érudition** amazing for his learning; **~ manque de temps** owing to lack of time; **~ habitude** out of *ou* from habit; **~ plaisir/pitié** for pleasure/out of pity; **~ hasard/erreur** by chance/mistake.
(**d**) *(lieu, état)* through. **il est sorti ~ la fenêtre** he went out by (way of) *ou* through the window; **nous sommes venus ~ l'Espagne** we came via *ou* through Spain; **se promener ~ les champs** to walk through *ou* across the fields; **~ tout le pays** throughout *ou* all over the (entire) country; **il habite ~ ici** he lives round here; **sortez ~ ici** go out this way; **~ où sont-ils entrés?** which way *ou* how did they get in?; **~ où est-il venu?** which way did he come (by)?; **passer ~ de dures épreuves** to go through some very trying times; **~ 5 mètres de fond** at a depth of 5 metres; **~ 10° de latitude sud** at a latitude of 10° south; **arriver ~ le nord** to arrive from the north.
(**e**) *(distribution, mesure)* a, per, by. **marcher 2 ~ 2** to walk 2 by 2 *ou* in 2's; **50 F ~ personne** 50 francs per person *ou* a head *ou* apiece; **3 fois ~ jour** 3 times daily *ou* a day; **6 étudiants ~ appartement** 6 students to a flat *ou* per flat; **~ an** a *ou* per year, per annum; **~ moments** at times; **ils sont venus ~ milliers** they came in their thousands; **il y en avait ~ milliers** there were thousands of them; **~ poignées** in handfuls, by the handful; **~ 3 fois, on lui a demandé** 3 times he has been asked.
(**f**) *(atmosphère)* in, on; *(moment)* on. **~ une belle nuit** one *ou* on a beautiful night; **~ ce froid/cette chaleur** in this cold/heat; **~ temps de pluie** in wet weather; **sortir ~ moins 10°** to go out when it's minus 10°.
(**g**) **commencer ~ qch/~ faire** to begin with sth/by doing; **il a fini ~ ennuyer tout le monde** he ended up *ou* finished up boring everyone; **~ où allons-nous commencer?** where shall we begin?
(**h**) *(exclamations)* by. **~ tout ce que j'ai de plus cher** by all that I hold most dear.
(**i**) **~ trop** far too, excessively; **de ~ le roi** in the name of the king, by order of the king; **de ~ le monde** throughout the world, the world over.

parabole [paʀabɔl] *nf (Math)* parabola; *(Rel)* parable. ◆ **parabolique 1** *adj* parabolic. **2** *nm (radiateur)* electric fire.

parachever [paʀaʃve] (5) *vt* to perfect, put the finishing touches to. ◆ **parachèvement** *nm* perfection.

parachute [paʀaʃyt] *nm* parachute. ◆ **para *** *nm* para *. ◆ **parachutage** *nm* parachuting. ◆ **parachuter** (1) *vt* to parachute. **ils m'ont parachuté à ce poste *** I was pitchforked into this job. ◆ **parachutisme** *nm* parachuting. **faire du ~** to go parachuting; **faire du ~ en chute libre** to skydive, do skydiving. ◆ **parachutiste** *nmf* parachutist; *(Mil)* paratrooper.

parade [paʀad] *nf* (**a**) *(ostentation)* show. **faire ~ de** to parade, show off; **de ~** *uniforme* ceremonial. (**b**) *(spectacle)* parade. **~ militaire/foraine** military/circus parade. (**c**) *(Escrime, Boxe)* parry; *(fig)* answer, reply. ◆ **parader** (1) *vi* to show off.

paradis [paʀadi] *nm (lit, fig)* paradise, heaven. **le P~ terrestre** *(Bible)* the Garden of Eden; *(fig)* heaven on earth; **~ fiscal** tax haven. ◆ **paradisiaque** *adj* heavenly.

paradoxe [paʀadɔks(ə)] *nm* paradox. ◆ **paradoxal, e,** *mpl* **-aux** *adj* paradoxical. ◆ **paradoxalement** *adv* paradoxically.

paraffine [paʀafin] *nf* paraffin wax.

parages [paʀaʒ] *nmpl* (**a**) **dans les** ~ in the area, in the vicinity; **dans les** ~ **de** round about, in the vicinity of. (**b**) *(Naut)* waters, region.

paragraphe [paʀagʀaf] *nm* paragraph.

Paraguay [paʀagwɛ] *nm* Paraguay. ◆ **paraguayen, -enne** *adj*, **P~(ne)** *nm (f)* Paraguayan.

paraître [paʀɛtʀ(ə)] (57) *vi* (**a**) *(se montrer)* to appear (*sur* on). **il n'a pas paru à la réunion** he didn't appear *ou* turn up at the meeting; ~ **en public** to appear in public, make a public appearance. (**b**) *(Presse)* to appear, come out. **faire** ~ **qch** *[éditeur]* to bring sth out; *[auteur]* to have sth published. (**c**) *(être visible)* to show (through). **il en paraît toujours qch** one can always see some sign of it *ou* traces of it; **laisser** ~ **son irritation** to let one's annoyance show; *(péj)* **chercher à** ~ to show off. (**d**) *(sembler)* to look, seem, appear. **cela me paraît une erreur** it looks *ou* seems like a mistake to me; **cette robe la fait** ~ **plus grande** that dress makes her look taller; **il lui paraissait impossible de refuser** he didn't see how he could refuse; **il paraît que oui** so it seems *ou* appears, apparently so.

parallèle [paʀalɛl] **1** *adj* (**a**) *(Math)* parallel (*à* to). (**b**) *(comparable)* similar; *(indépendant)* separate; *(non officiel)* unofficial; *énergie, société* alternative. **2** *nf (Math)* parallel line. *(Élec)* **en** ~ in parallel. **3** *nm (Géog, fig)* parallel. **mettre en** ~ *choses opposées* to compare; *choses semblables* to parallel. ◆ **parallèlement** *adv (lit)* parallel (*à* to); *(ensemble)* at the same time; *(similairement)* in the same way. ◆ **parallélisme** *nm (lit, fig)* parallelism; *(Aut)* wheel alignment. ◆ **parallélogramme** *nm* parallelogram.

paralyser [paʀalize] (1) *vt (Méd, fig)* to paralyse. ◆ **paralysé, -e 1** *adj* paralysed. *[aéroport]* ~ **par le brouillard** fogbound; ~ **par la neige** snowbound; ~ **par la grève** *[gare]* strike-bound; *[hôpital]* crippled by the strike. **2** *nm, f* paralytic. ◆ **paralysie** *nf* paralysis. ◆ **paralytique** *adj, nmf* paralytic.

paramédical, e, *mpl* **-aux** [paʀamedikal, o] *adj* paramedical.

paramètre [paʀamɛtʀ(ə)] *nm* parameter.

paranoïaque [paʀanɔjak] *adj, nmf* paranoiac.

parapet [paʀapɛ] *nm* parapet.

paraphe [paʀaf] *nm (trait)* flourish; *(initiales)* initial; *(signature)* signature. ◆ **parapher** (1) *vt (Admin)* to initial; to sign.

paraphrase [paʀafʀɑz] *nf* paraphrase. ◆ **paraphraser** (1) *vt* to paraphrase.

parapluie [paʀaplɥi] *nm* umbrella. ~ **atomique** nuclear shield *ou* umbrella.

parapsychologie [paʀapsikɔlɔʒi] *nf* parapsychology.

parascolaire [paʀaskɔlɛʀ] *adj* extracurricular.

parasite [paʀazit] **1** *nm (lit, fig)* parasite. *(Rad, TV)* **~s** interference, atmospherics, static. **2** *adj* parasitic(al). ◆ **parasiter** (1) *vt (Bot, Vét)* to live as a parasite on; *(Rad, TV)* to cause interference on.

parasol [paʀasɔl] *nm [plage]* beach umbrella, parasol; *[café]* sunshade, parasol.

paratonnerre [paʀatɔnɛʀ] *nm* lightning conductor.

paravent [paʀavɑ̃] *nm* folding screen *ou* partition.

parc [paʀk] **1** *nm (jardin public)* park; *[château]* grounds; *(Mil: entrepôt)* depot; *(fig, Écon: ensemble)* stock. **le** ~ **français des ordinateurs individuels** the total number of personal computers owned in France. **2** : ~ **à l'anglaise** landscaped garden; ~ **d'attractions** amusement park; ~ **automobile** *[pays]* number of vehicles on the road; *[entreprise]* car fleet; ~ **à bébé** playpen; ~ **à la française** formal garden (in the French style); ~ **à huîtres** oyster bed; ~ **à moutons** sheep pen, sheepfold; ~ **naturel** nature reserve; ~ **de stationnement** car park, parking lot *(US)*; ~ **zoologique** zoological gardens.

parcelle [paʀsɛl] *nf (lit)* fragment; *[vérité]* grain, scrap; *[bonheur]* bit; *(sur cadastre)* parcel *(of land)*. ~ **de terre** plot of land.

parce que [paʀsk(ə)] *conj* because.

parchemin [paʀʃəmɛ̃] *nm* (piece of) parchment.

parcimonie [paʀsimɔni] *nf* parsimony. ◆ **parcimonieusement** *adv* parsimoniously. ◆ **parcimonieux, -euse** *adj* parsimonious.

par-ci par-là [paʀsipaʀla] *adv (espace)* here and there; *(temps)* now and then.

parcmètre [paʀkmɛtʀ(ə)] *nm* (parking) meter.

parcourir [paʀkuʀiʀ] (11) *vt* (**a**) *distance* to cover, travel; *(en tous sens) lieu* to go all over; *pays* to travel up and down. ~ **les mers** to sail all over the seas; **un frisson parcourut tout son corps** a shiver ran through his body. (**b**) *livre* to glance *ou* skim through. **il parcourut la foule des yeux** he ran his eye over the crowd. ◆ **parcours** *nm* (**a**) *(distance)* distance; *(trajet)* journey; *(itinéraire)* route; *[fleuve]* course. **le prix du** ~ the fare. (**b**) *(Sport)* course. **sur un** ~ **difficile** over a difficult course; ~ **de golf** *(terrain)* golf course; *(partie, trajet)* round of golf; *(Mil)* **faire le** ~ **du combattant** to go round an assault course.

par-delà [paʀdəla] *prép* beyond.

par-derrière [paʀdɛʀjɛʀ] **1** *prép* (round) behind. **2** *adv passer* round the back; *attaquer* from behind, from the rear; *se boutonner* at the back. **dire du mal de qn** ~ to speak ill of sb behind his back.

par-dessous [paʀd(ə)su] *prép, adv* under(neath).

pardessus [paʀdəsy] *nm* overcoat.

par-dessus [paʀd(ə)sy] **1** *prép* over. ~ **tout** above all; **j'en ai** ~ **la tête** I'm sick and tired of it; ~ **le marché** into the bargain, on top of all that; ~ **bord** overboard. **2** *adv* over (the top).

par-devant [paʀd(ə)vɑ̃] **1** *prép*: ~ **notaire** in the presence of *ou* before a lawyer. **2** *adv passer* round the front; *attaquer* from the front; *se boutonner* at the front.

pardon [paʀdɔ̃] *nm* (**a**) *(grâce)* forgiveness, pardon *(Jur)*. (**b**) *(en Bretagne)* pardon *(religious festival)*. (**c**) **demander** ~ **à qn d'avoir fait qch** to apologize to sb for doing *ou* having done sth; **demande** ~! say you're sorry!; **(je vous demande)** ~ (I'm) sorry, I beg your pardon; ~ **Monsieur, avez-vous l'heure?** excuse me, could you tell me the time?; **et puis** ~! * **il travaille dur** he works hard I can tell you. ◆ **pardonnable** *adj* pardonable, forgivable. ◆ **pardonner** (1) **1** *vt* to forgive, pardon. ~ **qch à qn/à qn d'avoir fait qch** to forgive sb for sth/for doing *ou* having done sth; **pour se faire** ~ so as to be forgiven; **pardonnez-moi de vous avoir dérangé** I'm sorry to have disturbed you; **on lui pardonne tout** he gets away with everything; **je ne me le pardonnerai jamais** I'll never forgive myself. **2** *vi* to forgive. **erreur qui ne pardonne pas** fatal mistake.

pare- [paʀ] *préf V* **parer²**.

pareil, -eille [paʀɛj] **1** *adj* (**a**) *(identique)* similar. **il n'y en a pas deux ~s** there aren't two the same *ou* alike; ~ **que,** ~ **à** the same as, similar to, just like; **c'est toujours** ~ it's always the same; **il est** ~ **à lui-même** he's the same as ever; **j'en ai un** ~ I have one the same *ou* just like it; **l'an dernier à ~eille époque** this time last year. (**b**) *(tel)* such (a). **je n'ai jamais entendu un discours** ~ I've never heard such a speech *ou* a speech like it. **2** *nm, f*: **nos ~s** *(semblables)* our fellow men; *(égaux)* our equals *ou* peers; **ne pas avoir son** ~ to be second to none; **vous et vos ~s** people like you; **sans**

~ unparalleled, unequalled; **c'est du ~ au même** * it comes to the same thing. **3** *adv* (*) *s'habiller* the same, in the same way, alike. **faire ~** to do the same thing (*que* as). ◆ **pareillement** *adv (de la même manière)* in the same way (*à* as); *(également)* likewise, also, equally. **à vous ~!** the same to you!

parent, e [paʀɑ̃, ɑ̃t] **1** *adj* related (*de* to). **2** *nm, f* (**a**) relative, relation. **être ~ de qn** to be related to sb; *(fig)* **~ pauvre** poor relation. (**b**) *(Bio)* parent. **3** *nmpl*: **~s** *(père et mère)* parents; *(ancêtres)* ancestors, forefathers. ◆ **parenté** *nf (rapport)* relationship, kinship; *(famille)* relations, relatives.

parenthèse [paʀɑ̃tɛz] *nf (digression)* digression; *(signe)* bracket, parenthesis. **entre ~s** *(lit)* in brackets *ou* parentheses; *(fig)* incidentally, in parenthesis; **par ~** incidentally, in passing; *(fig)* **ouvrir une ~** to digress.

parer[1] [paʀe] (1) **1** *vt* (**a**) *(orner)* to adorn. **robe richement parée** richly trimmed dress. (**b**) *viande* to dress, trim; *cuir* to dress. **2 se ~** *vpr (se faire beau)* to put on all one's finery. **se ~ de** *bijoux* to adorn o.s. with; *faux titre* to assume.

parer[2] [paʀe] (1) **1** *vt coup* to ward off, stave off, fend off; *(Boxe, Escrime, fig)* to parry. **2 ~ à** *vt indir inconvénient* to deal with, remedy; *danger* to ward off; *éventualité* to be prepared for. **~ au plus pressé** to attend to the most urgent things first. ◆ **paré, e** *adj (prêt)* ready, all set; *(préparé)* prepared (*contre* against). ◆ **pare-balles** *adj inv* bulletproof. ◆ **pare-brise** *nm inv* windscreen, windshield *(US)*. ◆ **pare-chocs** *nm inv (Aut)* bumper, fender *(US)*. ◆ **pare-soleil** *nm inv* sun visor.

paresseux, -euse [paʀɛsø, øz] **1** *adj personne* lazy, idle; *esprit* slow; *allure* lazy; *estomac, intestin* sluggish; *fleuve* lazy, sluggish. **~ comme une couleuvre** * *ou* **un loir** * *ou* **un lézard** * bone-idle *, lazy. **2** *nm, f* lazy *ou* idle person, lazybones *. ◆ **paresse** *nf* laziness; idleness; slowness; sluggishness; *(péché)* sloth. ◆ **paresser** (1) *vi* to laze about *ou* around. ◆ **paresseusement** *adv* lazily.

parfait, e [paʀfɛ, ɛt] **1** *adj (gén)* perfect; *raisonnement, manières* flawless, faultless; *tranquillité* complete, total; *crétin* utter, downright. **(c'est) ~!** (that's) perfect! *ou* great! * **2** *nm* (**a**) *(Culin)* **~ au café** coffee parfait. (**b**) *(Ling)* perfect. ◆ **parfaire** (60) *vt* to perfect. ◆ **parfaitement** *adv* perfectly; completely, totally; utterly. **tu as fait ça tout seul? — ~!** you did it all on your own? — I certainly did! *ou* I did indeed!

parfois [paʀfwa] *adv* sometimes.

parfum [paʀfœ̃] *nm (substance)* perfume, scent; *(odeur)* scent, fragrance; *[café]* aroma; *[glace]* flavour. **être au ~** ⁑ to be in the know *; **mettre qn au ~** ⁑ to put sb in the picture *. ◆ **parfumé, e** *adj savon* scented; *air, fleur* fragrant, sweet-smelling. **~ au citron** *glace* lemon-flavour(ed); *savon* lemon-scented; **fraises très ~es** very sweet strawberries. ◆ **parfumer** (1) **1** *vt [fleurs]* to perfume, scent; *[café, tabac]* to fill with its aroma; *mouchoir* to put scent *ou* perfume on; *(Culin)* to flavour (*à* with). **2 se ~** *vpr* to use perfume *ou* scent. ◆ **parfumerie** *nf (gén)* perfumery; *(boutique)* perfume shop. ◆ **parfumeur, -euse** *nm, f* perfumer.

pari [paʀi] *nm* bet, wager; *(Sport)* bet. *(fig)* **les ~s sont ouverts** it's anyone's bet *. ◆ **parier** (7) *vt* (**a**) *(gager)* to bet, wager. **je (te) parie que c'est lui** I bet you it's him; **il y a gros à ~ que...** the odds are that...; **je l'aurais parié** I might have known; **tu as faim, je parie** I bet you're hungry. (**b**) *(Courses) argent* to bet, lay, stake. **~ sur un cheval** to bet on a horse. ◆ **parieur, -euse** *nm, f* punter.

Paris [paʀi] *n* Paris.

parisien, -ienne [paʀizjɛ̃, jɛn] **1** *adj (gén)* Paris; *ambiance* Parisian. **la vie ~ienne** Paris *ou* Parisian life. **2** *nm (f)*: **P~(ne)** Parisian.

parité [paʀite] *nf* parity. ◆ **paritaire** *adj commission* joint; *représentation* equal.

parjure [paʀʒyʀ] **1** *adj personne* faithless; *serment* false. **2** *nm (violation de serment)* betrayal. **3** *nmf* traitor. ◆ **parjurer (se)** (1) *vpr* to be faithless to one's promise.

parking [paʀkiŋ] *nm (lieu)* car park, parking lot *(US)*; *(action)* parking. **~ souterrain/à étages** underground/multistorey car park *ou* parking lot *(US)*.

parlement [paʀləmɑ̃] *nm* parliament. ◆ **parlementaire** **1** *adj* parliamentary. **2** *nmf (Pol)* member of Parliament; *(aux USA)* member of Congress; *(négociateur)* negociator, mediator. ◆ **parlementer** (1) *vi (négocier)* to parley.

parler [paʀle] (1) **1** *vi* (**a**) *(faculté physique)* to talk, speak. **votre perroquet parle?** can your parrot talk?; **parlez plus fort!** talk *ou* speak louder!, speak up! (**b**) *(exprimer sa pensée)* to speak; *(bavarder)* to talk. **~ franc** to speak frankly; **faire ~ un suspect** to make a suspect talk; **~ à tort et à travers** to talk through one's hat *; **voilà qui est bien parlé!** well said! (**c**) **~ à qn** to talk *ou* speak to sb; **nous ne nous parlons pas** we're not on speaking terms; **moi qui vous parle** I myself; *(fig)* **trouver à qui ~** to meet one's match; **se ~ à soi-même** to talk to o.s. (**d**) **~ de qch/qn** to talk about sth/sb; **~ de faire qch** to talk of doing sth; **faire ~ de soi** to get o.s. talked about; **~ mal de qn** to speak ill of sb; **toute la ville en parle** it's the talk of the town; **il n'en parle jamais** he never mentions it *ou* refers to it *ou* talks about it; **quand on parle du loup (on en voit la queue)** speak of the devil (and he will appear). (**e**) **~ de qch à qn** to tell sb about sth; **je lui parlerai de cette affaire** I'll speak to him *ou* I'll have a word with him about this business; **on m'a beaucoup parlé de vous** I've heard a lot about you. (**f**) **~ par gestes** to use sign language; **~ à l'imagination** to appeal to the imagination; **les faits parlent d'eux-mêmes** the facts speak for themselves; **de quoi ça parle, ton livre? — ça parle de bateaux** * what is your book about? — it's about ships. (**g**) *(locutions)* **vous parlez!** * *(bien sûr)* you're telling me! *, you bet! *; *(iro)* no chance! *, you must be joking! *; **tu parles d'une brute!** talk about a brute!; **n'en parlons plus!** let's forget (about) it, let's not mention it again; **sans ~ de...** not to mention..., to say nothing of..., let alone...; **vous n'avez qu'à ~** just say the word.

2 *vt langue* to speak. **~ (l')anglais** to speak English; **~ politique** to talk politics.

3 *nm* speech; *(régional)* dialect.

◆ **parlant, e** **1** *adj être* speaking, talking; *(fig) portrait* lifelike; *comparaison* graphic, vivid; *regard* eloquent, meaningful. **2** *adv*: **économiquement** *etc* **~** economically *etc* speaking. ◆ **parlé, e** *adj langue* spoken. ◆ **parleur, -euse** *nm, f* talker. **beau ~** fine talker. ◆ **parloir** *nm [école, prison]* visiting room; *[couvent]* parlour.

Parme [paʀm(ə)] *n* Parma.

parmi [paʀmi] *prép (gén)* among. **~ nous** among us, in our midst; **aller ~ les rues désertes** to go through the deserted streets.

parodie [paʀɔdi] *nf* parody. *(fig)* **une ~ de procès** a parody *ou* mockery of a trial. ◆ **parodier** (7) *vt* to parody.

paroi [paʀwa] *nf (gén)* wall; *[véhicule]* side; *(cloison)* partition. **~ rocheuse** rock face.

paroisse [paʀwas] *nf* parish. ◆ **paroissial, e,** *mpl* **-aux** *adj* parish. **salle ~e** church hall. ◆ **paroissien, -ienne** *nm, f* parishioner. **drôle de ~** * funny customer *.

parole [paʀɔl] *nf* (**a**) *(mot)* word; *(remarque)* remark. **comprenez-vous le sens de ses ~s?** can you understand (the meaning of) what he says?; **c'est ~ d'évangile** it's the gospel truth; *(iro)* **de belles ~s** fair *ou* fine words! *(iro)*; **ce sont des ~s en l'air** it's just idle talk; **assez de ~s, des actes!** enough talk *ou* enough said, let's have some action!; **tout cela est bien joli en ~s mais...** this sounds all very well but... (**b**) *[chanson]* **~s** words, lyrics; **histoire sans ~s** wordless cartoon; *(légende)* **'sans ~s'** 'no caption'. (**c**) *(promesse)* word. **tenir ~** to keep one's word; **manquer à sa ~** to fail to keep one's word, go back on one's word; **c'est un homme de ~** he's a man of his word; **je l'ai cru sur ~** I took his word for it; **~ d'honneur!** you have my word (of honour); **ma ~! *** (upon) my word! (**d**) *(faculté)* speech. **avoir la ~ facile** to be a fluent speaker; **la ~ est d'argent, le silence est d'or** speech is silver, silence is golden. (**e**) *(Ling)* speech, parole. (**f**) *(dans un débat)* **droit de ~** right to speak; **passer la ~ à qn** to hand over to sb; **prendre la ~** to speak; **prendre la ~ pour dire** to take the floor to say.

paroxysme [paʀɔksism(ə)] *nm [maladie]* crisis (point); *[sentiment]* paroxysm, height. **au ~ de la joie** beside o.s. with joy; **atteindre son ~** to be at its height.

parpaing [paʀpɛ̃] *nm (aggloméré)* breeze-block.

parquer [paʀke] (1) **1** *vt voiture* to park; *bétail* to pen (in *ou* up). **2 se ~** *vpr (Aut)* to park.

parquet [paʀkɛ] *nm* (**a**) *(plancher)* (wooden *ou* parquet) floor. (**b**) *(Jur)* public prosecutor's department *ou* office.

parrain [paʀɛ̃] *nm (Rel, fig)* godfather; *(dans une société)* sponsor. ◆ **parrainage** *nm* sponsorship. ◆ **parrainer** (1) *vt* to sponsor.

parricide [paʀisid] **1** *adj* parricidal. **2** *nmf* parricide. **3** *nm (crime)* parricide.

parsemer [paʀsəme] (5) *vt* (**a**) *(répandre)* **~ de** to sprinkle with, strew with; **~ un texte de citations** to scatter quotations through a text. (**b**) *(être répandu sur)* to be scattered *ou* sprinkled over. **ciel parsemé d'étoiles** sky sprinkled *ou* studded with stars; **parsemé de difficultés** riddled with difficulties.

part [paʀ] *nf* (**a**) *(portion)* *(gén, Fin)* share; *[légumes]* portion. **la ~ du lion** the lion's share.
(**b**) *(participation)* part. **prendre ~ à** *travail, manifestation* to take part in, join in; *frais* to share in, contribute to; *débat* to participate in, take part in; *douleur* to share in; **cela prend une grande ~ dans sa vie** it plays a great part in his life; **faire la ~ de la fatigue** to take tiredness into account, make allowances for tiredness; **faire la ~ belle à qn** to give sb more than his (*ou* her) due.
(**c**) *(partie)* part, portion, fraction. **pour une large ~** to a great extent; **pour une petite ~** in a small way.
(**d**) **à ~** *(de côté)* aside, on one side; *(séparément)* separately, on its (*ou* their) own; *(excepté)* except for, apart from; **prendre qn à ~** to take sb aside; **plaisanterie à ~** joking apart *ou* aside; **c'est un homme à ~** he's an exceptional man, he's in a class of his own; **un cas à ~** a special case.
(**e**) **faire ~ de qch à qn** to inform sb of sth, tell sb about sth; **de la ~ de** *(provenance)* from; *(au nom de)* on behalf of; **cela m'étonne de sa ~** I'm surprised at that (coming) from him; **pour ma ~** as for me, as far as I'm concerned; **c'est gentil de sa ~** that's nice of him; *(Téléc)* **c'est de la ~ de qui?** who's calling? *ou* speaking?; **prendre qch en bonne ~** to take sth in good part; **prendre qch en mauvaise ~** to take offence at sth; **de toute(s) ~(s)** from all sides; **d'autre ~** *(de plus)* moreover; **d'une ~... d'autre ~** on the one hand... on the other hand; **de ~ et d'autre** on both sides; **de ~ en ~** right through; **membre à ~ entière** full member; **Français à ~ entière** person with full French citizenship, fully-fledged French citizen.

partage [paʀtaʒ] *nm* (**a**) *(division)* division; *[gâteau]* cutting. **faire le ~ de qch** to divide sth up. (**b**) *(distribution)* sharing out. **le ~ n'est pas juste** it isn't fairly shared out. (**c**) *(participation)* sharing. **il y a ~ des responsabilités** the responsibility is shared; **fidélité sans ~** undivided loyalty. (**d**) *(part)* share; *(fig: sort)* portion, lot. *(Jur)* **recevoir qch en ~** to receive sth in a will.

partager [paʀtaʒe] (3) **1** *vt* (**a**) *(fractionner)* to divide up; *(distribuer)* to share out. **~ en 2/en 2 bouts** to divide in 2/into 2 pieces *ou* bits; **~ son temps entre** to divide one's time between. (**b**) *héritage, sort* to share (*avec* with). **les torts sont partagés** both (*ou* all) parties are at fault, there are faults on both (*ou* all) sides. (**c**) *bonheur, goûts* to share (in); *idée* to share, agree with. **amour partagé** mutual love. (**d**) *[conflit]* to divide. **partagé entre l'amour et la haine** torn between love and hatred. **2 se ~** *vpr*: **ça peut facilement se ~ en 3** it can easily be divided in 3; **le pouvoir ne se partage pas** power is not sth which can be shared; *(fig)* **se ~ le gâteau** to share out the cake; **ils se sont partagé le butin** they shared the booty between them. ◆ **partagé, e** *adj* (**a**) *opinions* divided. (**b**) *(littér: doté)* endowed. **il est bien ~ par le sort** fate has been kind to him.

partance [paʀtɑ̃s] *nf*: **en ~** *train* due to leave; *avion* outward bound; *bateau* sailing, outward bound; **en ~ pour Londres** for London.

partant [paʀtɑ̃] *nm* (**a**) *(coureur)* starter; *(cheval)* runner. **tous ~s** all horses running; **non ~** non-runner. (**b**) *(personne)* person leaving. **je suis ~** I'm quite prepared to join in; **il est toujours ~ pour un bon repas *** he's always ready for a good meal.

partenaire [paʀtənɛʀ] *nmf* partner. **~s sociaux** ≃ unions and management, management and labour; **~s commerciaux** trading partners.

parterre [paʀtɛʀ] *nm* (**a**) *(plate-bande)* border, (flower) bed. (**b**) *(Théât)* stalls, orchestra *(US)*; *(public)* audience.

parti [paʀti] *nm* (**a**) *(groupe)* party. **prendre le ~ de qn, prendre ~ pour qn** to stand up for sb, take sb's side; **prendre ~ (dans une affaire)** *(se rallier)* to take sides (on *ou* in a matter); *(dire ce qu'on pense)* to take a stand (on a matter). (**b**) *(solution)* option, course of action. **prendre le ~ de faire** to make up one's mind to do, decide to do; **prendre son ~ de qch** to come to terms with sth. (**c**) *(personne à marier)* match. (**d**) **tirer ~ de** *situation* to take advantage of, turn to (good) account; *ressources* to put to good use; **faire un mauvais ~ à qn** to beat sb up. (**e**) **~ pris** prejudice, bias; **juger sans ~ pris** to take an unbiased *ou* objective view.

partial, e, *mpl* **-aux** [paʀsjal, o] *adj jugement* biased, prejudiced. **être ~** to be biased *ou* partial. ◆ **partialement** *adv* in a biased way. ◆ **partialité** *nf*: **~** *(en faveur de qn)* partiality (for sb); **~** *(contre qn)* bias (against sb).

participer [paʀtisipe] (1) **1 ~ à** *vt indir (gén)* to take part in; *discussion, jeu* to participate in, join in; *concours* to enter; *complot* to be involved in; *frais* to share in, contribute to; *profits* to share in. *[artiste]* **~ à un spectacle** to appear in a show; **~ à la joie de qn** to share sb's joy; **~ (financièrement) à** *projet* to cooperate in; **on demande aux élèves de ~ davantage pendant le cours** pupils are asked to be more actively involved during the class. **2 ~ de** *vt indir (littér)* to partake of *(littér)*. ◆ **participant, e 1** *adj* participant, participating. **2** *nm, f [concours, course]* entrant (*à* in); *[débat]* participant; *[association]* member (*à* of). **les ~s à la cérémonie** those taking part in the ceremony.

◆ **participation** *nf* (**a**) *[débat]* participation; *[spectacle]* appearance; *[complot]* involvement (*à* in). **c'est la ~ qui compte** what counts is taking part *ou* joining in; '**~ aux frais: 50 F**' 'cost: 50 francs'; **~ électorale** turnout at the polls, voter turnout *(US)*. (**b**) *(Écon) (détention d'actions)* interest. **la ~ (ouvrière)** worker participation; **~ aux bénéfices** profit-sharing; **~ du personnel à la marche d'une entreprise** staff participation *ou* involvement in the running of a firm. ◆ **participe** *nm* participle.

particulariser [paʀtikylaʀize] (1) **1** *vt* to particularize. **2 se ~** *vpr* to be distinguished *ou* characterized (*par* by). ◆ **particularité** *nf* particularity, distinctive characteristic *ou* feature.

particule [paʀtikyl] *nf (Ling, Phys)* particle. **nom à ~** title.

particulier, -ière [paʀtikylje, jɛʀ] **1** *adj* (**a**) *(spécifique)* particular; *style* distinctive. **dans ce cas ~** in this particular case; **cette habitude lui est ~ière** this habit is peculiar to him. (**b**) *(inhabituel)* unusual. **rien de ~ à signaler** nothing in particular *ou* unusual to report; **avec un soin tout ~** with very special care, with particular care. (**c**) *(étrange)* peculiar, odd. (**d**) *(privé)* private. **leçons ~ières** private lessons *ou* tuition. (**e**) **en ~** *(en privé) parler* in private; *(séparément) examiner* separately; *(surtout, entre autres choses)* in particular. **2** *nm* (**a**) *(personne)* person; *(Admin)* private individual. **comme un simple ~** like any ordinary person; **vente de ~ à ~** private sale; **drôle de ~** * odd character *ou* individual. (**b**) *(chose)* **du général au ~** from the general to the particular. ◆ **particulièrement** *adv* particularly. **tout ~** especially, specially.

partie [paʀti] *nf* (**a**) *(fraction)* part. **une petite ~ de l'argent** a small part *ou* amount of the money; **la majeure ~ du temps** most of *ou* the greater part of the time; **en ~** partly, in part; **en majeure ~** largely, for the most part; **faire ~ de** *ensemble, risques* to be part of; *club* to belong to; *gagnants* to be among; **faire ~ intégrante de** to be an integral part of, be part and parcel of. (**b**) *(spécialité)* field, subject. **il n'est pas de la ~** it's not his line *ou* field. (**c**) *(Cartes, Sport)* game; *(Golf)* round. *(fig)* **abandonner la ~** to give up the fight; **la ~ n'est pas égale** it's not an even *ou* a fair match. (**d**) *(Jur) [contrat]* party; *[procès]* litigant; *(Mil: adversaire)* opponent. **se porter ~ civile** to associate in a court action with the public prosecutor; **avoir affaire à forte ~** to have a tough opponent to contend with; **être ~ prenante dans une négociation** to be a party to a negotiation. (**e**) *(Mus)* part. *(Ling)* **les ~s du discours** the parts of speech; *(Anat)* **~s sexuelles** private parts. (**f**) *(sortie, réunion)* party. **~ de pêche** fishing party *ou* expedition; **~ de campagne** outing in the country; **ce n'est pas une ~ de plaisir!** it's not my idea of fun! (**g**) *(locutions)* **ils ont la ~ belle** it's easy for them; **se mettre de la ~** to join in; **je veux être de la ~** I want to be in on this *; **ce n'est que ~ remise** it will be for another time; **prendre qn à ~** to attack sb; **comptabilité en ~ simple/double** single-/double-entry book-keeping.

partiel, -elle [paʀsjɛl] **1** *adj (gén)* partial. **paiement ~** part payment. **2** *nm (Univ)* class exam. ◆ **partiellement** *adv* partially, partly.

partir [paʀtiʀ] (16) *vi* (**a**) *(gén)* to go (*dans, pour* to); *(quitter un lieu)* to leave (*pour* for); *(se mettre en route)* to set off, set out (*pour* for); *(s'éloigner)* to go away *ou* off. **il est parti chercher du pain/faire des courses/en vacances** he has gone to buy some bread/gone (out) shopping/gone (off) on holiday; **allez, je pars** I'm off now; **sa femme est partie de la maison** his wife has left home; **faire ~ qn** to drive sb *ou* chase sb away; *(fig)* **~ en fumée** to go up in smoke; **fais ~ le chat de ma chaise** get the cat off my chair.

(**b**) *[moteur]* to start; *[avion]* to take off; *[train]* to leave; *[coureur]* to be off; *[plante]* to take. **~ en courant** to dash off; **la voiture partit** the car drove off; **~ battu d'avance/gagnant** to begin as if one is already beaten/as if one is sure of success; **attention, prêts? partez!** ready, steady, go!, on your marks, get set, go!; **c'est parti mon kiki!** * here we go! *; **faire ~ une voiture** to start (up) a car.

(**c**) *[fusée, coup de feu]* to go off; *[bouchon]* to pop *ou* shoot out. **ces cris partaient de la foule** these cries came from the crowd; **faire ~** *fusée* to launch; *pétard* to set off.

(**d**) *(être engagé)* **~ sur une idée fausse** to start off with the wrong idea; *[affaire]* **~ bien/mal** to get off to a good/bad start, start (off) well/badly; **le pays est mal parti** the country is in a bad way *ou* in a mess *ou* in a sorry state; **il est bien parti pour gagner** he's all set to win; **~ dans des digressions** to launch into digressions; **~ d'un éclat de rire** to burst out laughing; **la pluie est partie pour toute la journée** the rain has set in for the day; **on est parti pour ne pas déjeuner** at this rate *ou* the way things are going, we won't get any lunch.

(**e**) **~ de** *[contrat, vacances]* to begin on, run from; *[course]* to start *ou* leave from; *[analyse]* to be based on; **un chemin qui part de l'église** a path going from the church; **si tu pars du principe que tu as toujours raison** if you start from the notion that you're always right; **cela part d'un bon sentiment** that comes from his (*ou* her *etc*) kindness.

(**f**) *(disparaître) (gén)* to go; *[tache]* to come out; *[bouton, crochet]* to come off; *[odeur]* to clear. **toute la couleur est partie** all the colour has gone *ou* faded; **faire ~** *tache* to remove; *odeur* to clear, get rid of.

(**g**) **à ~ de** from; **à ~ d'aujourd'hui** from today onwards; **à ~ de maintenant** from now on; **à ~ de** *ou* **en partant de la gauche, c'est le troisième** it is (the) third along from the left; **pantalons à ~ de 300 F** trousers from 300 francs (upwards).

partisan, e [paʀtizɑ̃, an] **1** *adj* (**a**) *(partial)* partisan. (**b**) **être ~ de qch/de faire qch** to be in favour of sth/of doing sth; **être ~ du moindre effort** to be a believer in (taking) the line of least resistance. **2** *nm, f (gén)* supporter; *(Mil)* partisan.

partitif, -ive [paʀtitif, iv] *adj* partitive.

partition [paʀtisjɔ̃] *nf* (**a**) *(Mus)* score. (**b**) *(division)* partition.

partout [paʀtu] *adv* everywhere, everyplace *(US)*. **~ où** wherever; **avoir mal ~** to ache all over; **tu as mis des papiers ~** you've put papers all over the place; *(Sport)* **2/15 ~** 2/15 all; *(Tennis)* **40 ~** deuce.

partouze ‡ [paʀtuz] *nf* orgy.

parure [paʀyʀ] *nf (toilette)* costume; *(bijoux)* jewels; *(fig littér)* finery. **~ de lit** set of bed linen.

parution [paʀysjɔ̃] *nf* appearance, publication.

parvenir [paʀvəniʀ] (22) **1 ~ à** *vt indir* (**a**) *(arriver) (gén)* to reach; *sommet* to get to; *honneurs* to achieve. **~ à maturité** to become ripe; **faire ~ qch à qn** to send sth to sb; **~ à ses fins** to achieve one's ends. (**b**) *(réussir)* **~ à faire qch** to manage to do sth, succeed in doing sth; **il y est parvenu** he managed it. **2** *vi (faire fortune)* to succeed *ou* get on in life. ◆ **parvenu, e 1** *adj* upstart. **2** *nm, f (péj)* parvenu, upstart.

parvis [paʀvi] *nm* square *(in front of church)*.

pas[1] [pɑ] *nm* (**a**) *(gén)* step; *(bruit)* footstep; *(trace)* footprint; *(démarche)* tread. **faire un ~ en arrière** to step back, take a step back; **marcher à grands ~** to stride along; **revenir** *ou* **retourner sur ses ~** to retrace one's steps *ou* path; *(lit, fig)* **~ à ~** step by step; **ne le quittez pas d'un ~** follow him wherever he goes; **arriver sur les ~ de qn** to follow close on sb's heels. (**b**) *(distance)* pace. **c'est à deux**

~ **d'ici** it's just a stone's throw from here. (**c**) *(vitesse)* pace; *(Mil, Danse)* step; *[cheval]* walk. **d'un bon** ~ at a good *ou* brisk pace; **marcher d'un** ~ **lent** to walk slowly; **marcher au** ~ to march; **mettre son cheval au** ~ to walk one's horse; *(Aut)* **rouler au** ~ to drive dead slow, go at a walking pace; **au** ~ **cadencé** in quick time; **au** ~ **de charge** at the charge; **au** ~ **de course** at a run; **au** ~ **de gymnastique** at a jog trot; **faire le** ~ **de l'oie** to goose-step. (**d**) *[montagne]* pass; *[mer]* strait. **le** ~ **de Calais** the Straits of Dover. (**e**) ~ **(de vis)** thread. (**f**) **le** ~ **de la porte** the doorstep; *(Jur)* ~ **de porte** key money *(for shop etc)*. (**g**) **avancer à** ~ **de géant** to take gigantic steps forward; **à** ~ **de loup, à** ~ **feutrés** stealthily; **j'y vais de ce** ~ I'll go straightaway *ou* at once; **mettre qn au** ~ to bring sb to heel, make sb toe the line; **avoir le** ~ **sur qn** to rank before sb; **prendre le** ~ **sur** *considérations* to override; *méthode* to supplant; *personne* to steal a lead over; **sauter le** ~ to take the plunge; **du mensonge à la calomnie il n'y a qu'un** ~ it's a short *ou* small step from lies to slander.

pas² [pɑ] *adv nég* (**a**) *(avec ne)* not. **ce n'est** ~ **vrai, c'est** ~ **vrai** * it isn't *ou* it's not *ou* it is not true; **je ne trouve** ~ **mon sac** I can't *ou* cannot find my bag; **ils n'ont** ~ **de voiture** they don't have *ou* haven't got a car, they have no car; **il m'a dit de ne** ~ **le faire** he told me not to do it; **il n'y a** ~ **que ça** it's not just that; **il n'y a** ~ **que lui** he's not the only one; **je n'en sais** ~ **plus que vous** I know no more *ou* I don't know any more about it than you (do); **il n'est** ~ **moins intelligent que vous** he is no less intelligent than you. (**b**) *(opposition)* **elle travaille, mais lui** ~ she works, but he doesn't; **ils sont 4 et non** ~ **3** there are 4 of them, not 3. (**c**) *(réponses négatives)* ~ **de sucre, merci!** no sugar, thanks!; ~ **du tout** not at all; ~ **encore** not yet; ~ **des masses** ‡ not a lot; **qui l'a prévenu? —** ~ **moi** who told him? — not me *ou* I didn't. (**d**) *(excl)* ~ **un n'est venu** not one *ou* none (of them) came; ~ **possible!** no!, you don't say! *; ~ **de chance!** * hard *ou* bad luck!, too bad! *; **tu es content,** ~ **vrai?** * you're pleased, aren't you?; ~ **d'histoires** no nonsense; **(c'est)** ~ **bête!** that's not a bad idea!; ~ **de ça!** none of that!; **ce n'est** ~ **trop tôt!** it's not before time! (**e**) *(locutions)* ~ **plus tard qu'hier** only *ou* just yesterday; **ils ont** ~ **mal d'argent** they have quite a lot of money.

passable [pɑsabl(ə)] *adj* passable, reasonable, tolerable; *(sur copie d'élève)* fair. *(Univ)* **mention** ~ ≃ pass(mark). ◆ **passablement** *adv travailler* reasonably well; *irritant, long* rather, fairly; *(beaucoup)* quite a lot *ou* a bit * (*de* of).

passade [pɑsad] *nf* passing fancy.

passage [pɑsaʒ] **1** *nm* (**a**) *(venue)* **attendre le** ~ **de l'autobus** to wait for the bus to come (by *ou* past); **observer le** ~ **des oiseaux** to watch the birds fly by *ou* over; **lors de votre** ~ **à la douane** when you go *ou* pass through customs; **l'autobus fait 4** ~**s par jour** the bus goes past 4 times a day; '~ **de troupeaux**' 'cattle crossing'; **commerçant qui travaille avec le** ~ shopkeeper catering for the casual *ou* passing trade; **il est de** ~ **à Paris** he is in *ou* visiting *ou* passing through Paris at the moment; **je l'ai saisi au** ~ I grabbed him as I went by *ou* past. (**b**) *(transfert)* **le** ~ **de l'enfance à l'adolescence** the transition *ou* passage from childhood to adolescence; **le** ~ **du jour à la nuit** the change from day to night; **le** ~ **de l'alcool dans le sang** the entry of alcohol into the bloodstream; ~ **à l'acte** taking action, acting. (**c**) *(lieu)* passage; *(chemin)* way, passage; *(itinéraire)* route; *(rue)* passage(way), alley(way). **on se retourne sur son** ~ people turn round and look when he goes past; **barrer le** ~ **à qn** to block sb's way; **laisser le** ~ **à qn** to let sb pass *ou* past, make way for sb. (**d**) *(Naut)* **payer son** ~ to pay for one's passage, pay one's fare. (**e**) *[livre, symphonie]* passage. (**f**) *(traversée) [rivière, limite]* crossing. (**g**) *(loc)* **il a eu un** ~ **à vide** *(syncope)* he felt a bit faint; *(baisse de forme)* he went through a bad patch *ou* spell. **2** : ~ **clouté** pedestrian crossing; '~ **interdit**' 'no entry'; ~ **à niveau** level crossing, grade crossing *(US)*; ~ **souterrain** subway, underpass; ~ **à tabac** beating up.

passager, -ère [pɑsaʒe, ɛʀ] **1** *adj* (**a**) *hôte* temporary, making a short stay. (**b**) *malaise etc* passing; *inconvénient* temporary; *bonheur, beauté* transient. **pluies** ~**ères** intermittent *ou* occasional showers *ou* rain. (**c**) *rue* busy. **2** *nm, f* passenger. ~ **clandestin** stowaway. ◆ **passagèrement** *adv* temporarily.

passant, e [pɑsɑ̃, ɑ̃t] **1** *adj rue* busy. **2** *nm, f* passer-by. **3** *nm [ceinture]* loop.

passation [pɑsasjɔ̃] *nf [contrat]* signing. ~ **de pouvoirs** transfer of power.

passe [pɑs] **1** *nf (gén)* pass; *(Roulette)* passe; *(chenal)* pass, channel. **être en** ~ **de faire** to be on the way to doing; **être dans** *ou* **traverser une mauvaise** ~ to go through a bad patch, have a rough time; *(fig)* ~ **d'armes** heated exchange. **2** *nm* (*) skeleton *ou* master key. ◆ **passe-droit,** *pl* **passe-droits** *nm* undeserved privilege. ◆ **passe-montagne,** *pl* **passe-montagnes** *nm* balaclava. ◆ **passe-partout** **1** *nm inv* skeleton *ou* master key. **2** *adj inv*: **formule** *etc* ~ all-purpose phrase *etc*. ◆ **passe-plat,** *pl* **passe-plats** *nm* serving hatch. ◆ **passe-temps** *nm inv* pastime.

passé, e [pɑse] **1** *adj* (**a**) *(dernier)* last. **le mois** ~ last month; **au cours des années** ~**es** over the past years. (**b**) *(révolu)* past. ~ **de mode** out of fashion, out of date; **sa gloire** ~**e** his past *ou* former glory; **cette époque est** ~**e maintenant** that era is now over; **il se rappelait le temps** ~ he was thinking back to days *ou* time gone by. (**c**) *(fané)* faded. (**d**) *(plus de)* **il est 8 heures** ~**es** it's past *ou* gone 8 o'clock; **ça fait une heure** ~**e que je t'attends** I've been waiting for you for more than *ou* over an hour. **2** *nm* (**a**) *(gén)* past. **c'est du** ~ it's (all) in the past now. (**b**) *(Gram)* past tense. ~ **antérieur** past anterior; ~ **composé** perfect; ~ **simple** past historic. **3** *prép* after. ~ **6 heures/cette maison** after 6 o'clock/this house.

passementerie [pasmɑ̃tʀi] *nf (objets)* braid, trimmings.

passeport [pɑspɔʀ] *nm* passport.

passer [pɑse] (1) **1** *vi (avec aux être)* (**a**) *(gén)* to pass; *[train]* to come *ou* go past; *[démarcheur]* to call. ~ **en courant** to run past; **il passait dans la rue** he was walking down the street; **où passe la route?** where does the road go?; **la Seine passe à Paris** the Seine flows through Paris; **faire** ~ **qn d'abord** to let sb go first; **une lueur passa dans son regard** a gleam came into his eyes; ~ **au bureau** to call (in *ou* by) *ou* drop in *ou* by at the office; ~ **prendre qn** to call for sb; **le facteur est passé** the postman has been; **j'irai le voir en passant** I'll call to see him on my way past; *(fig)* **soit dit en passant** let me say in passing *ou* by the way. (**b**) *(changer)* to go. ~ **d'une pièce dans une autre** to go from one room to another; ~ **d'un état à l'autre** to change *ou* pass from one state to another; ~ **du rire aux larmes** to switch from laughter to tears; ~ **à l'ennemi** to go over to the enemy; **la photo passa de main en main** the photo was passed *ou* handed round; ~ **dans la langue** to pass *ou* come into the language; **son argent de poche passe en bonbons** his pocket money (all) goes on sweets. (**c**) *[temps]* to go by, pass. **comme le temps passe!** how time flies!; **cela fait** ~ **le temps** it passes the time. (**d**) *[liquide]* to go through; *[courant électrique]* to get through. (**e**) *(être accepté) [proposition, candidat]* to pass, get through; *[plaisanterie, erreur]* to be acceptable; *[aliment]* to go down. **mon déjeuner ne passe pas** my lunch hasn't settled; **il est passé dans la classe supérieure** he's moved up to the next class, he's passed *ou* been promoted to the next grade *(US)*; ~ **directeur** to become *ou* be appointed director; **qu'il soit menteur, passe encore, mais voleur, c'est plus grave** it's one thing if he's a liar, but it's more serious if he's a thief; **passe pour cette fois** I'll let you off this time. (**f**) *[film]* to be showing, be on; *(TV) [émission]* to be on; *[personne]* to be on, appear. ~ **à la télé** * to be on TV *. (**g**) *(dépasser) [oreilles, queue]* to stick out. **son manteau est trop court, la robe passe** her coat is too short — her dress shows underneath (it); **ne laisse pas ~ ton bras par la portière** don't put your arm out of the window. (**h**) *[couleur, beauté]* to fade; *[mode]* to die out; *[douleur]* to pass (off), wear off; *[colère, orage]* to die down; *[jeunesse]* to pass; *(mourir)* to pass on *ou* away. **faire ~ à qn l'envie de faire** to cure sb of doing; **cela fera ~ votre rhume** that will get you over your cold *ou* get rid of your cold for you; **le plus dur est passé** the worst is over now; **ça lui passera!** * *(habitude)* he'll get over it!; *(sentiment)* he'll grow out of it! (**i**) *(Cartes)* to pass. (**j**) *(Aut)* ~ **en première** to go into first (gear); ~ **en seconde** to change into second; **les vitesses passent mal** the gears are stiff. (**k**) ~ **par** *(lit, fig)* to go through; **par où êtes-vous passé?** which way did you go?; ~ **par des difficultés** to have difficulties *ou* a difficult time; **nous sommes tous passés par là** we've all been through that; **il faudra bien en ~ par là** there's no way round it, we'll have to put up with it; **une idée m'est passée par la tête** an idea occurred to me; **elle dit tout ce qui lui passe par la tête** she says whatever comes into her head. (**l**) ~ **pour un imbécile/pour un Allemand** to be taken for a fool/for a German; ~ **pour un séducteur** to be regarded as a lady's man; **il passe pour intelligent** he is supposed to be intelligent; **cela passe pour vrai** it's thought to be true; **se faire ~ pour** to pass o.s. off as; **faire ~ qn pour** to make sb out to be. (**m**) ~ **sous/sur/derrière** *etc* to go under/over/behind *etc*; ~ **devant la maison de qn** to pass *ou* go past sb's house; **l'air passe sous la porte** a draught comes in under the door; **passez donc devant** you go first; ~ **devant une juridiction** to come before a court; **il est passé sous l'autobus** he was run over by the bus; **le travail passe avant les loisirs** work comes before leisure; **ma famille passe en premier** my family comes first; **le confort, ça passe après** comfort is less important *ou* comes second; **les poissons sont passés au travers du filet** the fish slipped through the net; ~ **sur** *faute, détail* to pass over. (**n**) **y** ~ *: **tout le monde y a** *ou* **y est passé** everybody got it, nobody escaped it; **toute sa fortune y a passé** *ou* **y est passée** his whole fortune went on it. (**o**) **laisser ~** *air* to let in; *personne* to let through *(ou* past, in, out *etc)*; *erreur* to overlook, miss; *occasion* to let slip, miss; **nous ne pouvons pas laisser ~ cette affaire sans protester** we cannot let this matter pass without a protest.

2 *vt (avec aux avoir)* (**a**) *frontière* to cross; *porte* to go through; *obstacle* to get through; *haie* to jump *ou* get over. ~ **une rivière à la nage** to swim across a river. (**b**) *examen* to sit, take; *douane* to go through, clear. *visite médicale* to have. (**c**) *temps* to spend *(à faire* doing). **pour ~ le temps** to while away *ou* pass the time. (**d**) *(assouvir)* ~ **sa colère sur qn** to work off *ou* vent one's anger on sb. (**e**) *(omettre) mot* to miss *ou* leave out. ~ **son tour** to miss one's turn; **et j'en passe!** and that's not all!; **j'en passe, et des meilleures!** and that's not all — I could go on!, and that's the least of them! (**f**) *(permettre)* ~ **une faute à qn** to overlook sb's mistake; ~ **un caprice à qn** to indulge sb's whim; **on lui passe tout** he gets away with anything; **passez-moi l'expression** (if you'll) pardon the expression. (**g**) *consigne, maladie* to pass on; *objet* to pass, give, hand; *faux billets* to pass; *(Sport) ballon* to pass *(à* to). ~ **(en fraude) de l'alcool** to smuggle spirits; **tu (le) fais ~** pass *ou* hand it round; **passe-moi du feu** give me a light; *(au téléphone)* **je vous passe M. X** *(gén)* here's Mr X; *(standard)* I'm putting you through to Mr X; **passe-lui un coup de fil** give him a ring *ou* call. (**h**) *pull* to slip on; *robe* to slip into. ~ **une bague au doigt de qn** to slip a ring on sb's finger; ~ **un lacet dans qch** to thread a lace through sth; ~ **la corde au cou de qn** to put the rope round sb's neck. (**i**) ~ **la tête à la porte** to poke one's head round the door; ~ **la main à la fenêtre** to stick one's hand out of the window. (**j**) *(dépasser) maison* to pass, go past. ~ **les bornes** to go too far; **tu as passé l'âge (de ces jeux)** you are too old (for these games); **il ne passera pas la nuit** he won't last the night. (**k**) *thé* to strain; *café* to pour the water on. ~ **la soupe** *(à la passoire)* to strain the soup; *(au mixer)* to blend the soup. (**l**) *(Aut)* ~ **la seconde** to go *ou* change (up *ou* down) into second (gear). (**m**) *film* to show; *disque* to put on, play. **que passent-ils au cinéma?** what's on *ou* showing at the cinema? (**n**) *(Comm) écriture* to enter; *commande* to place; *accord* to reach, come to; *contrat* to sign. *(lit, fig)* ~ **qch aux profits et pertes** to write sth off. (**o**) ~ **le balai** to sweep up; ~ **l'aspirateur** to hoover ®, vacuum; **passe le chiffon dans le salon** dust the sitting room, give the sitting room a dust; ~ **une couche de peinture sur qch** to give sth a coat of paint; **elle lui passa la main dans les cheveux** she ran her hand through his hair; **se ~ les mains à l'eau** to rinse one's hands; **qu'est-ce qu'il lui a passé (comme savon)!** * he gave him a really rough time! *

3 se ~ *vpr* (**a**) *(avoir lieu)* to take place; *(arriver)* to happen. **qu'est-ce qu'il se passe?** what's going on?; **ça ne s'est pas passé comme je l'espérais** it didn't work out as I'd hoped; **tout s'est bien passé** everything went off smoothly; **ça s'est mal passé** it turned out badly, it went off badly; **cela ne se passera pas ainsi!** I shan't let it rest at that!; **il ne se passe pas un seul jour sans qu'il ne pleuve** not a day goes by without rain. (**b**) *(finir) [douleur, orage]* to pass off, be over. (**c**) **se ~ de qch/de faire** to do without sth/doing; **se ~ de qn** to manage without sb; **la citation se passe de commentaires** the quotation needs no comment *ou* speaks for itself.

passerelle [pɑsʀɛl] *nf (pont)* footbridge; *(Aviat, Naut)* gangway; *(du commandant)* bridge; *(fig: passage)* (inter)link.

passeur [pɑsœʀ] *nm [rivière]* ferryman; *[frontière]* smuggler.

passible [pasibl(ə)] *adj*: ~ **d'une amende** *personne* liable to a fine; *délit* punishable by a fine; ~ **d'un impôt** liable for (a) tax.

passif, -ive [pasif, iv] **1** *adj (gén)* passive. **2** *nm (Ling)* passive; *(Fin)* liabilities. ◆ **passivement** *adv* passively. ◆ **passivité** *nf* passivity, passiveness.

passing-shot [pasiŋʃɔt] *nm* passing shot.

passion [pɑsjɔ̃] *nf* passion. **avoir la ~ du jeu** to have a passion for gambling; **aimer/discuter avec ~** to love/argue passionately *ou* heatedly; **sans ~** dispassionately, coolly; *(Rel)* **la P~** the Passion. ◆ **passionnant, e** *adj personne* fascinating; *film* fascinating, gripping, exciting. ◆ **passionné, e 1** *adj personne, haine* passionate; *orateur, jugement* impassioned. **être ~ de** to have a passion for; **débat ~** heated *ou* impassioned debate. **2** *nm, f*: **un ~ de voitures** a car fanatic. ◆ **passionnel, -elle** *adj sentiment* passionate; *crime* of passion. ◆ **passionnément** *adv* passionately. ◆ **passionner** (1) **1** *vt personne* to fascinate, grip; *débat* to inflame. **la musique le passionne** music is his passion, he has a passion for music. **2 se** ~ *vpr*: **se** ~ **pour** *livre* to be fascinated by; *sport, science* to have a passion for.

passoire [pɑswaʀ] *nf (gén, fig)* sieve; *[thé]* strainer; *[légumes]* colander. **avoir la tête comme une** ~ to have a head like a sieve.

pastel [pastɛl] *nm, adj inv* pastel.

pastèque [pastɛk] *nf* watermelon.

pasteur [pastœʀ] *nm (prêtre)* minister, pastor, clergyman, preacher *(US)*; *(littér, Rel: berger)* shepherd.

pasteuriser [pastœʀize] (1) *vt* to pasteurize. ◆ **pasteurisation** *nf* pasteurization.

pastiche [pastiʃ] *nm* pastiche. ◆ **pasticher** (1) *vt* to write a pastiche of.

pastille [pastij] *nf (bonbon)* pastille, lozenge; *[couleur]* block; *[papier]* disc. **~s de menthe** mints; **~s pour la toux** cough pastilles *ou* lozenges *ou* drops.

pastoral, e, *mpl* **-aux** [pastɔʀal, o] **1** *adj (gén)* pastoral. **2** *nf (gén)* pastoral; *(Mus)* pastorale.

Patagonie [patagɔni] *nf* Patagonia.

patate [patat] *nf (*: pomme de terre)* spud ⁑; *(⁑: imbécile)* fathead ⁑, chump *. ~ **(douce)** sweet potato.

patati * [patati] *excl*: **et** ~ **et patata** and so on and so forth.

patatras [patatʀa] *excl* crash!

pataud, e [pato, od] *adj* lumpish, clumsy.

patauger [patoʒe] (3) *vi (avec effort)* to wade about; *(avec plaisir)* to splash about; *(fig: être perdu)* to flounder. ◆ **pataugeoire** *nf* paddling pool.

patchwork [patʃwœʀk] *nm* patchwork.

pâte [pɑt] **1** *nf* (**a**) *(à tarte)* pastry; *(à gâteaux)* mixture; *(à pain)* dough; *(à frire)* batter. (**b**) *[fromage]* cheese. (**c**) **~s (alimentaires)** pasta; *(dans la soupe)* noodles. (**d**) *(gén: substance)* paste; *(crème)* cream. **2** : ~ **d'amandes** almond paste; ~ **brisée** shortcrust *ou* pie crust *(US)* pastry; ~ **dentifrice** toothpaste; ~ **feuilletée** puff *ou* flaky pastry; ~ **de fruits** crystallized fruit; ~ **à modeler** modelling clay, Plasticine ®; ~ **à papier** paper pulp; ~ **sablée** sablé *ou* sugar crust *(US)* pastry. ◆ **pâté** *nm (Culin)* pâté; *(d'encre)* inkblot. ~ **en croûte** ≃ meat pie; ~ **de campagne** pâté de campagne, farmhouse pâté; ~ **de foie** liver pâté; ~ **de maisons** block (of houses); ~ **(de sable)** sandpie, sandcastle. ◆ **pâtée** *nf* (**a**) *[chien, volaille]* mash, feed; *[porcs]* swill. (**b**) *(*: correction)* hiding *.

patelin * [patlɛ̃] *nm* village.

patent, e[1] [patɑ̃, ɑ̃t] *adj* obvious, patent.

patente[2] [patɑ̃t] *nf* (trading) licence. ◆ **patenté, e** *adj* licensed.

patère [patɛʀ] *nf* (hat- *ou* coat-)peg.

paternel, -elle [patɛʀnɛl] **1** *adj* paternal; *(bienveillant)* fatherly. **quitter le domicile** ~ to leave one's father's house; **ma tante** ~**elle** my aunt on my father's side, my paternal aunt. **2** *nm* (⁑) old man ⁑. ◆ **paternalisme** *nm* paternalism. ◆ **paternaliste** *adj* paternalistic. ◆ **paternellement** *adv* paternally; in a fatherly way. ◆ **paternité** *nf* paternity.

pâteux, -euse [pɑtø, øz] *adj (gén)* pasty; *langue* coated; *voix* thick, husky.

pathétique [patetik] **1** *adj* moving, pathetic; *(Anat)* pathetic. **2** *nm* pathos.

pathogène [patɔʒɛn] *adj* pathogenic.

pathologique [patɔlɔʒik] *adj* pathological. ◆ **pathologiquement** *adv* pathologically.

patibulaire [patibylɛʀ] *adj* sinister.

patience [pasjɑ̃s] *nf (gén)* patience. **prendre** ~ to be patient, have patience; **il faut avoir une** ~ **d'ange** it takes the patience of a saint *ou* of Job; **ma** ~ **a des limites!** there are limits to my patience!; *(Cartes)* **faires des ~s** to play patience; ~, **j'arrive!** wait a minute! *ou* hang on! *, I'm coming. ◆ **patiemment** *adv* patiently. ◆ **patient, e** **1** *adj* patient. **2** *nm, f (Méd)* patient. ◆ **patienter** (1) *vi* to wait. **faites-le** ~ ask him to wait; ~ **un instant** to wait *ou* hang on * a moment; **pour** ~ **il regardait les tableaux** to fill in *ou* pass the time he looked at the paintings.

patin [patɛ̃] *nm [patineur]* skate; *[luge]* runner; *(pour le parquet)* cloth pad. ~ **(de frein)** brake block; **~s à glace** iceskates; **~s à roulettes** roller skates; **faire du** ~ **à glace** to go ice-skating. ◆ **patinage** *nm* skating. ~ **artistique** figure skating. ◆ **patiner**[1] (1) *vi (Sport)* to skate; *(Aut) [roue]* to spin; *[embrayage]* to slip. ◆ **patinette** *nf* scooter. ◆ **patineur, -euse** *nm, f* skater. ◆ **patinoire** *nf* skating rink, ice rink.

patine [patin] *nf* patina, sheen. ◆ **patiner**[2] (1) *vt (naturellement)* to give a sheen to; *(artificiellement)* to give a patina to.

pâtir [pɑtiʀ] (2) *vi (littér)* to suffer (*de* because of).

pâtisserie [pɑtisʀi] *nf (magasin)* cake shop, confectioner's; *(gâteau)* cake, pastry; *(art ménager)* cakemaking, pastry-making, baking; *(commerce)* confectionery. ◆ **pâtissier, -ière** *nm, f* confectioner, pastrycook.

patois [patwa] *nm* patois.

patraque * [patʀak] *adj* peaky *, out of sorts.

pâtre [pɑtʀ(ə)] *nm (littér)* shepherd.

patriarche [patʀijaʀʃ(ə)] *nm* patriarch.

patricien, -ienne [patʀisjɛ̃, jɛn] *adj, nm, f* patrician.

patrie [patʀi] *nf (gén)* homeland, fatherland. **Limoges,** ~ **de la porcelaine** Limoges, the home of porcelain.

patrimoine [patʀimwan] *nm (gén)* inheritance; *(Jur)* patrimony; *(Fin: biens)* property; *(fig)* heritage. ~ **national** national heritage.

patriote [patʀiɔt] **1** *adj* patriotic. **2** *nmf* patriot. ◆ **patriotique** *adj* patriotic. ◆ **patriotisme** *nm* patriotism.

patron [patʀɔ̃] *nm* (**a**) *(propriétaire)* owner, boss *; *(gérant)* manager, boss *; *(employeur)* employer, boss *; *(Hist, Rel: protecteur)* patron. ~ **de presse** press baron *ou* tycoon *ou* magnate; **saint** ~ patron saint; ~ **(pêcheur)** skipper. (**b**) *(Couture)* pattern. **taille demi-~/~/grand~** small/medium/large size. ◆ **patronne** *nf* boss *, lady owner (*ou* manager *ou* employer); *(sainte)* patron saint. ◆ **patronage** *nm* (**a**) *(protection)* patronage. (**b**) *(organisation)* youth club. ◆ **patronal, e,** *mpl* **-aux** *adj* employer's. ◆ **patronat** *nm*: **le** ~ the employers. ◆ **patronner** (1) *vt* to sponsor, support.

patrouille [patʀuj] *nf* patrol. ◆ **patrouiller** (1) *vi* to patrol, be on patrol. ~ **dans les rues** to patrol the streets. ◆ **patrouilleur** *nm (soldat)* patroller; *(Naut)* patrol boat.

patte [pat] **1** *nf* (**a**) *(jambe)* leg; *(pied) [chat]* paw; *[oiseau]* foot; *(*: main)* hand, paw *. **~s de devant** forelegs; forefeet; **~s de derrière** hind legs; hind feet; **le chat retomba sur ses ~s** the cat fell on its feet; *[chat]* **faire** ~ **de velours** to draw in *ou* sheathe its claws; **court sur ~s** *personne* short-legged; *table* low; **il est toujours dans mes ~s** * he's always under my feet; **s'il me tombe sous la** ~ * if I get my hands *ou* paws * on him; **tomber dans les ~s de qn** * to fall into sb's clutches. (**b**) *[ancre]* fluke; *(languette)* tongue; *[vêtement]* strap; *(sur l'épaule)* epaulette. (**c**) *(favoris)* **~s (de lapin)** sideburns. **2** : **pantalon à ~s d'éléphant** bell-bottom trousers; **~s de mouche** spidery scrawl; **~-d'oie** *nf, pl* **~s-~** *(à l'œil)* crow's-foot; *(carrefour)* branching crossroads.

pâturer [pɑtyʀe] (1) *vti* to graze. ◆ **pâturage** *nm (lieu)* pasture; *(action)* grazing. ◆ **pâture** *nf (nourriture)* food; *(pâturage)* pasture.

paume [pom] *nf [main]* palm.

paumer ‡ [pome] (1) **1** *vt (perdre)* to lose. **2 se** ~ *vpr* to get lost. ◆ **paumé, e** ‡ **1** *adj* lost. **habiter un bled** ~ to live in a godforsaken hole ‡. **2** *nmf* dropout *.

paupière [popjɛʀ] *nf* eyelid.

paupiette [popjɛt] *nf*: ~ **de veau** veal olive.

pause [poz] *nf (arrêt)* break; *(en parlant, Mus)* pause; *(Sport)* half-time.

pauvre [povʀ(ə)] **1** *adj (gén)* poor; *végétation* sparse; *mobilier* cheap-looking; *excuse, orateur, sourire* weak. **minerai** ~ **en cuivre** ore with a low copper content, ore poor in copper; **air** ~ **en oxygène** air low in oxygen; **pays** ~ **en ressources** country short of *ou* lacking resources; **de** ~**s chances de succès** only a slim *ou* slender chance of success; **elle avait un** ~ **petit air** she looked miserable *ou* wretched. (**b**) ~ **crétin** ‡ stupid ass ‡; ~ **hère** poor wretch; ~ **d'esprit** half-wit; **mon** ~ **mari** my poor husband; ~ **de moi!** poor (little) me!; **mon** ~ **ami** my dear friend. **2** *nmf* poor man *ou* woman. **les** ~**s** the poor, poor people; **mon** ~! my dear fellow; **le** ~! the poor guy! * ◆ **pauvrement** *adv* poorly; *vêtu* shabbily. ◆ **pauvreté** *nf (gén)* poverty; *[mobilier]* cheapness.

pavaner (se) [pavane] (1) *vpr* to strut about.

pavé [pave] *nm [chaussée]* cobblestone; *[cour]* paving stone; *(viande)* thick piece of steak; *(péj: livre)* hefty tome *. **être sur le** ~ *(sans domicile)* to be on the streets; *(sans emploi)* to be out of a job; **mettre qn sur le** ~ to throw sb out; **jeter un** ~ **dans la mare** to set the cat among the pigeons. ◆ **paver** (1) *vt cour* to pave; *chaussée* to cobble. ◆ **pavage** *nm (revêtement)* paving; cobbles.

pavillon [pavijɔ̃] *nm* (**a**) *(villa)* house; *(de gardien)* lodge; *(d'hôpital)* ward, pavilion. ~ **de banlieue** house in the suburbs; ~ **de chasse** hunting lodge. (**b**) *(Naut)* flag. (**c**) *[instrument]* bell; *[phonographe]* horn; *[oreille]* pavilion, pinna. ◆ **pavillonnaire** *adj*: **lotissement** ~ private housing estate; **banlieue** ~ residential suburb with exclusively low-rise housing.

pavoiser [pavwaze] (1) **1** *vt navire* to dress; *monument* to deck with flags. **2** *vi* to put out flags; *(fig)* to rejoice, exult.

pavot [pavo] *nm* poppy.

payer [peje] (8) **1** *vt* (**a**) *somme, employé* to pay; *dette* to pay, settle; *entrepreneur* to pay, settle up with. ~ **comptant** to pay cash; ~ **qn de promesses** to fob sb off with promises; *(fig)* **il est payé pour le savoir** he has learnt that to his cost. (**b**) *travail, marchandise* to pay for. **je l'ai payé de ma poche** I paid for it out of my own pocket; **il m'a fait** ~ **50F** he charged me 50 francs (*pour* for); **travail bien/mal payé** well-paid/badly-paid work. (**c**) *(*: offrir)* ~ **qch à qn** *(gén)* to buy sth for sb; *restaurant, apéritif* to treat sb to sth, stand sb sth; ~ **un voyage à qn** to pay for sb to go on a trip; **sa mère lui a payé une voiture** his mother bought him a car. (**d**) *(récompenser)* to reward (*de* for). (**e**) *faute, crime* to pay for. **il l'a payé de sa vie** it cost him his life; **il me le paiera!** he'll pay for this!
2 *vi* (**a**) *[effort]* to pay off; *[métier]* to be well-paid. **le crime ne paie pas** crime doesn't pay; ~ **pour qn** *(lit)* to pay for sb; *(fig)* to pick up the pieces (for sb), carry the can for sb *. (**b**) ~ **de sa personne** to give of o.s., sacrifice o.s.; **ça ne paie pas de mine, mais** it isn't much to look at but; ~ **d'audace** to take a gamble *ou* a risk.
3 se ~ *vpr* (**a**) **tout se paie** everything must be paid for. (**b**) *(*: s'offrir) objet* to buy o.s., treat o.s. to; *maladie* to get. **se** ~ **une pinte de bon sang** to have a good laugh *; **se** ~ **la tête de qn** to make a fool of sb. (**c**) **se** ~ **d'illusions** to delude o.s. ◆ **payable** *adj*: ~ **en 3 fois** payable in 3 instalments; **l'impôt est** ~ **par tous** taxes must be paid by everyone. ◆ **payant, e** *adj* (**a**) *spectateur* who pays (for his seat). **spectacle** ~ show for which there is an admission charge. (**b**) *(rentable) affaire* profitable; *politique, conduite* which pays off. ◆ **paye** *nf* = **paie.** ◆ **payement** *nm* = **paiement.** ◆ **payeur, -euse 1** *adj*: **service** ~ payments office. **2** *nm, f* payer; *(Mil, Naut)* paymaster. **mauvais** ~ bad debtor.

pays [pei] **1** *nm* (**a**) *(contrée)* country. **des** ~ **lointains** far-off countries *ou* lands. (**b**) *(région)* region. **gens/vin du** ~ local people/wine; **revenir au** ~ to go back home; ~ **de légumes/d'élevage** vegetable-growing/cattle-breeding region; **le** ~ **du vin** the wine country. (**c**) *(village)* village. (**d**) **voir du** ~ to travel around (a lot); **être en** ~ **de connaissance** *(dans une réunion)* to be among familiar faces; *(sur un sujet)* to be on home ground *ou* on familiar territory. **2** : ~ **d'accueil** *[conférences, jeux]* host country; *[réfugiés]* country of refuge; ~ **de Cocagne** land of plenty; ~ **développé** developed country *ou* nation; **le** ~ **de Galles** Wales; ~ **industrialisé** industrialized country *ou* nation; ~ **en voie de développement** developing country.

paysage [peizaʒ] *nm (gén)* landscape, scenery; *(Peinture)* landscape painting. **le** ~ **urbain** the urban landscape; **le** ~ **politique** the political scene; *(gén iro)* **ça fait bien dans le** ~! it adds a nice touch! ◆ **paysagiste** *nmf (Peinture)* landscape painter. *(Agr)* **(jardinier)** ~ landscape gardener.

paysan, -anne [peizɑ̃, an] **1** *adj problème* farming; *revendications* farmers'; *coutumes* country; *(péj) manières* peasant. **2** *nm* countryman, farmer; *(péj)* peasant, rustic. **3** *nf* peasant woman, countrywoman; *(péj)* peasant. ◆ **paysannerie** *nf* peasantry, farmers.

Pays-Bas [peiba] *nmpl*: **les** ~ the Netherlands.

péage [peaʒ] *nm (droit)* toll; *(barrière)* tollgate. **autoroute à** ~ toll motorway, expressway *(US)*; **pont à** ~ toll bridge; **poste de** ~ tollbooth.

peau, *pl* ~**x** [po] **1** *nf* (**a**) *(gén)* skin. **n'avoir que la** ~ **et les os** to be all skin and bones; **attraper qn par la** ~ **du cou** to grab sb by the scruff of his *ou* her neck; **faire** ~ **neuve** *[administration]* to find a new image; *(en changeant d'habit)* to change (one's clothes). (**b**) *(*: corps, vie)* **risquer sa** ~ to risk one's neck * *ou* hide *; **sauver sa** ~ to save one's skin *ou* hide *; **j'aurai sa** ~! I'll have his hide for this! *; **être bien/mal dans sa** ~ *(physiquement)* to feel great */awful; *(mentalement)* to feel quite at ease/ill-at-ease, be at peace/at odds with o.s.; **avoir qn dans la** ~ to be crazy about sb *; **avoir le jeu** *etc* **dans la** ~ to have gambling *etc* in one's blood; **se mettre dans la** ~ **de qn** to put o.s in sb's place *ou* shoes. (**c**) *(cuir)* hide; *(fourrure)* pelt. **gants de** ~ leather gloves. (**d**) *[fromage]* rind; *(épluchure)* peel. **2** : ~ **de chamois** chamois leather, shammy; ~ **de mouton** sheepskin; ~ **de porc** pigskin; **P~-Rouge** *nmf, pl* **P~x-R~s** Red Indian, redskin; ~ **de vache** ‡ *(homme)* bastard ‡; *(femme)* bitch ‡.

peaufiner [pofine] (1) *vt* to polish up, put the finishing touches to.

pébroque * [pebʀɔk] *nm* brolly *, umbrella.

pécari [pekaʀi] *nm* peccary.

peccadille [pekadij] *nf (vétille)* trifle; *(délit)* peccadillo.

pêche¹ [pɛʃ] *nf (fruit)* peach; *(‡: coup)* slap, clout. ~**-abricot/blanche** yellow/white peach; **avoir la** ~ * to be on top form. ◆ **pêcher¹** *nm* peach tree.

pêche² [pɛʃ] *nf* (**a**) *(activité)* fishing; *(saison)* fishing season. **la** ~ **à la ligne** *(mer)* line fishing; *(rivière)* angling; **grande ~ au large** deep-sea fishing; **la ~ aux moules** the gathering of mussels; **aller à la ~** to go fishing; **barque de ~** fishing boat. (**b**) *(poissons)* catch. ◆ **pêcher²** (1) **1** *vt (être pêcheur de)* to fish for; *(attraper)* to catch, land; *coquillages* to gather. ~ **la baleine/la crevette** to go whaling/ shrimping; **où as-tu été ~ cette idée?** * where did you dig that idea up from? * **2** *vi* to go fishing; to go angling. ~ **à l'asticot** to fish with maggots. ◆ **pêcherie** *nf* fishery, fishing ground. ◆ **pêcheur 1** *nm* fisherman; angler. ~ **de crevettes** shrimper; ~ **de corail** coral fisherman; ~ **de perles** pearl diver. **2** *adj bateau* fishing. ◆ **pêcheuse** *nf* fisherwoman; *(à la ligne)* (woman) angler.

péché [peʃe] *nm* sin. ~ **capital** *ou* **mortel** deadly sin; ~ **de jeunesse** youthful indiscretion; **c'est son ~ mignon** he has a weakness for it. ◆ **pécher** (6) *vi (Rel)* to sin. ~ **par imprudence** to be too reckless; ~ **par ignorance** to err through ignorance; ~ **par excès de prudence** to be over-careful; **ça pèche par bien des points** it has a lot of weaknesses *ou* shortcomings. ◆ **pécheur, pécheresse** *nm, f* sinner.

pécule [pekyl] *nm (économies)* savings; *[détenu, soldat]* earnings, wages.

pécuniaire [pekynjɛʀ] *adj* financial.

pédagogie [pedagɔʒi] *nf (éducation)* education; *(art d'enseigner)* teaching skills; *(méthodes d'enseignement)* educational methods. ◆ **pédagogique** *adj méthodes* educational; *(clair) exposé* clear. **stage (de formation)** ~ teacher-training course. ◆ **pédagogue** *nmf* teacher.

pédale [pedal] *nf (gén)* pedal; *[machine à coudre, tour]* treadle. ◆ **pédaler** (1) *vi* to pedal. ◆ **pédalier** *nm* pedal and gear mechanism. ◆ **pédalo** *nm* pedal-boat.

pédant, e [pedɑ̃, ɑ̃t] **1** *adj* pedantic. **2** *nm, f* pedant. ◆ **pédantisme** *nm* pedantry.

pédéraste [pedeʀast(ə)] *nm* homosexual.

pédiatre [pedjatʀ(ə)] *nmf* paediatrician. ◆ **pédiatrie** *nf* paediatrics *(sg)*.

pédicure [pedikyʀ] *nmf* chiropodist.

pedigree [pedigʀe] *nm* pedigree.

pègre [pɛgʀ(ə)] *nf*: **la ~** the underworld; **membre de la ~** gangster, mobster.

peigne [pɛɲ] *nm [cheveux]* comb; *(Tex)* card. ~ **de poche** pocket comb; **passer qch au ~ fin** to go through sth with a fine-tooth comb. ◆ **peignée** * *nf (raclée)* thrashing, hiding. ◆ **peigner** (1) **1** *vt cheveux* to comb; *enfant* to comb the hair of; *(Tex)* to card. **mal peigné** dishevelled, tousled. **2 se ~** *vpr* to comb one's hair.

peignoir [pɛɲwaʀ] *nm* dressing gown. ~ **(de bain)** bathrobe.

peinard, e * [pɛnaʀ, aʀd(ə)] *adj travail, vie* cushy ‡. **être ~** *(pour se reposer)* to take it easy; *(pour agir)* to be left in peace.

peindre [pɛ̃dʀ(ə)] (52) *vt (gén)* to paint; *(fig: décrire)* to portray, depict. ~ **qch en jaune** to paint sth yellow; **se faire ~ par X** to have one's portrait painted by X; **le désespoir se peignait sur leur visage** despair was written on their faces.

peine [pɛn] *nf* (**a**) *(chagrin)* sorrow, sadness. **avoir de la ~** to be sad *ou (moins fort)* upset; **elle m'a fait de la ~** *(pitié)* I felt sorry for her; *(chagrin)* she upset me *ou* made me sad; **avoir des ~s de cœur** to have an unhappy love life; **cela fait ~ à voir** it hurts to see it; **il faisait ~ à voir** he looked a pitiful sight. (**b**) *(effort)* effort, trouble. **cela demande de la ~** that requires an effort; **se donner de la ~ pour faire** to go to a lot of trouble to do; **si tu te donnais seulement la ~ d'essayer** if you would only bother to try; **donnez-vous donc la ~ d'entrer** do come in; **ne vous donnez pas la ~ de venir me chercher** please don't bother to come and collect me; **est-ce que c'est la ~ d'y aller?** is it worth going?; **ce n'est pas la ~ de me le répéter** there's no point in repeating that, you've no need to repeat that; **ce n'est pas la ~** don't bother; **c'était bien la ~ de sortir!** it was a waste of time going out; **tu as été sage, pour la ~, tu auras un bonbon** here's a sweet for being good; **en être pour sa ~** to get nothing for one's pains *ou* trouble; **ne vous mettez pas en ~ pour moi** don't go to *ou* put yourself to any trouble for me. (**c**) *(difficulté)* difficulty. **avoir de la ~ à faire** to have difficulty in doing, find it difficult *ou* hard to do; **sans ~** without difficulty, easily; **il n'est pas en ~ pour trouver des secrétaires** he has no difficulty finding secretaries; **je serais bien en ~ de vous le dire** I'd be hard pushed *ou* hard pressed to tell you. (**d**) *(punition)* punishment, penalty; *(Jur)* sentence. ~ **capitale** *ou* **de mort** capital punishment, death sentence *ou* penalty; ~ **de prison** prison sentence; **sous ~ de mort** on pain of death; **défense d'afficher sous ~ d'amende** billposters will be fined; **pour la ~ tu mettras la table** for that you can set the table. (**e**) **à ~** hardly; **il est à ~ 2 heures** it's only just 2 o'clock; **il gagne à ~ de quoi vivre** he hardly earns enough to keep body and soul together; **à ~ rentré, il a dû ressortir** he had hardly *ou* scarcely got in when he had to go out again, no sooner had he got in than he had to go out again; **il était à ~ aimable** he was barely *ou* scarcely civil. ◆ **peiner** (1) **1** *vi [personne]* to work hard, toil; *[moteur]* to labour. ~ **sur un problème** to toil *ou* struggle with a problem. **2** *vt* to sadden, distress. **ton peiné** *(gén)* sad tone; *(vexé)* aggrieved tone; **il avait l'air peiné** he looked upset.

peintre [pɛ̃tʀ(ə)] *nmf (lit)* painter; *(fig: écrivain)* portrayer. ~ **en bâtiment** house painter. ◆ **peinture** *nf (action, art)* painting; *(ouvrage)* painting, picture; *(surface peinte)* paintwork; *(matière)* paint; *(fig) (action)* portrayal; *(résultat)* portrait. **faire de la ~ (à l'huile/à l'eau)** to paint (in oils/watercolours); **attention à la ~!, ~ fraîche!** wet paint!; ~ **à l'huile** *(tableau)* oil painting; *(matière)* oil paint; *(pour le bâtiment)* oil-based paint; ~ **au pistolet** spray painting. ◆ **peinturlurer** (1) *vt* to daub (with paint). **visage peinturluré** painted face; **se ~ le visage** to plaster make-up on one's face.

péjoratif, -ive [peʒɔʀatif, iv] *adj* derogatory, pejorative.

Pékin [pekɛ̃] *n* Peking. ◆ **pékinois, e** *adj, nm,* **P~(e)** *nm (f)* Pekinese.

pelage [pəlaʒ] *nm* coat, fur.

pêle-mêle [pɛlmɛl] *adv* higgledy-piggledy.

peler [pəle] (5) *vti (gén)* to peel. ◆ **pelé, e 1** *adj personne* bald(-headed); *animal* hairless; *vêtement* threadbare; *terrain* bare. **2** *nm*: **il n'y avait que quatre ~s et un tondu** * there was hardly anyone there.

pèlerin [pɛlʀɛ̃] *nm* pilgrim. ◆ **pèlerinage** *nm* pilgrimage. **faire un ~ à** to go on a pilgrimage to.

pèlerine [pɛlʀin] *nf* cape.

pélican [pelikɑ̃] *nm* pelican.

pelle [pɛl] *nf (gén)* shovel; *[enfant]* spade. ~ **à ordures** dustpan; ~ **à tarte** cake *ou* pie server; **il y en a à la ~** * there are loads of them *; **prendre une ~** ‡ to come a cropper *. ◆ **pelletée** *nf* shovelful; spadeful. ◆ **pelleteuse** *nf* mechanical shovel *ou* digger, excavator. ◆ **pelleteur** *nm* workman *who does the digging*.

pellicule [pelikyl] *nf (gén, Phot)* film. *(Méd)* **~s** dandruff.

Péloponnèse [pelɔpɔnɛz] *nm*: **le ~** the Peloponnese.

pelote [p(ə)lɔt] *nf [laine]* ball. *(fig)* **faire sa ~** to feather one's nest; **~ d'épingles** pin cushion; *(fig)* **c'est une vraie ~ d'épingles** he *(ou* she) is really prickly. **~ (basque)** pelota.

peloter * [p(ə)lɔte] (1) *vt* to pet *, paw *.

peloton [p(ə)lɔtɔ̃] *nm (Mil)* platoon; *(Sport)* pack. **~ d'exécution** firing squad; **être dans le ~ de tête** *(Sport)* to be up with the leaders; *(en classe)* to be among the top few; *[pays, entreprise]* to be one of the front runners.

pelouse [p(ə)luz] *nf* lawn; *(Ftbl, Rugby)* field, ground.

peluche [p(ə)lyʃ] *nf (Tex)* plush; *(poil)* bit of fluff. **jouets en ~** soft *ou* fluffy toys; **chien en ~** fluffy *ou* stuffed dog.

pelure [p(ə)lyʀ] *nf (épluchure)* peeling, piece of peel; *(*‡*: manteau)* (over)coat. *(Bot)* **~ d'oignon** onion skin.

pénal, e, *mpl* **-aux** [penal, o] *adj* penal. **le droit ~** (the) criminal law. ◆ **pénaliser** (1) *vt* to penalize. ◆ **pénalité** *nf (Fin, Sport)* penalty. ◆ **penalty,** *pl* **~ies** *nm (Ftbl)* penalty (kick).

pénates [penat] *nmpl (Myth)* Penates; *(fig hum)* home.

penaud, e [pəno, od] *adj* sheepish.

penchant [pɑ̃ʃɑ̃] *nm (tendance)* tendency, propensity *(à faire* to do); *(faible)* liking, fondness *(pour qch* for sth). **avoir un ~ pour la boisson** to be partial to drink.

pencher [pɑ̃ʃe] (1) **1** *vt objet* to tip up, tilt. **~ la tête** *(en avant)* to bend one's head forward; *(sur le côté)* to lean *ou* tilt one's head to one side. **2** *vi* (**a**) *[mur, arbre]* to lean over; *[navire]* to list; *[objet]* to tilt, tip (to one side). *(fig)* **faire ~ la balance** to tip the scales. (**b**) **~ pour qch** to favour sth; **~ à croire que** to be inclined to believe that. **3 se ~** *vpr* (**a**) to lean over; *(se baisser)* to bend down. **défense de se ~ au dehors** do not lean out of the window. (**b**) **se ~ sur un cas** to look into *ou* study a case; **se ~ sur les malheurs de qn** to turn one's attention to sb's misfortunes. ◆ **penché, e** *adj tableau, poteau* slanting; *objet* tilting, tipping; *écriture* sloping. **être ~ sur ses livres** to be bent over one's books.

pendaison [pɑ̃dɛzɔ̃] *nf* hanging. **~ de crémaillère** house-warming party.

pendant[1]**, e** [pɑ̃dɑ̃, ɑ̃t] **1** *adj* (**a**) *jambes* hanging, dangling; *oreilles* drooping; *branches* hanging, drooping. **la langue ~e** with his *(ou* its) tongue hanging out. (**b**) *(Admin) question* outstanding; *affaire, procès* pending. **2** *nm* (**a**) **~ (d'oreille)** drop earring. (**b**) *(contrepartie)* **le ~ de** *meuble* the matching piece to; *personne* the counterpart of; **faire ~ à, se faire ~** to match.

pendant[2] [pɑ̃dɑ̃] **1** *prép (au cours de)* during; *(durée)* for. **~ la journée/la guerre** during the day/the war; **~ ce temps** meanwhile, in the meantime; *[médicament]* **à prendre ~ le repas** to be taken at mealtimes *ou* during meals; **marcher ~ des kilomètres/des heures** to walk for miles/for hours. **2** : **~ que** *conj* while; **~ que vous serez à Paris, pourriez-vous aller le voir?** while you're in Paris could you go and see him?; *(iro)* **finissez le plat ~ que vous y êtes** why don't you eat it all (up) while you're at it *(iro)*.

pendentif [pɑ̃dɑ̃tif] *nm (bijou)* pendant.

penderie [pɑ̃dʀi] *nf (meuble)* wardrobe.

pendre [pɑ̃dʀ(ə)] (41) **1** *vt objet* to hang up; *criminel* to hang. **~ le linge au dehors** to hang the washing out to dry; **~ la crémaillère** to have a house-warming party; **qu'il aille se faire ~ ailleurs!** * he can go hang! * **2** *vi [objet]* to hang (down) *(de* from); *[bras, jambes]* to dangle; *[joue]* to sag. **laisser ~ ses jambes** to dangle one's legs; **cela lui pend au nez** * he's got it coming to him *. **3 se ~** *vpr (se tuer)* to hang o.s. **se ~ à** *branche* to hang from; **se ~ au cou de qn** to throw one's arms round sb's neck. ◆ **pendu, e 1** *adj* (**a**) *chose* hung up, hanging up. **~ à** hanging from. (**b**) **être ~ au téléphone** * to spend all one's time on the telephone; **être ~ aux lèvres de qn** to hang on sb's every word. **2** *nm, f* hanged man *(ou* woman). **le (jeu du) ~** (the game of) hangman; **jouer au ~** to play hangman.

pendule [pɑ̃dyl] **1** *nf* clock. *(fig)* **remettre les ~s à l'heure** to set the record straight. **2** *nm* pendulum. ◆ **pendulette** *nf* small clock.

pénétrer [penetʀe] (6) **1** *vi* (**a**) *[personne, véhicule]* **~ dans** *bâtiment* to enter; *groupe* to penetrate; **faire ~ qn dans le salon** to show *ou* let sb into the lounge; **des voleurs ont pénétré dans la maison** thieves broke into the house. (**b**) *[air, liquide]* to come *ou* get in. **le soleil pénètre dans la pièce** the sun is shining into the room; **~ dans le bois** *[balle]* to penetrate the wood; *[vernis]* to soak into the wood; **faire ~ de l'air (dans)** to let fresh air in(to); **faire ~ une crème (dans la peau)** to rub a cream in(to the skin). **2** *vt (gén, fig)* to penetrate; *[odeur, sentiment]* to fill. **le froid les pénétrait jusqu'aux os** the cold cut *ou* went right through them; **~ les intentions de qn** to fathom sb's intentions; **pénétré de pitié** filled with pity. **3 se ~** *vpr*: **se ~ d'une idée** to get an idea firmly fixed *ou* set in one's mind, become convinced of an idea. ◆ **pénétrable** *adj* penetrable *(à* by). ◆ **pénétrant, e** *adj pluie* drenching; *froid* piercing, biting; *odeur, regard, esprit, crème* penetrating. ◆ **pénétration** *nf (gén)* penetration. ◆ **pénétré, e** *adj air, ton* earnest. **être ~ de** *sa propre importance* to be full of; *ses obligations* to be highly conscious of.

pénible [penibl(ə)] *adj travail* tiresome, tedious; *personne* tiresome; *nouvelle, maladie* painful *(à* to). **~ à lire** hard *ou* difficult to read; **l'hiver a été ~** the winter has been unpleasant; **il est vraiment ~** * he's a thorough nuisance; **la lumière violente lui est ~** bright light hurts his eyes; **ce bruit est ~ à supporter** this noise is unpleasant *ou* painful to listen to; **il m'est ~ de constater que** I am sorry to find that. ◆ **péniblement** *adv (difficilement)* with difficulty; *(tristement)* painfully.

péniche [peniʃ] *nf* barge.

pénicilline [penisilin] *nf* penicillin.

péninsule [penɛ̃syl] *nf* peninsula.

pénitence [penitɑ̃s] *nf (gén)* punishment; *(Rel) (repentir)* penitence; *(peine, sacrement)* penance. **faire ~** to repent *(de* of); **mettre qn en ~** to make sb stand in the corner. ◆ **pénitencier** *nm* (**a**) *(prison)* prison, penitentiary *(US)*. (**b**) *(Rel)* penitentiary. ◆ **pénitent, e** *adj, nm, f* penitent. ◆ **pénitentiaire** *adj* prison. **établissement ~** penal establishment.

Pennsylvanie [pɛnsilvani] *nf* Pennsylvania.

pénombre [penɔ̃bʀ(ə)] *nf (faible clarté)* half-light; *(obscurité)* darkness.

pensable [pɑ̃sabl(ə)] *adj* thinkable. **ce n'est pas ~** it's unthinkable.

pensée[1] [pɑ̃se] *nf (gén)* thought. **si vous voulez connaître le fond de ma ~** if you want to know what I really think (about it) *ou* how I really feel about it; **venir à la ~ de qn** to occur to sb; **les soucis qui hantent sa ~** the worries that haunt his thoughts *ou* his mind; **la ~ marxiste** Marxist thinking.

pensée[2] [pɑ̃se] *nf (Bot)* pansy.

penser [pɑ̃se] (1) **1** *vi* to think. **~ tout haut** to think out loud; **~ à qch/à faire** *(réfléchir)* to think about sth/about doing; *(prévoir)* to think of sth/of doing; *(se souvenir)* to remember sth/to do; **pensez-y avant d'accepter** think it over *ou* give it some thought before you accept; **il me fait ~ à**

mon père he makes me think of *ou* he reminds me of my father; **fais m'y** ~ don't let me forget, remind me about that; **faire qch sans y** ~ to do sth without thinking (about it); **n'y pensons plus!** let's forget it!; **il vient? — pensez-vous!** is he coming? — you must be joking! *; **il va accepter? — je pense bien!** will he accept? — of course he will!
2 *vt* (**a**) *(avoir une opinion)* to think. **il en pense du bien/du mal** he has a high/poor opinion of it; **que pensez-vous de ce projet?** what do you think *ou* how do you feel about this plan?; **que penseriez-vous d'un voyage à Rome?** what would you say to *ou* how would you fancy a trip to Rome? (**b**) *(supposer)* to think. **je pense que oui/non** I think so/don't think so; **ce n'est pas si bête qu'on le pense** it's not such a silly idea as you might think; **ils pensent avoir trouvé une maison** they think they've found a house; **vous pensez bien qu'elle a refusé** you can well imagine that she refused; **j'ai pensé mourir** I thought I was going to die; **tout laisse à** ~ **qu'elle l'a quitté** there is every indication that she has left him. (**c**) ~ **faire** *(avoir l'intention de)* to be thinking of doing, consider doing, intend to do; *(espérer)* to hope *ou* expect to do. (**d**) *(concevoir) projet, machine* to think out. ◆ **penseur** *nm* thinker. ◆ **pensif, -ive** *adj* pensive, thoughtful. ◆ **pensivement** *adv* pensively, thoughtfully.

pension [pɑ̃sjɔ̃] *nf* (**a**) *(allocation)* pension. ~ **de retraite** retirement *ou* old age pension; ~ **alimentaire** *[étudiant]* living allowance; *[divorcée]* alimony. (**b**) *(hôtel)* boarding house; *(Scol)* boarding school; *(hébergement)* board and lodging. ~ **de famille** ≃ boarding house, guesthouse. **être en** ~ **chez qn** to board with sb; **chambre sans/avec demi-**~ room *(with no meals provided)*/with half-board; ~ **complète** full board. ◆ **pensionnaire** *nmf (Scol)* boarder; *[famille]* lodger; *[hôtel]* resident. ◆ **pensionnat** *nm* boarding school. ◆ **pensionné, e** *nm, f* pensioner. ◆ **pensionner** (1) *vt* to give a pension to.

pentagone [pɛ̃tagɔn] *nm* pentagon.

pente [pɑ̃t] *nf* slope; **être en** ~ **douce/raide** to slope (down) gently/steeply; **la** ~ **d'un toit** the pitch *ou* slope of a roof; **en** ~ *toit* sloping; *allée* on a slope. **rue en** ~ steep street; **suivre sa** ~ **naturelle** to follow one's natural tendency; **être sur une mauvaise** ~ to be going downhill; *(fig)* **remonter la** ~ to get on one's feet again; *(fig)* ~ **glissante** slippery slope. ◆ **pentu, e** *adj* sloping.

Pentecôte [pɑ̃tkot] *nf (dimanche)* Whit Sunday; *(période)* Whitsun.

pénurie [penyʀi] *nf* shortage. ~ **de** shortage *ou* lack of.

pépé * [pepe] *nm* grandad *, grandpa *.

pépée ‡ [pepe] *nf (fille)* bird ‡, chick *.

pépère * [pepɛʀ] **1** *nm (pépé)* grandad *, grandpa *; *(homme)* (old) man. **2** *adj vie, endroit* quiet; *travail* cushy *.

pépie [pepi] *nf*: **avoir la** ~ * to be parched *.

pépier [pepje] (7) *vi* to chirp, chirrup, tweet.

pépin [pepɛ̃] *nm* (**a**) *(Bot)* pip. **sans** ~**s** seedless. (**b**) *(*: ennui)* snag, hitch. **avoir un** ~ to hit a snag *. (**c**) *(*: parapluie)* brolly *, umbrella.

pépinière [pepinjɛʀ] *nf (lit)* tree nursery; *(fig)* breeding-ground, nursery (*de* for). ◆ **pépiniériste** *nm* nurseryman.

perception [pɛʀsɛpsjɔ̃] *nf* (**a**) *(sensation)* perception. (**b**) *[impôt]* collection; *(bureau)* tax (collector's) office. ◆ **percepteur** *nm* tax collector, tax man *. ◆ **perceptible** *adj* (**a**) *son, ironie* perceptible (*à* to). (**b**) *impôt* collectable.

percer [pɛʀse] (3) **1** *vt* (**a**) *(trouer)* to pierce; *(avec perceuse)* to drill *ou* bore through; *chaussette* to wear a hole in; *coffre-fort* to break open; *abcès* to lance; *tympan* to burst; *nuages, lignes ennemies* to pierce, break through. **avoir une poche percée** to have a hole in one's pocket; **percé de trous** full of holes. (**b**) *trou, ouverture* to pierce, make; *canal* to build; *tunnel* to bore, drive (*dans* through). **mur percé de petites fenêtres** wall with small windows set in it. (**c**) *mystère* to penetrate. ~ **qch à jour** to see (right) through sth. (**d**) ~ **une dent** to cut a tooth.
2 *vi [abcès]* to burst; *[plante]* to come up; *[soleil, armée]* to break through; *[émotion]* to show; *[vedette]* to become famous. **il a une dent qui perce** he's cutting a tooth; *(Comm)* ~ **sur un nouveau marché** to break into a new market; **rien n'a percé des négociations** no news of the negotiations has filtered through.
◆ **perçant, e** *adj (gén)* piercing; *vue* sharp, keen. ◆ **perce** *nf*: **mettre en** ~ *tonneau* to broach, tap. ◆ **percée** *nf [forêt]* opening, clearing; *[mur]* breach, gap; *(Mil, Sci, Écon)* breakthrough; *(Rugby)* break. ◆ **percement** *nm [trou]* piercing; *(avec perceuse)* drilling, boring; *[rue]* building, driving; *[fenêtre]* making. ◆ **perce-neige** *nm inv* snowdrop. ◆ **perceur** *nm* driller. ~ **de coffre-fort** * safe-breaker. ◆ **perceuse** *nf* drill. ~ **à percussion** hammer drill.

percevoir [pɛʀsəvwaʀ] (28) *vt* (**a**) *(ressentir)* to perceive, detect, make out. (**b**) *taxe* to collect; *indemnité* to receive, get. ◆ **percevable** *adj impôt* collectable, payable.

perche [pɛʀʃ(ə)] *nf* (**a**) *(poisson)* perch. (**b**) *(bâton)* pole; *(*: personne)* beanpole *.

percher [pɛʀʃe] (1) **1** *vi [oiseau]* to perch; *[volailles]* to roost; *(‡: habiter)* to live; *(pour la nuit)* to stay, kip *. **2** *vt (*: mettre)* to stick. **3 se** ~ *vpr (lit, fig)* to perch. **être perché sur** to be perched upon. ◆ **perchoir** *nm (lit, fig)* perch; *[volailles]* roost.

percolateur [pɛʀkɔlatœʀ] *nm* commercial (coffee) percolating machine.

percuter [pɛʀkyte] (1) **1** *vt (gén)* to strike. **2** *vi*: ~ **contre** *[avion, voiture]* to crash into. ◆ **percussion** *nf (gén)* percussion. ◆ **percussionniste** *nmf* percussionist. ◆ **percutant, e** *adj discours* forceful, powerful. ◆ **percuteur** *nm* firing pin, hammer.

perdre [pɛʀdʀ(ə)] (41) **1** *vt* (**a**) *(gén)* to lose; *nom, date* to forget; *habitude* to get out of. *(lit, fig)* ~ **qn de vue** to lose sight of sb; **j'ai perdu le goût de rire** I don't feel like laughing any longer; ~ **son chemin** to lose one's way; ~ **l'équilibre** to lose one's balance; ~ **espoir/l'appétit/la vie** to lose hope/one's appetite/one's life; **l'arbre perd ses feuilles** the tree is shedding *ou* losing its leaves. (**b**) *temps, argent* to waste (*à qch* on sth, *à faire* doing); *occasion* to lose, miss; *aliment* to spoil. **tu ne l'as jamais vu? tu n'y perds rien!** you've never seen him? you haven't missed anything!; **il a perdu l'occasion de se taire** he'd have done better to keep quiet, it was a pity he didn't keep quiet; **il ne perd rien pour attendre!** I'll be quits with him yet! (**c**) *(causer préjudice à)* to ruin. **son ambition l'a perdu** ambition was his downfall *ou* the ruin of him. **2** *vi* (**a**) *(gén)* to lose (*sur* on). **tu as perdu en ne venant pas** you missed something by not coming; **tu ne perds pas au change** you get the better of the deal; **il a perdu au change** he lost out (on the deal), he came off worst. (**b**) *[réservoir]* to leak. **3 se** ~ *vpr* (**a**) *(s'égarer)* to get lost, lose one's way. **se** ~ **dans les détails** to get bogged down *ou* get lost in the details; **il y a trop de chiffres, je m'y perds** there are too many figures, I'm all confused. (**b**) *(disparaître)* to disappear, vanish; *[coutume]* to die out; *(Naut)* to sink. **se** ~ **dans la foule** to disappear *ou* vanish into the crowd; **son cri s'est perdu dans le vacarme** his shout was lost in the din. (**c**) *(devenir inutilisable)* to be wasted; *[denrées]* to go bad. **il y a des gifles qui se perdent** he *(ou* she *etc)* deserves a good slap. ◆ **perdant, e 1** *adj numéro, cheval* losing. **je suis ~** *(gén)* I lose out *; *(financièrement)* I'm out of pocket. **2** *nm, f* loser. ◆ **perdition** *nf* (**a**) *(Rel)* perdition. **lieu de ~** den of vice *ou* iniquity. (**b**) *(Naut)* **en ~** in distress. ◆ **perdu, e** *adj* (**a**) *(gén)* lost; *malade* done for; *balle, chien* stray. **je suis ~** *(égaré)* I'm lost; *(désespéré)* I'm done for; *(embrouillé)* I'm lost *ou* all at sea; **c'est de l'argent ~** it's money down the drain, it's a waste of money; **pendant ses moments ~s** in his spare time; **ma récolte est ~e** my harvest is ruined. (**b**) *endroit* out-of-the-way, isolated. (**c**) *emballage* non-returnable.

perdrix [pɛʀdʀi] *nf* partridge. ◆ **perdreau,** *pl* **~x** *nm* (young) partridge.

père [pɛʀ] *nm* (**a**) father. **~ de famille** father; **Martin (le) ~** Martin senior; **de ~ en fils** from father to son. (**b**) *(ancêtres)* **~s** forefathers, ancestors. (**c**) *(Zool) [animal]* sire. (**d**) *(Rel)* father. **le P~ X** Father X; **mon P~** Father; **le P~ éternel** the Heavenly Father; **les P~s de l'Église** the Church Fathers. (**e**) *(*: monsieur)* **le ~ Benoit** old (man) Benoit *; **un ~ tranquille** a quiet fellow; **le ~ Noël** Father Christmas, Santa Claus.

péremptoire [peʀɑ̃ptwaʀ] *adj* peremptory.

perfection [pɛʀfɛksjɔ̃] *nf* perfection. **à la ~** to perfection. ◆ **perfectionné, e** *adj* sophisticated. ◆ **perfectionnement** *nm* perfection, perfecting *(de* of), improvement *(de* in). **cours de ~** proficiency course. ◆ **perfectionner** (1) **1** *vt* to improve, perfect. **2 se ~** *vpr [chose]* to improve; *[personne]* to improve o.s. **se ~ en anglais** to improve one's English.

perfide [pɛʀfid] *adj (littér)* perfidious. ◆ **perfidie** *nf (vice)* perfidy; *(acte)* perfidious act.

perforer [pɛʀfɔʀe] (1) *vt (trouer)* to pierce; *(poinçonner)* to punch; *(Méd)* to perforate. **carte perforée** punch card; **bande perforée** punched tape. ◆ **perforateur, -trice 1** *nm, f (ouvrier)* punch-card operator. **2** *nf (Ordin)* card punch. ◆ **perforation** *nf (Méd)* perforation; *(Ordin)* punch.

performance [pɛʀfɔʀmɑ̃s] *nf* (**a**) *(résultat)* result, performance; *(exploit)* feat, achievement. (**b**) *[voiture, machine]* **~s** performance. (**c**) *(Ling)* **la ~** performance. ◆ **performant, e** *adj machine* high-performance; *résultat* outstanding, impressive; *investissement* high-return; *administrateur* effective.

perfusion [pɛʀfyzjɔ̃] *nf* drip, perfusion. **mettre qn/être sous ~** to put sb/be on the drip.

péricliter [peʀiklite] (1) *vi [affaire]* to collapse.

péril [peʀil] *nm (littér)* peril, danger. **mettre en ~** to imperil, endanger; **au ~ de sa vie** at the risk of one's life; **le ~ jaune** the yellow peril. ◆ **périlleux, -euse** *adj* perilous.

périmé, e [peʀime] *adj*: **être ~** *[billet]* to be out-of-date *ou* no longer valid; *[idée]* to be outdated.

périmètre [peʀimɛtʀ(ə)] *nm (Math)* perimeter; *(zone)* area.

période [peʀjɔd] *nf (gén)* period. **une ~ de chaleur** a hot spell, a heat wave; **pendant la ~ électorale** at election time. ◆ **périodicité** *nf* periodicity. ◆ **périodique 1** *adj* periodic. **2** *nm (Presse)* periodical. ◆ **périodiquement** *adv* periodically.

péripétie [peʀipesi] *nf* event, episode. **les ~s d'une révolution** the turns taken by a revolution; **après bien des ~s** after all sorts of incidents; **voyage plein de ~s** eventful journey.

périphérie [peʀifeʀi] *nf (limite)* periphery; *(banlieue)* outskirts. ◆ **périphérique 1** *adj (Anat, Math)* peripheral; *quartier* outlying. **poste** *ou* **radio** *ou* **station ~** private radio station *(broadcasting from a neighbouring country)*. **2** *nm (Ordin)* peripheral. **(boulevard) ~** ring road, circular route *(US)*; *(Ordin)* **~ entrée-sortie** input-output device.

périphrase [peʀifʀɑz] *nf* circumlocution.

périple [peʀipl(ə)] *nm (par mer)* voyage; *(par terre)* tour, trip, journey.

périr [peʀiʀ] (2) *vi (littér)* to perish *(littér)*, die; *[navire]* to go down, sink. **~ noyé** to drown; **faire ~** to kill. ◆ **périssable** *adj* perishable.

périscolaire [peʀiskɔlɛʀ] *adj* extracurricular.

périscope [peʀiskɔp] *nm* periscope.

péritonite [peʀitɔnit] *nf* peritonitis.

perle [pɛʀl(ə)] *nf (bijou)* pearl; *(boule)* bead; *[eau, sang]* drop; *[sueur]* bead; *(fig: trésor, hum: erreur)* gem. **~ fine/de culture** natural/cultured pearl.

permanence [pɛʀmanɑ̃s] *nf* (**a**) *(durée)* permanence. **en ~** *siéger* permanently; *crier* continuously. (**b**) *(service)* **être de ~** to be on duty *ou* on call; **une ~ est assurée le dimanche** there is someone on duty *ou* on call on Sundays. (**c**) *(bureau)* (duty) office; *(Pol)* committee room; *(Scol)* study room *ou* hall *(US)*. ◆ **permanent, e 1** *adj (gén)* permanent; *armée, comité* standing; *spectacle* continuous. *(Ciné)* **~ de 2 heures à minuit** continuous showings from 2 o'clock to midnight. **2** *nm (Pol)* (party) official. **3** *nf (Coiffure)* perm.

perméable [pɛʀmeabl(ə)] *adj* permeable. **~ à l'air** air permeable.

permettre [pɛʀmɛtʀ(ə)] (56) **1** *vt* (**a**) *(gén)* to allow, permit. **~ à qn de faire** *(autoriser)* to allow *ou* permit sb to do, let sb do; *(donner la possibilité)* to enable sb to do; *(donner le droit)* to entitle sb to do; **il se croit tout permis** he thinks he can do what he likes *ou* as he pleases; **est-il permis d'être aussi bête!** how can anyone be so stupid!; **mes moyens ne me le permettent pas** I cannot afford it; **mes occupations ne me le permettent pas** I'm too busy to be able to do it. (**b**) *(sollicitation)* **vous permettez?** may I?; **permettez-moi de vous dire que** may I say that, let me tell you that; **vous permettez que je fume?** do you mind if I smoke?; **permettez! je ne suis pas d'accord** if you don't mind! *ou* pardon me! I disagree.

2 se ~ *vpr (gén)* to allow o.s.; *fantaisie* to indulge o.s. in. **je ne peux pas me ~ d'acheter ce manteau** I can't afford to buy this coat; **il s'est permis de partir sans permission** he took the liberty of going without permission; **je me permettrai de vous dire que** let me tell you that; **je me permets de vous écrire au sujet de...** I am writing to you in connection with...

◆ **permis, e 1** *adj limites* permitted. **il est ~ d'en douter** one might *ou* may well doubt this. **2** *nm* permit, licence. **~ (de conduire)** *(carte)* driving licence, driver's license *(US)*; *(épreuve)* driving test; **~ de construire** planning permission; **~ d'inhumer** burial certificate; **~ moto** motorbike licence; **~ poids lourds** heavy-goods vehicle licence; **~ de séjour** residence permit; **~ de travail** work permit. ◆ **permissif, -ive** *adj* permissive. ◆ **permission** *nf* (**a**) permission. **demander/donner la ~** to ask/give permission *(de* to). (**b**) *(Mil) (congé)* leave; *(certificat)* pass. **en ~** on leave; **~ de minuit** late pass. ◆ **permissionnaire** *nm* soldier on leave. ◆ **permissivité** *nf* permissiveness.

permuter [pɛʀmyte] (1) **1** *vt (gén)* to change round, permutate; *(Math)* to permutate. **2** *vi* to change, swap (seats *ou* jobs *etc*). ◆ **permutation** *nf* permutation.

pernicieux, -euse [pɛʀnisjø, øz] *adj* pernicious.

pérorer [peʀɔʀe] (1) *vi* to hold forth *(péj)*, declaim *(péj)*.

Pérou [peʀu] *nm* Peru. **ce n'est pas le ~ *** it's no great fortune.

perpendiculaire [pɛʀpɑ̃dikylɛʀ] *adj, nf* perpendicular *(à* to). ◆ **perpendiculairement** *adv* perpendicularly. ~ **à** at right angles to, perpendicular to.

perpétrer [pɛʀpetʀe] (6) *vt* to perpetrate.

perpétuel, -elle [pɛʀpetɥɛl] *adj (gén)* perpetual; *secrétaire* permanent; *rente* life. ◆ **perpétuellement** *adv* perpetually. ◆ **perpétuer** (1) **1** *vt* to perpetuate. **2 se** ~ *vpr [usage]* to be perpetuated; *[espèce]* to survive. ◆ **perpétuité** *nf* perpetuity. **à** ~ *condamnation* for life; *concession* in perpetuity.

perplexe [pɛʀplɛks(ə)] *adj* perplexed, puzzled. **laisser** ~ to perplex, puzzle. ◆ **perplexité** *nf* perplexity.

perquisition [pɛʀkizisjɔ̃] *nf (Police)* search. ◆ **perquisitionner** (1) *vi* to carry out a search. ~ **au domicile de qn** to search sb's house.

perron [pɛʀɔ̃] *nm* steps *(leading to entrance)*.

perroquet [pɛʀɔkɛ] *nm (Orn, fig)* parrot.

perruche [peʀyʃ] *nf (Orn)* budgerigar, budgie *; *(bavard)* chatterbox *.

perruque [peʀyk] *nf* wig.

persan, e [pɛʀsɑ̃, an] *adj, nm,* **P~(e)** *nm(f)* Persian.

perse [pɛʀs(ə)] **1** *adj, nm,* **P~** *nmf* Persian. **2** *nf:* **la P~** Persia.

persécuter [pɛʀsekyte] (1) *vt* to persecute. ◆ **persécuteur, -trice** *nm, f* persecutor. ◆ **persécution** *nf* persecution.

persévérer [pɛʀseveʀe] (6) *vi* to persevere. ◆ **persévérance** *nf* perseverance.

persienne [pɛʀsjɛn] *nf* (metal) shutter.

persiflage [pɛʀsiflaʒ] *nm* mockery.

persil [pɛʀsi] *nm* parsley.

persister [pɛʀsiste] (1) *vi* to persist. ~ **dans qch/à faire** to persist in sth/in doing; ~ **dans son opinion** to stick to one's opinion; **je persiste à croire que...** I still believe that...; **il persiste un doute** a doubt remains. ◆ **persistance** *nf* persistence (*à faire* in doing). **avec** ~ *(tout le temps)* persistently; *(avec obstination)* persistently, doggedly, stubbornly. ◆ **persistant, e** *adj* persistent.

personne [pɛʀsɔn] **1** *nf* (**a**) *(être humain)* person. **deux ~s** two people, two persons *(US)*; **le respect de la ~ humaine** respect for human dignity; **les ~s qui...** those who..., the people who...; **100 F par** ~ 100 francs per head *ou* per person; **par ~ interposée** through an intermediary, through a third party. (**b**) *(corps)* **être bien (fait) de sa** ~ to be good-looking; **toute sa ~ inspire confiance** his whole being inspires confidence; **il prend soin de sa petite** ~ he looks after himself; **je l'ai vu en** ~ I saw him in person; **je m'en occupe en** ~ I'll see to it personally; **c'est la bonté en** ~ he's (*ou* she's) kindness itself *ou* personified. (**c**) *(Gram)* person. **à la première** ~ in the first person. **2** *pron (quelqu'un)* anyone, anybody; *(aucun)* no one, nobody. **elle le sait mieux que** ~ she knows that better than anyone *ou* anybody (else); **elle sait faire le café comme** ~ she makes better coffee than anyone (else); **presque** ~ hardly anyone *ou* anybody, practically no one *ou* nobody; **il n'y a** ~ there's no one *ou* nobody there, there isn't anyone *ou* anybody there; **ce n'est la faute de** ~ it's no one's *ou* nobody's fault. **3** : ~ **âgée** elderly person; ~ **à charge** dependent; *(Jur)* ~ **civile** *ou* **morale** legal entity; *(Jur)* ~ **physique** individual. ◆ **personnage** *nm (individu)* character, individual; *(célébrité)* personage, (very) important person; *[roman]* character; *[tableau]* figure. ~ **influent** influential person; *(lit, fig)* **jouer un** ~ to play a part. ◆ **personnalité** *nf (gén)* personality. **avoir une forte ~/de la** ~ to have a strong personality/lots of personality.

personnel, -elle [pɛʀsɔnɛl] **1** *adj (gén, Gram)* personal; *(égoïste)* selfish, self-centred. **fortune ~elle** personal *ou* private fortune; **mon opinion ~elle** my own *ou* personal opinion. **2** *nm [école, château]* staff; *[usine, service public]* personnel, employees. **faire partie du** ~ to be on the staff; ~ **en civil/en tenue** plain-clothes/uniformed staff; **chef du** ~ personnel officer *ou* manager. ◆ **personnellement** *adv* personally.

personnifier [pɛʀsɔnifje] (7) *vt* to personify, embody. **être la bêtise personnifiée** to be stupidity itself *ou* personified. ◆ **personnification** *nf* personification, embodiment.

perspective [pɛʀspɛktiv] *nf* (**a**) *(Art)* perspective. (**b**) *(point de vue) (lit)* view; *(fig)* angle, viewpoint. (**c**) *(idée, possibilité)* prospect. **en** ~ in prospect; **à la ~ de** at the prospect of.

perspicace [pɛʀspikas] *adj* perspicacious. ◆ **perspicacité** *nf* insight, perspicacity.

persuader [pɛʀsɥade] (1) *vt* to persuade, convince (*qn de qch* sb of sth). **j'en suis persuadé** I'm quite sure *ou* convinced (of it); **se ~ de qch** to convince o.s. of sth, be convinced of sth. ◆ **persuasif, -ive** *adj* persuasive, convincing. ◆ **persuasion** *nf (action, art)* persuasion; *(croyance)* conviction, belief.

perte [pɛʀt(ə)] *nf (gén)* loss; *(ruine)* ruin. ~ **de** *chaleur* loss of; *temps* waste of; **vendre à** ~ to sell at a loss; *(Mil)* **de lourdes ~s** heavy losses; **il court à sa** ~ he is on the road to ruin; **à ~ de vue** as far as the eye can see; *(Fin)* ~ **sèche** dead loss, absolute loss; ~ **de connaissance** loss of consciousness, fainting; ~ **de mémoire** loss of memory, memory loss; *(lit, fig)* **être en ~ de vitesse** to lose momentum.

pertinent, e [pɛʀtinɑ̃, ɑ̃t] *adj remarque* pertinent, relevant; *analyse, esprit* judicious, discerning; *(Ling)* significant. ◆ **pertinemment** *adv parler* pertinently, to the point. **savoir ~ que** to know full well that. ◆ **pertinence** *nf* pertinence, relevance.

perturber [pɛʀtyʀbe] (1) *vt services publics, réunion* to disrupt, disturb; *personne* to perturb, disturb. ◆ **perturbateur, -trice** **1** *adj* disruptive. **2** *nm, f (gén)* troublemaker; *(dans un débat)* heckler. ◆ **perturbation** *nf* disruption; disturbance; perturbation. ~ **(atmosphérique)** (atmospheric) disturbance.

péruvien, -ienne [peʀyvjɛ̃, jɛn] *adj, nm,* **P~(ne)** *nm(f)* Peruvian.

pervenche [pɛʀvɑ̃ʃ] *nf (Bot)* periwinkle; *(*: contractuelle)* female traffic warden, meter maid *(US)*.

pervers, e [pɛʀvɛʀ, ɛʀs(ə)] **1** *adj joie* perverse; *personne* perverted. **2** *nm, f* pervert. ◆ **perversion** *nf* perversion. ◆ **perversité** *nf* perversity. ◆ **pervertir** (2) **1** *vt* to pervert. **2 se** ~ *vpr* to become perverted.

peser [pəze] (5) **1** *vt (lit)* to weigh; *(fig: évaluer)* to weigh up. **tout bien pesé** everything considered. **2** *vi* to weigh. ~ **lourd** *[objet]* to be heavy; *[argument, homme politique]* to carry weight; *(fig)* **il n'a pas pesé lourd devant son adversaire** he was no match for his opponent; ~ **sur** *objet* to press on; *estomac, conscience* to lie heavy on; *décision* to influence; **le soupçon/la menace qui pèse sur lui** the suspicion/the threat which hangs over him; **toute la responsabilité pèse sur ses épaules** all the responsibility rests on his shoulders, he has to shoulder all the responsibility; **le temps lui pèse** time hangs heavy on his hands; **ses responsabilités lui pèsent** he feels weighed down by his responsibilities, his responsibilities weigh heavy on him.

◆ **pesamment** *adv* heavily. ◆ **pesant, e** **1** *adj (gén: lit, fig)* heavy; *sommeil* deep; *architecture* massive; *style* ponderous; *présence* burdensome. **2** *nm:* **valoir son ~ d'or** to be worth its (*ou* one's) weight in gold. ◆ **pesanteur** *nf (Phys)* gravity; *(lourdeur)* heaviness; weightiness; massiveness; ponderousness. ◆ **pesée** *nf [objet]* weighing; *(poussée)* push, thrust. ◆ **pèse-bébé,** *pl* **pèse-bébés** *nm* baby scales. ◆ **pèse-lettre,** *pl* **pèse-lettres** *nm* letter scales. ◆ **pèse-personne,** *pl* **pèse-personnes** *nm* scales.

pessimisme [pesimism(ə)] *nm* pessimism. ◆ **pessimiste 1** *adj* pessimistic (*sur* about). **2** *nmf* pessimist.

peste [pɛst(ə)] *nf (Méd)* plague; *(fig: personne)* pest, nuisance, menace. *(fig)* **fuir qch comme la ~** to avoid sth like the plague.

pester [pɛste] (1) *vi* to curse. **~ contre qn/qch** to curse sb/sth.

pesticide [pɛstisid] **1** *adj* pesticidal. **2** *nm* pesticide.

pestilence [pɛstilɑ̃s] *nf* stench. ◆ **pestilentiel, -elle** *adj* stinking.

pet [pɛ] *nm* (**a**) (‡) fart ‡. (**b**) **faire le ~** * to be on (the) watch *ou* on (the) look-out.

pétale [petal] *nm* petal.

pétarader [petaʀade] (1) *vi [moteur]* to backfire.

pétard [petaʀ] *nm* (**a**) banger, firecracker; *(Rail)* detonator, torpedo *(US)*. (**b**) (‡: *tapage)* din, racket. **faire du ~** to kick up a stink ‡; **être en ~** to be raging mad * (*contre* at). (**c**) (‡: *revolver)* gun. (**d**) (‡: *derrière)* bottom *.

péter [pete] (6) **1** *vi* (**a**) (‡) to fart ‡. (**b**) (*) *[détonation]* to go off; *[tuyau, ballon]* to burst; *[ficelle]* to bust *, snap. **2** *vt* (*) *ficelle* to bust *, snap; *objet* to bust *. *(tomber)* **se ~ la gueule** ‡ to fall flat on one's face; *(saoul)* **il est complètement pété** ‡ he's pissed out of his brains ‡; **~ la** *ou* **de santé** to be bursting with health.

pétiller [petije] (1) *vi [feu]* to crackle; *[liquide]* to bubble; *[yeux, joie]* to sparkle. ◆ **pétillant, e** *adj eau* bubbly, fizzy; *vin* sparkling. ◆ **pétillement** *nm*: **~(s)** crackling; bubbling; sparkling.

petit, e [p(ə)ti, it] **1** *adj* (**a**) *objet, pointure etc* small; *(nuance affective)* little. *(fig)* **se faire tout ~** to make o.s. inconspicuous; **être de ~e taille** to be short *ou* small. (**b**) *(mince) taille* slim, slender; *membre* thin, slender. **une ~e pluie fine** a fine drizzle. (**c**) *(jeune)* small, young; *(nuance affective)* little. **son ~ frère** his younger *ou* little brother; *(bébé)* his baby brother; **~ chat/chien** (little) kitten/puppy; **un ~ Anglais** an English boy; **les ~s Anglais** English children; **dans sa ~e enfance** when he was very small, in his early childhood; **le ~ Jésus** baby Jesus. (**d**) *voyage, distance, lettre* short, little. **par ~es étapes** in short *ou* easy stages; **il en a pour une ~e heure** it won't take him more than an hour; **j'en ai pour un ~ moment** *(longtemps)* it'll take me quite a while; *(peu de temps)* it won't take me long. (**e**) *bruit, espoir* faint, slight; *coup* light, gentle; *opération, détail, fonctionnaire* minor; *rhume* slight; *cadeau* little. **~e robe d'été** light summer dress; **il a un ~ appétit** he has a small appetite, he hasn't much of an appetite; **avoir une ~e santé** to be in poor health; **ce n'est pas une ~e affaire que de le faire obéir** getting him to obey is no easy matter; **la ~e industrie** light industry; **le ~ commerce** small businesses; **les ~es et moyennes entreprises** small and medium-sized businesses; **les ~es gens** ordinary people; **la ~e histoire** the footnotes of history. (**f**) *(péj: mesquin)* mean, petty, low. (**g**) *(affectif, intensif)* little. **'juste une ~e signature'** 'can I just have your signature'; **ma ~e maman** my (dear) mummy; **mon ~ chou** *etc* (my little) pet *, darling; **un ~ coin tranquille** a nice quiet spot; **un bon ~ souper** a nice little supper; *(euph)* **le ~ coin** *ou* **endroit** the bathroom *(euph)*; **être/ne pas être dans les ~s papiers de qn** to be in sb's good/bad books; **mettre les ~s plats dans les grands** to lay on a first rate meal; **être aux ~s soins pour qn** to dance attendance on sb; **être dans ses ~s souliers** to be shaking in one's shoes.

2 *adv*: **~ à ~** little by little.

3 *nm (enfant)* (little) boy; *(Scol)* junior (boy); *(homme petit)* small man; *(personne inférieure)* little man. **les ~s** children; **viens ici, ~** come here, son; **pauvre ~** poor little thing; **le ~ Durand** young Durand, the Durand boy; **les tout ~s** the very young, the tiny tots; **la chatte et ses ~s** the cat and her kittens; **la lionne et ses ~s** the lioness and her young *or* cubs; **faire des ~s** to have kittens (*ou* puppies *ou* lambs *etc*); *(fig)* **son argent a fait des ~s** his money has made more money; **c'est le monde en ~** it is the world in miniature.

4 *nf (enfant)* (little) girl; *(femme)* small woman. **la ~e Durand** the Durand's daughter.

5 : **~ ami** boyfriend; **~e amie** girlfriend ; **~-beurre** *nm, pl* **~s-~** petit beurre biscuit, butter cookie *(US)*; **le P~ Chaperon Rouge** Little Red Riding Hood; **~ cousin** *(enfant)* little *ou* young cousin; *(parent éloigné)* distant cousin; **~ déjeuner** breakfast; **le ~ doigt** the little finger; **le ~ écran** television, TV; **~-enfant** *nm, pl* **~s-~s** grandchild; **~e fille** *nf, pl* **~es-~s** granddaughter; **~-fils** *nm, pl* **~s-~** grandson; **~-neveu** *nm, pl* **~s-~s** great-nephew; **~e-nièce** *nf, pl* **~es-~s** great-niece; **~ nom** * Christian name, first name; **~-pois** *nm, pl* **~s-~** (garden) pea; **le P~ Poucet** Tom Thumb; *(Culin)* **~ salé** salted pork; **~-suisse** *nm, pl* **~s-~s** petit-suisse *(kind of cream cheese eaten as a dessert)*.

◆ **petitement** *adv (chichement)* poorly; *(mesquinement)* meanly, pettily. **nous sommes ~ logés** our accommodation is cramped. ◆ **petitesse** *nf [taille, endroit]* smallness, small size; *[somme]* smallness; *[acte]* meanness, pettiness.

pétition [petisjɔ̃] *nf* petition. **faire une ~ auprès de qn** to petition sb. ◆ **pétitionnaire** *nmf* petitioner.

pétrifier [petʀifje] (7) *vt (Géol)* to petrify; *personne* to paralyze, transfix (*de* with). ◆ **pétrification** *nf* petrification.

pétrin [petʀɛ̃] *nm* (**a**) (*: *ennui)* mess *. **être dans le ~** to be in a mess * *ou* jam * *ou* fix *. (**b**) *(Boulangerie)* kneading-trough. ◆ **pétrir** (2) *vt* to knead.

pétrole [petʀɔl] *nm (brut)* oil, petroleum. **~ (lampant)** paraffin (oil), kerosene *(US)*; **lampe à ~** paraffin *ou* kerosene *(US) ou* oil lamp. ◆ **pétrochimie** *nf* petrochemistry. ◆ **pétrodollar** *nm* petrodollar. ◆ **pétrolier, -ière 1** *adj* petroleum, oil; *pays* oil-producing. **2** *nm (navire)* (oil) tanker; *(financier)* oil magnate. ◆ **pétrolifère** *adj* oil-bearing.

peu [pø] **1** *adv* (**a**) *(petite quantité)* little, not much; *(petit nombre)* few, not many. **il gagne très ~** he doesn't earn very much, he earns very little; **il se contente de ~** he is satisfied with little; **il mange trop ~** he doesn't eat (nearly) enough. (**b**) *(modifiant adj etc)* (a) little, not very. **il est ~ sociable** he is not very sociable; **il conduit ~ prudemment** he doesn't drive very carefully; **ils sont trop ~ nombreux** there are too few of them; **c'est un ~ grand** it's a little *ou* a bit (too) big. (**c**) **~ de** *(quantité)* little, not much; *(nombre)* few, not (very) many; **nous avons eu (très) ~ de soleil/d'orages** we had (very) little sunshine/(very) few storms, we didn't have (very) much sunshine/(very) many storms; **il est ici pour ~ de temps** he is here for (only) a short time *ou* while. (**d**) *(locutions)* **il l'a battu de ~** he just beat him; **à ~ près terminé** almost *ou* nearly *ou* more or less finished; **à ~ près 10 kilos** roughly *ou* approximately 10 kilos; **rester dans l'à ~ près** to remain vague; **à ~ de chose près** more or less, just about; **(c'est) ~ de chose** it's nothing; **~ à ~** gradually, little by little, bit by bit.

2 *nm* (**a**) little. **le ~ (d'argent)** qu'elle a what little (money) *ou* the little (money) she has; **son ~ de patience lui a nui** his lack of patience has done him harm; **le ~ d'amis qu'elle avait** the few friends she had; **le ~ de cheveux qui lui restent sont blancs**

the bit of hair he has left is white. (**b**) **un** ~ a little; **un petit** ~ a little bit; **il boite un** ~ he limps slightly *ou* a little *ou* a bit, he is slightly *ou* a bit lame; **il est un** ~ **artiste** he's a bit of an artist, he's something of an artist; **nous avons un** ~ **moins de clients** we have slightly fewer customers; **pour un** ~ *ou* **un** ~ **plus il écrasait le chien** he all but *ou* he very nearly ran over the dog. (**c**) **un** ~ **d'eau** a little water; **un** ~ **de patience** a little patience, a bit of patience; **un** ~ **de silence!** let's have some quiet *ou* a bit of quiet!; **il a un** ~ **de sinusite** he has a touch of sinusitis. (**d**) *(*: intensif)* **un** ~**!, un** ~ **mon neveu!** ‡ you bet! *, and how! *; **montre-moi un** ~ **comment tu fais** just show me how you do it; **comme menteur il est un** ~ **là!** as liars go, he'd be hard to beat!; **un** ~ **partout** just about everywhere; **c'est un** ~ **beaucoup** * that's a bit much *.

peuple [pœpl(ə)] *nm (gén)* people; *(foule)* crowd (of people). **les gens du** ~ the common people, ordinary people. ◆ **peuplade** *nf* (small) tribe, people. ◆ **peuplé, e** *adj* populated. ◆ **peupler** (1) **1** *vt* (**a**) *(pourvoir) colonie* to populate; *étang* to stock; *forêt* to plant out; *(fig) esprit* to fill (*de* with). (**b**) *(habiter) terre, maison* to inhabit. **2 se** ~ *vpr [région]* to become populated; *(fig: s'animer)* to fill (up), be filled (*de* with). ◆ **peuplement** *nm* (**a**) *(action)* populating; stocking; planting (with trees). (**b**) *(population)* population.

peuplier [pøplije] *nm* poplar (tree).

peur [pœʀ] *nf* fear. **être vert** *ou* **mort de** ~ to be frightened *ou* scared out of one's wits; **prendre** ~ to take fright; **sans** ~ *(adj)* fearless (*de* of); *(adv)* fearlessly; **avoir une** ~ **bleue de qch** to be scared stiff * of sth; **il m'a fait une de ces** ~**s!** he gave me a dreadful fright *ou* scare; **avoir** ~ to be frightened *ou* afraid *ou* scared (*de* of); **je n'ai pas** ~ **des mots** I'm not afraid of using plain language; *(fig)* **j'ai bien** ~**/très** ~ **qu'il ne pleuve** I'm afraid/very much afraid it's going to rain; **il y a eu plus de** ~ **que de mal** it caused more fright than real harm, it was more frightening than anything else; **faire** ~ **à qn** to frighten *ou* scare sb; **cette pensée fait** ~ it's a frightening thought; **le travail ne lui fait pas** ~ he's not scared *ou* afraid of hard work; **laid à faire** ~ frightfully ugly; **il a couru de** ~ **de manquer le train** he ran for fear of missing the train. ◆ **peureusement** *adv* fearfully, timorously. ◆ **peureux, -euse** *adj* fearful, timorous.

peut-être [pøtɛtʀ(ə)] *adv* perhaps, maybe. ~ **bien qu'il pleuvra** it may *ou* might well rain; ~ **que oui** perhaps so; **tu le sais mieux que moi** ~**?** so (you think) you know more about it than I do, do you?

pèze ‡ [pɛz] *nm (argent)* dough ‡, bread ‡.

phalange [falɑ̃ʒ] *nf* phalanx.

pharaon [faʀaɔ̃] *nm* Pharaoh.

phare [faʀ] *nm* (**a**) *(tour)* lighthouse; *(Aviat, fig)* beacon. (**b**) *(Aut)* headlight, headlamp. **rouler pleins** ~**s** to drive on full beam *ou* high beams *(US)*; ~**s code** dipped headlights, low beams *(US)*; ~ **antibrouillard** fog lamp; ~**s longue portée** high intensity lights; ~ **de recul** reversing light, back-up light *(US)*.

pharmacie [faʀmasi] *nf* (**a**) *(magasin)* chemist's (shop), pharmacy, drugstore *(Can, US)*. (**b**) *(science)* pharmacology; *(profession)* pharmacy. (**c**) *(produits)* pharmaceuticals, medicines. **(armoire à)** ~ medicine cabinet; ~ **portative** first-aid kit. ◆ **pharmaceutique** *adj* pharmaceutical. ◆ **pharmacien, -ienne** *nm, f* (dispensing) chemist, pharmacist, druggist *(US)*. ◆ **pharmacodépendance** *nf* drug dependency.

pharynx [faʀɛ̃ks] *nm* pharynx.

phase [fɑz] *nf* phase. *(Élec)* **la** ~ the live wire; **être en** ~ *(Phys)* to be in phase; *(fig)* to be on the same wavelength.

phénol [fenɔl] *nm* carbolic acid, phenol.

phénomène [fenɔmɛn] *nm (gén)* phenomenon; *(excentrique)* character; *(anormal)* freak. ◆ **phénoménal, e,** *mpl* **-aux** *adj (gén)* phenomenal. ◆ **phénoménalement** *adv* phenomenally.

phénotype [fenɔtip] *nm* phenotype.

philanthrope [filɑ̃tʀɔp] *nmf* philanthropist. ◆ **philanthropie** *nf* philanthropy. ◆ **philanthropique** *adj* philanthropic(al).

philatélie [filateli] *nf* philately, stamp collecting. ◆ **philatélique** *adj* philatelic. ◆ **philatéliste** *nmf* philatelist, stamp collector.

philharmonique [filaʀmɔnik] *adj* philharmonic.

philippin, e [filipɛ̃, in] **1** *adj* Philippine. **2** *nm, f:* **P**~**(e)** Filipino. ◆ **Philippines** *nfpl:* **les** ~ the Philippines.

philodendron [filɔdɛ̃dʀɔ̃] *nm* philodendron.

philosophie [filɔzɔfi] *nf* philosophy. ◆ **philosophe** **1** *nmf* philosopher. **2** *adj* philosophical. ◆ **philosopher** (1) *vi* to philosophize. ◆ **philosophique** *adj* philosophical. ◆ **philosophiquement** *adv* philosophically.

phlébite [flebit] *nf* phlebitis. ◆ **phlébologue** *nmf* vein specialist.

phobie [fɔbi] *nf* phobia.

phonétique [fɔnetik] **1** *nf* phonetics *(sg)*. **2** *adj* phonetic. **système** ~ sound system. ◆ **phonétiquement** *adv* phonetically.

phonique [fɔnik] *adj* phonic.

phonographe [fɔnɔgʀaf] *nm* (wind-up) gramophone, phonograph *(US)*.

phoque [fɔk] *nm (animal)* seal; *(fourrure)* sealskin.

phosphate [fɔsfat] *nm* phosphate.

phosphore [fɔsfɔʀ] *nm* phosphorus. ◆ **phosphorer** * (1) *vi* to beaver away, work hard. ◆ **phosphorescence** *nf* luminosity, phosphorescence. ◆ **phosphorescent, e** *adj* luminous, phosphorescent.

photo [fɔto] *nf* photo, snap(shot). **prendre qn en** ~ to take a photo *ou* snap(shot) of sb.

photocomposition [fɔtɔkɔ̃pozisjɔ̃] *nf* photocomposition, filmsetting. ◆ **photocomposeuse** *nf (machine)* photocomposer, filmsetter. ◆ **photocomposer** (1) *vt* to photocompose, filmset.

photocopie [fɔtɔkɔpi] *nf (action)* photocopying, photostatting; *(copie)* photocopy, photostat (copy). ◆ **photocopier** (7) *vt* to photocopy, photostat. ◆ **photocopieur** *nm*, **photocopieuse** *nf* photocopier, photostat.

photo-électrique [fɔtoelɛktʀik] *adj* photoelectric. **cellule** ~ photoelectric cell, photocell.

photographie [fɔtɔgʀafi] *nf (art)* photography; *(image)* photograph. **faire de la** ~ to take photographs, do photography; ~ **d'identité** passport photograph. ◆ **photographe** *nmf (artiste)* photographer; *(commerçant)* camera dealer. *(boutique)* **chez un** ~ at a camera shop *ou* store *(US)*. ◆ **photographier** (7) *vt* to photograph. **se faire** ~ to have one's photo(graph) taken. ◆ **photographique** *adj* photographic.

photogravure [fɔtɔgʀavyʀ] *nf* photoengraving.

photomaton [fɔtɔmatɔ̃] *nm* ® automatic photo booth, five-minute photo machine.

photosensible [fɔtɔsɑ̃sibl(ə)] *adj* photosensitive. **dispositif** ~ photosensor.

phrase [fʀɑz] *nf (Ling)* sentence; *(Mus, fig: expression)* phrase. **faire des** ~**s** to talk in flowery language; ~ **toute faite** stock phrase.

phtisie [ftizi] *nf* consumption.

physicien, -ienne [fizisjɛ̃, jɛn] *nm, f* physicist.

physiologie [fizjɔlɔʒi] *nf* physiology. ◆ **physiologique** *adj* physiological. ◆ **physiologiste** *nmf* physiologist.

physionomie [fizjɔnɔmi] *nf (lit, fig)* face. ◆ **physionomiste** *adj, nmf*: **il est** ~ he has a good memory for faces.

physique [fizik] **1** *adj (gén)* physical. **2** *nm* physique. **au** ~ physically; **avoir un** ~ **agréable** to be quite good-looking; **avoir le** ~ **de l'emploi** to look the part. **3** *nf* physics *(sg)*. ◆ **physiquement** *adv* physically.

pi [pi] *nm (lettre, Math)* pi.

piaffer [pjafe] (1) *vi [cheval]* to stamp, paw the ground. ~ **d'impatience** to fidget with impatience.

piailler [pjɑje] (1) *vi (lit, péj)* to squawk. ◆ **piaillement** *nm*: ~**(s)** squawking.

piano [pjano] **1** *nm* piano. ~ **droit/à queue** upright/grand piano. **2** *adv (Mus)* piano; *(* fig)* gently. ◆ **pianiste** *nmf* pianist.

pic [pik] *nm* (**a**) *(cime)* peak. (**b**) *(pioche)* pick(axe). ~ **à glace** ice pick. (**c**) *(oiseau)* ~ **(vert)** (green) woodpecker. (**d**) **à** ~ *falaise* sheer; **couler à** ~ to go straight down; **arriver à** ~ * to come just at the right time *ou* in the nick of time.

Picardie [pikaʀdi] *nf* Picardy.

pichet [piʃɛ] *nm* pitcher, jug.

picoler * [pikɔle] (1) *vi* to booze ‡, tipple *.

picorer [pikɔʀe] (1) *vti* to peck; *(manger très peu)* to nibble.

picoter [pikɔte] (1) **1** *vt* (**a**) *gorge* to tickle; *peau* to make smart; *yeux* to sting; *(avec une épingle)* to prick. (**b**) *(picorer)* to peck at. **2** *vi [gorge]* to tickle; *[peau]* to smart, prickle; *[yeux]* to smart, sting. ◆ **picotement** *nm*: ~**(s)** tickling; smarting; prickling; stinging.

picrate ‡ [pikʀat] *nm* plonk *, (cheap) wine.

pie [pi] **1** *nf (oiseau)* magpie; *(bavard)* chatterbox *. **2** *adj inv cheval* piebald; *vache* black and white.

pièce [pjɛs] **1** *nf* (**a**) *(fragment)* piece. **en** ~**s** in pieces; *(lit, fig)* **mettre en** ~**s** to pull *ou* tear to pieces; **c'est inventé de toutes** ~**s** it's a complete fabrication; **fait d'une seule** ~ made in one piece; **il est tout d'une** ~ he's very cut and dried about things. (**b**) *(objet, pion)* piece; *(Mil)* gun; *(Chasse, Pêche: prise)* specimen. **se vendre à la** ~ to be sold separately *ou* individually; **2 F** ~ 2 francs each *ou* apiece; **travail à la** ~ *ou* **aux** ~**s** piecework; *(costume)* **un deux** ~**s** a two-piece (suit). (**c**) *(Tech)* ~ **(détachée)** part, component; ~**s (de rechange)** spares, spare parts; ~ **d'origine** guaranteed genuine spare part; **livré en** ~**s détachées** delivered in kit form. (**d**) *(document)* paper, document. ~ **d'identité** identity paper; ~ **à conviction** exhibit; **juger sur** ~**s** to judge on actual evidence; **avec** ~**s à l'appui** with supporting documents. (**e**) *(Couture: reprise)* patch. (**f**) *[maison]* room. **un deux-**~**s** a 2-room(ed) flat *ou* apartment *(US)*. (**g**) *(Littérat, Mus)* piece. ~ **(de théâtre)** play. (**h**) ~ **(de monnaie)** coin; **une** ~ **de 5 francs** a 5-franc piece *ou* coin; **donner la** ~ **à qn** * to give *ou* slip sb a tip.
2 : ~ **de bétail** head of cattle; ~ **de blé** wheat field; ~ **d'eau** ornamental lake *ou* pond; *(Culin)* ~ **montée** ≃ tiered cake; *(noce)* wedding cake; ~ **de musée** museum piece; ~ **de terre** piece *ou* patch of land; ~ **de vin** cask of wine.

pied [pje] *nm* (**a**) *(gén)* foot. **aller** ~**s nus** *ou* **nu-pieds** to go barefoot(ed); **avoir les** ~**s plats** to have flat feet, be flatfooted; **à** ~**s joints** with one's feet together; **le** ~ **lui a manqué** he lost his footing, his foot slipped; **aller à** ~ to go on foot, walk; *(lit, fig)* ~**s et poings liés** bound hand and foot. (**b**) *[arbre, mur etc]* foot, bottom; *[table]* leg; *[appareil-photo, lampadaire]* stand, tripod; *[lampe]* base; *[verre]* stem; *[colonne]* base, foot. (**c**) *[salade, tomate]* plant. ~ **de céleri** head of celery; ~ **de vigne** vine; **blé sur** ~ standing corn *ou* wheat *(US)*. (**d**) *(Culin) [porc, veau]* trotter. (**e**) *(mesure)* foot. **un poteau de 6** ~**s** a 6-foot pole. (**f**) *(Poésie)* foot. (**g**) *(niveau)* **vivre sur un grand** ~ to live in (great *ou* grand) style; **sur un** ~ **d'amitié/d'égalité** on a friendly/equal footing. (**h**) *(‡: idiot)* twit *, idiot. **il chante comme un** ~ he's a useless * *ou* lousy ‡ singer. (**i**) *(avec prép)* ~ **à** ~ *lutter* every inch of the way; **au** ~ **de la lettre** literally; **remplacer qn au** ~ **levé** to stand in for s.o. at a moment's notice; **à** ~ **d'œuvre** ready to get down to the job; **à** ~ **sec** without getting one's feet wet; **de** ~ **ferme** resolutely; **des** ~**s à la tête** from head to foot; **sur le** ~ **de guerre** ready for action. (**j**) *(avec verbes)* **avoir** ~ to be able to touch the bottom *(in swimming)*; **perdre** ~ to be *ou* get out of one's depth; **avoir bon** ~ **bon œil** to be as fit as a fiddle; **avoir le** ~ **marin** to be a good sailor; **avoir les** ~**s sur terre** to have one's feet firmly on the ground; *(fig)* **avoir un** ~ **dans une société** to have a foothold *ou* a toehold in a firm; **avoir un** ~ **dans la tombe** to have one foot in the grave; **être sur** ~ *[projet]* to be under way; *[malade]* to be up and about; **faire du** ~ **à qn** *(prévenir)* to give sb a (warning) kick; *(galamment)* to play footsy with sb *; **faire le** ~ **de grue** * to kick one's heels; **faire des** ~**s et des mains pour faire qch** * to move heaven and earth to do sth; **faire un** ~ **de nez à qn** to thumb one's nose at sb; **cela lui fera les** ~**s** * that'll teach him (a thing or two) *; **mettre qn à** ~ to dismiss sb; **mettre** ~ **à terre** to dismount; **mettre les** ~**s chez qn** to set foot in sb's house; **mettre qn au** ~ **du mur** to put sb to the test; **mettre les** ~**s dans le plat** * *(se fâcher)* to put one's foot down; *(gaffer)* to put one's foot in it; *(intervenir)* to put one's foot down; **mettre qch sur** ~ to set sth up; **remettre qn sur** ~ to set sb back on his feet again; *(mourir)* **partir** *ou* **sortir les** ~**s devant** * to go out feet first; **prendre** ~ **dans/sur** to get a foothold in/on; **c'est le** ~! ‡ it's a real turn-on! ‡, it's great! * ◆ **pied-noir,** *pl* **pieds-noirs** *nm* pied-noir *(Algerian-born Frenchman)*. ◆ **pied-plat** *nm,pl* **pieds-plats** *(littér)* lout. ◆ **pied-de-poule 1** *nm, pl* **pieds-de-poule** hound's-tooth cloth. **2** *adj inv* hound's tooth. ◆ **pied-à-terre** *nm inv* pied-à-terre.

piédestal, *pl* **-aux** [pjedɛstal, o] *nm (lit, fig)* pedestal.

piège [pjɛʒ] *nm (lit, fig)* trap; *(fosse)* pit; *(collet)* snare. **les** ~**s d'une dictée** the pitfalls of a dictation; **pris à son propre** ~ caught in one's own trap; **tendre un** ~ **à qn** to set a trap for sb; ~ **à loups** mantrap. ◆ **piégé, e** *adj*: **engin** ~ booby trap; **colis** ~ parcel *ou* mail bomb; **voiture/lettre** ~**e** car/letter bomb. ◆ **piéger** (3) *vt* (**a**) *animal, personne* to trap. **se faire** ~ to be trapped; **se faire** ~ **par un radar** to get caught in a radar trap. (**b**) *objet* to set a trap in; *(avec explosifs)* to booby-trap.

pierre [pjɛʀ] **1** *nf (gén, Méd)* stone. **cœur de** ~ heart of stone; **faire d'une** ~ **deux coups** to kill two birds with one stone; ~ **qui roule n'amasse pas mousse** a rolling stone gathers no moss; **c'est une** ~ **dans son jardin** it's a dig at him; **jour à marquer d'une** ~ **blanche/noire** red-letter/black day; **aimer les vieilles** ~**s** to like old buildings. **2** : ~ **d'achoppement** stumbling block; ~ **à aiguiser** whetstone; ~ **à briquet** flint; ~ **ponce** pumice stone; ~ **précieuse** precious stone, gem; **mur en** ~**s sèches** drystone wall *ou* dyke; ~ **de taille** freestone; ~ **tombale** tombstone, gravestone; *(lit, fig)* ~ **de touche** touchstone. ◆ **pierraille** *nf* loose stones, chippings. ◆ **pierreries** *nfpl* gems, precious stones. ◆ **pierreux, -euse** *adj* stony.

pierrot [pjɛʀo] *nm* (**a**) *(Théât)* pierrot. (**b**) *(Orn)* sparrow.

pietà [pjeta] *nf* pietà.

piété [pjete] *nf* piety. **articles/livre de** ~ devotional articles/book.

piétiner [pjetine] (1) **1** *vi (trépigner)* to stamp (one's foot *ou* feet); *(ne pas avancer) [personne]* to stand about; *[discussion, enquête]* to be at a standstill, hang fire; *[science]* to be at a standstill. ~ **dans la boue** to trudge through the mud. **2** *vt sol* to trample *ou* tread on; *(fig) adversaire* to trample underfoot. ◆ **piétinement** *nm (marche sur place)* standing about; *(bruit)* stamping. **le ~ de la discussion** the fact that the discussion is not making progress.

piéton[1] [pjetɔ̃] *nm* pedestrian. ◆ **piéton**[2], **-onne** *ou* ◆ **piétonnier, -ière** *adj* pedestrian. **rue ~ne** *ou* **~ière** pedestrianized street; **zone ~ne** *ou* **~ière** pedestrian precinct, mall *(US)*.

piètre [pjɛtʀ(ə)] *adj* very poor, mediocre. **c'est une ~ consolation** it's small *ou* little comfort; **avoir ~ allure** to be a sorry sight.

pieu, *pl* **~x**[1] [pjø] *nm* (**a**) post; *(pointu)* stake; *(Constr)* pile. (**b**) *(‡: lit)* bed. **se mettre au ~** to turn in *.

pieuvre [pjœvʀ(ə)] *nf* octopus.

pieux[2], **-euse** [pjø, øz] *adj* pious, devout. ~ **mensonge** white lie. ◆ **pieusement** *adv* piously.

pif ‡ [pif] *nm (nez)* beak ‡, nose. **au ~** at a rough guess.

pigeon [piʒɔ̃] *nm (oiseau)* pigeon; *(*: dupe)* mug ‡. ~ **ramier** woodpigeon; ~ **voyageur** carrier *ou* homing pigeon; **par ~ voyageur** by pigeon post. ◆ **pigeonnier** *nm* dovecote.

piger ‡ [piʒe] (3) *vi* to twig ‡, understand. **je ne pige pas** I don't get it *, I don't twig ‡.

pigment [pigmɑ̃] *nm* pigment. ◆ **pigmentation** *nf* pigmentation. ◆ **pigmenter** (1) *vt* to pigment.

pignon [piɲɔ̃] *nm (Archit)* gable; *(roue dentée)* gearwheel; *(petite roue)* pinion. *(fig)* **avoir ~ sur rue** to be prosperous and highly respected.

pile [pil] **1** *nf* (**a**) *(tas)* pile, stack. (**b**) *[pont]* pile, pier. (**c**) *(Élec)* battery. **à ~(s)** battery-operated; ~ **rechargeable** rechargeable battery; ~ **solaire** solar cell; **appareil à ~s** *ou* **fonctionnant sur ~s** battery-operated *ou* battery-driven appliance, cordless appliance; ~ **atomique** nuclear reactor. (**d**) *[pièce]* ~ **ou face?** heads or tails?; **tirer à ~ ou face pour savoir si...** to toss up to find out if ... **2** *adv* (*) *(net)* dead *; *(juste)* just, right. **s'arrêter ~** to stop dead *; **ça tombe ~!** that's just *ou* exactly what I (*ou* we *etc*) need(ed)!; **arriver ~** to come just at the right time; **à 2 heures ~** (at) dead on 2 *, at 2 on the dot *.

piler [pile] (1) **1** *vt (lit)* to crush, pound. ~ **qn** * *(rosser)* to give sb a hammering ‡; *(vaincre)* to beat sb hollow *. **2** *vi (*: freiner)* to jam on the brakes.

pilier [pilje] *nm* pillar; *(Rugby)* prop (forward).

piller [pije] (1) *vt ville, maison* to loot, ransack, pillage; *personne* to fleece; *(fig: plagier)* to plagiarize. ◆ **pillage** *nm* looting, ransacking, pillaging; fleecing; plagiarizing. ◆ **pillard, e** **1** *adj* pillaging, looting. **2** *nm, f* looter.

pilon [pilɔ̃] *nm (instrument)* pestle; *(jambe)* wooden leg; *[poulet]* drumstick. ◆ **pilonner** (1) *vt (Culin)* to pound; *(Mil)* to pound, shell, bombard. ◆ **pilonnage** *nm* pounding; shelling, bombardment.

pilori [pilɔʀi] *nm* pillory, stocks *(pl)*. **mettre au ~** *(lit)* to put in the stocks; *(fig)* to pillory.

pilote [pilɔt] **1** *adj ferme* experimental; *magasin* cut-price. **projet ~** pilot project. **2** *nm (Aviat, Naut)* pilot; *(Aut)* driver; *(fig: guide)* guide. ~ **automatique/d'essai/de ligne** automatic/test/airline pilot; ~ **de course** racing driver. ◆ **pilotage** *nm* piloting, flying. **véhicule à ~ automatique** self-steering vehicle; ~ **sans visibilité** flying blind. ◆ **piloter** (1) *vt avion* to pilot, fly; *navire* to pilot; *voiture* to drive. ~ **qn** to show *ou* guide *ou* pilot sb round.

pilotis [pilɔti] *nm* pile.

pilule [pilyl] *nf* pill. **prendre la ~** *(contraceptive)* to be on *ou* take the pill; *(‡ fig)* to take a hammering ‡.

piment [pimɑ̃] *nm* chilli (pepper); *(fig)* spice. ~ **doux** pepper, capsicum; **avoir du ~** to be spicy. ◆ **pimenté, e** *adj plat* hot; *récit* spicy.

pimpant, e [pɛ̃pɑ̃, ɑ̃t] *adj* spruce.

pin [pɛ̃] *nm (arbre)* pine (tree); *(bois)* pine(wood). ~ **maritime/parasol** maritime/umbrella pine.

pinard ‡ [pinaʀ] *nm* plonk *, (cheap) wine.

pince [pɛ̃s] *nf* (**a**) *(outil)* **~(s)** *(gén)* pliers; *(à sucre, charbon, de forgeron)* tongs; ~ **à cheveux** hair clip, bobby pin *(US)*; ~ **à épiler** tweezers; ~ **à linge** clothes peg. (**b**) *(levier)* crowbar. (**c**) *[crabe]* pincer, claw. (**d**) *(Couture)* dart. **faire des ~s à** to put darts in. (**e**) *(‡: main)* mitt ‡, paw ‡. **je lui ai serré la ~** I shook hands with him. (**f**) *(‡: jambe)* leg. **aller à ~s** to foot it *. ◆ **pince-monseigneur,** *pl* **pinces-monseigneur** *nf* jemmy.

pinceau, *pl* **~x** [pɛ̃so] *nm (Peinture)* (paint)brush; *(‡: pied)* foot, hoof ‡. ~ **lumineux** pencil of light.

pincer [pɛ̃se] (3) **1** *vt* (**a**) *(pour faire mal)* to pinch, nip; *[froid, chien]* to nip; *(Agr)* to pinch out; *(Mus)* to pluck. **se ~ le doigt dans la porte** to trap *ou* catch one's finger in the door; **il s'est fait ~ par un crabe** he was nipped by a crab. (**b**) *(serrer)* to grip. ~ **les lèvres** to purse (up) one's lips; **se ~ le nez** to hold one's nose; **robe qui pince la taille** dress which is tight at the waist. (**c**) *(Couture) veste* to put darts in. (**d**) *(* fig: arrêter)* to catch, cop ‡. (**e**) **en ~ pour qn** ‡ to be stuck on sb ‡, be mad about sb *. **2** *vi* (‡) **ça pince** *(dur)* it's freezing (cold). ◆ **pincé, e**[1] *adj air, ton* stiff. *(Mus)* **instrument à cordes ~es** plucked stringed instrument. ◆ **pincée**[2] *nf [sel, poivre]* pinch. ◆ **pincement** *nm*: **elle a eu un ~ de cœur** she felt a twinge of sorrow. ◆ **pince-sans-rire** *nm inv*: **c'est un ~** he's the deadpan type.

pincettes [pɛ̃sɛt] *nfpl* (fire) tongs; *[horloger]* tweezers. **il n'est pas à toucher avec des ~s** *(sale)* he's filthy dirty; *(mécontent)* he's like a bear with a sore head.

pinçon [pɛ̃sɔ̃] *nm* pinch-mark.

pinède [pinɛd] *nf* pinewood, pine forest.

pingouin [pɛ̃gwɛ̃] *nm [arctique]* auk; *(gén)* penguin.

ping-pong [piŋpɔ̃g] *nm* table tennis.

pingre [pɛ̃gʀ(ə)] *(péj)* **1** *adj* stingy, niggardly. **2** *nmf* skinflint, niggard. ◆ **pingrerie** *nf (péj)* stinginess, niggardliness.

pinson [pɛ̃sɔ̃] *nm* chaffinch.

pintade [pɛ̃tad] *nf* guinea-fowl.

pioche [pjɔʃ] *nf* mattock, pickaxe. ◆ **piocher** (1) **1** *vt terre* to dig up; (*) *sujet* to cram for; *(Jeu) carte* to take (from the pile). **2** *vi (creuser)* to dig; *(Jeu)* to take a card. ~ **dans le tas** *(nourriture)* to dig in; *(objets)* to dig into the pile.

piolet [pjɔlɛ] *nm* ice axe.

pion [pjɔ̃] *nm* (**a**) *(Échecs)* pawn; *(Dames)* piece, draught, checker *(US)*. *(fig)* **n'être qu'un ~ (sur l'échiquier)** to be nothing but a pawn. (**b**) *(Scol: péj)* ≃ supervisor.

pioncer ‡ [pjɔ̃se] (3) *vi* to have a kip ‡, sleep.

pionnier [pjɔnje] *nm (lit, fig)* pioneer.

pipe [pip] *nf* pipe. ~ **de bruyère** briar pipe.

pipeau [pipo] *nm (Mus)* (reed-)pipe.

pipelet, -ette * [piplɛ, ɛt] *nm, f (péj)* concierge.

pipe-line, *pl* **pipe-lines** [pajplajn, piplin] *nm* pipeline.

pipi * [pipi] *nm* wee(wee) *. **faire ~** to go to the toilet.

piquant, e [pikɑ̃, ɑ̃t] **1** *adj barbe* prickly; *(Bot) tige* thorny; *froid* biting; *critique* biting, cutting; *détail* titillating, spicy; *moutarde* hot; *goût, fromage* pungent; *vin* sour, tart. *(Culin)* **sauce ~e** piquant sauce. **2** *nm [hérisson, oursin]* spine; *[rosier]* thorn; *[chardon]* prickle; *[barbelé]* barb; *[conversation]* piquancy; *[aventure]* spice. **et, détail qui ne manque pas de ~,...** the most entertaining thing (about it) is that...

pique [pik] **1** *nf (arme)* pike; *(critique)* cutting remark; *[picador]* lance. **2** *nm (carte)* spade; *(couleur)* spades.

piqué, e [pike] **1** *adj* (**a**) *(Couture) (cousu)* (machine-)stitched; *couvre-lit* quilted. (**b**) *glace, linge* mildewed; *meuble* worm-eaten; *vin* sour. **~ par la rouille** *métal* pitted with rust; *linge* covered in rust spots. (**c**) *(*: fou)* nuts *, barmy *. **2** *nm* (**a**) *(Aviat)* dive. (**b**) *(tissu)* piqué.

piquer [pike] (1) **1** *vt* (**a**) *[guêpe]* to sting; *[moustique, serpent]* to bite; *(avec une pointe)* to prick; *(Méd)* to give an injection to. **se faire ~** to have an injection; *(euph)* **faire ~ un chat** to have a cat put to sleep *(euph)*. (**b**) *aiguille* to stick, stab, jab (*dans* into). **~ la viande avec une fourchette** to prick the meat with a fork; **~ qch au mur** to put *ou* stick *ou* pin sth up on the wall. (**c**) *(Couture)* **~ qch** *(***à la machine***)* to (machine) stitch sth, sew sth up. (**d**) *[barbe]* to prick, prickle; *[ortie]* to sting; *[froid]* to bite, sting. **ça (me) pique** *[démangeaison]* it itches; *[barbe, tissu]* it's prickly; *[liqueur]* it burns; *[ronces]* it prickles; *[alcool sur une plaie]* it stings *ou* burns; **les yeux me piquent** my eyes are smarting *ou* stinging. (**e**) *(exciter) curiosité* to arouse, excite; *(vexer)* to pique, nettle. **~ qn au vif** to cut sb to the quick. (**f**) *(*: faire)* **~ un cent mètres** to put on a burst of speed; **~ une crise de larmes** to have a fit of tears; **~ une colère** to fly into a rage; **~ une suée** to break out in a sweat; **~ un plongeon** to dive. (**g**) *(*: prendre) accent* to pick up; *manie, maladie* to pick up, catch, get; *portefeuille* to pinch *, whip ‡; *idée* to pinch * (*à* from); *voleur* to nab ‡, nick ‡. **~ dans le tas** to choose *ou* pick at random.
2 *vi* (**a**) *[avion]* to go into a dive; *[oiseau]* to swoop down. **il faudrait ~ vers le village** we'll have to head towards the village; **~ du nez** *[avion]* to go into a nose-dive; *[bateau]* to dip her head; *[fleurs]* to droop; *[personne]* to fall headfirst. (**b**) *[moutarde, radis]* to be hot; *[vin]* to be sour; *[fromage]* to be pungent.
3 se ~ *vpr* (**a**) *(avec une aiguille)* to prick o.s.; *(dans les orties)* to get stung; *(Méd)* to give o.s. an injection, inject o.s. (**b**) *[miroir, linge]* to go mildewed; *[métal]* to be pitted; *[vin, cidre]* to go *ou* turn sour. (**c**) **se ~ de littérature** to pride o.s. on one's knowledge of literature; **se ~ de faire qch** to pride o.s. on one's ability to do sth. (**d**) *(se vexer)* to take offence. (**e**) **il s'est piqué au jeu** it grew on him; **se ~ le nez** ‡ to booze ‡. ◆ **pique-assiette** * *nmf inv* scrounger *, sponger * *(for a free meal)*. ◆ **pique-feu** *nm inv* poker. ◆ **pique-nique,** *pl* **pique-niques** *nm* picnic. ◆ **pique-niquer** (1) *vi* to have a picnic, picnic.

piquet [pikɛ] *nm (pieu)* post, stake; *[tente]* peg; *(Ski)* (marker) pole. **~** *(de grève)* (strike-)picket; *(Scol)* **mettre qn au ~** to put sb in the corner.

piqueter [pikte] (4) *vt (moucheter)* to dot (*de* with).

piquette [pikɛt] *nf (vin)* (cheap) wine; *(‡: défaite)* hammering ‡, thrashing *. **prendre une ~** to be hammered ‡ *ou* thrashed *.

piqûre [pikyʀ] *nf* (**a**) *[épingle]* prick; *[guêpe, ortie]* sting; *[moustique]* bite; *(trace, trou)* hole. **~ d'amour-propre** injury to one's pride. (**b**) *(Méd)* injection, shot *. **faire/se faire faire une ~** to give/have an injection. (**c**) *(Couture) (point)* (straight) stitch; *(rang)* (straight) stitching.

piranha [piʀana] *nm* piranha.

pirate [piʀat] **1** *adj* pirate. **2** *nm* pirate; *(fig: escroc)* swindler, shark *. **~ de l'air** hijacker, skyjacker *; **~ informatique** hacker *. ◆ **pirater** (1) *vt* to pirate. ◆ **piraterie** *nf* piracy; *(acte)* act of piracy. **~ aérienne** hijacking, skyjacking *; **c'est de la ~!** it's daylight robbery!

pire [piʀ] **1** *adj* (**a**) *(comp)* worse. **c'est ~ que jamais** it's worse than ever. (**b**) *(superl)* **le ~, la ~** the worst. **2** *nm*: **le ~** the worst; **le ~ c'est que...** the worst thing *ou* the worst of it is that...; **pour le meilleur et pour le ~** for better and for worse; **au ~** at (the very) worst.

Pirée [piʀe] *nm*: **le ~** Piraeus.

pirogue [piʀɔg] *nf* dugout (canoe), pirogue.

pirouette [piʀwɛt] *nf (lit)* pirouette; *(fig: volte-face)* about-turn *(fig)*; *(faux-fuyant)* evasive reply.

pis¹ [pi] *nm [vache]* udder.

pis² [pi] *(littér)* **1** *adj* worse. **qui ~ est** what is worse. **2** *adv* worse. **de ~ en ~** worse and worse; **dire ~ que pendre de qn** to sling mud at sb *(fig)*, have nothing good to say about sb. **3** *nm*: **le ~** the worst (thing); **au ~ aller** if the worst comes to the worst. ◆ **pis-aller** *nm inv (personne, solution)* stopgap; *(chose)* makeshift.

pisciculture [pisikyltyʀ] *nf* fish breeding.

piscine [pisin] *nf* swimming pool.

Pise [piz] *n* Pisa.

pissenlit [pisɑ̃li] *nm* dandelion. **manger les ~s par la racine** to be pushing up the daisies.

pisser ‡ [pise] (1) **1** *vi [personne]* to pee ‡; *[récipient]* to gush out. **2** *vt*: **ça pisse le sang/l'eau** it's gushing blood/water, there's blood/water gushing from it. ◆ **pisse** ‡ *nf* pee ‡.

pistache [pistaʃ] *nf* pistachio (nut).

piste [pist(ə)] *nf* (**a**) *[animal, suspect]* track, trail; *(Police: indice)* lead. **être sur la bonne ~** to be on the right track; **perdre la ~ du meurtrier** to lose the murderer's trail. (**b**) *[hippodrome]* course; *[stade]* track; *[patinage]* rink; *[danse]* (dance)floor; *[skieurs]* (ski)run; *[cirque]* ring; *(Aviat)* runway. **~ cavalière** bridle path; **~ cyclable** cycle track; *(Athlétisme)* **~ 3** lane 3; **en ~!** *(lit)* into the ring!; *(fig)* set to it! (**c**) *(sentier)* track; *[désert]* trail. (**d**) *[magnétophone]* track. *(Ciné)* **~ sonore** sound track. ◆ **pister** (1) *vt* to track, trail.

pistolet [pistɔlɛ] *nm (arme)* pistol, gun; *[peintre]* spray gun. **peindre au ~** to spray-paint; **~ à air comprimé** airgun; **~ mitrailleur** submachine gun.

piston [pistɔ̃] *nm (Tech)* piston; *(Mus)* valve; *(*: aide)* string-pulling *. ◆ **pistonner** * (1) *vt* to pull strings for * (*auprès de* with). **se faire ~** to get sb to pull (some) strings (for one) *.

piteux, -euse [pitø, øz] *adj (minable)* pitiful, pathetic; *(honteux)* shamefaced. **en ~ état** in a sorry *ou* pitiful state. ◆ **piteusement** *adv* pathetically.

pitié [pitje] *nf* (**a**) *(compassion)* pity. **avoir ~ de qn** to pity sb, feel pity for sb; **prendre qn en ~** to take pity on sb; **il me fait ~** I feel sorry for him, I pity him; **quelle ~ de voir ça** it's pitiful to see (that). (**b**) *(miséricorde)* pity, mercy. **avoir ~ d'un ennemi** to have pity *ou* mercy on an enemy; **~!** *(lit: grâce)* (have) mercy!; *(*: assez)* for goodness' *ou* pity's sake!; **sans ~** *agir* pitilessly, mercilessly, ruthlessly; *personne* pitiless, merciless, ruthless.

piton [pitɔ̃] *nm* (**a**) *(à anneau)* eye; *(à crochet)* hook; *[alpiniste]* piton, peg. (**b**) *(Géog)* peak.

pitoyable [pitwajabl(ə)] *adj (gén)* pitiful, pitiable.

pitre [pitʀ(ə)] *nm (lit, fig)* clown. **faire le ~** to clown *ou* fool about. ◆ **pitrerie** *nf* tomfoolery. **il n'arrête pas de faire des ~s** he's always clowning around *ou* acting the fool.

pittoresque [pitɔʀɛsk(ə)] **1** *adj* picturesque; *récit* colourful, vivid. **2** *nm*: **le ~ de qch** the picturesque quality of sth.

pivert [pivɛʀ] *nm* green woodpecker.

pivoine [pivwan] *nf* peony.

pivot [pivo] *nm (gén)* pivot; *[dent]* post. ◆ **pivotant, e** *adj panneau* pivoting, revolving; *fauteuil* swivel. ◆ **pivoter** (1) *vi [porte]* to revolve, pivot. *[personne]* ~ **(sur ses talons)** to turn *ou* swivel round; **faire ~ qch** to pivot *ou* swivel sth round.

placage [plakaʒ] *nm (en bois)* veneer; *(en pierre)* facing.

placard [plakaʀ] *nm* (**a**) *(armoire)* cupboard. (**b**) *(affiche)* poster, notice. ~ **publicitaire** display advertisement. (**c**) *(*: couche)* thick layer. ◆ **placarder** (1) *vt affiche* to stick up, put up; *mur* to stick posters on, placard.

place [plas] *nf* (**a**) *(esplanade)* square. **la ~ Rouge** Red Square; *(fig)* **sur la ~ publique** in public. (**b**) *[objet]* place. **remettre qch en ~** to put sth back where it belongs *ou* in its proper place; **changer qch de ~** to move *ou* shift sth. (**c**) *[personne] (lit, fig)* place; *(assise)* seat. ~ **d'honneur** place *ou* seat of honour; **prenez ~** take your place *ou* seat; *(lit, fig)* **prendre la ~ de qn** to take sb's place; **il ne tient pas en ~** he can't keep still; *(fig)* **remettre qn à sa ~** to put sb in his place; **laisser la ~ à qn** *(lit)* to give (up) one's seat to sb; *(fig)* to hand over to sb; **il n'est pas à sa ~ dans ce milieu** he is out of place in this setting; **se faire une ~ au soleil** to find o.s. a place in the sun *(fig)*; **être en bonne ~ pour gagner** to be well-placed *ou* in a good position to win; **se mettre à la ~ de qn** to put o.s. in sb's place *ou* in sb's shoes; **à votre ~** if I were you, in your place. (**d**) *(espace libre)* room, space. **prendre/faire de la ~** to take up/make room *ou* space. (**e**) *(siège, billet)* seat; *(prix d'un trajet)* fare; *(emplacement réservé)* space. **louer** *ou* **réserver sa ~** to book one's seat; **payer ~ entière** *(au cinéma etc)* to pay full price; *(dans le bus etc)* to pay full fare; ~ **de parking** parking space; **cinéma de 400 ~s** cinema seating 400 (people) *ou* with a seating capacity of 400; ~ **assise** seat; **tente à 4 ~s** tent that sleeps 4, 4-man tent; **une voiture de 4 ~s** a 4-seater car; **j'ai 3 ~s dans ma voiture** I've room for 3 in my car. (**f**) *(rang) (Scol)* place (in class); *(Sport)* place, placing. **il a eu une ~ de 2ᵉ en histoire** he came *ou* was 2nd in history. (**g**) *(emploi)* job; *[domestique]* position, situation. **une ~ d'employé** a job as a clerk; *(Pol)* **les gens en ~** influential people. (**h**) *(Mil)* ~ **(forte)** fortified town; *(lit, fig)* **s'introduire dans la ~** to get on the inside; ~ **d'armes** parade ground. (**i**) *(Comm, Fin)* market. ~ **financière** money market. (**j**) **de ~ en ~** here and there, in places; **rester sur/se rendre sur ~** to stay on/go to the spot; **être cloué sur ~** to be *ou* stand rooted on the spot; **à la ~ (de)** *(en échange)* instead (of), in place (of); **répondre à la ~ de qn** to reply in sb's place *ou* on sb's behalf; **être en ~** *[plan]* to be ready; *[forces de l'ordre]* to be in place *ou* stationed; **mettre qch en ~** *plan* to set up, organize; *service d'ordre* to deploy; *mécanisme* to install; **faire ~ à qn** *(lit)* to let sb pass; *(fig)* to give way to sb; **faire ~ nette** to make a clean sweep.

placement [plasmɑ̃] *nm (Fin)* investment.

placer [plase] (3) **1** *vt* (**a**) *(mettre) (gén)* to place, put; *invité, spectateur* to seat; *sentinelle* to post, station; *(Boxe) coup* to land, place; *parole* to put in, get in; *(Tech: installer)* to put in, fit in. **vous me placez dans une situation délicate** you're placing *ou* putting me in a tricky position; **il a placé l'action de son roman en Provence** he has set *ou* situated the action of his novel in Provence. (**b**) *malade, écolier* to place (*dans* in). ~ **qn comme vendeur** to get *ou* find sb a job as a salesman; ~ **qn comme apprenti (chez X)** to apprentice sb (to X); **l'orchestre est placé sous la direction de...** the orchestra is conducted by... (**c**) *(Comm: vendre)* to place, sell; *argent (Bourse)* to invest; *(Caisse d'Épargne)* to deposit; *(sur son compte)* to put, pay (*sur* into).

2 se ~ *vpr* (**a**) *[personne]* to take up a position; *(debout)* to stand; *(assis)* to sit (down); *[événement]* to take place, occur, happen. **si nous nous plaçons dans cette perspective** if we look at things from this point of view *ou* angle; **plaçons-nous dans cette hypothèse** let us suppose that this happens. (**b**) *(Scol, Sport)* **se ~ 2ᵉ** to be *ou* come 2nd, be in 2nd place; **il s'est bien placé** he was well placed. (**c**) *[ouvrier]* to get *ou* find a job; *[retraité]* to find a place in a home.

◆ **placé, e** *adj*: **la fenêtre est ~e à gauche** the window is (situated) on the left; **être bien/mal ~** *[terrain]* to be well/badly situated; *[objet, concurrent]* to be well/badly placed; *[spectateur]* to have a good/a poor seat; **sa fierté est mal ~e** his pride is misplaced *ou* out of place; **je suis bien/mal ~ pour vous répondre** I'm in a/in no position to answer.

placide [plasid] *adj* placid. ◆ **placidité** *nf* placidity.

plafond [plafɔ̃] *nm (gén, fig)* ceiling; *[voiture, caverne]* roof. **prix ~** ceiling *ou* maximum price. ◆ **plafonner** (1) **1** *vi [prix, écolier, salaire]* to reach a ceiling *ou* maximum. **2** *vt (Constr)* to put a ceiling in; *salaires* to put an upper limit on. ◆ **plafonnier** *nm [voiture]* courtesy light; *[chambre]* ceiling light.

plage [plaʒ] *nf [mer, lac]* beach; *[disque]* track; *(ville)* (seaside) resort; *(fig: zone)* area. *(Scol)* ~ **horaire** slot (in timetable); ~ **de prix** price range *ou* bracket; ~ **arrière** *(Naut)* quarter-deck; *(Aut)* parcel *ou* back shelf.

plagiat [plaʒja] *nm* plagiarism. ◆ **plagier** (7) *vt* to plagiarize.

plaider [plede] (1) **1** *vt* to plead. ~ **la légitime défense** to plead self-defence; ~ **la cause de qn** *(fig)* to plead sb's cause; *(Jur)* to plead sb's case; **l'affaire s'est plaidée à Paris** the case was heard in Paris. **2** *vi [avocat]* to plead (*pour* for; *contre* against); *(intenter un procès)* to go to court. *(fig)* ~ **pour qn** *[personne]* to speak for sb; *[qualités]* to be a point in sb's favour. ◆ **plaideur, -euse** *nm, f* litigant. ◆ **plaidoirie** *nf (Jur)* defence speech; *(fig)* plea, appeal (*en faveur de* on behalf of). ◆ **plaidoyer** *nm (Jur)* speech for the defence; *(fig)* defence, plea.

plaie [plɛ] *nf (gén)* wound; *(coupure)* cut; *(fig: fléau)* scourge. **quelle ~!** * what a bind! * *ou* pest! * *ou* nuisance!; **remuer le fer dans la ~** to twist the knife in the wound; *(Bible)* **les ~s d'Égypte** the plagues of Egypt.

plaignant, e [plɛɲɑ̃, ɑ̃t] **1** *adj partie* litigant. **2** *nm, f* plaintiff.

plaindre [plɛ̃dʀ(ə)] (52) **1** *vt* (**a**) *personne* to pity, feel sorry for. **elle n'est pas à ~** *(c'est bien fait)* she doesn't deserve to be pitied; *(elle a de la chance)* she's got nothing to complain about; **je vous plains** I pity you (*de faire* for doing). (**b**) *(*: donner chichement)* to begrudge. **2 se ~** *vpr (gémir)* to moan; *(protester)* to complain, grumble, moan * (*de* about); *(Jur: réclamer)* to make a complaint (*de* about, *auprès de* to). **se ~ de** *maux de tête etc* to complain of.

plaine [plɛn] *nf* plain.

plain-pied [plɛ̃pje] *adv*: **de ~** *(pièce)* on the same level (*avec* as); *(maison)* (built) at street-level; *(fig)* **entrer de ~ dans le sujet** to come straight to the point.

plainte [plɛ̃t] *nf (gémissement)* moan, groan; *(protestation)* complaint. **porter ~ contre qn** to lodge a complaint against *ou* about sb. ◆ **plaintif, -ive**

adj plaintive, doleful. ◆ **plaintivement** *adv* plaintively, dolefully.

plaire [plɛʀ] (54) **1** *vi [personne]* ~ **à qn** to be liked by sb; **ça me plaît** *[livre, spectacle, travail]* I like *ou* enjoy it; *[plan]* it suits me; *[sport, activité]* I'm keen on it, I enjoy it; **ce genre de musique ne me plaît pas beaucoup** I'm not keen on *ou* I don't care for that kind of music, that kind of music doesn't appeal to me very much; **c'est une chose qui me plairait beaucoup à faire** it's something I'd very much like to do *ou* I'd love to do; **il cherche à ~ à tout le monde** he tries to please everyone; **ça te plairait d'aller au cinéma?** would you like to go to the pictures?, do you fancy * going *ou* do you feel like going to the pictures?; **quand ça me plaît** when I feel like it, when it suits me, when the fancy takes me *; **je fais ce qui me plaît** I do what I like *ou* as I please; *[idée, repas]* **cela plaît toujours** it always goes down well, it's always popular. **2** *vb impers*: **et s'il me plaît d'y aller?** and what if I want to go?; **comme il vous plaira** just as you like *ou* please; **s'il te plaît, s'il vous plaît** please; **plaît-il?** I beg your pardon? **3 se ~** *vpr*: **il se plaît à Londres** he likes *ou* enjoys being in London; **les fougères se plaisent dans les sous-bois** ferns do well *ou* thrive in the undergrowth; **tu te plais avec ton chapeau?** do you like *ou* fancy * yourself in your hat?; **ces deux-là se plaisent** those two get on well together; **se ~ à lire** to take pleasure in reading.

plaisance [plɛzɑ̃s] *nf*: **la navigation de ~** boating; *(à voile)* sailing, yachting; **bateau de ~** yacht; **maison de ~** country cottage. ◆ **plaisancier** *nm* yachtsman.

plaisant, e [plɛzɑ̃, ɑ̃t] *adj (agréable)* pleasant, agreeable; *(amusant)* amusing, funny; *(ridicule)* laughable, ridiculous. ◆ **plaisamment** *adv* pleasantly; agreeably; amusingly; laughably.

plaisanter [plɛzɑ̃te] (1) **1** *vi* to joke (*sur* about). **et je ne plaisante pas!** and I'm not joking!; **vous plaisantez** you must be joking; **pour ~** for fun *ou* a joke *ou* a laugh *; **il ne plaisante pas sur la discipline** there's no joking with him over matters of discipline. **2** *vt*: **~ qn sur qch** to tease sb about sth. ◆ **plaisanterie** *nf* (**a**) *(blague, raillerie)* joke (*sur* about); *(farce)* practical joke, prank. **aimer la ~** to be fond of a joke; **il est en butte aux ~s de ses amis** his friends are always making fun of him *ou* poking fun at him; **mauvaise ~** (nasty) practical joke. ◆ **plaisantin** *nm (blagueur)* joker; *(fumiste)* phoney *.

plaisir [pleziʀ] *nm* (**a**) *(joie)* pleasure. **prendre ~ à faire qch** to find *ou* take pleasure in doing sth, delight in doing sth; **j'ai le ~ de vous annoncer que...** I have pleasure in announcing that...; **ranger pour le ~ de ranger** to tidy up just for the sake of it; *(iro)* **je vous souhaite bien du ~!** good luck to you! *(iro)*; **au ~ de vous revoir, au ~ *** (I'll) see you again sometime. (**b**) *(distraction)* pleasure; *(dada)* hobby. (**c**) *(littér: volonté)* pleasure *(littér)*, wish. **si c'est votre (bon) ~** if such is your will *ou* wish. (**d**) **faire ~ à qn** to please sb; **cela me fait ~ de vous voir** I'm pleased *ou* delighted to see you; **ça fait ~ à voir** it is a pleasure to see; **fais-moi ~: mange ta soupe** do me a favour, eat your soup; **voulez-vous me faire le ~ de venir dîner?** would you do me the pleasure of dining with me?; **fais-moi le ~ de te taire!** would you mind just being quiet!, do me a favour and be quiet!; **il se fera un ~ de vous reconduire** he'll be (only too) pleased *ou* glad to drive you back; **bon, c'est bien pour vous faire ~** all right, if it will make you happy.

plan[1] [plɑ̃] *nm* (**a**) *[maison, machine]* plan; *[ville, région]* map. **faire des ~s** to draw up plans. (**b**) *(Math etc: surface)* plane. *(dans cuisine)* **~ de travail** work-top; **~ incliné** inclined plane; **en ~ incliné** sloping; **~ d'eau** *(lac)* lake; *(sur un cours d'eau)* stretch of water. (**c**) *(Ciné)* shot. **premier ~** foreground; **dernier ~** background; *(Peinture)* **au deuxième ~** in the middle distance. (**d**) *(fig: niveau)* plane. **mettre qch au deuxième ~** to consider sth of secondary importance; **ce problème vient au premier ~ de nos préoccupations** this problem is uppermost in our minds; **personnalité de premier/second ~** key/minor figure; **au premier ~ de l'actualité** in the forefront of the news. (**e**) *(projet, Écon)* plan. **~ de travail** work plan *ou* programme *ou* schedule; **~ d'action** plan of action; **avoir/exécuter un ~** to have/carry out a plan. (**f**) *[livre, dissertation]* plan, outline, framework. (**g**) **laisser en ~ *** *personne* to leave in the lurch *ou* stranded; *affaires, voiture* to abandon, ditch *; **il a tout laissé en ~ *** he dropped everything; **rester en ~ *** *[projet]* to be left in mid air.

plan[2], plane [plɑ̃, plan] *adj (gén)* flat; *(Math)* plane.

planche [plɑ̃ʃ] *nf* (**a**) *(en bois)* plank; *(plus large)* board; *(rayon)* shelf; *(Naut: passerelle)* gangplank; *(plongeoir)* diving board; *(*: ski)* ski. **~ à dessin/à repasser** drawing/ironing board; **~ à laver** washboard; **~ à roulettes** *(objet)* skateboard; *(sport)* skateboarding; *(fig)* **~ de salut** last hope; **~ à voile** *(objet)* sailboard; *(sport)* windsurfing; *(Théât)* **monter sur les ~s** to go on the stage; *(Natation)* **faire la ~** to float on one's back; **cabine en ~s** wooden hut. (**b**) *(Typ, illustration)* plate. (**c**) *(Horticulture)* bed. ◆ **plancher** *nm (Constr)* floor. **(prix) ~** minimum *ou* floor *ou* bottom price.

plancton [plɑ̃ktɔ̃] *nm* plankton.

planer [plane] (1) *vi [oiseau]* to glide, soar; *(en tournoyant)* to hover; *[avion]* to glide; *[fumée]* to float, hover; *(fig) [rêveur]* to have one's head in the clouds. **~ sur** *[regard]* to look down on *ou* over; *[danger, soupçons]* to hang over.

planète [planɛt] *nf* planet. ◆ **planétaire** *adj (Astron, Tech)* planetary. ◆ **planétarium** *nm* planetarium.

planeur [planœʀ] *nm (Aviat)* glider.

planifier [planifje] (7) *vt* to plan. ◆ **planification** *nf* (economic) planning. ◆ **planning** *nm (Écon, Ind)* programme, schedule. **~ familial** family planning.

planque ‡ [plɑ̃k] *nf (cachette)* hideaway, hideout; *(travail)* cushy ‡ *ou* soft * job. ◆ **planquer** ‡ (1) **1** *vt* to hide *ou* stash * away. **2 se ~** *vpr* to take cover.

plant [plɑ̃] *nm (plante)* seedling, young plant; *(plantation)* bed; *[arbres]* plantation. **un ~ de vigne** a young vine.

plantation [plɑ̃tɑsjɔ̃] *nf (action)* planting; *(culture)* plant; *(terrain)* bed; *[arbres]* plantation; *(exploitation agricole)* plantation. **faire des ~s de fleurs** to plant flowers (out).

plante [plɑ̃t] *nf* (**a**) *(Bot)* plant. **~ fourragère** fodder plant; **~ grasse** succulent (plant); **~ grimpante** creeper; **~ verte** green (foliage) plant. (**b**) *(Anat)* **~** *(des pieds)* sole (of the foot).

planter [plɑ̃te] (1) *vt* (**a**) *plante* to plant, put in; *jardin* to put plants in; *(repiquer)* to plant out. **avenue plantée d'arbres** tree-lined avenue. (**b**) *clou* to hammer in, knock in; *pieu* to drive in; *aiguille* to stick in. **~ un poignard dans le dos de qn** to knife *ou* stab sb in the back; **se ~ une épine dans le doigt** to get a thorn stuck in one's finger; **la flèche se planta dans la cible** the arrow sank into the target. (**c**) *(mettre) objet* to stick, put. **il se planta devant moi** he planted himself in front of me; **rester planté devant une vitrine** * to stand looking at a shop window; **~ là *** *personne, voiture* to dump *, ditch *; *outils* to dump *, drop; *métier* to pack in *; *(se tromper)* **se ~ *** to get it all wrong. (**d**) *tente* to put up, pitch; *(Théât) décors* to set up. **~ une échelle contre un mur** to stand a ladder (up) against a wall. ◆ **planteur** *nm (colon)* planter. ◆ **plantoir** *nm* dibble.

planton [plɑ̃tɔ̃] *nm (Mil)* orderly. **faire le** ~ * to hang about *.

plantureux, -euse [plɑ̃tyʀø, øz] *adj repas* copious; *région* fertile. **récolte** ~**euse** bumper crop.

plaquage [plakaʒ] *nm (Rugby)* tackle.

plaque [plak] *nf [métal, verre]* sheet, plate; *[marbre, chocolat]* slab; *(de verglas, sur la peau)* patch; *(Élec, Phot, de revêtement)* plate; *(portant une inscription)* plaque; *(insigne)* badge. ~ **chauffante** *ou* **de cuisson** hotplate; ~ **d'identité** identity disc; *(Aut)* ~ **minéralogique** number *ou* license *(US)* plate; ~ **tournante** *(Rail)* turntable; *(fig)* centre.

plaquer [plake] (1) *vt* (**a**) *bois* to veneer; *bijoux* to plate. (**b**) *(‡: abandonner) personne* to ditch *; *emploi* to chuck (in *ou* up) ‡, pack in *. (**c**) *(aplatir) cheveux* to plaster down. ~ **qn au sol** to pin sb to the ground; **se** ~ **contre un mur** to flatten o.s. against a wall. (**d**) *(Rugby)* to tackle, bring down. (**e**) *(Mus) accord* to play. ◆ **plaqué, e 1** *adj*: ~ *(or etc)* (gold *etc*) plated; ~ **chêne** oak veneered. **2** *nm* plate. **c'est du** ~ it's plated.

plasma [plasma] *nm (Anat, Phys)* plasma.

plastic [plastik] *nm* gelignite. ◆ **plasticage** *nm* bombing (*de* of); bomb attack (*de* on).

plasticien [plastisjɛ̃] *nm (chirurgien)* plastic surgeon.

plastifier [plastifje] (7) *vt* to coat with plastic.

plastique [plastik] **1** *adj* plastic. **en matière** ~ plastic; **chirurgie** ~ plastic surgery. **2** *nm* plastic. **3** *nf* plastic art.

plastiquer [plastike] (1) *vt* to blow up, carry out a bomb attack on.

plastron [plastʀɔ̃] *nm [chemise]* shirt front; *[escrimeur]* plastron.

plastronner [plastʀɔne] (1) *vi* to swagger.

plat[1], plate [pla, plat] **1** *adj* (**a**) *(gén)* flat; *eau* plain, non-fizzy; *angle, cheveux* straight; *style* flat, dull; *(obséquieux)* obsequious. **bateau à fond** ~ flat-bottomed boat; **chaussure à talon** ~ flat(-heeled) shoe. (**b**) **poser qch à** ~ to lay sth (down) flat; **être à** ~ *[pneu, batterie]* to be flat; *[automobiliste]* to have a flat tyre; (*) *[personne]* to be washed out *; **la grippe l'a mis à** ~ * he was laid low by (the) flu; **tomber à** ~ *[plaisanterie]* to fall flat; **tomber à** ~ **ventre** to fall flat on one's face; **se mettre à** ~ **ventre** to lie face down; *(fig)* **se mettre à** ~ **ventre devant qn** to crawl to sb. **2** *nm (partie plate)* flat (part). **course de** ~ flat race; *(fig)* **faire du** ~ **à** * *supérieur* to crawl to; *femme* to sweet-talk *. ◆ **plate-bande,** *pl* **plates-bandes** *nf (Horticulture)* flower bed. **piétiner les** ~**s-**~**s de qn** * to tread on sb else's patch. ◆ **plate-forme,** *pl* **plates-formes** *nf (gén, fig)* platform; *(Rail: wagon)* flat wagon *ou* car *(US)*. ~ *(de forage en mer)* (off-shore) oil rig; ~ **flottante** floating rig.

plat[2] [pla] *nm (récipient, mets)* dish; *(partie du repas)* course. **il en a fait tout un** ~ * he made a great fuss about it; **mettre les petits** ~**s dans les grands** to lay on a first-rate meal; ~ **du jour** today's special; ~ **de résistance** *[repas]* main course; *(fig)* pièce de résistance.

platane [platan] *nm* plane tree.

plateau, *pl* ~**x** [plato] *nm (de serveur)* tray; *[balance]* pan; *[électrophone]* turntable, deck; *[table]* top; *[graphique]* plateau; *(Géog)* plateau; *(Théât)* stage; *(Ciné, TV)* set; *(Rail: wagon)* flat wagon *ou* car *(US)*; *(plate-forme roulante)* trailer. ~ **de fromages** cheeseboard; ~**-repas** tray meal; *(Ciné)* ~ **de tournage** film set.

platine [platin] **1** *nm, adj inv* platinum. **2** *nf [électrophone]* deck, turntable.

platitude [platityd] *nf [livre]* dullness; *(propos)* platitude.

plâtre [plɑtʀ(ə)] *nm (matière)* plaster; *(objet)* plaster cast. *(Constr)* **les** ~**s** the plasterwork; *(Chirurgie)* ~ **de marche** walking plaster *ou* cast *(US)*. ◆ **plâtras** *nm (débris)* rubble. ◆ **plâtrer** (1) *vt mur* to plaster; *jambe* to set *ou* put in plaster. ◆ **plâtrier** *nm* plasterer.

plausible [plozibl(ə)] *adj* plausible.

playback [plɛbak] *nm* miming. **chanter en** ~ to mime to a prerecorded tape.

plébiscite [plebisit] *nm* plebiscite. ◆ **plébisciter** (1) *vt (Pol)* to elect by plebiscite. *(fig)* **se faire** ~ to be elected by an overwhelming majority.

pléiade [plejad] *nf (gén)* pleiad. **une** ~ **d'artistes** a whole host of stars.

plein, pleine [plɛ̃, plɛn] **1** *adj* (**a**) *(rempli)* full; *vie, journée* full, busy. ~ **à déborder** full to overflowing; ~ **à craquer** full to bursting, crammed full; **un** ~ **panier de pommes** a whole basketful of apples; **avoir le ventre** ~ * to be full, have eaten one's fill; **être** ~ **aux as** ‡ to be rolling in money *; *(péj)* **un gros** ~ **de soupe** ‡ a big fat slob ‡ *(péj)*; ~ **comme une barrique** ‡ as drunk as a lord; ~ **de** *(gén)* full of; *taches* covered in *ou* with; *idées* bursting with; **salle pleine de monde** room full of people, crowded room; **remarque pleine de finesse** very shrewd remark; **être** ~ **d'égards pour qn** to shower attention on sb. (**b**) *succès, confiance* complete, total. **accord** ~ **et entier** wholehearted consent; **absent un jour** ~ absent for a whole day; **à** ~ **temps** full-time; **avoir les** ~**s pouvoirs** to have full powers; **politique de** ~**-emploi** policy of full employment; **être membre de** ~ **droit** to be a member in one's own right. (**c**) *lune* full. **la mer est pleine** the tide is in, it is high tide; **en pleine mer** on the open sea. (**d**) *paroi* solid; *trait* unbroken, continuous; *voix* rich, sonorous. (**e**) *(Vét)* pregnant, in calf (*ou* foal, lamb *etc*). (**f**) *(intensité)* **la pleine lumière** the bright light; **avoir pleine conscience de qch** to be fully aware of sth; **être en pleine forme** * to be in *ou* on top form; **de son** ~ **gré** of one's own free will; **réclamer qch de** ~ **droit** to claim sth as one's right; **heurter qch de** ~ **fouet** to crash headlong into sth; *[usine]* **marcher à** ~ **rendement** to work at full capacity; **ça sent l'ammoniaque à** ~ **nez** there's a terrible smell *ou* stench of ammonia; **respirer à** ~**s poumons** to take deep breaths; **prendre qch à pleines mains** to grasp sth firmly. (**g**) ~ **air** open air; **les enfants ont** ~ **air le mercredi** the children have games *ou* sport on Wednesdays; **jeux de** ~ **air** outdoor games; **en** ~ **air** *spectacle, cirque* open-air; *s'asseoir* in the open (air). (**h**) **en** ~ **milieu** right *ou* bang * *ou* slap * in the middle; **en pleine tête** right in the head; **oiseau en** ~ **vol** bird in full flight; **en pleine jeunesse** in the bloom of youth; **en** ~ **jour** in broad daylight; **le jardin est en** ~ **soleil** the garden is in full sun; **enfant en pleine croissance** child who is growing fast *ou* shooting up; **affaire en pleine croissance** rapidly expanding *ou* growing business; **en pleine saison** at the height *ou* peak of the season; **je suis en** ~ **travail** I'm in the middle of work *ou* working; **en pleine obscurité** in complete darkness; **arriver en** ~ **drame** to arrive in the middle of a crisis.

2 *adv* (**a**) **avoir de l'encre** ~ **les mains** to have ink all over one's hands, have one's hands covered in ink; **il a des jouets** ~ **un placard** he's got a cupboardful *ou* a cupboard full of toys; **se diriger** ~ **ouest** to head due west; **en avoir** ~ **le dos de qch** * to be fed up with sth *; **en avoir** ~ **les jambes** * to be all-in *; **il a voulu nous en mettre** ~ **la vue** * he wanted to dazzle us. (**b**) ~ **de** * *argent, gens etc* lots of, loads of *; **il a mis** ~ **de chocolat sur sa veste** he has got chocolate all over his jacket. (**c**) **en** ~: **la lumière frappait son visage en** ~ the light was shining straight into his face; **en** ~ **devant toi** right *ou* straight in front of you.

(**d**) **à** ~ *fonctionner* at full capacity; *utiliser* to the full; **les légumes donnent à** ~ it is the height of the vegetable season.
3 *nm* (**a**) **faire le** ~ *(Aut)* to fill up; *(Théât)* to have a full house; **le** ~ **, s'il vous plaît** fill it up please. (**b**) *[animation, fête]* height.

pleinement [plɛnmɑ̃] *adv vivre* to the full; *approuver* wholeheartedly, fully; *responsable* wholly, entirely, fully. **utiliser qch** ~ to make full use of sth.

plénipotentiaire [plenipɔtɑ̃sjɛʀ] *adj, nm* plenipotentiary.

pléonasme [pleɔnasm(ə)] *nm* pleonasm.

pléthore [pletɔʀ] *nf* overabundance, plethora. ◆ **pléthorique** *adj nombre* excessive; *effectifs* overabundant.

pleurer [plœʀe] (1) **1** *vi* (**a**) *[personne]* to cry, weep (*sur* over); *[yeux]* to water, run. ~ **de rire/de rage** to shed tears of laughter/rage; **faire** ~ **qn** *[peine]* to make sb cry; *[oignons]* to make sb's eyes water; ~ **comme une madeleine** to cry one's eyes *ou* one's heart out; **sur le point de** ~ almost in tears, on the verge of tears; **triste à** ~ terribly sad; **bête à** ~ pitifully stupid. (**b**) *(péj: réclamer)* to moan. **2** *vt* (**a**) *personne* to mourn (for); *chose* to bemoan. ~ **des larmes de joie** to weep *ou* shed tears of joy; ~ **toutes les larmes de son corps** to cry one's eyes out. (**b**) *(péj) (quémander)* to beg for; *(lésiner sur)* to begrudge, stint. ~ **misère** to moan about one's lot. ◆ **pleur** *nm*: **en** ~**s** in tears.

pleurésie [plœʀezi] *nf* pleurisy.

pleurnicher [plœʀniʃe] (1) *vi* to snivel *. ◆ **pleurnicherie** *nf*: ~**(s)** snivelling *. ◆ **pleurnicheur, -euse** **1** *adj* snivelling *. **2** *nm, f* crybaby *.

pleuviner [pløvine] (1) *vi* to drizzle.

pleuvoir [pløvwaʀ] (23) **1** *vb impers* to rain. **il pleut** it's raining; **il pleut à torrents, il pleut des cordes** it's pouring (down). **2** *vi [coups, projectiles]* to rain down; *[critiques, invitations]* to shower down. **faire** ~ **des coups sur qn** to rain blows (up)on sb.

plexiglas [plɛksiglas] *nm* ® plexiglass ®.

pli [pli] *nm* (**a**) *[rideau etc]* fold; *(Couture)* pleat. **(faux)** ~ crease; ~ **de pantalon** trouser crease; **ton manteau fait un** ~ **dans le dos** your coat creases (up) at the back; **garder un bon** ~ to keep its shape; *[vêtement]* **prendre un mauvais** ~ to get crushed; **les** ~**s et les replis de sa cape** the many folds of his cloak; *(fig)* **cela ne fait pas un** ~ * there's no doubt about it. (**b**) *[genou, bras]* bend; *[menton, ventre]* (skin-)fold; *[bouche, yeux]* crease; *[front]* crease, furrow, line. (**c**) *(habitude)* habit. **prendre le** ~ **de faire** to get into the habit of doing; **mauvais** ~ bad habit. (**d**) *(enveloppe)* envelope; *(lettre)* letter. (**e**) *(Cartes)* trick. **faire un** ~ to win *ou* take a trick. (**f**) *(Géol)* fold. ~ **de terrain** fold in the ground, undulation.

pliant, e [plijɑ̃, ɑ̃t] **1** *adj table etc* collapsible, folding. **2** *nm* folding *ou* collapsible stool, campstool.

plie [pli] *nf* plaice.

plier [plije] (7) **1** *vt* (**a**) *(gén)* to fold; *(ranger)* to fold up; *volets* to fold back. *(fig)* ~ **bagage** to pack up and go. (**b**) *branche, genou* to bend. *(fig)* ~ **le genou devant qn** to bow before sb; **plié par l'âge** bent (double) with age; **plié (en deux) de rire/par la douleur** doubled up with laughter/pain; ~ **qn à une discipline** to force a discipline upon sb. **2** *vi* (**a**) *[branche]* to bend (over); *[plancher]* to sag. ~ **sous le poids des ans** to be weighed down by years. (**b**) *[personne]* to yield, give in; *[armée]* to give way, lose ground. **faire** ~ **qn** to make sb give in. **3 se** ~ *vpr [chaise]* to fold (up). **se** ~ **à** *règle* to submit to; *circonstances* to bow to, yield to; *désirs* to give in to.

plinthe [plɛ̃t] *nf* skirting board.

plisser [plise] (1) **1** *vt jupe* to pleat; *papier* to fold (over); *(en chiffonnant)* to crease; *lèvres* to pucker (up); *yeux* to screw up; *front* to crease, wrinkle; *(Géol)* to fold. **2** *vi* to become creased. **3 se** ~ *vpr [front]* to crease, furrow; *[lèvres]* to pucker (up). ◆ **plissé, e** *adj jupe* pleated; *peau* creased, wrinkled. ◆ **plissement** *nm*: ~ **de terrain** fold. ◆ **plissure** *nf* pleats.

pliure [plijyʀ] *nf (gén)* fold; *[bras, genou]* bend.

plomb [plɔ̃] *nm (métal)* lead; *(Pêche)* sinker; *(Chasse)* piece of (lead) shot; *(Typ)* type; *(Élec: fusible)* fuse. **avec** ~ *essence* leaded; **de** ~ *tuyau* lead; *soldat* tin; *ciel* leaden; *soleil* blazing; *sommeil* deep, heavy; **avoir du** ~ **dans l'aile** to be in a bad way; **avoir du** ~ **dans la tête** to have common sense; **le soleil tombe à** ~ the sun is blazing straight down; **les** ~**s ont sauté** the fuses have blown; **sans** ~ *essence* lead-free.

plomber [plɔ̃be] (1) *vt canne, ligne* to weight (with lead); *dent* to fill; *colis* to seal (with lead). ◆ **plombage** *nm [dent]* filling. ◆ **plombé, e** *adj couleur* leaden. ◆ **plomberie** *nf (métier, installations)* plumbing; *(atelier)* plumber's (work)shop. ◆ **plombier** *nm* plumber.

plonger [plɔ̃ʒe] (3) **1** *vi [personne, sous-marin, avion]* to dive (*dans* into, *sur* on, onto); *[route, terrain]* to plunge down; *[racines]* to go down. **il plongea dans sa poche pour prendre son mouchoir** he plunged his hand *ou* he dived into his pocket to get his handkerchief out. **2** *vt (lit, fig)* ~ **qch/qn dans** to plunge *ou* thrust sth/sb into; ~ **qn dans la surprise** to surprise sb greatly; ~ **qn dans le désespoir** to throw *ou* plunge sb into despair; ~ **son regard sur/vers** to cast one's eyes at/towards; **il plongea son regard dans mes yeux** he looked deeply into my eyes. **3 se** ~ *vpr*: **se** ~ **dans** *lecture* to bury *ou* immerse o.s. in; *eau* to plunge into. ◆ **plongé, e**[1] *adj*: ~ **dans** *obscurité, misère* plunged in; *vice* steeped in; *méditation* immersed in, deep in; *livre* buried *ou* immersed in; ~ **dans le sommeil** sound asleep, in a deep sleep. ◆ **plongeant, e** *adj décolleté, tir* plunging. **vue** ~**e** view from above. ◆ **plongée**[2] *nf (action)* diving; *(exercice)* dive; *[sous-marin]* submersion. ~ **sous-marine** *(gén)* diving; *(sans scaphandre)* skin diving, scuba diving; ~ **de haut vol** platform high diving. ◆ **plongeoir** *nm* diving board. ◆ **plongeon** *nm* dive. **faire un** ~ to dive; *(fig)* **faire le** ~ to make heavy losses. ◆ **plongeur, -euse** *nm, f* (**a**) *(Sport)* diver; *(sans scaphandre)* skin diver. (**b**) *[restaurant]* dish-washer.

plouf [pluf] *nm, excl* splash.

ployer [plwaje] (8) *(littér)* **1** *vi (lit, fig)* to bend; *[poutre]* to sag; *[armée]* to yield, give in. **2** *vt* to bend.

pluie [plɥi] *nf* (**a**) rain; *(averse)* shower. **le temps est à la** ~ it looks like rain; **temps de** ~ wet *ou* rainy weather; ~ **battante** driving *ou* lashing rain; ~ **diluvienne** downpour; ~ **fine** drizzle. (**b**) *[cadeaux]* shower; *[coups]* hail, shower. **verser qch en** ~ to sprinkle sth in *ou* on. (**c**) **faire la** ~ **et le beau temps** to rule the roost; **il n'est pas né de la dernière** ~ he wasn't born yesterday.

plumage [plymaʒ] *nm* plumage, feathers.

plumard ‡ [plymaʀ] *nm* bed.

plume [plym] *nf* (**a**) *[oiseau]* feather. **chapeau à** ~**s** feathered hat; **oreiller de** ~**s** feather pillow; **soulever qch comme une** ~ to lift sth up as if it were a featherweight; **il y a laissé des** ~ **s** * *(gén)* he came off badly; *(financièrement)* he got his fingers burnt. (**b**) *(pour écrire)* pen; *(pour vacciner)* vaccine point. **il a la** ~ **facile** writing comes easily to him; **prendre la** ~ **pour...** to take up one's pen to... ◆ **plumeau,** *pl* ~**x** *nm* feather duster. ◆ **plumer** (1) *vt volaille* to pluck; (‡ *fig) personne* to fleece *. ◆ **plumet** *nm* plume.

plumier [plymje] *nm* pencil box.

plupart [plypaʀ] *nf*: **la ~ des gens** most people, the majority of people; **la ~ des gens qui se trouvaient là** most of the people there; **dans la ~ des cas** in most cases, in the majority of cases; **pour la ~** for the most part; **la ~ du temps** most of the time.

pluriel, -elle [plyʀjɛl] **1** *adj* plural. **2** *nm* plural. **au ~** in the plural; **la première personne du ~** the first person plural.

plus **1** *adv nég* [ply] (**a**) *(temps)* no longer. **il n'en a ~ besoin** he doesn't need it any longer, he no longer needs it; **il n'a ~ dit un mot** he didn't say another word; *(euph)* **son père n'est ~** his father has passed away *(euph)*; **elle n'est ~ très jeune** she's not as young as she was; **~ de doute** no doubt now; **il n'y a ~ d'enfants!** children aren't what they used to be. (**b**) *(quantité)* no more. **elle n'a ~ de pain** she hasn't (got) any more bread, she's got no (more) bread left; **des fruits? il n'y en a ~** fruit? there is none left; **il n'y a ~ personne** there's no one left; **il n'y a ~ rien** there's nothing left; **il n'y a ~ rien d'autre à faire** there's nothing else to do; **on n'y voit ~ guère** *ou* **presque ~ rien** you can hardly see anything now. (**c**) *(avec que: seulement)* **il n'y a ~ que des miettes** there are only crumbs left; **~ que huit jours avant les vacances** only a week to go before the holidays; **~ que 5 km à faire** only another 5 km to go.
2 *adv emploi comparatif* [ply(s)] (**a**) *travailler etc* more (*que* than). **il est ~ intelligent/âgé (que moi)** he is more intelligent/he is older (than me *ou* than I am); **trois fois ~ cher/souvent que...** three times as expensive/often as...; **il est ~ qu'intelligent** he's clever to say the least; **j'aime dix fois ~ le théâtre que le cinéma** I like the theatre ten times better than the cinema. (**b**) **~ de pain** *etc* more bread *etc*; **il n'y aura pas ~ de monde demain** there won't be any more people tomorrow; **il y aura ~ de 100 personnes** there will be more than *ou* over 100 people; **les enfants de ~ de 4 ans** children over 4; **il n'y avait pas ~ de 10 personnes** there were no more than 10 people; **il est ~ de 9 heures** it's after *ou* past 9 o'clock; **~ d'un** more than one. (**c**) **~ on est de fous, ~ on rit** the more the merrier; **~ on boit, ~ on a soif** the more you drink, the thirstier you get; **~ il gagne, moins il est content** the more he earns, the less happy he is. (**d**) **elle a 10 ans de ~ (que lui)** she's 10 years older (than him); **il y a 10 personnes de ~ qu'hier** there are 10 more people than yesterday; **une fois de ~** once more, once again; **les faux frais sont en ~** the incidental expenses are not included *ou* are extra; **deux verres de ~** *ou* **en ~** two more *ou* extra glasses; *(de trop)* two glasses too many; **en ~ de son travail** on top of *ou* in addition to his work. (**e**) **de ~ en ~** more and more; **aller de ~ en ~ vite** to go faster and faster; **~ ou moins** more or less; **~ que jamais** more than ever; **qui ~ est, de plus** furthermore, what is more, moreover.
3 *adv emploi superlatif* [ply(s)]: **le film le ~ long/beau que j'aie vu** the longest/most beautiful film I've ever seen; **le ~ intelligent des deux** the cleverer *ou* the more intelligent of the two; **le ~ intelligent de tous** the cleverest *ou* most intelligent of all; **la ~ grande partie de son temps** most of his time; **le livre que je lis le ~ souvent** the book I read most often; **il a couru le ~ vite** he ran the fastest; **ce que j'aime le ~** what I like (the) most *ou* (the) best; **c'est le samedi qu'il y a le ~ de monde** it's on Saturdays that there are (the) most people; **prends le ~ possible de livres/de beurre** take as many books/as much butter as possible *ou* as you can; **au ~** at the most, at the outside; **tout au ~** at the very most.
4 *conj* [plys] plus. **les voisins, ~ leurs enfants** the neighbours, plus *ou* and their children; *(degré)* **il fait ~ deux** it's plus two (degrees), it's two above freezing.
5 *nm* [plys] *(Math)* **(signe) ~** plus (sign).
◆ **plus-que-parfait** [plyskəpaʀfɛ] *nm* pluperfect (tense), past perfect. ◆ **plus-value,** *pl* **plus-values** [plyvaly] *nf (bénéfice)* profit; *(imposable)* capital gains.

plusieurs [plyzjœʀ] *adj et pron indéf pl* several. **nous nous sommes mis à ~ pour...** several of us got together to...

plutonium [plytɔnjɔm] *nm* plutonium.

plutôt [plyto] *adv* (**a**) *(de préférence)* rather; *(à la place)* instead. **prends ce livre ~ que celui-là** take this book rather than *ou* instead of that one; **cette maladie affecte ~ les enfants** this illness affects children for the most part *ou* tends to affect children; **~ souffrir que mourir** it is better to suffer than to die. (**b**) *(plus exactement)* rather. **il est ignorant ~ que sot** he's ignorant rather *ou* more than stupid. (**c**) *(assez) chaud, bon* rather, quite, fairly, pretty *. **c'est ~ bon signe** that's quite *ou* rather a good sign; **il est ~ petit** he is rather *ou* somewhat on the small side, he is rather *ou* fairly small.

pluvieux, -euse [plyvjø, øz] *adj* rainy, wet.

pneu [pnø] *nm* (*abrév de* **pneumatique**) *[véhicule]* tyre, tire *(US)*; *(message)* letter sent by pneumatic despatch *ou* tube. **~ clouté** *ou* **à clous** studded tyre *ou* tire *(US)*; **~-neige** snow tyre *ou* tire *(US)*.

pneumatique [pnømatik] **1** *adj (Sci)* pneumatic; *(gonflable)* inflatable. **2** *nm* = **pneu.**

pneumonie [pnømɔni] *nf*: **la ~** pneumonia; **une ~** an attack *ou* a bout of pneumonia; **faire une ~** to have pneumonia.

Pô [po] *nm*: **le ~** the Po.

poche [pɔʃ] *nf (gén)* pocket; *[kangourou]* pouch; *(sac)* bag. **~ revolver/intérieure** hip/inside pocket; **~ de pantalon/d'air** trouser/air pocket; *(Méd)* **~ des eaux** amniotic sac; **de ~** *mouchoir* pocket; *livre* paperback; **format de ~** pocket-size; **j'avais 10 F en ~** I had 10 francs on me; **en être de sa ~** * to be out of pocket; **il a payé de sa ~** he paid for it out of his (own) pocket; **mettre qn dans sa ~** * to twist sb round one's little finger; **c'est dans la ~!** * it's in the bag! *; **faire les ~s à qn** * to go through sb's pockets; **connaître un endroit comme sa ~** to know a place like the back of one's hand; *[veste]* **faire des ~s** to bag, go out of shape.

pocher [pɔʃe] (1) *vt (Culin)* to poach. **~ un œil à qn** to give sb a black eye.

pochette [pɔʃɛt] *nf (mouchoir)* pocket handkerchief; *(petite poche)* breast pocket; *(enveloppe)* envelope; *(étui)* case; *[disque]* sleeve. **~ surprise** lucky bag; **~ d'allumettes** book of matches.

podium [pɔdjɔm] *nm* podium. **monter sur le ~** to mount the podium.

podologie [pɔdɔlɔʒi] *nf* chiropody, podiatry *(US)*. ◆ **podologue** *nmf* chiropodist, podiatrist *(US)*.

poêle[1] [pwal] *nf*: **~ (à frire)** frying pan; **passer à la ~** to fry.

poêle[2], **poële** [pwal] *nm* stove.

poème [pɔɛm] *nm* poem. **c'est tout un ~** * *(compliqué)* it's a real palaver *; *(indescriptible)* it defies description. ◆ **poésie** *nf (art)* poetry; *(poème)* poem. ◆ **poète** **1** *nm* poet. **2** *adj tempérament* poetic. **être ~** to be a poet. ◆ **poétesse** *nf* poetess. ◆ **poétique** *adj* poetic(al). ◆ **poétiquement** *adv* poetically.

pognon ‡ [pɔɲɔ̃] *nm* dough ‡, lolly ‡.

poids [pwa] **1** *nm* (**a**) *(lit, fig)* weight. **prendre du ~** to gain *ou* put on weight; **vendu au ~** sold by weight; **quel ~ pèse-t-il?** what weight is he?, what does he weigh?; **plier sous le ~ des sacs/des soucis** to be weighed down with bags/by worries; **il ne fait pas le ~** *[acteur, homme politique]* he doesn't measure up; *[lutteur]* he's no match for his opponent; **enlever un ~ (de la conscience) à qn** to take a weight *ou* a load off sb's mind; **avoir un ~ sur l'estomac** to have something lying heavy on one's stomach; **argument de ~** weighty *ou* forceful argument. (**b**) *(Sport)* shot. **lancer le ~** to put(t) the shot. (**c**) *(boxeur)* **~ lourd** heavyweight; **~ mouche** flyweight; **~ moyen** middleweight; **~ plume** featherweight. **2** : *(Sport)* **~s et haltères** weight lifting; **~ lourd** *(camion)* lorry, truck *(US)*; *(Tech, fig)* **~ mort** dead weight; **~ spécifique** specific gravity; *[véhicule]* **~ à vide** tare.

poignant, e [pwaɲɑ̃, ɑ̃t] *adj* poignant, heart-rending.

poignard [pwaɲaʀ] *nm* dagger. **coup de ~** stab. ◆**poignarder** (1) *vt* to stab, knife.

poigne [pwaɲ] *nf (étreinte)* grip; *(main)* hand. **avoir de la ~** *(lit)* to have a strong grip; *(fig)* to be firm-handed.

poignée [pwaɲe] *nf (quantité)* handful; *[porte etc]* handle. **~ de main** handshake; **donner une ~ de main à qn** to shake hands with sb.

poignet [pwaɲɛ] *nm (Anat)* wrist; *(Habillement)* cuff.

poil [pwal] **1** *nm* (**a**) *(Anat)* hair; *[brosse]* bristle; *[étoffe]* strand. **avoir du ~** *ou* **des ~s sur la poitrine** to have hairs on one's chest; **manteau en ~ de lapin/de chameau** rabbit-skin/camel-hair coat; *(pelage)* **chat qui a un beau ~** cat with a sleek coat *ou* with sleek fur; **caresser dans le sens du ~** *chat* to stroke the right way; *(fig) personne* to rub up the right way; **les ~s d'un tapis/d'un tissu** the pile of a carpet/of a fabric. (**b**) (*: *un peu*) **ça mesure un mètre, à un ~ près** it measures roughly one metre; **il n'y a pas un ~ de différence entre les deux** there isn't the slightest difference between the two (of them); **il s'en est fallu d'un ~** it was a near thing *ou* a close shave. (**c**) **être à ~** ⁑ to be in the altogether * *ou* in one's birthday suit *; **se mettre à ~** ⁑ to strip off; **c'est au (quart de) ~** * it's great * *ou* fantastic *; **avoir un ~ dans la main** * to be bone-idle *; **être de bon/de mauvais ~** * to be in a good/bad mood; **tomber sur le ~ à qn** * to go for * *ou* lay into * sb; **reprendre du ~ de la bête** * to regain strength. **2** : **~ de carotte** *personne* red-haired; *cheveux* red; **~ à gratter** itching powder. ◆**poilu, e** **1** *adj* hairy. **2** *nm* poilu *(French soldier in First World War)*.

poinçon [pwɛ̃sɔ̃] *nm* (**a**) *[cordonnier]* awl; *[graveur]* style; *(pour estampiller)* die, stamp. (**b**) *(estampille)* hallmark. ◆**poinçonner** (1) *vt marchandise* to stamp; *or etc* to hallmark; *billet* to punch. ◆**poinçonneur, -euse** **1** *nm, f (personne)* ticketpuncher. **2** *nf (machine)* punching machine.

poindre [pwɛ̃dʀ(ə)] (49) *vi (littér) [jour]* to break; *[plante]* to come up, peep through.

poing [pwɛ̃] *nm* fist. **taper du ~ sur la table** to thump the table; **mettre son ~ dans la figure de qn** to punch sb in the face; **revolver au ~** revolver in hand; **menacer qn du ~** to shake one's fist at sb.

point¹ [pwɛ̃] **1** *nm* (**a**) *(endroit, degré)* point. **pour aller d'un ~ à un autre** to go from one point *ou* place *ou* spot to another; **avoir atteint le ~ où...** to have reached the point *ou* stage where...; **nous en sommes toujours au même ~** we haven't got any further; **au ~ où on en est** considering the situation we're in; **~ d'ébullition** boiling point; **jusqu'à un certain ~** up to a point, to a certain extent; **au plus haut ~** extremely; **au plus haut ~ de la gloire** at the height *ou* peak *ou* summit of glory; **est-il possible d'être bête à ce ~(-là)!** how stupid can you get? *; **sa colère avait atteint un ~ tel que...** he was so angry that..., his anger was such that...; **il a mangé au ~ de se rendre malade** he ate so much (that) he was sick.
(**b**) *(détail, subdivision)* point. **~ de philosophie** point of philosophy; **passons au ~ suivant de l'ordre du jour** let us move on to the next item on the agenda; **~ de détail** minor point, point of detail; **ils sont d'accord sur ce ~** they agree on this point *ou* score; **se ressembler en tout ~** to resemble each other in every respect.
(**c**) *(position) (Aviat, Naut)* position. *(Naut)* **faire le ~** to plot one's position; **faire le ~ de la situation** *(analyse)* to take stock of the situation, review the situation; *(résumé)* to sum up the situation.
(**d**) *(marque) (en morse, sur i etc)* dot; *(ponctuation)* full stop, period; *(tache)* spot, speck; *[dé]* pip. *(fig)* **mettre les ~s sur les i** to dot one's i's (and cross one's t's), spell it out; **mettre un ~ final à qch** to put an end to sth; **tu n'iras pas, un ~ c'est tout** you're not going — period *ou* full stop.
(**e**) *(score) (Cartes, Sport)* point; *(Scol, Univ)* mark, point; *[retraite]* unit; *[salaire]* point. *(Boxe)* **aux ~s** on points; **bon/mauvais ~** *(Scol)* good/bad mark *(for conduct etc)*; *(fig)* plus/minus (mark); **enlever un ~ par faute** to take a mark *ou* point off for every mistake.
(**f**) *(Couture)* stitch. **faire un ~ à qch** to put a stitch in sth.
(**g**) *(Typ)* point.
(**h**) **à ~** *viande* medium; **arriver à ~ (nommé)** to arrive just at the right moment; **au ~** *photo* in focus; *procédé* perfected; *discours* up to scratch; **mettre au ~** to (bring into) focus; to perfect; **mettre une affaire au ~ avec qn** to finalize *ou* settle all the details of a matter with sb; *[machine, spectacle]* **ce n'est pas encore au ~** it isn't quite up to scratch yet; **j'étais sur le ~ de faire du café** I was just going to *ou* (just) about to make some coffee.
2 : **~ d'appui** *[levier]* fulcrum; *[personne]* **chercher un ~ d'appui** to look for sth to lean on; **~s cardinaux** cardinal points; **~ chaud** *(Mil)* trouble spot; *(de l'actualité)* talking point, major issue; **~ de côté** stitch *(pain in the side)*; **~ culminant** *[gloire, épidémie]* height; *[scandale]* climax; *[montagne]* peak, summit; **~ de départ** *[train]* point of departure; *[aventure]* starting point; *(Sport)* start; *(fig)* **nous voilà revenus au ~ de départ** (so) we're back to square one *, we're back where we started; **~ d'eau** *(source)* watering place; *[camping]* water (supply) point; **~ d'exclamation** exclamation mark *ou* point *(US)*; **~ faible** weak point; **~ fort** strong point; **~ d'honneur** point of honour; **~ d'interrogation** question mark; **le ~ du jour** daybreak; **~ de mire** *(lit)* target; *(fig)* focal point; *(Aut)* **~ mort** neutral; *[négociations, affaires]* **au ~ mort** at a standstill; **~ névralgique** *(Méd)* nerve centre; *(fig)* sensitive spot; **~ de non-retour** point of no return; **~ de rencontre** meeting point; **~ de repère** *(dans l'espace)* landmark; *(dans le temps)* point of reference; **~ stratégique** key point; **~s de suspension** suspension points; *(Méd)* **~ de suture** stitch; **~ de vente** point of sale; **liste des ~s de vente** list of stockists *ou* retailers; **~ virgule** semi-colon; **~ de vue** *(lit)* view(point); *(fig)* point of view, standpoint; **du** *ou* **au ~ de vue argent** from the financial point of view.

point² [pwɛ̃] *adv (littér, hum)* = **pas²**.

pointage [pwɛ̃taʒ] *nm* (**a**) *(sur une liste)* ticking *ou* checking *ou* marking off; *[employé]* checking in; *(à la sortie)* checking out; *[canon]* aiming. (**b**) *(contrôle)* check.

pointe [pwɛ̃t] **1** *nf* (**a**) *(pointue)* point; *[montagne]* peak, top; *[chaussure]* toe; *[grille]* spike. **à la ~ de l'île** at the tip of the island; **la côte s'avance en ~** the coast forms a headland; **objet qui forme une ~** object that tapers to a point; *(Danse)* **faire des ~s** to dance on points; *(Danse)* **chausson à ~** point *ou* block shoe; **en ~** *barbe* in a point, pointed. (**b**) *(clou)* tack; *(Sport) [chaussure]* spike;

(outil pointu) point. (c) (foulard) triangular (neck)scarf. (d) ~ de ail, ironie, jalousie touch ou hint of; accent hint of. (e) (maximum) peak. ~ de vitesse burst of speed; à la ~ de actualité etc in the forefront of; de ~ industrie leading, high tech; technique latest; vitesse top, maximum; [circulation] heure de ~ rush ou peak hour; faire une ~ jusqu'à Paris to push ou press on as far as Paris. 2 : ~ d'asperge asparagus tip ou spear; la ~ des pieds the toes; (se mettre) sur la ~ des pieds (to stand) on tiptoe; ~ de terre spit of land.

pointer [pwɛ̃te] (1) 1 vt (a) (cocher) to tick off, check off, mark off. (Naut) ~ (sa position) to plot one's position. (b) (Ind) employé (à l'arrivée) to clock ou check in; (au départ) to clock ou check out. (c) fusil to aim (vers, sur at); jumelles to train (vers, sur on); lampe to direct (vers, sur towards); doigt to point (sur at). (d) [chien] ~ les oreilles to prick up its ears. 2 vi (a) [employé] (arrivée) to clock in, check in; (départ) to clock out, check out. (b) (apparaître) (gén) to appear; [plante] to peep out; (fig) [ironie] to pierce through; [jour] to break, dawn. (c) (s'élever) [tour] to soar up. 3 se ~ * vpr (arriver) to turn up *, show up *.

pointillé, e [pwɛ̃tije] 1 adj dotted. 2 nm dotted line.

pointilleux, -euse [pwɛ̃tijø, øz] adj particular, pernickety (sur about).

pointu, e [pwɛ̃ty] adj pointed; (aiguisé) sharp; (fig) analyse in-depth; sujet specialized.

pointure [pwɛ̃tyʀ] nf size. quelle est votre ~? what size are you?

poire [pwaʀ] nf (fruit) pear; (*: tête) face, mug **; (*: dupe) mug **, sucker *. ~ électrique (pear-shaped) switch.

poireau, pl ~x [pwaʀo] nm leek. faire le ~ * to hang about *. ◆ poireauter * (1) vi to hang about *.

poirier [pwaʀje] nm pear tree. (fig) faire le ~ to do a headstand.

pois [pwa] 1 nm (légume) pea; (dessin) (polka) dot, spot. petits ~ (garden) peas; robe à ~ dotted ou spotted dress. 2 : ~ cassés split peas; ~ chiche chickpea; ~ de senteur sweet pea.

poison [pwazɔ̃] nm (lit, fig) poison. quel ~! * what a pest * ou nuisance!

poisse ** [pwas] nf bad ou rotten * luck. avoir la ~ to have bad ou rotten * luck.

poisser [pwase] (1) vt (a) (**: attraper) to nab **. (b) (salir) to make sticky. ◆ poisseux, -euse adj sticky.

poisson [pwasɔ̃] nm fish. 2/3 ~s 2/3 fish ou fishes; comme un ~ dans l'eau in one's element; (Astron, Astrol) P ~s Pisces; (blague) ~ d'avril April fool's trick; ~ rouge goldfish. ◆ poissonnerie nf (boutique) fishmonger's (shop); (métier) fish trade. ◆ poissonneux, -euse adj full of fish. ◆ poissonnier, -ière nm, f fishmonger.

poitrine [pwatʀin] nf (gén) chest, breast (littér); (seins) bust, bosom; (Culin) [veau, mouton] breast. [porc] ~ (salée ou fumée) streaky bacon. ◆ poitrail nm (Zool) breast; (hum: poitrine) chest.

poivre [pwavʀ(ə)] nm pepper. ~ en grains whole pepper, peppercorns; ~ et sel cheveux pepper-and-salt; ~ vert green pepper (spice). ◆ poivré, e adj plat peppery; histoire spicy, juicy *. ◆ poivrer (1) vt to pepper. ◆ poivrier nm (Bot) pepper plant; (objet) pepperpot, pepper shaker (US).

poivron [pwavʀɔ̃] nm: ~ (vert) green pepper, capsicum; ~ rouge red pepper, capsicum.

poivrot, e * [pwavʀo, ɔt] nm, f drunkard.

poix [pwa] nf pitch (tar).

poker [pɔkɛʀ] nm (Cartes) (jeu) poker; (partie) game of poker. (fig) coup de ~ gamble.

pôle [pol] nm pole. P~ Nord/Sud North/South Pole; (fig) ~ d'attraction centre of attraction. ◆ polaire adj polar. ◆ polariser (1) vt (Élec, Phys) to polarize; (fig: attirer) to attract. ~ son attention ou se ~ sur qch to focus ou centre one's attention on sth.

polémique [pɔlemik] 1 adj controversial. 2 nf controversy, argument, polemic. (débat) une grande ~ s'est engagée sur... a great debate has been started about ou on....

poli, e [pɔli] 1 adj (a) polite (avec to). soyez ~! don't be so rude. (b) bois, métal polished; caillou smooth. 2 nm shine. ◆ poliment adv politely.

police [pɔlis] 1 nf (a) (corps) police, police force. voiture de ~ police car; être dans ou de la ~ to be in the police (force), be a policeman; la ~ est à ses trousses the police are after him ou are on his tail. (b) (maintien de l'ordre) policing, enforcement of law and order. faire la ~ to keep law and order (dans in). (c) (règlements) regulations. (d) ~ (d'assurance) (insurance) policy; ~ d'assurance vie life insurance policy. 2 : ~ de l'air et des frontières border police; ~ judiciaire ≃ Criminal Investigation Department; ~ des mœurs ≃ vice squad; ~ parallèle unofficial government police, parapolice; ~ de la route traffic police; ~ secours police (special service for emergencies), ≃ emergency services. ◆ policier, -ière 1 adj (gén) police; roman detective. 2 nm policeman.

Polichinelle [pɔliʃinɛl] nm (marionnette) Punch; (péj) buffoon.

policlinique [pɔliklinik] nf out-patients' clinic.

polio(myélite) [pɔljɔ(mjelit)] nf polio(myelitis).

polir [pɔliʀ] (2) vt (gén, fig) to polish; discours to polish (up); manières to polish, refine.

polisson, -onne [pɔlisɔ̃, ɔn] 1 adj (espiègle) naughty; (grivois) naughty, saucy. 2 nm, f (enfant) (little) devil *. ◆ polissonnerie nf naughty trick.

politesse [pɔlitɛs] nf politeness; (parole) polite remark; (action) polite gesture.

politique [pɔlitik] 1 adj political; (littér: habile) diplomatic, politic. homme ~ politician; compte-rendu de la semaine ~ report on the week in politics. 2 nf (a) (science, carrière) politics (sg). faire de la ~ (militantisme) to be a political activist; (métier) to be in politics. (b) (ligne de conduite) policy; (manière de gouverner) policies. ~ extérieure foreign policy; la ~ du gouvernement the government's policies; pratiquer la ~ de l'autruche to bury one's head in the sand. ◆ politicien, -ienne (péj) 1 adj politicking (péj). (péj) la politique ~ne politicking, politics for its own sake. 2 nm, f political schemer. ◆ politiquement adv (lit) politically; (fig littér) diplomatically. ◆ politisation nf politicization. ◆ politiser (1) vt to politicize. ◆ politologie nf political science. ◆ politologue nmf political pundit ou analyst ou expert.

polka [pɔlka] nf polka.

pollen [pɔlɛn] nm pollen.

polluer [pɔlɥe] (1) vt to pollute. ◆ polluant, e 1 adj polluting. 2 nm pollutant. produit ~ pollutant. ◆ pollueur, -euse 1 adj polluting. 2 nm, f pollutant, polluting agent. ◆ pollution nf pollution.

polo [pɔlo] nm (a) (Sport) polo. (b) (chemise) sports shirt.

polochon * [pɔlɔʃɔ̃] nm bolster. sac ~ duffel bag.

Pologne [pɔlɔɲ] nf Poland. ◆ polonais, e 1 adj Polish. 2 nm (a) P~ Pole. (b) (Ling) Polish. 3 nf (a) P~e Pole. (b) (Mus, Culin) polonaise.

poltron, -onne [pɔltʀɔ̃, ɔn] 1 adj cowardly. 2 nm, f coward. ◆ poltronnerie nf cowardice.

poly... [pɔli] préf poly...

polychrome [pɔlikʀom] adj polychrome, polychromatic.

polyclinique [pɔliklinik] *nf* private general hospital.

polycopier [pɔlikɔpje] (7) *vt* to duplicate, stencil. **machine à** ~ duplicator.

polyculture [pɔlikyltyʀ] *nf* mixed farming.

polyester [pɔliɛstɛʀ] *nm* polyester.

polygame [pɔligam] **1** *adj* polygamous. **2** *nm* polygamist. ◆ **polygamie** *nf* polygamy.

polyglotte [pɔliglɔt] *adj, nmf* polyglot.

polygone [pɔligɔn] *nm (Math)* polygon; *(fig: zone)* area, zone. *(Mil)* ~ **de tir** rifle range.

Polynésie [pɔlinezi] *nf* Polynesia. ◆ **polynésien, -ienne** *adj*, **P~(ne)** *nm(f)* Polynesian.

polysémie [pɔlisemi] *nf* polysemy.

polystyrène [pɔlistiʀɛn] *nm* polystyrene. ~ **expansé** expanded polysterene.

polyvalent, e [pɔlivalɑ̃, ɑ̃t] *adj (Chim, Méd)* polyvalent; *rôle* varied; *usages* various, many; *personne* versatile. **enseignement** ~ comprehensive education. ◆ **polyvalence** *nf* polyvalency.

pommade [pɔmad] *nf [peau]* ointment; *[cheveux]* cream, pomade. *(fig)* **passer de la** ~ **à qn** * to butter sb up *, soft-soap sb *.

pomme [pɔm] **1** *nf* (**a**) *(fruit)* apple. **tomber dans les** ~**s** * to faint, pass out *. (**b**) *[laitue]* heart; *[canne]* knob; *[arrosoir]* rose. (**c**) (*) *(tête)* head, nut *; *(visage)* face. **c'est pour ma** ~ it's for my own sweet self *.
2 : ~ **d'Adam** Adam's apple; **(~s) chips** (potato) crisps *ou* chips *(US)*; ~**s frites** chips, French fries; ~ **de pin** pine *ou* fir cone; ~ **de terre** potato.

pommeau, *pl* ~**x** [pɔmo] *nm [épée, selle]* pommel; *[canne]* knob.

pommelé, e [pɔmle] *adj cheval* dappled; *ciel* mackerel, flecked with clouds. **gris** ~ dapple-grey.

pommette [pɔmɛt] *nf* cheekbone. ~**s saillantes** high cheekbones.

pommier [pɔmje] *nm* apple tree.

pompe [pɔ̃p] *nf* (**a**) *(machine)* pump; (‡: *chaussure)* shoe. ~ **à air** air pump; **à toute** ~ ‡ at top speed, flat out *; *(Sport)* **faire des** ~**s** to do press-ups *ou* push-ups *(US)*. ~ **à essence** *(distributeur)* petrol *ou* gasoline *(US)* pump; *(station)* petrol *ou* gas *(US)* station; ~ **à incendie** fire engine *(apparatus)*. (**b**) *(littér: solennité)* pomp. **en grande** ~ with great pomp. (**c**) ~**s funèbres** funeral director's, undertaker's, mortician's *(US)*; **entreprise de** ~**s funèbres** funeral director's, funeral parlor *(US)*; **employé des** ~**s funèbres** undertaker's *ou* mortician's *(US)* assistant. ◆ **pomper** (1) *vt* to pump; *(évacuer)* to pump out; *[éponge, buvard]* to soak up; *(arg Scol: copier)* to crib * *(sur* from); (‡: *boire)* to drink, knock back ‡; (‡: *épuiser)* to wear *ou* tire out. ◆ **pompeusement** *adv* pompously. ◆ **pompeux, -euse** *adj (ampoulé)* pompous, pretentious; *(imposant)* solemn. ◆ **pompier** **1** *adj* (*) *style* pompous, pretentious. **2** *nm* fireman. **appeler les** ~**s** to call the fire brigade. ◆ **pompiste** *nmf* petrol *ou* gasoline *(US)* pump attendant.

Pompéi [pɔ̃pei] *n* Pompeii.

pompon [pɔ̃pɔ̃] *nm* pompon, bobble. **c'est le** ~! * it's the last straw!, that beats everything! *

pomponner [pɔ̃pɔne] (1) **1** *vt* to titivate, doll up *. **2 se** ~ *vpr* to titivate (o.s.), get dolled up *.

poncer [pɔ̃se] (3) *vt* to sand, rub down. ◆ **ponçage** *nm* sanding, rubbing down. ◆ **ponce** *nf*: **pierre** ~ pumice (stone). ◆ **ponceuse** *nf* sander.

ponction [pɔ̃ksjɔ̃] *nf (lombaire)* puncture; *(pulmonaire)* tapping; *[argent]* withdrawal. **faire une** ~ **dans ses économies** to dip into one's savings.

ponctuel, -elle [pɔ̃ktɥɛl] *adj* punctual. **ces terroristes se livrent à des actions** ~**les** these terrorists strike selectively. ◆ **ponctualité** *nf* punctuality. ◆ **ponctuellement** *adv* punctually.

ponctuer [pɔ̃ktɥe] (1) *vt (lit, fig)* to punctuate *(de* with). ◆ **ponctuation** *nf* punctuation.

pondérer [pɔ̃deʀe] (6) *vt (équilibrer)* to balance; *(Écon)* to weight. ◆ **pondéré, e** *adj personne* levelheaded. *(Écon)* **indice** ~ weighted index. ◆ **pondération** *nf* level-headedness; balancing; weighting.

pondéreux, -euse [pɔ̃deʀø, øz] *adj* heavy.

pondre [pɔ̃dʀ(ə)] (41) **1** *vt œuf* to lay; (*) *enfant, devoir* to produce. **œuf frais pondu** new-laid egg. **2** *vi* to lay.

poney [pɔnɛ] *nm* pony.

pont [pɔ̃] **1** *nm (Constr)* bridge; *(fig: lien)* bridge, link; *(Naut)* deck; *(Aut)* axle. **vivre sous les** ~**s** to be a tramp; **faire un** ~ **d'or à qn** to offer sb a fortune to take on a job; *(vacances)* **on a un** ~ **de 3 jours** we have 3 days (off); **faire le** ~ to make a long weekend of it. **2** : ~ **basculant/ suspendu/ tournant/transbordeur** bascule/ suspension/swing/ transporter bridge; ~ **aérien** airlift; **les P~s et chaussées** the department of civil engineering; ~ **de graissage** ramp *(in a garage)*; ~**-levis** *nm*, *pl* ~**s-**~ drawbridge. ◆ **pontage** *nm* decking *(Naut)*. *(Méd)* ~ *(cardiaque)* (heart) bypass operation.

ponte[1] [pɔ̃t] *nf (action)* laying (of eggs); *(saison)* (egg-)laying season.

ponte[2] * [pɔ̃t] *nm* big shot *, big noise *.

pontife [pɔ̃tif] *nm (Rel)* pontiff. ◆ **pontifical, e,** *mpl* **-aux** *adj messe* pontifical; *gardes, états* papal. ◆ **pontificat** *nm* pontificate. ◆ **pontifier** * (7) *vi* to pontificate.

ponton [pɔ̃tɔ̃] *nm* pontoon, landing stage.

pop [pɔp] *adj inv* pop.

pop-corn [pɔpkɔʀn] *nm* popcorn.

pope [pɔp] *nm* (Orthodox) priest.

popeline [pɔplin] *nf* poplin.

popote * [pɔpɔt] **1** *nf (cuisine)* cooking. **2** *adj inv* stay-at-home, home-loving.

populace [pɔpylas] *nf (péj)* rabble, mob.

populaire [pɔpylɛʀ] *adj (gén, fig)* popular; *quartier* working-class; *(Ling) expression* colloquial. **république** ~ people's republic; **manifestation** ~ mass demonstration.
◆ **populariser** (1) *vt* to popularize. ◆ **popularité** *nf* popularity.

population [pɔpylɑsjɔ̃] *nf (gén)* population. ◆ **populeux, -euse** *adj pays* densely populated; *rue* crowded.

porc [pɔʀ] *nm (animal)* pig, hog *(US)*; *(viande)* pork; *(péj: personne)* pig; *(peau)* pigskin.

porcelaine [pɔʀsəlɛn] *nf (matière)* porcelain, china; *(objet)* piece of porcelain.

porcelet [pɔʀsəlɛ] *nm* piglet.

porc-épic, *pl* **porcs-épics** [pɔʀkepik] *nm* porcupine.

porche [pɔʀʃ(ə)] *nm* porch.

porcherie [pɔʀʃəʀi] *nf (lit, fig)* pigsty.

pore [pɔʀ] *nm* pore. ◆ **poreux, -euse** *adj* porous.

pornographie [pɔʀnɔgʀafi] *nf* pornography. ◆ **pornographique** *adj* pornographic.

port[1] [pɔʀ] *nm* harbour, port. ~ **d'attache** *(Naut)* port of registry; *(fig)* home base; **arriver à bon** ~ to arrive safe and sound.

port[2] [pɔʀ] *nm* (**a**) **le** ~ **de la barbe** *etc* wearing a beard *etc*; ~ **d'armes prohibées** illegal carrying of firearms. (**b**) *(prix) (poste)* postage; *(transport)* carriage. **franco de** ~ carriage paid; **(en)** ~ **dû** postage due. (**c**) *(comportement)* bearing, carriage.

portable [pɔʀtabl(ə)] **1** *nm (Ordin)* laptop. **2** *adj (Ordin)* portable.

portail [pɔʀtaj] *nm* portal.

portant, e [pɔʀtɑ̃, ɑ̃t] *adj*: **être bien/mal** ~ to be in good/poor health.

portatif, -ive [pɔʀtatif, iv] *adj* portable.

porte [pɔʀt(ə)] **1** *nf* (**a**) *(gén)* door; *[forteresse, jardin, écluse, ski]* gate; *(seuil)* doorstep; *(embrasure)* doorway. ~ **pliante/coulissante** folding/sliding door; **sonner à la** ~ to ring the (door)bell; **c'est à ma** ~ it's on the doorstep; **le bus me descend à ma** ~ the bus takes me to my door; **faire du** ~ **à** ~ to sell from door to door, be a door-to-door salesman; **Dijon,** ~ **de la Bourgogne** Dijon, the gateway to Burgundy. (**b**) **être à la** ~ to be locked out; **mettre qn à la** ~ *(licencier)* to sack sb, fire sb *; *(éjecter)* to throw sb out; **être mis à la** ~ to get the chop ⁑; **claquer la** ~ **au nez de qn** to slam the door in sb's face; **frapper à la bonne/mauvaise** ~ to get hold of the right/wrong person; **laisser la** ~ **ouverte à** *compromis, abus* to leave the door open to; **parler à qn entre deux** ~**s** to have a quick word with sb, speak to sb very briefly; **prendre la** ~ to go away, leave; **aimable comme une** ~ **de prison** like a bear with a sore head.
2 : ~ **cochère** carriage entrance; ~ **à deux battants** double door; ~ **d'embarquement** departure gate; ~ **d'entrée** front door; ~**-fenêtre** *nf, pl* ~**s-**~**s** French window; ~ **de secours** emergency exit; ~ **de service** tradesman's entrance; *(lit, fig)* ~ **de sortie** way out.

porte- [pɔʀt(ə)] *préf formant nm*: ~**-avions** *inv* aircraft carrier; ~**-bagages** *inv* (luggage) rack; ~**-bébé** *nm, pl* ~**-**~**s** baby-sling, baby-carrier; ~**-bonheur** *inv* lucky charm; ~**-clefs** *inv (anneau)* key ring; *(étui)* key case; ~**-couteau,** *pl* ~**-**~**(x)** knife rest; ~**-documents** *inv* brief case, attaché case; *(lit, fig)* ~**-drapeau,** *pl* ~**-**~**(x)** standard bearer; **en** ~**-à-faux** *objet* precariously balanced; *situation* awkward ; ~**-mine,** *pl* ~**-**~**(s)** propelling pencil; ~**-monnaie** *inv (gén)* purse, coin purse *(US)*; *(pour hommes)* wallet; ~**-parapluies** *inv* umbrella stand; ~**-parole** *inv (gén)* spokesperson; *(homme)* spokesman; *(femme)* spokeswoman; *(revue politique etc)* mouthpiece; ~**-plume** *inv* penholder; ~**-revues** *inv* magazine rack; ~**-savon,** *pl* ~**-**~**(s)** soapdish; ~**-serviettes** *inv* towel rail; ~**-voix** *inv* megaphone; *(électrique)* loudhailer.

porté, e¹ [pɔʀte] *adj*: **être** ~ **à faire** to be inclined to do, tend to do; **être** ~ **à la colère** to be prone to anger; **être** ~ **sur qch** to be partial to sth.

portée² [pɔʀte] *nf* (**a**) *(distance)* range, reach; *[fusil, radar]* range. **canon à faible/longue** ~ short-/long-range gun; **missile de moyenne** ~ intermediate-range weapon; **à** ~ **de voix** within earshot; **restez à** ~ **de vue** don't go out of sight; **c'est à la** ~ **de toutes les bourses** it's within everyone's means; **hors de** ~ out of reach (*de* of). (**b**) *[intelligence]* reach, scope, capacity. **se mettre à la** ~ **des enfants** to come down to a child's level. (**c**) *[parole]* impact, import; *[acte]* significance. (**d**) *(Archit) (poussée)* loading; *(distance)* span. (**e**) *(Mus)* stave, staff. (**f**) *(Vét)* litter.

portefeuille [pɔʀtəfœj] *nm [argent]* wallet; *(Bourse, Pol)* portfolio.

portemanteau, *pl* ~**x** [pɔʀtmɑ̃to] *nm* coat hanger; *(accroché au mur)* coat rack; *(sur pied)* hat stand.

porter [pɔʀte] (1) **1** *vt* (**a**) *paquet* to carry; *responsabilité* to bear, carry. **pouvez-vous me** ~ **ma valise?** can you carry my case for me?; ~ **la tête droite** to hold one's head up; **cette poutre porte tout le poids** this beam bears *ou* carries *ou* takes the whole weight. (**b**) *(amener)* to take. **porte-lui ce livre** take this book to him, take him this book; **il s'est fait** ~ **à manger** he had food brought to him; ~ **la main sur qn** to raise one's hand to sb; ~ **qch à sa bouche** to lift *ou* put sth to one's lips; ~ **une œuvre à l'écran** to transfer a work to the screen; ~ **bonheur/malheur (à qn)** to be lucky/unlucky (for sb), bring (sb) (good) luck/misfortune. (**c**) *vêtement* to wear; *barbe* to have, wear; *nom* to have, bear; *blessure, inscription* to bear; *trace* to show. ~ **les cheveux longs** to wear one's hair long, have long hair; ~ **le nom de Jérôme** to be called Jerome; **elle porte bien le pantalon** trousers suit her; **elle porte bien son âge** she's wearing well; **cela ne se porte plus** that's out of fashion, nobody wears that any more; *(fig)* **je ne veux pas** ~ **le chapeau** * I don't want to carry the can * *ou* take the rap * (*pour* for). (**d**) *(inscrire)* to write down, put down (*sur* on, in); *(Comm) somme* to enter (*sur* in). ~ **de l'argent au crédit/débit d'un compte** to credit/debit an account with a sum; **se faire** ~ **absent** to go absent; **se faire** ~ **malade** to report *ou* go sick; **porté disparu** reported missing. (**e**) *sentiment* to have, feel (*à* for); *coup* to deal (*à* to); *accusation, attaque* to make (*contre* against); *pas* to turn (*vers* towards). **faire** ~ *regard, choix, effort* to direct (*sur* towards); *attention* to focus, turn (*sur* on). (**f**) *(faire arriver)* to bring. ~ **au pouvoir/à la perfection** to bring to power/to perfection; ~ **la température/le nombre à** to bring the temperature/the number up to. (**g**) *(inciter)* ~ **qn à (faire) qch** to prompt *ou* lead sb to do sth; **tout (nous) porte à croire que...** everything leads us to believe that... (**h**) *(Méd) enfant* to carry; *intérêts, récolte* to yield; *fruit* to bear. **je ne le porte pas dans mon cœur** I am not exactly fond of him. (**i**) *(conduire)* to carry; *[foi]* to carry along; *[vent, foule]* to carry away.
2 *vi* (**a**) *[bruit]* to carry. **le son a porté à 500 mètres** the sound carried 500 metres. (**b**) *[conseil]* to be effective. *[reproche, coup]* ~ **(juste)** to hit *ou* strike home; **tous les coups portaient** every blow told. (**c**) *(Vét) [animal]* to carry its young. (**d**) ~ **sur** *[édifice, pilier]* to be supported by *ou* on; *[débat]* to turn on, be about; *[revendications]* to concern; *[étude, action]* to focus on; *[accent]* to fall on; **faire** ~ **son exposé sur qch** to focus on sth in one's talk; **sa tête a porté sur le trottoir** his head struck the pavement.
3 se ~ *vpr* (**a**) **se** ~ **bien/mal** to be well/unwell; **se** ~ **mieux/plus mal** to feel better/worse; **se** ~ **comme un charme** to be fighting fit, be as fit as a fiddle. (**b**) **se** ~ **candidat** to stand *ou* run as a candidate; **se** ~ **acquéreur (de)** to put in a bid (for). (**c**) *[regard, soupçon, choix]* **se** ~ **sur** to fall on; **son attention se porta sur ce point** he focused *ou* concentrated his attention on this point. (**d**) **se** ~ **à** *violences* to commit; **se** ~ **à la rencontre de qn** to go to meet sb.

porteur, -euse [pɔʀtœʀ, øz] **1** *adj fusée* booster; *courant* carrier; *(Écon) marché, créneau* strong, buoyant. **2** *nm, f [colis]* porter; *[message, chèque]* bearer; *[actions]* (share)holder. ~ **d'eau/de germes** water/germ carrier; **il était** ~ **de faux papiers** he was carrying forged papers; **le** ~ **du ballon** the holder of the (foot)ball; *(Fin)* **payable au** ~ payable to bearer.

portier [pɔʀtje] *nm* commissionnaire, janitor.

portière [pɔʀtjɛʀ] *nf (Aut, Rail)* door.

portillon [pɔʀtijɔ̃] *nm* gate.

portion [pɔʀsjɔ̃] *nf (gén)* portion; *(Culin)* helping. ~ **congrue** smallest share; ~ **de route** stretch of road.

portique [pɔʀtik] *nm (Archit)* portico; *(Sport)* crossbar and stands *(for holding gymnastic apparatus)*.

porto [pɔʀto] **1** *nm* port (wine). **2** : **P**~ *n (Géog)* Oporto.

Porto Rico [pɔʀtɔʀiko] *nf* Puerto Rico. ◆ **portoricain, e** *adj,* **P**~**(e)** *nm(f)* Puerto Rican.

portrait [pɔʀtʀɛ] *nm (peinture, description)* portrait; *(photo)* photograph. ~**-robot** Identikit picture ®, Photofit ® (picture); **faire le** ~**-robot du Français moyen** to draw the profile of the average Frenchman; ~ **en pied** full-lenght portrait; **c'est tout le**

~ **de son père** he's the spitting image of his father; **faire le ~ de qn** to paint sb's portrait.

portuaire [pɔʀtɥɛʀ] *adj* port, harbour.

Portugal [pɔʀtygal] *nm* Portugal. ◆ **portugais, e** *adj, nm,* **P~(e)** *nm (f)* Portuguese.

pose [poz] *nf* (**a**) *(installation)* installation. **la ~ d'une serrure** fitting a lock. (**b**) *(Art, attitude)* pose; *(affectation)* posing. **prendre une ~** to strike a pose. (**c**) *(Phot)* exposure; *(bouton)* time exposure. **indice de ~** exposure index; **prendre une photo en ~** to take a photo in time exposure.

posé, e [poze] *adj personne* calm, level-headed; *attitude* steady, sober. ◆ **posément** *adv parler* calmly, steadily.

poser [poze] (1) **1** *vt* (**a**) *(placer)* to put (down), lay (down), set down (*sur* on); *(debout)* to stand, put (*contre* against); *(Math) opération* to write, set down. ~ **son manteau** to take off one's coat; ~ **son regard sur qch** to look at sth; **réussir à ~ son avion** to manage to land one's plane; ~ **un lapin à qn** * to stand sb up *. (**b**) *carrelage, fondations etc* to lay; *gaz* to install; *rideaux* to hang, put up; *tapis, vitre* to put in; *moquette, serrure* to fit (*sur* on); *bombe* to plant. ~ **des jalons** *(lit)* to put stakes up; *(fig)* to prepare the ground. (**c**) *principe, condition* to lay down, set out, state; *devinette* to set. **le prof nous a posé un problème difficile** the teacher set us a difficult problem; *(formuler)* **il a bien su ~ le problème** he put *ou* formulated the problem well; **ce retard pose un problème** this delay poses a problem *ou* confronts us with a problem; ~ **une question à qn** to ask sb a question, put a question to sb; *(à l'examen)* to set sb a question; ~ **la question de confiance** to ask for a vote of confidence; ~ **sa candidature** to apply (*à* for); *(Pol)* to put o.s. up *ou* stand *ou* run *(US)* for election; **posons que...** let us suppose *ou* assume that... (**d**) *(donner de l'importance)* to give standing to; *(professionnellement)* to establish the reputation of.

2 *vi* (**a**) *(Art, Phot)* to pose, sit (*pour* for); *(se vanter)* to show off. ~ **à l'artiste** to play *ou* act the artist. (**b**) *[poutre]* ~ **sur** to bear *ou* rest on.

3 se ~ *vpr* (**a**) *[oiseau]* to alight (*sur* on); *[avion]* to land, touch down; *[regard]* to settle, fix (*sur* on). *(Aviat)* **se ~ sur le ventre** to make a belly-landing. (**b**) **se ~ comme victime** to pretend *ou* claim to be a victim; **comme menteur, il se pose là** * he's a terrible liar; *(poids)* **il se pose là!** * he's enormous. (**c**) *[question]* to come up, crop up, arise. **le problème qui se pose** the problem we are faced with; **il commence à se ~ des questions** he's beginning to wonder; **il y a une question que je me pose** there's one thing I'd like to know.

poseur, -euse [pozœʀ, øz] **1** *adj* affected. **2** *nm, f* (**a**) *(péj)* show-off, poseur. (**b**) *(ouvrier)* ~ **de tuyaux** *etc* pipe *etc* layer; ~ **de bombes** bomb planter.

positif, -ive [pozitif, iv] *adj, nm (gén)* positive. ◆ **positivement** *adv (gén)* positively.

position [pozisjɔ̃] *nf (gén)* position. *(lit, fig)* **rester sur ses ~s** to stand one's ground; **avoir une ~ de repli** *(Mil)* to have a position to fall back on; *(fig)* to have other proposals to fall back on; **prendre ~** *(gén, Mil)* to take up (one's) position; *(se déclarer)* to take a stand; **être en première/seconde/dernière ~** to be first/second/last; **dormir dans une mauvaise ~** to sleep in the wrong position; **être dans une ~ fausse** to be in a false position; **être en ~ de force pour négocier** to be bargaining from (a position of) strength; **le gouvernement doit définir sa ~ sur cette question** the government must make its position *ou* stance on this question clear; **prendre (fermement) ~ en faveur de qch** to come down (strongly) in favour of sth; *(Fin)* **demander sa ~** to ask for the balance of one's account. ◆ **positionnement** *nm* positioning. ◆ **positionner** (1) *vt* to position.

posologie [pozɔlɔʒi] *nf* directions for use.

posséder [pɔsede] (6) **1** *vt* (**a**) *(gén)* to have; *fortune, qualité* to possess; *maison* to own; *diplôme* to hold. **bien ~ une langue** to have a thorough knowledge of a language. (**b**) *[démon]* to possess. **la jalousie le possède** he is consumed with jealousy. (**c**) *(*: duper)* ~ **qn** to take sb in *; **se faire ~** to be had *. **2 se ~** *vpr* to control o.s. **elle ne se possédait plus de joie** she was beside herself *ou* was overcome with joy.

◆ **possédant, e 1** *adj* propertied. **2** *nmpl*: **les ~s** the wealthy. ◆ **possédé, e 1** *adj* possessed (*de* by). **2** *nm, f* person possessed. ◆ **possesseur** *nm* possessor, owner; holder. **être ~ de** *objet* to have. ◆ **possessif, -ive** *adj, nm* possessive. ◆ **possession** *nf* (**a**) *(gén)* possession; *[bien]* ownership. **la ~ d'une arme** possessing *ou* having a weapon; **avoir qch en sa ~** to have sth in one's possession; **prendre ~ de** *fonction* to take up; *appartement* to take possession of; **en ~ de toutes ses facultés** in possession of all one's faculties. (**b**) *(chose possédée)* possession; *(Rel: envoûtement)* possession. *(maîtrise)* ~ **de soi** self-control.

possibilité [pɔsibilite] *nf (gén)* possibility; *[projet]* feasibility. **ai-je la ~ de faire cela?** is it possible for me to do that?, can I do that?; **quelles sont vos ~s financières?** how much money can you put up?, what is your financial situation?; **quelles sont vos ~s de logement?** how many people can you accommodate *ou* put up?

possible [pɔsibl(ə)] **1** *adj (gén)* possible; *projet* feasible. **lui serait-il ~ d'arriver plus tôt?** could he possibly *ou* would it be possible for him to come earlier?; **arrivez tôt si (c'est) ~** arrive early if possible *ou* if you can; **ce n'est pas ~ autrement** there's no other way; **il est ~ qu'il vienne** he may *ou* might (possibly) come, it's possible (that) he'll come; **il a eu toutes les difficultés ~s et imaginables à obtenir un visa** he had all kinds of problems *ou* every imaginable problem getting a visa; **venez aussitôt que ~** come as soon as possible *ou* as soon as you (possibly) can; **il a acheté la valise la plus légère ~** he bought the lightest possible suitcase; **cette situation n'est plus ~** this situation has become impossible *ou* intolerable; **ce n'est pas ~** *(faux)* that can't be true; *(étonnant)* well I never!; *(irréalisable)* it's impossible; **c'est (bien) ~** (quite) possibly, maybe. **2** *nm*: **dans le ~, dans les limites du ~** within the realms of possibility; **faire tout son ~** to do one's utmost, do all one can (*pour* to); **énervant au ~** extremely annoying.

post- [pɔst] *préf* post-.

postal, e, *mpl* **-aux** [pɔstal, o] *adj (gén)* postal; *train, avion* mail; *colis* sent by post *ou* mail.

postcure [pɔstkyʀ] *nf* aftercare.

postdater [pɔstdate] (1) *vt* to postdate.

poste[1] [pɔst(ə)] *nf* (**a**) *(administration, bureau)* post office. **les Postes, Télécommunications et Télédiffusion** *the French post office and telephone service;* **la ~ principale** the main *ou* head post office. (**b**) *(service)* postal *ou* mail service. **envoyer qch par la ~** to send sth by post *ou* mail; **mettre une lettre à la ~** to post *ou* mail a letter; ~ **aérienne** airmail; ~ **restante** poste restante.

poste[2] [pɔst(ə)] **1** *nm* (**a**) *(emplacement)* post. ~ **de douane** *etc* customs *etc* post; **à vos ~s!** to your stations! *ou* posts! (**b**) *(emploi) (gén)* job; *[fonctionnaire]* post; *(dans une hiérarchie)* position; *(nomination)* appointment. **toujours fidèle au ~?** * still manning the fort? * (**c**) *(Rad, TV)* set. ~ **émetteur/récepteur** transmitting/receiving set, transmitter/receiver; **éteindre le ~** to turn the set off. (**d**) *(Téléc)* ~ **23** extension 23. (**e**) *[budget]* item. (**f**)

(Ind) shift. ~ **de 8 heures** 8-hour shift. **2** : ~ **d'aiguillage** signal box; ~ **de commandement** headquarters; ~ **de contrôle** checkpoint; ~ **d'équipage** crew's quarters; ~ **d'essence** petrol *ou* gas *(US)* station; ~ **d'incendie** fire point; ~ **de pilotage** cockpit; ~ **de police** police station; *(Ordin)* ~ **de travail** work station.

poster[1] [pɔste] (1) **1** *vt lettre* post, mail; *sentinelle* to post, station. **2 se** ~ *vpr* to position *ou* station o.s.

poster[2] [pɔstɛʀ] *nm* poster.

postérieur, e [pɔsteʀjœʀ] **1** *adj (dans le temps)* later; *(dans l'espace)* back. ~ **à 1800** after 1800. **2** *nm* (*) behind *. ◆ **postérieurement** *adv* later. ~ **à** after.

postérité [pɔsteʀite] *nf* posterity.

posthume [pɔstym] *adj* posthumous.

postiche [pɔstiʃ] **1** *adj (gén)* false. **2** *nm (pour homme)* toupee; *(pour femme)* hairpiece, postiche.

postier, -ière [pɔstje, jɛʀ] *nm, f* post office worker.

postillon [pɔstijɔ̃] *nm (Hist)* postilion; *(*: salive)* sputter.

postopératoire [pɔstɔpeʀatwaʀ] *adj* postoperative.

postposition [pɔstpozisjɔ̃] *nf* postposition. **verbe à** ~ phrasal verb.

postscolaire [pɔstskɔlɛʀ] *adj enseignement* further, continuing.

post-scriptum [pɔstskʀiptɔm] *nm inv* postscript.

postsonoriser [pɔstsɔnɔʀize] (1) *vt* to dub.

postsynchroniser [pɔstsɛ̃kʀɔnize] (1) *vt* to dub *(a film)*.

postuler [pɔstyle] (1) *vt* (**a**) *emploi* to apply for, put in for. (**b**) *principe* to postulate. ◆ **postulant, e** *nm, f* applicant. ◆ **postulat** *nm* postulate.

posture [pɔstyʀ] *nf* posture, position. **en bonne** ~ in a good position; **être en très mauvaise** ~ to be in a really bad position *ou* a tight corner.

pot [po] **1** *nm* (**a**) *(en verre)* jar; *(en terre)* pot; *(en carton)* carton. **mettre en** ~ *fleur* to pot; *confiture* to put in jars; **mettre un enfant sur le** ~ to put a child on the potty; **tu viens boire un** ~? * are you coming for a drink? (**b**) *(*: chance)* luck. **avoir du/manquer de** ~ to be lucky/unlucky; **coup de** ~ stroke of luck. (**c**) *(Cartes) (enjeu)* kitty; *(restant)* pile.
2 : ~ **de chambre** chamberpot; ~ **de colle** *(lit)* pot of glue; *(péj: crampon)* leech; ~ **à eau** water jug; ~ **d'échappement** exhaust pipe; ~ **catalytique** catalytic converter; ~**-au-feu** *(nm inv) (plat)* (beef) stew; *(viande)* stewing beef; ~ **de fleurs** *(récipient)* flowerpot; *(fleurs)* flowering plant; ~ **à lait** *(pour transporter)* milk can; *(sur la table)* milk jug; *(Mus)* ~**-pourri** *nm, pl* ~**s**-~**s** potpourri, medley; ~**-de-vin** *nm, pl* ~**s**-~-~ bribe, backhander *, payola *(US)*.

potable [pɔtabl(ə)] *adj (lit)* drinkable; *(*fig)* decent. **eau** ~ drinking water; **eau non** ~ water which is not for drinking, non-drinking water.

potage [pɔtaʒ] *nm* soup.

potager, -ère [pɔtaʒe, ɛʀ] **1** *adj* vegetable. **2** *nm* kitchen *ou* vegetable garden.

potasser * [pɔtase] (1) *vt* to cram for.

pote * [pɔt] *nm* pal *, mate *.

poteau, *pl* ~**x** [pɔto] *nm* post. **au** ~! * down with him!; ~ **(d'exécution)** execution post; ~ **d'arrivée/de départ** finishing/starting post; ~ **de but** goalpost; ~ **indicateur** signpost; ~ **télégraphique** telegraph post *ou* pole.

potelé, e [pɔtle] *adj enfant* plump, chubby; *bras* plump.

potence [pɔtɑ̃s] *nf (gibet)* gallows *(sg)*; *(support)* bracket.

potentiel, -elle [pɔtɑ̃sjɛl] *adj, nm (gén)* potential. ◆ **potentiellement** *adv* potentially.

poterie [pɔtʀi] *nf (atelier, art)* pottery; *(objet)* piece of pottery. ◆ **potiche** *nf* oriental vase; *(fig)* figurehead. ◆ **potier** *nm* potter.

poterne [pɔtɛʀn(ə)] *nf* postern.

potin * [pɔtɛ̃] *nm* (**a**) *(vacarme)* din, racket. **faire du** ~ *(lit)* to make a noise; *(fig)* to kick up a fuss *. (**b**) *(commérage)* ~**s** gossip.

potion [posjɔ̃] *nf* potion. *(fig)* ~ **amère** bitter pill.

potiron [pɔtiʀɔ̃] *nm* pumpkin.

pou, *pl* ~**x** [pu] *nm* louse. **couvert de** ~**x** covered in lice.

pouah [pwa] *excl* ugh!

poubelle [pubɛl] *nf [ordures]* (dust)bin, trash can *(US)*. **mettre à la** ~ to throw away.

pouce [pus] *nm* (**a**) *[main]* thumb; *[pied]* big toe. **se tourner les** ~**s** to twiddle one's thumbs; *(au jeu)* ~! pax!, truce!; **manger sur le** ~ * to have a quick snack. (**b**) *(mesure)* inch.

poudre [pudʀ(ə)] *nf (gén)* powder; *(poussière)* dust; *(fard)* (face) powder; *(explosif)* (gun)powder; *(arg Drogue: héroïne)* stuff *, smack ‡, H *(arg)*. **réduire qch en** ~ to grind sth to a powder; **en** ~ *lait* dried, powdered; *chocolat* drinking; *sucre* granulated; **prendre la** ~ **d'escampette** * to take to one's heels; ~ **à laver/à récurer** soap/scouring powder. ◆ **poudrer** (1) *vt* to powder. ◆ **poudrerie** *nf* gunpowder *ou* explosives factory. ◆ **poudreux, -euse** *adj (poussiéreux)* dusty. **neige** ~**euse** powder snow. ◆ **poudrier** *nm* (powder) compact. ◆ **poudrière** *nf* powder magazine; *(fig)* powder keg *(fig)*.

pouf [puf] **1** *nm* pouffe. **2** *excl* thud! **faire** ~ to tumble (over).

pouffer [pufe] (1) *vi*: ~ **(de rire)** to giggle.

pouilleux, -euse [pujø, øz] **1** *adj (lit)* lousy, verminous; *quartier* squalid, seedy; *personne* dirty, filthy. **2** *nm, f (pauvre)* down-and-out.

poulailler [pulɑje] *nm* henhouse. *(Théât)* **le** ~ * the gods *, the gallery.

poulain [pulɛ̃] *nm* foal; *(fig)* promising young athlete; *(protégé)* protégé.

poularde [pulaʀd(ə)] *nf* fatted chicken.

poule[1] [pul] **1** *nf* (**a**) *(Zool)* hen; *(Culin)* (boiling) fowl. **se lever/se coucher avec les** ~**s** to get up/go to bed early; **quand les** ~**s auront des dents** when pigs can fly. (**b**) (*) *(maîtresse)* mistress; *(prostituée)* whore. **ma** ~ (my) pet. **2** : ~ **de batterie** battery hen; ~ **d'eau** moorhen; ~ **faisane** hen pheasant; ~ **mouillée** * coward, softy *; **la** ~ **aux œufs d'or** the goose that lays the golden eggs; *(Culin)* ~ **au pot** boiled chicken.

poule[2] [pul] *nf* (**a**) *(enjeu)* pool, kitty. (**b**) *(tournoi) (gén)* tournament; *(Escrime)* pool; *(Rugby)* group.

poulet [pulɛ] *nm* chicken; *(‡: flic)* cop ‡.

pouliche [puliʃ] *nf* filly.

poulie [puli] *nf* pulley; *(avec sa caisse)* block.

poulpe [pulp(ə)] *nm* octopus.

pouls [pu] *nm* pulse. **prendre le** ~ **de qn** to take sb's pulse.

poumon [pumɔ̃] *nm* lung. ~ **d'acier** iron lung.

poupe [pup] *nf (Naut)* stern.

poupée [pupe] *nf (jouet)* doll, dolly; *(*: femme jolie)* doll *; *(‡: fille)* bird *; *(pansement)* finger bandage.

poupon [pupɔ̃] *nm* little baby. ◆ **pouponner** (1) *vi* to play mother. ◆ **pouponnière** *nf* day nursery, crèche.

pour [puʀ] **1** *prép* (**a**) *(direction)* for, to. **il part** ~ **l'Espagne demain** he leaves for Spain *ou* he is off to Spain tomorrow; **le train** ~ **Londres** the London train, the train for London.
(**b**) *(temps)* for. **il lui faut sa voiture** ~ **demain** he must have his car for *ou* by tomorrow; ~ **l'instant**

for the moment; ~ **toujours** for ever; **gardez le meilleur ~ la fin** keep the best till the end.
(**c**) *(intention)* for. **il ferait tout ~ sa mère** he would do anything for his mother *ou* for his mother's sake; **faire qch ~ la gloire** to do sth for the glory of it; **c'est fait** ~ that's what it's meant *ou* made for; **son amour ~ les bêtes** his love of animals; **coiffeur ~ dames** ladies' hairdresser; **c'est mauvais/bon ~ vous** it's bad/good for you; **il a été très gentil ~ ma mère** he was very kind to my mother; **sirop ~ la toux** cough mixture *ou* syrup *(US)*; **le plombier est venu ~ la chaudière** the plumber came about the boiler; ~ **le meilleur et ~ le pire** for better or for worse.
(**d**) *(approbation)* for, in favour of. **je suis ~!** * I'm all for it *, I'm all in favour (of it).
(**e**) *(point de vue)* ~ **moi** *(à mon avis)* in my opinion, in my view; *(en ce qui me concerne)* personally, for my part; **sa fille est tout ~ lui** his daughter is everything to him.
(**f**) *(cause)* **condamné ~ vol** convicted for theft; **puni ~ avoir menti** punished for lying *ou* having lied; **félicité ~ son audace** congratulated on his boldness; **fermé ~ cause de maladie** closed because of *ou* on account of illness; **pourquoi se faire du souci ~ cela?** why worry about that?; **il y est ~ qch/~ beaucoup** he is partly/largely responsible for it.
(**g**) *(à la place de)* **payer ~ qn** to pay for sb; *(Comm etc)* ~ **le directeur** p.p. Manager; **il a parlé ~ nous** he spoke on our behalf; **donnez-moi ~ 200 F d'essence** give me 200 francs' worth of petrol; **il l'a eu ~ 5 F** he got it for 5 francs.
(**h**) *(rapport)* for. ~ **cent** per cent; **petit ~ son âge** small for his age; **jour ~ jour** to the (very) day; **mourir ~ mourir, je préfère que ce soit ici** if I have to die I should prefer it to be here.
(**i**) *(comme)* for, as. **prendre qn ~ un imbécile** to take sb for an idiot; **il a ~ adjoint son cousin** he has his cousin as his deputy; **il passe ~ filou** he's said to be a crook; **il a ~ principe de faire...** his principle is to do...; ~ **de bon** * truly, really.
(**j**) *(emphatique)* ~ **(ce qui est de) notre voyage** as for our journey, as far as our journey goes *ou* is concerned; ~ **une malchance c'est une malchance!** this is a most unfortunate thing indeed!
(**k**) *(but)* to. **nous avons assez d'argent ~ l'aider** we have enough money to help him; **je n'ai rien dit ~ ne pas le blesser** I didn't say anything in order not to *ou* so as not to hurt him; **il étendit le bras ~ prendre la boîte** he reached (out) for the box; **le travail n'est pas ~ l'effrayer** he's not afraid of hard work; **il a dit ça ~ rire** he said it in fun *ou* as a joke; **il est parti ~ ne plus revenir** he left never to return; **j'étais ~ partir** * I was just going, I was just about to go.
(**l**) ~ **que** + *subj* so that, in order that; **écris ta lettre ~ qu'elle parte ce soir** write your letter so that it leaves this evening; **il est trop tard ~ qu'on le prévienne** it's too late to warn him.
(**m**) *(restriction)* ~ **riche qu'il soit, il n'est pas généreux** rich though he is, he's not generous; ~ **peu qu'il soit sorti sans sa clef...** if he should have come out without his key...; ~ **autant que je sache** as far as I know *ou* am aware.
2 *nm*: **le ~ et le contre** the arguments for and against, the pros and the cons.

pourboire [puRbwaR] *nm* tip.

pourcentage [puRsɑ̃taʒ] *nm*, percentage. **travailler au** ~ to work on commission.

pourchasser [puRʃase] (1) *vt [ennemi]* to pursue, hunt down; *[créancier, importun]* to hound. ~ **le crime** to hunt out crime.

pourlécher (se) [puRleʃe] (6) *vpr* to lick one's lips.

pourparlers [puRpaRle] *nmpl* talks, negotiations, discussions. **être en ~ avec** to have talks with.

pourpre [puRpR(ə)] **1** *adj, nm (couleur)* crimson. **2** *nf (matière, étoffe, symbole)* purple.

pourquoi [puRkwa] **1** *conj* why. ~ **est-il venu?** why did he come?, what did he come for? **2** *adv* why. **tu viens? — ~ pas?** are you coming? — why not? *ou* why shouldn't I?; **allez savoir ~ *!** I don't know why! **3** *nm inv (raison)* reason (*de* for); *(question)* question.

pourrir [puRiR] (2) **1** *vi [fruit]* to go rotten *ou* bad; *[bois, cadavre]* to rot away. ~ **en prison** to rot in prison; **laisser ~ la situation** to let the situation deteriorate *ou* get worse. **2** *vt fruit* to make rotten, rot; *(fig) enfant etc* to spoil, ruin. ◆ **pourri, e 1** *adj* (**a**) *(gén)* rotten; *feuille, cadavre* rotting; *viande* bad. **être ~** to have gone rotten *ou* bad. (**b**) *temps* wet, rainy; *société* rotten; *enfant* spoilt. **2** *nm* (**a**) *(morceau)* rotten *ou* bad part; *odeur* putrid smell. (**b**) (*⁑: crapule)* swine ⁑, bastard ⁑. ◆ **pourrissement** *nm [situation]* deterioration, worsening (*de* in, of). ◆ **pourriture** *nf* (**a**) *(lit, Agr)* rot; *[société]* rottenness. (**b**) *(péj: personne)* swine ⁑.

poursuivre [puRsɥivR(ə)] (40) **1** *vt* (**a**) *(courir après) (gén)* to pursue; *animal* to hunt down; *malfaiteur* to chase (after). (**b**) *[importun, souvenir]* to hound; *[idée]* to haunt. ~ **qn de sa colère** to hound sb through anger. (**c**) *rêve etc* to pursue; *gloire* to seek (after); *idéal* to strive towards. (**d**) *(continuer) (gén)* to continue, go *ou* carry on with; *avantage* to follow up, pursue. ~ **sa marche** to keep going, walk on. (**e**) *(Jur)* ~ **qn (en justice)** *(au criminel)* to prosecute sb; *(au civil)* to sue sb. **2** *vi (continuer)* to carry on, go on, continue; *(persévérer)* to keep at it, keep it up. **3 se ~** *vpr* to go on, continue. ◆ **poursuite** *nf* (**a**) *[fugitif]* chase (*de* after), pursuit (*de* of); *[gloire]* pursuit (*de* of). **se mettre à la ~ de qn** to go in pursuit of sb. (**b**) **~s (judiciaires)** legal proceedings; **engager des ~s contre** to take legal action against; **s'exposer à des ~s** to run the risk of prosecution. (**c**) *(continuation)* continuation. (**d**) *(Sport)* **(course)** ~ track race. ◆ **poursuivant, e** *nm, f (ennemi)* pursuer.

pourtant [puRtɑ̃] *adv* yet, nevertheless. **frêle mais ~ résistant** frail but nevertheless *ou* yet resilient; **il n'est ~ pas très intelligent** (and) yet he's not very clever, he's not very clever though.

pourtour [puRtuR] *nm [cercle]* circumference; *[rectangle]* perimeter; *(bord)* surround. **sur le ~ de** around.

pourvoir [puRvwaR] (25) **1** *vt*: ~ **qn de qch** to provide *ou* equip *ou* supply sb with sth, provide sth for sb; ~ **sa cave de vin** to stock one's cellar with wine. **2 ~ à** *vt indir éventualité, besoins* to provide for, cater for; *emploi* to fill. **j'y pourvoirai** I'll see to it *ou* deal with it. **3 se ~** *vpr*: **se ~ de** *argent* to provide o.s. with. ◆ **pourvoyeur, -euse** *nm, f* supplier. ◆ **pourvu¹, e** *adj emploi* filled. ~ **de** *intelligence* gifted *ou* endowed with; *dispositif* equipped *ou* fitted with; **nous voilà ~s pour l'hiver** we're well provided for *ou* stocked up for the winter; **feuille de papier ~e d'une marge** sheet of paper with a margin.

pourvu² [puRvy] *conj*: ~ **que** *(souhait)* let's hope; *(condition)* provided (that), so long as; ~ **que ça dure!** let's hope it lasts!, here's hoping it lasts! *

pousse [pus] *nf* (**a**) *(bourgeon)* shoot. (**b**) *(action) [feuilles]* sprouting; *[cheveux]* growth.

poussé, e¹ [puse] *adj études* advanced; *enquête* exhaustive. **très ~** *technique, dessin* elaborate.

pousse-café * [puskafe] *nm inv* liqueur.

poussée² [puse] *nf* (**a**) *(pression)* pressure; *(coup)* push, shove; *(Tech, Mil)* thrust. **sous la ~** under the pressure. (**b**) *[acné]* attack; *[prix]* rise, upsurge; *(électorale)* upsurge. ~ **de fièvre** (sudden) high temperature.

pousser [puse] (1) **1** *vt* (**a**) *(gén)* to push; *verrou* to slide; *objet gênant* to move, push aside; *(du* *coude)* to nudge; *(en bousculant)* to jostle. ~ **la porte** *(fermer)* to push the door to *ou* shut; *(ouvrir)* to push the door open; ~ **l'aiguille** to sew; ~ **un caillou du pied** to kick a stone (along); **le vent nous poussait vers la côte** the wind was blowing *ou* pushing us towards the shore; *(balançoire)* **peux-tu me** ~**?** can you give me a push? (**b**) *cheval* to ride hard, push; *moteur* to drive hard; *feu* to stoke up; *chauffage* to turn up; *élève (stimuler)* to urge on, push; *(mettre en valeur)* to push. **c'est l'ambition qui le pousse** he is driven by ambition; **poussé par ses amis** pushed *ou* persuaded by his friends. (**c**) ~ **qn à faire qch** *[faim, curiosité]* to drive sb to do sth; *[personne] (inciter)* to urge *ou* press sb to do sth; *(persuader)* to persuade *ou* induce sb to do sth; **son échec nous pousse à croire que...** his failure leads us to think that...; ~ **qn au crime** to drive sb to crime; ~ **qn à la dépense** to encourage sb to spend money. (**d**) *études, marche* to continue; *avantage* to press (home), follow up. ~ **la plaisanterie un peu loin** to carry *ou* take the joke a bit far; ~ **qch à la perfection** to carry *ou* bring sth to perfection; **il a poussé la gentillesse jusqu'à faire** he was kind enough to do; ~ **qn dans ses derniers retranchements** to drive sb into a corner; ~ **qn à bout** to push sb to breaking point. (**e**) *cri* to let out, utter, give; *soupir* to heave, give. ~ **des cris** to shout, scream; ~ **des rugissements** to roar.

2 *vi* (**a**) *(grandir) (gén)* to grow; *[graine]* to sprout. **faire** ~ **des tomates** to grow tomatoes; **ça pousse comme du chiendent** they grow like weeds; **se laisser** ~ **la barbe/les cheveux** to grow a beard/one's hair; **il a une dent qui pousse** he's cutting a tooth, he's got a tooth coming through; **de nouvelles villes poussaient comme des champignons** new towns were springing up *ou* mushrooming. (**b**) *(faire un effort)* to push. *(fig)* ~ **à la roue** to do a bit of pushing, push a bit; **faut pas** ~**!** ⁂ this is going a bit far! (**c**) *(aller)* ~ **jusqu'à Lyon** to go on *ou* push on as far as Lyons.

3 se ~ *vpr (se déplacer)* to move, shift.

poussette [pusɛt] *nf* push chair. ~**-canne** baby buggy, (folding) stroller *(US)*.

poussière [pusjɛʀ] *nf* dust. **faire de la** ~ to raise a dust; **avoir une** ~ **dans l'œil** to have a speck of dust in one's eye; **3 F et des** ~**s** * just over 3 francs; **tomber en** ~ to crumble into dust. ◆ **poussiéreux, -euse** *adj* dusty.

poussif, -ive [pusif, iv] *adj personne* shortwinded; *moteur* puffing, wheezing.

poussin [pusɛ̃] *nm* chick. **mon** ~**!** * pet!

poussoir [puswaʀ] *nm [sonnette]* button.

poutre [putʀ(ə)] *nf (en bois)* beam; *(en métal)* girder; *(Gym)* beam. ◆ **poutrelle** *nf* girder.

pouvoir¹ [puvwaʀ] (33) **1** *vb aux* (**a**) *(permission)* can, may, to be allowed to. **peut-il venir?** can he *ou* may he come?; **il peut ne pas venir** he doesn't have to come, he needn't come, he's not bound to come; **il pourrait venir s'il nous prévenait** he could come *ou* he would be able *ou* allowed to come if he notified us; **est-ce qu'on peut fermer la fenêtre?** may we *ou* do you mind if we shut the window? (**b**) *(possibilité)* can, to be able to. **il ne peut pas ne pas venir** he can't not come, he has to *ou* he must come; **il n'a (pas) pu venir** he couldn't *ou* wasn't able to *ou* was unable to come; **il ne peut pas s'empêcher de tousser** he can't help coughing; **comme il pouvait comprendre la fiche technique, il a pu réparer le poste** since he could understand the technical information he was able to *ou* he managed to repair the set; **pourriez-vous nous apporter du thé?** could you bring us some tea? (**c**) *(éventualité)* **il peut être français** he may *ou* might *ou* could be French; **il ne peut pas être français** he can't be French; **quel âge peut-il avoir?** how old might he be?; **qu'est-ce que cela peut bien lui faire?** * what's that (got) to do with him? *; **il peut être très méchant, parfois** he can be very nasty at times; **où ai-je bien pu mettre mon stylo?** where on earth can I have put my pen?; **cela pourrait se faire** that might *ou* could be arranged. (**d**) *(suggestion)* **elle pourrait arriver à l'heure!** she might *ou* could (at least) be punctual! (**e**) *(littér: souhait)* **puisse Dieu les aider!** may God help them!; **puissiez-vous dire vrai!** let us pray *ou* hope you're right!

2 *vb impers*: **il peut** *ou* **pourrait pleuvoir** it may *ou* might *ou* could rain, it is possible that it will rain.

3 *vt* can. **il partira dès qu'il le pourra** he will leave as soon as he can *ou* is able (to); **que puis-je pour vous?** what can I do for you?; **il a été on ne peut plus aimable** he couldn't have been kinder, he was as kind as could be; **je n'en peux plus** I can't stand it any longer; **je n'en peux plus d'attendre** I can wait no longer; **il n'en peut plus** *(fatigué)* he's all-in * *ou* tired out; *(à bout)* he can't take any more; **on n'y peut rien** there's nothing we can do (about it), it can't be helped.

4 se ~ *vpr*: **il se peut/se pourrait qu'elle vienne** she may *ou* could/might *ou* could (well) come; **cela se pourrait bien** that's quite possible, that might *ou* could well be.

pouvoir² [puvwaʀ] *nm* (**a**) *(gén)* power. ~ **absorbant** absorption power; ~ **d'achat** purchasing power; **avoir le** ~ **de faire** *(capacité)* to have the power *ou* ability to do; *(autorisation)* to have authority *ou* power to do; **ce n'est pas en mon** ~ it is not within *ou* in my power, it is beyond my power; **avoir du** ~ **sur qn** to have influence *ou* power over sb; **avoir du** ~ **sur soi-même** to have self-control; **dépasser ses** ~**s** to exceed one's powers. (**b**) *(Pol)* **le** ~ *(direction)* power; *(dirigeants)* the government; **le parti au** ~ the party in power *ou* in office; **avoir le** ~ to hold power, rule, govern; **prendre le** ~ *(légalement)* to come to power *ou* into office; *(illégalement)* to seize power; **le** ~ **exécutif** the executive power; **les** ~**s publics** the authorities. (**c**) *(Jur: procuration)* proxy. **donner** ~ **à qn de faire** to give sb proxy to do.

praesidium [pʀezidjɔm] *nm* praesidium. **le** ~ **suprême** the praesidium of the Supreme Soviet.

Prague [pʀag] *n* Prague.

praire [pʀɛʀ] *nf* clam.

prairie [pʀeʀi] *nf* meadow.

praline [pʀalin] *nf* sugared almond. ◆ **praliné, e 1** *adj* praline-flavoured. **2** *nm* praline-flavoured ice cream.

pratique [pʀatik] **1** *adj* (**a**) *(non théorique, réaliste)* practical. **avoir le sens** ~ to be practical-minded. (**b**) *(commode) (gén)* practical; *instrument* handy; *emploi du temps* convenient. **2** *nf* (**a**) *(application, procédé)* practice; *(expérience)* practical experience. **en** ~ in practice; **mettre qch en** ~ to put sth into practice; **dans la** ~ **de tous les jours** in the ordinary run of things, in the normal course of events; **il a une longue** ~ **des élèves** he has a long practical experience of teaching; **il a perdu la** ~ he is out of practice; **des** ~**s malhonnêtes** dishonest practices. (**b**) *[règle]* observance; *[sport]* practising; *[vertu]* exercise, practice. **la** ~ **du golf** golfing, (playing) golf; **la** ~ **du yoga** the practice of yoga; ~ **(religieuse)** church attendance; **la** ~ **de la médecine** the practising of medicine. ◆ **pratiquement** *adv (en pratique)* in practice; *(presque)* practically. ◆ **praticable** *adj (gén)* practicable; *projet* feasible; *chemin* passable, negotiable. ◆ **praticien, -ienne** *nm, f (gén, Méd)* practitioner. ◆ **pratiquant, e 1** *adj* practising. **il est très** ~ he goes to church regularly. **2** *nm, f (d'une foi)* follower; *(assidu)* regular churchgoer.

il a pu (he was able/could)

pratiquer [pʀatike] (1) **1** *vt* (**a**) *art etc* to practise, practice *(US)*; *règle* to observe; *vertu* to exercise; *football* to play. ~ **l'escrime** to go in for fencing; **il est recommandé de ~ un sport** it is considered advisable to play *ou* practise *ou* do a sport. (**b**) *ouverture* to make; *trou* to pierce, bore; *route* to build, open up; *(Méd) intervention* to carry out (*sur* on). (**c**) *méthode* to use. **2** *vi (Rel)* to go to church; *(Méd)* to be in practice. **3 se** ~ *vpr [méthode]* to be the practice; *[religion]* to be practised. **les prix qui se pratiquent à Paris** prices which prevail *ou* are current in Paris.

pré [pʀe] *nm* meadow.

pré... [pʀe] *préf* pre...

préalable [pʀealabl(ə)] **1** *adj entretien, condition* preliminary; *accord, avis* prior, previous. ~ **à** preceding, prior to. **2** *nm* precondition, prerequisite. **au** ~ first, beforehand. ◆ **préalablement** *adv* first, beforehand. ~ **à** prior to.

préambule [pʀeɑ̃byl] *nm [loi]* preamble (*de* to); *[contrat]* recitals *(pl)*; *(fig: prélude)* prelude (*à* to). **sans** ~ without any preliminaries, straight off.

préau, *pl* ~**x** [pʀeo] *nm [école]* covered playground; *[prison]* (exercise) yard; *[couvent]* inner courtyard.

préavis [pʀeavi] *nm* (advance) notice. ~ **de grève** strike notice; **déposer un ~ de grève** to give notice *ou* warning of strike action; **sans** ~ without advance *ou* previous notice.

précaire [pʀekɛʀ] *adj (gén)* precarious; *santé* shaky.

précaution [pʀekosjɔ̃] *nf* (**a**) *(disposition)* precaution. **prendre ses ~s** to take precautions; **faire qch avec les plus grandes ~s** to do sth with the utmost care *ou* the greatest precautions. (**b**) *(prudence)* caution, care. **par** ~ as a precaution; **pour plus de** ~ to be on the safe side; **avec** ~ cautiously. ◆ **précautionneux, -euse** *adj (prudent)* cautious; *(soigneux)* careful.

précéder [pʀesede] (6) **1** *vt* (**a**) *(venir avant)* to precede, come before; *(dans une file)* to be in front *ou* ahead of, precede. **faire ~ son discours d'une remarque** to precede one's speech by a remark. (**b**) *(devancer)* to precede, get ahead of. **il m'a précédé de 5 minutes** he got there 5 minutes before me *ou* ahead of me, he preceded me by 5 minutes.
2 *vi* to precede. **tout ce qui a précédé** all that has been said *etc* before *ou* so far; **dans le chapitre qui précède** in the preceding chapter. ◆ **précédemment** *adv* before, previously. ◆ **précédent, e 1** *adj* previous. **un discours** ~ a previous *ou* an earlier speech; **le film** ~ the preceding *ou* previous film. **2** *nm* precedent. **sans** ~ unprecedented; **créer un** ~ to create *ou* set a precedent.

précepte [pʀesɛpt(ə)] *nm* precept.

précepteur [pʀesɛptœʀ] *nm* private tutor.

prêcher [pʀeʃe] (1) **1** *vt (Rel, fig)* to preach; *personne* to preach to. *(hum)* ~ **la bonne parole** to spread the good word. **2** *vi* to preach. ~ **d'exemple** to preach by example.

précieux, -euse [pʀesjø, øz] *adj (lit, fig, péj)* precious; *conseil* invaluable; *ami* valued, precious. ◆ **précieusement** *adv* preciously.

précipice [pʀesipis] *nm (gouffre)* chasm; *(fig)* abyss. *(paroi)* **au bord du** ~ at the brink of the precipice.

précipiter [pʀesipite] (1) **1** *vt* (**a**) *(jeter)* to throw *ou* hurl down; *(dans le malheur)* to plunge (*dans* into). (**b**) *(hâter) pas, événement* to hasten. **il ne faut rien** ~ we mustn't rush things. **2** *vti (Chim)* to precipitate. **3 se** ~ *vpr* (**a**) *(se ruer)* to rush forward. **se ~ vers/sur** to rush towards/at; **se ~ contre** *[personne]* to rush at, throw o.s. against; *[voiture]* to smash into; **se ~ dans le vide** to hurl o.s. into space; **se ~ sur l'ennemi** to rush at *ou* hurl o.s. at the enemy; **il se précipita au-dehors** he raced *ou* dashed *ou* rushed outside. (**b**) *(s'accélérer)* to speed up; *[pouls]* to quicken. **les choses se précipitaient** events started to move faster. (**c**) *(se dépêcher)* to hurry, rush. ◆ **précipitamment** *adv* hastily. **sortir** ~ to rush out. ◆ **précipitation** *nf (hâte)* haste. *(Mét)* ~**s** precipitation. ◆ **précipité, e 1** *adj départ, pas, décision* hasty; *fuite* headlong; *rythme* swift. **2** *nm (Chim)* precipitate.

précis, e [pʀesi, iz] **1** *adj (juste)* precise, accurate; *(défini)* precise, definite; *(net) contours* distinct, precise. **je ne pense à rien de** ~ I'm not thinking of anything in particular; **à cet instant** ~ at that precise *ou* very moment; **à 4 heures ~es** at 4 o'clock sharp *ou* on the dot *. **2** *nm (résumé)* précis, summary; *(manuel)* handbook. ◆ **précisément** *adv (gén)* precisely; *(avec exactitude)* accurately; *(distinctement)* distinctly. **je venais ~ de sortir** in fact *ou* as a matter of fact I had just gone out, as it happened I'd just gone out; **il est arrivé ~ à ce moment-là** he arrived right *ou* just at that moment *ou* at that very moment; **ce n'est pas ~ beau** it's not exactly beautiful. ◆ **préciser** (1) **1** *vt intention* to specify, make clear, clarify; *fait* to be more specific about. **je vous préciserai la date plus tard** I'll let you know the exact date later; **je dois ~ que...** I must point out *ou* add *ou* explain that..., I must be specific that... **2 se** ~ *vpr [idée]* to take shape; *[danger]* to become clear *ou* clearer. ◆ **précision** *nf* (**a**) precision; accuracy; distinctness. **outil de** ~ precision tool. (**b**) *(détail)* point, piece of information; *(explication)* explanation.

précoce [pʀekɔs] *adj* early; *sénilité* premature; *enfant* precocious, advanced for his *ou* her age. ◆ **précocement** *adv* precociously. ◆ **précocité** *nf* earliness; precocity, precociousness.

préconçu, e [pʀekɔ̃sy] *adj* preconceived.

préconiser [pʀekɔnize] (1) *vt remède* to recommend; *méthode* to advocate; *plan, solution* to advocate, push. ◆ **préconisation** *nf* recommendation.

précuit, e [pʀekɥi, it] *adj* precooked.

précurseur [pʀekyʀsœʀ] **1** *adj m* precursory. ~ **de** preceding. **2** *nm* forerunner, precursor.

prédateur, -trice [pʀedatœʀ, tʀis] **1** *adj* predatory. **2** *nm* predator. ◆ **prédation** *nf* predation.

prédécesseur [pʀedesesœʀ] *nm* predecessor.

prédestiner [pʀedɛstine] (1) *vt* to predestine (*à qch* for sth, *à faire* to do). ◆ **prédestination** *nf* predestination.

prédicateur [pʀedikatœʀ] *nm* preacher.

prédiction [pʀediksjɔ̃] *nf* prediction.

prédilection [pʀedilɛksjɔ̃] *nf* predilection, partiality (*pour* for). **de** ~ favourite.

prédire [pʀediʀ] (37) *vt [prophète]* to foretell; *(gén)* to predict. ~ **l'avenir** to tell *ou* predict the future; **il m'a prédit que je...** he predicted (that) I..., he told me (that) I...

prédisposer [pʀedispoze] (1) *vt* to predispose (*à* to). ◆ **prédisposition** *nf* predisposition (*à* to).

prédominer [pʀedɔmine] (1) *vi (gén)* to predominate. ◆ **prédominance** *nf* predominance. ◆ **prédominant, e** *adj* predominant.

prééminence [pʀeeminɑ̃s] *nf* pre-eminence. ◆ **prééminent, e** *adj* pre-eminent.

préencollé, e [pʀeɑ̃kɔle] *adj* pre-pasted. **papier peint** ~ pre-pasted *ou* ready-pasted wallpaper.

préexister [pʀeɛgziste] (1) *vi* to pre-exist. ◆ **préexistant, e** *adj* pre-existent. ◆ **préexistence** *nf* pre-existence.

préfabriqué, e [pʀefabʀike] **1** *adj* prefabricated. **2** *nm (maison)* prefabricated house.

préface [pʀefas] *nf* preface.

préfecture [pʀefɛktyʀ] *nf* prefecture. ~ **de police** Paris police headquarters. ◆ **préfectoral, e,** *mpl* **-aux** *adj* prefectural.

préférer [pʀefeʀe] (6) *vt* to prefer (*à* to). **je te préfère avec les cheveux courts** I like you better *ou* I prefer you with short hair; **je préfère aller au cinéma** I prefer to go *ou* I would rather go to the cinema; **nous avons préféré attendre (plutôt que)** we preferred to wait *ou* thought it better to wait (rather than); **si tu préfères** if you prefer, if you like; **comme vous préférez** as you prefer *ou* like *ou* wish *ou* please. ◆ **préférable** *adj* preferable (*à qch* to sth), better (*à qch* than sth). **il serait** ~ **d'y aller** it would be better if you (*ou* we *etc*) went, it would be better for you (*ou* us *etc*) to go. ◆ **préféré, e** *adj, nm, f* favourite, pet *. ◆ **préférence** *nf* preference. **de** ~ preferably; **de** ~ **à** in preference to, rather than; **je n'ai pas de** ~ I don't mind; **par ordre de** ~ in order of preference. ◆ **préférentiel, -ielle** *adj* preferential. **tarif** ~ preferential *ou* special rate. ◆ **préférentiellement** *adv* preferentially.

préfet [pʀefɛ] *nm* prefect.

préfigurer [pʀefigyʀe] (1) *vt* to foreshadow.

préfixe [pʀefiks] *nm* prefix.

préhistoire [pʀeistwaʀ] *nf* prehistory. ◆ **préhistorique** *adj* prehistoric; *(péj)* antediluvian, ancient.

préjudice [pʀeʒydis] *nm (matériel)* loss; *(moral)* harm, damage, wrong. **porter** ~ **à qn** *(gén)* to harm sb; *[décision]* to be detrimental to sb; **au** ~ **de sa santé** at the expense of his health. ◆ **préjudiciable** *adj* prejudicial, detrimental, harmful (*à* to).

préjugé [pʀeʒyʒe] *nm* prejudice. **avoir un** ~ **contre** to be prejudiced *ou* biased against; ~**s de classe** class bias; ~ **de race** racial prejudice.

préjuger [pʀeʒyʒe] (3) *vt,* ~ **de** *vt indir* to prejudge.

prélasser (se) [pʀelɑse] (1) *vpr* to lounge.

prélavage [pʀelavaʒ] *nm* pre-wash.

prélat [pʀela] *nm* prelate.

prélever [pʀelve] (5) *vt échantillon* to take (*sur* from); *impôt* to levy (*sur* on); *retenue* to deduct *sur* from); *argent sur un compte* to withdraw (*sur* from). ◆ **prélèvement** *nm* taking; levying; deduction; withdrawal. **faire un** ~ **de sang** to take a blood sample; ~ **bancaire** standing *ou* banker's order, automatic deduction *(US)*.

préliminaire [pʀeliminɛʀ] **1** *adj (gén)* preliminary; *(discours)* introductory. **2** *nmpl*: ~**s** preliminaries.

prélude [pʀelyd] *nm* prelude (*à* to). ◆ **préluder à** (1) *vt indir* to be a prelude to.

prématuré, e [pʀematyʀe] **1** *adj (gén)* premature; *mort* untimely. **2** *nm, f* premature baby. ◆ **prématurément** *adv* prematurely.

préméditer [pʀemedite] (1) *vt* to premeditate. ~ **de faire** to plan to do. ◆ **préméditation** *nf* premeditation. **avec** ~ *crime* premeditated; *tuer* with intent.

premier, -ière [pʀəmje, jɛʀ] **1** *adj* (**a**) *(gén)* first; *impression* initial; *enfance* early; *rang* front; *ébauche* rough; *branche* lower, bottom. **être** ~ to be first; *(Sport)* **être en ~ière position** to be in the lead; *(Presse)* **en ~ière page** on the front page; **les 100 ~ières pages** the first 100 pages; **la ~ière marche de l'escalier** *(en bas)* the bottom step; *(en haut)* the top step; **le** ~ **mouchoir de la pile** the first *ou* top handkerchief in the pile; **ses ~s poèmes** his first *ou* early poems; **lire qch de la ~ière à la dernière ligne** to read sth from beginning to end; *(lit, fig)* **poser la ~ière pierre** to lay the foundation stone *ou* first stone; **au** ~ **signe de résistance** at the first sign of resistance. (**b**) *(dans un ordre)* first; *(à un examen)* first, top; *(en importance)* leading, foremost. ~ **secrétaire** first secretary; ~ **commis** chief shop assistant; ~ **danseur/rôle** leading dancer/part; **de ~ière qualité** top-quality; **de** ~ **ordre** first-rate; **c'est de ~ière urgence** it's a matter of the utmost urgency, it's (a) top priority; ~ **en classe** top of the class, first in the class; **de ~ière importance** of paramount *ou* prime *ou* the first importance; **de ~ière nécessité** absolutely essential; **cela m'intéresse au** ~ **chef** it's of the greatest *ou* utmost interest to me; **c'est le** ~ **écrivain français vivant** he's the leading *ou* foremost French writer alive today; **le** ~ **personnage de l'État** the country's leading *ou* most senior statesman. (**c**) *(du début) grade, prix* bottom. **c'était le** ~ **prix** it was the cheapest; **les ~s rudiments** the first *ou* basic rudiments. (**d**) *(après n: (fondamental) cause* basic; *objectif, qualité* prime; *état* initial, original. (**e**) **au** ~ **abord** at first sight; **au** *ou* **du** ~ **coup** at the first go *ou* try; **il n'est plus de la ~ière jeunesse** he's not as young as he used to be; **en** ~ **lieu** in the first place; *(fig)* **être aux ~ières loges** to have a front seat; **il n'en sait pas le** ~ **mot** he doesn't know the first thing about it; **~ière nouvelle!** it's news to me!; **à la ~ière occasion** at the first opportunity, as soon as one can; **faire ses ~s pas** to take one's first steps; **faire les ~s pas** to make the first move; **dans un** ~ **temps** as a first step, at first; **dans les ~s temps** at first, at the outset; **à ~ière vue** at first sight.

2 *nm, f* first (one). **passer le** ~ to go first; **il a été le** ~ **à le dire** he was the first to say so; **il a été reçu dans les ~s** he was in the first few.

3 *nm (gén)* first; *(étage)* first floor, second floor *(US)*; *(enfant)* first child. **le** ~ **de l'an** New Year's Day; **en** ~ *arriver* first; *dire* first(ly).

4 *nf (gén)* first; *(Rail etc)* first class; *(Théât)* first night; *(Ciné)* première; *(Alpinisme)* first ascent; *(Scol)* ≃ lower sixth, junior year *(US)*. *(Aut)* **passer en ~ière** to go into first gear; **c'est de ~ière!** * it's first-class!

5 : **le** ~ **âge** the first 3 months of life; **le** ~ **avril** the first of April, April Fool's Day; **~ière communion** first communion; ~ **jour** *[exposition]* first *ou* opening day; **le P~ Mai** the first of May, May Day; **P~ ministre** Prime Minister, Premier; ~ **né** first *ou* eldest child; ~ **plan** *(Phot)* foreground; *(fig)* forefront; **rôle de** ~ **plan** principal role; **les ~s secours** first aid; **le** ~ **venu** *(lit)* the first to come; *(fig)* anybody; *(chef)* ~ **violon** leader, concert master *(US)*; *(groupe)* **les ~s violons** the first violins.

premièrement [pʀəmjɛʀmɑ̃] *adv (d'abord)* first(ly); *(en premier lieu)* in the first place, to start with; *(objection)* firstly, for a start.

prémonition [pʀemɔnisjɔ̃] *nf* premonition. ◆ **prémonitoire** *adj* premonitory.

prémunir [pʀemyniʀ] (2) **1** *vt* to protect (*contre* against). **2 se** ~ *vpr* to protect o.s. (*contre* from).

prenant, e [pʀənɑ̃, ɑ̃t] *adj film, activité* absorbing, engrossing; *voix* fascinating, captivating.

prénatal, e, *mpl* ~**s** [pʀenatal] *adj* antenatal; *allocation* maternity.

prendre [pʀɑ̃dʀ(ə)] (58) **1** *vt* (**a**) *(saisir)* to take. **il l'a pris dans le tiroir** he took *ou* got it out of the drawer; **il prit un journal sur la table** he picked up *ou* took a newspaper from the table; **prends tes lunettes pour lire** put your glasses on to read; **il la prit par le cou** he put his arms round her neck. (**b**) *(aller chercher) chose* to get, fetch; *personne* to pick up; *(emmener)* to take. **je ne veux plus de ce manteau, tu peux le** ~ I don't want this coat any more so you can take *ou* have it; **prends ta chaise et viens ici** bring *ou* fetch your chair over here; **prends du beurre dans le frigo** get some butter out of the fridge.

(**c**) *(s'emparer de) (gén)* to take; *poisson, voleur* to catch. **le voleur s'est fait ~** the robber was caught; *(Tennis)* **~ le service de qn** to break sb's service.
(**d**) *(surprendre)* to catch; *(duper)* to take in. **~ qn à faire qch** to catch sb doing sth; **~ qn sur le fait** to catch sb in the act *ou* red-handed; **se laisser ~ à des paroles aimables** to let o.s. be taken in by soft talk.
(**e**) *repas* to have; *médicament* to take; *bain, repos* to take, have. **est-ce que vous prendrez du café?** will you have *ou* would you like (some) coffee?; **fais-lui ~ son médicament** give him his medicine; **il a pris son temps!** he took his time (over *ou* about it)!
(**f**) *métro, direction* to take. **il a pris le train** he took the train *ou* went by train; **je prends le train de 4 heures** I'm catching the 4 o'clock train; **il a pris sa voiture/l'avion pour aller à Lyon** he drove/flew to Lyons, he went by car/air to Lyons.
(**g**) *billet, essence* to get; *assurance-vie* to take out; *couchette* to book. **nous avons pris une maison** *(loué)* we have taken *ou* rented a house; *(acheté)* we have bought a house.
(**h**) *client, pensionnaire* to take; *passager* to pick up; *locataire* to take (in); *personnel* to take on.
(**i**) *renseignement, adresse* to write down, make a note of; *mesures, température* to take; *(sous la dictée)* to take (down). **~ des notes** to take notes; **~ qn en photo** to take a photo *ou* snap * of sb.
(**j**) *risque etc* to take; *air, ton* to put on, assume; *décision* to take, make, come to.
(**k**) *autorité* to gain. **~ du ventre** to get fat; **~ du poids** to put on weight; **les feuilles prenaient une couleur dorée** the leaves were turning golden-brown.
(**l**) *(coûter, prélever) temps, place, argent* to take; *(faire payer)* to charge. **cela me prend tout mon temps** it takes up all my time; **ce spécialiste prend très cher** this specialist charges very high fees; **~ de l'argent à la banque** to draw (out) *ou* withdraw money from the bank; **la cotisation est prise sur le salaire** the contribution is taken off *ou* deducted from one's salary; **il a dû ~ sur ses économies** he had to dip into his savings.
(**m**) *coup* to get; *maladie* to catch; *nouvelle, plaisanterie* to take. **~ froid/un rhume** to catch cold/ a cold; **qu'est-ce qu'on a pris!** *(reproches)* we didn't half catch it! *; *(défaite)* we took a beating *; *(averse)* we got drenched!
(**n**) *(manier) personne, problème* to handle, tackle. **~ qn par la douceur** to use gentle persuasion on sb; **elle m'a pris par les sentiments** she appealed to my feelings.
(**o**) **~ qn/qch pour** *(considérer)* to take sb/sth for; *(se servir de)* to take *ou* use sb/sth as; **pour qui me prenez-vous?** what do you take me for?, who do you think I am?; **~ qn pour un autre** to mistake sb for sb else.
(**p**) *[fièvre, remords]* to strike; *[doute, colère]* to seize, sweep over. **être pris de panique** to be panic-stricken; **il me prend l'envie de faire** I feel like doing, I've got an urge to do; **qu'est-ce qui te prend?** * what's the matter with you?, what's come over you?; **quand le froid vous prend** when the cold hits you.
(**q**) *(coincer)* to catch, trap. **j'ai pris mon manteau** *ou* **mon manteau s'est pris dans la porte** I caught *ou* trapped my coat in the door, my coat got stuck *ou* caught in the door.
(**r**) *(locutions)* **à tout ~** on the whole, all in all; **c'est à ~ ou à laisser** take it or leave it; **il faut en ~ et en laisser** you have to take it with a pinch of salt; **c'est toujours ça de pris** that's something at least; **~ sur soi de faire qch** to take it upon o.s. to do sth.
2 *vi* (**a**) *[ciment, pâte]* to set.
(**b**) *[plante]* to take root; *[vaccin]* to take; *[mode]* to catch on; *[spectacle]* to be a success. **avec moi, ça ne prend pas *** it doesn't work with me *.
(**c**) *[feu de bûches]* to go; *[incendie]* to start; *[bois]* to catch fire.
(**d**) *(se diriger)* to go. **~ à gauche** to go *ou* turn *ou* bear left.
3 se ~ *vpr* (**a**) **se ~ au sérieux** to take o.s. seriously; **il se prend pour un intellectuel** he thinks *ou* likes to think he's an intellectual.
(**b**) **s'y ~** to set about (doing) it; **s'y ~ bien/mal pour faire qch** to set about doing sth the right/ wrong way; **s'y ~ à deux fois pour faire qch** to try twice to do sth, take two attempts to do sth; **il faut s'y ~ à deux** it needs two of us (to do it); **je ne sais pas comment tu t'y prends, mais...** I don't know how you manage it but...; **il faut s'y ~ à l'avance** you have to do it ahead of time *ou* in advance.
(**c**) **s'en ~ à** *(agresser)* to lay into, set about; *(passer sa colère sur)* to take it out on; *(blâmer)* to lay *ou* put the blame on.
(**d**) *(se solidifier)* to set hard. **se ~ en glace** to freeze over.

preneur, -euse [pʀənœʀ, øz] *nm, f (acheteur)* buyer; *(locataire)* tenant. **je suis ~ à 100 F** I'll buy *ou* take it for 100 francs.

prénom [pʀenɔ̃] *nm* Christian name, first name; *(Admin)* forename, given name *(US)*. ◆ **prénommer** (1) *vt* to call, name. **le prénommé Paul** the said Paul; **se ~** to be called *ou* named.

préoccuper [pʀeɔkype] (1) **1** *vt (inquiéter)* to worry, bother; *(absorber)* to preoccupy. **l'avenir le préoccupe** he is concerned *ou* anxious *ou* bothered about the future; **tu as l'air préoccupé** you look worried, you look as though you've got sth on your mind; **il est uniquement préoccupé de sa petite personne** he only thinks about himself *ou* number one *. **2 se ~** *vpr (s'occuper)* to concern o.s. (*de* with); *(s'inquiéter)* to worry (*de* about). **il ne s'en préoccupe guère** he doesn't bother very much about it. ◆ **préoccupant, e** *adj* worrying. ◆ **préoccupation** *nf (inquiétude)* worry, anxiety; *(ennui)* worry; *(problème à résoudre)* preoccupation, concern.

préparer [pʀepaʀe] (1) **1** *vt* (**a**) *(gén)* to prepare; *repas* to make; *complot* to hatch; *plan* to draw up; *bagages* to get ready; *peaux, poisson* to dress; *voyage* to get ready for; *examen* to prepare for, study for. **~ l'avenir** to prepare for the future; **il a préparé la rencontre des 2 ministres** he organized *ou* he set up the meeting of the 2 ministers; *(Mil, fig)* **~ le terrain** to prepare the ground. (**b**) **~ qn à qch/à faire qch** to prepare sb for sth/to do sth; **~ qn à un examen** to prepare *ou* coach sb for an exam; **je n'y étais pas préparé** I wasn't prepared for it, I wasn't expecting it. (**c**) **~ qch à qn** to have sth in store for sb; **il nous prépare une surprise** he has a surprise in store for us, he's got a surprise up his sleeve.
2 se ~ *vpr* (**a**) *(s'apprêter)* to prepare (o.s.), get ready; *[athlète]* to train (*à qch* for sth, *à faire* to do). **elle se prépare** she's getting ready; **préparez-vous à venir** be prepared to come; **vous vous préparez des ennuis** you are storing up problems for yourself. (**b**) *(lit, fig) [orage]* to be brewing. **il se prépare une bagarre** there's going to be a fight; **il se prépare qch de louche** there's sth fishy in the air.
◆ **préparateur, -trice** *nm, f (gén)* assistant; *(Univ)* demonstrator. **~ en pharmacie** pharmaceutical *ou* chemist's assistant. ◆ **préparatifs** *nmpl* preparations (*de* for). ◆ **préparation** *nf (gén)* preparation (*d'un repas etc* of a meal *etc*, *d'un voyage etc* for a trip *etc*); *[peaux, poisson]* dressing (*de* of); *(à épreuve sportive)* training (*à* for). **annoncer qch sans ~** to announce sth abruptly *ou* without

preparation; **avoir qch en** ~ to have sth in hand *ou* preparation. ◆ **préparatoire** *adj* preparatory, preliminary.

prépondérance [pʀepɔ̃deʀɑ̃s] *nf [nation, théorie]* supremacy; *[trait de caractère]* domination. ◆ **prépondérant, e** *adj rôle* dominating, preponderant.

préposer [pʀepoze] (1) *vt* to appoint (*à* to). **être préposé à** to be in charge of. ◆ **préposé** *nm (Postes)* postman (*ou* woman), mailman (*ou* woman) *(US)*; *(gén)* employee; *[vestiaire]* attendant.

préposition [pʀepozisjɔ̃] *nf* preposition.

préretraite [pʀeʀ(ə)tʀɛt] *nf (état)* early retirement; *(pension)* early retirement pension. **être mis en** ~ to be given early retirement. ◆ **préretraité, e** *nm, f* person who takes early retirement.

prérogative [pʀeʀɔgativ] *nf* prerogative.

près [pʀɛ] *adv* (**a**) *(espace)* near(by), close (by), near *ou* close at hand; *(temps)* near, close. **c'est plus/moins** ~ **que je ne croyais** it's nearer *ou* closer than I thought/not as near *ou* close as I thought. (**b**) ~ **de** *(dans le temps)* close to; *(dans l'espace)* close to, near (to); *(presque)* nearly, almost; **le moins** ~ **possible de Noël** as far away as possible from Christmas; **ils étaient très** ~ **l'un de l'autre** they were very close to each other; **elle est** ~ **de sa mère** she's with her mother; **il est** ~ **de la retraite** he is close to *ou* nearing retirement; **il en a dépensé** ~ **de la moitié** he has spent nearly *ou* almost half of it; **il a été** ~ **de refuser** he was on the point of refusing *ou* about to refuse; *(iro)* **je ne suis pas** ~ **de partir** at this rate, I'm not likely to, be going (yet); *(fig)* **être** ~ **de son argent** to be close-fisted, be tight-fisted. (**c**) **de** ~ *(gén)*, *examiner* closely; *surveiller* carefully; **le coup a été tiré de** ~ the shot was fired at close range; **il voit mal de** ~ he can't see very well close to; **il a vu la mort de** ~ he has stared *ou* looked death in the face, he has come within an inch of death. (**d**) **à peu de chose** ~ more or less; **ce n'est pas aussi bon, à beaucoup** ~ it's nothing like as good, it's nowhere near as good; **ils sont identiques, à la couleur** ~ they are identical apart from *ou* except for the colour; **à cela** ~ **que...** apart from *ou* aside from the fact that...; **je vais vous donner le chiffre à un franc** ~ I'll give you the figure to within about a franc; **il a raté le bus à une minute** ~ he missed the bus by a minute or so; **il n'est pas à 10 minutes/à un kilo de sucre** ~ he can spare 10 minutes/a kilo of sugar.

présage [pʀezaʒ] *nm* omen, sign. **mauvais** ~ ill omen. ◆ **présager** (3) *vt (annoncer)* to be a sign *ou* an omen of; *(prévoir)* to predict, foresee. **rien ne laissait** ~ **que** there was nothing to hint that.

presbyte [pʀɛsbit] *adj* long-sighted, far-sighted *(US)*, presbyopic.

presbytère [pʀɛsbitɛʀ] *nm* presbytery.

prescience [pʀesjɑ̃s] *nf* prescience, foresight.

prescrire [pʀɛskʀiʀ] (39) *vt (Méd, Jur)* to prescribe; *(stipuler)* to stipulate; *(ordonner)* to order, command. ◆ **prescription** *nf* prescription; stipulation; order.

préséance [pʀeseɑ̃s] *nf* precedence.

présélectionner [pʀeselɛksjɔne] (1) *vt (Rad)* to preset; *candidats* to short-list. ◆ **présélection** *nf (gén)* preselection; *[candidats]* short-listing.

présence [pʀezɑ̃s] *nf (gén)* presence; *(au bureau, à l'école)* attendance. **avoir de la** ~ to have great presence; **en** ~ *armées* opposing; **mettre deux personnes en** ~ to bring two people together *ou* face to face; **en** ~ **de** in the presence of; **hors de ma** ~ while I was not there, in my absence; **en** ~ **de tels incidents** faced with such incidents; ~ **d'esprit** presence of mind.

présent¹, e [pʀezɑ̃, ɑ̃t] **1** *adj (gén)* present. **ici** ~ here present; **être** ~ **à une cérémonie** to be present at *ou* attend a ceremony; **métal** ~ **dans un minerai** metal present *ou* found in an ore; **avoir qch** ~ **à l'esprit** to have sth fresh in one's mind, not to forget about sth. **2** *nm (Gram)* present tense. *(époque)* **le** ~ the present; *(personnes)* **les** ~**s** those present; **il y avait 5** ~**s** there were 5 people present *ou* there; **à** ~ at present, presently *(US)*, now; *(de nos jours)* nowadays; **les gens d'à** ~ people of today.

présent² [pʀezɑ̃] *nm (littér)* gift, present.

présentation [pʀezɑ̃tɑsjɔ̃] *nf (gén)* presentation; *[nouveau venu]* introduction. **sur** ~ **du billet** on presentation of the ticket; **faire les** ~**s** to make the introductions; ~ **de mode** fashion show; *[personne]* **avoir une bonne/mauvaise** ~ to have a good/poor appearance. ◆ **présentable** *adj* presentable. ◆ **présentateur, -trice** *nm, f (Rad, TV) [spectacle]* introducer, presenter; *[nouvelles]* newscaster, newsreader.

présentement [pʀezɑ̃tmɑ̃] *adv* at present, presently *(US)*.

présenter [pʀezɑ̃te] (1) **1** *vt* (**a**) *(gén) tableau, pièce de théâtre* to present; *personne* to introduce (*à* to, *dans* into); *marchandises* to display (*à* to), set out (*à* before); *(TV) nouvelles* to present; *émission* to present, compere. (**b**) *facture etc* to present, submit; *passeport* to present, show; *requête, candidat* to put in; *plat* to hold out. ~ **le flanc à l'ennemi** to turn one's flank towards the enemy; ~ **sa candidature à un poste** to apply for *ou* put in for a job; **présentez armes!** present arms! (**c**) *excuses, félicitations* to present, offer; *respects* to present, pay; *objection* to raise. (**d**) *(exposer) problème, idée, théorie* to set out, expound. **travail bien/mal présenté** well-/badly presented *ou* laid-out piece of work; ~ **qch sous un jour favorable** to present sth in a favourable light; **il nous a présenté son ami comme un héros** he spoke of his friend as a hero. (**e**) *(laisser paraître) avantage, symptôme, danger, obstacle* to show. **cette route présente beaucoup de détours** there are a lot of bends on this road; **ce vase présente de nombreux défauts** this vase has *ou* shows a number of flaws. (**f**) *(Tech: placer)* to position, line up.
2 *vi [personne]* ~ **bien/mal** to have a good/poor appearance.
3 se ~ *vpr* (**a**) *(se rendre)* to go, come, appear. **se** ~ **chez qn** to go to sb's house; **il ne s'est présenté personne** no one came *ou* appeared *ou* turned up. (**b**) *[candidat]* to come forward. **se** ~ **pour un emploi** to apply for *ou* put in for a job; **se** ~ **à** *élection* to stand *ou* put o.s. up *ou* run *(US)* for; *examen* to sit, take; *concours* to go in for, enter for. (**c**) *(donner son nom)* to introduce o.s. (**d**) *[solution etc]* to present itself; *[occasion]* to arise, present itself; *[difficulté]* to crop *ou* come up. **un problème se présente à nous** we are faced with a problem; **si une nouvelle occasion se présente** if another opportunity arises; **se** ~ **à l'esprit** to come *ou* spring to mind. (**e**) *(apparaître)* **se** ~ **sous forme de cachets** to come in the form of tablets; **l'affaire se présente bien/mal** things are looking good/aren't looking too good; **se** ~ **sous un nouveau jour** to appear in a new light; **comment cela se présente-t-il?** *(lit)* what does it look like?; *(* fig)* how's it going? *

présentoir [pʀezɑ̃twaʀ] *nm (étagère)* display shelf.

préserver [pʀezɛʀve] (1) *vt* to protect (*de* from, against). **se** ~ **du soleil** to protect o.s. from the sun; **Dieu m'en préserve!** Heaven preserve me! ◆ **préservation** *nf* preservation, protection.

président [pʀezidɑ̃] *nm [pays, club]* president; *[comité, firme]* chairman; *[commission]* convener; *[université]* vice-chancellor, president *(US)*; *[tri-*

bunal] presiding judge *ou* magistrate. ~ **du jury** *(Scol)* chief examiner; *(Jur)* foreman of the jury; ~ **du conseil** prime minister; ~**-directeur général** chairman and managing director; ~ **à vie** life president; **Monsieur le** ~ *(gén)* Mr President; *(Jur)* your Honour. ◆ **présidence** *nf* presidency; chairmanship; vice-chancellorship; *(résidence)* presidential residence *ou* palace. *(Pol)* **candidat à la** ~ presidential candidate. ◆ **présidente** *nf* *(en titre)* (lady *ou* woman) president *etc*; *(épouse)* president's *etc* wife. ◆ **présidentiable** *adj*: **être** ~ to be in the running as a candidate for the presidency. ◆ **présidentiel, -elle** *adj* presidential.

présider [pʀezide] (1) **1** *vt (gén)* to preside over; *débat* to chair. ~ **un dîner** to be the guest of honour at a dinner; **c'est X qui préside** *(séance)* X is in the chair. **2** ~ **à** *vt indir*: ~ **à qch** to govern sth.

présomption [pʀezɔ̃psjɔ̃] *nf (supposition)* presumption; *(prétention)* presumptuousness. ◆ **présomptueux, -euse** *adj* presumptuous.

presque [pʀɛsk(ə)] *adv* almost, nearly, virtually; *(négatif)* hardly, scarcely. **c'est** ~ **de la folie** it's little short of madness; ~ **rien** hardly *ou* scarcely anything, next to nothing; **la** ~ **totalité des lecteurs** almost *ou* nearly all the readers.

presqu'île [pʀɛskil] *nf* peninsula.

pressant, e [pʀɛsɑ̃, ɑ̃t] *adj besoin, danger* pressing; *travail, désir* urgent; *demande* insistent.

presse [pʀɛs] *nf* (**a**) *(institution)* press; *(journaux)* (news)papers. ~ **d'opinion** papers specializing in political *etc* analysis and commentary; **la** ~ **périodique** periodicals, journals; ~ **automobile** car magazines; *(lit, fig)* **avoir bonne/mauvaise** ~ to be well/badly thought of; **agence** *etc* **de** ~ press agency *etc*. (**b**) *(appareil) (gén)* press; *(Typ)* (printing) press. **mettre sous** ~ *livre* to send to press; *journal* to put to bed. (**c**) *(littér: foule)* throng *(littér)*, press *(littér)*. (**d**) *(urgence)* **il n'y a pas de** ~ * there's no rush *ou* hurry. ◆ **presse-citron** *nm inv* lemon squeezer. ◆ **presse-papiers** *nm inv* paperweight. ◆ **presse-purée** *nm inv* potato-masher.

pressentir [pʀesɑ̃tiʀ] (16) *vt* (**a**) *danger* to sense. ~ **que...** to have a feeling *ou* a premonition that...; **rien ne laissait** ~ **sa mort** there was nothing to forewarn of *ou* to hint at his death. (**b**) *personne* to sound out, approach. ◆ **pressentiment** *nm* *(intuition)* presentiment, premonition; *(idée)* feeling.

presser [pʀese] (1) **1** *vt* (**a**) *éponge, fruit, objet* to squeeze; *bouton* to press, push; *raisin, disque* to press. **les gens étaient pressés les uns contre les autres** people were squashed up *ou* crushed up against one another; *(fig)* **on presse l'orange** *ou* **le citron et on jette l'écorce** you use people as long as they can be of service to you and then you cast them aside. (**b**) ~ **qn de faire** to urge *ou* press sb to do. (**c**) *départ* to hasten, speed up. **(faire)** ~ **qn** to hurry sb (up); **(faire)** ~ **les choses** to speed things up; ~ **le pas** to speed up; **rien ne vous presse** there's no hurry, we're in no rush. (**d**) *débiteur, ennemi* to press. **pressé par le besoin** driven *ou* pressed by need; ~ **qn de questions** to bombard *ou* ply sb with questions. **2** *vi [affaire]* to be urgent. **le temps presse** time is short, time presses; **rien ne presse** there's no hurry *ou* rush. **3** **se** ~ *vpr* (**a**) **se** ~ **contre qn** to squeeze up against sb; **se** ~ **autour de qn** to press *ou* crowd round sb; **les gens se pressaient pour entrer** people were pushing to get in. (**b**) *(se hâter)* to hurry (up). **sans se** ~ without hurrying.
◆ **pressé, e** *adj pas* hurried. **être** ~ **(de partir)** to be in a hurry (to leave); **il faut parer au plus** ~ we must do the most urgent thing(s) first, first things first.

pressing [pʀesiŋ] *nm* (**a**) *(repassage)* steampressing; *(établissement)* dry-cleaner's. (**b**) *(Sport)* pressure.

pression [pʀɛsjɔ̃] *nf* (**a**) *(gén, fig, Sci)* pressure. *(Tech)* **mettre sous** ~ to pressurize; **faire** ~ **sur** *objet* to press on; *personne* to put pressure on; **être soumis à des** ~**s** to be under pressure; ~ **sociale/fiscale** social/tax pressure; **bière à la** ~ draught *ou* draft *(US)* beer. (**b**) *(bouton)* press stud, snap (fastener) *(US)*.

pressoir [pʀɛswaʀ] *nm (appareil)* press; *(local)* presshouse.

pressurer [pʀesyʀe] (1) *vt fruit* to press; *(fig: exploiter) personne* to squeeze.

pressuriser [pʀesyʀize] (1) *vt* to pressurize. ◆ **pressurisation** *nf* pressurization.

prestance [pʀɛstɑ̃s] *nf* imposing bearing, presence. **avoir de la** ~ to have great presence.

prestation [pʀɛstɑsjɔ̃] *nf* (**a**) *(allocation)* benefit, allowance. ~**s sociales** social security benefits, welfare payments; ~ **en nature** payment in kind. (**b**) *[hôtel]* ~**(s)** service. (**c**) *[artiste, sportif]* performance.

preste [pʀɛst(ə)] *adj (littér)* nimble.

prestidigitation [pʀɛstidiʒitɑsjɔ̃] *nf* conjuring. ◆ **prestidigitateur, -trice** *nm, f* conjurer, magician.

prestige [pʀɛstiʒ] *nm* prestige. **voiture** *etc* **de** ~ prestige car *etc*. ◆ **prestigieux, -euse** *adj* prestigious.

présumer [pʀezyme] (1) **1** *vt* to presume, assume. **2** ~ **de** *vt indir*: **trop** ~ **de** to overestimate, overrate.

présupposer [pʀesypoze] (1) *vt* to presuppose.

prêt[1], e [pʀɛ, ɛt] *adj* (**a**) *(préparé)* ready (*à qch* for sth, *à faire* to do). **poulet** ~ **à cuire** oven-ready chicken; **tout est** ~ everything is ready, everything is in readiness; *[criminel]* **il est** ~ **à tout** he will do anything, he will stop at nothing. (**b**) *(disposé)* ~ **à** ready *ou* prepared *ou* willing to. ◆ **prêt-à-porter** *nm* ready-to-wear (clothes).

prêt[2] [pʀɛ] *nm (action)* loaning, lending; *(somme)* loan; *(sur salaire)* advance. ~ **bancaire** bank loan; ~ **à la construction** building loan; ~ **privilégié** guaranteed loan.

prétendant, e [pʀetɑ̃dɑ̃, ɑ̃t] **1** *nm (prince)* pretender; *(amoureux)* suitor. **2** *nm, f (candidat)* candidate (*à* for).

prétendre [pʀetɑ̃dʀ(ə)] (41) **1** *vt* (**a**) *(affirmer)* to claim, maintain, assert. **il se prétend médecin** he makes out *ou* claims he's a doctor; **on le prétend très riche** he is said *ou* alleged to be very rich; **à ce qu'il prétend** according to him *ou* to what he says. (**b**) *(avoir la prétention de)* to claim, pretend. **tu ne prétends pas le faire tout seul?** you don't pretend *ou* expect to do it on your own? (**c**) *(littér) (vouloir)* to want; *(avoir l'intention de)* to mean, intend. **2** ~ **à** *vt indir* to lay claim to, aspire to. ~ **à faire** to aspire to do. ◆ **prétendu, e** *adj chose* alleged; *personne* so-called, would-be. ◆ **prétendument** *adv* supposedly, allegedly.

prétention [pʀetɑ̃sjɔ̃] *nf* (**a**) *(exigence)* claim. **avoir des** ~**s sur** to lay claim to. (**b**) *(ambition)* pretension, claim (*à* to). **avoir la** ~ **de faire** to claim to be able to do; **sans** ~ *maison, repas* unpretentious; *robe* simple. (**c**) *(vanité)* pretentiousness, pretension. ◆ **prétentieusement** *adv* pretentiously. ◆ **prétentieux, -euse** *adj* pretentious.

prêter [pʀete] (1) **1** *vt* (**a**) *objet, argent* to lend. ~ **qch à qn** to lend sth to sb, lend sb sth; ~ **sur gages** to lend against security; *(Prov)* **on ne prête qu'aux riches** reputations shape reactions; *(fig)* **c'est un prêté pour un rendu** it's tit for tat. (**b**) *sentiment, intention* to attribute, ascribe (*à* to). **on lui prête l'intention de démissionner** he is alleged *ou* claimed *ou* supposed to be going to resign. (**c**) *aide* to give, lend. ~ **main forte à qn** to lend sb a hand, go to sb's help; ~ **la main à un complot** to get involved in *ou* take part in a plot. (**d**) *(locutions)* ~ **attention à** to pay attention to, take notice of; ~ **le flanc à la critique** to lay o.s. open to criticism, invite criticism; ~ **l'oreille** to listen (*à* to); ~ **serment** to take an *ou* the oath; **faire ~ serment à qn** to administer the oath to sb; ~ **de l'importance à qch** to accord importance to sth, consider sth to be important. **2** ~ **à** *vt indir:* ~ **à la critique** to be open to *ou* give rise to criticism; ~ **à rire** to be ridiculous *ou* laughable. **3 se** ~ *vpr* (**a**) *(gén)* **se ~ à qch** to lend o.s. to sth. (**b**) *[chaussures, cuir]* to give, stretch. ◆ **prêteur, -euse 1** *adj* unselfish. **il n'est pas** ~ he doesn't like lending his things. **2** *nm, f* (money)lender. ~ **sur gages** pawnbroker. ◆ **prête-nom,** *pl* **prête-noms** *nm* figurehead.

prétérit [pʀeteʀit] *nm* preterite.

prétexte [pʀetɛkst(ə)] *nm* pretext, excuse. **mauvais** ~ poor *ou* lame excuse; **sous** ~ **de/que** on the pretext *ou* pretence of/that; **sous aucun** ~ on no account. ◆ **prétexter** (1) *vt:* ~ **qch** to give sth as a pretext *ou* an excuse.

prêtre [pʀɛtʀ(ə)] *nm* priest. ◆ **prêtresse** *nf* priestess. ◆ **prêtrise** *nf* priesthood.

preuve [pʀœv] *nf* (**a**) *(gén, Jur, Math)* proof. **pouvez-vous apporter la ~ de ce que vous dites?** can you prove what you're saying?, can you produce proof *ou* evidence of what you're saying?; **j'avais prévu cela, la ~, j'ai déjà mon billet** * I'd thought of that and to prove it I've already got my ticket; **je n'ai pas de ~s** I have no proof *ou* evidence; **il y a 3 ~s irréfutables qu'il ment** there are 3 definite pieces of evidence to show that he's lying. (**b**) *(locutions)* **faire ~ de** to show; **faire ses ~s** *[personne]* to prove o.s.; *[technique]* to be well-tried; **professeur qui a fait ses ~s** experienced teacher.

prévaloir [pʀevalwaʀ] (29) **1** *vi* to prevail (*sur* over, *contre* against). **faire ~ ses droits** to insist upon one's rights; **faire ~ son opinion** to win acceptance for one's opinion. **2 se** ~ *vpr:* **se ~ de** *(se flatter)* to pride o.s. on; *(profiter)* to take advantage of.

prévenance [pʀɛvnɑ̃s] *nf:* ~**(s)** thoughtfulness, consideration, kindness. ◆ **prévenant, e** *adj* considerate, kind (*envers* to), thoughtful.

prévenir [pʀɛvniʀ] (22) *vt* (**a**) *(menacer)* to warn (*de qch* about *ou* against sth); *(aviser)* to inform, tell, let know (*de qch* about sth). ~ **le médecin** to call the doctor; **partir sans** ~ to leave without telling anyone. (**b**) *accident, malheur* to prevent, avoid. **mieux vaut ~ que guérir** prevention is better than cure. (**c**) *besoin, désir* to anticipate; *objection* to forestall. (**d**) ~ **qn contre qn/en faveur de qn** to prejudice sb against sb/in sb's favour. ◆ **préventif, -ive** *adj* preventive. **à titre** ~ as a preventive. ◆ **prévention** *nf* (**a**) *[accident, crime]* prevention. ~ **routière** road safety. (**b**) *(Jur)* custody, detention. (**c**) *(préjugé)* prejudice (*contre* against). ◆ **préventivement** *adv agir* preventively. ◆ **préventorium** *nm* sanatorium. ◆ **prévenu, e** *(Jur)* **1** *adj* charged (*de* with). **2** *nm, f* defendant, accused (person).

prévoir [pʀevwaʀ] (24) *vt* (**a**) *événement, conséquence* to foresee, anticipate; *temps* to forecast. ~ **le pire** to expect the worst; **tout laisse ~ une issue rapide** everything points to a rapid solution; **rien ne faisait** *ou* **ne laissait ~ que...** there was nothing to suggest *ou* to make one think that...; **on ne peut pas tout** ~ you can't think of everything; **plus tôt que prévu** earlier than expected *ou* anticipated. (**b**) *voyage, construction* to plan. ~ **de faire qch** to plan to do sth; **au moment prévu** at the appointed *ou* scheduled *ou* prescribed time; **comme prévu** as planned; **prévu pour lundi** scheduled for Monday. (**c**) *temps, place, argent* to allow; *équipements, repas* to provide. **tout est prévu pour l'arrivée de nos hôtes** everything is organized for the arrival of our guests; **cette voiture est prévue pour 4 personnes** this car is designed to take 4 people; **déposez vos lettres dans la boîte prévue à cet effet** put your letters in the box provided. (**d**) *[loi]* to provide for, make provision for. ◆ **prévisibilité** *nf* foreseeable nature. ◆ **prévisible** *adj* foreseeable. ◆ **prévision** *nf (gén)* prediction; *(attente)* expectation. ~**s budgétaires** budget estimates; ~**s météorologiques** weather forecast; ~ **à court/long terme** short-term/long-term forecast; **il a réussi au-delà de toute** ~ he has succeeded beyond all *ou* the wildest expectations; *(action)* **la ~ du temps** weather forecasting; **en ~ de son arrivée** in anticipation *ou* expectation of his arrival.

prévoyance [pʀevwajɑ̃s] *nf* foresight, forethought. **société de** ~ provident society. ◆ **prévoyant, e** *adj* provident.

prier [pʀije] (7) **1** *vt (Rel)* to pray to; *(implorer)* to beg. **il m'a prié de venir** *(demande)* he begged me to come; *(invitation)* he asked *ou* invited me to come; *(ordre)* he requested me to come; **je vous prie de sortir** will you please leave the room; **je vous en prie** *(faites donc)* please do, of course; *(après vous)* after you; *(idée d'irritation)* would you mind!; *(de rien)* don't mention it, not at all; **voulez-vous ouvrir la fenêtre je vous prie?** would you mind opening the window please?; **il s'est fait** ~ he needed coaxing *ou* persuading; **sans se faire** ~ without hesitation. **2** *vi* to pray (*pour* for). ◆ **prière** *nf (Rel)* prayer; *(demande)* request; *(supplication)* plea, entreaty. **être en** ~ to be at prayer *ou* praying; **à la ~ de qn** at sb's request; ~ **de ne pas fumer** no smoking (please); ~ **de ne pas se pencher à la fenêtre** (please) do not lean out of the window.

primaire [pʀimɛʀ] **1** *adj (gén)* primary; *(péj) personne* simple-minded; *raisonnement* simplistic. **2** *nm (Géol)* Primary, Palaeozoic. *(Scol)* **être en** ~ to be in primary school.

primate [pʀimat] *nm (Zool)* primate.

primauté [pʀimote] *nf* primacy.

prime[1] [pʀim] *nf* (**a**) *(cadeau)* free gift. (**b**) *(bonus)* bonus; *(subvention)* premium, subsidy; *(indemnité)* allowance. ~ **de transport** transport allowance. (**c**) *(Assurance, Bourse)* premium.

prime[2] [pʀim] *adj:* **de ~ abord** at first glance; ~ **jeunesse** earliest youth; *(Math)* **n** ~ n prime.

primer [pʀime] (1) **1** *vt (surpasser)* to prevail over, take precedence over; *(récompenser)* to award a prize to. **2** *vi* to be of prime importance.

primeur [pʀimœʀ] **1** *nfpl (Comm)* ~**s** early fruit and vegetables; **marchand de ~s** greengrocer. **2** *nf:* **avoir la ~ d'une nouvelle** to be the first to hear a piece of news.

primevère [pʀimvɛʀ] *nf (sauvage)* primrose; *(cultivée)* primula.

primitif, -ive [pʀimitif, iv] **1** *adj (gén, Sociol)* primitive; *(originel)* original, first; *couleur* primary; *(sommaire) installation* primitive, crude. **2** *nm, f* primitive. ◆ **primitivement** *adv* originally.

primo [pʀimo] *adv* first (of all), firstly.

primordial, e, *mpl* **-aux** [pʀimɔʀdjal, o] *adj* essential, primordial.

prince [pʀɛ̃s] *nm* prince. **être bon** ~ to be generous; **habillé comme un** ~ dressed like a prince; ~ **charmant** Prince Charming; ~ **consort** Prince Consort; ~ **héritier** crown prince. ◆ **princesse** *nf* princess. ◆ **princier, -ière** *adj (lit, fig)* princely.

principal, e, *mpl* **-aux** [pʀɛ̃sipal, o] **1** *adj bâtiment* main; *employé* chief, head; *question, raison* principal, main. **il a eu l'un des rôles ~aux** he played a major role, he was one of the leading *ou* main figures. **2** *nm (Fin)* principal; *(Scol)* head(master), principal *(of a college)*; *(Admin)* chief clerk. **c'est le ~** that's the main thing. **3** *nf* (**a**) *(Gram)* main clause. (**b**) *(Scol)* head(mistress), principal *(of a college)*. ◆ **principalement** *adv* principally, mainly, chiefly.

principauté [prɛ̃sipote] *nf* principality.

principe [prɛ̃sip] *nm* principle. **partir du ~ que** to work on the principle *ou* assumption that; **avoir pour ~ de faire** to make it a principle to do, make a point of doing; **il a manqué à ses ~s** he has failed to stick to his principles; **par ~** on principle; **en ~** *(d'habitude)* as a rule; *(théoriquement)* in principle; **de ~** *opposition etc* mechanical, automatic; **faire qch pour le ~** to do sth on principle.

printemps [prɛ̃tɑ̃] *nm* spring. **au ~** in (the) spring(time). ◆ **printanier, -ière** *adj soleil* spring; *temps, vêtement* spring-like.

priorité [prijɔrite] *nf (gén)* priority. **en ~** as a (matter of) priority; **venir en ~** to come first; *(Aut)* **avoir la ~** to have right of way (*sur* over). ◆ **prioritaire** *adj* having priority; *(Aut)* having right of way.

pris, prise[1] [pri, priz] *adj* (**a**) *place* taken. **avoir les mains prises** to have one's hands full; **tous les billets sont ~** the tickets are sold out; **toute ma journée est prise** I'm busy all day, I have engagements all day. (**b**) *personne* busy, engaged. **si vous n'êtes pas ~ ce soir...** if you're free *ou* if you're not busy this evening... (**c**) *(Méd) nez* stuffed-up; *gorge* hoarse. **les poumons sont ~** the lungs are affected. (**d**) *crème* set; *(gelé) eau* frozen. (**e**) **~ de peur/remords** stricken with *ou* by fear/remorse; **~ de boisson** under the influence of drink.

prise[2] [priz] **1** *nf* (**a**) *(pour empoigner)* hold, grip; *(pour soulever)* purchase; *(Judo, Alpinisme)* hold. **cette construction offre trop de ~ au vent** this building catches the wind very badly. (**b**) *(Chasse, Pêche)* catch; *(Mil, Dames, Échecs)* capture. **la ~ de la Bastille** the storming of the Bastille. (**c**) *(Aut)* **être en ~** to be in gear; **en ~ (directe)** in direct drive; *(fig)* **en ~ directe avec** *ou* **sur** tuned in to. (**d**) *(Méd)* dose. (**e**) *(locutions)* **avoir ~ sur** to have a hold on *ou* over; **son attitude donne ~ aux soupçons** his attitude gives rise to *ou* lays him open to suspicion; **aux ~s avec qn/qch** battling *ou* grappling with sb/sth. **2** : **~ d'air** air inlet *ou* intake; **~ de bec** * row *, set-to *; **~ de conscience** awareness, realization; **~ de contact** initial contact *ou* meeting; **~ de courant** *(mâle)* plug; *(femelle)* socket; **~ d'eau** water (supply) point; *(robinet)* tap, faucet *(US)*; **~ d'otages** taking *ou* seizure of hostages; **~ de position** stand; *(Pol)* **~ du pouvoir** seizure of power, political takeover; **~ pour rasoir électrique** razor point. **~ de sang** blood test; *(Ciné)* **~ de son** sound recording; *(Élec, Rad)* **~ de terre** earth, ground *(US)*; **~ de vue** *(opération)* filming, shooting; *(photo)* shot.

priser [prize] (1) **1** *vt tabac* to take; *(fig: apprécier)* to prize, value. **2** *vi* to take snuff.

prisme [prism(ə)] *nm* prism.

prison [prizɔ̃] *nf (lieu)* prison, jail, penitentiary *(US)*; *(peine)* imprisonment. **mettre/être en ~** to send to/be in prison *ou* jail; **peine de ~** prison sentence; **condamné à 3 mois de ~ ferme** sentenced to 3 months' imprisonment; **faire de la ~ préventive** to be remanded in custody. ◆ **prisonnier, -ière 1** *adj soldat* captive. **être ~** to be a prisoner (*de* of); **~ de ses vêtements** imprisoned in one's clothes. **2** *nm, f* prisoner. **~ d'opinion** prisoner of conscience; **~ politique** political prisoner; **faire/retenir qn ~** to take/hold sb prisoner.

prisunic [prizynik] *nm* ® department store *(for inexpensive goods)*, ≃ Woolworth's ® ≃, five and ten *(US)*.

privation [privasjɔ̃] *nf (suppression)* deprivation; *(gén pl: sacrifice)* privation, hardship. **la ~ de la vue** the loss of one's sight.

privatiser [privatize] (1) *vt entreprise* to privatize. ◆ **privatisation** *nf* privatization.

privautés [privote] *nfpl* liberties.

privé, e [prive] **1** *adj (gén)* private; *(Presse) source* unofficial; *(Jur) droit* civil. **personne ~e** private person; **en séjour (à titre) ~** on a private visit. **2** *nm (vie)* private life; *(Comm: secteur)* private sector. **en ~** in private.

priver [prive] (1) **1** *vt*: **~ qn de qch** to deprive sb of sth; **~ qch d'un élément** to remove an element from sth, strip sth of one of its elements; **privé de connaissance** unconscious; **privé de voix** speechless, unable to speak; **il a été privé de sommeil** he didn't get any sleep; **cela ne me prive pas** *(de vous le donner)* I can spare it; *(de ne plus en manger)* I don't miss it; *(de ne pas y aller)* I don't mind. **2 se ~** *vpr* to go *ou* do without. **se ~ de qch** to go *ou* do without sth, manage without sth; **se ~ de dessert** to do without dessert, forego the dessert; **se ~ de cigarettes** to deny o.s. cigarettes; **se ~ inutilement de qch** to deprive o.s. of sth unnecessarily; **il ne s'est pas privé de le dire** he had no hesitation in saying so; **si tu veux y aller, ne t'en prive pas pour moi** if you want to go don't hold back for me.

privilège [privilɛʒ] *nm (gén)* privilege. **j'ai eu le ~ de faire** I had the privilege of doing, I was privileged to do. ◆ **privilégié, e** *adj (gén)* privileged; *(par le sort)* favoured. ◆ **privilégier** (7) *vt* to favour.

prix [pri] **1** *nm* (**a**) *(gén, fig)* price; *[location, transport]* cost. **le ~ du pain** the price of bread. **quel est le ~ du billet de métro?** how much does a ticket on the underground cost?, what is the fare on the underground?; **menu à ~ fixe** set price menu; **votre ~ sera le mien** name *ou* state your price; **acheter qch à ~ d'or** to pay a (small) fortune for sth; **ça n'a pas de ~** it is priceless; **je vous fais un ~ (d'ami)** I'll let you have it at a reduced price, I'll knock a bit off for you *; **'~ sacrifiés', '~ écrasés'** 'prices slashed', 'rock-bottom prices'; **~ imbattable** *ou* **défiant toute concurrence** unbeatable price; **y mettre le ~** to pay a lot for sth; **c'est dans mes ~** that's within my price-range; *(enchères)* **mettre qch à ~** to set a reserve price *ou* an upset price *(US)* on sth; **mettre à ~ la tête de qn** to put a price on sb's head; **objet de ~** expensive *ou* pricey object; **j'apprécie votre geste à son juste ~** I appreciate your gesture for what it's worth; **donner du ~ à qch** to make sth more precious; **à tout ~** at all costs; **à aucun ~** on no account; **au ~ de grands efforts** at the expense of great effort. (**b**) *(récompense)* prize. **le ~ Nobel de la paix** the Nobel Peace Prize. (**c**) *(vainqueur) (personne)* prizewinner; *(livre)* prize winning book. (**d**) *(Courses)* race. *(Aut)* **Grand ~ (automobile)** Grand Prix. **2** : **~ coûtant** cost price; **~ de détail** retail price; **~ forfaitaire** contract price; **~ de gros** wholesale price; **~ à la production** *ou* **au producteur** farm gate price; **~ de revient** cost price; **~ sortie d'usine** factory price.

pro [pro] *nm, préf* pro-.

probable [prɔbabl(ə)] *adj* probable, likely. **il est peu ~ qu'il vienne** he is unlikely to come, there is little chance of his coming. ◆ **probabilité** *nf* probability, likelihood; *(chance)* probability. ◆ **probablement** *adv* probably.

probant, e [prɔbɑ̃, ɑ̃t] *adj* convincing.

probité [prɔbite] *nf* probity, integrity.

problème [prɔblɛm] *nm* problem; *(à débattre)* issue; *(Math)* problem, sum. **enfant à ~s** problem child; **faire ~** to pose problems; **(il n'y a) pas de ~!** * no problem. ◆ **problématique 1** *adj* problematic(al). **2** *nf (problème)* problem; *(science)* problematics *(sg)*.

procéder [pʀɔsede] (6) **1** *vi (agir)* to proceed; *(moralement)* to behave. **2** ~ **à** *vt indir enquête etc* to conduct, carry out. ~ **à l'ouverture de qch** to proceed to open sth; ~ **au vote (sur)** to take a vote (on); ~ **à une élection** to hold an election. **3** ~ **de** *vt indir (littér)* to come from, proceed from. ◆ **procédé** *nm (méthode)* process. *(conduite)* ~**(s)** behaviour, conduct.

procédure [pʀɔsedyʀ] *nf (gén, Jur)* procedure; *(procès)* proceedings.

procès [pʀɔsɛ] *nm (civil)* (legal) proceedings, (court) action, lawsuit; *(criminel)* trial. **engager un** ~ **contre qn** to take (court) action against sb, take sb to court, sue sb; **gagner/perdre son** ~ to win/lose one's case; *(fig)* **faire le** ~ **de qn** to put sb on trial *(fig)*. ◆ **procès-verbal**, *pl* **procès-verbaux** *nm (compte-rendu)* minutes; *(constat)* report; *(de contravention)* statement. **dresser un** ~ **contre qn** to book *ou* give a ticket to sb.

processeur [pʀɔsɛsœʀ] *nm* processor.

procession [pʀɔsesjɔ̃] *nf (gén)* procession.

processus [pʀɔsesys] *nm (gén)* process; *[maladie]* progress.

prochain, e [pʀɔʃɛ̃, ɛn] **1** *adj* (**a**) *(suivant)* next. **le mois** ~ next month; **le 8 septembre** ~ on the 8th September of this year; **la** ~**e fois** next time; **à la** ~**e occasion** at the next *ou* first opportunity; **au revoir, à une** ~**e fois!** goodbye, see you again!; **ce sera pour une** ~**e fois** it'll have to be some other time; **je descends à la** ~**e** * I'm getting off at the next stop. (**b**) *(proche) arrivée* imminent; *avenir* near, immediate. **un jour** ~ soon, in the near future. **2** *nm* fellow man. ◆ **prochainement** *adv* soon, shortly.

proche [pʀɔʃ] **1** *adj* (**a**) *village* neighbouring, nearby. **être** ~ to be near, be close (by); ~ **de** near, close to; **le magasin le plus** ~ the nearest shop; **de** ~ **en** ~ gradually; **le P**~**-Orient** the Near-East. (**b**) *mort* close, at hand; *départ* imminent. **dans un** ~ **avenir** in the near future; **être** ~ to be drawing near, be at hand; **être** ~ **de** to be close to. (**c**) *événement* close, recent. (**d**) *parent* close, near. **2** *nmpl*: ~**s** close relations, next of kin.

proclamer [pʀɔklame] (1) *vt (gén)* to proclaim; *décret* to publish; *résultats d'élection* to declare; *résultats d'examen* to announce. ◆ **proclamation** *nf* proclamation; declaration; announcement.

procréer [pʀɔkʀee] (1) *vt* to procreate. ◆ **procréation** *nf* procreation.

procuration [pʀɔkyʀɑsjɔ̃] *nf* proxy; *(Fin)* power of attorney.

procurer [pʀɔkyʀe] (1) **1** *vt* to bring, give. ~ **qch à qn** to get *ou* obtain sth for sb, provide sb with sth. **2 se** ~ *vpr* to get, find, obtain (for o.s.); *(acheter)* to buy (o.s.).

procureur [pʀɔkyʀœʀ] *nm: (Jur)* ~ **(de la République)** public *ou* state prosecutor.

prodigalité [pʀɔdigalite] *nf (gén)* prodigality, extravagance; *(fig: profusion)* profusion. ~**s** extravagance.

prodige [pʀɔdiʒ] **1** *nm (événement)* marvel, wonder; *(personne)* prodigy. **tenir du** ~ to be extraordinary; **faire des** ~**s** to work wonders; **grâce à des** ~**s de courage** thanks to his (*ou* her *etc*) prodigious *ou* extraordinary courage. **2** *adj*: **enfant** ~ child prodigy. ◆ **prodigieusement** *adv* fantastically, incredibly, prodigiously. ◆ **prodigieux, -euse** *adj (gén)* fantastic, incredible; *effort, personne* prodigious.

prodigue [pʀɔdig] **1** *adj (dépensier)* extravagant, wasteful, prodigal; *(généreux)* generous. **être** ~ **de** *compliments, argent* to be free with; *temps* to be unsparing of; *(Rel)* **le fils** ~ the prodigal son. **2** *nmf* spendthrift.

prodiguer [pʀɔdige] (1) *vt énergie* to be unsparing of; *conseils* to give; *argent* to be lavish with. ~ **qch à qn** to lavish sth on sb.

produire [pʀɔdɥiʀ] (38) **1** *vt (gén, Ciné, Jur)* to produce; *voitures etc* to produce, make; *(Agr)* to produce, grow; *intérêt* to yield, return. **2 se** ~ *vpr* (**a**) *(survenir)* to happen, occur, take place. (**b**) *[acteur]* to give a performance, appear. ◆ **producteur, -trice** **1** *adj (gén, Agr)* producing. **pays** ~ **de pétrole** oil-producing country, oil producer. **2** *nm, f (gén, Ciné, TV, Agr)* producer. **du** ~ **au consommateur** from the producer to the consumer; *(TV)* ~**-réalisateur** producer and director. ◆ **productif, -ive** *adj* productive. *(Fin)* ~ **d'intérêts** interestbearing. ◆ **production** *nf* (**a**) *(action)* production. (**b**) *(rendement) (Ind)* production, output; *(Agr)* production, yield. (**c**) *(produit)* product. ~**s** *(Agr)* produce; *(Comm, Ind)* goods. (**d**) *(Ciné)* production. ◆ **productique** *nf* factory *ou* industrial automation. ◆ **productivité** *nf* productivity.

produit [pʀɔdɥi] *nm* (**a**) *(article)* product; *(Chim)* chemical. ~**s** *(Agr)* produce; *(Comm, Ind)* goods, products; ~**s finis** finished goods *ou* products; ~ **de substitution** alternative product; ~ **de consommation** consumable; ~ **de consommation courante** basic consumable; ~**s alimentaires** foodstuffs; ~**s de beauté** cosmetics; ~ **pharmaceutique** pharmaceutical (product). (**b**) *(rapport)* product, yield; *(bénéfice)* profit; *(revenu)* income. **le** ~ **de la collecte** the proceeds *ou* takings from the collection; ~ **intérieur brut** gross domestic product; ~ **national brut** gross national product. (**c**) *(Math)* product.

proéminent, e [pʀɔeminɑ̃, ɑ̃t] *adj* prominent.

prof * [pʀɔf] *abrév de* **professeur.**

profane [pʀɔfan] **1** *adj fête etc* secular. **2** *nmf* (**a**) *(gén)* layman, lay person. (**b**) *(Rel)* non-believer. **3** *nm (Rel)* **le** ~ the secular. ◆ **profaner** (1) *vt église* to desecrate, profane; *souvenir* to defile. ◆ **profanateur, -trice** **1** *adj* profaning. **2** *nm, f* profaner. ◆ **profanation** *nf* desecration, profanation ; defilement.

proférer [pʀɔfeʀe] (6) *vt parole* to utter.

professer [pʀɔfese] (1) *vt* (**a**) *opinion etc* to profess, declare. (**b**) *(Scol)* to teach.

professeur [pʀɔfɛsœʀ] *nm (gén)* teacher; *[lycée, collège]* (school)teacher; *(Univ)* ≃ lecturer, instructor *(US)*; *(avec chaire)* professor. ~ **de piano** piano teacher *ou* master (*ou* mistress).

profession [pʀɔfɛsjɔ̃] *nf (gén)* occupation; *(manuelle)* trade; *(libérale)* profession. *(Admin)* **'sans** ~**'** 'occupation: none'; **faire** ~ **d'être artiste** to profess *ou* declare o.s. an artist; *(Rel, fig)* ~ **de foi** profession of faith. ◆ **professionnel, -elle** **1** *adj activité, maladie* occupational; *école* technical; *formation* vocational; *sportif, secret, faute* professional. **2** *nm, f (gén, Sport)* professional. **les** ~**s du tourisme** people working in the tourist industry.

professoral, e, *mpl* **-aux** [pʀɔfɛsɔʀal, o] *adj ton* professorial. ◆ **professorat** *nm*: **le** ~ teaching.

profil [pʀɔfil] *nm (gén, fig)* profile; *[voiture]* line. **de** ~ in profile. ◆ **profilé, e** **1** *adj (gén)* shaped; *(aérodynamique)* streamlined. **2** *nm (Tech)* ~ **(métallique)** metal section. ◆ **profiler** (1) **1** *vt (Tech) (dessiner)* to profile; *(fabriquer)* to shape. **2 se** ~ *vpr [objet]* to stand out, be outlined (*sur, contre* against); *[ennuis, solution]* to emerge.

profit [pʀɔfi] *nm (Comm, Fin)* profit; *(avantage)* benefit, advantage, profit. **être d'un grand** ~ **à qn** to be of great benefit to sb; **faire du** ~ *(gén)* to be economical; *[vêtement]* to wear well; *[rôti]* to go a long way; **vous avez** ~ **à faire cela** it's in your interest *ou* to your advantage to do that; **tirer**

~ **de, mettre à** ~ *leçon* to profit *ou* benefit from; *malheur des autres* to take advantage of; *invention* to turn to good account; *jeunesse, temps libre* to make the most of; **collecte au** ~ **des aveugles** collection in aid of the blind. ◆ **profitable** *adj (utile)* beneficial, of benefit; *(lucratif)* profitable (*à* to). ◆ **profiter** (1) **1** ~ **de** *vt indir* to take advantage of; *jeunesse, vacances* to make the most of. **2** ~ **à** *vt indir*: ~ **à qn** *[repas, conseil]* to benefit sb; **cette affaire lui a profité** he benefited by that business; **à qui cela profite-t-il?** who stands to gain by it? **3** *vi* (*) *[enfant]* to thrive, grow; *(être économique)* to be economical. ◆ **profiteur, -euse** *nm, f* profiteer.

profond, e [pRɔfɔ̃, ɔ̃d] **1** *adj* (**a**) *(lit)* deep. **peu** ~ shallow; ~ **de 3 mètres** 3 metres deep. (**b**) *nuit, couleur, voix* deep; *soupir* deep, heavy; *sommeil* deep, sound; *silence, mystère, réflexion* deep, profound; *erreur, intérêt, sentiment* profound; *révérence* deep, low; *cause, signification* underlying, deeper; *tendance* deep-seated, underlying. **la France ~e** the broad mass of French people. **2** *nm*: **au plus** ~ **de** *(gén)* in the depths of; **au plus** ~ **de la nuit** at dead of night. **3** *adv creuser* deep; *planter* deep (down). ◆ **profondément** *adv* deeply; profoundly; *creuser* deep; *s'incliner* low. ~ **différent** vastly *ou* profoundly different; **il dort** ~ he is sound *ou* fast asleep; **idée** ~ **ancrée dans les esprits** idea deeply rooted in people's minds; **ça m'est** ~ **égal** I really couldn't care less. ◆ **profondeur** *nf* (**a**) *(lit)* depth. **à cause du peu de** ~ because of the shallowness; **creuser en** ~ to dig deep; **avoir 10 mètres de** ~ to be 10 metres deep *ou* in depth; **les ~s** the depths (*de* of). (**b**) *[personne, remarque]* profundity; *[sentiment, regard]* depth; *[couleur, voix]* deepness. **en** ~ *agir* in depth; *réforme* radical.

profusion [pRɔfyzjɔ̃] *nf (gén)* profusion; *[idées]* wealth. **il y a des fruits à** ~ there is fruit galore * *ou* in plenty, there is plenty of fruit.

progéniture [pRɔʒenityR] *nf* offspring.

progiciel [pRɔʒisjɛl] *nm* software package.

programme [pRɔgRam] *nm* (**a**) *(gén)* programme, program *(US)*; *(emploi du temps)* timetable; *(Ordin)* program. **au** ~ in the programme. (**b**) *(Scol) (d'une matière)* syllabus; *(d'une classe, d'une école)* curriculum. **les œuvres du** ~ the set *ou* assigned *(US)* books, the books on the syllabus. ◆ **programmable** *adj* programmable. **touche** ~ user-definable key. ◆ **programmation** *nf* programming. ◆ **programmer** (1) *vt émission* to bill; *ordinateur* to program; *(*: prévoir)* to plan. ◆ **programmeur, -euse** *nm, f* (computer) programmer.

progrès [pRɔgRɛ] *nm (gén)* progress. **faire des** ~ to make progress; **élève en** ~ pupil who is making progress *ou* who is getting on (well); ~ **scolaires** academic progress; **il y a du** ~ there is some progress *ou* improvement; **suivre les** ~ **de** to follow the progress of; **c'est le** ~! that's progress! ◆ **progresser** (1) *vi* (**a**) *(s'améliorer)* to progress, get *ou* come on well. (**b**) *(avancer)* to advance, progress; *[théorie]* to gain ground, make headway. ◆ **progressif, -ive** *adj* progressive. ◆ **progression** *nf* (**a**) *(gén)* progress; *[ennemi]* advance; *[maladie]* progression. (**b**) *(Math, Mus)* progression. ◆ **progressiste** *adj, nmf* progressive. ◆ **progressivement** *adv* progressively.

prohiber [pRɔibe] (1) *vt* to prohibit, ban, forbid. ◆ **prohibitif, -ive** *adj* prohibitive. ◆ **prohibition** *nf (gén, Hist USA)* prohibition (*de* on). **la** ~ **du port d'armes** a ban on the carrying of weapons.

proie [pRwa] *nf (lit, fig)* prey. **être la** ~ **de** to fall prey to, be the prey of; **être en** ~ **à** *maladie* to be a victim of; *douleur* to be tortured by; *émotion* to be prey to.

projecteur [pRɔʒɛktœR] *nm* (**a**) *[film]* projector. (**b**) *(lampe) [théâtre]* spotlight; *[bateau]* searchlight; *[monument]* floodlight; *(Aut)* headlamp unit *ou* assembly, headlight.

projectile [pRɔʒɛktil] *nm* missile, projectile.

projection [pRɔʒɛksjɔ̃] *nf* (**a**) *[film] (action)* projection; *(séance)* showing. **appareil de** ~ projector; **salle de** ~ film theatre; **cabine de** ~ projection room. (**b**) *[pierres etc]* throwing; *[vapeur]* discharge. ◆ **projectionniste** *nmf* projectionist.

projet [pRɔʒɛ] *nm* (**a**) *(dessein)* plan. **faire le** ~ **de faire** to make plans to do; **ce** ~ **de livre** this plan for a book; **c'est encore en** ~ it's still only at the planning stage. (**b**) *(ébauche) [roman]* (preliminary) draft; *[maison]* plan. ~ **de loi** bill; **établir un** ~ **de contrat** to draft a contract. ◆ **projeteur** *nm* project manager.

projeter [pRɔʒte] (4) **1** *vt* (**a**) *(envisager)* to plan (*de faire* to do). (**b**) *(jeter) (gén)* to throw, fling; *gravillons* to throw up; *étincelles* to throw off; *fumée* to send out, discharge. (**c**) *ombre, reflet* to cast, project, throw; *diapositive* to project, show. **2 se** ~ *vpr [ombre]* to be cast, fall (*sur* on).

prolétaire [pRɔletɛR] **1** *adj* proletarian. **2** *nmf* proletarian. **les enfants de ~s** children of working-class people; **~s de tous les pays unissez-vous!** workers of the world unite! ◆ **prolétariat** *nm* proletariat. ◆ **prolétarien, -ienne** *adj* proletarian.

prolifération [pRɔlifeRɑsjɔ̃] *nf* proliferation. ◆ **proliférer** (6) *vi* to proliferate. ◆ **prolifique** *adj* prolific.

prologue [pRɔlɔg] *nm* prologue (*à* to).

prolonger [pRɔlɔ̃ʒe] (3) **1** *vt (gén)* to prolong; *billet* to extend; *rue, mur* to extend, continue. **2 se** ~ *vpr (gén)* to go on, carry on, continue; *[effet]* to last, persist.

◆ **prolongateur** *nm* extension cable *ou* lead. ◆ **prolongation** *nf* prolongation; extension. *(Ftbl)* **~s** extra time. ◆ **prolongé, e** *adj* prolonged. ◆ **prolongement** *nm [route]* continuation; *[bâtiment, affaire]* extension. **être dans le** ~ **de qch** to run *ou* lead straight on from sth; *(suites)* **~s** repercussions, effects.

promenade [pRɔmnad] *nf* (**a**) *(à pied)* walk, stroll; *(en voiture)* drive, ride; *(en bateau)* sail; *(en vélo, à cheval)* ride. **faire une ~/être en** ~ to go out/be out for a walk (*ou* a drive *etc*). (**b**) *(avenue)* walk, esplanade. ◆ **promener** (5) **1** *vt*: **(emmener)** ~ **qn** to take sb (out) for a walk *ou* stroll; ~ **le chien** to walk the dog, take the dog out (for a walk); **cela te promènera** that will get you out for a while; *(péj)* ~ **qch/qn partout** * to trail sb/sth everywhere; ~ **ses regards/ses doigts sur qch** to run one's eyes/one's fingers over sth. **2 se** ~ *vpr* to go for a walk (*ou* drive *etc*); *[regards, doigts]* to wander. **ses affaires se promènent toujours partout** * his things are always lying around all over the place. ◆ **promeneur, -euse** *nm, f* walker, stroller.

promesse [pRɔmɛs] *nf* promise; *(Comm)* commitment, undertaking. ~ **en l'air** empty *ou* vain promise; ~ **d'achat** commitment to buy; **faire une** ~ to make a promise, give one's word; **j'ai sa** ~ I have his word for it; *(fig)* **plein de ~s** very promising.

prometteur, -euse [pRɔmɛtœR, øz] *adj début, signe* promising; *acteur, politicien* up-and-coming, promising.

promettre [pRɔmɛtR(ə)] (56) **1** *vt (gén, fig)* to promise. **je te le promets** I promise (you); **il a promis de venir** he promised to come; **il m'a promis de venir** *ou* **qu'il viendrait** he promised me that he would come; ~ **la lune** to promise the moon *ou* the earth; ~ **son cœur** to pledge one's heart; **on nous promet du beau temps** we are promised *ou* we are in for * some fine weather; **le dîner promet d'être réussi** the dinner promises to be a success; **cet enfant promet** this child shows promise *ou* is

promising; *(iro)* **ça promet!** that's a good start! *(iro)*, that's promising! *(iro)*.
2 se ~ *vpr*: **se** ~ **de faire** to mean *ou* resolve to do; **se** ~ **du bon temps** to promise o.s. a good time. ◆ **promis, e** *adj*: **être** ~ **à qch** to be destined for sth.

promiscuité [pʀɔmiskɥite] *nf* lack of privacy (*de* in).

promo [pʀɔmo] *nf* (*abrév de* **promotion**) year, class *(US)*.

promontoire [pʀɔmɔ̃twaʀ] *nm* headland, promontory.

promotion [pʀɔmosjɔ̃] *nf [employé, produit]* promotion; *(Scol: année)* year, class *(US)*. ~ **sociale** social advancement; **(article en)** ~ (item on) special offer. ◆ **promoteur, -trice** *nm, f (instigateur)* promoter. ~ **(immobilier)** property developer. ◆ **promotionnel, -elle** *adj article* on (special) offer; *vente* promotional. ◆ **promouvoir** (27) *vt* to promote, upgrade (*à* to).

prompt, prompte [pʀɔ̃, pʀɔ̃t] *adj (gén)* swift, rapid, quick; *réaction* prompt, swift; *départ, changement* sudden. ~ **rétablissement!** get well soon!; ~ **à agir** swift *ou* quick to act; *(Comm)* **dans l'espoir d'une prompte réponse** hoping for an early reply. ◆ **promptement** *adv* swiftly; rapidly; quickly; promptly; suddenly. ◆ **promptitude** *nf* swiftness; rapidity; quickness; promptness; suddenness.

promulguer [pʀɔmylge] (1) *vt* to promulgate.

prôner [pʀone] (1) *vt (vanter)* to extol; *(préconiser)* to advocate.

pronom [pʀɔnɔ̃] *nm* pronoun. ◆ **pronominal, e,** *mpl* **-aux** *adj* pronominal. **verbe** ~ reflexive verb.

prononcer [pʀɔnɔ̃se] (3) **1** *vt* (**a**) *(articuler)* to pronounce. **mal** ~ **un mot** to mispronounce a word; ~ **distinctement** to speak clearly. (**b**) *(dire) parole, nom* to utter; *discours* to make, deliver. (**c**) *sentence, dissolution* to pronounce. **2 se** ~ *vpr* (**a**) to reach *ou* come to a decision, give a verdict (*sur* on). **se** ~ **en faveur de** to pronounce o.s. in favour of. (**b**) *[mot]* to be pronounced. ◆ **prononçable** *adj* pronounceable. ◆ **prononcé, e** *adj accent, goût, trait* marked, pronounced, strong. ◆ **prononciation** *nf* pronunciation. **il a une bonne** ~ he speaks clearly; *(langue étrangère)* he has a good pronunciation; **défaut de** ~ speech impediment *ou* defect.

pronostic [pʀɔnɔstik] *nm* forecast. **se tromper dans ses** ~**s** to get one's forecasts wrong. ◆ **pronostiquer** (1) *vt (prédire)* to forecast; *(être le signe de)* to foretell, be a sign of. ◆ **pronostiqueur, -euse** *nm, f (gén)* forecaster; *(Courses)* tipster.

propagande [pʀɔpagɑ̃d] *nf* propaganda. **faire de la** ~ **pour qch/qn** to push *ou* plug * sth/sb; ~ **électorale** electioneering propaganda.

propager [pʀɔpaʒe] (3) **1** *vt foi, idée* to propagate; *nouvelle, maladie* to spread. **2 se** ~ *vpr (gén)* to spread; *(Phys) [onde]* to be propagated; *(Bio) [espèce]* to propagate. ◆ **propagateur, -trice** *nm, f* propagator; spreader. ◆ **propagation** *nf* propagation; spreading.

propane [pʀɔpan] *nm* propane.

propension [pʀɔpɑ̃sjɔ̃] *nf* propensity (*à qch* for sth, *à faire* to do).

prophète [pʀɔfɛt] *nm* prophet. ◆ **prophétesse** *nf* prophetess. ◆ **prophétie** *nf* prophecy. ◆ **prophétique** *adj* prophetic. ◆ **prophétiser** (1) *vt* to prophesy.

propice [pʀɔpis] *adj (gén)* favourable (*à* to); *circonstance* auspicious, propitious. **moment** ~ opportune moment.

proportion [pʀɔpɔʀsjɔ̃] *nf (gén)* proportion. *(rapport)* **la** ~ **entre hauteur et largeur** the proportion *ou* relation of height to width, the ratio between height and width; **réduire qch à de plus justes** ~**s** to cut sth down to size; **en** ~ in proportion (*de* to); **hors de** ~ out of proportion (*avec* to); **toutes** ~**s gardées** relatively speaking, making due allowance(s). ◆ **proportionné, e** *adj*: ~ **à** proportional *ou* proportionate to; **bien** ~ well-proportioned. ◆ **proportionnel, -elle** *adj* proportional. ~ **à** proportional *ou* proportionate to; **représentation** ~**elle** proportional representation. ◆ **proportionnellement** *adv* proportionally, proportionately (*à* to). ◆ **proportionner** (1) *vt* to proportion.

propos [pʀɔpo] *nm* (**a**) *(paroles)* talk, remarks, words. (**b**) *(littér: intention)* intention. **de** ~ **délibéré** deliberately, on purpose. (**c**) *(sujet)* subject. **à quel** ~ **voulait-il me voir?** what did he want to see me about?; **à** ~ **de ta voiture** about your car, on the subject of your car; **je vous écris à** ~ **de l'annonce** I am writing regarding *ou* concerning the advertisement *ou* in connection with the advertisement; **il se plaint à tout** ~ he complains at the slightest (little) thing; **à ce** ~ in this connection. (**d**) *(lit, fig)* **arriver à** ~ to come at the right moment *ou* time; *[fait]* **arriver mal à** ~ to happen (just) at the wrong moment *ou* time; **juger à** ~ **de faire qch** to see fit to do sth; **à** ~**, dis-moi...** incidentally *ou* by the way, tell me...

proposer [pʀɔpoze] (1) **1** *vt* (**a**) *(suggérer) (gén)* to suggest, propose (*de faire* doing); *solution, candidat* to put forward. ~ **qch à qn** to suggest *ou* put sth to sb; **je vous propose de passer me voir** I suggest that you come round and see me. (**b**) *(offrir) aide, prix, situation* to offer. ~ **de faire** to offer to do; ~ **qch à qn** to offer sth to sb, offer sb sth.
2 se ~ *vpr* (**a**) *(offrir ses services)* to offer one's services. **se** ~ **pour faire qch** to offer to do sth. (**b**) *but, tâche* to set o.s. **se** ~ **de faire qch** to intend *ou* mean *ou* propose to do sth.
◆ **proposition** *nf* (**a**) *(suggestion, offre)* proposal, proposition. *(Pol)* ~ **de loi** private bill; **sur** ~ **de** on the proposal of. (**b**) *(Math, Philos, déclaration)* proposition. (**c**) *(Gram)* clause. ~ **principale** main clause.

propre[1] [pʀɔpʀ(ə)] **1** *adj* (**a**) *(pas sali)* clean; *(net) personne, vêtement* neat, tidy; *travail, cahier* neat. ~ **comme un sou neuf** as neat *ou* clean as a new pin; **ce n'est pas** ~ **de manger avec les doigts** it's messy to eat with your fingers; **nous voilà** ~**s!** * now we're in a fine *ou* proper mess! * (**b**) *(qui ne salit pas) chien* house-trained; *enfant* toilet-trained. (**c**) *(honnête)* honest, decent. **2** *nm*: **sentir le** ~ to smell clean; **recopier qch au** ~ to make a fair copy of sth; **c'est du** ~**!** * *(gâchis)* what a mess!; *(comportement)* what a way to behave!, it's an absolute disgrace!

propre[2] [pʀɔpʀ(ə)] **1** *adj* (**a**) *(possessif)* own. **par ses** ~**s moyens** *réussir* on one's own; *rentrer* under one's own steam; **ce sont ses** ~**s mots** those are his own *ou* his very *ou* his actual words; **de son** ~ **chef** on his own initiative. (**b**) *(spécifique)* ~ **à** peculiar to, characteristic of; **c'est un trait qui lui est** ~ it's a distinctive *ou* specific characteristic of his; *(Jur)* **biens** ~**s** personal property. (**c**) *(qui convient)* suitable, appropriate (*à* for). **le mot** ~ the right *ou* proper word. (**d**) *(de nature à)* **un poste** ~ **à lui apporter des satisfactions** a job likely to bring him satisfaction. (**e**) *(Ling) sens d'un mot* literal. **2** *nm* (**a**) *(qualité)* **c'est le** ~ **de qch** it's a peculiarity *ou* (distinctive) feature of sth; **avoir qch en** ~ to have exclusive possession of sth; **cette caractéristique que la France possède en** ~ this feature which is peculiar *ou* exclusive to France. (**b**) *(Ling)* **au** ~ in the literal sense, literally.

propre-à-rien, *pl* **propres-à-rien** [pʀɔpʀaʀjɛ̃] *nmf* good-for-nothing.

proprement [pʀɔpʀəmɑ̃] *adv* (**a**) *(avec propreté)* cleanly; *(avec netteté)* neatly, tidily; *(comme il faut)* properly; *(fig: décemment)* decently. **mange ~!** eat properly! (**b**) *(exactement)* exactly, literally; *(exclusivement)* specifically, strictly. **à ~ parler** strictly speaking; **le village ~ dit** the actual village, the village itself; **c'est ~ scandaleux** it's absolutely disgraceful.

propreté [pʀɔpʀəte] *nf (V* **propre**[1]*)* cleanliness, cleanness; neatness; tidiness; *(hygiène)* hygiene.

propriété [pʀɔpʀijete] *nf* (**a**) *(droit)* ownership, property. **~ artistique** artistic copyright; **posséder en toute ~** to have sole ownership of. (**b**) *(maison)* property; *(terres)* property, land. **~ bâtie/non bâtie** developed/undeveloped property; **~ privée** private property. (**c**) *(qualité)* property. (**d**) *(correction) [mot]* appropriateness, suitability. ◆ **propriétaire 1** *nm (gén)* owner; *[entreprise]* proprietor; *[appartement loué]* landlord. **il est ~** he owns his house; **~ récoltant** grower; **~ terrien** landowner; **~ foncier** property owner. **2** *nf* owner; proprietress; landlady.

propulser [pʀɔpylse] (1) *vt* (**a**) *voiture* to propel, drive; *missile* to propel, power. (**b**) *(projeter)* to hurl, fling. ◆ **propulseur 1** *adj* propulsive, driving. **2** *nm* propeller. ◆ **propulsion** *nf* propulsion. **à ~ atomique** atomic-powered.

prorata [pʀɔʀata] *nm inv*: **au ~ de** in proportion to.

proroger [pʀɔʀɔʒe] (3) *vt durée* to extend; *échéance* to put back, defer; *séance* to adjourn; *(Parl)* to prorogue. ◆ **prorogation** *nf* extension; deferment; adjournment; prorogation.

prosaïque [pʀozaik] *adj* mundane, prosaic. ◆ **prosaïquement** *adv* mundanely, prosaically.

proscrire [pʀɔskʀiʀ] (39) *vt chose* to ban, prohibit, proscribe; *personne (mettre hors la loi)* to outlaw, proscribe; *(exiler)* to banish, exile. **~ une expression de son style** to banish an expression from one's style. ◆ **proscription** *nf* banning; prohibition; proscription; banishment. ◆ **proscrit, e** *nm, f (hors-la-loi)* outlaw; *(exilé)* exile.

prose [pʀoz] *nf (gén)* prose; *(hum: lettre)* letter. **poème en ~** prose poem.

prosélytisme [pʀozelitism(ə)] *nm* proselytism. **faire du ~** to proselytize, preach.

prospecter [pʀɔspɛkte] (1) *vt (Min)* to prospect; *(Comm)* to canvass. ◆ **prospecteur, -trice** *nm, f* prospector. ◆ **prospection** *nf* prospecting; canvassing.

prospectus [pʀɔspɛktys] *nm (tract)* leaflet, handout; *(dépliant)* prospectus, brochure, leaflet.

prospère [pʀɔspɛʀ] *adj commerce, pays, collectivité* prosperous, thriving, flourishing; *santé* flourishing. ◆ **prospérer** (6) *vi* to prosper; to thrive; to flourish. ◆ **prospérité** *nf (matérielle, économique)* prosperity; *[finances]* thriving *ou* flourishing state.

prostate [pʀɔstat] *nf* prostate (gland).

prosterner [pʀɔstɛʀne] (1) **1** *vt (littér)* to bow low. **2 se ~** *vpr (s'incliner)* to bow down, prostrate o.s. *(devant* before); *(fig: s'humilier)* to grovel *(devant* before). ◆ **prosterné, e** *adj* prostrate.

prostituer [pʀɔstitɥe] (1) **1** *vt* to prostitute. **2 se ~** *vpr (lit, fig)* to prostitute o.s. ◆ **prostituée** *nf* prostitute. ◆ **prostitution** *nf (lit, fig)* prostitution.

prostration [pʀɔstʀɑsjɔ̃] *nf* prostration. ◆ **prostré, e** *adj* prostrate.

protagoniste [pʀɔtagɔnist(ə)] *nm* protagonist.

protection [pʀɔtɛksjɔ̃] *nf (défense)* protection; *(patronage)* patronage; *(blindage)* armour-plating. **mesures de ~** protective measures; **prendre qn sous sa ~** to give sb one's protection *(ou* patronage); **assurer la ~ rapprochée du chef de l'État** to ensure the personal safety of the head of state; **il a demandé à bénéficier d'une ~ rapprochée** he asked for 24-hour police protection; **~ de l'enfance** child welfare; **~ de la nature** preservation *ou* protection of the countryside. ◆ **protecteur, -trice 1** *adj (gén)* protective *(de* of); *ton, air* patronizing. **2** *nm, f (défenseur)* protector, guardian; *[arts]* patron. **3** *nm (souteneur)* pimp *(péj)*. ◆ **protectionnisme** *nm* protectionism. ◆ **protectionniste** *adj, nmf* protectionist. ◆ **protectorat** *nm* protectorate.

protéger [pʀɔteʒe] (6) *et* (3) **1** *vt (gén)* to protect; *(moralement)* to guard, shield; *(des éléments)* to protect, shelter *(de* from); *(fig: patronner)* to patronize. **2 se ~** *vpr* to protect o.s. ◆ **protégé, e** *nm, f* protégé; protégée; *(*: favori)* favourite, pet *. ◆ **protège-cahier,** *pl* **protège-cahiers** *nm* exercise-book cover.

protéine [pʀɔtein] *nf* protein.

protestant, e [pʀɔtɛstɑ̃, ɑ̃t] *adj, nm, f* Protestant. ◆ **protestantisme** *nm* Protestantism.

protester [pʀɔtɛste] (1) *vti* to protest *(contre* against, about). **~ de son innocence** to protest one's innocence. ◆ **protestataire 1** *adj personne* protesting; *marche* protest. **2** *nmf* protester. ◆ **protestation** *nf (plainte)* protest; *(déclaration)* protestation, profession.

prothèse [pʀɔtɛz] *nf* prosthesis. **~ (dentaire)** dentures. ◆ **prothésiste** *nmf* dental technician.

protide [pʀɔtid] *nm* protein.

proto... [pʀɔtɔ] *préf* proto...

protocole [pʀɔtɔkɔl] *nm* (**a**) *(étiquette)* etiquette; *(Pol, Ordin)* protocol. (**b**) *(procès-verbal)* protocol. **~ d'accord** draft treaty. ◆ **protocolaire** *adj cérémonie* formal.

prototype [pʀɔtɔtip] *nm* prototype. **~ d'avion** prototype aircraft.

protubérance [pʀɔtybeʀɑ̃s] *nf* bulge, protuberance. ◆ **protubérant, e** *adj* bulging, protuberant, protruding.

proue [pʀu] *nf* bow, bows, prow.

prouesse [pʀuɛs] *nf (littér)* feat. *(fig)* **faire des ~s** to work miracles.

prouver [pʀuve] (1) *vt (gén)* to prove. **cela prouve que...** it proves *ou* shows that...; **cela n'est pas prouvé** there's no proof of it, that hasn't been proved; **il a voulu se ~ qu'il en était capable** he wanted to prove to himself that he was capable of it; **son efficacité n'est plus à ~** its effectiveness is no longer in doubt *ou* in question.

Provence [pʀɔvɑ̃s] *nf* Provence.

provenir [pʀɔvniʀ] (22) **~ de** *vt indir pays* to come from; *cause* to be due to, be the result of. ◆ **provenance** *nf [objet]* origin; *[coutume]* source. **j'ignore la ~ de cette lettre** I don't know where this letter comes from; **en ~ de l'Angleterre** from England.

proverbe [pʀɔvɛʀb(ə)] *nm* proverb. **comme dit le ~** as the saying goes; *(Bible)* **le livre des P~s** (the Book of) Proverbs. ◆ **proverbial, e,** *mpl* **-aux** *adj* proverbial.

providence [pʀɔvidɑ̃s] *nf (Rel)* providence; *(fig: sauveur)* guardian angel. *(fig)* **ça a été notre ~** it was our salvation. ◆ **providentiel, -elle** *adj* providential. ◆ **providentiellement** *adv* providentially.

province [pʀɔvɛ̃s] *nf* province. **vivre en ~** to live in the provinces; **ville de ~** provincial town; *(Hist: Hollande)* **les P~s Unies** the United Provinces. ◆ **provincial, e,** *mpl* **-aux** *adj, nm, f* provincial.

proviseur [pʀɔvizœʀ] *nm* head(master), principal *(of a lycée)*.

provision [pʀɔvizjɔ̃] *nf* (**a**) *(réserve)* stock, supply. **faire ~ de** to stock up with, get in a stock *ou* supply of. (**b**) **~s** *(vivres)* provisions, food; *(courses)* groceries; **faire ses ~s** to go shopping; **filet à ~s** shopping bag. (**c**) *(arrhes)* deposit.

(Banque) **y a-t-il ~ au compte?** are there sufficient funds in the account?

provisoire [pRɔvizwaR] *adj mesure, gouvernement* provisional, temporary; *bonheur, installation* temporary. **à titre ~** temporarily, provisionally; **c'est du ~** it's a temporary *ou* provisional arrangement. ◆ **provisoirement** *adv* for the time being.

provoquer [pRɔvɔke] (1) *vt* (**a**) *(inciter)* **~ qn à** to incite sb to. (**b**) *(défier)* to provoke. **~ qn en duel** to challenge sb to a duel. (**c**) *accident, révolte etc* to cause; *réaction* to provoke, produce; *gaieté, commentaires* to give rise to; *colère, curiosité* to arouse. **le malade est sous sommeil provoqué** the patient is in an induced sleep. ◆ **provocant, e** *adj* provocative. ◆ **provocateur, -trice 1** *adj* provocative. **2** *nm* agitator. ◆ **provocation** *nf* provocation.

proxénète [pRɔksenɛt] *nm* procurer.

proximité [pRɔksimite] *nf* proximity. **à ~** close by, near at hand; **à ~ de** near (to), in proximity to.

prude [pRyd] **1** *adj* prudish. **2** *nf* prude.

prudent, e [pRydɑ̃, ɑ̃t] *adj (circonspect)* cautious, prudent; *(sage)* wise, sensible; *(réservé)* cautious. **il serait ~ de faire** you would be well-advised to do, it is advisable to do; **ce n'est pas ~** it's not advisable; **c'est plus ~** it's wiser *ou* safer; **soyez ~!** be careful!, take care! ◆ **prudemment** *adv* cautiously, prudently; wisely, sensibly. ◆ **prudence** *nf* caution, cautiousness, prudence; wisdom. **par ~** as a precaution, to be on the safe side; **il a eu la ~ de partir** he had the good sense *ou* he was wise enough to leave; *(Prov)* **~ est mère de sûreté** safety is born of caution.

prune [pRyn] **1** *nf (fruit)* plum; *(alcool)* plum brandy. **pour des ~s** ⁑ for nothing; **des ~s!** ⁑ not likely! * **2** *adj inv* plum-coloured. ◆ **pruneau,** *pl* **~x** *nm* prune; *(*: balle)* slug *. ◆ **prunier** *nm* plum tree.

prunelle [pRynɛl] *nf* (**a**) *(Bot)* sloe; *(eau-de-vie)* sloe gin. (**b**) *(pupille)* pupil. **il y tient comme à la ~ de ses yeux** it's the apple of his eye.

psalmodier [psalmɔdje] (7) *vt* to chant.

psaume [psom] *nm* psalm. *(Bible)* **le livre des P~s** the Book of Psalms.

pseudo- [psødɔ] *préf (gén)* pseudo-; *(péj)* bogus *(péj)*.

pseudonyme [psødɔnim] *nm (gén)* assumed name; *[écrivain]* pen name; *[comédien]* stage name; *(Jur, hum)* alias.

psychanalyse [psikanaliz] *nf* psychoanalysis. ◆ **psychanalyser** (1) *vt* to psychoanalyze. ◆ **psychanalyste** *nmf* psychoanalyst. ◆ **psychanalytique** *adj* psychoanalytic(al).

psychiatre [psikjatR(ə)] *nmf* psychiatrist. ◆ **psychiatrie** *nf* psychiatry. ◆ **psychiatrique** *adj troubles* psychiatric; *hôpital* psychiatric, mental.

psychique [psiʃik] *adj* psychological, psychic(al). ◆ **psychisme** *nm* psyche.

psychodrame [psikɔdRam] *nm* psychodrama.

psychologie [psikɔlɔʒi] *nf* psychology. ◆ **psychologique** *adj* psychological. ◆ **psychologiquement** *adv* psychologically. ◆ **psychologue** *nmf* psychologist. *(fig)* **être ~** to be a good psychologist. ◆ **psychopathe** *nmf* person who is mentally ill; *(agressif, criminel)* psychopath. ◆ **psychose** *nf (Psych)* psychosis; *(fig: obsession)* obsessive fear (*de* of). ◆ **psychothérapie** *nf* psychotherapy.

puant, e [pɥɑ̃, ɑ̃t] *adj (lit)* stinking, foul-smelling; *(fig) personne* obnoxious. ◆ **puanteur** *nf* stink, stench.

pub[1] [pœb] *nm (bar)* pub.

pub[2] * [pyb] *nf (annonce)* ad *, advert *; *(ciné, TV)* commercial, ad *, advert *. *(métier)* **la ~** advertising; **faire de la ~ pour qch** to plug sth *, give sth a plug *.

puberté [pybɛRte] *nf* puberty.

public, -ique [pyblik] **1** *adj (gén)* public. **danger ~** public danger; **rendre ~** *nouvelle* to make public. **2** *nm (population)* (general) public; *(assistance)* audience. **des huées s'élevèrent du ~** boos rose from the audience *ou* public; **cet acteur a son ~** this actor has his fans *ou* followers; **un ~ clairsemé assistait au match** the match was attended by very few spectators; **le ~ est informé que...** the public is advised that...; **en ~** in public; **roman destiné au grand ~** novel written for the general reader *ou* public; **appareils électroniques grand ~** consumer electronics.

publication [pyblikɑsjɔ̃] *nf (gén)* publication.

publicité [pyblisite] *nf* (**a**) *(méthode, profession)* advertising. *(Comm, fig)* **faire de la ~ pour qch** to advertise sth. (**b**) *(annonce)* advertisement, ad *, advert *; *(Ciné, TV)* commercial, advertisement. (**c**) *(révélations)* publicity. **faire de la ~ autour de qch** to give sth a lot of publicity. ◆ **publicitaire 1** *adj (gén)* advertising; *film, voiture* promotional. **vente ~** promotional sale. **2** *nmf* adman *, advertising executive.

publier [pyblije] (7) *vt* to publish. **ça vient d'être publié** it has just come out *ou* been published; **~ un communiqué (au sujet de** *ou* **concernant)** to release a statement (about).

publiphone [pyblifɔn] *nm* public telephone, payphone. **~ à carte à mémoire** card phone.

publiquement [pyblikmɑ̃] *adv* publicly.

puce [pys] *nf (Zool)* flea; *(Ordin)* (silicon) chip. **cela m'a mis la ~ à l'oreille** that started me thinking; **les ~s, le marché aux ~s** the flea market; **oui, ma ~** * yes, pet *; **jeu de ~s** tiddlywinks. ◆ **puceron** *nm* greenfly.

pudeur [pydœR] *nf (sexuelle)* sense of modesty *ou* decency; *(délicatesse)* sense of propriety. ◆ **pudibond, e** *adj* prudish. ◆ **pudibonderie** *nf* prudishness. ◆ **pudique** *adj (chaste)* modest; *(discret)* discreet. ◆ **pudiquement** *adv* modestly; discreetly.

puer [pɥe] (1) **1** *vi* to stink, reek. **2** *vt* to stink *ou* reek of.

puéricultrice [pɥeRikyltRis] *nf (infirmière)* paediatric nurse; *(institutrice)* nursery nurse. ◆ **puériculture** *nf* paediatric nursing; nursery nursing.

puéril, e [pɥeRil] *adj* puerile, childish. ◆ **puérilité** *nf (caractère)* puerility, childishness; *(acte)* childish act.

pugilat [pyʒila] *nm* (fist)fight.

puis [pɥi] *adv* then. *(en outre)* **et ~** and besides; **et ~ c'est tout** and that's all; **et ~ après?** *(ensuite)* and what next?, and then what?; *(et alors?)* so what?, what of it?

puisard [pɥizaR] *nm* cesspool.

puiser [pɥize] (1) *vt* to draw (*dans* from). **~ dans son sac** to dip into one's bag.

puisque [pɥisk(ə)] *conj* as, since, seeing that. *(intensif)* **~ je te le dis!** I'm telling you (so)!

puissance [pɥisɑ̃s] *nf (gén, fig, Pol, Sci)* power; *[vent]* strength, force. **avoir une grande ~ de travail** to have a great capacity for work; **avoir une grande ~ d'imagination** to have a very powerful imagination *ou* great powers of imagination; *(Aut)* **~ fiscale** engine rating; *(Jur)* **~ paternelle** parental rights *ou* authority; *(Math)* **10 ~ 4** 10 to the power of 4, 10 to the 4th; **exister en ~** to have a potential existence; **c'est là en ~** it is potentially present. ◆ **puissamment** *adv (fortement)* powerfully; *(beaucoup)* greatly. ◆ **puissant, e 1** *adj (gén)* powerful. **2** *nm*: **les ~s** the mighty *ou* powerful.

puits [pɥi] *nm [eau, pétrole]* well; *(Min)* shaft; *(Constr)* well, shaft. ~ **d'aération/d'extraction** ventilation/winding shaft; *(Min)* ~ **à ciel ouvert** opencast mine; ~ **de science** well of learning.

pull(-over) [pul(ɔvœʀ)] *nm* sweater, jersey, pullover.

pulluler [pylyle] (1) *vi (se reproduire)* to proliferate, multiply; *(grouiller)* to swarm (*de* with); *[erreurs]* to abound.

pulmonaire [pylmɔnɛʀ] *adj* pulmonary, lung.

pulpe [pylp(ə)] *nf [fruit, dent, bois]* pulp.

pulsation [pylsɑsjɔ̃] *nf (action)* beating. ~**s** heartbeats.

pulsé [pylse] *adj m:* **chauffage à air** ~ warm-air heating.

pulsion [pylsjɔ̃] *nf (Psych)* drive, urge.

pulvériser [pylveʀize] (1) *vt solide, adversaire* to pulverize; *liquide* to spray; *record* to smash *. ◆ **pulvérisable** *adj* pulverable. ◆ **pulvérisateur** *nm* spray. ◆ **pulvérisation** *nf* pulverization; spraying. *(Méd)* **ordonner des** ~**s** to prescribe a nasal spray.

puma [pyma] *nm* puma.

punaise [pynɛz] *nf (Zool)* bug; *(clou)* drawing pin, thumbtack *(US)*. ◆ **punaiser** (1) *vt* to pin up.

punch[1] [pɔ̃ʃ] *nm (boisson)* punch.

punch[2] [pœnʃ] *nm (Boxe)* punching ability; *(fig)* punch.

punching-ball, *pl* **punching-balls** [pœnʃiŋbol] *nm* punchball.

punir [pyniʀ] (2) *vt (gén)* to punish (*pour* for). **être puni de prison** to be sentenced to prison; **c'est puni par la loi** it is punishable by law. ◆ **punissable** *adj* punishable (*de* by). ◆ **punitif, -ive** *adj expédition* punitive. ◆ **punition** *nf* punishment (*de qch* for sth). **pour ta** ~ for your punishment.

punk [pœnk] *adj inv, nmf inv* punk.

pupille[1] [pypij] *nf (Anat)* pupil.

pupille[2] [pypij] *nmf (enfant)* ward. ~ **de la Nation** war orphan.

pupitre [pypitʀ(ə)] *nm (Scol)* desk; *(Rel)* lectern; *[musicien]* music stand; *[piano]* music rest; *[chef d'orchestre]* rostrum; *(Ordin)* console. ◆ **pupitreur, -euse** *nm, f* computer operator, keyboard operator, keyboarder.

pur, e [pyʀ] *adj* (**a**) *(gén, fig)* pure; *personne* pure-hearted; *ciel* clear; *vin* undiluted; *whisky, gin* neat, straight; *diamant* flawless. (**b**) *(intensif)* **c'est de la folie** ~**e** it's pure *ou* sheer madness; **c'est de l'insubordination** ~**e et simple** it's insubordination pure and simple; **c'était du racisme** ~ **et simple** *ou* **à l'état** ~ it was straight *ou* plain racism; **par** ~ **hasard** by sheer chance, purely by chance; **c'est la** ~**e vérité** it's the plain *ou* simple truth; **en** ~**e perte** for absolutely nothing, fruitlessly. ◆ **purement** *adv* purely. ~ **et simplement** purely and simply. ◆ **pureté** *nf (gén)* purity; *[diamant]* flawlessness. ◆ **pur-sang** *nm inv* thoroughbred, purebred.

purée [pyre] *nf [tomates etc]* purée. ~ **(de pommes de terre)** mashed potatoes; **être dans la** ~ ‡ to be in the soup *.

purgatoire [pyʀgatwaʀ] *nm (Rel, fig)* purgatory.

purge [pyʀʒ(ə)] *nf (Méd, Pol)* purge. ◆ **purgatif, -ive** *adj, nm* purgative. ◆ **purger** (3) **1** *vt radiateur* to bleed, flush (out), drain; *freins* to bleed; *(Méd, fig)* to purge; *(Jur) peine* to serve. **2 se** ~ *vpr* to take a purgative.

purifier [pyʀifje] (7) **1** *vt (gén)* to purify, cleanse; *métal* to refine. **2 se** ~ *vpr* to cleanse o.s. ◆ **purification** *nf* purification, cleansing; refinement.

purin [pyʀɛ̃] *nm* liquid manure.

purisme [pyʀism(ə)] *nm* purism. ◆ **puriste** *adj, nmf* purist.

puritain, e [pyʀitɛ̃, ɛn] **1** *adj* puritan(ical). **2** *nm, f* puritan. ◆ **puritanisme** *nm* puritanism.

pus [py] *nm* pus.

pustule [pystyl] *nf* pustule.

putain ‡ [pytɛ̃] *nf* whore. **ce** ~ **de réveil!** that goddamn ‡ alarm clock!

putois [pytwa] *nm* polecat.

putréfier *vt,* **se** ~ *vpr* [pytʀefje] (7) to putrefy. ◆ **putréfaction** *nf* putrefaction.

putsch [putʃ] *nm* putsch. ◆ **putschiste** *nm* putschist.

puzzle [pœzl(ə)] *nm* jigsaw (puzzle).

pygmée [pigme] *nm* pygmy, pigmy.

pyjama [piʒama] *nm* pyjamas, pajamas *(US)*. **un** ~ a pair of pyjamas.

pylône [pilon] *nm* pylon.

pyramide [piʀamid] *nf (gén)* pyramid.

Pyrénées [piʀene] *nfpl:* **les** ~ the Pyrenees.

pyromane [piʀɔman] *nmf* arsonist, fire-raiser. ◆ **pyromanie** *nf* pyromania.

python [pitɔ̃] *nm* python.

Q, q [ky] *nm (lettre)* Q, q.

qu' [k(ə)] *V* **que.**

quadragénaire [kwadʀaʒenɛʀ] **1** *adj*: **être** ~ to be forty years old. **2** *nmf* forty-year-old man (*ou* woman).

quadrangle [kwadʀɑ̃gl(ə)] *nm (Géom)* quadrangle.

quadrature [kwadʀatyʀ] *nf (gén)* quadrature. *(Math)* ~ **du cercle** quadrature *ou* squaring of the circle; *(fig)* **c'est la** ~ **du cercle** it's like trying to square the circle, it's attempting the impossible.

quadrilatère [kadʀilatɛʀ] *nm (Géom, Mil)* quadrilateral.

quadriller [kadʀije] (1) *vt (Mil, Police)* to cover, control. ◆ **quadrillage** *nm* (**a**) *(Mil, Police)* covering, control. (**b**) *[papier]* square *ou* grid pattern. ◆ **quadrillé, e** *adj papier* squared.

quadrimoteur [kadʀimɔtœʀ] *nm* four-engined plane.

quadripartite [kwadʀipaʀtit] *adj (Pol)* **conférence** ~ four-power conference.

quadriréacteur [kadʀiʀeaktœʀ] *nm* four-engined jet.

quadrupède [kadʀypɛd] *adj, nm* quadruped.

quadruple [kadʀypl(ə)] **1** *adj quantité* quadruple. **en** ~ **partie** in four parts. **2** *nm (Math, gén)* quadruple. **je l'ai payé le** ~ I paid four times as much for it; **augmenter au** ~ to increase fourfold. ◆ **quadrupler** (1) *vti* to quadruple, increase fourfold. ◆ **quadruplés, -ées** *nm, fpl* quadruplets, quads *.

quai [ke] *nm [port]* quay; *(pour marchandises)* wharf; *[gare]* platform; *[rivière]* embankment. **être à** ~ *[bateau]* to be alongside (the quay); *[train]* to be in (the station).

qualifier [kalifje] (7) **1** *vt* (**a**) *(décrire)* to describe (*de* as). ~ **qn de menteur** to call *ou* label sb a liar. (**b**) *(Sport, gén: rendre apte)* to qualify (*pour* for). (**c**) *(Gram)* to qualify. **2 se** ~ *vpr (Sport)* to qualify (*pour* for). *(hum)* **il se qualifie d'artiste** he labels *ou* calls himself an artist. ◆ **qualificateur** *nm (Ling)* qualifier. ◆ **qualificatif, -ive 1** *adj adjectif* qualifying. **2** *nm (Gram)* qualifier; *(fig: terme)* term. ◆ **qualification** *nf* description; label; qualification. *(Sport)* **obtenir sa** ~ to qualify. ◆ **qualifié, e** *adj* (**a**) *(compétent)* qualified; *ouvrier* skilled. **non** ~ unskilled. (**b**) *vol* aggravated. *(fig)* **c'est du vol** ~ it's daylight *ou* sheer robbery.

qualité [kalite] *nf* (**a**) *(gén)* quality. **de mauvaise** ~ of bad *ou* poor quality; **produits de** ~ high-quality products; **il a les** ~**s requises pour faire ce travail** he has the necessary skills for this job. (**b**) *(fonction)* position; *(†: noblesse)* quality; *(Admin: métier)* occupation. **en sa** ~ **de maire** in his capacity as mayor; *(Jur)* **avoir** ~ **pour** to have authority to. ◆ **qualitatif, -ive** *adj* qualitative. ◆ **qualitativement** *adv* qualitatively.

quand [kɑ̃] **1** *conj* when. ~ **ce sera fini, nous irons prendre un café** when it's finished we'll go and have a coffee; ~ **je te le disais!** didn't I tell you so!, I told you so!; ~ **bien même** even though *ou* if; **malgré tous ses défauts elle est** ~ **même gentille** in spite of all her faults she's still nice; ~ **même, il exagère!** really, he overdoes it!; **tu aurais pu venir** ~ **même** even so you could have come, you could have come all the same. **2** *adv* when. ~ **pars-tu?** when are you leaving?; **c'est pour** ~**?** *[devoir]* when is it for?; *[rendez-vous]* when is it?; *[naissance]* when is it to be?; **ça date de** ~**?** *[événement]* when did it take place?

quant [kɑ̃] *adv*: ~ **à** as for, as to; ~ **à moi** as for me; ~ **à cela, je n'en sais rien** as to that *ou* as regards that *ou* as far as that goes, I know nothing about it.

quantité [kɑ̃tite] *nf* quantity, amount. **la** ~ **de gens qui** the number of people who; **en** ~**s industrielles** in massive *ou* huge amounts; **(une)** ~ **de** *argent, eau* a great deal of, a lot of; *gens, objets* a great many, a lot of, a great number of; **des fruits en** ~ fruit in plenty; *(fig)* **considérer qn comme** ~ **négligeable** to consider sb as totally insignificant. ◆ **quantificateur** *nm* quantifier. ◆ **quantifier** (7) *vt* to quantify. ◆ **quantitatif, -ive** *adj* quantitative.

quarante [kaʀɑ̃t] *adj, nm inv* forty. **les Q**~ *the members of the French Academy; (disque)* **un** ~**-cinq tours** a forty-five, an EP; *V* **soixante.** ◆ **quarantaine** *nf* (**a**) *(nombre)* about forty; *V* **soixantaine.** (**b**) *(Méd)* quarantine. **mettre en** ~ *(lit)* to quarantine; *(fig)* to send to Coventry. ◆ **quarantième** *adj, nmf,* fortieth.

quart [kaʀ] *nm* (**a**) *(fraction)* quarter. **un** ~ **de poulet** a quarter chicken; **un** ~ **de vin** a quarter-litre bottle of wine; *(Sport)* ~**s de finale** quarter finals; **un kilo un** ~ *ou* **et** ~ a kilo and a quarter; **on n'a pas fait le** ~ **du travail** we haven't done a quarter of the work; **donner un** ~ **de tour à un bouton** to give a knob a quarter turn; *(Aut)* **partir au** ~ **de tour** to start first time; **le** ~**-monde** the Fourth World. (**b**) *(Mil: gobelet)* beaker *(of 1/4 litre capacity)*. (**c**) ~ **d'heure** quarter of an hour; **3 heures moins le** ~ (a) quarter to 3; **3 heures et** ~ *ou* **un** ~ (a) quarter past 3; **il est le** ~**/moins le** ~ it's (a) quarter past/(a) quarter to; **passer un mauvais** ~ **d'heure** to have a bad *ou* nasty time of it. (**d**) *(Naut)* watch. **être de** ~ to keep the watch; **de** ~ *homme* on watch.

quarté [kaʀte] *nm French system of forecast betting on four horses in a race.*

quartette [kwaʀtɛt] *nm (Mus)* jazz quartet(te).

quartier [kaʀtje] *nm* (**a**) *[ville]* district, area, quarter. **les gens du** ~ the local people, the people of the area; **de** ~ *cinéma, épicier* local; **le** ~ **est de la ville** the east end *ou* side of (the) town. (**b**) *(Mil)* ~**(s)** quarters; **avoir** ~**(s) libre(s)** to be free *ou* off (for a few hours); *(lit, fig)* **prendre ses** ~**s d'hiver** to go into winter quarters; **grand** ~ **général** general headquarters; *[prison]* ~ **de haute surveillance** high *ou* maximum *ou* top security wing. (**c**) *[bœuf]* quarter; *[viande]* chunk; *[fruit]* piece, segment. *(lit, fig)* **mettre en** ~**s** to tear to pieces; **ne pas faire de** ~ to give no quarter †.

quartz [kwaʀts] *nm* quartz. **montre** *etc* **à** ~ quartz watch *etc.*

quasi [kazi] **1** *adv* almost, nearly. **2** *préf* near. ~**-certitude** near certainty; **la** ~**-totalité de** the near total of. ◆ **quasiment** *adv* almost, nearly.

quatorze [katɔʀz(ə)] *adj, nm inv* fourteen. **la guerre de** ~ the First World War; **le** ~ **Juillet** the Fourteenth of July, Bastille Day *(French national holi-*

day). ◆ **quatorzième** *adj, nmf* fourteenth; *V* **sixième.**

quatrain [katʀɛ̃] *nm* quatrain.

quatre [katʀ(ə)] *adj, nm inv* four. **une robe de ~ sous** a cheap dress; *(lit, fig)* **aux ~ coins de** in the four corners of; **à ~ pattes** on all fours; **être tiré à ~ épingles** to be dressed up to the nines; **un de ces ~ (matins)** * one of these (fine) days; **faire les ~ cents coups** to sow one's wild oats; to get into a lot of trouble; **faire ses ~ volontés** to do exactly as one pleases; **dire à qn ses ~ vérités** to tell sb a few plain *ou* home truths; **monter (l'escalier) ~ à ~** to rush up the stairs four at a time; **manger comme ~** to eat like a wolf; **se mettre en ~ pour qn** to go out of one's way for sb, put o.s. out for sb; **ne pas y aller par ~ chemins** not to beat about the bush. ◆ **quatre heures** *nm inv* (children's) afternoon tea *ou* snack. ◆ **quatre-quarts** *nm inv (Culin)* pound cake. ◆ **quatre-vingt-dix** *adj, nm inv* ninety. ◆ **quatre-vingt-dixième** *adj, nmf* ninetieth. ◆ **quatre-vingt-onze** *adj, nm inv* ninety-one. ◆ **quatre-vingt-onzième** *adj, nmf* ninety-first. ◆ **quatre-vingts** *adj, nm inv* eighty. ◆ **quatrième 1** *adj* fourth. *(fig)* **en ~ vitesse** * at great speed. **2** *nmf (Jeux)* fourth player. **3** *nf (Aut)* fourth gear; *(Scol: classe)* ≃ third form *ou* year, third year (in junior high school) *(US)*; *V* **sixième.** ◆ **quatrièmement** *adv* fourthly, in the fourth place.

quatuor [kwatɥɔʀ] *nm* quartet(te).

que [k(ə)] **1** *conj* (**a**) *(introduisant subordonnée)* that. **elle sait ~ tu es prêt** she knows (that) you're ready; **je veux qu'il vienne** I want him to come; **venez que nous causions** come along so that we can have a chat. (**b**) *(remplaçant si, quand etc: non traduit)* **si vous êtes sages et qu'il fasse beau** if you are good and the weather is fine; **quand il rentrera et qu'il aura déjeuné** when he comes home and he's had a meal. (**c**) *(temps)* **elle venait à peine de sortir qu'il se mit à pleuvoir** she had no sooner gone out than it started raining, she had hardly gone out when it started raining; **ça fait 2 ans qu'il est là** he has been here (for) 2 years; **ça fait 2 ans qu'il est parti** it is 2 years since he left, he left 2 years ago. (**d**) *(ordre, souhait etc)* **qu'il le veuille ou non** whether he likes it or not; **~ la guerre finisse!** if only *ou* I wish the war would end!; **qu'il vienne!** let him come!; **~ m'importe!** what do I care?, I don't care! (**e**) *(comparaison) (avec plus, moins)* than; *(avec aussi, autant, tel)* as. **il est plus petit qu'elle** he's smaller than her *ou* than she is; **elle est tout aussi capable ~ vous** she's just as capable as you (are).

2 *adv*: **ce ~ tu es lent!** * you're so slow!, how slow you are!; **~ de monde!** what a crowd (there is)!, what a lot of people!; **~ n'es-tu venu me voir?** why didn't you come to see me?

3 *pron* (**a**) *(relatif direct) (personne)* that, whom; *(chose, animal)* which, that *(gén omis)*; *(temps)* when. **les enfants ~ tu vois dans la rue** the children (that *ou* whom) you see in the street; **la raison qu'il a donnée** the reason (that *ou* which) he gave; **un jour ~** one day when. (**b**) *(attribut)* **quel homme charmant ~ votre voisin!** what a charming man your neighbour is; **distrait qu'il est, il n'a rien vu** dreamy as he is, he didn't notice anything; **c'est un inconvénient ~ de ne pas avoir de voiture** it's inconvenient not having a car; **en bon fils qu'il est** being the good son (that) he is. (**c**) *(interrog)* what; *(discriminatif)* which. **~ fais-tu?** what are you doing?; **qu'est-ce qu'il y a?** what's the matter?; **je pense ~ non** I don't think so; **mais il n'a pas de voiture! — il dit ~ si** but he has no car! — he says he has; **qu'est-ce ~ tu préfères, le rouge ou le noir?** which (one) do you prefer, the red or the black? (**d**) **je ne l'y ai pas autorisé, ~ je sache** I didn't give him permission to do so, as far as I know, I'm not aware that I gave him permission to do so; **qu'il dit!** * that's what he says!; **~ oui!** yes indeed!; **~ non!** certainly not!

Québec [kebɛk] **1** *n (ville)* Quebec. **2** *nm (province)* **le ~** Quebec. ◆ **québécois, e 1** *adj* Quebec. **2** *nm (Ling)* Quebec French. **3** *nm, f*: **Q~(e)** Quebecker, Quebecer.

quel, quelle [kɛl] **1** *adj* (**a**) *(interrog)* what; *(être animé: attribut)* who. **~ est cet auteur?** who is that author?; **sur ~ auteur/sujet va-t-il parler?** what author/subject is he going to talk about? (**b**) *(discriminatif)* which. **~ acteur préférez-vous?** which actor do you prefer? (**c**) *(excl)* what. **quelle surprise!** what a surprise!; **j'ai remarqué avec quelle attention ils écoutaient** I noticed how attentively they were listening. (**d**) *(relatif) (être animé)* whoever; *(chose)* whatever; *(discriminatif)* whichever, whatever. **~ que soit le train que vous preniez** whichever *ou* whatever train you take; **les hommes, ~s qu'ils soient** men, whoever they may be. **2** *pron interrog* which. **des deux solutions, quelle est la meilleure?** of the two solutions, which (one) is better?

quelconque [kɛlkɔ̃k] *adj* (**a**) *(n'importe quel)* some (or other), any; *(moindre)* any. **pour une raison ~** for some reason (or other); **à partir d'un point ~ du cercle** from any point on the circle; **il n'a pas manifesté un désir ~ d'y aller** he didn't show the slightest *ou* least desire *ou* any desire to go. (**b**) *(médiocre)* poor, indifferent; *(laid)* plain-looking; *(ordinaire)* ordinary.

quelque [kɛlk(ə)] **1** *adj indéf* (**a**) *(sans pl)* some. **cela fait ~ temps que je ne l'ai vu** I haven't seen him for some time *ou* for a while; **avez-vous ~ idée de?** have you any idea about?; **j'ai ~ peine à croire cela** I find it rather *ou* somewhat difficult to believe; **par ~ temps qu'il fasse** whatever the weather (may be *ou* is like); **en ~ sorte** *(pour ainsi dire)* as it were, so to speak; *(bref)* in a word; *(d'une certaine manière)* in a way. (**b**) *(pl)* **~s** a few, some; **reste-t-il ~s places?** are there any *ou* some *ou* a few seats left?; **les ~s enfants qui étaient venus** the few children who had come. **2** *adv* (**a**) *(environ)* some, about. **ça a augmenté de ~ 50 F** it's gone up by about *ou* by some 50 francs; **20 kg et ~(s)** * a bit over 20 kg *. (**b**) **~ peu déçu** rather *ou* somewhat disappointed; **il est ~ peu menteur** he is something of *ou* a bit of a liar; **~ lourde que soit la tâche** however heavy the task may be.

◆ **quelque chose** *pron indéf* something; *(avec interrog)* anything, something. **~ d'autre** something else; **il a ~ qui ne va pas** there's something the matter with him; **ça y est pour ~** it has got something to do with it; **il y a ~ comme une semaine** something like a week ago; **il a plu ~!** * it rained something dreadful! *, it didn't half rain! *; *(lit, fig)* **faire ~ à qn** to have an effect on sb; **ça alors, c'est ~!** that's a bit stiff! ◆ **quelquefois** *adv* sometimes, occasionally, at times. ◆ **quelque part** *adv* somewhere. ◆ **quelques-uns, -unes** *pron indéf pl* some, a few. ◆ **quelqu'un** *pron indéf* somebody, someone; *(avec interrog)* anybody, anyone. **c'est ~ de sûr** he's a reliable person, he's someone reliable; **~ pourrait-il répondre?** could somebody answer?; **c'est ~** *[savant]* he is (a) somebody; *(excl)* that's a bit stiff!

quémander [kemɑ̃de] (1) *vt* to beg for.

qu'en-dira-t-on [kɑ̃diʀatɔ̃] *nm inv* gossip.

quenelle [kənɛl] *nf (Culin)* quenelle.

quenotte * [kənɔt] *nf* tooth, toothy-peg *.

querelle [kəʀɛl] *nf* quarrel. **~ d'amoureux** lovers' tiff; *(Pol)* **la ~ sur l'avortement** the abortion debate *ou* issue; **chercher une mauvaise ~ à qn** to pick a quarrel with sb for nothing. ◆ **quereller**

(1) **1** *vt* to scold. **2 se** ~ *vpr* to quarrel (with one another). **se** ~ **au sujet** *ou* **à propos de qch** to quarrel *ou* squabble over *ou* about sth. ◆ **querelleur, -euse** *adj* quarrelsome.

question [kɛstjɔ̃] *nf* (**a**) *(demande) (gén)* question; *(pour lever un doute)* query, question. ~ **subsidiaire** tiebreaker *(decisive question in a competition)*; *(Pol)* **poser la** ~ **de confiance** to ask for a vote of confidence. (**b**) *(problème)* question, matter, issue. **la** ~ **sociale** the social question *ou* issue; **la** ~ **n'est pas là** that's not the point; **cela ne fait pas** ~ there's no question about it; **c'est une** ~ **de temps** it's a question *ou* matter of time; *(ordre du jour)* **'autres** ~ **s'** 'any other business'. (**c**) *(locutions)* ~ **argent** as far as money goes, money-wise *; **de quoi est-il** ~? what is it about?; **il fut d'abord** ~ **du budget** first they spoke about *ou* discussed the budget; **il est** ~ **de lui comme ministre** there's some question *ou* talk of his being *ou* becoming a minister; **il n'en est pas** ~! there's no question of it!; **hors de** ~ out of the question; **la personne en** ~ the person in question; **remettre en** ~ *autorité* to question, challenge; *science* to question, call into question; *projets* to put a question mark over, cast doubt over; **c'est notre vie même qui est en** ~ it's our very lives that are at stake. ◆ **questionnaire** *nm* questionnaire. *(Scol etc)* ~ **à choix multiple** multiple choice question paper. ◆ **questionner** (1) *vt (interroger)* to question, ask (*sur* about).

quête [kɛt] *nf (collecte)* collection. *(littér: recherche) [Graal]* quest (*de* for); *[absolu]* pursuit (*de* of). **en** ~ **de** *(gén)* in search of; **être en** ~ **de travail** to be looking for *ou* seeking work. ◆ **quêter** (1) **1** *vi (à l'église)* to take the collection; *(dans la rue)* to collect money. **2** *vt* to seek. ◆ **quêteur, -euse** *nm, f* collector.

quetsche [kwɛtʃ(ə)] *nf kind of dark-red plum.*

queue [kø] **1** *nf* (**a**) *(gén)* tail; *[classement]* bottom; *[poêle]* handle; *[fruit, feuille]* stalk; *[fleur]* stem; *[train]* rear. **commencer par la** ~ to begin at the end. (**b**) *(file)* queue, line *(US)*. (**c**) *(locutions)* **la** ~ **entre les jambes** * with one's tail between one's legs; **à la** ~ **leu leu** *marcher* in single file; *se plaindre* one after the other; **il n'y en avait pas la** ~ **d'un** * there wasn't the sniff *ou* glimmer of one *; *(Aut)* **faire une** ~ **de poisson à qn** to cut in front of sb; **finir en** ~ **de poisson** to finish up in the air; **histoire sans** ~ **ni tête** * cock-and-bull story. **2** : ~ **de billard** (billiard) cue; ~ **de cheval** ponytail; ~**-de-pie** *nf, pl* **queues-de-pie** tails.

qui [ki] **1** *pron* (**a**) *(interrog) (sujet)* who; *(objet)* who, whom. ~ **(est-ce)** ~ **l'a vu?** who saw him?; ~ **d'entre eux/parmi vous?** which of them/of you?; ~ **a-t-elle vu?** who *ou* whom did she see?; **à** ~ **voulez-vous parler?** who do you wish to speak to?, who is it you want to speak to?; **à** ~ **est ce sac?** whose bag is this?, whose is this bag?; **elle ne sait à** ~ **se plaindre** she doesn't know who to complain to *ou* to whom to complain. (**b**) *(relatif sujet) (être animé)* who, that *; *(chose)* which, that. **Paul,** ~ **traversait le pont, trébucha** Paul, who was crossing the bridge, tripped, Paul was crossing the bridge and tripped; **il a un perroquet** ~ **parle** he's got a talking parrot, he's got a parrot which *ou* that talks; **je la vis** ~ **nageait vers le rivage** I saw her (as she was) swimming towards the bank; **montre-nous, toi** ~ **sais tout** show us, since you know it all *ou* since you're so clever. (**c**) *(relatif avec prép)* **le patron pour** ~ **il travaille** the employer (that *ou* who * *ou* whom) he works for, the employer for whom he works. (**d**) *(relatif sans antécédent)* whoever, anyone who. **amenez** ~ **vous voulez** bring along whoever *ou* anyone you like; ~ **vous savez** you-know-who *; **c'est à** ~ **des deux mangera le plus vite** each tries to eat faster than the other, they try to outdo each other in the speed they eat; **je le dirai à** ~ **de droit** I will tell whoever is concerned; **j'interdis à** ~ **que ce soit d'entrer ici** I forbid anyone to come in here; **à** ~ **mieux mieux** *(gén)* each one more so than the other; *crier* each one louder than the other; **ils ont pris tout ce qu'ils ont pu:** ~ **une chaise,** ~ **une radio** they took whatever they could: some took a chair, others a radio. (**e**) ~ **va lentement va sûrement** more haste less speed; ~ **vivra verra** what will be will be; ~ **a bu boira** once a thief always a thief; ~ **se ressemble s'assemble** birds of a feather flock together; ~ **veut la fin veut les moyens** he who wills the end wills the means. **2** : **qui-vive?** *excl* who goes there?; **être sur le** ~ to be on the alert.

quiconque [kikɔ̃k] **1** *pron rel* whoever, anyone who. **2** *pron indéf* anyone, anybody.

quiétude [kjetyd] *nf [lieu]* quiet; *[personne]* peace (of mind). **en toute** ~ in (complete) peace.

quignon [kiɲɔ̃] *nm:* ~ **(de pain)** *(croûton)* crust (of bread), heel of the loaf; *(morceau)* hunk *ou* chunk of bread.

quille [kij] *nf (jouet)* skittle; *(*: jambe)* pin *; *(Naut)* keel. **(jeu de)** ~**s** ninepins, skittles.

quincaillerie [kɛ̃kɑjʀi] *nf (ustensiles, métier)* hardware, ironmongery; *(magasin)* hardware shop *ou* store, ironmonger's (shop); *(fig péj: bijoux)* jewellery. ◆ **quincaillier, -ière** *nm, f* hardware dealer, ironmonger.

quinconce [kɛ̃kɔ̃s] *nm*: **en** ~ in staggered rows.

quinine [kinin] *nf* quinine.

quinquagénaire [kɛ̃kaʒenɛʀ] **1** *adj*: **être** ~ to be fifty years old. **2** *nmf* fifty-year-old man (*ou* woman).

quinquennal, e *mpl* **-aux** [kɛ̃kenal, o] *adj* five-year, quinquennial.

quintal, *pl* **-aux** [kɛ̃tal, o] *nm* quintal *(100 kg)*.

quinte [kɛ̃t] *nf* (**a**) *(Méd)* ~ **(de toux)** coughing fit. (**b**) *(Mus)* fifth; *(Escrime)* quinte; *(Cartes)* quint.

quintessence [kɛ̃tesɑ̃s] *nf* quintessence.

quintette [kɛ̃tɛt] *nm* quintet(te). ~ **à cordes/à vent** string/wind quintet.

quintuple [kɛ̃typl(ə)] **1** *adj* quintuple. **en** ~ **partie** in five parts. **2** *nm* quintuple (*de* of). **je l'ai payé le** ~ I paid five times as much for it. ◆ **quintupler** (1) *vti* to quintuple, increase fivefold. ◆ **quintuplés, -ées** *nm, fpl* quintuplets, quins *, quints * *(US)*.

quinze [kɛ̃z] **1** *nm inv* fifteen; *V* **six**. **2** *adj inv* fifteen. **le** ~ **août** the 15th August, Assumption; **demain en** ~ a fortnight tomorrow, two weeks from tomorrow *(US)*; **lundi en** ~ a fortnight on Monday, two weeks from Monday *(US)*; **dans** ~ **jours** in a fortnight, in two weeks; **tous les** ~ **jours** every fortnight, every two weeks. ◆ **quinzaine** *nf* about fifteen, fifteen or so. **une** ~ **(de jours)** a fortnight, two weeks; ~ **publicitaire** (two-week) sale; *V* **soixantaine**. ◆ **quinzième** *adj, nmf* fifteenth; *V* **sixième**.

quiproquo [kipʀɔko] *nm (sur personne)* mistake; *(sur sujet)* misunderstanding.

quittance [kitɑ̃s] *nf (reçu)* receipt; *(facture)* bill.

quitte [kit] *adj*: **être** ~ **(envers qn)** to be quits *ou* all square (with sb); **tu es** ~ *ou* **je t'en tiens** ~ **pour cette fois** I'll let you off this time; **être** ~ **d'une dette** to be rid *ou* clear of a debt; **nous en sommes** ~**s pour la peur** we got off with a fright; ~ **à s'ennuyer, ils préfèrent rester chez eux** they prefer to stay (at) home even if it means *ou* although it may mean getting bored; *(fig)* **c'est du** ~ **ou double** it's a big gamble.

quitter [kite] (1) *vt* (**a**) *lieu, personne* to leave. **ne pas** ~ **la chambre** to be confined to one's room; **les clients sont priés de** ~ **la chambre avant 11 heures** guests are requested to vacate their rooms before 11 o'clock; **se ~** to part. (**b**) *espoir* to give up. *[crainte, énergie]* ~ **qn** to leave *ou* desert sb. (**c**) *vêtement* to take off. (**d**) **si je le quitte des yeux une seconde** if I take my eyes off him for a second; *(Téléc)* **ne quittez pas** hold the line; **ils ne se quittent pas** they are always together, you never see them apart.

quoi [kwa] *pron* (**a**) *(interrog)* what. **de ~ parles-tu?** what are you talking about?; **en ~ puis-je vous aider?** how can I help you?; **c'est fait en ~?** what is it made of?; **~ faire?** what are we (going) to do?; **à ~ bon?** what's the use? (*faire* of doing); **et puis ~ encore!** what next! (**b**) *(relatif)* **la chose à ~ tu fais allusion** what you're referring to; **c'est en ~ tu te trompes** that's where you're wrong. (**c**) **il n'y a pas de ~ rire** it's no laughing matter, there's nothing to laugh about; **il n'y a pas de ~ fouetter un chat** it's not worth making a fuss about; **ils ont de ~ occuper leurs vacances** they've got enough *ou* plenty to occupy their holiday; **avoir de ~ écrire** to have sth to write with; **il n'a pas de ~ se l'acheter** he can't afford it, he hasn't the means to buy it; **si vous avez besoin de ~ que ce soit** if there's anything (at all) you need; **merci beaucoup! — il n'y a pas de ~** many thanks! — don't mention it *ou* (it's) a pleasure *ou* not at all *ou* you're welcome. (**d**) **~ qu'il arrive** whatever happens; **~ qu'il en soit** be that as it may, however that may be; **~ qu'on en dise** whatever *ou* no matter what people say.

quoique [kwak(ə)] *conj (bien que)* although, though. **quoiqu'il soit malade** although he is ill.

quolibet † [kɔlibɛ] *nm* gibe, jeer.

quote-part, *pl* **quotes-parts** [kɔtpaʀ] *nf (lit, fig)* share.

quotidien, -ienne [kɔtidjɛ̃, jɛn] **1** *adj (journalier)* daily; *(banal)* everyday; *existence* humdrum. **dans la vie ~ienne** in everyday *ou* daily life. **2** *nm* daily (paper). *(routine)* **le ~** everyday life. ◆ **quotidiennement** *adv* daily, every day.

quotient [kɔsjɑ̃] *nm* quotient. **~ intellectuel** intelligence quotient, IQ.

R

R, r [ɛʀ] *nm (lettre)* R, r.

rabâcher [ʀabɑʃe] (1) **1** *vt* to rehearse, harp on *, keep (on) repeating. **2** *vi* to keep repeating o.s. ◆ **rabâcheur, -euse** *nm, f* repetitive bore.

rabais [ʀabɛ] *nm* reduction, discount. **au ~** *vendre* at a reduced price, (on the) cheap; *(péj)* **enseignement/médecine au ~** cheap-rate teaching/ medicine, teaching/medicine on the cheap.

rabaisser [ʀabese] (1) **1** *vt (dénigrer)* to belittle, disparage; *(réduire)* to reduce. **2 se ~** *vpr* to belittle o.s.

rabattre [ʀabatʀ(ə)] (41) **1** *vt* (**a**) *capot* to close; *col* to turn down; *strapontin (ouvrir)* to pull down; *(fermer)* to put up. **le vent rabat la fumée** the wind blows the smoke back down; **les cheveux rabattus sur les yeux** with his hair brushed down over his eyes; **~ les couvertures** *(se couvrir)* to pull the blankets up; *(se découvrir)* to push back the blankets. (**b**) *(diminuer)* to reduce; *(déduire)* to deduct, take off. **~ l'orgueil de qn** to humble sb's pride; *[prétentieux]* **en ~** to climb down. (**c**) *gibier* to drive; *terrain* to beat. **~ des clients** * to tout for customers. **2 se ~** *vpr* (**a**) *[voiture, coureur]* to cut in. **se ~ devant qn** to cut in front of sb. (**b**) **se ~ sur** *marchandise, personne* to fall back on, make do with. (**c**) *[porte]* to fall *ou* slam shut; *[couvercle]* to close; *[dossier]* to fold down, fold away. ◆ **rabat** *nm [table, poche]* flap. ◆ **rabat-joie** *nm inv* killjoy, spoilsport, wet blanket. ◆ **rabattage** *nm (Chasse)* beating. ◆ **rabatteur, -euse** *nm, f (Chasse)* beater; *(fig péj)* tout.

rabbin [ʀabɛ̃] *nm* rabbi. **grand ~** chief rabbi.

rabibocher * [ʀabibɔʃe] (1) **1** *vt* to reconcile. **2 se ~** *vpr* to make it up (*avec* with).

rabiot ⁑ [ʀabjo] *nm [nourriture]* extra (food); *[temps]* extra time. **5 minutes de ~** 5 minutes' extra time, 5 minutes extra. ◆ **rabioter** ⁑ (1) *vt nourriture* to scrounge * (*à qn* from sb); *temps, argent* to fiddle * (*à qn* off sb).

râblé, e [ʀɑble] *adj* well-set, heavy-set *(US)*, stocky.

rabot [ʀabo] *nm* plane. ◆ **raboter** (1) *vt (Menuiserie)* to plane (down); *(*: égratigner)* to scrape. ◆ **raboteux, -euse** *adj* uneven, rough.

rabougri, e [ʀabugʀi] *adj (chétif)* stunted, puny; *(desséché)* shrivelled.

rabrouer [ʀabʀue] (1) *vt* to snub, rebuff.

racaille [ʀakɑj] *nf* rabble, riffraff.

raccommoder [ʀakɔmɔde] (1) **1** *vt* (**a**) *(réparer)* to mend, repair; *chaussette* to darn. (**b**) (*) *ennemis* to reconcile. **2 se ~** * *vpr* to make it up. ◆ **raccommodage** *nm* (**a**) *(action)* mending, repairing; darning. (**b**) *(endroit réparé)* mend, repair; darn.

raccompagner [ʀakɔ̃paɲe] (1) *vt* to take *ou* see back (*à* to). **~ qn en voiture** to drive sb back (home); **~ qn (jusqu')à la porte** to see sb to the door.

raccord [ʀakɔʀ] *nm* (**a**) *[papier peint]* join. **~ (de maçonnerie)** pointing; **~ (de peinture)** touch up. (**b**) *[discours]* link, join; *(Ciné) (scène)* link scene. (**c**) *(pièce, joint)* link.

raccorder [ʀakɔʀde] (1) *vt (gén)* to link up, join (up); *(Téléc)* to connect (*à* with, to). *(fig)* **~ à** *faits* to link (up) with, tie up with. ◆ **raccordement** *nm (action)* linking; joining; connecting; *(résultat)* join; connection.

raccourcir [ʀakuʀsiʀ] (2) **1** *vt (gén)* to shorten; *vacances, textes* to curtail, cut short. **2** *vi [jours]* to get shorter; *(au lavage)* to shrink. ◆ **raccourci** *nm (chemin)* short cut; *(résumé)* summary. **en ~** *(en miniature)* in miniature; *(en bref)* in a nutshell. ◆ **raccourcissement** *nm* shortening.

raccrocher [ʀakʀɔʃe] (1) **1** *vi (Téléc)* to hang up, ring off. **2** *vt vêtement* to hang back up; *écouteur* to put down; *personne, bonne affaire* to grab *ou* get hold of; *wagons, faits* to link, connect (*à* to, with). **3 se ~** *vpr*: **se ~ à** *branche* to catch *ou* grab (hold of); *espoir, personne* to cling to, hang on to.

race [ʀas] *nf (ethnique)* race; *(Zool)* breed. **la ~ humaine** the human race; **de ~** *(gén)* pedigree, purebred; *cheval* thoroughbred; **de ~ noble** of noble stock *ou* race; *(péj)* **lui et les gens de sa ~** him and people of his type; **les cordonniers, c'est une ~ qui disparaît** cobblers are a dying breed *ou* race. ◆ **racé, e** *adj animal* purebred, pedigree; *cheval, personne, voiture* thoroughbred.

racheter [ʀaʃte] (5) **1** *vt* (**a**) *objet qu'on possédait avant* to buy back; *nouvel objet* to buy another; *pain, lait* to buy some more; *firme* to take over; *parts de société* to buy up; *objet d'occasion* to buy (*à* from); *dette* to redeem; *otage* to ransom; *(Rel) pécheur* to redeem. (**b**) *crime* to atone for, expiate; *faute, imperfection* to make up for (*par* by). **2 se ~** *vpr [pécheur]* to redeem o.s.; *[criminel, fautif]* to make amends. ◆ **rachat** *nm* buying (back); takeover; redemption; ransom; atonement, expiation.

rachitisme [ʀaʃitism(ə)] *nm* rickets *(sg)*. **faire du ~** to have rickets. ◆ **rachitique** *adj (Méd)* rickety; *(péj)* scraggy, scrawny.

racial, e, *mpl* **-aux** [ʀasjal, o] *adj* racial.

racine [ʀasin] *nf (gén, Math, fig)* root. **prendre ~** to take root; **~ carrée** square root.

racisme [ʀasism(ə)] *nm* racialism, racism. ◆ **raciste** *adj, nmf* racialist, racist.

racket [ʀakɛt] *nm (action)* racketeering; *(vol)* racket *(extortion through blackmail etc)*.

raclée * [ʀɑkle] *nf (coups)* hiding, thrashing; *(défaite)* hiding *, thrashing *, licking.

racler [ʀɑkle] (1) *vt (gén)* to scrape; *tache* to scrape away; *écailles* to scrape off. **se ~ la gorge** to clear one's throat.

racoler [ʀakɔle] (1) *vt [prostituée]* to accost; *[vendeur]* to solicit, tout for. ◆ **racolage** *nm* soliciting; touting. ◆ **racoleur, -euse** *adj slogan, publicité (gén)* eye-catching, enticing; *(Pol)* vote-catching.

raconter [ʀakɔ̃te] (1) *vt histoire* to tell, relate, recount; *malheurs* to tell about, recount. **~ qch à qn** to tell sb sth, relate sth to sb; **~ ce qui s'est passé** to say *ou* relate *ou* recount what happened; **qu'est-ce que tu racontes?** what are you talking about? *ou* saying?; **~ des histoires** to tell stories. ◆ **racontar** *nm* story, lie.

racorni, e [ʀakɔʀni] *adj (durci)* hardened; *(desséché)* shrivelled (up).

radar [ʀadaʀ] *nm* radar. **système/écran ~** radar system/screen.

rade [ʀad] *nf* (natural) harbour, roads. **en ~ de Brest** in Brest harbour; **laisser en ~** * *personne* to leave stranded *ou* in the lurch; *projet* to drop, shelve; *voiture* to leave behind.

radeau, *pl* **~x** [ʀado] *nm* raft.

radiateur [ʀadjatœʀ] *nm (à eau, huile, Aut)* radiator; *(à gaz)* heater.

radiation [ʀadjɑsjɔ̃] *nf* (**a**) *(Phys)* radiation. (**b**) *[nom]* crossing *ou* striking off.

radical, e, *mpl* **-aux** [ʀadikal, o] *adj, nm (gén)* radical. ◆ **radicalement** *adv (gén)* radically. **~ faux** completely wrong. ◆ **radicaliser** *vt*, **se ~** *vpr* (1) *position* to toughen, harden.

radier [ʀadje] (7) *vt* to cross off, strike off (a list).

radieux, -euse [ʀadjø, øz] *adj personne* beaming *ou* radiant with joy; *air* radiant, beaming; *soleil* radiant; *journée, temps* brilliant, glorious.

radin, e * [ʀadɛ̃, in] **1** *adj* stingy, tight-fisted. **2** *nm, f* skinflint. ◆ **radinerie** * *nf* stinginess.

radio [ʀadjo] **1** *nf* (**a**) *(poste)* radio (set). **mets la ~** turn *ou* put on the radio. (**b**) *(radiodiffusion)* **la ~** (the) radio; **avoir la ~** to have a radio; **parler à la ~** to speak on the radio, broadcast; **travailler à la ~** to work in broadcasting *ou* on the radio. (**c**) *(station)* radio station. **~ libre** independent local radio station; **~ pirate** pirate radio station. (**d**) *(radiographie)* X-ray (photograph). **passer une ~** to have an X-ray (taken), be X-rayed. **2** *nm (opérateur)* radio operator; *(message)* radiogram, radiotelegram. ◆ **radioactif, -ive** *adj* radioactive. ◆ **radioactivité** *nf* radioactivity. ◆ **radioamateur** *nm* radio ham *. ◆ **radiocassette** *nm* cassette radio, radio cassette player. ◆ **radiodiffuser** (1) *vt* to broadcast *(by radio)*. ◆ **radiodiffusion** *nf* broadcasting *(by radio)*. ◆ **radiographie** *nf (technique)* radiography, X-ray photography; *(photographie)* X-ray (photograph), radiograph. ◆ **radiographier** (7) *vt* to X-ray. ◆ **radiographique** *adj* X-ray. ◆ **radioguidage** *nm (Aviat)* radio control. ◆ **radiologie** *nf* radiology. ◆ **radiologique** *adj* radiological. ◆ **radiologue** *nmf* radiologist. ◆ **radiophonie** *nf* radiotelephony. ◆ **radiophonique** *adj* radio. ◆ **radioreportage** *nm* radio report. ◆ **radioreporter** *nm* radio reporter. ◆ **radio-réveil,** *pl* **~-~s** *nm* alarm-radio, clock-radio. ◆ **radioscopie** *nf* radioscopy. ◆ **radio-taxi,** *pl* **~-~s** *nm* radio taxi, radio cab. ◆ **radiotélévisé, e** *adj* broadcast and televised. ◆ **radiothérapie** *nf* radiotherapy.

radis [ʀadi] *nm* radish; *(‡: sou)* penny *(Brit)*, cent *(US)*. **~ noir** horseradish.

radium [ʀadjɔm] *nm* radium.

radoter [ʀadɔte] (1) *vi (péj)* to ramble on *ou* drivel (on). ◆ **radotage** *nm (péj)* **~(s)** drivel. ◆ **radoteur, -euse** *nm, f (péj)* (old) driveller.

radoucir [ʀadusiʀ] (2) **1** *vt ton* to soften. **2 se ~** *vpr [personne]* to calm down; *[voix]* to soften; *[temps]* to become milder. ◆ **radoucissement** *nm (Mét)* **le ~** the milder weather; **un ~** a milder spell (of weather).

rafale [ʀafal] *nf [vent, pluie]* gust; *[mitrailleuse]* burst; *[neige]* flurry. **en** *ou* **par ~s** in gusts; **~s de balles** hail of bullets; **~ de vent** squall.

raffermir [ʀafɛʀmiʀ] (2) **1** *vt (gén)* to strengthen; *peau* to tone up; *voix* to steady. **2 se ~** *vpr (gén)* to grow stronger; *[voix]* to become steadier.

raffiner [ʀafine] (1) **1** *vt (gén)* to refine; *langage* to polish. **2** *vi* to be meticulous. ◆ **raffinage** *nm* refining. ◆ **raffiné, e** *adj (gén)* refined; *mœurs* polished, sophisticated. ◆ **raffinement** *nm (caractère)* refinement, sophistication; *(détail)* refinement. ◆ **raffinerie** *nf* refinery. ◆ **raffineur, -euse** *nm, f* refiner.

raffoler [ʀafɔle] (1) **~ de** *vt indir* to be very keen on.

raffut * [ʀafy] *nm* row, racket, din. **faire du ~** to kick up * a row.

rafiot [ʀafjo] *nm (péj: bateau)* (old) tub *(péj)*.

rafistoler * [ʀafistɔle] (1) *vt* to patch up.

rafle [ʀɑfl(ə)] *nf* (police) roundup *ou* raid. ◆ **rafler** * (1) *vt* to swipe. **elle a raflé tous les prix** she ran away *ou* off with all the prizes, she made a clean sweep of the prizes.

rafraîchir [ʀafʀeʃiʀ] (2) **1** *vt* (**a**) *(refroidir)* to cool, make cooler. **fruits rafraîchis** fruit salad. (**b**) **~ qn** *[bain]* to freshen sb (up); *[boisson]* to refresh sb. (**c**) *vêtement, couleur* to brighten up; *appartement* to do up; *connaissances* to brush up. **se faire ~ les cheveux** to have a trim; **~ la mémoire de qn** to jog *ou* refresh sb's memory. **2** *vi [vin etc]* to cool (down). **mettre à ~** to chill. **3 se ~** *vpr* (**a**) *[temps]* to get cooler *ou* colder. (**b**) *(en se lavant)* to freshen (o.s.) up; *(en buvant)* to refresh o.s. ◆ **rafraîchissant, e** *adj* refreshing. ◆ **rafraîchissement** *nm* (**a**) *[température]* cooling. (**b**) *(boisson)* cool *ou* cold drink. *(glaces, fruits)* **~s** refreshments.

ragaillardir [ʀagajaʀdiʀ] (2) *vt* to perk up, buck up *.

rage [ʀaʒ] *nf* (**a**) *(colère)* rage, fury. **mettre qn en ~** to infuriate *ou* enrage sb; **ivre de ~** mad with rage. (**b**) *(manie)* maddening habit. *(passion)* **avoir la ~ de faire/de qch** to have a mania for doing/for sth. (**c**) **faire ~** *[incendie, tempête]* to rage. (**d**) *(Méd)* **la ~** rabies *(sg)*. (**e**) **~ de dents** raging toothache. ◆ **rager** (3) *vi* to fume. **ça (me) fait ~!** it makes me fume! *ou* mad! ◆ **rageur, -euse** *adj (coléreux)* bad-tempered; *(furieux)* furious. ◆ **rageusement** *adv* angrily.

ragot * [ʀago] *nm* piece of gossip. **~s** gossip, tittle-tattle.

ragoût [ʀagu] *nm* stew.

ragoûtant, e [ʀagutɑ̃, ɑ̃t] *adj: (lit, fig)* **peu ~** unsavoury, unappetizing.

raid [ʀɛd] *nm (Mil)* raid, hit-and-run attack. *(Sport)* **~ automobile** long-distance car rally.

raide [ʀɛd] **1** *adj* (**a**) *(rigide) (gén)* stiff; *cheveux* straight; *câble* taut, tight. (**b**) *(abrupt)* steep, abrupt. (**c**) *morale* rigid, inflexible; *manières, démarche* stiff. (**d**) *alcool* rough; *(fig: osé) propos* daring, bold. **elle est ~ celle-là** * *(incrédulité)* that's a bit hard to swallow, that's a bit far-fetched; *(indignation)* that's a bit steep *ou* stiff. (**e**) **être ~ (comme un passe-lacet)** * to be (stony *ou* stone *(US) ou* flat) broke *. **2** *adv* (**a**) **ça montait ~** *[ascension]* it was a steep climb; *[pente]* it climbed steeply. (**b**) **tomber ~** to drop to the ground; **~ mort** stone dead; **il l'a étendu ~ (mort)** * he laid him out cold *. ◆ **raideur** *nf* stiffness; straightness; tautness, tightness; steepness, abruptness; rigidity, inflexibility. **avec ~** stiffly. ◆ **raidillon** *nm* steep path.

raidir [ʀediʀ] (2) **1** *vt (gén)* to stiffen; *corde* to tighten; *(fig) position* to harden, toughen. **2 se ~** *vpr* (**a**) *[tissu]* to stiffen; *[corde]* to grow taut; *[position]* to harden. (**b**) *[personne] (perdre sa souplesse)* to become stiff(er); *(bander ses muscles)* to tense *ou* stiffen o.s.; *(s'entêter)* to take a hard *ou* tough line. ◆ **raidissement** *nm (gén)* stiffening; *[prise de position]* hard line.

raie [ʀɛ] *nf* (**a**) *(trait)* line; *(éraflure)* mark, scratch. (**b**) *(bande)* stripe. (**c**) *(Coiffure)* parting. (**d**) *(Zool)* skate, ray.

raifort [ʀɛfɔʀ] *nm* horseradish.

rail [ʀɑj] *nm* rail. *(voie)* **les ~s** the rails; **~ conducteur** live rail; *(transport)* **le ~** the railway, the railroad *(US)*; **transport ~-route** road-rail transport; *(lit, fig)* **remettre sur les ~s** to put back on the rails.

railler [ʀɑje] (1) *vt* to scoff at, mock at. ◆ **raillerie** *nf (action)* mockery; *(parole)* mocking remark. ◆ **railleur, -euse** **1** *adj* mocking. **2** *nmpl*: **les** ~**s** the mockers.

rainure [ʀenyʀ] *nf* groove; *(courte)* slot. ◆ **rainurage** *nm* grooved surface. ◆ **rainurer** (1) *vt* to groove.

raisin [ʀɛzɛ̃] *nm (espèce)* grape. **le** ~, **les** ~**s** grapes; ~**s de Corinthe** currants; ~**s secs** raisins; ~**s de table** dessert grapes.

raison [ʀɛzɔ̃] **1** *nf* (**a**) *(faculté)* reason. **il a perdu la** ~ he has lost his reason, he has taken leave of his senses, he is not in his right mind; **boire plus que de** ~ to drink more than is sensible *ou* more than is good for one. (**b**) *(motif)* reason. **pour quelles** ~**s l'avez-vous renvoyé?** on what grounds did you sack him?, what were your reasons for sacking him?; **il n'y a pas de** ~ **de s'arrêter** there's no reason to stop; **il a refusé pour la simple** ~ **que...** he refused simply on the grounds that..., he refused simply because...; **ce n'est pas une** ~! that's no excuse! *ou* reason!; **avec (juste)** ~ with good reason; ~ **de plus** all the more reason (*pour faire* for doing); **comme de** ~ as one might expect; **rire sans** ~ to laugh for no reason; **non sans** ~ not without reason. (**c**) **avoir** ~ to be right (*de faire* in doing, to do); **avoir** ~ **de qn/qch** to get the better of sb/sth; **donner** ~ **à qn** *[événement]* to prove sb right; *[personne]* to side with sb; **se faire une** ~ to put up with it; **en** ~ **du froid** because of *ou* owing to the cold weather; **payé en** ~ **du travail fourni** paid according to the work produced; **à** ~ **de 5 F par caisse** at the rate of 5 francs per crate; *(Math)* ~ **directe/indirecte** direct/inverse ratio *ou* proportion. **2** : ~ **d'État** reason of State; ~ **d'être** raison d'être; *(Comm)* ~ **sociale** corporate name.

raisonnable [ʀɛzɔnabl(ə)] *adj* (**a**) *(sensé) personne* sensible, reasonable; *conseil* sensible, sound, sane. (**b**) *(décent)* reasonable, fair. ◆ **raisonnablement** *adv* sensibly, reasonably; *dépenser* moderately.

raisonner [ʀɛzɔne] (1) **1** *vi (penser)* to reason; *(discourir, ergoter)* to argue (*sur* about). **il raisonne juste** his reasoning is sound. **2** *vt* (**a**) ~ **qn** to reason with sb, make sb see reason. (**b**) *conduite* to reason out. **explication bien raisonnée** well-reasoned explanation. **3 se** ~ *vpr* to reason with o.s., try to be reasonable. ◆ **raisonné, e** *adj (gén)* reasoned. **bien** ~! well argued!, well reasoned! ◆ **raisonnement** *nm* (**a**) *(façon de réfléchir)* reasoning. **ses** ~**s m'étonnent** his reasoning surprises me. (**b**) *(argumentation)* argument. **un** ~ **logique** a logical argument, a logical line of reasoning. (**c**) *(péj: ergotages)* ~**s** argument, quibbling. ◆ **raisonneur, -euse** *(péj)* **1** *adj* argumentative. **2** *nm, f* arguer, quibbler.

rajeunir [ʀaʒœniʀ] (2) **1** *vt* (**a**) ~ **qn** *[cure]* to rejuvenate sb; *[repos, expérience etc]* to make sb feel (*ou* look) younger. (**b**) *manuel* to update, bring up to date; *institution* to modernize; *installation, vieux habits* to give a new look to, brighten up; *personnel* to recruit younger people into; *thème* to inject new life into. **2** *vi [personne]* to feel (*ou* look) younger; *[quartier]* to be modernized. **3 se** ~ *vpr (se prétendre moins âgé)* to make o.s. younger. ◆ **rajeunissant, e** *adj traitement, crème* rejuvenating. ◆ **rajeunissement** *nm* rejuvenation; updating; modernization.

rajouter [ʀaʒute] (1) *vt sel* to add (some) more; *commentaire* to add another. **il rajouta que...** he added that...; *(fig)* **en** ~ * to overdo it, exaggerate. ◆ **rajout** *nm* addition.

rajuster [ʀaʒyste] (1) **1** *vt mécanisme* to readjust; *vêtement* to straighten, tidy. **2 se** ~ *vpr [personne]* to tidy *ou* straighten o.s. up, rearrange o.s. ◆ **rajustement** *nm* adjustment.

râle [ʀɑl] *nm* (**a**) *[blessé]* groan; *[mourant]* death rattle. (**b**) *(Méd)* rale. (**c**) *(Orn)* rail.

ralentir [ʀalɑ̃tiʀ] (2) **1** *vt* to slow down. ~ **sa marche** to slacken one's pace, slow down. **2** *vi [marcheur]* to slow down, slacken one's pace; *[automobiliste]* to slow down, reduce speed. **3 se** ~ *vpr [production]* to slow down *ou* up, slacken off; *[ardeur]* to flag. ◆ **ralenti, e** **1** *adj* slow. **2** *nm (Ciné)* slow motion; *(Aut)* tick-over. **au** ~ slow motion; *(Aut, Ind)* **tourner au** ~ to tick over, idle; **vivre au** ~ to live at a slower pace. ◆ **ralentissement** *nm* slowing down; slackening off ; flagging.

râler [ʀɑle] (1) *vi* (**a**) *[blessé]* to groan, moan; *[mourant]* to give the death rattle. (**b**) *(*: rouspéter)* to grouse *, moan *. **faire** ~ **qn** to infuriate sb, make sb fume. ◆ **râleur, -euse** *nm, f* grouser *, moaner *.

rallier [ʀalje] (7) **1** *vt (grouper)* to rally; *(unir)* to unite; *(rejoindre)* to rejoin; *suffrages* to bring in, win. ~ **qn à son avis** to bring sb round *ou* win sb over to one's opinion. **2 se** ~ *vpr (se regrouper)* to rally. **se** ~ **à** *parti* to join; *ennemi* to go over to; *chef* to rally round; *avis* to come round to. ◆ **ralliement** *nm* rallying. **son** ~ **à notre cause** his joining *ou* the fact that he joined our cause; **cri de** ~ rallying cry.

rallonger [ʀalɔ̃ʒe] (3) **1** *vt (gén)* to lengthen, make longer; *vacances, bâtiment* to extend. **2** *vi* (*) *[jours]* to get longer. ◆ **rallonge** *nf [table]* (extra) leaf; *[fil électrique]* extension cord *ou* flex; *[perche]* extension piece. **une** ~ **d'argent/de temps** some extra money/time; **obtenir une** ~ **de crédit** to get an extension of credit.

rallumer [ʀalyme] (1) **1** *vt feu* to light (up) again, relight; *courage, conflit* to revive, rekindle. ~ **(la lumière)** to switch *ou* turn the light(s) on again. **2 se** ~ *vpr [incendie, guerre]* to flare up again; *[lampe]* to come on again; *[haine, courage]* to revive, be revived.

rallye [ʀali] *nm*: ~ **(automobile)** (car) rally.

RAM [ʀam] *nf (Ordin)* RAM.

ramadan [ʀamadɑ̃] *nm*: **(R)**~ Ramadan.

ramage [ʀamaʒ] *nm (chant)* song. *(branchages, dessin)* ~**(s)** foliage.

ramasser [ʀamɑse] (1) **1** *vt (lit, fig: prendre)* to pick up; *copies, ordures* to collect; *fruits* to gather; *objets épars* to gather up *ou* together; *cartes* to pick up; *pommes de terre* to dig up; *maladie, amende* to get, pick up. ~ **une bûche** * to come a cropper *; *(fig)* ~ **ses forces** to gather *ou* muster one's strength. **2 se** ~ *vpr (se pelotonner)* to curl up; *(pour bondir)* to crouch; *(*: tomber, échouer)* to come a cropper *. **se faire** ~ *[candidat]* to come a cropper *, take a flat beating * *(US)*. ◆ **ramassage** *nm* picking up; collection; gathering. ~ **scolaire** school bus service. ◆ **ramassé, e** *adj (trapu)* squat, stocky; *(concis)* compact, condensed. ◆ **ramasseur, -euse** *nm, f (gén)* collector. ~ **de balles (de tennis)** ballboy; ~ **de pommes de terre** potato-picker. ◆ **ramassis** *nm (péj)* ~ **de** *voyous* pack *ou* bunch of; *doctrines, objets* jumble of.

rambarde [ʀɑ̃baʀd(ə)] *nf* guardrail.

ramdam * [ʀamdam] *nm* row, racket. **faire du** ~ to kick up * a row.

rame [ʀam] *nf (aviron)* oar; *(Rail)* train; *(Typ)* ream; *(Agr)* stake, stick.

rameau, *pl* ~**x** [ʀamo] *nm* (small) branch. *(Rel)* **les R**~**x** Palm Sunday.

ramener [ʀamne] (5) **1** *vt* (**a**) *(lit, fig: faire revenir)* to bring back; *paix* to restore. **je vais te** ~ **(en voiture)** I'll drive *ou* take you back (home); **cela**

nous ramène 20 ans en arrière it takes us back 20 years; ~ **à la vie** to bring back to *ou* restore to life. (**b**) *couverture* to pull. ~ **ses cheveux en arrière** to brush one's hair back; ~ **ses jambes en arrière** to draw back one's legs. (**c**) *(réduire à)* ~ **qch à** to reduce sth to. **2 se** ~ *vpr* (**a**) *[problèmes]* **se** ~ **à** to come down to, boil down to. (**b**) *(‡: arriver)* to roll up *, turn up *.

ramer [Rame] (1) *vi* to row. ◆ **rameur, -euse** *nm, f (sportif)* oarsman (*ou* oarswoman), rower.

ramette [Ramɛt] *nf [papier à lettres]* ream.

rameuter [Ramøte] (1) *vt foule, partisans* to gather together, round up; *chiens* to round up, form into a pack again.

rami [Rami] *nm* rummy.

ramier [Ramje] *nm*: **(pigeon)** ~ woodpigeon.

ramifier (se) [Ramifje] (7) *vpr [veines]* to ramify; *[routes, branches]* to branch out (*en* into). ◆ **ramification** *nf (gén)* ramification.

ramollir [RamɔliR] (2) **1** *vt* to soften. **2 se** ~ *vpr (lit, fig)* to get *ou* go soft; *(Méd)* to soften. ◆ **ramolli, e** *adj* soft. ◆ **ramollissement** *nm* softening.

ramoner [Ramɔne] (1) *vt cheminée* to sweep; *pipe* to clean out; *(Alpinisme)* to climb. ◆ **ramonage** *nm* chimney-sweeping; *(Alpinisme)* chimney-climbing. ◆ **ramoneur** *nm* (chimney) sweep.

rampe [Rɑ̃p] *nf* (**a**) *(voie d'accès)* ramp; *(côte)* slope. ~ **de lancement** launching pad. (**b**) *[escalier]* banister(s); *[chemin]* handrail. (**c**) *(projecteurs)* **la** ~ the footlights.

ramper [Rɑ̃pe] (1) *vi [serpent]* to crawl, slither, slide (along); *[homme]* to crawl; *[plante, ombre]* to creep; *[sentiment, maladie]* to lurk. *(péj)* ~ **devant qn** to grovel before *ou* crawl to sb.

ramure [RamyR] *nf [cerf]* antlers; *[arbre]* boughs, foliage.

rancard ‡ [Rɑ̃kaR] *nm (tuyau)* tip; *(rendez-vous)* date. **donner** ~ **à qn** to make a date with sb. ◆ **rancarder** ‡ (1) *vt* to tip off.

rancart ‡ [Rɑ̃kaR] *nm*: **mettre au** ~ to chuck out ‡, scrap.

rance [Rɑ̃s] *adj beurre* rancid; *odeur* rank, rancid. ◆ **rancir** (2) *vi* to go rancid.

ranch [Rɑ̃tʃ] *nm* ranch.

rancœur [Rɑ̃kœR] *nf* rancour, resentment.

rançon [Rɑ̃sɔ̃] *nf (lit)* ransom. **la** ~ **de la gloire** the price of fame. ◆ **rançonner** (1) *vt voyageurs* to demand *ou* exact a ransom from; *(fig) contribuables, clients* to fleece.

rancune [Rɑ̃kyn] *nf* grudge, rancour. **garder** ~ **à qn** to hold a grudge against sb, bear sb a grudge (*de qch* for sth); **sans** ~! no hard feelings! ◆ **rancunier, -ière** *adj*: **être** ~ to bear a grudge.

randonnée [Rɑ̃dɔne] *nf*: ~ **(en voiture)** drive, ride; ~ **(à bicyclette)** ride; ~ **(à pied)** walk, ramble; *(grande)* hike; ~ **(à ski)** cross-country ski run; **faire une** ~ to go for a drive (*ou* a ride *etc*). ◆ **randonneur, -euse** *nm, f* walker, rambler, hiker.

rang [Rɑ̃] *nm* (**a**) *(rangée)* row, line; *(Mil, fig)* rank. **en** ~ **d'oignons** in a row *ou* line; **en** ~**s serrés** in close order, in serried ranks; **en** ~ **par 2** 2 abreast; **sur 4** ~**s** 4 deep; **se mettre sur un** ~ to get into *ou* form a line; **se mettre en** ~**s par 4** to get into *ou* form rows of 4; **plusieurs personnes sont sur** *ou* **se sont mises sur les** ~**s pour l'acheter** several people are in the running to buy it. (**b**) *(noblesse)* station, rank. (**c**) *(hiérarchique)* rank; *[classement]* place. **avoir** ~ **de** to hold the rank of; **avoir** ~ **parmi** to rank among; **par** ~ **d'âge** in order of age; **mettre un écrivain au** ~ **des plus grands** to rank a writer among the greatest; **c'est au premier** ~ **de mes préoccupations** that's uppermost in *ou* in the forefront of my mind. ◆ **rangée**¹ *nf* row, line.

ranger [Rɑ̃ʒe] (3) **1** *vt* (**a**) *(mettre en ordre) maison, papiers* to tidy (up); *mots* to arrange, order. (**b**) *(mettre à sa place) (gén)* to put away; *véhicule* to park. **où se rangent les tasses?** where do the cups go? *ou* belong?; **je le range parmi les meilleurs** I rank it among the best. (**c**) *écoliers* to line up, put into rows; *invités* to place. **2 se** ~ *vpr* (**a**) *[automobiliste] (stationner)* to park; *(venir s'arrêter)* to pull in, draw up; *[piéton]* to step *ou* stand aside. (**b**) *(se mettre en rang)* to line up, get into rows. (**c**) *(se rallier à)* **se** ~ **à** *décision, avis* to fall in with; **se** ~ **du côté de qn** to side with sb. (**d**) *(*: se marier)* to settle down. ◆ **rangé, e**² *adj pièce* tidy; *vie* well-ordered; *personne (ordonné)* orderly; *(sans excès)* settled. **il est** ~ **maintenant** he has settled down now; **jeune fille** ~**e** well-behaved young lady; **mal** ~ untidy. ◆ **rangement** *nm* (**a**) *[objets]* putting away. **faire du** ~ to do some tidying (up). (**b**) *(espace) [appartement]* cupboard space; *[remise]* storage space. (**c**) *(arrangement)* arrangement.

ranimer [Ranime] (1) **1** *vt blessé* to revive, bring round; *souvenir, querelle, douleur* to revive; *feu, sentiment* to rekindle; *forces, ardeur* to revive, restore. **2 se** ~ *vpr* to revive; to come round; to rekindle; to be restored.

rapace [Rapas] **1** *nm (Orn)* bird of prey. **2** *adj (Orn)* predatory; *(fig)* rapacious, grasping. ◆ **rapacité** *nf (lit, fig)* rapaciousness, rapacity.

rapatrier [RapatRije] (7) *vt personne* to repatriate; *objet* to bring back (home). ◆ **rapatrié, e** *nm, f* repatriate. ◆ **rapatriement** *nm* repatriation.

râper [Rɑpe] (1) *vt carottes, fromage* to grate; *bois* to rasp. ◆ **râpe** *nf* grater; rasp. ◆ **râpé, e** **1** *adj (usé)* threadbare; *carottes, fromage* grated. *(*: raté)* **c'est** ~ **pour ce soir** we've had it for tonight *. **2** *nm (fromage)* grated cheese.

rapetisser [Raptise] (1) **1** *vt (raccourcir)* to shorten; *(dénigrer)* to belittle. *(faire paraître plus petit)* ~ **qch** to make sth seem *ou* look small(er). **2** *vi*, **se** ~ *vpr [vieillard]* to shrink, get smaller; *[jours]* to get shorter.

râpeux, -euse [Rɑpø, øz] *adj (gén)* rough.

raphia [Rafja] *nm* raffia.

rapiat, e [Rapja, at] *(péj)* **1** *adj* niggardly, tight-fisted. **2** *nm, f* niggard, skinflint.

rapide [Rapid] **1** *adj (gén)* quick, rapid, swift; *coureur* fast; *guérison* speedy; *mouvement* brisk; *intelligence* lively; *pente* steep, abrupt; *film* fast; *ciment* quick-setting. ~ **comme l'éclair** (as) quick as a flash. **2** *nm* (**a**) *(train)* express (train), fast train. (**b**) *[rivière]* rapid. ◆ **rapidement** *adv (gén)* fast, quickly, rapidly, swiftly, speedily; *marcher* briskly; *descendre en pente* steeply, abruptly. ◆ **rapidité** *nf (gén)* speed, rapidity, speediness, swiftness, quickness; *[mouvement]* briskness; *[intelligence]* liveliness.

rapiécer [Rapjese] (3) *et* (6) *vt* to patch (up).

rappel [Rapɛl] *nm* (**a**) *[ambassadeur, réservistes]* recall; *[marchandises défectueuses]* callback; *(Théât)* curtain call. (**b**) *(évocation, avertissement)* reminder; *(Comm: référence)* quote; *(somme due)* back pay; *(vaccination)* booster. ~ **à l'ordre** call to order. (**c**) *(Alpinisme)* **faire un** ~ to abseil, rope down.

rappeler [Raple] (4) **1** *vt* (**a**) *(faire revenir)* to call back; *réservistes, diplomate* to recall. *(Ordin)* ~ **un dossier à l'écran** to call up a file on the screen. (**b**) ~ **qch** *(mentionner)* to mention sth; *(Comm) référence* to quote sth; *(être similaire)* to be reminiscent of sth; ~ **qch à qn** to remind sb of sth; **cela ne te rappelle rien?** doesn't that remind you of anything?, doesn't that ring a bell? (**c**) ~ **qn à la vie** to bring sb back to life, revive sb; ~ **qn à l'ordre** to call sb to order; ~ **qn à son devoir**

to remind sb of his duty. (**d**) *(retéléphoner à)* to call *ou* ring *ou* phone back. **2 se** ~ *vpr* to remember, recollect, recall.

rappliquer ⁑ [Raplike] (1) *vi (revenir)* to come back; *(arriver)* to turn up, show up *.

rapport [Rapɔʀ] *nm* (**a**) *(lien)* connection, relationship, link. **avoir beaucoup de ~/n'avoir aucun ~ avec qch** to have a lot to do/nothing to do with sth, be closely related/be unrelated to sth. (**b**) *(relations)* **~s** relations, relationships; **entretenir de bons/mauvais ~s avec qn** to be on good/bad terms *ou* have good/bad relations with sb; **~s (sexuels)** sexual relations. (**c**) *(compte rendu)* report; *(Mil)* conference. **~ de police** police report. (**d**) *(profit)* yield, return. **être d'un bon ~** to give a good profit *ou* return; **immeuble de ~** residential property (for renting), investment property. (**e**) *(Math, Tech)* ratio. **~ de 1 à 100** ratio of 1 to 100; **le ~ qualité-prix** the quality-price ratio; **ce n'est pas d'un bon ~ qualité-prix** it's not good value for money. (**f**) *(locutions)* **être en ~ avec qch** *(en harmonie)* to be in keeping *ou* in line with sth; **être en ~ avec qn** to be in touch with sb, have dealings with sb; **mettre/se mettre en ~ avec qn** to put/get in touch *ou* contact with sb; **par ~ à** in relation to; **la force de la livre par ~ au dollar** the strength of the pound against the dollar; **sous le ~ de l'honnêteté** from the point of view of honesty; **sous tous les ~s** in every respect; *(équilibre)* **le ~ des forces** the balance of power; *(lutte)* **des ~s de force** power struggle.

rapporter [Rapɔʀte] (1) **1** *vt* (**a**) *objet, réponse* to bring *ou* take back (*à* to). (**b**) *(Fin, fig) profit* to bring in. **placement qui rapporte 5%** investment that yields (a return of) 5% *ou* that brings in (a yield *ou* revenue of) 5%. (**c**) *fait (gén)* to report; *(mentionner)* to mention; *(citer)* to quote. **on nous a rapporté que** we were told that, it was reported to us that. (**d**) *(ajouter)* to add. **c'est un élément rapporté** this element has been added on. (**e**) *(établir un lien entre)* **~ qch à** to relate sth to. (**f**) *(annuler)* to revoke. **2** *vi* (**a**) *(Chasse)* to retrieve. (**b**) *(Fin)* to give a good return *ou* yield. **ça rapporte gros** it brings in a lot of money, it pays very well. (**c**) *(arg Scol: moucharder)* **~ (sur ses camarades)** to tell on * *ou* sneak on * *ou* tattle on * *(US)* one's friends. **3 se ~** *vpr* (**a**) **se ~ à qch** to relate to sth; **ça se rapporte à ce que je disais tout à l'heure** that ties up with *ou* links up with *ou* relates to what I was saying just now. (**b**) **s'en ~ à qn/au jugement de qn** to rely on sb/on sb's judgment.

rapporteur, -euse [RapɔʀtœR, øz] **1** *nm, f (mouchard)* telltale, sneak *, tattler * *(US)*. **2** *nm (Admin)* reporter; *(Géom)* protractor.

rapprocher [RapRɔʃe] (1) **1** *vt* (**a**) *(approcher)* to bring closer *ou* nearer (*de* to). **~ sa chaise (de la table)** to pull *ou* draw one's chair up (to the table). (**b**) *(réconcilier, réunir)* to bring together. (**c**) *indices, textes (confronter)* to put *ou* bring together; *(assimiler)* to establish a connection *ou* link between. **c'est à ~ de ce qu'on disait tout à l'heure** that ties up *ou* connects with what was being said earlier. **2 se ~** *vpr* (**a**) *(approcher)* to get closer *ou* nearer (*de* to). **rapproche-toi** come *ou* move *ou* draw closer; **se ~ de la vérité** to get near *ou* close to the truth. (**b**) *(en fréquence)* to become more frequent. (**c**) *[ennemis]* to come together; *[points de vue]* to draw closer together. **se ~ de** to move *ou* draw closer to. (**d**) *(s'apparenter à)* to be close to. **ça se rapproche de ce qu'on disait** that's close to, *ou* that ties up with what was being said. ◆ **rapproché, e** *adj*: **être ~** *(proche)* to be close *ou* near (*de* to); *(répété)* to be frequent. ◆ **rapprochement** *nm (réconciliation)* reconciliation; *(comparaison)* comparison; *(rapport)* link, connection. **le ~ des 2 objets** *(action)* bringing the 2 objects (closer) together; *(résultat)* the fact that the 2 objects are close together.

rapt [Rapt] *nm (enlèvement)* abduction.

raquette [Rakɛt] *nf (Tennis)* racket; *(Ping-Pong)* bat; *(à neige)* snowshoe.

rare [RaR] *adj* (**a**) *(peu commun) (gén)* rare; *énergie* exceptional, singular; *imprudence* singular. **ça n'a rien de ~** there's nothing uncommon *ou* unusual about it; **il était ~ qu'il ne sache pas** he rarely *ou* seldom did not know. (**b**) *(peu nombreux)* few, rare. **les ~s voitures qui passaient** the few *ou* odd cars that went by; **les clients sont ~s** customers are scarce *ou* are few and far between. (**c**) *(peu abondant) (gén)* scarce; *barbe* thin; *végétation* sparse; *gaz* rare. *[légumes]* **se faire ~** to become scarce, be in short supply. ◆ **se raréfier** (7) *vpr (gén)* to become scarce; *[air]* to rarefy, get thin. ◆ **rarement** *adv* rarely, seldom. ◆ **rareté** *nf* (**a**) *[objet, cas]* rarity; *[vivres, argent]* scarcity; *[visites]* infrequency. (**b**) *(objet)* rarity; *(événement)* rare *ou* unusual occurrence. ◆ **rarissime** *adj* extremely rare.

ras, e [Rɑ, Rɑz] *adj* (**a**) *poil, herbe* short; *cheveux* close-cropped; *mesure* full. **à poil ~** *chien* short-haired; *étoffe* with a short pile; **cheveux coupés (à) ~** hair cut short. (**b**) *(locutions)* **à ~ de terre** level with the ground; **coupé à ~ de terre** cut down to the ground; **voler au ~ de l'eau** to skim the water; **à ~ bords** to the brim; **en ~e campagne** in open country; **pull ~ du cou** crew-neck sweater, round-neck sweater; **j'en ai ~ le bol** * I'm fed up to the back teeth ⁑; **le ~-le-bol étudiant** * the students' discontent *ou* dissatisfaction, student unrest.

rasade [Rɑzad] *nf* glassful.

raser [Rɑze] (1) **1** *vt* (**a**) *barbe* to shave off; *menton, malade etc* to shave. (**b**) *[projectile]* to graze, scrape; *[oiseau, balle de tennis]* to skim (over). **~ les murs** to hug the walls. (**c**) *(abattre)* to raze (to the ground). (**d**) *(*: ennuyer)* to bore. **2 se ~** *vpr* (**a**) *(toilette)* to shave. **se ~ les jambes** to shave one's legs. (**b**) *(*: s'ennuyer)* to be bored stiff *ou* to tears. ◆ **rasage** *nm* shaving. ◆ **rasant, e** *adj* (**a**) *(*: ennuyeux)* boring. (**b**) *lumière* low-angled. **tir ~** grazing fire. ◆ **rasé, e** *adj menton* (clean-)shaven; *tête* shaven. **mal ~** unshaven; **~ de près** close-shaven. ◆ **rase-mottes** *nm inv*: **faire du ~** to hedgehop. ◆ **raseur, -euse** * *nm, f* bore. ◆ **rasoir 1** *nm* (**a**) razor. **~ électrique** (electric) shaver, electric razor; **~ à main** *ou* **de coiffeur** cut-throat *ou* straight razor. (**b**) *(*: importun)* bore. **2** *adj* (*) boring.

rassasier [Rasazje] (7) **1** *vt faim, désirs* to satisfy. **~ qn** to satisfy sb *ou* sb's hunger (*de* with); **être rassasié** to be satisfied, have eaten one's fill; *(dégoûté)* to have had more than enough (*de* of). **2 se ~** *vpr* to satisfy one's hunger. **je ne me rassasierai jamais de...** I'll never tire of...

rassembler [Rasɑ̃ble] (1) **1** *vt (gén)* to gather, assemble; *troupes* to rally; *troupeau* to round up; *objets, notes* to gather together, collect; *(après démontage)* to put back together, reassemble; *idées* to collect; *courage* to summon up. **2 se ~** *vpr* to gather, assemble. ◆ **rassemblement** *nm* (**a**) gathering, assembling *etc. (Mil)* ~! fall in! (**b**) *(groupe)* gathering; *(parti)* union. ◆ **rassembleur** *nm* unifier.

rasseoir [RaswaR] (26) **1** *vt bébé* to sit back up (straight); *objet* to put back up straight. **2 se ~** *vpr* to sit down again.

rasséréner (se) [RaseRene] (6) *vpr* to become serene again.

rassir *vi*, **se ~** *vpr* [RasiR] (2) to go stale. ◆ **rassis, e** *adj (lit, péj)* stale.

rassurer [RasyRe] (1) **1** *vt*: **~ qn** to put sb's mind at ease, reassure sb. **2 se ~** *vpr* to put one's mind at ease, reassure o.s. ◆ **rassurant, e** *adj* reassuring, comforting, cheering.

rat [Ra] *nm* rat. **il est fait comme un** ~ he's cornered, he has no escape; ~ **de bibliothèque** bookworm; ~ **des champs** fieldmouse; ~ **d'hôtel** hotel thief; ~ **musqué** muskrat, musquash; **(petit)** ~ **de l'Opéra** pupil of the Opéra ballet class.

ratatiner [Ratatine] (1) **1** *vt* (**a**) *pomme* to dry up, shrivel; *visage* to wrinkle. (**b**) *(‡: détruire)* to wreck. **se faire** ~ *(battre)* to get thrashed; *(tuer)* to get done in ‡ *ou* bumped off ‡. **2 se** ~ *vpr [pomme]* to shrivel *ou* dry up; *[visage, personne]* to become wrinkled *ou* shrivelled.

rate[1] [Rat] *nf (Anat)* spleen.

rate[2] [Rat] *nf (animal)* she-rat.

râteau, *pl* ~**x** [Rɑto] *nm (Agr, Roulette)* rake.

râtelier [Rɑtəlje] *nm* rack; *(*: dentier)* (set of) false teeth.

rater [Rate] (1) **1** *vi [coup]* to misfire, fail to go off; *[projet]* to fail, go wrong, backfire. **tout faire** ~ to ruin everything; **ça ne va pas** ~ * it's dead certain *. **2** *vt* (*) *cible, occasion, train* to miss; *travail* to mess up, spoil, botch; *mayonnaise, sauce* to spoil; *examen* to fail, flunk *. **raté!** missed!; *(iro)* **il n'en rate pas une** he's always putting his foot in it *; **je ne te raterai pas!** you won't get away with it!; ~ **son effet** to spoil one's effect; **il a raté son coup** he didn't pull it off. ◆ **raté, e 1** *nm, f (personne)* failure. **2** *nm (Aut) [arme]* misfire. **avoir des** ~**s** to misfire; *(fig)* **il y a eu des** ~**s dans la conduite de cette affaire** there were some hiccups in the handling of this matter.

ratiboiser ‡ [Ratibwaze] (1) *vt maison* to wreck; *personne* to do in *. ~ **qch à qn** *(au jeu)* to clean sb out of sth *; *(en le volant)* to nick ‡ *ou* pinch * *ou* swipe * sth from sb.

raticide [Ratisid] *nm* rat poison.

ratifier [Ratifje] (7) *vt* to ratify. ◆ **ratification** *nf (Admin, Jur)* ratification.

ratio [Rasjo] *nm* ratio.

ration [Rɑsjɔ̃] *nf (gén)* ration; *(fig: part)* share; *[soldat]* rations.

rationaliser [Rasjɔnalize] (1) *vt* to rationalize. ◆ **rationnel, -elle** *adj* rational. ◆ **rationnellement** *adv* rationally.

rationner [Rasjɔne] (1) **1** *vt charbon, personne* to ration. **2 se** ~ *vpr* to ration o.s. ◆ **rationnement** *nm* rationing.

ratisser [Ratise] (1) *vt gravier* to rake; *feuilles* to rake up; *(Mil, Police)* to comb; *(*: au jeu)* to clean out *. **il s'est fait** ~ **(au jeu)** he was cleaned out * *ou* he lost everything at the gambling table. ◆ **ratissage** *nm* raking; combing.

raton [Ratɔ̃] *nm*: ~ **laveur** racoon.

raton(n)ade [Ratɔnad] *nf*: ~**s** attacks on immigrants.

rattacher [Rataʃe] (1) *vt prisonnier* to tie up again; *lacets* to do up *ou* fasten again; *territoire, service* to join (*à* to), unite (*à* with); *problème* to link, connect, tie up (*à* with); *fait* to relate (*à* to). **rien ne le rattache plus à sa famille** nothing binds *ou* ties him to his family any more. ◆ **rattachement** *nm* uniting (*à* with), joining (*à* to). **quel est votre service de** ~**?** which service are you attached to?

rattraper [RatRape] (1) **1** *vt* (**a**) *prisonnier* to recapture; *objet, enfant qui tombe* to catch (hold of); *voiture, coureur, (fig) leçon en retard* to catch up with. **on ne m'y rattrapera plus** I won't be caught (at it) again. (**b**) *mayonnaise* to salvage; *erreur, temps perdu* to make up for; *argent perdu* to recover, get back, recoup; *sommeil* to catch up on. (**c**) *(Scol: repêcher)* ~ **qn** to allow sb to pass, let sb get through. **2 se** ~ *vpr (reprendre son équilibre)* to stop o.s. falling; *(fig: récupérer)* to make up for it, make good (one's losses *ou* one's mistakes). **se** ~ **à une branche** to catch hold of a branch to stop o.s. falling. ◆ **rattrapable** *adj* which can be put right. ◆ **rattrapage** *nm [candidat]* passing. **le** ~ **d'un oubli/du retard** making up for an omission/for lost time; ~ **scolaire** remedial teaching; **cours de** ~ remedial class *ou* course.

raturer [RatyRe] (1) *vt (corriger)* to make an alteration to; *(barrer)* to erase, delete. ◆ **rature** *nf* alteration; erasure, deletion.

rauque [Rok] *adj voix (enrouée)* hoarse; *(éraillée)* husky, throaty; *cri* raucous.

ravage [Ravaʒ] *nm*: **faire des** ~**s** to wreak havoc (*dans* in). ◆ **ravagé, e** *adj (tourmenté) visage* harrowed, haggard; *(‡: fou)* nuts *, bonkers ‡. ◆ **ravager** (3) *vt pays* to lay waste, ravage, devastate; *visage [maladie]* to ravage; *[soucis]* to harrow. ◆ **ravageur, -euse** *adj* devastating.

ravaler [Ravale] (1) *vt* (**a**) *(nettoyer)* to clean, give a face-lift * to; *(réparer)* to restore. **se faire** ~ **la façade** * to have a face-lift. (**b**) *sanglots, colère* to choke back. (**c**) *dignité, personne* to lower. ◆ **ravalement** *nm* cleaning; restoration; face-lift *. ◆ **ravaleur** *nm (maçon)* stone restorer.

ravauder [Ravode] (1) *vt vêtement* to repair, mend; *chaussette* to darn.

rave [Rav] *nf (Bot)* rape.

ravi, e [Ravi] *adj (enchanté)* delighted. ~ **de vous connaître** delighted *ou* pleased to meet you.

ravier [Ravje] *nm* hors d'œuvres dish.

ravigoter * [Ravigɔte] (1) *vt* to buck up *.

ravin [Ravɛ̃] *nm (gén)* gully; *(encaissé)* ravine. ◆ **ravinement** *nm* gullying. ◆ **raviner** (1) *vt (Géog)* to gully; *visage* to furrow.

ravioli [Ravjɔli] *nmpl* ravioli.

ravir [RaviR] (2) *vt* (**a**) *(charmer)* to delight. **cela lui va à** ~ that suits her beautifully. (**b**) *(enlever)* ~ **qch à qn** to rob sb of sth, take sth (away) from sb. ◆ **ravissant, e** *adj* ravishing, delightful. ◆ **ravissement** *nm* rapture. **plongé dans le** ~ in raptures; **regarder qn avec** ~ to look at sb rapturously. ◆ **ravisseur, -euse** *nm, f* kidnapper, abductor.

raviser (se) [Ravize] (1) *vpr* to change one's mind, decide otherwise, think better of it.

ravitailler [Ravitɑje] (1) **1** *vt (en vivres)* to provide with fresh supplies; *(en carburant)* to refuel. **2 se** ~ *vpr [armée]* to get fresh supplies; *[ménagère]* to stock up (*à* at); *[véhicule]* to refuel. ◆ **ravitaillement** *nm (action)* resupplying; refuelling; *(réserves)* supplies. **aller au** ~ to go for fresh supplies.

raviver [Ravive] (1) *vt feu, sentiment* to revive, rekindle; *couleur* to brighten up.

ravoir [RavwaR] *vt (recouvrer)* to have *ou* get back; *(obtenir davantage)* to get more *ou* another; *(*: nettoyer)* to get clean.

rayer [Reje] (8) *vt (marquer)* to rule, line; *(érafler)* to scratch; *(biffer)* to cross *ou* score out, delete. ~ **qn d'une liste** to cross sb *ou* sb's name off a list, delete sb's name from a list. ◆ **rayé, e** *adj tissu, pelage* striped; *disque* scratched, scratchy.

rayon [Rɛjɔ̃] *nm* (**a**) *(gén, Opt, Phys: faisceau)* ray; *[jour]* ray, beam; *[phare]* beam. *(radiations)* ~**s** radiation; ~**s infrarouges/ultraviolets** infrared/ultraviolet rays; ~**s X** X-rays; ~ **laser** laser beam; *(lit, fig)* ~ **de soleil** ray of sunshine; ~ **de lune** moonbeam; ~ **d'espoir** ray *ou* gleam of hope. (**b**) *[roue]* spoke. (**c**) *(planche)* shelf; *[bibliothèque]* (book)shelf. (**d**) *(Comm) (section)* department; *(comptoir)* counter. **c'est son** ~ *(spécialité)* that's his line; *(responsabilité)* that's his concern *ou* responsibility *ou* department *; *(fig)* **il en connaît un** ~ * he knows masses about it *, he's really clued up about it *. (**e**) *[ruche]* (honey)comb. (**f**) *(Math, fig)* radius. **dans un ~ de 10 km** within a radius of 10 km *ou* a 10-km radius; ~ **d'action** *(lit)* range; *(fig)* scope, range; **à grand ~ d'action** long-range; *(Aut)* ~ **de braquage** lock. ◆ **rayonnage** *nm*: ~**(s)** set of shelves, shelving.

rayonne [ʀɛjɔn] *nf* rayon.

rayonner [ʀɛjɔne] (1) *vi* (**a**) *[influence, joie, astre]* to radiate. *[prestige etc]* ~ **sur/dans** to extend over/in; ~ **de bonheur** to be radiant *ou* glowing with happiness. (**b**) *(Phys) [chaleur, énergie]* to radiate. (**c**) ~ **dans une région** *[touristes]* to tour around a region (from a base); *[cars]* to service a region. (**d**) *[avenues, lignes]* to radiate (*autour de* from, out from). ◆ **rayonnant, e** *adj (Phys, fig)* radiant; *(Méd) douleur* spreading. ◆ **rayonnement** *nm [culture]* influence; *[influence]* extension; *[personnalité, beauté, astre]* radiance; *(Phys: radiation)* radiation.

rayure [ʀejyʀ] *nf (dessin)* stripe; *(éraflure)* scratch. **papier à ~s** striped paper.

raz-de-marée [ʀɑdmaʀe] *nm inv (Géog, fig)* tidal wave. ~ **électoral** landslide.

razzia [ʀazja] *nf* raid, foray. *(fig)* **faire une ~ dans qch** * to raid *ou* plunder sth.

ré [ʀe] *nm (Mus)* D; *(en chantant)* re, ray.

réabonner [ʀeabɔne] (1) **1** *vt*: ~ **qn** to renew sb's subscription (*à* to). **2 se** ~ *vpr* to renew one's subscription (*à* to). ◆ **réabonnement** *nm* renewal of subscription.

réaccoutumer [ʀeakutyme] (1) **1** *vt* to reaccustom. **2 se** ~ *vpr* to reaccustom o.s. (*à* to).

réacteur [ʀeaktœʀ] *nm (Aviat)* jet engine; *(Chim, Phys nucléaire)* reactor.

réaction [ʀeaksjɔ̃] *nf (gén)* reaction. **être sans** ~ to show no reaction; ~ **en chaîne** chain reaction ; *(Aviat)* **moteur à** ~ jet engine. ◆ **réactionnaire** *adj, nmf* reactionary.

réadapter [ʀeadapte] (1) **1** *vt personne* to readjust (*à* to); *(Méd)* to rehabilitate; *muscle* to re-educate. **2 se** ~ *vpr* to readjust (*à* to). ◆ **réadaptation** *nf* readjustment; rehabilitation; re-education.

réaffirmer [ʀeafiʀme] (1) *vt* to reaffirm, reassert.

réagir [ʀeaʒiʀ] (2) *vi* to react (*à* to, *contre* against, *sur* upon).

réaliser [ʀealize] (1) **1** *vt* (**a**) *rêve* to achieve, fulfil; *effort* to make, exercise; *exploit* to achieve, carry off; *projet* to carry out. (**b**) *(*: se rendre compte de)* to realize. (**c**) *(Ciné)* to produce. (**d**) *vente, bénéfice* to make. (**e**) *(Fin) capital* to realize. **2 se** ~ *vpr [rêve]* to come true; *[personnalité]* to fulfil o.s. ◆ **réalisateur, -trice** *nm, f (Ciné, Rad, TV)* director. ◆ **réalisation** *nf* (**a**) *(action)* realization; fulfilment, achievement. **plusieurs projets sont déjà en cours de** ~ several projects are already in the pipeline *ou* are already under way. (**b**) *(ouvrage)* achievement, creation. (**c**) *(Ciné)* production.

réalisme [ʀealism(ə)] *nm* realism. ◆ **réaliste 1** *adj* realistic. **2** *nmf* realist.

réalité [ʀealite] *nf* reality. **en** ~ in (actual) fact, in reality; **la ~ dépasse la fiction** truth is stranger than fiction; **son rêve est devenu (une)** ~ his dream became (a) reality *ou* came true.

réanimer [ʀeanime] (1) *vt* to resuscitate, revive. ◆ **réanimateur, -trice 1** *nm, f (personne)* resuscitator. **2** *nm (respirateur)* ventilator, respirator. ◆ **réanimation** *nf* resuscitation. **être en (service de)** ~ to be in the intensive care unit, be in intensive care.

réapparaître [ʀeapaʀɛtʀ(ə)] (57) *vi* to reappear. ◆ **réapparition** *nf* reappearance.

réapprendre [ʀeapʀɑ̃dʀ(ə)] (58) *vt (gén)* to relearn, learn again. ~ **qch à qn** to teach sth to sb again.

réapprovisionner [ʀeapʀɔvizjɔne] (1) **1** *vt* to restock. **2 se** ~ *vpr* to stock up again (*en* with).

réarmer [ʀeaʀme] (1) **1** *vt fusil, appareil-photo* to reload; *bateau* to refit. **2** *vi,* **se** ~ *vpr [pays]* to rearm. ◆ **réarmement** *nm (Pol)* rearmament.

réassortir [ʀeasɔʀtiʀ] (2) **1** *vt magasin* to restock (*en* with); *stock* to replenish; *verres* to match (up). **2 se** ~ *vpr (Comm)* to stock up again (*de* with). ◆ **réassortiment** *nm* replenishment.

rébarbatif, -ive [ʀebaʀbatif, iv] *adj mine* forbidding, unprepossessing; *sujet, tâche* daunting, forbidding.

rebâtir [ʀ(ə)bɑtiʀ] (2) *vt* to rebuild.

rebattre [ʀ(ə)batʀ(ə)] (41) *vt*: ~ **les oreilles de qn de qch** to keep harping about sth *. ◆ **rebattu, e** *adj citation* hackneyed.

rebelle [ʀəbɛl] **1** *adj soldat* rebel; *enfant, esprit* rebellious; *maladie* stubborn; *virus* resistant; *cheveux* unruly. ~ **à** *discipline* unamenable to; *maths, latin* unable to understand; **il est ~ à la poésie** poetry is a closed book to him. **2** *nmf* rebel. ◆ **se rebeller** (1) *vpr* to rebel (*contre* against). ◆ **rébellion** *nf (révolte)* rebellion. *(rebelles)* **la** ~ the rebels.

rebiffer (se) * [ʀ(ə)bife] (1) *vpr* to hit *ou* strike back (*contre* at).

reboiser [ʀ(ə)bwaze] (1) *vt* to reafforest.

rebondir [ʀ(ə)bɔ̃diʀ] (2) *vi* (**a**) *(sur le sol)* to bounce; *(contre un mur etc)* to rebound. (**b**) *[conversation, action]* to get going *ou* moving again, spring to life again; *[scandale]* to take a new turn. **faire** ~ to set *ou* get going again. ◆ **rebond** *nm* bounce; rebound. ◆ **rebondi, e** *adj objet* potbellied; *croupe* rounded; *ventre* fat; *visage* chubby; *porte-monnaie* well-lined. ◆ **rebondissement** *nm [affaire]* (sudden new) development (*de* in).

rebord [ʀ(ə)bɔʀ] *nm [assiette, pot]* rim; *[puits, falaise, table]* edge. **le ~ de la fenêtre** the windowsill, the window ledge.

reboucher [ʀ(ə)buʃe] (1) **1** *vt trou* to fill in again; *bouteille* to recork; *carafe* to restopper; *tube* to put the cap back on. **2 se** ~ *vpr [tuyau]* to get blocked again.

rebours [ʀ(ə)buʀ] *nm*: **à** ~ *(à rebrousse-poil)* the wrong way; *(à l'envers)* the other way round; **compter à** ~ to count backwards; **faire tout à** ~ to do everything the wrong way round; *(à l'opposé de)* **à ~ de** against.

rebouteux, -euse [ʀ(ə)butø, øz] *nm, f* bonesetter.

rebrousser [ʀ(ə)bʀuse] (1) *vt poil* to brush up. ~ **chemin** to turn back, retrace one's steps; *(lit, fig)* **à rebrousse-poil** the wrong way.

rebuffade [ʀ(ə)byfad] *nf* rebuff. **essuyer une** ~ to suffer a rebuff.

rébus [ʀebys] *nm* rebus.

rebut [ʀəby] *nm (déchets)* scrap. **mettre au** ~ to scrap, throw out, discard; *(péj: racaille)* **le ~ de la société** the scum *ou* dregs of society; *(Poste)* ~**s** dead letters.

rebuter [ʀ(ə)byte] (1) **1** *vt (décourager)* to put off, dishearten, discourage; *(répugner)* to repel; *(littér: repousser)* to repulse. **2 se** ~ *vpr* to be discouraged. ◆ **rebutant, e** *adj* repellent; off-putting; disheartening.

récalcitrant, e [ʀekalsitʀɑ̃, ɑ̃t] *adj, nm, f* recalcitrant.

recaler [ʀ(ə)kale] (1) *vt (Scol)* to fail. **se faire ~ (en histoire)** to fail *ou* flunk * (history).

récapituler [ʀekapityle] (1) *vt* to recapitulate, sum up. ◆ **récapitulatif, -ive** *adj* recapitulatory, summary. ◆ **récapitulation** *nf* recapitulation, summing-up.

recauser * [ʀ(ə)koze] (1) *vi*: ~ **de qch** to talk about sth again.

receler [ʀəs(ə)le] (5) *vt objet volé* to receive; *voleur* to harbour; *trésor* to conceal. ◆ **recel** *nm*: ~ **(d'objets volés)** *(action)* receiving stolen goods, receiving; *(résultat)* possession of stolen goods. ◆ **receleur, -euse** *nm, f* receiver.

récemment [ʀesamɑ̃] *adv* recently. **l'as-tu vu ~?** have you seen him lately? *ou* recently?

recenser [ʀ(ə)sɑ̃se] (1) *vt population* to take a census of; *objets* to make an inventory of; *futurs conscrits* to compile a register of. ◆ **recensement** *nm* census; inventory; registration. ◆ **recenseur** *adj m, nm*: **(agent)** ~ census taker.

récent, e [ʀesɑ̃, ɑ̃t] *adj événement* recent; *propriétaire* new.

recentrage [ʀ(ə)sɑ̃tʀaʒ] *nm [parti]* movement towards the centre. **le ~ de notre politique** adopting more centrist policies.

récépissé [ʀesepise] *nm* receipt.

réception [ʀesɛpsjɔ̃] *nf* (**a**) *(gala)* reception. (**b**) *(accueil)* reception, welcome. **discours de ~** welcoming speech. (**c**) *(salon)* reception room; *[hôtel] (hall)* entrance hall, lobby; *(bureau)* reception desk. **salle de ~** function room. (**d**) *[paquet, lettre]* receipt; *(Bio, Rad, TV)* reception. (**e**) *(Sport) [ballon]* trapping, catching; *[sauteur]* landing. (**f**) *(Constr)* ~ **des travaux** acceptance of work done *(after verification)*. ◆ **récepteur, -trice 1** *adj* receiving. **2** *nm (gén, Téléc)* receiver. ◆ **réceptif, -ive** *adj* receptive (*à* to). ◆ **réceptionnaire** *nmf [marchandises]* receiving clerk. ◆ **réceptionner** (1) *vt marchandises* to receive, take delivery of; *ballon* to trap, catch. ◆ **réceptionniste** *nmf* receptionist. ◆ **réceptivité** *nf (gén)* receptivity, receptiveness.

récession [ʀesesjɔ̃] *nf* recession. **de ~** recessionary; ~ **avec inflation** slumpflation. ◆ **récessif, -ive** *adj* recessive.

recette [ʀ(ə)sɛt] *nf* (**a**) *(Culin)* recipe; *(Chim)* formula; *(fig: truc)* formula, recipe (*de* for). (**b**) *(recouvrement)* collection; *(encaisse)* takings. **faire ~** to be a big success, be a winner; *(rentrées d'argent)* **~s** receipts; *(Impôts)* **~-perception** tax office; ~ **municipale** rates office.

recevabilité [ʀəsvabilite] *nf (Jur)* admissibility. ◆ **recevable** *adj* admissible.

receveur, -euse [ʀəsvœʀ, øz] *nm, f (Méd)* recipient. ~ **(d'autobus)** bus conductor (*ou* conductress); ~ **(des contributions)** tax collector *ou* officer; ~ **(des postes)** postmaster (*ou* mistress); ~ **municipal** rate collector.

recevoir [ʀəsvwaʀ] (28) **1** *vt* (**a**) *(gén)* to receive, get; *refus* to meet with. **nous avons bien reçu votre lettre du 15 courant** we acknowledge *ou* confirm receipt of your letter of the 15th instant *ou* of this month; *(Rad, fig)* **je vous reçois 5 sur 5** I'm reading *ou* receiving you loud and clear; **je n'ai d'ordre à ~ de personne** I don't take orders from anyone; **je n'ai pas de leçon à ~ de lui!** I don't need to take any lessons from him!; **il a reçu un coup de pied/de poing** he got kicked/punched; **c'est lui qui a tout reçu** he got the worst of it; **recevez l'expression de mes sentiments distingués** yours faithfully *ou* truly *(US) ou* sincerely. (**b**) *invité (accueillir)* to receive, welcome, greet; *(à dîner)* to entertain; *(pour coucher)* to take in; *(Admin) demandeur* to see. **le docteur reçoit de 10h à 12h** the doctor's surgery *ou* office *(US)* is from 10 a.m. till noon; ~ **la visite de qn** to receive *ou* have a visit from sb. (**c**) *candidat* to pass. **être reçu à un examen** to pass an exam; **il a été reçu premier** he came first. (**d**) *(contenir) [hôtel]* to take, hold, accommodate; *(récolter) [gouttière]* to collect. **2 se ~** *vpr (en sautant)* to land.

rechange [ʀ(ə)ʃɑ̃ʒ] *nm* (**a**) ~ **(de vêtements)** change of clothes. (**b**) **de ~** *solution* alternative; *outil* spare; **j'ai apporté des chaussures de ~** I brought a spare *ou* an extra pair of shoes.

réchapper [ʀeʃape] (1) *vi*: ~ **de** *ou* **à** *accident* to come through.

recharge [ʀ(ə)ʃaʀʒ(ə)] *nf [arme]* reload; *[stylo]* refill. ◆ **rechargeable** *adj* reloadable; refillable; rechargeable. ◆ **rechargement** *nm* reloading; refilling; recharging. ◆ **recharger** (3) *vt véhicule, arme, appareil-photo* to reload; *briquet* to refill; *accumulateur* to recharge.

réchauffer [ʀeʃofe] (1) **1** *vt* (**a**) *(Culin)* **(faire** *ou* **mettre à)** ~ to reheat, heat *ou* warm up again. (**b**) *personne* to warm up; *cœur* to warm; *courage* to revive, rekindle. (**c**) *[soleil]* to heat up, warm up. **2 se ~** *vpr [temps]* to get warmer; *[personne]* to warm o.s. (up). ◆ **réchaud** *nm* stove. ◆ **réchauffé, e** *adj (lit)* reheated, warmed-up; *(péj: fig)* rehashed *(péj)*; *plaisanterie* stale, old hat. ◆ **réchauffement** *nm* warming (up). **un ~ de la température** a rise *ou* an increase in the temperature.

rêche [ʀɛʃ] *adj* rough, harsh.

rechercher [ʀ(ə)ʃɛʀʃe] (1) *vt* (**a**) *objet égaré* to look for, search for, hunt for; *honneurs, danger* to seek; *succès, plaisir* to pursue; *cause d'accident* to look for, try to determine. ~ **comment** to try to find out how; *(Ordin)* ~ **un mot dans un dossier** to search a file for a word; **'on recherche femme de ménage'** 'cleaning lady required'; **recherché pour meurtre** wanted for murder; **la police recherche...** the police want to interview...; ~ **la perfection** to strive for *ou* seek perfection; ~ **l'amitié de qn** to seek sb's friendship. (**b**) *(chercher à nouveau)* to search for *ou* look for again. ◆ **recherche** *nf* (**a**) *(gén)* search (*de* for); *[plaisirs, gloire]* pursuit (*de* of); *[perfection]* quest (*de* for). **se mettre à la ~ de qch** to go in search of sth, look *ou* hunt *ou* search for sth; *(enquête)* **faire des ~s** to make investigations. (**b**) *(Scol, Univ)* **la ~** research; **faire des ~s sur un sujet** to do *ou* carry out research into a subject; **travail de ~** piece of research; ~ **fondamentale** basic research. (**c**) *[tenue, ameublement]* meticulousness, studied elegance; *(péj: affectation)* affectation. (**d**) *(Ordin)* search. ◆ **recherché, e** *adj (très demandé)* in great demand, much sought-after; *(de qualité)* choice, exquisite; *style* mannered; *tenue* meticulous; *(péj)* affected, studied.

rechigner [ʀ(ə)ʃiɲe] (1) *vi* to balk, jib (*à qch* at sth, *à faire* at doing).

rechute [ʀ(ə)ʃyt] *nf (Méd)* relapse. **faire une ~** to have a relapse. ◆ **rechuter** (1) *vi* to have a relapse.

récidive [ʀesidiv] *nf (Jur)* second *ou* subsequent offence *ou* offense *(US)*; *(Méd)* recurrence; *(fig)* repetition. ◆ **récidivant, e** *adj (Méd)* recurring. ◆ **récidiver** (1) *vi (Jur)* to reoffend, commit a second *ou* subsequent offence *ou* offense *(US)*; *(fig)* to do it again; *(Méd)* to recur. ◆ **récidiviste** *nmf* recidivist. ◆ **récidivité** *nf (Méd)* recurring nature.

récif [ʀesif] *nm* reef. ~ **de corail** coral reef ; **~-barrière** barrier reef.

récipient [ʀesipjɑ̃] *nm* container, receptacle.

réciproque [ʀesipʀɔk] **1** *adj* reciprocal. **2** *nf*: **la ~** *(l'inverse)* the opposite, the reverse; *(la pareille)* the same. ◆ **réciprocité** *nf* reciprocity. ◆ **réciproquement** *adv (l'un l'autre)* each other, one another; *(vice versa)* vice versa.

récit [ʀesi] *nm (action, histoire)* account; *(genre)* narrative; *(Théât)* monologue. **faire le ~ de** to give an account of.

récital, *pl* **~s** [ʀesital] *nm* recital.

réciter [ʀesite] (1) *vt* to recite. ◆ **récitation** *nf (poème)* recitation; *(action)* recital.

réclamation [ʀeklamɑsjɔ̃] *nf* complaint. **faire une ~** to make *ou* lodge a complaint; *(Téléc)* **téléphonez aux ~s** ring the engineers.

réclame [ʀeklam] *nf (annonce)* advertisement, advert, ad *. *(publicité)* **la ~** advertising, publicity; **faire de la ~ pour** to advertise *ou* publicize; **article (en) ~** special offer; **~ lumineuse** neon sign.

réclamer [ʀeklame] (1) **1** *vt aide, argent etc* to ask for; *droit, part* to claim; *patience, soin* to call for, require, demand. **~ l'indulgence de qn** to beg *ou* crave sb's indulgence; **je réclame la parole!** I ask *ou* beg to speak!; **il se réclame de l'école romantique** he claims to draw his inspiration from the romantic school. **2** *vi* to complain.

reclasser [ʀ(ə)klɑse] (1) *vt chômeur* to redeploy; *ex-prisonnier* to rehabilitate; *fonctionnaire* to regrade.

reclus, e [ʀəkly, yz] **1** *adj* cloistered. **2** *nm, f* recluse. ◆ **réclusion** *nf*: **~ (criminelle)** imprisonment.

recoiffer [ʀ(ə)kwafe] (1) **1** *vt*: **~ qn** to do sb's hair. **2 se ~** *vpr* to do one's hair.

recoin [ʀəkwɛ̃] *nm (lit)* nook; *(fig)* hidden *ou* innermost recess.

récolter [ʀekɔlte] (1) *vt (Agr)* to harvest, gather (in); *signatures, argent* to collect; (*) *coups* to get, collect *. ◆ **récoltant, e** *nm, f* grower. ◆ **récolte** *nf (action)* harvesting, gathering (in); *(lit, fig: produit)* crop; *[blé]* harvest.

recommander [ʀ(ə)kɔmɑ̃de] (1) **1** *vt* (**a**) *(gén)* to recommend (*à* to). **~ à qn de faire** to recommend *ou* advise sb to do; **il est recommandé de** it's advisable to, you would be well-advised to. (**b**) *lettre (pour attester sa remise)* to record; *(pour assurer sa valeur)* to register. **2 se ~** *vpr*: **se ~ de qn** to give sb's name as a reference; **il se recommande par son talent** his talent commends him. ◆ **recommandable** *adj* commendable. ◆ **recommandation** *nf* recommendation; recording; registration. ◆ **recommandé, e** *adj* (**a**) **envoyer qch en ~** to send sth recorded delivery (*ou* by registered mail). (**b**) *(conseillé)* recommended. **ce n'est pas très ~** it's not very *ou* really advisable, it's not really recommended.

recommencer [ʀ(ə)kɔmɑ̃se] (3) **1** *vt récit, travail* to begin *ou* start (over) again; *erreur* to make again, repeat; *combat* to renew, resume. **2** *vi (gén)* to begin *ou* start again; *[combat]* to start afresh, resume. **~ à** *ou* **de faire** to begin *ou* start to do *ou* doing again. ◆ **recommencement** *nm* new beginning, renewal.

recomparaître [ʀ(ə)kɔ̃paʀɛtʀ(ə)] (57) *vi (Jur)* to appear (in court) again.

récompense [ʀekɔ̃pɑ̃s] *nf* reward; *(prix)* award. **en ~ de** in return for. ◆ **récompenser** (1) *vt* to reward, recompense (*de* for).

recompter [ʀ(ə)kɔ̃te] (1) *vt* to count again, recount.

réconcilier [ʀekɔ̃silje] (7) **1** *vt* to reconcile (*avec* with). **2 se ~** *vpr* to be *ou* become reconciled (*avec* with). **ils se sont réconciliés** they have been reconciled, they have made their peace with one another; **se ~ avec soi-même** to feel *ou* be at peace with o.s. ◆ **réconciliation** *nf* reconciliation.

reconduire [ʀ(ə)kɔ̃dɥiʀ] (38) *vt* (**a**) *politique, bail* to renew. (**b**) **~ qn chez lui** to see *ou* take sb (back) home; **il m'a reconduit à la porte** he showed me to the door. ◆ **reconductible** *adj* renewable. ◆ **reconduction** *nf* renewal.

réconfort [ʀekɔ̃fɔʀ] *nm* comfort. ◆ **réconfortant, e** *adj parole* comforting; *aliment* fortifying. ◆ **réconforter** (1) *vt* to comfort; to fortify.

reconnaître [ʀ(ə)kɔnɛtʀ(ə)] (57) **1** *vt* (**a**) *(gén: identifier)* to recognize. **ces jumeaux sont impossibles à ~** these twins are impossible to tell apart; **on reconnaît un fumeur à ses doigts jaunis** you can tell *ou* recognize *ou* spot a smoker by his stained fingers; **je le reconnais bien là** that's just like him *ou* typical of him, that's him all over! (**b**) *(admettre) (gén)* to recognize; *torts* to admit; *supériorité, dette* to acknowledge. **il faut ~ qu'il faisait très froid** admittedly it was very cold, you must admit it was very cold; **il a reconnu s'être trompé** he admitted *ou* acknowledged making a mistake; *(Jur)* **~ qn coupable** to find sb guilty; **il ne reconnaît à personne le droit d'intervenir** he doesn't recognize in anyone the right to intervene, he doesn't acknowledge that anyone has the right to intervene. (**c**) *terrain* to reconnoitre. **~ les lieux** to see how the land lies, reconnoitre (the ground). **2 se ~** *vpr (dans la glace)* to recognize o.s.; *(entre personnes)* to recognize each other; *(lit, fig: trouver son chemin)* to find one's way about *ou* around. **je ne m'y reconnais plus** I'm completely lost; **je commence à me ~** I'm beginning to find my bearings; **le pêcher se reconnaît à ses fleurs roses** the peach tree is recognizable by its pink flowers, you can tell a peach tree by its pink flowers; **se ~ vaincu** to admit *ou* acknowledge defeat. ◆ **reconnaissable** *adj* recognizable (*à* by, from). ◆ **reconnaissance** *nf* (**a**) *(gratitude)* gratitude, gratefulness (*à qn* to *ou* towards sb). (**b**) *(gén, Pol: fait de reconnaître)* recognition; *(Jur: d'un droit)* recognition, acknowledgement; *(littér: aveu)* acknowledgement, admission. **il lui fit un petit signe de ~** he gave her a little sign of recognition; **il tenait un journal en signe de ~** he was carrying a newspaper so that he could be recognized *ou* identified; **~ de dette** note of hand. (**c**) *(exploration)* reconnaissance, survey; *(Mil)* reconnaissance, recce *. **partir en ~** to make a reconnaissance, go on a recce *; **mission de ~** reconnaissance mission. (**d**) *(Ordin)* recognition. **~ de parole** speech recognition. ◆ **reconnaissant, e** *adj* grateful (*à qn de qch* to sb for sth). **je vous serais ~ de me dire** I would be grateful if you could tell me. ◆ **reconnu, e** *adj* recognized.

reconquérir [ʀ(ə)kɔ̃keʀiʀ] (21) *vt (Mil)* to reconquer; *liberté* to recover, win back. ◆ **reconquête** *nf* reconquest; recovery.

reconsidérer [ʀ(ə)kɔ̃sideʀe] (6) *vt* to reconsider, rethink.

reconstituer [ʀ(ə)kɔ̃stitɥe] (1) *vt parti, texte* to reconstitute; *fortune* to build up again; *édifice* to reconstruct; *faits, puzzle, crime, histoire* to reconstruct, piece together; *(Bio) organisme* to regenerate. ◆ **reconstituant, e 1** *adj* energizing. **2** *nm* energy-giving food, energizer. ◆ **reconstitution** *nf* reconstitution; rebuilding; reconstruction; piecing together; regeneration. **~ historique** reconstruction of history.

reconstruire [ʀ(ə)kɔ̃stʀɥiʀ] (38) *vt* to rebuild, reconstruct. ◆ **reconstruction** *nf* reconstruction.

reconvertir [ʀ(ə)kɔ̃vɛʀtiʀ] (2) **1** *vt usine* to reconvert (*en* to); *personnel* to redeploy. **2 se ~** *vpr [personne]* to move into *ou* turn to a new type of employment. **nous nous sommes reconvertis dans le textile** we have moved (over) into textiles. ◆ **reconversion** *nf* reconversion; redeployment.

recopier [ʀ(ə)kɔpje] (7) *vt* to copy out *ou* write out (again). **~ ses notes au propre** to make a fair copy of one's notes.

record [ʀ(ə)kɔʀ] *nm, adj inv* record. **en un temps ~** in record time. ◆ **recordman** [ʀ(ə)kɔʀdman], *pl* **recordmen** [ʀ(ə)kɔʀdmɛn] *nm* record holder.

recorder [ʀ(ə)kɔʀde] (1) *vt raquette* to restring.

recoucher [ʀ(ə)kuʃe] (1) **1** *vt enfant* to put back to bed. **2 se ~** *vpr* to go back to bed.

recouper [R(ə)kupe] (1) **1** *vt (à nouveau)* to cut again; *(davantage)* to cut more; *route* to intersect; *témoignage* to tie up *ou* match up with. **2 se** ~ *vpr [faits]* to tie *ou* match up; *[chiffres, résultats]* to add up. ◆ **recoupement** *nm* crosscheck. **faire un** ~ to crosscheck.

recourbé, e [R(ə)kuRbe] *adj (gén)* curved; *bec* hooked. **nez** ~ hooknose.

recourir [R(ə)kuRiR] (11) ~ **à** *vt indir moyen, force* to resort to; *personne* to turn to, appeal to. ◆ **recours** *nm* resort, recourse; *(Jur)* appeal. **en dernier** ~ as a last resort; **la situation est sans** ~ there's no solution to the situation; **avoir** ~ **à** *moyen, force* to resort to; *personne* to turn to, appeal to; ~ **en grâce** appeal for mercy.

recouvrer [R(ə)kuvRe] (1) *vt santé* to recover; *liberté* to regain; *cotisation* to collect. ◆ **recouvrement** *nm* recovery; collection.

recouvrir [R(ə)kuvRiR] (18) **1** *vt (gén, fig)* to cover; *(à nouveau)* to re-cover. **recouvert d'eau** covered in *ou* with water; ~ **une casserole** to put a lid on a saucepan. **2 se** ~ *vpr (se superposer)* to overlap.

récréation [RekReɑsjɔ̃] *nf* (**a**) *(lycée)* break; *(école primaire)* playtime, break, recess *(US)*. **aller/être en** ~ to go out for/have one's break. (**b**) *(amusement)* recreation, relaxation.

recréer [R(ə)kRee] (1) *vt* to re-create.

récrier (se) [RekRije] (7) *vpr* to exclaim.

récriminer [RekRimine] (1) *vi* to recriminate (*contre* against). ◆ **récrimination** *nf* recrimination.

récrire [RekRiR] (39) *vt (à nouveau)* to rewrite; *(davantage)* to write again.

recroqueviller (se) [R(ə)kRɔkvije] (1) *vpr [papier]* to shrivel up, curl up; *[personne]* to huddle *ou* curl o.s. up.

recrudescence [R(ə)kRydesɑ̃s] *nf* (fresh) upsurge, new wave *ou* outburst.

recrue [R(ə)kRy] *nf* recruit. ◆ **recrutement** *nm* recruitment. ◆ **recruter** (1) *vt* to recruit. ~ **des cadres pour une entreprise** to headhunt for a company.

rectangle [Rɛktɑ̃gl(ə)] *nm* rectangle. *(TV)* ~ **blanc** 'suitable for adults only' sign. ◆ **rectangulaire** *adj* rectangular.

rectifier [Rɛktifje] (7) *vt (corriger)* to correct; *(ajuster)* to adjust; *erreur* to rectify, put right; *tracé* to straighten. ~ **le tir** *(lit)* to adjust the fire; *(fig)* to adjust one's sights. ◆ **rectificatif** *nm* correction. ◆ **rectification** *nf* rectification; correction.

rectiligne [Rɛktiliɲ] *adj (gén)* straight; *mouvement* rectilinear; *(Géom)* rectilinear.

rectitude [Rɛktityd] *nf (morale)* rectitude; *[ligne]* straightness.

recto [Rɛkto] *nm* front (of a page), first side. ~ **verso** on both sides (of the page).

reçu, e [R(ə)sy] **1** *adj usages* accepted; *candidat* successful. **2** *nm (quittance)* receipt, chit.

recueil [R(ə)kœj] *nm (gén)* book, collection.

recueillir [R(ə)kœjiR] (12) **1** *vt suffrages etc* to get; *graines* to gather, collect; *argent* to collect; *réfugié* to take in; *déposition* to take down, take note of; *opinion* to record. *[orateur, discours]* ~ **de vifs applaudissements** to be enthusiastically *ou* warmly applauded. **2 se** ~ *vpr (Rel, gén)* to collect *ou* gather one's thoughts. **se** ~ **sur la tombe de qn** to meditate at sb's grave. ◆ **recueillement** *nm (Rel, gén)* meditation, contemplation. **écouter avec** ~ to listen reverently. ◆ **recueilli, e** *adj* meditative.

recul [R(ə)kyl] *nm* (**a**) *(lit, fig: retraite)* retreat. **avoir un mouvement de** ~ to recoil, start *ou* shrink back (*par rapport à* from). (**b**) *[maladie]* recession; *[civilisation, valeur boursière]* decline. **être en** ~ *(gén)* to be on the decline; *[monnaie]* to be falling; *[parti]* to be losing ground; *(Pol)* ~ **de la majorité** fall *ou* drop in government support. (**c**) *(éloignement)* distance. **avec le** ~ *(du temps)* with the passing of time; *(dans l'espace)* from a distance, from further away; **prendre du** ~ to stand back (*par rapport à* from); **avec du** ~ with (the benefit of) hindsight; **cette salle n'a pas assez de** ~ there isn't enough room to move back in this room. (**d**) *[arme à feu]* recoil, kick. (**e**) *[échéance]* deferment. (**f**) *[véhicule]* backward movement. ◆ **reculade** *nf* retreat.

reculer [R(ə)kyle] (1) **1** *vi* (**a**) *[personne]* to move *ou* step back; *(par peur)* to draw back, back away; *[automobiliste]* to reverse; *(Mil)* to retreat. ~ **de 2 pas** to take 2 paces back, retreat 2 paces; **faire** ~ *foule* to move *ou* force back; *cheval* to move back; *ennemi* to push *ou* force back. (**b**) *(hésiter)* to shrink back; *(changer d'avis)* to back out. ~ **devant la dépense** to shrink from the expense; **rien ne me fera** ~ I'll stop *ou* stick at nothing, nothing will stop me. (**c**) *(diminuer) (gén)* to decline; *[incendie]* to subside; *[eaux]* to subside, recede, go down. **faire** ~ **l'épidémie** to reduce the epidemic. (**d**) *[arme à feu]* to recoil. **2** *vt meuble, frontière* to push back; *véhicule* to reverse; *date, décision* to defer, postpone; *échéance* to defer. **3 se** ~ *vpr* to step back, retreat. **se** ~ **d'horreur** to draw back *ou* back away in horror. ◆ **reculé, e** *adj époque* remote, distant; *ville* remote, out-of-the-way. ◆ **reculons** *loc adv*: **aller à** ~ to go backwards; **sortir à** ~ **d'une pièce** to back out of a room.

récupérer [RekypeRe] (6) **1** *vt argent, forces* to recover, get back; *ferraille* to salvage; *chiffons* to reprocess; *délinquant* to rehabilitate; *journées de travail* to make up; *(Pol: péj) mouvement* to take over; *(*: prendre)* to get. **regarde si tu peux** ~ **qch dans ces vieux habits** have a look and see if there's anything you can rescue *ou* retrieve from among these old clothes; ~ **son enfant à la sortie de l'école** to pick up *ou* collect one's child when school finishes for the day. **2** *vi [coureur]* to recover, recuperate. ◆ **récupération** *nf* recovery; salvage; reprocessing; rehabilitation; takeover; recuperation.

récurer [RekyRe] (1) *vt* to scour.

récuser [Rekyze] (1) **1** *vt (Jur)* to challenge. *(Jur)* ~ **un argument** to make objection to an argument. **2 se** ~ *vpr* to decline to give an opinion. ◆ **récusable** *adj* challengeable. ◆ **récusation** *nf* challenge.

recycler [R(ə)sikle] (1) **1** *vt élève* to reorientate; *ingénieur (perfectionner)* to send on a refresher course; *(reconvertir)* to retrain; *matière* to recycle. **2 se** ~ *vpr* to retrain; to go on a refresher course. ◆ **recyclable** *adj* recyclable. ◆ **recyclage** *nm* reorientation; retraining; recycling.

rédaction [Redaksjɔ̃] *nf* (**a**) *[contrat]* drafting; *[thèse]* writing; *[dictionnaire]* compilation; *(Jur, Admin)* wording. (**b**) *(Presse) (personnel)* editorial staff; *(bureaux)* editorial offices. (**c**) *(Scol)* essay, composition, theme *(US)*. ◆ **rédacteur, -trice** *nm, f (Presse)* (sub-)editor; *[article]* writer; *[loi]* drafter; *[encyclopédie]* compiler. ~ **en chef** chief editor; ~ **sportif** sportswriter, sports editor.

reddition [Redisjɔ̃] *nf (Mil)* surrender. ~ **sans conditions** unconditional surrender.

redécoupage [Rədekupaʒ] *nm*: **effectuer un** ~ **électoral** to make boundary changes.

redemander [Rədmɑ̃de] (1) *vt adresse* to ask again for; *aliment* to ask for more.

redémarrer [RədemaRe] (1) *vi [économie]* to get going again, take off again. ◆ **redémarrage** *nm [économie]* takeoff, resurgence.

rédemption [ʀedɑ̃psjɔ̃] *nf* redemption. ◆ **rédempteur, -trice** **1** *adj* redemptive, redeeming. **2** *nm, f* redeemer.

redéployer [ʀədeplwaje] (1) *vt effectifs* to redeploy.

redescendre [ʀ(ə)desɑ̃dʀ(ə)] (41) **1** *vt (avec aux avoir) escalier* to go *ou* come (back) down again; *objet* to take downstairs again. **2** *vi (avec aux être) [personne]* to go *ou* come (back) down again; *[ascenseur, chemin]* to go down again; *[baromètre, fièvre]* to fall again.

redevable [ʀədvabl(ə)] *adj*: **être ~ à qn de** *argent* to owe sb; *aide* to be indebted to sb for.

redevance [ʀədvɑ̃s] *nf (gén: impôt)* tax; *(Rad, TV)* licence fee; *(Téléc)* rental charge; *(bail, rente)* dues, fees.

rédhibitoire [ʀedibitwaʀ] *adj défaut* damning.

rediffuser [ʀədifyze] (1) *vt émission* to repeat, rerun. ◆ **rediffusion** *nf* repeat, rerun.

rédiger [ʀediʒe] (3) *vt lettre* to write; *dictionnaire* to compile, write; *contrat* to draw up, draft.

redire [ʀ(ə)diʀ] (37) *vt* to repeat. **~ qch à qn** to say sth to sb again, tell sb sth again, repeat sth to sb; **elle ne se le fait pas ~ deux fois** she doesn't need telling *ou* to be told twice; **trouver à ~ à qch** to find fault with sth; **je ne vois rien à ~ (à cela)** I've no complaint with that, I can't see anything wrong with that.

redite [ʀ(ə)dit] *nf* (needless) repetition.

redondance [ʀ(ə)dɔ̃dɑ̃s] *nf*: **la ~** superfluity. ◆ **redondant, e** superfluous.

redonner [ʀ(ə)dɔne] (1) *vt objet* to give back, return; *confiance, énergie* to restore; *renseignement* to give again; *pain* to give more; *couche, tranche* to give another. **cela te redonnera des forces** that will build your strength back up *ou* put new strength into you.

redoubler [ʀ(ə)duble] (1) **1** *vt joie, douleur* to increase, intensify; *efforts* to step up, redouble. **frapper à coups redoublés** to bang twice as hard; **~ (une classe)** to repeat a year *ou* a grade *(US)*. **2 ~ de** *vt indir*: **~ d'efforts** to step up *ou* redouble one's efforts; **~ de prudence** to be extra *ou* doubly careful; **~ de larmes** to cry even harder. **3** *vi (gén)* to increase, intensify; *[vent]* to become twice as strong; *[cris]* to get even louder *ou* twice as loud. ◆ **redoublant, e** *nm, f* pupil who is repeating a year at school. ◆ **redoublement** *nm* increase (*de* in), intensification (*de* of). **avec un ~ d'attention** with increased attention; *(Scol)* **le ~** repeating a year.

redouter [ʀ(ə)dute] (1) *vt* to dread. ◆ **redoutable** *adj* fearsome, formidable.

redoux [ʀ(ə)du] *nm (temps plus chaud)* spell of milder weather; *(dégel)* thaw.

redresser [ʀ(ə)dʀese] (1) **1** *vt* (**a**) *poteau* to set upright; *tige* to straighten (up); *tôle cabossée* to straighten out; *(Élec) courant* to rectify; *(Opt) image* to straighten; *personne couchée* to sit *ou* prop up. **~ la tête** *(lit)* to hold up *ou* lift one's head; *(être fier)* to hold one's head up high; *(se révolter)* to show signs of rebellion. (**b**) *bateau* to right; *avion, voiture* to straighten up. (**c**) *situation, économie* to redress. **~ le pays** to get *ou* put the country on its feet again. (**d**) *erreur, torts, abus* to right, redress. **2 se ~** *vpr* (**a**) *(se mettre assis)* to sit up; *(se mettre droit)* to stand up straight; *(être fier)* to hold one's head up high. (**b**) *[bateau]* to right itself; *[avion, voiture]* to straighten up; *[économie]* to recover; *[situation]* to correct itself. (**c**) *[cheveux]* to stick up. ◆ **redressement** *nm [économie, situation]* recovery. **~ fiscal** payment of back taxes. ◆ **redresseur** *nm (Élec)* rectifier. **~ de torts** righter of wrongs.

réduire [ʀedɥiʀ] (38) **1** *vt* (**a**) *(diminuer) (gén)* to reduce; *prix* to cut, bring down; *pression* to lessen; *texte* to shorten, cut; *production* to cut (back), lower; *dépenses* to cut down *ou* back (on); *inflation* to curb; *dessin* to scale down; *photographie* to make smaller. **~ petit à petit l'autorité de qn/la portée d'une loi** to chip away at sb's authority/a law. (**b**) **~ à** *(contraindre à)* to reduce to; *(ramener à)* to bring down to, reduce to; *(limiter à)* to limit *ou* confine to; **il en est réduit à mendier** he has been reduced to begging; **~ qch à néant** to reduce sth to nothing. (**c**) **~ en** *poudre etc* to reduce to; **~ qch en morceaux** to smash sth to pieces; **~ qch en bouillie** to crush *ou* reduce sth to (a) pulp; **réduit en cendres** reduced to ashes, burnt to a cinder. (**d**) *(Méd)* to set, reduce; *(Chim)* to reduce. (**e**) *place forte* to capture; *rebelles* to quell. **~ l'opposition** to silence the opposition. **2** *vi (Culin) [sauce]* to reduce. **faire ~** to reduce. **3 se ~** *vpr (financièrement)* to cut down on *ou* reduce one's spending. **se ~ à** *[incident]* to boil down to, amount to; *[somme, quantité]* to amount to; **je me réduirai à quelques exemples** I'll limit *ou* confine myself to a few examples; **se ~ en cendres** to be burnt to a cinder, be reduced to ashes. ◆ **réduction** *nf (gén, Culin, Sci)* reduction; *(diminution)* reduction, cut (*de* in); *(rabais)* discount, reduction; *(Mil) [ville]* capture; *[rebelles]* quelling. *(Comm)* **carte de ~** discount card; **bénéficier d'une carte de ~ dans les transports** to have a concessionary fare *ou* a discount travel card; **un monde en ~** a world in miniature. ◆ **réduit, e** **1** *adj* (**a**) *objet (à petite échelle)* small-scale, scaled-down; *(en miniature)* miniature; *(miniaturisé)* miniaturized. (**b**) *prix, vitesse* reduced; *moyens, débouchés* limited. **livres à prix ~s** cut-price books, books at reduced prices. **2** *nm (pièce)* tiny room; *(péj)* cubbyhole; *(recoin)* recess; *(Mil) [maquisards]* hideout.

rééchelonner [ʀeeʃlɔne] (1) *vt dettes* to recycle. ◆ **rééchelonnement** *nm [dettes]* recycling.

rééditer [ʀeedite] (1) *vt (Typ)* to republish; *(* fig)* to repeat. ◆ **réédition** *nf (Typ)* new edition; *(* fig)* repetition, repeat.

rééduquer [ʀeedyke] (1) *vt (gén)* to reeducate; *délinquant, malade* to rehabilitate. ◆ **rééducation** *nf* re-education; rehabilitation. **centre de ~** rehabilitation centre; **faire de la ~ (fonctionnelle)** to have physiotherapy, have physical therapy *(US)*.

réel, -elle [ʀeɛl] **1** *adj (gén)* real; *plaisir, amélioration* real, genuine; *(Fin) valeur, salaire* real, actual. **faire de ~elles économies** to make genuine *ou* real savings; **taux d'intérêt ~** effective interest rate. **2** *nm*: **le ~** reality. ◆ **réellement** *adv* really.

réélire [ʀeeliʀ] (43) *vt* to re-elect. **ne pas ~ qn** to vote sb out. ◆ **réélection** *nf* re-election. ◆ **rééligible** *adj* re-eligible.

réembaucher [ʀeɑ̃boʃe] (1) *vt* to take on again, re-employ.

rééquilibrer [ʀeekilibʀe] (1) *vt* to restabilize, find a new equilibrium for. ◆ **rééquilibrage** *nm (gén, Pol)* readjustment.

réescompter [ʀeɛskɔ̃te] (1) *vt* to rediscount. ◆ **réescompte** *nm* rediscount.

réévaluer [ʀeevalɥe] (1) *vt monnaie* to revalue; *salaire* to upgrade. ◆ **réévaluation** *nf* revaluation.

réexaminer [ʀeɛgzamine] (1) *vt* to re-examine. ◆ **réexamen** *nm* re-examination.

réexpédier [ʀeɛkspedje] (7) *vt (à l'envoyeur)* to return, send back; *(au destinataire)* to send on, forward.

refaire [ʀ(ə)fɛʀ] (60) **1** *vt* (**a**) *(recommencer) (gén)* to redo, make *ou* do again; *pansement* to renew; *devoir* to rewrite; *nœud* to do up again, tie again, retie. **~ sa vie** to start a new life; **il m'a refait une visite** he paid me another call; **il va falloir ~ de la soupe** we'll have to make some more soup; **son éducation est à ~** he'll have to be re-educated; **si c'était à** ~! if I had to do it again! *ou* begin again! (**b**) *toit* to redo, renew; *meuble, chambre* to do up, renovate. ~ **qch à neuf** to do sth up like new; *(fig)* ~ **ses forces** to recover one's strength. (**c**) *(*: duper)* to take in. **je me suis fait ~ de 5 F** he did me out of 5 francs *. **2 se** ~ *vpr (santé)* to recover; *(argent)* to make up one's losses. **on ne se refait pas!** you can't change your own character!

réfection [ʀefɛksjɔ̃] *nf (action)* repairing; *(résultat)* repairs.

réfectoire [ʀefɛktwaʀ] *nm (Scol)* dining hall, canteen; *(Rel)* refectory; *[usine]* canteen.

référence [ʀefeʀɑ̃s] *nf* (**a**) *(renvoi)* reference; *(en bas de page)* footnote. **par** ~ **à** in reference to; **ouvrage de** ~ reference book; **point de** ~ point of reference; **faire** ~ **à** to refer to, make reference to; *(Fin)* **année de** ~ base year. (**b**) *[employé]* reference, testimonial. *(iro)* **ce n'est pas une** ~ that's no recommendation; **lettre de** ~ letter of reference *ou* testimonial.

référendum [ʀefeʀɛ̃dɔm] *nm* referendum. ◆ **référendaire 1** *adj (pour un référendum)* referendum. **2** *nm:* **(conseiller)** ~ ≃ public auditor.

référer [ʀefeʀe] (6) **1 en** ~ **à** *vt indir*: **en** ~ **à qn** to refer *ou* submit a matter to sb. **2 se** ~ *vpr*: **se** ~ **à** *(consulter)* to consult; *(s'en remettre à)* to refer to.

refermer [ʀ(ə)fɛʀme] (1) **1** *vt* to close *ou* shut again. **2 se** ~ *vpr* to close up. **le piège se referma sur lui** the trap closed *ou* shut on him.

refiler ⁑ [ʀ(ə)file] (1) *vt (gén)* to give; *maladie* to pass on (*à* to); *fausse pièce* to palm off * (*à* on).

réfléchir [ʀefleʃiʀ] (2) **1** *vi* to think (*à* about). **prends le temps de** ~ take time to reflect *ou* to think about it *ou* to consider it; **cela donne à** ~ that makes you think; *(péj)* **sans** ~ thoughtlessly, without thinking; **réfléchissez-y** think about it, think it over. **2** *vt* (**a**) ~ **que** to realize that. (**b**) *lumière, son* to reflect. **3 se** ~ *vpr* to be reflected. ◆ **réfléchi, e** *adj (Gram)* reflexive; *(Opt)* reflected; *action* well thought-out; *personne, air* thoughtful. **tout bien** ~ after careful consideration *ou* thought, having weighed all the pros and cons; **c'est tout** ~ my decision is made, my mind is made up. ◆ **réfléchissant, e** *adj* reflective. ◆ **réflecteur, -trice 1** *adj* reflecting. **2** *nm (gén)* reflector.

reflet [ʀ(ə)flɛ] *nm* (**a**) *(éclat) (gén)* reflection; *[cheveux] (naturel)* light; *(artificiel)* highlight. ~**s du soleil sur la mer** reflection *ou* glint *ou* flash of the sun on the sea. (**b**) *(lit, fig: image)* reflection. **c'est le** ~ **de son père** he's the image of his father. ◆ **refléter** (6) **1** *vt* to reflect. **2 se** ~ *vpr* to be reflected.

réflexe [ʀeflɛks(ə)] **1** *adj* reflex. **2** *nm* reflex. ~ **conditionné** conditioned reflex; **il eut le** ~ **de couper l'électricité** he instinctively switched off the electricity; **manquer de** ~ to be slow to react.

réflexif, -ive [ʀeflɛksif, iv] *adj (Math)* reflexive; *(Psych)* introspective.

réflexion [ʀeflɛksjɔ̃] *nf* (**a**) *(méditation)* thought. **la** ~ reflection; **ceci donne matière à** ~ this gives (you) food for thought; *[offre]* **ceci mérite** ~ this is worth thinking about *ou* considering; **ceci nécessite une** ~ **plus approfondie sur les problèmes** further thought needs to be given to the problems; **avec** ~ thoughtfully; ~ **faite** on reflection, on second thoughts; **à la** ~ when you think about it; *(Pol)* **centre** *ou* **cellule** *ou* **cercle de** ~ think tank. (**b**) *(remarque)* remark, comment, reflection; *(idée)* thought; *(plainte)* complaint. (**c**) *(Phys)* reflection.

refluer [ʀ(ə)flye] (1) *vi [liquide]* to flow back; *[foule]* to pour *ou* surge back; *[sang]* to rush back. ◆ **reflux** *nm [foule]* backward surge; *[marée]* ebb.

refondre [ʀ(ə)fɔ̃dʀ(ə)] (41) *vt cloche, texte* to recast; *système, programme* to overhaul. ◆ **refonte** *nf (gén)* recasting; overhaul; *[enseignement]* restructuring.

réforme [ʀefɔʀm(ə)] *nf* reform; *(Rel)* reformation. **mettre à la** ~ *objets* to scrap; *soldat* to discharge. ◆ **réformateur, -trice 1** *adj* reforming. **2** *nm, f* reformer. ◆ **réformé, e 1** *adj (Rel)* reformed; *(Mil) appelé* declared unfit for service; *soldat* discharged. **2** *nm, f (Rel)* Protestant. ◆ **réformer** (1) **1** *vt loi, mœurs, administration* to reform; *abus* to (put) right; *jugement* to reverse, quash; *(Mil) appelé* to declare unfit for service; *soldat* to discharge; *matériel* to scrap. **2 se** ~ *vpr* to change one's ways, turn over a new leaf. ◆ **réformette** * *nf* so-called reform. ◆ **réformisme** *nm* reformism. ◆ **réformiste** *adj, nmf* reformist.

reformer *vt*, **se** ~ *vpr* [ʀ(ə)fɔʀme] (1) to reform.

refouler [ʀ(ə)fule] (1) *vt envahisseur* to drive back, repulse; *immigrant* to turn back; *larmes, liquide* to force back; *désir, colère* to repress. ◆ **refoulé, e** *adj personne* repressed, frustrated, inhibited. ◆ **refoulement** *nm* driving (*ou* turning *ou* forcing) back; *(Psych: complexe)* repression.

réfractaire [ʀefʀaktɛʀ] **1** *adj* (**a**) ~ **à** *autorité, virus* resistant to; *musique* impervious to; **maladie** ~ stubborn illness; **je suis** ~ **à la poésie** poetry is a closed book to me. (**b**) *métal* refractory; *brique* fire; *plat* ovenproof, heat-resistant. **2** *nm (Mil)* draft evader.

réfracter [ʀefʀakte] (1) *vt* to refract. ◆ **réfraction** *nf* refraction.

refrain [ʀ(ə)fʀɛ̃] *nm* refrain, chorus. **c'est toujours le même** ~ * it's always the same old story; **change de** ~ *! put another record on! *

refréner [ʀ(ə)fʀene] (6) *vt* to curb, (hold in) check.

réfrigérateur [ʀefʀiʒeʀatœʀ] *nm* refrigerator, fridge *. ◆ **réfrigérant, e** *adj fluide* refrigerating; *accueil* icy, frosty. ◆ **réfrigération** *nf* refrigeration; *(Tech)* cooling. ◆ **réfrigérer** (6) *vt (gén)* to refrigerate; *(Tech)* to cool; *enthousiasme* to put a damper on, cool. **je suis réfrigéré** * I'm frozen stiff *.

refroidir [ʀ(ə)fʀwadiʀ] (2) **1** *vt nourriture* to cool (down); *zèle* to cool, put a damper on; *personne (dégoûter)* to put off; (⁑: *tuer)* to do in ⁑, bump off ⁑. **2** *vi* to cool (down); *(devenir trop froid)* to get cold. **faire** ~ to leave to cool, let cool. **3 se** ~ *vpr [ardeur]* to cool (off); *[temps]* to get cooler *ou* colder; *[personne]* to get *ou* catch cold. ◆ **refroidissement** *nm [air, liquide]* cooling; *(Méd)* chill. ~ **de la température** drop in the temperature.

refuge [ʀ(ə)fyʒ] *nm (gén)* refuge; *(pour piétons)* (traffic) island; *(en montagne)* mountain hut *ou* shelter. ◆ **réfugié, e** *adj, nm, f* refugee. ◆ **se réfugier** (7) *vpr (lit, fig)* to take refuge.

refuser [ʀ(ə)fyze] (1) **1** *vt* (**a**) *(gén)* to refuse; *offre* to decline, turn down, reject; *marchandise, routine* to refuse to accept. ~ **de faire** to refuse to do; ~ **le risque** to refuse to take risks; ~ **à qn la permission de faire** to refuse sb permission to do; ~ **l'entrée à qn** to refuse admittance *ou* entry to sb, turn sb away; **je lui refuse toute compétence** I deny him any ability. (**b**) *client* to turn away; *candidat (à un examen)* to fail; *(à un poste)* to turn down. **2 se** ~ *vpr plaisir* to refuse o.s., deny o.s. *(iro)* **tu ne te refuses rien!** you don't let yourself go short! *(iro)*; **ça ne se refuse pas** it is not to be refused, I wouldn't say no (to it); **se** ~ **à** *solution* to refuse (to accept), reject; *commentaire* to refuse to make; **se** ~ **à faire qch** to refuse to do sth. ◆ **refus** *nm* refusal. *(Aut)* ~ **de priorité** refusal to give way; **ce n'est pas de** ~ * I won't say no (to that).

réfuter [ʀefyte] (1) *vt* to refute. ◆ **réfutable** *adj* refutable, which can be disproved *ou* refuted. ◆ **réfutation** *nf* refutation.

regagner [ʀ(ə)gaɲe] (1) *vt amitié* to regain; *argent* to win *ou* get back; *lieu* to get back to. ~ **le temps perdu** to make up for lost time; *(Mil, fig)* ~ **du terrain** to regain ground; ~ **sa place** to regain one's place, return to one's place.

regain [ʀ(ə)gɛ̃] *nm* (**a**) ~ **de** *jeunesse* renewal of; *popularité* revival of. (**b**) *(Agr)* second crop of hay.

régaler [ʀegale] (1) **1** *vt personne* to treat to a delicious meal. **2 se** ~ *vpr (bien manger)* to have a delicious meal; *(fig: profiter)* to make a handsome *ou* fat * profit. **on s'est bien régalé** it was delicious; **se** ~ **de qch** to have a feast on sth. ◆ **régal,** *pl* ~**s** *nm* delight, treat.

regard [ʀ(ə)gaʀ] *nm* (**a**) *(vue)* eye, glance, gaze; *(fixe)* stare. **parcourir qch du** ~ to cast a glance *ou* an eye over sth; **soustraire qch aux** ~**s** to hide sth from sight *ou* view; **cela attire les** ~**s** it catches people's eye *ou* attention. (**b**) *(expression)* look *ou* expression (in one's eye). **dévorer/menacer qn du** ~ to look hungrily/threateningly at sb, fix sb with a hungry/threatening look *ou* stare. (**c**) *(coup d'œil)* look, glance. **échanger des** ~**s d'intelligence** to exchange knowing looks; **lancer un** ~ **de colère à qn** to cast an angry look *ou* glare *ou* glance at sb; **au premier** ~ at first glance *ou* sight; ~ **en coulisse** sideways *ou* sidelong glance; ~ **noir** black look. (**d**) *[égout]* manhole; *[four]* peephole, window. (**e**) **au** ~ **de la loi** in the eyes of the law; **texte avec photos en** ~ text with photos on the opposite page *or* with photos facing; **en** ~ **de ce qu'il gagne** in comparison with what he earns.

regardant, e [ʀ(ə)gaʀdɑ̃, ɑ̃t] *adj* careful with money. **il n'est pas** ~ he's quite free with his money.

regarder [ʀ(ə)gaʀde] (1) **1** *vt* (**a**) *paysage, objet* to look at; *action en déroulement* to watch. ~ **la télévision** to watch television; ~ **le journal** to look at *ou* have a look at the paper; ~ **par la fenêtre** to look out of the window; **regarde où tu marches** * watch *ou* look where you're going; **regarde voir dans l'armoire** have a look in the wardrobe; **regardez-moi ça!** * just (take a) look at that!; **vous ne m'avez pas regardé!** ‡ what do you take me for! *; **regardez-le faire** watch him do it; **elles sont allées** ~ **les vitrines** they've gone to do some window-shopping; **sans** ~ *traverser* without looking; *payer* regardless of the expense. (**b**) *(rapidement)* to glance at; *(longuement)* to gaze at; *(fixement)* to stare at. ~ **(qch) par le trou de la serrure** to peep (at sth) through the keyhole; ~ **de près** to have a close look at; ~ **bouche bée** to gape at; ~ **à la dérobée** to steal a glance at; ~ **qn avec colère** to glare angrily at sb; ~ **qn de travers** to scowl at sb; ~ **qch d'un bon/mauvais œil** to look on sth *ou* view sth favourably/unfavourably; ~ **qn de haut** to give sb a scornful look, look scornfully at sb; *(lit, fig)* ~ **qn/qch en face** to look sb/sth in the face. (**c**) *(vérifier)* to (have a) look at; *essence* to check. ~ **un mot dans le dictionnaire** to look up *ou* check a word in the dictionary. (**d**) *(envisager) problème, avenir* to view. **ne** ~ **que son propre intérêt** to be only concerned with one's own interests; ~ **qn comme un ami** to look upon *ou* regard *ou* consider sb as a friend. (**e**) *(concerner)* to concern. **la suite me regarde** what happens next is my concern *ou* business; **mêlez-vous de ce qui vous regarde** mind your own business. (**f**) *[maison]* ~ **(vers)** to face.
2 ~ **à** *vt indir*: **y** ~ **à deux fois avant de faire qch** to think twice before doing sth; **il n'y regarde pas de si près** he's not that fussy *ou* particular; **à y bien** ~ on thinking it over; **c'est qn qui va** ~ **à 2 F** he's the sort of person who worries about 2 francs; **il ne regarde pas à la dépense** he doesn't worry how much he spends, he spares no expense, expense is no object for him.
3 se ~ *vpr (dans une glace)* to look at o.s.; *(l'un l'autre)* to look at each other *ou* at one another. *(iro)* **il ne s'est pas regardé!** * he should take a look at himself!

régate [ʀegat] *nf*: ~**(s)** regatta.

régence [ʀeʒɑ̃s] *nf* regency.

régénérer [ʀeʒeneʀe] (6) *vt (Bio, Rel)* to regenerate; *personne, forces* to revive, restore.

régent, e [ʀeʒɑ̃, ɑ̃t] *nm, f* regent. ◆ **régenter** (1) *vt (gén)* to rule over; *personne* to dictate to.

reggae [ʀege] *nm* reggae.

régie [ʀeʒi] *nf (Ciné, Théât, TV)* production department; *(Rad, TV: salle de contrôle)* control room. *(compagnie)* ~ **(d'État)** state-owned company, government corporation.

regimber [ʀ(ə)ʒɛ̃be] (1) *vi (gén)* to baulk, jib (*contre* at).

régime [ʀeʒim] *nm* (**a**) *(Pol) (mode)* system (of government); *(gouvernement)* government; *(péj)* régime. (**b**) *(Admin) (système)* scheme, system; *(règlements)* regulations. ~ **de la Sécurité sociale** Social Security system; ~ **(matrimonial)** marriage settlement. (**c**) *(Méd)* diet. **être au** ~ to be on a diet. (**d**) *[moteur]* (engine *ou* running) speed. ~ **de croisière** cruising speed; *(Tech, fig)* **marcher à plein** ~ to go (at) full speed; *(fig)* **à ce** ~ at this rate. (**e**) *(Gram)* object. (**f**) *[dattes, bananes]* bunch.

régiment [ʀeʒimɑ̃] *nm* regiment. **être au** ~ * to be doing (one's) military service.

région [ʀeʒjɔ̃] *nf (gén, fig)* region; *(limitée)* area. ◆ **régional, e,** *mpl* **-aux** *adj* regional. ◆ **régionalisme** *nm* regionalism. ◆ **régionaliste** *adj, nmf* regionalist.

régir [ʀeʒiʀ] (2) *vt (gén, Ling)* to govern.

régisseur [ʀeʒisœʀ] *nm* (**a**) *(Théât)* stage manager; *(Ciné, TV)* assistant director. ~ **de plateau** studio director. (**b**) *[propriété]* steward.

registre [ʀəʒistʀ(ə)] *nm (gén, Ling, Mus)* register. ~ **de l'état civil** register of births, marriages and deaths; *(Scol)* ~ **de notes** mark book, grades register *ou* book *(US)*; *(Scol)* ~ **d'absences** attendance register.

réglage [ʀeglaʒ] *nm* adjustment; *[moteur]* tuning. ◆ **réglable** *adj* adjustable.

règle [ʀɛgl(ə)] *nf (gén, Rel, loi)* rule; *(instrument)* ruler. *(lit, fig)* **c'est la** ~ **du jeu** those are the rules of the game; ~**s de sécurité** safety regulations; ~ **de conduite/de 3** rule of conduct/of 3; ~ **à calculer** slide rule; **avoir pour** ~ **de faire** to make it a rule to do; *(menstruation)* **avoir ses** ~**s** to have one's period(s); **il est de** ~ **qu'on fasse un cadeau** it's usual *ou* it's standard practice *ou* the done thing to give a present; **en** ~ *comptabilité* in order; *réclamation* made according to the rules; **bataille en** ~ proper *ou* right old * fight; **se mettre en** ~ **avec les autorités** to sort out *ou* straighten out one's position with the authorities; **je ne suis pas en** ~ my papers *etc* are not in order; **en** ~ **générale** as a (general) rule; *(hum)* **dans les** ~**s de l'art** according to the rule book.

réglé, e [ʀegle] *adj vie* (well-)ordered, regular; *personne* steady, stable; *papier* ruled, lined.

règlement [ʀɛgləmɑ̃] *nm* (**a**) *(règle)* regulation; *(réglementation)* rules, regulations. *(Scol)* ~ **intérieur** school rules. (**b**) *[conflit, facture]* settlement. ~ **par chèque** payment by cheque; *(fig)* ~ **de compte(s)** settling of scores; *(de gangsters)* gangland killing. ◆ **réglementaire** *adj uniforme* regulation; *procédure* statutory. **dans le temps** ~ in the prescribed time; **ce n'est pas** ~ it doesn't conform to the regulations.

réglementer [ʀɛgləmɑ̃te] (1) *vt* to regulate, control. ◆ **réglementation** *nf (règles)* regulations; *(contrôle)* control, regulation. ~ **des changes** exchange control regulations.

régler [ʀegle] (6) *vt* (**a**) *conflit* to settle; *problème* to settle, sort out. (**b**) *dette* to settle (up), pay; *compte* to settle; *commerçant* to settle up with, pay; *travaux* to settle up for, pay for. ~ **par chèque** to pay by cheque; **j'ai un compte à** ~ **avec lui** I've got a score to settle with him, I've got a bone to pick with him; **on lui a réglé son compte** * they've settled his hash ⁑. (**c**) *débit, machine* to regulate, adjust; *tir, poste de T.V.* to adjust; *moteur* to tune; *thermostat* to set. (**d**) *(fixer) modalités* to settle (on), fix, decide on; *conduite* to determine. ~ **le sort de qn** to decide *ou* determine sb's fate. (**e**) *(imiter)* ~ **qch sur** to model sth on; **se** ~ **sur qn d'autre** to model o.s. on sb else. (**f**) *papier* to rule (lines on).

réglisse [ʀeglis] *nf ou nm* liquorice.

règne [ʀɛɲ] *nm (Pol, fig)* reign; *(Bot, Min, Zool)* kingdom. **sous le** ~ **de Louis XIV** *(période)* in the reign of Louis XIV; *(domination)* under the reign *ou* rule of Louis XIV. ◆ **régnant, e** *adj* reigning; prevailing. ◆ **régner** (6) *vi (Pol, fig)* to reign; *(exercer sa domination)* to rule; *[silence]* to reign; *[confiance, confusion]* to prevail (*sur* over). **faire** ~ **l'ordre** to maintain law and order; **faire** ~ **la terreur** to make terror reign.

regorger [ʀ(ə)gɔʀʒe] (3) *vi*: ~ **de** *[pays]* to abound in, overflow with; *[magasin]* to be packed *ou* crammed with; **le marché regorge de fruits** there is plenty of fruit *ou* there is an abundance of fruit on the market.

régresser [ʀegʀese] (1) *vi [science, enfant]* to regress; *[épidémie]* to recede, diminish, decrease. ◆ **régressif, -ive** *adj* regressive. ◆ **régression** *nf (gén)* regression. **en (voie de)** ~ on the decline *ou* decrease.

regret [ʀ(ə)gʀɛ] *nm [décision, faute]* regret (*de* for); *[passé]* regret (*de* about). **le** ~ **d'avoir échoué** the regret that he had failed *ou* at having failed; **j'ai le** ~ **de vous le dire, c'est avec** ~ **que je vous le dis** I'm sorry *ou* I regret to have to tell you this; **sans** ~ with no regrets; **à** ~ *partir* with regret, regretfully; *donner* with regret, reluctantly. ◆ **regrettable** *adj* regrettable, unfortunate. ◆ **regretter** (1) *vt (gén)* to regret; *(être désolé)* to be sorry; *personne, jeunesse* to miss. **notre regretté président** our late lamented president; **on le regrette beaucoup dans le village** he is greatly *ou* sadly missed in the village; **je ne regrette rien** I have no regrets; **je regrette mon geste** I'm sorry I did that, I regret doing that; **je regrette de ne pas lui avoir écrit** I'm sorry *ou* I regret that I didn't write to him, I regret not writing *ou* not having written to him.

regrouper [ʀ(ə)gʀupe] (1) **1** *vt (gén)* to group *ou* gather together; *(de nouveau) armée* to reassemble; *parti* to regroup; *bétail* to round up. **2 se** ~ *vpr* to gather (together), assemble (*autour de* round, *derrière* behind). ◆ **regroupement** *nm* grouping *ou* gathering together; reassembly; round-up. *(Fin, Jur)* ~**s de sociétés** groupings of companies; ~ **familial** family reunion.

régulariser [ʀegylaʀize] (1) *vt position* to regularize, straighten out, sort out; *passeport* to put in order; *débit* to regulate. ◆ **régularisation** *nf* regularization; straightening out; putting in order; regulation.

régularité [ʀegylaʀite] *nf (V* **régulier***)* regularity; steadiness; evenness. **contester la** ~ **d'une opération** to question the lawfulness *ou* legality of an operation.

régulation [ʀegylɑsjɔ̃] *nf (gén)* regulation; *[circulation, naissances]* control. ◆ **régulateur, -trice 1** *adj* regulating. **2** *nm (Tech, fig)* regulator. ~ **de vitesse/de température** speed/temperature control *ou* regulator.

régulier, -ière [ʀegylje, jɛʀ] **1** *adj* (**a**) *(gén, Mil, Rel)* regular; *élève, qualité, vitesse* steady; *répartition, ligne, paysage* even; *humeur* equable. **à intervalles** ~**s** at regular intervals; **il est** ~ **dans son travail** he's steady in his work; *(Aviat)* **ligne** ~**ière** scheduled service; **vol** ~ scheduled flight; **armée** ~**ière** regular *ou* standing army; **il faut que la pression soit bien** ~**ière** the pressure must be evenly distributed. (**b**) *gouvernement* legitimate; *élection, procédure* in order; *tribunal* legal, official; *opération, homme d'affaires* aboveboard, on the level. **être en situation** ~**ière** to be in line with *ou* straight with the law; **ce n'est pas très** ~ it is not quite on the level *ou* aboveboard; ~ **en affaires** straight *ou* honest in business. **2** *nm (Mil, Rel)* regular. ◆ **régulièrement** *adv* (**a**) regularly; steadily; evenly. **élu** ~ properly elected. (**b**) *(normalement)* normally.

réhabiliter [ʀeabilite] (1) **1** *vt condamné* to rehabilitate; *art* to restore to favour; *mémoire, droits de qn* to restore; *quartier de ville, immeuble* to restore, rehabilitate, give a facelift to. ~ **qn dans ses fonctions** to reinstate sb (in his job). **2 se** ~ *vpr [criminel]* to rehabilitate o.s.; *[candidat etc]* to redeem o.s. ◆ **réhabilitation** *nf* rehabilitation; restoring; reinstatement.

rehausser [ʀəose] (1) *vt mur, plafond* to raise, heighten; *beauté, couleur* to set off, enhance; *goût, détail* to emphasize, bring out; *mérite* to enhance, increase; *tableau, robe* to brighten up, liven up. **rehaussé de** embellished with.

réimprimer [ʀeɛ̃pʀime] (1) *vt* to reprint. ◆ **réimpression** *nf (action)* reprinting; *(livre)* reprint.

Reims [ʀɛ̃s] *n* Rheims.

rein [ʀɛ̃] *nm* (**a**) *(organe)* kidney. ~ **artificiel** kidney machine. (**b**) *(région)* ~**s** small of the back; **avoir mal aux** ~**s** to have backache; *(fig)* **avoir les** ~**s solides** to be on a sound financial footing; *(fig)* **casser les** ~**s à qn** to ruin *ou* break sb.

réincarner (se) [ʀeɛ̃kaʀne] (1) *vpr* to be reincarnated. ◆ **réincarnation** *nf* reincarnation.

reine [ʀɛn] **1** *nf (Échecs, Pol, Zool, fig)* queen. **la** ~ **d'Angleterre** the Queen of England; **la** ~ **Élisabeth** Queen Elizabeth; ~ **de beauté** beauty queen. **2** : ~**-claude** *nf, pl* ~**(s)-**~**s** greengage ; ~**-marguerite** *nf, pl* ~**s-**~**s** (China) aster.

reinette [ʀənɛt] *nf* rennet, pippin. ~ **grise** russet.

réinscrire [ʀeɛ̃skʀiʀ] (39) **1** *vt nom* to put down again; *élève* to re-enrol, reregister. **2 se** ~ *vpr* to re-enrol, reregister. ◆ **réinscription** *nf* re-enrolment, reregistration.

réinsérer [ʀeɛ̃seʀe] (6) *vt publicité* to reinsert; *délinquant* to reintegrate, rehabilitate. **se** ~ **dans la société** to rehabilitate o.s. *ou* become reintegrated in society. ◆ **réinsertion** *nf* reinsertion; reintegration, rehabilitation. **la** ~ **sociale des anciens détenus** the (social) rehabilitation of ex-prisoners.

réinstaller [ʀeɛ̃stale] (1) **1** *vt objet* to put back, reinstall; *(dans ses fonctions)* to reinstate. **2 se** ~ *vpr (dans un fauteuil)* to settle down again (*dans* in); *(dans une maison)* to settle back (*dans* into). ◆ **réinstallation** *nf* putting back; reinstallation; settling back.

réintégrer [ʀeɛ̃tegʀe] (6) *vt* (**a**) *(dans ses fonctions)* to reinstate. (**b**) *lieu* to return to, go back to. ◆ **réintégration** *nf* reinstatement (*dans* in); return (*de* to).

réitérer [ʀeiteʀe] (6) *vt ordre, question* to reiterate, repeat; *exploit* to repeat.

rejaillir [ʀ(ə)ʒajiʀ] (2) *vi [liquide]* to splash back *ou* up (*sur* onto, at). ~ **sur qn** *[scandale]* to rebound on sb; *[gloire]* to be reflected on sb; *[bienfaits]* to fall upon sb.

rejeter [Rəʒte] (4) **1** *vt* (**a**) *(relancer)* to throw back (*à* to). (**b**) *nourriture* to bring *ou* throw up, vomit; *lave* to spew *ou* throw out; *déchets, fumée* to discharge. **cadavre rejeté par la mer** corpse cast up *ou* washed up by the sea. (**c**) *envahisseur* to drive back, repulse; *indésirable* to cast out, expel; *domination, projet de loi* to reject; *offre* to turn down; *hypothèse* to dismiss. **la machine rejette les mauvaises pièces de monnaie** the machine rejects *ou* refuses invalid coins. (**d**) ~ **une faute sur qn/qch** to shift *ou* transfer the blame *ou* responsibility for a mistake onto sb/sth. (**e**) *(placer)* **la préposition est rejetée à la fin** the preposition is put at the end; ~ **en arrière** *tête* to throw *ou* toss back; *cheveux* to push (*ou* comb *ou* brush) back; *épaules* to pull back; *chapeau* to tilt back. (**f**) *(Ordin)* to reject.
2 se ~ *vpr*: **se** ~ **sur qch** to fall back on sth. ◆ **rejet** *nm* (**a**) *(action)* bringing *ou* throwing up *etc*; discharge; repulsion; expulsion; rejection; dismissal. (**b**) *(Bot)* shoot; *(Littérat)* enjambment; *(Méd) [greffe]* rejection. (**c**) *(Ordin)* reject. ◆ **rejeton** *nm (*: enfant)* kid *; *(Bot)* shoot.

rejoindre [R(ə)ʒwɛ̃dR(ə)] (49) **1** *vt* (**a**) *(retrouver) lieu* to get (back) to; *personne* to (re)join, meet (again); *poste* to rejoin, return to. **la route rejoint la voie ferrée à X** the road meets (up with) *ou* (re)joins the railway line at X. (**b**) *(rattraper)* to catch up (with). (**c**) *(se rallier à) parti* to join; *point de vue* to agree with. **mon idée rejoint la vôtre** my idea is closely akin to yours *ou* is very similar to yours. (**d**) *(réunir)* to bring together (again). **2 se** ~ *vpr [routes]* to join, meet; *[idées]* to be similar *ou* closely akin to each other; *[personnes] (pour rendez-vous)* to meet (up) (again); *(sur point de vue)* to agree.

rejouer [R(ə)ʒwe] (1) **1** *vt (gén)* to play again; *match* to replay; *pièce* to perform again. **on rejoue une partie?** shall we have *ou* play another game? **2** *vi* to play again; *[musicien]* to perform again.

réjouir [Reʒwir] (2) **1** *vt* to delight. **ça ne me réjouit pas beaucoup** I don't find it particularly appealing. **2 se** ~ *vpr* to be delighted *ou* thrilled (*de faire* to do, *de qch* about *ou* at sth). **se** ~ **du malheur de qn** to take delight in *ou* rejoice over sb's misfortunes; **je m'en réjouis pour vous** I'm delighted for you; **je me réjouis à l'avance de les voir** I am greatly looking forward to seeing them; **réjouissez-vous!** rejoice! ◆ **réjoui, e** *adj air* joyful, joyous. ◆ **réjouissance** *nf* rejoicing. ~**s** festivities. ◆ **réjouissant, e** *adj histoire* amusing, entertaining; *nouvelle* cheering; *(iro) perspective* delightful, heartening. *(iro)* **c'est** ~! that's great! * *(iro)*.

relâche [R(ə)lɑʃ] **1** *nm ou nf* (**a**) *(littér: répit)* respite, rest. **sans** ~ without a break, non-stop. (**b**) *(Théât)* closure. **faire** ~ to be closed. **2** *nf (Naut)* port of call. **faire** ~ **dans un port** to put in at *ou* call at a port.

relâcher [R(ə)lɑʃe] (1) **1** *vt* (**a**) *étreinte, muscle* to relax; *lien* to loosen, slacken (off); *ressort* to release; *discipline, effort* to relax, slacken. (**b**) *(libérer) prisonnier, otage, gibier* to release, let go, set free. (**c**) *(refaire tomber)* to let go of again. **2** *vi (Naut)* ~ **(dans un port)** to put into port. **3 se** ~ *vpr* (**a**) *[courroie]* to go loose *ou* slack; *[muscle]* to relax. (**b**) *[surveillance, discipline, mœurs]* to become *ou* get lax; *[style]* to become loose; *[attention]* to flag; *[effort, zèle]* to slacken, flag. **ne te relâche pas maintenant!** don't let up *ou* slacken off now!; **il se relâche dans son travail** he's growing lax *ou* slack in his work. ◆ **relâché, e** *adj style* loose; *mœurs* loose, lax; *discipline* lax, slack. ◆ **relâchement** *nm* relaxation; loosening; slackening; release; laxity; flagging. ~ **des mœurs** loosening *ou* slackening of moral standards.

relais [R(ə)lɛ] *nm (Sport)* relay (race); *(Alpinisme)* stance; *(Ind: équipe)* shift; *(Téléc) (action)* relaying; *(dispositif)* relay; *(chevaux)* relay; *(restaurant)* restaurant; *(Hist: auberge)* coaching inn; *(Mil)* staging post. **prendre le** ~ to take over (*de* from); ~ **de télévision** television relay station.

relancer [R(ə)lɑ̃se] (3) *vt ballon* to throw back (again); *idée* to revive, relaunch; *économie* to boost, stimulate; *débiteur* to harass, pester, badger. ◆ **relance** *nf* boosting, stimulation; revival, relaunching. *(résultat)* **la** ~ **de l'économie** the boost (given) to the economy; **mesures/politique de** ~ reflationary measures/policy.

relater [R(ə)late] (1) *vt* to relate, recount.

relatif, -ive [R(ə)latif, iv] **1** *adj (gén)* relative; *silence, luxe* relative, comparative. ~ **à** relative *ou* relating to, connected with. **2** *nm* (**a**) *(Gram)* relative pronoun. (**b**) **avoir le sens du** ~ to have a sense of proportion. **3** *nf (Gram)* relative clause.

relation [R(ə)lɑsjɔ̃] *nf* (**a**) *(gén, Math, Philos)* relation(ship). **c'est sans** ~ **avec** it has no connection with, it bears no relation to. (**b**) *(rapports)* ~**s** *(gén)* relations; ~**s amoureuses** love affair; **avoir de bonnes** ~**s avec qn** to be on good terms with sb, have a good relationship with sb; **être en** ~**s d'affaires avec qn** to have business relations *ou* dealings with sb; ~**s patrons-ouvriers** labour-management relations; **être en** ~**(s) avec qn** to be in touch *ou* contact with sb; **entrer** *ou* **se mettre en** ~**(s) avec qn** to get in touch *ou* make contact with sb; **être dans les** ~**s publiques** to be in public relations. (**c**) *(connaissance)* acquaintance. **avoir des** ~**s** to have (influential) connections. (**d**) *(récit)* account, report. ◆ **relationnel, -elle** *adj grammaire* relational; *(Psych) problèmes* relationship.

relativement [R(ə)lativmɑ̃] *adv* relatively, comparatively. ~ **à** *(par comparaison)* in relation to, compared to; *(concernant)* with regard to, concerning.

relativité [R(ə)lativite] *nf* relativity. ◆ **relativiser** (1) *vt* to relativize.

relaxer [R(ə)lakse] (1) **1** *vt* (**a**) *(acquitter)* to acquit, discharge; *(relâcher)* to release. (**b**) *muscles* to relax. **2 se** ~ *vpr* to relax. ◆ **relaxant, e** *adj* relaxing. ◆ **relaxation** *nf* relaxation. ◆ **relaxe**[1] *nf* acquittal, discharge; release. ◆ **relaxe**[2] * *adj (gén)* relaxed; *tenue* informal, casual.

relayer [R(ə)leje] (8) **1** *vt ouvrier etc* to relieve, take over from; *(Téléc)* to relay. **se faire** ~ to hand over to somebody else. **2 se** ~ *vpr* to take turns (*pour faire* to do); *(Sport)* to take over from one another. ◆ **relayeur, -euse** *nm, f* relay runner.

reléguer [R(ə)lege] (6) *vt* to relegate (*en, à* to). ◆ **relégation** *nf* relegation.

relent [R(ə)lɑ̃] *nm* foul smell, stench. **des** ~**s de** the stench *ou* reek of.

relever [Rəlve] (5) **1** *vt* (**a**) *meuble* to stand up again; *véhicule* to right; *personne* to help (back) up, help (back) to his feet; *blessé* to pick up. *(lit, fig)* ~ **la tête** to raise one's head. (**b**) *(gén)*, *niveau* to raise; *col* to turn up; *chaussettes* to pull up; *jupe* to raise, lift; *manche* to roll up; *vitre (en poussant)* to push up; *(avec manivelle)* to wind up; *siège* to tip up, fold away. ~ **les yeux** to lift *ou* raise one's eyes, look up. (**c**) *mur en ruines* to rebuild; *pays, entreprise* to put back on its feet; *économie* to rebuild, restore. (**d**) *salaire, note* to raise, increase, put up; *niveau de vie* to raise. (**e**) *sauce* to season, add seasoning *ou* spice to; *goût* to bring out. (**f**) *sentinelle* to relieve, take over from. ~ **la garde** to change the guard. (**g**) *(remarquer) (gén)* to find; *faute* to pick out. (**h**) *(inscrire) renseignement* to take down, note (down); *plan* to copy out, sketch; *(Naut) point* to plot; *compteur* to read. ~ **une cote**

to plot an altitude. (**i**) *injure* to react to; *défi* to accept, take up, answer. **je n'ai pas relevé cette insinuation** I ignored this insinuation. (**j**) *(ramasser) copies* to collect (in), take in. (**k**) ~ **qn de** *promesse* to release sb from; *fonctions* to relieve sb of.

2 ~ **de** *vt indir (être du ressort de)* to be a matter for, be the concern of; *(être sous la tutelle de)* to come under. **cette affaire ne relève pas de ma compétence** this matter does not come within my remit; **ça relève de l'imagination la plus fantaisiste** that is a product of the wildest imagination; ~ **de maladie** to recover from *ou* get over an illness.

3 *vi [vêtement]* to pull up, go up.

4 se ~ *vpr* (**a**) *(se remettre debout)* to stand *ou* get up (again), get back (on)to one's feet; *(sortir du lit)* to get up (again). (**b**) *[col]* to turn up; *[strapontin]* to tip up, fold away; *[couvercle]* to lift up. (**c**) *[pays, économie]* to pick up again, recover. **se** ~ **de** *chagrin* to recover from, get over; *ruines* to rise from.

◆ **relève** *nf (gén)* relief; *(troupe)* relief (troops). **la** ~ **de la garde** the changing of the guards; *(lit, fig)* **prendre la** ~ to take over (*de* from). ◆ **relevé, e 1** *adj virage* banked; *sauce* spicy, highly seasoned; *style* elevated, lofty, refined. **chapeau à bords** ~**s** hat with a turned-up brim. **2** *nm [dépenses]* summary, statement; *[cote]* plotting; *[adresses]* list; *[compteur]* reading; *(facture)* bill. ~ **de compte** bank statement; ~ **de notes** marks sheet, grade sheet *(US)*. ◆ **relèvement** *nm [note, prix] (action)* raising, increasing, putting up; *(résultat)* rise, increase (*de* in); *[pays, économie]* recovery (*de* of); *(Naut) [position]* plotting (*de* of). ◆ **releveur** *nm* (gas *ou* electricity *etc*) meter man.

relief [Rəljɛf] *nm* (**a**) *(gén, Art, Géog)* relief. **au** ~ **accidenté** hilly; *(lit, fig)* **manquer de** ~ to be flat; **portrait qui a beaucoup de** ~ portrait which has plenty of depth. (**b**) **en** ~ *motif* in relief; *caractères* raised, embossed; *photographie* three-dimensional; **carte en** ~ relief map; **mettre en** ~ *intelligence, détail* to bring out; *qualités* to set *ou* show off, enhance; *point à débattre* to underline, stress, emphasize; **essayer de se mettre en** ~ to try to draw attention to o.s. *ou* to get o.s. noticed. (**c**) *(†: restes)* ~**s** remains, left-overs.

relier [Rəlje] (7) *vt (gén)* to link (*à* to); *(ensemble)* to link *ou* join up *ou* together; *faits* to connect *ou* link together; *livre* to bind. **livre relié** bound volume, hard-back (book). ◆ **relieur, -euse** *nm, f* (book)binder.

religion [R(ə)liʒjɔ̃] *nf (gén, fig)* religion; *(foi)* (religious) faith; *(vie monastique)* monastic life. **se faire une** ~ **de qch** to make a religion of sth; **entrer en** ~ to take one's vows. ◆ **religieusement** *adv* religiously. ◆ **religieux, -euse 1** *adj (gén)* religious; *art* sacred; *école, mariage, musique* church. **l'habit** ~ the monk's (*ou* nun's) habit. **2** *nm* monk, friar. **3** *nf* (**a**) *(nonne)* nun. (**b**) *(Culin)* iced *ou* frosted *(US)* cream puff *(made with choux pastry)*.

reliquaire [R(ə)likɛR] *nm* reliquary.

reliquat [R(ə)lika] *nm [compte]* balance; *[somme]* remainder.

relique [R(ə)lik] *nf (Rel, fig)* relic. **garder qch comme une** ~ to treasure sth.

relire [R(ə)liR] (43) *vt* to read again, reread. **je n'arrive pas à me** ~ I can't manage to reread *ou* to read back what I've written.

reliure [RəljyR] *nf (couverture)* binding; *(art, action)* (book)binding.

reloger [R(ə)lɔʒe] (3) *vt* to rehouse. ◆ **relogement** *nm* rehousing.

reluire [RəlɥiR] (38) *vi* to shine, gleam; *(sous la pluie)* to glisten. **faire** ~ **qch** to polish *ou* shine sth up, make sth shine. ◆ **reluisant, e** *adj* shining, shiny, gleaming (*de* with). *(iro)* **peu** ~ *avenir, résultat* far from brilliant; *personne* despicable.

reluquer ‡ [R(ə)lyke] (1) *vt* to eye (up) *.

remâcher [R(ə)mɑʃe] (1) *vt [ruminant]* to ruminate; *échec* to ruminate *ou* brood over.

remake [Rimɛk] *nm (Ciné)* remake.

remanger [R(ə)mɑ̃ʒe] (3) **1** *vt (de nouveau)* to have again; *(davantage)* to have *ou* eat some more. **2** *vi* to eat again.

remanier [R(ə)manje] (7) *vt (gén)* to revise; *livre* to reshape, recast; *programme* to reorganize; *ministère* to reshuffle. ◆ **remaniement** *nm* revision; reshaping, recasting; reorganization; reshuffle.

remarcher [R(ə)maRʃe] (1) *vi [personne]* to walk again; *[appareil]* to work again.

remarier *vt*, **se** ~ *vpr* [R(ə)maRje] (7) to remarry. ◆ **remariage** *nm* second marriage, remarriage.

remarquable [R(ə)maRkabl(ə)] *adj personne, exploit* remarkable, outstanding; *fait* striking, noteworthy. ~ **par sa taille** notable for his height ; **elle est** ~ **par son intelligence** she is outstandingly intelligent. ◆ **remarquablement** *adv doué* remarkably, outstandingly; *jouer* remarkably *ou* outstandingly well.

remarque [R(ə)maRk(ə)] *nf (observation)* remark, comment; *(critique)* critical remark; *(annotation)* note. **il m'en a fait la** ~ he remarked *ou* commented on it to me, he made a remark *ou* a comment about it to me.

remarquer [R(ə)maRke] (1) *vt* (**a**) *(apercevoir)* to notice. **sans se faire** ~ unnoticed, without being noticed, without attracting attention; **cette tache se remarque beaucoup/à peine** this stain is quite/hardly noticeable; **sa jalousie se remarque beaucoup** his jealousy is very obvious *ou* noticeable; **ça ne se remarquera pas** no one will notice it; **se faire** ~ to make o.s. conspicuous, draw attention to o.s.; **je remarque que vous avez une cravate** I notice *ou* see *ou* note that you are wearing a tie. (**b**) *(faire une remarque)* to remark, observe, comment. **remarquez (bien) que je n'en sais rien** mark you *ou* mind you I don't know; **faire** ~ *détail, erreur* to point out (*à qn* to sb). ◆ **remarqué, e** *adj entrée, absence* conspicuous. **elle a fait un discours très** ~ she made a speech which attracted considerable attention.

remballer [Rɑ̃bale] (1) *vt* to pack (up) again; *(dans du papier)* to rewrap.

rembarquer *vti*, **se** ~ *vpr* [Rɑ̃baRke] (1) to re-embark.

rembarrer [Rɑ̃baRe] (1) *vt* to rebuff.

remblai [Rɑ̃blɛ] *nm (Rail, pour route)* embankment; *(Constr)* cut. **(terre de)** ~ *(Rail)* ballast; *(pour route)* hard core; *(Constr)* backfill; *(Aut)* ~**s récents** soft verges. ◆ **remblayer** (8) *vt route, voie ferrée* to bank up; *fossé* to fill in *ou* up.

rembobiner [Rɑ̃bɔbine] (1) *vt* to rewind.

remboîter [Rɑ̃bwate] (1) *vt tuyaux* to fit together again; *os* to put back into place.

rembourrer [Rɑ̃buRe] (1) *vt fauteuil* to stuff; *vêtement* to pad. ◆ **rembourrage** *nm* stuffing; padding.

rembourser [Rɑ̃buRse] (1) *vt (gén)* to reimburse, repay, pay back; *dette* to settle; *billet* to refund. **se faire** ~ to get one's money back, get reimbursed; **je veux être remboursé** I want my money back; ~ **qn de ses dépenses** to refund *ou* reimburse sb's expenses; **je te rembourserai demain** I'll pay you back *ou* square up with you tomorrow. ◆ **remboursable** *adj billet* refundable; *emprunt* repayable. ◆ **remboursement** *nm* reimbursement, repayment; settlement; refund. **envoi contre** ~ cash with order.

rembrunir (se) [rɑ̃bʀyniʀ] (2) *vpr [visage]* to darken; *[ciel]* to darken, cloud over.

remède [ʀ(ə)mɛd] *nm (Méd, fig: traitement)* remedy, cure; *(médicament)* medicine. ~ **de bonne femme** old wives' *ou* folk cure *ou* remedy; ~ **universel** cure-all; **porter ~ à qch** to cure *ou* remedy sth; **la situation est sans ~** the situation cannot be remedied *ou* is beyond remedy. ◆ **remédier à** (7) *vt indir maladie* to cure; *situation* to remedy, put right; *difficulté* to solve.

remembrer [ʀ(ə)mɑ̃bʀe] (1) *vt terres* to regroup. ◆ **remembrement** *nm* regrouping of lands.

remémorer (se) [ʀ(ə)memɔʀe] (1) *vpr* to recall, recollect.

remercier [ʀ(ə)mɛʀsje] (7) *vt* (**a**) *(dire merci)* to thank (*de qch* for sth, *d'avoir fait* for doing). **il me remercia d'un sourire** he thanked me with a smile, he smiled his thanks; **je vous remercie** thank you, thanks. (**b**) *(refuser)* **vous voulez boire? — je vous remercie** would you like a drink? — no thank you. (**c**) *employé* to dismiss *(from his job)*. ◆ **remerciement** *nm* (**a**) ~**s** thanks; *(dans un livre)* acknowledgements. (**b**) *(action)* thanking. **lettre de ~** thank-you letter.

remettre [ʀ(ə)mɛtʀ(ə)] (56) **1** *vt* (**a**) *(à nouveau) objet* to put back; *vêtement* to put back on, put on again; *radio, chauffage* to put *ou* turn *ou* switch on again. ~ **un bouton à une veste** to sew *ou* put a button back on a jacket; **je ne veux plus ~ les pieds ici!** I never want to set foot in here again!; ~ **un enfant insolent à sa place** to put an insolent child in his place; ~ **un appareil en marche** to restart a machine, start a machine (up) again, set a machine going again; ~ **le moteur en marche** to start up the engine again; ~ **en question** *autorité* to (call into) question, challenge; *accord* to cast doubt over, throw back into question; ~ **une pendule à l'heure** to put *ou* set a clock right; ~ **qch à neuf** to make sth as good as new again; ~ **qch en état** to repair *ou* mend sth; **le repos l'a remise (sur pied)** the rest has set her back on her feet; ~ **de l'ordre dans qch** to sort sth out. (**b**) *(davantage) chaise* to add; *tricot* to put on another; *sel, argent* to put in some more. ~ **de l'huile dans le moteur** to top up the engine with oil. (**c**) *lettre, rançon, criminel* to hand over; *devoir, clefs* to hand in, give in; *objet prêté ou volé* to return; *récompense* to present; *démission* to hand in, tender (*à* to). **il s'est fait ~ les clefs** he got *ou* had the keys given to him; ~ **un enfant à ses parents** to return a child to his parents; ~ **son sort entre les mains de qn** to put one's fate into sb's hands. (**d**) *réunion* to put off, postpone (*à* until); *date* to put back, postpone (*à* to). **il ne faut jamais ~ au lendemain ce qu'on peut faire le jour même** never put off till tomorrow what you can do today. (**e**) *(se rappeler)* to remember. ~ **qch en mémoire à qn** to remind sb of sth, recall sth to sb. (**f**) *peine, péché* to remit. ~ **une dette à qn** to remit sb's debt, let sb off a debt. (**g**) ~ **ça** * *(démarches)* to go through it all again; *(au café)* to have another drink; *(travail)* to get down to it again; *(bruit)* **les voilà qui remettent ça!** there they go again!, they're at it again! *
2 se ~ *vpr* (**a**) *(recouvrer la santé)* to recover, get better, pick up. **se ~ d'une maladie** to recover from *ou* get over an illness; **remettez-vous!** pull yourself together! (**b**) *(recommencer)* **se ~ à (faire) qch** *(gén)* to start (doing) sth again; *(sport, habitude)* to take up sth again; **il se remet à faire froid** the weather *ou* it is getting *ou* turning cold again; **se ~ debout** to get back to one's feet. (**c**) *(se confier)* **se ~ entre les mains de qn** to put o.s. in sb's hands; **je m'en remets à vous** I'll leave it (up) to you. (**d**) *(se réconcilier)* **se ~ avec qn** to make it up with sb; **ils se sont remis ensemble** they've come back together again.

réminiscence [ʀeminisɑ̃s] *nf* reminiscence. **quelques ~s de** some vague recollections of.

remise [ʀ(ə)miz] **1** *nf* (**a**) *[lettre, rançon, clefs]* delivery; *[rançon, clefs]* handing over; *[récompense]* presentation; *[devoir]* handing in. (**b**) *[péchés, dette]* remission; *[peine]* remission, reduction (*de* of, in). (**c**) *(rabais)* discount, reduction. (**d**) *(local)* shed. (**e**) *(ajournement)* postponement, putting off *ou* back. **2** : ~ **en cause** calling into question; ~ **en état** *[machine]* repair(ing); *[tableau]* restoration; ~ **en jeu** *(Hockey)* face-off; *(Ftbl)* throw-in; ~ **à jour** updating; ~ **en marche** restarting; ~ **en ordre** reordering; ~ **en place** putting back in place; ~ **en question** calling into question.

remiser [ʀ(ə)mize] (1) *vt (ranger)* to put away.

rémission [ʀemisjɔ̃] *nf (gén)* remission. **sans ~** *travailler* unremittingly, relentlessly; *mal* irremediable.

remontage [ʀ(ə)mɔ̃taʒ] *nm [montre]* rewinding, winding up; *[meuble]* reassembly, putting back together.

remontant, e [ʀ(ə)mɔ̃tɑ̃, ɑ̃t] **1** *adj* (**a**) *boisson* invigorating, fortifying. (**b**) *rosier* reflowering, remontant *(T)*; *fraisier* double-cropping *ou* -fruiting. **2** *nm* tonic, pick-me-up *.

remontée [ʀ(ə)mɔ̃te] *nf [côte, rivière]* ascent; *[prix]* rise; *[candidat]* recovery. *(Sport)* ~ **mécanique** ski lift.

remonte-pente, *pl* **remonte-pentes** [ʀ(ə)mɔ̃tpɑ̃t] *nm* ski tow.

remonter [ʀ(ə)mɔ̃te] (1) **1** *vi (avec aux être)* (**a**) *(à nouveau) [personne]* to go *ou* come back up; *[marée]* to come in again; *[prix, baromètre, route]* to rise again, go up again. **il remonta sur la table** he climbed back (up) onto the table; ~ **en voiture** to get back into one's car, get into one's car again; **il est remonté de la 7ᵉ à la 3ᵉ place** he has come up *ou* recovered from 7th to 3rd place. (**b**) *[vêtement]* to go up, pull up. (**c**) *(revenir) [souvenir]* to come back; *[odeur]* to come up. **sous-marin qui remonte en surface** submarine which is coming back up to the surface *ou* which is resurfacing; ~ **jusqu'au coupable** to trace back to the guilty man; ~ **à la source** to go back *ou* return to the source; **aussi loin que remontent ses souvenirs** as far back as he can remember; ~ **dans le temps** to go back in time; **cette histoire remonte à plusieurs années** this story dates back *ou* goes back several years; **tout cela remonte au déluge!** all that's as old as the hills!
2 *vt (avec aux avoir)* (**a**) *étage, côte* to go *ou* climb back up; *rue* to go *ou* come back up. ~ **le courant** *(en barque)* to sail *ou* row (back) upstream; *(fig)* to begin to get back on one's feet again. (**b**) *adversaire* to catch up with. **il a 15 points à ~** he has 15 marks to catch up. (**c**) *mur, jupe, note* to raise; *vitre (en poussant)* to push up; *(avec manivelle)* to wind up; *manche* to roll up; *col* to turn up. (**d**) *(reporter) objet* to take *ou* bring back up. (**e**) *montre* to wind up. *(fig)* **il est remonté à bloc aujourd'hui** he's on top form today. (**f**) *(réinstaller) machine, meuble* to put together again, put back together (again), reassemble; *usine* to set up again. (**g**) *(réassortir) garde-robe* to renew; *magasin* to restock. (**h**) *(remettre en état) personne (physiquement)* to set up (again); *(moralement)* to cheer *ou* buck * up (again); *entreprise* to put *ou* set back on its feet.
3 se ~ *vpr* (**a**) **se ~ en boîtes de conserves** to get in (further) stocks of canned food; **se ~ en chaussures** to get some new shoes. (**b**) *(physiquement)* to set o.s. up (again); *(moralement)* to cheer *ou* buck * o.s. up.

remontoir [ʀ(ə)mɔ̃twaʀ] *nm* winder.

remontrance [ʀ(ə)mɔ̃tʀɑ̃s] *nf* (**a**) remonstrance, reproof, reprimand. **faire des ~s à qn (au sujet**

de qch) to remonstrate with sb (about sth), reprimand sb (for sth). (**b**) *(Hist)* remonstrance.

remontrer [R(ə)mɔ̃tRe] (1) *vt* (**a**) *(de nouveau)* to show again. (**b**) **en ~ à qn: il pourrait t'en ~** he could teach you a thing or two; **il a voulu m'en ~** he wanted to show he knew better than me.

remords [R(ə)mɔR] *nm*: **le ~, les ~** remorse; **avoir un** *ou* **des ~** to feel remorse, be conscience-stricken; **j'ai eu un ~ de conscience** I had second thoughts.

remorque [R(ə)mɔRk(ə)] *nf (véhicule)* trailer; *(câble)* tow-rope, towline. **prendre une voiture en ~** to tow a car; **avoir qn en ~** to have sb in tow; *(lit, fig)* **être à la ~ de** to tag behind. ◆ **remorquer** (1) *vt voiture, bateau* to tow; *train* to pull, haul; *(fig) personne* to have in tow, trail *ou* drag along. ◆ **remorquage** *nm* towing; pulling, hauling. ◆ **remorqueur** *nm* tug(boat).

remous [R(ə)mu] *nm*: **le ~, les ~** *[bateau]* the (back)wash; *[eau]* the swirl, the eddies; *[air]* the eddy; *[foule]* the bustle; *[scandale]* the stir.

rempailler [Rɑ̃pɑje] (1) *vt chaise* to reseat, rebottom *(with straw)*.

rempart [Rɑ̃paR] *nm (Mil, fig)* rampart. **sur les ~s** on the ramparts *ou* battlements; **faire à qn un ~ de son corps** to shield sb with one's (own) body.

remplacer [Rɑ̃plase] (3) *vt (gén)* to replace *(par* with); *objet usagé* to change *(par* for); *directeur à la retraite* to take over from; *professeur malade* to stand in for, substitute for. **se faire ~** to find o.s. a stand-in *ou* replacement; **le miel peut ~ le sucre** honey can be used in place of *ou* as a substitute for sugar. ◆ **remplaçable** *adj* replaceable. ◆ **remplaçant, e** *nm, f (gén)* replacement, substitute; *(Méd)* locum; *(Sport)* reserve; *(pendant un match)* substitute; *(Scol)* supply *ou* substitute *(US)* teacher, stand-in. ◆ **remplacement** *nm* replacement. *(intérim)* **assurer le ~ de qn** to stand in *ou* deputize for sb; **faire des ~s** to do temporary (replacement) work; **en ~ de qch** instead of sth, as a replacement *ou* substitute for sth; **solution de ~** alternative solution, alternative; **produit de ~** substitute (product).

remplir [Rɑ̃pliR] (2) **1** *vt* (**a**) *(gén)* to fill *(de* with); *récipient* to fill (up); *(à nouveau)* to refill; *questionnaire* to fill in. **~ qch à moitié** to half fill sth, fill sth half full. (**b**) *promesse, fonction, condition* to fulfil; *travail* to carry out, do; *contrat, mission* to fulfil, carry out; *rôle* to fill, play; *besoin* to fulfil, meet, satisfy. **~ ses fonctions** to carry out *ou* perform one's duties. **2 se ~** *vpr [récipient, salle]* to fill (up) *(de* with). **se ~ les poches *** to line one's pockets. ◆ **rempli, e** *adj (gén)* full *(de* of), filled *(de* with); *visage* full, plump; *journée, vie* full, busy. **avoir l'estomac bien ~** to have a full stomach, have eaten one's fill; **texte ~ de fautes** text riddled *ou* packed with mistakes. ◆ **remplissage** *nm [tonneau]* filling (up); *[discours]* padding.

remplumer * (se) [Rɑ̃plyme] (1) *vpr (physiquement)* to fill out again; *(financièrement)* to get back on one's feet.

remporter [Rɑ̃pɔRte] (1) *vt* (**a**) *objet* to take away (again), take back. (**b**) *victoire* to win; *prix* to carry off; *succès* to achieve.

remuer [R(ə)mɥe] (1) **1** *vt* (**a**) *tête, bras, lèvres* to move; *oreille* to twitch; *hanches* to sway. **~ la queue** *[vache]* to flick its tail; *[chien]* to wag its tail; *(fig)* **il n'a pas remué le petit doigt** he didn't lift a finger (to help). (**b**) **(faire) ~** *branches* to stir; *objet (déplacer)* to move, shift; *(secouer)* to shake. (**c**) *café, sauce* to stir; *salade* to toss; *terre* to dig *ou* turn over; *souvenirs* to stir up, arouse. **il a remué la sauce/ les braises** he stirred the sauce/poked the fire; **~ de l'argent (à la pelle)** to make a fortune, handle vast amounts of money; **~ ciel et terre pour** to move heaven and earth (in order) to. (**d**) *(émouvoir)* to move. **2** *vi [personne]* to move; *[dent, tuile]* to be loose. **cesse de ~!** keep still!, stop fidgeting! **3 se ~** *vpr* (**a**) *(bouger)* to move; *(se déplacer)* to move about. (**b**) (*: *s'activer)* to bestir o.s., get a move on *. ◆ **remuant, e** *adj* restless. ◆ **remue-ménage** *nm inv (bruit)* commotion; *(activité)* hurly-burly, bustle. **faire du ~** to make a commotion.

rémunérer [Remyneʀe] (6) *vt personne* to remunerate, pay. **~ le travail de qn** to remunerate *ou* pay sb for his work. ◆ **rémunérateur, -trice** *adj emploi* remunerative, lucrative. ◆ **rémunération** *nf* remuneration, payment *(de* for).

renâcler [R(ə)nɑkle] (1) *vi [animal]* to snort; *[personne]* to grumble, show (one's) reluctance. **~ à faire qch** to jib at having to do sth, do sth reluctantly; **faire qch en renâclant** to do sth grudgingly *ou* with (a) bad grace.

renaissance [R(ə)nɛsɑ̃s] **1** *nf (Rel, fig)* rebirth. *(Hist)* **la R~** the Renaissance. **2** *adj inv mobilier* Renaissance.

renaître [R(ə)nɛtR(ə)] (59) *vi* (**a**) *[sentiment, intérêt]* to be revived *(dans* in); *[plante, conflit]* to spring up again; *[difficulté]* to recur, crop up again; *[économie]* to revive, recover; *[sourire]* to return *(sur* to); *[jour]* to dawn, break. **faire ~** to bring back, revive. (**b**) *(revivre)* to come to life again. **~ de ses cendres** to rise from one's ashes; **je me sens ~** I feel as if I've been given a new lease of life; *(littér)* **~ au bonheur** to find happiness again.

rénal, e, *mpl* **-aux** [Renal, o] *adj* renal, kidney.

renard [R(ə)naR] *nm (Zool)* fox. *(fig)* **fin ~** crafty *ou* sly fox *ou* dog. ◆ **renarde** *nf* vixen.

renchérir [Rɑ̃ʃeRiR] (2) *vi* (**a**) *[personne]* to go further. **~ sur ce que qn dit** to add something to what sb says, go further *ou* one better *(péj)* than sb. (**b**) *[prix]* to get dearer *ou* more expensive. ◆ **renchérissement** *nm [marchandises]* rise *ou* increase in the price *(de* of).

rencontre [Rɑ̃kɔ̃tR(ə)] *nf (gén)* meeting; *(imprévue)* encounter; *(Mil)* encounter; *[éléments]* conjunction; *[routes]* junction; *(Athlétisme)* meeting; *(Ftbl etc)* fixture, game. **faire la ~ de qn** to meet sb; **aller à la ~ de qn** to go and meet sb, go to meet sb; **faire une mauvaise ~** to have an unpleasant encounter; **~ au sommet** summit meeting; **~ de boxe** boxing match.

rencontrer [Rɑ̃kɔ̃tRe] (1) **1** *vt* (**a**) *(gén)* to meet; *(par hasard)* to run *ou* bump into; *(en réunion)* to have a meeting with. (**b**) *(trouver) expression, village, passant* to find, come across; *occasion* to meet with; *obstacle* to meet with, encounter, come up against. (**c**) *(heurter)* to strike; *(toucher)* to meet (with). (**d**) *équipe* to meet, play (against); *boxeur* to meet, fight (against). **2 se ~** *vpr* (**a**) *(gén)* to meet; *(en réunion)* to have a meeting; *[équipes]* to meet, play (each other); *[véhicules]* to collide (with each other). (**b**) *(avoir les mêmes idées)* to be at one *(avec* with), be of the same opinion *ou* mind *(avec* as). (**c**) *[coïncidence, curiosité]* to be found.

rendement [Rɑ̃dmɑ̃] *nm [champ]* yield; *[machine, personne]* output; *[entreprise] (productivité)* productivity; *(production)* output *(de* of); *[investissement]* return *(de* on); *(Phys)* efficiency.

rendez-vous [Rɑ̃devu] *nm inv* (**a**) *(rencontre)* appointment; *(d'amoureux)* date. **donner un ~ à qn** to make an appointment with sb, arrange to see *ou* meet sb; **~ spatial** docking (in space); **prendre un ~ chez le coiffeur** to make a hair appointment; **le médecin ne reçoit que sur ~** the doctor only sees patients by appointment. (**b**) *(lieu)* meeting place. **~ de chasse** meet.

rendormir (se) [Rɑ̃dɔRmiR] (16) *vpr* to go back to sleep, fall asleep again.

rendre [ʀɑ̃dʀ(ə)] (41) **1** *vt* (**a**) *objet, argent* to give back, return; *(Scol) devoir* to hand *ou* give in; *réponse* to give. ~ **à qn sa parole** to release sb from a promise, let sb off (his promise); ~ **la liberté à qn** to set sb free, give sb his freedom; ~ **la santé à qn** to restore sb to health; ~ **la vue à qn** to restore sb's sight; *(fig)* ~ **son tablier** to give (in) one's notice; ~ **à César ce qui est à César** to render unto Caesar the things which are Caesar's. (**b**) *justice* to administer, dispense; *jugement* to pronounce, render; *verdict* to return. *(fig)* ~ **justice à qn** to do justice to sb. (**c**) *hospitalité, invitation* to return, repay; *salut, coup* to return. **il m'a joué un sale tour, mais je le lui rendrai** he played a dirty trick on me, but I'll get even with him *ou* I'll pay him back; **il la déteste, et elle le lui rend bien** he hates her and she feels exactly the same (way) about him; ~ **la monnaie à qn** to give sb his change; *(fig)* ~ **à qn la monnaie de sa pièce,** ~ **la pareille à qn** to pay sb back in his own coin; **je lui rendrai la monnaie de sa pièce** I'll be quits *ou* even with him yet. (**d**) (+ *adj*) to make. ~ **qn heureux** *etc* to make sb happy *etc*; **c'est à vous** ~ **fou!** it's enough to drive you mad! (**e**) *expression, traduction* to render. (**f**) *(produire) liquide* to give out; *son* to produce. *(fig)* **l'enquête n'a rien rendu** the inquiry drew a blank *ou* didn't come to anything. (**g**) *(vomir)* to vomit, bring up. (**h**) *(locutions)* ~ **l'âme** *ou* **le dernier soupir** to breathe one's last, give up the ghost; ~ **les armes** to lay down one's arms; ~ **des comptes à qn** to be accountable to sb; ~ **compte de qch à qn** to give sb an account of sth; ~ **gloire à Dieu** to glorify God; ~ **grâces à** to give thanks to; ~ **hommage à** to pay tribute to; *(Sport) [cheval]* ~ **du poids** to have a weight handicap; ~ **service à qn** to be of service *ou* help to sb; ~ **visite à qn** to visit sb, call on sb, pay sb a visit.
2 *vi* (**a**) *[arbres, terre]* to yield, be productive. **la pêche a bien rendu** we have got a good catch (of fish). (**b**) *(vomir)* to be sick, vomit.
3 se ~ *vpr* (**a**) *(céder) [soldat, criminel]* to give o.s. up, surrender. **se** ~ **à l'avis de qn** to bow to sb's opinion; **se** ~ **à l'évidence** to face (the) facts; **se** ~ **aux prières de qn** to give in *ou* yield to sb's pleas. (**b**) *(aller)* **se** ~ **à** to go to; **alors qu'il se rendait à...** as he was on his way to... *ou* going to...; **la police s'est rendue sur les lieux** the police went to *ou* arrived on the scene. (**c**) **se** ~ **compte de qch** to realize sth, be aware of sth; **se** ~ **compte que** to realize that, be aware that; **rendez-vous compte!** just imagine! *ou* think! (**d**) (+ *adj*) to make o.s. **se** ~ **ridicule** to make o.s. ridiculous, make a fool of o.s.

rendu, e [ʀɑ̃dy] **1** *adj* (**a**) *(arrivé)* **être** ~ to have arrived. (**b**) *(remis)* ~ **à domicile** delivered to the house. (**c**) *(fatigué)* exhausted, tired out, worn out. **2** *nm (Comm)* return.

rêne [ʀɛn] *nf* rein. **tenir les ~s du gouvernement** to hold the reins of government, be in the saddle.

renégat, e [ʀənega, at] *nm, f* renegade.

renfermer [ʀɑ̃fɛʀme] (1) **1** *vt* to contain, hold. **2 se** ~ *vpr*: **se** ~ **(en soi-même)** to withdraw (into o.s.). ◆ **renfermé, e 1** *adj* withdrawn, uncommunicative. **2** *nm*: **odeur de** ~ fusty *ou* stale smell.

renflé, e [ʀɑ̃fle] *adj* bulging. ◆ **renflement** *nm* bulge.

renflouer [ʀɑ̃flue] (1) *vt entreprise, bateau* to refloat; *personne* to set back on his feet again, bail out.

renfoncement [ʀɑ̃fɔ̃smɑ̃] *nm* recess.

renforcer [ʀɑ̃fɔʀse] (3) **1** *vt objet, argument, équipe* to reinforce; *paix* to consolidate; *effort* to add to, intensify; *position, amitié* to strengthen. ~ **qn dans une opinion** to confirm sb in an opinion. **2 se** ~ *vpr [craintes, amitié]* to strengthen; *[pression]* to intensify.

renfort [ʀɑ̃fɔʀ] *nm* (**a**) *(Mil)* ~**s** *(hommes)* reinforcements; *(matériel)* (further) supplies. (**b**) *(Tech)* reinforcement, strengthening piece. (**c**) **de** ~ *barre, toile* strengthening; *armée* back-up, supporting; *personnel* extra, additional; **envoyer qn en** ~ to send sb as an extra; **à grand** ~ **de gestes** accompanied by a great many gestures.

renfrogner (se) [ʀɑ̃fʀɔɲe] (1) *vpr* to scowl. ◆ **renfrogné, e** *adj* sullen, sulky.

rengager [ʀɑ̃gaʒe] (3) **1** *vt discussion* to start up again; *fonds* to reinvest; *combat, ouvrier* to re-engage. **2 se** ~ *vpr (Mil)* to join up again, re-enlist.

rengaine [ʀɑ̃gɛn] *nf*: **(vieille)** ~ (old) folk song; **c'est toujours la même** ~ * it's always the same old song *.

rengainer [ʀɑ̃gene] (1) *vt épée* to sheathe, put up; *revolver* to put back in its holster; (*) *compliment* to save, withhold.

rengorger (se) [ʀɑ̃gɔʀʒe] (3) *vpr [oiseau]* to puff out its throat; *[personne]* to puff o.s. up.

renier [ʀənje] (7) **1** *vt foi, Dieu* to renounce; *signature* to disown, repudiate; *promesse* to go back on, break. **2 se** ~ *vpr* to go back on what one has said *ou* done. ◆ **reniement** *nm* renunciation; disowning, repudiation; breaking.

renifler [ʀ(ə)nifle] (1) **1** *vt* to sniff (at). **2** *vi [personne]* to sniff; *[cheval]* to snort. ◆ **reniflement** *nm (action)* sniffing; *(bruit)* sniff.

renne [ʀɛn] *nm* reindeer.

renom [ʀ(ə)nɔ̃] *nm (notoriété)* renown, repute, fame; *(réputation)* reputation. **de grand** ~, **en** ~ renowned, famous; **avoir du** ~ to be famous *ou* renowned. ◆ **renommé, e**[1] *adj* celebrated, renowned, famous. ~ **pour** renowned *ou* famed for. ◆ **renommée**[2] *nf* (**a**) *(célébrité)* fame, renown. **de** ~ **mondiale** world-famous. (**b**) *(opinion publique)* public report. (**c**) *(réputation)* reputation. **bonne/mauvaise** ~ good/bad reputation *ou* name.

renoncer [ʀ(ə)nɔ̃se] (3) ~ **à** *vt indir (gén)* to give up, renounce. ~ **à qn** to give sb up; **je** *ou* **j'y renonce** I give up. ◆ **renoncement** *nm* renunciation. ◆ **renonciation** *nf* giving up, renunciation.

renouer [ʀənwe] (1) **1** *vt lacet* to tie (up) again, re-tie; *conversation* to renew. **2** *vi*: ~ **avec** *habitude* to take up again; ~ **avec qn** to take up with sb again.

renouveau, *pl* **~x** [ʀ(ə)nuvo] *nm (transformation)* revival. *(regain)* ~ **de succès/faveur** renewed success/favour.

renouveler [ʀ(ə)nuvle] (4) **1** *vt (gén)* to renew; *stock* to replenish; *conseil d'administration* to re-elect; *congé* to re-grant; *offre, exploit, erreur* to repeat; *douleur, théorie* to revive. ~ **l'air d'une salle** to air a room; **cette découverte a complètement renouvelé notre vision des choses** this discovery has given us a whole new insight into things *ou* has cast a whole new light on things for us; ~ **sa confiance à qn** to reassert one's confidence in sb. **2 se** ~ *vpr (se répéter) [erreur, fait]* to recur, be repeated; *(être remplacé) [personnel]* to be renewed; *(innover) [auteur]* to try sth new. ◆ **renouvelable** *adj passeport* renewable; *assemblée* that must be re-elected. ◆ **renouvellement** *nm* renewal; replenishment; repetition; revival; recurrence. *(Pol)* **solliciter le** ~ **de son mandat** to stand *ou* run for re-election.

rénover [ʀenɔve] (1) *vt maison* to renovate, modernize; *quartier* to redevelop, renovate; *meuble* to restore; *institutions, méthodes* to reform, regenerate; *science* to renew. ◆ **rénovateur, -trice** *adj, nm, f*: **être** ~ to have a reforming *ou* regenerative influence. ◆ **rénovation** *nf* renovation, modernization; redevelopment; restoration; reform; renewal.

renseignement [rɑ̃sɛɲmɑ̃] *nm*: **~(s)** information; **un ~ intéressant** an interesting piece of information, some interesting information; **demander des ~s sur qn** to make inquiries *ou* ask for information *ou* for particulars about sb; **avoir de bons ~s sur qn** to have good reports about *ou* on sb; **pourriez-vous me donner un ~?** could you give me some information?, could you tell me something?; **veuillez m'envoyer de plus amples ~s sur...** please send me further details of... *ou* further information about...; **'~s'** *(panneau)* 'inquiries', 'information'; *(Téléc)* directory inquiries, information *(US)*. (**b**) *(Mil)* **~(s)** intelligence; **agent de ~s** intelligence agent; **travailler dans le ~** to work in intelligence.

renseigner [rɑ̃seɲe] (1) **1** *vt* to give information to. **qui pourrait me ~ sur lui?** who could tell me sth about him?, who could give me some information *ou* particulars about him?; **il a l'air bien renseigné** he seems to be well informed; **on vous a mal renseigné** you have been misinformed. **2 se ~** *vpr* to make inquiries, ask for information *ou* particulars (*sur* about). **je vais me ~ auprès de lui** I'll ask him about it; **j'essaierai de me ~** I'll try to find out.

rentable [rɑ̃tabl(ə)] *adj* profitable. **c'est très ~** it really pays; *(fig)* **ce n'est plus du tout ~** it has become a losing proposition, it is no longer financially viable. ◆ **rentabilisation** *nf [ligne aérienne]* making profitable. **la ~ d'une invention** the marketing *ou* commercializing of an invention. ◆ **rentabilité** *nf* profitability. **~ des investissements** return on investments.

rente [rɑ̃t] *nf (pension)* annuity, pension; *(fournie par la famille)* allowance; *(emprunt d'État)* government stock *ou* bond. **avoir des ~s** to have a private income, have private *ou* independent means. ◆ **rentier, -ière** *nm, f* person of independent *ou* private means.

rentrant, e [rɑ̃trɑ̃, ɑ̃t] *adj train d'atterrissage* retractable; *(Math) angle* reflex.

rentrée [rɑ̃tre] *nf* (**a**) **~ (scolaire)** start of the new school year; *(Univ)* start of the new academic year; *(du trimestre)* start of the new (school *ou* university) term; **la ~ aura lieu lundi** the new term begins on Monday, school starts again on Monday; **la ~ s'est bien passée** the term began well; *(Comm)* **'les affaires de la ~'** 'back-to-school bargains'; **à la ~ de Noël** at the start of (the) term after the Christmas holidays. (**b**) *[tribunaux]* reopening; *[parlement]* reassembly; *[députés]* return. **c'est la ~ des théâtres parisiens** it's the start of the theatrical season in Paris; *(après les vacances)* **faire sa ~ politique** to start the new political season, begin one's autumn campaign; **la mode de la ~** the autumn fashions; **on verra ça à la ~** we'll see about that after the holidays. (**c**) *[acteur, sportif]* comeback. **faire sa ~ politique** to make a political comeback. (**d**) *(retour)* return. **à l'heure des ~s dans Paris** when everyone is coming back into Paris *ou* returning to Paris; *(Espace)* **~ dans l'atmosphère** re-entry into the atmosphere; **effectuer sa ~ dans l'atmosphère** to re-enter the atmosphere. (**e**) *(Comm)* **~s** income; **~ d'argent** (incoming) sum of money.

rentrer [rɑ̃tre] (1) **1** *vi (avec aux être)* (**a**) *(à nouveau) (aller)* to go back in; *(venir)* to come back in. **~ (chez soi)** to return home, go (*ou* get *ou* come) back home; **est-ce qu'il est rentré?** is he (back) home?; **~ à Paris/de Paris** to go back *ou* come back *ou* return to Paris/from Paris; **je rentre en voiture** I'm driving back, I'm going back by car. (**b**) *(reprendre ses activités) [élèves]* to go back to school, start school again; *[université]* to start again; *[tribunaux]* to reopen; *[parlement]* to reassemble; *[députés]* to return. **le trimestre prochain, on rentrera un lundi** next term we start on a Monday. (**c**) *(entrer) [personne]* to go in; to come in; *[chose]* to go in. **nous sommes rentrés dans un café** we went into a café; **cette clef ne rentre pas dans la serrure** this key doesn't fit (into) the lock. (**d**) **~ dans** *(travailler dans)* to join, go into; *(s'écraser contre)* to crash into, collide with; *(être compris dans)* to be included in, be part of; **il l'a fait ~ dans la firme** he helped him to get a job in the firm; **furieux, il lui est rentré dedans ‡** he was furious and he pitched * *ou* laid * into him; **~ dans une catégorie** to fall into *ou* come into a category. (**e**) *[argent]* to come in. **faire ~ l'argent** to get the money in. (**f**) (*) *[connaissances]* **les maths, ça ne rentre pas** he can't take maths in, he can't get the hang of maths *; **faire ~ qch dans la tête de qn** to drum *ou* get sth into sb's head. (**g**) *(locutions)* **~ dans sa coquille** to go back into one's shell; **~ dans son argent** to recover *ou* get back one's money; **~ dans ses fonds** to recoup one's costs; **tout est rentré dans l'ordre** *(dans son état normal)* everything is back to normal again; *(dans le calme)* order has been restored; *(tout a été clarifié)* everything is sorted out now; **~ dans le rang** to come *ou* fall back into line; **~ en grâce auprès de qn** to get back into sb's good graces; **j'aurais voulu ~ sous terre** I wished the ground could have opened and swallowed me up.

2 *vt (avec aux avoir)* (**a**) *foins, marchandises, animaux* to bring in. **~ sa voiture au garage** to put the car away in the garage. (**b**) *train d'atterrissage* to raise; *(lit, fig) griffes* to draw in. **~ sa chemise (dans son pantalon)** to tuck one's shirt in (one's trousers); **ne me rentre pas ton coude dans le ventre** don't jab *ou* stick your elbow in(to) my stomach; **~ le ventre** to pull one's stomach in; **~ sa rage** to hold back *ou* suppress one's anger.

renverser [rɑ̃vɛrse] (1) **1** *vt* (**a**) *(faire tomber) personne* to knock over *ou* down; *objet* to knock over, upset, overturn; *liquide* to spill, upset; *grains* to scatter. (**b**) *(mettre à l'envers)* to turn upside down. (**c**) *(abattre) obstacles (lit)* to knock down; *(fig)* to overcome; *ordre établi, royauté* to overthrow. **~ le gouvernement** *(coup d'État)* to overthrow *ou* overturn the government; *(vote)* to defeat the government. (**d**) **~ la tête en arrière** to tip *ou* tilt one's head back; **~ le corps en arrière** to lean back. (**e**) *(inverser) ordre des mots, courant* to reverse; *(Opt) image* to invert, reverse. **~ la situation** to reverse the situation, turn things (a)round; **~ la vapeur** *(lit)* to reverse steam; *(fig)* to change course. (**f**) (*: *étonner*) to bowl over, stagger. **2 se ~** *vpr* (**a**) **se ~ en arrière** to lean back. (**b**) *[voiture]* to overturn; *[bateau]* to overturn, capsize; *[vase]* to fall over, be overturned. ◆ **renversant, e** * *adj nouvelle* staggering, astounding; *personne* amazing, incredible. ◆ **renverse** *nf*: **tomber à la ~** to fall backwards. ◆ **renversement** *nm [ordre des mots]* inversion, reversal; *[situation, valeurs]* reversal; *(Pol) (par un coup d'État)* overthrow; *(par vote)* defeat. **un ~ de tendance de l'opinion publique** a shift *ou* swing (in the opposite direction) in public opinion.

renvoi [rɑ̃vwa] *nm* (**a**) (*V* **renvoyer**) dismissal; sacking; expulsion; suspension; return; discharge; referral; postponement. (**b**) *(référence)* cross-reference; *(en bas de page)* footnote. (**c**) *(rot)* belch. **ça me donne des ~s** it gives me wind, it makes me belch.

renvoyer [rɑ̃vwaje] (8) *vt* (**a**) *(congédier) employé* to dismiss, sack; *élève (définitivement)* to expel; *(temporairement)* to suspend. **se faire ~** to be dismissed (*ou* expelled). (**b**) *lettre, ballon, personne* to send back; *cadeau* to return. **~ les soldats dans**

leurs foyers to discharge soldiers, send soldiers back home; ~ **la balle** *(Sport)* to return the ball; **il m'a renvoyé la balle** *(argument)* he threw the *ou* my argument back at me; *(responsabilité)* he tried to pass the buck (to me) *; *(fig)* ~ **l'ascenseur** to return a favour. (**c**) *(référer) lecteur* to refer (*à* to). (**d**) *(différer) rendez-vous* to postpone, put off (*à plus tard* until later). *(Jur)* **l'affaire a été renvoyée à huitaine** the case was postponed *ou* deferred for a week. (**e**) *(réfléchir) son* to echo; *lumière, chaleur, image* to reflect.

réorganiser [ReɔRganize] (1) **1** *vt* to reorganize. **2 se** ~ *vpr [pays, parti]* to be reorganized. ◆ **réorganisation** *nf* reorganization.

réouverture [ReuvɛRtyR] *nf* reopening.

repaire [R(ə)pɛR] *nm (Zool)* den, lair; *(fig)* den, hideout. ~ **de brigands** thieves' den.

repaître (se) [RəpɛtR(ə)] (57) *vpr*: **se** ~ **de** *aliments* to gorge o.s. on; *lectures* to revel in.

répandre [Repɑ̃dR(ə)] (41) **1** *vt* (**a**) *(accidentellement) liquide* to spill; *grains* to scatter. (**b**) *(gén, fig) (volontairement)* to spread; *dons* to lavish; *sang, larmes, lumière* to shed; *odeur* to give off; *chaleur, fumée* to give out. **2 se** ~ *vpr [liquide]* to spill, be spilled; *[grains]* to scatter, be scattered; *[odeur, lumière, doctrine]* to spread (*sur* over); *[son]* to carry (*dans* through); *[opinion, méthode]* to become widespread (*dans* among); *[coutume, pratique]* to take hold, become widespread. **la foule se répand dans les rues** the crowd spills out *ou* pours out into the streets; **la nouvelle se répandit comme une traînée de poudre** the news spread like wildfire; **se** ~ **en menaces** *etc* to pour out threats *etc*. ◆ **répandu, e** *adj opinion* widespread. **idée très ~e** widely held *ou* widespread idea.

reparaître [R(ə)paRɛtR(ə)] (57) *vi* to reappear.

réparer [RepaRe] (1) *vt* (**a**) *(remettre en état) (gén)* to mend, repair, fix; *forces, santé* to restore. *(lit, fig)* ~ **les dégâts** to repair the damage; **faire** ~ **qch** to get *ou* have sth mended *ou* repaired; ~ **qch sommairement** to patch sth up. (**b**) *(corriger) erreur, négligence* to put right. (**c**) *(compenser) faute* to make up for, make amends for; *perte* to make good, make up for, compensate for. ◆ **réparable** *adj objet* repairable, which can be repaired; *erreur* which can be put right. ◆ **réparateur, -trice 1** *adj sommeil* refreshing. **2** *nm, f* repairer. ~ **de télévision** television repairman *ou* engineer. ◆ **réparation** *nf* (**a**) *(remise en état)* mending, repairing, fixing; restoration; *(résultat)* repair. **en** ~ under repair; **faire des ~s** to do some repairs; **l'atelier de** ~ the repair shop. (**b**) *(correction)* putting right. (**c**) *(compensation)* compensation (*de* for). **en** ~ **du dommage** to make up for *ou* to compensate for the harm; **obtenir** ~ **(d'un affront)** to obtain redress (for an insult). (**d**) *(dommages-intérêts)* damages, compensation. *(Hist)* **~s** reparations.

reparler [R(ə)paRle] (1) *vi*: ~ **de qch** to talk about sth again; ~ **à qn** to speak to sb again.

repartie [RəpaRti] *nf* retort. **avoir de la** ~ to be good *ou* quick at repartee.

repartir [R(ə)paRtiR] (16) *vi [voyageur]* to set off *ou* leave again; *[machine]* to start (up) again; *[affaire, discussion]* to get going again. ~ **chez soi** to go back home; ~ **à zéro** to start from scratch again; *[discussion]* **c'est reparti!** * they're off again! *

répartir [RepaRtiR] (2) **1** *vt* (**a**) *(diviser) somme, travail* to share out, divide up (*en* into, *entre* among), distribute (*entre* among). ~ **les joueurs en 2 groupes** to divide *ou* split (up) the players into 2 groups. (**b**) *(égaliser) masses, chaleur* to distribute; *(étaler) paiement, horaire* to spread (*sur* over). **les troupes sont réparties le long de la frontière** troops are spread out *ou* distributed *ou* scattered along the frontier. **2 se** ~ *vpr (se diviser)* to be divided (up); *(s'égaliser)* to be distributed. **se** ~ **le travail** to share out the work (among themselves *ou* ourselves *etc*). ◆ **répartition** *nf (action)* sharing out, division, distribution; spreading; *(résultat)* distribution.

repas [R(ə)pɑ] *nm* meal. ~ **léger** light meal, snack; ~ **scolaire** school lunch; ~ **de noces** wedding breakfast; **aux heures des** ~ at mealtimes; **panier-**~ picnic basket; **plateau-**~ meal tray; **ticket-**~ luncheon voucher, meal ticket *(surtout US)*.

repasser [R(ə)pɑse] (1) **1** *vt* (**a**) *frontière* to cross again; *examen* to resit, take again; *film* to show again. ~ **un plat au four** to put a dish in the oven again *ou* back in the oven. (**b**) *(au fer)* to iron. **ça ne se repasse pas** it doesn't need ironing; **planche à** ~ ironing board. (**c**) *couteau, lame* to sharpen (up). (**d**) *leçon* to go (back) over, go over again (*dans son esprit* in one's mind). (**e**) *(*: transmettre) affaire* to hand over *ou* on; *maladie* to pass on (*à qn* to sb). *(au téléphone)* **je te repasse ta mère** I'm handing you back to your mother. **2** *vi (dans un endroit)* to come back, go back; *(devant un même lieu)* to go *ou* come past again; *(sur un même trait)* to go over again, go back over. **tu peux toujours** ~ ‡ nothing doing ‡, you've got a hope *. ◆ **repassage** *nm [linge]* ironing; *[couteau]* sharpening. *(sur une étiquette)* ~ **superflu** wash-and-wear, non-iron.

repayer [R(ə)peje] (8) *vt* to pay again.

repêcher [R(ə)peʃe] (1) *vt* (**a**) *corps* to recover, fish out. (**b**) *(Scol) candidat* to let through, pass *(with less than the official pass mark)*; *athlète* to give a second chance to. ◆ **repêchage** *nm* recovery, fishing out; passing. **question de** ~ question to give candidates a second chance.

repeindre [R(ə)pɛ̃dR(ə)] (52) *vt* to repaint.

repenser [R(ə)pɑ̃se] (1) **1** ~ **à** *vt indir:* ~ **à qch** to think about sth again. **2** *vt concept* to rethink; *question* to rethink, think out again.

repentir[1] (se) [R(ə)pɑ̃tiR] (16) *vpr (Rel)* to repent. **se** ~ **de qch/d'avoir fait qch** to regret sth/having done sth, be sorry for sth/for having done sth; *(Rel)* to repent of sth/of having done sth. ◆ **repentant, e** *ou* **repenti, e** *adj* repentant, penitent. ◆ **repentir[2]** *nm (Rel)* repentance; *(regret)* regret.

répercuter [RepɛRkyte] (1) **1** *vt son* to echo; *écho* to send *ou* throw back; *lumière* to reflect. ~ **une augmentation sur le client** to pass an increase in cost on to the customer. **2 se** ~ *vpr [son]* to reverberate, echo; *[lumière]* to be reflected, reflect. *(fig)* **se** ~ **sur** to have repercussions on. ◆ **répercussion** *nf (gén)* repercussion (*sur, dans* on).

repérer [R(ə)peRe] (6) **1** *vt (Mil)* to locate; (*) *personne, erreur* to spot, pick out; *coin tranquille* to discover, locate, find. **se faire** ~ to be spotted, be picked out. **2 se** ~ *vpr (se diriger)* to find one's way about *ou* around; *(lit, fig: savoir où l'on est)* to find *ou* get one's bearings. ◆ **repérable** *adj* which can be spotted. ◆ **repérage** *nm (Aviat, Mil)* location. **le** ~ **d'un point sur la carte** locating a point on the map. ◆ **repère** *nm (marque)* line, mark; *(jalon)* marker, indicator; *(monument etc)* landmark; *(événement)* landmark; *(date)* reference point.

répertoire [RepɛRtwaR] *nm* (**a**) *(carnet)* index notebook; *(liste)* (alphabetical) list; *(catalogue)* catalogue. ~ **des rues** street index. (**b**) *(Théât)* repertoire, repertory; *[chanteur] (fig)* repertoire. **pièce du** ~ stock play.

répertorier [RepɛRtɔRje] (7) *vt* to itemize, list.

répéter [Repete] (6) **1** *vt* (**a**) *parole, essai etc* to repeat. **je l'ai répété/je te l'ai répété dix fois** I've said that/I've told you that a dozen times; **il ne se l'est pas fait** ~ he didn't have to be told *ou* asked twice; **tentatives répétées** repeated attempts. (**b**) *pièce de théâtre* to rehearse; *rôle, leçon* to learn, go over; *morceau de piano* to practise. **2 se** ~ *vpr [personne]* to repeat o.s.; *[événement]* to be repeated, recur. **que cela ne se répète pas!** (just) don't let that happen again!; **l'histoire ne se répète jamais** history never repeats itself. ◆ **répétitif, -ive** *adj* repetitive. ◆ **répétition** *nf* repetition; *(Théât, fig)* rehearsal. ~ **générale** (final) dress rehearsal; **fusil à** ~ repeater rifle.

repeupler [Rəpœple] (1) **1** *vt région* to repopulate; *bassin, chasse* to restock (*de* with); *forêt* to replant (*de* with). **2 se** ~ *vpr* to be *ou* become repopulated. ◆ **repeuplement** *nm* repopulation; restocking; replanting.

repiquer [R(ə)pike] (1) *vt* (**a**) *(Bot)* to plant out. **plantes à** ~ bedding plants. (**b**) *disque* to record, tape. (**c**) *[moustique]* to bite again; *[épine]* to prick again. ◆ **repiquage** *nm* planting out; recording.

répit [Repi] *nm (rémission)* respite; *(repos)* respite, rest; *(pour payer)* respite, breathing space. **sans** ~ *travailler* continuously, without respite; *harceler* relentlessly.

replacer [R(ə)plase] (3) *vt objet* to replace, put back (in its place).

replanter [R(ə)plɑ̃te] (1) *vt plante* to replant, plant out; *forêt, arbre* to replant.

replâtrer [R(ə)plɑtRe] (1) *vt* (**a**) *mur* to replaster. (**b**) (*) *amitié, gouvernement* to patch up. ◆ **replâtrage** *nm* patching up.

replet, -ète [Rəplɛ, ɛt] *adj personne* podgy, fat; *visage* chubby.

repleuvoir [R(ə)plœvwaR] (23) *vb impers* to rain again, start raining again.

replier [R(ə)plije] (7) **1** *vt* (**a**) *journal* to fold up, fold back up; *manche* to roll up, fold up; *coin de feuille* to fold over; *ailes* to fold; *jambes* to tuck up; *couteau* to close. (**b**) *troupes* to withdraw. **2 se** ~ *vpr (Mil)* to fall back, withdraw (*sur* to). **se** ~ **(sur soi-même)** to withdraw into oneself. ◆ **repli** *nm [terrain, papier]* fold; *[conscience]* hidden *ou* innermost recess; *(Mil)* withdrawal, falling back. ~ **sur soi-même** withdrawal into oneself.

réplique [Replik] *nf* (**a**) *(réponse)* reply, retort, rejoinder. **et pas de** ~! and don't answer back!; **obéis sans** ~! do as you're told without a word *ou* without argument!; **argument sans** ~ unanswerable *ou* irrefutable argument. (**b**) *(contre-attaque)* counter-attack. (**c**) *(Théât)* line; *(signal)* cue. **donner la** ~ **à qn** *(pour répéter)* to give sb his cue; *(dans une scène)* to play opposite sb; *(fig)* **je saurai lui donner la** ~ I can match him (in an argument). (**d**) *(Art, objet identique)* replica. *(fig)* **il est la** ~ **de son jumeau** he is the image of his twin brother. ◆ **répliquer** (1) **1** *vt* to reply. ~ **que** to reply *ou* retort that; **il n'y a rien à** ~ **à cela** there's no answer to that. **2** *vi (répondre)* to reply; *(protester)* to protest; *(être insolent)* to answer back; *(contre-attaquer)* to counter-attack, retaliate.

répondant, e [Repɔ̃dɑ̃, ɑ̃t] **1** *nm, f* guarantor, surety. **servir de** ~ **à qn** *(Fin)* to stand surety for sb, be sb's guarantor; *(fig)* to vouch for sb. **2** *nm*: **avoir du** ~ to have a lot of money.

répondeur [Repɔ̃dœR] *nm*: ~ **(téléphonique)** (telephone) answering machine; ~ **(enregistreur)** Ansafone ®.

répondre [Repɔ̃dR(ə)] (41) **1** *vt bêtise, insulte* to reply with. ~ **que** to answer *ou* reply that; **il m'a répondu qu'il viendrait** he told me (in reply) *ou* he replied that he would come; ~ **présent à l'appel** *(lit)* to answer present at roll call; *(fig)* to come forward, volunteer; **bien répondu!** well answered *ou* said!; **qu'est-ce que vous voulez** ~ **à cela?** what can you reply *ou* say to that?

2 *vi* (**a**) to answer, reply. ~ **à qn/à une question** *etc* to reply to *ou* answer sb/a question *etc*; ~ **à une invitation** to reply to *ou* acknowledge an invitation; ~ **(à la porte/à la sonnette)** to answer the door/the bell; ~ **(au téléphone)** to answer the telephone; **il répond au nom de Dick** he answers to the name of Dick; ~ **par oui** to reply *ou* answer *ou* say yes; ~ **par un sourire** to smile in reply; ~ **par des injures** to reply with a string of insults. (**b**) *(être impertinent)* to answer back. (**c**) *(réagir) commandes, membres* to respond (*à* to).

3 ~ **à** *vt indir* (**a**) *besoin* to answer; *signalement* to answer, fit; *désirs* to meet. **ça répond à mon attente** it comes up to *ou* meets my expectations. (**b**) *attaque, avances, appel* to respond to; *amour, salut* to return; *politesse, invitation* to repay, pay back. **s'ils lancent une attaque, nous saurons y** ~ if they launch an attack we'll fight back *ou* retaliate. (**c**) *dessin, façade* to match. **les 2 ailes du bâtiment se répondent** the 2 wings of the building match (each other).

4 ~ **de** *vt indir (garantir)* to answer *ou* vouch for. **il viendra, je vous en réponds!** he'll come all right, you can take it from me! *ou* you can take my word for it!; **si vous agissez ainsi, je ne réponds plus de rien** if you behave like that, I'll accept no further responsibility; *(Jur)* ~ **de ses crimes** to answer for one's crimes.

réponse [Repɔ̃s] *nf (gén)* answer, reply; *(Physiol, Tech, fig)* response (*à, de* to). **en** ~ **à votre question** in answer *ou* reply to your question; **le droit de** ~ the right of reply; **ma lettre est restée sans** ~ my letter remained unanswered; **sa demande est restée sans** ~ there has been no reply *ou* response to his request; **coupon-**~ reply coupon; **avoir** ~ **à tout** to have an answer for everything; **c'est la** ~ **du berger à la bergère** it's tit for tat; ~ **de Normand** evasive answer.

report [R(ə)pɔR] *nm (V* **reporter**[1]*)* postponement, deferment; transfer; carrying over. *(Fin)* ~ **d'échéance** extension of due date; *(sur livre de compte)* **'** ~ **'** *(en bas de page)* 'carried forward'; *(en haut de page)* 'brought forward'.

reportage [R(ə)pɔRtaʒ] *nm* report (*sur* on); *(métier)* (news) reporting. ~ **en direct** live commentary; **faire le** ~ **d'une cérémonie** to cover a ceremony, do the coverage of a ceremony; **le grand** ~ the coverage of major international events; **il a fait plusieurs grands** ~**s pour...** he has covered several big stories for...

reporter[1] [R(ə)pɔRte] (1) **1** *vt* (**a**) *objet* to take back; *(par la pensée)* to take back (*à* to). (**b**) *match* to postpone, put off; *date* to put back, defer (*à* until). (**c**) *indications, vote, affection* to transfer (*sur* to). ~ **une somme sur la page suivante** to carry an amount over to the next page. **2 se** ~ *vpr*: **se** ~ **à** to refer to; *(par la pensée)* to think back to, cast one's mind back to; **reportez-vous à la page 5** turn to *ou* refer to *ou* see page 5.

reporter[2] [R(ə)pɔRtɛR] *nm* reporter. **grand** ~ international reporter; ~ **photographe** reporter and photographer; ~**-cameraman** news reporter and cameraman.

repos [R(ə)po] *nm* (**a**) *(détente)* rest. **prendre du** ~ to take *ou* have a rest; **rester en** ~ to rest; **après une journée de** ~ after a day's rest. (**b**) *(congé)* **jour de** ~ day off; **le médecin lui a donné du** ~ the doctor has given him some time off. (**c**) *(tranquillité)* peace and quiet; *(moral)* peace of mind; *(littér: sommeil, mort)* rest, sleep. **avoir la conscience en** ~ to have an easy *ou* a clear conscience; **pour avoir l'esprit en** ~ to put my (*ou* your *etc*) mind at rest; **laisse ton frère en** ~ leave your brother in peace. (**d**) *(pause) [discours]* pause; *[vers]* rest; *(Mus)* cadence. (**e**) *(locutions) (Mil)* ~! (stand) at ease!; **au** ~ *machine, animal* at rest; **sans** ~ *poursuivre* relentlessly; *quête* relentless; **de tout** ~ *situa-*

tion, entreprise secure, safe; *placement* gilt-edged, safe.

reposer [ʀ(ə)poze] (1) **1** *vt* (**a**) *verre etc* to put back down, put down again; *objet démonté* to refit, put back. *(Mil)* **reposez armes!** order arms! (**b**) *yeux, membres* to rest; *esprit* to rest, relax. ~ **sa tête sur un coussin** to rest one's head on a cushion; **elle avait le visage reposé** she looked rested. (**c**) *question* to repeat, ask again; *problème* to bring up again, raise again. **2** ~ **sur** *vt indir [bâtiment]* to be built on; *[supposition]* to rest on. **3** *vi* (**a**) *(littér) (être étendu, enterré, endormi)* to rest. **l'épave repose par 20 mètres de fond** the wreck is lying 20 metres down. (**b**) **laisser** ~ *liquide* to leave to settle; *pâte à crêpes* to leave to stand; **laisser** ~ **la terre** to let the land lie fallow; **faire** ~ **son cheval** to rest one's horse. **4 se** ~ *vpr* (**a**) *(se délasser)* to rest. (**b**) **se** ~ **sur qn** to rely on sb. (**c**) *(à nouveau) [oiseau]* to settle again; *[problème]* to crop up again. ◆ **reposant, e** *adj sommeil* refreshing; *lieu, couleur* restful; *vacances* restful, relaxing. ◆ **repose-bras** *nm inv* armrest. ◆ **repose-pieds** *nm inv* footrest. ◆ **repose-tête,** *pl* **repose-têtes** *nm* headrest.

repousser [ʀ(ə)puse] (1) **1** *vt* (**a**) *objet encombrant, personne* to push away; *ennemi* to repel, drive back; *coups* to ward off; *quémandeur* to turn away, repulse. (**b**) *(fig: refuser) (gén)* to reject; *demande, aide* to turn down; *hypothèse* to reject, dismiss, rule out; *objections, arguments* to brush aside, dismiss. (**c**) *(remettre en place) meuble* to push back; *tiroir* to push back in; *porte* to push to. (**d**) *(différer) date, réunion* to put off *ou* back, postpone, defer (*à plus tard* until later). (**e**) *(dégoûter)* to repel, repulse. (**f**) *(Tech) cuir, métal* to emboss (by hand). **en cuir repoussé** in repoussé leather. **2** *vi [feuilles, cheveux]* to grow again. **laisser** ~ **sa barbe** to let one's beard grow again. ◆ **repoussant, e** *adj* repulsive.

répréhensible [ʀepʀeɑ̃sibl(ə)] *adj acte, personne* reprehensible. **ce n'est pas** ~! there's nothing wrong with that!

reprendre [ʀ(ə)pʀɑ̃dʀ(ə)] (58) **1** *vt* (**a**) *(récupérer) ville, prisonnier* to recapture; *employé, objet prêté* to take back; *espoir, forces* to regain, recover. ~ **des couleurs** to get some colour back in one's cheeks; *[humour etc]* ~ **ses droits** to reassert itself; ~ **le dessus** *[malade]* to fight back; *[équipe]* to get back on top; ~ **haleine** *ou* **son souffle** to regain one's breath, get one's breath back; ~ **sa place** *(à table)* to go back to one's seat, resume one's seat; *(dans un groupe)* to take one's place again; **j'irai** ~ **mon manteau chez le teinturier** I'll go and get *ou* fetch my coat (back) from the cleaner's. (**b**) *(Comm) marchandises* to take back; *(contre un nouvel achat)* to take in part exchange; *usine* to take over. **les articles en solde ne sont pas repris** sale goods cannot be returned *ou* exchanged. (**c**) *pain, viande* to have *ou* take (some) more; *légumes* to have a second helping of. (**d**) *travaux, récit etc* to resume; *livre* to pick up again, go back to; *hostilités* to reopen, start again; *lutte, habitudes, idée* to take up again; *pièce de théâtre* to put on again; *refrain* to take up; *argument, critique* to repeat. **reprenez votre histoire au début** start your story from the beginning again; **reprenons les faits un par un** let's go over the facts one by one again; ~ **le travail** to go back to work, start work again; ~ **la route** to go on *ou* set off on one's way again; **la vie reprend son cours** life goes on again as before *ou* as usual. (**e**) *(saisir à nouveau) (gén)* to catch again. **son mal de gorge l'a repris** he's suffering from a sore throat again; *(iro)* **voilà que ça le reprend!** there he goes again!, he's off again! *; **ses doutes le reprirent** he was seized with doubts once more. (**f**) *(fig)* **on ne m'y reprendra plus** I won't let myself be caught (out) *ou* had * again; *(menace)* **que je ne t'y reprenne pas!** don't let me catch you doing that again! (**g**) *(Sport: rattraper) balle* to catch. (**h**) *(retoucher) tableau* to touch up; *chapitre* to go over again; *manteau (gén)* to alter; *(trop grand)* to take in; *(trop petit)* to let out; *(trop long)* to take up; *(trop court)* to let down. **il y a beaucoup de choses à** ~ **dans ce travail** there are lots of improvements to be made to this work. (**i**) *(réprimander)* to reprimand, tell off *; *(pour faute de langue)* to pull up; *(corriger)* to correct. **2** *vi* (**a**) *(retrouver la vigueur) [plante]* to take again; *[affaires]* to pick up. (**b**) *(recommencer)* to start again. (**c**) *(dire)* **'ce n'est pas moi' reprit-il** 'it's not me' he went on. **3 se** ~ *vpr* (**a**) *(se corriger)* to correct o.s.; *(s'interrompre)* to stop o.s. (**b**) *(recommencer)* **se** ~ **à plusieurs fois pour faire qch** to make several attempts to do sth *ou* at doing sth; **se** ~ **à espérer** to find o.s. hoping again. (**c**) *(réagir)* to take a grip on o.s., pull o.s. together (again), take o.s. in hand. **le coureur s'est bien repris sur la fin** the runner made a good recovery towards the end.

repreneur [ʀ(ə)pʀənœʀ] *nm (Ind)* (company) rescuer.

représailles [ʀ(ə)pʀezɑj] *nfpl (Pol, fig)* reprisals, retaliation. **user de** ~ to take reprisals (*envers* against); **en** ~ as a reprisal, in retaliation (*de* for).

représenter [ʀ(ə)pʀezɑ̃te] (1) **1** *vt* (**a**) *[peintre, romancier]* to depict, portray, show; *[photographie]* to represent, show. ~ **fidèlement les faits** to describe the facts faithfully. (**b**) *(symboliser, signifier)* to represent. **ça va** ~ **beaucoup de travail** that will mean *ou* represent *ou* involve a lot of work; **ça représente une part importante des dépenses** it accounts for *ou* represents a large part of the costs. (**c**) *(Théât) (jouer)* to perform, play; *(mettre à l'affiche)* to perform, put on, stage; *adaptation* to stage. (**d**) *(agir au nom de)* to represent. **il s'est fait** ~ **par son notaire** he was represented by his lawyer, he sent his lawyer to represent him. (**e**) *(littér: insister sur)* ~ **qch à qn** to point sth out to sb. **2** *vi (en imposer)* **il représente bien** he cuts a fine figure. **3 se** ~ *vpr* (**a**) *(s'imaginer)* to imagine. (**b**) *(survenir à nouveau) [idée, situation]* to occur again; *[occasion]* to present itself again, arise again; *[problème]* to crop up again. (**c**) **se** ~ **à un examen** to resit an exam; **se** ~ **à une élection** to stand *ou* run for election again, stand *ou* run for re-election.
◆ **représentant, e** *nm, f (gén)* representative. ~ **de commerce** sales representative *ou* rep *, travelling salesman; ~ **des forces de l'ordre** police officer. ◆ **représentatif, -ive** *adj (gén)* representative (*de* of). ◆ **représentation** *nf* (**a**) *(notation) (gén, fig)* representation; *[paysage, société]* portrayal; *[faits]* description. (**b**) *(Théât)* performance. (**c**) *[pays, mandant]* representation; *(groupe de délégués)* representatives. (**d**) *(Comm) (métier)* commercial travelling. **faire de la** ~ to be a (sales) representative *ou* a commercial traveller. (**e**) *(réception)* **avoir des frais de** ~ to get an entertainment allowance. ◆ **représentativité** *nf* representativeness.

répression [ʀepʀesjɔ̃] *nf [crime, abus]* suppression; *[pulsions]* repression; *[révolte]* suppression; quelling, repression. *(Pol)* **la** ~ repression; **prendre des mesures de** ~ **contre le crime** to crack down on crime. ◆ **répressible** *adj* repressible. ◆ **répressif, -ive** *adj* repressive.

réprimande [ʀepʀimɑ̃d] *nf* reprimand, rebuke. ◆ **réprimander** (1) *vt* to reprimand, rebuke.

réprimer [ʀepʀime] (1) *vt (gén)* to suppress; *insurrection* to quell, put down; *larmes, colère* to hold back, swallow.

repris de justice [ʀ(ə)pʀidʒystis] *nm inv* ex-prisoner, ex-convict.

reprise [ʀ(ə)pʀiz] *nf* (**a**) *[activité]* resumption; *[hostilités]* re-opening, renewal; *[froid]* return; *(Théât)* revival; *(Ciné)* rerun; *(Rad, TV: rediffusion)* repeat. **les ouvriers ont décidé la ~ du travail** the men have decided to go back *ou* return to work; **~ (économique)** (economic) revival *ou* recovery. (**b**) *(Aut)* **avoir de bonnes ~s** to have good acceleration. (**c**) *(Boxe)* round; *(Tennis)* return. *(Ftbl)* **à la ~** at the start of the second half. (**d**) *(Comm) [marchandise]* taking back; *(pour nouvel achat)* part exchange, trade-in; *(pour occuper des locaux)* key money. **valeur de ~ d'une voiture** part-exchange value *ou* trade-in value of a car; **~ des bouteilles vides** return of empties. (**e**) *[chaussette]* darn; *[drap, chemise]* mend. (**f**) **à 2 ou 3/à plusieurs ~s** on 2 or 3/on several occasions, 2 or 3/several times.

repriser [ʀ(ə)pʀize] (1) *vt chaussette, lainage* to darn; *drap, accroc* to mend.

réprobation [ʀepʀɔbɑsjɔ̃] *nf* reprobation. ◆ **réprobateur, -trice** *adj* reproving.

reproche [ʀ(ə)pʀɔʃ] *nm* reproach. **faire des ~s à qn** to reproach *ou* blame sb; **conduite qui mérite des ~s** reprehensible behaviour; **avec ~** reproachfully; **ton de ~** reproachful tone; **homme sans ~** man beyond *ou* above reproach.

reprocher [ʀ(ə)pʀɔʃe] (1) *vt* (**a**) **~ qch à qn** to blame *ou* reproach sb for sth; **~ à qn de faire qch** to reproach sb for *ou* with doing sth; *(Jur)* **les faits qui lui sont reprochés** the charges against him; **je ne te reproche rien** I'm not blaming you for anything; **je n'ai rien à me ~** I've nothing to reproach myself with. (**b**) *(critiquer)* **qu'as-tu à ~ à mon plan/à ce tableau?** what have you got against my plan/this picture?; **je reproche à ce tissu d'être salissant** the fault I find with that material is that it gets dirty; **il n'y a rien à ~ à cela** there's nothing wrong with that.

reproduire [ʀ(ə)pʀɔdɥiʀ] (38) **1** *vt (gén)* to reproduce; *modèle* to copy; *erreur* to repeat. **2 se ~** *vpr (Bio, Bot)* to reproduce, breed; *[phénomène]* to recur. **et que ça ne se reproduise plus!** and don't let that happen again! ◆ **reproducteur, -trice** *adj* reproductive. ◆ **reproductible** *adj* which can be reproduced, reproducible. ◆ **reproduction** *nf (action)* reproduction; copy; repeat; *(photo)* reproduction. **organes de ~** reproductive organs; *(sur un livre)* **'~ interdite'** 'all rights (of reproduction) reserved'.

reprographier [ʀəpʀɔgʀafje] (7) *vt* to (photo)copy, duplicate. ◆ **reprographie** *nf* reprography *(T)*, reprographics *(T)*, repro *(T)*. **le service de ~** the photocopying department.

réprouver [ʀepʀuve] (1) *vt personne* to reprove; *action* to condemn; *projet* to disapprove of; *(Rel)* to damn, reprobate. ◆ **réprouvé, e** *nm, f* reprobate.

reptile [ʀɛptil] *nm (Zool)* reptile; *(serpent)* snake; *(péj: personne)* creep * *(péj)*.

repu, e [ʀəpy] *adj animal* sated, satisfied. **je suis ~** I'm full, I've eaten my fill.

république [ʀepyblik] *nf* republic. **on est en ~!** * this is *ou* it's a free country; **la R~ française** the French Republic; **la R~ d'Irlande** the Irish Republic; **la R~ démocratique allemande** the German Democratic Republic; **la R~ fédérale d'Allemagne** the Federal Republic of Germany; **la R~ populaire de Chine** the Chinese People's Republic; *(péj)* **~ bananière** banana republic. ◆ **républicain, e** *adj, nm, f* republican; *(US Pol)* Republican.

répudier [ʀepydje] (7) *vt conjoint* to repudiate; *foi, engagement* to renounce. ◆ **répudiation** *nf* repudiation; renouncement.

répugnance [ʀepyɲɑ̃s] *nf* (**a**) *(répulsion)* repugnance, disgust (*pour* for), loathing (*pour* of). **avoir de la ~ pour les épinards** to loathe spinach. (**b**) *(hésitation)* reluctance (*à faire qch* to do sth). **éprouver de la ~ à faire** to be loath *ou* reluctant to do; **avec ~** reluctantly, unwillingly. ◆ **répugnant, e** *adj individu* repugnant; *laideur* revolting; *travail, odeur, nourriture* disgusting, revolting, loathsome. ◆ **répugner** (1) **~ à** *vt indir* (**a**) *(dégoûter)* to repel, disgust, be repugnant to. **ça me répugne** I am repelled by *ou* disgusted with it, I find it disgusting. (**b**) *(hésiter)* **~ à faire qch** to be loath *ou* reluctant to do sth.

répulsion [ʀepylsjɔ̃] *nf (gén, Phys)* repulsion (*pour* for). ◆ **répulsif, -ive** *adj* repulsive.

réputation [ʀepytɑsjɔ̃] *nf (honneur)* reputation, good name; *(renommée)* reputation. **avoir bonne/mauvaise ~** to have a good/bad reputation; **sa ~ n'est plus à faire** his (*ou* her) reputation is not in doubt, his (*ou* her) reputation is firmly established; **connaître qn de ~** to know sb by repute; **il a la ~ d'être avare** he has a reputation for *ou* of being miserly, he is reputed to be miserly. ◆ **réputé, e** *adj* (**a**) *(célèbre)* reputable, renowned. **hautement ~** of great repute *ou* renown; **~ pour** renowned *ou* famous for. (**b**) *(prétendu)* **remède ~ infaillible** cure which is reputed *ou* supposed *ou* said to be infallible.

requérir [ʀəkeʀiʀ] (21) *vt (exiger)* to call for, require; *(solliciter)* to request; *police* to call on; *(Jur) peine* to call for, demand.

requête [ʀəkɛt] *nf (Jur)* petition; *(supplique)* request, petition. **adresser une ~ à un juge** to petition a judge; **à** *ou* **sur la ~ de qn** at sb's request.

requiem [ʀekɥijɛm] *nm inv* requiem.

requin [ʀ(ə)kɛ̃] *nm (Zool, fig)* shark. *(fig)* **les ~s de la finance** the sharks of the business world.

requinquer * [ʀ(ə)kɛ̃ke] (1) **1** *vt* to pep up *, buck up *. **2 se ~** *vpr* to perk up *.

requis, e [ʀəki, iz] *adj conditions* requisite, required. *(réquisitionné)* **les ~** labour conscripts *(civilians)*.

réquisitionner [ʀekizisjɔne] (1) *vt biens* to requisition, commandeer; *hommes* to requisition, conscript. ◆ **réquisition** *nf* requisition; conscription.

réquisitoire [ʀekizitwaʀ] *nm (plaidoirie)* closing speech for the prosecution; *(fig)* indictment (*contre* of).

rescapé, e [ʀɛskape] **1** *adj personne* surviving. **2** *nm, f* survivor (*de* of).

rescousse [ʀɛskus] *nf*: **venir à la ~** to come to the rescue; **appeler qn à la ~** to call on *ou* to sb for help.

réseau, *pl* **~x** [ʀezo] *nm (gén, fig)* network. **~ fluvial** river system, network of rivers; **~ d'espionnage** spy network *ou* ring; **~ express régional** *high-speed suburban branch of the Paris métro;* **~ d'intrigues** web of intrigue; **~ d'habitudes** pattern of habits.

réservation [ʀezɛʀvɑsjɔ̃] *nf (à l'hôtel)* reservation; *(des places)* reservation, booking. *(Tourisme)* **~ de groupes** group booking; **bureau de ~** booking office.

réserve [ʀezɛʀv(ə)] *nf* (**a**) *(provision)* reserve. **faire des ~s de sucre** to get in *ou* lay in a stock of *ou* reserves of sugar; **mettre qch en ~** to put sth by, put sth in reserve; **avoir/tenir qch en ~** *(gén)* to have/keep sth in reserve; *(Comm)* to have/keep sth in stock. (**b**) *(restriction)* reservation, reserve. **émettre des ~s sur qch** to have reservations *ou* reserves about sth; **sous toutes ~s** *publier* with all reserve; *dire* with reservations; **sous ~ de** subject to; **sans ~** *admiration* unreserved; *approuver* unreservedly. (**c**) *(prudence, discrétion)* reserve. (**d**) *(Mil)* **la ~** the reserve; **armée de ~** reserve army. (**e**) *(territoire) [nature, animaux]* reserve; *[Indiens]* reservation. **~ de pêche/chasse** fishing/ hunting preserve; **~ naturelle** nature reserve *ou* sanctuary.

(**f**) *[bibliothèque]* reserve collection. (**g**) *(entrepôt)* storehouse, storeroom.

réserver [ʀezɛʀve] (1) **1** *vt* (**a**) *(mettre à part) (gén)* to keep, save, reserve; *marchandises* to put aside *ou* on one side (*à, pour* for). ~ **le meilleur pour la fin** to keep *ou* save the best till last. (**b**) *(louer) place, table* to book, reserve. (**c**) *(fig: destiner) accueil, châtiment* to have in store, reserve (*à* for). **nous ne savons pas ce que l'avenir nous réserve** we don't know what the future has in store for us *ou* holds for us; **il lui était réservé de mourir jeune** he was destined to die young. (**d**) *(retarder) réponse, opinion* to reserve. **2 se** ~ *vpr*: **se** ~ **le meilleur morceau** to keep *ou* save *ou* reserve the best bit for o.s.; **se** ~ **pour plus tard** to save *ou* reserve o.s. for later; **se** ~ **pour une autre occasion** to wait for another opportunity; **se** ~ **le droit/la possibilité de faire qch** to reserve the right to do sth/the possibility of doing sth. ◆ **réservé, e** *adj place* reserved (*à* for); *personne, caractère* reserved. **pêche** ~**e** private fishing; **les médecins sont très** ~**s à son sujet** the doctors are very guarded *ou* cautious in their opinions about him; **tous droits** ~**s** all rights reserved; **voie** ~**e aux autobus** bus lane.

réserviste [ʀezɛʀvist(ə)] *nm* reservist.

réservoir [ʀezɛʀvwaʀ] *nm (cuve)* tank; *(plan d'eau)* reservoir; *[poissons]* fishpond; *[usine à gaz]* gasometer, gasholder.

résider [ʀezide] (1) *vi [personne]* to live, reside; *[problème]* to lie, reside (*dans* in). ◆ **résidant, e** *adj* resident. ◆ **résidence** *nf (gén)* residence. **changer de** ~ to move (house); **en** ~ **surveillée** under house arrest; *(Diplomatie)* **la** ~ the residency; ~ **principale** main home; ~ **secondaire** second home; ~ **universitaire** (university) hall(s) of residence, residence hall *(US)*, dormitory *(US)*. ◆ **résident, e** *nm, f (étranger)* foreign national *ou* resident; *(diplomate)* resident. **ministre** ~ resident minister; **avoir le statut de** ~ **permanent en France** to have permanent resident status in France. ◆ **résidentiel, -ielle** *adj* residential.

résidu [ʀezidy] *nm* (**a**) *(reste) (Chim, fig)* residue ; *(Math)* remainder. (**b**) *(déchets)* ~**s** remnants, residue; ~**s industriels** industrial waste. ◆ **résiduel, -elle** *adj* residual.

résigner (se) [ʀeziɲe] (1) *vpr* to resign o.s. (*à* to). **il faudra s'y** ~ we'll have to resign ourselves to it *ou* put up with it. ◆ **résignation** *nf* resignation (*à* to). **avec** ~ with resignation, resignedly. ◆ **résigné, e** *adj* resigned (*à* to).

résilier [ʀezilje] (7) *vt contrat* to terminate. ◆ **résiliation** *nf* termination.

résine [ʀezin] *nf* resin. ◆ **résineux, -euse 1** *adj* resinous. **2** *nm* coniferous tree.

résistance [ʀezistɑ̃s] *nf* (**a**) *(gén)* resistance (*à* to). **en appuyant, je sentis une** ~ when I pressed I felt some resistance; **opposer une** ~ **farouche à un projet** to put up fierce resistance to a project, make a very determined stand against a project; **il a une grande** ~ he has great resistance *ou* stamina; **coureur qui a de la** ~ runner who has lots of staying power; **ça offre une grande** ~ **au feu/aux chocs** it is very heat-/shock-resistant. (**b**) *(Élec) (mesure)* resistance; *[réchaud, radiateur]* element. ◆ **résistant, e 1** *adj personne* robust, tough; *plante* hardy; *tissu* strong, hard-wearing; *couleur* fast; *métal* resistant, strong. ~ **à la chaleur** heatproof, heat-resistant. **2** *nm, f (Hist)* (French) Resistance worker *ou* fighter. ◆ **résister** (1) ~ **à** *vt indir (gén)* to resist; *fatigue, sécheresse* to stand up to, withstand; *douleur* to stand; *attaque* to hold out against. ~ **au courant d'une rivière** to hold one's own against the current of a river; ~ **à l'épreuve du temps** to stand the test of time; **le plancher ne pourra pas** ~ **au poids** the floor won't support *ou* take the weight; **ça n'a pas résisté longtemps** it didn't resist *ou* hold out for long; **couleur qui résiste au lavage** colour which is fast in the wash; **cette vaisselle résiste au feu** this crockery is heat-resistant *ou* heatproof; **ça ne résiste pas à l'analyse** it does not stand up to analysis.

résolu, e [ʀezɔly] *adj personne, air* resolute. ~ **à faire** resolved *ou* determined to do, set on doing. ◆ **résolument** *adv* resolutely. ◆ **résolution** *nf (gén, Pol: décision)* resolution; *(énergie)* resolve, resolution; *(solution)* solution. **prendre la** ~ **de faire** to make a resolution to do, resolve to do, make up one's mind to do.

résonner [ʀezɔne] (1) *vi [son]* to resonate, reverberate, resound; *[salle]* to be resonant; *[objet]* to resound. **ça résonne** the noise resonates *ou* reverberates *ou* echoes; ~ **de** to resound *ou* ring *ou* resonate with. ◆ **résonance** *nf (gén, Élec, Phys, Phon)* resonance; *(fig)* echo; **être en** ~ to be resonating. ◆ **résonateur** *nm* resonator. ◆ **résonnant, e** *adj* resonant.

résorber [ʀezɔʀbe] (1) **1** *vt (Méd)* to resorb; *chômage* to bring down, reduce (gradually); *surplus* to absorb; *inflation* to curb. **2 se** ~ *vpr* to be resorbed; to be brought down *ou* reduced; to be absorbed. ◆ **résorption** *nf* resorption; gradual reduction (*de* in); absorption.

résoudre [ʀezudʀ(ə)] (51) **1** *vt* (**a**) *problème etc* to solve; *difficultés* to resolve, settle, sort out. (**b**) *(décider) exécution* to decide on, determine on. ~ **de faire qch** to decide *ou* resolve to do sth, make up one's mind to do sth; ~ **qn à faire qch** to induce sb to do sth. **2 se** ~ *vpr* (**a**) **se** ~ **à faire qch** *(se décider)* to resolve *ou* decide to do sth, make up one's mind to do sth; *(se résigner)* to resign *ou* reconcile o.s. to doing sth; **il n'a pas pu se** ~ **à la quitter** he couldn't bring himself to leave her. (**b**) **se** ~ **en pluie** to resolve into rain.

respect [ʀɛspɛ] *nm* (**a**) respect (*de, pour* for). **il n'a aucun** ~ **pour le bien d'autrui** he has no respect *ou* consideration *ou* regard for other people's property; **sauf votre** ~ with all due respect; ~ **de soi** self-respect. (**b**) *(formule de politesse)* **présentez mes** ~**s à votre femme** give my regards *ou* pay my respects to your wife; **mes** ~**s, mon colonel** good day to you, sir. (**c**) **tenir qn en** ~ *(avec une arme)* to keep sb at a respectful distance *ou* at bay. ◆ **respectabilité** *nf* respectability. ◆ **respectable** *adj (honorable)* respectable; *(important)* respectable, sizeable. ◆ **respecter** (1) **1** *vt* to respect, have respect for. **se faire** ~ to be respected (*par* by), command respect (*par,* from); **la jeunesse ne respecte rien** young people show no respect for anything *ou* do not respect anything; ~ **l'ordre alphabétique** to keep things in alphabetical order; **faire** ~ **la loi** to enforce the law; ~ **les termes d'un contrat** to abide by *ou* respect the terms of a contract. **2 se** ~ *vpr* to respect o.s. *(hum)* **tout professeur qui se respecte** any self-respecting teacher.

respectif, -ive [ʀɛspɛktif, iv] *adj* respective. ◆ **respectivement** *adv* respectively.

respectueux, -euse [ʀɛspɛktɥø, øz] *adj* respectful (*envers* to, *de* of). **se montrer** ~ **du bien d'autrui** to show respect *ou* consideration for other people's property; ~ **de la loi** respectful of the law, law-abiding; **veuillez agréer mes salutations** ~**euses** yours respectfully. ◆ **respectueusement** *adv* respectfully.

respirer [ʀɛspiʀe] (1) **1** *vi* (**a**) *(lit, Bio)* to breathe. ~ **par le nez** to breathe through one's nose; ~ **profondément** to breathe deeply, take a deep breath. (**b**) *(fig) (se détendre)* to get one's breath, have a break; *(se rassurer)* to breathe again. **2** *vt* (**a**) *(inhaler)* to breathe (in), inhale. **faire** ~ **qch à qn** to make sb inhale sth. (**b**) *calme, bonheur* to radiate; *honnêteté* to exude, emanate; *joie* to glow with. ◆ **respirable** *adj (lit, fig)* breathable. ◆ **respirateur** *nm:* ~ **(artificiel)** *(gén)* respirator; *(pour malade dans le coma)* ventilator. ◆ **respiration** *nf (fonction)* breathing, respiration; *(souffle)* breath. **avoir la ~ difficile** to have difficulty (in) breathing; **retenir sa ~** to hold one's breath; **faites 3 ~s complètes** breathe in and out 3 times. ◆ **respiratoire** *adj* breathing, respiratory.

resplendir [ʀɛsplɑ̃diʀ] (2) *vi (gén, fig)* to shine; *[astre]* to beam; *[surface métallique]* to gleam; *[lac, neige]* to glisten, glitter. ~ *ou* **être resplendissant de bonheur** to be aglow *ou* radiant with happiness; **soleil resplendissant** radiant *ou* beaming sun.

responsable [ʀɛspɔ̃sabl(ə)] **1** *adj* (**a**) *(de dégâts)* liable, responsible (*de* for); *(de délits)* responsible (*de* for); *(moralement)* responsible, accountable (*de* for, *devant qn* to sb). **civilement ~** liable in civil law. (**b**) *(chargé de)* ~ **de** responsible for, in charge of. (**c**) *(coupable)* responsible. **les freins défectueux sont ~s (de l'accident)** the faulty brakes are to blame *ou* are responsible for the accident. (**d**) *(sérieux) attitude, étudiant* responsible. **agir de manière ~** to behave responsibly. **2** *nmf* (**a**) *(coupable)* **le ~** the person responsible *ou* who is to blame, the culprit; **le seul ~ est l'alcool** alcohol alone is to blame. (**b**) *(chef) [service]* person in charge; *[parti, syndicat]* official. **des ~s de l'industrie** representatives *ou* leaders of industry; **~ politique** political leader. ◆ **responsabiliser** (1) *vt:* ~ **qn** to make sb aware of his responsibilities. ◆ **responsabilité** *nf (gén)* responsibility (*de* for). **de lourdes ~s** heavy responsibilities; **avoir la ~ de qch** to be responsible for sth; **avoir la ~ de qn** to take *ou* have responsibility for sb; **avoir un poste à ~** to have *ou* hold a position of responsibility; ~ **civile** civil liability.

resquiller [ʀɛskije] (1) *vi (dans l'autobus)* to sneak a free seat; *(au cinéma)* to get in on the sly, sneak in; *(ne pas faire la queue)* to jump the queue. ◆ **resquilleur, -euse** *nm, f (dans une queue)* queue-jumper; *(dans l'autobus)* fare-dodger.

ressac [ʀəsak] *nm:* **le ~** *(mouvement)* the backwash, the undertow; *(vague)* the surf.

ressaisir [ʀ(ə)seziʀ] (2) **1** *vt* (**a**) *objet* to catch hold of again; *fuyard* to recapture; *prétexte* to seize on again. (**b**) *[peur]* to grip (once) again; *[désir]* to take hold of again. **2 se ~** *vpr* (**a**) to regain one's self-control; *[athlète]* to rally, recover. **ressaisissez-vous!** pull yourself together! (**b**) **se ~ de** *pouvoir* to seize again. ◆ **ressaisissement** *nm* recovery.

ressasser [ʀ(ə)sɑse] (1) *vt pensées* to keep rehearsing *ou* turning over; *conseil* to keep trotting out.

ressembler [ʀ(ə)sɑ̃ble] (1) **1 ~ à** *vt indir* to resemble, be *ou* look like. **à quoi ressemble-t-il?** * what does he look like?, what's he like?; **ça ne ressemble à rien!** * *(attitude)* it makes no sense at all; *(peinture)* it's like nothing on earth!; **à quoi ça ressemble de crier comme ça!** * what do you mean by shouting like that!; **cela lui ressemble bien de dire ça** it's just like him *ou* it's typical of him to say that. **2 se ~** *vpr* to look *ou* be alike, resemble each other. **ils se ressemblent comme deux gouttes d'eau** they're as like as two peas (in a pod). ◆ **ressemblance** *nf (visuelle)* resemblance, likeness; *(de composition)* similarity. **avoir une ~ avec qch** to bear a resemblance *ou* likeness to sth. ◆ **ressemblant, e** *adj photo* lifelike, true to life.

ressemeler [ʀ(ə)səmle] (4) *vt* to resole. ◆ **ressemelage** *nm* resoling.

ressentiment [ʀ(ə)sɑ̃timɑ̃] *nm* resentment (*contre* against, *de* at). **éprouver du ~** to feel resentful (*envers* towards).

ressentir [ʀ(ə)sɑ̃tiʀ] (16) **1** *vt (gén)* to feel; *sensation* to experience. **2 se ~** *vpr:* **se ~ de** *[travail, qualité]* to show the effects of; *[personne]* to feel the effects of.

resserre [ʀ(ə)sɛʀ] *nf (cabane)* shed; *(réduit)* storeroom.

resserrer [ʀ(ə)seʀe] (1) **1** *vt (gén)* to tighten; *amitié* to strengthen; *crédits* to squeeze. **2 se ~** *vpr [étreinte]* to tighten; *[liens affectifs]* to grow stronger; *[groupe]* to draw in; *[pores, mâchoire]* to close; *[vallée]* to narrow. **le filet se resserrait autour de lui** the net was closing in on him. ◆ **resserré, e** *adj vallée* narrow. **maison ~e entre des immeubles** house squeezed between high buildings. ◆ **resserrement** *nm* (**a**) *(action)* strengthening; narrowing. **le ~ du crédit** the tightening of *ou* squeeze on credit. (**b**) *(partie étroite)* narrow part.

resservir [ʀ(ə)sɛʀviʀ] (14) **1** *vt plat* to serve (up) again (*à* to); *dîneur* to give a second helping to (*de, en* of); *(fig) histoire* to trot out again *(péj)*. **2** *vi [vêtement, outil]* to serve again, do again, be useful again. **3 se ~** *vpr [dîneur]* to help o.s. again (*de* to), take another helping (*de* of). **se ~ de** *outil* to use again.

ressort [ʀ(ə)sɔʀ] *nm* (**a**) *(de métal)* spring. **~ à boudin** spiral spring; **faire ~** to spring back; **à ~** spring-loaded. (**b**) *(énergie)* spirit. **avoir du ~** to have spirit. (**c**) *(littér: motivation)* **les ~s qui le font agir** the motivating forces behind his actions. (**d**) *(Jur: circonscription)* jurisdiction. *(compétence)* **être du ~ de** to fall within the competence of; *(fig)* **ce n'est pas de mon ~** this is not my responsibility.

ressortir [ʀ(ə)sɔʀtiʀ] (2) **1** *vi (avec aux être)* (**a**) *(à nouveau) [personne]* to go out again, leave again; *[objet]* to come out again. **souvenirs qui ressortent** memories which resurface; **ce film ressort sur nos écrans** this film is showing again *ou* has been re-released. (**b**) *(contraster) [détail, qualité]* to stand out. **faire ~ qch** to make sth stand out, bring out sth. **2 ~ de** *vt indir (résulter)* to emerge from, be the result of. **3 ~ à** *vt indir (Jur)* to come under the jurisdiction of. **4** *vt (avec aux avoir) vêtements, outil etc* to take *ou* bring out again; *film* to re-release, bring out again; *(Comm) modèle* to bring out again. *(fig)* **~ un vieux projet d'un tiroir** to get out an old plan again, disinter an old plan.

ressortissant, e [ʀ(ə)sɔʀtisɑ̃, ɑ̃t] *nm, f* national. **~ français** French national *ou* citizen.

ressouder [ʀ(ə)sude] (1) **1** *vt objet* to solder together again; *amitié* to patch up. **2 se ~** *vpr [os]* to knit, mend.

ressource [ʀ(ə)suʀs(ə)] *nf* (**a**) **~s** *(gén)* resources; *[art, technique]* possibilities; *(finances personnelles)* means; **famille sans ~s** family with no means of support *ou* no resources; **~s en hommes** manpower resources; **être à bout de ~s** to have exhausted all the possibilities, be at the end of one's resources; **homme de ~(s)** man of resource, resourceful man. (**b**) *(recours)* **n'ayant pas la ~ de lui parler** having no means *ou* possibility of speaking to him; **sa seule ~ était de** the only way *ou* course open to him was to; **vous êtes ma dernière ~** you are my last resort; **en dernière ~** as a last resort. (**c**) **avoir de la ~** *[sportif, cheval]* to have strength in reserve.

ressouvenir (se) [ʀ(ə)suvniʀ] (22) *vpr:* **se ~ de** to remember, recall; **faire se ~ qn de qch** to remind sb of sth.

ressusciter [ʀesysite] (1) **1** *vi (Rel)* to rise (from the dead); *(fig)* to come back to life, revive. **2** *vt (Rel)* to raise (from the dead); *(fig)* to bring back to life, revive; *mourant* to resuscitate; *(péj) passé, coutume* to resurrect *(péj)*.

restant, e [ʀɛstɑ̃, ɑ̃t] **1** *adj* remaining. **2** *nm* (**a**) *(l'autre partie)* **le ~** the rest, the remainder. (**b**) *(ce* *qui est en trop)* **faire une écharpe dans un ~ de tissu** to make a scarf out of some left-over material.

restaurant [ʀɛstɔʀɑ̃] *nm* restaurant. **on va au ~?** shall we have a meal out?; **~ d'entreprise** staff canteen *ou* dining room; **~ libre-service** self-service restaurant, cafeteria; **~ rapide** fast-food restaurant; **~ universitaire** university refectory *ou* canteen *ou* cafeteria.

restaurer [ʀɛstɔʀe] (1) **1** *vt tableau, paix* to restore; *(nourrir)* to feed. **2 se ~** *vpr* to have sth to eat. ◆ **restaurateur, -trice** *nm, f* (**a**) *(Art, Pol)* restorer. (**b**) *(aubergiste)* restaurant owner. ◆ **restauration** *nf* (**a**) *(Art, Pol)* restoration *[ville, bâtiment]* restoration, rehabilitation. *(Hist)* **la R~** the Restoration. (**b**) *(hôtellerie)* catering. **la ~ rapide** the fast-food industry *ou* trade.

reste [ʀɛst(ə)] *nm* (**a**) *(l'autre partie)* **le ~** the rest; **le ~ du lait** the rest *ou* remainder *ou* remains of the milk, what is left of the milk. (**b**) *(ce qui est en trop)* **il y a un ~ de fromage** there's some cheese left over; **s'il y a un ~ de laine** if there's some spare wool *ou* some wool to spare; **un ~ de tendresse le poussa à rester** a last trace *ou* a remnant of tenderness moved him to stay. (**c**) **les ~s** *(nourriture)* the left-overs; *(dépouille mortelle)* the (mortal) remains; **les ~s de** the remains of, what is left of. (**d**) *(Math: différence)* remainder. (**e**) **avoir de l'argent/du temps de ~** to have money/time left over *ou* in hand *ou* to spare; **il ne voulait pas être en ~ avec eux** he didn't want to be outdone by them *ou* indebted to them; **au ~, du ~** besides, moreover; **partir sans demander son ~** to leave without further ado; **pour le ~** (as) for the rest; **et (tout) le ~** and everything else, and all the rest.

rester [ʀɛste] (1) **1** *vi* (**a**) *(dans un lieu)* to stay, remain; *(*: habiter)* to live. **~ à la maison** to stay *ou* remain indoors; **~ (à) dîner** to stay for *ou* to dinner; **je ne peux ~ que 10 minutes** I can only stay *ou* stop * 10 minutes; **un os lui est resté dans la gorge** a bone was caught *ou* got stuck in his throat; **~ à regarder la télévision** to stay watching television; **naturellement ça reste entre nous** of course we shall keep this to ourselves *ou* this is just between ourselves; *[nerveux]* **il ne peut pas ~ en place** he can't keep still. (**b**) *(dans un état)* to stay, remain. **~ sans rien dire** to stay *ou* keep *ou* remain silent; **~ dans l'ignorance** to remain in ignorance; **~ debout** to stand, remain standing; *(ne pas se coucher)* to stay up; **je suis resté assis toute la journée** I spent the whole day sitting; **ne reste pas là les bras croisés** don't just stand there with your arms folded; **~ en carafe** ‡ to be left stranded. (**c**) *(subsister)* to be left, remain. **rien ne reste de l'ancien château** nothing is left *ou* remains of the old castle; **le seul parent qui leur reste** their only remaining relative; **l'argent qui leur reste** the money they have left; **10 km restaient à faire** there were still 10 km to go. (**d**) *(durer) [sentiments, œuvre]* to last, live on. **le surnom lui est resté** the nickname stayed with him, the nickname stuck. (**e**) **~ sur une impression** to retain an impression; **je suis resté sur ma faim** *(après un repas)* I still felt hungry; *(à la fin d'une histoire)* I was left unsatisfied, I was left hanging *; **ça m'est resté sur le cœur** I still feel sore about it *, it still rankles with me. (**f**) **ils en sont restés à des discussions préliminaires** they have got no further than *ou* they are still at the stage of preliminary discussions; **où en étions-nous restés?** where did we leave off?; **restons-en là** let's leave off there, let's leave it at that. (**g**) *(*: mourir)* **y ~** to meet one's end.
2 *vb impers*: **il reste encore un peu de pain** there's still a little bread left; **il me reste à faire ceci** I still have this to do; **il reste beaucoup à faire** much remains *ou* there's a lot left to do *ou* to be done; **il ne me reste que toi** you're all I have left; **il ne me reste qu'à vous remercier** it only remains for me to thank you; **il restait à faire 50 km** there were 50 km still *ou* left to go; **reste à savoir si** it remains to be seen whether; **il n'en reste pas moins que** the fact remains (nonetheless) that.

restituer [ʀɛstitɥe] (1) *vt objet volé* to return, restore (*à qn* to sb); *somme d'argent* to return, refund (*à qn* to sb); *texte reconstitué* to restore; *(Tech) énergie, chaleur* to release; *sons* to reproduce. ◆ **restitution** *nf* return; restoration; release; reproduction. **la ~ des objets volés** the return *ou* restitution of the stolen goods.

restreindre [ʀɛstʀɛ̃dʀ(ə)] (52) **1** *vt (gén)* to restrict, limit; *dépenses* to cut down. **2 se ~** *vpr* (**a**) *(dans ses dépenses)* to cut down. (**b**) *[production]* to decrease, go down; *[espace]* to decrease, diminish; *[ambition, champ d'action]* to narrow; *[sens d'un mot]* to become more restricted. ◆ **restreint, e** *adj* limited, restricted (*à* to).

restriction [ʀɛstʀiksjɔ̃] *nf* (**a**) *(limitation)* restriction, limiting, limitation. **~s** restrictions. (**b**) *(condition)* qualification. *(réticence)* **~ (mentale)** mental reservation; **approuver qch sans ~s** to give one's unqualified approval to sth, accept sth without reservation. ◆ **restrictif, -ive** *adj* restrictive.

restructurer [ʀəstʀyktyʀe] (1) *vt* to restructure. ◆ **restructuration** *nf* restructuring.

résultat [ʀezylta] *nm (gén)* result. **cette tentative a eu des ~s désastreux** this attempt had disastrous results *ou* a disastrous outcome; **c'est un ~ remarquable** it's a remarkable result *ou* achievement; **~s sportifs** sports results. ◆ **résultante** *nf (Sci)* resultant; *(fig: conséquence)* outcome, result, consequence. ◆ **résulter** (1) **1** *vi*: **~ de** to result from; **rien de bon ne peut en ~** no good can come of it *ou* result from it. **2** *vb impers*: **il résulte de tout ceci que** the result of all this is that; **qu'en résultera-t-il?** what will be the result? *ou* outcome?

résumer [ʀezyme] (1) **1** *vt (abréger)* to summarize; *(récapituler, aussi Jur)* to sum up; *(reproduire en petit)* to epitomize, typify. **2 se ~** *vpr* (**a**) *[personne]* to sum up (one's ideas). (**b**) *(se réduire à)* **se ~ à** to amount to, come down to, boil down to. ◆ **résumé** *nm* summary, résumé. **en ~** *(en bref)* in short, in brief; *(pour conclure)* to sum up; *(en miniature)* in miniature.

resurgir [ʀ(ə)syʀʒiʀ] (2) *vi* to reappear, re-emerge.

résurrection [ʀezyʀɛksjɔ̃] *nf (Rel)* resurrection; *(fig)* revival.

rétablir [ʀetabliʀ] (2) **1** *vt (gén)* to restore; *fait, vérité* to re-establish. **~ qn dans son emploi** to reinstate sb in *ou* restore sb to his post; *(guérir)* **~ qn** to restore sb to health, bring about sb's recovery. **2 se ~** *vpr [malade]* to recover; *[calme]* to return, be restored; *(faire un rétablissement)* to pull o.s. up *(onto a ledge etc)*. ◆ **rétablissement** *nm (action)* restoring; re-establishment; *(guérison)* recovery. *(Sport)* **faire un ~** to do a pull-up *(onto a ledge etc)*.

rétamer [ʀetame] (1) *vt* (**a**) *casseroles* to re-coat, re-tin. (**b**) (‡) *(fatiguer)* to wear out *; *(rendre ivre)* to knock out ‡; *(démolir)* to wipe out; *(au jeu)* to clean out *. **se ~ (par terre)** to take a dive *, crash to the ground.

retape ‡ [ʀ(ə)tap] *nf*: **faire (de) la ~** to tout for business.

retaper [ʀ(ə)tape] (1) **1** *vt* (**a**) (*) *maison, vêtement* to do up; *voiture* to fix up; *lit* to straighten; *malade* to set up (again), buck up *. (**b**) *(dactylographier)* to retype, type again. **2 se ~** *vpr* (**a**) *(*: guérir)* to get back on one's feet. (**b**) *(‡: à nouveau)* to do again. **se ~ un verre** to have o.s. another drink *.

retapisser [ʀ(ə)tapise] (1) *vt* to re-paper.

retard [ʀ(ə)taʀ] *nm* (**a**) *[personne attendue]* lateness. **être/mettre qn en** ~ to be/make sb late; *(Scol)* **il a eu quatre ~s** he was late four times; **vous avez 2 heures de** ~ you're 2 hours late; **après plusieurs ~s** after being late several times. (**b**) *[train etc]* delay. **en** ~ **sur l'horaire** behind schedule; **léger** ~ slight delay; **combler son** ~ to make up for the delay; *(Sport)* **être en** ~ **(de 2 km) sur le peloton** to be (2 km) behind the pack. (**c**) *[montre]* **cette montre a du** ~ this watch is slow; **la pendule prend du** ~ the clock goes slow; **prendre un** ~ **de 3 minutes par jour** to lose 3 minutes a day. (**d**) *(sur des délais)* delay. **paiement en** ~ *(effectué)* late payment; *(non effectué)* overdue payment; **il est toujours en** ~ **sur les autres pour payer** he is always behind the others *ou* later than the others in paying; **sans** ~ without delay. (**e**) *(sur un programme)* delay. **en** ~ **sur le programme** behind schedule; **j'ai du courrier en** ~ I'm behind *ou* behind-hand with my mail, I have a backlog of mail; **il doit combler son** ~ **en anglais** he has a lot of ground to make up in English. (**f**) *(infériorité) [peuple, pays]* backwardness. **il est en** ~ **pour son âge** he's backward for his age; ~ **de croissance** slow development; **pays qui a un siècle de** ~ **économique** country whose economy is a century behind; ~ **industriel** industrial backwardness; ~ **mental** backwardness; **être en** ~ **sur son temps** to be behind the times. (**g**) *(Aut)* ~ **à l'allumage** retarded ignition.
◆ **retardataire 1** *adj arrivant* late; *théorie* obsolete, outmoded. **2** *nmf* latecomer. ◆ **retardement** *nm*: **à** ~ *dispositif* delayed action; *(Phot) mécanisme* self-timing; *comprendre* after the event; **bombe à** ~ time bomb.

retarder [ʀ(ə)taʀde] (1) **1** *vt* (**a**) *(mettre en retard) (gén)* to delay; *opération, automobiliste* to hold up; *programme* to hinder, set back. **ne te retarde pas** don't make yourself late; **ça l'a retardé dans ses études** this has set him back in *ou* hindered him in his studies. (**b**) *(remettre) opération* to delay; *date* to put back. ~ **son départ d'une heure** to put back one's departure by an hour, delay one's departure for an hour. (**c**) *montre* to put back. ~ **l'horloge d'une heure** to put the clock back an hour. **2** *vi [montre]* to be slow; *(d'habitude)* to lose. **je retarde de 10 minutes** I'm 10 minutes slow; *(fig) [personne]* ~ **(sur son époque)** to be behind the times, be out of touch. ◆ **retardé, e** *adj enfant* backward.

retéléphoner [ʀ(ə)telefɔne] (1) *vi* to phone again, call back.

retenir [ʀətniʀ] (22) **1** *vt* (**a**) *(empêcher de tomber, de passer etc)* to hold back; *chien* to check; *cheval* to rein in, hold back. **la timidité le retenait** shyness held him back; ~ **qn de faire qch** to keep sb from doing sth, stop sb doing sth. (**b**) *(garder) personne* to keep. ~ **qn à dîner** to have sb stay for dinner, keep sb for dinner; **j'ai été retenu** I was kept back *ou* detained *ou* held up; ~ **qn prisonnier** to hold sb prisoner. (**c**) *humidité, odeur, chaleur* to retain. (**d**) *(fixer) [clou, nœud etc]* to hold. *(fig)* ~ **l'attention de qn** to hold sb's attention. (**e**) *(réserver) place, table* to book, reserve. (**f**) *(se souvenir de) leçon, nom* to remember; *impression* to retain. **j'en retiens qu'il est borné** the thing that stands out *ou* that sticks in my mind *ou* the thing I've learnt is that he's narrow-minded; **celui-là, je le retiens!** * I'll remember him all right!, I shan't forget him in a hurry! * (**g**) *(réprimer) larmes, cri* to hold *ou* choke back *ou* in; *colère* to hold back, restrain. ~ **son souffle** to hold one's breath; **il ne put** ~ **un sourire** he could not hold back *ou* suppress a smile, he could not help smiling. (**h**) *(garder) salaire* to stop, withhold; *bagages d'un client* to retain; *(prélever) somme d'argent* to deduct, keep back. *(Math)* **je pose 4 et je retiens 2** put down 4 and carry 2. (**i**) *(accepter) proposition, plan* to accept; *nom, candidature* to retain, accept.
2 se ~ *vpr (s'accrocher)* to hold o.s. back; *(se contenir)* to restrain o.s.; *(besoins naturels)* to hold on. **se** ~ **de pleurer** to stop o.s. crying; **se** ~ **à qch** to hold *ou* cling on to sth.

rétention [ʀetɑ̃sjɔ̃] *nf (Jur, Méd)* retention.

retentir [ʀ(ə)tɑ̃tiʀ] (2) *vi [sonnerie]* to ring. ~ **de** to ring *ou* resound with; *(affecter)* ~ **sur** to have an effect upon, affect. ◆ **retentissant, e** *adj voix* ringing; *claque, bruit, succès* resounding; *scandale* tremendous; *discours* which causes a great stir. ◆ **retentissement** *nm [nouvelle, œuvre]* stir, effect. *(répercussions)* **~s** repercussions.

retenue [ʀətny] *nf* (**a**) *(prélèvement)* deduction, stoppage *. (**b**) *(modération)* self-control, (self-) restraint; *(réserve)* reserve. **avoir de la** ~ to be reserved; **sans** ~ without restraint, unrestrainedly. (**c**) *(Math)* **n'oublie pas la** ~ don't forget what to carry (over). (**d**) *(Scol)* detention. **être en** ~ to be in detention, be kept in.

réticence [ʀetisɑ̃s] *nf* reluctance. **~s** hesitations, reservations; **avec** ~ reluctantly; **sans** ~ without (any) hesitation *ou* reservation(s). ◆ **réticent, e** *adj (hésitant)* hesitant, reluctant; *(réservé)* reticent, reserved.

rétif, -ive [ʀetif, iv] *adj animal* stubborn; *personne* rebellious, restive.

rétine [ʀetin] *nf* retina.

retirer [ʀ(ə)tiʀe] (1) **1** *vt* (**a**) *(lit, fig: enlever) manteau etc* to take off, remove; *candidature* to withdraw; *plainte* to withdraw, take back. **il retira vite sa main** he quickly took away *ou* removed *ou* withdrew his hand; ~ **qch à qn** *(gén)* to take sth away from sb; *emploi, amitié* to deprive sb of sth; **je retire ce que j'ai dit** I take back what I said; **retire-lui ses chaussures** take his shoes off (for him); ~ **son permis de conduire à qn** to disqualify sb from driving; ~ **à qn sa confiance** to withdraw one's confidence in sb. (**b**) *(faire sortir)* to take out, remove (*de* from). ~ **un bouchon** to pull out *ou* take out *ou* remove a cork; **je ne peux pas** ~ **la clef de la serrure** I can't get the key out of the lock; **on ne peut pas lui** ~ **ça de la tête** we can't get it out of his head. (**c**) *bagages, billets réservés* to collect, pick up; *argent en dépôt* to withdraw, take out; *gage* to redeem. *(Comm)* **votre commande est prête à être retirée** your order is now awaiting collection *ou* ready for collection. (**d**) *(obtenir)* ~ **des avantages de qch** to get *ou* gain *ou* derive advantages from sth; **il n'en a retiré que des ennuis** it brought him nothing but worry. (**e**) *(extraire) minerai, huile* to obtain.
2 se ~ *vpr (partir)* to retire, withdraw; *(se coucher)* to retire (to bed); *(prendre sa retraite)* to retire; *(ôter sa candidature)* to withdraw, stand down (*en faveur de* in favour of); *(pour laisser passer qn etc)* to move out of the way; *(Mil) [troupes]* to withdraw; *[marée]* to recede, go back, ebb; *[eaux d'inondation]* to recede, go down. **se** ~ **de** *compétition etc* to withdraw from.
◆ **retiré, e** *adj lieu* remote, out-of-the-way; *vie* secluded. **il vivait** ~ **du reste du monde** he lived withdrawn *ou* cut off from the rest of the world; ~ **des affaires** retired from business.

retombée [ʀ(ə)tɔ̃be] *nf* (**a**) *(fig: gén pl) (répercussions)* consequences, effects; *[invention etc]* spin-off. **~s** *[bombe]* fallout. (**b**) *(Archit)* spring, springing.

retomber [ʀ(ə)tɔ̃be] (1) *vi* (**a**) *(à nouveau) [personne, neige]* to fall again. ~ **dans** *erreur, guerre* to lapse into; *oubli* to sink into; ~ **en enfance** to lapse into second childhood; ~ **amoureux/malade** to fall in love/fall ill again. (**b**) *(redescendre) [fusée, personne]* to land; *[chose lancée, liquide]* to come down; *[capot]* to fall back down; *[conversation, intérêt]* to fall away. *(lit, fig)* ~ **sur ses pieds** to fall *ou* land on one's feet; *(fig)* **ça lui est retombé sur le nez** it has rebounded on him; **se laisser ~ sur son oreiller** to fall back *ou* sink back onto one's pillow. (**c**) *(pendre) [cheveux, rideaux]* to fall, hang (down) (*sur* onto). (**d**) *[responsabilité]* ~ **sur qn** to fall *ou* land on sb; **les frais retombèrent sur nous** we were landed * *ou* saddled * with the expense; **faire ~ sur qn la responsabilité de qch** to pass the responsibility for sth on to sb.

rétorquer [RetɔRke] (1) *vt* to retort.

rétorsion [RetɔRsjɔ̃] *nf (Jur, Pol)* retortion, retaliation.

retoucher [R(ə)tuʃe] (1) **1** *vt* (**a**) *photo, peinture* to touch up; *vêtement, texte* to alter, make alterations to. (**b**) *(toucher de nouveau)* to touch again; *(blesser de nouveau)* to hit again. **2** *vi*: ~ **à qch** to touch sth again. ◆ **retouche** *nf [texte, vêtement]* alteration. **faire une ~ *ou* des ~s à une photo** to touch up a photograph.

retour [R(ə)tuR] **1** *nm* (**a**) *(gén, Comm, Tech)* return; *(Tennis)* return; *(billet)* return (ticket). **être sur le (chemin du) ~** to be on one's way back; **pendant le ~** on the way *ou* journey back, during the return journey; **à leur ~ (d'Afrique), ils trouvèrent la maison vide** when they got back *ou* on their return (from Africa) they found the house empty; **de ~ à la maison** back home; **le ~ à une vie normale** the return *ou* reversion to (a) normal life; **le ~ (périodique) de ce phénomène/thème** the recurrence of this phenomenon/theme; **on prévoit un ~ du froid** a return of the cold weather is forecast; **un ~ offensif de la grippe** a renewed outbreak of flu; **~ à l'envoyeur** return to sender. (**b**) **en ~** in return; **choc *ou* effet en ~** backlash; **c'est un juste ~ des choses** it's poetic justice; **par ~ (du courrier)** by return (of post); **sans ~** *partir* for ever; *voyage* final; **faire un ~ sur soi-même** to take stock of o.s., do some soul-searching. **2** : **~ d'âge** change of life; **~ en arrière** *(Littérat, Ciné)* flashback; *(souvenir)* look back; *(mesure rétrograde)* retreat; **~ de flamme** blowback; **~ en force** return in strength; **~ de manivelle** *(lit)* kick; *(fig)* backlash.

retournement [R(ə)tuRnəmɑ̃] *nm [situation, opinion publique]* reversal (*de* of), turnaround (*de* in).

retourner [R(ə)tuRne] (1) **1** *vt (avec aux avoir)* (**a**) *(dans l'autre sens) caisse* to turn upside down; *matelas* to turn (over); *carte* to turn up *ou* over; *viande, omelette* to turn over. **~ un tableau contre le mur** to turn a picture against the wall; *(fig)* **elle l'a retourné comme une crêpe *** she soon changed his mind for him; **~ la situation** to reverse the situation, turn the situation round. (**b**) *(en remuant) foin, terre* to turn over; *salade* to toss. **~ qch dans sa tête** to turn sth over in one's mind; *(fig)* **~ le couteau dans la plaie** to twist the knife in the wound. (**c**) *(mettre l'intérieur à l'extérieur) sac, gant* to turn inside out; *(Couture) col* to turn. *(fig)* **~ sa veste** to turn one's coat; **son col est retourné** *(par mégarde)* his collar is turned up. (**d**) *(dans le sens opposé) phrase* to turn round; *argument* to turn back (*contre* against); *compliment, critique* to return. **il retourna le pistolet contre lui-même** he turned the gun on himself. (**e**) *(renvoyer) marchandise, lettre* to return, send back. (**f**) *(fig*: bouleverser) pièce, maison* to turn upside down; *personne* to shake. **ce spectacle m'a retourné *** the sight of this shook me *ou* gave me quite a turn *.
2 *vi (avec aux être)* to return, go back (*à, chez* to). **~ sur ses pas** to turn back, retrace one's steps.
3 *vb impers*: **nous voudrions bien savoir de quoi il retourne** we should really like to know what is going on *ou* what it's all about.
4 se ~ *vpr* (**a**) *[personne couchée]* to turn over; *[véhicule]* to turn over, overturn. **se ~ dans son lit** to toss and turn in bed; **il doit se ~ dans sa tombe** he must be turning in his grave; *(fig)* **laissez-lui le temps de se ~** give him time to sort himself out *ou* turn himself round *ou* find his feet; *(fig)* **il sait se ~** he knows how to cope. (**b**) *(tourner la tête)* to turn round; *(tourner les yeux)* to look back. (**c**) *(fig) [situation]* to be reversed, be turned round. **se ~ contre qn** *[personne]* to turn against sb; *[situation]* to backfire on sb, rebound on sb; *(Jur: poursuivre)* to take (court) action *ou* proceedings against sb; **il ne savait vers qui se ~** he didn't know who to turn to. (**d**) *(tordre) pouce* to wrench, twist. (**e**) *(partir)* **s'en ~** to go back.

retracer [R(ə)tRase] (3) *vt vie, histoire* to relate, recount; *trait effacé* to redraw, draw again.

rétracter [RetRakte] (1) **1** *vt griffe* to draw in, retract; *parole* to retract, withdraw, take back. **2 se ~** *vpr [griffe, antenne]* to retract; *(se dédire)* to retract, withdraw one's statement. **je ne veux pas avoir l'air de me ~** I don't want to appear to back down. ◆ **rétractation** *nf* retraction, withdrawal. ◆ **rétractile** *adj* retractile. ◆ **rétraction** *nf* retraction.

retrait [R(ə)tRɛ] *nm* (**a**) *[mer]* ebb; *[eaux, glacier]* retreat; *[troupes, candidat, somme d'argent]* withdrawal; *[bagages]* collection; *[objet en gage]* redemption. **~ du permis de conduire** disqualification from driving. (**b**) **situé en ~** set back (*de* from); **se tenant en ~** standing back; *(fig)* **rester en ~** to stand aside.

retraite [R(ə)tRɛt] *nf* (**a**) *(fuite)* retreat. **~ aux flambeaux** torchlight procession. (**b**) *[travailleur] (état)* retirement; *(pension)* retirement pension. **être en ~** to be retired *ou* in retirement; **mettre qn à la ~** to pension sb off; **mise à la ~** retirement; **mettre qn à la ~ d'office** to make sb take compulsory retirement; **mise à la ~ d'office** compulsory retirement; **prendre sa ~** to retire, go into retirement; **prendre une ~ anticipée** to retire early; **~ complémentaire** supplementary pension. (**c**) *(littér: refuge)* retreat; *[animal]* lair; *[voleurs]* hideout, hiding place. (**d**) *(Rel)* retreat. **faire une ~** to be in retreat. ◆ **retraité, e 1** *adj personne* retired; *déchets* reprocessed. **2** *nm, f* (old age) pensioner.

retraitement [R(ə)tRɛtmɑ̃] *nm* reprocessing. **usine de ~ des déchets nucléaires** nuclear reprocessing plant. ◆ **retraiter** (1) *vt* to reprocess.

retranchement [R(ə)tRɑ̃ʃmɑ̃] *nm (Mil)* entrenchment, retrenchment. *(fig)* **poursuivre qn jusque dans ses derniers ~s** to drive sb into a corner.

retrancher [R(ə)tRɑ̃ʃe] (1) **1** *vt quantité, nombre* to take away, subtract; *somme d'argent* to deduct, dock, take off; *passage, mot* to take out, remove, omit (*de* from). *(littér)* **son argent le retranchait des autres** his money cut him off from other people. **2 se ~** *vpr (Mil)* **se ~ derrière/dans** to entrench o.s. behind/in; **se ~ dans son mutisme/derrière la loi** to take refuge in silence/behind the law; **se ~ dans sa douleur** to draw back into one's pain, shut o.s. off with one's pain.

retranscrire [R(ə)tRɑ̃skRiR] (39) *vt* to retranscribe. ◆ **retranscription** *nf* retranscription.

retransmettre [R(ə)tRɑ̃smɛtR(ə)] (56) *vt* to broadcast, relay. ◆ **retransmission** *nf* broadcast. **~ en direct/différé** live/recorded broadcast.

rétrécir [RetResiR] (2) **1** *vt vêtement* to take in; *tissu* to shrink; *pupille* to contract; *rue, orifice* to make narrower; *bague* to tighten, make smaller; *esprit* to narrow. **faire ~** *tissu* to shrink. **2** *vi*, **se ~** *vpr [tissu]* to shrink; *[pupille]* to contract; *[vallée]* to narrow, get narrower; *[esprit]* to grow narrow; *[cercle d'amis]* to grow smaller, dwindle. ◆ **rétrécissement** *nm [tricot]* shrinkage; *[pupille]* contraction; *[vallée]* narrowing.

rétribuer [RetRibɥe] (1) *vt ouvrier* to pay. **~ le travail de qn** to pay sb for his work. ◆ **rétribution** *nf* payment.

rétro [ʀetʀo] **1** *adj inv*: **la mode** ~ the pre-1940s fashions. **2** *nm*: **le** ~ the pre-1940s style.

rétroactif, -ive [ʀetʀɔaktif, iv] *adj* retrospective; *(Jur)* retroactive. *(Admin)* **augmentation avec effet** ~ backdated pay rise. ◆ **rétroaction** *nf* retrospective effect. ◆ **rétroactivement** *adv (gén)* retrospectively; *(Jur)* retroactively. ◆ **rétroactivité** *nf* retroactivity.

rétrofusée [ʀetʀɔfyze] *nf* retrorocket.

rétrograde [ʀetʀɔgʀad] *adj idées, politique* retrograde, reactionary; *mouvement, sens* backward, retrograde. *(Billard)* **effet** ~ screw-back stroke.

rétrograder [ʀetʀɔgʀade] (1) **1** *vi (Aut)* to change down; *(dans une hiérarchie)* to regress, move down; *(perdre son avance)* to fall back; *(reculer)* to move back. **2** *vt fonctionnaire* to demote, downgrade.

rétroprojecteur [ʀetʀɔpʀɔʒɛktœʀ] *nm* overhead projector.

rétrospectif, -ive [ʀetʀɔspɛktif, iv] *adj, nf* retrospective. ◆ **rétrospectivement** *adv* in retrospect.

retrousser [ʀ(ə)tʀuse] (1) **1** *vt jupe* to hitch up, tuck up; *manche* to roll up; *lèvres* to curl up. *(lit, fig)* ~ **ses manches** to roll up one's sleeves. **2** **se** ~ *vpr [bords]* to turn outwards. ◆ **retroussé, e** *adj nez* turned-up, retroussé; *moustaches* curled up.

retrouvailles [ʀ(ə)tʀuvɑj] *nfpl* reunion.

retrouver [ʀ(ə)tʀuve] (1) **1** *vt* (**a**) *(récupérer) objet, situation, chemin* to find again; *santé, calme* to regain; *secret, recette* to rediscover; *nom, date* to think of, remember, recall. **on a retrouvé le corps** the body has been found; **une telle occasion ne se retrouvera jamais** an opportunity like this will never occur again *ou* crop up again; **une chienne n'y retrouverait pas ses petits** it's in absolute chaos. (**b**) *(rencontrer) personne* to meet (up with) again; *(pour rendez-vous)* to join, meet *ou* see again; *endroit* to be back in, see again; *caractéristique, phénomène* to find, encounter. **et que je ne te retrouve pas ici!** and don't let me catch *ou* find you here again!; **on retrouve chez Jacques le sourire de son père** you can see *ou* recognize his father's smile in Jacques; **je retrouve bien là mon fils!** that's my son all right!; **on retrouve sans cesse les mêmes tournures dans ses romans** you are constantly coming across *ou* meeting the same expressions in his novels.
2 se ~ *vpr* (**a**) *(se réunir)* to meet; *(après une absence)* to meet again. **on se retrouvera!** I'll get even with you!; **comme on se retrouve!** fancy *ou* imagine meeting *ou* seeing you here! (**b**) *(dans même endroit, situation)* to find o.s. back (*dans* in). (**c**) *(*: finir)* **il s'est retrouvé en prison/dans le fossé** he ended up *ou* landed (up) * in prison/in the ditch. (**d**) **s'y** ~ *(trouver son chemin)* to find one's way; *(*: rentrer dans ses frais)* to break even; *(*: tirer un profit)* to make a profit; **on a de la peine à s'y** ~, **dans ces digressions** it's hard to find one's way through *ou* to make sense of these digressions; **je ne m'y retrouve plus** I'm completely lost.

rétroviseur [ʀetʀɔvizœʀ] *nm* rear-view mirror, (driving) mirror. ~ **(d'aile)** wing mirror, side-view mirror *(US)*.

Réunion [ʀeynjɔ̃] *nf*: **la** ~, **l'île de la** ~ Réunion Island.

réunir [ʀeyniʀ] (2) **1** *vt* (**a**) *objets* to gather *ou* collect (together); *preuves* to put together; *fonds* to raise; *pièces de collection* to collect; *tendances, styles* to combine. (**b**) *participants* to gather, collect; *membres d'un parti* to call together, call a meeting of; *amis, famille* to entertain, have round, have in; *personnes brouillées* to bring together, reunite. (**c**) *(raccorder) [couloir, fil]* to join, link. ~ **deux fils** to tie *ou* join two threads together; ~ **à** *province etc* to unite to. **2 se** ~ *vpr* (**a**) *(se rencontrer)* to meet, get together. **se** ~ **entre amis** to have a friendly get-together. (**b**) *[compagnies]* to combine; *[états]* to unite; *[fleuves]* to merge. ◆ **réuni, e** *adj*: ~**s** *(pris ensemble)* (put) together, combined; *(Comm: associés)* associated. ◆ **réunification** *nf* reunification. ◆ **réunifier** (7) *vt* to reunify. ◆ **réunion** *nf* (**a**) *(action)* collection, gathering; raising; combination; reunion. ~ **d'une province à un État** union of a province with a state. (**b**) *(séance)* meeting. **dans une** ~ at *ou* in a meeting; ~ **cycliste** cycle rally; ~ **hippique** gymkhana, horse show; ~ **de famille** family gathering; ~ **sportive** sports meeting; ~ **syndicale** union meeting. ◆ **réunionite** * *nf* mania for meetings.

réussir [ʀeysiʀ] (2) **1** *vi* (**a**) *[projet]* to succeed, be a success, be successful; *[culture]* to thrive, do well; *[manœuvre, ruse]* to pay off. **tout lui réussit** everything goes *ou* comes right for him, everything works for him; **cela ne lui a pas réussi** that didn't do him any good. (**b**) *[personne]* to succeed, be successful, be a success; *(à un examen)* to pass; *(dans les affaires, ses études)* to do well (*dans* in). **ont-ils réussi?** did they succeed?, did they pull it off?; **il a réussi à son examen** he passed his exam; **il réussit bien en maths** he does well *ou* he's a success at maths; ~ **à faire** to succeed in doing, manage to do. (**c**) *[climat, aliment]* ~ **à qn** to agree with sb. **2** *vt entreprise, plat* to make a success of, make a good job of; *but* to bring off, pull off *; *photo* to manage successfully. ~ **son coup** * to pull it off *; **elle a réussi son effet** she achieved the effect she wanted. ◆ **réussi, e** *adj (gén)* successful; *mouvement* good, well executed. **c'était très** ~ it was a great success *ou* very successful. ◆ **réussite** *nf (succès)* success; *(Cartes)* patience. **faire une** ~ *ou* **des** ~**s** to play patience.

réutiliser [ʀeytilize] (1) *vt* to re-use.

revaloir [ʀ(ə)valwaʀ] (29) *vt*: **je te revaudrai ça** *(hostile)* I'll pay you back for this; *(reconnaissant)* I'll repay you some day.

revaloriser [ʀ(ə)valɔʀize] (1) *vt monnaie* to revalue; *salaire* to raise; *méthode* to promote again. ◆ **revalorisation** *nf* revaluation; raising; fresh promotion.

revanche [ʀ(ə)vɑ̃ʃ] *nf* revenge; *(Jeux, Sport)* return match; *(Boxe)* return fight *ou* bout. **prendre sa** ~ **(sur qn)** to take one's revenge (on sb), get one's own back (on sb) *; **en** ~ on the other hand.

rêvasser [ʀɛvase] (1) *vi* to daydream. ◆ **rêvasserie** *nf*: ~**(s)** daydreaming.

rêve [ʀɛv] *nm (lit, fig)* dream; *(éveillé)* daydream. **faire des** ~**s** to dream, have dreams; **il est dans un** ~ he's (day)dreaming; **voiture/silence de** ~ dream car/silence; **son** ~ **de jeunesse** his youthful dream; **la femme de ses** ~**s** the woman of his dreams, his dream woman; **disparaître** *ou* **s'évanouir comme un** ~ to vanish *ou* fade like a dream; **disparaître comme dans un** ~ to disappear in a trice; **ça, c'est le** ~ * that would be ideal, that would be (just) perfect.

revêche [ʀəvɛʃ] *adj* surly, sour-tempered.

réveil [ʀevɛj] *nm* (**a**) *[dormeur]* waking (up), wakening; *(retour à la réalité)* awakening; *[nature, sentiment, souvenir]* reawakening; *[volcan]* fresh stirrings; *[douleur]* return. **dès le** ~, **il chante** as soon as he's awake *ou* he wakes up he starts singing. (**b**) *(Mil)* reveille. (**c**) *(réveille-matin)* alarm (clock).

réveiller [ʀeveje] (1) **1** *vt dormeur* to wake (up), waken; *personne évanouie* to bring round, revive; *appétit, courage, sentiment* to rouse, awaken; *douleur (physique)* to start up again; *(mentale)* to revive, reawaken. **2 se** ~ *vpr [dormeur]* to wake (up), awake; *[personne évanouie]* to come round, come to, regain consciousness; *[appétit, courage, sentiment]* to be roused; *[douleur, souvenir]* to return; *[nature]* to reawaken; *[volcan]* to stir again. **se**

réveillant de sa torpeur rousing himself from his lethargy. ◆ **réveillé, e** *adj* awake; *(*: dégourdi)* bright. **à moitié** ~ half asleep. ◆ **réveille-matin** *nm inv* alarm clock.

réveillon [ʀevɛjɔ̃] *nm* Christmas Eve *ou* New Year's Eve dinner. ◆ **réveillonner** (1) *vi* to celebrate Christmas *ou* New Year's Eve *(with a dinner and a party)*.

révéler [ʀevele] (6) **1** *vt* (**a**) *secret* to disclose, give away, reveal; *opinion* to make known. (**b**) *aptitude, caractère* to reveal, display; *sentiments* to show. (**c**) *artiste [impresario]* to discover; *[œuvre]* to bring to fame. **2 se** ~ *vpr [vérité, talent, tendance]* to be revealed, reveal itself; *(Rel)* to reveal o.s.; *[artiste]* to show *ou* display one's talent. **se** ~ **cruel** to show o.s. *ou* prove to be cruel; **se** ~ **difficile** to prove difficult. ◆ **révélateur, -trice 1** *adj indice* revealing. **c'est** ~ **d'un malaise** it reveals a malaise. **2** *nm (Phot)* developer; *(expérience)* revelation. ◆ **révélation** *nf* revelation; disclosure. **ce jeune auteur a été la** ~ **de l'année** this young author was the discovery of the year; **faire des** ~**s** to make disclosures *ou* revelations. ◆ **révélé, e** *adj (Rel)* revealed.

revenant, e [ʀəvnɑ̃, ɑ̃t] *nm, f* ghost. **tiens, un** ~! * hello stranger! *

revendeur, -euse [ʀ(ə)vɑ̃dœʀ, øz] *nm, f (détaillant)* retailer; *(d'occasion)* secondhand dealer.

revendiquer [ʀ(ə)vɑ̃dike] (1) *vt droits* to claim, demand; *responsabilité* to claim; *explosion, attentat* to claim responsibility for. ◆ **revendicatif, -ive** *adj mouvement etc* of protest. ◆ **revendication** *nf (action)* claiming; *(demande)* claim, demand.

revendre [ʀ(ə)vɑ̃dʀ(ə)] (41) *vt (d'occasion)* to resell; *(au détail)* to sell. *(davantage)* **j'en ai revendu 4** I sold another 4; **avoir de l'énergie à** ~ to have energy enough and to spare; **des tableaux, on en a à** ~ pictures, we've got them by the score.

revenir [ʀəvniʀ] (22) **1** *vi* (**a**) *[personne] (repasser de nouveau)* to come back, come again; *(rentrer)* to come back, return; *[saison, mode, lettre]* to come back, return; *[fête, date]* to come (round) again; *[calme, soleil]* to return; *[thème, idée]* to recur, reappear. **cette expression revient souvent dans sa conversation** that expression often crops up in his conversation; ~ **chez soi/de voyage/dans son pays** to come back *ou* return home/from a journey/to one's country; ~ **en bateau/avion** to sail/fly back; **je reviens dans un instant** I'll be back in a minute, I'll be right back *. (**b**) ~ **à** *études, sujet* to go back to, return to; *méthode* to revert to; ~ **à la charge** to return to the attack; **revenons à nos moutons** let's get back to the subject; **nous y reviendrons dans un instant** we'll come back to that in a moment; **il n'y a pas à y** ~ there's no going back on it; ~ **en arrière** *(gén)* to go back; *(dans le temps)* **on ne peut pas** ~ **en arrière** you can't turn *ou* put back the clock. (**c**) ~ **à** *(équivaloir à)* to come down to, amount to, boil down to; *(coûter)* to amount to, come to; **cela revient à dire que** that amounts to saying that; **cela revient au même** it amounts to *ou* comes to the same thing; **ça revient cher** it's expensive; **à combien est-ce que cela va vous** ~? how much will that cost you? (**d**) ~ **à qn** *[souvenir oublié]* to come back to sb, recur to sb; *[courage, appétit, parole]* to come back to sb, return (to sb); *[prérogative, honneur]* to fall to sb; *[héritage]* to come *ou* go *ou* pass to sb; *[ragots]* to reach sb's ears; **il a une tête qui ne me revient pas** I don't like the look of him; **tout le mérite vous revient** all the credit goes to you, the credit is all yours; **il lui revient de décider** it's for him *ou* it's up to him to decide; **ce titre lui revient de droit** this title is his by right; **là-dessus, 100 F me reviennent** 100 francs of that comes to me. (**e**) ~ **sur** *passé, problème* to go back over; *promesse* to go back on; **ne revenons pas là-dessus** let's not go back over that. (**f**) ~ **de** *maladie* to recover from, get over; *syncope* to come round from; *surprise* to get over; *illusions* to lose, shake off; *erreurs, théories* to leave behind, cast aside; **elle est revenue de tout** she's seen it all before; **crois-tu qu'il en reviendra?** do you think he'll pull through?; **il revient de loin** it was a close shave *ou* a near thing for him, he had a close shave; **je n'en reviens pas!** I can't get over it! (**g**) ~ **à soi** to come round; ~ **à la vie** to come back to life. (**h**) *(Culin)* **faire** ~ to brown. **2 s'en** ~ *vpr* to come back (*de* from).

revente [ʀ(ə)vɑ̃t] *nf* resale.

revenu [ʀəvny] *nm [particulier]* income; *[état]* revenue (*de* from); *[investissement]* yield, revenue (*de* from, on). ~ **intérieur brut** gross domestic income; ~ **national** gross national product; ~ **net d'impôts** disposable income.

rêver [ʀeve] (1) **1** *vi* (**a**) *(gén, fig)* to dream (*de, à* of, about); *(rêvasser)* to daydream. **tu m'as appelé? — moi? tu rêves!** did you call me? — me? you must have been dreaming! *ou* you're imagining things!; **on croit** ~! * I can hardly believe it!, the mind boggles! * (**b**) *(désirer)* ~ **de qch/de faire** to dream of sth/of doing; ~ **de réussir** to long to succeed, long for success. **2** *vt (en dormant)* to dream; *(imaginer)* to dream up; *(désirer)* to dream of. **il se rêve conquérant** he dreams of being a conqueror. ◆ **rêvé, e** *adj* ideal, perfect.

réverbérer [ʀevɛʀbeʀe] (6) *vt son* to send back, reverberate; *chaleur, lumière* to reflect. ◆ **réverbération** *nf* reverberation; reflection. ◆ **réverbère** *nm* street lamp *ou* light.

révérence [ʀeveʀɑ̃s] *nf* (**a**) *[homme]* bow; *[femme]* curtsey. **faire une** ~ to bow; to curtsey (*à qn* to sb); *(fig: partir)* **tirer sa** ~ **(à qn)** to take one's leave (of sb). (**b**) *(respect)* reverence (*envers* for). ◆ **révérencieux, -ieuse** *adj* reverent.

révérend, e [ʀeveʀɑ̃, ɑ̃d] *adj, nm* reverend. **le R~ Père Martin** Reverend Father Martin.

révérer [ʀeveʀe] (6) *vt* to revere.

rêverie [ʀɛvʀi] *nf (état)* daydreaming; *(rêve, chimère)* daydream.

revérifier [ʀ(ə)veʀifje] (7) *vt* to double-check.

revers [ʀ(ə)vɛʀ] *nm* (**a**) *[papier, main]* back; *[étoffe]* wrong side; *[médaille]* reverse side. **prendre l'ennemi à** ~ to take the enemy from *ou* in the rear; *(fig)* **c'est le** ~ **de la médaille** that's the other side of the coin; **d'un** ~ **de main** with the back of one's hand. (**b**) *(Tennis)* backhand. **faire un** ~ to play a backhand shot. (**c**) *[veste]* lapel; *[pantalon]* turn-up, cuff *(US)*; *[bottes]* top; *[manche]* (turned-back) cuff. (**d**) *(coup du sort)* setback. ~ **(de fortune)** reverse (of fortune); ~ **économiques** economic setbacks *ou* reverses.

reverser [ʀ(ə)vɛʀse] (1) *vt liquide* to pour out some more; *somme* to put back, pay back (*dans, sur* into).

réversible [ʀevɛʀsibl(ə)] *adj* reversible; *(Jur)* revertible (*sur* to). ◆ **réversion** *nf (Bio, Jur)* reversion.

revêtir [ʀ(ə)vetiʀ] (20) **1** *vt* (**a**) *habit* to don, put on. (**b**) *caractère, importance, forme* to assume, take on. (**c**) ~ **qn de** *habit* to array sb in; *autorité, dignité* to endow *ou* invest sb with; *(déguiser)* ~ **qch de** to cloak sth in, cover sth with; ~ **un document de sa signature** to append one's signature to a document. (**d**) *(enduire)* to coat; *route* to surface; *mur, sol* to cover (*de* with). ~ **de plâtre** to plaster; **montagnes revêtues de neige** mountains covered in snow, snow-covered mountains. **2 se** ~ *vpr (mettre)* **se** ~ **de** *habit* to array o.s. in, don, dress o.s. in; *neige, feuilles* to be covered in. ◆ **revêtement** *nm (enduit)* coating; *[route]* surface; *[mur extérieur]* facing; *[mur intérieur]* covering; *[sol]* flooring, floor-covering. ~ **mural** wall-covering. ◆ **revêtu, e** *adj [personne]* ~ **de** dressed in, wearing.

rêveur, -euse [ʀɛvœʀ, øz] **1** *adj air* dreamy. **ça vous laisse** ~ * the mind boggles *, it makes you wonder. **2** *nm, f (lit, péj)* dreamer. ◆ **rêveusement** *adv* dreamily.

revigorer [ʀ(ə)vigɔʀe] (1) *vt [vent]* to invigorate; *[repas]* to revive, buck up *; *[discours]* to cheer. **ça revigore** it's bracing *ou* invigorating.

revirement [ʀ(ə)viʀmɑ̃] *nm (gén)* reversal (*de* of); *[goûts]* (abrupt) change (*de* in); *[opinions]* change, U-turn, turnaround (*de* in).

réviser [ʀevize] (1) *vt procès, règlement* to review; *opinion* to review, reappraise; *comptes* to audit; *liste, leçons, manuscrit* to revise; *moteur* to overhaul, service; *montre* to service. ~ **en hausse/en baisse** *estimation* to revise up/down; **faire** ~ **sa voiture** to have one's car serviced. ◆ **révision** *nf (action)* review; reappraisal; auditing; revision; overhaul; servicing. *(Scol)* **faire ses ~s** to do one's revision; *(Aut)* **prochaine** ~ **après 10 000 km** next major service after 10,000 km.

revivifier [ʀ(ə)vivifje] (7) *vt* to revive.

revivre [ʀəvivʀ(ə)] (46) **1** *vi (être ressuscité)* to live again; *(être revigoré)* to come alive again; *[coutumes]* to be revived. **faire** ~ *(ressusciter)* to bring back *ou* restore to life; *(revigorer)* to revive, put new life into; *mode, époque* to revive. **2** *vt* to relive, live again.

révocation [ʀevɔkɑsjɔ̃] *nf [fonctionnaire]* removal (from office), dismissal; *[contrat]* revocation, repeal. *(Hist)* **la** ~ **de l'Édit de Nantes** the Revocation of the Edict of Nantes. ◆ **révocable** *adj* removable, dismissible; revocable.

revoici * [ʀ(ə)vwasi] *prép*, **revoilà** * [ʀ(ə)vwala] *prép:* ~ **Paul!** Paul's back (again)!, here's Paul again!; **le** ~ **qui se plaint!** there he goes complaining again!

revoir [ʀ(ə)vwaʀ] (30) *vt* (**a**) *(gén, fig)* to see again; *photos* to have another look at. **quand le revois-tu?** when are you seeing *ou* meeting him again?, when are you meeting again?; **au** ~ **Monsieur** goodbye Mr X; **dire au** ~ **à qn** to say goodbye to sb; **faire au** ~ **de la main** to wave goodbye; **ce n'est qu'un au** ~ it's only a temporary farewell *ou* parting. (**b**) *(réviser) édition* to revise; *(Scol) leçons* to revise, go over again.

révolter [ʀevɔlte] (1) **1** *vt* to revolt, outrage, appal. **2 se** ~ *vpr (s'insurger)* to revolt, rise up (*contre* against); *(protester)* to rebel (*contre* against); *(s'indigner)* to be revolted *ou* outraged *ou* appalled (*contre* by). ◆ **révoltant, e** *adj* revolting, outrageous, appalling. ◆ **révolte** *nf* revolt. **en** ~ **contre** in revolt *ou* up in arms against. ◆ **révolté, e** **1** *adj* (**a**) rebellious, in revolt. (**b**) *(outré)* outraged, appalled. **2** *nm, f* rebel.

révolu, e [ʀevɔly] *adj* past. **des jours ~s** past *ou* bygone days, days gone by; *(Admin)* **âgé de 20 ans ~s** over 20 years of age; **après 2 ans ~s** when two full years had (*ou* have) passed.

révolution [ʀevɔlysjɔ̃] *nf (gén)* revolution. *[rue]* **être en** ~ to be in an uproar. ◆ **révolutionnaire** *adj, nmf* revolutionary. ◆ **révolutionner** (1) *vt (transformer radicalement)* to revolutionize; *(*: bouleverser)* to stir up.

revolver [ʀevɔlvɛʀ] *nm (gén)* gun; *(à barillet)* revolver.

révoquer [ʀevɔke] (1) *vt fonctionnaire* to remove from office, dismiss; *contrat, édit* to revoke, repeal.

revue [ʀ(ə)vy] *nf* (**a**) *(gén, Mil: examen)* review. ~ **de presse** review of the press; *(lit, fig)* **passer en** ~ to pass in review. (**b**) *(magazine)* magazine; *(spécialisée)* journal; *(érudite)* review. (**c**) *(spectacle)* *(satirique)* revue; *(de variétés)* variety show *ou* performance. ~ **à grand spectacle** revue spectacular.

révulser (se) [ʀevylse] (1) *vpr [visage]* to contort; *[yeux]* to roll upwards. ◆ **révulsif, -ive** *adj, nm* revulsant. ◆ **révulsion** *nf (Méd, fig)* revulsion.

rez-de-chaussée [ʀedʃose] *nm inv* ground floor, first floor *(US)*. **habiter un** ~ to live in a ground-floor flat *ou* in a first-floor apartment *(US)*.

rez-de-jardin [ʀedʒaʀdɛ̃] *nm inv* garden level. **appartement en** ~ garden flat *ou* apartment *(US)*.

rhabiller [ʀabije] (1) **1** *vt:* ~ **qn** to dress sb again; *(lui racheter des habits)* to fit sb out again, reclothe sb. **2 se** ~ *vpr* to put one's clothes back on, dress (o.s.) again. **tu peux aller te** ~! ⁑ you've had it! *

rhapsodie [ʀapsɔdi] *nf* rhapsody.

rhésus [ʀezys] *nm (Méd)* Rhesus.

rhétorique [ʀetɔʀik] **1** *nf* rhetoric. **2** *adj* rhetorical.

Rhin [ʀɛ̃] *nm:* **le** ~ the Rhine.

rhinocéros [ʀinɔseʀɔs] *nm* rhinoceros.

rhinopharyngite [ʀinɔfaʀɛ̃ʒit] *nf* sore throat, throat infection.

Rhodes [ʀɔd] *n* Rhodes. **l'île de** ~ the island of Rhodes.

Rhodésie [ʀɔdezi] *nf* Rhodesia.

rhododendron [ʀɔdɔdɛ̃dʀɔ̃] *nm* rhododendron.

Rhône [ʀon] *nm:* **le** ~ *(fleuve, département)* the Rhone.

rhubarbe [ʀybaʀb(ə)] *nf* rhubarb.

rhum [ʀɔm] *nm* rum.

rhumatisme [ʀymatism(ə)] *nm:* ~**(s)** rheumatism. ◆ **rhumatisant, e** *adj, nm, f* rheumatic. ◆ **rhumatismal, e,** *mpl* **-aux** *adj* rheumatic. ◆ **rhumatologie** *nf* rheumatology. ◆ **rhumatologiste** *nmf,* **rhumatologue** *nmf* rheumatologist.

rhume [ʀym] *nm* cold. **attraper un** ~ to catch a cold; ~ **de cerveau** head cold; ~ **des foins** hay fever.

riant, e [ʀijɑ̃, ɑ̃t] *adj paysage* smiling; *atmosphère, perspective* cheerful, pleasant, happy.

ribambelle [ʀibɑ̃bɛl] *nf:* ~ **de** *enfants* swarm *ou* herd *ou* flock of; *noms* string of.

ribouldingue * † [ʀibuldɛ̃g] *nf* spree, binge *. **faire la** ~ to go on the spree *ou* the binge *.

ricain, e ⁑ [ʀikɛ̃, ɛn] *adj,* **R~(e)** *nm(f) (péj)* Yank(ee) * *(péj)*.

ricaner [ʀikane] (1) *vi (méchamment)* to snigger; *(bêtement)* to giggle. ◆ **ricanement** *nm* snigger; giggle.

riche [ʀiʃ] **1** *adj (gén, fig)* rich; *personne* rich, wealthy, well-off. ~ **à millions** enormously wealthy; **faire un** ~ **mariage** to marry (into) money; **ce n'est pas un** ~ **cadeau** it's not much of a gift; **ça fait** ~ * it looks plush(y) * *ou* expensive *ou* posh *; **c'est une** ~ **idée** that's a great * *ou* grand idea; **il y a une documentation très** ~ **sur ce sujet** there is a wealth of *ou* a vast amount of information on this subject; ~ **en** *calories, gibier* rich in; ~ **de** *possibilités, espérances* full of; ~ **en protéines** with a high protein content, rich in protein; **alimentation** ~ **en protéines** high-protein diet; **je ne suis pas** ~ **en sucre** I'm not very well-off for sugar. **2** *nmf* rich *ou* wealthy person. **les ~s** the rich, the wealthy. ◆ **richard, e** * *nm, f (péj)* moneybags *. ◆ **richement** *adv* richly. ◆ **richesse** *nf* (**a**) *[personne, pays]* wealth; *[ameublement, décor]* richness; *[sol, texte, collection]* richness. **la** ~ **en calcium de cet aliment** the high calcium content of this food; **la** ~ **en pétrole du pays** the country's abundant *ou* vast oil resources; **la santé est une** ~ good health is a great blessing *ou* is a boon. (**b**) **~s** *(argent)* riches, wealth; *(ressources)* wealth; *(fig: trésors)* treasures; **~s naturelles** natural resources. ◆ **richissime** *adj* fabulously rich *ou* wealthy.

ricin [ʀisɛ̃] *nm* castor oil plant.

ricocher [ʀikɔʃe] (1) *vi [balle de fusil]* to rebound, ricochet; *[pierre etc]* to rebound; *(sur l'eau)* to bounce (*sur qch* off sth). ◆ **ricochet** *nm* rebound; ricochet; bounce. **faire** ~ to rebound *ou* ricochet *ou* bounce (*sur* off); *(fig)* to rebound; **faire des ~s** to skim pebbles.

rictus [ʀiktys] *nm (moqueur, cruel)* grin; *[animal, dément]* grimace.

ride [ʀid] *nf [peau, pomme]* wrinkle (*de* in); *[eau, sable]* ripple (*de* on, in), ridge (*de* in).

rideau, *pl* **~x** [ʀido] *nm (gén, Théât)* curtain; *[boutique]* shutter; *[cheminée]* blower; *[classeur]* roll shutter; *[appareil-photo]* shutter. **tirer les ~x** to draw the curtains *ou* drapes *(US)*; ~ **de** *arbres* screen of; *pluie* sheet of; ~ **de fer** *[boutique]* metal shutter(s); *[théâtre]* (metal) safety curtain; *(Pol)* **le** ~ **de fer** the Iron Curtain.

rider [ʀide] (1) **1** *vt peau, fruit* to wrinkle; *eau* to ripple; *sable* to ruffle the surface of. **2 se** ~ *vpr* to become wrinkled; to become rippled.

ridicule [ʀidikyl] **1** *adj (gén)* ridiculous; *personne, vêtement* ludicrous, absurd; *prétentions* laughable; *quantité* ridiculously small. **se rendre** ~ to make o.s. (look) ridiculous, make a fool of o.s. **2** *nm* (**a**) **le** ~ *(grotesque)* ridicule; *(absurdité)* **le** ~ **de qch** the ridiculousness *ou* the absurdity of sth; **se donner le** ~ **de...** to be ridiculous enough to...; **tomber dans le** ~ to become ridiculous; **le** ~ **ne tue pas** ridicule never killed anyone; **tourner qn en** ~ to ridicule sb, make sb an object of ridicule. (**b**) *(travers)* **~s** ridiculous *ou* silly ways, absurdities. ◆ **ridiculement** *adv* ridiculously. ◆ **ridiculiser** (1) **1** *vt* to ridicule, hold up to ridicule. **2 se** ~ *vpr* to make o.s. (look) ridiculous, make a fool of o.s.

rien [ʀjɛ̃] **1** *pron indéf* (**a**) *(avec ne)* nothing. **je n'ai** ~ **entendu** I didn't hear anything, I didn't hear a thing, I heard nothing; **il n'y a plus** ~ there's nothing left; **je ne crois plus à** ~ I don't believe in anything any more. (**b**) ~ **de** + *adj, ptp* nothing; ~ **de plus** nothing more *ou* else *ou* further; **il n'est** ~ **de tel qu'une bonne pêche** there's nothing like *ou* nothing to beat a good peach; ~ **de plus facile** nothing easier. (**c**) ~ **que la chambre coûte très cher** the room alone costs a great deal; **la vérité,** ~ **que la vérité** the truth and nothing but the truth; **je voudrais vous voir,** ~ **qu'une minute** could I see you just for a minute. (**d**) *(= quelque chose)* anything. **as-tu jamais lu** ~ **de plus drôle?** have you ever read anything funnier? (**e**) *(intensif)* ~ **au monde** nothing on earth *ou* in the world; ~ **du tout** nothing at all; ~ **de** ~ * nothing, absolutely nothing; **trois fois** ~ next to nothing. (**f**) *(Sport)* nil, nothing. ~ **partout** nothing all; *(Tennis)* **15 à** ~ 15 love. (**g**) *(avec avoir, être, faire)* **n'avoir** ~ **contre qn** to have nothing against sb; **il n'a** ~ **d'un dictateur** he's got nothing of the dictator about him; **n'être** ~ *[personne]* to be a nobody; *[chose]* to be nothing; **il ne nous est** ~ he's nothing to do with us; **n'être pour** ~ **dans une affaire** to have no hand in *ou* have nothing to do with an affair; **il n'en est** ~ it's not so at all, it's nothing of the sort; **élever 4 enfants, ça n'est pas** ~ bringing up 4 children is no mean feat; **il ne fait (plus)** ~ he doesn't work (any more); **il ne nous a** ~ **fait** he hasn't done anything to us; **cela ne lui fait** ~ he doesn't mind, it doesn't matter to him; **ça ne fait** ~ * it doesn't matter, never mind; ~ **à faire!** it's no good!, nothing doing! * (**h**) *(locutions)* ~ **à déclarer/signaler** nothing to declare/report; **je vous remercie — de** ~ * thank you — you're welcome *ou* don't mention it *ou* not at all; **c'est cela ou** ~ it's that or nothing; **c'est mieux que** ~ it's better than nothing; ~ **n'y fait!** nothing's any good!; **c'est à moi,** ~ **qu'à moi** it's mine and mine alone; **une blessure de** ~ **(du tout)** a trifling *ou* trivial injury, a mere scratch; **une fille de** ~ a worthless girl; **cela ne nous gêne en** ~ **(du tout)** it doesn't bother us in any way *ou* in the least *ou* at all; **pour** ~ *(peu cher)* for a song, for next to nothing; *(inutilement)* for nothing; **ce n'est pas pour** ~ **que...** it is not without cause *ou* good reason that..., it's not for nothing that...; **il ne s'agit de** ~ **moins qu'un crime** it's nothing less than a crime.
2 *nm* (**a**) *(néant)* nothingness. (**b**) **un** ~ a mere nothing; **des ~s** trivia; **il a peur d'un** ~ every little thing *ou* anything *ou* the slightest thing frightens him; **avec un** ~ **d'ironie** with a hint *ou* touch of irony; **en un** ~ **de temps** in no time (at all), in next to no time; **c'est un** ~ **bruyant ici** it's a bit *ou* a shade *ou* a fraction noisy in here.
3 *adv* (‡) *(très)* not half *, really. **il fait** ~ **froid ici** it isn't half cold here *.

rieur, rieuse [ʀijœʀ, ʀijøz] **1** *adj personne* cheerful, merry; *expression* cheerful, laughing. **2** *nm, f*: **les ~s** people who are (*ou* were) laughing.

rigide [ʀiʒid] *adj armature* rigid, stiff; *muscle, carton* stiff; *règle, politique* strict, rigid. **livre à couverture** ~ hardback (book). ◆ **rigidement** *adv* strictly, rigidly. ◆ **rigidifier** (7) *vt (lit)* to make rigid *ou* stiff; *(fig)* to rigidify. ◆ **rigidité** *nf* rigidity, stiffness; strictness.

rigole [ʀigɔl] *nf (canal)* channel; *(filet d'eau)* rivulet; *(Agr: sillon)* furrow. ~ **d'irrigation** irrigation channel; ~ **d'écoulement** drain.

rigoler * [ʀigɔle] (1) *vi (rire)* to laugh; *(s'amuser)* to have fun, have a laugh *; *(plaisanter)* to joke. *(iro)* **tu me fais** ~ you make me laugh; **on a bien rigolé** we had great fun *ou* a good laugh *; **tu rigoles!** you're kidding! * *ou* joking!; **il ne faut pas** ~ **avec ce genre de maladie** you mustn't fool around with an illness like this *; **j'ai dit ça pour** ~ it was only a joke, I only said it in fun *ou* for a laugh *. ◆ **rigolade** * *nf*: **aimer la** ~ to like a bit of fun *ou* a laugh *; **il prend tout à la** ~ he thinks everything's a big joke *ou* laugh *, he makes a joke of everything; **c'est de la** ~ *(c'est facile)* it's child's play *ou* a cinch *; *(c'est une parodie)* it's a big joke *ou* farce; *(c'est un attrape-nigaud)* it's a complete con ‡. ◆ **rigolo, -ote** * **1** *adj personne, histoire* funny, killing *. **ce n'est pas** ~ it's no joke, it's not funny; **c'est** ~**, je n'avais jamais remarqué cela** that's funny, *ou* odd, I had never noticed that. **2** *nm, f (amusant)* comic, wag; *(péj: fumiste)* fraud, phoney.

rigueur [ʀigœʀ] *nf* (**a**) *[discipline, climat]* harshness, rigour. **les ~s du sort/de l'hiver** the rigours of fate/winter. (**b**) *[morale, personne]* strictness. **la politique de** ~ **du gouvernement** the government's austerity measures; **la** ~ **économique** economic austerity. (**c**) *[définition, classification]* strictness, rigour. **manquer de** ~ to lack rigour. (**d**) **tenir** ~ **à qn de n'être pas venu** to hold it against sb that he didn't come; **à la** ~ *(si nécessaire)* at a pinch, if need be; *(peut-être)* possibly; **Il est de** ~ **d'envoyer un mot de remerciement** it is the done thing to send a note of thanks; **'tenue de soirée de** ~**'** 'evening dress', 'dress: formal'. ◆ **rigoureusement** *adv punir* harshly; *démontrer* rigorously; *appliquer* rigorously, strictly; *exact* rigorously; *interdit, vrai* strictly. ◆ **rigoureux, -euse** *adj (gén)* rigorous; *punition, climat* harsh; *moraliste, interdiction, définition* strict.

rime [ʀim] *nf* rhyme. **faire qch sans** ~ **ni raison** to do sth without either rhyme or reason. ◆ **rimer** (1) **1** *vi [mot]* to rhyme (*avec* with); *[poète]* to write verse. *(fig)* **cela ne rime à rien** it does not make sense, there's no sense *ou* point in it. **2** *vt* to put into verse.

rimmel [ʀimɛl] *nm* ® mascara.

rincer [ʀɛ̃se] (3) **1** *vt* to rinse (out). **se faire** ~ * *(par la pluie)* to get drenched *ou* soaked; *(au jeu)* to get cleaned out *. **2 se** ~ *vpr*: **se** ~ **la bouche**

to rinse out one's mouth; **se ~ l'œil** ‡ to get an eyeful *. ◆ **rinçage** *nm (action)* rinsing (out). **cette machine à laver fait 3 ~s** this washing machine does 3 rinses. ◆ **rince-doigts** *nm inv (bol)* finger-bowl; *(en papier)* (disposable) finger wipe.

ring [Riŋ] *nm* (boxing) ring.

ringard, e * [Rɛ̃gaR, aRd(ə)] *adj (démodé)* corny *, rinky-dink * *(US)*. **c'est ~** it's corny * *ou* old hat *.

riper [Ripe] (1) *vi* to slip. **faire ~** to slide along.

riposter [Ripɔste] (1) **1** *vi* (**a**) *(répondre)* to answer back, retaliate. **~ à une insulte** to reply to an insult; **~ par une insulte** to retort *ou* retaliate with an insult. (**b**) *(contre-attaquer)* to counter-attack, retaliate. **~ à une attaque** to counter an attack (*par* by). **2** *vt*: **~ que** to retort *ou* answer back that. ◆ **riposte** *nf (réponse)* retort, riposte; *(contre-attaque)* counter-attack, reprisal.

riquiqui * [Rikiki] *adj inv portion* tiny, mean, stingy *; *vêtement, objet* tiny.

rire [RiR] (36) **1** *vi* (**a**) to laugh. **~ aux éclats** to roar with laughter, laugh one's head off; **~ bruyamment** to guffaw; **~ dans sa barbe** to laugh to o.s.; **~ jaune** to laugh on the other side of one's face; *(iro)* **laissez-moi ~!** don't make me laugh!, you make me laugh! *(iro)*; **c'est à mourir de ~** it's hilarious, it's awfully funny; **ça ne me fait pas ~** I don't find it funny; **nous avons bien ri** we had a good laugh *; **il a pris les choses en riant** *(avec bonne humeur)* he saw the funny side of it; *(à la légère)* he laughed it off; **rira bien qui rira le dernier** he who laughs last laughs longest *ou* best *(US)*. (**b**) *[yeux, visage]* to shine with happiness. (**c**) *(s'amuser)* to have fun, have a laugh *. **il aime bien ~** he likes a bit of fun *ou* a good laugh *. (**d**) *(plaisanter)* **vous voulez ~!** you must be joking!; **il a dit cela pour ~** he was only joking, he said it in fun; **il a fait cela pour ~** he did it for a joke *ou* laugh *; **c'était une bagarre pour ~** it wasn't a real fight.
2 ~ de *vt indir* to laugh at, scoff at. **il fait ~ de lui** he makes himself a laughing stock.
3 se ~ *vpr*: **se ~ de** *difficultés* to make light of; *menaces, personne* to laugh at.
4 *nm (façon, éclat)* laugh. **le ~** laughter; **un gros ~** a loud laugh, a guffaw; **un ~ moqueur** a mocking *ou* scornful laugh; *(TV, Rad)* **~s préenregistrés** *ou* **en boîte** * canned laughter; **un petit ~ de satisfaction** a little chuckle of satisfaction; **un petit ~ bête** a stupid giggle *ou* titter; **il y eut des ~s** there was laughter; **elle eut un ~ méchant** she gave a wicked laugh, she laughed wickedly.

ris [Ri] *nm*: **~ de veau** calf sweetbread.

risée [Rize] *nf*: **s'exposer à la ~ générale** to lay o.s. open to ridicule; **être la ~ de toute l'Europe** to be *ou* make o.s. the laughing stock of Europe.

risette [Rizɛt] *nf*: **faire (une) ~ à qn** to give sb a nice *ou* little smile.

risible [Rizibl(ə)] *adj (ridicule)* laughable, ridiculous, silly; *aventure* laughable, funny.

risque [Risk(ə)] *nm* (**a**) *(gén, Jur: danger)* risk. **le goût du ~** a taste for danger; **une entreprise pleine de ~s** a high-risk business; **prendre tous les ~s** to take any number of risks; **à cause du ~ d'incendie** because of the fire risk *ou* the risk of fire; **~ pour la santé** health hazard *ou* risk; *(Sociol)* **à ~** *population* at risk; *(Fin) placement* risky; **à haut ~** high-risk; *(fig)* **ne prendre aucun ~** to play (it) safe, take no risks. (**b**) **ce sont les ~s du métier** that's an occupational hazard *(hum)*; **il n'y a pas de ~ qu'il refuse** there's no risk *ou* chance of his refusing; **au ~ de le mécontenter** at the risk of displeasing him; **c'est à tes ~s et périls** it's at your own risk.

risquer [Riske] (1) **1** *vt* (**a**) *réputation, vie* to risk. **~ le tout pour le tout** to risk *ou* chance the lot; **risquons le coup** * let's chance it; **qui ne risque rien n'a rien** nothing ventured, nothing gained. (**b**) *prison, ennuis* to risk. **tu risques gros** you're taking a big risk; **tu risques qu'on te le vole** you risk having it stolen; **bien emballé, ce vase ne risque rien** packed like this the vase is quite safe *ou* won't come to any harm; **ce vieux chapeau ne risque rien** this old hat doesn't matter at all, it doesn't matter what happens to this old hat. (**c**) *allusion, regard* to venture, hazard. (**d**) **tu risques de le perdre** *(éventualité)* you might (well) *ou* could (well) lose it; *(probabilité)* you're likely to lose it; **avec ces embouteillages, il risque d'être en retard** with these traffic jams he's likely to be late, these traffic jams could well make him late; **pourquoi ~ de tout perdre?** why should we risk losing *ou* take the risk of losing everything?; **ça ne risque pas d'arriver!** there's no chance *ou* danger of that happening!, that's not likely to happen. **2 se ~** *vpr*: **se ~ dans** *grotte* to venture into; *entreprise* to venture (up)on, launch o.s. into; **se ~ à faire qch** to venture *ou* dare to do sth, have a try *ou* a go at doing sth. ◆ **risqué, e** *adj (hasardeux)* risky; *(licencieux)* risqué, daring. ◆ **risque-tout** *nmf inv* daredevil.

rissoler [Risɔle] (1) *vti (aussi*: **faire ~***)* to brown.

ristourne [RistuRn(ə)] *nf* rebate, discount. ◆ **ristourner** (1) *vt* to give a rebate of.

rite [Rit] *nm (gén, Rel)* rite; *(fig: habitude)* ritual.

ritournelle [RituRnɛl] *nf (Mus)* ritornello. *(fig)* **c'est toujours la même ~** it's always the same (old) story *ou* tune *ou* theme.

rituel, -elle [Ritɥɛl] *adj, nm (gén)* ritual. ◆ **rituellement** *adv* ritually; *(invariablement)* invariably, unfailingly.

rivage [Rivaʒ] *nm* shore.

rival, e, *mpl* **-aux** [Rival, o] *adj, nm, f* rival. **sans ~** unrivalled. ◆ **rivaliser** (1) *vi*: **~ avec** *[personne]* to rival, compete *ou* vie with; *[chose]* to rival, hold its own against; **ils rivalisaient de générosité** they vied with each other *ou* they tried to outdo each other in generosity. ◆ **rivalité** *nf* rivalry.

rive [Riv] *nf [mer, lac]* shore; *[rivière]* bank.

river [Rive] (1) *vt clou* to clinch; *plaques* to rivet together. **~ son clou à qn** * to shut sb up *; **~ qch au sol** to nail sth to the floor. ◆ **rivé, e** *adj*: **~ à** *(gén)* riveted to; *travail* tethered *ou* tied to; **~ sur place** rooted to the spot; **~ à la télé** * glued to the TV *.

riverain, e [RivRɛ̃, ɛn] **1** *adj (d'un lac)* waterside. *(d'une route)* **les propriétés ~es** the houses along the road. **2** *nm, f* lakeside (*ou* riverside) resident. *[rue]* **les ~s** the residents of *ou* in the street; **'interdit sauf aux ~s'** 'no entry except for access', 'residents only'.

rivet [Rivɛ] *nm* rivet. ◆ **rivetage** *nm* riveting. ◆ **riveter** (4) *vt* to rivet (together).

rivière [Rivjɛr] *nf (lit, fig)* river; *(Équitation)* water jump. **~ de diamants** diamond rivière.

rixe [Riks(ə)] *nf* brawl, fight, scuffle.

Riyad [Rijad] *n* Riyadh.

riz [Ri] *nm* rice. **~ brun** *ou* **complet** brown rice; **~ au lait** rice pudding. ◆ **rizière** *nf* paddy-field, ricefield.

robe [Rɔb] *nf [femme, fillette]* dress, frock; *[magistrat, prélat]* robe; *[professeur]* gown; *[cheval, fauve]* coat; *(couleur) [vin]* colour. **~ bain de soleil** sundress; **~ de chambre** dressing gown; **pommes de terre en ~ de chambre** *ou* **des champs** jacket *ou* baked potatoes; **~ de grossesse** maternity dress; **~ de mariée** wedding dress *ou* gown; **~ du soir** evening dress *ou* gown.

robinet [Rɔbinɛ] *nm* tap, faucet *(US)*. ◆ **robinetterie** *nf (installations)* taps; *(usine)* tap factory; *(commerce)* tap trade.

robot [ʀɔbo] *nm (lit, fig)* robot. ~ **ménager** food-processor; **avion** ~ remote-controlled aircraft. ◆ **robotique** *nf* robotics *(sg)*. ◆ **robotisation** *nf* automation. ◆ **robotiser** (1) *vt* to automate.

robuste [ʀɔbyst(ə)] *adj personne, voiture* robust, sturdy; *santé* robust, sound; *plante* robust, hardy; *foi* firm, strong. ◆ **robustesse** *nf* robustness; sturdiness; soundness; hardiness; firmness, strength.

roc [ʀɔk] *nm (lit, fig)* rock.

rocade [ʀɔkad] *nf (route)* bypass.

rocaille [ʀɔkɑj] *nf (cailloux)* loose stones; *(terrain)* rocky *ou* stony ground; *(jardin)* rockery, rock garden. ◆ **rocailleux, -euse** *adj terrain* rocky, stony; *voix* harsh, grating.

rocambolesque [ʀɔkɑ̃bɔlɛsk(ə)] *adj* fantastic, incredible.

roche [ʀɔʃ] *nf* rock. ◆ **rocher** *nm* rock. ◆ **rocheux, -euse** *adj* rocky. **paroi ~euse** rock face.

rock (and roll) [ʀɔk(ɛnʀɔl)] *nm (musique)* rock-'n'-roll; *(danse)* jive. ◆ **rocker** *nm (chanteur)* rock musician; *(admirateur)* rock fan.

roder [ʀɔde] (1) *vt moteur, spectacle etc* to run in, break in *(US)*; *soupape* to grind. **il faut ~ ce spectacle** we have to let this show get into its stride; *[personne]* **il n'est pas encore rodé** he is not yet broken in. ◆ **rodage** *nm* running in, breaking in *(US)* ; grinding.

rôder [ʀode] (1) *vi (au hasard)* to roam *ou* wander about; *(de façon suspecte)* to lurk *ou* prowl about. ~ **autour d'un magasin** to hang *ou* lurk around a shop. ◆ **rôdeur, -euse** *nm, f* prowler.

rogne * [ʀɔɲ] *nf* anger. **être/se mettre en** ~ to be/get (hopping) mad *.

rogner [ʀɔɲe] (1) *vt ongle, page* to trim; *aile* to clip; *salaire* to cut *ou* whittle down. ~ **sur** *dépense* to cut down *ou* back on.

rognon [ʀɔɲɔ̃] *nm (Culin)* kidney.

rognures [ʀɔɲyʀ] *nfpl [métal, ongles]* clippings; *[viande]* scraps.

roi [ʀwa] *nm* king. **les R~s mages** the Magi, the Three Wise Men; **le R~-Soleil** the Sun King; **le jour des R~s** *(gén)* Twelfth Night; *(Rel)* Epiphany; **tirer les ~s** to eat Twelfth Night cake; **un des ~s de la presse** one of the press barons *ou* kings *ou* magnates *ou* tycoons; **X, le ~ des fromages** X, the leading *ou* first name in cheese(s); **c'est le ~ de la resquille!** * he's a master *ou* an ace at getting something for nothing; **tu es le ~ (des imbéciles)!** * you're the world's biggest idiot! *

roide [ʀwad], **roideur** [ʀwadœʀ], **roidir** [ʀwadiʀ] = **raide, raideur, raidir.**

roitelet [ʀwatlɛ] *nm (péj)* kinglet; *(Orn)* wren.

rôle [ʀol] *nm* (**a**) *(Théât, fig)* role, part. **premier/petit** ~ leading/minor role *ou* part; **jouer un** ~ to play a part, act a role; *(fig)* **il joue les seconds ~s** he plays second fiddle; **ce n'est pas mon ~ de vous sermonner mais...** it isn't my job *ou* place to lecture you but...; **la télévision a pour ~ de...** the role *ou* function of television is to... (**b**) *(registre)* roll, list.

ROM [ʀɔm] *nf (Ordin)* ROM.

romain, e [ʀɔmɛ̃, ɛn] **1** *adj (gén)* Roman. **2** *nm(f)* **R~(e)** Roman. **3** *nf*: **(laitue) ~e** cos (lettuce), romaine (lettuce) *(US)*; **(balance) ~e** steelyard.

roman[1] [ʀɔmɑ̃] *nm (livre)* novel; *(genre médiéval)* romance; *(fig: récit)* story. **ils ne publient que des ~s** they only publish novels *ou* fiction; *(lit, fig)* ~ **d'amour** love story; ~ **d'aventures** adventure story; ~ **de cape et d'épée** historical romance; ~ **de chevalerie** tale of chivalry; ~ **courtois** courtly romance; ~ **d'épouvante** horror story; ~ **d'espionnage** spy thriller *ou* story; **~-feuilleton** *(lit)* serialized novel, serial; *(fig)* saga; **~-photo** photo romance, photo love story; ~ **policier** detective novel *ou* story; ~ **de science-fiction** science fiction novel; ~ **(de) série noire** thriller.

roman[2]**, e** [ʀɔmɑ̃, an] *adj (Ling)* Romance, Romanic; *(Archit)* Romanesque.

romance [ʀɔmɑ̃s] *nf* sentimental ballad, lovesong.

romancer [ʀɔmɑ̃se] (3) *vt (sous forme de roman)* to make into a novel; *(agrémenter)* to romanticize.

romancier, -ière [ʀɔmɑ̃sje, jɛʀ] *nm, f* novelist.

romanesque [ʀɔmanɛsk(ə)] **1** *adj histoire* fabulous, fantastic; *amours, aventures* storybook; *personne, imagination* romantic; *mode littéraire* novelistic. **œuvres ~s** novels, fiction. **2** *nm [personne]* romantic side; *(imagination)* fancy.

romanichel, -elle [ʀɔmaniʃɛl] *nm, f* gipsy.

romantique [ʀɔmɑ̃tik] *adj, nmf* romantic. ◆ **romantisme** *nm* romanticism. **le** ~ the Romantic Movement.

romarin [ʀɔmaʀɛ̃] *nm* rosemary.

Rome [ʀɔm] *n* Rome.

rompre [ʀɔ̃pʀ(ə)] (41) **1** *vt (gén, fig)* to break; *fiançailles, pourparlers* to break off. ~ **l'équilibre** to upset the balance; ~ **le front de l'ennemi** to break through the enemy front; ~ **qn à un exercice** to break sb in to an exercise; ~ **des lances contre qn** to cross swords with sb; *(Mil)* ~ **les rangs** to fall out, dismiss. **2** *vi [corde]* to break, snap; *[digue]* to burst, break; *[fiancés]* to break it off; *(Boxe, Escrime)* to break. *(Mil)* ~ **le combat** to withdraw from the engagement; ~ **avec** *personne, habitude* to break with. **3 se** ~ *vpr [corde, branche]* to break, snap; *[digue]* to burst, break; *[veine]* to burst, rupture. **il va se ~ le cou** he's going to break his neck. ◆ **rompu, e** *adj* (**a**) *(fourbu)* exhausted, worn-out, tired out. (**b**) *(expérimenté)* ~ **à qch** experienced in sth; ~ **aux affaires** with wide business experience; ~ **aux privations** accustomed *ou* inured to hardship.

romsteck [ʀɔmstɛk] *nm (viande)* rumpsteak; *(tranche)* piece of rumpsteak.

ronce [ʀɔ̃s] *nf (branche)* bramble branch. *(buissons)* **~s** brambles.

ronchonner * [ʀɔ̃ʃɔne] (1) *vi* to grumble, grouse *, grouch * *(après* at). ◆ **ronchon** * **1** *adj* grumpy, grouchy *. **2** *nm* grumbler, grouch(er) *, grouser *. ◆ **ronchonnement** * *nm*: **~(s)** grumbling, grousing *, grouching *.

rond, e [ʀɔ̃, ʀɔ̃d] **1** *adj* (**a**) *forme* round. (**b**) *(gras) visage* round, chubby, plump; *mollet, poitrine* (well-)rounded; *ventre, personne* plump, tubby. (**c**) *(net)* round. **chiffre** ~ round number *ou* figure; **ça fait 50 F tout** ~ it comes to a round 50 francs; **pour faire un compte** ~ to make a round figure; **être ~ en affaires** to be straight(forward) *ou* on the level * in business matters. (**d**) *(*: soûl)* drunk, tight *.

2 *nm* (**a**) *(cercle dessiné)* circle, ring; *(tranche)* slice; *(objet)* ring. ~ **de serviette** serviette *ou* napkin ring; **en** ~ in a circle *ou* ring. (**b**) *(*: sou)* **~s** lolly *, cash; **il n'a pas le** *ou* **un** ~ he hasn't got a penny *ou* a cent; **il n'a plus le** ~ he's broke *; **ça doit valoir des ~s!** that must cost a lot! *ou* a packet! *

3 *adv*: **avaler qch tout** ~ to swallow sth whole.

4 *nf* (**a**) *[gardien, soldats]* rounds; *[policier]* beat, patrol, rounds; *(patrouille)* patrol. **faire sa ~e** to be on one's rounds *ou* on the beat *ou* on patrol. (**b**) *(danse)* round (dance), dance in a ring; *(danseurs)* circle, ring. **faites la ~e** dance round in a circle *ou* ring. (**c**) *(Mus: note)* semibreve, whole note *(US)*. (**d**) *(Écriture)* roundhand. (**e**) **à des kilomètres à la ~e** for miles around; **passer qch à la ~e** to pass sth round.

◆ **rondelet, -ette** *adj femme* plumpish; *somme* tidy. ◆ **rondelle** *nf (tranche)* slice; *(disque)* disc; *[boulon]* washer. ◆ **rondement** *adv (efficacement)* briskly; *(franchement)* frankly. ◆ **rondeur** *nf* (**a**) *[forme] (gén)* roundness; *[bras, visage]* plumpness, chubbiness. *(hum)* **les ~s d'une femme** *(formes)* a woman's curves; *(embonpoint)* a woman's plumpness. (**b**) *(bonhomie)* friendly straightforwardness, easy-going directness. ◆ **rondin** *nm* log. ◆ **rondouillard, e** * *adj (péj)* tubby, podgy, pudgy *(US)*. ◆ **rond-point,** *pl* **ronds-points** *nm (carrefour)* roundabout, traffic circle *(US)*.

ronéoter [ʀɔneɔte] (1) *vt* to duplicate, roneo ®, mimeo. ◆ **ronéo** *nf* ® mimeo, roneo ®.

ronfler [ʀɔ̃fle] (1) *vi* (**a**) *[dormeur]* to snore; *[toupie]* to hum; *[poêle] (sourdement)* to hum; *(fort)* to roar; *[moteur] (sourdement)* to purr, throb; *(fort)* to roar. **faire ~ son moteur** to rev up one's engine. (**b**) *(*: dormir)* to snore away. ◆ **ronflant, e** *adj (péj) promesse* high-flown; *titre* pompous, grand(-sounding). ◆ **ronflement** *nm*: **~(s)** snore(s); hum; roar; purr, throb. ◆ **ronfleur, -euse** *nm, f* snorer.

ronger [ʀɔ̃ʒe] (3) **1** *vi [souris, chagrin]* to gnaw *ou* eat away at; *[acide, vers]* to eat into; *[mer]* to wear away, eat into. **~ un os** to gnaw (at) a bone; **rongé par les vers** worm-eaten; **rongé par la rouille** rust-eaten; *(lit, fig)* **~ son frein** to champ at the bit; **rongé par la maladie** sapped by illness. **2 se ~** *vpr*: **se ~ les ongles** to bite one's nails; **se ~ les sangs** to worry o.s., eat one's heart out. ◆ **rongeur, -euse** *adj, nm* rodent.

ronronner [ʀɔ̃ʀɔne] (1) *vi [chat]* to purr; *[moteur]* to purr, hum. ◆ **ronronnement** *nm*: **~(s)** purr; hum.

roquet [ʀɔkɛ] *nm (péj)* (nasty little) dog.

roquette [ʀɔkɛt] *nf (Mil)* rocket.

rosace [ʀozas] *nf [cathédrale]* rose window; *[plafond]* (ceiling) rose; *(Géom)* rosette.

rosaire [ʀozɛʀ] *nm* rosary.

rosâtre [ʀozatʀ(ə)] *adj* pinkish.

rosbif [ʀɔsbif] *nm*: **du ~** *(rôti)* roast beef; *(à rôtir)* roasting beef; **un ~** a joint of (roast) beef.

rose [ʀoz] **1** *nf (fleur)* rose; *(vitrail)* rose window; *(diamant)* rose diamond. **pas de ~s sans épines** no rose without a thorn; **~ de Noël** Christmas rose; **~ pompon** button rose; **~ des sables** gypsum flower; **~ trémière** hollyhock; **~ des vents** compass card. **2** *nm (couleur)* pink. **3** *adj (gén)* pink; *(plein de santé)* rosy. **~ bonbon** candy-pink; **tout n'est pas ~** it's not all roses *ou* all rosy, it's not a bed of roses; **voir la vie en ~** to see everything through rose-coloured spectacles.

rosé, e[1] [ʀoze] **1** *adj couleur* pinkish; *vin* rosé. **2** *nm* rosé (wine).

roseau, *pl* **~x** [ʀozo] *nm* reed.

rosée[2] [ʀoze] *nf* dew.

roseraie [ʀozʀɛ] *nf* rose garden.

rosette [ʀozɛt] *nf (nœud)* bow; *(insigne, Archit, Bot)* rosette.

rosier [ʀozje] *nm* rosebush, rose tree. **~ nain/grimpant** dwarf/climbing rose.

rosir [ʀoziʀ] (2) *vti* to turn pink.

rosse [ʀɔs] **1** *nf* (**a**) *(† péj: cheval)* nag. (**b**) *(* péj) (homme)* beast *, swine ‡; *(femme)* beast *, bitch ‡. **2** *adj (péj)* horrid, nasty, rotten *. ◆ **rosserie** *nf* nastiness; *(propos)* nasty remark; *(acte)* nasty trick.

rosser [ʀɔse] (1) *vt* to thrash. **se faire ~** to get a (good) hiding *ou* a thrashing.

rossignol [ʀɔsiɲɔl] *nm* (**a**) *(Orn)* nightingale. (**b**) *(*: invendu)* unsaleable article. (**c**) *(clef)* picklock.

rot [ʀo] *nm* belch, burp *; *[bébé]* burp.

rotation [ʀɔtɑsjɔ̃] *nf* (**a**) *(mouvement)* rotation. **mouvement de ~** rotating *ou* rotary movement. (**b**) *[matériel]* turnover; *[avions, bateaux]* frequency (of service); *[cultures, équipes de travail]* rotation. **par ~** in rotation. ◆ **rotatif, -ive** **1** *adj* rotary. **2** *nf* rotary press. ◆ **rotatoire** *adj* rotary.

roter * [ʀɔte] (1) *vi* to burp *, belch.

rotin [ʀɔtɛ̃] *nm* rattan (cane). **chaise de ~** cane chair.

rôtir [ʀotiʀ] (2) **1** *vt (Culin: aussi* **faire ~** *)* to roast. **agneau rôti** roast, lamb. **2** *vi (lit, fig)* to roast. **3 se ~** *vpr*: **se ~ au soleil** to bask in the sun. ◆ **rôti** *nm*: **du ~** roasting meat; *(cuit)* roast meat; **un ~** a joint. ◆ **rôtisserie** *nf (restaurant)* steakhouse, grill and griddle; *(boutique)* shop selling roast meat. ◆ **rôtisseur, -euse** *nm, f* seller of roast meat; steakhouse proprietor. ◆ **rôtissoire** *nf* (roasting) spit.

rotonde [ʀɔtɔ̃d] *nf (Archit)* rotunda.

rotophare [ʀɔtɔfaʀ] *nm (Aut)* revolving *ou* flashing light *(on police car etc)*.

rotor [ʀɔtɔʀ] *nm* rotor.

Rotterdam [ʀɔtɛʀdam] *n* Rotterdam.

rotule [ʀɔtyl] *nf (Anat)* kneecap. **être sur les ~s** * to be dead beat * *ou* all in.

rouage [ʀwaʒ] *nm [engrenage]* cog(wheel), gearwheel; *[montre]* part; *(fig)* cog. **les ~s** *[montre]* the works *ou* parts; *[organisme]* the workings; **les ~s de l'État** the wheels of State; **les ~s administratifs** the administrative machinery.

roublard, e * [ʀublaʀ, aʀd(ə)] *adj* crafty, wily, artful.

rouble [ʀubl(ə)] *nm* rouble.

roucouler [ʀukule] (1) **1** *vi [oiseau]* to coo; *[amoureux]* to bill and coo; *[chanteur]* to warble. **2** *vt (péj) chanson* to warble; *mots d'amour* to coo. ◆ **roucoulade** *nf ou* ◆ **roucoulement** *nm*: **~(s)** cooing, warbling.

roue [ʀu] *nf (gén)* wheel; *[engrenage]* cog(wheel), (gear)wheel. **~ à aubes** paddle wheel; **~ de secours** spare wheel; **véhicule à deux ~s** two-wheeled vehicle; **faire la ~** *[paon]* to spread *ou* fan its tail; *[personne] (se pavaner)* to strut about; *(Gymnastique)* to do a cartwheel; **faire ~ libre** to freewheel; *(fig: ne pas se surmener)* **il s'est mis en ~ libre** * he's taking it easy.

roué, e [ʀwe] *adj* cunning, wily, sly.

rouer [ʀwe] (1) *vt* (**a**) **~ qn de coups** to give sb a beating *ou* thrashing. (**b**) *(supplice)* to put on the wheel.

rouerie [ʀuʀi] *nf* cunning, wiliness, slyness; *(tour)* cunning *ou* wily *ou* sly trick.

rouet [ʀwɛ] *nm (à filer)* spinning wheel.

rouflaquettes * [ʀuflakɛt] *nfpl* sideburns.

rouge [ʀuʒ] **1** *adj (gén)* red; *(porté à l'incandescence) fer* red-hot. **~ de colère/honte** red *ou* flushed with anger/shame; **devenir ~ comme une cerise** to blush, go red in the face; **il est ~ comme une pivoine** he's as red as a beetroot *ou* a lobster. **2** *nm (couleur)* red; *(vin)* red wine; *(fard)* rouge (†), blusher. **~ à lèvres** lipstick; *(Pol)* **voter ~** to vote Communist; *(Aut)* **le feu est au ~** the lights are red; **le ~ lui monta aux joues** his cheeks flushed, he blushed, he went red in the face; **fer porté au ~** red-hot iron. **3** *nmf (péj: communiste)* Red * *(péj)*, Commie * *(péj)*. ◆ **rougeâtre** *adj* reddish. ◆ **rougeaud, e** *adj* red-faced. ◆ **rouge-gorge,** *pl* **rouges-gorges** *nm* robin (redbreast).

rougeole [ʀuʒɔl] *nf*: **la ~** (the) measles *(sg)*; **une ~** a bout of measles.

rougeoyer [ʀuʒwaje] (8) *vi [feu]* to glow red; *[ciel]* to turn red. ◆ **rougeoiement** *nm* red *ou* reddish glow. ◆ **rougeoyant, e** *adj ciel* reddening; *cendres* glowing.

rouget [ʀuʒɛ] *nm*: **~ (barbet)** red mullet; **~ (grondin)** gurnard.

rougeur [ʀuʒœʀ] *nf (teinte)* redness; *(Méd: tache)* red blotch *ou* patch; *[visage]* redness. **sa ~ a trahi sa**

gêne her red face *ou* her blushes betrayed her embarrassment.

rougir [ʀuʒiʀ] (2) **1** *vi* (**a**) *[personne] (gén)* to go red, redden; *(émotion)* to flush; *(honte)* to blush (*de* with). ~ **jusqu'aux oreilles** to go bright red, blush to the roots of one's hair; *(lit, fig)* **faire ~ qn** to make sb blush; **dire qch sans** ~ to say sth without blushing *ou* unblushingly. (**b**) *(fig: avoir honte)* ~ **de** to be ashamed of; **il ne rougit de rien** he is quite shameless, he has no shame; **j'en rougis pour lui** I blush for him, I'm ashamed for him. (**c**) *[ciel, tomate, feuille]* to go *ou* turn red, redden; *[métal]* to get red-hot. **2** *vt ciel, feuilles* to turn red; *métal* to make red-hot. ◆ **rougissant, e** *adj visage* blushing; *feuille, ciel* reddening. ◆ **rougissement** *nm (de honte etc)* blush; *(d'émotion)* flush.

rouille [ʀuj] **1** *nf* rust. **2** *adj inv* rust(-coloured), rusty. ◆ **rouillé, e** *adj métal* rusty, rusted; *mémoire, athlète* rusty; *muscles* stiff. **tout** ~ rusted over. ◆ **rouiller** (1) **1** *vi* to rust, go *ou* get rusty. **2** *vt métal, esprit* to make rusty. **3 se** ~ *vpr [métal]* to go *ou* get rusty, rust; *[athlète, mémoire]* to become rusty; *[muscles]* to get stiff.

roulade [ʀulad] *nf* (**a**) *(Mus)* roulade, run; *[oiseau]* trill. (**b**) *(Culin)* rolled meat. (**c**) *(Sport)* roll.

roulant, e [ʀulɑ̃, ɑ̃t] **1** *adj* (**a**) *meuble* on wheels. *(Rail)* **matériel** ~ rolling stock; **personnel** ~ train crews. (**b**) *(‡: drôle)* killing *. **2** *nf (arg Mil)* field kitchen.

roulé, e [ʀule] **1** *adj* (**a**) **être bien** ~ * to have a good *ou* shapely figure. (**b**) *bord de chapeau* curved; *bord de foulard, morceau de boucherie* rolled. (**c**) *(Ling)* rolled. **r** ~ trilled *ou* rolled r. **2** *nm (gâteau)* Swiss roll; *(pâte)* ≃ turnover; *(viande)* rolled meat. ◆ **roulé-boulé,** *pl* **roulés-boulés** *nm* roll.

rouleau, *pl* ~**x** [ʀulo] *nm (gén, Sport)* roll; *(outil, vague)* roller; *[machine à écrire]* platen, roller; *(pour se coiffer)* curler, roller. ~ **compresseur** steam-roller, roadroller; ~ **à pâtisserie** rolling pin; ~ **de papier** roll of paper; **passer une pelouse au** ~ to roll a lawn.

roulement [ʀulmɑ̃] *nm* (**a**) *(rotation)* rotation. **travailler par** ~ to work on a rota system, work in rotation. (**b**) **avoir des ~s d'épaules/de hanches** to sway one's shoulders/wiggle one's hips; **faire des ~s d'yeux** to roll one's eyes. (**c**) *(circulation)* movement. **pneu usé par le** ~ tyre worn through use. (**d**) *(bruit) [train, camion]* rumble; *[charrette]* rattle. ~ **de tonnerre** rumble *ou* peal *ou* roll of thunder; ~ **de tambour** drum roll. (**e**) *[capitaux]* circulation. (**f**) ~ **(à billes)** ball bearings.

rouler [ʀule] (1) **1** *vt* (**a**) *meuble, tonneau* to roll along; *brouette* to wheel along, trundle along. ~ **qch dans la farine** to roll sth in flour; ~ **des projets dans sa tête** to turn plans over (and over) in one's mind. (**b**) *tapis, manches* to roll up; *cigarette* to roll; *ficelle* to wind up, roll up. ~ **qn dans une couverture** to wrap *ou* roll sb (up) in a blanket. (**c**) *(Culin) pâte* to roll out. (**d**) *(*: duper)* to con ‡; *(sur le prix, le poids)* to diddle *, do * (*sur* over). **Il s'est fait ~ dans la farine** * he was had *. (**e**) *épaules* to sway; *hanches* to wiggle; *yeux* to roll. **il a roulé sa bosse** he has knocked about the world *; *(Ling)* ~ **les 'r'** to roll one's r's.

2 *vi* (**a**) *[voiture, train]* to go, run; *[conducteur]* to drive. **cette voiture a très peu roulé** this car has a very low mileage; **les voitures ne roulent pas bien sur le sable** cars don't run well on sand; **le véhicule roulait à gauche** the vehicle was driving (along) on the left; ~ **au pas** *(prudence)* to go dead slow, go at a walking pace; *(dans un embouteillage)* to crawl along; ~ **à 80 km à l'heure** to do 80 km per hour, drive at 80 km per hour; **on a bien roulé** * we kept up a good speed; **ça roule bien** the traffic is flowing well; **il roule en Rolls** he drives around in a Rolls; *(fig: être à la solde de)* ~ **pour qn** * to work for sb. (**b**) *[bille, dé]* to roll. **une larme roula sur sa joue** a tear rolled down his cheek; **un coup de poing l'envoya ~ dans la poussière** a punch sent him rolling in the dust; **faire** ~ *boule* to roll; *cerceau* to roll along. (**c**) *[bateau]* to roll. (**d**) *[tambour]* to roll; *[tonnerre]* to roll, rumble, peal. (**e**) *(fig) [aventurier]* to knock about, drift around. *[conversation]* ~ **sur** to turn on, be centred on; ~ **sur l'or** to be rolling in money *, have pots of money *.

3 se ~ *vpr*: **se ~ par terre** to roll on the ground; *(fig)* to fall about * (laughing), roll on the ground with laughter *(US)*; **se ~ dans une couverture** to roll *ou* wrap o.s. up in a blanket; **se ~ en boule** to roll o.s. (up) into a ball.

roulette [ʀulɛt] *nf* (**a**) *[meuble]* castor. **ça a été comme sur des ~s** * it went very smoothly. (**b**) ~ **de dentiste** dentist's drill. (**c**) *(jeu)* roulette; *(instrument)* roulette wheel. ~ **russe** Russian roulette.

roulis [ʀuli] *nm* roll(ing). **il y a du** ~ the ship is rolling a lot.

roulotte [ʀulɔt] *nf* caravan, trailer *(US)*.

Roumanie [ʀumani] *nf* Rumania, Romania. ◆ **roumain, e** *adj, nm*, **R~(e)** *nm(f)* Rumanian, Romanian.

round [ʀund] *nm (Boxe)* round.

roupie [ʀupi] *nf (Fin)* rupee.

roupiller * [ʀupije] (1) *vi (dormir)* to sleep; *(faire un somme)* to have a snooze *ou* a kip ‡ *ou* a nap; *(fig)* to doze, be half asleep. **je vais** ~ I'll be turning in *. ◆ **roupillon** * *nm* snooze, kip ‡, nap.

rouquin, e * [ʀukɛ̃, in] **1** *adj personne* red-haired; *cheveux* red, carroty *. **2** *nm, f* redhead.

rouspéter * [ʀuspete] (6) *vi* to grouse *, grouch * (*après* at). ◆ **rouspétance** * *nf* grousing *, grouching *. ◆ **rouspéteur, -euse** * **1** *adj* grumpy. **2** *nm, f* grouser *, grouch *.

roussir [ʀusiʀ] (2) **1** *vt [fer à repasser]* to scorch, singe; *[flamme]* to singe. *[chaleur]* ~ **l'herbe** to scorch the grass. **2** *vi* (**a**) *[feuilles]* to turn brown *ou* russet. (**b**) *(Culin)* **faire** ~ to brown. ◆ **rousse** *adj f V* **roux.** ◆ **rousseur** *nf [cheveux]* redness; *[feuilles]* russet colour. *(sur la peau)* ~**s** brown blotches, freckles. ◆ **roussi** *nm*: **ça sent le ~!** *(lit)* there's a smell of burning; *(fig *)* I can smell trouble.

routage [ʀutaʒ] *nm* sorting and mailing. **entreprise de** ~ mailing firm *ou* service.

routard * [ʀutaʀ] *nm* (young) traveller *ou* globe-trotter.

route [ʀut] *nf* (**a**) road. ~ **nationale/départementale** ≃ trunk *ou* main/secondary road ; **faire de la** ~ to do a lot of mileage; **accidents de la** ~ road accidents. (**b**) *(chemin à suivre)* way; *(Naut: cap)* course. **montrer la ~ à qn** to show the way to sb; **la ~ sera longue** *(gén)* it'll be a long journey; *(en voiture)* it'll be a long drive; **ce n'est pas ma** ~ it's not on my way. (**c**) *(ligne de communication)* route. ~ **aérienne/maritime** air/sea route; **la ~ de l'opium** the opium route *ou* trail. (**d**) *(fig)* path, road, way. **être sur la bonne** ~ *(dans la vie)* to be on the right road *ou* path; *(dans un problème)* to be on the right track. (**e**) *(locutions)* **faire ~ vers** *(gén)* to head towards *ou* for; *[bateau]* **en ~ pour** bound for; **faire ~ avec qn** to travel with sb; **prendre la ~, se mettre en** ~ to set off *ou* out; **en** ~ on the way; **en ~!** let's go!, let's be off!; *(hum)* **en ~, mauvaise troupe!** off we go!; **bonne ~!** have a good journey! *ou* trip!; **mettre en** ~ *moteur* to start (up); *affaire* to set in motion, get under way; **mise en** ~ starting up; setting in motion; **carnet de** ~ travel diary; **tenir la** ~ *[voiture]* to hold the road; *[matériel]* to be well-made *ou* serviceable; *[plan]* to hold together. ◆ **routier, -ière 1** *adj* road. **2** *nm (camionneur)* long-distance lorry *ou* truck *(US)* driver; *(restaurant)* ≃ transport café, roadside café.

routine [ʀutin] *nf* routine. **visite de** ~ routine visit. ◆ **routinier, -ière** *adj travail, vie* humdrum, routine; *personne* routine-minded.

rouvrir *vti*, **se** ~ *vpr* [ʀuvʀiʀ] (18) to reopen, open again.

roux, rousse [ʀu, ʀus] **1** *adj personne* red-haired; *cheveux* red, auburn; *(orangé)* ginger; *pelage, feuilles* russet, reddish-brown. **2** *nm* (**a**) *(couleur)* red, auburn; ginger; russet, reddish-brown. (**b**) *(Culin)* roux. **3** *nm, f* redhead.

royal, e, *mpl* **-aux** [ʀwajal, o] *adj (lit)* royal; *magnificence* kingly, regal; *repas, cadeau* fit for a king; *salaire* princely; *mépris* majestic, regal; *paix* blissful. ◆ **royalement** *adv vivre, traiter* royally. **il s'en moque** ~ * he couldn't care less *; *(iro)* **il m'a** ~ **offert 3 F d'augmentation** * he offered me a princely 3-franc rise *(iro)*. ◆ **royaliste** *adj, nmf* royalist. ◆ **royaume** *nm (lit)* kingdom, realm; *(fig)* realm. **le R~-Uni (de Grande-Bretagne et d'Irlande du Nord)** the United Kingdom (of Great Britain and Northern Ireland). ◆ **royauté** *nf (régime)* monarchy; *(fonction, dignité)* kingship.

ruade [ʀyad] *nf* kick *(of a horse's hind legs)*. **lancer une** ~ to lash *ou* kick out.

ruban [ʀybɑ̃] *nm (gén, fig)* ribbon; *[téléscripteur]* tape; *[ourlet]* binding, tape. ~ **d'acier** steel band *ou* strip; ~ **adhésif** adhesive tape, sticky tape; ~ **de chapeau** hat band; ~ **isolant** insulating tape; *(Ordin)* ~ **perforé** paper tape.

rubéole [ʀybeɔl] *nf* German measles *(sg)*, rubella.

rubis [ʀybi] **1** *nm (pierre, couleur)* ruby; *[montre]* jewel. **2** *adj inv* ruby(-coloured).

rubrique [ʀybʀik] *nf (article)* column; *(titre, catégorie)* heading, rubric.

ruche [ʀyʃ] *nf (lit, fig)* (bee)hive.

rude [ʀyd] *adj* (**a**) *(au toucher)* rough; *(à l'ouïe)* harsh. (**b**) *métier, climat, adversaire* tough; *montée* stiff. **être mis à** ~ **épreuve** *[personne]* to be severely tested, be put through the mill; *[tissu]* to get rough treatment; **il a été à** ~ **école** he learned life the hard way; **en faire voir de ~s à qn** to give sb a hard *ou* tough time. (**c**) *(fruste) manières* unpolished, crude; *traits* rugged; *montagnards* rugged, tough. (**d**) *(bourru) personne* harsh, hard; *manières* rough. (**e**) *(intensif) gaillard, appétit* hearty; *peur, coup* real. ◆ **rudement** *adv* (**a**) *frapper* hard; *répondre* harshly; *traiter* roughly, harshly. (**b**) (*) *content, mauvais, cher* terribly *, awfully *; *travailler* terribly *ou* awfully hard *. ~ **bien** terribly *ou* awfully well; **ça change** ~ it's a real change; **il est** ~ **plus généreux** he's a great deal *ou* darned sight * more generous; **j'ai eu** ~ **peur** I had a dreadful *ou* an awful scare *ou* fright. ◆ **rudesse** *nf* roughness; harshness; toughness; crudeness; ruggedness.

rudiments [ʀydimɑ̃] *nmpl [discipline]* rudiments; *[théorie]* principles. **avoir quelques** ~ **d'anglais** to have a smattering of English *ou* some basic knowledge of English. ◆ **rudimentaire** *adj* rudimentary.

rudoyer [ʀydwaje] (8) *vt* to treat harshly.

rue [ʀy] *nf* street. *(péj: populace)* **la** ~ the mob; ~ **à sens unique** one-way street; ~ **piétonnière** pedestrianized street; **être à la** ~ to be out on the street.

ruée [ʀɥe] *nf* rush; *(péj)* stampede, (mad) scramble. **la** ~ **vers l'or** the gold rush.

ruelle [ʀɥɛl] *nf (rue)* alley(-way).

ruer [ʀɥe] (1) **1** *vi [cheval]* to kick (out). *(fig)* ~ **dans les brancards** to rebel. **2 se** ~ *vpr*: **se** ~ **sur** to pounce on; **se** ~ **vers/dans** to dash *ou* rush towards/into; **se** ~ **à l'assaut** to hurl *ou* fling o.s. into the attack.

rugby [ʀygbi] *nm* Rugby (football), rugger *. ~ **à quinze** Rugby Union; ~ **à treize** Rugby League. ◆ **rugbyman,** *pl* **rugbymen** *nm* rugby player.

rugir [ʀyʒiʀ] (2) **1** *vi (gén)* to roar (*de* with); *[vent]* to howl, roar. **2** *vt* to roar out. ◆ **rugissement** *nm* roar; howl.

rugueux, -euse [ʀygø, øz] *adj (gén)* rough; *(grossier)* coarse; *sol* rugged, bumpy. ◆ **rugosité** *nf* roughness; coarseness; ruggedness, bumpiness; *(aspérité)* rough patch, bump.

ruine [ʀɥin] *nf (lit, fig)* ruin. *(péj)* ~ **(humaine)** (human) wreck; **en** ~ in ruins, ruined; **c'est la** ~ **de tous mes espoirs** that puts paid to *ou* that means the ruin of all my hopes; **menacer** ~ to be threatening to collapse; **tomber en** ~ to fall in ruins; *(financièrement)* **cette voiture est une vraie** ~ that car will ruin me. ◆ **ruiner** (1) **1** *vt (lit, fig)* to ruin. **ça ne va pas te** ~! * it won't break * *ou* ruin you! **2 se** ~ *vpr* to ruin *ou* bankrupt o.s.; *(fig: dépenser trop)* to spend a fortune. ◆ **ruineux, -euse** *adj goût* ruinously expensive; *dépense* ruinous.

ruisseau, *pl* **~x** [ʀɥiso] *nm (cours d'eau)* stream, brook; *(lit, fig: caniveau)* gutter. **des ~x de** *larmes* floods of; *lave, sang* streams of.

ruisseler [ʀɥisle] (4) *vi [liquide]* to flow, stream; *[mur]* to run with water, stream (with water). ~ **de** *eau, lumière etc* to stream with. ◆ **ruissellement** *nm*: **le** ~ **de la pluie sur le mur** the rain streaming *ou* running *ou* flowing down the wall; ~ **de lumière** stream of light.

rumba [ʀumba] *nf* rumba.

rumeur [ʀymœʀ] *nf* (**a**) *(nouvelle imprécise)* rumour. **selon certaines ~s, elle...** rumour has it that she..., it is rumoured that she... (**b**) *[vagues, vent]* murmur, murmuring; *[rue, conversation]* hum; *[émeute]* hubbub. (**c**) *(protestation)* rumblings. ~ **de mécontentement** rumblings of discontent.

ruminer [ʀymine] (1) **1** *vt (Zool)* to ruminate; *projet* to ruminate *ou* chew over; *chagrin* to brood over; *vengeance* to ponder, meditate. **2** *vi (Zool)* to ruminate, chew the cud. ◆ **ruminant** *nm* ruminant. ◆ **rumination** *nf* rumination.

rumsteck [ʀɔmstɛk] *nm* = **romsteck.**

rupin, e ‡ [ʀypɛ̃, in] *adj quartier* ritzy ‡, plush(y) *; *personne* stinking *ou* filthy rich ‡.

rupture [ʀyptyʀ] *nf* (**a**) *(annulation) [contrat]* breach (*de* of); *[relations diplomatiques]* severance, rupture (*de* of); *[pourparlers]* breakdown (*de* of, in). *(action)* **la** ~ **des pourparlers entre les 2 pays** the breaking off of talks between the 2 countries; **après la** ~ **des négociations** after negotiations broke down *ou* were broken off. (**b**) *(séparation amoureuse)* break-up, split. (**c**) *[câble, poutre]* breaking; *[digue]* bursting; *[organe]* rupture; *[tendon]* tearing. **limite de** ~ breaking point; ~ **entre le passé et le présent** break between the past and the present; ~ **de rythme** (sudden) break in (the) rhythm; ~ **d'équilibre** *(lit)* loss of balance; *(fig)* upsetting of the balance; ~ **d'essieu** broken axle; **être en** ~ **de stock** to be out of stock. (**d**) *(Ordin)* ~ **de séquence** jump.

rural, e, *mpl* **-aux** [ʀyʀal, o] **1** *adj* country, rural. **2** *nm, f* country person.

ruse [ʀyz] *nf* (**a**) **la** ~ *(pour gagner)* cunning, craftiness, slyness; *(pour tromper)* trickery, guile. (**b**) *(subterfuge)* trick, ruse. *(lit, fig)* ~ **de guerre** stratagem, tactics. ◆ **rusé, e** *adj personne* cunning, crafty, sly. ◆ **ruser** (1) *vi* to use cunning; to use trickery.

rush [ʀœʃ] *nm (afflux, Ciné)* rush.

russe [ʀys] *adj, nm,* **R~** *nmf* Russian. ◆ **Russie** *nf* Russia.

rustaud, e [ʀysto, od] **1** *adj* coarse. **2** *nm, f* country bumpkin, yokel.

rustine [Rystin] *nf* ® rubber repair, patch *(for bicycle tyre)*.

rustique [Rystik] **1** *adj (gén)* rustic; *vie* country; *(Agr)* hardy. **2** *nm (style)* rustic style.

rustre [RystR(ə)] **1** *nm (péj: brute)* lout, boor; *(†: paysan)* peasant. **2** *adj* boorish.

rut [Ryt] *nm [mâle]* rut; *[femelle]* heat; *(période)* rutting *ou* heat period. **être en** ~ to be rutting; to be in *ou* on heat.

rutabaga [Rytabaga] *nm* swede, rutabaga *(US)*.

rutiler [Rytile] (1) *vi* to gleam, shine brightly. ◆ **rutilant, e** *adj* brightly shining, gleaming. ◆ **rutilement** *nm* gleam.

rythme [Ritm(ə)] *nm* (**a**) *(Art, fig: cadence)* rhythm. *(Mus)* **au** ~ **de** to the beat *ou* rhythm of; *(Théât)* **pièce qui manque de** ~ play which lacks tempo, slow-moving play. (**b**) *(vitesse) (gén)* rate; *[vie, travail]* tempo, pace. ~ **cardiaque** (rate of) heartbeat; **à ce ~-là** at that rate; **suivre le** ~ to keep up (the pace); **au** ~ **de 1 000 par jour** at the rate of 1,000 a *ou* per day. ◆ **rythmé, e** *adj* rhythmic(al). ◆ **rythmer** (1) *vt* to give rhythm to, punctuate. ◆ **rythmique 1** *adj* rhythmic(al). **danse** ~ rhythmics *(sg)*. **2** *nf* rhythmics *(sg)*.

S

S, s [ɛs] *nm (lettre)* S, s. **en s** *route* zigzagging, winding; *barre* S-shaped.

s' [s] *V* **se, si**[1].

sa [sa] *adj poss V* **son**[1].

sabbat [saba] *nm (Rel)* Sabbath; *(*: bruit)* racket, row *.

sable [sɑbl(ə)] **1** *nm* sand. **de ~** *dune, vent* sand; *plage* sandy; **~s mouvants** quicksands; **mer de ~** sea of sand; **tempête de ~** sandstorm. **2** *adj inv* sandy, sand-coloured. ◆ **sablage** *nm [allée]* sanding; *[façade]* sandblasting. ◆ **sablé** *nm* shortbread biscuit *ou* cookie *(US)*. ◆ **sabler** (1) *vt* (**a**) *route* to sand; *façade* to sandblast. (**b**) **~ le champagne** *(lit)* to drink *ou* have champagne; *(fig: fêter quelque chose)* to celebrate. ◆ **sableux, -euse** *ou* ◆ **sablonneux, -euse** *adj* sandy. ◆ **sablier** *nm (gén)* hourglass, sandglass; *(Culin)* egg timer. ◆ **sablière** *nf (carrière)* sand quarry.

sabord [sabɔʀ] *nm* scuttle *(Naut)*. ◆ **sabordage** *nm (Naut)* scuppering, scuttling; *(fig)* winding up, shutting down. ◆ **saborder** (1) **1** *vt navire, projet* to scupper, scuttle; *entreprise* to wind up, shut down. **2 se ~** *vpr (Naut)* to scupper *ou* scuttle one's ship; *[patron]* to wind up, shut down; *[candidat]* to write o.s. off, scupper o.s.

sabot [sabo] *nm (chaussure)* clog; *(Zool)* hoof; *(péj: machine)* useless heap *. **il travaille comme un ~** he's a hopeless worker; **~ de frein** brake shoe; **~ de Denver** Denver shoe.

saboter [sabɔte] (1) *vt* (**a**) *(Mil, Pol, fig)* to sabotage. (**b**) *(bâcler)* to make a (proper) mess of, botch; *(abîmer)* to mess up, ruin. ◆ **sabotage** *nm* (**a**) *(Mil, Pol, fig)* sabotage; *(acte)* act of sabotage. (**b**) *(bâclage)* botching. ◆ **saboteur, -euse** *nm, f (Mil, Pol)* saboteur; *(bâcleur)* shoddy worker, botcher.

sabre [sɑbʀ(ə)] *nm* sabre. **~ d'abordage** cutlass; **mettre ~ au clair** to draw one's sword. ◆ **sabrer** (1) *vt (Mil)* to sabre, cut down; *(*: recaler à l'examen)* to plough *; *(*: critiquer)* to tear to pieces; *(*: biffer)* to score out; *projet* to axe, chop *. **cette nouvelle m'a sabré (le moral)** I was really shattered by the news *.

sac [sak] **1** *nm* (**a**) *(gén)* bag; *(de grande taille, en toile)* sack; *(cartable)* (school) bag; *(à bretelles)* satchel. (**b**) *(contenu)* bag, bagful; sack, sackful. (**c**) *(‡: argent)* ten francs. (**d**) *[ville]* sack(ing). **mettre à ~** *ville* to sack; *maison* to ransack. (**e**) *(locutions)* **mettre dans le même ~** * to lump together; **l'affaire est dans le ~** * it's in the bag *. (**f**) *(Anat)* sac. **2** : **~ de couchage** sleeping bag; **~ à dos** rucksack, knapsack; **~ à main** handbag, purse *(US)*; **~ à provisions** shopping bag; *(en papier)* (paper) carrier; **~ reporter** organizer bag; **~ de voyage** overnight *ou* travelling bag.

saccade [sakad] *nf* jerk. **avancer par ~s** to move forward *ou* along in fits and starts *ou* jerkily; **rire par ~s** to give a jerky laugh. ◆ **saccadé, e** *adj gestes, style* jerky; *respiration* spasmodic, halting; *bruit* staccato; *sommeil* fitful.

saccager [sakaʒe] (3) *vt* (**a**) *(dévaster) pièce* to turn upside down; *jardin* to create havoc in, wreck. **saccagé par la grêle** devastated by the hail. (**b**) *(piller) ville* to sack, lay waste; *maison* to ransack. ◆ **saccage** *nm* havoc (*de* in).

saccharine [sakaʀin] *nf* saccharin(e).

sacerdoce [sasɛʀdɔs] *nm (Rel)* priesthood; *(fig)* calling, vocation. ◆ **sacerdotal, e,** *mpl* **-aux** *adj* priestly, sacerdotal.

sachet [saʃɛ] *nm [bonbons]* bag; *[poudre]* sachet; *[soupe]* packet. **de la soupe en ~** packet soup; **~ de thé** tea bag.

sacoche [sakɔʃ] *nf (gén)* bag; *(pour outils)* toolbag; *[cycliste] (de selle)* saddlebag; *(de porte-bagages)* pannier; *[écolier]* (school)bag; *(à bretelles)* satchel.

sacquer * [sake] (1) *vt* (**a**) *employé* to fire, give the sack * *ou* push ‡ to. **se faire ~** to get the sack *, get fired *. (**b**) *élève (mauvaise note)* to give a lousy mark to ‡; *(recaler)* to plough *, fail. (**c**) *(détester)* **je ne peux pas le ~** I can't stand him.

sacrer [sakʀe] (1) **1** *vt roi* to crown; *évêque* to consecrate. **2** *vi* (* †) to curse, swear. ◆ **sacraliser** (1) *vt* to regard as sacred, make sacred. ◆ **sacre** *nm [roi]* coronation; *[évêque]* consecration. *(Mus)* **le S~ du Printemps** the Rite of Spring. ◆ **sacré, e 1** *adj* (**a**) *(Rel)* sacred, holy; *art, droit, repas* sacred; *terreur* holy. (**b**) (*) *(maudit)* blasted *, confounded *, damned ‡. *(considérable)* **c'est un ~ menteur** he's one heck * *ou* hell ‡ of a liar; **ce ~ Paul a encore gagné** that devil Paul has gone and won again *. **2** *nm*: **le ~** the sacred. ◆ **sacrement** *nm* sacrament. ◆ **sacrément** * *adv froid etc* fearfully, damned ‡. **ça m'a ~ plu** I liked it ever so much *.

sacrifice [sakʀifis] *nm (Rel, fig)* sacrifice. **faire le ~ de sa vie** to sacrifice one's life. ◆ **sacrifier** (7) **1** *vt (gén)* to sacrifice (*à* to, *pour* for); *(abandonner)* to give up; *(Comm) marchandises* to give away (at a knockdown price). **'prix ~s'** 'giveaway prices', 'rock bottom prices', 'prices slashed'. **2 ~ à** *vt indir mode* to conform to. **3 se ~** *vpr* to sacrifice o.s.

sacrilège [sakʀilɛʒ] **1** *adj (Rel, fig)* sacrilegious. **2** *nm* sacrilege. **3** *nmf* sacrilegious person.

sacripant [sakʀipɑ̃] *nm (†, hum)* rogue, scoundrel.

sacristie [sakʀisti] *nf (catholique)* sacristy; *(protestante)* vestry. ◆ **sacristain** *nm [sacristie]* sacristan; *[église]* sexton.

sacro-saint, e [sakʀosɛ̃, ɛ̃t] *adj (lit, iro)* sacrosanct.

sacrum [sakʀɔm] *nm* sacrum.

sadique [sadik] **1** *adj* sadistic. **2** *nmf* sadist. ◆ **sadiquement** *adv* sadistically. ◆ **sadisme** *nm* sadism.

sadomasochiste [sadɔmazɔʃist(ə)] **1** *adj* sadomasochistic. **2** *nmf* sadomasochist. ◆ **sadomasochisme** *nm* sadomasochism.

safari [safaʀi] *nm* safari. **faire un ~** to go on safari; **~-photo** photographic safari.

safran [safʀɑ̃] *nm, adj inv* saffron.

sagace [sagas] *adj (littér)* sagacious, shrewd. ◆ **sagacité** *nf* sagacity, shrewdness.

sagaie [sagɛ] *nf* assegai.

sage [saʒ] **1** *adj (avisé)* wise, sensible; *(chaste)* good, well-behaved; *(docile)* good, well-behaved; *(modéré) goûts etc* sober, moderate. **~ comme une image** (as) good as gold. **2** *nm* wise man; *(Antiq)* sage. ◆ **sage-femme,** *pl* **sages-femmes** *nf* midwife. ◆ **sagement** *adv* wisely, sensibly; properly; moderately. **il est resté ~ assis** he sat quietly, he sat like a good child (*ou* boy). ◆ **sagesse** *nf* wisdom, (good) sense; properness; good behaviour; moderation.

Sagittaire [saʒitɛʀ] *nm*: **le** ~ Sagittarius; **être (du)** ~ to be Sagittarius *ou* a Sagittarian.

sagouin ‡ [sagwɛ̃] *nm (sale)* dirty *ou* filthy pig *; *(salopard)* swine ‡, slob ‡, bastard ‡; *(incompétent)* bungling idiot ‡.

Sahara [saaʀa] *nm*: **le** ~ the Sahara (desert).

Sahel [saɛl] *nm*: **le** ~ the Sahel.

saigner [seɲe] (1) **1** *vi* to bleed. **il saignait du nez** he had a nosebleed, his nose was bleeding. **2** *vt* to bleed. ~ **qn à blanc** to bleed sb white. **3 se** ~ *vpr*: **se** ~ **(aux quatre veines) pour qn** to bleed o.s. white for sb. ◆ **saignant, e** *adj plaie (lit)* bleeding; *(fig)* raw; *viande* rare, underdone; (‡) *critique* scathing, savage, biting; *mésaventure* damned nasty ‡. ◆ **saignée** *nf* (**a**) *(Méd)* bleeding. **faire une** ~ **à qn** to bleed sb, let sb's blood. (**b**) *[budget]* savage cut (*à, dans* in). **les** ~**s faites par la guerre** the heavy losses incurred by the war. (**c**) *(Anat)* **la** ~ **du bras** the bend of the arm. (**d**) *(sillon) [sol]* trench, ditch; *[mur]* groove. ◆ **saignement** *nm* bleeding. ~ **de nez** nosebleed.

saillir[1] [sajiʀ] (13) *vi [corniche]* to jut out, stick out, project; *[menton, veine, muscle]* to protrude ; *[pommette]* to be prominent; *[yeux]* to bulge ◆ **saillant, e** *adj* jutting, projecting; protruding ; prominent; bulging; *événement* salient, outstanding. ◆ **saillie**[1] *nf* (**a**) *(aspérité)* projection. **faire** ~ to project, jut out; **rocher qui s'avance en** ~ rock which sticks *ou* juts out. (**b**) *(boutade)* witticism.

saillir[2] [sajiʀ] (2) **1** *vi (littér: jaillir)* to gush forth. **2** *vt (Zool)* to cover, serve. **saillie**[2] *nf (Zool)* covering, serving.

sain, saine [sɛ̃, sɛn] *adj* (**a**) *personne* healthy; *constitution, dents* healthy, sound. ~ **et sauf** safe and sound. (**b**) *climat, nourriture* healthy, wholesome. **il est** ~ **de faire** it is good for you *ou* healthy to do. (**c**) *fondations, fruit* sound; *viande* good; *gestion* healthy. (**d**) *(moralement) personne* sane; *politique, jugement* sound, sane; *goûts* healthy; *lectures* wholesome. ◆ **sainement** *adv* healthily; soundly; wholesomely; sanely.

saindoux [sɛ̃du] *nm* lard.

saint, e [sɛ̃, sɛ̃t] **1** *adj* (**a**) *(sacré)* holy. **la** ~**e Famille** the Holy Family; **le vendredi** ~ Good Friday; **le jeudi** ~ Maundy Thursday; **le mardi** ~ Tuesday of Holy Week; **le samedi** ~ Easter Saturday; **toute la** ~**e journée** * the whole blessed day *; **avoir une** ~**e terreur de qch** * to have a holy terror of sth *. (**b**) *(devant prénom)* Saint. *(apôtre)* ~ **Pierre** Saint Peter; *(église)* **S~-Pierre** Saint Peter's; *(fête)* **la S~-Pierre** the feast of Saint Peter; *(jour)* **à la S~-Pierre** on Saint Peter's day; **à la S~-Michel/Martin** at Michaelmas/Martinmas. (**c**) *personne* saintly, godly; *action* pious, saintly, holy.
2 *nm, f (lit, fig)* saint; *(statue)* statue of a saint. **la fête de tous les** ~**s** All Saints' Day.
3 : ~**-bernard** *nm inv (chien)* St Bernard; *(fig)* good Samaritan; **S~-Domingue** Santo Domingo; **le S~-Esprit** the Holy Spirit *ou* Ghost; ~**-frusquin** * clobber *, gear *; **et tout le** ~**-frusquin** * and the whole caboodle; **à la** ~**-glinglin** never in a month of Sundays; **attendre jusqu'à la** ~**-glinglin** to wait till the cows come home; **on ne va pas rester là jusqu'à la** ~**-glinglin** we're not going to hang around here forever *; **S~e-Hélène** St Helena; **le S~-Laurent** the St Lawrence (river); *(péj)* ~**e nitouche** (pious *ou* saintly) hypocrite; ~ **patron** patron saint; **S~-Père** Holy Father; **S~-Pierre-et-Miquelon** Saint Pierre and Miquelon; **le** ~ **sacrement** the Blessed Sacrament; *(Rel, fig)* **le S~ des S~s** the Holy of Holies; **le S~ Suaire** the Holy Shroud; **le S~-Siège** the Holy See; **la S~-Sylvestre** New Year's Eve; **la S~e Vierge** the Blessed Virgin.

◆ **saintement** *adv* like a saint. ◆ **sainteté** *nf [personne]* saintliness; *[Évangile, Vierge]* holiness; *[lieu, mariage]* sanctity. **Sa S~ (le pape)** His Holiness (the Pope).

saisir [seziʀ] (2) **1** *vt* (**a**) *(prendre)* to take hold of, catch hold of; *(s'emparer de)* to seize, grab (hold of); *prétexte* to seize. ~ **qn à la gorge** to grab *ou* seize sb by the throat; ~ **une occasion au vol** to jump at the opportunity. (**b**) *mot, nom* to catch, get; *explications* to grasp, understand, get. (**c**) *[sentiment]* to take hold of, seize, grip; *[malaise]* to come over. *(surprendre)* ~ **qn** to bring sb up with a start; **saisi de joie** overcome with joy; **saisi de panique** seized with panic, panic-stricken; **être saisi par** *horreur* to be gripped by, be transfixed with; *ressemblance, froid* to be struck by; **elle fut tellement saisie que...** she was so overcome that... (**d**) *(Jur) personne, chose* to seize; *juridiction* to submit *ou* refer to. ~ **la Cour de Justice** to complain to the Court of Justice. (**e**) *(Culin)* to seal, fry briskly. (**f**) *(Ordin)* to capture, keyboard. **2 se** ~ *vpr*: **se** ~ **de qch/qn** to seize *ou* grab sth/sb. ◆ **saisie** *nf [biens, journal]* seizure. *(Ordin)* ~ **de données** data capture *ou* keyboarding; ~**-arrêt** distraint. ◆ **saisissant, e** *adj spectacle* gripping; *ressemblance* startling, striking. ◆ **saisissement** *nm (froid)* sudden chill; *(émotion)* (rush of) emotion; *(surprise)* surprise.

saison [sɛzɔ̃] *nf* season; *(cure)* cure. **la belle** ~ the summer months; **en cette** ~ at this time of year; **en toutes** ~**s** all (the) year round; **temps de** ~ seasonable weather; **la** ~ **des pluies** the rainy *ou* wet season; **la** ~ **littéraire/théâtrale** the literary/theatre season; *(Tourisme)* **haute/basse** ~ high/low *ou* off-season; **hors** ~ *plante* out of season. ◆ **saisonnier, -ière 1** *adj* seasonal. **2** *nm, f* seasonal worker.

saké [sake] *nm* sake.

salade [salad] *nf* (**a**) *(laitue)* lettuce; *(scarole)* curly endive; *(plat)* green salad. ~ **de tomates** *etc* tomato *etc* salad; ~ **niçoise** salade niçoise; ~ **composée** mixed salad; **haricots en** ~ bean salad. (**b**) *(* fig) (confusion)* tangle, muddle. *(mensonges)* ~**s** stories *; *[représentant]* **vendre sa** ~ to sell one's line. ◆ **saladier** *nm* salad bowl.

salaire [salɛʀ] *nm* (**a**) wage(s), salary, pay. ~ **de famine** *ou* **de misère** starvation wage; ~ **brut/net** gross/net wage, ≃ before-tax/tax-deducted *ou* disposable income. (**b**) *(fig: récompense, châtiment)* reward (*de* for).

salaison [salɛzɔ̃] *nf (procédé)* salting; *(aliment)* salt meat (*ou* fish).

salamandre [salamɑ̃dʀ(ə)] *nf (Zool)* salamander; *(poêle)* slow-combustion stove.

salami [salami] *nm* salami.

salarié, e [salaʀje] **1** *adj travailleur* salaried, wage-earning; *travail* paid. **2** *nm, f* salaried employee, wage-earner.

salaud ‡ [salo] *nm* bastard, swine ‡.

sale [sal] *adj* (**a**) *(crasseux)* dirty. ~ **comme un cochon** filthy (dirty). (**b**) *(ordurier)* dirty, filthy. (**c**) *(*: avant n : mauvais) (gén)* nasty; *temps, caractère* rotten *, foul, lousy *. ~ **tour** dirty trick; **faire une** ~ **tête** * to be damned annoyed ‡.

salé, e [sale] **1** *adj* (**a**) *saveur, mer* salty; *amande, plat, beurre* salted; *gâteau (non sucré)* savoury; *(au goût ~)* salty; *(conservé au sel) poisson, viande* salt. (**b**) *(*: grivois)* spicy, juicy. (**c**) (*) *punition* stiff; *facture* steep. **2** *nm (nourriture)* salty food; *(porc salé)* salt pork. **préférer le** ~ **au sucré** to prefer savoury *ou* salty *(US)* foods to sweet. **3** *adv*: **manger** ~ to like a lot of salt on one's food.

salement [salmɑ̃] *adv* dirtily; (‡: *très*) damned ‡. **j'ai eu** ~ **peur** I had a hell of a fright ‡, I was damned scared ‡.

saler [sale] (1) *vt* (**a**) *(lit)* to put salt in, salt. (**b**) (*) *client* to do *, fleece; *facture* to bump up *; *inculpé* to be tough on *.

saleté [salte] *nf* (**a**) *(malpropreté) [lieu, personne]* dirtiness; *(crasse)* dirt, filth. **il y a une ~ par terre** there's some dirt on the floor; **tu as fait des ~s** *ou* **de la ~ partout** you've made a mess all over the place. (**b**) (*) **de la ~ , une ~** *(objet)* rubbish, junk; *(nourriture)* rubbish, muck *; **ce réfrigérateur est une ~** *ou* **de la ~** this fridge is a load of old rubbish *; **acheter une ~** to buy some (old) junk *ou* rubbish *ou* trash. (**c**) (*) *(maladie)* nasty bug *; *(obscénité)* dirty *ou* filthy remark; *(méchanceté)* dirty *ou* filthy trick *; *(salaud)* nasty piece of work *, nasty character.

salière [saljɛʀ] *nf* saltcellar.

saligaud ⁑ [saligo] *nm* *(malpropre)* dirty *ou* filthy pig *; *(salaud)* swine ⁑, bastard ⁑.

salin, e [salɛ̃, in] *adj* saline.

salir [saliʀ] (2) **1** *vt lieu* to (make) dirty, mess up. **~ qn** to soil *ou* tarnish sb's reputation. **2 se ~** *vpr [tissu]* to get dirty *ou* soiled; *[personne]* to get dirty, dirty o.s. *(lit, fig)* **se ~ les mains** to get one's hands dirty, dirty one's hands. ◆ **salissant, e** *adj étoffe* which shows the dirt; *travail* dirty, messy.

salive [saliv] *nf* saliva, spittle. ◆ **saliver** (1) *vi* to salivate; *[animal]*, *(péj)* to drool. **ça le faisait ~** *[nourriture]* it made his mouth water; *[spectacle]* it made him drool.

salle [sal] **1** *nf* (**a**) *[musée, café]* room; *[château]* hall; *[restaurant]* (dining) room; *[hôpital]* ward. (**b**) *(Ciné, Théât) (auditorium)* auditorium, theatre; *(public)* audience; *(cinéma)* cinema, movie theater *(US)*. **faire ~ comble** to have a full house, pack the house; **cinéma à plusieurs ~s** film-centre with several cinemas; **film projeté dans la ~ 3** film showing in cinema 3. **2** : **~ d'attente** waiting room; **~ de bain(s)** bathroom; **~ de classe** classroom; **~ de concert** concert hall; **~ d'eau** shower-room; *(Aviat)* **~ d'embarquement** departure lounge; **~ des fêtes** village hall; **~ à manger** *(pièce)* dining room; *(meubles)* dining room suite; **~ d'opération** operating theatre *ou* room *(US)*; **~ des professeurs** staff room; **~ de réanimation** *ou* **de réveil** recovery room; **~ de rédaction** (newspaper) office; **~ de séjour** living room; **~ de soins** treatment room; **~ de spectacle** theatre; cinema; **~ des ventes** saleroom, auction room.

salon [salɔ̃] **1** *nm* (**a**) *[maison]* lounge, sitting room; *[hôtel]* lounge; *[navire]* saloon, lounge. (**b**) *(hôtel) (pour les clients)* lounge; *(pour conférences)* function room. (**c**) *(meubles)* lounge *ou* living-room suite. **~ de jardin** set of garden furniture. (**d**) *(exposition)* exhibition, show. (**e**) *(cercle littéraire)* salon. *(hum)* **faire ~** to have a natter *. **2** : **S~ de l'Auto** Motor *ou* Car Show; **~ de coiffure** hairdressing salon; **~ de thé** tearoom.

salopard ⁑ [salɔpaʀ] *nm* bastard ⁑, swine ⁑.

salope ⁑ [salɔp] *nf (méchante)* bitch ⁑; *(dévergondée)* whore, tart ⁑; *(sale)* slut.

saloper ⁑ [salɔpe] (1) *vt (bâcler)* to botch, bungle; *(salir)* to mess up *, muck up *.

saloperie ⁑ [salɔpʀi] *nf* (**a**) **de la ~** *(nourriture)* rubbish, muck *; *(objet)* trash, junk, rubbish; **acheter une ~** to buy some (old) trash *ou* junk *ou* rubbish. (**b**) *(maladie)* nasty bug *; *(action)* dirty trick *; *(obscénité)* dirty *ou* filthy remark. (**c**) *(crasse)* filth. **ça fait de la ~** *ou* **des ~s partout** it makes a mess everywhere.

salopette [salɔpɛt] *nf (gén)* dungarees; *[ouvrier]* overall(s); *(Ski)* salopette.

salpêtre [salpɛtʀ(ə)] *nm* saltpetre.

salsa [salsa] *nf* salsa.

salsifis [salsifi] *nm* salsify, oyster-plant.

saltimbanque [saltɛ̃bɑ̃k] *nmf* (travelling) acrobat.

salubre [salybʀ(ə)] *adj* healthy, salubrious. ◆ **salubrité** *nf* healthiness, salubrity. **~ publique** public health.

saluer [salɥe] (1) *vt (gén, fig)* to greet; *(Mil, Naut)* to salute. *(dire au revoir)* **~ qn** to take one's leave of sb; **~ qn de la main** to wave (one's hand) to sb (in greeting); **~ qn d'un signe de tête** to nod (a greeting) to sb; **saluez-le de ma part** give him my regards; **~ (le public)** to bow to the audience; **'je vous salue, Marie'** 'Hail, Mary'.

salut [saly] **1** *nm* (**a**) *(de la main)* wave (of the hand); *(de la tête)* nod (of the head); *(du buste)* bow; *(Mil, Naut)* salute. (**b**) *(sauvegarde)* safety. **mesures de ~ public** state security measures, measures to protect national security; **ancre** *ou* **planche de ~** sheet anchor. (**c**) *(Rel: rédemption)* salvation. **2** *excl* (**a**) (*) *(bonjour)* hi (there)! *, hello!; *(au revoir)* see you! *, bye! *. (**b**) *(littér)* **~ (à toi)** (all) hail (to thee).

salutaire [salytɛʀ] *adj (gén)* salutary; *air* healthy; *remède* beneficial. **ça m'a été ~** it did me good *ou* was good for me.

salutation [salytɑsjɔ̃] *nf* salutation, greeting. **veuillez agréer, Monsieur, mes ~s distinguées** yours faithfully *ou* truly.

Salvador [salvadɔʀ] *nm*: **le ~** El Salvador. ◆ **salvadorien, -ienne** *adj,* **S~(ne)** *nm(f)* Salvadorian.

salve [salv(ə)] *nf* salvo.

samba [sɑ̃mba] *nf* samba.

samedi [samdi] *nm* Saturday. **~ nous irons** on Saturday we'll go; **~ qui vient** this Saturday, next Saturday; **un ~ sur deux** every other *ou* second Saturday; **~ , le 18 décembre** Saturday December 18th; **le ~ 23 janvier** on Saturday January 23rd; **~ soir** Saturday evening *ou* night.

sanatorium [sanatɔʀjɔm] *nm* sanatorium, sanitarium *(US)*.

sanctifier [sɑ̃ktifje] (7) *vt* to sanctify, hallow, bless. ◆ **sanctification** *nf* sanctification. ◆ **sanctifié, e** *adj* blessed.

sanction [sɑ̃ksjɔ̃] *nf* (**a**) *(condamnation)* sanction, penalty; *(Scol)* punishment; *(fig: conséquence)* penalty (*de* for). **prendre des ~s contre qn** to take action against sb; **imposer des ~s contre qn** to impose sanctions on sb. (**b**) *(ratification)* sanction, approval. ◆ **sanctionner** (1) *vt (punir)* to punish; *(consacrer)* to sanction, approve.

sanctuaire [sɑ̃ktɥɛʀ] *nm* sanctuary.

sandale [sɑ̃dal] *nf* sandal. ◆ **sandalette** *nf* sandal.

sandow [sɑ̃do] *nm* ® *(attache)* luggage elastic; *(Aviat)* catapult.

sandwich [sɑ̃dwitʃ] *nm* sandwich. **(pris) en ~ (entre)** * sandwiched (between).

sang [sɑ̃] *nm (lit, fig)* blood. **animal à ~ froid/ chaud** cold-blooded/warm-blooded animal; **être en ~** to be bleeding; **du même ~** of the same flesh and blood; **avoir le ~ chaud** to be hot-blooded; **il a le jeu dans le ~** he's got gambling in his blood; **mon ~ n'a fait qu'un tour** *(peur)* my heart missed *ou* skipped a beat; *(colère)* I saw red; **se faire un ~ d'encre** * to be worried stiff *; **se ronger les ~s** to worry (o.s.), fret. ◆ **sang-froid** *nm inv* sang-froid, self-control. **garder/perdre son ~-~** to keep/ lose one's head; **faire qch de ~-~** to do sth in cold blood *ou* cold-bloodedly; **répondre avec ~-~** to reply coolly *ou* calmly. ◆ **sanglant, e** *adj (gén)* bloody; *insulte, défaite* savage.

sangle [sɑ̃gl(ə)] *nf (gén)* strap; *[selle]* girth. *[siège]* **~s** webbing. ◆ **sangler** (1) *vt cheval* to girth; *colis, corps* to strap up.

sanglier [sɑ̃glije] *nm* (wild) boar.

sanglot [sɑ̃glo] *nm* sob. ◆ **sangloter** (1) *vi* to sob.

sangsue [sɑ̃sy] *nf (lit, fig)* leech.

sanguin, e [sɑ̃gɛ̃, in] **1** *adj caractère* fiery; *visage* ruddy; *(Anat)* blood. **2** *nf (Bot)* blood orange; *(dessin)* red chalk drawing.

sanguinaire [sɑ̃ginɛʀ] *adj personne* bloodthirsty; *combat* bloody.

sanguinolent, e [sɑ̃ginɔlɑ̃, ɑ̃t] *adj linge* streaked with blood; *plaie* slightly bleeding.

sanitaire [sanitɛʀ] **1** *adj* (**a**) *(Méd) services, mesures* health; *conditions* sanitary. (**b**) *(Plomberie)* **l'installation ~** the bathroom plumbing; **appareil ~** bathroom *ou* sanitary appliance. **2** *nmpl*: **les ~s** *(lieu)* the bathroom; *(appareils)* the bathroom suite; *(plomberie)* the bathroom plumbing.

sans [sɑ̃] **1** *prép* (**a**) *(gén)* without. **je suis sorti ~ chapeau ni manteau** I went out without a hat or coat *ou* with no hat or coat; **repas à 60 F ~ le vin** meal at 60 francs exclusive of wine *ou* not including wine; **être ~ abri** to be homeless; **être ~ travail** *ou* **~ emploi** to be unemployed *ou* out of work; **manger ~ fourchette/faim** to eat without a fork/without feeling hungry; **non ~ mal** not without difficulty; **marcher ~ chaussures** to walk barefoot; **marcher ~ but** to walk aimlessly; **il est ~ scrupules** he is unscrupulous, he has no scruples, he is devoid of scruples; **robe ~ manches** sleeveless dress; **~ père** fatherless, with no father; **dictée ~ fautes** error-free dictation; **demain ~ faute** tomorrow without fail; **je le connais, ~ plus** I know him but no more than that. (**b**) *(cause négative)* but for. **~ cette réunion, il aurait pu partir ce soir** if it had not been for *ou* were it not for *ou* but for this meeting he could have left tonight. (**c**) *(avec infin ou subj)* without. **vous n'êtes pas ~ savoir que** you must be aware that; **je n'irai pas ~ être invité** *ou* **~ que je sois invité** I won't go without being invited *ou* unless I am invited; **~ plus attendre** without further delay; **j'y crois ~ y croire** I believe it and I don't; **je ne suis pas ~ avoir des doutes** I have my doubts *ou* I am not without some doubts; **il ne se passe pas de jour ~ qu'il lui écrive** not a day passes without his writing to him; **il va ~ dire que** it goes without saying that. (**d**) (*) **~ ça, ~ quoi** otherwise; if not; **sois sage, ~ ça...!** be good or else...!, be good — otherwise...! **2** *adv* (*) **votre parapluie! vous alliez partir ~** your umbrella! you were going to go off without it. **3** : **~-abri** *nmf inv* homeless person; **~-emploi** *nmf inv* unemployed person; **les ~-emploi** *nmpl* the jobless, the unemployed, those out of work; **~ faute** *loc adv* without fail; **faire un ~ fautes** *(Équitation)* to do a clear round; *(fig: Pol etc)* not to put a foot wrong; **~-gêne** *(adj inv)* inconsiderate; *(nm inv)* lack of consideration (for others); *(nmf inv)* inconsiderate type; **~-soin** *(adj inv)* careless; *(nmf inv)* careless person; **~-le-sou** *adj inv* penniless; **~-souci** *adj inv* carefree; **~-travail** *nmf inv* = **~-emploi**.

santé [sɑ̃te] *nf* health. **avoir la ~** to be healthy, be in good health; **meilleure ~** get well soon; *(Admin)* **services de ~** health services; *(en trinquant)* **à votre ~!** cheers! *; **à la ~ de Paul!** here's to Paul!; **boire à la ~ de qn** to drink (to) sb's health.

saoul, e [su, sul] = **soûl**.

sape [sap] *nf* (**a**) *(lit, fig: action)* undermining, sapping; *(tranchée)* approach *ou* sapping trench. (**b**) *(habits)* **~s** ⁑ gear *, clobber ⁑. ◆ **saper** (1) **1** *vt (lit, fig)* to undermine, sap. **2 se ~** ⁑ *vpr* to do o.s. up *. **bien sapé** well turned out *ou* got up *. ◆ **sapeur** *nm (Mil)* sapper. **~-pompier** fireman.

saphir [safiʀ] *nm (pierre)* sapphire; *(aiguille)* sapphire, needle.

sapin [sapɛ̃] *nm (arbre)* fir (tree); *(bois)* fir. **~ de Noël** Christmas tree. ◆ **sapinière** *nf* fir plantation *ou* forest.

saquer * [sake] (1) *vt* = **sacquer** *.

sarabande [saʀabɑ̃d] *nf (danse)* saraband; (*: *tapage)* racket, hullabaloo *. **faire la ~** * to make a racket; **~ de chiffres** jumble of figures.

sarbacane [saʀbakan] *nf (arme)* blowpipe, blowgun; *(jouet)* peashooter.

sarcasme [saʀkasm(ə)] *nm (ironie)* sarcasm; *(remarque)* sarcastic remark. ◆ **sarcastique** *adj* sarcastic.

sarcler [saʀkle] (1) *vt jardin* to weed; *mauvaise herbe* to hoe. ◆ **sarclette** *nf*, **sarcloir** *nm* spud, weeding hoe.

sarcome [saʀkom] *nm* sarcoma.

sarcophage [saʀkɔfaʒ] *nm (cercueil)* sarcophagus.

Sardaigne [saʀdɛɲ] *nf* Sardinia. ◆ **sarde** *adj, nm*, **S~** *nmf* Sardinian.

sardine [saʀdin] *nf* sardine.

sardonique [saʀdɔnik] *adj* sardonic. ◆ **sardoniquement** *adv* sardonically.

sarment [saʀmɑ̃] *nm*: **~ (de vigne)** vine shoot.

sarrasin [saʀazɛ̃] *nm (Bot)* buckwheat.

sas [sɑ] *nm* (**a**) *(Espace, Naut)* airlock; *[écluse]* lock. (**b**) *(tamis)* sieve, screen.

Satan [satɑ̃] *nm* Satan. ◆ **satané, e** * *adj* blasted *, confounded *. ◆ **satanique** *adj* satanic.

satellite [satelit] *nm (lit, fig)* satellite. **~ de communication/de télécommunications/de radiodiffusion** communications/telecommunications/broadcast satellite. ◆ **satelliser** (1) *vt fusée* to put into orbit; *pays* to make into a satellite.

satiété [sasjete] *nf* satiety, satiation. **à ~** *manger* to satiety *ou* satiation; *répéter* ad nauseam; **j'en ai à ~** I've more than enough.

satin [satɛ̃] *nm* satin. ◆ **satiné, e** *adj tissu, aspect* satiny, satin-like; *peinture* with a silk finish. ◆ **satiner** (1) *vt étoffe* to put a satin finish on; *photo* to put a silk finish on.

satire [satiʀ] *nf* satire. ◆ **satirique** *adj* satirical. ◆ **satiriquement** *adv* satirically. ◆ **satiriser** (1) *vt (gén)* to satirize.

satisfaction [satisfaksjɔ̃] *nf* satisfaction; *[désir]* satisfaction, gratification. **je vois avec ~ que** I'm gratified to see that; **à la ~ de tous** to everybody's satisfaction; **leur fils ne leur a donné que des ~s** their son has been a (source of) great satisfaction to them; **donner ~ à qn/obtenir ~** to give sb/get satisfaction (*de qch* for sth). ◆ **satisfaire** (60) **1** *vt (gén)* to satisfy; *désir, besoin* to satisfy, gratify; *demande* to satisfy, meet. **~ l'attente de qn** to come up to sb's expectations; *(Ind)* **arriver à ~ la demande** to keep up with demand. **2 ~ à** *vt indir* to satisfy; to gratify; to meet; *promesse, condition* to fulfil. **3 se ~** *vpr* to be satisfied (*de* with); *(euph)* to relieve o.s. ◆ **satisfaisant, e** *adj (acceptable)* satisfactory; *(qui fait plaisir)* satisfying. ◆ **satisfait, e** *adj* satisfied. **être ~ de** *décision* to be satisfied with, be happy with *ou* about; *soirée* to be pleased with; **~ de soi** self-satisfied.

saturer [satyʀe] (1) *vt* (**a**) *(gén, Sci)* to saturate (*de* with). **saturé d'eau** *terre* waterlogged; *(lit, fig)* **j'en suis saturé** I've had my fill of it. (**b**) *(Téléc)* **être saturé** *[réseau]* to be overloaded *ou* saturated; *[standard]* to be jammed; *[lignes]* to be engaged *ou* busy *(US)*. ◆ **saturation** *nf (gén, Sci)* saturation (*de* of). **être à ~** to be at saturation point.

Saturne [satyʀn(ə)] **1** *nm (Myth)* Saturn. **2** *nf (Astron)* Saturn.

satyre [satiʀ] *nm (*: obsédé)* sex maniac; *(Myth)* satyr.

sauce [sos] *nf (Culin)* sauce; *[salade]* dressing; *(jus de viande)* gravy. **~ blanche** *etc* white *etc* sauce; **à quelle ~ allons-nous être mangés?** I wonder what fate has in store for us; **mettre de la ~ dans un discours** to pad out *ou* add some padding to a speech; **mettre un exemple à toutes les ~s** to turn *ou* adapt an example to fit any case; **recevoir la ~ *** to get soaked *ou* drenched. ◆ **saucer** (3) *vt assiette* to wipe (the sauce off). **se faire ~ *** to get soaked *ou* drenched. ◆ **saucière** *nf* sauce-boat; *[jus de viande]* gravy boat.

saucisse [sosis] *nf* sausage. ~ **de Francfort** frankfurter. ◆ **saucisson** *nm* (slicing) sausage.

sauf¹, sauve [sof, sov] *adj personne* unharmed, unhurt; *honneur* saved, intact. ◆ **sauf-conduit,** *pl* **sauf-conduits** *nm* safe-conduct.

sauf² [sof] *prép (à part)* except; *(à moins de)* unless. **tout le monde ~ lui** everyone except *ou* but him; **~ si** except if, unless; **~ avis contraire** unless you hear otherwise *ou* to the contrary; **~ erreur de ma part** if I'm not mistaken.

sauge [soʒ] *nf (Culin)* sage; *(ornementale)* salvia.

saugrenu, e [sogʀəny] *adj* preposterous, ludicrous.

saule [sol] *nm* willow (tree). **~ pleureur** weeping willow.

saumâtre [somɑtʀ(ə)] *adj goût* brackish, briny; *(fig)* unpleasant.

saumon [somɔ̃] **1** *nm* salmon. **2** *adj inv* salmon pink.

saumure [somyʀ] *nf* brine.

sauna [sona] *nm* sauna.

saupoudrer [sopudʀe] (1) *vt (gén)* to sprinkle; *(Culin)* to dredge, dust, sprinkle (*de* with).

saut [so] *nm (lit, fig: bond)* jump, leap; *(Sport: épreuve, spécialité)* jumping. **faire qch au ~ du lit** to do sth on getting up *ou* getting out of bed; **faire un ~ chez qn** to pop over *ou* round to sb's (place) *, drop in on sb; **il a fait un ~ jusqu'à Bordeaux** he paid a flying visit to Bordeaux; **~ avec/sans élan** running/standing jump; **~ en hauteur** high jump; **~ en longueur** long jump; **~ en parachute** *(sport)* parachuting, parachute jumping; *(bond)* parachute jump; **~ à la perche** *(sport)* pole vaulting; *(bond)* (pole) vault; **~ périlleux** somersault. ◆ **saute** *nf*: **~ de** *humeur* sudden change of; *température* jump in; **~ de vent** (sudden) change of wind direction; *(TV)* **pour empêcher les ~s d'images** to stop the picture flickering, keep the picture steady. ◆ **sauté, e** *adj, nm* sauté.

sauter [sote] (1) **1** *vi* (**a**) *(gén, fig)* to jump, leap; *[oiseau]* to hop. **~ à pieds joints** to make a standing jump; **~ à cloche-pied** to hop; **~ à la corde** to skip *(with a rope)*; **~ en parachute** *(gén, Sport)* to parachute; *(en cas d'accident)* to bale out, bail out *(US)*, make an emergency (parachute) jump; **~ à la perche** to pole-vault; **il sauta de la table** he jumped *ou* leapt (down) off *ou* from the table; **~ en l'air** to jump *ou* leap *ou* spring up; *(de colère)* to hit the roof *; *(de peur)* to jump, start; **~ de joie** to jump for joy; **~ à la gorge/au cou de qn** to fly at sb's throat/into sb's arms; *(fig)* **~ sur une occasion** to jump *ou* leap at an opportunity; **~ d'un sujet à l'autre** to jump *ou* leap *ou* skip from one subject to another; **il m'a sauté dessus** he pounced on me, he leapt at me; **va faire tes devoirs, et que ça saute!** * go and do your homework and get a move on! * *ou* be quick about it!; **cela saute aux yeux** it sticks out a mile, it's (quite) obvious. (**b**) *[bouchon]* to pop *ou* fly off; *[chaîne de vélo]* to come off; *[bombe, pont]* to blow up, explode; *(Élec) [circuit]* to fuse; *[fusible]* to blow; (*) *[employé, ministère]* to get fired, get the sack *, get kicked out ‡; *[cours]* to be cancelled. (**c**) **faire ~** *train, caserne* to blow up; *(Élec) plombs* to blow; *crêpe* to toss; *serrure* to break open; *(*: annuler)* to cancel; *(Culin)* to sauté, shallow-fry; **faire ~ un enfant sur ses genoux** to bounce *ou* dandle a child on one's knee; *(Casino)* **faire ~ la banque** to break the bank; **se faire ~ la cervelle** * to blow one's brains out. (**d**) *(clignoter) [paupière]* to twitch; *[télévision]* to flicker.
2 *vt obstacle* to jump (over), leap (over); *page, repas* to skip, miss (out). *(fig)* **~ le pas** to take the plunge; **on la saute ici!** ‡ we're starving to death here! *
◆ **saute-mouton** *nm* leapfrog. ◆ **sauterelle** *nf (gén)* grasshopper; *(criquet)* locust. *(lit, fig)* **nuage** *ou* **nuée de ~s** plague *ou* swarm of locusts; **(grande) ~ *** beanpole. ◆ **sauterie** *nf* party. ◆ **sauteur, -euse** **1** *nm, f* jumper. **~ à la perche** pole-vaulter. **2** *nf (Culin)* high-sided frying pan.

sautiller [sotije] (1) *vi [oiseau]* to hop; *[enfant]* to skip; *(sur un pied)* to hop. ◆ **sautillant, e** *adj mouvement* hopping, skipping; *musique* bouncy, bouncing. ◆ **sautillement** *nm*: **~(s)** hopping, skipping.

sautoir [sotwaʀ] *nm (Bijouterie)* chain. **porter qch en ~** to wear sth (on a chain) round one's neck.

sauvage [sovaʒ] **1** *adj* (**a**) *(gén)* wild; *peuplade, combat* savage; *(fig: insociable)* unsociable. **vivre à l'état ~** to live wild. (**b**) *vente* unauthorized; *concurrence* unfair; *grève, école* unofficial; *urbanisation* unplanned. **faire du camping ~** *(illégal)* to camp on unauthorized sites; *(dans la nature)* to camp in the wild, camp rough. **2** *nmf (solitaire)* unsociable type, recluse; *(brute)* brute, savage; *(indigène)* savage. ◆ **sauvagement** *adv* savagely, wildly. ◆ **sauvagerie** *nf* savagery.

sauve [sov] *adj f V* **sauf¹**.

sauvegarde [sovgard(ə)] *nf (gén)* safeguard; *(Ordin)* backup. **sous la ~ de** under the protection of; *(Ordin)* **faire la ~ d'un programme** to save a program, make a backup of a program. ◆ **sauvegarder** (1) *vt (gén)* to safeguard; *(Ordin)* to save.

sauve-qui-peut [sovkipø] *nm inv (panique)* stampede, mad rush.

sauver [sove] (1) **1** *vt (gén)* to save; *(en portant secours)* to rescue (*de* from); *(en retirant des décombres) meubles* to salvage. **ce sont les illustrations qui sauvent le livre** it's the illustrations which save *ou* redeem the book; **~ la vie à** *ou* **de qn** to save sb's life; *(fig)* **~ les meubles** to salvage *ou* save sth from the wreckage *(fig)*; **~ la situation** to retrieve the situation; **~ les apparences** to keep up appearances; **~ la face** to save face; **il m'a sauvé la mise** he bailed me out, he got me out of a tight corner. **2 se ~** *vpr* (**a**) **se ~ de** *danger* to save o.s. from. (**b**) *(s'enfuir)* to run away (*de* from); *(*: partir)* to be off, get going; *[lait]* to boil over. ◆ **sauvetage** *nm* rescue; *(moral)* salvation; *[biens]* salvaging. **~ en montagne** mountain-rescue; **cours de ~** life-saving lessons; *(Écon)* **proposer un plan de ~ de la firme** to put forward a rescue plan for the firm. ◆ **sauveteur** *nm* rescuer. ◆ **sauveur** *adj m, nm* saviour.

sauvette * [sovɛt] *nf*: **à la ~** hastily, hurriedly; **vendre à la ~** to hawk *ou* peddle on the streets *(without authorization)*.

savane [savan] *nf* savannah.

savant, e [savɑ̃, ɑ̃t] **1** *adj (érudit)* learned, scholarly; *(habile)* clever, skilful; *chien, puce* performing. *(hum)* **c'est trop ~ pour moi** it's too learned *ou* highbrow for me. **2** *nm (sciences)* scientist; *(lettres)* scholar. ◆ **savamment** *adv* learnedly; skilfully, cleverly. *(par expérience)* **j'en parle ~** I speak knowingly.

savate * [savat] *nf (pantoufle)* worn-out old slipper; *(soulier)* worn-out old shoe. **être en ~s** to be in one's slippers.

saveur [savœʀ] *nf* flavour; *(fig)* savour.

Savoie [savwa] *nf* Savoy. ◆ **savoyard, e** *adj*, **S~(e)** *nm(f)* Savoyard.

savoir [savwaʀ] (32) **1** *vt* (**a**) *adresse, nom, leçon* to know; *nouvelle* to hear, learn of. **je la savais malade** I knew (that) she was ill, I knew her to be ill; **elle sait cela par** *ou* **de son boucher** she heard it from her butcher; **personne ne savait sur quel pied danser/où se mettre** nobody knew what to do/where to put themselves; **je crois ~ que** I believe *ou* understand that; **il ment — qu'en savez-vous?** he is lying — how do you know? *ou* what do you know about it?; **il nous a fait ~ que** he informed us *ou* let us know that; **ça finira bien par se ~** it will surely end up getting out *ou* getting known, it'll get out in the end. (**b**) *(avec infin : être capable de)* to know how to. **elle sait lire** she can read, she knows how to read; **~ plaire** to know how to please; **il sait parler aux enfants** he's good at talking to children; **elle saura bien se défendre** she'll be quite able to look after herself, she'll be quite capable of looking after herself; **~ y faire** *ou* **s'y prendre** to know how to go about things (the right way); **il faut ~ attendre** you have to learn to be patient; **je ne saurais pas vous répondre** I'm afraid I couldn't answer you. (**c**) *(se rendre compte)* to know. **il ne sait plus ce qu'il dit** he doesn't know *ou* realize what he's saying, he isn't aware of what he's saying; **il se savait très malade** he knew he was very ill; **sans le ~** unknowingly. (**d**) *(locutions)* **qui sait?** who knows?; **et que sais-je encore** and I don't know what else; **il nous a emmenés je ne sais où** he took us goodness knows where; **elle ne sait pas quoi faire pour l'aider** she's at a loss to know how to help him; **on ne sait jamais** you never know, you can never tell; **pas que je sache** not as far as I know, not to my knowledge; **sachons-le bien, si...** let's be quite clear, if...; **sachez que** you should know that, let me tell you that; *(énumération)* **à ~** that is, namely, i.e.; *(hum)* **la personne que vous savez** you-know-who; **vous n'êtes pas sans ~ que** you are not unaware (of the fact) that; **il ne savait à quel saint se vouer** he didn't know which way to turn; **elle ne savait où donner de la tête** she didn't know what to do first; **si j'avais su** had I known, if I had known. **2** *nm* learning, knowledge. **~-faire** know-how *; **~-vivre** savoir-faire, mannerliness; **avoir du ~-vivre** to know how to behave.

savon [savɔ̃] *nm (matière)* soap; *(morceau)* bar *ou* cake of soap. **~ à barbe/de Marseille** shaving/household soap; **~ en poudre** soap powder; **il m'a passé un ~** * he gave me a ticking-off * *ou* dressing-down *. ◆ **savonnage** *nm* soaping. ◆ **savonner** (1) *vt* to soap. ◆ **savonnette** *nf* bar *ou* cake of (toilet) soap. ◆ **savonneux, -euse** *adj* soapy.

savourer [savuʀe] (1) *vt* to savour. ◆ **savoureux, -euse** *adj plat* tasty, flavoursome; *anecdote* juicy, spicy.

Saxe [saks(ə)] *nf* Saxony.

saxophone [saksɔfɔn] *nm* saxophone. ◆ **saxophoniste** *nmf* saxophonist.

sbire [sbiʀ] *nm (péj)* henchman *(péj)*.

scabreux, -euse [skabʀø, øz] *adj (indécent)* improper, shocking; *(dangereux)* risky.

scalp [skalp] *nm (action)* scalping; *(chevelure)* scalp. ◆ **scalper** (1) *vt* to scalp.

scalpel [skalpɛl] *nm* scalpel.

scandale [skɑ̃dal] *nm* (**a**) *(fait choquant)* scandal. **ce livre a fait ~** that book scandalized people *ou* provoked an uproar; **crier au ~** to cry out in indignation; **à ~** *livre, couple* controversial. (**b**) *(tapage)* scene, fuss. **faire un** *ou* **du ~** to make a scene, kick up a fuss *. ◆ **scandaleusement** *adv se comporter* scandalously, outrageously, shockingly; *cher* scandalously, prohibitively; *laid, mauvais* appallingly; *sous-estimé, exagéré* grossly. ◆ **scandaleux, -euse** *adj* scandalous, outrageous, shocking. ◆ **scandaliser** (1) *vt* to scandalize. **se ~ de qch** to be scandalized by sth.

scander [skɑ̃de] (1) *vt vers* to scan; *nom, slogan* to chant.

Scandinavie [skɑ̃dinavi] *nf* Scandinavia. ◆ **scandinave** *adj*, **S~** *nmf* Scandinavian.

scanner [skanɛʀ] *nm* body scanner. ◆ **scannographie** *nf (science)* (body) scanning. *(photo)* **~ du cerveau** brain scan.

scaphandre [skafɑ̃dʀ(ə)] *nm [plongeur]* diving suit; *[cosmonaute]* space-suit. **~ autonome** aqualung. ◆ **scaphandrier** *nm* (underwater) diver.

scarabée [skaʀabe] *nm* beetle.

scarlatine [skaʀlatin] *nf* scarlet fever.

scarole [skaʀɔl] *nf* curly endive.

sceau, *pl* **~x** [so] *nm* seal; *(fig)* stamp, mark. **sous le ~ du secret** under the seal of secrecy.

scélérat, e [seleʀa, at] **1** *adj* (†) villainous, wicked. **2** *nm, f* (†) villain, blackguard †. **petit ~! *** (you) little rascal!

sceller [sele] (1) *vt pacte, sac* to seal; *(Constr)* to embed. ◆ **scellement** *nm* sealing; embedding. ◆ **scellés** *nmpl* seals.

scénario [senaʀjo] *nm (Ciné, fig: plan)* scenario; *(dialogues)* screenplay, (film) script, scenario. *(évolution possible)* **il y a plusieurs ~s possibles** there are several possible scenarios; *(fig)* **ça s'est déroulé selon le ~ habituel** it followed the usual pattern. ◆ **scénariste** *nmf (Ciné)* scriptwriter.

scène [sɛn] *nf* (**a**) *(gén)* scene. *(Théât)* **dans la première ~** in the first scene, in scene one; **changement de ~** scene change; **la ~ se passe à Rome** the action takes place in Rome, the scene is set in Rome; **sur la ~ internationale** on the international scene; **j'ai assisté à toute la ~** I was present at *ou* during the whole scene; **~ de ménage** domestic fight *ou* scene; **faire une ~ (à qn)** to make a scene. (**b**) *(estrade)* stage. **en ~, sur ~** on stage; *(le théâtre)* **la ~** the stage; **mettre en ~** *personnage* to present; *pièce de théâtre* to stage, direct; *film* to direct.

sceptique [sɛptik] **1** *adj* sceptical. **2** *nmf* sceptic. ◆ **scepticisme** *nm* scepticism. ◆ **sceptiquement** *adv* sceptically.

sceptre [sɛptʀ(ə)] *nm (lit, fig)* sceptre.

schéma [ʃema] *nm (diagramme)* diagram, sketch; *(résumé)* outline. **~ de montage** assembly diagram *ou* instructions. ◆ **schématique** *adj dessin* diagrammatic(al), schematic; *(péj) conception* oversimplified. ◆ **schématiquement** *adv* diagrammatically, schematically. **expliquer qch ~** to outline sth; **très ~ , voici de quoi il s'agit...** briefly this is what it's all about... ◆ **schématisation** *nf* schematization; *(péj)* (over)simplification. ◆ **schématiser** (1) *vt* to schematize; *(péj)* to (over)simplify.

schisme [ʃism(ə)] *nm (Rel)* schism; *(Pol)* split.

schiste [ʃist(ə)] *nm* schist.

schizophrène [skizɔfʀɛn] *adj, nmf* schizophrenic. ◆ **schizophrénie** *nf* schizophrenia.

schnoque ‡ [ʃnɔk] *nm*: **vieux ~** old fathead ‡.

sciage [sjaʒ] *nm [bois, métal]* sawing.

sciatique [sjatik] **1** *nf* sciatica. **2** *adj* sciatic.

scie [si] *nf* (**a**) saw. **couteau-~** saw-edged knife, knife with a saw-edged blade; **~ à découper** fretsaw; **~ électrique** power saw; **~ à métaux** hacksaw; **~ à ruban** bandsaw; **~ sauteuse** jigsaw. (**b**) *(péj) (chanson)* catch-tune; *(personne)* bore.

sciemment [sjamɑ̃] *adv* knowingly, wittingly, on purpose.

science [sjɑ̃s] *nf* (**a**) *(domaine)* science. **~s appliquées/humaines** applied/social sciences; *(Scol)* **~s naturelles** biology; **les ~s de la vie** the life sciences. (**b**) *(art)* art. **sa ~ des couleurs** his skill *ou* technique in the use of colour. (**c**) *(érudition)* knowledge. **avoir la ~ infuse** to have innate knowledge. ◆ **science-fiction** *nf* science fiction. ◆ **scientifique** **1** *adj* scientific. **2** *nmf* scientist. ◆ **scientifiquement** *adv* scientifically.

scier [sje] (7) *vt (gén)* to saw; *bûche* to saw (up); *partie en trop* to saw off. **ça m'a scié!** * it bowled me over!, it staggered me! ◆ **scierie** *nf* sawmill. ◆ **scieur** *nm* sawyer.

scinder *vt*, **se ~** *vpr* [sɛ̃de] (**1**) to split (up) (*en* in, into).

scintiller [sɛ̃tije] (**1**) *vi [diamant, lumières]* to sparkle, glitter; *[étoile]* to twinkle; *[yeux]* to sparkle, glitter (*de* with); *[goutte d'eau]* to glisten; *[esprit]* to sparkle, scintillate. ◆ **scintillement** *nm*: ~**(s)** sparkling; glittering; twinkling; glistening; scintillating.

scission [sisjɔ̃] *nf* split, scission. **faire ~** to split away, secede. ◆ **scissionniste** *adj, nmf* secessionist.

sciure [sjyʀ] *nf*: ~ **(de bois)** sawdust.

sclérose [skleʀoz] *nf (Méd)* sclerosis; *(fig)* ossification. ~ **en plaques** multiple sclerosis. ◆ **scléroser (se)** (**1**) *vpr (Méd)* to become sclerosed, sclerose; *(fig)* to become ossified.

scolaire [skɔlɛʀ] *adj (gén)* school; *(péj)* schoolish. **ses succès ~s** his success in *ou* at school, his scholastic achievements; **progrès ~s** academic progress. ◆ **scolarisation** *nf* schooling. **taux de ~** percentage of children in full-time education. ◆ **scolariser** (**1**) *vt* to provide with schooling, send to school. ◆ **scolarité** *nf (gén)* schooling; *(âge limite)* school-leaving age. **pendant mes années de ~** during my school years; ~ **obligatoire** compulsory school attendance, compulsory schooling; *(Univ)* **service de la ~** registrar's office.

scoliose [skɔljoz] *nf* curvature of the spine, scoliosis.

sconse [skɔ̃s] *nm* skunk (fur).

scoop * [skup] *nm (Presse)* scoop.

scooter [skutœʀ] *nm* (motor) scooter.

scorbut [skɔʀbyt] *nm* scurvy.

score [skɔʀ] *nm (gén, Sport)* score. *(Pol)* **faire un bon/mauvais ~** to have a good/bad result.

scories [skɔʀi] *nfpl (Ind)* slag; *(Géol)* (volcanic) scoria.

scorpion [skɔʀpjɔ̃] *nm* (**a**) *(Zool)* scorpion. (**b**) *(Astron)* **le S~** Scorpio, the Scorpion; **être (du) S~** to be Scorpio.

scotch [skɔtʃ] *nm* (**a**) *(boisson)* scotch (whisky). (**b**) ® *(adhésif)* sellotape ®, Scotchtape ® *(US)*.

scout, e [skut] *adj, nm* (boy) scout. ◆ **scoutisme** *nm (mouvement)* (boy) scout movement; *(activités)* scouting.

scribe [skʀib] *nm (Hist)* scribe. ◆ **scribouillard, e** *nm, f (péj)* penpusher *(péj)*.

script [skʀipt] *nm*: **(écriture)** ~ printing. ◆ **script-girl,** *pl* **script-girls** *nf* continuity girl.

scrupule [skʀypyl] *nm* scruple. **avoir des ~s à faire qch** to have scruples *ou* misgivings *ou* qualms about doing sth; **sans ~s** *personne* unscrupulous, without scruples; *agir* without scruple, unscrupulously; **par un ~ d'honnêteté** in scrupulous regard for honesty. ◆ **scrupuleusement** *adv* scrupulously. ◆ **scrupuleux, -euse** *adj* scrupulous. **peu ~** unscrupulous.

scrutateur, -trice [skʀytatœʀ, tʀis] **1** *adj regard* searching. **2** *nm (Pol)* scrutineer, teller, canvasser *(US)*.

scruter [skʀyte] (**1**) *vt* to scrutinize, examine; *pénombre* to peer into, search.

scrutin [skʀytɛ̃] *nm (vote)* ballot; *(élection)* poll; *(système)* (election) system. **au ~ secret** by secret ballot; **au 3e tour de ~** on *ou* at the third ballot *ou* round; **dépouiller le ~** to count the votes; **le jour du ~** polling day; ~ **majoritaire** election on a majority basis; ~ **proportionnel** voting using the system of proportional representation; ~ **uninominal** uninominal system.

sculpter [skylte] (**1**) *vt marbre* to sculpture, sculpt; *bois* to carve (*dans* out of). ◆ **sculpteur** *nm (homme)* sculptor; *(femme)* sculptress. ~ **sur bois** woodcarver. ◆ **sculptural, e,** *mpl* **-aux** *adj (Art)* sculptural; *beauté* statuesque. ◆ **sculpture** *nf* sculpture. ~ **sur bois** woodcarving.

se [s(ə)] *pron* (**a**) *(réfléchi) (sg) (indéfini)* oneself; *(mâle)* himself; *(femelle)* herself; *(non humain)* itself; *(pl)* themselves. ~ **regarder dans la glace** to look at o.s. in the mirror; ~ **raser/laver** to shave/wash; ~ **mouiller/salir** to get wet/dirty. (**b**) *(réciproque)* each other, one another. **deux personnes qui s'aiment** two people who love each other *ou* one another. (**c**) *(possessif)* ~ **casser la jambe** to break one's leg; **il ~ lave les mains** he is washing his hands. (**d**) *(passif)* **cela ne ~ fait pas** that's not done; **cela ~ répare facilement** it can easily be repaired again; **l'anglais ~ parle dans le monde entier** English is spoken throughout the world; **cela ~ vend bien** it sells well. (**e**) *(impersonnel)* **il ~ peut que** it may be that; **comment ~ fait-il que...?** how is it that...? (**f**) *(changement)* **s'améliorer** to get better; ~ **boucher** to become *ou* get blocked; *V aussi le verbe en question.*

séance [seɑ̃s] *nf* (**a**) *[conseil municipal]* meeting, session; *[tribunal, parlement]* session, sitting; *[comité]* séance. **être en ~** to be in session, sit; ~ **extraordinaire** extraordinary meeting. (**b**) *(période)* session. ~ **de gymnastique** gymnastics session; ~ **de pose** sitting. (**c**) *(Théât)* performance. ~ **de cinéma** film show; *(Ciné)* **première/dernière ~** first/last showing. (**d**) ~ **tenante** forthwith.

séant[1] [seɑ̃] *nm (hum)* posterior *(hum)*. **se mettre sur son ~** to sit up.

séant[2], e [seɑ̃, ɑ̃t] *adj (convenable)* seemly, fitting.

seau, *pl* ~**x** [so] *nm (récipient)* bucket, pail; *(contenu)* bucket(ful), pail(ful). **il pleut à ~x** it's pouring down in buckets *; ~ **hygiénique** slop pail.

sébile [sebil] *nf* (offering) bowl.

sec, sèche[1] [sɛk, sɛʃ] **1** *adj (gén, fig)* dry; *raisins, figue* dried; *(maigre) bras, personne* thin; *cœur* hard, cold; *réponse* curt; *(sans eau) alcool* neat, straight. *(fig)* **avoir la gorge sèche** * to be parched *ou* dry; **il est ~ comme un coup de trique** * he's as thin as a rake; *(Sport)* **placage ~** hard tackle; **bruit ~** sharp snap; **je suis ~ sur ce sujet** * I draw a blank on that subject. **2** *adv frapper, boire* hard. **démarrer ~** *(sans douceur)* to start (up) with a jolt *ou* jerk; *(fig)* **ça démarre ~ ce soir** it's getting off to a good start this evening; **aussi ~** ⁑ straight off, straight away. **3** *nm*: **au ~** *conserver* in a dry place; *rester* in the dry; **être à ~** *[torrent, puits]* to be dry *ou* dried-up; *(*: sans argent) [personne]* to be broke *; *[caisse]* to be empty; **mettre à ~ un étang** to drain a pond.

sécateur [sekatœʀ] *nm* (pair of) secateurs, (pair of) pruning shears.

sécession [sesesjɔ̃] *nf* secession. **faire ~** to secede. ◆ **sécessionniste** *adj, nmf* secessionist.

sèche[2] * [sɛʃ] *nf (cigarette)* fag *, cigarette.

sécher [seʃe] (**6**) **1** *vt* (**a**) *(gén)* to dry; *flaque* to dry (up). **se ~ au soleil** to dry o.s. in the sun. (**b**) *(arg Scol) cours* to skip *. **2** *vi* (**a**) *[surface, peinture]* to dry (off); *[pâte, éponge]* to dry (out); *[linge]* to dry; *[fleur]* to dry up *ou* out. **faire** *ou* **laisser ~ qch** to leave sth to dry (off *ou* out); *fruits, viande* to dry sth; **'faire ~ à plat'** 'dry flat'; **le caoutchouc a séché** the rubber has dried up *ou* gone dry. (**b**) *(arg Scol) (rester sec)* to be stumped *, dry up *; *(être absent)* to skip classes. ◆ **sèche-cheveux** *nm* *inv* hair-drier. ◆ **sèche-linge** *nm inv* drying cabinet; *(machine)* tumble-dryer. ◆ **sèche-mains** *nm inv* hand-dryer *ou* blower. ◆ **sèchement** *adv (gén)* drily; *répondre* curtly. ◆ **sécheresse** *nf (gén)* dryness; *[réponse]* curtness; *[cœur]* coldness, hardness; *(absence de pluie)* drought. ◆ **séchoir** *nm (local)* drying shed; *(appareil)* drier; *(pliant)* clothes-horse. ~ **à cheveux** hair-drier; ~ **à tambour** tumble-dryer.

second, e[1] [s(ə)gɔ̃, ɔ̃d] **1** *adj* (**a**) *(gén)* second. **en ~ lieu** second(ly), in the second place; **il a obtenu ces renseignements de ~e main** he got this information secondhand; *[chercheur]* **travailler sur des ouvrages de ~e main** to work from secondary sources; ~ **chapitre, chapitre ~** chapter two; **de ~ choix** *(péj)* low-quality, low-grade; *(Comm)* class two; **articles de ~ choix** seconds; **voyager en ~e classe** to travel second-class; **passer en ~** to come second; **commander en ~** to be second in command; **jouer les ~s rôles** *(Ciné)* to play minor parts *ou* supporting roles; *(fig: en politique etc)* to play second fiddle (*auprès de* to); **chez lui, c'est une ~e nature** with him it's second nature; **doué de ~e vue** gifted with second sight; **être dans un état ~** to be in a sort of trance. (**b**) *(dérivé) cause* secondary. **2** *nm, f* second. *(Alpinisme)* ~ **(de cordée)** second (on the rope). **3** *nm* (**a**) *(adjoint)* second in command; *(Naut)* first mate; *(en duel)* second. (**b**) *(étage)* second floor, third floor *(US)*. **4** *nf (transport)* second class; *(billet)* second-class ticket; *(Scol)* ≃ fifth form, tenth grade *(US)*; *(Aut)* second (gear).

secondaire [s(ə)gɔ̃dɛʀ] **1** *adj (gén)* secondary. *(gén, Méd)* **effets ~s** side effects. **2** *nm (Scol)* **le ~** secondary (school) *ou* high-school *(US)* education.

seconde[2] [s(ə)gɔ̃d] *nf (gén, Géom)* second.

seconder [s(ə)gɔ̃de] (1) *vt (lit, fig)* to assist, aid, help.

secouer [s(ə)kwe] (1) **1** *vt* (**a**) *(lit)* to shake; *poussière, paresse, oppression* to shake off; *tapis* to shake (out). ~ **la tête** *(pour dire oui)* to nod (one's head); *(pour dire non)* to shake one's head; **on est drôlement secoué** *(dans un autocar)* you're terribly shaken about; *(dans un bateau)* you're terribly tossed about. (**b**) *[deuil, professeur]* ~ **qn** to shake sb up; ~ **les puces à qn*** *(réprimander)* to give sb a ticking-off * *ou* telling-off; *(stimuler)* to give sb a good shake(-up). **2 se ~** *vpr (lit)* to shake o.s.; *(*: faire un effort)* to shake o.s. up; *(*: se dépêcher)* to get a move on.

secours [s(ə)kuʀ] *nm* (**a**) *(aide)* help, aid, assistance. **crier au ~** to shout *ou* call (out) for help; **au ~!** help!; **porter ~ à qn** to give sb help *ou* assistance; *(en montagne etc)* to rescue sb; ~ **aux blessés** aid *ou* assistance for the wounded; **le ~ en mer** sea rescue; **équipe de ~** rescue party *ou* team; **cela m'a été d'un grand ~** this has been a *ou* of great help to me; **sortie de ~** emergency exit; **roue de ~** spare wheel. (**b**) *(Mil)* **le ~, les ~** relief. (**c**) *(aumône)* **un ~, des ~** aid. ◆ **secourable** *adj personne* helpful. ◆ **secourir** (11) *vt* to help, assist, aid. ◆ **secourisme** *nm* first aid. ◆ **secouriste** *nmf* first-aid worker.

secousse [s(ə)kus] *nf (choc)* jerk, jolt; *(traction)* tug, pull; *(morale)* jolt, shock. **sans une ~** smoothly; ~ **(électrique)** (electric) shock; ~ **sismique** earth tremor; ~ **politique** political upheaval.

secret, -ète [səkʀɛ, ɛt] **1** *adj (gén)* secret; *(renfermé) personne* reserved. **garder qch ~** to keep sth secret *ou* dark; **des informations classées ~ètes** classified information.

2 *nm* (**a**) secret. ~ **de fabrication/d'État/de Polichinelle** trade/state *ou* official/open secret; **ce n'est un ~ pour personne que...** it's no secret that...; **une sauce dont il a le ~** a sauce of which he (alone) has the secret; **mettre qn dans le ~** to let sb into *ou* in on the secret, let sb in on it *; **être dans le ~ des dieux** to share the secrets of the powers that be; **faire ~ de tout** to be secretive about everything; **en ~** secretly; *(Prison)* **au ~** in solitary confinement. (**b**) *(discrétion, silence)* secrecy. **promettre le ~ (absolu)** to promise (absolute) secrecy; **le ~ professionnel** professional secrecy; **le gouvernement a gardé le ~ sur les négociations** the government has maintained silence *ou* remained silent about the negotiations. ◆ **secrètement** *adv* secretly.

secrétaire [s(ə)kʀetɛʀ] **1** *nmf (gén)* secretary. ~ **médicale/commerciale** medical/business *ou* commercial secretary; ~ **de direction** executive secretary; ~ **d'État** junior minister (*de* in); *(US Pol: ministre des Affaires étrangères)* Secretary of State, State Secretary; **le ~ d'État américain au Trésor** the Treasury Secretary; ~ **général** secretary-general. **2** *nm (meuble)* writing desk, secretaire, secretary *(US)*. ◆ **secrétariat** *nm* (**a**) *(travail)* secretarial work. **école de ~** secretarial college. (**b**) *(bureaux d'une école)* (secretary's) office; *(d'une firme)* secretarial offices; *(d'un organisme)* secretariat. (**c**) *(personnel)* secretarial staff. (**d**) ~ **d'État** *(fonction)* post of junior minister; *(bureau)* junior minister's office.

sécréter [sekʀete] (6) *vt (Bio)* to secrete; *ennui* to exude. ◆ **sécrétion** *nf* secretion.

secte [sɛkt(ə)] *nf* sect. ◆ **sectaire** *adj, nmf* sectarian. ◆ **sectarisme** *nm* sectarianism.

secteur [sɛktœʀ] *nm* (**a**) *(gén, Mil)* sector; *(Admin)* district; *(gén: zone)* area; *[agent de police]* beat; *(fig) (domaine)* area; *(partie)* part. **dans le ~ *** *(ici)* round here; *(là-bas)* round there; **changer de ~ *** to move elsewhere; *(Scol)* ~ **géographique** *ou* **de recrutement scolaire** catchment area. (**b**) *(Élec) (zone)* local supply area. *(circuit)* **le ~** the mains (supply). (**c**) *(Écon)* ~ **public/privé** public *ou* state/private sector; ~ **d'activité** branch of industry; ~ **primaire/secondaire/tertiaire** primary/manufacturing *ou* secondary/tertiary industry. ◆ **sectorisation** *nf* division into sectors. ◆ **sectoriser** (1) *vt* to divide into sectors, sector.

section [sɛksjɔ̃] *nf (gén)* section; *(Admin)* section, department; *(en autobus)* fare stage; *(Mil)* platoon. ◆ **sectionnement** *nm* severance. ◆ **sectionner** (1) **1** *vt* to sever. **2 se ~** *vpr* to be severed.

séculaire [sekylɛʀ] *adj (très vieux)* age-old. **forêts 4 fois ~s** 4-century-old forests.

séculier, -ière [sekylje, jɛʀ] *adj* secular.

sécuriser [sekyʀize] (1) *vt* : ~ **qn** to give (a feeling of) security to sb, make sb feel secure. ◆ **sécurisant, e** *adj climat* of security, reassuring. **attitude ~e** reassuring attitude, attitude which makes one feel secure.

sécurité [sekyʀite] *nf (absence de danger)* safety; *(absence de troubles)* security. **être en ~** to be safe, be secure; **la ~ de l'emploi** security of employment, job security; **mesures de ~** strict security measures; *(contre accident)* safety measures; *(contre attentat)* security measures; **de ~** *dispositif* safety; *(Aut)* **(porte à) ~ enfants** childproof (door) lock, child lock; **la ~ routière** road safety; **la S~ sociale** ≃ Social Security.

sédatif, -ive [sedatif, iv] *adj, nm* sedative.

sédentaire [sedɑ̃tɛʀ] *adj* sedentary. ◆ **sédentariser** (1) *vt* to settle.

sédiment [sedimɑ̃] *nm* sediment. ◆ **sédimentaire** *adj* sedimentary. ◆ **sédimentation** *nf* sedimentation.

séditieux, -euse [sedisjø, øz] **1** *adj troupes* insurrectionary; *propos* seditious. **2** *nm, f* insurrectionary. ◆ **sédition** *nf* insurrection; sedition.

séduire [sedɥiʀ] (38) *vt* (**a**) *(abuser de)* to seduce. (**b**) *[femme]* to charm, captivate; *[charlatan]* to win over, charm; *[style, qualité, projet]* to appeal to. ◆ **séducteur, -trice 1** *adj* seductive. **2** *nm* seducer; *(péj: Don Juan)* womanizer *(péj)*. **3** *nf* seductress. ◆ **séduction** *nf* (**a**) seduction, seducing; charming; captivation; winning over. (**b**) *(attirance)* appeal; charm. **les ~s de la vie estudiantine** the attractions *ou* appeal of student life. ◆ **séduisant, e** *adj femme, beauté* enticing, seductive; *homme, visage* (very) attractive; *projet* appealing, attractive.

segment [sɛgmɑ̃] *nm (gén)* segment. ◆ **segmentation** *nf* segmentation. ◆ **segmenter** *vt,* **se ~** (1) *vpr* to segment.

ségrégation [segʀegɑsjɔ̃] *nf* segregation. ◆ **ségrégatif, -ive** *adj* segregative. ◆ **ségrégationnisme** *nm* racial segregation, segregationism. ◆ **ségrégationniste** *adj, nmf* segregationist.

seiche [sɛʃ] *nf (Zool)* cuttlefish.

seigle [sɛgl(ə)] *nm* rye.

seigneur [sɛɲœʀ] *nm* lord. *(Rel)* **le S~** the Lord; **se montrer grand ~ avec qn** to behave in a lordly fashion towards sb. ◆ **seigneurial, e,** *mpl* **-aux** *adj château* seigniorial; *allure* lordly, stately. ◆ **seigneurie** *nf* (**a**) **votre/sa S~** your/his Lordship. (**b**) *(terre)* seigniory.

sein [sɛ̃] *nm (mamelle)* breast; *(littér, fig) (giron)* bosom *(littér)*; *(matrice)* womb. **donner le ~ à un bébé** to breast-feed (a baby); **dans le ~ de la terre** in the bosom of the earth; **au ~ de** *équipe* within; *bonheur, flots* in the midst of.

Seine [sɛn] *nf:* **la ~** the Seine.

séisme [seism(ə)] *nm (Géog)* earthquake.

seize [sɛz] *adj inv, nm* sixteen; *V* **six.** ◆ **seizième** *adj, nmf* sixteenth. ◆ **seizièmement** *adv* in the sixteenth place.

séjour [seʒuʀ] *nm* (**a**) *(arrêt)* stay. **faire un ~ forcé** to have an enforced stay. (**b**) *(salon)* living room. (**c**) *(littér: endroit)* abode *(littér)*, dwelling place. ◆ **séjourner** (1) *vi [personne]* to stay; *[neige, eau]* to lie.

sel [sɛl] *nm (gén, Chim)* salt; *(humour)* wit; *(piquant)* spice. **~s de bain** bath salts; **~ fin** *ou* **de table** table salt; **~ gemme** rock salt.

select * [selɛkt] *adj inv* posh *.

sélectionner [selɛksjɔne] (1) *vt* to select, pick. *[joueur international]* **3 fois sélectionné** capped *ou* selected 3 times. ◆ **sélecteur** *nm* selector. ◆ **sélectif, -ive** *adj* selective. ◆ **sélection** *nf* selection; *(Scol, Univ)* selective entry *ou* admission *(US)*. **faire une ~ parmi** to make a selection from among; **épreuve de ~** (selection) trial. ◆ **sélectionné, e 1** *adj* specially selected. **2** *nm, f* selected player *ou* competitor. ◆ **sélectionneur, -euse** *nm, f (Sport)* selector. ◆ **sélectivement** *adv* selectively.

self [sɛlf] **1** *nm (*: restaurant)* self-service (restaurant), cafeteria. **2** *nf (Élec) (propriété)* self-induction; *(bobine)* self-induction coil.

self-made-man [sɛlfmɛdman] *nm, pl* **self-made-men** [sɛlfmɛdmɛn] self-made man.

self-service, *pl* **self-services** [sɛlfsɛʀvis] *nm* self-service (restaurant), cafeteria.

selle [sɛl] *nf* (**a**) saddle. **se mettre en ~** to mount, get into the saddle. (**b**) *(Méd)* **~s** stools, motions; **êtes-vous allé à la ~?** have you had a motion? ◆ **seller** (1) *vt* to saddle. ◆ **sellerie** *nf* saddlery. ◆ **sellier** *nm* saddler.

sellette [sɛlɛt] *nf (support)* stand. *(fig)* **être/mettre qn sur la ~** to be/put sb in the hot seat.

selon [s(ə)lɔ̃] *prép (conformément à)* in accordance with; *(en fonction de, suivant l'opinion de)* according to. **vivre ~ ses moyens** to live according to one's means; **c'est ~ le cas** it all depends on the individual case; **~ moi** in my opinion, to my mind, according to me; **~ toute vraisemblance** in all probability; **~ que** according to *ou* depending on whether.

semailles [s(ə)mɑj] *nfpl (opération)* sowing; *(période)* sowing period; *(graine)* seed, seeds.

semaine [s(ə)mɛn] *nf (gén)* week; *(salaire)* week's *ou* weekly pay. **en ~** during the week, on weekdays; **dans 2 ~s** in 2 weeks *ou* a fortnight; **~ publicitaire** publicity week; **la ~ sainte** Holy Week; **il te le rendra la ~ des quatre jeudis** he'll never give it back to you in a month of Sundays; **faire la ~ anglaise** to work *ou* do a five-day week; **officier de ~** officer on duty *(for the week)*.

sémantique [semɑ̃tik] **1** *adj* semantic. **2** *nf* semantics *(sg)*.

sémaphore [semafɔʀ] *nm (Naut)* semaphore.

semblable [sɑ̃blabl(ə)] **1** *adj* (**a**) *(similaire)* similar. **~ à** like, similar to. (**b**) *(tel)* such. **de ~s erreurs sont inacceptables** such errors *ou* errors of this kind are unacceptable. (**c**) *(qui se ressemblent) [jumeaux, objets]* **être ~s** to be alike. **2** *nm* fellow creature, fellow man. *(péj)* **toi et tes ~s** you and your kind *(péj)*, you and people like you *(péj)*.

semblant [sɑ̃blɑ̃] *nm* (**a**) **un ~ de** *calme, vie, vérité* a semblance of; *soleil* a glimmer of; **un ~ de réponse** some vague attempt at a reply, a sort of a reply *. (**b**) **faire ~ de faire qch** to pretend to do sth; **il fait ~** he's pretending.

sembler [sɑ̃ble] (1) **1** *vb impers*: **il semble** it seems; **il me semble que** *(j'estime)* it seems *ou* appears to me that, it looks to me as though; *(je crois)* I think that, I have a feeling that; **comme bon te semble** as you see fit, as you think best; **prenez ce que bon vous semble** take what you please *ou* wish; **il me semble revoir mon grand-père** it's as though I see my grandfather again. **2** *vi* to seem (*à qn* to sb). **il semblait content** he seemed (to be) *ou* appeared happy; **vous me semblez pessimiste** you sound *ou* seem *ou* look pessimistic.

semelle [s(ə)mɛl] *nf* sole. **~s intérieures** insoles; **~s compensées** platform soles; **leur viande était de la vraie ~ *** their meat was like leather; **il n'a pas reculé d'une ~** he hasn't moved back an inch; **il ne m'a pas quitté d'une ~** he never left me by so much as an inch.

semence [s(ə)mɑ̃s] *nf (Agr, fig)* seed; *(sperme)* seed; *(clou)* tack. **blé de ~** seed corn.

semer [s(ə)me] (5) *vt* (**a**) *graines, peur* to sow; *clous* to scatter, strew; *faux bruits* to spread. (**b**) *(*: perdre)* to lose; *poursuivant* to shake off. ◆ **semé, e** *adj*: **~ de** *pièges* bristling with; *difficultés* plagued with; *anecdotes* interspersed *ou* sprinkled with; *arbres* dotted with; *fleurs, diamants, étoiles* studded with; **la vie est ~e de joies et de peines** life is strewn with joys and troubles. ◆ **semeur, -euse** *nm, f* sower.

semestre [s(ə)mɛstʀ(ə)] *nm (période)* half-year, six-month period; *(loyer)* half-yearly rent; *(Univ)* semester. **payé par ~** paid half-yearly; **le premier ~** the first half of the year. ◆ **semestriel, -elle** *adj* half-yearly, six-monthly; semestral.

semi- [səmi] *préf inv* semi-. **~-automatique** semiautomatic; **~-circulaire** semicircular; **~-conducteur, -trice** *(adj)* semiconducting; *(nm)* semiconductor; **~-conserve** *nf* semi-preserve; **~-fini, e** semifinished; **~-remorque** *(nf : remorque)* trailer, semi-trailer *(US)*; *(nm : camion)* articulated lorry, trailer truck *(US)*.

sémillant, e [semijɑ̃, ɑ̃t] *adj (vif)* vivacious; *(fringant)* dashing.

séminaire [seminɛʀ] *nm (Rel)* seminary; *(Univ)* seminar. ◆ **séminariste** *nm* seminarist.

semis [s(ə)mi] *nm (plante)* seedling; *(opération)* sowing; *(terrain)* seedbed.

semonce [səmɔ̃s] *nf* reprimand. *(Naut, fig)* **coup de ~** shot across the bows.

semoule [s(ə)mul] *nf* semolina.

sempiternel, -elle [sɛ̃pitɛʀnɛl] *adj* eternal, never-ending.

sénat [sena] *nm* senate. ◆ **sénateur** *nm* senator. ◆ **sénatorial, e,** *mpl* **-aux** *adj* senatorial.

Sénégal [senegal] *nm* Senegal. ◆ **sénégalais, e** *adj,* **S~(e)** *nm(f)* Senegalese.

sénile [senil] *adj* senile. ◆ **sénilité** *nf* senility.

sens [sɑ̃s] *nm* (**a**) *(instinct, conscience)* sense. **les 5 ~** the 5 senses; **reprendre ses ~** to regain consciousness; **avoir le ~ des réalités** to be a realist; **avoir le ~ de l'orientation** to have a (good) sense of direction. (**b**) *(raison, avis)* sense. **c'est plein de ~** it is very sensible; **cela n'a pas de ~** that doesn't make (any) sense; **~ commun** common sense; **à mon ~** to my mind, in my opinion, the way I see it. (**c**) *(signification)* meaning. **au ~ propre/figuré** in the literal/figurative sense *ou* meaning; **dépourvu de ~** meaningless; **en un ~** in a way *ou* sense; **en ce ~ que** in the sense that. (**d**) *(direction)* direction. **aller dans le mauvais ~** to go in the wrong direction, go the wrong way; **dans le ~ de la longueur/largeur** lengthwise *ou* lengthways/widthwise; **dans le ~ (du bois)** with the grain (of the wood); **venir en ~ contraire** to come from the opposite direction; **dans le ~ des aiguilles d'une montre** clockwise; **dans le ~ contraire des aiguilles d'une montre** anticlockwise, counterclockwise *(US)*; **dans le ~ de la marche** facing the engine; **il a retourné la boîte dans tous les ~** he turned the box this way and that; *(lit, fig)* **mettre ~ dessus dessous** to turn upside down. (**e**) *(ligne directrice)* line. **il a agi dans le même ~** he acted along the same lines; **j'ai donné des directives dans ce ~** I've given instructions to that effect *ou* end. (**f**) *(Aut)* **être en ~ giratoire** to form a roundabout *ou* traffic circle *(US)*; **~ interdit** *ou* **unique** one-way street; '**~ interdit**' 'no entry'; **à ~ unique** *(Aut)* one-way; *(fig: concession)* one-sided.

sensation [sɑ̃sɑsjɔ̃] *nf* feeling, sensation. **j'ai la ~ de l'avoir déjà vu** I have a feeling I've seen him before; **faire ~** to cause *ou* create a sensation; **roman à ~** sensational novel; **la presse à ~** the gutter press. ◆ **sensationnel, -elle** *adj (*: merveilleux)* fantastic *, terrific *, sensational *; *(qui fait sensation)* sensational.

sensé, e [sɑ̃se] *adj* sensible.

sensibiliser [sɑ̃sibilize] (1) *vt*: **~ qn** to make sb sensitive *ou* alive (*à* to); **~ l'opinion publique au problème de** to heighten public awareness of the problem of, make the public aware of the problem of. ◆ **sensibilisation** *nf*: **la ~ de l'opinion publique à ce problème est récente** public opinion has only become sensitive *ou* alive to this problem in recent years; *(Pol)* **campagne de ~** awareness *ou* consciousness-raising campaign.

sensible [sɑ̃sibl(ə)] *adj* (**a**) *personne, blessure, balance etc* sensitive (*à* to). **pas recommandé aux personnes ~s** not recommended for people of (a) nervous disposition; **elle a le cœur ~** she is tenderhearted; **être ~ au froid** to feel the cold, be sensitive to the cold. (**b**) *(perceptible) (gén)* perceptible (*à* to); *progrès, différence* appreciable, noticeable. ◆ **sensibilité** *nf (gén, Tech)* sensitivity. ◆ **sensiblement** *adv (presque)* approximately, more or less; *(notablement)* appreciably, noticeably, markedly. ◆ **sensiblerie** *nf (sentimentalité)* sentimentality, mawkishness; *(impressionnabilité)* squeamishness.

sensitif, -ive [sɑ̃sitif, iv] **1** *adj (Anat)* sensory. **2** *nf (Bot)* sensitive plant.

sensoriel, -elle [sɑ̃sɔʀjɛl] *adj* sensory.

sensuel, -elle [sɑ̃sɥɛl] *adj* sensuous; *(sexuellement)* sensual. ◆ **sensualité** *nf* sensuousness; sensuality. ◆ **sensuellement** *adv* sensuously; sensually.

sentence [sɑ̃tɑ̃s] *nf (verdict)* sentence; *(adage)* maxim. ◆ **sentencieux, -euse** *adj* sententious.

senteur [sɑ̃tœʀ] *nf* scent, perfume.

senti, e [sɑ̃ti] *adj*: **bien ~** *sentiment, discours* heartfelt; *mots* well-chosen; **quelques vérités bien ~es** a few home truths.

sentier [sɑ̃tje] *nm (lit)* (foot)path; *(fig)* path. *(lit, fig)* **hors des ~s battus** off the beaten track; *(lit, fig)* **sur le ~ de la guerre** on the warpath.

sentiment [sɑ̃timɑ̃] *nm* (**a**) *(émotion, opinion)* feeling. **~ de culpabilité** guilt *ou* guilty feeling; **prendre qn par les ~s** to appeal to sb's feelings. (**b**) *(sensibilité)* **le ~** feeling, emotion; *(péj)* **faire du ~** to sentimentalize, be sentimental. (**c**) *(conscience)* **avoir le ~ de** to be aware of; **avoir le ~ que qch va arriver** to have a feeling that sth is going to happen. (**d**) *(formules de politesse)* **recevez, Monsieur, mes ~s distingués** yours faithfully, yours truly *(US)*; **transmettez-lui nos meilleurs ~s** give him our best wishes. ◆ **sentimental, e,** *mpl* **-aux 1** *adj (gén)* sentimental; *(péj)* soppy *; *aventure* love. **il a des problèmes ~aux** he has problems with his love life. **2** *nm, f* sentimentalist. ◆ **sentimentalement** *adv* sentimentally. ◆ **sentimentalité** *nf* sentimentality.

sentinelle [sɑ̃tinɛl] *nf* sentry. **être en ~** *(Mil)* to be on sentry duty; *(fig)* to stand guard *ou* keep watch at the window.

sentir [sɑ̃tiʀ] (16) **1** *vt* (**a**) *(par l'odorat)* to smell; *(au goût)* to taste; *(au toucher, contact)* to feel. **il ne peut pas ~ la différence** he can't tell (*ou* taste *ou* smell) the difference; **elle sentit une odeur de brûlé** she smelt *ou* smelled *(US)* burning; *(fatigue)* **je ne sens plus mes jambes** my legs are dropping off *, my legs are folding under me *(US)*; **il ne peut pas le ~ *** he can't stand *ou* bear (the sight of) him. (**b**) *(dégager une odeur)* to smell. **~ bon/mauvais** to smell good *ou* nice/bad; **~ des pieds** to have smelly feet; **ce thé sent le jasmin** *(goût)* this tea tastes of jasmine; *(odeur)* this tea smells of jasmine; **la pièce sent le renfermé/le moisi** the room smells stale/musty; **ça ne sent pas la rose! *** it's not a very nice smell, is it? (**c**) *(fig: dénoter) autoritarisme, hypocrisie* to smack of. **ça sent le piège** there's a trap *ou* catch in it; **ça sent la pluie** it looks *ou* feels like rain; **ça sent l'orage** there's a storm in the air; **ça sent le roussi *** there's going to be trouble. (**d**) *changement, fatigue* to feel, be aware *ou* conscious of; *beauté de qch* to appreciate; *danger, difficulté* to sense. **~ que** to feel *ou* be aware *ou* conscious that; *(pressentir)* to sense that; **il ne sent pas sa force** he doesn't know *ou* realize his own strength. (**e**) **faire ~ son autorité** to make one's authority felt; **faire ~ la beauté de qch** to bring out *ou* demonstrate *ou* show the beauty of sth; **les effets commencent à se faire ~** the effects are beginning to be felt *ou* to make themselves felt.
2 se ~ *vpr* (**a**) **se ~ mieux** *etc* to feel better *etc*; **se ~ revivre** to feel o.s. coming alive again; **il ne se sent pas le courage de le lui dire** he doesn't feel brave enough to tell him. (**b**) *(effet, changements)* to be felt, show. (**c**) **ne pas se ~ de joie** to be beside o.s. with joy; **il ne se sent plus! *** he's off his head! * *ou* out of his mind! *

seoir [swaʀ] (26) **1** *vi*: **~ à qn** to become sb. **2** *vb impers*: **il sied de/que** it is proper *ou* fitting to/that.

Séoul [seul] *n* Seoul.

séparer [sepaʀe] (1) **1** *vt (gén)* to separate (*de* from); *combattants* to pull apart, part; *questions, aspects* to distinguish between. **~ l'écorce du tronc** to pull the bark off *ou* away from the trunk; **~ qch en 2** to split *ou* divide sth in 2; **~ les cheveux par une raie** to part one's hair; **ils avaient séparé l'enfant de sa mère** they had separated *ou* parted the child from its mother; **un seul obstacle le séparait du but** only one obstacle stood between him and his goal; *(fig)* **tout les séparait** they were worlds apart, they had nothing in common. **2 se ~** *vpr* (**a**) **se ~ de** *employé, objet* to part with. (**b**) *(s'écarter)* to divide, part (*de* from); *(se détacher)* to split off, separate off (*de* from). **le premier étage de la fusée s'est séparé** the first stage of the rocket has split off *ou* separated (off); **le fleuve se sépare en deux** the river divides in(to) two. (**c**) *[adversaires]* to separate, break apart; *[manifestants]* to disperse; *[assemblée]* to break up; *[convives]* to leave each other, part; *[époux]* to part, split up, separate. **se ~ de sa femme** to part *ou* separate from one's wife.

◆ **séparable** *adj* separable (*de* from). ◆ **séparation** *nf* (**a**) *(gén, Jur, Pol)* separation. **au moment de la ~** *[manifestants]* when they dispersed; *[convives]* when they parted; **mur de ~** separating *ou* dividing wall; **~ de corps** legal separation; **des ~s déchirantes** heartrending partings. (**b**) *(cloison)* division, partition. *(fig)* **faire une ~ nette entre 2 problèmes** to draw a clear dividing line between 2 problems. ◆ **séparatisme** *nm* separatism. ◆ **séparatiste** *adj, nmf* separatist. ◆ **séparé, e** *adj sons, notions* separate; *personnes (Jur: désuni)* separated; *(gén: éloigné)* apart. **vivre ~** to live apart (*de* from). ◆ **séparément** *adv* separately.

sept [sɛt] *adj inv, nm inv* seven; *V* **six**.

septante [sɛptɑ̃t] *adj inv († ou dial)* seventy.

septembre [sɛptɑ̃bʀ(ə)] *nm* September. **arriver le premier ~** to arrive on the first of September; **en ~** in September; **à la mi-~** in mid-September; **vers la fin de ~** in late September; **en ~ prochain/dernier** next/last September.

septennat [sɛptena] *nm [président]* seven-year term (of office).

septentrional, e, *mpl* **-aux** [sɛptɑ̃tʀijɔnal, o] *adj* northern.

septicémie [sɛptisemi] *nf* blood poisoning, septicaemia.

septième [sɛtjɛm] *adj, nmf* seventh. **le ~ art** the cinema; **être au ~ ciel** to be in (the) seventh heaven; *V* **sixième**. ◆ **septièmement** *adv* seventhly; *V* **sixièmement**.

septuagénaire [sɛptɥaʒenɛʀ] **1** *adj* septuagenarian, seventy-year-old. **2** *nmf* septuagenarian, seventy-year-old man (*ou* woman).

sépulcre [sepylkʀ(ə)] *nm* sepulchre. ◆ **sépulcral, e,** *mpl* **-aux** *adj* sepulchral.

sépulture [sepyltyʀ] *nf (tombeau)* burial place.

séquelles [sekɛl] *nfpl [maladie]* after-effects; *[guerre]* aftermath.

séquence [sekɑ̃s] *nf* sequence.

séquestrer [sekɛstʀe] (**1**) *vt personne* to confine illegally. ◆ **séquestration** *nf* illegal confinement. ◆ **séquestre** *nm*: **mettre sous ~** to sequester.

séquoia [sekɔja] *nm* sequoia, redwood.

sérail [seʀaj] *nm* seraglio.

séraphin [seʀafɛ̃] *nm* seraph.

serein, e [səʀɛ̃, ɛn] *adj ciel* serene, clear; *visage* serene, calm; *jugement* calm, dispassionate. ◆ **sereinement** *adv* serenely; clearly; calmly; dispassionately. ◆ **sérénissime** *adj* Serene. ◆ **sérénité** *nf* serenity; clarity; calmness; dispassionateness.

sérénade [seʀenad] *nf* (**a**) *(Mus)* serenade. **donner une ~ à qn** to serenade sb. (**b**) *(* hum: vacarme)* racket, hullabaloo *.

serf, serve [sɛʀ(f), sɛʀv(ə)] *nm, f* serf.

sergent [sɛʀʒɑ̃] *nm (Mil)* sergeant. **~-chef** staff sergeant; **~ de ville †** policeman; **~-major** ≃ quartermaster sergeant.

série [seʀi] *nf* (**a**) *[objets, timbres]* set; *[ennuis]* series, string *. *(beaucoup)* **(toute) une ~ de *...** a (whole) series *ou* string * of...; **ouvrages de ~ noire** crime thrillers. (**b**) *(catégorie) (Naut)* class; *(Sport)* rank; *(éliminatoire)* qualifying heat *ou* round. **film de ~ B** B (grade) film *ou* movie. (**c**) *(Ind, fig)* **fabrication en ~** mass production; **article de ~** standard article. (**d**) *(Chim, Math, Mus, Phon)* series. *(Élec)* **monté en ~** connected in series.

sérieux, -euse [seʀjø, øz] **1** *adj* (**a**) *personne (ne plaisantant pas)* serious, earnest; *(réfléchi)* serious-minded; *(digne de confiance)* reliable, dependable; *(moralement) jeune fille* responsible, trustworthy. **~ comme un pape** sober as a judge; **ce n'est vraiment pas ~!** it's not taking a very responsible *ou* serious attitude. (**b**) *acquéreur, promesses, menace* genuine, serious. **non, il était ~** no, he was serious *ou* he meant it; **'pas ~ s'abstenir'** 'only genuine inquirers need apply'. (**c**) *conversation, situation, maladie, études* serious; *travail, artisan* careful, painstaking. (**d**) *(intensif) raison, avance, chances* strong, good; *coup* serious; *différence* serious, considerable. **2** *nm* seriousness; earnestness; serious-mindedness; reliability; dependability; trustworthiness; carefulness; genuineness. **garder son ~** to keep a straight face; **(se) prendre au ~** to take (o.s.) seriously. ◆ **sérieusement** *adv* seriously; responsibly; genuinely; considerably. **il l'a dit ~** he meant it seriously, he was in earnest.

serin [s(ə)ʀɛ̃] *nm (Orn)* canary.

seriner [s(ə)ʀine] (**1**) *vt (péj)* **~ qch à qn** to drum *ou* din sth into sb.

seringue [s(ə)ʀɛ̃g] *nf* syringe.

serment [sɛʀmɑ̃] *nm* (**a**) *(solennel)* oath. **faire un ~** to take an oath; **sous ~** on *ou* under oath. (**b**) *(promesse)* pledge. **des ~s (d'amour)** vows *ou* pledges of love; **je te fais le ~ de venir** I swear to you that I'll come.

sermon [sɛʀmɔ̃] *nm (Rel, fig)* sermon. ◆ **sermonner** (**1**) *vt*: **~ qn** to lecture sb, sermonize sb.

serpe [sɛʀp(ə)] *nf* billhook, bill. **visage taillé à coups de ~** craggy *ou* rugged face.

serpent [sɛʀpɑ̃] *nm (Zool)* snake, serpent; *(Mus)* bass horn; *(fig: ruban)* ribbon. *(Écon)* **le ~ (monétaire)** the (currency) snake; **~ à sonnettes** rattlesnake. ◆ **serpenter** (**1**) *vi [rivière, chemin]* to snake, meander, wind; *[vallée]* to wind. ◆ **serpentin** *nm (ruban)* streamer; *(Chim)* coil.

serpillière [sɛʀpijɛʀ] *nf* floorcloth.

serpolet [sɛʀpɔlɛ] *nm* wild thyme.

serre [sɛʀ] *nf* (**a**) *(Agr) (gén)* greenhouse, glasshouse; *(attenant à une maison)* conservatory. **effet de ~** greenhouse effect; **~ chaude** hothouse. (**b**) *(griffe)* talon, claw.

serrer [seʀe] (**1**) **1** *vt* (**a**) *(avec la main)* to grip, hold tight. **~ qn dans ses bras** to clasp sb in one's arms; **~ la main à qn** *(la donner à qn)* to shake sb's hand, shake hands with sb; *(presser)* to squeeze *ou* press sb's hand; **se ~ la main** to shake hands; **~ qn à la gorge** to grab sb by the throat. (**b**) *poing, mâchoires* to clench; *lèvres* to set. **les lèvres serrées** with tight lips; **avoir la gorge serrée par l'émotion** to be choked by emotion; **cela serre le cœur** it wrings your heart; **~ les dents** *(lit)* to clench one's teeth; *(fig)* to grit one's teeth. (**c**) *[chaussures, vêtements] (comprimer)* to be too tight; *(mouler)* to fit tightly. (**d**) *vis* to tighten; *joint* to clamp; *robinet* to turn off tight; *nœud, ceinture* to tighten, pull tight. **~ qch dans un étau** to grip sth in a vice; **~ le frein à main** to put on the handbrake; **~ la vis à qn *** to crack down harder on sb *. (**e**) *véhicule, piéton (par derrière)* to keep close behind; *(latéralement)* to squeeze (*contre* up against). **~ qn dans un coin** to wedge sb in a corner; **~ le trottoir** to hug the kerb; *(fig)* **~ une question de plus près** to study a question more closely; *(Naut)* **~ la côte**

to sail close to the shore, hug the shore. (**f**) *(rapprocher) objets, mots* to close up, put close together; *convives* to squeeze up *ou* together. *(Mil)* ~ **les rangs** to close ranks. (**g**) *(†: ranger)* to put away.
2 *vi (Aut)* ~ **à droite** to move in to the right.
3 se ~ *vpr*: **se** ~ **contre qn** to huddle (up) against sb; *(tendrement)* to cuddle *ou* snuggle up to sb; **se** ~ **autour du feu** to squeeze *ou* crowd round the fire; **serrez-vous un peu** squeeze up a bit; **son cœur se serra** he felt a pang of anguish; **se** ~ **les coudes** ‡ to back one another up; **se** ~ **la ceinture** to tighten one's belt.
◆ **serrage** *nm [vis]* tightening; *[joint]* clamping.
◆ **serré, e 1** *adj* (**a**) *vêtement* tight. (**b**) *spectateurs* (tightly) packed. (**c**) *tissu* closely woven; *réseau, herbe* dense; *mailles, écriture* close. (**d**) *(bloqué)* **trop** ~ too tight; **pas assez** ~ not tight enough. (**e**) *(contracté)* **avoir le cœur** ~ to feel a pang of anguish; **avoir la gorge** ~**e** to feel a tightening *ou* a lump in one's throat. (**f**) *discussion* closely conducted, closely argued; *lutte, match* tight, close-fought; *budget* tight. **2** *adv*: **écrire** ~ to write a cramped hand; *(fig)* **jouer** ~ to play a tight game. ◆ **serrement** *nm*: ~ **de main** handshake; ~ **de cœur** pang of anguish.

serrure [sɛʀyʀ] *nf* lock. ~ **à pompe** spring lock; ~ **de sûreté** safety lock; ~ **trois points** three-point security lock. ◆ **serrurerie** *nf (métier)* locksmith's trade; *(travail)* ironwork. ◆ **serrurier** *nm* locksmith.

sertir [sɛʀtiʀ] (2) *vt bijou* to set.

sérum [seʀɔm] *nm* serum. *(fig)* ~ **de vérité** truth drug.

servant [sɛʀvɑ̃] *nm (Rel, Mil)* server. ◆ **servante** *nf* (maid) servant.

serveur [sɛʀvœʀ] *nm* (**a**) *[restaurant]* waiter; *[bar]* barman. (**b**) *(Tennis)* server; *(Cartes)* dealer. (**c**) *(Ordin)* **centre** ~ service centre. ◆ **serveuse** *nf* waitress; barmaid.

serviable [sɛʀvjabl(ə)] *adj* obliging, willing to help. ◆ **serviabilité** *nf* obligingness.

service [sɛʀvis] **1** *nm* (**a**) *(travail)* duty. **heures de** ~ hours of service *ou* duty; **prendre son/être de** ~ to come on/be on duty; **pompier de** ~ duty fireman, fireman on duty; *(Admin, Mil)* **être en** ~ **commandé** to be acting under orders, be on an official assignment; **avoir 25 ans de** ~ to have completed 25 years' service. (**b**) *(gén, Écon: prestations)* ~**s** services; *(Écon)* **les** ~**s** the service industries; **offrir ses** ~**s à qn** to offer sb one's services. (**c**) *(domesticité)* (domestic) service. **entrer en** ~ **chez qn** to go into service with sb; **être au** ~ **de** to be in the service of; **escalier de** ~ backstairs, servants' stairs; **entrée de** ~ service *ou* tradesman's entrance. (**d**) *(Mil)* **le** ~ **(militaire)** military *ou* national service; **faire son** ~ to do one's military *ou* national service; ~ **armé** combatant service. (**e**) *(organisme public)* service; *(section)* department, section. **les** ~**s postaux** the postal services; ~ **des achats/des urgences** buying/casualty department; ~ **de réanimation** intensive care unit; **les** ~**s publics** the (public) utilities. (**f**) *(Rel)* service. ~ **funèbre** funeral service. (**g**) *(faveur, aide)* service. **rendre un** ~ **à qn** to do sb a favour *ou* a service; **rendre** ~ **à qn** *(aider)* to do sb a service *ou* a good turn; *(s'avérer utile)* to come in useful *ou* handy for sb, be of use to sb; **il aime rendre** ~ he likes to be helpful; **rendre un mauvais** ~ **à qn** to do sb a disservice; **qu'y a-t-il pour votre** ~? how can I be of service to you?; **je suis à votre** ~ I am at your service. (**h**) *(au restaurant)* service; *(pourboire)* service (charge). ~ **compris/non compris** service included/not included, inclusive/exclusive of service; **premier/deuxième** ~ first/second sitting. (**i**) *[vaisselle, linge]* service, set. ~ **à liqueurs** set of liqueur glasses. (**j**) *(fonctionnement)* **mettre en** ~ to put *ou* bring into service, bring on stream *ou* line; **entrer en** ~ to come on stream *ou* line *ou* into service; **hors de** ~ out of order *ou* commission. (**k**) *(transport)* service. ~ **d'autobus/d'hiver** bus/winter service; **le** ~ **est interrompu sur la ligne 3** (the) service is suspended on line 3. (**l**) *(Tennis)* service. **être au** ~ to have the service. **2** : ~ **après-vente** after-sales service; ~ **d'ordre** *(policiers)* police patrol; *(manifestants)* team of stewards *(responsible for crowd control etc)*; ~**s secrets** secret service.

serviette [sɛʀvjɛt] *nf* (**a**) ~ **(de toilette)** (hand) towel; ~ **(de table)** serviette, (table) napkin; ~ **de bain** bath towel; ~**-éponge** towel; ~ **périodique** sanitary towel. (**b**) *(cartable)* briefcase.

servile [sɛʀvil] *adj homme, obéissance* servile, cringing; *imitation* slavish. ◆ **servilement** *adv* servilely, cringingly; slavishly. ◆ **servilité** *nf* servility; slavishness.

servir [sɛʀviʀ] (14) **1** *vt* (**a**) *(être au service de)* to serve. ~ **qn** *(dans un magasin)* to attend to *ou* serve sb; *(au restaurant)* to wait on *ou* serve sb; ~ **la messe** to serve mass; **elle aime se faire** ~ she likes to be waited on; **le boucher m'a bien servi** *(en qualité)* the butcher has sold me good meat; *(en quantité)* the butcher has given me a good amount for my money; **'Madame est servie'** 'dinner is served'; **il sert dans un café** he is a waiter in a café; **ils voulaient la pluie, ils ont été servis!** they wanted rain — well, they've got what they asked for *ou* wanted!; **en fait d'ennuis, elle a été servie** as regards troubles, she's had her share (and more) *ou* she's had more than her fair share. (**b**) *plat* to serve. ~ **qch à qn** to serve sb with sth, help sb to sth; **'~ frais'** 'serve cool'; ~ **à boire à qn** to serve a drink to sb; **à table, c'est servi!** come and sit down now, it's ready!; **il nous sert toujours les mêmes plaisanteries** he always trots out the same old jokes *ou* treats us to the same old jokes. (**c**) *(aider) personne, ambitions* to serve (well), aid. **sa prudence l'a servi** his caution served him well (*auprès de* with); **il a été servi par une bonne mémoire** he was aided by a good memory. (**d**) *(être utile)* ~ **à** *personne* to be of use *ou* help to; *usage* to be of use in, be useful for; ~ **à faire** to be used for doing; **ça m'a servi à réparer le lit** I used it to mend the bed; **cela ne sert à rien** it's no use, it's useless; **cela ne sert à rien de pleurer** it's no use *ou* there's no point crying, crying doesn't help; **à quoi sert cet objet?** what is this object used for?; **à quoi servirait de réclamer?** what use would complaining be?, what would be the point of complaining? (**e**) ~ **de qch** *[objet]* to serve as sth, be used as sth, *[personne]* **elle lui a servi d'interprète** she acted as his interpreter; ~ **de leçon à qn** to be a lesson to sb. (**f**) *(verser)* to pay. ~ **des intérêts à qn** to pay sb interest. (**g**) *(Cartes)* to deal; *(Tennis)* to serve; *(Mil) canon* to serve.
2 se ~ *vpr* (**a**) *(distribution)* to help o.s. *(chez un fournisseur)* **se** ~ **chez X** to shop at X's. (**b**) **se** ~ **de qch** to use sth; **se** ~ **de ses relations** to make use of *ou* use one's contacts; **il s'est servi de moi** he used me.

serviteur [sɛʀvitœʀ] *nm (gén)* servant.

servitude [sɛʀvityd] *nf* (**a**) *(esclavage)* servitude. (**b**) *(gén pl: contrainte)* constraint.

servofrein [sɛʀvɔfʀɛ̃] *nm (Tech)* servo(-assisted) brake.

ses [se] *adj poss V* **son**[1].

session [sesjɔ̃] *nf (Jur, Parl)* session, sitting. ~ **(d'examen)** university exam session.

seuil [sœj] *nm (marche)* doorstep; *(entrée)* doorway, threshold †; *(fig)* threshold; *(Géog, Tech)* sill. *(fig)*

au ~ de la mort on the threshold *ou* brink of death.

seul, e [sœl] **1** *adj* (**a**) *(non accompagné)* alone, on one's (*ou* its *etc*) own, by oneself (*ou* itself *etc*); *(isolé)* lonely. **ils se retrouvèrent enfin ~s** they were alone (together) *ou* on their own *ou* by themselves at last; **une femme ~e peut très bien se débrouiller** a woman on her own *ou* a single woman can manage perfectly well. (**b**) *(avant n: unique)* **un ~ livre** *(et non plusieurs)* one book, a single book; *(à l'exception de tout autre)* only one book; **le ~ homme** the one man, the only man, the sole man; **pour cette ~e raison** for this reason alone *ou* only, for this one reason; **une ~e fois** only once. (**c**) *(en apposition)* only, alone. **~ le résultat compte** the result alone counts, only the result counts. (**d**) *(locutions)* **~ et unique** one and only; **c'est la ~e et même personne** it's one and the same person; **d'un ~ coup** *(subitement)* suddenly; *(ensemble, à la fois)* in *ou* at one go; **d'un ~ tenant** *terrain* all in one piece; **vous êtes ~ juge** you alone can judge; **à ~e fin de** with the sole purpose of; **du ~ fait que...** by the mere *ou* very fact that...; **parler à qn ~ à ~** to speak to sb in private *ou* privately *ou* alone; **se retrouver ~ à ~ avec qn** to find o.s. alone with sb; *(fig)* **comme un ~ homme** as one man; **d'une ~e voix** with one voice.
2 *adv parler, rire* to oneself; *vivre* alone, by oneself, on one's own. *(sans aide)* **faire qch (tout) ~** to do sth (all) on one's own *ou* unaided *ou* single-handed.
3 *nm, f*: **un ~** *(gén)* only one; **le ~ que j'aime** the only one I love; **il n'en reste pas un ~** there isn't a single one left.

seulement [sœlmã] *adv* (**a**) *(gén)* only; *(exclusivement)* only, solely; *(toutefois)* only, but. **nous serons ~ 4** there will be only 4 of us; **on ne vit pas ~ de pain** you can't live on bread alone *ou* only *ou* solely on bread; **ce n'est pas ~ sa maladie qui le déprime** it's not only *ou* just his illness that depresses him; **il vient ~ d'entrer** he's only just (now) come in; **c'est bien, ~ c'est cher** it's fine only *ou* but it's expensive. (**b**) *(locutions)* **non ~ il a plu, mais (encore) il a fait froid** it didn't only rain but it was cold too; **on ne nous a pas ~ donné un verre d'eau** we were not even given a glass of water, we were not given so much as a glass of water; **si ~** if only.

sève [sɛv] *nf* sap.

sévère [sevɛʀ] *adj (gén)* severe; *juge, climat* harsh; *parent, ton* stern. ◆ **sévèrement** *adv* severely; harshly; sternly. ◆ **sévérité** *nf* severity; harshness; sternness.

sévices [sevis] *nmpl* (physical) cruelty, ill treatment.

Séville [sevil] *n* Seville.

sévir [seviʀ] (2) *vi* (**a**) *(punir)* to act ruthlessly. **~ contre** to deal ruthlessly with. (**b**) *[fléau, doctrine]* to rage, hold sway; *[pauvreté]* to be rampant *ou* rife. **il sévit à la télé depuis 20 ans** he's been doing his worst on TV for 20 years now *(hum)*.

sevrer [səvʀe] (5) *vt nourrisson* to wean. *(fig)* **~ qn de qch** to deprive sb of sth. ◆ **sevrage** *nm* weaning.

sexe [sɛks(ə)] *nm* sex; *(organes)* sex organs. **enfant du ~ masculin** child of male sex, male child; **le beau ~** the fair sex. ◆ **sexisme** *nm* sexism. ◆ **sexiste** *adj, nmf* sexist. ◆ **sexualité** *nf* sexuality. ◆ **sexué, e** *adj* sexual. ◆ **sexuel, -elle** *adj (gén)* sexual; *éducation, hormone, organe* sexual, sex. ◆ **sexuellement** *adv* sexually. **maladie ~ transmissible** sexually transmitted disease. ◆ **sexy** * *adj inv* sexy *.

sextant [sɛkstã] *nm* sextant.

seyant, e [sɛjã, ãt] *adj vêtement* becoming.

Seychelles [seʃɛl] *nfpl*: **les ~** the Seychelles.

shah [ʃa] *nm* shah.

shaker [ʃɛkœʀ] *nm* cocktail shaker.

shakespearien, -ienne [ʃɛkspiʀjɛ̃, jɛn] *adj* Shakespearian.

shampooing [ʃãpwɛ̃] *nm* shampoo. **faire un ~ à qn** to shampoo sb's hair; **~ colorant** tint, rinse. ◆ **shampooiner** (1) *vt* to shampoo. ◆ **shampooineur, -euse 1** *nm, f* (hairdressing) junior. **2** *nf* carpet shampooing-machine.

shérif [ʃeʀif] *nm* sheriff.

shetland [ʃɛtlãd] *nm* (**a**) *(laine)* Shetland wool; *(tricot)* Shetland pullover. (**b**) **les îles S~** the Shetland Islands.

shooter [ʃute] (1) **1** *vi (Ftbl)* to shoot, make a shot. **2 se ~** *vpr (arg)* to mainline *. ◆ **shoot** *nm* shot.

shopping [ʃɔpiŋ] *nm* shopping. **faire du ~** to go shopping.

short [ʃɔʀt] *nm*: **~(s)** pair of shorts, shorts.

si[1] [si] **1** *conj* (**a**) *(hypothèse)* if. **~ j'avais de l'argent** if I had any money, had I any money; **~ j'étais riche** if I were rich; **~ j'avais su!** if I had only known!, had I only *ou* but known!; **et s'il refusait?** and what if he refused?; **~ tu lui téléphonais?** how *ou* what about phoning him?, supposing you phoned him? (**b**) *(répétition)* if, when. **~ je sors sans parapluie, il pleut** if *ou* when(ever) I go out without an umbrella, it always rains. (**c**) *(opposition)* while. **~ lui est aimable, sa femme est arrogante** while *ou* whereas he is very pleasant, his wife is arrogant. (**d**) *(exposant un fait)* **c'est un miracle ~ la voiture n'a pas pris feu** it's a miracle (that) the car didn't catch fire; **excusez-nous ~ nous n'avons pas pu venir** please excuse us for not being able to come. (**e**) *(interrogation indirecte)* if, whether. **il se demande ~ elle viendra** he is wondering whether *ou* if she will come; **vous imaginez s'ils étaient fiers!** you can imagine how proud they were!; **~ je veux y aller! quelle question!** do I want to go! what a question! (**f**) **qui peut le savoir, ~ ce n'est lui?** who will know if not him? *ou* apart from him? *ou* but him?; **~ ce n'était la crainte de les décourager** if it were not *ou* were it not for the fear of putting them off; **une des plus belles, ~ ce n'est la plus belle** one of the most beautiful, if not the most beautiful; **elle va bien, ~ ce n'est qu'elle est fatiguée** she's quite well apart from the fact that she is tired. (**g**) *(locutions)* **il te répondra ~ tant est qu'il le sache** he'll tell you, that is if he knows; **s'il te** *ou* **vous plaît** please; **~ je ne me trompe** if I am not mistaken, unless I'm mistaken; **~ j'ose dire** if I may say so, if I may put it like that; **~ l'on peut dire** in a way, as it were, so to speak; **~ l'on veut** in a way; **~ c'est ça *, je m'en vais** if that's how it is, I'm off *. **2** *nm inv* if. **avec des ~ on mettrait Paris en bouteille** if ifs and ands were pots and pans there'd be no need for tinkers.

si[2] [si] *adv* (**a**) *(affirmatif)* **vous ne venez pas? — ~/mais ~** aren't you coming? — yes I am/of course I am; **~, ~, il faut venir** oh but you must come!; **il n'a pas voulu, moi ~** he didn't want to, but I did. (**b**) *(tellement)* so. **un ami ~ gentil** such a kind friend; **j'ai ~ faim** I'm so hungry. (**c**) **~ bien que** so that. (**d**) *(concessif)* however. **~ bête qu'il soit, il comprendra** stupid as he is *ou* however stupid he is he will understand; **~ peu que ce soit** however little it may be. (**e**) *(égalité)* as, so. **elle n'est pas ~ timide que vous croyez** she's not so *ou* as shy as you think.

si[3] [si] *nm inv (Mus)* B; *(en chantant)* ti, te, si.

siamois, e [sjamwa, waz] **1** *adj* Siamese. **2** *nm, f pl*: **~, ~es** Siamese twins. **3** *nm (chat)* Siamese.

Sibérie [sibeʀi] *nf* Siberia. ◆ **sibérien, -ienne** *adj*, **S~(ne)** *nm(f)* Siberian.

sic [sik] *adv* sic.

Sicile [sisil] *nf* Sicily. ◆ **sicilien, -ienne** *adj, nm*, **S~(ne)** *nm(f)* Sicilian.

sida, SIDA [sida] *nm (abrév de* **syndrome immuno-déficitaire acquis***)* aids, AIDS.

sidéral, e, *mpl* **-aux** [sideʀal, o] *adj* sidereal.

sidérer * [sideʀe] (6) *vt* to stagger, shatter *.

sidérurgie [sideʀyʀʒi] *nf (fabrication)* iron and steel metallurgy; *(industrie)* iron and steel industry. ◆ **sidérurgique** *adj procédé* (iron and) steelmaking. ◆ **sidérurgiste** *nmf* (iron and) steel worker.

siècle [sjɛkl(ə)] *nm* century; *(époque)* age, century. **être de son ~/d'un autre ~** to live with the times/ be behind the times; **le ~ de Périclès** the age of Pericles; **il y a des ~s que nous ne nous sommes vus** * it's years *ou* ages since we last saw each other.

siège [sjɛʒ] *nm* (**a**) *(objet)* seat. **~ de jardin** garden chair; **prenez un ~** take a seat; **~ éjectable** ejector seat. (**b**) *(Méd: postérieur)* seat. (**c**) *(Pol: fonction)* seat. (**d**) *(Jur) [magistrat]* bench. (**e**) *[firme]* head office; *[parti]* headquarters; *[assemblée]* seat. **~ social** registered office; **~ épiscopal** episcopal see. (**f**) *[maladie, rébellion]* seat; *[faculté, sensation]* centre. (**g**) *[place forte]* siege. *(lit, fig)* **faire le ~ de** to lay siege to; **lever le ~** *(lit)* to raise the siege; *(fig)* to get up and go. ◆ **siéger** (3) *et* (6) *vi [assemblée]* to sit. **voilà où siège le mal** that's where the trouble lies.

sien, sienne [sjɛ̃, sjɛn] **1** *pron poss*: **le ~, la sienne, les ~s, les siennes** *[homme]* his (own); *[femme]* hers, her own; *[chose]* its own; *(indéf)* one's own; **ce sac est le ~** this bag is hers; **mes enfants sont sortis avec les 2 ~s** my children have gone out with his (*ou* her) 2. **2** *nm* (**a**) **y mettre du ~** to give and take. (**b**) **les ~s** *(famille)* one's family; *(partisans)* one's own people. **3** *nf*: **il a encore fait des siennes** * he has (gone and) done it again *. **4** *adj poss (littér)* **un ~ cousin** a cousin of his (*ou* hers); **faire sienne une théorie** to adopt a theory, make a theory one's own.

Sienne [sjɛn] *n* Siena.

Sierra Leone [sjɛʀaleɔn] *nf* Sierra Leone.

sieste [sjɛst(ə)] *nf (gén)* nap, snooze; *(en Espagne etc)* siesta. **faire la ~** to have a nap *ou* siesta.

siffler [sifle] (1) **1** *vi (gén, fig)* to whistle; *(avec un sifflet)* to blow one's *ou* a whistle; *[gaz, serpent]* to hiss; *[respiration]* to wheeze. **2** *vt* (**a**) *(appeler) chien* to whistle for; *(pour infraction)* to blow one's whistle at; *départ, faute* to blow one's whistle for. *(Ftbl)* **~ la fin du match** to blow the final whistle, blow for time. (**b**) *acteur, pièce* to hiss, boo. **se faire ~** to get hissed *ou* booed. (**c**) *chanson* to whistle. (**d**) (**‡**: *avaler)* to guzzle *, knock back **‡**. ◆ **sifflant, e** *adj sonorité* whistling; *toux* wheezing; *prononciation* hissing, whistling. **(consonne) ~e** sibilant. ◆ **sifflement** *nm*: **~(s)** whistling; hissing; wheezing; **un ~** a whistle; **~ d'oreilles** whistling in the ears. ◆ **sifflet** *nm* whistle. *(huées)* **~s** hissing, booing, cat calls. ◆ **siffleur, -euse** **1** *adj merle* whistling; *serpent* hissing. **2** *nm, f* whistler; hisser, booer. ◆ **sifflotement** *nm* whistling. ◆ **siffloter** (1) *vti* to whistle.

sigle [sigl(ə)] *nm* (set of) initials, acronym.

sigma [sigma] *nm* sigma.

signal, *pl* **-aux** [siɲal, o] *nm* signal. **donner le ~ de** *(lit)* to give the signal for; *(fig: déclencher)* to be the signal *ou* sign for, signal; **à mon ~ tous se levèrent** when I gave the signal *ou* sign everyone got up; **~ de détresse** distress signal; *(Aut)* **signaux (lumineux)** traffic signals *ou* lights; *(Rail)* **~ automatique** automatic signal; **tirer le ~ d'alarme** to pull the alarm. ◆ **signalé, e** *adj service* signal. ◆ **signalement** *nm* description, particulars. ◆ **signaler** (1) **1** *vt (être l'indice de)* to indicate, be a sign of; *(avertir)* to signal; *(mentionner)* to indicate; *fait, vol* to report; *erreur, détail* to point out. **signalez que vous allez tourner à droite** indicate *ou* signal that you are turning right; **rien à ~** nothing to report; **~ qn à l'attention de qn** to bring sb to sb's attention; **nous vous signalons que...** we would point out to you that...; **nous vous signalons qu'il...** for your information, he... **2 se ~** *vpr (s'illustrer)* to distinguish o.s., stand out; *(attirer l'attention)* to draw attention to o.s. **se ~ à l'attention de qn** to attract sb's attention, bring o.s. to sb's attention.

signaliser [siɲalize] (1) *vt route* to put up (road) signs on; *voie* to put signals on. ◆ **signalisation** *nf* (**a**) *(action)* erection of (road)signs (*ou* signals) (*de* on). **erreur de ~** signposting (*ou* signalling) error; **panneau de ~** roadsign; **moyens de ~** means of signalling. (**b**) *(signaux)* signals. **~ routière** roadsigns.

signature [siɲatyʀ] *nf (action)* signing; *(marque)* signature. ◆ **signataire** *nmf* signatory.

signe [siɲ] **1** *nm* (**a**) *(gén)* sign. **un ~ de tête affirmatif/négatif** a nod/a shake of the head; **c'est un ~ de pluie** it's a sign it's going to rain; **c'est bon/ mauvais ~** it's a good/bad sign; *(lit, fig)* **ne pas donner ~ de vie** to give no sign of life; **donner des ~s de fatigue** to show signs of tiredness; **en ~ de respect** as a sign *ou* mark *ou* token of respect; **'~s particuliers: néant'** 'special peculiarities: none'; *(fig)* **rencontre placée sous le ~ de l'amitié franco-britannique** meeting where the keynote *ou* where the dominant theme was Franco-British friendship. (**b**) **faire ~ à qn** *(lit)* to make a sign to sb, sign to sb (*de faire* to do); *(fig: contacter)* to get in touch with sb, contact sb; **faire ~ du doigt à qn** to beckon (to) sb with one's finger; *(de la tête)* **faire ~ que oui** to nod in agreement; **faire ~ que non** to shake one's head. **2** : **~ de croix/du zodiaque** *etc* sign of the cross/of the Zodiac *etc*; **~s extérieurs de richesse** outward signs of wealth; *(clin d'œil)* **~ d'intelligence** knowing look; **~ de ponctuation** punctuation mark; **~ (typographique)** character; **~ précurseur** omen, portent; **~ de ralliement** rallying symbol.

signer [siɲe] (1) **1** *vt* to sign. **tableau non signé** unsigned painting; *(fig)* **c'est signé!** * it's absolutely characteristic, it's written all over it! * **2 se ~** *vpr (Rel)* to cross o.s.

signet [siɲɛ] *nm* bookmark.

signifier [siɲifje] (7) *vt* (**a**) *(avoir pour sens)* to mean, signify. **bonté ne signifie pas forcément faiblesse** kindness does not necessarily mean *ou* signify *ou* imply weakness; **qu'est-ce que cela signifie?** what's the meaning of this? (**b**) *(faire connaître)* to make known; *(Jur)* to serve notice of (*à* on), notify (*à* to). **~ sa volonté à qn** to make one's wishes known to sb, inform sb of one's wishes; **~ son congé à qn** to give sb his notice.

silence [silɑ̃s] *nm* (**a**) silence. *(lit, fig)* **garder le ~** to keep silent (*sur* on); **faire ~** to be silent; **passer qch sous ~** to pass over sth in silence; **en ~** in silence; **sortez vos cahiers et en ~!** get out your books and no talking!; **un ~ de mort** a deathly hush *ou* silence. (**b**) *(dans la conversation, un récit)* pause; *(Mus)* rest. **à son entrée il y eut un ~** there was a hush when he came in. (**c**) *(paix)* silence, stillness. ◆ **silencieusement** *adv* silently; noiselessly. ◆ **silencieux, -euse** **1** *adj (gén)* silent; *(paisible)* still; *moteur* noiseless. **2** *nm (Tech)* silencer.

silex [silɛks] *nm* flint.

silhouette [silwɛt] *nf (profil)* outline, silhouette; *(allure, dessin)* figure. **~s de tir** figure targets.

silice [silis] *nf* silica.

silicium [silisjɔm] *nm* silicon.

silicone [silikon] *nf* silicone.

sillage [sijaʒ] *nm [bateau]* wake; *[avion]* slipstream. *(lit, fig)* **dans son ~** in his (*ou* its *etc*) wake *ou* trail.

sillon [sijɔ̃] *nm (Agr, fig)* furrow; *[disque]* groove. ◆ **sillonner** (1) *vt [bateau, routes]* to cut across, cross; *[rides, ravins]* to furrow. **~ les routes** to travel the roads.

silo [silo] *nm* silo.

simagrées [simagʀe] *nfpl* fuss. **faire des ~** to make a fuss *ou* a to-do *.

simiesque [simjɛsk(ə)] *adj (V* **singe***)* monkey-like; ape-like.

similaire [similɛʀ] *adj* similar. ◆ **similarité** *nf* similarity. ◆ **simili** *préf* imitation. ◆ **similitude** *nf* similarity.

simple [sɛ̃pl(ə)] **1** *adj* (**a**) *(non complexe)* simple; *(non multiple) billet, fleur* single; *(facile)* straightforward. **en ~ épaisseur** in a single thickness; **réduit à sa plus ~ expression** reduced to a minimum; **~ comme bonjour** * easy as pie *. (**b**) *(modeste)* plain, simple. **il a su rester ~** he has managed to stay unaffected *ou* simple; *(hum)* **dans le plus ~ appareil** in one's birthday suit. (**c**) *(naïf)* simple. **~ d'esprit** *(adj)* simple-minded; *(nmf)* simpleton. (**d**) *(restrictif)* simple. **un ~ particulier** an ordinary citizen; **un ~ soldat** a private; **une ~ formalité** a simple *ou* mere formality; **un ~ regard la déconcertait** just a *ou* a mere *ou* simple look would upset her. **2** *nm* (**a**) **passer du ~ au double** to double. (**b**) *(† Bot)* simple †. (**c**) *(Tennis)* singles. **~ dames** ladies' singles. ◆ **simplement** *adv* simply; straightforwardly; plainly; unaffectedly. **je veux ~ dire que...** I simply *ou* merely *ou* just want to say that... ◆ **simplet, -ette** *adj personne* simple; *raisonnement* simplistic. ◆ **simplicité** *nf* simplicity; straightforwardness; plainness; unaffectedness; *(naïveté)* simpleness. ◆ **simplification** *nf* simplification. ◆ **simplifier** (7) *vt (gén, Math)* to simplify. **trop ~** to oversimplify. ◆ **simpliste** *adj (péj)* simplistic.

simuler [simyle] (1) *vt (gén, Tech, Ordin)* to simulate; *sentiment, attaque* to feign, sham. **~ une maladie** to feign illness, pretend to be ill. ◆ **simulacre** *nm (action simulée)* enactment. *(péj)* **un ~ de justice** a pretence of justice; **un ~ de procès** a sham trial, a mockery of a trial. ◆ **simulateur, -trice** **1** *nm, f* shammer, pretender; *(Mil: faux malade)* malingerer. **2** *nm*: **~ de vol** flight simulator. ◆ **simulation** *nf* simulation, feigning. **c'est de la ~** it's all sham, it's all put on. ◆ **simulé, e** *adj* feigned, sham.

simultané, e [simyltane] *adj* simultaneous. ◆ **simultanéité** *nf* simultaneity. ◆ **simultanément** *adv* simultaneously.

Sinaï [sinai] *nm*: **le ~** Sinai.

sinapisme [sinapism(ə)] *nm* mustard plaster.

sincère [sɛ̃sɛʀ] *adj (gén)* sincere; *partisan, sentiment* sincere, genuine, true. ◆ **sincèrement** *adv* sincerely; genuinely; truly; *(pour parler franchement)* honestly, really. ◆ **sincérité** *nf* sincerity; genuineness.

sinécure [sinekyʀ] *nf* sinecure. **ce n'est pas une ~** * it's not exactly a rest cure.

Singapour [sɛ̃gapuʀ] *nm* Singapore.

singe [sɛ̃ʒ] *nm (Zool)* monkey; *(de grande taille)* ape; *(personne laide)* horror; *(enfant espiègle)* monkey. **faire le ~** to monkey about; **malin comme un ~** as crafty *ou* artful as a monkey. ◆ **singer** (3) *vt attitude* to ape, mimic, take off; *sentiments* to feign. ◆ **singeries** *nfpl (pitreries)* antics, clowning; *(simagrées)* airs and graces. **faire des ~** to clown about, play the fool.

singulier, -ière [sɛ̃gylje, jɛʀ] **1** *adj (Ling)* singular; *(étonnant)* remarkable, singular. **2** *nm (Ling)* singular. ◆ **singulariser** (1) **1** *vt* to mark out, make conspicuous. **2 se ~** *vpr* to call attention to o.s., make o.s. conspicuous. ◆ **singularité** *nf* (**a**) remarkable nature; singularity. (**b**) *(exception)* peculiarity. ◆ **singulièrement** *adv* remarkably, singularly; peculiarly; *(en particulier)* particularly, especially.

sinistre [sinistʀ(ə)] **1** *adj* sinister, ominous. *(avant n: intensif)* **un ~ imbécile** an utter idiot. **2** *nm (catastrophe)* disaster; *(incendie)* blaze; *(Assurances: cas)* accident. **déclarer un ~** to put in *ou* submit an accident claim. ◆ **sinistré, e** **1** *adj* (disaster-)stricken. **le département du Gard a été déclaré zone ~e après les incendies** the department of the Gard was declared a disaster area after the fires. **2** *nm, f* disaster victim. ◆ **sinistrement** *adv* in a sinister way.

sinon [sinɔ̃] *conj* (**a**) *(sauf)* except, other than. **à quoi sert cette manœuvre ~ à nous intimider?** what is the purpose of this manoeuvre other than *ou* if not to intimidate us?; **je ne sais pas grand-chose, ~ qu'il a démissionné** I don't know much about it, except that *ou* only that he has resigned. (**b**) *(concession)* if not. **il avait leur approbation, ~ leur enthousiasme** he had their approval, if not their enthusiasm. (**c**) *(autrement)* otherwise, or else. *(menace)* **fais-le, ~...** do it, or else...

sinueux, -euse [sinɥø, øz] *adj route* winding; *rivière* winding, meandering; *ligne* sinuous; *pensée* tortuous. ◆ **sinuosité** *nf (aspect)* winding; *(courbe)* curve, loop.

sinus [sinys] *nm (Anat)* sinus; *(Math)* sine. ◆ **sinusite** *nf* sinusitis. ◆ **sinusoïdal, e**, *mpl* **-aux** *adj* sinusoidal. ◆ **sinusoïde** *nf* sinusoid.

sionisme [sjɔnism(ə)] *nm* Zionism. ◆ **sioniste** *adj, nmf* Zionist.

siphon [sifɔ̃] *nm (tube, bouteille)* siphon; *[évier, W.-C.]* U-bend; *(Spéléologie)* sump. ◆ **siphonné, e** ‡ *adj* cracked ‡. ◆ **siphonner** (1) *vt* to siphon.

sire [siʀ] *nm* (**a**) *(au roi)* **S~** Sire. (**b**) *(seigneur)* lord. (**c**) **triste ~** unsavoury individual.

sirène [siʀɛn] *nf* (**a**) *(Myth, fig)* siren, mermaid. (**b**) *[bateau, ambulance]* siren; *[usine]* hooter, siren *(US)*. *(incendie)* **~ d'alarme** fire alarm.

sirop [siʀo] *nm (pharmaceutique)* syrup, mixture; *(pour boisson)* syrup, squash, cordial. **~ de menthe** mint cordial *ou* beverage *(US)*; **~ d'érable** maple syrup.

siroter [siʀɔte] (1) *vt* to sip.

sirupeux, -euse [siʀypø, øz] *adj (lit, péj)* syrupy.

sis, sise [si, siz] *adj (Admin, Jur)* located.

sismique [sismik] *adj* seismic. ◆ **sismographe** *nm* seismograph.

site [sit] *nm (environnement)* setting; *(endroit pittoresque)* beauty spot; *(Constr: emplacement)* site. **~ naturel** natural site; **un ~ classé** a conservation area; **la protection des ~s** the conservation of places of interest.

sitôt [sito] **1** *adv*: **~ (après qu'elle fut) couchée, elle s'endormit** as soon as *ou* immediately she was in bed she fell asleep, she was no sooner in bed than she fell asleep; **~ dit, ~ fait** no sooner said than done; **~ qu'il sera guéri** as soon as he is better; **~ après la guerre** straight *ou* right *(US) ou* immediately after the war; **il ne reviendra pas de ~** he won't be back for quite a while *ou* for (quite) some time; *(hum)* he won't be back in a hurry. **2** *prép*: **~ les vacances, elle partait** she went away as soon as the holidays started.

situation [sitɥasjɔ̃] *nf (circonstances)* situation; *(emplacement)* situation, position, location;

(emploi) job, position, situation; *(Fin: état)* statement of finances. **être en ~ de faire** to be in a position to do; **~ de fait** de facto situation; **~ de famille** marital status; **dans une ~ désespérée** in a desperate plight; **se faire une belle ~** to work up to a good position.

situer [sitɥe] (1) **1** *vt (construire)* to site, situate, locate; *(par la pensée: localiser)* to set, place; *(*: catégoriser) personne* to place, pin down. **2 se ~** *vpr* (**a**) *(emploi réfléchi)* to place o.s. *(par rapport à* in relation to). (**b**) *(dans l'espace)* to be situated; *(dans le temps)* to take place; *(par rapport à des notions)* to stand. **bien/mal situé** well/ badly situated; **l'action se situe à Paris** the action is set *ou* takes place in Paris; **la hausse des prix se situera entre 5% et 10%** prices will rise between 5% and 10%.

six [sis], *devant consonne* [si], *devant voyelle ou h muet* [siz] **1** *adj cardinal inv* six. **~ mille** six thousand; **les ~ huitièmes de cette somme** six eighths of this sum; **il a ~ ans** he is six (years old); **un enfant de ~ ans** a six-year-old (child), a child of six; **un objet de ~ F** a six-franc article; **à ~ faces** six-sided; **il est trois heures moins ~** it is six minutes to three; **cinq fois sur ~** five times out of six; **tous les ~** all six of them; **ils ont porté la table à eux ~** the six of them carried the table; **ils viennent à ~ pour déjeuner** there are six coming to lunch; **on peut s'asseoir à ~ autour de cette table** this table can seat six (people); **se battre à ~ contre un** to fight six against one; **entrer ~ par ~** to come in six at a time *ou* six by six; **se mettre en rangs par ~** to form rows of six.
2 *adj ordinal inv* sixth, six. **arriver le ~ septembre** to arrive on the sixth of September *ou* (on) September (the) sixth; **Louis ~** Louis the Sixth; **page ~** page six; **il habite au numéro ~** he lives at number six; **il est ~ heures du soir** it's six in the evening *ou* p.m.
3 *nm inv* six. **quarante-~** forty-six; **quatre et deux font ~** four and two are *ou* make six; **il fait mal ses ~** he writes his sixes badly; *(numéro)* **le ~** number six; **il habite ~ rue de Paris** he lives at six Rue de Paris; **nous sommes le ~ aujourd'hui** it's the sixth today; *(Cartes)* **le ~ de cœur** the six of hearts; *(Dominos)* **le ~ et deux** the six-two; **la facture est datée du ~** the bill is dated the 6th.
4 : *(Mus)* **~-huit** *nm inv* six-eight (time); **mesure à ~-huit** bar in six-eight (time); *(Naut)* **~-mâts** *nm inv* six-master.
◆ **sixième 1** *adj* sixth. **vingt-~** twenty-sixth; **dans le ~ (arrondissement)** in the sixth arrondissement *(in Paris)*; **au ~ (étage)** on the sixth floor. **2** *nmf (gén)* sixth (person). **se classer ~** to come sixth. **3** *nm (portion)* sixth. **calculer le ~ d'un nombre** to work out the sixth of a number; **recevoir le ~ d'une somme** to receive a sixth of a sum; **(les) deux ~s du budget** two sixths of the budget. **4** *nf (Scol)* first form, sixth grade *(US)*. **entrer en (classe de) ~** ≃ to go into the first form *ou* sixth grade *(US)*; **élève de ~** ≃ first form *ou* sixth grade *(US)* pupil. ◆ **sixièmement** *adv* in the sixth place, sixthly.

skaï [skɑj] *nm* ® Skai (fabric) ®, leatherette.

sketch, *pl* **sketches** [skɛtʃ] *nm* (variety) sketch.

ski [ski] *nm (objet)* ski; *(sport)* skiing. **~ acrobatique** hot-dogging, free-styling; **~ alpin** Alpine skiing; **~ de fond** cross-country skiing, ski touring *(US)*, langlauf; **~ nautique** water-skiing; **~ hors piste** off-piste skiing; **faire du ~** to ski, go skiing; **chaussures de ~** ski boots. ◆ **skier** (7) *vi* to ski. ◆ **skieur, -euse** *nm, f* skier.

skipper [skipœʀ] *nm (course à la voile)* skipper.

slalom [slalɔm] *nm* slalom; *(fig)* zigzag. ◆ **slalomer** (1) *vi (Ski)* to slalom; *(fig: obstacles)* to zigzag. ◆ **slalomeur, -euse** *nm, f* slalom skier.

slave [slav] **1** *adj* Slavic, Slavonic. **2** *nmf*: **S~** Slav.

slip [slip] *nm* briefs, pants. **~ de bain** *[homme]* (bathing) trunks; *(du bikini)* bikini briefs; **2 ~s** 2 pairs of briefs *ou* pants.

slogan [slɔgɑ̃] *nm* slogan.

slow [slo] *nm* slow number.

smala * [smala] *nf (troupe)* tribe *.

smicard, e * [smikaʀ, aʀd(ə)] *nm, f* minimum wage earner.

smoking [smɔkiŋ] *nm (costume)* dinner suit; *(veston)* dinner jacket, tuxedo *(US)*.

snack(-bar) [snak(baʀ)] *nm* snack bar.

snob [snɔb] **1** *nmf* snob. **2** *adj* snobbish, snobby, posh *. ◆ **snober** (1) *vt*: **~ qn** to snub sb, give sb the cold shoulder. ◆ **snobisme** *nm* snobbishness, snobbery.

sobre [sɔbʀ(ə)] *adj personne* sober, temperate, abstemious; *style* sober. **~ de paroles** sparing of words; **~ comme un chameau** as sober as a judge. ◆ **sobrement** *adv* soberly, temperately; frugally. ◆ **sobriété** *nf* sobriety, temperance; frugality.

sobriquet [sɔbʀikɛ] *nm* nickname.

sociable [sɔsjabl(ə)] *adj caractère* sociable; *milieu* hospitable. ◆ **sociabilité** *nf* sociability; hospitality.

social, e, *mpl* **-aux** [sɔsjal, o] *adj (gén)* social. **prestations ~es** social security benefits. ◆ **social-démocrate,** *mpl* **sociaux-démocrates** *adj, nmf* Social Democrat. ◆ **social-démocratie** *nf, pl* **social-démocraties** social democracy. ◆ **socialement** *adv* socially. ◆ **socialisation** *nf* socialization. ◆ **socialiser** (1) *vt* to socialize. ◆ **socialisme** *nm* socialism. ◆ **socialiste** *adj, nmf* socialist.

société [sɔsjete] *nf* (**a**) *(groupe)* society. **la ~** society; **la bonne/haute ~** polite/high society; **la ~ de consommation** the consumer society. (**b**) *(club)* *(littéraire)* society; *(sportive)* club. **la S~ protectrice des animaux** ≃ the Royal Society for the Prevention of Cruelty to Animals, the American Society for the Prevention of Cruelty to Animals *(US)*. (**c**) *(Comm)* company, firm. **~ par actions/ anonyme** joint stock/limited company. (**d**) *(assemblée)* company, gathering. **une ~ d'artistes** a company *ou* gathering of artists; **toute la ~ se leva** the whole company rose. (**e**) *(compagnie)* company. **rechercher la ~ de qn** to seek sb's company. ◆ **sociétaire** *nmf* member *(of a society)*.

socio- [sɔsjɔ] *préf* socio. **~-éducatif/-économique** *etc* socioeducational/economic *etc*.

sociologie [sɔsjɔlɔʒi] *nf* sociology. ◆ **sociologique** *adj* sociological. ◆ **sociologiquement** *adv* sociologically. ◆ **sociologue** *nmf* sociologist.

socle [sɔkl(ə)] *nm [statue]* plinth, pedestal; *[lampe]* base.

socquette [sɔkɛt] *nf* ankle sock.

soda [sɔda] *nm* fizzy drink. **~ à l'orange** orangeade.

sodium [sɔdjɔm] *nm* sodium.

sœur [sœʀ] *nf (gén, Rel)* sister. **avec un dévouement de ~** with a sister's *ou* with sisterly devotion; **et ta ~?** ⁑ get lost ⁑; **~ Jeanne** Sister Jeanne; **mis en pension chez les ~s** sent to a convent (boarding) school.

sofa [sɔfa] *nm* sofa.

Sofia [sɔfja] *n* Sofia.

soft(ware) [sɔft(wɛʀ)] *nm* software.

soi [swa] **1** *pron pers (gén)* oneself. **n'aimer que ~** to love only oneself; **il faut regarder devant ~** you must look in front of you; **rester chez ~** to stay at home; *(faire un effort)* **prendre sur ~** to take a grip on o.s.; **prendre sur ~ de faire qch** to take it upon o.s. to do sth; **il n'agit que pour ~** he is only acting for himself; **se rendre service entre ~** to help each other *ou* one another (out); **cela**

va de ~ it's obvious, it stands to reason, it goes without saying (*que* that); *(intrinsèquement)* **en** ~ in itself; ~**-même** oneself; **le respect de** ~**-même** self-respect; *(hum)* **Monsieur X? — ~-même!** Mr X? — in person! **2** *nm (Philos)* self; *(Psych)* id. ◆ **soi-disant 1** *adj inv:* **un** ~ **poète** a so-called *ou* would-be poet. **2** *adv* supposedly. **il était** ~ **parti** he had supposedly left, he was supposed to have left.

soie [swa] *nf (Tex)* silk; *[sanglier etc]* bristle. ◆ **soierie** *nf (tissu)* silk; *(commerce)* silk trade.

soif [swaf] *nf* (**a**) *(lit)* **avoir** ~ to be thirsty; **le sel donne** ~ salt makes you thirsty, salt gives one a thirst; **jusqu'à plus** ~ * till one can take no more. (**b**) *(fig: désir)* ~ **de qch** thirst *ou* craving for sth; ~ **de faire qch** craving to do sth.

soigné, e [swaɲe] *adj* (**a**) *personne, tenue, chevelure* tidy, well-groomed, neat; *ongles* well-groomed, well-kept; *mains* well-cared-for; *travail, présentation* neat, careful, meticulous; *jardin* well-kept, neat; *repas* carefully-prepared. **peu** ~ *personne* untidy; *cheveux* unkempt, untidy. (**b**) *(*: intensif) note* massive *, whopping *; *punition* stiff *. **avoir un rhume** ~ to have a whopper * of a cold.

soigner [swaɲe] (1) **1** *vt* (**a**) *[médecin]* to treat; *[infirmière]* to look after, nurse. **se faire** ~ to have treatment; ~ **les blessés** to tend *ou* nurse the injured; **il faut te faire** ~**!** * you need your head examined! * (**b**) *plantes, invité, ongles* to look after, take (good) care of; *tenue, travail, repas* to take care over. **2 se** ~ *vpr (lit, fig) [personne]* to take good care of o.s., look after o.s. **cette maladie se soigne** this disease can be treated. ◆ **soigneur** *nm (Boxe)* second; *(Cyclisme, Ftbl)* trainer.

soigneux, -euse [swaɲø, øz] *adj personne* tidy, neat; *travail* careful, meticulous. ~ **de sa personne/de ses vêtements** careful about one's appearance/with one's clothes. ◆ **soigneusement** *adv* tidily, neatly; carefully, meticulously. ~ **préparé** carefully prepared.

soin [swɛ̃] *nm* (**a**) *(application)* care; *(ordre et propreté)* tidiness, neatness. **sans** ~ *(adj)* careless; untidy; *(adv)* carelessly; untidily; **avec (grand)** ~ with (great) care, (very) carefully. (**b**) *(charge)* care. **confier à qn le** ~ **de faire** to entrust sb with the job of doing; **je vous laisse ce** ~ I leave this to you, I leave you to take care of this; **son premier** ~ **fut de faire...** his first concern was to do... (**c**) ~**s** care; *(traitement)* attention, treatment; **les** ~**s du ménage** the care of the home; **les** ~**s du visage** face-care, care of the complexion; ~**s médicaux** medical *ou* health care; ~**s dentaires** dental treatment; **le blessé a reçu les premiers** ~**s** the injured man has been given first aid; **confier qn/qch aux (bons)** ~**s de** to leave sb/sth in the hands *ou* care of; *(sur lettre)* **aux bons** ~**s de** care of, c/o; **être aux petits** ~**s pour qn** to wait on sb hand and foot. (**d**) **avoir** *ou* **prendre** ~ **de faire** to take care to do; **avoir** *ou* **prendre** ~ **de qn/qch** to take care of *ou* look after sb/sth; **prenez** ~ **d'éteindre** take care *ou* be sure to turn out the lights.

soir [swaʀ] *nm* evening. **journal du** ~ evening paper; **5 heures du** ~ 5 (o'clock) in the afternoon *ou* evening, 5 p.m.; **11 heures du** ~ 11 (o'clock) at night, 11 p.m.; **le** ~ in the evening; **j'y vais ce** ~ I'm going this evening *ou* tonight; **hier** ~ last night, yesterday evening; **demain** ~ tomorrow evening *ou* night; **la veille au** ~ the previous evening, in the evening of the previous day. ◆ **soirée** *nf (soir)* evening; *(réception)* party; *(Théât)* evening performance. ~ **dansante** dance.

soit [swa] **1** *adv (oui)* very well, well and good. **2** *conj* (**a**) *(d'alternative)* ~ **l'un** ~ **l'autre** (either) one or the other; ~ **avant** ~ **après** (either) before or after; ~ **qu'il soit fatigué,** ~ **qu'il en ait assez** whether he is tired or whether he has had enough. (**b**) *(à savoir)* that is to say. (**c**) *(Math: posons)* ~ **un rectangle ABCD** let ABCD be a rectangle.

soixante [swasɑ̃t] *adj inv, nm inv* sixty. **les années** ~ the sixties, the 60s; ~ **et un** sixty-one; ~ **et unième** sixty-first; ~**-dix** seventy; ~**-dixième** seventieth; ~ **et onze** seventy-one; *(jeu, rue)* **le (numéro)** ~ number sixty. ◆ **soixantaine** *nf* (**a**) *(environ soixante)* sixty or so, (round) about sixty, sixty-odd *. **la** ~ **de spectateurs qui étaient là** the sixty or so *ou* the sixty-odd * people there; **ils étaient une bonne** ~ there were a good sixty of them; **ça doit coûter une** ~ **de mille (francs)** that must cost sixty thousand or so francs *ou* (round) about sixty thousand francs. (**b**) *(soixante)* sixty. (**c**) *(âge)* sixty. **d'une** ~ **d'années** *personne* of about sixty; *arbre* sixty or so years old; **elle a la** ~ she is sixtyish *ou* in her sixties. ◆ **soixantième** *adj, nmf* sixtieth.

soja [sɔʒa] *nm (plante)* soya.

sol¹ [sɔl] **1** *nm (gén)* ground; *(d'une maison)* floor; *(Agr, Géol)* soil. **sur le** ~ **français** on French soil; **vitesse au** ~ ground speed; *(Sport)* **exercices au** ~ floor exercises. **2** : *(Mil)* ~**-air** *adj inv* ground-to-air; ~**-**~ *adj inv* ground-to-ground.

sol² [sɔl] *nm inv (Mus)* G; *(en chantant)* so(h).

solaire [sɔlɛʀ] **1** *adj (Astrol, Astron), énergie, panneaux* solar; *crème* sun. **2** *nm (énergie)* **le** ~ solar energy.

soldat [sɔlda] *nm (gén)* soldier. **simple** ~ private; ~ **d'infanterie** infantryman; **le S**~ **inconnu** the Unknown Soldier *ou* Warrior; ~ **de plomb** tin soldier.

solde¹ [sɔld(ə)] *nf (salaire)* pay. *(péj)* **être à la** ~ **de** to be in the pay of.

solde² [sɔld(ə)] *nm* (**a**) *(Fin)* balance; *(à payer)* balance outstanding. ~ **créditeur** credit balance; **pour** ~ **de tout compte** in settlement. (**b**) **(article en)** ~ sale(s) article; ~ **de lainages** sale of woollens, woollen sale; **acheter qch en** ~ to buy sth at sale price; **les** ~**s** the sales.

solder [sɔlde] (1) **1** *vt* (**a**) *compte (arrêter)* to wind up; *(acquitter)* to settle, balance. (**b**) *marchandises* to sell (off) at sale price. **je vous le solde à 40 F** I'll let you have it for 40 francs. **2 se** ~ *vpr (Fin)* **se** ~ **par un bénéfice** to show a profit; *(fig)* **se** ~ **par un échec** to end in failure.

sole [sɔl] *nf (poisson)* sole.

solécisme [sɔlesism(ə)] *nm* solecism *(in language)*.

soleil [sɔlɛj] *nm* (**a**) *(astre)* sun; *(lumière)* sunshine, sunlight; *(chaleur)* sunshine. **le** ~ **levant/couchant/de minuit** the rising/setting/midnight sun; **se mettre au** ~ to go out into the sun(shine) *ou* sunlight; **il fait du** ~ the sun is shining, it's sunny; **il fait un** ~ **de plomb** the sun is blazing down; **des jours sans** ~ sunless days. (**b**) *(feu d'artifice)* Catherine wheel; *(acrobatie)* grand circle; *(fig: culbute)* somersault; *(fleur)* sunflower. (**c**) *(locutions)* **rien de nouveau sous le** ~ there's nothing new under the sun; **avoir du bien au** ~ to be the owner of property; *(fig)* **se faire une place au** ~ to find o.s. a place in the sun.

solennel, -elle [sɔlanɛl] *adj (gén)* solemn; *promesse, ton, occasion* solemn, formal; *séance* ceremonious. ◆ **solennellement** *adv* solemnly; ceremoniously. ◆ **solennité** *nf* solemnity.

Solex [sɔlɛks] *nm* ® ≃ moped.

solfège [sɔlfɛʒ] *nm* musical theory.

solidaire [sɔlidɛʀ] *adj* (**a**) *[personnes]* **être** ~**s** to show solidarity, stand *ou* stick together; **être** ~ **de** to stand by, back, support. (**b**) *mécanismes* interdependent. **cette pièce est** ~ **de l'autre** this part is firmly *ou* immovably attached to the other. (**c**) *(Jur) engagement* binding all parties; *débiteurs* jointly liable. ◆ **solidairement** *adv* jointly. ◆ **se solidariser** (1) *vpr:* **se** ~ **avec** to show solidarity with. ◆ **solidarité** *nf* solidarity; interdependence; joint liability. **faire une grève de** ~ to come out in sympathy *ou* stop work in sympathy with the strikers.

solide [sɔlid] **1** *adj* (**a**) *(non liquide)* solid. (**b**) *(robuste) objet, muscles* solid, sturdy, strong; *qualité, connaissances, santé, esprit* sound; *personne* sturdy; *(sérieux)* reliable, solid. **c'est du** ~ it's solid stuff; **être** ~ **sur ses jambes** to be steady on one's legs; **cela ne repose sur rien de** ~ it has no solid *ou* sound foundation; **avoir la tête** ~ *(lit)* to have a hard head; *(fig: équilibré)* to have a good head on one's shoulders. (**c**) *coup de poing* hefty *; *revenus* substantial; *repas* (good) solid. **2** *nm (Géom, Phys)* solid. ◆ **solidement** *adv fixer* firmly; *fabriquer* solidly; *s'installer* securely. ◆ **solidification** *nf* solidification. ◆ **solidifier** *vt*, **se** ~ *vpr* (7) to solidify. ◆ **solidité** *nf* solidity; sturdiness; soundness; reliability.

soliloque [sɔlilɔk] *nm* soliloquy.

soliste [sɔlist(ə)] *nmf* soloist.

solitaire [sɔlitɛʀ] **1** *adj (gén)* solitary, lonely; *caractère* solitary. **un passant** ~ a solitary *ou* lone passer-by. **2** *nmf (ermite)* recluse, hermit; *(fig: ours)* lone wolf, loner. **travailler en** ~ to work on one's own. **3** *nm (sanglier)* old boar; *(diamant)* solitaire; *(jeu)* solitaire. ◆ **solitude** *nf* (**a**) *(tranquillité)* solitude; *(manque de compagnie)* loneliness, lonesomeness *(US)*; *[endroit]* loneliness. (**b**) *(désert)* solitude.

solliciter [sɔlisite] (1) *vt faveur, audience* to seek, request, solicit (*de qn* from sb); *poste* to seek; *curiosité* to appeal to; *attention* to attract, entice; *cheval, voiture* to coax forward. **il est très sollicité** he's very much in demand; **les attractions qui sollicitent le touriste** the attractions that are there to tempt *ou* entice the tourist. ◆ **sollicitation** *nf (démarche)* entreaty, appeal; *(tentation)* temptation, solicitation. ◆ **solliciteur, -euse** *nm, f* supplicant.

sollicitude [sɔlisityd] *nf* concern, solicitude.

solo [sɔlo] *adj inv, nm* solo.

solstice [sɔlstis] *nm* solstice.

soluble [sɔlybl(ə)] *adj substance* soluble; *problème* soluble, solvable. **café** ~ instant coffee. ◆ **solubilité** *nf* solubility.

solution [sɔlysjɔ̃] *nf (réponse)* solution (*de* to); *(Math, Chim)* solution. **c'est une** ~ **de facilité** that's an easy answer *ou* the easy way out; ~ **de continuité** solution of continuity.

solvable [sɔlvabl(ə)] *adj (Fin)* solvent, creditworthy. ◆ **solvabilité** *nf* solvency, creditworthiness.

solvant [sɔlvɑ̃] *nm (Chim)* solvent.

Somalie [sɔmali] *nf (région)* Somaliland; *(État)* Somalia. ◆ **somalien, -ienne** *adj*, **S~(ne)** *nm(f)* Somalian.

sombre [sɔ̃bʀ(ə)] *adj* (**a**) *(foncé)* dark. **il fait** ~ it's dark; **bleu** ~ dark blue. (**b**) *pensées, avenir* sombre, gloomy, dark, dismal. (**c**) ~ **idiot** utter idiot; **une** ~ **histoire d'enlèvement** a murky story of abduction. ◆ **sombrement** *adv* darkly; sombrely, gloomily, dismally.

sombrer [sɔ̃bʀe] (1) *vi [bateau]* to sink, go down, founder; *[raison]* to give way; *[empire]* to founder. ~ **dans le désespoir** to sink into despair; ~ **corps et biens** to go down with all hands.

sommaire [sɔmɛʀ] **1** *adj exposé, réponse* brief, summary; *examen* cursory; *réparation, repas* basic; *tenue, décoration* scanty; *justice* summary. **2** *nm* summary. ◆ **sommairement** *adv* briefly; summarily; cursorily; basically; scantily.

sommation [sɔmɑsjɔ̃] *nf (Jur)* summons; *(injonction)* demand; *(Mil)* warning.

somme¹ [sɔm] *nm* nap, snooze. **faire un** ~ to have a nap *ou* a snooze.

somme² [sɔm] *nf (Math)* sum; *(quantité)* amount. **la** ~ **totale** the grand total, the total sum; **faire la** ~ **de** to add up; ~ **(d'argent)** sum *ou* amount (of money); **en** ~ in sum, in short; ~ **toute** when all's said and done.

sommeil [sɔmɛj] *nm (gén, fig)* sleep; *(envie de dormir)* drowsiness, sleepiness. **avoir** ~ to be *ou* feel sleepy; **8 heures de** ~ 8 hours' sleep; ~ **de plomb** heavy *ou* deep sleep; **premier** ~ first hours of sleep; **nuit sans** ~ sleepless night; **laisser une affaire en** ~ to leave a matter (lying) dormant, leave a matter in abeyance; *(littér)* **le** ~ **éternel** eternal rest. ◆ **sommeiller** (1) *vi [personne]* to doze; *[qualité, nature]* to lie dormant.

sommelier [sɔməlje] *nm* wine waiter.

sommer [sɔme] (1) *vt*: ~ **qn de faire** to charge *ou* enjoin sb to do.

sommet [sɔmɛ] *nm* (**a**) *(gén)* top; *[montagne]* summit; *[vague]* crest; *[crâne]* crown; *[angle]* vertex. **les ~s de la gloire** the summits *ou* heights of fame. (**b**) *(montagne)* summit, mountain top.

sommier [sɔmje] *nm* bedsprings; *(avec pieds)* divan base, box springs *(US)*. ~ **à lattes** slatted bed base.

sommité [sɔmite] *nf* leading light (*de* in).

somnambule [sɔmnɑ̃byl] *nmf* sleepwalker, somnambulist. ◆ **somnambulisme** *nm* sleepwalking, somnambulism.

somnifère [sɔmnifɛʀ] **1** *nm* sleeping drug, soporific; *(pilule)* sleeping pill *ou* tablet. **2** *adj* soporific.

somnolence [sɔmnɔlɑ̃s] *nf* sleepiness, drowsiness, somnolence. ◆ **somnolent, e** *adj* sleepy, drowsy, somnolent. ◆ **somnoler** (1) *vi (lit)* to doze; *(fig)* to lie dormant.

somptueux, -euse [sɔ̃ptɥø, øz] *adj habit, résidence* sumptuous, magnificent; *train de vie* lavish; *cadeau* handsome; *repas* sumptuous, lavish. ◆ **somptueusement** *adv* sumptuously, magnificently; lavishly; handsomely. ◆ **somptuosité** *nf* sumptuousness, magnificence; lavishness; handsomeness.

son¹ [sɔ̃], **sa** [sa], **ses** [se] *adj poss* (**a**) *[homme]* his; *[femme]* her; *[objet]* its. **Sa Majesté** *(roi)* His Majesty; *(reine)* Her Majesty; **ce n'est pas** ~ **genre** he (*ou* she) is not that sort, it's not like him (*ou* her); *(emphatique)* ~ **jardin à lui est une vraie jungle** his *ou* his own garden is a real jungle; **à sa vue, elle poussa un cri** she screamed at the sight of him (*ou* her) *ou* on seeing him (*ou* her); **un de ses amis** one of his (*ou* her) friends, a friend of his (*ou* hers); ~ **idiote de sœur** * that stupid sister of his (*ou* hers); **ça a** ~ **importance** that has its *ou* a certain importance. (**b**) *(à valeur d'indéfini)* one's. **faire ses études** to study; **être satisfait de sa situation** to be satisfied with one's situation; **chacun selon ses possibilités** each according to his (own) capabilities. (**c**) *(*: valeur intensive)* **il doit gagner** ~ **million par an** he must be earning a million a year; **il a passé tout** ~ **dimanche à travailler** he spent the whole of *ou* all Sunday working.

son² [sɔ̃] *nm (gén, Ling, Phys)* sound. **défiler au** ~ **d'une fanfare** to march past to the music of a band; **le** ~ **d'une cloche** the sound *ou* ringing of a bell; *(fig)* **entendre un autre** ~ **de cloche** to hear another side of the story; **(spectacle)** ~ **et lumière** son et lumière (display).

son³ [sɔ̃] *nm (Agr)* bran.

sonate [sɔnat] *nf* sonata.

sonde [sɔ̃d] *nf (Naut)* sounding line; *(Tech: de forage)* borer, drill; *(Méd)* probe; *(à canal central)* catheter; *(d'alimentation)* feeding tube; *(Mét)* sonde; *(spatiale)* probe. **mettre une** ~ **à qn** to put a catheter in sb. ◆ **sondage** *nm* boring, drilling; sounding; probing; catheterization. ~ **(d'opinion)** (opinion) poll. ◆ **sonder** (1) *vt* (**a**) *(Naut)* to sound; *(Mét)* to probe; *terrain* to bore, drill; *plaie* to probe; *vessie, malade* to catheterize. (**b**) *personne (gén)* to sound out; *(par sondage d'opinion)* to poll; *avenir* to probe.

songer [sɔ̃ʒe] (3) **1** *vi (littér)* to dream. **2** *vt*: ~ **que** *(réfléchir)* to reflect *ou* consider that; *(imaginer)* to imagine that; **songe que...** remember that... **3** ~ **à** *vt indir (évoquer)* to think over, reflect upon; *(s'occuper de)* to think of. **songez-y** think it over, consider it; ~ **à faire qch** to contemplate doing sth, think of doing sth. ◆ **songe** *nm (littér)* dream. ◆ **songerie** *nf (littér)* reverie. ◆ **songeur, -euse** **1** *adj* pensive. **cela me laisse** ~ I just don't know what to think. **2** *nm, f* dreamer.

sonner [sɔne] (1) **1** *vt* (**a**) *cloche* to ring; *glas* to sound, toll; *clairon, réveil, retraite* to sound; *infirmière* to ring for. ~ **l'alarme** to sound the alarm; **la pendule sonne 3 heures** the clock strikes 3 (o'clock); **on ne t'a pas sonné!** * nobody asked you!; **se faire** ~ **les cloches** * to get a good telling-off *; ~ **les cloches à qn** * to give sb a telling-off *. (**b**) *(*: étourdir) [chute]* to knock out; *[nouvelle]* to stagger *, take aback. **2** *vi [cloches, téléphone]* to ring; *[réveil]* to ring, go off; *[clairon]* to sound; *[glas]* to sound, toll; *[heure]* to strike; *[clefs, monnaie]* to jangle, jingle. ~ **creux** *(lit)* to sound hollow; *(fig)* to ring hollow; ~ **faux** *(lit)* to sound out of tune; *(fig)* to ring false; *(fig)* ~ **bien/mal** to sound good/bad; ~ **à toute volée** to peal out; **on a sonné** the bell has just gone, sb just rang (the bell). **3** ~ **de** *vt indir clairon, cor* to sound. ◆ **sonnant, e** *adj*: **à 4 heures** ~**(es)** on the stroke of 4. ◆ **sonné, e** *adj* (**a**) **il est midi** ~ it's gone *ou* past twelve; **avoir trente ans bien** ~**s** * to be on the wrong side of thirty *. (**b**) (‡: *fou)* cracked *. (**c**) *(*: assommé)* groggy. ◆ **sonnerie** *nf* (**a**) *(son) [cloche]* ringing; *[téléphone]* bell; *[clairon]* sound. (**b**) *(Mil: air)* call. (**b**) *(mécanisme) [réveil]* alarm (mechanism); *[pendule]* chimes; *(sonnette)* bell. ◆ **sonnette** *nf* bell. ~ **de nuit** night-bell; ~ **d'alarme** alarm bell; *(fig)* **tirer la** ~ **d'alarme** to set off *ou* sound the alarm (bell). ◆ **sonneur** *nm*: ~ **(de cloches)** bell ringer.

sonore [sɔnɔʀ] *adj objet* resonant; *voix* resonant, ringing, sonorous; *baiser, gifle* resounding; *salle, voûte* echoing; *(Ling)* voiced; *(Acoustique) vibrations* sound. **onde** ~ sound wave; **fond** ~ background noise; **bande** ~ sound track. ◆ **sonorisation** *nf ou* ◆ **sono** * *nf (équipement) [salle de conférences]* public address system, P.A. system; *[discothèque]* sound system. **la** ~ **est trop forte** the sound's too loud. ◆ **sonorité** *nf [instrument de musique]* tone; *[salle]* acoustics *(pl)*; *[grotte]* resonance. ~**s** tones.

sophistiqué, e [sɔfistike] *adj (gén)* sophisticated.

soporifique [sɔpɔʀifik] *adj, nm* soporific.

soprano [sɔpʀano] *nmf* soprano.

sorbet [sɔʀbɛ] *nm* water ice, sorbet, sherbet *(US)*. ◆ **sorbetière** *nf* ice cream churn.

sorcellerie [sɔʀsɛlʀi] *nf* witchcraft, sorcery. **c'est de la** ~! it's magic! ◆ **sorcier** *nm (lit)* sorcerer. **il ne faut pas être** ~ **pour...** you don't have to be a wizard to... ◆ **sorcière** *nf* witch, sorceress; *(fig péj)* (old) witch, (old) hag.

sordide [sɔʀdid] *adj quartier* sordid, squalid; *action* base, sordid; *gains* sordid. ◆ **sordidement** *adv* sordidly; squalidly; basely.

Sorlingues [sɔʀlɛ̃g] *nfpl*: **les (îles)** ~ the Scilly Isles, the Isles of Scilly, the Scillies.

sornettes † [sɔʀnɛt] *nfpl* twaddle, balderdash. ~! fiddlesticks!

sort [sɔʀ] *nm* (**a**) *(condition)* lot, fate. **envier le** ~ **de qn** to envy sb's lot. (**b**) *(destinée)* fate. **le (mauvais)** ~ fate; **abandonner qn à son triste** ~ to abandon sb to his sad fate; **faire un** ~ **à un plat** * to polish off a dish *. (**c**) *(hasard)* fate. **le** ~ **est tombé sur lui** he was chosen by fate, it fell to his lot; **tirer (qch) au** ~ to draw lots (for sth). (**d**) *(sorcellerie)* curse, spell. **jeter un** ~ **sur** to put a curse *ou* spell on.

sortable * [sɔʀtabl(ə)] *adj*: **tu n'es pas** ~! you're not presentable!

sorte [sɔʀt(ə)] *nf* (**a**) *(espèce)* sort, kind. **toutes** ~**s de gens** all kinds *ou* sorts of people; **une** ~ **de** a sort *ou* kind of; *(péj)* **une** ~ **de médecin** a doctor of sorts. (**b**) **accoutré de la** ~ dressed in that fashion *ou* way; **il n'a rien fait de la** ~ he did nothing of the kind *ou* no such thing; **de** ~ **à** so as to, in order to; **en quelque** ~ in a way, as it were; **de (telle)** ~ **que** *(de façon à ce que)* so that, in such a way that; *(si bien que)* so much so that; **faites en** ~ **d'avoir fini demain** see to it *ou* arrange it so that you will have finished tomorrow; **faire en** ~ **que** to see to it that.

sortie [sɔʀti] *nf* (**a**) *(action) [personne]* leaving, exit; *[véhicule]* departure; *(Théât)* exit. **à sa** ~ when he went out *ou* left; **il a fait une** ~ **discrète** he made a discreet exit, he left discreetly; **faire une** ~ *(Mil)* to make a sortie; **à la** ~ **de l'école** after school; **c'est sa première** ~ **depuis sa maladie** it's his first day *ou* time out since his illness. (**b**) *(promenade etc)* outing; *(le soir: au théâtre etc)* evening *ou* night out. **jour de** ~ *[domestique]* day off; *[pensionnaire]* day out; *(Scol)* ~ **éducative** *ou* **scolaire** school (educational) outing, school visit, field trip. (**c**) *(lieu)* exit, way out. *(lit, fig)* **(porte de)** ~ way out; ~ **de secours** emergency exit; ~ **des artistes** stage door; **attention,** ~ **d'usine/de garage** caution, factory/garage entrance *ou* exit; ~ **de camions** vehicle exit; **garé devant la** ~ **de l'école** parked in front of the school gates *ou* entrance; **les** ~**s de Paris** the roads out of Paris. (**d**) *(paroles) (indignée)* outburst; *(drôle)* sally; *(incongrue)* odd remark. (**e**) *(Comm) [voiture, modèle]* launching; *[livre]* appearance; *[disque, film]* release; *(pour l'exportation)* export. ~ **(de capitaux)** outflow (of capital). (**f**) *(somme dépensée)* outlay. ~**s** outgoings. (**g**) *(Ordin)* output, readout. ~ **sur imprimante** printout. (**h**) *(Sport)* ~ **en touche** going into touch; *[gardien de but]* **faire une** ~ to leave the goal mouth, come out of goal; **lors de la dernière** ~ **de l'équipe de France contre l'Angleterre** when France last played a match against England, during the last French-English encounter *ou* match. (**i**) ~ **de bain** bathrobe.

sortilège [sɔʀtilɛʒ] *nm* (magic) spell.

sortir [sɔʀtiʀ] (16) **1** *vi (avec aux être)* (**a**) *[personne] (aller)* to go out, leave; *(venir)* to come out, leave; *(à pied)* to walk out; *(le soir)* to go out; *(Ordin)* to exit, log out; *(Théât)* to exit, leave (the stage). ~ **acheter du pain** to go out to buy some bread *ou* for some bread; **faites** ~ **ces gens** make these people go *ou* leave, get these people out; **sors (d'ici)!** get out (of here)!; **laisser** ~ **qn** to let sb out, let sb leave. (**b**) *[objet] (gén)* to come out; *[disque, film]* to be released; *(à la loterie)* to come up *ou* out. *(Comm)* **tout ce qui sort (du pays) doit être déclaré** everything going out *ou* leaving (the country) must be declared. (**c**) *(dépasser)* to stick out; *(pousser) [plante]* to come up; *[dent]* to come through. (**d**) *(quitter)* ~ **de** *lieu* to go *ou* come out of, leave; *indifférence* to overcome; *silence* to break out of; ~ **de l'eau** to come out of the water; ~ **du lit** to get out of bed, get up; *[fleuve]* ~ **de son lit** to overflow its banks; ~ **des rails** to go off the rails; **la voiture est sortie de la route** the car left *ou* came off the road; *(Sport)* ~ **en touche** to go into touch. (**e**) *(passé immédiat)* **on sortait de l'hiver** it was getting near the end of winter; **il sort d'ici/du lit** he's just left/just got up. (**f**) *(s'écarter de)* ~ **de** *légalité, limites* to go beyond, overstep; *compétences* to be outside; ~ **du sujet** to go *ou* get off the subject; *[balle]* ~ **du jeu** to go out of play;

cela sort de l'ordinaire that's out of the ordinary; **il n'y a pas à ~ de là, nous avons besoin de lui** there's no getting away from it *ou* round it — we need him; **il ne veut pas ~ de là** he won't budge. (**g**) *(provenir de)* ~ **de** *lieu, bonne famille* to come from; **il sort du Lycée X** he was educated at the Lycée X; **officier sorti du rang** officer who has come up through the ranks *ou* risen from the ranks; **sait-on ce qui sortira de ces entrevues!** who knows what'll come (out) of these talks!; **de la fumée sortait par les fenêtres** smoke was pouring out of the windows; *(lit, fig)* **d'où sors-tu!** where have you been! (**h**) *(locutions)* ~ **de ses gonds** *(lit)* to come off its hinges; *(fig)* to fly off the handle; **je sors d'en prendre** * I've had quite enough thank you *(iro)*; **il est sorti d'affaire** he has got over it; **on n'est pas sorti de l'auberge** * we're not out of the wood yet; **se croire sorti de la cuisse de Jupiter** * to think a lot of o.s.; **ça me sort par les yeux (et les oreilles)** * I've had more than I can take (of it); **cela lui est sorti de la mémoire** that slipped his mind; **cela m'est sorti de la tête** it went right out of my head.
2 *vt (avec aux avoir) (gén)* to take out; *(expulser)* to throw out; *(mettre en vente)* to bring out; *film* to release; *(Aviat) train d'atterrissage* to lower. ~ **qch de sa poche** to take *ou* bring *ou* pull sth out of one's pocket; *(lit, fig)* **il faut le ~ de là** we have to get him out of there; *(dire)* **qu'est-ce qu'il va encore nous ~?** * what will he come out with next? *
3 se ~ *vpr*: **se ~ d'une situation difficile** to manage to get out of a difficult situation; **tu crois qu'il va s'en ~?** *(travail)* do you think he'll ever see the end of it?; *(procès, maladie)* do you think he'll come through all right?
4 *nm*: **au ~ de l'hiver** as winter draws (*ou* drew) to a close; **au ~ de la réunion** at the end of the meeting, when the meeting broke up.

S.O.S. [ɛsoɛs] *nm* SOS. *(Aviat, Naut)* **lancer un ~** to put out an SOS; ~ **médecins/dépannage** *etc* emergency medical/repair *etc* service.

sosie [sozi] *nm* double *(person)*.

sot, sotte [so, sɔt] *adj* silly, foolish, stupid. ◆ **sottement** *adv* foolishly, stupidly. ◆ **sottise** *nf* stupidity, foolishness; *(parole, action)* silly *ou* foolish remark (*ou* action).

sou [su] *nm (monnaie)* sou; *(fig)* penny. **machine à ~s** *(jeu)* one-armed bandit, fruit-machine; *(distributeur)* slot machine; **économiser ~ à** *ou* **par ~** to save penny by penny; **il est sans le ~** he's penniless; **il n'a pas pour un ~ de bon sens** he hasn't an ounce of common sense (in him); **il n'est pas menteur pour un ~** he isn't the least bit untruthful; **propre comme un ~ neuf** (as) neat as a new pin, spick and span; **un ~ est un ~** every penny counts.

soubassement [subasmɑ̃] *nm [maison]* base.

soubresaut [subʀəso] *nm (cahot)* jolt; *(de peur)* start; *(d'agonie)* convulsive movement. **avoir un ~** to give a start; to make a convulsive movement.

soubrette [subʀɛt] *nf (†, hum)* maid.

souche [suʃ] *nf* (**a**) *[arbre]* stump; *[vigne]* stock. **rester planté comme une ~** to stand stock-still. (**b**) *[famille]* founder. **de vieille ~** of old stock. (**c**) *(Ling)* root. (**d**) *[microbes]* colony, clone. (**e**) *(talon)* counterfoil, stub. **carnet à ~s** counterfoil book.

souci [susi] *nm* (**a**) *(tracas)* worry. **donner du ~ à, se faire du ~** to worry; **être sans ~** to be free of worries *ou* care(s); **~s d'argent** money worries. (**b**) *(préoccupation)* concern (*de* for). **avoir ~ du bien-être de son prochain** to have concern for the well-being of one's neighbour; **c'est le cadet de mes ~s** that's the least of my worries. (**c**) *(fleur)* marigold. ◆ **se soucier** (7) *vpr*: **se ~ de** *chose* to care about; *personne* to care about, show concern for; **il s'en soucie comme de l'an quarante** * he doesn't give *ou* care a *fig* (about it) *, he couldn't care less (about it). ◆ **soucieux, -euse** *adj (inquiet)* concerned, worried. **peu ~** unconcerned; **être ~ de qch** to be concerned *ou* preoccupied about sth; **être ~ de faire** to be anxious to do. ◆ **soucieusement** *adv* with concern.

soucoupe [sukup] *nf* saucer. ~ **volante** flying saucer.

soudain, e [sudɛ̃, ɛn] **1** *adj (gén)* sudden; *mort* sudden, unexpected. **2** *adv (tout à coup)* suddenly, all of a sudden. ◆ **soudainement** *adv* suddenly. ◆ **soudaineté** *nf* suddenness.

Soudan [sudɑ̃] *nm*: **le ~** (the) Sudan. ◆ **soudanais, e** *adj*, **S~(e)** *nm(f)* Sudanese.

soude [sud] *nf (industrielle)* soda. ~ **caustique** caustic soda.

souder [sude] (1) **1** *vt métal* to solder; *(soudure autogène)* to weld; *os* to knit; *organismes* to fuse (together); *êtres* to bind together. **soudé au sol** glued to the spot. **2 se ~** *vpr [os]* to knit together. ◆ **soudeur** *nm* solderer; welder. ◆ **soudure** *nf (opération)* soldering; welding; knitting; *(endroit)* soldered joint; weld; *(substance)* solder. ~ **à l'arc** arc welding; ~ **autogène** welding; **faire la ~ (entre)** to bridge the gap (between).

soudoyer [sudwaje] (8) *vt* to bribe, buy over.

souffle [sufl(ə)] *nm* (**a**) *(expiration) (en soufflant)* blow, puff; *(en respirant)* breath. **murmurer un nom dans un ~** to breathe a name; **le dernier ~ d'un agonisant** the last breath of a dying man. (**b**) *(respiration)* breathing; *(capacité)* breath. ~ **régulier** regular breathing; **manquer de ~** to be short of breath; **avoir le ~ court** to be short-winded; **reprendre son ~** to get one's breath back, regain one's breath; **n'avoir plus de ~ , être à bout de ~** to be out of breath; *(lit)* **avoir le ~ coupé** to be winded; *(fig)* **il en a eu le ~ coupé** it took his breath away; **c'est à vous couper le ~** it's enough to take your breath away *ou* to make you gasp. (**c**) *[ventilateur, explosion]* blast. (**d**) *(vent)* puff *ou* breath of air, puff of wind. **un ~ d'air** a slight breeze. (**e**) *(inspiration)* inspiration. (**f**) ~ **au cœur** cardiac *ou* heart murmur.

souffler [sufle] (1) **1** *vi* (**a**) *[vent, personne]* to blow. **le vent soufflait en rafales** the wind was blowing in gusts. (**b**) *(respirer avec peine)* to puff (and blow). (**c**) *(se reposer)* to get one's breath back. **laisser ~ qn** to give sb a breather, let sb get his breath back. **2** *vt* (**a**) *bougie, feu* to blow out. (**b**) ~ **de la fumée au nez de qn** to blow smoke in(to) sb's face. (**c**) *(*: prendre)* to pinch *, nick ‡. (**d**) *[bombe, explosion]* to destroy. (**e**) *conseil, réponse* to whisper (*à qn* to sb). *(Théât)* ~ **son rôle à qn** to prompt sb; **ne pas ~ mot** not to breathe a word. (**f**) *(*: étonner)* to flabbergast *, stagger. (**g**) *(Tech)* ~ **le verre** to blow glass. ◆ **soufflant, e 1** *adj (*: étonnant)* staggering, stunning. **2** *nm (radiateur)* fan heater. ◆ **soufflé** *nm (Culin)* soufflé. ◆ **soufflerie** *nf [orgue, forge]* bellows; *(d'aération)* ventilating fan; *(Ind)* blowing engine; *(Aviat)* wind tunnel. ◆ **soufflet** *nm* (**a**) *[forge, appareil photo]* bellows *(pl)*; *(Rail)* vestibule; *(Couture)* gusset. (**b**) *(gifle)* slap (in the face). ◆ **souffleur, -euse** *nm, f (Théât)* prompter. ~ **de verre** glassblower.

souffrir [sufʀiʀ] (18) **1** *vi (gén, fig)* to suffer (*de* from). **il souffre beaucoup** he is suffering a great deal, he is in great pain; **faire ~ qn** *(physiquement)* to hurt sb; *(moralement)* to make sb suffer; *[événement]* to cause sb pain; **ça fait ~** it hurts, it is painful; ~ **de l'estomac** to have stomach trouble; **je souffre de le voir si affaibli** it pains *ou* grieves me to see him so weakened; **j'en souffrais pour**

lui I felt bad for him. **2** *vt* (**a**) *pertes, mépris, tourments* to endure, suffer. ~ **le martyre** to go through agonies. (**b**) *(supporter)* to bear. **il ne peut pas** ~ **les épinards/cet individu** he can't stand *ou* bear spinach/that individual. (**c**) *(permettre) retard, exception* to admit of, allow of. ~ **que** to allow *ou* permit that; **je ne souffrirai pas que mon fils en pâtisse** I will not allow my son to suffer from it.
◆ **souffrance** *nf* (**a**) *(douleur)* suffering. (**b**) **être en** ~ *[colis]* to be awaiting delivery, be held up; *[dossier]* to be pending. ◆ **souffrant, e** *adj personne* unwell. **l'humanité ~e** suffering humanity. ◆ **souffre-douleur** *nmf inv* scapegoat, underdog. ◆ **souffreteux, -euse** *adj* sickly.

soufre [sufʀ(ə)] *nm* sulphur. *(fig)* **sentir le** ~ to smack of heresy.

souhait [swɛ] *nm* wish. **les ~s de bonne année** New Year greetings; **à tes ~s!** bless you!; **tout marchait à** ~ everything went as well as one could wish *ou* went perfectly. ◆ **souhaitable** *adj* desirable. ◆ **souhaiter** (1) *vt réussite, changements* to wish for. ~ **que** to hope that; **je souhaite réussir** I hope to succeed; **je souhaiterais vous aider** I wish I could help you; ~ **à qn le bonheur** to wish sb happiness; **je vous souhaite bien des choses** all good wishes; ~ **la bonne année/bonne chance à qn** to wish sb a happy New Year/luck.

souiller [suje] (1) *vt (littér) vêtement, atmosphère* to dirty; *réputation, âme* to soil, dirty, sully, tarnish. **souillé de boue** spattered with mud; *(fig)* ~ **ses mains** to stain one's hands. ◆ **souillon** *nf* slattern, slut. ◆ **souillure** *nf (lit, fig)* stain.

souk [suk] *nm (lit)* souk. *(fig)* **c'est le** ~ **ici!** * it's like a cattle market in here.

soûl, soûle [su, sul] **1** *adj* drunk. ~ **comme un Polonais** * (as) drunk as a lord, blind drunk *. **2** *nm*: **manger tout son** ~ to eat one's fill; **elle a ri tout son** ~ she laughed till she could laugh no more.

soulager [sulaʒe] (3) **1** *vt (gén)* to relieve (*de* of); *douleur* to relieve, soothe; *conscience* to ease. **buvez, ça vous soulagera** drink this — it'll give you relief *ou* make you feel better. **2 se** ~ *vpr* to find relief; *(apaiser sa conscience)* to ease one's conscience; *(*: euph)* to relieve o.s. ◆ **soulagement** *nm* relief.

soûler [sule] (1) **1** *vt*: ~ **qn** *[personne]* to get sb drunk; *[boisson]* to make sb drunk; *[fatigue, vitesse etc]* to make sb's head spin *ou* reel; ~ **qn de** *théories, promesses* to intoxicate sb with, make sb's head spin *ou* reel with. **2 se** ~ *vpr* to get drunk. *(fig)* **se** ~ **de** *bruit, vent* to intoxicate o.s. with. ◆ **soûlard, e** ‡ *nm, f ou* ◆ **soûlaud, e** ‡ *nm, f* drunkard. ◆ **soûlerie** *nf (péj)* drunken binge.

soulever [sulve] (5) **1** *vt* (**a**) *poids* to lift (up); *poussière* to raise. **cela me soulève le cœur** it makes me feel sick; **le bateau soulevait de grosses vagues** the boat was sending up great waves. (**b**) *foule* to stir up, rouse; *enthousiasme, colère* to arouse; *protestations, applaudissements* to raise; *difficultés, problème* to raise, bring up. **2 se** ~ *vpr [malade]* to lift o.s. up; *[véhicule, couvercle, rideau]* to lift; *[vague]* to swell (up); *[rebelles]* to rise up. **à cette vue, son cœur se souleva** his stomach turned at the sight. ◆ **soulèvement** *nm (révolte)* uprising; *(Géol)* upthrust.

soulier [sulje] *nm* shoe. **~s montants** boots; **être dans ses petits ~s** to feel awkward.

souligner [suliɲe] (1) *vt (lit)* to underline; *silhouette* to emphasize; *détail, problème* to underline, stress, emphasize.

soumettre [sumɛtʀ(ə)] (56) **1** *vt* (**a**) *(asservir, astreindre) (gén)* to subject (*à* to); *rebelles* to put down, subdue, subjugate. (**b**) *idée, cas* to submit (*à* to). **2 se** ~ *vpr (gén)* to submit (*à* to). **se** ~ **à un régime** to submit *ou* subject o.s. to a diet. ◆ **soumis, e** *adj* submissive. ◆ **soumission** *nf* submission (*à* to). **faire sa** ~ to submit.

soupape [supap] *nf* valve. *(lit, fig)* ~ **de sûreté** safety valve.

soupçon [supsɔ̃] *nm* (**a**) *(suspicion)* suspicion. **avoir des ~s** to have one's suspicions; **au-dessus de tout** ~ above suspicion; **difficultés dont il n'avait pas** ~ difficulties of which he had no inkling *ou* no suspicion. (**b**) *[assaisonnement, maquillage, vulgarité]* hint, touch, suggestion; *[vin, lait]* drop. ◆ **soupçonner** (1) *vt* to suspect (*de* of). **vous ne soupçonnez pas ce que ça demande comme travail** you haven't an inkling *ou* you've no idea how much work that involves. ◆ **soupçonneux, -euse** *adj* suspicious.

soupe [sup] *nf (Culin)* soup; *(*: Ski)* porridge *. ~ **aux légumes** vegetable soup; **à la** ~! ‡ grub's up! ‡; **il est** ~ **au lait** he's very quick-tempered; ~ **populaire** *(lit)* soup kitchen; *(fig)* **être réduit à la** ~ **populaire** to be on one's uppers *.

souper [supe] **1** *nm* supper. **2** *vi* (1) to have supper. **j'en ai soupé de ces histoires!** * I'm sick and tired * of all this fuss!

soupeser [supəze] (5) *vt (lit)* to weigh in one's hands; *(fig)* to weigh up.

soupière [supjɛʀ] *nf* (soup) tureen.

soupir [supiʀ] *nm* (**a**) sigh. ~ **de soulagement** sigh of relief; **pousser un** ~ **de soulagement** to heave a sigh of relief. (**b**) *(Mus)* crotchet rest, quarter (-note) rest *(US)*. ◆ **soupirant** *nm* suitor. ◆ **soupirer** (1) *vi (lit)* to sigh. *(littér)* ~ **après qch** to sigh *ou* yearn for sth.

soupirail, *pl* **-aux** [supiʀaj, o] *nm* (small) basement window.

souple [supl(ə)] *adj membres* supple; *tige* pliable, supple; *lentilles cornéennes* soft; *caractère, discipline* flexible; *silhouette, démarche, taille* lithe. ◆ **souplesse** *nf* suppleness; pliability; flexibility; litheness. **faire qch en** ~ to do sth smoothly; **un démarrage en** ~ a smooth start.

source [suʀs(ə)] *nf* (**a**) *(point d'eau)* spring; *(début de cours d'eau)* source. ~ **thermale** thermal spring; **prendre sa** ~ **dans** to have its source in. (**b**) *(fig)* source. ~ **de** *ridicule, chaleur etc* source of; **l'argent est la** ~ **de tous nos maux** money is the root of all our ills; **tenir qch de** ~ **sûre** to have sth on good authority, get sth from a reliable source; **de** ~ **autorisée** from an official source; *(Ordin)* **langage/programme** ~ source language/program.

sourcil [suʀsi] *nm* (eye)brow. ◆ **sourciller** (1) *vi*: **il n'a pas sourcillé** he didn't turn a hair *ou* bat an eyelid. ◆ **sourcilleux, -euse** *adj (pointilleux)* finicky.

sourd, e [suʀ, suʀd(ə)] **1** *adj* (**a**) *personne* deaf. **être** ~ **comme un pot** * to be as deaf as a post; **faire la ~e oreille** to turn a deaf ear; ~ **à** *conseils* deaf to; *vacarme* oblivious to. (**b**) *son* muffled, muted; *couleur* toned-down, subdued; *(Phonétique) consonne* voiceless; *douleur* dull; *désir, inquiétude* muted, gnawing; *hostilité* veiled; *lutte, manigances* silent, hidden. **2** *nm, f* deaf person. **les ~s** the deaf; **taper comme un** ~ to bang with all one's might; **crier comme un** ~ to yell at the top of one's voice. ◆ **sourdement** *adv (avec un bruit assourdi)* dully; *(secrètement)* silently. ◆ **sourdine** *nf* mute. **jouer en** ~ to play softly *ou* quietly; *(fig)* **mettre une** ~ **à** *enthousiasme* to damp; *prétentions* to tone down. ◆ **sourd-muet,** *f* **sourde-muette 1** *adj* deaf-and-dumb. **2** *nm, f* deaf-mute.

sourdre [suʀdʀ(ə)] *vi [source]* to rise.

souriant, e [suʀjɑ̃, ɑ̃t] *adj visage* smiling; *personne* cheerful; *(fig) pensée, philosophie* benign, agreeable.

souricière [suʀisjɛʀ] *nf (lit)* mousetrap; *(fig)* trap.

sourire [suʀiʀ] **1** *nm* smile. **avec le** ~ *(accueillir qn)* with a smile; *(travailler)* cheerfully; **gardez le** ~! keep smiling!; **faire un** ~ **à qn** to give sb a smile. **2** (36) *vi* to smile (*à qn* at sb). **faire** ~ **qn** to make sb smile; **cette idée ne me sourit guère** that idea doesn't appeal to me, I don't fancy that idea *; **la chance lui souriait** luck smiled on him.

souris [suʀi] *nf* (**a**) *(Zool)* mouse. ~ **blanche** white mouse; *(fig: pour espionner)* **je voudrais bien être une petite** ~ I wish I were a fly on the wall. (**b**) (‡*: femme)* bird *, chick * *(US)*.

sournois, e [suʀnwa, waz] *adj personne, regard, air* deceitful, sly, shifty; *méthode, propos* sly, underhand. ◆ **sournoisement** *adv* deceitfully; slyly; shiftily; in an underhand manner. ◆ **sournoiserie** *nf* deceitfulness; slyness; shiftiness; underhand manner.

sous [su] **1** *prép* (**a**) *(position)* under, underneath, beneath. **s'abriter** ~ **un arbre** to shelter under *ou* underneath *ou* beneath a tree; **se promener** ~ **la pluie** to take a walk in the rain; **le pays était** ~ **la neige** the country was covered with *ou* in snow; **dormir** ~ **la tente** to sleep under canvas *ou* in a tent; ~ **terre** underground, under the ground; **cela s'est passé** ~ **nos yeux** it happened before *ou* under our very eyes; ~ **le feu de l'ennemi** under enemy fire; ~ **une apparence paisible** beneath his (*ou* her *etc*) peaceful exterior. (**b**) *(à l'époque de)* under, during; *(dans un délai de)* within. ~ **le règne de** under *ou* during the reign of; ~ **peu** shortly, before long; ~ **huitaine** within the *ou* a week. (**c**) *(cause, dépendance etc)* under. ~ **l'influence/les ordres/la direction de** under the influence/orders/management of; ~ **l'empire de la terreur** in the grip of terror; **elle est encore** ~ **le coup de l'émotion** she's still in a state of shock; **examiner une question** ~ **tous ses angles** to look at a question from every angle; ~ **certaines conditions** on certain conditions; **voir qch** ~ **un jour nouveau** to see sth in a new light; ~ **ce rapport** on that score, in this respect; **il a été peint** ~ **les traits d'un berger** he was painted as a shepherd *ou* in the guise of a shepherd; **l'affaire est** ~ **sa responsabilité** the affair is his responsibility. (**d**) *(Méd)* ~ **anesthésie** under anaesthetic; **malade** ~ **perfusion** patient on the drip. (**e**) *(Tech)* **(emballé)** ~ **plastique** plastic-wrapped; ~ **tube** in (a) tube; **(emballé)** ~ **vide** vacuum-packed.

2 *préf* (**a**) *(infériorité)* **c'est du** ~**-art** it's pseudo-art ; ~**-homme** subhuman. (**b**) *(subordination)* sub-. ~**-directeur** assistant *ou* sub-manager; ~**-chef de bureau** deputy chief clerk; ~**-officier** non-commissioned officer, N.C.O.; ~**-secrétaire d'État** Undersecretary of State; ~**-louer** to sublet; ~**-titrer** to subtitle; ~**-agence** sub-branch. (**c**) *(insuffisance)* under. ~**-alimenté** undernourished, underfed; ~**-employer** to underuse; ~**-équipé** underequipped; ~**-équipement** lack of equipment; ~**-développement** underdevelopment; **pays** ~**-développés** underdeveloped *ou* developing *ou* emergent countries; ~**-évaluer** to underestimate, underrate; ~**-peuplé** underpopulated; ~**-peuplement** underpopulation.

◆ **sous-bois** *nm inv* undergrowth. ◆ **sous-entendre** (41) *vt* to imply, infer. ◆ **sous-entendu, e** **1** *adj* implied, understood. **2** *nm* innuendo, insinuation. ◆ **sous-estimer** *vt* to underestimate, underrate. ◆ **sous-fifre** * *nm* underling. ◆ **sous-jacent, e** *adj* underlying. ◆ **sous-main** *nm inv* desk blotter. *(fig)* **en** ~**-main** secretly. ◆ **sous-marin, e** **1** *adj chasse* underwater; *faune* submarine. **2** *nm* submarine. ◆ **sous-sol** *nm* *[terre]* subsoil, substratum; *[maison]* basement. **les richesses de notre** ~**-sol** our mineral resources. ◆ **sous-tendre** *vt (Géom)* to subtend; *(fig)* to underlie. ◆ **sous-vêtement** *nm* undergarment. ~**-vêtements** underwear, undergarments.

souscrire [suskʀiʀ] (39) **1** ~ **à** *vt indir (Fin, fig)* to subscribe to. ~ **pour 100 F à qch** to subscribe 100 francs to sth. **2** *vt (Comm) billet* to sign. ◆ **souscripteur, -trice** *nm, f* subscriber (*de* to). ◆ **souscription** *nf* subscription. **ouvrir une** ~ **en faveur de...** to start a fund in aid of...

soussigné, e [susiɲe] *adj, nm, f* undersigned. **je** ~ **X déclare que...** I the undersigned, X, certify that...

soustraire [sustʀɛʀ] (50) **1** *vt (défalquer)* to subtract, take away (*de* from); *(dérober)* to remove, abstract; *(cacher)* to conceal, shield (*à* from). **2** **se** ~ *vpr*: **se** ~ **à** *devoir* to shirk; *autorité* to elude, escape from; *curiosité* to conceal o.s. from. ◆ **soustraction** *nf (Math)* subtraction; *(vol)* removal, abstraction.

soutane [sutan] *nf* cassock, soutane.

soute [sut] *nf [navire]* hold. ~ **(à bagages)** baggage hold; ~ **à charbon** coal-bunker; ~ **à mazout** oil-tank.

souteneur [sutnœʀ] *nm* procurer.

soutenir [sutniʀ] (22) **1** *vt* (**a**) *(physiquement)* to support, hold up; *[médicament etc]* to sustain. (**b**) *parti, candidat* to support, back; *famille* to support. *(moralement)* **il m'a beaucoup soutenu** he was a real support *ou* prop to me; **elle soutient les enfants contre leur père** she takes the children's part *ou* she stands up for the children against their father. (**c**) *attention, effort* to keep up, sustain; *réputation* to keep up, maintain. (**d**) *assaut, choc* to stand up to, withstand; *regard* to bear, support. ~ **la comparaison avec** to bear *ou* stand comparison with. (**e**) *opinion* to uphold, support. *(Univ)* ~ **sa thèse** to attend one's viva; ~ **que** to maintain that. **2 se** ~ *vpr (sur ses jambes)* to hold o.s. up, support o.s.; *(s'entraider)* to stand by each other. *(fig)* **ça peut se** ~ it's a tenable point of view. ◆ **soutenu, e** *adj style* elevated; *effort* sustained, unflagging; *marché* buoyant.

souterrain, e [sutɛʀɛ̃, ɛn] **1** *adj* underground, subterranean. **2** *nm* underground *ou* subterranean passage.

soutien [sutjɛ̃] *nm* support. *(Scol)* **cours de** ~ remedial course; ~ **en français** extra teaching in French. ◆ **soutien-gorge,** *pl* **soutiens-gorge** *nm* bra.

soutirer [sutiʀe] (1) *vt* (**a**) ~ **qch à qn** *argent* to squeeze *ou* get sth out of sb; *promesse* to extract sth from sb. (**b**) *vin* to decant.

souvenir [suvniʀ] **1** *nm* (**a**) *(réminiscence)* memory, recollection; *(fait de se souvenir)* recollection, remembrance. **mauvais** ~ bad memory; **vague** ~ vague *ou* dim recollection; ~**s d'enfance** childhood memories; **avoir le** ~ **de qch** to have a memory of sth, remember sth; **je n'ai pas** ~ **d'avoir...** I have no recollection of having...; **en** ~ **de** *personne disparue* in memory *ou* remembrance of; *occasion* in memory of. (**b**) *(mémoire)* memory. (**c**) *(objet)* keepsake, memento; *(trace, pour touristes)* souvenir. **magasin de** ~**s** souvenir shop. (**d**) *(formules de politesse)* **amical** ~ yours (ever); **mon bon** ~ **à X** remember me to X, (my) regards to X.

2 se ~ (22) *vpr*: **se** ~ **de qn** to remember sb; **se** ~ **de qch/d'avoir fait qch/que...** to remember *ou* recall *ou* recollect sth/doing sth/that...; **il s'en souviendra!** he won't forget it!; **souvenez-vous qu'il est très puissant** bear in mind *ou* remember that he is very powerful; **souviens-toi de ta promesse!** remember your promise!; **tu m'as fait me** ~ **que...** you have reminded me that...

3 *vb impers (littér)* **il me souvient d'avoir fait** I recollect *ou* recall *ou* remember having done.

souvent [suvɑ̃] *adv* often. **le plus** ~ more often than not; **peu** ~ seldom.

souverain, e [suvʀɛ̃, ɛn] **1** *adj (Pol)* sovereign; *juge, mépris* supreme. **le ~ pontife** the Supreme Pontiff; **remède ~ contre qch** sovereign remedy against sth. **2** *nm, f (Pol, fig)* sovereign. ◆ **souverainement** *adv (intensément)* supremely, intensely; *(en tant que souverain)* with sovereign power. ◆ **souveraineté** *nf* sovereignty.

soviet [sɔvjɛt] *nm* soviet. **le S~ suprême** the Supreme Soviet; **les S~s** the Soviets. ◆ **soviétique** **1** *adj* Soviet. **2** *nmf*: **S~** Soviet citizen.

soyeux, -euse [swajø, øz] **1** *adj* silky. **2** *nm* (Lyons) silk manufacturer.

spacieux, -euse [spasjø, øz] *adj* spacious, roomy.

sparadrap [spaʀadʀa] *nm* adhesive *ou* sticking plaster, band-aid ® *(US)*.

spartiate [spaʀsjat] *adj*, **S~** *nmf* Spartan.

spasme [spasm(ə)] *nm* spasm. ◆ **spasmodique** *adj* spasmodic.

spatial, e, *mpl* **-aux** [spasjal, o] *adj* spatial; *(Espace)* space.

spationaute [spasjɔnot] *nmf* astronaut, spaceman, spacewoman.

spatule [spatyl] *nf* spatula.

speaker [spikœʀ] *nm*, **speakerine** [spikʀin] *nf (Rad, TV) (annonceur)* announcer; *(journaliste)* newscaster, newsreader.

spécial, e, *mpl* **-aux** [spesjal, o] *adj (gén)* special; *(bizarre)* peculiar. ◆ **spécialement** *adv (particulièrement)* especially, particularly; *(exprès)* specially.

spécialiser (se) [spesjalize] (1) *vpr* to specialize *(dans* in). ◆ **spécialisation** *nf* specialization. ◆ **spécialisé, e** *adj travail, personne* specialized. **être ~ dans** *[personne]* to be a specialist in; *[firme]* to specialize in. ◆ **spécialiste** *nmf (gén, Méd)* specialist. ◆ **spécialité** *nf (gén, Culin)* speciality; *(Univ etc: branche)* specialism, special field. **il a la ~ de faire...** * he has a special *ou* particular knack of doing...

spécieux, -euse [spesjø, øz] *adj* specious.

spécifier [spesifje] (7) *vt* to specify, state. ◆ **spécification** *nf* specification. ◆ **spécificité** *nf* specificity. ◆ **spécifique** *adj* specific. ◆ **spécifiquement** *adv (tout exprès)* specifically; *(typiquement)* typically.

spécimen [spesimɛn] *nm (gén)* specimen; *(publicitaire)* specimen copy, sample copy.

spectacle [spɛktakl(ə)] *nm* (**a**) *(vue)* sight; *(grandiose)* spectacle. **au ~ de** at the sight of; *(péj)* **se donner en ~ (à qn)** to make a spectacle *ou* an exhibition of o.s. (in front of sb); **assister à un ~ imprévu** to see a happening. (**b**) *(Ciné, Théât) (représentation)* show. *(branche)* **le ~** show business, entertainment; *(rubrique)* **'~s'** 'entertainment'; **aller au ~** to go to a show. ◆ **spectaculaire** *adj* spectacular, dramatic. ◆ **spectateur, -trice** *nm, f [événement]* onlooker, witness; *(Sport)* spectator; *(Ciné, Théât)* member of the audience. **les ~s** the audience.

spectre [spɛktʀ(ə)] *nm (fantôme)* ghost; *(fig)* spectre; *(Phys)* spectrum. ◆ **spectral, e,** *mpl* **-aux** *adj (gén)* spectral. ◆ **spectroscopie** *nf* spectroscopy.

spéculer [spekyle] (1) *vi (Philos)* to speculate *(sur* on, about); *(Fin)* to speculate *(sur* in). *(fig: tabler sur)* **~ sur** to bank on, rely on. ◆ **spéculateur, -trice** *nm, f* speculator. ◆ **spéculatif, -ive** *adj (Fin, Philos)* speculative. ◆ **spéculation** *nf* speculation.

spéléologie [speleɔlɔʒi] *nf (étude)* speleology; *(exploration)* potholing. ◆ **spéléologique** *adj* speleological; potholing. ◆ **spéléologue** *nmf* speleologist; potholer.

sperme [spɛʀm(ə)] *nm* semen, sperm.

sphère [sfɛʀ] *nf (Astron, fig)* sphere. ◆ **sphérique** *adj* spherical.

sphincter [sfɛ̃ktɛʀ] *nm* sphincter.

sphinx [sfɛ̃ks] *nm* sphinx.

spirale [spiʀal] *nf* spiral.

spirite [spiʀit] *adj, nmf* spiritualist. ◆ **spiritisme** *nm* spiritualism, spiritism. ◆ **spiritualité** *nf* spirituality.

spirituel, -elle [spiʀitɥɛl] *adj* (**a**) *(fin)* witty. (**b**) *(Philos, Rel, gén)* spiritual. **concert ~** concert of sacred music. ◆ **spirituellement** *adv* wittily; spiritually.

spiritueux [spiʀitɥø] *nm (alcool)* spirit.

splendeur [splɑ̃dœʀ] *nf (gén)* splendour. **c'est une ~** it is quite magnificent *ou* splendid; *(iro)* **dans toute sa ~** in all its splendour *ou* glory. ◆ **splendide** *adj* splendid, magnificent. ◆ **splendidement** *adv* splendidly, magnificently.

spolier [spɔlje] (7) *vt* to despoil. ◆ **spoliation** *nf* despoilment *(de* of).

spongieux, -euse [spɔ̃ʒjø, øz] *adj* spongy.

sponsor [spɔ̃sɔʀ] *nm* sponsor.

spontané, e [spɔ̃tane] *adj* spontaneous. ◆ **spontanéité** *nf* spontaneity. ◆ **spontanément** *adv* spontaneously.

sporadique [spɔʀadik] *adj* sporadic. ◆ **sporadiquement** *adv* sporadically.

sport [spɔʀ] **1** *nm* sport. **~s d'équipe** team sports; **faire du ~** to do sport; **aller aux ~s d'hiver** to go on a winter sports holiday, go winter sporting; **voiture** *etc* **de ~** sports car *etc*; **il va y avoir du ~!** * we'll see some fun! * *ou* action! * **2** *adj inv vêtement* casual. ◆ **sportif, -ive** **1** *adj épreuve, résultats* sports; *pêche* competitive; *jeunesse, allure* athletic; *mentalité* sporting, sportsmanlike. **2** *nm* sportsman. **3** *nf* sportswoman. ◆ **sportivement** *adv* sportingly. ◆ **sportivité** *nf* sportsmanship.

spot [spɔt] *nm (Phys)* light spot; *(Théât etc)* spotlight, spot. **~ (publicitaire)** commercial, advert *.

square [skwaʀ] *nm* public garden(s).

squash [skwaʃ] *nm* squash.

squelette [skəlɛt] *nm (lit, fig)* skeleton. ◆ **squelettique** *adj personne, arbre* scrawny, skeleton-like; *exposé* sketchy, skimpy; *(Anat)* skeletal; *effectifs* minimal. **d'une maigreur ~** all skin and bone.

Sri Lanka [sʀilɑ̃ka] *nf* Sri Lanka. ◆ **sri-lankais, e** *adj*, **Sri-Lankais(e)** *nm(f)* Sri-Lankan.

stable [stabl(ə)] *adj (gén)* stable; *position, échelle* steady. ◆ **stabilisateur, -trice** **1** *adj* stabilizing. **2** *nm [véhicule]* anti-roll device; *[navire, vélo]* stabilizer; *[avion] (horizontal)* tailplane; *(vertical)* fixed fin; *(Chim)* stabilizer. ◆ **stabilisation** *nf* stabilization. ◆ **stabiliser** *vt*, **se ~** *vpr* (1) to stabilize. ◆ **stabilité** *nf* stability.

stade [stad] *nm* (**a**) *(sportif)* stadium. (**b**) *(période)* stage.

staff [staf] *nm* (**a**) *(personnel)* staff. (**b**) *(plâtre)* staff.

stage [staʒ] *nm (période)* training period; *(cours)* training course. **~ de formation (professionnelle)** vocational (training) course; **faire un ~** to go on a (training) course; *[employé]* **faire un ~ d'informatique** *(gén)* to go on a computing course; *(pris sur le temps de travail)* to have in-service *ou* in-house training in computing. ◆ **stagiaire** *nmf, adj* trainee.

stagner [stagne] (1) *vi (lit, fig)* to stagnate. ◆ **stagnant, e** *adj* stagnant. ◆ **stagnation** *nf* stagnation.

stalactite [stalaktit] *nf* stalactite.

stalagmite [stalagmit] *nf* stalagmite.

stand [stɑ̃d] *nm [exposition]* stand; *[foire]* stall. **~ (de tir)** *(Sport)* shooting range; *(Mil)* firing range; **~ de ravitaillement** pit.

standard [stɑ̃daʀ] **1** *nm (norme)* standard; *(Téléc)* switchboard. ~ **de vie** standard of living. **2** *adj inv* standard. ◆ **standardisation** *nf* standardization. ◆ **standardiser** (1) *vt* to standardize. ◆ **standardiste** *nmf* switchboard operator.

standing [stɑ̃diŋ] *nm* standing. **immeuble de grand** ~ block of luxury flats *ou* apartments *(US)*.

star [staʀ] *nf (Ciné)* star. ◆ **starlette** *nf* starlet.

starter [staʀtɛʀ] *nm (Aut)* choke. **mettre le** ~ to pull the choke out.

station [stɑsjɔ̃] *nf* (**a**) ~ **(de métro)** (underground *ou* subway *(US)*) station; ~ **(d'autobus)** (bus) stop; ~ **(de chemin de fer)** halt; ~ **de taxis** taxi rank. (**b**) *(poste, lieu)* station. ~ **orbitale** orbiting station; ~ **de radio** radio station, network; ~**-service** service *ou* petrol *ou* filling station, gas station *(US)*; ~ **spatiale** space station. (**c**) *(de vacances)* resort. ~ **balnéaire** sea *ou* seaside resort; ~ **thermale** thermal spa. (**d**) *(posture)* posture, stance. **la** ~ **debout** an upright posture *ou* stance. (**e**) *(halte)* stop. ◆ **stationnaire** *adj* stationary.

stationner [stasjɔne] (1) *vi (être garé)* to be parked; *(se garer)* to park. ◆ **stationnement** *nm (Aut)* parking. '~ **interdit**' 'no parking'; *(sur autoroute)* 'no stopping'.

statique [statik] *adj* static. ◆ **statiquement** *adv* statically.

statistique [statistik] **1** *nf (science)* statistics *(sg)*. *(données)* **des** ~**s** statistics; **une** ~ a statistic. **2** *adj* statistical. ◆ **statisticien, -ienne** *nm, f* statistician. ◆ **statistiquement** *adv* statistically.

statue [staty] *nf* statue. ◆ **statuette** *nf* statuette.

statuer [statɥe] (1) *vi* to give a verdict. ~ **sur** to rule on; ~ **sur le cas de qn** to decide sb's case.

statu quo [statykwo] *nm* status quo.

stature [statyʀ] *nf* stature.

statut [staty] *nm (position)* status. *(règlement)* ~**s** statutes. ◆ **statutaire** *adj* statutory. ◆ **statutairement** *adv* in accordance with the statutes *ou* regulations, statutoriiy.

stencil [stɛnsil] *nm (Typ)* stencil.

sténo(dactylo) [steno(daktilo)] *nf (personne)* shorthand typist; *(travail)* shorthand typing. ◆ **sténo(graphie)** *nf* shorthand. **prendre une lettre en** ~ to take a letter (down) in shorthand. ◆ **sténographier** (7) *vt* to take down in shorthand. ◆ **sténographique** *adj* shorthand.

stentor [stɑ̃tɔʀ] *nm*: **une voix de** ~ a stentorian voice.

steppe [stɛp] *nf* steppe.

stère [stɛʀ] *nm* stere.

stéréo [steʀeo] *nf, adj* stereo. ◆ **stéréophonie** *nf* stereophony. ◆ **stéréophonique** *adj* stereophonic.

stéréotype [steʀeɔtip] *nm (lit, fig)* stereotype. ◆ **stéréotypé, e** *adj* stereotyped.

stérile [steʀil] *adj (gén)* sterile; *terre* barren; *discussion, effort* fruitless. ◆ **stérilet** *nm* coil, loop. ◆ **stérilisateur** *nm* sterilizer. ◆ **stérilisation** *nf* sterilization. ◆ **stériliser** (1) *vt* to sterilize. ◆ **stérilité** *nf* sterility; barrenness; fruitlessness.

sternum [stɛʀnɔm] *nm* breastbone, sternum.

stéthoscope [stetɔskɔp] *nm* stethoscope.

steward [stiwaʀt] *nm (Aviat)* steward, flight attendant.

stick [stik] *nm [colle etc]* stick. **déodorant en** ~ stick deodorant.

stigmate [stigmat] *nm (marque)* mark. *(Rel)* ~**s** stigmata. ◆ **stigmatisation** *nf* stigmatization. ◆ **stigmatiser** (1) *vt* to stigmatize.

stimuler [stimyle] (1) *vt* to stimulate. ◆ **stimulant, e** **1** *adj* stimulating. **2** *nm (physique)* stimulant; *(intellectuel)* stimulus, spur, incentive. ◆ **stimulateur** *nm*: ~ **cardiaque** pacemaker. ◆ **stimulation** *nf* stimulation. ◆ **stimulus,** *pl* **stimuli** *nm* stimulus.

stipuler [stipyle] (1) *vt* to stipulate. ◆ **stipulation** *nf* stipulation.

stock [stɔk] *nm* stock. ◆ **stockage** *nm (Comm)* stocking. **le** ~ **des déchets radio-actifs** the storage *ou* stockpiling of nuclear waste. ◆ **stocker** (1) *vt (Comm)* to stock; *(péj)* to stockpile.

Stockholm [stɔkɔlm] *n* Stockholm.

stoïque [stɔik] *adj* stoical, stoic. ◆ **stoïquement** *adv* stoically.

stomacal, e, *mpl* **-aux** [stɔmakal, o] *adj* stomach, gastric.

stop [stɔp] **1** *excl* stop. **2** *nm (panneau)* stop *ou* halt sign; *(feu arrière)* brake-light. **faire du** ~ * to hitch-hike, hitch *; **faire le tour de l'Europe en** ~ to hitch round Europe. ◆ **stoppage** *nm* invisible mending. ◆ **stopper** (1) **1** *vti* to halt, stop. **2** *vt (Couture) bas* to mend. **faire** ~ **un vêtement** to get a garment (invisibly) mended. ◆ **stoppeur, -euse** *nm, f* (**a**) *(Couture)* invisible mender. (**b**) *(*: auto-stoppeur)* hitchhiker.

store [stɔʀ] *nm [fenêtre]* blind, shade; *(voilage)* net curtain; *[magasin]* awning, shade. ~ **vénitien** Venetian blind.

strabisme [stʀabism(ə)] *nm* squint.

strapontin [stʀapɔ̃tɛ̃] *nm* jump seat, foldaway seat.

Strasbourg [stʀazbuʀ] *n* Strasbourg.

stratagème [stʀataʒɛm] *nm* stratagem.

strate [stʀat] *nf* stratum.

stratège [stʀatɛʒ] *nm (Mil, fig)* strategist. ◆ **stratégie** *nf* strategy. ◆ **stratégique** *adj* strategic.

stratifier [stʀatifje] (7) *vt* to stratify. ◆ **stratification** *nf* stratification.

stratosphère [stʀatɔsfɛʀ] *nf* stratosphere.

stress [stʀɛs] *nm (gén, Méd)* stress. ◆ **stressant, e** *adj situation* stress-inducing, stressful. ◆ **stresser** (1) *vt* to cause stress in. **la femme stressée d'aujourd'hui** today's stress-ridden woman; **cette réunion m'a complètement stressé** this meeting made me feel very tense.

strict, e [stʀikt(ə)] *adj discipline, maître, sens* strict; *costume* plain; *interprétation* literal. **c'est la** ~**e vérité** it is the plain *ou* simple truth; **c'est son droit le plus** ~ it is his most basic right; **le** ~ **nécessaire/minimum** the bare essentials/minimum; **dans la plus** ~**e intimité** strictly in private. ◆ **strictement** *adv* strictly; plainly.

strident, e [stʀidɑ̃, ɑ̃t] *adj* shrill, strident.

strie [stʀi] *nf (de couleur)* streak; *(en relief)* ridge; *(en creux)* groove; *(Anat, Géol)* stria. ◆ **strier** (7) *vt* to streak; to ridge; to striate.

stroboscope [stʀɔbɔskɔp] *nm* stroboscope. ◆ **stroboscopique** *adj* stroboscopic, strobe. **lumière** ~ strobe lighting.

strophe [stʀɔf] *nf* verse, stanza.

structure [stʀyktyʀ] *nf* structure. ~**s d'accueil** reception facilities. ◆ **structural, e,** *mpl* **-aux** *adj* structural. ◆ **structuralement** *adv* structurally. ◆ **structurel, -elle** *adj* structural. ◆ **structurer** (1) *vt* to structure.

stuc [styk] *nm* stucco.

studieux, -euse [stydjø, øz] *adj personne* studious; *vacances* study. ◆ **studieusement** *adv* studiously.

studio [stydjo] *nm (d'artiste, de prise de vues)* studio; *(auditorium)* film theatre, arts cinema; *(d'habitation)* bedsitter, studio apartment *(US)*. ~ **à louer** bedsitter to let, studio apartment for rent *(US)*.

stupéfaire [stypefɛʀ] (60) *vt* to stun, astound, dumbfound. ◆ **stupéfaction** *nf* stupefaction, amazement. ◆ **stupéfait, e** *adj* stunned, dumbfounded, astounded (*de qch* at sth).

stupéfier [stypefje] (7) *vt* to stun, stagger, astound. ◆ **stupéfiant, e 1** *adj* stunning, astounding, staggering. **2** *nm* drug, narcotic. ◆ **stupeur** *nf* astonishment, amazement; *(Méd)* stupor.

stupide [stypid] *adj (inepte)* stupid, silly, foolish; *(hébété)* stunned. ◆ **stupidement** *adv* stupidly. ◆ **stupidité** *nf* stupidity; *(parole, acte)* stupid *ou* silly *ou* foolish remark (*ou* action).

style [stil] *nm* **(a)** *(genre, classe)* style. **meubles de** ~ period furniture. **(b)** *(pointe)* style, stylus. **(c)** *(Ling)* ~ **direct/indirect** direct/indirect *ou* reported speech; ~ **journalistique** journalistic style, journalese *(péj)*; ~ **télégraphique** telegraphese. ◆ **styler** (1) *vt domestique etc* to train. **(bien) stylé** well-trained. ◆ **stylisation** *nf* stylization. ◆ **styliser** (1) *vt* to stylize.

stylo [stilo] *nm* pen. ~**(-bille** *ou* **à bille)** ball-point (pen); ~ **(à encre)** (fountain) pen.

su [sy] *nm*: **au** ~ **de** with the knowledge of.

suaire [sɥɛʀ] *nm (littér)* shroud.

suant, e ⁑ [sɥɑ̃, ɑ̃t] *adj (ennuyeux)* deadly (dull) *.

suave [sɥav] *adj personne, manières* suave, smooth; *musique, parfum* sweet; *couleurs* mellow; *formes* smooth. ◆ **suavement** *adv s'exprimer* suavely. ◆ **suavité** *nf* suavity; smoothness; sweetness; mellowness.

subalterne [sybaltɛʀn(ə)] **1** *adj rôle* subordinate, subsidiary; *employé, poste* junior. **officier** ~ subaltern. **2** *nmf* subordinate, inferior.

subconscient, e [sypkɔ̃sjɑ̃, ɑ̃t] *adj, nm* subconscious.

subdiviser [sybdivize] (1) **1** *vt* to subdivide (*en* into). **2 se** ~ *vpr* to be subdivided (*en* into). ◆ **subdivision** *nf* subdivision.

subir [sybiʀ] (2) *vt attaque, critique* to undergo, suffer, be subjected to; *perte, défaite* to suffer, sustain; *corvée, importun* to put up with, endure; *examen, modifications* to undergo, go through; *peine de prison, opération* to undergo; *charme* to be subject to, be under the influence of; *influence* to be under. ~ **les effets de qch** to experience the effects of sth; **faire** ~ **à qn** *torture* to subject sb to; *défaite* to inflict upon sb; *influence* to exert over sb; *examen* to put sb through.

subit, e [sybi, it] *adj* sudden. ◆ **subitement** *adv* suddenly, all of a sudden.

subjectif, -ive [sybʒɛktif, iv] *adj* subjective. ◆ **subjectivement** *adv* subjectively. ◆ **subjectivité** *nf* subjectivity.

subjonctif, -ive [sybʒɔ̃ktif, iv] *adj, nm* subjunctive.

subjuguer [sybʒyge] (1) *vt auditoire* to captivate, enthrall; *esprits* to render powerless; *vaincu* to subjugate.

sublime [syblim] *adj* sublime. ◆ **sublimation** *nf* sublimation. ◆ **sublimement** *adv* sublimely. ◆ **sublimer** (1) *vt* to sublimate.

submerger [sybmɛʀʒe] (3) *vt terres* to flood, submerge; *barque* to submerge. ~ **qn** *[foule]* to engulf sb; *[ennemi, émotion]* to overcome *ou* overwhelm sb; **submergé de** *travail, commandes* snowed under *ou* swamped with. ◆ **submersible** *adj, nm* submarine. ◆ **submersion** *nf* flooding, submersion.

subordonner [sybɔʀdɔne] (1) *vt*: ~ **qn/qch à** to subordinate sb/sth to; *(faire dépendre de)* **leur départ est subordonné au résultat des examens** their departure is subject to *ou* depends on the exam results. ◆ **subordination** *nf* subordination. ◆ **subordonné, e 1** *adj* subordinate (*à* to). *(Ling)* **proposition** ~**e** dependent *ou* subordinate clause. **2** *nm, f* subordinate. **3** *nf (Ling)* dependent *ou* subordinate clause.

suborner [sybɔʀne] (1) *vt témoins* to bribe; *jeune fille* to seduce.

subreptice [sybʀɛptis] *adj* surreptitious. ◆ **subrepticement** *adv* surreptitiously.

subside [sypsid] *nm* grant. ~**s** allowance.

subsidiaire [sypsidjɛʀ] *adj* subsidiary. ◆ **subsidiairement** *adv* subsidiarily.

subsistance [sybzistɑ̃s] *nf* subsistence. **assurer la** ~ **de qn** to support *ou* maintain *ou* keep sb; **ma** ~ **était assurée** I had enough to live on; **moyen de** ~ means of subsistence. ◆ **subsistant, e** *adj* remaining. ◆ **subsister** (1) *vi (ne pas périr)* to live on, survive; *(se nourrir)* to subsist; *[doute, vestiges]* to remain, subsist.

substance [sypstɑ̃s] *nf* substance. **en** ~ in substance; ~ **alimentaire** food. ◆ **substantiel, -elle** *adj* substantial. ◆ **substantiellement** *adv* substantially.

substantif [sypstɑ̃tif] *nm* noun, substantive.

substituer [sypstitɥe] (1) **1** *vt*: ~ **qch/qn à** to substitute sth/sb for. **2 se** ~ *vpr*: **se** ~ **à qn** *(en évinçant)* to substitute o.s. for sb; *(en le représentant)* to substitute for sb. ◆ **substitut** *nm (magistrat)* deputy public prosecutor; *(succédané)* substitute (*de* for). *(Psych)* ~ **maternel** surrogate mother. ◆ **substitution** *nf (intentionnelle)* substitution (*à* for); *(accidentelle)* mix-up (*de* of, in).

subterfuge [syptɛʀfyʒ] *nm* subterfuge.

subtil, e [syptil] *adj (sagace) esprit, réponse* subtle; *distinction* subtle, fine, nice. ◆ **subtilement** *adv* subtly. ◆ **subtilité** *nf* subtlety; nicety.

subtiliser [syptilize] (1) *vt* to spirit away *(hum)*. ◆ **subtilisation** *nf* spiriting away.

subvenir [sybvəniʀ] (22) ~ **à** *vt indir besoins* to provide for, meet; *frais* to meet, cover. ~ **à ses besoins** to support o.s.

subvention [sybvɑ̃sjɔ̃] *nf (gén)* grant; *(aux agriculteurs, à un théâtre)* subsidy. ◆ **subventionner** (1) *vt* to grant funds to; to subsidize.

subversion [sybvɛʀsjɔ̃] *nf* subversion. ◆ **subversif, -ive** *adj* subversive.

suc [syk] *nm (gén, Anat)* juice.

succédané [syksedane] *nm* substitute (*de* for).

succéder [syksede] (6) **1** ~ **à** *vt indir (gén)* to succeed, follow; *roi* to succeed; *titres* to succeed to. **2 se** ~ *vpr* to follow *ou* succeed one another.

succès [syksɛ] *nm (gén)* success; *(livre)* bestseller; *(disque)* hit; *(film, pièce)* box-office success, hit. *(conquête)* ~ **(féminin)** conquest; **avoir du** ~ to be a success, be successful (*auprès de* with); **avec** ~ successfully; **sans** ~ unsuccessfully, without success; **à** ~ *auteur* successful; **film à** ~ hit film *, blockbuster, box-office success; **chanson à** ~ hit (song).

succession [syksesjɔ̃] *nf (gén)* succession; *(Jur: patrimoine)* estate, inheritance. **prendre la** ~ **de** *directeur* to succeed, take over from; *roi* to succeed; *maison de commerce* to take over. ◆ **successeur** *nm* successor. ◆ **successif, -ive** *adj* successive. ◆ **successivement** *adv* successively.

succinct, e [syksɛ̃, ɛ̃t] *adj écrit* succinct; *repas* frugal. **soyez** ~ be brief. ◆ **succinctement** *adv* succinctly; frugally.

succion [syksjɔ̃] *nf* suction. **bruit de** ~ sucking noise.

succomber [sykɔ̃be] (1) *vi (mourir)* to die, succumb. ~ **sous le nombre** to be overcome by numbers; ~ **à** *tentation, fatigue etc* to succumb to.

succulent, e [sykylɑ̃, ɑ̃t] *adj* delicious, succulent.

succursale [sykyʀsal] *nf (Comm)* branch.

sucer [syse] (3) *vt* to suck. ◆ **sucette** *nf (bonbon)* lollipop; *(tétine)* dummy.

sucre [sykʀ(ə)] *nm (substance)* sugar; *(morceau)* lump of sugar. **cet enfant n'est pas en** ~ **quand même!** for goodness sake, the child won't break!; **être tout** ~ **tout miel** to be all sweetness and light;

~ **de canne** cane sugar; ~ **cristallisé** (coarse) granulated sugar; ~ **en morceaux** lump sugar; ~ **d'orge** *(substance)* barley sugar; *(bâton)* stick of barley sugar; ~ **en poudre,** ~ **semoule** caster sugar. ◆ **sucré, e** **1** *adj fruit, saveur* sweet; *jus de fruits* sweetened; *(péj) ton* sugary, honeyed. **trop** ~ too sweet; **bien** ~ well-sweetened; **non** ~ unsweetened. **2** *nm*: **le** ~ sweet things. ◆ **sucrer** (1) **1** *vt* (**a**) *boisson* to sugar, put sugar in, sweeten. ~ **les fraises** ‡ to be a bit doddery *. (**b**) *(‡: supprimer) argent, avantage* to stop. **2 se** ~ *vpr (lit)* to help o.s. to sugar; *(‡ fig: s'enrichir)* to line one's pocket(s) *. ◆ **sucrerie** *nf* (**a**) ~**s** sweets, sweet things; **aimer les** ~**s** to have a sweet tooth. (**b**) *(usine)* sugar house; *(raffinerie)* sugar refinery. ◆ **sucrier, -ière** **1** *adj industrie, betterave* sugar; *région* sugar-producing. **2** *nm* (**a**) *(récipient)* sugar basin *ou* bowl. ~ **(verseur)** sugar shaker. (**b**) *(industriel)* sugar producer.

sud [syd] **1** *nm* south. **vent du** ~ south(erly) wind; **regarder vers le** ~ to look south(wards) *ou* towards the south; **au** ~ **de** (to the) south of; **l'Europe du** ~ Southern Europe; **le S**~ **de la France** the South of France. **2** *adj inv région, partie* southern; *entrée* south; *côte* south(ern); *côté* south(ward); *direction* southward, southerly *(Mét)*. **3** : ~**-africain** *etc* South African *etc*; ~**-est/-ouest** south-east/-west. ◆ **sudiste** *(Hist US)* **1** *nmf* Southerner. **2** *adj* Southern.

Suède [sɥɛd] **1** *nf* Sweden. **2** *nm (peau)* **s** ~ suede. ◆ **suédine** *nf* suedette. ◆ **suédois, e** **1** *adj, nm* Swedish. **2** *nm(f)*: **S**~**(e)** Swede.

suer [sɥe] (1) **1** *vi (transpirer)* to sweat; *(fig: peiner)* to sweat * (*sur* over). ~ **à grosses gouttes** to sweat profusely; **faire** ~ **qn** *(lit)* to make sb sweat; **tu me fais** ~ * you're a pain (in the neck) *; **on se fait** ~ **ici** * what a drag it is here *. **2** *vt sueur* to sweat; *humidité* to ooze; *pauvreté* to exude. ~ **sang et eau pour faire qch** to sweat blood to get sth done. ◆ **suée** * *nf* sweat. **prendre une bonne** ~ to work up a good sweat *; **quelle** ~**!** what a drag! * *ou* pain! * ◆ **sueur** *nf* sweat. **en** ~ in a sweat, sweating; **j'en avais des** ~**s froides** I was in a cold sweat.

suffire [syfiʀ] (37) **1** *vi* to be enough, be sufficient, suffice. ~ **à** *besoins* to meet; *personne* to be enough for; **5 hommes me suffisent (pour ce travail)** 5 men will do me *ou* will be sufficient (for me) (for this job); **il ne peut** ~ **à tout** he can't manage (to do) everything, he can't cope with everything; **ça suffit** that's enough, that'll do; **ça ne te suffit pas de l'avoir cassé?** isn't it enough for you to have broken it?
2 *vb impers:* **il suffit de s'inscrire pour devenir membre** enrolling is enough *ou* sufficient to become a member, you just *ou* only have to enrol to become a member; **il suffit d'un rien pour l'inquiéter** it only takes the smallest thing to worry him, the smallest thing is enough to worry him; **il suffit d'une fois** once is enough.
3 se ~ *vpr (Écon)* **se** ~ **(à soi-même)** to be self-sufficient.
◆ **suffisamment** *adv* sufficiently, enough. ~ **fort** sufficiently strong, strong enough; **être** ~ **vêtu** to have sufficient *ou* enough clothes on, be adequately dressed; ~ **de nourriture** sufficient *ou* enough food. ◆ **suffisance** *nf* (**a**) *(vanité)* self-importance, bumptiousness. (**b**) **avoir qch en** ~ to have sth in plenty, have a sufficiency of sth. ◆ **suffisant, e** *adj* (**a**) *(adéquat)* sufficient; *(Scol) résultats* satisfactory. **c'est** ~ **pour qu'il se mette en colère** it's enough to make him lose his temper; **je n'ai pas la place** ~**e** I haven't got sufficient *ou* enough room; **500 F, c'est amplement** ~ 500 francs is more than enough. (**b**) *(prétentieux)* self-important, bumptious. **faire le** ~ to give o.s. airs and graces.

suffixe [syfiks(ə)] *nm* suffix.

suffoquer [syfɔke] (1) **1** *vi (lit)* to choke, suffocate, stifle (*de* with). *(fig)* ~ **de** to choke with. **2** *vt [fumée]* to suffocate, choke, stifle; *[colère, joie]* to choke; *(étonner) [nouvelle]* to stagger. ◆ **suffocant, e** *adj* suffocating, stifling; staggering. ◆ **suffocation** *nf (sensation)* suffocating feeling.

suffrage [syfʀaʒ] *nm (Pol: voix)* vote; *(approbation)* approval, approbation. ~**s exprimés** valid votes; ~ **universel** universal suffrage *ou* franchise; **le parti obtiendra peu de/beaucoup de** ~**s** the party will poll badly/heavily; **remporter tous les** ~**s** to meet with universal approval *ou* approbation.

suggérer [sygʒeʀe] (6) *vt (gén)* to suggest; *solution* to suggest, put forward. **j'ai suggéré d'aller** *ou* **que nous allions au cinéma** I suggested going *ou* that we went to the cinema.

suggestion [sygʒɛstjɔ̃] *nf* suggestion. ◆ **suggestif, -ive** *adj* suggestive.

suicide [sɥisid] *nm (lit, fig)* suicide. ◆ **suicidaire** *adj (lit, fig)* suicidal. ◆ **suicidé, e** *nm, f (personne)* suicide. ◆ **se suicider** (1) *vpr* to commit suicide.

suie [sɥi] *nf* soot.

suif [sɥif] *nm* tallow.

suinter [sɥɛ̃te] (1) *vi* to ooze. ◆ **suintement** *nm*: ~**(s)** oozing.

Suisse [sɥis] **1** *nf (pays)* Switzerland. ~ **romande** French-speaking Switzerland. **2** *nmf (habitant)* Swiss. **3** *adj*: **s**~ Swiss. **4** *nm*: **s**~ *((bedeau)* ≃ verger; *(fromage)* **(petit-)**~ petit-suisse. ◆ **Suissesse** *nf* Swiss (woman).

suite [sɥit] *nf* (**a**) *(escorte)* retinue, suite. (**b**) *(nouvel épisode)* continuation, following episode; *(second roman, film)* sequel; *(rebondissement d'une affaire)* follow-up; *(reste)* remainder, rest. **la** ~ **au prochain numéro** to be continued (in the next issue); ~ **et fin** concluding *ou* final episode; **la** ~ **des événements devait lui donner raison** what followed was to prove him right; **attendons la** ~ let's see what comes next. (**c**) *(aboutissement)* result. *(prolongements)* ~**s** *[maladie]* after-effects; *[accident]* results; *[incident]* consequences, repercussions; **la** ~ **logique de** the logical result of. (**d**) *(succession) (Math)* series; *(Ling)* sequence. ~ **de** *maisons etc* succession *ou* string *ou* series of; *événements* train of; *(Comm)* **article sans** ~ discontinued line. (**e**) *(cohérence)* coherence. **des propos sans** ~ disjointed talk; **avoir de la** ~ **dans les idées** to show great single-mindedness *ou* singleness of purpose, not to be easily put off. (**f**) *(appartement)* suite. (**g**) *(Mus)* suite. (**h**) *(locutions)* **(comme)** ~ **à votre lettre** further to your letter; **à la** ~ *(successivement)* one after the other; *(derrière)* **mettez-vous à la** ~ join on at the back; **à la** ~ **de** *(derrière)* behind; *(en conséquence de)* **à la** ~ **de sa maladie** following his illness; **de** ~ *(immédiatement)* at once; **pendant 3 jours de** ~ (for) 3 days on end *ou* in a row *ou* running; **par** ~ **de** owing to, as a result of; *(par conséquent)* **par** ~ consequently, therefore; **par la** ~, **dans la** ~ afterwards, subsequently; **donner** ~ **à** to follow up; **faire** ~ **à** to follow; **prendre la** ~ **de** *firme, directeur* to succeed, take over from.

suivant[1]**, e** [sɥivɑ̃, ɑ̃t] **1** *adj* following, next. **le mardi** ~ the following *ou* next Tuesday; **pas jeudi prochain, le** ~ not Thursday *ou* Thursday coming *, the one after (that); **voir page** ~**e** see next page; **faites l'exercice** ~ do the following exercise. **2** *nm, f* following (one), next (one). **(au)** ~ ! next (please)!

suivant[2] [sɥivɑ̃] *prép (selon)* according to. ~ **l'usage** in keeping with the custom; ~ **l'expression** as the saying goes; ~ **les jours** according to *ou* depending on the day; **découper** ~ **le pointillé** cut (out) along the dotted line; ~ **que** according to whether.

suivi, e [sɥivi] **1** *adj travail* steady; *correspondance* regular; *qualité* consistent; *conversation, politique* consistent; *(Comm) article* in general production. **très ~** *cours* well-attended; *mode* widely adopted; *feuilleton* widely followed. **2** *nm:* **assurer le ~ de** *affaire* to follow through; *produit en stock* to go on stocking.

suivisme [sɥivism(ə)] *nm (Pol)* follow-my-leader attitude. ◆ **suiviste** *adj attitude, politique* follow-my-leader.

suivre [sɥivʀ(ə)] (40) **1** *vt* (**a**) *(espace, temps, série)* to follow. **il me suit comme mon ombre** he follows me about like my shadow; **je ne peux pas vous ~** I can't keep up (with you); *(iro)* **certains députés, suivez mon regard, ont...** certain deputies, without mentioning any names, have...; **~ qn de près** *[garde du corps]* to stick close to sb; *[voiture]* to follow close behind sb; **~ qn à la trace** to follow sb's tracks; **faire ~ qn** to have sb followed; **suivez le guide!** this way, please!; **suivez la N7 sur 10 km** keep to *ou* follow the N7 (road) for 10 km ; *(Police)* **~ une piste** to follow up a clue. (**b**) *exemple, instinct, conseil* to follow. **~ un traitement** to follow a course of treatment; **~/faire ~ un régime** to be/put on a diet; **l'enquête suit son cours** the inquiry is running *ou* taking its course; **~ le mouvement** to follow the crowd, follow the general trend. (**c**) *(Scol) (être inscrit à)* to attend, go to; *(être attentif à)* to follow, attend to; *(assimiler) programme* to keep up with. (**d**) *affaire, match* to follow; *feuilleton, actualité* to follow, keep up with. **~ un élève** to follow *ou* monitor the progress of a pupil; **il est suivi par un médecin** he's having treatment from a doctor; **à ~** to be continued. (**e**) *(Comm) article* to (continue to) stock. (**f**) *(comprendre) argument, personne* to follow. **jusqu'ici je vous suis** I'm with you *ou* I follow you so far.

2 *vi* (**a**) *[élève] (être attentif)* to attend, pay attention; *(assimiler le programme)* to keep up, follow. (**b**) **faire ~ son courrier** to have one's mail forwarded; **'faire ~'** 'please forward'. (**c**) *(venir après)* to follow. **ce qui suit** what follows.

3 *vb impers*: **il suit que...** it follows that...; **comme suit** as follows.

4 se ~ *vpr [personnes, événements]* to follow one behind the other; *[pages, nombres]* to be in (the right) order; *[argument, pensée]* to be coherent, be consistent. **3 démissions qui se suivent** 3 resignations running *ou* in a row *ou* in quick succession.

sujet, -ette [syʒɛ, ɛt] **1** *adj*: **~ à** *maladie etc* liable to, subject to, prone to; **~ à faire** liable *ou* prone to do; **il n'est pas ~ à faire des imprudences** he is not one to do anything imprudent; **~ à caution** *nouvelle* unconfirmed; *moralité* questionable. **2** *nm, f (gouverné)* subject. **3** *nm* (**a**) *(matière)* subject (*de* for). **~ de conversation** topic of conversation, subject (for conversation); **c'était devenu un ~ de plaisanterie** it had become a standing joke *ou* sth to joke about; **~ d'examen** examination question. (**b**) *(motif)* **~ de** *mécontentement etc* cause for, ground(s) for; **avoir ~ de faire** to have cause *ou* grounds for doing; **ayant tout ~ de croire à sa bonne foi** having every reason to believe in his good faith. (**c**) *(individu)* subject. *(Scol)* **brillant ~** brilliant pupil; **un mauvais ~** *(enfant)* a bad boy; *(jeune homme)* a bad lot. (**d**) *(Ling, Mus, Philos)* subject. (**e**) *(à propos de)* **au ~ de** about, concerning; **à ce ~, je voulais vous dire que...** on that subject I wanted to tell you that...

sujétion [syʒesjɔ̃] *nf (asservissement)* subjection; *(contrainte)* constraint.

sulfamides [sylfamid] *nmpl* sulpha drugs.

sulfate [sylfat] *nm* sulphate.

sulfure [sylfyʀ] *nm* sulphide. ◆ **sulfureux, -euse** *adj* sulphurous. ◆ **sulfurique** *adj* sulphuric. ◆ **sulfurisé, e** *adj*: **papier ~** greaseproof paper.

sultan [syltɑ̃] *nm* sultan. ◆ **sultane** *nf (épouse)* sultana; *(canapé)* (sort of) couch.

Sumatra [symatʀa] *nf* Sumatra.

summum [sɔmɔm] *nm* height.

super [sypɛʀ] **1** *nm*: **~(carburant)** super, four-star (petrol), premium *(US)*. **2** *préf* (*) **~ chic** ultra-chic *ou* smart, fantastically smart *. **3** *adj inv* (*) terrific *, great *, fantastic *, super *.

superbe [sypɛʀb(ə)] *adj (gén)* superb, magnificent. ◆ **superbement** *adv* superbly, magnificently.

superbénéfice [sypɛʀbenefis] *nm* immense profit.

supercherie [sypɛʀʃəʀi] *nf* trick. **la ~** trickery.

superficie [sypɛʀfisi] *nf (gén)* area.

superficiel, -ielle [sypɛʀfisjɛl] *adj (gén)* superficial; *esprit* shallow; *blessure* superficial, skin-deep; *(sans valeur) solution* cosmetic. ◆ **superficiellement** *adv* superficially.

superflu, e [sypɛʀfly] **1** *adj* superfluous. **2** *nm*: **le ~** *(excédent)* the surplus; *(accessoire)* the superfluity.

super-grand [sypɛʀgʀɑ̃] *nm* superpower.

supérieur, e [sypeʀjœʀ] **1** *adj* (**a**) *(les plus importants) niveaux, branches, classes etc* upper; *planètes* superior; *animaux, végétaux* higher; *vitesse, nombre* higher, greater. **la partie ~e de l'objet** the upper *ou* top part of the object; **montez à l'étage ~** go to the next floor up *ou* to the floor above; **mâchoire/lèvre ~e** upper jaw/lip; *(Rel)* **Père ~** Father Superior. (**b**) *(plus important) (gén)* higher; *intelligence, qualité* superior; *quantité, somme* larger. **forces ~es en nombre** forces superior in number; **~ à** *nombre* greater *ou* higher than, above; *production* superior to; **intelligence ~e à la moyenne** above-average *ou* higher than average intelligence; **hiérarchiquement ~ à qn** above sb in the hierarchy. (**c**) *(hautain)* superior. (**d**) *(à la hauteur)* **~ à sa tâche** more than equal to the task; **restant ~ à la situation** remaining master of *ou* in control of the situation. **2** *nm, f* (**a**) superior. **~ hiérarchique** immediate superior, senior. (**b**) *(Univ)* **le ~** higher education. ◆ **supérieurement** *adv* exceptionally well. **~ doué** exceptionally gifted. ◆ **supériorité** *nf (gén)* superiority. **nous avons la ~ du nombre** we outnumber them.

superlatif, -ive [sypɛʀlatif, iv] *adj, nm* superlative.

supermarché [sypɛʀmaʀʃe] *nm* supermarket.

superposer [sypɛʀpoze] (1) **1** *vt objets* to superpose (*à* on); *clichés, (fig) visions* to superimpose. **2 se ~** *vpr* to be superposed; to be superimposed (on one another). ◆ **superposition** *nf* superposition; superimposition.

superproduction [sypɛʀpʀɔdyksjɔ̃] *nf (Ciné)* spectacular.

superprofit [sypɛʀpʀɔfi] *nm* immense profit.

superpuissance [sypɛʀpɥisɑ̃s] *nf* superpower.

supersonique [sypɛʀsɔnik] *adj* supersonic.

superstition [sypɛʀstisjɔ̃] *nf* superstition. ◆ **superstitieusement** *adv* superstitiously. ◆ **superstitieux, -euse** *adj* superstitious.

superstructure [sypɛʀstʀyktyʀ] *nf (gén)* superstructure.

superviser [sypɛʀvize] (1) *vt* to supervise, oversee. ◆ **supervision** *nf* supervision.

supplanter [syplɑ̃te] (1) *vt* to supplant.

suppléance [sypleɑ̃s] *nf (poste)* supply post; *(action)* temporary replacement. ◆ **suppléant, e** **1** *adj (gén)* deputy, substitute *(US)*; *professeur* supply, substitute *(US)*. **médecin ~** locum. **2** *nm, f (professeur)* supply *ou* substitute teacher; *(juge)* deputy (judge); *(Pol)* deputy; *(médecin)* locum.

suppléer [syplee] (1) **1** *vt* (**a**) *(ajouter)* to supply. (**b**) *lacune* to fill; *défaut* to make up for. (**c**) *(remplacer) (gén)* to replace; *professeur* to stand in for; *juge* to deputize for. **2 ~ à** *vt indir défaut, manque* to make up for, compensate for; *qualité, faculté* to substitute for.

supplément [syplemɑ̃] *nm (gén)* supplement; *(au restaurant)* extra charge; *(dans le train)* excess fare. **un ~ de travail** extra *ou* additional work; **un ~ d'information** supplementary *ou* additional information; **~ de prix** additional charge, surcharge; **payer un ~ pour excès de bagages** to pay extra for excess luggage; **le fromage est en ~** cheese is extra. ◆ **supplémentaire** *adj crédits, retards* additional, further; *travail* additional, extra; *trains* relief; *angle* supplementary.

suppliant, e [syplijɑ̃, ɑ̃t] **1** *adj* beseeching, imploring. **2** *nm, f* suppliant, supplicant. ◆ **supplication** *nf (gén)* plea, entreaty; *(Rel)* supplication.

supplice [syplis] *nm* (**a**) *(peine)* **le ~** torture; **un ~** a form of torture; **le ~ de la roue** (torture on) the wheel; **~ chinois** Chinese torture; **~ de Tantale** torment of Tantalus. (**b**) *(souffrance)* torture. **~s moraux** moral tortures *ou* torments; **le ~ de l'incertitude** the ordeal *ou* torture of uncertainty; **être au ~** *(appréhension)* to be in agonies; *(douleur)* to be in misery; **mettre qn au ~** to torture sb. ◆ **supplicié, e** *nm, f* torture victim. ◆ **supplicier** (7) *vt (lit, fig)* to torture.

supplier [syplije] (7) *vt* to beseech, implore, entreat (*de faire* to do). **n'insistez pas, je vous en supplie** I beg of you not to insist.

supplique [syplik] *nf* petition.

supporter[1] [sypɔʀte] (1) *vt* (**a**) *(soutenir)* to support, hold up. (**b**) *(subir, endurer) (gén)* to bear; *conséquences, malheur* to suffer; *maladie, solitude* to endure; *conduite* to tolerate, put up with. **elle supporte tout de son fils** she puts up with *ou* takes anything from her son; **je ne peux pas ~ l'hypocrisie** I can't bear *ou* abide hypocrisy; **je ne peux pas les ~** I can't bear *ou* stand them; **je ne supporte pas qu'elle fasse cela** I won't stand for *ou* tolerate her doing that; **on supporte un gilet, par ce temps** * you can do with a cardigan in this weather. (**c**) *(résister à) température, épreuve* to withstand. **verre qui supporte la chaleur** heatproof *ou* heat-resistant glass; **il a bien supporté l'opération** he took the operation well; **il ne supporte pas l'alcool** he can't take alcohol; **il ne supporte pas la chaleur/les épinards** heat/spinach doesn't agree *ou* disagrees with him, he can't stand *ou* bear the heat/spinach; **lait facile à ~** easily-digested milk. ◆ **support** *nm* (**a**) *(soutien) (gén)* support; *(béquille)* prop. (**b**) *(moyen)* medium. **~ publicitaire** advertising medium; **conférence faite à l'aide d'un ~ écrit** lecture given with the help of a written text; **~ audio-visuel** audio-visual aids; **~ visuel** visual aids, visuals *. ◆ **supportable** *adj douleur, chaleur* bearable ; *conduite* tolerable.

supporter[2] [sypɔʀtɛʀ] *nm (Sport)* supporter.

supposer [sypoze] (1) *vt* (**a**) *(présumer)* to suppose, assume. **à ~ que** supposing *ou* assuming (that); **je suppose que tu es contre** I take it *ou* I assume *ou* I suppose you are against it. (**b**) *(présupposer)* to presuppose; *(suggérer)* to imply. **ta réponse suppose que tu n'as rien compris** your reply implies *ou* indicates that you haven't understood a thing. ◆ **supposé, e** *adj auteur* supposed; *nombre* estimated; *(Jur) meurtrier* alleged. ◆ **supposition** *nf* supposition, assumption.

suppositoire [sypozitwaʀ] *nm* suppository.

supprimer [sypʀime] (1) **1** *vt objet, obstacle* to remove (*de* from); *mot, paragraphe* to delete (*de* from); *trains* to cancel; *permis de conduire* to withdraw, take away (*de* from); *emplois, témoin gênant* to do away with; *douleur, fatigue* to eliminate; *loi, concurrence* to abolish; *publication, effets nocifs* to suppress; *abus* to put an end to; *allocation* to stop. **~ qch à qn** to deprive sb of sth; **~ qch de son alimentation** to cut sth out of one's diet, eliminate sth from one's diet; **cette technique supprime des opérations inutiles** this technique does away with *ou* cuts out some unnecessary operations. **2 se ~** *vpr* to do away with o.s., take one's own life. ◆ **suppression** *nf* removal; deletion; cancellation; withdrawal; elimination; abolition; suppression. **faire des ~s dans un texte** to make some deletions in a text; **7 000 ~s d'emploi** 7,000 jobs axed *ou* lost.

suppurer [sypyʀe] (1) *vi* to suppurate. ◆ **suppuration** *nf* suppuration.

supputer [sypyte] (1) *vt* to calculate. ◆ **supputation** *nf* calculation.

supra... [sypʀa] *préf* supra...

suprême [sypʀɛm] **1** *adj (gén)* supreme. **2** *nm (Culin)* supreme. ◆ **suprématie** *nf* supremacy. ◆ **suprêmement** *adv* supremely.

sur[1] [syʀ] **1** *prép* (**a**) *(position)* on, upon; *(sur le haut de)* on (top of); *(avec mouvement)* on, onto; *(dans)* on, in; *(par-dessus)* over; *(au-dessus)* above. **il y a un sac ~ la table** there's a bag on the table; **~ ma route** on my way; **elle rangea ses chapeaux ~ l'armoire** she put her hats away on top of the wardrobe; **elle a jeté son sac ~ la table** she threw her bag onto the table; **une chambre (qui donne) ~ la rue** a room that looks out onto the street; **il n'est jamais monté ~ un bateau** he's never been in *ou* on a boat; **~ la place** in the square; **lire qch ~ le journal** to read sth in the paper; **un pont ~ la rivière** a bridge across *ou* on *ou* over the river; **l'avion est passé ~ nos têtes** the aircraft flew over *ou* above our heads; **retire tes livres de ~ la table** take your books (from) off the table; **je n'ai pas d'argent ~ moi** I haven't (got) any money on *ou* with me; **elle a acheté des poires ~ le marché** she bought pears at the market; **s'étendre ~ 3 km** to spread over 3 kms; **travaux ~ 5 km** roadworks for 5 kms; *(fig)* **vivre les uns ~ les autres** to live one on top of the other.

(**b**) *(direction)* to, towards. **tourner ~ la droite** to turn (to the) right; **l'église est ~ votre gauche** the church is on *ou* to your left; **fermez bien la porte ~ vous** be sure and close the door behind *ou* after you.

(**c**) *(temps)* **il est arrivé ~ les 2 heures** he came (at) about *ou* (at) around 2; **il va ~ ses quinze ans** he's getting on for *ou* going on *(US)* fifteen; **l'acte s'achève ~ une réconciliation** the act ends with a reconciliation; **il est ~ le départ** he's just going, he's (just) about to leave; **~ ce, il est sorti** whereupon *ou* upon which he went out; **~ ce, il faut que je vous quitte** and now I must leave you; **boire du café ~ de la bière** to drink coffee on top of beer; **~ une période de 3 mois** over a period of 3 months; **juger les résultats ~ une année** to assess the results over a year.

(**d**) *(cause)* on, by. **~ commande** by order; **~ présentation d'une pièce d'identité** on presentation of identification; **~ la recommandation de X** on X's recommendation.

(**e**) *(manière)* on. **ils vivent ~ son traitement** they live on *ou* off his salary; **ne le prends pas ~ ce ton** don't take it like that; **chanter qch ~ l'air de** to sing sth to the tune of.

(**f**) *(sujet)* on, about. **causerie ~ la Grèce** talk on *ou* about Greece; **être ~ un travail** to be occupied with a job, be (in the process of) doing a job; **être ~ une bonne affaire/une piste** to be on to a bargain/on a trail.

(**g**) *(proportion)* out of, in; *(mesure)* by; *(accumulation)* after. **~ 12 verres, 6 sont ébréchés** out of 12 glasses 6 are chipped; **un homme ~ 10** one man in (every) *ou* out of 10; *(note)* **9 ~ 10** 9 out

of 10; **la cuisine fait 2 mètres ~ 3** the kitchen is *ou* measures 2 metres by 3; **un vendredi ~ trois** every third Friday; **un jour ~ deux** every other day; **faire faute ~ faute** to make one mistake after another.
(**h**) *(influence)* over, on. **elle ne peut rien ~ lui** she has no control over him; **savoir prendre ~ soi** to keep a grip on o.s.; **prendre ~ soi de faire qch** to take it upon o.s. to do sth.
2 *préf* over. **~excité** overexcited; **~production** overproduction.
3 : **~-le-champ, ~ l'heure** *(littér) adv* immediately, at once, straightaway, right away *(US)*.

sur², e [syʀ] *adj (aigre)* sour.

sûr, e [syʀ] *adj* (**a**) *(certain)* certain, sure (*de* of, about). **il est ~ de son fait** he's sure *ou* confident he'll do it; **~ de soi** self-assured, self-confident; **j'en étais ~!** I knew it!, just as I thought!; **j'en suis ~ et certain** I'm positive (about it), I'm absolutely sure *ou* certain (of it); **la chose est ~e** that's certain, that's for sure *ou* certain. (**b**) *(sans danger)* safe. **peu ~** unsafe; **le plus ~ est de...** the safest thing is to...; **en lieu ~** in a safe place. (**c**) *(digne de confiance) (gén)* reliable; *personne, firme* trustworthy; *instinct, raisonnement* sound; *remède, moyen* safe, sure. **avoir la main ~e** to have a steady hand; **peu ~** *(gén)* unreliable; *allié* untrustworthy; *méthode* unsafe; *bases* unsound.

surabonder [syʀabɔ̃de] (**1**) *vi* to be overabundant, be superabundant. ◆ **surabondance** *nf* overabundance, superabundance. ◆ **surabondant, e** *adj* overabundant, superabundant.

suranné, e [syʀane] *adj* outmoded, outdated.

surarmement [syʀaʀməmɑ̃] *nm* massive stock of weapons.

surcharger [syʀʃaʀʒe] (**3**) *vt voiture* to overload. **~ qn de travail** to overload *ou* overburden sb with work; **je suis surchargé de travail** I'm overloaded *ou* snowed under with work; **manuscrit surchargé de corrections** manuscript covered *ou* littered with corrections. ◆ **surcharge** *nf* (**a**) *(action)* overloading; *(poids en excédent)* extra load, excess load. **une tonne de ~** an extra *ou* excess load of a ton; **prendre des passagers en ~** to take on excess passengers; **une ~ de travail** extra work. (**b**) *[document]* alteration; *[timbre-poste, voyage, hôtel]* surcharge.

surchauffer [syʀʃofe] (**1**) *vt pièce* to overheat; *(Phys, Tech)* to superheat.

surchoix [syʀʃwa] *adj inv* top-quality.

surclasser [syʀklɑse] (**1**) *vt* to outclass.

surcroît [syʀkʀwa] *nm*: **donner un ~ de travail** to give extra *ou* additional work; **par (un) ~ d'honnêteté** through an excess of honesty; **pour ~ de malheur...** to add to his (*ou* her *etc*) misfortune...; **avare et paresseux de** *ou* **par ~** miserly and idle to boot.

surdité [syʀdite] *nf* deafness.

surdoué, e [syʀdwe] **1** *adj enfant* gifted, exceptional *(US)*. **2** *nm, f* gifted *ou* exceptional child.

sureau, *pl* **~x** [syʀo] *nm* elder (tree).

sureffectifs [syʀefɛktif] *nmpl* overmanning.

surélever [syʀɛlve] (**5**) *vt* to raise, heighten (*de* by). **rez-de-chaussée surélevé** raised ground floor.

sûrement [syʀmɑ̃] *adv* (**a**) *progresser* in safety; *attacher* securely; *fonctionner* safely. (**b**) *(certainement)* certainly. **viendra-t-il? — ~!/~ pas!** will he be coming? — certainly!/certainly not!; **il viendra ~** he'll certainly come, he's sure to come.

surenchère [syʀɑ̃ʃɛʀ] *nf (sur prix fixé)* overbid; *(enchère plus élevée)* higher bid. **une ~ de violence** an increasing build-up of violence; *(fig)* **faire de la ~** to use outbidding tactics. ◆ **surenchérir** (**2**) *vi* to bid higher (*sur* than); *(élection etc)* to try to outmatch *ou* outbid each other (*de* with). **~ sur qn** to bid higher than sb, outbid sb.

surestimer [syʀɛstime] (**1**) *vt importance* to overestimate; *maison à vendre* to overvalue. ◆ **surestimation** *nf* overestimation; overvaluation.

sûreté [syʀte] *nf* (**a**) *(sécurité)* safety; *(précaution)* precaution. **la ~ de l'État** state security; **pour plus de ~** as an extra precaution, to be on the safe side; **être en ~** to be in safety, be safe; **mettre en ~** to put in a safe *ou* secure place; **serrure** *etc* **de ~** safety lock *etc*. (**b**) *(exactitude) (gén)* reliability; *[coup d'œil, geste]* steadiness; *[jugement]* soundness. **il a une grande ~ de main** he has a very sure hand; **~ d'exécution** sureness of touch. (**c**) *(dispositif)* safety device. (**d**) *(garantie)* assurance, guarantee. (**e**) *(Police)* **la S~ (nationale)** the (French) criminal investigation department, ≃ the CID *(Brit)*, ≃ the FBI *(US)*.

surévaluer [syʀevalɥe] (**1**) *vt* to overvalue.

surexciter [syʀɛksite] (**1**) *vt* to overexcite. ◆ **surexcitation** *nf* overexcitement.

surf [sœʀf] *nm* surfing, surfboarding. **faire du ~** to go surfing *ou* surfboarding.

surface [syʀfas] *nf (gén)* surface; *[champ, chambre]* surface area. **faire ~** to surface; *(lit, fig)* **refaire ~** to resurface; **de ~** *politesse* superficial; *modifications* cosmetic; *grammaire* surface; **en ~** *nager* at the surface, near the surface; *apprendre* superficially; *(Ftbl)* **~ de but** goal area; *(Ftbl)* **~ de réparation** penalty area.

surfait, e [syʀfɛ, ɛt] *adj* overrated.

surfin, e [syʀfɛ̃, in] *adj* superfine.

surgelé, e [syʀʒəle] *adj* deep-frozen. **(aliments) ~s** (deep-)frozen food. ◆ **surgeler** (**5**) *vt* to deep-freeze, fast-freeze.

surgir [syʀʒiʀ] (**2**) *vi (lit)* to appear suddenly; *[difficultés]* to arise, crop up. *[plante, immeuble]* **~ de terre** to shoot up, spring up.

surhomme [syʀɔm] *nm* superman. ◆ **surhumain, e** *adj* superhuman.

Surinam [syʀinam] *nm* Surinam.

surinfection [syʀɛ̃fɛksjɔ̃] *nf* additional infection.

surir [syʀiʀ] (**2**) *vi [lait, vin]* to turn *ou* go sour.

surlendemain [syʀlɑ̃dmɛ̃] *nm*: **le ~ de son arrivée** two days after his arrival; **il est mort le ~** he died two days later.

surligneur [syʀliɲœʀ] *nm* highlighter (pen).

surmener [syʀməne] (**5**) **1** *vt* to overwork, overtax. **2 se ~** *vpr* to overwork, overtax (o.s.). ◆ **surmenage** *nm (action)* overworking, overtaxing; *(état)* overwork. **le ~ intellectuel** mental fatigue, brain-fag *.

surmonter [syʀmɔ̃te] (**1**) **1** *vt (dans l'espace)* to surmount, top; *(vaincre)* to overcome, get over, surmount. **2 se ~** *vpr* to master o.s., control o.s.

surnager [syʀnaʒe] (**3**) *vi [objet]* to float (on the surface); *[souvenir]* to linger on.

surnaturel, -elle [syʀnatyʀɛl] **1** *adj (gén)* supernatural; *ambiance inquiétante* uncanny, eerie. **2** *nm*: **le ~** the supernatural.

surnom [syʀnɔ̃] *nm* nickname; *(d'un héros)* name.

surnombre [syʀnɔ̃bʀ(ə)] *nm*: **en ~** too many; **j'étais en ~** I was one too many; **ils ont fait sortir les spectateurs en ~** they asked the excess spectators to leave.

surnommer [syʀnɔme] (**1**) *vt*: **~ qn 'le gros'** to nickname sb 'fatty'; **le roi Richard surnommé 'le Courageux'** King Richard known as *ou* named 'the Brave'.

surnoter [syʀnɔte] (**1**) *vt (Scol)* to overmark, overgrade *(US)*.

surpasser [syʀpɑse] (**1**) **1** *vt (gén)* to surpass; *rival* to surpass, outdo (*en* in). **2 se ~** *vpr* to surpass o.s., excel o.s.

surpeuplé, e [syʀpœple] *adj* overpopulated. ◆ **surpeuplement** *nm* overpopulation.

surplis [syʀpli] *nm* surplice.

surplomb [syʀplɔ̃] *nm* overhang. **en** ~ overhanging. ◆ **surplomber** (1) *vt* to overhang.

surplus [syʀply] *nm* (**a**) *(gén, Comm)* surplus. **marchandises en** ~ surplus goods; **il me reste un** ~ **de clous** I've got some nails left over *ou* some surplus nails; **avec le** ~ **(du bois)** with the leftover *ou* surplus (wood). (**b**) *(d'ailleurs)* **au** ~ moreover, what is more.

surpopulation [syʀpɔpylɑsjɔ̃] *nf* overpopulation.

surprendre [syʀpʀɑ̃dʀ(ə)] (**58**) *vt* (**a**) *ennemi* to surprise; *voleur* to surprise, catch in the act; *(par visite imprévue)* to catch unawares *ou* on the hop *. **se** ~ **à faire qch** to find o.s. doing sth; **je vais aller le** ~ **au travail** I'm going to drop in (unexpectedly) on him at work. (**b**) *secret* to discover; *conversation* to overhear; *regard* to intercept. (**c**) *[pluie, marée, nuit]* to catch out. **se laisser** ~ **par la nuit** to be overtaken by nightfall. (**d**) *(étonner)* to amaze, surprise. ◆ **surprenant, e** *adj* amazing, surprising. ◆ **surpris, e**[1] *adj* surprised. ~ **de qch** surprised *ou* amazed at sth. ◆ **surprise**[2] *nf (gén)* surprise. **avoir la** ~ **de voir que** to be surprised to see that; **prix sans** ~**s** (all-)inclusive price; **par** ~ *attaquer* by surprise; **il m'a pris par** ~ he caught me off guard *ou* unawares, he caught me on the hop *; **visite-/attaque-**~ surprise visit/attack; **grève-**~ unofficial strike; *[homme politique]* **voyage-**~ surprise *ou* unexpected trip *ou* visit. ◆ **surprise-partie, *pl* surprises-parties** *nf* party.

surproduction [syʀpʀɔdyksjɔ̃] *nf* overproduction.

surpuissant, e [syʀpɥisɑ̃, ɑ̃t] *adj voiture, moteur* ultra-powerful.

surréalisme [syʀʀealism(ə)] *nm* surrealism. ◆ **surréaliste 1** *adj (Art)* surrealist; *(bizarre)* surrealistic. **2** *nmf* surrealist.

sursaut [syʀso] *nm* start, jump. *(fig)* ~ **d'énergie** (sudden) burst *ou* fit of energy; **se réveiller en** ~ to wake up with a start *ou* jump. ◆ **sursauter** (1) *vi* to start, jump, give a start. **faire** ~ **qn** to make sb start *ou* jump, startle sb.

surseoir [syʀswaʀ] (**26**) ~ **à** *vt indir publication* to defer, postpone; *(Jur) jugement etc* to stay. ~ **à l'exécution d'un condamné** to grant a reprieve to a condemned man. ◆ **sursis** *nm [condamnation à mort]*, *(fig)* reprieve. **peine avec** ~ suspended *ou* deferred sentence; **il a eu 2 ans avec** ~ he was given a 2-year suspended *ou* deferred sentence; ~ **(d'incorporation)** deferment. ◆ **sursitaire** *adj (Mil)* deferred.

surtaxe [syʀtaks(ə)] *nf* surcharge. ◆ **surtaxer** (1) *vt* to surcharge.

surtout [syʀtu] *adv (avant tout)* above all; *(spécialement)* especially, particularly. **j'aime** ~ **les romans** I particularly like novels, I like novels above all; **dernièrement, j'ai** ~ **lu des romans** I have read mostly *ou* mainly novels of late; ~ **que** * especially as *ou* since; ~ **pas (maintenant)** certainly not (now); ~ **ne vous mettez pas en frais** please *ou* above all don't go to any expense.

surveiller [syʀveje] (1) **1** *vt (gén)* to watch, keep an eye on; *prisonnier, malade, territoire* to (keep) watch over; *locaux, ennemi* to keep watch on; *études de qn* to supervise; *réparation* to supervise; oversee; *(Scol) examen* to invigilate. ~ **qn du coin de l'œil** to keep half an eye on sb; ~ **sa ligne** to watch one's figure. **2 se** ~ *vpr* to keep a check *ou* a watch on o.s. ◆ **surveillance** *nf* watch; supervision; invigilation. **sous la** ~ **de la police** under police surveillance; *(lit, fig)* **mettre qch sous haute** ~ to keep a close *ou* tight watch on sth; **société de** ~ security firm; **mission de** ~ surveillance mission; ~ **médicale** medical supervision. ◆ **surveillant, e** *nm, f [prison]* warder, guard *(US)*; *[usine, chantier]* supervisor, overseer; *[magasin]* shopwalker; *[hôpital]* nursing officer; *(Scol) (pion)* supervisor; *(aux examens)* invigilator. *(Scol)* ~ **d'internat** supervisor of boarders.

survenir [syʀvəniʀ] (**22**) *vi [événement]* to take place; *[incident, retards]* to occur, arise.

survêtement [syʀvɛtmɑ̃] *nm (sportif)* tracksuit; *[skieur]* overgarments.

sur-vitrage [syʀvitʀaʒ] *nm* double-glazing.

survivre [syʀvivʀ(ə)] (**46**) *vi (lit, fig)* to survive. ~ **à** *accident, humiliation* to survive; *personne, époque* to outlive; **se** ~ **dans** *œuvre, enfant* to live on in. ◆ **survie** *nf* survival. *(Rel)* **la** ~ afterlife; **équipement** *etc* **de** ~ survival equipment *etc.* ◆ **survivance** *nf* survival. ◆ **survivant, e 1** *adj* surviving. **2** *nm, f* survivor.

survoler [syʀvɔle] (1) *vt (lit)* to fly over; *livre* to skim *ou* skip through; *question* to skim over. ◆ **survol** *nm*: **le** ~ **de** flying over; skimming *ou* skipping through; skimming over.

survolté, e [syʀvɔlte] *adj* (**a**) *(surexcité)* worked up, over-excited. (**b**) *(Élec)* stepped up, boosted.

sus [sy(s)] *adv (Admin)* **en** ~ in addition (*de* to).

susceptible [sysɛptibl(ə)] *adj* (**a**) *(ombrageux)* touchy, thin-skinned, sensitive. (**b**) **être** ~ **de faire qch** *(aptitude)* to be in a position *ou* be able to do sth; *(éventualité)* to be likely *ou* liable to do sth; ~ **d'être démontré** susceptible of proof ; **texte** ~ **d'améliorations** text open to improvement *ou* that can be improved upon; **il est** ~ **de gagner** he may well win, he is liable to win. ◆ **susceptibilité** *nf* touchiness, sensitiveness. ~**s** susceptibilities, sensibilities.

susciter [sysite] (1) *vt intérêt* to arouse; *passions* to arouse, incite; *controverse* to give rise to, provoke; *obstacles* to create.

suspect, e [syspɛ(kt), ɛkt(ə)] **1** *adj individu, conduite* suspicious; *opinion, citoyen* suspect. **être** ~ **de qch** to be suspected of sth. **2** *nm, f* suspect. ◆ **suspecter** (1) *vt personne* to suspect (*de faire* of doing); *bonne foi* to suspect, have (one's) suspicions about, question.

suspendre [syspɑ̃dʀ(ə)] (**41**) **1** *vt* (**a**) *vêtements* to hang up (*à* on); *lampe* to hang, suspend (*à* from); *hamac* to sling (up). (**b**) *(interrompre) (gén)* to suspend; *récit* to break off; *séance* to adjourn. (**c**) *jugement* to suspend, defer; *décision* to postpone, defer. (**d**) *fonctionnaire, joueur* to suspend. ~ **qn de ses fonctions** to suspend sb from office. **2 se** ~ *vpr*: **se** ~ **à qch** to hang from sth. ◆ **suspendu, e** *adj* (**a**) ~ **à qch** *vêtement, lustre* hanging *ou* suspended from sth; *(fig)* **être** ~ **aux lèvres de qn** to hang upon sb's every word; *(fig)* **chalets** ~**s au-dessus d'une gorge** chalets suspended *ou* perched over a gorge. (**b**) *(Aut)* **voiture bien/mal** ~**e** car with good/poor suspension.

suspens [syspɑ̃] *nm*: **en** ~ *affaire, projet* in abeyance; *poussière* in suspension; *(dans l'incertitude)* in suspense; **tenir les lecteurs en** ~ to keep the reader in suspense; **en** ~ **dans l'air** suspended in the air.

suspense [syspɑ̃s] *nm [film, roman]* suspense. **un moment de** ~ a moment's suspense; **film à** ~ suspense film, thriller.

suspension [syspɑ̃sjɔ̃] **1** *nf* (**a**) *(action: V* **suspendre***)* hanging; suspending; breaking off; adjournment; suspension, deferment; postponement. (**b**) *(Aut)* suspension. (**c**) *(lustre)* chandelier. (**d**) *(Chim)* suspension. (**e**) **en** ~ *poussière* in suspension; **en** ~ **dans l'air** suspended in the air. **2** : ~ **d'armes** suspension of fighting; ~ **de paiement** suspension of payment(s); ~ **de séance** adjournment.

suspicion [syspisjɔ̃] *nf* suspicion.

susurrer [sysyʀe] (1) *vti* to whisper, murmur.

suture [sytyʀ] *nf* suture. ◆ **suturer** (1) *vt* to suture *(Méd)*, stitch up.

suzerain, e [syzʀɛ̃, ɛn] *adj, nm, f* suzerain. ◆ **suzeraineté** *nf* suzerainty.

svelte [svɛlt(ə)] *adj* slender. ◆ **sveltesse** *nf* slenderness.

Swaziland [swazilɑ̃d] *nm* Swaziland.

sweater [switœʀ] *nm* sweater.

sweat-shirt, *pl* **sweat-shirts** [switʃœʀt] *nm* sweatshirt.

sycomore [sikɔmɔʀ] *nm* sycamore (tree).

syllabe [silab] *nf* syllable. ◆ **syllabique** *adj* syllabic.

syllogisme [silɔʒism(ə)] *nm* syllogism.

sylviculture [silvikyltyʀ] *nf* forestry. ◆ **sylvicole** *adj* forestry.

symbole [sɛ̃bɔl] *nm (gén)* symbol. ◆ **symbolique** *adj (gén)* symbolic(al); *(fig: très modique)* token, nominal; *(sans valeur) solution* cosmetic. **geste** ~ symbolic *ou* token gesture. ◆ **symboliquement** *adv* symbolically. ◆ **symbolisation** *nf* symbolization. ◆ **symboliser** (1) *vt* to symbolize.

symétrie [simetʀi] *nf (gén)* symmetry (*par rapport à* in relation to). ◆ **symétrique** *adj* symmetrical (*de* to, *par rapport à* in relation to). ◆ **symétriquement** *adv* symmetrically.

sympa * [sɛ̃pa] *adj inv (abrév de* **sympathique***)* nice, friendly. **sois ~, prête-le-moi** be a pal * and lend it to me.

sympathie [sɛ̃pati] *nf* (**a**) *(inclination)* liking; *(affinité)* fellow feeling, warmth, friendship. **j'ai beaucoup de ~ pour lui** I have a great liking for him, I like him a great deal; **des relations de ~ les unissaient** they were united by a fellow feeling. (**b**) *(compassion)* sympathy. **croyez à notre** ~ you have our deepest sympathy. ◆ **sympathique** *adj* (**a**) *(agréable)* nice, friendly; *ambiance* pleasant; *plat* good; *appartement* nice, pleasant. **je le trouve** ~ I like him, I find him likeable *ou* friendly *ou* nice. (**b**) *(Anat)* sympathetic. ◆ **sympathiquement** *adv accueillir* in a friendly manner. ◆ **sympathisant, e** *nm, f (Pol)* sympathizer. ◆ **sympathiser** (1) *vi (bien s'entendre)* to get on (well) (*avec* with); *(se prendre d'amitié)* to make friends (*avec* with). *(fréquenter)* **ils ne sympathisent pas avec les voisins** they don't have much contact with the neighbours; **ils ont tout de suite sympathisé** they took to each other immediately.

symphonie [sɛ̃fɔni] *nf* symphony. ◆ **symphonique** *adj* symphonic; *orchestre* symphony.

symposium [sɛ̃pozjɔm] *nm* symposium.

symptôme [sɛ̃ptom] *nm (Méd)* symptom; *(signe)* sign, symptom. ◆ **symptomatique** *adj (Méd)* symptomatic; *(révélateur)* significant. ~ **de** symptomatic of.

synagogue [sinagɔg] *nf* synagogue.

synchronie [sɛ̃kʀɔni] *nf* synchrony. ◆ **synchronique** *adj* synchronic. ◆ **synchronisation** *nf* synchronization. ◆ **synchronisé, e** *adj* synchronized. ◆ **synchroniser** (1) *vt* to synchronize. ◆ **synchronisme** *nm [oscillations, dates]* synchronism; *(Philos)* synchronicity. *(fig)* **avec un ~ parfait** with perfect synchronization.

syncope [sɛ̃kɔp] *nf* (**a**) *(évanouissement)* blackout, fainting fit. **tomber en** ~ to faint, pass out. (**b**) *(Mus)* syncopation. ◆ **syncopé, e** *adj (Mus)* syncopated.

syndic [sɛ̃dik] *nm*: ~ **(d'immeuble)** managing agent.

syndicat [sɛ̃dika] *nm [travailleurs]* (trade) union; *[employeurs]* union, syndicate; *[producteurs agricoles]* union; *(non professionnel)* association. ~ **d'initiative** tourist (information) office *ou* bureau; ~ **de propriétaires** *(gén)* association of property owners; *(d'un même immeuble)* householders' association. ◆ **syndical, e,** *mpl* **-aux** *adj* (trade-) union. **conseil ~ d'un immeuble** ≃ management committee of a block of flats *ou* an apartment house *(US)*. ◆ **syndicalisation** *nf* union membership. ◆ **syndicalisme** *nm (mouvement)* trade unionism; *(doctrine politique)* syndicalism. *(activité)* **faire du** ~ to participate in unionist activities. ◆ **syndicaliste 1** *nmf (responsable d'un syndicat)* (trade-)union official, trade unionist; *(doctrinaire)* syndicalist. **2** *adj chef* trade-union; *doctrine* unionist. ◆ **syndiqué, e 1** *adj*: **être** ~ to be a union member; **travailleurs non ~s** non-union *ou* non-unionized workers. **2** *nm, f* union member. ◆ **syndiquer** (1) **1** *vt* to unionize. **2 se** ~ *vpr (se grouper)* to form a trade union, unionize; *(adhérer)* to join a trade union.

syndrome [sɛ̃dʀom] *nm* syndrome. ~ **immuno-déficitaire acquis** acquired immuno-deficiency syndrome.

synode [sinɔd] *nm* synod.

synonyme [sinɔnim] **1** *adj* synonymous (*de* with). **2** *nm* synonym. ◆ **synonymie** *nf* synonymy.

syntagme [sɛ̃tagm(ə)] *nm* (word) group, phrase, syntagm. ~ **nominal** nominal group, noun phrase; ~ **verbal** verb phrase.

syntaxe [sɛ̃taks(ə)] *nf* syntax. ◆ **syntactique** *adj ou* ◆ **syntaxique** *adj* syntactic.

synthèse [sɛ̃tɛz] *nf* synthesis. **faire la ~ de qch** to synthesize sth. ◆ **synthétique** *adj* synthetic. ◆ **synthétiquement** *adv* synthetically. ◆ **synthétiser** (1) *vt* to synthesize. ◆ **synthétiseur** *nm* synthesizer. *(Ordin)* ~ **de (la) parole** speech synthesizer.

syphilis [sifilis] *nf* syphilis. ◆ **syphilitique** *adj, nmf* syphilitic.

Syrie [siʀi] *nf* Syria. ◆ **syrien, -ienne** *adj,* **S~(ne)** *nm(f)* Syrian.

système [sistɛm] *nm (gén)* system. ~ **métrique/nerveux** metric/nervous system; ~ **de gestion de bases de données** database management system; ~ **de traitement de texte** word-processing package; *(institution etc)* **faire partie du** ~ to be part of the system; **il connaît le** ~ he knows the system; **il me tape sur le** ~ ‡ he gets on my nerves *; **le ~ D** * resourcefulness. ◆ **systématique** *adj (gén)* systematic. **il est trop** ~ he's too rigid *ou* dogmatic in his thinking. ◆ **systématiquement** *adv* systematically. ◆ **systématisation** *nf* systematization. ◆ **systématiser** (1) **1** *vt* to systematize. **2 se** ~ *vpr* to become the rule.

T

T, t [te] *nm (lettre)* T, t. **en T** *table etc* T-shaped; **équerre en T** T-square.

t' [t(ə)] *V* **te, tu.**

ta [ta] *adj poss V* **ton**¹.

tabac [taba] **1** *nm* (**a**) *(produit)* tobacco; *(couleur)* buff, tobacco (brown); *(magasin)* tobacconist's (shop). ~ **blond** light *ou* mild *ou* Virginia tobacco; ~ **brun** dark tobacco; ~ **à priser** snuff. (**b**) (*) **passer qn à** ~ to beat sb up; *(arg Théât)* **faire un** ~ to be a great hit; **c'est toujours le même** ~ it's always the same old thing. **2** *adj inv* buff, tobacco (brown). ◆ **tabagie** *nf* smoke den. ◆ **tabagisme** *nm* addiction to smoking, nicotine addiction.

tabasser * [tabase] (1) **1** *vt*: ~ **qn** to beat sb up; **se faire** ~ to be given a beating, get one's face smashed in * (*par* by). **2 se** ~ *vpr* to have a punch-up *.

tabatière [tabatjɛʀ] *nf* (**a**) *(boîte)* snuffbox. (**b**) *(lucarne)* skylight.

tabernacle [tabɛʀnakl(ə)] *nm* tabernacle.

table [tabl(ə)] **1** *nf* (**a**) *(meuble)* table. *(fig)* **faire** ~ **rase** to make a clean sweep (*de* of). (**b**) *(pour le repas)* table. **être à** ~ to be having a meal, be at table; **nous étions 8 à** ~ there were 8 of us at *ou* round the table; **à** ~! come and eat!; **mettre la** ~ to lay *ou* set the table; **se mettre à** ~ to sit down to eat, sit down at the table; *(arg Police)* to talk, come clean ⁑; **toute la** ~ **éclata de rire** the whole table burst out laughing; **avoir une bonne** ~ to keep a good table; **aimer (les plaisirs de) la** ~ to enjoy one's food. (**c**) *(gén, Math: liste)* table. ~ **alphabétique** alphabetical table. (**d**) *(Géol: plateau)* tableland, plateau. **2** : ~ **basse** coffee table, occasional table; ~ **de conférence** conference table; ~ **de cuisson** cooking surface; ~ **à dessin** drawing board; ~ **d'écoute** wire-tapping set; **mettre qn sur** ~ **d'écoute** to tap sb's phone; ~ **des matières** (table of) contents; ~ **de nuit** bedside table; ~ **d'opération** operating table; ~ **d'orientation** viewpoint indicator; ~ **à repasser** ironing board; *(lit, fig)* ~ **ronde** round table; ~ **roulante** trolley; *(Ordin)* ~ **traçante** (graph) plotter; ~ **de travail** work table *ou* desk.

tableau, *pl* ~**x** [tablo] *nm* (**a**) *(peinture)* painting; *(reproduction, gravure)* picture. *(lit, fig)* ~ **de chasse** *[chasseur]* bag; *(fig)* tally; **ajouter qch à son** ~ **de chasse** to add sth to one's list of successes; ~ **de maître** masterpiece. (**b**) *(fig)* *(scène)* picture, scene; *(description)* picture. **un** ~ **tragique** a tragic picture *ou* scene; **pour compléter le** ~ * to cap it all; **gagner sur les 2/sur tous les** ~**x** to win on both/all counts. (**c**) *(Théât)* scene. (**d**) *(Scol)* ~ **(noir)** (black)board. (**e**) *(panneau)* *(gén)* board; *[fusibles]* box; *[clefs]* rack, board. ~ **des horaires** timetable; ~ **d'affichage** notice board; ~ **de bord** dashboard, instrument panel; ~ **électronique** tote board; ~ **d'honneur** merit *ou* prize list, honor roll *(US)*; ~ **de service** duty roster. (**f**) *(carte, graphique)* table, chart; *(Ordin: fait par tableur)* spreadsheet; *(Admin: liste)* register, roll, list. **présenter qch sous forme de** ~ to show sth in tabular form.

tablée [table] *nf* table *(of people)*.

tabler [table] (1) *vi*: ~ **sur qch** to count *ou* reckon *ou* bank on sth.

tablette [tablɛt] *nf* (**a**) *[chocolat]* bar; *[chewing-gum]* stick; *[métal]* block. (**b**) *[lavabo, étagère]* shelf; *[secrétaire]* flap. (**c**) *(Hist: pour écrire)* tablet. *(hum)* **marquer qch sur ses** ~**s** to make a note of sth. (**d**) *(Ordin)* tablet.

tableur [tablœʀ] *nm (Ordin)* spreadsheet (program).

tablier [tablije] *nm* (**a**) *(gén)* apron; *[ménagère]* *(sans manches)* apron, pinafore; *(avec manches)* overall; *[écolier]* overall, smock. (**b**) *[pont]* roadway. (**c**) *[cheminée]* (flue-)shutter; *[magasin]* (iron *ou* steel) shutter.

tabou [tabu] *nm, adj* taboo.

tabouret [tabuʀɛ] *nm* stool; *(pour les pieds)* footstool.

tac [tak] *nm* (**a**) *(bruit)* tap. (**b**) **il lui a répondu du** ~ **au** ~ he came back at him immediately *ou* quick as a flash. (**c**) *(jeu) type of national lottery played in France.*

tache [taʃ] *nf* (**a**) *[fruit]* mark; *[plumage, pelage]* spot; *[peau]* blotch, mark. ~ **de rousseur** freckle ; *(fig)* **faire** ~ to jar, stick out like a sore thumb. (**b**) *(salissure)* stain, mark. ~ **d'encre** *(sur les doigts)* ink stain; *(sur le papier)* ink blot *ou* blotch; ~ **d'huile** oily mark, oil stain; *(fig)* **faire** ~ **d'huile** to spread, gain ground; ~ **de sang** bloodstain; **sa robe n'avait pas une** ~ her dress was spotless. (**c**) *(sur réputation)* blot, stain. **sans** ~ *conduite* spotless, unblemished. (**d**) *(impression visuelle)* patch, spot. ~ **de couleur/d'ombre** patch of colour/shadow. (**e**) *(Peinture)* spot, dot, blob.

tâche [tɑʃ] *nf (travail)* task, work; *(mission)* task, job. **s'atteler à une** ~ to get down to work, get stuck in *; **mourir à la** ~ to die in harness; **à la** ~ *payer* by the piece; **travail à la** ~ piecework.

tacher [taʃe] (1) **1** *vt* (**a**) *[encre, vin]* to stain; *[graisse]* to mark, stain. **taché de sang** bloodstained. (**b**) *(colorer) pré, robe* to spot, dot; *peau, fourrure* to spot, mark. (**c**) *réputation* to stain. **2 se** ~ *vpr* *[personne]* to get stains on one's clothes; *[tissu]* to get stained *ou* marked; *(s'abîmer)* *[fruits]* to become marked.

tâcher [tɑʃe] (1) *vi*: ~ **de faire** to try to do; **tâchez de venir avant samedi** try to *ou* try and come before Saturday; **et tâche de ne pas recommencer** * and see to it that *ou* mind it doesn't happen again.

tacheter [taʃte] (4) *vt* to spot, dot, speckle.

tacite [tasit] *adj* tacit. ◆ **tacitement** *adv* tacitly.

taciturne [tasityʀn(ə)] *adj* taciturn, silent.

tacot * [tako] *nm (voiture)* banger *, crate *.

tact [takt] *nm* tact. **avoir du** ~ to have tact, be tactful; **avec** ~ tactfully; **sans** ~ *(adj)* tactless; *(adv)* tactlessly.

tactile [taktil] *adj* tactile.

tactique [taktik] **1** *adj* tactical. **2** *nf (gén)* tactics.

Tahiti [taiti] *nf* Tahiti. ◆ **tahitien, -ienne** *adj*, **T~(ne)** *nm(f)* Tahitian.

taie [tɛ] *nf* (**a**) ~ **(d'oreiller)** pillowcase, pillowslip; ~ **de traversin** bolster case. (**b**) *(Méd)* opaque spot.

taillader [tɑjade] (1) *vt* to slash, gash. ◆ **taillade** *nf* slash, gash, cut, wound.

taille[1] [tɑj] (**a**) *(hauteur) [personne, cheval, objet]* height. **homme de haute/petite** ~ tall/short man; **ils sont de la même** ~ they are the same height. (**b**) *(grosseur)* size. **de petite/moyenne** ~ small-/ medium-sized; **c'est de la** ~ **d'un crayon** it's the size of a pencil. (**c**) *(Comm: mesure)* size. **la** ~ **40** size 40; **ce pantalon n'est pas à sa** ~ these trousers aren't his size; **si je trouvais qn de ma** ~ if I found sb my size. (**d**) *(fig)* **c'est un poste à sa** ~ it's a job in keeping with *ou* which matches his capabilities; **il a trouvé un adversaire à sa** ~ he's met his match; **être de** ~ **à faire** to be up to doing, be quite capable of doing; **il n'est pas de** ~ *(face à un concurrent)* he doesn't measure up; **de** ~ *erreur, enjeu* considerable, sizeable. (**e**) *(ceinture)* waist. **avoir la** ~ **fine** to have a slim waist, be slim-waisted; **avoir la** ~ **mannequin** to have a perfect figure; **ils se tenaient par la** ~ they had their arms round each other's waist; **pantalon (à)** ~ **basse** low-waisted trousers, hipsters.

taille[2] [tɑj] *nf (action: V* **tailler***)* cutting; carving; engraving; pruning; trimming; clipping. *(résultat)* **de** ~ **hexagonale** with a six-sided cut. ◆**taille-crayon(s)** *nm inv* pencil sharpener.

tailler [taje] (1) **1** *vt* (**a**) *pierre* to cut; *bois* to carve; *verre* to engrave; *crayon* to sharpen; *tissu* to cut (out); *arbre* to prune, cut back; *haie* to trim, clip, cut; *barbe* to trim. ~ **qch en biseau** to bevel sth; ~ **qch en pointe** to cut *ou* sharpen sth to a point. (**b**) *vêtement* to make; *statue* to carve; *tartines* to cut, slice. *(fig)* **il a un rôle taillé à sa mesure** this role is tailor-made for him; ~ **une bavette** * to have a natter *; ~ **une armée en pièces** to hack an army to pieces; **il se ferait** ~ **en pièces pour elle** he'd go through fire *ou* he'd suffer tortures for her. **2** *vi*: ~ **dans la chair** to cut into the flesh. **3 se** ~ *vpr* (**a**) (⁂: *partir)* to beat it ⁂, clear off ⁂. (**b**) **se** ~ **un franc succès** to be a great success; **se** ~ **la part du lion** to take the lion's share; **se** ~ **un empire** to carve out an empire for o.s. ◆**taillé, e** *adj personne* **bien** ~ well-built; **il est** ~ **en athlète** he has an athletic build; *(fig)* **être** ~ **pour qch/pour faire qch** to be cut out for sth/to do sth. ◆**tailleur** *nm* (**a**) *(couturier)* tailor. **en** ~ *assis* cross-legged. (**b**) *(costume)* (woman's) suit. (**c**) ~ **de pierre(s)** stone-cutter.

taillis [taji] *nm* copse, coppice, thicket.

tain [tɛ̃] *nm [miroir]* silvering. **glace sans** ~ two-way mirror.

taire [tɛʀ] (54) **1 se** ~ *vpr* (**a**) *[personne]* to be silent *ou* quiet; *[nature, forêt]* to be silent; *[bruit]* to disappear. **ils ne voulaient pas se** ~ they wouldn't stop talking *ou* keep quiet; **l'orchestre s'était tu** the orchestra had fallen silent. (**b**) *(être discret)* to keep quiet, remain silent (*sur qch* about sth). **tais-toi!** * *(ne m'en parle pas)* don't talk to me about it! **2** *vt fait, vérité* to hush up, not to tell; *raisons* to conceal, say nothing about; *chagrin* to stifle, keep to o.s. **une personne dont je tairai le nom** a person who shall remain nameless *ou* whose name I shan't mention *ou* reveal. **3** *vi*: **faire** ~ *opposition* to silence; *craintes, désirs* to stifle, suppress; **fais** ~ **les enfants** make the children keep *ou* be quiet, make the children shut up *.

Taiwan [tajwan] *n* Taiwan.

talc [talk] *nm* talcum powder, talc.

talent [talɑ̃] *nm* talent. *(hum)* **montrez-nous vos** ~**s** * show us what you can do; **avoir du** ~ to have talent, be talented; **encourager les jeunes** ~**s** to encourage young talent; *(iro)* **il a le** ~ **de se faire des ennemis** he has a gift for making enemies. ◆**talentueux, -euse** *adj* talented.

taler [tale] (1) *vt fruits* to bruise.

talisman [talismɑ̃] *nm* talisman.

talkie-walkie [tɔkiwɔki] *nm* walkie-talkie.

taloche * [talɔʃ] *nf* clout, cuff. ◆**talocher** * (1) *vt* to clout, cuff.

talon [talɔ̃] *nm (gén, Anat)* heel; *[chèque]* stub, counterfoil; *(Cartes)* talon. **tourner les** ~**s** to turn on one's heel and leave; **être sur les** ~**s de qn** to be (hot) on sb's heels; ~ **d'Achille** Achilles' heel; ~**-minute** heel bar, on-the-spot shoe repairs. ◆**talonner** (1) *vt fugitifs* to follow (hot) on the heels of; *débiteur* to hound; *cheval* to kick; *[faim]* to gnaw at. *(Rugby)* ~ **(le ballon)** to heel (the ball). ◆**talonneur** *nm (Rugby)* hooker.

talquer [talke] (1) *vt* to put talcum powder *ou* talc on.

talus [taly] *nm [route]* embankment; *[rivière]* bank.

tambouille * [tɑ̃buj] *nf* grub *. **faire la** ~ to cook the grub *.

tambour [tɑ̃buʀ] *nm* (**a**) *(instrument)* drum. ~ **de basque** tambourine; ~ **battant** briskly; **sans** ~ **ni trompette** without any fuss, unobtrusively; **il est parti sans** ~ **ni trompette** he left quietly, he slipped away unobtrusively. (**b**) *(musicien)* drummer. ~**-major** drum major. (**c**) *(à broder)* embroidery hoop. (**d**) *(porte) (sas)* tambour; *(à tourniquet)* revolving door. (**e**) *[machine, à laver]* drum; *[moulinet]* spool. ~ **de frein** brake drum. ◆**tambourin** *nm* tambourine. ◆**tambouriner** (1) **1** *vi [personne, pluie]* to drum (*sur* on). **2** *vt musique* to drum out; *(fig) nouvelle* to broadcast.

tamis [tami] *nm (gén)* sieve; *(à sable)* riddle, sifter. **passer au** ~ *farine, plâtre* to sieve; *sable* to riddle, sift; *personne* to screen; *dossier* to sift through. ◆**tamisage** *nm* sieving; riddling, sifting; filtering. ◆**tamiser** (1) *vt farine* to sieve; *sable* to riddle, sift; *(fig) lumière* to filter. ◆**tamisé, e** *adj terre* sifted, sieved; *lumière (artificielle)* subdued; *(du jour)* soft, softened.

Tamise [tamiz] *nf*: **la** ~ the Thames.

tampon [tɑ̃pɔ̃] *nm* (**a**) *(pour boucher) (gén)* plug; *(en coton)* wad; *(pour nettoyer une plaie)* swab; *(pour étendre un liquide, un vernis)* pad. ~ **buvard** blotter; ~ **encreur** inking-pad; ~ **à récurer** scouring pad; **rouler qch en** ~ to roll sth (up) into a ball. (**b**) *(timbre)* stamp. **le** ~ **de la poste** the postmark. (**c**) *(Rail, fig: amortisseur)* buffer. **état** ~ buffer state. ◆**tamponner** (1) **1** *vt* (**a**) *(essuyer)* to mop up, dab; *yeux* to dab (at). (**b**) *(collision)* to ram (into), crash into. (**c**) *(avec un timbre)* to stamp. **faire** ~ **un reçu** to have a receipt stamped. **2 se** ~ *vpr* (**a**) *[trains]* to crash into each other, ram each other. (**b**) **se** ~ **de qch** ⁂ not to give a damn about sth ⁂.

tam-tam, *pl* **tams-tams** [tamtam] *nm* tomtom. **faire du** ~ **autour de** * *affaire* to make a lot of fuss *ou* a hullaballoo about.

tancer [tɑ̃se] (3) *vt (littér)* to scold, berate *(littér)*.

tandem [tɑ̃dɛm] *nm (bicyclette)* tandem; *(fig: duo)* pair, duo.

tandis [tɑ̃di] *conj*: ~ **que** *(simultanéité)* while; *(opposition)* whereas, while.

tangage [tɑ̃gaʒ] *nm (Naut)* pitching.

tangent, e [tɑ̃ʒɑ̃, ɑ̃t] **1** *adj (Géom)* tangent, tangential (*à* to). *(*: juste)* **c'était** ~ it was a close thing, it was touch-and-go; **il était** ~ he was a borderline case; **il a eu son examen mais c'était** ~ he passed his exam by the skin of his teeth *ou* but it was a near thing. **2** *nf (Géom)* tangent. **prendre la** ~**e** * *(partir)* to make off *, make o.s. scarce ; *(éluder)* to dodge the issue.

tangible [tɑ̃ʒibl(ə)] *adj* tangible.

tango [tɑ̃go] *nm* tango.

tanguer [tɑ̃ge] (1) *vi [navire, avion]* to pitch; *(fig)* to reel.

tanière [tanjɛʀ] *nf (lit, fig)* den, lair.

tank [tɑ̃k] *nm* tank.

tanker [tɑ̃kɛʀ] *nm* tanker.

tanner [tane] (1) *vt cuir* to tan; *visage* to weather. ~ **le cuir à qn** ‡ to tan sb's hide *; ~ **qn** * to pester sb. ◆ **tannage** *nm* tanning. ◆ **tannant, e** * *adj (ennuyeux)* maddening *. ◆ **tannerie** *nf (endroit)* tannery; *(activité)* tanning. ◆ **tanneur** *nm* tanner.

tant [tɑ̃] *adv* (**a**) *(intensité: avec vb)* so much. **il mange** ~! he eats so much! *ou* such a lot!; **vous m'en direz** ~! is that really so! (**b**) *(quantité)* ~ **de** *temps, eau* so much; *arbres, gens* so many; *habileté* such, so much; ~ **de fois** so many times, so often. (**c**) *(avec adj, participe)* so. **il est rentré** ~ **le ciel était menaçant** he went home (because) the sky looked so overcast; **cet enfant** ~ **désiré** this child they had longed for so much; ~ **il est vrai que...** since..., as... ; **le jour** ~ **attendu** the long-awaited day. (**d**) *(quantité imprécise)* so much. **gagner** ~ **par mois** to earn so much a month; ~ **pour cent** so many per cent. (**e**) *(comparaison)* **ce n'est pas** ~ **leur maison qui me plaît que leur jardin** it's not so much their house that I like as their garden; **il criait** ~ **qu'il pouvait** he shouted as much as he could *ou* for all he was worth; ~ **filles que garçons** both girls and boys, girls as well as boys, girls and boys alike. (**f**) ~ **que** *(aussi longtemps que)* as long as; *(pendant que)* while; ~ **qu'elle aura de la fièvre** while *ou* as long as she has a temperature; ~ **que vous y êtes** * while you are about it. (**g**) ~ **bien que mal** so-so, after a fashion; **s'il est** ~ **soit peu intelligent** if he is at all *ou* in the least bit intelligent; ~ **mieux** so much the better, that's fine; ~ **mieux pour lui** good for him; ~ **pis** *(conciliant)* never mind, (that's) too bad; *(indifférent)* (that's just) too bad; ~ **pis pour lui** (that's just) too bad for him; ~ **et si bien que** to such an extent that, so much so that; **il y en a** ~ **et plus** *[eau]* there is ever so much; *[objets]* there are ever so many; **il a protesté** ~ **et plus** he protested for all he was worth; ~ **qu'à faire, on va payer maintenant** we might *ou* may as well pay now; ~ **qu'à marcher, allons en forêt** if we have to walk let's go to the forest; ~ **que ça?** * that much?, as much as that?; **pas** ~ **que ça** * not that much; ~ **s'en faut** far from it.

tante [tɑ̃t] *nf (parente)* aunt, aunty *; *(‡: homosexuel)* poof ‡, queer ‡.

tantinet * [tɑ̃tinɛ] *nm*: **un** ~ **fatigant** a tiny *ou* weeny * bit tiring.

tantôt [tɑ̃to] *adv* (**a**) *(cet après-midi)* this afternoon. (**b**) *(parfois)* ~ **à pied,** ~ **en voiture** sometimes on foot, sometimes by car.

Tanzanie [tɑ̃zani] *nf* Tanzania. ◆ **tanzanien, -ienne** *adj,* **T~(ne)** *nm(f)* Tanzanian.

taon [tɑ̃] *nm* horsefly, gadfly.

tapage [tapaʒ] *nm* (**a**) *(vacarme)* din, uproar, row. **faire du** ~ to create a din *ou* an uproar, make a row; ~ **nocturne** disturbance of the peace *(at night)*. (**b**) *(battage)* fuss, talk *(autour de* about, over). ◆ **tapageur, -euse** *adj* (**a**) *(bruyant)* noisy, rowdy. (**b**) *publicité* obtrusive; *toilette* flashy, loud, showy.

tapant, e * [tapɑ̃, ɑ̃t] *adj*: **à 8 heures** ~**(es)** at 8 o'clock sharp *ou* on the dot *.

tape [tap] *nf (coup)* slap.

taper [tape] (1) **1** *vt* (**a**) *tapis* to beat; *enfant* to slap, clout; *porte* to bang, slam. ~ **un coup à la porte** to knock once at the door, give a knock at the door. (**b**) ~ **(à la machine)** *lettre* to type (out); **elle tape 60 mots par minute** her typing speed is 60 words a minute; **tapé à la machine** typed, typewritten. (**c**) *(‡: emprunter)* ~ **qn (de 10 F)** to touch sb * (for 10 francs), cadge (10 francs) off sb *. **2** *vi* (**a**) ~ **sur** *clou* to hit; *table* to bang *ou* rap on; ~ **sur qn** * *(coups)* to thump sb *; *(critiques)* to run sb down *; ~ **à la porte** to knock on the door; ~ **dans un ballon** to kick a ball about; ~ **dur** to hit hard. (**b**) *(‡: entamer)* ~ **dans** *provisions, caisse* to dig into *. (**c**) *[soleil]* to beat down. (**d**) ~ **des pieds** to stamp one's feet; ~ **des mains** to clap one's hands; *(fig)* **se faire** ~ **sur les doigts** * to be rapped over the knuckles; **il a tapé à côté** * he was wide of the mark; ~ **sur les nerfs de qn** * to get on sb's nerves *; ~ **dans l'œil de qn** * to take sb's fancy *; ~ **dans le tas** *(bagarre)* to pitch into the crowd; *(repas)* to tuck in *, dig in *. **3 se** ~ *vpr* (**a**) *(‡: s'envoyer) repas* to put away *; *marche* to do; *corvée* to get landed with *. (**b**) **c'est à se** ~ **la tête contre les murs** it's enough to drive you up the wall *; **se** ~ **la cloche** * to feed one's face *.

◆ **tape-à-l'œil** **1** *adj inv* flashy, showy. **2** *nm* show, flash *.

tapette [tapɛt] *nf* (**a**) *(pour tapis)* carpet beater; *(pour mouches)* flyswatter; *(pour souris)* mousetrap. (**b**) *(langue)* **elle a une (bonne)** ~ she's a real chatterbox *. (**c**) *(‡: homosexuel)* poof ‡, queer *.

tapeur, -euse * [tapœʀ, øz] *nm, f (emprunteur)* cadger *.

tapin ‡ [tapɛ̃] *nm*: **faire le** ~ to be on the game ‡, be a prostitute.

tapinois [tapinwa] *nm*: **en** ~ furtively.

tapioca [tapjɔka] *nm* tapioca.

tapir (se) [tapiʀ] (2) *vpr (se blottir)* to crouch; *(se cacher)* to hide away; *(s'embusquer)* to lurk.

tapis [tapi] *nm* (**a**) *(gén, fig)* carpet; *(petit)* rug; *(natte, dans un gymnase)* mat; *(sur un meuble)* cloth. ~ **vert** *(tissu)* green baize; *(table de jeu)* gambling table; ~**-brosse** doormat; ~ **roulant** *(pour colis etc)* conveyor belt; *(pour piétons)* moving walkway, travelator; *(pour bagages)* carousel. (**b**) **aller au** ~ to go down for the count; **envoyer qn au** ~ to floor sb; **mettre sur le** ~ *affaire* to lay on the table, bring up for discussion; **revenir sur le** ~ to come back up for discussion. ◆ **tapisser** (1) *vt* (**a**) *[personne] (de papier peint)* to (wall)paper; *(de tentures)* to hang, cover; *(d'affiches)* to plaster, cover *(de* with). (**b**) *[tenture, papier]* to cover, line; *[mousse, neige]* to carpet, cover; *(Anat, Bot)* to line. **tapissé de lierre** ivy-clad, covered in ivy. ◆ **tapisserie** *nf* (**a**) *(tenture)* tapestry; *(papier peint)* wallpaper, wall covering; *(activité)* tapestry-making. **faire de la** ~ to do tapestry work; *[danseur]* **faire** ~ to sit out. (**b**) *(broderie)* tapestry; *(activité)* tapestrywork. ◆ **tapissier, -ière** *nm, f (fabricant)* tapestry-maker; *(commerçant)* upholsterer; *(décorateur)* interior decorator.

taquin, e [takɛ̃, in] **1** *adj* teasing. **il est** ~ he is a tease *ou* teaser. **2** *nm, f* tease, teaser. ◆ **taquiner** (1) *vt [personne]* to tease; *[fait, douleur]* to bother, worry. ◆ **taquinerie** *nf*: ~**(s)** teasing.

tarabiscoté, e [taʀabiskɔte] *adj* (over-)ornate, fussy.

tarabuster [taʀabyste] (1) *vt [personne]* to badger, pester; *[fait, idée]* to bother, worry.

tarama [taʀama] *nm* taramasalata.

taratata [taʀatata] *excl* nonsense!, rubbish!

tard [taʀ] **1** *adv* late. **il se fait** ~ it's getting late; ~ **dans la matinée** late in the morning, in the late morning; **plus** ~ later (on); **jeudi au plus** ~ on Thursday at the latest; **pas plus** ~ **qu'hier** only yesterday; **pas plus** ~ **que la semaine dernière** just *ou* only last week, as recently as last week; **remettre qch à plus** ~ to put sth off till later (on). **2** *nm*: **sur le** ~ *(dans la vie)* late (on) in life. ◆ **tarder** (1) **1** *vi* (**a**) *(différer, traîner)* to delay. ~ **à entreprendre qch** to put off *ou* delay starting sth; **ne tardez pas (à le faire)** don't be long doing it; ~ **en chemin** to loiter on the way; **sans (plus)** ~ without (further) delay. (**b**) *[réaction, moment, lettre]* to be a long time coming. **ça n'a pas tardé** it wasn't long (in) coming; **ils ne vont pas** ~ they won't be long (now); **il n'a pas tardé à s'en apercevoir** it didn't take him long to notice, he noticed soon enough; **l'élève ne tarda pas à dépasser le maître** the pupil soon outstripped the teacher. **2** *vb impers*: **il me tarde de le revoir** I am longing *ou* I can't wait to see him again. ◆ **tardif, -ive** *adj (gén)* late; *regrets, remords* belated. ◆ **tardivement** *adv rentrer* late; *s'apercevoir* belatedly.

tare [taʀ] *nf* (**a**) *(contrepoids)* tare. **faire la** ~ to allow for the tare. (**b**) *[personne]* defect (*de* in, of); *[système]* flaw (*de* in), defect (*de* of). ◆ **taré, e 1** *adj régime* tainted, corrupt; *enfant* sickly, with a defect. **2** *nm, f (Méd)* degenerate; *(péj)* cretin *.

targette [taʀʒɛt] *nf* bolt *(on a door)*.

targuer (se) [taʀge] (1) *vpr*: **se ~ de qch/de faire qch** to boast about sth/that one can do sth, pride *ou* preen o.s. on sth/on doing sth.

tarif [taʀif] *nm (tableau)* price list, tariff; *(barème)* rate, tariff; *(taux)* rate. **les ~s postaux vont augmenter** postage rates are going up; **quels sont vos ~s?** *(réparateur)* how much do you charge?; *(profession libérale)* what are your fees?, what fee do you charge?; **voyager à plein ~/à ~ réduit** to travel at full/ reduced fare; *(hum)* **50 F d'amende, c'est le ~!** * a 50-franc fine is what you get! ◆ **tarifaire** *adj* tariff. ◆ **tarifer** (1) *vt* to fix the price *ou* rate for. **marchandises tarifées** fixed-price goods. ◆ **tarification** *nf* fixing of a price scale (*de* for).

tarir [taʀiʀ] (2) **1** *vi (gén)* to dry up; *[imagination, puits]* to run dry, dry up. **il ne tarit pas sur ce sujet** he can't stop talking about that. **2** *vt (lit, fig)* to dry up. **3 se ~** *vpr* to run dry, dry up. ◆ **tarissement** *nm* drying up.

tartare [taʀtaʀ] **1** *adj (Hist)* Tartar; *(Culin)* tartar(e). **2** *nmf*: **T~** Tartar.

tarte [taʀt(ə)] **1** *nf (Culin)* tart; *(‡: gifle)* clout. **c'est pas de la ~ ‡** it's no easy matter. **2** *adj inv* (*) *(bête)* daft *, stupid; *(laid)* plain-looking. ◆ **tartelette** *nf* tartlet, tart.

tartine [taʀtin] *nf* (**a**) slice of bread; *(beurrée)* slice of bread and butter. (**b**) *(*fig: lettre, article)* screed. ◆ **tartiner** (1) *vt pain* to spread (*de* with); *beurre* to spread. **fromage à ~** cheese spread.

tartre [taʀtʀ(ə)] *nm [dents]* tartar; *[chaudière]* fur.

tas [tɑ] *nm* (**a**) *(amas)* pile, heap. **mettre en ~** to put into a heap, heap *ou* pile up; **~ de fumier** manure heap. (**b**) *(*: beaucoup de)* **un** *ou* **des ~ de** loads of *, heaps of *, lots of; **un ~ de mensonges** a pack of lies; **~ de crétins** * you load of idiots! * (**c**) **tirer dans le ~** to fire into the crowd; **dans le ~, il n'y en a que 3 de bons** out of that lot there are only 3 that are any good; **j'ai acheté des cerises, tape** *ou* **pioche dans le ~** I've bought some cherries so dig in * *ou* so help yourself; **former qn sur le ~** to train sb on the job; **formation sur le ~** on-the-job training, in-house training.

Tasmanie [tasmani] *nf* Tasmania.

tasse [tɑs] *nf* cup. **~ à thé** teacup; **~ de thé** cup of tea; *(fig)* **boire une ~** * *(en nageant)* to swallow a mouthful.

tasser [tɑse] (1) **1** *vt (gén)* to pack; *passagers* to pack, cram; *sol* to pack down. **2 se ~** *vpr* (**a**) *[terrain]* to settle, sink, subside; *[vieillard]* to shrink. (**b**) *(se serrer)* to bunch *ou* squeeze up. (**c**) (*) **ça va se ~** things will settle down. ◆ **tassé, e** *adj*: **bien ~** * *(fort) whisky* stiff; *(bien rempli) verre* well-filled; **café bien ~** good strong coffee, coffee that is good and strong; **3 kilos bien ~s** a good 3 kilos. ◆ **tassement** *nm* (**a**) packing; settling, subsidence. **~ de la colonne (vertébrale)** compression of the spinal cord. (**b**) *(diminution)* **un ~ de l'activité économique** a downturn *ou* a slowing down in economic activity.

tata [tata] *nf (*: tante)* auntie *; *(‡: homosexuel)* poof ‡, queer ‡.

tâter [tɑte] (1) **1** *vt (palper)* to feel; *(fig: sonder)* to sound out. **marcher en tâtant les murs** to feel *ou* grope one's way along the walls; *(fig)* **~ le terrain** to see how the land lies. **2** *vi*: **~ de** *(gén)* to try; *mets* to taste; *prison* to sample. **3 se ~** *vpr* to feel o.s.; *(‡: hésiter)* to be in two minds.

tatillon, -onne [tatijɔ̃, ɔn] *adj* finicky, pernickety.

tâtonner [tɑtɔne] (1) *vi (lit, fig)* to grope around; *(par méthode)* to proceed by trial and error. ◆ **tâtonnement** *nm*: ~(**s**) trial and error, experimentation. ◆ **tâtons** *adv (lit, fig)* **avancer à ~** to grope along; **chercher qch à ~** to grope *ou* feel around for sth.

tatouage [tatwaʒ] *nm (action)* tattooing; *(dessin)* tattoo. ◆ **tatouer** (1) *vt* to tattoo.

taudis [todi] *nm* hovel. **quartier de ~** slum area.

taule ‡ [tol] *nf (prison)* nick ‡, clink ‡. **il a fait de la ~** he's done time, he has been inside *. ◆ **taulard, -arde ‡** *nm, f (arg crime)* convict, con *(arg)*.

taupe [top] *nf (animal, fig: espion)* mole; *(fourrure)* moleskin. *(péj)* **vieille ~** old crone. ◆ **taupinière** *nf* molehill.

taureau, *pl* **~x** [tɔʀo] *nm (Zool)* bull. *(Astron)* **le T~** Taurus, the Bull; *(fig)* **prendre le ~ par les cornes** to take the bull by the horns; **être (du) T~** to be Taurus *ou* a Taurean.

tautologie [totɔlɔʒi] *nf* tautology. ◆ **tautologique** *adj* tautological.

taux [to] *nm (gén, Fin, Statistique)* rate; *[infirmité]* degree; *[cholestérol]* level. **~ de change** exchange rate, rate of exchange.

taverne [tavɛʀn(ə)] *nf* inn, tavern.

taxe [taks(ə)] *nf (impôt)* tax; *(à la douane)* duty. **toutes ~s comprises** inclusive of tax; **~ à la valeur ajoutée** value added tax, VAT. ◆ **taxable** *adj (gén)* taxable; *(à la douane)* liable to duty, dutiable. ◆ **taxation** *nf* taxing, taxation; fixing the price. ◆ **taxer** (1) *vt* (**a**) *(imposer)* to tax; *(à la douane)* to impose *ou* put duty on. (**b**) *produit* to fix the price of. (**c**) **~ qn de qch** *(qualifier de)* to call sb sth; *(accuser de)* to accuse sb of sth.

taxi [taksi] *nm (voiture)* taxi, (taxi)cab; *(*: chauffeur)* cabby *, taxi driver.

taximètre [taksimɛtʀ(ə)] *nm* (taxi)meter.

taxiphone [taksifɔn] *nm* pay phone, public (tele)phone.

Tchad [tʃad] *nm*: **le ~** Chad; **le lac ~** Lake Chad. ◆ **tchadien, -ienne** *adj*, **T~(ne)** *nm(f)* Chad.

tchao [tʃao] *excl* bye!, cheerio!

Tchécoslovaquie [tʃekɔslɔvaki] *nf* Czechoslovakia. ◆ **tchécoslovaque** *adj* Czechoslovak(ian). ◆ **tchèque** *adj, nm,* **T~** *nmf* Czech.

tchin-(tchin) * [tʃin(tʃin)] *excl* cheers!

te [t(ə)] *pron* you; *(réfléchi)* yourself.

technicolor [tɛknikɔlɔʀ] *nm* technicolor.

technique [tɛknik] **1** *nf* technique. **2** *adj* technical. ◆ **technicien, -ienne** *nm, f* technician. ◆ **technicité** *nf* technical nature. ◆ **technico-commercial, e** *mpl* **-aux** *adj*: **(agent) ~** technical salesman. ◆ **techniquement** *adv* technically.

technocrate [tɛknɔkʀat] *nmf* technocrat. ◆ **technocratie** *nf* technocracy. ◆ **technocratique** *adj* technocratic. ◆ **technologie** *nf* technology. **~ de pointe** *ou* **avancée** frontier *ou* leading-edge *ou* advanced *ou* high technology. ◆ **technologique** *adj* technological. ◆ **technologue** *nmf* technologist.

teck [tɛk] *nm* teak.

teckel [tekɛl] *nm* dachshund.

Téhéran [teeʀɑ̃] *n* Teheran.

teigne [tɛɲ] *nf (Méd)* ringworm; *(péj: personne)* pest.

teindre [tɛ̃dʀ(ə)] (52) **1** *vt* to dye. **2 se ~** *vpr*: **se ~ (les cheveux)** to dye one's hair. ◆ **teint** *nm* *(permanent)* complexion, colouring; *(momentané)* colour. ◆ **teinte** *nf (nuance)* shade, tint; *(couleur)* colour; *(fig)* tinge, hint. ◆ **teinter** (1) *vt (gén)* to tint; *bois* to stain; *(fig)* to tinge. ◆ **teinture** *nf (colorant)* dye; *(action)* dyeing; *(Pharm)* tincture. *(fig)* **une ~ de maths** a smattering of maths. ◆ **teinturerie** *nf (métier)* dyeing; *(magasin)* (dry) cleaner's. ◆ **teinturier, -ière** *nm, f (qui nettoie)* dry cleaner; *(qui teint)* dyer.

tel, telle [tɛl] **1** *adj* (**a**) *(similitude, quantité)* such; *(dans comparaison)* like. **une telle ignorance/réponse** such ignorance/such an answer; **~ père, ~ fils** like father like son; **as-tu jamais rien vu de ~?** have you ever seen such a thing? *ou* anything like it?; **en tant que ~, comme ~** as such; **~ il était enfant, ~ je le retrouve** so he was as a child and so he has remained; *(littér)* **le lac ~ un miroir** the lake like a mirror. (**b**) *(indéfini)* such-and-such. **venez ~ jour** come on such-and-such a day; **telle quantité d'alcool** a given quantity of alcohol; **telle ou telle personne vous dira que** someone or other will tell you that. (**c**) **~ que** like, such as; **il est resté ~ que je le connaissais** he is still the same *ou* just as he used to be; **un homme ~ que lui** a man like him, such a man; **~ que je le connais, il ne viendra pas** if I know him, he won't come; **~ que vous me voyez, j'ai 72 ans** you wouldn't think it to look at me but I'm 72; **les métaux ~s que l'or et le platine** metals like *ou* such as gold and platinum; **laissez tous ces dossiers ~s quels** *ou* **~s que** * leave all those files as they are *ou* as you find them; *(sur objet en solde)* **'à vendre ~ quel'** 'sold as seen', 'sold as is'. (**d**) *(conséquence)* **de telle façon que** in such a way that; **de telle sorte que** so that; **à telle(s) enseigne(s) que** so much so that. **2** *pron indef*: **~ vous dira oui, ~ autre...** one will say yes, another...; **~ ou ~** somebody (or other); **~ est pris qui croyait prendre** (it's) the biter bitten.

télé * [tele] *nf (abrév de* **télévision***)* (**a**) *(organisme)* TV. **il travaille à la ~** he works on TV. (**b**) *(programmes)* TV. **qu'est-ce qu'il y a à la ~ ce soir?** what's on TV *ou* telly * tonight?; **la ~ du matin** breakfast TV. (**c**) *(chaîne)* TV channel. (**d**) *(poste)* TV. **allume la ~** turn on the TV *ou* the telly *.

téléboutique [telebutik] *nf* telephone shop.

télécommande [telekɔmɑ̃d] *nf* remote control. ◆ **télécommander** (1) *vt (Tech)* to operate by remote control. *(fig)* **ça a été télécommandé** it was initiated from elsewhere.

télécommunications [telekɔmynikɑsjɔ̃] *nfpl* telecommunications.

télécopie [telekɔpi] *nf* facsimile transmission, fax, telefax. **transmettre par ~** to send by fax *ou* facsimile. ◆ **télécopleur** *nm* facsimile *ou* fax machine.

télédiffusion [teledifyzjɔ̃] *nf* television broadcasting. ◆ **télédiffuser** (1) *vt* to broadcast by television.

téléenseignement [teleɑ̃sɛɲmɑ̃] *nm* television teaching, teaching by television.

téléférique [telefeʀik] *nm (installation)* cableway; *(cabine)* cable-car.

téléfilm [telefilm] *nm* television *ou* TV film.

télégramme [telegʀam] *nm* telegram, wire, cable.

télégraphe [telegʀaf] *nm* telegraph. ◆ **télégraphie** *nf* telegraphy. ◆ **télégraphier** (7) **1** *vt message* to telegraph, wire, cable. **2** *vi*: **~ à qn** to wire *ou* cable sb. ◆ **télégraphique** *adj fils* telegraph; *alphabet* Morse; *message, adresse, (fig) style* telegraphic. ◆ **télégraphiste** *nmf (messager)* telegraph boy.

téléguidage [telegidaʒ] *nm* radio control. ◆ **téléguider** (1) *vt (Tech)* to radio-control. *(fig)* **ça a été téléguidé** it was initiated from elsewhere.

téléinformatique [teleɛ̃fɔʀmatik] *nf* remote-access computing.

télématique [telematik] **1** *adj* telematic. **2** *nf* telematics *(sg)*.

téléobjectif [teleɔbʒɛktif] *nm* telephoto lens.

télépathie [telepati] *nf* telepathy. ◆ **télépathique** *adj* telepathic.

téléphone [telefɔn] *nm (système)* telephone; *(appareil)* (tele)phone. **avoir le ~** to be on the (tele)phone; **~ arabe** bush telegraph; **~ automatique** automatic telephone system; **~ à carte (magnétique)** cardphone; *(Pol)* **le ~ rouge** the hot line; **~ sans fil** cordless (tele)phone. ◆ **téléphoner** (1) **1** *vt* to (tele)phone. **téléphone-lui de venir** phone *ou* call him and tell him to come. **2** *vi* to phone, be on the phone. **~ à qn** to telephone sb, phone *ou* ring *ou* call sb (up). ◆ **téléphonique** *adj* telephone. ◆ **téléphoniste** *nmf* (telephone) operator.

téléprompteur [telepʀɔ̃ptœʀ] *nm* teleprompter.

téléreportage [teleʀ(ə)pɔʀtaʒ] *nm (activité)* television reporting. **un ~** a television report; **le car de ~** the outside-broadcast coach.

télescope [telɛskɔp] *nm* telescope. ◆ **télescopique** *adj (gén)* telescopic.

télescoper [telɛskɔpe] (1) **1** *vt véhicule* to smash up; *faits, idées* to mix up, jumble together. **2 se ~** *vpr [véhicules]* to telescope, concertina; *[souvenirs]* to become confused *ou* mixed up. ◆ **télescopage** telescoping, concertinaing.

téléscripteur [teleskʀiptœʀ] *nm* teleprinter.

télésiège [telesjɛʒ] *nm* chairlift.

téléski [teleski] *nm* (ski) lift, (ski) tow.

téléspectateur, -trice [telespɛktatœʀ, tʀis] *nm, f* (television *ou* TV) viewer. **les ~s** the viewing audience, the viewers.

Télétel [teletɛl] *nm* ® electronic telephone directory.

télétexte [teletekst] *nm* teletext, viewdata.

télétraitement [teletʀɛtmɑ̃] *nm* remote processing.

télétransmission [teletʀɑ̃smisjɔ̃] *nf* remote transmission.

télétype [teletip] *nm* teleprinter.

télévision [televizjɔ̃] *nf* (**a**) *(organisme, technique)* television. **la ~ par satellite** satellite television; **la ~ câblée** *ou* **par câble** cable television, cable vision *(US)*; **il travaille pour la ~ allemande** he works for German television. (**b**) *(programmes)* television. **à la ~** on television; **regarder la ~** to watch television; **la ~ du matin** breakfast television. (**c**) *(chaîne)* television channel. **les ~s étrangères** foreign channels. (**d**) *(poste)* television (set). ◆ **téléviser** (1) *vt* to televise. ◆ **téléviseur** *nm* television (set). ◆ **télévisuel, -elle** *adj* television.

télex [telɛks] *nm* telex. **envoyer par ~** to telex. ◆ **télexer** (1) *vt* to telex. ◆ **télexiste** *nmf* telex operator.

tellement [tɛlmɑ̃] *adv* (**a**) *(si)* so; *(avec comp)* so much. **il est ~ gentil** he's so (very) nice (*que* that); **~ mieux** so much better (*que l'autre* than the other). (**b**) *(tant)* so much. **~ de gens** so many people; **~ de temps** so much time, so long; **on ne le comprend pas, ~ il parle vite** he talks so quickly (that) you can't understand him; **il dort à peine, ~ il travaille** he hardly sleeps, he works so much *ou* hard. (**c**) *(avec nég)* **pas ~ fort** not (all) that strong, not so (very) strong; **il ne travaille pas ~** he doesn't work (all) that much *ou* so (very) much; **tu aimes le cinéma? — pas ~** do you like the cinema? — not (all) that much *ou* — not (very) much; **on ne la voit plus ~** we don't really see (very) much of her any more.

téméraire [temeʀɛʀ] *adj action, personne* rash, reckless, foolhardy; *jugement* rash. ◆ **témérairement** *adv* rashly; recklessly; foolhardily. ◆ **témérité** *nf* rashness; recklessness; foolhardiness.

témoignage [temwaɲaʒ] *nm* (**a**) *(gén, Jur)* testimony, evidence; *(fig: récit, reportage)* account, testimony. **ces ~s sont contradictoires** these are contradictory pieces of evidence; **porter ~ de qch** to testify to sth, bear witness to sth. (**b**) *(preuve)* **~ de** *bonne conduite* evidence *ou* proof of; *confiance* expression of; **~ d'amitié** *(geste)* expression of friendship: *(cadeau)* token *ou* mark *ou* sign of friendship; **en ~ de ma reconnaissance** as a token *ou* mark of my gratitude; **en ~ de quoi...** in witness whereof...

témoigner [temwaɲe] (1) **1** *vi (Jur)* to testify, give evidence. **2** *vt* (**a**) *goût, intérêt* to show, display. (**b**) **~ que** *[témoin]* to testify that; *[attitude, situation]* to attest *ou* reveal *ou* show that. **3 ~ de** *vt indir [conduite, évolution]* to attest, show. *[personne]* **je peux en ~** I can testify to that, I can bear witness to that.

témoin [temwɛ̃] **1** *nm* (**a**) *(gén, Jur)* witness; *[duel]* second. **~ oculaire** eyewitness; **~ à charge/à décharge** witness for the prosecution/for the defence; **être ~ de** to witness, be a witness to; **prendre qn à ~ (de qch)** to call sb to witness (to *ou* of sth); **faire qch sans ~** to do sth unwitnessed; **que Dieu m'en soit ~** as God is my witness. (**b**) *(preuve)* evidence, testimony. **les ~s d'une époque révolue** the surviving evidence of a bygone age. (**c**) *(Sport)* baton. **passer le ~** to hand on *ou* pass the baton. **2** *adj sujet, échantillon* control. **appartement ~** show-flat, model apartment *(US)*; **réalisation ~** pilot *ou* test development; **lampe ~** warning light.

tempe [tɑ̃p] *nf (Anat)* temple.

tempérament [tɑ̃peʀamɑ̃] *nm* (**a**) *(physique)* constitution; *(caractère)* disposition, temperament, nature. (**b**) *(Comm)* **vente à ~** sale on deferred (payment), terms; **acheter qch à ~** to buy sth on hire purchase *ou* on an installment plan *(US)*.

tempérance [tɑ̃peʀɑ̃s] *nf* temperance. ◆ **tempérant, e** *adj* temperate.

température [tɑ̃peʀatyʀ] *nf* temperature. **avoir** *ou* **faire de la ~** to have a temperature; **prendre la ~ de** *malade* to take the temperature of; *auditoire, public* to gauge the temperature of.

tempérer [tɑ̃peʀe] (16) *vt climat, ardeur, sévérité* to temper; *douleur* to soothe, ease. ◆ **tempéré, e** *adj climat* temperate.

tempête [tɑ̃pɛt] *nf (lit, fig)* storm. **~ de sable** sandstorm; **vent qui souffle en ~** gale force wind; **une ~ dans un verre d'eau** a storm in a teacup; **une ~ d'applaudissements** a storm of applause, thunderous applause. ◆ **tempêter** (1) *vi* to rant and rave, rage. ◆ **tempétueux, -euse** *adj* tempestuous, stormy.

temple [tɑ̃pl(ə)] *nm (Hist, littér)* temple; *(protestant)* (Protestant) church.

temporaire [tɑ̃pɔʀɛʀ] *adj* temporary. ◆ **temporairement** *adv* temporarily.

temporel, -elle [tɑ̃pɔʀɛl] *adj* (**a**) *(Rel) (non spirituel)* worldly, temporal; *(non éternel)* temporal. (**b**) *(Ling, Philos)* temporal.

temporiser [tɑ̃pɔʀize] (1) *vi* to temporize, delay, stall, play for time. ◆ **temporisateur, -trice 1** *adj* temporizing, delaying, stalling. **2** *nm, f* temporizer. ◆ **temporisation** *nf* temporization, delaying, stalling, playing for time.

temps¹ [tɑ̃] *nm* (**a**) *(durée)* **le ~** time; **il a mis beaucoup de ~ à se préparer** he took a long time to get ready; **avec le ~** with *ou* in time; **la jeunesse n'a qu'un ~** youth will not endure; **travailler à plein ~/à ~ partiel** to work full-time/part-time; **peu de ~ avant/après** shortly before/after, a short while *ou* time before/after; **dans quelque ~** before too long, in a (little) while; **pour un ~** for a time *ou* while; **durant (tout) ce ~ (là)** all this time; **je ne le vois plus depuis quelque ~** I haven't seen him for a (little) while *ou* some (little) time.
(**b**) *(portion de temps)* time. **~ d'arrêt** pause, halt; **marquer un ~ d'arrêt** to pause (momentarily); **~ mort** *(dans le travail)* slack period; *(dans la conversation)* lull; **s'accorder un ~ de réflexion** to give o.s. time for reflection; **la plupart du ~** most of the time; **avoir le ~ (de faire)** to have time (to do); **il avait du ~ devant lui** he had time to spare; **prendre le ~ de vivre** to make time to enjoy o.s.; **prenez votre ~** take your time; **passer son ~ à lire** to spend one's time reading; **donnez-moi le ~ de m'habiller** just give me time *ou* a moment to get dressed; **je me suis arrêté juste le ~ de prendre un verre** I stopped just long enough for a drink; **le ~ perdu ne se rattrape jamais** time and tide wait for no man; *[soldat, prisonnier]* **faire son ~** to serve one's time; *(fig) [personne]* **il a fait son ~** he has had his day.
(**c**) *(moment précis)* time. **il est grand ~ qu'il parte** it's high time he went, it's time for him to go; **le ~ est venu de...** the time has come to...; **il était ~!** *(pas trop tôt)* none too soon!, not before time!; *(c'était juste)* it came in the nick of time!; **il n'est plus ~ de se lamenter** the time for bemoaning one's lot is past *ou* over.
(**d**) *(époque)* time, times, days. **en ~ de guerre** in wartime; **en ~ de crise** in times of crisis; **par les ~ qui courent** these days, nowadays; **c'était le bon ~** those were the good times, those were the days; **dans le ~** at one time; **dans le bon vieux ~** in the good old days; **en ce ~ là** at that time; **en ~ normal** in normal circumstances; **les premiers ~** at the beginning, at first; **ces derniers ~** lately, recently, latterly; **dans un premier ~** at first; **dans un deuxième ~** subsequently; **au ~ des Tudors** in Tudor times, in the days of the Tudors; **de mon ~** in my day *ou* time; **dans mon jeune ~** in my younger days; **être de son ~** to move with *ou* keep up with the times; **les jeunes de notre ~** young people of our time *ou* (of) today; **le ~ des vacances** holiday time.
(**e**) *(Mus)* beat; *(Gym) [mouvement]* stage. **~ fort/faible** strong/weak beat; *(fig)* **les ~ forts d'un roman** the powerful moments of a novel; **à deux/trois ~** in double/triple time.
(**f**) *(Ling) [verbe]* tense. **~ simple/composé** simple/compound tense.
(**g**) *(Tech)* stroke. **moteur à 4 ~** 4-stroke engine.
(**h**) *(Sport) [coureur]* time.
(**i**) *(locutions)* **à ~** in time; **de ~ en ~, de ~ à autre** from time to time, now and again; **de tout ~** from time immemorial; **au ~ où** in the days when, at the time when; **en ~ voulu** *ou* **utile** in due time *ou* course; **à ~ perdu** in one's spare time; **cela fait passer le ~** it passes the time; **le ~ c'est de l'argent** time is money.

temps² [tɑ̃] *nm (conditions atmosphériques)* weather. **quel ~ fait-il?** what's the weather like?; **il fait beau/mauvais ~** the weather's fine/bad; **avec le ~ qu'il fait!** in this weather!, with the weather we are having!; **~ de chien *** rotten * *ou* lousy * weather; **le ~ est lourd aujourd'hui** it's close today; *(fig)* **prendre le ~ comme il vient** to take things as they come.

tenable [t(ə)nabl(ə)] *adj*: **ce n'est pas ~** it's unbearable.

tenace [tənas] *adj* (**a**) *(persistant) (gén)* stubborn, persistent; *volonté* tenacious, stubborn. (**b**) *colle* firmly adhesive, strong. ◆ **tenacement** *adv* stubbornly; persistently; tenaciously. ◆ **ténacité** *nf* stubbornness; persistence; tenacity.

tenaille [t(ə)nɑj] *nf*: **~(s)** *[menuisier]* pliers, pincers; *[forgeron]* tongs; *(Mil)* **prendre en** ~ to catch in a pincer movement.

tenailler [tənɑje] (1) *vt [inquiétude]* to torture, torment. **la faim le tenaillait** he was gnawed by hunger.

tenancier [tənɑ̃sje] *nm [bar]* manager. ◆ **tenancière** *nf [bar]* manageress.

tenant [tənɑ̃] *nm* (**a**) *[doctrine]* supporter, upholder (*de* of); *(Sport) [coupe]* holder. **le** ~ **du titre** the title holder, the reigning champion. (**b**) **les ~s et (les) aboutissants d'une affaire** the ins and outs of a question; **d'un (seul)** ~ *terrain* all in one piece.

tendance [tɑ̃dɑ̃s] *nf* (**a**) *(inclination, Psych)* tendency. ~ **à l'exagération** tendency to exaggerate. (**b**) *(opinions) [parti, artiste]* leanings; *[livre]* drift, tenor. **quelle est sa** ~ **(politique)?** what are his (political) leanings? *ou* sympathies? (**c**) *(évolution) [art, économie, public]* trend. ~ **à la hausse** upward trend. (**d**) **avoir** ~ **à faire qch** to have a tendency *ou* tend *ou* be inclined to do sth.

tendancieux, -ieuse [tɑ̃dɑ̃sjø, jøz] *adj* tendentious.

tendon [tɑ̃dɔ̃] *nm* tendon, sinew. ~ **d'Achille** Achilles' tendon.

tendre[1] [tɑ̃dʀ(ə)] (41) **1** *vt* (**a**) *(raidir) corde* to tighten, tauten; *ressort* to set; *muscles* to tense, brace; *pièce de tissu* to stretch, pull *ou* draw tight. (**b**) *(installer) tenture* to hang; *piège, filet* to set. ~ **une bâche sur une remorque** to stretch *ou* pull a tarpaulin over a trailer; ~ **un fil entre deux points** to stretch a thread between two points; ~ **une pièce de tissu** to hang a room with material. (**c**) *(avancer) cou* to crane; *joue* to offer; *main* to hold out; *bras* to stretch out (*à* to). ~ **une main secourable** to hold out *ou* offer a helping hand; ~ **l'oreille** to prick up one's ears. (**d**) ~ **qch à qn** *(donner)* to hold sth out to sb; *(offrir)* to offer sth to sb; *(fig)* ~ **une perche à qn** to throw sb a line. **2 se** ~ *vpr [corde]* to become taut, tighten; *[rapports]* to become strained. **3** *vi*: ~ **à qch/à faire** *(avoir tendance à)* to tend towards sth/to do; *(viser à)* to aim at sth/to do; *(Math)* ~ **vers l'infini** to tend towards infinity.

tendre[2] [tɑ̃dʀ(ə)] *adj* (**a**) *peau, pierre* soft; *haricots, viande* tender. **l'herbe** ~ the sweet grass; **depuis sa plus** ~ **enfance** from his earliest days; **c'est** ~ **comme la rosée** it melts in the mouth. (**b**) *(affectueux) ami, amour, regard* fond, tender, loving. **ne pas être** ~ **pour qn** to be hard on sb. (**c**) *couleurs* soft, delicate. ◆ **tendrement** *adv* tenderly; lovingly; fondly. ◆ **tendresse** *nf* tenderness; fondness. ~ **maternelle** maternal love; **combler qn de ~s** to overwhelm sb with tenderness *ou* with tokens of (one's) love; **n'avoir aucune** ~ **pour** to have no fondness for. ◆ **tendreté** *nf [viande]* tenderness; *[bois, métal]* softness.

tendu, e [tɑ̃dy] *adj corde, toile* tight, taut; *muscles* tensed, braced; *ressort* set; *(Ling) voyelle, prononciation* tense; *rapports* strained, fraught; *personne* tense, strained; *situation* tense, fraught. **les bras ~s** with arms outstretched; ~ **de** *velours, soie* hung with.

ténèbres [tenɛbʀ(ə)] *nfpl* darkness, gloom. ◆ **ténébreux, -euse** *adj (obscur)* dark, gloomy; *(mystérieux)* dark; *époque* obscure.

teneur [tənœʀ] *nf (gén)* content; *[lettre]* content, terms; *[solution]* content.

tenir [t(ə)niʀ] (22) **1** *vt* (**a**) *(maintenir) (avec les mains, une ficelle)* to hold; *(en position)* to hold, keep; *(dans un état)* to keep; *(Mus) note* to hold. ~ **les yeux fermés** to keep one's eyes shut; **une robe qui tient chaud** a dress which keeps you warm; **elle tient ses enfants très propres** she keeps her children very neat; ~ **qch en place** to hold *ou* keep sth in place; **ses affaires le tiennent** he is tied *ou* tied up *(US)* by his business; **l'envie me tenait de...** I was gripped by the desire to... (**b**) *voleur,* (*) *rhume etc* to have, have caught; *vérité, preuve* to hold, have. *(menace)* **si je le tenais!** if I could get my hands on him! *ou* lay hands on him!; **nous le tenons** we've got him; **nous tenons un bon filon** we're on to a good thing; **mieux vaut** ~ **que courir** a bird in the hand is worth two in the bush. (**c**) *(avec autorité) enfant, classe* to have *ou* keep under control; *pays* to have under one's control. (**d**) *(gérer) hôtel, magasin* to run, keep; *registre* to keep; *(Comm) marchandise* to stock, keep; *conférence, emploi* to hold; *maison, ménage* to keep. (**e**) ~ **de qn** *renseignement, bijou* to have (got) from sb; **il tient cela de son père** he gets that from his father. (**f**) *(occuper) place, largeur* to take up. **tu tiens trop de place!** you are taking up too much room!; *(Aut)* **il ne tenait pas sa droite** he was not keeping to the right. (**g**) *(contenir) [récipient]* to hold. (**h**) *(résister) [souliers]* ~ **l'eau** to keep out the water; *(Naut)* ~ **la mer** to be seaworthy; *(Aut)* ~ **la route** to hold the road. (**i**) *promesse* to keep; *pari (accepter)* to take on; *(respecter)* to keep to, honour. (**j**) *discours* to give; *langage* to use. ~ **des propos désobligeants à l'égard de qn** to make *ou* pass offensive remarks about sb, say offensive things about sb; **si tu tiens ce raisonnement** if this is the view you hold *ou* take, if this is how you think. (**k**) ~ **qn/qch pour** to regard sb/sth as, consider sb/sth (as), hold sb/sth to be; ~ **pour certain que...** to regard it as certain that... (**l**) **tiens!** *(en donnant)* take this, here (you are); *(de surprise)* ah!; *(pour attirer l'attention)* look!; **tiens, tiens** * well, well!, fancy that!; **tenez, ça m'écœure** you know, that sickens me.

2 *vi* (**a**) *[objet, fixe, nœud]* to hold; *[échafaudage]* to stay up, hold (up). **l'armoire tient au mur** the cupboard is held *ou* fixed to the wall; **ce chapeau ne tient pas sur ma tête** this hat won't stay on (my head); ~ **debout** *[objet]* to be upright, be standing; *[personne]* to be standing; **son histoire ne tient pas debout** his story doesn't make sense *ou* doesn't hold together *ou* doesn't hold water; **il tient bien sur ses jambes** he is very steady on his legs; **cet enfant ne tient pas en place** this child cannot keep *ou* stay still. (**b**) *(être valable)* to be on. **il n'y a pas de bal qui tienne** there's no question of going to any dance; **ça tient toujours, notre pique-nique?** * is our picnic still on? *, does our picnic still stand? (**c**) *(Mil, gén: résister)* ~ (**bon** *ou* **ferme**) to hold *ou* stand firm; **je n'ai pas pu** ~ *(chaleur)* I couldn't stand it; *(colère)* I couldn't contain myself. (**d**) *(être contenu dans)* ~ **dans** to fit in(to); **nous tenons à 4 à cette table** this table seats 4, we can get 4 round this table; **son discours tient en quelques pages** his speech is just a few pages long; **ma réponse tient en un seul mot: non** my answer is just one word long: no. (**e**) *[accord, beau temps]* to hold; *[couleur]* to be fast; *[mariage]* to last; *[fleurs]* to last (well); *[mise en plis]* to hold, stay in.

3 ~ **à** *vt indir* (**a**) *(aimer) réputation* to value, care about; *objet, personne* to be attached to, be fond of; *vie* to care about. **un peu de vin? — je n'y tiens pas** would you like some wine? — not really, not particularly. (**b**) *(vouloir)* **il tient beaucoup à vous connaître** he is very anxious to meet you *ou* keen *ou* eager to meet you; **il tient à ce que nous sachions...** he insists *ou* is anxious that we should know...; **si vous y tenez** if you really want to, if you insist. (**c**) *(avoir pour cause)* to be due to, stem from. **ça tient au climat** it's because of the climate, it's due to the climate.

4 ~ **de** *vt indir (ressembler à) parent* to take after. **il a de qui** ~ it runs in the family; **sa réussite tient du prodige** his success is something of a miracle.

5 *vb impers* to depend. **il ne tient qu'à elle** it's up to her, it depends on her; **à quoi cela tient-il qu'il**

n'écrive pas? how is it *ou* why is it that he doesn't write?; **qu'à cela ne tienne** never mind (that), that needn't matter; **cela tient à peu de chose** it's touch and go, it's in the balance.
6 se ~ *vpr* (**a**) **se** ~ **la tête** to hold one's head; **se** ~ **par la main** to hold hands; **se** ~ **à qch** to hold on to sth; **il se tenait le ventre de douleur** he was clutching *ou* holding his stomach in pain; **se** ~ **debout/couché/à genoux** to be standing (up)/lying (down)/kneeling (down); **tenez-vous prêts à partir** be ready to leave; **elle se tenait à sa fenêtre** she was standing at her window; **tiens-toi tranquille** keep still; **tiens-toi bien** *ou* **droit** *(debout)* stand up straight; *(assis)* sit up (straight). (**b**) *(se conduire)* to behave. **tiens-toi bien!** behave yourself! (**c**) *(réunion etc: avoir lieu)* to be held. (**d**) *[faits etc] (être liés)* to hang *ou* hold together. (**e**) *(se retenir)* **il ne peut se** ~ **de rire** he can't help laughing; **il ne se tenait pas de joie** he couldn't contain his joy; **se** ~ **à quatre pour ne pas faire qch** to struggle to stop o.s. (from) doing sth. (**f**) **s'en** ~ **à qch** *(se limiter à)* to confine o.s. to sth; *(se satisfaire de)* to content o.s. with sth; **nous nous en tiendrons là pour aujourd'hui** we'll leave it at that for today; **il aimerait savoir à quoi s'en** ~ he'd like to know where he stands; **je sais à quoi m'en** ~ **sur son compte** I know exactly who I'm dealing with. (**g**) *(se considérer)* **il ne se tient pas pour battu** he doesn't consider himself beaten; **tenez-vous-le pour dit** consider yourself told *ou* warned once and for all.

tennis [tenis] **1** *nm* (**a**) *(sport)* tennis. ~ **sur gazon/terre battue** lawn/hard-court tennis; ~ **de table** table tennis. (**b**) *(terrain)* (tennis) court. **2** *nmpl (chaussures)* gym shoes, sneakers; *(pour jouer au tennis)* tennis shoes. ◆ **tennisman,** *pl* **tennismen** *nm* tennis player. ◆ **tenniswoman,** *pl* **tenniswomen** *nf* tennis player.

ténor [tenɔʀ] **1** *nm (Mus)* tenor; *(fig)* big name (*de* in). **2** *adj* tenor.

tension [tɑ̃sjɔ̃] *nf* (**a**) *[ressort etc]* tension. (**b**) *(Élec)* voltage, tension. **à haute/basse** ~ high-/low-voltage *ou* tension; **sous** ~ *(lit)* live; *(fig)* under stress; **chute de** ~ voltage, drop; **mettre un appareil sous** ~ to switch on a piece of equipment. (**c**) *(Méd)* ~ **(artérielle)** blood pressure; **avoir de la** ~ to have (high) blood pressure; ~ **nerveuse** nervous tension; *(fig)* ~ **d'esprit** sustained mental effort. (**d**) *(fig) [relations]* tension (*de* in); *[situation]* tenseness (*de* of). ◆ **tensiomètre** *nm* tensiometer.

tentacule [tɑ̃takyl] *nm (Zool, fig)* tentacle. ◆ **tentaculaire** *adj (Zool)* tentacular; *(fig)* sprawling.

tente [tɑ̃t] *nf (gén)* tent. **coucher sous la** ~ to sleep under canvas, sleep out, camp out; ~ **à oxygène** oxygen tent.

tenter [tɑ̃te] (1) *vt* (**a**) *(séduire)* to tempt. **se laisser** ~ to yield to temptation; ~ **le diable** to tempt fate, ask for trouble. (**b**) *(essayer)* to try, attempt. ~ **l'impossible pour...** to attempt the impossible to...; ~ **le tout pour le tout** to risk one's all; ~ **sa chance** to try one's luck; ~ **le coup** * to have a go *, give it a try; ~ **de faire** to attempt *ou* try to do. ◆ **tentant, e** *adj (gén)* tempting; *offre, projet* attractive, enticing. ◆ **tentateur, -trice 1** *adj (gén)* tempting; *beauté* alluring, enticing. **2** *nm* tempter. **3** *nf* temptress. ◆ **tentation** *nf* temptation. ◆ **tentative** *nf (gén)* attempt, endeavour; *(sportive, style journalistique)* bid, attempt. ~ **de meurtre** *(gén)* murder attempt; *(Jur)* attempted murder.

tenture [tɑ̃tyʀ] *nf (tapisserie)* hanging; *(rideau)* curtain. ~ **murale** wall covering.

tenu, e[1] [t(ə)ny] *adj* (**a**) **bien/mal** ~ *enfant* well/poorly turned out; *maison* well/poorly kept *ou* looked after. (**b**) *(surveillé)* **leurs filles sont très** ~**es** their daughters are kept on a tight rein. (**c**) *(obligé)* **être** ~ **de faire** to be obliged to do, have to do; **être** ~ **au secret professionnel** to be bound by professional secrecy.

tenue[2] [t(ə)ny] *nf* (**a**) *[maison]* upkeep, running; *[magasin]* running; *[classe]* handling, control; *[séance]* holding. **la** ~ **des livres de comptes** the book-keeping. (**b**) *(conduite)* (good) manners, good behaviour. **un peu de** ~! behave yourself!, watch your manners!; *(Fin)* **la bonne** ~ **du franc face au dollar** the good performance of the franc against the dollar. (**c**) *(qualité) [journal]* standard, quality. **publication de haute** ~ quality publication. (**d**) *(maintien)* posture. (**e**) *(apparence)* appearance; *(vêtements)* dress, clothes; *(uniforme)* uniform. ~ **d'intérieur** indoor clothes; **en** ~ **légère** *(d'été)* wearing light clothing; *(osée)* scantily dressed; **en grande** ~ in full dress (uniform); **les policiers en** ~ uniformed policemen, policemen in uniform; ~ **de combat/de soirée** battle/evening *ou* formal dress; '~ **de soirée de rigueur**' ≃ 'black tie'. (**f**) *(Aut)* ~ **de route** road holding.

ténu, e [teny] *adj point, fil* fine; *brume, voix* thin; *raisons, nuances* tenuous.

ter [tɛʀ] *adj (numéro)* **10** ~ (number) 10 B.

térébenthine [teʀebɑ̃tin] *nf* turpentine.

tergal [tɛʀgal] *nm* ® Terylene ®.

tergiverser [tɛʀʒivɛʀse] (1) *vi* to procrastinate. ◆ **tergiversations** *nfpl* procrastinations.

terme [tɛʀm(ə)] *nm* (**a**) *(mot)* term. **en** ~**s clairs** in clear terms; **en d'autres** ~**s** in other words. (**b**) *[équation, contrat]* term. (**c**) *(date limite)* time limit, deadline; *[vie, voyage, récit]* end, term. **arriver à** ~ *[délai]* to expire; *[opération]* to reach its conclusion; *[paiement]* to fall due; **mettre un** ~ **à qch** to put an end *ou* a stop to sth; **mener qch à** ~ to bring sth to completion; **à court/long** ~ *emprunt, projet* short-/long-term; *(Bourse)* **marché à** ~ † forward market. (**d**) *(Méd)* **à** ~ *accouchement* full-term; *naître* at term; **avant** ~ *naître* prematurely; *naissance* premature; **un bébé né 2 mois avant** ~ a baby born 2 months premature. (**e**) *[loyer] (date)* term; *(période)* quarter (year); *(somme)* (quarterly) rent. (**f**) *(relations)* ~**s** terms; **en bons/mauvais** ~**s avec qn** on good/bad terms with sb.

terminer [tɛʀmine] (1) **1** *vt* (**a**) *séance* to bring to an end *ou* to a close, terminate; *travail* to finish (off), complete; *repas, récit* to finish, end. ~ **un repas par un café** to finish off *ou* end a meal with a coffee; **j'en ai terminé avec eux** I am *ou* have finished with them, I have done with them; **pour** ~ **je dirais que...** in conclusion *ou* to conclude I would say that.... (**b**) *(dernier élément)* **le café termina le repas** the meal finished *ou* ended with coffee; **un bourgeon termine la tige** the stalk ends in a bud. **2 se** ~ *vpr (gén)* to end (*par* with, *en* in); *[repas, vacances]* to (come to an) end. **se** ~ **en pointe** to end in a point. ◆ **terminaison** *nf* ending. ◆ **terminal, e,** *mpl* **-aux 1** *adj élément, bourgeon, phase de maladie* terminal. *(Scol)* **classe** ~**e** final year, ≃ upper sixth (form), senior year *(US)*; **malade au stade** ~ terminally ill patient. **2** *nm (aérogare) (air)* terminal; *[pétrole, marchandises]* terminal; *(ordinateur)* terminal. ~ **intelligent/passif** smart *ou* intelligent/dumb terminal. **3 terminale** *nf (Scol) V* **1**.

terminologie [tɛʀminɔlɔʒi] *nf* terminology.

terminus [tɛʀminys] *nm* terminus.

termite [tɛʀmit] *nm* termite, white ant. ◆ **termitière** *nf* ant-hill.

terne [tɛʀn(ə)] *adj (gén)* dull, drab; *regard* lifeless.

ternir [tɛʀniʀ] (2) **1** *vt métal* to tarnish; *glace* to dull; *réputation* to stain, tarnish. **2 se** ~ *vpr* to become tarnished; to become dull.

terrain [tɛʀɛ̃] **1** *nm* (**a**) *(relief)* ground; *(sol)* soil, ground; *(Géol: formation)* formation. ~ **lourd** heavy soil *ou* ground. (**b**) *(Ftbl, Rugby)* pitch, field;

(avec les installations) ground; *(Courses, Golf)* course; *(Basketball)* basketball court. **sur le ~** on the field; **disputer un match sur ~ adverse/sur son propre ~** to play an away/a home match. (**c**) *(parcelle)* plot (of land), piece of land; *(à bâtir)* site. **maison avec 2 hectares de ~** house with 2 hectares of land; **le prix du ~** the price of land. (**d**) *(Mil) (lieu d'opérations)* terrain; *(gagné ou perdu)* ground. *(lit, fig)* **gagner/perdre du ~** to gain/lose ground; **reconnaître le ~** *(lit)* to reconnoitre the terrain; *(fig)* to see how the land lies; *(fig)* **tâter le ~** to test the ground; **préparer/déblayer le ~** to prepare/clear the ground; *(Sociol etc)* **sur le ~** in the real world, in the field. (**e**) *(fig: sujet)* ground. **être sur son ~** to be on home ground *ou* territory; **trouver un ~ d'entente** to find common ground *ou* an area of agreement; **je ne le suivrai pas sur ce ~** I can't go along with him there *ou* on that; **sur un ~ glissant** on slippery *ou* dangerous ground. (**f**) *[épidémie]* breeding ground. **2** : **~ d'aviation** airfield; **~ de camping** campsite, camping ground; **~ de sport** sports ground; **un ~ vague** a piece of *ou* some waste ground.

terrasse [tɛʀas] *nf [parc, appartement]* terrace; *(sur le toit]* terrace roof; *[café]* terrace, pavement (area). **à la ~ (du café)** at the terrace of the café, outside (the café).

terrasser [tɛʀase] (1) *vt* (**a**) *[adversaire]* to floor, bring down; *[fatigue]* to overcome; *[attaque]* to bring down; *[émotion]* to overwhelm; *[maladie]* to strike down. (**b**) *(Tech)* to excavate, dig out. ◆ **terrassement** *nm (action)* excavation. *(remblais)* **~s** excavations, earthworks; *[voie ferrée]* embankments. ◆ **terrassier** *nm* unskilled road worker, navvy.

terre [tɛʀ] **1** *nf* (**a**) **la ~** *(planète)* the earth; *(monde)* the world; **parcourir la ~ entière** to travel the world over *ou* all over the globe; **sur la ~** on (the) earth, in the world; *(fig)* **redescendre sur ~** to come back to earth. (**b**) *(sol)* ground; *(matière)* earth, soil; *(pour poterie)* clay. **vase en ~** clay vase; **à** *ou* **par ~** *poser* (down) on the ground; *jeter* to the ground; **cela fiche tous nos projets par ~** * that really messes up all our plans *; **mettre qn en ~** to bury sb; **(5 mètres) sous ~** (5 metres) underground; *(fig: de honte)* **j'aurais voulu rentrer sous ~** I wished the earth would swallow me up. (**c**) *(étendue, campagne)* land. **une langue de ~** a strip *ou* tongue of land; **aimer la ~** to love the land; **des ~s à blé** corn-growing land; **lopin de ~** piece *ou* patch *ou* plot of land. (**d**) *(opp à mer)* land. **sur la ~ ferme** on dry land; *(Naut)* **aller à ~** to go ashore; **dans les ~s** inland; **voyager par voie de ~** to travel by land *ou* overland. (**e**) *(domaine)* **la ~** land; **une ~** an estate. (**f**) *(pays)* land, country. **la T~ promise** the Promised Land. (**g**) *(Élec)* earth, ground *(US)*. **mettre à la ~** to earth, ground *(US)*.
2 : **la ~ Adélie** the Adélie Coast, Adélie Land; **~ battue** hard-packed surface; **politique de la ~ brûlée** scorched earth policy; **~ de bruyère** heath-peat; **~ cuite** *(pour tuiles)* baked clay; *(pour statuettes)* terracotta; **la T~ de Feu** Tierra del Fuego; **~ glaise** clay; **la T~ Sainte** the Holy Land.
◆ **Terre-Neuve** **1** *nf* Newfoundland. **2** *nm inv*: **t~-n~** *(chien)* Newfoundland terrier. ◆ **terre-plein,** *pl* **terre-pleins** *nm (Mil)* terreplein; *(Constr)* platform; *(sur chaussée)* central reservation, center divider strip *(US)*. ◆ **terre-à-terre** *adj inv* esprit down-to-earth, matter-of-fact.

terreau [tɛʀo] *nm* compost. **~ de feuilles** leaf mould.

terrer (se) [tɛʀe] (1) *vpr [criminel, renard] (en fuite)* to crouch down; *(dans une tanière)* to go to ground *ou* earth; *[timide, insociable]* to hide (o.s.) away.

terrestre [tɛʀɛstʀ(ə)] *adj faune, transports* land; *surface* earth's, terrestrial; *biens, plaisirs, vie* earthly, terrestrial.

terreur [tɛʀœʀ] *nf* terror. **avec ~** with terror *ou* dread; **vaines ~s** empty fears; *(*hum)* **jouer les ~s** to play the tough guy *.

terreux, -euse [tɛʀø, øz] *adj goût* earthy; *sabots* muddy; *mains, salade* dirty; *teint* sallow.

terrible [tɛʀibl(ə)] *adj (*: excellent)* terrific *, tremendous *; *(horrible)* terrible, dreadful, awful. **c'est ~ ce qu'il peut manger** * it's incredible what he can eat *; **ce film n'est pas ~** * this film is nothing special. ◆ **terriblement** *adv* terribly, dreadfully, awfully.

terrien, -ienne [tɛʀjɛ̃, jɛn] **1** *adj propriétaire* landed; *origine* country. **2** *nm (paysan)* countryman; *(habitant de la Terre)* Earthman; *(non-marin)* landsman. **3** *nf* countrywoman; Earthwoman; landswoman.

terrier [tɛʀje] *nm* (**a**) *[lapin]* burrow, hole. (**b**) *(chien)* terrier.

terrifier [tɛʀifje] (7) *vt* to terrify. ◆ **terrifiant, e** *adj (effrayant)* terrifying; *progrès, appétit* fearsome, incredible.

terrine [tɛʀin] *nf (récipient)* terrine; *(pâté)* pâté.

territoire [tɛʀitwaʀ] *nm (gén, Pol, Zool)* territory; *[commune]* area; *[évêque, juge]* jurisdiction. **~s d'outre-mer** (French) overseas territories. ◆ **territorial, e,** *mpl* **-aux** **1** *adj* territorial. **2** *nf* Territorial Army.

terroir [tɛʀwaʀ] *nm (Agr)* soil. **accent du ~** country *ou* rural accent.

terroriser [tɛʀɔʀize] (1) *vt* to terrorize. ◆ **terrorisme** *nm* terrorism. ◆ **terroriste** *adj, nmf* terrorist.

tertiaire [tɛʀsjɛʀ] *adj (Géol, Méd)* tertiary. *(Écon)* **(secteur) ~** service industries, tertiary sector.

tertio [tɛʀsjo] *adv* third(ly).

tertre [tɛʀtʀ(ə)] *nm* mound.

tes [te] *adj poss V* **ton**[1].

tesson [tesɔ̃] *nm*: **~ (de bouteille)** shard, piece of broken bottle.

test [tɛst] **1** *nm (gén)* test. **faire passer un ~ à qn** to give sb a test, put sb through a test; **le ~ du SIDA** the test for AIDS. **2** *adj*: **région-~** test area. ◆ **tester**[1] (1) *vt* to test.

testament [tɛstamɑ̃] *nm (Jur)* will, testament; *(fig)* legacy. **ceci est mon ~** this is my last will and testament; *(Rel)* **Ancien/Nouveau T~** Old/New Testament. ◆ **testamentaire** *adj*: **dispositions ~s** provisions of a will. ◆ **testateur** *nm* testator. ◆ **testatrice** *nf* testatrix. ◆ **tester**[2] (1) *vi* to make (out) one's will.

testicule [tɛstikyl] *nm* testicle.

tétanos [tetanos] *nm (Méd)* tetanus, lockjaw; *(Physiol)* tetanus. **vaccin contre le ~** tetanus vaccine.

têtard [tɛtaʀ] *nm* tadpole.

tête [tɛt] **1** *nf* (**a**) *[homme, animal, objet, plante]* head; *(chevelure)* hair. **être ~ nue** to be bareheaded; **avoir la ~ sale** to have dirty hair; **de la ~ aux pieds** from head to foot; **gagner d'une ~** to win by a head; **20 ~s de bétail** 20 head of cattle; **50 F par ~** 50 francs a head *ou* apiece *ou* per person. (**b**) *(fig: vie)* head, neck. **risquer sa ~** to risk one's neck. (**c**) *(visage)* face. **il a une ~ sympathique** he has a friendly face; **faire une drôle de ~** to pull a (wry *ou* long) face; **faire la ~** to sulk, have the sulks *; **c'est une ~ à claques** * he has got the sort of face you itch to smack. (**d**) *(début) [train, procession]* front, head; *(Mil) [colonne]* head; *[page, liste, classe]* top, head. **en ~ de phrase** at the beginning of the sentence; *(Rail)* **monter en ~** to get on at the front; *[coureur etc]* **être en/prendre la ~** to be in/take the lead; **être en ~** *ou* **à la ~ de qch** to be at the head of sth, head (up) sth. (**e**) *(facultés* *mentales)* **avoir (toute) sa** ~ to have (all) one's wits about one; **n'avoir rien dans la** ~ to be empty-headed; **où ai-je la ~?** whatever am I thinking of?; **avoir une petite** ~ to be dim-witted; ~ **sans cervelle** *ou* **en l'air** *ou* **de linotte** scatterbrain; **avoir la** ~ **sur les épaules** to be level-headed; **femme de** ~ capable woman; **calculer qch de** ~ to work sth out in one's head; **je n'ai plus le nom en** ~ I can't recall the name, the name has gone (clean) out of my head; **chercher qch dans sa** ~ to search one's memory for sth; **mettre qch dans la** ~ **de qn** to put *ou* get sth into sb's head; **se mettre dans la** ~ **que** *(s'imaginer)* to get it into one's head that; **se mettre dans la** *ou* **en** ~ **de faire qch** *(se décider)* to take it into one's head to do sth; **avoir la** ~ **ailleurs** to have one's mind elsewhere; **se creuser la** ~ to rack one's brains; **ils ne se sont pas cassé la** ~! they didn't exactly overexert themselves!; **n'en faire qu'à sa** ~ to do (exactly) as one pleases; **faire qch à** ~ **reposée** to do sth in a more leisurely moment; **c'est lui la** ~ **du complot** he's the leader of the plot. (**f**) *(tempérament)* **avoir la** ~ **chaude/froide/dure** to be hot-/cool-/thick-headed; **il fait sa mauvaise** ~ he's being awkward; **c'est une forte** ~ he's a rebel. (**g**) *(Ftbl)* header. **faire une** ~ to head the ball. (**h**) *(locutions)* **marcher la** ~ **haute** to walk with one's head held high; **avoir la** ~ **basse** to hang one's head; *(lit, fig)* **courir** ~ **baissée** to rush headlong (*dans* into); **garder la** ~ **froide** to keep a cool head, remain cool; **tomber la** ~ **la première** to fall headfirst; **jeter** *ou* **lancer à la** ~ **de qn que...** to hurl in sb's face that...; **en avoir par-dessus la** ~ to be fed up to the back teeth *; **j'en donnerais ma** ~ **à couper** I would stake my life on it; **ne plus savoir où donner de la** ~ not to know which way to turn; **tenir** ~ **à** to stand up to; **mettre la** ~ **de qn à prix** to put a price on sb's head; **se trouver à la** ~ **d'une petite fortune** to find o.s. the owner *ou* possessor of a small fortune.

2 *(Théât)* ~ **d'affiche** top of the bill; *(Aut)* ~ **de bielle** big end; ~ **brûlée** wild adventurer; ~ **chaude** hothead; ~ **chercheuse** homing device; *(Aut)* ~ **de Delco** ® distributor cap; *(Ordin)* ~ **d'écriture** writing head; ~ **d'épingle** pinhead; ~ **de lard** * *ou* **de mule** * pigheaded so and so *; ~ **de lecture** *[pick-up]* pickup head; *[magnétophone]* play-back head; *(Ordin)* reading head; *(Ordin)* ~ **de lecture-écriture** read-write head; ~ **de ligne** terminus, end of the line *(Rail)*; ~ **de mort** *(emblème)* death's-head; *[pavillon]* skull and crossbones, Jolly Roger; *(Culin)* Gouda cheese; ~ **nucléaire** nuclear warhead; ~ **de pont** *(fleuve)* bridgehead; *(mer)* beachhead; ~ **de Turc** whipping boy, Aunt Sally. ◆ **tête-bêche** *adv* head to foot *ou* tail. ◆ **tête-de-nègre** *adj inv* dark brown. ◆ **tête-à-queue** *nm inv (Aut)* spin. ◆ **tête-à-tête** *nm inv (conversation)* tête-a-tête, private conversation. **en** ~-~-~ alone together; **dîner en** ~-~-~ intimate dinner for two.

téter [tete] (6) *vt lait, pouce* to suck; *biberon, sein, pipe* to suck at. ~ **sa mère** to suck at one's mother's breast; **donner à** ~ **à un bébé** to feed a baby. ◆ **tétée** *nf (action)* sucking; *(repas)* feed, nursing *(US)*; *(moment)* feeding *ou* nursing time. ◆ **tétine** *nf [vache, biberon]* teat; *(sucette)* dummy, pacifier *(US)*. ◆ **téton** * *nm* breast.

têtu, e [tety] *adj* stubborn, pigheaded.

texte [tɛkst(ə)] *nm (gén)* text; *(morceau choisi)* passage, piece; *(énoncé de devoir)* subject, topic. **erreur dans le** ~ textual error; *(Théât)* **apprendre son** ~ to learn one's lines; **amender un** ~ **de loi** to amend a law. ◆ **textuel, -elle** *adj traduction* literal, word for word; *citation* verbatim, exact; *analyse, sens* textual. ◆ **textuellement** *adv* literally, word for word; exactly, verbatim. **il me l'a dit** ~ those were his very words.

textile [tɛkstil] **1** *nm* (**a**) *(matière)* textile. ~**s synthétiques** synthetic *ou* man-made fibres. (**b**) *(Ind)* **le** ~ the textile industry, textiles. **2** *adj* textile.

texture [tɛkstyʀ] *nf (lit, fig)* texture.

Thaïlande [tailɑ̃d] *nf* Thailand. ◆ **thaïlandais, e** **1** *adj* Thai. **2** *nm, f:* **T~(e)** Thai, Thailander. ◆ **thaï** *adj inv, nm* Thai.

thé [te] **1** *nm* tea; *(plante)* tea plant; *(réunion)* tea party. ~ **à la menthe** mint tea. **2** *adj inv:* **rose** ~ tea rose.

théâtre [teɑtʀ(ə)] *nm* (**a**) **le** ~ *(technique)* the theatre; *(profession)* the stage *ou* theatre; **faire du** ~ to be on the stage, be an actor; **s'intéresser au** ~ to be interested in drama *ou* the theatre; **je n'aime pas le** ~ **à la télévision** I do not like televised stage dramas *ou* stage productions on television; ~ **d'essai** experimental theatre *ou* drama; ~ **d'amateurs** amateur dramatics *ou* theatricals; **roman adapté pour le** ~ novel adapted for the stage *ou* the theatre. (**b**) *(lieu)* theatre. ~ **de marionnettes/de verdure** puppet/open-air theatre; **il ne va jamais au** ~ he never goes to the theatre, he is not a theatregoer; **le** ~ **était plein** there was a full house. (**c**) **homme de** ~ man of the theatre *ou* stage; **accessoires de** ~ stage props; **directeur de** ~ theatre *ou* theatrical *ou* stage director; **troupe de** ~ theatre *ou* drama company. (**d**) *(genre littéraire)* theatre. **le** ~ **de Sheridan** Sheridan's plays *ou* dramatic works, the theatre of Sheridan; **le** ~ **classique** the classical theatre, classical drama; **le** ~ **de boulevard** light comedies. (**e**) *(fig péj) (exagération)* theatricals, histrionics; *(simulation)* playacting. (**f**) *[crime]* scene. *(Mil)* **le** ~ **des opérations** the theatre of operations. ◆ **théâtral, e,** *mpl* **-aux** *adj* (**a**) *œuvre* theatrical, dramatic; *rubrique, saison* theatre; *représentation* stage, theatrical. (**b**) *(péj) attitude* theatrical, histrionic, dramatic. ◆ **théâtralement** *adv (lit)* theatrically; *(péj)* histrionically.

théière [tejɛʀ] *nf* teapot.

thème [tɛm] *nm* (**a**) *(sujet)* theme. (**b**) *(Scol: traduction)* prose (composition).

théologie [teɔlɔʒi] *nf* theology. ◆ **théologien** *nm* theologian, theologist. ◆ **théologique** *adj* theological.

théorème [teɔʀɛm] *nm* theorem.

théorie [teɔʀi] *nf* theory. **en** ~ in theory. ◆ **théoricien, -ienne** *nm, f* theoretician, theorist. ◆ **théorique** *adj* theoretical. ◆ **théoriquement** *adv* theoretically.

thérapeutique [teʀapøtik] **1** *adj* therapeutic. **2** *nf (science)* therapeutics *(sg)*; *(traitement)* therapy.

thermal, e, *mpl* **-aux** [tɛʀmal, o] *adj:* **cure** ~**e** water cure; **établissement** ~ hydropathic *ou* water-cure establishment; **source** ~**e, eaux** ~**es** thermal *ou* hot springs; **station** ~**e** spa.

thermique [tɛʀmik] *adj unité* thermal; *énergie* thermic. **centrale** ~ power station.

thermoélectrique [tɛʀmɔelɛktʀik] *adj* thermoelectric(al).

thermomètre [tɛʀmɔmɛtʀ(ə)] *nm* thermometer. ~ **médical** clinical thermometer; *(fig)* **le** ~ **de l'opinion publique** the barometer *ou* gauge of public opinion.

thermonucléaire [tɛʀmɔnykleɛʀ] *adj* thermonuclear.

thermos [tɛʀmos] *nm ou nf* (®: *aussi* **bouteille** ~) vacuum *ou* Thermos ® flask *ou* bottle *(US)*.

thermostat [tɛʀmɔsta] *nm* thermostat.

thésauriser [tezɔʀize] (1) **1** *vi* to hoard money. **2** *vt* to hoard (up).

thèse [tɛz] *nf (gén)* thesis; *(Univ)* ≃ Ph.D. thesis; *(Police: théorie)* theory, possibility. **écarter la ~ du suicide** to rule out the theory of suicide.

thon [tɔ̃] *nm* tunny (fish), tuna(-fish).

thorax [tɔʀaks] *nm* thorax. ◆ **thoracique** *adj cavité* thoracic. **cage ~** rib-cage; **capacité ~** respiratory *ou* vital capacity.

thrombose [tʀɔ̃boz] *nf* thrombosis.

thym [tɛ̃] *nm* thyme.

thyroïde [tiʀɔid] *adj, nf* thyroid. ◆ **thyroïdien, -ienne** *adj* thyroid.

tiare [tjaʀ] *nf* tiara.

Tibet [tibɛ] *nm* Tibet. ◆ **tibétain, e** *adj, nm,* **T~(e)** *nm(f)* Tibetan.

tibia [tibja] *nm* shinbone, tibia.

tic [tik] *nm (nerveux)* twitch, tic; *(manie)* habit, mannerism. **c'est un ~ chez lui** *(manie)* it's a habit with him; *(geste)* it's a tic he has.

ticket [tikɛ] *nm* ticket. **~ de caisse** sales slip *ou* receipt; **~ de quai** platform ticket; **~ de rationnement** (ration) coupon; **~-repas** *ou* **-restaurant** luncheon voucher.

tic-tac [tiktak] *nm* ticking, tick-tock. **faire ~** to tick, go tick tock.

tiède [tjɛd] **1** *adj liquide, foi, accueil* lukewarm; *vent, temps* mild, warm. **2** *nmf (péj)* lukewarm *ou* half-hearted individual. **3** *adv*: **boire qch ~** to drink sth when it's lukewarm *ou* not very hot *ou* not very cold. ◆ **tièdement** *adv (péj)* in a lukewarm way, half-heartedly. ◆ **tiédeur** *nf* lukewarmness, half-heartedness; mildness, warmth. ◆ **tiédir** (2) **1** *vi* (**a**) *(devenir moins chaud)* to cool down; *(se réchauffer)* to grow warm(er). **faire ~ de l'eau** to warm *ou* heat up some water. (**b**) *[foi, ardeur]* to cool (off). **2** *vt [soleil]* to warm (up); *[air frais]* to cool (down).

tien, tienne [tjɛ̃, tjɛn] **1** *pron poss*: **le ~, la tienne, les ~s, les tiennes** yours, your own; **à la tienne!** * your (good) health!, cheers! * **2** *nm*: **le ~** what's yours; **les ~s** *(famille)* your family; *(groupe)* your set. **3** *adj poss*: **un ~ cousin** a cousin of yours; *V* **sien.**

tiens [tjɛ̃] *excl V* **tenir**; **un ~ vaut mieux que deux tu l'auras** a bird in the hand is worth two in the bush.

tiers, tierce [tjɛʀ, tjɛʀs(ə)] **1** *adj* third. **une tierce personne** a third party; **le T~-Monde** the Third World; **le T~-État** the third estate. **2** *nm* (**a**) *(fraction)* third. **j'ai lu le** *ou* **un ~/les deux ~ du livre** I have read a third/two thirds of the book; **les deux ~ des gens pensent que** the majority of people think that. (**b**) *(personne)* third party. **3** *nf (Mus)* third; *(Cartes, Escrime)* tierce. ◆ **tiercé** *nm* tiercé, *French system of forecast betting on three horses.*

tif ‡ [tif] *nm* hair. **~s** hair.

tige [tiʒ] *nf [fleur]* stem; *[céréales]* stalk; *[botte, chaussette]* leg (part); *(en métal)* shaft.

tignasse * [tiɲas] *nf* shock of hair, mop (of hair).

tigre [tigʀ(ə)] *nm* tiger. ◆ **tigré, e** *adj (tacheté)* spotted; *(rayé)* striped, streaked. ◆ **tigresse** *nf* tigress.

tilleul [tijœl] *nm (arbre)* lime (tree); *(infusion)* lime tea.

tilt [tilt] *nm (billard électrique)* electronic billiards. **faire ~** *(lit)* to mark the end of the game; *(fig: échouer)* to fail; *(fig: inspirer)* **ce mot a fait ~ dans mon esprit** this word rang a bell (in my mind).

timbale [tɛ̃bal] *nf* (**a**) *(Mus)* **les ~s** the timpani, the kettledrums. (**b**) *(gobelet)* (metal) cup *ou* tumbler; *(Culin)* timbale. ◆ **timbalier** *nm* timpanist.

timbre [tɛ̃bʀ(ə)] *nm* (**a**) *(objet, vignette)* stamp. **~(-poste)** (postage) stamp; **~ fiscal** excise *ou* revenue stamp. (**b**) *(marque)* stamp; *(cachet de la poste)* postmark. (**c**) *(son)* timbre, tone. (**d**) *(sonnette)* bell. ◆ **timbrage** *nm* stamping; postmarking. **dispensé de ~** postage paid. ◆ **timbré, e** * **1** *adj (fou)* cracked *, dotty *, nuts *, loony *. **2** *nm, f* (* *fou*) loony *, nut-case ‡. ◆ **timbrer** (1) *vt (apposer un cachet sur) acte* to stamp; *lettre* to postmark; *(affranchir)* to stamp, put a stamp on.

timide [timid] *adj (timoré)* timid, timorous; *(emprunté) amoureux* shy, timid, bashful. **faussement ~** coy; **c'est un grand ~** he's very shy; **une ~ amélioration de l'économie** a slight *ou* faint improvement in the economy. ◆ **timidement** *adv* timidly; timorously; shyly; bashfully. ◆ **timidité** *nf* timidity; timorousness; shyness; bashfulness.

timonier [timɔnje] *nm (Naut)* helmsman, steersman.

timoré, e [timɔʀe] *adj* timorous.

tintamarre [tɛ̃tamaʀ] *nm* din, racket. **faire du ~** to make a din *ou* racket.

tinter [tɛ̃te] (1) *vi [cloche]* to ring, chime; *[clochette]* to tinkle; *[objets métalliques]* to jingle, chink; *[verres]* to chink. **faire ~** *cloche* to ring; *verres* to make chink; **les oreilles me tintent** my ears are ringing. ◆ **tintement** *nm*: **~(s)** ringing; chiming; tinkling; jingling; chinking.

tintin ‡ [tɛ̃tɛ̃] *excl* nothing doing! *, no go! **faire ~** to go without.

tintouin * [tɛ̃twɛ̃] *nm* bother.

tique [tik] *nf (parasite)* tick.

tiquer [tike] (1) *vi* to pull *ou* make a face, raise an eyebrow. **sans ~** without turning a hair.

tir [tiʀ] *nm* (**a**) *(Sport)* shooting. **~ au pistolet** pistol shooting; **~ à l'arc** archery. (**b**) *(action)* firing. **déclencher le ~** to open the firing. (**c**) *(trajectoire)* fire. **régler le ~** to regulate the fire; **~ groupé** grouped fire; *(fig)* combined attack; **angle de ~** angle of fire. (**d**) *(rafales)* fire. **un ~** *ou* **des ~s de barrage/d'artillerie** barrage/artillery fire. (**e**) *(Boules, Ftbl)* shot. (**f**) *(stand)* **~ (forain)** shooting gallery, rifle range.

tirade [tiʀad] *nf* soliloquy.

tirage [tiʀaʒ] *nm* (**a**) *(Phot) (action)* printing; *(photo)* print. (**b**) *[journal]* circulation; *[livre]* edition. **quel est le ~ de cet ouvrage?** how many copies of this work were printed?; **~ de 2 000 exemplaires** run *ou* impression of 2,000 copies; **~ à part** off-print. (**c**) *[cheminée]* draught. (**d**) *(Loterie)* draw. **le ~ des numéros gagnants** the draw for the winning numbers; **procéder par ~ au sort** to draw lots. (**e**) *(*: désaccord)* friction.

tirailler [tiʀɑje] (1) **1** *vt* (**a**) *corde, manche* to pull at, tug at. (**b**) *[douleurs]* to gnaw at, stab at; *[doutes]* to plague. **tiraillé entre plusieurs possibilités** torn between several possibilities. **2** *vi (Mil)* to fire. ◆ **tiraillement** *nm (douleur)* gnawing *ou* stabbing pain; *(doute)* doubt. **~(s)** *(conflit)* friction; *(sur une corde)* tugging. ◆ **tirailleur** *nm (Mil, fig)* skirmisher.

tirant [tiʀɑ̃] *nm*: **~ d'eau** draught, draft *(US)*; **avoir 6 mètres de ~ d'eau** to draw 6 metres of water.

tire[1] ‡ [tiʀ] *nf (voiture)* car.

tire[2] [tiʀ] *nf*: **voleur à la ~** pick-pocket; *V aussi* **tirer.**

tiré, e[1] [tiʀe] *adj traits, visage* drawn, haggard. **~ à quatre épingles** done up *ou* dressed up to the nines *; *(fig)* **~ par les cheveux** far-fetched.

tirée[2] * [tiʀe] *nf (trajet)* long haul *ou* trek. *(quan- tité)* **une ~ de** a load * of, heaps * of.

tirelire [tiʀliʀ] *nf* (**a**) moneybox, piggy bank. (**b**) (‡) *(tête)* nut *; *(visage)* face.

tirer [tiʀe] (1) **1** *vt* (**a**) *poignée, corde* to pull; *manche, robe* to pull down; *chaussette* to pull up; *véhicule, charge* to pull, draw; *remorque, navire* to tow. **~ qn par la manche** to tug at sb's sleeve; **~ qn à**

l'écart to draw sb aside; **ne tire pas** don't pull; ~ **les cheveux à qn** to pull sb's hair. (**b**) *rideaux* to draw, pull; *tiroir* to pull open; *verrou* to slide to, shoot. **tire la porte** pull the door to. (**c**) *vin, idée etc* to draw; *épée* to draw, pull out; *plaisir* to draw, get, derive; *jus, substance* to extract; *mot, citation, passage* to take (*de* from). ~ **un son d'un instrument** to get a sound out of *ou* draw a sound from an instrument; ~ **un objet d'un tiroir** to pull an object out of a drawer; ~ **son chapeau à qn** to raise one's hat to sb; ~ **de l'argent d'une activité** to make *ou* get money from an activity; ~ **son origine de qch** to have sth as its origin; ~ **son nom de qch** to take its name from sth; ~ **qn du sommeil** to arouse sb from sleep; ~ **qn du lit** to get *ou* drag sb out of bed; **on ne peut rien en** ~ *(enfant têtu)* you can't do anything with him; *(qui refuse de parler)* you can't get anything out of him; **encore une heure à** ~ **avant la fin** * another hour to get through before the end. (**d**) *(délivrer)* ~ **qn de** *prison etc* to get sb out of; *misère* to rescue sb from; ~ **qn du doute** to remove *ou* dispel sb's doubts; ~ **qn de l'erreur** to disabuse sb; **il faut le** ~ **de là** we'll have to help him out. (**e**) *numéro* to draw; *carte* to take, draw. (**f**) *(Phot, Typ)* to print. **se faire** ~ **le portrait** * to have one's picture taken. (**g**) *(tracer) trait* to draw; *plan* to draw up. (**h**) *coup de feu* to fire; *feu d'artifice* to set off; *gibier* to shoot. **il a tiré plusieurs coups de revolver sur l'agent** he shot *ou* fired at the policeman several times; ~ **le canon** to fire the cannon. (**i**) *chèque* to draw. ~ **de l'argent sur son compte** to draw money out of one's account, withdraw money from one's account.

2 *vi* (**a**) *(faire feu)* to fire, shoot; *(Ftbl)* to shoot; *(Boules)* to throw. ~ **à vue** to shoot on sight; ~ **à balles/à blanc** to fire bullets/blanks; **apprendre à** ~ to learn to shoot. (**b**) *(Presse)* ~ **à 10 000 exemplaires** to have a circulation of 10,000. (**c**) *[cheminée]* to draw; *[voiture]* to pull. (**d**) ~ **au flanc** * to skive *, shirk; ~ **dans les jambes** *ou* **pattes** * **de qn** to make life difficult for sb.

3 ~ **sur** *vt indir* (**a**) *corde, poignée* to pull *ou* tug at. *(fig)* ~ **sur la ficelle** * to push one's luck *, go too far, overstep the mark. (**b**) *couleur* to border on, verge on; *âge* to be getting on for *ou* going on *(US) ou* verging on. (**c**) *(faire feu sur)* to shoot at, fire at. (**d**) *pipe* to pull at, draw on; *cigarette* to puff at, draw on.

4 ~ **à** *vt indir*: ~ **à sa fin** to be drawing to a close; ~ **à conséquence** to matter.

5 se ~ *vpr* (**a**) **se** ~ **de** *danger, situation* to get (o.s.) out of; *travail, examen* to manage, cope with, get through; **s'en** ~ * *[malade]* to pull through; *[délinquant]* to get off with it; *(financièrement)* to manage, get by; **il s'en est bien tiré** *(procès)* he got off lightly; *(épreuve)* he coped well with it, he made a good job of it; **il s'en est tiré avec une amende** he got off with a fine. (**b**) (*‡*: *déguerpir*) to push off, clear off ‡. (**c**) (*: *toucher à sa fin*) to drag towards its close. (**d**) *[traits, visage]* to become drawn.

◆ **à tire d'ailes** *loc adv voler* swiftly. ◆ **tire-bouchon,** *pl* **tire-bouchons** *nm* corkscrew. **en** ~ corkscrew; **cochon avec la queue en** ~ pig with a corkscrew *ou* curly tail; **pantalon en** ~ crumpled trousers. ◆ **tire-fesses** * *nm inv* ski tow. ◆ **tire-au-flanc** * *nmf inv* skiver *, shirker. ◆ **à tire-larigot** * *loc adv* to one's heart content.

tiret [tiʀɛ] *nm (trait)* dash; *(en fin de ligne)* hyphen.

tireur [tiʀœʀ] *nm* (**a**) ~ **isolé** sniper; ~ **d'élite** marksman, sharpshooter; **c'est un bon** ~ he is a good shot. (**b**) *(Fin)* drawer.

tireuse [tiʀøz] *nf* (**a**) ~ **de cartes** fortuneteller. (**b**) *(pompe)* (hand) pump. **bière/vin à la** ~ hand-drawn beer/wine.

tiroir [tiʀwaʀ] *nm* drawer. ◆ **tiroir-caisse,** *pl* **tiroirs-caisses** *nm* till, cash register.

tisane [tizan] *nf* herb(al) tea. ~ **de menthe** mint tea.

tison [tizɔ̃] *nm* brand. ◆ **tisonner** (1) *vt* to poke. ◆ **tisonnier** *nm* poker.

tisser [tise] (1) *vt (lit, fig)* to weave; *[araignée]* to spin. ◆ **tissage** *nm* weaving. ◆ **tisserand, e** *nm, f ou* ◆ **tisseur, -euse** *nm, f* weaver.

tissu [tisy] *nm (Tex)* cloth, fabric, material; *(Anat)* tissue. *(péj)* **un** ~ **de** *mensonges, intrigues* a web of; *obscénités, inepties* a jumble *ou* farrago of. *(Sociol)* **le** ~ **industriel/urbain** the industrial/urban fabric. ◆ **tissu-éponge,** *pl* **tissus-éponge** *nm* (terry) towelling.

titre [titʀ(ə)] *nm* (**a**) *[livre etc]* title; *[chapitre]* heading, title. *(Presse)* **les (gros)** ~**s** the headlines. (**b**) *(honorifique, sportif etc)* title; *(appellation)* title, name. ~ **de noblesse** title; *(Admin)* **en** ~ titular. (**c**) *(document)* title. ~ **de pension** pension book; ~ **de propriété** title deed; ~ **de transport** ticket. (**d**) *(Bourse)* security. ~**s** securities, stocks; ~ **au porteur** bearer bond (*ou* share); ~**s d'État** government securities. (**e**) *(diplôme)* qualification. ~**s universitaires** academic *ou* university qualifications; **avoir les** ~**s requis** to be fully qualified, have all the necessary qualifications. (**f**) *(littér: prétentions)* **ses** ~**s de gloire** his claims to fame. (**g**) *[or, argent]* fineness; *[solution]* titre. ~ **d'alcool** alcohol content. (**h**) **à ce** ~ *(en cette qualité)* as such; *(pour cette raison)* therefore; **à quel** ~? on what grounds?; **au même** ~ in the same way (*que* as); **à aucun** ~ on no account; **à double** ~ on two accounts; **à** ~ **privé/personnel** in a private/ personal capacity; **à** ~ **permanent/provisoire** on a permanent/temporary basis; **à** ~ **exceptionnel** in exceptional cases; **à** ~ **d'ami** as a friend; **à** ~ **gratuit** *ou* **gracieux** free of charge; **à** ~ **d'exemple** as an example, by way of example; **à** ~ **indicatif** for information only; **à** ~ **d'indemnité** by way of indemnity, as an indemnity. ◆ **titré, e** *adj personne* titled. ◆ **titrer** (1) *vt* (**a**) *(ennoblir)* to confer a title on. (**b**) *(Presse)* to run as a headline. (**c**) *(Chim) solution* to titrate. ~ **10°** to be 10° proof *(on the Gay Lussac scale)*.

tituber [titybe] (1) *vi* to stagger *ou* totter *ou* stumble (along); *(d'ivresse)* to reel (along).

titulaire [titylɛʀ] **1** *adj professeur* tenured. **être** ~ to have tenure; **être** ~ **de** *poste, permis* to hold. **2** *nmf [poste]* incumbent; *[carte]* holder. ◆ **titulariser** (1) *vt* to give tenure to. **être titularisé** to get *ou* be given tenure.

toast [tost] *nm (pain)* slice *ou* piece of toast; *(discours)* toast. **porter un** ~ **en l'honneur de qn** to toast sb.

toboggan [tɔbɔgɑ̃] *nm (jeu)* slide; *(traîneau)* toboggan; *(Aut)* flyover, overpass *(US)*.

toc [tɔk] **1** *excl (bruit)* **toc toc**! knock knock!, rat-a-tat! **2** *nm*: **c'est du** ~ * *(faux)* it's a fake; *(camelote)* it's rubbish *ou* trash; **en** ~ imitation, fake.

tocsin [tɔksɛ̃] *nm* alarm (bell), tocsin.

toge [tɔʒ] *nf (Hist)* toga; *(Jur, Scol)* gown.

Togo [tɔgo] *nm* Togo. ◆ **togolais, e** *adj*, **T~(e)** *nm(f)* Togolese.

tohu-bohu [tɔybɔy] *nm* hubbub.

toi [twa] *pron pers* (**a**) *(sujet, objet)* you. **si j'étais** ~ if I were you; **il a accepté,** ~ **non** he accepted but you didn't *ou* but not you; ~**, tu n'as pas à te plaindre** you have no cause to complain; ~**, je te connais** I know you. (**b**) *(avec vpr)* **assieds-**~ sit down; **tais-**~! you be quiet! (**c**) *(avec prép)* **cette maison est-elle à** ~? is this house yours?; **tu n'as même pas une chambre à** ~ **tout seul?** you haven't even a room of your own? *ou* a room to yourself?

toile [twal] **1** *nf* (**a**) *(tissu)* cloth; *(grossière)* canvas; *(pour pneu)* canvas. **grosse** ~ (rough *ou* coarse) canvas; ~ **de lin/coton** linen/cotton (cloth); **en** ~, **de** ~ *draps* linen; *pantalon* (heavy) cotton; *sac* canvas; ~ **imprimée** printed cotton. (**b**) *(morceau)* piece of cloth. *(*: draps)* **se mettre dans les** ~**s** to hit the hay * *ou* the sack *. (**c**) *(Art) (support)* canvas; *(œuvre)* canvas, painting. (**d**) *[araignée]* web. **la** ~ **de l'araignée** the spider's web; **plein de** ~**s d'araignées** full of cobwebs. (**e**) *(*: film)* film, movie *(surtout US)*. **2** : ~ **cirée** oilcloth; ~ **émeri** emery cloth; *(Théât, fig)* ~ **de fond** backdrop; ~ **goudronnée** tarpaulin; ~ **de jute** hessian; ~ **à matelas** ticking; ~ **de tente** tent canvas.

toilette [twalɛt] *nf* (**a**) *(action)* washing; *[voiture]* cleaning; *(chien)* grooming. **faire sa** ~ to have a wash, get washed; *[chat]* to wash itself; ~ **intime** intimate hygiene; **elle passe des heures à sa** ~ she spends hours getting ready *ou* washing and dressing; **la** ~ **des enfants prend toujours du temps** it always takes a long time to get children washed *ou* ready; **nécessaire de** ~ toilet bag; **faire la** ~ **de** *voiture* to clean; *chien* to groom; *[animal]* **faire sa** ~ to wash itself. (**b**) *(meuble)* washstand. (**c**) *(vêtements)* clothes; *(costume)* outfit. **en** ~ **de bal** dressed for a dance; ~ **de mariée** wedding *ou* bridal dress *ou* gown. (**d**) *(W.-C.)* ~**s** toilet; *(publiques)* public conveniences *ou* lavatory, restroom *(US)*; **aller aux** ~**s** to go to the toilet.

toiser [twaze] (1) *vt* to look up and down, eye scornfully (up and down).

toison [twazɔ̃] *nf* (**a**) *[mouton]* fleece. (**b**) *(chevelure) (épaisse)* mop; *(longue)* mane. (**c**) *(poils)* abundant growth.

toit [twa] *nm (lit)* roof; *(fig: maison)* home, roof. **habiter sous les** ~**s** to live under the eaves; *(fig)* **crier qch sur les** ~**s** to shout sth from the rooftops; **voiture à** ~ **ouvrant** car with a sunroof; **vivre sous le** ~ **paternel** to live in the parental home. ◆ **toiture** *nf* roof, roofing.

Tokyo [tokjo] *n* Tokyo.

tôle [tol] *nf (matériau)* sheet metal; *(morceau)* steel (*ou* iron) sheet. ~ **ondulée** corrugated iron.

tolérer [tɔleʀe] (6) *vt (gén, Méd, Tech)* to tolerate; *comportement* to put up with; *douleur* to bear, endure, stand; *excédent de bagages etc* to allow. **il ne tolère pas qu'on le contredise** he won't stand (for) *ou* tolerate being contradicted. ◆ **tolérable** *adj* tolerable, bearable. ◆ **tolérance** *nf* tolerance. **c'est une** ~, **pas un droit** it is tolerated rather than allowed as of right; *(Douane)* **il y a une** ~ **de 200 cigarettes** there's an allowance of 200 cigarettes. ◆ **tolérant, e** *adj* tolerant.

tôlerie [tolʀi] *nf (commerce)* sheet metal trade; *(atelier)* sheet metal workshop; *(carcasse)* plates, steelwork. ◆ **tôlier** *nm* sheet metal worker. ~ **en voitures** panel beater.

tollé [tɔle] *nm*: ~ **(général)** general outcry.

tomahawk [tɔmaok] *nm* tomahawk.

tomate [tɔmat] *nf* tomato. ~**s farcies** stuffed tomatoes; *(fig)* **il va recevoir des** ~**s** he'll have a hostile reception, he'll get booed.

tombe [tɔ̃b] *nf (gén, fig)* grave; *(avec monument)* tomb; *(pierre)* gravestone, tombstone. **suivre qn dans la** ~ to follow sb to the grave. ◆ **tombale** *adj f*: **pierre** ~ tombstone. ◆ **tombeau,** *pl* ~**x** *nm (lit)* tomb; *(fig)* grave. **mettre au** ~ to commit to the grave, entomb; **mise au** ~ entombment; *(secret)* **je serai un vrai** ~ my lips are sealed, I'll be as silent as the grave; **à** ~ **ouvert** at breakneck speed.

tombée [tɔ̃be] *nf*: **(à) la** ~ **de la nuit** (at) nightfall; **(à) la** ~ **du jour** (at) the close of the day.

tomber [tɔ̃be] (1) **1** *vi (avec aux être)* (**a**) *[personne, objet]* to fall (over *ou* down). ~ **de vélo/d'un arbre** to fall off one's bike/down from a tree; ~ **par terre** to fall down, fall to the ground; ~ **raide mort** to fall down *ou* drop (down) dead; ~ **à genoux** to fall on(to) one's knees; *(fig)* ~ **aux pieds de qn** to fall at sb's feet; ~ **de tout son long** to fall headlong, go sprawling; ~ **de tout son haut** *ou* **de toute sa hauteur** to fall *ou* crash *ou* topple to the ground; **faire** ~ **qn/qch** to knock sb/sth over *ou* down; **faire** ~ *(en lâchant)* to drop; ~ **de fatigue** to drop from exhaustion; ~ **de sommeil** to be falling asleep on one's feet; *(fig)* ~ **(bien) bas** to sink (very) low; **la nouvelle vient de** ~ the news has just broken *ou* come through. (**b**) *[feuilles, lumière, nuit]* to fall; *[cheveux]* to fall (out); *[pluie]* to fall, come down; *[foudre]* to strike; *[brouillard]* to come down. **il tombe de la neige** snow is falling. (**c**) *[soldat, régime, garnison]* to fall. **faire** ~ **le gouvernement** to bring down the government. (**d**) *[température, prix, nombre]* to drop, fall; *[vent, fièvre]* to drop; *[baromètre]* to fall; *[jour]* to draw to a close; *[voix]* to drop, fall away; *[colère, conversation]* to die down; *[enthousiasme]* to fall away. **le dollar est tombé à 5 F** the dollar has fallen *ou* dropped to 5 francs; **faire** ~ *vent, prix etc* to bring down. (**e**) *[obstacle, objection]* to disappear; *[projet]* to fall through. (**f**) *[draperie, robe, chevelure]* to fall, hang; *[moustaches, épaules]* to droop. **ce pantalon tombe bien** these trousers hang well. (**g**) *[date, choix, sort]* to fall (*sur* on). **Noël tombe un mardi** Christmas falls on a Tuesday; **et il a fallu que ça tombe sur moi** it (just) had to be me. (**h**) *(inopinément)* **il est tombé en pleine réunion** he walked in right in the middle of a meeting. (**i**) *(devenir: V aussi noms etc en question)* ~ **malade** *etc* to fall ill *etc.* (**j**) *(se trouver: V aussi noms en question)* ~ **dans un piège** *etc* to fall into a trap *etc.* (**k**) **laisser** ~ *objet*, (*) *amis, métier, activité* to drop; *fiancé* to jilt; *vieux parents* to let down. **laisse** ~! * *(gén)* forget it! *; *(nuance d'irritation)* give it a rest! *; **se laisser** ~ **dans un fauteuil** to drop *ou* fall into an armchair. (**l**) *(locutions)* **bien/mal** ~ *(avoir de la chance/malchance)* to be lucky/unlucky; *(se produire)* to come at the right/wrong moment; ~ **de Charybde en Scylla** to jump out of the frying pan into the fire; ~ **juste** *(en devinant)* to be right; *[calculs]* to come out right; ~ **de haut** to be bitterly disappointed; **il n'est pas tombé de la dernière pluie** he wasn't born yesterday; **ce n'est pas tombé dans l'oreille d'un sourd** it didn't fall on deaf ears; **il est tombé sur la tête!** * he's got a screw loose! *; *[aubaine]* ~ **du ciel** to be heaven-sent; ~ **des nues** to be completely taken aback; *[projet]* ~ **à l'eau** to fall through; *[plaisanterie]* ~ **à plat** to fall flat; **cela tombe sous le sens** it's obvious, it stands to reason.

2 ~ **sur** *vt indir (avec aux être)* (**a**) *ami* to run into; *détail* to come across *ou* upon. (**b**) *[regard]* to fall *ou* light upon; *[conversation]* to come round to. (**c**) *(*: attaquer, critiquer)* to go for *. **ils nous sont tombés dessus à 8 contre 3** 8 of them laid into the 3 of us; *(*: s'inviter)* **il nous est tombé dessus hier** he landed on us yesterday.

3 *vt (avec aux avoir)*: ~ **la veste** * to slip off one's jacket.

tombereau, *pl* ~**x** [tɔ̃bʀo] *nm (charrette)* tipcart; *(contenu)* cartload.

tombola [tɔ̃bɔla] *nf* tombola, raffle.

Tombouctou [tɔ̃buktu] *n* Timbuktu.

tome [tɔm] *nm (division)* part, book; *(volume)* volume.

ton[1] [tɔ̃], **ta** [ta], **tes** [te] *adj poss* your, your own.

ton[2] [tɔ̃] *nm* (**a**) *(hauteur de la voix)* pitch; *(timbre)* tone. ~ **aigu** shrill pitch; ~ **nasillard** nasal tone; **hausser/baisser le** ~ to raise/lower one's voice; *(fig)* **il devra changer de** ~ he'll have to sing a different tune; **ne le prenez pas sur ce** ~ don't take it that way *ou* like that; *(fig)* **dire qch sur tous les**

~**s** to say sth in every possible way. (**b**) *(Mus) (intervalle)* tone; *(clef)* key. **donner le** ~ to give the pitch; **être dans le** ~ to be in tune. (**c**) *(Ling)* tone. (**d**) *(manière de s'exprimer)* tone. **des plaisanteries de bon** ~ jokes in good taste; **il est de bon** ~ **de faire** it is good form to do; **être dans le** ~ to fit in; **donner le** ~ to set the tone; *(mode)* to set the fashion. (**e**) *(couleur)* shade, tone. **être dans le** ~ to tone in, match; **la ceinture n'est pas du même** ~ **que la robe** the belt does not match the dress. ◆ **tonalité** *nf (gén)* tone; *(Mus: système)* tonality; *(Mus: clef)* key; *(Téléc)* dialling tone.

tondre [tɔ̃dʀ(ə)] (41) *vt* (**a**) *mouton, (hum) personne* to shear; *gazon* to mow; *haie* to clip, cut; *caniche* to clip; *cheveux* to crop. (**b**) *(*: escroquer)* to fleece. **il ne faut pas te faire** ~ **la laine sur le dos** you shouldn't just allow people to fleece you *ou* to get the better of you. ◆ **tondeuse** *nf (à cheveux)* clippers; *(pour les moutons)* shears. ~ **(à gazon)** (lawn)mower. ◆ **tondu, e** *adj cheveux, pelouse* closely-cropped.

tongs [tɔ̃g] *nfpl (sandales)* flip-flops, thongs *(US)*.

tonifier [tɔnifje] (7) *vt muscles* to tone up; *esprit* to invigorate, stimulate. ◆ **tonifiant, e** *adj air* bracing, invigorating; *lotion* toning; *lecture* invigorating, stimulating. ◆ **tonique** **1** *adj boisson* tonic; *lotion* toning; *air, froid* invigorating, bracing; *lecture* invigorating, stimulating; *(Ling)* tonic. **2** *nm (Méd, fig)* tonic; *(lotion)* toning lotion.

tonitruant, e [tɔnitʀyɑ̃, ɑ̃t] *adj voix* thundering, booming.

tonnage [tɔnaʒ] *nm* tonnage.

tonnant, e [tɔnɑ̃, ɑ̃t] *adj voix* thunderous, thundering.

tonne [tɔn] *nf* (metric) ton, tonne. **des** ~**s de** * tons of *, loads of *.

tonneau, *pl* ~**x** [tɔno] *nm* (**a**) *(récipient)* barrel, cask. (**b**) *(Aviat)* hestitation flick roll; *(Aut)* somersault. **faire un** ~ to somersault, roll over. (**c**) *(Naut)* ton. ◆ **tonnelet** *nm* keg, (small) cask. ◆ **tonnelier** *nm* cooper.

tonnelle [tɔnɛl] *nf* bower, arbour.

tonner [tɔne] (1) **1** *vi [canon]* to thunder, boom, roar; *[personne]* to thunder, rage, inveigh (*contre* against). **2** *vb impers*: **il tonne** it is thundering.

tonnerre [tɔnɛʀ] **1** *nm* (**a**) thunder. **le** ~ **gronde** there is a rumble of thunder; **un bruit de** ~ a noise like thunder, a thunderous noise; **un** ~ **d'applaudissements** thunderous applause, a thunder of applause. (**b**) **du** ~ * terrific *, fantastic *, stupendous, great *. **2** *excl*: ~! * hell's bells! *

tonsure [tɔ̃syʀ] *nf (Rel)* tonsure; *(*: calvitie)* bald patch.

tonte [tɔ̃t] *nf [moutons]* shearing; *[haie]* clipping; *[gazon]* mowing; *(époque)* shearing-time.

tonton * [tɔ̃tɔ̃] *nm* uncle.

tonus [tɔnys] *nm (musculaire)* tone; *(fig: dynamisme)* energy, dynamism.

top [tɔp] **1** *nm* (**a**) *(signal électrique)* pip. *(Rad)* **au 4ᵉ** ~ at the 4th pip *ou* stroke. (**b**) *(Courses)* **donner le** ~ to give the starting signal; **attention,** ~**, partez!,** ~ **départ!** on your marks, get set, go! **2** *adj*: ~ **secret** top secret; *[athlète, chercheur]* **être au** ~ **niveau** to be a top level athlete (*ou* researcher *etc*).

topaze [tɔpaz] **1** *nf* topaz. **2** *adj inv (couleur)* topaz.

topinambour [tɔpinɑ̃buʀ] *nm* Jerusalem artichoke.

topo * [tɔpo] *nm (exposé)* spiel *.

topographie [tɔpɔgʀafi] *nf* topography. ◆ **topographique** *adj* topographic(al).

toquade [tɔkad] *nf (péj) (pour qn)* infatuation; *(pour qch)* fad, craze.

toque [tɔk] *nf [femme]* fur hat; *[juge, jockey]* cap. ~ **de cuisinier** chef's hat.

toqué, e * [tɔke] **1** *adj* crazy *, cracked *, nuts * (*de* about). **2** *nm, f* loony ⁑, nutcase *.

torche [tɔʀʃ(ə)] *nf* torch. ~ **électrique** (electric) torch, flashlight *(US)*; *(Parachutisme)* **se mettre en** ~ to candle. ◆ **torchère** *nf (Ind)* flare.

torcher * [tɔʀʃe] (1) *vt* to wipe.

torchis [tɔʀʃi] *nm* cob *(for walls)*.

torchon [tɔʀʃɔ̃] *nm* (**a**) *(gén)* cloth; *(pour épousseter)* duster; *(à vaisselle)* tea towel, dish towel. **le** ~ **brûle entre eux** they're at daggers drawn. (**b**) *(péj) (devoir mal présenté)* mess; *(mauvais journal)* rag.

tordant, e * [tɔʀdɑ̃, ɑ̃t] *adj* killing *, screamingly funny *, hilarious. **il est** ~ he's a scream * *ou* a kill *.

tordre [tɔʀdʀ(ə)] (41) **1** *vt (gén)* to wring; *(pour essorer)* to wring (out); *barre de fer, bras* to twist; *cuiller* to bend; *(déformer) visage* to contort, twist. **je vais lui** ~ **le cou** I'll wring his neck (for him). **2 se** ~ *vpr* (**a**) *[personne] (de douleur, de rire)* to be doubled up (*de* with). **se** ~ **le bras** to sprain *ou* twist one's arm. (**b**) *[barre]* to bend; *[roue]* to buckle, twist. ◆ **tordu, e** **1** *adj jambes* bent, crooked; *tronc* twisted; *barre* bent; *roue* buckled, twisted; *idée, raisonnement* weird, twisted; *esprit* warped. *(péj)* **être** ~ ⁑ to be round the bend *. **2** *nm, f* (⁑*: fou)* nutcase *; *(crétin)* twit ⁑.

toréador [tɔʀeadɔʀ] *nm* toreador, bullfighter.

tornade [tɔʀnad] *nf* tornado.

Toronto [tɔʀɔ̃to] *n* Toronto. ◆ **torontois, e** *adj,* **T~(e)** *nm(f)* Torontonian.

torpeur [tɔʀpœʀ] *nf* torpor.

torpille [tɔʀpij] *nf (Mil, Zool)* torpedo. ◆ **torpillage** *nm* torpedoing. ◆ **torpiller** (1) *vt* to torpedo. ◆ **torpilleur** *nm* torpedo boat.

torréfier [tɔʀefje] (7) *vt café* to roast.

torrent [tɔʀɑ̃] *nm (lit, fig)* torrent. **il pleut à** ~**s** the rain is coming down in torrents; *(fig)* **des** ~**s de** streams *ou* floods of. ◆ **torrentiel, -elle** *adj* torrential.

torride [tɔʀid] *adj région* torrid; *chaleur* scorching.

torsade [tɔʀsad] *nf [fils]* twist. ◆ **torsader** (1) *vt* to twist.

torse [tɔʀs(ə)] *nm (gén)* chest; *(Anat, Sculp)* torso. ~ **nu** stripped to the waist.

torsion [tɔʀsjɔ̃] *nf (action)* twisting; *(Phys, Tech)* torsion. **exercer une** ~ **sur qch** to twist sth.

tort [tɔʀ] *nm* (**a**) *(action blâmable)* fault. **il a le** ~ **d'être trop jeune** his trouble is that he's too young; **ils ont tous les** ~**s de leur côté** the fault *ou* wrong is entirely on their side, they're entirely at fault *ou* in the wrong; **avoir des** ~**s envers qn** to have wronged sb; **regretter ses** ~**s** to be sorry for one's wrongs; **vous avez refusé? c'est un** ~ did you refuse? — you were wrong (to do so); **tu ne le savais pas? c'est un** ~ you didn't know? — you should have *ou* that was a mistake. (**b**) *(préjudice)* wrong. **faire (du)** ~ **à qn** to harm sb, do sb harm; **ça va faire du** ~ **aux produits laitiers** it will harm *ou* be harmful to *ou* be detrimental to the dairy industry. (**c**) **à** ~ wrongly; **c'est à** ~ **qu'on l'avait dit malade** he was wrongly *ou* mistakenly said to be ill; **à** ~ **ou à raison** rightly or wrongly; **dépenser à** ~ **et à travers** to spend wildly; **parler à** ~ **et à travers** to talk wildly. (**d**) **être/se mettre dans son** ~ to be/put o.s. in the wrong; **être en** ~ to be in the wrong *ou* at fault; **avoir** ~ to be wrong (*de faire* to do); **donner** ~ **à qn** *[témoin]* to lay the blame on sb, blame sb; *[événements]* to show sb to be wrong, prove sb wrong.

torticolis [tɔʀtikɔli] *nm* stiff neck.

tortiller [tɔʀtije] (1) **1** *vt mouchoir* to twist; *moustache* to twirl. **2** *vi*: ~ **des hanches** to wiggle one's hips; **il n'y a pas à** ~ * there's no wriggling round it. **3 se** ~ *vpr [serpent]* to writhe; *[ver, personne]* to wiggle, squirm.

tortionnaire [tɔRsjɔnɛR] *nm* torturer.

tortue [tɔRty] *nf (Zool)* tortoise; *(fig)* slowcoach, slowpoke *(US)*, tortoise. ~ **d'eau** terrapin; ~ **de mer** turtle; **avancer comme une** ~ to crawl along at a snail's pace.

tortueux, -euse [tɔRtɥø, øz] *adj chemin, rivière* winding; *discours* tortuous; *manœuvres* devious.

torture [tɔRtyR] *nf*: ~**(s)** torture. ◆**torturer** (1) *vt* to torture. **se** ~ **l'esprit** to rack *ou* cudgel one's brains.

tory [tɔRi] *nmf* Tory.

Toscane [tɔskan] *nf* Tuscany.

tôt [to] *adv* (**a**) *(de bonne heure)* early. **il se lève** ~ he is an early riser, he gets up early; ~ **dans la matinée** early in the morning, in the early morning; **l'avenir appartient à ceux qui se lèvent** ~ the early bird catches the worm. (**b**) *(vite)* soon, early. **il est un peu** ~ **pour le juger** it's a little too soon *ou* early to judge him; ~ **ou tard** sooner or later; **il a eu** ~ **fait de s'en apercevoir!** he was quick to notice it!, it wasn't long before he noticed it!; **si seulement vous me l'aviez dit plus** ~! if only you had told me sooner! *ou* earlier!; **ce n'est pas trop** ~! it's not a moment too soon!, it's not before time!; **il n'était pas plus** ~ **parti que la voiture est tombée en panne** no sooner had he set off than the car broke down. (**c**) **venez le plus** ~ **possible** come as early *ou* as soon as you can; **le plus** ~ **sera le mieux** the sooner the better; **il peut venir jeudi au plus** ~ Thursday is the earliest *ou* soonest he can come.

total, e, *mpl* **-aux** [tɔtal, o] **1** *adj (gén)* total; *ruine, désespoir* utter, total; *pardon* absolute. **grève** ~**e** all-out strike. **2** *adv*: ~, **il a tout perdu** * the net result *ou* outcome was that he lost everything. **3** *nm* total. **le** ~ **de la population** the total (number of the) population; *(fig)* **si on fait le** ~ if you add it all up *ou* together; **au** ~ *(lit)* in total; *(fig)* on the whole, all in all. ◆**totalement** *adv* totally. ◆**totalisation** *nf* adding up, addition. ◆**totaliser** (1) *vt* to total. ◆**totalitaire** *adj (Pol) régime* totalitarian. ◆**totalitarisme** *nm* totalitarianism. ◆**totalité** *nf* (**a**) *(gén)* **la** ~ **de** all of; **la** ~ **de son salaire** his whole *ou* entire salary, all of his salary; **vendu en** ~ **aux États-Unis** all sold to the USA; **pris dans sa** ~ taken as a whole *ou* in its entirety. (**b**) *(Philos)* totality.

totem [tɔtɛm] *nm (gén)* totem; *(poteau)* totem pole.

toubib * [tubib] *nm* doctor, doc *.

toucan [tukɑ̃] *nm* toucan.

touchant[1] [tuʃɑ̃] *prép* concerning, about.

touchant[2]**, e** [tuʃɑ̃, ɑ̃t] *adj (émouvant)* touching, moving.

touche [tuʃ] *nf* (**a**) *[piano etc]* key; *[guitare]* fret. *(Ordin)* ~ **de fonction/programmable** function/user-defined key. (**b**) *(de couleur)* touch, stroke; *(d'ironie)* touch. **une** ~ **de gaieté** a touch *ou* note of gaiety; **avec une** ~ **d'humour** with a hint *ou* suggestion *ou* touch of humour. (**c**) *(Pêche)* bite; *(Escrime)* hit. **faire une** ~ *(lit)* to have a bite; *(*: flirter)* to make a hit. (**d**) *(Ftbl, Rugby) (ligne)* touch-line; *(sortie)* touch; *(remise en jeu) (Ftbl)* throw-in; *(Rugby)* line-out. **sortir en** ~ to go into touch; **rester sur la** ~ *(lit)* to stay on the touch-lines; *(fig)* to be left on the sidelines. (**e**) *(*: allure)* look, appearance. **quelle drôle de** ~! what a sight! *, what does he (*ou* she *etc*) look like! *

touche-à-tout [tuʃatu] *nmf inv (gén enfant)* (little) meddler; *(inventeur)* dabbler.

toucher [tuʃe] (1) **1** *vt* (**a**) *(gén)* to touch; *(pour palper) tissu etc* to feel. ~ **qch du doigt** to touch sth with one's finger; **je n'avais pas touché une raquette depuis 6 mois** I hadn't had a racket in my hands for 6 months; **il ne faut pas que ça touche (le mur)** it mustn't touch (the wall); ~ **le fond** *(lit)* to touch the bottom; *(fig) [récession, productivité]* to bottom out; *(fig)* ~ **le fond de l'abîme** to be utterly destitute, be in abject poverty; ~ **le fond du désespoir** to be in the depths of despair; ~ **terre** to land; **l'avion toucha le sol** the plane touched down *ou* landed. (**b**) *(jouxter)* to adjoin. **son jardin touche le nôtre** his garden (ad)joins ours *ou* is adjacent to ours. (**c**) *adversaire, objectif* to hit. **touché d'une balle en plein cœur** hit by a bullet in the heart. (**d**) *(contacter)* to reach, get in touch with, contact. (**e**) *(faire escale à) port* to put in at, call at. (**f**) *salaire* to draw, get, be paid; *prime* to get, receive; *chèque* to cash; *gros lot* to win. (**g**) *(émouvoir) [drame, deuil]* to affect, shake; *[cadeau, bonté]* to touch, move; *[reproche]* to have an effect on. ~ **qn au vif** to cut sb to the quick. (**h**) *(concerner) [problème]* to affect, concern. **touché par la dévaluation** affected *ou* hit by devaluation. (**i**) **je vais lui en** ~ **un mot** I'll have a word with him about it, I'll mention it to him; **touchons du bois!** * touch wood! *, knock on wood! * *(US)* , let's keep our fingers crossed!

2 se ~ *vpr [lignes, cercles]* to touch; *[terrains]* to be adjacent (to each other), adjoin.

3 ~ **à** *vt indir* (**a**) *objet* to touch; *économies* to break into, touch. ~ **à tout** *(lit)* to meddle with everything; *(faire plusieurs métiers)* to dabble in everything; **on n'a pas touché au fromage** we haven't touched the cheese, the cheese has been left untouched. (**b**) *(malmener) enfant* to touch, lay a finger on; *réputation* to question. (**c**) *(modifier) règlement* to meddle with; *mécanisme* to tamper with; *monument* to touch. *(Pol)* ~ **aux intérêts d'un pays** to interfere with a country's interests. (**d**) *(concerner) intérêts* to affect; *problème, domaine* to touch, have to do with. (**e**) *(aborder) période, but* to near, approach; *sujet* to broach, come onto; *activité* to try one's hand at. *(fig)* **sans avoir l'air d'y** ~ looking as if butter wouldn't melt in his mouth; **l'hiver touche à sa fin** winter is nearing its end *ou* is drawing to a close. (**f**) *(être en contact avec)* to touch; *(être contigu à)* to border on, adjoin. **cela touche à la folie** that verges *ou* borders on madness.

4 *nm (sens)* (sense of) touch; *(impression produite)* feel. **doux au** ~ soft to the touch.

touffe [tuf] *nf [herbe, poils]* tuft; *[arbres, fleurs]* clump (*de* of).

touffu, e [tufy] *adj barbe* bushy; *arbres* leafy; *haie, bois* thick; *roman, style* dense.

touiller * [tuje] (1) *vt* to stir.

toujours [tuʒuR] *adv* (**a**) *(continuité)* always; *(répétition)* forever, always. ~ **à l'heure** always on time; **la vie se déroule** ~ **pareille** life goes on the same as ever *ou* forever the same; **il est** ~ **en train de critiquer** he is always *ou* forever criticizing, he keeps on criticizing; **comme** ~ as ever, as always; **les jeunes veulent** ~ **plus d'indépendance** young people want more and more *ou* still more independence; **ce sont des amis de** ~ they are lifelong friends; **il est parti pour** ~ he's gone forever *ou* for good. (**b**) *(encore)* still. **il travaille** ~ he is still working; **j'espère** ~ **qu'elle viendra** I keep hoping *ou* I'm still hoping she'll come; **ils n'ont** ~ **pas répondu** they still haven't replied, they have not yet replied. (**c**) *(intensif)* anyway, anyhow. **écrivez** ~, **il vous répondra peut-être** write anyway *ou* anyhow, he (just) might answer you; **où est-elle? — pas chez moi** ~! where is she? — not at my place anyway! *ou* at any rate!; **je trouverai** ~ **(bien) une excuse** I can always think up an excuse; **tu trouveras** ~ **(bien) une poste** you're sure *ou* bound to find a post office; **tu peux** ~ **courir!** * you've got some hope! *(iro)*; **vous pouvez** ~ **crier, il n'y a per-**

sonne shout as much as you like, there's no one about; ~ **est-il que** the fact remains that, that does not alter the fact that.

toupet [tupɛ] *nm* (**a**) ~ **(de cheveux)** quiff, tuft (of hair). (**b**) *(*: culot)* sauce *, nerve, cheek. **avoir du** ~ to have a nerve *ou* a cheek.

toupie [tupi] *nf (jouet)* (spinning) top. **vieille** ~ ‡ silly old trout ‡.

tour[1] [tuʀ] *nf* (**a**) tower; *(immeuble)* tower block, high-rise block. ~ **de contrôle** control tower; *(fig péj)* **c'est une vraie** ~, **il est gros comme une** ~ he is massive *ou* enormous. (**b**) *(Échecs)* castle, rook.

tour[2] [tuʀ] *nm* (**a**) *(parcours, exploration)* **faire le** ~ **de** *parc etc* to go round; *possibilités* to explore; *magasins* to go round, look round; *problème* to consider from all angles; ~ **de ville** *(pour touristes)* city tour; **si on faisait le** ~? shall we go round (it)?; **faire le** ~ **du cadran** *[aiguille]* to go round the clock; *[dormeur]* to sleep (right) round the clock; **faire le** ~ **du monde** to go round the world; **faire un** ~ **d'Europe** to tour Europe; ~ **d'horizon** (general) survey; ~ **de chant** song recital; ~ **de piste** *(Sport)* lap; *(Cirque)* circuit; **la bouteille a fait le** ~ **de la table** the bottle went round the table; *(dans un débat)* **procéder à un** ~ **de table** to seek the views of all those seated round the table.
(**b**) *(excursion)* trip, outing; *(balade) (à pied)* walk, stroll; *(en voiture)* run, drive. **faire un** ~ **de manège** to have a ride on a merry-go-round; **faire un** ~ **en ville** to go for a walk round town; **je vais te faire faire le** ~ **du propriétaire** I'll show you over *ou* round the place.
(**c**) *(succession)* turn, go. ~ **de garde** spell *ou* turn of duty; **c'est votre** ~ it's your turn; **à ton** ~ **(de jouer)** *(gén)* (it's) your turn *ou* go; *(Échecs, Dames)* (it's) your move; **attendre son** ~ to wait one's turn; **chacun son** ~ everyone will have his turn; **nous le faisons chacun à notre** ~ *ou* ~ **à** ~ *ou* **à** ~ **de rôle** we do it in turn, we take turns at it; **à qui le** ~? whose turn *ou* go is it?, who is next?
(**d**) *(Pol)* ~ **(de scrutin)** ballot; **au premier** ~ in the first ballot *ou* round.
(**e**) *[partie du corps]* measurement; *[tronc, colonne]* girth; *[visage]* contour, outline; *[surface]* circumference; *[bouche]* outline. ~ **de taille** *etc* waist *etc* measurement; **la table fait 3 mètres de** ~ the table measures 3 metres round (the edge).
(**f**) *(rotation)* turn; *(Tech)* revolution. **un** ~ **de vis** a (turn of a) screw; *(fig)* **donner un** ~ **de vis au crédit** to freeze credit, put a squeeze on credit; **donner un** ~ **de vis aux libertés** to crack down *ou* clamp down on freedom; *(Aut)* **régime de 2 000** ~**s** speed of 2,000 revs *ou* revolutions; **donner un** ~ **de clef** to turn the key, give the key a turn; **faire un** ~ **sur soi-même** to spin round once; **souffrir d'un** ~ **de reins** to suffer from a sprained *ou* strained back; **à** ~ **de bras** *frapper* with all one's strength; *produire* prolifically; *critiquer* with a vengeance.
(**g**) *(disque)* **un 33** ~**s** an LP; **un 45** ~**s** a single; **un 78** ~**s** a 78.
(**h**) *(tournure) [situation, conversation]* turn, twist. ~ **d'esprit** turn *ou* cast of mind; ~ **(de phrase)** turn of phrase.
(**i**) *[acrobate]* feat, stunt; *[jongleur, escroc, plaisantin]* trick. ~ **d'adresse/de cartes** skilful/card trick; ~ **de force** *(lit)* feat of strength; *(fig)* amazing feat; **en un** ~ **de main** in next to no time; **et le** ~ **est joué!** and there you have it!; **par un** ~ **de passe-passe** by sleight of hand; **c'est un** ~ **à prendre** it's just a knack one picks up; **avoir plus d'un** ~ **dans son sac** to have more than one trick up one's sleeve; **jouer un** ~ **à qn** to play a trick on sb; **un** ~ **de cochon** * a dirty *ou* lousy trick *.
(**j**) *(Tech)* lathe. ~ **de potier** potter's wheel.

tourbe [tuʀb(ə)] *nf* peat. ◆ **tourbeux, -euse** *adj* peaty. ◆ **tourbière** *nf* peat bog.

tourbillon [tuʀbijɔ̃] *nm (dans l'eau)* whirlpool; *(de vent)* whirlwind; ~ **de fumée/neige** swirl *ou* eddy of smoke/snow; ~ **de plaisirs** whirl of pleasure; **le** ~ **de la vie** the hurly-burly *ou* hustle and bustle of life. ◆ **tourbillonnement** *nm* whirling, swirling, eddying. ◆ **tourbillonner** (1) *vi [poussière etc]* to whirl, swirl, eddy; *[danseurs, idées]* to swirl *ou* whirl round.

tourelle [tuʀɛl] *nf (gén)* turret; *[sous-marin]* conning tower.

tourisme [tuʀism(ə)] *nm*: **le** ~ tourism; **faire du** ~ to go touring *ou* sightseeing; **le** ~ **d'hiver** the winter tourist trade *ou* industry; **avion/voiture de** ~ private plane/car; **office du** ~ tourist office; **agence de** ~ tourist agency. ◆ **touriste** *nmf* tourist. ◆ **touristique** *adj (gén)* tourist; *région* with great tourist attractions, popular with (the) tourists, touristic *(péj)*.

tourment [tuʀmɑ̃] *nm* agony, torment.

tourmente [tuʀmɑ̃t] *nf (lit)* storm, gale; *(fig)* storm, turmoil. ~ **de neige** blizzard.

tourmenter [tuʀmɑ̃te] (1) **1** *vt (gén)* to torment; *[remords, doute]* to rack, plague. ~ **qn de questions** to plague *ou* harass sb with questions; **ce qui me tourmente dans cette affaire** what worries *ou* bothers me in this business. **2 se** ~ *vpr* to fret, worry (o.s.). ◆ **tourmenté, e** *adj personne, visage* tormented, tortured; *formes* tortured; *vie, mer* stormy.

tournage [tuʀnaʒ] *nm (Ciné)* shooting; *(Menuiserie)* turning.

tournant, e [tuʀnɑ̃, ɑ̃t] **1** *adj fauteuil* swivel; *scène* revolving; *(Mil) mouvement* encircling; *escalier* spiral. **2** *nm (virage)* bend; *(changement)* turning point. *(fig)* ~ **décisif** watershed; **cette entreprise a bien su prendre le** ~ this company has managed the change *ou* switch well; **avoir qn au** ~ * to get even with sb; **attendre qn au** ~ * to wait for the chance to catch sb out.

tourné, e[1] [tuʀne] *adj* (**a**) **bien** ~ *personne, jambes* shapely; *taille* neat, trim; *compliment* well-turned; *article, lettre* well-worded, well-phrased; **mal** ~ *lettre* badly worded *ou* phrased; **avoir l'esprit mal** ~ to have a dirty mind. (**b**) *lait, vin* sour. (**c**) *(Menuiserie)* turned.

tournebouler * [tuʀnəbule] (1) *vt personne* to put in a whirl.

tournebroche [tuʀnəbʀɔʃ] *nm* roasting jack *ou* spit, rotisserie.

tourne-disque, *pl* **tourne-disques** [tuʀnə disk(ə)] *nm* record player.

tournedos [tuʀnədo] *nm* tournedos.

tournée[2] [tuʀne] *nf* (**a**) *[conférencier, artiste]* tour; *[inspecteur, livreur]* round. **être en** ~ to be on tour; to be on one's rounds; **faire la** ~ **de** *magasins* to do the rounds of, go round; **faire la** ~ **des grands ducs** to go out on a spree. (**b**) *(consommations)* round (of drinks). **c'est la** ~ **du patron** the drinks are on the house.

tournemain [tuʀnəmɛ̃] *nm*: **en un** ~ in next to no time.

tourner [tuʀne] (1) **1** *vt* (**a**) *clef, regard etc* to turn; *sauce* to stir; *page* to turn (over). ~ **et retourner** to turn over and over; **quand il m'a vu, il a tourné la tête** when he saw me he looked away *ou* he turned his head away; *(lit, fig)* ~ **le dos à** to turn one's back on; **le dos tourné à la fenêtre** with one's back to the window; **dès que j'ai le dos tourné** as soon as my back is turned; ~ **ses pensées/efforts vers** to turn *ou* bend one's thoughts/efforts towards *ou* to. (**b**) *armée* to turn, outflank; *obstacle* to round; *difficulté* to get round *ou* past. (**c**) *phrase, compliment* to turn; *demande, lettre* to phrase, express. (**d**) *(Ciné) scène* to shoot, film; *film (faire les prises de vue)* to shoot; *(en être producteur ou* *acteur)* to make. **ils ont dû ~ en studio** they had to do the filming in the studio; **scène tournée en extérieur** scene shot on location. (**e**) *bois, ivoire* to turn; *pot* to throw. (**f**) *(locutions)* **~ qch en ridicule** to make sth a laughing stock, ridicule sth, hold sth up to ridicule; **il a tourné l'incident en plaisanterie** he made a joke out of the incident; **il tourne tout à son avantage** he turns everything to his (own) advantage; *(fig)* **~ la page** to turn over a new leaf; *(lit, fig)* **se ~ les pouces** to twiddle one's thumbs; **~ la tête à qn** *[vin]* to go to sb's head; *[succès]* to go to *ou* turn sb's head.

2 *vi* (**a**) *(gén)* to turn; *[aiguilles]* to go round; *(Tech) [roue]* to revolve; *[toupie]* to spin; *[taximètre]* to tick away; *[usine, moteur]* to run. **~ sur soi-même** to turn round on o.s.; *(très vite)* to spin round; **l'heure tourne** time is passing *ou* is going by *ou* on; **j'ai vu tout ~** my head began to spin *ou* swim; **faire ~ le moteur** to run the engine; **~ au ralenti** to tick over. (**b**) *[programme d'ordinateur]* to work. **arriver à faire ~ un programme** to get a program working *ou* to work. (**c**) **~ autour de** *(gén)* to turn *ou* go round; *[terre, roue]* to revolve *ou* go round; *[prix]* to be around *ou* about; *[oiseau, mouches]* to fly round; **~ autour de qn** *(péj: importuner)* to hang round sb; *(par curiosité)* to hover round sb; *[enquête, conversation]* **~ autour de qch** to centre on sth. (**d**) *(changer) [vent, opinion]* to turn, shift, veer (round); *[chemin, promeneur]* to turn; *[chance]* to turn. **bien/mal ~** to turn out well/badly; **ça va mal ~** * that'll lead to trouble, it'll turn nasty; **~ au froid/au rouge** to turn cold/red; **~ à l'avantage de qn** to turn to sb's advantage; **~ à la bagarre** to turn *ou* degenerate into a fight; **sa bronchite a tourné en pneumonie** his bronchitis has turned *ou* developed into pneumonia; **~ au drame** to take a dramatic turn. (**e**) *[lait]* to turn (sour); *[poisson, viande]* to go off, go bad; *[fruits]* to go rotten *ou* bad. **faire ~** to turn sour. (**f**) *(locutions)* **~ à l'aigre** to turn sour; **~ court** to come to a sudden end; **~ de l'œil** * to pass out, faint; **~ en rond** *(lit)* to walk round and round; *[discussion]* to go round in circles; **~ rond** to run smoothly; **elle ne tourne pas rond** * she must be a bit touched *; **qu'est-ce qui ne tourne pas rond?** * what's the matter?, what's wrong?, what's up? *; **~ autour du pot** * to beat about the bush; **il tourne comme un ours** *ou* **comme une bête en cage** he paces about like a caged animal; *(Spiritisme)* **faire ~ les tables** to do table-turning; **faire ~ qn en bourrique** to drive sb round the bend *.

3 se ~ *vpr (lit, fig)* **se ~ vers** to turn to; **se ~ contre qn** to turn against sb; **tourne-toi (de l'autre côté)** turn round *ou* the other way.

tournesol [tuʀnəsɔl] *nm* sunflower.

tourneur [tuʀnœʀ] *nm (Tech)* turner.

tournevis [tuʀnəvis] *nm* screwdriver.

tourniquet [tuʀnikɛ] *nm (barrière)* turnstile; *(porte)* revolving door; *(d'arrosage)* sprinkler hose; *(présentoir)* revolving stand; *(Méd)* tourniquet.

tournis * [tuʀni] *nm*: **donner le ~ à qn** to make sb feel dizzy *ou* giddy.

tournoi [tuʀnwa] *nm* tournament.

tournoyer [tuʀnwaje] (**8**) *vi [eau, fumée]* to whirl, swirl, eddy; *[oiseaux]* to wheel (round); *[feuilles mortes]* to swirl around. **faire ~ qch** to whirl sth round. ◆ **tournoiement** *nm*: **~(s)** whirling; swirling; eddying; wheeling.

tournure [tuʀnyʀ] *nf* (**a**) *(tour de phrase)* turn of phrase; *(forme)* form. **~ négative** negative form. (**b**) *[événements]* turn. **la situation a pris une mauvaise/meilleure ~** the situation took a turn for the worse/for the better; **prendre ~** to take shape. (**c**) **~ d'esprit** turn *ou* cast of mind.

tourteau, *pl* **~x** [tuʀto] *nm* (sort of) crab.

tourterelle [tuʀtəʀɛl] *nf* turtledove.

tous [tu] *V* **tout.**

Toussaint [tusɛ̃] *nf*: **la ~** All Saints' Day.

tousser [tuse] (**1**) *vi [personne]* to cough; *[moteur]* to splutter, cough, hiccup. ◆ **toussoter** (**1**) *vi* to cough, have a slight cough. ◆ **toussotement** *nm* (slight) coughing.

tout [tu], **toute** [tut], *mpl* **tous** [tu] *(adj) ou* [tus] *(pron)*, *fpl* **toutes** [tut] **1** *adj* (**a**) *(complet)* all (of), the whole (of). **~ le, toute la** all (the), the whole (of the); **lire ~ Balzac** to read the whole of *ou* all of Balzac; **il a plu toute la nuit/toute une nuit** it rained the whole (of the) night *ou* all night (long)/for a whole night; **~ le monde** everybody, everyone; **~ le reste** (all) the rest; **~ le temps** all the time; **toute la France** the whole of *ou* all France; **donner toute satisfaction** to give complete satisfaction; **en toute franchise** in all sincerity; **c'est toute une affaire** it's quite a business.

(**b**) *(tout à fait)* quite. **c'est ~ le contraire** it's quite the opposite *ou* the very opposite; **lui ~ le premier** him *ou* he first of all; **c'est ~ autre chose** that's quite another matter; **avec toi c'est ~ l'un ou ~ l'autre** with you it's either all black or all white; **c'est ~ le portrait de son père** he is the spitting image of his father.

(**c**) *(seul)* only. **c'est ~ l'effet que cela lui fait** that's all the effect *ou* the only effect it has on him; **c'est là ~ le problème** that's the whole problem; **cet enfant est toute ma joie** this child is all my joy.

(**d**) *(n'importe quel)* any, all. **toute personne** any person, anyone; **toute trace d'agitation a disparu** all *ou* any trace of agitation has gone; **il me dérange à ~ instant** he keeps on disturbing me, he's constantly *ou* continually disturbing me; **ça peut se produire à ~ instant** it can happen (at) any time *ou* moment; **à ~ âge** at any age, at all ages; **pour ~ renseignement, téléphoner...** for all information, ring...; **(véhicule) ~ terrain** all-purpose *ou* all-roads vehicle.

(**e**) *(complètement)* **il était ~ à son travail** he was entirely taken up by his work; **habillé ~ en noir** dressed all in black; **un style ~ en nuances** a very subtle style, a style full of nuances.

(**f**) **tous, toutes** *(l'ensemble)* all, every; **toutes les personnes** all the people, everyone; **courir dans tous les sens** to run in all directions *ou* in every direction; **film pour tous publics** film suitable for all audiences; **toutes sortes de** all sorts of, every kind of; **tous azimuts** *attaquer* on all fronts.

(**g**) **tous** *ou* **toutes les** *(chaque)* every; **tous les ans** every year; **tous les deux jours** every other *ou* second *ou* alternate day, every two days; **tous les 10 mètres** every 10 metres; **tous les trente-six du mois** once in a blue moon; **tous (les) deux** both (of them), the two of them, **tous (les) 3/4** all 3/4 (of them).

(**h**) *(locutions)* **en ~ bien ~ honneur** with the most honourable (of) intentions; **à ~ bout de champ** every now and then; **en ~ cas** anyway, in any case, at any rate; **~ un chacun** every one of us; **de ~ côté** *chercher* on all sides, everywhere; **à tous égards** in every respect; **en ~ état de cause, de toute façon** in any case, anyway, anyhow; **il s'est enfui à toutes jambes** he ran away as fast as his legs could carry him, he showed a clean pair of heels; **en tous lieux** everywhere; **faire ~ son possible** to do one's utmost; **toutes proportions gardées** relatively speaking, making due allowances; **à ~ propos** every other minute; **de ~ cœur** wholeheartedly; **de toute beauté** most beautiful, of the utmost beauty; **de ~ temps, de toute éternité** from time immemorial, since the beginning of time; **ce n'est pas un travail de ~ repos** it's not an easy job; **c'est un placement de ~ repos** it's an absolutely secure investment; **à ~ prix** at all costs; **à toute vitesse** at full *ou* top speed; **il a une**

patience/un courage à toute épreuve his patience/courage will stand any test, he has limitless patience/unshakeable courage; **selon toute apparence** to all appearances.

2 *pron indéf* (**a**) *(gén)* everything, all; *(n'importe quoi)* anything. **il a ~ organisé** he organized everything, he organized it all; **il vend de ~** he sells anything and everything; **c'est ~ ou rien** it's all or nothing.

(**b**) **tous, toutes** all; **vous tous** all of you; **tous ensemble** all together; **film pour tous** film suitable for all audiences.

(**c**) **~ ce qui, ~ ce que**: **~ ce que je sais, c'est qu'il est parti** all I know is that he's gone; **ne croyez pas ~ ce qu'il raconte** don't believe everything *ou* all he tells you; **~ ce qui lui appartient** everything *ou* all that belongs to him; **~ ce qui brille n'est pas or** all that glitters is not gold; **il a été ~ ce qu'il y a de gentil** he was most kind, he couldn't have been kinder.

(**d**) *(locutions)* **~ est bien qui finit bien** all's well that ends well; ... **et ~ et ~ *** ... and all that sort of thing, ... and so on and so forth; **~ est là** that's the whole point; **c'est ~** that's all; **c'est ~ dire** I need say no more; **et ce n'est pas ~!** and that's not all!, and there's more to come; **ce n'est pas ~ de partir, il faut arriver** it's not enough to set off, one must arrive as well; **il y avait des gens ~ ce qu'il y a de plus distingué** there were the most distinguished people there; **à ~ prendre, ~ bien considéré** all things considered, taking everything into consideration; *(Comm)* **~ compris** inclusive, all-in; **avoir ~ d'un brigand** to be an absolute *ou* a real outlaw; **en ~** in all; **en ~ et pour ~** all in all.

3 *adv* (**a**) *(tout à fait)* very, quite; *surpris, déçu* very, most; *cru* quite, completely. **les toutes premières années** the very first *ou* early years; **c'est une ~ autre histoire** that's quite another story; **c'est ~ naturel** it's perfectly *ou* quite natural; **la ville ~ entière** the whole town; **~ nu** stark naked; **~ neuf** brand new.

(**b**) *(quoique)* **~ médecin qu'il soit** even though *ou* although he is a doctor; **toute malade qu'elle se dise** however *ou* no matter how ill she says she is.

(**c**) *(intensif)* **~ près** very near *ou* close; **~ là-bas/au bout** right over there/at the end; **~ simplement** quite simply; **je le sais ~ autant que toi** I know it as well as you do, I'm as aware of it as you are; **j'aime ça ~ aussi peu que lui** I like that as little as he does; **parler ~ bas** to speak very low; **il était ~ en sueur** he was in a lather of sweat *ou* running with sweat; **elle était ~ en larmes** she was in floods of tears; **le jardin est ~ en fleurs** the garden is a mass of flowers.

(**d**) **~ en +** *participe présent*: **~ en marchant** as *ou* while you walk, while walking; **~ en prétendant le contraire il voulait être élu** (al)though he pretended otherwise he wanted to be elected.

(**e**) *(avec n)* **être ~ yeux/oreilles** to be all eyes/ears; **être ~ sucre ~ miel** to be all sweetness and light; **~ laine** all wool; **être ~ feu ~ flammes** to be fired with enthusiasm.

(**f**) *(déjà)* **~ prêt, ~ préparé** ready-made; **formules toutes faites** ready-made *ou* set *ou* standard phrases; **idées toutes faites** preconceived ideas; **vendu ~ cuit** sold ready-cooked *ou* pre-cooked; **c'est du ~ cuit *** it's a cinch * *ou* a pushover *; **c'est ~ vu *** it's a foregone conclusion, it's a dead cert *.

(**g**) *(locutions)* **~ à coup** all of a sudden, suddenly; **~ à fait** quite, entirely; **~ à l'heure** *(futur)* in a moment; *(passé)* a moment ago; **~ de suite** straightaway, at once, immediately; **~ au plus** at the (very) most; **~ au moins** at (the very) least; **~ d'abord** first of all, in the first place; **~ de même** *(en dépit de cela)* all the same, for all that; *(très)* quite, really; *(indignation)* **~ de même!** well really!; **il est gentil ~ plein *** he is really very *ou* really awfully * nice; **~ nouveau ~ beau** (just) wait till the novelty wears off; **c'est ~ comme *** it comes to the same thing really; **c'est ~ un** it's all one, it's one and the same thing.

4 *nm* (**a**) *(ensemble)* whole. **vendre le ~** to sell the (whole) lot.

(**b**) **le ~ est qu'il parte à temps** the main *ou* most important thing is that he leaves in time; **il avait changé du ~ au ~** he had changed completely; **ce n'est pas le ~ *, il faut se dépêcher** this isn't good enough, we'll have to hurry; **(pas) du ~** not at all; **il n'y a plus du ~ de pain** there's no bread left at all.

◆ **tout-à-l'égout** *nm inv* mains drainage. ◆ **tout-petit,** *pl* **tout-petits** *nm* toddler, tiny tot. ◆ **toute-puissance** *nf* omnipotence. ◆ **tout-puissant,** *f* **toute-puissante 1** *adj* omnipotent, all-powerful. **2** *nm*: **le T~-P~** the Almighty. ◆ **tout-venant** *nm inv (charbon)* raw coal. *(articles, marchandises)* **le ~** the run-of-the-mill *ou* ordinary stuff.

toutefois [tutfwa] *adv* however.

toutou * [tutu] *nm* doggie *, bow-wow *. **obéir à qn comme un ~** to obey sb as meekly as a lamb.

toux [tu] *nf* cough.

toxique [tɔksik] **1** *adj* toxic, poisonous. **2** *nm* toxin, poison. ◆ **toxicologie** *nf* toxicology. ◆ **toxicologique** *adj* toxicological. ◆ **toxicologue** *nmf* toxicologist. ◆ **toxicomane** *nmf* drug addict. ◆ **toxicomanie** *nf* drug addiction. ◆ **toxine** *nf* toxin.

trac [tʀak] *nm (Théât, en public)* stage fright; *(aux examens etc)* nerves. **avoir le ~** to get stage fright; to get nerves; **donner le ~ à qn** to give sb a fright.

tracas [tʀaka] *nm* worry. **donner du** *ou* **des ~ à qn** to give sb trouble, worry sb. ◆ **tracasser** (1) **1** *vt (gén)* to worry, bother; *[administration]* to harass, bother. **2 se ~** *vpr* to worry, fret.

trace [tʀas] *nf* (**a**) *(gén, fig: marque)* mark; *(empreinte d'animal, de pneu)* tracks; *(vestige de civilisation)* trace; *(indice)* sign. **~s de pas** footprints; **~s de doigt** finger marks; **~s d'effraction** signs of a break-in. (**b**) *(quantité minime) [poison, substance]* trace. **sans une ~ d'accent étranger** without a *ou* any trace of a foreign accent. (**c**) **disparaître sans laisser de ~s** *[personne]* to disappear without trace; *[tache]* to disappear completely without leaving a mark; **il n'y avait pas ~ des documents** there was no trace of the documents; **être sur la ~ de** to be on the track of; **perdre la ~ d'un fugitif** to lose track of *ou* lose the trail of a fugitive; *(fig)* **marcher sur les ~s de qn** to follow in sb's footsteps.

tracé [tʀase] *nm* (**a**) *(plan)* layout, plan. (**b**) *(parcours) [autoroute]* route; *[rivière]* line, course; *[côte, crête]* line. (**c**) *(graphisme)* line.

tracer [tʀase] (3) *vt (dessiner) ligne, plan* to draw; *courbe graphique* to plot; *(écrire)* to write, trace; *(frayer) route* to open up. *(fig)* **~ la voie à qn** to show sb the way. ◆ **traceur** *nm (Ordin)* **~ de courbes** (graph) plotter.

trachée [tʀaʃe] *nf*: **~(-artère)** windpipe.

tract [tʀakt] *nm* leaflet.

tractation [tʀaktɑsjɔ̃] *nf* dealings, bargaining, negotiation.

tracter [tʀakte] (1) *vt* to tow.

tracteur [tʀaktœʀ] *nm* tractor.

traction [tʀaksjɔ̃] *nf (gén)* traction. *(Aut)* **~ avant** car with front-wheel drive.

tradition [tʀadisjɔ̃] *nf (gén)* tradition. **il est de ~ que** it is a tradition *ou* traditional that. ◆ **traditionnel, -elle** *adj* traditional; *(*: habituel)* **sa**

~**elle robe noire** * her good old * *ou* usual black dress. ◆ **traditionnellement** *adv* traditionally; *(habituellement)* as usual.

traduire [tʀadɥiʀ] (38) **1** *vt* (**a**) *texte, auteur* to translate (*en* into); *sentiment* to convey, render, express. **cela traduit notre inquiétude** this shows *ou* conveys our anxiety. (**b**) ~ **qn en justice** to bring sb before the courts. **2 se** ~ *vpr (gén)* to be translated. **ça va se** ~ **par une augmentation des impôts** the visible outcome will be an increase in taxes, it will be translated into an increase in taxes. ◆ **traducteur, -trice** *nm, f* translator. ◆ **traduction** *nf* translation; expression. **la** ~ **de ce texte en anglais** the translation of *ou* translating this text into English; ~ **littérale** literal translation. ◆ **traduisible** *adj* translatable.

trafic [tʀafik] *nm* (**a**) *(péj)* traffic; *(†: commerce)* trade (*de* in). ~ **d'armes** arms dealing, gunrunning; ~ **de la drogue** drug trafficking. (**b**) *(activités suspectes)* dealings; *(*: micmac)* funny business *, goings-on *. (**c**) *(Aut, Aviat, Rail)* traffic. ◆ **trafiquant, e** *nm, f (péj)* trafficker. ~ **d'armes** arms dealer, gunrunner. ◆ **trafiquer** (1) **1** *vi (péj)* to traffic, trade (illicitly). **2** *vt (*: péj) vin* to doctor *; *moteur* to tamper *ou* fiddle with.

tragédie [tʀaʒedi] *nf (gén, Théât)* tragedy. ◆ **tragédien, -ienne** *nm, f* tragic actor *ou* actress. ◆ **tragique 1** *adj (Théât, fig)* tragic. **ce n'est pas** ~ it's not the end of the world. **2** *nm (auteur)* tragic author; *(tragédie)* **le** ~ tragedy. **prendre qch au** ~ to make a tragedy out of sth. ◆ **tragiquement** *adv* tragically.

trahir [tʀaiʀ] (2) *vt ami, patrie* to betray; *secret, émotion* to betray, give away. **sa rougeur l'a trahie** her blushes gave her away *ou* betrayed her; **ses nerfs l'ont trahi** his nerves failed him; **ces mots ont trahi ma pensée** those words misrepresented my thoughts. ◆ **trahison** *nf (gén)* betrayal, treachery; *(Jur, Mil: crime)* treason.

train [tʀɛ̃] *nm* (**a**) *(Rail)* train. ~ **omnibus/direct** slow *ou* stopping/fast *ou* non-stop train; ~ **de marchandises/voyageurs** goods/passenger train; ~ **auto-couchettes** car-sleeper train, ≃ Motorail; ~ **à grande vitesse** high-speed train; **il est dans ce** ~ he's on *ou* aboard this train; **mettre qn dans le** ~ *ou* **au** ~ to see sb to the train; **prendre le** ~ to take the train; **prendre le** ~ **en marche** *(lit)* to get on the moving train; *(fig)* to jump on the bandwagon. (**b**) *(allure)* pace. **aller son petit** ~ to go along at one's own pace; **aller bon** ~ *[affaire, voiture]* to make good progress; *[commentaires]* to be rife; *(fig: dépenser beaucoup)* **mener grand** ~ to live in grand style, spend money like water; **il allait à un** ~ **d'enfer** he was going flat out, he was racing along; **au** ~ **où il travaille** (at) the rate he is working; **au** *ou* **du** ~ **où vont les choses** at this rate. (**c**) **être en** ~ *(en forme)* to be in good form; *(gai)* to be in good spirits; **mettre un travail en** ~ to get a job under way *ou* started; **mise en** ~ *[travail]* starting (up), start; *(exercices de gym)* warm-up; **elle ne se sent pas très en** ~ she doesn't feel too good *ou* too bright *. (**d**) **être en** ~ **de faire qch** to be doing sth; **être en** ~ **de manger** to be (busy) eating. (**e**) *(ensemble) [bateaux, mulets]* train, line; *[réformes, mesures]* set, batch. ~ **de pneus** set of (four) tyres; *(Aut)* ~ **avant/arrière** front/rear wheel-axle unit; *[animal]* ~ **de devant** forequarters; ~ **de derrière** hindquarters; ~ **d'atterrissage** undercarriage, landing gear. (**f**) ~ **de vie** style of living, life style; **le** ~ **de vie de l'État** the government's rate of expenditure.

traînant, e [tʀɛnɑ̃, ɑ̃t] *adj voix* drawling; *démarche* shuffling.

traînard, e [tʀɛnaʀ, aʀd(ə)] *nm, f (péj) (gén)* slowcoach *; *(toujours en queue d'un groupe)* straggler.

traîne [tʀɛn] *nf [robe]* train. *(fig)* **être à la** ~ *(en remorque)* to be in tow; *(*: en retard)* to lag behind.

traîneau, *pl* ~**x** [tʀɛno] *nm* sleigh, sledge, sled *(US)*.

traînée [tʀene] *nf (sur le sol)* trail, tracks; *(sur un mur, dans le ciel)* streak. **se répandre comme une** ~ **de poudre** to spread like wildfire.

traîner [tʀene] (1) **1** *vt objet lourd, personne* to drag (along). ~ **les pieds** to drag one's feet, shuffle along; ~ **la jambe** to limp, hobble; ~ **qn dans la boue** to drag sb through the mud; *(fig)* ~ **un boulet** to have a millstone round one's neck; **elle est obligée de** ~ **ses enfants partout** she has to trail *ou* drag her children along (with her) everywhere; **elle traîne un mauvais rhume** she has a bad cold she can't get rid of. **2** *vi* (**a**) *[personne] (rester en arrière)* to lag *ou* trail behind; *(aller lentement)* to dawdle; *(péj: errer, s'attarder)* to hang about. ~ **en chemin** to dawdle on the way. (**b**) *[chose] (être éparpillé)* to lie about *ou* around. **des idées qui traînent partout** ideas that float around everywhere; **elle attrape tous les microbes qui traînent** *ou* **tout ce qui traîne** she catches anything that's going. (**c**) *[conversation, procès, maladie]* ~ **(en longueur)** to drag on; **ça n'a pas traîné!** * that wasn't long coming!; **faire** ~ **qch** to drag sth out; **doctrine où traînent des relents de fascisme** doctrine with a lingering whiff of fascism about it. (**d**) *[robe]* to trail. ~ **par terre** to trail *ou* hang *ou* drag on the ground. **3 se** ~ *vpr* (**a**) *[personne]* to drag o.s. (about *ou* along); *[train, voiture]* to crawl along. **se** ~ **par terre** to crawl on the ground; *(fig)* **se** ~ **aux pieds de qn** to grovel at sb's feet. (**b**) *[conversation, journée, hiver]* to drag on.

training [tʀɛniŋ] *nm* (**a**) *(entraînement)* training. (**b**) *(chaussures)* trainer. *(®: survêtement)* **T**~tracksuit top.

train-train [tʀɛ̃tʀɛ̃] *nm* humdrum routine.

traire [tʀɛʀ] (**50**) *vt vache* to milk; *lait* to draw.

trait [tʀɛ] *nm* (**a**) *(ligne)* line. **faire un** ~ to draw a line; *(fig)* **tirer un** ~ **sur son passé** to make a complete break with one's past; ~ **de plume/de crayon** stroke of the pen/of the pencil; ~ **d'union** *(Typ)* hyphen; *(fig)* link; **biffer qch d'un** ~ to score *ou* cross sth out; *(lit, fig)* **à grands** ~**s** roughly; *(fig)* **ça lui ressemble** ~ **pour** ~ that's just *ou* exactly like him. (**b**) *(caractéristique)* feature, trait; *(acte)* act. **avoir des** ~**s de ressemblance avec** to have certain features in common with; ~ **de courage** act of courage. (**c**) *(physionomie)* ~**s** features. (**d**) *(†: projectile)* arrow, dart; *(littér: critique)* taunt, gibe. **filer comme un** ~ to be off like an arrow *ou* a shot; ~ **d'esprit** flash *ou* shaft of wit; ~ **de génie** brainwave, flash of genius. (**e**) *(courroie)* trace. **animal de** ~ draught animal. (**f**) *(gorgée)* draught, draft *(US)*, gulp. **d'un** ~ *dire* in one breath; *boire* in one gulp; *dormir* uninterruptedly, without a break. (**g**) *(rapport)* **avoir** ~ **à** to relate to, be connected with, have to do with, concern.

traite [tʀɛt] *nf* (**a**) *(trafic)* ~ **des Noirs** slave trade. (**b**) *(Comm: billet)* draft, bill. (**c**) *(parcours)* stretch. **d'une (seule)** ~ *parcourir* in one go, without stopping on the way; *dire* in one breath, *boire* in one gulp; *dormir* uninterruptedly, without waking. (**d**) *[vache]* milking.

traité [tʀete] *nm (livre)* treatise; *(convention)* treaty.

traitement [tʀɛtmɑ̃] *nm* (**a**) *[personne]* treatment; *(Méd)* course of treatment. **mauvais** ~**s** ill-treatment; **être en** ~ to be having treatment (*à l'hôpital* in hospital). (**b**) *(rémunération)* salary, wage; *(Rel)* stipend. (**c**) *[matières premières]* processing, treating. *(Ordin)* ~ **de texte** *(technique)* wordprocessing; *(logiciel)* word-processing package; **machine** *ou* **système de** ~ **de texte (dédié)** word processor.

traiter [tʀete] (1) **1** *vt* (**a**) *personne, animal* to treat; *(Méd)* to treat; (†) *invités* to entertain. ~ **qn bien/**

mal to treat sb well/badly; ~ **qn durement** to be hard with *ou* on sb; ~ **qn en enfant** to treat sb as *ou* like a child; **se faire** ~ **pour** to undergo treatment for, be treated for. (**b**) *(qualifier)* to call. ~ **qn de menteur** to call sb a liar. (**c**) *question* to treat, deal with; *(Art) thème* to treat; *(Comm) affaire* to handle, deal with. (**d**) *(Tech)* to treat, process. **non traité** untreated. **2** ~ **de** *vt indir sujet, problème* to deal with, treat of. **3** *vi (négocier)* to negotiate, make *ou* do * a deal.

traiteur [tʀɛtœʀ] *nm* caterer.

traître, traîtresse [tʀɛtʀ(ə), tʀɛtʀɛs] **1** *adj (lit, fig)* treacherous. **ne pas dire un** ~ **mot** not to breathe a (single) word. **2** *nm (gén)* traitor; *(Théât)* villain. **prendre/attaquer qn en** ~ to take/attack sb off-guard, play an underhand trick/make an insidious attack on sb. **3** *nf* traitress. ◆ **traîtreusement** *adv* treacherously. ◆ **traîtrise** *nf*: **la** ~ treacherousness; **une** ~ a treachery.

trajectoire [tʀaʒɛktwaʀ] *nf* trajectory.

trajet [tʀaʒɛ] *nm (à parcourir)* distance; *(itinéraire)* route; *(voyage)* journey; *(par mer)* voyage; *(Anat) [nerf, artère]* course. **quel** ~ **il a parcouru depuis son dernier roman!** what a distance *ou* a long way he has come since his last novel!

tralala * [tʀalala] *nm (luxe, apprêts)* fuss.

trame [tʀam] *nf [tissu]* weft, woof; *[roman]* framework; *[vie]* web; *(Géog)* network, system. **la** ~ **urbaine** the urban network *ou* system; **usé jusqu'à la** ~ threadbare.

tramer [tʀame] (1) *vt évasion* to plot; *complot* to hatch. **il se trame qch** there's sth brewing.

trampoline [tʀɑ̃pɔlin] *nm* trampoline. **faire du** ~ to go *ou* do trampolining.

tramway [tʀamwɛ] *nm (moyen de transport)* tram(way); *(voiture)* tram(car), streetcar *(US)*.

tranchant, e [tʀɑ̃ʃɑ̃, ɑ̃t] **1** *adj* (**a**) *couteau, arête* sharp. **du côté** ~ with the sharp *ou* cutting edge. (**b**) *personne* sharp, cutting. **2** *nm* sharp *ou* cutting edge.

tranche [tʀɑ̃ʃ] *nf* (**a**) *[pain, jambon]* slice; *[bacon]* rasher. ~ **de bœuf** beefsteak; **couper en** ~**s** to slice. (**b**) *(bord) [livre, planche]* edge. (**c**) *(section)* section; *[crédit, prêt]* instalment; *(Admin) [revenus]* bracket. *(Admin)* ~ **d'âge/de salaires** age/wage bracket; **la première** ~ **des travaux** the first phase of the work; ~ **de temps** period of time; **une** ~ **de vie** a part of sb's life.

trancher [tʀɑ̃ʃe] (1) **1** *vt* (**a**) *corde* to cut, sever. ~ **le cou à qn** to cut off sb's head; ~ **la gorge à qn** to cut *ou* slit sb's throat. (**b**) *discussion* to conclude, bring to a close; *question, difficulté* to settle, decide. ~ **court** *ou* **net** to bring things to an abrupt conclusion; **il faut** ~ we have to take a decision. **2** *vi [couleur]* to stand out clearly (*sur, avec* against); *[trait, qualité]* to contrast strongly *ou* sharply (*sur, avec* with). ◆ **tranché, e**[1] *adj couleurs* clear, distinct; *limite* clear-cut, definite; *opinion* clear-cut, cut-and-dried. ◆ **tranchée**[2] *nf (fossé)* trench.

tranquille [tʀɑ̃kil] *adj* (**a**) *(calme)* quiet, tranquil *(littér)*; *(paisible)* peaceful. **aller d'un pas** ~ to walk calmly; **se tenir** ~ to be quiet; **nous étions bien** ~**s** we were having a nice quiet *ou* peaceful time; **j'aime être** ~ I like (to have) some peace; **laisser qn** ~ to leave sb alone, to leave sb in peace; **laisser qch** ~ to leave sth alone *ou* in peace. (**b**) *(rassuré)* **être** ~ to be easy in one's mind; **tu peux être** ~ you needn't worry; **pour avoir l'esprit** ~ to set one's mind at rest *ou* at ease; **avoir la conscience** ~ to be at peace with one's conscience, have a clear conscience; **tu peux être** ~ **que...** you may be sure that..., rest assured that... (**c**) *(emploi adverbial)* (*: *facilement)* easily. **il l'a fait en 3 heures** ~ he did it in 3 hours easily *ou* no trouble; *(sans risques)* **tu peux y aller** ~ you can go there quite safely. ◆ **tranquillement** *adv* quietly; tranquilly; peacefully. ◆ **tranquillisant, e** **1** *adj nouvelle* reassuring; *effet, produit* soothing, tranquillizing. **2** *nm (Méd)* tranquillizer. ◆ **tranquilliser** (1) *vt*: ~ **qn** to reassure sb; **se** ~ to set one's mind at rest. ◆ **tranquillité** *nf* quietness; tranquillity; peacefulness. **en toute** ~ *agir* without being bothered *ou* disturbed; *partir* with complete peace of mind; **troubler la** ~ **publique** to disturb the peace; **travailler dans la** ~ to work in peace (and quiet); ~ **(d'esprit)** peace of mind; ~ **matérielle** material security.

trans... [tʀɑ̃z] *préf* trans...

transaction [tʀɑ̃zaksjɔ̃] *nf (Comm)* transaction.

transatlantique [tʀɑ̃zatlɑ̃tik] **1** *adj* transatlantic. **course** ~ transatlantic race. **2** *nm (paquebot)* transatlantic liner; *(fauteuil)* deckchair.

transbahuter * [tʀɑ̃zbayte] (1) *vt* to shift, lug along *.

transborder [tʀɑ̃sbɔʀde] (1) *vt (Naut)* to tran(s)-ship; *(Rail)* to transfer. ◆ **transbordement** *nm* tran(s)shipment; transfer. ◆ **transbordeur** *nm*: **pont** ~ transporter bridge.

transcendance [tʀɑ̃sɑ̃dɑ̃s] *nf* transcendence. ◆ **transcendant, e** *adj (sublime)* transcendent; *(Philos, Math)* transcendental. ◆ **transcendantal, e,** *mpl* **-aux** *adj* transcendental. ◆ **transcender** (1) **1** *vt* to transcend. **2 se** ~ *vpr* to transcend o.s.

transcrire [tʀɑ̃skʀiʀ] (39) *vt (copier)* to copy out; *(Mus, Ling)* to transcribe. ◆ **transcription** *nf* copying out; transcription.

transe [tʀɑ̃s] *nf* (**a**) *(état second)* trance. **être/ entrer en** ~ to be in/to go into a trance. (**b**) *(affres)* ~**s** agony; **dans les** ~**s** in agony; **dans les** ~**s de l'attente** in agonies of anticipation.

transférer [tʀɑ̃sfeʀe] (6) *vt* to transfer. ◆ **transfert** *nm* transfer; *(Psych)* transference.

transfigurer [tʀɑ̃sfigyʀe] (1) *vt* to transfigure.

transformer [tʀɑ̃sfɔʀme] (1) **1** *vt (gén)* to change, alter; *(radicalement)* to transform; *magasin, essai de rugby* to convert; *matière première* to convert, process. **le bonheur l'a transformé** happiness has transformed him *ou* made a new man of him; ~ **qch en** to turn *ou* convert sth into; **elle a fait** ~ **son manteau en veste** she's had her coat made *ou* converted into a jacket. **2 se** ~ *vpr [embryon]* to be transformed, transform itself; *[énergie, matière]* to be converted; *[personne, pays]* to change, alter; *(radicalement)* to be transformed (*en* into). ◆ **transformable** *adj structure, canapé* convertible; *aspect* transformable. ◆ **transformateur** *nm* transformer. ◆ **transformation** *nf* change; alteration; transformation; conversion; processing. **industries de** ~ processing industries.

transfuge [tʀɑ̃sfyʒ] *nmf (Mil, Pol)* renegade.

transfusion [tʀɑ̃sfyzjɔ̃] *nf*: ~ **(sanguine)** (blood) transfusion.

transgresser [tʀɑ̃sgʀese] (1) *vt règle* to infringe, contravene; *ordre* to disobey, go against. ~ **la loi** to break the law. ◆ **transgression** *nf* infringement, contravention; disobedience; breaking.

transiger [tʀɑ̃ziʒe] (3) *vi* to compromise (*avec* with).

transir [tʀɑ̃ziʀ] (2) *vt [froid]* to chill to the bone, numb; *[peur]* to paralyze, numb. ◆ **transi, e** *adj* numb (with cold).

transistor [tʀɑ̃zistɔʀ] *nm* transistor. ◆ **transistoriser** (1) *vt* to transistorize. **transistorisé** transistorized.

transit [tʀɑ̃zit] *nm* transit. **en** ~ in transit; **de** ~ transit. ◆ **transiter** (1) *vti* to pass in transit.

transitif, -ive [tʀɑ̃zitif, iv] *adj* transitive.

transition [tʀɑ̃zisjɔ̃] *nf* transition. **de** ~ *période, mesure* transitional; **sans** ~ without any transition.

transitoire [tʀɑ̃zitwaʀ] *adj* transitional.

translucide [tʀɑ̃slysid] *adj* translucent.

transmettre [tʀɑ̃smɛtʀ(ə)] (56) *vt* (**a**) *(lit, fig: léguer)* to transmit, pass on; *biens* to hand down; *fonctions, titre* to hand over. (**b**) *message* to pass on; *lettre* to send on, forward; *(Téléc)* to transmit, send; *(Rad, TV)* to broadcast. (**c**) *(Sport) ballon* to pass; *témoin, flambeau* to hand over, pass on. (**d**) *(Sci) énergie, impulsion* to transmit; *(Méd) maladie* to pass on, transmit. ◆ **transmetteur** *nm* transmitter. ◆ **transmissible** *adj* transmissible, transmittable; *maladie* communicable. **maladie sexuellement** ~ sexually transmitted disease. ◆ **transmission** *nf* transmission; passing on; handing down; handing over; sending on, forwarding; broadcasting. *(Pol)* ~ **des pouvoirs** handing over *ou* transfer of power; *(Ordin)* ~ **de données** data transmission; *(Mil: service)* **les** ~**s** ≃ the Signals (corps); ~ **de pensée** thought transfer, telepathy.

transparaître [tʀɑ̃spaʀɛtʀ(ə)] (57) *vi* to show (through). ◆ **transparence** *nf* transparency, transparence; limpidity, clearness; openness. **regarder qch par** ~ to look at sth against the light; **voir qch par** ~ to see sth showing through; **la** ~ **de cette allusion** the transparency of this allusion; **société dotée de la** ~ **fiscale** ≃ partnership. ◆ **transparent, e** *adj (lit, fig)* transparent; *eau, ciel, yeux* transparent, limpid, clear; *(sans secret) négociation, comptes* open.

transpercer [tʀɑ̃spɛʀse] (3) *vt (lit, fig)* to go through, pierce; *(d'un coup de couteau)* to stab. ~ **qn du regard** to give sb a piercing look; **je suis transpercé (par la pluie)** I'm soaked through *ou* drenched (by the rain).

transpirer [tʀɑ̃spiʀe] (1) *vi* (**a**) *(lit)* to perspire, sweat. **il transpire des mains** his hands perspire *ou* sweat, he has sweaty hands; ~ **à grosses gouttes** to be running *ou* streaming with sweat; ~ **sur un devoir** * to sweat over an exercise *. (**b**) *[secret]* to come to light, leak out, transpire. ◆ **transpiration** *nf* perspiration. **être en** ~ to be perspiring *ou* sweating *ou* in a sweat.

transplanter [tʀɑ̃splɑ̃te] (1) *vt (Bot, Méd, fig)* to transplant. ◆ **transplantation** *nf (action)* transplantation; *(Méd: intervention)* transplant. ~ **cardiaque** heart transplant.

transport [tʀɑ̃spɔʀ] *nm* (**a**) *(action) (gén)* carrying; *(par véhicule)* transport(ation), conveyance. **un train se chargera du** ~ **des bagages** the luggage will be taken *ou* transported by train; **endommagé pendant le** ~ damaged in transit; ~ **par train** rail transport(ation); **frais de** ~ transportation costs. (**b**) **les** ~**s** transport; ~**s publics** *ou* **en commun** public transport; ~**(s) routier(s)** road haulage *ou* transport; ~**s aériens** air transport; **mal des** ~**s** travel-sickness, motion sickness *(US)*; **entreprise de** ~**s** haulage company. (**c**) *(émotion)* transport. **avec des** ~**s de joie** with transports of delight; ~ **au cerveau** seizure, stroke.

transporter [tʀɑ̃spɔʀte] (1) **1** *vt* (**a**) *(gén, fig)* to carry; *(avec véhicule)* to transport, carry, convey; *énergie, son* to carry. **transporté d'urgence à l'hôpital** rushed to hospital; **ils ont dû** ~ **le matériel à bras** they had to move the equipment by hand; **cette musique nous transporte dans un autre monde** this music transports us into another world. (**b**) *(exalter)* to carry away, send into raptures. ~ **qn de joie** to send sb into raptures; **être transporté de joie** to be in transports of delight, be carried away with delight. **2 se** ~ *vpr (littér: se déplacer)* to betake o.s., repair (*à, dans* to). ◆ **transporteur** *nm (entrepreneur)* haulage contractor, carrier; *(appareil)* conveyor. ~ **aérien** airline company; ~ **routier** road haulage contractor.

transposer [tʀɑ̃spoze] (1) *vti* to transpose. ◆ **transposition** *nf* transposition.

transvaser [tʀɑ̃svɑze] (1) *vt* to decant.

transversal, e, *mpl* **-aux** [tʀɑ̃svɛʀsal, o] *adj coupe, barre* cross; *mur, rue* which runs across; *vallée* transverse. ◆ **transversalement** *adv* across, crosswise.

trapèze [tʀapɛz] *nm* (**a**) *(Géom)* trapezium, trapezoid *(US)*. (**b**) *(Sport)* trapeze. ~ **volant** flying trapeze. ◆ **trapéziste** *nmf* trapeze artist.

trappe [tʀap] *nf* trap door; *(Tech)* hatch; *(pour parachute)* exit door; *(piège)* trap.

trappeur [tʀapœʀ] *nm* trapper, fur trader.

trapu, e [tʀapy] *adj* (**a**) *personne* squat, stocky, thickset; *maison* squat. (**b**) *(arg Scol) élève* brainy *; *problème* tough, hard, stiff. ~ **en maths** terrific at maths *.

traquenard [tʀaknaʀ] *nm (lit)* trap; *(fig)* pitfall, trap.

traquer [tʀake] (1) *vt gibier, fugitif* to track down, hunt down; *abus* to hunt down; *débiteur, vedette* to hound, pursue. **bête traquée** hunted animal. ◆ **traque** *nf*: **la** ~ **(du gibier)** the tracking (of game).

traumatiser [tʀomatize] (1) *vt* to traumatize. ◆ **traumatisme** *nm* traumatism.

travail, *pl* **-aux** [tʀavaj, o] *nm* (**a**) *(activité)* **le** ~ work; ~ **manuel/scolaire** manual/school work; **c'est le** ~ **de l'électricien** that's the electrician's job; **observer qn au** ~ to watch sb at work, watch sb working; **séance de** ~ working session; **avoir du** ~**/beaucoup de** ~ to have (some) work/a lot of work to do; **se mettre au** ~ to set to *ou* get down to work. (**b**) *(tâche)* **un** ~ work, a job; **c'est un** ~ **de spécialiste** *(difficile à faire)* it's work for a specialist, it's a specialist's job; *(bien fait)* it's the work of a specialist; **commencer un** ~ to start a piece of work *ou* a job; **un** ~ **de Romain** a Herculean task. (**c**) ~**aux** work; ~**aux pratiques/ scientifiques/de réparation/de plomberie** practical/scientific/repair/plumbing work; ~**aux d'approche** *(Mil)* sapping *ou* approach works; *(pour faire la cour)* initial overtures (*auprès de* to); *(pour demander qch)* preliminary manœuvres *ou* moves (*auprès de* with); **faire faire des** ~**aux dans la maison** to have some work *ou* some jobs done in the house; **les** ~**aux des champs** farm work; **les** ~**aux pénibles** the heavy work *ou* tasks; ~**aux ménagers** housework; *(Scol)* ~**aux manuels** handicrafts; *(Admin)* ~**aux publics** civil engineering; *(Comm)* **'pendant les** ~**aux'** 'during alterations'; **attention!** ~**aux!** caution! work in progress!; *(sur la route)* road works ahead!; ~**aux d'utilité collective** community work, ≃ YTS. (**d**) *(métier)* **le** ~ work; **un** ~ a job, an occupation; **être sans** ~ to be out of work *ou* without a job *ou* unemployed; **accident du** ~ industrial accident; ~ **d'équipe/en usine** team/factory work; ~ **à la pièce** piecework; ~ **à la chaîne** assembly line *ou* production line work; ~ **au noir** * moonlighting *; **cesser le** ~ to stop work, down tools; **reprendre le** ~ to go back to work. (**e**) *(Écon: opposé au capital)* labour. **le monde du** ~ the workers. (**f**) *[pierre, bois, cuir] (façonnage)* working; *(facture)* work. **dentelle d'un** ~ **très fin** finely-worked lace; **c'est un très joli** ~ it's a very nice piece of handiwork *ou* craftsmanship *ou* work. (**g**) *[machine, organe]* work. ~ **musculaire** work of the muscles. (**h**) *[gel, érosion]* work; *[bois]* warp, warping; *[vin, cidre]* working. **le** ~ **du temps** the work of time. (**i**) *(Phys)* work. **unité de** ~ unit of work. (**j**) *(Méd) [femme]* labour; **femme en** ~ woman in labour. **entrer en** ~ to go into *ou* start labour; **salle de** ~ labour ward. (**k**) ~**aux forcés** hard labour; **c'est un** ~ **de forçat** it's hard labour;

(fig) **dans cette entreprise c'est vraiment les ~aux forcés** it's real slave labour in this company.

travaillé, e [tʀavaje] *adj bois, cuivre* worked, wrought; *style* polished; *meuble, ornement* finely-worked. *(tourmenté)* ~ **par** tormented by.

travailler [tʀavaje] (1) **1** *vi* (**a**) *(gén)* to work; *[artiste] (s'exercer)* to practise, train. **commencer à/finir de** ~ to start/stop work; **je vais** ~ **un peu** I'm going to do some work; **faire** ~ **sa tête** to set one's mind to work; **fais** ~ **ta tête!** use your head!; **faire** ~ **ses bras** to exercise one's arms; **va** ~ (go and) get on with your work; ~ **à domicile** to work at home; ~ **au noir** to moonlight, do moonlighting; **sa femme travaille** his wife works *ou* goes out to work; **le temps travaille pour/contre eux** time is on their side/against them; ~ **sans filet** *(lit)* to work without a safety net; *(fig)* to work in the dark, work without any backup. (**b**) *[métal, bois]* to warp; *[vin, imagination]* to work. **2** *vt* (**a**) *(façonner) verre, cuir* to work; *discipline, style* to work on. ~ **la terre** to work the land; *(Culin)* ~ **la pâte** to work the mixture; ~ **le chant/piano** to practise singing/the piano; ~ **les esprits** to work on people's minds. (**b**) *[doutes]* to distract, worry; *[douleur]* to distract, torment. **cette idée le travaille** this idea is on his mind *ou* is preying on his mind. **3** ~ **à** *vt indir projet* to work on; *but* to work for. ~ **à la perte de qn** to work towards sb's downfall.

travailleur, -euse [tʀavajœʀ, øz] **1** *adj* hardworking, painstaking, diligent. **2** *nm, f* worker. **les ~s** the workers, working people; **~s étrangers** immigrant workers; ~ **agricole** agricultural *ou* farm worker; ~ **de force** labourer; ~ **indépendant** self-employed person, freelance worker; ~ **au noir** moonlighter.

travailliste [tʀavajist(ə)] **1** *adj* Labour. **2** *nmf* Labour Party member. **il est** ~ he is Labour; **les ~s** Labour, the Labour Party.

travée [tʀave] *nf* (**a**) *(section) [mur]* bay; *[pont]* span. (**b**) *(rangée)* row (of benches *ou* seats).

travers¹ [tʀavɛʀ] *nm (défaut)* failing, fault, shortcoming.

travers² [tʀavɛʀ] *nm* (**a**) **en** ~ across, crosswise; **en** ~ **de** across; **le véhicule se mit en** ~ **de la route** the vehicle stopped sideways on *ou* stopped across the road; **se mettre en** ~ **des projets de qn** to stand in the way of sb's plans; **en** ~**, par le** ~ *navire* abeam, on the beam. (**b**) **au** ~ **(de)** through; **le vent passe au** ~ the wind comes (right) through; *(fig)* **passer au** ~ to escape. (**c**) **de** ~ *nez* crooked; **comprendre de** ~ to misunderstand; **marcher de** ~ *(lit)* to stagger *ou* totter along; *(fig)* to be going wrong; **il répond toujours de** ~ he never gives a straight *ou* proper answer; **elle a mis son chapeau de** ~ she has put her hat on crooked, her hat is not on straight; **il a l'esprit un peu de** ~ he's slightly odd; **il l'a regardé de** ~ he looked askance at him, he gave him a funny look; **il a avalé sa soupe de** ~ his soup has gone down the wrong way; **prendre qch de** ~ to take sth the wrong way, take sth amiss. (**d**) **à** ~ *(lit, fig)* through; *campagne* across, through; **à** ~ **le grillage/les siècles** through the fence/the centuries; **à** ~ **champs** through *ou* across the fields; *(lit, fig)* **passer à** ~ **(les mailles du filet)** to slip through the net. (**e**) *(Boucherie)* ~ **(de porc)** sparerib of pork.

traverse [tʀavɛʀs(ə)] *nf (Rail)* sleeper; *(barre transversale)* strut, crosspiece.

traversée [tʀavɛʀse] *nf (gén)* crossing. **la** ~ **de la ville en voiture** going through *ou* crossing the town by car; **faire la** ~ **d'un fleuve à la nage** to swim across a river.

traverser [tʀavɛʀse] (1) *vt* (**a**) *rue, pont, mer* to cross; *forêt, tunnel, (fig) crise* to go through. ~ **une rivière à la nage** to swim across a river; ~ **(une rivière) à gué** to ford a river; ~ **la foule** to make one's way through the crowd. (**b**) *[pont, route]* to cross, run across; *[tunnel]* to cross under; *[barre, trait]* to run across; *[projectile, infiltration]* to go *ou* come through. ~ **qch de part en part** to go right through sth; **une idée lui traversa l'esprit** an idea passed through his mind *ou* occurred to him.

traversin [tʀavɛʀsɛ̃] *nm [lit]* bolster.

travestir [tʀavɛstiʀ] (2) *vt personne* to dress up; *vérité, paroles* to travesty, misrepresent, parody. ◆ **travesti** *nm (acteur)* drag artist; *(Psych: homosexuel)* transvestite; *(déguisement)* fancy dress.

trébucher [tʀebyʃe] (1) *vi (lit, fig)* to stumble. **faire** ~ **qn** to trip sb up; ~ **sur** *ou* **contre** *pierre* to stumble over, trip against; *mot* to stumble over.

trèfle [tʀɛfl(ə)] *nm (Bot)* clover; *(Cartes)* clubs. ~ **à quatre feuilles** four-leaf clover; **le 8 de** ~ the 8 of clubs; *(emblème de l'Irlande)* **le** ~ the shamrock; *(Rugby)* **l'équipe du** ~ the Irish team.

tréfonds [tʀefɔ̃] *nm*: **le** ~ **de** the inmost depths of; **dans le** ~ **de mon cœur** deep down in my heart.

treillage [tʀɛjaʒ] *nm (sur un mur)* lattice work, trellis(work); *(clôture)* trellis fence.

treille [tʀɛj] *nf (tonnelle)* vine arbour; *(vigne)* climbing vine.

treillis [tʀeji] *nm* (**a**) *(en bois)* trellis; *(en métal)* wire-mesh; *(Constr)* lattice work. (**b**) *(Tex)* canvas; *(Mil: tenue)* combat uniform.

treize [tʀɛz] *adj inv, nm inv* thirteen. ~ **à la douzaine** baker's dozen; *V* **six.** ◆ **treizième** *adj, nmf* thirteenth; *V* **sixième.** ◆ **treizièmement** *adv* in the thirteenth place.

tréma [tʀema] *nm* dieresis. **i** ~ i dieresis.

tremble [tʀɑ̃bl(ə)] *nm* aspen.

tremblement [tʀɑ̃bləmɑ̃] *nm (frisson)* shiver. **~(s)** trembling; **avec des ~s dans la voix** with a trembling *ou* quavering *ou* shaky voice; **tout le** ~ * the whole caboodle *; ~ **de terre** earthquake; **léger** ~ **de terre** earth tremor.

trembler [tʀɑ̃ble] (1) *vi* to tremble; *(de froid, fièvre)* to shiver, shake (*de* with); *[feuille]* to flutter; *[lumière]* to flicker; *[voix]* to quaver. **tremblant de tout son corps** shaking *ou* trembling all over; **faire** ~ **le sol** to make the ground tremble; **la terre a tremblé** there has been an earth tremor; *(fig: avoir peur)* ~ **pour qn/qch** to fear for *ou* tremble for sb/sth. ◆ **tremblote** * *nf*: **avoir la** ~ *(froid)* to have the shivers *; *(peur)* to have the jitters *; *(vieillesse)* to have the shakes *. ◆ **tremblotement** *nm*: **~(s)** trembling. ◆ **trembloter** (1) *vi* to tremble *ou* shake *ou* flutter *ou* flicker slightly.

trémolo [tʀemɔlo] *nm [instrument]* tremolo; *[voix]* quaver, tremor. **avec des ~s dans la voix** with a quaver *ou* tremor in one's voice.

trémousser (se) [tʀemuse] (1) *vpr (sur sa chaise)* to jig about, wriggle; *(en marchant)* to wiggle.

trempe [tʀɑ̃p] *nf* (**a**) *[acier] (processus)* quenching; *(qualité)* temper. (**b**) *[personne, âme]* calibre. (**c**) (*) *(gifle)* slap; *(râclée)* hiding *.

tremper [tʀɑ̃pe] (1) **1** *vt* (**a**) *[pluie]* to soak, drench. **se faire** ~ to get drenched. (**b**) *(plus gén* **faire** ~*) linge* to soak; *aliments* to soak, steep; *papier* to damp, wet; *tiges de fleurs* to stand in water. (**c**) *(plonger)* to dip (*dans* into, in). ~ **sa main dans l'eau** to dip one's hand in the water. (**d**) *(Tech) métal, lame* to quench; *(littér) caractère* to steel, strengthen. **2** *vi* (**a**) *[tige de fleur]* to stand in water; *[linge, graines]* to soak. (**b**) *(péj)* ~ **dans** *crime* to take part in, have a hand in, be involved in. **3 se** ~ *vpr (bain rapide)* to have a quick dip; *(se mouiller)* to get (o.s.) soaked, get drenched. ◆ **trempé, e** *adj* (**a**) *(mouillé)* soaked, drenched. ~ **de sueur** bathed in perspiration; ~ **jusqu'aux os** wet through, soaked to the skin. (**b**) *(Tech)* tempered. ◆ **trempette** * *nf (baignade)* (quick) dip. **faire** ~ to have a (quick) dip.

tremplin [tʀɑ̃plɛ̃] *nm [piscine]* diving-board, spring-board; *[gymnase]* springboard; *[ski]* ski-jump; *(fig)* springboard.

trente [tʀɑ̃t] *adj inv, nm inv* thirty. **il y en a ~-six modèles** * there are umpteen * models; **il n'y a pas ~-six possibilités** * there aren't all that many choices; **tous les ~-six du mois** once in a blue moon; **voir ~-six chandelles** * to see stars; **se mettre sur son ~ et un** * to put on one's Sunday best; *V* **six, soixante.** ◆ **trentaine** *nf* about thirty, thirty or so; *V* **soixantaine.** ◆ **trentième** *adj, nmf* thirtieth; *V* **sixième, soixantième.**

trépan [tʀepɑ̃] *nm* trepan. ◆ **trépanation** *nf* trepanation. ◆ **trépaner** (1) *vt* to trepan.

trépas [tʀepɑ] *nm (littér)* demise, death. ◆ **trépassé, e** *adj, nm, f (littér)* deceased. ◆ **trépasser** (1) *vi (littér)* to pass away.

trépider [tʀepide] (1) *vi* to vibrate, reverberate. ◆ **trépidant, e** *adj* vibrating; *rythme* pulsating; *vie* hectic, busy. ◆ **trépidation** *nf* vibration, reverberation.

trépied [tʀepje] *nm* tripod.

trépigner [tʀepiɲe] (1) *vi* to stamp one's feet (*de* with). ◆ **trépignement** *nm*: **~(s)** stamping (of feet).

très [tʀɛ] *adv* very; *(avec ptp)* (very) much. **~ difficile** very *ou* most difficult; **~ admiré** greatly *ou* highly *ou* (very) much admired; **~ peu de gens** very few people; **avoir ~ peur** to be very much afraid *ou* very frightened; **c'est ~ nécessaire** it's most essential; **ils sont ~ amis** they are great friends; **il est ~ en avant** *(sur le chemin)* he is well *ou* a long way ahead; **un jeune homme ~ comme il faut** a well brought-up young man, a very respectable young man; **~ bien, si vous insistez** all right *ou* very well, if you insist.

trésor [tʀezɔʀ] *nm* (**a**) *(gén, fig)* treasure. **découvrir un ~** to find some treasure *ou* a treasure-trove; **chasse au ~** treasure hunt; **des ~s de** *renseignements, patience* a wealth of; **dépenser des ~s d'ingéniosité** to expend boundless ingenuity. (**b**) *(musée)* treasure-house, treasury. (**c**) *(Fin) [roi, état]* exchequer, finances. *(service)* **T~ (public)** public revenue department. ◆ **trésorerie** *nf (bureaux) [Trésor public]* public revenue office; *[firme]* accounts department; *(gestion)* accounts; *(argent disponible)* finances, funds. ◆ **trésorier, -ière** *nm, f* treasurer. *(Admin)* **~-payeur général** paymaster.

tressaillir [tʀesajiʀ] (13) *vi* (**a**) *(de plaisir)* to thrill, quiver; *(de peur)* to shudder, shiver; *(de douleur)* to wince. **son cœur tressaillait** his heart was fluttering. (**b**) *(sursauter)* to start, give a start. **faire ~ qn** to startle sb, make sb jump. (**c**) *(s'agiter) [personne, animal]* to quiver, twitch; *[plancher, véhicule]* to shake, vibrate. ◆ **tressaillement** *nm* thrill, quiver; shudder; wince; start; twitch; vibration.

tressauter [tʀesote] (1) *vi* (**a**) *(sursauter)* to start, give a start. **faire ~ qn** to startle sb, make sb jump. (**b**) *(être secoué) [voyageurs]* to be jolted *ou* tossed about; *[objets]* to shake about, jump about. ◆ **tressautement** *nm* start; jump; jolt.

tresser [tʀese] (1) *vt cheveux, rubans* to plait, braid; *paille* to plait; *panier, guirlande* to weave; *câble* to twist. ◆ **tressage** *nm* plaiting; braiding; weaving; twisting. ◆ **tresse** *nf (cheveux)* plait, braid; *(cordon)* braid.

tréteau, *pl* **~x** [tʀeto] *nm* trestle. *(Théât fig)* **les ~x** the boards, the stage.

treuil [tʀœj] *nm* winch, windlass.

trêve [tʀɛv] *nf (Mil, Pol)* truce; *(fig: répit)* respite, rest. **~ de plaisanteries** enough of this joking; **sans ~** unremittingly, unceasingly, relentlessly.

tri [tʀi] *nm (gén)* sorting out; *[fiches]* sorting; *[volontaires]* selection; *[wagons]* marshalling, shunting; *[lentilles]* picking over; *(calibrage)* grading; *(tamisage)* sifting. **faire le ~ de** to sort out; to sort; to select; to marshal; to pick over; to grade; to sift; *(Poste)* **le (bureau de) ~** the sorting office. ◆ **triage** *nm* = **tri;** *V* **gare.**

tri... [tʀi] *préf* tri...

triangle [tʀijɑ̃gl(ə)] *nm (Géom, Mus)* triangle. **en ~** in a triangle. ◆ **triangulaire 1** *adj (gén)* triangular; *débat, tournoi* three-cornered. **2** *nf:* **(élection) ~** three-cornered (election) contest *ou* fight.

triathlon [tʀi(j)atlɔ̃] *nm* triathlon.

tribal, e, *mpl* **-aux** [tʀibal, o] *adj* tribal.

tribord [tʀibɔʀ] *nm* starboard. **à ~** to starboard.

tribu [tʀiby] *nf* tribe.

tribulations [tʀibylɑsjɔ̃] *nfpl* tribulations, troubles.

tribunal, *pl* **-aux** [tʀibynal, o] *nm* court. **~ pour enfants/de police** juvenile/police court; **~ militaire** military tribunal; **porter une affaire devant les ~aux** to bring a case before the courts; *(fig)* **le ~ des hommes** the justice of men.

tribune [tʀibyn] *nf* (**a**) *(pour le public)* gallery; *(sur un stade)* stand. **~ d'honneur** grandstand. (**b**) *(pour un orateur)* platform, rostrum. (**c**) *(fig: débat)* forum. **~ libre d'un journal** opinion column of a newspaper.

tribut [tʀiby] *nm (lit, fig)* tribute.

tributaire [tʀibytɛʀ] *adj: (dépendant)* **être ~ de** to be dependant *ou* reliant on.

tricentenaire [tʀisɑ̃tnɛʀ] **1** *adj* three-hundred-year-old. **2** *nm* tercentenary, tricentennial.

tricher [tʀiʃe] (1) *vi (gén)* to cheat. **~ sur son âge** to lie about *ou* cheat over one's age. ◆ **triche** * *nf* cheating. ◆ **tricherie** *nf*: **la ~** cheating; **une ~** a trick. ◆ **tricheur, -euse** *nm, f* cheater, cheat.

tricolore [tʀikɔlɔʀ] *adj* three-coloured. **le drapeau ~** the (French) tricolour; *(Sport)* **l'équipe ~** * the French team.

tricot [tʀiko] *nm* (**a**) *(vêtement)* jumper, sweater. **~ de corps** vest, undershirt *(US)*; **emporte des ~s** take some woollens *ou* woollies * with you. (**b**) *(technique)* knitting; *(Comm)* knitwear. **faire du ~** to knit. (**c**) *(tissu)* knitted fabric. **en ~** knitted. ◆ **tricoter** (1) *vti* to knit.

tricycle [tʀisikl(ə)] *nm* tricycle.

trident [tʀidɑ̃] *nm* trident.

triennal, e, *mpl* **-aux** [tʀiɛnal, o] *adj prix, foire* triennal, three-yearly; *mandat, plan* three-year; *président* elected *ou* appointed for three years. *(Agr)* **assolement ~** 3-year rotation of crops.

trier [tʀije] (7) *vt (classer)* to sort (out); *(sélectionner)* to select, pick; *(en calibrant)* to grade; *(en tamisant)* to sift. *(fig)* **trié sur le volet** hand-picked. ◆ **trieur, -euse 1** *nm, f (personne)* sorter; grader. **2** *nm (machine)* sorter. **3 trieuse** *nf (machine) (gén)* sorter; *[ordinateur, photocopieur]* sorting machine.

trigonométrie [tʀigɔnɔmetʀi] *nf* trigonometry.

trilatéral, e, *mpl* **-aux** [tʀilateʀal, o] *adj (Géom)* trilateral, three-sided; *(Écon) accords* tripartite. **la (commission) ~e** the Trilateral Commission.

trilingue [tʀilɛ̃g] *adj secrétaire* trilingual. **elle est ~** she is trilingual, she speaks three languages.

trille [tʀij] *nm [oiseau, flûte]* trill.

trilogie [tʀilɔʒi] *nf* trilogy.

trimaran [tʀimaʀɑ̃] *nm* trimaran.

trimbal(l)er [tʀɛ̃bale] (1) **1** *vt* (*) *bagages* to lug * *ou* cart * around; *(péj) personne* to trail along. **2 se ~** ‡ *vpr* to trail along.

trimer * [tʀime] (1) *vi* to slave away. **faire ~ qn** to drive sb hard, keep sb hard at it *.

trimestre [tʀimɛstʀ(ə)] *nm* (**a**) *(période)* quarter; *(Scol)* term. (**b**) *(loyer)* quarter, quarter's rent;

(frais de scolarité) term's fees; *(salaire)* quarter's income. ◆ **trimestriel, -elle** *adj publication* quarterly; *paiement* three-monthly, quarterly; *(Scol) bulletin, examen* end-of-term.

tringle [tʀɛ̃gl(ə)] *nf* rod. ~ **à rideaux** curtain rod *ou* rail.

trinité [tʀinite] *nf* (**a**) trinity. **à la T~** on Trinity Sunday; **la Sainte T~** the Holy Trinity. (**b**) *(Géog)* **T~ et Tobago** Trinidad and Tobago; **(l'île de) la T~** Trinidad.

trinquer [tʀɛ̃ke] (1) *vi* (**a**) *(porter un toast)* to clink glasses. ~ **à qch** to drink to sth. (**b**) *(*: écoper)* to cop it ‡, take the rap *. **il a trinqué pour les autres** he took the rap for the others *.

triomphe [tʀijɔ̃f] *nm (gén)* triumph; *[maladie, mode]* victory. **en** ~ in triumph; **air de** ~ air of triumph, triumphant air; **remporter un** ~ to have *ou* be a triumphant success. ◆ **triomphal, e,** *mpl* **-aux** *adj succès* triumphal; *entrée, air* triumphant. ◆ **triomphalement** *adv saluer* in triumph; *annoncer* triumphantly. ◆ **triomphant, e** *adj* triumphant. ◆ **triomphateur, -trice** *nm, f* triumphant victor. ◆ **triompher** (1) **1** *vi* (**a**) *(gén, Mil)* to triumph; *[raison]* to prevail, be triumphant; *[maladie]* to claim its victim. **faire** ~ **une cause** to bring *ou* give victory to a cause. (**b**) *(crier victoire)* to exult, rejoice. **2** ~ **de** *vt indir (gén)* to triumph over; *peur, timidité* to conquer, overcome.

tripatouiller * [tʀipatuje] (1) *vt (péj) (toucher)* to fiddle about with *; *(truquer)* to fiddle *.

tripes [tʀip] *nfpl (Culin)* tripe; *(*: intestins)* guts *. **rendre ~s et boyaux** to be as sick as a dog *. ◆ **triperie** *nf (boutique)* tripe shop; *(commerce)* tripe trade. ◆ **tripier, -ière** *nm, f* tripe butcher.

tripette * [tʀipɛt] *nf*: **ça ne vaut pas** ~ that's a load of rubbish *.

triple [tʀipl(ə)] *adj* (**a**) triple. *(péj)* ~ **menton** row of chins; *(Sport)* ~ **saut** triple jump; **au** ~ **galop** hell for leather *; **faire qch en** ~ **exemplaire** to make three copies of sth, do sth in triplicate; **l'inconvénient en est** ~, **il y a un** ~ **inconvénient** there are three disadvantages, the disadvantages are threefold; **prendre une** ~ **dose (de)** to take a triple dose (of). (**b**) *(intensif)* **c'est un** ~ **idiot** he is a prize idiot; ~ **idiot!** you great idiot! *ou* fool! **2** *nm*: **manger le** ~ **(de qn)** to eat three times as much (as sb); **9 est le** ~ **de 3** 9 is three times 3; **c'est le** ~ **du prix normal** it's three times *ou* treble the normal price. ◆ **triplé, e** **1** *nm* (**a**) *(Courses de chevaux)* betting on 3 different horses in 3 different races. (**b**) *(Sport) [athlète]* triple success. *(fig iro)* **c'est un beau** ~! that's a fine catalogue of disasters. **2** ~**(e)s** *nm(f)pl (bébés)* triplets. ◆ **triplement** **1** *adv (pour trois raisons)* in three ways; *(à un degré triple)* trebly. **2** *nm* trebling, tripling (*de* of); threefold increase (*de* in). ◆ **tripler** (1) **1** *vt* to treble, triple. **2** *vi* to triple, treble, increase threefold (*de* in).

triporteur [tʀipɔʀtœʀ] *nm* delivery tricycle.

tripot [tʀipo] *nm (péj)* dive *, joint *.

tripoter * [tʀipɔte] (1) *(péj)* **1** *vt* to fiddle with. **se** ~ **le nez** to fiddle with one's nose. **2** *vi (fouiller)* to root about, rummage about (*dans* in). *(trafiquer)* ~ **dans qch** to get involved in sth. ◆ **tripotage** * *nm (manigances)* ~**(s)** jiggery-pokery *. ◆ **tripotée** * *nf* (**a**) *(correction)* belting ‡, hiding *. (**b**) *(grand nombre)* **une** ~ **de...** loads * of...; lots of... ◆ **tripoteur, -euse** * *nm, f (affairiste)* shark *, shady dealer *.

trique [tʀik] *nf* cudgel. **mener qn à la** ~ to bully sb along, drive sb like a slave; **donner des coups de** ~ **à** to cudgel, thrash; **sec comme un coup de** ~ as skinny as a rake.

trisomie 21 [tʀizɔmivɛ̃teɛ̃] *nf* = **mongolisme.**

triste [tʀist(ə)] *adj* (**a**) *(gén)* sad; *personne, sort* unhappy; *regard, sourire* sorrowful; *nécessité, devoir* painful; *pensée* gloomy; *couleur, temps, paysage* dreary, dismal, miserable. **chanson** ~ sad *ou* melancholy song; **il est** ~ **comme un bonnet de nuit** he's as miserable as sin; **faire** ~ **figure** *ou* **mine** to give a cool reception to, greet unenthusiastically; **être dans un** ~ **état** to be in a sad *ou* sorry state. (**b**) *(péj: lamentable) résultats* wretched, deplorable; *personne, époque* dreadful; *réputation, affaire* sorry. **un** ~ **sire** *ou* **personnage** an unsavoury *ou* dreadful individual. ◆ **tristement** *adv* sadly; sorrowfully; gloomily. **se rendre** ~ **célèbre par ses crimes** to gain an unenviable reputation because of one's crimes. ◆ **tristesse** *nf (gén)* sadness; *[pensée]* gloominess; *[paysage]* bleakness, dreariness; *(chagrin)* sorrow.

triton [tʀitɔ̃] *nm (Zool)* triton.

triturer [tʀityʀe] (1) *vt pâte* to knead; *objet* to manipulate. **se** ~ **la cervelle** * to rack *ou* cudgel one's brains.

trivial, e, *mpl* **-aux** [tʀivjal, o] *adj (vulgaire)* coarse, crude; *(littér: ordinaire)* mundane, commonplace. ◆ **trivialement** *adv* coarsely, crudely; in a mundane *ou* commonplace way. ◆ **trivialité** *nf* coarseness, crudeness; mundane *ou* commonplace nature; *(remarque)* coarse *ou* crude remark.

troc [tʀɔk] *nm (échange)* exchange; *(système)* barter. **faire un** ~ **avec qn** to make an exchange with sb.

troène [tʀɔɛn] *nm* privet.

troglodyte [tʀɔglɔdit] *nm* cave dweller.

trogne * [tʀɔɲ] *nf (péj: visage)* mug ‡ *(péj)*, face.

trognon [tʀɔɲɔ̃] *nm [fruit]* core; *[chou]* stalk, core. **il s'est fait avoir jusqu'au** ~ ‡ he was well and truly had *; **mon petit** ~ * sweetie pie *.

trois [tʀwɑ] *adj, nm* three. *[égratignure, cadeau]* **c'est** ~ **fois rien** it's nothing at all, it's hardly anything; **ça coûte** ~ **fois rien** it costs next to nothing; **en** ~ **coups de cuiller à pot** * in next to no time; **à** ~ **dimensions** three-dimensional; *(travail)* **faire les** ~**-huit** to operate three eight-hour shifts; *V* **six.** ◆ **trois étoiles** *nm inv* three-star hotel (*ou* restaurant). ◆ **trois-mâts** *nm inv* three-master. ◆ **trois-pièces** *nm inv (complet)* three-piece suit; *(appartement)* three-room flat *ou* apartment *(US)*. ◆ **trois-portes** *nf inv (Aut)* two-door hatchback. ◆ **trois-quarts** **1** *nmpl* three-quarters. **manteau** ~**-**~ three-quarter (length) coat; **les** ~**-**~ **du travail** three-quarters of the work; **aux** ~**-**~ **détruit** almost totally destroyed. **2** *nm inv (Rugby)* three-quarter. ◆ **troisième** **1** *adj, nmf* third. **le** ~ **âge** *(période)* the years of retirement; *(groupe social)* senior citizens; *V* **sixième.** **2** *nf (Scol)* **(classe de)** ~ fourth form *ou* year, 8th grade *(US)*. ◆ **troisièmement** *adv* third(ly), in the third place.

trolleybus [tʀɔlɛbys] *nm* trolley bus.

trombe [tʀɔ̃b] *nf (Mét)* waterspout. *(fig: pluie)* **des** ~**s d'eau** a cloudburst, a downpour; **entrer en** ~ to sweep in like a whirlwind.

trombine ‡ [tʀɔ̃bin] *nf (visage)* face, mug ‡ *(péj)*; *(tête)* nut *.

trombone [tʀɔ̃bɔn] *nm* (**a**) *(Mus) (instrument)* trombone; *(artiste)* trombonist, trombone (player). ~ **à coulisse/à pistons** slide/valve trombone; ~ **basse** bass trombone. (**b**) *(agrafe)* paper clip.

trompe [tʀɔ̃p] *nf* (**a**) *(Mus)* horn. ~ **de chasse** hunting horn. (**b**) *[éléphant]* trunk; *[insecte]* proboscis. *(Anat)* ~ **d'Eustache** Eustachian tube.

tromper [tʀɔ̃pe] (1) **1** *vt* (**a**) *(duper) (gén)* to deceive (*sur* about, over); *(sans le faire exprès)* to mislead; *poursuivant, vigilance* to elude; *époux* to be unfaithful to, deceive. **mari trompé** husband who has been deceived; **cette manœuvre les a trompés** this move tricked *ou* fooled them; **les apparences trompent** appearances are deceptive *ou* misleading; **c'est ce qui vous trompe** that's where you are mistaken *ou* wrong; **c'est un signe qui ne trompe pas** it's a clear *ou* an unmistakable sign. (**b**) *attente* to while away; *faim, soif* to stave off; *espoirs* to fall short of, fail to come up to, disappoint. **pour ~ le temps** to kill *ou* pass time, to while away the time. **2 se ~** *vpr* to make a mistake, be mistaken. **se ~ de 5 F dans un calcul** to be 5 francs out *ou* off *(US)* in one's calculations; **on pourrait s'y ~** you'd hardly know the difference; **si je ne me trompe** if I am not mistaken; **se ~ de route** to take the wrong road; **se ~ de jour** to get the day wrong, make a mistake about the day. ◆**trompe-l'œil** *nm inv (Art)* trompe-l'œil; *(fig)* eye-wash *. ◆**tromperie** *nf (duperie)* deception, deceit. ◆**trompeur, -euse 1** *adj personne, paroles* deceitful; *apparences* deceptive, misleading; *distance, profondeur* deceptive. **2** *nm, f* deceiver. ◆**trompeusement** *adv* deceitfully; deceptively.

trompette [tʀɔ̃pɛt] **1** *nf* trumpet. **2** *nm* trumpeter, trumpet (player); *(Mil)* bugler. ◆**trompettiste** *nmf* trumpet player, trumpeter.

tronc [tʀɔ̃] *nm (gén)* trunk; *(pour aumônes)* (collection) box. *(Scol)* **~ commun** common-core syllabus.

tronche ‡ [tʀɔ̃ʃ] *nf (visage)* mug ‡ *(péj)*, face; *(tête)* nut *.

tronçon [tʀɔ̃sɔ̃] *nm* section. ◆**tronçonner** (1) *vt* to cut into sections. ◆**tronçonneuse** *nf* chain saw.

trône [tʀon] *nm* throne. **monter sur le ~** to come to *ou* ascend the throne. ◆**trôner** (1) *vi [roi, invité]* to sit enthroned; *[chose]* to sit imposingly.

tronquer [tʀɔ̃ke] (1) *vt colonne* to truncate; *texte* to truncate, curtail, cut down, shorten.

trop [tʀo] **1** *adv* (**a**) *(devant adv, adj)* too; *(avec vb) (gén)* too much; *attendre, durer* (for) too long. **il a ~ bu** he has had too much to drink, he has drunk too much; **un ~ grand effort l'épuiserait** too great an effort would exhaust him; **c'est ~ loin pour que j'y aille à pied** it's too far for me to walk there; **c'est ~ beau pour être vrai** it's too good to be true; **elle en a déjà bien** *ou* **beaucoup** *ou* **par ~ dit** she has said far *ou* much too much already; **vous êtes ~ (nombreux)/~ peu (nombreux)** there are too many/too few of you; **une ~ forte dose** an overdose; **insister ~** to be overinsistent *ou* too pressing; **c'est ~ chauffé** it's overheated.
(**b**) **~ de** *pain, eau* too much; *objets* too many; *gentillesse, sévérité* excessive; **s'il te reste ~ de dollars, vends-les-moi** if you have dollars left over *ou* to spare, sell them to me; **nous avons ~ de personnel/de travail** we are overstaffed/overworked; **il y a ~ de monde dans la salle** the hall is overcrowded *ou* overfull.
(**c**) *(superl, intensif)* too, so (very). **c'est ~ bête/drôle** how stupid/funny, it's too stupid/funny for words; **nous n'avons pas ~ de place chez nous** we haven't got (so) very much room *ou* (all) that much room at our place; **vous êtes ~ aimable** you are too *ou* most kind; **il n'aime pas ~ ça *** he isn't too keen *ou* overkeen (on it), he doesn't like it overmuch *ou* (all) that much; **je ne le sais que ~** I know only too well; **c'est ~!** that's going too far!, enough is enough!; **cela ne va pas ~ bien** things are not going so *ou* terribly well; **je n'en sais ~ rien** I don't really know.
(**d**) **de ~, en ~: il y a une personne de ~** *ou* **en ~ dans l'ascenseur** there is one person too many in the lift; **s'il y a du pain en ~, j'en emporterai** if there is any bread (left) over *ou* any bread extra *ou* any surplus bread I'll take some away; **il m'a rendu 2 F de ~** he gave me back 2 francs too much; **l'argent versé en ~** the excess payment; **il pèse 3 kg de ~** he is 3 kg overweight; **si je suis de ~, je peux m'en aller!** if I'm in the way *ou* not welcome I can always leave!; **cette remarque est de ~** that remark is uncalled for; **il a bu un verre de ~** he's had a drink too many.
2 *nm (excédent)* excess, surplus; *(reste)* extra. **le ~ d'importance accordé à** the excessive importance attributed to.
◆**trop-perçu,** *pl* **trop-perçus** *nm* excess (tax) payment. ◆**trop-plein,** *pl* **trop-pleins** *nm* excess; *(d'eau)* overflow. **~ d'énergie** surplus *ou* boundless energy.

trophée [tʀɔfe] *nm* trophy.

tropique [tʀɔpik] *nm* tropic. **~ du cancer/capricorne** tropic of Cancer/Capricorn; **les ~s** the tropics; **vivre sous les ~s** to live in the tropics. ◆**tropical, e,** *mpl* **-aux** *adj* tropical.

troquer [tʀɔke] (1) *vt*: **~ qch contre qch d'autre** to swap sth for sth else; *(Écon)* to barter *ou* exchange *ou* trade sth for sth else.

troquet ‡ [tʀɔkɛ] *nm* small café.

trot [tʀo] *nm* trot. **petit/grand ~** jog/full trot; **course de ~** trotting race; *(fig)* **au ~ *** at the double. ◆**trotte *** *nf*: **il y a une ~ (d'ici au village)** it's a fair distance (from here to the village). ◆**trotter** (1) *vi [cheval, cavalier]* to trot; *[personne] (à petits pas)* to trot along; *(beaucoup)* to run around; *[souris, enfants]* to scurry *ou* scamper (about); *[bébé]* to toddle along. **un air/une idée qui vous trotte dans la tête** a tune/an idea which keeps running through your head. ◆**trotteur, -euse 1** *nm, f (cheval)* trotter, trotting horse. **2** *nm (chaussure)* flat shoe. **3** *nf (aiguille)* (sweep) second hand. ◆**trottiner** (1) *vi [cheval]* to jog along; *[personne]* to trot along; *[souris]* to scurry *ou* scamper along; *[bébé]* to toddle along. ◆**trottinette** *nf* (child's) scooter.

trottoir [tʀɔtwaʀ] *nm* pavement, sidewalk *(US)*. **~ roulant** moving walkway, travellator; *(péj)* **faire le ~ *** to walk the streets, be on the game *.

trou [tʀu] *nm* (**a**) *(lit)* hole. **~ d'aération** airhole, air vent; **~ d'air** air pocket; **le ~ de la serrure** the keyhole; *(Théât)* **le ~ du souffleur** the prompt box; *(fig: désespoir)* **c'était le ~ noir** I (*ou* he *etc*) was in the depths of despair; **faire un ~** *(gén)* to dig *ou* make a hole; *(déchirure)* to tear a hole; *(usure)* to wear a hole (*dans* in). (**b**) *(moment de libre)* gap; *(déficit)* deficit. **un ~ dans ses économies** a hole in his savings; **j'ai eu un ~ (de mémoire)** my memory failed me for a moment, my mind went blank; *[professeur]* **j'ai un ~** *ou* **une heure de ~** I have a free period *ou* an hour's free time. (**c**) *(péj: localité)* place, hole * *(péj)*, dump * *(péj)*. **il n'est jamais sorti de son ~** he has never been out of his own backyard.

troubadour [tʀubaduʀ] *nm* troubadour.

troublant, e [tʀublɑ̃, ɑ̃t] *adj (gén)* disturbing.

trouble¹ [tʀubl(ə)] **1** *adj* (**a**) *eau, vin* unclear, cloudy; *regard, image* blurred, misty; *photo* blurred, out of focus. (**b**) *affaire* shady, murky; *personnage, rôle* fishy, suspicious; *désir* dark. **2** *adv*: **voir ~** to have blurred vision.

trouble² [tʀubl(ə)] *nm* (**a**) *(remue-ménage)* tumult, turmoil; *(désunion)* discord, trouble. *(émeute)* **~s** unrest, disturbances, troubles; **~s politiques** political unrest *ou* disturbances *ou* upheavals. (**b**) *(émoi)* (inner) turmoil, agitation; *(inquiétude)* distress; *(gêne, perplexité)* confusion, embarrassment. **semer le ~ dans l'esprit des gens** to sow confusion in peoples' minds. (**c**) *(gén pl: Méd)* disorder. **~s psychiques** psychological trouble *ou* disorders; **~s du comportement** behavioural problems; **~s du langage** speech difficulties.

trouble-fête [tʀubləfɛt] *nmf inv* spoilsport, killjoy.

troubler [tʀuble] (1) **1** *vt* (**a**) *ordre etc* to disturb, disrupt; *esprit* to cloud. **en ces temps troublés** in these troubled times. (**b**) *personne (impressionner)* to disturb; *(inquiéter, gêner)* to trouble, bother. (**c**) *(brouiller) eau* to make cloudy; *atmosphère, ciel* to cloud. **les larmes lui troublaient la vue** tears clouded *ou* blurred her vision. **2 se ~** *vpr* (**a**) *[eau]* to cloud, become cloudy; *[temps, ciel]* to become cloudy *ou* overcast. (**b**) *[personne]* to become flustered. **sans se ~** unperturbed.

trouer [tʀue] (1) *vt* (**a**) *(transpercer)* to pierce; *vêtement (usure)* to wear a hole in; *(déchirure)* to tear a hole in; *(brûlure)* to burn a hole in. **sac troué** bag with a hole *ou* with holes in it; **tout troué** full of holes; **corps troué comme une passoire** body riddled with bullets; **~ la peau à qn** ‡ to put a bullet into sb; **~ qch de part en part** to pierce sth through. (**b**) *(fig: traverser) silence, nuit* to pierce. ◆ **trouée** *nf [haie, nuages]* gap, break; *(Mil)* breach (*dans* in).

troufion * [tʀufjɔ̃] *nm* soldier.

trouille ‡ [tʀuj] *nf*: **avoir la ~** to be scared stiff; **flanquer la ~ à qn** to put the wind up sb *. ◆ **trouillard, e** ‡ **1** *adj* chicken *, yellow-bellied ‡. **2** *nm, f* chicken, yellowbelly ‡.

troupe [tʀup] *nf* (**a**) *(Mil)* troop. **la ~** *(l'armée)* the army; *(les simples soldats)* the troops, the rank and file. (**b**) *[chanteurs, danseurs]* troupe. *[acteurs]* **~ (de théâtre)** (theatrical) company. (**c**) *[gens, animaux]* band, group, troop.

troupeau, *pl* **~x** [tʀupo] *nm [bœufs, chevaux] (dans un pré)* herd; *(transhumant)* drove; *[éléphants, buffles, etc]* herd; *[moutons]* flock; *[oies]* gaggle; *(péj) [touristes]* herd *(péj)*.

trousse [tʀus] *nf* (**a**) *(étui) (gén)* case, kit; *[médecin]* instrument case; *[écolier]* pencil case *ou* wallet. **~ de maquillage** make-up *ou* vanity case; **~ à outils** toolkit; **~ de toilette** *(sac)* toilet bag, sponge bag; *(mallette)* travelling case. (**b**) **aux ~s de** (hot) on the heels of, on the tail of.

trousseau, *pl* **~x** [tʀuso] *nm* (**a**) **~ de clefs** bunch of keys. (**b**) *[mariée]* trousseau; *[écolier]* outfit.

trouvaille [tʀuvɑj] *nf (objet)* find; *(fig: idée, métaphore, procédé)* brainwave, stroke of inspiration; *mot* coinage.

trouver [tʀuve] (1) **1** *vt* (**a**) *(en cherchant)* to find; *(par hasard)* to find, come upon *ou* across; *difficultés* to meet with, come up against. **~ un emploi à qn** to find sb a job, find a job for sb; **je ne le trouve pas** I can't find it; **où peut-on le ~?** where can he be found?, where is he to be found?; **aller/venir ~ qn** to go/come and see sb; *(énigme)* **comment as-tu fait pour ~?** how did you manage to find out?, how did you work it out?; **j'ai trouvé!** I've got it!; **formule bien trouvée** clever *ou* happy phrase; **où est-il allé ~ ça?** where (on earth) did he get that idea from?, whatever gave him that idea? (**b**) *(avec à + infin)* **~ à redire (à tout)** to find fault with everything, find sth to criticize (in everything); **~ à manger** to find sth to eat; **~ à se distraire** to find a way to amuse o.s.; **on ne peut rien ~ à redire là-dessus** there's nothing to say *ou* you can say to that. (**c**) *(éprouver)* **~ du plaisir à qch/à faire qch** to take pleasure in sth/in doing sth; **~ de la difficulté à faire** to find *ou* have difficulty (in) doing. (**d**) *(estimer)* **~ que** to find *ou* think that; **je le trouve fatigué** I think he looks tired, I find him tired-looking; **vous trouvez?** (do) you think so?; **il a trouvé bon de nous écrire** he thought *ou* saw fit to write to us. (**e**) *(locutions)* **il a trouvé à qui parler** he met his match; **~ son maître** to find one's master; **cet objet n'avait pas trouvé preneur** the object had had no takers; **~ la mort** to meet one's death; **je la trouve mauvaise!** * I think it's a bit off *, I don't like it at all; **~ le sommeil** to get to sleep; **~ chaussure à son pied** to find a suitable match; **il a trouvé son compte dans cette affaire** he got something out of this bit of business; **il a trouvé le moyen de s'égarer** he managed *ou* contrived to get (himself) lost.

2 se ~ *vpr* (**a**) *(être dans une situation) [personne]* to find o.s; *[chose]* to be; *(être situé) [personne, chose]* to be. **où se trouve la poste?** where is the post office?; **ça ne se trouve pas sur la carte** it isn't *ou* doesn't appear on the map; **ça ne se trouve pas sous le pas** *ou* **le sabot d'un cheval** it's not easy to find *ou* to come by; **je me trouvais près de l'entrée** I was (standing *ou* sitting *etc*) near the entrance; **je me suis trouvé dans l'impossibilité de répondre** I found myself unable to reply. (**b**) *(se sentir)* to feel. **se ~ bien** *(dans un fauteuil etc)* to feel comfortable; *(dans une atmosphère)* to feel happy *ou* at ease; *(santé)* **se ~ bien/mieux** to feel well/better; **se ~ mal** to faint, pass out; **se ~ bien/mal d'avoir fait qch** to be pleased/displeased at having done sth, have reason to be glad/to regret having done sth. (**c**) *(coïncidence)* **se ~ être/avoir...** to happen to be/have...; **elles se trouvaient avoir le même chapeau** it turned out that they had *ou* they happened to have the same hat.

3 *vpr impers* (**a**) *(le fait est)* **il se trouve que c'est moi** it happens *ou* it turns out to be me, it's me as it happens; **il se trouvait que j'étais là** I happened to be there; **comme il se trouve parfois** as is sometimes the case, as sometimes happens. (**b**) *(il y a)* **il se trouve toujours des gens pour dire...** you'll always find people who will say... (**c**) (*) **ils sont sortis, si ça se trouve** they may well be out, they're probably out.

truand [tʀyɑ̃] *nm (gangster)* gangster; *(escroc)* crook. ◆ **truander** ‡ (1) *vt* to swindle, do ‡.

trublion [tʀyblijɔ̃] *nm* troublemaker, agitator.

truc * [tʀyk] *nm (moyen)* way, trick; *(tour, artifice)* trick; *(dispositif)* thingummy *, whatsit *. **trouver le ~ (pour faire)** to find a way (of doing). (**b**) *(chose, idée)* thing. **j'ai pensé (à) un ~** I've thought of sth, I've had a thought; **il y a un tas de ~s à faire** there's a heap of things to do *; **méfie-toi de ces ~s-là** be careful of those things. (**c**) *(personne)* **(Machin-) ~** what's-his-(*ou* -her-) name *. ◆ **trucage** *nm* = **truquage**.

truchement [tʀyʃmɑ̃] *nm*: **par le ~ de qn** through (the intervention of) sb; **par le ~ de qch** by means of sth.

truculent, e [tʀykylɑ̃, ɑ̃t] *adj* colourful. ◆ **truculence** *nf* colourfulness.

truelle [tʀyɛl] *nf* trowel.

truffe [tʀyf] *nf (Culin)* truffle; *(nez du chien)* nose. ◆ **truffer** (1) *vt* to garnish with truffles. *(fig)* **truffé de** *citations* peppered *ou* larded with; *pièges* bristling with; *fautes* packed full of, riddled with.

truie [tʀɥi] *nf (Zool)* sow.

truite [tʀɥit] *nf* trout.

truquer [tʀyke] (1) *vt (gén)* to fix *; *élections* to rig; *comptes* to fiddle *. ◆ **truquage** *nm* (**a**) fixing; rigging *; fiddling *. (**b**) *(Ciné)* special effect.

trust [tʀœst] *nm (Écon: cartel)* trust; *(grande entreprise)* corporation. ◆ **truster** (1) *vt (lit, fig)* to monopolize.

tsar [dzaʀ] *nm* tsar.

tsé-tsé [tsetse] *nf*: **(mouche) ~** tsetse fly.

tsigane [tsigan] **1** *adj* (Hungarian) gypsy, tzigane. **2** *nmf*: **T~** (Hungarian) Gypsy, Tzigane.

tu [ty] *pron pers* you *(used to address a child, close relation or friend)*; *(Rel)* thou †. **dire ~ à qn** to address sb as 'tu'; **être à ~ et à toi avec qn** * to be on first-name terms with sb.

tuant, e [tɥɑ̃, ɑ̃t] *adj (fatigant)* exhausting; *(énervant)* exasperating.

tuba [tyba] *nm (Mus)* tuba; *(Sport)* snorkel, breathing tube.

tubage [tybaʒ] *nm (Méd)* intubation, cannulation.

tube [tyb] *nm* (**a**) *(gén)* tube; *(canalisation)* pipe. ~ **à essai** test tube; *(TV)* ~**-image** cathode ray tube; *(Élec)* ~ **au néon** neon tube; *(Élec, TV, Ordin)* ~ **cathodique** cathode ray tube; ~ **de rouge (à lèvres)** lipstick; ~ **digestif** digestive tract. (**b**) *(*: chanson à succès)* hit song (*ou* record). (**c**) *(locutions) [moteur]* **marcher à pleins** ~**s** * to be running full throttle; *(fig)* **délirer à pleins** ~**s** * to be raving mad *, be off one's head *.

tubercule [tybɛʀkyl] *nm (Anat, Méd)* tubercle; *(Bot)* tuber.

tuberculose [tybɛʀkyloz] *nf* tuberculosis. ◆**tuberculeux, -euse 1** *adj* tuberculous, tubercular. **être** ~ to have tuberculosis *ou* TB. **2** *nm, f* tuberculosis *ou* tubercular *ou* TB patient.

tubulure [tybylyʀ] *nf (tube)* pipe. ◆**tubulaire** *adj* tubular.

tuer [tɥe] (1) **1** *vt (gén)* to kill; *(à la chasse)* to shoot; *(fig: exténuer)* to exhaust, wear out. ~ **qn à coups de couteau** to stab *ou* knife sb to death; ~ **qn d'une balle** to shoot sb dead; **l'alcool tue** alcohol can kill *ou* is a killer; **cet enfant me tuera** this child will be the death of me; ~ **la poule aux œufs d'or** to kill the goose that lays the golden eggs; ~ **qch dans l'œuf** to nip sth in the bud; ~ **le temps** to kill time. **2 se** ~ *vpr (accident)* to be killed; *(suicide)* to kill o.s. **se** ~ **à travailler** to work o.s. to death, kill o.s. with work; **se** ~ **à répéter qch à qn** to wear o.s. out repeating sth to sb. ◆**tué, e** *nm, f* person killed. **les** ~**s** the dead. ◆**tuerie** *nf (carnage)* slaughter, carnage. ◆**tue-tête** *adv*: **crier à** ~ to shout at the top of one's voice, shout one's head off *. ◆**tueur, -euse 1** *nm, f* killer. ~ **(à gages)** hired *ou* contract killer, hitman *. **2** *nm (d'abattoir)* slaughterman, slaughterer.

tuile [tɥil] *nf* (**a**) *(Constr)* tile. (**b**) *(*: malchance)* blow. **quelle** ~! what a blow! (**c**) *(Culin)* wafer.

tulipe [tylip] *nf* tulip. ◆**tulipier** *nm* tulip tree.

tuméfié, e [tymefje] *adj* puffed-up, swollen.

tumeur [tymœʀ] *nf* tumour.

tumulte [tymylt(ə)] *nm* (**a**) *(bruit) [foule, rue]* commotion; *[voix]* hubbub; *[acclamations]* thunder, tumult. (**b**) *(agitation) [affaires]* hurly-burly; *[passions]* turmoil, tumult. ◆**tumultueux, -euse** *adj séance, époque* stormy, turbulent; *foule* turbulent, agitated; *passion* tumultuous, turbulent.

tuner [tynɛʀ] *nm (amplificateur)* tuner.

tunique [tynik] *nf* tunic.

Tunisie [tynizi] *nf* Tunisia. ◆**tunisien, -ienne** *adj*, **T~(ne)** *nm(f)* Tunisian.

tunnel [tynɛl] *nm* tunnel. **le** ~ **sous la Manche** the Chunnel, the Channel Tunnel.

turban [tyʀbɑ̃] *nm* turban.

turbine [tyʀbin] *nf* turbine.

turboréacteur [tyʀboʀeaktœʀ] *nm* turbojet (engine).

turbulent, e [tyʀbylɑ̃, ɑ̃t] *adj enfant* boisterous; *(Sci)* turbulent. ◆**turbulence** *nf (Sci: remous)* ~**(s)** turbulence.

turc, turque [tyʀk(ə)] **1** *adj* Turkish. **2** *nm* (**a**) *(personne)* **T**~ Turk; *(fig)* **jeune T**~ Young Turk. (**b**) *(Ling)* Turkish. **3** *nf*: **Turque** Turkish woman.

turfiste [tyʀfist(ə)] *nmf* racegoer.

turlupiner * [tyʀlypine] (1) *vt* to bother, worry.

turne [tyʀn(ə)] *nf (arg Scol: chambre)* room.

Turquie [tyʀki] *nf* Turkey.

turquoise [tyʀkwaz] *nf, adj inv* turquoise.

tutelle [tytɛl] *nf (Jur) [mineur, aliéné]* guardianship. **mettre qn en** ~ to put sb in the care of a guardian; **sous la** ~ **de qn** *(dépendance)* under sb's supervision; *(protection)* in sb's tutelage *ou* guardianship; **sous** ~ **administrative/de l'État** under administrative/state supervision; **territoires sous** ~ trust territories.

tuteur, -trice [tytœʀ, tʀis] **1** *nm, f (Jur)* guardian. **2** *nm (Agr)* stake, support, prop.

tutorat [tytɔʀa] *nm (Scol)* pastoral care, guidance (teaching); *(Univ)* student counselling.

tutoyer [tytwaje] (**8**) *vt*: ~ **qn** to address sb as 'tu', ≃ be on first-name terms with sb. ◆**tutoiement** *nm* use of (the familiar) 'tu'.

tutu [tyty] *nm* tutu, ballet skirt.

tuyau, *pl* ~**x** [tɥijo] *nm* (**a**) *(gén, rigide)* pipe, length of piping; *(flexible)* length of rubber (*ou* plastic *etc*) tubing; *[pipe]* stem. ~ **d'arrosage** hosepipe, garden hose; ~ **de cheminée** chimney pipe; ~ **d'échappement** exhaust (pipe); *(fig)* **il me l'a dit dans le** ~ **de l'oreille** * he whispered it to me. (**b**) *(*: conseil)* tip. ◆**tuyauter** * (1) *vt*: ~ **qn** *(conseiller)* to give sb a tip; *(mettre au courant)* to put sb in the know *. ◆**tuyauterie** *nf*: ~**(s)** piping; *[orgue]* pipes.

tweed [twid] *nm* tweed.

twist [twist] *nm (danse)* twist.

tympan [tɛ̃pɑ̃] *nm (Anat)* eardrum.

type [tip] **1** *nm* (**a**) *(modèle)* type. **une pompe du** ~ **réglementaire** a regulation-type pump; **avoir le** ~ **oriental** to be Oriental-looking, have Oriental looks; **ce** *ou* **il n'est pas mon** ~ * he is not my type *ou* sort; **c'est le** ~ **(parfait** *ou* **même) de l'intellectuel** he's a perfect example *ou* he's the epitome of the intellectual. (**b**) *(*: individu)* bloke *, guy *. **quel sale** ~! what a nasty customer! **2** *adj inv* typical, classic; *(Statistique)* standard. **l'exemple** ~ the typical *ou* classic example.

typhoïde [tifɔid] *adj* typhoid. **la (fièvre)** ~ typhoid (fever).

typhon [tifɔ̃] *nm* typhoon.

typhus [tifys] *nm* typhus (fever).

typique [tipik] *adj* typical. **sa réaction est** ~ his reaction is typical (of him). ◆**typiquement** *adv* typically.

typographe [tipɔgʀaf] *nmf* typographer. ◆**typographie** *nf* typography. ◆**typographique** *adj opérations, art* typographic(al). **erreur** ~ typographic(al) *ou* printer's error, misprint.

typologie [tipɔlɔʒi] *nf* typology.

tyran [tiʀɑ̃] *nm (lit, fig)* tyrant. ◆**tyrannie** *nf* tyranny. **exercer sa** ~ **sur qn** to tyrannize sb. ◆**tyrannique** *adj* tyrannical. ◆**tyranniser** (1) *vt* to tyrannize.

U

U, u [y] *nm (lettre)* U, u.

Ukraine [ykʀɛn] *nf* Ukraine. ◆ **ukrainien, -ienne** *adj, nm,* **U~(ne)** *nm(f)* Ukrainian.

ulcère [ylsɛʀ] *nm* ulcer. ◆ **ulcération** *nf* ulceration. ◆ **ulcérer** (6) **1** *vt (révolter)* to sicken, appal; *(Méd)* to ulcerate. **être ulcéré (par l'attitude de qn)** to be sickened *ou* appalled (by sb's attitude); **plaie ulcérée** festering *ou* ulcerated wound. **2 s'** ~ *vpr* to ulcerate. ◆ **ulcéreux, -euse** *adj* ulcerated, ulcerous.

ultérieur, e [ylteʀjœʀ] *adj* later, subsequent, ulterior. **à une date ~e** at a later *ou* subsequent date. ◆ **ultérieurement** *adv* later, subsequently.

ultimatum [yltimatɔm] *nm* ultimatum. **envoyer** *ou* **adresser un ~ à qn** to present sb with an ultimatum.

ultime [yltim] *adj* ultimate, final.

ultra [yltʀa] *préf* ultra. **~-rapide** *etc* ultrafast *etc*; *(Aviat)* ~ **léger motorisé** *nm* ultra-light.

ultra-confidentiel, -ielle [yltʀakɔ̃fidɔ̃sjɛl] *adj* top secret.

ultramoderne [yltʀamɔdɛʀn(ə)] *adj (gén)* ultramodern; *équipement* high tech, state-of-the-art.

ultra(-)son [yltʀasɔ̃] *nm* ultrasonic sound. **les ~s** ultrasonic sound, ultrasonics. ◆ **ultra(-)sonique** *adj* ultrasonic.

ultra(-)violet [yltʀavjɔlɛ] **1** *adj* ultraviolet. **2** *nm* ultraviolet ray.

un, une [œ̃, yn] **1** *adj indéf* (**a**) a, an *(devant voyelle)*; *(un, une quelconque)* some; *(avec noms abstraits) non traduit.* **ne venez pas ~ dimanche** don't come on a Sunday; **retrouvons-nous dans ~ café** let's meet in a café *ou* in some café (or other); **~ jour sur deux** every other day; **une semaine sur trois** one week in every three, every third week; **~ jour, tu comprendras** one day *ou* some day you'll understand; **avec une grande sagesse** with great wisdom; **cet enfant sera ~ Paganini** this child will be another Paganini; **Monsieur Un tel** Mr So-and-So; **~ certain Mr X** a (certain) Mr X, one Mr X. **ce n'est pas ~ génie** he's no genius. (**b**) *(intensif)* **elle a fait une de ces scènes!** she made a dreadful scene! *ou* such a scene!; **j'ai une de ces faims!** I'm so hungry!; **il est d'~ sale!** he's so dirty!

2 *pron* (**a**) one. **prêtez-m'en ~** lend me one (of them); **j'en connais ~ qui sera content!** I know someone *ou* somebody *ou* one person who'll be pleased! (**b**) *(avec art déf)* **l' ~** one; **les ~s** some; **l'une et l'autre solution sont acceptables** either solution is acceptable, both solutions are acceptable; **ils se regardaient l' ~ l'autre** they looked at one another *ou* at each other; *(à tout prendre)* **l' ~ dans l'autre** on balance, by and large; *(loc)* **à la une, à la deux, à la trois** with a one and a two and a three.

3 *adj* one. **~ seul** one only, only one; **pas ~ (seul)** not one; *(emphatique)* not a single one; **~ à ~, ~ par ~** one by one, one after another; **sans ~ sou *** penniless, broke *.

4 *nm, f* one. **j'ai tiré le (numéro) ~** I picked (number) one; **(d'abord) et d'une! *** for a start!; **il n'a fait ni une ni deux, il a accepté** he accepted without a second's hesitation; *(TV)* **la une** channel one; *(Presse)* **la une** the front page, page one; *(Presse)* **sur cinq colonnes à la une** in banner headlines on the front page.

unanime [ynanim] *adj* unanimous. ◆ **unanimement** *adv* unanimously. ◆ **unanimité** *nf* unanimity. **élu à l' ~** elected unanimously; **cette décision a fait l' ~** this decision was approved unanimously; **il y a ~ pour dire que** the unanimous opinion is that, everybody agrees that.

uni, e [yni] *adj* (**a**) *tissu* plain, self-coloured; *couleur* plain. (**b**) *couple, amis* close; *famille* close (-knit). **présenter un front ~ contre** to present a united front to. (**c**) *surface* smooth, even.

unicité [ynisite] *nf* uniqueness, unicity.

unième [ynjɛm] *adj*: **vingt/trente et ~** twenty-/ thirty-first.

unifier [ynifje] (7) **1** *vt (gén)* to unify. **2 s' ~** *vpr [pays]* to become unified. ◆ **unificateur, -trice** *adj* unifying. ◆ **unification** *nf* unification.

uniforme [ynifɔʀm(ə)] **1** *adj (gén)* uniform; *surface* even. **2** *nm (vêtement)* uniform. **en (grand) ~** in (dress) uniform, in full regalia. ◆ **uniformément** *adv* uniformly; evenly. ◆ **uniformisation** *nf* standardization. ◆ **uniformiser** (1) *vt (standardiser)* to standardize; *teinte* to make uniform. ◆ **uniformité** *nf* uniformity; evenness.

unijambiste [yniʒɑ̃bist(ə)] **1** *adj* one-legged. **2** *nmf* one-legged man (*ou* woman).

unilatéral, e, *mpl* **-aux** [ynilateʀal, o] *adj* unilateral. ◆ **unilatéralement** *adv* unilaterally.

unilingue [ynilɛ̃g] *adj* unilingual.

union [ynjɔ̃] **1** *nf (alliance, mariage)* union; *(groupe)* association, union; *[éléments, couleurs]* combination, blending. *(fig)* **ils ont fait l' ~ sacrée** they presented a united front; **l' ~ fait la force** strength through unity. **2** : **~ de consommateurs** consumers' association; **U~ des Républiques Socialistes Soviétiques** Union of Soviet Socialist Republics; **l'U~ Soviétique** the Soviet Union.

Uniprix [ynipʀi] *nm* ® department store *(for inexpensive goods)*, ≃ Woolworth's®, five and ten *(US)*.

unique [ynik] *adj* (**a**) *(seul)* only. **mon ~ espoir** my only *ou* sole *ou* one hope; **fils ~** only son; **route à voie ~** single-lane road; **tiré par un cheval ~** drawn by only one *ou* by a single horse; **~ en France** unique *ou* the only one of its kind in France; **deux aspects d'un même et ~ problème** two aspects of one and the same problem; *(dans un cinéma)* **'places: prix ~ 30 francs'** 'all seats 30 F'. (**b**) *(après n: exceptionnel) livre, talent* unique. **~ en son genre** unique of its kind; **~ au monde** absolutely unique. (**c**) *(*: impayable)* priceless *. ◆ **uniquement** *adv* (**a**) *(exclusivement)* only, solely. **pas ~** not only *ou* not just that; **il pense ~ à l'argent** he thinks only of money. (**b**) *(simplement)* only, merely, just. **c'était ~ par curiosité** it was only *ou* just *ou* merely out of curiosity.

unir [yniʀ] (2) **1** *vt* (**a**) *(associer)* to unite (*à* with). **le sentiment qui les unit** the feeling which binds them together *ou* unites them; **~ en mariage** to unite *ou* join in marriage. (**b**) *(combiner) couleurs, qualités* to combine (*à* with). (**c**) *(relier) continents, villes* to link, join up. **2 s' ~** *vpr (s'associer)* to unite (*à, avec* with, *contre* against); *(se marier)* to be joined in marriage; *(se combiner)* to combine (*à, avec* with).

unisexe [ynisɛks] *adj inv* unisex.

unisson [ynisɔ̃] *nm (Mus)* unison. **à l'** ~ *chanter* in unison; *(fig) penser* with one mind, identically.

unitaire [ynitɛʀ] *adj (Comm, Math, Phys)* unitary; *(Pol)* unitarian. **prix** ~ unit price.

unité [ynite] *nf* (**a**) *(cohésion)* unity. ~ **de vues** unity of views. (**b**) *(gén, Comm, Math: élément)* unit. ~ **de mesure** unit of measure; ~ **monétaire** monetary unit; **prix de vente à l'** ~ unit selling price; **nous ne les vendons pas à l'** ~ we don't sell them singly *ou* individually. (**c**) *(troupe)* unit; *(bateau)* ship. ~ **mobile de police** police mobile unit; ~ **de réanimation** resuscitation unit. (**d**) *(Univ)* ~ **de formation et de recherches** university department. (**e**) *(Ordin)* ~ **centrale** mainframe, central processing unit; ~ **de commande** control unit; ~ **de (lecteur de) disquettes** disk drive unit. (**f**) *(*: 10 000 F)* ten thousand francs.

univers [ynivɛʀ] *nm (gén)* universe. ◆ **universalité** *nf* universality. ◆ **universel, -elle** *adj (gén)* universal; **esprit** ~ polymath; **un produit de réputation** ~**le** a world-famous product. ◆ **universellement** *adv* universally.

universitaire [ynivɛʀsitɛʀ] **1** *adj vie, restaurant* university; *études, milieux, diplôme* university, academic. **2** *nmf* academic.

université [ynivɛʀsite] *nf* university. ~ **d'été** summer school.

uranium [yʀanjɔm] *nm* uranium.

urbain, e [yʀbɛ̃, ɛn] *adj* (**a**) *(de la ville)* urban, city. (**b**) *(littér: poli)* urbane. ◆ **urbanisation** *nf* urbanization. ◆ **urbaniser** (1) **1** *vt* to urbanize. **2 s'** ~ *vpr* to become urbanized. ◆ **urbanisme** *nm* town planning. ◆ **urbaniste** *nmf* town planner. ◆ **urbanité** *nf (littér)* urbanity.

urée [yʀe] *nf* urea. ◆ **urémie** *nf* uraemia.

urgence [yʀʒɑ̃s] *nf* (**a**) *[décision, situation]* urgency. **y a-t-il** ~ **à ce que nous fassions...?** is it urgent for us to do...?; **d'** ~ *mesures, situation* emergency; **faire qch d'** ~ to do sth as a matter of urgency; **transporté d'** ~ **à l'hôpital** rushed to hospital; **à envoyer d'** ~ to be sent immediately, for immediate dispatch; **le patron l'a convoqué d'**~ the boss requested to see him urgently *ou* immediately. (**b**) *(cas urgent)* emergency. **salle des** ~**s** emergency ward. ◆ **urgent, e** *adj* urgent. **rien d'** ~ nothing urgent; **l'** ~ **est de** the most urgent thing is to; **c'est plus qu'** ~ it's desperately urgent. ◆ **urger *** (3) *vi*: **ça urge!** it's urgent!

urine [yʀin] *nf*: ~**(s)** urine. ◆ **uriner** (1) *vi* to urinate. ◆ **urinoir** *nm* (public) urinal.

urne [yʀn(ə)] *nf* (**a**) *(Pol)* ~ **(électorale)** ballot box; **aller aux** ~**s** to vote, go to the polls. (**b**) *(vase)* urn.

urticaire [yʀtikɛʀ] *nf* nettle rash, hives, urticaria.

Uruguay [yʀygwɛ] *nm* Uruguay. ◆ **uruguayen, -enne** *adj,* **U**~**(ne)** *nm(f)* Uruguayan.

us [ys] *nmpl*: ~ **(et coutumes)** (habits and) customs.

usage [yzaʒ] *nm* (**a**) *(utilisation)* use. **perdre l'** ~ **de ses yeux/membres** to lose the use of one's eyes/limbs; **perdre l'** ~ **de la parole** to lose the power of speech; **outil à** ~**s multiples** multipurpose tool; **faire** ~ **de** *(gén)* to use, make use of; *droit* to exercise; **faire un bon/mauvais** ~ **de qch** to put sth to good/bad use; **avoir l'** ~ **de qch** to have the use of sth; **ces souliers ont fait de l'**~ I've (*ou* we've *etc*) had good use out of these shoes; **à l'** ~ with use; **à l'** ~ **de** for; **en** ~ in use. (**b**) *(coutume, habitude)* custom. **c'est l'** ~ it's the custom, it's what's done; **entrer dans l'** ~ **(courant)** *[objet, mot]* to come into common *ou* current use; *[mœurs]* to become common practice; **contraire aux** ~**s** contrary to common practice *ou* to custom; **il était d'** ~ **de** it was customary *ou* a custom *ou* usual to; **formule d'** ~ set formula; **après les compliments d'** ~ after the usual *ou* customary compliments. (**c**) *(Ling)* **l'** ~ usage; **l'** ~ **écrit** written usage. ◆ **usagé, e** *adj* worn, old. ◆ **usager, -ère** *nm, f* user. ~ **de la route** roaduser.

user [yze] (1) **1** *vt* (**a**) *(détériorer) outil, roches* to wear away; *vêtements, personne* to wear out; *nerfs* to wear down. (**b**) *(consommer) (gén)* to use; *essence, charbon* to use, burn. **il use 2 paires de chaussures par mois** he goes through 2 pairs of shoes (in) a month. **2** *vi (littér)* **en** ~ **bien/mal avec qn** to deal well/badly by sb, treat sb well/ badly. **3** ~ **de** *vt indir (gén)* to make use of, use; *droit* to exercise. **il en a usé et abusé** he has used and abused it. **4 s'** ~ *vpr [tissu]* to wear out. **s'** ~ **les yeux** to strain one's eyes (à *faire* by doing). ◆ **usé, e** *adj* (**a**) *objet* worn; *(fig) personne* worn-out. ~ **jusqu'à la corde** threadbare. (**b**) *(banal) thème* hackneyed, trite; *plaisanterie* well-worn, stale.

usine [yzin] *nf (gén)* factory; *(importante)* plant; *(textile)* mill; *(métallurgique)* works. ~ **automatisée** automated factory; ~ **à gaz** gasworks. ◆ **usiner** (1) *vt (traiter)* to machine; *(fabriquer)* to manufacture.

usité, e [yzite] *adj* in common use, common.

ustensile [ystɑ̃sil] *nm (gén)* implement. ~ **(de cuisine)** (kitchen) utensil.

usuel, -elle [yzɥɛl] **1** *adj objet* everyday, ordinary; *mot* everyday; *nom* common. **2** *nm (livre)* book on the open shelf.

usufruit [yzyfʀɥi] *nm* usufruct. ◆ **usufruitier, -ière** *adj, nm, f* usufructuary.

usure[1] [yzyʀ] *nf* (**a**) *(processus) [vêtement]* wear (and tear); *[roche]* wearing away; *[forces]* wearing out. **on l'aura à l'** ~ we'll wear him down in the end. (**b**) *(état) [objet]* worn state.

usure[2] [yzyʀ] *nf (intérêt)* usury. ◆ **usuraire** *adj* usurious. ◆ **usurier, -ière** *nm, f* usurer.

usurper [yzyʀpe] (1) *vt* to usurp. ◆ **usurpateur, -trice** **1** *adj* usurping. **2** *nm, f* usurper. ◆ **usurpation** *nf* usurpation.

ut [yt] *nm (Mus)* (the note) C.

utérus [yteʀys] *nm* womb.

utile [ytil] *adj (gén)* useful; *conseil* useful, helpful (*à qn* to *ou* for sb). **livre** ~ **à lire** useful book to read; **cela vous sera** ~ that'll be of use to you; **ton parapluie m'a été bien** ~ **ce matin** your umbrella came in very handy this morning; **est-il vraiment** ~ **que j'y aille?** do I really need to go?; **puis-je vous être** ~**?** can I be of help?, can I do anything for you? ◆ **utilement** *adv* profitably, usefully.

utiliser [ytilize] (1) *vt (gén)* to use, make use of. ◆ **utilisable** *adj* usable. ◆ **utilisateur, -trice** *nm, f* user. *(Ordin)* ~ **final** end user. ◆ **utilisation** *nf* use.

utilitaire [ytilitɛʀ] **1** *adj* utilitarian. **2** *nm (Ordin)* utility.

utilité [ytilite] *nf (caractère utile)* usefulness; *(utilisation possible)* use. **cet outil peut avoir son** ~ this tool has its uses *ou* may come in handy *ou* useful; **d'aucune** ~ (of) no use *ou* help, useless; **déclaré d'** ~ **publique** state-approved.

utopie [ytɔpi] *nf* utopian view (*ou* idea *etc*). **c'est de l'** ~ that's sheer utopianism. ◆ **utopique** *adj* utopian.

V, v [ve] *nm (lettre)* V, v. **en V** V-shaped.

vacance [vakɑ̃s] **1** *nf (Admin: poste)* vacancy. **2** *nfpl*: **~s** holidays, vacation *(US)*. **les ~s de Noël** the Christmas holidays *ou* vacation; **partir/être en ~s** to go/be away on holiday *ou* on vacation; **prendre ses ~s en une fois** to take (all) one's holiday(s) *ou* vacation at once; **j'ai besoin de ~s** I need a holiday *ou* vacation; **~s de neige** winter sports holiday *ou* vacation; **lieu de ~s** holiday place. ◆ **vacancier, -ière** *nm, f* holiday-maker, vacationist *(US)*, vacationer *(US)*.

vacant, e [vakɑ̃, ɑ̃t] *adj (gén)* vacant; *appartement* unoccupied.

vacarme [vakaʀm(ə)] *nm* din, racket, row. **faire du ~** to make a din.

vaccin [vaksɛ̃] *nm (substance)* vaccine; *(vaccination)* vaccination, inoculation. **faire un ~ à qn** to give sb a vaccination *ou* inoculation. ◆ **vaccination** *nf* vaccination, inoculation. ◆ **vacciner** (1) *vt (Méd)* to vaccinate, inoculate (*contre* against). **se faire ~** to have a vaccination, get vaccinated.

vache [vaʃ] **1** *nf* (**a**) *(Zool)* cow; *(cuir)* cowhide. **~ laitière** dairy cow. (**b**) (⁑: *méchant) (femme)* bitch ⁑, cow ⁑; *(homme)* swine ⁑. (**c**) **~ à eau** canvas waterbag. (**d**) *(locutions)* **période de ~s grasses/maigres** good *ou* prosperous/lean *ou* hard times; **c'est une ~ à lait** * he's a mug * *ou* sucker *; **il parle français comme une ~ espagnole** he absolutely murders the French language; **manger de la ~ enragée** to go through hard *ou* lean times; **faire un coup en ~ à qn** to do the dirty on sb ⁑; **ah la ~!** ⁑ *(douleur, indignation)* hell! ⁑, damn! ⁑; **une ~ de surprise** ⁑ a hell of a surprise ⁑. **2** *adj* (⁑: *méchant)* rotten *, mean. ◆ **vachement** ⁑ *adv* (**a**) *crier etc* like mad *. **~ bon/difficile** damned ⁑ good/hard. (**b**) *(méchamment)* in a rotten * *ou* mean way. ◆ **vacher** *nm* cowherd. ◆ **vacherie** *nf* (**a**) (⁑: *méchanceté)* rottenness *, meanness. **une ~** *(action)* a dirty trick *; *(remarque)* a nasty remark. (**b**) (⁑: *intensif)* **c'est de la ~** it's rubbish *ou* junk *; **quelle ~ de temps** *etc*! what damned ⁑ awful weather *etc*!

vaciller [vasije] (1) *vi* (**a**) *(lit) [personne, mur]* to sway (to and fro); *[blessé, ivrogne]* to totter, reel, stagger; *[bébé, meuble]* to wobble. **~ sur ses jambes** to stand shakily *ou* unsteadily on one's legs; **s'avancer en vacillant** to totter *ou* reel along. (**b**) *[lumière]* to flicker; *[voix]* to shake; *[résolution, courage]* to falter, waver; *[raison, santé, mémoire]* to be shaky, be failing. ◆ **vacillant, e** *adj démarche* shaky, wobbly; *flamme* flickering; *santé, mémoire, raison* shaky, failing; *courage* wavering, faltering; *caractère* indecisive. ◆ **vacillement** *nm*: **~(s)** swaying; wobbling, flickering; faltering, wavering.

vadrouille * [vadʀuj] *nf* ramble. **être en ~** to be out on a ramble. ◆ **vadrouiller** * (1) *vi* to be out on a ramble.

va-et-vient [vaevjɛ̃] *nm inv [personnes etc]* comings and goings, to-ings and fro-ings; *[piston]* to and fro (motion), backwards and forwards motion. **faire le ~ entre** to go to and fro between; *(Élec)* **(interrupteur de) ~** two-way switch.

vagabond, e [vagabɔ̃, ɔ̃d] **1** *adj peuple, vie* wandering; *imagination, humeur* restless. **2** *nm, f (péj: rôdeur)* tramp, vagrant, vagabond. ◆ **vagabondage** *nm* wandering, roaming; *(Jur, péj)* vagrancy. **le ~ de son imagination** the rovings of his imagination. ◆ **vagabonder** (1) *vi [personne, imagination]* to roam, wander.

vagin [vaʒɛ̃] *nm* vagina.

vagir [vaʒiʀ] (2) *vi [bébé]* to cry, wail. ◆ **vagissement** *nm* cry, wail.

vague[1] [vag] **1** *adj (gén)* vague; *idée* hazy; *regard* faraway; *robe, manteau* loose(-fitting). **un ~ cousin** some sort of distant cousin; **il avait un ~ diplôme** he had a degree of sorts *ou* some kind of degree. **2** *nm* vagueness. **il est resté dans le ~** he kept it all rather vague; **regarder dans le ~** to gaze (vacantly) into space; **avoir du ~ à l'âme** to feel vaguely melancholic. ◆ **vaguement** *adv* vaguely.

vague[2] [vag] *nf (lit, fig)* wave. **~(s) de fond** ground swell; **~ d'enthousiasme** wave *ou* surge of enthusiasm; **premières ~s de touristes** first influxes of tourists; **~ de chaleur** heatwave; **~ de froid** cold spell *ou* snap; **~ de criminalité** crime wave.

vaillant, e [vajɑ̃, ɑ̃t] *adj* (**a**) *(courageux)* brave, courageous; *(au combat)* valiant, gallant. (**b**) *(vigoureux)* vigorous, robust. **je ne me sens pas très ~** I don't feel particularly great today *. ◆ **vaillamment** *adv* bravely, courageously; valiantly, gallantly. ◆ **vaillance** *nf* courage, bravery; valour, gallantry.

vain, e [vɛ̃, vɛn] *adj* (**a**) *promesse, espoir* vain, empty; *tentative, attente* vain, futile, fruitless; *regrets, discussion* vain, useless, idle. **en ~** in vain; **son sacrifice n'aura pas été ~** his sacrifice will not have been in vain; **il est ~ d'essayer de...** it is futile to try to... (**b**) *(vaniteux)* vain. ◆ **vainement** *adv* vainly.

vaincre [vɛ̃kʀ(ə)] (42) *vt rival* to defeat, beat; *ennemi* to defeat, vanquish, conquer; *obstacle etc* to overcome; *timidité, sentiment, maladie* to overcome, triumph over, conquer. **nous vaincrons** we shall overcome. ◆ **vaincu, e** *adj* beaten, defeated, vanquished. **s'avouer ~** to admit defeat, confess o.s. beaten; **les ~s** the vanquished, the defeated. ◆ **vainqueur 1** *nm (à la guerre)* conqueror, victor; *(en sport)* winner. **2** *adj m* victorious, triumphant.

vaisseau, *pl* **~x** [vɛso] *nm* (**a**) *(Naut)* ship, vessel. **~ amiral** flagship; **~ de guerre** warship; *(Aviat)* **~ spatial** spaceship. (**b**) *(Anat)* vessel.

vaisselle [vɛsɛl] *nf (plats)* crockery; *(plats à laver)* dishes; *(lavage)* washing-up, dishes. **faire la ~** to wash up, do the washing-up *ou* the dishes. ◆ **vaisselier** *nm* dresser.

val, *pl* **~s** *ou* **vaux** [val, vo] *nm* valley.

valable [valabl(ə)] *adj contrat, passeport, raison, motif* valid; *œuvre, solution, équipements* decent, worthwhile. *(Comm)* **offre ~ une semaine** firm offer for a week. ◆ **valablement** *adv* validly. **pour en parler ~...** to be able to say anything worthwhile *ou* valid about it...

valdinguer ⁑ [valdɛ̃ge] (1) *vi*: **aller ~** *[personne]* to go sprawling; *[objet]* to come crashing down; **envoyer ~ qch** to send sth flying *.

Valence [valɑ̃s] *n (en Espagne)* Valencia; *(en France)* Valence.

valet [valɛ] *nm (domestique)* (man)servant; *(Cartes)* jack, knave. ~ **de chambre** manservant, valet; ~ **de ferme** farmhand; ~ **de pied** footman; *(cintre)* ~ **(de nuit)** valet.

valeur [valœʀ] *nf* (**a**) *(prix)* value, worth; *(Fin) [devise, action]* value, price. ~ **marchande/vénale** market/monetary value; **prendre/perdre de la** ~ to go up/down in value, lose/gain in value; **ça a beaucoup de/n'a aucune** ~ it is worth a lot/worthless. (**b**) *(titre boursier)* security. ~**s (boursières)** securities, stocks and shares; ~**s (mobilières)** transferable securities; ~**s disponibles** liquid assets; ~**s de tout repos** *ou* **de père de famille** gilt-edged *ou* blue-chip securities. (**c**) *(qualité) [personne]* worth, merit; *[roman]* value, merit; *[science, théorie]* value. **acteur de** ~ actor of considerable merit; **juger qn/qch à sa (juste)** ~ to judge sb/sth at his/its true value *ou* worth; ~**s morales** moral values. (**d**) *(mesure)* value. ~ **relative/absolue d'un terme** relative/absolute value of a term; **en** ~ **absolue/relative** in absolute/relative terms; **donnez-lui la** ~ **d'une cuiller à café** give him the equivalent of a teaspoonful, give him a teaspoon's worth. (**e**) *(locutions)* **objets de** ~ valuables, articles of value; **sans** ~ *objet* valueless, worthless; *témoignage* invalid, valueless; **mettre en** ~ *terrain* to exploit; *détail* to bring out, highlight; *objet décoratif* to set off; **mettre qn en** ~ *[conversation, esprit]* to show sb to advantage, bring out sb's personal qualities; **se mettre en** ~ to show o.s. off to advantage.

valeureux, -euse [valœʀø, øz] *adj* valorous. ◆**valeureusement** *adv* valorously.

valide [valid] *adj* (**a**) *(non blessé)* able, able-bodied; *(en bonne santé)* fit, well; *membre* good. (**b**) *billet, carte d'identité* valid. ◆**valider** (**1**) *vt passeport, billet* to validate; *document* to authenticate. ◆**validation** *nf* validation; authentication. ◆**validité** *nf* validity.

valise [valiz] *nf* (suit)case, bag. *(lit, fig)* **faire ses** ~**s** to pack one's bags; **la** ~ **(diplomatique)** the diplomatic bag.

vallée [vale] *nf* valley. ◆**vallon** *nm* small valley. ◆**vallonné, e** *adj* undulating. ◆**vallonnement** *nm* undulation.

valoir [valwaʀ] (**29**) **1** *vi* (**a**) *[objet]* ~ **qch** to be worth sth; **ça vaut combien?** how much is it (worth)?; **ça vaut 10 F** it's worth 10 francs; ~ **cher** to be worth a lot, be expensive; **acompte à** ~ **sur...** deposit to be deducted from...; **cette montre vaut-elle plus cher que l'autre? — elles se valent à peu près** is this watch worth more than the other one? — they are worth about the same (amount). (**b**) *(qualité)* **que vaut cet auteur/cette pièce?** is this author/this play any good?; **ils ne valent pas mieux l'un que l'autre** there's nothing to choose between them, they are two of a kind; **il ne vaut pas cher!** *ou* **pas grand-chose!** he's a bad lot; **il a conscience de ce qu'il vaut** he is aware of his worth, he knows his value *ou* worth; **ça ne vaut rien** *ou* **pas un clou** * *(gén)* it's no good *(pour* for); *[marchandise]* it's rubbish; *[argument]* it's worthless; *[outil]* it's useless *ou* no use; **ne faire rien qui vaille** to do nothing useful *ou* worthwhile *ou* of any use; **cela ne me dit rien qui vaille** I don't like the look of that, it seems rather ominous to me. (**c**) *(s'appliquer)* to hold, apply, be valid. **ceci ne vaut que dans certains cas** this only holds *ou* applies *ou* is only valid in certain cases. (**d**) *(être aussi bon)* ~ **qn/qch** to be as good as sb/sth; *(revenir au même)* ~ **qch** to be equivalent to sth, be worth sth; **rien ne vaut la mer** there's nothing like *ou* nothing to beat the sea; **cette méthode en vaut une autre** it's as good a method as any (other); *(en mal)* **ces deux frères se valent** these two brothers are two of a kind; **ça se vaut** * it's six of one and half a dozen of the other *. (**e**) *(justifier)* to be worth. **le musée valait le détour/d'être vu** the museum was worth the detour/was worth seeing; **cela vaut la peine** *ou* **le coup** * it's worth it, it's worth the trouble. (**f**) **faire** ~ *domaine* to exploit; *droits* to assert; *fait, argument* to emphasize; *(mettre en vedette) caractéristique* to highlight, bring out; *personne* to show off to advantage ; **je lui fis** ~ **que...** I impressed upon him that..., I pointed out to him that... (**g**) **cet auteur/ce film ne vaut pas un clou** * this author/this film is a dead loss * *ou* is a waste of time *; **il vaut/vaudrait mieux refuser, mieux vaut/vaudrait refuser** it is better/would be better to refuse; **il vaudrait mieux que vous refusiez** you had better refuse, you would do better to refuse; **mieux vaut trop de travail que pas assez** too much work is better than not enough.
2 *vt*: **ceci lui a valu des reproches** *etc* this earned *ou* brought him reproaches *etc*; **qu'est ce qui nous vaut l'honneur de cette visite?** to what do we owe the honour of this visit?

valoriser [valɔʀize] (**1**) *vt (Écon) région* to develop (the economy of); *produit* to enhance the value of. ◆**valorisation** *nf* (economic) development; enhanced value.

valse [vals(ə)] *nf (danse)* waltz; *(fig: carrousel)* musical chairs. **la** ~ **des étiquettes** constant price rises; ~**-hésitation** pussyfooting *. ◆**valser** (**1**) *vi* (**a**) *(danser)* to waltz. (**b**) *(* fig)* **envoyer** ~ **qch/qn** to send sth/sb flying; **il est allé** ~ **contre le mur** he went flying against the wall; **faire** ~ **l'argent** to spend money like water. ◆**valseur, -euse** *nm, f* waltzer.

valve [valv(ə)] *nf* valve.

vampire [vɑ̃piʀ] *nm (gén)* vampire; *(Zool)* vampire bat.

van [vɑ̃] *nm (véhicule)* horse-box, horse trailer *(US)*.

vandale [vɑ̃dal] *adj, nmf* vandal, hooligan. ◆**vandalisme** *nm* vandalism, hooliganism.

vanille [vanij] *nf* vanilla.

vanité [vanite] *nf* (**a**) *(amour-propre)* pride, vanity, conceit; *(frivolité)* shallowness, superficiality. **sans** ~ without false modesty; **tirer** ~ **de** to pride o.s. on. (**b**) *(futilité) [promesse, espoir]* emptiness, vanity; *[tentative]* futility, fruitlessness; *[regrets, discussion]* uselessness, idleness. ◆**vaniteusement** *adv* vainly, conceitedly. ◆**vaniteux, -euse** *adj* vain, conceited.

vanne [van] *nf (canalisation)* gate; *[écluse, digue]* (sluice) gate.

vanner [vane] (**1**) *vt* (**a**) *(Agr)* to winnow. (**b**) *(‡: fatiguer)* to exhaust, do in *. **je suis vanné** I'm dead-beat *.

vannerie [vanʀi] *nf* basketwork. ◆**vannier** *nm* basket maker.

vantail, *pl* **-aux** [vɑ̃taj, o] *nm [porte]* leaf. **porte à double** ~ Dutch door.

vanter [vɑ̃te] (**1**) **1** *vt auteur, endroit, qualités* to praise, speak highly of, speak in praise of; *méthode, avantages, marchandises* to vaunt. **film dont on vante les mérites** much-praised film. **2 se** ~ *vpr* (**a**) *(fanfaronner)* to boast, brag. **sans me** ~ without false modesty, without wishing to boast *ou* brag. (**b**) *(se targuer)* **se** ~ **de qch/d'avoir fait qch** to pride o.s. on sth/on having done sth; **il se vante de (pouvoir) faire...** he boasts he can do...; **il n'y a pas de quoi se** ~ there's nothing to be proud of *ou* to boast about. ◆**vantard, e 1** *adj* boastful, bragging, boasting. **2** *nm, f* braggart, boaster. ◆**vantardise** *nf (caractère)* boastfulness; *(propos)* boast.

va-nu-pieds [vanypje] *nmf inv (péj)* tramp, beggar.

vapes ‡ [vap] *nfpl*: **tomber dans les** ~ to fall into a dead faint, pass out; **être dans les** ~ *(évanoui)* to be out cold *; *(drogué, après un choc)* to be woozy * *ou* in a daze.

vapeur [vapœʀ] **1** *nf* (**a**) *(brouillard)* haze, vapour; *(Chim: émanation)* vapour. *(nocives)* **~s** fumes; **~s d'essence** petrol *ou* gasoline *(US)* fumes; **~ (d'eau)** steam, (water) vapour; **machine** *etc* **à ~** steam engine *etc*; **(cuit à la) ~** steamed; **aller à toute ~** to go full steam ahead. (**b**) *(†: malaises)* **~s** vapours †; **avoir ses ~s** *(bouffées de chaleur)* to have hot flushes; *(†: malaise)* to have the vapours †. **2** *nm (bateau)* steamship, steamer.

vaporeux, -euse [vapɔʀø, øz] *adj tissu* filmy; *atmosphère* misty, vaporous; *cheveux* gossamer.

vaporiser [vapɔʀize] (1) **1** *vt* to spray. **2 se ~** *vpr (Phys)* to vaporize. ◆ **vaporisateur** *nm* spray.

vaquer [vake] (1) **1 ~ à** *vt indir* to attend to, see to. **~ à ses occupations** to go about one's business. **2** *vi (Admin: être en vacances)* to be on vacation.

varappe [vaʀap] *nf* rock-climbing.

varech [vaʀɛk] *nm* wrack, kelp.

vareuse [vaʀøz] *nf [marin]* pea jacket; *(d'uniforme)* tunic.

varice [vaʀis] *nf* varicose vein. **bas à ~s** support stockings.

varicelle [vaʀisɛl] *nf* chickenpox.

varier [vaʀje] (7) *vti* to vary. ◆ **variable 1** *adj (gén)* variable; *temps* changeable, unsettled; *humeur* changeable. **le baromètre est au ~** the barometer reads 'change'; **les réactions sont très ~s** reactions are very varied *ou* vary greatly. **2** *nf* variable. ◆ **variante** *nf (gén)* variant (*de* of). ◆ **variateur** *nm: (Élec)* **~ (électronique)** dimmer. ◆ **variation** *nf* variation (*de* in). ◆ **varié, e** *adj* (**a**) *(non monotone) style, paysage, menu* varied. **un travail très ~** a very varied job. (**b**) *(divers) sujets, objets, produits* various. **hors-d'œuvre ~s** selection of hors d'œuvres; **on rencontre les opinions les plus ~es** you come across the most varied *ou* diverse opinions on the subject. ◆ **variété** *nf (gén)* variety. *(Music-hall)* **(spectacle de) ~s** variety show.

variole [vaʀjɔl] *nf* smallpox.

Varsovie [vaʀsɔvi] *n* Warsaw.

vase¹ [vɑz] *nm* vase, bowl. *(fig)* **en ~ clos** in isolation *ou* seclusion; **~s communicants** communicating vessels; **~ de nuit** chamberpot.

vase² [vɑz] *nf* silt, mud, sludge.

vaseline [vazlin] *nf* vaseline, petroleum jelly.

vaseux, -euse [vɑzø, øz] *adj* (**a**) (*) *(fatigué)* woozy *, in a daze *; *(confus) raisonnement* woolly *, hazy. (**b**) *(boueux)* silty, muddy, sludgy.

vasistas [vazistɑs] *nm* fanlight.

vasque [vask(ə)] *nf (bassin, lavabo)* basin; *(coupe)* bowl.

vassal, e, *mpl* **-aux** [vasal, o] *nm, f (Hist, fig)* vassal.

vaste [vast(ə)] *adj (gén)* vast, huge, immense. **c'est une ~ fumisterie** * it's a huge *ou* gigantic hoax *ou* joke *ou* farce.

va-t-en-guerre [vatɑ̃gɛʀ] *nm inv* warmonger.

Vatican [vatikɑ̃] *nm*: **le ~** the Vatican.

va-tout [vatu] *nm*: **jouer son ~** to stake *ou* risk one's all.

vaudeville [vodvil] *nm* vaudeville, light comedy. *(fig)* **ça tourne au ~** it's turning into a farce.

vaudou [vodu] **1** *nm*: **le (culte du) ~** voodoo. **2** *adj inv* voodoo.

vau-l'eau [volo] *adv*: **aller à ~** to be on the road to ruin.

vaurien, -ienne [voʀjɛ̃, jɛn] *nm, f (voyou)* good-for-nothing; *(garnement)* little devil *.

vautour [votuʀ] *nm (Zool, fig)* vulture.

vautrer (se) [votʀe] (1) *vpr*: **se ~ dans** *boue, vice* to wallow in; *fauteuil* to loll *ou* slouch in; **se ~ sur** *tapis* to sprawl on; **vautré dans l'herbe** sprawling *ou* sprawled in the grass.

va-vite * [vavit] *adv*: **à la ~** in a rush *ou* hurry.

veau, *pl* **~x** [vo] *nm* (**a**) *(Zool)* calf; *(Culin)* veal; *(cuir)* calfskin. **côte de ~** veal chop; **foie de ~** calf's liver. (**b**) *(* péj) (personne)* sheep; *(voiture)* tank * *(péj)*.

vecteur [vɛktœʀ] *nm (Math)* vector; *(Bio: d'un virus)* carrier, vector.

vécu, e [veky] **1** *adj* real(-life). **2** *nm*: **le ~** real-life experience.

vedette [vədɛt] *nf* (**a**) *[spectacle]* star. **une ~ de la politique** a leading light *ou* figure in politics; **produit-~** leading product; **avoir la ~** *[artiste]* to top the bill, have star billing; *[événement, criminel]* to be in the spotlight, make the headlines; *[orateur etc]* to be in the limelight; **mettre qn en ~** *(Ciné)* to give sb star billing; *(fig)* to push sb into the limelight, put the spotlight on sb; *(fig)* **ravir la ~** to steal the show (*à qn* from sb); **en ~ américaine** as a special guest star. (**b**) *(embarcation)* launch; *(Mil)* patrol boat; *(munie de canons)* gunboat. ◆ **vedettariat** *nm (état)* stardom; *(vedettes)* stars *(pl)*.

végétal, e, *mpl* **-aux** [veʒetal, o] **1** *adj graisses, teintures* vegetable; *biologie, cellules* plant. **2** *nm* vegetable, plant.

végétalien, -ienne [veʒetaljɛ̃, jɛn] *adj, nm, f* vegan.

végétarien, -ienne [veʒetaʀjɛ̃, jɛn] *adj, nm, f* vegetarian.

végéter [veʒete] (6) *vi (péj) [personne]* to vegetate; *[affaire]* to stagnate; *(Agr) (être chétif)* to grow poorly, be stunted. ◆ **végétatif, -ive** *adj* vegetative. ◆ **végétation** *nf* (**a**) *(Bot)* vegetation. (**b**) *(Méd)* **~s** adenoids.

véhémence [veemɑ̃s] *nf* vehemence. ◆ **véhément, e** *adj* vehement.

véhicule [veikyl] *nm* (**a**) *(Aut)* vehicle. **~ automobile/utilitaire** motor/commercial vehicle; **~ tout terrain** all-purpose *ou* all-roads vehicle. (**b**) *[pensée]* vehicle, medium. ◆ **véhiculer** (1) *vt (Aut)* to convey, transport; *substance, idées* to convey.

veille [vɛj] *nf* (**a**) *(état)* wakefulness. **en état de ~** in waking state, awake. (**b**) *(garde)* (night) watch. (**c**) *(jour précédent)* **la ~** the day before; **la ~ au soir** the previous evening, the evening before; **la ~ de cet examen** the day before that exam; **la ~ de Noël/du jour de l'an** Christmas/New Year's Eve; **la ~ de sa mort** on the eve of his death, on the day before his death. (**d**) *(fig)* **à la ~ de** *guerre* on the eve of; **être à la ~ de faire qch** to be on the brink *ou* point of doing sth.

veiller [veje] (1) **1** *vi ne pas se coucher* to stay up, sit up; *(être de garde)* to be on watch; *(rester vigilant)* to be watchful; *(faire la veillée)* to spend the evening in company. **2** *vt mort, malade* to watch over, sit up with. *(fig: obscurité)* **on veille les morts ici!** it's pitch dark in here. **3** *vt indir* (**a**) **~ à** *intérêts, approvisionnement etc* to attend to, see to, look after. **~ à ce que...** to see to it that..., make sure that...; **~ au grain** to keep an eye open for trouble. (**b**) **~ sur** to watch over, keep a watchful eye on. ◆ **veillée** *nf (réunion)* evening gathering *ou* meeting. **~ (funèbre)** wake, watch. ◆ **veilleur** *nm* (**a**) **~ (de nuit)** (night) watchman. (**b**) *(Mil)* look-out. ◆ **veilleuse** *nf (lampe)* night light; *(Aut)* sidelight. *(fig)* **mettre qch en ~** to soft-pedal on sth; **mets-la en ~!** ⁑ belt up! ⁑

veine [vɛn] *nf* (**a**) *(gén, Anat, Méd)* vein; *[houille]* seam, vein; *[minerai de fer]* lode, vein. (**b**) *(fig: inspiration)* inspiration. **de la même ~** in the same vein; **être en ~** to be inspired; **être en ~ de**

patience to be in a patient mood *ou* frame of mind. (**c**) *(*: chance)* luck. **c'est une** ~ that's a bit of luck; **coup de** ~ stroke of luck; **pas de** ~**!** hard *ou* bad *ou* rotten * luck!; **avoir de la** ~ to be lucky; **il n'a pas eu de** ~ **aux examens** his luck was out at the exams; *(iro)* **c'est bien ma** ~ that's just my (rotten *) luck. ◆**veinard, e** * **1** *adj* lucky. **2** *nm, f* lucky devil *. ◆**veiner** (1) *vt (donner l'aspect du bois)* to grain; *(donner l'aspect du marbre)* to vein.

velcro [vɛlkʀo] *nm* ® velcro.

vêler [vele] (1) *vi* to calve. ◆**vêlage** *nm* calving.

vélin [velɛ̃] *nm* vellum.

véliplanchiste [veliplɑ̃ʃist(ə)] *nmf* windsurfer.

velléité [veleite] *nf* vague desire, vague impulse. ◆**velléitaire** **1** *adj* irresolute, wavering. **2** *nmf* waverer.

vélo [velo] *nm* bike, cycle. ~ **de course** racing cycle; ~ **d'appartement** exercise bike; ~**-cross** *(Sport)* stunt-riding; *(vélo)* stunt bike; **faire du** ~**-cross** to go stunt-riding. **venir en** ~ to come by bike; **il sait faire du** ~ he can ride a bike; **je fais beaucoup de** ~ I cycle a lot, I do a lot of cycling. ◆**vélodrome** *nm* velodrome. ◆**vélomoteur** *nm* small motorbike *(under 125 cc)*.

vélocité [velɔsite] *nf* swiftness.

véloski [velɔski] *nm* skibob.

velours [v(ə)luʀ] *nm* (**a**) *(tissu)* velvet. ~ **côtelé** corduroy, cord. (**b**) *(velouté) (gén)* velvet; *[pêche]* bloom. **peau de** ~ velvet(y) skin.

velouté, e [vəlute] **1** *adj joues, crème, vin* smooth, velvety; *lumière, voix* mellow. **2** *nm* (**a**) *(douceur)* velvetiness, smoothness. (**b**) *(sauce)* velouté sauce; *(potage)* velouté. ~ **de tomates** cream of tomato soup.

velu, e [vəly] *adj* hairy.

venaison [vənɛzɔ̃] *nf* venison.

vénal, e, *mpl* **-aux** [venal, o] *adj* venal. ◆**vénalité** *nf* venality.

vendange [vɑ̃dɑ̃ʒ] *nf*: ~**(s)** grape harvest, vintage; **faire la** ~ to harvest *ou* pick the grapes. ◆**vendanger** (3) **1** *vt vigne* to harvest *ou* pick grapes from; *raisins* to pick, harvest. **2** *vi* to harvest *ou* pick the grapes. ◆**vendangeur, -euse** *nm, f* grape-picker.

vendetta [vɑ̃deta] *nf* vendetta.

vendre [vɑ̃dʀ(ə)] (41) **1** *vt* (**a**) *(lit, fig)* to sell (*à* to). ~ **qch à qn** to sell sb sth *ou* sth to sb; **il m'a vendu un tableau 900 F** he sold me a picture for 900 francs; **il vend cher** he is expensive *ou* dear, his prices are high; ~ **qch aux enchères** to sell sth by auction; **maison à** ~ house for sale. (**b**) *(*: trahir)* to sell. (**c**) *(locutions)* ~ **chèrement sa vie** to sell one's life dearly; ~ **la peau de l'ours (avant de l'avoir tué)** to count one's chickens (before they are hatched); ~ **la mèche** * to give the game *ou* show away *.

2 se ~ *vpr* (**a**) *[marchandise]* **se** ~ **à la pièce/douzaine** to be sold singly/by the dozen; **ça se vend bien/comme des petits pains** that sells well/like hot cakes. (**b**) *(péj: se laisser corrompre)* to sell o.s. ◆**vendeur, -euse** *nm, f (gén)* salesman (*ou* saleswoman), salesclerk *(US)*, shop *ou* sales assistant; *(Jur)* vendor, seller. ~ **de journaux** news vendor; **je ne suis pas** ~ I'm not selling; **il serait** ~ he'd be ready *ou* willing to sell. ◆**vendu** *nm (péj)* Judas.

vendredi [vɑ̃dʀədi] *nm* Friday. ~ **saint** Good Friday; *V* **samedi**.

vénéneux, -euse [venenø, øz] *adj* poisonous.

vénérer [veneʀe] (6) *vt* to venerate, revere. ◆**vénérable** *adj* venerable. ◆**vénération** *nf* veneration, reverence.

Venezuela [venezyɛla] *nm* Venezuela. ◆**vénézuélien, -ienne** *adj,* **V~(ne)** *nm(f)* Venezuelan.

vengeance [vɑ̃ʒɑ̃s] *nf* vengeance, revenge. **ce forfait crie** ~ this crime cries out for revenge; **de petites** ~**s** petty acts of vengeance *ou* revenge. ◆**venger** (3) **1** *vt* to avenge (*de qch* for sth). **2 se** ~ *vpr* to take (one's) revenge *ou* vengeance, to avenge o.s. **se** ~ **de qn** to take revenge on sb; **se** ~ **de qch** to take one's revenge for sth. ◆**vengeur, -geresse** **1** *adj personne* (re)vengeful; *bras, lettre* avenging. **2** *nm, f* avenger.

véniel, -elle [venjɛl] *adj* venial.

venin [vənɛ̃] *nm (lit, fig)* venom. ◆**venimeux, -euse** *adj (lit, fig)* venomous.

venir [v(ə)niʀ] (22) **1** *vi* (**a**) *[personne]* to come. **il vint vers moi** he came up to me *ou* towards me; **ils sont venus en voiture** they came by car, they drove (here); **je viens!** I'm coming!, I'm on my way!; **je viens dans un instant** I'll be there in a moment; **le voisin est venu** the man from next door came round *ou* called; **il vient chez nous tous les jeudis** he comes (round) to our house *ou* to us every Thursday. (**b**) **faire** ~ *médecin* to call, send for; **tu nous as fait** ~ **pour rien** you got us to come *ou* you made us come for nothing; **faire** ~ **son vin de Provence** to get one's wine sent from Provence. (**c**) *(fig)* to come. **le bruit est venu jusqu'à nous que...** word has reached us *ou* come to us that...; **ça ne me serait pas venu à l'idée** *ou* **à l'esprit** that would never have occurred to me *ou* entered my head, I should never have thought of that; **une idée m'est venue (à l'esprit)** an idea crossed my mind, an idea occurred to me; **la semaine qui vient** the coming week; **cette plante vient bien** this plant is coming along *ou* is doing well *ou* nicely; **les années à** ~ the years to come, future years. (**d**) ~ **de** *(provenance, cause)* to come from; *(Ling)* to derive from; **l'épée lui vient de son oncle** the sword has been passed down to him by his uncle; **ces troubles viennent du foie** this trouble stems *ou* comes from the liver; **d'où vient cette hâte soudaine?** what's the reason for this sudden haste?, how come * *ou* why this sudden haste?; **ça vient de ce que...** it comes *ou* results *ou* stems from the fact that... (**e**) *(atteindre)* ~ **(jusqu')à** *(vers le haut)* to come up to, reach (up to); *(vers le bas)* to come down to, reach (down to); *(en longueur, en superficie)* to come out to, reach; **l'eau nous vient aux genoux** the water comes up to *ou* reaches (up to) our knees, we are knee-deep in (the) water; ~ **au monde** to come into the world, be born; ~ **à bout de** *travail, gâteau* to get through; *adversaire* to get the better of, overcome; **je n'en viendrai jamais à bout** I'll never manage it, I'll never get through it, I'll never see the end of it. (**f**) **en** ~ **à: j'en viens maintenant à votre question** I shall now come *ou* turn to your question; **venons-en au fait** let's get to the point; **j'en viens à la conclusion que...** I have come to *ou* reached the conclusion that...; **j'en viens à leur avis** I'm coming round to their opinion; **j'en viens à me demander si...** I'm beginning to wonder if...; **comment les choses en sont-elles venues là?** how did things come to this? *ou* get to this stage?; **en** ~ **aux mains** to come to blows; **où voulez-vous en** ~**?** what are you getting *ou* driving at?

2 *vb aux* (**a**) *(se déplacer pour)* **je suis venu travailler** I have come to work; **il va** ~ **la voir** he's going to come to *ou* and see her; **viens m'aider** come and help me; **ne viens pas te plaindre!** don't (you) come and complain *ou* come complaining. (**b**) *(passé récent)* **il vient d'arriver** he has just arrived; **elle venait de se lever** she had just got up. (**c**) *(éventualité)* **s'il venait à mourir** if he were to die *ou* if he should (happen to) die.

3 *vb impers* (**a**) **il vient beaucoup d'enfants** a lot of children are coming; **il lui est venu des boutons** he came out in spots; **il ne lui viendrait pas à l'idée**

que... it wouldn't occur to him *ou* cross his mind *ou* enter his head that...; **il vient une heure où...** the hour comes when... (**b**) *(éventualité)* **s'il vient à pleuvoir** if it should (happen to) rain. **4 s'en** ~ *vpr (littér)* to come.

Venise [vəniz] *n* Venice.

vent [vɑ̃] *nm* (**a**) wind. ~ **du nord** North wind; ~ **coulis** draught; **un** ~ **de révolte** a wind of revolt; *(Naut)* ~ **contraire** headwind; **au** ~**/sous le** ~ **(de)** to windward/to leeward (of); **bon** ~**!** *(Naut)* fair journey!; *(*: fichez le camp)* good riddance!; **être en plein** ~ to be exposed to the wind; **il y a** *ou* **il fait du** ~ it is windy; **coup de** ~ gust of wind. (**b**) *(Méd)* **avoir des** ~**s** to have wind. (**c**) *(locutions) (lit, fig)* **observer d'où vient le** ~ to see how the wind blows; **le** ~ **est à l'optimisme** there is optimism in the air; *(fig)* **il a le** ~ **en poupe** he has the wind in his sails; **à tous les** ~ **s, aux quatre** ~**s** to the four winds; **être dans le** ~ * to be with it * *ou* hip *, be trendy *; **jeune fille dans le** ~ * trendy *ou* with it * girl *; *(péj)* **c'est du** ~ * it's all wind *ou* hot air *; **avoir** ~ **de** to get wind of; **quel bon** ~ **vous amène?** to what do I (*ou* we) owe the pleasure of seeing you?; **elle l'a fait contre** ~**s et marées** she did it against all the odds *ou* despite all the obstacles.

ventail, pl -aux [vɑ̃taj, o] *nm* ventail.

vente [vɑ̃t] *nf* sale. **bureau/promesse de** ~ sales office/agreement; **être en** ~ **libre** *(gén)* to be freely sold, have no sales restrictions; **en** ~ **chez votre libraire** available *ou* on sale at your local bookshop; **mettre en** ~ *produit* to put on sale; *maison* to put up for sale; **nous n'en avons pas la** ~ we have no demand *ou* sale for that; **la livre vaut 10 F à la** ~ the selling rate for sterling is 10 francs ; ~ **(aux enchères)** (auction) sale, auction; ~ **de charité** charity bazaar, jumble sale, sale of work; ~ **par correspondance** mail-order; ~ **à domicile** door-to-door selling; ~ **à tempérament** hire purchase, installment plan *(US)*.

venter [vɑ̃te] (1) *vb impers*: **il vente** the wind blows. ◆ **venté, e** *adj* windswept, windy.

ventiler [vɑ̃tile] (1) *vt* (**a**) *(aérer)* to ventilate. (**b**) *total* to break down; *crédits, travail* to allocate. (**c**) *(répartir) touristes, élèves* to divide up (into groups). ◆ **ventilateur** *nm (gén)* fan; *(dans un mur, une fenêtre)* ventilator, fan. ◆ **ventilation** *nf* ventilation; breaking down; allocation. *(Méd)* ~ **respiratoire** respiratory ventilation.

ventouse [vɑ̃tuz] *nf (Méd)* cupping glass; *(Zool)* sucker; *(dispositif adhésif)* suction pad; *(pour déboucher)* plunger. **faire** ~ to cling, adhere.

ventre [vɑ̃tʀ(ə)] *nm* (**a**) *(abdomen)* stomach, tummy *. **être étendu sur le** ~ to be lying on one's stomach *ou* front; **avoir/prendre du** ~ to have/be getting rather a paunch; *(fig)* **passer sur le** ~ **de qn** to ride roughshod over sb; **courir** ~ **à terre** to run at top speed. (**b**) *(estomac)* stomach. **avoir le** ~ **creux** to have an empty stomach; **avoir le** ~ **plein** to be full; **avoir mal au** ~ to have stomach ache *ou* (a) tummy ache *; *(fig)* **ça me ferait mal au** ~ ⁑ it would make me sick; *(fig)* **voyons ce que ça a dans le** ~ * let's see what's inside it; *(courage)* **il n'a rien dans le** ~ * he's got no guts *. (**c**) *(utérus)* womb. (**d**) *[animal]* (under)belly; *[vase]* bulb; *[bateau, avion]* belly. ◆ **ventricule** *nm* ventricle. ◆ **ventriloque** *nmf* ventriloquist. ◆ **ventripotent, e** *adj* potbellied. ◆ **ventru, e** *adj personne* potbellied; *objet* bulbous.

venu, e [v(ə)ny] *adj* (**a**) **être bien** ~ **de faire** to have (good) grounds for doing; **être mal** ~ **de faire** to have no grounds for doing, be in no position to do. (**b**) **bien** ~ *remarque* timely, apposite; **mal** ~ *question* untimely, inapposite; **sa remarque était plutôt mal** ~**e** his remark was rather out of place *ou* uncalled-for; **il serait mal** ~ **de lui poser cette question** it would be unseemly to ask him this question. (**c**) **bien** ~ *enfant* sturdy; *plante* sturdy, well-developed, fine. (**d**) *(arrivé)* **tard** ~ late; **tôt** ~ early. ◆ **venue** *nf* coming. **lors de ma** ~ **au monde** when I came into the world.

vêpres [vɛpʀ(ə)] *nfpl* vespers.

ver [vɛʀ] *nm (gén)* worm; *(larve)* grub; *[viande, fruits]* maggot. *[bois]* ~**s** woodworm; ~ **luisant** glowworm; ~ **à soie** silkworm; ~ **solitaire** tapeworm; ~ **de terre** earthworm; **tirer les** ~**s du nez à qn** * to worm information out of sb.

véracité [veʀasite] *nf* veracity, truthfulness.

véranda [veʀɑ̃da] *nf* veranda(h).

verbal, e, *mpl* **-aux** [vɛʀbal, o] *adj (gén)* verbal. **groupe** ~ verb phrase. ◆ **verbalement** *adv* verbally.

verbaliser [vɛʀbalize] (1) *vi*: **l'agent a dû** ~ the officer had to book * *ou* report him (*ou* me *etc*).

verbe [vɛʀb(ə)] *nm* (**a**) *(Gram)* verb. ~ **d'action/d'état** verb of action/state; ~ **fort** strong verb; ~ **à particule** phrasal verb. (**b**) *(Rel, littér: langage)* **le** ~ the word; **avoir le** ~ **haut** to speak in a high and mighty tone.

verbiage [vɛʀbjaʒ] *nm* verbiage.

verdâtre [vɛʀdɑtʀ(ə)] *adj* greenish.

verdeur [vɛʀdœʀ] *nf* (**a**) *(jeunesse)* vigour, vitality. (**b**) *[fruit]* tartness, sharpness; *[vin]* acidity. (**c**) *[langage]* forthrightness.

verdict [vɛʀdik(t)] *nm (Jur, gén)* verdict.

verdir [vɛʀdiʀ] (2) *vti* to turn green.

verdoyant, e [vɛʀdwajɑ̃, ɑ̃t] *adj* green, verdant *(littér)*.

verdure [vɛʀdyʀ] *nf (végétation)* greenery; *(légumes verts)* green vegetables.

véreux, -euse [veʀø, øz] *adj* (**a**) *aliment* maggoty, worm-eaten. (**b**) *financier, affaire* dubious, shady.

verge [vɛʀʒ(ə)] *nf (baguette)* rod; *(Anat)* penis.

verger [vɛʀʒe] *nm* orchard.

verglas [vɛʀgla] *nm* (black) ice *(on road etc)*. ◆ **verglacé, e** *adj* icy, iced-over.

vergogne [vɛʀgɔɲ] *nf*: **sans** ~ *(adj)* shameless; *(adv)* shamelessly.

vergue [vɛʀg(ə)] *nf (Naut)* yard.

véridique [veʀidik] *adj récit, témoin* truthful, veracious; *repentir* genuine, authentic.

vérifier [veʀifje] (7) *vt* (**a**) *(contrôler) (gén)* to check, verify; *(Fin) comptes* to audit. **cela a été vérifié et revérifié** it has been checked and doublechecked. (**b**) *(confirmer, prouver)* to establish *ou* confirm (the truth of), prove to be true; *soupçons, conjecture* to bear out, confirm. **cet accident a vérifié mes craintes** this accident has borne out *ou* confirmed my fears; **ça peut se** ~ **tous les jours** it is borne out every day. ◆ **vérifiable** *adj* verifiable. ◆ **vérificateur, -trice 1** *adj* checking, verifying. **2** *nm, f* controller, checker, inspector. **3** *nf (Tech)* verifier. ◆ **vérification** *nf* (**a**) *(contrôle)* check; *(action)* checking; verification; auditing. ~ **faite** on checking; ~ **d'identité** identity check. (**b**) *(preuve)* proof; *(confirmation)* confirmation.

vérin [veʀɛ̃] *nm* jack.

véritable [veʀitabl(ə)] *adj (gén)* real; *raisons, sentiment, ami* true, genuine; *cuir, perles* genuine. **sous son jour** ~ in its (*ou* his *etc*) true light; **un** ~ **coquin** a real *ou* a downright rogue; **c'est une** ~ **folie** it's absolute *ou* sheer madness. ◆ **véritablement** *adv* really; truly; genuinely. **il l'a** ~ **fait** he actually *ou* really did it; **c'est** ~ **délicieux** it's absolutely *ou* positively *ou* really delicious.

vérité [veʀite] *nf* (**a**) **la** ~ *(connaissance du vrai)* truth; *(conformité aux faits)* the truth; **nul n'est dépositaire de la** ~ no one has a monopoly of truth; **c'est l'entière** ~ it is the whole truth; **dire la** ~ to tell *ou* speak the truth; **la** ~**, c'est qu'il est paresseux**

the truth (of the matter) is, he's lazy. (**b**) *(ressemblance) [portrait]* lifelikeness, trueness to life; *[tableau]* trueness to life. (**c**) *(sincérité)* truthfulness, sincerity. **un air de** ~ an air of sincerity *ou* truthfulness, a truthful *ou* sincere look. (**d**) *(fait vrai)* truth. **~s éternelles/premières** eternal/first truths. (**e**) **c'est (bien) peu de chose, en** ~ it's really *ou* actually nothing very much; **à la** ~ *ou* **en** ~ **il préfère s'amuser** to tell the truth *ou* to be honest he prefers to enjoy himself.

verlan [vɛʀlɑ̃] *nm* (back) slang.

vermeil, -eille [vɛʀmɛj] **1** *adj tissu* vermilion, bright red; *bouche* ruby, cherry; *teint* rosy. **2** *nm (métal)* vermeil.

vermicelle [vɛʀmisɛl] *nm*: **~(s)** vermicelli.

vermifuge [vɛʀmifyʒ] *adj, nm* vermifuge. **poudre** ~ worm powder.

vermillon [vɛʀmijɔ̃] *adj inv, nm* vermilion.

vermine [vɛʀmin] *nf (lit, fig)* vermin.

vermoulu, e [vɛʀmuly] *adj* worm-eaten.

vernir [vɛʀniʀ] (2) *vt* to varnish; *poterie* to glaze. ◆ **verni, e** *adj* (**a**) *bois* varnished; *(luisant)* shiny, glossy. **souliers ~s** patent (leather) shoes. (**b**) *(*: chanceux)* lucky. ◆ **vernis** *nm* varnish; glaze; *(éclat)* shine, gloss. ~ **(à ongles)** nail varnish *ou* polish; **un** ~ **de culture** a veneer of culture. ◆ **vernissage** *nm* (**a**) varnishing; glazing. (**b**) *(exposition)* private viewing, preview *(at art gallery)*.

vérole ⁑ [veʀɔl] *nf* pox ⁑.

verre [vɛʀ] **1** *nm* (**a**) *(substance)* glass. **cela se casse comme du** ~ it's as brittle as glass. (**b**) *[vitre, cadre]* glass; *[lunettes]* lens. **mettre qch sous** ~ to put sth under glass; **porter des ~s** to wear glasses. (**c**) *(récipient, contenu)* glass. ~ **à bière** beer glass; ~ **de bière** glass of beer. (**d**) *(boisson)* drink. **boire** *ou* **prendre un** ~ to have a drink; **un petit** ~ * a quick one *, a dram *; **avoir bu un** ~ **de trop** *, **avoir un** ~ **dans le nez** * to have had one too many *, have had a drop too much *. **2** : ~ **blanc** plain glass; **~s de contact (souples/durs)** (soft/hard) contact lenses; **~s correcteurs (de la vue)** corrective lenses; ~ **à dents** tooth mug *ou* glass; ~ **dépoli** frosted glass; **~s fumés** tinted lenses; ~ **incassable** unbreakable glass; ~ **de montre** watch glass; ~ **à pied** stemmed glass. ◆ **verrerie** *nf (usine)* glassworks, glass factory; *(objets)* glassware; *(commerce)* glass trade *ou* industry. ◆ **verrier** *nm (ouvrier)* glassworker; *(artiste)* glass artist. ◆ **verrière** *nf (fenêtre)* window; *(toit vitré)* glass roof; *(paroi vitrée)* glass wall. ◆ **verroterie** *nf*: **bijoux en** ~ glass jewellery.

verrou [vɛʀu] *nm* (**a**) *[porte]* bolt. **mettre le** ~ to bolt the door; **mettre qn sous les ~s** to put sb behind bars *ou* under lock and key; **être sous les ~s** to be behind bars; *(fig)* **faire sauter le** ~ to break the deadlock. (**b**) *(Ordin)* lock. ◆ **verrouillage** *nm (action)* bolting; locking; *(dispositif)* locking mechanism. *(Aut)* ~ **automatique des portes** central (door) locking. ◆ **verrouiller** (1) *vt porte* to bolt; *culasse* to lock; *(Ordin)* to lock. *(lit, fig)* **ses parents le verrouillent** his parents keep him locked in.

verrue [vɛʀy] *nf* wart. ~ **plantaire** verruca.

vers¹ [vɛʀ] *prép* (**a**) *(direction)* toward(s), to. **en allant** ~ **la gare** going to *ou* towards the station; **il tendit la main** ~ **la bouteille** he reached out for the bottle, he stretched out his hand toward(s) the bottle. (**b**) *(approximation)* around, about. **c'est** ~ **Aix que nous avons eu une panne** it was (somewhere) near Aix *ou* round about Aix that we broke down; ~ **quelle heure doit-il venir?** (at) around *ou* (at) about what time is he due?; **il était** ~ **(les) 3 heures** it was about *ou* around 3; ~ **le début du siècle** toward(s) *ou* about the turn of the century.

vers² [vɛʀ] *nm* (**a**) *(sg: ligne)* line. **au 3e** ~ in line 3, in the 3rd line. (**b**) *(pl: poésie)* verse. **traduction en** ~ verse translation; **faire** *ou* **écrire des** ~ to write verse; ~ **blancs/libres** blank/free verse.

versant [vɛʀsɑ̃] *nm [vallée]* side; *[massif]* slopes.

versatile [vɛʀsatil] *adj* fickle, changeable. ◆ **versatilité** *nf* fickleness, changeability.

verse [vɛʀs(ə)] *adv*: **à** ~ in torrents; **il pleut à** ~ it is pouring down.

versé, e [vɛʀse] *adj*: **~/peu ~ dans qch** (well-) versed/ill-versed in sth.

Verseau [vɛʀso] *nm (Astron)* **le** ~ Aquarius, the Water-carrier; **être (du)** ~ to be Aquarius *ou* an Aquarian.

versement [vɛʀsəmɑ̃] *nm* payment (*sur un compte* into an account); *(échelonné)* instalment. ~ **en espèces** cash deposit; ~ **à une œuvre** donation to a charity.

verser [vɛʀse] (1) **1** *vt* (**a**) *liquide, grains* to pour, tip (*dans* into, *sur* onto); *(servir) thé etc* to pour (out), (*dans* into). **verse-toi à boire** pour yourself a drink. (**b**) *larmes, sang, clarté* to shed. (**c**) *(classer)* ~ **une pièce à un dossier** to add an item to a file. (**d**) *(payer)* to pay. ~ **qch à qn** to pay sb sth; ~ **une somme à un compte** to pay a sum of money into an account; ~ **des arrhes** to put down *ou* pay a deposit. (**e**) *(incorporer)* ~ **qn dans** to assign *ou* attach sb to. **2** *vi* (**a**) *[véhicule]* to overturn. **il va nous faire** ~ **dans le fossé** he'll tip us into the ditch. (**b**) ~ **dans** *sentimentalité* to lapse into. ◆ **verseur, -euse 1** *adj*: **bec** ~ (pouring) lip; **bouchon** ~ pour-through stopper. **2** *nm* pourer.

verset [vɛʀsɛ] *nm (Rel)* verse.

version [vɛʀsjɔ̃] *nf* (**a**) *(traduction)* translation *(into the mother tongue)*, unseen (translation). ~ **anglaise** English unseen (translation), translation from English. (**b**) *(variante)* version. **film en** ~ **originale** film in the original language *ou* version; **film italien en** ~ **française** Italian film dubbed in French; *(Aut)* ~ **4 portes** 4-door model. (**c**) *(interprétation)* version. **donner sa** ~ **des faits** to give one's (own) version of the facts.

verso [vɛʀso] *nm* back. **au** ~ on the back (of the page); **'voir au ~'** 'see over(leaf)'.

vert, verte [vɛʀ, vɛʀt(ə)] **1** *adj* (**a**) *(couleur)* green. ~ **de peur** green with fear. (**b**) *céréale, fruit* unripe, green; *vin* young; *bois* green. (**c**) *vieillard* sprightly, spry. (**d**) *réprimande* sharp, stiff. (**e**) *propos* spicy, saucy. **il en a dit des vertes (et des pas mûres)** * he said some pretty spicy *ou* saucy things. (**f**) *(de la campagne)* **tourisme** ~ country holidays; **classe ~e** school camp; **l'Europe ~e** European agriculture. **2** *nm* (**a**) *(couleur)* green; *(Golf)* green. ~ **olive** *etc* olive *etc* (-green); **mettre un cheval au** ~ to put a horse out to grass *ou* to pasture; *[gangster]* **se mettre au** ~ to hole up * in the country. (**b**) *(Pol: écologistes)* **les V~s** the Greens. ◆ **vert-de-gris 1** *nm inv* verdigris. **2** *adj inv* grey(ish)-green. ◆ **vertement** *adv réprimander* sharply.

vertèbre [vɛʀtɛbʀ(ə)] *nf* vertebra. ◆ **vertébral, e,** *mpl* **-aux** *adj* vertebral. ◆ **vertébré, e** *adj, nm* vertebrate.

vertical, e, *mpl* **-aux** [vɛʀtikal, o] **1** *adj (gén)* vertical; *position du corps* upright. **2** *nf (ligne)* vertical line. *(direction)* **la ~e** the vertical; **à la ~e** *s'élever* vertically. ◆ **verticalement** *adv monter* vertically, straight up; *descendre* vertically, straight down. ◆ **verticalité** *nf* verticalness, verticality.

vertige [vɛʀtiʒ] *nm* (**a**) *(peur du vide)* **le** ~ vertigo; **avoir le** ~ to suffer from vertigo, get dizzy *ou* giddy; **être pris de** ~ to feel dizzy *ou* giddy, have a fit of vertigo; **cela me donne le** ~ it makes me feel dizzy *ou* giddy, it gives me vertigo. (**b**) *(étourdissement)* dizzy *ou* giddy spell *ou* turn. (**c**) *(fig: égarement)* fever. **gagné par le** ~ **de l'expansion...**

having caught the expansion fever... ◆ **vertigineusement** *adv*: ~ **haut** vertiginously *ou* breathtakingly high, of a dizzy height; **les prix montent** ~ prices are rising at a dizzy *ou* breathtaking rate, prices are rocketing. ◆ **vertigineux, -euse** *adj (gén)* breathtaking; *précipice* breathtakingly high; *hauteur* dizzy, giddy.

vertu [vɛʀty] *nf (gén: morale)* virtue; *(littér) (pouvoir)* virtue *(littér)*, power; *(courage)* courage, bravery. **en ~ de** in accordance with. ◆ **vertueusement** *adv* virtuously. ◆ **vertueux, -euse** *adj* virtuous.

verveine [vɛʀvɛn] *nf (plante)* vervain, verbena; *(tisane)* verbena tea; *(liqueur)* vervain liqueur.

vésicule [vezikyl] *nf* vesicle. **la ~ (biliaire)** the gall-bladder.

vespa [vɛspa] *nf* ® Vespa ®.

vespasienne [vɛspazjɛn] *nf* urinal.

vessie [vesi] *nf* bladder. **prendre des ~s pour des lanternes** to believe that the moon is made of green cheese.

veste [vɛst(ə)] *nf* jacket. ~ **droite/croisée** single-/double-breasted jacket; ~ **de pyjama** pyjama jacket *ou* top; **retourner sa ~ *** to turn one's coat; **ramasser une ~ *** *(gén)* to come a cropper *; *(dans une élection)* to be beaten hollow.

vestiaire [vɛstjɛʀ] *nm [théâtre, restaurant]* cloakroom; *[stade, piscine]* changing-room. **(armoire-) ~** locker.

vestibule [vɛstibyl] *nm* hall, vestibule.

vestige [vɛstiʒ] *nm (objet)* relic; *(fragment)* trace; *[coutume, gloire]* vestige, remnant, relic. **~s** *[ville]* remains, vestiges; *[passé]* vestiges, remnants, relics.

vestimentaire [vɛstimɑ̃tɛʀ] *adj*: **élégance ~** sartorial elegance; **fantaisies ~s** eccentricities of dress; **détails ~s** details of one's dress.

veston [vɛstɔ̃] *nm* jacket.

vêtement [vɛtmɑ̃] *nm* (**a**) *(article d'habillement)* garment, item *ou* article of clothing. *(tenue)* **son ~** his clothes; *(Comm: industrie)* **le ~** the clothing industry. (**b**) **~s** clothes; **~s de sport** sports clothes; *(dans magasin)* sportswear; **~s de dessous** underclothes.

vétéran [veteʀɑ̃] *nm (Mil)* veteran; *(fig)* veteran, old hand *.

vétérinaire [veteʀinɛʀ] **1** *nm* vet, veterinary surgeon, veterinarian *(US)*. **2** *adj* veterinary.

vétille [vetij] *nf* trifle, triviality.

vêtir [vetiʀ] (20) **1** *vt (habiller)* to clothe, dress. **2 se ~** *vpr* to dress (o.s.). ◆ **vêtu, e** *adj* dressed. **bien/mal ~** well-/badly-dressed; **~ de** dressed in, wearing.

vétiver [vetivɛʀ] *nm* vetiver.

veto [veto] *nm (Pol, gén)* veto. **opposer son ~ à qch** to veto sth; **je mets mon ~** I veto that; **droit de ~** right of veto.

vétuste [vetyst(ə)] *adj* ancient, dilapidated. ◆ **vétusté** *nf* dilapidation.

veuf, veuve [vœf, vœv] **1** *adj* widowed. **il est deux fois ~** he has been twice widowed, he is a widower twice over. **2** *nm* widower. **3** *nf (gén)* widow. ◆ **veuvage** *nm [femme]* widowhood; *[homme]* widowerhood.

vexer [vɛkse] (1) **1** *vt* to hurt, upset. **être vexé par qch** to be hurt by sth, be upset at sth. **2 se ~** *vpr* to be hurt (*de* by), be upset (*de* at). ◆ **vexant, e** *adj (contrariant)* annoying; *(blessant) paroles* hurtful (*pour* to). ◆ **vexation** *nf* humiliation.

via [vja] *prép* via.

viabilité [vjabilite] *nf* (**a**) *[chemin]* practicability. **avec/sans ~** *terrain* with/without services (laid on), serviced/unserviced. (**b**) *[entreprise]* viability. ◆ **viable** *adj situation, enfant* viable.

viaduc [vjadyk] *nm* viaduct.

viager, -ère [vjaʒe, ɛʀ] **1** *adj*: **rente ~ère** life annuity. **2** *nm (rente)* life annuity; *(bien) property mortgaged for a life annuity.* **mettre un bien en ~** *to sell a property in return for a life annuity.*

viande [vjɑ̃d] *nf* meat. ~ **rouge/blanche** red/white meat; ~ **de boucherie** (butcher's *ou* fresh) meat; ~ **hachée** minced meat, hamburger *(US)*.

vibrer [vibʀe] (1) *vi (gén, Phys)* to vibrate; *[voix]* to quiver, be vibrant *ou* resonant; *[personne]* to thrill (*de* with), be stirred (*de* by). **faire ~** *objet* to vibrate; *auditoire* to stir, thrill; **~ d'enthousiasme** to be vibrant with enthusiasm. ◆ **vibrant, e** *adj membrane* vibrating; *voix* vibrant, resonant; *discours, nature* emotive. **~ de** vibrant with. ◆ **vibration** *nf (gén, Phys)* vibration. ◆ **vibratoire** *adj* vibratory.

vicaire [vikɛʀ] *nm [paroisse]* curate. *[évêque]* **~ général** vicar-general.

vice [vis] *nm* (**a**) *(moral)* vice. **vivre dans le ~** to live a life of vice. (**b**) *(défectuosité)* fault, defect; *(Jur)* defect. ~ **de construction** fault *ou* defect in construction; ~ **de forme** legal flaw *ou* irregularity; ~ **caché** latent defect.

vice- [vis] *préf* vice-. **~-amiral** *nm, pl* **~-~aux** vice-admiral; **~-président, e** *nm, f, mpl* **~-~s** vice-president, vice-chairman; **~-roi** *nm, pl* **~-~s** viceroy.

vice versa [visevɛʀsa] *adv* vice versa.

vicier [visje] (7) *vt atmosphère* to pollute, taint; *sang* to contaminate, taint; *rapports* to taint. ◆ **vicieusement** *adv* pervertedly. ◆ **vicieux, -euse 1** *adj personne, penchant* perverted, depraved; *cheval* restive, unruly; *attaque, balle* well-disguised, nasty *; *prononciation, expression* incorrect, wrong. **2** *nm, f* pervert.

vicinal, e, *mpl* **-aux** [visinal, o] *adj*: **chemin ~** by-road, byway.

vicissitudes [visisityd] *nfpl (gén)* vicissitudes.

vicomte [vikɔ̃t] *nm* viscount. ◆ **vicomtesse** *nf* viscountess.

victime [viktim] *nf (gén)* victim; *[accident]* casualty, victim; *(Jur)* aggrieved party, victim. **être ~ de** to be the victim of.

victoire [viktwaʀ] *nf (gén)* victory; *(Sport)* win, victory. ~ **aux points** win on points; **crier ~** to crow (over one's victory). ◆ **victorieusement** *adv* victoriously; triumphantly. ◆ **victorieux, -euse** *adj armée* victorious; *équipe* winnning, victorious; *air* triumphant.

victuailles [viktɥɑj] *nfpl* provisions.

vidange [vidɑ̃ʒ] *nf* (**a**) *[réservoir]* emptying; *(Aut)* oil change. *(Aut)* **faire la ~** to change the oil. (**b**) *(dispositif) [lavabo]* waste outlet. ◆ **vidanger** (3) *vt réservoir* to empty; *liquide* to empty out.

vide [vid] **1** *adj (lit, fig)* empty; *appartement* empty, vacant. **avoir l'estomac** *ou* **le ventre ~** to have an empty stomach; *(Comm)* **bouteilles ~s** empty bottles, empties *; **sa vie était ~** his life was empty *ou* a void; **~ de** *(gén)* empty *ou* (de)void of; **~ de sens** *mot* meaningless; **les rues ~s de voitures** the streets empty *ou* devoid of cars. **2** *nm* (**a**) *(absence d'air)* vacuum. **sous ~** under vacuum; **emballé sous ~** vacuum-packed; **emballage sous ~** vacuum packing. (**b**) *(trou) (entre objets)* gap, empty space; *(Archit)* void. *(Constr)* **~ sanitaire** underfloor space. (**c**) *(abîme)* drop. *(l'espace)* **le ~** the void; **être au-dessus du ~** to be over *ou* above a drop; **tomber dans le ~** to fall into empty space *ou* into the void; **avoir peur du ~** to be afraid of heights, have no head for heights. (**d**) *(néant)* emptiness. **le ~ de l'existence** the emptiness of life; **regarder dans le ~** to gaze *ou* stare into space *ou* emptiness. (**e**) *(fig: manque)* **un ~ douloureux dans son cœur** an aching void in one's heart; **~ juridique** gap in the law. (**f**) *(loc)* **faire le ~ autour**

de soi to isolate o.s.; **faire le ~ dans son esprit** to make one's mind a blank; **parler dans le ~** *(sans objet)* to talk vacuously; *(personne n'écoute)* to waste one's breath; *[camion]* **repartir à ~** to go off again empty.

vidéo [video] **1** *adj inv* video. **caméra/jeu ~** video camera/game. **2** *nf* video.

vidéocassette [videokasɛt] *nf* video cassette.

vidéoclip [videɔklip] *nm (chanson)* video.

vidéoclub [videɔklœb] *nm* videoclub.

vidéodisque [videɔdisk(ə)] *nm* videodisk.

vidéothèque [videɔtɛk] *nf* video library.

vider [vide] (1) **1** *vt* (**a**) *récipient, meuble, pièce* to empty; *étang, citerne* to empty, drain; *contenu* to empty (out). **~ un appartement de ses meubles** to empty *ou* clear a flat of its furniture; **il vida son verre** he emptied *ou* drained his glass; **ils ont vidé tous les tiroirs** they cleaned out *ou* emptied all the drawers. (**b**) *poisson, poulet* to gut, clean out; *pomme* to core. (**c**) *querelle* to settle. (**d**) *cavalier* to throw. **~ les étriers** to leave the stirrups. (**e**) *(*: expulser)* to throw out *, chuck out * (*de* of). (**f**) *(*: épuiser)* to wear out. (**g**) *(locutions)* **~ son sac *** to come out with it *; **~ l'abcès** to root out the evil; **~ son cœur** to pour out one's heart; **~ les lieux** to quit *ou* vacate the premises. **2 se ~** *vpr* to empty. ◆ **vide-ordures** *nm inv* (rubbish) chute. ◆ **vide-poches** *nm inv* tidy; *(Aut)* glove compartment.

vie [vi] *nf* (**a**) *(gén)* life. **être en ~** to be alive; **être bien en ~** to be well and truly alive, be alive and kicking *; **donner la ~** to give birth (*à* to); **plein de ~** full of life; **rappeler qn à la ~** to bring sb back to life; **attends de connaître la ~ pour juger** wait until you know (something) about life before you pass judgment; **sa présence met de la ~ dans la maison** he brings some life *ou* a bit of life into the house. (**b**) *(activités)* life. **dans la ~ courante** in everyday life; **(mode de) ~** way of life, life style; **la ~ de garçon** a bachelor's life *ou* existence; **la ~ d'un professeur n'est pas toujours drôle** a teacher's life *ou* the life of a teacher isn't always fun; **la ~ des animaux** animal life; **~ de bohème** bohemian way of life *ou* life style; **mener la ~ de château** to live a life of luxury. (**c**) *(moyens matériels)* living. **(le coût de) la ~** the cost of living; **la ~ chère** the high cost of living. (**d**) *(durée)* life(time). **toute sa ~** all his life; **ça n'arrive qu'une seule fois dans la ~** it only happens once in a lifetime. (**e**) *(biographie)* life (story). **elle m'a raconté sa ~** she told me her life story *ou* the story of her life. (**f**) *(locutions)* **à ~, pour la ~** for life; **passer de ~ à trépas** to pass on; **faire passer qn de ~ à trépas** to dispatch sb into the next world; **une question de ~ ou de mort** a matter of life and death; **c'était la belle ~!** those were the days!; **il a la belle ~** he has an easy *ou* cushy * life; **c'est la belle ~!** this is the life!; **ce n'est pas une ~!** it's a rotten * *ou* hard life!; **c'est une ~ de chien! *** it's a rotten *ou* a dog's life! *; **c'est la ~!** that's life!; **jamais de ma ~** never in my life; **jamais de la ~!** never!, not on your life! *; **être entre la ~ et la mort** to be at death's door; **avoir la ~ dure** *[personne]* to have nine lives; *[superstitions]* to die hard; **mener la ~ dure à qn** to give sb a hard time of it; **sans ~** *(mort)* lifeless; *(évanoui)* unconscious; *(amorphe)* lifeless, listless; **refaire sa ~ (avec qn)** to make a new life (with sb); **faire la ~** *(se débaucher)* to live it up, lead a life of pleasure; *(*: faire une scène)* to kick up * a row, make a scene; **laisser la ~ sauve à qn** to spare sb's life; **voir la ~ en rose** to see life through rose-coloured glasses, take a rosy view of life.

vieillesse [vjɛjɛs] *nf [personne]* old age; *[chose]* age, oldness. **aide à la ~** help for the old *ou* the elderly *ou* the aged. ◆ **vieil, vieille** *V* **vieux.** ◆ **vieillard** *nm* old man. **les ~s** the elderly, old people. ◆ **vieillerie** *nf* old-fashioned thing. ◆ **vieillir** (2) **1** *vi (prendre de l'âge)* to grow *ou* get old; *(paraître plus vieux)* to age; *[mot, doctrine]* to become (out)dated; *[vin, fromage]* to age. **je la trouve très vieillie** I find she has aged a lot. **2** *vt*: **~ qn** *[coiffure, maladie]* to age sb, put years on sb; *(par fausse estimation)* to make sb older than he (really) is. **3 se ~** *vpr* to make o.s. older. ◆ **vieillissant, e** *adj* ageing. ◆ **vieillissement** *nm [personne, vin]* ageing; *[doctrine, œuvre]* becoming (out)dated. ◆ **vieillot, -otte** *adj (démodé)* antiquated, quaint.

Vienne [vjɛn] *n (en Autriche)* Vienna.

vierge [vjɛʀʒ(ə)] **1** *nf* (**a**) virgin. **la (Sainte) V~** the (Blessed) Virgin; **la V~ (Marie)** the Virgin (Mary). (**b**) *(Astron)* **la V~** Virgo, the Virgin; **être de la V~** to be Virgo *ou* a Virgoan. **2** *adj* (**a**) *personne* virgin. **être ~** to be a virgin. (**b**) *feuille de papier* blank, virgin; *film* unexposed; *bande magnétique, disquette d'ordinateur* blank; *casier judiciaire* clean; *terre, neige* virgin. (**c**) **~ de** free from.

Viet-Nam, Vietnam [vjɛtnam] *nm* Vietnam. **~ du Nord/du Sud** North/South Vietnam. ◆ **vietnamien, -ienne** *adj, nm,* **V~(ne)** *nm (f)* Vietnamese.

vieux [vjø], *f* **vieille** [vjɛj], *msg* **vieil** [vjɛj] *devant voyelle ou h muet, mpl* **vieux** [vjø] **1** *adj* (**a**) *(âgé)* old. **très ~** ancient, very old; **la vieille génération** the older generation; **les vieilles gens** old people, old folk, the aged *ou* elderly; **il est plus ~ que moi** he is older than I am; **~ comme le monde** as old as the hills; **il commence à se faire ~** he is getting on (in years), he's beginning to get old; **sur ses ~ jours** in his old age; **il n'a pas fait de ~ os** he didn't last *ou* live long. (**b**) *(de longue date) ami, habitude* old, long-standing; *coutumes, famille* old, ancient. **de vieille race** of ancient lineage; **connaître qn de vieille date** to have known sb for a very long time. (**c**) *(précédent)* old, former, previous. **ma vieille voiture était plus rapide que la nouvelle** my old *ou* previous car was quicker than the new one; **il est de la vieille école** he belongs to the old school; **dans le bon ~ temps** in the good old days *ou* times. (**d**) *(expérimenté) marin, soldat* old, seasoned. **un ~ renard** a sly old dog *ou* fox; **un ~ routier de la politique** a wily old politician.

2 *nm* (**a**) old man. **les ~** the old *ou* aged *ou* elderly, old people, old folk *; **un ~ de la vieille *** one of the old brigade; *(père)* **le ~ ‡** my old man ‡; *(parents)* **ses ~ ‡** his folks *; **mon ~ *** old man * *ou* chap * *ou* boy * *ou* buddy * *(US)*. (**b**) **préférer le ~ au neuf** to prefer old things to new.

3 *nf* old woman. *(mère)* **la vieille ‡** my old woman ‡ *ou* lady ‡; **ma vieille *** old girl *; *(à un homme)* old man * *ou* chap * *ou* boy *.

4 *adv vivre* to a ripe old age; *s'habiller* old.

5 : **vieille bique ‡** old bag ‡; *(hum)* **vieille branche** old bean *; **vieille fille** spinster, old maid; **~ garçon** bachelor; **~ gâteux** old dodderer *; **~ jeton *** *ou* **schnock ‡** old misery *; **~ jeu** *adj inv* old-fashioned, old hat; **vieille noix *** (silly) old twit ‡ *ou* fathead ‡.

vif, vive[1] [vif, viv] **1** *adj* (**a**) *personne (plein de vie)* lively, vivacious; *(alerte)* sharp, quick; *rythme* lively; *imagination, intelligence* lively, keen. **il a l'œil ~** he has a sharp *ou* keen eye; **à l'esprit ~** quick-witted; **eau vive** running water. (**b**) *(emporté) personne* sharp, brusque, quick-tempered ; *ton, propos* sharp, brusque, curt. (**c**) *(profond) émotion, plaisir, déception etc* keen, intense; *souvenirs, impression* vivid; *satisfaction* deep, great; *critiques, réprobation* strong, severe; *impatience* great; *penchant* strong; *lumière, éclat* bright, brilliant; *couleur* vivid, brilliant; *froid* biting, bitter; *douleur* sharp; *vent* keen. **à vive allure** at a brisk pace; **avec mes plus ~s remerciements** with my most profound

thanks; **c'est avec un ~ plaisir que...** it is with very great pleasure that...; **l'air ~ les revigorait** the bracing *ou* sharp air gave them new life. (**d**) *(à nu) pierre* bare; *joints* dry; *(acéré) arête* sharp. (**e**) *(locutions)* **brûler ~ qn** to burn sb alive; **de vive voix** *renseigner, remercier* personally, in person.
2 *nm* (**a**) **à ~** *chair* bared; *plaie* open; **avoir les nerfs à ~** to be on edge; **piqué au ~** cut *ou* hurt to the quick; **couper dans le ~** to cut into the living flesh; **entrer dans le ~ du sujet** to get to the heart of the matter; **prendre qn en photo sur le ~** to photograph sb in a real-life situation; **faire un reportage sur le ~** to do a live *ou* on-the-spot broadcast; **les réactions de qn sur le ~** sb's instant *ou* on-the-spot reactions. (**b**) *(Pêche)* live bait. **pêcher au ~** to fish with live bait. (**c**) *(Jur: personne)* living person. **donation entre ~s** donation inter vivos.

vigie [viʒi] *nf (matelot)* look-out, watch; *(poste)* look-out post.

vigilant, e [viʒilɑ̃, ɑ̃t] *adj personne, œil* vigilant, watchful; *soins* vigilant. ◆ **vigilance** *nf* vigilance; watchfulness.

vigile [viʒil] *nm (Hist)* watch; *(veilleur de nuit)* (night) watchman; *[police privée]* vigilante.

vigne [viɲ] *nf (plante)* vine; *(vignoble)* vineyard. **~ vierge** Virginia creeper. ◆ **vigneron, -onne** *nm, f* wine grower. ◆ **vignoble** *nm* vineyard.

vignette [viɲɛt] *nf (Art: motif)* vignette; *(illustration)* illustration; *(Comm: timbre)* label. *(Aut)* **la ~** ≃ the (road) tax disc, (annual) licence tag *(US)*.

vigoureux, -euse [viguʀø, øz] *adj (gén)* vigorous, robust; *bras, mains* strong, powerful; *style* vigorous, energetic; *résistance* vigorous, strenuous. ◆ **vigoureusement** *adv* vigorously. ◆ **vigueur** *nf* (**a**) vigour; robustness; strength; energy. (**b**) **en ~** *loi* in force; *formule* current, in use; **entrer en ~** to come into force *ou* effect; **en ~ depuis hier** in force as of *ou* from yesterday; **cesser d'être en ~** to cease to apply.

vil, e [vil] *adj* (**a**) *(méprisable)* vile, base. (**b**) **à ~ prix** at a very low price.

vilain, e [vilɛ̃, ɛn] **1** *adj* (**a**) *(laid) personne* ugly (-looking); *vêtement* ugly, unattractive; *couleur* nasty. **le V~ petit canard** the Ugly Duckling. (**b**) *temps* nasty, bad, lousy *; *odeur, blessure, affaire* nasty, bad. (**c**) *(méchant) enfant, conduite* naughty; *action, pensée* wicked. **jouer un ~ tour à qn** to play a nasty *ou* mean trick on sb; **c'est un ~ monsieur** he's a nasty customer. **2** *nm* (**a**) *(Hist)* villain. (**b**) (*) **il va y avoir du ~** it's going to turn nasty.

vilebrequin [vilbʀəkɛ̃] *nm (outil)* (bit-)brace; *(Aut)* crankshaft.

villa [villa] *nf* villa, (detached) house.

village [vilaʒ] *nm* village. **~ de toile** tent village. ◆ **villageois, e** **1** *adj* village. **2** *nm, f* villager.

ville [vil] **1** *nf* (**a**) town; *(plus importante)* city. **en ~, à la ~** in town, in the city; **aller en ~** to go into town; **les gens de la ~** townspeople; *(vie)* **aimer la ~** to like town *ou* city life; *(quartier)* **la vieille ~** the old (part of) town. (**b**) *(municipalité)* ≃ local authority, town *ou* city council. **2** : **~ champignon** mushroom town; **~ d'eaux** spa (town); **~ satellite** satellite town.

villégiature [vileʒjatyʀ] *nf*: **aller en/être en ~ quelque part** to go on/be on holiday *ou* vacation *(US)* somewhere; **(lieu de) ~** (holiday *ou* vacation *(US)*) resort.

vin [vɛ̃] *nm* wine. **~ chaud** mulled wine; **~ cuit** liqueur wine; *(réunion)* **~ d'honneur** reception *(where wine is served)*; **être entre deux ~s** to be tipsy.

vinaigre [vinɛgʀ(ə)] *nm* vinegar. **tourner au ~ *** to turn sour. ◆ **vinaigré, e** *adj*: **trop** *etc* **~** with too much *etc* vinegar. ◆ **vinaigrette** *nf* French dressing, vinaigrette, oil and vinegar dressing.

vindicatif, -ive [vɛ̃dikatif, iv] *adj* vindictive.

vingt [vɛ̃] *([vɛ̃t] en liaison et dans les nombres de 22 à 29) adj inv, nm inv* twenty. **je te l'ai dit ~ fois** I've told you a hundred times; **il n'avait plus ses jambes de ~ ans** he no longer had the legs of a young man; **il mérite ~ sur ~** he deserves full marks; **~-quatre heures sur ~-quatre** round the clock, twenty-four hours a day; *V* **six, soixante.** ◆ **vingtaine** *nf*: **une ~** about twenty, twenty or so, (about) a score. ◆ **vingtième** *adj, nmf* twentieth. ◆ **vingtièmement** *adv* in the twentieth place.

vinicole [vinikɔl] *adj industrie* wine; *région* wine-growing, wine-producing; *établissement* wine-making.

vinyle [vinil] *nm* vinyl.

viol [vjɔl] *nm [femme]* rape; *[temple]* violation, desecration.

violacé, e [vjɔlase] *adj* purplish, mauvish.

violent, e [vjɔlɑ̃, ɑ̃t] *adj (gén)* violent; *effort* violent, strenuous; *besoin* intense, urgent. ◆ **violemment** *adv* violently. ◆ **violence** *nf* violence. **commettre des ~s contre qn** to assault sb, commit acts of violence against sb; **se faire ~** to force o.s.; **faire ~ à** to do violence to. ◆ **violenter** (1) *vt femme* to assault (sexually).

violer [vjɔle] (1) *vt (gén)* to violate; *promesse* to break; *temple* to desecrate; *femme* to rape. ◆ **violation** *nf (gén)* violation; *[promesse]* breaking; *[sépulture]* desecration. *(Jur)* **~ de domicile** forcible entry *(into a person's home)*; **~ du secret professionnel** breach *ou* violation of professional secrecy.

violet, -ette [vjɔlɛ, ɛt] **1** *adj* purple; *(pâle)* violet. **2** *nm (couleur)* purple; *(pâle)* violet. **3** *nf (Bot)* violet.

violon [vjɔlɔ̃] *nm* (**a**) *(instrument, musicien)* violin, fiddle *. *(personne)* **premier ~** leader. (**b**) *(*: prison)* cells *(pl)*, jug ‡. (**c**) **~ d'Ingres** (artistic) hobby. ◆ **violoniste** *nmf* violonist, violin-player, fiddler *.

violoncelle [vjɔlɔ̃sɛl] *nm* cello. ◆ **violoncelliste** *nmf* cellist, cello-player.

vipère [vipɛʀ] *nf* adder, viper. **langue de ~** viper's tongue.

virage [viʀaʒ] *nm [véhicule, coureur]* turn; *[politique]* change in policy *ou* direction; *(Aut: tournant)* bend, turn *(US)*. **prendre un ~ à la corde** to hug the bend; *(Ski)* **~ parallèle** parallel turn; **~ en épingle à cheveux** hairpin bend; **~ relevé** banked corner; **un ~ à 180 degrés de la politique française** a U-turn in French politics.

virée * [viʀe] *nf (en voiture)* drive, run; *(à pied)* walk; *(en vélo)* run; *(de plusieurs jours)* trip, tour; *(dans les cafés etc)* tour. **faire une ~** to go for a run (*ou* walk, drive *etc*).

virement [viʀmɑ̃] *nm*: **~ (bancaire)** credit transfer; **~ postal** ≃ (National) Giro transfer.

virer [viʀe] (1) **1** *vi* (**a**) *(changer de direction)* to turn. **~ sur l'aile** to bank; **~ de bord** to tack. (**b**) *[couleur]* to turn, change; *(Phot) [épreuves]* to tone; *(Méd) [cuti-réaction]* to come up positive. **bleu qui vire au violet** blue which is turning purple *ou* changing to purple; **~ à l'aigre** to turn sour; *[temps]* **~ au froid/au beau** to turn cold/fine *ou* fair. **2** *vt* (**a**) *(Fin)* to transfer *(à un compte* (in)to an account). (**b**) *(*: expulser)* to kick out *, chuck out *. **se faire ~** to get (o.s.) kicked * *ou* chucked out *. (**c**) *(Méd)* **il a viré sa cuti** he gave a positive skin test.

virevolter [viʀvɔlte] (1) *vi [danseuse]* to twirl around; *[cheval]* to do a demivolt. ◆ **virevolte** *nf* twirl; demivolt.

virginité [viʀʒinite] *nf [femme]* virginity, maidenhood; *[âme]* purity.

virgule [viʀgyl] *nf (ponctuation)* comma; *(Math)* (decimal) point. **5 ~ 2** 5 point 2; **~ flottante** floating decimal.

viril, e [viʀil] *adj attributs* male, masculine; *attitude, traits* manly, virile; *prouesses* virile. ◆ **virilement** *adv* in a manly *ou* virile way. ◆ **virilité** *nf* masculinity; manliness; virility.

virtuel, -elle [viʀtɥɛl] *adj (gén)* potential; *(Philos, Phys)* virtual. ◆ **virtuellement** *adv (en puissance)* potentially; *(pratiquement)* virtually.

virtuose [viʀtɥoz] *nmf (Mus)* virtuoso; *(fig: artiste)* master, virtuoso. ◆ **virtuosité** *nf* virtuosity.

virulence [viʀylɑ̃s] *nf* virulence. ◆ **virulent, e** *adj* virulent.

virus [viʀys] *nm (lit)* virus. *(fig)* **le ~ du jeu** the gambling bug.

vis [vis] *nf* screw. **escalier à ~** spiral staircase; **~ sans fin** worm, endless screw; *(Aut)* **~ platinées** (contact) points.

visa [viza] *nm (gén)* stamp; *[passeport]* visa. **~ de censure** (censor's) certificate; *(fig)* **~ pour...** passport to...; *(Fin)* **carte ~** ® Visa ® card.

visage [vizaʒ] *nm* face. **au ~ pâle** pale-faced; **V~ pâle** paleface; **agir à ~ découvert** to act openly; **faire bon ~ à qn** to put on a show of friendliness for sb. ◆ **visagiste** *nmf* beautician.

vis-à-vis [vizavi] **1** *prép*: **~ de** *(en face de)* opposite, vis-à-vis; *(comparé à)* beside, vis-à-vis, next to; *(envers)* towards, vis-à-vis; **sincère ~ de soi-même** frank with o.s.; **j'en ai honte ~ de lui** I'm ashamed of it in front of *ou* before him. **2** *adv (face à face)* face to face. **se faire ~** to be facing *ou* opposite each other. **3** *nm inv (personne)* person opposite; *(maison)* house opposite. **immeuble sans ~** building with an open *ou* unimpeded outlook.

viscères [visɛʀ] *nmpl* intestines. ◆ **viscéral, e,** *mpl* **-aux** *adj (Anat)* visceral; *peur* visceral, deep-seated, deep-rooted. ◆ **viscéralement** *adv*: **détester ~ qch** to have a gut * *ou* visceral hatred of sth; **~ jaloux** pathologically jealous.

viscose [viskoz] *nf* viscose.

viscosité [viskozite] *nf* viscosity.

viser [vize] (1) **1** *vt* (**a**) *cible, effet, carrière* to aim at. (**b**) *(concerner) [mesure, remarque]* to be aimed at, be directed at. **cette mesure vise tout le monde** this measure applies to everyone; **se sentir visé** to feel one is being got at *. (**c**) (*: *regarder)* to take a look at. (**d**) *(Admin) passeport* to visa; *document* to stamp. **faire ~ un passeport** to have a passport visaed. **2** *vi [tireur]* to aim, take aim. **~ juste** to aim accurately; **~ à la tête** to aim for the head; *(fig: ambitionner)* **~ haut** to set one's sights high, aim high. **3 ~ à** *vt indir*: **~ à qch/à faire** *[personne]* to aim at sth/at doing *ou* to do; *[mesures]* to be aimed at sth/at doing. ◆ **visée** *nf* (**a**) *(avec une arme)* aiming. **pour faciliter la ~** to help one's aim, help in taking aim. (**b**) *(desseins)* **~s** aim, design; **avoir des ~s sur** to have designs on. ◆ **viseur** *nm [arme]* sights; *[caméra, appareil photo]* viewfinder; *(Astron: lunette)* telescopic sight.

visible [vizibl(ə)] *adj (gén)* visible; *embarras* obvious, evident, visible; *progrès* clear, perceptible. **il est ~ que...** it is obvious *ou* apparent *ou* clear that...; **Monsieur est-il ~?** is Mr X seeing *ou* is Mr X receiving visitors?; **elle n'est pas ~ le matin** she's not at home to visitors in the morning. ◆ **visibilité** *nf* visibility. **sans ~** *pilotage, virage* blind. ◆ **visiblement** *adv* visibly, obviously, clearly.

visière [vizjɛʀ] *nf [casquette]* peak; *(en celluloïd)* eyeshade; *[armure]* visor.

vision [vizjɔ̃] *nf* (**a**) *(vue)* (eye)sight, vision. **champ de ~** field of view *ou* vision; **~ nette** clear vision; **porter des lunettes pour la ~ de loin** to wear glasses for seeing at a distance. (**b**) *(conception)* vision. (**c**) *(apparition)* vision. **tu as des ~s *** you're seeing things. ◆ **visionnaire** *adj, nmf* visionary. ◆ **visionner** (1) *vt* to view. ◆ **visionneuse** *nf (Ciné, Phot)* viewer.

visite [vizit] *nf* (**a**) *(action) [pays etc]* visiting; *[bagages]* examination, inspection. *(à l'hôpital)* **heures de ~** visiting hours; **la ~ du château a duré 2 heures** it took 2 hours to go round the castle. (**b**) *(tournée) (gén)* visit; *[ami, représentant]* visit, call; *[inspecteur]* visit, inspection. **~ guidée** guided tour; **en ~ officielle en France** on an official visit to France; **rendre ~ à qn** to pay sb a visit, call on sb, visit sb; **avoir la ~ de qn** to have a visit from sb. (**c**) *(visiteur)* visitor. **nous attendons de la ~** *ou* **des ~s** we are expecting visitors *ou* company *ou* guests. (**d**) *(Méd)* **~ médicale** medical examination; **~ (à domicile)** (house)call, visit; **~ de contrôle** follow-up visit; **la ~** *(chez le médecin)* (medical) consultation; *(Mil)* sick parade; *[recrue etc]* **passer à la ~ (médicale)** to have a medical *ou* physical *(US)* examination. ◆ **visiter** (1) *vt* (**a**) *pays* to visit; *château* to go round, visit; *maison à vendre* to go *ou* look over, view. **il nous a fait ~ la maison** he showed us round the house. (**b**) *bagages* to examine, inspect; *recoins* to search (in); *navire* to inspect; *(hum) coffre-fort* to visit. (**c**) *[médecin, représentant]* to visit, call on. ◆ **visiteur, -euse** *nm, f* visitor.

vison [vizɔ̃] *nm* mink; *(manteau)* mink (coat).

visqueux, -euse [viskø, øz] *adj (gén)* viscous; *surface* sticky; *(fig) personne, manière* smarmy, slimy.

visser [vise] (1) *vt* (**a**) to screw on. **ce n'est pas bien vissé** it's not screwed down *ou* up properly; *(fig)* **rester vissé sur sa chaise** to be rooted *ou* glued to one's chair. (**b**) (*: *surveiller) élève, employé* to keep a tight rein on.

visu [vizy] *adv*: **de ~** with one's own eyes.

visuel, -elle [vizɥɛl] **1** *adj (gén)* visual. **troubles ~s** eye trouble. **2** *nm (Ordin)* visual display unit, VDU. **~ graphique** graphical display unit. ◆ **visuellement** *adv* visually.

vital, e, *mpl* **-aux** [vital, o] *adj* vital. ◆ **vitalité** *nf* vitality.

vitamine [vitamin] *nf* vitamin. ◆ **vitaminé, e** *adj* with added vitamins.

vite [vit] *adv* (**a**) *(rapidement)* quickly, fast; *(en hâte)* in a rush *ou* hurry. **c'est ~ fait** it doesn't take long, it's done in a jiffy *; **ça ne va pas ~** it's slow work; **fais ~!** be quick about it!; **le temps passe ~** time flies; **vous allez un peu ~ en besogne *** you're working too fast, you're a bit too quick off the mark; **aller plus ~ que la musique** to jump the gun. (**b**) *(tôt)* soon, in no time. **on a ~ fait de dire que...** it's easy to say that...; **il eut ~ fait de découvrir que...** he soon *ou* quickly discovered that..., he discovered in no time that... (**c**) *(toute de suite)* quick. **lève-toi ~!** get up quick!; **eh, pas si ~!** hey, not so fast!, hey, hold on (a minute)!; **il faut le prévenir au plus ~** he must be warned as quickly *ou* as soon as possible; **~! un médecin** quick! a doctor; **et plus ~ que ça!** and get a move on! *, and be quick about it!

vitesse [vitɛs] *nf* (**a**) *(promptitude)* speed, quickness. **en ~** *(rapidement)* quickly; *(en hâte)* in a hurry *ou* rush; **faites-moi ça en ~** do this for me quickly; **faites-moi ça, et en ~!** do this for me and be quick about it!; **écrire un petit mot en ~** to scribble a hasty note; **à toute ~, en quatrième ~** at full *ou* top speed. (**b**) *[véhicule, courant]* speed. **~ acquise** momentum; **~ de croisière** cruising speed; **à quelle ~ allait-il?** what speed was he going at? *ou* doing?; **faire de la ~** to go *ou* drive fast; **prendre de la ~** to pick up *ou* gather speed; **gagner qn de ~** *(lit)* to beat sb; *(fig)* to beat sb to it; **il est parti à la ~ grand V *** he went tearing off *, he left like a bullet from a gun; *(Rail)* **expédier un colis en petite/grande ~** to send a parcel by slow/express goods service. (**c**) *(Aut)* gear. **changer de ~** to change gear; **en 2ᵉ/4ᵉ ~** in 2nd/4th gear; **passer les ~s** to go *ou* run through the gears.

viticole [vitikɔl] *adj industrie* wine; *région* wine-growing *ou* -producing; *établissement* wine-making. ◆ **viticulteur** *nm* wine grower. ◆ **viticulture** *nf* wine growing.

vitre [vitʀ(ə)] *nf [fenêtre, vitrine]* (window) pane; *[voiture]* window. **les camions font trembler les ~s** the lorries make the window panes *ou* the windows rattle; **casser une ~** to break a window (pane); *(Aut)* **la ~ arrière** the rear window. ◆ **vitrage** *nm (vitres)* windows; *(cloison)* glass partition. **double ~** double glazing. ◆ **vitrail,** *pl* **-aux** *nm* stained-glass window. ◆ **vitré, e** *adj* glass. ◆ **vitrer** (1) *vt* to glaze, put glass in. ◆ **vitrerie** *nf (activité)* glaziery, glazing; *(marchandise)* glass. ◆ **vitreux, -euse** *adj (Anat, Géol)* vitreous; *yeux* glassy, dull; *eau* dull. ◆ **vitrier** *nm* glazier.

vitrifier [vitʀifje] (7) *vt (par fusion)* to vitrify; *(par enduit)* to glaze, put a glaze on; *parquet* to seal, varnish. ◆ **vitrification** *nf* vitrification; glazing.

vitrine [vitʀin] *nf* (**a**) *(devanture)* (shop) window. **en ~** in the window. (**b**) *(armoire)* display cabinet.

vitriol [vitʀijɔl] *nm* vitriol.

vitupérer [vitypeʀe] (6) *vi* to vituperate (*contre* against), rant and rave (*contre* about). ◆ **vitupérations** *nfpl* vituperations.

vivable [vivabl(ə)] *adj personne* livable-with *; *milieu, monde* fit to live in. **ce n'est pas ~!** it's unbearable! *ou* intolerable!

vivace [vivas] *adj arbre* hardy; *préjugé* inveterate, indestructible. **plante ~** (hardy) perennial.

vivacité [vivasite] *nf* (**a**) *(rapidité, vie) [personne]* liveliness, vivacity; *[intelligence]* sharpness, quickness, keenness; *[mouvement]* liveliness. **~ d'esprit** quick-wittedness. (**b**) *(brusquerie)* **~ d'humeur** brusqueness, quick-temperedness. (**c**) *[lumière]* brightness, brilliance; *[couleur]* vividness; *[froid]* bitterness; *[douleur]* sharpness. (**d**) *[émotion]* keenness, intensity; *[souvenir, impression]* vividness.

vivant, e [vivɑ̃, ɑ̃t] **1** *adj* (**a**) *(en vie)* living. **il est encore ~** he's still alive *ou* living; **expériences sur des animaux ~s** experiments on live *ou* living animals. (**b**) *(plein de vie) enfant, rue, récit* lively; *portrait* lifelike. **c'est le portrait ~ de sa mère** he's the (living) image of his mother. (**c**) *(en usage) expression, croyance* living. **expression encore très ~e** expression which is still very much alive. **2** *nm (personnes)* **les ~s** the living; *(vie)* **de son ~** in his lifetime, while he was alive.

vivats [viva] *nmpl* cheers.

vive² [viv] *excl*: **~ le roi!** long live the king!; **vivent les vacances!** three cheers for *ou* hurrah for the holidays!

vivement [vivmɑ̃] *adv* (**a**) *(avec brusquerie)* sharply, brusquely. (**b**) *regretter* deeply, greatly; *désirer* keenly. **s'intéresser ~ à** to take a keen *ou* deep interest in. (**c**) *éclairer etc* brilliantly, vividly, brightly. (**d**) *(souhait)* **~ les vacances!** roll on the holidays! *; **~ que ce soit fini!** I'll be glad when it's all over!

viveur [vivœʀ] *nm* high liver.

vivier [vivje] *nm (étang)* fishpond; *(réservoir)* fishtank.

vivifier [vivifje] (7) *vt* to invigorate. ◆ **vivifiant, e** *adj air* invigorating, bracing.

vivisection [vivisɛksjɔ̃] *nf* vivisection.

vivoter [vivɔte] (1) *vi [personne]* to rub *ou* get along (somehow), live from hand to mouth.

vivre [vivʀ(ə)] (46) **1** *vi* (**a**) *(être vivant)* to live, be alive. **il avait cessé de ~** he was dead; **~ vieux/centenaire** to live to a ripe old age/to be a hundred; **ce manteau a vécu *** this coat is finished *ou* has had its day; **il fait bon ~** it's good to be alive, it's a good life. (**b**) *(habiter)* to live. **~ à Londres** to live in London; **~ avec qn** to live with sb. (**c**) *(se comporter)* to live. **se laisser ~** to take life as it comes; **être facile/difficile à ~** to be easy/difficult to live with *ou* to get on with. (**d**) *(exister)* to live. **on vit bien en France** life is good in France; **il a beaucoup vécu** he has seen a lot of life; **elle ne vit plus depuis que son fils est pilote** she lives on her nerves since her son became a pilot. (**e**) *(subsister)* to live; *de laitages, de son traitement* to live on. **avoir (juste) de quoi ~** to have (just) enough to live on; **travailler pour ~** to work for a living; **faire ~ qn** to provide (a living) for sb, support sb; **~ de l'air du temps** to live on air. (**f**) *[idée, rue]* to be alive; *[portrait]* to be lifelike *ou* lively. **2** *vt*: **~ des jours heureux** to live through *ou* spend happy days; **nous vivons des temps troublés** we are living in *ou* through troubled times; **il vivait une belle aventure** he was living out an exciting adventure; **~ sa vie** to live one's own life, live as one pleases *ou* sees fit. **3** *nm*: **le ~ et le couvert** board and lodging. **4** *nmpl:* **les ~s** supplies, provisions.

vlan, v'lan [vlɑ̃] *excl* wham!, bang!

vocabulaire [vɔkabylɛʀ] *nm* vocabulary. *(péj)* **quel ~!** what language!

vocal, e, *mpl* **-aux** [vɔkal, o] *adj* vocal. ◆ **vocalement** *adv* vocally.

vocation [vɔkɑsjɔ̃] *nf* vocation. **avoir la ~ de l'enseignement** to be cut out to be a teacher, have a vocation for teaching; **la ~ industrielle du Japon** the industrial vocation of Japan.

vociférer [vɔsifeʀe] (6) **1** *vi* to utter cries of rage, vociferate. **~ contre qn** to scream at sb. **2** *vt* to shout (out), scream. ◆ **vocifération** *nf* cry of rage, vociferation.

vodka [vɔdka] *nf* vodka.

vœu, *pl* **~x** [vø] *nm* (**a**) *(promesse)* vow. **faire (le) ~ de faire** to vow to do, make a vow to do. (**b**) *(souhait)* wish. **faire un ~** to make a wish; **tous nos ~x (de bonheur)** all good wishes for your happiness; **meilleurs ~x** best wishes.

vogue [vɔg] *nf* fashion, vogue. **être en ~** to be in fashion *ou* vogue; **c'est la grande ~ maintenant** it's all the rage now.

voguer [vɔge] (1) *vi (littér)* to sail; *[pensées]* to drift, wander. **~ au fil de l'eau** to float *ou* drift along.

voici [vwasi] *prép* (**a**) here *ou* this is; *(pl)* here *ou* these are. **~ mon bureau** here is *ou* this is my office; **~ vos livres** here *ou* these are your books; **~ la pluie** here comes the rain; **me** *etc* **~** here I am *etc*; **les ~ prêts à partir** they're ready to leave; **la maison que ~** this (particular) house; **M. Dupont, que ~** Mr Dupont here; **il m'a raconté l'histoire que ~** he told me the following story; **~ qu'il se met à pleuvoir maintenant** and now it's starting to rain; **~ pourquoi je l'avais supprimé** that was why I'd eliminated it. (**b**) *(il y a)* **~ 5 ans que je ne l'ai pas vu** it's 5 years (now) since I last saw him, I haven't seen him for the past 5 years; **il est parti ~ une heure** he left an hour ago, it's an hour since he left.

voie [vwa] *nf* (**a**) *(chemin)* way; *(Admin: route, rue)* road; *(itinéraire)* route. **par la ~ des airs** by air; **~ d'accès** access; **~s de communication** communication routes; **~ express** motorway, freeway *(US)* , express way; **~ à double sens** two-way road; **~s navigables** waterways; **la ~ publique** the public highway; **~ de raccordement** slip road; **~ sans issue** no through road, cul-de-sac. (**b**) *(partie d'une route)* lane. **route à ~ unique** single-lane *ou* single-track road; **route à 3/4 ~s** 3-/4-lane road; **~ réservée aux autobus** bus lane; **~ à contresens** contraflow lane. (**c**) *(Rail)* **~(s)** track, line. **~ ferrée** railway *ou* railroad *(US)* line; **~ de garage** siding; *(fig)* **mettre sur une ~ de garage** *affaire* to shelve; *personne* to shunt to one side; **ligne à ~ unique** single-track line; **ligne à ~ étroite** narrow-gauge line; **le train est annoncé sur la ~ 2** the train will arrive at platform 2. (**d**) *(Anat)* **~s digestives** *etc* digestive *etc* tract; **par ~ orale** orally. (**e**) *(fig)* way. **la ~ du bien** the path of good; **montrer la ~** to show the way; **l'affaire est en bonne ~** the matter is shaping *ou* going well; **mettre qn sur la ~** to put sb on the right track. (**f**) *(filière)* **par des ~s détournées** by devious *ou* roundabout means; **par la ~ hiérarchique/diplomatique** through official/diplomatic channels; **par ~ de conséquence** in consequence, as a result. (**g**) **en ~ d'exécution** in (the) process of being carried out; **pays en ~ de développement** developing country; **en ~ de guérison** getting better, on the road to recovery; **en ~ d'achèvement** (well) on the way to completion, nearing completion. (**h**) **~ d'eau** leak; **se livrer à des ~s de fait sur qn** to assault sb; **la ~ lactée** the Milky Way.

voilà [vwala] **1** *prép* (**a**) *(même sens que voici)* here *ou* this is; *(pl)* here *ou* these are; *(opposé à voici)* there *ou* that is; *(pl)* there *ou* those are. **~ mon frère** this is *ou* here is my brother; **voici mon frère et ~ ma sœur** this is my brother and that is my sister, here is my brother and there is my sister; **voici mes valises et ~ les vôtres** here *ou* these are my bags and there *ou* those are yours; **~ le printemps** here comes spring; **le ~, c'est lui** there he is, that's him; **le ~ prêt à partir** he's ready to leave; **~ ce dont il s'agit** that's *ou* this is what it's all about; **~ comment il faut faire** that's how it's done; **l'homme que ~** that man (there); **M. Dupont que ~** Mr Dupont there; **il m'a raconté l'histoire que ~** he told me the following story; **~ qu'il se met à pleuvoir** it's starting to rain, here comes the rain; **~ qui est louche** that's a bit odd *ou* suspicious. (**b**) *(il y a)* **~ 5 ans que je ne l'ai pas vu** it's 5 years since I last saw him, I haven't seen him for the past 5 years; **il est parti ~ une heure** he left an hour ago, it's an hour since he left. (**c**) *(locutions)* **en ~ une histoire/blague!** what a story/joke!; **en ~ assez!** that's enough!, that'll do!; **veux-tu de l'argent? — en ~** do you want some money? — here's some *ou* here you are; **~ le hic** there's *ou* that's the hitch; **~ tout** that's all; **~ bien les Français!** how like the French!, isn't that just like the French!, that's the French all over! * **2** *excl*: **~! j'arrive!** there — I'm coming!; **ah! ~! je comprends!** oh, (so) that's it; **~! ça devait arriver!** there you are, it was bound to happen!; **~, je vais vous expliquer** right (then), I'll explain to you.

voilage [vwalaʒ] *nm* *(rideau)* net curtain. *(tissu)* **acheter du ~** to buy some net.

voile¹ [vwal] *nf* (**a**) *[bateau]* sail. **faire ~ vers** to sail towards; **toutes ~s dehors** with full sail on; **mettre les ~s** ‡ to clear off ‡, push off ‡. (**b**) *(sport)* sailing, yachting. **faire de la ~** to sail, go sailing *ou* yachting.

voile² [vwal] *nm* (**a**) *(gén)* veil. *(Rel)* **prendre le ~** to take the veil; **sous le ~ de** under the veil of; **~ de brume** veil of mist; **avoir un ~ devant les yeux** to have a film before one's eyes. (**b**) *(tissu)* net. **~ de tergal** ® Terylene ® net. (**c**) *(Méd)* **~ au poumon** shadow on the lung; *(Anat)* **~ du palais** soft palate, velum. (**d**) *(Phot)* fog. **un ~ sur la photo** a shadow on the photo. ◆ **voilé, e** *adj* (**a**) *femme, allusion* veiled. **accusation à peine ~e** thinly disguised accusation. (**b**) *lumière, ciel, contour* misty, hazy; *éclat* dimmed; *regard* misty; *photo* fogged. **avoir la voix ~e** to have a husky voice. ◆ **voiler¹** (1) **1** *vt (lit, fig)* to veil. **2 se ~** *vpr* (**a**) *[musulmane]* **se ~ le visage** to wear a veil; *(fig)* **se ~ la face** to hide one's face. (**b**) *[horizon, soleil, regard]* to mist over; *[ciel]* to grow hazy *ou* misty. ◆ **voilette** *nf* (hat) veil.

voiler² *vt*, **se ~** *vpr* [vwale] (1) *[roue]* to buckle; *[planche]* to warp.

voilier [vwalje] *nm* sailing ship; *(de plaisance)* sailing dinghy *ou* boat, yacht. ◆ **voilure** *nf [bateau]* sails. **une ~ de 1 000m²** 1,000m² of sail.

voir [vwaʀ] (30) **1** *vt* (**a**) to see. **on n'y voit rien** you can't see a thing; **c'est un film à ~** it's a film worth seeing; **il a vu du pays** he has been around *ou* knocked about a bit; **~ qn faire qch** to see sb do sth; **j'ai vu bâtir ces maisons** I saw these houses being built; **je l'ai vu naître** I've known him since he was born; **le pays qui l'a vu naître** his native country; **il a vu deux guerres** he has lived through *ou* seen two wars; **à le ~ si joyeux/triste** seeing him look so happy/sad; *(fig)* **on commence à y ~ plus clair** things are beginning to come clear. (**b**) *(se représenter)* to see. **je le vois mal habitant la banlieue** I (somehow) can't see *ou* imagine him living in the suburbs; **ne ~ que par qn** to see only *ou* see everything through sb's eyes; **~ la vie en rose/les choses en noir** to take a rosy/black view of things; **~ loin** to see ahead; **~ le problème sous un autre jour** to see *ou* view the problem in a different light; **on n'en voit pas le bout** there seems to be no end to it; **façon de ~** view of things, outlook; **il a vu petit/grand** he planned things on a small/big scale; **ne ~ que son intérêt** to consider only one's own interest. (**c**) *(étudier) problème, dossier* to look at; *leçon* to look *ou* go over; *circulaire* to see, read. **je verrai** I'll have to see, I'll think about it; **c'est à vous de ~** it's up to you to see *ou* decide. (**d**) *(découvrir)* to see, find (out). **aller ~ s'il y a quelqu'un** to go and see *ou* go and find out if there is anybody there; **vous verrez que ce n'est pas leur faute** you will see *ou* find that it's not their fault; **c'est à ~** *(à prouver)* that remains to be seen; **(attendons) on verra bien** let's wait and see. (**e**) *(rendre visite à) médecin, avocat* to see. **aller ~ qn** *(gén)* to go and see sb; *ami* to call on *ou* visit sb. (**f**) *(faire l'expérience de)* **il en a vu de dures** *ou* **de toutes les couleurs** he has been through the mill *ou* through some hard times; **en faire ~ (de dures) à qn** to give sb a hard time; **j'en ai vu d'autres!** I've been through *ou* seen worse!; **on n'a jamais vu ça!** did you ever see *ou* hear the like?; **il ne voit pas ce que vous voulez dire** he doesn't see *ou* grasp what you mean. (**g**) **laisser ~, faire ~** to show; **faites-moi ~ ce dessin** let me see *ou* show me this picture; **elle ne peut pas le ~** * she can't stand him; **se faire mal ~ (de qn)** to be frowned on (by sb); **se faire bien ~ (de qn)** to make o.s. popular (with sb); **vous aurez du mal à lui faire ~ que...** you will find it difficult to make him see *ou* realise that... (**h**) *(locutions)* **voyons** *(réflexion)* let's see now; *(irritation)* come (on) now, come, come; **dis-moi ~** tell me; **je voudrais t'y ~** I'd like to see you try; **essaie ~!** * just you try it!; **c'est ce que nous verrons** we'll see about that; **regarde ~ ce qu'il a fait** * just look what he has done!; **pour ~** just to see; **c'est tout vu** it's a foregone conclusion; **qu'il aille se faire ~!** he can go to hell!; **il ferait beau ~ qu'il...** it would be a fine thing if he...; **cela n'a rien à ~ avec...** this has got nothing to do with...; **n'y ~ que du feu** to be completely hoodwinked *ou* taken in; *(être ivre)* **~ double** to see double; **~ trente-six chandelles** to see stars; **ne pas ~ plus loin que le bout de son nez** to see no further than the end of one's nose; **~ venir** to wait and see; **je te vois venir** * I can see what you're leading up to *ou* getting at.

2 ~ à *vt indir* to make sure that, see (to it) that. **voyez à être à l'heure** see *ou* make sure that you are on time.

3 se ~ *vpr* (**a**) *(être visible)* *[tache etc]* to show. **cela se voit!** that's obvious! (**b**) **se ~ forcé de** to find o.s. forced to; **cela se voit tous les jours** it happens *ou* can be seen *ou* found every day; **il s'est vu**

interdire l'accès he found himself *ou* he was refused admission.

voire [vwaʀ] *adv* or even, indeed.

voirie [vwaʀi] *nf (enlèvement des ordures)* refuse collection; *(entretien des routes)* highway maintenance.

voisin, e [vwazɛ̃, in] **1** *adj* (**a**) *(proche)* neighbouring; *(adjacent)* next. **les rues ~es** the neighbouring streets; **une maison ~e de l'église** a house next to *ou* adjoining the church. (**b**) *idées, espèces, cas* connected. **~ de** akin to, related to; **dans un état ~ de la folie** in a state bordering on *ou* akin to madness. **2** *nm, f* neighbour. **nos ~s d'à-côté** our next-door neighbours, the people next door; **mon ~ de dortoir** the person in the bed next to mine (in the dormitory); *(pays)* **notre ~ allemand** our neighbour, Germany, our German neighbours. ◆ **voisinage** *nm* (**a**) *(voisins)* neighbourhood. **être en bon ~ avec qn** to be on neighbourly terms with sb. (**b**) *(environs)* vicinity; *(proximité)* proximity, closeness. **les villages du ~** the villages in the vicinity; **le ~ de la montagne** the proximity *ou* closeness of the mountains. ◆ **voisiner** (1) *vi*: **~ avec qch** to be (placed) side by side with sth.

voiture [vwatyʀ] *nf* (**a**) *(automobile)* car, motor car, automobile *(US)*. **~ particulière** private car; **~ école** driving school car; **~ piégée** car bomb, booby-trapped car; **~ de location** hired *ou* rented car; **~ de sport** sportscar; **~ de tourisme** saloon, sedan *(US)*. (**b**) *(wagon)* carriage, coach, car *(US)*. **~-bar** buffet car; **~-couchette** couchette; **~-restaurant** dining car; **en ~!** all aboard! (**c**) *(attelée ou poussée) (pour marchandises)* cart; *(pour voyageurs)* carriage, coach. **~ à bras** handcart; **~ d'enfant** pram, perambulator, baby carriage *(US)*; **~ d'infirme** wheelchair, invalid carriage; **~ de pompiers** fire engine; **~-radio** radio car.

voix [vwa] *nf* (**a**) voice. **à ~ basse/haute** in a low *ou* hushed/loud voice; **à haute et intelligible ~** loud and clear; **rester sans ~** to be speechless *(devant* before, at); *[chien]* **donner de la ~** to bay, give tongue; **la ~ du sang** the call of the blood. (**b**) *(opinion)* voice; *(Pol: suffrage)* vote. **mettre qch aux ~** to put sth to the vote; **avoir ~ consultative** to have consultative powers *ou* a consultative voice; **donner sa ~ à qn** to vote for sb; **le parti obtiendra peu de/beaucoup de ~ en Écosse** the party will poll badly/heavily in Scotland; **avoir ~ au chapitre** to have a say in the matter. (**c**) *(Mus)* voice. **chanter à 2/3 ~** to sing in 2/3 parts; **chanter d'une ~ juste** to sing in tune; **être en ~** to be in good voice. (**d**) *(Ling)* voice.

vol¹ [vɔl] *nm* (**a**) *(gén)* flight. **faire un ~ plané** *[oiseau]* to glide through the air; *(fig: tomber)* to fall flat on one's face; **~ régulier** scheduled flight; **il y a 8 heures de ~ entre...** it's an 8-hour flight between...; **conditions de ~** flying conditions; **~ libre** hang-gliding; **~ à voile** gliding. (**b**) **un ~ de perdrix** a covey *ou* flock of partridges; **un ~ de moucherons** a cloud of gnats. (**c**) *(locutions)* **en (plein)** ~ in (full) flight; **prendre son ~** to take wing, fly off *ou* away; **attraper au ~** *autobus* to leap onto as it moves off; *ballon* to catch as it flies past, catch in midair; *occasion* to leap at, seize; **à ~ d'oiseau** as the crow flies. ◆ **voler¹** (1) *vi (lit, fig)* to fly. **~ de ses propres ailes** to fend for o.s.; **~ en éclats** to fly *ou* smash into pieces; **~ au vent** to fly in the wind, float on the wind; **~ vers qn/au secours de qn** to fly to sb/to sb's assistance; **~ dans les plumes de qn *** to fly at sb.

vol² [vɔl] *nm* theft. *(fig)* **c'est du ~!** it's daylight robbery!; **~ à l'arraché** bagsnatching; **~ à l'étalage** shoplifting; **~ à main armée** armed robbery; **~ à la tire** pickpocketing. ◆ **voler²** (1) *vt* (**a**) **~ qch à qn** to steal sth from sb; **se faire ~ ses bagages** to have one's luggage stolen; *(fig)* **il ne l'a pas volé!** he asked for it! (**b**) **~ qn** to rob sb; **~ les clients sur le poids** to cheat customers over (the) weight, give customers short measure; **on n'est pas volé *** you get your money's worth all right *. ◆ **voleur, -euse 1** *adj*: **être ~** *(gén)* to be light-fingered, be (a bit of) a thief; *[commerçant]* to be a cheat *ou* swindler, be dishonest; *[animal]* to be a thief. **2** *nm, f (malfaiteur)* thief; *(commerçant)* swindler. **~ de grand chemin** highwayman; **au ~!** stop thief!

volage [vɔlaʒ] *adj époux* flighty, fickle.

volaille [vɔlɑj] *nf*: **une ~** a fowl; **la ~** poultry. ◆ **volailler** *nm* poulterer.

volant¹ [vɔlɑ̃] *nm* (**a**) *(Aut)* steering wheel. **prendre le ~** to take the wheel; **un brusque coup de ~** a sharp turn of the wheel; **as du ~** crack *ou* ace driver; **la femme au ~** the woman driver, women drivers. (**b**) *(Tech) (régulateur)* flywheel; *(de commande)* (hand)wheel. (**c**) *[rideau, robe]* flounce. **jupe à ~s** flounced skirt. (**d**) *(Badminton)* shuttlecock.

volant², e [vɔlɑ̃, ɑ̃t] *adj* flying. *(Aviat)* **le personnel ~** the flight *ou* flying staff.

volatil, e¹ [vɔlatil] *adj (Chim)* volatile. ◆ **volatiliser** (1) **1** *vt (Chim)* to volatilize. **2 se ~** *vpr (Chim)* to volatilize; *(fig)* to vanish (into thin air).

volatile² [vɔlatil] *nm (volaille)* fowl; *(oiseau)* bird.

vol-au-vent [vɔlovɑ̃] *nm inv* vol-au-vent.

volcan [vɔlkɑ̃] *nm (Géog)* volcano; *(personne)* spitfire; *(situation)* powder keg, volcano. ◆ **volcanique** *adj (lit, fig)* volcanic.

volée [vɔle] *nf* (**a**) **~ de** *moineaux* flock *ou* flight of; *enfants* swarm of; *flèches* flight *ou* volley of; *coups* volley of; **recevoir une bonne ~** to get a sound thrashing *ou* beating. (**b**) *(Ftbl, Tennis)* volley. **de ~** on the volley. (**c**) **~ d'escalier** flight of stairs. (**d**) **jeter qch à la ~** to fling sth about; **semer à la ~** to sow broadcast; **à toute ~** *gifler, lancer* vigorously, with full force; **les cloches sonnaient à toute ~** the bells were pealing out.

voler [vɔle] *V* **vol¹, vol²**.

volet [vɔlɛ] *nm* (**a**) *(persienne)* shutter; *(Aut: panneau articulé)* flap. (**b**) *[triptyque]* volet, wing; *[carte]* section; *[reportage]* part. (**c**) *(fig: aspect)* facet.

voleter [vɔlte] (4) *vi* to flutter about.

voleur, -euse [vɔlœʀ, øz] *V* **vol²**.

volière [vɔljɛʀ] *nf (cage)* aviary. *(fig)* **c'est une ~** it's a proper henhouse *.

volley-ball [vɔlɛbol] *nm* volleyball. ◆ **volleyeur, -euse** *nm, f* volleyball player.

volontaire [vɔlɔ̃tɛʀ] **1** *adj* (**a**) *(voulu) (gén)* voluntary; *oubli* intentional. (**b**) *(décidé) personne* self-willed; *expression, menton* determined. **2** *nmf (Mil, gén)* volunteer. ◆ **volontairement** *adv (de son plein gré)* voluntarily, of one's own free will; *(exprès)* intentionally, deliberately; *(d'une manière décidée)* determinedly. **il a dit ça ~** he said it on purpose *ou* deliberately. ◆ **volontariste** *adj, nmf* voluntarist.

volonté [vɔlɔ̃te] *nf* (**a**) *(intention)* wish, will. **manifester sa ~ de faire qch** to show one's intention of doing sth; **respecter la ~ de qn** to respect sb's wishes; **la ~ nationale** the will of the nation; **~ de puissance/de réussir** will for power/to succeed. (**b**) **bonne ~** goodwill, willingness; **mauvaise ~** unwillingness; **il fait preuve de bonne/mauvaise ~** his attitude is positive/negative; **il y met de la mauvaise ~** he does it unwillingly *ou* grudgingly *ou* with a bad grace; **faire appel aux bonnes ~s pour construire qch** to appeal to volunteers to construct sth; **avec la meilleure ~ du monde** with the best will in the world. (**c**) *(énergie)* willpower, will. **une ~ de fer** a will of iron; **réussir à force de ~** to succeed through sheer willpower *ou* determination. (**d**) **à ~** at will; **servez-vous de pain à ~** take as much bread as you like; **'sucrer à**

~' 'sweeten to taste'; **il en fait toujours à sa** ~ he always does as he pleases *ou* likes, he always suits himself.

volontiers [vɔlɔ̃tje] *adv* (**a**) *(de bonne grâce)* with pleasure, gladly, willingly. **voulez-vous dîner chez nous? —** ~ would you like to eat with us? — I'd love to *ou* with pleasure. (**b**) *(naturellement)* readily. **on croit** ~ **que...** people readily believe that...

volt [vɔlt] *nm* volt. ◆ **voltage** *nm* voltage.

volte-face [vɔltəfas] *nf inv* (**a**) *(lit)* **faire** ~ to turn round. (**b**) *(fig)* volte-face, about-turn.

voltige [vɔltiʒ] *nf (Équitation)* trick riding; *(Aviat)* aerobatics. *(Gym)* **faire de la** ~ to do acrobatics.

voltiger [vɔltiʒe] (3) *vi* to flutter about.

volubile [vɔlybil] *adj* voluble. ◆ **volubilité** *nf* volubility.

volubilis [vɔlybilis] *nm* convolvulus, morning glory.

volume [vɔlym] *nm (gén)* volume. *[gros objets]* **faire du** ~ to be bulky, take up space. ◆ **volumineux, -euse** *adj* voluminous, bulky.

volupté [vɔlypte] *nf* sensual *ou* voluptuous pleasure. ◆ **voluptueusement** *adv* voluptuously. ◆ **voluptueux, -euse** *adj* voluptuous.

volute [vɔlyt] *nf (Archit)* volute; *[fumée]* curl.

vomir [vɔmiʀ] (2) *vt* (**a**) *aliments* to vomit, bring up; *flammes, injures* to spew out; *(fig: détester)* to loathe, abhor. (**b**) *(emploi absolu)* to be sick, vomit. **il a vomi partout** he was sick everywhere; **avoir envie de** ~ to want to be sick; *(fig)* **c'est à** ~ it's enough to make you sick. ◆ **vomi** *nm* vomit. ◆ **vomissement** *nm*: ~**(s)** vomiting.

vorace [vɔʀas] *adj* voracious. ◆ **voracement** *adv* voraciously. ◆ **voracité** *nf* voracity, voraciousness.

vos [vo] *adj poss V* **votre.**

voter [vɔte] (1) **1** *vi* to vote. **2** *vt projet de loi* to vote for; *loi* to pass; *crédits* to vote. ~ **la censure** to pass a vote of censure; **ne pas** ~ *amendement* to pass out. ◆ **votant, e** *nm, f* voter. ◆ **vote** *nm* (**a**) *(action) (gén)* voting (*de* for); *[loi]* passing. (**b**) *(suffrage)* vote; *(ensemble des votants)* voters. ~ **de confiance** vote of confidence; ~ **à main levée** vote by a show of hands; ~ **secret/par correspondance/par procuration** secret/postal/proxy vote.

votre [vɔtʀ(ə)], *pl* **vos** [vo] *adj poss* your; *V* **son**[1], **ton**[1].

vôtre [votʀ(ə)] **1** *pron poss*: **le** ~, **la** ~, **les** ~**s** yours, your own; **à la (bonne)** ~ ! your (good) health!, cheers! * **2** *nmf* (**a**) **j'espère que vous y mettrez du** ~ I hope you'll pull your weight. (**b**) **les** ~**s** your family; *(péj)* **vous et tous les** ~**s** you and your ilk *ou* all those like you; **nous pourrons être des** ~**s ce soir** we shall be able to join you tonight; *V* **sien. 3** *adj poss* yours; *V* **sien.**

vouer [vwe] (1) *vt temps, argent* to devote; *amour, fidélité* to vow; *(Rel)* to dedicate (à to). **se** ~ **à une cause** to dedicate o.s. *ou* devote o.s. to a cause; **projet voué à l'échec** plan doomed to *ou* destined for failure.

vouloir [vulwaʀ] (31) **1** *vt* (**a**) *(gén)* to want. **je veux de vous une réponse** I want an answer from you; *[vendeur]* **j'en veux 10 F** I want 10 francs for it; **je veux que tu te laves les mains/que tes mains soient lavées** I want you to wash your hands/your hands to be washed; **que lui voulez-vous?** what do you want with him?; **qu'il le veuille ou non** whether he likes *ou* wants it or not; **il veut absolument venir** he is absolutely set on coming, he is determined to come.

(**b**) *(sens affaibli: désirer)* **voulez-vous à boire?** would you like *ou* do you want a drink?; **je voudrais/j'aurais voulu du pain** I would like/I would have liked some bread; **je voudrais bien y aller** I'd love to go; **je voulais vous dire** I meant to tell you; **elle voulut se lever mais retomba** she tried to get up but fell back; **je voulais vous dire/lui écrire** I meant to tell you/to write to him; **ça va comme tu veux? *** is everything going all right *ou* O.K. (for you)? *; ~ **du bien à qn** to wish sb well; **je voudrais que vous voyiez sa tête!** I wish you could see his face!; **si tu veux** if you like; **s'il voulait, il pourrait être ministre** if he wanted (to), he could be a minister; **comme vous voulez** as you like *ou* wish *ou* please.

(**c**) *(consentir)* **ils ne voulurent pas nous recevoir** they wouldn't see us, they weren't willing to see us; **le moteur ne veut pas partir** the engine won't start; **il joue bien quand il veut** he plays well when he wants to *ou* has a mind (to); **voudriez-vous avoir l'obligeance de** would you be so kind as to; **veuillez croire à toute ma sympathie** please accept my deepest sympathy; **voulez-vous me prêter ce livre?** will you lend me this book?; **voudriez-vous fermer la fenêtre?** would you mind closing the window?; **veux-tu (bien) te taire!** will you be quiet!; **veuillez quitter la pièce immédiatement** please leave the room at once; **je veux bien le faire/qu'il vienne** *(volontiers)* I'm happy *ou* I'll be happy to do it/for him to come; *(s'il le faut vraiment)* I don't mind doing it/if he comes; **moi je veux bien le croire mais...** I'm quite willing *ou* prepared to believe him but...; **moi je veux bien, mais...** fair enough *, but...

(**d**) *[choses] (requérir)* to want, require. **ces plantes veulent de l'eau** these plants want *ou* need water; **l'usage veut que...** custom requires that...; **le hasard voulut que...** chance decreed that..., as fate would have it...

(**e**) *(s'attendre à)* to expect. **comment voulez-vous que je sache?** how do you expect me to know?, how should I know?; **et vous voudriez que nous acceptions?** and you expect us to agree?, and you would have us agree?

(**f**) **en** ~ **à qn** to have sth against sb, have a grudge against sb; **en** ~ **à qn de qch** to hold sth against sb; **il m'en veut d'avoir fait cela** he holds a grudge against me for having done that; **ne m'en veuillez pas** don't hold it against me; **tu ne m'en veux pas?** no hard feelings?; **en** ~ **à qch** to be after sth; **il en veut à mon argent** he is after my money.

(**g**) ~ **dire** *(signifier)* to mean; **qu'est-ce que cela veut dire?** what does that mean?

(**h**) *(locutions)* **que voulez-vous (qu'on y fasse)!** what can we do?, what can *ou* do you expect!; **je veux être pendu si...** I'll be hanged *ou* damned if...; **sans le** ~ unintentionally, inadvertently; **tu l'as voulu** you asked for it; **tu l'auras voulu** it'll have been your own fault; **il y a eu des discours en veux-tu en voilà** there were speeches galore; **elle fait de lui ce qu'elle veut** she twists him round her little finger.

2 ~ **de** *vt indir*: ~ **de qn/qch** to want sb/sth; **on ne veut plus de lui au bureau** they don't want him *ou* won't have him in the office any more; **il en veut** *(lit) (gâteau)* he wants some; *(fig: il veut réussir)* he's dead keen *, he wants to win.

3 *nm* will. **bon** ~ goodwill; **mauvais** ~ ill will, reluctance; **attendre le bon** ~ **de qn** to wait on sb's pleasure.

voulu, e [vuly] *adj* (**a**) *(requis)* required, requisite. **l'argent** ~ the required *ou* requisite money, the money required. (**b**) *(volontaire)* deliberate, intentional. **c'est** ~ * it's done on purpose, it's intentional *ou* deliberate.

vous [vu] **1** *pron pers* (**a**) you. **si j'étais** ~ if I were you; **eux ont accepté,** ~ **pas** they accepted but you didn't *ou* but not you; ~ **parti** once you've gone; **qui l'a vu?,** ~**?** who saw him?, (did) you? *ou* was it you?; **pourquoi ne le ferais-je pas:** ~ **l'avez bien fait,** ~! why shouldn't I do it — you did (it)!; ~ **tous qui m'écoutez** all of you listening to me;

cette maison est-elle à ~? does this house belong to you?, is this house yours? *ou* your own?; **vous ne pensez qu'à ~** you think only of yourself (*ou* yourselves). (**b**) *(dans comparaisons)* you. **il est aussi fort que ~** he is as strong as you (are); **je vais faire comme ~** I'll do the same as you (do). (**c**) *(avec vpr)* **~ êtes-~ bien amusé(s)?** did you have a good time?; **je crois que ~ ~ connaissez** I believe you know each other; **servez-~ donc** do help yourself (*ou* yourselves); **ne ~ disputez pas** don't fight. **2** *nm*: **le ~** the 'vous' form; **dire ~ à qn** to call sb 'vous'.

voûte [vut] *nf (Archit)* vault; *(porche)* archway. **la ~ céleste** the vault *ou* canopy of heaven; **~ plantaire** arch of the foot. ◆ **voûter** (1) *vt* (**a**) *(Archit)* to arch, vault. (**b**) *personne, dos* to make stooped. **dos voûté** bent back; **il s'est voûté** he has become stooped.

vouvoyer [vuvwaje] (8) *vt*: **~ qn** to address sb as 'vous'. ◆ **vouvoiement** *nm* addressing sb as 'vous'.

vox populi [vɔkspɔpyli] *nf* vox populi, voice of the people.

voyage [vwajaʒ] *nm* journey, trip; *(par mer)* voyage. *(action)* **le ~, les ~s** travelling; **les ~s de Gulliver** Gulliver's Travels; **il revient de ~** he's just come back from a journey *ou* a trip; **il est en ~** he's away; **au moment de partir en ~** just as he was setting off on his journey *ou* travels; **frais/souvenirs de ~** travel expenses/souvenirs; **~ d'affaires** *etc* business *etc* trip; **~ de noces** honeymoon; **~ organisé** package tour *ou* holiday. ◆ **voyager** (3) *vi* to travel. **aimer ~** to be fond of travelling; **cette malle a beaucoup voyagé** this trunk has travelled a great deal *ou* has done a lot of travelling. ◆ **voyageur, -euse 1** *adj tempérament* wayfaring. **2** *nm, f* traveller. **~ de commerce** commercial traveller, sales representative. ◆ **voyagiste** *nm* tour operator.

voyant, e [vwajɑ̃, ɑ̃t] **1** *adj couleurs* loud, gaudy, garish. **2** *nm (signal)* **~ (lumineux)** light; **~ d'huile** oil warning light. **3** *nf*: **~e (extra-lucide)** clairvoyant.

voyelle [vwajɛl] *nf* vowel.

voyeur, -euse [vwajœʀ, øz] *nm, f (péj)* peeping Tom, voyeur.

voyou [vwaju] **1** *nm (enfant)* rascal; *(délinquant)* lout, hoodlum, hooligan. **2** *adj inv air* loutish.

vrac [vʀak] *adv*: **en ~** *(sans emballage) (au détail)* loose; *(en gros)* in bulk *ou* quantity; *(fig: en désordre)* in a jumble.

vrai, vraie [vʀɛ] **1** *adj (gén)* true; *(réel)* real; *(authentique)* genuine. **c'est dangereux, c'est ~, mais...** it's dangerous, it's true *ou* certainly, but...; **il n'en est pas moins ~ que** it's nonetheless *ou* nevertheless true that; **ce n'est que trop ~** it's only too true; **ce sont ses ~s cheveux** that's his real *ou* own hair; **un ~ Picasso** a real *ou* genuine Picasso; **son ~ nom est Charles** his real *ou* true name is Charles; **un ~ de ~ *** the real thing, the genuine article; **c'est un ~ fou!** he's really mad!, he's downright mad!; **c'est une vraie mère pour moi** she's a real mother to me. **2** *nm*: **le ~** the truth; **il y a du ~ dans ce qu'il dit** there's some truth in what he says; **être dans le ~** to be right. **3** *adv*: **il dit ~** he's right, what he says is right *ou* true; **à dire ~, à ~ dire** to tell (you) the truth, in (actual) fact; **pour de ~ *** for real *; *[décor, perruque]* **faire ~** to look real *ou* like the real thing. ◆ **vraiment** *adv (gén)* really. **nous voulons ~ la paix** we really (and truly) want peace; **il est ~ idiot** he's a real idiot.

vraisemblable [vʀɛsɑ̃blabl(ə)] *adj hypothèse* likely; *intrigue* plausible, convincing. **peu ~** *histoire* improbable, unlikely; **il est ~ que** it's likely *ou* probable that. ◆ **vraisemblablement** *adv* in all likelihood *ou* probability, probably. ◆ **vraisemblance** *nf [hypothèse]* likelihood; *[situation romanesque]* plausibility. **selon toute ~** in all likelihood *ou* probability.

vrille [vʀij] *nf (Tech)* gimlet; *(spirale)* spiral; *(Aviat)* (tail)spin. **escalier en ~** spiral staircase.

vrombir [vʀɔ̃biʀ] (2) *vi [moteur]* to hum, roar. **faire ~ son moteur** to rev one's engine. ◆ **vrombissement** *nm*: **~(s)** humming.

vroum [vʀum] *excl* brum! brum!

vu, vue¹ [vy] **1** *adj* (**a**) *(*: compris)* **c'est ~?** all right?, got it? *, understood?; **c'est tout ~** it's a foregone conclusion. (**b**) *(considéré)* **bien ~** *personne* well thought of; *chose* good form; **mal ~** *personne* poorly thought of; *chose* bad form. **2** *nm*: **au ~ et au su de tous** openly and publicly. **3** *prép* in view of. **~ la situation** in view of *ou* considering *ou* given the situation. **4** *conj* (*) **~ que** in view of the fact that, seeing *ou* considering that.

vue² [vy] *nf* (**a**) *(sens)* (eye)sight. **il a la ~ basse** he is short-sighted *ou* near-sighted *(US)*; **don de seconde** *ou* **double ~** gift of second sight.
(**b**) *(regard)* **détourner la ~** to look away; **s'offrir à la ~ de tous** to present o.s. for all to see; *(lit, fig)* **perdre de ~** to lose sight of; **il lui en a mis plein la ~ *** he dazzled him (*ou* her).
(**c**) *(panorama)* view. **avec ~ imprenable** with an open *ou* unobstructed view *ou* outlook; **cette pièce a ~ sur la mer** this room looks out onto the sea.
(**d**) *(spectacle)* sight. **la ~ du sang l'a fait s'évanouir** the sight of the blood made him faint; **à sa ~ elle s'est mise à rougir** when she saw him she began to blush.
(**e**) *(image)* view; *(photo)* photograph, photo. **un film de 36 ~s** a 36-exposure film.
(**f**) *(conception)* view. **c'est une ~ de l'esprit** that's a purely theoretical view; **~s** *(opinion)* views; *(projet)* plans; *(sur qn ou ses biens)* designs (*sur* on).
(**g**) *(locutions)* **je le connais de ~** I know him by sight; **à ~** *payable etc* at sight; *atterrir* visually; *atterrissage* visual; **à ~ d'œil** *diminuer etc* before one's very eyes; **à ~ de nez *** roughly, at a rough guess; **en ~** *(lit, fig: proche)* in sight; *(en évidence)* **(bien) en ~** conspicuous; *(célèbre)* **très en ~** very much in the public eye; **avoir un poste en ~** to have one's sights on a job; **avoir un collaborateur en ~** to have an associate in mind; **avoir en ~ de faire** to have it in mind to do, plan to do; **il a acheté une maison en ~ de son mariage** he has bought a house with his marriage in mind; **il a dit cela en ~ de le décourager** he said that with the idea of *ou* with a view to discouraging him.

vulgaire [vylgɛʀ] *adj (grossier)* vulgar, coarse; *(commun)* common. **de la ~ matière plastique** ordinary plastic, common or garden plastic. ◆ **vulgairement** *adv* vulgarly, coarsely. ◆ **vulgarisation** *nf* popularization. ◆ **vulgariser** (1) *vt* to popularize. ◆ **vulgarité** *nf* vulgarity, coarseness. **des ~s** vulgarities.

vulnérable [vylneʀabl(ə)] *adj* vulnerable. ◆ **vulnérabilité** *nf* vulnerability.

vulve [vylv(ə)] *nf* vulva.

W, w [dublәve] *nm (lettre)* W, w.

wagon [vagɔ̃] *nm (de marchandises)* truck, wagon, freight car *(US)*; *(de voyageurs)* carriage, car *(US)*; *(contenu)* truckload, wagonload. ~ **à bestiaux** cattle truck; ~**-citerne** *nm, pl* ~**s**-~**s** tanker, tank wagon; ~ **frigorifique** refrigerated van; ~**-lit** *nm, pl* ~**s**- ~**s** sleeper, Pullman *(US)*; ~**-restaurant** *nm, pl* ~**s**-~**s** restaurant *ou* dining car. ◆ **wagonnet** *nm* small truck.

walkman [wɔkman] *nm* ® walkman ®, personal stereo.

wallon, -onne [walɔ̃, ɔn] *adj, nm,* **W**~**(ne)** *nm (f)* Walloon.

wassingue [wasɛ̃g] *nf* floorcloth.

water-polo [watɛʀpɔlo] *nm* water polo.

waters [watɛʀ] *nmpl* toilet, lavatory, restroom *(US)*. **où sont les** ~**?** where is the toilet?

watt [wat] *nm* watt.

week-end, *pl* **week-ends** [wikɛnd] *nm* weekend. **partir en** ~ to go away for the weekend; **partir en** ~ **prolongé** to go away on *ou* for a long weekend.

western [wɛstɛʀn] *nm* western.

whisky, *pl* ~**ies** [wiski] *nm* whisky. ~ **américain** bourbon.

white-spirit [wajtspiʀit] *nm* white-spirit.

X, x [iks] *nm (lettre)* X, x. **ça fait x temps que je ne l'ai pas vu *** I haven't seen him for n months; **je te l'ai dit x fois** I've told you innumerable times; **plainte contre X** action against person or persons unknown; **Monsieur X** Mr X; **film classé X** 18 film.

xénophobe [ksenɔfɔb] **1** *adj* xenophobic. **2** *nmf* xenophobe. ◆ **xénophobie** *nf* xenophobia.

xérès [gzeʀɛs] *nm (vin)* sherry.

xylophène [ksilɔfɛn] *nm* ® woodworm and pesticide fluid.

xylophone [ksilɔfɔn] *nm* xylophone.

Y

Y, y[1] [igʀɛk] *nm (lettre)* Y, y.

y[2] [i] **1** *adv* there. **restez-**~ stay there; **il avait une feuille de papier et il** ~ **dessinait un bateau** he had a sheet of paper and he was drawing a ship on it; **j'** ~ **suis, j'** ~ **reste** here I am and here I stay. **2** *pron pers* it. **elle s'** ~ **connaît** she knows all about it, she's an expert; **il faudra vous** ~ **faire** you'll just have to get used to it; **je n'** ~ **suis pour rien** it is nothing to do with me; **ça** ~ **est! c'est fait!** that's it, it's done!

yacht [jɔt] *nm* yacht. ~**-club** yacht club.

yaourt [jauʀ(t)] *nm* yog(h)urt. ◆ **yaourtière** *nf* yoghurt maker.

Yemen [jemɛn] *nm:* **le** ~ the Yemen. ◆ **yéménite** *adj,* **Y**~ *nmf* yemenite.

yen [jɛn] *nm (Fin)* yen.

yeux [jø] *nmpl de* **oeil.**

yoga [jɔga] *nm* yoga. **faire du** ~ to do yoga.

yoghourt [jɔguʀ(t)] *nm* = **yaourt.**

Yougoslavie [jugɔslavi] *nf* Yugoslavia. ◆ **yougoslave** *adj,* **Y**~ *nmf* Yugoslav(ian).

youpi [jupi] *excl* yippee.

youyou [juju] *nm* dinghy.

yo-yo [jojo] *nm inv* yo-yo.

yucca [juka] *nm* yucca.

Z

Z, z [zɛd] *nm (lettre)* Z, z.

Zaïre [zaiʀ] *nm* Zaire. ◆ **zaïrois, oise** *adj,* **Z**~**(e)** *nm(f)* Zairese.

Zambèze [zɑ̃bɛz] *nm:* **le** ~ the Zambezi.

Zambie [zɑ̃bi] *nf* Zambia.

zèbre [zɛbʀ(ә)] *nm (Zool)* zebra; *(*: individu)* bloke *, guy *. **courir comme un** ~ to run like a hare *ou* the wind.

zébrer [zebʀe] (6) *vt* to stripe, streak (*de* with).

zébu [zeby] *nm* zebu.

zèle [zɛl] *nm* zeal. *(péj)* **faire du** ~ to be overzealous, overdo it. ◆ **zélé, e** *adj* zealous.

zénith [zenit] *nm (lit, fig)* zenith.

zéro [zeʀo] **1** *nm* (**a**) *(gén, Math)* zero, nought; *(compte à rebours)* zero; *(dans un numéro de téléphone)* O, zero *(US)*. **recommencer à** ~ to start from scratch again, go back to square one; **taux de croissance** ~ zero growth; **3 degrés au-dessus de** ~ 3 degrees above freezing (point) *ou* above zero. (**b**) *(Rugby, Ftbl)* nil, zero, nothing *(US)*; *(Tennis)* love. ~ **à** ~ *ou* ~ *partout à la mi-temps* no score at half time; **gagner par 2 (buts) à ~** to win by 2 goals to nil *ou* zero. (**c**) *(Scol)* zero, nought. **~ de conduite** bad mark for behaviour *ou* conduct; *(fig)* **mais en cuisine, ~ (pour la question)** * but as far as cooking goes he's (*ou* she's) useless *ou* a dead loss *. (**d**) *(*: personne)* nonentity, dead loss *, washout *. **2** *adj:* **~ heure** *(gén)* midnight; *(heure GMT)* zero hour; **il a fait ~ faute** he didn't make any mistakes; **ça m'a coûté ~ franc ~ centime** * I got it for precisely *ou* exactly nothing.

zeste [zɔst(ə)] *nm:* **~ de citron** piece of lemon peel.

zézayer [zezeje] (8) *vi* to lisp. ◆ **zézaiement** *nm* lisp.

zibeline [ziblin] *nf* sable.

zig * [zig] *nm,* **zigomar** * [zigɔmaʀ] *nm,* **zigoto** * [zigɔto] *nm* bloke *, guy *.

zigouiller * [ziguje] **1** *vt* to do in *.

zigzag [zigzag] *nm* zigzag. **route en ~** winding *ou* zigzagging road. ◆ **zigzaguer 1** *vi* to zigzag (along).

Zimbabwe [zimbabwe] *nm* Zimbabwe.

zinc [zɛ̃g] *nm (métal)* zinc; *(*: avion)* plane; *(*: comptoir)* bar, counter. ◆ **zinguer** (1) *vt toiture* to cover with zinc; *acier* to coat with zinc.

zinzin * [zɛ̃zɛ̃] **1** *adj* cracked *, nuts *, barmy *. **2** *nm* what's-it *.

zip [zip] *nm* zip.

zizanie [zizani] *nf* ill-feeling, discord.

zizi * [zizi] *nm* willy *.

zodiaque [zɔdjak] *nm* zodiac.

zombi [zɔ̃bi] *nm* zombie.

zona [zona] *nm* shingles *(sg).*

zonard ‡ [zonaʀ] *nm (marginal)* dropout *.

zone [zon] *nf* zone, area. **~ bleue** ≃ restricted parking zone *ou* area; **~ dangereuse** danger zone; **~ franche** free zone; **~ franc** franc area; **~ industrielle** industrial park *ou* estate; **~ piétonnière** pedestrian precinct; *(fig)* **de deuxième/troisième ~** second-/third-rate; *(bidonville)* **la ~** the slum belt.

zoo [zoo] *nm* zoo. ◆ **zoologie** *nf* zoology. ◆ **zoologique** *adj* zoological. ◆ **zoologiste** *nmf ou* ◆ **zoologue** *nmf* zoologist.

zoom [zum] *nm (objectif)* zoom lens; *(effet)* zoom.

zouave [zwav] *nm* Zouave, zouave. **faire le ~** * to play the fool, fool around.

zozoter [zɔzɔte] (1) *vi* to lisp.

zut * [zyt] *excl (c'est embêtant)* dash (it)! *; *(tais-toi)* (do) shut up! *

ENGLISH - FRENCH
ANGLAIS - FRANÇAIS

A, a¹ [eɪ] *n* A, a *m*; *(Mus)* la *m*. **to know sth from A to Z** connaître qch de A à Z; *(houses)* **24a** le 24 bis; *(Aut)* **on the A4** ≃ sur la nationale 4. ◆ **A-1,** *(US)* **A number 1** *adj* champion *. ◆ **ABC** *n* abc *m*, alphabet *m*; **as easy as ABC** simple comme bonjour. ◆ **A-bomb** *n* bombe *f* atomique. ◆ **A-levels** *npl* ≃ baccalauréat *m*.

a² [eɪ, ə], **an** *indef art* un, une. ~ **tree** un arbre; **an apple** une pomme; **he smokes** ~ **pipe** il fume la pipe; ~ **third of the book** le tiers du livre; ~ **woman hates violence** les femmes détestent la violence; **she was** ~ **doctor** elle était médecin; **as** ~ **soldier** en tant que soldat; **my uncle,** ~ **sailor** mon oncle, qui est marin; **what** ~ **pleasure!** quel plaisir!; **I have heard of** ~ **Mr Martin** j'ai entendu parler d'un certain M. Martin; **they are of** ~ **size** ils sont de la même grandeur; **at** ~ **blow** d'un seul coup; **£4** ~ **person** 4 livres par personne; **3 francs** ~ **kilo** 3 F le kilo; **twice** ~ **month** deux fois par mois; **80 km an hour** 80 kilomètres-heure.

aback [ə'bæk] *adv*: **to be taken** ~ être interloqué (*by* par), en rester tout interdit.

abacus ['æbəkəs] *n* boulier *m* (compteur).

abandon [ə'bændən] **1** *vt (gen)* abandonner; *right* renoncer à; *lawsuit* se désister de. **to** ~ **ship** abandonner le navire. **2** *n*: **with** *(gay)* ~ avec (une belle) désinvolture. ◆ **abandoned** *adj* abandonné; *(dissolute)* débauché.

abase [ə'beɪs] *vt* abaisser; *(humiliate)* humilier. **to** ~ **o.s. so far as to do** s'abaisser jusqu'à faire.

abashed [ə'bæʃt] *adj* confus.

abate [ə'beɪt] *vi [storm, emotions, pain]* s'apaiser; *[flood, fever, noise]* baisser; *[pollution]* diminuer; *[wind]* se modérer. ◆ **abatement** *n [noise, pollution]* suppression *f*, réduction *f*.

abattoir ['æbətwɑːʳ] *n* abattoir *m*.

abbey ['æbɪ] *n* abbaye *f*.

abbot ['æbət] *n* abbé *m*, supérieur *m*.

abbreviate [ə'briːvɪeɪt] *vt* abréger. ◆ **abbreviation** *n* abréviation *f*.

abdicate ['æbdɪkeɪt] **1** *vt right* abdiquer; *responsibility, post* se démettre de. **to** ~ **the throne** abdiquer. **2** *vi* abdiquer. ◆ **abdication** *n [monarch]* abdication *f*.

abdomen ['æbdəmen] *n* abdomen *m*. ◆ **abdominal** [æb'dɒmɪnl] *adj* abdominal.

abduct [æb'dʌkt] *vt* enlever, kidnapper. ◆ **abduction** *n* enlèvement *m*. ◆ **abductor** *n* ravisseur *m*.

abed † [ə'bed] *adv* au lit. **to lie** ~ rester couché.

aberrant [ə'ber(ə)nt] *adj* aberrant, anormal. ◆ **aberration** *n* aberration *f*.

abet [ə'bet] *vt* encourager (*sb in a crime* qn à commettre un crime).

abeyance [ə'be(ɪ)əns] *n* suspension *f* temporaire. **to be in** ~ rester en suspens.

abhor [əb'hɔːʳ] *vt* abhorrer, avoir en horreur. ◆ **abhorrence** *n* horreur *f* (*of* de). ◆ **abhorrent** *adj* odieux (*to* à).

abide [ə'baɪd] *vt* **I can't** ~ **her** je ne peux pas la supporter; **I can't** ~ **living here** je ne supporte pas de vivre ici. ◆ **abide by** *vt fus rule, decision* se conformer à; *promise* rester fidèle à; *resolve* s'en tenir à. ◆ **abiding** *adj* éternel.

ability [ə'bɪlɪtɪ] *n* aptitude *f* (*to do* à faire), compétence *f* (*in* en; *to do* pour faire); *(skill)* talent *m*, don *m*. **to the best of one's** ~ de son mieux; **a person of great** ~ une personne très douée; **a certain artistic** ~ un certain talent artistique.

abject ['æbdʒekt] *adj person, action* abject; *state* misérable; *apology* servile; *poverty* extrême. ◆ **abjectly** *adv* abjectement; avec servilité.

abjure [əb'dʒʊəʳ] *vt* renoncer (publiquement) à.

ablaze [ə'bleɪz] *adj, adv*: **to be** ~ flamber; ~ **with** *anger* enflammé de; *light* resplendissant de.

able ['eɪbl] *adj (having means)* capable (*to do* de faire); *(clever)* capable, compétent; *(physically)* valide. **to be** ~ **to do** *(be capable of)* pouvoir faire; *(know how to)* savoir faire; ~ **to pay** en mesure de payer; **you are better** ~ **to do it** *(easier for you)* vous êtes mieux à même de le faire; *(better qualified)* vous êtes mieux désigné pour le faire; **I was** ~ **to catch the bus** j'ai réussi à attraper l'autobus. ◆ **able-bodied** *adj* robuste. ◆ **able(-bodied) seaman** *n* matelot breveté. ◆ **ably** *adv* habilement, de façon très compétente.

abnormal [æb'nɔːm(ə)l] *adj* anormal. ◆ **abnormality** *n (state)* caractère anormal; *(instance: gen, Bio, Psych)* anomalie *f*; *(Med)* malformation *f*. ◆ **abnormally** *adv formed* d'une manière anormale; *long, quiet etc* exceptionnellement.

aboard [ə'bɔːd] **1** *adv (Aviat, Naut)* à bord. **to go** ~ monter à bord; **to take** ~ embarquer; **all** ~! *(Rail)* en voiture!; *(Naut)* tout le monde à bord! **2** *prep (Aviat, Naut)* à bord de. ~ **ship** à bord; ~ **the train** dans le train.

abode [ə'bəʊd] *n* demeure *f*; *(Jur)* domicile *m*.

abolish [ə'bɒlɪʃ] *vt death penalty, law* abolir; *practice, custom, ignorance* supprimer. ◆ **abolishment** *or* ◆ **abolition** *n* abolition *f*; suppression *f*.

abominable [ə'bɒmɪnəbl] *adj* abominable. ◆ **abominably** *adv* abominablement.

abominate [ə'bɒmɪneɪt] *vt* abominer, exécrer. ◆ **abomination** *n* abomination *f*.

aborigine [,æbə'rɪdʒɪnɪ] *n* aborigène *mf*. ◆ **aboriginal** *adj, n* aborigène (*mf*).

abort [ə'bɔːt] **1** *vi (Med, fig)* avorter; *(Mil, Space)* échouer. **2** *vt (Med, fig)* faire avorter; *(Mil, Space)* abandonner (pour raisons de sécurité); *(Comput)* abandonner; *(* fig) deal* faire capoter. ◆ **abortion** *n (Med)* avortement *m*; **to have an ~ion** avorter; **to get an ~ion** se faire avorter. ◆ **abortionist** *n* avorteur *m*, -euse *f*. ◆ **abortive** *adj plan, invasion, coup* manqué, raté; *attempt* infructueux. ◆ **abortively** *adv* en vain.

abound [ə'baʊnd] *vi* abonder (*in* en).

about [ə'baʊt] **1** *adv* (**a**) *(approximately)* vers, à peu près, environ. ~ **11 o'clock** vers 11 heures; **it's** ~ **11 o'clock** il est environ 11 heures; **it's** ~ **time to go** il est presque temps de partir; **there are** ~ **30** il y en a une trentaine; **she's** ~ **as old as you** elle est à peu près de votre âge; **I've had** ~ **enough!** * je commence à en avoir marre! * (**b**) *(here and there)* çà et là, ici et là, de tous côtés. **shoes lying** ~ des chaussures dans tous les coins *or* traînant çà et là. (**c**) *(near)* près, par ici, par là. **there was nobody** ~ il n'y avait personne; **he's somewhere** ~ il est par ici quelque part; **there's**

a lot of flu ~ il y a beaucoup de cas de grippe en ce moment. (**d**) *(all round)* autour. **to glance** ~ jeter un coup d'œil autour de soi. (**e**) *(opposite direction)* à l'envers. *(fig)* **it's the other way** ~ c'est tout le contraire; *(Mil)* ~ **turn!** demi-tour, marche!; *(Naut)* **to go** ~ virer de bord. (**f**) **to be** ~ **to do** être sur le point de faire, aller faire. **2** *prep* (**a**) *(concerning)* au sujet de, à propos de. **I heard nothing** ~ **it** je n'en ai pas entendu parler; **what is it** ~? de quoi s'agit-il?; **I know what it's all** ~ je sais de quoi il retourne; **to speak** ~ **sth** parler de qch; **how** ~ * *or* **what** ~ * **going to the pictures?** si on allait au cinéma? (**b**) *(near to)* vers, près de; *(somewhere in)* en, dans. ~ **here** par ici, près d'ici; ~ **the house** quelque part dans la maison; **to wander** ~ **the town/the streets** errer dans la ville/par les rues. (**c**) *(occupied with)* **what are you** ~? que faites-vous?; **while we're** ~ **it** pendant que nous y sommes; **mind what you're** ~! faites un peu attention!; **how does one go** ~ **it?** comment est-ce qu'on s'y prend? (**d**) *(with, on)* **I've got it** ~ **me somewhere** je l'ai quelque part sur moi; **there is something interesting** ~ **him** il a un côté intéressant. (**e**) **(round)** ~ autour de. ◆ **about-face** *or* ◆ **about-turn** **1** *n (Mil)* demi-tour *m*; *(fig)* volte-face *f*; **2** *vi* faire un demi-tour ; faire volte-face.

above [əˈbʌv] **1** *adv* (**a**) *(overhead, higher up)* au-dessus, en haut. **from** ~ d'en haut; **the flat** ~ l'appartement au-dessus *or* du dessus; *(fig)* **a warning from** ~ un avertissement (venu) d'en haut. (**b**) *(more)* **boys of 6 and** ~ les garçons à partir de 6 ans. (**c**) *(earlier: in document etc)* ci-dessus, plus haut. **the address** ~ l'adresse ci-dessus. **2** *prep* (**a**) *(higher or better than)* au-dessus de. ~ **all** surtout. (**b**) *(more than)* plus de. **children** ~ **7 years of age** les enfants de plus de 7 ans *or* au-dessus de 7 ans; **over and** ~ **the cost of...** en plus de ce que coûte... (**c**) *(beyond)* au-delà de. **to get** ~ **o.s.** avoir des idées de grandeur; ~ **one's means** au-delà de *or* au-dessus de ses moyens; **that is quite** ~ **me** * c'est trop compliqué pour moi; **he is** ~ **such behaviour** il est au-dessus d'une pareille conduite; **he's not** ~ **stealing** il irait jusqu'à voler; **he's not** ~ **playing with the children** il ne dédaigne pas de jouer avec les enfants. **3** *adj (in text)* ci-dessus mentionné.
◆ **aboveboard** **1** *adj person, action* régulier, correct; **it's all quite** ~**board** *(not unfair)* c'est franc jeu; *(not illegal)* c'est régulier; **2** *adv* cartes sur table, ouvertement. ◆ **aboveground** *adv* au-dessus du sol, à la surface; *(US fig)* déclaré. ◆ **above-mentioned** *adj* ci-dessus mentionné. ◆ **above-named** *adj* susnommé.

abrasion [əˈbreɪʒ(ə)n] *n* frottement *m*; *(Med)* écorchure *f*; *(Geol)* érosion *f*; *(Tech)* abrasion *f*. ◆ **abrasive** *adj substance* abrasif; *voice* caustique; *wit* corrosif.

abreast [əˈbrest] *adv* de front. **3** ~ 3 de front; *(Naut)* **in line** ~ en ligne de front; ~ **of** *(at level of)* à la hauteur de; *(aware of)* au courant de; **to be** ~ **of the times** marcher avec son temps.

abridge [əˈbrɪdʒ] *vt book, edition, speech* abréger; *interview* écourter; *text* réduire. ◆ **abridgement** *n (short version)* abrégé *m*.

abroad [əˈbrɔːd] *adv* (**a**) *(in foreign land)* à l'étranger. **news from** ~ nouvelles de l'étranger. (**b**) *(far and wide)* au loin; *(in all directions)* de tous côtés, dans toutes les directions. **there is a rumour** ~ **that...** le bruit circule que...

abrupt [əˈbrʌpt] *adj person, conduct* brusque; *turn* soudain; *style, speech* heurté; *slope* raide. ◆ **abruptly** *adv turn, move* brusquement; *speak, behave* avec brusquerie; *rise* en pente raide. ◆ **abruptness** *n [person]* brusquerie *f*; *[departure]* soudaineté *f*; *(steepness)* raideur *f*.

abscess [ˈæbsɪs] *n* abcès *m*.

abscond [əbˈskɒnd] *vi* s'enfuir *(from* de). ◆ **absconder** *n* évadé(e) *m(f)*. **to be an** ~**er** être en cavale *.

abseil [ˈæpsaɪl] **1** *vi* descendre en rappel. **2** *n* rappel *m*.

absence [ˈæbs(ə)ns] *n* (**a**) absence *f*. *(Jur)* **sentenced in his** ~ condamné par contumace. (**b**) *(lack)* manque *m*, défaut *m*. **in the** ~ **of information** faute de renseignements.

absent [ˈæbs(ə)nt] **1** *adj* absent; *(absent-minded)* distrait. *(Mil)* ~ **without leave** absent sans permission. **2** [æbˈsent] *vt*: **to** ~ **o.s.** s'absenter *(from* de). ◆ **absentee** **1** *n* absent(e) *m(f)*; *(habitual)* absentéiste *mf*; **2** *adj* absentéiste. ◆ **absenteeism** *n* absentéisme *m*. ◆ **absently** *adv* distraitement. ◆ **absent-minded** *adj person* distrait; *air, manner* absent, distrait. ◆ **absent-mindedly** *adv* d'un air distrait *or* absent. ◆ **absent-mindedness** *n* distraction *f*, absence *f*.

absolute [ˈæbs(ə)luːt] **1** *adj (gen)* absolu. **the divorce was made** ~ le jugement en divorce a été prononcé; **it's an** ~ **scandal** c'est un véritable scandale; ~ **idiot** * parfait crétin *; **it's an** ~ **fact that...** c'est un fait indiscutable que...; ~ **proof** preuve *f* irréfutable. **2** *n* absolu *m*. ◆ **absolutely** *adv* absolument.

absolution [ˌæbsəˈluːʃ(ə)n] *n* absolution *f*.

absolve [əbˈzɒlv] *vt (from sin etc)* absoudre *(from, of* de); *(Jur)* acquitter *(of* de); *(from obligation, oath)* délier *(from* de).

absorb [əbˈsɔːb] *vt (lit, fig)* absorber; *sound, shock* amortir. **to become** ~**ed in one's work/in a book** s'absorber dans son travail/dans la lecture d'un livre; **to be** ~**ed in a book** être plongé dans un livre; **to be completely** ~**ed in one's work** être tout entier à son travail. ◆ **absorbed** *adj* absorbé *(in* dans). ◆ **absorbency** *n* pouvoir absorbant; *(Chem, Phys)* absorptivité *f*. ◆ **absorbent** *adj* absorbant; *(US)* ~**ent cotton** coton *m* hydrophile. ◆ **absorbing** *adj book, film* captivant; *work* absorbant. ◆ **absorption** *n* absorption *f*.

abstain [əbˈsteɪn] *vi* s'abstenir *(from* de; *from doing* de faire); *(be teetotaller)* s'abstenir complètement des boissons alcoolisées. ◆ **abstainer** *n (Pol)* abstentionniste *mf*; *(teetotaller)* personne *f* qui s'abstient de toute boisson alcoolisée.

abstemious [əbˈstiːmɪəs] *adj* frugal. ◆ **abstemiousness** *n* frugalité *f*.

abstention [əbˈstenʃ(ə)n] *n* abstention *f (from* de).

abstinent [ˈæbstɪnənt] *adj* sobre, tempérant. ◆ **abstinence** *n* abstinence *f*.

abstract [ˈæbstrækt] **1** *adj* abstrait. **2** *n (summary)* résumé *m*; *(work of art)* œuvre abstraite. **in the** ~ dans l'abstrait. **3** [æbˈstrækt] *vt (remove)* retirer *(from* de); *(summarize)* résumer. ◆ **abstracted** *adj* préoccupé. ◆ **abstraction** *n (removing)* extraction *f*; *(abstract concept)* abstraction *f*.

abstruse [æbˈstruːs] *adj* abstrus.

absurd [əbˈsɜːd] *adj, n* absurde (*m*). ◆ **absurdity** *n* absurdité *f*. ◆ **absurdly** *adv* absurdement.

abundant [əˈbʌndənt] *adj* abondant. **there is** ~ **proof that he is guilty** les preuves de sa culpabilité abondent. ◆ **abundance** *n* abondance *f*; **in abundance** en abondance. ◆ **abundantly** *adv supply etc* abondamment; *grow* à foison; *clear* tout à fait; **he made it** ~**ly clear to me that...** il m'a bien fait comprendre que...

abuse [əˈbjuːz] **1** *vt privilege* abuser de; *person (insult)* injurier; *(ill-treat)* maltraiter. **2** [əˈbjuːs] *n (gen)* abus *m*; *(curses, insults)* insultes *fpl*, injures *fpl*; *(ill-treatment)* mauvais traitements *mpl (of* infligés à). **child** ~ mauvais traitements infligés aux enfants. ◆ **abusive** *adj language* injurieux, offensant; *person* grossier.

abut [ə'bʌt] *vi*: **to ~ on** être contigu à.

abysmal [ə'bɪzm(ə)l] *adj ignorance* sans bornes; *mistake* énorme; *work* exécrable. ◆ **abysmally** *adv* abominablement, atrocement.

abyss [ə'bɪs] *n* abîme *m*, gouffre *m*.

acacia [ə'keɪʃə] *n* acacia *m*.

academic [ˌækə'demɪk] **1** *adj affairs, career* universitaire; *freedom* de l'enseignement; *progress* scolaire; *(scholarly) style, approach* intellectuel; *(theoretical)* théorique. *(US)* ~ **advisor** directeur *m*, -trice *f* des études; ~ **standards** niveaux *mpl* d'instruction; ~ **year** année *f* universitaire; **that's quite ~** ça n'a aucun intérêt pratique; **it's ~ now** ça n'a plus d'importance. **2** *n (person)* universitaire *mf*.

academy [ə'kædəmɪ] *n* académie *f*; *(Scol etc)* école *f*, collège *m*. **the Royal A~** l'Académie Royale *(de Londres)*; **military ~** école militaire. ◆ **academician** *n* académicien(ne) *m(f)*.

accede [æk'si:d] *vi*: **to ~ to a request** agréer une demande; **to ~ to the throne** monter sur le trône.

accelerate [æk'seləreɪt] **1** *vt movement* accélérer; *work* activer; *events* précipiter. **2** *vi (esp Aut)* accélérer. ◆ **acceleration** *n* accélération *f*. ◆ **accelerator** *n* accélérateur *m*.

accent ['æks(ə)nt] **1** *n (all senses)* accent *m*. **2** [æk'sent] *vt* accentuer. ◆ **accentuate** *vt* accentuer. ◆ **accentuation** *n* accentuation *f*.

accept [ək'sept] *vt (gen)* accepter; *goods* prendre livraison de. **I ~ that...** je conviens que... ◆ **acceptable** *adj gift, suggestion* acceptable; **the money was most ~able** l'argent était vraiment le bienvenu. ◆ **acceptance** *n* acceptation *f*. ◆ **accepted** *adj fact, method, principle* reconnu; *idea* répandu; *behaviour, pronunciation* admis; *sense, meaning* usuel.

access ['ækses] **1** *n* accès *m* (*to sth* à qch; *to sb* auprès de qn); *(Jur: in divorce)* droit *m* de visite; *(Comput)* **random ~** accès aléatoire. **2** *adj: (Comput)* ~ **time** temps *m* d'accès; ~ **road** route *f* d'accès; *(to motorway)* bretelle *f* d'accès. ◆ **accessibility** *n* accessibilité *f*. ◆ **accessible** *adj* accessible (*to* à).

accession [æk'seʃ(ə)n] *n [monarch]* avènement *m*.

accessory [æk'sesərɪ] **1** *adj* accessoire, auxiliaire. **2** *n* (**a**) *(Dress, Theat, Comm etc)* accessoire *m*. **toilet accessories** objets *mpl* de toilette. (**b**) *(Jur)* complice *mf* (*before the fact* par instigation; *after the fact* par assistance).

accident ['æksɪd(ə)nt] **1** *n* accident *m*. **by ~** *injure etc* accidentellement; *meet etc* par hasard. **2** *adj statistics etc* des accidents; *insurance* contre les accidents. ~ **prevention** prévention *f* des accidents; *(Aut)* prévention routière. ◆ **accidental** *adj death* accidentel; *meeting* fortuit; *effect, benefit* accessoire. ◆ **accidentally** *adv meet etc* par hasard; *injure etc* accidentellement; **it was done quite ~ally** on ne l'a pas fait exprès. ◆ **accident-prone** *adj* prédisposé aux accidents.

acclaim [ə'kleɪm] **1** *vt (applaud)* acclamer; *(proclaim)* proclamer. **2** *n* acclamations *fpl*. ◆ **acclamation** *n* acclamation *f*.

acclimatize [ə'klaɪmətaɪz], *(US)* **acclimate** [ə'klaɪmət] **1** *vt* acclimater (*to* à); *(fig)* accoutumer (*to* à). **2** *vi (also* **become ~d***)* s'acclimater; *(fig)* s'accoutumer. ◆ **acclimatization,** *(US)* **acclimation** *n* acclimatation *f*; *(fig)* accoutumance *f* (*to* à).

accommodate [ə'kɒmədeɪt] *vt* (**a**) *(lodge) [landlady, town council]* loger; *[car, house]* contenir; *[hotel]* recevoir. (**b**) *(supply)* fournir (*sb with sth* qch à qn); *demand* accéder à. **to ~ sb with a loan** consentir un prêt à qn. (**c**) *(reconcile) differences* concilier; *(adapt) plans, wishes* adapter (*to* à). ◆ **accommodating** *adj* accommodant, obligeant.

accommodation [əˌkɒmə'deɪʃ(ə)n] **1** *n* (**a**) *(also US* **~s***)* logement *m*. '**~ (to let)**' 'chambres *fpl* à louer'; **we have no ~ available** nous n'avons pas de place; **there is no ~ for children** on n'accepte pas les enfants. (**b**) *(compromise)* compromis *m*. **2** *adj*: ~ **address** *adresse utilisée pour la correspondance*; ~ **bureau** agence *f* de logement; ~ **officer** responsable *mf* de l'hébergement; *(US)* ~ **train** (train *m*) omnibus *m*.

accompany [ə'kʌmp(ə)nɪ] *vt* accompagner (*Mus: on* à). **accompanied by** accompagné de. ◆ **accompaniment** *n* accompagnement *m*. ◆ **accompanist** *n* accompagnateur *m*, -trice *f*.

accomplice [ə'kʌmplɪs] *n* complice *mf* (*in a crime* d'un crime).

accomplish [ə'kʌmplɪʃ] *vt* accomplir, exécuter; *task, mission* accomplir, achever; *desire* réaliser; *aim* arriver à; *journey* effectuer. ◆ **accomplished** *adj* accompli. ◆ **accomplishment** *n (achievement)* œuvre accomplie; *(skill)* talent *m*; *(completion)* réalisation *f*, accomplissement *m*.

accord [ə'kɔ:d] **1** *vt* accorder (*to* à). **2** *vi* s'accorder (*with* avec). **3** *n* (**a**) *(agreement)* consentement *m*, accord *m*. **of his own ~** de lui-même, de son propre chef; **with one ~** d'un commun accord. (**b**) *(treaty)* traité *m*. ◆ **accordance** *n* accord *m* (*with* avec); **in ~ance with** conformément à.

according [ə'kɔ:dɪŋ] *adv*: ~ **to** selon, suivant; **everything went ~ to plan** tout s'est passé comme prévu; ~ **to what he says** d'après ce qu'il dit; ~ **to him** selon lui. ◆ **accordingly** *adv* (**a**) *(and so)* en conséquence; (**b**) **to act ~ly** faire le nécessaire.

accordion [ə'kɔ:dɪən] *n* accordéon *m*. ◆ **accordionist** *n* accordéoniste *mf*.

accost [ə'kɒst] *vt* accoster.

account [ə'kaʊnt] **1** *n* (**a**) *(reckoning, bill)* compte *m*. **put it on my ~** vous le mettrez sur mon compte; **in ~ with** en compte avec; **to ~ rendered** facture non payée; **on ~** à compte; **to pay £50 on ~** verser un acompte de 50 livres; *(Advertising)* **they have the Michelin ~** ce sont eux qui détiennent la publicité de Michelin; **to keep the ~s** tenir la comptabilité *or* les comptes. (**b**) *(benefit)* profit *m*, avantage *m*. **to turn sth to ~** mettre qch à profit. (**c**) *(report)* compte rendu *m*. **to give an ~ of** faire le compte rendu de; **to call sb to ~ for having done** demander des comptes à qn pour avoir fait; **he gave a good ~ of himself** il s'en est bien tiré; **by all ~s** d'après l'opinion générale; **by her own ~** d'après ce qu'elle dit. (**d**) *(phrases)* **of no ~** sans importance; **to take sth into ~** tenir compte de qch; **on ~ of** à cause de; **on no ~** en aucun cas, sous aucun prétexte; **on her ~** à cause d'elle, pour elle. **2** *adj*: ~ **book** livre *m* de comptes; **~s department** (service *m* de) comptabilité *f*. **3** *vt* estimer, juger. **to ~ o.s. lucky** s'estimer heureux.

◆ **account for** *vt fus expenses* rendre compte de; *one's conduct* justifier; *circumstances* expliquer; *(Hunting etc: kill)* tuer. **there's no ~ing for tastes** chacun son goût; **everyone is ~ed for** on n'a oublié personne; *(after air crash etc)* tous les passagers ont été retrouvés.

◆ **accountability** *n* responsabilité *f*. ◆ **accountable** *adj*: **to be ~able for sth** avoir à répondre de qch (*to sb* devant qn). ◆ **accountancy** *n* comptabilité *f*. ◆ **accountant** *n* comptable *mf*; **~ant's office** agence *f* comptable. ◆ **accounting** *n* comptabilité *f*.

accoutrements [ə'ku:trəmənts], *(US)* **accouterments** [ə'ku:tərmənts] *npl (gen)* attirail *m*; *(Mil)* équipement *m*.

accredit [ə'kredɪt] *vt* accréditer (*to* auprès de).

accretion [ə'kri:ʃ(ə)n] *n* accroissement *m*.

accrue [ə'kru:] *vi [money, advantages]* revenir (*to* à); *[interest]* courir.

accumulate [ə'kjuːmjʊleɪt] **1** *vt* accumuler. **2** *vi* s'accumuler. ◆ **accumulation** *n (act)* accumulation *f*; *(heap of objects etc)* tas *m*. ◆ **accumulator** *n* accumulateur *m*.

accurate ['ækjʊrɪt] *adj figures, clock* exact; *report, story, shot* précis; *aim, judgment, assessment* juste; *memory, translation* fidèle. ◆ **accuracy** *n* exactitude *f*; précision *f*; justesse *f*; fidélité *f*. ◆ **accurately** *adv* exactement; avec précision; avec justesse; fidèlement.

accursed, accurst [ə'kɜːst] *adj (liter) (damned)* maudit; *(hateful)* détestable, exécrable.

accusative [ə'kjuːz(ə)tɪv] *adj, n* accusatif (*m*). **in the** ~ à l'accusatif.

accuse [ə'kjuːz] *vt* accuser (*of* de; *of doing* de faire). ◆ **accusal** *or* ◆ **accusation** *n* accusation *f*. ◆ **accused** *n* accusé(e) *m(f)*. ◆ **accuser** *n* accusateur *m*, -trice *f*. ◆ **accusing** *adj* accusateur. ◆ **accusingly** *adv* d'une manière accusatrice.

accustom [ə'kʌstəm] *vt* habituer, accoutumer (*to* à; *to doing* à faire). ◆ **accustomed** *adj* (**a**) *(used)* habitué, accoutumé (*to* à; *to do, to doing* à faire). **to become ~ed to** s'habituer *or* s'accoutumer à ; **I am not ~ed to such treatment** je n'ai pas l'habitude qu'on me traite *(subj)* de cette façon. (**b**) *(usual) kindness etc* habituel, coutumier.

ace [eɪs] *n* as *m (also fig: of sportsman etc)*. *(fig)* **to keep an ~ up one's sleeve,** *(US)* **to have an ~ in the hole** avoir une carte maîtresse; *(fig)* **to play one's ~** jouer sa meilleure carte; **within an ~ of** à deux doigts de.

acerbity [ə'sɜːbɪtɪ] *n* âpreté *f*, aigreur *f*.

acetate ['æsɪteɪt] *n* acétate *m*.

acetic [ə'siːtɪk] *adj* acétique.

acetone ['æsɪtəʊn] *n* acétone *f*.

acetylene [ə'setɪliːn] **1** *n* acétylène *m*. **2** *adj*: ~ **burner** chalumeau *m* à acétylène; ~ **welding** soudure *f* autogène.

ache [eɪk] **1** *vi* faire mal, être douloureux. **my head ~s** j'ai mal à la tête; **to be aching all over** *(after exercise)* être courbaturé; *(from illness)* avoir mal partout; **it makes my heart** ~ cela me fend le cœur; *(fig)* **to be aching to do** mourir d'envie de faire. **2** *n* douleur *f*, souffrance *f*. **stomach** ~ mal *m* de ventre; **I've got stomach** ~ j'ai mal au ventre; **all his ~s and pains** toutes ses douleurs. ◆ **aching** *adj* douloureux; *tooth, limb* malade; **to have an aching heart** avoir le cœur gros.

achieve [ə'tʃiːv] *vt aim* atteindre, arriver à; *success* obtenir; *fame* parvenir à. **I feel I've ~d sth** je crois que j'ai fait qch d'utile. ◆ **achievement** *n* réussite *f*, exploit *m*; *(Scol)* **the level of ~ment** le niveau des élèves.

acid ['æsɪd] **1** *n* acide *m*; *(*: LSD)* acide *. **2** *adj* acide; *(fig) person* revêche; *voice* aigre; *remark* mordant. ~ **rain** pluies *fpl* acides; *(fig)* ~ **test** épreuve décisive. ◆ **acidity** *n* acidité *f*.

acknowledge [ək'nɒlɪdʒ] *vt* (**a**) avouer, admettre (*that* que); *child, error* reconnaître. **to ~ sb as leader** reconnaître qn pour chef. (**b**) *greeting* répondre à; *(also ~* **receipt of***) letter, parcel* accuser réception de; *sb's action, services, help* manifester sa gratitude pour; *source of quotation etc* mentionner ; *applause, cheers* saluer pour répondre à. **I smiled at him but he didn't even ~ me** je lui ai souri mais il a fait comme s'il ne me voyait pas. ◆ **acknowledged** *adj* reconnu. ◆ **acknowledgement** *n [money]* reçu *m*; *[letter]* accusé *m* de réception; *(in preface etc)* remerciements *mpl*. **in ~ment of your help** en reconnaissance de votre aide.

acme ['ækmɪ] *n* point *m* culminant.

acne ['æknɪ] *n* acné *f*.

acorn ['eɪkɔːn] *n (Bot)* gland *m*.

acoustic [ə'kuːstɪk] *adj* acoustique. ◆ **acoustics** *n* (*sg or pl*) acoustique *f*.

acquaint [ə'kweɪnt] *vt* aviser (*sb with sth* qn de qch), renseigner (*sb with sth* qn sur qch). **to ~ sb with the situation** mettre qn au courant de la situation; **to be ~ed with** *person, subject* connaître; *fact* savoir, être au courant de; **to become ~ed with** *person* faire la connaissance de; *facts* prendre connaissance de. ◆ **acquaintance** *n* connaissance *f* ; **to make sb's ~ance** faire la connaissance de qn; **to improve upon ~ance** gagner à être connu; **old ~ances** de vieilles connaissances; **she's an ~ance of mine** c'est une de mes relations.

acquiesce [ˌækwɪ'es] *vi* consentir, acquiescer (*in* à). ◆ **acquiescence** *n* consentement *m*. ◆ **acquiescent** *adj* consentant.

acquire [ə'kwaɪə^r] *vt knowledge, money, fame* acquérir; *language* apprendre; *habit* prendre; *reputation* se faire; *car, house* faire l'acquisition de. **to ~ a taste for** prendre goût à. ◆ **acquired** *adj characteristic* acquis; *taste* qui s'acquiert. ◆ **acquirement** *n* acquisition *f* (*of* de); *(skill)* connaissance *f*.

acquisition [ˌækwɪ'zɪʃ(ə)n] *n* acquisition *f*. ◆ **acquisitive** *adj (for money)* âpre au gain; *(greedy)* avide (*of* de). ◆ **acquisitiveness** *n* instinct *m* de possession.

acquit [ə'kwɪt] *vt* (**a**) *(Jur)* acquitter (*of* de). (**b**) **to ~ o.s. well** bien s'en tirer. ◆ **acquittal** *n* acquittement *m*.

acre ['eɪkə^r] *n* ≃ demi-hectare *m*. **a few ~s of land** quelques hectares de terrain; *(fig)* **~s of** * des kilomètres et des kilomètres de.

acrid ['ækrɪd] *adj smell* âcre; *remark* acerbe.

Acrilan ['ækrɪlæn] *n* ® Acrilan *m* ®.

acrimonious [ˌækrɪ'məʊnɪəs] *adj* acrimonieux. ◆ **acrimony** *n* acrimonie *f*.

acrobat ['ækrəbæt] *n* acrobate *mf*. ◆ **acrobatic** *adj* acrobatique. ◆ **acrobatics** *npl [gymnast etc]* acrobatie *f*; *[child etc]* acrobaties *fpl*.

acronym ['ækrənɪm] *n* acronyme *m*.

across [ə'krɒs] **1** *prep* (**a**) *(from one side to other of)* d'un côté à l'autre de. **bridge ~ the river** pont sur le fleuve; **to walk ~ the road** traverser la route. (**b**) *(on other side of)* de l'autre côté de. **the shop ~ the road** le magasin d'en face, le magasin de l'autre côté de la rue; **lands ~ the sea** terres d'outre-mer. (**c**) *(crosswise over)* en travers de, à travers. **to go ~ the fields** *or* ~ **country** aller à travers champs; **plank ~ a door** planche en travers d'une porte; ~ **his chest** sur la poitrine. **2** *adv*: **the river is 5 km ~** le fleuve a 5 km de large; **to help sb ~** aider qn à traverser; *(fig)* **to get sth ~ to sb** faire comprendre qch à qn; ~ **from** en face de.

acrylic [ə'krɪlɪk] *adj,n* acrylique *(m)*.

act [ækt] **1** *n* (**a**) *(deed)* acte *m*. **in the ~ of doing** en train de faire; **caught in the ~** pris en flagrant délit; **A~s of the Apostles** Actes des Apôtres. (**b**) *(Jur: ~* **of Parliament***)* loi *f*. (**c**) *[play]* acte *m*; *(in circus etc)* numéro *m*. **he's just putting on an ~** il joue la comédie; **to get in on the ~** * (parvenir à) participer aux opérations; **to get one's ~ together** * se reprendre en main.
2 *vi* (**a**) *(gen)* agir. **to ~ like a fool** agir comme un imbécile; *[drug]* **to ~ on sth** agir sur qch; **the table ~s as a desk** la table sert de bureau; **he ~s as my assistant** il me sert d'assistant. (**b**) *(Theat)* jouer. **have you ever ~ed before?** avez-vous déjà fait du théâtre?; *(fig)* **she's only ~ing** elle joue la comédie.
3 *vt (Theat) part* jouer. *(Theat, fig)* **to ~ the part of** tenir le rôle de; *(fig)* **to ~ the fool** * faire l'idiot. ◆ **act out** *vt sep event* faire un récit mimé de; *fantasies* vivre. ◆ **act up** * *vi [person]* se conduire mal; *[car etc]* faire des caprices. ◆ **act (up)on** *vt fus advice* suivre, se conformer à; *order* exécuter.

I ~ed (up)on your letter j'ai fait le nécessaire quand j'ai reçu votre lettre.

acting ['æktɪŋ] **1** *adj* suppléant, par intérim. **2** *n*: **his ~ is very good** il joue très bien; **I like his ~** j'aime son jeu; **he has done some ~** il a fait du théâtre (*or* du cinéma).

action ['ækʃ(ə)n] **1** *n* (**a**) action *f*. **to put into ~** *plan* mettre à exécution; *principles, suggestion* mettre en action; *machine* mettre en marche; **the time has come for ~** il est temps d'agir; **they want a piece of the ~ *** ils veulent être dans le coup; **to take ~** agir; **to go into ~** passer à l'action; **out of ~** *machine etc* en dérangement, détraqué; *person* hors de combat; **to put out of ~** *machine* mettre hors d'usage, détraquer; *person* mettre hors de combat. (**b**) *(deed)* acte *m*, action *f*. **to suit the ~ to the word** joindre le geste à la parole; **~s speak louder than words** les actes sont plus éloquents que les paroles. (**c**) *(Jur)* procès *m*, action *f* en justice. **to bring an ~ against sb** intenter une action *or* un procès contre qn. (**d**) *(Tech)* mécanisme *m*; *[clock etc]* mécanique *f*. (**e**) *(Mil)* combat *m*, engagement *m*. **to go into ~** *[unit, person]* aller au combat; *[army]* engager le combat; **to see ~** combattre; **killed in ~** tué à l'ennemi. **2** *adj*: *(TV)* **~ replay** répétition immédiate *(d'une séquence)*; **~ stations!** à vos postes! **3** *vt (Admin)* exécuter. ◆ **actionable** *adj (Jur) claim* recevable; *person* passible de poursuites. ◆ **action-packed** *adj film* plein d'action.

activate ['æktɪveɪt] *vt* activer.

active ['æktɪv] *adj person, life, imagination* actif; *file, case* en cours; *volcano* en activité. **to take an ~ part in** prendre une part active à; **we're giving it ~ consideration** nous l'examinons sérieusement; *(Mil)* **on ~ service** en campagne; **on the ~ list** en activité; *(Gram)* **in the ~** à l'actif. ◆ **actively** *adv* activement. ◆ **activist** *n* militant(e) *m(f)*. ◆ **activity** *n (gen)* activité *f*; *[town, port]* mouvement *m*; **activity holiday** vacances *fpl* actives.

actor ['æktəʳ] *n* acteur *m*. ◆ **actress** *n* actrice *f*.

actual ['æktjʊəl] *adj figures, result* réel, véritable; *example* concret; *fact* positif. **in ~ fact** en fait; **his ~ words were...** il a dit très exactement... ◆ **actuality** *n* réalité *f*. ◆ **actually** *adv* (**a**) *(in reality)* effectivement, véritablement, en fait; **the person ~ly in charge is...** la personne véritablement responsable *or* responsable en fait, c'est...; **~ly I don't know him** à vrai dire *or* en fait, je ne le connais pas; **what did he ~ly say?** qu'est-ce qu'il a dit exactement *or* au juste? (**b**) *(even: often showing surprise)* vraiment; **it's ~ly taking place now** ça se produit en ce moment même.

actuary ['æktjʊərɪ] *n* actuaire *mf*.

actuate ['æktjʊeɪt] *vt* faire agir. **~d by** animé de.

acumen ['ækjʊmen] *n* flair *m*. **business ~** sens *m* aigu des affaires.

acupuncture ['ækjʊpʌŋktʃəʳ] *n* acupuncture *f*. ◆ **acupuncturist** *n* acupuncteur *m*.

acute [ə'kju:t] *adj pain, accent, angle* aigu (*f* -guë); *remorse* intense; *shortage, situation* critique, grave; *person, mind* pénétrant, perspicace; *hearing* fin. ◆ **acutely** *adv* (**a**) *(intensely) suffer* vivement, intensément; **~ly aware that** profondément conscient du fait que; (**b**) *(shrewdly) observe* avec perspicacité.

ad [æd] *n abbr of* **advertisement.**

Adam ['ædəm] *n* Adam *m*. **~'s apple** pomme *f* d'Adam; **I don't know him from ~ *** je ne le connais ni d'Ève ni d'Adam.

adamant ['ædəmənt] *adj* inflexible.

adapt [ə'dæpt] **1** *vt* adapter (*to* à, *for* pour). **2** *vi* s'adapter. ◆ **adaptability** *n* faculté *f* d'adaptation. ◆ **adaptable** *adj* adaptable; **he's very ~able** il s'adapte à tout. ◆ **adaptation** *n* adaptation *f* (*of* de, *to* à). ◆ **adapter** *or* ◆ **adaptor** *n (person)* adaptateur *m*, -trice *f*; *(device)* adaptateur *m*; *(Elec)* prise *f* multiple.

add [æd] *vt* (**a**) ajouter (*to* à, *that* que). **~ some more pepper** rajoutez un peu de poivre; **to ~ insult to injury** porter l'insulte à son comble; **~ed to which...** ajoutez à cela que...; **an ~ed advantage** un avantage supplémentaire. (**b**) *(Math) figures* additionner; *column of figures* totaliser. ◆ **add in** *vt sep* inclure, ajouter. ◆ **add to** *vt fus* ajouter à, accroître. ◆ **add together** *vt sep* additionner. ◆ **add up 1** *vi (fig)* **it all ~s up *** tout s'explique; **it doesn't ~ up *** il y a qch qui cloche *. **2** *vt sep figures* additionner; *column of figures* totaliser; *advantages, reasons* faire la somme de. ◆ **add up to** *vt fus [figures]* s'élever à; *(* fig: mean)* signifier. ◆ **adding machine** *n* machine *f* à calculer. ◆ **additive** *n* additif *m;* **~-free** sans additif.

adder ['ædəʳ] *n* vipère *f*.

addict ['ædɪkt] *n* intoxiqué(e) *m(f)*. **heroin ~** héroïnomane *mf*; **he's an ~** il ne peut plus s'en passer; **he's a yoga ~ *** c'est un fanatique du yoga. ◆ **addicted** *adj* adonné (*to* à); **to become ~ed to** s'adonner à; **he's ~ed to cigarettes** c'est un fumeur invétéré. ◆ **addiction** *n* penchant *m* très fort (*to* pour); *(Med)* dépendance *f* (*to* à). ◆ **addictive** *adj* qui crée une dépendance.

Addis Ababa ['ædɪs'æbəbə] *n* Addis-Abeba.

addition [ə'dɪʃ(ə)n] *n (Math etc)* addition *f*; *(fact of adding)* adjonction *f*; *(increase)* augmentation *f* (*to* de); *(to tax, income, profit)* surcroît *m* (*to* de). **in ~** de plus; **in ~ to** en plus de; **there's been an ~ to the family** la famille s'est agrandie; **this is a welcome ~ to the series** ceci enrichit la série. ◆ **additional** *adj* additionnel; *(extra)* de plus, supplémentaire. ◆ **additionally** *adv* de plus, en sus.

address [ə'dres] **1** *n* (**a**) *(US)* ['ædres] *(on letter etc, also Comput)* adresse *f*. (**b**) *(talk)* discours *m*, allocution *f*. **2** *vt* (**a**) *(direct) letter, speech, writing* adresser (*to* à). **this is ~ed to you** *[letter etc]* ceci vous est adressé; *[words, comment]* ceci s'adresse à vous; **to ~ o.s. to sth** se mettre à qch. (**b**) *(speak to)* s'adresser à. **he ~ed the meeting** il a pris la parole (devant l'assistance); **don't ~ me as 'Colonel'** ne m'appelez pas 'Colonel'. ◆ **addressee** *n* destinataire *mf*.

adenoids ['ædɪnɔɪdz] *npl* végétations *fpl* (adénoïdes). ◆ **adenoidal** *adj*: **in an adenoidal voice** en parlant du nez.

adept ['ædept] **1** *n* expert *m* (*in, at* en). **2** [ə'dept] *adj* expert (*in, at* à, en, dans; *at doing* à faire).

adequate ['ædɪkwit] *adj amount, supply, reward, description* suffisant (*for* pour, *to do* pour faire); *tool etc* adapté (*to* à); *essay, performance* satisfaisant; *person* compétent. ◆ **adequately** *adv warm* suffisamment; *do etc* convenablement.

adhere [əd'hɪəʳ] *vi* adhérer (*to* à). **to ~ to** *party* adhérer à; *rule* obéir à; *promise* tenir; *resolve* persister dans. ◆ **adherence** *n* adhésion *f* (*to* à). ◆ **adherent** *n* adhérent(e) *m(f)*; *(Rel)* adepte *mf*. ◆ **adhesion** *n* adhérence *f*. ◆ **adhesive** *adj, n* adhésif *(m)* ; **adhesive plaster** pansement adhésif; **adhesive tape** *(Med)* sparadrap *m*; *(stationery)* ruban adhésif.

adieu [ə'dju:] *n, excl* adieu *m*.

ad infinitum [,ædɪnfɪ'naɪtəm] *adv* à l'infini.

adjacent [ə'dʒeɪs(ə)nt] *adj (gen)* voisin (*to* de); *(Math)* adjacent.

adjective ['ædʒektɪv] *n* adjectif *m*. ◆ **adjectival** *adj* adjectival.

adjoin [ə'dʒɔɪn] *vt* être contigu à. ◆ **adjoining** *adj* voisin.

adjourn [ə'dʒɜ:n] **1** *vt* ajourner, reporter (*to, until* à; *for a month* à un mois); *(Jur) case* renvoyer (*to* à). **to ~ a meeting** *(break off)* suspendre la séance; *(close)* lever la séance. **2** *vi (break off)* suspendre la séance; *(close)* lever la séance; *[Parliament]* s'ajourner. **to ~ to the drawing room** passer au salon. ◆ **adjournment** *n* ajournement *m*; renvoi *m*; suspension *f*.

adjudicate [ə'dʒu:dɪkeɪt] *vt case, competition* juger; *claim* décider. ◆ **adjudication** *n* jugement *m*; décision *f*. ◆ **adjudicator** *n* juge *m*.

adjunct ['ædʒʌŋkt] *n* accessoire *m*.

adjust [ə'dʒʌst] **1** *vt speed, tool, lever* ajuster; *machine, brakes* régler; *production, terms* ajuster; *wages, prices* rajuster; *(correct) figures* rectifier; *differences* régler; *clothes* rajuster. **2** *vi [person] (to circumstances)* s'adapter; *(to new demands)* faire face à; *[machine]* se régler. ◆ **adjustable** *adj height, tool* ajustable, réglable; *shape* ajustable; *rate, hours* flexible; **~ spanner** clé *f* universelle. ◆ **adjustment** *n (to height, speed)* ajustage *m*, réglage *m*; *(to machine)* réglage *m*; *(to plan, terms)* ajustement *m*; *(to wages, prices)* rajustement *m*; **to make ~ments** *(to circumstances)* s'adapter.

ad lib [æd'lɪb] **1** *adv continue* à volonté. **there was food ~** il y avait à manger à discrétion. **2 ad-lib** *n* improvisation *f*. **3** *adj* improvisé. **4 ad-lib** *vti* improviser.

adman * ['ædmæn] *n* publicitaire *m*.

admass ['ædmæs] **1** *n* masses *fpl*. **2** *adj* de masse.

admin * ['ædmɪn] *n abbr of* **administration.**

administer [əd'mɪnɪstəʳ] *vt (gen)* administrer (*to* à); *funds* gérer. **to ~ an oath to sb** faire prêter serment à qn. ◆ **administration** *n* administration *f*; *[funds]* gestion; *(Pol)* **under previous administrations** sous des gouvernements précédents. ◆ **administrative** *adj* administratif. ◆ **administrator** *n* administrateur *m*, -trice *f*.

admiral ['ædm(ə)rəl] *n* amiral *m* (d'escadre). **A~ of the Fleet** ≃ Amiral *m* de France. ◆ **Admiralty Board** *n (Brit)* ≃ ministère *m* de la Marine.

admire [əd'maɪəʳ] *vt* admirer. ◆ **admirable** ['ædm(ə)rəbl] *adj* admirable. ◆ **admirably** *adv* admirablement. ◆ **admiration** *n* admiration *f* (*of, for* pour); **to be the admiration of** faire l'admiration de. ◆ **admirer** *n* admirateur *m*, -trice *f*; *(†: suitor)* soupirant † *m*. ◆ **admiring** *adj* admiratif. ◆ **admiringly** *adv* avec admiration.

admissible [əd'mɪsəbl] *adj plan* acceptable; *evidence* recevable.

admission [əd'mɪʃ(ə)n] *n* (**a**) *(entry)* admission *f*, entrée *f* (*to* à). **~ free** entrée gratuite; **to gain ~ to** *person* trouver accès auprès de; *place* être admis dans. (**b**) *(confession)* aveu *m*. **by one's own ~** de son propre aveu.

admit [əd'mɪt] *vt* (**a**) *(let in)* laisser entrer. **children not ~ted** entrée interdite aux enfants; **this ticket ~s 2** ce billet est valable pour 2 personnes. (**b**) *(acknowledge)* reconnaître, admettre (*that* que); *[criminal]* avouer (*that* que); *crime* reconnaître avoir commis; *one's guilt* reconnaître. **I must ~ that...** je dois avouer *or* admettre que...; **I was wrong I ~** j'ai eu tort, j'en conviens.
◆ **admit of** *vt fus* admettre, permettre. ◆ **admit to** *vt fus crime* reconnaître avoir commis. **to ~ to having done** reconnaître avoir fait; **to ~ to a feeling of** avouer avoir un sentiment de.
◆ **admittance** *n* droit *m* d'entrée, admission *f* (*to sth* à qch); accès *m* (*to sth* à qch; *to sb* auprès de qn); **I gained ~tance** on m'a laissé entrer ; **no ~tance except on business** accès interdit à toute personne étrangère au service. ◆ **admittedly** *adv*: **~tedly this is true** je reconnais *or* il faut reconnaître que c'est vrai.

admonish [əd'mɒnɪʃ] *vt (reprove)* réprimander (*for doing* pour avoir fait; *about, for* pour, à propos de); *(warn)* avertir (*against doing* de ne pas faire); *(exhort)* exhorter (*to do* à faire). ◆ **admonition** *n* réprimande *f*; avertissement *m*.

ad nauseam [ˌæd'nɔ:sɪæm] *adv* à satiété.

ado [ə'du:] *n*: **much ~ about nothing** beaucoup de bruit pour rien; **without more ~** sans plus de cérémonies.

adolescent [ˌædə(ʊ)'lesnt] *adj, n* adolescent(e) *m(f)*. ◆ **adolescence** *n* adolescence *f*.

adopt [ə'dɒpt] *vt child, method, (Pol) motion* adopter; *candidate, career* choisir. ◆ **adopted** *adj child* adopté; *country* d'adoption; *son, family* adoptif. ◆ **adoption** *n* adoption *f*; choix *m*. ◆ **adoptive** *adj parent, child* adoptif; *country* d'adoption.

adore [ə'dɔ:ʳ] *vt* adorer. ◆ **adorable** *adj* adorable. ◆ **adoration** *n* adoration *f*. ◆ **adoringly** *adv* avec adoration.

adorn [ə'dɔ:n] *vt room* orner; *dress* parer (*with* de). **to ~ o.s.** se parer. ◆ **adornment** *n* ornement *m*; parure *f*.

adrenalin(e) [ə'drenəlɪn] *n* adrénaline *f*. *(fig)* **he felt the ~ rising** il a senti son pouls s'emballer.

Adriatic (Sea) [ˌeɪdrɪ'ætɪk('si:)] *n* (mer *f*) Adriatique *f*.

adrift [ə'drɪft] *adv, adj (Naut)* à la dérive. **to turn ~** *boat* abandonner à la dérive; *(fig) person* laisser se débrouiller tout seul; **to come ~** * *[wire etc]* se détacher; *[plans]* tomber à l'eau.

adroit [ə'drɔɪt] *adj* adroit. ◆ **adroitly** *adv* adroitement. ◆ **adroitness** *n* adresse *f*.

adulate ['ædjʊleɪt] *vt* aduler. ◆ **adulation** *n* adulation *f*.

adult ['ædʌlt] **1** *n* adulte *mf*. *(Cine etc)* **~s only** interdit aux moins de 18 ans. **2** *adj person, animal* adulte; *film, book, classes* pour adultes. **~ education** enseignement *m* pour adultes.

adulterate [ə'dʌltəreɪt] *vt* frelater.

adultery [ə'dʌltərɪ] *n* adultère *m*. ◆ **adulterous** *adj* adultère.

advance [əd'vɑ:ns] **1** *n* (**a**) *(gen, Mil)* avance *f*; *[ideas, science]* progrès *mpl*. **to make ~s in technology** faire des progrès *mpl* en technologie; **to make ~s to sb** faire des avances *fpl* à qn; **in ~** *prepare, thank, book* à l'avance; *decide, announce* d'avance; **to be in ~ of one's time** être en avance sur son époque; **a week in ~** une semaine à l'avance; **luggage in ~** bagages enregistrés. (**b**) *(sum of money)* avance *f* (*on* sur). **2** *adj payment* anticipé; *copy of speech etc* distribué à l'avance. **~ guard** avant-garde *f*; **~ notice** préavis *m*; *(Mil)* **~ party** pointe *f* d'avant-garde; **~ post** poste avancé. **3** *vt (gen)* avancer; *work* faire avancer; *cause* promouvoir. **4** *vi* avancer, s'avancer (*on* sur, *towards* vers); *[troops]* se porter en avant; *[work, civilization, mankind]* progresser, faire des progrès. **he ~d upon me** il est venu vers *or* a marché sur moi.
◆ **advanced** *adj ideas, age, child* avancé; *studies, class* supérieur; *work* poussé; *technology, equipment* de pointe; **~d mathematics** hautes études *fpl* mathématiques. ◆ **advancement** *n* avancement *m*.

advantage [əd'vɑ:ntɪdʒ] *n* avantage *m*. **to have an ~ over sb** avoir un avantage sur qn; **to have the ~ of numbers** avoir l'avantage du nombre; **to take ~ of** *occasion* profiter de; *person* exploiter; **to turn sth to ~** tourner qch à son avantage ; **I find it to my ~** j'y trouve mon compte; **it is to his ~ to do it** c'est son intérêt de le faire; **this dress shows her off to ~** cette robe l'avantage. ◆ **advantageous** *adj* avantageux (*to* pour).

advent ['ædvənt] *n* avènement *m*. *(Rel)* **A~** l'Avent *m*.

adventure [əd'ventʃəʳ] **1** *n* aventure *f*. **2** *adj story, film* d'aventures; **~ playground** aire *f* de jeux. ◆ **adventurer** *n* aventurier *m*. ◆ **adventuress** *n* aventurière *f*. ◆ **adventurous** *adj* aventureux.

adverb ['ædvɜːb] *n* adverbe *m*. ◆ **adverbial** *adj* adverbial.

adversary ['ædvəs(ə)rɪ] *n* adversaire *mf*.

adverse ['ædvɜːs] *adj factor, report, circumstances* défavorable; *wind* contraire. ◆ **adversity** *n* adversité *f*.

advert * ['ædvɜːt] *n abbr of* **advertisement.**

advertise ['ædvətaɪz] **1** *vt (Comm etc) goods* faire de la publicité *or* de la réclame pour. **I've seen that ~d on television** j'ai vu une publicité pour ça à la télévision; **to ~ a flat for sale** mettre une annonce pour vendre un appartement; **try not to ~ the fact that...** essaie de ne pas trop laisser voir que...; **don't ~ your ignorance!** inutile d'afficher votre ignorance! **2** *vi (Comm)* faire de la publicité *or* de la réclame. **it pays to ~** la publicité paie; **to ~ for a flat** faire paraître une annonce pour trouver un appartement. ◆ **advertiser** *n* annonceur *m* (publicitaire). ◆ **advertising** **1** *n* publicité *f* ; **2** *adj (gen)* publicitaire; *agency* de publicité.

advertisement [əd'vɜːtɪsmənt] *n* (**a**) *(Comm)* réclame *f*, publicité *f*; *(TV)* spot *m* publicitaire. *(Cine, Press, Rad, TV)* **~s** publicité; *(TV)* **during the ~s** pendant que passait la publicité; **he's not a good ~ for his school** il ne constitue pas une bonne réclame pour son école. (**b**) *(private: in paper etc)* annonce *f*. **~ column** petites annonces; **to put an ~ in a paper** mettre une annonce dans un journal.

advice [əd'vaɪs] *n* avis *m*, conseils *mpl*; *(Comm: notification)* avis. **a piece of ~** un avis, un conseil; **to seek ~ from sb** demander conseil à qn; **to take medical ~** consulter un médecin; **to follow sb's ~** suivre le(s) conseil(s) de qn.

advise [əd'vaɪz] *vt* (**a**) *(give advice to)* conseiller (*sb on/about sth* qn sur/à propos de qch). **to ~ sb to do** conseiller à qn de faire; **to ~ sb against sth** déconseiller qch à qn; **to ~ sb against doing** conseiller à qn de ne pas faire; **you would be well/ ill ~d to do that** vous feriez bien de/vous auriez tort de faire cela. (**b**) *(recommend) course of action* recommander. (**c**) *(inform)* aviser (*sb of sth* qn de qch). ◆ **advisability** *n* opportunité *f* (*of* de, *of doing* de faire). ◆ **advisable** *adj* recommandé, conseillé; **I do not think it advisable for you to come** je ne vous conseille pas de venir. ◆ **advisedly** *adv* en toute connaissance de cause. ◆ **adviser, advisor** *n* conseiller *m*, -ère *f*. ◆ **advisory** *adj* consultatif; **in an advisory capacity** à titre consultatif.

advocate ['ædvəkɪt] **1** *n* (**a**) *[cause etc]* défenseur *m*, avocat(e) *m(f)*. **to be an ~ of** être partisan de. (**b**) *(Scot Jur)* avocat *m* (plaidant). **2** ['ædvəkeɪt] *vt* recommander, préconiser.

Aegean (Sea) [iː'dʒiːən('siː)] *n* mer *f* Égée.

aegis ['iːdʒɪs] *n*: **under the ~ of** sous l'égide *f* de.

aeons ['iːənz] *npl* éternités *fpl*.

aerate ['ɛəreɪt] *vt liquid* gazéifier; *blood* oxygéner; *room* aérer; *soil* retourner. **~d water** eau *f* gazeuse.

aerial ['ɛərɪəl] **1** *adj* aérien. **~ railway** téléphérique *m*. **2** *n (Telec etc)* antenne *f*.

aero... ['ɛərəʊ] *pref* aéro... ◆ **aerobatics** *npl* acrobatie *f* aérienne. ◆ **aerobics** *n* aérobic *m*. ◆ **aerodrome** *n* aérodrome *m*. ◆ **aerodynamic** *adj* aérodynamique. ◆ **aerodynamics** *nsg* aérodynamique *f*. ◆ **aero-engine** *n* aéromoteur *m*. ◆ **aerogramme** *n* aérogramme *m*. ◆ **aeronaut** *n* aéronaute *mf*. ◆ **aeronautic(al)** *adj* aéronautique. ◆ **aeronautics** *nsg* aéronautique *f*. ◆ **aeroplane** *n* avion *m*. ◆ **aerosol** **1** *n (system)* aérosol *m*; *(spray)* bombe *f* ; **2** *adj* en bombe. ◆ **aerospace** *adj*: **~space industry** industrie aérospatiale.

aesthete ['iːsθiːt] *n* esthète *mf*. ◆ **aesthetic(al)** *adj* esthétique. ◆ **aesthetically** *adv* esthétiquement. ◆ **aestheticism** *n* esthétisme *m*. ◆ **aesthetics** *nsg* esthétique *f*.

afar [ə'fɑːʳ] *adv* au loin. **from ~** de loin.

affable ['æfəbl] *adj* affable. ◆ **affability** *n* affabilité *f*. ◆ **affably** *adv* avec affabilité.

affair [ə'fɛəʳ] *n (gen)* affaire *f*; *(love ~)* liaison *f* (*with* avec). **the Suez ~** l'affaire de Suez; **this is not her ~** ce n'est pas son affaire, cela ne la regarde pas; **state of ~s** situation *f*; **~s of state** affaires d'État.

affect [ə'fekt] *vt* (**a**) *(have effect on) result* avoir un effet sur, modifier; *decision* influer sur; *(harm) person* atteindre, toucher; *health, conditions* détériorer; *(concern)* concerner, toucher; *(move)* affecter. **don't let it ~ you** ne te laisse pas décourager par ça. (**b**) *[disease]* attaquer, atteindre; *[drug]* agir sur. (**c**) *(feign)* affecter, feindre. ◆ **affectation** *n* affectation *f*. ◆ **affected** *adj* affecté. ◆ **affectedly** *adv* avec affectation.

affection [ə'fekʃ(ə)n] *n* affection *f* (*for* pour). **I have a great ~ for her** j'ai beaucoup d'affection pour elle. ◆ **affectionate** *adj* affectueux; *(letter-ending)* **your ~ate daughter** votre fille affectionnée. ◆ **affectionately** *adv* affectueusement; **yours ~ately** (bien) affectueusement à vous.

affidavit [ˌæfɪ'deɪvɪt] *n (Jur)* déclaration *f* par écrit sous serment. **to swear an ~ to the effect that** déclarer sous serment que.

affiliate [ə'fɪlɪeɪt] *vt* affilier (*to, with* à). **~d company** filiale *f*. ◆ **affiliation** *n* affiliation *f*.

affinity [ə'fɪnɪtɪ] *n (gen)* affinité *f* (*with, to* avec; *between* entre). *[people]* **there is a certain ~ between them** ils ont des affinités.

affirm [ə'fɜːm] *vt* affirmer (*that* que). ◆ **affirmation** *n* affirmation *f*. ◆ **affirmative** *adj, n* affirmatif *(m)*; **in the ~ative** *(Gram)* à l'affirmatif; *answer* affirmativement; *(US)* **~ative action** mesures *fpl* antidiscriminatoires en faveur des minorités. ◆ **affirmatively** *adv* affirmativement.

affix [ə'fɪks] **1** *vt seal, signature* apposer (*to* à); *stamp* coller (*to* à). **2** ['æfɪks] *n* affixe *m*.

afflict [ə'flɪkt] *vt* affliger. **~ed with** affligé de. ◆ **affliction** *n* affliction *f*.

affluent ['æflʊənt] *adj person* riche; *society* d'abondance. ◆ **affluence** *n (wealth)* richesse *f*; *(plenty)* abondance *f*.

afford [ə'fɔːd] *vt* (**a**) *(gen)* avoir les moyens (*to do* de faire); *object, car* s'offrir, se payer *. **he can't ~ (to make) a mistake** il ne peut pas se permettre (de faire) une erreur; **I can't ~ the time to do it** je n'ai pas le temps de le faire. (**b**) *(provide) opportunity* fournir; *pleasure* procurer.

afforestation [æˌfɒrɪs'teɪʃ(ə)n] *n* (re)boisement *m*.

affray [ə'freɪ] *n* échauffourée *f*.

affront [ə'frʌnt] **1** *vt (insult)* faire un affront à; *(face)* affronter. **2** *n* affront *m*.

Afghanistan [æf'gænɪstæn] *n* Afghanistan *m*. ◆ **Afghan** **1** *adj* afghan; **2** Afghan(e) *m(f)*.

afield [ə'fiːld] *adv*: **far ~** très loin; **further ~** plus loin.

afloat [ə'fləʊt] *adv* à flot *(also fig)*; *(Naut: on board ship)* en mer. **to stay ~** *[ship]* rester à flot; *[person] (in water)* surnager; *(fig)* rester à flot.

afoot [ə'fʊt] *adv*: **there is sth ~** il se prépare qch; **there is a plan ~ to do** on envisage de faire.

afraid [ə'freɪd] *adj*: **to be ~ of sb/sth** avoir peur de qn/qch, craindre qn/qch; **don't be ~** n'ayez pas peur, ne craignez rien; **I am ~ of hurting him** j'ai peur *or* je crains de lui faire mal; **I am ~ he will hurt me** je crains *or* j'ai peur qu'il (ne) me fasse mal; **I am ~ to go** je n'ose pas y aller, j'ai peur d'y aller; **he is not ~ of work** le travail ne lui fait pas peur; *(regret)* **I'm ~ I can't do it** je regrette *or* je suis désolé, mais je ne pourrai pas le faire; **I'm ~ that...** je regrette de vous dire que...; **I'm ~ not/so** hélas non/oui; **there are too many people, I'm ~** je regrette, mais il y a trop de monde.

afresh [ə'freʃ] *adv* de nouveau. **to start ~** recommencer.

Africa ['æfrɪkə] *n* Afrique *f*. ◆ **African** **1** *n* Africain(e) *m(f)*; **2** *adj (gen)* africain; *elephant* d'Afrique.

Afrikaans [ˌæfrɪ'kɑːns] *n* afrikaans *m*. ◆ **Afrikaaner** *n* Afrikander *mf*.

afro * ['æfrəʊ] *adj* afro * *inv*.

Afro- ['æfrəʊ] *pref:* **~-American** afro-américain; **~-Asian** afro-asiatique.

aft [ɑːft] *adv (Naut)* sur *or* à *or* vers l'arrière.

after ['ɑːftəʳ] **1** *prep* après. **~ dinner** après le dîner; **the day ~ tomorrow** après-demain; **shortly ~ 10 o'clock** peu après 10 heures; **it was ~ 2 o'clock** il était plus de 2 heures; *(US)* **it was 20 ~ 3** il était 3 heures 20; **~ all** après tout; **~ hours** * après la fermeture; **~ seeing her** après l'avoir vue; **~ you** après vous; **~ you with the salt** * passez-moi le sel, s'il vous plaît; **to run ~ sb** courir après qn; **he shut the door ~ her** il a refermé la porte sur elle; **shut the door ~ you** fermez la porte (derrière vous); **day ~ day** jour après jour; **for kilometre ~ kilometre** sur des kilomètres et des kilomètres; **you tell me lie ~ lie** tu me racontes mensonge sur mensonge; **time ~ time** maintes et maintes fois; **they went out one ~ the other** ils sont sortis *(individually)* les uns après les autres *or (in a line)* à la file; *(according to)* **~ El Greco** d'après Le Gréco; **she takes ~ her mother** elle tient de sa mère; **to name a child ~ sb** donner à un enfant le nom de qn; **to be ~ sb/sth** chercher qn/qch; *(after loss, robbery etc)* rechercher qn/qch; **the police are ~ him** il est recherché par la police; **what are you ~?** *(want)* qu'est-ce que vous désirez?; *(thinking of)* où voulez-vous en venir?; *(nagging)* **she's always ~ her children** * elle est toujours après ses enfants *.
2 *adv* après, ensuite. **for years ~** pendant des années après cela; **soon ~** bientôt après; **the week ~** la semaine d'après, la semaine suivante.
3 *conj* après (que). **~ he had closed the door, she spoke** après qu'il eut fermé la porte, elle parla; **~ he had closed the door, he spoke** après avoir fermé la porte, il a parlé.
4 *adj*: **in ~ life** *or* **~ years** plus tard (dans la vie).
5 *npl (dessert)* **~s** * dessert *m*.
◆ **afterbirth** *n* placenta *m*. ◆ **aftercare** *n [convalescent]* post-cure *f*; *[ex-prisoner]* assistance *f* (aux anciens détenus). ◆ **after-dinner drink** *n* digestif *m*. ◆ **after-dinner speaker** *n* orateur *m* (de fin de banquet). ◆ **after-effect** *n [events etc]* suite *f*, répercussion *f*; *[treatment]* réaction *f*; *[illness]* séquelle *f*; *(Psych)* after-effect *m*. ◆ **afterlife** *n* vie future. ◆ **after-lunch** *adj*: **to have an ~-lunch nap** faire la sieste. ◆ **aftermath** *n* suites *fpl*, séquelles *fpl*. ◆ **afternoon** **1** *n* après-midi *m or f*; **in the ~noon** l'après-midi; **at 3 o'clock in the ~noon** à 3 heures de l'après-midi; **on Sunday ~noon(s)** le dimanche après-midi; **on the ~noon of December 2nd** l'après-midi du 2 décembre, le 2 décembre dans l'après-midi; **good ~noon!** *(on meeting sb)* bonjour!; *(on leaving sb)* au revoir!; **2** *adj lecture, class, train, meeting* (de) l'après-midi; **~noon performance** matinée *f*; **~noon tea** thé *m* (de cinq heures). ◆ **after-sales service** *n* service *m* après-vente. ◆ **after-shave** *n* lotion *f* après-rasage. ◆ **aftertaste** *n* arrière-goût *m*. ◆ **afterthought** *n* pensée *f* après coup; **I had an ~thought** cela m'est venu après coup; **I had ~thoughts about my decision** j'ai eu après coup des doutes sur ma décision; **added as an ~thought** ajouté après coup. ◆ **afterwards** *adv* après, plus tard, par la suite.

again [ə'gen] *adv* de nouveau, encore une fois, une fois de plus. **here we are ~!** nous revoilà!; **~ and ~, time and ~** maintes et maintes fois; **I've told you ~ and ~** je te l'ai dit et répété; **she is home ~** elle est rentrée chez elle; **what's his name ~?** comment s'appelle-t-il déjà?; **to begin ~** recommencer; **I won't do it ~** je ne le ferai plus; **never ~** plus jamais; **never ~!** c'est bien la dernière fois!; *(iro)* **not ~!** encore! *(iro)*; **as much ~** deux fois autant; **then ~, and ~** d'autre part, d'un autre côté; **~ it is not certain that** et d'ailleurs il n'est pas sûr que.

against [ə'genst] *prep* (**a**) *(opposition etc)* contre. **to be ~ capital punishment** être contre la peine de mort; **I'm ~ helping him at all** je ne suis pas d'avis qu'on l'aide *(subj)*; **I've got nothing ~ him** je n'ai rien contre lui; **to be dead ~ sth** s'opposer absolument à qch; *(Pol)* **to run ~ sb** se présenter contre qn; **now we're up ~ it!** nous voici au pied du mur!, c'est maintenant qu'on va s'amuser! *; **~ my will** malgré moi; **to work ~ the clock** travailler contre la montre; **(as) ~** contre, en comparaison de; **~ that, it might be said...** en revanche *or* par contre on pourrait dire... (**b**) *(support, impact)* contre. **to lean ~ a wall** s'appuyer contre un mur; **to hit one's head ~ the mantelpiece** se cogner la tête contre la cheminée; **the truck ran ~ a tree** le camion s'est jeté sur un arbre. (**c**) *(in contrast to)* sur. **~ the light** à contre-jour; **the trees stood out ~ the sunset** les arbres se détachaient sur le couchant; **it shows up ~ the white background** cela ressort sur le fond blanc. (**d**) **tickets are available ~ this voucher** on peut obtenir des billets contre remise de ce bon.

age [eɪdʒ] **1** *n* (**a**) âge *m*. **what's her ~?, what ~ is she?** quel âge a-t-elle?; **he is 10 years of ~** il a 10 ans; **you don't look your ~** vous ne faites pas votre âge; **of an ~** du même âge; **to come of ~** atteindre sa majorité; **to be of ~** être majeur; **to be under ~** être mineur; **~ of consent** âge à partir duquel les rapports sexuels entre parties consentantes sont licites. (**b**) **I haven't seen him for ~s** il y a une éternité que je ne l'ai vu; **she stayed for ~s** elle est restée un temps fou. **2** *vti* vieillir. **3** *adj*: **~ bracket, ~ group** tranche *f* d'âge; **the 40-50 ~ group** la tranche d'âge de 40 à 50 ans, les 40 à 50 ans; **~ limit** limite *f* d'âge.
◆ **aged** [eɪdʒd] **1** *adj* (**a**) âgé de; **a boy ~d 10** un garçon (âgé) de 10 ans; (**b**) ['eɪdʒɪd] *(old)* âgé, vieux; **2** *npl*: **the ~d** les personnes âgées; **the ~d and infirm** les gens âgés et infirmes. ◆ **ageing** **1** *adj person* vieillissant; *hairstyle, dress* qui fait paraître vieux; **2** *n* vieillissement *m*. ◆ **ageless** *adj* toujours jeune. ◆ **age-old** *adj* séculaire.

agency ['eɪdʒ(ə)nsɪ] *n* (**a**) agence *f*. **tourist ~** agence de tourisme. (**b**) **through the ~ of friends** par l'intermédiaire *m* d'amis, grâce à des amis.
◆ **agent** *n (gen)* agent *m* (*of, for* de); *(dealer)* **the Citroën ~** le concessionnaire Citroën.

agenda [ə'dʒendə] *n* ordre *m* du jour. **on the ~** à l'ordre du jour.

agglomeration [əˌglɒmə'reɪʃ(ə)n] *n* agglomération *f*.

aggravate ['ægrəveɪt] *vt* aggraver; *(annoy)* exaspérer, agacer. ◆ **aggravating** *adj* exaspérant, agaçant. ◆ **aggravation** *n* aggravation *f*; *(annoyance)* exaspération *f*, agacement *m*.

aggregate ['ægrɪgɪt] **1** *n* ensemble *m*, total *m*. **in the ~** dans l'ensemble; *(Sport)* **on ~** ≃ au total des points *(dans le groupe de sélection)*. **2** *adj* global, total.

aggression [ə'greʃ(ə)n] *n* agression *f*; *(aggressiveness)* agressivité *f*. ◆ **aggressive** *adj* agressif. ◆ **aggressively** *adv* d'une manière agressive, agressivement. ◆ **aggressiveness** *n* agressivité *f*. ◆ **aggressor** *n* agresseur *m*.

aggrieved [əˈgriːvd] *adj* chagriné (*at, by* par).

aggro * [ˈægrəʊ] (*n abbr of* **aggression**) (*emotion*) agressivité *f*; (*physical violence*) grabuge * *m*.

aghast [əˈgɑːst] *adj* atterré (*at* de).

agile [ˈædʒaɪl] *adj* agile. ◆ **agility** *n* agilité *f*.

agitate [ˈædʒɪteɪt] **1** *vt* agiter. **2** *vi* (*Pol etc*) mener une campagne (*for* en faveur de; *against* contre). ◆ **agitated** *adj* agité. ◆ **agitation** *n* agitation *f*; (*campaign*) campagne *f* (*for* pour; *against* contre). ◆ **agitator** *n* agitateur *m*, -trice *f*.

agnostic [ægˈnɒstɪk] *adj, n* agnostique (*mf*). ◆ **agnosticism** *n* agnosticisme *m*.

ago [əˈgəʊ] *adv*: **a week** ~ il y a huit jours; **how long** ~? il y a combien de temps?; **a little while** ~ tout à l'heure; **as long** ~ **as 1950** déjà en 1950.

agog [əˈgɒg] *adj*: **to be (all)** ~ être en émoi; **to be** ~ **to do** brûler de faire; ~ **for news** impatient d'avoir des nouvelles.

agonize [ˈægənaɪz] *vi*: **to** ~ **over sth** se tourmenter à propos de qch. ◆ **agonized** *adj* déchirant. ◆ **agonizing** *adj situation* angoissant; *cry* déchirant; **agonizing reappraisal** révision déchirante.

agony [ˈægənɪ] **1** *n* (*mental pain*) angoisse *f*; (*physical pain*) douleur *f* atroce. **death** ~ agonie *f*; **to suffer agonies, to be in** ~ souffrir le martyre; **to be in an** ~ **of impatience** se mourir d'impatience. **2** *adj*: ~ **aunt** *journaliste qui tient la rubrique du courrier du cœur;* ~ **column** courrier *m* du cœur.

agrarian [əˈgrɛərɪən] *adj* agraire.

agree [əˈgriː] **1** *vt* (**a**) (*consent*) consentir (*to do* à faire), accepter (*to do* de faire); (*accept*) *statement, report* accepter (la véracité de); (*fix*) *price, date* se mettre d'accord sur. (**b**) (*admit*) reconnaître, admettre (*that* que). (**c**) (*come to agreement*) convenir (*to do* de faire), se mettre d'accord (*to do* pour faire); (*be of same opinion*) être d'accord (*that* que). **everyone** ~**s that we should stay** tout le monde s'accorde à reconnaître que nous devrions rester; **it was** ~**d** c'était convenu; **to** ~ **to differ** rester sur ses positions.
2 *vi* (**a**) (*be in agreement*) être d'accord (*with* avec), être du même avis (*with* que). **they all** ~**d in finding the play dull** tous ont été d'accord pour trouver la pièce ennuyeuse; **she** ~**s with me that it is unfair** elle trouve comme moi que c'est injuste; **I quite** ~ je suis tout à fait d'accord; **I can't** ~ **with you there** je ne suis absolument pas d'accord avec vous sur ce point. (**b**) (*come to terms*) se mettre d'accord (*with sb* avec qn; *about, on sth* sur qch); (*get on well*) s'entendre (bien). (**c**) (*consent*) consentir (*to sth* à qch; *to doing* à faire). **to** ~ **to a proposal** accepter une proposition; **I** ~ **to your going** je consens à ce que vous y alliez. (**d**) [*ideas, stories*] concorder (*with* avec). (**e**) (*Gram*) s'accorder (*with* avec). (**f**) (*suit the health of*) réussir à. **onions don't** ~ **with me** les oignons ne me réussissent pas.
◆ **agreeable** *adj* (*pleasant*) *person* agréable; (*willing*) **to be** ~**able to (doing) sth** consentir volontiers à (faire) qch. ◆ **agreeably** *adv* agréablement. ◆ **agreed** *adj* (**a**) **to be** ~**d** être d'accord (*about* au sujet de; *on* sur); (**b**) *time, place, amount* convenu; **it's all** ~**d** c'est tout décidé; **it's** ~**d that** il est convenu que + *indic;* ~**d!** entendu!, d'accord! ◆ **agreement** *n* (*all senses*) accord *m*; **to be in** ~**ment on** être d'accord sur; **to come to an** ~**ment** parvenir à un accord; **by mutual** ~**ment** d'un commun accord; (*without quarrelling*) à l'amiable.

agribusiness [ˈægrɪˌbɪznɪs] *n* agro-industries *fpl*.

agriculture [ˈægrɪkʌltʃəʳ] *n* agriculture *f*. **Ministry of A**~ ministère *m* de l'Agriculture. ◆ **agricultural** *adj* (*gen*) agricole; *engineer, expert* agronome; **agricultural college** école *f* d'agriculture. ◆ **agriculture(al)ist** *n* (*scientist*) agronome *mf*; (*farmer*) agriculteur *m*.

aground [əˈgraʊnd] *adj* échoué. **to run** ~ s'échouer.

ahead [əˈhed] *adv* (**a**) (*in space*) en avant, devant. **to draw** ~ gagner de l'avant; **I'll go on** ~ moi, je vais en avant; (*lit, fig*) **to get** ~ prendre de l'avance. (**b**) (*in time*) *book, plan* à l'avance. ~ **of time** *decide, announce* d'avance; *arrive, be ready* avant l'heure, en avance; **2 hours** ~ **of the next car** en avance de 2 heures sur la voiture suivante; **he's 2 hours** ~ **of you** il a 2 heures d'avance sur vous; (*fig*) ~ **of one's time** en avance sur son époque; **to plan** ~ faire des projets à l'avance; **to think** ~ penser à l'avenir.

ahoy [əˈhɔɪ] *excl* ohé! **ship** ~! ohé du navire!

aid [eɪd] **1** *n* (**a**) (*help*) aide *f*. **with the** ~ **of** *sb* avec l'aide de; *sth* à l'aide de; **in** ~ **of the blind** au profit des aveugles; (*fig*) **what is the meeting in** ~ **of?** * c'est dans quel but, cette réunion? (**b**) (*helper*) aide *mf*, assistant(e) *m(f); (apparatus)* aide *f*, moyen *m*. **audio-visual** ~**s** support audio-visuel, moyens audio-visuels; **teaching** ~**s** outils *mpl* pédagogiques. **2** *vt person* aider (*to do* à faire); *progress, recovery* contribuer à. (*Jur*) **to** ~ **and abet sb** être complice de qn.

aide [eɪd] *n* aide *mf*.

AIDS, aids [eɪdz] *n* (*abbr of* **acquired immune deficiency syndrome**) SIDA *m*.

ailing [ˈeɪlɪŋ] *adj* souffrant; *company* qui périclite. ◆ **ailment** *n* ennui *m* de santé.

aim [eɪm] **1** *n* (**a**) **to miss one's** ~ manquer son coup; **to take** ~ viser (*at sb/sth* qn/qch); **his** ~ **is bad** il vise mal. (**b**) (*purpose*) but *m*. **with the** ~ **of doing** dans le but de faire; **her** ~ **is to do** elle a pour but de faire. **2** *vt gun* braquer (*at* sur); *missile* pointer (*at* sur); *stone* lancer (*at* sur); *blow* décocher (*at* à); *remark* diriger (*at* contre). **3** *vi* viser. **to** ~ **at sth** viser qch; **to** ~ **at doing** *or* **to do** viser à faire; (*less formally*) avoir l'intention de faire. ◆ **aimless** *adj* sans but. ◆ **aimlessly** *adv wander* sans but; *stand around* sans trop savoir que faire; *chat, kick ball about* pour passer le temps.

air [ɛəʳ] **1** *n* (**a**) air *m*. **to go out for a breath of (fresh)** ~ sortir prendre l'air; **by** ~ par avion; **to throw sth (up) into the** ~ jeter qch en l'air; **the balloon rose up into the** ~ le ballon s'est élevé (dans les airs); (*fig*) **there's sth in the** ~ il se prépare qch; **it's still all in the** ~ ce ne sont encore que des projets en l'air; **all her plans were up in the** ~ (*vague*) tous ses projets étaient vagues; (*destroyed*) tous ses projets étaient tombés à l'eau; **to be up in the** ~ **about** * être (*angry*) en rogne * *or* (*excited*) très excité à l'idée de; **I can't live on** ~ je ne peux pas vivre de l'air du temps; **to walk on** ~ être aux anges. (**b**) (*Rad, TV*) **on the** ~ à l'antenne; **you're on the** ~ vous avez l'antenne; **he's on the** ~ **every day** il parle à la radio tous les jours; **the station is on the** ~ la station émet; **the programme goes on the** ~ **every week** l'émission passe (sur l'antenne) toutes les semaines; **to go off the** ~ quitter l'antenne. (**c**) (*manner*) air *m*. **with an** ~ **of bewilderment** d'un air perplexe; **she has an** ~ **about her** elle a de l'allure; **to put on** ~**s** se donner de grands airs; ~**s and graces** minauderies *fpl*. (**d**) (*Mus*) air *m*.
2 *vt linen, room, bed* aérer; *anger* exhaler; *opinion* faire connaître; *idea* mettre sur le tapis.
3 *adj bubble* d'air; *hole* d'aération; *cushion, mattress* pneumatique; *pressure, current* atmosphérique; (*Mil*) *superiority, base* aérien. ~ **bed** matelas *m* pneumatique; ~ **brake** (*Aut*) frein *m* à air comprimé; (*Aviat*) aérofrein *m*; ~ **force** armée *f* de l'air; **by** ~ **freight** par voie aérienne; ~ **lane** couloir aérien; ~ **letter** lettre *f* par avion; ~ **pocket** trou *m* d'air; ~ **pump** compresseur *m*; ~ **rifle**

carabine *f* à air comprimé; ~ **show** *(Comm etc)* salon *m* de l'aéronautique; *(flying display)* meeting *m* d'aviation; ~ **space** espace *m* aérien; ~ **terminal** aérogare *f*; ~ **traffic control** contrôle *m* de la navigation aérienne; ~ **traffic controller** contrôleur *m*, -euse *f* de la navigation aérienne.
◆ **airborne** *adj*: ~**borne troops** troupes aéroportées; **the plane was** ~**borne** l'avion avait décollé. ◆ **airbrush** *n* aérographe *m*. ◆ **airbus** *n* airbus *m*. ◆ **air-conditioned** *adj* climatisé. ◆ **air-conditioner** *n* climatiseur *m*. ◆ **air-conditioning** *n* climatisation *f*. ◆ **air-cooled** *adj* à refroidissement par air. ◆ **aircraft** *n (pl inv)* avion *m*. ◆ **aircraft-carrier** *n* porte-avions *m inv*. ◆ **aircrew** *n* équipage *m (d'un avion)*. ◆ **airdrome** *n* aérodrome *m*. ◆ **airdrop** **1** *vt* parachuter ; **2** *n* parachutage *m*. ◆ **airfield** *n* terrain *m* d'aviation. ◆ **airgun** *n* fusil *m* à air comprimé. ◆ **air-hostess** *n* hôtesse *f* de l'air. ◆ **airily** *adv* d'un ton dégagé, avec désinvolture. ◆ **airing** *n [linen]* aération *f*; **to give an idea an** ~**ing** mettre une idée sur le tapis. ◆ **airing cupboard** *n* placard-séchoir *m*. ◆ **airless** *adj room* privé d'air. ◆ **airlift** **1** *n* pont aérien; **2** *vt* évacuer (*or* amener *etc*) par pont aérien. ◆ **airline** *n (Aviat)* compagnie *f* d'aviation. ◆ **airliner** *n* avion *m* (de ligne). ◆ **airlock** *n [spacecraft, caisson etc]* sas *m*; *(in pipe)* bouchon *m* d'air. ◆ **airmail** **1** *n*: **by** ~**mail** par avion; **2** *adj letter, edition* par avion; **3** *vt* expédier par avion. ◆ **airman** *n* aviateur *m*; *(in Air Force)* soldat *m* (de l'armée de l'air). ◆ **airplane** *n* avion *m*. ◆ **airport** *n* aéroport *m*. ◆ **air-raid** *n* attaque aérienne, raid aérien. ◆ **air-sea rescue** *n* sauvetage *m* en mer *(par hélicoptère etc)*. ◆ **airship** *n* (ballon *m*) dirigeable *m*. ◆ **airsick** *adj*: **to be** ~**sick** avoir le mal de l'air. ◆ **airstrip** *n* piste *f* d'atterrissage. ◆ **airtight** *adj* hermétique, étanche (à l'air). ◆ **air-to-air** *adj* avion-avion *inv*. ◆ **air-to-ground** *or* ◆ **air-to-surface** *adj* air-sol *inv*. ◆ **airwaves** *npl* ondes *fpl* (hertziennes). ◆ **airway** *n (route)* voie aérienne; *(company)* compagnie *f* d'aviation. ◆ **airwoman** *n* aviatrice *f*; *(in Air Force)* auxiliaire *f* (de l'armée de l'air). ◆ **airworthiness** *n* navigabilité *f*. ◆ **airworthy** *adj* en état de navigation. ◆ **airy** *adj room* clair; *manner* désinvolte, dégagé; *promise* en l'air. ◆ **airy-fairy** * *adj* farfelu.

aisle [aɪl] *n [church]* nef latérale; *(between pews)* allée centrale; *[theatre]* allée *f*; *[train, coach]* couloir *m* (central).

ajar [əˈdʒɑːʳ] *adj* entrouvert.

akimbo [əˈkɪmbəʊ] *adj*: **with arms** ~ les poings sur les hanches.

akin [əˈkɪn] *adj*: ~ **to** qui tient de, qui ressemble à.

alabaster [ˈæləbɑːstəʳ] *n* albâtre *m*.

alacrity [əˈlækrɪtɪ] *n* empressement *m*.

alarm [əˈlɑːm] **1** *n (gen)* alarme *f*; *(clock)* réveil *m*. **to raise the** ~ donner l'alarme *or* l'alerte. **2** *vt person* alarmer; *animal, bird* effaroucher. **to become** ~**ed** prendre peur. **3** *adj bell, signal, call* d'alarme. ~ **clock** réveil *m*, réveille-matin *m inv*. ◆ **alarming** *adj* alarmant. ◆ **alarmingly** *adv* d'une manière alarmante. ◆ **alarmist** *adj, n* alarmiste *(mf)*.

alas [əˈlæs] *excl* hélas!

Albania [ælˈbeɪnɪə] *n* Albanie *f*. ◆ **Albanian** **1** *adj* albanais; **2** *n* Albanais(e) *m(f)*.

albatross [ˈælbətrɒs] *n* albatros *m*.

albino [ælˈbiːnəʊ] *n* albinos *mf*. ~ **rabbit** lapin *m* albinos.

album [ˈælbəm] *n* album *m*. **photo/stamp** ~ album de photos/de timbres.

albumen, albumin [ˈælbjʊmɪn] *n* albumen *m*; *(Physiol)* albumine *f*.

alchemy [ˈælkɪmɪ] *n* alchimie *f*. ◆ **alchemist** *n* alchimiste *m*.

alcohol [ˈælkəhɒl] *n* alcool *m*. ◆ **alcoholic** **1** *adj (gen)* alcoolique; *drink* alcoolisé; **2** *n* alcoolique *mf*. ◆ **alcoholism** *n* alcoolisme *m*.

alcove [ˈælkəʊv] *n* alcôve *f*.

alder [ˈɔːldəʳ] *n* aulne *m*.

alderman [ˈɔːldəmən] *n* ≃ conseiller *m*, -ère *f* municipal(e).

ale [eɪl] *n* bière *f*, ale *f*.

alert [əˈlɜːt] **1** *n* alerte *f*. **to give the** ~ donner l'alerte; **on the** ~ *person* sur le qui-vive; *troops* en état d'alerte. **2** *adj (watchful)* vigilant; *(bright)* alerte, vif; *(child)* éveillé. **3** *vt* alerter (*to* sur). **we are now** ~**ed to...** notre attention est maintenant éveillée sur... ◆ **alertness** *n* vigilance *f*; esprit éveillé.

alfalfa [ælˈfælfə] *n* luzerne *f*.

alfresco [ælˈfreskəʊ] *adj, adv* en plein air.

algae [ˈældʒiː] *npl* algues *fpl*.

algebra [ˈældʒɪbrə] *n* algèbre *f*.

Algeria [ælˈdʒɪərɪə] *n* Algérie *f*. ◆ **Algiers** *n* Alger.

ALGOL [ˈælgɒl] *n (Comput)* ALGOL *m*.

alias [ˈeɪlɪæs] **1** *adv* alias. **2** *n* faux nom *m*.

alibi [ˈælɪbaɪ] *n* alibi *m*.

alien [ˈeɪlɪən] **1** *n (foreign)* étranger *m*, -ère *f*; *(non human)* extra-terrestre *mf*. **2** *adj* étranger (*to* à); extra-terrestre. ◆ **alienate** *vt* aliéner; **this has** ~**ated his friends** ceci a aliéné ses amis; **she has** ~**ated her friends** elle s'est aliéné ses amis (*by doing* en faisant). ◆ **alienation** *n* aliénation *f*.

alight[1] [əˈlaɪt] *vi [person]* descendre (*from* de); *[bird]* se poser (*on* sur).

alight[2] [əˈlaɪt] *adj, adv fire* allumé; *building* en feu. **to set sth** ~ mettre le feu à qch.

align [əˈlaɪn] **1** *vt* aligner (*on, with* sur). **non-**~**ed** non-aligné. **2** *vi [persons]* s'aligner; *[object]* être aligné. ◆ **alignment** *n* alignement *m*.

alike [əˈlaɪk] **1** *adj* semblable. **to be** ~ se ressembler; **it's all** ~ **to me** cela m'est tout à fait égal. **2** *adv dress, treat* de la même façon. **winter and summer** ~ été comme hiver; **they think** ~ ils sont souvent du même avis.

alimentary [ˌælɪˈmentərɪ] *adj* alimentaire. ~ **canal** tube *m* digestif.

alimony [ˈælɪmənɪ] *n (Jur)* pension *f* alimentaire.

alive [əˈlaɪv] *adj (living)* vivant, en vie. **to bury sb** ~ enterrer qn vivant; **to burn** ~ brûler vif; **it's good to be** ~ il fait bon vivre; **no man** ~ personne au monde; **as well as anyone** ~ aussi bien que n'importe qui; **to keep** ~ *person* maintenir en vie; *tradition* préserver; *memory* garder; **to stay** ~ rester en vie, survivre; ~ **to** *honour* sensible à; *danger* conscient de; ~ **and kicking** * *(living)* bien en vie; *(energy)* plein de vie; **look** ~**!** * remuez-vous! *; ~ **with insects** grouillant d'insectes.

alkali [ˈælkəlaɪ] *n* base *f*. ◆ **alkaline** *adj* basique.

all [ɔːl] **1** *adj* tout. ~ **the country** tout le pays, le pays tout entier; ~ **my life** toute ma vie; ~ **the others** tous (*or* toutes) les autres; ~ **you boys** vous (tous) les garçons; ~ **three** tous les trois; ~ **three men** les trois hommes; ~ **day** toute la journée; ~ **that** tout cela; **why me of** ~ **people?** pourquoi moi?; **with** ~ **(possible) care** avec tout le soin possible.

2 *pron* (**a**) tout *m*. ~ **is well** tout va bien; **that is** ~ c'est tout; **if that's** ~ **then it's not important** s'il n'y a que cela, ce n'est pas important; **and I don't know what** ~ * et je ne sais quoi encore; ~ **of it was lost** (le) tout a été perdu; **he drank** ~ **of it** il a tout bu, il l'a bu en entier; ~ **of Paris** Paris tout entier; **that is** ~ **he said** c'est tout ce qu'il a dit; ~ **that is in the box** tout ce qui est dans la boîte; **bring it** ~ apportez le tout. (**b**) *(pl)* tous *mpl*, toutes *fpl*. **we** ~ **sat down** nous nous sommes tous assis (*or* toutes assises); ~ **of the boys came**

tous les garçons sont venus, les garçons sont tous venus; **one and** ~ tous sans exception; ~ **who knew him** tous ceux qui l'ont connu; **the score was two** ~ le score était *(Tennis)* deux partout *or (other sports)* deux à deux. (**c**) *(in phrases)* **if she comes at** ~ si tant est qu'elle vienne; **very rarely if at** ~ très rarement (si tant est); **I don't know at** ~ je n'en sais rien; **if there is any water at** ~ si seulement il y a de l'eau; **if at** ~ **possible** dans la mesure du possible; **not at** ~ pas du tout; *(after thanks)* il n'y a pas de quoi; **it was** ~ **I could do not to laugh** c'est à peine *or* tout juste si j'ai pu m'empêcher de rire; **it's not as bad as** ~ **that** ce n'est pas si mal que ça; **that's** ~ **very well but...** tout cela est bien beau mais...; **taking it** ~ **in** ~ à tout prendre; **she is** ~ **in** ~ **to him** elle est tout pour lui; ~ **but** presque; **he** ~ **but lost it** il a bien failli le perdre; **for** ~ **I know** autant que je sache; **for** ~ **his wealth he was unhappy** malgré sa fortune il était malheureux; **for** ~ **he may say** quoi qu'il en dise; **once and for** ~ une fois pour toutes; **most of** ~ surtout.

3 *adv* (**a**) tout, tout à fait. ~ **of a sudden** tout à coup, soudain; ~ **too soon it was time to go** malheureusement il a bientôt fallu partir; **dressed** ~ **in white** habillé tout en blanc; ~ **along the road** tout le long de la route; **I feared that** ~ **along** je l'ai craint depuis le début; **he won the race** ~ **the same** il a néanmoins *or* tout de même gagné la course; **it's** ~ **the same** *or* ~ **one to me** cela m'est tout à fait égal; ~ **over** *(everywhere)* partout, d'un bout à l'autre; *(finished)* fini; **to be** ~ **for sth** * être tout à fait en faveur de qch; **to be** ~ **there** * avoir toute sa tête; **she's not quite** ~ **there** * il lui manque une case *; **it is** ~ **up with him** * il est fichu *; ~ **the better!** tant mieux!; ~ **the more so since...** d'autant plus que... (**b**) ~ **right** (très) bien; *(in approval, exasperation)* ça va! *; *(in agreement)* entendu!, c'est ça!; **it's** ~ **right** ça va *, tout va bien; **he's** ~ **right** *(doubtful)* il n'est pas mal *; *(approving)* c'est un type bien *; *(reassuring)* il est très bien; *(healthy)* il va bien; *(safe)* il est sain et sauf; **I'm** ~ **right Jack** * moi en tout cas je suis peinard *; *(comfortably off)* **we're** ~ **right for the rest of our lives** nous sommes tranquilles pour le restant de nos jours.

4 *n* : **my** ~ tout ce que j'ai.

◆ **all-American** *adj* cent pour cent américain. ◆ **all-day** *adj* qui dure toute la journée. ◆ **all-embracing** *adj* compréhensif. ◆ **all-important** *adj* de la plus haute importance, capital. ◆ **all-in** *adj (exhausted)* éreinté; *(inclusive) price* net; *cost* tout compris; *insurance policy* tous risques *inv*; *tariff* inclusif. ◆ **all-night** *adj*: ~**-night service** permanence *f* de nuit. ◆ **all-out 1** *adj effort* maximum; *strike, war* total; **2** *adv*: **to go** ~**-out** aller à la limite de ses forces. ◆ **allover** *adj* (qui est) sur toute la surface. ◆ **all-powerful** *adj* tout-puissant. ◆ **all-purpose** *adj* qui répond à tous les besoins; *knife, spanner* universel. ◆ **all-round** *adj sportsman* complet; *improvement* général, sur toute la ligne. ◆ **all-rounder** *n*: **to be a good** ~**-rounder** être bon en tout. ◆ **allspice** *n* poivre *m* de la Jamaïque. ◆ **all-star** *adj*: *(Theat)* ~**-star show** plateau *m* de vedettes. ◆ **all-time** *adj record* sans précédent; **an** ~**-time low** un record de médiocrité. ◆ **all-weather** *adj* de toute saison, tous temps *inv*. ◆ **all-the-year-round** *adj sport* que l'on pratique toute l'année; *resort* ouvert toute l'année.

Allah ['ælə] *n* Allah *m*.

allay [ə'leɪ] *vt (gen)* apaiser. **to** ~ **suspicion** dissiper les soupçons.

allege [ə'ledʒ] *vt* alléguer, prétendre (*that* que). **to** ~ **illness** prétexter *or* alléguer une maladie; **he is** ~**d to have said** il aurait dit. ◆ **allegation** *n* allégation *f*. ◆ **alleged** *adj reason* allégué; *thief, author* présumé. ◆ **allegedly** *adv* à ce que l'on prétend.

allegiance [ə'li:dʒ(ə)ns] *n* allégeance *f* (*to* à).

allegory ['ælɪgərɪ] *n* allégorie *f*. ◆ **allegoric(al)** *adj* allégorique.

allergy ['ælədʒɪ] *n* allergie *f* (*to* à). ◆ **allergic** *adj* allergique (*to* à). ◆ **allergist** *n* allergologue *mf*.

alleviate [ə'li:vɪeɪt] *vt pain* soulager; *sorrow* adoucir; *thirst* apaiser.

alley ['ælɪ] **1** *n (between buildings: also* ~ **way***)* ruelle *f*; *(in garden)* allée *f*. **this is right up my** ~ * *(my speciality)* c'est tout à fait mon rayon; *(just what I wanted)* c'est tout à fait ce que j'espérais. **2** *adj*: ~ **cat** chat *m* de gouttière.

alliance [ə'laɪəns] *n* alliance *f*.

allied ['ælaɪd] *adj (gen, Pol)* allié (*to* à, *with* avec); *(Bio)* de la même famille *or* espèce. **history and** ~ **subjects** l'histoire et sujets apparentés.

alligator ['ælɪgeɪtə^r] *n* alligator *m*.

alliteration [əˌlɪtə'reɪʃ(ə)n] *n* allitération *f*.

allocate ['ælə(ʊ)keɪt] *vt money, task* allouer, attribuer (*to sb* à qn); *money* affecter (*to sth* à qch). ◆ **allocation** *n* allocation *f*.

allot [ə'lɒt] *vt* attribuer, assigner (*sth to sb* qch à qn). **in the time** ~**ted** dans le temps qui est assigné. ◆ **allotment** *n* parcelle *f* de terre *(louée pour la culture)*.

allow [ə'laʊ] *vt* (**a**) *(permit)* permettre (*sb sth* qch à qn; *sb to do* à qn de faire), autoriser (*sb to do* qn à faire); *(tolerate)* tolérer (*sb to do* que qn fasse). **she was not** ~**ed to do it** elle n'était pas autorisée à le faire; **to** ~ **sb in** *etc* permettre à qn d'entrer *etc*; **to** ~ **sth to happen** laisser se produire qch; **smoking/dogs not** ~**ed** interdit de fumer/aux chiens. (**b**) *(grant) money* accorder, allouer; *(Jur)* accorder. **to** ~ **sb a discount** consentir une remise à qn; ~ **an hour to cross the city** comptez une heure pour traverser la ville; ~ **5 cm for shrinkage** prévoyez 5 cm de plus pour le cas où le tissu rétrécirait. (**c**) *(concede)* admettre, reconnaître (*that* que); *claim* admettre. ~**ing that...** en admettant que... + *subj*.

◆ **allow for** *vt fus* tenir compte de. ~**ing for the circumstances** compte tenu des circonstances; **to** ~ **for all possibilities** parer à toute éventualité. ◆ **allow of** *vt fus* admettre, souffrir.

allowable [ə'laʊəbl] *adj* permis, admissible; *(Tax) expenses* déductible.

allowance [ə'laʊəns] *n* (**a**) *(money given to sb)* pension *f*, rente *f*; *(for lodgings, food etc)* indemnité *f*, *(Admin)* allocation *f*; *(from separated husband)* pension *f* alimentaire; *(salary)* appointements *mpl*; *(food)* ration *f*. **rent** ~ allocation de logement; **she has a dress** ~ *(from father)* elle reçoit une certaine somme pour ses vêtements; *(from employers)* elle touche une allocation vestimentaire. (**b**) *(Comm, Fin: discount)* réduction *f*, rabais *m*. **tax** ~**s** sommes *fpl* déductibles. (**c**) **you must learn to make** ~**s** tu dois apprendre à faire la part des choses; **to make** ~ **(s) for** *(excuse) person, fault* se montrer indulgent envers; *(allow for) shrinkage etc* tenir compte de.

alloy ['ælɔɪ] *n* alliage *m*. *(Aut)* ~ **wheels** roues *fpl* en alliage léger.

allude [ə'lu:d] *vi* faire allusion (*to* à).

allure [ə'ljʊə^r] **1** *vt* attirer. **2** *n* charme *m*, attrait *m*. ◆ **alluring** *adj* attrayant, séduisant.

allusion [ə'lu:ʒən] *n* allusion *f*.

alluvial [ə'lu:vɪəl] *adj ground* alluvial; *deposit* alluvionnaire.

ally [ə'laɪ] **1** *vt*: **to** ~ **o.s. with** s'allier avec. **2** ['ælaɪ] *n* allié(e) *m(f)*.

almanac ['ɔ:lmənæk] *n* almanach *m*.

almighty [ɔ:l'maɪtɪ] **1** *adj* (**a**) *(Rel)* tout-puissant. **A**~ **God** Dieu Tout-Puissant. (*) *row, scandal* formidable, fantastique. **an ~ din *** un vacarme du diable. **2** *n*: **the A~** le Tout-Puissant.

almond ['ɑːmənd] *n* amande *f*; (**~tree**) amandier *m*. ◆ **almond-shaped** *adj* en amande.

almost ['ɔːlməʊst] *adv* presque. **it is ~ midnight** il est presque *or* bientôt minuit; **he ~ fell** il a failli tomber.

alms [ɑːmz] *n* aumône *f*. **to give ~** faire l'aumône; **~ box** tronc *m* pour les pauvres.

aloft [ə'lɒft] *adv* (**up ~**) en l'air; *(Naut)* dans la mâture.

alone [ə'ləʊn] *adj, adv* seul. **all ~** tout(e) seul(e); **leave them ~ together** laissez-les seuls ensemble; **he ~ could tell you** lui seul pourrait vous le dire; **we are not ~ in thinking** nous ne sommes pas les seuls à penser; **he lives on bread ~** il ne vit que de pain; **to let** *or* **leave ~** *person* laisser tranquille; *book etc* ne pas toucher à; *business, scheme* ne pas se mêler de; **he can't read, let ~ write** il ne sait pas lire, encore moins écrire.

along [ə'lɒŋ] **1** *adv*: **come ~!** venez donc!; *(remonstrating)* allons, allons!; **she'll be ~ tomorrow** elle viendra demain; **come ~ with me** venez avec moi; **bring your friend ~** amène ton camarade (avec toi); **~ here** dans cette direction-ci, par ici; **get ~ with you! *** *(go away)* fiche le camp! *; *(you can't mean it)* allons donc!; **all ~** *(space)* d'un bout à l'autre; *(time)* depuis le début. **2** *prep* le long de. **to walk ~ the beach** se promener le long de la plage; **the trees ~ the road** les arbres qui sont au bord de la route; **somewhere ~ the way** quelque part en chemin; *(fig: at some time)* à un moment donné; **~ the lines suggested** conformément à la ligne d'action proposée. ◆ **alongside** **1** *prep (along)* le long de; *(beside)* à côté de; **to come ~side the quay** accoster le quai; **the railway runs ~side the beach** la ligne de chemin de fer longe la plage; **2** *adv (Naut)* bord à bord. **to come ~side** accoster.

aloof [ə'luːf] *adj* distant (*towards* à l'égard de). ◆ **aloofness** *n* réserve *f*, attitude *f* distante.

aloud [ə'laʊd] *adv read* à haute voix; *think, wonder* tout haut.

alphabet ['ælfəbet] *n* alphabet *m*. ◆ **alphabetic(al)** *adj* alphabétique. ◆ **alphabetically** *adv* par ordre alphabétique. ◆ **alphabetize** *vt* classer par ordre alphabétique.

Alps [ælps] *npl* Alpes *fpl*. ◆ **alpine** *adj* des Alpes, alpestre; **alpine hut** (chalet-)refuge *m*. ◆ **alpinism** *n* alpinisme *m*. ◆ **alpinist** *n* alpiniste *mf*.

already [ɔːl'redɪ] *adv* déjà.

alright ['ɔːl,raɪt] = **all right;** *V* **all 3b.**

Alsatian [æl'seɪʃ(ə)n] *n (dog)* chien *m* loup, berger *m* allemand.

also ['ɔːlsəʊ] *adv* (**a**) *(too)* aussi, également. **her cousin ~ came** son cousin aussi est venu *or* est venu également. (**b**) *(moreover)* de plus, en outre, également. **~ I must explain** de plus *or* en outre, je dois expliquer, je dois également expliquer. ◆ **also-ran** *n (Horse-racing)* cheval non classé; *(*: person)* perdant(e) *m(f)*.

altar ['ɒltəʳ] *n* autel *m*.

alter ['ɒltəʳ] **1** *vt* (**a**) *(gen)* changer, modifier; *plans* modifier; *painting, poem, speech etc* remanier; *garment* retoucher; *(stronger)* transformer. **to ~ one's attitude** changer d'attitude (*to* envers); **that ~s the case** voilà qui change tout; **to ~ sth for the better/worse** changer qch en mieux/en mal. (**b**) *(falsify) date, evidence* falsifier; *text* altérer. **2** *vi* changer. ◆ **alteration** *n* (**a**) *(act of altering)* changement *m*, modification *f*, remaniement *m*, retouchage *m*, transformation *f*; **timetable subject to ~ation** horaire sujet à des modifications; (**b**) *(to plan, rules etc)* modification *f*, changement *m* (*to, in* apporté à); *(to painting etc)* retouche *f* *(major)* remaniement *m*; *(to garment)* retouche, *(major)* transformation *f*; *(Archit)* transformation (*to* apportée à); **they're having ~ations made to their house** ils font des travaux dans leur maison.

altercation [,ɒltə'keɪʃ(ə)n] *n* altercation *f*.

alter ego ['æltər'iːgəʊ] *n* alter ego *m*.

alternate [ɒl'tɜːnɪt] **1** *adj (by turns)* alterné; *(every second)* tous les deux. **on ~ days** tous les deux jours, un jour sur deux; **they work on ~ days** ils travaillent un jour sur deux à tour de rôle. **2** ['ɒltɜːneɪt] *vt* faire alterner; *crops* alterner. **3** *vi (occur etc in turns)* alterner (*with* avec); *(change over regularly)* se relayer. ◆ **alternately** *adv* alternativement, tour à tour; **~ly with** en alternance avec. ◆ **alternating** *adj* alternant; *(Elec)* alternatif.

alternative [ɒl'tɜːnətɪv] **1** *adj possibility, answer* autre; *(Philos) proposition* alternatif; *(Mil) position* de repli; *(non-traditional) medicine* parallèle, alternatif; *(Tech)* de rechange. **~ proposal** contre-proposition *f*; **the only ~ method** la seule autre méthode; **~ theatre** anti-théâtre *m*; *(Aut)* **~ route** itinéraire *m* de délestage. **2** *n (choice) (between two)* alternative *f*, choix *m*; *(among several)* choix; *(solution) (only one)* alternative, seule autre solution; *(one of several)* autre solution. **she had no ~ but to accept** elle n'avait pas d'autre solution que d'accepter; **there is no ~** il n'y a pas le choix. ◆ **alternatively** *adv* comme alternative.

although [ɔːl'ðəʊ] *conj* bien que + *subj*, quoique + *subj*. **~ it's raining** bien qu'il pleuve, malgré la pluie; **even ~ he might agree to go** quand bien même il accepterait d'y aller.

altimeter ['æltɪmiːtəʳ] *n* altimètre *m*.

altitude ['æltɪtjuːd] *n* altitude *f*. **at these ~s** à cette altitude.

alto ['æltəʊ] *n (female)* contralto *m*; *(male)* haute-contre *f*; *(instrument)* alto *m*. **~ saxophone** saxophone *m* alto.

altogether [,ɔːltə'geðəʳ] **1** *adv* (**a**) *(wholly)* entièrement, tout à fait, complètement. **it is ~ out of the question** il n'en est absolument pas question. (**b**) *(on the whole)* somme toute, tout compte fait. **~ it wasn't very pleasant** somme toute ce n'était pas très agréable. (**c**) *(with everything included)* en tout. **what do I owe you ~?** je vous dois combien en tout?; **taken ~** à tout prendre. **2** *n (hum)* **in the ~ ‡** tout nu, à poil ‡.

altruism ['æltrʊɪz(ə)m] *n* altruisme *m*. ◆ **altruist** *n* altruiste *mf*. ◆ **altruistic** *adj* altruiste.

aluminium [,æljʊ'mɪnɪəm], *(US)* **aluminum** [ə'luːmɪnəm] *n* aluminium *m*.

alveolar [æl'vɪələʳ] *adj* alvéolaire.

always ['ɔːlweɪz] *adv* toujours. **as ~** comme toujours; **for ~** pour toujours; **office ~ open** bureau ouvert en permanence.

amalgam [ə'mælgəm] *n* amalgame *m*. ◆ **amalgamate** **1** *vt metals* amalgamer; *companies* fusionner. **2** *vi* s'amalgamer; fusionner. ◆ **amalgamation** *n* amalgamation *f*; fusion *f*.

amanuensis, *pl* **-enses** [ə,mænjʊ'ensɪs, ensɪz] *n* secrétaire *mf*.

amass [ə'mæs] *vt* amasser.

amateur ['æmətəʳ] **1** *n* amateur *m*. **2** *adj painter, player, sport* amateur *inv*; *photography etc* d'amateur; *(pej) work* d'amateur. **~ dramatics** théâtre *m* amateur; **~ status** statut *m* d'amateur. ◆ **amateurish** *adj (pej)* d'amateur.

amaze [ə'meɪz] *vt* stupéfier, ébahir. ◆ **amazed** *adj* ébahi; **to be ~d at (seeing) sth** être stupéfait *or* stupéfié de (voir) qch. ◆ **amazement** *n* stupéfaction *f*, ébahissement *m*. ◆ **amazing** *adj* stupéfiant, ahurissant; *bargain, offer* sensationnel. ◆ **amazingly** *adv* étonnamment; **amazingly enough, he...** chose étonnante *or* par miracle, il...

Amazon ['æməz(ə)n] *n (river)* Amazone *m*; *(woman)* Amazone *f*. ◆ **Amazonia** *n (Geog)* Amazonie. ◆ **Amazonian** *adj* amazonien.

ambassador [æm'bæsədəʳ] *n (lit, fig)* ambassadeur *m*. **French ~** ambassadeur de France; **~-at-large** ambassadeur extraordinaire. ◆ **ambassadorial** *adj* d'ambassadeur. ◆ **ambassadress** *n* ambassadrice *f*.

amber ['æmbəʳ] **1** *n* ambre *m*. **2** *adj (colour)* couleur d'ambre *inv*. *(Aut)* **~ light** feu *m* orange. ◆ **ambergris** *n* ambre *m* gris.

ambidextrous [ˌæmbɪ'dekstrəs] *adj* ambidextre.

ambiguous [æm'bɪgjʊəs] *adj phrase* ambigu (*f* -uë); *past* équivoque. ◆ **ambiguity** *n* ambiguïté *f*. ◆ **ambiguously** *adv* de façon ambiguë.

ambition [æm'bɪʃ(ə)n] *n* ambition *f*. **it is my ~ to do** mon ambition est de faire. ◆ **ambitious** *adj* ambitieux; **to be ambitious to do** ambitionner de faire. ◆ **ambitiously** *adv* ambitieusement.

ambivalent [æm'bɪvələnt] *adj* ambivalent. ◆ **ambivalence** *n* ambivalence *f*.

amble ['æmbl] *vi [horse]* aller l'amble; *[person]* aller d'un pas tranquille *or* sans se presser.

ambulance ['æmbjʊləns] **1** *n* ambulance *f*. **2** *adj*: **~ driver** ambulancier *m*, -ière *f*.

ambush ['æmbʊʃ] **1** *n* embuscade *f*, guet-apens *m*. **to lie in ~** se tenir en embuscade; **to lie in ~ for sb** tendre une embuscade à qn. **2** *vt* tendre une embuscade à.

ameliorate [ə'mi:lɪəreɪt] **1** *vt* améliorer. **2** *vi* s'améliorer. ◆ **amelioration** *n* amélioration *f*.

amen ['ɑ:'men] *excl* amen.

amenable [ə'mi:nəbl] *adj* maniable, conciliant. **~ to argument** prêt à se laisser convaincre; **~ to kindness** sensible à la douceur; **~ to reason** raisonnable; **~ to treatment** guérissable.

amend [ə'mend] *vt law, document* amender; *text, wording* modifier; *habits* réformer. ◆ **amendment** *n* amendement *m*. ◆ **amends** *npl*: **to make ~s** *(apologize)* faire amende honorable; *(by doing sth)* se racheter; **to make ~s to sb for sth** *(apologize)* s'excuser auprès de qn de qch; *(compensate)* dédommager qn de qch.

amenity [ə'mi:nɪtɪ] **1** *n (gen)* agrément *m*. **amenities** *[town etc]* aménagements *mpl*; *(courtesies)* politesses *fpl*. **2** *adj*: *(Brit Med)* **~ bed** lit 'privé' (dans un hôpital).

America [ə'merɪkə] *n* Amérique *f*. ◆ **American** **1** *adj* américain; **~n English** anglais américain; **~n Indian** **~** Indien(ne) *m(f)* d'Amérique; *(adj)* des Indiens d'Amérique; **2** *n* Américain(e) *m(f)*; *(Ling)* américain *m*. ◆ **americanism** *n* américanisme *m*. ◆ **americanize** *vt* américaniser.

amethyst ['æmɪθɪst] **1** *n* améthyste *f*. **2** *adj (colour)* violet d'améthyste *inv*.

amiable ['eɪmɪəbl] *adj* aimable. ◆ **amiability** *n* amabilité *f* (*to, towards* envers). ◆ **amiably** *adv* aimablement.

amicable ['æmɪkəbl] *adj* amical; *(Jur) settlement* à l'amiable. ◆ **amicably** *adv* amicalement; *(Jur)* à l'amiable.

amid(st) [ə'mɪd(st)] *prep* parmi, au milieu de. ◆ **amidships** *adv* au milieu du navire.

amiss [ə'mɪs] **1** *adv*: **to take sth ~** prendre qch de travers, s'offenser de qch; **nothing comes ~ to him** il tire parti de tout; **a little courtesy wouldn't come ~** un peu de politesse ne ferait pas de mal. **2** *adj*: **there's sth ~** il y a qch qui ne va pas; **to say sth ~** dire qch mal à propos.

ammonia [ə'məʊnɪə] *n (gas)* ammoniac *m*; *(liquid)* ammoniaque *f*.

ammunition [ˌæmjʊ'nɪʃ(ə)n] **1** *n* munitions *fpl*. **2** *adj*: **~ belt** ceinturon *m*; **~ dump** dépôt *m* de munitions.

amnesia [æm'ni:zɪə] *n* amnésie *f*.

amnesty ['æmnɪstɪ] **1** *n* amnistie *f*. **under an ~** en vertu d'une amnistie. **2** *vt* amnistier.

amoeba [ə'mi:bə] *n* amibe *f*. ◆ **amoebic** *adj* amibien.

amok [ə'mɒk] *adv* = **amuck.**

among(st) [ə'mʌŋ(st)] *prep* entre, parmi. **this is ~ the things we must do** ceci fait partie des choses que nous avons à faire; **~ yourselves** entre vous; **~ other things** entre autres (choses); **to count sb ~ one's friends** compter qn parmi *or* au nombre de ses amis; **~ friends** entre amis.

amoral [eɪ'mɒrəl] *adj* amoral.

amorous ['æmərəs] *adj* amoureux. ◆ **amorously** *adv* amoureusement.

amorphous [ə'mɔ:fəs] *adj* amorphe.

amount [ə'maʊnt] *n* (**a**) *(total)* montant *m*; *(sum of money)* somme *f*. **the ~ of a bill** le montant d'une facture; **there is a small ~ still to pay** il reste une petite somme à payer. (**b**) *(quantity)* quantité *f*. **an enormous ~ of, any ~ of** énormément de; **any ~ of time** tout le temps qu'il faut. ◆ **amount to** *vt fus [sums, debts]* s'élever à; *(fig)* revenir à, représenter. **it ~s to the same thing** cela revient au même; **it ~s to stealing/a change in policy** cela revient à du vol/un changement de politique; **this ~s to very little** cela ne représente pas grand-chose; **he will never ~ to much** il ne fera jamais grand-chose.

amp(ère) ['æmp(εəʳ)] *n* ampère *m*. **a 13-amp plug** une fiche de 13 ampères.

ampersand ['æmpəsænd] *n* esperluète *f*.

amphetamine [æm'fetəmi:n] *n* amphétamine *f*.

amphibian [æm'fɪbɪən] **1** *adj* amphibie. **2** *n (Zool)* amphibie *m*; *(car/tank etc)* voiture *f*/char *m* amphibie. ◆ **amphibious** *adj* amphibie.

amphitheatre, *(US)* **amphitheater** ['æmfɪˌθɪətəʳ] *n (gen)* amphithéâtre *m*; *(in mountains)* cirque *m*.

ample ['æmpl] *adj* (**a**) *(enough) money etc* bien *or* largement assez de; *reason, motive* solide; *means, resources* gros. **there is ~ room for** il y a largement la place pour; *(fig)* **there is ~ room for improvement** il y a encore bien des progrès à faire; **to have ~ time** avoir largement le temps (*to do* de *or* pour faire). (**b**) *(large) garment* ample. ◆ **amply** *adv* amplement.

amplify ['æmplɪfaɪ] *vt sound, story* amplifier; *statement, idea* développer. ◆ **amplification** *n* amplification *f*. ◆ **amplifier** *n* amplificateur *m*.

amputate ['æmpjʊteɪt] *vt* amputer. **to ~ sb's leg** amputer qn de la jambe. ◆ **amputation** *n* amputation *f*.

Amsterdam ['æmstədæm] *n* Amsterdam.

amuck [ə'mʌk] *adv*: **to run ~** être pris d'un accès de folie meurtrière; *[crowd]* se déchaîner.

amuse [ə'mju:z] *vt* (**a**) *(cause mirth to)* amuser, divertir, faire rire. **it ~d us** cela nous a fait rire; **to be ~d at** *or* **by** s'amuser de; **he was not ~d** il n'a pas trouvé ça drôle. (**b**) *(entertain)* amuser, distraire. **to ~ o.s. with sth/by doing** s'amuser avec qch/à faire; **you'll have to ~ yourselves** il va vous falloir trouver de quoi vous distraire *or* vous occuper. ◆ **amusement** **1** *n* (**a**) amusement *m*; **to my ~ment** à mon grand amusement; **look of ~ment** regard amusé; **to hide one's ~ment** dissimuler son envie de rire; (**b**) *(diversion)* distraction *f*, amusement *m*; **a town with plenty of ~ments** une ville qui offre beaucoup de distractions; **2** *adj*: **~ment arcade** galerie *f* de jeux; **~ment park** parc *m* d'attractions. ◆ **amusing** *adj* amusant, drôle. ◆ **amusingly** *adv* d'une manière amusante.

an [æn, ən, n] *indef art V* **a²**.

anachronism [əˈnækrənɪzəm] *n* anachronisme *m*. ◆ **anachronistic** *adj* anachronique.

anaemia [əˈniːmɪə] *n* anémie *f*. ◆ **anaemic** *adj* anémique.

anaesthesia [ˌænɪsˈθiːzɪə] *n* anesthésie *f*. ◆ **anaesthetic** [ˌænɪsˈθetɪk] **1** *n* anesthésique *m*; **under the anaesthetic** sous anesthésie; **2** *adj* anesthésique. ◆ **anaesthetist** [æˈniːsθɪtɪst] *n* anesthésiste *mf*. ◆ **anaesthetize** [æˈniːsθɪtaɪz] *vt* anesthésier.

anagram [ˈænəgræm] *n* anagramme *f*.

analgesia [ˌænælˈdʒiːzɪə] *n* analgésie *f*. ◆ **analgesic** *adj, n* analgésique *(m)*.

analog, analogue [ˈænəlɒg] *n* analogue *m*. ~ **computer** calculateur *m* analogique. ◆ **analogic(al)** *adj* analogique. ◆ **analogous** *adj* analogue *(to, with* à). ◆ **analogy** *n* analogie *f*.

analyse, *(US)* **analyze** [ˈænəlaɪz] *vt* analyser, faire l'analyse de; *(Psych)* psychanalyser. ◆ **analysis** *pl* **analyses** *n* analyse *f*; *(Psych)* psychanalyse *f*; **in the last** *or* **final analysis** en dernière analyse. ◆ **analyst** *n (Psych)* (psych)analyste *mf*. ◆ **analytic(al)** *adj* analytique.

anarchy [ˈænəkɪ] *n* anarchie *f*. ◆ **anarchic(al)** *adj* anarchique. ◆ **anarchism** *n* anarchisme *m*. ◆ **anarchist** *n* anarchiste *mf*.

anathema [əˈnæθɪmə] *n* anathème *m*. **it was ~ to him** il l'avait en abomination.

anatomy [əˈnætəmɪ] *n (Sci)* anatomie *f*; *[country etc]* structure *f*. **he had spots all over his ~** il avait des boutons partout. ◆ **anatomical** *adj* anatomique. ◆ **anatomist** *n* anatomiste *mf*.

ancestor [ˈænsɪstəʳ] *n* ancêtre *m*. ◆ **ancestral** *adj* ancestral; **ancestral home** château ancestral. ◆ **ancestry** *n* ascendance *f*; *(ancestors collectively)* ancêtres *mpl*.

anchor [ˈæŋkəʳ] **1** *n* ancre *f*. **to be at ~** être à l'ancre. **2** *vt (Naut)* mettre à l'ancre; *(fig)* ancrer. **3** *vi (Naut)* jeter l'ancre. **4** *adj*: ~ **man** *(Rad, TV)* présentateur-réalisateur *m*; *(in team, organization)* pilier *m*. ◆ **anchorage** *n* ancrage *m*; *(Aut)* **~age point** point *m* d'ancrage.

anchovy [ˈæntʃəvɪ] *n* anchois *m*.

ancient [ˈeɪnʃ(ə)nt] **1** *adj* (**a**) *world, painting* antique; *document, custom, history* ancien; *monument* historique; *rock etc* très vieux. **in ~ days** dans les temps anciens; ~ **Rome** la Rome antique. (**b**) *person* très vieux; *clothes, object* antique, très vieux. **this is positively ~** cela remonte à Mathusalem. **2** *n*: **the ~s** les anciens *mpl*.

ancillary [ænˈsɪlərɪ] *adj (gen)* auxiliaire. ~ **to** subordonné à; ~ **workers** personnel *m* des services auxiliaires.

and [ænd, ənd, nd, ən] *conj* et. **his table ~ chair** sa table et sa chaise; **~?** et alors?; **on Saturday ~/or Sunday** *(Admin)* samedi et/ou dimanche; *(gen)* samedi ou dimanche ou les deux; **three hundred ~ ten** trois cent dix; **two thousand ~ eight** deux mille huit; **two pounds ~ six pence** deux livres (et) six pence; **an hour ~ twenty minutes** une heure vingt (minutes); **five ~ three quarters** cinq trois quarts; **try ~ come** tâchez de venir; **for hours ~ hours** pendant des heures et des heures; **I rang ~ rang** j'ai sonné et resonné; **he talked ~ talked** il a parlé pendant des heures; **~ so on, ~ so forth** et ainsi de suite; **uglier ~ uglier** de plus en plus laid; **eggs ~ bacon** œufs au bacon; **summer ~ winter (alike)** été comme hiver.

Andes [ˈændiːz] *npl*: **the ~** les Andes *fpl*.

Andorra [ˌænˈdɔːrə] *n* Andorre.

anecdote [ˈænɪkdəʊt] *n* anecdote *f*. ◆ **anecdotal** *adj* anecdotique.

anemia *etc* = **anaemia** *etc*.

anemone [əˈnemənɪ] *n* anémone *f*.

anesthesia *etc* = **anaesthesia** *etc*.

aneurism [ˈænjʊrɪz(ə)m] *n* anévrisme *m*.

anew [əˈnjuː] *adv* de nouveau. **to begin ~** recommencer.

angel [ˈeɪn(d)ʒ(ə)l] *n* ange *m*. **be an ~ and fetch me my gloves** apporte-moi mes gants, tu seras un ange. ◆ **angelic** *adj* angélique.

angelica [ænˈdʒelɪkə] *n* angélique *f*.

angelus [ˈændʒɪləs] *n (prayer, bell)* angélus *m*.

anger [ˈæŋgəʳ] **1** *n* colère *f*. **in ~** sous le coup de la colère. **2** *vt* mettre en colère

angina [ænˈdʒaɪnə] *n* angine *f*; *[heart]* angine de poitrine.

angle¹ [ˈæŋgl] **1** *n (also Math)* angle *m*. **at an ~ of** formant un angle de; **at an ~** en biais (*to* par rapport à); **cut at an ~** coupé en biseau; **to study a topic from every ~** étudier un sujet sous tous les angles; **from the parents' ~** du point de vue des parents; **let's have your ~ on it *** dites-nous votre point de vue là-dessus. **2** *vt lamp* diriger la lumière de (*towards* sur); (*) *information, report* présenter sous un certain angle. ◆ **Anglepoise** ® **lamp** *n* lampe *f* d'architecte.

angle² [ˈæŋgl] *vi (lit)* pêcher à la ligne. **to ~ for** *trout* pêcher; *compliments* chercher; **to ~ for an invitation** chercher à se faire inviter. ◆ **angler** *n* pêcheur *m*, -euse *f* (à la ligne). ◆ **angling** *n* pêche *f* (à la ligne).

Anglican [ˈæŋglɪkən] *adj, n* anglican(e) *m(f)*. ◆ **Anglicanism** *n* anglicanisme *m*.

anglicism [ˈæŋglɪsɪz(ə)m] *n* anglicisme *m*. ◆ **anglicist** *n* angliciste *mf*. ◆ **anglicize** *vt* angliciser.

Anglo- [ˈæŋgləʊ] *pref* anglo-. **~-French** *adj* anglo-français; **~-Catholic** *adj, n* anglo-catholique *(mf)*; **~-Saxon** *adj, n* anglo-saxon *(m)*.

anglophile [ˈæŋgləʊˈfaɪl] *adj, n* anglophile *(mf)*.

anglophobe [ˈæŋgləʊˈfəʊb] *adj, n* anglophobe *(mf)*.

Angola [æŋˈgəʊlə] *n* Angola. ◆ **Angolan 1** *adj* angolais ; **2** *n* Angolais(e) *m(f)*.

angora [æŋˈgɔːrə] **1** *n* angora *m*. **2** *adj* angora *inv*.

angry [ˈæŋgrɪ] *adj person* en colère (*with sb* contre qn, *at sth* à cause de qch, *about sth* à propos de qch); *(annoyed)* irrité, fâché (*with sb* contre qn, *at sth* de qch, *about sth* à cause de qch); *look, reply* irrité, plein de colère; *(fig) sea* mauvais; *wound* enflammé. **to get ~** se fâcher, se mettre en colère; **to make sb ~** mettre qn en colère; **he was ~ at being dismissed** il était furieux qu'on l'ait renvoyé; **you won't be ~ if I tell you?** vous n'allez pas vous fâcher si je vous le dis?; **an ~ mark on his forehead** une vilaine meurtrissure au front. ◆ **angrily** *adv leave* en colère; *talk* avec colère, avec emportement.

anguish [ˈæŋgwɪʃ] *n* angoisse *f*. ◆ **anguished** *adj* angoissé.

angular [ˈæŋgjʊləʳ] *adj* anguleux.

animal [ˈænɪməl] **1** *n* animal *m*; *(*pej: person)* brute *f*. **2** *adj (gen)* animal. ~ **husbandry** élevage *m*; ~ **kingdom** règne animal; ~ **lover** personne *f* qui aime les animaux; ~ **rights** les droits des animaux; ~ **spirits** entrain *m*.

animate [ˈænɪmɪt] **1** *adj* animé. **2** [ˈænɪmeɪt] *vt* animer. ◆ **animated** *adj* animé; **to become ~d** s'animer; **~d cartoon** dessin(s) animé(s). ◆ **animatedly** *adv talk* d'un ton animé, avec animation; *behave* avec entrain. ◆ **animation** *n (gen, Cine)* animation *f*; *[person]* entrain *m*. ◆ **animator** *n (Cine)* animateur *m*, -trice *f*.

animism [ˈænɪmɪz(ə)m] animisme *m*. ◆ **animist** *adj, n* animiste *(mf)*.

animosity [ˌænɪˈmɒsɪtɪ], **animus** [ˈænɪməs] *n* animosité *f* (*against, towards* contre).

aniseed [ˈænɪsiːd] **1** *n* graine *f* d'anis. **2** *adj* à l'anis.

ankle ['æŋkl] **1** *n (Anat)* cheville *f.* **2** *adj*: ~ **sock** socquette *f*; ~ **strap** bride *f.* ◆ **anklebone** *n* astragale *m.* ◆ **anklet** *n* bracelet *m* de cheville.

annals ['æn(ə)lz] *npl* annales *fpl.*

annex [ə'neks] **1** *vt* annexer. **2** ['æneks] *n (also* **annexe***)* annexe *f.* ◆ **annexation** *n* annexation *f (of* de).

annihilate [ə'naɪəleɪt] *vt army, fleet* anéantir; *effect, argument* annihiler. ◆ **annihilation** *n* anéantissement *m.*

anniversary [ˌænɪ'vɜːs(ə)rɪ] **1** *n* anniversaire *m (d'une date).* **2** *adj*: ~ **dinner** dîner commémoratif.

Anno Domini ['ænəʊ'dɒmɪnaɪ] *(abbr* **A.D.***)*: **in 53** ~ en 53 après Jésus-Christ (*abbr* ap. J.-C.); **it's just** ~ * c'est le poids des ans *(hum).*

annotate ['ænəʊ'teɪt] *vt* annoter. ◆ **annotation** *n* annotation *f.*

announce [ə'naʊns] *vt (gen)* annoncer. **to** ~ **the birth/death of** faire part de la naissance de/du décès de; **it is** ~**d from London** on apprend de Londres. ◆ **announcement** *n (gen)* annonce *f*; *(esp Admin)* avis *m*; *[birth, marriage, death]* avis; *(privately inserted or circulated)* faire-part *m inv.* ◆ **announcer** *n (Rad, TV) (linking programmes)* speaker(ine) *m(f)*; *(within a programme)* présentateur *m*, -trice *f.*

annoy [ə'nɔɪ] *vt (vex)* agacer, ennuyer, contrarier; *(deliberately irritate)* agacer, énerver; *(inconvenience)* ennuyer. **to be/get** ~**ed with sb** être/se mettre en colère contre qn; **to be** ~**ed about** *or* **over sth** être contrarié par qch; **to be** ~**ed with sb about sth** être mécontent de qn à propos de qch; **to get** ~**ed with a machine** se mettre en colère *or* s'énerver contre une machine; **don't get** ~**ed!** ne vous fâchez pas!; **I am very** ~**ed that he hasn't come** je suis très ennuyé *or* contrarié qu'il ne soit pas venu. ◆ **annoyance** *n* (**a**) contrariété *f*, mécontentement *m*; **with a look of** ~**ance** d'un air contrarié; **to his great** ~**ance** à son grand mécontentement; (**b**) *(cause of* ~*ance)* ennui *m.* ◆ **annoying** *adj* agaçant, énervant; *(stronger)* ennuyeux, fâcheux. ◆ **annoyingly** *adv* d'une façon agaçante *etc.*

annual ['ænjʊəl] **1** *adj* annuel. ~ **general meeting** assemblée générale annuelle. **2** *n (Bot)* plante annuelle; *(book)* publication annuelle; *(children's)* album *m.* ◆ **annually** *adv* annuellement, tous les ans; **£5** ~**ly** 5 livres par an.

annuity [ə'njuːɪtɪ] *n (income)* rente *f*; *(for life)* rente viagère; *(investment)* viager *m.*

annul [ə'nʌl] *vt (gen)* annuler; *law* abroger. ◆ **annulment** *n* annulation *f*; abrogation *f.*

Annunciation [əˌnʌnsɪ'eɪʃ(ə)n] *n* Annonciation *f.*

anode ['ænəʊd] *n* anode *f.*

anodyne ['ænəʊ'daɪn] *adj (Med)* analgésique; *(fig)* apaisant.

anoint [ə'nɔɪnt] *vt* oindre (*with* de). **to** ~ **sb king** sacrer qn.

anomalous [ə'nɒmələs] *adj* anormal. ◆ **anomaly** *n* anomalie *f.*

anon [ə'nɒn] *adj abbr of* **anonymous.**

anonymous [ə'nɒnɪməs] *adj* anonyme. **to remain** ~ garder l'anonymat. ◆ **anonymity** [ænə'nɪmɪtɪ] *n* anonymat *m.* ◆ **anonymously** *adv* anonymement.

anorak ['ænəræk] *n* anorak *m.*

anorexia [ænə'reksɪə] *n* anorexie *f.* ~ **nervosa** anorexie mentale. ◆ **anorexic** *adj, n* anorexique *(mf).*

another [ə'nʌðə'] **1** *adj* (**a**) *(one more)* un... de plus, encore un. ~ **10** 10 de plus, encore 10; **not** ~ **minute!** pas une minute de plus!; **without** ~ **word** sans ajouter un mot; **and** ~ **thing, ...** et de plus, ... , et d'ailleurs, ... ; **in** ~ **20 years** dans 20 ans d'ici. (**b**) *(similar)* un autre, un second. **there is not** ~ **book like it** ce livre est unique dans son genre; ~ **Hitler** un second Hitler. (**c**) *(different)* un autre. **that's quite** ~ **matter** c'est une tout autre question. **2** *pron* (**a**) un(e) autre, encore un(e). **many** ~ bien d'autres. (**b**) **one** ~ = **each other;** *V* **each.**

answer ['ɑːnsə'] **1** *n* (**a**) *(reply)* réponse *f*; *(to prayer)* exaucement *m (to* de). **there's no** ~ *(gen)* on ne répond pas; *(Telec)* ça ne répond pas; **in** ~ **to your letter** en réponse à votre lettre; **she's always got an** ~ elle a réponse à tout; *(hum)* **it's the** ~ **to a maiden's prayer** * c'est ce dont j'ai toujours rêvé; **the poor man's** ~ **to caviar** le caviar du pauvre. (**b**) *(solution)* solution *f.* **there is no easy** ~ c'est un problème difficile à résoudre. **2** *vt* (**a**) *question* répondre à; *charge, argument* réfuter. ~ **me** répondez-moi; **to** ~ **the bell** *or* **door** aller ouvrir; **to** ~ **the phone** répondre (au téléphone). (**b**) *description, need* répondre à; *prayer* exaucer; *problem* résoudre. **it** ~**s the purpose** cela fait l'affaire. **3** *vi* répondre.
◆ **answer back** *vi* répondre (avec impertinence) (*to* à). ◆ **answer for** *vt fus sb's safety etc* répondre de; *truth of sth* garantir. **he has a lot to** ~ **for** il a bien des comptes à rendre. ◆ **answer to** *vt fus name, description* répondre à.
◆ **answerable** *adj* (**a**) *question* susceptible de réponse; *charge, argument* réfutable; *problem* soluble; (**b**) *(responsible)* responsable (*to sb* devant qn, *for sth* de qch); **I am** ~**able to no one** je n'ai de comptes à rendre à personne. ◆ **answerback code** *n* indicatif *m.* ◆ **answering machine** *n* répondeur *m* automatique. ◆ **answering service** *n* permanence *f* téléphonique.

ant [ænt] *n* fourmi *f.* ◆ **anteater** *n* fourmilier *m.* ◆ **anthill** *n* fourmilière *f.*

antagonize [æn'tægənaɪz] *vt* éveiller l'hostilité de, contrarier. **I don't want to** ~ **him** je ne veux pas le contrarier *or* me le mettre à dos. ◆ **antagonism** *n* antagonisme *m* (*between* entre), opposition *f* (*to* à). ◆ **antagonist** *n* antagoniste *mf.* ◆ **antagonistic** *adj* opposé (*to sth* à qch).

Antarctic [ænt'ɑːktɪk] **1** *n* Antarctique *m.* **2** *adj* antarctique. ~ **Circle/Ocean** cercle *m*/océan *m* Antarctique. ◆ **Antarctica** *n* Antarctique *m.*

ante... ['æntɪ] *pref* anté..., anti... ◆ **antechamber** *n* antichambre *f.* ◆ **antedate** *vt document* antidater; *event* précéder. ◆ **antediluvian** *adj* antédiluvien. ◆ **antenatal** *adj* prénatal; ~**natal clinic** service *m* de consultation prénatale. ◆ **anteroom** *n* antichambre *f.*

antecedent [ˌæntɪ'siːd(ə)nt] **1** *adj* antérieur (*to* à). **2** *n* antécédent *m.*

antelope ['æntɪləʊp] *n* antilope *f.*

antenna, *pl* **-ae** [æn'tenə, iː] *n* antenne *f.*

anterior [æn'tɪərɪə'] *adj* antérieur (*to* à).

anthem ['ænθəm] *n* motet *m.*

anthology [æn'θɒlədʒɪ] *n* anthologie *f.* ◆ **anthologist** *n* anthologiste *mf.*

anthracite ['ænθrəsaɪt] *n* anthracite *m.*

anthropoid ['ænθrəʊ'pɔɪd] *adj, n* anthropoïde *(m).*

anthropology [ˌænθrə'pɒlədʒɪ] *n* anthropologie *f.* ◆ **anthropological** *adj* anthropologique. ◆ **anthropologist** *n* anthropologiste *mf.*

anti... ['æntɪ] *pref* anti..., contre... **he's rather** ~ * il est plutôt contre. ◆ **anti-abortionist** *n* adversaire *m* de l'avortement. ◆ **anti-aircraft** *adj gun* antiaérien. ◆ **antiballistic** *adj missile* antibalistique. ◆ **antibiotic** *adj, n* antibiotique *(m).* ◆ **antibody** *n* anticorps *m.* ◆ **Antichrist** *n* Antéchrist *m.* ◆ **anticlerical** *adj* anticlérical. ◆ **anticlimax** *n [style, thought]* chute *f* (dans le trivial); **it was an** ~**climax** cela n'a pas répondu à l'attente; **what an** ~**climax!** quelle retombée! ◆ **anticlockwise** *adv* dans le sens inverse des aiguilles d'une montre. ◆ **anticyclone** *n* anticyclone *m*. ◆ **antidote** *n* antidote *m* (*for, to* à, contre). ◆ **anti-establishment** *adj* contestataire. ◆ **antifreeze** *n* antigel *m*. ◆ **antigen** *n* antigène *m*. ◆ **antihistamine** *n* antihistaminique *m*. ◆ **anti-lock** *adj:* **~-lock device** dispositif *m* anti-blocage. ◆ **antipodes** [æn'tɪpədi:z] *npl* antipodes *mpl*; **the A~podes** les Antipodes, l'Australie et la Nouvelle-Zélande. ◆ **anti-rust** *adj* antirouille *inv*. ◆ **antisemitic** *adj* antisémite, antisémitique. ◆ **antisemitism** *n* antisémitisme *m*. ◆ **antisepsis** *n* antisepsie *f*. ◆ **antiseptic** *adj, n* antiseptique (*m*). ◆ **anti-skid** *adj* antidérapant. ◆ **antislavery** *adj* antiesclavagiste. ◆ **antisocial** *adj tendency, behaviour* antisocial; **don't be ~social** * ne sois pas si sauvage. ◆ **anti-tank** *adj* antichar. ◆ **anti-theft** *adj*: **~-theft device** *(Aut)* antivol *m*; *(gen)* dispositif *m* antivol. ◆ **antithesis,** *pl* **-eses** *n (direct opposite)* opposé *m*, contraire *m* (*to, of* de); *(contrast)* antithèse *f*. ◆ **antivivisectionist** *n* adversaire *mf* de la vivisection.

antic ['æntɪk] *n [child, animal]* cabriole *f*; *[clown]* bouffonnerie *f*. *(pej)* **all his ~s** tout le cinéma * qu'il a fait.

anticipate [æn'tɪsɪpeɪt] *vt* (**a**) *(expect, foresee)* prévoir, s'attendre à; *attack, events* anticiper sur; *question* prévoir. **we don't ~ any trouble** nous ne prévoyons pas d'ennuis; **I ~ that he will come** je m'attends à ce qu'il vienne; **I ~ seeing him tomorrow** je pense le voir demain; **as ~d** comme prévu. (**b**) *(use etc before due time) pleasure* savourer à l'avance; *event, profits, income* anticiper sur; *grief, pain* souffrir à l'avance; *success* escompter; *wishes, objections, command, needs* aller au-devant de. **they ~d Columbus' discovery of America** ils ont découvert l'Amérique avant Christophe Colomb. ◆ **anticipation** *n*: **in anticipation** par anticipation; *(Comm)* **thanking you in anticipation** avec mes remerciements anticipés; **in anticipation of** en prévision de; **with growing anticipation** avec une impatience grandissante.

antimony ['æntɪmənɪ] *n* antimoine *m*.

antipathetic [ˌæntɪpə'θetɪk] *adj* antipathique (*to* à). ◆ **antipathy** [æn'tɪpəθɪ] *n* antipathie *f*.

antiquarian [ˌæntɪ'kwɛərɪən] **1** *adj* d'antiquaire. **~ bookseller** libraire *mf* spécialisé(e) dans le livre ancien. **2** *n* amateur *m* d'antiquités; *(Comm)* antiquaire *mf*. ◆ **antiquary** *n (Comm)* antiquaire *mf*.

antiquated ['æntɪkweɪtɪd] *adj* vieillot; *person* vieux jeu *inv; building* vétuste.

antique [æn'ti:k] **1** *adj (very old)* ancien; *(pre-medieval)* antique; *(*: hum)* antédiluvien *. **2** *n (sculpture, ornament etc)* objet *m* d'art (ancien); *(furniture)* meuble *m* ancien. **~ dealer** antiquaire *mf*; **~ shop** magasin *m* d'antiquités; **it's a genuine ~** c'est un objet (*or* un meuble) d'époque. ◆ **antiquity** *n* antiquité *f*.

antirrhinum [ˌæntɪ'raɪnəm] *n* gueule-de-loup *f*.

antler ['æntlə^r] *n* merrain *m*. **the ~s** les bois *mpl*.

antonym ['æntənɪm] *n* antonyme *m*.

anus ['eɪnəs] *n* anus *m*.

anvil ['ænvɪl] *n* enclume *f*.

anxiety [æŋ'zaɪətɪ] *n (anxiousness: also Psych)* anxiété *f*. **deep ~** angoisse *f*; **this is a great ~ to me** ceci m'inquiète énormément; **in his ~ to be gone** dans son souci de partir au plus vite; **his biggest ~ was** son plus grand sujet d'inquiétude était; **~ to do well** grand désir *m* de réussir.

anxious ['æŋ(k)ʃəs] *adj* (**a**) *(troubled)* anxieux, (très) inquiet, angoissé. **to be over-~** être d'une anxiété maladive; **she is ~ about my health** mon état de santé la préoccupe *or* l'inquiète beaucoup. (**b**) *(causing anxiety) news* inquiétant, angoissant; *moment* d'anxiété. (**c**) *(desirous)* anxieux, impatient (*for* de). **~ to start** pressé *or* impatient de commencer; **he is ~ to see you** il tient beaucoup à vous voir; **I am ~ that he should do it** je tiens beaucoup à ce qu'il le fasse; **I am not very ~ to do** j'ai peu envie de faire. ◆ **anxiously** *adv (with concern)* avec inquiétude, anxieusement; *(eagerly)* avec impatience.

any ['enɪ] **1** *adj* (**a**) *(neg etc)* **I haven't ~ money/books** je n'ai pas d'argent/de livres; **without ~ difficulty** sans la moindre difficulté. (**b**) *(interrog etc)* **have you ~ butter?** avez-vous du beurre?; **can you see ~ birds?** voyez-vous des oiseaux?; **are there ~ others?** y en a-t-il d'autres?; **if you see ~ children** si vous voyez des enfants; **if you have ~ money** si vous avez de l'argent. (**c**) *(no matter which)* n'importe quel, quelconque; *(each and every)* tout. **take ~ two points** prenez deux points quelconques; **take ~ dress you like** prenez n'importe quelle robe; **come at ~ time** venez à n'importe quelle heure; **~ day now** d'un jour à l'autre; **at ~ hour of the day** à toute heure du jour; **~ amount** *or* **number of** n'importe quelle quantité de; *(fig: a lot)* beaucoup de; **~ person who** toute personne qui.

2 *pron* (**a**) **I haven't ~** je n'en ai pas; **I have hardly ~ left** il ne m'en reste presque plus; **have you got ~?** en avez-vous? (**b**) **if ~ of you can sing** si quelqu'un parmi vous sait chanter; **few, if ~** peu de gens, et peut-être même personne; **~ of those books will do** n'importe lequel de ces livres fera l'affaire.

3 *adv*: **I can't hear him ~ more** je ne l'entends plus; **not ~ further** pas plus loin; **not ~ longer** pas plus longtemps; **they didn't behave ~ too well** ils ne se sont pas tellement bien conduits; **are you feeling ~ better?** vous sentez-vous un peu mieux?; **do you want ~ more soup?** voulez-vous encore de la soupe?; **it didn't help them ~** * cela ne leur a pas servi à grand-chose.

anybody ['enɪbɒdɪ] *pron* (**a**) *(neg etc)* **I can't see ~** je ne vois personne; **there is hardly ~ there** il n'y a presque personne; **without ~ seeing him** sans que personne le voie. (**b**) *(interrog etc)* quelqu'un. **did ~ see you?** est-ce que quelqu'un t'a vu?; **~ want my sandwich?** * quelqu'un veut mon sandwich? * (**c**) *(no matter who)* **~ could tell you** n'importe qui pourrait vous le dire; **~ would have thought he had lost** on aurait pu croire qu'il avait perdu; **bring ~ you like** amenez qui vous voudrez; **~ who had heard him speak** quiconque l'a entendu parler; **~ with any sense would know that!** le premier venu saurait cela pourvu qu'il ait un minimum de bon sens!; **~ but Robert** n'importe qui d'autre que Robert; **~ else would have refused** un autre aurait refusé; **bring ~ else you like** amenez n'importe qui d'autre; **is there ~ else I can talk to?** est-ce qu'il y a quelqu'un d'autre à qui je puisse parler?; **work harder if you want to be ~** il faut travailler plus si vous voulez devenir quelqu'un; **he's not just ~** ce n'est pas n'importe qui.

anyhow ['enɪhaʊ] *adv* (**a**) *(any way whatever)* **do it ~ you like** faites-le comme vous voulez ; **I couldn't get in ~** je n'avais aucun moyen d'entrer; **I finished my essay ~** j'ai fini ma dissertation n'importe comment *or* à la va-vite; **the books were all ~** * **on the floor** les livres étaient tous en désordre *or* en vrac *or* n'importe comment par terre. (**b**) *(in any case)* en tout cas, de toute façon, quand même. **whatever you say, they'll do it ~** vous pouvez dire ce que vous voulez, ils le feront de toute façon *or* quand même; **you can try ~** vous pouvez toujours essayer.

anyone ['enɪwʌn] *pron* = **anybody.**

anyplace * ['enɪpleɪs] *adv (US)* = **anywhere.**

anything ['enɪθɪŋ] *pron* (**a**) *(neg etc)* **we haven't seen ~** nous n'avons rien vu; **hardly ~** presque rien; **this is ~ but pleasant** ceci n'a vraiment rien d'agréable; *(reply to question)* ~ **but!** pas du tout! (**b**) *(interrog etc)* **did you see ~?** avez-vous vu quelque chose?; **is there ~ in this idea?** peut-on tirer quoi que ce soit de cette idée?; **can ~ be done?** peut-on faire quelque chose?; ~ **else?** c'est tout?; **is there ~ more tiring than...** y a-t-il rien de plus fatigant que...; ~ **between 15 and 20 apple trees** quelque chose comme 15 ou 20 pommiers; **if ~ it's an improvement** ce serait plutôt une amélioration. (**c**) *(no matter what)* **say ~ (at all)** dites n'importe quoi; **take ~ you like** prenez ce que vous voudrez; ~ **else would disappoint her** s'il en était autrement, elle serait déçue; **I'll try ~ else** j'essaierai n'importe quoi d'autre; **I'd give ~ to know the secret** je donnerais n'importe quoi pour connaître le secret; *(intensive)* **he ran** *etc* **like ~** * il a drôlement * couru *etc.*

anyway ['enɪweɪ] *adv* = **anyhow (b).**

anywhere ['enɪwɛəʳ] *adv* (**a**) *(affirmative)* n'importe où, partout. **I'd live ~ in France** j'habiterais n'importe où en France; **put it down ~** pose-le n'importe où; **you can find that soap ~** ce savon se trouve partout; **go ~ you like** allez où vous voulez; ~ **you go it's the same** où que vous alliez c'est la même chose; ~ **else** partout ailleurs. (**b**) *(neg)* nulle part. **they didn't go ~** ils ne sont allés nulle part; **not ~ else** nulle part ailleurs; *(fig)* **it won't get you ~** cela ne vous mènera à rien. (**c**) *(interrog)* quelque part. **have you seen it ~?** l'avez-vous vu quelque part?

aorta [eɪ'ɔːtə] *n* aorte *f.*

apace [ə'peɪs] *adv* rapidement.

apart [ə'pɑːt] *adv* (**a**) *(separated)* **2 houses a long way ~** 2 maisons à une grande distance l'une de l'autre; **birthdays 2 days ~** anniversaires à 2 jours d'intervalle; **to stand with one's feet ~** se tenir les jambes écartées. (**b**) *(on one side)* à part, à l'écart. **to hold o.s. ~** se tenir à l'écart *(from* de); ~ **from these difficulties** en dehors de *or* à part ces difficultés, ces difficultés mises à part; ~ **from the fact that** outre que. (**c**) *(separately)* séparément. **they are living ~** ils sont séparés; **he lives ~ from his wife** il est séparé de sa femme; **to tell ~** distinguer l'un(e) de l'autre; **to keep ~** séparer; **to come ~** *[two objects]* se séparer, se détacher; *[small object]* se défaire; *[furniture]* se démonter; *(break)* s'en aller en morceaux; **to take ~** démonter; *(fig)* **they are in a class ~** ils sont tout à fait à part.

apartheid [ə'pɑːteɪt] *n* apartheid *m.*

apartment [ə'pɑːtmənt] *n* (**a**) *(Brit: room)* pièce *f.* **a 5-~ house** une maison de 5 pièces; **'~s'** 'chambres *fpl* à louer'; **furnished ~(s)** meublé *m.* (**b**) *(US: flat)* appartement *m*, logement *m.* ~ **building, ~ house** immeuble *m (de résidence).*

apathy ['æpəθɪ] *n* apathie *f*, indifférence *f.* ◆ **apathetic** *adj* apathique.

ape [eɪp] **1** *n* (grand) singe *m.* **2** *vt* singer.

aperient [ə'pɪərɪənt] *adj, n* laxatif *(m).*

aperitif [ə'perɪtɪv] *n* apéritif *m.*

aperture ['æpətʃjʊəʳ] *n* ouverture *f (also Phot).*

apex ['eɪpeks] *n* sommet *m.*

aphid ['eɪdɪd] *n* puceron *m* (des plantes).

aphis, *pl* **aphides** ['eɪfɪs,'eɪfɪdiːz] *n* aphis *m.*

aphorism ['æfərɪz(ə)m] *n* aphorisme *m.*

aphrodisiac [ˌæfrəʊ'dɪzɪæk] *n* aphrodisiaque *m.*

apiary ['eɪpɪərɪ] *n* rucher *m.*

apiece [ə'piːs] *adv* chacun(e).

aplomb [ə'plɒm] *n* sang-froid *m.*

Apocalypse [ə'pɒkəlɪps] *n* Apocalypse *f.* ◆ **apocalyptic** *adj* apocalyptique.

Apocrypha [ə'pɒkrɪfə] *npl* apocryphes *mpl.* ◆ **apocryphal** *adj* apocryphe.

apogee ['æpəʊ'dʒiː] *n* apogée *m.*

apolitical [ˌeɪpə'lɪtɪk(ə)l] *adj* apolitique.

apologetic [əˌpɒlə'dʒetɪk] *adj smile etc* d'excuse. **she was very ~ for not coming/about her mistake** elle s'est beaucoup excusée de n'être pas venue/de son erreur. ◆ **apologetically** *adv* en s'excusant, pour s'excuser.

apologize [ə'pɒlədʒaɪz] *vi* s'excuser *(to sb for sth* de qch auprès de qn; *for having done* d'avoir fait). **to ~ profusely** se confondre en excuses.

apology [ə'pɒlədʒɪ] *n* (**a**) *(regrets)* excuses *fpl.* **to make an ~ for sth/for having done** faire ses excuses pour qch/pour avoir fait; **to send one's apologies** envoyer une lettre d'excuse; *(pej)* **it was an ~ for a bed** comme lit c'était plutôt minable *. (**b**) *(defence: for beliefs etc)* apologie *f (for* de).

apoplexy ['æpəpleksɪ] *n* apoplexie *f.* ◆ **apoplectic** *adj* apoplectique; **apoplectic fit** attaque *f* d'apoplexie.

apostle [ə'pɒsl] *n* apôtre *m.* **A~s' Creed** Credo *m.* ◆ **apostolic** *adj* apostolique.

apostrophe [ə'pɒstrəfɪ] *n* apostrophe *f.*

appal, *(US)* **appall** [ə'pɔːl] *vt* consterner; *(stronger)* épouvanter. ◆ **appalling** *adj destruction* épouvantable; *ignorance* consternant. ◆ **appallingly** *adv* épouvantablement.

apparatchik [ˌæpə'rættʃiːk] *n* apparatchik *m.*

apparatus [ˌæpə'reɪtəs] *n (for heating etc: also Anat)* appareil *m*; *[laboratory]* instruments *mpl*; *[gym]* agrès *mpl*; *[filming, camping etc]* équipement *m.*

apparent [ə'pær(ə)nt] *adj* (**a**) *(obvious)* évident, apparent, manifeste. (**b**) *(not real)* apparent. **his ~ weakness** son air de faiblesse. ◆ **apparently** *adv* apparemment; *(according to rumour)* à ce qu'il paraît.

apparition [ˌæpə'rɪʃ(ə)n] *n* apparition *f.*

appeal [ə'piːl] **1** *vi* (**a**) *(request publicly)* lancer un appel *(on behalf of* en faveur de; *for sb* pour qn; *for sth* pour obtenir qch). *(Fin)* **to ~ for funds** faire un appel de fonds; **he ~ed for silence** il a demandé le silence; *(Pol)* **to ~ to the country** en appeler au pays. (**b**) *(beg)* faire appel *(to sb's generosity* à la générosité de qn). **to ~ to sb for money/help** demander de l'argent/des secours à qn; **I ~ to you!** je vous en supplie! (**c**) *(Jur)* se pourvoir en appel. **to ~ to the supreme court** se pourvoir en cassation; **to ~ against** *judgment* appeler de; *decision* faire opposition à. (**d**) *(attract)* **to ~ to** plaire à; **it doesn't ~ to me** cela ne me dit rien *; **it ~s to the imagination** cela parle à l'imagination.
2 *n* (**a**) *(public call)* appel *m.* *(Fin)* ~ **for funds** appel de fonds; **he made a public ~ for the blind** il a lancé un appel au profit des aveugles. (**b**) *(by individual: for help etc)* appel *m (for* à); *(for money)* demande *f (for* de). **with a look of ~** d'un air suppliant. (**c**) *(Jur)* appel *m.* **acquitted on ~** acquitté en seconde instance; **A~ Court** cour *f* d'appel. (**d**) *(attraction) [person, object]* attrait *m*, charme *m*; *[plan, idea]* intérêt *m.*
◆ **appealing** *adj (moving)* émouvant; *look* pathétique; *(begging)* suppliant; *(attractive)* attirant. ◆ **appealingly** *adv* de façon émouvante; d'un air suppliant; *(charmingly)* avec beaucoup de charme.

appear [ə'pɪəʳ] *vi* (**a**) *[person, sun etc]* apparaître, se montrer; *[ghost, vision]* apparaître, se manifester *(to sb* à qn); *[publication]* paraître. *(Theat)* **to ~ in 'Hamlet'** jouer dans 'Hamlet'; **to ~ as Hamlet** jouer Hamlet; **to ~ on TV** passer à la télévision. (**b**) *(arrive)* arriver, se présenter. **he ~ed from nowhere** il est apparu comme par miracle. (**c**) *(Jur etc)* comparaître *(before* devant). **to ~ on a charge of** être jugé pour; **to ~ for sb** plaider pour qn. (**d**) *(seem: physical aspect)* paraître, avoir l'air. **they ~ (to be) ill** ils ont l'air malades. (**e**) *(seem: on evidence)* paraître *(that* que + *indic).* **so it ~s, so it would ~** à ce qu'il paraît; *(iro)* on dirait! (**f**) *(seem: by surmise)* sembler *(that* que *gen* + *subj)*, sembler bien *(that* que + *indic).* **there ~s to be**

a mistake il semble qu'il y ait une erreur; **it ~s he did say that** il semble bien qu'il a dit cela; **it ~s to me they are mistaken** il me semble qu'ils ont tort; **how does it ~ to you?** qu'en pensez-vous?

appearance [ə'pɪər(ə)ns] *n* (**a**) *(act)* apparition *f* ; *(arrival)* arrivée *f*; *(Jur)* comparution *f*; *[publication]* parution *f*. **to make a personal ~** apparaître en personne; **to put in an ~** faire acte de présence; *(Theat)* **in order of ~** par ordre d'entrée en scène. (**b**) *(look)* apparence *f*; *[house etc]* aspect *m*. **his ~ worried us** la mine qu'il avait nous a inquiétés; **~s are deceptive, you shouldn't go by ~s** il ne faut pas se fier aux apparences; **in order to keep up ~s** pour sauver les apparences; **to all ~s** selon toute apparence.

appease [ə'pi:z] *vt* apaiser. ◆ **appeasement** *n* apaisement *m*.

append [ə'pend] *vt document* joindre; *signature* apposer. ◆ **appendage** *n* appendice *m*.

appendix, *pl* **-ices** [ə'pendɪks,-ɪsi:z] *n* (**a**) *(Anat)* appendice *m*. **to have one's ~ out** se faire opérer de l'appendicite. (**b**) *[book]* appendice *m*; *[document]* annexe *f*. ◆ **append(ic)ectomy** *n* appendicectomie *f*. ◆ **appendicitis** *n* appendicite *f*.

appertain [,æpə'teɪn] *vi* se rapporter (*to* à).

appetite ['æpɪtaɪt] *n* appétit *m*; *(fig)* goût *m* (*for* pour). **to have a good ~** avoir bon appétit. ◆ **appetizer** *n (drink)* apéritif *m*; *(food)* amuse-gueule * *m inv*. ◆ **appetizing** *adj* appétissant.

applaud [ə'plɔ:d] *vt person, victory* applaudir; *decision, efforts* approuver. ◆ **applause** *n* applaudissements *mpl*.

apple ['æpl] **1** *n* pomme *f*; (*~ tree)* pommier *m*. **he's the ~ of my eye** je tiens à lui comme à la prunelle de mes yeux; *(US)* **the big A~** * New York. **2** *adj*: **~ blossom** fleur *f* de pommier; **~ core** trognon *m* de pomme; **~ orchard** champ *m* de pommiers; **~ pie** tourte *f* aux pommes; **in ~-pie order** en ordre parfait; **~ sauce** compote *f* de pommes; **~ tart** tarte *f* aux pommes; *(individual)* tartelette aux pommes.

apply [ə'plaɪ] **1** *vt paint, ointment, dressing* appliquer, mettre (*to* sur); *theory, rule, law* appliquer (*to* à). **to ~ a match to sth** allumer qch avec une allumette; **to ~ the brakes** actionner les freins; **to ~ one's mind** *or* **o.s. to (doing) sth** s'appliquer à (faire) qch; **applied sciences** sciences appliquées. **2** *vi* s'adresser (*to sb for sth* à qn pour obtenir qch). **~ at the office** adressez-vous au bureau.

◆ **apply for** *vt fus scholarship, money, assistance* demander. **to ~ for a job** faire une demande d'emploi (*to sb* auprès de qn); **to ~ for a divorce** formuler une demande en divorce. ◆ **apply to** *vt fus* s'appliquer à. **this does not ~ to you** ceci ne s'applique pas à vous.

◆ **appliance** *n* appareil *m*; *(smaller)* dispositif *m*. ◆ **applicable** *adj* applicable (*to* à). ◆ **applicant** *n (for job)* candidat(e) *m(f)* (*for* à); *(Admin: for benefits etc)* demandeur *m*, -euse *f*. ◆ **application** *n* (**a**) *(act of applying)* application *f* (*to* à); *(request)* demande *f*; **application for membership** demande d'adhésion; **application for a job** demande d'emploi, candidature *f* à un poste; **on application** sur demande; **details may be had on application to the secretary** s'adresser au secrétaire pour tous renseignements; **application form** formulaire *m* de demande; *(for job)* formulaire de demande d'emploi; *(Univ)* dossier d'inscription; **application software** logiciels *mpl* d'application; (**b**) *(diligence)* application *f*, attention *f*. ◆ **applicator** *n* applicateur *m*.

appliqué [æ'pli:keɪ] **1** *vt* coudre (en application). **2** *n* (*~ work)* travail *m* d'application.

appoint [ə'pɔɪnt] *vt* nommer (*sb to a post* qn à un emploi *or* poste); *(fix) date, place* fixer; *(ordain)* prescrire (*that* que + *subj*). **at the ~ed time** à l'heure dite *or* convenue; **to ~ sb manager** nommer qn directeur; **to ~ a new secretary** engager une nouvelle secrétaire; **a well-~ed house** une maison bien aménagée. ◆ **appointee** *n* candidat *m* retenu; *(esp US)* délégué *m (or* ambassadeur *m etc)* nommé pour des raisons politiques.

appointment [ə'pɔɪntmənt] *n* (**a**) *(arrangement to meet)* rendez-vous *m*. **to make an ~ with sb** prendre rendez-vous avec qn; **to keep an ~** aller à un rendez-vous; **have you an ~?** avez-vous pris rendez-vous?; **to meet sb by ~** rencontrer qn sur rendez-vous. (**b**) *(act of appointing)* nomination *f* (*to a post* à un emploi *or* poste); *(office assigned)* poste *m*; *(posting)* affectation *f*. *(Comm)* **'By ~ to Her Majesty the Queen'** 'fournisseur de S.M. la Reine'; *(Press)* **' ~s (vacant)'** 'offres *fpl* d'emploi'; **~s bureau** agence *f* de placement.

apposite ['æpəzɪt] *adj* juste, pertinent. ◆ **apposition** *n* apposition *f*.

appraise [ə'preɪz] *vt* évaluer, estimer. ◆ **appraisal** *n* évaluation *f*, estimation *f*.

appreciate [ə'pri:ʃɪeɪt] **1** *vt* (**a**) *(be aware of) difficulty, fact, sb's attitude* se rendre compte de, être conscient de. **to ~ sth at its true value** estimer qch à sa juste valeur; **yes, I ~ that** oui, je m'en rends bien compte. (**b**) *(value) music, person* apprécier; *honour* être sensible à; *sb's help, work, kindness* être reconnaissant de. **he felt that nobody ~d him** il ne se sentait pas apprécié à sa juste valeur. **2** *vi [currency]* monter; *[object, property]* prendre de la valeur. ◆ **appreciable** *adj* appréciable. ◆ **appreciably** *adv* de façon appréciable. ◆ **appreciation** *n* estimation *f*; *(gratitude)* reconnaissance *f*; *(Art etc: critique)* critique *f*; *(Fin)* hausse *f*; **in appreciation of...** en remerciement de... ◆ **appreciative** *adj person* sensible (*of* à); *(admiring)* admiratif; *(grateful)* reconnaissant; *comment* élogieux; **an appreciative glance** un regard connaisseur *or* admiratif.

apprehend [,æprɪ'hend] *vt (arrest)* appréhender, arrêter; *(fear)* redouter, appréhender. ◆ **apprehension** *n (fear)* appréhension *f*; *(arrest)* arrestation *f*. ◆ **apprehensive** *adj* plein d'appréhension. ◆ **apprehensively** *adv* avec appréhension.

apprentice [ə'prentɪs] **1** *n* apprenti(e) *m(f)*. **~ plumber, plumber's ~** apprenti plombier. **2** *vt* mettre en apprentissage (*to sb* chez qn). **to be ~d to** être en apprentissage chez. ◆ **apprenticeship** *n* apprentissage *m*.

apprise [ə'praɪz] *vt* informer (*sb of sth* qn de qch).

appro * ['æprəʊ] *n (Comm) abbr of* **approval.**

approach [ə'prəʊtʃ] **1** *vi [person, vehicle]* (s')approcher; *[date, season, death, war]* approcher, être proche. **2** *vt place* s'approcher de, s'avancer vers; *topic* aborder; *(fig) perfection etc* atteindre presque à. **it all depends on how one ~es it** tout dépend de la façon dont on s'y prend; **to ~ sb about sth** s'adresser à qn à propos de qch; **a man ~ed me in the street** un homme m'a abordé dans la rue; **I saw him ~ing me** je l'ai vu qui venait vers moi; **she is ~ing 30** elle approche de la trentaine; **it was ~ing midnight** il était près de *or* presque minuit.

3 *n [person, vehicle]* approche *f*. **at the ~ of** à l'approche de; **his ~ to the problem** sa façon d'aborder le problème; **a new ~ to teaching French** une nouvelle façon d'enseigner le français; **to make ~es to sb** faire des avances à qn; **to make an ~ to sb** faire une proposition à qn; **all the ~es to the town** tous les abords *mpl or* toutes les approches de la ville; **the ~ to the top of the hill** le chemin qui mène au sommet de la colline; **the station ~** les abords de la gare.

4 *adj*: *(Aviat)* ~ **lights** balisage *m*; ~ **road** *(gen)* route *f* d'accès; *(to motorway)* voie *f* de raccordement.
◆ **approachable** *adj* approchable. ◆ **approaching** *adj date, car* qui approche; *oncoming car* venant en sens inverse.

approbation [ˌæprəˈbeɪʃ(ə)n] *n* approbation *f*. **a nod of** ~ un signe de tête approbateur.

appropriate [əˈprəʊprɪɪt] **1** *adj moment, decision, ruling* opportun; *remark* opportun, juste; *word* juste, propre; *name* bien choisi; *authority, department* compétent. ~ **for** *or* **to** propre à, approprié à; **it would not be** ~ **for me to comment** ce n'est pas à moi de faire des commentaires; **he is the** ~ **person to ask** c'est à lui qu'il faut le demander. **2** [əˈprəʊprɪeɪt] *vt* s'approprier. ◆ **appropriately** *adv speak, comment* pertinemment; *design* convenablement; *situated* au bon endroit; ~**ly named** au nom bien choisi. ◆ **appropriation** *n (act: also Jur)* appropriation *f*; *(funds assigned)* dotation *f*; *(US Pol)* crédit *m* budgétaire.

approve [əˈpruːv] *vt (gen)* approuver; *decision* ratifier; *request* agréer. ◆ **approve of** *vt fus behaviour, idea* approuver, être partisan de; *person* avoir bonne opinion de. **she doesn't** ~ **of drinking** elle n'approuve pas qu'on boive; **he doesn't** ~ **of me** il désapprouve ma façon d'être; **we** ~ **of our new neighbours** nos nouveaux voisins nous plaisent. ◆ **approval** *n* approbation *f*, assentiment *m*; *(Comm)* **on approval** sous condition, à l'essai; **a nod of approval** un signe de tête approbateur; **has it got your approval?** l'approuvez-vous? ◆ **approving** *adj* approbateur. ◆ **approvingly** *adv* d'un air *or* d'un ton approbateur.

approximate [əˈprɒks(ɪ)mɪt] **1** *adj* approximatif. ~ **to** proche de. **2** [əˈprɒksɪmeɪt] *vi* s'approcher (*to* de). ◆ **approximately** *adv* approximativement. ◆ **approximation** *n* approximation *f*.

apricot [ˈeɪprɪkɒt] *n* abricot *m*; *(~ tree)* abricotier *m*.

April [ˈeɪpr(ə)l] **1** *n* avril *m*; *for phrases V* **September**. **2** *adj*: **to make an** ~ **fool of sb** faire un poisson d'avril à qn; ~ **Fools' Day** le premier avril; ~ **showers** ≃ giboulées *fpl* de mars.

apron [ˈeɪpr(ə)n] **1** *n* tablier *m*; *(Aviat)* aire *f* de stationnement. **2** *adj*: **tied to his mother's** ~ **strings** pendu aux jupes de sa mère; *(Theat)* ~ **stage** avant-scène *f*.

apropos [ˌæprəˈpəʊ] *adj, adv* à propos (*of* de).

apse [æps] *n* abside *f*.

apt [æpt] *adj* (**a**) *person* enclin, porté, disposé (*to do* à faire); *thing* susceptible (*to do* de faire). **one is ~ to believe that...** on a tendance à croire que...; **he's** ~ **to be out in the afternoons** il a tendance à ne pas être chez lui l'après-midi. (**b**) *comment, reply* approprié, juste; *pupil* doué. ◆ **aptitude** *n* aptitude *f* (*for* à), disposition *f* (*for* pour). ◆ **aptly** *adv answer* avec justesse; *behave* avec propos; ~**ly named** bien nommé. ◆ **aptness** *n* à-propos *m*, justesse *f*.

aqualung [ˈækwəlʌŋ] *n* scaphandre *m* autonome.

aquamarine [ˌækwəməˈriːn] **1** *n* aigue-marine *f*. **2** *adj (colour)* bleu vert *inv*.

aquaplane [ˈækwəpleɪn] *vi (Sport)* faire de l'aquaplane; *(Aut)* faire de l'aquaplaning.

aquarium [əˈkwɛərɪəm] *n* aquarium *m*.

Aquarius [əˈkwɛərɪəs] *n* le Verseau.

aquatic [əˈkwætɪk] *adj animal, plant* aquatique; *sport* nautique.

aqueduct [ˈækwɪdʌkt] *n* aqueduc *m*.

aquiline [ˈækwɪlaɪn] *adj* aquilin.

Arab [ˈærəb] **1** *n* Arabe *mf*; *(horse)* (cheval *m*) arabe *m*. **2** *adj* arabe. ◆ **Arabia** *n* Arabie *f*. ◆ **Arabian** *adj* arabe; *desert, sea* d'Arabie; ~**ian Gulf** golfe *m* Arabique; **the** ~**ian Nights** les Mille et Une Nuits. ◆ **Arabic** **1** *n* arabe *m*; **written** ~ l'arabe littéral; **2** *adj* arabe; ~**ic numerals** chiffres *mpl* arabes.

arable [ˈærəbl] *adj* arable.

arbitrary [ˈɑːbɪtrərɪ] *adj* arbitraire. ◆ **arbitrarily** *adv* arbitrairement.

arbitrate [ˈɑːbɪtreɪt] *vti* arbitrer. ◆ **arbitration** **1** *n* arbitrage *m*; **to go to arbitration** recourir à l'arbitrage; **2** *adj*: **arbitration tribunal** instance *f* chargée d'arbitrer les conflits sociaux. ◆ **arbitrator** *n* arbitre *m (Ind, Jur)*.

arc [ɑːk] **1** *n* arc *m*. **2** *adj*: ~ **light** lampe *f* à arc, *(Cine, TV)* sunlight *m*; ~ **welding** soudure *f* à l'arc voltaïque.

arcade [ɑːˈkeɪd] *n (arches)* arcade *f*; *(shopping precinct)* galerie *f* marchande.

arch[1] [ɑːtʃ] **1** *n [church etc]* arc *m*, voûte *f*; *[bridge etc]* arche *f*; *[eyebrows]* arcade *f*; *[foot]* voûte *f* plantaire. **2** *vt* arquer. ~**ed** *foot, back* cambré ; *window* cintré. ◆ **archway** *n* voûte *f* (d'entrée), porche *m*.

arch[2] [ɑːtʃ] *adj (teasing)* coquin.

arch[3] [ɑːtʃ] **1** *adj (gen)* grand, par excellence. **an** ~ **traitor/villain** un grand traître/scélérat; **the** ~ **villain** le principal scélérat. **2** *pref* arch(i)... ◆ **archangel** [ˈɑːkˌeɪn(d)ʒ(ə)l] *n* archange *m*. ◆ **archbishop** *n* archevêque *m*. ◆ **archduke** *n* archiduc *m*. ◆ **arch-enemy** *n* ennemi *m* par excellence. ◆ **arch-priest** *n* archiprêtre *m*.

archaeology [ˌɑːkɪˈɒlədʒɪ] *n* archéologie *f*. ◆ **archaeological** *adj* archéologique. ◆ **archaeologist** *n* archéologue *mf*.

archaic [ɑːˈkeɪɪk] *adj* archaïque. ◆ **archaism** *n* archaïsme *m*.

archeology *etc (US)* = **archaeology** *etc*.

archer [ˈɑːtʃə[r]] *n* archer *m*. ◆ **archery** *n* tir *m* à l'arc.

archetype [ˈɑːkɪtaɪp] *n* archétype *m*. ◆ **archetypal** *adj* archétype.

archipelago [ˌɑːkɪˈpelɪgəʊ] *n* archipel *m*.

architect [ˈɑːkɪtekt] *n* architecte *m*. ◆ **architectural** *adj* architectural. ◆ **architecture** *n* architecture *f*.

archives [ˈɑːkaɪvz] *npl* archives *fpl*. ◆ **archivist** *n* archiviste *mf*.

Arctic [ˈɑːktɪk] **1** *adj* arctique. *(fig: very cold)* **a**~ glacial; ~ **Circle/Ocean** cercle *m*/océan *m* Arctique. **2** *n*: **the** ~ l'Arctique *m*.

ardent [ˈɑːdənt] *adj* ardent; *admirer* fervent. ◆ **ardently** *adv* ardemment.

ardour, *(US)* **ardor** [ˈɑːdə[r]] *n* ardeur *f*.

arduous [ˈɑːdjʊəs] *adj* ardu. ◆ **arduously** *adv* laborieusement. ◆ **arduousness** *n* difficulté *f*.

area [ˈɛərɪə] **1** *n* (**a**) *(surface measure)* aire *f*, superficie *f*. **an** ~ **of 800 m²** une superficie de 800 m², 800 m² de superficie. (**b**) *(region)* région *f*; *(Mil, Pol)* territoire *m* ; *(smaller)* secteur *m*, zone *f*; *(fig: of knowledge, enquiry)* domaine *m*, champ *m*. ~ **of outstanding natural beauty** site *m* naturel; **the** ~**s of disagreement** les zones *fpl* de désaccord; *(fig)* **in this** ~ à ce propos; **dining/sleeping** ~ coin *m* salle-à-manger/chambre. **2** *adj*: ~ **code** *(Brit Post)* code *m* postal; *(US Telec)* indicatif *m* de zone ; ~ **manager** directeur régional; ~ **office** agence régionale.

arena [əˈriːnə] *n* arène *f*.

Argentina [ˌɑːdʒ(ə)nˈtiːnə] *n (also* **the Argentine***)* Argentine *f*. ◆ **Argentinian** **1** *n* Argentin(e) *m(f)* ; **2** *adj* argentin.

argue [ˈɑːgjuː] **1** *vi* (**a**) *(dispute)* se disputer (*with sb* avec qn, *about sth* au sujet de qch). **don't** ~! pas de discussion! (**b**) *(reason)* argumenter (*about* sur; *against sb* contre qn). **he** ~**d against going** il a donné les raisons qu'il avait de ne pas vouloir y aller; **to** ~ **from sth** tirer argument de qch. (**c**) *[fact, evidence]* témoigner (*against* contre, *in favour of* en faveur de). **2** *vt* (**a**) **to ~ sb into/out of doing** persuader/dissuader qn de faire. (**b**) *(debate) case* discuter, débattre; *(maintain)* soutenir, affirmer (*that* que). **a well-~d case** un cas étayé de bons arguments; **to ~ the toss** * discuter le coup *. (**c**) *(show evidence of)* dénoter, indiquer. **it ~s a certain lack of feeling** cela dénote *or* indique une certaine insensibilité. ◆ **arguable** *adj*: **it is arguable that** on peut soutenir que. ◆ **arguably** *adv*: **it is arguably...** on peut soutenir que c'est...

argument ['ɑ:gjʊmənt] *n* (**a**) *(debate)* discussion *f*, débat *m*. **one side of the ~** une seule version de l'affaire; **for ~'s sake** à titre d'exemple; **it is open to ~ that** on peut soutenir que. (**b**) *(dispute)* dispute *f*, discussion *f*. **to have an ~** se disputer (*with sb* avec qn). (**c**) *(reasons)* argument *m*. **his ~ is that...** il soutient que... ◆ **argumentative** *adj* raisonneur, ergoteur *(pej)*.

argy-bargy * ['ɑ:dʒɪ'bɑ:dʒɪ] *n* discutailleries * *fpl*.

aria ['ɑ:rɪə] *n* aria *f*.

arid ['ærɪd] *adj* aride. ◆ **aridity** *n* aridité *f*.

Aries ['ɛəri:z] *n* le Bélier.

aright [ə'raɪt] *adv* bien, correctement.

arise [ə'raɪz] *pret* **arose,** *ptp* **arisen** [ə'rɪzn] *vi* (**a**) *[difficulty]* survenir, surgir; *[question]* se présenter, se poser; *[cry]* s'élever; *[occasion]* se présenter. **should the need ~** en cas de besoin. (**b**) *(result)* résulter, provenir (*from* de). (**c**) *(†: rise)* se lever.

aristocracy [,ærɪs'tɒkrəsɪ] *n* aristocratie *f*. ◆ **aristocrat** ['ærɪstəkræt] *n* aristocrate *mf*. ◆ **aristocratic** [,ærɪstə'krætɪk] *adj* aristocratique.

arithmetic [ə'rɪθmətɪk] *n* arithmétique *f*. ◆ **arithmetical** *adj* arithmétique.

ark [ɑ:k] *n* arche *f*. **Noah's ~** l'arche de Noé; *(fig)* **it's out of the ~** * ça date du déluge.

arm¹ [ɑ:m] *n (gen)* bras *m*; *[garment]* manche *f*; *[spectacle frames]* branche *f*. **in one's ~s** dans ses bras; **he had a coat over his ~** il avait un manteau sur le bras; **take my ~** prenez mon bras; **on her husband's ~** au bras de son mari; **to put one's ~ round sb** passer son bras autour des épaules de qn; **~ in ~** bras dessus bras dessous; **within ~'s reach** à portée de la main; **at ~'s length** à bout de bras; *(fig)* à distance; **to cost an ~ and a leg** * coûter les yeux de la tête *; **the (long) ~ of the law** le bras de la justice; *(fig)* **to have a long ~** avoir le bras long. ◆ **armband** *n* brassard *m*. ◆ **armchair** **1** *n* fauteuil *m*; **2** *adj*: **~chair general** *etc* général *m etc* en chambre. ◆ **armful** *n* brassée *f*. ◆ **armhole** *n* emmanchure *f*. ◆ **armlet** *n* brassard *m*. ◆ **armpit** *n* aisselle *f*. ◆ **armrest** *n* accoudoir *m*. ◆ **arm-twisting** * *n* pressions *fpl* directes *(fig)*. ◆ **arm-wrestling** *n* bras *m* de fer.

arm² [ɑ:m] **1** *n* (**a**) *(weapon)* arme *f*. **under ~s** sous les armes; **in ~s** armé; **to ~s!** aux armes!; **to be up in ~s against** *sb, the authorities* être en rébellion ouverte contre; *decision etc* partir en guerre contre; **she was up in ~s about it** cela la mettait hors d'elle-même. (**b**) *(Her)* **~s** armes *fpl*. **2** *adj*: **~s control** contrôle *m* des armements; **~s factory** fabrique *f* d'armes; **~s manufacturer** fabricant *m* d'armes; **~s race** course *f* aux armements. **3** *vt person, nation* armer; *missile* munir d'une (tête d')ogive.
4 *vi* (s')armer (*against* contre).
◆ **armaments** *npl* armement *m*; **~aments race** course *f* aux armements. ◆ **armed** *adj (lit, fig)* armé (*with* de); *missile* muni d'une (tête d')ogive; *conflict, neutrality* armé; **~ed to the teeth** armé jusqu'aux dents; **the ~ed forces** les (forces) armées *fpl*; **~ed robbery** vol *m* à main armée.

Armenia [ɑ:'mi:nɪə] *n* Arménie *f*. ◆ **Armenian** **1** *adj* arménien; **2** *n* Arménien(ne) *m(f)*.

armistice ['ɑ:mɪstɪs] *n* armistice *m*. *(Brit)* **A~ Day** le onze novembre.

armour, *(US)* **armor** ['ɑ:məʳ] *n* (**a**) *[knight]* armure *f*. **in full ~** armé de pied en cap. (**b**) *(Mil: ~-plating)* blindage *m*; *(vehicles)* blindés *mpl*; *(forces)* forces blindées. ◆ **armour-clad** *or* ◆ **armour-plated** *adj* blindé. ◆ **armoured car** *n* voiture blindée. ◆ **armour-piercing** *adj shell, bullet* perforant. ◆ **armour-plate** *or* ◆ **armour-plating** *n (Mil)* blindage *m*; *(Naut)* cuirasse *f*. ◆ **armoury** *n* dépôt *m* d'armes; *(US: factory)* fabrique *f* d'armes.

army ['ɑ:mɪ] **1** *n* armée *f* (de terre); *(fig)* foule *f*, armée. **to be in the ~** être dans l'armée, être militaire; **to join the ~** s'engager; **to go into the ~** *[professional]* devenir militaire *m* (de carrière); *[conscript]* partir au service. **2** *adj life, nurse, uniform* militaire. **~ corps** corps *m* d'armée; **~ officer** officier *m* (de l'armée de terre).

aroma [ə'rəʊmə] *n* arôme *m*. ◆ **aromatic** *adj* aromatique.

arose [ə'rəʊz] *pret of* **arise.**

around [ə'raʊnd] **1** *adv* (**a**) autour. **all ~** tout autour, de tous côtés; **for miles ~** sur un rayon de plusieurs kilomètres. (**b**) *(nearby)* dans les parages. **he is somewhere ~** il est dans les parages; **is he ~?** * est-ce qu'il est là?; **there's a lot of flu ~** il y a beaucoup de cas de grippe en ce moment; **he's been ~** * *(travelled)* il a pas mal roulé sa bosse *; *(experienced)* il n'est pas né d'hier; **it's been ~** * **for 20 years** ça existe depuis 20 ans. **2** *prep* (**a**) *(round)* autour de. **~ the fire** autour du feu; **to go ~ an obstacle** contourner un obstacle; **the country ~ the town** les environs *mpl or* alentours *mpl* de la ville; **~ the corner** après le coin. (**b**) *(about)* **to wander ~ the city** errer dans la ville; **they are somewhere ~ the house** ils sont quelque part dans la maison. (**c**) *(approximately)* environ, à peu près, vers. **~ 2 kilos** environ *or* à peu près 2 kilos; **~ 10 o'clock/1890** vers 10 heures/1890.

arouse [ə'raʊz] *vt* (**a**) *(awaken)* réveiller; *(stir to action)* pousser à agir. **that ~d him to protest** cela l'a poussé à protester. (**b**) *(cause) suspicion, curiosity etc* éveiller; *contempt, anger* provoquer. ◆ **arousal** *n* excitation *f* sexuelle.

arrange [ə'reɪn(d)ʒ] **1** *vt* (**a**) *(order) room, clothing, hair, flowers* arranger; *(Mus)* arranger (*for* pour); *books, objects* ranger, mettre en ordre. **room ~d as a laboratory** pièce aménagée en laboratoire. (**b**) *(decide on) meeting* arranger, organiser; *date* fixer; *plans, programme* arrêter, convenir de. **it was ~d that** il a été arrangé *or* décidé *or* convenu que; **I have sth ~d for tonight** j'ai qch de prévu pour ce soir; **to ~ a marriage** faire un mariage. **2** *vi* s'arranger (*to do* pour faire; *for sb to do* pour que qn fasse; *with sb about sth* avec qn au sujet de qch). **to ~ for sb's luggage to be sent up** faire monter les bagages de qn; **to ~ with sb to do** s'entendre avec qn pour faire.

arrangement [ə'reɪn(d)ʒmənt] *n (gen: also Mus)* arrangement *m*; *(something decided)* décision *f*, arrangement. **larger sizes by ~** tailles supérieures sur demande; **price by ~** prix *m* à débattre; **by ~ with Covent Garden** avec l'autorisation *f* de Covent Garden; *(plans, preparations)* **~s** mesures *fpl*, dispositions *fpl*, préparatifs *mpl;* **the ~s we made** les dispositions que nous avons prises; **to make ~s to do** s'arranger pour faire; **to make ~s for a holiday** faire des préparatifs *mpl* pour des vacances; **to make ~s for sth to be done** prendre des mesures *fpl or* dispositions *fpl* pour faire faire qch.

array [ə'reɪ] **1** *vt*: **~ed in** revêtu de. **2** *n [objects]* ensemble impressionnant; *[people]* assemblée *f*; *(Comput)* tableau *m*.

arrears [ə'rɪəz] *npl* arriéré *m*. **rent in ~** (loyer) arriéré; **to get into ~** s'arriérer; **to be 3 months in ~ with the rent** devoir 3 mois de loyer.

arrest [ə'rest] **1** *vt* (**a**) *[police etc]* arrêter. (**b**) *growth etc (stop)* arrêter; *(hinder)* entraver; *(retard)* retarder; *disease* enrayer. **~ed development** *(Med)* arrêt *m* de croissance; *(Psych)* atrophie *f* de la personnalité. **2** *n [police etc]* arrestation *f*. **under ~** en état d'arrestation; *(Mil)* aux arrêts; **to put sb under ~** arrêter qn; *(Mil)* mettre qn aux arrêts; **to make an ~** procéder à une arrestation. ◆ **arresting** *adj (fig)* frappant, saisissant.

arrival [ə'raɪv(ə)l] *n* (**a**) *(gen)* arrivée *f*; *(Comm) [goods in bulk]* arrivage *m*. **on ~** à l'arrivée. (**b**) *(consignment)* arrivage *m*. *(person)* **the first ~** le premier arrivé; **a new ~** un nouveau venu; *(baby)* un(e) nouveau-né(e).

arrive [ə'raɪv] *vi* arriver (*at* à); *(succeed)* arriver, réussir. **to ~ on the scene** arriver; **the moment has ~d when we must go** le moment est venu pour nous de partir. ◆ **arrive at** *vt fus decision, solution* aboutir à, parvenir à; *perfection* atteindre. **to ~ at a price** *[one person]* fixer un prix; *[2 people]* se mettre d'accord sur un prix; **they finally ~d at the idea of doing** ils en sont finalement venus à l'idée de faire.

arrogant ['ærəgənt] *adj* arrogant. ◆ **arrogance** *n* arrogance *f*.

arrow ['ærəʊ] **1** *n* flèche *f*. **2** *vt route, direction* flécher; *item on list etc* cocher. ◆ **arrowhead** *n* pointe *f* de flèche.

arsenal ['ɑːsɪnl] *n* arsenal *m*.

arsenic ['ɑːsnɪk] *n* arsenic *m*.

arson ['ɑːsn] *n* incendie *m* volontaire. ◆ **arsonist** *n* incendiaire *mf*.

art [ɑːt] **1** *n* art *m*. **~ for ~'s sake** l'art pour l'art; **to study ~** *(gen)* faire des études d'art; *(Univ)* faire les beaux-arts; **~s and crafts** artisanat *m* (d'art); *(Univ)* **Faculty of A~s** faculté *f* des Lettres; **he's doing A~s** il fait des lettres. **2** *adj*: **~ collection** collection *f* de tableaux (*or* d'objets d'art *etc*); **~ college** ≃ école *f* des beaux-arts; **~ exhibition** exposition *f* (de peinture *or* de sculpture); **~ form** moyen *m* d'expression artistique; **~ gallery** *(museum)* musée *m* d'art; *(shop)* galerie *f* (de tableaux *or* d'art); **~ paper** papier couché; **~ school** école *f* des beaux-arts; *(Univ)* **A~s degree** licence *f* ès lettres; **~ student** étudiant(e) *m(f)* des *or* en beaux-arts; **A~s student** étudiant(e) *m(f)* en *or* de Lettres.
◆ **artful** *adj* rusé, astucieux; **he's an ~ful one** * c'est un petit malin *; **~ful dodger** roublard(e) * *m(f)*. ◆ **artfully** *adv (cunningly)* astucieusement; *(skilfully)* habilement. ◆ **artfulness** *n (cunning)* astuce *f*; *(skill)* habileté *f*. ◆ **artless** *adj* naturel. ◆ **artlessly** *adv* ingénument. ◆ **arty** * *adj person* qui a le genre artiste *or* bohème; *clothes* de style bohème; *decoration, style* (d'un art) apprêté. ◆ **art(s)y-craft(s)y** * *adj (pej) object, style* exagérément artisanal; *person* qui affiche un genre artiste *or* bohème.

artefact ['ɑːtɪfækt] *n* objet *m* fabriqué.

artery ['ɑːtərɪ] *n* artère *f (also fig: road)*. ◆ **arterial** *adj (Anat)* artériel; **arterial road** route *f* à grande circulation. ◆ **arteriosclerosis** *n* artériosclérose *f*.

artesian [ɑː'tiːzɪən] *adj*: **~ well** puits *m* artésien.

arthritis [ɑː'θraɪtɪs] *n* arthrite *f*. ◆ **arthritic** *adj, n* arthritique *(mf)*.

artichoke ['ɑːtɪtʃəʊk] *n (globe ~)* artichaut *m*; *(Jerusalem ~)* topinambour *m*.

article ['ɑːtɪkl] *n (Admin, Jur, Gram, Press etc)* article *m; (Comm)* article, marchandise *f*; *(object)* objet *m*. **~s of clothing** vêtements *mpl*; **~ of food** denrée *f*; **~s of value** objets de valeur.

articulate [ɑː'tɪkjʊlɪt] **1** *adj speech* bien articulé; *person* qui s'exprime bien; *book* clair; *(Anat)* articulé. **2** [ɑː'tɪkjʊleɪt] *vti* articuler. **to ~ a plan** expliquer clairement un plan; **~d lorry** semi-remorque *m*. ◆ **articulately** *adv* avec facilité. ◆ **articulation** *n* articulation *f*.

artifact ['ɑːtɪfækt] *n* = **artefact.**

artifice ['ɑːtɪfɪs] *n (stratagem)* artifice *m*; *(cunning)* adresse *f*.

artificial [ˌɑːtɪ'fɪʃ(ə)l] *adj* artificiel *(also fig)*. **~ intelligence** intelligence *f* artificielle; **~ teeth** fausses dents; **it was a very ~ situation** la situation manquait de naturel. ◆ **artificiality** *n* manque *m* de naturel. ◆ **artificially** *adv* artificiellement.

artillery [ɑː'tɪlərɪ] *n* artillerie *f*.

artisan ['ɑːtɪzæn] *n* artisan *m*.

artist ['ɑːtɪst] *n* artiste *mf*. ◆ **artiste** *n (Cine, Theat, TV)* artiste *mf*. ◆ **artistic** *adj arrangement, activity, sense* artistique; *temperament* artiste; *person* qui a un sens artistique très développé. ◆ **artistically** *adv* artistiquement, avec art. ◆ **artistry** *n* art *m*, talent *m* artistique.

Aryan ['ɛərɪən] *adj* aryen.

as [æz, əz] **1** *conj* (**a**) *(when, while)* comme, alors que, tandis que, pendant que. **~ she was resting she heard it** tandis qu'elle *or* comme elle se reposait elle l'entendit; **I saw him ~ he came out** je l'ai vu comme *or* au moment où il sortait; **he got deafer ~ he got older** il devenait plus sourd à mesure qu'il vieillissait. (**b**) *(since, because)* comme, puisque. (**c**) *(in comparisons)* **as tall ~** aussi grand que; **not so** *or* **not as tall ~** pas aussi *or* pas si grand que; **as much ~** autant que; **twice as rich ~** deux fois plus riche que; **by day (as well) ~ by night** de jour comme de nuit. (**d**) *(concessive)* **big ~ the box is...** si grande que soit la boîte...; **try ~ he would, he couldn't do it** il a eu beau essayer, il n'y est pas arrivé. (**e**) *(manner)* comme. **do ~ you like** faites comme vous voudrez; **M ~ in Marcel** M comme Marcel; **~ usual** comme d'habitude; **~ often happens** comme il arrive souvent; **~ is her brother** comme son frère, ainsi que son frère, de même que son frère; **~ it were** pour ainsi dire; **~ it is, I can't come** les choses étant ce qu'elles sont, je ne peux pas venir; **leave it ~ it is** laisse ça tel quel. (**f**) **such people ~ knew him** les gens qui le connaissaient; **such a book ~ you gave him** un livre comme celui que tu lui as donné; **the same day ~** le même jour que; **a man such ~ he is** un homme tel que lui; **~ if, ~ though** comme (si); **~ if he'd been drinking** comme s'il avait bu; **he rose ~ if to go out** il s'est levé comme pour sortir; **~ for, ~ to, ~ regards** quant à; **~ of yesterday** depuis hier; **~ of today** à partir d'aujourd'hui. (**g**) **so ~ to +** *infin* pour, de façon à, afin de + *infin*. **2** *adv* aussi, si. **~ tall as** aussi grand que; **not ~ tall as** pas si *or* pas aussi grand que. **3** *prep* (**a**) *(in the capacity of)* comme, en tant que. **sold ~ a slave** vendu comme esclave; **~ a bachelor he...** en tant que célibataire il...; **Olivier ~ Hamlet** Olivier dans le rôle de Hamlet. (**b**) **to treat sb ~ a child** traiter qn comme un enfant *or* en enfant; **to acknowledge sb ~ leader** reconnaître qn pour chef.

asbestos [æz'bestəs] *n* amiante *f*. **~ mat** plaque *f* d'amiante. ◆ **asbestosis** *n* asbestose *f*.

ascend [ə'send] **1** *vi* monter; *(esp Rel)* s'élever (*to* à, jusqu'à). **2** *vt ladder* monter à; *mountain* gravir, faire l'ascension de; *river* remonter; *staircase* monter; *throne* monter sur. ◆ **ascendancy** *n* ascendant *m* (*over* sur). ◆ **ascendant** *adj, n* ascendant *(m)*. ◆ **ascension** *n* ascension *f*. ◆ **ascent** *n* ascension *f*, *(in rank)* montée *f*.

ascertain [ˌæsə'teɪn] *vt* établir (*that* que); *truth, what happened* établir; *sb's age, name, address etc* vérifier.

ascetic [ə'setɪk] **1** *adj* ascétique. **2** *n* ascète *mf*. ◆ **asceticism** *n* ascétisme *m*.

ascribe [ə'skraɪb] *vt virtue, work* attribuer (*to* à); *fault* imputer (*to* à).

aseptic [eɪ'septɪk] *adj* aseptique.

asexual [eɪ'seksjʊəl] *adj* asexué.

ash¹ [æʃ] *n (~ tree)* frêne *m*.

ash² [æʃ] **1** *n* cendre *f*. **~es to ~es, dust to dust** tu es poussière et tu retourneras en poussière. **2** *adj*: ~ **blond(e)** blond cendré *inv*; **A~ Wednesday** mercredi *m* des Cendres. ◆ **ashcan** *n* boîte *f* à ordures, poubelle *f*. ◆ **ashen** *adj face* terreux. ◆ **ashman** *n (US)* éboueur *m*. ◆ **ashtray** *n* cendrier *m*.

ashamed [ə'ʃeɪmd] *adj* honteux, confus. **to be** *or* **feel** ~ **(of o.s.)** avoir honte; **to be** ~ **of** avoir honte de; **I am** ~ **to say** à ma honte je dois dire.

ashore [ə'ʃɔːʳ] *adv* à terre; *(to the shore)* vers la rive, vers le rivage. **to go** ~ descendre à terre; **to put sb** ~ débarquer qn.

Asia ['eɪʃə] *n* Asie *f*. ◆ **Asian** *or* ◆ **Asiatic** **1** *adj* asiatique ; **2** *n* Asiatique *mf*.

aside [ə'saɪd] **1** *adv* de côté, à l'écart, à part. **to put sth** ~ mettre qch de côté; **to take sb** ~ prendre qn à part; **joking** ~ plaisanterie *or* blague * à part; ~ **from** à part. **2** *n (esp Theat)* aparté *m*. **in an** ~ en aparté.

asinine ['æsɪnaɪn] *adj* stupide, idiot.

ask [ɑːsk] **1** *vt* (**a**) *(inquire)* demander (*sb sth* qch à qn). **to** ~ **sb about sth** interroger qn *or* poser des questions à qn au sujet de qch; **to** ~ **(sb) a question** poser une question (à qn); ~ **him if he has seen her** demande-lui s'il l'a vue; **don't** ~ **me!** * allez savoir! *; **I** ~ **you!** * je vous demande un peu! * (**b**) *(request)* demander (*sb to do* à qn de faire; *that sth be done* que qch soit fait; *sb for sth* qch à qn). **he ~ed to go on the picnic** il a demandé s'il pouvait se joindre au pique-nique; **that's ~ing a lot!** c'est beaucoup en demander!; *(Comm)* **he is ~ing £80,000 for the house** il demande 80 000 livres *or* veut 80 000 livres pour la maison; **~ing price** prix *m* de départ. (**c**) *(invite)* inviter (*sb to sth* qn à qch; *sb to do* qn à faire). **to** ~ **sb in/out** *etc* inviter qn à entrer/sortir *etc*. **2** *vi* demander. **to** ~ **about sth** s'informer de qch, se renseigner sur qch; **it's there for the ~ing** il suffit de le demander (pour l'obtenir). ◆ **ask after** *vt fus person* demander des nouvelles de; *sb's health* s'informer de. ◆ **ask along** *vt sep* inviter. ◆ **ask back** *vt sep (for a second visit)* réinviter; *(on reciprocal visit)* rendre son invitation à. ◆ **ask for** *vt fus help, permission, money* demander; *person* demander à voir. **he ~ed for his pen back** il a demandé qu'on lui rende son stylo; **they are ~ing for trouble** * ils cherchent les ennuis *or* les embêtements *; **she was ~ing for it!** * elle l'a bien cherché! *

askance [ə'skɑːns] *adv*: **to look** ~ **at** *(sideways)* regarder de côté; *(suspiciously/disapprovingly)* regarder d'un air soupçonneux/d'un œil désapprobateur.

askew [ə'skjuː] *adv* de travers. *(US fig)* **something is** ~ il y a quelque chose qui ne tourne pas rond.

asleep [ə'sliːp] *adj* endormi. **to be** ~ dormir, être endormi; **to be fast** *or* **sound** ~ dormir profondément *or* à poings fermés; **my finger is** ~ j'ai le doigt engourdi; **to fall** ~ s'endormir.

asparagus [əs'pærəgəs] *n (Bot)* asperge *f*; *(Culin)* asperges. ~ **fern** asparagus *m*; ~ **tips** pointes *fpl* d'asperges.

aspect ['æspekt] *n* (**a**) *(gen; also Gram)* aspect *m*. **to study every** ~ **of a question** étudier une question sous tous ses aspects; **seen from this** ~ vu sous cet angle. (**b**) *[building etc]* exposition *f*. **house with a southerly** ~ maison exposée au midi.

asperity [æs'perɪtɪ] *n* rudesse *f*.

aspersion [əs'pɜːʃ(ə)n] *n* calomnie *f*. **to cast ~s on sth/sb** dénigrer qch/qn.

asphalt ['æsfælt] **1** *n* asphalte *m*. **2** *vt* asphalter. **3** *adj* asphalté.

asphyxia [æs'fɪksɪə] *n* asphyxie *f*. ◆ **asphyxiate** **1** *vt* asphyxier ; **2** *vi* s'asphyxier. ◆ **asphyxiation** *n* asphyxie *f*.

aspic ['æspɪk] *n*: **chicken in** ~ aspic *m* de volaille.

aspidistra [ˌæspɪ'dɪstrə] *n* aspidistra *m*.

aspirate ['æsp(ə)rɪt] **1** *n* aspirée *f*. **2** *adj* aspiré.

aspire [əs'paɪəʳ] *vi* aspirer (*to sth* à qch; *to do* à faire). **we can't** ~ **to that** nos prétentions ne vont pas jusque-là. ◆ **aspiration** *n* aspiration *f*. ◆ **aspiring** *adj* ambitieux.

aspirin ['æsprɪn] *n* aspirine *f*.

ass [æs] *n (Zool)* âne *m*; *(fool)* idiot(e) *m(f)*, imbécile *mf*. **to make an** ~ **of o.s.** se rendre ridicule; **don't be an ~!** *(action)* ne fais pas l'imbécile!; *(speech)* ne dis pas de sottises!

assail [ə'seɪl] *vt* assaillir (*with* de). ◆ **assailant** *n* agresseur *m*.

assassin [ə'sæsɪn] *n* assassin *m (Pol etc)*. ◆ **assassinate** *vt* assassiner. ◆ **assassination** *n* assassinat *m*.

assault [ə'sɔːlt] **1** *n (Mil)* assaut *m* (*on* de); *(Jur)* agression *f*. **the** ~ **on the man** l'agression dont l'homme a été victime; ~ **and battery** coups *mpl* et blessures *fpl*. **2** *vt (Jur)* agresser; *(sexually)* violenter; *(Mil)* donner l'assaut à. **3** *adj*: *(Mil)* ~ **course** parcours *m* du combattant.

assemble [ə'sembl] **1** *vt objects, ideas* assembler; *people* rassembler; *(Tech) machine* monter. **2** *vi* s'assembler; se rassembler; se monter. ◆ **assemblage** *n [things]* collection *f*; *[people]* assemblée *f*. ◆ **assembler** *n (Comput)* assembleur *m*. ◆ **assembly** **1** *n* (**a**) *(meeting)* assemblée *f*; *(Scol)* réunion *f* de tous les élèves de l'établissement. **in open assembly** en séance publique; **the general assembly of the U.N.** l'assemblée générale de l'ONU; (**b**) *(Tech)* montage *m*; **the engine assembly** le bloc moteur; *(Comput)* assemblage *m* ; **2** *adj*: **assembly language** *(Comput)* langage *m* d'assemblage; **assembly line** chaîne *f* de montage.

assent [ə'sent] **1** *n* assentiment *m*. **2** *vi* donner son assentiment (*to* à).

assert [ə'sɜːt] *vt* affirmer, soutenir (*that* que); *one's innocence* protester de; *claim* défendre; *one's rights* faire valoir. ◆ **assertion** *n* affirmation *f*, assertion *f*. ◆ **assertive** *adj* assuré.

assess [ə'ses] *vt (gen)* estimer, évaluer; *payment, damages, tax* déterminer le montant de; *rateable property* calculer la valeur imposable de; *situation, time, amount* évaluer; *candidate* juger (la valeur de). ◆ **assessment** *n* estimation *f*; évaluation *f*; détermination *f* (du montant); calcul *m* (de la valeur imposable); jugement *m* (*of* sur); *(Educ)* contrôle *m* des connaissances; *(on pupil's report)* appréciation *f* du professeur; *(Scol, Univ)* **continuous ~ment** contrôle *m* continu. ◆ **assessor** *n [property]* expert *m*; *(US)* **~or of taxes** contrôleur *m* des contributions directes.

asset ['æset] *n*: **~s** *(Fin)* actif *m*; *(gen)* biens *mpl*; **~s and liabilities** actif et passif *m*; *(fig)* **his greatest** ~ son meilleur atout. ◆ **asset-stripper** *n* spécialiste de la cannibalisation. ◆ **asset-stripping** cannibalisation *f* (d'une compagnie).

assiduous [ə'sɪdjʊəs] *adj* assidu. ◆ **assiduity** *n* assiduité *f*. ◆ **assiduously** *adv* assidûment.

assign [ə'saɪn] *vt task, office, date* assigner (*to* à); *meaning* attribuer (*to* à); *employee* affecter (*to* à); *(Jur) property, right* céder (*to sb* à qn). ◆ **assignation** *n (appointment)* rendez-vous *m inv*. ◆ **assignment** *n (task)* mission *f*.

assimilate [ə'sɪmɪleɪt] *vt* assimiler (*to* à). ◆ **assimilation** *n* assimilation *f*.

assist [ə'sɪst] **1** *vt* aider, assister (*to do, in doing* à faire). **to ~ sb in/out** *etc* aider qn à entrer/sortir *etc*; **~ed by** avec le concours de; *(Travel)* **~ed passage** billet subventionné. **2** *vi* aider, prêter secours (*in* à).
◆ **assistance** *n* assistance *f*; **to come to sb's ~ance** venir à l'aide de qn; **can I be of ~ance?** puis-je vous aider? ◆ **assistant 1** *n* aide *mf*, auxiliaire *mf*; *(foreign language ~) (Scol)* assistant(e) *m(f)*; *(Univ)* lecteur *m*, -trice *f*; **2** *adj* adjoint; **~ant librarian** bibliothécaire *mf* adjoint(e); *(Scol)* **~ant master** *or* **mistress** professeur *m (qui n'a pas la responsabilité d'une section)*; *[primary school]* instituteur *m*, -trice *f*.

assizes [ə'saɪzɪz] *npl (Jur)* assises *fpl*.

associate [ə'səʊʃɪɪt] **1** *adj* associé, allié. **2** *n* (**a**) associé(e) *m(f)*, collègue *mf*; *(accomplice)* complice *mf*. (**b**) *[a society]* associé *m*; *[learned body]* (membre *m*) correspondant *m*. **3** [ə'səʊʃɪeɪt] *vt* associer (*with* avec). *(in undertaking etc)* **to be ~ed with sth** être associé à qch; **I should like to ~ myself with what has been said** je voudrais me faire l'écho de cette opinion; **I don't wish to be ~d with it** je préfère que mon nom ne soit pas mêlé à ceci. **4** *vi*: **to ~ with sb** fréquenter qn.
◆ **association** [ə,səʊsɪ'eɪʃ(ə)n] **1** *n (most senses)* association *f*; **full of historic associations** riche en souvenirs historiques ; **2** *adj*: **association football** football *m* (association).

assorted [ə'sɔːtɪd] *adj* assorti. **well-/ill-~** bien/mal assortis; **in ~ sizes** de différentes tailles.
◆ **assortment** *n [objects]* assortiment *m*; **this shop has a good assortment** ce magasin a un grand choix; **an assortment of people** des gens (très) divers.

assuage [ə'sweɪdʒ] *vt* calmer.

assume [ə'sjuːm] *vt* (**a**) *(suppose)* supposer, présumer, admettre. **let us ~ that** admettons *or* supposons que + *subj*; **you resigned, I ~** vous avez démissionné, je suppose *or* présume; **you are assuming a lot** vous faites bien des suppositions. (**b**) *(take) (gen)* prendre; *responsibility, burden, role* assumer; *title, right, authority* s'approprier; *name, air, attitude* adopter; *innocence, indifference* affecter un air de. **to ~ control of** prendre en main la direction de; **under an ~d name** sous un nom d'emprunt. ◆ **assumption** *n* (**a**) *(supposition)* supposition *f*, hypothèse *f*; **on the assumption that** en supposant que + *subj*; **to go on the assumption that** présumer que; (**b**) *[power etc]* appropriation *f*; *[indifference]* affectation *f*; *(Rel)* **A~** Assomption

assure [ə'ʃʊə^r] *vt (all senses)* assurer (*sb of sth* qn de qch). ◆ **assurance** *n (all senses)* assurance *f*; **in the assurance that** avec l'assurance que; **you have my assurance that** je vous promets formellement que. ◆ **assuredly** *adv* assurément.

aster ['æstə^r] *n* aster *m*.

asterisk ['æst(ə)rɪsk] *n* astérisque *m*.

astern [ə'stɜːn] *adv (Naut)* à *or* sur l'arrière.

asteroid ['æstərɔɪd] *n* astéroïde *m*.

asthma ['æsmə] *n* asthme *m*. ◆ **asthmatic** *adj, n* asthmatique *(mf)*.

astigmatism [æs'tɪgmətɪz(ə)m] *n* astigmatisme *m*.
◆ **astigmatic** *adj* astigmate.

astonish [ə'stɒnɪʃ] *vt* étonner; *(stronger)* ahurir. **you ~ me!** non! pas possible! ◆ **astonished** *adj* étonné, stupéfait; **I am ~ed that** cela m'étonne *or* m'ahurit que + *subj*. ◆ **astonishing** *adj* étonnant; ahurissant. ◆ **astonishingly** *adv* incroyablement. ◆ **astonishment** *n* étonnement *m*; ahurissement *m*; **look of ~ment** regard stupéfait; **to my ~ment** à mon grand étonnement.

astound [ə'staʊnd] *vt* stupéfier, abasourdir.
◆ **astounded** *adj* abasourdi, ébahi. ◆ **astounding** *adj* stupéfiant, ahurissant.

astrakhan [,æstrə'kæn] *n* astrakan *m*.

astray [ə'streɪ] *adv*: **to go ~** s'égarer; **to lead sb ~** détourner qn du droit chemin.

astride [ə'straɪd] **1** *adv* à califourchon, à cheval. **2** *prep* à califourchon *or* à cheval sur.

astringent [əs'trɪn(d)ʒənt] **1** *adj* astringent; *(fig)* dur. **2** *n* astringent *m*.

astrology [əs'trɒlədʒɪ] *n* astrologie *f*. ◆ **astrologer** *n* astrologue *m*. ◆ **astrological** *adj* astrologique.

astronaut ['æstrənɔːt] *n* astronaute *mf*.

astronomy [əs'trɒnəmɪ] *n* astronomie *f*. ◆ **astronomer** *n* astronome *m*. ◆ **astronomic(al)** *adj (lit, fig)* astronomique.

astrophysics ['æstrə(ʊ)'fɪzɪks] *nsg* astrophysique *f*. ◆ **astrophysicist** *n* astrophysicien(ne) *m(f)*.

Astroturf ['æstrəʊtɜːf] *n* ® gazon *m* artificiel.

astute [əs'tjuːt] *adj* fin, astucieux. ◆ **astutely** *adv* avec finesse, astucieusement. ◆ **astuteness** *n* finesse *f*, astuce *f*.

asylum [ə'saɪləm] *n* asile *m*.

at [æt] *prep* (**a**) *(place)* à. **~ the table** à la table; **~ my brother's** chez mon frère; **~ the baker's** chez le boulanger; **~ home** à la maison, chez soi; **to dry o.s. ~ the fire** se sécher devant le feu; **to stand ~ the window** se tenir à *or* devant la fenêtre. (**b**) *(time)* à. **~ 10 o'clock** à 10 heures; **3 ~ a time** 3 par 3, 3 à la fois, *(stairs)* 3 à 3; **~ a time like this** à un moment pareil; **~ my time of life** à mon âge. (**c**) *(activity)* **to play ~ football** jouer au football; **while we are ~ it *** pendant que nous y sommes; **let me see you ~ it again! *** que je t'y reprenne!; **they are ~ it all day *** ils font ça toute la journée; **she was (on) ~ her husband to buy a new car *** elle a harcelé son mari pour qu'il achète *(subj)* une nouvelle voiture; **he's always (on) ~ me *** il est toujours après moi *; **good ~ languages** bon en langues; **~ war** en guerre. (**d**) *(manner)* **~ full speed** à toute allure; **~ 80 km/h** à 80 km/h; **he drove ~ 80 km/h** il faisait du 80 (à l'heure). (**e**) *(cause)* **surprised ~** étonné de; **annoyed ~** contrarié par; **angry ~** en colère contre. (**f**) *(rate, value, degree)* à, dans, en. **he sells them ~ 2 francs a kilo** il les vend 2 F le kilo; **let's leave it ~ that** restons-en là!; **~ a stroke** d'un seul coup; **he's only a teacher and a poor one ~ that** ce n'est qu'un professeur et encore assez piètre. ◆ **at-home** *n* réception *f (chez soi)*.

ate [et, *(US)* eɪt] *pret of* **eat**.

atheism ['eɪθɪɪz(ə)m] *n* athéisme *m*. ◆ **atheist** *n* athée *mf*. ◆ **atheistic(al)** *adj* athée.

Athens ['æθɪnz] *n* Athènes.

athlete ['æθliːt] *n (in competitions)* athlète *mf*. *(gen)* **he's a fine ~** il est très sportif; *(Med)* **~'s foot** mycose *f*. ◆ **athletic** [æθ'letɪk] *adj activity* athlétique; *meeting* sportif, d'athlétisme; *person (sporty)* sportif; *(muscular)* athlétique; *(US Scol, Univ)* **~ coach** entraîneur *m* (sportif). ◆ **athletics** *nsg (Brit)* athlétisme *m*; *(US)* sport *m*.

Atlantic [ət'læntɪk] *adj winds, currents* de l'Atlantique. **the ~ (Ocean)** l'Atlantique *m*, l'océan *m* Atlantique; **~ liner** transatlantique *m*.

atlas ['ætləs] *n* atlas *m*.

atmosphere ['ætməsfɪə^r] *n* atmosphère *f*.
◆ **atmospheric** [,ætməs'ferɪk] *adj* atmosphérique.
◆ **atmospherics** *nsg (Telec)* parasites *mpl*.

atom ['ætəm] **1** *n* atome *m*. *(fig)* **smashed to ~s** réduit en miettes; **not an ~ of truth** pas un grain de vérité. **2** *adj*: **~ bomb** *n* bombe *f* atomique.
◆ **atomic** *adj* atomique; **~ reactor** réacteur *m* nucléaire. ◆ **atomize** *vt* atomiser. ◆ **atomizer** *n* atomiseur *m*.

atone [ə'təʊn] *vi*: **to ~ for** *sin* expier; *mistake* réparer. ◆ **atonement** *n* expiation *f (Rel)*; réparation *f*.

atrocious [ə'trəʊʃəs] *adj* atroce. ◆ **atrociously** *adv* atrocement. ◆ **atrocity** [ə'trɒsɪtɪ] *n* atrocité *f*.

atrophy ['ætrəfɪ] **1** *n* atrophie *f*. **2** *vi* s'atrophier. **3** *vt* atrophier.

attach [ə'tætʃ] *vt (gen)* attacher (*to* à); *document* joindre (*to* à); *troops* affecter (*to* à); *employee* attacher (*to* à). **the ~ed letter** la lettre ci-jointe; **to ~ credence to** ajouter foi à; **to ~ o.s. to a group** se joindre à un groupe; *(fond of)* **to be ~ed to sb/sth** être attaché à qn/qch; **he's ~ed** * *(married etc)* il n'est pas libre. ◆ **attaché** [ə'tæʃeɪ] *n* attaché(e) *m(f)*; **~é case** mallette *f*, attaché-case *m*. ◆ **attachment** *n (for tool etc: accessory)* accessoire *m*; *(affection)* attachement *m* (*to* à); *(temporary transfer)* stage *m* (*to* chez).

attack [ə'tæk] **1** *n* (**a**) *(gen, Mil, Sport)* attaque *f* (*on* contre). **to return to the ~** revenir à la charge; **~ on sb's life** attentat *m* contre qn; *(fig)* **to leave o.s. open to ~** prêter le flanc à la critique; **to be under ~** *(Mil)* être attaqué (*from* par); *(fig)* être en butte aux attaques (*from* de). (**b**) *(Med)* crise *f*. **~ of fever** accès *m* de fièvre; **an ~ of migraine** une migraine. **2** *vt person, enemy* attaquer; *task, problem* s'attaquer à; *(Chem) metal* attaquer. ◆ **attacker** *n* attaquant(e) *m(f)*, agresseur *m*.

attain [ə'teɪn] *vti* (**a**) *aim, rank, age* atteindre, parvenir à. (**b**) *(also ~* **to**) *knowledge* acquérir; *happiness* atteindre à; *perfection etc* toucher à; *power, prosperity* parvenir à. ◆ **attainable** *adj* accessible (*by* à), à la portée (*by* de). ◆ **attainment** *n* réussite *f*, résultat *m* obtenu.

attempt [ə'tem(p)t] **1** *vt* essayer, tenter (*to do* de faire); *task* entreprendre. **~ed escape/murder** *etc* tentative *f* d'évasion/de meurtre *etc*; **to ~ suicide** tenter de se suicider. **2** *n* tentative *f* (*at sth* de qch), effort *m*; *(unsuccessful)* essai *m*. **an ~ at escape** une tentative d'évasion; **first ~** coup *m* d'essai; **to make an ~ at doing** essayer de faire; **to be successful at the first ~** réussir du premier coup; **to make an ~ on the record** essayer de battre le record; **it was a good ~ on his part** il a vraiment essayé; **~ on sb's life** attentat *m* contre qn.

attend [ə'tend] **1** *vt* (**a**) *meeting, lecture* assister à; *classes, course* suivre; *church, school* aller à. **the meeting was well ~ed** il y avait beaucoup de monde à la réunion. (**b**) *[lady-in-waiting]* accompagner; *[doctor]* soigner. **method ~ed by great risks** méthode qui comporte de grands risques. **2** *vi (pay attention)* faire attention (*to* à); *(be present)* être présent *or* là.

◆ **attend to** *vt fus speech, lesson* faire attention à; *advice* prêter attention à; *business, customer* s'occuper de.

◆ **attendance** **1** *n (being present)* présence *f*; *(number of people present)* assistance *f*; **he was in ~ance on the queen** il escortait la reine; **to be in ~ance** être de service; *(Med)* **~ance on a patient** visites *fpl* à un malade ; **2** *adj*: *(Brit Jur)* **~ance centre** prison *f* de week-end; *(Scol)* **~ance officer** ≃ inspecteur *m* (chargé de faire respecter l'obligation scolaire). ◆ **attendant** **1** *n [museum etc]* gardien(ne) *m(f)*; *(US: in hospital)* garçon *m* de salle; *(servant)* serviteur *m*; **the prince and his ~ants** le prince et sa suite ; **2** *adj* qui accompagne (qch); **the ~ant rise in prices** la hausse des prix correspondante; **old age and its ~ant ills** la vieillesse et les infirmités qui l'accompagnent.

attention [ə'tenʃ(ə)n] **1** *n* attention *f*. **to pay ~ to** faire attention à; **to call (sb's) ~ to sth** attirer l'attention (de qn) sur qch; **it has come to my ~ that** j'ai appris que; **for the ~ of** à l'attention de; **it needs daily ~** il faut s'en occuper tous les jours; *(kindness)* **~s** attentions *fpl*; *(Mil)* **~!** garde-à-vous!; **to stand at/come to ~** être/se mettre au garde-à-vous; **to jump** *or* **spring to ~** se mettre vivement au garde-à-vous. **2** *adj*: **his ~ span is too short** il ne peut pas se concentrer assez longtemps.

◆ **attention-seeking** *adj* cherchant à se faire remarquer. ◆ **attentive** *adj* prévenant (*to sb* envers qn); soucieux (*to sth* de qch); *audience, spectator* attentif; **attentive to sb's advice** attentif aux conseils de qn. ◆ **attentively** *adv* attentivement. ◆ **attentiveness** *n* attention *f*.

attenuate [ə'tenjʊeɪt] *vt* atténuer.

attest [ə'test] *vt* attester. ◆ **attestation** *n* attestation *f* (*that* que).

attic ['ætɪk] *n* grenier *m*. **~ room** mansarde *f*.

attire [ə'taɪə[r]] **1** *vt* vêtir (*in* de). **2** *n* vêtements *mpl*.

attitude ['ætɪtju:d] *n* attitude *f* (*towards* envers, à l'égard de). **~ of mind** état *m* d'esprit; **if that's your ~** si c'est ainsi que vous le prenez. ◆ **attitudinize** *vi* se donner des attitudes.

attorney [ə'tɜ:nɪ] *n* mandataire *m*; *(US: lawyer)* avoué *m*. **A~ General** *(Brit)* ≃ Procureur général; *(US)* ≃ Ministre *m* de la Justice.

attract [ə'trækt] *vt* attirer. ◆ **attraction** *n [magnet]* attraction *f*; *[plan]* attrait *m*; *[person, place]* attraits, charmes *mpl*. ◆ **attractive** *adj person, manner* attrayant, attirant; *price, idea, offer* attrayant, intéressant. ◆ **attractively** *adv* d'une manière attrayante; **~ively dressed woman** femme élégamment habillée.

attribute [ə'trɪbju:t] **1** *vt* attribuer (*to* à). **2** ['ætrɪbju:t] *n* attribut *m*; *(Gram)* attribut *m*. ◆ **attributable** *adj* attribuable (*to* à). ◆ **attribution** *n* attribution *f*. ◆ **attributive** **1** *adj* attributif; *(Gram)* attributif ; **2** *n* attribut *m*; *(Ling)* attribut *m*.

attrition [ə'trɪʃ(ə)n] *n* usure *f (par frottement)*. **war of ~** guerre *f* d'usure.

attuned [ə'tju:nd] *adj*: **~ to** *person* habitué à; *methods, tastes* en accord avec.

aubergine ['əʊbəʒi:n] *n* aubergine *f*.

auburn ['ɔ:bən] *adj* auburn *inv*.

auction ['ɔ:kʃ(ə)n] **1** *n* (vente *f* aux) enchères *fpl*. **2** *vt* vendre aux enchères. **3** *adj*: **~ bridge** bridge *m* aux enchères; **~ room** salle *f* des ventes; **~ sale** (vente *f* aux) enchères *fpl*. ◆ **auctioneer** *n* commissaire-priseur *m*.

audacious [ɔ:'deɪʃəs] *adj* audacieux. ◆ **audacity** *n* audace *f*.

audible ['ɔ:dɪbl] *adj words* audible, perceptible; *voice* distinct. **she was hardly ~** on l'entendait à peine; **there was ~ laughter** des rires se firent entendre. ◆ **audibility** *n* audibilité *f*. ◆ **audibly** *adv* distinctement.

audience ['ɔ:dɪəns] **1** *n* (**a**) *(Theat)* spectateurs *mpl*, public *m*; *[speaker]* auditoire *m*; *(Mus, Rad)* auditeurs *mpl*; *(TV)* téléspectateurs *mpl*. **the whole ~ applauded** toute la salle a applaudi; **those in the ~** les gens dans la salle. (**b**) *(formal interview)* audience *f*. **2** *adj*: **~ participation** participation *f* de l'assistance *(à ce qui se passe sur scène)*; *(Rad, TV)* **~ rating** indice *m* d'audience; **~ research** études *fpl* d'opinion.

audio ['ɔ:dɪəʊ] **1** *adj equipment* acoustique. **~ system** système *m* audio. **2** *n* (*) partie *f* son. ◆ **audiotyping** *n* audiotypie *f*. ◆ **audiotypist** *n* audiotypiste *mf*. ◆ **audio-visual** *adj* audio-visuel. **~-visual aids** (support *m*) audio-visuel *m*.

audit ['ɔ:dɪt] **1** *n* vérification *f* des comptes. **2** *vt accounts* vérifier; *(US Univ) lecture course* assister comme auditeur libre à. ◆ **auditor** *n* expert-comptable *m*, vérificateur *m* (de comptes).

audition [ɔ:'dɪʃ(ə)n] **1** *n* audition *f*. **2** *vti* auditionner (*for a part* pour un rôle).

auditorium [ˌɔːdɪ'tɔːrɪəm] *n* salle *f*.

aught [ɔːt] *n*: **for ~ I know** (pour) autant que je sache; **for ~ I care** pour ce que cela me fait.

augment [ɔːg'ment] *vti* augmenter (*by* de). ◆ **augmentation** *n* augmentation *f*.

augur ['ɔːgəʳ] **1** *vi*: **to ~ well/ill** être de bon/de mauvais augure (*for* pour). **2** *vt* présager. ◆ **augury** *n* augure *m*.

August ['ɔːgəst] *n* août *m*; *for phrases V* **September**.

august [ɔː'gʌst] *adj* auguste.

auk [ɔːk] *n* pingouin *m*.

aunt [ɑːnt] *n* tante *f*. **yes ~** oui, ma tante; **A~ Sally** *(game)* jeu *m* de massacre; *(person)* tête *f* de Turc. ◆ **auntie *, aunty *** *n* tata * *f*.

au pair ['əʊ'pɛə] **1** *adj, adv* au pair. **2** *n* jeune fille *f* au pair.

aura ['ɔːrə] *n (lit)* aura *f*; *(fig: of place)* atmosphère *f*. **he has an ~ of** il donne une impression de.

aurora borealis [ɔː'rɔːrəbɔːrɪ'eɪlɪs] *n* aurore *f* boréale.

auspices ['ɔːspɪsɪz] *npl*: **under the ~ of** sous les auspices *mpl* de. ◆ **auspicious** [ɔːs'pɪʃəs] *adj sign* de bon augure; *occasion* propice; *start* bon. ◆ **auspiciously** *adv* sous d'heureux auspices; **to start ~ly** prendre un bon départ.

Aussie * ['ɒzɪ] = **Australian**.

austere [ɒs'tɪəʳ] *adj* austère. ◆ **austerely** *adv* avec austérité. ◆ **austerity** *n* austérité *f*; **years of austerity** années *fpl* de restrictions.

Australasia [ˌɔːstrə'leɪsjə] *n* Australasie *f*. ◆ **Australasian** **1** *n* habitant(e) *m(f)* d'Australasie; **2** *adj* d'Australasie.

Australia [ɒs'treɪlɪə] *n* Australie *f*. ◆ **Australian** **1** *n* Australien(ne) *m(f)* ; **2** *adj* australien.

Austria ['ɒstrɪə] *n* Autriche *f*. ◆ **Austrian** **1** *n* Autrichien(ne) *m(f)* ; **2** *adj* autrichien.

authentic [ɔː'θentɪk] *adj* authentique. ◆ **authenticate** *vt* établir l'authenticité de. ◆ **authenticity** *n* authenticité *f*.

author ['ɔːθəʳ] **1** *n* auteur *m*. **2** *vt* être l'auteur de. ◆ **authoress** *n* femme *f* auteur.

authority [ɔː'θɒrɪtɪ] *n (power)* autorité *f*; *(permission)* autorisation *f*. **I'm in ~ here** c'est moi qui commande ici; **to be in ~ over sb** avoir autorité sur qn; **those in ~** ceux qui nous gouvernent; **he did it without ~, he had no ~ to do it** il l'a fait sans autorisation; **he has no ~ to do it** il n'a pas le droit de le faire; **on her own ~** de sa propre autorité; **the proper authorities** les autorités compétentes; **the health authorities** les services *mpl* de la santé publique; *[person, book]* **to be an ~** faire autorité (*on* en matière de); **I have it on good ~ that...** je sais de source sûre que... ◆ **authoritarian** *adj* autoritaire. ◆ **authoritative** *adj opinion, source* autorisé; *person* autoritaire; *treatise, edition* qui fait autorité. ◆ **authorization** *n* autorisation *f* (*of, for* pour; *to do* de faire). ◆ **authorize** *vt* autoriser (*sb to do* qn à faire); **authorized dealer** distributeur *m* agréé; **the Authorized Version** la Bible de 1611.

autism ['ɔːtɪz(ə)m] *n* autisme *m*. ◆ **autistic** *adj* autistique.

auto ['ɔːtəʊ] *n (US)* auto *f*. **~ worker** ouvrier *m* de l'industrie automobile. ◆ **autocade** *n* cortège *m* d'automobiles.

auto... ['ɔːtəʊ] *pref* auto... ◆ **auto-immune** *adj disease* auto-immune. ◆ **autopilot** *n* pilote *m* automatique. ◆ **auto-teller** *n* distributeur *m* automatique de billets. ◆ **autotimer** *n [oven]* programmateur *m* (de four).

autobiography [ˌɔːtəʊbaɪ'ɒgrəfɪ] *n* autobiographie *f*. ◆ **autobiographic(al)** *adj* autobiographique.

autocrat ['ɔːtəʊkræt] *n* autocrate *m*. ◆ **autocratic** *adj* autocratique.

autocue ['ɔːtəʊkjuː] *n* autocue *m or f*.

autocycle ['ɔːtəʊsaɪkl] *n* cyclomoteur *m*; *(bigger)* vélomoteur *m*.

autograph ['ɔːtəgrɑːf] **1** *n* autographe *m*. **2** *adj*: **~ album** album *m* d'autographes; **~ hunter** collectionneur *m*, -euse *f* d'autographes. **3** *vt* dédicacer.

automat ['ɔːtəmæt] *n* cafétéria *f* à distributeurs automatiques.

automatic [ˌɔːtə'mætɪk] **1** *adj* automatique. *(Comput)* **~ data processing** traitement *m* automatique de l'information; **on ~ pilot** en pilotage automatique. **2** *n (gun)* automatique *m*; *(car)* voiture *f* (à transmission) automatique. ◆ **automatically** *adv* automatiquement. ◆ **automation** *n* automatisation *f*. ◆ **automaton**, *pl* **-ta** [ɔː'tɒmət(ə)n, tə] *n* automate *m*.

automobile ['ɔːtəməbiːl] *n* automobile *f*, auto *f*.

automotive [ˌɔːtə'məʊtɪv] *adj (Aut)* (de l') automobile; *(self-propelled)* automoteur.

autonomy [ɔː'tɒnəmɪ] *n* autonomie *f*. ◆ **autonomous** *adj* autonome.

autopsy ['ɔːtɒpsɪ] *n* autopsie *f*.

autosuggestion ['ɔːtəʊsə'dʒestʃ(ə)n] *n* autosuggestion *f*.

autumn ['ɔːtəm] **1** *n* automne *m*. **in ~** en automne. **2** *adj* d'automne. **~ leaves** feuilles mortes. ◆ **autumnal** *adj* d'automne.

auxiliary [ɔːg'zɪlɪərɪ] **1** *adj* auxiliaire. *(US)* **~ police** corps *m* de policiers auxiliaires volontaires. **2** *n (person)* auxiliaire *mf*; *(verb)* auxiliaire *m*.

avail [ə'veɪl] **1** *vt*: **to ~ o.s. of** *opportunity* profiter de; *right* user de; *service* utiliser. **2** *n*: **to no ~** sans résultat; **it is of no ~** cela ne sert à rien. ◆ **availability** *n* disponibilité *f*. ◆ **available** *adj* disponible; **to make sth ~able to sb** mettre qch à la disposition de qn; **every ~able means** tous les moyens possibles; **he is not ~able just now** il n'est pas libre en ce moment; **he is not ~able for comment** il se refuse à toute déclaration.

avalanche ['ævəlɑːnʃ] **1** *n* avalanche *f*. **2** *adj precautions* anti-avalanche *inv*. **'avalanche warning'** *(on sign)* 'risque d'avalanches'.

avant-garde [ˌævɒŋ'gɑːd] **1** *n* avant-garde *f*. **2** *adj* d'avant-garde.

avarice ['ævərɪs] *n* avarice *f*. ◆ **avaricious** *adj* avare.

avenge [ə'ven(d)ʒ] *vt* venger. **to ~ o.s. on** se venger de. ◆ **avenger** *n* vengeur *m*. ◆ **avenging** *adj* vengeur (*f* -geresse).

avenue ['ævənjuː] *n* avenue *f*; *(fig)* route *f*.

aver [ə'vɜːʳ] *vt* déclarer.

average ['ævərɪdʒ] **1** *n* moyenne *f*. **on ~** en moyenne; **above/below ~** au-dessus/en-dessous de la moyenne. **2** *adj* moyen. **3** *vt (find the ~ of)* établir *or* faire la moyenne de; *(reach an ~ of)* atteindre la moyenne de. **we ~ 8 hours' work** *or* **our working hours ~ (out at) 8 per day** nous travaillons en moyenne 8 heures par jour; **the sales ~ 200 copies a month** la vente moyenne est de 200 exemplaires par mois; *(Aut)* **we ~d 50 the whole way** nous avons fait (du) 50 de moyenne pendant tout le trajet.

averse [ə'vɜːs] *adj* opposé (*to* à). **to be ~ to doing** répugner à *or (less formal)* avoir horreur de faire; **I am not ~ to an occasional drink** je ne refuse pas un verre de temps en temps. ◆ **aversion** *n* aversion *f*, répugnance *f*. **to take an aversion to** se mettre à détester; **my greatest** *or* **pet aversion** ce que je déteste le plus.

avert [ə'vɜːt] *vt danger, accident* prévenir, éviter; *blow, eyes, thoughts* détourner (*from* de).

aviary [ˈeɪvɪ(ə)rɪ] *n* volière *f*.

aviation [ˌeɪvɪˈeɪʃ(ə)n] *n* aviation *f*. ~ **fuel** kérosène *m*; ~ **glasses** lunettes *fpl* sport; ~ **industry** aéronautique *f*. ◆ **aviator** *n* aviateur *m*, -trice *f*.

avid [ˈævɪd] *adj* avide (*for* de). ◆ **avidity** *n* avidité *f*. ◆ **avidly** *adv* avidement.

avocado [ˌævəˈkɑːdəʊ] *n*: ~ **(pear)** avocat *m (fruit)*.

avoid [əˈvɔɪd] *vt (gen)* éviter (*doing* de faire). **to ~ tax** *(legally)* se soustraire à l'impôt; *(illegally)* frauder le fisc; ~ **being seen** évitez qu'on ne vous voie; **to ~ sb's eye** fuir le regard de qn; **to ~ notice** échapper aux regards; **I can't ~ going now** je ne peux plus me dispenser d'y aller; ~ **it like the plague** il faut fuir cela comme la peste. ◆ **avoidable** *adj* évitable. ◆ **avoidance** *n*: **his ~ance of me** le soin qu'il met à m'éviter; **tax ~ance** fraude *f* fiscale.

avoirdupois [ˌævədəˈpɔɪz] *n* système *m* des poids commerciaux; *(*: overweight)* embonpoint *m*.

avow [əˈvaʊ] *vt* avouer. **he is an ~ed atheist** il avoue être athée; **~ed enemy** ennemi déclaré. ◆ **avowal** *n* aveu *m*. ◆ **avowedly** *adv* de son propre aveu.

await [əˈweɪt] *vt* attendre. **long-~ed** longtemps attendu.

awake [əˈweɪk] *pret* **awoke** *or* **~d,** *ptp* **awoken** *or* **~d** **1** *vi* s'éveiller, se réveiller. *(fig)* **to ~ to sth** prendre conscience de qch; **to ~ to the fact that** se rendre compte que. **2** *vt person* éveiller, réveiller; *suspicion, hope, curiosity* éveiller; *memories* réveiller. **3** *adj* (**a**) *(not asleep)* éveillé, réveillé. **he was still ~** il ne s'était pas encore endormi; **to lie ~** ne pas pouvoir dormir; **to stay ~ all night** *(deliberately)* veiller toute la nuit; *(involuntarily)* passer une nuit blanche; **it kept me ~** cela m'a empêché de dormir. (**b**) *(alert)* en éveil, vigilant. **to be ~ to** avoir conscience de. ◆ **awaken** *vti* = **awake.** ◆ **awakening** **1** *n* réveil *m*; **a rude ~ning** un réveil brutal ; **2** *adj interest* naissant.

award [əˈwɔːd] **1** *vt prize etc* décerner (*to* à); *money* attribuer (*to* à); *dignity, honour* conférer (*to* à); *damages* accorder (*to* à). **2** *n* prix *m*; *(for bravery)* récompense *f*; *(scholarship)* bourse *f*. ◆ **award-winner** *n (person)* lauréat(e) *m(f)*; *(book etc)* livre *etc* primé. ◆ **award-winning** *adj* primé.

aware [əˈwɛəʳ] *adj* (**a**) *(conscious)* conscient (*of* de); *(informed)* au courant (*of* de). **to become ~ of sth/that sth is happening** prendre conscience *or* se rendre compte de qch/que qch se passe; **to be ~ of/that** être conscient de/que; **I am quite ~ of it** je m'en rends bien compte; **as far as I am ~** autant que je sache; **not that I am ~ of** pas que je sache; **to make sb ~ of sth** rendre qn conscient de qch. (**b**) *(knowledgeable)* informé. **politically ~** politisé; **socially ~** au courant des problèmes sociaux. ◆ **awareness** *n* conscience *f* (*of* de). **~ness programme** programme *m* de sensibilisation.

awash [əˈwɒʃ] *adj* inondé (*with* de).

away [əˈweɪ] **1** *adv* (**a**) au loin, loin. ~ **from** loin de; **far ~** au loin, très loin; **the lake is 3 km ~** le lac est à 3 km de distance *or* à une distance de 3 km; ~ **back** *(distance)* très loin derrière; ~ **back in prehistoric times** dans les temps reculés de la préhistoire; ~ **back in 1600** il y a bien longtemps en 1600; ~ **back in the 40s** il y a longtemps déjà dans les années 40; ~ **over there** là-bas au loin, loin là-bas. (**b**) *(absent)* **he's ~ just now** il n'est pas là en ce moment; **he is ~ in London** il est (parti) à Londres; **when I have to be ~** lorsque je dois m'absenter; **she was ~ before I could speak** elle était partie avant que j'aie pu parler; ~ **with you!** allez-vous-en! (**c**) *(continuously)* sans arrêt. **to work ~** travailler sans arrêt. (**d**) *(loss etc)* **to gamble ~ one's money** perdre son argent au jeu; **the snow has melted ~** la neige a fondu complètement. **2** *adj (Sport)* ~ **match** match *m* à l'extérieur.

awe [ɔː] **1** *n* crainte *f* révérentielle. **to be in ~ of sb** être intimidé par qn. **2** *vt* inspirer un respect mêlé de crainte à. ◆ **awed** *adj* respectueux et intimidé. ◆ **awe-inspiring** *or* ◆ **awesome** *adj* impressionnant, imposant. ◆ **awe-struck** *adj (frightened)* frappé de terreur; *(astounded)* stupéfait.

awful [ˈɔːf(ə)l] *adj* affreux, terrible; *(stronger)* épouvantable; *(imposing)* imposant. **an ~ lot of** *cars, dogs, people* un nombre incroyable de; *butter, flowers* une quantité incroyable de. ◆ **awfully** *adv* vraiment, très, terriblement; **thanks ~ly *** merci infiniment; **~ly sorry** vraiment désolé; **an ~ly big house** une très grande maison.

awhile [əˈwaɪl] *adv* (pendant) quelque temps. **wait ~** attendez un peu.

awkward [ˈɔːkwəd] *adj* (**a**) *tool, shape* peu commode; *path* difficile; *(Aut) bend* difficile à négocier; *problem, task, question, situation* délicat; *silence* embarrassé. **at an ~ time** au mauvais moment; **an ~ moment** *(embarrassing)* un moment gênant; **he's an ~ customer *** c'est un type pas facile *; **it's a bit ~** *(inconvenient)* ce n'est pas très commode; *(annoying)* c'est un peu ennuyeux; **he's being ~ about it** il ne se montre pas très coopératif à ce sujet. (**b**) *(clumsy) person, movement* maladroit; *style* gauche. **the ~ age** l'âge ingrat. ◆ **awkwardly** *adv speak* d'un ton embarrassé; *behave, handle, move* maladroitement, peu élégamment; *place* à un endroit difficile; *express* gauchement. ◆ **awkwardness** *n [person, movement]* maladresse *f*; *[situation etc]* côté *m* délicat; *(embarrassment)* embarras *m*.

awl [ɔːl] *n* alêne *f*, poinçon *m*.

awning [ˈɔːnɪŋ] *n (Naut)* taud *m*; *[shop]* banne *f*; *[hotel door]* marquise *f*; *[tent]* auvent *m*; *(in garden)* vélum *m*.

awoke(n) [əˈwəʊk(ən)] *pret (ptp) of* **awake.**

awry [əˈraɪ] *adv* de travers. **to go ~** *[plan etc]* s'en aller à vau-l'eau; *[undertaking]* mal tourner.

ax *(US)*, **axe** [æks] **1** *n* hache *f*. *(fig)* **I've no ~ to grind** ce n'est pas mon intérêt personnel que j'ai en vue; *(fig)* **when the ~ fell** quand le coup fut porté. **2** *vt* **to ~ expenditure** réduire les dépenses, faire *or* opérer des coupes sombres dans le budget; **to ~ sb** mettre qn à la porte *(pour raisons économiques)*.

axiom [ˈæksɪəm] *n* axiome *m*. ◆ **axiomatic** *adj* axiomatique; *(clear)* évident.

axis, *pl* **axes** [ˈæksɪs, sɪːz] *n* axe *m (Geom etc)*.

axle [ˈæksl] **1** *n [wheel]* axe *m*; *(Aut:* **~-tree***)* essieu *m*. **front/rear ~** essieu avant/arrière. **2** *adj*: ~ **grease** graisse *f* à essieux; ~ **pin** clavette *f* d'essieu.

ay(e) [aɪ] **1** *particle* oui. **2** *n* oui *m*. *(in voting)* **the ~s and noes** les voix *fpl* pour et contre; **the ~s have it** les oui l'emportent.

azalea [əˈzeɪlɪə] *n* azalée *f*.

azure [ˈeɪʒəʳ] **1** *n* azur *m*. **2** *adj* d'azur.

B

B, b [biː] *n* B, b *m*; *(Mus)* si *m*. *(house numbers)* **24b** le 24 ter.

babble [ˈbæbl] **1** *n [voices]* rumeur *f*; *[baby, stream]* gazouillement *m*. **2** *vi (indistinctly)* bredouiller; *(chatter)* bavarder; *[baby, stream]* gazouiller. **3** *vt* bredouiller. ◆ **babbling** *adj* babillard.

babe [beɪb] *n* bébé *m*, petit(e) enfant *m(f)*. ~ **in arms** enfant au berceau.

babel [ˈbeɪbəl] *n* brouhaha *m*.

baboon [bəˈbuːn] *n* babouin *m*.

baby [ˈbeɪbɪ] **1** *n* bébé *m*. ~ **of the family** benjamin(e) *m(f)*; **don't be such a** ~! ne fais pas l'enfant!; *(fig)* **he was left holding the** ~ tout lui est retombé dessus; *(fig)* **to throw out the** ~ **with the bathwater** jeter le bébé avec l'eau du bain; **come on,** ~! * *(to woman)* viens ma belle!; *(to man)* viens mon gars! *; **the new system is his** ~ le nouveau système est son affaire. **2** *vt* (*) *person* dorloter. **3** *adj clothes etc* de bébé; *rabbit etc* bébé-. ~ **boom** baby boom *m*; ~ **boy** petit garçon; ~ **girl** petite fille; *(US)* ~ **carriage** voiture *f* d'enfant; ~ **face** visage *m* poupin; ~ **grand (piano)** (piano *m*) demi-queue *m*; ~ **linen** layette *f*; ~ **scales** pèse-bébé *m*; ~ **seat** siège *m* pour bébés; ~ **talk** langage *m* de bébé. ◆ **baby-batterer** *n* bourreau *m* d'enfants. ◆ **baby-battering** *n* mauvais traitements infligés aux enfants. ◆ **babyhood** *n* petite enfance *f*. ◆ **babyish** *adj clothes* de bébé; *behaviour, speech* puéril. ◆ **baby-minder** *n* nourrice *f (gardant les enfants dont les mères travaillent)*. ◆ **baby-sit** *vi* garder les bébés *or* les enfants. ◆ **baby-sitter** *n* baby-sitter *mf*. ◆ **baby-sitting** *n* baby-sitting *m*; **to go** ~**-sitting** faire du baby-sitting. ◆ **baby-walker** *n* trotte-bébé *m inv*.

baccalaureate [ˌbækəˈlɔːrɪɪt] *n (US)* licence *f*.

baccara(t) [ˈbækərɑː] *n* baccara *m*.

bachelor [ˈbætʃ(ə)ləʳ] *n, adj* célibataire *(m)*. **B~ of Arts/of Science/of Law** licencié(e) *m(f)* ès lettres/ès sciences/en droit; ~ **flat** garçonnière *f*; ~ **girl** célibataire *f*.

bacillus, *pl* **bacilli** [bəˈsɪləs, bəˈsɪlɪ] *n* bacille *m*.

back [bæk] **1** *n* (**a**) *[person, animal, book]* dos *m*; *[chair]* dossier *m*. **to fall on one's** ~ tomber à la renverse; *(fig)* **behind his mother's** ~ derrière le dos de sa mère; *(lit, fig)* ~ **to** ~ dos à dos; **with one's** ~ **to the light** le dos à la lumière; **he had his** ~ **to the houses** il tournait le dos aux maisons; **he stood with his** ~ **(up) against the wall** il était adossé au mur; *(fig)* **to have one's** ~ **to the wall** être au pied du mur; **to put one's** ~ **into doing** mettre toute son énergie à faire; **to put sb's** ~ **up** braquer qn; **to get off sb's** ~ laisser qn en paix. (**b**) *(as opp to front) (gen)* dos *m*, derrière *m*; *[hand, hill, medal]* revers *m*; *[record]* deuxième face *f*; *[dress]* dos; *[head, house]* derrière; *[page, cheque]* verso *m*; *[material]* envers *m*. ~ **to front** (sens) devant derrière; **at the** ~ **of the book** à la fin du livre; **to have an idea at the** ~ **of one's mind** avoir une idée derrière la tête; **in the** ~ **(of a car)** à l'arrière (d'une voiture); *(US)* **in** ~ **of the house** derrière la maison; **I know Paris like the** ~ **of my hand** je connais Paris comme ma poche. (**c**) *(furthest from front) [cupboard, garden, stage]* fond *m*. **at the very** ~ tout au fond; **at the** ~ **of beyond** * au diable vauvert *. (**d**) *(Ftbl etc)* arrière *m*.

2 *adj* (**a**) *(not front) seat, wheel* arrière *inv; door, garden* de derrière; *(Ling) vowel* postérieur. *(fig)* **to enter through the** ~ **door** entrer par la petite porte; ~**room** chambre *f* du fond; *(fig)* **the** ~**room boys** * ceux qui restent dans la coulisse; *(fig)* **to take a** ~ **seat** * passer au second plan; *(fig)* **he's a** ~**seat driver** * il est toujours à donner des conseils au conducteur; ~ **streets** *(lit)* petites rues; **he grew up in the** ~ **streets of Leeds** il a grandi dans les quartiers pauvres de Leeds; ~ **tooth** molaire *f*; ~ **number** *[magazine etc]* vieux numéro; *(fig)* **to be a** ~ **number** * ne plus être dans le coup. (**b**) *(overdue) taxes* arriéré. ~ **pay** rappel *m* de salaire *or (Mil)* de solde; ~ **rent** arriéré *m* de loyer.

3 *adv* (**a**) *(to the rear)* en arrière, à *or* vers l'arrière. **(stand)** ~! rangez-vous!, reculez!; **far** ~ loin derrière; **the house stands** ~ **from the road** la maison est en retrait par rapport à la route; ~ **and forth** en allant et venant; *(in mechanism)* par un mouvement de va-et-vient. (**b**) *(in return)* **to give** ~ rendre. (**c**) *(again: often re-+vb in French)* **to come** ~ revenir; **to be** ~ être de retour, être rentré; **he's not** ~ **yet** il n'est pas encore rentré *or* revenu; **he went to Paris and** ~ il a fait le voyage de Paris aller et retour; **to go there and** ~ faire l'aller et retour. (**d**) *(in time phrases)* **as far** ~ **as 1800** déjà en 1800; **a week** ~ il y a une semaine.

4 *vt* (**a**) *(support) wall, map* renforcer; *book* endosser; *picture* maroufler; *(fig) singer* accompagner; *person* soutenir; *candidate* pistonner *; *(finance) person, enterprise* financer; *bill* endosser. (**b**) *(bet on) horse* parier sur. **to** ~ **a horse each way** jouer un cheval gagnant et placé; **to** ~ **a loser** *(Sport, fig)* parier sur un perdant; *(Comm)* mal placer son argent. (**c**) *(reverse) horse, cart* faire reculer; *train* refouler. **he** ~**ed the car out** il a sorti la voiture en marche arrière; **to** ~ **the oars** culer.

5 *vi [person, animal]* reculer; *[vehicle]* faire marche arrière. **to** ~ **in/out** *etc [vehicle]* entrer/sortir *etc* en marche arrière; *[person]* entrer/sortir *etc* à reculons.

◆ **back away** *vi* reculer (*from* devant). ◆ **back down** *vi (fig)* se dégonfler *. ◆ **back off** *vi* ne pas insister; *(US: withdraw)* tirer son épingle du jeu. ◆ **back on to** *vt fus [house etc]* donner par derrière sur. ◆ **back out** *vi (of duty)* se dérober (*of* à); *(of deal)* se dégager (*of* de). ◆ **back up** **1** *vi (Aut)* faire marche arrière. **2** *vt sep (support)* soutenir; *(reverse) vehicle* faire reculer. *(Comput)* **to** ~ **up a file** sauvegarder un fichier.

◆ **backache** *n* mal *m* de *or* aux reins. ◆ **backbencher** *n* membre *m* du Parlement sans portefeuille; **the** ~**benchers** le gros des députés. ◆ **backbiting** *n* médisance *f*. ◆ **backbone** *n* colonne vertébrale; *[fish]* arête centrale; **English to the** ~**bone** anglais jusqu'à la moelle (des os); **to be the** ~**bone of an organisation** être le pivot d'une organisation; **he's got no** ~**bone** c'est un mollusque. ◆ **back-breaking** *adj work* éreintant. ◆ **backchat** * *n* impertinence *f*. ◆ **backcloth** *n* toile *f* de fond. ◆ **backcomb** *vt* crêper. ◆ **backdate** *vt cheque etc* antidater; *(increase etc)* ~**dated to** avec rappel à compter de. ◆ **backdrop** *n* = **backcloth**. ◆ **backer** *n (supporter)* partisan *m* ; *[play etc]* commanditaire *m*. ◆ **backfire** *vi (Aut)* avoir un raté (d'allumage);*[plan etc]* échouer. ◆ **back-**

gammon *n* trictrac *m*. ◆ **background** *V below*. ◆ **backhand** **1** *adj blow* en revers; *writing* penché à gauche ; **2** *n (Tennis)* revers *m*. ◆ **backhanded** *adj (fig) action* déloyal; *compliment* équivoque. ◆ **backing** *n (gen, Fin, Pol)* soutien *m*; *(Mus)* accompagnement *m*; *[picture]* marouflage *m*. ◆ **backkitchen** *n* arrière-cuisine *f*. ◆ **backlash** *n (fig)* réaction *f* (brutale). ◆ **backlog** *n [rent etc]* arriéré *m*; ~**log of work** accumulation *f* de travail (en retard). ◆ **backpacking** *n*: **to go ~packing** faire de la randonnée (sac au dos). ◆ **backpedal** *vi* pédaler en arrière; *(fig)* faire marche arrière *(fig)*. ◆ **backrest** *n* dossier *m*. ◆ **back-shop** *n* arrière-boutique *f*. ◆ **backside** *n* arrière *m*; *(*: buttocks)* postérieur * *m*. ◆ **backslapping** * *n* grandes démonstrations d'amitié. ◆ **backslide** *vi* ne pas tenir bon. ◆ **backspace** *vi (Typ)* rappeler le chariot. ◆ **backstage** *adv, adj* dans les coulisses. ◆ **backstairs** **1** *n* escalier *m* de service ; **2** *adj (fig) gossip, plot* d'antichambre. ◆ **backstroke** *n (Swim)* dos *m* crawlé. ◆ **back-to-back** *adj*: **~-to-~ houses** maisons adossées les unes aux autres. ◆ **backtrack** *vi* faire marche arrière *(fig)*. ◆ **backup** **1** *n* appui *m*; *(reserves)* réserves *fpl; [personne]* remplaçants *mpl ;* **2** *adj vehicle etc* supplémentaire; *person* remplaçant; **~up (file)** sauvegarde *f*. ◆ **backward** *V below*. ◆ **backwash** *n (lit, fig)* remous *m* (*from* provoqué par). ◆ **backwater** *n [river]* bras mort; *(fig)* petit coin tranquille; *(pej)* trou perdu *(pej)*. ◆ **backwoods** *npl* région (forestière) inexploitée; *(pej)* **in the ~woods** en plein bled *. ◆ **backyard** *n* arrière-cour *f*; *(US)* jardin *m* (de derrière).

background ['bækgraʊnd] **1** *n* (**a**) *[picture, fabric]* fond *m*; *[photograph]* arrière-plan *m*; *(Theat)* arrière *m* du décor; *(fig)* arrière-plan. **in the ~** dans le fond, à l'arrière-plan; **on a blue ~** sur fond bleu; **to keep sb in the ~** tenir qn à l'écart. (**b**) *(circumstances etc)* antécédents *mpl*; *(Soc)* milieu *m* (socioculturel); *(Pol)* climat *m* politique; *(basic knowledge)* éléments *mpl* de base; *(experience)* formation *f*. **family ~** milieu familial; **what is his ~?** *(social)* de quel milieu est-il?; *(professional)* qu'est-ce qu'il a comme formation?; *(to case etc)* **to fill in the ~** compléter la documentation; **what is the ~ to these events?** quel est le contexte de ces événements? **2** *adj music, noise* de fond. **~ reading** lectures générales (autour du sujet).

backward ['bækwəd] **1** *adj look, step* en arrière; *(retarded)* retardé; *(reluctant)* lent, peu disposé (*in doing* à faire). **2** *adv (also ~s) look* en arrière; *fall* à la renverse. **to walk ~ and forwards** aller et venir; **to walk ~** marcher à reculons; **I know the poem ~** * je sais le poème sur le bout des doigts; **I know this road ~** * je connais cette route comme ma poche. ◆ **backward-looking** *adj project* rétrograde. ◆ **backwardness** *n (Med)* retard *m* mental; *(Econ)* état *m* arriéré; *(reluctance, shyness)* manque *m* d'empressement (*in doing* à faire).

bacon ['beɪkən] *n* bacon *m*. **fat ~** lard *m*; **~ and eggs** œufs *mpl* au jambon; *(fig)* **to bring home the ~** * décrocher la timbale *. ◆ **bacon-slicer** *n* coupe-jambon *m inv*.

bacteria [bæk'tɪərɪə] *n (pl of* **bacterium***)* bactéries *fpl*. ◆ **bacterial** *adj* bactérien. ◆ **bacteriological** *adj* bactériologique. ◆ **bacteriologist** *n* bactériologiste *mf*. ◆ **bacteriology** *n* bactériologie *f*.

bad [bæd] **1** *adj, comp* **worse,** *superl* **worst** *(gen)* mauvais; *person* méchant; *child, dog* vilain; *tooth* carié; *coin, money* faux; *mistake, accident, wound* grave. **~ language** gros mots; **he's a ~ lot** * c'est un sale type *; **it was a ~ thing to do** ce n'était pas bien de faire cela; **you ~ boy!** vilain!; **it is not so ~** ce n'est pas si mal; **too ~!** *(indignant)* c'est un peu fort!; *(sympathetic)* quel dommage!; **it's too ~ of you** ce n'est vraiment pas bien de votre part; **how is he? — not so ~** comment va-t-il? — pas trop mal; **~ for the health** mauvais pour la santé; **this is ~ for you** cela ne vous vaut rien; *(Med)* **to feel ~** se sentir mal; **I feel very ~ about it** * ça m'embête *; **from ~ to worse** de mal en pis; **business is ~** les affaires vont mal; **she speaks ~ English** elle parle un mauvais anglais; **to go ~** *[food]* se gâter; *[milk]* tourner; *[bread etc]* moisir; *[teeth]* se carier; *(fig)* **~ blood** animosité *f*; **it's a ~ business** *(sad)* c'est une triste affaire ; *(unpleasant)* c'est une mauvaise histoire; **a ~ cold** un gros rhume; **to come to a ~ end** mal finir; **~ headache** violent mal *m* de tête; **her ~ leg** sa jambe malade; *(Ling)* **in a ~ sense** dans un sens péjoratif; **there is a ~ smell** ça sent mauvais; **it wouldn't be a ~ thing (to do)** ce ne serait pas une mauvaise idée (de faire); **to have a ~ time of it** *(poverty)* manger de la vache enragée; *(pain)* avoir très mal; *(trouble)* être dans une mauvaise passe; **to be in a ~ way** *(in a fix)* être dans le pétrin; *(very ill)* être très mal. **2** *n*: **the ~** le mauvais; **he's gone to the ~** * il a mal tourné. **3** *adv*: **he's got it ~** *(hobby etc)* c'est une marotte chez lui; *(person)* il l'a dans la peau *. ◆ **baddie** ‡ *n* méchant *m*. ◆ **baddish** *adj* pas fameux. ◆ **badly** *adv* **(worse, worst)** (**a**) mal; **he did ~ly** ça a mal marché (pour lui); **things are going ~ly** les choses vont mal; **he took it ~ly** il a mal pris la chose; **to be ~ly off** être dans la gêne; **he is ~ly off for space** il manque de place; (**b**) *(seriously) wound* grièvement; **~ly defeated** battu à plate couture; **the ~ly disabled** les grands invalides; (**c**) *(very much)* **to want sth ~ly** avoir grande envie de qch; **I need it ~ly** j'en ai absolument besoin; **he ~ly needs a beating** * il a sérieusement besoin d'une correction. ◆ **bad-mannered** *adj* mal élevé. ◆ **bad-mouth** * *(US) vt* débiner *. ◆ **badness** *n (wickedness)* méchanceté *f*. ◆ **bad-tempered** *adj*: **to be ~-tempered** avoir mauvais caractère; *(in bad temper)* être de mauvaise humeur.

bade [bæd, beɪd] *pret of* **bid.**

badge [bædʒ] *n (gen, also Mil)* insigne *m*; *[an order, police]* plaque *f*; *(sew-on, stick-on)* badge *m*; *(fig)* signe *m* (distinctif). **his ~ of office** l'insigne de sa fonction.

badger ['bædʒəʳ] **1** *n* blaireau *m (animal)*. **2** *vt* harceler (*sb to do* qn pour qu'il fasse; *with* de).

badminton ['bædmɪntən] *n* badminton *m*.

baffle ['bæfl] *vt person* déconcerter; *pursuers* semer *; *description* défier. ◆ **baffling** *adj* déconcertant.

bag [bæg] **1** *n* sac *m*. **~s** *(luggage)* bagages *mpl*, valises *fpl*; **~s of** * des masses de *; **paper~** sac en papier; **~s under the eyes** * poches *fpl* sous les yeux; **with ~ and baggage** avec armes et bagages; **the whole ~ of tricks** * tout le bataclan *; *(fig)* **it's in the ~** * c'est dans le sac *; *(pej)* **she's an old ~** ‡ *(ugly)* c'est un vieux tableau *; *(grumpy)* c'est une vieille teigne. **2** *vt* (**a**) *(Hunting)* tuer; *(*: get, grab)* empocher. **I ~s that!** ‡ c'est à moi! (**b**) **(~ up)** *flour, goods* mettre en sac. **3** *vi [garment]* goder. ◆ **bagful** *n* sac *m* plein. ◆ **baggy** *adj jacket* flottant; *trousers* ample, *(pej)* trop ample. ◆ **bagpipes** *npl* cornemuse *f*. ◆ **bag-snatching** *n*: **to be accused of ~-snatching** être accusé d'avoir arraché son sac à qn.

bagel ['beɪgl] *n petit pain en couronne.*

baggage ['bægɪdʒ] **1** *n* bagages *mpl*; *(Mil)* équipement *m*. **2** *adj*: *(esp US)* **~ car** fourgon *m*; **~ check** bulletin *m* de consigne; *(US)* **~ checkroom** consigne *f*; **~ elastic** pieuvre *f*; **~ handler** bagagiste *m*; **~ reclaim** livraison *f* des bagages; **~ room** consigne *f*.

Baghdad [bæg'dæd] *n* Baghdâd, Bagdad.

Bahamas [bə'hɑːməz] *npl*: **the ~** les Bahamas *fpl*.

Bahrain [bɑː'reɪn] *n* Bahreïn *m*.

bail[1] [beɪl] **1** *n (Jur)* caution *f*. **on ~** sous caution; **to free** *or* **release sb on ~** mettre qn en liberté provisoire sous caution; **to stand ~ for sb** se porter garant de qn; **to ask for ~** demander la mise en liberté sous caution. **2** *vt* **(~ out)** *(Jur)* faire mettre en liberté provisoire sous caution; *(fig)* sortir d'affaire.

bail[2] [beɪl] *vt*: **to ~ out** *boat* écoper; *water* vider.

bailiff ['beɪlɪf] *n (Jur)* huissier *m*; *[estate]* régisseur *m*.

bait [beɪt] **1** *n* appât *m*; *(fig)* appât, leurre *m*. *(lit, fig)* **to swallow the ~** mordre à l'hameçon. **2** *vt hook, trap* appâter; *(torment) animal, person* tourmenter.

baize [beɪz] *n* serge *f*; *(Snooker)* tapis *m*. **~ door** porte matelassée.

bake [beɪk] **1** *vt (Culin)* faire cuire au four; *bricks etc* cuire. **to ~ a cake** *(make)* faire un gâteau; *(actually cook)* faire cuire un gâteau; **~d potatoes** pommes *fpl* de terre au four; **~d beans** haricots blancs à la sauce tomate.

2 *vi [bread, cakes]* cuire (au four). **she ~s every Tuesday** elle fait du pain (*or* de la pâtisserie *etc*) tous les mardis.

◆ **baker** *n* boulanger *m*, -ère *f*; **~r's shop** boulangerie *f*; **~r's dozen** treize à la douzaine. ◆ **bakery** *or* ◆ **bakehouse** *n* boulangerie(-pâtisserie) *f*. ◆ **baking 1** *n* cuisson *f*; **the bread is our own baking** nous faisons le pain nous-mêmes; **2** *adj*: **baking dish** plat *m* allant au four; **baking powder** ≃ levure alsacienne; **baking sheet** *or* **tray** plaque *f* à gâteau; **baking soda** bicarbonate *m* de soude; **baking-tin** *[cakes]* moule *m* (à gâteaux); *[tarts]* tourtière *f*; **it's baking (hot)!** * il fait une de ces chaleurs!

balaclava [ˌbæləˈklɑːvə] *n*: **~ (helmet)** passe-montagne *m*.

balance ['bæləns] **1** *n* (**a**) *(equilibrium)* équilibre *m*; *(scales)* balance *f*. *(fig)* **to hang in the ~** être en balance; *(fig)* **to hold the ~** faire pencher la balance; **to keep/lose one's ~** garder/perdre son équilibre; *(lit, fig)* **off ~** mal équilibré; **to throw sb off ~** *(lit)* faire perdre l'équilibre à qn; *(fig)* couper le souffle à qn; **the ~ of power** l'équilibre des forces; **to strike a ~** trouver le juste milieu; **on ~** tout compte fait; *(Jur)* **when the ~ of his mind was disturbed** alors qu'il n'était pas responsable de ses actes; **a nice ~ of humour and pathos** un délicat dosage d'humour et de pathétique. (**b**) *(Comm, Fin)* solde *m*; **(bank ~)** solde *m* (d'un compte); *(remainder: of holidays etc)* reste *m*. **credit ~, ~ in hand** solde créditeur; **~ carried forward** solde reporté *or* à reporter; *(Econ)* **~ of trade/payments** balance commerciale/des paiements; **sterling ~s** balances sterling.

2 *adj*: **~ sheet** bilan *m*.

3 *vt* (**a**) tenir en équilibre; *(fig: counterbalance)* équilibrer, compenser. *[2 objects]* **they ~ each other** ils se font contrepoids. (**b**) *(weigh up)* balancer, peser; *arguments, solutions* comparer. **this must be ~d against that** il faut peser le pour et le contre. (**c**) *account* balancer; *budget* équilibrer. **to ~ the books** dresser le bilan; **to ~ the cash** faire la caisse.

4 *vi [acrobat etc]* se maintenir en équilibre; *[scales, accounts]* être en équilibre; *(waver)* balancer (*between* entre). **to ~ on one foot** se tenir en équilibre sur un pied.

◆ **balanced** *adj person, diet* équilibré; *views* sensé, mesuré. ◆ **balancing** *adj*: *(fig)* **to do a balancing act** jongler *(fig)*.

balcony ['bælkənɪ] *n* balcon *m*; *(Theat)* fauteuils *mpl* de deuxième balcon.

bald [bɔːld] *adj person* chauve; *tyre* lisse; *lie* flagrant, non déguisé. **~ patch** *[person]* (petite) tonsure *f*; *[animal]* place *f* dépourvue de poils; *[carpet etc]* coin *m* pelé; **a ~ statement** une simple exposition de faits. ◆ **bald-headed** *adj* chauve. ◆ **balding** *adj* qui devient chauve. ◆ **baldly** *adv* abruptement. ◆ **baldness** *n [person]* calvitie *f*; *[tyre]* état *m* lisse.

balderdash ['bɔːldədæʃ] *n* balivernes *fpl*.

bale[1] [beɪl] *n* balle *f (de coton etc)*.

bale[2] [beɪl] *vi*: **to ~ out** *(Aviat)* sauter (en parachute).

Balearic [ˌbælɪˈærɪk] *adj*: **the ~ Islands** les (îles *fpl*) Baléares *fpl*.

baleful ['beɪlf(ʊ)l] *adj* sinistre. **to give sb/sth a ~ look** regarder qn/qch d'un œil torve. ◆ **balefully** *adv* sinistrement; *look* d'un œil torve.

balk [bɔːk] **1** *vt person, plan* contrecarrer. **2** *vi [person]* regimber (*at* contre); *[horse]* se dérober (*at* devant).

Balkan ['bɔːlkən] *n*: **the ~s** les Balkans *mpl*.

ball[1] [bɔːl] *n* (**a**) *(gen)* balle *f*; *(inflated: Ftbl etc)* ballon *m*; *(Billiards)* bille *f*, boule *f*; *(Croquet)* boule. **as round as a ~** rond comme une boule; **cat curled up in a ~** chat pelotonné (en boule); *(fig)* **to keep the ~ rolling** soutenir la conversation (*or* l'intérêt *etc*); **to start the ~ rolling** * faire démarrer une affaire (*or* une conversation *etc*); *(fig)* **the ~ is in your court** (c'est) à vous de jouer; **to be on the ~** * *(competent)* être à la hauteur; *(alert)* ouvrir l'œil et le bon *; **~ of fire** globe *m* de feu; *(fig)* **he's a real ~ of fire** * il est débordant d'activité; **~ of the foot** plante *f* du pied; **~ and chain** boulet *m*. (**b**) *[wool, string]* pelote *f*, peloton *m*. (**c**) *[meat, fish]* boulette *f*; *[potato]* croquette *f*. ◆ **ball bearings** *npl* roulement *m* à billes. ◆ **ballcock** *n* robinet *m* à flotteur. ◆ **ball game** *n (US)* partie *f* de baseball; **it's a whole new ~ game** * c'est une toute autre histoire. ◆ **ballpark** *n (US)* stade *m* de baseball; **~park figure** * chiffre approximatif. ◆ **ballpoint (pen)** *n* stylo *m* à bille.

ball[2] [bɔːl] *n (dance)* bal *m*. *(fig)* **to have a ~** * faire la bringue *. ◆ **ballroom** *n* salle *f* de bal; **~room dancing** danse *f* (de salon).

ballad ['bæləd] *n (Mus)* romance *f*; *(Literat)* ballade *f*.

ballast ['bæləst] *n (Naut etc)* lest *m*.

ballerina [ˌbæləˈriːnə] *n* ballerine *f*.

ballet ['bæleɪ] **1** *n* ballet *m*. **2** *adj*: **~ dancer** danseur *m*, -euse *f* de ballet.

ballistic [bəˈlɪstɪk] *adj* balistique. **~ missile** engin *m* balistique. ◆ **ballistics** *nsg* balistique *f*.

balloon [bəˈluːn] **1** *n* ballon *m*. **to go up in a ~** monter en ballon; *(fig)* **the ~ went up** * l'affaire a éclaté; **weather ~** ballon-sonde *m*. **2** *adj*: **~ glass** verre *m* ballon; **~ tyre** pneu *m* ballon. **3** *vi*: **to go ~ing** faire une *or* des ascension(s) en ballon. ◆ **balloonist** *n* aéronaute *mf*.

ballot ['bælət] **1** *n (Pol etc)* scrutin *m*; *(drawing lots)* tirage *m* au sort. **first ~** premier tour de scrutin. **2** *vi (Pol etc)* voter au scrutin secret; *(draw lots)* tirer au sort. **3** *vt members* faire voter. **4** *adj*: **~ box** urne *f* (électorale); **~ paper** bulletin *m* de vote.

ballyhoo * [ˌbælɪˈhuː] *n* balivernes *fpl*.

balm [bɑːm] *n* baume *m*. ◆ **balmy** *adj (mild)* doux; *(*: silly)* timbré *.

baloney * [bəˈləʊnɪ] *n* balivernes *fpl*.

balsa ['bɔːlsə] *n*: **~ (wood)** balsa *m*.

Baltic ['bɔːltɪk] *adj port* de la Baltique; *state* balte. **the ~ (Sea)** la (mer) Baltique.

balustrade [ˌbæləsˈtreɪd] *n* balustrade *f*.

bamboo [bæmˈbuː] *n* bambou *m*. **~ shoots** pousses *fpl* de bambou.

bamboozle * [bæmˈbuːzl] *vt (deceive)* avoir *, embobiner *; *(perplex)* déboussoler *.

ban [bæn] **1** *n* interdit *m*. **2** *vt (gen)* interdire (*sth* qch, *sb from doing* à qn de faire); *person* exclure (*from* de).

banal [bəˈnɑːl] *adj* banal. ◆ **banality** *n* banalité *f*.

banana [bəˈnɑːnə] **1** *n* banane *f*; *(tree)* bananier *m*. **2** *adj*: ~ **boat** bananier *m (cargo)*; ~ **republic** république *f* bananière; ~ **skin** peau *f* de banane.

band¹ [bænd] *n (gen)* bande *f*; *[cigar]* bague *f*; *[hat]* ruban *m*; *[gramophone record]* plage *f*. **elastic** ~ élastique *m*.

band² [bænd] *n* (**a**) *(group)* bande *f*, troupe *f*. (**b**) *(Mus)* orchestre *m*; *(Mil)* fanfare *f*. ◆ **band together** *vi* former une bande. ◆ **bandsman** *n* musicien *m*. ◆ **bandstand** *n* kiosque *m* (à musique). ◆ **bandwagon** *n*: *(fig)* **to climb on the ~wagon** prendre le train en marche *.

bandage [ˈbændɪdʒ] **1** *n (strip)* bande *f*; *(dressing)* bandage *m*; *(of gauze)* pansement *m*; *[blindfolding]* bandeau *m*. **2** *vt* (~ **up**) *limb* bander; *wound* mettre un pansement *or* un bandage sur.

Band-Aid [ˈbændeɪd] *n* ® pansement *m* adhésif.

bandan(n)a [bænˈdænə] *n* foulard *m* (à pois).

bandit [ˈbændɪt] *n* bandit *m*. ◆ **banditry** *n* banditisme *m*.

bandolier [ˌbændəˈlɪəʳ] *n* cartouchière *f*.

bandy¹ [ˈbændɪ] *vt ball, reproaches* se renvoyer; *blows, jokes* échanger. **to ~ words** discuter. ◆ **bandy about** *vt sep story, report* faire circuler. **to ~ sb's name about** parler de qn.

bandy² [ˈbændɪ] *adj leg* arqué; *(also* **~-legged**) *person* bancal; *horse* arqué.

bane [beɪn] *n*: **he's the ~ of my life** * il m'empoisonne la vie *. ◆ **baneful** *adj* funeste.

bang¹ [bæŋ] **1** *n (noise) [gun, explosives]* détonation *f*, fracas *m*; *(Aviat)* bang *m* (supersonique); *[door]* claquement *m*; *(blow)* coup *m* (violent). **2** *excl* pan! **3** *adv* (*) **to go ~** éclater; **~ in the middle** en plein milieu; **his answer was ~ on** sa réponse est tombée pile; **~ on time** à l'heure pile; **~ went a £10 note!** et pan, voilà un billet de 10 livres fichu! * **4** *vt* frapper violemment. **to ~ one's fist on the table** frapper la table du poing; **to ~ one's head against sth** se cogner la tête contre qch; *(fig)* **you're ~ing your head against a brick wall** tu perds ton temps!; **to ~ the door** (faire) claquer la porte. **5** *vi [door]* claquer, battre; *[fireworks]* éclater; *[gun]* détoner. **to ~ on the door** donner de grands coups dans la porte; **to ~ into sth** heurter qch; **to ~ about** *or* **around** faire du bruit.
◆ **bang down** *vt sep* poser brusquement; *lid* rabattre violemment. *(Telec)* **to ~ down the receiver** raccrocher brutalement. ◆ **bang together** *vt sep objects* cogner l'un(e) contre l'autre. **I could have ~ed their heads together!** * j'en aurais pris un pour taper sur l'autre!

bang² [bæŋ] *n [hair] (also US* **bangs**) frange *f* (droite).

banger * [ˈbæŋəʳ] *n* (**a**) *(sausage)* saucisse *f*. **~s and mash** saucisses à la purée. (**b**) *(old car)* (vieux) tacot * *m*.

Bangkok [bæŋˈkɒk] *n* Bangkok.

Bangladesh [ˈbæŋgləˈdeʃ] *n* Bangladesh *m*.

bangle [ˈbæŋgl] *n* bracelet *m (rigid)* jonc *m*.

bang-up ‡ [bæŋʌp] *adj (US)* formidable, impec *.

banish [ˈbænɪʃ] *vt person* exiler (*from* de; *to* en, à), bannir (*from* de); *cares* bannir. ◆ **banishment** *n* bannissement *m*, exil *m*.

banister [ˈbænɪstəʳ] *n* = **bannister.**

banjo [ˈbændʒəʊ] *n* banjo *m*.

bank¹ [bæŋk] **1** *n* (**a**) *(mound) [earth, snow]* talus *m*; *(embankment)* remblai *m*; *(on road, racetrack)* bord relevé; *[sand, sea, river]* banc *m*. (**b**) *(edge) [river, lake]* bord *m*, rive *f*; *[canal]* bord. *[Paris]* **the Left B~** la Rive gauche. **2** *vt* (~ **up**) *road* relever *(dans un virage)*; *earth* amonceler; *fire* couvrir. **3** *vi (Aviat)* virer (sur l'aile).

bank² [bæŋk] *n [oars, switches]* rangée *f*.

bank³ [bæŋk] **1** *n (Fin, Betting, Med)* banque *f*. **the B~ of France** la Banque de France; **it is as safe as the B~ of England** ça ne court aucun risque; **to break the ~** faire sauter la banque. **2** *adj*: **~ account** compte *m* en banque; **~ balance** état *m* de compte (bancaire); **~ book** livret *m* de banque; **~ card** carte *f* d'identité bancaire; **~ charges** frais *mpl* de banque; **~ clerk** employé(e) *m(f)* de banque; **~ holiday** jour férié; **~note** billet *m* de banque; **~ rate** taux *m* d'escompte; **~ statement** relevé *m* de compte. **3** *vt* déposer en banque. **4** *vi*: **to ~ with Lloyds** avoir un compte à la Lloyds; **where do you ~?** quelle est votre banque?
◆ **bank (up)on** *vt fus (fig)* compter sur.
◆ **banker** *n* banquier *m*; **~er's card** carte *f* d'identité bancaire; **~er's order** ordre *m* de virement bancaire *(pour paiements réguliers)*. ◆ **banking** **1** *n*: **to study ~ing** faire des études bancaires; **he's in ~ing** il est banquier; **2** *adj*: **~ing hours** heures *fpl* d'ouverture des banques; **~ing house** banque *f*. ◆ **bankrupt** **1** *n* failli(e) *m(f)* ; **2** *adj (Jur)* failli; (**fig: penniless)* fauché *; **to go ~rupt** faire faillite; **to be ~rupt** être en faillite ; **3** *vt* mettre en faillite; (*: *fig)* ruiner. ◆ **bankruptcy** **1** *n* faillite *f* ; **2** *adj*: **B~ruptcy Court** ≃ tribunal *m* de commerce; **~ruptcy proceedings** procédure *f* de faillite.

banner [ˈbænəʳ] *n* bannière *f*. *(Press)* **~ headline** manchette *f*.

bannister [ˈbænɪstəʳ] *n* rampe *f* (d'escalier). **to slide down the ~(s)** descendre sur la rampe.

banns [bænz] *npl* bans *mpl (de mariage)*. **to call the ~** publier les bans.

banquet [ˈbæŋkwɪt] *n* banquet *m*; *(fig: lavish meal)* festin *m*. ◆ **banquet(ing) hall** *n* salle *f* des banquets.

banshee [ˈbænˈʃiː] *n* fée *f (aux cris funestes)*.

bantam [ˈbæntəm] *n* coq *m* nain, poule *f* naine.

banter [ˈbæntəʳ] **1** *n* badinage *m*. **2** *vi* badiner. ◆ **bantering** *adj* badin.

baptize [bæpˈtaɪz] *vt* baptiser. ◆ **baptism** *n* baptême *m*. ◆ **baptismal** *adj* baptismal. ◆ **baptist** *n, adj (Rel)* **B~** baptiste *(mf)*.

bar¹ [bɑːʳ] **1** *n* (**a**) *(slab) [metal]* barre *f*; *[wood]* planche *f*; *[gold]* lingot *m*; *[chocolate]* tablette *f*. **~ of soap** savonnette *f*. (**b**) *(rod) [window, cage]* barreau *m*; *[grate, door, also Sport]* barre *f*. **behind ~s** sous les verrous; **to be a ~ to progress** faire obstacle au progrès. (**c**) *(Jur)* barreau *m*. **to be called** *or (US)* **admitted to the ~** s'inscrire au barreau; **the prisoner at the ~** l'accusé(e) *m(f)*. (**d**) *(in hotel etc)* bar *m*; *(at open-air shows etc)* buvette *f*; *(counter)* comptoir *m*. **to have a drink at the ~** prendre un verre au comptoir; *(Comm)* **stocking ~** rayon *m* des bas. (**e**) *(Mus)* mesure *f*. **the opening ~s** les premières mesures.
2 *vt* (**a**) *road* barrer; *door* mettre la barre à. **to ~ sb's way** barrer le passage à qn, couper la route à qn; *(lit, fig)* **to ~ the door against sb** barrer la porte à qn; **five-~red gate** barrière *f* à cinq barreaux. (**b**) *(exclude) person* exclure (*from* de); *action, thing* défendre.
◆ **barbell** *n (US)* barre *f* à disques. ◆ **bar code** *n* code *m* barres. ◆ **barmaid** *n* serveuse *f (de bar)*. ◆ **barman** *or* ◆ **bartender** *n* barman *m*.

bar² [bɑːʳ] *prep* sauf. **~ none** sans exception.

barb [bɑːb] *n [fish hook]* barbillon *m*; *[arrow]* barbelure *f*; *[feather]* barbe *f*; *(fig) [wit etc]* trait *m*. ◆ **barbed** *adj arrow* barbelé; *words, wit* acéré ; **~(ed) wire** fil *m* de fer barbelé; **~(ed)-wire fence** haie *f* barbelée.

Barbados [bɑːˈbeɪdɒs] *n* Barbade *f*.

barbarian [bɑːˈbɛərɪən] *adj, n* barbare *(mf)*. ◆ **barbaric** *adj* barbare, de barbare. ◆ **barbarism** *n (Ling)* barbarisme *m*. ◆ **barbarity** *n* barbarie *f*. ◆ **barbarous** *adj* barbare. ◆ **barbarously** *adv* cruellement.

barbecue [ˈbɑːbɪkjuː] **1** *n* barbecue *m*. **2** *vt steak* griller au charbon de bois; *animal* rôtir tout entier. **3** *adj*: ~ **sauce** sauce *f* barbecue.

barber [ˈbɑːbəʳ] *n* coiffeur *m (pour hommes)*. ~**'s pole** enseigne *f* de coiffeur.

barbiturate [bɑːˈbɪtjʊrɪt] *n* barbiturique *m*. ~ **poisoning** dose *f* excessive de barbituriques.

Barcelona [ˌbɑːsɪˈləʊnə] *n* Barcelone.

bard[1] [bɑːd] *n* barde *m*; *(poet)* poète *m*.

bard[2] [bɑːd] *vt (Culin)* barder.

bare [bɛəʳ] **1** *adj (gen)* nu; *hill* pelé; *countryside, tree, style* dépouillé; *(Elec) wire* dénudé; *cupboard, room* vide; *wall* nu. **with his ~ hands** à mains nues; ~ **patch** *[grass]* place pelée; *[carpet]* coin pelé; **with his head ~** nu-tête *inv*; **to sleep on ~ boards** coucher sur la dure; **to lay ~** mettre à nu; ~ **statement of facts** simple énoncé *m* des faits; **the ~ necessities/minimum** le strict nécessaire/minimum; **to earn a ~ living** gagner tout juste de quoi vivre; ~ **majority** faible majorité *f*. **2** *vt* mettre à nu. **to ~ one's teeth** montrer les dents *(at* à); **to ~ one's head** se découvrir (la tête). ◆ **bareback** *adv* à cru. ◆ **barefaced** *adj* éhonté. ◆ **barefoot(ed)** *adv* nu-pieds; *adj* aux pieds nus. ◆ **bareheaded** *adv* nu-tête *inv*; *adj* nu-tête *inv*; *woman* en cheveux. ◆ **barelegged** *adj* aux jambes nues. ◆ **barely** *adv* à peine. ◆ **bareness** *n [person]* nudité *f*; *[room]* dénuement *m*.

bargain [ˈbɑːgɪn] **1** *n* (**a**) *(transaction)* marché *m*, affaire *f*. **to make a ~** conclure un marché *(with* avec); **it's a ~! *** c'est convenu!; **a bad ~** une mauvaise affaire; *(fig)* **into the ~** par-dessus le marché. (**b**) *(good buy)* occasion *f*. **it's a (real) ~!** c'est une véritable occasion! **2** *adj offer, price* avantageux. ~ **basement** coin *m* des (bonnes) affaires; ~ **hunter** chercheur *m*, -euse *f* d'occasions; ~ **sale** soldes *mpl*. **3** *vi*: **to ~ with sb** *(haggle)* marchander avec qn; *(negotiate)* négocier avec qn; *(fig)* **I did not ~ for that** je ne m'attendais pas à cela; **I got more than I ~ed for** j'ai eu du fil à retordre. ◆ **bargaining** **1** *n* marchandage *m* ; **2** *adj*: **that gives us more ~ing power** ceci nous donne plus d'atouts dans les négociations.

barge [bɑːdʒ] **1** *n (on river, canal)* chaland *m*; *(large)* péniche *f*; *(with sail)* barge *f*; *[admiral]* vedette *f*; *(ceremonial)* barque *f*. **2** *adj*: **I wouldn't touch it with a ~ pole *** *(revolting)* je n'y toucherais pas avec des pincettes; *(risky)* je ne m'y frotterais pas. **3** *vi*: **to ~ into a room** faire irruption dans une pièce, entrer sans façons dans une pièce. ◆ **barge in** *vi (enter)* faire irruption; *(interrupt)* interrompre; *(interfere)* se mêler de ce qui ne vous regarde pas.
◆ **bargee** *or* ◆ **bargeman** *n* batelier *m*, marinier *m*.

baritone [ˈbærɪtəʊn] **1** *n* baryton *m*. **2** *adj* de baryton.

barium [ˈbɛərɪəm] *n*: ~ **meal** sulfate *m* de baryum.

bark[1] [bɑːk] **1** *n [tree]* écorce *f*. **to strip the ~ off a tree** écorcer un arbre. **2** *vt*: **to ~ one's shins** s'écorcher les jambes.

bark[2] [bɑːk] **1** *n [dog]* aboiement *m*; *[fox]* glapissement *m*. **the ~ of a gun** un coup de canon; **his ~ is worse than his bite** il fait plus de bruit que de mal. **2** *vi [dog]* aboyer *(at* après); *[fox]* glapir; *[gun]* aboyer, tonner; *(speak sharply)* crier. *(fig)* **to ~ up the wrong tree** faire fausse route.
◆ **bark out** *vt sep order* glapir.
◆ **barker** *n [fairground]* bonimenteur *m*. ◆ **barking** **1** *n* aboiements *mpl* ; **2** *adj*: ~**ing cough** toux *f* sèche.

barley [ˈbɑːlɪ] **1** *n* orge *f*. **2** *adj*: ~ **sugar** sucre *m* d'orge; ~ **water** orgeat *m*.

bar mitzvah [bɑːˈmɪtsvə] *n* bar-mitzva *f*.

barmy * [ˈbɑːmɪ] *adj* timbré *.

barn [bɑːn] *n* grange *f*; *(US) [horses]* écurie *f*; *[cattle]* étable *f*; *(huge house)* énorme bâtisse *f*. ~ **dance** soirée *f* de danses paysannes. ◆ **barnyard** *n* basse-cour *f*; ~**yard fowls** volaille *f*.

barnacle [ˈbɑːnəkl] *n* anatife *m*.

barney * [ˈbɑːnɪ] *n* prise *f* de bec.

barometer [bəˈrɒmɪtəʳ] *n* baromètre *m*. ◆ **barometric** *adj* barométrique.

baron [ˈbærən] *n* baron *m*; *(fig)* magnat *m*. ◆ **baroness** *n* baronne *f*. ◆ **baronet** *n* baronnet *m*. ◆ **baronial hall** *n* demeure *f* seigneuriale.

baroque [bəˈrɒk] *adj, n* baroque *(m)*.

barrack[1] [ˈbærək] **1** *n*: ~**s** caserne *f*; **in ~s** à la caserne. **2** *adj*: ~ **square** cour *f* de caserne. ◆ **barrack room** **1** *n* chambrée *f* ; **2** *adj language* de caserne; *(fig)* **to be a ~-room lawyer** se promener toujours avec le code sous le bras.

barrack[2] [ˈbærək] *vt* chahuter.

barracuda [ˌbærəˈkjuːdə] *n* barracuda *m*.

barrage [ˈbærɑːʒ] **1** *n* (**a**) *[river]* barrage *m*. (**b**) *(Mil)* tir *m* de barrage; *[questions]* pluie *f*; *[words]* flot *m*. **2** *adj*: ~ **balloon** ballon *m* de barrage.

barrel [ˈbærəl] **1** *n* (**a**) *[wine, beer]* tonneau *m*; *[cider]* futaille *f*; *[herring]* caque *f*; *[oil, tar]* baril *m*. (**b**) *[firearm, key]* canon *m*; *[fountain pen]* corps *m*. **to give sb both ~s *** lâcher ses deux coups sur qn *. **2** *adj*: ~ **organ** orgue *m* de Barbarie.

barren [ˈbær(ə)n] *adj* stérile; *(fig)* aride. ◆ **barrenness** *n* stérilité *f*.

barrette [bæˈret] *n (US)* barrette *f*.

barricade [ˌbærɪˈkeɪd] **1** *n* barricade *f*. **2** *vt* barricader.

barrier [ˈbærɪəʳ] **1** *n* barrière *f*; *(in station)* portillon *m* (d'accès); *(fig)* obstacle *m (to* à). **2** *adj*: ~ **cream** crème *f* isolante.

barring [ˈbɑːrɪŋ] *prep* excepté, sauf.

barrister [ˈbærɪstəʳ] *n* avocat *m*.

barrow[1] [ˈbærəʊ] *n (wheel~)* brouette *f*; *(coster's)* voiture *f* des quatre saisons; *(Rail: luggage ~)* diable *m*; *(Min)* wagonnet *m*. ◆ **barrow-boy** *n* marchand *m* des quatre saisons.

barrow[2] [ˈbærəʊ] *n (Archeol)* tumulus *m*.

barter [ˈbɑːtəʳ] **1** *n* échange *m*, troc *m*. **2** *vt* échanger, troquer *(for* contre). ◆ **barter away** *vt sep rights* vendre *(for* pour).

basalt [ˈbæsɔːlt] *n* basalte *m*.

base[1] [beɪs] **1** *n (gen; also Mil)* base *f*; *[tree]* pied *m*; *(of paint: ~ coat)* première couche. **2** *adj camp, rate* de base. **3** *vt opinion* baser *(on* sur); *troops* baser *(at* à). **post ~d on London** poste centré sur Londres; **London- ~d** dont le centre d'opérations est Londres; **I am ~d on Glasgow** j'opère à partir de Glasgow.
◆ **baseball** *n* base-ball *m*. ◆ **baseless** *adj* sans fondement.

base[2] [beɪs] *adj* (**a**) *(vile: gen)* bas; *behaviour, motive* ignoble; *metal* vil. (**b**) *(US)* = **bass**[1]. ◆ **basely** *adv* bassement; ignoblement. ◆ **baseness** *n* bassesse *f*.

basement [ˈbeɪsmənt] *n* sous-sol *m*.

bash [bæʃ] **1** *n* coup *m*. **the bumper has had a ~** le pare-choc est cabossé; **I'll have a ~ (at it) *** je vais essayer un coup *. **2** *vt* frapper, cogner. **to ~ sb on the head** assommer qn.
◆ **bash in** *vt sep door* enfoncer; *car* cabosser; *cover* défoncer. **to ~ sb's head in** défoncer le crâne à

qn *. ◆ **bash up** *vt sep car* bousiller *; *person* tabasser *.

bashful ['bæʃf(ʊ)'l] *adj* timide. ◆ **bashfully** *adv* timidement. ◆ **bashfulness** *n* timidité *f*.

basic ['beɪsɪk] **1** *adj (fundamental) principle, problem, French* fondamental; *salary, vocabulary* de base; *(elementary) rules, precautions* élémentaire. **2** *n*: **the ~s** l'essentiel *m*. ◆ **basically** *adv* au fond, essentiellement.

BASIC ['beɪsɪk] *n (Comput)* BASIC *m*.

basil ['bæzl] *n (Bot)* basilic *m*.

basilica [bə'zɪlɪkə] *n* basilique *f*.

basin ['beɪsn] *n (gen)* cuvette *f*, bassine *f*; *(for food)* saladier *m*; *(smaller)* bol *m*; *(wash~)* cuvette, *(plumbed in)* lavabo *m*; *[fountain]* vasque *f*; *[river]* bassin *m*.

basis, *pl* **bases** ['beɪsɪs, 'beɪsi:z] *n* base *f*. **on that ~** dans ces conditions; **on the ~ of what you've told me** par suite de ce que vous m'avez dit.

bask [bɑ:sk] *vi (in sun)* se dorer (*in* à). **to ~ in sb's favour** jouir de la faveur de qn.

basket ['bɑ:skɪt] **1** *n (gen)* corbeille *f*; *(one-handled; also for bicycle etc)* panier *m*. **2** *adj*: **~ chair** chaise *f* en osier. ◆ **basketball** *n* basket(-ball) *m*. ◆ **basketwork** *n* vannerie *f*.

Basque [bæsk] **1** *n* Basque *mf*; *(Ling)* basque *m*. **2** *adj* basque. **~ Country** Pays *m* basque.

bass[1] [beɪs] *(Mus)* **1** *(part, singer) n* basse *f*; *(double bass)* contrebasse *f*. **2** *adj* bas; *clef* de fa. **~ baritone** baryton-basse *m*; **~ drum** grosse caisse.

bass[2] [bæs] *n (freshwater)* perche *f*; *(sea)* bar *m*.

basset ['bæsɪt] *n*: **~ (hound)** basset *m*.

bassoon [bə'su:n] *n* basson *m*.

bastard ['bɑ:stəd] **1** *n* bâtard(e) *m(f)*; *(‡ pej)* salaud ‡ *m*. **poor ~ ‡** pauvre type *. **2** *adj child* bâtard; *language* abâtardi.

baste [beɪst] *vt (Culin)* arroser; *(Sewing)* bâtir.

bat[1] [bæt] *n (Zool)* chauve-souris *f*. *(fig)* **to have ~s in the belfry** * avoir une araignée au plafond *.

bat[2] [bæt] **1** *n (Baseball, Cricket)* batte *f*; *(Table Tennis)* raquette *f*. *(fig)* **off one's own ~** de sa propre initiative. **2** *vi* manier la batte.

bat[3] [bæt] *vt*: **he didn't ~ an eyelid** il n'a pas sourcillé; **without ~ting an eyelid** sans sourciller.

batch [bætʃ] *n [loaves]* fournée *f*; *[people]* groupe *m*; *[letters]* paquet *m*; *[goods]* lot *m*. *(Comput)* **~ processing** traitement *m* par lots.

bated ['beɪtəd] *adj*: **with ~ breath** en retenant son souffle.

bath [bɑ:θ] **1** *n, pl* **~s** [bɑ:ðz] *(gen)* bain *m*; *(~tub)* baignoire *f*. **to have a ~** prendre un bain; **to give sb a ~** donner un bain à qn; **room with ~** chambre *f* avec salle de bains; **~s** *(washing)* (établissement *m* de) bains-douches *mpl*; *(swimming)* piscine *f*. **2** *vt* donner un bain à. **3** *vi* prendre un bain. **4** *adj towel, sheet, salts* de bain. ◆ **bathchair** *n* fauteuil roulant. ◆ **bathmat** *n* tapis *m* de bain. ◆ **bathrobe** *n* peignoir *m* de bain. ◆ **bathroom** **1** *n* salle *f* de bains ; **2** *adj*: **~room cabinet** armoire *f* de toilette; **~room scales** pèse-personne *m*. ◆ **bathtub** *n* baignoire *f*. ◆ **bathwater** *n* eau *f* du bain.

bathe [beɪð] **1** *vt* baigner; *wound* laver. **~d in sweat** en nage; **~d in light** baigné de lumière. **2** *vi* se baigner *(dans la mer etc)*; *(US)* prendre un bain *(dans une baignoire)*. **3** *n*: **to have a ~** se baigner. ◆ **bather** *n* baigneur *m*, -euse *f*. ◆ **bathing** **1** *n* baignade *f* ; **2** *adj*: **bathing beauty** belle baigneuse; **bathing cap** bonnet *m* de bain; **bathing costume** *or* **suit** *or* **trunks** maillot *m* (de bain).

baton ['bætən] *n (Mil, Mus, French Police)* bâton *m*; *(Brit Police)* matraque *f*; *[relay race]* témoin *m*. **~ charge** charge *f* à la matraque.

bats ‡ [bæts] *adj* toqué *, timbré *.

batsman ['bætsmən] *n (Cricket)* batteur *m*.

battalion [bə'tælɪən] *n (Mil, fig)* bataillon *m*.

batten[1] ['bætn] *n (Carpentry)* latte *f*.

batten[2] ['bætn] *vi* s'engraisser (*on sb* aux dépens de qn; *on sth* de qch).

batter[1] ['bætə'] **1** *n (Culin) (for frying)* pâte *f* à frire; *(for pancakes)* pâte à crêpes. **fried fish in ~** poisson frit (enrobé de pâte à frire). **2** *vt* battre; *baby* martyriser. **3** *vi*: **to ~ at the door** cogner à la porte à coups redoublés. ◆ **batter down, batter in** *vt sep* défoncer. ◆ **battered** *adj hat, car* cabossé; *face* meurtri; *furniture, house* délabré; **~ed babies** enfants martyrs. ◆ **battering** *adj*: **~ing ram** bélier *m*.

batter[2] ['bætə'] *n (US Sport)* batteur *m*.

battery ['bætərɪ] **1** *n* (**a**) *(guns)* batterie *f*. (**b**) *[torch, radio]* pile *f*; *[vehicle]* accumulateurs *mpl*. (**c**) *(row of similar objects)* batterie *f*; *[questions etc]* pluie *f*. (**d**) *(Agr)* batterie *f*. **2** *adj radio* à piles; *farming* intensif; **~ hen** poule *f* en batterie; *(Elec)* **~ charger** chargeur *m*.

battle ['bætl] **1** *n* bataille *f*, combat *m*; *(fig)* lutte *f*, combat (*for sth* pour obtenir qch; *to do* pour faire). **killed in ~** tué à l'ennemi; *(fig)* **to fight sb's ~s** se battre à la place de qn; **we are fighting the same ~** nous nous battons pour la même cause; **~ royal** bataille en règle; **that's half the ~** * c'est déjà pas mal *. **2** *adj cry* de guerre; *zone* de combat. **~ dress** tenue *f* de campagne. **3** *vi* se battre, lutter (*for sth* pour obtenir qch; *to do* pour faire). ◆ **battle-axe** * *n (woman)* virago *f*. ◆ **battlefield** *or* ◆ **battleground** *n* champ *m* de bataille. ◆ **battlements** *npl* remparts *mpl*. ◆ **battle-scarred** *adj* marqué par les combats. ◆ **battleship** *n* cuirassé *m*.

bauble ['bɔ:bl] *n* babiole *f*.

baulk [bɔ:lk] = **balk.**

bauxite ['bɔ:ksaɪt] *n* bauxite *f*.

Bavaria [bə'vɛərɪə] *n* Bavière *f*. ◆ **Bavarian** **1** *n* Bavarois(e) *m(f)*; **2** *adj* bavarois.

bawdy ['bɔ:dɪ] *adj* paillard.

bawl [bɔ:l] *vti* brailler (*at* contre). ◆ **bawl out ‡** *vt sep (scold)* engueuler ‡.

bay[1] [beɪ] *n (Geog: gen)* baie *f*. **the B~ of Biscay** le golfe de Gascogne.

bay[2] [beɪ] *n (~ tree)* laurier(-sauce) *m*. **~ leaf** feuille *f* de laurier.

bay[3] [beɪ] *n (for parking)* lieu *m* de stationnement (autorisé). **~ window** fenêtre *f* en saillie.

bay[4] [beɪ] **1** *n*: **to be at ~** être aux abois; **to keep sb/sth at ~** tenir qn/qch en échec. **2** *vi [dog]* aboyer (*at* à, après).

bay[5] [beɪ] *adj horse* bai.

bayonet ['beɪənɪt] **1** *n* baïonnette *f*. **2** *vt* passer à la baïonnette. **3** *adj charge* à la baïonnette.

bayou ['baɪju:] *n (US)* bayou *m*, marécages *mpl*.

bazaar [bə'zɑ:'] *n (market; shop)* bazar *m*; *(sale of work)* vente *f* de charité.

bazooka [bə'zu:kə] *n* bazooka *m*.

be [bi:] *pret* **was, were,** *ptp* **been** **1** *copulative vb* (**a**) être. **he is a soldier** il est soldat; **she is an Englishwoman** c'est une Anglaise, elle est anglaise; **who is that? — it's me!** qui est-ce? — c'est moi!; **~ good** sois sage. (**b**) *(health)* aller. **how are you?** comment allez-vous?; **I am better** je vais mieux; **she is well** elle va bien. (**c**) *(age)* **how old is he?** quel âge a-t-il?; **he is 3** il a 3 ans; **I would take her to ~ 40** je lui donnerais 40 ans. (**d**) *(cost)* coûter. **how much is it?** combien cela coûte-t-il?, ça fait combien? *; **it is 10 francs** cela coûte 10F. (**e**) *(Math)* faire. **2 and 2 are 4** 2 et 2 font 4.

2 *aux vb* (**a**) *(+ prp = continuous tense)* **what are you doing? — I am reading a book** qu'est-ce que vous faites? — je lis *or* je suis en train de lire un livre; **what have you been doing this week?** qu'avez-vous fait cette semaine?; **I have been waiting for you for an hour** je t'attends depuis une heure. (**b**) *(+ ptp = passive)* être. **he was killed** il a été tué, on l'a tué; **he is to ~ pitied** il est à plaindre; **the car is to ~ sold** la voiture doit être vendue; **peaches are sold by the kilo** les pêches se vendent au kilo. (**c**) *(in tag questions, short answers)* **he's always late, isn't he? — yes, he is** il est toujours en retard, n'est-ce pas? — oui, toujours; **it's all done, is it?** tout est fait, alors? (**d**) *(+ to + infin)* **he is to do it** il doit le faire; **they are to ~ married** ils vont se marier; **she was never to return** elle ne devait jamais revenir; **the telegram was to warn us** le télégramme était pour nous avertir; **I am not to speak to him** je ne dois pas lui parler, on m'a défendu de lui parler; **I wasn't to tell you** je ne devais pas vous le dire; **it is not to ~ opened** il est interdit de l'ouvrir. (**e**) *(modal 'were')* **if we were in London** si nous étions à Londres; **if I were to tell him** et à supposer (même) que je lui dise; **if I were you** à votre place, si j'étais vous.

3 *vi* (**a**) être, exister. **to ~ or not to ~** être ou ne pas être; **the best artist that ever was** le meilleur peintre qui ait jamais existé; **that may ~** cela se peut; **~ that as it may** quoi qu'il en soit; **how is it that...?** comment se fait-il que + *indic or subj*; **let me ~** laissez-moi tranquille; **the bride-/mother-to-be** la future mariée/maman. (**b**) **there is, there are** il y a; **there was once a castle here** il y avait autrefois un château ici; **there will ~ dancing** on dansera; **there were three of us** nous étions trois; **there is no knowing...** il est impossible de savoir...; **let there ~ light** que la lumière soit. (**c**) *(presenting, pointing out)* **here is, here are** voici; **there is, there are** voilà; **there he was, sitting at the table** il était là, assis à la table. (**d**) *(come, go: esp in perfect tense)* aller, venir, être. **I have been to see my aunt** je suis allé voir ma tante; **I have already been to Paris** j'ai déjà été *or* je suis déjà allé à Paris; **he has been and gone** il est venu et reparti.

4 *impers vb* (**a**) *(time)* être. **it is morning** c'est le matin; **it is 6 o'clock** il est 6 heures; **it is the 14th June today** nous sommes *or* c'est aujourd'hui le 14 juin; **it is a long time since I saw you** il y a longtemps que je ne vous ai vu; **it is you who did it** c'est vous qui l'avez fait; **were it not that** si ce n'était que; **were it not for my friendship for him** sans mon amitié pour lui; **had it not been for him we...** sans lui, nous...; **as it were** pour ainsi dire. (**b**) *(weather etc)* faire. **it is fine/cold** il fait beau/froid; **it is windy** il fait du vent.

◆ **be-all** *n*: **the ~-all and end-all** le but suprême (*of* de). ◆ **being** *n* (**a**) existence *f*; **to come into ~ing** *[idea]* prendre naissance; *[society]* être créé; **to bring into ~ing** faire naître; **then in ~ing** qui existait alors; (**b**) être *m*; **human ~ings** êtres humains; **all my ~ing revolts at** tout mon être se révolte à.

beach [biːtʃ] **1** *n [sea]* plage *f*; *(shore)* grève *f*; *[lake]* rivage *m*. **2** *vt* échouer. **3** *adj*: **~ ball** ballon *m* de plage; **~ buggy** buggy *m*; **~ umbrella** parasol *m*. ◆ **beachcomber** *n* ramasseur *m* d'épaves. ◆ **beachhead** *n* tête *f* de pont. ◆ **beachwear** *n* tenue *f* de plage.

beacon ['biːk(ə)n] *n (gen, fig)* phare *m*; *(Aviat, Naut)* balise *f*; *(on hills)* feu *m* (d'alarme). **Belisha ~** lampadaire *m (indiquant un passage clouté)*.

bead [biːd] *n (gen)* perle *f*; *[rosary]* grain *m*; *[dew]* perle; *[sweat]* goutte *f*. **(string of) ~s** collier *m*. ◆ **beady-eyed** *adj (glittering)* aux yeux en boutons de bottines; *(pej)* aux yeux de fouine.

beak [biːk] *n* bec *m*; *(⁑: nose)* nez *m* crochu.

beaker ['biːkəʳ] *n* gobelet *m*; *(Chem)* vase *m* à bec.

beam [biːm] **1** *n* (**a**) *(Archit)* poutre *f*. (**b**) *(Naut)* **on the port ~** à bâbord. (**c**) *[light, sunlight]* rayon *m*, trait *m*; *[headlight, searchlight, etc]* faisceau *m* (lumineux); *(Phys)* faisceau; *(Aviat, Naut)* chenal *m* de radio-guidage. *(fig)* **to be on (the) ~** * être sur la bonne voie; *(fig)* **to be off (the) ~** * dérailler *. (**d**) *(smile)* sourire *m* épanoui. **2** *vi [sun]* rayonner. **she ~ed** son visage s'est épanoui en un large sourire; **she ~ed at me** elle a levé vers moi un visage épanoui; **face ~ing with joy** visage rayonnant de joie. **3** *vt (Rad, Telec) message* transmettre par émission dirigée; *programme* diffuser (*to* à l'intention de). ◆ **beam-ends** *npl*: **on one's ~-ends** * dans la gêne.

bean [biːn] *n* haricot *m*; *(green ~)* haricot vert; *(broad ~)* fève *f*; *[coffee]* grain *m*. **full of ~s** * en pleine forme; **he hasn't a ~** ⁑ il n'a pas le sou. ◆ **beanbag** *n (for throwing)* balle lestée; *(chair)* sacco *m*. ◆ **beanpole** *n (lit, fig)* perche *f*. ◆ **beanshoots** *or* ◆ **beansprouts** *npl* germes *mpl* de soja.

bear¹ [bɛəʳ] *pret* **bore,** *ptp* **borne** **1** *vt* (**a**) *(carry) burden, message, signature, name* porter. **to ~ away** emporter; **to ~ back** rapporter; **to ~ no relation to** être sans rapport avec; **he bore himself like a soldier** *(carried himself)* il avait une allure militaire *or* de soldat; *(conducted himself)* il se comportait en soldat; **it was borne in on me that...** il m'est apparu de plus en plus évident que...; **the love he bore her** l'amour qu'il lui portait; **to ~ sb ill-will** *or* **a grudge** garder rancune à qn. (**b**) *(support) weight* supporter; *comparison* soutenir; *responsibility* assumer; *(endure)* supporter, tolérer. **I cannot ~ that man** je ne peux pas souffrir cet homme; **she cannot ~ being laughed at** elle ne supporte pas qu'on se moque *(subj)* d'elle. (**c**) *(produce) child* donner naissance à; *crop* produire; *(Fin) interest* rapporter. *(lit, fig)* **to ~ fruit** porter des fruits.

2 *vi* (**a**) **to ~ right** prendre à droite; **~ towards the church** allez vers l'église; **~ north at the windmill** prenez la direction nord au moulin. (**b**) *[ice etc]* porter, supporter. (**c**) *[fruit tree etc]* donner, produire. (**d**) **to bring to ~** *pressure* exercer (*on sth* sur qch); *gun* pointer (*on* sur); *energy* consacrer (*on* à); **to bring one's mind to ~ on sth** porter son attention sur qch.

◆ **bear down** *vi [ship]* venir (*on* sur); *(fig) [person]* foncer (*on* sur); *(press)* appuyer fermement, peser (*on* sur). ◆ **bear out** *vt sep suspicions* confirmer; *statement* corroborer. **to ~ sb out** corroborer ce que qn dit. ◆ **bear up** *vi* ne pas se laisser abattre, tenir le coup *. **~ up!** * courage!; **how are you? — ~ing up!** * comment ça va? — on fait aller *. ◆ **bear with** *vt fus* supporter patiemment. **~ with me** je vous demande un peu de patience.

◆ **bearable** *adj* supportable, tolérable. ◆ **bearer** *n [letter, coffin, title, cheque]* porteur *m*, -euse *f*; *[passport]* titulaire *mf*; *(servant)* serviteur *m*. ◆ **bearing** *n* (**a**) *(posture)* maintien *m*; **noble ~ing** maintien noble; (**b**) *(relation)* rapport *m*; **to have a ~ing on** avoir un rapport avec; (**c**) **to take a compass ~ing** prendre un relèvement au compas ; **to take a ship's ~ings** faire le point; *(fig)* **to get one's ~ings** se repérer; *(fig)* **to lose one's ~ings** être désorienté; (**d**) *(Tech)* palier *m*, coussinet *m*.

bear² [bɛəʳ] **1** *n* ours(e) *m(f)*; *(St Ex)* baissier *m*. **like a ~ with a sore head** * d'une humeur massacrante; *(Astron)* **the Great B~** la Grande Ourse. **2** *adj*: **~ cub** ourson *m*; *(fig)* **~ garden** pétaudière *f*.

beard [bɪəd] **1** *n* barbe *f*. **to have a ~** porter la barbe; **a man with a ~** un (homme) barbu. **2** *vt* braver. *(fig)* **to ~ the lion in his den** aller braver le lion dans sa tanière. ◆ **bearded** *adj* barbu; **a ~ed man** un barbu; **the ~ed lady** la femme à barbe. ◆ **beardless** *adj* imberbe.

bearish ['bɛərɪʃ] *adj (St Ex)* ~ **tendency** tendance *f* baissière *or* à la baisse.

beast [bi:st] *n* bête *f*, animal *m*; *(cruel person)* brute *f*; *(*: disagreeable)* chameau * *m*. **the king of the ~s** le roi des animaux; ~ **of burden** bête de somme; *(Agr)* **~s** bétail *m*; *[greedy person]* **to make a ~ of o.s.** se goinfrer. ◆ **beastly** *adj person, conduct* brutal; *language* obscène; *food, sight* dégoûtant; *(*: less strong) weather, person* infect *; *child, trick, business* sale *(before n)*.

beat [bi:t] *(vb: pret* **beat,** *ptp* **beaten***)* **1** *n* (**a**) *[heart, drums]* battement *m*; *(Mus)* temps *m*; *[conductor]* battement; *(Jazz)* rythme *m*. *(Mus)* **strong** ~ temps fort. (**b**) *[policeman, sentry]* ronde *f*. **on the** ~ faisant sa *(etc)* ronde.
2 *adj* (**a**) *(*: **dead-~***)* éreinté, claqué *. (**b**) **the ~ * generation** la génération beatnik.
3 *vt* (**a**) *(strike)* battre. **to ~ sb with a stick** donner des coups de bâton à qn; **to ~ a drum** battre du tambour; **to ~ a retreat** battre en retraite; **~ it!** ‡ fiche le camp! *; **to ~ one's breast** se frapper la poitrine; **to ~ time** battre la mesure; **off the ~en track** hors des sentiers battus. (**b**) *(defeat)* battre, vaincre. **to be ~en** être vaincu; **to ~ sb to the top of a hill** arriver au sommet d'une colline avant qn; *(fig)* **to ~ sb to it** * devancer qn; **to ~ sb hollow** battre qn à plates coutures; **coffee ~s tea any day** * le café vaut tout le thé du monde; **that ~s me, that's got me ~en** *or* ~ * ça me dépasse complètement; **it ~s me how...** ça me dépasse que * + *subj*; **that takes some ~ing! *, can you ~ it!** * faut le faire! *
4 *vi (gen)* battre. **to ~ at the door** cogner à la porte; **he doesn't ~ about the bush** il n'y va pas par quatre chemins; *(Naut)* **to ~ (to windward)** louvoyer au plus près.
◆ **beat back** *vt, sep* repousser. ◆ **beat down 1** *vi [sun]* taper *. **the rain was ~ing down** il pleuvait à torrents. **2** *vt sep prices* faire baisser; *person* faire baisser ses prix à. **I ~ him down to £2** je l'ai fait descendre à 2 livres. ◆ **beat in** *vt sep door* défoncer. **to ~ sb's brains in** défoncer le crâne à qn *. ◆ **beat off** *vt sep* repousser. ◆ **beat out** *vt sep fire* étouffer; *metal* marteler; *rhythm* marquer. ◆ **beat up** *vt sep eggs, cream* battre; *(assault) person* passer à tabac; *(find) recruits, customers* racoler.
◆ **beater** *n (carpet ~)* tapette *f*; *(egg whisk)* fouet *m*; *(rotary)* batteur *m*. ◆ **beating** *n* (**a**) *(whipping)* correction *f*; **to give/get a ~ing** flanquer/recevoir une correction; (**b**) *[drums, wings, heart]* battement *m*; (**c**) *(defeat)* défaite *f*; **the car takes a ~ing on that road** * la voiture en voit de dures * sur cette route. ◆ **beatnik** *n, adj* beatnik *(mf)*. ◆ **beat-up** * *adj* bousillé *.

beatify [bi:'ætɪfaɪ] *vt* béatifier. ◆ **beatific** [,bi:ətɪ fɪk] *adj* béatifique; *smile* béat.

beauty ['bju:tɪ] **1** *n* beauté *f*. ~ **is only skin-deep** la beauté n'est pas tout; ~ **is in the eye of the beholder** il n'y a pas de laides amours; **the ~ of it is that** *... ce qui est formidable, c'est que *...; **she is no ~** * ce n'est pas une beauté; **B~ and the Beast** la Belle et la Bête; **isn't this car a ~!** * quelle merveille que cette voiture!
2 *adj cream, preparations, salon* de beauté. ~ **competition** *or* **contest** concours *m* de beauté; ~ **queen** reine *f* de beauté; **you need your ~ sleep** tu as besoin de bien dormir; ~ **specialist** esthéticien(ne) *m(f)*; ~ **spot** *(on skin)* grain *m* de beauté; *(in countryside)* site *m* superbe; *(in tourist guide etc)* site *m* touristique; ~ **treatment** soins *mpl* de beauté.
◆ **beauteous** *adj (liter)* = **beautiful.** ◆ **beautician** *n* esthéticien(ne) *m(f)*. ◆ **beautiful** *adj (gen)* beau *(f* belle*)*; *weather, dinner* magnifique. ◆ **beautifully** *adv (very well) work, sew* à la perfection; *fit, adapt* parfaitement; *(pleasantly) hot, calm* merveilleusement. ◆ **beautify** *vt* embellir.

beaver ['bi:vəʳ] *n* castor *m*. **to work like a ~** travailler d'arrache-pied.

becalmed [bɪ'kɑ:md] *adj* encalminé.

became [bɪ'keɪm] *pret of* **become.**

because [bɪ'kɒz] *conj (gen)* parce que. **the more surprising** ~ d'autant plus surprenant que; ~ **he lied, he was punished** il a été puni pour avoir menti; ~ **of** à cause de, en raison de.

beck [bek] *n*: **to be at sb's ~ and call** être (constamment) à la disposition de qn; **to have sb at one's ~ and call** faire marcher qn au doigt et à l'œil.

beckon ['bek(ə)n] *vti* faire signe (*to sb* à qn; *to do* de faire). **he ~ed me in/over** *etc* il m'a fait signe d'entrer/d'approcher *etc*.

become [bɪ'kʌm] *pret* **became,** *ptp* **become 1** *vi* devenir. **to ~ famous** devenir célèbre; **to ~ a doctor** devenir *or* se faire médecin; **to ~ thin** maigrir; **to ~ accustomed to** s'accoutumer à. **2** *impers vb*: **what has ~ of him?** qu'est-il devenu? **3** *vt*: **it does not ~ him** cela ne lui sied pas. ◆ **becoming** *adj behaviour* bienséant; *clothes* seyant.

bed [bed] **1** *n* (**a**) lit *m*. **room with 2 ~s** chambre *f* à 2 lits; **to go to ~** se coucher; **to go to ~ with sb** * coucher avec qn *; **to get out of ~** se lever; *(fig)* **to get out of ~ on the wrong side** se lever du pied gauche; **to put to ~** *person* coucher; *newspaper* boucler; **to make the ~** faire le lit; **to be in ~** être couché; *(through illness)* garder le lit; **to give sb a ~ for the night** loger qn pour la nuit; **before ~** avant de se coucher; ~ **of sickness** lit de douleur; **'~ and breakfast'** 'chambres'; **to book in for ~ and breakfast** prendre une chambre avec le petit déjeuner; **we stayed at ~-and-breakfast places** nous avons pris une chambre chez des particuliers; ~ **and board** le vivre et le couvert; **it's not a ~ of roses** ce n'est pas une partie de plaisir; ~ **of nails** lit à clous. (**b**) *(layer) [coal, ore]* gisement *m*; *[clay]* couche *f*; *[coral, oysters]* banc *m*; *[mortar]* bain *m*. (**c**) *(bottom) [sea]* fond *m*; *[river]* lit *m*. (**d**) *[vegetables]* planche *f*; *(square)* carré *m*; *[flowers]* parterre *m*; *(strip)* plate-bande *f*. **2** *adj*: ~ **bath** grande toilette *f* (d'un malade); ~ **jacket** liseuse *f*; ~ **linen** draps *mpl* de lit (et taies *fpl* d'oreillers).
◆ **bed down** *vi* (aller) se coucher; *(spend nights)* coucher. ◆ **bed out** *vt sep plants* repiquer.
◆ **bed-bug** *n* punaise *f*. ◆ **bedclothes** *npl* couvertures *fpl* et draps *mpl* (de lit). ◆ **bedoover** *n* couvre-lit *m*. ◆ **bedding** *n* literie *f*; *(Mil etc)* matériel *m* de couchage; *[animals]* litière *f*. ◆ **bedfellow** *n*: *(fig)* **they are strange ~fellows** ils forment une drôle de paire. ◆ **bedhead** *n* tête *f* de lit. ◆ **bedpan** *n* bassin *m* (hygiénique). ◆ **bedpost** *n* colonne *f* de lit. ◆ **bedridden** *adj* alité, cloué au lit. ◆ **bedrock** *n (Geol)* soubassement *m*; *(fig)* base *f*. ◆ **bedroom 1** *n* chambre *f* (à coucher) ; **2** *adj*: *(Theat)* **~room farce** comédie *f* de boulevard; **~room slipper** pantoufle *f* ; **~room suite** chambre *f* à coucher *(mobilier)*. ◆ **bedsettee** *n* divan-lit *m*. ◆ **bedside 1** *n*: **at his ~side** à son chevet ; **2** *adj book, lamp* de chevet; **~side rug** descente *f* de lit; *[doctor]* **he has a good ~side manner** il sait parler à ses malades. ◆ **bedsitter** *or* ◆ **bed-sitting room** *or* ◆ **bedsit** * *n* chambre meublée. ◆ **bedsocks** *npl* chaussettes *fpl* (de lit). ◆ **bedsore** *n* escarre *f*. ◆ **bedspread** *n* dessus-de-lit *m inv*. ◆ **bedstead** *n* bois *m* de lit. ◆ **bedtime 1** *n*: **it is ~time** il est l'heure d'aller se coucher; **his ~time is 7 o'clock** il se couche à 7 heures; **it's past your ~time** tu devrais être déjà couché ; **2** *adj*: **to tell a child a ~time story** raconter une histoire à un enfant avant qu'il ne s'endorme. ◆ **bedwetting** *n* incontinence *f* nocturne.

bedeck [bɪ'dek] *vt* parer (*with* de).

bedevil [bɪ'devl] *vt* embrouiller. **~led by** *person* accablé par; *plan* qui a souffert de.

bedlam ['bedləm] *n* ramdam ‡ *m*, chahut * *m*.

bedraggled [bɪ'drægld] *adj clothes, person* débraillé; *hair* embroussaillé; *(wet)* trempé.

bee [bi:] *n* (**a**) abeille *f*. **to have a ~ in one's bonnet** * avoir une idée fixe (*about* en ce qui concerne); **like ~s round a honeypot** comme des mouches sur un pot de confiture. (**b**) **to have a sewing ~** se réunir pour coudre. ◆ **beehive** *n* ruche *f*. ◆ **beekeeper** *n* apiculteur *m*, -trice *f*. ◆ **beeline** *n*: **to make a ~line for** filer droit sur. ◆ **beeswax** *n* cire *f* d'abeille.

beech [bi:tʃ] *n* hêtre *m*. ◆ **beechnut** *n* faine *f*.

beef [bi:f] **1** *n (Culin)* bœuf *m*. **roast ~** rosbif *m*. **2** *adj*: **~ cattle** bœufs *mpl* de boucherie; **~ olive** paupiette *f* de bœuf; **~ tea** bouillon *m* (de viande). **3** *vi* (‡: *complain*) râler * (*about* contre). ◆ **beefburger** *n* hamburger *m*. ◆ **beefeater** *n* hallebardier *m (de la Tour de Londres)*. ◆ **beefsteak** *n* bifteck *m*, steak *m*. ◆ **beefy** * *adj* costaud * *f inv*.

been [bi:n] *ptp of* **be**.

beep [bi:p] **1** *n* bip *m*. **2** *vi* faire bip.

beer [bɪəʳ] **1** *n* bière *f*. **life's not all ~ and skittles** tout n'est pas qu'une partie de rigolade * en ce monde. **2** *adj*: **~ bottle** canette *f*; **~ can** boîte *f* de bière; **~ glass** bock *m*, chope *f*.

beet [bi:t] **1** *n* betterave *f*. **2** *adj sugar* de betterave. ◆ **beetroot** *n* betterave *f* (potagère).

beetle ['bi:tl] **1** *n (gen)* scarabée *m; (Zool)* coléoptère *m*. **there's a huge ~ in the bath!** il y a un énorme cafard dans la baignoire! **2** *vi* (‡) **to ~ in/out** *etc* entrer/sortir *etc* en vitesse. ◆ **beetle-browed** *adj* aux sourcils broussailleux.

befall [bɪ'fɔ:l] *pret* **befell,** *ptp* **befallen** **1** *vi* arriver, advenir. **2** *vt* arriver à.

befit [bɪ'fɪt] *vt (impers)* convenir à. **it ill ~s him** il lui sied mal (*to do* de faire). ◆ **befitting** *adj* convenable.

before [bɪ'fɔ:ʳ] **1** *prep* (**a**) *(time, order, rank)* avant. **~ Christ** avant Jésus-Christ; **the year ~ last** il y a deux ans; **not ~ next week** pas avant la semaine prochaine; **~ then** avant, auparavant; **~ now** déjà; **~ long** avant peu, d'ici peu; **~ doing** avant de faire. (**b**) *(place, position)* devant. **he stood ~ me** il était là devant moi; **the question ~ us** la question qui nous occupe; **the task ~ him** la tâche qu'il a devant lui; **to appear ~ a judge** comparaître devant un juge. (**c**) *(rather than)* plutôt que. **to put death ~ dishonour** préférer la mort au déshonneur; **he would die ~ betraying...** il mourrait plutôt que de trahir...
2 *adv* (**a**) *(time)* avant, auparavant. **the day ~** la veille; **the evening ~** la veille au soir; **the week ~** la semaine d'avant *or* précédente; **I have read it ~** je l'ai déjà lu; **it has never happened ~** cela n'est jamais arrivé jusqu'ici; **it had never happened ~** cela n'était jamais arrivé jusqu'alors; **long ~** longtemps auparavant; **to continue as ~** faire comme par le passé. (**b**) *(place)* en avant, devant. (**c**) *(order)* avant. **that chapter and the one ~** ce chapitre et celui d'avant.
3 *conj* (**a**) *(time)* avant de + *infin*, avant que + ne + *subj*. **I did it ~ going out** je l'ai fait avant de sortir; **go and see him ~ he goes** allez le voir avant son départ *or* avant qu'il ne parte; **it will be 6 weeks ~ the boat returns** le bateau ne reviendra pas avant 6 semaines; **~ I forget...** avant que je n'oublie *(subj)*... (**b**) *(rather than)* plutôt que de + *infin*. **he will die ~ he surrenders** il mourra plutôt que de se rendre.
◆ **beforehand** *adv* à l'avance.

befriend [bɪ'frend] *vt* donner son amitié à.

befuddled [bɪ'fʌdld] *adj (confused)* embrouillé; *(tipsy)* éméché.

beg [beg] **1** *vt* (**a**) *money, food* mendier; *favour* solliciter. **to ~ sb's pardon** demander pardon à qn; **I ~ your pardon** *(apologizing)* je vous demande pardon; *(not having heard)* pardon?; **I ~ to state that** je me permets de faire remarquer que; **I ~ to differ** permettez-moi d'être d'un autre avis; **I ~ to inform you that** j'ai l'honneur de vous faire savoir que; **to ~ leave to do** solliciter l'autorisation de faire; **to ~ sb to do** supplier qn de faire; **I ~ you!** je vous en supplie! (**b**) **this ~s the question** c'est présumer la question résolue. **2** *vi* mendier. **to ~ for money** mendier; **to ~ for food** mendier de la nourriture; **to ~ for help** demander de l'aide; *[dog]* **to sit up and ~** faire le beau; **it's going ~ging** * personne n'en veut.
◆ **beg off** * *vi* se faire excuser (*from* de).
◆ **beggar** **1** *n* mendiant(e) *m(f)*; **~gars can't be choosers** nécessité fait loi; **~gar's opera** opéra *m* de quat' sous; **poor ~gar!** * pauvre diable! *; **a lucky ~gar** un veinard *; **a queer little ~gar** * un drôle de petit bonhomme; **2** *vt (fig: ruin)* ruiner; **to ~gar description** défier toute description. ◆ **beggarly** *adj amount, meal* piètre *(before n)*; *wage* dérisoire. ◆ **beggar-my-neighbour** *n* bataille *f (Cartes)*.

began [bɪ'gæn] *pret of* **begin**.

beget [bɪ'get] *pret* **begot,** *ptp* **begotten** *vt* engendrer.

begin [bɪ'gɪn] *pret* **began,** *ptp* **begun** **1** *vt* commencer (*to do, doing* à faire, de faire), se mettre (*to do, doing* à faire); *work, song, bottle, book* commencer; *conversation* engager; *quarrel, rumour* faire naître; *reform, war, series of events* déclencher; *fashion* lancer; *custom, policy* inaugurer. **to ~ a journey** partir en voyage; **he began the day with a glass of milk** il a bu un verre de lait pour bien commencer la journée; **to ~ life as** débuter dans la vie comme; **that doesn't even ~ to compare with...** c'est loin d'être comparable à...; **it soon began to rain** il n'a pas tardé à pleuvoir; **to ~ again** recommencer (*to do* à faire).
2 *vi* commencer (*with* par; *by doing* par faire), s'y mettre; *[river]* prendre sa source; *[road]* partir (*at* de); *[political party, movement, custom]* commencer, naître. **to ~ at the beginning** commencer par le commencement; **it's ~ning rather well** cela s'annonce plutôt bien; **just where the hair ~s** à la naissance des cheveux; **before October ~s** avant le début d'octobre; **to ~ again** recommencer; *[classes]* reprendre; **~ning from Monday** à partir de lundi; **he began in the sales department** il a débuté dans le service des ventes; **he began as a Marxist** il a commencé par être marxiste; **he began with the intention of writing a thesis** au début son intention était d'écrire une thèse; **to ~ with, there were only 3 of them** d'abord, ils n'étaient que 3; **~ on a new page** prenez une nouvelle page; **to ~ on sth** commencer qch; **since the world began** depuis que le monde est monde.
◆ **beginner** *n* débutant(e) *m(f)*; **it's just ~ner's luck** aux innocents les mains pleines. ◆ **beginning** *n* commencement *m*, début *m*; **to make a ~ning** commencer, débuter; **the ~ning of the academic year** la rentrée (universitaire *or* scolaire); **in the ~ning** au commencement, au début; **to start again at** *or* **from the ~ning** recommencer au commencement; **the ~ning of negotiations** l'ouverture *f* des négociations; **the ~ning of the end** le commencement de la fin; **the ~nings of science** les rudiments *mpl* de la science; **the shooting was the ~ning of the rebellion** la fusillade a été à l'origine de la révolte; **fascism had its ~nings...** le fascisme prit naissance...

begone [bɪ'gɒn] *excl* partez!

begonia [bɪ'gəʊnɪə] *n* bégonia *m*.

begot(ten) [bɪ'gɒt(n)] *pret (ptp) of* **beget.**

begrudge [bɪ'grʌdʒ] *vt* = **grudge.**

beguile [bɪ'gaɪl] *vt (deceive)* tromper; *(entertain)* distraire; *(charm)* captiver. ◆ **beguiling** *adj* séduisant.

begun [bɪ'gʌn] *ptp of* **begin.**

behalf [bɪ'hɑ:f] *n*: **on ~ of sb** *attend, accept* de la part de qn, pour qn; *plead* en faveur de qn; **he was worried on my ~** il s'inquiétait pour moi.

behave [bɪ'heɪv] *vi* (**~ o.s.**) *(conduct o.s.)* se conduire; *(conduct o.s. well)* bien se tenir; *[child]* être sage; *[machine]* marcher. **to ~ well towards sb** bien agir envers qn; **~ yourself!** tiens-toi bien! ◆ **behaviour,** *(US)* **behavior** *n* conduite *f*, comportement *m* (*to, towards* envers); *[machine]* fonctionnement *m*; **to be on one's best behaviour** se conduire de son mieux; *[child]* se montrer d'une sagesse exemplaire. ◆ **behavio(u)ral** *adj sciences, studies* behavioriste; *pattern* de comportement; **behavioural problems** troubles *mpl* du comportement. ◆ **behavio(u)rism** *n* behaviorisme *m*. ◆ **behavio(u)rist** *adj, n* behavioriste *(mf)*.

behead [bɪ'hed] *vt* décapiter.

beheld [bɪ'held] *pret, ptp of* **behold.**

behest [bɪ'hest] *n*: **at the ~ of** sur l'ordre de.

behind [bɪ'haɪnd] **1** *adv come* derrière; *stay, look* en arrière. **to leave ~** laisser derrière soi; **to be ~ with sth** être en retard dans qch. **2** *prep* derrière. **from ~ the door** de derrière la porte; **walk close ~ me** suivez-moi de près; *(fig)* **to put sth ~ one** oublier qch, refuser de penser à qch; *(fig)* **what is ~ this?** qu'y a-t-il là-dessous?; **he is ~ the other pupils** il est en retard sur les autres élèves; **~ time** en retard; **~ the times** en retard sur son temps. **3** *n (*: buttocks)* derrière *m*, postérieur * *m*. ◆ **behindhand** *adv, adj* en retard (*with sth* dans qch).

behold [bɪ'həʊld] *pret, ptp* **beheld** *vt* voir, apercevoir. **behold!** voici!

beholden [bɪ'həʊld(ə)n] *adj* redevable (*to* à, *for* de).

behove [bɪ'həʊv], *(US)* **behoove** [bɪ'hu:v] *impers vt* incomber (*sb to do* à qn de faire).

beige [beɪʒ] *adj, n* beige *(m)*.

Beijing ['beɪ'dʒɪŋ] *n* Pékin.

Beirut [beɪ'ru:t] *n* Beyrouth.

bejewelled, *(US)* **bejeweled** [bɪdʒu:əld] *adj* couvert de bijoux.

belabour, *(US)* **belabor** [bɪ'leɪbə^r] *vt* rouer de coups.

belated [bɪleɪtɪd] *adj* tardif. ◆ **belatedly** *adv* tardivement.

belch [beltʃ] **1** *vi* faire un renvoi. **2** *vt* (**~ forth**) *smoke etc* vomir. **3** *n* renvoi *m*.

beleaguered [bɪ'li:gəd] *adj city* assiégé; *army* cerné.

Belfast ['bɛlfɑ:st] *n* Belfast.

belfry ['belfrɪ] *n* beffroi *m*.

Belgium ['beldʒəm] *n* Belgique *f*. ◆ **Belgian** **1** *n* Belge *mf*; **2** *adj* belge.

Belgrade [bɛl'gre(ɪ)d] *n* Belgrade.

belie [bɪ'laɪ] *vt* démentir.

belief [bɪ'li:f] *n* (**a**) croyance *f* (*in* en, à). **~ in God/in ghosts** croyance en Dieu/aux revenants; **beyond ~** *(adj)* incroyable; **wealthy beyond ~** incroyablement riche. (**b**) conviction *f*. **in the ~ that** persuadé que; **it is my ~ that** je suis convaincu que; **to the best of my ~** autant que je sache.

believe [bɪ'li:v] **1** *vt statement, evidence, person* croire (*that* que). **I don't ~ a word of it** je n'en crois pas un mot; **don't you ~ it!** ne va pas croire ça!; **he could hardly ~ his eyes** il en croyait à peine ses yeux; **if he is to be ~d** à l'en croire; **I ~ I'm right** je crois avoir raison; **I don't ~ he will come** je ne crois pas qu'il viendra *or* qu'il vienne; **he is ~d to be ill** on le croit malade; **I ~ so/not** je crois que oui/non. **2** *vi* croire. **to ~ in** *God* croire en; *ghosts, promises, antibiotics* croire à; *friend* avoir confiance en; *method* être partisan de; **I don't ~ in borrowing** je ne suis pas d'avis qu'il faille faire des emprunts. ◆ **believable** *adj* croyable. ◆ **believer** *n (Rel)* croyant(e) *m(f)*; *(gen)* **he is a great ~er in** il est très partisan de.

belittle [bɪ'lɪtl] *vt* déprécier.

Belize [bɛ'li:z] *n* Bélize *m*.

bell [bel] *n [church, school, cows]* cloche *f*; *(hand~)* clochette *f*; *[toys, cats etc]* grelot *m*; *[goats, sheep]* clochette; *[door]* sonnette *f*; *(electric, also telephone)* sonnerie *f*; *[cycle, typewriter]* timbre *m*. **there's the ~!** on sonne!; *(Naut)* **eight ~s** huit coups piqués. ◆ **bell-bottomed** *adj*: **~-bottomed trousers** pantalon *m* de marine. ◆ **bellboy** *or* ◆ **bellhop** *n* groom *m*. ◆ **bell-push** *n* bouton *m* de sonnette. ◆ **bell-ringer** *n* sonneur *m*. ◆ **bell-tent** *n* tente *f* conique. ◆ **bell-tower** *n* clocher *m*.

belladonna [ˌbelə'dɒnə] *n* belladonne *f*.

belle [bel] *n* beauté *f*. **the ~ of the ball** la reine du bal.

bellicose ['belɪkəʊs] *adj* belliqueux.

belligerent [bɪ'lɪdʒər(ə)nt] *adj, n* belligérant(e) *m(f)*. ◆ **belligerence** *or* ◆ **belligerency** *n* belligérance *f*.

bellow ['beləʊ] **1** *vi [animals]* mugir; *[person]* brailler, beugler * (*with* de). **2** *vt* (**~ out**) *song, order* brailler, beugler *. **3** *n* mugissement *m*; beuglement * *m*.

bellows ['beləʊz] *npl [forge, organ]* soufflerie *f*; *[fire]* soufflet *m*.

belly ['belɪ] **1** *n* ventre *m*. **2** *vi* (**~ out**) se gonfler. **3** *adj*: **~ button** nombril *m*; **~ dancer** danseuse orientale; **~ laugh** gros rire gras. ◆ **bellyache** **1** *n* mal *m* de *or* au ventre ; **2** *vi* (⁂: *complain)* ronchonner *. ◆ **bellyflop** *n (Swimming)* plat-ventre *m*. ◆ **bellyful** *n*: **he had had a ~ful** ⁂ il en avait plein le dos *. ◆ **belly-landing** * *n (Aviat)* atterrissage *m* sur le ventre.

belong [bɪ'lɒŋ] *vi* appartenir (*to* à). **this book ~s to me** ce livre m'appartient, ce livre est à moi; **the lid ~s to this box** le couvercle va avec cette boîte; **to ~ to a society** faire partie *or* être membre d'une société; **to ~ to a town** *[native]* être originaire d'une ville; *[inhabitant]* habiter une ville; **to feel that one doesn't ~** se sentir étranger; **to ~ together** aller ensemble; **put it back where it ~s** remets-le à sa place. ◆ **belongings** *npl* affaires *fpl*, possessions *fpl*; **personal ~ings** objets personnels.

beloved [bɪ'lʌvɪd] *adj, n* bien-aimé(e) *m(f)*.

below [bɪ'ləʊ] **1** *prep (under)* sous; *(lower than)* au-dessous de. **~ the bed** sous le lit; **on the bed and ~ it** sur le lit et en dessous; **skirt well ~ the knee** jupe bien au-dessous du genou; **~ average** au-dessous de la moyenne; **the Thames ~ Oxford** la Tamise en aval d'Oxford. **2** *adv* en bas, en dessous, plus bas; *(Naut)* en bas. **the tenants ~** les locataires du dessous; **they live 2 floors ~** ils habitent 2 étages en dessous; **voices from ~** des voix venant d'en bas; **the road ~** la route en contrebas; *(on earth)* **here ~** ici-bas; *(in hell)* **down ~** en enfer; *[documents]* **see ~** voir ci-dessous.

belt [belt] **1** *n* (**a**) *(gen)* ceinture *f*; *(Tech)* courroie *f*; *(corset)* gaine *f*. **(shoulder) ~** baudrier *m*; **that was below the ~** c'était un coup bas; **he's got 10 years' experience under his ~** il a 10 ans d'expérience à son acquis; *(fig)* **to tighten one's ~** se serrer la ceinture; *(Judo)* **to be a Black B~** être ceinture noire. (**b**) *(Geog)* zone *f*; *(Agr)* région *f*. **industrial ~** zone industrielle; **the cotton ~** la

région de culture du coton. **2** *vt (thrash)* administrer une correction à. **she ~ed him one in the eye** ‡ elle lui a flanqué un gnon ‡ dans l'œil. **3** *vi (‡: rush)* **to ~ in/out/across** *etc* entrer/sortir/ traverser *etc* à toutes jambes.
◆ **belt out** * *vt sep song* chanter à pleins poumons. ◆ **belt up** *vi* (**a**) *(seat belts)* attacher sa ceinture. (**b**) *(‡: quiet)* la boucler ‡. ~ **up!** boucle-la! ‡
◆ **beltway** *n (US)* périphérique *m.*

bemoan [bɪ'məʊn] *vt* pleurer, déplorer.

bemuse [bɪ'mju:z] *vt* stupéfier, hébéter.

bench [ben(t)ʃ] **1** *n (gen, Parl)* banc *m*; *(in tiers)* gradin *m*; *(padded)* banquette *f*; *[workshop, factory]* établi *m*. **to be on the B~** *(permanent office)* être juge (*or* magistrat); *(when in court)* siéger au tribunal. **2** *adj*: ~ **mark** *(Surv)* repère *m* de nivellement; *(fig: reference point)* point *m* de référence, repère; *(Comput)* jeu *m* d'essai.

bend [bend] *(vb: pret, ptp* **bent***)* **1** *n [river, tube, pipe]* coude *m*; *[arm, knee]* pli *m*; *[road]* coude, virage *m*. **~s for 8 km** virages sur 8 km; *[car]* **to take a ~** prendre un virage; *(fig)* **round the ~** ‡ cinglé *; *(Med)* **the ~s** * la maladie des caissons.
2 *vt* (**a**) *back, body, head, branch, rail* courber; *leg, arm* plier; *bow* bander; *(fig *) rule* faire une entorse à. **to ~ at right angles** couder; **to ~ out of shape** fausser; **to go down on ~ed knee** se mettre à genoux. (**b**) **to be bent on doing** vouloir absolument faire.
3 *vi [person]* se courber; *[branch, instrument etc]* être courbé; *[river, road]* faire un coude. **to ~ backward/forward** se pencher en arrière/en avant.
◆ **bend back** *vt sep* replier, recourber. ◆ **bend down** *vi* se courber. ◆ **bend over 1** *vi* se pencher. *(fig)* **to ~ over backwards to help sb** * se mettre en quatre pour aider qn. **2** *vt sep* replier.

beneath [bɪ'ni:θ] **1** *prep (under)* sous; *(lower than)* au-dessous de. ~ **the table** sous la table; **town ~ the castle** ville (située) au-dessous du château; **it is ~ my notice** cela ne mérite pas mon attention; **it is ~ her to interfere** elle ne daignerait pas intervenir. **2** *adv*: **the flat ~** l'appartement au-dessous *or* du dessous.

benediction [ˌbenɪ'dɪkʃ(ə)n] *n* bénédiction *f.*

benefactor ['benɪfæktəʳ] *n* bienfaiteur *m*. ◆ **benefactress** *n* bienfaitrice *f.*

benefice ['benɪfɪs] *n* bénéfice *m (Rel).*

beneficent [bɪ'nefɪs(ə)nt] *adj person* bienfaisant; *thing* salutaire. ◆ **beneficence** *n* bienfaisance *f.*

beneficial [ˌbenɪ'fɪʃ(ə)l] *adj* salutaire (*to* pour). ~ **to the health** bon pour la santé. ◆ **beneficially** *adv* avantageusement.

beneficiary [ˌbenɪ'fɪʃ(ə)rɪ] *n* bénéficiaire *mf.*

benefit ['benɪfɪt] **1** *n* (**a**) *(advantage)* avantage *m*. **for the ~ of your health** dans l'intérêt de votre santé; **it is for his ~ that...** c'est pour lui que... ; **it is to your ~** c'est dans votre intérêt; **it wasn't (of) much ~ to me** cela ne m'a pas beaucoup aidé; **he's just crying for your ~** * il pleure pour se faire remarquer; **to give sb the ~ of the doubt** laisser à qn le bénéfice du doute; **the ~s of a good education** les bienfaits *mpl or* les avantages *mpl* d'une bonne éducation. (**b**) *(money)* allocation *f*, prestation *f*. **unemployment ~** allocation de chômage. **2** *vt* faire du bien à, profiter à. **3** *vi* gagner (*from, by doing* à faire). **he will ~ from a holiday** des vacances lui feront du bien. **4** *adj (Sport)* ~ **match** match *m* au profit d'un joueur.

Benelux ['benɪlʌks] *adj*: **the ~ countries** les pays *mpl* du Bénélux.

benevolent [bɪ'nevələnt] *adj (kind)* bienveillant (*to* envers); *(charitable)* bienfaisant, charitable (*to* envers); *society* de bienfaisance. ◆ **benevolence** *n (kindness)* bienveillance *f*; *(generosity)* bienfaisance *f.*

benign [bɪ'naɪn], **benignant** [bɪ'nɪgnənt] *adj* bienveillant; *(Med)* bénin.

bent¹ [bent] *(pret, ptp of* **bend***) adj wire, pipe* tordu; *(‡: dishonest)* véreux; *(‡: homosexual)* homosexuel. ◆ **bentwood** *adj hatstand* en bois courbé; *chair* bistrot *inv.*

bent² [bent] *n (aptitude)* dispositions *fpl* (*for* pour); *(liking)* penchant *m* (*for* pour). **to follow one's ~** suivre son inclination *f.*

benumbed [bɪ'nʌmd] *adj limb* engourdi; *person (cold, fear)* transi; *(shock)* paralysé.

Benzedrine ['benzɪdri:n] *n* ® benzédrine *f.*

benzine ['benzi:n] *n* benzine *f.*

bequeath [bɪ'kwi:ð] *vt* léguer (*to* à). ◆ **bequest** *n* legs *m.*

berate [bɪ'reɪt] *vt* réprimander.

bereave [bɪ'ri:v] *pret, ptp* **bereft** *vt (deprive)* priver (*of* de). ◆ **bereaved 1** *adj* endeuillé ; **2** *n*: **the ~d** la famille du disparu. ◆ **bereavement** *n* deuil *m*; **owing to a recent ~ment** en raison d'un deuil récent.

beret ['bereɪ] *n* béret *m.*

Berlin [bɜ:'lɪn] *n* Berlin. **East/West ~** Berlin Est/ Ouest.

berm [bɜ:m] *n (US Aut)* accotement *m*, bas-côté *m.*

Bermuda [bɜ:'mju:də] *n* Bermudes *fpl*. ~ **shorts** bermuda *m.*

Bern [bɜ:n] *n* Berne.

berry ['berɪ] *n* baie *f.*

berserk [bə'sɜ:k] *adj* fou furieux (*f* folle furieuse). **to go ~** *(lit)* devenir fou furieux; *(fig: with anger)* se mettre en rage.

berth [bɜ:θ] **1** *n* (**a**) *(in plane, train, ship)* couchette *f*. *(easy job)* **a soft ~** ‡ une bonne planque ‡. (**b**) *(place for ship)* poste *m* d'amarrage. *(fig)* **to give sb a wide ~** éviter qn à tout prix. **2** *vi* s'amarrer. **3** *vt* amarrer.

beryl ['berɪl] *n* béryl *m.*

beseech [bɪ'si:tʃ] *pret, ptp* **besought** *vt* implorer (*sb to do* qn de faire). ◆ **beseeching** *adj* implorant. ◆ **beseechingly** *adv* d'un air implorant.

beset [bɪ'set] *pret, ptp* **beset** *vt [difficulties, doubts]* assaillir; *[temptations]* entourer. **enterprise ~ with difficulties** entreprise hérissée de difficultés. ◆ **besetting** *adj*: **his ~ting sin** son plus grand défaut.

beside [bɪ'saɪd] *prep (at the side of)* à côté de, auprès de; *(compared with)* à côté de, comparé à. **that's ~ the point** cela n'a rien à voir avec la question; **it's quite ~ the point to suggest that...** il est tout à fait inutile de suggérer que...; **to be ~ o.s.** *(with anger)* être hors de soi; *(with excitement)* ne plus se posséder; ~ **himself with joy** fou de joie.

besides [bɪ'saɪdz] **1** *adv* (**a**) *(in addition)* en outre, en plus. **many more ~** bien d'autres encore; **there is nothing ~** il n'y a rien de plus *or* d'autre. (**b**) *(moreover)* d'ailleurs, du reste, en outre. **2** *prep* (**a**) *(in addition to)* en plus de. **others ~ ourselves** d'autres que nous; **there were 3 of us ~ Mary** nous étions 3 sans compter Marie; ~ **which...** et pardessus le marché... (**b**) *(except)* excepté, hormis, en dehors de. **no one ~ you** personne en dehors de vous, personne d'autre que vous; **who ~ them** qui si ce n'est eux.

besiege [bɪ'si:dʒ] *vt* assiéger; *(fig)* assaillir.

besom ['bi:zəm] *n* balai *m* de bouleau.

besotted [bɪ'sɒtɪd] *adj (drunk)* hébété (*with* de); *(infatuated)* entiché (*with* de).

besought [bɪ'sɔ:t] *pret, ptp of* **beseech.**

bespatter [bɪ'spætəʳ] *vt* éclabousser (*with* de).

bespectacled [bɪ'spektɪkld] *adj* à lunettes.

bespoke [bɪ'spəʊk] *adj garment* fait sur commande; *tailor* à façon.

best [best] **1** *adj (superl of* **good***)* le meilleur, la meilleure. **the ~ pupil in the class** le meilleur élève de la classe; **the ~ thing about her is...** ce qu'il y a de meilleur chez elle c'est...; **the ~ thing to do is to wait** le mieux c'est d'attendre; **the ~ years of one's life** les plus belles années de sa vie; **in one's ~ clothes** vêtu de ses plus beaux vêtements; **may the ~ man win!** que le meilleur gagne!; **her ~ friend** sa meilleure amie; *(biggest)* **the ~ part of** la plus grande partie de; **for the ~ part of an hour** pendant près d'une heure; *(on product)* **~ before...** à consommer de préférence avant...; **~ man** *(at wedding)* garçon *m* d'honneur.
2 *n*: **to do one's ~** faire tout son possible (*to do* pour faire); **do the ~ you can** faites de votre mieux; **to get the ~ out of** tirer le maximum de; **to get the ~ of it** l'emporter; **he wants the ~ of both worlds** il veut tout avoir; **to make the ~ of sth** profiter au maximum de qch; **to make the ~ of a bad job** faire contre mauvaise fortune bon cœur; **the ~ of it is that...** le plus beau de l'affaire c'est que...; **it's all for the ~** c'est pour le mieux; **to the ~ of my knowledge/recollection** *etc* autant que je sache/que je me souvienne *etc*; **to look one's ~** être resplendissant; *[woman]* être en beauté; *(on form)* **to be at one's ~** être en pleine forme *; **that is Racine at his ~** voilà du meilleur Racine; **even at the ~ of times he's not very patient but...** il n'est jamais particulièrement patient mais...; **at ~** au mieux; **he can sing with the ~ of them** il sait chanter comme pas un *.
3 *adv (superl of* **well***)* le mieux, le plus. **the ~ dressed** le mieux habillé; **the ~ loved** le plus aimé; **I like strawberries ~** je préfère les fraises; **as ~ I can** *or* **could** de mon mieux; **to think it ~ to do** croire qu'il vaudrait mieux faire; **do as you think ~** faites pour le mieux; **you know ~** c'est vous le mieux placé pour en décider; **you had ~ go** tu ferais mieux de t'en aller.
4 *vt* battre, l'emporter sur.
◆ **bestseller** *n (book, goods)* best-seller *m*; *(author)* auteur *m* à succès.

bestial ['bestɪəl] *adj* bestial. ◆ **bestiality** *n* bestialité *f*.

bestow [bɪ'stəʊ] *vt (gen)* accorder (*on* à); *title* conférer (*on* à).

bet [bet] *pret, ptp* **bet** *or* **betted** **1** *vi* parier (against contre; *on* sur; *with* avec). **to ~ 10 to 1** parier (à) 10 contre 1; **to ~ on horses** parier *or* jouer aux courses; **to ~ on a horse** jouer un cheval. **2** *vt (fig)* **I ~ he'll come!** * je te parie qu'il viendra!; **you ~!** * tu parles! *; **~ you can't!** * chiche! *; **you can ~ your life that** *... tu peux parier tout ce que tu veux que... **3** *n* pari *m* (*on* sur). ◆ **better**[1] *or* ◆ **bettor** *n* parieur *m*, -euse *f*; *(at races)* turfiste *mf*. ◆ **betting** **1** *n* paris *mpl*; **the ~ting was 2 to 1** la cote était 2 contre 1; *(fig)* **the ~ting is that...** il y a des chances que...; **2** *adj*: **~ting shop** bureau *m* de P.M.U.; **~ting slip** ≃ P.M.U. *m*.

beta-blocker ['bi:tə'blɒkə[r]] *n* bêta-bloquant *m*.

betel ['bi:t(ə)l] *n* bétel *m*.

bethink [bɪ'θɪŋk] *pret, ptp* **bethought** *vt*: **to ~ o.s. of sth/to do/that...** s'aviser de qch/de faire/que...

betimes [bɪ'taɪmz] *adv (early)* tôt; *(quickly)* promptement.

betoken [bɪ'təʊk(ə)n] *vt* être signe de.

betray [bɪ'treɪ] *vt (gen)* trahir; *(disclose) age, fears etc* révéler (*to* à), trahir. **to ~ sb to the police** livrer qn à la police; **his speech ~ed the fact that...** on devinait à l'écouter que... ◆ **betrayal** *n* trahison *f*; **~al of trust** abus *m* de confiance.

betrothal [bɪ'trəʊð(ə)l] *n (liter)* fiançailles *fpl* (*to* avec). ◆ **betrothed** *adj, n* fiancé(e) *m(f)*.

better[2] ['betə[r]] **1** *adj (comp of* **good***)* meilleur (*than* que). **she is ~ at dancing than at singing** elle danse mieux qu'elle ne chante; **he's a ~ man than his brother** il est mieux que son frère; *(hum)* **you're a ~ man than I am!** vous êtes plus doué que moi! *; **he's no ~ than a thief** c'est un voleur ni plus ni moins; **he's no ~ than he should be!** ce n'est pas l'honnêteté qui l'étouffe! *; *(Med)* **he is much ~ now** il va bien mieux maintenant; **to get ~** *(gen)* s'améliorer; *(Med)* se remettre (*from* de); **~ and ~!** de mieux en mieux!; **that's ~!** voilà qui est mieux!; **it couldn't be ~** ça ne pourrait pas mieux tomber; **it would be ~ to stay at home** il vaudrait mieux rester à la maison; **a ~ class of hotel** un hôtel de catégorie supérieure; **his ~ nature** ses bons sentiments; **to go one ~ than sb** damer le pion à qn; **the ~ part of a year** près d'un an; **to hope for ~ things** espérer mieux.
2 *adv (comp of* **well***)* mieux (*than* que). **he sings ~ than he dances** il chante mieux qu'il ne danse; **all the ~, so much the ~** tant mieux (*for* pour); **he was all the ~ for it** il s'en est trouvé mieux; **it would be all the ~ for a drop of paint** un petit coup de peinture ne lui ferait pas de mal; **they are ~ off than we are** *(richer)* ils ont plus d'argent que nous; *(more fortunate)* ils sont dans une meilleure position que nous; **he is ~ off at his sister's** il est mieux chez sa sœur; **I had ~ go** il faudrait que je m'en aille; **hadn't you ~ speak to him?** ne vaudrait-il pas mieux que tu lui parles *(subj)*?; **~ dressed** mieux habillé; **~ known** plus connu.
3 *n*: **a change for the ~** une amélioration, un changement en mieux; **for ~ or worse** pour le meilleur ou pour le pire; **to get the ~ of sb** triompher de qn; **one's ~s** ses supérieurs *mpl*.
4 *vt sb's achievements* dépasser; *record, score* améliorer. **to ~ o.s.** améliorer sa condition.

between [bɪ'twi:n] **1** *prep (gen)* entre. **no one can come ~ us** personne ne peut nous séparer; **~ the wars** entre les deux guerres; **the ferry goes ~ Dover and Calais** le ferry fait la navette entre Douvres et Calais; **~ here and London** d'ici (à) Londres; **~ now and next week** d'ici la semaine prochaine; **the match ~ A and B** le match qui oppose A à B; **they have 5 oranges ~ them** ils ont 5 oranges en tout; **~ ourselves, he...** entre nous, il...; **the 2 boys managed to lift the box ~ them** à eux deux les garçons sont arrivés à soulever la caisse. **2** *adv* au milieu, dans l'intervalle. **few and far ~** très espacés, très rares; **rows of trees with grass in ~** des rangées d'arbres séparées par de l'herbe.

betwixt [bɪ'twɪkst] *adv*: **~ and between** entre les deux.

bevel ['bev(ə)l] **1** *n (~ edge)* biseau *m*; *(tool: ~ square)* fausse équerre *f*. **2** *vt* biseauter.

beverage ['bevərɪdʒ] *n* boisson *f*.

bevy ['bevɪ] *n* bande *f*, troupe *f*.

bewail [bɪ'weɪl] *vt* se lamenter sur.

beware [bɪ'wɛə[r]] *vti*: **to ~ (of)** prendre garde (*sb/sth* à qn/à qch; *doing* de faire), se garder (*doing* de faire), se méfier (*sth* de qch); **~ of falling** prenez garde de tomber; **~ of listening to him** gardez-vous de l'écouter; **'~ of the dog!'** 'attention, chien méchant'; **'~ of pickpockets!'** 'attention aux pickpockets!'; **'~ of imitations'** 'se méfier des contrefaçons'.

bewilder [bɪ'wɪldə[r]] *vt* dérouter; *(stronger)* confondre. ◆ **bewildered** *adj person* dérouté, ahuri; *look* perplexe. ◆ **bewildering** *adj* déroutant; *(stronger)* ahurissant. ◆ **bewilderingly** *adv* d'une façon déroutante *or* ahurissante. ◆ **bewilderment** *n* confusion *f*; *(stronger)* ahurissement *m*.

bewitch [bɪ'wɪtʃ] *vt* ensorceler; *(fig)* charmer. ◆ **bewitching** *adj* charmant. ◆ **bewitchingly** *adv* d'une façon séduisante; **~ingly beautiful** belle à ravir.

beyond [bɪ'jɒnd] **1** *prep (in space)* au-delà de, de l'autre côté de; *(in time)* plus de; *(exceeding)* au-dessus de; *(except)* sauf. **this work is quite ~ him** ce travail le dépasse complètement; **it's ~ me * why he hasn't left her** ça me dépasse * qu'il ne l'ait pas quittée; **~ my reach** hors de ma portée; **he is ~ caring** il ne s'en fait plus du tout; **that's ~ a joke** cela dépasse les bornes; **~ his means** au-dessus de ses moyens; **he gave her no answer ~ a grunt** il ne lui a répondu que par un grognement. **2** *adv* au-delà, plus loin, là-bas. **the room ~** la pièce d'après; **the lands ~** les terres lointaines.

bezique [bɪ'zi:k] *n* bésigue *m*.

bi... [baɪ] *pref* bi... ◆**biannual** *adj* semestriel. ◆**bicentenary** *adj, n* bicentenaire *(m)*. ◆**biennial** *adj* biennal. ◆**bifocals** *npl* verres *mpl* à double foyer. ◆**bilateral** *adj* bilatéral. ◆**bilingual** *adj* bilingue. ◆**bimonthly** *adj* bimensuel. ◆**biped** *adj, n* bipède *(m)*. ◆**biplane** *n* biplan *m*. ◆**bisexual** *adj (Bio)* bisexué; *(Psych)* (sexuellement) ambivalent. ◆**biweekly** *adj* bihebdomadaire.

bias ['baɪəs] **1** *n* (**a**) *(inclination)* tendance *f (towards* à); *(prejudice)* préjugé *m (towards* pour ; *against* contre). (**b**) *(Sewing)* **on the ~** dans le biais; **~ binding** biais *m (ruban)*. **2** *vt* influencer; *(pej)* prévenir *(towards* en faveur de; *against* contre). ◆**bias(s)ed** *adj* partial; **to be ~(s)ed against** avoir un préjugé contre.

bib [bɪb] *n [child]* bavoir *m*; *[apron]* bavette *f*. **in her best ~ and tucker *** sur son trente et un.

Bible ['baɪbl] **1** *n* Bible *f*. **2** *adj oath* sur la Bible; *story* tiré de la Bible. **~ thumper *** évangéliste *m* de carrefour. ◆**biblical** ['bɪblɪk(ə)l] *adj* biblique.

bibliography [,bɪblɪ'ɒgrəfɪ] *n* bibliographie *f*. ◆**bibliographer** *n* bibliographe *mf*. ◆**bibliographic(al)** *adj* bibliographique. ◆**bibliomaniac** *n* bibliomane *mf*.

bibulous ['bɪbjʊləs] *adj* adonné à la boisson; *look* aviné; *evening* bien arrosé.

bicarbonate [baɪ'kɑ:bənɪt] *n*: **~ of soda** bicarbonate *m* de soude.

biceps ['baɪseps] *n* biceps *m*.

bicker ['bɪkə^r] *vi* se chamailler *. ◆**bickering** *n* chamailleries * *fpl*.

bicycle ['baɪsɪkl] **1** *n* bicyclette *f*, vélo *m*. **to ride a ~** faire de la bicyclette *or* du vélo. **2** *adj bell, chain* de bicyclette; *pump* à bicyclette; *path* cyclable; *race* cycliste. **~ clip** pince *f* de cycliste. **~ rack** râtelier *m* à bicyclettes. **~ shed** abri *m* à bicyclettes.

bid [bɪd] *pret* **bade** *or* **bid**, *ptp* **bidden** *or* **bid** **1** *vt* (**a**) *(command)* ordonner *(sb to do* à qn de faire). (**b**) *(say)* dire. **to ~ sb good morning** dire bonjour à qn; **to ~ sb welcome** souhaiter la bienvenue à qn. (**c**) *(offer) amount* offrir; *(at auction)* faire une enchère de; *(Cards)* demander. **2** *vi* faire une offre *or (at auction)* une enchère *(for* pour). **to ~ against sb** renchérir sur qn; **to ~ for power** viser le pouvoir; **to ~ fair to do** promettre de faire. **3** *n* (**a**) offre *f*; *(at auction)* enchère *f*; *(Cards)* demande *f*. **'no ~'** 'parole'. (**b**) *(attempt)* tentative *f*. **suicide ~** tentative de suicide; **to make a ~ for power/ freedom** tenter de s'emparer du pouvoir/ de s'évader. ◆**biddable** *adj child* docile; *(Cards) suit* demandable. ◆**bidder** *n* enchérisseur *m*, offrant *m*; **the highest ~der** le plus offrant. ◆**bidding** *n* (**a**) *(at sale, also Cards)* enchère(s) *f(pl)*; **the ~ding is closed** l'enchère est faite; (**b**) **I did his ~ding** j'ai fait ce qu'il m'a dit.

bide [baɪd] *vt*: **to ~ one's time** attendre le bon moment.

bidet ['bi:deɪ] *n* bidet *m*.

bier [bɪə^r] *n* bière *f (pour enterrement)*.

biff * [bɪf] *vt* flanquer * un coup de poing à.

big [bɪg] **1** *adj (in height, age) person, building, tree* grand; *(in bulk, amount) fruit, parcel, book, lie* gros *(f* grosse). **my ~ brother** mon grand frère, mon frère aîné; *(Aut)* **~ end** tête *f* de bielle; **a ~ man** un homme grand et fort; *(important)* un grand homme, un homme marquant; *(Pol)* **the B~ Four** les quatre Grands; **~ game** gros gibier; **~ game hunter** chasseur *m* de gros gibier; **~ game hunting** chasse *f* au gros gibier; **~ toe** gros orteil; **~ top** *(circus)* cirque *m*; *(main tent of it)* grand chapiteau *m*; **to grow ~** *or* **~ger** grandir *(or* grossir); **to look ~** faire l'important; **~ noise *, ~ shot *** grosse légume *; **the B~ Bang** le big bang; **~ business** les grandes entreprises; **to have ~ ideas** voir grand; **what's the ~ idea? *** ça ne va pas, non? *; **to do things in a ~ way** faire les choses en grand; **that's rather a ~ word** c'est un bien grand mot; **~ talk** beaux discours *(pej)*; **he's too ~ for his boots** il a des prétentions; **he's got a ~ head *** il est crâneur *; **he's got a ~ mouth *** il ne sait pas se taire; **why can't you keep your ~ mouth shut! *** tu aurais mieux fait de la boucler! ‡; **to make the ~ time *** réussir; *(iro)* **~ deal! *** tu parles! *; *(iro)* **that's ~ of you! *** quelle générosité! **2** *adv*: **to talk ~ *** fanfaronner, se faire mousser *; **to go over ~ ‡** avoir un succès monstre *; **his speech went down ~ * with his audience** ses auditeurs ont été emballés * par son discours. ◆**big-boned** *adj* fortement charpenté. ◆**bighead *** *n* crâneur * *m*, -euse * *f*. ◆**bigheaded *** *adj* crâneur *. ◆**big-hearted** *adj* au grand cœur; **to be ~-hearted** avoir du cœur. ◆**bigmouth *** *n* hâbleur *m*, -euse *f*. ◆**big-sounding** *adj idea, plan etc* prétentieux; *name* ronflant. ◆**bigwig ‡** *n* grosse légume * *f*.

bigamy ['bɪgəmɪ] *n* bigamie *f*. ◆**bigamist** *n* bigame *mf*. ◆**bigamous** *adj* bigame.

bigot ['bɪgət] *n (Rel)* bigot(e) *m(f)*; *(Pol etc)* fanatique *mf*. ◆**bigoted** *adj* bigot; fanatique. ◆**bigotry** *n* bigoterie *f*; fanatisme *m*.

bike [baɪk] **1** *n* (*) vélo *m*; *(motorbike)* moto *f*. **2** *vi* (‡) aller à vélo.

bikini [bɪ'ki:nɪ] *n* bikini *m*.

bilberry ['bɪlb(ə)rɪ] *n* myrtille *f*.

bile [baɪl] *n (Anat)* bile *f*; *(anger)* mauvaise humeur. **~ stone** calcul *m* biliaire.

bilge [bɪldʒ] *n (water)* eau *f* de cale; *(*: nonsense)* idioties *fpl*.

bilious ['bɪlɪəs] *adj* bilieux. **~ attack** crise *f* de foie. ◆**biliousness** *n* affection *f* hépatique.

bill[1] [bɪl] **1** *n* (**a**) *(account)* facture *f*; *[hotel, also gas etc]* note *f*; *[restaurant]* addition *f*. **have you paid the milk ~?** as-tu payé le lait?; **a pile of ~s in the post** une pile de factures dans le courrier; **may I have the ~ please** l'addition *(or* la note) s'il vous plaît. (**b**) **~ of fare** menu *m*, carte *f* (du jour); **~ of indictment** acte *m* d'accusation; **~ of lading** connaissement *m*; **~ of rights** déclaration *f* des droits; **~ of exchange** lettre *f* de change; **~ of sale** acte *m* de vente. (**c**) *(US: banknote)* billet *m* (de banque). **5-dollar ~** billet de 5 dollars. (**d**) *(Parl)* projet *m* de loi. (**e**) *(poster)* placard *m*; *(Theat etc)* affiche *f*. **to top the ~** être en tête d'affiche. **2** *vt* (**a**) *goods* facturer. **to ~ sb for sth** envoyer la facture de qch à qn. (**b**) **he is ~ed to play Hamlet** il est à l'affiche dans le rôle de Hamlet. ◆**billboard** *n* panneau *m* d'affichage. ◆**billfold** *n* portefeuille *m*. ◆**billing[1]** *n (Theat)* **to get top/ second ~ing** figurer en tête d'affiche/en deuxième place à l'affiche. ◆**billposter** *or* ◆**billsticker** *n* colleur *m* d'affiches.

bill[2] [bɪl] **1** *n [bird]* bec *m*. **2** *vi*: **to ~ and coo** roucouler. ◆**billing[2]** *n*: **~ing and cooing** roucoulements *mpl* (d'amoureux).

billet ['bɪlɪt] *(Mil)* **1** *n* cantonnement *m* (chez l'habitant). **2** *vt* cantonner (*on sb* chez qn).

billhook ['bɪlhuk] *n* serpette *f*.

billiard ['bɪljəd] **1** *n*: ~**s** (jeu *m* de) billard *m*. **2** *adj*: ~ **ball/cue** boule *f*/queue *f* de billard; ~**(s) saloon** (café-)billard *m*; ~ **table** (table *f* de) billard *m*.

billion ['bɪljən] *n (Brit)* billion *m*; *(US)* milliard *m*.

billow ['bɪləʊ] **1** *n* flot *m*. **2** *vi [sea]* se soulever; *[sail]* se gonfler; *[cloth]* onduler.

billy can ['bɪlɪkæn] *n* gamelle *f*.

billy goat ['bɪlɪgəʊt] *n* bouc *m*.

billy-ho * ['bɪlɪ(hə)ʊ] *n*: **like** ~ *laugh* à gorge déployée; *run* à toutes jambes.

bimbo ‡ ['bɪmbaʊ] *n* minette * *f (superficielle)*.

bin [bɪn] *n [coal, corn]* coffre *m*; *[bread]* boîte *f*; *(larger)* huche *f*; *[wine]* casier *m* (à bouteilles); *(dust ~, rubbish ~)* boîte *f* à ordures, poubelle *f*.

binary ['baɪnərɪ] *adj* binaire.

bind [baɪnd] *pret, ptp* **bound** **1** *vt* (**a**) *(fasten) thing* attacher; *2 or more things* attacher, lier; *person, animal* lier, attacher (*to* à); *prisoner* ligoter; *(Culin)* lier. **bound hand and foot** pieds et poings liés. (**b**) *(encircle)* entourer (*with* de); *artery* ligaturer; *wound* bander; *material, hem* border (*with* de); *book* relier (*in* en). (**c**) *(oblige)* obliger (*sb to do* qn à faire). **2** *vi* (**a**) *[agreement]* engager. (**b**) (‡*: complain)* rouspéter *. **3** *n* (‡*: nuisance)* scie * *f*.

◆ **bind over** *vt sep (Jur)* mettre en liberté conditionnelle. ◆ **bind together** *vt sep sticks* lier; *(fig) people* unir. ◆ **bind up** *vt sep wound* bander. **to be totally bound up with** *person* se dévouer entièrement à; *work, hobby* se donner corps et âme à; **it's all bound up with whether...** tout dépend si...

◆ **binder** *n (Agr)* lieuse *f*; *(for papers)* classeur *m*; *(Med etc)* bandage *m*. ◆ **binding** **1** *n [book]* reliure *f*; *[skis]* fixation *f*; *(tape)* extra-fort *m*; **2** *adj rule* obligatoire; *agreement, promise* qui lie; **to be ~ing on sb** lier qn. ◆ **bindweed** *n* liseron *m*.

binge ‡ [bɪn(d)ʒ] *n*: **to have a** ~ faire la bombe *.

bingo ['bɪŋgəʊ] *n* loto *m (joué collectivement pour de l'argent)*.

binoculars [bɪ'nɒkjʊləz] *npl* jumelles *fpl*.

biochemistry ['baɪə(ʊ)'kemɪstrɪ] *n* biochimie *f*. ◆ **biochemical** *adj* biochimique. ◆ **biochemist** *n* biochimiste *mf*.

biodegradable ['baɪəʊdɪ'greɪdəbl] *adj* biodégradable.

bioengineering [ˌbaɪəʊˌendʒɪ'nɪərɪŋ] *n* bioingénierie *f*.

biography [baɪ'ɒgrəfɪ] *n* biographie *f*. ◆ **biographer** *n* biographe *mf*. ◆ **biographic(al)** *adj* biographique.

biology [baɪ'ɒlədʒɪ] *n* biologie *f*. ◆ **biologist** *n* biologiste *mf*. ◆ **biological** *adj reason, warfare* biologique; *soap powder* aux enzymes.

biomass ['baɪəʊmæs] *n* biomasse *f*.

bionic [baɪ'ɒnɪk] *adj* bionique.

biophysics [ˌbaɪəʊ'fɪzɪks] *nsg* biophysique *f*. ◆ **biophysical** *adj* biophysique. ◆ **biophysicist** *n* biophysicien(ne) *m(f)*.

biopsy ['baɪɒpsɪ] *n* biopsie *f*.

biorhythm ['baɪəʊrɪð(ə)m] *n* biorythme *m*.

biotechnology [ˌbaɪaʊtek'nɒlədʒɪ] *n* biotechnologie *f*.

birch [bɜːtʃ] **1** *n (tree, wood)* bouleau *m*; *(for whipping)* verge *f*, fouet *m*. **2** *vt* fouetter. ◆ **birching** *n* peine *f* du fouet.

bird [bɜːd] **1** *n* oiseau *m*; *(game)* pièce *f* de gibier (à plume); *(Culin)* volaille *f*; (‡*: fellow)* type * *m*; (‡*: girl)* nana ‡ *f*. ~ **of passage/prey** oiseau de passage/proie; ~**'s nest** nid *m* d'oiseau; **a ~ in the hand is worth two in the bush** un tiens vaut mieux que deux tu l'auras; **they're ~s of a feather** ils sont à mettre dans le même sac; **a little ~ told me** * mon petit doigt me l'a dit; **to give sb the** ~ ‡ envoyer paître qn ‡; **that's strictly for the ~s** ‡ ça c'est bon pour les imbéciles. **2** *adj*: ~ **bath** vasque *f* pour les oiseaux; ~ **brain** ‡ tête *f* de linotte; ~ **cage** cage *f* à oiseaux; ~ **call** cri *m* d'oiseau; **to go ~ nesting** aller dénicher les oiseaux; ~ **sanctuary** réserve *f* d'oiseaux; **a ~'s eye view of Paris** Paris (vu) à vol d'oiseau; *(fig)* **~'s-eye view** vue *f* d'ensemble; ~ **watcher** ornithologue *mf* amateur; **to go ~ watching** aller observer les oiseaux.

Biro ['baɪ(ə)rəʊ] *n* ® ≃ (pointe *f*) Bic *m* ®.

birth [bɜːθ] **1** *n [baby, idea etc]* naissance *f*; *(childbirth)* accouchement *m*. **during the** ~ pendant l'accouchement; **to give ~ to** *[woman]* donner naissance à; *[animal]* mettre bas; **from ~, by ~** de naissance; **of good ~** de bonne famille. **2** *adj*: ~ **certificate** acte *m* de naissance; ~ **control** régulation *f* des naissances; ~ **pill** pilule *f* (anticonceptionnelle); ~ **rate** (taux *m* de) natalité *f*.

◆ **birthday** **1** *n* anniversaire *m* ; **2** *adj cake, card, present* d'anniversaire; **she is having a ~day party** on a organisé une petite fête pour son anniversaire; *(hum)* **in one's ~day suit** * dans le costume d'Adam (*or* d'Ève) *. ◆ **birthmark** *n* tache *f* de vin *(sur la peau)*. ◆ **birthplace** *n (gen, Admin)* lieu *m* de naissance; *(house)* maison natale; *(fig: of civilisation etc)* berceau *m*. ◆ **birthright** *n* droit *m* acquis en naissant.

biscuit ['bɪskɪt] **1** *n (Brit)* petit gâteau sec, biscuit *m*; *(US)* petit pain au lait. **he takes the ~!** ‡ il est marrant! ‡ **2** *adj (colour)* biscuit *inv*.

bisect [baɪ'sekt] *vt* couper en deux (parties égales).

bishop ['bɪʃəp] *n* évêque *m*; *(Chess)* fou *m*. ◆ **bishopric** *n* évêché *m*.

bismuth ['bɪzməθ] *n* bismuth *m*.

bison ['baɪsn] *n* bison *m*.

bit[1] [bɪt] **1** *pret of* **bite**. **2** *n* (**a**) *[horse]* mors *m*. **to take the ~ between one's teeth** prendre le mors aux dents. (**b**) *[tool]* mèche *f*.

bit[2] [bɪt] **1** *n [bread]* morceau *m*; *[paper, string]* bout *m*; *[book, talk etc]* passage *m*; *(Comput)* bit *m*. **a ~ of** *(gen)* un peu de; **a ~ of garden** un bout de jardin; **a tiny little ~** un tout petit peu; **a ~ of advice** un petit conseil; **a ~ of news** une nouvelle; **a ~ of luck** une chance; **he's got a ~ of money put aside** il a un peu d'argent en réserve; **the ~ of money he had left** le peu d'argent qui lui restait; **a ~/a little ~/a good ~ late** un peu/un petit peu/très en retard; **a good ~ bigger** bien *or* beaucoup plus grand; **I'm a ~ of a socialist** * je suis plutôt socialiste; **it was a ~ of a shock** ça nous a plutôt fait un choc; **not a ~** pas du tout; **bring all your ~s and pieces** apporte toutes tes petites affaires; **in ~s and pieces** *(broken)* en morceaux, en miettes; *(dismantled)* en pièces détachées; *(fig) plan, scheme* en ruines; **to come to ~s** *(break)* s'en aller en morceaux; *(dismantle)* se démonter; *(fig)* **he went to ~s** * il a craqué *; ~ **by** ~ petit à petit; **to do one's ~** fournir sa part d'effort; **when it comes to the ~** en fin de compte; *(of time)* **after a good ~** après un bon bout de temps *; **wait a ~** attendez un instant; **to pay a good ~ for sth** payer qch assez cher. **2** *adj (Theat)* ~ **part** petit rôle. ◆ **bitty** * *adj* décousu.

bitch [bɪtʃ] **1** *n [dog]* chienne *f*; *[canines generally]* femelle *f*; (‡ *pej: woman)* garce ‡ *f*. **terrier ~** terrier *m* femelle. **2** *vi* (‡*: complain)* râler * (*about* contre). ◆ **bitchy** ‡ *adj* rosse *, vache ‡.

bite [baɪt] *vb: pret* **bit,** *ptp* **bitten** **1** *n [dog, snake etc]* morsure *f*; *[insect]* piqûre *f*; *(Fishing)* touche *f*; *(piece bitten off)* bouchée *f*; *(something to eat)* morceau *m*. **in two ~s** en deux bouchées; **there's not a ~ to eat** il n'y a rien à manger; **come and have**

a ~ venez manger un morceau. **2** *vt (gen)* mordre; *[insect]* piquer. **to ~ one's nails** se ronger les ongles; **to ~ one's tongue/fingers** se mordre la langue/les doigts; **to ~ the dust** mordre la poussière; *(fig)* **to ~ the hand that feeds you** être d'une ingratitude monstrueuse; **once bitten twice shy** chat échaudé craint l'eau froide; **to be bitten with * the desire to do** mourir d'envie de faire; **what's biting you?** ‡ qu'est-ce que tu as à râler? * **3** *vi (gen)* mordre; *[insect]* piquer; *[cogs]* s'engrener. **to ~ into sth** *[person]* mordre (dans) qch; *[acid]* mordre sur qch.

◆ **bite off** *vt sep* couper d'un coup de dents. **she bit off a piece of apple** elle a mordu dans la pomme; *(fig)* **he has bitten off more than he can chew** il a eu les yeux plus grands que le ventre; *(fig)* **to ~ sb's head off *** rembarrer qn (brutalement). ◆ **bite through** *vt fus lip* mordre (de part en part); *thread* couper avec les dents.

◆ **biting** *adj cold* perçant; *wind* cinglant; *wit, remarks* mordant. ◆ **bitingly** *adv speak* d'un ton mordant.

bitter ['bɪtəʳ] **1** *adj* (**a**) *taste* amer, âpre. *(fig)* **it was a ~ pill to swallow** la pilule était amère; **~ lemon** Schweppes *m* ® au citron; **~ orange** *(fruit)* orange *f* amère. (**b**) *weather* glacial; *winter* rude. (**c**) *person, reproach, tears* amer; *critic, criticism* acerbe; *fate, sorrow, suffering* cruel; *hatred* acharné; *opposition, protest* violent; *remorse* cuisant. **to the ~ end** jusqu'au bout; **I feel very ~ about the whole business** toute cette histoire m'a rempli d'amertume. **2** *n (Brit: beer)* bière anglaise *(pression)*. *(drink)* **~s** bitter *m*.

◆ **bitterly** *adv speak, complain, weep* amèrement; *criticize, reproach* âprement; *oppose, resist* avec acharnement; *disappointed* cruellement; *jealous* profondément; *(Met)* **it was ~ly cold** il faisait un froid de loup. ◆ **bitterness** *n* amertume *f*.

◆ **bittersweet** *adj* aigre-doux.

bitumen ['bɪtjʊmɪn] *n* bitume *m*.

bivouac ['bɪvʊæk] **1** *n* bivouac *m*. **2** *vi* bivouaquer.

bizarre [bɪ'zɑːʳ] *adj* bizarre.

blab [blæb], **blabber** ['blæbə] **1** *vi (tell secret)* tout raconter; *(chatter)* jaser. **2** *vt* (**~ out**) aller raconter.

black [blæk] **1** *adj (lit, fig)* noir. **~ and blue** couvert de bleus; **~ art(s), ~ magic** magie noire; **~ beetle** cafard *m*; *(Aviat)* **~ box** boîte noire; **the B~ Country** le Pays Noir (de l'Angleterre); **the B~ Death** la peste noire; **~ economy** économie noire; **~ eye** œil *m* au beurre noir *; **to give sb a ~ eye** pocher l'œil à qn; **~ Forest** Forêt-Noire; **~ hole** trou noir; **~ gold** or noir; **~ ice** verglas *m*; **B~ Maria *** panier *m* à salade *; **on the ~ market** au marché noir; **~ marketeer** profiteur *m*, -euse *f*; **~ mass** messe noire; **the B~ Prince** le Prince Noir; **~ pudding** boudin *m*; **B~ Sea** mer Noire; **~ sheep (of the family)** brebis galeuse (de la famille); **(accident) ~ spot** point noir *(Aut)*; **'~ tie'** *(on invitation)* 'smoking'; **~ man** Noir *m*; **~ woman** Noire *f*; **the ~ Americans** les Noirs américains; **'~ is beautiful'** ≃ 'nous sommes fiers d'être noirs'; **B~ Power** *(movement)* Black Power *m*; **it is as ~ as pitch** il fait noir comme dans un four; **his hands were ~** il avait les mains noires; *(fig)* **he looked as ~ as thunder** il avait l'air furibond; **you can scream till you're ~ in the face but...** tu peux toujours t'égosiller, mais...; **a ~ deed** un crime; **things are looking ~** les choses se présentent très mal; **a ~ day on the roads** une sombre journée sur les routes; **a ~ day for England** un jour bien triste *or (stronger)* un jour de deuil pour l'Angleterre; *(during strike)* **to declare a cargo ~** boycotter une cargaison; **~ goods** marchandises boycottées.

2 *n (colour)* noir *m*; *(person)* Noir(e) *m(f)*; *(darkness)* obscurité *f*. **dressed in ~** habillé de noir; **there it is in ~ and white** c'est écrit noir sur blanc; **two ~s don't make a white** la faute de l'un n'excuse pas celle de l'autre; **to swear that ~ is white** *[obstinate person]* se refuser à l'évidence; *[liar]* mentir effrontément.

3 *vt (gen)* noircir; *shoes* cirer; *(Ind) goods, firm* boycotter. **to ~ sb's eye (for him)** pocher l'œil à qn.

◆ **black out** **1** *vi (Med)* s'évanouir. **2** *vt sep (in wartime) town, building* faire le black-out dans; *[power cut]* plonger dans l'obscurité totale; *(Theat) stage* faire l'obscurité sur.

◆ **black-ball** **1** *n* vote *m* contraire; **2** *vt* blackbouler. ◆ **blackberry** **1** *n* mûre *f*; *(bush)* mûrier *m* ; **2** *vi*: **to go ~berrying** aller cueillir des mûres. ◆ **blackbird** *n* merle *m*. ◆ **blackboard** *n* tableau *m* (noir). ◆ **blackcurrant** *n* cassis *m*. ◆ **blacken** *vti* noircir. ◆ **blackguard** ['blægɑːd] *n* fripouille *f*. ◆ **blackguardly** *adj* ignoble. ◆ **blackhead** *n* point noir *(sur la peau)*. ◆ **black-hearted** *adj* mauvais. ◆ **blacking** *n [shoes]* cirage *m* (noir); *[stoves]* pâte *f* à noircir; *[cargo etc]* boycottage *m*. ◆ **blackish** *adj* tirant sur le noir, noirâtre *(pej)*. ◆ **blackjack** *n (flag)* pavillon noir *(des pirates)*; *(weapon)* matraque *f*; *(Cards)* vingt-et-un *m*. ◆ **blacklead** *vt* frotter à la mine de plomb. ◆ **blackleg** *(Ind)* **1** *n* jaune *m* ; **2** *vi* briser la grève. ◆ **blacklist** **1** liste noire ; **2** *vt person* mettre sur la liste noire; *book* mettre à l'index. ◆ **blackmail** **1** *n* chantage *m*; **2** *vt* faire chanter; **to ~mail sb into doing** forcer qn par le chantage à faire. ◆ **blackmailer** *n* maître-chanteur *m*. ◆ **blackness** *n [colour, substance]* couleur noire, noirceur *f*; *(darkness)* obscurité *f*; *(dirtiness)* saleté *f*. ◆ **blackout** *n [lights]* panne *f* d'électricité; *(during war)* black-out *m*; *(amnesia)* trou *m* de mémoire; *(fainting)* évanouissement *m*. ◆ **blackshirt** *n (Pol)* chemise noire *(fasciste)*. ◆ **blacksmith** *n (shoes horses)* maréchal-ferrant *m*; *(forges iron)* forgeron *m*.

bladder ['blædəʳ] *n* vessie *f*; *(Bot)* vésicule *f*.

blade [bleɪd] *n [knife, tool, weapon, razor]* lame *f*; *[chopper, guillotine]* couperet *m*; *[tongue]* dos *m; [oar]* plat *m*; *[spade]* fer *m*; *[propeller]* pale *f*; *[windscreen wiper]* caoutchouc *m*; *[grass]* brin *m*.

blah ‡ [blɑː] *n* blablabla * *m*.

blame [bleɪm] **1** *vt* (**a**) *(fix responsibility on)* **to ~ sb for sth, to ~ sth on sb *** rejeter la responsabilité de qch sur qn, mettre qch sur le dos de qn *; **I'm not to ~** ce n'est pas ma faute; **you have only yourself to ~** tu l'as bien cherché; **whom/what are we to ~ for this accident?** à qui/à quoi attribuer cet accident? (**b**) *(censure)* reprocher (*sb for doing* à qn de faire; *sb for sth* qch à qn), blâmer (*sb for doing* qn de faire; *sb for sth* qn de qch). **to ~ o.s. for sth/for having done** se reprocher qch/ d'avoir fait; **he was greatly to ~ for doing that** il a eu grand tort de faire cela. **2** *n* (**a**) *(responsibility)* responsabilité *f*. **to put** *or* **lay the ~ for sth on sb** rejeter la responsabilité de qch sur qn. (**b**) *(censure)* blâme *m*. ◆ **blamable** *adj* blâmable.

◆ **blameless** *adj* irréprochable. ◆ **blamelessly** *adv* d'une manière irréprochable. ◆ **blameworthy** *adj* blâmable.

blanch [blɑːn(t)ʃ] **1** *vt vegetables* blanchir; *almonds* monder. **2** *vi [person]* blêmir.

blancmange [blə'mɒnʒ] *n* blanc-manger *m*.

bland [blænd] *adj air, flavour* doux; *manner* affable.

◆ **blandly** *adv* avec affabilité.

blandishments ['blændɪʃmənts] *npl* flatteries *fpl*.

blank [blæŋk] **1** *adj paper, page* blanc; *map* muet; *cheque* en blanc; *cartridge* à blanc; *wall* aveugle; *silence, darkness* profond; *refusal, denial* absolu; *life etc* dépourvu d'intérêt, vide; *face, look (expressionless)* sans expression, vide; *(puzzled)* déconcerté, dérouté. *(fig)* **to give sb a ~ cheque (to do)** donner à qn carte blanche (pour faire); **~ space** blanc *m*, espace *m* vide; **~ form** formulaire *m* (à remplir); *(on form)* **please leave ~** laisser en blanc s.v.p.; **a look of ~ astonishment** un regard ébahi;

his mind went ~ il a eu un passage à vide; ~ **verse** vers *mpl* blancs. **2** *n* (**a**) *(void)* blanc *m*, espace *m* vide. **she left several ~s in her answers** elle a laissé plusieurs de ses réponses en blanc; **my mind was a** ~ j'avais la tête vide. (**b**) *(~ form)* formulaire *m*, fiche *f*; *[coin, medal, record]* flan *m*. *(fig)* **to draw a** ~ faire chou blanc. ◆ **blankly** *adv say, announce* carrément; *look (expressionlessly)* sans expression; *(without understanding)* sans comprendre.

blanket ['blæŋkɪt] **1** *n* couverture *f*; *[snow etc]* couche *f*; *[fog]* nappe *f*; *[smoke]* nuage *m*. **2** *adj statement, condemnation etc* global. *[insurance policy]* **to give** ~ **cover** être tous risques.

blare [blɛəʳ] **1** *n* vacarme *m*. **2** *vi [music, horn etc]* retentir; *[loud voice]* claironner; *[radio]* beugler. **3** *vt music* faire retentir.

blarney * ['blɑːnɪ] *n* boniment * *m*.

blasé ['blɑːzeɪ] *adj* blasé.

blaspheme [blæs'fiːm] *vti* blasphémer (*against* contre). ◆ **blasphemer** *n* blasphémateur *m*, -trice *f*. ◆ **blasphemous** ['blæsfɪməs] *adj person* blasphémateur; *words* blasphématoire. ◆ **blasphemously** *adv* avec impiété. ◆ **blasphemy** ['blæsfɪmɪ] *n* blasphème *m*.

blast [blɑːst] **1** *n* (**a**) *(sound) [bomb, quarrying]* explosion *f*; *[space rocket]* grondement *m*; *[trumpets etc]* fanfare *f*; *[whistle, carhorn]* coup *m* strident. ~ **on the siren** coup *m* de sirène; **to blow a** ~ **on the bugle** donner un coup de clairon; **the radio was going at full** ~ la radio marchait à plein volume. (**b**) *(explosion)* explosion *f*; *(shock wave) [bomb, furnace etc]* souffle *m*. *(lit, fig)* **at full** ~ à plein; ~ **of air/steam** jet *m* d'air/de vapeur; ~ **of wind** coup *m* de vent, rafale *f*; *(wind)* **the icy** ~ le souffle glacé (du vent). (**c**) *(US)* fête *f*, foire *f*. **2** *adj*: ~ **furnace** haut fourneau *m*. **3** *vt rocks* faire sauter; *[lightning]* foudroyer; *hopes, future* anéantir. **4** *excl* (*) la barbe! * ~ **him!** il est embêtant! *

◆ **blast off** *vi [rocket etc]* être mis à feu.

◆ **blasted** * *adj* fichu * *(before n)*. ◆ **blasting** *n (Tech)* minage *m*; **'~ing in progress'** 'attention, tir de mines'. ◆ **blast-off** *n (Space)* lancement *m*.

blatant ['bleɪt(ə)nt] *adj injustice, lie etc* criant, flagrant; *bully, social climber* éhonté; *coward, thief, liar* fieffé *(before n)*. ◆ **blatantly** *adv* d'une manière flagrante.

blather ['blæðəʳ] *vi* raconter des bêtises.

blaze¹ [bleɪz] **1** *n (fire)* feu *m*, flambée *f*; *(conflagration)* incendie *m*; *[gems, beauty etc]* éclat *m*. ~ **of light** torrent *m* de lumière; ~ **of colour** flamboiement *m* de couleur(s); **a** ~ **of anger** une explosion de colère; **go to ~s!** * va te faire voir! *; **how the ~s!** * comment diable!; **like~s** * comme un fou (*f* une folle). **2** *vi [fire]* flamber; *[sun, colour]* flamboyer; *[jewel, light]* resplendir; *[anger]* éclater. **blazing with colour** resplendissant de couleur.

◆ **blaze away** *vi [soldiers, guns]* maintenir un feu nourri (*at* contre). ◆ **blaze up** *vi [fire]* s'enflammer; *[person, anger]* éclater.

◆ **blazing** *adj* (**a**) *building etc* en feu, en flammes; *torch* enflammé; *sun* éclatant, ardent; *(fig) eyes* qui jette des éclairs; *jewel* étincelant; *colour* très vif; (**b**) *(*: angry)* furibard *; (**c**) *(fig) indiscretion, lie* flagrant.

blaze² [bleɪz] **1** *n (mark) [horse etc]* étoile *f*; *[tree]* marque *f*. **2** *vt*: **to** ~ **a trail** *(lit)* frayer un chemin; *(fig)* montrer la voie.

blazer ['bleɪzəʳ] *n* blazer *m*.

bleach [bliːtʃ] **1** *n* décolorant *m*; *(liquid)* eau *f* oxygénée. **(household)** ~ eau de Javel. **2** *vt linen, bones etc* blanchir; *hair* décolorer. **to** ~ **one's hair** se décolorer (les cheveux). ◆ **bleach out** *vt sep colour* enlever.

bleak [bliːk] *adj country, landscape* exposé au vent, désolé; *room* nu, austère; *weather, wind* froid; *existence* sombre; *prospect* lugubre; *smile* triste. **things look rather** ~ **for him** les choses se présentent plutôt mal pour lui. ◆ **bleakly** *adv look* sombrement; *speak* d'un ton morne. ◆ **bleakness** *n* aspect désolé; austérité *f*; froid *m*; aspect sombre; tristesse *f*.

bleary ['blɪərɪ] *adj eyes (from sleep, fatigue)* voilé; *(from illness)* chassieux; *(from tears)* larmoyant. ◆ **bleary-eyed** *adj* aux yeux voilés *etc*.

bleat [bliːt] **1** *vi* bêler; *(‡: complain)* se plaindre (*about* de). **2** *n* bêlement *m*.

bleed [bliːd] *pret, ptp* **bled** [bled] **1** *vi* saigner. **his nose is ~ing** il saigne du nez; **he is ~ing to death** il perd tout son sang; *(iro)* **my heart ~s for you** tu me fends le cœur. **2** *vt brakes, radiator* purger; *person* saigner. **to** ~ **sb white** saigner qn à blanc. ◆ **bleeding** **1** *n* saignement *m*; *(more serious)* hémorragie *f*; **2** *adj wound* saignant; *person* qui saigne; *(fig) heart* brisé.

bleep [bliːp] **1** *n (Rad, TV)* top *m*; *[pocket call radio]* bip *m*. **2** *vi* émettre des signaux. **3** *vt* biper. ◆ **bleeper** *n* bip *m*.

blemish ['blemɪʃ] *n* défaut *m*; *(on fruit, reputation)* tache *f*.

blench [blen(t)ʃ] *vi (flinch)* sursauter; *(turn pale)* blêmir. **without ~ing** sans broncher.

blend [blend] **1** *n (gen)* mélange *m*; *[qualities]* alliance *f*. **excellent** ~ **of tea** thé *m* d'excellente qualité; *[coffee]* **Brazilian** ~ café *m* du Brésil; **'our own ~'** 'mélange (spécial de la) maison'. **2** *vt (gen)* mélanger (*with* à, avec); *qualities* joindre (*with* à); *colours, styles* fondre. **3** *vi* (~ **in**) *(gen)* se mélanger (*with* à, avec); *[voices, perfumes]* se confondre; *[styles]* se marier; *[ideas, political parties, races]* fusionner; *[colours] (shade in)* se fondre; *(go together)* aller bien ensemble. ◆ **blender** *n (Tech)* malaxeur *m*; *(Culin)* mixeur *m*.

bless [bles] *pret, ptp* **blessed** [blest] *or* **blest** *vt* bénir. **God** ~ **the king!** Dieu bénisse le roi!; **I was never ~ed with children** je n'ai jamais connu le bonheur d'avoir des enfants; *(iro)* **she'll** ~ **you for this!** elle va te bénir!; ~ **you!** vous êtes un ange!; *(sneezing)* à vos souhaits!; **and Paul,** ~ **his heart, had no idea that...** et ce brave Paul dans son innocence ne savait pas que...; ~ **his little heart!** qu'il est mignon!; ~ **my soul!** *, **well I'm blest!** * ça alors! * ◆ **blessed** ['blesɪd] *adj* (**a**) *(Rel) (holy)* béni, saint; *(happy)* bienheureux; **B~ed Virgin** Sainte Vierge; **B~ed Sacrament** Saint Sacrement; **the B~ed Antony Bennet** le bienheureux Antony Bennet; (**b**) (*) fichu * *(before n)*, satané *(before n)*; **that ~ed child** ce fichu * gosse; **the whole ~ed day** toute la sainte journée; **every ~ed evening** tous les soirs que le bon Dieu fait *. ◆ **blessing** *n* (**a**) *(prayer)* bénédiction *f*; **with God's ~ing** par la grâce de Dieu; **the plan had his ~ing** * il avait donné sa bénédiction à ce projet; *(at meal)* **to ask a ~ing** dire le bénédicité; (**b**) *(benefit)* bienfait *m*; **the ~ings of civilization** les bienfaits *or* les avantages *mpl* de la civilisation; **what a ~ing that...** quelle chance que... + *subj*; **this rain has been a real ~ing** * cette pluie a été une vraie bénédiction *; **it was a ~ing in disguise** c'était malgré les apparences un bien.

blew [bluː] *pret of* **blow¹**.

blight [blaɪt] **1** *n [cereals, rose]* rouille *f*; *[potato]* mildiou *n*; *[fruit trees]* cloque *f*; *(fig)* fléau *m*. **urban** ~ dégradation urbaine. **2** *vt plants* rouiller; *hopes* anéantir; *career, life, future* gâcher.

blighter * ['blaɪtəʳ] *n* type * *m*, bonne femme. **silly** ~ imbécile *mf*; **lucky** ~! quel(le) veinard(e) *!; **you** ~! espèce de chameau! *

blimey ‡ ['blaɪmɪ] *excl* mince alors! *

blind [blaɪnd] **1** *adj person, obedience* aveugle; *corner, flying* sans visibilité; *passage* sans issue; *door, window* faux. **a ~ man/woman** un/une aveugle; **~ man's buff** colin-maillard *m*; **a ~ boy** un jeune aveugle; **~ in one eye** borgne; **as ~ as a bat** myope comme une taupe *; **it was approaching on his ~ side** cela approchait dans son angle mort; **~ spot** *(Med)* point *m* aveugle; *(Aut, Aviat)* angle *m* mort; *(fig)* **that was his ~ spot** sur ce point il refusait d'y voir clair; **she was ~ to his faults** elle ne voyait pas ses défauts; **to turn a ~ eye to** fermer les yeux sur; **~ alley** impasse *f*; **a ~-alley job** une situation sans avenir; **~ date** rencontre arrangée; **not a ~ bit of use** ‡ qui ne sert strictement à rien.
2 *vt* aveugler; *(fig)* aveugler (*to* sur). **the war-~ed** les aveugles *mpl* de guerre.
3 *n* (**a**) **the ~** les aveugles *mpl*; **it's the ~ leading the ~** c'est comme l'aveugle qui conduit l'aveugle. (**b**) *[window]* store *m*. (**c**) *(pretence)* feinte *f*, masque *m*. (**d**) **to go on a ~** ‡ (aller) se soûler la gueule ‡.
4 *adv fly* sans visibilité. **~ drunk** ‡ complètement rond *.
◆ **blindfold** **1** *vt* bander les yeux à *or* de ; **2** *n* bandeau *m*; **3** *adj* aux yeux bandés ; **4** *adv* les yeux bandés. ◆ **blinding** *adj* aveuglant. ◆ **blindly** *adv* aveuglément. ◆ **blindness** *n* cécité *f*; *(fig)* aveuglement *m* (*to* devant); **~ness to the truth** refus *m* de voir la vérité.

blink [blɪŋk] **1** *n* clignotement *m* (des yeux). **my telly's on the ~** * ma télé est détraquée. **2** *vi* cligner des yeux; *[light]* vaciller. **3** *vt*: **to ~ one's eyes** cligner des yeux; **to ~ back the tears** refouler les larmes (d'un battement de paupières).
◆ **blinkers** *npl [horse]* œillères *fpl*; *(Aut)* feux *mpl* de détresse. ◆ **blinking** * *adj* fichu * *(before n)*; **~ing idiot** espèce *f* d'idiot.

bliss [blɪs] *n (Rel)* béatitude *f*; *(gen)* félicité *f*. **what ~! *, it's ~! *** c'est merveilleux!, c'est divin!
◆ **blissful** *adj (Rel, gen)* bienheureux; (*) divin, merveilleux. ◆ **blissfully** *adv smile* d'un air béat; *happy, unaware* parfaitement.

blister ['blɪstə^r] **1** *n [skin]* ampoule *f*; *[paint]* boursouflure *f*; *[metal, skin]* soufflure *f*; (‡ *pej: person)* plaie * *f*. **2** *vi* former une *or* des ampoule(s); *[paint]* se boursoufler. ◆ **blistering** *adj heat, day* étouffant; *sun* brûlant; *attack* cinglant. ◆ **blister-pack** *n (Comm: for pills)* plaquette *f*; *(for display)* emballage *m* pelliculé.

blithe [blaɪð] *adj* joyeux. ◆ **blithely** *adv* joyeusement.

blithering * ['blɪð(ə)rɪŋ] *adj*: **~ idiot** espèce *f* d'idiot(e).

blitz [blɪts] **1** *n (Mil)* attaque *f* éclair *inv*; *(Aviat)* bombardement *m* (aérien). **the B~** le Blitz; *(fig)* **to have a ~ on sth** s'attaquer à qch. **2** *vt* bombarder. ◆ **blitzkrieg** *n* guerre-éclair *f*.

blizzard ['blɪzəd] *n* tempête *f* de neige.

bloated ['bləʊtɪd] *adj (gen)* gonflé; *face* bouffi; *stomach* ballonné; *(with pride etc)* bouffi (*with* de).

bloater ['bləʊtə^r] *n* (hareng *m*) bouffi *m*.

blob [blɒb] *n (drop)* grosse goutte *f*; *(spot, stain)* tache *f*.

bloc [blɒk] *n* bloc *m (Pol)*. **en ~** en bloc.

block [blɒk] **1** *n* (**a**) *[stone]* bloc *m*; *[wood]* bille *f*; *[butcher, blacksmith, executioner]* billot *m*; *[chocolate]* plaque *f*. *(toys)* **~s** (jeu *m* de) cubes *mpl*. (**b**) *[buildings]* pâté *m* (de maisons). **a ~ of flats, an apartment ~** un immeuble; **to walk round the ~** faire le tour du pâté de maisons; *(US)* **3 ~s away** 3 rues plus loin. (**c**) *[prison, hospital]* quartier *m*, pavillon *m*; *[factory]* bâtiment *m*. (**d**) *(obstruction) [traffic]* embouteillage *m*, encombrement *m*; *[pipe]* obstruction *f*; *(Med, Psych)* blocage *m*. (**e**) *(unit) [tickets]* série *f*; *[shares]* tranche *f*; *[seats]* groupe *m*. (**f**) *(Tech)* **~ and tackle** palan *m*. **2** *adj*: **in ~ capitals** *or* **letters** en majuscules *fpl* d'imprimerie. **3** *vt (gen)* bloquer; *pipe etc* boucher; *(Ftbl) opponent* gêner. **to ~ sb's way** barrer le chemin à qn.
◆ **block off** *vt sep part of road etc* interdire; *(accidentally)* obstruer. ◆ **block out** *vt sep* (**a**) *(obscure) view* boucher; *(censor) passage* caviarder. (**b**) *(sketch roughly) scheme* ébaucher. ◆ **block up** *vt sep gangway* encombrer; *pipe* bloquer; *window, entrance* murer, condamner; *hole* boucher, bloquer.
◆ **blockade** **1** *n* blocus *m*; **2** *vt* bloquer. ◆ **blockage** *n (gen)* obstruction *f*; *(Med, Psych)* blocage *m*; *(fig)* bouchon *m*. ◆ **blockbuster** * *n* bombe *f* de gros calibre; *(film, TV series)* superproduction *f* ; *(argument)* argument *m* massue *inv*. ◆ **blockhead** * *n* imbécile *mf*. ◆ **blockhouse** *n* blockhaus *m*.

bloke * [bləʊk] *n* type * *m*.

blond(e) [blɒnd] *adj, n* blond(e) *m(f)*.

blood [blʌd] **1** *n* sang *m*. **till the ~ comes** jusqu'au sang; **it's like trying to get ~ out of a stone** c'est comme si on parlait à un mur; **bad ~** désaccord *m*; **his ~ will be on your head** vous aurez sa mort sur la conscience; **my ~ was boiling** je bouillais (de rage); **his ~ is up** il est très monté; **he's out for ~** * il cherche qn sur qui passer sa colère; **she is out for his ~** * elle veut sa peau *; **his ~ ran cold** son sang s'est figé *or* s'est glacé dans ses veines; **~ is thicker than water** la voix du sang est la plus forte; **it's in his ~** il a cela dans le sang; **of Irish ~** de sang irlandais; *(fig)* **new ~** sang nouveau.
2 *adj temperature* du sang; *group, plasma, transfusion* sanguin. **~ bank** banque *f* du sang; **~ bath** massacre *m*; **~ blister** pinçon *m*; **~ brother** frère *m* de sang; **~ cell** cellule *m* sanguine; **~ corpuscle** globule *m* sanguin; **~ count** numération *f* globulaire; **~ donor** donneur *m*, -euse *f* de sang; **~ grouping** recherche *f* du groupe sanguin; **~ heat** température *f* du sang; **~ lust** soif *f* de sang; **~ money** prix *m* du sang; **~ orange** (orange *f*) sanguine *f*; **~ poisoning** empoisonnement *m* du sang; **~ pressure** tension *f* (artérielle); **to have high/low ~ pressure** faire de l'hypertension/ hypotension; **to take sb's ~ pressure** prendre la tension de qn; **his ~ pressure went up** sa tension a monté; *(fig)* il a failli avoir une attaque; **~ relation** parent(e) *m(f)* par le sang; **~ sports** sports *mpl* sanguinaires; **~ test** analyse *f* du sang; **~ vessel** vaisseau *m* sanguin.
◆ **blood-and-thunder** *adj novel* à sensation; **a ~-and-thunder play** *or* **film** un sombre mélodrame. ◆ **bloodcurdling** *adj* à vous figer le sang. ◆ **bloodhound** *n* limier *m*. ◆ **bloodless** *adj complexion* anémié; *victory* sans effusion de sang. ◆ **bloodlessly** *adv* sans effusion de sang. ◆ **bloodletting** *n* saignée *f (Med)*. ◆ **blood-red** *adj* rouge sang *inv*. ◆ **bloodshed** *n* effusion *f* de sang. ◆ **bloodshot** *adj* injecté (de sang); **to become ~shot** s'injecter. ◆ **bloodstain** *n* tache *f* de sang. ◆ **bloodstained** *adj* taché de sang, ensanglanté. ◆ **bloodstock** *n* bêtes *fpl* de sang. ◆ **bloodstream** *n* sang *m*, système *m* sanguin. ◆ **bloodthirsty** *adj* sanguinaire.

bloody ['blʌdɪ] **1** *adj* (**a**) *hands, weapon* taché de sang, ensanglanté; *battle* sanglant; *nose* en sang. (**b**) (‡) foutu ‡ *(before n)*. **it's a ~ nuisance** ce que c'est emmerdant ‡. **2** *adv* (‡) vachement ‡. **not ~ likely!** tu te fous de moi! ‡ ◆ **bloody-minded** ‡ *adj* mauvais coucheur. ◆ **bloody-mindedness** *n*: **out of sheer ~-mindedness** ‡ (rien que) pour emmerder le monde ‡.

bloom [blu:m] **1** *n* (**a**) *(flower)* fleur *f*. **in ~** *flower* éclos; *tree* en fleurs; **in full ~** *flower* épanoui; *tree* en pleine floraison. (**b**) *[fruit, skin]* velouté *m*. **2** *vi [flower]* éclore; *[tree]* fleurir; *[person]* être florissant. ~**ing with health** resplendissant de santé. ◆**bloomer** *n* (**a**) (*‡: mistake)* gaffe *f*; (**b**) *(Dress)* ~**ers** culotte *f* bouffante. ◆**blooming** * *adj* fichu * *(before n)*.

blossom ['blɒsəm] **1** *n* fleurs *fpl*; *(one flower)* fleur *f*. **a spray of** ~ une petite branche fleurie; **peach** ~ fleur de pêcher. **2** *vi* fleurir; *(fig)* s'épanouir. *(fig)* **to** ~ **(out) into** devenir.

blot [blɒt] **1** *n* tache *f*. **a** ~ **on his character** une tache à sa réputation; **to be a** ~ **on the landscape** déparer le paysage. **2** *vt* (**a**) *(spot with ink)* tacher d'encre. *(fig)* **to** ~ **one's copybook** faire un accroc à sa réputation. (**b**) *(dry) ink, page* sécher.
◆**blot out** *vt sep words* rayer; *memories* effacer; *[fog etc] view* masquer; *(destroy) city* annihiler.
◆**blotter** *n* buvard *m*; *(desk pad)* sous-main *m inv*; *(US: record)* registre *m*. ◆**blotting paper** *n* (papier *m*) buvard *m*.

blotch [blɒtʃ] **1** *n* tache *f*. **2** *vt* tacher. ◆**blotchy** *adj face* marbré; *paint* couvert de taches.

blotto ‡ ['blɒtəʊ] *adj* bourré ‡, rond ‡.

blouse [blaʊz] *n* chemisier *m*.

blouson ['blu:zɒn] *n* blouson *m*.

blow[1] [bləʊ] *pret* **blew**, *ptp* **blown** **1** *vt* (**a**) *[wind] ship* pousser; *leaves* chasser. **the wind blew the ship off course** le vent a fait dévier le navire; **the wind blew the door open** un coup de vent a ouvert la porte. (**b**) *fire* souffler sur; *bellows* faire marcher; *egg* vider. **to** ~ **one's nose** se moucher. (**c**) *bubbles* faire; *glass* souffler; *kiss* envoyer. (**d**) *trumpet, horn* jouer de, souffler dans. **to** ~ **a whistle** siffler; **to** ~ **one's own trumpet** chanter ses propres louanges. (**e**) *fuse, safe* faire sauter. **to** ~ **a gasket** griller un joint de culasse; **the whole plan has been** ~**n sky-high** tout le projet a sauté; **I blew £5 on a new hat** * j'ai claqué * 5 livres pour un nouveau chapeau. (**f**) *(*: spoil)* rater, gâcher. (**g**) *(phrases)* **to** ~ **one's top** ‡ piquer une colère *; **to** ~ **the gaff** ‡ vendre la mèche; **he realized he was** ~**n** ‡ il a compris qu'il était brûlé *; ~ **the expense!** * tant pis pour la dépense!; **well, I'm** ~**ed!** * ça alors! *; ~ **it!** * la barbe! *, zut! *
2 *vi* (**a**) *[wind, person, animal]* souffler. **to** ~ **on one's fingers/one's soup** souffler dans ses doigts/sur sa soupe; **it was** ~**ing a gale** le vent soufflait en tempête; **it's** ~**ing great guns** * il fait un vent à décorner les bœufs *; *(fig)* **to see which way the wind** ~**s** regarder de quel côté souffle le vent; **to** ~ **hot and cold** *[person]* souffler le chaud et le froid; *[enthusiasm]* avoir des hauts et des bas; **the door blew open** un coup de vent a ouvert la porte; **his hat blew out of the window** son chapeau s'est envolé par la fenêtre. (**b**) *[trumpet]* sonner; *[whistle]* retentir; *[foghorn]* mugir. **when the whistle** ~**s** au coup de sifflet. (**c**) *[fuse, light bulb]* sauter; *[tyre]* éclater.
◆**blow down** **1** *vi [tree etc]* être abattu par le vent. **2** *vt sep [person]* abattre (en soufflant); *[wind]* faire tomber. ◆**blow in** **1** *vi (*: arrive)* débarquer *. **2** *vt sep door, window* enfoncer. **look what the wind's** ~**n in!** * regardez qui s'amène! *
◆**blow off** **1** *vi [hat]* s'envoler. **2** *vt sep hat* emporter. **that blew the lid off the whole business** * c'est cela qui a fait découvrir le pot aux roses; **to** ~ **off steam** lâcher de la vapeur; *(*: fig)* se défouler *. ◆**blow out** **1** *vi [lamp]* s'éteindre; *[tyre]* éclater; *[fuse]* sauter. **2** *vt sep lamp* éteindre; *candle* souffler; *one's cheeks* gonfler. **to** ~ **one's brains out** se brûler la cervelle. ◆**blow over** **1** *vi [storm, dispute]* passer. **2** *vt sep tree* renverser.
◆**blow up** **1** *vi [bomb]* exploser; *(*: get angry)* sauter au plafond; *[wind]* se lever; *[storm] (gather)* se préparer; *(begin)* éclater; *[affair, crisis]* se déclencher. **2** *vt sep building* faire sauter; *tyre* gonfler; *photo* agrandir; *event* exagérer; *(‡: reprimand)* passer un (bon) savon à *.
◆**blow dryer** *n* sèche-cheveux *m inv*. ◆**blow-dry** *n* brushing *m*. ◆**blower** ‡ *n (loudspeaker)* haut-parleur *m*; *(telephone)* téléphone *m*. ◆**blow-fly** *n* mouche *f* à viande. ◆**blowhole** *n* évent *m*. ◆**blowlamp** *n* lampe *f* à souder. ◆**blow-out** *n [tyre]* éclatement *m*; *(Elec)* court-circuit *m*; *(‡: feast)* gueuleton ‡ *m*. ◆**blowtorch** *n* lampe *f* à souder. ◆**blow-up** *n* explosion *f*; *(‡: quarrel)* engueulade ‡ *f*; *(Phot *)* agrandissement *m*.
◆**blowy** *adj* éventé.

blow[2] [bləʊ] *n (gen)* coup *m*; *(with fist)* coup de poing. **to come to** ~**s** en venir aux mains; **at one** ~ du premier coup; **he gave me a** ~**-by-**~ **account** il ne m'a fait grâce d'aucun détail; **it was a terrible** ~ **for him** cela a été un coup terrible pour lui.

blowzy ['blaʊzɪ] *adj hair* mal peigné; *woman* débraillé.

blubber ['blʌbəʳ] **1** *n [whale]* blanc *m* de baleine. **2** *vi (cry)* pleurer comme un veau.

bludgeon ['blʌdʒ(ə)n] **1** *n* matraque *f*. **2** *vt* matraquer. *(fig)* **he** ~**ed me into doing it** il m'a forcé la main (pour que je le fasse).

blue [blu:] **1** *adj* (**a**) bleu. ~ **with cold** bleu de froid; **you may talk till you are** ~ **in the face** * tu peux toujours parler; ~ **baby** enfant bleu; ~ **blood** sang bleu; ~ **cheese** (fromage *m*) bleu *m*; ~ **jeans** blue-jean *m*; ~ **whale** baleine bleue; **once in a** ~ **moon** * tous les trente-six du mois; **like a** ~ **streak** * au triple galop; **to have a** ~ **fit** ‡ piquer une crise *; *(fig)* **to feel** ~ * avoir le cafard *; **to be in a** ~ **funk** * avoir la frousse *. (**b**) *(obscene) joke* grivois; *book, film* porno * *inv*.
2 *n (colour)* bleu *m*. **the** ~ *(sky)* l'azur *m*; *(sea)* les flots *mpl*; *(fig)* **to come out of the** ~ être complètement inattendu; **to go off into the** ~ *(into the sky)* disparaître dans le ciel; *(into the unknown)* partir à l'aventure; *(out of touch)* disparaître de la circulation *; **the** ~**s** * *(depression)* le cafard *; *(Mus)* le blues; *(Univ)* **he is a rugby** ~ il a représenté son université au rugby.
3 *vt (*: squander)* gaspiller, claquer ‡.
◆**bluebell** *n* jacinthe *f* des bois. ◆**bluebird** *n* oiseau *m* bleu. ◆**bluebottle** *n* mouche *f* bleue.
◆**blue-eyed** *adj* aux yeux bleus; *(fig)* **the** ~**-eyed boy** le chouchou *. ◆**blueprint** *n (fig)* plan *m*, schéma *m* directeur (*for* de). ◆**bluestocking** *n* bas-bleu *m*.

bluff[1] [blʌf] **1** *adj person* direct. **2** *n (headland)* falaise *f* avancée.

bluff[2] [blʌf] **1** *vti* bluffer *. **2** *n* bluff * *m*. **to call sb's** ~ prouver que qn bluffe *. ◆**bluffer** *n* bluffeur * *m*, -euse * *f*.

blunder ['blʌndəʳ] **1** *n* gaffe *f*; *(error)* grosse faute. **2** *vi (make mistake)* faire une gaffe *or* une grosse faute. **to** ~ **in/out** *etc* entrer/sortir *etc* à l'aveuglette; **to** ~ **against** *or* **into sth** se cogner contre qch. ◆**blunderer** *n* gaffeur *m*, -euse *f*. ◆**blundering** *adj* maladroit.

blunt [blʌnt] **1** *adj* (**a**) *blade, knife, point, needle* émoussé; *pencil* mal taillé. *(Jur)* **with a** ~ **instrument** avec un instrument contondant. (**b**) *(outspoken) person, speech* carré, brusque *(slightly pej)*; *fact* brutal. **he was very** ~ il n'a pas mâché ses mots. **2** *vt blade, pencil etc* émousser; *palate, feelings* blaser. ◆**bluntly** *adv speak* carrément. ◆**bluntness** *n* état émoussé *etc*; *(outspokenness)* franc-parler *m*, brusquerie *f (slightly pej)*.

blur [blɜ:ʳ] **1** *n (vague form)* masse *f* confuse, tache *f* floue; *(mist: on mirror etc)* buée *f*. **2** *vt shining surface* embuer, troubler; *inscription, view, outline* estomper. **eyes** ~**red with tears** yeux voilés de larmes. ◆**blurred** *adj (TV, Phot etc)* flou; *eyesight* troublé.

blurb [blɜ:b] *n (gen)* baratin * *m* publicitaire; *(on book jacket)* texte *m* de présentation *or* de couverture.

blurt [blɜːt] *vt* (~ **out**) *word* lâcher; *information* laisser échapper.

blush [blʌʃ] **1** *vi* rougir (*with* de). **I ~ for him** j'ai honte pour lui; **I ~ to say so** je rougis de le dire. **2** *n* rougeur *f*. **with a ~** en rougissant; **without a ~** sans rougir. ◆ **blusher** *n* fard *m* à joues. ◆ **blushing** *adj (with shame)* le rouge au front; *(from embarrassment)* le rouge aux joues; *bride* rougissant.

bluster ['blʌstəʳ] *vi [wind, storm]* faire rage; *[person] (rage)* tempêter, fulminer (*at sb* contre qn); *(boast)* fanfaronner. ◆ **blustering** **1** *adj* fanfaron ; **2** *n* fanfaronnades *fpl*. ◆ **blustery** *adj wind* qui souffle en rafales; *weather, day* à bourrasques.

boa ['bəʊə] *n* boa *m*. ~ **constrictor** boa constricteur *m*.

boar [bɔːʳ] *n (wild)* sanglier *m*; *(male pig)* verrat *m*. **~'s head** hure *f*. ◆ **boarhound** *n* vautre *m*.

board [bɔːd] **1** *n* (**a**) *(piece of wood)* planche *f*. *(Theat)* **the ~s** les planches, la scène; *(fig)* **above ~** tout ce qu'il y a de plus régulier; *(fig)* **across the ~** *(adv)* systématiquement; *(adj)* de portée générale. (**b**) *(meals)* pension *f*. ~ **and lodging** (chambre *f* avec) pension; **full ~** pension complète. (**c**) *(group of officials)* conseil *m*, commission *f*. ~ **of directors** conseil d'administration; **he has a seat on the ~** il siège au conseil d'administration; *(Brit)* **B~ of Trade** ministère *m* du Commerce; **medical ~** commission *f* médicale; *(Mil)* conseil de révision; ~ **of inquiry** commission *f* d'enquête; ~ **of examiners** jury *m* (d'examen). (**d**) *(Aviat, Naut)* **to go on ~** monter à bord (*a ship etc* d'un navire *etc*); **to take on ~** embarquer; *(fig)* prendre note de; **on ~ (ship)** à bord; **to go by the ~** *[plan, attempt]* échouer; *[business]* aller à vau-l'eau; *[principles, dreams]* être abandonné. (**e**) *(cardboard)* carton *m*; *(for games)* tableau *m*. **2** *adj decision, meeting* du conseil d'administration. ~ **game** jeu *m* de société; ~ **room** salle *f* de conférence; ~ **walk** passage *m* en planches. **3** *vt* (**a**) *ship, plane* monter à bord de; *train, bus* monter dans; *(Naut) (in attack)* monter à l'abordage de, prendre à l'abordage; *(for inspection)* arraisonner. (**b**) *(lodge)* prendre en pension. **4** *vi*: **to ~ with sb** être en pension chez qn.

◆ **board out** *vt sep person* mettre en pension (*with* chez). ◆ **board up** *vt sep window* boucher, clouer des planches en travers de.

◆ **boarder** *n* pensionnaire *mf*. ◆ **boarding** *adj*: **~ing card** *or* **pass** carte *f* d'embarquement; **~ing house** pension *f* (de famille); **~ing school** pension *f*, pensionnat *m*; **to send a child to ~ing school** mettre un enfant en pension.

boast [bəʊst] **1** *n* fanfaronnade *f*. **it is their ~ that they succeeded** ils se vantent d'avoir réussi. **2** *vi* se vanter (*about, of* de). **3** *vt* (être fier de) posséder.

◆ **boaster** *n* vantard(e) *m(f)*. ◆ **boastful** *adj* vantard. ◆ **boastfully** *adv* en se vantant. ◆ **boasting** *n* vantardise *f*.

boat [bəʊt] **1** *n (gen)* bateau *m*; *(small, light)* embarcation *f*; *(ship)* navire *m*; *(rowing ~)* barque *f*, canot *m*; *(ship's ~)* canot, chaloupe *f*; *(sailing ~)* voilier *m*; *(barge)* péniche *f*. **to go by ~** prendre le bateau; **to cross by ~** traverser en bateau; *(fig)* **we're all in the same ~** nous sommes tous logés à la même enseigne. **2** *vi*: **to go ~ing** aller faire une partie de canot. **3** *adj*: ~ **hook** gaffe *f*; ~ **people** gens *mpl* de la mer *(réfugiés du Vietnam etc)*; ~ **race** course *f* d'aviron; ~ **train** *train qui assure la correspondance avec le ferry*.

◆ **boatbuilder** *n* constructeur *m* de bateaux. ◆ **boatbuilding** *n* construction *f* de bateaux. ◆ **boater** *n (hat)* canotier *m*. ◆ **boathouse** *n* abri *m* à bateaux. ◆ **boating** **1** *n* canotage *m*; **2** *adj club, accident* de canotage; *holiday, trip* en bateau. ◆ **boatload** *or* ◆ **boatful** *n [goods etc]* cargaison *f*; *[people]* plein bateau *m*. ◆ **boatswain** ['bəʊsn] *n* maître *m* d'équipage. ◆ **boatyard** *n* chantier *m* de construction de bateaux.

bob¹ [bɒb] **1** *vi* monter et descendre. **to ~ up and down** *(in the air)* pendiller; *(in water)* danser sur l'eau; **he ~bed * up again in London** il s'est repointé * à Londres. **2** *n (curtsy)* petite révérence *f*.

bob² * † [bɒb] *n, pl inv (Brit)* shilling *m*.

bob³ [bɒb] **1** *n (haircut)* coiffure courte; *(straight)* coiffure à la Jeanne d'Arc. **2** *vt* couper court.

bob⁴ [bɒb] *n* (**~sled, ~sleigh**) bobsleigh *m*.

bobbin ['bɒbɪn] *n (gen)* bobine *f*; *[lace]* fuseau *m*.

bobby * ['bɒbɪ] *n (policeman)* flic * *m*.

bod ⁑ [bɒd] *n* type * *m*; *(US)* corps *m*.

bode [bəʊd] *vi*: **to ~ well/ill** être de bon/mauvais augure (*for* pour).

bodice ['bɒdɪs] *n* corsage *m (d'une robe)*.

bodkin ['bɒdkɪn] *n* grosse aiguille *f*.

body ['bɒdɪ] **1** *n* (**a**) corps *m*. **(dead) ~** cadavre *m*, corps; **just enough to keep ~ and soul together** juste assez pour subsister; **he's a pleasant little ~** c'est un gentil petit bonhomme; ~ **of troops** corps de troupes; **the main ~ of the army** le gros de l'armée; **the great ~ of readers** la masse des lecteurs; **a large ~ of people** une masse de gens; **in a ~** en masse; **the ~ politic** le corps politique; **legislative ~** corps législatif; **a large ~ of water** une grande masse d'eau; *(Phys)* **heavenly ~** corps céleste. (**b**) *[car]* carrosserie *f*; *[plane]* fuselage *m*; *[ship]* coque *f*; *[camera]* boîtier *m*; *[speech, document]* fond *m*. **in the ~ of the hall** au centre de la salle. (**c**) *[wine, paper]* corps *m*. **to give one's hair ~** donner du volume à ses cheveux. **2** *adj*: ~ **stocking** body *m*; ~ **warmer** gilet matelassé.

◆ **bodily** **1** *adv carry* dans ses bras; *lift* à bras-le-corps ; **2** *adj need, comfort* matériel; *pain* physique; **bodily harm** blessure *f*. ◆ **bodybuilder** *n (food)* aliment *m* énergétique; *(person)* culturiste *mf*. ◆ **body-building** *n* culturisme *m*. ◆ **bodyguard** *n (group)* gardes *mpl* du corps; *(person)* garde *m* du corps. ◆ **bodywork** *n (Aut)* carrosserie *f*.

boffin * ['bɒfɪn] *n* chercheur *m (scientifique)*.

bog [bɒg] *n* marécage *m*; *[peat]* tourbière *f*; (⁑: *lavatory)* W.-C. *mpl*. ◆ **bog down** *vt sep*: **to get ~ged down** s'enliser (*in* dans). ◆ **boggy** *adj* marécageux, tourbeux.

bogey ['bəʊgɪ] *n (frightening)* épouvantail *m*, démon *m*; *(bugbear)* bête *f* noire. *(fig)* **it is a ~ for them** cela leur fait peur. ◆ **bogeyman** *n* croquemitaine *m*.

boggle ['bɒgl] *vi (be amazed)* être ahuri (*at* par); *(hesitate)* hésiter (*at* à). **the mind ~s!** c'est ahurissant!; **his mind ~d when he heard the news** la nouvelle l'a plongé dans l'ahurissement.

Bogota [ˌbəʊgə'tɑː] *n* Bogota.

bogus ['bəʊgəs] *adj* faux *(before n)*, simulé.

bohemian [bə(ʊ)'hiːmɪən] *adj, n (gipsy)* bohémien(ne) *m(f)*; *(artist, writer etc)* bohème *mf*.

boil¹ [bɔɪl] *n (Med)* furoncle *m*.

boil² [bɔɪl] **1** *vi* (**a**) *[water etc]* bouillir. **the kettle is ~ing** l'eau bout (dans la bouilloire); **to ~ fast/gently** bouillir à gros bouillons/à petits bouillons; **to let the kettle ~ dry** laisser s'évaporer complètement l'eau de la bouilloire. (**b**) *[sea]* bouillonner; *[person]* bouillir (*with* de). **2** *vt water* faire bouillir; *food* (faire) cuire à l'eau, (faire) bouillir. **3** *n*: **on the ~** bouillant, qui bout; **off the ~** qui ne bout plus.

◆ **boil away** *vi* s'évaporer. ◆ **boil down** **1** *vi (fig)* revenir (*to* à). **2** *vt sep sauce etc* faire réduire; *text* réduire. ◆ **boil over** *vi* déborder. ◆ **boil up** *vi [milk]* monter. **they are ~ing up * for a row** (*or* **confrontation** *etc*) le torchon brûle!

◆ **boiled** *adj bacon, beef* bouilli; *ham* cuit; *egg* à la coque; *vegetables* cuit à l'eau; *potatoes* à l'anglaise, à l'eau; *sweet* à sucer. ◆ **boiler** **1** *n (gen)* chaudière *f*; *(for clothes)* lessiveuse *f*; *(pan)* casserole *f* ; **2** *adj*: **~er house** bâtiment *m* des chaudières; **~er room** salle *f* des chaudières; *(Naut)* chaufferie *f*; **~er suit** bleu(s) *m(pl)* de travail. ◆ **boilermaker** *n* chaudronnier *m*. ◆ **boilermaking** *n* grosse chaudronnerie *f*. ◆ **boiling** *adj water, oil* bouillant; *beef* pour pot-au-feu; *chicken* à faire au pot; **at ~ing point** *(lit)* au point d'ébullition; *(fig)* à ébullition; **it's ~ing (hot)** il fait une chaleur terrible; **I'm ~ing hot *** je crève * de chaleur!; **he is ~ing (with rage)** il bout de colère.

boisterous ['bɔɪst(ə)rəs] *adj sea, meeting* houleux; *wind* violent; *person, evening* (gai et) bruyant. ◆ **boisterously** *adv* bruyamment.

bold [bəʊld] *adj* (**a**) *(brave) person, action, look* hardi, audacieux, intrépide. **to grow ~** s'enhardir. (**b**) *(impudent)* hardi, effronté. **to be ~ enough to do** avoir l'audace de faire; **as ~ as brass** d'une impudence peu commune. (**c**) *(Art, Literat: striking)* hardi, vigoureux. **to paint in ~ strokes** avoir une touche puissante; **~ type** caractères *mpl* gras. ◆ **boldly** *adv* hardiment, avec audace; effrontément; avec vigueur. ◆ **boldness** *n* hardiesse *f*, audace *f*; effronterie *f*; vigueur *f*.

bolero [*(Mus)* bə'lɛərəʊ, *(Dress)* 'bɒlərəʊ] *n* boléro *m*.

Bolivia [bə'lɪvɪə] *n* Bolivie *f*. ◆ **Bolivian** **1** *n* Bolivien(ne) *m(f)* ; **2** *adj* bolivien.

bollard ['bɒləd] *n* borne *f*.

boloney ⁑ [bə'ləʊnɪ] *n* idioties *fpl*.

Bolshevik ['bɒlʃəvɪk], **Bolshevist** ['bɒlʃəvɪst] **1** *n* Bolchevique *mf*. **2** *adj* bolchevique. ◆ **Bolshevism** *n* bolchevisme *m*. ◆ **bolshie** * *adj (Pol)* rouge; *(gen)* querelleur.

bolster ['bəʊlstəʳ] **1** *n* traversin *m*. **2** *vt* (**~up**) soutenir (*with* par).

bolt [bəʊlt] **1** *n* (**a**) *[door, window]* verrou *m*; *[lock]* pêne *m*; *(for nut)* boulon *m*; *[cloth]* rouleau *m*; *(lightning)* éclair *m*. *(fig)* **a ~ from the blue** un coup de tonnerre dans un ciel bleu. (**b**) *(dash)* **he made a ~ for the door** il a fait un bond vers la porte; **to make a ~ for it *** se sauver à toutes jambes. **2** *adv*: **~ upright** droit comme un piquet. **3** *vi* (**a**) *(run away) [horse]* s'emballer; *[person]* se sauver. (**b**) *(move quickly)* se précipiter. **to ~ in/out** *etc* entrer/sortir *etc* comme un ouragan. **4** *vt* (**a**) *food* engouffrer. (**b**) *door, window* verrouiller. **~ the door!** mettez les verrous! (**c**) *(Tech:* **~ together***)* *beams* boulonner.

bomb [bɒm] **1** *n* bombe *f*; *(US *: film etc)* fiasco *m*, bide * *m*. **the B~** la bombe atomique. **letter/parcel ~** lettre *f*/paquet *m* piégé(e); **his party went like a ~ *** sa réception a été (un succès) du tonnerre *; **this car goes like a ~ *** elle file, cette bagnole *; **it cost a ~ *** cela a coûté les yeux de la tête. **2** *adj*: **~ crater** entonnoir *m*; **~ disposal squad** équipe *f* de déminage; **~ disposal expert** artificier *m*; **~ scare** alerte *f* à la bombe; **~ shelter** abri *m* (anti-aérien); **~ site** lieu *m* bombardé. **3** *vt town* bombarder. **4** *vi (US *: fail)* être un fiasco *or* un bide *.

◆ **bomb out** *vt sep house* détruire par un bombardement. **the family was ~ed out** la famille a dû abandonner sa maison bombardée.

◆ **bomber** *n (aircraft)* bombardier *m*; *(terrorist)* plastiqueur *m*. ◆ **bombing** **1** *n* bombardement *m*; *[terrorists]* attentat *m* au plastic *or* à la bombe ; **2** *adj raid, plane* de bombardement. ◆ **bombproof** *adj* blindé. ◆ **bombshell** *n (Mil)* obus *m*; *(fig)* **to come like a ~shell** faire l'effet d'une bombe; **she's a real ~shell! *** c'est une fille sensass! *

bombard [bɒm'bɑːd] *vt* bombarder (*with* de). ◆ **bombardment** *n* bombardement *m*.

bombast ['bɒmbæst] *n (pej)* grandiloquence *f*. ◆ **bombastic** *adj* grandiloquent. ◆ **bombastically** *adv* avec grandiloquence.

bona fide ['bəʊnə'faɪdɪ] *adj traveller* véritable; *offer* sérieux. ◆ **bona fides** *n* bonne foi *f*.

bonanza [bə'nænzə] *n (money etc)* filon *m*, mine *f* d'or; *(boon)* aubaine *f*.

bond [bɒnd] **1** *n* (**a**) *(agreement)* engagement *m*. **to enter into a ~** s'engager (*to do* à faire). (**b**) *(link)* lien(s) *m(pl)*. **~s** *(chains)* fers *mpl*, chaînes *fpl*; *(fig: ties)* liens. (**c**) *(Fin)* bon *m*, titre *m*. (**d**) *(Comm)* **to put sth into ~** entreposer qch en douane. (**e**) *(adhesion between surfaces)* adhérence *f*. **2** *vt bricks* liaisonner; *[strong glue]* coller, souder. **~ed warehouse** entrepôt *m* des douanes. ◆ **bondage** *n* esclavage *m*. ◆ **bondsman** *n* esclave *m*.

bone [bəʊn] **1** *n (gen)* os *m*; *[fish]* arête *f*; *[corset]* baleine *f*. **chilled to the ~** glacé jusqu'à la moelle (des os); **I feel it in my ~s** j'en ai le pressentiment; **~ of contention** pomme *f* de discorde; **to have a ~ to pick with sb** avoir un compte à régler avec qn; **he made no ~s about saying what he thought** il n'a pas hésité à dire ce qu'il pensait; **there are no ~s broken** il n'y a rien de cassé; *(fig)* il n'y a rien de grave; **(made) of ~** en os. **2** *adj buttons etc* en os. **~ china** porcelaine *f* tendre; **~ meal** engrais *m* (de cendres d'os). **3** *vt meat, fowl* désosser; *fish* ôter les arêtes de.

◆ **bone up** ⁑ *vt sep*, **bone up on** ⁑ *vt fus* potasser *.

◆ **boned** *adj meat* désossé; *fish* sans arêtes; *corset* baleiné. ◆ **bone-dry** *adj* absolument sec. ◆ **bonehead** ⁑ *n* crétin(e) *m(f)*. ◆ **bone-idle** * *or* ◆ **bone-lazy** * *adj* fainéant. ◆ **bone-shaker** * *n (car)* vieille guimbarde *f*. ◆ **bony** *adj tissue* osseux; *knee, person* anguleux; *fish* plein d'arêtes; *meat* plein d'os.

bonfire ['bɒnfaɪəʳ] *n* feu *m* (de joie); *(for rubbish)* feu (de jardin).

bonkers ⁑ ['bɒŋkəz] *adj* cinglé *.

Bonn [bɒn] *n* Bonn.

bonnet ['bɒnɪt] *n* bonnet *m*; *(Brit) [car]* capot *m*.

bonny ['bɒnɪ] *adj (esp Scot)* joli.

bonus ['bəʊnəs] *n* prime *f*, gratification *f*. **~ of 500 francs** 500 F de prime; *(fig)* **as a ~** en prime; *(Fin)* **~ issue** émission *f* d'actions gratuites.

boo [buː] **1** *excl* hou!, peuh! **he wouldn't say ~ to a goose *** il n'ose jamais ouvrir le bec *. **2** *vti* huer. **to be ~ed off the stage** sortir de scène sous les huées. **3** *n*: **~s** *(also* **~ing***)* huées *fpl*.

boob ⁑ [buːb] **1** *n (mistake)* gaffe *f*; *(breast)* sein *m*, nichon ⁑ *m*. **2** *vi* gaffer. ◆ **boobtube** *n (US: TV)* télé *f*; *(Dress)* bustier *m (en forme de tube)*.

booby ['buːbɪ] **1** *n* nigaud(e) *m(f)*. **2** *adj*: **~ prize** prix *m* de consolation *(décerné au dernier)*; **~ trap** traquenard *m*; *(Mil)* objet *m* piégé.

book [bʊk] **1** *n* livre *m*, bouquin * *m*; *[Bible etc]* livre; *(exercise ~)* cahier *m*; *(libretto)* livret *m*; *[samples etc]* album *m*; *[tickets etc]* carnet *m*; *[matches]* pochette *f*. **(account) ~s** livre *m* de comptes; **to keep the ~s** tenir la comptabilité; **to be on the ~s of an organization** être inscrit à une organisation; **to take one's name off the ~s** donner sa démission; *(Betting)* **to make (a) ~** inscrire les paris; **to bring sb to ~** obliger qn à rendre des comptes; **by the ~** selon les règles; **to go by the ~, to stick to the ~** appliquer strictement le règlement; **to be in sb's good/bad ~s** être bien/mal vu de qn; *(fig)* **in my ~ *** à mon avis; **that's one for the ~! *** c'est à marquer d'une pierre blanche! **2** *adj*: **~ club** club *m* du livre; **~ learning** connaissances *fpl* livresques; **~ lover** bibliophile *mf*; **~**

post tarif *m* imprimés *inv*; ~ **token** bon-cadeau *m (négociable en librairie)*.
3 *vt* (**a**) *seat* louer; *room, sleeper* retenir, réserver; *ticket* prendre. *(Theat)* **we're fully ~ed** on joue à guichets fermés; **the hotel is fully ~ed** l'hôtel est complet; **I'm ~ed for lunch** * je suis pris à déjeuner; *(Rail)* **to ~ sb through to Birmingham** assurer à qn une réservation jusqu'à Birmingham. (**b**) *(Comm, Fin) order* inscrire, enregistrer. (**c**) *(Police) driver etc* donner un procès-verbal *or* P.-V. * à; *(Ftbl) player* prendre le nom de. **to be ~ed for speeding** attraper une contravention pour excès de vitesse.
◆ **book in 1** *vi (at hotel etc)* prendre une chambre. **2** *vt sep person* réserver une chambre *etc* à. ◆ **book up** *vt sep* retenir, réserver. **the tour is ~ed up** on ne prend plus d'inscriptions pour l'excursion; **the hotel is ~ed up** l'hôtel est complet; **I'm very ~ed up** * je suis très pris.
◆ **bookable** *adj seat etc* qu'on peut retenir; **all seats ~able in advance** toutes les places peuvent être retenues à l'avance; **seats ~able from 6th June** location ouverte dès le 6 juin. ◆ **bookbinder** *n* relieur *m*, -euse *f*. ◆ **bookcase** *n* bibliothèque *f (meuble)*. ◆ **bookends** *npl* presse-livres *m inv*. ◆ **bookie** * *n* bookmaker *m*. ◆ **booking 1** *n* réservation *f*; **2** *adj*: **~ing clerk** préposé(e) *m(f)* aux réservations; **~ing office** (bureau *m* de) location *f*. ◆ **bookish** *adj* qui aime les livres. ◆ **bookkeeper** *n* comptable *mf*. ◆ **bookkeeping** *n* comptabilité *f*. ◆ **booklet** *n* petit livre, brochure *f*. ◆ **bookmaker** *n* bookmaker *m*. ◆ **bookmark** *n* signet *m*. ◆ **bookmobile** *n (US)* bibliobus *m*. ◆ **bookplate** *n* ex-libris *m inv*. ◆ **bookrest** *n* support *m* à livres. ◆ **bookseller** *n* libraire *mf*. ◆ **bookshelf** *n* rayon *m* (de bibliothèque). ◆ **bookshop** *n* librairie *f*. ◆ **bookstall** *n [station etc]* kiosque *m* à journaux; *[secondhand ~s]* étalage *m* de bouquiniste. ◆ **bookstore** *n* librairie *f*. ◆ **bookworm** *n* rat *m* de bibliothèque.

boom¹ [bu:m] *n* (**a**) *(across river etc)* barrage *m*. (**b**) *[mast]* gui *m*; *[crane]* flèche *f*; *[microphone, camera]* perche *f*.

boom² [bu:m] **1** *n (sound) [sea, waves, wind]* mugissement *m*; *[guns, thunder, voices, storm]* grondement *m*; *[organ]* ronflement *m*. **sonic ~** bang *m* supersonique. **2** *vi [wind]* mugir; *[thunder, sea, guns]* gronder; *[organ]* ronfler; *[voice]* retentir; *[person]* tonitruer. **3** *vt* (**~ out**) dire d'une voix tonitruante. ◆ **booming** *adj sound, noise* retentissant; *voice* tonitruant.

boom³ [bu:m] **1** *vi [trade]* être en expansion; *[business, sales]* être en plein essor; *[books, goods]* se vendre comme des petits pains; *[prices]* être en forte hausse. **2** *n [business, prices, shares]* montée *f* en flèche, forte hausse *f*; *[product]* popularité *f*; *[sales]* progression *f*; *(Econ:* ~ **period***)* boom *m*. ~ **town** ville *f* en plein développement.

boomerang ['bu:məræŋ] **1** *n* boomerang *m*. **2** *vi* faire boomerang.

boon [bu:n] **1** *n (godsend)* bénédiction * *f*; *(good luck)* aubaine *f*. **2** *adj*: ~ **companion** joyeux compère.

boor [bʊəʳ] *n* rustre *m*. ◆ **boorish** *adj* rustre, grossier. ◆ **boorishly** *adv behave* en rustre; *speak* grossièrement. ◆ **boorishness** *n* rudesse *f*, manque *m* de savoir-vivre.

boost [bu:st] **1** *n*: **to give sb a ~ (up)** *(help him up)* soulever qn par derrière *or* par en dessous; *(raise his morale)* remonter le moral à qn; *(do publicity for him)* faire du battage pour qn. **2** *vt (Elec)* survolter; *engine* suralimenter; *spacecraft* propulser; *price* faire monter; *output, productivity* accroître; *sales* augmenter; *product* promouvoir; *the economy* donner du tonus à; *confidence etc* renforcer.
◆ **booster** *n (Elec)* survolteur *m*; *(Rad)* amplificateur *m*; *(~er rocket)* booster *m*; *(~er shot, ~er dose)* (piqûre *f* de) rappel *m*.

boot¹ [bu:t] *n*: **to ~** par-dessus le marché.

boot² [bu:t] **1** *n* (**a**) *(gen)* botte *f*; *(ankle ~)* bottillon *m*; *[soldier]* brodequin *m*; *[workman etc]* grosse chaussure (montante). *(fig)* **the ~ is on the other foot** les rôles sont renversés; **to give sb the ~** ‡ flanquer * qn à la porte. (**b**) *[car]* coffre *m*. **2** *vt*: **to ~ sb out** flanquer * qn à la porte.
◆ **boot up** *vi* démarrer.
◆ **bootee** *n* petit chausson. ◆ **bootlace** *n* lacet *m* (de chaussure). ◆ **bootleg** * **1** *vi* faire la contrebande de l'alcool; **2** *adj* de contrebande. ◆ **bootlegger** *n* bootlegger *m*. ◆ **bootlicker** *n* lèche-bottes * *mf inv*. ◆ **bootmaker** *n* bottier *m*. ◆ **bootpolish** *n* cirage *m*. ◆ **bootstrap** *n*: **to pull o.s. up by one's (own) ~straps** se faire tout seul.

booth [bu:ð] *n [fair]* baraque *f* (foraine); *[language lab, telephone etc]* cabine *f*; *(voting ~)* isoloir *m*.

booty ['bu:tɪ] *n* butin *m*.

booze * [bu:z] **1** *n* alcool *m (boissons)*. **to buy some ~** acheter à boire. **2** *vi* biberonner *.
◆ **boozer** ‡ *n (drunkard)* pochard(e) ‡ *m(f)*; *(pub)* bistro * *m*. ◆ **booze-up** ‡ *n* partie *f* de soûlographie * *f*. ◆ **boozy** ‡ *adj person* qui a la dalle en pente ‡; *evening* où l'on boit beaucoup.

borage ['bɒrɪdʒ] *n* bourrache *f*.

borax ['bɔ:ræks] *n* borax *m*. ◆ **boracic** *adj* borique.

Bordeaux [bɔ:'dəʊ] *n (wine)* bordeaux *m*.

border ['bɔ:dəʳ] **1** *n* (**a**) *[lake, carpet, dress]* bord *m*; *[woods]* lisière *f*; *[picture]* bordure *f*; *(in garden)* bordure. (**b**) *(frontier)* frontière *f*. **to escape over the ~** s'enfuir en passant la frontière; *(Brit)* **the B~s** la région frontière du sud-est de l'Écosse. **2** *adj town, state* frontière *inv; patrol* frontalier. ~ **dispute** différend *m* sur une question de frontière(s); ~ **incident** incident *m* de frontière; ~ **raid** incursion *f*; ~ **town** ville *f* frontière. **3** *vt [trees etc]* border.
◆ **border (up)on** *vt fus [country]* être limitrophe de; *[estate]* toucher; *(fig: come near to being)* être voisin de, frôler.
◆ **borderer** *n* frontalier *m*, -ière *f*. ◆ **borderland** *n (fig)* **on the ~ land of** aux frontières de. ◆ **borderline** *n* ligne *f* de démarcation; **~line case** cas *m* limite.

bore¹ [bɔ:ʳ] **1** *vt hole, tunnel* percer; *well, rock* forer. **to ~ one's way through** se frayer un chemin en creusant à travers. **2** *n [tube, gun]* calibre *m*. **a 12-~ shotgun** un fusil de (calibre) 12. ◆ **borehole** *n* trou *m* de sonde.

bore² [bɔ:ʳ] **1** *n (person)* raseur * *m*, -euse * *f*; *(event, situation)* ennui *m*, corvée *f*. **2** *vt* ennuyer, raser *.
◆ **bored** *adj person* qui s'ennuie; *look* d'ennui; **to be ~d stiff** *or* **to death** *or* **to tears** s'ennuyer ferme *or* à mourir; **he was ~d with reading** il en avait assez de lire. ◆ **boredom** *n* ennui *m*. ◆ **boring** *adj* ennuyeux, rasant *.

bore³ [bɔ:ʳ] *pret of* **bear¹**.

bore⁴ [bɔ:ʳ] *n (tidal wave)* mascaret *m*.

born [bɔ:n] *adj* né. **to be ~** naître; **to be ~ again** renaître; **he was ~ in 1920** il est né *or* il naquit en 1920; **3 sons ~ to her** 3 fils nés d'elle; **every baby ~ into the world** tout enfant qui vient au monde; **a Parisian ~ and bred** un Parisien de souche; **he wasn't ~ yesterday** * il n'est pas né de la dernière pluie; **in all my ~ days** * de toute ma vie; **poets are ~, not made** on naît poète, on ne le devient pas; **a ~ poet** un poète né; ~ **fool** parfait idiot; **misfortunes ~ of war** malheurs dus à la guerre; **Chicago-~** natif de Chicago, né à Chicago; **Australian-~** d'origine australienne.

borne [bɔ:n] *ptp of* **bear¹**.

Borneo ['bɔ:nɪəʊ] *n* Bornéo *f*.

borough ['bʌrə] *n* municipalité *f*; *(in London)* ≃ arrondissement *m*; *(Brit Parl)* circonscription *f* électorale urbaine.

borrow ['bɒrəʊ] *vt* emprunter (*from* à). **a ~ed word** un mot d'emprunt; *(Math)* ~ **10** ≃ j'ajoute 10. ◆ **borrower** *n* emprunteur *m*, -euse *f*. ◆ **borrowing** *n* emprunt *m*.

Borstal ['bɔːstl] *n (Brit)* maison *f* de redressement.

bosh * [bɒʃ] *n* blague(s) * *f(pl)*, bêtises *fpl*.

bos'n ['bəʊsn] *n* = **bosun**.

bosom ['bʊzəm] *n [person]* poitrine *f*, seins *mpl*; *[dress]* corsage *m*; *(fig)* sein. **in the ~ of the family** au sein de la famille; **~ friend** ami(e) *m(f)* intime.

boss * [bɒs] **1** *n* patron(ne) *m(f)*, chef *m*; *[gang etc]* caïd ‡ *m*. **2** *vt* mener. ◆ **boss about *, boss around** * *vt sep* mener à la baguette, régenter. ◆ **bossy** * *adj* autoritaire.

boss-eyed [bɒs'aɪd] *adj* qui louche.

bosun ['bəʊsn] *n* maître *m* d'équipage.

botany ['bɒtənɪ] *n* botanique *f*. **~ wool** laine *f* mérinos. ◆ **botanic(al)** *adj* botanique. ◆ **botanist** *n* botaniste *mf*. ◆ **botanize** *vi* herboriser.

botch [bɒtʃ] *vt* (**~ up**) *(repair)* rafistoler *; *(bungle)* saboter, bousiller *.

both [bəʊθ] **1** *adj* les deux, l'un(e) et l'autre. **~ (the) books are his** les deux livres sont à lui; **you can't have it ~ ways *** il faut choisir.
2 *pron* tous *or* toutes (les) deux, l'un(e) et l'autre. **~ (of them) were there, they were ~ there** ils étaient là tous les deux; **~ of us agree** nous sommes d'accord tous les deux; **~ alike** l'un comme l'autre.
3 *adv*: **~ this and that** non seulement ceci mais aussi cela, aussi bien ceci que cela; **~ you and I saw him** nous l'avons vu vous et moi, vous et moi (nous) l'avons vu; **~ Paul and I came** Paul et moi sommes venus tous les deux; **she was ~ laughing and crying** elle riait et pleurait à la fois.

bother ['bɒðəʳ] **1** *vt (annoy)* ennuyer, embêter *; *(pester)* harceler; *(worry)* inquiéter, ennuyer. **don't ~ me!** laisse-moi tranquille!; **I'm sorry to ~ you** excusez-moi de vous déranger; **does it ~ you if I smoke?** ça vous dérange que je fume *subj or* si je fume?; **to ~ o.s.** *or* **one's head about sth** se tracasser au sujet de qch; **to get (all hot and) ~ed *** se mettre dans tous ses états (*about* au sujet de); **I can't be ~ed going out** *or* **to go out** je n'ai pas le courage de sortir; **his leg ~s him** sa jambe le fait pas mal * souffrir.
2 *vi* se donner la peine (*to do* de faire). **you needn't ~ to come** ce n'est pas la peine de venir; **don't ~ about me/about my lunch** ne vous occupez pas de moi/de mon déjeuner; **please don't ~** ce n'est pas la peine.
3 *n* ennui *m*, barbe * *f*. **what a ~ it all is!** quel ennui *or* quelle barbe * que tout cela!; *(excl)* **bother!** zut *, la barbe! *; **she's having a spot of ~** elle a des ennuis; **we had a bit of ~ with the car** on a eu un petit embêtement * avec la voiture.
◆ **botheration** * *excl* zut! * ◆ **bothersome** *adj* ennuyeux, embêtant *.

Botswana [bɒt'swɑːnə] *n* Botswana *m*.

bottle ['bɒtl] **1** *n* bouteille *f*; *(small)* flacon *m*; *(wide-mouthed)* bocal *m*; *(of stone)* cruche *f*; *(for beer)* canette *f*; *(baby's ~)* biberon *m*. **wine ~** bouteille à vin; **~ of wine** bouteille de vin; **to take to the ~ *** se mettre à boire. **2** *adj*: **~ bank** conteneur *m* (pour le verre usagé); **~ party** surprise-party *f* où chacun apporte une bouteille; **~ rack** casier *m* à bouteilles. **3** *vt wine* mettre en bouteilles; *fruit* mettre en bocaux.
◆ **bottle up** *vt sep feelings etc* refouler.
◆ **bottlebrush** *n* rince-bouteilles *m inv*.
◆ **bottled** *adj beer* en canette; *wine* en bouteilles; *fruit* en bocaux. ◆ **bottle-fed** *adj* nourri au biberon. ◆ **bottle-green** *adj* vert bouteille *inv*.
◆ **bottleneck** *n [road]* rétrécissement *m* de la chaussée; *[traffic]* bouchon *m*; *[production etc]* goulet *m* d'étranglement. ◆ **bottle-opener** *n* ouvre-bouteille(s) *m*.

bottom ['bɒtəm] **1** *n [box] (outside)* bas *m*; *(inside)* fond *m*; *[well, garden, sea]* fond; *[dress, heap, page]* bas *m*; *[tree, hill]* pied *m*; *[table]* bout *m*; *[chair]* siège *m*; *[ship]* carène *f*; *(buttocks)* derrière *m*; *(fig: origin)* base *f*, fondement *m*. **at the ~ of page 10** en *or* au bas de la page 10; **at the ~ of the hill** au pied *or* au bas de la colline; **the name at the ~ of the list** le nom en bas de la liste; **he's at the ~ of the list** il est en queue de liste; **to be ~ of the class** être le dernier de la classe; **~s up!** ‡ cul sec!; **from the ~ of my heart** du fond de mon cœur; **at ~** au fond; **to knock the ~ out of an argument** démolir un argument; **the ~ fell out of his world *** son monde s'est effondré; *(fig)* **to be at the ~ of sth** être à l'origine de qch; **we can't get to the ~ of it** impossible de découvrir le fin fond de cette histoire.
2 *adj shelf* du bas, inférieur; *step, gear* premier; *part of garden etc* du fond. *(fig)* **her ~ drawer** son trousseau; **~ half** *[box]* partie *f* inférieure; *[class, list]* deuxième moitié *f*; **the ~ line** *(Fin)* le résultat financier; *(fig)* l'essentiel.
◆ **bottomless** *adj pit* sans fond; *mystery* insondable; *supply* inépuisable. ◆ **bottommost** *adj* le plus bas.

botulism ['bɒtjʊlɪz(ə)m] *n* botulisme *m*.

bouclé [buː'kleɪ] *adj* en bouclette.

bougainvill(a)ea [ˌbuːgən'vɪlɪə] *n* bougainvillée *f*.

bough [baʊ] *n* rameau *m*, branche *f*.

bought [bɔːt] *pret, ptp of* **buy**.

boulder ['bəʊldəʳ] *n* rocher *m* (rond), grosse pierre.

bounce [baʊns] **1** *vi [ball]* rebondir; *[child, car]* faire des bonds; (*) *[cheque]* être sans provision. *[person]* **to ~ in/out** *etc* entrer/sortir *etc* avec entrain. **2** *vt ball* faire rebondir; (*) *cheque* refuser; (‡) *rowdy customer* vider ‡, flanquer * à la porte. **3** *n [ball]* rebond *m*. *(fig)* **he's got plenty of ~ *** il est très dynamique.
◆ **bouncer** ‡ *n* videur ‡ *m*. ◆ **bouncing** *adj*: **bouncing baby** beau bébé *m* (florissant de santé).
◆ **bouncy** *adj ball, mattress* élastique; *hair* vigoureux; *person* dynamique.

bound[1] [baʊnd] **1** *n*: **~s** limite(s) *f(pl)*, bornes *fpl*; **to know no ~s** être sans bornes; **to keep within ~s** rester dans la juste mesure; **within the ~s of possibility** dans les limites du possible; **out of ~s** dont l'accès est interdit; *(Scol)* défendu aux élèves. **2** *vt*: **~ed by** borné *or* limité par.
◆ **boundless** *adj space* infini; *trust* illimité; *devotion* sans bornes.

bound[2] [baʊnd] **1** *n* bond *m*, saut *m*. **2** *vi [person, horse]* bondir, faire un bond *or* des bonds. **to ~ in/away** *etc* entrer/partir *etc* d'un bond; **the horse ~ed over the fence** le cheval a sauté la barrière (d'un bond).

bound[3] [baʊnd] *(pret, ptp of* **bind***) adj* (**a**) *prisoner* lié, attaché. (**b**) *book* relié. (**c**) **I am ~ to confess** je suis forcé d'avouer; **you're ~ to do it** *(obliged to)* vous êtes tenu *or* obligé de le faire; *(sure to)* vous le ferez sûrement; **it was ~ to happen** cela devait arriver, c'était à prévoir. (**d**) *(destined)* **~ for** *person* en route pour; *parcel, train* à destination de; *ship, plane* en route pour; *(about to leave)* en partance pour; **where are you ~ for?** où allez-vous?; **Australia-~** à destination de l'Australie.
◆ **bounden** *adj duty* impérieux.

boundary ['baʊnd(ə)rɪ] *n* limite *f*, frontière *f*; *(Sport)* limites *fpl* du terrain.

bounty ['baʊntɪ] *n (generosity)* générosité *f*; *(gift)* don *m*; *(Mil)* prime *f*. ◆ **bounteous** *or* ◆ **bountiful** *adj harvest* abondant; *rain* bienfaisant; *person* généreux.

bouquet ['bʊkeɪ] *n* bouquet *m*.

bourbon ['bɜːbən] *n (whisky)* bourbon *m*.

bourgeois ['bʊəʒwɑː] *adj, n* bourgeois(e) *m(f)*. ◆ **bourgeoisie** *n* bourgeoisie *f*.

bout [baʊt] *n* (**a**) *[fever, malaria etc]* accès *m*; *[rheumatism]* crise *f*. **a ~ of flu** une grippe; **he's had several ~s of illness** il a été malade plusieurs fois; **a ~ of work** une période de travail intensif; **drinking ~** beuverie *f*. (**b**) *(Boxing, Wrestling)* combat *m*; *(Fencing)* assaut *m*.

boutique [buː'tiːk] *n* boutique *f (de mode etc)*.

bovine ['bəʊvaɪn] *adj* bovin.

bow[1] [bəʊ] **1** *n (weapon)* arc *m*; *(Mus)* archet *m*; *[rainbow etc]* arc; *(knot)* nœud *m*. **2** *adj*: **~ tie** nœud *m* papillon; **~ window** fenêtre *f* en saillie. ◆ **bow-legged** *adj* aux jambes arquées. ◆ **bowstring** *n* corde *f*.

bow[2] [baʊ] **1** *n* salut *m*. **to make one's ~ (as a pianist** *etc*) faire ses débuts (de pianiste *etc*); **to take a ~** saluer. **2** *vi* (**a**) *(in greeting)* saluer, incliner la tête. **to ~ to sb** saluer qn; **~ing and scraping** salamalecs *mpl*. (**b**) **(~ down)** *[branch etc]* fléchir, se courber; *[person]* se courber; *(fig: submit)* s'incliner (before, to devant; *under* sous). **3** *vt back* courber; *head* pencher. **to ~ one's back** courber le dos; **to ~ one's knee** fléchir le genou. ◆ **bow out** *vi (fig)* tirer sa révérence.

bow[3] [baʊ] *n [ship]* ~(**s**) avant *m*, proue *f*. **in the ~s** à l'avant, en proue; **on the port ~** par bâbord devant.

bowdlerize ['baʊdləraɪz] *vt* expurger.

bowels ['baʊəlz] *npl* intestins *mpl*. **~ of the earth** entrailles *fpl* de la terre.

bowl[1] [bəʊl] *n* bol *m*, jatte *f*; *(for water, washing up)* cuvette *f*; *(for fruit)* coupe *f*; *(for salad)* saladier *m*; *(for punch)* bol; *(for sugar)* sucrier *m*; *[spoon]* creux *m*; *[lamp]* globe *m*; *[lavatory, sink]* cuvette.

bowl[2] [bəʊl] **1** *n* boule *f*. *(game)* **~s** *(Brit)* (jeu *m* de) boules; *(US: skittles)* bowling *m*. **2** *vi* (**a**) **to go ~ing** jouer aux boules (*or* au bowling). (**b**) *[person, car]* **to go ~ing down the street** descendre la rue à bonne allure. **3** *vt bowl, ball* lancer; *hoop* faire rouler; *(Cricket) ball* servir; *batsman* **(~ out)** mettre hors jeu.
◆ **bowl down** * *vt sep* renverser. ◆ **bowl over** *vt sep* renverser. *(fig)* **to be ~ed over by** *(surprise)* rester stupéfait devant; *(emotion)* être bouleversé par.
◆ **bowler** *n* joueur *m*, -euse *f* de boules (*or* de bowling); *(Cricket)* lanceur *m*, -euse *f* (de la balle); *(hat)* (chapeau *m*) melon *m*. ◆ **bowling** **1** *n (Brit)* jeu *m* de boules; *(US)* bowling *m*; **2** *adj*: **~ing alley** bowling *m*; **~ing green** terrain *m* de boules *(sur gazon)*; **~ing match** concours *m* de boules (*or* de bowling).

box[1] [bɒks] **1** *n* (**a**) boîte *f*; *(crate; also for cash)* caisse *f*; *(cardboard ~)* carton *m*. *(TV)* **on the ~** * à la télé *. (**b**) *(Theat)* loge *f*; *(Jur) [jury, press]* banc *m*; *[witness]* barre *f*; *[stable]* box *m*. **2** *adj*: **~ calf** box(-calf) *m*; **~ number** numéro *m* d'annonce; **~ office** bureau *m* de location; **it's good ~ office** cela fait recette; **~-office attraction** *or* **success** spectacle *m* à (grand) succès; **~ room** (cabinet *m* de) débarras *m*. **3** *vt goods* mettre en boîte *or* en caisse *etc*. *(Naut)* **to ~ the compass** réciter les aires du vent. ◆ **box in** *vt sep bath, sink* encastrer. *(fig)* **to feel ~ed in** se sentir confiné *or* à l'étroit. ◆ **Boxing Day** *n* le lendemain de Noël.

box[2] [bɒks] **1** *vi (Sport)* faire de la boxe. **2** *vt (Sport)* boxer avec. **to ~ sb's ears** gifler qn. **3** *n*: **a ~ on the ear** une gifle. ◆ **boxer** *n (Sport)* boxeur *m*; *(dog)* boxer *m*; **~er shorts** *npl* boxer short *m*. ◆ **boxing** **1** *n* boxe *f* ; **2** *adj gloves, match* de boxe; **~ing ring** ring *m*.

box[3] [bɒks] *n (~ wood)* buis *m*.

boy [bɔɪ] *n* garçon *m*. **little ~** petit garçon, garçonnet *m*; **English ~** petit *or* jeune Anglais *m*; **come, my ~** viens ici, mon petit *or* mon grand; **the Jones ~** le petit Jones; **when I was a ~** quand j'étais petit *or* enfant; **~s will be ~s!** les garçons, on ne les changera jamais!; **he was as much a ~ as ever** il était toujours aussi gamin; **my dear ~** mon cher (ami); **a night out with the ~s** une sortie avec les copains *; *(excl)* **~!** * bigre! * ◆ **boyfriend** *n* petit ami. ◆ **boyhood** *n* enfance *f*, adolescence *f*. ◆ **boyish** *adj behaviour* d'enfant, de garçon; *(pej)* puéril; *smile, look* gamin; *girl* garçonnier.

boycott ['bɔɪkɒt] **1** *vt* boycotter. **2** *n* boycottage *m*.

bra [brɑː] *n* soutien-gorge *m*.

brace [breɪs] **1** *n* (**a**) *(gen)* attache *f*; *(Med)* appareil *m* orthopédique; *(dental)* appareil (dentaire *or* orthodontique); *(Constr)* entretoise *f*. *(Brit Dress)* **~s** bretelles *fpl*; **~ and bit** vilebrequin *m (à main)*. (**b**) *(pl inv: pair) [animals etc]* paire *f*. **2** *vt (support)* soutenir, consolider; *beam* armer. **to ~ o.s.** s'arc-bouter; *(fig)* rassembler ses forces (*to do* pour faire); **~ yourself for the news!** tenez-vous bien que je vous raconte *(subj)* la nouvelle! ◆ **bracing** *adj air, climate* tonifiant; *wind* vivifiant.

bracelet ['breɪslɪt] *n* bracelet *m*.

bracken ['bræk(ə)n] *n* fougère *f*.

bracket ['brækɪt] **1** *n* (**a**) *(angled support)* support *m*; *(for shelf)* tasseau *m*; *(shelf itself)* (petite) étagère *f*; *(for lamp)* fixation *f*. **~ lamp** applique *f*. (**b**) *(Typ) (round)* parenthèse *f*; *(square)* crochet *m*; *(Mus, Typ)* **brace ~** accolade *f*; **in ~s** entre parenthèses; **the lower income ~** la tranche des petits revenus. **2** *vt (Typ)* mettre entre parenthèses *etc*; *(fig:* **~ together**) *names, persons* mettre dans le même groupe; *candidates etc* mettre ex aequo. *(Scol, Sport etc)* **~ed first** premiers ex aequo.

brackish ['brækɪʃ] *adj* saumâtre.

bradawl ['brædɔːl] *n* poinçon *m (de menuisier)*.

brag [bræg] *vti* se vanter (about, of de; *about or of doing* de faire; *that one has done* d'avoir fait). ◆ **braggart** *n* vantard(e) *m(f)*. ◆ **bragging** **1** *n* vantardise *f* ; **2** *adj* vantard.

braid [breɪd] **1** *vt hair* tresser. **2** *n (on dress)* ganse *f*; *(Mil)* galon *m*; *[hair]* tresse *f*.

Braille [breɪl] *n, adj* braille *(m) inv*.

brain [breɪn] **1** *n (Anat, fig)* cerveau *m*. **~s** *(Anat, Culin)* cervelle *f*; *(fig)* **he's got that on the ~** * il ne pense qu'à ça! *; **his ~ reeled** la tête lui a tourné; **he's got ~s** il est intelligent; **he's the ~(s) of the family** c'est le cerveau de la famille. **2** *adj (Med) disease, operation* cérébral. **~ damage** lésions cérébrales; *(Med)* **~ dead** dans un coma dépassé; **~ drain** exode *m* des cerveaux; **~s trust** réunion-débat *f*; *(US)* **~ trust** brain-trust *m*. **3** *vt (*: knock out)* assommer.
◆ **brain-child** *n* invention *f* personnelle. ◆ **brainless** *adj* sans cervelle, stupide. ◆ **brainstorm** *n (Med)* congestion cérébrale; *(fig)* idée *f* géniale; *(pej)* moment *m* d'aberration. ◆ **brainstorming** *n* remue-méninges *m (hum)*, brain-storming *m*. ◆ **brainwash** *vt* faire un lavage de cerveau à; *(fig)* **he was ~washed into believing that...** on a réussi à lui faire croire que... ◆ **brainwashing** *n* lavage *m* de cerveau; *[the public etc]* bourrage *m* de crâne *. ◆ **brainwave** *n* idée *f* géniale. ◆ **brainwork** *n* travail *m* intellectuel. ◆ **brainy** * *adj* intelligent, doué.

braise [breɪz] *vt (Culin)* braiser.

brake[1] [breɪk] *n (vehicle)* break *m*.

brake² [breɪk] **1** *n (Aut etc)* frein *m*. *(fig)* **to act as a ~ on** mettre un frein à. **2** *vi* freiner. **3** *adj pedal, drum, lining* de frein. **~ fluid** liquide *m* de freins; **~ light** feu *m* de stop; **~ pad** plaquette *f* de frein. ◆ **braking** **1** *n* freinage *m* ; **2** *adj distance, power* de freinage.

bramble ['bræmbl] *n (thorny shrub)* roncier *m*; *(blackberry bush)* mûrier *m* sauvage; *(berry)* mûre *f* (sauvage).

bran [bræn] *n* son *m (de blé)*. **~ mash** son mouillé.

branch [brɑːn(t)ʃ] **1** *n* (**a**) *(gen: lit, fig)* branche *f*; *[river]* bras *m*; *[mountain chain]* ramification *f*; *[road, pipe, railway]* embranchement *m*; *(Ling)* rameau *m*; *(Admin)* section *f*. *(Mil)* **their ~ of the service** leur arme *f*. (**b**) *[store, company]* succursale *f*; *[bank]* agence *f*. **2** *adj (Rail)* **~ line** ligne *f* secondaire; **~ office** succursale *f* (locale). **3** *vi* se ramifier. **the road ~es off the main road** la route quitte la grand-route. ◆ **branch out** *vi [businessman, company]* étendre ses activités (*into* à).

brand [brænd] **1** *n* (**a**) *(Comm: of goods)* marque *f*. (**b**) *(mark) [cattle, property]* marque *f*; *[prisoner]* flétrissure *f*. (**c**) *(burning wood)* tison *m*. **2** *vt cattle, property* marquer (au fer rouge). **~ed goods** produits *mpl* de marque; *(fig: stigmatize)* **to ~ sb a criminal** flétrir qn du nom de criminel. **3** *adj*: **~ image** image *f* de marque; **~ name** (nom *m* de) marque *f*. ◆ **branding-iron** *n* fer *m* à marquer. ◆ **brand-new** *adj* flambant neuf (*f* flambant neuve).

brandish ['brændɪʃ] *vt* brandir.

brandy ['brændɪ] *n* cognac *m*. **~ and soda** fine *f* à l'eau; **plum ~** eau-de-vie *f* de prune.

brash [bræʃ] *adj (reckless)* impétueux; *(impudent)* effronté; *(tactless)* indiscret.

Brasilia [brə'zɪlɪə] *n* Brasilia.

brass [brɑːs] **1** *n* (**a**) *(metal)* cuivre *m* (jaune); (‡: *money)* pognon ‡ *m*. (**b**) *(tablet)* plaque *f* (en cuivre); *(object/ornament)* objet *m*/ornement *m* en cuivre. **to clean the ~** astiquer les cuivres; *(Mus)* **the ~** les cuivres *mpl*; *(Mil)* **the (top) ~** * les huiles * *fpl*. **2** *adj ornament etc* en *or* de cuivre. **~ band** fanfare *f*; **it's not worth a ~ farthing** * cela ne vaut pas un clou *; *(Mil)* **~ hat** * huile * *f*; **he's got a ~ neck** * il a du toupet *; **~ plate** plaque *f* de cuivre; **~ rubbing** *(activity)* décalquage *m* par frottement; *(object)* décalque; **to get down to ~ tacks** * en venir aux choses sérieuses. ◆ **brassware** *n* chaudronnerie *f* d'art. ◆ **brassy** *adj* cuivré.

brassière ['bræsɪəʳ] *n* soutien-gorge *m*; *(strapless)* bustier *m*.

brat [bræt] *n (pej)* moutard * *m*, gosse * *mf*.

bravado [brə'vɑːdəʊ] *n* bravade *f*.

brave [breɪv] **1** *adj* courageux, brave. **be ~!** du courage!; **be ~ and tell her** prends ton courage à deux mains et va lui dire; *(iro)* **it's a ~ new world!** on n'arrête pas le progrès! **2** *vt* braver. **to ~ it out** faire face à la situation. ◆ **bravely** *adv* courageusement, bravement. ◆ **bravery** *n* courage *m*.

bravo ['brɑː'vəʊ] *excl, n* bravo *(m)*.

bravura [brə'vʊərə] *n* bravoure *f*.

brawl [brɔːl] **1** *vi* se bagarrer *. **2** *n* rixe *f*, bagarre *f*. ◆ **brawling** **1** *adj* bagarreur *; **2** *n* rixe *f*, bagarre *f*.

brawn [brɔːn] *n* muscle *m*; *(Culin)* fromage *m* de tête. ◆ **brawny** *adj arm* musculeux; *person* musclé.

bray [breɪ] **1** *n* braiement *m*. **2** *vi* braire.

brazen ['breɪzn] **1** *adj (~-faced)* effronté. **2** *vt*: **to ~ it out** payer d'effronterie. ◆ **brazenly** *adv* effrontément.

brazier ['breɪzɪəʳ] *n* brasero *m*.

Brazil [brə'zɪl] *n* Brésil *m*. **~ nut** noix *f* du Brésil. ◆ **Brazilian** **1** *n* Brésilien(ne) *m(f)*; **2** *adj* brésilien, du Brésil.

breach [briːtʃ] **1** *n* (**a**) *[law, secrecy]* violation *f*; *[rules]* infraction *f* (*of* à); *[friendship, manners]* manquement *m* (*of* à). **~ of contract** rupture *f* de contrat; **~ of the peace** attentat *m* à l'ordre public; **~ of promise** violation de promesse de mariage; **~ of trust** abus *m* de confiance. (**b**) *(gap: in wall etc)* brèche *f*; *(estrangement)* brouille *f* (*between* entre). **2** *vt wall* ouvrir une brèche dans; *enemy lines, defences* percer.

bread [bred] **1** *n* pain *m*; (‡: *money)* fric ‡ *m*. **~ and milk** pain au lait; **~ and butter** tartine *f* (beurrée *or* de beurre); *(fig)* **it's his ~ and butter** c'est son gagne-pain; **he knows which side his ~ is buttered** il sait où est son intérêt; **to put sb on ~ and water** mettre qn au pain et à l'eau; *(Rel)* **the ~ and wine** les (deux) espèces *fpl*. **2** *adj*: **to be on the ~ line** * être sans le sou; **~ sauce** sauce *f* à la mie de pain. ◆ **bread-and-butter letter** *n* lettre *f* de remerciements *(pour hospitalité reçue)*. ◆ **breadbasket** *n* corbeille *f* à pain. ◆ **breadbin** *n* boîte *f* à pain, *(larger)* huche *f* à pain. ◆ **breadboard** *n* planche *f* à pain. ◆ **breadcrumbs** *npl* miettes *fpl* de pain; *(Culin)* chapelure *f*; **fried in ~crumbs** pané. ◆ **breadfruit** *n* fruit *m* de l'arbre à pain. ◆ **breadknife** *n* couteau *m* à pain. ◆ **breadwinner** *n* soutien *m* (de famille).

breadth [bretθ] *n* largeur *f (also fig: of thought etc)*. **this field is 100 metres in ~** ce champ a 100 mètres de large. ◆ **breadthwise** *adv* dans la *or* en largeur.

break [breɪk] *(vb: pret* **broke,** *ptp* **broken***)* **1** *n* (**a**) *(gen)* cassure *f*; *[relationship]* rupture *f*, brouille *f*; *[wall]* trouée *f*; *[line, conversation, transmission]* interruption *f*; *[journey]* arrêt *m*; *(Scol)* récréation *f*. **to take a ~** *(few minutes)* s'arrêter cinq minutes; *(holiday)* prendre des vacances; *(change)* se changer les idées; **6 hours without a ~** 6 heures de suite; *(Elec)* **~ in circuit** rupture *f* de circuit; **a ~ in the clouds** une éclaircie; **a ~ in the weather** un changement de temps; **with a ~ in her voice** d'une voix entrecoupée; **at ~ of day** au point du jour; **to make a ~ for it** * *(escape)* prendre la fuite; **to have a good/bad ~** * avoir une période de veine/de déveine *; **give me a ~!** * donnez-moi ma chance! (**b**) *(vehicle)* break *m*.

2 *vt* (**a**) *(gen)* casser; *(into small pieces)* briser; *stick* casser, rompre; *bone, limb* casser, fracturer; *skin* écorcher. **to ~ one's leg/back** se casser la jambe/la colonne vertébrale; *(fig)* **to ~ the back of a task** faire le plus dur d'une tâche; **to ~ open** *door* enfoncer; *packet* ouvrir; *lock, safe* fracturer; *(fig)* **to ~ new ground** faire œuvre de pionnier; **to ~ cover** *[animal]* débusquer; *[hunted person]* sortir à découvert; **to ~ ranks** rompre les rangs; *(Aviat)* **to ~ the sound barrier** franchir le mur du son; *(Sport etc)* **to ~ a record** battre un record; **to ~ one's heart over sth** avoir le cœur brisé par qch; **to ~ sb's heart** briser le cœur à *or* de qn; *(lit, fig)* **to ~ the ice** briser la glace. (**b**) *promise* manquer à; *vow* rompre; *treaty, law, the sabbath* violer; *commandment* désobéir à. **to ~ faith with sb** manquer de parole à qn; **to ~ an appointment with sb** faire faux bond à qn. (**c**) *health* détériorer; *strike, rebellion, courage, spirit* abattre, briser; *horse* dresser. **to ~ sb** *(morally)* causer la perte de qn; *(financially)* ruiner qn; **to ~ sb of a habit** faire perdre une habitude à qn; *(Betting)* **to ~ the bank** faire sauter la banque. (**d**) *silence, spell, fast* rompre; *journey* interrompre; *(Elec)* couper. (**e**) *fall, blow* amortir. **the wall ~s the force of the wind** le mur coupe le vent. (**f**) *news* annoncer (*to* à). **try to ~ it to her gently** essayez de le lui annoncer avec ménagement.

3 *vi* (**a**) *(gen)* se casser, se briser; *[stick, rope]* se casser, se rompre; *[bone, limb]* se casser, se fracturer; *[wave]* déferler; *[clouds]* se dissiper; *[ranks]* se rompre; *[heart]* se briser. **to ~ into little pieces** se casser en mille morceaux; *(fig)* **to ~ with a friend** rompre avec un ami; **to ~ even** *[individual]* s'y retrouver; *[company]* atteindre l'équilibre financier; **to ~ free** *or* **loose** se libérer (*from* de); **to ~ for lunch** faire une pause pour le déjeuner. (**b**) *[dawn, day]* poindre; *[news, story, storm]* éclater. (**c**) *[health, weather]* se détériorer; *[heatwave etc]* toucher à sa fin; *[voice]* (*boy's*) muer; *(in emotion)* se briser (*with* de). **he broke under torture** il a craqué sous la torture; **his spirit broke** son courage l'a abandonné.

◆ **break away** **1** *vi (gen)* se détacher (*from* de); *(Ftbl, Racing)* s'échapper. **to ~ away from routine** sortir de la routine. **2** *vt sep* détacher (*from* de).

◆ **break down** **1** *vi [vehicle, machine]* tomber en panne; *[health]* se détériorer; *[argument]* s'effondrer; *[resistance]* céder; *[negotiations, plan]* échouer; *(weep)* éclater en sanglots. **2** *vt sep* (**a**) *(demolish)* démolir; *door* enfoncer; *opposition* briser. (**b**) *(analyse: gen)* décomposer (*into* en); *accounts* détailler; *sales figures, costs* ventiler; *(Chem) substance* décomposer. ◆ **break in** **1** *vi* (**a**) *(interrupt)* interrompre. **to ~ in on sb/sth** interrompre qn/qch. (**b**) *[burglar]* entrer par effraction. **2** *vt sep* (**a**) *door* enfoncer. (**b**) *horse* dresser; *(US) engine, car* roder. **it will take you 6 months before you're broken in** * vous mettrez 6 mois à vous faire au métier. ◆ **break into** *vt fus house* entrer par effraction dans; *safe, cashbox* forcer; *savings, new box* entamer. **he broke into a long explanation** il s'est lancé dans une longue explication; **to ~ into a trot** se mettre à trotter. ◆ **break off** **1** *vi* (**a**) *[twig etc]* se détacher net. (**b**) *(stop)* s'arrêter (*doing* de faire). **to ~ off from work** interrompre le travail; **to ~ off with sb** rompre avec qn. **2** *vt sep piece of chocolate etc* casser, détacher; *engagement, negotiations* rompre; *habit* se défaire de; *work* interrompre. ◆ **break out** *vi* (**a**) *[epidemic, fire, storm, war]* éclater. **to ~ out into a sweat** commencer à suer. (**b**) *(escape)* s'évader (*of* de). ◆ **break through** **1** *vi (Mil)* faire une percée; *[sun]* percer (les nuages). **2** *vt fus defences, obstacles, sb's reserve* percer; *crowd* se frayer un passage à travers; *sound barrier* franchir. ◆ **break up** **1** *vi [ice]* craquer; *[road]* être défoncé; *[ship in storm]* se disloquer; *[partnership]* prendre fin; *[marriage]* se briser; *[health, weather]* se détériorer; *[clouds, crowd, group, meeting]* se disperser; *[friends]* se quitter; *[school, college]* entrer en vacances. **the schools ~ up tomorrow** les vacances (scolaires) commencent demain. **2** *vt sep object* mettre en morceaux; *house* démolir; *ground* ameublir; *road* défoncer; *coalition* briser; *empire* démembrer; *marriage* désunir; *crowd, meeting* disperser.

◆ **breakable** **1** *adj* cassable, fragile ; **2** *n*: **~ables** objets *mpl* fragiles. ◆ **breakage** *n* casse *f*, bris *m*; **to pay for ~ages** payer la casse. ◆ **breakaway** **1** *n [group, movement]* rupture *f*; *(Sport)* échappée *f*; *(Boxing)* dégagement *m* ; **2** *adj group, movement* séparatiste, dissident; *state* dissident. ◆ **breakdown** **1** *n [machine, vehicle, electricity]* panne *f*; *[communications etc]* rupture *f*; *[railway system etc]* interruption *f* (subite) de service; *(in health)* délabrement *m*; *(mental)* dépression nerveuse; *(analysis)* analyse *f*; *(into categories etc)* décomposition *f* (*into* en) ; **2** *adj*: **~down gang/service** équipe *f*/service *m* de dépannage; **~down truck** dépanneuse *f*. ◆ **breaker** *n* (**a**) *(wave)* brisant *m*; (**b**) **to send to the ~er's** *ship* envoyer à la démolition; *car* envoyer à la casse. ◆ **break-even** *adj*: **~-even point** seuil *m* de rentabilité. ◆ **breakfast** ['brekfəst] **1** *n* petit déjeuner *m* ; **2** *vi* déjeuner (*off, on* de) ; **3** *adj*: **~fast cereals** céréales *fpl*, flocons *mpl* d'avoine (*or* de maïs *etc*); **~fast cup** déjeuner *m (tasse)*; **~fast room** petite salle à manger; **~fast TV** la télévision du matin. ◆ **break-in** *n* cambriolage *m*. ◆ **breaking** **1** *n [cup, chair, seal]* bris *m*; *[bone, limb]* fracture *f*; *[promise]* manquement *m* (*of* à); *[treaty, law]* violation *f* (*of* de); *[commandment]* désobéissance *f* (*of* à); *[silence, spell]* rupture *f*; *[journey]* interruption *f* (*of* de); *(Jur)* **~ing and entering** effraction *f* ; **2** *adj*: **at ~ing point** *rope, political situation* au point de rupture; *person, sb's patience* à bout. ◆ **breakneck** *adj*: **at ~neck speed** à fond de train. ◆ **breakout** *n* évasion *f (de prison)*. ◆ **break point** *n* point *m* d'avantage. ◆ **breakthrough** *n (Mil)* percée *f*; *[research etc]* découverte *f* sensationnelle. ◆ **break-up** *n [ship]* dislocation *f*; *[ice, political party]* débâcle *f*; *[friendship]* rupture *f*; *[empire]* démembrement *m*. ◆ **breakwater** *n* brise-lames *m inv*.

bream [bri:m] *n* brème *f*.

breast [brest] **1** *n [woman]* sein *m*; *(chest)* poitrine *f*; *(Culin) [chicken etc]* blanc *m*. **2** *vt hill* atteindre le sommet de. ◆ **breast-fed** *adj* nourri au sein. ◆ **breast-feed** *vti* allaiter. ◆ **breast-feeding** *n* allaitement *m* au sein. ◆ **breast-pocket** *n* poche *f* de poitrine. ◆ **breast-stroke** *n*: **to swim ~-stroke** nager la brasse.

breath [breθ] *n* haleine *f*, souffle *m*. **bad ~** mauvaise haleine; **to get one's ~ back** reprendre haleine; **out of ~** essoufflé, hors d'haleine; **to take a deep ~** respirer à fond; **to take sb's ~ away** couper le souffle à qn; **save your ~!** inutile de gaspiller ta salive!; **to be short of ~** avoir le souffle court; **under one's ~** tout bas; **in the same ~** dans la même seconde; **all in one ~** tout d'un trait; **with one's dying ~** en mourant; **there wasn't a ~ of air** *or* **wind** il n'y avait pas un souffle d'air; **to go out for a ~ of air** sortir prendre l'air.

◆ **breathalyse,** *(US)* **breathalyze** *vt* faire subir l'alcootest à. ◆ **breathalyser,** *(US)* **breathalyzer** *n* alcootest *m*. ◆ **breathless** *adj (from exertion)* hors d'haleine; *(through illness)* qui a de la peine à respirer; *(with excitement)* le souffle coupé par l'émotion; *silence* ému. ◆ **breathlessly** *adv* en haletant; *(fig)* en grande hâte. ◆ **breathtaking** *adj* stupéfiant, à vous couper le souffle.

breathe [bri:ð] **1** *vi* respirer. **to ~ deeply** *or* **hard** *(after running)* souffler (fort); *(in illness)* respirer péniblement; **to ~ freely, to ~ again** (pouvoir) respirer; **she is still breathing** elle vit encore. **2** *vt air* respirer; *sigh* laisser échapper; *prayer* murmurer. **to ~ air into sth** insuffler de l'air dans qch; **don't ~ a word (about it)!** n'en dis rien à personne!

◆ **breathe in** *vi, vt sep* aspirer, inspirer.

◆ **breathe out** *vi, vt sep* expirer.

◆ **breather** * *n* moment *m* de répit; **to give sb a ~r** laisser souffler qn; **to go out for a ~r** sortir prendre l'air. ◆ **breathing** **1** *n* respiration *f*; **heavy breathing** respiration bruyante ; **2** *adj apparatus* respiratoire; **a breathing space** un moment de répit.

bred [bred] *(pret, ptp of* **breed***) adj*: **well-/ill-~** bien/mal élevé.

breech [bri:tʃ] **1** *n [gun]* culasse *f*. **2** *adj*: **~ birth** accouchement *m* par le siège.

breeches ['brɪtʃɪz] *npl (riding ~)* culotte *f* (de cheval); *(knee ~)* haut-de-chausses *m*. **his wife wears the ~** c'est sa femme qui porte la culotte.

breed [bri:d] *pret, ptp* **bred** **1** *vt animals* élever, faire l'élevage de; *hate, suspicion* faire naître, engendrer. **to ~ sth in/out** faire acquérir/perdre qch *(par la sélection)*. **2** *vi* se reproduire, se multiplier. **3** *n* race *f*, espèce *f*; *(fig)* espèce. ◆ **breeder** *n* (**a**) *(Phys: ~er reactor)* sur(ré)générateur *m;* (**b**) *(Agr etc: person)* éleveur *m*, -euse *f*. ◆ **breeding** *n* (**a**) *(Agr)* élevage *m*; *(reproduction)* reproduction *f*;

~**ing season** saison *f* des accouplements; (**b**) **(good)** ~**ing** (bonne) éducation *f*, savoir-vivre *m*.

breeze [bri:z] **1** *n (wind)* brise *f*. **gentle** ~ petite brise; **stiff** ~ vent frais. **2** *vi*: **to** ~ **in/out** entrer/sortir *(jauntily)* d'un air dégagé *or (briskly)* en coup de vent. ◆ **breezily** *adv (jauntily)* d'un air dégagé; *(briskly)* brusquement; *(jovially)* jovialement. ◆ **breezy** *adj weather, day* frais; *corner, spot* éventé; *person (jaunty)* dégagé; *(brisk)* brusque; *(jovial)* jovial.

breeze-block ['bri:zblɒk] *n* parpaing *m*.

Bren gun ['bren gʌn] *n* fusil *m* mitrailleur.

brethren ['breðrɪn] *npl (Rel) pl of* **brother.**

Breton ['bret(ə)n] **1** *adj* breton. **2** *n* Breton(ne) *m(f)*; *(Ling)* breton *m*.

brevity ['brevɪtɪ] *n* brièveté *f*; *(conciseness)* concision *f*.

brew [bru:] **1** *n* décoction *f*. **witch's** ~ brouet *m* de sorcière. **2** *vt beer* brasser; *tea, scheme, mischief* préparer. **3** *vi [brewer]* brasser; *[beer]* fermenter; *[tea]* infuser; *[storm]* se préparer; *[plot]* se tramer. **there's trouble** ~**ing** il y a de l'orage dans l'air *(fig)*; **sth's** ~**ing** il se trame qch. ◆ **brew up** *vi* (**a**) *(*: make tea)* faire du thé. (**b**) *[storm, dispute]* se préparer. ◆ **brewer** *n* brasseur *m*. ◆ **brewery** *n* brasserie *f (fabrique)*. ◆ **brewing** *n* brassage *m*.

briar ['braɪəʳ] *n* = **brier.**

bribe [braɪb] **1** *n* pot-de-vin *m*. **to take/offer a** ~ accepter/offrir un pot-de-vin (*from sb* de qn; *to* à). **2** *vt* suborner, soudoyer; *witness* suborner. **to** ~ **sb to do sth** soudoyer qn pour qu'il fasse qch. ◆ **bribery** *n* corruption *f*.

brick [brɪk] *n* brique *f*; *(toy)* cube *m (de construction)*. **you can't make** ~**s without straw** à l'impossible nul n'est tenu; **he came down on me like a ton of** ~**s** * il m'a passé un de ces savons! *; **you might as well talk to a** ~ **wall** * autant parler à un mur; **to come up against a** ~ **wall** se heurter à un mur; **a** ~ **of ice cream** une glace pour plusieurs personnes; **he's a** ~ * il est sympa *.
◆ **brick in, brick up** *vt sep* murer.
◆ **brickbat** *n (fig)* critique *f*. ◆ **brick-built** *adj* en brique(s). ◆ **bricklayer** *n* ouvrier-maçon *m*. ◆ **brick-red** *adj* (rouge) brique *inv*. ◆ **brickwork** *n* briquetage *m*. ◆ **brickworks** *npl* briqueterie *f*.

bride [braɪd] *n* (future *or* jeune) mariée *f*. **the** ~ **and groom** les mariés. ◆ **bridal** *adj feast* de noce; *procession* nuptial; *veil, gown* de mariée; *suite* réservé aux jeunes mariés. ◆ **bridegroom** *n* (futur *or* jeune) marié *m*. ◆ **bridesmaid** *n* demoiselle *f* d'honneur.

bridge¹ [brɪdʒ] **1** *n (gen)* pont *m* (*across* sur); *(Naut)* passerelle *f* (de commandement); *[nose]* arête *f*; *(Dentistry)* bridge *m*. **2** *vt river* construire un pont sur. *(fig)* **to** ~ **a gap** établir un rapprochement (*between* entre); *(in knowledge)* combler une lacune (*in* dans); *(in budget)* combler un trou (*in* dans).
◆ **bridge-building** *n (fig)* efforts *mpl* de rapprochement. ◆ **bridgehead** *n* tête *f* de pont. ◆ **bridging** *adj*: **bridging loan** prêt-relais *m*.

bridge² [brɪdʒ] *n (Cards)* bridge *m*. ◆ **bridge-player** *n* bridgeur *m*, -euse *f*.

bridle ['braɪdl] **1** *n* bride *f*. ~ **path** sentier *m (pour chevaux)*. **2** *vt* mettre la bride à. **3** *vi (in anger)* regimber; *(in scorn)* lever le menton *(de mépris)*.

brief [bri:f] **1** *adj life, meeting* bref; *interval, period, stay* court; *speech* bref, concis, laconique *(pej)*; *account* sommaire. **in** ~ *or* **to be** ~**, he didn't come** bref *or* en deux mots, il n'est pas venu. **2** *n* (**a**) *(Jur)* dossier *m*, affaire *f*. *(fig)* **I hold no** ~ **for him** je ne prends pas sa défense; **to have a watching** ~ **for** veiller (en justice) aux intérêts de. (**b**) *(Mil: instructions)* briefing *m*; *(gen)* instructions *fpl*. **his** ~ **is to...** la tâche qui lui a été assignée consiste à... (**c**) *(Dress)* ~**s** slip *m*. **3** *vt barrister* confier une cause à; *pilots, soldiers* donner des instructions à; *person (give orders to)* donner des instructions à; *(bring up to date)* mettre au courant (*on sth* de qch). ◆ **briefcase** *n* serviette *f*. ◆ **briefing** *n* briefing *m*. ◆ **briefly** *adv visit* en coup de vent; *reply* laconiquement; *speak* brièvement. ◆ **briefness** *n* brièveté *f*; courte durée *f*; concision *f*, laconisme *m*.

brier ['braɪəʳ] *n* (racine *f* de) bruyère *f*; *(~ pipe)* pipe *f* de bruyère.

brigade [brɪ'geɪd] *n* brigade *f*. **one of the old** ~ un vieux de la vieille *. ◆ **brigadier** *n* général *m* de brigade. *(US)* **brigadier-general** *(Mil)* général *m* de brigade; *(Aviat)* général *m* de brigade aérienne.

brigand ['brɪgənd] *n* brigand *m*.

bright [braɪt] *adj* (**a**) *eyes, star, gem* brillant; *light, fire* vif; *sunshine* éclatant; *day, weather, room* clair; *colour* vif, éclatant; *metal* poli. *(Met)* **to become** ~**(er)** s'éclaircir; *(Met)* ~ **intervals** éclaircies *fpl*; **the outlook is** ~**er** *(Met)* on prévoit une amélioration (du temps); *(fig)* l'avenir se présente mieux. (**b**) *(cheerful) person* gai, animé; *face, expression* gai, radieux; *prospects, future* brillant, splendide. **as** ~ **as a button** gai comme un pinson; ~ **and early** de bon matin; **to look on the** ~ **side** essayer d'être optimiste. (**c**) *(intelligent) person* intelligent, doué; *child* éveillé. **he's a** ~ **spark** * il est vraiment futé.
◆ **brighten 1** *vt* (~ **up**) *metal* faire reluire; *colour* aviver; *room, person* égayer; *prospects, situation* améliorer; **2** *vi [weather, sky]* se dégager; *[eyes, expression]* s'éclairer; *[person]* s'animer; *[prospects, future]* s'améliorer. ◆ **brightly** *adv shine* avec éclat; *behave* gaiement; *say* avec animation; **the sun shone** ~**ly** le soleil brillait d'un vif éclat. ◆ **brightness** *n (gen)* éclat *m*; *[light]* intensité *f*; *(intelligence)* intelligence *f*.

brill * [brɪl] *adj* sensass * *inv*, super * *inv*.

brilliant ['brɪljənt] *adj light* éclatant; *person, idea, wit* brillant. ◆ **brilliance** *n* éclat *m*; *[person]* intelligence *f* supérieure. ◆ **brilliantly** *adv shine* avec éclat; *suggest etc* brillamment.

Brillo ['brɪləʊ] *adj* ®: ~ **pad** ≃ tampon *m* Jex ®.

brim [brɪm] *n* bord *m*. ◆ **brim over** *vi (lit, fig)* déborder (*with* de). ◆ **brimful** *adj* plein à déborder; *(fig)* débordant (*with* de).

brine [braɪn] *n* eau *f* salée; *(Culin)* saumure *f*.

bring [brɪŋ] *pret, ptp* **brought** *vt object, news, information* apporter; *person, animal, vehicle, storm, consequences* amener; *evidence* fournir. **to** ~ **sb up/down** *etc* faire monter/faire descendre *etc* qn (avec soi); **to** ~ **sth up/down** monter/descendre qch; **it brought him a good income** cela lui rapportait bien; *(Jur)* **to** ~ **an action against sb** intenter un procès à qn; **to** ~ **luck** porter bonheur; **to** ~ **tears to sb's eyes** faire venir les larmes aux yeux de qn; **to** ~ **sth (up)on o.s.** s'attirer qch; **to** ~ **sth to a close** *or* **an end** mettre fin à qch; **to** ~ **sth to light** mettre qch en lumière; **he brought him to understand that...** il l'a amené à comprendre que...; **I cannot** ~ **myself to speak to him** je ne peux me résoudre à lui parler.
◆ **bring about** *vt sep* (**a**) *reforms, review* amener, provoquer; *war, accident* causer, provoquer. (**b**) *boat* faire virer de bord. ◆ **bring along** *vt sep object* apporter; *person, car* amener. ◆ **bring back** *vt sep* (**a**) *person* ramener; *object* rapporter; *spacecraft* récupérer. (**b**) *(call to mind)* rappeler (à la mémoire). ◆ **bring down** *vt sep kite etc* ramener au sol; *plane* faire atterrir; *animal, bird, enemy plane* descendre; *tree, opponent* abattre; *dictator, government* faire tomber; *temperature, prices* faire baisser; *swelling* réduire. **the play brought the house down** * la pièce a fait crouler la salle sous les applaudissements. ◆ **bring forward** *vt sep person* faire avancer; *chair etc* avancer; *witness* produire; *evi-*

dence avancer; *(advance time of) meeting* avancer; *(Book-keeping) figure* reporter. ◆ **bring in** *vt sep person* faire entrer; *chair* rentrer; *police, troops* faire intervenir; *fashion* lancer; *custom, legislation* introduire; *income, interest* rapporter; *[jury] verdict* rendre; *(Parl) bill* présenter. ◆ **bring off** *vt sep people from wreck* sauver; *plan, aim* réaliser; *deal* mener à bien; *attack, hoax* réussir. **he didn't ~ it off** il n'a pas réussi son coup. ◆ **bring on** *vt sep illness, quarrel* provoquer, causer; *crops, flowers* faire pousser; *(Theat) person* amener; *thing* apporter sur la scène. ◆ **bring out** *vt sep person* faire sortir; *object* sortir; *meaning, colour* faire ressortir; *qualities* mettre en valeur; *book* publier, faire paraître; *new product* lancer. ◆ **bring round** *vt sep person* amener; *object* apporter; *conversation* ramener (*to* sur); *unconscious person* ranimer; *(convert)* convertir (*to* à). ◆ **bring together** *vt sep people (introduce)* faire se rencontrer; *(reconcile)* réconcilier. ◆ **bring up** *vt sep person* faire monter; *object* monter; *(vomit)* vomir, rendre; *(mention) fact, problem* mentionner; *question* soulever; *(rear) child, animal* élever. **well brought-up** bien élevé; **to ~ sb up short** arrêter qn net; **to ~ sb up before a court** faire comparaître qn devant un tribunal.
◆ **bring-and-buy sale** *n* vente *f* de charité.

brink [brɪŋk] *n* bord *m*. **on the ~ of (doing) sth** à deux doigts de (faire) qch. ◆ **brinkmanship** * *n* stratégie *f* du bord de l'abîme.

brisk [brɪsk] *adj person, voice* vif, animé; *(abrupt)* brusque; *movement* vif, rapide; *attack* vigoureux; *trade, trading* actif; *air* frais. **at a ~ pace** d'un bon pas; **business is ~** les affaires marchent (bien). ◆ **briskly** *adv move* vivement; *walk* d'un bon pas; *speak* brusquement; *act* sans tarder; *sell* très bien. ◆ **briskness** *n* vivacité *f*; animation *f*; brusquerie *f*; rapidité *f*; activité *f*; fraîcheur *f*.

bristle ['brɪsl] **1** *n [beard, brush, plant]* poil *m*; *[boar etc]* soie *f*. **brush with nylon ~s** brosse en nylon; **pure ~ brush** brosse pur sanglier *inv*. **2** *vi [animal, hair, person]* se hérisser (*at* à). **bristling with** *pins, difficulties* hérissé de; *policemen* grouillant de. ◆ **bristly** *adj chin* qui pique; *hair, beard* hérissé.

Britain ['brɪtən] *n*: **(Great) ~** Grande-Bretagne *f*. ◆ **Briticism** *n* anglicisme *m*. ◆ **British** **1** *adj economy, team* britannique, anglais; *ambassador* de Grande-Bretagne; **the British Commonwealth** le Commonwealth; **British English** l'anglais d'Angleterre; **British Isles** îles *fpl* Britanniques ; **2** *n*: **the British** les Britanniques *mpl*, les Anglais *mpl*. ◆ **Britisher** *or* ◆ **Briton** *n* Britannique *mf*, Anglais(e) *m(f)*.

Brittany ['brɪtənɪ] *n* Bretagne *f*.

brittle ['brɪtl] *adj* cassant, fragile.

broach [brəʊtʃ] *vt* entamer.

broad [brɔ:d] *adj road, smile* large; *hint* transparent; *mind, ideas* large, libéral; *accent* prononcé. **to grow ~(er)** s'élargir; **to make ~(er)** élargir; **~ bean** fève *f*; *(fig)* **he's got a ~ back** il a bon dos; **the lake is 200 metres ~** le lac a 200 mètres de largeur *or* de large; *(fig)* **it's as ~ as it is long** c'est du pareil au même *; **in ~ daylight** au grand jour; **the ~ outlines** les grandes lignes; **in the ~est sense** au sens le plus large.
◆ **broadcast** *V below*. ◆ **broaden (~ out)** **1** *vt* élargir ; **2** *vi* s'élargir. ◆ **broadly** *adv*: **~ly (speaking)** en gros. ◆ **broad-minded** *adj* qui a les idées (très) larges. ◆ **broad-mindedness** *n* largeur *f* d'esprit. ◆ **broadness** *n* largeur *f*. ◆ **broadsheet** *n* placard *m*. ◆ **broad-shouldered** *adj* large d'épaules. ◆ **broadside** *n (Naut)* bordée *f*; *(fig: insults etc)* bordée d'injures *etc*; **~side on** par le travers. ◆ **broadways** *or* ◆ **broadwise** *adv* en largeur.

broadcast ['brɔ:dkɑ:st] *pret, ptp* **broadcast** **1** *vt (Rad)* (radio)diffuser, émettre; *(TV)* téléviser, émettre. *(fig)* **don't ~ it!** * ne va pas le crier sur les toits! **2** *vi [station]* émettre; *[actor, interviewee]* participer à une émission; *[interviewer]* faire une émission. **3** *n* émission *f*. **4** *adj (Rad)* (radio)diffusé; *(TV)* télévisé. ◆ **broadcaster** *n* personnalité *f* de la radio *or* de la télévision. ◆ **broadcasting** *n (Rad)* radiodiffusion *f*; *(TV)* télévision *f*; *(broadcasts)* émissions *fpl*.

brocade [brə(ʊ)'keɪd] *n* brocart *m*.

broccoli ['brɒkəlɪ] *n* brocoli *m*.

brochure ['brəʊʃjʊəʳ] *n (Scol etc)* prospectus *m*; *(Tourism)* brochure *f*, dépliant *m*.

brogue [brəʊg] *n (shoe)* chaussure *f* de marche; *(accent)* accent *m* irlandais.

broil [brɔɪl] *vti (also fig)* griller.

broke [brəʊk] *(pret of* **break***) adj (*: penniless)* à sec *, fauché *. **to go ~** * faire faillite.

broken ['brəʊk(ə)n] *(ptp of* **break***) adj* (**a**) *window, rib* cassé; *neck, leg* fracturé, cassé; *heart, marriage* brisé; *promise* rompu, violé; *appointment* manqué. **~ bones** fractures *fpl*; **~ home** foyer brisé; **he is a ~ reed** on ne peut jamais compter sur lui; **a spell of ~ weather** un temps variable. (**b**) *(uneven) ground* accidenté; *road* défoncé; *surface* raboteux; *line* brisé; *coastline* dentelé. (**c**) *(interrupted) journey* interrompu; *sleep (disturbed)* interrompu; *(restless)* agité; *gestures* incohérent; *voice* brisé; *words* haché. **to speak ~ English** parler un mauvais anglais; **~ nights** mauvaises nuits. (**d**) *(spoilt) health* délabré; *spirit* abattu. **he is a ~ man** il est brisé. ◆ **broken-down** *adj car* en panne; *machine* détraqué; *house* délabré, en ruines. ◆ **broken-hearted** *adj* au cœur brisé. ◆ **brokenly** *adv say* d'une voix entrecoupée; *sob* par à-coups.

broker ['brəʊkəʳ] *n* courtier *m*.

brolly * ['brɒlɪ] *n (Brit)* pépin * *m*, parapluie *m*.

bromide ['brəʊmaɪd] *n* bromure *m*; *(fig)* banalité *f* euphorisante.

bronchial ['brɒŋkɪəl] *adj infection* des bronches. **~ tubes** bronches *fpl*.

bronchitis [brɒŋ'kaɪtɪs] *n* bronchite *f*.

bronze [brɒnz] **1** *n* bronze *m*. **2** *vi* se bronzer. **3** *vt skin* faire bronzer. **4** *adj (made of ~)* en bronze; *(colour)* bronze *inv*. **B~ Age** âge *m* du bronze. ◆ **bronzed** *adj* bronzé.

brooch [brəʊtʃ] *n* broche *f (bijou)*.

brood [bru:d] **1** *n* nichée *f*. **2** *vi [storm, danger]* couver; *[person]* broyer du noir. *[person]* **to ~ on** *misfortune* remâcher; *plan* ruminer; *the past* ressasser. ◆ **broody** *adj person* distrait; *(depressed)* cafardeux *. **~ hen** couveuse *f*.

brook[1] [brʊk] *n (stream)* ruisseau *m*.

brook[2] [brʊk] *vt (tolerate)* souffrir, admettre.

broom [brʊm] *n* (**a**) *(Bot)* genêt *m*. (**b**) *(brush)* balai *m*. *(fig)* **this firm needs a new ~** cette compagnie a besoin de sang nouveau. ◆ **broomstick** *n* (manche *m* à) balai *m*.

broth [brɒθ] *n* bouillon *m* de viande et de légumes.

brothel ['brɒθl] *n* bordel ‡ *m*.

brother ['brʌðəʳ] **1** *n (gen, Rel)* frère *m*; *(in trade unions etc)* camarade *m*. **2** *adj*: **his ~ officers** ses compagnons *mpl* d'armes. ◆ **brotherhood** *n* fraternité *f*; *(association)* confrérie *f*. ◆ **brother-in-law** *n* beau-frère *m*. ◆ **brotherly** *adj* fraternel.

brought [brɔ:t] *pret, ptp of* **bring**.

brow [braʊ] *n (forehead)* front *m*; *(arch above eye)* arcade *f* sourcilière; *(eyebrow)* sourcil *m*; *[hill]* sommet *m*; *[cliff]* bord *m*. ◆ **browbeat** *(pret* **browbeat**, *ptp* **browbeaten***) vt* intimider, brusquer; **to ~beat sb into doing sth** forcer qn à faire qch par l'intimidation.

brown [braʊn] **1** *adj (gen)* brun; *hair* châtain; *shoes, material, leather* marron *inv*; *(tanned)* bronzé, bruni; *(dusky-skinned)* brun de peau. **~ ale** bière brune;

~ **bread** pain bis; ~ **bear** ours brun; ~ **paper** papier *m* d'emballage; ~ **rice** riz complet; **in a ~ study** plongé dans ses pensées; ~ **sugar** cassonade *f*, sucre brun; **to go** ~ *[person]* brunir; *[leaves]* roussir; **as ~ as a berry** tout bronzé. **2** *n* brun *m*, marron *m*. **3** *vt [sun]* bronzer, brunir; *(Culin) meat, potatoes* faire dorer; *sauce* faire roussir. **to be ~ed off** ‡ en avoir marre *. ◆ **brownie** *n* lutin *m*; **B~ie (Guide)** jeannette *f*. ◆ **brownish** *adj* qui tire sur le brun, brunâtre *(pej)*. ◆ **brown-out** *n (US Elec)* panne *f* partielle. ◆ **brownstone (house)** *n (US)* bâtiment *m* de grès brun.

browse [braʊz] *vi [animal]* brouter; *[person in bookshop]* feuilleter les livres; *(in other shops)* regarder.

bruise [bru:z] **1** *vt person* faire un bleu à; *fruit* abîmer, taler; *lettuce* froisser. **to ~ one's foot** se faire un bleu au pied; **to be ~d all over** être couvert de bleus. **2** *n [person]* bleu *m*, ecchymose *f*; *[fruit]* talure *f*. **body covered with ~s** corps couvert d'ecchymoses. ◆ **bruiser** * *n* malabar * *m*.

brunch [brʌn(t)ʃ] *n* (grand) petit déjeuner *m*.

brunt [brʌnt] *n*: **the ~** *[attack, blow]* le choc; *[argument, displeasure]* le poids; *[work, expense]* le (plus) gros; **he bore the ~ of it all** c'est lui qui a porté le poids de l'affaire.

brush [brʌʃ] **1** *n* (**a**) *(gen)* brosse *f*; *(paint ~)* pinceau *m*, brosse; *(broom)* balai *m*; *(hearth ~ etc)* balayette *f*; *(scrubbing ~)* brosse (dure); *(shaving ~)* blaireau *m*. **hair/shoe ~** brosse à cheveux/à chaussures; **give your coat a ~** donne un coup de brosse à ton manteau. (**b**) *(light touch)* effleurement *m*. **to have a ~ with the law** avoir des démêlés *mpl* avec la police; *(quarrel)* **to have a ~ with sb** avoir un accrochage avec qn. (**c**) *(undergrowth)* broussailles *fpl*. **2** *vt* (**a**) *carpet* balayer; *clothes, hair etc* brosser. **to ~ one's teeth** se laver les dents; **to ~ one's hair** se brosser les cheveux; **hair ~ed back** cheveux ramenés en arrière. (**b**) *(touch lightly)* effleurer; *the ground* raser. (**c**) *(Tex) wool* gratter. **~ed cotton** pilou *m*; **~ed nylon** nylon gratté. **3** *vi*: **to ~ against sb/sth** effleurer *or* frôler qn/qch; **to ~ past sb/sth** frôler qn/qch en passant.

◆ **brush aside** *vt sep objections* balayer; *objector* repousser. ◆ **brush away** *vt sep mud, dust (on clothes)* brosser; *(on floor)* balayer; *tears* essuyer; *insects* chasser. ◆ **brush down** *vt sep person, garment* donner un coup de brosse à; *horse* brosser. ◆ **brush off** *vt sep mud, snow, fluff* enlever; *insect* balayer. ◆ **brush up** *vt sep crumbs, dirt* ramasser avec une brosse *or* à la balayette; *(*: revise)* se remettre à, réviser.

◆ **brush-off** ‡ *n*: **to give sb the ~-off** ‡ envoyer promener * qn; **to get the ~-off** ‡ se faire envoyer promener *. ◆ **brush-stroke** *n* coup *m* de pinceau. ◆ **brushwood** *n (undergrowth)* broussailles *fpl*; *(cuttings)* brindilles *fpl*. ◆ **brushwork** *n (Art)* facture *f*.

brusque [bru:sk] *adj* brusque. ◆ **brusquely** *adv* avec brusquerie. ◆ **brusqueness** *n* brusquerie *f*.

Brussels ['brʌslz] *n* Bruxelles. ~ **sprouts** choux *mpl* de Bruxelles.

brute [bru:t] **1** *n (animal)* brute *f*, bête *f*; *(person)* brute. **this machine is a ~!** * quelle vache que cette machine! ‡ **2** *adj strength, passion* brutal; *matter* brut. **by (sheer) ~ force** par la force. ◆ **brutal** *adj* brutal, cruel. ◆ **brutality** *n* brutalité *f*. ◆ **brutally** *adv* brutalement. ◆ **brutish** *adj (animal-like)* bestial; *(unfeeling)* grossier.

bubble ['bʌbl] **1** *n* bulle *f*; *(in hot liquid)* bouillon *m*; *(in paint)* boursouflure *f*. **to blow ~s** faire des bulles; **soap ~** bulle de savon. **2** *adj*: ~ **bath** bain moussant. **3** *vi [liquid]* bouillonner; *[champagne]* pétiller; *[gas]* barboter; *(gurgle)* faire glouglou, glouglouter. **to ~ out** sortir à gros bouillons; **to ~ up** monter en bouillonnant; *(lit, fig)* **to ~ over** déborder (*with* de). ◆ **bubble-car** *n* petite voiture *(à toit transparent)*. ◆ **bubble-gum** *n* chewing-gum *m* (qui fait des bulles).

bubonic [bju:'bɒnɪk] *adj* bubonique.

buccaneer [ˌbʌkə'nɪə^r] *n* boucanier *m*.

Bucharest [bu:kə'rɛst] *n* Bucarest.

buck [bʌk] **1** *n* (**a**) *(Zool)* mâle *m*. (**b**) *(US *)* dollar *m*. (**c**) **to pass the ~** refiler * la responsabilité aux autres. (**d**) *(Gymnastics)* cheval *m* d'arçons. **2** *adj rabbit* mâle. **3** *vi [horse]* lancer une ruade. *(US)* **to ~ for sth** * rechercher qch.

◆ **buck up** * **1** *vi (hurry up)* se grouiller *; *(cheer up)* se secouer. **2** *vt sep* remonter le moral de. ◆ **bucked** ‡ *adj* tout content. ◆ **buckshot** *n* chevrotines *fpl*. ◆ **buckskin** *n* peau *f* de daim. ◆ **buck-toothed** *adj*: **to be ~-toothed** avoir des dents de lapin.

bucket ['bʌkɪt] **1** *n (gen)* seau *m*; *[dredger etc]* godet *m*. ~ **of water** seau d'eau; **chain of ~s** pompe *f* à chapelet; **to weep ~s** * pleurer toutes les larmes de son corps. **2** *vi*: **the rain is ~ing (down)** ‡ il pleut à seaux, il tombe des cordes *. **3** *adj*: ~ **seat** (siège-)baquet *m*; ~ **shop** agence vendant des billets d'avion à prix réduit. ◆ **bucketful** *n* plein seau; **I've had a ~ful** ‡ j'en ai ras le bol ‡ (*of* de).

buckle ['bʌkl] **1** *n* boucle *f*. **2** *vt* (**a**) *belt* boucler, attacher. (**b**) *wheel* voiler; *metal* gauchir. **3** *vi* (**a**) se boucler. (**b**) se voiler; gauchir. ◆ **buckle down** * *vi* se coller au boulot *. **to ~ down to a job** s'atteler à un boulot *. ◆ **buckle on** *vt sep armour* revêtir; *sword* ceindre.

buckram ['bʌkrəm] *n* bougran *m*.

buckshee ‡ [bʌk'ʃi:] *adj, adv* gratis *(inv)*.

bud [bʌd] **1** *n [tree, plant]* bourgeon *m*; *[flower]* bouton *m*. **in ~** *tree* bourgeonnant; *flower* en bouton. **2** *vi [tree]* bourgeonner; *[flower]* former des boutons. ◆ **budding** *adj plant* bourgeonnant; *flower* en bouton; *poet etc* en herbe; *passion* naissant.

Budapest [ˌbju:də'pɛst] *n* Budapest.

Buddha ['bʊdə] *n* Bouddha *m*. ◆ **Buddhism** *n* bouddhisme *m*. ◆ **Buddhist** **1** *n* Bouddhiste *mf*; **2** *adj monk* bouddhiste; *religion* bouddhique.

buddy * ['bʌdɪ] *n (US)* copain * *m*, copine * *f*.

budge [bʌdʒ] **1** *vi* bouger; *(fig)* changer d'avis. **2** *vt* faire bouger; *(fig)* faire changer d'avis. ◆ **budge over** *, **budge up** * *vi* se pousser.

budgerigar ['bʌdʒərɪgɑ:^r] *n* perruche *f*.

budget ['bʌdʒɪt] **1** *n* budget *m*. **2** *adj* (**a**) *(Econ) spending, credit* budgétaire. *(Comm)* ~ **account** compte-crédit *m*; ~ **cuts** compressions *fpl* budgétaires; ~ **deficit** déficit *m* budgétaire; *(Parl)* ~ **day** jour *m* de la présentation du budget; *(US Comm)* ~ **plan** système *m* de crédit; ~ **surplus** excédent *m* budgétaire. (**b**) *(cut-price)* pour petits budgets, économique. **3** *vi* dresser un budget. **to ~ for sth** *(Econ)* porter qch au budget; *(gen)* inscrire qch à son budget. **4** *vt* budgétiser. ◆ **budgetary** *adj* budgétaire; **~ary year** exercice *m* budgétaire.

budgie * ['bʌdʒɪ] *n abbr of* **budgerigar**.

Buenos Aires ['bweɪnɒs'aɪrɪz] *n* Buenos Aires.

buff[1] [bʌf] **1** *n (for polishing)* polissoir *m*; *(colour)* (couleur *f*) chamois *m*. **in the ~** ‡ à poil ‡. **2** *adj (~-coloured)* (couleur) chamois *inv*. **3** *vt metal* polir.

buff[2] * [bʌf] *n (enthusiast)* mordu(e) * *m(f)*. **film ~** mordu(e) * du cinéma.

buffalo, *pl* ~ *or* **~es** ['bʌfələʊ, z] *n (wild ox)* buffle *m*, bufflesse *f*; *(esp in US)* bison *m*.

buffer ['bʌfə^r] **1** *n (gen, also Rail)* tampon *m*; *(US Aut)* pare-chocs *m inv*; *(Comput)* mémoire *f* tampon. **2** *adj*: ~ **state** état *m* tampon.

buffet[1] ['bʌfɪt] **1** *n* gifle *f*. *(fig)* **the ~s of fate** les coups *mpl* du sort. **2** *vt [waves]* battre, ballotter; *[wind]* secouer. ◆ **buffeting** **1** *n [wind, rain etc]* assaut *m* ; **2** *adj wind* violent.

buffet[2] ['bʊfeɪ] **1** *n* buffet *m (repas)*. *(in menu)* **cold ~** viandes froides. **2** *adj (Rail)* **~ car** voiture-buffet *f*, buffet *m*; **~ lunch** lunch *m*; **~ supper** souper-buffet *m*.

buffoon [bə'fu:n] *n* bouffon *m*. ◆ **buffoonery** *n* bouffonneries *fpl*.

bug [bʌg] **1** *n* (**a**) punaise *f*; *(*: any insect)* insecte *m*, bestiole * *f*; *(*: germ)* microbe *m*. **the flu ~** le virus de la grippe. (**b**) *(*: microphone)* micro *m* (caché). (**c**) *(Comput)* défaut *m*. **2** *vt* (**a**) (*) *phone* brancher sur table d'écoute; *room etc* poser des micros dans. (**b**) *(‡: annoy)* embêter *. ◆ **bugbear** *n* épouvantail *m*, cauchemar *m*. ◆ **bug-eyed** ‡ *adj* aux yeux à fleur de tête. ◆ **bugging** * *adj*: **~ging device** appareil *m* d'écoute *(clandestine)*. ◆ **bug-ridden** *adj* infesté de punaises.

buggy ['bʌgɪ] *n (for beach)* buggy *m*; *(for moon)* jeep *f* lunaire; *(‡: car)* bagnole * *f*. **(baby) ~** *(Brit: push chair)* poussette *f*; *(US: pram)* voiture *f* d'enfant.

bugle ['bju:gl] *n* clairon *m*. **~ call** sonnerie *f* de clairon. ◆ **bugler** *n* (joueur *m* de) clairon *m*.

build [bɪld] *(vb: pret, ptp* **built***)* **1** *n [person]* carrure *f*. **2** *vt house, town* bâtir, construire; *bridge, ship, machine* construire; *temple* bâtir, édifier; *nest* faire, bâtir; *theory, plan, empire* bâtir; *(Games) words* former. **the house is being built** la maison se bâtit; **to ~ sth into a wall** encastrer qch dans un mur; *[person]* **to be solidly built** être puissamment charpenté; **pine-built house** maison en bois de pin; **French-built ship** navire de construction française. ◆ **build in** *vt sep wardrobe* encastrer; *safeguards* intégrer (*into* à). ◆ **build on** *vt sep* ajouter (*to* à). ◆ **build up** **1** *vi [pressure]* s'accumuler; *[interest]* monter. **2** *vt sep* (**a**) *(establish) reputation* bâtir; *business* créer, monter; *theory* échafauder; *(increase) production, forces* accroître; *pressure* accumuler; *tension, excitement* faire monter. (**b**) *(cover with houses) area, land* urbaniser.
◆ **builder** *n [houses etc] (worker)* maçon *m*; *(owner)* entrepreneur *m*; *[ships, machines]* constructeur *m*; *(fig)* fondateur *m*, -trice *f*; **~er's labourer** ouvrier-maçon *m*. ◆ **building** **1** *n* bâtiment *m*, construction *f*; *(imposing)* édifice *m*; *(habitation or offices)* immeuble *m* ; **2** *adj*: **~ing block** *(toy)* cube *m*; *(fig)* composante *f*; **~ing contractor** entrepreneur *m* (de bâtiment); **~ing industry** (industrie *f* du) bâtiment *m*; **~ing land** terrain *m* à bâtir; **~ing materials** matériaux *mpl* de construction; **~ing site** chantier *m* (de construction); **~ing society** ≃ société *f* d'investissement immobilier; **~ing workers** ouvriers *mpl* du bâtiment. ◆ **build-up** *n [pressure, gas]* accumulation *f*; *(Mil) [troops]* rassemblement *m*; *[tension, excitement]* montée *f*; *(fig)* **to give sb/sth a good ~-up** faire une bonne publicité pour qn/qch. ◆ **built-in** *adj bookcase* encastré; *desire* inné.
◆ **built-up** *adj* urbanisé; **~-up area** agglomération *f* (urbaine).

bulb [bʌlb] *n* (**a**) *[plant]* bulbe *m*, oignon *m*. **~ of garlic** tête *f* d'ail. (**b**) *(Elec)* ampoule *f*; *[thermometer]* cuvette *f*. ◆ **bulbous** *adj* bulbeux.

Bulgaria [bʌl'gɛərɪə] *n* Bulgarie *f*.

bulge [bʌldʒ] **1** *n [surface, metal]* bombement *m*; *[cheek]* gonflement *m*; *[plaster]* bosse *f*; *[tyre]* hernie *f*; *[pocket, jacket]* renflement *m*; *[numbers]* augmentation *f* temporaire; *[sales, birth rate]* poussée *f*. **the postwar ~** l'explosion *f* démographique de l'après-guerre. **2** *vi* **(~ out)** *(swell)* bomber; *(stick out)* faire saillie; *[plaster]* être bosselé; *[pocket, sack, cheek]* être gonflé (*with* de). ◆ **bulging** *adj forehead, wall* bombé; *stomach, eyes* protubérant; *pockets, suitcase* bourré (*with* de).

bulk [bʌlk] *n [thing]* grosseur *f*, grandeur *f*; *[person]* corpulence *f*; *(in food)* fibre *f* (végétale). **the ~ of** *[people, community]* la plus grande partie de; *[work]* le plus gros de; **in ~** *(in large quantities)* en gros; *(not pre-packed)* en vrac. ◆ **bulk-buying** *n* achat *m* en gros. ◆ **bulkiness** *n [parcel, luggage]* grosseur *f*; *[person]* corpulence *f*. ◆ **bulky** *adj parcel, suitcase* volumineux; *book* épais; *person* corpulent.

bull[1] [bʊl] **1** *n* (**a**) taureau *m*; *(male of elephant etc)* mâle *m*; *(St Ex)* haussier *m*. *(fig)* **to take the ~ by the horns** prendre le taureau par les cornes; **like a ~ in a china shop** comme un éléphant dans un magasin de porcelaine; **it's like a red rag to a ~** ça lui *(etc)* fait monter la moutarde au nez; **to go at it like a ~ at a gate** foncer tête baissée. (**b**) *(Mil sl)* fourbissage *m*. **2** *adj elephant etc* mâle.
◆ **bulldog** **1** *n* bouledogue *m* ; **2** *adj*: **~dog clip** pince *f* (à dessin). ◆ **bulldoze** *vt* passer au bulldozer; *(fig)* **to ~doze sb into doing sth** * employer les grands moyens pour faire faire qch à qn. ◆ **bulldozer** *n* bulldozer *m*. ◆ **bullfight** *n* course *f* de taureaux, corrida *f*. ◆ **bullfighter** *n* matador *m*, torero *m*. ◆ **bullfighting** *n* courses *fpl* de taureaux; *(art)* tauromachie *f*. ◆ **bullfinch** *n* bouvreuil *m*. ◆ **bullfrog** *n* grosse grenouille *f* d'Amérique. ◆ **bullish** *adj (St Ex)* haussier. ◆ **bull-necked** *adj* au cou de taureau. ◆ **bullock** *n* bœuf *m*; *(young)* bouvillon *m*. ◆ **bullring** *n* arène *f (pour courses de taureaux)*. ◆ **bull's-eye** *n* centre *m* (de la cible); **to hit the ~'s-eye** mettre dans le mille.
◆ **bullterrier** *n* bullterrier *m*.

bull[2] [bʊl] *n (Rel)* bulle *f*.

bullet ['bʊlɪt] *n* balle *f*. **~ hole** trou *m* d'une balle; **~ wound** blessure *f* par balle. ◆ **bulletheaded** *adj* à (la) tête ronde. ◆ **bulletproof** **1** *adj garment etc* pare-balles *inv*; *car etc* blindé ; **2** *vt* blinder.

bulletin ['bʊlɪtɪn] *n* bulletin *m*.

bullion ['bʊljən] *n (gold)* or *m* en lingot(s); *(silver)* argent *m* en lingot(s).

bully ['bʊlɪ] **1** *n* brute *f*. **2** *vt* persécuter, brutaliser, brimer. **to ~ sb into doing sth** contraindre qn par la menace à faire qch. ◆ **bullying** **1** *adj* brutal ; **2** *n* brimades *fpl*, brutalités *fpl*.

bully-beef ['bʊlɪbi:f] *n* corned-beef *m*.

bulrush ['bʊlrʌʃ] *n* jonc *m*.

bulwark ['bʊlwək] *n* rempart *m*.

bum [bʌm] **1** *n* (**a**) (*) *(vagrant)* clochard * *m*; *(good-for-nothing)* bon à rien *m*. (**b**) *(‡: bottom)* derrière *m*. **2** *vi* (**~ about** *or* **around**) fainéanter. **3** *vt*: **to ~ a meal off sb** * taper * qn d'un repas.

bumblebee ['bʌmblbi:] *n (Zool)* bourdon *m*.

bumbling ['bʌmblɪŋ] *adj* empoté.

bumf [bʌmf] *n (*: forms etc)* paperasses *fpl*; *(‡: toilet paper)* papier *m* de cabinets.

bump [bʌmp] **1** *n* (**a**) *(blow)* choc *m*, heurt *m*; *(jolt)* cahot *m*, secousse *f*; *(Boat-racing)* heurt. (**b**) *(swelling etc: on road, car, head etc)* bosse *f*. **~ of locality** * sens *m* de l'orientation. **2** *vt car, boat* heurter. **to ~ one's head** se cogner la tête (*against* contre). **3** *vi*: **to ~ along** cahoter; **to ~ into** *[vehicle]* entrer en collision avec, rentrer dans *; *[person]* se cogner contre; *(*: meet)* rencontrer par hasard, tomber sur; **the car ~ed up onto the pavement** la voiture a grimpé sur le trottoir. ◆ **bump off** ‡ *vt sep* liquider *, supprimer.
◆ **bumper** **1** *n [car]* pare-chocs *m inv* ; **2** *adj crop* exceptionnel. ◆ **bumping** *adj*: **~ing cars** autos *fpl* tamponneuses. ◆ **bumpy** *adj road* bosselé, inégal; **we had a ~y flight/crossing** nous avons été très secoués pendant le vol/la traversée.

bumptious ['bʌm(p)ʃəs] *adj* suffisant, prétentieux.

bun [bʌn] *n (Culin)* petit pain au lait; *[hair]* chignon *m*. ◆ **bun-fight** * *n* thé *m (servi pour un grand nombre de gens)*.

bunch [bʌn(t)ʃ] *n [flowers]* bouquet *m*; *[bananas]* régime *m*; *[feathers]* touffe *f*; *[radishes, asparagus]* botte *f*; *[twigs]* paquet *m*; *[keys]* trousseau *m*; *[ribbons]* nœud *m*, flot *m*; *[people]* groupe *m*, bande *f*. ~ **of grapes** grappe *f* de raisin; *[hair]* ~**es** couettes *fpl*; *(fig)* **the pick** *or* **the best of the** ~ le *or* la meilleur(e), les meilleur(e)s; **the best of a bad** ~ * le *or* la moins médiocre, les moins médiocres; **what a** ~! quelle équipe! * ◆ **bunch together** **1** *vi* se grouper. **2** *vt sep* grouper.

bundle ['bʌndl] **1** *n [clothes, goods]* paquet *m*, ballot *m*; *[hay]* botte *f*; *[letters, papers]* liasse *f*; *[linen]* paquet; *[firewood]* fagot *m*; *[rods, sticks]* poignée *f*, paquet. **he is a** ~ **of nerves** c'est un paquet de nerfs; **a** ~ **of mischief** un sac à malices; *(money)* **to make a** ~ * faire son beurre *. **2** *vt* (**a**) (~ **up**) mettre en paquet; *clothes* faire un ballot de; *papers* mettre en liasse. (**b**) **to** ~ **sth into a corner** fourrer qch dans un coin; **to** ~ **sb into the house** pousser qn dans la maison sans cérémonie; **he was** ~**d off to Australia** on l'a expédié * en Australie.

bung [bʌŋ] **1** *n* bonde *f*. **2** *vt* (**a**) (~**up**) *pipe etc* boucher, obstruer. ~**ed up** * *nose* bouché; *person* très enrhumé. (**b**) (✱: *throw*) envoyer *, jeter.

bungalow ['bʌŋgələʊ] *n* bungalow *m*, petit pavillon *m*. ◆ **bungaloid growth** *n (hum, pej)* extension *f* pavillonnaire.

bungle ['bʌŋgl] *vt* bousiller *, saboter. ◆ **bungler** *n* bousilleur * *m*, -euse * *f*. ◆ **bungling** **1** *adj* maladroit; **2** *n* gâchis *m*.

bunion ['bʌnjən] *n (Med)* oignon *m*.

bunk [bʌŋk] *n* (**a**) *(bed)* couchette *f*. (**b**) **to do a** ~ ✱ mettre les voiles *. (**c**) (✱: *also* **bunkum**) blagues * *fpl*, balivernes *fpl*. ◆ **bunk-beds** *npl* lits *mpl* superposés. ◆ **bunk-up** * *n*: **to give sb a** ~**-up** * soulever qn par derrière *or* par en dessous.

bunker ['bʌŋkə^r] *n [coal]* coffre *m*; *(Naut)* soute *f* (à charbon); *(Mil)* blockhaus *m*; *(Golf)* bunker *m*. **(nuclear)** ~ abri *m* anti-nucléaire.

bunny ['bʌnɪ] *n* (~ **rabbit)** Jeannot *m* lapin; (~ **girl)** hôtesse *f (du Club Playboy)*.

Bunsen ['bʌnsn] *n*: ~ **burner** bec *m* Bunsen.

bunting ['bʌntɪŋ] *n (flags etc)* drapeaux *mpl*, pavoisement *m*.

buoy [bɔɪ] *n* bouée *f*, balise *f* flottante. ◆ **buoy up** *vt sep* maintenir à flot; *(fig)* soutenir. ◆ **buoyancy** *n [ship, object]* flottabilité *f*; *[liquid]* poussée *f*; *(lightheartedness)* entrain *m*; ~**ancy aid** gilet *m* de sauvetage. ◆ **buoyant** *adj ship, object* flottable; *liquid* dans lequel les objets flottent; *person* plein d'entrain; *mood* optimiste; *step* léger; *(Fin) market* ferme. ◆ **buoyantly** *adv walk, float* légèrement; *answer* avec entrain, avec optimisme.

bur [bɜː^r] *n* (**a**) *(Bot)* bardane *f*. (**b**) **to speak with a** ~ grasseyer.

burble ['bɜːbl] *vi [stream]* murmurer; *[person]* marmonner.

burden ['bɜːdn] **1** *n* fardeau *m*, charge *f*; *[taxes, years]* poids *m*. **to be a** ~ **to** être un fardeau pour; **to make sb's life a** ~ rendre la vie intenable à qn; **the** ~ **of the expense** les frais *mpl* à charge; **the** ~ **of proof lies with him** la charge de la preuve lui incombe; **the** ~ **of their complaint** leur principal sujet de plainte. **2** *vt person* accabler (*with* de); *object, memory, essay* surcharger (*with* de). ◆ **burdensome** *adj* pénible.

bureau [bjʊə'rəʊ] *n (writing desk)* secrétaire *m (bureau)*; *(chest of drawers)* commode *f*; *(office)* bureau *m*; *(government department)* service *m* (gouvernemental). ◆ **bureaucracy** *n* bureaucratie *f*. ◆ **bureaucrat** *n* bureaucrate *mf*. ◆ **bureaucratic** *adj* bureaucratique.

burg * [bɜːg] *n (US pej)* bled *m*, patelin *m*.

burger ['bɜːgə^r] *n* hamburger *m*.

burglar ['bɜːglə^r] **1** *n* cambrioleur *m*, -euse *f*. **2** *adj*: ~ **alarm** sonnerie *f* d'alarme. ◆ **burglarize** *vt (US)* cambrioler. ◆ **burglar-proof** **1** *vt house* munir d'un dispositif d'alarme ; **2** *adj lock* incrochetable. ◆ **burglary** *n* cambriolage *m*. ◆ **burgle** *vt* cambrioler.

Burgundy ['bɜːg(ə)ndɪ] *n* Bourgogne *f*. *(wine)* **b**~ bourgogne *m*.

burial ['berɪəl] **1** *n* enterrement *m*. **2** *adj*: ~ **ground** cimetière *m*; ~ **place** lieu *m* de sépulture.

Burkina-Faso [bɜː'kiːnə'fæsəʊ] *n* Burkina Faso *m*.

burlesque [bɜː'lesk] **1** *n (Literat)* burlesque *m*; *(US: striptease)* revue déshabillée *(souvent vulgaire)*; *[book, poem etc]* parodie *f*; *[society, way of life]* caricature *f*. **2** *vt* tourner en ridicule; *(parody)* parodier.

burly ['bɜːlɪ] *adj* de forte carrure. **a** ~ **policeman** un grand gaillard d'agent.

burn [bɜːn] *(vb: pret, ptp* **burned** *or* **burnt**) **1** *n (gen)* brûlure *f*; *[space rocket]* (durée *f* de) combustion *f*. **2** *vt (gen)* brûler; *town, building* incendier; *meat, toast* laisser brûler. ~**t to a cinder** carbonisé; **to be** ~**t to death** *or* ~**t alive** être brûlé vif; **to** ~ **one's fingers** se brûler les doigts; ~**t offering** holocauste *m*; ~**t orange** orange foncé *inv*; **money** ~**s a hole in my pocket** l'argent me fond dans les mains; *(fig)* **to** ~ **one's boats** brûler ses vaisseaux; **to** ~ **the candle at both ends** brûler la chandelle par les deux bouts. **3** *vi (gen)* brûler; *[wound]* cuire. **you left all the lights** ~**ing** vous avez laissé toutes les lumières allumées; **a** ~**ing question** une question brûlante; **he was** ~**ing for revenge** il brûlait du désir de se venger.

◆ **burn down** **1** *vi [house etc]* brûler complètement; *[fire, candle]* baisser. **2** *vt sep building* incendier. ◆ **burn off** *vt sep paint etc* brûler (au chalumeau). ◆ **burn out** **1** *vi [fire, candle]* s'éteindre; *[light bulb]* griller. **2** *vt sep*: **to be** ~**t out** *[candle]* être mort; *[student]* être usé (à force de travail). ◆ **burn up** **1** *vi [fire etc]* flamber, monter; *[rocket in atmosphere]* se désintégrer. **2** *vt sep rubbish* brûler. ~**ed up with envy** dévoré d'envie.

◆ **burner** *n [cooker]* brûleur *m*; *[lamp, science lab]* bec *m* (de gaz). ◆ **burning** **1** *adj town, forest* en flammes, incendié; *fire, candle* allumé; *coals, faith* ardent; *feeling* cuisant; *thirst, fever, question, topic* brûlant; *indignation* violent; *words* véhément; **the** ~**ing bush** le buisson ardent; **with a** ~**ing face** *(shame)* le rouge au front; *(embarrassment)* le rouge aux joues; **it's a** ~**ing * shame that...** c'est un scandale que + *subj* ; **2** *n (setting, on fire)* incendie *m*; **there is a smell of** ~**ing** ça sent le brûlé *or* le roussi; **I could smell** ~**ing** je sentais une odeur de brûlé.

burnish ['bɜːnɪʃ] *vt* polir.

burp * [bɜːp] **1** *vi* faire un rot *. **2** *vt baby* faire faire son rot * à. **3** *n* rot * *m*.

burr [bɜː^r] *n* = **bur**.

burrow ['bʌrəʊ] **1** *n* terrier *m*. **2** *vi [rabbits]* creuser un terrier; *[dog]* creuser. *[person]* **to** ~ **under** *(in earth)* se creuser un chemin sous; *(under blanket etc)* se réfugier sous.

bursar ['bɜːsə^r] *n [small institution]* économe *mf*; *[large institution]* administrateur *m*, -trice *f*. ◆ **bursary** *n* bourse *f* (d'études).

burst [bɜːst] *(vb: pret, ptp* **burst**) **1** *n [shell, anger, indignation]* explosion *f*; *[laughter]* éclat *m*; *[affection, eloquence, enthusiasm]* élan *m*; *[activity]* vague *f*; *[applause]* salve *f*; *[flames]* jaillissement *m*. ~ **of rain** averse *f*; **to put on a** ~ **of speed** faire une pointe de vitesse; ~ **of gunfire** rafale *f* de tir.
2 *vi* (**a**) *[bomb, shell, boiler]* éclater; *[bubble, balloon, abscess]* crever; *[tyre] (blow out)* éclater; *(puncture)* crever. **to** ~ **open** *[door]* s'ouvrir violemment; *[container]* s'éventrer; *[sack etc]* **to be** ~**ing at the seams** être plein à crever (*with* de); **filled to** ~**ing point** rempli à craquer; **she's** ~**ing out of that dress**

elle éclate de partout dans cette robe; **to be ~ing with** *health, joy* déborder de; *impatience* brûler de; *pride* éclater de; **I was ~ing * to tell you** je mourais d'envie de vous le dire. (**b**) *(rush)* **to ~ in/out** *etc* entrer/sortir *etc* en trombe; **he ~ into/out of the room** il s'est précipité dans/hors de la pièce; **to ~ into tears** fondre en larmes; **to ~ out laughing** éclater de rire; **to ~ out singing/ crying** se mettre tout d'un coup à chanter/à pleurer; **to ~ into flames** prendre feu (soudain). **3** *vt balloon, bubble, tyre* crever; *bag* crever; *(by blowing)* faire éclater; *boiler* faire sauter. **to ~ open** *door* ouvrir violemment; *container* éventrer; **the river has ~ its banks** le fleuve a rompu ses digues; **to ~ a blood vessel** (se) rompre un vaisseau; *(fig: with anger etc)* en avoir une attaque *.

Burundi [bə'rʊndɪ] *n* Burundi *m*.

bury ['berɪ] *vt body, treasure, quarrel* enterrer; *(conceal)* enfouir; *[avalanche etc]* ensevelir; *(plunge) hands, knife* enfoncer, plonger (*in* dans). **he was buried at sea** son corps fut immergé en haute mer; *(fig)* **to ~ one's head in the sand** pratiquer la politique de l'autruche; *(fig)* **to ~ the hatchet** enterrer la hache de guerre; **to ~ one's face in one's hands** se couvrir la figure de ses mains; **village buried in the country** village enfoui en pleine campagne; **buried in thought** plongé dans une rêverie *or* dans ses pensées.

bus [bʌs] **1** *n* autobus *m*, bus * *m*; *(long-distance)* autocar *m*, car *m*. **2** *vi* (*) prendre l'autobus *or* le car. **3** *vt*: **to ~ children to school** transporter des enfants à l'école en car. **4** *adj driver, depot, service, ticket* d'autobus. **~ lane** couloir *m* d'autobus; **the house is on a ~ route** la maison est sur un trajet d'autobus; **~ service** réseau *m or* service *m* d'autobus; **~ shelter** abribus *m*; **~ station** gare *f* d'autobus; *[coaches]* gare routière; **~ stop** arrêt *m* d'autobus. ◆ **busload** *n* car entier (*of* de); **by the ~load, in ~loads** par cars entiers. ◆ **busman** *n (fig)* **to take a ~man's holiday** passer ses vacances à travailler; **the ~men's strike** la grève des employés des autobus. ◆ **bussing** *n* ramassage *m* scolaire *(comme mesure de déségrégation)*.

bush [bʊʃ] *n (shrub)* buisson *m*; *(thicket)* taillis *m*, fourré *m*. *[Africa, Australia]* **the ~** la brousse. ◆ **bushed** ‡ *adj (exhausted)* crevé *, claqué *. ◆ **bushfighting** *n* guérilla *f*. ◆ **bushfire** *n* feu *m* de brousse. ◆ **bush telegraph** * *n (fig)* téléphone *m* arabe. ◆ **bushy** *adj* touffu.

business ['bɪznɪs] **1** *n* (**a**) *(commerce)* affaires *fpl*. **to be in ~** être dans les affaires; **to be in the grocery ~** être dans l'épicerie; **to be in ~ for o.s.** travailler pour son propre compte; **to set up in ~ as a butcher** s'établir boucher; **to do ~ with sb** faire des affaires avec qn; **to go out of ~** fermer; **to put out of ~** faire fermer; **~ is ~** les affaires sont les affaires; **on ~** pour affaires; *(fig)* **what's his line of ~?** * qu'est-ce qu'il fait (dans la vie)?; **to know one's ~** s'y connaître; **to get down to ~** passer aux choses sérieuses; **now we're in ~!** * tout devient possible!; **he means ~** * il ne plaisante pas; **to mix ~ with pleasure** joindre l'utile à l'agréable; **our ~ has doubled** notre chiffre d'affaires a doublé; **he gets a lot of ~ from the Americans** il travaille beaucoup avec les Américains. (**b**) *(commercial enterprise)* commerce *m*. **a grocery ~** un commerce d'alimentation. (**c**) *(task, duty)* affaire *f*. **it's all part of the day's ~** cela fait partie de la routine journalière; **to make it one's ~ to do** se charger de faire; **that's none of his ~** ce n'est pas son affaire, cela ne le regarde pas; **it's your ~ to do it** c'est à vous de le faire; **you've no ~ to do that** ce n'est pas à vous de faire cela; **mind your own ~** mêlez-vous de vos affaires *or* de ce qui vous regarde; **finding a flat is quite a ~** c'est toute une affaire de trouver un appartement; **she made a terrible ~ of helping him** elle a fait toute une histoire * pour l'aider; **it's a bad ~** c'est une sale affaire *or* histoire; **I am tired of this protest ~** j'en ai assez de cette histoire de contestation; **there's some funny ~ going on** il se passe qch de louche.
2 *adj lunch, trip, meeting* d'affaires; *college, studies* commercial; *hours, day* ouvrable. **his ~ address** l'adresse *f* de son bureau; **~ associate** collègue *mf*; **~ centre** centre *m* d'affaires; **~ cycle** cycle *m* économique; **the ~ end of a knife** le côté opérant d'un couteau; **~ expenses** frais généraux; **~ girl** jeune femme *f* d'affaires; **~ manager** *(Comm, Ind)* directeur commercial; *(Cine, Sport, Theat)* manager *m*; **~ reply service** service-lecteurs *m*; **to have ~ sense** avoir du flair pour les affaires; **~ suit** complet *m* (veston).
◆ **businesslike** *adj person, method* pratique, efficace; *firm, transaction, manner* sérieux; **this is a very ~like knife!** * ça, c'est un couteau sérieux! * ◆ **businessman** *n* homme *m* d'affaires. ◆ **businesswoman** *n* femme *f* d'affaires.

busker ['bʌskə^r] *n* musicien *m* ambulant.

bust¹ [bʌst] *n (Anat, Sculp)* buste *m*. **~ measurement** tour *m* de poitrine.

bust² * [bʌst] **1** *adj (broken)* fichu *, cassé. *(bankrupt)* **to go ~** faire faillite. **2** *vt* (**a**) = **burst 3.** (**b**) *(break)* casser. (**c**) (*) *(denounce)* choper *; *(of police: break up) crime ring* démanteler; *(arrest)* arrêter; *(search) place* perquisitionner. ◆ **bust up** ‡ *vt sep marriage, friendship* briser, flanquer en l'air *. ◆ **bust-up** ‡ *n* engueulade ‡ *f*; **to have a ~-up** ‡ **with sb** s'engueuler ‡ avec qn *(et rompre)*.

bustle ['bʌsl] **1** *vi*: **to ~ about** s'affairer; **to ~ in/out** *etc* entrer/sortir *etc* d'un air affairé. **2** *n* remue-ménage *m inv*. ◆ **bustling** *adj person* empressé, affairé; *place* bruyant.

busy ['bɪzɪ] **1** *adj* (**a**) *(occupied) person* occupé (*with sth* à qch). **she's ~ cooking** elle est en train de faire la cuisine; **he's ~ playing with the children** il est occupé à jouer avec les enfants; **~ at his work** absorbé dans son travail. (**b**) *person (active)* énergique; *(having a lot to do)* affairé; *day* chargé; *period* de grande activité; *place street, town* animé. **as ~ as a bee** très occupé; **to keep o.s. ~** trouver à s'occuper; **to get ~** s'y mettre; **the shop is at its busiest in summer** c'est en été qu'il y a le plus d'affluence dans le magasin. (**c**) *(Telec) line* occupé. **~ signal** tonalité *f* occupé *inv*.
2 *vt*: **to ~ o.s.** s'occuper, s'appliquer (*doing* à faire; *with sth* à qch).
◆ **busily** *adv* activement; *(pej)* avec trop de zèle; **to be busily engaged in (doing) sth** être très occupé à (faire) qch. ◆ **busybody** *n* mouche *f* du coche.

but [bʌt] **1** *conj (gen)* mais. **never a week passes ~ she is ill** il ne se passe jamais une semaine qu'elle ne soit malade; *(fig)* **it never rains ~ it pours** un malheur n'arrive jamais seul.
2 *adv* seulement, ne... que. **she's ~ a child** ce n'est qu'une enfant; **I cannot ~ think that...** je ne peux m'empêcher de penser que...; **you can ~ try** vous pouvez toujours essayer.
3 *prep* sauf, excepté. **they've all gone ~ me** ils sont tous partis sauf *or* excepté moi; **no one, ~ him** personne d'autre que lui; **anything ~ that** tout mais pas ça; **there was nothing for it ~ to jump** il n'y avait plus qu'à sauter; **the last house ~ one** l'avant-dernière maison; **the next house ~ one** la seconde maison à partir d'ici; **~ for you** sans vous; **it was all ~** * c'était tout juste.
4 *n*: **no ~s about it!** il n'y a pas de mais (qui tienne)!

butane ['bju:teɪn] *n* butane *m*; *(US: for camping)* butagaz *m* ®. **~ gas** gaz *m* butane, butagaz *m* ®.

butcher ['bʊtʃə^r] **1** *n* boucher *m*. **at the ~'s** chez le boucher; **~'s shop** boucherie *f*; **~ meat** viande *f* de boucherie. **2** *vt animal* tuer, abattre; *person* massacrer.

butler ['bʌtləʳ] *n* maître *m* d'hôtel.

butt¹ [bʌt] *n (barrel)* (gros) tonneau *m*.

butt² [bʌt] *n (end)* bout *m*; *[rifle]* crosse *f*. **cigarette** ~ mégot *m*.

butt³ [bʌt] *n (Shooting)* **the** ~**s** le champ de tir; **to be a** ~ **for ridicule** être un objet de risée, être en butte au ridicule; **the** ~ **of a practical joker** la victime d'un farceur.

butt⁴ [bʌt] **1** *n* coup *m* de tête; *[goat etc]* coup de corne. **2** *vt* donner un coup de tête *or* de corne à. ◆ **butt in** *vi* intervenir dans les affaires des autres; *(speaking)* dire son mot. **I don't want to** ~ **in** je ne veux pas m'immiscer dans la conversation.

butter ['bʌtəʳ] **1** *n* beurre *m*. **he looks as if** ~ **wouldn't melt in his mouth** on lui donnerait le bon Dieu sans confession. **2** *adj*: ~ **bean** (gros) haricot blanc; ~ **dish** beurrier *m*; ~ **knife** couteau *m* à beurre. **3** *vt bread etc* beurrer. ◆ **butter up** * *vt sep* passer de la pommade à * *(fig)*. ◆ **buttercup** *n* bouton *m* d'or. ◆ **butter-fingered** *adj*: **he is** ~**-fingered** tout lui glisse des mains. ◆ **butterfingers** *n* maladroit(e) *m(f)*; *(excl)* ~**fingers!** espèce d'empoté(e)! * ◆ **butterfly** **1** *n* papillon *m*; **to have** ~ **flies in the stomach** * avoir le trac ; **2** *adj net* à papillons; ~**fly nut** papillon *m (écrou)*; ~**fly stroke** brasse *f* papillon *inv*. ◆ **buttermilk** *n* babeurre *m*. ◆ **butterscotch** *n* caramel dur.

buttock ['bʌtək] *n* fesse *f*.

button ['bʌtn] **1** *n* bouton *m*. **chocolate** ~**s** pastilles *fpl* de chocolat. **2** *vt* (~ **up**) *garment* boutonner. **3** *vi* se boutonner. **4** *adj*: ~ **mushroom** (petit) champignon *m* de couche. ◆ **button-down** *adj collar* boutonné. ◆ **buttonhole** **1** *n* boutonnière *f*; **to wear a** ~**hole** avoir une fleur à sa boutonnière; **2** *vt person* accrocher *, attirer l'attention de. ◆ **button-through** *adj*: ~**-through dress** robe *f* chemisier.

buttress ['bʌtrɪs] **1** *n (Archit)* contrefort *m*; *(flying* ~*)* arc-boutant *m*. **2** *vt* arc-bouter; *(fig)* étayer.

buxom ['bʌksəm] *adj* bien en chair.

buy [baɪ] *pret, ptp* **bought** **1** *vt* acheter (*sth from sb* qch à qn; *sth for sb* qch pour *or* à qn); *petrol, tickets* prendre. **victory dearly bought** victoire chèrement payée; **he won't** ~ * **that explanation** il n'avalera * jamais cette explication; **all right, I'll** ~ **it** * bon, je marche *; *(die)* **he's bought it** ‡ il y est resté *. **2** *n*: **a good/bad** ~ * une bonne/mauvaise affaire.
◆ **buy back** *vt sep* racheter. ◆ **buy in** *vt sep* s'approvisionner en. ◆ **buy off** *vt sep* person acheter (le silence de). ◆ **buy out** *vt sep business partner* désintéresser. *(Mil)* **to** ~ **o.s. out** se racheter. ◆ **buy up** *vt sep* acheter tout ce qu'il y a de. ◆ **buyer** *n* acheteur *m*, -euse *f*; ~**er's market** marché *m* acheteur; **house** ~**ers** les gens *mpl* qui achètent un logement. ◆ **buying** *n* achat *m*; ~**ing power** pouvoir *m* d'achat.

buzz [bʌz] **1** *n* bourdonnement *m*; *(Rad etc: extraneous noise)* friture *f*. *(Telec)* **to give sb a** ~ * passer un coup de fil * à qn. **2** *adj*: ~ **saw** scie *f* mécanique; ~ **word** * mot *m* à la mode. **3** *vi [insect, ears]* bourdonner. **my head is** ~**ing** j'ai des bourdonnements; *(fig)* ~**ing with** bourdonnant de. **4** *vt* (**a**) *person* appeler (par interphone); *(*: telephone)* passer un coup de fil * à. (**b**) *(Aviat) plane* frôler; *building* raser.
◆ **buzz off** ‡ *vi* ficher le camp *.
◆ **buzzer** *n (phone)* interphone *m*; *(hooter)* sirène *f*; *(on timer)* sonnerie *f*. ◆ **buzzing** **1** *n* bourdonnement *m* ; **2** *adj insect* bourdonnant; *sound* confus.

buzzard ['bʌzəd] *n* buse *f*.

BVDS [ˌbi:vi:'di:z] *npl (US)* sous-vêtements *mpl* (d'homme).

by [baɪ] **1** *adv* près. **close** *or* **hard** ~ tout près; **to go** *or* **pass** ~ passer; **he'll be** ~ **any minute** il sera là dans un instant; **we'll get** ~ on y arrivera; **to put** *or* **lay** ~ mettre de côté; ~ **and** ~ bientôt, (un peu) plus tard; ~ **and large** généralement.
2 *prep* (**a**) *(close to)* à côté de, près de. ~ **the fire** près du feu; **the house** ~ **the church** la maison à côté de l'église; ~ **the sea** au bord de la mer; **I've got it** ~ **me** je l'ai sous la main; **(all)** ~ **himself** (tout) seul.
(**b**) *(through, along)* par. **I went** ~ **Dover** j'y suis allé par Douvres; **he came in** ~ **the window** il est entré par la fenêtre; *(fig)* ~ **the way,** ~ **the by(e)** à propos, au fait.
(**c**) *(past)* à côté de, devant. **I go** ~ **the church every day** je passe devant l'église tous les jours; **he went** ~ **me** il est passé à côté de moi.
(**d**) *(during)* ~ **day** le jour, de jour; ~ **night** la nuit, de nuit.
(**e**) *(not later than)* avant. **I'll be back** ~ **midnight** je rentrerai avant minuit *or* pas plus tard que minuit; ~ **tomorrow I'll be in France** d'ici demain je serai en France; ~ **1999** d'ici à 1999; ~ **the time I got there** lorsque je suis arrivé; ~ **30th September we had paid...** au 30 septembre nous avions payé... ; ~ **then I knew** à ce moment-là je savais déjà.
(**f**) *(amount)* à. **to sell** ~ **the metre/the kilo** vendre au mètre/au kilo; ~ **the hour** à l'heure; ~ **degrees** par degrés, graduellement; **one** ~ **one** un à un; **little** ~ **little** petit à petit, peu à peu.
(**g**) *(agent, cause)* par, de. **he was warned** ~ **his neighbour** il a été prévenu par son voisin; **killed** ~ **lightning** tué par la foudre; **a painting** ~ **Van Gogh** un tableau de Van Gogh; **surrounded** ~ **soldiers** entouré de soldats.
(**h**) *(method, means, manner)* par. ~ **land and sea** par terre et par mer; ~ **bus/car** en autobus/ voiture; ~ **rail** *or* **train** par le train, en train; ~ **electric light** à la lumière électrique; **made** ~ **hand** fait à la main; **to lead** ~ **the hand** conduire par la main; ~ **cheque** par chèque; **a daughter** ~ **his first wife** une fille de sa première femme.
(**i**) *(according to)* d'après, suivant, selon. ~ **what he says** d'après *or* selon ce qu'il dit; **to judge** ~ **appearances** juger d'après les apparences; ~ **my watch** à ma montre; **to do one's duty** ~ **sb** remplir son devoir envers qn; **to call sth** ~ **its proper name** appeler qch de son vrai nom; **it's all right** ~ **me** * je n'ai rien contre *.
(**j**) *(measuring difference)* de. **broader** ~ **a metre** plus large d'un mètre; **it missed me** ~ **10 centimetres** cela m'a manqué de 10 centimètres.
(**k**) *(Math, Measure)* **to divide** ~ diviser par; **room 3 metres** ~ **4** pièce de 3 mètres sur 4.
(**l**) *(points of compass)* **south** ~ **south-west** sud quart sud-ouest.
(**m**) *(in oaths)* par. ~ **all I hold sacred** par tout ce que j'ai de plus sacré; ~ **God!** * nom d'un chien! *
◆ **by-election** *n* élection (législative) partielle. ◆ **bygone** **1** *adj*: **in** ~**gone days** jadis ; **2** *n*: **let** ~**gones be** ~**gones** oublions le passé. ◆ **by-law** *n* arrêté *m* (municipal). ◆ **bypass** **1** *n* (**a**) *(road)* route *f* de contournement *m*; **the Carlisle** ~**pass** la route qui contourne Carlisle; (**b**) *(Tech: pipe etc)* conduit *m* de dérivation; (**c**) *(Elec)* dérivation *f*; (**d**) *(Med)* ~**pass (operation)** pontage *m*; **2** *vt town, village* contourner, éviter; *pipe;* éviter; *fluid, gas* amener (en dérivation); *supplier* se passer de; *procedure* omettre; *regulations* contourner; *(fig)* **he** ~**passed his foreman and went straight to the manager** il est allé trouver le directeur sans passer par le contremaître. ◆ **by-product** *n (Ind etc)* sous-produit *m*, dérivé *m*; *(fig)* conséquence *f*

(secondaire). ◆ **by-road** *n* chemin *m* de traverse. ◆ **bystander** *n* spectateur *m*, -trice *f*. ◆ **byway** *n* chemin *m* (écarté). ◆ **byword** *n*: **his name was a ~word for meanness** son nom était devenu synonyme d'avarice.

bye * [baɪ] *excl (also* **bye-bye***)* salut! * ◆ **bye-law** *n* = **by-law** *(V above)*.

byte [baɪt] *n (Comput)* octet *m*.

C

C, c [siː] *n* C, c *m*; *(Mus)* do *m*, ut *m*.

cab [kæb] **1** *n* (**a**) taxi *m*. **by** ~ en taxi. (**b**) *[truck, engine]* cabine *f*. **2** *adj*: ~ **rank** station *f* de taxis. ◆ **cabby** * *or* ◆ **cab-driver** *or* ◆ **cabman** *n* chauffeur *m* de taxi, taxi * *m*.

cabal [kəˈbæl] *n* cabale *f*.

cabana [kəˈbɑːnə] *n (US)* cabine *f* (de plage).

cabaret [ˈkæbəreɪ] *n* cabaret *m*.

cabbage [ˈkæbɪdʒ] **1** *n* chou *m*. **she's just a** ~ * elle végète. **2** *adj*: ~ **lettuce** laitue *f* pommée.

cabin [ˈkæbɪn] **1** *n (hut)* cabane *f*, hutte *f*; *(on ship)* cabine *f*; *(driver's ~)* cabine. **2** *adj*: ~ **boy** mousse *m*; ~ **cruiser** cruiser *m*; ~ **trunk** malle-cabine *f*.

cabinet [ˈkæbɪnɪt] **1** *n* meuble *m* (de rangement); *(glass-fronted)* vitrine *f*; *(filing ~)* classeur *m*; *(medicine ~)* armoire *f* à pharmacie; *(Parl)* cabinet *m*. **2** *adj (Parl) crisis, decision* ministériel. ~ **meeting** réunion *f* du cabinet; ~ **minister** ministre *m* siégeant au cabinet. ◆ **cabinetmaker** *n* ébéniste *m*. ◆ **cabinetmaking** *n* ébénisterie *f*.

cable [ˈkeɪbl] **1** *n* câble *m*. **by** ~ par câble. **2** *vt* câbler (*to* à). **3** *adj*: ~ **television** télévision *f* par câble; ~ **release** *(Phot)* déclencheur *m* souple. ◆ **cablecar** *n* téléphérique *m*; *(on rail)* funiculaire *m*. ◆ **cablecast** **1** *n* émission *f* de télévision par câble ; **2** *vt* transmettre par câble. ◆ **cablegram** *n* câblogramme *m*. ◆ **cable-laying** **1** *n* pose *f* de câbles ; **2** *adj*: ~**-laying ship** câblier *m*. ◆ **cable-railway** *n* funiculaire *m*. ◆ **cablevision** *n* télévision *f* par câble.

caboodle ‡ [kəˈbuːdl] *n*: **the whole** ~ tout le tremblement *.

cacao [kəˈkɑːəʊ] *n* cacao *m*.

cache [kæʃ] *n (place)* cachette *f*. **a** ~ **of guns** des fusils cachés.

cachet [ˈkæʃeɪ] *n* cachet *m*.

cackle [ˈkækl] **1** *n [hen]* caquet *m*; *(laugh)* gloussement *m*; *(talking)* caquetage *m*. **2** *vi* caqueter; glousser.

cacophony [kæˈkɒfənɪ] *n* cacophonie *f*.

cactus, *pl* **-ti** [ˈkæktəs, taɪ] *n* cactus *m*.

cadaver [kəˈdeɪvəʳ] *n* cadavre *m*. ◆ **cadaverous** *adj* cadavérique.

caddie [ˈkædɪ] *n* caddie *m*.

caddy [ˈkædɪ] *n (tea ~)* boîte *f* à thé; *(US: for shopping)* caddie *m*.

cadence [ˈkeɪd(ə)ns] *n* cadence *f*.

cadet [kəˈdet] *n (Mil etc)* élève *m* officier. ~ **force** peloton *m* de préparation militaire; ~ **school** école *f* militaire.

cadge [kædʒ] *vt*: **to** ~ **10 francs from sb** taper * qn de 10 F; **to** ~ **lunch from sb** se faire inviter à déjeuner par qn; **to** ~ **a lift from sb** se faire emmener en voiture par qn; **he's always cadging** il est toujours à quémander. ◆ **cadger** *n* parasite *m*; *[money]* tapeur * *m*, -euse * *f*; *[meals]* pique-assiette *mf inv*.

cadre [ˈkædrɪ] *n (Mil, fig)* cadre *m*.

Caesarean, Caesarian [siːˈzɛərɪən] *adj, n (Med)* ~ **(section)** césarienne *f*.

café [ˈkæfeɪ] *n* snack *m*. ◆ **cafeteria** *n* cafétéria *f*.

caffein(e) [ˈkæfiːn] *n* caféine *f*. ~**-free** décaféiné.

caftan [ˈkæftæn] *n* caftan *m*.

cage [keɪdʒ] **1** *n* cage *f*; *[elevator]* cabine *f*; *(Min)* cage. **2** *adj*: ~ **bird** oiseau *m* de volière. **3** *vt* (~ **up**) mettre en cage. ~**d bird** oiseau *m* en cage.

cagey * [ˈkeɪdʒɪ] *adj* peu communicatif, dissimulé *(pej)*. **she is** ~ **about her age** elle n'aime pas avouer son âge.

cagoule [kəˈguːl] *n* anorak *m (long)*.

cahoots * [kəˈhuːts] *npl*: **in** ~ de mèche * (*with* avec).

cairn [kɛən] *n* cairn *m*. ◆ **cairngorm** *n* quartz *m* fumé.

Cairo [ˈkaɪərəʊ] *n* Le Caire.

cajole [kəˈdʒəʊl] *vt* cajoler. **to** ~ **sb into doing sth** faire faire qch à qn à force de cajoleries. ◆ **cajolery** *n* cajolerie *f*.

cake [keɪk] **1** *n* (**a**) gâteau *m*; *(small)* pâtisserie *f*; *(fruit ~)* cake *m*; *(sponge ~ etc)* génoise *f*. **it's selling like hot ~s** * cela se vend comme des petits pains; **it's a piece of** ~ * c'est du gâteau *. (**b**) *[chocolate]* tablette *f*; *[wax, tobacco]* pain *m*. ~ **of soap** savonnette *f*. **2** *adj*: ~ **shop** pâtisserie *f (magasin)*. **3** *vi [mud]* durcir, faire croûte; *[blood]* se coaguler. ◆ **caked** *adj blood* coagulé; *mud* séché; **clothes** ~**d with mud** vêtements raidis par la boue.

calamity [kəˈlæmɪtɪ] *n* calamité *f*. ◆ **calamitous** *adj* catastrophique.

calcify [ˈkælsɪfaɪ] **1** *vt* calcifier. **2** *vi* se calcifier. ◆ **calcification** *n* calcification *f*.

calcium [ˈkælsɪəm] *n* calcium *m*.

calculate [ˈkælkjʊleɪt] **1** *vt cost, numbers, dates* calculer; *distance* évaluer; *chances* estimer. **this was not** ~**d to reassure me** cela n'était pas fait pour me rassurer. **2** *vi* calculer, faire des calculs. **to** ~ **for sth** prévoir qch. ◆ **calculable** *adj* calculable. ◆ **calculated** *adj action, decision, insult* délibéré; *risk* pris en toute connaissance de cause. ◆ **calculating** *adj (scheming)* calculateur; **calculating machine** machine *f* à calculer. ◆ **calculation** *n* calcul *m*. ◆ **calculator** *n* calculatrice *f*. ◆ **calculus** *n* calcul *m*.

calendar [ˈkæləndəʳ] **1** *n* calendrier *m*. **university** ~ ≃ livret *m* de l'étudiant. **2** *adj*: ~ **month** mois *m* (de calendrier); ~ **year** année *f* civile.

calf[1] [kɑːf] **1** *npl* **calves** *(animal)* veau *m*; *(skin)* veau; *(for shoes, bags)* box(-calf) *m*. **cow in** ~ vache pleine; **elephant** ~ éléphanteau *m*. **2** *adj*: ~ **love** amour *m* juvénile.

calf[2], *pl* **calves** [kɑːf, kɑːvz] *n (Anat)* mollet *m*.

calibre, *(US)* **caliber** [ˈkælɪbəʳ] *n (lit, fig)* calibre *m*. ◆ **calibrate** *vt* calibrer. ◆ **calibration** *n* calibrage *m*.

calipers [ˈkælɪpəz] *npl (Math)* compas *m*; *(leg-irons)* appareil *m* orthopédique.

calisthenics [ˌkælɪsˈθenɪks] *nsg* gymnastique *f* suédoise.

call [kɔːl] **1** *n* (**a**) *(shout)* appel *m*, cri *m*; *[bird]* cri; *[duty]* appel *n*; *(Theat) (during play)* appel *n*; *(curtain ~)* rappel *m*; *(vocation)* vocation *f*; *(Bridge)* annonce *f*. *(telephone ~)* coup *m* de téléphone, coup de fil *, communication *f (Admin)*. **within** ~ à portée de (la) voix; **a** ~ **for help** un appel au secours; *(Telec)* **to make a** ~ téléphoner, donner *or* passer un coup de fil *; **I'd like a** ~ **at 7**

a.m. j'aimerais qu'on me réveille *(subj)* à 7 heures; **to be on ~** être de garde; **the ~ of the unknown** l'attrait *m* de l'inconnu; **the ~ of the sea** l'appel du large; **there's not much ~ for these articles** ces articles ne sont pas très demandés; **repayable on ~/at 3 months'** ~ remboursable sur demande/à 3 mois; **I have many ~s on my time** je suis très pris; **I have many ~s on my purse** j'ai beaucoup de dépenses; **there is no ~ for you to worry** vous n'avez pas besoin de vous inquiéter; **there was no ~ to say that** vous n'aviez aucune raison de dire cela. (**b**) *(visit: also Med)* visite *f.* **to make a ~ on sb** rendre visite à qn, aller voir qn; **I have several ~s to make** j'ai plusieurs visites à faire; **port of ~** (port *m* d') escale *f.*
2 *adj:* ~ **girl** call-girl *f*; *(Telec)* ~ **sign,** *(US)* ~ **letters** indicatif *m* (d'appel).
3 *vt* (**a**) *(gen)* appeler; *(Telec)* téléphoner à; *(waken)* réveiller; *(summon)* appeler, convoquer; *doctor, taxi* appeler, faire venir; *(Bridge)* annoncer, demander. **to ~ sb in/out** *etc* crier à qn d'entrer/de sortir *etc*; ~ **me at eight** réveillez-moi à huit heures; *(Rad)* **London ~ing** ici Londres; **duty ~s** le devoir m'appelle; **to ~ a meeting** convoquer une assemblée; **to ~ sb as a witness** *(Jur)* avoir qn comme témoin. (**b**) *(give name to)* appeler. **what are you ~ed?** comment vous appelez-vous?; **he is ~ed after his father** on lui a donné le nom de son père; **he ~s himself a colonel** il se prétend colonel; **are you ~ing me a liar?** dites tout de suite que je suis un menteur; **he ~ed her a liar** il l'a traitée de menteuse; **would you ~ French a difficult language?** diriez-vous que le français est difficile?; **I ~ that a shame** j'estime que c'est une honte; **shall we ~ it £1?** disons 1 livre?; **let's ~ it a day!** * ça suffira (pour aujourd'hui)! (**c**) *(US Sport) game* arrêter, suspendre.
4 *vi* (**a**) *[person]* appeler, crier; *[birds]* pousser un cri. **to ~ (out) to sb** appeler qn; *(from afar)* héler qn. (**b**) *(visit:* ~ **in***)* passer. **he was out when I ~ed** il n'était pas là quand je suis passé chez lui; *(Naut)* **to ~ (in) at Dover** faire escale à Douvres. ◆ **call aside** *vt sep person* prendre à part. ◆ **call away** *vt sep*: **to be ~ed away on business** être obligé de s'absenter pour affaires; **to be ~ed away from a meeting** devoir quitter une réunion *(pour affaires plus pressantes).* ◆ **call back** *vi, vt sep (Telec)* rappeler. ◆ **call for** *vt fus* (**a**) *(summon) person* appeler; *food, drink* demander; *courage* demander, exiger. **that was not ~ed for** ce n'était pas justifié; **strict measures are ~ed for** des mesures strictes sont nécessaires. (**b**) *(collect) person, thing* passer prendre. ◆ **call in** **1** *vi* = **call 4b. 2** *vt sep* (**a**) *doctor* faire venir, appeler; *police* appeler. **he was ~ed in to arbitrate** on a fait appel à lui pour arbitrer. (**b**) *money, library books* faire rentrer; *banknotes* retirer de la circulation; *faulty machines etc* rappeler. ◆ **call off** **1** *vi* se décommander. **2** *vt sep* (**a**) *appointment* annuler; *agreement, deal* résilier. **to ~ off a strike** annuler un ordre de grève. (**b**) *dog* rappeler. ◆ **call out** **1** *vi* pousser un *or* des cri(s). **to ~ out for sth** demander qch à haute voix; **to ~ out to sb** héler qn. **2** *vt sep doctor, troops, fire brigade* appeler. **to ~ workers out (on strike)** donner la consigne de grève. ◆ **call round** *vi* passer *(to see sb* voir qn). ◆ **call up** *vt sep* (**a**) *(Mil)* appeler, mobiliser. (**b**) *(esp US: Telec)* téléphoner à. (**c**) *memories* évoquer. ◆ **call (up)on** *vt fus* (**a**) *person* rendre visite à. (**b**) **to ~ (up)on sb to do** *(invite)* inviter qn à faire; *(demand)* sommer qn de faire; **I now ~ (up)on Mr Brown to speak** je laisse maintenant la parole à M. Brown.
◆ **callbox** *n (Brit)* cabine *f* (téléphonique); *(US)* téléphone *m* de police-secours. ◆ **callboy** *n (Theat)* avertisseur *m.* ◆ **caller** *n (visitor)* visiteur *m*, -euse *f*; *(Telec)* demandeur *m*, -euse *f.* ◆ **call-in** *n (US Rad)* programme *m* à ligne ouverte. ◆ **calling-card** *n (US)* carte *f* de visite. ◆ **call-up** **1** *n (Mil)* appel *m* (sous les drapeaux) ; **2** *adj:* **~-up papers** feuille *f* de route.

calligraphy [kə'lɪgrəfɪ] *n* calligraphie *f.*

callipers ['kælɪpəz] *npl* = **calipers.**

callisthenics [ˌkælɪs'θenɪks] *n* = **calisthenics.**

callous ['kæləs] *adj* dur, sans cœur. ◆ **callously** *adv act, speak* avec dureté; *decide, suggest* cyniquement. ◆ **callousness** *n* dureté *f*, manque *m* de cœur.

callow ['kæləʊ] *adj* inexpérimenté, novice.

calm [kɑːm] **1** *adj* calme, tranquille. **keep ~!** du calme!; **to grow ~** se calmer; **~ and collected** maître (*f* maîtresse) de soi. **2** *n* (**a**) *(period)* période *f* de calme *or* de tranquillité; *(after agitation)* accalmie *f.* **the ~ before the storm** le calme qui précède la tempête. (**b**) *(calmness)* calme *m.* **3** *vt* (**~ down**) calmer, apaiser.
◆ **calm down** *vi* se calmer.
◆ **calmly** *adv* calmement, avec calme. ◆ **calmness** *n* calme *m.*

Calor ['kælə^r] *n* ®: ~ **gas** butane *m*, butagaz *m* ®.

calorie ['kælərɪ] *n* calorie *f.* **to be ~-conscious** * avoir la hantise des calories. ◆ **calorific** *adj* calorifique.

calumny ['kæləmnɪ] *n* calomnie *f*; *(Jur)* diffamation *f.*

calve [kɑːv] *vi* vêler.

calves [kɑːvz] *npl of* **calf.**

cam [kæm] *n (Tech)* came *f.* ~ **shaft** arbre *m* à cames.

camber ['kæmbə^r] **1** *n [road]* bombement *m.* **2** *vt* bomber.

Cambodia [kæm'bəʊdɪə] *n* Cambodge *m.* ◆ **Cambodian** **1** *adj* cambodgien ; **2** *n* Cambodgien(ne) *m(f).*

camcorder ['kæmˌkɔːdə^r] *n* caméscope *m.*

came [keɪm] *pret of* **come.**

camel ['kæm(ə)l] **1** *n* chameau *m.* **2** *adj (colour)* (de couleur) fauve *inv.* ◆ **camel-hair** *adj brush* en poil de chameau.

camellia [kə'miːlɪə] *n* camélia *m.*

cameo ['kæmɪəʊ] *n* camée *m. (Cine)* ~ **part** brève apparition (d'une grande vedette).

camera ['kæm(ə)rə] *n* (**a**) appareil *m* (photographique), appareil-photo *m*; *(movie ~)* caméra *f.* (**b**) *(Jur)* **in ~** à huis clos. ◆ **cameraman** *n* cameraman *m*, opérateur *m* de prise de vue. ◆ **camerawork** *n* prise *f* de vue.

Cameroon [kæmə'ruːn] *n* Cameroun *m.*

camomile ['kæmə(ʊ)maɪl] *n* camomille *f.*

camouflage ['kæməflɑːʒ] **1** *n* camouflage *m.* **2** *vt* camoufler.

camp[1] [kæmp] **1** *n* camp *m ; (less permanent)* campement *m.* **to go to ~** partir camper; *(fig)* **in the same ~** du même bord; **a foot in both ~s** un pied dans chaque camp.
2 *adj (US Scol)* ~ **counselor** animateur *m*, -trice *f* (de camp de vacances); *(fig)* ~ **follower** sympathisant(e) *m(f)*; **~(ing) chair** chaise pliante (de camping); **~(ing) ground** *or* **site** *(commercialized)* camping *m*; *(clearing etc)* endroit *m* où camper; *(with tent on it)* camp *m*; **~(ing) stool** pliant *m*; **~(ing) stove** réchaud *m* de camping.
3 *vi* camper. **to go ~ing** (aller) faire du camping.
◆ **camp out** *vi* camper *(also fig).*
◆ **campbed** *n* lit *m* de camp. ◆ **camper** *n (person)* campeur *m*, -euse *f*; *(van)* camping-car *m; (US)* caravane pliante. ◆ **campfire** *n* feu *m* de camp.
◆ **camping** *n* camping *m (activité)*; **~ing gas** ® *(Brit: gas)* butane *m; (US: stove)* camping-gaz *m inv.*

camp[2] * [kæmp] **1** *adj (affected)* maniéré; *(overdramatic)* cabotin; *(homosexual) man* (qui fait) pédé ‡; *manners, clothes* de pédé ‡; *(vulgar)* vulgaire. **2** *vt*: **to ~ it up** cabotiner.

campaign [kæm'peɪn] **1** *n* campagne *f*. *(Pol)* **~ worker** membre *m* de l'état major *(d'un candidat)*. **2** *vi* faire campagne (*also fig: for* pour, *against* contre). ◆ **campaigner** *n (Mil)* **old ~er** vétéran *m*; *(fig)* **a ~er for/against sth** un(e) militant(e) *m(f)* pour/contre qch.

camphor ['kæmfəʳ] *n* camphre *m*. ◆ **camphorated** *adj* camphré.

campus ['kæmpəs] *n* campus *m*.

can¹ [kæn] *modal aux vb: neg* **cannot, can't;** *cond and pret* **could.** (**a**) *(am etc able to)* (je) peux *etc*. **he ~ lift the suitcase** il peut soulever la valise; **he will do what he ~** il fera ce qu'il pourra, il fera son possible; **he will help you all he ~** il vous aidera de son mieux; **he couldn't speak because he had a bad cold** il ne pouvait pas parler parce qu'il était très enrhumé; **he could have helped us** il aurait pu nous aider; **it could be true** cela pourrait être vrai; **you could be making a big mistake** tu es peut-être en train de faire une grosse erreur; **could you be hiding sth from us?** est-il possible que vous nous cachiez *(subj)* qch?; **he could have changed his mind** il aurait pu changer d'avis; **he could have forgotten** il a peut-être oublié; **you can't be serious!** vous ne parlez pas sérieusement!; **he can't have known about it** il est impossible qu'il l'ait su; **she can't be very clever** elle ne doit pas être très intelligente; **where CAN he be?** où peut-il bien être?; **as big as ~** *or* **could be** aussi grand que possible; **it ~ be very cold here** il arrive qu'il fasse très froid ici.
(**b**) *(know how to)* (je) sais *etc*. **he ~ read and write** il sait lire et écrire; **he ~ speak Italian** il parle italien, il sait l'italien; **she could not swim** elle ne savait pas nager.
(**c**) *(not translated)* **I ~ see you** je vous vois; **they could hear him** ils l'entendaient; **~ you smell it?** tu le sens?
(**d**) *(have permission to)* (je) peux *etc*. **you ~ go** vous pouvez partir; **~ I have some milk? — yes, you ~** puis-je avoir du lait? — mais oui, bien sûr; **could I have a word with you?** est-ce que je pourrais vous parler un instant?; **I can't go out** je n'ai pas le droit de sortir.
◆ **can-do** * *adj (US) person, organization* dynamique.

can² [kæn] **1** *n [milk, oil, water]* bidon *m*; *[garbage]* boîte *f* à ordures, poubelle *f*; *(for foodstuffs)* boîte *f* (de conserve). **a ~ of fruit/beer** une boîte de fruits/bière. **2** *vt food* mettre en boîte(s) *or* en conserve.
◆ **canned** *adj fruit, salmon* en boîte, en conserve; (*: *recorded) music* enregistré; (*: *drunk)* rétamé ‡, soûl ; **~ned goods** conserves *fpl*; *(Rad etc)* **~ned laughter** rires préenregistrés. ◆ **cannery** *or* ◆ **canning factory** *n* conserverie *f* *(fabrique)*. ◆ **canning industry** *n* conserverie *f* *(industrie)*. ◆ **can-opener** *n* ouvre-boîtes *m inv*.

Canada ['kænədə] *n* Canada *m*. ◆ **Canadian** **1** *adj* canadien ; **2** *n* Canadien(ne) *m(f)*.

canal [kə'næl] *n* canal *m*.

canary [kə'nɛərɪ] **1** *n (bird)* canari *m*. **2** *adj*: **~ yellow** jaune canari *inv*. ◆ **Canary Islands** *npl* (îles *fpl*) Canaries *fpl*.

Canberra ['kænbərə] *n* Canberra.

cancel ['kæns(ə)l] *vt agreement, contract* résilier; *order, arrangement, meeting, debt* annuler; *cheque* faire opposition à; *taxi, appointment, party* décommander, annuler; *decree, will* révoquer; *train* annuler; *(permanently)* supprimer; *application* retirer; *(cross out)* barrer, biffer; *stamp* oblitérer; *(Math) figures* éliminer. ◆ **cancel out** *vt sep (Math) noughts* barrer; *amounts etc* annuler; *(fig)* neutraliser. **they ~ each other out** ils se neutralisent.
◆ **cancellation** *n* résiliation *f*; annulation *f*; révocation *f*; suppression *f*; retrait *m*; biffage *m*; oblitération *f*; *(Math)* élimination *f*; **~lations will not be accepted after...** *(travel, hotel)* les réservations *or (Theat)* les locations ne peuvent être annulées après...; **I have 2 ~lations for tomorrow** j'ai 2 personnes qui se sont décommandées pour demain.

cancer ['kænsəʳ] **1** *n* (**a**) cancer *m*. **lung** *etc* **~** cancer du poumon *etc*. (**b**) *(Astron, Geog)* **C~** Cancer *m*. **2** *adj*: **~ patient** cancéreux *m*, -euse *f*; **~ research** cancérologie *f*; *(in appeals)* la lutte contre le cancer; **~ specialist** cancérologue *mf*. ◆ **cancerous** *adj* cancéreux. ◆ **cancer-producing** *adj* cancérigène.

candelabra [ˌkændɪ'lɑːbrə] *n* candélabre *m*.

candid ['kændɪd] *adj* franc, sincère. ◆ **candidly** *adv* franchement, sincèrement. ◆ **candidness** *or* ◆ **candour,** *(US)* **candor** *n* franchise *f*, sincérité *f*.

candidate ['kændɪdeɪt] *n* candidat(e) *m(f)*. ◆ **candidacy** *or* ◆ **candidature** *n* candidature *f*.

candied ['kændɪd] *adj* confit. **~ peel** écorce confite.

candle ['kændl] **1** *n [wax]* bougie *f*; *[tallow]* chandelle *f*; *(in church)* cierge *m*. **the game is not worth the ~** le jeu n'en vaut pas la chandelle. **2** *adj*: **~ grease** suif *m*. ◆ **candlelight** **1** *n*: **by ~ light** à la lueur d'une bougie *etc* ; **2** *adj*: **~ light dinner** dîner *m* aux chandelles. ◆ **Candlemas** *n* la Chandeleur. ◆ **candlestick** *n (flat)* bougeoir *m*; *(tall)* chandelier *m*. ◆ **candlewick** *n* chenille *f* (de coton).

candy ['kændɪ] *n* sucre *m* candi; *(US: sweets)* bonbon(s) *m(pl)*. ◆ **candy-floss** *n* barbe *f* à papa. ◆ **candy-striped** *adj* à rayures multicolores.

cane [keɪn] **1** *n (gen)* canne *f*; *[officer, rider]* badine *f*; *(for chairs, baskets)* rotin *m*, jonc *m*; *(for punishment)* trique *f*; *(Scol)* verge *f*. **2** *vt* donner des coups de trique à; *(Scol)* fouetter. **3** *adj*: **~ chair** chaise cannée; **~ sugar** sucre *m* de canne. ◆ **caning** *n*: **to get a caning** *(lit)* recevoir la trique *or (Scol)* le fouet; (*: *fig)* recevoir une bonne volée.

canine ['kænaɪn] **1** *adj* canin. **2** *n (tooth)* canine *f*.

canister ['kænɪstəʳ] *n* boîte *f (en métal)*.

cannabis ['kænəbɪs] *n* cannabis *m*.

cannibal ['kænɪb(ə)l] *adj, n* cannibale *(mf)*, anthropophage *(mf)*. ◆ **cannibalism** *n* cannibalisme *m*, anthropophagie *f*. ◆ **cannibalize** *vt machine, car* démonter pour en réutiliser les pièces. **~ized parts** pièces récupérées.

cannon ['kænən] **1** *n* canon *m*. **2** *adj*: **~ fodder** * chair *f* à canown *. **3** *vi*: **to ~ into** *or* **against** *object* percuter; *person* se heurter contre. ◆ **cannonball** *n* boulet *m* de canon.

canoe [kə'nuː] **1** *n* canoë *m*. **2** *vi*: **to go ~ing** faire du canoë *or* du kayac. ◆ **canoeing** *n* canoë-kayac *m*. ◆ **canoeist** *n* canoéiste *mf*.

canon ['kænən] **1** *n (Mus, Rel, also gen: law etc)* canon *m*; *(cleric)* chanoine *m*. **2** *adj*: **~ law** droit *m* canon. ◆ **canonization** *n* canonisation *f*. ◆ **canonize** *vt* canoniser.

canoodle ‡ † [kə'nuːdl] *vi* se faire des mamours *.

canopy ['kænəpɪ] *n [bed]* baldaquin *m*; *[throne etc]* dais *m*; *[tent etc]* marquise *f*.

cant¹ [kænt] *n (pej) (insincere talk)* paroles *fpl* hypocrites; *(clichés)* phrases toutes faites; *(jargon)* jargon *m*.

cant² [kænt] *vti (tilt)* pencher.

can't [kɑːnt] *abbr of* **cannot;** *V* **can¹.**

cantankerous [kæn'tæŋk(ə)rəs] *adj (ill-tempered)* acariâtre; *(aggressive)* hargneux.

canteen [kæn'tiːn] *n* (**a**) *(restaurant)* cantine *f*. (**b**) **a ~ of cutlery** une ménagère *(couverts de table)*.

canter ['kæntəʳ] **1** *n* petit galop. **2** *vi* aller au petit galop.

Canterbury ['kæntəb(ə)rɪ] *n* Cantorbéry. ~ **bell** campanule *f*.

cantilever ['kæntɪli:vəʳ] *n*: ~ **bridge** pont *m* cantilever *inv*.

canton ['kæntɒn] *n* canton *m*. ◆ **cantonal** *adj* cantonal.

canvas ['kænvəs] *n* toile *f*. **under** ~ *(in a tent)* sous la tente; *(Naut)* sous voiles.

canvass ['kænvəs] **1** *vt* (**a**) *(Pol) district* faire du démarchage électoral dans; *person* solliciter le suffrage de; *(US: scrutinize votes)* pointer; *(Comm) district* prospecter; *(gen) people* sonder. **to** ~ **opinions** sonder l'opinion (*about* à propos de). (**b**) *matter, question* examiner à fond. **2** *vi (Pol)* solliciter des suffrages; *(Comm) (door to door)* faire du démarchage. **to** ~ **for sb** *(Pol)* solliciter des voix pour qn; *(gen)* faire campagne pour qn. ◆ **canvasser** *n (Pol)* agent électoral *(qui sollicite les voix des électeurs)*; *(US: checking votes)* scrutateur *m*, -trice *f*; *(Comm)* démarcheur *m*. ◆ **canvassing** *n (Pol)* démarchage électoral *(pour solliciter les suffrages)*; *(when applying for job etc)* **no** ~**ing allowed** ≃ s'abstenir de toute démarche personnelle.

canyon ['kænjən] *n* cañon *m*, gorge *f*.

cap [kæp] **1** *n* (**a**) *(gen)* casquette *f*; *[baby, sailor]* bonnet *m*; *[officer]* képi *m*; *[soldier]* calot *m*. *(fig)* ~ **in hand** chapeau bas, humblement; **if the** ~ **fits, put it on** qui se sent morveux qu'il se mouche; *(Sport)* **he's got his** ~ **for England** il a été sélectionné pour l'équipe d'Angleterre. (**b**) *[bottle]* capsule *f*; *[fountain pen]* capuchon *m*; *[radiator, tyre-valve]* bouchon *m*; *(Med: contraceptive)* diaphragme *m*. (**c**) *(for toy gun)* amorce *f*. **2** *vt bottle etc* couvrir d'une capsule *etc*; *sb's words* renchérir sur; *achievements* surpasser. **he** ~**ped this story** il a trouvé une histoire encore meilleure que celle-ci; **to** ~ **it all** * pour couronner le tout. ◆ **capful** *n*: **one** ~**ful to 4 litres of water** une capsule pleine pour 4 litres d'eau.

capable ['keɪpəbl] *adj person* capable (*of doing* de faire); *event, situation* susceptible (*of* de); *(competent)* capable. ◆ **capability** *n* capacité *f* (*to do, for doing* de faire); **capabilities** moyens *mpl*. ◆ **capably** *adv* habilement, avec compétence.

capacity [kə'pæsɪtɪ] **1** *n* (**a**) *(gen, Elec, Phys)* capacité *f*; *[factory]* moyens *mpl* de production. **filled to** ~ absolument plein; **the hall has a seating** ~ **of 400** la salle a 400 places assises; *[machine, factory]* **to work at full** ~ produire à plein rendement. (**b**) *(ability)* aptitude *f* (*for sth* à qch; *for doing* à faire). **capacities** capacité(s) *f(pl)*, moyens *mpl*. (**c**) *[machine]* potentiel *m*. (**d**) *(legal power)* pouvoir légal (*to do* de faire); *(position)* qualité *f*. **in my** ~ **as a doctor** en ma qualité de médecin; **in his official** ~ dans l'exercice de ses fonctions; **in an advisory** ~ à titre consultatif; **we must not employ him in any** ~ **whatsoever** il ne faut pas l'employer à quelque titre que ce soit. **2** *adj*: **there was** ~ **booking** on jouait à guichets fermés; **there was a** ~ **crowd** il n'y avait plus une place (de) libre. ◆ **capacious** *adj* d'une grande capacité.

cape¹ [keɪp] *n (full length)* cape *f*; *(policeman's, cyclist's)* pèlerine *f*.

cape² [keɪp] *n (Geog)* cap *m*. *(in South Africa)* **C**~ **Coloureds** métis sud-africains; **the C**~ **(of Good Hope)** le cap de Bonne Espérance; **C**~ **Town** Le Cap.

caper¹ ['keɪpəʳ] **1** *vi* (~ **about**) *[child]* gambader; *(fool around)* faire l'idiot. **2** *n (pej)* **that was quite a** ~ * ça a été toute une histoire *.

caper² ['keɪpəʳ] *n (Culin)* câpre *f*.

capillary [kə'pɪlərɪ] *adj, n* capillaire *(m)*.

capital ['kæpɪtl] **1** *adj* (**a**) *(gen, also Jur)* capital. ~ **offence** crime capital; ~ **punishment** peine capitale; *(excl)* ~! excellent!; **of** ~ **importance** d'une importance capitale; ~ **A** A majuscule. (**b**) *(Fin)* ~ **expenditure** dépense *f* d'investissement; ~ **gains tax** impôt *m* sur les plus-values; ~ **goods** biens *mpl* d'équipement; ~ **reserves** réserves *fpl* et provisions *fpl*; ~ **sum** capital *m*. **2** *n (~ city)* capitale *f*; *(~ letter)* majuscule *f*; *(Fin)* capital *m*. ~ **invested** mise *f* de fonds; *(fig)* **to make** ~ **out of** tirer parti *or* profit de. ◆ **capital-intensive** *adj industry etc* à forte intensité de capital. ◆ **capitalism** *n* capitalisme *m*. ◆ **capitalist** *adj, n* capitaliste *(mf)*. ◆ **capitalization** *n* capitalisation *f*. ◆ **capitalize** **1** *vt property, plant* capitaliser; *company* constituer le capital social de *(par émission d'actions)*; *(Fin)* **over-/ under-**~**ized** sur-/sous-capitalisé ; **2** *vi (fig)* **to** ~**ize on** tirer parti de.

capitulate [kə'pɪtjʊleɪt] *vi* capituler. ◆ **capitulation** *n* capitulation *f*.

cappucino [ˌkæpʊ'tʃi:nəʊ] *n* cappucino *m*.

caprice [kə'pri:s] *n* caprice *m*. ◆ **capricious** *adj* capricieux, fantasque. ◆ **capriciously** *adv* capricieusement.

Capricorn ['kæprɪkɔ:n] *n* Capricorne *m*.

capsicum ['kæpsɪkəm] *n (sweet)* poivron *m*; *(hot)* piment *m*.

capsize [kæp'saɪz] **1** *vi [boat]* chavirer; *[object]* se renverser. **2** *vt* faire chavirer; renverser.

capstan ['kæpstən] *n* cabestan *m*.

capsule ['kæpsju:l] *n* capsule *f*.

captain ['kæptɪn] **1** *n* capitaine *m*. ~ **of industry** capitaine d'industrie; *(US Police)* **(precinct)** ~ ≃ commissaire *m* (de police) de quartier. **2** *vt team* être le capitaine de; *ship* commander; *(fig)* diriger.

caption ['kæpʃ(ə)n] **1** *n (Press) (heading)* sous-titre *m*; *(under illustration)* légende *f*; *(Cine)* sous-titre. **2** *vt* mettre une légende à; sous-titrer.

captious ['kæpʃəs] *adj person* chicanier; *remark* critique.

captivate ['kæptɪveɪt] *vt* captiver. ◆ **captivating** *adj* captivant.

captive ['kæptɪv] **1** *n* captif *m*, -ive *f*. **to take sb** ~ faire qn prisonnier; **to hold** ~ garder en captivité. **2** *adj* captif. **she had a** ~ **audience** son auditoire était bien obligé de l'écouter. ◆ **captivity** *n* captivité *f*; **in captivity** en captivité.

capture ['kæptʃəʳ] **1** *vt animal, soldier* capturer; *escapee* reprendre; *city* s'emparer de; *(fig) attention* captiver; *interest* gagner; *(Art)* rendre; *(Comput)* saisir. **2** *n [town, treasure, escapee]* capture *f*; *(Comput)* saisie *f*. ◆ **captor** *n (unlawful)* ravisseur *m*; *(lawful)* personne *f* qui capture.

car [kɑ:ʳ] *n (Aut)* voiture *f*, automobile *f*, auto *f*; *(US Rail)* wagon *m*, voiture; *(tramcar)* tramway *m*. **2** *adj wheel etc* de voiture; *travel etc* en voiture. ~ **allowance** indemnité *f* de déplacements (en voiture); ~ **bomb** voiture piégée; ~ **chase** poursuite *f*; ~ **radio** autoradio *f*; ~ **transporter** *(Aut)* camion *m or (Rail)* wagon *m* pour transport d'automobiles; ~ **wash** *(place)* lave-auto *m*. ◆ **car-ferry** *n* ferry *m*. ◆ **carhop** *n (US: serving food)* serveur *m*, -euse *f*; *(parking cars)* gardien *m* de parking. ◆ **carpark** *n* parking *m*. ◆ **carphone** *n* téléphone *m* de voiture. ◆ **carport** *n* auvent *m* (pour voiture). ◆ **car-sick** *adj*: **to be** ~**-sick** avoir le mal de la route. ◆ **car-worker** *n (Ind)* ouvrier *m*, -ière *f* de l'industrie automobile.

Caracas [kə'rækəs] *n* Caracas.

caramel ['kærəm(ə)l] *n* caramel *m*.

carat ['kærət] *n* carat *m*. **22** ~ **gold** or *m* à 22 carats.

caravan ['kærəvæn] *n (Aut)* caravane *f*; *[gipsy]* roulotte *f*; *(group: in desert etc)* caravane. ~ **site** camping *m* pour caravanes. ◆ **caravanette** *n* autocamping *f*.

caraway [ˈkærəweɪ] *n* cumin *m*.

carbohydrate [ˌkɑːbə(ʊ)ˈhaɪdreɪt] *n* hydrate *m* de carbone. *(in diets etc)* **~s** féculents *mpl*.

carbolic [kɑːˈbɒlɪk] *adj*: **~ acid** phénol *m*.

carbon [ˈkɑːbən] **1** *n* carbone *m*. **2** *adj*: **~ copy** *[typing etc]* carbone *m*; *(fig)* réplique *f*; **~ dating** datation *f* au carbone; **~ dioxide** gaz *m* carbonique; **~ fibre** fibre *f* de carbone; **~ monoxide** oxyde *m* de carbone; **~ paper** (papier *m*) carbone *m*. ◆ **carbonate** *n* carbonate *m*. ◆ **carbonic** *adj* carbonique. ◆ **carboniferous** *adj* carbonifère. ◆ **carbonization** *n* carbonisation *f*. ◆ **carbonize** *vt* carboniser.

carborundum [ˌkɑːbəˈrʌndəm] *n* carborundum *m*.

carboy [ˈkɑːbɔɪ] *n* bonbonne *f*.

carbuncle [ˈkɑːbʌŋkl] *n (jewel)* escarboucle *f*; *(Med)* furoncle *m*.

carburet(t)or [ˌkɑːbjʊˈretəʳ] *n* carburateur *m*.

carcass [ˈkɑːkəs] *n* carcasse *f*.

carcinogen [kɑːˈsɪnədʒen] *n* substance *f* cancérigène. ◆ **carcinogenic** *adj* cancérigène.

carcinoma [ˈkɑːsɪˈnəʊmə] *n* carcinome *m*.

card [kɑːd] **1** *n (gen)* carte *f*; *(index ~)* fiche *f*; *(cardboard)* carton *m*. **identity ~** carte d'identité; **to play ~s** jouer aux cartes; *(fig)* **to play one's ~s well** manœuvrer habilement; **to put one's ~s on the table** jouer cartes sur table; **it's (quite) on the ~s that *...** il y a de grandes chances pour que... + *(subj)*; *(Ind etc)* **to get one's ~s** être mis à la porte; *(Ind etc)* **to ask for one's ~s** quitter son travail.
2 *adj*: **~ game** *(e.g. bridge etc)* jeu *m* de cartes; *(game of cards)* partie *f* de cartes.
3 *vt* (**a**) *information* mettre sur fiches. (**b**) *(US: check)* **to ~ sb** demander à voir les pièces d'identité de qn.
◆ **cardboard 1** *n* carton *m* ; **2** *adj* de *or* en carton; **~board box** (boîte *f* en) carton *m*. ◆ **card-carrying** *adj*: **~-carrying member** membre *m*, adhérent(e) *m(f)*. ◆ **card-index** *n* fichier *m*. ◆ **cardphone** *n* téléphone *m* à carte. ◆ **card-player** *n* joueur *m*, -euse *f* de cartes. ◆ **cardsharp(er)** *n* tricheur *m*, -euse *f (professionnel)*. ◆ **card-table** *n* table *f* de jeu *or* à jouer. ◆ **card-trick** *n* tour *m* de cartes.

cardamom [ˈkɑːdəməm] *n* cardamome *f*.

cardiac [ˈkɑːdɪæk] *adj* cardiaque. **~ arrest** arrêt *m* du cœur.

cardigan [ˈkɑːdɪgən] *n* cardigan *m*.

cardinal [ˈkɑːdɪnl] *adj, n* cardinal *(m)*.

cardiology [ˌkɑːdɪˈɒlədʒɪ] *n* cardiologie *f*. ◆ **cardiological** *adj* cardiologique. ◆ **cardiologist** *n* cardiologue *mf*.

care [kɛəʳ] **1** *n* (**a**) *(heed)* attention *f*, soin *m*; *(charge)* charge *f*, garde *f*. **with the greatest ~** avec le plus grand soin; *(on parcels)* **'with ~'** 'fragile'; **take ~ not to catch cold** faites attention de *or* à ne pas prendre froid; **take ~** (fais) attention; *(as good wishes)* fais bien attention (à toi); **to take (great) ~ with sth** faire très attention à qch; **you should take more ~ with your work** vous devriez apporter plus d'attention à votre travail; **you should take more ~ of yourself** tu devrais faire plus attention (à ta santé); *(Jur)* **driving without due ~ and attention** conduite négligente; **he took ~ to explain why...** il a pris soin d'expliquer pourquoi...; **to take ~ of** s'occuper de; **to take good ~ of** *person* bien s'occuper de; *object* prendre grand soin de; *(threateningly)* **I'll take ~ of him!** je vais m'occuper de lui!; **he can take ~ of himself** il sait se débrouiller tout seul; **that can take ~ of itself** cela s'arrangera tout seul; **I leave** *or* **put it in your ~** je vous le confie; *(on letters)* **~ of** *(abbr* **c/o***)* aux bons soins de; **he was left in his aunt's ~** on l'a laissé à la garde de sa tante; *(Sociol)* **children in ~** enfants retirés de la garde de leurs parents. (**b**) *(anxiety)* souci *m*. **he hasn't a ~ in the world** il n'a pas le moindre souci; **the ~s of State** les responsabilités *fpl* de l'État.
2 *vi* (**a**) se soucier (*about* de), s'intéresser (*about* à). **money is all he ~s about** il n'y a que l'argent qui l'intéresse *(subj)*; **to ~ deeply about** *thing* être profondément concerné par; *person* être profondément attaché à; **not to ~ about** se moquer de; **he really ~s about this** c'est vraiment important pour lui; **I don't ~** ça m'est égal; **as if I ~d!** je m'en fiche! *; **what do I ~?** qu'est-ce que cela peut me faire?; **for all I ~** pour ce que cela me fait; **I couldn't ~ less what people say** je me fiche pas mal * de ce que les gens peuvent dire; **he doesn't ~ a damn *** il s'en fiche comme de l'an quarante *; **who ~s!** qu'est-ce que cela peut bien faire! (**b**) *(like)* vouloir, aimer. **would you ~ to sit down?** voulez-vous vous asseoir?; **I shouldn't ~ to meet him** je n'aimerais pas le rencontrer; **I don't much ~ for it** cela ne me dit pas grand-chose; **I don't ~ for him** il ne me plaît pas beaucoup; **would you ~ for a cup of tea?** voulez-vous (prendre) une tasse de thé?
◆ **care for** *vt fus invalid* soigner; *child* s'occuper de. **well-~d for** *invalid* qu'on soigne bien; *child* dont on s'occupe bien; *hands, hair* soigné; *garden* bien entretenu; *house* bien tenu.
◆ **carefree** *adj* insouciant. ◆ **careful,** ◆ **careless** *V below*. ◆ **caretaker 1** *n* gardien(ne) *m(f)*, concierge *mf* ; **2** *adj government* intérimaire. ◆ **careworn** *adj* rongé par les soucis. ◆ **caring** *adj parent* aimant; *teacher* bienveillant; *society* humanitaire; **a child needs a caring environment** un enfant a besoin d'être entouré d'affection; **the caring professions** les professions à vocation sociale.

career [kəˈrɪəʳ] **1** *n* carrière *f*. **journalism is his ~** il fait carrière dans le journalisme; **he is making a ~ (for himself) in advertising** il est en train de faire carrière dans la publicité. **2** *adj soldier, diplomat* de carrière. **~ girl** jeune fille *f* qui veut faire une carrière; **~ guidance** orientation professionnelle; **~s officer**, *(US)* **~s counselor** conseiller *m*, -ère *f* d'orientation professionnelle; **~ prospects** possibilités *fpl* d'avancement. **3** *vi* (**~ along**) aller à toute allure. ◆ **careerist** *n* carriériste *mf*.

careful [ˈkɛəf(ʊ)l] *adj (painstaking) writer, worker* consciencieux, soigneux; *work* soigné; *(cautious)* prudent, circonspect; *(acting with care)* soigneux. **to be ~** faire attention (*of, with sth* à qch; *to do* à faire); **(be) ~ !** (fais) attention!; **be ~ not to let it fall** faites attention à ne pas le laisser tomber; **be ~ to shut the door** n'oubliez pas de fermer la porte; **be ~ what you do** faites attention à ce que vous faites; **be ~ (that) he doesn't hear you** faites attention à ce qu'il ne vous entende pas; **he was ~ to point out that** il a pris soin de faire remarquer que; **you can't be too ~** *(gen)* on n'est jamais trop prudent; *(when double-checking sth)* deux précautions valent mieux qu'une; **he is very ~ with (his) money** il regarde à la dépense. ◆ **carefully** *adv (painstakingly) work, cut, choose* soigneusement, avec soin; *(cautiously) proceed, announce* prudemment, avec précaution; *reply* avec circonspection; *(fig)* **we must go ~ly here** il faut nous montrer prudents là-dessus. ◆ **carefulness** *n* soin *m*, attention *f*.

careless [ˈkɛəlɪs] *adj worker* qui manque de soin; *driver, driving* négligent. **~ mistake** faute *f* d'inattention. ◆ **carelessly** *adv (inattentively)* négligemment, sans faire attention; *(in carefree way)* avec insouciance. ◆ **carelessness** *n* manque *m* de soin; négligence *f*; manque d'attention; *(carefreeness)* insouciance *f*.

caress [kə'res] **1** *n* caresse *f.* **2** *vt* caresser.

cargo ['kɑːgəʊ] *n* cargaison *f.* ~ **boat** cargo *m.*

Caribbean [ˌkærɪ'biːən] *adj, n*: **the** ~ **(Sea)** la mer des Antilles *or* des Caraïbes.

caricature ['kærɪkətjʊəʳ] **1** *n* caricature *f.* **2** *vt* caricaturer. ◆ **caricaturist** *n* caricaturiste *mf.*

caries ['kɛərɪiːz] *n* carie *f.* ◆ **carious** *adj* carié.

carmine ['kɑːmaɪn] *adj, n* carmin *(m).*

carnage ['kɑːnɪdʒ] *n* carnage *m.*

carnal ['kɑːnl] *adj (of the flesh)* charnel; *(sensual)* sensuel; *(sexual)* sexuel.

carnation [kɑː'neɪʃ(ə)n] *n* œillet *m.*

carnival ['kɑːnɪv(ə)l] *n* carnaval *m.*

carnivore ['kɑːnɪvɔːʳ] *n* carnivore *m.* ◆ **carnivorous** [kɑː'nɪv(ə)rəs] *adj* carnivore.

carol ['kær(ə)l] *n*: **(Christmas)** ~ chant *m* de Noël.

carouse [kə'raʊz] *vi* faire ribote *. ◆ **carousal** *n* beuverie *f.*

carp¹ [kɑːp] *n (fish)* carpe *f.*

carp² [kɑːp] *vi* critiquer sans cesse. **to** ~ **at sb/sth** critiquer sans cesse qn/qch. ◆ **carping** **1** *adj person, manner* chicanier; *criticism* mesquin; *voice* malveillant ; **2** *n* critique *f* (malveillante).

carpenter ['kɑːpɪntəʳ] *n* charpentier *m*; *(joiner)* menuisier *m.* ◆ **carpentry** *n* charpenterie *f*; menuiserie *f.*

carpet ['kɑːpɪt] **1** *n* tapis *m*; *(fitted)* moquette *f.* *(fig)* **to be on the** ~ * *[subject]* être sur le tapis; *[person scolded]* être sur la sellette. **2** *adj*: ~ **slippers** pantoufles *fpl*; ~ **sweeper** *(mechanical)* balai *m* mécanique; *(vacuum cleaner)* aspirateur *m.* **3** *vt floor* recouvrir d'un tapis *or* d'une moquette; *(*: scold)* houspiller. ◆ **carpetbagger** * *n* profiteur *m*, -euse *f.* ◆ **carpeting** *n* moquette *f.*

carriage ['kærɪdʒ] *n* **(a)** *(horse-drawn)* voiture *f* (de maître), équipage *m*; *(Rail)* voiture, wagon *m* (de voyageurs). **(b)** *(Comm: conveyance of goods)* transport *m.* ~ **free** franco de port; ~ **paid** (en) port payé. **(c)** *[person] (bearing)* maintien *m*, port *m.* ◆ **carriage return** *n* retour-charriot *m.*

carrier ['kærɪəʳ] *n* **(a)** *(company)* entreprise *f* de transports; *(truck owner etc)* transporteur *m.* **by** ~ *(Aut)* par camion; *(Rail)* par chemin de fer. **(b)** *(on cycle etc)* porte-bagages *m inv*; *(~ bag)* sac *m* (en plastique). **(c)** *(Med)* porteur *m*, -euse *f.* **(d)** *(aircraft ~)* porte-avions *m inv*; *(troop ~) (plane)* appareil *m* transporteur (de troupes); *(ship)* transport *m.* ◆ **carrier-bag** *n* sac *m* (en plastique). ◆ **carrier-pigeon** *n* pigeon *m* voyageur.

carrion ['kærɪən] *n* charogne *f.*

carrot ['kærət] *n* carotte *f.* ◆ **carroty** *adj hair* carotte *inv* roux.

carry ['kærɪ] **1** *vt* **(a)** *(gen)* porter; *goods, passengers* transporter; *identity card, cigarettes, money* avoir (sur soi); *umbrella, gun* porter; *message, news* porter; *[sea, river]* emporter; *[pillar]* supporter, soutenir; *[pipe]* amener; *[wire]* conduire. **they carried the pipes under the street** ils ont fait passer les tuyaux sous la rue; *(fig)* **to** ~ **sth too far** pousser qch trop loin; **she carries herself very well** elle se tient très droite; **he carries himself like a soldier** il a le port d'un militaire; **to** ~ **in one's head** retenir dans sa tête; *(Math)* **and** ~ **3** et je retiens 3; *(fig)* **to** ~ **coals to Newcastle** porter de l'eau à la rivière; **to** ~ **the can** * (devoir) payer les pots cassés; **he carries his life in his hands** il risque sa vie; **£5 won't** ~ **you far** on ne va pas loin avec 5 livres; **enough food to** ~ **us through the winter** assez de provisions pour nous durer tout l'hiver; **he can't** ~ **his liquor** l'alcool lui monte à la tête.
(b) *consequences* entraîner; *(Fin) interest* rapporter; *responsibility, pay* comporter. **it carries a penalty of** cela est passible d'une amende de.
(c) *(Comm) goods* stocker. **we don't** ~ **that article** nous ne faisons pas cet article.
(d) *(win)* gagner, remporter; *fortress* enlever; *motion* voter. **to** ~ **the day** l'emporter; *(Mil)* être vainqueur; **to** ~ **all before one** l'emporter sur tous les tableaux.
(e) *[newspaper etc] story, details* rapporter. **all the papers carried (the story of) the murder** tous les journaux ont parlé du meurtre.
(f) *label* porter; *warning* comporter.
2 *vi [voice, sound]* porter.
◆ **carry away** *vt sep* emporter. *(fig)* **to get carried away by sth** * s'emballer * *or* s'enthousiasmer pour qch. ◆ **carry back** *vt sep things* rapporter; *person* ramener; *(fig: remind)* reporter (*to* à). ◆ **carry forward** *vt sep* reporter (*to* à). ◆ **carry off** *vt sep (gen)* emporter, enlever; *(kidnap)* enlever; *prizes* remporter. **to** ~ **it off** *(succeed)* réussir (son coup). ◆ **carry on** **1** *vi* continuer (*with sth* qch); *(*: make a scene)* faire des histoires *; *(*: have an affair)* avoir une liaison (*with sb* avec qn). **2** *vt sep (conduct) business, trade* diriger; *correspondence* entretenir; *conversation* soutenir; *negotiations* mener; *(continue)* continuer (*doing* à *or* de faire). ◆ **carry out** *vt sep (lit)* emporter; *(fig) plan, order* exécuter; *idea* mettre à exécution; *one's duty, obligation* s'acquitter de; *experiment* se livrer à; *search, investigation, inquiry* mener; *reform* effectuer; *the law, regulations* appliquer; *promise* tenir. ◆ **carry over** *vt sep* reporter (*to* à). ◆ **carry through** *vt sep plan* mener à bonne fin. **his courage carried him through** son courage lui a permis de surmonter l'épreuve.
◆ **carryall** *n* fourre-tout *m inv (sac).* ◆ **carrycot** *n* porte-bébé *m.* ◆ **carryings-on** *npl* façons *fpl* de se conduire. ◆ **carry-on** * *n* histoires * *fpl*; **what a ~-on about nothing!** * que d'histoires * pour rien! ◆ **carry-out** *adj meal* à emporter.

cart [kɑːt] **1** *n (horse-drawn)* charrette *f*; *(tip ~)* tombereau *m*; *(hand ~)* voiture *f* à bras; *(US: for luggage, shopping)* chariot *m.* *(fig)* **to put the** ~ **before the horse** mettre la charrue devant *or* avant les bœufs; *(fig)* **to be in the** ~ * être dans le pétrin. **2** *vt (in truck)* transporter (par camion); *(*: carry) shopping, books* trimballer *. ◆ **carter** *n* camionneur *m.* ◆ **cart-horse** *n* cheval *m* de trait. ◆ **cartload** *n* charretée *f*; tombereau *m*; voiturée *f.* ◆ **cart-track** *n* chemin *m* rural. ◆ **cartwheel** *n*: **to turn a ~wheel** faire la roue *(en gymnastique etc).*

cartilage ['kɑːtɪlɪdʒ] *n* cartilage *m.*

cartography [kɑː'tɒgrəfɪ] *n* cartographie *f.* ◆ **cartographer** *n* cartographe *mf.*

carton ['kɑːtən] *n [yogurt, cream]* pot *m*; *[milk, squash]* carton *m*; *[ice cream]* boîte *f*; *[cigarettes]* cartouche *f.*

cartoon [kɑː'tuːn] *n [newspaper etc]* dessin *m* (humoristique); *(Cine, TV)* dessin animé; *(Art: sketch)* carton *m.* ◆ **cartoonist** *n [newspaper etc]* caricaturiste *mf*; *(Cine, TV)* dessinateur *m*, -trice *f* de dessins animés.

cartridge ['kɑːtrɪdʒ] **1** *n [rifle, pen]* cartouche *f*; *[camera]* chargeur *m.* **2** *adj*: ~ **paper** papier *m* à cartouche, papier fort.

carve [kɑːv] *vt* tailler (*in, out of* dans); *(sculpt)* sculpter (*in, out of* dans); *(Culin)* découper. **to** ~ **one's initials on** graver ses initiales sur. ◆ **carve out** *vt sep piece* découper (*from* dans); *land* prendre (*from* à); *statue, tool* tailler (*of* dans). **to** ~ **out a career for o.s.** se tailler une carrière. ◆ **carve up** *vt sep meat* découper; *(fig) country* morceler; *(*: disfigure) person* amocher ‡ (à coups de couteau); *sb's face* taillader. ◆ **carver** *or* ◆ **carving knife** *n* couteau *m* à découper.

Casablanca [kæsə'blæŋkə] *n* Casablanca.

cascade [kæs'keɪd] **1** *n* cascade *f.* **2** *vi* tomber en cascade.

cascara [kæs'kɑːrə] *n* cascara sagrada *f.*

case[1] [keɪs] **1** *n* (**a**) *(gen, also Gram, Med, Soc)* cas *m.* **is it the ~ that...?** est-il vrai que...?; **that's not the ~** ce n'est pas le cas; **if that's the ~** en ce cas, dans ce cas-là; **put the ~ that** admettons que + *subj*; **as the ~ may be** selon le cas; **a clear ~ of lying** un exemple manifeste de mensonge; **in ~ he comes** au cas où il viendrait; **in ~ of** en cas de; **(just) in ~** à tout hasard; **in any ~** en tout cas; **in this ~** dans *or* en ce cas; **in that ~** dans ce cas-là; **in the ~ in point** en l'occurrence; **here is a ~ in point** en voici un bon exemple; **in nine ~s out of ten** neuf fois sur dix; **that alters the whole ~** cela change tout; **he's a hard ~** c'est un dur *; **she's a real ~!** * c'est un cas * *or* un numéro! *
(**b**) *(Jur)* affaire *f*, procès *m.* **to try a ~** juger une affaire; **to win one's ~** *(Jur)* gagner son procès; *(fig)* avoir gain de cause; **the ~ for the defendant** les arguments *mpl* en faveur de l'accusé; **there is no ~ against...** il n'y a pas lieu à poursuites contre...; **he's working on the Smith ~** il s'occupe de l'affaire Smith.
(**c**) *(reasoning)* arguments *mpl.* **to make out a good ~ for sth** réunir *or* présenter de bons arguments en faveur de qch; **to make out a good ~ for doing** bien expliquer pourquoi il faudrait faire; **there is a strong ~ for/against...** il y a beaucoup à dire en faveur de/contre...; **a ~ of conscience** un cas de conscience; **to have a strong ~** avoir de solides arguments.
2 *adj (Jur, Med, Soc)* **~ file** dossier *m*; **~ history** *(Soc)* évolution *f* du cas social; *(Med)* antécédents médicaux; **to have a heavy ~ load** avoir beaucoup de dossiers (sur les bras).
◆ **case-hardened** *adj* endurci. ◆ **casework** *n (Soc)* travail *m* avec des cas individuels. ◆ **caseworker** *n* ≃ assistante *f* sociale, auxiliaire *mf* social(e).

case[2] [keɪs] *n (suitcase)* valise *f*; *(packing ~, crate)* caisse *f*; *(for lettuce etc)* cageot *m*; *(box)* boîte *f*; *(chest)* coffre *m*; *(for goods on display)* vitrine *f*; *(for jewels)* coffret *m*; *(for watch etc)* écrin *m*; *(for camera, violin etc)* étui *m*; *(covering)* enveloppe *f*; *(Tech)* boîte.

cash [kæʃ] **1** *n* (**a**) *(notes and coins)* argent *m.* **how much ~ is there in the till?** combien d'argent y a-t-il dans la caisse?; **paid in ~ and not by cheque** payé en espèces et non pas par chèque; **ready ~** (argent *m*) liquide *m*; **~ in hand** encaisse *f.* (**b**) *(immediate payment)* **~ down** argent comptant; **to pay ~ (down)** payer comptant *or* cash *; **discount for ~** escompte *m* au comptant; **~ with order** payable à la commande; **~ on delivery** paiement *m* à la livraison. (**c**) *(*: money in general)* argent *m.* **to be short of ~** être à court (d'argent); **I've no ~** je suis sans le rond *.
2 *adj terms, sale, transaction* au comptant; *payment, price* comptant *inv*; *prize* en espèces; *problems* d'argent. **~ card** carte *f* de retrait; **~ dispenser** distributeur *m* (automatique de billets); **~ flow** cash-flow *m*; **~ offer** offre *f* d'achat avec paiement comptant; **~ receipts** recettes *fpl* de caisse.
3 *vt cheque* encaisser; *banknote* changer. **to ~ sb a cheque** donner à qn de l'argent contre un chèque; *[bank]* payer un chèque à qn.
◆ **cash in** *vt sep* réaliser. ◆ **cash in on** * *vt fus* tirer profit de.
◆ **cash-and-carry** *n* libre-service *m* de gros. ◆ **cashbook** *n* livre *m* de caisse. ◆ **cashbox** *n* caisse *f.* ◆ **cashdesk** *n [shop, restaurant]* caisse *f*; *[cinema, theatre]* guichet *m.* ◆ **cash-register** *n* caisse *f* (enregistreuse).

cashew [kæ'ʃuː] *n (~ nut)* noix *f* de cajou.

cashier[1] [kæ'ʃɪəʳ] *n (Fin etc)* caissier *m*, -ière *f.*

cashier[2] [kæ'ʃɪəʳ] *vt officer* casser.

cashmere [kæʃ'mɪəʳ] *n* cachemire *m.*

cashomat ['kæʃəʊmæt] *n (US)* distributeur *m* (automatique de billets).

casino [kə'siːnəʊ] *n* casino *m.*

cask [kɑːsk] *n* tonneau *m*, fût *m.*

casket ['kɑːskɪt] *n (gen)* coffret *m*; *(coffin)* cercueil *m.*

cassava [kə'sɑːvə] *n* manioc *m.*

casserole ['kæsərəʊl] **1** *n (utensil)* cocotte *f*; *(food)* ragoût *m* (en cocotte). **2** *vt* faire cuire à la cocotte.

cassette [kæ'set] **1** *n (Sound Recording)* cassette *f*; *(Phot)* cartouche *f.* **2** *adj*: **~ deck** platine *f* à cassettes; **~ player** lecteur *m* de cassettes; **~ recorder** magnétophone *m* à cassettes.

cassock ['kæsək] *n* soutane *f.*

cast [kɑːst] *(vb: pret, ptp* **cast***)* **1** *n* (**a**) *(Fishing)* lancer *m.* (**b**) *(mould)* moule *m*; *(in plaster, metal etc)* moulage *m*; *[medallion etc]* empreinte *f.* *(Med)* **leg in a ~** jambe *f* dans le plâtre; **~ of features** traits *mpl* (du visage); **~ of mind** tournure *f* d'esprit. (**c**) *(Theat) (actors)* acteurs *mpl*; *(list on programme etc)* distribution *f.* (**d**) *(Med: squint)* strabisme *m.* **to have a ~ in one eye** loucher d'un œil.
2 *vt* (**a**) *(throw) (gen)* jeter; *net, fishing line, stone* lancer, jeter; *shadow, light* projeter; *horoscope* tirer; *doubt* émettre; *blame* rejeter. **to ~ a vote** voter; **to ~ one's eye(s) towards** porter ses regards du côté de. (**b**) *(shed)* se dépouiller de; *horseshoe* perdre. *[snake]* **to ~ its skin** muer. (**c**) *(Art, Tech) plaster, metal* couler; *statue* mouler. (**d**) *(Theat) play* distribuer les rôles de. **he was ~ as Hamlet** on lui a donné le rôle de Hamlet.
◆ **cast about, cast around** *vi*: **to ~ about for sth** chercher qch. ◆ **cast away** *vt sep (Naut)* **to be ~ away** être naufragé. ◆ **cast down** *vt sep object* jeter par terre; *eyes* baisser. **to be ~ down** *(depressed)* être abattu. ◆ **cast off 1** *vi (Naut)* larguer les amarres; *(Knitting)* arrêter les mailles. **2** *vt sep (Naut)* larguer les amarres de; *(Knitting)* arrêter; *chains* se libérer de. ◆ **cast on** *(Knitting)* **1** *vi* monter les mailles. **2** *vt sep* monter. ◆ **cast up** *vt sep (reproach)* reprocher *(sth to sb* qch à qn).
◆ **castaway** *n* naufragé(e) *m(f).* ◆ **casting** *adj*: **to have a ~ing vote** avoir voix prépondérante. ◆ **cast-iron 1** *n* fonte *f*; **2** *adj* de *or* en fonte; *(fig) case* solide. ◆ **cast-off clothes** *or* ◆ **cast-offs** *npl* vêtements *mpl* dont on ne veut plus; *(pej)* vieilles nippes * *fpl.*

castanets [ˌkæstə'nets] *npl* castagnettes *fpl.*

caste [kɑːst] **1** *n* caste *f.* **2** *adj mark* de caste.

caster ['kɑːstəʳ] *n (wheel)* roulette *f.* ◆ **caster sugar** *n* sucre *m* en poudre.

castigate ['kæstɪgeɪt] *vt person* châtier; *book etc* critiquer sévèrement.

castle ['kɑːsl] **1** *n* château *m* (fort); *(Chess)* tour *f.* **~s in the air** châteaux en Espagne. **2** *vi (Chess)* roquer.

castor[1] ['kɑːstəʳ] *n* = **caster.**

castor[2] ['kɑːstəʳ] *n*: **~ oil** huile *f* de ricin.

castrate [kæs'treɪt] *vt (Anat)* châtrer; *(fig) text, film* expurger. ◆ **castration** *n* castration *f.*

casual ['kæʒjʊl] **1** *adj* (**a**) *(by chance) error* fortuit; *fall, spark* accidentel; *meeting* de hasard; *glance* jeté au hasard; *walk, stroll* sans but précis; *caller* venu par hasard; *remark* fait en passant. **a ~ acquaintance (of mine)** qn que je connais un peu; **a ~ (love) affair** une aventure; **to have ~ sex** faire l'amour au hasard d'une rencontre. (**b**) *(informal) person, manners* sans-gêne *inv*; *tone, voice* désinvolte; *clothes* sport *inv.* **to sound ~** parler avec désinvolture; **he was very ~ about it** il a pris tout ça avec beaucoup de désinvolture. (**c**) *work* intermittent; *worker* temporaire. **~ conversation** conversation *f* à bâtons rompus; **~ labourer** *(on*

building sites) ouvrier *m* sans travail fixe; *(on a farm)* journalier *m*.
2 *n (shoes)* **~s** chaussures *fpl* de sport.
◆ **casually** *adv (by chance)* par hasard, fortuitement; *(informally)* avec sans-gêne, avec désinvolture; *mention* en passant.

casualty ['kæʒjʊltɪ] **1** *n* (**a**) *(Mil) (dead)* mort(e) *m(f); (wounded)* blessé(e) *m(f)*. **casualties** les morts *mpl* et blessés *mpl*; *(dead)* les pertes *fpl*. (**b**) *(accident victim)* victime *f*; *(accident)* accident *m*. **2** *adj*: ~ **department** service *m* des urgences; ~ **list** *(Mil)* état *m* des pertes; *(Aviat, gen)* liste *f* des victimes; ~ **ward** salle *f* de traumatologie.

cat [kæt] *n* chat(te) *m(f); (species)* félin *m*; *(* pej: woman)* rosse * *f*. **to let the ~ out of the bag** vendre la mèche; **the ~'s out of the bag** ce n'est plus un secret maintenant; **to fight like ~ and dog** s'entendre comme chien et chat; **to be like a ~ on hot bricks** être sur des charbons ardents; **when the ~'s away the mice will play** quand le chat n'est pas là les souris dansent; **that set the ~ among the pigeons** ça a été le pavé dans la mare.
◆ **cat-and-mouse** *adj*: **to play a ~-and-mouse game with sb** jouer avec qn comme un chat avec une souris. ◆ **cat-burglar** *n* monte-en-l'air * *m inv*. ◆ **catcall** *n (Theat)* sifflet *m*. ◆ **catfish** *n* poisson-chat *m*. ◆ **catgut** *n (Mus, Sport)* boyau *m* (de chat); *(Med)* catgut *m*. ◆ **catlike** **1** *adj* félin ; **2** *adv* comme un chat. ◆ **catnap** *n*: **to take a ~nap** faire un (petit) somme. ◆ **cat-o'nine-tails** *n* martinet *m*. ◆ **cat's-eyes** *npl (Aut)* cataphotes *mpl*. ◆ **cat's-paw** *n* dupe *f (qui tire les marrons du feu)*. ◆ **catsuit** *n* combinaison-pantalon *f*. ◆ **cattiness** *n* méchanceté *f*, rosserie * *f*. ◆ **catty** *adj* méchant, rosse *; **~ty remark** rosserie * *f*; **to be ~ty about sb/sth** dire des rosseries * de qn/qch. ◆ **catwalk** *n* passerelle *f*.

cataclysm ['kætəklɪz(ə)m] *n* cataclysme *m*.

catalogue, *(US)* **catalog** ['kætəlɒg] **1** *n* catalogue *m*; *[library]* fichier *m*. **2** *vt* cataloguer.

catalyst ['kætəlɪst] *n* catalyseur *m*.

catalytic [ˌkætə'lɪtɪk] *adj*: ~ **converter** pot *m* catalytique.

catamaran [ˌkætəmə'ræn] *n* catamaran *m*.

catapult ['kætəpʌlt] **1** *n (slingshot)* lance-pierres *m inv*; *(Aviat, Mil)* catapulte *f*. **2** *vt* catapulter.

cataract ['kætərækt] *n (Geog, Med)* cataracte *f*.

catarrh [kə'tɑːʳ] *n* catarrhe *m*.

catastrophe [kə'tæstrəfɪ] *n* catastrophe *f*. ◆ **catastrophic** [ˌkætə'strɒfɪk] *adj* catastrophique.

catch [kætʃ] *(vb: pret, ptp* **caught***)* **1** *n (thing caught)* prise *f*, capture *f*; *(person caught)* capture; *(game)* jeu *m* de balle; *(Fishing)* pêche *f; (single fish)* prise; *(drawback)* attrape *f*, entourloupette * *f*. **where's the ~?** qu'est-ce qui se cache là-dessous?; **with a ~ in one's voice** d'une voix entrecoupée.
2 *adj*: ~ **question** colle * *f*.
3 *vt* (**a**) *(gen)* attraper; *fish, mice, thief* prendre, attraper. **to ~ sb by the arm** prendre *or* saisir qn par le bras; **you can usually ~ me (in) around noon** * en général on peut m'avoir * *or* me trouver vers midi; **to ~ sb doing sth** surprendre qn à faire qch; **if I ~ you at it again!** que je t'y reprenne!; **you won't ~ me doing that again** il n'y a pas de danger que je recommence *(subj)*; **caught in the act** pris en flagrant délit; **caught in a storm** pris dans un orage; **to get caught by sb** se laisser attraper par qn; **I must ~ the train** il ne faut pas que je manque le train; **he caught his train** il a eu son train; **to ~ the post** arriver à temps pour la levée; **to ~ a programme** réussir à voir (*or* entendre) une émission; **to ~ one's foot in sth** se prendre le pied dans qch. (**b**) *(understand, hear)* saisir, comprendre. (**c**) *flavour* sentir; *sound* percevoir; *tune, disease* attraper; *attention* attirer. **to ~ a cold** attraper un rhume; **to ~ cold** prendre froid; **to ~ one's death** ‡ attraper la crève ‡; **to ~ one's breath** retenir son souffle (un instant); **to ~ fire** prendre feu; **to ~ sight of** apercevoir; **you'll ~ it!** * tu vas prendre quelque chose! * (**d**) *(hit or snag)* **the branch caught my skirt, I caught my skirt on the branch** ma jupe s'est accrochée à la branche.
4 *vi [fire, wood, ice]* prendre. **her dress caught in the door/on a nail** sa robe s'est prise dans la porte/s'est accrochée à un clou.
◆ **catch at** *vt fus object* (essayer d')attraper; *opportunity* sauter sur. ◆ **catch on** *vi [fashion]* prendre; *[song]* marcher; *(understand)* comprendre (*to sth* qch). ◆ **catch out** *vt sep (catch sb napping)* prendre en défaut; *(catch sb in the act)* prendre sur le fait. **to ~ sb out in a lie** surprendre qn en train de mentir. ◆ **catch up** **1** *vi (gen)* se rattraper; *(with news)* se remettre au courant. **to ~ up on one's work** se mettre à jour dans son travail; **to ~ up with sb** rattraper qn. **2** *vt sep* (**a**) *person* rattraper. (**b**) *(pick up quickly)* ramasser vivement. (**c**) **to be** *or* **get caught up in sth** *(in net etc)* être pris dans qch; *(in activity etc)* être pris dans *or* mêlé à qch.
◆ **catch-22** *adj*: **it's a ~-22 * situation** il n'y a pas moyen de s'en sortir. ◆ **catch-as-catch-can** *n* catch *m*. ◆ **catcher** *n (Baseball)* attrapeur *m*; **~er's mitt** gant *m* de baseball. ◆ **catching** *adj* contagieux. ◆ **catchment** *n*: **~ment area** *[hospital]* circonscription *f* hospitalière; *[school]* aire *f* de recrutement. ◆ **catch-phrase** *n* cliché *m*, scie *f*; *(striking phrase)* slogan *m* accrocheur. ◆ **catchword** *n* slogan *m*. ◆ **catchy** *adj*: **~y tune** air entraînant.

catechism ['kætɪkɪz(ə)m] *n* catéchisme *m*. ◆ **catechist** *n* catéchiste *mf*. ◆ **catechize** *vt* catéchiser.

category ['kætɪg(ə)rɪ] *n* catégorie *f*. ◆ **categoric(al)** *adj* catégorique. ◆ **categorically** *adv* catégoriquement. ◆ **categorize** *vt* classer par catégories.

cater ['keɪtəʳ] *vi (provide food)* préparer un *or* des repas (*for* pour). **to ~ for** *sb's needs* pourvoir à; *sb's tastes* satisfaire; **this magazine ~s for all ages** ce magazine s'adresse à tous les âges. ◆ **caterer** *n (providing meals)* traiteur *m*; *(providing supplies)* fournisseur *m (en alimentation)*. ◆ **catering** **1** *n (providing supplies)* approvisionnement *m*; *(providing meals)* restauration *f*; **the ~ing was done by...** le buffet a été confié à... ; **2** *adj*: **~ing trade** restauration *f*.

caterpillar ['kætəpɪləʳ] **1** *n (Zool, Tech)* chenille *f*. **2** *adj vehicle* à chenilles. ~ **tractor** autochenille *f*.

caterwaul ['kætəwɔːl] *vi [cat]* miauler; *[person]* brailler. ◆ **caterwauling** *n* miaulement *m*; braillements *mpl*.

cathedral [kə'θiːdr(ə)l] *n* cathédrale *f*. ~ **city** évêché *m*.

catheter ['kæθɪtəʳ] *n (Med)* sonde *f* creuse.

cathode ['kæθəʊd] *n* cathode *f*. ~ **ray tube** tube *m* cathodique.

catholic ['kæθ(ə)lɪk] **1** *adj* (**a**) *(Rel)* **C~** catholique; **the C~ Church** l'Église *f* catholique. (**b**) *(universal)* universel; *(broad-minded)* libéral. ~ **tastes** goûts *mpl* éclectiques; ~ **views** opinions libérales. **2** *n*: **C~** catholique *mf*. ◆ **Catholicism** *n* catholicisme *m*.

catkin ['kætkɪn] *n (Bot)* chaton *m*.

cattle ['kætl] **1** *collective n* bétail *m*, bestiaux *mpl*. **herded like ~** parqués comme du bétail. **2** *adj*: ~ **breeder** éleveur *m* (de bétail); **'~ crossing'** 'passage *m* de troupeaux'; ~ **shed** étable *f*; ~ **show** concours *m* agricole; ~ **truck** fourgon *m* à bestiaux. ◆ **cattleman** *n* bouvier *m*.

caucus ['kɔːkəs] *n (US: committee)* comité *m* électoral; *(pej)* coterie *f* politique.

caught [kɔːt] *pret, ptp of* **catch**.

cauldron ['kɔːldr(ə)n] *n* chaudron *m*.

cauliflower ['kɒlɪflaʊəʳ] **1** *n* chou-fleur *m*. **2** *adj (Culin)* ~ **cheese** chou-fleur *m* au gratin; *(fig)* ~ **ear** oreille *f* en chou-fleur.

cause [kɔːz] **1** *n* cause *f*. ~ **and effect** la cause et l'effet *m*; **the relation of** ~ **and effect** la relation de cause à effet; **to be the** ~ **of** être cause de; **she has no** ~ **to be angry** elle n'a aucune raison de se fâcher; **there's no** ~ **for anxiety** il n'y a pas de raison de s'inquiéter *or* pas de quoi s'inquiéter; **with** ~ à juste titre; **without good** ~ sans raison valable; ~ **for complaint** sujet *m* de plainte; **in the** ~ **of justice** pour (la cause de) la justice; **it's all in a good** ~ * c'est pour le bien de la communauté; **to plead sb's** ~ plaider la cause de qn. **2** *vt* causer. **to** ~ **trouble to sb** *(problems)* créer des ennuis à qn; *(disturbance)* déranger qn; **to** ~ **sb to do sth** faire faire qch à qn; **to** ~ **sth to be done** faire faire qch. ◆ **causal** *adj* causal. ◆ **causality** *or* ◆ **causation** *n* causalité *f*. ◆ **causative** *adj* causatif.

causeway ['kɔːzweɪ] *n* chaussée *f*.

caustic ['kɔːstɪk] *adj* caustique.

cauterize ['kɔːtəraɪz] *vt* cautériser.

caution ['kɔːʃ(ə)n] **1** *n (gen)* prudence *f*, circonspection *f*; *(warning)* avertissement *m*; *(rebuke)* réprimande *f*. *(Aut)* **proceed with** ~ avancez lentement. **2** *vt* avertir. *(Police)* **to** ~ **sb** informer qn de ses droits; **to** ~ **sb against sth/against doing sth** déconseiller qch à qn/à qn de faire qch. ◆ **cautionary** *adj*: ~**ary tale** récit *m* édifiant.

cautious ['kɔːʃəs] *adj* prudent, circonspect. **to be** ~ **about doing sth** longuement réfléchir avant de faire qch. ◆ **cautiously** *adv* prudemment, avec circonspection. ◆ **cautiousness** *n* prudence *f*, circonspection *f*.

cavalier [ˌkævə'lɪəʳ] **1** *n* cavalier *m*; *(Hist)* royaliste *m*. **2** *adj* cavalier.

cavalry ['kæv(ə)lrɪ] *n* cavalerie *f*.

cave [keɪv] **1** *n* caverne *f*, grotte *f*. **2** *adj*: ~ **painting** peinture *f* rupestre. **3** *vi*: **to go caving** faire de la spéléologie.
◆ **cave in** *vi [floor, building]* s'effondrer; *[wall, beam]* céder; *(*: yield)* se dégonfler *.
◆ **cave-in** *n* effondrement *m*. ◆ **caveman** *n* homme *m* des cavernes. ◆ **caving** *n* spéléologie *f*.

caveat ['kævɪæt] *n* avertissement *m*.

cavern ['kævən] *n* caverne *f*. ◆ **cavernous** *adj darkness* épais; *eyes* cave; *voice* caverneux; *yawn* profond.

caviar(e) ['kævɪɑːʳ] *n* caviar *m*.

cavil ['kævɪl] *vi* ergoter (*about, at* sur).

cavity ['kævɪtɪ] *n* cavité *f*. ~ **wall insulation** isolation *f* des murs creux.

cavort * [kə'vɔːt] *vi* faire des gambades.

caw [kɔː] **1** *vi* croasser. **2** *n* croassement *m*.

cayenne ['keɪen] *n (pepper)* (poivre *m* de) cayenne *m*.

cease [siːs] **1** *vi* cesser, s'arrêter. **2** *vt* cesser, arrêter (*doing* de faire). **to** ~ **fire** cesser le feu. ◆ **cease-fire** *n* cessez-le-feu *m inv*. ◆ **ceaseless** *adj* incessant. ◆ **ceaselessly** *adv* sans cesse, sans arrêt.

cedar ['siːdəʳ] *n* cèdre *m*.

cede [siːd] *vt* céder.

cedilla [sɪ'dɪlə] *n* cédille *f*.

ceiling ['siːlɪŋ] **1** *n* plafond *m*. **to hit the** ~ * *(get angry)* piquer une crise *; *[prices]* crever le plafond. **2** *adj lamp, covering* de plafond; *price* plafond *inv*.

celebrate ['selɪbreɪt] *vt (gen)* célébrer; *event* fêter; *mass* célébrer. **let's** ~! * il faut fêter ça!; *(with drink)* il faut arroser ça! * ◆ **celebrated** *adj* célèbre. ◆ **celebration** *n (occasion)* festivités *fpl*; *(act)* célébration *f*; **we must have a celebration** il faut fêter cela. ◆ **celebrity** *n* célébrité *f*.

celeriac [sə'lerɪæk] *n* céleri(-rave) *m*.

celery ['selərɪ] *n* céleri *m* (à côtes). **head/stick of** ~ pied *m*/côte *f* de céleri.

celestial [sɪ'lestɪəl] *adj (lit, fig)* céleste.

celibacy ['selɪbəsɪ] *n* célibat *m*. ◆ **celibate** *adj, n* célibataire *(mf)*.

cell [sel] *n (gen)* cellule *f*; *(Elec)* élément *m (de pile)*. ◆ **cellular** *adj (Anat, Bio)* cellulaire; *blanket* en cellular. ◆ **Celluloid** *n* Ⓡ celluloïd *m* Ⓡ.

cellar ['seləʳ] *n [wine, coal]* cave *f*; *[food etc]* cellier *m*.

cello ['tʃeləʊ] *n* violoncelle *m*. ◆ **cellist** *n* violoncelliste *mf*.

cellophane ['seləfeɪn] *n* Ⓡ cellophane *f* Ⓡ.

cellulose ['seljʊləʊs] *n* cellulose *f*.

Celsius ['selsɪəs] *adj* Celsius *inv*.

Celt [kelt, selt] *n* Celte *mf*. ◆ **Celtic** ['keltɪk, 'seltɪk] **1** *adj* celtique, celte ; **2** *n* celtique *m*.

cement [sə'ment] **1** *n* ciment *m*. **2** *vt* cimenter. **3** *adj*: ~ **mixer** bétonnière *f*.

cemetery ['semɪtrɪ] *n* cimetière *m*.

cenotaph ['senətɑːf] *n* cénotaphe *m*.

censor ['sensəʳ] **1** *n* censeur *m*. **2** *vt* censurer. ◆ **censorship** *n* censure *f*.

censure ['senʃəʳ] **1** *vt* blâmer. **2** *n* blâme *m*.

census ['sensəs] *n* recensement *m*.

cent [sent] *n* (**a**) **per** ~ pour cent. (**b**) *(money)* cent *m*. **not a** ~ * pas un sou.

centenary [sen'tiːnərɪ] *adj, n* centenaire *(m)*. ◆ **centenarian** *adj, n* centenaire *(mf)*.

centennial [sen'tenɪəl] **1** *adj (100 years old)* centenaire; *(every 100 years)* séculaire. **2** *n* centenaire *m*.

center ['sentəʳ] *n (US)* = **centre.**

centigrade ['sentɪgreɪd] *adj* centigrade.

centimetre, *(US)* **centimeter** ['sentɪˌmiːtəʳ] *n* centimètre *m*.

centipede ['sentɪpiːd] *n* mille-pattes *m inv*.

central ['sentr(ə)l] **1** *adj* central. **C**~ **America/Europe** Amérique/Europe centrale; **C**~ **African Republic** République *f* Centrafricaine; **C**~ **European** (habitant(e) *m(f)*) de l'Europe centrale; ~ **heating** chauffage central; *(Comput)* ~ **processing unit** *(abbr* **CPU)** unité *f* centrale (*abbr* CU); *(Aut)* ~ **reservation** bande médiane. **2** *n (US)* central *m* téléphonique. ◆ **centralization** *n* centralisation *f*. ◆ **centralize** **1** *vt* centraliser ; **2** *vi* se centraliser. ◆ **centrally** *adv*: ~**ly heated** doté du chauffage central.

centre, *(US)* **center** ['sentəʳ] **1** *n* centre *m*. **in the** ~ au centre. **2** *vt* centrer. **3** *vi* tourner (*on* autour de). ◆ **centre-board** *n* dérive *f (d'un bateau)*. ◆ **centre-fold** *n* double page *f* (détachable); *(pinup)* photo *f* de pin up *(au milieu d'un magazine)*. ◆ **centre-forward** *n* avant-centre *m*. ◆ **centre-half** *n* demi-centre *m*.

centrifugal [sen'trɪfjʊg(ə)l] *adj* centrifuge. ◆ **centrifuge** *n* centrifugeuse *f*.

century ['sentjʊrɪ] *n* siècle *m*. **in the twentieth** ~ au vingtième siècle. ◆ **centuries-old** *adj* séculaire.

ceramic [sɪ'ræmɪk] **1** *adj art* céramique; *vase* en céramique. **2** *n*: ~**s** céramique *f*.

cereal ['sɪərɪəl] *n (plant)* céréale *f*; *(grain)* grain *m (de céréale)*. **baby** ~ blédine *f* Ⓡ; **breakfast** ~ flocons *mpl* de céréales.

ceremony ['serɪmənɪ] *n (event)* cérémonie *f*; *(pomp)* cérémonies *fpl*, façons *fpl*. **to stand on** ~ faire des cérémonies *or* des façons; **without** ~ sans cérémonies. ◆ **ceremonial** **1** *adj rite* cérémoniel; *dress* de cérémonie ; **2** *n* cérémonial *m*. ◆ **ceremonially** *adv* selon le cérémonial d'usage. ◆ **ceremonious** *adj* solennel; *(slightly pej)* cérémonieux. ◆ **ceremoniously** *adv* solennellement; *(slightly pej)* cérémonieusement.

cert ‡ [sɜːt] *n*: **it's a dead** ~ c'est sûr et certain *.

certain ['sɜːtən] *adj* (**a**) *(sure)* certain, sûr; *death, success* certain, inévitable; *remedy* infaillible. **he is** ~ **to go** il est certain qu'il ira; **that's for** ~ * c'est sûr et certain *; **I cannot say for** ~ **that...** je ne peux pas affirmer que...; **I don't know for** ~ je n'en suis pas sûr; **I am** ~ **he didn't do it** je suis certain qu'il n'a pas fait cela; **be** ~ **to go** allez-y sans faute, ne manquez pas d'y aller; **you can be** ~ **of success** vous êtes sûr de réussir; **to make** ~ **of sth/that...** s'assurer de qch/que... (**b**) *(particular)* certain *(before n)*. **a** ~ **gentleman** un certain monsieur. ◆ **certainly** *adv* certainement, sans aucun doute; ~**ly!** bien sûr!; ~**ly not!** certainement pas!; **I shall** ~**ly be there** j'y serai sans faute; **you may** ~**ly leave** vous pouvez partir, bien sûr. ◆ **certainty** *n* certitude *f*.

certify ['sɜːtɪfaɪ] **1** *vt* (**a**) certifier *(that* que). **certified as a true copy** certifié conforme; **to** ~ **sb (insane)** déclarer qn atteint d'aliénation mentale. (**b**) *(Comm) goods* garantir. *(US)* **to send by certified mail** ≃ envoyer avec avis de réception. **2** *vi*: **to** ~ **to sth** attester qch. ◆ **certifiable** *adj* qu'on peut certifier; *(*: mad)* bon à enfermer. ◆ **certificate** [sə'tɪfɪkɪt] *n (legal)* certificat *m*; *(academic)* diplôme *m*. ◆ **certificated** *adj* diplômé. ◆ **certification** *n* certification *f*.

certitude ['sɜːtɪtjuːd] *n* certitude *f*.

cervix ['sɜːvɪks] *n* col *m* de l'utérus. ◆ **cervical** *adj*: **cervical smear** frottis *m* vaginal.

cessation [se'seɪʃ(ə)n] *n* cessation *f*.

cesspit ['sespɪt] *n* fosse *f* à purin.

cesspool ['sespuːl] *n* fosse *f* d'aisance.

Chad [tʃæd] *n* Tchad *m*.

chafe [tʃeɪf] **1** *vt (rub)* frotter, frictionner; *(rub against)* frotter contre, gratter; *(wear through)* user (en frottant). *(from cold)* ~**d lips/hands** lèvres/mains gercées. **2** *vi* s'user; *(fig)* s'impatienter, s'irriter *(at, against* de).

chaff[1] [tʃɑːf] *n [grain]* balle *f*; *(cut straw)* menue paille *f*.

chaff[2] [tʃɑːf] *vt (tease)* taquiner.

chaffinch ['tʃæfɪn(t)ʃ] *n* pinson *m*.

chagrin ['ʃægrɪn] *n* vive déception, vif dépit. **much to my** ~ à mon vif dépit.

chain [tʃeɪn] **1** *n* (**a**) *(gen)* chaîne *f*. **in** ~**s** enchaîné; *[lavatory]* **to pull the** ~ tirer la chasse (d'eau). (**b**) *[mountains, atoms, shops]* chaîne *f*; *[ideas]* enchaînement *m*; *[events]* série *f*, suite *f*. *[people]* **to make a** ~ faire la chaîne. **2** *adj*: ~ **letters** chaîne *f* (de lettres); ~ **mail** cotte *f* de mailles; ~ **reaction** réaction *f* en chaîne; ~ **saw** tronçonneuse *f*; ~ **smoke** fumer cigarette sur cigarette; ~ **smoker** fumeur *m*, -euse *f* invétéré(e); ~ **store** grand magasin (à succursales multiples). **3** *vt* enchaîner; *dog* mettre à l'attache.

chair [tʃɛəʳ] **1** *n* (**a**) *(gen)* chaise *f*; *(arm~)* fauteuil *m*; *(seat)* siège *m*; *(Univ)* chaire *f*; *(wheel ~)* fauteuil roulant. **to take a** ~ s'asseoir; **dentist's** ~ fauteuil de dentiste; *(US: electric ~)* **to go to the** ~ passer à la chaise électrique; *(at meeting)* **to be in the** ~ présider; ~! ~! à l'ordre! (**b**) *(of committee)* président(e) *m(f)*. **2** *vt meeting* présider; *hero* porter en triomphe. ◆ **chairlift** *n* télésiège *m*. ◆ **chairman** *n* président *m (d'un comité etc)*. ◆ **chairmanship** *n* présidence *f*. ◆ **chairperson** * *n* président(e) *m(f)*.

chalet ['ʃæleɪ] *n (gen)* chalet *m*; *[motel]* bungalow *m*.

chalice ['tʃælɪs] *n* calice *m*.

chalk [tʃɔːk] **1** *n* craie *f*. **a (piece of)** ~ une craie, un morceau de craie; **they're as different as** ~ **from cheese** c'est le jour et la nuit; **by a long** ~ de beaucoup, de loin; **not by a long** ~ loin de là. **2** *vt* écrire à la craie; *luggage* marquer à la craie. ◆ **chalk up** *vt sep achievement, victory* remporter. *(amount owed)* ~ **it up** mettez-le sur mon compte; **he** ~**ed it up to experience** il l'a mis au compte de l'expérience. ◆ **chalkpit** *n* carrière *f* de craie. ◆ **chalky** *adj* crayeux.

challenge ['tʃælɪn(d)ʒ] **1** *n* défi *m*; *(by sentry)* sommation *f*. **to put out a** ~ lancer un défi; **to take up the** ~ relever le défi; **the** ~ **of new ideas** la stimulation qu'offrent de nouvelles idées; **the** ~ **of the 20th century** le défi du XXᵉ siècle; **Smith's** ~ **for leadership** la tentative qu'a faite Smith pour s'emparer du pouvoir; **the job was a great** ~ **to him** il a pris cette tâche comme une gageure. **2** *vt* défier *(sb to do* qn de faire); *(Sport)* inviter *(sb to a game* qn à faire une partie); *statement* mettre en question, contester; *[sentry]* faire une sommation à; *juror, jury* récuser. **to** ~ **sb to a duel** provoquer qn en duel; **to** ~ **sb's authority to do** contester à qn le droit de faire; **to** ~ **the wisdom of a plan** mettre en question la sagesse d'un projet. ◆ **challenger** *n* provocateur *m*, -trice *f*; *(Sport)* challenger *m*. ◆ **challenging** *adj remark* provocateur; *look, tone* de défi; *book* stimulant; **this is a very challenging situation** cette situation est une véritable gageure.

chamber ['tʃeɪmbəʳ] **1** *n (hall)* chambre *f*; *(†: room)* pièce *f*; *(bed ~)* chambre. ~**s** *[barrister, judge, magistrate]* cabinet *m*; *[solicitor]* étude *f*; **C~ of Commerce** Chambre de commerce; *(Parl)* **the Upper/Lower C~** la Chambre Haute/Basse; **the C~ of Horrors** la Chambre d'épouvante. **2** *adj*: ~ **music** musique *f* de chambre. ◆ **chambermaid** *n* femme *f* de chambre *(dans un hôtel)*. ◆ **chamberpot** *n* pot *m* de chambre.

chamberlain ['tʃeɪmbəlɪn] *n* chambellan *m*.

chameleon [kə'miːlɪən] *n* caméléon *m*.

chamois ['ʃæmwɑː] *n* (**a**) *(Zool)* chamois *m*. (**b**) ['ʃæmɪ] *(~ cloth)* chamois *m*. ~ **leather** peau *f* de chamois.

champ [tʃæmp] *vti* mâchonner. **to** ~ **at the bit** ronger son frein.

champagne [ʃæm'peɪn] *n* champagne *m*.

champion ['tʃæmpjən] **1** *n* champion(ne) *m(f)*. **world** ~ champion(ne) du monde; **skiing** ~ champion(ne) de ski. **2** *adj* sans rival, de première classe; *show animal* champion. ~ **swimmer** champion(ne) *m(f)* de natation. **3** *vt* défendre, soutenir. ◆ **championship** *n (Sport)* championnat *m*; *[cause etc]* défense *f*.

chance [tʃɑːns] **1** *n* (**a**) *(luck)* hasard *m*. **by** ~ par hasard; **have you a pen by (any)** ~**?** auriez-vous par hasard un stylo?; **a game of** ~ un jeu de hasard; **he left nothing to** ~ il n'a rien laissé au hasard. (**b**) *(possibility)* chances *fpl*, possibilité *f*. **he hasn't much** ~ **of winning** il n'a pas beaucoup de chances de gagner; **the** ~**s are that** il y a de grandes chances que + *subj*, il est très possible que + *subj*; **the** ~**s are against that happening** il y a peu de chances pour que cela arrive *(subj)*; **there is little** ~ **of his coming** il est peu probable qu'il vienne; **you'll have to take a** ~ **on his coming** vous verrez bien s'il vient ou non; **he's taking no** ~**s** il ne veut prendre aucun risque. (**c**) *(opportunity)* occasion *f*, chance *f*. **I had the** ~ **to go** *or* **of going** j'ai eu l'occasion d'y aller; **if there's a** ~ **of buying it** s'il y a une possibilité d'achat; **she was waiting for her** ~ elle attendait son heure; **now's your** ~! vas-y!, saute sur l'occasion!; **this is his big** ~ c'est le grand moment pour lui; **give him another** ~ laisse-lui encore sa chance; **he**

never had a ~ in life il n'a jamais eu sa chance dans la vie; **give me a ~ to show you...** donnez-moi la possibilité de vous montrer...
2 *adj error, remark* fortuit; *companion* rencontré par hasard; *discovery* accidentel; *meeting* de hasard.
3 *vt (happen)* **to ~ to do** faire par hasard; *(risk)* **to ~ doing** prendre le risque de faire; **to ~ it, to ~ one's arm** * risquer le coup *.
◆ **chance upon** *vt fus person* rencontrer par hasard; *thing* trouver par hasard.
◆ **chancy** * *adj* risqué.

chancel ['tʃɑ:ns(ə)l] *n* chœur *m (d'une église).*

chancellor ['tʃɑ:nsələʳ] *n* chancelier *m*. **C~ of the Exchequer** Chancelier *m* de l'Échiquier.

chandelier [ˌʃændəˈlɪəʳ] *n* lustre *m*.

chandler ['tʃɑ:ndləʳ] *n*: **ship's ~** shipchandler *m*, marchand *m* de fournitures pour bateaux.

change [tʃeɪn(d)ʒ] **1** *n* (**a**) changement *m* (*from* de, *into* en). **a ~ for the better/worse** un changement en mieux/en pire; **~ in the weather** changement de temps; **just for a ~** pour changer un peu; **to have a ~ of heart** changer d'avis; **it makes a ~** * ça change un peu; **it will be a nice ~** cela nous fera un changement; **the ~ of life** le retour d'âge; **~ of address** changement d'adresse; **a ~ of clothes** des vêtements de rechange; **~ of air** *or* **scene** changement d'air; **she likes ~** elle aime le changement *or* la variété.
(**b**) *(money)* monnaie *f*. **small** *or* **loose ~** petite monnaie; **can you give me ~ of £1?** pouvez-vous me faire la monnaie d'une livre?; **you don't get much ~ from a fiver** il ne reste pas grand-chose d'un billet de cinq livres; *(fig)* **you won't get much ~ out of him** * tu perds ton temps avec lui.
2 *vt* (**a**) *(by substitution) clothes, one's address, trains, one's name* changer de. **to ~ colour** changer de couleur; **to ~ hands** changer de main; **a sum of money ~d hands** une somme d'argent a été échangée; **to ~ the guard** faire la relève de la garde; *(Theat)* **to ~ the scene** changer le décor; **let's ~ the subject** parlons d'autre chose; **to ~ one's tune** changer de ton; **to ~ one's opinion** *or* **mind** changer d'avis; **to ~ gear** changer de vitesse; *(Aut)* **to ~ a wheel** changer une roue.
(**b**) *(exchange)* échanger (*sth for sth else* qch contre qch d'autre). **to ~ places (with sb)** changer de place (avec qn); *(fig)* **I wouldn't like to ~ places with you** je n'aimerais pas être à votre place; **to ~ ends** *(Tennis)* changer de côté; *(Ftbl etc)* changer de camp; **to ~ sides** changer de camp.
(**c**) *banknote, coin* faire la monnaie de, changer; *foreign currency* changer, convertir (*into* en).
(**d**) *(alter)* changer, transformer (*sth into sth else* qch en qch d'autre). **the witch ~d him into a cat** la sorcière l'a changé en chat.
3 *vi* (**a**) *(become different)* changer (*into* en). **you've ~d a lot** tu as beaucoup changé; **the prince ~d into a swan** le prince s'est changé en cygne.
(**b**) *(~ clothes)* se changer. **she ~d into an old skirt** elle s'est changée et a mis une vieille jupe.
(**c**) *(Rail etc)* changer. **all ~!** tout le monde descend!
◆ **change down** *vi (Aut)* rétrograder. ◆ **change over** *vi* passer (*from* de, *to* à); *[2 people, teams etc]* faire l'échange; *(Sport: change ends)* changer de côté. ◆ **change up** *vi (Aut)* monter les vitesses. ◆ **changeable** *adj person, character, colour* changeant; *weather* variable. ◆ **changeless** *adj rite* immuable; *character* inaltérable. ◆ **changeling** *n* enfant *mf* changé(e) *(substitué à un enfant volé)*. ◆ **change machine** *n* distributeur *m* de monnaie. ◆ **changeover** *n* changement *m* (*from* de, *to* à); *[guard]* relève *f*. ◆ **change purse** *n (US)* porte-monnaie *m inv*. ◆ **changing** **1** *adj wind* variable; *expression* mobile ; **2** *n*: **the changing of the guard** la relève de la garde. ◆ **changing-room** *n* vestiaire *m*.

channel ['tʃænl] **1** *n (navigable passage)* chenal *m*; *(between land masses)* bras *m* de mer; *[irrigation]* rigole *f*; *(in street)* caniveau *m*; *(groove in surface)* rainure *f*; *(Archit)* cannelure *f*; *(TV)* chaîne *f*. **the (English) C~** la Manche; **he directed the conversation into a new ~** il a fait prendre à la conversation une nouvelle direction; **~ of communication** voie *f* de communication; **to go through the usual ~s** suivre la filière (habituelle). **2** *adj (Geog)* **the C~ Isles** *or* **Islands** les îles Anglo-Normandes; **the C~ tunnel** le tunnel sous la Manche. **3** *vt* canaliser (*into* dans, *towards* vers).

chant [tʃɑ:nt] **1** *n (Mus)* chant *m*; *(Rel Mus)* psalmodie *f*; *[demonstrators, audience etc]* chant scandé. **2** *vt (gen)* chanter; *(recite)* réciter; *(Rel)* psalmodier; *[demonstrators etc]* scander. **3** *vi* chanter; psalmodier; scander des slogans.

chaos ['keɪɒs] *n* chaos *m*. ◆ **chaotic** *adj* chaotique.

chap¹ [tʃæp] **1** *n (in skin)* gerçure *f*. **2** *vi* se gercer.

chap² * [tʃæp] *n (man)* homme *m*, type * *m*. **old ~** mon vieux *; **a nice ~** un chic type *; **poor little ~** pauvre petit.

chapel ['tʃæp(ə)l] *n* chapelle *f*; *(nonconformist church)* église *f*, temple *m*. **~ of rest** chapelle ardente.

chaperon(e) ['ʃæpərəʊn] **1** *n* chaperon *m*. **2** *vt* chaperonner.

chaplain ['tʃæplɪn] *n (gen)* aumônier *m*; *(to nobleman etc)* chapelain *m*.

chapter ['tʃæptəʳ] *n* chapitre *m*. **in ~ 4** au chapitre 4; **to quote ~ and verse** citer ses références; **a ~ of accidents** une succession de mésaventures.

char¹ [tʃɑ:ʳ] *vt (burn black)* carboniser.

char² * [tʃɑ:ʳ] **1** *n (~lady, ~woman)* femme *f* de ménage. **2** *vi* faire des ménages.

character ['kærɪktəʳ] **1** *n (most senses)* caractère *m*; *(Literat, Theat)* personnage *m*. **he has the same ~ as his brother** il a le même caractère que son frère; **it's very much in ~ (for him)** cela lui ressemble tout à fait; **it takes ~ to do...** il faut avoir du caractère pour faire...; **he's quite a ~** c'est un numéro *; **he's a queer ~** c'est un type * curieux; **of good ~** qui a une bonne réputation; **Gothic ~s** caractères gothiques. **2** *adj*: **~ actor/actress** acteur *m*/actrice *f* de genre; **~ assassination** diffamation *f (destinée à ruiner la réputation d'une personne)*; **~ comedy** comédie *f* de caractère; **~ part** rôle *m* de composition; **~ sketch** portrait *m or* description *f* rapide.
◆ **characteristic** **1** *adj* caractéristique, typique; **with (his) ~istic enthusiasm** avec l'enthousiasme qui le caractérise ; **2** *n* caractéristique *f*. ◆ **characteristically** *adv* d'une façon caractéristique, typiquement. ◆ **characterization** *n* caractérisation *f*; *(Theat)* représentation *f* des caractères; *(Literat)* peinture *f* des caractères. ◆ **characterize** *vt* caractériser. ◆ **characterless** *adj* sans caractère, fade.

charcoal ['tʃɑ:kəʊl] **1** *n* charbon *m* de bois. **2** *adj sketch* au charbon; *(colour)* gris anthracite *inv*.

charge [tʃɑ:dʒ] **1** *n* (**a**) *(Jur etc)* accusation *f*. **to bring a ~ against sb** porter plainte contre qn; **arrested on a ~ of murder** arrêté sous l'inculpation de meurtre. (**b**) *(Mil)* charge *f*, attaque *f*. (**c**) *(cost)* prix *m*. **to make a ~ for sth** faire payer qch; **is there a ~?** y a-t-il qch à payer?; **free of ~** gratuit; **at a ~ of...** moyennant...; **extra ~** supplément *m*; **~ for admission** droit *m* d'entrée; **~ for delivery** (frais *mpl* de) port *m*. (**d**) *(responsibility)* charge *f*, responsabilité *f*. **he took ~** il a assumé la responsabilité (*or* les fonctions *etc*); **who takes ~ when...?** qui est-ce qui est responsable quand...?; **to take ~ of** se charger de; **to be in ~ of** avoir la garde de; **in his ~** à sa garde; **to put sb in ~ of sb/sth** charger qn de la garde de qn/qch; **to leave sb in ~ of sb/sth** confier qn/qch à la garde

de qn; **the man in ~** le responsable; **the nurse and her ~s** l'infirmière et ses malades. (**e**) *[firearm, battery etc]* charge *f*.
2 *adj*: ~ **account** compte *m*.
3 *vt* (**a**) **to ~ sb with sth** *(Jur)* inculper qn de qch; *(gen)* accuser qn de qch. (**b**) *(Mil)* charger. (**c**) *customer* faire payer; *amount* prendre, demander *(for* pour); *commission* prélever. **I ~d him £2 for this table** je lui ai fait payer cette table 2 livres; **how much do you ~ for mending shoes?** combien prenez-vous pour réparer des chaussures? (**d**) (**~ up**) *amount owed* mettre sur le compte (*to sb* de qn). (**e**) *firearm, battery* charger. (**f**) *(command)* **to ~ sb to do** sommer qn de faire.
4 *vi* (**a**) *(rush)* **to ~ in/out** entrer/sortir en coup de vent; **to ~ up/down** grimper/descendre à toute vitesse. (**b**) *[battery]* se recharger.
◆ **chargehand** *n* chef *m* d'équipe. ◆ **charger** *n* *[battery]* chargeur *m*; *(horse)* cheval *m* (de bataille).

chariot ['tʃærɪət] *n* char *m*.

charisma [kæ'rɪzmə] *n* charisme *m*, magnétisme *m*. ◆ **charismatic** *adj* charismatique, magnétique.

charity ['tʃærɪtɪ] *n* (**a**) charité *f*. **~ begins at home** charité bien ordonnée commence par soi-même; **to live on ~** vivre d'aumônes; **to collect for ~** faire une collecte pour une œuvre charitable. (**b**) *(charitable society)* œuvre *f* de bienfaisance. ◆ **charitable** *adj* charitable; **charitable institution** fondation *f* charitable. ◆ **charitably** *adv* charitablement.

charm [tʃɑ:m] **1** *n* charme *m*. **it worked like a ~** ça a marché à merveille. **2** *adj*: ~ **bracelet** bracelet *m* à breloques. **3** *vt* charmer. **to lead a ~ed life** être béni des dieux; **to ~ sth out of sb** obtenir qch de qn par le charme. ◆ **charmer** *n* charmeur *m*, -euse *f*. ◆ **charming** *adj* charmant. ◆ **charmingly** *adv* d'une façon charmante.

chart [tʃɑ:t] **1** *n* (**a**) *(map)* carte *f* (marine). (**b**) *(graph etc)* graphique *m*, tableau *m*; *(Med)* courbe *f*. **temperature ~** feuille *f* or courbe *f* de température; **the ~s** le hit-parade. **2** *vt route* porter sur la carte; *sales, results* faire le graphique *or* la courbe de. **this graph ~s...** ce graphique montre...

charter ['tʃɑ:təʳ] **1** *n* (**a**) *(document)* charte *f*; *[society, organization]* statuts *mpl*. (**b**) *(hiring)* *[plane, coach etc]* affrètement *m*. **on ~** sous contrat d'affrètement. **2** *adj*: ~ **flight** (vol *m* en) charter *m*; **by ~ flight** en charter; ~ **plane** charter *m*; ~ **train** train affrété. **3** *vt plane etc* affréter. ◆ **chartered** *adj*: **~ed accountant** expert-comptable *m*; **~ed surveyor** expert *m* immobilier.

chary ['tʃɛərɪ] *adj* circonspect. **~ of praise** avare de compliments; **to be ~ of doing** hésiter à faire. ◆ **charily** *adv* avec circonspection.

chase [tʃeɪs] **1** *n* chasse *f*. **to give ~ to** donner la chasse à; **in ~ of** à la poursuite de. **2** *vt* poursuivre, donner la chasse à. **3** *vi*: **to ~ up/down** *etc* monter/descendre *etc* au grand galop; **to ~ after sb** courir après qn.
◆ **chase away, chase off** *vt sep* chasser, faire partir. ◆ **chase up** *vt sep information* rechercher; *sth already asked for* réclamer. **to ~ sb up for sth** rappeler à qn de donner qch; **I'll ~ it** *or* **him up for you** je vais essayer d'activer les choses.

chasm ['kæz(ə)m] *n* gouffre *m*, abîme *m*.

chassis ['ʃæsɪ] *n* châssis *m*.

chaste [tʃeɪst] *adj* chaste; *style* sobre. ◆ **chastely** *adv behave* chastement; *dress* avec sobriété. ◆ **chastity** *n* chasteté *f*.

chasten ['tʃeɪsn] *vt (punish)* châtier; *(subdue)* assagir. ◆ **chastening** *adj thought* qui fait réfléchir; **it had a very ~ing effect on him** cela l'a fait réfléchir *or* l'a assagi.

chastise [tʃæs'taɪz] *vt (punish)* châtier; *(beat)* battre, corriger. ◆ **chastisement** *n* châtiment *m*; correction *f*.

chat [tʃæt] **1** *n* causette *f*, petite conversation. **to have a ~** bavarder, parler (*with, to* avec). **2** *adj* *(Rad/TV)* ~ **show** conversation *f* à bâtons rompus avec un(e) invité(e) célèbre. **3** *vi* bavarder, causer (*with* avec).
◆ **chat up** * *vt sep girl* baratiner *.
◆ **chatty** * *adj person* bavard; *style* familier; *letter* plein de bavardages.

chatter ['tʃætəʳ] **1** *vi [people]* bavarder, causer; *[children, monkeys, birds]* jacasser. **his teeth were ~ing** il claquait des dents. **2** *n* bavardage *m*; jacassement *m*. ◆ **chatterbox** *n* moulin *m* à paroles, bavard(e) *m(f)*.

chauffeur ['ʃəʊfəʳ] *n* chauffeur *m* (de maître).

chauvinism ['ʃəʊvɪnɪz(ə)m] *n (gen)* chauvinisme *m*; *(male ~)* machisme *m*.

chauvinist ['ʃəʊvɪnɪst] **1** *n (gen)* chauvin(e) *m(f)*; *(male ~)* macho *m*. **2** *adj (gen)* chauvin; *(male ~)* macho *inv*, machiste.

cheap [tʃi:p] **1** *adj* bon marché *inv*, peu cher; *tickets* à prix réduit; *fare* réduit; *money* bon marché; *(pej: poor quality)* de mauvaise qualité; *success, joke* facile. **on the ~** à bon marché, pour pas cher; **it's ~ at the price** c'est bon marché à ce prix-là; *(fig)* les choses auraient pu être pires; **~er** meilleur marché, moins cher; **it's ~er in the long run** cela revient moins cher à la longue; **this stuff is ~ and nasty** c'est de la camelote *; **his behaviour was very ~** il s'est très mal conduit; **to feel ~** avoir honte (*about* de). **2** *adv* bon marché; *(cut-price)* au rabais. ◆ **cheapen** *vt* baisser le prix de; *(fig)* déprécier; **to ~en o.s.** *[woman]* être facile; *(gen)* se déconsidérer. ◆ **cheapjack** *adj* de camelote. ◆ **cheaply** *adv* à bon marché, pour pas cher; **to get off ~ly** s'en tirer à bon compte. ◆ **cheapness** *n* bas prix *m*; *(fig)* médiocrité *f*. ◆ **cheapshot** * *vt (US)* débiner *, dénigrer.

cheat [tʃi:t] **1** *vt* tromper; *(swindle)* escroquer. **to ~ sb out of sth** escroquer qch à qn. **2** *vi (at games)* tricher (*at* à); *(defraud)* frauder. **3** *n* tricheur *m*, -euse *f*; *(crook)* escroc *m*. ◆ **cheating** **1** *n* tromperie *f*; escroquerie *f*; tricherie *f* ; **2** *adj* tricheur.

check¹ [tʃek] *n (US)* = **cheque.**

check² [tʃek] **1** *n* (**a**) *(setback)* *[movement]* arrêt *m* brusque; *[plans etc]* empêchement *m*; *(Mil)* revers *m*. **to hold** *or* **keep in ~** tenir en échec; **to put a ~ on** mettre un frein à; **to act as a ~ upon** freiner. (**b**) *(examination)* *[papers, passport, ticket]* contrôle *m*; *[luggage]* vérification *f*; *(mark)* marque *f* de contrôle. **to keep a ~ on** surveiller; *(US)* **~!** * d'accord!, O.K.! *. (**c**) *(Chess)* **in ~** en échec; *(excl)* **~!** échec au roi! (**d**) *(receipt)* *[left luggage]* bulletin *m* de consigne; *(Theat)* contremarque *f*; *[restaurant]* addition *f*. **2** *vt* (**a**) *(examine) figures, quality* vérifier; *tickets, passports* contrôler. **to ~ a copy against the original** vérifier une copie sur l'original. (**b**) *(stop) enemy* arrêter; *advance* enrayer; *(restrain)* maîtriser. **to ~ o.s.** se contrôler. (**c**) *(rebuke)* réprimander.
◆ **check in** **1** *vi (in hotel) (arrive)* arriver; *(register)* remplir une fiche (d'hôtel); *(Aviat)* se présenter à l'enregistrement. **2** *vt sep luggage* enregistrer.
◆ **check off** *vt sep* pointer, cocher. ◆ **check on** *vt fus* vérifier. ◆ **check out** **1** *vi (from hotel)* régler sa note. **2** *vt sep luggage* retirer. ◆ **check over** *vt sep* examiner, vérifier. ◆ **check up** *vi* se renseigner, vérifier. **to ~ up on** *fact* vérifier; *person* se renseigner sur.
◆ **checker** *n* contrôleur *m*, -euse *f*; *(US: in supermarket)* caissier *m*, -ière *f*; *(US: in cloakroom)* préposé(e) *m(f)* au vestiaire. ◆ **check-in** *adj*: *(Aviat)* **your ~-in time is...** présentez-vous à l'enregistrement des bagages à... ◆ **checking** *adj*: *(US)* **~ing account** compte *m* courant. ◆ **checklist** *n* liste

f de contrôle. ◆ **checkmate** **1** *n (Chess)* échec et mat *m*; *(fig)* impasse *f* ; **2** *vt* faire échec et mat à; *(fig)* coincer. ◆ **check-out** *n (Comm)* caisse *f (dans un libre-service)*. ◆ **checkpoint** *n* contrôle *m*. ◆ **checkroom** *n (US)* vestiaire *m*. ◆ **checkup** *n*: *(Med)* **to go for** *or* **have a ~up** se faire faire un bilan de santé.

check³ [tʃek] *n*: **~s** *(pattern)* carreaux *mpl*, damier *m*. ◆ **checked** *adj* à carreaux. ◆ **checkerboard** *n (US)* damier *m*. ◆ **checkered** *adj (US)* = **chequered.**
◆ **checkers** *npl (US)* jeu *m* de dames.

cheddar ['tʃedəʳ] *n* (fromage *m* de) cheddar *m*.

cheek [tʃi:k] **1** *n* (**a**) joue *f*. ~ **by jowl** côte à côte; ~ **by jowl with** tout près de; **to dance** ~ **to** ~ danser joue contre joue; ~ **bone** pommette *f*. (**b**) *(*: impudence)* toupet *m*, culot * *m*. **to have the** ~ **to do** avoir le toupet *or* le culot * de faire; **of all the** ~! quel culot! *, quel toupet! **2** *vt* être insolent avec. ◆ **cheekily** *adv* effrontément, avec insolence. ◆ **cheekiness** *n* effronterie *f*, toupet *m*, culot * *m*. ◆ **cheeky** *adj child* effronté, insolent, culotté *; *remark* impertinent.

cheep [tʃi:p] **1** *n [bird]* piaulement *m*. **2** *vi* piauler.

cheer [tʃɪəʳ] **1** *n*: **~s** acclamations *fpl*, hourras *mpl*; **to give three ~s for** acclamer; **three ~s for...!** un ban pour...!; **three ~s!** hourra!; **~s!** * *(drinking)* à la vôtre! *, à la tienne! *; *(goodbye)* au revoir!, tchao *! **2** *adj*: ~ **leader** meneur *m* (qui rythme les cris des supporters). **3** *vt* (**a**) (~ **up**) *(gladden)* égayer, dérider; *(comfort)* donner du courage à, remonter le moral à; *room* égayer. (**b**) *(applaud)* acclamer, applaudir. **4** *vi* applaudir, pousser des hourras.
◆ **cheer on** *vt sep person, team* encourager *(par des cris etc)*. ◆ **cheer up** **1** *vi* prendre courage, prendre espoir. ~ **up!** courage! **2** *vt sep* = **cheer 3a**. ◆ **cheerful** *adj person, smile, conversation* joyeux, gai; *place, colour* gai, riant; *prospect* attrayant; *news* réconfortant. ◆ **cheerfully** *adv* gaiement, joyeusement. ◆ **cheerfulness** *n* gaieté *f*. ◆ **cheerily** *adv* gaiement, joyeusement. ◆ **cheering** **1** *n* acclamations *fpl*, hourras *mpl* ; **2** *adj news, sight* réconfortant, qui remonte le moral. ◆ **cheerio** * *excl (goodbye)* au revoir!, salut! *; *(your health)* à la vôtre! *, à la tienne! * ◆ **cheerless** *adj* morne, triste. ◆ **cheery** *adj* gai, joyeux.

cheese [tʃi:z] **1** *n* fromage *m*. *(for photograph)* **'say** ~' 'un petit sourire'. **2** *adj sandwich* au fromage. ~ **board** plateau *m* à *or* de fromage(s); ~ **dip** ≃ fondue *f*. ◆ **cheeseburger** *n* ≃ croque-monsieur *m*. ◆ **cheesecake** *n* flan *m* au fromage blanc. ◆ **cheesecloth** *n* toile *f* à beurre. ◆ **cheesed** *adj*: **to be ~d off** * en avoir marre * (*with* de). ◆ **cheeseparing** **1** *n* économies *fpl* de bouts de chandelles ; **2** *adj* pingre.

cheetah ['tʃi:tə] *n* guépard *m*.

chef [ʃef] *n* chef *m* (de cuisine).

chemical ['kemɪk(ə)l] **1** *adj* chimique. **2** *n* produit *m* chimique. ◆ **chemically** *adv* chimiquement.

chemist ['kemɪst] *n (researcher etc)* chimiste *mf*; *(pharmacist)* pharmacien(ne) *m(f)*. **~'s shop** pharmacie *f*. ◆ **chemistry** *n* chimie *f*.

chemotherapy ['kɪ:məʊ'θerəpɪ] *n* chimiothérapie *f*.

cheque [tʃek] *n* chèque *m* (*for £10* de 10 livres). **bad** ~ chèque sans provision; ~ **book** carnet *m* de chèques; ~ **card** carte *f* d'identité bancaire.

chequered ['tʃekəd] *adj* à carreaux, à damier; *(fig)* varié. **he had a** ~ **career** sa carrière a connu des hauts et des bas.

cherish ['tʃerɪʃ] *vt person, memory* chérir; *feelings, opinion* entretenir; *hope, illusions* caresser. ◆ **cherished** *adj* très cher.

cherry ['tʃerɪ] **1** *n* cerise *f*; (~ *tree)* cerisier *m*. **2** *adj pie, tart* aux cerises. ~ **brandy** cherry-brandy *m*; ~ **orchard** cerisaie *f*; ~ **red** (rouge) cerise *inv*.

cherub ['tʃerəb] *n* chérubin *m*. ◆ **cherubic** *adj* angélique.

chervil ['tʃ3:vɪl] *n* cerfeuil *m*.

chess [tʃes] *n* échecs *mpl*. ◆ **chessboard** *n* échiquier *m*. ◆ **chessman** *n* pièce *f* (de jeu d'échecs). ◆ **chessplayer** *n* joueur *m*, -euse *f* d'échecs.

chest¹ [tʃest] *n (box)* coffre *m*, caisse *f*; *(tea ~)* caisse. ~ **of drawers** commode *f*.

chest² [tʃest] **1** *n (Anat)* poitrine *f*. **to get something off one's** ~ * déballer * ce qu'on a sur le cœur. **2** *adj cold* de poitrine; *specialist* des voies respiratoires. ◆ **chesty** *adj person* fragile de la poitrine; *cough* de poitrine.

chestnut ['tʃesnʌt] **1** *n* châtaigne *f*; *(Culin)* châtaigne, marron *m*; (~ *tree)* châtaignier *m*, marronnier *m*; *(horse)* alezan *m*; *(old joke etc)* vieille histoire rabâchée. **2** *adj*: ~ **hair** cheveux châtains.

chew [tʃu:] *vt* mâcher, mastiquer. **to** ~ **tobacco** chiquer; **to** ~ **the cud** ruminer. ◆ **chew over** *vt sep facts, problem* ruminer. ◆ **chew up** *vt sep* mâchonner. ◆ **chewing** *adj*: **~ing gum** chewing-gum *m*.

chic [ʃi:k] *adj, n* chic *(m) inv*.

Chicano [tʃɪ'kɑ:nəʊ] *n (US)* Mexicain(e)-Américain(e) *m(f)*.

chichi * ['ʃi:ˌʃi:] *adj (US: too stylish)* trop recherché.

chick [tʃɪk] **1** *n (chicken)* poussin *m*; *(nestling)* oisillon *m*. **come here** ~ * viens ici mon petit poulet. **2** *adj*: ~ **pea** pois *m* chiche. ◆ **chickweed** *n* mouron *m* des oiseaux.

chicken ['tʃɪkɪn] **1** *n* poulet *m*; *(very young)* poussin *m*. **she's no** ~ * elle n'est plus toute jeune. **2** *adj*: ~ **farmer** éleveur *m* de volailles; ~ **farming** élevage *m* de volailles; ~ **liver** foie(s) *m(pl)* de volaille.
◆ **chicken out** ⁑ *vi* se dégonfler *.
◆ **chicken-feed** *n (fig)* somme *f* dérisoire.
◆ **chicken-hearted** *adj* peureux. ◆ **chickenpox** *n* varicelle *f*. ◆ **chicken-wire** *n* grillage *m*.

chicory ['tʃɪkərɪ] *n [coffee]* chicorée *f*; *(for salads)* endive *f*.

chide [tʃaɪd] *vt* gronder.

chief [tʃi:f] **1** *n (gen)* chef *m*; *(boss)* patron *m*. **in** ~ principalement, surtout; ~ **of staff** chef d'état-major. **2** *adj assistant, inspector* principal, en chef. **C~ Constable** ≃ directeur *m* (de police); ~ **of police** ≃ préfet *m* de police; *(US Pol)* **C~ of Staff** secrétaire *m* général (de la Maison-Blanche); ~ **priest** archiprêtre *m*. ◆ **chiefly** *adv* principalement, surtout. ◆ **chieftain** *n* chef *m (de clan)*.

chiffon ['ʃɪfɒn] *n* mousseline *f* de soie.

chilblain ['tʃɪlbleɪn] *n* engelure *f*.

child [tʃaɪld] **1** *n, pl* **children** ['tʃɪldr(ə)n] enfant *mf*. **don't be such a** ~ ne fais pas l'enfant; **the** ~ **of his imagination** le produit de son imagination. **2** *adj labour* des enfants; *psychology, psychiatry* de l'enfant, infantile; *psychologist, psychiatrist* pour enfants. ~ **abuse** mauvais traitements à enfant; ~ **care** protection *f* de l'enfance; *(US)* ~ **care center** crèche *f*, garderie *f*; ~ **guidance centre** centre *m* psycho-pédagogique; ~ **minder** gardienne *f* d'enfants; ~ **prodigy** enfant *mf* prodige; **it's ~'s play** c'est un jeu d'enfant (*to sb* pour qn); ~ **welfare** protection *f* de l'enfance. ◆ **child-bearing** *n*: **constant ~-bearing** grossesses répétées; **of ~-bearing age** en âge d'avoir des enfants. ◆ **childbirth** *n* accouchement *m*; **in ~birth** en couches. ◆ **childhood** *n* enfance *f*; **in his ~hood he...** tout enfant il...; **to be in one's second ~hood** retomber en enfance. ◆ **childish** *adj behaviour* puéril *(pej)*; *ailment* infantile; *games* d'enfants; **don't be so ~ish** ne fais pas l'enfant. ◆ **childishly** *adv* comme un enfant. ◆ **childishness** *n* puérilité *f (pej)*.

◆ **childless** *adj* sans enfants. ◆ **childlike** *adj* d'enfant, innocent. ◆ **childproof** *adj door etc* sans danger pour les enfants; ~**proof (door) lock** serrure *f* de sécurité enfants.

Chile ['tʃɪlɪ] *n* Chili *m*.

chill [tʃɪl] **1** *n* froid *m*; *(fig)* froideur *f*; *(Med)* refroidissement *m*. **there's a ~ in the air** il fait un peu froid; **to take the ~ off** *wine* chambrer; *water* dégourdir; *room* réchauffer un peu; *(fig)* **to cast a ~ over** jeter un froid sur; **a ~ down one's spine** un frisson; **to catch a ~** prendre froid. **2** *adj* (assez) froid. **3** *vt person* donner froid à; *wine, melon* faire rafraîchir; *meat* frigorifier, réfrigérer; *dessert* mettre au frais. ~**ed to the bone** *or* **marrow** transi jusqu'aux os *or* jusqu'à la moelle; **to ~ sb's blood** glacer le sang de qn. ◆ **chill(i)ness** *n (cold)* froid *m*; *(coolness)* fraîcheur *f*; *(fig)* froideur *f*. ◆ **chilling** *adj wind, look* froid; *thought* qui donne le frisson. ◆ **chilly** *adj person* frileux; *weather, wind* froid; *manner, look, smile* glacé, froid; *[person]* **to feel ~y** avoir froid; **it's rather ~y** il fait frais.

chilli ['tʃɪlɪ] *n* piment *m* (rouge).

chime [tʃaɪm] **1** *n* carillon *m*. **2** *vi [bells, voices]* carillonner; *[clock]* sonner. ◆ **chime in** *vi [person]* faire chorus.

chimney ['tʃɪmnɪ] **1** *n* cheminée *f*. **2** *adj*: ~ **breast** manteau *m* de (la) cheminée; ~ **corner** coin *m* du feu; ~**piece** (dessus *m or* tablette *f* de) cheminée *f*; ~ **pot** tuyau *m* de cheminée; ~ **stack** *[factory]* tuyau de cheminée (d'usine); ~ **sweep** ramoneur *m*.

chimpanzee [ˌtʃɪmpæn'ziː] *n* chimpanzé *m*.

chin [tʃɪn] *n* menton *m*. **keep your ~ up!** * courage! ◆ **chinstrap** *n* jugulaire *f*.

China ['tʃaɪnə] *n* Chine *f*. ~ **tea** thé *m* de Chine. ◆ **Chinatown** *n* le quartier chinois *(d'une ville)*. ◆ **Chinese** **1** *adj* chinois; **Chinese People's Republic** République *f* populaire de Chine; **C~ leaves** bette *f* ; **2** *n (person: pl inv)* Chinois(e) *m(f)*; *(Ling)* chinois *m*.

china ['tʃaɪnə] **1** *n* porcelaine *f*. **a piece of ~** une porcelaine. **2** *adj* de *or* en porcelaine; *industry* de la porcelaine. ◆ **chinaware** *n* (objets *mpl* de) porcelaine *f*.

chink[1] [tʃɪŋk] *n (slit) [wall]* fente *f*; *[door]* entrebâillement *m*. *(fig)* **the ~ in the armour** le défaut de la cuirasse.

chink[2] [tʃɪŋk] **1** *n (sound)* tintement *m*. **2** *vt* faire tinter. **3** *vi* tinter.

chintz [tʃɪnts] *n* chintz *m*.

chip [tʃɪp] **1** *n* (**a**) *(gen: piece)* fragment *m*; *[wood, glass, stone]* éclat *m*; *(Electronics)* microplaquette *f*. **he's a ~ off the old block** c'est bien le fils de son père; **to have a ~ on one's shoulder** être aigri. (**b**) *(Culin)* ~**s** *(Brit)* frites *fpl*; *(US)* chips *fpl*. (**c**) *(Comput)* puce *f*. (**d**) *(break) [stone, crockery]* ébréchure *f*; *[furniture]* écornure *f*. **this cup has a ~** cette tasse est ébréchée. (**e**) *(Poker etc)* jeton *m*. **he's had his ~s** ‡ il est fichu *; **when the ~s are down** * dans les moments cruciaux. **2** *vt (damage) cup, plate* ébrécher; *furniture, stone* écorner; *varnish, paint* écailler; *(cut deliberately)* tailler. ~**ped potatoes** (pommes *fpl* de terre) frites *fpl*.

◆ **chip away, chip off** **1** *vi [paint etc]* s'écailler. **2** *vt sep paint etc* enlever petit à petit. ◆ **chip in** * *vi (interrupt)* dire son mot; *(contribute)* contribuer. **he ~ped in with 10 francs** il y est allé de (ses) 10 F *.

◆ **chipboard** *n (US)* carton *m*; *(Brit)* bois aggloméré. ◆ **chippings** *npl* gravillons *mpl*.

chiropody [kɪ'rɒpədɪ] *n (science)* podologie *f*; *(treatment)* soins *mpl* du pied. ◆ **chiropodist** *n* pédicure *mf*.

chirp [tʃɜːp], **chirrup** ['tʃɪrəp] **1** *vi [birds]* pépier; *[crickets]* chanter. **2** *n* pépiement *m*; chant *m*. ◆ **chirpy** * *adj* gai.

chisel ['tʃɪzl] **1** *n (Tech)* ciseau *m*; *(for engraving)* burin *m*. **2** *vt* ciseler; buriner. **finely ~led features** traits finement ciselés; **to ~ sb out of sth** ‡ carotter * qch à qn.

chit[1] [tʃɪt] *n*: **she's a mere ~ of a girl** ce n'est qu'une gamine *.

chit[2] [tʃɪt] *n (gen)* bulletin *m* de livraison; *(receipt)* reçu *m*; *(note)* note *f*.

chitchat ['tʃɪttʃæt] *n* bavardage *m*.

chivalry ['ʃɪv(ə)lrɪ] *n* (**a**) *(Hist)* chevalerie *f*. (**b**) *(quality)* générosité *f*, galanterie *f*. ◆ **chivalresque** *adj* chevaleresque. ◆ **chivalrous** *adj (courteous)* chevaleresque; *(gallant)* galant. ◆ **chivalrously** *adv* de façon chevaleresque; galamment.

chives [tʃaɪvz] *npl* ciboulette *f*.

chivvy * ['tʃɪvɪ] *vt* (~ **along**) pourchasser; *(pester)* harceler (*sb into doing* qn jusqu'à ce qu'il fasse).

chlorate ['klɔːreɪt] *n* chlorate *m*.

chloride ['klɔːraɪd] *n* chlorure *m*.

chlorine ['klɔːriːn] *n* chlore *m*. ◆ **chlorinate** *vt water* javelliser; *(Chem)* chlorurer.

chloroform ['klɒrəfɔːm] **1** *n* chloroforme *m*. **2** *vt* chloroformer.

chlorophyll ['klɒrəfɪl] *n* chlorophylle *f*.

choc-ice ['tʃɒkaɪs] *n* esquimau *m (glace)*.

chock [tʃɒk] *n* cale *f*. ◆ **chock-a-block** *or* ◆ **chock-full** *adj container* plein à déborder (*with, of* de); *room* plein à craquer (*with, of* de).

chocolate ['tʃɒklɪt] **1** *n* chocolat *m*. **2** *adj egg* en chocolat; *biscuit, éclair* au chocolat; *(colour)* chocolat *inv*.

choice [tʃɔɪs] **1** *n* choix *m*. **a wide ~** un grand choix; **to take one's ~** faire son choix; **he had no ~** il n'avait pas le choix; **he had no ~ but to obey** il ne pouvait qu'obéir; **it's Hobson's ~** c'est à prendre ou à laisser; **from ~** de préférence; **he did it from ~** il a choisi de le faire; **this book would be my ~** c'est ce livre que je choisirais. **2** *adj goods, fruit* de choix; *word, phrase* bien choisi.

choir ['kwaɪəʳ] *n* chœur *m*. **to sing in the ~** faire partie du chœur. ◆ **choirboy** *n* jeune choriste *m*. ◆ **choirstall** *n* stalle *f* (du chœur).

choke [tʃəʊk] **1** *vt person* étrangler; *fire, flower* étouffer; (~ **up**) *pipe, tube* boucher. **street ~d with traffic** rue embouteillée. **2** *vi* étouffer, s'étrangler. **3** *n (Aut)* starter *m*.

◆ **choke back** *vt sep feelings, tears* refouler; *words* contenir. ◆ **choke off** * *vt sep suggestions etc* étouffer dans l'œuf; *discussion* empêcher; *person* envoyer promener *.

◆ **choker** *n (scarf)* foulard *m*; *(necklace)* collier *m* (de chien).

cholera ['kɒlərə] *n* choléra *m*.

cholesterol [kə'lestəˌrɒl] *n* cholestérol *m*.

choose [tʃuːz] *pret* **chose,** *ptp* **chosen** **1** *vt* (**a**) *(select)* choisir; *(elect)* élire. *(Rel)* **the chosen (people)** les élus *mpl*; **there is nothing to ~ between them** ils se valent; **in a few well-chosen words** en quelques mots choisis. (**b**) décider, juger bon (*to do* de faire). **he chose not to speak** il a jugé bon de se taire, il a préféré se taire. **2** *vi* choisir. **as you ~** comme vous voulez; **if you ~** si cela vous dit; **he'll do it when he ~s** il le fera quand il voudra; **to ~ between** faire un choix entre; **there's not too much to ~ from** il n'y a pas tellement de choix. ◆ **choos(e)y** * *adj* difficile (à satisfaire); **I'm ~y about the people I go out with** je ne sors pas avec n'importe qui.

chop[1] [tʃɒp] **1** *n* (**a**) *(Culin)* côtelette *f*. **pork ~** côtelette de porc. (**b**) *(blow)* coup *m* (de hache *etc*).

to get the ~ ‡ se faire mettre à la porte. **2** *vt wood* couper; *meat, vegetables* hacher. ◆ **chop down** *vt sep tree* abattre. ◆ **chop off** *vt sep* trancher, couper. **they** ~**ped off his head** on lui a tranché la tête. ◆ **chop up** *vt sep wood* couper en morceaux; *(Culin)* hacher menu. ◆ **chopper** *n* hachoir *m*; *(Aviat *)* hélico * *m*. ◆ **chopping** *adj*: ~**ping board** planche *f* à hacher; ~**ping knife** hachoir *m (couteau)*. ◆ **chopsticks** *npl* baguettes *fpl*.

chop² [tʃɒp] *vi*: **to** ~ **and change** changer constamment d'avis. ◆ **choppy** *adj lake* clapoteux; *sea* un peu agité; *wind* variable.

chopsuey [tʃɒp'suːɪ] *n* ragoût *m* (à la chinoise).

choral ['kɔːr(ə)l] *adj* choral. ~ **society** chorale *f*.

chord [kɔːd] *n (gen)* corde *f*; *(Mus)* accord *m*. *(fig)* **to touch the right** ~ toucher la corde sensible.

chore [tʃɔːʳ] *n (everyday)* travail *m* de routine; *(unpleasant)* corvée *f*. **the** ~**s** les travaux du ménage; **to do the** ~**s** faire le ménage.

choreography [ˌkɒrɪ'ɒgrəfɪ] *n* chorégraphie *f*. ◆ **choreographer** *n* chorégraphe *mf*.

chorister ['kɒrɪstəʳ] *n (Rel)* choriste *mf*.

chortle ['tʃɔːtl] **1** *vi* glousser, rire (*about* de). **2** *n* gloussement *m*.

chorus ['kɔːrəs] **1** *n* (**a**) *(musical work, people)* chœur *m*. **in** ~ en chœur; **she's in the** ~ *(at concert)* elle chante dans les chœurs; *(Theat)* elle fait partie de la troupe; **a** ~ **of objections** un concert de protestations. (**b**) *(part of song)* refrain *m*. **to join in the** ~ reprendre le refrain. **2** *adj*: ~ **girl** girl *f*. **3** *vt song* chanter *or* réciter en chœur. **'yes' they** ~**sed** 'oui' répondirent-ils en chœur.

chose [tʃəʊz], **chosen** ['tʃəʊzn] *pret, ptp of* **choose**.

chow [tʃaʊ] *n* chow-chow *m*.

chowder ['tʃaʊdəʳ] *n* soupe épaisse de palourdes.

Christ [kraɪst] *n* (le) Christ, Jésus-Christ. **the** ~ **Child** l'enfant Jésus. ◆ **Christendom** *n* chrétienté

christen ['krɪsn] *vt (Rel)* baptiser; *(gen: name)* appeler; *(nickname)* surnommer. **he was** ~**ed Robert but everyone calls him Bob** son nom de baptême est Robert mais tout le monde l'appelle Bob. ◆ **christening** *n* baptême *m*.

Christian ['krɪstɪən] **1** *adj* chrétien; *(fig)* charitable. ~ **name** prénom *m*, nom *m* de baptême; ~ **scientist** scientiste *mf* chrétien(ne). **2** *n* chrétien(ne) *m(f)*. ◆ **Christianity** *n* christianisme *m*.

Christmas ['krɪsməs] **1** *n* Noël *m*. **at** ~ à Noël. **2** *adj card, tree, present, cake* de Noël. ~ **box** étrennes *fpl*; ~ **Day** le jour de Noël; ~ **Eve** la veille de Noël; ~ **party** fête *f or* arbre *m* de Noël; **I got it in my** ~ **stocking** ≃ je l'ai trouvé sous l'arbre (de Noël); ~ **time** période *f* de Noël; **at** ~ **time** à Noël.

chromatic [krə'mætɪk] *adj* chromatique.

chrome [krəʊm] **1** *n* chrome *m*. **2** *adj fittings* chromé.

chromium ['krəʊmɪəm] *n* acier *m* chromé. ◆ **chromium-plated** *adj* chromé.

chromosome ['krəʊməsəʊm] *n* chromosome *m*.

chronic ['krɒnɪk] *adj disease, state* chronique; *liar, smoker etc* invétéré; (*) *weather, person* épouvantable.

chronicle ['krɒnɪkl] **1** *n* chronique *f*. *(fig)* **a** ~ **of disasters** une succession de catastrophes. **2** *vt* faire la chronique de.

chronology [krə'nɒlədʒɪ] *n* chronologie *f*. ◆ **chronological** *adj* chronologique; **in chronological order** par ordre chronologique. ◆ **chronologically** *adv* chronologiquement.

chronometer [krə'nɒmɪtəʳ] *n* chronomètre *m*.

chrysalis ['krɪsəlɪs] *n* chrysalide *f*.

chrysanthemum [krɪ'sænθ(ə)məm] *n* chrysanthème *m*.

chubby ['tʃʌbɪ] *adj* potelé. ~**-cheeked** joufflu.

chuck¹ [tʃʌk] *vt* (**a**) *(*: throw)* lancer, jeter; (‡: ~ **in** *, ~ **up** *) *job, girlfriend* laisser tomber *. (**b**) **he** ~**ed her under the chin** il lui a pris le menton. ◆ **chuck away** * *vt sep (throw out) old clothes, books* jeter, balancer *; *(waste) money* jeter par les fenêtres; *opportunity* laisser passer. ◆ **chuck out** * *vt sep useless article* jeter, balancer *; *person* vider *, sortir *.

chuck² [tʃʌk] *n (~ steak)* morceau *m* dans le paleron.

chuckle ['tʃʌkl] **1** *n* gloussement *m*, petit rire. **2** *vi* rire (*over, at* de), glousser.

chuffed ‡ [tʃʌft] *adj* tout content (*about* de).

chug [tʃʌg] *vi [machine]* souffler; *[train]* faire teuf-teuf. ◆ **chug along** *vi [train]* avancer en faisant teuf-teuf.

chum * [tʃʌm] *n* copain * *m*, copine * *f*. ◆ **chummy** * *adj* sociable; **she is very** ~**my with him** elle est très copine avec lui *.

chunk [tʃʌŋk] *n (gen)* gros morceau; *[bread]* quignon *m*. ◆ **chunky** *adj person* trapu; *knitwear* de grosse laine.

Chunnel * ['tʃʌnl] *n*: **the** ~ le tunnel sous la Manche.

church [tʃɜːtʃ] *n* église *f*. **to go to** ~ aller à l'église *f*; **in** ~ à l'église; **in the** ~ dans l'église; **after** ~ après l'office; *(for Catholics)* après la messe; **the C**~ **of England** l'Église anglicane; **he has gone into the C**~ il est entré dans les ordres. ◆ **churchgoer** *n* pratiquant(e) *m(f)*. ◆ **church-hall** *n* salle *f* paroissiale. ◆ **churchyard** *n* cimetière *m (autour d'une église)*.

churlish ['tʃɜːlɪʃ] *adj (ill-mannered)* grossier; *(bad-tempered)* hargneux, de mauvaise humeur. ◆ **churlishly** *adv* grossièrement; avec humeur. ◆ **churlishness** *n* grossièreté *f*; mauvaise humeur *f*.

churn [tʃɜːn] **1** *n* baratte *f*; *(milk can)* bidon *m*. **2** *vt butter* baratter; (~ **up**) *water* battre. ◆ **churn out** *vt sep objects, letters, books* produire en série.

chute [ʃuːt] *n (for coal etc)* descente *f*; *(Sport, for toboggans)* piste *f*; *(Brit: children's slide)* toboggan *m*.

chutney ['tʃʌtnɪ] *n* condiment *m (à base de fruits)*.

cicada [sɪ'kɑːdə] *n* cigale *f*.

cider ['saɪdəʳ] **1** *n* cidre *m*. **2** *adj apple, press* à cidre. ~ **vinegar** vinaigre *m* de cidre.

cigar [sɪ'gɑːʳ] **1** *n* cigare *m*. **2** *adj box etc* à cigares. ~ **case** étui *m* à cigares; ~ **lighter** allume-cigare *m inv*.

cigarette [ˌsɪgə'ret] **1** *n* cigarette *f*. **2** *adj box, paper etc* à cigarettes; *ash* de cigarette. ~ **case** porte-cigarettes *m inv*; ~ **end** mégot *m*; ~ **holder** fume-cigarette *m inv*; ~ **lighter** briquet *m*.

cinch [sɪntʃ] *n*: **it's a** ~ ‡ c'est du gâteau *.

cinder ['sɪndəʳ] **1** *n* cendre *f*. **burnt to a** ~ *(gen)* réduit en cendres; *food* carbonisé. **2** *adj*: ~ **track** (piste *f*) cendrée *f*.

Cinderella [ˌsɪndə'relə] *n* Cendrillon *f*.

cinema ['sɪnəmə] *n* cinéma *m*. ◆ **cine-camera** *n* caméra *f*. ◆ **cine-film** *n* film *m*. ◆ **cine-projector** *n* projecteur *m* de cinéma.

cinnamon ['sɪnəmən] *n* cannelle *f*.

cipher ['saɪfəʳ] *n (numeral code)* chiffre *m*; *(zero)* zéro *m*. **he's a mere** ~ c'est un zéro; **in** ~ en chiffre, en code.

circle ['sɜːkl] **1** *n (gen)* cercle *m*; *(Theat)* balcon *m*. **to stand in a** ~ faire (un) cercle; **an inner** ~ **of advisers** un groupe de proches conseillers; **in political** ~**s** dans les milieux *mpl* politiques; **to come full** ~ revenir à son point de départ. **2** *vt (go round)* contourner; *(move round)* tourner autour de; *(draw ~ round)* entourer d'un cercle. **3** *vi (~* **about** *or*

around) *[birds]* décrire des cercles; *[aircraft]* tourner (en rond).

◆ **circular** **1** *adj* circulaire ; **2** *n (letter)* circulaire *f*; *(as advertisement etc)* prospectus *m*. ◆ **circularize** *vt* envoyer des circulaires *or* des prospectus à.

circuit ['sɜːkɪt] *n (journey)* tour *m*, circuit *m*; *[judge, theatre company]* tournée *f*; *(group of cinemas etc)* groupe *m*; *(Elec, Sport)* circuit. **to make a ~ of** faire le tour de; **to make a ~ round** faire un détour *or* un circuit autour de; *(Jur)* **he is on the eastern ~** il fait la tournée de l'est. ◆ **circuit-breaker** *n* disjoncteur *m*. ◆ **circuitous** *adj route, method* indirect; *means* détourné. ◆ **circuitously** *adv reach* en faisant un détour; *(fig)* indirectement.

circulate ['sɜːkjʊleɪt] **1** *vi* circuler. **2** *vt* faire circuler. ◆ **circulation** **1** *n (gen)* circulation *f*; *[newspaper etc]* tirage *m*; *(Med)* **he has poor circulation** il a une mauvaise circulation; *(Fin)* **to put into circulation** mettre en circulation; **to withdraw from circulation** retirer de la circulation; **in circulation** en circulation; **he's now back in circulation *** il est à nouveau dans le circuit * ; **2** *adj (Press)* **circulation manager** directeur *m* du service de la diffusion.

circumcise ['sɜːkəmsaɪz] *vt* circoncire. ◆ **circumcision** *n* circoncision *f*.

circumference [s(ə)'kʌmf(ə)r(ə)ns] *n* circonférence *f*.

circumflex ['sɜːk(ə)mfleks] *n* accent *m* circonflexe.

circumlocution [ˌsɜːkəmlə'kjuːʃ(ə)n] *n* circonlocution *f*.

circumnavigate [ˌsɜːkəm'nævɪgeɪt] *vt cape* doubler; *globe* faire naviguer tout autour de. ◆ **circumnavigation** *n* circumnavigation *f*.

circumscribe ['sɜːkəmskraɪb] *vt* circonscrire; *powers* limiter.

circumspect ['sɜːkəmspekt] *adj* circonspect. ◆ **circumspection** *n* circonspection *f*. ◆ **circumspectly** *adv* avec circonspection.

circumstance ['sɜːkəmstəns] *n* circonstance *f*. **in the present ~s** dans les circonstances actuelles, vu l'état des choses; **under no ~s** en aucun cas; *(financial)* **~s** situation financière; **in easy/poor ~s** dans l'aisance/la gêne. ◆ **circumstantial** *adj report, statement* circonstancié; **circumstantial evidence** preuve indirecte. ◆ **circumstantiate** *vt* confirmer en donnant des détails sur.

circus ['sɜːkəs] *n (animals etc)* cirque *m*; *(in town)* rond-point *m*.

cirrhosis [sɪ'rəʊsɪs] *n* cirrhose *f*.

cissy * ['sɪsɪ] *n* = **sissy**.

cistern ['sɪstən] *n* citerne *f*; *[WC]* chasse *f* d'eau.

citadel ['sɪtədl] *n* citadelle *f*.

cite [saɪt] *vt* citer. **to ~ as an example** citer en exemple; *(Jur)* **to ~ sb to appear** citer qn. ◆ **citation** *n* citation *f*.

citizen ['sɪtɪzn] *n* citoyen(ne) *m(f)*; *[town]* habitant(e) *m(f)*. **C~'s Band Radio** *fréquence réservée au public*. ◆ **citizenship** *n* citoyenneté *f*.

citrus ['sɪtr(ə)s] *n* citrus *mpl*. **~ fruits** agrumes *mpl*. ◆ **citric** *adj* citrique.

city ['sɪtɪ] **1** *n* (grande) ville *f*. *[London]* **the C~** la Cité (de Londres); **he's (something) in the C~ *** il est dans les affaires. **2** *adj (Press) editor, page, news* financier. **~ centre** centre *m* (de la) ville; **~ dweller** citadin(e) *m(f)*; **the ~ fathers** les élus *mpl* locaux; *(US)* **~ hall** hôtel *m* de ville; **~ planner** urbaniste *mf*; **~ planning** urbanisme *m*; **~ slicker *** citadin mielleux et habile.

civic ['sɪvɪk] *adj rights, virtues* civique; *guard, authorities* municipal. **~ centre** centre administratif (municipal). ◆ **civics** *n* instruction *f* civique.

civil ['sɪvl] *adj* (**a**) *law, war, marriage* civil. **the American C~ War** la guerre de Sécession; **~ commotion** émeute *f*; **~ defence** défense passive; **~ disobedience** résistance passive *(à la loi)*; **~ engineer** ingénieur *m* des travaux publics; **~ engineering** travaux publics; **~ liberties** libertés *fpl* civiques; **~ rights movement** campagne *f* pour les droits *mpl* civiques; **~ servant** fonctionnaire *mf*; **~ service** fonction *f* publique, administration *f*. (**b**) *(polite)* civil, poli. ◆ **civilian** *n, adj* civil(e) *m(f)* *(opposé à militaire)*. ◆ **civility** *n* civilité *f*. ◆ **civilization** *n* civilisation *f*. ◆ **civilize** *vt* civiliser. ◆ **civilized** *adj* civilisé; **to become ~ized** se civiliser. ◆ **civilly** *adv* poliment.

clad [klæd] *adj* habillé (*in* de).

claim [kleɪm] **1** *vt property, prize, right* revendiquer (*from* à); *diplomatic immunity, damages* réclamer (*from* à); *attention* demander, solliciter; *(maintain)* prétendre (*that* que). **to ~ acquaintance with sb** prétendre connaître qn.
2 *n* revendication *f*, réclamation *f*; *(Insurance)* demande *f* d'indemnité; *(Min etc)* concession *f*. **to lay ~ to** prétendre à; **there are many ~s on my time** mon temps est très pris; **there are many ~s on my purse** on fait beaucoup appel à ma bourse; **that's a big ~ to make!** la prétention est de taille!; **his ~ that he acted legally** son affirmation d'avoir agi d'une manière licite; *(Insurance)* **the ~s were all paid** les dommages ont été intégralement payés; *(Ind)* **a ~ for an extra £5 per week** une demande d'augmentation de 5 livres par semaine; **expenses ~** note *f* de frais. **his ~ to the throne** son titre *or* droit à la couronne.
3 *adj*: **~ form** *(gen)* formulaire *m* de demande; *(for expenses)* feuille *f* de note de frais.
◆ **claimant** *n [throne]* prétendant(e) *m(f)* (*to* à); *[social benefits]* demandeur *m*, -eresse *f*.

clairvoyant(e) [klɛə'vɔɪənt] **1** *n* voyant(e) *m(f)*. **2** *adj* doué de seconde vue. ◆ **clairvoyance** *n* voyance *f*.

clam [klæm] *n* palourde *f*. **~ chowder** soupe *f* épaisse de palourdes. ◆ **clam up *** *vi* se taire. **he ~med up on me** il ne m'a plus dit un mot (là-dessus).

clamber ['klæmbəʳ] *vi* grimper (avec difficulté). **to ~ over a wall** escalader un mur.

clammy ['klæmɪ] *adj hand* moite (et froid); *wall* suintant; *climate* humide.

clamour, *(US)* **clamor** ['klæməʳ] **1** *n (shouts)* clameurs *fpl*, vociférations *fpl*; *(demands)* revendications bruyantes. **2** *vi*: **to ~ for sth/sb** réclamer qch/qn à grands cris. ◆ **clamorous** *adj crowd* vociférant; *demand* impérieux.

clamp [klæmp] **1** *n (gen)* attache *f*; *(bigger)* crampon *m*; *(Med)* clamp *m*; *(Carpentry)* valet *m* d'établi; *[stone, china]* agrafe *f*; *(Elec)* serre-fils *m inv*; *(on car wheel)* sabot *m* (de Denver). **2** *vt* fixer (*onto* à); *stones, china* agrafer; *carwheel* mettre un sabot (de Denver) à. ◆ **clamp down on *** *vt fus person* serrer la vis à *; *expenditure* mettre un frein à; *information* supprimer; *the press, opposition* bâillonner. ◆ **clampdown** *n (gen)* répression *f* (*on sth* de qch, *on sb* contre qn); **a ~down on arms sales** un renforcement des restrictions sur les ventes d'armes.

clan [klæn] *n* clan *m*. ◆ **clannish** *adj group* fermé; *person* qui a l'esprit de clique.

clandestine [klæn'destɪn] *adj* clandestin.

clang [klæŋ] **1** *n* son *m or (louder)* fracas *m* métallique. **2** *vi* émettre un son métallique. **the gate ~ed shut** la grille s'est refermée bruyamment. ◆ **clanger ⁑** *n* gaffe *f*. ◆ **clangorous** *adj noise* métallique. ◆ **clangour**, *(US)* **clangor** *n* fracas *m* métallique.

clank [klæŋk] **1** *n* cliquetis *m*. **2** *vi* cliqueter.

clap [klæp] **1** *n [hands]* battement *m*; *(action)* tape *f*; *(applause)* applaudissements *mpl*. **a ~ on the back**

une tape dans le dos; **a ~ of thunder** un coup de tonnerre. **2** *vt* (**a**) frapper, taper; *dog* donner des tapes amicales à; *(applaud)* applaudir. **to ~ one's hands** battre des mains; **to ~ sb on the back** donner à qn une tape dans le dos; **he ~ped his hand over my mouth** il a mis sa main sur ma bouche. (**b**) mettre, jeter. **to ~ sb into prison** mettre qn en prison; **to ~ eyes on** voir. **3** *vi* applaudir. ◆ **clap on** *vt sep one's hat* enfoncer sur sa tête. **to ~ on the brakes** freiner brusquement. ◆ **clapped-out** * *adj person, car* crevé *; *horse* fourbu. ◆ **clapping** *n* applaudissements *mpl*. ◆ **claptrap** * *n* boniment * *m*.

claret ['klærət] *n* bordeaux *m* (rouge).

clarify ['klærɪfaɪ] *vt* clarifier. ◆ **clarification** *n* clarification *f*.

clarinet [ˌklærɪ'net] *n* clarinette *f*. ◆ **clarinettist** *n* clarinettiste *mf*.

clarity ['klærɪtɪ] *n* clarté *f*, précision *f*.

clash [klæʃ] **1** *vi [metallic objects]* s'entrechoquer; *[cymbals]* résonner; *[armies]* se heurter; *[interests, personalities]* être incompatible (*with* avec); *[colours]* jurer (*with* avec); *[two events, invitations etc]* tomber en même temps (*or* le même jour *etc*). **they ~ over the question of...** ils sont en désaccord total en ce qui concerne...; **the dates ~** les deux événements tombent le même jour. **2** *vt metallic objects* heurter bruyamment; *cymbals* faire résonner; *(Aut) gears* faire grincer. **3** *n (sound)* choc *m or* fracas *m* métallique; *[armies, weapons]* heurt *m*; *(between people, parties)* accrochage *m*; *(with police, troops)* échauffourée *f*; *[interests]* conflit *m*; *[colours]* discordance *f*; *[dates, events, invitations]* coïncidence *f* (fâcheuse). **a ~ with the police** une échauffourée avec la police; **a ~ of personalities** une incompatibilité de caractères.

clasp [klɑːsp] **1** *n (gen)* fermoir *m*; *[belt]* boucle *f*. **2** *adj*: **~ knife** grand couteau *m* pliant. **3** *vt* étreindre, serrer; *sb's hand* serrer. **to ~ one's hands (together)** joindre les mains; **to ~ sb in one's arms** serrer qn dans ses bras.

class [klɑːs] **1** *n (gen)* classe *f*. **~ of ship** type *m* de vaisseau; **they are just not in the same ~** il n'y a pas de comparaison (possible) entre eux; **in a ~ by itself** hors concours; **a good ~ (of) hotel** un très bon hôtel; **first ~ honours in history** ≃ licence *f* d'histoire avec mention très bien; **to give/attend a ~** faire/suivre un cours; **the French ~** la classe *or* le cours de français; **an evening ~** un cours du soir; *(US)* **the ~ of 1970** la promotion de 1970; **to have ~** avoir de la classe. **2** *vt* classer, classifier. **~ed as** classé comme. **3** *adj*: **~ distinction** distinction sociale; **~ war(fare)** lutte *f* des classes. ◆ **class-conscious** *adj* conscient des distinctions sociales; *(snobbish)* snob *inv*. ◆ **classmate** *n* camarade *mf* de classe. ◆ **classroom** *n* salle *f* de classe. ◆ **classy** * *adj object* chic *inv*; *person* ultra-chic *inv*.

classic ['klæsɪk] **1** *adj* classique. **it was ~!** * c'était le coup classique! * **2** *n (author, work)* classique *m*; *(Racing)* classique *f*. **to study ~s** étudier les humanités *fpl*; **a ~ of its kind** un classique du genre. ◆ **classical** *adj* classique; **~al scholar** humaniste *mf*. ◆ **classicism** *n* classicisme *m*.

classify ['klæsɪfaɪ] *vt* classifier. **classified advertisement** petite annonce *f*; **classified information** renseignements *mpl* secrets. ◆ **classifiable** *adj* qu'on peut classifier. ◆ **classification** *n* classification *f*.

clatter ['klætəʳ] **1** *n* cliquetis *m*; *(louder)* fracas *m*. **the ~ of cutlery** le bruit de couverts entrechoqués. **2** *vi [keys, typewriter]* cliqueter; *[large falling object, cymbals]* résonner. **to ~ in/out** entrer/sortir bruyamment. **3** *vt* entrechoquer bruyamment.

clause [klɔːz] *n (Gram)* proposition *f*; *[contract, law, treaty]* clause *f*; *[will]* disposition *f*.

claustrophobia [ˌklɔːstrə'fəʊbɪə] *n* claustrophobie *f*. ◆ **claustrophobic** *adj person* claustrophobe; *feeling* de claustrophobie; *situation, atmosphere* claustrophobique.

claw [klɔː] **1** *n [cat, lion, small bird etc]* griffe *f*; *[bird of prey]* serre *f*; *[lobster etc]* pince *f*. **2** *vt (scratch)* griffer; *(rip)* déchirer avec ses griffes *or* ses serres; *(clutch)* agripper. ◆ **claw-hammer** *n* marteau *m* à pied-de-biche.

clay [kleɪ] **1** *n* argile *f*. **2** *adj*: **~ pigeon shooting** ball-trap *m*; **~ pipe** pipe *f* en terre.

clean [kliːn] **1** *adj (gen)* propre; *sheet of paper* blanc, neuf; *reputation, shape, line, cut, stroke* net; *joke, story* qui n'a rien de choquant; *contest, game* loyal. **to wipe sth ~** essuyer qch; **keep it ~** ne le salissez pas; *(fig)* pas d'inconvenances!; **as ~ as a new pin** propre comme un sou neuf; **to make a ~ breast of it** dire ce qu'on a sur la conscience; **to make a ~ sweep** faire table rase (*of* de); **~ living** une vie saine; *(Jur)* **a ~ record** un casier judiciaire vierge; **a ~ driving licence** un permis de conduire où n'est portée aucune contravention; **the doctor gave him a ~ bill of health** le médecin l'a trouvé en parfait état de santé; **he's ~** * *(carrying nothing incriminating)* il n'a rien sur lui; *(innocent)* il n'a rien fait.

2 *adv* complètement, tout à fait. **he got ~ away** il a décampé sans laisser de traces; **to cut ~ through sth** couper qch de part en part; **he jumped ~ over the fence** il a sauté la barrière sans la toucher; **the car went ~ through the hedge** la voiture est carrément passée à travers la haie; **to break off ~** casser net; **to come ~ about sth** ‡ tout dire sur qch.

3 *n*: **to give sth a good ~** bien nettoyer qch.

4 *vt clothes, room* nettoyer; *vegetables* laver; *blackboard* essuyer. **to ~ one's teeth** se brosser les dents; **to ~ one's nails** se nettoyer les ongles; **to ~ the windows** faire les vitres.

◆ **clean off** *vt sep (from blackboard)* essuyer; *(from floor, wall)* enlever. ◆ **clean out** *vt sep* nettoyer à fond; *(*: leave penniless etc)* ruiner, nettoyer *. ◆ **clean up** **1** *vi* tout nettoyer; *(tidy)* remettre en ordre; *(*: make profit)* faire son beurre * (*on a deal* dans une affaire). **2** *vt sep room* nettoyer; *(fig) a town, television etc* épurer. **to ~ o.s. up** se laver, se débarbouiller.

◆ **clean-cut** *adj* bien délimité, net. ◆ **cleaner** *n (Comm)* teinturier *m*, -ière *f*; *(charwoman)* femme *f* de ménage; *(man: in office etc)* agent *m* de service; *(device)* appareil *m* de nettoyage; *(household ~er)* produit *m* d'entretien; *(stain-remover)* détachant *m*; **the ~er's shop** la teinturerie. ◆ **cleaning** *n* nettoyage *m*; *(housework)* ménage *m*; **~ing fluid** détachant *m*; **~ing woman** femme *f* de ménage. ◆ **clean-limbed** *adj* bien proportionné. ◆ **cleanliness** ['klenlɪnɪs] *n* (habitude *f* de la) propreté *f*. ◆ **clean-living** *adj* honnête. ◆ **cleanly** ['kliːnlɪ] **1** *adv* proprement, nettement ; **2** ['klenlɪ] *adj* propre. ◆ **cleanness** *n* propreté *f*. ◆ **clean-out** *n* nettoyage *m* à fond. ◆ **clean-shaven** *adj*: **to be ~-shaven** n'avoir ni barbe ni moustache. ◆ **clean-up** *n [room]* nettoyage *m*; *[person]* débarbouillage *m*.

cleanse [klenz] *vt* nettoyer; *ditch, drain etc* curer; *(fig)* laver (*of* de); *soul etc* purifier. ◆ **cleanser** *n (detergent)* détergent *m*; *(for complexion)* démaquillant *m*. ◆ **cleansing** **1** *adj*: **cleansing cream** crème *f* démaquillante; **cleansing department** service *m* de voirie ; **2** *n* nettoyage *m*.

clear [klɪəʳ] **1** *adj* (**a**) *piece of glass, plastic* transparent; *water, lake, stream* limpide; *sky, weather, complexion* clair; *photograph, outline* net; *honey* liquide; *majority, profit* net. **on a ~ day** par temps clair; **~ red** rouge vif; **~ soup** bouillon *m*; **he left with a ~ conscience** il est parti la conscience tranquille. (**b**) *sound* clair; *words* distinct. **you're not very ~**

je ne vous entends pas bien. (**c**) *explanation, account, style* clair; *reasoning* clair, lucide; *intelligence* pénétrant; *proof, sign, consequence, motive* évident, clair. ~ **thinker** esprit *m* lucide; **I want to be quite ~ on this point** *(understand clearly)* je veux savoir exactement ce qu'il en est; *(explain unambiguously)* je veux bien me faire comprendre; **a ~ case of murder** un cas d'assassinat manifeste; **to make o.s. ~** se faire bien comprendre; **to make it ~ to sb that** bien faire comprendre à qn que; **I wish to make it ~ that** je tiens à préciser que; **as ~ as day** clair comme le jour; **it is ~ to me that** il me paraît hors de doute que. (**d**) *road, path* libre; *route* sans obstacles. **all ~!** *(Mil)* fin d'alerte!; **we had a ~ view** rien ne gênait la vue; **we were ~ of the town** nous étions hors de l'agglomération; **~ of debts** libre de dettes; **three ~ days** trois jours entiers.

2 *n*: **to send a message in ~** envoyer un message en clair; **in the ~ *** *(above suspicion)* au-dessus de tout soupçon; *(no longer suspected)* blanchi de tout soupçon; *(out of danger)* hors de danger.

3 *adv* (**a**) **loud and ~** très distinctement. (**b**) entièrement, complètement. **the thief got ~ away** le voleur a disparu sans laisser de traces. (**c**) **~ of** à l'écart de, à distance de; **to keep ~ of sth/sb** éviter qch/qn; **to stand ~** s'écarter; **stand ~ of the doors!** dégagez les portes!; **to get ~ of** *(go away from)* s'éloigner *or* s'écarter de; *(rid o.s. of)* se débarrasser de.

4 *vt* (**a**) *liquid* clarifier; *blood* dépurer; *bowels* purger; *situation, account* éclaircir. **to ~ the air** aérer; *(fig)* détendre l'atmosphère; **to ~ one's throat** s'éclaircir la voix; **to ~ one's head** se dégager le cerveau. (**b**) *canal, path, road, railway line* dégager, déblayer; *pipe* déboucher; *land* défricher. **to ~ the table** débarrasser la table; *(fig)* **to ~ the decks** tout déblayer; **to ~ sth of rubbish** déblayer qch; **to ~ the way for** faire place à; *(fig)* ouvrir la voie à; **to ~ a way through** ouvrir un passage à travers; **to ~ a room** *(of people)* faire évacuer une salle; *(of things)* débarrasser une salle; *(Jur)* **to ~ the court** faire évacuer la salle; *(Ftbl)* **to ~ the ball** dégager le ballon. (**c**) *(find innocent etc) person* disculper (*of* de). **to ~ o.s.** se disculper; **to ~ sb of suspicion** laver qn de tout soupçon; **you will have to be ~ed by our security department** il faudra que nos services de sécurité donnent *(subj)* le feu vert en ce qui vous concerne; **we've ~ed it with him** nous avons obtenu son accord. (**d**) *hedge, fence* franchir, sauter; *obstacle, rocks* éviter; *harbour* quitter. **he ~ed the gate by 10 cm** il a sauté la barrière avec 10 cm de marge; **raise the car till the wheel ~s the ground** soulevez la voiture jusqu'à ce que la roue ne touche *(subj)* plus le sol. (**e**) *cheque* compenser; *account, goods* liquider; *debt* s'acquitter de; *profit* gagner net; *(Customs) goods* dédouaner; *ship* expédier; *one's conscience* décharger; *doubts* dissiper. *(Comm)* **'half price to ~'** 'solde à moitié prix pour liquider'; **I've ~ed £100 on this business** cette affaire m'a rapporté 100 livres net.

5 *vi [weather]* s'éclaircir; *[sky]* se dégager; *[fog]* se dissiper; *[face, expression]* s'éclairer.

◆ **clear away** **1** *vi [mist etc]* se dissiper; *(clear the table)* desservir. **2** *vt sep* enlever. ◆ **clear off** **1** *vi* (*) filer *, décamper. **2** *vt sep things on desk* enlever; *debts* s'acquitter de; *stock, goods* liquider. ◆ **clear out** **1** *vi* (*) = **clear off 1**. **2** *vt sep cupboard* vider; *room* débarrasser; *unwanted objects* enlever. **he ~ed everyone out of the room** il a fait évacuer la pièce. ◆ **clear up** **1** *vi (tidy)* ranger; *[weather]* se lever. **2** *vt sep mystery, matter* éclaircir; *room, clothes* ranger. **to ~ up the mess** *(lit)* tout nettoyer; *(fig)* tout arranger.

◆ **clearance** **1** *n [road, path, land]* déblaiement *m*; *[room, court]* évacuation *f*; *[cupboard, passage]* dégagement *m*; *[accused]* disculpation *f*; *[litter, objects, rubbish]* enlèvement *m*; *[cheque]* compensation *f*; *(Customs)* dédouanement *m*; *(permission etc)* autorisation *f*; **sent to the Foreign Office for ~ance** soumis au ministère des Affaires étrangères pour contrôle; *(Aviat)* **~ance for takeoff** autorisation de décoller; **2 metre ~ance** espace *m* de 2 mètres ; **2** *adj*: **~ance sale** soldes *mpl*. ◆ **clearcut** *adj outline* net; *attitude, situation* précis. ◆ **clearheaded** *adj* lucide, perspicace. ◆ **clearing** **1** *n (in forest)* clairière *f*; *[liquid]* clarification *f*; *[bowels]* purge *f*; *[rubbish, objects]* enlèvement *m*; *[land]* défrichement *m*; *[pipe etc]* débouchage *m*; *[road]* dégagement *m* ; **2** *adj*: **~ing bank** banque *f* (appartenant à une chambre de compensation); **~ing house** *(Banking)* chambre *f* de compensation; *(for documents etc)* bureau *m* central. ◆ **clearly** *adv (distinctly) see, state* clairement; *hear* distinctement; *understand* bien; *(obviously)* manifestement; **~ly visible** bien visible. ◆ **clearness** *n [air, glass]* transparence *f*; *[liquid]* limpidité *f*; *[sound, sight, print, thought etc]* clarté *f*, netteté *f*. ◆ **clear-sighted** *adj (fig)* clairvoyant. ◆ **clearway** *n* route *f* à stationnement interdit.

cleave [kliːv] *pret* **cleft** *or* **clove,** *ptp* **cleft** *or* **cloven** *vt* fendre. **in a cleft stick** dans une impasse; **cleft palate** palais *m* fendu. ◆ **cleavage** *n*: **a dress which showed her cleavage** * une robe qui laissait voir la naissance des seins. ◆ **cleaver** *n* couperet *m*.

clef [klef] *n (Mus)* clef *f*.

cleft [kleft] *n (in rock)* crevasse *f (V also* **cleave***)*.

clematis ['klemətɪs] *n* clématite *f*.

clement ['klemənt] *adj* clément. ◆ **clemency** *n* clémence *f*.

clench [klen(t)ʃ] *vt object* serrer dans ses mains; *fists, teeth* serrer.

clergy ['klɜːdʒɪ] *collective n* clergé *m*. ◆ **clergyman** *n* ecclésiastique *m*.

clerical ['klerɪk(ə)l] *adj* (**a**) *(Rel)* clérical; *collar* de pasteur. (**b**) *(Comm etc) job* d'employé; *work, worker* de bureau. ~ **error** erreur *f* d'écriture.

clerk [klɑːk, *(US)* klɜːrk] *n* employé(e) *m(f) (de bureau, de commerce)*, commis *m*; *(US: shop assistant)* vendeur *m*, -euse *f*. **bank ~** employé(e) de banque; *(in hotel)* **desk ~** réceptionniste *mf*; *(Jur)* **C~ of the Court** greffier *m* (du tribunal); **~ of works** conducteur *m* de travaux.

clever ['klevəʳ] *adj person* intelligent; *(smart)* astucieux; *book* intelligemment écrit; *play, film* intelligemment fait; *machine, invention, trick, explanation* ingénieux; *idea, joke, story* astucieux; *(skilful)* habile (*at doing* à faire). **to be ~ at French** être fort en français; **~ with one's hands** adroit de ses mains; **he's very ~ with cars** il s'y connaît en voitures; **he was too ~ for me** il m'a eu *; **~ Dick** petit malin *m*. ◆ **cleverly** *adv* intelligemment; astucieusement; ingénieusement; habilement. ◆ **cleverness** *n* intelligence *f*; astuce *f*; ingéniosité *f*; habileté *f* (*at* à).

clew [kluː] *n (US)* = **clue.**

click [klɪk] **1** *n* déclic *m*, petit bruit sec; *[tongue]* claquement *m*; *[wheel]* cliquet *m*. **2** *vi [lid, device]* faire un bruit sec; *[heels, typewriter]* cliqueter. **the door ~ed shut** la porte s'est refermée avec un déclic; *(fig)* **suddenly it ~ed** * j'ai compris tout à coup; *(fig)* **the product ~ed** * le produit a bien marché. **3** *vt*: **to ~ one's heels** claquer des talons; **to ~ one's tongue** faire claquer sa langue. ◆ **clicking** *n* cliquetis *m*.

client ['klaɪənt] *n* client(e) *m(f)*. ◆ **clientele** *n* clientèle *f*.

cliff [klɪf] *n [seashore]* falaise *f*; *[mountains]* escarpement *m*. ◆ **cliff-hanger** * *n* récit *m* (*or* situation *f etc*) à suspense.

climate ['klaɪmɪt] *n* climat *m*. **the ~ of opinion** les courants *mpl* de l'opinion. ◆ **climatic** *adj* climatique. ◆ **climatology** *n* climatologie *f*.

climax ['klaɪmæks] *n* point *m* culminant; *[career etc]* apogée *m*; *(sexual)* orgasme *m*. **to bring sth to/to come to a ~** porter qch à/atteindre son point culminant; **to work up to a ~** *[story, events]* tendre vers son point culminant; *[speaker]* amener le point culminant.

climb [klaɪm] **1** *vt* (**~ up**) *stairs, steps, slope* monter; *hill* grimper; *tree, ladder* monter sur *or* à; *rope* monter à; *cliff, wall* escalader; *mountain* faire l'ascension de. **2** *vi* (**a**) (*~* **up**: *gen)* monter; *[persons, plants]* grimper; *[road, sun]* monter; *[aircraft, rocket]* monter, prendre de l'altitude. (**b**) **to ~ down sth** descendre de qch; **to ~ over sth** escalader qch; **to ~ into an aircraft** monter à bord d'un avion; **to ~ out of a hole** se hisser hors d'un trou; *(Sport)* **to go ~ing** faire de l'alpinisme; *(rock-~ing)* faire de la varappe. **3** *n [hill]* montée *f*, côte *f* ; *(Alpinism, Aviat)* ascension *f*. ◆ **climb down** *vi* descendre; *(fig)* en rabattre.
◆ **climber** *n* grimpeur *m*, -euse *f*; *(mountaineer)* alpiniste *mf*; *(also* **rock-~er***)* varappeur *m*, -euse *f*; *(social etc ~er)* arriviste *mf*; *(plant)* plante *f* grimpante. ◆ **climbing** *n (Sport)* alpinisme *m*; *(also* **rock- ~ing***)* varappe *f*; **~ing frame** cage *f* à poules.

clinch [klɪntʃ] **1** *vt argument* consolider, confirmer; *bargain, deal* conclure. **that ~es it** comme ça c'est réglé. **2** *n (embrace)* **in a ~** ** enlacés.

cling [klɪŋ] *pret, ptp* **clung** *vi* (**a**) *(hold tight)* **to ~ to** *rope, sb's hand* se cramponner à; *opinion* maintenir envers et contre tout; *belief* se raccrocher à; **to ~ to one another** *(lovingly)* se tenir étroitement enlacés; *(fearfully)* se cramponner l'un à l'autre. (**b**) *(stick)* coller (*to* à). ◆ **clingfilm** *n* scellofrais *m* ®. ◆ **clinging** *adj garment, person* collant; *odour* tenace.

clinic ['klɪnɪk] *n (nursing home; teaching session)* clinique *f*; *[G.P., hospital]* service *m* de consultation. ◆ **clinical** *adj (Med)* clinique; *thermometer* médical; *(fig) attitude, approach* objectif.

clink [klɪŋk] **1** *vt* faire tinter. **to ~ glasses with sb** trinquer avec qn. **2** *vi* tinter. **3** *n* tintement *m*.

clip[1] [klɪp] *n (paper ~)* trombone *m*; *(bulldog ~)* pince *f* à dessin; *(for tube)* collier *m*; *(cartridge ~)* chargeur *m*; *(brooch)* clip *m*. ◆ **clip on** *vt sep brooch* fixer (*to* sur); *document* attacher. ◆ **clip together** *vt sep* attacher. ◆ **clipboard** *n* écritoire *f* (panneau).

clip[2] [klɪp] **1** *vt* (**a**) *(cut: gen)* couper; *hedge* tailler; *sheep, dog* tondre; *ticket* poinçonner; *article from newspaper* découper. *(fig)* **to ~ sb's wings** rogner les ailes à qn; *(fig)* **in a ~ped voice** en détachant bien les syllabes. (**b**) *(*: hit)* flanquer une taloche à *.
2 *n (Cine)* extrait *m*.
◆ **clipper** *n (Aviat, Naut)* clipper *m*. ◆ **clippers** *npl (for hair)* tondeuse *f*; *(for hedge)* sécateur *m*; *(for nails)* pince *f* à ongles. ◆ **clipping** *n [newspaper etc]* coupure *f* de presse.

clique [kli:k] *n* clique *f*, coterie *f*. ◆ **cliquey** *or* ◆ **cliquish** *adj* qui a l'esprit de clique.

cloak [kləʊk] **1** *n* grande cape. **as a ~ for sth** pour cacher qch. **2** *vt (fig)* masquer, cacher. **~ed with mystery** empreint de mystère. ◆ **cloak-and-dagger** *adj* clandestin, mystérieux. ◆ **cloakroom** *n [coats etc]* vestiaire *m*; *(W.C.) (public)* toilettes *fpl*; *(in house)* cabinets *mpl*; **~room ticket** numéro *m* de vestiaire.

clock [klɒk] **1** *n* (**a**) *(large)* horloge *f*; *(smaller)* pendule *f*. **by the church ~** à l'horloge *or* au clocher de l'église; **2 hours by the ~** 2 heures d'horloge; **round the ~** vingt-quatre heures d'affilée; **to work against the ~** travailler contre la montre. (**b**) *[taxi]* compteur *m*. *(Aut)* **50,000 miles on the ~** 50 000 milles au compteur. **2** *vt runner* chronométrer. **he ~ed 4 minutes for the mile** il a fait le mille en 4 minutes. **3** *vi*: **to ~ in** *or* **on** pointer (à l'arrivée); **to ~ out** *or* **off** pointer (à la sortie).
◆ **clock up** *vt sep work, distance* faire.
◆ **clock-golf** *n* jeu *m* de l'horloge. ◆ **clock-maker** *n* horloger *m*, -ère *f*. ◆ **clock-radio** *n* radio-réveil *m*. ◆ **clock-tower** *n* clocher *m*.
◆ **clock-watcher** *n*: **he's a terrible ~-watcher** il ne fait que guetter l'heure de sortie. ◆ **clockwise** *adv, adj* dans le sens des aiguilles d'une montre. ◆ **clockwork** **1** *n*: **to go like ~work** aller comme sur des roulettes ; **2** *adj toy* mécanique.

clog [klɒg] **1** *n* sabot *m (chaussure)*. **2** *vt* (**~ up**) *pipe* boucher; *wheel, passage* bloquer. **3** *vi* (**~ up**) se boucher.

cloister ['klɔɪstər] *n* cloître *m*. ◆ **cloistered** *adj*: **~ed life** vie *f* monacale.

clone [kləʊn] **1** *n* clone *m*. **2** *vt* cloner. ◆ **cloning** *n* clonage *m*.

close[1] [kləʊs] **1** *adj* (**a**) *(near) date, relative* proche; *friend* intime; *resemblance* exact, fidèle; *connection* étroit; *contact* direct; *encounter* face à face. **house ~ to the shops** maison près *or* proche des magasins; **sit here ~ to me** asseyez-vous ici près de moi; **~ to tears** au bord des larmes; **at ~ quarters** tout près; **to have a ~ call * or shave *** l'échapper belle, y échapper de justesse; **that was ~!** on l'a échappé belle! (**b**) *handwriting, rank, election, reasoning* serré; *grain* fin; *account* proche de la vérité; *argument* précis; *control, surveillance* étroit; *questioning, investigation* serré, minutieux; *examination, study* attentif; *attention* soutenu; *translation* fidèle; *silence* impénétrable; *(secretive) person* peu communicatif. **to keep a ~ watch on** surveiller de près; **~ combat** corps à corps *m*; **in ~ confinement** en détention surveillée; **she was very ~ to her brother** *(in age)* son frère et elle étaient d'âges très rapprochés; *(in friendship)* elle était très proche de son frère. (**c**) *(airless) room* mal aéré; *weather* lourd, étouffant. **it's very ~ in here** il n'y a pas d'air ici; **it's ~ today** il fait lourd aujourd'hui. (**d**) *(Sport)* **~ season** fermeture *f* de la chasse (*or* de la pêche).
2 *adv* étroitement, de près. **to hold sb ~** serrer qn dans ses bras; **~ by** tout près, tout proche; **~ by, ~ to, ~ up(on)** tout près de; **~ to the ground** très bas, au ras du sol; **~ by us** tout à côté de nous; **~ at hand** tout près; **he followed ~ behind me** il me suivait de près; **~ together** serrés les uns contre les autres; **to come ~r together** se rapprocher.
3 *n [cathedral]* enceinte *f*.
◆ **close-cropped** *adj* coupé ras. ◆ **close-fisted** *adj* grippe-sou *inv*. ◆ **close-fitting** *adj* ajusté. ◆ **close-knit** *adj (fig)* très uni. ◆ **closely** *adv guard* étroitement; *grasp* en serrant fort; *resemble* beaucoup; *watch, follow, study* de près; *listen* attentivement; *connected* étroitement; **they are ~ly related** ils sont proches parents. ◆ **close-mouthed** *adj* taciturne. ◆ **closeness** *n [weave]* texture *f* serrée; *[friendship]* intimité *f*; *[resemblance etc]* fidélité *f*; *[pursuers]* proximité *f*; *[weather, atmosphere]* lourdeur *f*; *[room]* manque *m* d'air. ◆ **close-run** *adj*: **~-run race** course très serrée. ◆ **close-set** *adj eyes* rapprochés. ◆ **closeshaven** *adj* rasé de près. ◆ **close-up** *n* gros plan *m*; **in ~-up** en gros plan.

close[2] [kləʊz] **1** *n (end)* fin *f*. **to come to a ~** se terminer; **to draw to a ~** tirer à sa fin; **to bring sth to a ~** mettre fin à qch. **2** *vt* (**a**) *(shut: gen)* fermer; *pipe, opening* boucher; *road* barrer. **~d to traffic** interdit à la circulation; **the shop is ~d** le magasin est fermé; **the shop is ~d on Sundays** le magasin ferme le dimanche; **to ~ a gap between 2 objects** réduire l'intervalle qui sépare 2 objets; **to ~ ranks** serrer les rangs. (**b**) *(end) proceedings, discussion* terminer, mettre fin à; *account* arrêter, clore; *bargain* conclure. **to ~ the meeting** lever la séance. **3** *vi* (**a**) *[door, box, lid]* fermer, se fermer; *[museum, shop]* fermer; *[eyes]* se fermer. **the door ~d** la porte s'est fermée; **the door ~s badly** la porte ferme mal; **the shop ~s on Sundays** le magasin ferme le dimanche; **his fingers ~d around the pencil** ses doigts se sont refermés sur le crayon; **to ~ with sb** se prendre corps à corps avec qn. (**b**) *(end) [meeting etc]* se terminer, prendre fin; *[speaker etc]* terminer. *(St Ex)* **shares ~d at 120p** les actions étaient cotées à 120 pence en clôture.

◆ **close down** **1** *vi [business, shop]* fermer (définitivement); *(Rad, TV)* terminer les émissions. **2** *vt sep* fermer (définitivement). ◆ **close in** **1** *vi [hunters etc]* se rapprocher; *[evening, night]* tomber ; *[darkness, fog]* descendre. **the days are closing in** les jours raccourcissent; **to ~ in on sb** cerner qn. **2** *vt sep area* clôturer. ◆ **close on** *vt fus competitor, goal* rattraper. ◆ **close up** **1** *vi [people in line etc]* se rapprocher; *[wound]* se refermer. **2** *vt sep house, shop* fermer (complètement); *pipe, opening* boucher; *wound* refermer.

◆ **closed** *adj door, eyes* fermé; *road* barré; *pipe, opening etc* bouché; **'~d'** *(gen)* 'fermé'; *(Theat)* 'relâche'; **maths are a ~d book to me** je suis complètement rebelle aux maths; **~d-circuit television** télévision *f* en circuit fermé; *(Ind)* **~d shop** atelier *m* qui n'admet que des travailleurs syndiqués; **~d-shop policy** exclusion *f* des travailleurs non syndiqués. ◆ **close-down** *n [shop etc]* fermeture *f* (définitive); *(Rad, TV)* fin *f* des émissions. ◆ **closing** **1** *n (gen)* fermeture *f*; *[meeting]* clôture *f* ; **2** *adj* final, dernier; **closing speech** discours *m* de clôture; **when is closing time?** à quelle heure est-ce qu'on ferme?; *(St Ex)* **closing price** cours *m* en clôture. ◆ **closure** *n* fermeture *f*; *(Parl)* **to move the closure** demander la clôture.

closet ['klɒzɪt] **1** *n (cupboard)* armoire *f*, placard *m*; *(for clothes)* penderie *f*; *(room)* cabinet *m*; *(W.C.)* cabinets *mpl*. **to come out of the ~** * sortir de l'anonymat. **2** *vt*: **he was ~ed with his father for several hours** son père et lui sont restés plusieurs heures enfermés à discuter.

clot [klɒt] **1** *n* caillot *m*; *(*: fool)* imbécile *mf*. **a ~ on the brain/in the lung** une embolie cérébrale/pulmonaire; **a ~ in the leg** une thrombose. **2** *vti* coaguler. **~ted cream** crème *f* en grumeaux.

cloth [klɒθ] **1** *n* (**a**) *(material)* tissu *m*, étoffe *f*; *[linen, cotton]* toile *f*; *[wool]* drap *m*; *(Bookbinding, Naut)* toile *f*. (**b**) *(tablecloth)* nappe *f*; *(duster)* chiffon *m*; *(dishcloth)* torchon *m*. **2** *adj*: **~ cap** casquette *f* (d'ouvrier).

clothe [kləʊð] *vt* habiller, vêtir (*in, with* de). ◆ **clothes** **1** *npl* vêtements *mpl*; *(bed ~s)* draps *mpl* et couvertures *fpl*; **with one's ~s on** tout habillé; **with one's ~s off** déshabillé, tout nu; **to put on one's ~s** s'habiller; **to take off one's ~s** se déshabiller ; **2** *adj*: **~s basket** panier *m* à linge; **~s brush** brosse *f* à habits; **~s dryer** séchoir *m*, sèche-linge *m inv*; **~s hanger** cintre *m*; **~s horse** séchoir *m* à linge pliant; **~s line** corde *f* à linge; **~s peg** pince *f* à linge; **~s shop** magasin *m* d'habillement; *(US)* **~s tree** portemanteau *m*. ◆ **clothier** *n (clothes seller)* marchand *m* de confection; *(cloth dealer, maker)* drapier *m*. ◆ **clothing** *n* vêtements *mpl*; **an article of clothing** un vêtement; **clothing allowance** indemnité *f* vestimentaire.

cloud [klaʊd] **1** *n (Met)* nuage *m*; *[smoke, dust etc]* nuage; *[insects, arrows etc]* nuée *f*; *[gas]* nappe *f*. **to have one's head in the ~s** être dans les nuages; **to be on ~ nine** ‡ être aux anges; *(fig)* **under a ~** *(under suspicion)* en butte aux soupçons; *(in disgrace)* en disgrâce. **2** *vt liquid* rendre trouble; *mirror* embuer; *mind* obscurcir. **~ed sky** ciel couvert; **to ~ the issue** brouiller les cartes *(fig)*. **3** *vi* (**~ over**) *[sky]* se couvrir (de nuages); *[face, expression]* s'assombrir. ◆ **cloudburst** *n* déluge *m* de pluie. ◆ **cloud-cuckoo land** *n*: **she lives in ~-cuckoo land** elle plane complètement. ◆ **cloudiness** *n [sky]* aspect *m* nuageux; *[liquid]* aspect trouble; *[mirror]* buée *f*. ◆ **cloudless** *adj* sans nuages. ◆ **cloudy** *adj sky* couvert; *liquid* trouble; **it was ~y** le temps était couvert.

clout [klaʊt] **1** *n* (**a**) *(blow)* coup *m* de poing (*or* de canne *etc*). (**b**) *(*: influence)* influence *f*, poids *m*. **2** *vt* donner un coup de poing *etc* à.

clove¹ [kləʊv] *n* clou *m* de girofle. **oil of ~s** essence *f* de girofle; **~ of garlic** gousse *f* d'ail.

clove² [kləʊv] *pret of* **cleave.**

cloven ['kləʊvn] **1** *ptp of* **cleave.** **2** *adj*: **~ hoof** *[animal]* sabot *m* fendu; *[devil]* pied *m* fourchu.

clover ['kləʊvəʳ] *n* trèfle *m*. **to be in ~** * être comme un coq en pâte; **~leaf** *(Bot)* feuille *f* de trèfle; *(road intersection)* croisement *m* en trèfle.

clown [klaʊn] **1** *n* clown *m*. **2** *vi* (**~ about, ~ around**) faire le clown *or* le pitre. ◆ **clowning** *n* pitreries *fpl*.

cloy [klɔɪ] *vi* perdre son charme. ◆ **cloying** *adj* écœurant.

club [klʌb] **1** *n* (**a**) *(weapon)* matraque *f*; *(golf ~)* club *m*. *(Cards)* **~s** trèfles *mpl*; **the ace of ~s** l'as *m* de trèfle; **one ~** un trèfle; **he played a ~** il a joué trèfle. (**b**) *(society)* club *m*. **tennis ~** club de tennis; *(fig)* **join the ~!** * tu n'es pas le seul! **2** *adj*: *(US)* **~ car** wagon-restaurant *m*; **~ class** classe *f* club; **~ member** membre *m* du club; **~ sandwich** sandwich *m* à deux étages. **3** *vt person* matraquer. **to ~ sb with a rifle** assommer qn d'un coup de crosse. ◆ **club together** *vi* se cotiser (*to buy* pour acheter). ◆ **club-foot** *n* pied-bot *m*. ◆ **clubhouse** *n* pavillon *m*.

cluck [klʌk] **1** *vi* glousser. **2** *n* gloussement *m*.

clue [klu:] *n (gen)* indication *f*; *(police etc)* indice *m*; *[crosswords]* définition *f*. **to find the ~ to sth** découvrir la clef de qch; **to have a ~** être sur une piste; *(fig)* **I haven't a ~!** * je n'en ai pas la moindre idée! ◆ **clue up** ‡ *vt sep* renseigner (*on* sur). **he's very ~d up on politics** il est très calé * en politique. ◆ **clueless** * *adj* qui n'a pas la moindre idée.

clump¹ [klʌmp] *n [shrubs]* massif *m*; *[trees]* bouquet *m*; *[flowers, grass]* touffe *f*.

clump² [klʌmp] **1** *n (noise)* bruit *m* de pas lourds. **2** *vi* (**~ about**) marcher d'un pas lourd.

clumsy ['klʌmzɪ] *adj person, action, painting, forgery* maladroit; *tool etc* peu pratique; *shape, form* lourd; *(tactless) person, remark, apology, style* gauche, maladroit. ◆ **clumsily** *adv* maladroitement; gauchement. ◆ **clumsiness** *n* maladresse *f*; caractère *m* peu pratique; gaucherie *f*.

clung [klʌŋ] *pret, ptp of* **cling.**

clunk [klʌŋk] *n* bruit sourd.

clunker * ['klʌŋkəʳ] *n (US)* (vieille) guimbarde.

cluster ['klʌstəʳ] **1** *n [flowers, blossom, fruit]* grappe *f*; *[bananas]* régime *m*; *[trees]* bouquet *m*; *[persons, houses, islands]* (petit) groupe; *[stars]* amas *m*. **2** *vi [people]* se rassembler (*around* autour de); *[things]* former un groupe *etc* (*around* autour de).

clutch [klʌtʃ] **1** *n* (**a**) *(Aut)* embrayage *m*; *(~ pedal)* pédale *f* d'embrayage. **to let in the ~** embrayer; **to let out the ~** débrayer; **~ plate** disque *m* d'embrayage. (**b**) **to fall into sb's ~es** tomber sous les griffes de qn. **2** *vt (grasp)* empoigner, saisir; *(hold tightly)* serrer fort; *(hold on to)* se cramponner à. **3** *vi*: **to ~ at** essayer de saisir; *(fig)* **to ~ at a straw** se raccrocher à n'importe quoi.

clutter ['klʌtəʳ] **1** *n* désordre *m*, fouillis *m*. **in a ~** en désordre, en pagaille *. **2** *vt* (**~ up**) encombrer (*with* de).

co- [kəʊ] *pref* co-. ◆ **co-author** *n* co-auteur *m*. ◆ **co-driver** *n (in race)* copilote *m*; *[lorry]* deuxième chauffeur *m*. ◆ **coeducation** *n* éducation *f* mixte. ◆ **coeducational** *adj* mixte. ◆ **coexist** *vi* coexister (*with* avec). ◆ **coexistence** *n* coexistence *f*. ◆ **co-pilot** *n* copilote *m (Aviat)*. ◆ **co-respondent** *n* co-défendeur *m*, -deresse *f* (d'un adultère). ◆ **co-star** *n (Cine, Theat)* partenaire *mf*. ◆ **co-worker** *n* collègue *mf* de travail.

coach [kəʊtʃ] **1** *n* (**a**) *(Rail)* voiture *f*, wagon *m*; *(motor ~)* car *m*, autocar *m*; *(horse-drawn)* carrosse *m*. (**b**) *(tutor)* répétiteur *m*, -trice *f*; *(Sport)* entraîneur *m*. **2** *vt* donner des leçons particulières à; *(Sport)* entraîner. **to ~ sb for an exam** préparer qn à un examen; **he had been ~ed in what to say** on lui avait fait répéter ce qu'il aurait à dire. **3** *adj*: **~ trip** excursion *f* en car. ◆ **coachman** *n* cocher *m*. ◆ **coachwork** *n* carrosserie *f*.

coagulate [kəʊ'ægjʊleɪt] **1** *vt* coaguler. **2** *vi* se coaguler. ◆ **coagulant** *n* coagulant *m*. ◆ **coagulation** *n* coagulation *f*.

coal [kəʊl] **1** *n* charbon *m*; *(Ind)* houille *f*. *(fig)* **on hot ~s** sur des charbons ardents. **2** *adj fire, dust* de charbon; *box, stove, cellar* à charbon; *industry* houiller. **~ scuttle** seau *m* à charbon; **~ shed** réserve *f* à charbon. ◆ **coal-black** *adj* noir comme du charbon. ◆ **coal-face** *n* front *m* de taille. ◆ **coalfield** *n* bassin *m* houiller. ◆ **coal-gas** *n* gaz *m* (de houille). ◆ **coalman** *or* ◆ **coal-merchant** *n* charbonnier *m*. ◆ **coalmine** *n* houillère *f*, mine *f* de charbon. ◆ **coalminer** *n* mineur *m*. ◆ **coal-mining** *n* charbonnage *m*.

coalesce [,kəʊə'les] *vi* se grouper.

coalition [,kəʊə'lɪʃ(ə)n] *n* coalition *f*.

coarse [kɔːs] *adj material, cloth, texture* grossier; *linen, salt, sand* gros; *sandpaper* à gros grain; *skin* rude; *food* fruste; *manners, language, joke* grossier; *laugh* gras; *accent* vulgaire. **~ red wine** gros rouge *m*. ◆ **coarse-grained** *adj* à gros grain. ◆ **coarsely** *adv* grossièrement; grassement; vulgairement; **~ly woven** de texture grossière. ◆ **coarsen** **1** *vt* rendre grossier *or* vulgaire *etc*; **2** *vi* devenir rude *or* grossier *or* vulgaire *etc*. ◆ **coarseness** *n* caractère *m* grossier *or* rude; vulgarité *f*; grossièreté *f*.

coast [kəʊst] **1** *n* côte *f*; *(~ line)* littoral *m*. **the ~ is clear** la voie est libre. **2** *vi (Aut, Cycling)* avancer (*or* descendre) en roue libre. ◆ **coastal** *adj* côtier. ◆ **coaster** *n (Naut)* caboteur *m*; *(drip mat)* dessous *m* de verre. ◆ **coastguard** **1** *n (service)* ≃ gendarmerie *f* maritime; *(person)* membre *m* de la gendarmerie maritime ; **2** *adj*: **~guard station** (bureau *m* de la) gendarmerie maritime; **~guard vessel** (vedette *f*) garde-côte.

coat [kəʊt] **1** *n (gen)* manteau *m*; *[animal]* pelage *m*, poil *m*; *[horse]* robe *f*; *[paint, tar etc]* couche *f*. **~ of arms** armoiries *fpl*. **2** *vt* enduire, couvrir (*with* de); *(with egg)* dorer. **his tongue was ~ed** il avait la langue chargée. ◆ **coat-hanger** *n* cintre *m*. ◆ **coating** *n (gen)* couche *f (on saucepan etc)* revêtement *m*. ◆ **coatstand** *n* portemanteau *m*.

coax [kəʊks] *vt* enjôler. **to ~ sb into doing** amener qn à force de cajoleries à faire; **to ~ sth out of sb** obtenir qch de qn par des cajoleries. ◆ **coaxing** *n* cajolerie(s) *f(pl)*. ◆ **coaxingly** *adv* d'un ton câlin *or* enjôleur.

cobalt ['kəʊbɒlt] *n* cobalt *m*.

cobble ['kɒbl] **1** *n* (**~ stone**) pavé *m* rond. **2** *vt*: **to ~ together** bricoler. ◆ **cobbled** *adj*: **~d street** rue pavée.

cobbler ['kɒbləʳ] *n* cordonnier *m*.

COBOL ['kəʊbɒl] *n (Comput)* COBOL *m*.

cobra ['kəʊbrə] *n* cobra *m*.

cobweb ['kɒbweb] *n* toile *f* d'araignée.

Coca-Cola [,kəʊkə 'kəʊlə] *n* ® coca-cola *m inv*.

cocaine [kə'keɪn] *n* cocaïne *f*.

cochineal ['kɒtʃɪniːl] *n (Culin)* colorant *m* rouge.

cock [kɒk] **1** *n* coq *m*. **the ~ of the walk** le roi *(fig)*. **2** *vt gun* armer. **to ~ one's ear** dresser les oreilles; *(fig)* dresser l'oreille; **to ~ a snook at** faire un pied de nez à; *(fig)* faire fi de. **3** *adj*: **~ bird** (oiseau *m*) mâle *m*.
◆ **cock-a-doodle-doo** *n* cocorico *m*. ◆ **cock-a-hoop** **1** *adj* fier comme Artaban ; **2** *adv* d'un air de triomphe. ◆ **cockamamie** * *adj (US)* farfelu. ◆ **cockand-bull** *adj*: **~-and-bull story** histoire *f* à dormir debout. ◆ **cockcrow** *n*: **at ~crow** au premier chant du coq. ◆ **cocked** *adj*: **to knock sb into a ~ed hat** * battre qn à plate couture. ◆ **cockerel** *n* jeune coq *m*. ◆ **cock-eyed** *adj (*: cross-eyed)* qui louche; *(*: crooked)* de traviole *; *(*: absurd)* absurde; *(*: drunk)* soûl *. ◆ **cockfighting** *n* combats *mpl* de coqs. ◆ **cockiness** *n* outrecuidance *f*. ◆ **cockpit** *n [aircraft]* poste *m* de pilotage; *[racing car]* poste du pilote; *(fig)* arènes *fpl*. ◆ **cockroach** *n* cafard *m*. ◆ **cocksure** *adj* (trop) sûr de soi. ◆ **cocktail** **1** *n* cocktail *m (boisson)*; **fruit ~tail** salade *f* de fruits; **prawn ~tail** cocktail de crevettes ; **2** *adj*: **~tail bar** bar *m (dans un hôtel)*; **~tail cabinet** bar *m (meuble)*; **~tail party** cocktail *m (réunion)*. ◆ **cocky** *adj* trop sûr de soi, outrecuidant.

cockade [kɒ'keɪd] *n* cocarde *f*.

cockatoo ['kɒkə'tuː] *n* cacatoès *m*.

cocker ['kɒkəʳ] *n*: **~ (spaniel)** cocker *m*.

cockle ['kɒkl] *n (Zool)* coque *f*. **it warmed the ~s of his heart** cela lui a réchauffé le cœur.

cockney ['kɒknɪ] **1** *n* Cockney *mf (personne née dans l'"East End" de Londres)*; *(Ling)* cockney *m*. **2** *adj* cockney, londonien.

cocoa ['kəʊkəʊ] *n* cacao *m*.

coconut ['kəʊkənʌt] **1** *n* noix *f* de coco. **2** *adj*: **~ matting** tapis *m* de fibre; **~ palm** cocotier *m*; **~ shy** jeu *m* de massacre.

cocoon [kə'kuːn] *n* cocon *m*.

cod [kɒd] *n, pl inv* morue *f*; *(Culin)* cabillaud *m* ; *(salted, dried)* morue. **the C~ War** la guerre de la morue. ◆ **cod-liver oil** *n* huile *f* de foie de morue.

coddle ['kɒdl] *vt* dorloter; *(Culin)* cuire à feu doux.

code [kəʊd] **1** *n (all senses)* code *m*. **in ~** en code; **~ of practice** *(gen)* déontologie *f*.
2 *vt* coder.
3 *adj*: **~ letter** chiffre *m*; **~ name** nom *m* codé; *(Tax)* **~ number** ≃ indice *m* des déductions fiscales. ◆ **codify** *vt* codifier. ◆ **coding** *n [message]* mise *f* en code; *(Comput)* codage *m*.

codeine ['kəʊdiːn] *n* codéine *f*.

codicil ['kɒdɪsɪl] *n* codicille *m*.

coefficient [,kəʊɪ'fɪʃ(ə)nt] *n* coefficient *m*.

coerce [kəʊ'ɜːs] *vt* contraindre (*sb into doing* qn à faire). ◆ **coercion** *n* contrainte *f*. ◆ **coercive** *adj* coercitif.

coffee ['kɒfɪ] **1** *n* café *m*. **a ~** un café; **black ~** café noir; **white ~**, *(US)* **~ with milk** café au lait; **one white ~, please!** un (café-)crème s'il vous plaît! **2** *adj*: **~ bar** cafétéria *f*; **~ bean** grain *m* de café; **~ break** pause-café *f*; **~ cup** tasse *f* à café; *(smaller; also measure)* tasse à moka; **~ maker** cafetière *f*; **~ percolator** cafetière *f (à pression)*; **~ pot** *n* cafetière *f*; **~ spoon** cuiller *f* à moka; **~ table** (petite) table *f* basse; **a ~ table book** un beau livre grand format.

coffer ['kɒfəʳ] *n* coffre *m*.

coffin ['kɒfɪn] *n* cercueil *m*.

cog [kɒg] *n* dent *f (d'engrenage)*. *(fig)* **a ~ in the wheel** un simple rouage dans la machine.

cogent ['kəʊdʒ(ə)nt] *adj (compelling)* puissant; *(relevant)* pertinent. ◆ **cogency** *n* puissance *f*. ◆ **cogently** *adv* puissamment; pertinemment.

cogitate ['kɒdʒɪteɪt] *vti* méditer (*on* sur). ◆ **cogitation** *n* réflexion *f*.

cognac ['kɒnjæk] *n* cognac *m*.

cohabit [kəʊ'hæbɪt] *vi* cohabiter (*with* avec). ◆ **cohabitation** *n* cohabitation *f*.

coherent [kə(ʊ)'hɪərənt] *adj person, words* cohérent; *account, speech* facile à suivre; *behaviour* logique. ◆ **coherence** *n (fig)* cohérence *f*. ◆ **coherently** *adv* d'une façon cohérente.

coil [kɔɪl] **1** *vt* enrouler. **2** *vi [rope]* s'enrouler; *[snake]* se lover. **3** *n (roll: gen)* rouleau *m*; *(one loop)* spire *f*; *[snake, smoke]* anneau *m*; *[hair at back of head]* chignon *m*. *(contraceptive)* **the** ~ le stérilet.

coin [kɔɪn] **1** *n* pièce *f* de monnaie. **a 10p** ~ une pièce de 10 pence. **2** *vt money* frapper; *word* inventer. *(fig)* **he is ~ing money** il fait des affaires d'or; *(hum)* **to** ~ **a phrase** si je peux m'exprimer ainsi. ◆ **coin box** *n* cabine *f* téléphonique. ◆ **coin-op** * *n* laverie *f* automatique. ◆ **coin-operated** *adj* automatique.

coincide [ˌkəʊɪn'saɪd] *vi* coïncider (*with* avec). ◆ **coincidence** *n* coïncidence *f*. ◆ **coincidental** *adj* de coïncidence.

coke [kəʊk] *n* coke *m*.

Coke [kəʊk] *n* ® coca *m* ®.

colander ['kʌləndəʳ] *n* passoire *f*.

cold [kəʊld] **1** *adj (lit, fig)* froid. **as** ~ **as ice** *(gen)* glacé; *room* glacial; **it's as** ~ **as charity** il fait un froid de canard *; **it's a** ~ **morning** il fait froid ce matin; **the tea's** ~ le thé est froid; **I am** ~ j'ai froid; **my feet are** ~ j'ai froid aux pieds; *(fig)* **to have** ~ **feet** avoir la frousse *; **to get** ~ *[weather, room]* se refroidir; *[food]* refroidir; *[person]* commencer à avoir froid; *(catch a chill)* attraper froid; **that's** ~ **comfort** ce n'est pas tellement réconfortant; **that leaves me** ~ * ça ne me fait ni chaud ni froid; **in** ~ **blood** de sang-froid; **he was out** ~ * il était sans connaissance; ~ **cream** crème *f* de beauté; ~ **sore** bouton *m* de fièvre; ~ **start**, *(US)* ~ **starting** démarrage *m* à froid; **to put into** ~ **storage** *food* mettre en chambre froide; *scheme* mettre en attente; ~ **store** entrepôt *m* frigorifique; **the** ~ **war** la guerre froide.
2 *n* (**a**) *(Met etc)* froid *m*. **I am beginning to feel the** ~ je commence à avoir froid; **I never feel the** ~ je ne suis pas frileux; *(fig)* **to be left out in the** ~ rester en plan *. (**b**) *(Med)* rhume *m*. ~ **in the head** rhume de cerveau; **a bad** ~ un gros rhume; **to have a** ~ être enrhumé; **to get a** ~ s'enrhumer.
3 *adv (US *) (completely)* absolument; *(unexpectedly)* de façon complètement inattendue.
◆ **cold-blooded** *adj animal* à sang froid; *person* sans pitié. ◆ **cold-bloodedly** *adv* de sang froid. ◆ **cold-hearted** *adj* impitoyable. ◆ **coldly** *adv* avec froideur. ◆ **coldness** *n* froideur *f*. ◆ **cold-shoulder** * *vt* se montrer froid envers.

coleslaw ['kəʊlslɔː] *n* salade *f* de chou cru.

colic ['kɒlɪk] *n* coliques *fpl*; *(diarrhoea)* colique.

colitis [kɒ'laɪtɪs] *n* colite *f*.

collaborate [kə'læbəreɪt] *vi* collaborer (*with sb in sth* avec qn à qch). ◆ **collaboration** *n* collaboration *f* (*in* à). ◆ **collaborator** *n* collaborateur *m*, -trice *f*.

collapse [kə'læps] **1** *vi [person, building, roof, floor]* s'écrouler, s'effondrer; *[beam]* fléchir; *[government]* tomber; *[prices, defences, civilization, society]* s'effondrer; *[scheme]* s'écrouler; *(*: with laughter)* être plié en deux (de rire). **he ~d at work** il a eu un grave malaise à son travail. **2** *vt chair* plier; *paragraphs* comprimer. **3** *n* écroulement *m*; effondrement *m*; fléchissement *m*; *[lung etc]* collapsus *m*; *[government]* chute *f*. ◆ **collapsible** *adj* pliant.

collar ['kɒləʳ] **1** *n* col *m*; *(separate) (for men)* faux-col *m*; *(for women)* collerette *f*; *[dogs]* collier *m*; *(on pipe etc)* bague *f*. **to get hold of sb by the** ~ saisir qn au collet. **2** *vt* (*) *person* accrocher *, intercepter *; *book, object* faire main basse sur. ◆ **collarbone** *n* clavicule *f*. ◆ **collarstud** *n* bouton *m* de col.

collate [kɒ'leɪt] *vt* collationner (*with* avec). ◆ **collation** *n* collation *f*.

collateral [kɒ'læt(ə)r(ə)l] *adj (parallel)* parallèle; *(corresponding)* concomitant; *(Jur, Med)* collatéral; *(subordinate)* accessoire. *(Fin)* ~ **(security)** nantissement *m*.

colleague ['kɒliːg] *n* collègue *mf*.

collect [kə'lekt] **1** *vt* (**a**) *(assemble) valuables, wealth* accumuler; *facts, documents* rassembler, recueillir; *group of helpers* rassembler, réunir; *money, subscriptions* recueillir; *taxes, dues, fines* percevoir; *rents* encaisser. *(US)* ~ **on delivery** livraison *f* contre remboursement; **the ~ed works of Milton** les œuvres *fpl* complètes de Milton; *(fig)* **to** ~ **one's thoughts** se recueillir. (**b**) *(pick up) books etc* ramasser; *[bus or railway company] luggage etc* prendre à domicile; *[ticket collector]* ramasser. *(Post)* **to** ~ **letters** faire la levée du courrier; **the rubbish is ~ed twice a week** les ordures sont enlevées deux fois par semaine. (**c**) *(as hobby) stamps* collectionner. **she ~s * poets** elle collectionne * les poètes. (**d**) *(call for) person, books, one's mail* passer prendre. **the bus ~s the children** l'autobus ramasse les enfants.
2 *vi* (**a**) *[people]* se rassembler; *[things]* s'amasser; *[dust, water]* s'accumuler. (**b**) **to** ~ **for the injured** faire la quête pour les blessés.
3 *adv (US Telec)* **to call** ~ téléphoner en P.C.V.
◆ **collect call** *n (US Telec)* communication *f* en P.C.V. ◆ **collection** *n [information]* rassemblement *m*; *[taxes]* perception *f*; *[refuse]* enlèvement *m*; *[stamps etc]* collection *f*; *[miscellaneous objects]* amas *m*, ramassis *m (pej)*; *(in church)* quête *f*; *(Post)* levée *f*. ◆ **collective** **1** *adj* collectif; **~ive bargaining** ≃ convention *f* collective du travail ; **2** *n* association collective. ◆ **collectively** *adv* collectivement. ◆ **collectivism** *n* collectivisme *m*. ◆ **collector** *n [taxes]* percepteur *m*; *[stamps etc]* collectionneur *m*, -euse *f*.

college ['kɒlɪdʒ] *n (gen)* collège *m*. ~ **of agriculture** institut *m* agronomique; ~ **of art** école *f* des beaux-arts; ~ **of domestic science** école d'enseignement ménager; ~ **of education** *(for primary teachers)* ≃ école normale primaire; *(for secondary teachers)* ≃ centre pédagogique régional de formation des maîtres; ~ **of music** conservatoire *m* de musique; **technical** ~ collège technique; **to go to** ~ faire des études supérieures; **C~ of Physicians/Surgeons** Académie *f* de médecine/de chirurgie.

collide [kə'laɪd] *vi* entrer en collision; *(less violently)* se heurter. **to** ~ **with** entrer en collision avec, heurter. ◆ **collision** *n* collision *f*; **to be on a collision course** être sur une route de collision.

collie ['kɒlɪ] *n* colley *m*.

collier ['kɒlɪəʳ] *n* mineur *m*. ◆ **colliery** *n* mine *f* (de charbon), houillère *f*.

colloquial [kə'ləʊkwɪəl] *adj* familier, parlé. ◆ **colloquialism** *n* expression *f* familière. ◆ **colloquially** *adv* familièrement, dans la langue parlée.

collusion [kə'luːʒ(ə)n] *n* collusion *f*. **in** ~ **with** de connivence avec.

Cologne [kə'ləʊn] *n* Cologne.

Colombia [kə'lɒmbɪə] *n* Colombie *f*. ◆ **Colombian** **1** *adj* colombien ; **2** *n* Colombien(ne) *m(f)*.

colon ['kəʊlən] *n (Anat)* côlon *m*; *(Gram)* deux-points *m inv*.

colonel ['kɜ:nl] *n* colonel *m*. **C~ Smith** le colonel Smith.

colony ['kɒlənɪ] *n* colonie *f*. ◆ **colonial** *adj* colonial; **Colonial Office** ministère *m* des Colonies. ◆ **colonialism** *n* colonialisme *m*. ◆ **colonialist** *adj, n* colonialiste *(mf)*. ◆ **colonist** *n* colon *m*. ◆ **colonization** *n* colonisation *f*. ◆ **colonize** *vt* coloniser.

Colorado beetle [ˌkɒlə'rɑ:dəʊ 'bi:tl] *n* doryphore *m*.

colossus [kə'lɒsəs] *n* colosse *m*. ◆ **colossal** *adj* colossal.

colour, *(US)* **color** ['kʌləʳ] **1** *n* couleur *f*. **what ~ is it?** de quelle couleur est-ce?; **to take the ~ out of sth** décolorer qch; *(fig)* **let's see the ~ of your money *** fais voir la couleur de ton fric *; **under (the) ~ of** sous prétexte de; **to change ~** changer de couleur; **to lose (one's) ~** pâlir; **to get one's ~ back** reprendre des couleurs; **he looks an unhealthy ~** il a très mauvaise mine; **to have a high ~** avoir le teint vif; **to paint sth in bright/dark ~s** *(lit)* peindre qch de couleurs vives/sombres; *(fig)* peindre qch sous de belles couleurs/sous des couleurs sombres; **to see sth in its true ~s** voir qch sous son vrai jour; *(gen, Mil, Naut)* **~s** couleurs *fpl*; **to salute the ~s** saluer le drapeau; *(fig)* **he showed his true ~s** il s'est révélé tel qu'il est vraiment; **his ~ counted against him** sa couleur jouait contre lui; **it is not a question of ~** ce n'est pas une question de race.
2 *adj film, slide, photograph* en couleur; *problem etc* racial. **~ bar** discrimination raciale; **~ scheme** combinaison *f* de(s) couleurs; **to choose a ~ scheme** assortir les couleurs; *(Press)* **~ supplement** supplément illustré; **~ television** télévision *f* (en) couleur; **~ television (set)** téléviseur *m* couleur *inv*.
3 *vt (gen: lit, fig)* colorer; *(paint)* peindre; *(crayon)* colorier; *(dye)* teindre; *(tint)* teinter. **to ~ sth red** colorer *etc* qch en rouge; **~ing book** album *m* à colorier.
4 *vi [person]* rougir.
◆ **coloration** *n* coloration *f*. ◆ **colorcast** **1** *n* programme *m* (télévisé) en couleur ; **2** *vt* téléviser en couleur. ◆ **colour-blind** *adj* daltonien. ◆ **colour-blindness** *n* daltonisme *m*. ◆ **coloured** **1** *adj liquid* coloré; *drawing* colorié; *pencil* de couleur; *photograph etc* en couleur; *person, race* de couleur; **a highly ~ed tale** un récit très coloré; **a straw-~ed hat** un chapeau couleur paille; **muddy-~ed** couleur de boue ; **2** *n*: **~eds** personnes *fpl* de couleur; *(in South Africa)* métis *mpl*. ◆ **colourfast** *adj* grand teint *inv*. ◆ **colourful** *adj dress, tale* coloré; *personality* pittoresque. ◆ **colouring** *n* coloration *f*; *(complexion)* teint *m*; **high ~ing** teint coloré. ◆ **colourless** *adj* incolore. ◆ **colourway** *n* coloris *m*.

colt [kəʊlt] *n* poulain *m*.

column ['kɒləm] *n (all senses)* colonne *f*. ◆ **columnist** *n (Press)* chroniqueur *m*, échotier *m*, -ière *f*.

coma ['kəʊmə] *n* coma *m*. **in a ~** dans le coma. ◆ **comatose** *adj* comateux.

comb [kəʊm] **1** *n* peigne *m*. **to run a ~ through one's hair** se donner un coup de peigne. **2** *vt* (**a**) peigner. **to ~ one's hair** se peigner; **to ~ sb's hair** peigner qn. (**b**) *(search) area, town* ratisser; **(~ through)** *file* dépouiller.

combat ['kɒmbæt] **1** *n* combat *m*. **on ~ duty** en service commandé. **2** *adj* **~ car** (véhicule *m)* blindé *m* léger de campagne; **~ jacket** veste *f* de treillis; **~ troops** troupes *fpl* de combat. **3** *vti* combattre (*for* pour, *with, against* contre). ◆ **combatant** *adj, n* combattant(e) *m(f)*.

combine [kəm'baɪn] **1** *vt projects, objectives* combiner (*with* avec); *qualities* allier (*with* à); *forces, efforts* unir. **to ~ business with pleasure** joindre l'utile à l'agréable; **~d clock and radio** combiné *m* radio-réveil; **their ~d wealth** leurs richesses réunies; **a ~d effort** un effort conjugué; **~d forces** forces alliées; **~d operation** *(Mil)* opération *f* interarmes *inv*; *(by allies)* opération alliée; *(fig)* entreprise *f* faite en commun. **2** *vi (gen)* s'unir, s'associer; *[parties]* fusionner; *[workers]* se syndiquer; *(Chem)* se combiner; *(fig)* se liguer (*against* contre); *[events]* concourir (*to* à). **3** ['kɒmbaɪn] *n* association *f*; *(Comm, Fin)* trust *m*, cartel *m*; *(Jur)* corporation *f*; *(~ harvester)* moissonneuse-batteuse *f*. ◆ **combination** **1** *n (gen)* combinaison *f*; *[events]* concours *m*; **(motorcycle) combination** side-car *m* ; **2** *adj*: **combination lock** serrure *f* à combinaison.

combustion [kəm'bʌstʃ(ə)n] *n* combustion *f*. ◆ **combustible** *adj* combustible.

come [kʌm] *pret* **came,** *ptp* **come** *vi* (**a**) *(gen)* venir; *(arrive)* venir, arriver; *(have its place)* venir, se trouver. **~ with me** venez avec moi; **~ and see me soon** venez me voir bientôt; **he has ~ to mend the television** il est venu réparer la télévision; **he has ~ from Edinburgh** il est venu d'Édimbourg; **he has just ~ from Edinburgh** il arrive d'Édimbourg; *(originate from)* **to ~ from** venir de; **he has ~ a long way** il est venu de loin; *(fig)* il a fait du chemin; **they were coming and going all day** ils n'ont fait qu'aller et venir toute la journée; *(TV)* **the picture ~s and goes** l'image saute; **the pain ~s and goes** la douleur est intermittente; **to ~ running** arriver en courant; **to ~ home** rentrer (chez soi *or* à la maison); **to ~ for sb/sth** venir chercher qn/qch, venir prendre qn/qch; **I'll ~ after you** je vous suis; **coming!** j'arrive!; *(excl)* **~, ~!, ~ now!** voyons!; **they came to a town** ils sont arrivés à une ville, ils ont atteint une ville; **help came in time** les secours sont arrivés à temps; **it came into my head that** il m'est venu à l'esprit que; **it came as a shock to him** cela lui a fait un choc; **it came as a surprise to him** cela l'a (beaucoup) surpris; **when it ~s to mathematics** pour ce qui est des mathématiques; **when it ~s to choosing** quand il faut choisir; *(fig)* **he will never ~ to much** il ne sera *or* fera jamais grand-chose; **the time will ~ when...** il viendra un temps où...; **May ~s before June** mai vient avant *or* précède juin; **July ~s after June** juillet vient après *or* suit juin; **this passage ~s on page 10** ce passage se trouve à la page 10.
(**b**) *(happen)* arriver (*to* à), se produire. **~ what may** quoi qu'il arrive *(subj)*; **nothing came of it** il n'en est rien résulté; **that's what ~s of disobeying!** voilà ce que c'est que de désobéir!; **no good will ~ of it** il n'en sortira rien de bon; **how do you ~ to be so late?** comment se fait-il que vous soyez si en retard?
(**c**) *(be, become)* devenir, se trouver. **his dreams came true** ses rêves se sont réalisés; **the handle has ~ loose** le manche s'est desserré; **it ~s less expensive to shop in town** cela revient moins cher de faire ses achats en ville; **that ~s naturally to him** il est doué pour cela; **everything came right in the end** tout s'est arrangé à la fin; **this dress ~s in 3 sizes** cette robe existe en 3 tailles; **I have ~ to believe him** j'en suis venu à le croire; **he came to admit he was wrong** il a fini par reconnaître qu'il avait tort; **now I ~ to think of it** réflexion faite, quand j'y songe; *(liter)* **it came to pass that** il advint que *(liter)*; **to ~ undone** se défaire; **to ~ apart** *(come off)* se détacher; *(come unstuck)* se décoller.
(**d**) *(phrases)* **the life to ~** la vie future; **the years to ~** les années à venir; **if it ~s to that, you shouldn't have done it either** à ce compte-là *or* à ce moment-là *, tu n'aurais pas dû le faire non plus; **I've known him for 3 years ~ January** cela fera 3 ans en janvier que je le connais; **she is**

coming * **6** elle va sur ses 6 ans; **she had it coming to her** * elle l'a *or* l'avait (bien) cherché; **to ~ between two people** (venir) se mettre entre deux personnes; **she's as clever as they ~** * elle est futée comme pas une *; **you could see that coming** * on voyait venir ça de loin; **~ again?** * comment?, pardon?; **how ~?** * comment ça se fait?; **how ~ you can't find it?** * comment se fait-il que tu n'arrives *(subj)* pas à le trouver?

◆ **come about** *vi* se faire (*that* que + *subj*) arriver.

◆ **come across** **1** *vi* (**a**) *(gen)* traverser; *(be received)* faire de l'effet. **his speech came across very well/badly** son discours a fait beaucoup d'effet/n'a pas fait d'effet; **his true feelings came across** ses vrais sentiments se faisaient sentir. (**b**) *(US *: keep promise etc)* s'exécuter, tenir parole. **2** *vt fus (find, meet)* tomber sur.

◆ **come along** *vi* (**a**) **~ along!** *(impatiently)* (allons *or* voyons) dépêchez-vous!; *(in friendly tone)* (allez) venez! (**b**) *(accompany)* venir. (**c**) *(progress)* faire des progrès. **how is your broken arm? — it's coming along quite well** comment va votre bras cassé? — il *or* ça se remet bien; **how are your lettuces/plans coming along?** où en sont vos laitues/projets?

◆ **come away** *vi (leave)* partir, s'en aller; *[button etc]* se détacher, partir. **~ away from there!** sors de là!, écarte-toi de là!

◆ **come back** *vi* revenir. **I asked her to ~ back with me** je lui ai demandé de me raccompagner; **to ~ back to what I was saying** pour en revenir à ce que je disais; **I'll ~ back to you on that one** * nous en reparlerons plus tard; **his name is coming back to me** son nom me revient (à la mémoire).

◆ **come by** **1** *vi* passer (par là). **he came by yesterday** il est venu *or* passé (par là) hier. **2** *vt fus (obtain) object* se procurer; *idea, opinion* se faire.

◆ **come down** *vi* descendre (*from* de, *to* jusqu'à); *[buildings etc]* être démoli; *[prices]* baisser. **to ~ down in favour of sth** prendre position en faveur de qch; **to ~ down in the world** descendre dans l'échelle sociale; **he came down on me like a ton of bricks** * il m'est tombé dessus à bras raccourcis; **to ~ down with flu** attraper une grippe.

◆ **come forward** *vi* se présenter (*as* comme). **to ~ forward with** *help, money, suggestion* offrir; *answer* suggérer.

◆ **come in** *vi [person]* entrer; *[trains etc]* arriver; *[tide]* monter; *(in race)* arriver. **where does your brother ~ in?** et ton frère là-dedans?; **he came in fourth** il est arrivé quatrième; **the socialists came in at the last election** les socialistes sont arrivés au pouvoir aux dernières élections; **he has £5,000 coming in every year** il touche 5 000 livres chaque année; **to ~ in for** *criticism, reproach* être l'objet de, subir; *praise* recevoir; **to ~ into** *(inherit)* hériter de.

◆ **come off** **1** *vi* (**a**) *[button]* se détacher; *[stains, marks]* partir. (**b**) *[event etc]* avoir lieu; *[plans etc]* se réaliser; *[attempts, experiments]* réussir. (**c**) *(acquit o.s.)* s'en tirer, s'en sortir. **he came off well by comparison with his brother** il s'en est très bien tiré en comparaison de son frère; **to ~ off best** gagner. **2** *vt fus*: **a button came off his coat** un bouton s'est détaché de son manteau; **he came off his bike** il est tombé de son vélo; **~ off it!** * et puis quoi encore?, vraiment?

◆ **come on** **1** *vi* (**a**) *(follow)* suivre; *(continue to advance)* continuer d'avancer. (**b**) = **come along (a)**. (**c**) = **come along (c)**. (**d**) *(US *)* **he came on as a fine man** il a fait l'effet d'être un homme bien. (**e**) *(start) [illness]* se déclarer. **the rain came on** il s'est mis à pleuvoir; **I feel a cold coming on** je sens que je m'enrhume. (**f**) *(Theat) [actor]* entrer en scène. **'Hamlet' is coming on next week** on donne 'Hamlet' la semaine prochaine. **2** *vt fus* = **come upon**.

◆ **come out** *vi [person, object, flowers, car, drawer]* sortir (*of* de); *[sun, stars]* paraître; *[spots, rash]* sortir; *[secret, news]* être divulgué; *[truth]* se faire jour; *[books, magazines, films]* paraître, sortir; *[qualities]* se manifester; *[stains]* s'en aller; *[dyes, colours] (run)* déteindre; *(fade)* se faner; *(Math) [problems]* se résoudre; *[division etc]* tomber juste. **to ~ out on strike** se mettre en grève; **the photo came out well** la photo est très bonne; **the total ~s out at 500** le total s'élève à 500; **he came out third in French** il s'est classé troisième en français; **to ~ out in a rash** avoir une poussée de boutons; **to ~ out for/against sth** se déclarer ouvertement pour/contre qch; **you never know what she's going to ~ out with next** * on ne sait jamais ce qu'elle va dire *or* sortir *.

◆ **come over** **1** *vi* venir. **he came over to England for a few months** il est venu passer quelques mois en Angleterre; **he came over to our way of thinking** il s'est rangé à notre avis; **she came over faint** elle a failli s'évanouir; **his speech came over well** son discours a fait bonne impression. **2** *vt fus*: **a feeling of shyness came over her** la timidité la saisit; **what's ~ over you?** qu'est-ce qui vous prend?

◆ **come round** *vi* (**a**) faire le tour *or* un détour. **we had to ~ round by the farm** nous avons dû faire un détour par la ferme. (**b**) venir, passer. **do ~ round and see me one evening** passez me voir un de ces soirs. (**c**) *(recur regularly)* revenir périodiquement. **your birthday will soon ~ round again** ce sera bientôt à nouveau ton anniversaire. (**d**) *(change one's mind)* changer d'avis. (**e**) *(regain consciousness)* reprendre connaissance. (**f**) *(throw off bad mood etc)* **leave her alone, she'll soon ~ round** laissez-la tranquille, elle reviendra bientôt à d'autres sentiments.

◆ **come through** **1** *vi (survive)* s'en tirer. *(Telec)* **the call came through** on a eu la communication. **2** *vt fus (survive) danger, war* se tirer indemne de; *illness* survivre à.

◆ **come through with** *vt fus (US)* **come up with**.

◆ **come to** **1** *vi* = **come round (e)**. **2** *vt fus*: **how much does it ~ to?** cela fait combien?; **it ~s to much less per metre if you buy a lot** cela revient bien moins cher le mètre si vous en achetez beaucoup.

◆ **come together** *vi (assemble)* se rassembler; *(meet)* se rencontrer.

◆ **come under** *vt fus sb's influence, domination* tomber sous; *heading* être classé sous, se trouver sous.

◆ **come up** *vi* (**a**) monter. **he came up to me with a smile** il m'a abordé en souriant. (**b**) *[accused]* comparaître (*before* devant); *[law suit]* être entendu (*before* par); *[matters for discussion, question]* être soulevé. **he came up against total opposition to his plans** il s'est heurté à une opposition radicale à ses projets; **to ~ up against sb** entrer en conflit avec qn. (**c**) **the water came up to his knees** l'eau lui venait *or* arrivait jusqu'aux genoux; **my son ~s up to my shoulder** mon fils m'arrive à l'épaule; **his work has not ~ up to our expectation** son travail n'a pas répondu à notre attente.

◆ **come up with** *vt fus idea, plan* proposer, suggérer; *money, suggestion* offrir.

◆ **come upon** *vt fus (find, meet) object, person* tomber sur.

◆ **comeback** *n (Theat etc)* rentrée *f*; *(reaction)* réaction *f*; *(response)* réplique *f*. ◆ **comedown** * *n*: **it was rather a ~down for him to have to work** c'était assez humiliant pour lui d'avoir à travailler. ◆ **comer** *n*: **open to all ~rs** ouvert à tous; **the first ~r** le premier venu. ◆ **come-hither** * *adj*: **a ~-hither look** un regard aguichant. ◆ **come-on** * *n* attrape-nigaud *m*, truc * *m*. ◆ **comeup-**

pance * [ˌkʌm'ʌpəns] *n*: **he got his ~uppance** il a échoué (*or* perdu *etc*) et il ne l'a pas volé. ◆ **coming 1** *n* arrivée *f*, venue *f*; **coming and going** va-et-vient *m*; **comings and goings** allées *fpl* et venues; **2** *adj (future)* à venir, futur; *(next)* prochain; *(promising)* qui promet, d'avenir; **a coming politician** un homme politique d'avenir.

comedy ['kɒmɪdɪ] *n* comédie *f*. **low ~** farce *f*. ◆ **comedian** *n* (acteur *m*) comique *m*. ◆ **comedienne** *n* actrice *f* comique.

comely ['kʌmlɪ] *adj (liter)* beau, gracieux. ◆ **comeliness** *n* beauté *f*, grâce *f*.

comet ['kɒmɪt] *n* comète *f*.

comfort ['kʌmfət] **1** *n* (**a**) confort *m*, bien-être *m*. **to live in ~** vivre dans l'aisance; **every modern ~** tout le confort moderne; **he likes his ~s** il aime ses aises. (**b**) *(consolation)* consolation *f*, réconfort *m*. **to take ~ from sth** trouver du réconfort *or* une consolation dans qch; **you are a great ~ to me** vous êtes pour moi d'un grand réconfort; **if it's any ~ to you** si ça peut te consoler; **it is a ~ to know that...** il est consolant de savoir que...; **to take ~ from the fact/the knowledge that** trouver rassurant le fait que/de savoir que; **the fighting was too close for (my) ~** les combats étaient trop près pour mon goût.
2 *adj*: *(US)* **~ station** toilettes *fpl*.
3 *vt* consoler, soulager.
◆ **comfortable** *adj armchair, bed, win, majority* confortable; *temperature* agréable; *thought, idea, news* réconfortant; *income* très suffisant; **I am quite ~able here** je me trouve très bien ici; **to make o.s. ~able** *(in armchair etc)* s'installer confortablement; *(make o.s. at home)* se mettre à son aise; *(fig)* **I am not very ~able about it** cela m'inquiète un peu. ◆ **comfortably** *adv* confortablement; agréablement; *live* dans l'aisance; **they are ~ably off** ils sont à l'aise. ◆ **comforter** *n (person)* consolateur *m*, -trice *f (liter)*; *(scarf)* cache-nez *m inv*; *(dummy-teat)* tétine *f*; *(quilt)* édredon *m*. ◆ **comforting** *adj words, thoughts* consolant; *news* soulageant; **it is ~ing to think that...** il est réconfortant de penser que... ◆ **comfortless** *adj room* sans confort; *prospect* désolant. ◆ **comfy** * *adj chair, room* confortable; **are you comfy?** êtes-vous bien?

comic ['kɒmɪk] **1** *adj* comique. **~ opera** opéra *m* comique; **~ relief** moment *m* de détente comique; **~ verse** poésie *f* humoristique. **2** *n (person)* (acteur *m*) comique *m*, actrice *f* comique; *(magazine)* comic *m*. **~s, ~ strip** bande dessinée. ◆ **comical** *adj* comique. ◆ **comically** *adv* comiquement.

comma ['kɒmə] *n* virgule *f*.

command [kə'mɑːnd] **1** *vt* ordonner, commander (*sb to do* à qn de faire; *that* que + *subj*); *army, ship* commander; *money, services, resources* disposer de; *respect etc* imposer. **that ~s a high price** cela se vend très cher. **2** *vi* commander. **3** *n (order)* ordre *m*; *(Mil)* commandement *m*. **at** *or* **by the ~ of** sur l'ordre de; **at the word of ~** au commandement; **to be in ~ of** être à la tête de; **to have/take ~ of** avoir/prendre le commandement de; **under the ~ of** sous le commandement *or* les ordres de; **who's in ~ here?** qui est-ce qui commande ici?; **~ of the seas** maîtrise *f* des mers; **he has a ~ of 3 foreign languages** il possède 3 langues étrangères; **his ~ of English** sa maîtrise de l'anglais; **all the money at my ~** tout l'argent à ma disposition. **4** *adj*: **~ module** module *m* de commande; **~ performance** ≃ représentation *f* de gala *(à la requête du souverain)*; **~ post** poste *m* de commandement. ◆ **commandant** *n* commandant *m*. ◆ **commandeer** *vt* réquisitionner. ◆ **commander** *n* chef *m*; *(Mil)* commandant *m*; **~er-in-chief** commandant *m* en chef. ◆ **commanding** *adj air* imposant; *look, voice, tone* impérieux; **~ing officer** commandant *m*; **to be in a ~ing position** avoir une position dominante. ◆ **commandment** *n* commandement *m*. ◆ **commando** *n* commando *m*.

commemorate [kə'meməreɪt] *vt* commémorer. ◆ **commemoration** *n* commémoration *f*. ◆ **commemorative** *adj* commémoratif.

commence [kə'mens] *vti* commencer (*sth* qch; *to do, doing* à faire). ◆ **commencement** *n* commencement *m*.

commend [kə'mend] *vt (praise)* louer; *(recommend)* recommander; *(entrust)* confier (*to* à). **his scheme did not ~ itself to the public** son projet n'a pas été du goût du public; **his scheme has little to ~ it** son projet n'a pas grand-chose qui le fasse recommander. ◆ **commendable** *adj* louable; recommandable. ◆ **commendably** *adv*: **that was ~ably short** cela avait le mérite de la brièveté. ◆ **commendation** *n* louange *f*; recommandation *f*.

commensurate [kə'menʃ(ə)rɪt] *adj*: **~ with** proportionné à.

comment ['kɒment] **1** *n (spoken, written)* commentaire *m* (bref), remarque *f*; *(critical)* critique *f*. **he let it pass without ~** il ne l'a pas relevé; **'no ~'** 'je n'ai rien à dire'. **2** *vt* remarquer (*that* que); *text* commenter. **3** *vi* faire des remarques (*on* sur). ◆ **commentary** *n (gen)* commentaire *m*; *(Sport)* reportage *m*. ◆ **commentate 1** *vi (Rad, TV)* faire un reportage (*on* sur) ; **2** *vt (Rad, TV)* faire un reportage sur; *text* commenter. ◆ **commentator** *n (Rad, TV)* reporter *m*.

commerce ['kɒmɜːs] *n (Comm)* commerce *m*, affaires *fpl*; **Department of C~** ≃ ministère *m* du Commerce.
◆ **commercial 1** *adj (gen)* commercial; *world* du commerce; *value* marchand, commercial; *district* commerçant; **commercial college** école *f* de commerce; **commercial traveller** représentant *m* de commerce; **commercial vehicle** véhicule *m* utilitaire ; **2** *n (Rad, TV)* annonce *f* publicitaire, spot *m*. ◆ **commercialism** *n* mercantilisme *m*; *(on large scale)* affairisme *m*. ◆ **commercialization** *n* commercialisation *f*. ◆ **commercialize** *vt* commercialiser. ◆ **commercially** *adv* commercialement.

commiserate [kə'mɪzəreɪt] *vi (show commiseration for)* témoigner de la sympathie (*with* à); *(feel it)* éprouver de la commisération (*with* pour). ◆ **commiseration** *n* commisération *f*.

commissar ['kɒmɪsɑːʳ] *n* commissaire *m* du peuple. ◆ **commissariat** *n* commissariat *m*.

commission [kə'mɪʃ(ə)n] **1** *n* (**a**) *(Comm)* commission *f*. **on a ~ basis** à la commission; **he gets 10% ~** il reçoit une commission de 10%. (**b**) *(orders)* instructions *fpl*; *(to artist etc)* commande *f*. (**c**) *(Mil)* brevet *m*. **to get one's ~** être nommé officier. (**d**) *(body of people)* commission *f*, comité *m*. **~ of inquiry** commission d'enquête. (**e**) **out of ~** *machine, lift etc* hors service. **2** *vt* (**a**) donner pouvoir à. **he was ~ed to inquire into...** il a reçu mission de faire une enquête sur...; **I have been ~ed to say** j'ai été chargé de dire. (**b**) *book, painting* commander. (**c**) *(Mil etc)* **~ed officer** officier *m*; **he was ~ed in 1970** il a été nommé officier en 1970. ◆ **commissionaire** *n* commissionnaire *m (d'hôtel)*. ◆ **commissioner** *n* membre *m* d'une commission, commissaire *m*; *(Brit Police)* ≃ préfet *m* (de police); *(US)* (commissaire *m*) divisionnaire *m*.

commit [kə'mɪt] *vt* (**a**) *crime etc* commettre. **to ~ suicide** se suicider. (**b**) *(consign)* remettre (*to* à, aux soins de). **to ~ sb to prison** faire incarcérer qn; **to ~ sb for trial** mettre qn en accusation; **to ~ to writing** coucher par écrit; **to ~ to memory**

apprendre par cœur. (**c**) **to ~ o.s.** s'engager (*to* à); **to be ~ted to a policy** s'être engagé à poursuivre une politique. ◆ **commitment** *n (gen)* engagement *m*; *(obligation)* responsabilité(s) *f(pl)*; *(Fin)* engagement financier; *(Comm)* **'without ~ment'** 'sans obligation'; **teaching ~ments** (heures *fpl* d') enseignement *m*. ◆ **committal** *n* remise *f* (*to* à, aux soins de); *(to prison)* incarcération *f*; *(burial)* mise *f* en terre. ◆ **committed** *adj writer etc* engagé; *Christian etc* convaincu; *parent etc* dévoué, attentif; **a ~ted supporter** un supporter ardent.

committee [kə'mɪtɪ] **1** *n (gen)* comité *m*, commission *f*; *(Parl)* commission. **to be on a ~** faire partie d'une commission *or* d'un comité; **~ of inquiry** commission d'enquête. **2** *adj*: **~ meeting** réunion *f* de comité *or* de commission; **~ member** membre *m* d'un comité *or* d'une commission.

commodious [kə'məʊdɪəs] *adj* spacieux.

commodity [kə'mɒdɪtɪ] *n* produit *m*; *(food)* denrée *f*. **(staple) commodities** produits de base.

common ['kɒmən] **1** *adj* (**a**) *(affecting many) interest, cause, language* commun. **to make ~ cause with sb** faire cause commune avec qn; **by ~ consent** d'un commun accord; *(fig)* **~ ground** terrain *m* d'entente; **it's ~ knowledge that...** chacun sait que...; **~ land** terrain communal; **~ lodging house** asile *m* de nuit; **the C~ Market** le Marché commun; **~ wall** mur mitoyen. (**b**) *(usual, universal) method* commun, ordinaire; *sight* familier; *occurrence* fréquent; *belief* général; *(pej) accent, person* commun, vulgaire; *(Gram, Math)* commun. **it's quite ~** c'est très courant; **it's a ~ experience** cela arrive à tout le monde; **it is only ~ courtesy to apologise** la politesse la plus élémentaire veut qu'on s'excuse *(subj)*; *(pej)* **the ~ herd** la plèbe; **~ honesty** la simple honnêteté; **the ~ man** l'homme du commun *or* du peuple; **the ~ people** le peuple; **in ~ parlance** dans le langage courant; **out of the ~ run** hors du commun; **~ salt** sel *m* (ordinaire); **~ or garden** ordinaire.
2 *n* (**a**) *(land)* terrain communal. (**b**) **in ~** en commun (*with* avec); **they have nothing in ~** ils n'ont rien de commun.
◆ **commoner** *n* roturier *m*, -ière *f*. ◆ **common-law** *adj*: **~-law wife** épouse *f* de droit coutumier. ◆ **commonly** *adv (V above* **1b**) communément; ordinairement; fréquemment; généralement; *(vulgarly)* d'une façon vulgaire *or* commune. ◆ **commonness** *n* caractère *m* commun *or* ordinaire; fréquence *f*; généralité *f*; vulgarité *f*. ◆ **commonplace** **1** *adj* ordinaire; **2** *n* lieu *m* commun. ◆ **commonroom** *n* salle *f* commune; *(staffroom)* salle des professeurs. ◆ **commons** *npl (Parl)* **the C~s** les Communes *fpl*; *(gen)* **on short ~s** strictement rationné. ◆ **commonsense** **1** *n* sens *m* commun, bon sens ; **2** *adj* sensé, plein de bon sens. ◆ **Commonwealth** *n*: **the C~wealth** le Commonwealth; *(Hist)* la république de Cromwell; **Minister of C~wealth Affairs** ministre *m* du Commonwealth.

commotion [kə'məʊʃ(ə)n] *n* : **to make a ~** *(noise)* faire du tapage; **to cause a ~** *(upheaval)* semer la perturbation.

commune [kə'mju:n] **1** *vi* converser intimement (*with* avec). **to ~ with nature** communier avec la nature. **2** ['kɒmju:n] *n (Admin)* commune *f*; *(community)* communauté *f*. **to live in a ~** vivre en communauté. ◆ **communal** *adj facilities* commun; *life* collectif. ◆ **communally** *adv* en commun, collectivement.

communicable [kə'mju:nɪkəbl] *adj disease* transmissible.

communicate [kə'mju:nɪkeɪt] **1** *vt (gen)* communiquer (*to* à); *illness* transmettre (*to* à). **2** *vi* communiquer, se mettre en rapport (*with* avec); *[rooms]* communiquer; *(Rel)* communier. ◆ **communicant** *n (Rel)* communiant(e) *m(f)*. ◆ **communication** **1** *n* communication *f*; **to be in communication with sb** être en contact *or* rapport avec qn; **to be in radio communication with sb** communiquer avec qn par radio; **there has been no communication between them** il n'y a eu aucun contact entre eux ; **2** *adj (Rail)* **communication cord** sonnette *f* d'alarme; **communications satellite** satellite *m* de communication. ◆ **communicative** *adj* communicatif. ◆ **communion** *n (gen)* communion *f*; **to take communion** recevoir la communion. ◆ **communiqué** *n* communiqué *m*.

communism ['kɒmjʊnɪz(ə)m] *n* communisme *m*. ◆ **communist** *adj, n* communiste *(mf)*. ◆ **communistic** *adj* communisant.

community [kə'mju:nɪtɪ] **1** *n* communauté *f*. **the French ~ in Edinburgh** la colonie française d'Édimbourg; **the student ~** les étudiants *mpl*, le monde étudiant; *(Pol: EEC)* **the C~** la Communauté. **2** *adj*: *(Pol)* **C~ bodies/budget** instances *fpl*/budget *m* communautaire(s); **~ centre** foyer *m* socio-éducatif; *(US)* **~ chest** fonds *m* commun; **~ health centre** centre *m* médico-social; **~ singing** chants *mpl* en chœur *(improvisés)*; **~ spirit** esprit *m* civique; **~ worker** animateur *m*, -trice *f* socio-culturel(le).

commute [kə'mju:t] **1** *vt* substituer (*into* à); *(Elec, Jur)* commuer (*into* en). **2** *vi* faire un trajet journalier, faire la navette (*between* entre; *from* de). ◆ **commuter** *n* banlieusard(e) *m(f)*; *(Brit)* **I work in London but I'm a ~r** je travaille à Londres mais je fais la navette; **the ~r belt** la grande banlieue.

compact [kəm'pækt] **1** *adj* compact, serré. **the house is very ~** la maison n'a pas de place perdue. **2** ['kɒmpækt] *n (agreement)* contrat *m*, convention *f*; *(powder ~)* poudrier *m*. ◆ **compact disc** *n* disque *m* compact. ◆ **compactly** *adv build, design* sans perte de place. ◆ **compactness** *n [room etc]* économie *f* d'espace.

companion [kəm'pænjən] **1** *n* compagnon *m*, compagne *f*; *(lady ~)* dame *f* de compagnie; *(one of pair of objects)* pendant *m*; *(handbook)* manuel *m*. **2** *adj*: **~ volume** volume *m* qui va de pair (*to* avec). ◆ **companionable** *adj person* sociable; *presence* sympathique. ◆ **companionship** *n* compagnie *f*. ◆ **companionway** *n* escalier *m* des cabines.

company ['kʌmp(ə)nɪ] *n (gen, also Mil)* compagnie *f*; *(Comm, Fin)* société *f*, compagnie; *[actors]* troupe *f*, compagnie. **to keep sb ~** tenir compagnie à qn; **to part ~ with** se séparer de; **in ~ with** en compagnie de; **he is good ~** on ne s'ennuie pas avec lui; **it's ~ for her** ça lui fait une compagnie; **we are expecting ~** nous attendons des invités; **to be in good ~** être en bonne compagnie; **to get into bad ~** avoir de mauvaises fréquentations; **she is no fit ~ for your sister** ce n'est pas une fréquentation pour votre sœur; **Smith** *&* **C~** Smith et Compagnie; **shipping ~** compagnie de navigation; **~ car** voiture *f* de fonction; **~ secretary** secrétaire *m* général *(d'une société)*; **National Theatre C~** la troupe du Théâtre national; *(Naut)* **ship's ~** équipage *m*.

compare [kəm'pɛə[r]] **1** *vt* comparer (*with* à, avec; *to* à), mettre en comparaison (*with* avec). **~d with** en comparaison de, par comparaison avec; *(fig)* **to ~ notes with sb** échanger ses impressions avec qn. **2** *vi* être comparable (*with* à). **how do the cars ~ for speed?** quelles sont les vitesses respectives des voitures?; **how do the prices ~?** est-ce que les prix sont comparables?; **he can't ~ with you** il n'y a pas de comparaison entre vous et lui. **3** *n*: **beyond ~** *(adv)* incomparablement; *(adj)* sans pareil. ◆ **comparable** ['kɒmp(ə)rəbl] *adj* comparable (*with, to* à). ◆ **comparative** [kəm'pærətɪv] **1** *adj method* comparatif; *linguistics, literature* comparé; *(Gram)* comparatif; *cost, freedom, luxury* relatif; **he's a comparative stranger** je le connais relativement peu ; **2** *n*: **in the comparative** au comparatif. ◆ **comparatively** *adv* relativement. ◆ **comparison** *n* comparaison *f*; **in comparison with** en comparaison de; **by comparison (with)** par comparaison (avec).

compartment [kəm'pɑːtmənt] *n* compartiment *m*. ◆ **compartmentalize** *vt* compartimenter.

compass ['kʌmpəs] *n* boussole *f*; *(Naut)* compas *m*; *(of powers, voice)* étendue *f*. **within the ~ of** dans les limites *fpl* de; *(Math)* **~es** compas *m*.

compassion [kəm'pæʃ(ə)n] *n* compassion *f*. ◆ **compassionate** *adj person* compatissant; *reasons, grounds* de convenance personnelle; *leave* exceptionnel.

compatible [kəm'pætɪbl] *adj* compatible (*with* avec). ◆ **compatibility** *n* compatibilité *f*.

compatriot [kəm'pætrɪət] *n* compatriote *mf*.

compel [kəm'pel] *vt* contraindre (*sb to do* qn à faire). **to be ~led to do** être contraint de faire; **to ~ obedience from sb** contraindre qn à obéir. ◆ **compelling** *adj* irrésistible. ◆ **compellingly** *adv* irrésistiblement.

compendium [kəm'pendɪəm] *n (summary)* abrégé *m*. *(Brit)* **~ of games** boîte *f* de jeux.

compensate ['kɒmpenseɪt] **1** *vi*: **to ~ for sth** compenser qch; **then, to ~ for that, he...** puis, pour compenser, il... ; **2** *vt (gen)* compenser (*sb for sth* qn de qch); *(financially)* dédommager (*sb for sth* qn de qch). ◆ **compensation** *n* compensation *f*; dédommagement *m*; **in compensation** en compensation (*for* de).

compère ['kɒmpɛəʳ] **1** *n* animateur *m*, -trice *f*. **2** *vt show* animer.

compete [kəm'piːt] *vi* (**a**) *(gen)* rivaliser (*with sb* avec qn, *for sth* pour obtenir qch, *to do* pour faire). (**b**) *(Sport)* concourir (*against sb* avec qn, *for sth* pour obtenir qch, *to do* pour faire). **to ~ for a prize** se disputer un prix; **to ~ in a race** participer à une course. (**c**) *(Comm)* faire concurrence (*with* à, *for* pour). **to ~ with one another** se faire concurrence.

competent ['kɒmpɪtənt] *adj person, court* compétent (*for* pour, *to do* pour faire). **a ~ knowledge of** une connaissance suffisante de. ◆ **competence** *or* ◆ **competency** *n* compétence *f* (*for* pour, *in* en). ◆ **competently** *adv* avec compétence.

competition [ˌkɒmpɪ'tɪʃ(ə)n] *n* (**a**) compétition *f*, concurrence *f* (*for* pour); *(Comm)* concurrence. **in ~ with** en concurrence avec. (**b**) concours *m* (*for* pour); *(Sport)* compétition *f*; *(Aut)* course *f*. **to go in for a ~** se présenter à un concours; **beauty ~** concours de beauté; **I won it in a newspaper ~** je l'ai gagné en faisant un concours dans le journal. ◆ **competitive** *adj entry, selection* par concours; *person* qui a l'esprit de compétition; *price* concurrentiel; *goods* à prix concurrentiel; **competitive examination** concours *m*. ◆ **competitor** *n* concurrent(e) *m(f)*.

compile [kəm'paɪl] *vt material* compiler; *dictionary* composer (par compilation); *list, catalogue* dresser. ◆ **compiler** *n* compilateur *m*, -trice *f*.

complacent [kəm'pleɪs(ə)nt] *adj* satisfait de soi, suffisant. ◆ **complacence** *or* ◆ **complacency** *n* suffisance *f*. ◆ **complacently** *adv* avec suffisance.

complain [kəm'pleɪn] *vi* se plaindre (*to sb* à qn; *of, about* de; *that* que). ◆ **complaint** *n (expression of discontent)* plainte *f*; *(reason for ~)* sujet *m* de plainte; *(Comm)* réclamation *f*; *(Jur)* plainte; *(Med)* maladie *f*. *(Comm)* **to make a ~t** faire une réclamation (*about* au sujet de).

complected [kəm'plektɪd] *adj (US)* **dark-/light-~** au teint foncé/clair.

complement ['kɒmplɪmənt] **1** *n (gen, Gram, Math)* complément *m*; *[staff etc]* effectif *m* complet. **2** ['kɒmplɪment] *vt* être le complément de. ◆ **complementary** *adj* complémentaire.

complete [kəm'pliːt] **1** *adj* (**a**) *(total)* complet, total. **~ works** œuvres *fpl* complètes; **he's a ~ idiot *** il est complètement idiot; **~ with** doté de, pourvu de; **a house ~ with furniture** une maison meublée. (**b**) *(finished)* achevé, terminé. **2** *vt collection* compléter; *misfortune* mettre le comble à; *piece of work* achever, terminer; *order* exécuter; *form, questionnaire* remplir. **and to ~ his happiness** et pour comble de bonheur; **and just to ~ things** et pour couronner le tout. ◆ **completely** *adv* complètement. ◆ **completeness** *n* état complet. ◆ **completion** *n [work]* achèvement *m*; *[contract, sale]* exécution *f*; **near completion** près d'être achevé; **on completion of contract** à la signature du contrat.

complex ['kɒmpleks] **1** *adj (all senses)* complexe. **2** *n* (**a**) complexe *m*, ensemble *m*. **mining ~** complexe minier; **housing ~** (ensemble de) résidences *fpl*; *(high rise)* grand ensemble. (**b**) *(Psych)* complexe *m*. **he's got a ~ about it** il en fait un complexe. ◆ **complexity** *n* complexité *f*.

complexion [kəm'plekʃ(ə)n] *n [face]* teint *m*. *(fig)* **that puts a new ~ on it** ça change tout.

complicate ['kɒmplɪkeɪt] *vt* compliquer (*with* de; *by doing* en faisant). ◆ **complicated** *adj* compliqué. ◆ **complication** *n* complication *f*.

compliment ['kɒmplɪmənt] **1** *n* compliment *m*. **to pay sb a ~** faire un compliment à qn; **give him my ~s** faites-lui mes compliments; **the ~s of the season** tous mes vœux; **'with the ~s of Mr X'** 'avec les hommages *or* les bons compliments de Monsieur X'; **~s slip** ≈ papillon *m* (avec les bons compliments de l'expéditeur). **2** ['kɒmplɪment] *vt* faire des compliments à (*on* de, sur); féliciter (*on doing* d'avoir fait). ◆ **complimentary** *adj (praising)* flatteur; *(gratis)* à titre gracieux; *ticket* de faveur.

comply [kəm'plaɪ] *vi*: **to ~ with** *rules* respecter; *sb's wishes* se conformer à; *request* accéder à; *specifications* être conforme à. ◆ **compliance** *n*: **in compliance with** conformément à. ◆ **compliant** *adj* accommodant.

component [kəm'pəʊnənt] **1** *adj* constituant. **2** *n (Aut, Tech)* pièce *f*. **~s factory** usine *f* de pièces détachées.

compose [kəm'pəʊz] *vt* composer. **to be ~d of** se composer de; **to ~ o.s.** se calmer. ◆ **composed** *adj* calme, posé. ◆ **composedly** *adv* avec calme, posément. ◆ **composer** *n* compositeur *m*, -trice *f*. ◆ **composition** **1** *n (gen)* composition *f*; *(Scol: essay)* rédaction *f*; *[sentence]* construction *f*; *[word]* composition ; **2** *adj rubber* synthétique. ◆ **compositor** *n (Typ)* compositeur *m*, -trice *f*. ◆ **composure** *n* calme *m*, sang-froid *m*.

compos mentis ['kɒmpɒs'mentɪs] *adj* sain d'esprit.

compost ['kɒmpɒst] *n* compost *m*.

compound ['kɒmpaʊnd] **1** *n (Chem)* composé; *(Gram)* mot *m* composé; *(Tech)* compound *f*; *(enclosed area)* enclos *m*, enceinte *f*. **2** *adj (Chem)* composé; *number, sentence* complexe; *tense, word, interest* composé; *fracture* compliqué. **3** [kəm'paʊnd] *vt mixture* composer (*of* de); *ingredients* combiner; *(fig) problem, difficulties* aggraver.

comprehend [ˌkɒmprɪ'hend] *vt* comprendre. ◆ **comprehensible** *adj* compréhensible. ◆ **comprehension** *n* compréhension *f*; *(Scol)* exercice *m* de compréhension; *(inclusion)* inclusion *f*. ◆ **comprehensive** **1** *adj description, review* détaillé, complet; *knowledge* étendu; *rule* compréhensif; *measures* d'ensemble; *insurance* tous-risques *inv* ; **2** *n*: **comprehensive (school)** établissement *m* secondaire polyvalent.

compress [kəm'pres] **1** *vt substance* comprimer; *facts* condenser. **2** *vi* se comprimer; se condenser. **3** ['kɒmpres] *n (Med)* compresse *f*. ◆ **compression** *n* compression *f*; condensation *f*. ◆ **compressor** *n* compresseur *m*.

comprise [kəm'praɪz] *vt* comprendre.

compromise ['kɒmprəmaɪz] **1** *n* compromis *m*. **2** *vi* transiger (*over* sur), aboutir à un compromis. **3** *vt* compromettre. **4** *adj decision, solution* de compromis. ◆ **compromising** *adj* compromettant.

comptometer [kɒmp'tɒmɪtə[r]] *n* ® machine *f* comptable. ~ **operator** mécanographe *mf*.

compulsion [kəm'pʌlʃ(ə)n] *n* contrainte *f*. **under** ~ sous la contrainte; **you are under no** ~ vous n'êtes nullement obligé. ◆ **compulsive** *adj reason, demand* coercitif; *desire, behaviour* compulsif; *smoker, liar* invétéré; **she's a compulsive talker** parler est un besoin chez elle. ◆ **compulsively** *adv drink, smoke, talk* d'une façon compulsive. ◆ **compulsorily** *adv* obligatoirement, de force. ◆ **compulsory** *adj education, military service* obligatoire; *loan* forcé; **compulsory purchase** expropriation *f* pour cause d'utilité publique; **compulsory retirement** mise *f* à la retraite d'office.

compunction [kəm'pʌŋ(k)ʃ(ə)n] *n* scrupule *m* (*about sth* à propos de qch; *about doing* à faire).

compute [kəm'pju:t] *vt* calculer. ◆ **computation** *n* calcul *m*. ◆ **computer** **1** *n* ordinateur *m*; **he is in** ~**rs** il est dans l'informatique ; **2** *adj*: ~**r game** jeu *m* électronique; ~**r language** langage *m* de programmation; ~**r model** modèle calculé par ordinateur; ~**r operator** *n* opérateur *m*, -trice *f* de saisie; ~**r programmer** programmeur *m*, -euse *f*; ~**r programming** programmation *f*; ~**r science** informatique *f*; ~**r scientist** informaticien(ne) *m(f)*. ◆ **computerization** *n [facts, figures]* traitement *m* électronique; *[system, process]* automatisation *f* électronique; *[records]* mise *f* sur ordinateur. ◆ **computerize** *vt facts* informatiser; *system* automatiser; *records* mettre sur ordinateur.

comrade ['kɒmrɪd] *n* camarade *mf*. ◆ **comrade-in-arms** *n* compagnon *m* d'armes. ◆ **comradeship** *n* camaraderie *f*.

con * [kɒn] **1** *vt*: **to** ~ **sb into doing** amener qn à faire en le dupant; **I've been** ~**ned** je me suis fait avoir *. **2** *n*: **it was all a big** ~ c'était une vaste escroquerie. **3** *adj*: ~ **man** escroc *m*; ~ **game** escroquerie *f*.

concave ['kɒn'keɪv] *adj* concave.

conceal [kən'si:l] *vt object* cacher, dissimuler (*from sb* pour que qn ne le voie pas *etc*); *news, event* cacher (*from sb* à qn), garder secret; *emotions, thoughts* cacher (*from sb* à qn), dissimuler. ~**ed lighting** éclairage *m* indirect; *(Aut)* ~**ed turning** intersection *f* cachée. ◆ **concealment** *n* dissimulation *f*; *[facts]* non-divulgation *f*; *(place of ~ment)* cachette *f*.

concede [kən'si:d] *vt* concéder. **to** ~ **victory** s'avouer vaincu.

conceit [kən'si:t] *n* vanité *f*, suffisance *f*. ◆ **conceited** *adj* vaniteux, suffisant. ◆ **conceitedly** *adv* avec vanité, avec suffisance.

conceive [kən'si:v] **1** *vt child, idea* concevoir. **I cannot** ~ **why...** je ne comprends vraiment pas pourquoi... **2** *vi*: **to** ~ **of** concevoir. ◆ **conceivable** *adj* concevable; **it is conceivable that** il est concevable que + *subj*. ◆ **conceivably** *adv*: **she may conceivably be right** il est concevable qu'elle ait raison.

concentrate ['kɒnsəntreɪt] **1** *vt (gen)* concentrer (*on* sur); *hopes* reporter (*on* sur). **2** *vi* (**a**) *[troops, people]* se concentrer. (**b**) *(think hard)* se concentrer (*on* sur). **to** ~ **on doing** s'appliquer à faire; **I just can't** ~! je n'arrive pas à me concentrer!; **the terrorists** ~**d on the outlying farms** les terroristes ont concentré leurs attaques sur les fermes isolées; ~ **on getting well** occupe-toi d'abord de ta santé; *[speaker]* **I shall** ~ **on the 16th century** je traiterai en particulier le XVIe siècle. **3** *adj, n (Chem)* concentré *(m)*. ◆ **concentration** *n* concentration *f*; **concentration camp** camp *m* de concentration.

concept ['kɒnsept] *n* concept *m*.

conception [kən'sepʃ(ə)n] *n* conception *f*.

concern [kən'sɜ:n] **1** *vt (affect)* concerner; *(be the business of)* être l'affaire de; *(be about) [report]* se rapporter à. **as** ~**s** en ce qui concerne; **that doesn't** ~ **you** cela ne vous regarde pas, ce n'est pas votre affaire; **'to whom it may** ~**'** ≃ 'je soussigné(e) certifie que...'; **as far as he is** ~**ed** en ce qui le concerne; **the persons** ~**ed** les intéressés; **the department** ~**ed** *(under discussion)* le service en question; *(relevant)* le service compétent; **to be** ~**ed in** avoir un intérêt dans; **to** ~ **o.s. with** s'occuper de; **we are** ~**ed only with facts** nous ne nous occupons que des faits; **to be** ~**ed by** *or* **for** *or* **about** *or* **at** s'inquiéter de, être inquiet de; **I am** ~**ed about him** je m'inquiète à son sujet; **I am** ~**ed to hear that...** j'apprends avec inquiétude que...

2 *n* (**a**) **to have no** ~ **with** n'avoir rien à voir avec, être sans rapport avec; **it's no** ~ **of his, it's none of his** ~ cela ne le regarde pas; **what** ~ **is it of yours?** en quoi est-ce que cela vous regarde? (**b**) *(business* ~*)* entreprise *f*, affaire *f*. **he has a** ~ **in the business** il a des intérêts dans l'affaire. (**c**) *(anxiety)* inquiétude *f*, souci *m*. **a look of** ~ un regard inquiet.

◆ **concerned** *adj (worried)* inquiet, soucieux (*for* de). ◆ **concerning** *prep* en ce qui concerne, concernant.

concert ['kɒnsət] **1** *n* concert *m*. **in** ~ à l'unisson. **2** *adj ticket, pianist* de concert. ~ **performer** concertiste *mf*; ~ **tour** tournée *f* de concerts. ◆ **concerted** *adj action, effort* concerté. ◆ **concertgoer** *n* habitué(e) *m(f)* des concerts. ◆ **concert-hall** *n* salle *f* de concert.

concertina [ˌkɒnsə'ti:nə] **1** *n* concertina *m*. **2** *vi* se télescoper.

concerto [kən'tʃɛətəʊ] *n* concerto *m*.

concession [kən'seʃ(ə)n] *n* concession *f*. **price** ~ réduction *f*. ◆ **concessionary** *adj* concessionnaire; *ticket, fare* à prix réduit.

conch [kɒn(t)ʃ] *n* conque *f*.

conciliate [kən'sɪlɪeɪt] *vt person* apaiser; *opposing views* concilier. ◆ **conciliation** *n* apaisement *m*; conciliation *f*; *(Ind)* **conciliation board** conseil *m* d'arbitrage. ◆ **conciliator** *n* conciliateur *m*, -trice *f*; *(in negotiations)* médiateur *m*, -trice *f*. ◆ **conciliatory** *adj person, words, manner* conciliant; *spirit* de conciliation; *procedure* conciliatoire.

concise [kən'saɪs] *adj (short)* concis; *(shortened)* abrégé. ◆ **concisely** *adv* avec concision. ◆ **conciseness** *or* ◆ **concision** *n* concision *f*.

conclude [kən'klu:d] **1** *vt (all senses)* conclure. **'to be** ~**d'** 'suite et fin au prochain numéro'. **2** *vi [events]* se terminer (*with* par, sur); *[speaker]* conclure. ◆ **concluding** *adj* final. ◆ **conclusion** *n (all senses)* conclusion *f*; **in conclusion** pour conclure, en conclusion; **to come to the conclusion that** conclure que; **to try conclusions with sb** se mesurer contre qn. ◆ **conclusive** *adj* concluant. ◆ **conclusively** *adv* de façon concluante.

concoct [kən'kɒkt] *vt (Culin etc)* confectionner; *scheme, excuse* fabriquer. ◆ **concoction** *n (Culin etc)* mélange *m*, mixture *f (pej)*.

concord ['kɒŋkɔ:d] *n* concorde *f*.

concourse ['kɒŋkɔ:s] *n (crowd)* foule *f*; *(place)* lieu *m* de rassemblement; *(US: in park)* carrefour *m*; *(US: in building, station)* hall *m*; *(US: street)* boulevard *m*.

concrete ['kɒnkri:t] **1** *adj* (**a**) *object, proof, advantage* concret; *proposal, offer* précis. (**b**) *building* en béton. ~ **mixer** bétonnière *f*. **2** *n* (**a**) *(Constr)* béton *m*. (**b**) **the** ~ **and the abstract** le concret et l'abstrait. **3** *vt path* bétonner.

concur [kən'kɜ:ʳ] *vi (agree)* être d'accord (*with sb* avec qn, *in sth* sur qch); *[opinions]* converger; *[events]* coïncider, arriver en même temps; *(contribute)* concourir (*to* à). ◆ **concurrent** *adj* simultané. ◆ **concurrently** *adv* simultanément.

concussed [kən'kʌst] *adj* commotionné. ◆ **concussion** *n* commotion *f* cérébrale.

condemn [kən'dem] *vt person* condamner (*to* à); *building* condamner; *materials* déclarer inutilisable. **to** ~ **to death** condamner à mort; **the** ~**ed man** le condamné; **the** ~**ed cell** la cellule des condamnés. ◆ **condemnation** *n* condamnation *f*.

condense [kən'dens] *vt* condenser. ◆ **condensation** *n* condensation *f*. ◆ **condenser** *n* condensateur *m*.

condescend [,kɒndɪ'send] *vi* daigner (*to do* faire). **to** ~ **to sb** se montrer condescendant envers qn. ◆ **condescending** *adj* condescendant. ◆ **condescendingly** *adv* avec condescendance. ◆ **condescension** *n* condescendance *f*.

condiment ['kɒndɪmənt] *n* condiment *m*.

condition [kən'dɪʃ(ə)n] **1** *n (all senses)* condition *f*. **on** ~ **that** à condition que + *fut indic or subj*, à condition de + *infin*; **he made the** ~ **that no one should accompany him** il a stipulé que personne ne devait l'accompagner; **under** *or* **in the present** ~**s** dans les conditions actuelles; **working/living** ~**s** conditions de travail/de vie; **weather** ~**s** conditions météorologiques; **physical** ~ condition *or* état *m* physique; **in** ~ *thing* en bon état; *person* en forme; **it's out of** ~ c'est en mauvais état; **he's out of** ~ il n'est pas en forme; **she was not in a** ~ *or* **in any** ~ **to go out** elle n'était pas en état de sortir. **2** *vt (all senses)* conditionner (*into doing* à faire).
◆ **conditional** **1** *adj* conditionnel; **to be** ~**al (up)on** dépendre de ; **2** *n* conditionnel *m*; **in the** ~**al** au conditionnel. ◆ **conditionally** *adv* conditionnellement. ◆ **conditioner** *n (for hair)* baume démêlant; *(for skin)* crème traitante.

condole [kən'dəʊl] *vi* offrir ses condoléances (*with sb* à qn). ◆ **condolences** *npl* condoléances *fpl*.

condom ['kɒndəm] *n* préservatif *m*.

condone [kən'dəʊn] *vt (overlook)* fermer les yeux sur; *(forgive)* pardonner.

conduce [kən'dju:s] *vi*: **to** ~ **to** conduire à. ◆ **conducive** *adj*: **to be conducive to** conduire à.

conduct ['kɒndʌkt] **1** *n* conduite *f* (*towards* envers). **2** [kən'dʌkt] *vt person, group* conduire, mener; *heat* conduire; *business, orchestra* diriger; *enquiry* conduire. **he** ~**ed me round the gardens** il m'a fait faire le tour des jardins; ~**ed tour** *(gen)* voyage *m* organisé; *[building]* visite *f* guidée; **to** ~ **o.s.** se conduire, se comporter. ◆ **conduction** *n* conduction *f*. ◆ **conductivity** *n* conductivité *f*. ◆ **conductor** *n (Mus)* chef *m* d'orchestre; *[bus]* receveur *m*; *(US Rail)* chef de train; *[heat etc]* conducteur *m*. ◆ **conductress** *n* receveuse *f*.

cone [kəʊn] *n (gen)* cône *m*; *[ice cream]* cornet *m*.

confab ‡ ['kɒnfæb] *n* brin *m* de causette *.

confectioner [kən'fekʃ(ə)nəʳ] *n (sweetmaker)* confiseur *m*, -euse *f*; *(cakemaker)* pâtissier *m*, -ière *f*. ~**'s (shop)** confiserie *f* (-pâtisserie *f*); *(US)* ~**'s sugar** sucre *m* glace. ◆ **confectionery** *n* confiserie *f*; *(cakes etc)* pâtisserie *f*.

confederate [kən'fed(ə)rɪt] **1** *adj* confédéré. **2** *n* confédéré(e) *m(f)*; *(in criminal act)* complice *mf*. **3** [kən'fedəreɪt] *vt* confédérer. **4** *vi* se confédérer. ◆ **confederacy** *n* confédération *f*; *(US Hist)* **the Confederacy** les États *mpl* confédérés. ◆ **confederation** *n* confédération *f*.

confer [kən'fɜ:ʳ] **1** *vt* conférer (*on* à). **2** *vi* conférer (*with sb* avec qn; *about sth* de qch). ◆ **conference** ['kɒnf(ə)r(ə)ns] **1** *n (meeting)* conférence *f*, réunion *f*; *(especially academic)* congrès *m*; **in** ~**ence** en conférence; **the** ~**ence decided...** les participants à la conférence ont décidé... ; **2** *adj*: *(Telec)* ~ **call** audioconférence *f*; ~ **centre** *(town)* ville *f* de congrès; *(building)* palais *m* de congrès; ~ **room** salle *f* de conférences; ~**ence table** table *f* de conférence; ~**ence member** congressiste *mf*.

confess [kən'fes] **1** *vt* avouer, confesser (*that* que); *mistake* reconnaître; *(Rel)* confesser. **2** *vi* avouer (*to sth* qch; *to doing* avoir fait); *(Rel)* se confesser. ◆ **confession** *n* aveu *m*, confession *f* (*of* de); *(Rel)* confession; *(Jur)* **a full** ~**ion** des aveux complets; *(Rel)* **to hear sb's** ~**ion** confesser qn; **to go to** ~**ion** aller se confesser; **to make one's** ~**ion** se confesser. ◆ **confessional** *n* confessionnal *m*. ◆ **confessor** *n* confesseur *m*.

confetti [kən'feti:] *n* confettis *mpl*.

confide [kən'faɪd] **1** *vt* avouer en confidence (*that* que). **2** *vi*: **to** ~ **in sb** s'ouvrir à qn, se confier à qn; **to** ~ **in sb about sth** confier qch à qn; **to** ~ **in sb about what one is going to do** révéler à qn ce qu'on va faire. ◆ **confidant** *n* confident *m*. ◆ **confidante** *n* confidente *f*.

confidence ['kɒnfɪd(ə)ns] **1** *n* (**a**) *(trust)* confiance *f* (*in* en). **to have every** ~ **in sb** avoir pleine confiance en qn; **I have every** ~ **that** je suis sûr *or* certain que; **motion of no** ~ motion *f* de censure. (**b**) *(self-*~*)* confiance *f* en soi, assurance *f*. (**c**) *(secret)* confidence *f*. **to take sb into one's** ~ faire des confidences à qn; **this is in strict** ~ c'est strictement confidentiel; **'write in** ~ **to X'** 'écrire à X: discrétion garantie'. **2** *adj*: ~ **trick** escroquerie *f*; ~ **trickster** escroc *m*. ◆ **confident** *adj (self* ~*)* sûr de soi, assuré; *(sure)* sûr, persuadé (*of* de; *of doing* de faire; *that* que). ◆ **confidential** *adj letter, remark, information* confidentiel; *servant* de confiance; *secretary* particulier. ◆ **confidentiality** *n* confidentialité *f*. ◆ **confidentially** *adv* en confidence. ◆ **confidently** *adv* avec confiance; *predict* avec assurance.

confine [kən'faɪn] *vt* (**a**) *(imprison)* emprisonner; *(shut up)* enfermer (*in* dans). **to be** ~**d to the house** être obligé de rester chez soi; *(Mil)* ~**d to barracks** consigné. (**b**) *(limit)* limiter, borner. **to** ~ **o.s. to doing** se borner à faire; **the damage is** ~**d to the back of the car** seul l'arrière de la voiture est endommagé; **in a** ~**d space** dans un espace restreint. ◆ **confinement** *n (Med)* couches *fpl*; *(imprisonment)* emprisonnement *m*, réclusion *f (Jur)*.

confirm [kən'fɜ:m] *vt (gen, also Rel)* confirmer; *one's resolve* raffermir; *treaty, appointment* ratifier. ◆ **confirmation** *n* confirmation *f*; raffermissement *m*; ratification *f*. ◆ **confirmed** *adj smoker, habit, liar* invétéré; *bachelor* endurci; *admirer* fervent.

confiscate ['kɒnfɪskeɪt] *vt* confisquer (*sth from sb* qch à qn). ◆ **confiscation** *n* confiscation *f*.

conflict ['kɒnflɪkt] **1** *n* conflit *m*. **2** [kən'flɪkt] *vi* être *or* entrer en conflit (*with* avec); *[ideas]* s'opposer, se heurter (*with* à). **that** ~**s with what he told me** ceci est en contradiction avec ce qu'il m'a raconté. ◆ **conflicting** *adj views* incompatible; *reports, evidence* contradictoire.

conform [kən'fɔ:m] *vi* se conformer (*to, with* à); *[actions, sayings]* être en conformité (*to* avec). ◆ **conformist** *adj, n* conformiste *(mf)*. ◆ **conformity** *n*: **in ~ity with** conformément à.

confound [kən'faʊnd] *vt* (**a**) *(perplex)* déconcerter. (**b**) ~ **it!** * la barbe! *; ~ **him!** * qu'il aille au diable!

confront [kən'frʌnt] *vt* confronter (*sb with sb* qn avec qn); *enemy, danger* affronter. **to ~ sb with sth** présenter qch à qn; **problems which ~ us** problèmes auxquels nous devons faire face. ◆ **confrontation** *n* affrontement *m; (with situation etc)* confrontation *f*.

confuse [kən'fju:z] *vt* (**a**) *(throw into disorder) opponents* confondre; *(perplex)* déconcerter; *(embarrass)* confondre, embarrasser; *(mix up) persons, ideas* embrouiller. **you are just confusing me** tu m'embrouilles. (**b**) *(not distinguish between)* confondre (*with* avec). ◆ **confused** *adj person (muddled)* désorienté; *(embarrassed)* embarrassé; *(perplexed)* déconcerté; *opponent* confondu; *mind, sounds, memories, ideas, situation* confus; **to get ~d** *(muddled up)* ne plus savoir où on en est; *(embarrassed)* se troubler. ◆ **confusedly** *adv* confusément. ◆ **confusing** *adj* déroutant. ◆ **confusion** *n* confusion *f*; **he was in a state of confusion** la confusion régnait dans son esprit.

congeal [kən'dʒi:l] *vi [spilt blood, paint]* sécher; *[spilt oil, gravy]* se figer.

congenial [kən'dʒi:nɪəl] *adj* sympathique, agréable.

congenital [kən'dʒenɪtl] *adj* congénital.

congested [kən'dʒestɪd] *adj town, countryside* surpeuplé; *street, corridors* encombré; *telephone lines* embouteillé; *(Med)* congestionné. ~ **traffic** encombrements *mpl*. ◆ **congestion** *n* surpeuplement *m*; encombrement *m*; congestion *f*.

Congo ['kɒŋgəʊ] *n (state)* (république *f* du) Congo *m*. ◆ **Congolese 1** *adj* congolais ; **2** *n* Congolais(e) *m(f)*.

congratulate [kən'grætjʊleɪt] *vt* féliciter (*on* de, *on doing* de faire). ◆ **congratulations** *npl* félicitations *fpl* (*on* pour); **congratulations!** toutes mes félicitations!

congregate ['kɒŋgrɪgeɪt] *vi* se rassembler, s'assembler. ◆ **congregation** *n [worshippers]* assemblée *f* (des fidèles); *[cardinals etc]* congrégation *f*. ◆ **congregational** *adj*: **the Congregational Church** l'Église *f* congrégationaliste.

congress ['kɒŋgres] **1** *n* congrès *m*. *(US)* **C~** le Congrès. **2** *adj*: ~ **member** congressiste *mf*. ◆ **Congressional** *adj (US)* du Congrès; **C~ional Record** Journal *m* officiel du Congrès. ◆ **congressman** *or* ◆ **congresswoman** *n (US)* membre *m* du Congrès, ≃ député *m*; **C~man J. Smith said that...** Monsieur le député J. Smith a dit que...

conic(al) ['kɒnɪk(əl)] *adj* conique.

conifer ['kɒnɪfəʳ] *n* conifère *m*. ◆ **coniferous** *adj tree* conifère; *forest* de conifères.

conjecture [kən'dʒektʃəʳ] **1** *vti* conjecturer. **2** *n* conjecture *f*. ◆ **conjectural** *adj* conjectural.

conjugal ['kɒn(d)ʒʊgəl] *adj* conjugal.

conjugate ['kɒn(d)ʒʊgeɪt] **1** *vt* conjuguer. **2** *vi* se conjuguer. ◆ **conjugation** *n* conjugaison *f*.

conjunction [kən'dʒʌŋ(k)ʃ(ə)n] *n* conjonction *f*. **in ~ with** conjointement avec.

conjunctivitis [kən,dʒʌŋ(k)tɪ'vaɪtɪs] *n* conjonctivite *f*.

conjuncture [kən'dʒʌŋ(k)tʃəʳ] *n* conjoncture *f*.

conjure ['kʌn(d)ʒəʳ] **1** *vt* faire apparaître *(par la prestidigitation)*. **2** *vi* faire des tours de passe-passe; *(juggle)* jongler (*with* avec). **a name to ~ with** un nom prestigieux. ◆ **conjure up** *vt sep memories* évoquer. **to ~ up visions of...** évoquer... ◆ **conjurer** *or* ◆ **conjuror** *n* prestidigitateur *m*, -trice *f*. ◆ **conjuring** *n* prestidigitation *f*; **conjuring trick** tour *m* de passe-passe.

conk ‡ [kɒŋk] *vi* (~ **out**) tomber *or* rester en panne.

conker * ['kɒŋkəʳ] *n (Brit)* marron *m*.

connect [kə'nekt] **1** *vt (gen)* relier, rattacher (*with, to* à); *[roads, rail link, airline]* relier (*with, to* à); *(Telec) caller* mettre en communication (*with* avec); *pipes, drains* raccorder (*to* à); *(install) cooker, telephone* brancher, raccorder. *(Telec)* **we are trying to ~ you** nous essayons d'obtenir votre communication; *(Elec)* **to ~ to the mains** brancher sur le secteur; **I always ~ Paris with springtime** j'associe toujours Paris au printemps; **he is ~ed with that firm** il a des rapports *or* des contacts avec cette firme; **it is not ~ed with the murder** cela n'a aucun rapport avec *or* n'a rien à voir avec le meurtre; **well ~ed** de bonne famille. **2** *vi* se relier, se raccorder; *[trains]* assurer la correspondance (*with* avec). *(Aut)* **~ing rod** bielle *f*. ◆ **connected** *adj languages, species* connexe; *events* lié; *rooms* communicants. ◆ **connection** *or* ◆ **connexion** *n (gen)* rapport *m* (*with* avec), lien *m* (*between* entre); *(Elec)* contact *m*; *(Telec)* communication *f*; *(Rail)* correspondance *f* (*with* avec); **this has no ~ion with** ceci n'a aucun rapport avec; **in this ~ion** à ce sujet; **in ~ion with** à propos de; **in another ~ion** dans un autre ordre d'idées; **to build up a ~ion with a firm** établir des relations d'affaires avec une firme; **we have no ~ion with any other firm** toute ressemblance avec une autre compagnie est purement fortuite; **they have some family ~ion** ils ont un lien de parenté; *(Rail)* **to miss one's ~ion** manquer la correspondance.

conning tower ['kɒnɪŋ ,taʊəʳ] *n [submarine]* kiosque *m*; *[warship]* centre *m* opérationnel.

connive [kə'naɪv] *vi*: **to ~ at** *(pretend not to notice)* fermer les yeux sur; *(aid and abet)* être de connivence dans. ◆ **connivance** *n* connivence *f*.

connoisseur [,kɒnə'sɜ:ʳ] *n* connaisseur *m*, -euse *f* (*of* de, en).

conquer ['kɒŋkəʳ] *vt (lit) person, enemy* vaincre; *nation, country, castle* conquérir; *(fig) feelings, habits* surmonter. ◆ **conquering** *adj* victorieux. ◆ **conqueror** *n* conquérant *m*; *(fig)* vainqueur *m*. ◆ **conquest** *n* conquête *f*.

conscience ['kɒnʃ(ə)ns] *n* conscience *f*. **to have a clear ~** avoir la conscience tranquille; **to have sth on one's ~** avoir qch sur la conscience; **in (all) ~** en conscience; **for ~' sake** par acquit de conscience. ◆ **conscience-stricken** *adj* pris de remords. ◆ **conscientious** *adj person, work* consciencieux; **conscientious objector** objecteur *m* de conscience. ◆ **conscientiously** *adv* consciencieusement. ◆ **conscientiousness** *n* conscience *f*.

conscious ['kɒnʃəs] *adj* (**a**) conscient, ayant conscience (*of* de); *insult* délibéré; *guilt* ressenti clairement. **to be ~ of doing** avoir conscience de faire; **to become ~ of sth** prendre conscience de qch. (**b**) *(Med)* conscient. **to become ~** revenir à soi, reprendre connaissance. ◆ **consciously** *adv* consciemment. ◆ **consciousness** *n* conscience *f* (*of* de); *(Med)* connaissance *f*; **to lose/regain ~ness** perdre/reprendre connaissance; **~ness-raising** prise *f* de conscience.

conscript [kən'skrɪpt] **1** *vt* recruter (par conscription). **2** ['kɒnskrɪpt] *n* conscrit *m*. ◆ **conscription** *n* conscription *f*.

consecrate ['kɒnsɪkreɪt] *vt* consacrer (*to* à). ◆ **consecration** *n* consécration *f*.

consecutive [kən'sekjʊtɪv] *adj* consécutif, de suite. ◆ **consecutively** *adv* consécutivement; *(Jur)* ... **the sentences to be served ~ly** ... avec cumul *m* de peines.

consensus [kən'sensəs] *n*: ~ **of opinion** opinion *f* générale, consensus *m* d'opinion.

consent [kən'sent] **1** *vi* consentir (*to sth* à qch, *to do* à faire). *(Jur)* **~ing adults** adultes consentants. **2** *n* consentement *m*, assentiment *m*. **by common ~** de l'opinion de tous; **by mutual ~** *(general agreement)* d'un commun accord; *(private arrangement)* à l'amiable; **divorce by (mutual) ~** divorce *m* par consentement mutuel; **age of ~** âge *m* nubile légal.

consequence ['kɒnsɪkwəns] *n (result)* conséquence *f*. **in ~** par conséquent; **in ~ of which** par suite de quoi; **it's of no ~** cela n'a aucune importance; **as a ~ of sth** en conséquence de qch; **he's of no ~** c'est un homme de peu d'importance. ◆ **consequent** *adj* résultant (*on* de). ◆ **consequently** *adv* par conséquent, en conséquence.

conserve [kən'sɜːv] *vt* conserver, préserver; *strength* ménager; *electricity* économiser. ◆ **conservancy** *or* ◆ **conservation** *n* préservation *f*; *[nature]* défense *f* de l'environnement; *(Phys)* conservation *f*; **conservation area** secteur sauvegardé. ◆ **conservationist** *n* défenseur *m* de l'environnement. ◆ **conservatism** *n* conservatisme *m*. ◆ **conservative** **1** *adj (Pol)* conservateur; *(gen) assessment* modeste; *style, behaviour* traditionnel; **at a conservative estimate** au bas mot ; **2** *n* conservateur *m*, -trice *f*. ◆ **conservatory** *n (greenhouse)* serre *f*; *(Mus etc)* conservatoire *m*.

consider [kən'sɪdəʳ] *vt (gen)* considérer (*that* que); *(think about) problem, possibility* considérer, examiner; *question, matter, subject* réfléchir à; *(take into account) facts* prendre en considération; *person's feelings* avoir égard à; *cost, difficulties, dangers* tenir compte de. **I had not ~ed taking it with me** je n'avais pas envisagé de l'emporter; **all things ~ed** tout bien considéré; **it is my ~ed opinion that...** après avoir mûrement réfléchi je pense que...; **he is being ~ed for the post** on songe à lui pour le poste; **she ~s him very mean** elle le considère comme très avare, elle estime qu'il est très avare; **~ yourself lucky** * estimez-vous heureux. ◆ **considering** **1** *prep* étant donné, vu (*that* que); **2** *adj*: **he played very well, ~ing** tout compte fait, il a très bien joué.

considerable [kən'sɪd(ə)rəbl] *adj* considérable. **to a ~ extent** dans une large mesure; **we had ~ difficulty in finding you** nous avons eu beaucoup de mal à vous trouver. ◆ **considerably** *adv* considérablement.

considerate [kən'sɪd(ə)rɪt] *adj* prévenant (*towards* envers), plein d'égards (*towards* pour, envers). ◆ **considerately** *adv act* avec prévenance.

consideration [kənˌsɪdə'reɪʃ(ə)n] *n (all senses)* considération *f*. **out of ~ for** par égard pour; **to show ~ for sb's feelings** ménager les susceptibilités de qn; **to take sth into ~** prendre qch en considération, tenir compte de qch; **taking everything into ~** tout bien considéré; **the matter is under ~** l'affaire est à l'étude; **after due ~** après mûre réflexion; **money is the first ~** il faut considérer avant tout la question d'argent; **it's of no ~** cela n'a aucune importance; **money is no ~** l'argent n'entre pas en ligne de compte; **his age was an important ~** son âge constituait un facteur important; **to do sth for a ~** faire qch moyennant finance.

consign [kən'saɪn] *vt (send)* expédier; *(hand over)* remettre. ◆ **consignee** *n* consignataire *mf*. ◆ **consignment** *n (incoming)* arrivage *m*; *(outgoing)* envoi *m*.

consist [kən'sɪst] *vi* consister (*of* en; *in doing* à faire; *in sth* dans qch). ◆ **consistency** *n* consistance *f*; *(fig)* **to lack ~ency** manquer de logique *f*. ◆ **consistent** *adj person, behaviour* conséquent, logique; *argument* qui se tient; **~ent with** compatible avec. ◆ **consistently** *adv argue* avec logique; *happen* régulièrement, sans exception; **~ently with** conformément à.

console¹ [kən'səʊl] *vt* consoler (*sb for sth* qn de qch). ◆ **consolation** **1** *n* consolation *f* ; **2** *adj*: **consolation prize** prix *m* de consolation. ◆ **consoling** *adj* consolant.

console² ['kɒnsəʊl] *n* console *f; [aircraft]* tableau *m* de bord.

consolidate [kən'sɒlɪdeɪt] *vt* consolider. ◆ **consolidation** *n* consolidation *f*.

consonant ['kɒnsənənt] *n* consonne *f*.

consort ['kɒnsɔːt] **1** *n* époux *m*, épouse *f*. **prince ~** prince *m* consort. **2** [kən'sɔːt] *vi*: **to ~ with sb** fréquenter qn.

consortium [kən'sɔːtɪəm] *n* consortium *m*.

conspicuous [kən'spɪkjʊəs] *adj person, behaviour, clothes* voyant, qui attire la vue; *poster* qui attire les regards; *bravery* insigne; *difference, fact* notable, remarquable. **a ~ lack of...** un manque manifeste de...; **he was in a ~ position** il était bien en évidence; *(fig)* il occupait une situation très en vue; **to make o.s. ~** se faire remarquer; **to be ~ by one's absence** briller par son absence. ◆ **conspicuously** *adv behave* d'une manière à se faire remarquer; *angry* visiblement.

conspire [kən'spaɪəʳ] *vi* conspirer (*against* contre). **to ~ to do** *[people]* comploter pour faire; *[events]* conspirer à faire. ◆ **conspiracy** *n* conspiration *f*, conjuration *f*; **conspiracy of silence** conspiration du silence. ◆ **conspirator** *n* conspirateur *m*, -trice *f*.

constable ['kʌnstəbl] *n (police ~) (in town)* agent *m* de police, gardien *m* de la paix; *(in country)* gendarme *m*. ◆ **constabulary** *n* police *f*; gendarmerie *f*.

constant ['kɒnst(ə)nt] **1** *adj quarrels, interruptions* incessant, continuel; *affection* inaltérable, constant; *friend* fidèle. **2** *n (Math, Phys)* constante *f*. ◆ **constancy** *n* constance *f*. ◆ **constantly** *adv* constamment, sans cesse.

constellation [ˌkɒnstə'leɪʃ(ə)n] *n* constellation *f*.

consternation [ˌkɒnstə'neɪʃ(ə)n] *n* consternation *f*. **filled with ~** frappé de consternation, consterné.

constipate [ˌkɒnstɪpeɪt] *vt* constiper. ◆ **constipated** *adj* constipé. ◆ **constipation** *n* constipation *f*.

constituency [kən'stɪtjʊənsɪ] *n (place)* circonscription *f* électorale; *(people)* électeurs *mpl* (d'une circonscription). **~ party** section *f* locale (du parti). ◆ **constituent** **1** *adj* constituant ; **2** *n (element)* élément constitutif; *(Pol)* électeur *m*, -trice *f* (dans une circonscription).

constitute ['kɒnstɪtjuːt] *vt* constituer. ◆ **constitution** *n* constitution *f*. ◆ **constitutional** **1** *adj (Pol etc)* constitutionnel; *(Med)* diathésique. **2** *n* (*) petite promenade *f*. ◆ **constitutionally** *adv (Pol etc)* constitutionnellement; *(Med etc)* par nature.

constrain [kən'streɪn] *vt* contraindre (*sb to do* qn à faire). **to be ~ed to do** être contraint de faire. ◆ **constrained** *adj atmosphere* de gêne; *voice, manner* contraint. ◆ **constraint** *n* contrainte *f*.

constrict [kən'strɪkt] *vt (gen)* resserrer; *muscle etc* serrer; *movements* gêner. ◆ **constricted** *adj space, freedom* restreint; *point of view* borné; *movement* limité. ◆ **constriction** *n* resserrement *m*; constriction *f (esp Med)*.

construct [kən'strʌkt] *vt building, novel, play* construire; *theory, one's defence* bâtir. ◆ **construction** *n* construction *f*; **under ~ion** en construction; **~ion engineer** ingénieur *m* des travaux publics et des bâtiments; **to put a wrong ~ion on sb's words** mal interpréter les paroles de qn. ◆ **constructive** *adj* constructif. ◆ **constructively** *adv* d'une manière constructive. ◆ **constructor** *n* constructeur *m*, -trice *f*.

construe [kən'stru:] *vt sentence* analyser; *Latin poem* expliquer. **this was ~d as...** on a interprété ceci comme signifiant...

consul ['kɒnsəl] *n* consul *m*. **~ general** consul général. ◆ **consular** *adj* consulaire; **~ar section** service *m* consulaire. ◆ **consulate** *n* consulat *m*.

consult [kən'sʌlt] **1** *vt* consulter (*about* sur, au sujet de). **2** *vi* être en consultation (*with* avec). **to ~ together** se consulter. ◆ **consultant 1** *n* consultant *m*, expert-conseil *m* (*to sb* auprès de qn); *(Med)* médecin *m* consultant, spécialiste *m* ; **2** *adj* consultant. ◆ **consultation** *n* consultation *f*. ◆ **consultative** *adj* consultatif. ◆ **consulting** *adj engineer etc* conseil *(f inv)*; **~ing hours** heures *fpl* de consultation; **~ing room** cabinet *m* de consultation.

consume [kən'sju:m] *vt food, resources, fuel* consommer; *[fire]* consumer. **~d with** *grief* consumé de; *desire* brûlant de; *jealousy* rongé par. ◆ **consumables** *npl (Econ)* produits *mpl* de consommation. ◆ **consumer 1** *n* consommateur *m*, -trice *f*; *[telephone, gas, electricity]* abonné(e) *m(f)*; **2** *adj protection, resistance* du consommateur; **~r demand** demande *f* de consommation; **~r durables** biens *mpl* de consommation durable; **~r goods** biens *mpl* de consommation; **Ministry of C~r Protection** ≃ Secrétariat *m* d'État à la consommation; **~r research** études *fpl* de marchés; **~r society** société *f* de consommation. ◆ **consumerism** *n* consumérisme *m*. ◆ **consuming** *adj passion* dévorant, brûlant.

consummate [kən'sʌmɪt] **1** *adj* consommé. **2** ['kɒnsʌmeɪt] *vt* consommer. ◆ **consummation** *n* consommation *f (d'un mariage)*.

consumption [kən'sʌm(p)ʃ(ə)n] *n* (**a**) *[food, fuel]* consommation *f*. **not fit for human ~** non-comestible; *(pej)* immangeable. (**b**) *(†: tuberculosis)* phtisie † *f*.

contact ['kɒntækt] **1** *n (all senses)* contact *m*. **to be in ~ with sb** être en contact avec qn; **we have had no ~ with him** nous sommes sans contact avec lui; **I seem to make no ~ with him** je n'arrive pas à communiquer avec lui; **he has some ~s in Paris** il a des relations *fpl* à Paris. **2** *vt* se mettre en contact *or* en rapport avec, contacter. **we'll ~ you soon** nous nous mettrons en rapport avec vous sous peu. **3** *adj*: **~ lenses** verres *mpl* de contact.

contagion [kən'teɪdʒ(ə)n] *n* contagion *f*. ◆ **contagious** *adj* contagieux.

contain [kən'teɪn] *vt* contenir. **he couldn't ~ himself for joy** il ne se sentait pas de joie. ◆ **container 1** *n (goods transport)* conteneur *m*; *(jug, box etc)* récipient *m* ; **2** *adj train, ship* porte-conteneurs *inv*; *dock* pour la manutention de conteneurs; *terminal* à conteneurs; *transport* par conteneurs. ◆ **containerization** *n* conteneurisation *f*. ◆ **containerize** *vt* conteneuriser. ◆ **containment** *n (Pol)* endiguement *m*.

contaminate [kən'tæmɪneɪt] *vt* contaminer. ◆ **contamination** *n* contamination *f*.

contemplate ['kɒntempleɪt] *vt (look at)* contempler; *(consider)* envisager (*doing* de faire). ◆ **contemplation** *n* contemplation *f*. ◆ **contemplative** *adj* contemplatif.

contemporary [kən'temp(ə)rərɪ] *adj, n* contemporain(e) *m(f)* (*with* de).

contempt [kən'tem(p)t] *n* mépris *m*. **to hold in ~** mépriser; **it's beneath ~** c'est au-dessous de tout; **~ of court** outrage *m* à la Cour. ◆ **contemptible** *adj* méprisable. ◆ **contemptuous** *adj person* dédaigneux (*of* de); *manner* méprisant; *gesture* de mépris. ◆ **contemptuously** *adv* avec mépris, dédaigneusement.

contend [kən'tend] **1** *vi*: **to ~ with sb for sth** disputer qch à qn; **to have sth to ~ with** devoir faire face à qch; **to have sb to ~ with** avoir affaire à qn; **he has a lot to ~ with** il a beaucoup de problèmes. **2** *vt* soutenir, prétendre (*that* que). ◆ **contender** *n* concurrent(e) *m(f)*; *(for job, election)* candidat *m;* **~er for** prétendant(e) *m(f)* à. ◆ **contention** *n (dispute)* dispute *f*; *(assertion)* assertion *f*; **bone of contention** pomme *f* de discorde. ◆ **contentious** *adj person* querelleur; *issue* contesté.

content[1] [kən'tent] **1** *adj* content, satisfait (*with* de). **to be ~ with** *(accept)* se contenter de; **he is quite ~ to stay** il ne demande pas mieux que de rester. **2** *n* contentement *m*. **3** *vt* contenter. **to ~ o.s. with doing** se contenter de faire. ◆ **contented** *adj* content (*with* de). ◆ **contentedly** *adv* avec contentement. ◆ **contentedness** *or* ◆ **contentment** *n* contentement *m*.

content[2] ['kɒntent] *n [book, play]* contenu *m*; *[document, metal]* teneur *f*. *[box etc]* **~s** contenu; *[book]* **'~s'** 'table *f* des matières'; **oranges have a high vitamin C ~** les oranges sont riches en vitamine C; **gold ~** teneur en or.

contest [kən'test] **1** *vt matter, result, will* contester; *election, seat* disputer. **2** ['kɒntest] *n* combat *m*, lutte *f*; *(Sport)* lutte; *(Boxing, Wrestling)* rencontre *f*; *(competition)* concours *m*. ◆ **contestant** *n (for prize)* concurrent(e) *m(f)*; *(in fight)* adversaire *mf*.

context ['kɒntekst] *n* contexte *m*. **in/out of ~** dans le/sans contexte.

continent ['kɒntɪnənt] *n* continent *m*. *(Brit)* **the C~** l'Europe continentale; **on the C~** en Europe. ◆ **continental** *adj (gen)* continental; *drift* des continents; **~al breakfast** petit-déjeuner *m* à la française; **~al quilt** couette *f*.

contingency [kən'tɪdʒ(ə)nsɪ] **1** *n* événement *m* imprévu, éventualité *f*. **in a ~** en cas d'imprévu. **2** *adj*: **~ fund** caisse *f* de prévoyance; **~ plans** plans *mpl* d'urgence. ◆ **contingent 1** *adj* contingent; **to be contingent upon sth** dépendre de qch ; **2** *n* contingent *m*.

continue [kən'tɪnju:] **1** *vt (gen)* continuer (*to do* à *or* de faire); *tradition, policy* maintenir; *(after interruption)* reprendre. *[serial]* **to be ~d** à suivre; **to be ~d on page 10** suite page 10; **to ~ one's way** continuer son chemin; *(after pause)* se remettre en marche; **'and so', he ~d** 'et ainsi', reprit-il *or* poursuivit-il. **2** *vi (gen)* continuer; *(after interruption)* reprendre. **the forest ~s to the sea** la forêt s'étend jusqu'à la mer; **to ~ in one's job** garder *or* conserver son poste; **he ~d with his voluntary work** il a poursuivi son travail bénévole; **she ~d as his secretary** elle est restée sa secrétaire. ◆ **continual** *adj* continuel. ◆ **continually** *adv* continuellement, sans cesse. ◆ **continuance** *n (duration)* durée *f*; *(continuation)* continuation *f*; *(continuity)* continuité *f*. ◆ **continuation** *n* continuation *f*; *(after interruption)* reprise *f*; *[serial story]* suite *f*. ◆ **continuing** *adj argument* ininterrompu; *correspondence* soutenu. ◆ **continuity** *n* continuité *f*; **continuity girl** scripte *f*. ◆ **continuous** *adj* continu; *(Cine)* **continuous performance** spectacle *m* permanent; **continuous stationery** papier *m* en continu. ◆ **continuously** *adv (uninterruptedly)* sans interruption ; *(repeatedly)* continuellement, sans arrêt. ◆ **continuum** *n* continuum *m*.

contort [kən'tɔːt] *vt features* tordre; *words, story* déformer. ◆ **contortion** *n [esp acrobat]* contorsion *f*; *[features]* convulsion *f*. ◆ **contortionist** *n* contorsionniste *mf*.

contour ['kɒntʊəʳ] **1** *n* contour *m*. **2** *adj*: ~ **line** courbe *f* de niveau; ~ **map** carte *f* avec courbes de niveau.

contraband ['kɒntrəbænd] **1** *n* contrebande *f*. **2** *adj* de contrebande.

contraception [ˌkɒntrə'sepʃ(ə)n] *n* contraception *f*. ◆ **contraceptive** *adj, n* contraceptif *(m)*.

contract ['kɒntrækt] **1** *n* contrat *m*. **marriage** ~ contrat de mariage; **to enter into a** ~ **with sb for sth** passer un contrat avec qn pour qch; **to put work out to** ~ mettre du travail à l'entreprise; **by** ~ par *or* sur contrat; *(fig: by killer)* **there's a** ~ **out for him** ‡ sa tête a été mise à prix *(par un rival)*. **2** *adj*: ~ **bridge** bridge *m* contrat; ~ **work** travail *m* à l'entreprise. **3** [kən'trækt] *vt* (**a**) *debts, illness, vices, alliance* contracter. **to** ~ **to do** s'engager (par contrat) à faire; **to** ~ **with sb to do** passer un contrat avec qn pour faire. (**b**) *muscles, metal* contracter; *face* crisper; *word, phrase* contracter (*to* en). **4** *vi* se contracter.
◆ **contract in** *vi* s'engager (par contrat).
◆ **contract out** **1** *vi* se libérer, se dégager (*of* de). **to** ~ **out of a pension scheme** cesser de cotiser à une caisse de retraite. **2** *vt sep work* sous-traiter (*to sb* à qn).
◆ **contraction** *n* contraction *f*; *(word)* forme *f* contractée. ◆ **contractor** *n* entrepreneur *m*. ◆ **contractual** *adj* contractuel.

contradict [ˌkɒntrə'dɪkt] *vt* contredire. ◆ **contradiction** *n* contradiction *f*; **a** ~**ion in terms** une contradiction (dans les termes). ◆ **contradictory** *adj* contradictoire.

contraflow ['kɒntrəfləʊ] *adj (Aut)* ~ **lane** voie *f* à contresens.

contralto [kən'træltəʊ] **1** *n* contralto *m*. **2** *adj* de contralto.

contraption * [kən'træpʃ(ə)n] *n* machin * *m*, truc * *m*.

contrary ['kɒntrərɪ] **1** *adj* (**a**) *(gen)* contraire (*to* à). **in a** ~ **direction** en sens inverse *or* opposé; ~ **to nature** contre nature. (**b**) [kən'trɛərɪ] *(self-willed)* contrariant. **2** *adv* contrairement (*to* à). **3** *n* contraire *m*. **on the** ~ au contraire; **unless you hear to the** ~ sauf contrordre. ◆ **contrariness** *n* esprit *m* de contradiction. ◆ **contrariwise** *adv (on the contrary)* au contraire; *(in opposite direction)* en sens opposé.

contrast [kən'trɑːst] **1** *vt* mettre en contraste, contraster (*with* avec). **2** *vi* contraster, faire contraste (*with* avec). **3** ['kɒntrɑːst] *n* contraste *m* (*between* entre). **in** ~ par contraste (*to* avec). ◆ **contrasting** *adj opinions* opposé; *colours* contrasté.

contravene [ˌkɒntrə'viːn] *vt* enfreindre. ◆ **contravention** *n* infraction *f* (*of* à).

contribute [kən'trɪbjuːt] **1** *vt (gen)* contribuer; *specific sum* offrir, donner; *(Admin)* cotiser; *article to a newspaper* donner, envoyer. **2** *vi*: **to** ~ **to** *collection, charity, misunderstanding* contribuer à; *discussion* prendre part à, participer à; *newspaper* collaborer à; **to** ~ **to doing** contribuer à faire.
◆ **contribution** [ˌkɒntrɪ'bjuːʃ(ə)n] *n (gen)* contribution *f*; *(Admin)* cotisation *f*; *(to publication)* article *m*. ◆ **contributor** *n (to publication)* collaborateur *m*, -trice *f*; *[money, goods]* donateur *m*, -trice *f*. ◆ **contributory** *adj cause* accessoire; **it was a contributory factor in...** cela a contribué à...; **contributory pension scheme** caisse *f* de retraite (à laquelle cotisent les employés).

contrite ['kɒntraɪt] *adj* contrit. ◆ **contrition** *n* contrition *f*.

contrive [kən'traɪv] *vt plan, scheme* combiner, inventer. **to** ~ **a means of doing** trouver un moyen pour faire; **to** ~ **to do** s'arranger pour faire, trouver le moyen de faire; **can you** ~ **to be here at 3 o'clock?** est-ce que vous pouvez vous arranger pour être ici à 3 heures? ◆ **contrivance** *n (gen)* appareil *m*; *(device)* dispositif *m*. ◆ **contrived** *adj* forcé, qui manque de naturel.

control [kən'trəʊl] **1** *n* (**a**) *(gen)* contrôle *m* (*of* de); autorité *f* (*over* sur). **the** ~ **of** *[traffic]* la réglementation de; *[aircraft]* le contrôle de; *[pests]* la suppression de; *[disease, forest fires]* la lutte contre; *[the seas, the air]* la maîtrise de; **he has no** ~ **over his children** il n'a aucune autorité sur ses enfants; **to keep a dog under** ~ se faire obéir d'un chien; **to have a horse under** ~ maîtriser un cheval; **to lose** ~ **of** perdre le contrôle de; **to lose** ~ **of o.s.** perdre tout contrôle de soi; **to be in** ~ **of** être maître de; **to get** *or* **bring under** ~ *fire, inflation* maîtriser; *situation* dominer; *children, dog* mater; **the situation is under** ~ on a la situation bien en main; **everything's under** ~ * tout est en ordre; **his car went out of** ~ il a perdu le contrôle de sa voiture; **the children are quite out of** ~ les enfants sont déchaînés; **under French** ~ sous contrôle français; **circumstances beyond our** ~ circonstances indépendantes de notre volonté; **who is in** ~ **?** qui *or* quel est le responsable?; *(Sport)* **his** ~ **of the ball is not very good** il ne contrôle pas très bien la balle; **price** ~**s** le contrôle des prix. (**b**) ~**s** *[train, car, ship, aircraft]* commandes *fpl*; *[radio, TV]* boutons *mpl* de commande; **to be at the** ~**s** être aux commandes; *(Rad, TV)* **volume** ~ (bouton *m de*) réglage *m* de volume. (**c**) *(Phys, Psych etc: standard of comparison)* cas *m* témoin.
2 *vt emotions* maîtriser; *animal, child* se faire obéir de; *vehicle, machine* manier; *organization, business* diriger; *expenditure, traffic* régler; *prices, wages* mettre un frein à la hausse de; *inflation* maîtriser; *immigration* contrôler; *disease* enrayer. **to** ~ **o.s.** se contrôler, se maîtriser; **she can't** ~ **the children** elle n'a aucune autorité sur les enfants.
3 *adj: (Med etc)* ~ **case/group** cas *m*/groupe *m* témoin; ~ **knob** bouton *m* de commande *or* de réglage; ~ **panel** *[aircraft, ship]* tableau *m* de bord; *[TV, comput]* pupitre *m* de commande; ~ **room** *(Naut)* poste *m* de commande; *(Mil)* salle *f* de commande; *(Rad, TV)* régie *f*; *(Aviat)* ~ **tower** tour *f* de contrôle.
◆ **controlled** *adj emotion* contenu; **he was very** ~**led** il se dominait très bien; **...he said in a** ~**led voice** ...dit-il, en se contrôlant; *(Econ)* ~**led economy** économie dirigée. ◆ **controller** *n* contrôleur *m*. ◆ **controlling** *adj factor* déterminant; ~**ling interest** participation *f* majoritaire.

controversy [kən'trɒvəsɪ] *n* controverse *f*. **there was a lot of** ~ **about it** ça a provoqué beaucoup de controverses. ◆ **controversial** *adj (thought-provoking) speech, action, decision* discutable, sujet à controverse; *(talked about) person, book, suggestion* discuté.

contusion [kən'tjuːʒ(ə)n] *n* contusion *f*.

conundrum [kə'nʌndrəm] *n* énigme *f*.

conurbation [ˌkɒnɜː'beɪʃ(ə)n] *n* conurbation *f*.

convalesce [ˌkɒnvə'les] *vi* se remettre *(d'une maladie)*. **to be convalescing** être en convalescence.
◆ **convalescence** *n* convalescence *f*. ◆ **convalescent** *adj, n* convalescent(e) *m(f)*; ~**nt home** maison *f* de convalescence *or* de repos.

convection [kən'vekʃ(ə)n] *n* convection *f*. **convection heater** radiateur *m* à convection. ◆ **convector** *n* convecteur *m*.

convene [kən'viːn] **1** *vt* convoquer. **2** *vi* s'assembler. ◆ **convener** *or* ◆ **convenor** *n* président(e) *m(f) (de commission etc)*. ◆ **convening** *adj*: **convening country** pays *m* hôte.

convenient [kən'vi:nɪənt] *adj tool, device* commode; *time* qui convient; *place, position* bon; *event, occurrence* opportun. **if it is ~ to you** si vous n'y voyez pas d'inconvénient, si cela ne vous dérange pas; **will it be ~ for you to come tomorrow?** est-ce que cela vous arrange *or* vous convient de venir demain?; **is it ~ to see him now?** peut-on le voir tout de suite sans le déranger?; **it is not a very ~ time** le moment n'est pas très bien choisi; **the house is ~ for shops** la maison est bien située pour les magasins; **he put it down on a ~ chair** il l'a posé sur une chaise qui se trouvait à portée. ◆ **convenience 1** *n* (**a**) *[plan, apartment]* commodité *f*; **for convenience' sake** par souci de commodité; *(Comm)* **at your earliest convenience** dans les meilleurs délais; **do it at your own convenience** faites-le quand cela vous conviendra; *[house]* **conveniences** commodités; (**b**) *(lavatory)* W.C. *mpl* ; **2** *adj*: **convenience foods** aliments *mpl* tout préparés; *(dishes)* plats cuisinés; *(US)* **convenience store** épicerie *f* de dépannage. ◆ **conveniently** *adv happen* fort à propos; *situated etc* bien; **very ~ly he arrived late** heureusement il est arrivé en retard.

convent ['kɒnv(ə)nt] **1** *n* couvent *m*. **to go into a ~** entrer au couvent. **2** *adj*: **~ school** couvent *m*.

convention [kən'venʃ(ə)n] *n (meeting, agreement)* convention *f*; *(accepted behaviour)* usage *m*, convenances *fpl*. **there is a ~ that** l'usage veut que + *subj*. ◆ **conventional** *adj person, behaviour* conventionnel *(also slightly pej)*; *method* conventionnel, classique; *weapons* classique.

converge [kən'vɜ:dʒ] *vi* converger (*on* sur). ◆ **convergence** *n* convergence *f*. ◆ **convergent** *or* ◆ **converging** *adj* convergent.

conversant [kən'vɜ:s(ə)nt] *adj*: **to be ~ with** *car, machinery* s'y connaître en; *language, science, laws* connaître; *facts* être au courant de.

conversation [ˌkɒnvə'seɪʃ(ə)n] **1** *n* conversation *f*, entretien *m*. **in ~ with** en conversation avec; **what was your ~ about?** de quoi parliez-vous? **2** *adj*: **that was a ~ piece *** cela a fourni un grand sujet de conversation; **that was a ~ stopper *** cela a arrêté net la conversation. ◆ **conversational** *adj voice, words* de la conversation; *person* qui a la conversation facile. ◆ **conversationalist** *n* causeur *m*, -euse *f*; **she's a great ~alist** elle brille dans la conversation. ◆ **conversationally** *adv speak* sur le ton de la conversation; **'nice day' she said ~ally** 'il fait beau' dit-elle du ton de quelqu'un qui cherche à entamer une conversation.

converse[1] [kən'vɜ:s] *vi* converser. **to ~ with sb about sth** s'entretenir avec qn de qch.

converse[2] ['kɒnvɜ:s] *adj, n* inverse *(m)*. ◆ **conversely** [kɒn'vɜ:slɪ] *adv* inversement.

convert ['kɒnvɜ:t] **1** *n* converti(e) *m(f)*. **to become a ~ to** se convertir à. **2** [kən'vɜ:t] *vt* convertir (*into* en, *to* à); *(Rugby)* transformer; *house* aménager (*into* en).

◆ **conversion 1** *n (gen)* conversion *f* (*to* à, *into* en); *[house, room etc]* aménagement *m* (*into* en); *(Rugby)* transformation *f* ; **2** *adj*: **conversion table** table *f* de conversion. ◆ **converter** *n (Elec)* convertisseur *m*. ◆ **convertibility** *n* convertibilité *f*. ◆ **convertible 1** *adj* convertible ; **2** *n (Aut)* décapotable *f*.

convex ['kɒn'veks] *adj* convexe.

convey [kən'veɪ] *vt goods, passengers* transporter; *[pipeline etc]* amener; *sound, order, thanks, congratulations* transmettre (*to* à); *ideas* communiquer (*to* à). **to ~ to sb that...** faire comprendre à qn que...; **words cannot ~...** les paroles ne peuvent traduire...; **what does this music ~ to you?** qu'est-ce que cette musique évoque pour vous? ◆ **conveyance** *n [goods]* transport *m*; *(vehicle)* véhicule *m*. ◆ **conveyancing** *n* rédaction *f* d'actes translatifs. ◆ **conveyor** *n* transporteur *m*, convoyeur *m*; **~or belt** tapis *m* roulant.

convict ['kɒnvɪkt] **1** *n* forçat *m*, bagnard *m*. **2** [kən'vɪkt] *vt* reconnaître coupable (*sb of a crime* qn d'un crime). **a ~ed murderer** un homme reconnu coupable de meurtre. **3** *vi [jury]* rendre un verdict de culpabilité. ◆ **conviction** *n* (**a**) *(Jur)* condamnation *f*; (**b**) conviction *f* (*that* selon laquelle); **to carry ~ion** être convaincant.

convince [kən'vɪns] *vt* convaincre, persuader (*of* de). **he ~d her that she should leave** il l'a persuadée de partir, il l'a convaincue qu'elle devait partir. ◆ **convincing** *adj speaker, argument* persuasif, convaincant; *victory* décisif. ◆ **convincingly** *adv speak* d'une façon convaincante; *win* de façon décisive.

convivial [kən'vɪvɪəl] *adj* joyeux.

convoke [kən'vəʊk] *vt* convoquer. ◆ **convocation** *n (act)* convocation *f*; *(assembly)* assemblée *f*.

convoluted ['kɒnvəlu:tɪd] *adj shape* contourné; *argument* compliqué.

convolution [ˌkɒnvə'lu:ʃ(ə)n] *n* circonvolution *f*.

convolvulus [kən'vɒlvjʊləs] *n* liseron *m*.

convoy ['kɒnvɔɪ] **1** *n* convoi *m*. **in ~** en convoi. **2** *vt* convoyer.

convulse [kən'vʌls] *vt [earthquake, storm]* ébranler; *[war, riots]* bouleverser. **to be ~d (with laughter)** se tordre de rire; **~d with pain** *etc* convulsé par la douleur *etc*. ◆ **convulsion** *n* convulsion *f*. ◆ **convulsive** *adj* convulsif.

coo [ku:] *vti [doves etc]* roucouler; *[baby]* gazouiller.

cook [kʊk] **1** *n* cuisinier *m*, -ière *f*. **she is a good ~** elle fait bien la cuisine; **head ~ and bottle-washer *** *(in household)* bonne *f* à tout faire; *(elsewhere)* factotum *m*. **2** *vt* (**a**) *food* (faire) cuire. *(fig)* **to ~ sb's goose *** faire son affaire à qn. (**b**) *(*: falsify) figures* truquer. **to ~ the books *** truquer les comptes. **3** *vi [food]* cuire; *[person]* faire la cuisine. *(fig)* **what's ~ing? *** qu'est-ce qui se mijote? *

◆ **cook up *** *vt sep excuse, story* inventer, fabriquer.

◆ **cookbook** *n* livre *m* de cuisine. ◆ **cooker** *n* cuisinière *f (fourneau)*. ◆ **cookery** *n* cuisine *f (activité)* ; **~ery book** livre *m* de cuisine. ◆ **cookhouse** *n* cuisine *f (endroit)*. ◆ **cookie** *n* gâteau *m* sec. ◆ **cooking 1** *n* cuisine *f (activité, nourriture)* ; **2** *adj utensils* de cuisine; *apples, chocolate* à cuire; **~ing foil** papier *m* d'aluminium; **~ing salt** gros sel. ◆ **cookout** *n* grillade *f* en plein air.

cool [ku:l] **1** *adj (gen)* frais (*f* fraîche); *drink* rafraîchissant; *soup, hot drink* qui n'est plus chaud; *dress* léger; *(calm)* calme; *(impertinent)* effronté; *(unfriendly etc)* froid (*towards* envers). *(Met)* **it is ~** il fait frais; **it's turning ~er** le temps se rafraîchit; **to keep in a ~ place** tenir au frais; **I feel quite ~ now** j'ai bien moins chaud maintenant; **to keep ~** ne pas s'échauffer; *(fig: calm)* garder son sang-froid; **keep ~!** du calme!; **play it ~! *** pas de panique! *; **she was as ~ as a cucumber** elle n'avait pas chaud du tout; *(fig)* elle affichait un calme imperturbable; **to be ~ towards sb** traiter qn avec froideur; **he's a ~ customer *** il n'a pas froid aux yeux; **that was very ~ * of him** quel toupet! *; **he earns a ~ * £10,000 a year** il se fait la coquette somme de 10 000 livres par an.

2 *n*: **in the ~ of the evening** dans la fraîcheur du soir; **to keep sth in the ~** tenir qch au frais; **to keep/lose one's ~ *** garder/perdre son sang-froid *or* son calme.

3 *vt air* rafraîchir; *(stronger)* refroidir; *food* laisser refroidir. **to ~ one's heels** attendre, poireauter *; **~ it! *** calme-toi!

4 *vi [air, liquid] (from being warm)* (se) rafraîchir; *(from being hot)* refroidir.

◆ **cool down** **1** *vi* refroidir; *[anger, person]* se calmer; *[critical situation]* se détendre. **2** *vt sep* faire refroidir; *(fig)* calmer. ◆ **cool off** *vi (lose enthusiasm)* perdre son enthousiasme; *(change one's affections)* se refroidir (*towards sb* envers qn); *(become less angry)* se calmer.

◆ **cooler** *n* glacière *f*; (⁑: *prison)* taule ⁑ *f*. ◆ **cooling** *adj* rafraîchissant; ~**ing system** circuit *m* de refroidissement; ~**ing tower** refroidisseur *m*; ~**ing-off period** période *f* de détente. ◆ **coolly** *adv (calmly)* de sang-froid, calmement; *(unenthusiastically)* avec froideur; *(impertinently)* sans la moindre gêne. ◆ **coolness** *n* fraîcheur *f*; froideur *f*; calme *m*; effronterie *f*.

coop [ku:p] *n (hen ~)* poulailler *m*, cage *f* à poules. ◆ **coop up** *vt sep person* claquemurer; *feelings* refouler.

co-op ['kəʊ'ɒp] *n (abbr of* **cooperative***)* coop * *f*.

cooperate [kəʊ'ɒpəreɪt] *vi* coopérer (*with sb* avec qn; *in sth* à qch; *to do* pour faire). **I hope he'll** ~ j'espère qu'il va se montrer coopératif. ◆ **cooperation** *n* coopération *f*, concours *m*. ◆ **cooperative** **1** *adj* coopératif; *(US)* **cooperative apartment** appartement *m* en copropriété ; **2** *n* coopérative *f*.

coopt [kəʊ'ɒpt] *vt* coopter (*onto* à).

coordinate [kəʊ'ɔ:dnɪt] **1** *n* coordonnée *f*. **2** [kəʊ'ɔ:dɪneɪt] *vt* coordonner (*with* avec). ◆ **coordination** *n* coordination *f*. ◆ **coordinator** *n* coordinateur *m*, -trice *f*.

cop * [kɒp] **1** *n* (**a**) *(policeman)* flic * *m*. **to play at** ~**s and robbers** jouer aux gendarmes et aux voleurs. (**b**) **it's not much** ~ * ça ne vaut pas grand-chose. **2** *vt*: **to** ~ **it** écoper *, être puni. ◆ **cop out** ⁑ *vi* se défiler *, se dérober.

cope [kəʊp] *vi* se débrouiller, s'en tirer. **to** ~ **with** *task, person* s'occuper de; *situation* faire face à; *difficulties, problems (tackle)* affronter; *(solve)* venir à bout de; **they** ~ **with 500 applications a day** 500 formulaires leur passent entre les mains chaque jour; **can you** ~**?** ça ira?, vous y arriverez?; **leave it to me, I'll** ~ laissez cela, je m'en charge *or* je me débrouillerai; **he's coping pretty well** il se débrouille très bien; **she just can't** ~ **any more** *(overworked etc)* elle ne s'en sort plus; *(work too difficult)* elle est complètement dépassée.

Copenhagen [kəʊpn'heɪg(ə)n] *n* Copenhague.

copious ['kəʊpɪəs] *adj food* copieux; *amount, notes, harvest* abondant.

copper ['kɒpəʳ] *n* (**a**) cuivre *m*; *(money)* petite pièce *f*. ~**s** la petite monnaie. (**b**) (*: *policeman)* flic * *m*. ◆ **copper-coloured** *or* ◆ **coppery** *adj* cuivré. ◆ **copperplate** *adj*: ~**plate handwriting** écriture moulée.

coppice ['kɒpɪs], **copse** [kɒps] *n* taillis *m*.

copulate ['kɒpjʊleɪt] *vi* copuler. ◆ **copulation** *n* copulation *f*. ◆ **copulative** *adj* copulatif.

copy ['kɒpɪ] **1** *n* (**a**) *[painting, document]* copie *f* ; *(Phot: print)* épreuve *f*; *[book, newspaper]* exemplaire *m*. (**b**) *(material: for advertisement)* texte *m* (*for* de). *(Press)* **it makes good** ~ c'est un bon sujet d'article; **he handed in his** ~ il a remis son article. **2** *vt* copier. ◆ **copier** *n* machine *f* à polycopier. ◆ **copybook** *n* cahier *m*. ◆ **copying** *adj*: ~**ing ink** encre *f* à copier. ◆ **copyright** **1** *n* droits *mpl* d'auteur, copyright *m*; **out of** ~**right** dans le domaine public ; **2** *vt* obtenir les droits exclusifs sur. ◆ **copywriter** *n* rédacteur *m*, -trice *f* publicitaire.

coral ['kɒr(ə)l] **1** *n* corail *m*. **2** *adj necklace, reef* de corail; *island* coralien.

cord [kɔ:d] **1** *n* (**a**) *[curtains, pyjamas etc]* cordon *m*; *[windows]* corde *f*; *[parcel etc]* ficelle *f*; *(Elec)* cordon *or* fil *m* électrique. (**b**) *(corduroy)* velours *m* côtelé. ~**s** *npl* pantalon *m* en velours côtelé. **2** *adj*: ~ **carpet** tapis *m* de corde. ◆ **corded** *adj fabric* côtelé. ◆ **cordless** *adj telephone* sans fil.

cordial ['kɔ:dɪəl] *adj, n* cordial *(m)*. ◆ **cordiality** *n* cordialité *f*. ◆ **cordially** *adv* cordialement.

cordon ['kɔ:dn] **1** *n* cordon *m*. **2** *vt* (~ **off**) *crowd* tenir à l'écart; *area* interdire l'accès à.

corduroy ['kɔ:dərɔɪ] *n* velours *m* côtelé.

core [kɔ:ʳ] **1** *n [fruit]* trognon *m*; *[earth, cable]* noyau *m*; *[nuclear reactor]* cœur *m*; *[problem etc]* essentiel *m*. *(fig)* **rotten to the** ~ pourri jusqu'à l'os; **English to the** ~ anglais jusqu'à la moelle (des os). **2** *vt fruit* enlever le trognon de. ◆ **corer** *n* vide-pomme *m*.

coriander [,kɒrɪ'ændəʳ] *n* coriandre *f*.

cork [kɔ:k] **1** *n (substance)* liège *m*; *(in bottle etc)* bouchon *m*. **to pull the** ~ **out of** déboucher. **2** *vt* (~**up**) *bottle* boucher. **3** *adj*: ~ **oak** chêne-liège *m*. ◆ **corked** *adj wine* qui sent le bouchon. ◆ **corkscrew** *n* tire-bouchon *m*.

corn[1] [kɔ:n] **1** *n (gen)* grain *m*; *(Brit: wheat)* blé *m*; *(US: maize)* maïs *m*. ~ **on the cob** épi *m* de maïs. **2** *adj oil, cob* de maïs. ◆ **cornfield** *n (Brit)* champ *m* de blé; *(US)* champ de maïs. ◆ **cornflakes** *npl* céréales *fpl*, cornflakes *mpl*. ◆ **cornflour** *or* ◆ **cornstarch** *(US) n* maïzena *f* ®. ◆ **cornflower** *n* bleuet *m*.

corn[2] [kɔ:n] *n (Med)* cor *m*. **to tread on sb's** ~**s** toucher qn à l'endroit sensible; ~ **plaster** pansement *m* (pour cors).

cornea ['kɔ:nɪə] *n* cornée *f*.

corned beef [kɔ:nd 'bi:f] *n* corned-beef *m*.

cornelian [kɔ:'ni:lɪən] *n* cornaline *f*.

corner ['kɔ:nəʳ] **1** *n (gen)* coin *m*; *(Aut)* tournant *m*; *(Ftbl)* coup *m* (de pied) de coin. *(fig)* **to drive sb into a** ~ coincer * qn; **to be in a (tight)** ~ être dans le pétrin; **out of the** ~ **of one's eye** du coin de l'œil; **it's just round the** ~ *(lit)* c'est juste après le coin; *(fig: very near)* c'est à deux pas d'ici; *(in time)* c'est pour demain; **in odd** ~**s** dans des recoins; **in every** ~ dans tous les coins et recoins; **in every** ~ **of Europe** dans toute l'Europe; **in the four** ~**s of the earth** aux quatre coins du monde; **to make a** ~ **in wheat** accaparer le marché du blé. **2** *adj*: ~ **cupboard** placard *m* de coin; **the** ~ **house** la maison du coin; *(Rail)* ~ **seat** (place *f* de) coin *m*; ~ **shop** boutique *f* du coin. **3** *vt hunted animal etc* acculer; *(fig: catch to speak to etc)* coincer *. **to** ~ **the market** accaparer le marché. **4** *vi (Aut)* prendre un virage. ◆ **cornerstone** *n (lit, fig)* pierre *f* angulaire; *(foundation stone)* première pierre.

cornet ['kɔ:nɪt] *n* (**a**) *(Mus)* cornet *m* (à pistons). ~ **player** cornettiste *mf*. (**b**) *[sweets, ice cream]* cornet *m*.

Cornwall ['kɔ:nw(ə)l] *n* Cornouailles *f*. ◆ **Cornish** *adj* de Cornouailles.

corny * ['kɔ:nɪ] *adj* bébête.

corollary [kə'rɒlərɪ] *n* corollaire *m*.

coronary ['kɒrən(ə)rɪ] *adj, n*: ~ **(thrombosis)** infarctus *m*.

coronation [,kɒrə'neɪʃ(ə)n] *n* couronnement *m*.

coroner ['kɒrənəʳ] *n* coroner *m (officiel qui détermine les causes d'un décès)*.

corporal[1] ['kɔ:p(ə)r(ə)l] *n (Mil)* caporal-chef *m*.

corporal[2] ['kɔ:p(ə)r(ə)l] *adj* corporel. ~ **punishment** châtiment *m* corporel.

corporate ['kɔ:p(ə)rɪt] *adj* (**a**) *(Fin: of a corporation) property* appartenant à une corporation; ~ **body** personne morale; ~ **name** raison sociale. (**b**) *action, ownership* en commun; *responsibility* collectif. ◆ **corporation** *n [town]* conseil *m* municipal; *(Comm, Fin)* société *f* commerciale.

corps [kɔ:ʳ] *n* corps *m*. ~ **de ballet** corps de ballet.

corpse [kɔ:ps] *n* cadavre *m*, corps *m*.

corpulence ['kɔːpjʊləns] *n* corpulence *f*. ◆ **corpulent** *adj* corpulent.

corpus [kɔːpəs] *n* corpus *m*. **C~ Christi** la Fête-Dieu.

corpuscle ['kɔːpʌsl] *n* corpuscule *m*; *[blood]* globule *m*.

correct [kə'rekt] **1** *adj answer, amount* correct, exact, juste; *temperature, time* exact; *forecast, estimate, dress, behaviour* correct. **the predictions proved** ~ les prédictions se sont avérées justes; **you are** ~ vous avez raison; **it's the** ~ **thing** c'est ce qui se fait; **the** ~ **procedure** la procédure d'usage. **2** *vt work, error, proofs* corriger. **he ~ed me several times during the course of my speech** il m'a repris plusieurs fois pendant mon discours; **I stand ~ed** je reconnais mon erreur. ◆ **correction** *n* correction *f*; **~ion fluid** liquide correcteur. ◆ **correctly** *adv* correctement; d'une manière exacte; avec justesse. ◆ **correctness** *n* correction *f*; exactitude *f*; justesse *f*.

correlate ['kɒrɪleɪt] **1** *vi* être en corrélation (*with* avec). **2** *vt* mettre en corrélation (*with* avec). ◆ **correlation** *n* corrélation *f*.

correspond [ˌkɒrɪs'pɒnd] *vi* (**a**) *(agree; be equivalent)* correspondre (*with, to* à). **that does not** ~ **with what he said** cela ne correspond pas à ce qu'il a dit; **his job ~s roughly to mine** son poste est à peu près l'équivalent du mien. (**b**) *(exchange letters)* correspondre (*with* avec). **they** ~ ils correspondent. ◆ **correspondence** **1** *n* correspondance *f* (*between* entre, *with* avec) ; **2** *adj*: **~ence card** carte-lettre *f*; **~ence column** courrier *m* (des lecteurs); **~ence course** cours *m* par correspondance. ◆ **correspondent** *n* correspondant(e) *m(f)*; *(Press)* **foreign/sports ~ent** correspondant étranger/sportif. ◆ **corresponding** *adj (gen)* correspondant; **~ing to the original** conforme à l'original; **for a ~ing period** pendant une période analogue. ◆ **correspondingly** *adv (as a result)* en conséquence; *(proportionately)* proportionnellement.

corridor ['kɒrɪdɔːʳ] *n* couloir *m*, corridor *m*. ~ **train** train *m* à couloir.

corroborate [kə'rɒbəreɪt] *vt* corroborer. ◆ **corroboration** *n* corroboration *f*.

corrode [kə'rəʊd] **1** *vt* corroder. **2** *vi* se corroder. ◆ **corrosion** *n* corrosion *f*. ◆ **corrosive** *adj, n* corrosif *(m)*.

corrugated ['kɒrəgeɪtɪd] *adj* ondulé. ~ **iron** tôle *f* ondulée.

corrupt [kə'rʌpt] **1** *adj (evil)* corrompu; *(dishonest)* vénal. ~ **practices** *(dishonesty)* tractations *fpl* malhonnêtes; *(bribery etc)* trafic *m* d'influence, malversations *fpl*. **2** *vt* corrompre. ◆ **corruption** *n* corruption *f*.

corset ['kɔːsɪt] *n (Dress)* corset *m*; *(lightweight)* gaine *f*; *(Med)* corset.

Corsica ['kɔːsɪkə] *n* Corse *f*. ◆ **Corsican** **1** *adj* corse ; **2** *n* Corse *mf*.

cortisone ['kɔːtɪzəʊn] *n* cortisone *f*.

cosh [kɒʃ] **1** *vt* (*) taper sur. **2** *n* matraque *f*.

cosmetic [kɒz'metɪk] **1** *adj surgery* esthétique; *preparation* cosmétique; *changes* superficiel. **2** *n* cosmétique *m*, produit *m* de beauté.

cosmic ['kɒzmɪk] *adj* cosmique.

cosmographer [kɒz'mɒgrəfəʳ] *n* cosmographe *mf*. ◆ **cosmography** *n* cosmographie *f*.

cosmology [kɒz'mɒlədʒɪ] *n* cosmologie *f*.

cosmonaut ['kɒzmənɔːt] *n* cosmonaute *mf*.

cosmopolitan [ˌkɒzmə'pɒlɪt(ə)n] *adj, n* cosmopolite *(mf)*.

cosmos ['kɒzmɒs] *n* cosmos *m*.

cosset ['kɒsɪt] *vt* dorloter.

cost [kɒst] **1** *vt* (**a**) *(pret, ptp* **cost***)* coûter. **how much** *or* **what does it** ~? combien est-ce que cela coûte *or* vaut?; **what will it** ~ **to have it repaired?** combien est-ce que cela coûtera de le faire réparer?; **it** ~ **him a lot of money** cela lui a coûté cher; **it ~s the earth *** cela coûte les yeux de la tête; **it** ~ **him a great effort/a lot of trouble** cela lui a coûté un gros effort/causé beaucoup d'ennuis; **it will** ~ **you a present** vous en serez quitte pour un cadeau; **politeness ~s very little** il ne coûte rien d'être poli; *(fig)* **whatever it ~s** coûte que coûte.
(**b**) *(pret, ptp* **~ed***) articles for sale* établir le prix de revient de; *job etc* évaluer le coût de. **the job was ~ed at £200** le devis pour ces travaux s'élevait à 200 livres.
2 *n* coût *m*. ~ **of living** coût de la vie; **to bear the** ~ **of** faire face aux frais *mpl* or aux dépenses *fpl* de; *(fig)* faire les frais de; *(lit, fig)* **at great** ~ à grands frais; **at** ~ **(price)** au prix coûtant; *(Jur)* **to be ordered to pay ~s** être condamné aux dépens *mpl*; *(fig)* **at all ~s, at any** ~ coûte que coûte, à tout prix; *(fig)* **whatever the** ~ quoi qu'il en coûte; **at the** ~ **of his life/health** au prix de sa vie/santé; *(fig)* **to my** ~ à mes dépens.
◆ **cost-cutting** *n* réduction *f* des coûts. ◆ **cost-effective** *adj* rentable. ◆ **costing** *n* estimation *f* du prix de revient; évaluation *f* du coût. ◆ **costliness** *n (value)* grande valeur; *(high price)* cherté *f*. ◆ **costly** *adj furs, jewels* de grande valeur; *undertaking, trip* coûteux; *tastes* dispendieux. ◆ **cost-of-living** *adj*: **~-of-living allowance** indemnité *f* de vie chère ; **~-of-living index** index *m* du coût de la vie.

Costa Rica [kɒstə'riːkə] *n* Costa Rica *m*.

costermonger ['kɒstəˌmʌŋgəʳ] *n* marchand(e) *m(f)* des quatre saisons.

costume ['kɒstjuːm] **1** *n (gen)* costume *m*; *(†: lady's suit)* tailleur *m*. **national** ~ costume national; *(fancy dress)* **in** ~ déguisé. **2** *adj*: ~ **ball** bal *m* masqué; ~ **jewellery** bijoux *mpl* fantaisie.

cosy ['kəʊzɪ] **1** *adj room* douillet, confortable; *atmosphere* douillet. **we are very** ~ **here** nous sommes très bien ici; **it is** ~ **in here** il fait bon ici; **a** ~ **little corner** un petit coin intime. **2** *n (tea ~)* couvre-théière *m*; *(egg ~)* couvre-œuf *m*. ◆ **cosiness** *n* confort *m*.

cot [kɒt] *n* lit *m* d'enfant; *(US: folding bed)* lit *m* de camp. ~ **death** mort subite du nourrisson.

cottage ['kɒtɪdʒ] **1** *n* petite maison (à la campagne), cottage *m*; *(thatched)* chaumière *f*; *(in holiday village etc)* villa *f*.
2 *adj*: ~ **cheese** fromage *m* blanc (égoutté); ~ **hospital** petit hôpital *m*; ~ **industry** industrie artisanale.

cotton ['kɒtn] **1** *n (material)* coton *m*; *(sewing thread)* fil *m* (de coton). **2** *adj shirt, dress* de coton. *(US)* ~ **candy** barbe *f* à papa; ~ **goods** cotonnades *fpl*; ~ **industry** industrie *f* cotonnière; ~ **mill** filature *f* de coton; ~ **wool** ouate *f*, coton *m* hydrophile. ◆ **cotton on *** *vi* piger *. **to** ~ **on to sth** piger * qch.

couch [kaʊtʃ] **1** *n (gen)* divan *m*; *(in doctor's surgery)* lit *m*. **2** *vt (express)* formuler.

couchette [kuː'ʃet] *n* couchette *f*.

cougar ['kuːgəʳ] *n* couguar *m*.

cough [kɒf] **1** *n* toux *f*. **to give a warning** ~ tousser en guise d'avertissement; **he has a bad** ~ il tousse beaucoup. **2** *adj*: ~ **drop** pastille *f* pour la toux; ~ **mixture** sirop *m* pour la toux. **3** *vi* tousser. ◆ **cough up** *vt sep* cracher en toussant; *(*: fig) money* cracher *.

could [kʊd] *pret, cond of* **can¹**.

council ['kaʊnsl] **1** *n* conseil *m*. ~ **of war** conseil de guerre; **city** *or* **town** ~ conseil municipal; **the**

Security C~ le Conseil de Sécurité. **2** *adj*: ~ **flat** *or* **house** ≃ habitation *f* à loyer modéré, H.L.M. *m or f*; ~ **housing** logements *mpl* sociaux; ~ **housing estate** quartier *m* de logements sociaux. ◆ **councillor** *n* conseiller *m*, -ère *f*.

counsel ['kaʊns(ə)l] **1** *n* (**a**) *(pl inv: Jur)* avocat(e) *m(f)*. ~ **for the defence** avocat de la défense; ~ **for the prosecution** avocat du ministère public; **King's** *or* **Queen's C~** avocat de la couronne. (**b**) *(advice)* conseil *m*. **to keep one's own** ~ garder ses opinions pour soi. **2** *vt* conseiller (*sb to do* à qn de faire); *caution* recommander. ◆ **counselling** *n (advice)* conseils *mpl; (Psych, Soc)* assistance *f* socio-psychologique. ◆ **counsellor** *n* (**a**) *(Psych, gen)* conseiller *m*, -ère *f*; (**b**) *(Ir, US: Jur)* avocat(e) *m(f)*.

count[1] [kaʊnt] **1** *n* (**a**) compte *m*; *[votes at election]* dépouillement *m*. **at the last** ~ la dernière fois qu'on a compté; **to be out for the** ~ *(Boxing)* être (mis) knock-out; *(*: gen)* être K.-O. *; **to keep** ~ **of** tenir le compte de; **you make me lose** ~ je ne sais plus où j'en suis. (**b**) *(Jur)* chef *m* d'accusation. **guilty on 3 ~s** coupable à 3 chefs.
2 *vt* (**a**) *(gen)* compter; *inhabitants, injured, causes* compter, dénombrer; *one's change etc* compter, vérifier; *(consider)* estimer. **to** ~ **the votes** dépouiller le scrutin; **don't** ~ **your chickens before they're hatched** il ne faut pas vendre la peau de l'ours avant de l'avoir tué; *(fig)* **to** ~ **sheep** compter les moutons; **to** ~ **the cost** compter *or* calculer la dépense; *(fig)* faire le bilan; *(lit, fig)* **without ~ing the cost** sans compter; ~ **your blessings** estimez-vous heureux. (**b**) *(include)* compter (*among* parmi). **not ~ing the children** sans compter les enfants; **~ing him** lui inclus *or* compris; **will you** ~ **it against me?** m'en tiendrez-vous rigueur?; **we must** ~ **ourselves fortunate** nous devons nous estimer heureux; **I** ~ **it an honour** je m'estime honoré (*to do* de faire; *that* que + *subj*).
3 *vi* compter. **~ing from tonight** à compter de ce soir; **~ing from the left** à partir de la gauche; **two children** ~ **as one adult** deux enfants comptent pour un adulte; **that doesn't** ~ ça ne compte pas; **that ~s against him** cela est un désavantage; **it ~s for very little** ça n'a pas beaucoup de valeur. ◆ **count in** * *vt sep* compter. **you can** ~ **me in** je suis de la partie! ◆ **count out** *vt sep* (**a**) *(Boxing)* **to be ~ed out** être mis knock-out. (**b**) *money* compter pièce par pièce; *small objects* compter. (**c**) **you can** ~ **me out of it** * ne comptez pas sur moi là-dedans. ◆ **count up** *vt sep* faire le compte de, additionner. ◆ **count (up)on** *vt fus* compter sur. **I'm ~ing (up)on you** je compte sur vous; **to** ~ **(up)on doing** compter faire.
◆ **countable** *adj* qui peut être compté; **~able noun** substantif *m* distributif. ◆ **countdown** *n* compte *m* à rebours. ◆ **counting** *n (school subject)* calcul *m*. ◆ **countless** *adj* innombrable, sans nombre; **on ~less occasions** je ne sais combien de fois.

count[2] [kaʊnt] *n (nobleman)* comte *m*. ◆ **countess** *n* comtesse *f*.

countenance ['kaʊntɪnəns] **1** *n (expression)* mine *f*. **to keep one's** ~ rester impassible. **2** *vt* admettre (*sth* qch; *sb's doing* que qn fasse).

counter[1] ['kaʊntəʳ] **1** *n* (**a**) *(in shop, canteen)* comptoir *m*; *(position: in post office)* guichet *m*. *(fig)* **to buy under the** ~ acheter clandestinement. (**b**) *(disc)* jeton *m*. (**c**) *(Tech)* compteur *m*. **Geiger** ~ compteur Geiger. **2** *adj*: ~ **hand** *(in shop)* vendeur *m*, -euse *f*; *(in snack bar)* serveur *m*, -euse *f*.
◆ **counterman** *n (US)* serveur *m*.

counter[2] ['kaʊntəʳ] **1** *adv*: ~ **to** à l'encontre de. **2** *vt plans* contrecarrer; *blow* parer. **3** *vi* contre-attaquer, riposter; *(Boxing etc)* riposter (*with* par).

counter... ['kaʊntəʳ] *pref* contre... ◆ **counteract** *vt* neutraliser, contrebalancer. ◆ **counter-attack** **1** *n* contre-attaque *f* ; **2** *vti* contre-attaquer. ◆ **counter-attraction** *n* attraction rivale. ◆ **counterbalance** *vt* faire contrepoids à. ◆ **counterclockwise** *adv* en sens inverse des aiguilles d'une montre. ◆ **counter-espionage** *or* ◆ **counterintelligence** *n* contre-espionnage *m*. ◆ **countermeasure** *n* contre-mesure *f*. ◆ **counter-offensive** *n* contre-offensive *f*. ◆ **counterpart** *n* contrepartie *f*; *[person]* homologue *mf*. ◆ **counter-productive** *adj* inefficace. ◆ **Counter-Reformation** *n* Contre-Réforme *f*. ◆ **counter-revolution** *n* contre-révolution *f*. ◆ **countersign** *vt* contresigner. ◆ **countertenor** *n (singer)* haute-contre *m*; *(voice)* haute-contre *f*.

counterfeit ['kaʊntəfi:t] **1** *adj, n* faux *(m)*. **2** *vt* contrefaire.

counterfoil ['kaʊntəfɔɪl] *n* talon *m*, souche *f*.

counterpane ['kaʊntəpeɪn] *n* dessus-de-lit *m inv*.

countersink ['kaʊntəsɪŋk] *vt* noyer *(une vis)*.

country ['kʌntrɪ] **1** *n* (**a**) *(gen)* pays *m*; *(native land)* patrie *f*. *(Pol)* **to go to the** ~ appeler le pays aux urnes; **to die for one's** ~ mourir pour la patrie. (**b**) *(as opposed to town)* campagne *f*; *(region)* pays *m*, région *f*. **in the** ~ à la campagne; **there is some lovely** ~ **to the north** il y a de beaux paysages dans le nord; **mountainous** ~ une région montagneuse; *(fig)* **in unknown** ~ en terrain inconnu. **2** *adj life, people* de (la) campagne. *(music)* ~ **and western** country music *f*; ~ **bumpkin** cul-terreux * *m*; ~ **cottage** *[weekenders]* maison *f* de campagne; *(fig)* ~ **cousin** cousin(e) *m(f)* de province; ~ **dancing** danse *f* folklorique; ~ **dweller** campagnard(e) *m(f)*; ~ **house** manoir *m*; ~ **life** vie *f* de la *or* à la campagne; ~ **road** petite route (de campagne); ~ **seat** château *m*.
◆ **countrified** *adj* rustique. ◆ **countryman** *n*: **fellow ~man** compatriote *m*, concitoyen *m*. ◆ **countryside** *n* campagne *f*. ◆ **country-wide** *adj* national.

county ['kaʊntɪ] **1** *n* comté *m*, ≃ département *m*. **2** *adj*: ~ **town** chef-lieu *m*.

coup [ku:] *n* beau coup *m*; *(Pol)* coup d'État.

coupé ['ku:peɪ] *n (Aut)* coupé *m*.

couple ['kʌpl] *n [animals, people]* couple *m*. **a** ~ **of** deux; **a** ~ **of times** deux ou trois fois; **I did it in a** ~ **of hours** je l'ai fait en deux heures environ.

coupon ['ku:pɒn] *n [newspaper, advertisements etc]* coupon *m (détachable)*; *[cigarette packets etc]* bon *m*, vignette *f*; *(offering price reductions)* bon de réduction; *(rationing)* ticket *m*; *(Fin)* coupon.

courage ['kʌrɪdʒ] *n* courage *m*. **I haven't the** ~ **to refuse** je n'ai pas le courage de refuser, je n'ose pas refuser; **to have the** ~ **of one's convictions** avoir le courage de ses opinions. ◆ **courageous** *adj* courageux. ◆ **courageously** *adv* courageusement.

courgette [kʊə'ʒet] *n* courgette *f*.

courier ['kʊrɪəʳ] *n (messenger)* courrier *m*; *(tourist guide)* guide *m*.

course [kɔ:s] **1** *n* (**a**) *(duration) [life, disease]* cours *m*. **in the** ~ **of time** à la longue; **in the ordinary** ~ **of events** normalement, en temps normal *or* ordinaire; **in the** ~ **of conversation** au cours de la conversation; **in (the)** ~ **of construction** en cours de construction; **in the** ~ **of the next few months** au cours des prochains mois; **in the** ~ **of the week** dans le courant de la semaine.
(**b**) **of** ~ bien sûr, naturellement; **(yes) of** ~ (oui) bien sûr; **of** ~ **not!** *(answering; denying; disagreeing)* bien sûr que non!; *(refusing)* certainement pas!; **of** ~ **I won't do it** je ne vais évidemment pas faire ça.

(**c**) *(route) [river, planet]* cours *m*; *[ship]* route *f*. **to hold one's ~** poursuivre sa route; *(Naut)* **to set ~ for** mettre le cap sur; *(Naut)* **to change ~** changer de cap; **to go off ~** faire fausse route; **~ of action** ligne *f* de conduite; **we have no other ~ but to...** nous n'avons d'autre moyen *or* ressource que de...; **there are several ~s open to us** plusieurs partis s'offrent à nous; **the best ~ would be to leave** le mieux à faire serait de partir; **to let sth take its ~** laisser qch suivre son cours.
(**d**) *(Scol, Univ)* cours *m*. **to go to a French ~** suivre un cours *or* des cours de français; **a ~ of lectures on Proust** une série de conférences sur Proust; *(Med)* **~ of treatment** traitement *m*.
(**e**) *(Sport: for races etc)* parcours *m*; *(grounds: Golf etc)* terrain *m*.
(**f**) *(Culin)* plat *m*. **first ~** entrée *f*; **main ~** plat de résistance.
2 *vi [water etc]* couler à flots; *[tears]* ruisseler. **it sent the blood coursing through his veins** cela lui a fouetté le sang.

court [kɔːt] **1** *n* (**a**) *(Jur)* cour *f*, tribunal *m* ; *(~ room)* salle *f* du tribunal. **~ of appeal(s)** cour d'appel; **~ of inquiry** commission *f* d'enquête; **to settle a case out of ~** arranger une affaire à l'amiable; **to rule out of ~** déclarer inadmissible; **to take sb to ~ over sth** poursuivre qn en justice à propos de qch; **he was brought before the ~s** il est passé en jugement. (**b**) *[monarch]* cour *f* (royale); *(Tennis)* court *m*; *(Basketball)* terrain *m*; *(~ yard)* cour *f (de maison etc)*. **2** *adj*: **~ card** figure *f (de jeu de cartes)*; **~ order** décision *f* judiciaire; **~ shoe** escarpin *m*. **3** *vt woman* faire la cour à; *danger, defeat* aller au-devant de. **4** *vi*: **they are ~ing *** ils sortent ensemble.
◆ **courthouse** *n* palais *m* de justice, tribunal *m*. ◆ **courtier** *n* courtisan *m*, dame *f* de la cour. ◆ **courting** *adj*: **a ~ing couple** un couple d'amoureux. ◆ **court-martial** **1** *n*, *pl* **~s-martial** conseil *m* de guerre; **2** *vt* faire passer en conseil de guerre. ◆ **courtship** *n*: **during their ~ship** au temps où ils sortaient ensemble.

Courtelle [kɔːˈtel] *n* ® Courtelle *m* ®.

courteous [ˈkɜːtɪəs] *adj* courtois (*towards* envers). ◆ **courteously** *adv* courtoisement. ◆ **courtesy** [ˈkɜːtɪsɪ] **1** *n* courtoisie *f*, politesse *f*; **will you do me the courtesy of reading it?** auriez-vous l'obligeance de le lire?; **exchange of courtesies** échange *m* de politesses; **by courtesy of** avec la permission de ; **2** *adj visit* de politesse; *title* de courtoisie; *(free) coach etc* gratuit; **courtesy card** carte *f* de priorité *(dans les hôtels etc)*; *(Aut)* **courtesy light** plafonnier *m*.

cousin [ˈkʌzn] *n* cousin(e) *m(f)*.

cove [kəʊv] *n* crique *f*; *(cavern)* caverne naturelle; *(US)* vallon encaissé.

covenant [ˈkʌvɪnənt] **1** *n (gen)* convention *f*; *(Fin)* engagement contractuel. **2** *vt* s'engager (*to do* à faire). **to ~ £10 per annum to a charity** s'engager par obligation contractuelle à verser 10 livres par an à une œuvre.

Coventry [ˈkɒv(ə)ntrɪ] *n*: **to send sb to ~** mettre qn en quarantaine *(fig)*.

cover [ˈkʌvəʳ] **1** *n* (**a**) *[saucepan, bowl, dish]* couvercle *m*; *[table]* nappe *f*; *[furniture, typewriter]* housse *f*; *[merchandise, vehicle etc]* bâche *f*; *(bed~)* dessus-de-lit *m inv*; *[book]* couverture *f*; *(envelope)* enveloppe *f*; *[parcel]* emballage *m*. *(bedclothes)* **the ~s** les couvertures *fpl*; **to read a book from ~ to ~** lire un livre de la première à la dernière page; *(Comm)* **under separate ~** sous pli séparé. (**b**) *(shelter)* abri *m*; *(covering fire)* feu *m* de couverture. **the trees gave him ~** les arbres le cachaient; *(sheltered)* les arbres l'abritaient; **to take ~** *(hide)* se cacher; *(Mil)* s'embusquer; *(shelter)* s'abriter (*from* de); **under ~** à l'abri, à couvert; **under ~ of darkness** à la faveur de la nuit. (**c**) *(Fin, Insurance)* couverture *f* (*against* contre). *(Fin)* **without ~** à découvert; *(Insurance)* **full ~** garantie *f* tous risques; **fire ~** assurance-incendie *f*. (**d**) *(in espionage etc)* identité *f* d'emprunt. (**e**) *(at table)* couvert *m*.
2 *adj [restaurant]* **~ charge** couvert *m*; *(Insurance)* **~ note** ≃ récépissé *m* (d'assurance).
3 *vt* (**a**) *(gen)* couvrir (*with* de). **~ed with confusion** couvert de confusion; **to ~ o.s. with glory** se couvrir de gloire. (**b**) *(hide) feelings, facts* dissimuler, cacher; *noise* couvrir. (**c**) *(protect) person, retreat* couvrir. *(Insurance)* **~ed against fire** couvert contre l'incendie; **he only said that to ~ himself** il n'a dit cela que pour se couvrir. (**d**) *(point gun at)* braquer un revolver sur. **to keep sb ~ed** tenir qn sous la menace du revolver; **I've got you ~ed!** ne bougez pas ou je tire! (**e**) *(Sport) opponent* marquer. (**f**) *distance* parcourir, couvrir. **to ~ a lot of ground** faire beaucoup de chemin; *(fig)* faire du bon travail. (**g**) *(be sufficient for)* couvrir; *(include)* englober, traiter. **his work ~s many fields** son travail englobe *or* embrasse plusieurs domaines; **the book ~s the subject thoroughly** le livre traite le sujet à fond; **in order to ~ all possibilities** pour parer à toute éventualité; **to ~ one's expenses** rentrer dans ses frais; **£5 will ~ everything** 5 livres payeront tout. (**h**) *(Press) event* assurer le reportage de.
◆ **cover over** *vt sep* recouvrir. ◆ **cover up** **1** *vi (warmly)* se couvrir. *(fig)* **to ~ up for sb** couvrir qn, protéger qn. **2** *vt sep child, object* recouvrir, envelopper (*with* de); *(hide) truth, facts* dissimuler, cacher. **to ~ up one's tracks** couvrir sa marche.
◆ **coverage** *n (Press, Rad, TV)* reportage *m*; **to give full ~age to an event** assurer la couverture complète d'un événement; **the match got nationwide ~age** *(Rad)* le reportage du match a été diffusé *or (TV)* le match a été retransmis sur l'ensemble du pays. ◆ **coveralls** *npl* bleus *mpl* de travail. ◆ **covergirl** *n* cover-girl *f*. ◆ **covering** **1** *n* couverture *f*; *(of snow, dust etc)* couche *f* ; **2** *adj letter* explicatif; *(Mil) fire* de couverture. ◆ **coverlet** *n* dessus-de-lit *m inv*. ◆ **cover-up** *n*: **the ~-up** les tentatives *fpl* faites pour étouffer l'affaire.

covert [ˈkʌvət] *adj (gen)* caché; *attack* indirect; *glance* dérobé.

covet [ˈkʌvɪt] *vt* convoiter. ◆ **covetous** *adj person* avide; *look* de convoitise. ◆ **covetously** *adv* avidement; avec convoitise. ◆ **covetousness** *n* avidité *f*; convoitise *f*.

cow¹ [kaʊ] **1** *n* vache *f*; (‡: *woman)* rosse * *f*, vache ‡ *f*. *(fig)* **till the ~s come home *** jusqu'à la Trinité *(fig)*; **to wait till the ~s come home *** attendre la semaine des quatre jeudis *. **2** *adj*: **~ elephant/buffalo** *etc* éléphant *m*/buffle *m etc* femelle. ◆ **cowboy** *n* cow-boy *m*; *(pej)* fumiste *m*; **to play ~boys and Indians** jouer aux cow-boys; **~boy boots** rangers *mpl*. ◆ **cowherd** *or* ◆ **cowman** *n* vacher *m*, bouvier *m*. ◆ **cowhide** *n* (peau *f* de) vache *f*. ◆ **cowpox** *n* variole *f* de la vache. ◆ **cowpuncher *** *n* cow-boy *m*. ◆ **cowshed** *n* étable *f*. ◆ **cowslip** *n (Bot)* coucou *m*.

cow² [kaʊ] *vt person* intimider. **a ~ed look** un air de chien battu.

coward [ˈkaʊəd] *n* lâche *mf*. ◆ **cowardice** *or* ◆ **cowardliness** *n* lâcheté *f*. ◆ **cowardly** *adj* lâche.

cower [ˈkaʊəʳ] *vi* (**~ down**) se recroqueviller.

cowl [kaʊl] *n* capuchon *m*.

cowrie, cowry [ˈkaʊrɪ] *n* cauri *m*.

cox [kɒks] **1** *n* barreur *m*. **2** *vti* barrer.

coy [kɔɪ] *adj person* qui fait le *or* la timide; *smile* de sainte nitouche *(pej)*; *(coquettish) woman* qui fait la coquette. ◆ **coyly** *adv* avec une timidité feinte;

avec coquetterie. ◆ **coyness** *n* timidité *f* feinte; coquetterie *f*.

cozy ['kəʊzɪ] *(US)* = **cosy.**

crab [kræb] *n* crabe *m*; (~ **apple**) pomme *f* sauvage. ◆ **crabbed** *or* ◆ **crabby** *adj person* grincheux.

crack [kræk] **1** *n* (**a**) *(split, slit)* fente *f*; *(in glass, pottery, bone etc)* fêlure *f*; *(in wall)* fente, lézarde *f*; *(in ground, skin)* crevasse *f*; *(in paint)* craquelure *f*. **through the ~ in the door** *(slight opening)* par l'entrebâillement de la porte; **at the ~ of dawn** au point du jour. (**b**) *(noise) [twigs]* craquement *m*; *[whip]* claquement *m*; *[rifle, thunder]* coup *m*. (**c**) *(sharp blow)* **a ~ on the head** un grand coup sur la tête. (**d**) *(joke)* plaisanterie *f*. **that was a ~ * at your brother** ça, c'était pour votre frère; **that was a dirty ~ *** c'était vache ‡ de dire ça. (**e**) *(try)* **to have a ~ at (doing) sth** * essayer (de faire) qch.
2 *adj sportsman* de première classe. **a ~ tennis player/skier** un as du tennis/du ski; **~ shot** excellent fusil *m*; *(Mil, Police etc)* tireur *m* d'élite.
3 *vt* (**a**) *pottery, glass, bone* fêler; *wall* lézarder; *ground* crevasser; *nut etc* casser; (*) *safe* cambrioler; *bottle* déboucher. **to ~ one's skull** se fendre le crâne; **to ~ sb over the head** assommer qn. (**b**) *whip* faire claquer. **to ~ one's finger joints** faire craquer ses doigts; **to ~ jokes** * faire des astuces *. (**c**) *code etc* déchiffrer; *case* résoudre.
4 *vi [pottery, glass]* se fêler; *[ground, skin]* se crevasser; *[wall]* se fendiller; *[whip]* claquer; *[dry wood]* craquer. **to get ~ing** * s'y mettre, se mettre au boulot *.
◆ **crack down on** *vt fus person* sévir contre; *expenditure, sb's actions* mettre le frein à. ◆ **crack up** * **1** *vi* (**a**) ne pas tenir le coup, flancher *. *(hum)* **I must be ~ing up!** ça ne tourne plus rond chez moi! * (**b**) *(US) [vehicle, plane]* s'écraser. **2** *vt sep*: **he's not all he's ~ed up to be** * il n'est pas aussi sensationnel * qu'on le dit.
◆ **crack-brained** *or* ◆ **cracked** * *or* ◆ **crackers** * *adj* fou, cinglé *. ◆ **crackdown** *n* mesures *fpl* énergiques (*on* contre). ◆ **cracker** *n (biscuit)* craquelin *m*, cracker *m*; *(firework)* pétard *m*; *(at parties etc)* diablotin *m*. ◆ **cracker-barrel** *adj (US)* ≃ du café du commerce. ◆ **crackpot** * *n, adj* fou *m*, folle *f*, tordu(e) ‡ *m(f)*. ◆ **crack-up** * *n (gen)* effondrement *m*; *(mental)* dépression *f* nerveuse; *(US)* accident *m*.

crackle ['krækl] **1** *vi [twigs burning]* crépiter; *[sth frying]* grésiller. **2** *n* crépitement *m*; grésillement *m*; *(on telephone etc)* crépitement(s), friture * *f*; *[china, porcelain etc]* craquelure *f*. ◆ **crackling** *n (sound)* crépitement *m*; *(Rad)* friture * *f*; *(Culin)* couenne *f* rissolée *(de rôti de porc)*.

Cracow ['krækəʊ] *n* Cracovie.

cradle ['kreɪdl] **1** *n* berceau *m*; *(Constr)* pont *m* volant; *[telephone]* support *m*; *(Med)* arceau *m*. **2** *vt child* bercer; *object* tenir entre ses mains. ◆ **cradle-snatcher** * *n* personne *f* qui les prend au berceau *. ◆ **cradlesong** *n* berceuse *f*.

craft [krɑːft] *n* (**a**) *(skill)* art *m*, métier *m*; *(job)* métier; *(Scol)* travaux manuels. (**b**) *(pl inv: boat)* embarcation *f*; *(plane)* appareil *m*. (**c**) *(cunning)* astuce *f*, ruse *f (pej)*. ◆ **craftsman** *n* artisan *m*, homme *m* de métier. ◆ **craftsmanship** *n* connaissance *f* d'un métier; **a superb piece of ~smanship** un travail superbe.

crafty ['krɑːftɪ] *adj* malin, rusé *(pej)*; *gadget, action* astucieux. **he's a ~ one** * c'est un malin. ◆ **craftily** *adv* astucieusement, avec ruse *(pej)*. ◆ **craftiness** *n* astuce *f*, ruse *f (pej)*.

crag [kræg] *n* rocher *m* escarpé. ◆ **craggy** *adj rock* escarpé; *features* taillé à la serpe.

cram [kræm] **1** *vt (gen)* fourrer (*into* dans), bourrer (*with* de); *people, passengers* faire entrer (*into* dans); *pupil* faire bachoter. **we can ~ in another book** nous pouvons encore y faire tenir un autre livre; **to ~ food into one's mouth** enfourner * de la nourriture; **we were all ~med into one room** nous étions tous entassés dans une seule pièce; **he ~med his hat (down) over his eyes** il a enfoncé son chapeau sur ses yeux; **head ~med with odd ideas** tête farcie d'idées bizarres. **2** *vi [people]* s'entasser, s'empiler (*into* dans). **to ~ for an exam** bachoter. ◆ **cram-full** *adj room, bus* bondé; *case* bourré (*of* de).

cramp [kræmp] **1** *n* crampe *f* (*in* à). **2** *vt* gêner, entraver. **to ~ sb's style** enlever ses moyens à qn. ◆ **cramped** *adj handwriting* en pattes de mouche; *posture* inconfortable; *space* resserré; **we were very ~ed** on était à l'étroit.

cranberry ['krænb(ə)rɪ] *n* canneberge *f*. **turkey with ~ sauce** dinde *f* aux canneberges.

crane [kreɪn] **1** *n (Orn, Tech)* grue *f*. **2** *adj*: **~ driver** grutier *m*. **3** *vti*: **to ~ forward, to ~ one's neck** tendre le cou.

crank [kræŋk] **1** *n* (**a**) *(eccentric)* excentrique *mf*. **a religious ~** un fanatique religieux. (**b**) *(Tech)* manivelle *f*. **2** *vt* (**~ up**) *car* faire partir à la manivelle; *cine-camera* remonter; *barrel organ* tourner la manivelle de. ◆ **crankcase** *n* carter *m*. ◆ **crankshaft** *n* vilebrequin *m*. ◆ **cranky** *adj (eccentric)* excentrique, loufoque *; *(bad-tempered)* revêche.

crap ‡ [kræp] *n* merde ‡ *f*.

crape [kreɪp] *n* = **crêpe.**

crash [kræʃ] **1** *n* (**a**) *(noise)* fracas *m*; *[thunder]* coup *m*. **~!** patatras! (**b**) *(accident)* accident *m*. **in a car ~** dans un accident de voiture. (**c**) *[company, firm]* faillite *f*; *(St Ex)* krach *m*. **2** *vt car* avoir une collision *or* un accident avec. **he ~ed the car into a tree** il a percuté un arbre; **he ~ed the plane** il s'est écrasé (au sol). **3** *vi* (**a**) *[aeroplane]* s'écraser au sol; *[vehicle]* s'écraser; *[two vehicles]* se percuter, se rentrer dedans *. **to ~ into sth** rentrer dans qch *, percuter qch; **the plate ~ed to the ground** l'assiette s'est fracassée par terre; **the car ~ed through the gate** la voiture a enfoncé la barrière. (**b**) *[bank, firm]* faire faillite; *[stock market]* s'effondrer. **4** *adj*: **~ barrier** glissière *f* de sécurité; **~ course** cours *m* intensif; **~ helmet** casque *m* (protecteur); *(Aviat)* **~ landing** atterrissage en catastrophe. ◆ **crash in, crash down** *vi [roof etc]* s'effondrer (avec fracas).

crass [kræs] *adj* crasse.

crate [kreɪt] *n (gen)* caisse *f*; *(for peaches etc)* cageot *m*.

crater ['kreɪtəʳ] *n (gen)* cratère *m*; *[bomb, shell]* entonnoir *m*.

crave [kreɪv] *vti* (**a**) (**~ for**) *drink, tobacco etc* avoir un besoin maladif de; *affection* avoir soif de. (**b**) *pardon* implorer; *permission* solliciter. ◆ **craving** *n* besoin *m* maladif (*for* de); *[affection]* soif *f* (*for* de).

crawl [krɔːl] **1** *n* (**a**) *(Aut)* **to go at a ~** avancer au pas. (**b**) *(Swimming)* crawl *m*. **to do the ~** nager le crawl. **2** *vi (gen)* ramper; *[vehicles]* avancer au pas; *[child]* se traîner à quatre pattes. **to ~ in/out** *etc* entrer/sortir *etc* en rampant *or* à quatre pattes; *(fig)* **to ~ to sb** s'aplatir devant qn; **the fly ~ed up the wall/along the table** la mouche a grimpé le long du mur/a avancé le long de la table; **to make sb's skin ~** donner la chair de poule à qn; **to ~ with vermin** grouiller de vermine. ◆ **crawler** *adj (Aut)* **~er lane** voie *f* pour véhicules lents.

crayfish ['kreɪfɪʃ] *n (freshwater)* écrevisse *f*; *(saltwater)* langouste *f*.

crayon ['kre(ɪ)ən] *n* crayon *m* de couleur; *(Art)* pastel *m*.

craze [kreɪz] **1** *n* engouement *m* (*for* pour), manie *f* (*for* de). **it's all the ~** * cela fait fureur. **2** *vt* rendre fou. **3** *vi [pottery]* craqueler; *[windscreen]* s'étoiler. ◆ **crazed** *adj person* affolé, fou ; *glaze, pottery* craquelé. ◆ **crazily** *adv* follement. ◆ **crazy** *adj (mad)* fou (*f* folle), cinglé *; *angle, slope* incroyable; *price, height* incroyable; *(US: excellent)* terrible *; *(*: enthusiastic)* fou, fana * (*f inv*) (*about sb/sth* de qn/qch); **to go crazy** devenir fou; **crazy with anxiety** fou d'inquiétude; **it was a crazy idea** c'était une idée idiote; **you were crazy to do it** tu étais fou de faire ça; **I am not crazy about it** ça ne m'emballe * pas; **he's crazy about her** il l'aime à la folie; **crazy paving** dallage *m* irrégulier.

creak [kri:k] **1** *vi [door hinge]* grincer; *[shoes, floorboard]* craquer. **2** *n* grincement *m*; craquement *m*. ◆ **creaky** *adj* grinçant; qui craque.

cream [kri:m] **1** *n* (**a**) crème *f*. **single/double ~** crème fraîche liquide/épaisse; **to take the ~ off the milk** écrémer le lait; **the ~ of society** la crème de la société; **chocolate ~** chocolat *m* fourré; **~ of tartar** crème de tartre; **~ of tomato soup** crème de tomates. (**b**) *(face ~, shoe ~)* crème *f*. **2** *adj (~-coloured)* crème *inv*; *(made with ~)* à la crème. **~ cheese** fromage *m* frais; **~ jug** pot *m* à crème. **3** *vt butter* battre. **to ~ (together) sugar and butter** travailler le beurre en crème avec le sucre; **~ed potatoes** purée *f* de pommes de terre. ◆ **cream off** *vt sep best talents, part of profits* prélever, écrémer. ◆ **creamery** *n (making cream)* laiterie *f*; *(shop)* crémerie *f*. ◆ **creamy** *adj* crémeux.

crease [kri:s] **1** *n (gen)* pli *m*; *(unwanted)* faux pli; *(on face)* ride *f*. **~-resistant** infroissable. **2** *vt* plisser. **3** *vi* se froisser, prendre un faux pli. **his face ~d with laughter** le rire a plissé son visage.

create [kri:'eɪt] **1** *vt (gen)* créer; *new fashion* lancer; *impression, noise, din* faire; *problem, difficulty* créer, provoquer. **to ~ a sensation** faire sensation; **he was ~d baron** il a été fait baron. **2** *vi (‡: fuss)* faire une scène *or* des histoires * (*about* au sujet de). ◆ **creation** *n* création *f*; **since the creation** depuis la création du monde. ◆ **creative** *adj mind, power* créateur; *person, activity* créatif. ◆ **creativity** *n* imagination *f* créatrice, créativité *f*. ◆ **creator** *n* créateur *m*, -trice *f*. ◆ **creature** ['kri:tʃəʳ] **1** *n (gen)* créature *f*; **the creatures of the deep** les animaux marins ; **2** *adj*: **creature comforts** confort matériel.

credentials [krɪ'denʃ(ə)lʒ] *npl (identifying papers)* pièce *f* d'identité; *[diplomat]* lettres *fpl* de créance; *(references)* références *fpl*.

credible ['kredɪbl] *adj (gen)* plausible; *person* crédible; *witness* digne de foi. ◆ **credibility** **1** *n* crédibilité *f* ; **2** *adj*: **credibility gap** manque *m* de crédibilité.

credit ['kredɪt] **1** *n* (**a**) *(Banking etc)* crédit *m*. **to give sb ~** faire crédit à qn; **on ~** à crédit; **you have £10 to your ~** vous avez un crédit de 10 livres. (**b**) honneur *m*. **to his ~ we must point out that...** il faut faire remarquer à son honneur *or* à son crédit que...; **he is a ~ to his family** il fait honneur à sa famille, il est l'honneur de sa famille; **to give sb ~ for (doing) sth** reconnaître que qn a fait qch; **I gave him ~ for more sense** je lui supposais plus de bon sens; **to take ~ for sth** s'attribuer le mérite de qch; **it does you ~** cela est tout à votre honneur, cela vous fait grand honneur; *(Cine)* **~s** générique *m*. (**c**) *(Scol)* unité *f* de valeur, U.V. *f*. **2** *vt* (**a**) *(believe)* croire, ajouter foi à. (**b**) **to be ~ed with having done** passer pour avoir fait; **I ~ed him with more sense** je lui supposais plus de bon sens; **it is ~ed with having magic powers** on lui attribue des pouvoirs magiques. (**c**) *(Banking)* **to ~ £5 to sb, to ~ sb with £5** créditer (le compte de) qn de 5 livres. **3** *adj limits, agency* de crédit. **~ balance** solde *m* créditeur; **~ card** carte *f* de crédit; **~ entry** inscription *f* au crédit; **~ facilities** facilités *fpl* de paiement; **~ note** avoir *m; **on the ~ side** à l'actif; **~ squeeze** restrictions *fpl* de crédit; **~ worthiness** solvabilité *f*. ◆ **creditable** *adj* honorable, estimable. ◆ **creditably** *adv* honorablement. ◆ **creditor** *n* créancier *m*, -ière *f*.

credulity [krɪ'dju:lɪtɪ] *n* crédulité *f*. ◆ **credulous** *adj* crédule. ◆ **credulously** *adv* avec crédulité.

creed [kri:d] *n* credo *m*.

creek [kri:k] *n* crique *f*, anse *f*.

creep [kri:p] *pret, ptp* **crept** **1** *vi (gen)* ramper; *(move silently)* se glisser. **to ~ in** *[person]* entrer sans un bruit; *[error]* s'y glisser; **to ~ up on sb** *[person]* s'approcher de qn à pas de loup; *[old age etc]* prendre qn par surprise; **the traffic crept along** les voitures avançaient au pas; **a feeling of peace crept over me** un sentiment de paix me gagnait peu à peu; **it makes my flesh ~** cela me donne la chair de poule. **2** *n*: **it gives me the ~s *** cela me donne la chair de poule; **he's a ~ ‡** c'est un saligaud ‡. ◆ **creeper** *n (Bot)* plante rampante; *(US: rompers)* **~ers** barboteuse *f*. ◆ **creeping** *adj plant* grimpant, rampant; *(fig) person* lécheur; *change* larvé; *inflation* rampant; **~ing paralysis** paralysie progressive. ◆ **creepy** *adj* qui donne la chair de poule. ◆ **creepy-crawly** * *n* petite bestiole.

cremate [krɪ'meɪt] *vt* incinérer *(un cadavre)*. ◆ **cremation** *n* incinération *f*. ◆ **crematorium** *or* ◆ **crematory** *n* crématorium *m*.

creosote ['krɪəsəʊt] **1** *n* créosote *f*. **2** *vt* créosoter.

crêpe [kreɪp] **1** *n* crêpe *m*. **2** *adj*: **~ bandage** bande *f* Velpeau ®; **~ paper** papier *m* crêpon; **~ (soled) shoes** chaussures *fpl* à semelles de crêpe.

crept [krept] *pret, ptp of* **creep.**

crescent ['kresnt] *n (gen)* croissant *m*; *(street)* rue *f (en arc de cercle)*. **~ moon** croissant *m* de (la) lune.

cress [kres] *n* cresson *m*.

crest [krest] *n [bird, wave, mountain]* crête *f*; *[helmet]* cimier *m*; *[road]* haut *m* de côte. **family ~** armoiries *fpl* familiales; *(fig)* **he is on the ~ of the wave** tout lui réussit en ce moment. ◆ **crestfallen** *adj person* déçu, déconfit; **to look ~fallen** avoir l'oreille basse.

Crete [kri:t] *n* Crète *f*.

cretin ['kretɪn] *n* crétin(e) *m(f)*. ◆ **cretinous** *adj* crétin.

crevice ['krevɪs] *n* fissure *f*, fente *f*.

crew[1] [kru:] **1** *n (Aviat, Naut)* équipage *m*; *(Cine, Rowing etc)* équipe *f*; *(group, gang)* bande *f*, équipe. *(pej)* **what a ~! *** quelle engeance! **2** *vi (Sailing)* **to ~ for sb** être l'équipier de qn. ◆ **crew-cut** *n*: **to have a ~-cut** avoir les cheveux en brosse. ◆ **crew-neck** *adj*: **~-neck sweater** pull-over *m* ras du cou.

crew[2] [kru:] *pret of* **crow**[2].

crib [krɪb] **1** *n* (**a**) *(cot)* lit *m* d'enfant; *(Rel)* crèche *f*; *(manger)* mangeoire *f*. *(US)* **~ death** mort subite du nourrisson. (**b**) *(plagiarism)* plagiat *m*; *(Scol)* traduction *f (utilisée illicitement)*. **2** *vti (Scol)* copier.

crick [krɪk] **1** *n*: **~ in the neck** torticolis *m*; **~ in the back** tour *m* de reins. **2** *vt*: **to ~ one's neck** attraper un torticolis; **to ~ one's back** se faire un tour de reins.

cricket[1] ['krɪkɪt] *n (insect)* grillon *m*.

cricket[2] ['krɪkɪt] **1** *n (Sport)* cricket *m*. *(fig)* **that's not ~** ce n'est pas fair-play. **2** *adj ball, match* de cricket.

crime [kraɪm] **1** *n* crime *m*. **minor ~** délit *m*; **~ wave** vague *f* de crimes; **~ is on the increase/decrease** il y a un accroissement/une régression de la criminalité. **2** *adj*: **~ car** voiture de police banalisée; **~ prevention** la lutte contre le crime; **~ wave** vague *f* de criminalité. ◆ **criminal** ['krɪmɪnl] **1** *n* criminel(le) *m(f)* ; **2** *adj action,* *motive, law* criminel; *(fig)* **it's criminal * to stay indoors today** c'est un crime de rester enfermé aujourd'hui; **the Criminal Investigation Department** la police judiciaire, la P.J.; **criminal lawyer** avocat *m* au criminel; **criminal offence** délit *m;* **to take criminal proceedings against sb** poursuivre qn au pénal; **criminal record** casier *m* judiciaire; **Criminal Records Office** identité *f* judiciaire. ◆ **criminologist** *n* criminologiste *mf*. ◆ **criminology** *n* criminologie *f*.

crimp [krɪmp] *vt hair* frisotter; *pastry* pincer.

Crimplene ['krɪmpli:n] *n* ® ≃ crêpe *m* acrylique.

crimson ['krɪmzn] *adj, n* cramoisi *(m)*.

cringe [krɪn(d)ʒ] *vi* avoir un mouvement de recul (*from* devant); *(fig)* ramper (*before* devant). **the very thought of it makes me ~ *** rien qu'à y penser j'ai envie de rentrer sous terre. ◆ **cringing** *adj movement* craintif; *behaviour* servile.

crinkle ['krɪŋkl] *vt* froisser, chiffonner. ◆ **crinkly** *adj paper* gaufré; *hair* crêpelé.

cripple ['krɪpl] **1** *n (lame)* estropié(e) *m(f)*; *(disabled)* invalide *mf*; *(maimed)* mutilé(e) *m(f)*. **2** *vt* (**a**) estropier. (**b**) *ship, plane* désemparer; *[strikes etc] production, exports etc* paralyser. **crippling taxes** impôts écrasants. ◆ **crippled** *adj person* estropié, handicapé; *plane* accidenté; *factory* gravement accidenté; **~d with rhumatism** perclus de rhumatismes.

crisis, *pl* **crises** ['kraɪsɪs, 'kraɪsi:z] *n* crise *f*. **to come to a ~** atteindre un point critique; **we've got a ~ on our hands** nous avons un problème urgent ; **~ centre** *(after disaster)* cellule *f* de crise; *(for advice etc)* centre *m* d'aide.

crisp [krɪsp] **1** *adj biscuit, bread* croustillant; *vegetables* croquant; *snow, paper* craquant; *linen* apprêté; *weather* vif, piquant; *reply, style* vif, tranchant *(pej)*; *tone, voice* acerbe, cassant *(pej)*. **2** *n* **(potato) ~s** (pommes *fpl*) chips *fpl*; **packet of ~s** sachet *m* de chips. ◆ **crispbread** *n* pain *m* scandinave. ◆ **crisply** *adv say etc* d'un ton acerbe *or* cassant *(pej)*. ◆ **crispness** *n* croquant *m*.

criss-cross ['krɪskrɒs] **1** *adj lines* entrecroisés. **in a ~ pattern** en croisillons. **2** *n* entrecroisement *m*. **3** *vt* entrecroiser (*by* de). **4** *vi* s'entrecroiser.

criterion, *pl* **-ia** *or* **-s** [kraɪ'tɪərɪən, -ɪə] *n* critère *m*.

critic ['krɪtɪk] *n [books, painting, music, films etc]* critique *m*; *(faultfinder)* détracteur *m*, -trice *f*. **film ~** critique de cinéma. ◆ **critical** *adj (all senses)* critique. **to be ~al of** critiquer, trouver à redire à. ◆ **critically** *adv (discriminatingly) judge, consider, discuss* en critique, d'un œil critique; *(adversely) review, report* sévèrement; **~ally ill** gravement malade. ◆ **criticism** *n* critique *f*. ◆ **criticize** *vt* critiquer. ◆ **critique** [krɪ'ti:k] *n* critique *f*.

croak [krəʊk] **1** *vi [frog]* coasser; *[raven]* croasser; *[person]* parler d'une voix rauque. **2** *vt* dire d'une voix rauque. **3** *n* coassement *m*; croassement *m*.

crochet ['krəʊʃeɪ] **1** *n* travail *m* au crochet. **~ hook** crochet *m*. **2** *vt* faire au crochet. **3** *vi* faire du crochet.

crock [krɒk] *n (pot)* cruche *f*; *(*: car)* guimbarde * *f*. *(broken pieces)* **~s** débris *mpl* de faïence; **he's an old ~ *** c'est un croulant *. ◆ **crockery** *n (earthenware)* poterie *f*; *(cups, saucers, plates)* vaisselle *f*.

crocodile ['krɒkədaɪl] *n* crocodile *m*. **~ tears** larmes *fpl* de crocodile; **to walk in a ~** aller deux par deux.

crocus ['krəʊkəs] *n* crocus *m*.

croft [krɒft] *n* petite ferme *f*. ◆ **crofter** *n* petit fermier *m*.

crone [krəʊn] *n* vieille bique *f (femme)*.

crony * ['krəʊnɪ] *n* copain * *m*, copine * *f*.

crook [krʊk] **1** *n* (**a**) *[shepherd]* houlette *f*; *[bishop]* crosse *f*. (**b**) *[road, river]* angle *m*. (**c**) *(*: thief)* escroc *m*. **2** *vt finger* courber; *arm* plier. ◆ **crooked** ['krʊkɪd] *adj stick* courbé, tordu; *person* tout courbé; *path* tortueux; *smile* contraint; *method, action* malhonnête; **the picture is ~ed** le tableau est de travers. ◆ **crookedness** *n* courbure *f*; malhonnêteté *f*.

croon [kru:n] *vti* chantonner; *[crooner]* chanter. ◆ **crooner** *n* chanteur *m*, -euse *f* de charme.

crop [krɒp] **1** *n* (**a**) *(produce)* culture *f*; *(amount produced: of fruit, vegetables etc)* récolte *f*; *[cereals]* moisson *f*; *[problems, questions]* série *f*, tas * *m*. **the ~s** la récolte; **one of the basic ~s** l'une des cultures de base. (**b**) *[bird]* jabot *m*; *[whip]* manche *m*; *(riding ~)* cravache *f*. **2** *adj*: **~ spraying** pulvérisation *f* des cultures; **~ sprayer** *(device)* pulvérisateur *m*; *(plane)* avion-pulvérisateur *m*. **3** *vt* (**a**) *[animals]* brouter. (**b**) *hair* tondre. **~ped hair** cheveux coupés ras. ◆ **crop up** *vi [questions, problems, subject]* se présenter. **sth's ~ped up** il s'est passé qch; **ready for anything that might ~ up** prêt à toute éventualité.

cropper * ['krɒpəʳ] *n (lit, fig)* **to come a ~** se casser la figure *.

croquet ['krəʊkeɪ] *n* croquet *m*.

cross [krɒs] **1** *n* (**a**) croix *f*. **to sign with a ~** signer d'une croix; **we each have our ~ to bear** chacun porte sa croix. (**b**) *(Bio, Zool)* hybride *m*. **it's a ~ between a novel and a poem** cela tient du roman et du poème. (**c**) **cut on the ~** *material* coupé dans le biais; *skirt* en biais.

2 *adj* (**a**) *(angry)* de mauvaise humeur. **to be ~ with sb** être fâché contre qn; **it makes me ~ when...** cela m'agace quand...; **to get ~ with sb** se fâcher contre qn; **don't be ~ with me** ne m'en veuillez pas; **to be as ~ as a bear with a sore head** être d'une humeur massacrante; **they haven't had a ~ word** ils ne se sont pas disputés une seule fois. (**b**) *(diagonal)* transversal, diagonal.

3 *vt* (**a**) *room, street, sea, continent, line* traverser; *river, bridge* traverser, passer; *threshold, fence, ditch* franchir. **the bridge ~es the river** le pont enjambe la rivière; **it ~ed my mind that...** il m'est venu à l'esprit que...; **don't ~ your bridges before you come to them** chaque chose en son temps; *(fig)* **to ~ sb's path** se trouver sur le chemin de qn. (**b**) *letter T, cheque* barrer. **to ~ o.s.** se signer, faire le signe de (la) croix; **~ my heart! *** ≃ croix de bois croix de fer! * (**c**) *arms, legs* croiser. **to ~ swords with sb** croiser le fer avec qn; **keep your fingers ~ed for me *** fais une petite prière pour moi (ça me portera bonheur); *(Telec)* **the lines are ~ed** les lignes sont embrouillées; **they've got their lines ~ed *** il y a un malentendu quelque part. (**d**) *(thwart) person, plans* contrecarrer. (**e**) *animals, plants* croiser (*with* avec).

4 *vi* (**a**) **(~ over)** traverser. **to ~ from one place to another** passer d'un endroit à un autre; **to ~ from Newhaven to Dieppe** faire la traversée de Newhaven à Dieppe. (**b**) *[roads, letters, people]* se croiser.

◆ **cross off, cross out** *vt sep* barrer, rayer. **to ~ sb's name off a list** radier qn d'une liste.

◆ **crossbar** *n [bicycle]* barre *f*. ◆ **crossbow** *n* arbalète *f*. ◆ **crossbreed** *n* hybride *m*. ◆ **cross-Channel** *adj*: **~-Channel ferry** ferry *m* qui traverse la Manche. ◆ **cross-check** **1** *n* contre-épreuve *f*; **2** *vti* vérifier par recoupement. ◆ **cross-country** *adj*: **~-country race** cross-country *m*; **~-country skiing** ski *m* de randonnée. ◆ **cross-examination** *n* contre-interrogatoire *m*. ◆ **cross-examine** *vt (Jur)* faire subir un contre-interrogatoire à; *(gen)* interroger (de façon serrée). ◆ **cross-eyed** *adj* qui louche. ◆ **crossfire** *n* feux *mpl* croisés. ◆ **crossing** *n (esp by sea)* traversée *f*; *[equator]* passage *m*; *(road junction)* croisement *m*, carrefour *m*; *(level ~)* passage à niveau; *(pedestrian ~)* passage *m* clouté; **school ~ing patrol** contractuel(le) *m(f) (qui fait traverser la rue aux enfants)*; **cross at the ~ing** traversez sur le passage clouté *or* dans les clous *. ◆ **cross-legged** *adv* en tailleur. ◆ **crossly** *adv* avec humeur. ◆ **cross-patch** * *n* grincheux *m*, -euse *f*. ◆ **cross-ply** *adj (Aut)* à carcasse diagonale. ◆ **cross-purposes** *npl*: **to be at ~-purposes with sb** *(misunderstand)* comprendre qn de travers; *(disagree)* être en désaccord avec qn; **we were talking at ~-purposes** notre conversation tournait autour d'un quiproquo. ◆ **cross-question** *vt* faire subir un interrogatoire à. ◆ **cross-refer** *vt* renvoyer (*to* à). ◆ **cross-reference** *n* renvoi *m* (*to* à). ◆ **cross-roads** *n* carrefour *m*. ◆ **cross-section** *n (Bio etc)* coupe *f* transversale; *[population etc]* échantillon *m*. ◆ **crosswalk** *n (US)* passage *m* clouté. ◆ **crosswind** *n* vent *m* de travers. ◆ **crosswise** *adv* en travers, en croix. ◆ **crossword puzzle** *n* mots *mpl* croisés.

crotch [krɒtʃ] *n [body, tree]* fourche *f*; *[garment]* entre-jambes *m inv*.

crotchet ['krɒtʃɪt] *n (Mus)* noire *f*. ◆ **crotchety** *adj* grincheux.

crouch [kraʊtʃ] *vi* **(~ down)** *[person, animal]* s'accroupir, se tapir; *(before springing)* se ramasser.

croup [kru:p] *n (Med)* croup *m*.

crow[1] [krəʊ] *n (bird)* corneille *f*; *(generic term)* corbeau *m*. **as the ~ flies** à vol d'oiseau; *(US)* **to eat ~** * faire des excuses humiliantes; *(wrinkles)* **~'s feet** pattes *fpl* d'oie *(rides)*; *(Naut)* **~'s nest** nid *m* de pie. ◆ **crowbar** *n* pince *f* à levier.

crow[2] [krəʊ] *vi* (**a**) *pret* **crowed** *or* **crew**, *ptp* **crowed** *[cock]* chanter. (**b**) *pret, ptp* **crowed** *[baby]* gazouiller; *[victor]* chanter victoire (*over sb* sur qn). **he ~ed with delight** il poussait des cris de joie; **it's nothing to ~ about** il n'y a pas de quoi pavoiser.

crowd [kraʊd] **1** *n* foule *f*; *(disorderly)* cohue *f*. **in ~s** en foule, en masse; **a large ~** une foule immense; **there was quite a ~** il y avait beaucoup de monde; **how big was the ~?** est-ce qu'il y avait beaucoup de monde?; *(actors)* **the ~** les figurants *mpl*; **~ scene** scène *f* de foule; **that would pass in a ~** * ça peut passer si on n'y regarde pas de trop près; **~s of books/people** des masses * de livres/de gens; *(fig)* **to follow the ~** suivre la foule *or* le mouvement; **I don't like that ~ * at all** je n'aime pas du tout cette bande; **he's one of our ~** * il fait partie de notre bande.
2 *vi*: **to ~ into** s'entasser dans; **to ~ together** se serrer; **to ~ round sth** s'attrouper pour voir qch; **to ~ round sb** se presser autour de qn; **to ~ down/in** *etc* descendre/entrer *etc* en foule.
3 *vt objects* entasser (*into* dans); *(jostle) person* bousculer; *car* serrer. **the houses are ~ed together** les maisons sont les unes sur les autres; **~ed with** *people, facts, incidents* plein de, bourré de; *objects, furniture* encombré de; **to ~ on sail** mettre toutes voiles dehors.
◆ **crowd out** *vt sep* empêcher d'entrer (faute de place).
◆ **crowded** *adj room, train, café* bondé, plein; *town, profession* encombré; *streets* plein (de monde); *day* chargé; **the shops are too ~ed** il y a trop de monde dans les magasins; *(Theat)* **~ed house** salle *f* comble.

crown [kraʊn] **1** *n* (**a**) couronne *f*. *(Jur)* **the C~** la Couronne, ≃ le ministère public. (**b**) *[head]* sommet *m* de la tête; *[hat]* fond *m*; *[road]* milieu *m*; *[tooth]* couronne *f*; *[hill]* faîte *m*. **2** *adj (Jur)* **C~ court** ≃ cour *f* d'assises; **~ jewels** joyaux *mpl* de la couronne; **~ prince** prince *m* héritier. **3** *vt (gen, Dentistry, fig)* couronner (*with* de); *[draughts]* damer; *(*: hit)* flanquer * un coup sur la tête à. **he was ~ed king** il fut couronné roi; **to ~ it all** * **it began to snow** pour couronner le tout il s'est mis à neiger. ◆ **crowning 1** *n* couronnement *m* ; **2** *adj achievement, moment* suprême.

crucial ['kru:ʃ(ə)l] *adj* crucial.

crucifix ['kru:sɪfɪks] *n* crucifix *m*. ◆ **crucifixion** *n* crucifixion *f*. ◆ **crucify** *vt* crucifier.

crude [kru:d] *adj materials* brut; *sugar* non raffiné; *drawing* qui manque de fini; *piece of work* mal fini, sommaire; *object, tool* grossier, rudimentaire; *light, colour* cru, vif; *person, behaviour* grossier; *manners* fruste. **~ (oil)** pétrole *m* brut; **he made a ~ attempt at building...** il a essayé tant bien que mal de construire...; **a ~ word** une grossièreté. ◆ **crudely** *adv make, fashion* sommairement; *say, order, explain* grossièrement, brutalement; **to put it ~ly I think he's mad** pour dire les choses crûment je pense qu'il est fou. ◆ **crudeness** *or* ◆ **crudity** *n* état *m* brut, manque *m* de fini; caractère *m* rudimentaire; grossièreté *f*.

cruel ['krʊəl] *adj* cruel (*to* envers). ◆ **cruelly** *adv* cruellement. ◆ **cruelty** *n* cruauté *f* (*to* envers); *(Jur)* sévices *mpl* (*to* sur); **mental ~ty** cruauté mentale.

cruet ['kru:ɪt] *n (~ stand)* ≃ huilier *m*; *(~ set)* salière *f* et poivrier *m*.

cruise [kru:z] **1** *vi* (**a**) *[fleet, ship]* croiser; *[holiday-makers]* être en croisière. (**b**) *[cars]* **to ~ at 80 km/h** faire du 80 km/h sans effort; **we were cruising along when suddenly...** nous roulions tranquillement quand tout à coup...; *(Aut, Aviat)* **cruising speed** vitesse *f* de croisière. (**c**) *[taxi, patrol car]* marauder. **a cruising taxi** un taxi en maraude. **2** *n (Naut)* croisière *f*. **to go on** *or* **for a ~** faire une croisière. ◆ **cruiser** *n (warship)* croiseur *m*; *(cabin ~)* yacht *m* de croisière.

crumb [krʌm] *n* miette *f*; *(inside of loaf)* mie *f*. *(fig)* **a ~ of** *comfort* un brin de; *information* des miettes de; **~s!** * zut alors! *; **he's a ~** * c'est un pauvre type *. ◆ **crumble 1** *vt bread* émietter; *earth* effriter ; **2** *vi [bread]* s'émietter; *[buildings etc]* tomber en ruine; *[plaster, stones]* s'effriter; *[rock, ceiling]* s'ébouler; *[hopes etc]* s'effondrer. ◆ **crumbly** *adj* friable.

crummy ⁑ ['krʌmɪ] *adj* minable.

crumple ['krʌmpl] **1** *vt* froisser; **(~ up)** chiffonner. **he ~d the paper into a ball** il a fait une boule de la feuille de papier. **2** *vi* se froisser; se chiffonner.

crunch [krʌn(t)ʃ] **1** *vt (with teeth)* croquer; *(underfoot)* écraser, faire craquer. **to ~ sth up** broyer qch. **2** *vi*: **he ~ed across the gravel** il a traversé en faisant craquer le gravier sous ses pas. **3** *n [broken glass, gravel]* craquement *m*. *(fig)* **when it comes to the ~** * dans une situation critique, au moment crucial. ◆ **crunchy** *adj* croquant.

crusade [kru:'seɪd] **1** *n* croisade *f*. **2** *vi (fig)* faire une croisade (*against* contre, *for* pour). ◆ **crusader** *n (Hist)* croisé *m*; *(fig)* champion *m* (*for* de), militant(e) *m(f)* (*against* contre).

crush [krʌʃ] **1** *n* (**a**) *(crowd)* cohue *f*, foule *f*. **there was a great ~ to get in** c'était la bousculade pour entrer. (**b**) **to have a ~ on sb** * avoir le béguin * pour qn. (**c**) **orange ~** orange *f* pressée.
2 *adj*: **~ barrier** barrière *f or* rampe *f* de sécurité.
3 *vt stones, old cars* broyer; *grapes* écraser; *(crumple) clothes* froisser; *(fig) enemy, revolution, opponent* écraser; *hope* détruire; *(snub)* rabrouer. **to ~ to a pulp** réduire en pulpe; **to ~ clothes into a bag** fourrer des vêtements dans une valise; **we were very ~ed in the car** nous étions très tassés dans la voiture.
4 *vi [clothes]* se froisser. **to ~ round sb** se presser autour de qn; **they ~ed into the car** ils se sont entassés dans la voiture; **to ~ (one's way) into/through** *etc* se frayer un chemin dans/à travers *etc*.

◆ **crush out** *vt sep juice etc* presser; *cigarette end, revolt* écraser.

◆ **crushing** *adj defeat* écrasant; *reply* percutant.

◆ **crush-resistant** *adj* infroissable.

crust [krʌst] *n* croûte *f*. **a ~ of ice** une couche de glace; *(Geol)* **the earth's ~** la croûte terrestre. ◆ **crusty** *adj loaf* croustillant; (*) *person* hargneux.

crustacean [krʌs'teɪʃən] *n* crustacé *m*.

crutch [krʌtʃ] *n* (**a**) *(support)* soutien *m*; *(Med)* béquille *f*. **he gets about on ~es** il marche avec des béquilles. (**b**) = **crotch**.

crux [krʌks] *n (gen)* point *m* crucial; *[problem]* cœur *m*. **the ~ of the matter** le point capital dans l'affaire.

cry [kraɪ] **1** *n* (**a**) cri *m*. **to give a ~** pousser un cri; **he gave a ~ for help** il a appelé au secours; **'votes for women' was their ~** leur slogan *m* était 'le vote pour les femmes'. (**b**) *(weep)* **she had a good ~** * elle a pleuré un bon coup *. **2** *vt* (**a**) s'écrier, crier. **'here I am' he cried** 'me voici' s'écria-t-il; **'go away' he cried to me** 'allez-vous-en' me cria-t-il. (**b**) **to ~ o.s. to sleep** s'endormir à force de pleurer; **to ~ one's eyes out** pleurer toutes les larmes de son corps. **3** *vi* (**a**) *(weep)* pleurer (*about, over* sur; *for sth* pour avoir qch; *with rage etc* de rage *etc*). **to laugh till one cries** rire aux larmes; **I'll give him sth to ~ for!** * je vais lui apprendre à pleurnicher!; **it's no use ~ing over spilt milk** ce qui est fait est fait. (**b**) (**~ out**) *(inadvertently)* pousser un cri; *(deliberately)* s'écrier. **he cried out with pain** il a poussé un cri de douleur; **to ~ out for help** appeler à l'aide; **to ~ out for mercy** implorer la pitié; **that floor is just ~ing out to be washed** * ce plancher a grandement besoin d'être lavé.

◆ **cry off** * **1** *vi (from meeting)* se décommander; *(from promise)* se dédire. **I'm ~ing off!** je ne veux plus rien savoir! **2** *vt fus arrangement, deal* annuler ; *project* ne plus se mêler à; *meeting* décommander.

◆ **crying** **1** *adj child* qui pleure; *injustice* criant, flagrant; *need* pressant, urgent; **it's a ~ing shame** c'est une honte ; **2** *n (shouts)* cris *mpl*; *(weeping)* pleurs *mpl*.

crypt [krɪpt] *n* crypte *f*.

cryptic(al) ['krɪptɪk(əl)] *adj (mysterious)* énigmatique; *(terse)* laconique. ◆ **cryptically** *adv* énigmatiquement; laconiquement.

crystal ['krɪstl] **1** *n (gen)* cristal *m*; *(watch glass)* verre *m* de montre. **2** *adj vase, lake* de cristal. **~ ball** boule *f* de cristal. ◆ **crystal-clear** *adj* clair comme le jour. ◆ **crystal-gazing** *n* prédictions *fpl*, prophéties *fpl*. ◆ **crystalline** *adj* cristallin. ◆ **crystallize** **1** *vi* se cristalliser ; **2** *vt* cristalliser; **~lized fruits** fruits *mpl* confits *or* candis. ◆ **crystallography** *n* cristallographie *f*.

cub [kʌb] *n* petit(e) *m(f)*. **wolf ~** louveteau *m*, jeune loup *m*. **~ reporter** jeune reporter *m*; **~ scout** louveteau *m (scout)*.

Cuba ['kju:bə] *n* Cuba *m*. **in ~** à Cuba.

cubbyhole ['kʌbɪhəʊl] *n* cagibi *m*; *(Aut)* vide-poches *m inv*.

cube [kju:b] **1** *n* cube *m*. **~ root** racine *f* cubique; *(Culin)* **to cut into ~s** couper en dés. **2** *vt (Math)* cuber. ◆ **cubic** *adj shape, volume* cubique; *yard, metre* cube; **cubic capacity** volume *m*. ◆ **cubism** *n* cubisme *m*. ◆ **cubist** *adj, n* cubiste *(mf)*.

cubicle ['kju:bɪk(ə)l] *n [hospital, dormitory]* box *m* ; *[swimming baths]* cabine *f*.

cuckoo ['kʊku:] **1** *n (Orn)* coucou *m*. **~ clock** coucou *m (pendule)*. **2** *adj* (‡) toqué *, fou.

cucumber ['kju:kʌmbəʳ] *n* concombre *m*.

cuddle ['kʌdl] **1** *vt* caresser; *child* câliner. **2** *vi*: **to ~ down** se pelotonner; **to ~ up to sb** se pelotonner contre qn. ◆ **cuddly** *adj child* caressant; *animal* qui donne envie de le caresser; *toy* doux.

cudgel ['kʌdʒ(ə)l] **1** *n* gourdin *m*. **to take up the ~s on behalf of** prendre fait et cause pour. **2** *vt*: **to ~ one's brains** se creuser la cervelle.

cue [kju:] *n* (**a**) *(Theat: verbal)* réplique *f (indiquant à un acteur qu'il doit parler)*; *(sign: Theat, Mus etc)* signal *m*. *(Theat)* **to give sb his ~** donner la réplique à qn; *(fig)* **to take one's ~ from sb** emboîter le pas à qn *(fig)*. (**b**) *(Billiards)* queue *f* de billard. ◆ **cue in** *vt sep (Rad, TV)* donner le signal à; *(Theat)* donner la réplique à. **to ~ sb in on sth** mettre qn au courant de qch.

cuff [kʌf] **1** *n* (**a**) manchette *f*; *(US: trouser turn-up)* revers *m* de pantalon. **~ link** bouton *m* de manchette; *(fig)* **off the ~** à l'improviste. (**b**) *(blow)* gifle *f*. **2** *vt (strike)* gifler.

cul-de-sac ['kʌldə'sæk] *n* cul-de-sac *m*.

culinary ['kʌlɪn(ə)rɪ] *adj* culinaire.

cull [kʌl] *vt (sample)* sélectionner; *(kill) animals* supprimer, éliminer.

culminate ['kʌlmɪneɪt] *vi* culminer. **to ~ in** finir *or* se terminer par; *(be cause of)* mener à; **it ~d in his throwing her out** pour finir il l'a mise à la porte. ◆ **culminating** *adj* culminant. ◆ **culmination** *n [success, career]* apogée *m*; *[disturbance, quarrel]* point *m* culminant.

culpable ['kʌlpəbl] *adj* coupable (*of* de).

culprit ['kʌlprɪt] *n* coupable *mf*.

cult [kʌlt] *n (Rel, fig)* culte *m*. **to make a ~ of sth** avoir le culte de qch; **~ figure** objet *m* d'un culte, idole *f*.

cultivate ['kʌltɪveɪt] *vt* cultiver. ◆ **cultivable** *adj* cultivable. ◆ **cultivated** *adj land, person* cultivé; *voice* distingué. ◆ **cultivation** *n* culture *f*. ◆ **cultivator** *n (machine)* cultivateur *m*; *(power-driven)* motoculteur *m*.

culture ['kʌltʃəʳ] *n (all senses)* culture *f*. **~ shock** choc culturel. ◆ **cultural** *adj* culturel; *(Agr)* cultural. ◆ **cultured** *adj person* cultivé; *voice* distingué; *pearl* de culture.

cumbersome ['kʌmbəsəm] *adj (bulky)* encombrant; *(heavy)* pesant.

cumin ['kʌmɪn] *n* cumin *m*.

cumulative ['kju:mjʊlətɪv] *adj* cumulatif.

cunning ['kʌnɪŋ] **1** *n* astuce *f*, ruse *f (pej)*. **2** *adj* malin, rusé *(pej)*; (*: *clever)* astucieux. ◆ **cunningly** *adv* avec astuce, avec ruse; astucieusement.

cup [kʌp] **1** *n* tasse *f*; *(Sport etc: prize)* coupe *f*; *[brassière]* bonnet *m* (de soutien-gorge). **~ of tea** tasse de thé; **tea ~** tasse à thé; **that's just his ~ of tea** * c'est tout à fait à son goût; **it isn't everyone's ~ of tea** * ça ne plaît pas à tout le monde. **2** *vt one's hands* mettre en coupe. **to ~ one's hands round sth** mettre ses mains autour de qch; **to ~ one's hand round one's ear** mettre sa main en cornet.

◆ **cup final** *n (Ftbl)* finale *f* de la coupe. ◆ **cupful** *n* tasse *f (contenu)*. ◆ **cuppa** ‡ *n* tasse *f* de thé. ◆ **cup-tie** *n (Ftbl)* match *m* de coupe.

cupboard ['kʌbəd] *n (esp Brit)* placard *m*. *(Brit)* **~ love** amour *m* intéressé.

cupidity [kju:'pɪdɪtɪ] *n* cupidité *f*.

cur [kɜ:ʳ] *n* sale chien *m*, sale cabot * *m*.

curate ['kjʊərɪt] *n* vicaire *m*. **it's like the ~'s egg** il y a du bon et du mauvais.

curator [kjʊə'reɪtəʳ] *n* conservateur *m (d'un musée etc)*.

curb [kɜ:b] **1** *n (US)* = **kerb**. **2** *vt impatience, passion, tendency* refréner; *expenditure* réduire.

curdle ['kɜ:dl] **1** *vt milk* cailler; *mayonnaise* faire tomber. **2** *vi [milk]* se cailler; *[mayonnaise]* tomber. **it made my blood ~** cela m'a glacé le sang dans les veines.

curds [kɜ:dz] *npl* lait *m* caillé. ◆ **curd cheese** *n* fromage *m* blanc.

cure [kjʊəʳ] **1** *vt* (**a**) *disease, patient* guérir (*of* de); *poverty, unfairness* éliminer; *injustice* réparer; *an evil* remédier à. **to be ~d (of)** guérir (de); **to ~ sb of a habit** faire perdre une habitude à qn; **to ~ o.s. of smoking** se guérir de l'habitude de fumer. (**b**) *meat, fish (salt)* saler; *(smoke)* fumer; *(dry)* sécher; *skins* traiter. **2** *n (remedy)* remède *m*, cure *f*; *(recovery)* guérison *f*. **to take a ~** faire une cure; **beyond ~** *person* incurable; *state, injustice, evil* irrémédiable. ◆ **curable** *adj* guérissable, curable. ◆ **curative** *adj* curatif. ◆ **cure-all** *n (lit, fig)* panacée *f*.

curfew ['kɜːfjuː] *n* couvre-feu *m*.

curio ['kjʊərɪəʊ] *n* bibelot *m*, curiosité *f*.

curiosity [ˌkjʊərɪ'ɒsɪtɪ] *n* curiosité *f* (*about* de). **~ killed the cat** la curiosité est toujours punie; **~ shop** magasin *m* de curiosités. ◆ **curious** *adj (inquisitive)* curieux (*about* de, *to know* de savoir); *(odd)* curieux, bizarre. ◆ **curiously** *adv (inquisitively)* avec curiosité; *(oddly)* curieusement, singulièrement; **curiously enough, he...** chose bizarre, il...

curl [kɜːl] **1** *n [hair]* boucle *f*; *(gen)* courbe *f*; *[smoke]* volute *f*. **with a ~ of the lip** avec une moue méprisante. **2** *vt hair (loosely)* boucler; *(tightly)* friser. **she ~s her hair** elle frise (*or* boucle) ses cheveux; **he ~ed his lip in disdain** il a fait une moue méprisante. **3** *vi [hair]* boucler; friser. **it's enough to make your hair ~** * c'est à vous faire dresser les cheveux sur la tête.
◆ **curl up** *vi (gen)* s'enrouler; *[paper]* se recourber; *[person]* se pelotonner; *(*: from shame etc)* rentrer sous terre; *[cat]* se mettre en boule; *[dog]* se coucher en rond; *[leaves]* se recroqueviller; *[stale bread]* se racornir; *[smoke]* monter en volutes. **he lay ~ed up on the floor** il était couché en boule par terre; **to ~ up with laughter** se tordre de rire. ◆ **curler** *n* rouleau *m*, bigoudi *m*. ◆ **curling tongs** *npl* fer *m* à friser. ◆ **curly** *adj hair* bouclé; *(tightly)* frisé; *eyelashes* recourbé; *lettuce* frisé; **~y-haired, ~y-headed** aux cheveux bouclés (*or* frisés).

curlew ['kɜːluː] *n* courlis *m*.

currant ['kʌr(ə)nt] *n* groseille *f*; *(bush)* groseillier *m*; *(dried fruit)* raisin *m* sec *or* de Corinthe. **~ bun** petit pain *m* aux raisins.

currency ['kʌr(ə)nsɪ] *n* (**a**) monnaie *f*, devise *f*; *(money)* argent *m*. **the ~ is threatened** la monnaie est en danger; **foreign ~** devise *or* monnaie étrangère; **hard ~** devise forte; **paper ~** billets *mpl*; **~ restrictions** contrôle *m* des changes. (**b**) *[ideas etc]* **to gain ~** se répandre, s'accréditer.

current ['kʌr(ə)nt] **1** *adj opinion, phrase, price* courant; *fashion, tendency, popularity* actuel; *year, month, week* en cours. **in ~ use** d'usage courant; *(Bank)* **~ account** compte *m* courant; **~ affairs** actualité *f*; **~ events** événements *mpl* actuels, actualité ; *(Press)* **~ issue** dernier numéro *m*; **his ~ job** le travail qu'il fait en ce moment; **her ~ boyfriend** * le petit ami du moment. **2** *n [air, water]* courant *m (also Elec)*; *[events, opinions]* tendance *f*. *(fig)* **to go against the ~** aller à contre-courant. ◆ **currently** *adv* actuellement, en ce moment.

curriculum [kə'rɪkjʊləm] *n* programme *m* (d'études). **~ vitae** curriculum vitae *m*, C.V. *m*.

curry¹ ['kʌrɪ] *n* curry *m*. **beef ~** curry de bœuf; **~ powder** poudre *f* de curry.

curry² ['kʌrɪ] *vt*: **to ~ favour with sb** chercher à gagner la faveur de qn.

curse [kɜːs] **1** *n* malédiction *f*; *(swearword)* juron *m*, imprécation *f*. **~s!** * zut! *; **the ~ of poverty** le fléau de la pauvreté; **it has been the ~ of my life** c'est un sort qui m'a poursuivi toute ma vie; *(menstruation)* **she has the ~** * elle a ses règles *fpl*; **the ~ of it is that** l'embêtant *, c'est que. **2** *vt* maudire. *(fig)* **to be ~d with** être affligé de. **3** *vi* jurer, sacrer. ◆ **cursed** * ['kɜːsɪd] *adj* sacré *, maudit *(both before n)*.

cursor ['kɜːsəʳ] *n (Comput)* curseur *m*.

cursory ['kɜːs(ə)rɪ] *adj (superficial)* superficiel; *(hasty)* hâtif. **to take a ~ glance at** jeter un coup d'œil à. ◆ **cursorily** *adv* superficiellement; à la hâte.

curt [kɜːt] *adj (gen)* brusque, sec; *voice* cassant. **a ~ nod** un bref signe de tête. ◆ **curtly** *adv* sèchement; d'un ton cassant. ◆ **curtness** *n* brusquerie *f*, sécheresse *f*.

curtail [kɜː'teɪl] *vt (gen)* écourter; *wages, expenses* réduire. ◆ **curtailment** *n* raccourcissement *m*; réduction *f*.

curtain ['kɜːtn] **1** *n* rideau *m*. **to draw** *or* **pull the ~s** tirer les rideaux. **2** *adj (Theat)* **~ call** rappel *m*; **~ hook** crochet *m* de rideau; *(Theat)* **~ raiser** lever *m* de rideau *(pièce)*; **~ ring** anneau *m* de rideau; **~ rod** tringle *f* à rideaux; *(Theat)* **~-up** lever *m* du rideau. ◆ **curtain off** *vt sep room* diviser par un rideau; *bed, kitchen area* cacher derrière un rideau.

curts(e)y ['kɜːtsɪ] **1** *n* révérence *f*. **2** *vi* faire une révérence (*to* à).

curvaceous * [kɜː'veɪʃəs] *adj woman* bien balancée *, bien faite.

curve [kɜːv] **1** *n (gen)* courbe *f*; *[arch]* voussure *f*; *[beam]* cambrure *f*. **~ in the road** tournant *m*, virage *m*; **a woman's ~s** * les rondeurs *fpl* d'une femme. **2** *vt (gen)* courber; *arch, roof* cintrer. **3** *vi [surface, beam]* se courber; *[road, line etc]* faire une courbe. **the river ~s round the town** la rivière fait un méandre autour de la ville. ◆ **curvature** *n* courbure *f*; *(Med)* déviation *f*; **curvature of the spine** déviation de la colonne vertébrale; **the curvature of space** la courbure de l'espace. ◆ **curved** *adj line, space* courbe; *edge* arrondi; *road* en courbe; *(convex)* convexe.

cushion ['kʊʃ(ə)n] **1** *n* coussin *m*. **2** *vt seat* rembourrer; *shock, sb's fall* amortir. **to ~ sb against sth** protéger qn contre qch. ◆ **cushy** ‡ *adj*: **a cushy job** un petit travail tranquille; **to have a cushy time** se la couler douce *.

cuss * [kʌs] **1** *n (oath)* juron *m*. *(person)* **a queer ~** un drôle de type *. **2** *vi* jurer. ◆ **cussed** * ['kʌsɪd] *adj* têtu comme une mule *. ◆ **cussedness** * *n* esprit *m* de contradiction.

custard ['kʌstəd] **1** *n (pouring)* crème *f* anglaise; *(set)* crème renversée. **2** *adj*: **~ cream (biscuit)** biscuit *m* fourré; **~ powder** crème instantanée (en poudre); **~ tart** flan *m*.

custody ['kʌstədɪ] *n* (**a**) *(Jur etc)* garde *f*. **in safe ~** sous bonne garde; **in the ~ of** sous la garde de; *(Jur)* **she was given ~ of the children** elle a reçu la garde des enfants. (**b**) *(imprisonment)* emprisonnement *m*. **in ~** en captivité; **(police) ~** *(for short period)* garde *f* à vue; *(before trial)* détention préventive; **to take sb into ~** mettre qn en détention préventive ◆ **custodian** *n (gen)* gardien(ne) *m(f)*; *[museum]* conservateur *m*, -trice *f*.

custom ['kʌstəm] **1** *n* (**a**) coutume *f*, usage *m*, habitude *f*. **social ~s** usages sociaux, coutumes sociales; **it was his ~ to rest each morning** il avait l'habitude *or* la coutume de se reposer chaque matin. (**b**) *(Comm)* **to get sb's ~** obtenir la clientèle de qn; **he has lost a lot of ~** il a perdu beaucoup de clients. (**c**) **the ~s** la douane; **to go through the ~s** passer la douane. **2** *adj*: **~s duty** droits *mpl* de douane; **~s house** *or* **post** (poste *m or* bureaux *mpl* de) douane *f*; **~s inspection** visite *f* douanière; **~s officer** douanier *m*; **~s service** service *m* des douanes. ◆ **customary** *adj* habituel, coutumier. ◆ **custom-built** *adj* fait sur commande. ◆ **customer** *n* client(e) *m(f)*; **he's an awkward ~er** * il n'est pas commode; **ugly ~er** * sale type * *m*. ◆ **customize** *vt* fabriquer (*or* arranger *etc*) sur commande; *(Comput)* **~ized software** logiciel *m* sur mesure.

cut [kʌt] *(vb: pret, ptp* **cut***)* **1** *n* (**a**) *(stroke)* coup *m*; *[cards]* coupe *f*; *(mark, slit)* coupure *f*; *(notch)* entaille *f*; *(Med)* incision *f*. **a deep ~ in the leg** une profonde coupure à la jambe; **the ~ and thrust of politics** les estocades *fpl* de la politique; **that was a ~ at me** c'était une pierre dans mon jardin; **he is a ~ above the others** il vaut mieux que les autres.
(**b**) *(reduction)* réduction *f*, diminution *f* (*in* de); *(in staff)* compression *f* (*in* de). **power ~** coupure *f* de courant; **to take a ~ in salary** subir une réduction de salaire; **the ~s in education** les réductions dans les budgets scolaires; **to make ~s in a book** faire des coupures dans un livre.
(**c**) *[meat] (piece)* morceau *m*; *(slice)* tranche *f*; *(*: share)* **they all want a ~ in the profits *** ils veulent tous leur part du gâteau *.
(**d**) *[clothes]* coupe *f*; *[jewel]* taille *f*. **I like the ~ of this coat** j'aime la coupe de ce manteau.
2 *adj flowers* coupé; *tobacco* découpé. **~ glass** cristal *m* taillé; **~ prices** prix *mpl* réduits; **it was all ~ and dried** tout était déjà arrangé; **~ and dried opinions** opinions toutes faites.
3 *vt* (**a**) *(gen)* couper; *joint of meat, tobacco* découper; *(Med) abscess* inciser; *cards* couper. **to ~ one's finger** se couper le doigt *or* au doigt; **to ~ sb's throat** couper la gorge à qn; *(fig)* **he is ~ting his own throat** il prépare sa propre ruine; **to ~ in half** couper en deux; **to ~ in pieces** couper en morceaux; *army* tailler en pièces; *reputation* démolir; **to ~ open** ouvrir avec un couteau (*or* avec des ciseaux *etc*); **he ~ his arm open on a nail** il s'est ouvert le bras sur un clou; **to ~ sb free** délivrer qn en coupant ses liens; **it ~ me to the heart** cela m'a profondément blessé; **to ~ short** *story, proceedings* abréger; *visit* écourter; *speaker* couper la parole à; **to ~ a long story short, he came** bref *or* pour en finir, il est venu.
(**b**) *(shape)* couper; *steps, jewel, key, glass* tailler; *channel* creuser; *figure, statue* sculpter (*out of* dans); *(engrave)* graver; *record* graver. **to ~ one's way through** s'ouvrir un chemin à travers; *(fig)* **to ~ one's coat according to one's cloth** vivre selon ses moyens.
(**c**) *(clip, trim) hedge, trees* tailler; *corn, hay* faucher; *lawn* tondre. **to ~ one's nails/hair** se couper les ongles/les cheveux; **to get one's hair ~** se faire couper les cheveux.
(**d**) *(*: avoid) appointment* manquer exprès; *lecture, class* sécher *. **to ~ sb (dead)** faire semblant de ne pas voir qn.
(**e**) *(intersect)* couper.
(**f**) *(reduce) profits, wages, prices* réduire; *text, book, play* faire des coupures dans; *film* faire le montage de. *(Sport)* **he ~ 30 seconds off the record** il a amélioré le record de 30 secondes.
(**g**) *(Cine etc) film* monter.
(**h**) *(phrases) [child]* **to ~ a tooth** percer une dent; **he is ~ting teeth** il fait ses dents; *(fig)* **to ~ one's teeth on sth** se faire les dents sur qch; **she ~s a fine figure** elle a beaucoup d'allure; **to ~ a dash** faire de l'effet; **to ~ it fine** compter un peu juste, ne pas (se) laisser de marge; **that ~s no ice with me** ça ne m'impressionne guère, ça me laisse froid; **to ~ the ground from under sb's feet** couper l'herbe sous le pied de qn; **to ~ one's losses** sauver les meubles *; *(Aut)* **to ~ a corner** prendre un virage à la corde; *(fig)* **to ~ corners** prendre des raccourcis *(fig)*; **to ~ the Gordian knot** trancher le nœud gordien; **~ the cackle! ‡** assez bavardé comme ça! *
4 *vi* (**a**) *[person, knife]* couper, trancher. **he ~ into the cake** il a entamé le gâteau; **to ~ along the dotted line** découper suivant le pointillé; **that ~s both ways** c'est à double tranchant; **to ~ and run *** filer *; **to ~ loose** couper les amarres (*from* avec); **this piece will ~ into 4** ce morceau peut se couper en 4.
(**b**) *(hurry)* **to ~ across country** couper à travers champs; **to ~ through the lane** couper par la ruelle; **to ~ along** s'en aller.
(**c**) *(Cine, TV)* **they ~ from the street to the shop scene** ils ont passé de la rue à la scène du magasin; **cut!** coupez!
(**d**) *(Cards)* couper. **to ~ for deal** tirer pour la donne.
◆ **cut away** *vt sep branch* élaguer; *unwanted part* enlever (en coupant). ◆ **cut back** *vt sep plants* tailler; *production, expenditure* réduire. ◆ **cut down** *vt sep* (**a**) *tree* couper; *corn* faucher; *enemy* abattre. **~ down by pneumonia** terrassé par la *or* une pneumonie. (**b**) *(reduce) expenses* réduire; *article, essay* couper. *(fig)* **to ~ sb down to size *** remettre qn à sa place. ◆ **cut down on** *vt fus food* manger moins de; *cigarettes* fumer moins de; *expenditure* réduire. ◆ **cut in 1** *vi (into conversation)* se mêler à la conversation; *(Aut)* se rabattre. *(Aut)* **to ~ in on sb** faire une queue de poisson à qn. **2** *vt sep:* **to ~ sb in on a deal *** intéresser qn à une affaire. ◆ **cut off** *vt sep* (**a**) *piece of cloth, meat* couper (*from* dans); *limb* couper. **to ~ off sb's head** trancher la tête à qn; **to ~ off one's nose to spite one's face** scier la branche sur laquelle on est assis, par dépit. (**b**) *(disconnect) telephone, car engine, gas, electricity* couper. **our water supply has been ~ off** on nous a coupé l'eau; *(Telec)* **we were ~ off** nous avons été coupés. (**c**) *(isolate)* isoler (*sb from sth* qn de qch). **to ~ o.s. off from** rompre ses liens avec; **he feels very ~ off** il se sent très isolé; **to ~ off the enemy's retreat** couper la retraite à l'ennemi; **to ~ sb off with a shilling** déshériter qn. ◆ **cut out 1** *vi [engine]* caler. **2** *vt sep* (**a**) *picture, article* découper (*of, from* de); *statue, figure* tailler (*of* dans); *coat* couper (*of, from* dans). **to ~ out a path through the jungle** se frayer un chemin à travers la jungle; **to be ~ out for sth/to do** être fait pour qch/pour faire; **he had his work ~ out for him** il avait du pain sur la planche; **you'll have your work ~ out to do that** vous aurez du mal à faire cela. (**b**) *rival* supplanter. (**c**) *(remove)* enlever, ôter; *unnecessary detail* élaguer. **~ it out! *** ça suffit!; **~ out the tears! *** arrête de pleurnicher! (**d**) *(give up) tobacco* supprimer. **to ~ out smoking** arrêter de fumer. ◆ **cut up 1** *vi* (**a**) **to ~ up rough *** se mettre en rogne * *or* en colère. (**b**) *(US)* faire le pitre. **2** *vt sep* (**a**) *wood, food* couper; *meat (carve)* découper; *(chop up)* hacher; *enemy, army* tailler en pièces. (**b**) **to be ~ up about sth** *(hurt)* être affecté par qch; *(annoyed)* être très embêté par qch *.
◆ **cutback** *n (in expenditure, production)* réduction *f*, diminution *f* (*in* de); *(in staff)* compression *f* (*in* de); *(Cine: flashback)* flashback *m*. ◆ **cutoff** *n* arrêt *m*; **~off device** système *m* d'arrêt; **~off switch** interrupteur *m;* **~offs** jeans coupés. ◆ **cut-price** *adj goods* au rabais; *shop* à prix réduits. ◆ **cutter** *n* (**a**) *(person) [clothes]* coupeur *m*, -euse *f*; *[stones]* tailleur *m*; *[films]* monteur *m*, -euse *f*; (**b**) *(tool)* coupoir *m*; (**c**) *(motor boat)* vedette *f*. ◆ **cut-throat 1** *n* assassin *m* ; **2** *adj competition* acharné; *game* à trois; *razor* de coiffeur. ◆ **cutting 1** *n* (**a**) *(gen)* coupe *f*; *[diamond]* taille *f*; *[film]* montage *m*; (**b**) *(cleared way: for road, railway)* tranchée *f*; (**c**) (*press~*) coupure *f* ; **2** *adj knife* coupant, tranchant; *wind, cold* glacial; *rain* cinglant; *words, remark* cinglant, incisif; **the ~ting edge** le tranchant; *(Cine)* **~ting room** salle *f* de montage.

cute * [kjuːt] *adj (clever)* futé; *(attractive)* mignon.

cuticle ['kjuːtɪkl] *n [fingernail]* petites peaux *fpl*, envie *f*. **~ remover** repousse-peaux *m inv*.

cutlery ['kʌtlərɪ] *n* couverts *mpl*.

cutlet ['kʌtlɪt] *n* côtelette *f*; *(US: croquette)* croquette *f*.

cuttlefish ['kʌtlfɪʃ] *n* seiche *f*. ◆ **cuttlebone** *n* os *m* de seiche.

cyanide ['saɪənaɪd] *n* cyanure *m*.

cybernetics [ˌsaɪbə'netɪks] *n* cybernétique *f*.

cyclamen ['sɪkləmən] *n* cyclamen *m*.

cycle ['saɪkl] **1** *n* (**a**) bicyclette *f*, vélo *m*. **racing** ~ vélo de course. (**b**) *[poems, seasons etc]* cycle *m*. **2** *vi* faire de la bicyclette, faire du vélo. **he ~s to school** il va à l'école à bicyclette *or* en vélo. **3** *adj path* cyclable; *race* cycliste. ~ **clip** pince *f* à vélo; ~ **rack** râtelier *m* à bicyclettes; ~ **shed** abri *m* à bicyclettes.
◆ **cycling 1** *n* cyclisme *m* ; **2** *adj holiday* à bicyclette. **cycling clothes** tenue *f* cycliste. ◆ **cyclist** *n* cycliste *mf*.

cyclone ['saɪkləʊn] *n* cyclone *m*.

cyclostyle ['saɪkləstaɪl] *vt* polycopier *(avec des stencils)*.

cygnet ['sɪgnɪt] *n* jeune cygne *m*.

cylinder ['sɪlɪndəʳ] **1** *n (gen)* cylindre *m*; *[type writer]* rouleau *m*. **a 6-~ car** une 6-cylindres; **to fire on all 4 ~s** avoir les 4 cylindres qui donnent; *(fig)* fonctionner à pleins gaz *. **2** *adj*: ~ **block** bloc-cylindres *m*; ~ **head** culasse *f*. ◆ **cylindrical** *adj* cylindrique.

cymbal ['sɪmb(ə)l] *n* cymbale *f*.

cynic ['sɪnɪk] *n* cynique *mf*. ◆ **cynical** *adj* cynique. ◆ **cynically** *adv* cyniquement, avec cynisme. ◆ **cynicism** *n* cynisme *m*.

cypress ['saɪprɪs] *n* cyprès *m*.

Cyprus ['saɪprəs] *n* Chypre *f*. **in** ~ à Chypre. ◆ **Cypriot 1** *adj* cypriote ; **2** *n* Cypriote *mf*.

cyst [sɪst] *n* kyste *m*. ◆ **cystitis** *n* cystite *f*.

czar [zɑːʳ] *n* tsar *m*. ◆ **czarina** *n* tsarine *f*.

Czech [tʃek] **1** *adj* tchèque. **2** *n* Tchèque *mf*; *(Ling)* tchèque *m*. ◆ **Czechoslovakia** *n* Tchécoslovaquie *f*. ◆ **Czechoslovak(ian) 1** *adj* tchécoslovaque ; **2** *n* Tchécoslovaque *mf*.

D

D, d [diː] *n* D, d *m*; *(Mus)* ré *m*. **in 3-D** en relief; **D and C** * dilatation *f* et curetage *m*; **D-day** le jour J.

dab¹ [dæb] **1** *n* (**a**) **a ~ of** un petit peu de; *[glue]* une goutte de; *[paint]* un petit coup de. (**b**) *(fingerprints)* **~s** ‡ empreintes *fpl* digitales. **2** *vt (gen)* tamponner. **to ~ iodine** *etc* **on sth** appliquer de la teinture d'iode *etc* à petits coups sur qch.

dab² [dæb] *adj*: **to be a ~ hand * at sth/at doing** être doué en qch/pour faire.

dabble ['dæbl] **1** *vt*: **to ~ one's hands in the water** barboter dans l'eau avec les mains. **2** *vi (gen)* **to ~ in sth** faire qch en amateur; **to ~ in politics** donner dans la politique; **to ~ in stocks and shares** boursicoter.

Dacca ['dækə] *n* = **Dhaka.**

dachshund ['dækshʊnd] *n* teckel *m*.

Dacron ['dækrɒn] *n* ® tergal *m* ®.

dad * [dæd], **daddy** * ['dædɪ] *n* papa *m*. ◆ **daddy-long-legs** *n, pl inv (Zool)* faucheux *m*.

dado ['deɪdəʊ] *n* plinthe *f*; *[pedestal]* dé *m*; *[wall]* lambris *m* d'appui.

daffodil ['dæfədɪl] *n* jonquille *f*. **~ yellow** (jaune) jonquille *inv*.

daft [dɑːft] *adj* stupide, idiot. **to be ~ about sb/sth** * être fou de qn/qch.

dagger ['dægəʳ] *n* poignard *m*, dague *f*; *(Typ)* croix *f*. **to be at ~s drawn with sb** être à couteaux tirés avec qn; **to look ~s at sb** foudroyer qn du regard.

dago ['deɪgəʊ] *n* métèque *m*.

dahlia ['deɪlɪə] *n* dahlia *m*.

daily ['deɪlɪ] **1** *adj task, routine, walk, paper* quotidien; *consumption, output, wage* journalier; *(everyday)* de tous les jours. **our ~ bread** notre pain quotidien; **~ dozen** * gymnastique *f* quotidienne; **the ~ grind** * le train-train (quotidien). **2** *adv* quotidiennement, tous les jours. **twice ~** deux fois par jour. **3** *n (~ paper)* quotidien *m*; *(~ help, ~ woman)* femme *f* de ménage.

dainty ['deɪntɪ] *adj food* de choix, délicat; *figure, person* menu; *handkerchief, blouse, gesture* délicat; *child* mignon; *(difficult to please)* difficile. ◆ **daintily** *adv eat, hold* délicatement; *walk* à petits pas élégants. ◆ **daintiness** *n* délicatesse *f*.

dairy ['dɛərɪ] **1** *n (on farm)* laiterie *f*; *(shop)* crémerie *f*. **2** *adj cow, farm, produce* laitier; *herd* de vaches laitières; *ice cream* fait à la crème. **~ butter** beurre *m* fermier; **~ farming** industrie *f* laitière. ◆ **dairymaid** *n* fille *f* de laiterie. ◆ **dairyman** *n (on farm etc)* employé *m* de laiterie; *(in shop)* crémier *m*.

daisy ['deɪzɪ] *n* pâquerette *f*; *(cultivated)* marguerite *f*. **~ chain** guirlande *f* de pâquerettes; *(US fig)* série *f*, chapelet *m*; *(US Culin)* **~ (ham)** jambon fumé désossé; **~ wheel** marguerite *f*.

Dakar ['dækə] *n* Dakar.

dale [deɪl] *n* vallée *f*.

dally ['dælɪ] *vi (dawdle)* lanterner (*over sth* dans *or* sur qch). **to ~ with an idea** caresser une idée.

dalmatian [dæl'meɪʃ(ə)n] *n (dog)* dalmatien *m*.

dam¹ [dæm] **1** *n (wall)* barrage *m* (de retenue); *(water)* réservoir *m*. **2** *vt river* endiguer; *lake* construire un barrage sur; *flow of words, oaths* endiguer. **to ~ the waters of the Nile** construire un barrage pour contenir les eaux du Nil.

dam² [dæm] *n (animal)* mère *f*.

damage ['dæmɪdʒ] **1** *n* dommage(s) *m(pl)*; *(visible, eg to car)* dégâts *mpl*; *(to ship, cargo)* avaries *fpl*; *(fig)* préjudice *m*, tort *m*. **~ to property** dégâts matériels; **the bomb did a lot of ~** la bombe a causé des dommages importants *or* a fait de gros dégâts; **there was a lot of ~ to the house** la maison a beaucoup souffert; **there's no ~ done** il n'y a pas de mal; **what's the ~?** * *(how much is it?)* cela se monte à combien?; *(Jur)* **~s** dommages *mpl* et intérêts *mpl*; **liable for ~s** tenu des dommages et intérêts; **war ~** dommages de guerre. **2** *vt furniture, crops, machine* endommager; *food, eyesight, health* abîmer; *good relations, reputation* nuire à, porter atteinte à; *cause* faire du tort à. ◆ **damaging** *adj* nuisible (*to* à); *(Jur)* préjudiciable.

Damascus [də'mɑːskəs] *n* Damas.

dame [deɪm] *n* dame *f*; *(Theat)* vieille dame *(bouffonne jouée par un homme)*; *(US:* ‡*)* fille *f*, nana ‡ *f*.

damfool ‡ ['dæm'fuːl] *adj* fichu * *(before n)*.

dammit * ['dæmɪt] *excl* mince! * **as near as ~** à un poil * près.

damn [dæm] **1** *excl* (‡) merde! ‡ **2** *vt (Rel)* damner; *book, person* condamner; *plan* éreinter. **to ~ with faint praise** éreinter sous couleur d'éloge; **~ him!** ‡ qu'il aille se faire fiche! *; **well I'll be ~ed!** ‡ ça c'est trop fort!; **~ this machine!** ‡ au diable cette machine! **3** *n* (‡) **I don't care a ~** je m'en fiche pas mal *; **it's not worth a ~** cela ne vaut pas un clou *. **4** *adj* (‡*: also* **dam', ~ed**) fichu *, sacré * *(before n)*. **it is one ~ thing after another** quand ce n'est pas une chose, c'est l'autre. **5** *adv* (‡*: also* **dam', ~ed**) vachement ‡, rudement *. **~ all** strictement rien, fichtre * rien. ◆ **damnable** * *adj* détestable. ◆ **damnably** * *adv* rudement *. ◆ **damnation** **1** *n (Rel)* damnation *f*; **2** *excl* (‡) merde! ‡ ◆ **damnedest** ‡ *n*: **to do one's ~edest to help** faire l'impossible pour aider. ◆ **damning** *adj* accablant; **~ing criticism** éreintement *m*.

damp [dæmp] **1** *adj (gen)* humide; *skin* moite. **that was a ~ squib** * c'est tombé à plat *(fig)*. **2** *n* humidité *f*; *(fire~)* grisou *m*. **3** *vt a cloth, ironing* humecter; *enthusiasm, courage* refroidir; *(~ down) fire* couvrir. **to ~ sb's spirits** décourager qn. ◆ **damp-course** *n* couche *f* isolante. ◆ **damp-dry** *adj* prêt à repasser *(encore humide)*. ◆ **dampen** *vt* = **damp 3.** ◆ **damper** *or (US)* ◆ **dampener** *n [chimney]* registre *m*; *(fig)* **to put a ~er on** * jeter un froid sur. ◆ **dampness** *n* humidité *f*; moiteur *f*. ◆ **damp-proof** *adj* imperméable.

damson ['dæmz(ə)n] *n* prune *f* de Damas; *(tree)* prunier *m* de Damas.

dance [dɑːns] **1** *n* (**a**) *(movement)* danse *f*. **to lead sb a (pretty) ~** donner à qn du fil à retordre. (**b**) *(event)* bal *m*, soirée *f* dansante. **2** *vt waltz* danser. **to ~ attendance on sb** être aux petits soins pour qn. **3** *vi* danser. **he ~d with her** il l'a fait danser; **she ~d with him** elle a dansé avec lui; *(fig)* **to ~ in/out** *etc* entrer/sortir *etc* joyeusement; **to ~ about** gambader, sautiller. **4** *adj band, music* de danse. **~ hall** dancing *m*. ◆ **dancer** *n* danseur *m*, -euse *f.* ◆ **dancing** **1** *n* danse *f* ; **2** *adj master, school* de danse.

dandelion ['dændɪlaɪən] *n* pissenlit *m.*

dandruff ['dændrəf] *n* pellicules *fpl (du cuir chevelu).*

dandy ['dændɪ] **1** *n* dandy *m.* **2** *adj* (*) épatant *.

Dane [deɪn] *n* Danois(e) *m(f).* ◆ **Danish** **1** *adj* danois; **Danish blue cheese** bleu *m* du Danemark; **Danish pastry** feuilleté *m* fourré aux fruits *etc*; **2** *n* (**a**) danois *m.* (**b**) = **Danish pastry.**

danger ['deɪn(d)ʒəʳ] **1** *n* danger *m* (*to* pour). **in** ~ en danger; **he was in little** ~ il ne courait pas grand risque; **out of** ~ hors de danger; **in** ~ **of invasion** menacé d'invasion; **he was in** ~ **of losing his job** il risquait de perdre sa place; **there was no** ~ **that she would be recognized** elle ne courait aucun risque d'être reconnue; **a** ~ **of fire** un risque d'incendie; '~ **road up'** 'attention travaux'; '~ **keep out'** 'danger: défense d'entrer'. **2** *adj*: ~ **area,** ~ **zone** zone *f* dangereuse; *(Med)* **on the** ~ **list** dans un état critique; ~ **money** prime *f* de risque; ~ **point** cote *f* d'alerte; ~ **signal** signal *m* d'alarme. ◆ **dangerous** *adj (gen)* dangereux; *illness* grave. ◆ **dangerously** *adv (gen)* dangereusement; *ill* gravement; *wounded* grièvement.

dangle ['dæŋgl] **1** *vt object on string* balancer; *arm, leg* laisser pendre; *prospect, offer* faire miroiter (*before sb* aux yeux de qn). **2** *vi* pendre.

dank [dæŋk] *adj* humide et froid.

Danube ['dænju:b] *n* Danube *m.*

dapper ['dæpəʳ] *adj* fringant.

dare [dɛəʳ] **1** *vt* (**a**) oser (*do, to do* faire); *death* affronter, braver. ~ **you do it?** oserez-vous le faire?; **I daren't!** je n'ose pas!; **how** ~ **you!** comment osez-vous?, vous en avez du culot! *; **I** ~ **say he'll come** il viendra sans doute, j'imagine qu'il va venir; *(iro)* **I** ~ **say!** c'est bien possible! *(iro).* (**b**) **to** ~ **sb to do** mettre qn au défi de faire; **I** ~ **you!** chiche! * **2** *n* défi *m.* **to do sth for a** ~ faire qch pour relever un défi. ◆ **daredevil** **1** *n* casse-cou *mf inv* ; **2** *adj behaviour* de casse-cou ; *adventure* fou. ◆ **daring** **1** *adj* audacieux, hardi ; **2** *n* audace *f*, hardiesse *f.* ◆ **daringly** *adv* audacieusement, avec hardiesse.

Dar-es-Salaam [dɑ:ressə'lɑ:m] *n* Dar-es-Sala(a)m.

dark [dɑ:k] **1** *adj* (**a**) *room* sombre, obscur; *dungeon* noir, ténébreux. **it is** ~ il fait nuit *or* noir; **it is getting** ~ il commence à faire nuit; **the sky is getting** ~ le ciel s'assombrit; **the** ~ **side of the moon** la face cachée de la lune; *(Phot)* ~ **room** chambre *f* noire. (**b**) *colour* foncé, sombre; *complexion, hair, person* brun. ~ **blue** *etc* bleu *etc* foncé *inv*; ~ **brown hair** cheveux châtain foncé *inv*; ~ **glasses** lunettes *fpl* noires; ~ **chocolate** chocolat *m* à croquer. (**c**) *(sinister) plan* noir; *hint* sibyllin; *threat* sourd; *(gloomy) thoughts* sombre, triste. **to keep sth** ~ tenir qch secret; **keep it** ~! pas un mot!; **to look on the** ~ **side of things** voir tout en noir; *(fig)* ~ **horse** *(gen)* quantité inconnue; *(US Pol)* candidat inattendu; **the D~ Ages** le haut moyen âge.

2 *n* obscurité *f*, noir *m.* **after/until** ~ après/jusqu'à la tombée de la nuit; **to be afraid of the** ~ avoir peur du noir; **I am quite in the** ~ **about it** j'ignore tout de cette histoire; **to leave sb in the** ~ **about sth** laisser qn dans l'ignorance sur qch; *(fig)* **to work in the** ~ travailler à l'aveuglette.

◆ **darken** **1** *vt room, landscape* obscurcir, assombrir; *sky, future* assombrir; *colour* foncer ; **2** *vi* s'obscurcir; s'assombrir; foncer. ◆ **dark-eyed** *adj* aux yeux noirs. ◆ **darkly** *adv (gloomily)* tristement; *(sinisterly)* sinistrement. ◆ **darkness** *n* obscurité *f*; **in total** ~**ness** dans une complète obscurité; **the house was in** ~**ness** la maison était plongée dans l'obscurité. ◆ **dark-skinned** *adj person* brun (de peau); *race* de couleur.

darling ['dɑ:lɪŋ] **1** *n* favori(te) *m(f)*, bien-aimé(e) *m(f).* **the** ~ **of** la coqueluche de; **a mother's** ~ un chouchou *, une chouchoute *; **she's a little** ~ elle est adorable; **come here,** ~ viens, (mon) chéri; **be a** ~ *... sois un ange... **2** *adj child* chéri, bien-aimé; (*) *house etc* ravissant, adorable.

darn [dɑ:n] **1** *vt socks* repriser; *clothes etc* raccommoder. **2** *n* reprise *f.* **3** *excl* (*) *euph for* **damn.** ◆ **darning** **1** *n* reprise *f*, raccommodage *m*; *(things to be darned)* raccommodage *m*; **2** *adj needle, wool* à repriser.

dart [dɑ:t] **1** *n* (**a**) fléchette *f.* ~**s** *(game)* fléchettes *fpl*; ~ **board** cible *f.* (**b**) *(Sewing)* pince *f.* **2** *vi*: **to** ~ **in/out** *etc* entrer/sortir *etc* comme une flèche; **to** ~ **at sth** se précipiter sur qch. **3** *vt*: **to** ~ **a look at sth** jeter un regard sur qch.

dash [dæʃ] **1** *n* (**a**) **to make a** ~ se précipiter, se ruer, foncer * (*at* sur, *towards* vers); **he made a** ~ **for it** * il s'est enfui; **there was a** ~ **for the door** tout le monde se rua vers la porte; *(Sport)* **the 100 metre** ~ le sprint, le 100 mètres. (**b**) *(small amount)* petite quantité *f*; *[vinegar, flavouring]* goutte *f*; *[seasonings etc]* pointe *f*; *[colour]* tache *f.* **a** ~ **of soda** un peu d'eau de Seltz. (**c**) *(punctuation mark)* tiret *m*; *(Morse)* trait *m.* **2** *vt* (**a**) *(throw)* jeter violemment. **to** ~ **sth to pieces** casser qch en mille morceaux; **to** ~ **sth to the ground** jeter qch par terre; **to** ~ **one's head against** se cogner la tête contre. (**b**) *spirits* abattre; *person* démoraliser; *hopes* anéantir. **3** *vi* (**a**) *(rush)* **to** ~ **away/back** *etc* s'en aller/revenir *etc* à toute allure; **to** ~ **into a room** se précipiter dans une pièce; **I must** ~ * il faut que je file *. (**b**) *(crash) [waves]* se briser (*against* contre); *[car, bird, object]* se jeter (*against* contre). **4** *excl* (*) zut alors! *

◆ **dash off** *vt sep letter etc* faire en vitesse; *drawing* dessiner en un tour de main.

◆ **dashboard** *n (Aut)* tableau *m* de bord. ◆ **dashing** *adj behaviour* plein d'allant; *appearance* fringant, qui a grande allure.

data ['deɪtə] **1** *npl* données *fpl*, information *f* brute; *(Comput)* données. **2** *adj*: ~ **bank** banque *f* de données; ~ **base** base *f* de données; ~ **capture** saisie *f* des données; ~ **processing** traitement *m* des données; ~ **processor** unité *f* de traitement des données. **3** *vt (* US) person* ficher.

date¹ [deɪt] *n* datte *f*; ~ **palm** dattier *m.*

date² [deɪt] **1** *n* (**a**) *(gen)* date *f*; *(on coin etc)* millésime *m.* ~ **of birth** date de naissance; **what is today's** ~? quelle est la date aujourd'hui?, nous sommes le combien aujourd'hui?; **what** ~ **is he coming on?** à quelle date vient-il?; **what is the** ~ **of this letter?** de quand est cette lettre?; **to** ~ **we have...** jusqu'ici nous avons...; **to be out of** ~ *[document]* ne plus être applicable; *[building, object]* être démodé; *[person]* retarder; **to be up to** ~ *[document]* être à jour; *[building, person]* être moderne; *(in one's work etc)* être à jour; **to bring up to** ~ *accounts, correspondence etc* mettre à jour; *method etc* moderniser; **to bring sb up to** ~ mettre qn au courant (*about sth* de qch). (**b**) *(*: appointment)* rendez-vous *m*, rancard ⁑ *m*; *(⁑: person)* petit(e) ami(e) *m(f).* **to have/make a** ~ avoir/prendre rendez-vous.

2 *vt* (**a**) *document etc* dater; *(with machine)* composter. **letter** ~**d August 7th** lettre datée du 7 août; **a coin** ~**d 1390** une pièce au millésime de 1390. (**b**) *manuscripts, ruins etc* donner *or* assigner une date à, fixer la date de. **that** ~**s him** cela trahit son âge. (**c**) (*) *(go out with)* sortir avec; *(arrange meeting with)* prendre rendez-vous avec.

3 *vi* (**a**) **to** ~ **from** remonter à, dater de. (**b**) *(become old-fashioned)* dater.

◆ **date book** *n* agenda *m.* ◆ **dated** *adj* démodé, qui date. ◆ **dateless** *adj* qui ne date jamais. ◆ **date-line** *n* ligne *f* de changement de date. ◆ **date-stamp** **1** *n [library etc]* dateur *m*; *(post-*

mark) cachet *m* de la poste ; **2** *vt library book* tamponner; *document* apposer le cachet de la date sur.

dative ['deɪtɪv] *adj, n* datif *(m)*. **in the ~** au datif.

daub [dɔ:b] *vt* barbouiller (*with* de).

daughter ['dɔ:təʳ] *n* fille *f*. **~-in-law** belle-fille *f*, bru *f*.

daunt [dɔ:nt] *vt* intimider, démonter. **nothing ~ed he...** sans se démonter il... ◆ **daunting** *adj task, problem* décourageant; *person* intimidant. ◆ **dauntless** *adj person* intrépide; *courage* indomptable. ◆ **dauntlessly** *adv* avec intrépidité.

dawdle ['dɔ:dl] *vi* flâner, traîner *(pej)*. **to ~ over one's work** traînasser sur son travail. ◆ **dawdler** *n* flâneur *m*, -euse *f*. ◆ **dawdling** **1** *adj* traînard; **2** *n* flânerie *f*.

dawn [dɔ:n] **1** *n* aube *f*, point *m* du jour; *[civilization]* aube; *[idea, hope]* naissance *f*. **at ~** à l'aube, au point du jour; **from ~ to dusk** du matin au soir; **~ chorus** concert *m* matinal des oiseaux. **2** *vi [day]* poindre, se lever; *[hope]* naître. **the day will ~ when...** un jour viendra où...; **an idea ~ed upon him** une idée lui est venue à l'esprit; **the truth ~ed upon him** il a commencé à entrevoir la vérité; **it suddenly ~ed on him that...** il lui vint tout d'un coup à l'esprit que... ◆ **dawning** *adj* naissant, croissant.

day [deɪ] **1** *n* (**a**) *(24 hours)* jour *m*. **3 ~s ago** il y a 3 jours; **what ~ is it today?** quel jour sommes-nous aujourd'hui?; **what ~ of the month is it?** nous sommes le combien?; **the ~ that they...** le jour où ils...; **on that ~** ce jour-là; **on a ~ like this** un jour comme aujourd'hui; **twice a ~** deux fois par jour; **the ~ before yesterday** avant-hier *m*; **the ~ before/two ~s before her birthday** la veille/l'avant-veille de son anniversaire; **the ~ after, the following ~** le lendemain; **the ~ after tomorrow** après-demain; **this ~ week** d'aujourd'hui en huit; **2 years ago to the ~** il y a 2 ans jour pour jour; **any ~ now** d'un jour à l'autre; **every ~** tous les jours; **every other ~** tous les deux jours; **one of these ~s** un de ces jours, un jour ou l'autre; **~ by ~** jour après jour; **~ in ~ out** tous les jours que (le bon) Dieu fait; **for ~s on end** pendant des jours et des jours; **to live from ~ to ~** vivre au jour le jour; **the other ~** l'autre jour, il y a quelques jours; **to this ~** encore aujourd'hui; **he's fifty if he's a ~** * il a cinquante ans bien sonnés *; **the ~ of judgment** *or* **reckoning** le jour du jugement dernier; *(fig)* **the ~ of reckoning will come** un jour il faudra rendre des comptes.

(**b**) *(daylight hours)* jour *m*, journée *f*. **during the ~** pendant la journée; **to work all ~** travailler toute la journée; **to travel by ~** voyager de jour; **to work ~ and night** travailler jour et nuit; **it's a fine ~** il fait beau aujourd'hui; **one summer's ~** un jour d'été; **on a wet ~** par une journée pluvieuse.

(**c**) *(working hours)* journée *f*. **paid by the ~** payé à la journée; **it's all in the ~'s work** ça fait partie de la routine; **a ~ off** un jour de congé; **to work an 8-hour ~** faire une journée de 8 heures.

(**d**) *(period)* époque *f*, temps *m*. **these ~s, in the present ~** à l'heure actuelle, de nos jours, actuellement; **in this ~ and age** par les temps qui courent; **in ~s to come** dans l'avenir, dans les jours à venir; **in his working ~s** à l'époque où il travaillait; **in his younger ~s** quand il était plus jeune; **in Napoleon's ~** à l'époque *or* du temps de Napoléon; **famous in her ~** célèbre à son époque; **in the good old ~s** dans le bon vieux temps; **the happiest ~s of my life** les jours les plus heureux de ma vie; **during the early ~s of the war** tout au début *or* pendant les premiers temps de la guerre; **that has had its ~** cela est passé de mode.

2 *adj*: **~ bed** banquette-lit *f*; *(Scol)* **~ boy/girl** externe *m/f*; **~ care centre** ≃ garderie *f*; **~ centre** *centre spécialisé de jour pour le troisième âge, les handicapés etc;* **~ nursery** crèche *f*; **~ release course** ≃ cours professionnel *(de l'industrie etc)* à temps partiel; **~ return ticket** billet *m* d'aller et retour *(valable pour la journée)*; **to go to ~ school** être externe *mf*; **~ shift** *(workers)* équipe *f or* poste *m* de jour; **to be on ~ shift** être de jour; **~ trip** excursion *f* (d'une journée); **to go on a ~ trip to Calais** faire une excursion (d'une journée) à Calais; **~-tripper** excursionniste *mf*.

◆ **daybreak** *n*: **at ~break** au point du jour, à l'aube. ◆ **daydream** **1** *n* rêvasserie *f* ; **2** *vi* rêvasser. ◆ **daylight** **1** *n*: **in the ~light** à la lumière du jour, au grand jour; **it is still ~light** il fait encore jour; **I begin to see ~light** * *(understand)* je commence à voir clair; *(see the end appear)* j'en aperçois la fin ; **2** *adj attack* de jour; **it's ~light robbery** * c'est du vol caractérisé; **~light-saving time** l'heure *f* d'été. ◆ **daytime** **1** *n* jour *m*, journée *f* ; **2** *adj* de jour. ◆ **day-to-day** *adj routine* quotidien; *occurrence* journalier; **on a ~-to-~ basis** au jour le jour.

daze [deɪz] **1** *n*: **in a ~ = dazed.** **2** *vt [drug]* hébéter; *[blow]* étourdir; *[news etc]* abasourdir. ◆ **dazed** *adj* hébété; tout étourdi; abasourdi.

dazzle ['dæzl] *vt* éblouir. ◆ **dazzling** *adj* éblouissant.

deacon ['di:k(ə)n] *n* diacre *m*. ◆ **deaconess** *n* diaconesse *f*.

dead [ded] **1** *adj person, animal, plant* mort; *march* funèbre; *matter* inanimé; *limb* engourdi; *fingers* gourd; *custom* tombé en désuétude; *fire, town, language* mort; *cigarette* éteint. **~ or alive** mort ou vif; *(lit, fig)* **~ and buried** mort et enterré; **to drop down ~** tomber mort; **stone ~** raide mort; **as ~ as a doornail** tout ce qu'il y a de plus mort; **to wait for a ~ man's shoes** * attendre que qn veuille bien mourir pour prendre sa place; **over my ~ body!** * pas question! *; **~ men tell no tales** les morts ne parlent pas; **he's a ~ duck** * c'est un homme fini; **he was ~ to the world** * il dormait comme une souche; *(Telec)* **the line is ~** on n'entend rien (sur la ligne); **~ calm** calme plat; **in the ~ centre** au beau milieu, en plein milieu; **it's a ~ cert** ⁑ c'est sûr et certain *; **he's in ~ earnest** il ne plaisante pas; **the race was a ~ heat** ils sont arrivés ex aequo; **that is a ~ loss** * ça ne vaut rien; **D~ Sea** mer *f* Morte; **to make a ~ set at** * *thing* s'acharner pour avoir; *person* chercher à mettre le grappin sur *; *(Naut)* **by ~ reckoning** à l'estime *f*; **~ season** morte-saison *f*; **~ silence** silence *m* de mort; **~ weight** poids *m* mort.

2 *adv (completely) certain* absolument, complètement. **to stop ~** s'arrêter net; **~ ahead** tout droit; **~ broke** ⁑ fauché (comme les blés) *; **~ drunk** * ivre mort; **~ on time** juste à l'heure; **to be ~ set on doing** * vouloir faire à tout prix; **to be ~ set against sth** * s'opposer absolument à qch; *(order)* **~ slow** *(Aut)* allez au pas; *(Naut)* en avant lentement; **~ tired** éreinté, crevé *.

3 *n* (**a**) **the ~** les morts *mpl*. (**b**) **at ~ of night** au plus profond de la nuit.

◆ **dead-and-alive** *adj town* triste, mort. ◆ **deadbeat** * *adj (tired)* crevé *. ◆ **deaden** *vt shock, blow* amortir; *feeling* émousser; *sound* assourdir; *pain* calmer; *nerve* endormir. ◆ **dead-end** *n* impasse *f*; **a ~-end job** un travail sans débouchés. ◆ **deadhead** *vt* enlever les fleurs fanées de. ◆ **deadline** *n (Press, etc)* dernière limite; **to work to a ~line** travailler en vue d'une date *or* d'une heure limite. ◆ **deadlock** *n* impasse *f*. ◆ **deadly** **1** *adj (gen)* mortel; *aim* qui ne rate jamais; *weapon* meurtrier; *pallor* de mort; *(*: boring)* casse-pieds * *inv*, rasoir * *f inv*; ~**ly nightshade** belladone *f*; **seven ~ly sins** sept péchés *mpl* capitaux; **in ~ly earnest** tout à fait sérieux ; **2** *adv dull* mortellement, terriblement; *pale* comme la mort. ◆ **deadnettle** *n* ortie *f* blanche. ◆ **deadpan** *adj face* sans expression; *humour* pince-sans-rire *inv*. ◆ **deadwood** *n* bois *m* mort.

deaf [def] **1** *adj* sourd. ~ **in one ear** sourd d'une oreille; ~ **as a door post** sourd comme un pot *; **to be ~ to sth** rester sourd à qch; **to turn a ~ ear to sth** faire la sourde oreille à qch. **2** *n*: **the ~** les sourds *mpl*. ◆ **deaf-aid** *n* appareil *m* acoustique. ◆ **deaf-and-dumb** *adj* sourd-muet; *alphabet* des sourds-muets. ◆ **deafen** *vt* rendre sourd. ◆ **deafening** *adj* assourdissant. ◆ **deaf-mute** *n* sourd(e)-muet(te) *m(f)*. ◆ **deafness** *n* surdité *f*.

deal¹ [di:l] *n* (bois *m* de) sapin *m*, bois blanc.

deal² [di:l] *(vb: pret, ptp* **dealt***)* **1** *n* (**a**) **a (good** *or* **great)** ~ **of** beaucoup de, énormément de; **to have a great ~ to do** avoir beaucoup à faire; **a good ~ of the work** une bonne partie du travail; **that's saying a good ~** ce n'est pas peu dire; **there's a good ~ of truth in it** il y a beaucoup de vrai là-dedans; **to think a great ~ of sb** avoir beaucoup d'estime pour qn; **to mean a great ~ to sb** compter beaucoup pour qn; **a good ~ cleverer** beaucoup *or* nettement plus intelligent. (**b**) *(agreement, bargain)* marché *m*, affaire *f*; *(St Ex)* opération *f*, transaction *f*. **business ~** affaire, marché; **to do a ~ with sb** *(Comm)* faire une affaire avec qn; *(gen)* conclure un marché avec qn; **we might do a ~?** on pourrait peut-être s'arranger?; **it's a ~!** * d'accord!; *(Pol etc)* **a new ~** un programme de réformes; **he got a very bad ~ from them** ils se sont très mal conduits envers lui; *(iro)* **big ~!** la belle affaire! (**c**) *(Cards)* donne *f*. **it's your ~** à vous de donner.

2 *vt* (**a**) (**~ out***)* *cards* donner. (**b**) **to ~ sb a blow** porter *or* assener un coup à qn.

3 *vi* (**a**) *(Comm)* traiter, négocier (*with sb* avec qn). **I always ~ with that butcher** je vais *or* me fournis toujours chez ce boucher-là; **to ~ in wood** être dans le commerce du bois. (**b**) *(Cards)* donner. ◆ **deal out** *vt sep gifts, money* distribuer, partager (*between* entre). **to ~ out justice** rendre la justice. ◆ **deal with** *vt fus* (**a**) *(have to do with) person* avoir affaire à, traiter avec. **workers dealing with the public** les employés qui sont en contact avec le public *or* qui ont affaire au public. (**b**) *(be responsible for) person, task* s'occuper de, se charger de; *problem* venir à bout de; *(Comm) order* régler; *[book, film etc]* traiter de, avoir pour sujet; **I'll ~ with him** je me charge de lui; **I'll ~ with you later!** tu vas avoir affaire à moi tout à l'heure!; **to know how to ~ with sb** savoir s'y prendre avec qn; **he's not very easy to ~ with** il n'est pas commode; **to have to ~ with sb** avoir affaire à qn; **to ~ well/badly by sb** agir bien/mal avec qn. (**c**) *(be concerned with, cover) [book, film etc]* traiter de; *[speaker]* parler de.

◆ **dealer** *n (Comm)* marchand *m* (*in* de), négociant *m* (*in* en); **Citroën ~** concessionnaire *mf* Citroën; *(Cards)* donneur *m*. ◆ **dealings** *npl (gen)* relations *fpl* (*with sb* avec qn); *(Comm, St Ex)* transactions *fpl* (*in* en); *(trafficking)* trafic *m* (*in sth* de qch).

dean [di:n] *n* doyen *m*. *(US Scol)* conseiller *m*, -ère *f* (principal(e)) d'éducation.

dear [dɪəʳ] **1** *adj* (**a**) *(loved)* cher; *(lovable)* adorable. **she is very ~ to me** elle m'est très chère; **a ~ friend of mine** un de mes amis les plus chers; **to hold sb/sth ~** chérir qn/qch; **his ~est wish** son plus cher désir; **a ~ little dress** une ravissante petite robe; *(in letter-writing)* ~ **Daddy** (mon) cher papa; ~ **Sir** Monsieur; ~ **Sirs** Messieurs; ~ **Mr Smith** cher Monsieur; ~ **Mr and Mrs Smith** cher Monsieur, chère Madame. (**b**) *(expensive) prices, goods* cher, coûteux; *price* élevé; *shop* cher. **to get ~er** augmenter.

2 *excl*: **oh ~!** *(surprise)* mon Dieu!, pas possible!; *(regret)* oh mon Dieu!

3 *n*: **my ~** mon cher (ami); *(to child)* mon petit; **my ~est** mon chéri, mon amour; **poor ~** *(to child)* pauvre petit, pauvre chou *; *(to woman)* ma pauvre; **she is a ~** * c'est un amour; **give it to me, there's a ~** ⁑ sois gentil, donne-le-moi.

4 *adv buy, pay, sell* cher.

◆ **dearly** *adv*: **to love sb/sth ~ly** être très attaché à qn/qch; **I should ~ly like to live here** j'aimerais infiniment habiter ici; **to pay ~ly for sth** payer qch cher.

dearth [dɜ:θ] *n [food, ideas]* disette *f*; *[money, resources, water]* pénurie *f*. **there is no ~ of young men** les jeunes gens ne manquent pas.

death [deθ] **1** *n* mort *f*, décès *m (Jur, Admin)*; *[plans, hopes]* effondrement *m*. **to be burnt to ~** mourir carbonisé; **he drank himself to ~** c'est la boisson qui l'a tué; **at ~'s door** à l'article de la mort; **to sentence sb to ~** condamner qn à mort; **to put to ~** mettre à mort; **a fight to the ~** une lutte à mort; *(fig)* **to be in at the ~** assister au dénouement; *(lit)* **it will be the ~ of him** cela va l'achever; *(fig)* **he will be the ~ of me** il me fera mourir; **to be bored to ~** * crever * d'ennui; **you look tired to ~** * tu as l'air crevé *; **I'm sick to ~** * *or* **tired to ~ *of all this** j'en ai par-dessus la tête de tout ceci.

2 *adj*: ~ **cell** cellule *f* de condamné à mort; ~ **certificate** acte *m* de décès; ~ **duties** droits *mpl* de succession; ~ **march** marche *f* funèbre; ~ **mask** masque *m* mortuaire; ~ **penalty** peine *f* de mort; ~ **rate** (taux *m* de) mortalité *f*; ~ **rattle** râle *m* d'agonie; ~ **sentence** arrêt *m* de mort; ~ **squad** escadron *m* de la mort; ~ **throes** affres *fpl* de la mort, agonie *f*; ~ **toll** chiffre *m* des morts; ~ **warrant** ordre *m* d'exécution; ~ **wish** désir *m* de mort. ◆ **deathbed 1** *n* lit *m* de mort ; **2** *adj repentance* de la dernière heure. ◆ **death-blow** *n* coup *m* mortel *or* fatal. ◆ **deathless** *adj* immortel; **~less prose** *(iro, hum)* prose *f* impérissable. ◆ **deathly 1** *adj appearance* cadavérique; *silence* mortel, de mort ; **2** *adv*: **~ly pale** d'une pâleur mortelle. ◆ **death's-head** *n* tête *f* de mort. ◆ **deathtrap** *n* endroit *m* (*or* véhicule *m etc*) dangereux; **it's a real ~trap** c'est mortellement dangereux.

debar [dɪ'bɑ:ʳ] *vt* exclure (*from sth* de qch), interdire (*sb from doing* à qn de faire).

debase [dɪ'beɪs] *vt (Fin) coinage* déprécier; *word, object* dégrader; *person* avilir. **to ~ o.s. by doing** s'avilir en faisant. ◆ **debasement** *n* dépréciation *f*; dégradation *f*; avilissement *m*.

debate [dɪ'beɪt] **1** *vt* discuter, débattre. **2** *vi* discuter (*with* avec, *about* sur). **he was debating with himself whether to refuse or not** il se demandait s'il refuserait ou non. **3** *n* débat *m*, discussion *f*. **after much ~** après un long débat. ◆ **debatable** *adj* discutable, contestable; **it is debatable whether...** on est en droit de se demander si... ◆ **debating society** *n* société *f* de conférences contradictoires.

debauch [dɪ'bɔ:tʃ] *vt person* débaucher, corrompre; *morals, taste* corrompre. ◆ **debauched** *adj* débauché. ◆ **debauchery** *n* débauche *f*.

debilitate [dɪ'bɪlɪteɪt] *vt* débiliter. ◆ **debility** *n* débilité *f*.

debit ['debɪt] **1** *n (Comm)* débit *m*. **2** *adj account, balance* débiteur. **on the ~ side** au débit; *(fig)* au passif. **3** *vt*: **to ~ sb's account with a sum, to ~ sb with a sum** porter une somme au débit de qn, débiter qn d'une somme.

debonair [,debə'nɛəʳ] *adj* raffiné, doucereux.

debrief [,di:'bri:f] *vt* faire faire un compte rendu oral (de fin de mission) à; *freed hostages* recueillir le témoignage de. *(Mil)* **to be ~ed** faire rapport. ◆ **debriefing** *n* compte rendu *m* (de fin de mission); rapport *m*.

debris ['debri:] *n* débris *mpl*.

debt [det] *n (payment owed)* dette *f*, créance *f*. **bad ~s** créances irrécouvrables; ~ **of honour** dette d'honneur; **to be in** ~ avoir des dettes, être endetté; **I am £5 in** ~ je dois 5 livres; **to be out of sb's** ~ être quitte envers qn; **to get into** ~ faire des dettes, s'endetter; **to get out of** ~ s'acquitter de ses dettes; **to be out of** ~ n'avoir plus de dettes; **I am greatly in your** ~ **for sth/for having done** je vous suis très redevable de qch/d'avoir fait. ◆ **debt collector** *n* agent *m* de recouvrements. ◆ **debtor** *n* débiteur *m*, -trice *f*. ◆ **debt-ridden** *adj* criblé de dettes.

debug [di'bʌg] *vt* (**a**) *(Comput, fig)* mettre au point. (**b**) *(remove microphones from)* enlever les micros cachés dans. ◆ **debugging** *n (Comput)* mise *f* au point.

debunk * [ˌdi:'bʌŋk] *vt (gen)* démythifier; *person* déboulonner *; *claim* démentir; *institution* discréditer.

decade ['dekeɪd] *n* décennie *f*.

decadence ['dekəd(ə)ns] *n* décadence *f*. ◆ **decadent** *adj* décadent.

decaffeinated [ˌdi:'kæfɪneɪtɪd] *adj* décaféiné.

decamp * [dɪ'kæmp] *vi* décamper *.

decant [dɪ'kænt] *vt wine* décanter. ◆ **decanter** *n* carafe *f*.

decapitate [dɪ'kæpɪteɪt] *vt* décapiter.

decay [dɪ'keɪ] **1** *vi [work of art, stone]* s'altérer, se détériorer; *[food]* se gâter; *[flowers, vegetation, wood]* pourrir; *[tooth]* se carier; *[building]* se délabrer; *[radioactive nucleus]* se désintégrer; *[hopes]* s'enfuir; *[beauty]* se faner; *[civilization]* décliner; *[race, one's faculties]* s'affaiblir. **2** *n (gen)* pourriture *f*; *(Med)* carie *f*; *[building]* délabrement *m*; *(Phys)* désintégration *f*; *[hopes]* ruine *f*; *[civilization]* décadence *f*; *[race, faculties]* affaiblissement *m*. ◆ **decayed** *adj tooth* carié; *wood* pourri; *food* gâté; *building* délabré; *(Phys)* partiellement désintégré; *health, civilization* en déclin. ◆ **decaying** *adj vegetation* pourrissant; *flesh* en pourriture; *food* en train de s'avarier; *tooth* qui se carie; *building* en état de délabrement; *stone* qui s'altère; *civilization* en décadence.

decease [dɪ'si:s] *n* décès *m*. ◆ **deceased** **1** *adj* décédé ; **2** *n* défunt(e) *m(f)*.

deceit [dɪ'si:t] *n* tromperie *f*. ◆ **deceitful** *adj person* faux, trompeur; *words, conduct* trompeur, mensonger. ◆ **deceitfully** *adv* avec duplicité, faussement. ◆ **deceitfulness** *n* fausseté *f*, duplicité *f*.

deceive [dɪ'si:v] *vt* tromper, abuser; *spouse, hopes* tromper. **he ~d me into thinking that...** il m'a faussement fait croire que...; **I thought my eyes were deceiving me** je n'en croyais pas mes yeux; **to be ~d by appearances** être trompé par les apparences; **to ~ o.s.** s'abuser. ◆ **deceiver** *n* trompeur *m*, -euse *f*, imposteur *m*.

December [dɪ'sembəʳ] *n* décembre *m*; *for phrases V* **September.**

decent ['di:s(ə)nt] *adj* (**a**) *(respectable) person* convenable, bien * *inv; house, shoes* convenable; *(seemly) language, behaviour, dress* décent. (**b**) *(*: pleasant) person* bon, brave *(before n)*. **it was ~ of him** c'était chic * de sa part; **to do the ~ thing *** agir élégamment (*by sb* envers qn); **quite a ~ flat** un appartement qui n'est pas mal; **a ~ meal** un bon repas. (**c**) *(* US: great)* formidable. ◆ **decency** *n [dress, conversation]* décence *f*; *[person]* pudeur *f*; **to have a sense of decency** avoir de la pudeur; **the decencies** les convenances *fpl*; **common decency** la simple politesse; **to have the decency to do sth** avoir la décence de faire qch. ◆ **decently** *adv dressed etc* convenablement; *(*: well)* bien. **you can't ~ly ask him that** décemment vous ne pouvez pas lui demander cela.

decentralize [di:'sentrəlaɪz] *vt* décentraliser. ◆ **decentralization** *n* décentralisation *f*.

deception [dɪ'sepʃ(ə)n] *n (deceiving)* tromperie *f*; *(deceitful act)* supercherie *f*. ◆ **deceptive** *adj* trompeur. ◆ **deceptively** *adv*: **it looks deceptively near** *etc* ça donne l'illusion d'être proche *etc*. ◆ **deceptiveness** *n* caractère *m* trompeur.

decibel ['desɪbel] *n* décibel *m*.

decide [dɪ'saɪd] **1** *vt* décider (*to do* de faire; *that* que; *sb to do* qn à faire), se décider (*to do* à faire); *question, quarrel* décider; *piece of business* régler; *difference of opinion* juger; *sb's fate, future* décider de. **2** *vi* se décider (*on, for* pour; *against* contre; *on doing* à faire). **to ~ for/against sb** donner raison/tort à qn. ◆ **decided** *adj improvement* incontestable; *difference* marqué; *refusal* catégorique; *character, person, tone, look* résolu, décidé; *opinion* arrêté. ◆ **decidedly** *adv act, reply* avec décision; *lazy* incontestablement. ◆ **decider** *n (goal)* but *m* décisif; *(point)* point *m* décisif; *(factor)* facteur *m* décisif; *(game)* **the ~r** la belle. ◆ **deciding** *adj* décisif.

deciduous [dɪ'sɪdjʊəs] *adj tree* à feuilles caduques.

decimal ['desɪm(ə)l] **1** *adj (gen)* décimal. **to three ~ places** à la troisième décimale; ~ **point** virgule *f (de fraction décimale)*. **2** *n* décimale *f*. **~s** le calcul décimal. ◆ **decimalization** *n* décimalisation *f*. ◆ **decimalize** *vt* décimaliser.

decimate ['desɪmeɪt] *vt (lit, fig)* décimer.

decipher [dɪ'saɪfəʳ] *vt* déchiffrer. ◆ **decipherable** *adj* déchiffrable.

decision [dɪ'sɪʒ(ə)n] *n* décision *f*; *(Jur)* arrêt *m*. **to come to a ~** arriver à une décision, se décider. ◆ **decision-maker** *n* décideur *m*. ◆ **decisive** *adj battle, victory, factor* décisif; *manner, answer* décidé, catégorique; *person* qui a de la décision. ◆ **decisively** *adv speak* d'un ton décidé; *act* d'une façon décidée. ◆ **decisiveness** *n [person]* décision *f*, fermeté *f*.

deck [dek] **1** *n* (**a**) *[ship]* pont *m*. **to go up on ~** monter sur le pont; **below ~** sous le pont, en bas; **top ~, upper ~** *[bus]* impériale *f*; *[jumbo jet]* étage *m*. (**b**) *[record player etc]* platine *f*. (**c**) ~ **of cards** jeu *m* de cartes. **2** *vt* (~ **out**) orner (*with* de). ◆ **deckchair** *n* chaise *f* longue. ◆ **deck hand** *n* matelot *m*. ◆ **decklid** *n (US Aut)* capot *m* du coffre à bagages.

declaim [dɪ'kleɪm] *vti* déclamer (*against* contre). ◆ **declamation** *n* déclamation *f*. ◆ **declamatory** *adj* déclamatoire.

declare [dɪ'klɛəʳ] *vt (gen)* déclarer (*that* que); *results* proclamer. *(Customs)* **have you anything to ~?** avez-vous qch à déclarer?; **to ~ war** déclarer la guerre (*on* à); **to ~ o.s. for/against** se déclarer en faveur de/contre. ◆ **declaration** *n* déclaration *f*. ◆ **declared** *adj* déclaré, ouvert. ◆ **declaredly** *adv* ouvertement.

declassify [di:'klæsɪfaɪ] *vt* rayer de la liste des documents secrets.

declension [dɪ'klenʃ(ə)n] *n (Gram)* déclinaison *f*.

decline [dɪ'klaɪn] **1** *n (gen)* déclin *m*. ~ **in price** baisse *f* de prix; **these cases are on the ~** ces cas sont de moins en moins fréquents. **2** *vt (gen)* refuser (*to do* de faire); *invitation, honour, responsibility* décliner; *(Gram)* décliner. **3** *vi [health, influence]* décliner; *[empire]* tomber en décadence; *[prices, business]* être en baisse; *(Gram)* se décliner. **to ~ in importance** perdre de l'importance. ◆ **declining** *adj*: **in his declining years** au déclin de sa vie.

declutch ['di:'klʌtʃ] *vi* débrayer.

decode [ˈdiːˈkəʊd] *vt* décoder. ◆ **decoder** *n* décodeur *m*.

decoke [diːˈkəʊk] **1** *vt* décalaminer. **2** *n* décalaminage *m*.

decompose [ˌdiːkəmˈpəʊz] **1** *vt* décomposer. **2** *vi* se décomposer. ◆ **decomposition** *n* décomposition *f*.

decompression [ˌdiːkəmˈpreʃ(ə)n] **1** *n* décompression *f*. **2** *adj*: ~ **chamber** caisson *m* de décompression; ~ **sickness** maladie *f* des caissons.

decontaminate [ˌdiːkənˈtæmɪneɪt] *vt* décontaminer. ◆ **decontamination** *n* décontamination *f*.

decontrol [ˌdiːkənˈtrəʊl] *vt prices* libérer des contrôles gouvernementaux; *butter* lever le contrôle du prix de. ~**led road** route *f* non soumise à la limitation de vitesse.

decorate [ˈdekəreɪt] *vt* (**a**) orner, décorer (*with* de); *cake* décorer; *(paint etc) room* décorer, peindre (et tapisser). **to ~ with flags** pavoiser. (**b**) *soldier* décorer (*for gallantry* pour acte de bravoure). ◆ **decorating** *n*: **(painting and) decorating** décoration *f* intérieure; **they are doing some decorating** ils sont en train de refaire les peintures. ◆ **decoration** *n (state)* décor *m*; *(ornament, medal)* décoration *f*; **Christmas decorations** décorations de Noël. ◆ **decorative** *adj* décoratif. ◆ **decorator** *n* décorateur *m*, -trice *f*.

decorum [dɪˈkɔːrəm] *n* décorum *m*. **a breach of ~** une inconvenance; **a sense of ~** le sens des convenances. ◆ **decorous** [ˈdekərəs] *adj* comme il faut. ◆ **decorously** *adv* comme il faut.

decoy [ˈdiːkɔɪ] **1** *n (person)* compère *m*. **police ~** policier *m* en civil *(servant à attirer un criminel dans une souricière)*. **2** *also* [dɪˈkɔɪ] *vt* attirer dans un piège.

decrease [diːˈkriːs] **1** *vi [amount, numbers, supplies, birth rate, population]* diminuer, décroître; *[power, strength, intensity]* s'affaiblir, décroître; *[price, value, enthusiasm]* baisser; *(Knitting)* diminuer. **2** *vt* diminuer; affaiblir; baisser. **3** [ˈdiːkriːs] *n* diminution *f* (*in* de); affaiblissement *m* (*in* de); baisse *f* (*in* de). **~ in speed** ralentissement *m*; **~ in strength** affaiblissement. ◆ **decreasing** *adj* décroissant; qui s'affaiblit; en baisse. ◆ **decreasingly** *adv* de moins en moins.

decree [dɪˈkriː] **1** *n (Rel)* décret *m*; *[tribunal]* jugement *m*; *(municipal)* arrêté *m*. **by royal ~** par décret du roi; *[divorce]* **~ absolute/nisi** jugement définitif/provisoire de divorce. **2** *vt* décréter, arrêter (*that* que + *indic*).

decrepit [dɪˈkrepɪt] *adj structure, building* délabré; (*) *person* décrépit. ◆ **decrepitude** *n* délabrement *m*; décrépitude *f*.

decry [dɪˈkraɪ] *vt* décrier.

dedicate [ˈdedɪkeɪt] *vt* dédier (*to* à). **to ~ o.s.** *or* **one's life to sth/to doing** se consacrer à qch/à faire. ◆ **dedicated** *adj* consciencieux. ◆ **dedication** *n (in book)* dédicace *f*; *(devotion)* dévouement *m*.

deduce [dɪˈdjuːs] *vt* déduire, conclure (*from* de, *that* que). ◆ **deduction[1]** *n* déduction *f*. ◆ **deductive** *adj* déductif.

deduct [dɪˈdʌkt] *vt amount* déduire (*from* de); *numbers* soustraire (*from* de). **to ~ sth from the price** faire une réduction sur le prix; **to ~ 5% from the wages** faire une retenue de 5% sur les salaires; **after ~ing 5%** déduction faite de 5%. ◆ **deductible** *adj* à déduire (*from* de); *expenses* déductible. ◆ **deduction[2]** *n* déduction *f* (*from* de); *(from wage)* retenue *f* (*from* sur).

deed [diːd] *n* (**a**) action *f*, acte *m*. **brave ~** exploit *m*. **good ~** bonne action; **in ~** de fait, en fait. (**b**) *(Jur)* acte *m*. **~ of covenant** *or* **gift** (acte de) donation *f*; **to change one's name by ~ poll** changer de nom officiellement.

deejay [ˈdiːˌdʒeɪ] *n* disc-jockey *m*, animateur *m*.

deem [diːm] *vt* juger, estimer. **to ~ it prudent to do** juger prudent de faire.

deep [diːp] **1** *adj* (**a**) *water, hole, wound* profond; *snow* épais. **the pond was 4 metres ~** l'étang avait 4 mètres de profondeur; *(fig)* **to be in ~ water** être dans de vilains draps; *[swimming pool]* **the ~ end** le grand bain; **to go off (at) the ~ end** * *(excited)* se mettre dans tous ses états; *(angry)* se mettre en colère; *(fig)* **he was thrown in at the ~ end** ça a été le baptême du feu (pour lui); **he was ankle-~ in water** l'eau lui arrivait aux chevilles. (**b**) *shelf, cupboard* large, profond; *edge, border* large, haut. **the spectators stood 10 ~** il y avait 10 rangs de spectateurs debout; **~ space** espace *m* interstellaire. (**c**) *sound, voice, tones* grave; *(Mus) note, voice* bas, grave. (**d**) *sorrow, relief, colour, mystery, sleep* profond; *feeling* intense; *interest, concern* vif; *writer, thinker* profond. **~ in thought/in a book** absorbé dans ses pensées/dans un livre; **~ breathing (exercises)** exercices *mpl* respiratoires; *(Ling)* **~ structure** structure *f* profonde; **he's a ~ one** * il est plus malin qu'il n'en a l'air.

2 *adv breathe, penetrate* profondément; *drink* à longs traits. **don't go in too ~ if you can't swim** ne va pas trop loin si tu ne sais pas nager; **~ into the night** tard dans la nuit; **he's in it pretty ~** * il s'est engagé très loin là-dedans, *(pej)* il est dedans jusqu'au cou.

3 *n*: **the ~** (les grands fonds de) l'océan *m*.

◆ **deep-chested** *adj person* large de poitrine; *animal* à large poitrail. ◆ **deepen** **1** *vt hole, darkness* approfondir; *sorrow, interest* augmenter; *sound* rendre plus grave; *colour* foncer ; **2** *vi* devenir plus profond (*or* plus foncé *etc*); *[night, mystery]* s'épaissir; *[voice]* se faire plus grave. ◆ **deepening** *adj* de plus en plus profond *etc*. ◆ **deep-freeze** **1** *n (also* **deepfreezer***)* congélateur *m* ; **2** *vt* surgeler. ◆ **deep-freezing** *n* surgélation *f*. ◆ **deep-frozen** *adj* surgelé. ◆ **deep-fry** *vt* faire frire (en friteuse). ◆ **deeply** *adv dig, cut* profondément; *drink* à longs traits; *consider* profondément; *(very) grateful etc* infiniment ; *moving, concerned* extrêmement; *offended* profondément; **to regret ~ly** regretter vivement; **to go ~ly into sth** approfondir qch. ◆ **deep-rooted** *adj affection* profond; *prejudice* profondément enraciné; *habit* invétéré. ◆ **deep-sea** *adj animal, plant* pélagique; *diver* sous-marin; *fisherman, fishing* hauturier. ◆ **deep-seated** *adj prejudice, dislike* profondément enraciné; *conviction* fermement ancré ; *cough* caverneux. ◆ **deep-set** *adj eyes* très enfoncé.

deer [dɪəʳ] *n, pl inv* cerf *m*, biche *f*; *(red ~)* cerf ; *(fallow ~)* daim *m*; *(roe ~)* chevreuil *m*. **certain types of ~** certains types de cervidés *mpl*. ◆ **deerskin** *n* peau *f* de daim. ◆ **deer-stalking** *n* chasse *f* au cerf à pied.

de-escalate [diːˈeskəˌleɪt] *vt tension* faire baisser; *situation* décrisper. ◆ **de-escalation** *n (Mil, Pol)* désescalade *f*; *(in industrial relations)* décrispation *f*.

deface [dɪˈfeɪs] *vt monument, door* dégrader; *work of art* mutiler; *poster, inscription* barbouiller; *[thing] countryside* mutiler.

defame [dɪˈfeɪm] *vt* diffamer. ◆ **defamation** *n* diffamation *f*. ◆ **defamatory** *adj* diffamatoire.

default [dɪˈfɔːlt] **1** *n* (**a**) **in ~ of** à défaut de. (**b**) *(Comput: also* **~ value***)* valeur *f* par défaut. **2** *vi* manquer à ses engagements. ◆ **defaulter** *n* délinquant(e) *m(f)*. ◆ **defaulting** *adj* défaillant.

defeat [dɪˈfiːt] **1** *n [army, team]* défaite *f*; *[project, ambition]* échec *m*; *[legal case, appeal]* rejet *m*. **2** *vt opponent* vaincre; *army, team* battre; *hopes* ruiner; *ambitions, plans, efforts* faire échouer; *(Parl) party, group* mettre en minorité; *bill, amendment* rejeter. **to ~ one's own ends** aller à l'encontre du but que l'on s'est proposé; **that plan will ~ its own ends** ce plan sera auto-destructeur. ◆ **defeated** *adj* vaincu. ◆ **defeatism** *n* défaitisme *m*. ◆ **defeatist** *adj, n* défaitiste *(mf)*.

defecate ['defəkeɪt] *vi* déféquer.

defect ['di:fekt] **1** *n (gen)* défaut *m*. **physical ~** vice *m or* défaut de conformation; **mental ~** anomalie *f* mentale; **moral ~** défaut. **2** [dɪ'fekt] *vi (Pol)* faire défection. **to ~ from one country to another** s'enfuir d'un pays dans un autre pour raisons politiques; **to ~ to the enemy** passer à l'ennemi. ◆ **defection** *n (Pol)* défection *f*. ◆ **defective** *adj machine* défectueux; *reasoning* mauvais; *(Med)* déficient; *(Gram)* défectif; **to be ~ive in sth** manquer de qch. ◆ **defector** *n* transfuge *mf*.

defence [dɪ'fens] **1** *n (gen)* défense *f*, protection *f*; *[action, argument, belief]* justification *f*. **in ~ of** à la défense de; **Ministry** *or* **Department of D~** ministère *m* de la Défense nationale; *(Mil)* **~s** ouvrages *mpl* défensifs; **the body's ~s against disease** la défense de l'organisme contre la maladie; **as a ~ against** en guise de défense contre; **in his ~** à sa décharge; *(Jur)* **witness for the ~** témoin *m* à décharge; *(Jur)* **the case for the ~** la défense. **2** *adj* de défense. **~ counsel** avocat *m* de la défense; **~ expenditure** dépenses *fpl* militaires ; **the ~ forces** les forces *fpl* défensives, la défense; **~ mechanism** *(Physiol)* système *m* de défense; *(Psych)* défenses *fpl*. ◆ **defenceless** *adj* sans défense.

defend [dɪ'fend] *vt (gen)* défendre (*against* contre); *action, decision, opinion* défendre, justifier. **to ~ o.s.** se défendre (*against* contre). ◆ **defendant** *n (Jur)* défendeur *m*, -eresse *f*; *(in criminal case)* prévenu(e) *m(f)*, accusé(e) *m(f)*. ◆ **defender** *n (gen)* défenseur *m*; *[sport record, title]* détenteur *m*, -trice *f*; **~er of the faith** défenseur de la foi. ◆ **defending** *adj (Sport)* **~ing champion** champion(ne) *m(f)* en titre; *(Jur)* **~ing counsel** avocat *m* de la défense.

defense [dɪ'fens] *n (US)* = **defence.**

defensive [dɪ'fensɪv] **1** *adj* défensif. **2** *n* défensive *f*. **on the ~** sur la défensive.

defer¹ [dɪ'fɜ:ʳ] *vt (gen)* différer, remettre à plus tard (*doing* de faire); *meeting* reporter; *business* renvoyer; **~red payment** paiement *m* par versements échelonnés; *(Mil)* **his call-up's been ~red** il a été mis en sursis d'incorporation. ◆ **deferment** *n* report *m*; renvoi *m*.

defer² [dɪ'fɜ:ʳ] *vi (submit)* déférer (*to sb* à qn). **to ~ to sb's knowledge** s'en remettre aux connaissances de qn. ◆ **deference** *n* déférence *f*. ◆ **deferential** *adj person* plein de déférence; *tone* de déférence. ◆ **deferentially** *adv* avec déférence.

defiance [dɪ'faɪəns] *n* défi *m* (*of* à). **in ~ of** au mépris de. ◆ **defiant** *adj attitude, tone* de défi; *reply* provocant; *person* intraitable. ◆ **defiantly** *adv* d'un air *or* ton de défi.

deficiency [dɪ'fɪʃ(ə)nsɪ] *n* (**a**) *[goods]* manque *m*, insuffisance *f*; *[vitamins etc]* carence *f*; *(of liver etc)* déficience *f* (*of* de). (**b**) *(in character, system)* imperfection *f* (*in* dans). (**c**) *(Fin)* déficit *m*, découvert *m*. ◆ **deficient** *adj (defective)* défectueux; *(inadequate)* faible (*in* en); **to be deficient in sth** manquer de qch.

deficit ['defɪsɪt] *n (Fin etc)* déficit *m*.

defile¹ ['di:faɪl] **1** *n (procession; place)* défilé *m*. **2** [dɪ'faɪl] *vi (march in file)* défiler.

defile² [dɪ'faɪl] *vt (pollute)* souiller, salir. ◆ **defilement** *n* souillure *f*.

define [dɪ'faɪn] *vt* (**a**) *word, attitude, conditions, powers* définir. (**b**) *(outline)* **the tower was ~d against the sky** la tour se détachait sur le ciel. ◆ **definable** *adj* définissable. ◆ **definition** *n (gen)* définition *f*; *(Phot)* netteté *f*; *(TV)* définition *f*. ◆ **definitive** *adj* définitif. ◆ **definitively** *adv* définitivement.

definite ['defɪnɪt] *adj* (**a**) *(exact, clear) decision, agreement, plan* bien déterminé, précis; *stain, mark* très visible; *improvement* net, manifeste; *intention, order, sale* ferme. (**b**) *(certain)* certain, sûr; *manner, tone* assuré, positif. **it is ~ that** il est certain que + *indic*; **is it ~ that...?** est-il certain que...? + *subj*; **she was very ~ about it** elle a été catégorique *or* très nette sur la question. (**c**) *(Gram)* **~ article** article *m* défini; **past ~ tense** prétérit *m*. ◆ **definitely** *adv (certainly)* sans aucun doute, certainement; *(appreciably) better* nettement, manifestement; *(emphatically) state* catégoriquement; **~ly!** absolument!, bien sûr!; **she said very ~ly that...** elle a déclaré catégoriquement que...

deflate [di:'fleɪt] *vt tyre* dégonfler; *prices* faire baisser; (*) *person* rabattre le caquet à. ◆ **deflation** *n (Econ)* déflation *f*. ◆ **deflationary** *adj (Econ)* déflationniste.

deflect [dɪ'flekt] **1** *vt ball, projectile* faire dévier; *stream, person* détourner (*from* de). **2** *vi* dévier. ◆ **deflector** *n* déflecteur *m*.

defoliate [di:'fəʊlɪeɪt] *vt* défeuiller. ◆ **defoliant** *n* défoliant *m*. ◆ **defoliation** *n* défoliation *f*.

deforest [di:'fɒrɪst] *vt* déboiser. ◆ **deforestation** *n* déboisement *m*.

deform [dɪ'fɔ:m] *vt* déformer. ◆ **deformation** *n* déformation *f*. ◆ **deformed** *adj limb, body, person* difforme; *mind, structure* déformé. ◆ **deformity** *n [body]* difformité *f*; *[mind]* déformation *f*.

defraud [dɪ'frɔ:d] *vt Customs, state* frauder; *person* escroquer. **to ~ sb of sth** escroquer qch à qn.

defray [dɪ'freɪ] *vt cost* couvrir. **to ~ sb's expenses** défrayer qn.

defrock [di:'frɒk] *vt* défroquer.

defrost [di:'frɒst] **1** *vt refrigerator, windscreen* dégivrer; *meat, vegetables* décongeler. **2** *vi [fridge]* se dégivrer; *[frozen food]* se décongeler. ◆ **defroster** *n (Aut)* dégivreur *m; (US)* dispositif *m* antibuée.

deft [deft] *adj* adroit, preste. ◆ **deftly** *adv* adroitement, prestement. ◆ **deftness** *n* adresse *f*.

defuse [di:'fju:z] *vt (lit, fig)* désamorcer.

defy [dɪ'faɪ] *vt person, law, danger, death* braver, défier; *attack, description* défier; *efforts* résister à. **to ~ sb to do** défier qn de faire, mettre qn au défi de faire.

degenerate [dɪ'dʒenəreɪt] **1** *vi* dégénérer (*into* en). **2** [dɪ'dʒen(ə)rɪt] *adj, n* dégénéré(e) *m(f)*. ◆ **degeneracy** *or* ◆ **degeneration** *n* dégénérescence *f*.

degrade [dɪ'greɪd] *vt* dégrader. **he felt ~d** il se sentait dégradé; **I wouldn't ~ myself to do that** je n'irais pas m'avilir à faire cela. ◆ **degradation** *n (state)* déchéance *f*. ◆ **degrading** *adj* dégradant, avilissant.

degree [dɪ'gri:] *n* (**a**) *(gen, Geog, Math)* degré *m*. **it was 35 ~s in the shade** il faisait 35 (degrés) à l'ombre. (**b**) **by ~s** par degrés, petit à petit; **to a ~** extrêmement; **to some ~, to a certain ~** jusqu'à un certain point, dans une certaine mesure; **to such a ~ that** à un tel point que; **a high ~ of error** d'assez nombreuses erreurs; **a considerable ~ of doubt remains** des doutes considérables subsistent; **third-~ burns** brûlures *fpl* au troisième degré. (**c**) *(Univ)* diplôme *m* (universitaire). **first ~** ≃ licence *f*; **higher ~** ≃ doctorat *m*; **a science ~** une licence de sciences; **to have a ~ in** avoir une licence de; **to get one's ~** avoir sa licence; *(US pej)* **~ mill** usine *f* à diplômes.

dehumanize [di:'hju:mənaɪz] *vt* déshumaniser.

dehydrate [ˌdi:'haɪdreɪt] *vt* déshydrater. ◆ **dehydrated** *adj person, vegetables* déshydraté; *milk, eggs* en poudre. ◆ **dehydration** *n* déshydratation *f*.

de-ice ['diː'aɪs] *vt* dégivrer. ◆ **de-icer** *n* dégivreur *m*.

deify ['diːɪfaɪ] *vt* déifier. ◆ **deification** *n* déification *f*.

deign [deɪn] *vt* daigner (*to do* faire).

deity ['diːɪtɪ] *n* divinité *f*. **the D~** Dieu *m*.

dejected [dɪ'dʒektɪd] *adj* découragé. **to become ~** se décourager. ◆ **dejection** *n* découragement *m*.

delay [dɪ'leɪ] **1** *vt person* retarder, retenir; *train, plane, action, event* retarder; *traffic* ralentir, entraver; *payment* différer. **~ed-action bomb** bombe *f* à retardement; **to ~ doing sth** différer à faire qch. **2** *vi* s'attarder (*in doing* à faire). **don't ~!** dépêchez-vous! **3** *n (waiting)* délai *m*; *(stop)* arrêt *m*. **with as little ~ as possible** dans les plus brefs délais; **without ~** sans délai; **without further ~** sans plus tarder; **after 2 or 3 ~s** après 2 ou 3 arrêts; **there will be ~s to trains** on prévoit des retards *mpl* pour les trains; **there will be ~s to traffic** la circulation sera ralentie. ◆ **delayed-action** *adj* à retardement. ◆ **delaying** *adj* dilatoire.

delegate ['delɪgeɪt] **1** *vt* déléguer (*to sb* à qn; *to do* pour faire). **2** ['delɪgɪt] *n* délégué(e) *m(f)* (*to* à). ◆ **delegation** *n* délégation *f*.

delete [dɪ'liːt] *vt (gen)* effacer (*from* de); *(score out)* barrer, rayer (*from* de), effacer (*from* de). **'~ where inapplicable'** 'rayer les mentions inutiles'. ◆ **deletion** *n* suppression *f*; *(thing deleted)* rature *f*.

Delhi ['delɪ] *n* Delhi.

deli * ['delɪ] *n* épicerie fine.

deliberate [dɪ'lɪb(ə)rɪt] **1** *adj (intentional)* délibéré, voulu; *(cautious, thoughtful)* bien pesé, mûrement réfléchi; *(slow, purposeful) air, voice* décidé; *manner, walk* mesuré, posé. **it wasn't ~** ce n'était pas fait exprès. **2** [dɪ'lɪbəreɪt] *vi* délibérer (*upon* sur). **3** *vt (consider)* considérer, examiner; *(discuss)* délibérer sur. ◆ **deliberately** *adv (intentionally)* exprès, délibérément; *(slowly, purposefully)* posément. ◆ **deliberation** *n (gen)* délibération *f*; **after due deliberation** après mûre réflexion. ◆ **deliberative** *adj assembly* délibérant.

delicate ['delɪkɪt] *adj* délicat. ◆ **delicacy** *n* délicatesse *f*; *(tasty food)* mets *m* délicat. ◆ **delicately** *adv touch* délicatement; *act, express* avec délicatesse. ◆ **delicatessen** *n (shop)* épicerie *f* fine; *(food)* ≃ charcuterie *f*.

delicious [dɪ'lɪʃəs] *adj* délicieux.

delight [dɪ'laɪt] **1** *n* (**a**) *(joy)* grand plaisir *m*, joie *f*. **to my ~** à ma plus grande joie; **with great ~** *watch, taste* avec délices; *learn, wait* avec joie. (**b**) *(pleasant thing etc)* délice *m (f in pl)*, charme *m*. **the ~s of life in the open** les charmes *or* les délices de la vie en plein air; **this book is a great ~** ce livre est vraiment merveilleux; **a ~ to the eyes** un plaisir pour les yeux; **he's a ~ to watch** il fait plaisir à voir. **2** *vt person* réjouir, enchanter. **3** *vi* prendre plaisir, se délecter (*in sth* à qch; *in doing* à faire). ◆ **delighted** *adj* ravi, enchanté (*with, at, by* de, par; *to do* de faire; *that* que + *subj*); **I shall be ~ed** avec grand plaisir. ◆ **delightful** *adj person* charmant; *character, smile* délicieux, charmant; *place, object* ravissant; **it's ~ful** c'est merveilleux. ◆ **delightfully** *adv* délicieusement.

delineate [dɪ'lɪnɪeɪt] *vt outline* esquisser; *character* décrire.

delinquent [dɪ'lɪŋkwənt] *adj, n* délinquant(e) *m(f)*. ◆ **delinquency** *n* délinquance *f*.

delirious [dɪ'lɪrɪəs] *adj (Med, fig)* délirant (*with* de). **to become ~** *(Med)* être pris de délire; *(fig)* entrer en délire; *(Med, fig)* **to be ~** délirer. ◆ **deliriously** *adv (Med)* en délire; *(fig)* frénétiquement; **~ly happy** débordant de joie. ◆ **delirium** *n* délire *m*; **bout of delirium** accès *m* de délire; **delirium tremens** delirium *m* tremens.

deliver [dɪ'lɪvəʳ] *vt* (**a**) *(gen) message, object* remettre (*to sb* à qn); *[postman]* distribuer; *goods* livrer. **I will ~ the children to school tomorrow** j'emmènerai les enfants à l'école demain; **to ~ a child into sb's care** confier un enfant aux soins de qn ; *(fig)* **he ~ed the goods** * il a fait ce qu'on attendait de lui. (**b**) *(rescue)* délivrer, sauver (*sb from sth* qn de qch). **~ us from evil** délivrez-nous du mal. (**c**) *speech, sermon* prononcer; *ultimatum* lancer; *blow* porter, asséner. (**d**) *baby* mettre au monde; *woman* (faire) accoucher. ◆ **deliverance** *n* délivrance *f*. ◆ **deliverer** *n* sauveur *m*. ◆ **delivery** **1** *n [goods, parcels]* livraison *f*; *[letters]* distribution *f*; *(Med)* accouchement *m*; *[speaker]* débit *m*; **to take ~y of** prendre livraison de ; **2** *adj note, service, truck* de livraison; **~y man** livreur *m*; *(Med)* **~y room** salle *f* de travail.

delouse ['diː'laʊs] *vt* épouiller.

delta ['deltə] *n* delta *m*. **~-winged** à ailes en delta.

delude [dɪ'luːd] *vt* tromper, duper (*with* de). **to ~ sb into thinking that** faire croire à qn que; **to ~ o.s.** se faire des illusions. ◆ **deluded** *adj*: **to be ~d** être victime d'illusions; **the poor ~d boy said...** dans son erreur le pauvre garçon dit... ◆ **delusion** *n (false belief)* illusion *f*; *(Psych)* fantasme *m*.

deluge ['deljuːdʒ] **1** *n* déluge *m*. **a ~ of protests** un déluge de protestations; **a ~ of letters** une avalanche de lettres. **2** *vt (lit, fig)* inonder (*with* de).

delve [delv] *vi* : **to ~ into** *book* fouiller dans; *subject* creuser; *past* fouiller; *drawer, bag* fouiller dans.

demagogue ['deməgɒg] *n* démagogue *m*.

de-man [ˌdiː'mæn] *vt (Ind)* réduire les effectifs de.

demand [dɪ'mɑːnd] **1** *vt (gen)* exiger (*to do* de faire; *that* que + *subj*); *money, explanation, help, attention* exiger, réclamer (*from, of* de); *higher pay etc* revendiquer, réclamer. **2** *n* (**a**) *[person, situation etc]* exigence *f*; *(for better pay etc)* revendication *f*, réclamation *f*; *(for help, money)* demande *f*; (*Admin etc: letter*) avertissement *m*. **payable on ~** payable sur demande; **final ~ for payment** dernier avertissement d'avoir à payer; **to make great ~s on sb** exiger beaucoup de qn; *[child, work]* accaparer qn; **the ~s of the case** les nécessités *fpl* du cas. (**b**) *(Comm, Econ)* demande *f* (*for* pour). **to be in great ~** être très demandé; **the ~ for this product increases** ce produit est de plus en plus demandé; **there's no ~ for them** ils ne sont pas demandés. **3** *adj (Med)* **~ feeding** alimentation *f* libre. ◆ **demanding** *adj person* exigeant; *work* astreignant; **physically ~ing** qui demande beaucoup de résistance physique.

demarcation [ˌdiːmɑː'keɪʃ(ə)n] *n* démarcation *f*. **~ line** ligne *f* de démarcation; **~ dispute** conflit *m* d'attributions.

demean [dɪ'miːn] *vt*: **to ~ o.s.** s'abaisser (*to do* à faire). ◆ **demeaning** *adj* avilissant, abaissant.

demeanour, *(US)* **demeanor** [dɪ'miːnəʳ] *n* attitude *f*; *(bearing)* maintien *m*.

demented [dɪ'mentɪd] *adj* dément, fou. ◆ **dementedly** *adv* comme un fou.

demerara [ˌdemə'rɛərə] *n (~ sugar)* cassonade *f*.

demi... ['demɪ] *pref* demi-. **~god** demi-dieu *m* ; **~tasse** *(cup)* tasse *f* (à moka); *(coffee)* (tasse de) café *m* noir.

demijohn ['demɪdʒɒn] *n* dame-jeanne *f*.

demilitarize ['diː'mɪlɪtəraɪz] *vt* démilitariser. ◆ **demilitarization** *n* démilitarisation *f*.

demise [dɪ'maɪz] *n* décès *m*; *(of custom etc)* mort *f*.

demister [diː'mɪstəʳ] *n (Brit Aut)* dispositif *m* antibuée.

demo ‡ ['deməʊ] *n (Brit abbr of* **demonstration***)* manif * *f*.

demob * ['di:'mɒb] *abbr of* **demobilize, demobilization.**

demobilize [di:'məʊbɪlaɪz] *vt* démobiliser. ◆ **demobilization** *n* démobilisation *f*.

democracy [dɪ'mɒkrəsɪ] *n* démocratie *f*. **people's ~** démocratie populaire; **they are working towards ~** ils sont en train de se démocratiser. ◆ **democrat** *n* démocrate *mf*. ◆ **democratic** *adj institution, spirit* démocratique; *(believing in democracy)* démocrate; *(Pol) party* démocrate. ◆ **democratically** *adv* démocratiquement. ◆ **democratize** **1** *vt* démocratiser; **2** *vi* se démocratiser.

demography [dɪ'mɒgrəfɪ] *n* démographie *f*. ◆ **demographer** *n* démographe *mf*. ◆ **demographic** *adj* démographique.

demolish [dɪ'mɒlɪʃ] *vt (gen)* démolir; (*) *cake* liquider *. ◆ **demolisher** *n* démolisseur *m*. ◆ **demolition** **1** *n* démolition *f* ; **2** *adj*: **demolition squad** équipe *f* de démolition; **demolition worker** démolisseur *m;* **demolition zone** zone *f* de démolition.

demon ['di:mən] *n (gen)* démon *m*. **to be a ~ for work** être un bourreau de travail. ◆ **demoniac(al)** [ˌdi:mə'naɪək(əl)] *adj* démoniaque.

demonstrate ['demənstreɪt] **1** *vt truth, need* démontrer; *system* expliquer, décrire; *appliance* faire une démonstration de. **to ~ how sth works** montrer le fonctionnement de qch, faire une démonstration de qch; **to ~ how to do** montrer comment faire. **2** *vi (Pol etc)* manifester, faire une manifestation (*for* pour, *against* contre). ◆ **demonstrable** *adj* démontrable. ◆ **demonstrably** *adv* manifestement. ◆ **demonstration** **1** *n (gen)* démonstration *f*; *(Pol etc)* manifestation *f*; **to hold a demonstration** manifester; **2** *adj car, model* de démonstration. ◆ **demonstrative** *adj* démonstratif. ◆ **demonstrator** *n (Comm)* démonstrateur *m*, -trice *f*; *(Univ)* chargé(e) *m(f)* de travaux pratiques; *(Pol)* manifestant(e) *m(f)*.

demoralize [dɪ'mɒrəlaɪz] *vt* démoraliser. **to become ~d** perdre courage. ◆ **demoralization** *n* démoralisation *f*. ◆ **demoralizing** *adj* démoralisant.

demote [dɪ'məʊt] *vt* rétrograder. ◆ **demotion** *n* rétrogradation *f*.

demur [dɪ'mɜ:ʳ] **1** *vi* élever des objections (*at sth* contre qch). **2** *n*: **without ~** sans faire de difficultés.

demure [dɪ'mjʊəʳ] *adj* sage, modeste. ◆ **demurely** *adv* sagement, modestement. ◆ **demureness** *n* sagesse *f*, air *m* modeste.

demystify [di:'mɪstɪˌfaɪ] *vt* démystifier.

den [den] *n [animal]* antre *m*; *[thieves]* repaire *m*; *(*: room, study)* antre, turne * *f*. **~ of iniquity** lieu *m* de perdition.

denationalize [di:'næʃnəlaɪz] *vt* dénationaliser. ◆ **denationalization** *n* dénationalisation *f*.

denial [dɪ'naɪ(ə)l] *n [rights, guilt, truth]* dénégation *f*; *[authority]* reniement *m*. **~ of justice** déni *m* de justice; **to issue a ~** publier un démenti; **Peter's ~ of Christ** le reniement du Christ.

denier ['denɪəʳ] *n:* **25 ~ stockings** bas *mpl* de 25 deniers.

denigrate ['denɪgreɪt] *vt* dénigrer.

denim ['denɪm] **1** *n* toile *f* de jean; *(heavier)* treillis *m*. **~s** *(npl) (trousers)* blue-jean *m*; *(overalls)* bleus *mpl* de travail. **2** *adj jacket, skirt* en toile de jean.

Denmark ['denmɑ:k] *n* Danemark *m*.

denomination [dɪˌnɒmɪ'neɪʃ(ə)n] *n (Rel)* confession *f (secte)*; *[money]* valeur *f*.

denominator [dɪ'nɒmɪneɪtəʳ] *n* dénominateur *m*.

denote [dɪ'nəʊt] *vt (gen)* dénoter; *[word]* signifier.

denounce [dɪ'naʊns] *vt (gen)* dénoncer (*to* à). **to ~ sb as an impostor** accuser publiquement qn d'imposture.

dense [dens] *adj (gen)* dense; *(*: stupid)* bête, bouché *; *(US: meaningful)* profond. ◆ **densely** *adv*: **~ly wooded** couvert de forêts épaisses; **~ly populated** très peuplé. ◆ **density** *n* densité *f*.

dent [dent] **1** *n (in wood)* entaille *f*; *(in metal)* bosse *f*, bosselure *f*; *(*: in savings)* trou *m*. **to have a ~ in the bumper** avoir le pare-choc bosselé *or* cabossé. **2** *vt hat* cabosser; *car* bosseler, cabosser.

dental ['dentl] *adj* dentaire. **~ floss** fil *m* dentaire; **~ hygienist** assistant(e) *m(f)* de dentiste; **~ surgeon** chirurgien *m* dentiste; **~ technician** mécanicien *m* dentiste.

dentifrice ['dentɪfrɪs] *n* dentifrice *m*.

dentist ['dentɪst] *n* dentiste *mf*. **~'s chair** fauteuil *m* de dentiste; **~'s surgery** cabinet *m* de dentiste. ◆ **dentistry** *n*: **to study ~ry** faire l'école dentaire.

dentures ['den(t)ʃəz] *npl* dentier *m*.

denude [dɪ'nju:d] *vt* dénuder.

denunciation [dɪˌnʌnsɪ'eɪʃ(ə)n] *n* dénonciation *f*; *(in public)* accusation *f* publique.

deny [dɪ'naɪ] *vt* nier (*having done* avoir fait; *that* que + *indic or subj*); *fact, accusation* nier; *leader, religion* renier. **there is no ~ing it** c'est indéniable; **to ~ sb sth** refuser qch à qn; **to ~ o.s. cigarettes** se priver de cigarettes.

deodorant [di:'əʊdər(ə)nt] *adj, n* déodorant *(m)*. ◆ **deodorize** *vt* déodoriser.

depart [dɪ'pɑ:t] *vi (gen)* partir; *(from rule)* s'écarter (*from* de); *(from custom)* faire une entorse (*from* à). **to ~ from a city** quitter une ville, partir *or* s'en aller d'une ville; *(fig)* **to ~ from** *(gen)* s'écarter de; *(from habit, truth)* faire une entorse à. ◆ **departed** **1** *adj (dead)* défunt; *(bygone) glory, happiness* passé; *friends* disparu; **2** *n, pl inv* défunt(e) *m(f)*. ◆ **departure** **1** *n (gen)* départ *m*; *(from custom, principle, truth)* entorse *f* (*from* à); *(Comm: new type of goods)* nouveauté *f*; **a ~ure from the norm** une exception à la règle; **it's a new ~ure in biochemistry** c'est une nouvelle voie qui s'ouvre en biochimie ; **2** *adj preparations, gate, time* de départ; **~ure indicator** horaire *m* des départs; **~ure lounge** salle *f* de départ.

department [dɪ'pɑ:tmənt] **1** *n (government ~)* ministère *m*, département *m*; *(Ind)* service *m*; *[shop, store]* rayon *m*; *[smaller shop]* comptoir *m*; *(Scol)* section *f*; *(Univ)* ≃ U.E.R. *f (Unité d'études et de recherches)*, département; *(French Admin, Geog)* département; *(fig: field of activity)* domaine *m*, rayon. **D~ of Employment** ≃ ministère *m* du Travail; *(US)* **D~ of State** Département d'État; **which government ~?** quel ministère?; *(Comm)* **the shoe ~** le rayon des chaussures; **gardening is my wife's ~ *** le jardinage, c'est le rayon de ma femme. **2** *adj*: **~ store** grand magasin. ◆ **departmental** *adj* d'un *or* du département *or* ministère *or* service; d'une *or* de la section; *[France]* départemental; *[shop]* **~al manager** chef *m* de rayon.

depend [dɪ'pend] *vi* dépendre (*on sb/sth* de qn/qch). **it all ~s** ça dépend; **it ~s on whether he will do it or not** ça dépend s'il veut le faire ou non; **it ~s what you mean** ça dépend de ce que vous voulez dire (*by* par); **~ing on what happens tomorrow...** selon ce qui se passera demain...
◆ **depend (up)on** *vt fus* compter sur. **I'm ~ing on you to tell me what he wants** je compte sur vous pour savoir ce qu'il veut; **I'm ~ing on you for moral support** je compte sur votre soutien; **you can ~ (up)on it** soyez-en sûr, je vous le garantis; **he ~s (up)on his father for money** il dépend de son père pour son argent.
◆ **dependability** *n [machine]* sécurité *f* de fonctionnement; *[person]* sérieux *m*; **his ~ability is well-known** tout le monde sait qu'on peut compter sur lui. ◆ **dependable** *adj person*

sérieux, sur qui on peut compter; *mechanism* fiable; *vehicle* solide; *information* sûr. ◆ **dependant** *n* personne *f* à charge. ◆ **dependence** *n* dépendance *f* (*on* à l'égard de). ◆ **dependency** *n* dépendance *f*. ◆ **dependent 1** *adj (gen)* dépendant (*on* de); *child, relative* à charge; **to be ~ent on** dépendre de ; **2** *n* personne *f* à charge.

depersonalize [diːˈpɜːs(ə)nəlaɪz] *vt* dépersonnaliser.

depict [dɪˈpɪkt] *vt (in words)* dépeindre; *(in picture)* représenter.

depilatory [dɪˈpɪlət(ə)rɪ] *adj, n* dépilatoire *(m)*.

deplenish [dɪˈplenɪʃ] *vt* dégarnir.

deplete [dɪˈpliːt] *vt (reduce)* réduire; *(exhaust)* épuiser. **our stock is very ~d** nos stocks sont très bas; **numbers were greatly ~d** les effectifs étaient très réduits. ◆ **depletion** *n* réduction *f*; épuisement *m*.

deplore [dɪˈplɔːʳ] *vt* déplorer, regretter vivement. **to ~ the fact that** déplorer le fait que + *indic*, regretter vivement que + *subj*. ◆ **deplorable** *adj* déplorable. ◆ **deplorably** *adv* déplorablement.

deploy [dɪˈplɔɪ] *vt (Mil)* déployer; *(gen) equipment, staff* utiliser; *skills* déployer. ◆ **deployment** *n* déploiement *m*; *(fig)* utilisation *f*.

deponent [dɪˈpəʊnənt] *adj, n* déponent *(m)*.

depopulate [ˌdiːˈpɒpjʊleɪt] *vt* dépeupler. ◆ **depopulation** *n* dépeuplement *m*; **rural depopulation** exode *m* rural.

deport [dɪˈpɔːt] *vt* expulser; *(transport)* déporter; *(Hist) convict* déporter. ◆ **deportation** *n* expulsion *f*; déportation *f*; *(Jur)* **~ation order** arrêt *m* d'expulsion.

depose [dɪˈpəʊz] *vt king* déposer; *official* destituer. ◆ **deposition** *n* déposition *f*.

deposit [dɪˈpɒzɪt] **1** *vt (all senses)* déposer (*in or with the bank* à la banque; *sth with sb* qch chez qn). **2** *n* (**a**) *(in bank)* dépôt *m*. (**b**) *(part payment)* arrhes *fpl*, acompte *m*; *(in hire purchase)* premier versement *m* comptant; *(in hiring goods, against damage etc)* caution *f*; *(on bottle etc)* consigne *f*. **to leave a £2 ~ on a dress** verser 2 livres d'arrhes *or* d'acompte sur une robe; *(Pol)* **to lose one's ~** perdre son cautionnement. (**c**) *(Chem, Geol etc)* dépôt *m*; *[mineral, oil]* gisement *m*. **to form a ~** se déposer. **3** *adj*: **~ account** compte *m* de dépôt; **~ slip** bulletin *m* de versement. ◆ **depositor** *n* déposant(e) *m(f)*. ◆ **depository** *n* dépôt *m*.

depot [ˈdepəʊ, *(US)* ˈdiːpəʊ] *n* dépôt *m*.

deprave [dɪˈpreɪv] *vt* dépraver. ◆ **depraved** *adj* dépravé. ◆ **depravity** *n* dépravation *f*.

deprecate [ˈdeprɪkeɪt] *vt* désapprouver. ◆ **deprecating** *adj (disapproving)* désapprobateur; *(apologetic)* humble; **a deprecating smile** un sourire d'excuse. ◆ **deprecatingly** *adv* d'un ton désapprobateur; avec l'air de s'excuser.

depreciate [dɪˈpriːʃɪeɪt] **1** *vt* déprécier. **2** *vi* se déprécier. ◆ **depreciation** *n* dépréciation *f*.

depredations [ˌdeprɪˈdeɪʃ(ə)nz] *npl* déprédations *fpl*.

depress [dɪˈpres] *vt person* déprimer; *trade* réduire; *the market, prices* faire baisser; *(press down)* lever abaisser. ◆ **depressant** *adj, n* dépresseur *(m)*. ◆ **depressed** *adj industry, area* en déclin, touché par la crise; *(Fin) market, trade* en crise; *business* dans le marasme; *class, group* économiquement faible; *person* déprimé (*about* à cause de); **to feel ~ed** se sentir déprimé, avoir le cafard *; **to get ~ed** se décourager, se laisser abattre. ◆ **depressing** *adj* déprimant, décourageant; **I find it ~ing** ça me donne le cafard *. ◆ **depressingly** *adv* d'une manière déprimante *or* décourageante; **~ingly monotonous** d'une monotonie déprimante. ◆ **depression** *n (gen, Econ, Med, Met etc)* dépression *f*; *[lever, key etc]* abaissement *m*; **the D~ion** la crise de 1929; **the economy was in a state of ~ion** l'économie était dans le marasme *or* en crise. ◆ **depressive** *adj, n* dépressif *(m)*, -ive *(f)*.

deprive [dɪˈpraɪv] *vt* priver (*of* de). **to ~ o.s. of** se priver de; **~d child/family** enfant/famille déshérité(e). ◆ **deprivation** *n* privation *f*; *(Psych)* carence *f* affective.

depth [depθ] **1** *n (gen)* profondeur *f*; *[shelf, cupboard]* profondeur, largeur *f*; *[snow]* épaisseur *f*; *[edge, border]* largeur, hauteur *f*; *[knowledge, relief]* profondeur; *[feeling, sorrow, colour]* intensité *f*. **at a ~ of 3 metres** à 3 mètres de profondeur, par 3 mètres de fond; *(lit, fig)* **to get out of one's ~** perdre pied; *(fig)* **I am quite out of my ~** je nage complètement *; **the ~s of the ocean** les profondeurs océaniques; **to study in ~** étudier en profondeur; **to be in the ~s of despair** toucher le fond du désespoir; **I would never sink to such ~s as to do that** je ne tomberais jamais assez bas pour faire cela; **in the ~ of** *winter* au plus fort de; *night, forest* au plus profond de. **2** *adj*: **~ charge** grenade *f* sous-marine; **in-~ interview** interview *f* en profondeur.

depute [dɪˈpjuːt] *vt power, authority* déléguer; *person* députer (*sb to do* qn pour faire). ◆ **deputation** *n* députation *f*.

deputy [ˈdepjʊtɪ] **1** *n (second in command)* adjoint(e) *m(f)*; *(replacement)* suppléant(e) *m(f)*, remplaçant(e) *m(f)*; *(Pol)* député *m*. **2** *adj* adjoint. **~ chairman** vice-président *m*; **~ head** directeur *m* adjoint; *(US)* **~ (sheriff)** sherif adjoint. ◆ **deputize** *vi* assurer l'intérim (*for sb* de qn).

derail [dɪˈreɪl] *vt* faire dérailler. ◆ **derailment** *n* déraillement *m*.

derange [dɪˈreɪn(d)ʒ] *vt plan* déranger; *machine* dérégler; *(Med)* déranger. **~d person/mind** personne *f*/esprit *m* dérangé(e); **to be (mentally) ~d** avoir le cerveau dérangé.

derby [ˈdɑːbɪ, *(US)* dɜːbɪ] *n (Sport)* **local ~** match *m* entre équipes voisines; *(US: hat)* (chapeau *m*) melon *m*.

deregulate [dɪˈregjʊˌleɪt] *vt prices* libérer. ◆ **deregulation** *n [prices]* libération *f*.

derelict [ˈderɪlɪkt] *adj (abandoned)* abandonné; *(ruined)* en ruines. ◆ **dereliction** *n*: **~ion of duty** négligence *f* (dans le service).

derestricted [ˌdiːrɪˈstrɪktɪd] *adj (Aut)* sans limitation de vitesse.

deride [dɪˈraɪd] *vt* tourner en ridicule. ◆ **derision** *n* dérision *f*. ◆ **derisive** *adj smile, person* railleur; *amount, offer* dérisoire. ◆ **derisively** *adv* d'un ton railleur *or* de dérision. ◆ **derisory** *adj* dérisoire.

derive [dɪˈraɪv] **1** *vt profit, satisfaction* tirer (*from* de); *comfort, ideas* puiser (*from* dans); *name, origins* tenir (*from* de); *happiness* trouver (*from* dans). **2** *vi*: **to ~ from** (*also* **be ~d from**) dériver de; *[power, fortune]* provenir de; *[idea]* avoir sa source dans; **it all ~s from the fact that** tout cela tient au fait que. ◆ **derivation** *n* dérivation *f*. ◆ **derivative** *adj (Chem, Ling, Math)* dérivé; *literary work etc* peu original.

dermatitis [ˌdɜːməˈtaɪtɪs] *n* dermatite *f*. ◆ **dermatologist** *n* dermatologue *mf*. ◆ **dermatology** *n* dermatologie *f*.

derogatory [dɪˈrɒgət(ə)rɪ] *adj* désobligeant (*of, to* à).

derrick [ˈderɪk] *n (Naut)* mât *m* de charge; *(above oil well)* derrick *m*.

derv [dɜːv] *n (Brit)* gas-oil *m*.

descale [diːˈskeɪl] *vt* détartrer.

descend [dɪˈsend] **1** *vi (gen)* descendre (*from* de); *[property, customs, rights]* passer (*from* de, *to* à). *(Mil, fig)* **to ~ on** faire une descente sur; **sadness ~ed upon him** la tristesse l'a envahi; **in ~ing order of importance** par ordre d'importance décroissante; **visitors ~ed upon us** des gens sont arrivés chez nous sans crier gare; **to ~ to (doing) sth** s'abaisser à faire qch. **2** *vt stairs* descendre. **to be ~ed from sb** descendre de qn. ◆ **descendant** *n* descendant(e) *m(f)*. ◆ **descent** *n (gen)* descente *f* (*into* dans); *(fig: into crime etc)* chute *f*; *(ancestry)* origine *f*, famille *f*.

describe [dɪsˈkraɪb] *vt* (**a**) *scene, person* décrire, faire la description de. **~ what it is like** racontez *or* dites comment c'est; **~ him for us** décrivez-le-nous; **he ~s himself as a doctor** il se dit *or* se prétend docteur. (**b**) *(Math)* décrire. ◆ **description** *n* description *f*; *(Police)* signalement *m*; **beyond description** indescriptible; **vehicles of every description** véhicules de toutes sortes. ◆ **descriptive** *adj* descriptif.

descry [dɪsˈkraɪ] *vt* discerner, distinguer.

desecrate [ˈdesɪkreɪt] *vt* profaner. ◆ **desecration** *n* profanation *f*.

desegregate [ˌdiːˈsegrɪgeɪt] *vt* abolir la ségrégation raciale dans. **~d schools** écoles *fpl* où la ségrégation raciale n'est plus pratiquée. ◆ **desegregation** *n* déségrégation *f*.

desert¹ [ˈdezət] **1** *n* désert *m*. **2** *adj region, climate, animal, plant* désertique. **~ boot** chaussure *f* montante; **~ island** île *f* déserte.

desert² [dɪˈzɜːt] **1** *vt (gen)* déserter; *spouse, family, friend* abandonner. **his courage ~ed him** son courage l'a abandonné. **2** *vi (Mil)* déserter; *(from one's party)* faire défection. **to ~ to** passer du côté de. ◆ **deserted** *adj place* désert; *wife* abandonné. ◆ **deserter** *n (Mil)* déserteur *m*; *(to the enemy)* transfuge *m*. ◆ **desertion** *n* désertion *f*; abandon *m*; défection *f*.

deserts [dɪˈzɜːts] *npl*: **according to his ~** selon ses mérites; **to get one's (just) ~** recevoir ce que l'on mérite.

deserve [dɪˈzɜːv] *vt* mériter (*to do* de faire). **he ~s to be pitied** il mérite qu'on le plaigne, il est digne de pitié; **he got what he ~d** il n'a eu que ce qu'il méritait. ◆ **deservedly** *adv* à juste titre. ◆ **deserving** *adj person* méritant; *action, cause* méritoire; **she's a deserving case** c'est une personne méritante.

desiccate [ˈdesɪkeɪt] *vt* dessécher. **~d coconut** noix *f* de coco séchée.

design [dɪˈzaɪn] **1** *n* (**a**) *(intention)* dessein *m*, intention *f*. **by ~** à dessein, exprès; **to have ~s on sb/sth** avoir des visées sur qn/qch. (**b**) *(plan drawn in detail) [building, machine]* plan *m*, dessin *m* (*of, for* de); *[dress, hat]* croquis *m*, dessin *m* (*of, for* de); *(preliminary sketch)* ébauche *f*, étude *f* (*for* de). (**c**) *(way sth is planned and made) [building, book]* plan *m*, conception *f* (*of* de); *[dress]* style *m*, ligne *f* (*of* de); *[car, machine]* conception. **the ~ of the apartment facilitates...** le plan de l'appartement facilite...; **the overall ~** le plan d'ensemble; **this is a very practical design** c'est conçu de façon très pratique; **the latest ~ in...** le dernier modèle de... (**d**) *(subject for study) (for furniture, housing)* design *m*; *(for clothing etc)* stylisme *m*. **industrial ~** la création industrielle. (**e**) *(pattern: on pottery etc)* motif *m*, dessin *m* (*on* sur).
2 *vt* (**a**) *(think out) object, scheme* concevoir; *scheme* élaborer; *(draw on paper)* dessiner. **well-~ed** bien conçu; **~ed as sth** conçu pour être qch; **~ed to hold sth** fait pour contenir qch. (**b**) *(work out plans on paper for) object* dessiner; *scheme* élaborer. ◆ **designedly** *adv* à dessein, exprès. ◆ **designer** *n* **1** *[machine, car]* concepteur *m*; *[furniture]* designer *m*; *[dress etc]* styliste *mf*; *(famous)* couturier *m*; *[building]* architecte *m*; *[theatre sets]* décorateur *m*, -trice *f*; **2** *adj jeans, gloves* haute couture *inv*. ◆ **designing** *adj (scheming)* intrigant.

designate [ˈdezɪgneɪt] **1** *vt* désigner (*as* comme; *to do* pour faire). **2** [ˈdezɪgnɪt] *adj (après le nom)* désigné. ◆ **designation** *n* désignation *f*.

desire [dɪˈzaɪəʳ] **1** *n* désir *m* (*for* de; *to do* de faire). **I have no ~ to do it** je n'ai nullement envie de le faire. **2** *vt* (**a**) *(want)* désirer, vouloir (*sth* qch; *to do* faire; *that* que + *subj*). **his work leaves much to be ~d** son travail laisse beaucoup à désirer. (**b**) *(request)* prier (*sb to do* qn de faire). ◆ **desirability** *n [plan etc]* avantages *mpl*. ◆ **desirable** *adj* désirable; **it is desirable that** il est désirable *or* souhaitable que + *subj*; **'desirable residence'** 'belle propriété'. ◆ **desirous** *adj* désireux (*of* de).

desist [dɪˈzɪst] *vi* cesser (*from sth* qch; *from doing* de faire).

desk [desk] **1** *n (gen)* bureau *m*; *[pupil]* pupitre *m*; *(in shop, restaurant)* caisse *f*; *(in hotel, at airport)* réception *f*. *(Press)* **the news ~** le service des informations. **2** *adj lamp, diary* de bureau. **~ clerk** réceptionniste *mf*; **~ job** travail *m* de bureau.

deskill [dɪˈskɪl] *vt* déqualifier.

desolate [ˈdesəlɪt] *adj place* désolé, désert; *outlook, future* sombre, morne; *person (grief-stricken)* au désespoir; *(friendless)* délaissé; *cry* de désespoir. ◆ **desolately** *adv* d'un air désolé (*or* sombre *etc*). ◆ **desolation** *n* désolation *f*; *[landscape]* aspect *m* désert.

despair [dɪsˈpɛəʳ] **1** *n* désespoir *m* (*about, at, over* au sujet de; *at having done* d'avoir fait). **in ~** désespéré; **to drive sb to ~** réduire qn au désespoir. **2** *vi* (se) désespérer. **don't ~!** ne (te) désespère pas!; **to ~ of (doing) sth** désespérer de (faire) qch; **his life was ~ed of** on désespérait de le sauver. ◆ **despairing** *adj* désespéré; (*) *situation* catastrophique. ◆ **despairingly** *adv say* d'un ton désespéré; *look* d'un air désespéré; *agree, answer* avec désespoir; *look for* désespérément.

despatch [dɪsˈpætʃ] = **dispatch.**

desperate [ˈdesp(ə)rɪt] *adj (gen)* désespéré; *criminal* prêt à tout; *(*: very bad)* atroce *, abominable. **to feel ~** être désespéré; **to do something ~** commettre un acte de désespoir; **I am ~ for money** j'ai désespérément besoin d'argent. ◆ **desperately** *adv struggle, regret* désespérément; *say, look* avec désespoir; *cold, needy* terriblement; *ill* très gravement; **~ly in love** éperdument amoureux. ◆ **desperation** *n* désespoir *m*; **to be in desperation** être au désespoir; **to drive sb to desperation** pousser qn à bout; **in desperation she killed him** poussée à bout elle l'a tué; **in sheer desperation** en désespoir de cause.

despicable [dɪsˈpɪkəbl] *adj* ignoble, méprisable. ◆ **despicably** *adv* d'une façon ignoble *or* méprisable.

despise [dɪsˈpaɪz] *vt* mépriser (*for sth* pour qch; *for doing* pour avoir fait). ◆ **despisingly** *adv* avec mépris.

despite [dɪsˈpaɪt] *prep* malgré, en dépit de.

despondency [dɪsˈpɒndənsɪ] *n* découragement *m*, abattement *m*. ◆ **despondent** *adj* découragé, abattu (*about* par). ◆ **despondently** *adv* avec découragement.

despot [ˈdespɒt] *n* despote *m*. ◆ **despotic** *adj* despotique. ◆ **despotically** *adv* despotiquement. ◆ **despotism** *n* despotisme *m*.

dessert [dɪˈzɜːt] **1** *n* dessert *m*. **2** *adj*: **~ plate** assiette *f* à dessert; **~ spoon** cuiller *f* à dessert; **~ wine** vin doux.

destabilize [diːˈsteɪbɪˌlaɪz] *vt (Pol)* déstabiliser. ◆ **destabilization** *n* déstabilisation *f*.

destination [ˌdestɪˈneɪʃ(ə)n] *n* destination *f*.

destine [ˈdestɪn] *vt person, object* destiner (*for* à; *to do* à faire). **~d for** *[train etc]* à destination de; *[writer etc]* destiné à. ◆ **destiny** *n* destin *m*, destinée *f*, sort *m*.

destitute [ˈdestɪtjuːt] *adj* indigent, sans ressources. **utterly ~** dans le dénuement le plus complet. ◆ **destitution** *n* dénuement *m*, indigence *f*.

destroy [dɪs'trɔɪ] *vt (gen)* détruire; *toy, gadget* démolir; *dangerous animal, injured horse* abattre; *cat, dog* faire piquer. **to ~ o.s.** se suicider; **the village was ~ed by a fire** un incendie a ravagé le village. ◆ **destroyer** *n (ship)* contre-torpilleur *m*; *(person)* destructeur *m*, -trice *f*. ◆ **destruct** *vt* détruire volontairement. ◆ **destructible** *adj* destructible. ◆ **destruction** *n* destruction *f*; *(from war, fire)* dégâts *mpl*, dommages *mpl*; **destruction by fire** destruction par un incendie *or* par le feu. ◆ **destructive** *adj person, fire* destructeur; *(potentially so) power* destructif; *criticism* destructif. ◆ **destructively** *adv* de façon destructrice. ◆ **destructiveness** *n (gen)* caractère *or* effet destructeur; *[child etc]* penchant destructeur. ◆ **destructor** *n (refuse ~)* incinérateur *m* (à ordures).

desultory ['des(ə)lt(ə)rɪ] *adj reading* sans suite; *attempt* peu soutenu; *firing, contact* irrégulier. **to have a ~ conversation** échanger des propos décousus.

detach [dɪ'tætʃ] *vt* détacher (*from* de). ◆ **detachable** *adj* détachable (*from* de); *collar, lining* amovible. ◆ **detached** *adj part, section* détaché; *opinion* objectif; *manner* détaché, indifférent; **~ed house** ≃ pavillon *m*. ◆ **detachment** *n* détachement *m*.

detail ['di:teɪl] **1** *n* (**a**) détail *m*; *(information about sth)* renseignements *mpl*. **in ~** en détail; **in great ~** dans les moindres détails; **his attention to ~** l'attention qu'il apporte au détail; **to go into ~s** entrer dans les détails. (**b**) *(Mil)* détachement *m*. **2** *vt* (**a**) *reasons, facts* exposer en détail; *story, event* raconter en détail; *items, objects* énumérer. (**b**) *(Mil) troops* détacher (*for* pour, *to do* pour faire). ◆ **detailed** *adj* détaillé.

detain [dɪ'teɪn] *vt* retenir; *(in prison)* détenir.

detect [dɪ'tekt] *vt sadness* déceler; *object, movement, noise* distinguer; *mine, gas* détecter; *disease* dépister. ◆ **detectable** *adj* qu'on peut découvrir *or* discerner *or* détecter. ◆ **detection** *n* découverte *f*; détection *f*; **the ~ion of crime** la chasse aux criminels; **to escape ~ion** *[criminal]* échapper aux recherches; *[mistake]* passer inaperçu. ◆ **detective** *n* agent *m* de la sûreté, policier *m* en civil; *(private ~)* détective *m* (privé); **~ive story** roman *m* policier; **~ive work** *(fig)* enquêtes *fpl*. ◆ **detector** **1** *n* détecteur *m* ; **2** *adj (TV)* **~or van** voiture *f* gonio.

detention [dɪ'tenʃ(ə)n] *n [criminal, spy]* détention *f*; *(Mil)* arrêts *mpl*; *(Scol)* retenue *f*. *(Brit Jur)* **~ centre**, *(US)* **~ home** centre *m* de détention pour mineurs.

deter [dɪ'tɜ:ʳ] *vt (prevent)* détourner (*from sth* de qch), dissuader (*from doing* de faire); *(discourage)* décourager (*from doing* de faire); *(Mil) attack* prévenir; *enemy* dissuader. **a weapon which ~s no one** une arme qui ne dissuade personne.

detergent [dɪ'tɜ:dʒənt] *adj, n* détergent *(m)*.

deteriorate [dɪ'tɪərɪəreɪt] *vi (gen)* se détériorer; *[species, morals]* dégénérer; *[situation]* se dégrader; *[work]* devenir moins bon. ◆ **deterioration** *n* détérioration *f*; dégénération *f*; dégradation *f*.

determine [dɪ'tɜ:mɪn] *vt (gen)* déterminer; *frontier* délimiter; *sb's character, future* décider de; *(resolve)* décider (*to do* de faire); *(cause to decide) person* décider (*to do* à faire). ◆ **determine (up)on** *vt fus* décider de, résoudre de (*doing* faire); *course of action* se résoudre à; *alternative* choisir. ◆ **determinable** *adj* déterminable. ◆ **determination** *n* détermination *f* (*to do* de faire). ◆ **determinative** *adj* déterminant; *(Gram)* déterminatif. ◆ **determined** *adj* décidé; **to be ~d to do/that** être déterminé *or* décidé à faire/à ce que + *subj*. ◆ **determiner** *n* déterminant *m*. ◆ **determining** *adj* déterminant.

deterrent [dɪ'ter(ə)nt] *n* force *f* de dissuasion. **to act as a ~** exercer un effet de dissuasion.

detest [dɪ'test] *vt* détester, avoir horreur de (*doing* faire). ◆ **detestable** *adj* détestable. ◆ **detestably** *adv* détestablement. ◆ **detestation** *n* haine *f*.

dethrone [di:'θrəʊn] *vt* détrôner.

detonate ['detəneɪt] **1** *vi* détoner. **2** *vt* faire détoner. ◆ **detonation** *n* détonation *f*. ◆ **detonator** *n* détonateur *m*.

detour ['di:ˌtʊəʳ] *n (gen)* détour *m*; *(for traffic)* déviation *f*. *[person, road]* **to make a ~** faire un détour.

detoxification [di:ˌtɒksɪfɪ'keɪʃ(ə)n] *n* détoxification *f*.

detract [dɪ'trækt] *vi*: **to ~ from** *quality, pleasure, merit* diminuer; *reputation* porter atteinte à. ◆ **detractor** *n* détracteur *m*, -trice *f*.

detriment ['detrɪmənt] *n* détriment *m*, préjudice *m*. **to the ~ of** au détriment de; **without ~ to** sans porter préjudice à. ◆ **detrimental** *adj* nuisible; **to be ~al to** nuire à.

detritus [dɪ'traɪtəs] *n (Geol)* roches *fpl* détritiques; *(fig)* détritus *m*.

deuce [dju:s] *n (Cards etc)* deux *m*; *(Tennis)* égalité *f*.

devalue ['di:'vælju:] *vt* dévaluer. ◆ **devaluation** *n* dévaluation *f*.

devastate ['devəsteɪt] *vt place* dévaster, ravager; *opponent, opposition* anéantir; *(astound) person* foudroyer. ◆ **devastating** *adj wind, storm, power, passion* dévastateur; *news, grief, argument, effect* accablant; *wit, humour, charm, woman* irrésistible. ◆ **devastatingly** *adv beautiful, funny* irrésistiblement. ◆ **devastation** *n* dévastation *f*.

develop [dɪ'veləp] **1** *vt* (**a**) *(gen)* développer; *(change and improve) district etc* aménager (*as* en). **this ground is to be ~ed** on va bâtir sur ce terrain. (**b**) *cold* attraper; *symptoms, signs* présenter; *disease* commencer à souffrir de; *habit, taste* contracter; **to ~ a talent for** faire preuve de talent pour; **to ~ a tendency to** manifester une tendance à. **2** *vi [person, region, plot]* se développer; *[illness, tendency, talent]* se manifester; *[feeling]* se former; *(Phot)* se développer; *[event, situation]* se produire. **to ~ into** devenir; **it later ~ed that...** plus tard il est devenu évident que... ◆ **developer** *n (property ~)* promoteur *m* (de construction); *(Phot)* révélateur *m*. ◆ **developing** **1** *adj crisis, storm* qui se prépare; *country* en voie de développement; *industry* en expansion ; **2** *n (Phot)* développement *m*. ◆ **development** **1** *n (gen)* développement *m* (*of sth* de qch); aménagement *m* (*of sth as* de qch en); **(housing) ~ment** cité *f*; **(industrial) ~ment** zone industrielle; *(in situation etc)* **a new ~ment** un fait nouveau; **to await ~ments** attendre la suite des événements; **2** *adj*: **~ment area** zone *f* d'aménagement concerté; **~ment company** société *f* d'exploitation.

deviate ['di:vɪeɪt] *vi* (**a**) *(from truth, former statement etc)* dévier, s'écarter (*from* de). **to ~ from the norm** s'écarter de la norme. (**b**) *[ship, plane, projectile]* dévier. ◆ **deviance** *n* déviance *f* (*from* de). ◆ **deviant** **1** *adj behaviour* qui s'écarte de la norme; *development* anormal; *(sexually)* perverti ; **2** *n* déviant(e) *m(f)*. ◆ **deviation** *n* déviation *f* (*from* de).

device [dɪ'vaɪs] *n* (**a**) *(mechanical)* appareil *m*, mécanisme *m* (*for* pour). **nuclear ~** engin *m* nucléaire. (**b**) *(scheme)* formule *f* (*to do* pour faire). **to leave sb to his own ~s** laisser qn se débrouiller. (**c**) *(Her)* devise *f*.

devil ['devl] **1** *n* (**a**) diable *m*. **poor ~!** * pauvre diable!; **you little ~!** * petit monstre!; *(hum)* **be a ~!** laisse-toi tenter!; **between the ~ and the deep**

blue sea entre Charybde et Scylla; **go to the** ~! ‡ va te faire voir! *; **he is going to the** ~ * il court à sa perte; **his work has gone to the** ~ * son travail ne vaut plus rien; **talk of the** ~! quand on parle du loup on en voit la queue!; **to be the** ~**'s advocate** se faire l'avocat du diable; **to give the** ~ **his due...** pour être honnête, il faut reconnaître que...; **the luck of the** ~ * une veine de pendu *. (**b**) (*: *also* **dickens**) **it's the** ~ **of a job to do...** c'est un travail épouvantable de faire ...; **he had the** ~ **of a job to find it** il a eu un mal fou à le trouver; **it's the** ~ **of a job to...** c'est toute une affaire pour...; **why the** ~**...?** pourquoi diable...?; **to work/run** *etc* **like the** ~ travailler/courir *etc* comme un fou; **to be in a** ~ **of a mess** être dans un sacré pétrin *; **there will be the** ~ **to pay** ça va faire du grabuge *.
2 *vt (Culin) kidneys* (faire) griller au poivre et à la moutarde.
◆**devilish 1** *adj invention* diabolique; *(*: infuriating)* satané * *(before n)*; **2** *adv difficult* diablement. ◆**devilishly** *adv behave* diaboliquement; *difficult* diablement. ◆**devilishness** *n [invention]* caractère *m* diabolique; *[behaviour]* méchanceté *f* diabolique. ◆**devil-may-care** *adj* insouciant. ◆**devilment** *n (mischief)* espièglerie *f*; *(spite)* malice *f*. ◆**devilry** *or* ◆**deviltry** *(US) n (daring)* témérité *f*; *(mischief)* espièglerie *f*, *(stronger)* malice *f*.

devious ['di:vɪəs] *adj route, means, method* détourné; *path, mind* tortueux. **he's very** ~ il n'est pas franc. ◆**deviously** *adv act* d'une façon détournée. ◆**deviousness** *n [person]* sournoiserie *f*; *[scheme, method]* complexités *fpl*.

devise [dɪ'vaɪz] *vt scheme, style* inventer, concevoir; *plot* tramer; *escape* combiner.

devoid [dɪ'vɔɪd] *adj*: ~ **of** dénué de, dépourvu de.

devolution [,di:və'lu:ʃ(ə)n] *n (Pol etc)* décentralisation *f*.

devolve [dɪ'vɒlv] *vi [work, responsibility]* retomber (*on* sur); *[property]* passer (*on* à).

devote [dɪ'vəʊt] *vt* consacrer (*to* à). **to** ~ **o.s. to** *a cause, study, hobby* se consacrer à; *pleasure* se livrer à. ◆**devoted** *adj (gen)* dévoué; *admirer* fervent. ◆**devotedly** *adv* avec dévouement. ◆**devotee** *n [doctrine]* partisan *m*; *[religion]* adepte *mf*; *[sport, music, poetry]* passionné(e) *m(f)*. ◆**devotion** *n* dévouement *m* (*to sth* à qch; *to sb* à *or* envers qn); *(Rel)* dévotion *f*. ◆**devotional** *adj book* de dévotion.

devour [dɪ'vaʊəʳ] *vt* dévorer. ◆**devouring** *adj* dévorant.

devout [dɪ'vaʊt] *adj person* pieux, dévot; *prayer, hope* fervent. ◆**devoutly** *adv pray* avec dévotion; *hope* bien vivement.

dew [dju:] *n* rosée *f*. ◆**dewdrop** *n* goutte *f* de rosée. ◆**dewy** *adj* humide de rosée. ◆**dewy-eyed** *adj (credulous)* (trop) naïf; *(innocent)* aux grands yeux ingénus.

dexterity [deks'terɪtɪ] *n (skill: physical, mental)* adresse *f*, dextérité *f* (*in doing* à faire). ◆**dext(e)rous** *adj* adroit. ◆**dext(e)rously** *adv* adroitement, avec dextérité.

Dhaka ['dækə] *n* Dacca, Dhaka.

diabetes [,daɪə'bi:ti:z] *n* diabète *m*. ◆**diabetic** *adj, n* diabétique *(mf)*.

diabolic(al) [,daɪə'bɒlɪk(əl)] *adj (lit)* diabolique; *(*: dreadful)* épouvantable. ◆**diabolically** *adv* diaboliquement; (*) *hot, late* rudement *.

diacritic [,daɪə'krɪtɪk] *adj, n* diacritique *(m)*.

diadem ['daɪədem] *n* diadème *m*.

diaeresis [daɪ'erɪsɪs] *n (sign)* tréma *m*.

diagnose ['daɪəgnəʊz] *vt* diagnostiquer. **it was** ~**d as bronchitis** on a diagnostiqué une bronchite. ◆**diagnosis,** *pl* **-oses** *n* diagnostic *m*. ◆**diagnostician** *n* diagnostiqueur *m*.

diagonal [daɪ'ægənl] **1** *adj* diagonal. **2** *n* diagonale *f*. ◆**diagonally** *adv cut, fold* en diagonale; *opposite* diagonalement; **to go** ~**ly across** traverser en diagonale; **ribbon worn** ~**ly across the chest** ruban porté en écharpe sur la poitrine.

diagram ['daɪəgræm] *n* schéma *m*, diagramme *m*; *(Math)* figure *f*.

dial ['daɪ(ə)l] **1** *n* cadran *m*. **2** *vt (Telec) number* faire. **you must** ~ **336-1295** il faut faire le 336-1295; **to** ~ **999** ≃ appeler police secours; **can I** ~ **London from here?** est-ce que d'ici je peux avoir Londres par l'automatique? ◆**dialling** *adj*: ~**ling code** indicatif *m*; ~**ling tone** tonalité *f*.

dialect ['daɪəlekt] **1** *n* dialecte *m*. **local** ~ patois *m*. **2** *adj word* dialectal.

dialectic(s) [,daɪə'lektɪk(s)] *nsg* dialectique *f*.

dialogue ['daɪəlɒg] *n* dialogue *m*.

dialysis [daɪ'æləsɪs] *n* dialyse *f*.

diameter [daɪ'æmɪtəʳ] *n* diamètre *m*. **it is one metre in** ~ cela a un mètre de diamètre. ◆**diametrical** *adj* diamétral. ◆**diametrically** *adv* diamétralement.

diamond ['daɪəmənd] **1** *n (stone)* diamant *m*; *(shape)* losange *m*; *(Cards)* carreau *m*; *(Baseball)* terrain *m*. **the ace of** ~**s** l'as *m* de carreau; **he played a** ~ il a joué carreau. **2** *adj clip, ring* de diamant(s). ~ **jubilee** soixantième anniversaire *m (d'un événement)*; ~ **merchant** diamantaire *m*; ~ **necklace** rivière *f* de diamants; ~ **wedding** noces *fpl* de diamant. ◆**diamond-shaped** *adj* en losange.

diaper ['daɪəpəʳ] *n (US)* couche *f (de bébé)*.

diaphragm ['daɪəfræm] *n* diaphragme *m*.

diarrh(o)ea [,daɪə'ri:ə] *n* diarrhée *f*.

diary ['daɪərɪ] *n (record)* journal *m* (intime); *(for engagements)* agenda *m*. **I've got it in my** ~ je l'ai noté sur mon agenda.

diatribe ['daɪətraɪb] *n* diatribe *f* (*against* contre).

dice [daɪs] **1** *n, pl inv* dé *m* (à jouer). **to play** ~ jouer aux dés; **no** ~! * pas question. **2** *vi (fig)* **to** ~ **with death** jouer avec la mort. **3** *vt vegetables* couper en dés. ◆**dicey** * *adj* risqué.

dichotomy [dɪ'kɒtəmɪ] *n* dichotomie *f*.

dickens * ['dɪkɪnz] *n* = **devil b.**

Dictaphone ['dɪktəfəʊn] *n* ® dictaphone *m* ®. ~ **typist** dactylo *f* qui travaille au dictaphone.

dictate [dɪk'teɪt] **1** *vt* dicter (*to* à). **his action was** ~**d by circumstances** il a agi comme le lui dictaient les circonstances. **2** *vi*: **to** ~ **to sb** imposer sa volonté à qn. **3** ['dɪkteɪt] *n*: ~**s** préceptes *mpl*; *[conscience]* voix *f*. ◆**dictation** *n* dictée *f*; **to sb's dictation** sous la dictée de qn; **at dictation speed** à une vitesse de dictée. ◆**dictator** *n* dictateur *m*. ◆**dictatorial** *adj* dictatorial. ◆**dictatorially** *adv* dictatorialement, en dictateur. ◆**dictatorship** *n* dictature *f*.

diction ['dɪkʃ(ə)n] *n* diction *f*.

dictionary ['dɪkʃ(ə)nrɪ] *n* dictionnaire *m*. **French** ~ dictionnaire de français.

dictum, *pl* **dicta** ['dɪktəm, 'dɪktə] *n (maxim)* maxime *f*; *(pronouncement)* affirmation *f*.

did [dɪd] *pret of* **do¹**.

didactic [dɪ'dæktɪk] *adj* didactique.

diddle * ['dɪdl] *vt* rouler *, escroquer. **to** ~ **sb out of sth** soutirer qch à qn.

die¹, *pl* **dice** [daɪ, daɪs] *n* dé *m* (à jouer). **the** ~ **is cast** le sort en est jeté.

die² [daɪ] *vi (gen)* mourir (*of* de); *[engine, motor]* s'arrêter. **to be dying** être à l'agonie *or* à la mort; **to** ~ **a natural/violent death** mourir de sa belle mort/de mort violente; **he** ~**d a hero** il est mort

en héros; *(fig)* **never say** ~! il ne faut jamais désespérer; **I nearly ~d** * *(laughing)* j'ai failli mourir de rire; *(fear)* j'ai failli mourir de peur; *(embarrassment)* je voulais rentrer sous terre; **to be dying to do** * mourir d'envie de faire; **I'm dying * for a coffee** j'ai une envie folle d'un café; **the secret ~d with him** il a emporté le secret dans la tombe; **bad habits ~ hard** les mauvaises habitudes ont la vie dure. ◆ **die away** *vi [sound, voice]* s'éteindre. ◆ **die down** *vi [plant]* se flétrir; *[emotion, protest, wind]* se calmer; *[fire] (in blazing building)* diminuer; *(in grate etc)* baisser; *[noise]* diminuer. ◆ **die off** *vi* mourir les uns après les autres. ◆ **die out** *vi* disparaître.
◆ **diehard** **1** *n* réactionnaire *mf*; **2** *adj* intransigeant.

diesel ['di:z(ə)l] **1** *n* diesel *m*. **2** *adj*: ~ **engine** *(Aut)* moteur *m* diesel; *(Rail)* motrice *f*; ~ **fuel**, ~ **oil** gas-oil *m*; ~ **train** autorail *m*.

diet ['daɪət] **1** *n* (**a**) *(restricted food)* régime *m*. **milk** ~ régime lacté; **to go on a** ~ se mettre au régime. (**b**) *(customary food)* alimentation *f*. **to live on a** ~ **of** se nourrir de. **2** *vi* suivre un régime. ◆ **dietary** *adj* de régime, diététique; **~ary fibre** cellulose végétale. ◆ **dietetic** *adj* diététique. ◆ **dietetics** *nsg* diététique *f*. ◆ **dietician** *n* diététicien(ne) *m(f)*.

differ ['dɪfə^r] *vi (be different)* différer, être différent *(from* de); *(disagree)* ne pas être d'accord *(from sb* avec qn, *on or about sth* sur qch). **I beg to** ~ permettez-moi de ne pas partager cette opinion.

difference ['dɪfr(ə)ns] *n* différence *f (in* de, *between* entre). **that makes a big ~ to me** c'est très important pour moi, cela compte beaucoup pour moi; **to make a ~ in sb/sth** changer qn/qch; **that makes all the** ~ voilà qui change tout; **what ~ does it make if...?** qu'est-ce que cela peut faire que...? + *subj*; **it makes no** ~ cela ne change rien; **it makes no ~ to me** cela m'est égal; **for all the ~ it makes** pour ce que cela change; **with this ~ that** à ceci près que; **a car with a** ~ une voiture pas comme les autres *; ~ **of opinion** différence d'opinions; *(quarrel)* différend *m*.

different ['dɪfr(ə)nt] *adj* (**a**) différent *(from* de), autre. **he wore a ~ tie each day** il portait chaque jour une cravate différente; **go and put on a ~ tie** va mettre une autre cravate; **I feel a ~ person** je me sens tout autre; *(rested etc)* j'ai l'impression d'avoir fait peau neuve; **let's do sth** ~ faisons qch de nouveau; **quite a ~ way of doing** une tout autre manière de faire; **that's quite a ~ matter** c'est tout autre chose; **she's quite ~ from what you think** elle n'est pas du tout ce que vous croyez; **he wants to be** ~ il veut se singulariser. (**b**) *(various)* différent, divers, plusieurs. ~ **people noticed it** plusieurs personnes l'ont remarqué.
◆ **differential** **1** *adj* différentiel; **2** *n (Math)* différentielle *f*; *(Econ)* écart *m* salarial; *(Aut)* différentiel *m*. ◆ **differentiate** **1** *vt* différencier *(from* de); **2** *vi* faire la différence *(between* entre). ◆ **differentiation** *n* différenciation *f*. ◆ **differently** *adv* différemment, d'une manière différente *(from* de), autrement *(from* que); **he thinks ~ly** sa façon de penser n'est pas la même; *(doesn't agree)* il n'est pas de cet avis.

difficult ['dɪfɪk(ə)lt] *adj* difficile. ~ **to get on with** difficile à vivre; **it is ~ to know** il est difficile de savoir; **it's ~ to deny that...** on ne peut guère nier que... + *indic or subj*; **I find it ~ to believe** il m'est difficile de croire, j'ai de la peine à croire *(that* que); **the ~ thing is to begin** le plus difficile *or* dur c'est de commencer. ◆ **difficulty** *n* difficulté *f*; **she has ~y in walking** elle marche avec difficulté, elle a de la difficulté *or* du mal à marcher; **a slight ~y in breathing** un peu de gêne *f* dans la respiration; **there was some ~y in finding him** on a eu du mal à le trouver; **the ~y is to choose** le difficile, c'est de choisir; **to make ~ies for sb** créer des difficultés à qn; **to get into ~ies** se trouver en difficulté; **to get o.s. into ~y** se créer des ennuis; **I am in ~y** j'ai des difficultés, j'ai des problèmes *mpl*; **to be in (financial) ~ies** avoir des ennuis *mpl* d'argent; **he was in ~y over the rent** il était en difficulté pour son loyer; **he was working under great ~ies** il travaillait dans des conditions très difficiles; **I can see no ~y in what you suggest** je ne vois aucun obstacle à ce que vous suggérez; **he's having ~y** *or* **~ies with...** il a des ennuis *or* des problèmes avec...

diffident ['dɪfɪd(ə)nt] *adj person* qui manque d'assurance; *smile* embarrassé. **to be ~ about doing** hésiter à faire. ◆ **diffidence** *n* manque *m* d'assurance. ◆ **diffidently** *adv* avec timidité.

diffuse [dɪ'fju:z] **1** *vt* diffuser. **~d lighting** éclairage *m* indirect. **2** [dɪ'fju:s] *adj* diffus.

dig [dɪg] *(vb: pret, ptp* **dug***)* **1** *n* (**a**) **to give sb a ~ in the ribs** donner un coup de coude dans les côtes de qn; *(*: sly remark)* **to have a ~ at sb** donner un coup de patte *or* de griffe à qn; **that's a ~ at Paul** c'est une pierre dans le jardin de Paul. (**b**) *(Archeol)* fouilles *fpl*. **to go on a** ~ aller faire des fouilles. **2** *vt* (**a**) *(gen)* creuser; *(with spade)* bêcher; *potatoes* arracher. (**b**) *(thrust)* enfoncer *(sth into sth* qch dans qch). (**c**) (⁂) ~ **that guy!** vise un peu le type! *; **I ~ that!** ça me botte! *; **he really ~s jazz** il est vraiment fou de jazz; **I don't ~ that** ça me laisse froid. **3** *vi [dog, pig]* fouiller; *[person]* creuser *(into* dans); *(Tech)* fouiller; *(Archeol)* faire des fouilles. **to ~ for minerals** (creuser pour) extrai re du minerai; **to ~ into one's pockets/the past** fouiller dans ses poches/le passé.
◆ **dig in** **1** *vi (Mil)* se retrancher; *(*: eat)* attaquer * un repas *(or* un plat *etc)*. ~ **in!** * allez-y, mangez! **2** *vt sep compost etc* enterrer; *blade, knife* enfoncer. *(fig)* **to ~ one's heels in** se buter. ◆ **dig out** *vt sep* déterrer. **to ~ sb out of the snow** sortir qn de la neige (à coups de pelles); **where did he ~ out * that old hat?** où a-t-il déniché ce vieux chapeau? ◆ **dig over** *vt sep* retourner. ◆ **dig up** *vt sep weeds, vegetables* arracher; *treasure, body* déterrer; *earth* retourner; *garden* retourner; *(*: find) fact, idea* dénicher.
◆ **digger** *n (machine)* pelleteuse *f*. ◆ **diggings** *npl (Archeol)* fouilles *fpl*.

digest [daɪ'dʒest] **1** *vti (lit, fig)* digérer. **it is not easily ~ed** ça se digère mal. **2** ['daɪdʒest] *n (summary)* résumé *m*; *(magazine)* digest *m*. ◆ **digestible** *adj* facile à digérer. ◆ **digestion** *n* digestion *f*. ◆ **digestive** *adj* digestif; **~ive (biscuit)** sablé *m*.

digit ['dɪdʒɪt] *n (Math)* chiffre *m*; *(finger)* doigt *m*.
◆ **digital** *adj clock* à affichage numérique; *computer* numérique.

dignify ['dɪgnɪfaɪ] *vt* donner de la dignité à.
◆ **dignified** *adj* digne; **he is very dignified** il a beaucoup de dignité; **that is not very dignified** cela manque de dignité. ◆ **dignitary** *n* dignitaire *m*.
◆ **dignity** *n* dignité *f*.

digress [daɪ'gres] *vi* s'écarter *(from* de), faire une digression. ◆ **digression** *n* digression *f*.

digs * [dɪgz] *npl*: **to be in** ~ avoir une chambre chez un particulier; **I took him back to his** ~ je l'ai ramené chez lui.

dilapidated [dɪ'læpɪdeɪtɪd] *adj house* délabré; *clothes* dépenaillé; *book* déchiré. ◆ **dilapidation** *n [buildings]* délabrement *m*.

dilate [daɪ'leɪt] **1** *vt* dilater. **2** *vi* se dilater. ◆ **dilation** *n* dilatation *f*.

dilatory ['dɪlət(ə)rɪ] *adj person* lent; *action, policy* dilatoire. ◆ **dilatoriness** *n* lenteur *f (in doing* à faire).

dilemma [daɪ'lemə] *n* dilemme *m*. **on the horns of a ~** pris dans un dilemme.

diligent ['dɪlɪdʒ(ə)nt] *adj student, work* appliqué, assidu; *person, search* laborieux. ◆ **diligence** *n* zèle *m*, assiduité *f*. ◆ **diligently** *adv* avec application *or* assiduité.

dill [dɪl] *n* aneth *m*.

dilly * ['dɪlɪ] *n (US)* **it's/he's a ~** il est sensationnel; **a ~ of a storm** une sacrée tempête.

dillydally ['dɪlɪdælɪ] *vi* lanterner, lambiner *. **no ~ing!** ne traînez pas!

dilute [daɪ'lu:t] *vt (gen, also fig)* diluer; *sauce, colour* délayer. ◆ **dilution** *n* dilution *f*.

dim [dɪm] **1** *adj light, sight, lamp* faible; *room, forest etc* sombre, obscur; *colour, metal* terne, sans éclat; *sound, memory, outline* vague; imprécis; *(*: stupid)* stupide, borné. **to take a ~ view of sb** * avoir une piètre opinion de qn; **she took a ~ view of his selling the car** * elle n'a pas du tout apprécié qu'il ait vendu la voiture.

2 *vt light* baisser; *lamp* mettre en veilleuse; *colours, metals, beauty, glory* ternir; *sound* affaiblir; *memory, outline* effacer; *mind, senses* troubler. *(Theat)* **to ~ the lights** baisser les lumières; *(Aut)* **to ~ the headlights** se mettre en code.

3 *vi [light, sight]* baisser; *[metal, beauty, glory]* se ternir; *[colours]* devenir terne; *[outlines, memory]* s'effacer.

◆ **dimly** *adv shine, light* faiblement; *see, recollect* vaguement. ◆ **dimmer** *n (Elec)* variateur *m* (électronique); *(US Aut)* **~mers** phares *mpl* code *inv*; *(parking lights)* feux *mpl* de position. ◆ **dimness** *n* faiblesse *f*; obscurité *f*; imprécision *f*; stupidité *f*. ◆ **dim-sighted** *adj* à la vue faible. ◆ **dimwit** * *n* crétin(e) *m(f)*. ◆ **dim-witted** * *adj* idiot.

dime [daɪm] *n (Can, US)* pièce *f* de dix cents. **they're a ~ a dozen** * il y en a à la pelle; **~ store** ≃ prisunic *m*.

dimension [daɪ'menʃ(ə)n] *n (gen)* dimension *f*; *[problem, epidemic etc]* étendue *f*. ◆ **dimensional** *adj*: **two-~al** à deux dimensions.

diminish [dɪ'mɪnɪʃ] *vti* diminuer. ◆ **diminished** *adj (gen)* diminué; *workforce, staff, value* réduit; *(Jur) responsibility* atténué. ◆ **diminishing** *adj amount, importance, speed* qui diminue; *value, price* qui baisse; **law of ~ing returns** loi *f* des rendements décroissants. ◆ **diminutive** **1** *adj* tout petit, minuscule; *(Gram)* diminutif ; **2** *n* diminutif *m*.

dimple ['dɪmpl] *n* fossette *f* (*on* à); *[water]* ride *f*.

din [dɪn] **1** *n (from people)* vacarme *m*, tapage *m*; *(from battle)* fracas *m*; *(from factory, traffic)* vacarme; *(esp in classroom)* chahut *m*. **to kick up** * **a ~** faire un boucan monstre *, *(esp Scol)* chahuter. **2** *vt*: **to ~ into sb that...** répéter sans cesse à qn que...

dine [daɪn] *vi* dîner (*off, on* de). **to ~ out** dîner en ville. ◆ **diner** *n (person)* dîneur *m*, -euse *f*; *(Rail)* wagon-restaurant *m*; *(eating place)* petit restaurant *m*. ◆ **dining** *adj*: **dining car** wagon-restaurant *m*; **dining hall** réfectoire *m*; **dining room** salle *f* à manger.

dinghy ['dɪŋ(g)ɪ] *n* youyou *m*; *(rubber ~)* canot *m* pneumatique; *(sailing ~)* dériveur *m*.

dingy ['dɪn(d)ʒɪ] *adj* minable, miteux. ◆ **dinginess** *n* aspect minable *or* miteux.

dinner ['dɪnəʳ] **1** *n* dîner *m*; *(lunch)* déjeuner *m*; *(for dog, cat)* pâtée *f*. **we're having people to ~** nous avons du monde à dîner; **we had a good ~** nous avons bien dîné; **to go out to ~** *(restaurant)* dîner dehors *or* en ville; *(at friends')* dîner chez des amis. **2** *adj*: **~ jacket** smoking *m*; **to give a ~ party** avoir du monde à dîner, donner un dîner; **~ plate** (grande) assiette *f*; **~ service** service *m* de table; **at ~ time** à l'heure *f* du dîner.

dinosaur ['daɪnəsɔ:ʳ] *n* dinosaure *m*.

dint [dɪnt] *n*: **by ~of (doing) sth** à force de (faire) qch.

diocese ['daɪəsɪs] *n* diocèse *m*. ◆ **diocesan** [daɪ'ɒsɪs(ə)n] *adj* diocésain.

dioxin [daɪ'ɒksɪn] *n* dioxine *f*.

dip [dɪp] **1** *vt (into liquid)* tremper, plonger (*into* dans); *(into bag etc)* plonger; *sheep* laver. **to ~ the headlights** se mettre en code; **~ped headlights** codes *mpl*. **2** *vi* (**a**) *[ground, road]* descendre; *[temperature, prices, sun]* baisser; *[boat, raft]* tanguer. (**b**) **to ~ into** *pocket, savings* puiser dans; *book* feuilleter. **3** *n* (**a**) *(*: in sea etc)* baignade *f*. **to have a (quick) ~** prendre un bain rapide. (**b**) *(for cleaning animals)* bain *m* parasiticide. (**c**) *(in ground)* déclivité *f*. (**d**) *(cheese ~)* fondue *f* au fromage. ◆ **dipper** *n (ladle)* louche *f*; *(at fairground)* montagnes *fpl* russes; *(Aut: for headlamps)* basculeur *m* (de phares); *(Astron)* **the Big D~per** la Grande Ourse. ◆ **dipstick** *or* ◆ **diprod** *(US)* *n (Aut)* jauge *f* (de niveau d'huile).

diphtheria [dɪf'θɪərɪə] *n* diphtérie *f*.

diphthong ['dɪfθɒŋ] *n* diphtongue *f*.

diploma [dɪ'pləʊmə] *n* diplôme *m*. **to have a ~ in** être diplômé de *or* en.

diplomacy [dɪ'pləʊməsɪ] *n (Pol, fig)* diplomatie *f*. ◆ **diplomat** ['dɪpləmæt] *or* ◆ **diplomatist** [dɪ'pləʊ-] *n (Pol, fig)* diplomate *mf*. ◆ **diplomatic** [dɪplə'mæ-] *adj corps, immunity, service* diplomatique; *(tactful) person* diplomate; *action, answer* diplomatique; **diplomatic bag** *or (US)* **pouch** valise *f* diplomatique; **to be diplomatic in dealing with sth** s'occuper de qch en usant de diplomatie. ◆ **diplomatically** *adv* diplomatiquement.

dipsomania [ˌdɪpsə(ʊ)'meɪnɪə] *n* dipsomanie *f*. ◆ **dipsomaniac** *n* dipsomane *mf*.

dire ['daɪəʳ] *adj event* terrible, affreux; *poverty* extrême; *prediction* sinistre; *necessity* dur *(before n)*. **in ~ straits** dans une situation désespérée.

direct [daɪ'rekt] **1** *adj (gen)* direct; *refusal, denial* catégorique; *danger* immédiat; *(Gram) object, speech* direct. **to be a ~ descendant of sb** descendre de qn en ligne directe; *(Elec)* **~ current** courant *m* continu; **~ grant school** ≃ lycée *m* privé *(subventionné)*; **keep away from ~ heat** éviter l'exposition directe à la chaleur; **to make a ~ hit** porter un coup au but; *[bomb, projectile]* toucher son objectif.

2 *vt* (**a**) *(address etc) remark, letter* adresser (*to* à); *torch* diriger (*on* sur); *efforts* orienter (*towards* vers); *steps* diriger (*towards* vers); *attention* attirer (*to* sur). **can you ~ me to the town hall?** pourriez-vous m'indiquer le chemin de la mairie? (**b**) *(control) sb's work, conduct, business* diriger; *movements* guider; *(Theat) play* mettre en scène; *(Cine, Rad, TV) film, programme* réaliser; *group of actors* diriger. (**c**) *(instruct)* charger (*sb to do* qn de faire), ordonner (*sb to do* à qn de faire).

3 *adv go etc* directement.

◆ **directive** *n* directive *f*. ◆ **directly** **1** *adv go, involve, return, write* directement; *descended* en droite ligne; *speak* sans détours, franchement; *(completely) opposite* exactement; *opposed* diamétralement, directement; *(immediately)* tout de suite, immédiatement ; **2** *conj* aussitôt que, dès que; **he'll come ~ly he's ready** il viendra dès qu'il sera prêt. ◆ **directness** *n (frankness)* franchise *f*.

direction [dɪ'rekʃ(ə)n] **1** *n* (**a**) *(way)* direction *f*, sens *m*; *(fig)* direction, voie *f*. **in every ~** dans toutes les directions, en tous sens; *(fig)* **it's a step in the right ~** voilà un pas dans la bonne direction; **in the opposite ~** en sens inverse; **in the ~ of** dans la direction de, en direction de; **a sense of ~** le sens de l'orientation. (**b**) *(management)* direction *f*; *(Theat)* mise *f* en scène; *(Cine, Rad, TV)* réalisation *f*. (**c**) *(instruction)* indication *f*, instruction *f*. **~s for use** mode *m* d'emploi; **stage**

~s indications scéniques. **2** *adj*: ~ **finder** radiogoniomètre *m*. ◆ **directional** *adj* directionnel.

director [dɪ'rektəʳ] *n (gen, Comm etc)* directeur *m*, -trice *f*; *(Theat)* metteur *m* en scène; *(Cine, Rad, TV)* réalisateur *m*, -trice *f*. ~ **general** directeur général; ~ **of music** chef *m* de musique; **D ~of Public Prosecutions** ≃ procureur *m* général. ◆ **directory** **1** *n [addresses]* répertoire *m* (d'adresses); *(street ~)* guide *m* des rues; *(Telec)* annuaire *m* (des téléphones); *(Comm)* annuaire du commerce ; **2** *adj (Telec)* ~**y inquiries**, *(US)* ~**y assistance** (service *m* des) renseignements *mpl*.

dirge [dɜ:dʒ] *n* chant *m* funèbre.

dirndl ['dɜ:nd(ə)l] *adj, n*: ~ **(skirt)** large jupe froncée.

dirt [dɜ:t] **1** *n (on skin, clothes, objects)* saleté *f*, crasse *f*; *(earth)* terre *f*; *(mud)* boue *f*; *(excrement)* crotte *f*; *(Ind)* impuretés *fpl*; *(on machine, in engine)* encrassement *m*. **dog** ~ crotte de chien; **to treat sb like** ~ * traiter qn comme un chien; **to spread the** ~ * **about sb** calomnier qn; **what's the** ~ **on...?** * qu'est-ce qu'on raconte sur...? **2** *adj*: *(US)* ~ **farmer** petit fermier *(sans ouvriers)*; ~ **track** *(gen)* piste *f*; *(Sport)* cendrée *f*. ◆ **dirt-cheap** * *adj, adv* très bon marché *(inv)*.

dirty ['dɜ:tɪ] **1** *adj* (**a**) *(gen)* sale, crasseux; *job* salissant; *machine, plug* encrassé; *cut, wound* infecté. **to get** ~ se salir; **to get sth** ~ salir qch; **that coat gets** ~ **very easily** ce manteau est très salissant. (**b**) *(lewd) story, thought* sale, cochon *; *remark* ordurier. **to have a** ~ **mind** avoir l'esprit mal tourné; ~ **old man** vieux cochon * *m*; ~ **word** mot *m* grossier; *(fig)* **it's a** ~ **word * these days** ce mot est tabou de nos jours. (**c**) *(unpleasant) weather, business, trick* sale *(before n)*. ~ **crack** * vacherie ⁑ *f*; **to give sb a** ~ **look** regarder qn d'un sale œil; ~ **money** argent mal acquis; **he's a** ~ **rat** * c'est un sale type *; **he left the** ~ **work for me** il m'a laissé le plus embêtant du boulot *. **2** *vt* salir. ◆ **dirtily** *adv eat, live* salement; *(meanly) behave* bassement. ◆ **dirtiness** *n* saleté *f*. ◆ **dirty-faced** *adj* à la figure sale. ◆ **dirty-minded** *adj* à l'esprit mal tourné.

disable [dɪs'eɪbl] *vt [illness, accident, injury]* rendre infirme; *(stronger)* rendre impotent; *tank, gun* mettre hors d'action; *ship (gen)* mettre hors d'état; *(by enemy action)* mettre hors de combat; *(Jur: disqualify)* rendre inhabile *(from doing* à faire). ◆ **disability** *n (state)* incapacité *f (for* à); *(handicap)* infirmité *f*; *(disadvantage)* désavantage *m*; **disability allowance** pension *f* d'invalidité. ◆ **disabled** **1** *adj* infirme; *(Admin: unable to work)* invalide; *(through illness, old age)* impotent; ~**d ex-servicemen** invalides *mpl* de guerre ; **2** *n*: **the** ~**d** les invalides *mpl*. ◆ **disablement** *n* invalidité *f*; ~**ment pension** pension *f* d'invalidité.

disadvantage [ˌdɪsəd'vɑ:ntɪdʒ] **1** *n* désavantage *m*. **to be at a** ~ être dans une position désavantageuse; **you've got me at a** ~ vous avez l'avantage sur moi; **it would be to your** ~ cela vous ferait du tort. **2** *vt* désavantager. ◆ **disadvantaged** *adj child, minority* déshérité; **educationally** *etc* ~**d** défavorisé sur le plan scolaire *etc*. ◆ **disadvantageous** *adj* désavantageux *(to* à).

disaffected [ˌdɪsə'fektɪd] *adj* déçu.

disagree [ˌdɪsə'gri:] *vi* ne pas être d'accord, être en désaccord *(with sb/sth* avec qn/qch; *over* sur); *(quarrel)* se disputer *(with sb* avec qn; *over* à propos de); *[reports, figures]* ne pas concorder *(with* avec). **I** ~ je ne suis pas de cet avis, je ne suis pas d'accord; **to** ~ **with the suggestion** être contre la suggestion; **she** ~**s with everything he has done** elle se trouve en désaccord avec tout ce qu'il a fait; *[climate, food]* **to** ~ **with sb** ne pas convenir à qn; **mutton** ~**s with him** il ne digère pas le mouton. ◆ **disagreeable** *adj (gen)* désagréable; *person* désagréable, désobligeant *(towards* envers). ◆ **disagreeableness** *n [work, experience]* nature *f* désagréable; *[person]* manières *fpl* désagréables. ◆ **disagreeably** *adv* désagréablement. ◆ **disagreement** *n* désaccord *m*; **to have a** ~**ment with sb** se disputer avec qn *(about* à propos de).

disallow ['dɪsə'laʊ] *vt* rejeter; *(Sport) goal* refuser.

disappear [ˌdɪsə'pɪəʳ] *vi* disparaître. **he** ~**ed from sight** on l'a perdu de vue; **the ship** ~**ed over the horizon** le navire a disparu à l'horizon; **to do a** ~**ing trick** * s'éclipser *; **to make sth** ~ faire disparaître qch; *[conjurer]* escamoter qch. ◆ **disappearance** *n* disparition *f*.

disappoint [ˌdɪsə'pɔɪnt] *vt* décevoir, désappointer; *(after promising)* manquer de parole à; *hope* décevoir; *expectations* tromper. ◆ **disappointed** *adj person* déçu, désappointé; *hope, ambition* déçu; *plan* contrecarré; **I'm very** ~**ed with you** vous m'avez beaucoup déçu *or* désappointé. ◆ **disappointing** *adj* décevant. ◆ **disappointment** *n* déception *f*.

disapprove [ˌdɪsə'pru:v] *vi* désapprouver *(of sb/sth* qn/qch; *of sb's doing* que qn fasse). **your mother would** ~ ta mère ne trouverait pas ça bien; **he entirely** ~**s of drink** il est tout à fait contre la boisson. ◆ **disapproval** *n* désapprobation *f*. ◆ **disapproving** *adj* désapprobateur. ◆ **disapprovingly** *adv* avec désapprobation.

disarm [dɪs'ɑ:m] *vti* désarmer. ◆ **disarmament** *n* désarmement *m*; ~**ament talks** conférence *f* sur le désarmement. ◆ **disarming** *adj smile* désarmant. ◆ **disarmingly** *adv* d'une manière désarmante.

disarrange ['dɪsə'reɪn(d)ʒ] *vt* mettre en désordre.

disarray [ˌdɪsə'reɪ] *n*: **in (complete)** ~ *troops* en déroute; *party, movement* en plein désarroi; *thoughts* très confus; *clothes* en désordre.

disaster [dɪ'zɑ:stəʳ] **1** *n (gen, also fig)* désastre *m*, catastrophe *f*; *(air* ~, *sea* ~ *etc)* catastrophe. **doomed to** ~ voué à la catastrophe; **her hair was a** ~ * sa coiffure était une catastrophe *. **2** *adj*: ~ **area** région *f* sinistrée; ~ **fund** collecte *f* au profit des victimes. ◆ **disastrous** *adj* désastreux, catastrophique. ◆ **disastrously** *adv* désastreusement, catastrophiquement.

disband [dɪs'bænd] **1** *vt* disperser. **2** *vi* se disperser.

disbelieve ['dɪsbə'li:v] *vt person* ne pas croire; *news etc* ne pas croire à. ◆ **disbelief** *n* incrédulité *f*; **in disbelief** avec incrédulité. ◆ **disbelieving** *adj* incrédule.

disc [dɪsk] **1** *n (gen)* disque *m*; *(identity* ~*)* plaque *f* d'identité. **2** *adj brakes* à disque. ~ **jockey** animateur *m*, -trice *f* (de variétés), disc-jockey *m*.

discard [dɪs'kɑ:d] *vt (gen)* se débarrasser de; *(throw out)* jeter; *idea, plan* abandonner; *part of spacecraft* larguer; *(Cards)* se défausser de.

discern [dɪ'sɜ:n] *vt* discerner. ◆ **discernible** *adj object* visible; *likeness, fault* perceptible. ◆ **discerning** *adj person, look* perspicace; *taste* délicat. ◆ **discernment** *n* discernement *m*.

discharge [dɪs'tʃɑ:dʒ] **1** *vt ship, cargo* décharger; *liquid* déverser; *(Elec)* décharger; *employee* congédier; *soldier* rendre à la vie civile; *(for health reasons)* réformer; *prisoner* libérer; *jury* congédier; *accused* relaxer; *bankrupt* réhabiliter; *debt* acquitter; *obligation, duty* remplir; *patient* renvoyer (guéri) de l'hôpital; *gun* faire partir. **the patient** ~**d himself** le malade est sorti en signant une décharge. **to** ~ **pus** suppurer. **2** *vi [wound]* suinter. **3** ['dɪstʃɑ:dʒ] *n (Elec)* décharge *f*; *(Med) (gen)* suintement *m; (pus etc)* suppuration *f*; *(vaginal)* pertes *fpl* (blanches); *[employee, patient]* renvoi *m*; *[prisoner]* libération *f*. **he got his** ~ il a été congédié *or* libéré *etc*.

disciple [dɪ'saɪpl] *n* disciple *m*.

discipline ['dɪsɪplɪn] **1** *n* discipline *f*. **2** *vt (control)* discipliner; *(punish)* punir. ◆ **disciplinarian** *n* personne *f* stricte en matière de discipline. ◆ **disciplinary** *adj* disciplinaire.

disclaim [dɪs'kleɪm] *vt news, statement* démentir; *responsibility* rejeter; *authorship* nier; *paternity* désavouer. ◆ **disclaimer** *n* démenti *m*. **to issue a ~er** publier un démenti.

disclose [dɪs'kləʊz] *vt secret, news* divulguer, révéler; *intentions* révéler; *contents* exposer. ◆ **disclosure** *n* révélation *f*.

disco * ['dɪskəʊ] *n* disco *m*. **~ dancing** disco *m*.

discolour, *(US)* **discolor** [dɪs'kʌlə^r] **1** *vt* décolorer; *white object* jaunir. **2** *vi* se décolorer; jaunir. ◆ **discoloration** *n* décoloration *f*; jaunissement *m*.

discomfiture [dɪs'kʌmfɪtʃə^r] *n* embarras *m*.

discomfort [dɪs'kʌmfət] *n* gêne *f*. **I feel some ~ from it but not real pain** ça me gêne mais ça ne me fait pas vraiment mal; **this ~ will pass** cette gêne va passer.

disconcert [ˌdɪskən'sɜːt] *vt* déconcerter. ◆ **disconcerting** *adj* déconcertant, déroutant. ◆ **disconcertingly** *adv* d'une manière déconcertante.

disconnect ['dɪskə'nekt] *vt (gen)* détacher; *railway carriage* décrocher; *pipe, radio, television* débrancher; *gas, electricity, water supply, telephone* couper. *(Telec: in mid conversation)* **we've been ~ed** nous avons été coupés. ◆ **disconnected** *adj speech, thought* sans suite; *facts* sans rapport.

disconsolate [dɪs'kɒns(ə)lɪt] *adj* inconsolable. ◆ **disconsolately** *adv* inconsolablement.

discontent ['dɪskən'tent] *n* mécontentement *m*; *(Pol)* malaise *m* social. **cause of ~** grief *m*. ◆ **discontented** *adj* mécontent (*with, about* de).

discontinue ['dɪskən'tɪnjuː] *vt* cesser, interrompre; *production* abandonner; *series* interrompre; *story* interrompre la publication de. *(Comm)* **~d line** série *f* qui ne se fait plus; *(notice)* 'fin de série'. ◆ **discontinuous** *adj* discontinu.

discord ['dɪskɔːd] *n* discorde *f*; *(Mus)* dissonance *f*. ◆ **discordant** *adj* discordant; dissonant.

discotheque ['dɪskə(ʊ)'tek] *n* discothèque *f (dancing)*.

discount ['dɪskaʊnt] **1** *n* escompte *m*; *(on article)* remise *f*, rabais *m*. **to give a ~** faire une remise (*on* sur); **to buy at a ~** acheter au rabais; **~ for cash** escompte au comptant; *(fig)* **to be at a ~** être mal coté. **2** [dɪs'kaʊnt] *vt fact, remark* ne pas tenir compte de. **3** *adj*: **~ store** magasin *m* de vente au rabais.

discourage [dɪs'kʌrɪdʒ] *vt* (**a**) *(dishearten)* décourager, abattre. **to become ~d** se laisser décourager. (**b**) *(advise against)* décourager, dissuader (*sb from sth/from doing* qn de qch/de faire); *suggestion* déconseiller; *offer of friendship* repousser. ◆ **discouragement** *n (act)* désapprobation *f* (*of* de); *(depression)* découragement *m*. ◆ **discouraging** *adj* décourageant, démoralisant.

discourteous [dɪs'kɜːtɪəs] *adj* peu courtois (*towards* envers, avec). ◆ **discourteously** *adv* d'une manière peu courtoise. ◆ **discourtesy** *n* manque *m* de courtoisie.

discover [dɪs'kʌvə^r] *vt (gen)* découvrir; *mistake, loss* s'apercevoir de; *(after search) house, book* dénicher. **to ~ that** *(realize)* s'apercevoir que; *(learn)* apprendre que. ◆ **discoverer** *n*: **the ~er of penicillin** celui qui le premier a découvert la pénicilline. ◆ **discovery** *n (act)* découverte *f*; *(happy find)* trouvaille *f*.

discredit [dɪs'kredɪt] **1** *vt* discréditer. **2** *n* discrédit *m*. ◆ **discreditable** *adj* peu honorable.

discreet [dɪs'kriːt] *adj* discret. ◆ **discreetly** *adv* discrètement. ◆ **discretion** [dɪs'kreʃ(ə)n] *n* discrétion *f*; **use your own discretion** faites comme bon vous semblera; **the age of discretion** l'âge de raison. ◆ **discretionary** *adj powers* discrétionnaire.

discrepancy [dɪs'krep(ə)nsɪ] *n* contradiction *f*, divergence *f* (*between* entre). **there is a slight ~ between the explanations** les explications divergent légèrement.

discrete [dɪs'kriːt] *adj* discret *(distinct)*.

discriminate [dɪs'krɪmɪneɪt] **1** *vi* distinguer, faire un choix (*between* entre); *(unfairly)* établir une discrimination (against contre; *in favour of* en faveur de). **2** *vt* distinguer (*from* de). ◆ **discriminating** *adj judgment, mind* judicieux; *taste* fin; *tariff, tax* différentiel; **he's not very discriminating** il ne fait guère preuve d'esprit critique. ◆ **discrimination** *n (judgment)* discernement *m*; *(bias)* discrimination *f* (*against* contre, *in favour of* en faveur de).

discus ['dɪskəs] *n* disque *m*. **~ thrower** lanceur *m* de disque.

discuss [dɪs'kʌs] *vt (examine in detail) problem, project, price* discuter; *(talk about) topic, personality* discuter de. **we were ~ing him** nous parlions *or* discutions de lui; **I ~ed it with him** j'en ai discuté avec lui. ◆ **discussion** *n* discussion *f* (*of* sur); **under ~ion** en discussion.

disdain [dɪs'deɪn] **1** *vt* dédaigner (*to do* de faire). **2** *n* dédain *m*. ◆ **disdainful** *adj* dédaigneux. ◆ **disdainfully** *adv* dédaigneusement.

disease [dɪ'ziːz] *n* maladie *f*. ◆ **diseased** *adj* malade.

disembark [ˌdɪsɪm'bɑːk] *vti* débarquer. ◆ **disembarkation** *n* débarquement *m*.

disembodied ['dɪsɪm'bɒdɪd] *adj* désincarné.

disenchanted ['dɪsɪn'tʃɑːntɪd] *adj* désenchanté. ◆ **disenchantment** *n* désenchantement *m*.

disengage [ˌdɪsɪn'geɪdʒ] *vt (gen)* dégager (*from* de); *machine* débrayer. **to ~ the clutch** débrayer. ◆ **disengaged** *adj* libre, inoccupé; *(Tech)* débrayé. ◆ **disengagement** *n (Pol)* désengagement *m*.

disentangle ['dɪsɪn'tæŋgl] *vt (gen)* démêler; *plot* dénouer. **to ~ o.s. from** se dépêtrer de.

disfavour, *(US)* **disfavor** [dɪs'feɪvə^r] **1** *n* défaveur *f* (*with sb* auprès de qn). **to fall into ~** tomber en défaveur. **2** *vt (dislike)* désapprouver. *(US: disadvantage)* défavoriser.

disfigure [dɪs'fɪgə^r] *vt* défigurer. ◆ **disfigured** *adj* défiguré (*by* par). ◆ **disfigurement** *n* défigurement *m*.

disgorge [dɪs'gɔːdʒ] *vt* dégorger.

disgrace [dɪs'greɪs] **1** *n (dishonour)* honte *f*, déshonneur *m*; *(disfavour)* disgrâce *f*. **there is no ~ in doing** il n'y a aucune honte à faire; **to be in ~** *[politician etc]* être en disgrâce; *[child, dog]* être en pénitence; **it's a ~** c'est une honte; **it is a ~ to the country** cela déshonore le pays. **2** *vt family etc* faire honte à; *name, country* déshonorer. **he ~d himself by drinking too much** il s'est très mal conduit en buvant trop; *[officer, politician]* **to be ~d** être disgracié. ◆ **disgraceful** *adj* honteux, scandaleux. ◆ **disgracefully** *adv act* honteusement, scandaleusement; **~fully badly paid** scandaleusement mal payé.

disgruntled [dɪs'grʌntld] *adj person* mécontent (*about, with* à cause de); *expression* maussade.

disguise [dɪs'gaɪz] **1** *vt (gen)* déguiser (*as* en); *building, vehicle, ship* camoufler (*as* en). **to ~ o.s. as a woman** se déguiser en femme; **there is no disguising the fact that...** on ne peut pas se dissimuler que... **2** *n* déguisement *m*. **in ~** déguisé.

disgust [dɪs'gʌst] **1** *n* dégoût *m* (*for, at* pour). **he left in ~** il est parti dégoûté; **to my ~ he refused** j'ai trouvé dégoûtant qu'il refuse *(subj)*. **2** *vt* dégoûter. ◆ **disgusted** *adj* dégoûté (*at* de, par). ◆ **disgustedly** *adv* avec dégoût; **... he said ~edly**

... dit-il, dégoûté. ◆ **disgusting** *adj (gen)* dégoûtant; *behaviour* révoltant; *smell* nauséabond; **what a ~ing mess!** c'est dégoûtant! ◆ **disgustingly** *adv* d'une manière dégoûtante; **~ingly dirty** d'une saleté dégoûtante.

dish [dɪʃ] **1** *n* plat *m*; *(in laboratory etc)* récipient *m*; *(Phot)* cuvette *f*; *(food)* plat, mets *m*. **vegetable ~** plat à légumes; **the ~es** la vaisselle; **to do the ~es** faire la vaisselle. **2** *vt food* verser dans un plat; (‡) *sb's chances, hopes* flanquer par terre *. ◆ **dish out** *vt sep food* servir; *(*: fig) (money, books etc)* distribuer; *punishment* administrer. ◆ **dish up** *vt sep meal* servir; (*) *facts, statistics* sortir tout un tas de *.
◆ **dishcloth** *n (for washing)* lavette *f*; *(for drying)* torchon *m* à vaisselle. ◆ **dished wheel** *n* roue *f* désaxée. ◆ **dishmop** *n* lavette *f*. ◆ **dishpan** *n* bassine *f* (à vaisselle). ◆ **dishrack** *n* égouttoir *m* (à vaisselle). ◆ **dishtowel** *n* torchon *m* (à vaisselle). ◆ **dish-washer** *n (machine)* lave-vaisselle *m inv*; *(person: in restaurant)* plongeur *m*, -euse *f*. ◆ **dishwater** *n* eau *f* de vaisselle. ◆ **dishy** ‡ *adj person* excitant, sexy *.

dishearten [dɪs'hɑ:tn] *vt* décourager. **to get ~ed** se décourager. ◆ **disheartening** *adj* décourageant.

dishevelled [dɪ'ʃevəld] *adj person, hair* échevelé; *clothes* en désordre.

dishonest [dɪs'ɒnɪst] *adj (gen)* malhonnête; *(untruthful) person* menteur; *reply* mensonger. **to be ~ with sb** manquer de franchise envers qn. ◆ **dishonestly** *adv act* malhonnêtement; *say* en mentant. ◆ **dishonesty** *n* malhonnêteté *f*.

dishonour, *(US)* **dishonor** [dɪs'ɒnəʳ] **1** *n* déshonneur *m*. **2** *vt* déshonorer; *cheque* refuser d'honorer. ◆ **dishono(u)rable** *adj* peu honorable.

disillusion [ˌdɪsɪ'lu:ʒ(ə)n] **1** *vt* désillusionner. **to grow ~ed** perdre ses illusions. **2** *n* désillusion *f*.

disincentive [ˌdɪsɪn'sentɪv] *n*: **it's a real ~** cela a un effet de dissuasion; **this is a ~ to work** cela n'incite pas à travailler.

disinclination [ˌdɪsɪnklɪ'neɪʃ(ə)n] *n* manque *m* d'enthousiasme (*to do* à faire). ◆ **disinclined** *adj* peu disposé, peu enclin (*for* à, *to do* à faire).

disinfect [ˌdɪsɪn'fekt] *vt* désinfecter. ◆ **disinfectant** *adj, n* désinfectant *(m)*. ◆ **disinfection** *n* désinfection *f*.

disinformation [ˌdɪsɪnfə'meɪʃ(ə)n] *n* désinformation *f*.

disingenuous [ˌdɪsɪn'dʒenjʊəs] *adj* déloyal, peu sincère.

disinherit ['dɪsɪn'herɪt] *vt* déshériter.

disintegrate [dɪs'ɪntɪgreɪt] **1** *vi* se désintégrer. **2** *vt* désintégrer. ◆ **disintegration** *n* désintégration *f*.

disinterested [dɪs'ɪntrɪstɪd] *adj (impartial)* désintéressé; *(uninterested)* indifférent. ◆ **disinterestedness** *n* désintéressement *m*; indifférence *f*.

disjointed [dɪs'dʒɔɪntɪd] *adj* décousu.

disjunctive [dɪs'dʒʌŋktɪv] *adj* disjonctif.

disk [dɪsk] *n* (**a**) *(esp US)* = **disc.** (**b**) *(Comput)* disque *m*. **on ~** sur disque; **single-/double-sided ~** disque simple/double; **~ drive** lecteur *m* de disques.

diskette [dɪs'ket] *n (Comput)* disquette *f*.

dislike [dɪs'laɪk] **1** *vt* ne pas aimer (*doing* faire). **I don't ~ it** cela ne me déplaît pas; **I ~ her** je la trouve antipathique, elle ne me plaît pas; **I ~ this intensely** j'ai cela en horreur. **2** *n*: **his ~ of...** le fait qu'il n'aime pas...; **one's likes and ~s** ce que l'on aime et ce que l'on n'aime pas; **to take a ~ to sb/sth** prendre qn/qch en grippe.

dislocate ['dɪslə(ʊ)'keɪt] *vt (Med)* se disloquer; *[fall etc]* disloquer; *(fig) traffic, business* désorganiser; *plans* bouleverser. **he ~d his shoulder** il s'est disloqué l'épaule. ◆ **dislocation** *n* dislocation *f*; désorganisation *f*; bouleversement *m*.

dislodge [dɪs'lɒdʒ] *vt stone* déplacer; *cap, screw, nut* débloquer; *enemy* déloger; *person* faire bouger (*from* de).

disloyal ['dɪs'lɔɪ(ə)l] *adj* déloyal (*to* à, envers). ◆ **disloyally** *adv* déloyalement. ◆ **disloyalty** *n* déloyauté *f*.

dismal ['dɪzm(ə)l] *adj prospects, person* sombre, morne; *weather* morne; *failure* lamentable. ◆ **dismally** *adv say* d'un air sombre; *fail* lamentablement.

dismantle [dɪs'mæntl] *vt machine* démonter; *company* démanteler.

dismay [dɪs'meɪ] **1** *n* consternation *f*. **in ~** d'un air consterné. **2** *vt* consterner.

dismember [dɪs'membəʳ] *vt* démembrer.

dismiss [dɪs'mɪs] *vt* (**a**) *employee* licencier, congédier; *official, officer* destituer; *class, visitors* congédier; *troops* faire rompre les rangs à. *(Mil)* **~!** rompez (les rangs)!; *(Scol)* **class ~!** partez! (**b**) *thought, suggestion, possibility* écarter; *request* rejeter. (**c**) *(Jur) accused* relaxer; *appeal* rejeter; *jury* congédier. **to ~ a case** rendre une fin de non-recevoir; **to ~ a charge** rendre un non-lieu. ◆ **dismissal** *n* licenciement *m*; destitution *f*; congédiement *m*; rejet *m*; **he made a gesture of ~al** d'un geste il les a congédiés.

dismount [dɪs'maʊnt] **1** *vi* descendre (*from* de), mettre pied à terre. **2** *vt* démonter.

disobey ['dɪsə'beɪ] *vt person* désobéir à; *rule* enfreindre. ◆ **disobedience** *n* désobéissance *f* (*to* à). ◆ **disobedient** *adj* désobéissant (*to* à).

disobliging ['dɪsə'blaɪdʒɪŋ] *adj* désobligeant.

disorder [dɪs'ɔ:dəʳ] *n [room, plans etc]* désordre *m*, confusion *f*; *(Pol etc: rioting)* désordres *mpl*; *(Med)* troubles *mpl*. **in ~** en désordre; *(Mil)* en déroute; **speech ~** difficulté *f* de langage. ◆ **disordered** *adj room* en désordre; *imagination, existence* désordonné; *(Med) stomach, mind* malade. ◆ **disorderly** *adj room* en désordre; *flight, mind, crowd, behaviour, life* désordonné; *meeting* tumultueux; *(Jur)* **~ly conduct** conduite *f* contraire aux bonnes mœurs.

disorganize [dɪs'ɔ:gənaɪz] *vt* désorganiser. **she's very ~d** * elle est très désorganisée. ◆ **disorganization** *n* désorganisation *f*.

disorientate [dɪs'ɔ:rɪənteɪt] *vt* désorienter.

disown [dɪs'əʊn] *vt* renier.

disparage [dɪs'pærɪdʒ] *vt person, thing* dénigrer. ◆ **disparagement** *n* dénigrement *m*. ◆ **disparaging** *adj* désobligeant (*to* pour); **to be disparaging about** faire des remarques désobligeantes sur. ◆ **disparagingly** *adv* de façon désobligeante.

disparate ['dɪspərɪt] *adj* disparate. ◆ **disparity** *n* disparité *f*.

dispassionate [dɪs'pæʃ(ə)nɪt] *adj (unemotional)* calme; *(unbiased)* impartial. ◆ **dispassionately** *adv* avec calme; impartialement.

dispatch [dɪs'pætʃ] **1** *vt* (**a**) *(send) letter, goods* expédier; *messenger* dépêcher; *troops* faire partir. (**b**) *(finish off) job* expédier; *animal* tuer. **2** *n* (**a**) *(sending)* expédition *f*. (**b**) *(report: Mil, Press etc)* dépêche *f*. *(Mil)* **mentioned in ~es** cité à l'ordre du jour. (**c**) *(promptness)* promptitude *f*. **3** *adj*: **~ box** *(in Parliament)* ≃ tribune *f*; *(case)* valise officielle *(à documents)*; **~ case** serviette *f*, porte-documents *m inv*; **~ rider** estafette *f*.

dispel [dɪs'pel] *vt* dissiper, chasser.

dispense [dɪs'pens] *vt* (**a**) *food* distribuer; *justice, sacrament* administrer; *hospitality* accorder; *medicine, prescription* préparer. **dispensing chemist** *(person)* pharmacien(ne) *m(f)*; *(shop)* pharmacie *f*. (**b**) *(exempt)* dispenser (*sb from sth/from doing* qn de qch/de faire). ◆ **dispense with** *vt fus (do without)* se passer de; *(make unnecessary)* rendre superflu. ◆ **dispensable** *adj* dont on peut se passer. ◆ **dispensary** *n (in hospital)* pharmacie *f*; *(in chemist's)* officine *f*; *(clinic)* dispensaire *m*. ◆ **dispensation** *n (Jur, Rel)* dispense *f (from* de). ◆ **dispenser** *n (person)* pharmacien(ne) *m(f)*; *(device)* distributeur *m*.

disperse [dɪs'pɜːs] **1** *vt (gen)* disperser; *sorrow* dissiper; *knowledge* disséminer. **2** *vi* se disperser; se dissiper; se disséminer. ◆ **dispersal** *or* ◆ **dispersion** *n* dispersion *f*. ◆ **dispersant** *n* dispersant *m*.

dispirited [dɪs'pɪrɪtɪd] *adj* découragé, abattu. ◆ **dispiritedly** *adv* avec découragement.

displace [dɪs'pleɪs] *vt (move out of place) refugees, official* déplacer; *(replace)* remplacer. ~**d person** personne déplacée. ◆ **displacement** *n* déplacement *m*; remplacement *m*; *(Psych)* ~**ment activity** déplacement *m*.

display [dɪs'pleɪ] **1** *vt (gen)* montrer; *(ostentatiously)* faire parade de; *courage, ignorance* faire preuve de; *notice, results* afficher; *goods* exposer; *(Comput)* visualiser; *[electronic device]* afficher. **2** *n (act)* exposition *f*, déploiement *m*; *(ostentatious)* étalage *m*; *[paintings]* exposition; *(Comm)* étalage; *(Comput)* visuel *m*; *(visual information)* affichage *m*; *[courage, ignorance]* manifestation *f*; *[force etc]* déploiement. **on** ~ exposé; ~ **of gymnastics/dancing** *etc* exhibition *f* de gymnastique/de danse *etc;* **military** ~ parade *f* militaire; **air** ~ fête *f* aéronautique. **3** *adj goods* d'étalage. ~ **cabinet,** ~ **case** vitrine *f (meuble)*; ~ **panel** écran *m* de visualisation; ~ **window** vitrine *f (de magasin)*.

displease [dɪs'pliːz] *vt* déplaire à, mécontenter. ~**d with** mécontent de. ◆ **displeasing** *adj* déplaisant *(to* pour, à). ◆ **displeasure** [dɪs'pleʒəʳ] *n* mécontentement *m*.

dispose [dɪs'pəʊz] *vt* (**a**) *(arrange) papers, ornaments, troops* disposer; *forces* déployer. (**b**) *(make willing)* disposer *(sb to do* qn à faire).
◆ **dispose of** *vt fus* (**a**) *(get rid of)* se débarrasser de; *(by selling) item* vendre; *stock* écouler; *one's property, money* disposer de; *rubbish etc (remove)* enlever; *(destroy)* détruire; *bomb* désamorcer; *meal, question* expédier; *opponent* régler son compte à; *(kill)* liquider *. (**b**) *(control) time, money* disposer de.
◆ **disposable** *adj (available)* disponible; *(not reusable)* à jeter; **disposable income** revenu *m* net (d'impôts et de retenues); **disposable (nappy)** couche-culotte *f;* **disposable wrapping** emballage *m* perdu. ◆ **disposal** *n [rubbish]* enlèvement *m*, destruction *f*; *[bomb]* désamorçage *m*; *[property]* disposition *f*; **at sb's disposal** à la disposition de qn; **(waste) disposal unit** broyeur *m* (d'ordures). ◆ **disposed** *adj* disposé *(to do* à faire); **well** ~**d towards sb** bien disposé envers qn. ◆ **disposer** *n (waste ~)* broyeur *m* (d'ordures). ◆ **disposition** *n (temperament)* naturel *m*, tempérament *m*; *(readiness)* inclination *f (to do* à faire); *(arrangement)* disposition *f*.

dispossess ['dɪspə'zes] *vt* déposséder *(of* de).

disproportionate [ˌdɪsprə'pɔːʃnɪt] *adj* disproportionné *(to* à, avec). ◆ **disproportionately** *adv*: ~**ly large** *etc* d'une grandeur *etc* disproportionnée.

disprove [dɪs'pruːv] *vt* établir la fausseté de.

dispute [dɪs'pjuːt] **1** *n* (**a**) discussion *f*. **beyond** ~ incontestable; **without** ~ sans contredit; **there is some** ~ **about** on n'est pas d'accord sur; **in** *or* **under** ~ *matter* en discussion; *territory, facts, figures* contesté; *(Jur)* en litige. (**b**) *(quarrel)* dispute *f*; *(argument)* discussion *f*, débat *m*; *(Jur)* litige *m*; *(Ind, Pol)* conflit *m*. **industrial** ~ conflit social; **wages** ~ conflit salarial. **2** *vt* contester. **I do not** ~ **the fact that...** je ne conteste pas (le fait) que... + *subj*. ◆ **disputable** *adj* discutable, contestable. ◆ **disputably** *adv* de manière contestable. ◆ **disputed** *adj* contesté.

disqualify [dɪs'kwɒlɪfaɪ] *vt* rendre inapte *(from sth* à qch, *from doing* à faire); *(Sport)* disqualifier. **to** ~ **sb from driving** retirer à qn le permis de conduire *(for sth* pour qch). ◆ **disqualification** *n* disqualification *f (also Sport)*, exclusion *f (from* de); *(from driving)* retrait *m* du permis (de conduire).

disquieting [dɪs'kwaɪətɪŋ] *adj* inquiétant.

disregard ['dɪsrɪ'gɑːd] **1** *vt (gen)* ne tenir aucun compte de; *feelings* faire peu de cas de; *authority, rules, duty* passer outre à. **2** *n [difficulty, comments, feelings, money]* indifférence *f (for* à); *[danger]* mépris *m (for* de); *[safety]* négligence *f (for* en ce qui concerne); *[rule, law]* non-observation *f (for* de).

disrepair ['dɪsrɪ'pɛəʳ] *n* mauvais état. **in a state of** ~ *building* délabré; *road* en mauvais état; **to fall into** ~ *[building]* se délabrer; *[road]* se dégrader.

disrepute ['dɪsrɪ'pjuːt] *n* discrédit *m*, déshonneur *m*. **to fall into** ~ tomber en discrédit. ◆ **disreputable** [dɪs'repjʊtəbl] *adj person* peu recommandable; *behaviour* honteux; *clothes* miteux; *area* mal famé.

disrespect ['dɪsrɪs'pekt] *n* manque *m* de respect. ◆ **disrespectful** *adj* irrespectueux *(towards, to* envers); **to be** ~**ful to** manquer de respect envers.

disrupt [dɪs'rʌpt] *vt peace, relations, train service* perturber; *conversation, communications* interrompre; *plans* déranger. ◆ **disruption** *n* perturbation *f*; interruption *f*; dérangement *m*. ◆ **disruptive** *adj* perturbateur; *(Elec)* disruptif.

dissatisfaction ['dɪsˌsætɪs'fækʃ(ə)n] *n* mécontentement *m (at, with* devant, provoqué par). ◆ **dissatisfied** *adj* mécontent *(with* de).

dissect [dɪ'sekt] *vt* disséquer. ◆ **dissection** *n* dissection *f*.

dissemble [dɪ'sembl] *vti* dissimuler.

disseminate [dɪ'semɪneɪt] *vt* disséminer. ~**d sclerosis** sclérose *f* en plaques.

dissension [dɪ'senʃ(ə)n] *n* dissension *f*. ◆ **dissent** **1** *vi* différer *(from* de); *(Rel)* être dissident ; **2** *n* dissentiment *m*; *(Rel)* dissidence *f*. ◆ **dissenter** *n* dissident(e) *m(f)*.

dissertation [ˌdɪsə'teɪʃ(ə)n] *n* mémoire *m (on* sur); *(for doctorate)* thèse *f*.

disservice ['dɪs'sɜːvɪs] *n* mauvais service *m*. **to do sb a** ~ rendre un mauvais service à qn; *[appearance etc]* constituer un handicap pour qn.

dissidence ['dɪsɪd(ə)ns] *n* dissidence *f*. ◆ **dissident** *adj, n* dissident(e) *m(f)*.

dissimilar ['dɪ'sɪmɪləʳ] *adj* différent *(to* de). ◆ **dissimilarity** *n* différence *f (between* entre).

dissimulate [dɪ'sɪmjʊleɪt] *vti* dissimuler. ◆ **dissimulation** *n* dissimulation *f*.

dissipate ['dɪsɪpeɪt] *vt (gen)* dissiper; *energy, efforts* gaspiller. ◆ **dissipated** *adj life, behaviour* déréglé; *person* débauché, dissipé. ◆ **dissipation** *n* dissipation *f*.

dissociate [dɪ'səʊʃɪeɪt] *vt* dissocier *(from* de). ◆ **dissociation** *n* dissociation *f*.

dissolute ['dɪsəluːt] *adj person* débauché; *way of life* dissolu.

dissolution [ˌdɪsə'luːʃ(ə)n] *n* dissolution *f*.

dissolve [dɪ'zɒlv] **1** *vt (gen)* dissoudre; *[person] substance* faire dissoudre; *(Culin) sugar* faire fondre. **2** *vi* se dissoudre; *(Cine)* se fondre. **to** ~ **into thin air** s'en aller en fumée; **to** ~ **into tears** fondre en larmes.

dissuade [dɪ'sweɪd] *vt* dissuader *(sb from doing* qn de faire). ◆ **dissuasion** *n* dissuasion *f*. ◆ **dissuasive** *adj voice, person* qui cherche à dissuader; *powers* de dissuasion.

distance ['dɪst(ə)ns] **1** *n* distance *f* (*between* entre). **the ~ between the houses** la distance qui sépare les maisons; **the ~ between the eyes/rails** *etc* l'écartement *m* des yeux/des rails *etc*; **at a ~** à quelque distance; **at a ~ of 2 metres** à une distance de 2 mètres; **what ~ is it from here to London?** nous sommes à combien de Londres?; **it's a good ~** c'est assez loin; **in the ~** au loin, dans le lointain; **from a ~** de loin; **it's within walking ~** on peut y aller à pied; **a short ~ away** à une faible distance; **it's no ~ *** c'est tout près; **at a ~ of 400 years** à 400 ans d'écart; **at this ~ in time** après un tel intervalle de temps; **to keep sb at a ~** tenir qn à distance; **to keep one's ~** garder ses distances. **2** *vt*: **to ~ o.s. from sth** se distancier de qch. **3** *adj*: **~ race/runner** épreuve *f*/coureur *m* de fond.
◆ **distant** *adj (gen)* éloigné; *recollection, country* lointain; *(reserved)* distant, froid; **we had a distant view of the church** nous avons vu l'église de loin; **the school is 2 km distant from the church** l'école est à une distance de 2 km de l'église; **in the distant future/past** dans un avenir/un passé lointain. ◆ **distantly** *adv resemble* vaguement, un peu; *smile, say* froidement, d'une manière distante; **distantly related** d'une parenté éloignée.

distaste ['dɪs'teɪst] *n* répugnance *f* (*for* pour). ◆ **distasteful** *adj* déplaisant (*to* à).

distemper[1] [dɪs'tempəʳ] **1** *n (paint)* détrempe *f*, badigeon *m*. **2** *vt* badigeonner.

distemper[2] [dɪs'tempəʳ] *n [dogs]* maladie *f* des jeunes chiens *or* de Carré.

distend [dɪs'tend] **1** *vt* distendre. **2** *vi* se distendre.

distil(l) [dɪs'tɪl] *vt* distiller. *(Aut)* **~ed water** eau déminéralisée. ◆ **distiller** *n* distillateur *m*. ◆ **distillery** *n* distillerie *f*.

distinct [dɪs'tɪŋ(k)t] *adj* (**a**) *(clear) landmark, voice, memory* distinct, clair; *promise, offer* précis; *preference, likeness, increase, progress* net *(before n)*, marqué. (**b**) *(different)* distinct, différent (*from* de). **as ~ from** par opposition à. ◆ **distinction** *n (gen)* distinction *f*; *(Scol)* **he got a ~ion in French** il a été reçu en français avec mention *f* très bien. ◆ **distinctive** *adj* distinctif. ◆ **distinctly** *adv speak, hear, see* distinctement, clairement; *promise* sans équivoque; *stipulate* expressément; *better* incontestablement; *cool, friendly* vraiment.

distinguish [dɪs'tɪŋgwɪʃ] **1** *vt* (**a**) *(discern) landmark* distinguer, apercevoir; *change* discerner. (**b**) *(make different)* distinguer (*from* de); *(characterize)* caractériser. **to ~ o.s.** se distinguer (*as* en tant que). **2** *vi* distinguer (*between* entre). ◆ **distinguishable** *adj (discernible)* visible, perceptible; **easily ~able from each other** faciles à distinguer l'un de l'autre. ◆ **distinguished** *adj* distingué. ◆ **distinguishing** *adj* distinctif; **~ing mark** *(on passport)* signe *m* particulier.

distort [dɪs'tɔːt] *vt (gen)* déformer; *judgment* fausser. ◆ **distorted** *adj (lit)* déformé, altéré; *(fig) impression* faux, (*f* fausse); **he gave us a ~ed version of the events** il a dénaturé les événements en les racontant. ◆ **distortion** *n (gen)* distorsion *f*; *[facts]* déformation *f*.

distract [dɪs'trækt] *vt* distraire. ◆ **distracted** *adj* éperdu, égaré; **she was quite ~ed** elle était dans tous ses états. ◆ **distractedly** *adv behave, run* comme un fou; *love, weep* éperdument. ◆ **distracting** *adj* qui empêche de se concentrer, *(pej)* gênant. ◆ **distraction** *n* interruption *f*; **to love to ~ion** aimer à la folie; **to drive sb to ~ion** rendre qn fou.

distraught [dɪs'trɔːt] *adj* éperdu (*with* de), égaré.

distress [dɪs'tres] **1** *n* (**a**) peine *f*, *(stronger)* douleur *f*. **to be in great ~** être bouleversé. (**b**) *(poverty)* détresse *f*, misère *f*. (**c**) *(danger)* péril *m*, détresse *f*. **in ~** *ship* en perdition; *plane* en détresse; **comrades in ~** compagnons *mpl* d'infortune. **2** *vt* affliger, peiner. **3** *adj signal* de détresse. ◆ **distressed** *adj* affligé, peiné (*by* par, de); **very ~ed** bouleversé; **~ed area** zone *f* sinistrée. ◆ **distressing** *adj* pénible, affligeant.

distribute [dɪs'trɪbjuːt] *vt leaflets, prizes* distribuer; *money, load, weight* répartir. ◆ **distribution** *n* distribution *f*; répartition *f*. ◆ **distributive** *adj* distributif; **the distributive trades** le secteur de la distribution. ◆ **distributor** *n* (**a**) *(Comm: agent for goods)* concessionnaire *mf*; *[films]* distributeur *m*; (**b**) *(Aut, Tech)* distributeur *m*; *(Aut)* **distributor cap** tête *f* de delco ®.

district ['dɪstrɪkt] **1** *n (of a country)* région *f*; *(in town)* quartier *m*; *(US Pol)* circonscription électorale. **2** *adj manager etc* régional. *(US)* **~ attorney** ≃ procureur *m* de la République; *(US)* **~ court** cour *f* fédérale; **~ nurse** infirmière *f* visiteuse.

distrust [dɪs'trʌst] **1** *vt* se méfier de. **2** *n* méfiance *f* (*of* à l'égard de). ◆ **distrustful** *adj* méfiant (*of* de).

disturb [dɪs'tɜːb] *vt (inconvenience)* déranger; *(worry)* troubler, inquiéter; *silence, sleep, water* troubler; *atmosphere* perturber; *papers* déranger. **sorry to ~ you** excusez-moi de vous déranger; **'please do not ~'** 'prière de ne pas déranger'. ◆ **disturbance** *n (political, social)* troubles *mpl*, émeute *f*; *(in house, street)* tapage *m*; **to cause a ~ance** faire du tapage. ◆ **disturbed** *adj* troublé (*at, by* par); *(Psych)* perturbé. ◆ **disturbing** *adj (alarming)* inquiétant, troublant; *(distracting)* gênant.

disuse ['dɪs'juːs] *n* désuétude *f*. **to fall into ~** tomber en désuétude. ◆ **disused** ['dɪs'juːzd] *adj* désaffecté, abandonné.

ditch [dɪtʃ] **1** *n (gen)* fossé *m*; *(for irrigation)* rigole *f*. **2** *vt (*: get rid of) person* se débarrasser de, laisser tomber *; *car etc* abandonner.

dither * ['dɪðəʳ] **1** *n*: **to be in a ~** être dans tous ses états. **2** *vi* hésiter. **to ~ over a decision** se tâter pour prendre une décision.

ditto ['dɪtəʊ] *adv* idem.

divan [dɪ'væn] **1** *n* divan *m*. **2** *adj*: **~ bed** divan-lit *m*.

dive [daɪv] **1** *n [swimmer, goalkeeper]* plongeon *m*; *[submarine, deep-sea diver]* plongée *f*; *[aircraft]* piqué *m*. **2** *vi (gen: often ~ in)* plonger; *[aircraft]* descendre en piqué. **he ~d in head first** il a piqué une tête dans l'eau; **to ~ for pearls** pêcher des perles; **he ~d under the table** il s'est jeté sous la table; *(rush)* **to ~ in/out *** *etc* entrer/sortir *etc* tête baissée; **he ~d * for the exit** il a foncé tête baissée vers la sortie; **the goalie ~d for the ball** le gardien de but a plongé pour bloquer le ballon. ◆ **dive-bomb** *vt* bombarder en piqué. ◆ **dive-bombing** *n* bombardement *m* en piqué. ◆ **diver** *n* plongeur *m*; *(in suit)* scaphandrier *m*. ◆ **diving** *adj*: **diving bell** cloche *f* à plongeur; **diving board** plongeoir *m*; **diving suit** scaphandre *m*.

diverge [daɪ'vɜːdʒ] *vi* diverger. ◆ **divergence** *n* divergence *f*. ◆ **divergent** *adj* divergent.

diverse [daɪ'vɜːs] *adj* divers, différent. ◆ **diversification** *n* diversification *f*. ◆ **diversify** *vt* diversifier. ◆ **diversity** *n* diversité *f*.

diversion [daɪ'vɜːʃ(ə)n] *n* (**a**) *[traffic]* déviation *f*; *[stream]* dérivation *f*. (**b**) *(amusement)* distraction *f*, diversion *f*. (**c**) *(distraction)* diversion *f*. **to create a ~** *(Mil)* opérer une diversion; *(gen)* faire diversion. ◆ **diversionary** *adj* destiné à faire diversion.

divert [daɪ'vɜːt] *vt stream, conversation, attention, eyes* détourner; *train, plane, ship* dérouter; *traffic* dévier; *blow* écarter; *(amuse)* divertir, distraire, amuser. ◆ **diverting** *adj* divertissant.

divest [daɪ'vest] *vt* dépouiller (*of* de).

divide [dɪ'vaɪd] **1** *vt (gen: often* ~ **up***)* diviser (*into* en; *between, among* entre); *(*~ **out***)* répartir, distribuer (*among* entre); *(*~ **off***)* séparer (*from* de). **they ~d it (amongst themselves)** ils se le sont partagé; **she ~s her time between** elle partage son temps entre; **to ~ 36 by 6** diviser 36 par 6; **policy of ~ and rule** politique *f* consistant à diviser pour régner. **2** *vi [river]* se diviser; *[road]* bifurquer; *(*~ **up***)* se diviser (*into* en); *(Math)* être divisible (*by* par). *(Parl)* **the House ~d** la Chambre a procédé au vote. ◆**divided** *adj (lit)* divisé; *(Bot)* découpé; *(fig) people* divisés (*about, on* sur); *opinions etc* partagés (*on* sur); *couple, country* désuni; **I feel ~d in my own mind about this** je me sens indécis à cet égard; *(US)* **~d highway** route *f* à chaussées séparées *or* à quatre voies; **~d skirt** jupe-culotte *f*. ◆**dividing** *adj fence* mitoyen; *line* de démarcation.

dividend ['dɪvɪdend] *n* dividende *m*.

divine[1] [dɪ'vaɪn] *adj* divin. ◆**divinely** *adv* divinement. ◆**divinity** *n* divinité *f*; *(Univ)* théologie *f*.

divine[2] [dɪ'vaɪn] *vt the future* prédire; *sb's intentions* deviner; *water, metal* découvrir par la radiesthésie. ◆**diviner** *n* radiesthésiste *mf*. ◆**divining rod** *n* baguette *f* de sourcier.

division [dɪ'vɪʒ(ə)n] *n (gen)* division *f* (*into* en, *between, among* entre). ~ **of labour** division du travail; *(Parl)* **to call a** ~ passer au vote. ◆**divisible** *adj* divisible (*by* par). ◆**divisive** [dɪ'vaɪsɪv] *adj* qui sème la discorde. ◆**divisor** *n* diviseur *m*.

divorce [dɪ'vɔːs] **1** *n* divorce *m* (*from* d'avec). **2** *vt* divorcer avec *or* d'avec; *(fig)* séparer (*from* de). **3** *vi* divorcer. **4** *adj*: ~ **court** ≃ tribunal *m* de grande instance; **to start ~ proceedings** demander le divorce. ◆**divorced** *adj (Jur)* divorcé (*from* d'avec); *(fig)* séparé (*from* de). ◆**divorcee** *n* divorcé(e) *m(f)*.

divulge [daɪ'vʌldʒ] *vt* divulguer, révéler.

dizzy ['dɪzɪ] *adj person* pris de vertiges; *(heedless)* étourdi; *height, speed, rise in price* vertigineux. **to feel** ~ *(unwell)* être pris de vertiges; *(from fear of heights)* avoir le vertige; **it makes me** ~ cela me donne le vertige. ◆**dizzily** *adv walk* avec un sentiment de vertige; *rise, fall, spin* vertigineusement. ◆**dizziness** *n* vertiges *mpl*; **an attack of dizziness** un étourdissement.

Djakarta [dʒə'kɑːtə] *n* Djakarta.

do[1] [duː] *3rd person sg pres* **does,** *pret* **did,** *ptp* **done. 1** *aux vb*: ~ **you understand?** (est-ce que) vous comprenez?; **I don't understand** je ne comprends pas; **didn't you speak?** n'avez-vous pas parlé?; **DO come!** venez donc, je vous en prie!; **DO tell him that...** dites-lui bien que...; **but I DO like it!** mais si, je l'aime!; **he DID say it** bien sûr qu'il l'a dit; **so you DO know them!** alors c'est vrai que vous les connaissez!; **I DO wish I could come with you** je voudrais tant pouvoir vous accompagner; **you speak better than I** ~ vous parlez mieux que moi; **she says she will go but she never does** elle dit qu'elle ira, mais elle n'y va jamais; **so ~ I** moi aussi; **neither ~ I** moi non plus; **they said he would go and so he did** on a dit qu'il s'en irait et c'est bien ce qu'il a fait; **you know him, don't you?** vous le connaissez, n'est-ce pas?; **you know him, ~ you?** alors vous le connaissez?; **you DO agree, don't you?** vous êtes bien d'accord, n'est-ce pas?; **she said that, did she?** elle a vraiment dit ça?; **she said that, didn't she?** elle a bien dit ça, n'est-ce pas?; **I like them, don't you?** je les aime, pas vous?; ~ **they really?** vraiment?; **may I come in? — ~!** puis-je entrer? — bien sûr!; **who broke the mirror? — I did** qui est-ce qui a cassé le miroir? — c'est moi.

2 *vt* (**a**) *(gen)* faire. **what are you ~ing now?** qu'est-ce que tu fais?; **what are you ~ing these days?** qu'est-ce que tu deviens?; **what do you ~ for a living?** que faites-vous dans la vie?; **I've got plenty to** ~ j'ai beaucoup à faire; **I shall ~ nothing of the sort** je n'en ferai rien; **don't ~ too much!** n'en faites pas trop!; **he does nothing but complain** il ne fait que se plaindre; **what shall we ~ for money?** comment allons-nous faire pour trouver de l'argent?; **what have you done with my gloves?** qu'avez-vous fait de mes gants?; **what am I to ~ with you?** qu'est-ce que je vais bien pouvoir faire de toi?; **he didn't know what to ~ with himself all day** il ne savait pas quoi faire (de sa peau *) toute la journée; **I shan't know what to ~ with all my free time** je ne saurai pas quoi faire de mon temps libre; **I could ~ with a cup of tea** je prendrais bien une tasse de thé; **I can't ~ with whining children** je ne peux pas supporter les enfants qui pleurnichent; **to ~ without sth** se passer de qch.

(**b**) *(accomplish, produce etc) letter, copy, crossword, sum* faire. **I'll ~ all I can** je ferai tout mon possible; **what's to be done?** que faire?; **what can I ~ for you?** en quoi puis-je vous aider?; **what do you want me to ~ about it?** qu'est-ce que vous voulez que j'y fasse?; **to ~ sth again** refaire qch; **it's all got to be done again** tout est à refaire ; ~ **something for me, will you?** rends-moi (un) service, veux-tu?; **what's done cannot be undone** ce qui est fait est fait; **that's just not done!, that's not the done thing** * cela ne se fait pas!; **well done!** bravo!, très bien!; **that's done it!** * *(dismay)* il ne manquait plus que ça!; *(satisfaction)* ça y est!; **to ~ 6 years in jail** faire 6 ans de prison; *(Scol etc)* **to ~ Milton/German** faire Milton/de l'allemand; **to ~ the flowers** arranger les fleurs (dans les vases); **to ~ one's hair** se coiffer; **to ~ one's nails** se faire les ongles; **this room needs ~ing** cette pièce est à faire; **he's been badly done by** on s'est très mal conduit à son égard; **they ~ you very well at that restaurant** on mange rudement * bien dans ce restaurant; **she does her lodgers proud** elle dorlote ses pensionnaires; **to ~ o.s. well** ne se priver de rien.

(**c**) *(finished)* **the work's done** le travail est fait; **the soap is done** il ne reste plus de savon; **I haven't done * telling you** je n'ai pas fini de vous dire; **done!** entendu!; **to get done with sth** en finir avec qch; **to be done for** * être fichu *; **to be done in** * *(exhausted)* être éreinté.

(**d**) *(visit) city, museum* visiter, faire *.

(**e**) *(Aut etc)* **the car was ~ing 100** la voiture roulait à 100 à l'heure *or* faisait du 100 à l'heure; **we've done 200 km** nous avons fait *or* parcouru 200 km.

(**f**) *(suit)* aller à; *(be sufficient for)* suffire à. **that will ~ me nicely** *(what I want)* cela fera très bien mon affaire; *(enough)* cela me suffit.

(**g**) *(play role of)* faire, jouer le rôle de; *(pretend to be)* faire; *(mimic)* imiter. **she does the worried mother very convincingly** elle joue à la mère inquiète avec beaucoup de conviction.

(**h**) *(*: cheat)* avoir *, refaire *. **you've been done!** on vous a eu * *or* refait! *; **to ~ sb out of £10** refaire * qn de 10 livres; **to ~ sb out of a job** prendre à qn son travail.

(**i**) *(cook)* faire; *(prepare)* faire, préparer. **to ~ the cooking** faire la cuisine; **how do you like your steak done?** comment aimez-vous votre bifteck?; **steak well done** bifteck bien cuit; **done to a turn** à point.

3 *vi* (**a**) *(gen: act etc)* faire, agir. ~ **as your friends** ~ faites comme vos amis; **he did well to take advice** il a bien fait de demander des conseils; **she was up and ~ing at 6 o'clock** elle était à l'ouvrage dès 6 heures du matin.

(**b**) *(fare)* aller, marcher, être. **how do you ~?** *(greeting: gen)* comment allez-vous?; *(on being introduced)* enchanté de faire votre connaissance; **how**

are you ~ing? * comment ça va?; **his business is ~ing well** ses affaires vont *or* marchent bien.
(**c**) *(finish)* finir, terminer. **I've done** c'est fini; **I've done with all that** je ne veux plus rien avoir à faire avec tout ça; **have you done with that book?** vous n'avez plus besoin de ce livre?
(**d**) *(suit)* aller bien, convenir. **that will never ~!** ça ne peut pas aller!; **this room will ~** cette chambre ira bien *or* fera l'affaire; **will it ~ if I come back at 8?** ça va si je reviens à 8 heures?; **it doesn't ~ to tell him...** ce n'est pas la chose à faire que de lui dire...; **this coat will ~ for a cover** ce manteau servira de couverture; **to make ~** s'arranger, se débrouiller (*with* avec); **to make ~ and mend** faire des économies de bouts de chandelle.
(**e**) *(be sufficient)* suffire (*for* pour). **that will ~!** ça suffit!, assez!
(**f**) *(phrases)* **there's nothing ~ing * in this town** il n'y a rien d'intéressant dans cette ville; **£5? — nothing ~ing!** ‡ 5 livres? — rien à faire! * *or* pas question!; **it has to ~ with...** cela concerne...; **money has a lot to ~ with it** c'est surtout une question d'argent; **what has that got to ~ with it?** qu'est-ce que cela a à voir?; **that's got a lot to ~ with it!** cela y est pour beaucoup!; **that has nothing to ~ with the problem** cela n'a rien à voir avec le problème; **that has nothing to ~ with you!** cela ne vous regarde pas!; **I won't have anything to ~ with it** je ne veux pas m'en mêler; **to have to ~ with sb** avoir affaire à qn.
4 *n* (*) (**a**) *(party)* soirée *f*; *(ceremony)* fête *f*.
(**b**) **it's a poor ~** c'est plutôt minable; **the ~s and don'ts** ce qu'il faut faire ou ne pas faire.
◆ **do away with** *vt fus (abolish; kill)* supprimer. ◆ **do in** ‡ *vt sep (kill)* supprimer. ◆ **do out** *vt sep room* faire *or* nettoyer (à fond). ◆ **do up** *vt sep* (**a**) *buttons* boutonner; *zip* fermer; *dress, shoes* attacher; *parcel* faire. **books done up in paper** des livres emballés dans du papier. (**b**) *(renovate) house, room* remettre à neuf, refaire; *old dress etc* rafraîchir. **to ~ o.s. up** se faire beau.
◆ **do-gooder** * *n* pilier *m* de bonnes œuvres. ◆ **doing** *n*: **this is your ~ing** c'est vous qui avez fait cela; **that takes some ~ing** il faut le faire! * ◆ **doings** *n (pl: deeds)* faits *mpl* et gestes *mpl*; *(sg: thingummy)* machin * *m*, truc * *m*. ◆ **do-it-yourself** **1** *n* bricolage *m* ; **2** *adj shop* de bricolage; **~-it-yourself enthusiast** bricoleur *m*, -euse *f*; **the ~-it-yourself craze** la passion du bricolage.

do² [dəʊ] *n (Mus)* do *m*, ut *m*.

docile ['dəʊsaɪl] *adj* docile. ◆ **docility** *n* docilité *f*.

dock¹ [dɒk] **1** *n* dock *m*. *(fig)* **my car is in ~** * ma voiture est en réparation. **2** *vt* mettre à quai. **3** *vi [ship]* arriver à quai; *[two spacecraft]* s'amarrer. **the ship has ~ed** le bateau est à quai.
◆ **docker** *n* docker *m*. ◆ **docking** *n (Space)* amarrage *m*. ◆ **dockyard** *n* chantier naval.

dock² [dɒk] *n (Jur)* banc *m* des accusés.

dock³ [dɒk] *vt tail* couper; *(fig) wages* faire une retenue sur. **to ~ £5 off sb's wages** retenir 5 livres sur le salaire de qn.

dock⁴ [dɒk] *n (Bot)* patience *f*.

docket ['dɒkɪt] **1** *n (on document, parcel)* étiquette *f (indiquant le contenu)*; *(Customs certificate)* récépissé *m* de douane. **2** *vt contents* résumer; *information etc* consigner sommairement; *packet, document* étiqueter.

doctor ['dɒktəʳ] **1** *n* (**a**) *(Med)* docteur *m*, médecin *m*. **D~ Smith** le docteur Smith; **yes ~** oui docteur; **she is a ~** elle est médecin *or* docteur; **a woman ~** une femme docteur, une femme médecin; *(fig)* **it's just what the ~ ordered** * c'est exactement ce qu'il me fallait. (**b**) *(Univ)* **D~ of Law/of Science** *etc* docteur *m* en droit/ès sciences *etc*; **D~ of Philosophy** *(abbr* **PhD***)* docteur ès lettres. **2** *vt* (**a**) *sick person* soigner. (**b**) *(*: castrate)* châtrer *(un animal)*. (**c**) *(tamper with) wine* frelater; *food* altérer; *text, document* arranger; *accounts* falsifier. ◆ **doctorate** *n* doctorat *m* (*in science* ès sciences; *in geography* en géographie).

doctrine ['dɒktrɪn] *n* doctrine *f*. ◆ **doctrinaire** *adj* doctrinaire. ◆ **doctrinal** [dɒk'traɪnl] *adj* doctrinal.

document ['dɒkjʊmənt] **1** *n* document *m*. **~s relating to a case** dossier *m* d'une affaire. **2** ['dɒkjʊment] *vt* documenter. **3** *adj*: **~ case** porte-documents *m inv*. ◆ **documentary** *adj, n* documentaire *(m)*. ◆ **documentation** *n* documentation *f*.

dodder ['dɒdəʳ] *vi* ne pas tenir sur ses jambes. ◆ **dodderer** *n* vieux (*or* vieille) gaga * *m(f)*. ◆ **doddering** *adj* gâteux.

doddle ['dɒd(ə)l] *n*: **it's a ~** c'est simple comme bonjour *.

dodge [dɒdʒ] **1** *n (*: trick, scheme)* truc * *m*. **2** *vt blow, question, difficulty* esquiver; *pursuer* échapper à; *tax* éviter de payer; *work, duty* se dérober à; *acquaintance* éviter. **he ~d the issue** il est volontairement passé à côté de la question. **3** *vi (Boxing, Ftbl)* faire une esquive. **to ~ out of the way** s'esquiver; **to ~ behind a tree** disparaître derrière un arbre; **to ~ through the traffic** se faufiler entre les voitures; **to ~ about** aller et venir, remuer. ◆ **dodgems** *npl* autos *fpl* tamponneuses. ◆ **dodgy** * *adj* épineux, douteux; **in a very dodgy situation** dans une mauvaise passe.

doe [dəʊ] *n (deer)* biche *f*; *(rabbit)* lapine *f*. ◆ **doeskin** *n* peau *f* de daim.

dog [dɒg] **1** *n* chien(ne) *m(f)*; *[fox etc]* mâle *m*. **to lead a ~'s life** mener une vie de chien; *(Sport)* **the ~s** * les courses *fpl* de lévriers; *(fig)* **to go to the ~s** * *[person]* gâcher sa vie; *[institution, business]* aller à vau-l'eau; *(fig)* **it's a real ~'s dinner** *or* **breakfast** * ça a l'air de Dieu sait quoi; **he is being a ~ in the manger** il fait l'empêcheur de tourner en rond; **he hasn't a ~'s chance** * il n'a pas la moindre chance de réussir; **give a ~ a bad name and hang him** qui veut noyer son chien l'accuse de la rage; **lucky ~** * veinard(e) * *m(f)*; **dirty ~** * sale type * *m*. **2** *adj breed, show* canin; *collar* de chien; *food, biscuit* pour chien; *wolf, fox* mâle. **~ basket** panier *m* de chien; **~ breeder** éleveur *m*, -euse *f* de chiens; **~ guard** barrière *f* pour chien *(à l'arrière d'une voiture)*; **~ handler** maître-chien *m;* **~ licence** permis *m* de posséder un chien; **~ tag** *(US Mil)* plaque *f* d'identification *(portée au cou par les militaires)*. **3** *vt* suivre (de près). **he ~s my footsteps** il ne me lâche pas d'une semelle; **~ged by ill fortune** poursuivi par la malchance. ◆ **dog-eared** *adj* écorné. ◆ **dogged** *adj person* tenace; *courage* opiniâtre. ◆ **doggedly** *adv* avec ténacité *or* opiniâtreté. ◆ **doggo** * *adv*: **to lie ~go** se tenir coi; *[criminal]* se terrer. ◆ **doggy bag** *n* petit sac pour emporter les restes. ◆ **doghouse** *n*: **he is in the ~house** * il n'est pas en odeur de sainteté. ◆ **dogleg** *n (in road etc)* coude *m*, virage *m*. ◆ **doglike** *adj* de chien. ◆ **dog-paddle** *vi* nager en chien. ◆ **dogsbody** * *n* factotum *m*, bonne *f* à tout faire. ◆ **dog-tired** * *adj* claqué *, éreinté.

doggerel ['dɒg(ə)r(ə)l] *n* vers *mpl* de mirliton.

dogie ['dəʊgɪ] *n (US)* veau *m* sans mère.

dogma ['dɒgmə] *n* dogme *m*. ◆ **dogmatic** *adj person, attitude* dogmatique (*about* sur); *tone* autoritaire. ◆ **dogmatically** *adv* d'un ton autoritaire.

doh [dəʊ] *n (Mus)* = **do²**.

doldrums ['dɒldrəmz] *npl (fig)* **to be in the ~** *[person]* avoir le cafard *; *[business]* être dans le marasme.

dole [dəʊl] *n* indemnité *f* de chômage. **on the ~** au chômage. ◆ **dole out** *vt sep* distribuer au compte-gouttes.

doleful ['dəʊlf(ʊ)l] *adj* lugubre, morne. ◆ **dolefully** *adv* d'une manière lugubre *or* morne.

doll [dɒl] *n* (**a**) poupée *f*. **to play with ~s** jouer à la poupée; **~'s house/pram** maison *f*/voiture *f* de poupée. (**b**) (*‡: esp US: girl)* nana ‡ *f*, pépée ‡ *f*; *(pretty girl)* poupée *f*; *(attractive person)* **he's/she's a ~** il/elle est chou *. ◆ **doll up** * *vt sep*: **to ~ o.s. up** se faire (tout) beau *.

dollar ['dɒləʳ] **1** *n* dollar *m*. **2** *adj*: **~ area** zone *f* dollar; **~ bill** billet *m* d'un dollar.

dollop * ['dɒləp] *n [butter etc]* bon morceau *m*; *[cream, jam]* bonne cuillerée *f*.

dolphin ['dɒlfɪn] *n (Zool)* dauphin *m*.

dolt [dəʊlt] *n* balourd(e) *m(f)*. ◆ **doltish** *adj* gourde *, cruche *.

domain [dəʊ'meɪn] *n* domaine *m*.

dome [dəʊm] *n* dôme *m*. ◆ **domed** *adj forehead* bombé; *building* à dôme.

Domesday Book ['du:mzdeɪˌbʊk] *n* Domesday Book *m (recueil cadastral établi par Guillaume le Conquérant)*.

domestic [də'mestɪk] **1** *adj duty, happiness* familial, de famille; *(Econ, Pol) policy, affairs, flights* intérieur; *animal* domestique. **everything of a ~ nature** tout ce qui se rapporte au ménage; **~ chores** travaux *m* du ménage; **~ science** arts ménagers; **~ science college** école *f* d'art ménager; **~ science teaching** enseignement *m* ménager; **~ servants** employé(e)s *m(f)pl* de maison; **she was in ~ service** elle était domestique; **~ staff** *[hospital]* personnel *m* auxiliaire; *[house]* domestiques *mfpl*. **2** *n* domestique *mf*. ◆ **domesticate** *vt animal* domestiquer. ◆ **domesticated** *adj person* qui aime son intérieur; *animal* domestiqué; **she's very ~ated** elle est très femme d'intérieur. ◆ **domesticity** *n (home life)* vie *f* de famille.

domicile ['dɒmɪsaɪl] *n* domicile *m*. ◆ **domiciled** *adj* domicilié (*at* à). ◆ **domiciliary** *adj* domiciliaire.

dominate ['dɒmɪneɪt] *vti* dominer. ◆ **dominance** *n (gen, Pol)* prédominance *f*; *(Genetics, Psych)* dominance *f*. ◆ **dominant** **1** *adj (gen)* dominant; *(overbearing)* dominateur; *(Mus)* de dominante ; **2** *n (Mus)* dominante *f*. ◆ **domination** *n* domination *f*.

domineer [ˌdɒmɪ'nɪəʳ] *vi* se montrer autoritaire (*over* avec). ◆ **domineering** *adj* dominateur, autoritaire.

Dominican Republic [də'mɪnɪkənrɪ'pʌblɪk] *n* République *f* Dominicaine.

dominion [də'mɪnɪən] *n* (**a**) *(power)* domination *f*, empire *m* (*over* sur). (**b**) *(territory)* territoire *m*, possessions *fpl*; *(Brit Pol)* dominion *m*.

domino, *pl* **-es** ['dɒmɪnəʊ] *n* domino *m*. **~es** *(sg: game)* (jeu *m* de) dominos *mpl*; **~ effect** effet *m* d'entraînement.

don¹ [dɒn] *n* ≃ professeur *m* d'université.

don² [dɒn] *vt garment* revêtir, mettre.

donate [də(ʊ)'neɪt] *vt* faire don de. ◆ **donation** *n (act)* donation *f*; *(gift)* don *m*.

done [dʌn] *ptp of* **do¹**.

donkey ['dɒŋkɪ] **1** *n* âne(sse) *m(f)*; (*: *fool)* imbécile *mf*. **she hasn't been here for ~'s years** * il y a une éternité qu'elle n'est pas venue ici. **2** *adj*: **the ~ work** le gros du travail.

donor ['dəʊnəʳ] *n (gen)* donateur *m*, -trice *f*; *(Med)* donneur *m*, -euse *f*.

don't know ['dəʊnt'nəʊ] *n* sans opinion *mpl*.

donut ['dəʊnʌt] *n (US)* beignet *m*.

doodle ['du:dl] *vi* griffonner (distraitement).

doom [du:m] **1** *n (ruin)* ruine *f*; *(fate)* sort *m*. **2** *vt* condamner (*to* à). **~ed to failure** voué à l'échec. ◆ **doomed** *adj thing* voué à l'échec; *person* perdu d'avance. ◆ **doomsday** *n (fig)* **till ~sday** jusqu'à la fin des temps.

door [dɔ:ʳ] *n (gen)* porte *f*; *[railway carriage, car]* portière *f*. **he shut the ~ in my face** il m'a fermé la porte au nez; **'pay at the ~'** 'billets à l'entrée'; **2 ~s down the street** 2 portes plus loin; **out of ~s** (au-)dehors. ◆ **doorbell** *n* sonnette *f*; **there's the ~bell!** on sonne à la porte! ◆ **door chain** *n* chaîne *f* de sûreté. ◆ **door-handle** *or* ◆ **doorknob** *n* poignée *f* de porte (*or* de portière). ◆ **doorkeeper** *or* ◆ **doorman** *n [hotel]* portier *m*; *[block of flats]* concierge *m*. ◆ **door-knocker** *n* heurtoir *m*. ◆ **doormat** *n* paillasson *m* (d'entrée); (*: *person)* chiffe *f* molle. ◆ **doorstep** *n* pas *m* de porte; **at my ~step** à ma porte. ◆ **door-to-door** *adj salesman* à domicile ; **~-to-~ selling** porte à porte *m inv*. ◆ **doorway** *n* porte *f*; **in the ~way** dans l'embrasure *f* de la porte.

dope [dəʊp] **1** *n* (**a**) (*: *drugs)* drogue *f*; *(for athlete, horse)* dopant *m*. **to take ~** se droguer, se doper. (**b**) *(information)* tuyaux * *mpl*, renseignements *mpl*. **to give sb the ~** ‡ tuyauter * qn. (**c**) (*‡: stupid person)* andouille ‡ *f*, idiot(e) *m(f)*. **2** *vt horse, person* doper; *food* mettre une drogue *or* un dopant dans. ◆ **doping** *n* dopage *m*. ◆ **dope-peddler** * *or* ◆ **dope-pusher** * *n* revendeur *m*, -euse *f* de drogue. ◆ **dope-test** * *n* contrôle *m* anti-doping *inv*. ◆ **dopey** * *adj (drugged)* drogué; *(sleepy)* à moitié endormi; *(stupid)* abruti *.

dormant ['dɔ:mənt] *adj energy* en veilleuse; *(Bio, Bot)* dormant; *volcano* en sommeil; *rule* inappliqué. **to lie ~** rester en sommeil.

dormer window ['dɔ:mə'wɪndəʊ] *n* lucarne *f*.

dormitory ['dɔ:mɪtrɪ] **1** *n* dortoir *m*; *(US Univ)* résidence *f* universitaire. **2** *adj suburb, town* dortoir *f inv*.

Dormobile ['dɔ:məbi:l] *n* ® camping-car *m*.

dormouse, *pl* **-mice** ['dɔ:maʊs, maɪs] *n* loir *m*.

dose [dəʊs] **1** *n* (**a**) *(Pharm)* dose *f*. **give him a ~ of medicine** donne-lui son médicament; *(fig)* **to give sb a ~ of his own medicine** rendre à qn la monnaie de sa pièce; **in small ~s** à faible dose; (*: *fig)* à petites doses. (**b**) *(bout of illness)* attaque *f* (*of* de). **a ~ of flu** une bonne grippe *. **2** *vt person* administrer un médicament à. **she's always dosing herself** elle se bourre de médicaments. ◆ **dosage** *n (on medicine bottle)* posologie *f*.

doss [dɒs] *vi*: **to ~ down** * loger quelque part. ◆ **doss-house** *n* asile *m* (de nuit).

dossier ['dɒsɪeɪ] *n* dossier *m*.

dot [dɒt] **1** *n (gen)* point *m*; *(on material)* pois *m*. *(Morse)* **~s and dashes** points et traits *mpl*; *(in punctuation)* **~s** points de suspension; *(fig)* **on the ~** * à l'heure pile *. **2** *vt (fig)* **to ~ one's i's and cross one's t's** mettre les points sur les i; **field ~ted with flowers** champ parsemé de fleurs; **cars ~ted along the route** des voitures échelonnées sur le parcours; **~ted line** ligne pointillée; **to tear along the ~ted line** détacher suivant le pointillé; **to sign on the ~ted line** signer sur la ligne pointillée; *(fig)* accepter. ◆ **dot matrix printer** *n* imprimante matricielle. ◆ **dotty** ‡ *adj* toqué *, fou (*about* de).

dote [dəʊt] *vi*: **to ~ on sb/sth** aimer qn/qch à la folie; **her doting father** son père qui l'adore. ◆ **dotage** *n*: **in one's dotage** gâteux.

double ['dʌbl] **1** *adj (gen)* double; *door* à deux battants; *room* pour deux personnes; *bed* de deux personnes. **~ seven five four** *(7754)* deux fois sept cinq quatre; *(telephone number)* soixante-dix-sept cinquante-quatre; **spelt with a ~ 'p'** écrit avec deux 'p'; **~ agent** agent *m* double; *(Aut)* **~ bend**

virage *m* en S; ~ **bill** double programme *m;* ~ **bind** * situation *f* sans issue; ~ **consonant** consonne *f* double; ~ **chin** double menton *m*; ~ **glazing** double vitrage *m;* **with a** ~ **meaning** à double sens; ~ **saucepan** casserole *f* à double fond; *(Typ)* **in** ~ **spacing** à double interligne; **a** ~ **whisky** un double whisky; **to lead a** ~ **life** mener une double vie; **to play a** ~ **game** jouer un double jeu; **to have** ~ **standards** avoir deux poids, deux mesures; **to earn** ~ **time** être payé double; **to do a** ~ **take** * marquer un temps d'arrêt (par surprise).

2 *adv (twice)* deux fois; *(twofold) fold, bend* en deux; *see* double. **I've got** ~ **what you've got** j'en ai deux fois plus que toi, j'ai le double de ce que tu as.

3 *n* (**a**) *(twice sth)* double *m*. *(Tennis)* **mixed/ladies'** ~**s** double *m* mixte/dames; ~ **or quits** quitte ou double; *(running)* **at the** ~ au pas de course. (**b**) *(exactly similar thing)* réplique *f*; *(person)* sosie *m*; *(Cine: stand-in)* doublure *f*.

4 *vt (multiply by two)* doubler; *(fold:* ~ **over***)* plier en deux, replier. *(Theat)* **to** ~ **the parts of** jouer les deux rôles de; **to** ~ **sb's part** être la doublure de qn.

5 *vi [prices etc]* doubler; *(Cards)* contrer. *(Bridge)* ~! contre!; *(Theat)* **he** ~**d as...** il jouait aussi le rôle de...

◆ **double back 1** *vi* revenir sur ses pas; *[road]* faire un brusque crochet. **2** *vt sep* replier. ◆ **double up** *vi* (**a**) *(bend: also* ~ **over***)* se plier, se courber. **to** ~ **up with laughter/pain** être plié en deux de rire/de douleur. (**b**) *(share room)* partager une chambre (*with* avec).

◆ **double-barrelled** *adj gun* à deux coups; *surname* à rallonges *. ◆ **double bass** *n* contrebasse *f*. ◆ **double-blind** *adj experiment* en double aveugle; *method* à double insu. ◆ **double-breasted** *adj* croisé *(veston)*. ◆ **double-book** *vt room, seat* réserver pour deux personnes différentes. ◆ **double-check 1** *vti* revérifier ; **2** *n* revérification *f*. ◆ **double-cross** * *vt* trahir, doubler *. ◆ **double-dealer** *n* fourbe *m*. ◆ **double-dealing 1** *n* double jeu *m*, duplicité *f* ; **2** *adj* faux (comme un jeton *). ◆ **double-decker** *n (bus)* autobus *m* à impériale; *(sandwich)* sandwich *m* à deux garnitures superposées. ◆ **double-declutch** *vi* faire un double débrayage. ◆ **double-dutch** * *n* charabia * *m*. ◆ **double entendre** [ˌdu:blɒn'tɒndrə] *n* ambiguïté *f*. ◆ **double-glaze** *vt*: **to** ~**-glaze a window** poser une double fenêtre. ◆ **double-glazing** *n*: **to put in** ~**-glazing** faire installer des doubles fenêtres. ◆ **double-jointed** *adj* désarticulé. ◆ **double-knitting** *adj wool* sport *inv*. ◆ **double-lock** *vt* fermer à double tour. ◆ **double-park** *vi* stationner en double file. ◆ **double-quick** *adv run etc* au pas de course; *do, finish* en vitesse. ◆ **double-talk** *n (pej)* paroles *fpl* trompeuses. ◆ **doubly** *adv (gen)* doublement, deux fois plus; **to be doubly careful** redoubler de prudence.

doubt [daʊt] **1** *n* doute *m*. **to be in** ~ *[person]* être dans le doute (*about* au sujet de); *[sb's honesty etc]* être en doute; **there is room for** ~ il est permis de douter; **to cast** ~**(s) on** jeter le doute sur; **there is some** ~ **about** on ne sait pas très bien si + *indic*; **to have one's** ~**s about sth** avoir des doutes sur qch; **I have my** ~**s about whether** je doute que + *subj*; **I have no** ~**(s) about it** je n'en doute pas; **there is no** ~ **that** il n'y a pas de doute que + *indic*; **no** ~ sans doute; **no** ~ **he will come** sans doute qu'il viendra; **without (a)** ~ sans aucun doute; **beyond** ~ *(adj)* indubitable; *(adv)* indubitablement; **if in** ~ en cas de doute.

2 *vt* (**a**) *person, sb's honesty, statement* douter de. **I** ~ **it very much** j'en doute fort; **I** ~**ed my own eyes** je n'en croyais pas mes yeux; ~**ing Thomas** Thomas *m* l'incrédule.
(**b**) douter (*whether, if* que + *subj*). **I don't** ~ **that he will come** je ne doute pas qu'il vienne; **she didn't** ~ **that he would come** elle ne doutait pas qu'il viendrait; **I** ~ **he won't come now** je crains qu'il ne vienne pas maintenant.

◆ **doubter** *n* incrédule *mf*. ◆ **doubtful** *adj (undecided) person, look* indécis, peu convaincu; *question* douteux, discutable; *result* indécis; *(questionable) person, affair* suspect, louche; *taste* douteux; **to be** ~**ful about sb/sth** avoir des doutes sur qn/qch; **to be** ~**ful about doing** hésiter à faire; **I'm a bit** ~**ful** je n'en suis pas sûr; **it is** ~**ful whether** *or* **that** il est douteux que + *subj*. ◆ **doubtfully** *adv (unconvincedly)* d'un air de doute; *(hesitatingly)* d'une façon indécise. ◆ **doubtfulness** *n (hesitation)* indécision *f*; *(uncertainty)* incertitude *f*; *(suspicious quality)* caractère *m* louche. ◆ **doubtless** *adv* très probablement.

douche [du:ʃ] **1** *n (shower bath)* douche *f*; *(Med: internal)* lavage *m* interne. *(fig)* **it was like a cold** ~ cela a été une douche froide. **2** *vt* doucher.

dough [dəʊ] *n* (**a**) pâte *f*. **bread** ~ pâte à pain. (**b**) (‡: *money)* fric ‡ *m*, argent *m*. ◆ **doughnut** *n* beignet *m*. ◆ **doughy** *adj consistency* pâteux; *bread* mal cuit.

dour ['dʊə^r] *adj (hard)* austère; *(stubborn)* buté.

douse [daʊs] *vt (drench)* tremper; *flames* éteindre.

dove [dʌv] *n* colombe *f (also Pol)*. ◆ **dovecote** *n* colombier *m*. ◆ **dove-grey** *adj* gris perle *inv*. ◆ **dovetail 1** *vt plans etc* faire concorder, raccorder ; **2** *vi [piece of wood]* se raccorder (*into* à); *[plans]* concorder.

Dover ['dəʊvə^r] *n* Douvres.

dowager ['daʊədʒə^r] *n* douairière *f*.

dowdy ['daʊdɪ] *adj* sans chic. ◆ **dowdiness** *n* manque *m* de chic.

down[1] [daʊn] **1** *adv* (**a**) *move* en bas, vers le bas; *(to ground)* à terre, par terre. *(to dog)* ~! couché!; ~ **with traitors!** à bas les traîtres!; **to come** *or* **go** ~ descendre; **to fall** ~ tomber; ~ **and** ~ de plus en plus bas; **to run** ~ descendre en courant; **he came** ~ **from London yesterday** il est arrivé de Londres hier; **we're going** ~ **to the sea tomorrow** demain nous allons à la mer; *(Univ)* **he came** ~ **from Oxford in 1973** il est sorti d'Oxford en 1973; **from 1700** ~ **to the present** depuis 1700 jusqu'à nos jours; **from the biggest** ~ **to the smallest** du plus grand jusqu'au plus petit.
(**b**) *stay* en bas. ~ **there** en bas (là-bas); ~ **here** ici, en bas; ~ **under** aux Antipodes *(Australie etc)*; **don't hit a man when he is** ~ ne frappez pas un homme à terre; **the sun is** ~ le soleil est couché; **the blinds were** ~ les stores étaient baissés; **Paul isn't** ~ **yet** Paul n'est pas encore descendu; **I've been** ~ **with flu** j'ai été au lit avec une grippe; **the tyre is** ~ le pneu est dégonflé; **his temperature is** ~ sa température a baissé; **I'm £2** ~ **on what I expected** j'ai 2 livres de moins que je ne pensais; **I've got it** ~ **in my diary** je l'ai inscrit sur mon agenda; **did you get** ~ **what he said?** est-ce que vous avez noté ce qu'il a dit?; **let's get it** ~ **on paper** mettons-le par écrit; *[computer]* **to go** ~ tomber en panne; **it's** ~ **to him to do it** c'est à lui de le faire; **to be** ~ **for the next race** être inscrit dans la course suivante; **to be** ~ **on sb** * avoir une dent contre qn; **I am** ~ **on my luck** je n'ai pas de chance.

2 *prep roll* du haut en bas de; *drip* le long de. **he ran his finger** ~ **the list** il a parcouru la liste du doigt; **he went** ~ **the hill** il a descendu la colline; **he's** ~ **the hill** il est en bas de la côte; ~ **the street (from us)** plus bas *or* plus loin (que nous) dans la rue; **he was walking** ~ **the street** il descendait la rue; **he has gone** ~ **town** il est allé *or* descendu en ville; **looking** ~ **this street, you can see...** si vous

regardez le long de cette rue, vous verrez...; ~ **the ages** au cours des siècles.
3 *n*: **to have a ~ on sb** * avoir une dent contre qn.
4 *vt opponent* terrasser, abattre; *enemy plane* descendre *. **to ~ tools** *(stop work)* cesser le travail; *(strike)* se mettre en grève; **he ~ed * a glass of beer** il a vidé un verre de bière.
5 *adj* (**a**) *train, platform* en provenance de Londres. *(fig)* **on the ~ grade** sur le déclin; **~ payment** acompte *m*. (**b**) **to be** *or* **feel ~** avoir le cafard *. (**c**) *computer* en panne.
◆ **down-and-out** **1** *adj (Boxing)* hors de combat; *(destitute)* sur le pavé ; **2** *n (tramp)* clochard *m*; *(penniless)* sans-le-sou *m*. ◆ **down-at-heel** *adj person, appearance* miteux; *shoes* éculé. ◆ **downcast** *adj (discouraged)* abattu, démoralisé; *eyes* baissé. ◆ **downfall** *n* chute *f*, ruine *f*. ◆ **downgrade** *vt person* rétrograder; *thing* déclasser. ◆ **down-hearted** *adj* découragé; **don't be ~hearted** ne te laisse pas décourager! ◆ **downhill** **1** *adv*: **to go ~hill** *[road]* descendre; *[car]* descendre la pente; *(fig) [person]* être sur le déclin; *[business etc]* péricliter. **2** *adj (Ski)* **~hill race** descente *f*; **~hill racing** (ski *m* de) descente *f*. ◆ **down-in-the-mouth** *adj* abattu, démoralisé. ◆ **down-market** *adj goods* bas de gamme *inv*; **it's rather ~-market** *[programme etc]* c'est plutôt du genre grand public. ◆ **downpour** *n* pluie *f* torrentielle. ◆ **downright** **1** *adj person* franc, direct; *refusal* catégorique; *lie* effronté; *rudeness* flagrant; **it's a ~right lie to say...** c'est mentir effrontément que de dire... ; **2** *adv rude* carrément; *refuse* catégoriquement; *impossible* purement et simplement. ◆ **downstage** *adv* sur *or* vers le devant de la scène (*from* par rapport à). ◆ **downstairs** **1** *adj (on the ground floor)* du rez-de-chaussée; *(on the floor underneath)* de l'étage au-dessous; *(below)* d'en bas ; **2** *adv* au rez-de-chaussée; à l'étage inférieur; en bas; **to come** *or* **go ~stairs** descendre (l'escalier). ◆ **downstate** *(US)* **1** *n* campagne *f*, sud *m* de l'État ; **2** *adj* de campagne, du sud de l'État ; **3** *adv go* vers la campagne *or* le sud. ◆ **downstream** *adv* en aval. ◆ **down-to-earth** *adj* terre-à-terre *inv*. ◆ **downtown** **1** *adv* en ville ; **2** *adj*: **~town Chicago** le centre de Chicago. ◆ **downtrodden** *adj* opprimé, tyrannisé. ◆ **downward** **1** *adj movement, pull* vers le bas; *road* qui descend en pente; *glance* baissé; *trend* à la baisse ; **2** *adv (also* **~wards***) go, look* vers le bas, en bas; **face ~ward(s)** *person* face contre terre; *object* face en dessous; **from the 10th century ~ward(s)** à partir du Xᵉ siècle; **from the king ~ward(s)** depuis le roi (jusqu'au plus humble). ◆ **downwind** *adv* sous le vent (*of, from* par rapport à).

down² [daʊn] *n [bird, person, plant]* duvet *m*; *[fruit]* peau *f* (veloutée). ◆ **downie** *n (quilt)* couette *f*. ◆ **downy** *adj skin, leaf* duveté; *softness* duveteux; *peach* velouté.

down³ [daʊn] *n (hill)* colline *f (herbeuse)*.

Down's syndrome ['daʊnz,sɪndrəʊm] *n* trisomie *f* 21. **a Down's baby** un bébé trisomique.

dowry ['daʊrɪ] *n* dot *f*.

dowse [daʊz] *vi* faire de la radiesthésie (*for* pour trouver). ◆ **dowser** *n* radiesthésiste *mf*. ◆ **dowsing rod** *n* baguette *f* (de sourcier).

doze [dəʊz] **1** *n* somme *m*. **2** *vi* sommeiller, faire un petit somme. **to be dozing** être assoupi; **to ~ off** s'assoupir. ◆ **dozy** *adj (sleepy)* somnolent; *(*: stupid)* pas très dégourdi.

dozen ['dʌzn] *n* douzaine *f*. **a ~ shirts** une douzaine de chemises; **a round ~** une bonne douzaine; **half-a-~** une demi-douzaine; **20p a ~** 20 pence la douzaine; **~s of times** des dizaines *or* douzaines de fois; **~s of people** des dizaines de gens.

drab [dræb] *adj* terne. ◆ **drabness** *n* caractère *m or* aspect *m* terne.

drachm [dræm] *n* (**a**) *(Measure, Pharm)* drachme *f*. (**b**) = **drachma**.

drachma, *pl* **-s** *or* **drachmae** ['drækmə, 'drækmi:] *n (coin)* drachme *f*.

draconian [drə'kəʊnɪən] *adj* draconien.

draft [drɑ:ft] **1** *n* (**a**) *(gen)* avant-projet *m*; *[letter]* brouillon *m*; *[novel]* ébauche *f*. (**b**) *(for money)* traite *f*. (**c**) *(Mil: group)* détachement *m*; *(US Mil: conscript intake)* contingent *m*. (**d**) *(US)* = **draught**.
2 *adj letter, essay* au brouillon; *version* préliminaire. *(US Mil)* **~ board** conseil *m* de révision; **~ dodger** insoumis *m*. **3** *vt* (**a**) (**~ out**) *letter* faire le brouillon de; *speech* écrire, préparer; *bill, contract* rédiger; *plan, diagram* esquisser. (**b**) *(US Mil) conscript* appeler (sous les drapeaux). *(esp Mil)* **to ~ sb to a post/to do sth** détacher *or* désigner qn à un poste/pour faire qch. ◆ **draftee** *n (US: Mil, fig)* recrue *f*.

drag [dræg] **1** *n* (**a**) *(for dredging etc)* drague *f*; *(cluster of hooks)* araignée *f*; (**~ net**) drège *f*. (**b**) *(Aviat, Naut: resistance)* résistance *f*. *(nuisance)* **what a ~!** * quelle barbe! * (**c**) (*: *clothing)* travesti *m*. **in ~** en travesti. (**d**) *(US)* **the main ~** la grand-rue.
2 *adj (US)* **~ race** course *f* de hot-rods à départ arrêté; *(Theat)* **~ show** * spectacle *m* de travestis.
3 *vi (gen)* traîner (à terre); *[anchor]* chasser. **4** *vt* (**a**) *object* traîner, tirer; *person* traîner, entraîner. **to ~ one's feet** traîner les pieds; *(fig)* traîner (exprès); **to ~ the truth from sb** arracher la vérité à qn. (**b**) *river* draguer (*for* à la recherche de).
◆ **drag about** **1** *vi* traîner. **2** *vt sep* traîner, trimbaler *. **to ~ o.s. about (in pain** *etc***)** se traîner péniblement (sous l'effet de la douleur *etc*).
◆ **drag along** *vt sep person* entraîner (à contre-cœur); *toy etc* tirer. **to ~ o.s. along** se traîner.
◆ **drag away** *vt sep* arracher (*from* à), emmener de force (*from* de). ◆ **drag down** *vt sep* entraîner (en bas); *[illness]* affaiblir. *(fig)* **to ~ sb down to one's own level** rabaisser qn à son niveau. ◆ **drag in** *vt sep subject* tenir à placer. ◆ **drag on** *vi [meeting, conversation]* s'éterniser.

dragon ['dræg(ə)n] *n* dragon *m*. ◆ **dragonfly** *n* libellule *f*.

dragoon [drə'gu:n] **1** *n (Mil)* dragon *m*. **2** *vt*: **to ~ sb into doing** contraindre qn à faire.

dragster ['drægstəʳ] *n (US)* voiture *f* au moteur gonflé, hot-rod *m*.

drain [dreɪn] **1** *n* (**a**) *(in town)* égout *m*; *(in house)* canalisation *f* sanitaire, tuyau *m* d'écoulement; *(on washing machine etc)* tuyau d'écoulement; *(Agr, Med)* drain *m*; (**~ cover**) *(in street)* bouche *f* d'égout; *(beside house)* puisard *m*. **open ~** canal *m or* égout à ciel ouvert; *(fig)* **to throw one's money down the ~** jeter son argent par les fenêtres; **all his hopes have gone down the ~** * voilà tous ses espoirs à l'eau *. (**b**) *(on resources, manpower)* perte *f* (*on* en); *(on strength)* épuisement *m* (*on* de). **it has been a great ~ on her** cela l'a complètement épuisée.
2 *vt land, marshes* assécher; *vegetables* égoutter; *mine, wound* drainer; *reservoir, boiler* vider; *glass* vider complètement; *wine in glass* boire jusqu'à la dernière goutte. **to ~ a country of resources** saigner un pays. **3** *vi [liquid, stream]* s'écouler (*into* dans); *[vegetables, dishes]* s'égoutter.
◆ **drain away, drain off** **1** *vi [liquid]* s'écouler; *[strength]* s'épuiser. **2** *vt sep liquid* faire couler.
◆ **drainage** **1** *n (act of draining)* assèchement *m*, drainage *m*; *(system)* système *m* de fossés *(land) or* d'égouts *(town etc)* ; **2** *adj (Geog)* **~age basin** bassin *m* hydrographique; *(Med)* **~age tube** drain *m*. ◆ **drainer** *n* égouttoir *m*. ◆ **drain(ing) board** *n* égouttoir *m*, paillasse *f*. ◆ **drainpipe** *n* tuyau *m* d'écoulement *or* de drainage.

drake [dreɪk] *n* canard *m* (mâle).

drama ['drɑːmə] **1** *n (gen)* drame *m*; *(dramatic art)* théâtre *m*. **English ~** le théâtre anglais. **2** *adj*: **~ critic** critique *m* dramatique. ◆**dramatic** *adj art, criticism* dramatique; *news, situation, event* dramatique; *effect, entry* théâtral; *change* spectaculaire. ◆**dramatically** *adv* d'une manière dramatique *or* théâtrale *or* spectaculaire. ◆**dramatics** *npl* art *m* dramatique; *(*: fig)* comédie *f (fig)*. ◆**dramatis personae** *npl* personnages *mpl (d'une pièce etc)*. ◆**dramatist** *n* auteur *m* dramatique. ◆**dramatization** *n* adaptation *f* pour la scène *etc*. ◆**dramatize** *vt (gen)* dramatiser; *(adapt) novel etc* adapter pour la scène *or (Cine)* pour l'écran *or (TV)* pour la télévision; *episodes from sb's life* présenter sous forme de sketch.

drank [dræŋk] *pret of* **drink.**

drape [dreɪp] **1** *vt (gen)* draper (*with* de); *room, altar* tendre (*with* de). **2** *n*: **~s** tentures *fpl*; *(US)* rideaux *mpl*. ◆**draper** *n* marchand(e) *m(f)* de nouveautés. ◆**drapery** *n (material)* draperie *f*, étoffes *fpl*; *(hangings)* tentures *fpl*; *(shop)* magasin *m* de nouveautés.

drastic ['dræstɪk] *adj remedy* énergique; *effect, change* radical; *measures* énergique, draconien; *price reduction* massif. ◆**drastically** *adv* radicalement.

drat * [dræt] *excl* zut! * ◆**dratted** * *adj* sacré * *(before n)*.

draught [drɑːft] **1** *n* (**a**) courant *m* d'air; *(for fire)* tirage *m*; *(Naut)* tirant *m* d'eau. *(fig)* **to feel the ~** devoir se serrer la ceinture. (**b**) *[medicine]* breuvage *m*. **a ~ of cider** un coup de cidre; **to drink in long ~s** boire à longs traits. (**c**) **(game of) ~s** (jeu *m* de) dames *fpl*. **2** *adj animal* de trait; *beer* à la pression. **~ excluder** bourrelet *m (de porte etc)*. ◆**draughtboard** *n* damier *m*. ◆**draughtiness** *n* courants *mpl* d'air. ◆**draughtproof** **1** *adj* calfeutré ; **2** *vt* calfeutrer. ◆**draughtsman** *n (Art)* dessinateur *m*, -trice *f*; *(in drawing office)* dessinateur, -trice industriel(le). ◆**draughtsmanship** *n [artist]* talent *m* de dessinateur; *(in industry) art m* du dessin industriel. ◆**draughty** *adj room* plein de courants d'air; *street corner* exposé à tous les vents.

draw [drɔː] *(vb: pret* **drew,** *ptp* **drawn)** **1** *n* (**a**) *(lottery)* tombola *f*; *(act of ~ing)* tirage *m* au sort. (**b**) match *m* nul, partie *f* nulle. **the match ended in a ~** ils ont fini par faire match nul. (**c**) *(attraction)* attraction *f*. **Dirk Bogarde was the big ~** Dirk Bogarde était la grande attraction. (**d**) **to be quick on the ~** avoir la détente rapide; *(fig)* avoir la repartie facile.

2 *vt* (**a**) *(pull) object, bolt, curtains, cart, train* tirer; *caravan, trailer* remorquer. **to ~ a bow** tirer à l'arc; **to ~ one's hand over one's eyes** se passer la main sur les yeux; **I drew her arm through mine** j'ai passé son bras sous le mien; **to ~ one's finger along a surface** passer le doigt sur une surface; **to ~ one's hat over one's eyes** baisser son chapeau sur ses yeux; *(aim)* **to ~ a bead on sth** viser qch.

(**b**) *(extract) (from pocket, bag, tap, pump)* tirer (*from* de); *(from well)* puiser (*from* dans); *sword* dégainer; *teeth* arracher; *cork, money from bank* retirer (*from* de); *cheque* tirer (*on* sur); *salary* toucher; *(Culin) fowl* vider. *(fig)* **to ~ sb's teeth** mettre qn hors d'état de nuire; **he drew a gun on me** il a tiré un pistolet et l'a braqué sur moi; **to ~ a bath** faire couler un bain; **the stone drew blood** la pierre l'a fait saigner; **that remark drew blood** cette remarque a porté; **to ~ (a) breath** aspirer; *(fig)* souffler; **to ~ comfort from** puiser une consolation dans; **to ~ a smile from sb** faire sourire qn.

(**c**) *(attract etc) attention, customer, crowd* attirer. **to feel ~n towards sb** se sentir attiré par qn; **to ~ sb into a plan** entraîner qn dans un projet; **he refuses to be ~n** il refuse de réagir.

(**d**) *(sketch etc) picture* dessiner; *plan, line, circle* tracer; *portrait* faire; *map (Geog)* dresser; *(Scol)* dessiner; *situation* faire un tableau de; *character* dépeindre. *(fig)* **I ~ the line at (doing) that** je n'irai pas jusqu'à (faire) cela; **it's hard to know where to ~ the line** il n'est pas facile de savoir où fixer les limites.

(**e**) *(establish) conclusion* tirer (*from* de); *comparison, parallel, distinction,* établir (*between* entre).

(**f**) **to ~ a match/game** faire match nul/partie nulle.

3 *vi* (**a**) *(move)* se diriger (*towards* vers). **to ~ to one side, to ~ apart** s'écarter; **the train drew into the station** le train est entré en gare; **the car drew over towards...** la voiture a dévié vers...; **he drew ahead of the other runners** il s'est détaché des autres coureurs; **they drew level** ils sont arrivés à la hauteur l'un de l'autre; **to ~ near (to)** s'approcher (de); *[time, event]* approcher (de); **to ~ to an end** tirer à *or* toucher à sa fin.

(**b**) *(Cards)* tirer (*for* pour); *[chimney, pipe]* tirer; *[pump]* aspirer; *[tea]* infuser. **to ~ on one's savings** tirer sur ses économies.

(**c**) *(be equal) [two teams]* faire match nul; *(in exams, competitions)* être ex æquo *inv*. **to ~ for second place** remporter la deuxième place ex æquo.

(**d**) *(Art)* dessiner.

◆**draw along** *vt sep cart* tirer, traîner; *(fig) person* entraîner. ◆**draw aside** **1** *vi [people]* s'écarter. **2** *vt sep person* tirer à l'écart; *object* écarter. ◆**draw away** **1** *vi (go away)* s'éloigner (*from* de); *(move ahead)* prendre de l'avance (*from* sur). **2** *vt sep person* éloigner, emmener; *object* retirer, ôter. ◆**draw back** **1** *vi* se reculer (*from* de); *(fig)* reculer (*at, before, from* devant). **2** *vt sep person* faire reculer; *object, hand* retirer. ◆**draw down** *vt sep blind* baisser; *blame* attirer (*on* sur). ◆**draw in** **1** *vi* (**a**) *(Aut)* s'arrêter. (**b**) **the days are ~ing in** les jours raccourcissent. **2** *vt sep air* aspirer; *(pull back in) claws etc* rentrer; *reins* tirer sur; *crowds* attirer. ◆**draw off** *vt sep gloves, garment* retirer; *pint of beer* tirer; *(Med) blood* prendre. ◆**draw on** **1** *vi [time]* s'avancer. **2** *vt sep garment* enfiler; *shoes* mettre. ◆**draw out** **1** *vi*: **the days are ~ing out** les jours rallongent. **2** *vt sep* (**a**) *(bring out) handkerchief, purse* sortir (*from* de); *money from bank* retirer (*from* de); *secret, plan* soutirer (*from* à). **try and ~ him out** essayez de le faire parler. (**b**) *(stretch) wire* étirer; *speech, meeting* faire tirer en longueur; *meal* prolonger. ◆**draw up** **1** *vi [car etc]* s'arrêter. **2** *vt sep* (**a**) *chair* approcher; *troops* aligner. **to ~ o.s. up (to one's full height)** se redresser (fièrement). (**b**) *contract, agreement, list* dresser; *scheme* formuler, établir.

◆**drawback** *n* inconvénient *m*, désavantage *m* (*to* à). ◆**drawbridge** *n* pont-levis *m*. ◆**drawer** *n* (**a**) [drɔːr] *[furniture]* tiroir *m*; (**b**) ['drɔːər] *[cheque etc]* tireur *m*. ◆**drawing** **1** *n* dessin *m*; **to study ~ing** étudier le dessin; **pencil ~ing** dessin au crayon; **rough ~ing** ébauche *f* ; **2** *adj*: **~ing board** planche *f* à dessin; *(fig)* **the scheme is still on the ~ing board** le projet est encore à l'étude; **~ing office** bureau *m* de dessin industriel; **~ing pin** punaise *f (à papier)*; **~ing room** salon *m*. ◆**drawn** *adj* (**a**) *(haggard) features* tiré, crispé (*with pain* par la douleur); **to look ~n** avoir les traits tirés; (**b**) *(equal) game, match* nul; *battle* indécis. ◆**drawsheet** *n* alaise *f*. ◆**drawstring** *n* cordon *m*.

drawl [drɔːl] **1** *vi* parler d'une voix traînante. **2** *vt* dire d'une voix traînante. **3** *n* voix traînante. **an American ~** un accent américain.

dread [dred] **1** *vt* redouter (*doing* de faire; *that* que... ne + *subj*). **2** *n* terreur *f*, effroi *m*, épouvante *f*. **3** *adj (liter)* redoutable. ◆**dreadful** *adj crime, sight, suffering* épouvantable, atroce; *weapon, foe* redoutable; *(*: less strong) weather* affreux, atroce; *child* insupportable; **it's a ~ful thing but...**

c'est terrible, mais...; **I feel ~ful!** *(ill)* je ne me sens pas bien du tout!; *(ashamed)* j'ai vraiment honte! ◆ **dreadfully** *adv* terriblement, horriblement; **~fully sorry** absolument désolé.

dream [driːm] *(vb: pret, ptp* **dreamed** *or* **dreamt***)* **1** *n* rêve *m*. **to have a ~ about sth** faire un rêve sur qch, rêver de qch; **to have ~s of doing** rêver de faire; **I've had a bad ~** j'ai fait un mauvais rêve *or* un cauchemar; **it was like a ~ come true** c'était comme dans un rêve; **sweet ~s!** fais de beaux rêves!; **life is but a ~** la vie n'est qu'un songe; **she goes around in a ~** * elle est dans les nuages, elle rêvasse; **the house of his ~s** la maison de ses rêves; **idle ~s** rêvasseries *fpl*; **rich beyond his wildest ~s** plus riche qu'il n'aurait jamais pu rêver de l'être; **isn't he a ~?** * n'est-ce pas qu'il est adorable?
2 *adj*: **a ~ house** une maison de rêve; **his ~ house** la maison de ses rêves; **he lives in a ~ world** il plane complètement.
3 *vi* (**a**) rêver (*about, of* de; *about doing, of doing* qu'on a fait). **I'm sorry, I was ~ing** excusez-moi, j'étais dans la lune *or* je rêvais. (**b**) *(imagine)* songer, penser (*of* à; *of doing* à faire). **I shouldn't ~ of telling her!** jamais il ne me viendrait à l'idée de lui dire cela!; **I shouldn't ~ of it!** jamais de la vie!, pas question!
4 *vt* (**a**) *(in sleep)* rêver (*that* que). **to ~ a dream** faire un rêve. (**b**) *(imagine)* imaginer. **I didn't ~ that...** je n'ai jamais imaginé un instant que...
◆ **dream up** * *vt sep idea* imaginer.
◆ **dreamer** *n* rêveur *m*, -euse *f*; *(politically)* utopiste *mf*. ◆ **dreamily** *adv* d'un air rêveur, rêveusement. ◆ **dreamland** *n* pays *m* des rêves. ◆ **dreamy** *adj (gen)* rêveur; *music* langoureux; *(*: adorable)* ravissant.

dreary [ˈdrɪərɪ] *adj weather, landscape* morne; *life, work* monotone; *speech, person* ennuyeux. ◆ **dreariness** *n* caractère *m* morne *or* ennuyeux; monotonie *f*.

dredge¹ [dredʒ] **1** *n* drague *f*. **2** *vti* draguer (*for* pour trouver). ◆ **dredge up** *vt sep* draguer; *unpleasant facts* déterrer. ◆ **dredger** *n* dragueur *m*. ◆ **dredging** *n* dragage *m*.

dredge² [dredʒ] *vt sugar* saupoudrer (*with* de; *over* sur).

dregs [dregz] *npl* lie *f (also fig)*.

drench [dren(t)ʃ] *vt* tremper, mouiller. **to get ~ed to the skin** se faire tremper jusqu'aux os. ◆ **drenching** *adj rain* battant.

Dresden [ˈdrezd(ə)n] *n (~ china)* porcelaine *f* de Saxe. **a piece of ~** un saxe.

dress [dres] **1** *n (gown)* robe *f*; *(clothing)* tenue *f*. **in eastern ~** en tenue orientale. **2** *adj shirt* de soirée; *uniform* de cérémonie. *(Theat)* **~ circle** premier balcon *m*; **~ designer** styliste *mf (mode)*; *(famous)* couturier *m*; **~ designing** stylisme *m*; **~ length** *(of material)* hauteur *f* (de robe); **~ rehearsal** répétition *f* générale. **3** *vt* (**a**) habiller; *(Theat) play* costumer. **to ~ o.s., to get ~ed** s'habiller; **well-~ed** bien habillé; **~ed for the country/for tennis** en tenue de sport/de tennis; **~ed in black** habillé de *or* en noir; **~ed to kill** ‡ sur son trente et un. (**b**) *salad* assaisonner *(d'une vinaigrette etc)*; *food for table* apprêter, accommoder; *chicken, crab* préparer; *skins, material* apprêter; *wound* panser. **to ~ sb's wound** faire le pansement de qn; **to ~ a shop window** faire la vitrine; **to ~ sb's hair** coiffer qn. **4** *vi* s'habiller (*in black etc* de *or* en noir *etc*).
◆ **dress up** **1** *vi (smart clothes)* s'habiller, se mettre en grande toilette; *(fancy dress)* se déguiser (*as* en). **2** *vt sep* déguiser (*as* en).
◆ **dresser** *n* (**a**) *(Theat)* habilleur *m*, -euse *f*; *(window ~)* étalagiste *mf*; (**b**) *(sideboard)* vaisselier *m*; (**c**) *(US: dressing table)* coiffeuse *f*. ◆ **dressing** **1** *n* habillement *m*; *(Med)* pansement *m*; *(Culin)* assaisonnement *m*; **oil and vinegar ~ing** vinaigrette *f*; **2** *adj*: **~ing case** trousse *f* de toilette; **to give sb a ~ing down** * passer un savon à qn *; **~ing gown** robe *f* de chambre; *(in towelling)* peignoir *m*; **~ing room** *(in house)* dressing(-room) *m*; *(Theat)* loge *f (d'acteur)*; *(US: in shop)* cabine *f* d'essayage; **~ing table** coiffeuse *f*, (table *f* de) toilette *f*. ◆ **dressmaker** *n* couturière *f*. ◆ **dressmaking** *n* couture *f*. ◆ **dressy** * *adj person* chic *inv*, élégant; *party* habillé; *clothes* qui fait habillé.

drew [druː] *pret of* **draw**.

dribble [ˈdrɪbl] **1** *vi [liquids]* tomber goutte à goutte; *[person]* baver; *(Sport)* dribbler. *[people]* **to ~ back/in** *etc* revenir/entrer *etc* par petits groupes. **2** *vt* (**a**) *(Sport)* dribbler. (**b**) **he ~d his milk all down his chin** son lait lui dégoulinait le long du menton.

driblet [ˈdrɪblɪt] *n [liquid]* gouttelette *f*. **in ~s** goutte à goutte; *(fig)* petit à petit.

dribs and drabs [ˈdrɪbz(ə)nˈdræbz] *npl*: **in ~** *(gen)* petit à petit; *arrive* par petits groupes; *pay, give* au compte-gouttes.

dried [draɪd] *(pret, ptp of* **dry***) adj fruit, beans* sec; *vegetables, flowers* séché; *eggs, milk* en poudre.

drier [ˈdraɪəʳ] *n* = **dryer**.

drift [drɪft] **1** *vi (gen)* dériver; *(in wind, current)* être emporté; *[snow, sand etc]* s'amonceler; *[person, nation]* aller à la dérive; *[events]* tendre (*towards* vers). **to ~ downstream** descendre le courant à la dérive; *[person]* **to ~ away/out** *etc* s'en aller/sortir *etc* d'une allure nonchalante; **he was ~ing aimlessly about** il flânait (sans but); **to let things ~** laisser les choses aller à la dérive; **he ~ed into marriage** il s'est retrouvé marié. **2** *n* (**a**) *[snow, leaves]* amoncellement *m*. (**b**) *(deviation from course)* dérive *f*; *(gist: of questions etc)* portée *f*, sens *m* (général); *(direction: of conversation, events)* tournure *f*. **continental ~** dérive des continents. **3** *adj*: **~ ice** glaces *fpl* en dérive. ◆ **drifter** *n* personne *f* qui se laisse aller. ◆ **driftwood** *n* bois *m* flotté.

drill¹ [drɪl] **1** *n (cutting part)* mèche *f*; *(complete tool)* perceuse *f*; *[dentist]* roulette *f*; *(in mine, quarry)* foreuse *f*; *(pneumatic ~)* marteau-piqueur *m*; *(for oil well)* trépan *m*. **electric (hand) ~** perceuse électrique. **2** *vt wood etc* forer, percer; *tooth* fraiser; *oil well* forer. **3** *vi* effectuer des forages (*for* pour trouver). ◆ **drilling** **1** *n* forages *mpl* ; **2** *adj*: **~ing rig** derrick *m*; *(at sea)* plate-forme *f*; **~ing ship** navire *m* de forage.

drill² [drɪl] **1** *n (exercises)* exercice(s) *m(pl)*. *(fig)* **what's the ~?** * quelle est la marche à suivre? **2** *vt soldiers* faire faire l'exercice à; *pupils (in grammar etc)* faire faire des exercices à. **to ~ good manners into a child** dresser un enfant à bien se tenir; **I ~ed it into him that...** je lui ai bien fait entrer dans la tête que... **3** *vi* faire l'exercice.

drill³ [drɪl] *n (Tex)* coutil *m*, treillis *m*.

drily [ˈdraɪlɪ] *adv (coldly)* sèchement; *(with dry humour)* d'un air pince-sans-rire.

drink [drɪŋk] *(vb: pret* **drank**, *ptp* **drunk***)* **1** *n* (**a**) *(liquid to ~)* boisson *f*. **there's food and ~ in the kitchen** il y a de quoi boire et manger à la cuisine; **may I have a ~?** est-ce que je pourrais boire qch?; **to give sb a ~** donner à boire à qn. (**b**) *(alcoholic)* **a ~** un verre; *(before meal)* un apéritif; *(after meal)* un digestif; **let's have a ~** on va prendre *or* boire un verre; **I need a ~** il me faut à boire; **to ask friends in for ~s** inviter des amis à venir prendre un verre; **to stand a round of ~s** payer une tournée. (**c**) *(alcoholic liquor)* la boisson, l'alcool *m*. **to be under the influence of ~, to be the worse for ~** être en état d'ébriété; **to take to ~** s'adonner à la boisson; **to smell of ~** sentir l'alcool; **to drive sb to ~** pousser qn à la boisson.

2 *adj*: **the ~ problem** le problème de l'alcoolisme; **to have a ~ problem** boire (trop).
3 *vt (gen)* boire, prendre; *soup* manger. **would you like sth to ~?** voulez-vous boire qch?; **to ~ sb's health** boire à la santé de qn; **he ~s all his wages** il boit tout ce qu'il gagne; **to ~ sb under the table** faire rouler qn sous la table.
4 *vi* boire. **'don't ~ and drive'** 'attention, au volant l'alcool tue'; **to ~ like a fish** * boire comme un trou *; **to ~ to sb** boire à qn.
◆ **drink in** *vt sep [plants, soil]* boire; *[person] fresh air* respirer, humer; *story* avaler *. *(fig)* **the children were ~ing it all in** les enfants n'en perdaient pas une miette * *(fig)*. ◆ **drink up** **1** *vi* boire, vider son verre. **~ up** finis ton vin (*or* ton café *etc*). **2** *vt sep* boire (jusqu'au bout), finir.
◆ **drinkable** *adj (not poisonous)* potable; *(palatable)* buvable. ◆ **drinker** *n* buveur *m*, -euse *f*; **he's a heavy ~er** il boit sec. ◆ **drinking** **1** *n* fait *m* de boire; *(drunkenness)* boisson *f*; **eating and ~ing** manger et boire; **he wasn't used to ~ing** il n'avait pas l'habitude de boire; **his problem was ~ing** son problème c'était qu'il buvait; **2** *adj*: **~ing bout** beuverie *f*; **~ing chocolate** chocolat *m* en poudre; **~ing fountain** *(in street)* fontaine *f* publique; *(in toilets etc)* jet *m* d'eau potable; **~ing song** chanson *f* à boire; **~ing water** eau *f* potable.

drip [drɪp] **1** *vi [water, sweat, rain]* tomber goutte à goutte; *[tap]* couler, goutter; *[walls]* suinter; *[cheese, washing]* s'égoutter; *[hair, trees etc]* dégoutter (*with* de). **to be ~ping with sweat** ruisseler de sueur; **hands ~ping with blood** mains dégoulinantes de sang; **~ping wet** * trempé. **2** *vt liquid* faire tomber goutte à goutte. **you're ~ping paint all over the floor** tu mets de la peinture partout. **3** *n* **(a)** *(drop)* goutte *f*; *(*: spineless person)* lavette * *f*, mollasson *m*. **(b)** *(Med) (liquid)* perfusion *f*; *(device)* goutte-à-goutte *m inv*. **to be on a ~** être sous perfusion. ◆ **drip-dry** *adj shirt* qui ne nécessite aucun repassage; *(on label)* 'ne pas repasser'. ◆ **drip-feed** *vt (Med)* alimenter par perfusion. ◆ **drip mat** *n* dessous-de-verre *m inv*. ◆ **dripping** **1** *n (Culin)* graisse *f* (de rôti); **2** *adj tap* qui goutte; *washing, coat* trempé.

drive [draɪv] *(vb: pret* **drove**, *ptp* **driven***)* **1** *n* **(a)** *(Aut: journey)* promenade *f or* trajet *m* en voiture. **to go for a ~** faire une promenade en voiture; **it's one hour's ~ from London** c'est à une heure de voiture de Londres. **(b)** *(private road)* allée *f*. **(c)** *(energy)* dynamisme *m*, énergie *f*; *(Psych etc)* besoin *m*, instinct *m*. **sex ~** pulsions *fpl* sexuelles. **(d)** *(Pol etc)* campagne *f*, propagande *f*; *(Mil)* poussée *f*. **a ~ to boost sales** une promotion systématique de vente; **output ~** effort *m* de production. **(e)** *(Tech)* transmission *f*. *(Aut)* **front-wheel ~** traction *f* avant; **rear-wheel ~** propulsion *f* arrière; **left-hand ~** conduite *f* à gauche. **(f)** *(Comput) (for disk)* unité *f* de disques; *(for tape)* dérouleur *m*. **(g)** *(herding)* rassemblement *m*.
2 *vt* **(a)** *people, animals* chasser (devant soi); *(Hunting) game* rabattre; *clouds, leaves* chasser. **to ~ sb out of the country** chasser qn du pays; *(fig)* **to ~ sb into a corner** mettre qn au pied du mur; **the gale drove the ship off course** la tempête a fait dériver le navire; *(fig)* **to ~ sb hard** surcharger qn de travail; **to ~ sb mad** rendre qn fou; **to ~ sb to despair** réduire qn au désespoir; **to ~ sb to (do) sth** pousser qn à (faire) qch; **I was driven to it** j'y ai été poussé malgré moi, j'y ai été contraint. **(b)** *cart, car, train* conduire; *racing car* piloter; *passenger* conduire (en voiture). **he ~s a taxi** *(for a living)* il est chauffeur de taxi; **he ~s a Peugeot** il a une Peugeot; *(Aut)* **to ~ sb back** *etc* ramener *etc* qn en voiture. **(c)** *(operate) machine* actionner, commander. *(Rail)* **steam-driven engine** locomotive *f* à vapeur; **machine driven by electricity** machine fonctionnant à l'électricité. **(d)** *nail, stake* enfoncer; *rivet* poser; *(Golf, Tennis)* driver; *tunnel, well* percer. *(fig)* **to ~ a point home** réussir à faire comprendre un argument; **to ~ sth out of sb's head** faire complètement oublier qch à qn; **to ~ a bargain** conclure un marché.
3 *vi* **(a)** *(Aut)* conduire, aller en voiture. **to ~ away/back** *etc* partir/revenir *etc* en voiture; **to ~ down to the shops** aller faire des courses en voiture; **can you ~?** savez-vous conduire?; **to ~ at 50 km/h** rouler à 50 km/h; **to ~ on the right** rouler à droite; **by train? — no, we drove** par le train? — non, en voiture; **we have been driving all day** nous avons fait de la route toute la journée; **to ~ over sth** écraser qch. **(b)** *(fig)* **what are you driving at?** où voulez-vous en venir? ◆ **drive away, drive off** *vt sep* chasser. ◆ **drive back** *vt sep person, army* faire reculer. ◆ **drive in** *vt sep nail, idea* enfoncer. ◆ **drive on** **1** *vi* poursuivre *or (after stopping)* reprendre sa route. **2** *vt sep* pousser (*to* à, *to do* à faire). ◆ **drive out** *vt sep* chasser. ◆ **drive up** *vi [car]* arriver; *[person]* arriver (en voiture).
◆ **drive-in** *adj, n* drive-in *(m)*. ◆ **driveline** *n (Aut)* transmission *f*. ◆ **driver** *n [car, train]* conducteur *m*, -trice *f*; *[taxi, truck, bus]* chauffeur *m*, conducteur, -trice; *[racing car]* pilote *m*; **car ~rs** automobilistes *mpl*; **to be a good ~r** conduire bien; *(US)* **~r's license** permis *m* de conduire; **to be in the ~r's** *or* **driving seat** être au volant; *(fig)* être aux commandes. ◆ **driveshaft** *n (Aut)* arbre *m* de transmission. ◆ **drive-up window** *n (US)* guichet *m* pour automobilistes. ◆ **driveway** *n* allée *f*. ◆ **driving** **1** *n (Aut)* conduite *f*; **his driving is awful** il conduit très mal ; **2** *adj* **(a)** *necessity* impérieux, pressant; *force* agissant; *rain* battant; **(b)** *(Aut) lesson* de conduite; **driving instructor** moniteur *m*, -trice *f* d'auto-école; **driving licence** permis *m* de conduire; **driving mirror** rétroviseur *m*; **driving school** auto-école *f*; **to fail/pass one's driving test** être refusé à/avoir son permis.

drivel ['drɪvl] *n* sornettes *fpl*, imbécillités *fpl*.

drizzle ['drɪzl] **1** *n* bruine *f*. **2** *vi* bruiner. ◆ **drizzly** *adj* de bruine.

dromedary ['drɒmɪd(ə)rɪ] *n* dromadaire *m*.

drone [drəʊn] **1** *vi [bee]* bourdonner; *[engine, aircraft]* ronronner; *(louder)* vrombir; *(speak:* **~ away, ~ on***)* parler d'une façon monotone. **2** *n* **(a)** *(sound)* bourdonnement *m*; ronronnement *m*; *(louder)* vrombissement *m*; *(speech)* débit *m* monotone. **(b)** *(bee)* abeille *f* mâle; *(idler)* fainéant(e) *m(f)*.

drool [dru:l] *vi* baver; *(*: talk)* radoter (*about* au sujet de). *(fig)* **to ~ over sth** * baver d'admiration *or* s'extasier devant qch.

droop [dru:p] *vi [body]* s'affaisser; *[shoulders]* tomber; *[head]* pencher; *[eyelids]* s'abaisser; *[flowers]* commencer à se faner; *[feathers, one's hand]* retomber. **his spirits ~ed** il a été pris de découragement; **the heat made him ~** il était accablé par la chaleur.

drop [drɒp] **1** *n* **(a)** goutte *f*. **~ by ~** goutte à goutte; *(fig)* **a ~ in the ocean** une goutte d'eau dans la mer; **he's had a ~ too much** * il a un verre dans le nez. **(b)** *(fall: gen)* baisse *f* (*in* de). *(Elec)* **~ in voltage** chute *f* de tension; *(fig)* **at the ~ of a hat** sans hésitation. **(c)** *(abyss)* précipice *m*; *(fall)* chute *f*; *(distance of fall)* hauteur *f*; *(parachute jump)* saut *m* (en parachute); *[supplies, arms]* parachutage *m*; *[gallows]* trappe *f*. **sheer ~** descente *f* à pic.
2 *vt* **(a)** *(gen)* laisser tomber; *(release, let go)* lâcher; *bomb* lancer, larguer; *liquid* laisser tomber goutte à goutte; *stitch* sauter; *hem* ressortir; *eyes, voice, price* baisser; *(from car) person, thing* déposer; *(from boat) cargo, passengers* débarquer. **to ~ a letter in the postbox** mettre une lettre à la boîte; **to ~ by**

parachute parachuter; **to ~ anchor** jeter l'ancre; *(fig)* **to ~ a brick** * faire une gaffe; **to ~ a curtsy** faire une révérence. (**b**) *remark, clue* laisser échapper. **to ~ a hint about sth** suggérer qch; **to ~ a word in sb's ear** glisser un mot à l'oreille de qn. (**c**) *letter, card* envoyer, écrire (*to* à). **to ~ sb a line** écrire un (petit) mot à qn. (**d**) *(omit)* omettre; *(intentionally) thing* supprimer; *person* écarter (*from* de). **to ~ one's h's** ≃ avoir un accent vulgaire. (**e**) *(abandon) habit, idea, plan* renoncer à; *work, discussion, conversation* abandonner; *friend, boyfriend* lâcher, laisser tomber. **let's ~ the subject** ne parlons plus de cela; **~ it!** * laisse tomber! * (**f**) *(lose) money, game* perdre.

3 *vi* (**a**) *[object]* tomber, retomber; *[liquids]* tomber goutte à goutte; *[person]* se laisser tomber; *(collapse)* s'écrouler. **I'm ready to ~** * je tombe de fatigue, je ne tiens plus debout; **~ dead!** ‡ va te faire voir! * (**b**) *[wind]* tomber; *[temperature, voice, price]* baisser; *[numbers, attendance]* diminuer, tomber. (**c**) *(end) [conversation, correspondence]* en rester là.

◆ **drop back, drop behind** *vi* rester en arrière; *(in work etc)* prendre du retard. ◆ **drop down** *vi* tomber. ◆ **drop in** *vi*: **to ~ in on sb** passer chez qn. ◆ **drop off 1** *vi* (**a**) *(fall asleep)* s'endormir; *(doze)* faire un petit somme. (**b**) *[leaves]* tomber; *[sales, interest]* diminuer. **2** *vt sep (from car etc)* déposer, laisser. ◆ **drop out** *vi [contents etc]* tomber; *(fig)* se retirer (*of* de); *(from society)* choisir de vivre marginalement; *(from college etc)* abandonner.

◆ **drop-cloth** *n (US)* bâche *f* de protection. ◆ **drop-leaf table** *n* table *f* anglaise. ◆ **droplet** *n* gouttelette *f*. ◆ **drop-off** *n (in sales etc)* diminution *f*. ◆ **dropout** *n (from society)* marginal(e) *m(f)* ; *(from college etc)* étudiant(e) *m(f)* qui abandonne ses études. ◆ **dropper** *n (Med)* compte-gouttes *m inv*. ◆ **droppings** *npl [birds]* fiente *f*; *[animals, flies]* crottes *fpl*.

dross [drɒs] *n (fig)* rebut *m*.

drought [draʊt] *n* sécheresse *f*.

drove [drəʊv] (*pret of* **drive**) *n*: **~s of people** des foules *fpl* de gens; **in ~s** en foule.

drown [draʊn] **1** *vt (gen: lit, fig)* noyer; *land* inonder. **to be like a ~ed rat** * être trempé jusqu'aux os. **2** *vi* se noyer. ◆ **drowning 1** *adj* qui se noie (*or* noyait *etc*) ; **2** *n (death)* noyade *f*.

drowse [draʊz] *vi* être à moitié endormi. ◆ **drowsily** *adv* d'un air endormi. ◆ **drowsiness** *n* somnolence *f*. ◆ **drowsy** *adj person, smile, look* somnolent; *afternoon, atmosphere* soporifique; **to grow drowsy** s'assoupir; **to feel drowsy** avoir envie de dormir.

drudge [drʌdʒ] *n* bête *f* de somme *(fig)*. **the household ~** la bonne à tout faire *(fig)*. ◆ **drudgery** *n* corvées *fpl*, travail fastidieux; **it's sheer ~ry** c'est d'un fastidieux!

drug [drʌg] **1** *n* drogue *f*, stupéfiant *m*; *(Med, Pharm)* médicament *m*; *(fig)* drogue. **he's on ~s** *(gen)* il se drogue; *(Med)* il est sous médication; *(fig)* **a ~ on the market** une marchandise invendable. **2** *adj*: **~ addict** drogué(e) *m(f)*, toxicomane *mf*; **~ addiction** toxicomanie *f*; **~ peddler** *or* **pusher** revendeur *m*, -euse *f* de drogue; **~ runner** trafiquant(e) *m(f)* de drogue; **~ running** *or* **traffic** trafic *m* de la drogue *or* des stupéfiants. **3** *vt person* droguer *(also Med)*; *food, wine etc* mêler un narcotique à. **to be in a ~ged sleep** dormir sous l'effet d'un narcotique; **~ged with sleep** abruti de sommeil. ◆ **druggist** *n (Brit)* pharmacien(ne) *m(f)*; *(US)* droguiste-épicier *m*, -ière *f*. ◆ **drugstore** *n (US)* drugstore *m*. ◆ **drug-taker** *n* consommateur *m*, -trice *f* de drogue. ◆ **drug-taking** *n* usage *m* de la drogue.

drum [drʌm] **1** *n* (**a**) *(Mus)* tambour *m*. **the big ~** la grosse caisse; *(Mil Mus, Jazz)* **the ~s** la batterie. (**b**) *(for oil)* bidon *m*; *(cylinder, also machine part)* tambour *m*; *(Comput)* tambour magnétique; *(box of figs, sweets)* caisse *f*. **2** *vi (Mus)* battre le tambour; *[person, fingers]* tambouriner (*with* de, avec; *on* sur). **the noise was ~ming in my ears** le bruit me tambourinait aux oreilles. **3** *vt*: **to ~ one's feet on the floor** tambouriner des pieds sur le plancher; **to ~ sth into sb** enfoncer qch dans le crâne de qn.

◆ **drum out** *vt sep* expulser (à grand bruit) (*of* de). ◆ **drum up** *vt sep enthusiasm, support* susciter; *supporters* battre le rappel de; *customers* racoler. ◆ **drum kit** *n* batterie *f*. ◆ **drummer** *n* tambour *m*; *(Jazz)* batteur *m*; **~mer boy** petit tambour. ◆ **drumstick** *n* baguette *f* de tambour; *[chicken]* pilon *m*.

drunk [drʌŋk] *(ptp of* **drink***)* **1** *adj* ivre, soûl *; *(fig)* enivré (*with* de, par). **to get ~** s'enivrer, se soûler * (*on* de); *(Jur)* **~ and disorderly** ≃ en état d'ivresse publique; **as ~ as a lord** soûl comme une grive *. **2** *n* (*) ivrogne *m*, homme *or* femme soûl(e) *. ◆ **drunkard** *n* ivrogne *m*, alcoolique *mf*. ◆ **drunken** *adj (habitually)* ivrogne; *(intoxicated)* ivre, soûl *; *orgy, quarrel* d'ivrogne(s); *fury* d'ivrogne; *voice* aviné; **~en driving** conduite *f* en état d'ivresse. ◆ **drunkenly** *adv (gen)* comme un ivrogne; *sing* d'une voix avinée; *walk* en titubant. ◆ **drunkenness** *n (state)* ivresse *f*; *(problem, habit)* ivrognerie *f*. ◆ **drunkometer** *n (US)* alcootest *m*.

dry [draɪ] **1** *adj* (**a**) *(gen)* sec (*f* sèche); *day* sans pluie; *riverbed, well* à sec; *battery* à piles sèches; *bread* sec; *toast etc* sans beurre. **on ~ land** sur la terre ferme; **as ~ as a bone** tout sec; **to keep sth ~** tenir qch au sec; **'to be kept ~'** 'craint l'humidité'; **~ dock** cale *f* sèche; *(Comm)* **~ goods** tissus *mpl*, mercerie *f*; **~ ice** neige *f* carbonique; **~ rot** pourriture *f* sèche *(du bois)*; *(fig)* **~ run** *(trial)* essai *m*; *(rehearsal)* répétition *f*; **~ ski slope** piste *f* de ski artificielle; **the river ran ~** la rivière s'est asséchée; **his mouth was ~ with fear** la peur lui desséchait la bouche; *(thirsty)* **to be ~** * avoir le gosier sec *. (**b**) *humour* pince-sans-rire *inv*; *(dull) lecture, subject* aride. **as ~ as dust** ennuyeux comme la pluie. **2** *vt (gen)* sécher; *clothes* faire sécher. **to ~ one's eyes** sécher ses larmes; **to ~ the dishes** essuyer la vaisselle; **to ~ o.s.** s'essuyer, se sécher. **3** *vi* sécher.

◆ **dry off** *vi* sécher. ◆ **dry out 1** *vi* sécher; *[alcoholic]* se faire désintoxiquer. **2** *vt sep* sécher; désintoxiquer. ◆ **dry up** *vi* (**a**) *[stream, well]* se dessécher; *[moisture]* s'évaporer; *[source of supply]* se tarir. (**b**) *(dry the dishes)* essuyer la vaisselle. (**c**) *(*: fall silent)* se taire; *[actor]* sécher *.

◆ **dry-clean** *vt* nettoyer à sec; **to have sth ~-cleaned** donner qch à nettoyer. ◆ **dry-cleaner** *n* teinturier *m*. ◆ **dry-cleaning** *n* nettoyage *m* à sec. ◆ **dryer** *n (gen)* séchoir *m*; *(at hairdresser's)* **under the ~er** sous le casque. ◆ **dry-eyed** *adj*: **to be ~-eyed** avoir les yeux secs. ◆ **drying** *adj*: **~ing cupboard** *or* **room** séchoir *m*; **to do the ~ing-up** essuyer la vaisselle; **~ing-up cloth** torchon *m*. ◆ **dryness** *n* sécheresse *f*. ◆ **drysalter** *n* marchand *m* de couleurs.

dual ['djʊəl] *adj* double, à deux. **~ carriageway** route *f* à chaussées séparées; **~ controls** double commande *f*; **~ national** binational(e) *m(f)*; **~ nationality** double nationalité *f*; **~ personality** dédoublement *m* de la personnalité. ◆ **dual-control** *adj* à double commande. ◆ **dualism** *or* ◆ **duality** *n* dualisme *m*. ◆ **dual-purpose** *adj* à double usage.

dub [dʌb] *vt* (**a**) **to ~ sb 'Ginger'** qualifier qn de 'Poil de Carotte'. (**b**) *(Cine)* doubler *(dialogue)*. ◆ **dubbing** *n (Cine)* doublage *m*.

dubious ['dju:bɪəs] *adj (gen)* douteux; *person* qui doute, incertain (*of* de); *look, smile* de doute. **he was ~ about whether** il se demandait si; **I'm very ~ about it** j'en doute fort. ◆ **dubiety** *n* doute *m*, incertitude *f*. ◆ **dubiously** *adv* avec doute.

Dublin ['dʌblɪn] *n* Dublin.

duchess ['dʌtʃɪs] *n* duchesse *f*.

duchy ['dʌtʃɪ] *n* duché *m*.

duck [dʌk] **1** *n* canard *m*; *(female)* cane *f*; *(Mil: vehicle)* véhicule *m* amphibie. **wild ~** canard sauvage; **to play at ~s and drakes** faire des ricochets (sur l'eau); **he took to it like a ~ to water** c'était comme s'il l'avait fait toute sa vie. **2** *vi* (**~ down**) se baisser vivement; *(in fight etc)* esquiver un coup; *(under water)* plonger subitement. **3** *vt* (**a**) *one's head* baisser vivement; *blow, question* éviter, esquiver. (**b**) *(also* **give sb a ducking***)* plonger dans l'eau; *(as a joke)* faire faire le plongeon à; *(head only)* faire boire la tasse à *. ◆ **duckboard** *n* caillebotis *m*. ◆ **duck-egg blue** *adj* bleu-vert (pâle) *inv*. ◆ **duckling** *n* caneton *m*. ◆ **duckpond** *n* mare *f* aux canards.

duct [dʌkt] *n* conduite *f*; *(Anat)* conduit *m*.

ductile ['dʌktaɪl] *adj metal* ductile; *person* maniable, malléable, docile.

ductless ['dʌktlɪs] *adj*: **~ gland** glande *f* endocrine.

dud [dʌd] **1** *adj shell, bomb* qui a raté; *object, tool* mal fichu *; *note, coin* faux; *cheque* sans provision; *person* nul. **2** *n* (*person*) nullard(e) * *m(f)*. **this coin is a ~** cette pièce est fausse; **this watch is a ~** cette montre ne marche pas.

dudgeon ['dʌdʒən] *n*: **in high ~** offensé dans sa dignité, furieux.

due [dju:] **1** *adj* (**a**) *(owing) sum, money* dû (*f* due). **our thanks are ~ to him** nous aimerions le remercier; **to fall ~** venir à échéance; **~ on the 8th** payable le 8; **when is the rent ~?** quand faut-il payer le loyer?; **I am ~ 6 days' leave** on me doit 6 jours de permission; **he is ~ for a rise** il doit recevoir *or* en principe il va recevoir une augmentation; **the train is ~ at midday** le train doit arriver à midi; **I am ~ there tomorrow** je dois être là-bas demain. (**b**) *(proper)* **after ~ consideration** après mûre réflexion; **in ~ course** *(when the time is ripe)* en temps utile; *(in the long run)* à la longue; **with all ~ respect, I believe...** sans vouloir vous contredire, je crois... (**c**) **~ to** *(caused by)* dû à, attribuable à; *(because of)* à cause de; *(thanks to)* grâce à; **what's it ~ to?** comment cela se fait-il? **2** *adv*: **to go ~ west** aller droit vers l'ouest; **to face ~ north** *[house]* être (en) plein nord; *[person]* faire face au nord; **~ east of** plein est par rapport à.
3 *n* (**a**) **to give sb his ~** rendre justice à qn; **to give him his ~, he did try hard** il faut (être juste et) reconnaître qu'il a quand même fait tout son possible. (**b**) *(fees)* **~s** *[club etc]* cotisation *f*; *[harbour]* droits *mpl*.

duel ['djʊəl] **1** *n* duel *m*. **~ to the death** duel à mort. **2** *vi* se battre en duel (*with* contre, avec).

duet [dju:'et] *n* duo *m*. **to sing/play a ~** chanter/jouer en duo; **violin ~** duo de violon; **piano ~** morceau *m* à quatre mains.

duffel, duffle ['dʌf(ə)l] *adj*: **~ bag** sac *m* de paquetage; **~ coat** duffel-coat *m*.

dug [dʌg] *pret, ptp of* **dig**. ◆ **dugout** *n (Mil)* tranchée-abri *f*; *(canoe)* pirogue *f*.

duke [dju:k] *n* duc *m*.

dull [dʌl] **1** *adj* (**a**) *sight, hearing* faible; *(slow-witted) person, mind* borné, obtus; *pupil* peu doué; *(boring) book, evening* ennuyeux; *style, person* terne. **deadly ~ *** assommant *, mortel *; **as ~ as ditchwater** ennuyeux comme la pluie. (**b**) *(not bright) colour, eyes, mirror, metal* terne; *sound, pain* sourd; *weather, sky* couvert, maussade; *trade, business* lent; *person, mood* déprimé, las. **a ~ day** un jour maussade. **2** *vt senses, pleasure, blade* émousser; *mind* engourdir; *pain, impression, memory* atténuer; *sound* assourdir; *colour, mirror, metal* ternir. ◆ **dullard** *n* lourdaud(e) *m(f)*. ◆ **dullness** *n (slow-wittedness)* lourdeur *f* d'esprit; *(boredom)* caractère ennuyeux; **the ~ness of the weather** le temps couvert. ◆ **dully** *adv (depressedly) behave, walk* lourdement; *answer, listen* avec lassitude; *(boringly) talk, write* d'une manière ennuyeuse.

duly ['dju:lɪ] *adv (properly)* comme il faut, ainsi qu'il convient; *(Jur etc)* dûment; *(on time)* en temps voulu; *(in effect)* en effet. **everybody was ~ shocked** tout le monde a bien entendu été choqué.

dumb [dʌm] *adj* (**a**) muet; *(with surprise etc)* muet, abasourdi (*with, from* de). **a ~ person** un(e) muet(te); **~ animals** les animaux *mpl*; **our ~ friends** nos amis les bêtes *fpl*; **to be struck ~** rester muet; **in ~ show** en pantomime. (**b**) (*‡: stupid*) bête. **a ~ blonde** une blonde évaporée; **to act ~** faire l'innocent. ◆ **dumbbell** *n (Sport)* haltère *m*. ◆ **dumbfound** *vt* abasourdir. ◆ **dumbfounded** *adj* ahuri. ◆ **dumbness** *n (Med)* mutisme *m*; (*‡: stupidity*) bêtise *f*.

dummy ['dʌmɪ] **1** *n (Comm: sham object)* factice *m*; *[book]* maquette *f*; *(model)* mannequin *m*; *[ventriloquist]* pantin *m*; *(Fin etc: person)* prête-nom *m*; *(Bridge)* mort *m*; *(baby's teat)* tétine *f*. **2** *adj* faux, factice. **~ run** *(Aviat)* attaque *f* simulée; *(Comm, Ind)* essai *m*.

dump [dʌmp] **1** *n (pile of rubbish)* tas *m* d'ordures; *(place)* décharge *f* publique; *(Mil)* dépôt *m*; (**: unpleasant place*) trou *m*; (**: house, hotel*) baraque * *f*. **to be down in the ~s *** avoir le cafard *. **2** *vt* (**a**) *(get rid of) rubbish* déposer, jeter; *(Comm) goods* écouler à bas prix; (*) *person, thing* larguer. (**b**) *(put down) package* déposer; *sand, bricks* décharger, déverser; (*) *passenger* déposer. **~ your bag on the table** plante ton sac sur la table. ◆ **dumper** *or* ◆ **dump truck** *n* tombereau *m* automoteur. ◆ **dumping** *n [load, rubbish]* décharge *f*; *(Ecol: in sea etc)* déversement *m* (de produits nocifs); *(Comm)* dumping *m*. ◆ **dumpy** *adj* courtaud, boulot.

dumpling ['dʌmplɪŋ] *n (savoury)* boulette *f* (de pâte). **apple ~** ≃ chausson *m* aux pommes.

dun [dʌn] *vt* harceler *(pour lui faire payer ses dettes)*.

dunce [dʌns] *n (Scol)* âne *m*, cancre * *m* (*at* en).

dune [dju:n] *n* dune *f*.

dung [dʌŋ] *n (gen)* crotte *f*; *[cattle]* bouse *f*; *(manure)* fumier *m*. ◆ **dunghill** *n* (*tas m* de) fumier *m*.

dungarees [ˌdʌŋgə'ri:z] *npl [workman]* bleu *m* (de travail); *[child, woman]* salopette *f*.

dungeon ['dʌn(d)ʒ(ə)n] *n* cachot *m* (souterrain).

dunk [dʌŋk] *vt*: **to ~ one's bread in one's coffee** *etc* faire trempette.

Dunkirk [dʌn'kɜ:k] *n* Dunkerque.

duodenal [ˌdju:ə(ʊ)'di:nl] *adj ulcer* du duodénum.

dupe [dju:p] **1** *vt* duper, tromper. **to ~ sb into doing sth** amener qn à faire qch en le dupant. **2** *n* dupe *f*.

duplex ['dju:pleks] *adj (gen)* duplex *inv*. *(US)* **~ (house)** maison jumelée; *(US)* **~ (apartment)** duplex.

duplicate ['dju:plɪkeɪt] **1** *vt (gen)* faire un double de; *(on machine) document* polycopier; *film* faire un contretype de; *action etc* répéter exactement. **that is duplicating work already done** cela fait double emploi avec ce qu'on a déjà fait. **2** ['dju:plɪkɪt] *n* double *m*. **in ~** en deux exemplaires. **3** ['dju:plɪkɪt] *adj copy* en double; *coach* supplémentaire. **a ~ key** un double de la clef. ◆ **duplication** *n [efforts, work]* répétition *f*, reproduction *f*. ◆ **duplicator** *or* ◆ **duplicating machine** *n* duplicateur *m*.

duplicity [dju:'plɪsɪtɪ] *n* duplicité *f*, fausseté *f*.

durable ['djʊərəbl] **1** *adj material* solide, résistant; *friendship* durable. **2** *n (Comm)* **~s** biens *mpl* de consommation durables. ◆ **durability** *n* solidité *f*, résistance *f*; durabilité *f*.

duration [djʊ(ə)'reɪʃ(ə)n] *n (gen)* durée *f*. **for the ~ of the war** jusqu'à la fin de la guerre.

duress [djʊ(ə)'res] *n*: **under ~** sous la contrainte.

Durex ['djʊəreks] *n* ® préservatif *m*.

during ['djʊərɪŋ] *prep* pendant, durant; *(in the course of)* au cours de.

dusk [dʌsk] *n (twilight)* crépuscule *m*; *(gloom)* (semi-)obscurité *f*. **at ~** au crépuscule; **in the ~** dans la semi-obscurité. ◆ **dusky** *adj complexion* foncé; *person* au teint foncé.

dust [dʌst] **1** *n* poussière *f*. **thick ~** une épaisse couche de poussière; **I've got a speck of ~ in my eye** j'ai une poussière dans l'œil. **2** *adj cloud* de poussière. *(Geog)* **~ bowl** désert *m* de poussière; *(US)* **~ cloth** chiffon *m* (à poussière); **~ cover** *(of book: also* **~ jacket***)* jaquette *f (d'un livre)*; *(of furniture, also* **~ sheet***)* housse *f* de protection; **~ storm** tourbillon *m* de poussière. **3** *vt* (**a**) *furniture* épousseter; *room* essuyer la poussière dans. (**b**) *(sprinkle)* saupoudrer (*with* de). ◆ **dustbin** *n* poubelle *f*, boîte *f* à ordures. ◆ **dustcart** *n* tombereau *m* aux ordures. ◆ **duster** *n (Brit)* chiffon *m (à poussière, à effacer)*; *(esp US) (overgarment)* blouse *f* de protection; *(housecoat)* robe-tablier *f*. ◆ **dustheap** *n* poubelle *f*. ◆ **dusting** *adj:* **~ing powder** talc *m*. ◆ **dustman** *n* éboueur *m*. ◆ **dustpan** *n* pelle *f* à poussière. ◆ **dust-up** * *n*: **to have a ~-up with sb** * avoir un accrochage * avec qn. ◆ **dusty** *adj* poussiéreux; **to get ~y** se couvrir de poussière; **not so ~y** * pas mal; **to get a ~y answer** * en être pour ses frais.

Dutch [dʌtʃ] **1** *adj* hollandais, néerlandais, des Pays-Bas. **~ cheese** hollande *m*; *(fig)* **~ auction** enchères *fpl* au rabais; **~ cap** diaphragme *m*; **~ courage** courage *m* puisé dans la bouteille; **~ elm disease** champignon *m* parasite de l'orme; **to go ~** partager les frais. **2** *n (Ling)* hollandais *m*, néerlandais *m*. **the ~** les Hollandais *mpl*, les Néerlandais *mpl*; *(fig)* **it's all ~ to me** * c'est du chinois pour moi. ◆ **Dutchman** *n* Hollandais *m*. ◆ **Dutchwoman** *n* Hollandaise *f*.

duty ['dju:tɪ] **1** *n* (**a**) *(moral, legal)* devoir *m* (*to do* de faire; *to, by sb* envers qn). **I feel (in) ~ bound to say that...** il est de mon devoir de faire remarquer que...; *[employee, official etc]* **duties** fonctions *fpl*; **on ~** *(Mil)* de service; *(Med)* de garde; *(Admin, Scol)* de jour, de service; **to be off ~** *(gen)* être libre; *(Mil)* avoir quartier libre; **to go on/off ~** prendre/quitter le service (*or* la garde); **to do ~ for sb** remplacer qn; **the box does ~ for a table** la boîte fait fonction de table. (**b**) *(tax)* droit *m*, taxe *f* (indirecte). **to pay ~ on** payer un droit *or* une taxe sur. **2** *adj visit etc* de politesse. **~ officer** *(Mil etc)* officier *m* de service; *(Admin)* officiel *m* de service; **~ rota** tableau *m* de service. ◆ **dutiable** *adj (Customs)* soumis à des droits de douane. ◆ **dutiful** *adj child* respectueux; *husband* plein d'égards; *employee* consciencieux. ◆ **dutifully** *adv obey* respectueusement; *work* consciencieusement. ◆ **duty-free** *adj goods etc* exempté de douane; *shop* hors-taxe.

duvet ['du:veɪ] *n* couette *f (édredon)*. **~ cover** housse *f* de couette.

dwarf [dwɔ:f] **1** *adj, n* nain(e) *m(f)*. **2** *vt [skyscraper, person]* rapetisser, écraser; *[achievement]* éclipser.

dwell [dwel] *pret, ptp* **dwelt** *vi (liter)* demeurer. ◆ **dwell (up)on** *vt fus (think about)* s'arrêter sur; *(talk about)* s'étendre sur; *(emphasize)* appuyer sur. **don't let's ~ upon it** passons là-dessus. ◆ **dweller** *n* habitant(e) *m(f)*; **town ~er** citadin(e) *m(f)*. ◆ **dwelling** **1** *n* habitation *f* ; **2** *adj:* **~ing house** maison *f* d'habitation.

dwindle ['dwɪndl] *vi* diminuer (peu à peu). ◆ **dwindling** *adj interest, strength* décroissant; *resources* en diminution.

dye [daɪ] **1** *n* teinture *f*, colorant *m*. **hair ~** teinture pour les cheveux; **fast ~** grand teint. **2** *vt* teindre. **to ~ sth red** teindre qch en rouge; **to ~ one's hair** se teindre les cheveux. ◆ **dyed-in-the-wool** *adj* bon teint *inv (fig)*. ◆ **dyeing** *n* teinture *f*. ◆ **dyer** *n:* **~r's and cleaner's** teinturier *m*. ◆ **dyestuffs** *npl* matières *fpl* colorantes. ◆ **dyeworks** *npl* teinturerie *f*.

dying ['daɪɪŋ] **1** *adj* mourant; *custom etc* en train de disparaître. **to my ~ day** jusqu'à ma dernière heure. **2** *n (death)* mort *f*; *(just before death)* agonie *f*. **the ~** les mourants *mpl*.

dyke [daɪk] *n* (**a**) digue *f*; *(causeway)* levée *f*. (**b**) (‡: *lesbian)* gouine ‡ *f*.

dynamic [daɪ'næmɪk] *adj* dynamique. ◆ **dynamics** *nsg* dynamique *f*. ◆ **dynamism** *n* dynamisme *m*.

dynamite ['daɪnəmaɪt] **1** *n* dynamite *f*. **he's ~!** * *(terrific)* il est super! *; *(full of energy)* il est d'un dynamisme!; **that business is ~** * ça pourrait t'exploser dans les mains. **2** *vt* dynamiter.

dynamo ['daɪnəməʊ] *n* dynamo *f*.

dynasty ['dɪnəstɪ] *n* dynastie *f*. ◆ **dynastic** *adj* dynastique.

dysentery ['dɪsɪntrɪ] *n* dysenterie *f*.

dyslexia [dɪs'leksɪə] *n* dyslexie *f*. ◆ **dyslexic** *adj, n* dyslexique *(mf)*.

dyspepsia [dɪs'pepsɪə] *n* dyspepsie *f*.

dystrophy ['dɪstrəfɪ] *n* dystrophie *f*.

E

E, e [i:] *n* E, e *m*; *(Mus)* mi *m*.

each [i:tʃ] **1** *adj* chaque. ~ **day** chaque jour, tous les jours; ~ **one of us** chacun(e) de *or* d'entre nous. **2** *pron* (**a**) chacun(e) *m(f)*. ~ **of the boys** chacun des garçons; ~ **of us** chacun(e) de *or* d'entre nous; **a little of ~ please** un peu de chaque s'il vous plaît; **we gave them one apple ~** nous leur avons donné une pomme chacun; **they are £2 ~** ils coûtent 2 livres chacun *or* pièce. (**b**) ~ **other** l'un(e) l'autre *m(f)*; **they love ~ other** ils s'aiment; **they write to ~ other** ils s'écrivent; **they were sorry for ~ other** ils avaient pitié l'un de l'autre; **you must help ~ other** vous devez vous aider les uns les autres; **separated from ~ other** séparés l'un de l'autre.

eager [ˈi:gəʳ] *adj (keen)* désireux, avide (*for* de, *to do* de faire); *(impatient)* impatient (*to do* de faire); *scholar, supporter, desire* passionné; *search, glance* avide. **to be ~ for** *(gen)* désirer vivement; *happiness* rechercher avidement; *knowledge, affection* être avide de; *power, vengeance, pleasure* être assoiffé de; **to be ~ to do** *(keen)* désirer vivement faire; *(impatient)* être impatient de faire; ~ **beaver** * personne *f* enthousiaste et consciencieuse. ◆ **eagerly** *adv* avidement; avec impatience; passionnément. ◆ **eagerness** *n* vif désir *m* (*to do* de faire, *for* de); impatience *f* (*to do* de faire).

eagle [ˈi:gl] *n* aigle *mf (gen m)*. ◆ **eagle-eyed** *adj* qui a des yeux d'aigle.

ear¹ [ɪəʳ] **1** *n* oreille *f*. **to keep one's ~s open** ouvrir l'oreille; **to keep one's ~ to the ground** être aux écoutes; **to be all ~s** * être tout oreilles; **your ~s must have been burning** les oreilles ont dû vous tinter; **it goes in one ~ and out of the other** cela lui *etc* entre par une oreille et lui *etc* sort par l'autre; **to be up to the ~s in work** avoir du travail par-dessus la tête; *(Mus)* **to have a good ~** avoir de l'oreille; **to play by ~** jouer à l'oreille; *(fig)* **I'll play it by ~** je déciderai quoi faire le moment venu. **2** *adj operation* à l'oreille. *(Med)* **~, nose and throat department** service *m* d'oto-rhino-laryngologie; **~, nose and throat specialist** oto-rhino-laryngologiste *mf*; ~ **wax** cérumen *m*. ◆ **earache** *n* mal *m* d'oreille(s); **to have ~ache** avoir mal à l'oreille *or* aux oreilles. ◆ **eardrops** *npl* gouttes *fpl* pour les oreilles. ◆ **eardrum** *n* tympan *m (de l'oreille)*. ◆ **earmark** *vt object, seat* réserver (*for* à); *funds, person* assigner, destiner (*for* à). ◆ **earphone** *n (Rad, Telec etc)* écouteur *m*; **to listen on ~phones** écouter au casque. ◆ **earplugs** *npl (for sleeping)* boules *fpl* Quiès ®. ◆ **earring** *n* boucle *f* d'oreille. ◆ **earshot** *n*: **out of ~shot** hors de portée de voix; **within ~shot** à portée de voix. ◆ **ear-splitting** *adj sound, scream* strident; *din* fracassant. ◆ **earwig** *n* perce-oreille *m*.

ear² [ɪəʳ] *n [grain, plant]* épi *m*.

earl [3:l] *n* comte *m*.

early [ˈ3:lɪ] **1** *adj man, Church* primitif; *apple, plant* précoce; *death* prématuré. **it's still ~** il est encore tôt, il n'est pas tard; **you're ~!** vous arrivez de bonne heure!; **he is always ~** il est toujours en avance; **his ~ arrival** son arrivée de bonne heure, le fait qu'il arrive (*or* est arrivé *etc*) de bonne heure; **an ~ train** un train tôt le matin; **the ~ train** le premier train; **an ~ text** un texte très ancien; **to be an ~ riser** être matinal; **to keep ~ hours** se coucher tôt; **~ to bed, ~ to rise** tôt couché, tôt levé; **~ warning system** dispositif *m* de première alerte; *(Comm)* **it's ~ closing day** les magasins ferment l'après-midi; **it is too ~ yet to say** il est trop tôt pour dire; **~ fruit** *or* **vegetables** primeurs *fpl*; **at an ~ hour** de bonne heure, très tôt; **it was ~ in the morning** c'était tôt le matin; **in the ~ morning** de bon matin; **in the ~ afternoon/spring** au début de l'après-midi/du printemps; **she's in her ~ forties** elle a juste dépassé la quarantaine; **from an ~ age** dès l'enfance; **his ~ youth** sa première jeunesse; **his ~ life** sa jeunesse; **~ retirement** préretraite *f*, retraite *f* anticipée; **the ~ Victorians** les Victoriens *mpl* du début du règne; **an ~ Victorian table** une table du début de l'époque victorienne; **at the earliest possible moment** le plus tôt possible; *(Comm)* **at your earliest convenience** dans les meilleurs délais; *(Comm)* **to promise ~ delivery** promettre une livraison rapide.
2 *adv* de bonne heure, tôt. **too ~** trop tôt; **as ~ as possible** le plus tôt possible; **she left 10 minutes ~** elle est partie 10 minutes plus tôt; **10 minutes earlier** 10 minutes plus tôt; **not earlier than Thursday** pas avant jeudi; **earlier on** précédemment, plus tôt; **book ~** réservez longtemps à l'avance; **~ in the morning** de bon matin; **~ in the year** au début de l'année.

earn [3:n] *vt money* gagner; *salary* toucher; *interest* rapporter; *praise, rest* mériter. **to ~ one's living** gagner sa vie; **~ed income** revenus *mpl* salariaux. ◆ **earnings** *npl [person]* salaire *m*; *[business]* bénéfices *mpl*. ◆ **earnings-related** *adj* proportionnel au salaire.

earnest [ˈ3:nɪst] **1** *adj* sérieux, consciencieux; *(sincere)* sincère; *prayer* fervent; *desire, request* pressant. **2** *n*: **in ~** *(with determination)* sérieusement; *(without joking)* sans rire. **I am in ~** je ne plaisante pas; **it is snowing in ~** il neige pour de bon. ◆ **earnestly** *adv speak* avec sérieux; *work* consciencieusement; *beseech* instamment; *pray* avec ferveur. ◆ **earnestness** *n [person]* sérieux *m*; *[effort]* ardeur *f*; *[demand]* véhémence *f*.

earth [3:θ] **1** *n* (**a**) *(the world)* terre *f*, monde *m*. **(the) E~** la Terre; **on ~** sur terre; **to the ends of the ~** au bout du monde; **where/why on ~...?** mais où/pourquoi...?; **nothing on ~** rien au monde; **to promise sb the ~** promettre la lune à qn; **it must have cost the ~!** * ça a dû coûter les yeux de la tête! * (**b**) *(ground)* terre *f*, sol *m*; *(soil)* terre; *(Elec)* masse *f*. **to fall to ~** tomber à terre. (**c**) *[fox, badger etc]* terrier *m*, tanière *f*. **to run sth/sb to ~** dépister qch/qn. **2** *adj*: **~ mother** *(Myth)* déesse *f* de la fertilité; *(fig)* mère *f* nourricière; **~ tremor** secousse *f* sismique. **3** *vt (Elec) apparatus* mettre à la masse.
◆ **earthen** *adj* de terre, en terre. ◆ **earthenware** **1** *n* faïence *f*; **2** *adj* en faïence. ◆ **earthling** *n* terrien(ne) *m(f)*. ◆ **earthly** *adj* terrestre; **there is no ~ly reason to think** il n'y a pas la moindre raison de croire; **it's no ~ly use** ça ne sert absolument à rien. ◆ **earthman** *n* terrien *m*. ◆ **earthquake** *n* tremblement *m* de terre. ◆ **earth-shaking** *adj (fig)* stupéfiant. ◆ **earthward(s)** *adv* vers la terre. ◆ **earthwork** *n (Constr)* terrassement *m*; *(Mil, Archeol)* ouvrage *m* de terre. ◆ **earth-**

worm *n* ver *m* de terre. ◆ **earthy** *adj taste, smell* terreux; *person* terre-à-terre *inv*; *humour* truculent.

ease [i:z] **1** *n* (**a**) *(mental)* tranquillité *f*; *(physical)* bien-être *m*. **at** ~ à l'aise; *(Mil)* au repos; **to put sb at his** ~ mettre qn à l'aise; **to put sb's mind at** ~ tranquilliser qn; **ill at** ~ mal à l'aise; **to take one's** ~ prendre ses aises; **a life of** ~ une vie facile. (**b**) *(lack of difficulty)* aisance *f*, facilité *f*. **with** ~ sans difficulté. **2** *vt pain* soulager; *mind* calmer, tranquilliser; *strap* relâcher; *(alter) coat* donner plus d'ampleur à; *pressure, tension* diminuer; *speed* ralentir. **to** ~ **a key into a lock** introduire doucement *or* délicatement une clef dans une serrure; **to** ~ **in the clutch** embrayer en douceur; **he** ~**d himself through the gap in the fence** il s'est glissé par le trou de la barrière. **3** *vi (~* **off***) (slow down)* ralentir; *(work less hard)* se relâcher; *[situation]* se détendre; *[pressure, traffic]* diminuer; *[work, business]* devenir plus calme; *[pain]* se calmer; *[demand]* baisser. **the situation has** ~**d** une détente s'est produite. ◆ **ease up** *vi* se détendre. ~ **up a bit!** vas-y plus doucement!

easel ['i:zl] *n* chevalet *m*.

east [i:st] **1** *n* est *m*. *(Pol)* **the E**~ les pays *mpl* de l'Est; **the mysterious E**~ l'Orient *m* mystérieux; **to the** ~ **of** à l'est de; **in the** ~ **of** dans l'est de; **the wind is in the** ~**/is from the** ~ le vent est à l'est/vient de l'est; **to live in the** ~ habiter dans l'Est. **2** *adj side* est *inv*; *wind* d'est; *coast, door* est *inv*, oriental. *(in London)* **the E**~ **End** les quartiers *mpl* est de Londres *(quartiers pauvres)*; **E**~ **Africa** l'Afrique *f* orientale; **E**~ **Berlin** Berlin-Est; **E**~ **Germany** Allemagne *f* de l'Est. **3** *adv travel* en direction de l'est, vers l'est; *be* à *or* dans l'est. ~ **of the border** à l'est de la frontière; **to go due** ~ aller droit vers l'est. ◆ **eastbound** *adj traffic, vehicles* en direction de l'est; *carriageway* est *inv*. ◆ **easterly** *adj wind* d'est; *situation, aspect* à l'est; **in an** ~**erly direction** en direction de l'est. ◆ **eastern** *adj region* est *inv*, de l'est; *coast* est *inv*, oriental; *wall, side* exposé à l'est; **E**~**ern France** l'Est *m* de la France; *(Pol)* **the E**~**ern bloc** les pays *mpl* de l'Est; *(US)* **E**~**ern Standard Time** l'heure *f* normale de l'Est. ◆ **easterner** *n* homme *m or* femme *f* de l'Est. ◆ **easternmost** *adj* le plus à l'est. ◆ **eastward** **1** *adj* à l'est ; **2** *adv (also* ~**wards***)* vers l'est.

Easter ['i:stə^r] **1** *n* Pâques *msg or fpl*. **at** ~ à Pâques; **Happy** ~! joyeuses Pâques!; ~ **is celebrated between...** Pâques est célébré entre... **2** *adj egg, Monday* de Pâques; *holidays, week* pascal, de Pâques. ~ **Day** le jour de Pâques.

easy ['i:zɪ] **1** *adj* (**a**) *(not difficult)* facile. **it is** ~ **to see that...** on voit bien que...; **it is** ~ **for him to do that** il lui est facile de faire cela; **easier said than done!** c'est vite dit!; **you've got an** ~ **time of it** tu as une vie sans problèmes; **it's** ~ **money** c'est comme si on était payé à ne rien faire; **within** ~ **reach of** à distance commode de; **in** ~ **stages** *travel* par petites étapes; *learn* par degrés; **he is** ~ **to work with** il est agréable dans le travail; ~ **to get on with** facile à vivre; **I'm** ~ * ça m'est égal; **he came in an** ~ **first** il est arrivé bon premier. (**b**) *(relaxed) manners, style* aisé; *life* tranquille; *pace* modéré; *conditions* favorable; *relationship* cordial. **to feel** ~ **in one's mind** être tout à fait tranquille; ~ **chair** fauteuil *m* (rembourré); **in** ~ **circumstances** dans l'aisance; *(Comm)* **on** ~ **terms** avec facilités *fpl* de paiement.
2 *adv*: **to take things** *or* **it** ~ ne pas se fatiguer; **take it** ~! *(calm down)* ne vous en faites pas!; *(relax)* ne vous fatiguez pas!; *(go slow)* ne vous pressez pas!; **go** ~ **with the sugar** vas-y doucement avec le sucre; **to go** ~ **with sb** ne pas être trop dur envers qn; ~ **does it!** allez-y doucement!; *(Mil)* **stand** ~! repos!
◆ **easily** *adv enter, succeed* facilement, sans difficulté; *answer, agree, say* tranquillement; *(unquestionably)* sans aucun doute, de loin; **that's easily 4 km** cela fait facilement 4 km; **he may easily change his mind** il pourrait bien changer d'avis. ◆ **easiness** *n* facilité *f*, aisance *f*. ◆ **easy-going** *adj* accommodant; *attitude* complaisant.

eat [i:t] *pret* **ate,** *ptp* **eaten** **1** *vt food* manger. **to** ~ **(one's) lunch** déjeuner; **to** ~ **a meal** prendre un repas; **to have nothing to** ~ n'avoir rien à manger; **to** ~ **one's fill** manger à sa faim; **to** ~ **one's words** ravaler ses paroles; **I'll** ~ **my hat if...** * je veux bien être pendu si...; **he won't** ~ **you** * il ne va pas te manger; **what's** ~**ing you?** ‡ qu'est-ce qui ne va pas? **2** *vi* manger. **we** ~ **at 8** nous dînons à 20 heures; **to** ~ **like a horse** manger comme quatre; **he is** ~**ing us out of house and home** * son appétit va nous mettre à la rue; *(fig)* **I've got him** ~**ing out of my hand** il fait tout ce que je veux. ◆ **eat away** *vt sep [sea]* éroder; *[acid, mice]* ronger. ◆ **eat into** *vt fus [acid, insects]* ronger; *savings* entamer. ◆ **eat out** **1** *vi* aller au restaurant. **2** *vt sep*: **to** ~ **one's heart out** se ronger d'inquiétude. ◆ **eat up** *vt sep meal etc* finir; *(fig) profits* absorber; *savings* engloutir. ~**en up with envy** dévoré d'envie; **it** ~**s up the electricity** cela consomme beaucoup d'électricité.
◆ **eatable** **1** *adj (fit to eat)* mangeable; *(edible)* comestible ; **2** *npl*: ~**ables** * comestibles *mpl*. ◆ **eater** *n*: **a big** ~**er** un gros mangeur. ◆ **eatery** *n* café-restaurant *m*. ◆ **eating** *adj apple* à couteau; *(US)* ~**ing hall** réfectoire *m*; ~**ing place** restaurant *m*.

eaves [i:vz] *npl* avant-toit *m*. ◆ **eavesdrop** *vi* écouter en cachette (*on sth* qch). ◆ **eavesdropper** *n* oreille *f* indiscrète.

ebb [eb] **1** *n [tide]* reflux *m*. ~ **and flow** le flux et le reflux; **to be at a low** ~ *[person, spirits]* être bien bas; *[business]* aller mal. **2** *adj*: ~ **tide** marée *f* descendante. **3** *vi* (**a**) *[tide]* descendre. **to** ~ **and flow** monter et baisser. (**b**) *(~* **away***) [enthusiasm etc]* décliner.

ebony ['ebənɪ] *n* ébène *f*.

ebullient [ɪ'bʌlɪənt] *adj* exubérant. ◆ **ebullience** *n* exubérance *f*.

eccentric [ɪk'sentrɪk] *adj, n* excentrique *(mf)*. ◆ **eccentrically** *adv* avec excentricité. ◆ **eccentricity** *n* excentricité *f*.

ecclesiastic [ɪˌkli:zɪ'æstɪk] *n* ecclésiastique *m*. ◆ **ecclesiastical** *adj* ecclésiastique.

echo ['ekəʊ] **1** *n* écho *m*. **to cheer to the** ~ applaudir à tout rompre. **2** *vt [hills etc]* répercuter; *[person] sb's words* répéter. **3** *vi [sound]* se répercuter; *[place]* faire écho. **to** ~ **with music** retentir de musique. **4** *adj (Rad)* ~ **chamber** chambre *f* sonore. ◆ **echo-sounder** *n* sondeur *m* (à ultrasons).

eclectic [ɪ'klektɪk] *adj, n* éclectique *(mf)*. ◆ **eclecticism** *n* éclectisme *m*.

eclipse [ɪ'klɪps] **1** *n* éclipse *f*. **2** *vt* éclipser.

ecology [ɪ'kɒlədʒɪ] *n* écologie *f*. ◆ **ecological** *adj* écologique. ◆ **ecologist** *n* écologiste *mf*.

economy [ɪ'kɒnəmɪ] **1** *n (all senses)* économie *f (in* de). **economies of scale** économies d'échelle. **2** *adj*: ~ **class** classe *f* touriste; **to have an** ~ **drive** (s'efforcer de) faire des économies; ~ **pack/size** paquet *m*/taille *f* économique. ◆ **economic** *adj* (**a**) *development, geography, factor* économique; *management, performance* de l'économie; **the economic system of a country** l'économie *f* d'un pays; (**b**) *(profitable) business, rent, price* rentable; **it isn't an economic proposition, it doesn't make economic sense** cela n'est pas intéressant (financièrement). ◆ **economical** *adj person* économe; *method, appliance, speed* économique. ◆ **economically** *adv* économiquement; **to use sth economically** économiser qch. ◆ **economics** *n (sg: science)* économie *f* politique; **the economics** *(npl)* **of the situation** le côté économique de la situation. ◆ **economist** *n* économiste *mf*. ◆ **economize** **1** *vi* économiser (*on* sur), faire des économies ; **2** *vt* économiser.

ecosystem ['i:kəʊˌsɪstəm] *n* écosystème *m*.

ecstasy ['ekstəsɪ] *n* extase *f*. **to be in ecstasies over** *object* s'extasier sur; *person* être en extase devant. ◆ **ecstatic** *adj* extasié. ◆ **ecstatically** *adv* avec extase.

Ecuador ['ekwədɔ:ʳ] *n* Équateur *m*.

ecumenical [ˌi:kjʊ'menɪk(ə)l] *adj* œcuménique.

eczema ['eksɪmə] *n* eczéma *m*.

eddy ['edɪ] **1** *n* tourbillon *m*. **2** *vi [air, smoke, leaves]* tourbillonner; *[people]* tournoyer; *[water]* faire des tourbillons.

edge [edʒ] **1** *n (gen)* bord *m*; *[forest]* lisière *f*; *[town]* abords *mpl*; *[coin]* tranche *f*; *[cube, brick]* arête *f*; *(distance round ~)* pourtour *m*; *[knife, razor]* tranchant *m*, fil *m*. **a book with gilt ~s** un livre doré sur tranches; **the trees at the ~ of the road** les arbres en bordure de la route; **on the ~ of disaster** au bord du désastre; **to take the ~ off** *knife, sensation* émousser; *appetite* calmer; **it sets my teeth on ~** cela m'agace les dents; **he is on ~** il est énervé; *(fig)* **to have the ~ on sb/sth** être légèrement supérieur à qn/qch. **2** *vt (put a border on)* border (*with* de); *(sharpen)* aiguiser. **to ~ one's chair nearer the door** rapprocher sa chaise tout doucement de la porte. **3** *vi*: **to ~ through/into** *etc* se glisser à travers/dans *etc*; **to ~ forward** avancer petit à petit. ◆ **edgeways** *or* ◆ **edgewise** *adv* de côté; **I couldn't get a word in ~ways** * je n'ai pas réussi à placer un mot. ◆ **edginess** *n* nervosité *f*, énervement *m*. ◆ **edging** **1** *n* bordure *f*; *[ribbon, silk]* liseré *m*; **2** *adj*: **edging shears** cisaille *f* de jardinier. ◆ **edgy** *adj* énervé.

edible ['edɪbl] *adj (not poisonous)* comestible; *(fit to eat)* mangeable.

edict ['i:dɪkt] *n (Hist)* édit *m*; *(Jur, Pol)* décret *m*.

edifice ['edɪfɪs] *n* édifice *m*.

edify ['edɪfaɪ] *vt* édifier. ◆ **edification** *n* édification *f*.

Edinburgh ['edɪnb(ə)rə] *n* Édimbourg.

edit ['edɪt] *vt newspaper* être le rédacteur (*or* la rédactrice) en chef de; *magazine, review* diriger; *article, tape* mettre au point; *(cut)* couper; *series of texts* diriger la publication de; *text, author* éditer; *dictionary* rédiger; *(Rad, TV) programme* réaliser; *(Comput) file* éditer; *film* monter. ◆ **edition** *n* édition *f*. ◆ **editor** *n [daily newspaper]* rédacteur *m*, -trice *f* en chef; *[magazine, review]* directeur *m*, -trice *f*; *[series]* directeur, -trice de la publication; *[text]* éditeur *m*, -trice *f*; *[dictionary]* rédacteur, -trice; *[Rad, TV programme]* réalisateur *m*, -trice *f*; *(Press)* **political ~or** rédacteur, -trice politique. ◆ **editorial** **1** *adj* de la rédaction; **~orial staff** rédaction *f* ; **2** *n* éditorial *m*.

educate ['edjʊkeɪt] *vt pupil* instruire, donner de l'instruction à; *the public* éduquer; *mind, tastes* former; *(bring up) family, children* élever. **to ~ sb to believe that...** enseigner à qn que...; **he is being ~d in Paris** il fait ses études à Paris. ◆ **educable** *adj* éducable. ◆ **educated** *adj person* instruit, cultivé; *handwriting* distingué; *voice* cultivé; **well-~d** qui a reçu une bonne éducation. ◆ **educative** *adj* éducatif. ◆ **educator** *n* éducateur *m*, -trice *f*.

education [ˌedjʊ'keɪʃ(ə)n] *n* éducation *f*; *(teaching)* enseignement *m*, instruction *f*; *(studies)* études *fpl*; *(training)* formation *f*; *(knowledge)* culture *f*; *(Univ etc: subject)* pédagogie *f*. **Ministry of E~** ministère *m* de l'Éducation nationale ; **primary/secondary ~** enseignement primaire/ secondaire; **he had a good ~** il a reçu une bonne éducation; **physical/political ~** éducation physique/ politique; **his ~ was interrupted** ses études ont été interrompues; **literary/professional ~** formation littéraire/professionnelle; **diploma in ~** diplôme *m* de pédagogie; **the ~ system** le système d'éducation. ◆ **educational** *adj methods* pédagogique; *establishment, institution* d'enseignement; *system* d'éducation; *supplies* scolaire; *film, games, visit* éducatif; *role, function* éducateur; *experience, event* instructif; **~al psychology** psychopédagogie *f* ; **~al qualifications** diplômes *mpl;* **~al standards** le niveau d'instruction. ◆ **education(al)ist** *n* pédagogue *mf*. ◆ **educationally** *adv (as regards teaching methods)* du point de vue pédagogique; *(as regards education, schooling)* sous l'angle scolaire; **it is ~ally wrong** il est faux d'un point de vue pédagogique; **~ally subnormal** arriéré; **~ally deprived children** enfants sous-scolarisés.

Edwardian [ed'wɔ:dɪən] *adj (Brit) lady, architect, society* de l'époque du roi Édouard VII; *clothes, manners, design* dans le style 1900. **the ~ era** ≃ la Belle Époque.

eel [i:l] *n* anguille *f*.

eerie, eery ['ɪərɪ] *adj* sinistre, qui donne le frisson.

efface [ɪ'feɪs] *vt* effacer.

effect [ɪ'fekt] **1** *n* (**a**) *(result)* effet *m* (*on* sur), conséquence *f*; *[wind, chemical, drug]* action *f* (*on* sur); *(Phys)* effet. **to have an ~ on** produire un effet sur; *[wind etc]* agir sur; **to have no ~** ne produire aucun effet; **it will have the ~ of preventing** cela aura pour effet *or* conséquence d'empêcher; **the ~ of all this is that...** il résulte de tout ceci que...; **to no ~** en vain; **to such good ~ that** si bien que; **to put into ~** *project* mettre à exécution; *regulation* mettre en vigueur; **to take ~** *[drug]* agir; *[law]* entrer en vigueur; **in ~** en fait, en réalité. (**b**) *(impression)* effet *m*. **stage ~s** effets scéniques; **sound ~s** bruitage *m*; **to make an ~** faire de l'effet; **he said it for ~** il l'a dit pour faire de l'effet; **his letter is to the ~ that...** sa lettre nous apprend que...; **a letter to that ~** une lettre dans ce sens; **orders to the ~ that** ordres suivant lesquels; **or words to that ~** ou qch d'analogue. (**c**) *(property)* **~s** biens *mpl*. **2** *vt reform, reduction, payment, sale* effectuer; *cure* obtenir; *improvement* apporter; *transformation* opérer; *saving* réaliser; *reconciliation, reunion* amener. **to ~ an entry** entrer de force. ◆ **effective** *adj* (**a**) *(efficient) cure, measures, system* efficace; *word, remark, argument* qui porte; *(impressive)* frappant, qui fait de l'effet; **to become ~ive** *[regulation]* entrer en vigueur; *[ticket]* être valide; (**b**) *(actual) aid, contribution* effectif; **the ~ive head of the family** le chef réel de la famille. ◆ **effectively** *adv (efficiently)* efficacement; *(usefully)* utilement; *(strikingly)* d'une manière frappante; *(in reality)* effectivement. ◆ **effectiveness** *n (efficiency)* efficacité *f*; *(striking quality)* effet frappant. ◆ **effectual** *adj* efficace. ◆ **effectually** *adv* efficacement. ◆ **effectuate** *vt* effectuer.

effeminate [ɪ'femɪnɪt] *adj* efféminé. ◆ **effeminacy** *n* caractère *m* efféminé.

effervesce [ˌefə'ves] *vi [liquids]* être en effervescence; *[drinks]* mousser; *[person]* être tout excité. ◆ **effervescence** *n* effervescence *f*. ◆ **effervescent** *adj liquid, tablet* effervescent; *drink* gazeux; *person* plein d'entrain.

efficacious [ˌefɪ'keɪʃəs] *adj* efficace. ◆ **efficacy** ['efɪkəsɪ] *n* efficacité *f*.

efficient [ɪ'fɪʃ(ə)nt] *adj person* capable, compétent; *method, system, organization* efficace; *machine* qui fonctionne bien. ◆ **efficiency** *n* capacité *f*, compétence *f*; efficacité *f*; bon fonctionnement *m*. ◆ **efficiently** *adv* avec compétence; efficacement; *[machine]* **to work ~ly** bien fonctionner.

effluent ['eflʊənt] *adj, n* effluent *(m)*.

effort ['efət] *n* effort *m*. **to make an ~ to do** faire un effort pour faire, s'efforcer de faire; **to make every ~ to do** faire tout son possible pour faire; **he made no ~ to be polite** il ne s'est pas donné la peine d'être poli; **it's not worth the ~** cela ne vaut pas la peine; **in an ~ to solve the problem** pour essayer de résoudre le problème; **it's an awful ~ to get up!** il en faut du courage pour se lever!; **what do you think of his latest ~?** * qu'est-ce que tu penses de ce qu'il vient de faire?; **a first ~** un coup d'essai, une tentative; **that's a good ~** * ça n'est pas mal réussi; **it's a pretty poor ~** * ça n'est pas une réussite. ◆ **effortless** *adj success* facile; *movement* aisé. ◆ **effortlessly** *adv* sans effort, facilement.

effrontery [ɪ'frʌntərɪ] *n* effronterie *f*.

effusive [ɪ'fju:sɪv] *adj person* expansif; *welcome* chaleureux; *thanks, apologies* sans fin. ◆ **effusion** *n* effusion *f*. ◆ **effusively** *adv* avec effusion.

eft [eft] *n (Zool)* triton *m* crêté.

egalitarian [ɪ,gælɪ'tɛərɪən] **1** *n* égalitariste *mf*. **2** *adj person* égalitariste; *principle* égalitaire. ◆ **egalitarianism** *n* égalitarisme *m*.

egg [eg] **1** *n* œuf *m*. **~s and bacon** œufs au bacon; *(fig)* **to put all one's ~s in one basket** mettre tous ses œufs dans le même panier; *(fig)* **to have ~ on one's face** * avoir l'air plutôt ridicule. **2** *adj*: **~ white/yolk** blanc *m*/jaune *m* d'œuf; **~ custard** ≃ crème *f* renversée. **3** *vt* (**~ on**) inciter (*to do* à faire). ◆ **eggbeater** *n (rotary)* batteur *m* (à œufs); *(whisk)* fouet *m* (à œufs). ◆ **eggcup** *n* coquetier *m*. ◆ **eggflip** *or* ◆ **eggnog** *n* flip *m*. ◆ **egghead** ‡ *n* intellectuel(le) *m(f)*, cérébral(e) *m(f)*. ◆ **eggplant** *n* aubergine *f*. ◆ **egg-shaped** *adj* ovoïde. ◆ **eggshell** **1** *n* coquille *f* (d'œuf); **2** *adj paint* presque mat. ◆ **egg-timer** *n (sand)* sablier *m*; *(automatic)* minuteur *m*.

ego ['i:gəʊ] **1** *n (Psych)* **the ~** le moi, l'ego *m*. **2** *adj*: **to be on an ~ trip** planer *. ◆ **egocentric(al)** *adj* égocentrique. ◆ **egomania** *n* manie *f* égocentrique. ◆ **ego(t)ism** *n* égotisme *m*. ◆ **ego(t)ist** *n* égotiste *mf*. ◆ **ego(t)istic(al)** *adj* égotiste.

Egypt ['i:dʒɪpt] *n* Égypte *f*. ◆ **Egyptian** **1** *adj* égyptien ; **2** *n* Égyptien(ne) *m(f)*.

eiderdown ['aɪdədaʊn] *n* édredon *m*.

eight [eɪt] **1** *adj, n* huit *(m) inv*. **he's had one over the ~** * il a un verre dans le nez *. **2** *pron* huit *mfpl; for phrases V* **six**. ◆ **eighteen** *adj, n, pron* dix-huit *(m, mpl) inv*. ◆ **eighteenth** **1** *adj* dix-huitième ; **2** *n* dix-huitième *mf*; *(fraction)* dix-huitième *m*. ◆ **eighth** **1** *adj* huitième ; **2** *n* huitième *mf*; *(fraction)* huitième *m*. ◆ **eightieth** **1** *adj* quatre-vingtième ; **2** *n* quatre-vingtième *mf*; *(fraction)* quatre-vingtième *m*. ◆ **eighty** *adj, n, pron* quatre-vingts *(m, mfpl) inv*; **~y books** quatre-vingts livres; **~y-one** quatre-vingt-un; **~y-first** quatre-vingt-unième; **page ~y** page quatre-vingt.

Eire ['ɛərə] *n* République *f* d'Irlande, Irlande *f* du Sud.

either ['aɪðə'] **1** *adj* (**a**) *(one or other)* l'un ou l'autre, n'importe lequel (des deux). **~ day would suit me** l'un ou l'autre jour me conviendrait ; **I don't like ~ girl** je n'aime ni l'une ni l'autre de ces filles. (**b**) *(each)* chaque. **in ~ hand** dans chaque main; **on ~ side of the street** des deux côtés *or* de chaque côté de la rue; **on ~ side lay fields** de part et d'autre s'étendaient des champs. **2** *pron* l'un(e) ou l'autre, n'importe lequel (*or* laquelle) (des deux). **which bus will you take? — ~** quel bus prendrez-vous? — l'un ou l'autre *or* n'importe lequel (des deux); **I don't believe ~ of them** je ne les crois ni l'un ni l'autre; **give it to ~ of them** donnez-le soit à l'un soit à l'autre; **if ~ is attacked the other helps her** si l'une des deux est attaquée l'autre l'aide. **3** *adv* non plus. **he can't act ~** il ne sait pas jouer non plus; **no, I haven't ~** moi non plus. **4** *conj*: **~ ... or** ou (bien)... ou (bien), soit... soit; *(after neg)* ni... ni; **~ he or his sister** soit lui soit sa sœur, ou (bien) lui ou (bien) sa sœur; **I have never been ~ to Paris or to Rome** je ne suis jamais allé ni à Paris ni à Rome.

ejaculate [ɪ'dʒækjʊleɪt] *vti (cry out)* s'exclamer; *(Physiol)* éjaculer. ◆ **ejaculation** *n* exclamation *f*; éjaculation *f*.

eject [ɪ'dʒekt] **1** *vt (Aviat, Tech etc)* éjecter; *tenant, trouble-maker* expulser, vider *; *trespasser* chasser. **2** *vi [pilot]* utiliser le mécanisme d'éjection. ◆ **ejection** *n* éjection *f*; expulsion *f*. ◆ **ejector** *n* éjecteur *m*; **~or seat** siège *m* éjectable.

eke [i:k] *vt*: **to ~ out** *(by adding)* augmenter (*by doing* en faisant); *(by saving)* faire durer.

elaborate [ɪ'læb(ə)rɪt] **1** *adj (complicated)* complexe, compliqué; *(careful)* minutieux; *joke, meal, style, clothes* recherché; *work of art* travaillé. **with ~ care** très soigneusement, minutieusement. **2** [ɪ'læbəreɪt] *vt* élaborer. **3** *vi* donner des détails (*on* sur). ◆ **elaborately** *adv do, prepare, plan* minutieusement; *dress, write* avec recherche.

elapse [ɪ'læps] *vi* s'écouler, (se) passer.

elastic [ɪ'læstɪk] **1** *adj* élastique. **~ band** élastique *m*; **~ stockings** bas *mpl* à varices. **2** *n* élastique *m*. ◆ **elasticity** *n* élasticité *f*.

elate [ɪ'leɪt] *vt* transporter. ◆ **elated** *adj* transporté (de joie). ◆ **elation** *n* allégresse *f*.

elbow ['elbəʊ] **1** *n* coude *m*. **to lean one's ~s on** s'accouder à, être accoudé à; **at his ~** à ses côtés; **out at the ~s** *garment* percé aux coudes; *person* déguenillé. **2** *adj*: **to use a bit of ~ grease** * mettre de l'huile de coude *; **to have enough ~ room** avoir de la place pour se retourner; *(fig)* avoir les coudées franches. **3** *vt*: **to ~ sb aside** écarter qn du coude; **to ~ (one's way) through the crowd** se frayer un passage à travers la foule (en jouant des coudes).

elder[1] ['eldə'] *n (Bot)* sureau *m*. ◆ **elderberry** *n* baie *f* de sureau; **~berry wine** vin *m* de sureau.

elder[2] ['eldə'] **1** *adj* aîné *(de deux)*. **my ~ sister** ma sœur aînée; **~ statesman** homme *m* politique chevronné. **2** *n* aîné(e) *m(f)*. *[tribe]* **~s** anciens *mpl*; **one's ~s and betters** ses aînés. ◆ **elderly** *adj* assez âgé. ◆ **eldest** *adj* aîné *(de plusieurs)*; **their eldest child** l'aîné(e) de leurs enfants; **my eldest brother** l'aîné de mes frères.

elect [ɪ'lekt] **1** *vt (by vote)* élire (*to* à); *(more formally)* nommer (*to* à); *(choose)* choisir (*to do* de faire). **he was ~ed chairman** il a été élu président. **2** *adj* futur. **the president ~** le futur président. **3** *npl*: **the ~** les élus *mpl*. ◆ **election** **1** *n* élection *f*; **to hold an ~ion** procéder à une élection ; **2** *adj campaign, speech, agent* électoral; *day, results* du scrutin; *publication* de propagande électorale; *(US)* **~s judge** scrutateur *m*. ◆ **electioneer** *vi* mener une campagne électorale. ◆ **elective** **1** *adj committee* élu; *body, post* électif ; **2** *n (US)* matière *f* à option. ◆ **elector** *n* électeur *m*, -trice *f*. ◆ **electoral** *adj* électoral; **~oral district** circonscription *f* électorale; **~oral roll** liste *f* électorale. ◆ **electorate** *n* électorat *m*.

electric [ɪ'lektrɪk] *adj* électrique. **~ blanket** couverture *f* chauffante; **~ chair** chaise *f* électrique; **~ eye** cellule *f* photo-électrique; **~ fence** clôture électrifiée; **~ fire** radiateur *m* électrique; **~ light** lumière *f* électrique; **~ shock** décharge *f* électrique; **to get an ~ shock** recevoir une décharge électrique; *(Med)* **~ shock treatment** * électrochocs *mpl*; **~ storm** orage *m* magnétique; *(fig)* **the atmosphere was ~** il y avait de l'électricité dans l'air *. ◆ **electrical** *adj* électrique; **~al engineer** ingénieur *m* électricien; **~al engineering** électrotechnique *f*; **~al failure** panne *f* d'électricité. ◆ **electrician** *n* électricien *m*. ◆ **electricity** *n* électricité *f*; **to switch off/on the ~ity** couper/rétablir le courant; **~ity board** office *m* régional de l'électricité. ◆ **electrification** *n* électrification *f*. ◆ **electrify** *vt (Rail)* électrifier; *(charge with electricity)* électriser; *(fig) audience* électriser. ◆ **electrifying** *adj* électrisant.

electro... [ɪ'lektrəʊ] *pref* électro... ◆ **electrocardiogram** *n* électrocardiogramme *m*. ◆ **electrocardiograph** *n* électrocardiographe *m*. ◆ **electrochemical** *adj* électrochimique. ◆ **electrochemistry** *n* électrochimie *f*. ◆ **electroconvulsive** *adj*: **to give sb ~convulsive therapy** traiter qn par électrochocs. ◆ **electrocute** *vt* électrocuter. ◆ **electrocution** *n* électrocution *f*. ◆ **electrodynamics** *nsg* électrodynamique *f*. ◆ **electroencephalogram** *n* électro-encéphalogramme *m*. ◆ **electroencephalograph** *n* électro-encéphalographie *f*. ◆ **electrolysis** [ˌɪlek'trɒlɪsɪs] *n* électrolyse *f*. ◆ **electromagnetic** *adj* électromagnétique. ◆ **electroplated** *adj*: **~plated nickel silver** ruolz *m*. ◆ **electroshock treatment** *n (Med)* électrochocs *mpl*.

electrode [ɪ'lektrəʊd] *n* électrode *f*.

electron [ɪ'lektrɒn] **1** *n* électron *m*. **2** *adj microscope etc* électronique. **~ gun** canon *m* à électrons. ◆ **electronic** *adj (gen)* électronique; **~ic engineering** génie *m* électronique; **~ic mail** messagerie *f* électronique; **~ic surveillance** utilisation *f* d'appareils d'écoute. ◆ **electronics** *nsg* électronique *f*.

elegant ['elɪgənt] *adj* élégant. ◆ **elegance** *n* élégance *f*. ◆ **elegantly** *adv* élégamment, avec élégance.

elegy ['elɪdʒɪ] *n* élégie *f*.

element ['elɪmənt] *n (gen)* élément *m*; *[heater, kettle]* résistance *f*. **an ~ of danger/truth** une part de danger/de vérité; **the ~ of chance** le facteur chance; **to be in one's ~** être dans son élément; *(Rel)* **the E~s** les Espèces *fpl*. ◆ **elemental** *adj* élémentaire; *(basic)* essentiel. ◆ **elementary** *adj (gen)* élémentaire; *school, education* primaire; **~ary science** les rudiments *mpl* de la science.

elephant ['elɪfənt] *n* éléphant *m*. ◆ **elephantine** *adj* éléphantesque.

elevate ['elɪveɪt] *vt object* élever *(also fig, Rel)*. ◆ **elevated** *adj position* élevé; *railway* aérien; *rank* éminent; *style* soutenu; *thoughts* noble; *(US)* **~d railroad** métro *m* aérien. ◆ **elevating** *adj (fig)* exaltant. ◆ **elevation** *n (gen)* élévation *f*; *(altitude)* altitude *f*; *(Archit)* **front elevation** façade *f*; **sectional elevation** coupe *f* verticale. ◆ **elevator** *n* élévateur *m*; *(US: lift)* ascenseur *m*; *(hoist)* monte-charge *m inv*; *(US)* **elevator (shoe)** soulier *m* à talonnette.

eleven [ɪ'levn] *adj, n* onze *(m) inv*. *(Scol)* **the ~ plus** ≃ l'examen *m* d'entrée en sixième; *(Sport)* **the first ~** le onze, la première équipe; *for phrases V* **six**. ◆ **elevenses** * *npl* pause-café *f*. ◆ **eleventh** **1** *adj* onzième; *(fig)* **at the ~th hour** à la onzième heure ; **2** *n* onzième *mf*; *(fraction)* onzième *m*.

elf, *pl* **elves** [elf, elvz] *n* lutin *m*.

elicit [ɪ'lɪsɪt] *vt truth, secret* arracher *(from sb* à qn), découvrir; *facts of a case* tirer au clair; *(from sb)* obtenir *(from* de); *admission, reply, explanation* obtenir *(from* de).

eligible ['elɪdʒəbl] *adj (for membership, office)* éligible *(for* à); *(for job)* admissible *(for* à). **to be ~ for** *pension* avoir droit à; *promotion* remplir les conditions requises pour obtenir; **an ~ young man** un beau parti. ◆ **eligibility** *n* éligibilité *f*; admissibilité *f*.

eliminate [ɪ'lɪmɪneɪt] *vt (gen)* éliminer *(from* de); *possibility* exclure; *bad language, detail* supprimer; *(kill)* supprimer. ◆ **elimination** *n* élimination *f*; **by the process of elimination** en procédant par élimination.

elision [ɪ'lɪʒ(ə)n] *n* élision *f*.

élite [eɪ'li:t] **1** *n* élite *f*. **2** *adj troops* d'élite; *school* réservé à l'élite. ◆ **elitism** *n* élitisme *m*. ◆ **elitist** *adj, n* élitiste *(mf)*.

elixir [ɪ'lɪksə^r] *n* élixir *m*.

Elizabethan [ɪˌlɪzə'bi:θ(ə)n] *adj* élisabéthain.

elliptic(al) [ɪ'lɪptɪk(əl)] *adj* elliptique.

elm [elm] *n* orme *m*.

elocution [ˌelə'kju:ʃ(ə)n] *n* élocution *f*.

elongate ['i:lɒŋgeɪt] *vt* allonger. ◆ **elongation** *n* allongement *m*; *(Med)* élongation *f*.

elope [ɪ'ləʊp] *vi [couple]* s'enfuir. **to ~ with sb** *[woman]* se laisser enlever par qn; *[man]* enlever qn. ◆ **elopement** *n* fugue *f* (amoureuse).

eloquent ['eləkw(ə)nt] *adj (gen)* éloquent; *words* entraînant; *silence* qui en dit long. ◆ **eloquence** *n* éloquence *f*. ◆ **eloquently** *adv* avec éloquence.

else [els] *adv* autre, d'autre, de plus. **anybody ~ would have done it** tout autre *or* n'importe qui d'autre l'aurait fait; **is there anybody ~ there?** y a-t-il qn d'autre?; **I'd prefer anything ~** je préférerais n'importe quoi d'autre; **have you anything ~ to say?** avez-vous encore qch à dire?; **anything ~ sir?** *[shop assistant]* et avec ça *, monsieur?; **nothing ~, thank you** plus rien, merci; **anywhere ~ nobody would have noticed, but...** n'importe où ailleurs personne ne s'en serait aperçu, mais...; **can you do it anywhere ~?** pouvez-vous le faire ailleurs?; **how ~ can I do it?** comment est-ce que je peux le faire autrement?; **nobody ~, no one ~** personne d'autre; **nothing ~** rien d'autre; **nowhere ~** nulle part ailleurs; **sb ~** qn d'autre; **sth ~** autre chose, qch d'autre; **somewhere ~** ailleurs, autre part; **who ~?** qui encore?; **what ~ could I do?** que pouvais-je faire d'autre?; **and much ~** et bien d'autres choses (encore); **there is little ~ to be done** il n'y a pas grand-chose d'autre à faire; **or ~** ou bien, sinon, autrement; **do it or ~ go away** faites-le, ou bien allez-vous-en; **do it or ~!** * faites-le sinon...! ◆ **elsewhere** *adv* ailleurs.

elucidate [ɪ'lu:sɪdeɪt] *vt* élucider. ◆ **elucidation** *n* élucidation *f*.

elude [ɪ'lu:d] *vt enemy, pursuit, arrest* échapper à; *the law, question* éluder; *sb's gaze, police, responsibility* se dérober à; *blow* esquiver, éviter. **the name ~s me** le nom m'échappe; **success ~d him** le succès restait hors de sa portée. ◆ **elusive** *adj enemy, prey, thoughts* insaisissable; *word, happiness, success* qui échappe; *glance, personality* fuyant; *answer* évasif; *(gen)* **she's very elusive** il est impossible de la coincer.

emaciated [ɪ'meɪsɪeɪtɪd] *adj person, face* émacié; *limb* décharné. **to become ~** s'émacier, se décharner. ◆ **emaciation** *n* émaciation *f*.

emanate ['eməneɪt] *vi* émaner *(from* de). ◆ **emanation** *n* émanation *f*.

emancipate [ɪ'mænsɪpeɪt] *vt women* émanciper; *slaves* affranchir; *(fig)* émanciper, affranchir *(from* de). ◆ **emancipated** *adj* émancipé, libéré. ◆ **emancipation** *n* émancipation *f*; affranchissement *m*.

embalm [ɪm'bɑ:m] *vt* embaumer.

embankment [ɪm'bæŋkmənt] *n [path, railway]* talus *m*, remblai *m*; *[canal, dam]* digue *f*. *(fig)* **to sleep on the E~** ≃ coucher sous les ponts.

embargo [ɪm'bɑ:gəʊ] *n (Comm, Naut: prohibition)* embargo *m*; *(fig)* interdiction *f*. **to put an ~ on** mettre l'embargo sur; *(fig)* interdire.

embark [ɪm'bɑ:k] **1** *vt* embarquer. **2** *vi (Aviat, Naut)* s'embarquer *(on* à bord de, sur). **to ~ on** *journey* commencer; *business, undertaking, explanation* se lancer dans; *discussion* entamer. ◆ **embarkation** **1** *n [passengers]* embarquement *m*; *[cargo]* chargement *m* ; **2** *adj*: ~**ation card** carte *f* d'embarquement.

embarrass [ɪm'bærəs] *vt* embarrasser, gêner. **I feel ~ed about it** j'en suis gêné, cela m'embarrasse; **to be financially ~ed** avoir des embarras *mpl* d'argent. ◆ **embarrassing** *adj* embarrassant, gênant; **to get out of an ~ing situation** se tirer d'embarras. ◆ **embarrassment** *n* embarras *m*, gêne *f* (*at* devant); **to be an ~ment to sb** embarrasser qn.

embassy ['embəsɪ] *n* ambassade *f*. **the French E~** l'ambassade de France.

embed [ɪm'bed] *vt (in wood)* enfoncer; *(in cement, stone)* sceller; *jewel* enchâsser; *(Ling)* enchâsser.

embellish [ɪm'belɪʃ] *vt (gen)* embellir (*with* de); *manuscript, tale* enjoliver (*with* de); *truth* broder sur. ◆ **embellishment** *n* enjolivement *m*.

embers ['embəz] *npl* braise *f*. **the dying ~** les tisons *mpl*.

embezzle [ɪm'bezl] *vt* détourner *(des fonds)*. ◆ **embezzlement** *n* détournement *m* de fonds. ◆ **embezzler** *n* escroc *m*.

embitter [ɪm'bɪtəʳ] *vt person* aigrir; *relations, disputes* envenimer. ◆ **embittered** *adj* aigri.

emblem ['embləm] *n* emblème *m*.

embody [ɪm'bɒdɪ] *vt spirit, quality* incarner; *one's thoughts, theories* exprimer (*in* dans, en); *[machine] features* réunir. ◆ **embodiment** *n* incarnation *f*; **he is the embodiment of kindness** c'est la bonté incarnée.

embolism ['embəlɪz(ə)m] *n* embolie *f*.

emboss [ɪm'bɒs] *vt metal* travailler en relief ; *leather, cloth* gaufrer. ◆ **embossed** *adj wallpaper* gaufré; *writing paper* à en-tête en relief.

embrace [ɪm'breɪs] **1** *vt person* embrasser, étreindre; *religion, cause, theme, period* embrasser. **2** *vi* s'étreindre, s'embrasser. **3** *n* étreinte *f*.

embrocation [ˌembrə(ʊ)'keɪʃ(ə)n] *n* embrocation *f*.

embroider [ɪm'brɔɪdəʳ] *vt* broder; *facts, truth* broder sur. ◆ **embroidery** **1** *n* broderie *f*; **2** *adj silk* à broder.

embroiled [ɪm'brɔɪld] *adj*: **~ in** entraîné dans; **to get (o.s.) ~ in** se laisser entraîner dans.

embryo ['embrɪəʊ] *n* embryon *m*. **in ~** en germe. ◆ **embryonic** *adj* embryonnaire; *(fig)* en germe.

emend [ɪ'mend] *vt* corriger *(un texte)*. ◆ **emendation** *n* correction *f*.

emerald ['emər(ə)ld] **1** *n (stone)* émeraude *f*; *(colour)* émeraude *m*. **2** *adj necklace* d'émeraudes; *(~ **green**)* émeraude *inv*.

emerge [ɪ'mɜːdʒ] *vi (gen)* apparaître, surgir (*from* de, *from behind* de derrière); *(from water)* émerger, surgir (*from* de); *[truth, facts]* émerger (*from* de), apparaître; *[difficulties]* surgir, s'élever; *[new nation, theory, school of thought]* naître. **it ~s that** il ressort que, il apparaît que. ◆ **emergence** *n* apparition *f*; naissance *f*. ◆ **emergent** *adj*: **~nt nations** pays *mpl* en voie de développement.

emergency [ɪ'mɜːdʒ(ə)nsɪ] **1** *n* cas *m* urgent. **in an ~** en cas d'urgence *or* d'imprévu; **prepared for any ~** prêt à toute éventualité; **in this ~** dans cette situation critique; **to declare a state of ~** déclarer l'état d'urgence. **2** *adj measures, operation, repair* d'urgence; *brake, airstrip* de secours; *powers* extraordinaire; *rations* de réserve; *(improvised) mast* de fortune. *(Aut)* **~ blinkers** feux *mpl* de détresse ; *(Med)* **an ~ case** une urgence; **~ exit** sortie *f* de secours; *(Mil)* **~ force** force *f* d'intervention; *(Aviat)* **~ landing** atterrissage forcé; *(Med)* **~ service** service *m* des urgences; **~ services** ≃ police-secours *f*; **~ ward**, *(US)* **~ room** salle *f* des urgences.

emery ['emərɪ] **1** *n* émeri *m*. **2** *adj*: **~ cloth/paper** toile *f*/papier *m* d'émeri.

emetic [ɪ'metɪk] *adj, n* émétique *(m)*.

emigrate ['emɪgreɪt] *vi* émigrer. ◆ **emigrant** *n* émigrant(e) *m(f)*; *(established)* émigré(e) *m(f)*. ◆ **emigration** *n* émigration *f*.

eminent ['emɪnənt] *adj (gen)* éminent; *person* éminent, très distingué. ◆ **eminence** *n* distinction *f*; **to win eminence** acquérir un grand renom; **Your Eminence** Votre Éminence *f*. ◆ **eminently** *adv suited* éminemment; *respectable* parfaitement; *fair* admirablement.

emir [e'mɪəʳ] *n* émir *m*. ◆ **emirate** *n* émirat *m*.

emit [ɪ'mɪt] *vt (gen)* dégager, émettre; *sparks* jeter; *light, electromagnetic waves, banknotes, sound* émettre; *cry* laisser échapper. ◆ **emission** *n* dégagement *m*, émission *f*.

emolument [ɪ'mɒljʊmənt] *n* émoluments *mpl*.

emotion [ɪ'məʊʃ(ə)n] *n* (**a**) émotion *f*. **full of ~** ému. (**b**) *(jealousy, love etc)* sentiment *m*. ◆ **emotional** *adj shock, disturbance* émotif; *reaction, state* émotionnel; *moment* d'émotion profonde; *story, writing* qui fait appel aux sentiments; *person* facilement ému; **he was being very ~al about it** il prenait cela très à cœur. ◆ **emotionalism** *n* sensiblerie *f (pej)*. ◆ **emotionally** *adv speak* avec émotion; **~ally deprived** privé d'affection; **he is ~ally involved** ses sentiments sont en cause. ◆ **emotive** *adj word* chargé de connotations.

empathy ['empəθɪ] *n* empathie *f*.

emperor ['emp(ə)rəʳ] *n* empereur *m*.

emphasis ['emfəsɪs] *n (in word, phrase)* accentuation *f*, accent *m* d'intensité; *(fig)* accent. **to speak with ~** parler sur un ton d'insistance; *(fig)* **the ~ is on sport** on accorde une importance particulière au sport. ◆ **emphasize** *vt word, fact, point* appuyer sur, insister sur; *[garment etc] sb's height etc* accentuer; **I must emphasize that...** je dois souligner le fait que... ◆ **emphatic** *adj tone, manner, person* énergique; *denial, speech, condemnation* catégorique, énergique. ◆ **emphatically** *adv speak* énergiquement; *deny, refuse* catégoriquement; **yes, emphatically!** oui, absolument!; **I must say this emphatically** sur ce point je suis formel.

empire ['empaɪəʳ] **1** *n* empire *m*. **2** *adj*: **E~** *costume, furniture* Empire *inv*. ◆ **empire-builder** *n* bâtisseur *m* d'empires. ◆ **empire-build** *vi*: **he is ~-building** il joue les bâtisseurs d'empire.

empiric(al) [em'pɪrɪk(əl)] *adj* empirique. ◆ **empiricism** *n* empirisme *m*. ◆ **empiricist** *adj, n* empiriste *(mf)*.

employ [ɪm'plɔɪ] **1** *vt* employer (*as* comme; *to do* pour faire; *in doing* à faire). **to be ~ed in doing** être occupé à faire. **2** *n*: **in the ~ of** employé par; *domestic staff* au service de. ◆ **employee** *n* employé(e) *m(f)*. ◆ **employer** *n (gen)* patron(ne) *m(f)*; *(Admin)* employeur *m*, -euse *f*; *(Ind: collectively)* **~ers** le patronat; **~ers' federation/ contribution** fédération/cotisation patronale. ◆ **employment** **1** *n* emploi *m*; *(a job)* emploi, travail *m*; **full ~ment** le plein emploi; **to take up ~ment** prendre un emploi; **without ~ment** sans emploi, au chômage; **to find ~ment** trouver un emploi *or* du travail; **in sb's ~ment** employé par qn; *domestic staff* au service de qn; **conditions/place of ~ment** conditions *fpl*/lieu *m* de travail; **Ministry of E~ment** ministère *m* de l'Emploi ; **2** *adj*: **~ment agency** agence *f* de placement; **~ment exchange** bourse *f* du travail; *(US)* **E~ment service** agence nationale pour l'emploi.

empower [ɪm'paʊəʳ] *vt* autoriser (*sb to do* qn à faire).

empress ['emprɪs] *n* impératrice *f*.

empty ['em(p)tɪ] **1** *adj (gen)* vide; *house, room* inoccupé, vide; *post, job* vacant; *words* creux; *promise* en l'air; *threat* vain. **on an ~ stomach** à jeun; **an ~ gesture** un geste qui ne veut rien dire. **2** *npl*: **empties** bouteilles *fpl (or* boîtes *fpl etc)* vides. **3** *vt (gen)* vider; *(~* **out**) *pocket* vider; *bricks, books* sortir *(of, from* de; *into* dans); *liquid* vider *(from* de), verser *(from* de; *into* dans). **4** *vi [water]* se déverser; *[river]* se jeter *(into* dans); *[building, container]* se vider. ◆ **emptiness** *n* vide *m*; *[pleasures etc]* vanité *f*; **the emptiness of life** le vide de l'existence. ◆ **empty-handed** *adj*: **to be ~-handed** avoir les mains vides; **to arrive ~-handed** arriver les mains vides. ◆ **empty-headed** *adj* sot.

emu ['i:mju:] *n* émeu *m*.

emulate ['emjʊleɪt] *vt* (essayer d')égaler.

emulsify [ɪ'mʌlsɪfaɪ] *vt* émulsionner. ◆ **emulsion 1** *n* émulsion *f* ; **2** *adj paint* mat.

enable [ɪ'neɪbl] *vt*: **to ~ sb to do** permettre à qn de faire, donner à qn *(opportunity)* la possibilité *or (means)* le moyen de faire.

enact [ɪ'nækt] *vt* (**a**) *(Jur) (make into law)* promulguer; *(decree)* décréter. (**b**) *(perform) play* représenter. *(fig)* **the drama which was ~ed** le drame qui s'est déroulé.

enamel [ɪ'næm(ə)l] **1** *n (gen)* émail *m*. **nail ~** vernis *m* à ongles. **2** *vt* émailler. **3** *adj* en émail. **~ paint** ripolin *m* ®. ◆ **enamelled** *adj* en émail. ◆ **enamelware** *n* articles *mpl* en métal émaillé.

enamoured, *(US)* **enamored** [ɪ'næməd] *adj*: **to be ~ of** aimer beaucoup.

encampment [ɪn'kæmpmənt] *n* campement *m*.

encapsulate [ɪn'kæpsjʊleɪt] *vt (fig)* renfermer, résumer.

encase [ɪn'keɪs] *vt (contain)* enfermer *(in* dans); *(cover)* recouvrir *(in* de).

encephalitis [ˌensefə'laɪtɪs] *n* encéphalite *f*.

enchant [ɪn'tʃɑ:nt] *vt* enchanter, charmer. ◆ **enchanter** *n* enchanteur *m*. ◆ **enchanting** *adj* enchanteur, charmant. ◆ **enchantingly** *adv smile, dance* d'une façon ravissante; **~ingly beautiful** belle à ravir. ◆ **enchantment** *n* enchantement *m*. ◆ **enchantress** *n* enchanteresse *f*.

encircle [ɪn'sɜ:kl] *vt (gen)* entourer; *[people]* encercler, entourer. ◆ **encircling** *adj*: **encircling movement** manœuvre *f* d'encerclement.

enclose [ɪn'kləʊz] *vt* (**a**) *(fence in)* clôturer; *(surround)* entourer *(with* de). (**b**) *(with letter etc)* joindre *(in, with* à). **letter enclosing a receipt** lettre contenant un reçu; **please find ~d** veuillez trouver ci-joint. ◆ **enclosed** *adj space* clos; *(Rel) order* cloîtré; *(in letter) cheque etc* ci-joint. ◆ **enclosure** *n (act)* clôture *f*; *(piece of land)* enceinte *f*; *(at racecourse)* pesage *m*; *(document enclosed)* pièce *f* jointe.

encompass [ɪn'kʌmpəs] *vt (include)* inclure.

encore [ɒŋ'kɔ:ʳ] **1** *excl* bis! **2** ['ɒŋkɔ:ʳ] *n* bis *m*. **to give an ~** jouer *(or* chanter *etc)* un bis.

encounter [ɪn'kaʊntəʳ] **1** *vt person* rencontrer (à l'improviste); *enemy, difficulties* affronter, rencontrer; *danger* rencontrer; *opposition* se heurter à; *enemy fire* essuyer. **2** *n* rencontre *f*. **~ group** atelier relationnel.

encourage [ɪn'kʌrɪdʒ] *vt* encourager *(sb to do* qn à faire). ◆ **encouragement** *n* encouragement *m*. ◆ **encouraging** *adj* encourageant. ◆ **encouragingly** *adv* d'une manière encourageante.

encroach [ɪn'krəʊtʃ] *vi (on sb's land, time, rights)* empiéter *(on* sur). **the sea is ~ing on the land** la mer gagne du terrain.

encrusted [ɪn'krʌstəd] *adj*: **~ with** *earth etc* encroûté de; *jewels* incrusté de.

encumber [ɪn'kʌmbəʳ] *vt* encombrer *(with* de). ◆ **encumbrance** *n (burden)* fardeau *m*; *(preventing progress)* handicap *m*; *(furniture, clothes)* gêne *f*.

encyclical [ɪn'sɪklɪk(ə)l] *adj, n* encyclique *(f)*.

encyclop(a)edia [ɪnˌsaɪklə(ʊ)'pi:dɪə] *n* encyclopédie *f*. ◆ **encyclop(a)edic** *adj* encyclopédique.

end [end] **1** *n* (**a**) *(farthest part: gen)* bout *m*. **the southern ~ of the town** l'extrémité *f* sud de la ville; **the fourth from the ~** le quatrième avant la fin; **from ~ to ~** d'un bout à l'autre; **on ~** debout *(V also* **1b**); **to stand a box** *etc* **on ~** mettre une caisse *etc* debout; **his hair stood on ~** ses cheveux se dressèrent sur sa tête; **~ to ~** bout à bout; *(Sport)* **to change ~s** changer de côté; *(fig)* **to make (both) ~s meet** joindre les deux bouts; **to keep one's ~ up** * se défendre assez bien.

(**b**) *(conclusion)* fin *f*. **the ~ of the world** la fin du monde; **it's not the ~ of the world!** * ce n'est pas une catastrophe!; **it succeeded in the ~** cela a réussi à la fin *or* finalement; **he got used to it in the ~** il a fini par s'y habituer; **at the ~ of the day** à la fin de la journée; *(fig)* en fin de compte; **at the ~ of three weeks** au bout de trois semaines; **that was the ~ of my watch** ma montre était fichue *; **that was the ~ of that!** on n'en a plus reparlé; **there is no ~ to it all** cela n'en finit plus; **to be at an ~** *[action]* être terminé; *[time, period]* être écoulé; *[supplies]* être épuisé; *[patience]* être à bout; **at the ~ of one's patience/strength** à bout de patience/forces; **to bring to an ~** *speech, writing* achever; *work* terminer; *relations* mettre fin à; **to come to an ~** prendre fin, se terminer; **to get to the ~ of** *supplies, food* finir; *work, essay* venir à bout de; *holiday* arriver à la fin de; **to come to a bad ~** mal finir; **we shall never hear the ~ of it** on n'a pas fini d'en entendre parler; **no ~ * of** une masse * de, énormément de; **no ~** * *(adv)* énormément; **that's the (bitter) ~!** * il ne manquait plus que ça!, c'est la fin de tout!; **he's the ~!** * il est insupportable!; **for two hours on ~** deux heures de suite; **for days on ~** pendant des jours et des jours.

(**c**) *(remnant) [rope, candle]* bout *m*; *[loaf, meat]* reste *m*, restant *m*. **cigarette ~** mégot *m*.

(**d**) *(purpose)* but *m*, fin *f*. **with this ~ in view** dans ce but, à cette fin; **an ~ in itself** une fin en soi; **to no ~** en vain; **the ~ justifies the means** la fin justifie les moyens.

(**e**) *(US Ftbl)* ailier *m*.

2 *adj house* dernier *(before n)*; *result* final, définitif. **~ product** *(Comm, Ind)* produit fini; *(fig)* résultat *m*; *(US fig)* **~ run** moyen détourné.

3 *vt work* finir, achever; *period of service* accomplir; *speech, writing* conclure *(with* avec, par); *broadcast, series* terminer *(with* par); *speculation, rumour, quarrel, war* mettre fin à. **that was the lie to ~ all lies!** * comme mensonge on ne fait pas mieux! *

4 *vi* finir, se terminer *(in* par), s'achever. **the winter is ~ing** l'hiver tire à sa fin; **word ~ing in an s/in -re** mot se terminant par un s/en -re; **it ~ed in failure** ça s'est soldé par un échec.

◆ **end up** *vi* (**a**) finir, se terminer *(in* en, par); *[road]* aboutir *(in* à). (**b**) *(finally arrive at)* se retrouver *(in* à, en); *(finally become)* finir par devenir. ◆ **ending** *n (gen)* fin *f*; *(outcome)* issue *f*; *[speech etc]* conclusion *f*; *(Ling)* terminaison *f*; **story with a happy ~ing** histoire qui finit bien. ◆ **endless** *adj road, wait* interminable, sans fin; *(Tech) belt* sans fin; *times, attempts* innombrable; *discussion, argument* continuel, incessant; *patience* infini; *resources, supplies* inépuisable; *possibilities* illimité; **this job is ~less** on n'en voit pas la fin. ◆ **endlessly** *adv stretch out* interminablement, à perte de vue; *chatter, argue* continuellement; *repeat* sans cesse; **~lessly willing** d'une bonne volonté à toute épreuve. ◆ **endpapers** *npl (Typ)* gardes *fpl*. ◆ **endways** *or* ◆ **endwise** *adv (endways on)* en long; *(~ to ~)* bout à bout.

endanger [ɪn'deɪn(d)ʒəʳ] *vt life, interests* mettre en danger; *future, chances, health* compromettre; **~ed species** espèce *f* en voie de disparition.

endear [ɪn'dɪəʳ] *vt* faire aimer (*to* de). **what ~s him to me is...** ce qui me plaît en lui c'est... ◆ **endearing** *adj smile* engageant; *personality* attachant ; *characteristic* (qui rend) sympathique. ◆ **endearingly** *adv* de façon engageante *or* sympathique. ◆ **endearments** *npl (words)* paroles *fpl* affectueuses; *(acts)* marques *fpl* d'affection.

endeavour [ɪn'devəʳ] **1** *n* effort *m*, tentative *f* (*to do* pour faire). **to make an ~ to do** essayer *or* s'efforcer de faire; **to make every ~ to go** faire tout son possible pour y aller. **2** *vi* essayer, s'efforcer (*to do* de faire); *(stronger)* s'appliquer (*to do* à faire).

endemic [en'demɪk] *adj* endémique.

endive ['endaɪv] *n (curly)* chicorée *f*; *(smooth, flat)* endive *f*.

endorse [ɪn'dɔːs] *vt (sign) document, cheque* endosser; *(guarantee) bill* avaliser; *(approve) claim* appuyer; *opinion* souscrire à; *action, decision* approuver. *(Aut)* **he has had his licence ~d** ≃ il a eu une contravention portée sur son permis de conduire. ◆ **endorsement** *n (on cheque)* endos *m*; *(approval)* approbation *f*; *(on driving licence)* ≃ contravention *(portée sur un permis de conduire)*.

endow [ɪn'daʊ] *vt institution, church* doter (*with* de); *hospital bed, prize, chair* fonder. **~ed with brains** *etc* doté d'intelligence *etc*. ◆ **endowment** **1** *n* dotation *f*; fondation *f* ; **2** *adj*: **~ment assurance** assurance *f* à capital différé.

endure [ɪn'djʊəʳ] **1** *vt (gen)* supporter (*doing* de faire); *pain* supporter, endurer. **she can't ~ teasing** elle ne peut pas supporter *or* souffrir qu'on la taquine *(subj)*. **2** *vi [building, peace, friendship]* durer; *[book, memory]* rester. ◆ **endurable** *adj* supportable. ◆ **endurance** **1** *n* endurance *f*, résistance *f*; **he has come to the end of his endurance** il n'en peut plus; **beyond endurance** intolérable; **tried beyond endurance** excédé ; **2** *adj*: **endurance test** *(gen)* épreuve *f* de résistance; *(Aut)* épreuve d'endurance. ◆ **enduring** *adj* durable.

enema ['enɪmə] *n (Med)* lavement *m*.

enemy ['enəmɪ] **1** *n (gen)* ennemi(e) *m(f)*, adversaire *mf*; *(Mil)* ennemi *m*. **to make an ~ of sb** (se) faire un ennemi de qn; **he is his own worst ~** il est son pire ennemi. **2** *adj tanks, forces, tribes* ennemi; *morale, strategy* de l'ennemi. **~ action** une attaque ennemie; **killed by ~ action** tombé à l'ennemi; **~ alien** ressortissant(e) *m(f)* d'un pays ennemi. ◆ **enemy-occupied** *adj* occupé par l'ennemi.

energy ['enədʒɪ] **1** *n* énergie *f*. **Ministry of E~** ministère *m* de l'Énergie; **to save ~** faire des économies d'énergie; **with all one's ~** de toutes ses forces; **to put all one's ~ into (doing) sth** se consacrer tout entier à faire qch; **I haven't the ~ to go back** je n'ai pas l'énergie *or* le courage de retourner; **don't waste your ~** ne te donne pas du mal pour rien. **2** *adj crisis* énergétique, de l'énergie. **~ conservation** les économies *fpl* d'énergie. ◆ **energetic** *adj (gen)* énergique; **I've had a very energetic day** je me suis beaucoup dépensé aujourd'hui; **do you feel energetic enough to come for a walk?** est-ce que tu as assez d'énergie pour faire une promenade? ◆ **energetically** *adv move, behave* énergiquement, avec énergie; *speak* avec force. ◆ **energize** *vt* donner de l'énergie à; *(Elec)* alimenter (en courant). ◆ **energy-giving** *adj* énergétique.

enervate ['enɜːveɪt] *vt* affaiblir. ◆ **enervating** *adj* débilitant.

enforce [ɪn'fɔːs] *vt decision, policy* appliquer; *law* faire respecter; *discipline* imposer. **to ~ obedience** se faire obéir. ◆ **enforced** *adj* forcé, obligé.

enfranchise [ɪn'fræn(t)ʃaɪz] *vt (give vote to)* accorder le droit de vote à, admettre au suffrage; *(set free)* affranchir. ◆ **enfranchisement** *n* admission *f* au suffrage; affranchissement *m*.

engage [ɪn'geɪdʒ] **1** *vt servant* engager; *workers* embaucher; *lawyer* prendre; *sb's attention, interest* retenir; *(Mil) the enemy* attaquer; *(Tech)* engager. **to ~ sb in conversation** lier conversation avec qn; *(Aut)* **to ~ a gear** engager une vitesse; **to ~ gear** mettre en prise; **to ~ the clutch** embrayer. **2** *vi [person]* s'engager (*to do* à faire); *[wheels]* s'engrener. **the clutch didn't ~** l'embrayage n'a pas fonctionné; **to ~ in** *politics* se lancer dans; *controversy* s'embarquer dans; **to ~ in a discussion/conversation** entrer en discussion/conversation (*with* avec).

◆ **engaged** *adj* (**a**) *(gen) person, seat, phone number etc* occupé; **to be ~d in doing** être occupé à faire; **to be ~d on sth** s'occuper de qch; *(Telec)* **the ~d signal** la tonalité occupé *inv*; (**b**) *(betrothed)* fiancé (*to* à, avec); **to get ~d** se fiancer (*to* à, avec). ◆ **engagement** **1** *n* (**a**) *(appointment)* rendez-vous *m inv*; *[actor etc]* engagement *m*; **previous ~ment** engagement *m* antérieur; **I have an ~ment** je ne suis pas libre; (**b**) *[actor etc]* engagement *m*; (**c**) *(betrothal)* fiançailles *fpl*; **to break off one's ~ment** rompre ses fiançailles; (**d**) *(undertaking)* engagement *m*; **to give an ~ment to do sth** s'engager à faire qch; (**e**) *(Mil)* combat *m*, engagement *m* ; **2** *adj*: **~ment book** agenda *m*; **~ment ring** bague *f* de fiançailles. ◆ **engaging** *adj smile* engageant; *personality* attirant.

engender [ɪn'dʒendəʳ] *vt* engendrer *(fig)*.

engine ['en(d)ʒɪn] **1** *n (Tech)* machine *f*, moteur *m*; *[ship]* machine; *(Rail)* locomotive *f*; *(Aut, Aviat)* moteur. *(Rail)* **facing/with your back to the ~** dans le sens de/le sens contraire à la marche. **2** *adj (Aut)* **~ block** bloc-moteur *m; (Rail)* **~ driver** mécanicien *m*; *(Naut)* **~ room** salle *f* des machines; *(Aut)* **~ unit** bloc-moteur *m*. ◆ **-engined** *adj ending*: **twin-~d** à deux moteurs. ◆ **engineer** **1** *n (gen)* ingénieur *m*; *(Rail, Naut)* mécanicien *m*; *(tradesman)* technicien *m*; *(for domestic appliances etc)* dépanneur *m*; *(Mil)* **the E~ers** le génie; **the TV ~er came** le dépanneur est venu pour la télé * ; **2** *vt scheme* manigancer. ◆ **engineering** **1** *n* engineering *m*, ingénierie *f*; **to study ~ering** faire des études d'ingénieur ; **2** *adj*: **~ering factory** *or* **works** atelier *m* de construction mécanique; **~ering industries** industries *fpl* d'équipement.

England ['ɪŋglənd] *n* Angleterre *f*. ◆ **English** **1** *adj* anglais; *king* d'Angleterre; **the English Channel** la Manche; **English breakfast** petit déjeuner anglais ; **2** *n (Ling)* anglais *m*; *(people)* **the English** les Anglais *mpl*; **the King's** *or* **Queen's English** l'anglais correct; **in plain** *or* **simple English** ≃ en bon français. ◆ **Englishman** *n* Anglais *m*. ◆ **English-speaker** *n* anglophone *mf*. ◆ **English-speaking** *adj* qui parle anglais; *nation etc* anglophone. ◆ **Englishwoman** *n* Anglaise *f*.

engrave [ɪn'greɪv] *vt* graver. ◆ **engraver** *n* graveur *m*. ◆ **engraving** *n* gravure *f*.

engrossed [ɪn'grəʊst] *adj*: **~ in** *work* absorbé par; *reading, thoughts* plongé dans. ◆ **engrossing** *adj* absorbant.

engulf [ɪn'gʌlf] *vt* engouffrer.

enhance [ɪn'hɑːns] *vt attraction, beauty* mettre en valeur; *position, chances* améliorer; *prestige, reputation, powers* accroître.

enigma [ɪ'nɪgmə] *n* énigme *f*. ◆ **enigmatic** *adj* énigmatique. ◆ **enigmatically** *adv* d'une manière énigmatique.

enjoin [ɪn'dʒɔɪn] *vt* prescrire (*sb to do*, à qn de faire); *silence, obedience* imposer (*on* à); *discretion* recommander (*on* à).

enjoy [ɪn'dʒɔɪ] *vt* (**a**) *(gen)* aimer (*doing* faire), trouver agréable (*doing* de faire); *meal, wine* apprécier, trouver bon. **I ~ed doing it** cela m'a fait plaisir de le faire; **to ~ life** profiter de la vie; **to ~ a weekend** passer un bon week-end; **did you ~ the concert?** est-ce que le concert vous a plu?; **to ~ one's dinner** bien manger *or* dîner; **to ~ o.s.** (bien) s'amuser; **did you ~ yourself in Paris?** est-ce que tu t'es bien amusé à Paris?; **she always ~s herself in the country** elle se plaît toujours à la campagne. (**b**) *(benefit from) income, health* jouir de. ◆ **enjoyable** *adj visit* agréable; *meal* excellent. ◆ **enjoyment** *n* plaisir *m*; **to get ~ment from (doing) sth** trouver du plaisir à (faire) qch.

enlarge [ɪn'lɑːdʒ] **1** *vt (gen, also Phot)* agrandir; *(fig) empire, circle of friends* étendre. **2** *vi* (**a**) *(grow bigger)* s'agrandir; s'étendre. (**b**) **to ~ (up)on** s'étendre sur. ◆ **enlarged** *adj edition* augmenté; *majority* accru; *(Med) organ* hypertrophié; *pore* dilaté. ◆ **enlargement** *n (gen; Phot)* agrandissement *m*. ◆ **enlarger** *n (Phot)* agrandisseur *m*.

enlighten [ɪn'laɪtn] *vt* éclairer (*sb on sth* qn sur qch). ◆ **enlightened** *adj* éclairé.◆ **enlightening** *adj* révélateur (*about* au sujet de). ◆ **enlightenment** *n (explanations)* éclaircissements *mpl* (*on* sur); **the Age of E~ment** le Siècle des lumières.

enlist [ɪn'lɪst] **1** *vi (Mil etc)* s'engager (*in* dans). *(US Mil)* **~ed man** simple soldat *m*. **2** *vt supporters* recruter; *sb's support* s'assurer.

enliven [ɪn'laɪvn] *vt* animer.

enmeshed [ɪn'meʃt] *adj*: **to get ~ in** s'empêtrer dans.

enmity ['enmɪtɪ] *n* inimitié *f*, hostilité *f*.

enormous [ɪ'nɔːməs] *adj (gen)* énorme; *patience* immense; *strength* prodigieux; *stature* colossal. **an ~ quantity of** énormément de; **an ~ number of** *things* une masse * de; *people* une foule de. ◆ **enormously** *adv (+ vb or ptp)* énormément; (+ *adj*) extrêmement; **it has changed ~ly** cela a énormément changé; **an ~ly funny story** une histoire extrêmement drôle.

enough [ɪ'nʌf] **1** *adj, n* assez (de). **~ money/books** assez d'argent/de livres; **~ to eat** assez à manger; **he earns ~ to live on** il gagne de quoi vivre; **I've had ~** *(eating)* j'ai assez mangé; *(protesting)* j'en ai assez; **I've had ~ of (doing) this** j'en ai assez de (faire) cela; **you can never have ~ of this music** on ne se lasse jamais de cette musique; **it was ~ to show that...** cela a suffi à prouver que...; **that's ~** cela suffit; **it's ~ to drive you mad** c'est à vous rendre fou; **more than ~ wine** un peu trop de vin; **more than ~ for all** largement (assez) *or* plus qu'assez pour tous; **~'s ~!** ça suffit comme ça!
2 *adv* assez, suffisamment. **old ~ to go alone** suffisamment *or* assez grand pour y aller tout seul; **I was fool ~** *or* **~ of a fool to believe him** j'ai été assez bête pour le croire; **he knows well ~** il sait très bien; **he writes well ~** il écrit assez bien, il n'écrit pas mal; **oddly ~, I...** chose curieuse *or* c'est curieux, je...

enquire [ɪn'kwaɪəʳ] *etc* = **inquire** *etc.*

enrage [ɪn'reɪdʒ] *vt* mettre en rage.

enrapture [ɪn'ræptʃəʳ] *vt* enchanter.

enrich [ɪn'rɪtʃ] *vt (gen)* enrichir; *soil* fertiliser. **~ed uranium** uranium enrichi. ◆ **enrichment** *n* enrichissement *m*; fertilisation *f*.

enrol, *(US)* **enroll** [ɪn'rəʊl] **1** *vt (gen)* inscrire; *workers* embaucher; *soldiers* enrôler. **2** *vi* s'inscrire (*in* à; *for* pour); se faire embaucher (*as* comme) ; s'enrôler (*in* dans).

ensconce [ɪn'skɒns] *vt*: **to ~ o.s.** bien s'installer; **~d** bien installé.

ensign *n* (**a**) ['ensən] *(flag)* drapeau *m*, pavillon *m (Naut)*. *(Brit)* **red/white ~** pavillon de la marine marchande/de la marine de guerre. (**b**) ['ensaɪn] *(US Naut)* enseigne *m* de vaisseau de deuxième classe.

enslave [ɪn'sleɪv] *vt* asservir.

ensue [ɪn'sjuː] *vi* s'ensuivre (*from* de). ◆ **ensuing** *adj event, chaos* qui s'ensuit; *year, day* suivant.

en suite [ɑ̃'swiːt] *adj*: **with ~ bathroom** avec salle de bains attenante.

ensure [ɪn'ʃʊəʳ] *vt* assurer (*that* que).

entail [ɪn'teɪl] *vt (gen)* entraîner; *expense, work, delay* occasionner; *disadvantages, risk, difficulty* comporter; *suffering, hardship* entraîner. **it ~ed buying a car** cela nécessitait l'achat d'une voiture.

entangled [ɪn'tæŋgld] *adj thread etc* emmêlé; *(fig)* empêtré.

enter ['entəʳ] **1** *vt* (**a**) *(go into) house etc* entrer dans; *vehicle* monter dans; *path, road* s'engager dans; *profession, the army etc* entrer dans; *university* s'inscrire à. **to ~ the Church** se faire prêtre; **the thought never ~ed my head** cette pensée ne m'est jamais venue à l'esprit. (**b**) *(write down) amount, name, fact, order (on list etc)* inscrire; *(in notebook)* noter; *item in ledger* porter (*in* sur); *(Comput) data* introduire, entrer; *pupil, candidate, show dog* présenter (*for* à); *racehorse, runner* inscrire (*for, in* dans). *(Comm)* **~ these purchases to me** mettez ces achats à mon compte; **to ~ a protest** élever une protestation. **2** *vi* (**a**) entrer. *(Theat)* **~ Macbeth** entre Macbeth. (**b**) *(for race, exam etc)* s'inscrire (*for* pour).
◆ **enter into** *vt fus* (**a**) *explanation, apology* se lancer dans; *correspondence, conversation* entrer en; *plot* prendre part à; *negotiations* entamer; *alliance* conclure. (**b**) *sb's plans, calculations* entrer dans. **her money doesn't ~ into it at all** son argent n'y est pour rien.

enteritis [ˌentə'raɪtɪs] *n* entérite *f*.

enterprise ['entəpraɪz] *n* (**a**) *(undertaking, company)* entreprise *f*. (**b**) *(initiative)* esprit *m* d'initiative. ◆ **enterprising** *adj person* plein d'initiative, entreprenant; *venture* audacieux; **that was enterprising of you!** vous avez fait preuve d'initiative! ◆ **enterprisingly** *adv*: **to do sth enterprisingly** faire qch de sa propre initiative.

entertain [ˌentə'teɪn] *vt* (**a**) *audience* amuser, divertir; *guests* distraire. **to ~ sb to dinner** offrir un dîner à qn; *(at home)* recevoir qn à dîner; **they ~ a lot** ils reçoivent beaucoup. (**b**) *thought* méditer; *intention, doubt* nourrir; *proposal* accueillir favorablement. ◆ **entertainer** *n* artiste *mf* (de music-hall *etc*); **a well-known radio ~er** un(e) artiste bien connu(e) à la radio. ◆ **entertaining** **1** *adj* amusant, divertissant ; **2** *n*: **she does a lot of ~ing** elle reçoit beaucoup. ◆ **entertainingly** *adv* d'une façon amusante. ◆ **entertainment** **1** *n* (**a**) *(amusement) [audience]* amusement *m*; *[guests]* divertissement *m*; **for your ~ment we...** pour vous distraire nous...; **for my own ~ment** pour mon divertissement personnel; (**b**) *(performance)* spectacle *m*; **musical ~ment** soirée *f* musicale ; **2** *adj*: **~ment allowance** frais *mpl* de représentation; **the ~ment world** le monde du spectacle.

enthral(l) [ɪn'θrɔːl] *vt [book etc]* captiver, passionner; *[beauty]* ensorceler. ◆ **enthralling** *adj* passionnant; ensorcelant.

enthusiasm [ɪn'θuːzɪæz(ə)m] *n* enthousiasme *m* (*for* pour). ◆ **enthuse** *vi*: **to ~ over** parler avec beaucoup d'enthousiasme de.

enthusiast [ɪn'θuːzɪæst] *n* enthousiaste *mf*. **jazz** *etc* **~** passionné(e) *m(f)* de jazz *etc*; **a Vivaldi ~** un(e) fervent(e) de Vivaldi. ◆ **enthusiastic** *adj (gen)* enthousiaste; *swimmer etc* passionné; **I'm not very ~ic about it** ça ne me dit pas grand-chose; **to make sb ~ic** enthousiasmer qn; **to grow ~ic over** s'enthousiasmer pour. ◆ **enthusiastically** *adv* avec enthousiasme.

entice [ɪn'taɪs] *vt* attirer (*towards* vers); entraîner (*away from somewhere* à l'écart d'un endroit); éloigner (*sb away from sb* qn de qn); *(with food, prospects)* allécher. **to ~ sb to do** entraîner qn à faire. ◆ **enticing** *adj* alléchant.

entire [ɪn'taɪəʳ] *adj* (**a**) *(whole)* entier, tout. **the ~ week** la semaine entière, toute la semaine. (**b**) *(complete)* entier, complet; *(unreserved)* entier *(before n)*, total. **the ~ house** la maison (tout) entière; **my ~ confidence** mon entière confiance, ma confiance totale. ◆ **entirely** *adv* entièrement, tout à fait; *change* du tout au tout. ◆ **entirety** *n*: **in its ~ty** en (son) entier, intégralement.

entitle [ɪn'taɪtl] *vt* (**a**) *book* intituler. (**b**) **to ~ sb to sth** donner droit à qch à qn; **to ~ sb to do** donner à qn le droit de faire; **to be ~d to sth** avoir droit à qch; **to be ~d to do** *(by position, qualifications)* avoir qualité pour faire; *(by rules)* avoir le droit de faire; **he is quite ~d to believe that...** *(gen)* il a le droit de penser que...; *(has good reason)* il a tout lieu de croire que... ◆ **entitlement** *n* droit *m* (*to* à).

entity ['entɪtɪ] *n* entité *f*.

entomology [ˌentə'mɒlədʒɪ] *n* entomologie *f*. ◆ **entomological** *adj* entomologique. ◆ **entomologist** *n* entomologiste *mf*.

entrails ['entreɪlz] *npl* entrailles *fpl*.

entrance¹ [ɪn'trɑːns] *vt* transporter, ravir. ◆ **entranced** *adj* en extase. ◆ **entrancing** *adj* enchanteur. ◆ **entrancingly** *adv dance, sing* à ravir; *smile* d'une façon ravissante; **entrancingly beautiful** belle à ravir.

entrance² ['entr(ə)ns] **1** *n (act of entering; way in)* entrée *f* (*into* dans, *to* de); *(right to enter)* admission *f*. **to make an ~** faire son entrée; **'no ~'** 'défense d'entrer'; **to gain ~ to** (réussir à) entrer dans; *(to university etc)* être admis à *or* dans. **2** *adj card, ticket, examination* d'entrée. **~ fee** droit *m* d'inscription; *(US Aut)* **~ ramp** bretelle *f* d'accès. ◆ **entrant** *n (to profession)* débutant(e) *m(f)* (*to* dans, en); *(in race, competition)* concurrent(e) *m(f)*; *(in exam)* candidat(e) *m(f)*.

entreat [ɪn'triːt] *vt* supplier, implorer (*sb to do* qn de faire). **I ~ you** je vous en supplie. ◆ **entreating** *adj* suppliant, implorant. ◆ **entreaty** *n* prière *f*, supplication *f*; **at his earnest ~y** sur ses vives instances; **a look of ~y** un regard suppliant.

entrenched [ɪn'tren(t)ʃt] *adj*: **firmly ~** *(Mil)* solidement retranché; *(fig)* indélogeable; *attitude* très arrêté.

entrust [ɪn'trʌst] *vt* confier (*sth to sb, sb with sth* qch à qn).

entry ['entrɪ] **1** *n* (**a**) = **entrance² 1.** (**b**) *(item) [list]* inscription *f*; *[account book, ledger]* écriture *f*; *[dictionary, ship's log]* entrée *f*; *[encyclopedia]* article *m*. *(Book-keeping)* **single/double ~** comptabilité *f* en partie simple/double; **there are only 3 entries** *(for race, competition)* il n'y a que 3 concurrents *mpl*; *(for exam)* il n'y a que 3 candidats *mpl*. **2** *adj*: **~ form** feuille *f* d'inscription; **~ permit** visa *m* d'entrée; **~ phone** interphone *m*, portier *m* électrique.

entwine [ɪn'twaɪn] *vt (twist together)* entrelacer; *(twist around)* enlacer (*with* de).

enumerate [ɪ'njuːməreɪt] *vt* énumérer. ◆ **enumeration** *n* énumération *f*.

enunciate [ɪ'nʌnsɪeɪt] *vt sound, word* articuler; *principle, theory* énoncer. ◆ **enunciation** *n* articulation *f*; énonciation *f*.

enuresis [ˌenjʊ'riːsɪs] *n* énurésie *f*. ◆ **enuretic** *adj* énurétique.

envelop [ɪn'veləp] *vt* envelopper (*in a blanket* dans une couverture; *in clouds/mystery* de nuages/ mystère).

envelope ['envələʊp] *n* enveloppe *f*. **to put a letter in an ~** mettre une lettre sous enveloppe; **in a sealed ~** sous pli cacheté; **in the same ~** sous le même pli.

enviable ['envɪəbl] *adj* enviable.

envious ['envɪəs] *adj* envieux. **to be ~ of sth** être envieux de qch; **to be ~ of sb** envier qn. ◆ **enviously** *adv* avec envie.

environment [ɪn'vaɪər(ə)nmənt] *n (gen)* milieu *m*; *(Admin, Pol)* environnement *m*. *(fig)* **hostile ~** climat *m* d'hostilité, ambiance *f* hostile; **his normal ~** son cadre *or* son milieu normal; **working ~** conditions *fpl* de travail; **Ministry of the E~** ministère *m* de l'Environnement. ◆ **environmental** *adj conditions, changes* écologique, du milieu; *influence* exercé par le milieu *or* l'environnement; **~al studies** études *fpl* de l'environnement. ◆ **environmentalism** *n* science *f* de l'environnement. ◆ **environmentalist** *n* environnementaliste *mf*.

envisage [ɪn'vɪzɪdʒ] *vt (foresee)* prévoir; *(imagine)* envisager.

envision [ɪn'vɪʒən] *vt (conceive of)* imaginer; *(foresee)* prévoir.

envoy ['envɔɪ] *n (gen)* envoyé(e) *m(f)*; *(diplomat)* ministre *m* plénipotentiaire.

envy ['envɪ] **1** *n* envie *f*. **it was the ~ of everyone** cela faisait l'envie de tout le monde. **2** *vt* envier (*sb sth* qch à qn).

enzyme ['enzaɪm] *n* enzyme *f*.

eons ['iːənz] *npl* = **aeons.**

ephemeral [ɪ'femər(ə)l] *adj* éphémère.

epic ['epɪk] **1** *adj* épique. **2** *n* épopée *f*. **an ~ of the screen** un film à grand spectacle.

epicentre ['epɪsentəʳ] *n* épicentre *m*.

epicure ['epɪkjʊəʳ] *n* gourmet *m*. ◆ **epicurean** *adj* épicurien.

epidemic [ˌepɪ'demɪk] **1** *n* épidémie *f*. **2** *adj* épidémique.

epidural [ˌepɪ'djʊərəl] *adj, n*: **~ (anaesthetic)** péridurale *f*.

epiglottis [ˌepɪ'glɒtɪs] *n* épiglotte *f*.

epigram ['epɪgræm] *n* épigramme *f*.

epigraph ['epɪgrɑːf] *n* épigraphe *f*.

epilepsy ['epɪlepsɪ] *n* épilepsie *f*. ◆ **epileptic 1** *adj* épileptique; **epileptic fit** crise *f* d'épilepsie ; **2** *n* épileptique *mf*.

epilogue ['epɪlɒg] *n* épilogue *m*.

Epiphany [ɪ'pɪfənɪ] *n* Épiphanie *f*, fête *f* des Rois.

episcopal [ɪ'pɪskəp(ə)l] *adj* épiscopal. ◆ **Episcopalian 1** *adj* épiscopal *(de l'Église épiscopale)* ; **2** *n* membre *m* de l'Église épiscopale.

episode ['epɪsəʊd] *n* épisode *m*.

epistemology [ɪˌpɪstə'mɒlədʒɪ] *n* épistémologie *f*.

epistle [ɪ'pɪsl] *n* épître *f*.

epitaph ['epɪtɑːf] *n* épitaphe *f*.

epithet ['epɪθet] *n* épithète *f*.

epitome [ɪ'pɪtəmɪ] *n* modèle *m or* type *m* même. ◆ **epitomize** *vt* incarner, personnifier.

epoch ['iːpɒk] *n* époque *f*. ◆ **epoch-making** *adj* qui fait époque, qui fait date.

equable ['ekwəbl] *adj* égal, constant. **he is very ~** il a un tempérament très égal. ◆ **equably** *adv* tranquillement.

equal ['iːkw(ə)l] **1** *adj* égal (*to* à). **~ in number** égal en nombre; **to be ~ to sth** égaler qch; **~ pay for ~ work** à travail égal salaire égal; **~ opportunities** égalité *f* des chances; **~ rights** égalité *f* des droits; *(Rad, TV)* **~ time** droit *m* de réponse (à l'antenne); **other things being ~** toutes choses égales d'ailleurs; **an ~ sum of money** une même somme d'argent; **with ~ indifference** avec la même indifférence; **to talk to sb on ~ terms** parler à qn d'égal

à égal; **on an ~ footing** sur un pied d'égalité (*with* avec); **to be ~ to the task** être à la hauteur de la tâche; **she did not feel ~ to going out** elle ne se sentait pas capable de sortir; **~(s) sign** signe *m* d'égalité. **2** *n* égal(e) *m(f)*. **to treat sb as an ~** traiter qn d'égal à égal; **she has no ~** elle n'a pas sa pareille. **3** *vt* égaler (*in* en). **there is nothing to ~ it** il n'y a rien de comparable.
◆ **equality** *n* égalité *f*. ◆ **equalize** *vti* égaliser. ◆ **equalizer** *n (Sport)* but *m or* point *m* égalisateur. ◆ **equally** *adv guilty, clever* également; *divide* en parts *or* parties égales; **it would be ~ly wrong to suggest** il serait tout aussi faux de suggérer.

equanimity [ˌekwəˈnɪmɪtɪ] *n* sérénité *f*.

equate [ɪˈkweɪt] *vt (identify)* assimiler (*with* à); *(compare)* mettre sur le même pied (*with* que); *(make equal)* égaler. ◆ **equation** *n (Math)* équation *f*.

equator [ɪˈkweɪtəʳ] *n* équateur *m* (terrestre). **at the ~** sous l'équateur. ◆ **equatorial** *adj* équatorial.

equestrian [ɪˈkwestrɪən] *adj* équestre.

equidistant [ˈiːkwɪˈdɪst(ə)nt] *adj* équidistant (*from* de).

equilateral [ˌiːkwɪˈlætərəl] *adj* équilatéral.

equilibrium [ˌiːkwɪˈlɪbrɪəm] *n* équilibre *m*.

equine [ˈekwaɪn] *adj* chevalin.

equinox [ˈiːkwɪnɒks] *n* équinoxe *m*.

equip [ɪˈkwɪp] *vt* équiper (*with* de). **to ~ a room as a laboratory** aménager une pièce en laboratoire; **to ~ a ship with radar** installer le radar sur un bateau; **to be well ~ped with** être bien monté *or* pourvu en; **to be well ~ped to do** *(gen)* avoir tout ce qu'il faut pour faire; *[employee]* avoir toutes les compétences nécessaires pour faire.
◆ **equipment** *n (gen)* équipement *m*; *(for laboratory, office, lifesaving, camping etc)* matériel *m*; **electrical ~ment** appareillage *m* électrique; **sports ~ment** équipements *mpl* sportifs.

equity [ˈekwɪtɪ] *n* équité *f*. *(St Ex)* **equities** actions *fpl* (cotées en bourse). ◆ **equitable** *adj* équitable. ◆ **equitably** *adv* équitablement.

equivalent [ɪˈkwɪvələnt] *adj, n* équivalent *(m)* (*to* à; *in* en). ◆ **equivalence** *n* équivalence *f*.

equivocate [ɪˈkwɪvəkeɪt] *vi* user d'équivoques. ◆ **equivocal** *adj* équivoque. ◆ **equivocally** *adv* d'une manière équivoque. ◆ **equivocation** *n* paroles *fpl* équivoques.

era [ˈɪərə] *n (Geol, Hist)* ère *f*; *(gen)* époque *f*.

eradicate [ɪˈrædɪkeɪt] *vt (gen)* supprimer; *superstition* mettre fin à; *weeds* détruire.

erase [ɪˈreɪz] *vt (gen)* effacer; *(with rubber)* gommer. ◆ **eraser** *n (rubber)* gomme *f*; *(liquid: for typing)* liquide *m* correcteur. ◆ **erasure** *n* rature *f*.

erect [ɪˈrekt] **1** *adj (straight)* bien droit; *(standing)* debout. **with head ~** la tête haute. **2** *vt temple, statue* ériger; *wall, flats, factory* construire; *machinery, traffic signs* installer; *scaffolding, furniture* monter; *altar, tent, mast, barricade* dresser; *theory, obstacles* édifier. ◆ **erection** *n* érection *f (also Physiol)*; construction *f*; installation *f*; montage *m*; dressage *m*; édification *f*.

erode [ɪˈrəʊd] *vt (gen)* éroder; *[acid]* corroder; *(fig)* ronger. ◆ **erosion** *n* érosion *f*; corrosion *f*. ◆ **erosive** *adj* érosif; corrosif.

erotic [ɪˈrɒtɪk] *adj* érotique. ◆ **eroticism** *n* érotisme *m*.

err [ɜːʳ] *vi (be mistaken)* se tromper; *(sin)* pécher. **to ~ on the side of caution** pécher par excès de prudence. ◆ **erratum** , *pl* **-ata** *n* erratum *m*. ◆ **erroneous** *adj* erroné. ◆ **erroneously** *adv* erronément. ◆ **error** *n* erreur *f* (*of, in* de); **it would be an ~or to...** on aurait tort de...; **compass ~or** variation *f* du compas; **typing/spelling ~or** faute *f* de frappe/d'orthographe; **~ors and omissions excepted** sauf erreur ou omission; **in ~or** par erreur; **to see the ~or of one's ways** revenir de ses erreurs.

errand [ˈer(ə)nd] *n* commission *f*, course *f*. **to go on** *or* **run ~s** faire des commissions *or* des courses; **~ of mercy** mission *f* de charité; **~ boy** garçon *m* de courses.

erratic [ɪˈrætɪk] *adj person* capricieux; *record, results, performance* irrégulier; *mood* changeant; *(Geol, Med)* erratique. **his driving is ~** il conduit de façon déconcertante. ◆ **erratically** *adv* capricieusement; irrégulièrement; de façon déconcertante.

ersatz [ˈɛəzæts] **1** *n* ersatz *m*. **2** *adj*: **~ coffee** de l'ersatz de café.

erudite [ˈerʊdaɪt] *adj person, work* érudit, savant; *word* savant. ◆ **erudition** *n* érudition *f*.

erupt [ɪˈrʌpt] *vi [volcano]* entrer en éruption; *[spots]* sortir; *[anger]* exploser; *[war, fighting, quarrel]* éclater. **he ~ed into the room** il a fait irruption dans la pièce. ◆ **erupting** *adj volcano* en éruption. ◆ **eruption** *n [volcano, spots]* éruption *f*; *[anger, violence]* explosion *f*, accès *m*.

escalate [ˈeskəleɪt] **1** *vi [fighting, bombing, violence]* s'intensifier; *[costs]* monter en flèche. **the war is escalating** c'est l'escalade militaire; **prices are escalating** c'est l'escalade des prix. **2** *vt* intensifier; faire monter en flèche. ◆ **escalation** *n* intensification *f*; montée *f* en flèche, escalade *f*. ◆ **escalator** *n* escalier *m* roulant, escalator *m*.

escape [ɪsˈkeɪp] **1** *vi (gen)* échapper (*from sb* à qn), s'échapper (*from somewhere* de quelque part), s'enfuir (*to another place* dans un autre endroit); *[prisoner]* s'évader (*from* de); *[water, gas]* s'échapper; *(accidentally)* fuir. **an ~d prisoner** un évadé; *(fig)* **he ~d with a few scratches** il s'en est tiré avec quelques égratignures; **to ~ with a fright** en être quitte pour la peur; **to ~ from o.s.** se fuir.
2 *vt pursuit, danger, death* échapper à; *consequences* éviter; *punishment* se soustraire à. **he narrowly ~d being run over** il a failli être écrasé; **to ~ detection** ne pas se faire repérer; **nothing ~s him** rien ne lui échappe; **to ~ notice** passer inaperçu; **it had not ~d her notice that...** elle n'avait pas été sans s'apercevoir que...
3 *n [person, animal]* fuite *f*; *[prisoner]* évasion *f*; *[water, gas]* fuite; *[steam, gas in machine]* échappement *m*. **to plan an ~** combiner un plan d'évasion; **to have a lucky ~** l'échapper belle.
4 *adj valve, pipe* d'échappement; *plan, route* d'évasion; *device* de secours. **~ chute** toboggan *m* de secours; **~ clause** clause *f* de sauvegarde; **~ hatch** sas *m* de secours; *(Space)* **~ velocity** vitesse *f* de libération.
◆ **escapade** *n (misdeed)* fredaine *f*; *(adventure)* équipée *f*. ◆ **escapee** *n* évadé(e) *m(f)*. ◆ **escapism** *n* désir *m* d'évasion (de la réalité); **it's sheer escapism!** c'est simplement s'évader du réel! ◆ **escapist** **1** *n* personne *f* qui se complaît dans l'évasion ; **2** *adj* d'évasion. ◆ **escapologist** *n* virtuose *m* de l'évasion.

escarpment [ɪsˈkɑːpmənt] *n* escarpement *m*.

escort [ˈeskɔːt] **1** *n (Mil, Naut etc)* escorte *f*; *(male companion)* cavalier *m*; *(female)* hôtesse. **2** *adj duty, vessel* d'escorte. **~ agency** bureau *m* d'hôtesses (et de cavaliers). **3** [ɪsˈkɔːt] *vt (Mil, Naut, gen)* escorter. **to ~ sb in** *(Mil, Police)* faire entrer qn sous escorte; *(gen: accompany)* faire entrer qn.

escrow [ˈeskrəʊ] *n* dépôt *m* fiduciaire.

Eskimo [ˈeskɪməʊ] **1** *n* Esquimau(de) *m(f)*; *(Ling)* esquimau *m*. **2** *adj* esquimau.

esoteric [ˌesəʊˈterɪk] *adj* ésotérique.

especial [ɪsˈpeʃ(ə)l] *adj* particulier, spécial. ◆ **especially** *adv (particularly)* particulièrement; *(expressly)* exprès; **more ~ly as** d'autant plus que; **~ly as it's so late** d'autant plus qu'il est si tard;

why me ~ly? pourquoi moi en particulier?; **I came ~ly to see you** je suis venu exprès pour vous voir.

Esperanto [ˌespəˈræntəʊ] **1** *n* espéranto *m.* **2** *adj* en espéranto. ◆ **Esperantist** *n* espérantiste *mf.*

espionage [ˌespɪəˈnɑːʒ] *n* espionnage *m.*

espouse [ɪsˈpaʊz] *vt* épouser *(fig).*

espresso [esˈpresəʊ] *n* (café *m*) express *m.* ~ **bar** ≃ cafétéria *f.*

esquire [ɪsˈkwaɪəʳ] *n*: **B. Smith E~** Monsieur B. Smith.

essay [ˈeseɪ] *n (Literat)* essai *m* (*on* sur); *(Scol)* rédaction *f* (*on* sur); *(Brit Educ)* dissertation *f* (*on* sur); *(US Univ)* mémoire *m.* ◆ **essayist** *n* essayiste *mf.*

essence [ˈes(ə)ns] *n* essence *f*; *(Culin)* extrait *m.* **in** ~ essentiellement; **the ~ of what was said** l'essentiel *m* de ce qui a été dit; **speed is of the ~** la vitesse est essentielle; **the ~ of stupidity** * le comble de la stupidité; ~ **of violets** essence de violette; **meat** ~ extrait de viande. ◆ **essential 1** *adj* essentiel (*to* à); **it is essential that...** il est indispensable *or* essentiel que... + *subj* ; **2** *n* qualité *f* (*or* objet *m etc*) indispensable; **the essentials** *(necessities)* l'essentiel *m*; *(rudiments)* les éléments *mpl.* ◆ **essentially** *adv* essentiellement.

establish [ɪsˈtæblɪʃ] *vt* (**a**) *(set up) government, society, tribunal* constituer; *state, business, post* créer; *factory* monter; *laws, custom, sb's reputation, list, relations* établir; *power, authority* affermir; *peace, order* faire régner. **to ~ one's reputation as** se faire une réputation de. (**b**) *(prove) fact, identity, rights, innocence* établir; *necessity, guilt* prouver. ◆ **established** *adj (gen)* établi; *fact* acquis; *government* au pouvoir; **well-~ed business** maison *f* solide; **the ~ed Church** la religion d'État. ◆ **establishment** *n (institution etc)* établissement *m*; *(Admin, Mil, Naut etc: personnel)* effectifs *mpl*; **teaching ~ment** établissement d'enseignement; **the E~ment** les pouvoirs *mpl* établis, l'establishment *m*; **the values of the E~ment** les valeurs traditionnelles; **against the E~ment** anticonformiste; **he has joined the E~ment** il s'est rangé; **the literary E~ment** ceux qui font la loi dans le monde littéraire.

estate [ɪsˈteɪt] **1** *n* (**a**) *(land)* propriété *f*, domaine *m.* **country** ~ terres *fpl*; **housing** ~ lotissement *m*, cité *f.* (**b**) *(Jur: on death)* succession *f.* **he left a large** ~ il a laissé une grosse fortune. **2** *adj*: ~ **agency** agence *f* immobilière; ~ **agent** agent *m* immobilier; ~ **car** break *m*; ~ **duty,** *(US)* ~ **tax** droits *mpl* de succession.

esteem [ɪsˈtiːm] **1** *vt (think highly of) person* estimer; *quality* apprécier; *(consider)* estimer, considérer. **I ~ it an honour to do** je considère comme un honneur de faire. **2** *n* estime *f.* **he went up in my** ~ il a monté dans mon estime. ◆ **estimable** [ˈestɪməbl] *adj* estimable.

esthete [ˈiːsθiːt] *etc* = **aesthete** *etc.*

estimate [ˈestɪmɪt] **1** *n* évaluation *f*; *(Comm: for work to be done)* devis *m.* **give me an ~ of what your trip will cost** donnez-moi un état estimatif du coût de votre voyage; **this price is only a rough** ~ ce prix n'est que très approximatif; **at a rough** ~ approximativement; **at the lowest** ~ au bas mot; *(Admin, Pol)* **the ~s** le budget. **2** [ˈestɪmeɪt] *vt (all senses)* estimer (*that* que). ◆ **estimation** *n* (**a**) jugement *m*, opinion *f*; **in my estimation** à mon avis, selon moi; (**b**) *(esteem)* estime *f*; **he went up in my estimation** il a monté dans mon estime.

Estonia [eˈstəʊnɪə] *n* Estonie *f.*

estranged [ɪsˈtreɪn(d)ʒd] *adj*: **to become** ~ se brouiller (*from* avec); **the ~ couple** les époux désunis. ◆ **estrangement** *n* brouille *f* (*from* avec).

estrogen [ˈiːstrəʊˈdʒən] *n (US)* = **oestrogen.**

estuary [ˈestjʊərɪ] *n* estuaire *m.*

etch [etʃ] *vti* graver à l'eau forte. ◆ **etching** *n* gravure *f* à l'eau forte.

eternal [ɪˈtɜːnl] *adj (gen)* éternel; *(pej) complaints etc* continuel, perpétuel. *(fig)* **the ~ triangle** ≃ le ménage à trois. ◆ **eternally** *adv* éternellement; continuellement. ◆ **eternity** *n* éternité *f (also fig).*

ether [ˈiːθəʳ] *n* éther *m.* ◆ **ethereal** [ɪˈθɪərɪəl] *adj* éthéré.

ethic [ˈeθɪk] *n* morale *f*, éthique *f.* **the work** ~ l'attitude *f* moraliste envers le travail. ◆ **ethical** *adj* moral, éthique; **not ~al** contraire à la morale. ◆ **ethics** *n (sg: study)* éthique *f*; *(pl: system, principles)* morale *f.*

Ethiopia [iːθɪˈəʊpɪə] *n* Éthiopie *f.* ◆ **Ethiopian 1** *adj* éthiopien ; **2** *n* Éthiopien(ne) *m(f).*

ethnic [ˈeθnɪk] *adj* ethnique. ~ **minority** minorité *f* ethnique.

ethnology [eθˈnɒlədʒɪ] *n* ethnologie *f.* ◆ **ethnologist** *n* ethnologue *mf.*

ethos [ˈiːθɒs] *n* génie *m (d'un peuple, d'une culture).*

etiquette [ˈetɪket] *n* étiquette *f*, convenances *fpl.* **diplomatic** ~ protocole *m*; **court** ~ cérémonial *m* de cour; **that isn't** ~ c'est contraire aux convenances, cela ne se fait pas.

etymology [ˌetɪˈmɒlədʒɪ] *n* étymologie *f.* ◆ **etymological** *adj* étymologique. ◆ **etymologically** *adv* étymologiquement.

eucalyptus [ˌjuːkəˈlɪptəs] *n* eucalyptus *m.*

Eucharist [ˈjuːkərɪst] *n* Eucharistie *f.*

eugenics [juːˈdʒenɪks] *nsg* eugénique *f.*

eulogy [ˈjuːlədʒɪ] *n* panégyrique *m.* ◆ **eulogize** *vt* faire le panégyrique de.

eunuch [ˈjuːnək] *n* eunuque *m.*

euphemism [ˈjuːfəmɪz(ə)m] *n* euphémisme *m.* ◆ **euphemistic** *adj* euphémique. ◆ **euphemistically** *adv* par euphémisme.

euphonic [juːˈfɒnɪk] *adj* euphonique.

euphonium [juːˈfəʊnɪəm] *n* euphonium *m.*

euphoria [juːˈfɔːrɪə] *n* euphorie *f.* ◆ **euphoric** *adj* euphorique.

Eurasia [jʊ(ə)ˈreɪʃə] *n* Eurasie *f.* ◆ **Eurasian 1** *adj population* eurasien; *continent* eurasiatique ; **2** *n* Eurasien(ne) *m(f).*

euro... [ˈjʊərəʊ] *pref* euro... ◆ **eurocheque** *n* eurochèque *m.* ◆ **eurocrat** *n* eurocrate *mf.* ◆ **eurodollar** *n* eurodollar *m.* ◆ **euromarket** *or* ◆ **euromart** *n* Communauté *f* Économique Européenne. ◆ **eurosize** *n (Comm)* ~ **1** modèle *m* E1. ◆ **Eurovision** *n (TV)* Eurovision *f.*

Europe [ˈjʊərəp] *n* Europe *f.* *(Pol)* **to go into ~, to join** ~ entrer dans le Marché commun. ◆ **European 1** *adj* européen; **the ~an Economic Community** *(abbr* **EEC***)* la Communauté Économique Européenne (*abbr* CEE *f*); *(US: in hotel)* **~an plan** chambre *f* sans petit déjeuner ; **2** *n* Européen(ne) *m(f).* ◆ **Europeanize** *vt* européaniser.

euthanasia [ˌjuːθəˈneɪzɪə] *n* euthanasie *f.*

evacuate [ɪˈvækjʊeɪt] *vt (all senses)* évacuer. ◆ **evacuation** *n* évacuation *f.* ◆ **evacuee** *n* évacué(e) *m(f).*

evade [ɪˈveɪd] *vt blow, obligation, difficulty* éviter, esquiver; *pursuers, punishment* échapper à; *sb's gaze* éviter; *question* éluder; *law* tourner. **to ~ military service** se dérober à ses obligations militaires ; **to ~ taxation/customs duty** frauder le fisc/la douane.

evaluate [ɪˈvæljʊeɪt] *vt* évaluer (*at* à). ◆ **evaluation** *n* évaluation *f.*

evangelical [ˌiːvænˈdʒelɪk(ə)l] *adj, n* évangélique *(mf).* ◆ **evangelicalism** *n* évangélisme *m.* ◆ **evangelist** *n* évangéliste *m.* ◆ **evangelize 1** *vt* prêcher l'Évangile à ; **2** *vi* prêcher l'Évangile.

evaporate [ɪˈvæpəreɪt] **1** *vt* faire évaporer. **~d milk** lait concentré non sucré. **2** *vi* s'évaporer; *[hopes, fear]* s'évanouir. ◆ **evaporation** *n* évaporation *f*.

evasion [ɪˈveɪʒ(ə)n] *n [prisoner]* fuite *f*; *(excuse)* faux-fuyant *m*. ◆ **evasive** *adj* évasif; **to take evasive action** *(Mil)* effectuer une manœuvre dilatoire ; *(gen)* prendre la tangente. ◆ **evasively** *adv* évasivement.

eve [iːv] *n* veille *f*.

even [ˈiːv(ə)n] **1** *adj* (**a**) *(smooth) surface* uni, plat. **to make ~** égaliser, aplanir. (**b**) *(regular) progress* régulier; *breathing, temper* égal. (**c**) *(equal) quantities, values* égal. **they are an ~ match** *(Sport)* la partie est égale; *(fig)* ils sont bien assortis; **to get ~ with sb** se venger de qn; **I will get ~ with you for that** je vous revaudrai ça; **I'll give you ~ money that...** il y a une chance sur deux que... + *subj*. (**d**) *number, date* pair.
2 *adv* (**a**) même. **~ in the holidays** même pendant les vacances; **I have ~ forgotten his name** j'ai oublié jusqu'à son nom, j'ai même oublié son nom; **~ if** même si + *indic*; **~ though** quand (bien) même + *cond*, alors même que + *cond*; **if he ~ made an effort** si encore *or* si au moins il faisait un effort; **~ so** quand même, pourtant. (**b**) *(+ comp adj or adv)* encore. **~ better** encore mieux. (**c**) (+ *neg*) même, seulement. **without ~ saying goodbye** sans même *or* sans seulement dire au revoir; **he can't ~ swim** il ne sait même pas nager.
◆ **even out 1** *vi* s'égaliser. **2** *vt sep* égaliser.
◆ **even up** *vt sep* égaliser. **that will ~ things up** cela rétablira l'équilibre; *(financially)* cela compensera.
◆ **evenly** *adv spread, paint etc* de façon égale; *breathe, space* régulièrement; *divide* également.
◆ **even-tempered** *adj* d'humeur égale.

evening [ˈiːvnɪŋ] **1** *n* soir *m*; *(length of time)* soirée *f*. **in the ~** le soir; **let's have an ~ out** nous devrions sortir (un soir); **6 o'clock in the ~** 6 heures du soir; **on the ~ of the 29th** le 29 au soir; **the warm summer ~s** les chaudes soirées d'été; **all ~** toute la soirée; **to spend one's ~ reading** passer sa soirée à lire. **2** *adj paper, prayers, service* du soir. **~ class** cours *m* du soir; **in ~ dress** *man* en tenue de soirée; *woman* en robe du soir; **~ fixture** *or* **match** nocturne *f*; **~ performance** (représentation *f* en) soirée *f*; **~ star** étoile *f* du berger.

evensong [ˈiːv(ə)nsɒŋ] *n* ≃ vêpres *fpl*.

event [ɪˈvent] *n* (**a**) événement *m*. **course of ~s** suite *f* des événements; **in the course of ~s** par la suite; **in the normal course of ~s** normalement; **after the ~** après coup; **in the ~ of death** en cas de décès; **in the unlikely ~ that...** s'il arrivait par hasard que... + *subj*; **in the ~** en fait; **in that ~** dans ce cas; **in any ~, at all ~s** en tout cas, de toute façon; **in either ~** dans l'un ou l'autre cas. (**b**) *(Sport)* épreuve *f*; *(Racing)* course *f*. **field ~s** épreuves d'athlétisme *(à l'exception des épreuves de vitesse)*; **track ~s** épreuves de vitesse. ◆ **eventful** *adj (busy etc)* mouvementé; *(momentous)* mémorable.
◆ **eventing** *n* concours complet *(d'équitation)*.

eventual [ɪˈventʃʊəl] *adj (resulting)* qui s'ensuit; *(probably resulting)* éventuel. **it resulted in the ~ disappearance of...** cela a abouti finalement à la disparition de... ◆ **eventuality** *n* éventualité *f*.
◆ **eventually** *adv* finalement, en fin de compte; à la longue; **he ~ly did it** il a fini par le faire.
◆ **eventuate** *vi (US)* (finir par) se produire.

ever [ˈevəʳ] *adv* (**a**) jamais. **nothing ~ happens** il ne se passe jamais rien; **if you ~ see her** si jamais vous la voyez; **do you ~ see her?** est-ce qu'il vous arrive de la voir?; **have you ~ seen her?** l'avez-vous jamais *or* déjà vue?; **I haven't ~ seen her** je ne l'ai jamais vue; **seldom if ~** pour ainsi dire jamais; **now if ~ is the moment to...** c'est le moment ou jamais de...; **he's a liar if ~ there was one** c'est un menteur ou je ne m'y connais pas; **more beautiful than ~** plus beau que jamais; **the coldest night ~** la nuit la plus froide qu'on ait jamais connue.
(**b**) *(at all times)* toujours, sans cesse. **~ ready** toujours prêt; **~ increasing anxiety** inquiétude qui va croissant; **they lived happily ~ after** ils vécurent (toujours) heureux; **~ since I was a boy** depuis mon enfance; **for ~** *(for always) disappear* à jamais, pour toujours; *(a very long time) last, wait* une éternité; *(in letters)* **yours ~** bien amicalement à vous.
(**c**) *(intensive)* **as quickly as ~ you can** aussi vite que vous le pourrez; **the first ~** le tout premier; **~ so slightly drunk** tant soit peu ivre; **~ so pretty** vraiment joli; **thank you ~ so much** merci mille fois; **as if I ~ would!** comme si je ferais ça, moi!; **what ~ shall we do?** qu'est-ce que nous allons bien faire?; **why ~ not?** mais enfin, pourquoi pas?; **did you ~!** * ça par exemple!
◆ **evergreen** *adj, n* (arbre *m or* plante *f*) à feuilles persistantes; *(fig)* (chanson *f etc*) qui ne vieillit pas. ◆ **everlasting** *adj* éternel. ◆ **everlastingly** *adv* éternellement. ◆ **evermore** *adv*: **for ~more** à tout jamais.

every [ˈevrɪ] *adj* chaque, tout; tous les. **~ shop in the town** tous les magasins de la ville; **not ~ child has the same advantages** les enfants n'ont pas tous les mêmes avantages; **not ~ child has the advantages you have** tous les enfants n'ont pas les avantages que tu as; **I have ~ confidence in him** j'ai entièrement confiance en lui; **we wish you ~ success** nous vous souhaitons très bonne chance; **~ (single) one of them** chacun d'eux; **~ one had brought sth** chacun d'entre eux avait *or* ils avaient tous apporté qch; **from ~ country** de tous (les) pays; **of ~ sort** de toute sorte; **of ~ age** de tout âge; **~ fifth day, ~ five days** tous les cinq jours; **~ second** *or* **other child** un enfant sur deux; **~ quarter of an hour** tous les quarts d'heure; **~ other Wednesday** un mercredi sur deux; **~ few days** tous les deux ou trois jours; **his ~ action** chacune de ses actions; **his ~ wish** son moindre désir; **~ bit of the wall** le mur tout entier; **~ bit as clever as** tout aussi doué que; **~ now and then, ~ now and again, ~ so often** de temps en temps, de temps à autre; **~ time that** chaque fois que; **~ single time** chaque fois sans exception; **~ one of us is afraid of sth** nous craignons tous qch, tous tant que nous sommes nous craignons qch; **~ man for himself** chacun pour soi; *(excl)* sauve qui peut!
◆ **everybody** *pron* tout le monde, chacun; **~body has finished** tout le monde a fini; **~body has his** *or* **their * own ideas about it** chacun a ses (propres) idées là-dessus; **~body else** tous les autres. ◆ **everyday** *adj coat* de tous les jours; *occurrence* banal; *use, experience* ordinaire; **words in ~day use** mots d'usage courant; **it was not an ~day event** c'était un événement hors du commun. ◆ **everyone** *pron* = **everybody.** ◆ **everyplace** *adv (US)* = **everywhere.** ◆ **everything** *pron* tout; **~thing is ready** tout est prêt; **~thing you have** tout ce que vous avez; **stamina is ~thing** l'essentiel c'est d'avoir de la résistance. ◆ **everywhere** *adv (gen)* partout ; **~where you go you meet...** où qu'on aille on rencontre...

evict [ɪˈvɪkt] *vt* expulser *(from* de). ◆ **eviction** *n* expulsion *f*; **eviction notice** avis *m* d'expulsion.

evidence [ˈevɪdəns] *n (data)* preuves *fpl*; *(testimony)* témoignage *m (of sb* de qn). **the ~ of the senses** le témoignage des sens; **to give ~** témoigner *(for/against sb* en faveur de/contre qn); **to turn King's** *or* **Queen's ~** *or (US)* **state's ~** témoigner contre ses complices; **to show ~ of** témoigner de; **to be in ~** être en évidence; **he was nowhere in ~** il n'y avait pas trace de lui. ◆ **evident** *adj* évident, manifeste; **it was evident from the way he walked** cela se voyait à sa démarche; **it is evident from his speech that...** il ressort de son discours que... ◆ **evidently** *adv (obviously)* évidemment, manifestement; *(apparently)* à ce qu'il paraît; **he was evidently frightened** il était évident qu'il avait peur; **they are evidently going to change the rule** il paraît qu'ils vont changer le règlement.

evil ['i:vl] **1** *adj deed, person, example, reputation* mauvais; *influence* néfaste; *doctrine, spell, spirit* malfaisant; *hour, course of action, consequence* funeste. **the ~ eye** le mauvais œil. **2** *n* mal *m*. **the lesser ~** le moindre mal; **the ~s of drink** les conséquences *fpl* funestes de la boisson; **one of the great ~s of our time** un des grands fléaux de notre temps. ◆ **evildoer** *n* scélérat(e) *m(f)*. ◆ **evilly** *adv* avec malveillance. ◆ **evil-minded** *adj* malveillant.

evince [ɪ'vɪns] *vt* manifester.

evoke [ɪ'vəʊk] *vt memories* évoquer; *admiration* susciter. ◆ **evocation** *n* évocation *f*. ◆ **evocative** *adj* évocateur.

evolve [ɪ'vɒlv] **1** *vt system, theory, plan* élaborer. **2** *vi (gen, Bio)* évoluer. **to ~ from** se développer à partir de. ◆ **evolution** *n* évolution *f* (*from* à partir de).

ewe [ju:] *n* brebis *f*.

ex- [eks] **1** *pref (former)* ex-. **~president** ancien président, ex-président; **~husband** ex-mari *m*; **~serviceman** ancien combattant. **2** *n (*: ex-partner)* ex *mf*. **3** *prep (out of) (Comm, Ind)* **price ~ works** prix *m* départ usine; **~ officio** *(adj, adv)* ex officio.

exacerbate [eks'æsəbeɪt] *vt pain etc* exacerber; *situation* aggraver; *person* exaspérer.

exact [ɪg'zækt] **1** *adj (accurate) description, time, measurements, forecast* exact, juste; *copy* exact; *(precise) number, value* exact, précis; *meaning, time, place, instructions* précis; *instrument* de précision. **these were his ~ words** voilà textuellement ce qu'il a dit; **he's 44 to be ~** il a très exactement 44 ans; **to be ~ it was 4 o'clock** il était 4 heures, plus exactement; **can you be more ~?** pouvez-vous préciser un peu? **2** *vt* exiger (*from* de). ◆ **exacting** *adj person* exigeant; *profession, task, activity, work* astreignant. ◆ **exactitude** *n* exactitude *f*. ◆ **exactly** *adv answer, work, describe* avec précision; *obey, resemble, know* exactement; **~ly the same thing** exactement *or* précisément la même chose; **that's ~ly what I thought** c'est exactement *or* précisément ce que je pensais; **it is 3 o'clock ~ly** il est 3 heures juste(s). ◆ **exactness** *n* exactitude *f*; justesse *f*; précision *f*.

exaggerate [ɪg'zædʒəreɪt] *vt (overstate)* exagérer; *(in one's own mind)* s'exagérer; *(emphasize)* accentuer. **the dress ~d her paleness** la robe accentuait sa pâleur; **he ~s the importance of the task** il s'exagère l'importance de la tâche. ◆ **exaggerated** *adj* exagéré; **to have an ~d opinion of o.s.** avoir trop bonne opinion de soi-même. ◆ **exaggeration** *n* exagération *f*.

exalted [ɪg'zɔ:ltɪd] *adj (high) position* élevé; *person* haut placé; *(elated)* exalté.

examine [ɪg'zæmɪn] *vt* (**a**) *(gen, Med)* examiner; *machine* inspecter; *passport* contrôler; *(Customs) luggage* fouiller. (**b**) *pupil, candidate* examiner (*in* en); *(orally)* interroger (*on* sur); *witness, suspect, accused* interroger. ◆ **examination** *n (gen)* examen *m*; *[machine, premises]* inspection *f*; *[passports]* contrôle *m*; *(Customs)* fouille *f*; *(Scol etc: abbr* **exam***)* examen; *(one paper)* épreuve *f*; **on examination** après examen; **examination candidate** candidat(e) *m(f)* à un (*or* l' *etc*) examen. ◆ **examiner** *n* examinateur *m*, -trice *f* (*in* de).

example [ɪg'zɑ:mpl] *n* exemple *m*. **for ~** par exemple; **to set a good ~** donner l'exemple; **to take sb as an ~** prendre exemple sur qn; **to make an ~ of sb** faire un exemple en punissant qn; **to punish sb as an ~ to others** punir qn pour l'exemple; **to quote sth as an ~** citer qch en exemple.

exasperate [ɪg'zɑ:spəreɪt] *vt* exaspérer. ◆ **exasperated** *adj* exaspéré (*at sth* de qch; *with sb* par qn); **to become ~d** s'exaspérer. ◆ **exasperating** *adj* exaspérant. ◆ **exasperatingly** *adv* d'une manière exaspérante; **exasperatingly slow** d'une lenteur exaspérante. ◆ **exasperation** *n* exaspération *f*.

excavate ['ekskəveɪt] **1** *vt ground* creuser; *(Archeol)* fouiller; *remains* déterrer. **2** *vi (Archeol)* faire des fouilles. ◆ **excavation** *n (gen)* creusement *m*; *(Archeol)* fouilles *fpl*; **~ work** travaux *mpl* de creusement. ◆ **excavator** *n (machine)* pelleteuse *f*.

exceed [ɪk'si:d] *vt (gen)* dépasser (*in* en, *by* de); *powers, instructions* outrepasser. **to ~ the speed limit** dépasser la vitesse permise. ◆ **exceedingly** *adv* extrêmement, infiniment.

excel [ɪk'sel] **1** *vi* briller (*at, in* en), exceller (*at or in doing* à faire). **2** *vt* surpasser. **to ~ o.s.** se surpasser. ◆ **excellence** *n* excellence *f*. ◆ **Excellency** *n*: **His E~lency** Son Excellence *f*. ◆ **excellent** *adj* excellent, parfait. ◆ **excellently** *adv* admirablement, parfaitement.

excelsior [ek'selsjəʳ] *n (US)* copeaux *mpl* d'emballage.

except [ɪk'sept] **1** *prep* sauf, excepté. **~ for** à part, à l'exception de; **~ that/if/when** *etc* sauf que/si/quand *etc*; **what can they do ~ wait?** que peuvent-ils faire sinon attendre?
2 *vt* excepter (*from* de), faire exception de. **present company ~ed** exception faite des personnes présentes; **always ~ing...** à l'exception bien entendu de... ◆ **excepting** *prep* = **except 1**. ◆ **exception** *n* exception *f* (*to* à); **without ~ion** sans exception; **with the ~ion of** à l'exception de, exception faite de; **to take ~ion to** *(demur)* désapprouver; *(be offended)* s'offenser de; **to make an ~ion** faire une exception (*to sth* à qch, *for sb/sth* pour qn/qch); **the ~ion proves the rule** l'exception confirme la règle; **with this ~ion** à cette exception près, à ceci près. ◆ **exceptional** *adj* exceptionnel. ◆ **exceptionally** *adv* exceptionnellement.

excerpt ['eksɜ:pt] *n* extrait *m*.

excess [ɪk'ses] **1** *n* excès *m*. **to ~** à l'excès; **to carry to ~** pousser à l'excès; **in ~ of** dépassant; **the ~ of imports over exports** l'excédent *m* des importations sur les exportations. **2** *adj profit, weight, production* excédentaire. **~ fare** supplément *m*; **~ luggage** excédent *m* de bagages. ◆ **excessive** *adj* excessif; **~ive drinking** abus *m* de la boisson. ◆ **excessively** *adv (to excess) eat, drink, spend* avec excès; *optimistic* par trop; *proud* démesurément; *(extremely)* extrêmement, infiniment.

exchange [ɪks'tʃeɪn(d)ʒ] **1** *vt (gen)* échanger (*for* contre); *houses, cars, jobs* faire un échange de. **to ~ contracts** ≃ signer les contrats. **2** *n* (**a**) échange *m*. **in ~** en échange (*for* de); **to lose on the ~** perdre au change. (**b**) *(Fin)* change *m*. (**c**) *(telephone ~)* central *m*. **labour ~** bourse *f* du travail. **3** *adj teacher, student* participant à un échange. **~ control** contrôle *m* des changes; **~ rate** taux *m* de change. ◆ **exchangeable** *adj* échangeable (*for* contre).

exchequer [ɪks'tʃekəʳ] *n (Brit Parl)* Échiquier *m*; *(state treasury)* Trésor *or* trésor *m*; *(funds)* fonds *mpl*.

excise ['eksaɪz] *n* taxe *f* (*on* sur). **the E~** la Régie; **~ duties** ≃ contributions *fpl* indirectes.

excite [ɪk'saɪt] *vt person (gen)* exciter; *(rouse enthusiasm in)* passionner; *emotion* provoquer (*in sb* chez qn). **to ~ enthusiasm/interest in sb** enthousiasmer/intéresser qn. ◆ **excitable** *adj person* excitable, nerveux; *temperament* nerveux. ◆ **excited** *adj (gen)* excité; *laughter* énervé; *voice* animé; **to get ~d** s'exciter (*about* au sujet de); **don't get ~d!** ne t'énerve pas! ◆ **excitedly** *adv behave, speak* avec agitation; *laugh* d'excitation. ◆ **excitement** *n* excitation *f*; *(exhilaration)* exaltation *f*; **the ~ment of the departure/elections** la fièvre du départ/des élections; **the book caused great ~ment** le livre a fait sensation; **he likes ~ment** il aime les émotions *fpl* fortes *or* l'aventure *f*. ◆ **exciting** *adj events, story, film* passionnant; *account* saisissant; *holiday, experience* excitant.

exclaim [ɪks'kleɪm] **1** *vi* s'exclamer. **to ~ at sth** se récrier devant qch. **2** *vt* s'écrier (*that* que). ◆ **exclamation** **1** *n* exclamation *f* ; **2** *adj*: **exclamation mark** *or* **point** point *m* d'exclamation.

exclude [ɪks'klu:d] *vt (gen)* exclure (*from* de); *(from list)* écarter (*from* de). **he was ~d from taking part** il n'a pas eu le droit de participer. ◆ **exclusion** *n* exclusion *f* (*of, from* de).

exclusive [ɪks'klu:sɪv] *adj* (**a**) *(excluding others) group, gathering* choisi; *club, society* fermé; *hotel, restaurant* huppé; *person, friendship, interest, occupation* exclusif. (**b**) *(owned by one person, one firm) information, design, report* exclusif. **the ~ rights for** l'exclusivité *f* de; **an interview ~ to...** une interview accordée exclusivement à... (**c**) *(not including)* **from 15th to 20th ~** du 15 au 20 exclusivement; **~ of** non compris; **the price is ~ of transport charges** le prix ne comprend pas les frais de transport. ◆ **exclusively** *adv* exclusivement.

excommunicate [ˌekskə'mju:nɪkeɪt] *vt* excommunier. ◆ **excommunication** *n* excommunication *f*.

excrement ['ekskrɪmənt] *n* excrément *m*.

excrescence [ɪks'kresns] *n* excroissance *f*.

excrete [ɪks'kri:t] *vt* excréter. ◆ **excreta** *npl* excrétions *fpl*.

excruciating [ɪks'kru:ʃɪeɪtɪŋ] *adj pain* atroce; *suffering* déchirant; *noise* insupportable; *(*: unpleasant)* épouvantable, atroce. ◆ **excruciatingly** *adv* atrocement, affreusement; **~ly funny** * désopilant.

exculpate ['ekskʌlpeɪt] *vt person* disculper (*from* de).

excursion [ɪks'kɜ:ʃ(ə)n] **1** *n* excursion *f*; *(in car, on cycle)* randonnée *f*; *(fig: digression)* digression *f*. **2** *adj*: **~ ticket** billet *m* d'excursion; **~ train** train spécial *(pour excursions)*.

excuse [ɪks'kju:z] **1** *vt* (**a**) *(justify, pardon)* excuser (*sb for having done* qn d'avoir fait). **to ~ o.s.** s'excuser (*for* de, *for doing* de faire), présenter ses excuses; **if you will ~ the expression** passez-moi l'expression; **and now if you will ~ me, ...** maintenant, si vous permettez, ...; **~ me!** excusez-moi! (**b**) *(exempt)* exempter (*sb from sth* qn de qch), dispenser (*sb from sth* qn de qch, *sb from doing* qn de faire), excuser. *(to children)* **you are ~d** vous pouvez vous en aller; **to ask to be ~d** se faire excuser.
2 [ɪks'kju:s] *n* (**a**) *(reason, justification)* excuse *f*. **that is no ~ for his leaving so abruptly** cela ne l'excuse pas d'être parti si brusquement. (**b**) *(pretext)* excuse *f*, prétexte *m*. **he is only making ~s** il cherche tout simplement des prétextes; **to make an ~ for sth/for doing** trouver une excuse à qch/ pour faire; **he gave the bad weather as his ~ for not coming** il a prétexté le mauvais temps pour ne pas venir.
◆ **excusable** *adj* excusable, pardonnable.

ex-directory [ˌeksdɪ'rektərɪ] *adj (Telec)* qui ne figure pas dans l'annuaire, qui est sur la liste rouge.

execrate ['eksɪkreɪt] *vt* exécrer. ◆ **execrable** *adj* exécrable. ◆ **execrably** *adv* exécrablement. ◆ **execration** *n* exécration *f*.

execute ['eksɪkju:t] *vt* (**a**) *(put to death)* exécuter. (**b**) *(carry out) (gen)* exécuter; *work of art* réaliser; *purpose, sb's wishes, duties, task* accomplir. ◆ **execution** *n* exécution *f*; **in the execution of his duties** dans l'exercice de ses fonctions. ◆ **executioner** *n* bourreau *m*. ◆ **executive** [ɪg'zekjʊtɪv] **1** *adj powers, committee* exécutif; *job* de cadre; *director, secretary* général; *offices* de la direction; *post, car, plane* de direction; *unemployment* des cadres ; **2** *n (power)* (pouvoir *m*) exécutif *m*; *(person)* cadre *m*; *(group of managers)* bureau *m*; **senior/junior executive** cadre supérieur/moyen; **a sales executive** un cadre ventes. ◆ **executor** *n* [ɪg'zekjʊtə^r] exécuteur *m*, -trice *f* testamentaire.

exemplary [ɪg'zemplərɪ] *adj (gen)* exemplaire; *pupil etc* modèle.

exemplify [ɪg'zemplɪfaɪ] *vt (illustrate)* exemplifier; *(be example of)* servir d'exemple de.

exempt [ɪg'zem(p)t] **1** *adj* exempt (*from* de). **2** *vt* exempter (*from sth* de qch), dispenser (*from doing* de faire). ◆ **exemption** *n* exemption *f* (*from* de); *(Educ)* dispense *f*; *(Jur)* dérogation *f*.

exercise ['eksəsaɪz] **1** *n (gen)* exercice *m*. **in the ~ of his duties** dans l'exercice de ses fonctions; **physical ~** exercice physique; **(physical) ~s** la gymnastique; **to take ~** prendre de l'exercice; **a grammar ~** un exercice de grammaire; **NATO ~s** manœuvres *fpl* de l'OTAN; **an ~ in public relations** une opération de relations publiques; **a cost-cutting ~** une opération de réduction des coûts. **2** *vt limb, rights, influence* exercer; *(use) tact, restraint* faire preuve de; (*) *dog etc* promener. **the problem which is exercising my mind** le problème qui me préoccupe. **3** *vi* prendre de l'exercice. ◆ **exercise bike** *n* vélo *m* de santé. ◆ **exercise-book** *n (for writing)* cahier *m*.

exert [ɪg'zɜ:t] *vt (gen)* exercer; *force* employer. **to ~ o.s.** *(physically)* se dépenser; *(take trouble)* se donner du mal; *(iro)* **don't ~ yourself!** ne vous fatiguez pas! ◆ **exertion** *n* effort *m*; **by his own ~ions** par ses propres moyens *mpl*; **the day's ~ions** les fatigues *fpl* de la journée; **it doesn't require much ~ion** cela n'exige pas un grand effort.

exeunt ['eksɪʌnt] *vi (Theat)* ils sortent.

exhale [eks'heɪl] *vti (Physiol)* expirer.

exhaust [ɪg'zɔ:st] **1** *vt (all senses)* épuiser. **2** *n (~ system)* échappement *m*; *(~ pipe)* pot *m* d'échappement; *(~ fumes)* gaz *m* d'échappement. ◆ **exhausted** *adj* épuisé; **I'm ~ed** je n'en peux plus; **my patience is ~ed** ma patience est à bout. ◆ **exhausting** *adj* épuisant. ◆ **exhaustion** *n* épuisement *m*. ◆ **exhaustive** *adj account, report* complet; *study, description, list* exhaustif; *inquiry, inspection* minutieux. ◆ **exhaustively** *adv search, study* à fond; *list, describe* exhaustivement.

exhibit [ɪg'zɪbɪt] **1** *vt painting, handicrafts* exposer; *merchandise* exposer, étaler; *document, identity card* présenter; *courage, skill, ingenuity* faire preuve de. **2** *n (in exhibition)* objet *m* exposé; *(Jur)* pièce *f* à conviction. ◆ **exhibition** *n [paintings etc]* exposition *f*; *[articles for sale]* étalage *m*; **the Van Gogh ~ion** l'exposition Van Gogh; *(fig)* **to make an ~ion of o.s.** se donner en spectacle. ◆ **exhibitionism** *n* exhibitionnisme *m*. ◆ **exhibitionist** *adj, n* exhibitionniste *(mf)*. ◆ **exhibitor** *n* exposant(e) *m(f)*.

exhilarate [ɪg'zɪləreɪt] *vt [sea air etc]* vivifier; *[music, wine, good company]* stimuler. ◆ **exhilarated** *adj* stimulé. ◆ **exhilarating** *adj* vivifiant; stimulant. ◆ **exhilaration** *n* joie *f*, allégresse *f*.

exhort [ɪg'zɔ:t] *vt* exhorter (*to* à, *to do* à faire). ◆ **exhortation** *n* exhortation *f* (*to* à).

exhume [eks'hju:m] *vt* exhumer. ◆ **exhumation** *n* exhumation *f*.

exile ['eksaɪl] **1** *n (person)* exilé(e) *m(f)*; *(condition)* exil *m*. **in(to)** ~ en exil. **2** *vt* exiler (*from* de). ◆ **exiled** *adj* exilé, en exil.

exist [ɪg'zɪst] *vi* (**a**) *(be)* exister. **everything that ~s** tout ce qui existe *or* est; **doubt still ~s** le doute subsiste. (**b**) *(live)* vivre (*on* de), subsister. **we cannot ~ without water** nous ne pouvons pas vivre *or* subsister sans eau; **she ~s on very little** elle vit de très peu. ◆ **existence** *n* existence *f*; **to be in ~ence** exister; **to come into ~ence** être créé; **the only one in ~ence** le seul qui existe *(subj)*. ◆ **existent** *adj* existant. ◆ **existential** *adj* existentiel. ◆ **existentialism** *n* existentialisme *m*. ◆ **existentialist** *adj, n* existentialiste *(mf)*. ◆ **existing** *adj law* existant; *regime* actuel.

exit ['eksɪt] **1** *n* sortie *f*. **2** *vi* (**a**) *(Comput)* sortir. (**b**) *(Theat)* il sort. **3** *adj*: ~ **permit/visa** permis *m*/visa *m* de sortie; ~ **poll** sondage *m* à la sortie des bureaux de vote; *(US Aut)* ~ **ramp** bretelle *f* d'accès.

exodus ['eksədəs] *n* exode *m*. *(Bible)* **E~** l'Exode; *(fig)* **there was a general** ~ il y a eu un véritable exode.

exonerate [ɪg'zɒnəreɪt] *vt* disculper (*from* de), innocenter. ◆ **exoneration** *n* disculpation *f*.

exorbitant [ɪg'zɔːbɪt(ə)nt] *adj price* exorbitant; *demands* exorbitant, démesuré. ◆ **exorbitantly** *adv* démesurément.

exorcize ['eksɔːsaɪz] *vt* exorciser. ◆ **exorcism** *n* exorcisme *m*. ◆ **exorcist** *n* exorciste *m*.

exotic [ɪg'zɒtɪk] *adj* exotique. ◆ **exoticism** *n* exotisme *m*.

expand [ɪks'pænd] **1** *vt gas, metal, lungs* dilater; *business, ideas, notes, muscles* développer; *production* augmenter; *horizons, study* élargir; *influence, knowledge* étendre. **~ed polystyrene** polystyrène *m* expansé. **2** *vi* se dilater; se développer; augmenter; s'élargir; s'étendre. **the market is ~ing** les débouchés se multiplient. ◆ **expanding** *adj metal, market, universe* en expansion; *bracelet* extensible; **a rapidly ~ing industry** une industrie en pleine expansion; **~ing file** classeur extensible.

expanse [ɪks'pæns] *n* étendue *f*. ◆ **expansion** *n [gas]* dilatation *f*; *[business]* agrandissement *m*; *[trade, subject, idea]* développement *m*; *[production]* augmentation *f*; *(territorial, economic, colonial)* expansion *f*. ◆ **expansionism** *n* expansionnisme *m*. ◆ **expansive** *adj* expansif, communicatif; *smile* chaleureux; **in an expansive mood** en veine d'épanchements. ◆ **expansively** *adv (in detail)* avec abondance; *(warmly)* avec chaleur; **to smile expansively** arborer un large sourire; **to gesture expansively** faire de grands gestes.

expatiate [ɪks'peɪʃɪeɪt] *vi* discourir (*upon* sur).

expatriate [eks'pætrɪeɪt] *adj, n* expatrié(e) *m(f)*.

expect [ɪks'pekt] *vt* (**a**) *(anticipate)* s'attendre à; *(with confidence)* escompter; *(count on)* compter sur; *(hope for)* espérer. **to ~ to do** penser *or* compter *or* espérer faire, s'attendre à faire; **that was to be ~ed** c'était à prévoir, il fallait s'y attendre; **I ~ed as much** je m'y attendais; **I know what to ~** je sais à quoi m'attendre; **I did not ~ that from him** je n'attendais pas cela de lui; **to ~ that** s'attendre à ce que + *subj*, escompter que + *indic*; **it is ~ed that** il est vraisemblable que + *indic*, il y a des chances pour que + *subj*; **it is not as heavy as I ~ed** ce n'est pas aussi lourd que je le croyais; **as ~ed** comme prévu. (**b**) *(suppose)* penser, supposer. **I ~ so** je crois que oui; **yes, I ~ it is** oui, je m'en doute. (**c**) *(demand)* exiger, attendre (*sth from sb* qch de qn), demander (*sth from sb* qch à qn). **to ~ sb to do sth** exiger *or* demander que qn fasse qch; **you can't ~ too much from him** on ne peut pas trop exiger de lui; **I ~ you to tidy your own room** tu es censé ranger ta chambre toi-même; **what do you ~ me to do about it?** que voulez-vous que j'y fasse?; **England ~s that...** l'Angleterre compte que + *fut indic*. (**d**) *(await)* attendre. **I am ~ing them for dinner** je les attends à dîner; **we'll ~ you when we see you** * on ne t'attend pas à une heure précise; **she is ~ing a baby, she is ~ing** * elle attend un bébé. ◆ **expectancy** *n* attente *f*; *(hopefulness)* espoir *m*; **with eager ~ancy** avec une vive impatience; **look of ~ancy** regard plein d'espoir. ◆ **expectant** *adj person, crowd* qui attend qch; *attitude* d'expectative; *look* de qn qui attend qch; **~ant mother** femme *f* enceinte. ◆ **expectantly** *adv look, listen* avec l'air d'attendre qch; *wait* avec espoir. ◆ **expectation** *n* attente *f*; **in ~ation of** dans l'attente de, en prévision de; **~ation of life** espérance *f* de vie; **contrary to all ~ation** contre toute attente; **to come up to sb's ~ations** répondre à l'attente *or* aux espérances de qn; **beyond ~ation** au-delà de mes *etc* espérances.

expedient [ɪks'piːdɪənt] **1** *adj (convenient)* indiqué, opportun; *(politic)* politique, opportun. **it would be ~ to change the rule** il serait opportun de changer le règlement. **2** *n* expédient *m*. ◆ **expedience** *or* ◆ **expediency** *n (self-interest)* opportunisme *m*; *(advisability)* opportunité *f*.

expedite ['ekspɪdaɪt] *vt preparations, process* accélérer; *work, legal or official matters* activer, hâter; *business, deal* pousser; *task* expédier. ◆ **expedition** *n* expédition *f*. ◆ **expeditionary** *adj* expéditionnaire. ◆ **expeditious** *adj* expéditif. ◆ **expeditiously** *adv* promptement.

expel [ɪks'pel] *vt (gen)* expulser (*from* de); *(from school)* renvoyer; *enemy* chasser.

expend [ɪks'pend] *vt time, energy* consacrer (*on* à; *on doing* à faire); *money* dépenser (*on* pour; *on doing* à faire); *(use up)* épuiser. ◆ **expendable** *adj equipment* non-réutilisable; *troops* sacrifiable; *(of little value) person, object* facile à remplacer. ◆ **expenditure** *n* dépenses *fpl*; **an item of ~iture** une dépense.

expense [ɪks'pens] **1** *n* dépense *f*, frais *mpl*. **at my ~** à mes frais; *(fig)* à mes dépens; **at great ~** à grands frais; **to go to the ~ of buying a car** faire la dépense d'une voiture; **to go to great ~** faire beaucoup de frais (*to do* pour faire); **to go to some ~** faire des frais; **regardless of ~** sans regarder à la dépense; **to put sb to ~** causer des dépenses à qn; **to meet the ~ of sth** faire face aux frais de qch; **~s** frais; **after all ~s have been paid** tous frais payés. **2** *adj*: ~ **account** frais *mpl* de représentation; **to go on sb's ~ account** passer sur la note de frais de qn. ◆ **expensive** *adj* cher; *(costly)* coûteux; *tastes* de luxe; *journey* onéreux; **to be expensive** coûter cher *inv*; valoir cher *inv*. ◆ **expensively** *adv entertain* à grands frais; *dress* de façon coûteuse. ◆ **expensiveness** *n* cherté *f*.

experience [ɪks'pɪərɪəns] **1** *n* (**a**) *(knowledge etc)* expérience *f* (*of* de). **I know by ~** je le sais par expérience; **from my own *or* personal ~** d'après mon expérience personnelle; **I know from bitter ~ that...** j'ai appris à mes dépens que...; **he has no ~ of grief/of living in the country** il ne sait pas ce que c'est que le vrai chagrin/que de vivre à la campagne; **the greatest disaster in the ~ of this nation** le plus grand désastre que cette nation ait connu. (**b**) *(practice, skill)* pratique *f*, expérience *f*. **practical ~** pratique; **business/teaching/driving ~** expérience des affaires/de l'enseignement/du volant; **have you any previous ~?** avez-vous déjà fait ce genre de travail?; **I've no ~ of doing that** je n'ai jamais fait cela. (**c**) *(event ~d)* expérience *f*, aventure *f*, sensation *f*. **I had a pleasant/frightening ~** il m'est arrivé une chose *or* une aventure agréable/effrayante; **she's had some terrible ~s** elle en a vu de dures *; **it wasn't an ~ I would care to repeat** ça n'est pas une aventure

que je tiens à recommencer; **unfortunate** ~ mésaventure *f.*
2 *vt misfortune, hardship* connaître; *setbacks, losses* essuyer; *conditions* vivre dans; *ill treatment* subir; *difficulties* rencontrer; *sensation, terror, remorse* éprouver; *emotion* ressentir. **he has never ~d it** il n'en a jamais fait l'expérience, cela ne lui est jamais arrivé; **he ~s some difficulty in speaking** il éprouve de la difficulté à parler.
◆ **experienced** *adj (gen)* expérimenté, qui a de l'expérience (*in* en, en matière de); *eye, ear* exercé.

experiment [ɪks'perɪmənt] **1** *n* expérience *f (also Chem etc)*. **as an** ~ à titre d'essai *or* d'expérience. **2** [ɪks'perɪment] *vi (gen, fig)* faire une expérience. **to ~ with a new vaccine** expérimenter un nouveau vaccin; **to ~ on guinea pigs** faire des expériences sur des cobayes. ◆ **experimental** *adj (gen)* expérimental; *evidence* confirmé par l'expérience; *cinema, period* d'essai; **at the ~al stage** au stade expérimental; **this system is merely ~al** ce système est encore à l'essai; **~al chemist** chimiste *mf* de laboratoire. ◆ **experimentally** *adv prove etc* expérimentalement; *arrange, organize* à titre d'expérience. ◆ **experimentation** *n* expérimentation *f.*

expert ['ekspɜːt] **1** *n* spécialiste *mf* (*on, at sth* de qch); *(qualified)* expert *m* (*at sth* en qch; *at doing* à faire). **he is an ~ on wines** il est grand connaisseur en vins; **he is an ~ on the subject** c'est un expert en la matière. **2** *adj person* expert (*in sth* en qch; *in the art of* dans l'art de; *at, in doing* à faire); *knowledge, advice, evidence* d'expert; *(Jur) witness* expert. **he is ~** il s'y connaît; **with an ~ eye** *judge* en expert; *look at* d'un œil connaisseur ; **with an ~ touch** avec beaucoup d'habileté.
◆ **expertise** *n* compétence *f* (*in* en), adresse *f* (*in* à). ◆ **expertly** *adv* de façon experte, adroitement.

expire [ɪks'paɪəʳ] *vi [document]* expirer; *[period, time limit]* arriver à terme; *(die)* expirer. ◆ **expiration** *or* ◆ **expiry** *n* expiration *f*; **expiry date** *(gen)* date *f* de péremption; *(on label)* à utiliser avant...

explain [ɪks'pleɪn] *vt (gen)* expliquer; *mystery* éclaircir; *reasons, points of view* exposer. **to ~ o.s.** s'expliquer. ◆ **explain away** *vt sep* trouver une explication convaincante de. ◆ **explainable** *adj* explicable; **that is easily ~able** cela s'explique facilement. ◆ **explanation** *n* explication *f*; éclaircissement *m*; **to find an explanation for sth** trouver l'explication de qch; **has he something to say in explanation of his conduct?** est-ce qu'il peut fournir une explication de sa conduite?; **what have you to say in explanation?** qu'avez-vous à dire pour votre justification? ◆ **explanatory** *adj* explicatif.

expletive [ɪks'pliːtɪv] *n (oath)* juron *m.*

explicit [ɪks'plɪsɪt] *adj intention, statement* explicite; *denial* catégorique. ◆ **explicitly** *adv* explicitement; catégoriquement.

explode [ɪks'pləʊd] **1** *vi* exploser. **to ~ with laughter** éclater de rire. **2** *vt* faire exploser; *(fig) theory, rumour* montrer la fausseté de. **to ~ the myth that...** démolir le mythe selon lequel... ◆ **explosion** *n* explosion *f*; *(noise of explosion)* détonation *f.* ◆ **explosive** **1** *adj gas, matter* explosible; *mixture* détonant; *weapons, force, situation, temper* explosif; **2** *n* explosif *m.*

exploit ['eksplɔɪt] **1** *n* prouesse *f*; *(heroic)* exploit *m.* **~s** aventures *fpl.* **2** [ɪks'plɔɪt] *vt* exploiter.
◆ **exploitation** *n* exploitation *f.*

explore [ɪks'plɔːʳ] *vt (gen)* explorer; *(Med)* sonder; *issue* étudier sous tous ses aspects. **to go exploring** partir en exploration; **to ~ the ground** sonder le terrain; **to ~ every avenue** examiner toutes les possibilités. ◆ **exploration** *n* exploration *f.*
◆ **exploratory** *adj expedition* d'exploration; *step, discussion* préparatoire; *(Med)* **exploratory operation** sondage *m.* ◆ **explorer** *n* explorateur *m*, -trice *f.*

exponent [ɪks'pəʊnənt] *n [ideas]* interprète *m*; *[literary movement etc]* représentant(e) *m(f)*. ◆ **exponentially** *adv increase* de façon exponentielle.

export [ɪks'pɔːt] **1** *vt* exporter (*to* vers). **2** ['ekspɔːt] *n* exportation *f.* **for ~ only** réservé à l'exportation. **3** ['ekspɔːt] *adj goods, permit* d'exportation. **~ drive** campagne *f* pour encourager l'exportation; **~ duty** droit *m* de sortie; **~ reject** article *m* impropre à l'exportation. ◆ **exportation** *n* exportation *f.* ◆ **exporter** *n* exportateur *m*; *(country)* pays *m* exportateur.

expose [ɪks'pəʊz] *vt (gen, also Phot)* exposer (*to* à); *(uncover)* découvrir; *wire, nerve* mettre à nu; *(display) goods, pictures* exposer; *one's ignorance* afficher; *(unmask, reveal) vice* mettre à nu; *scandal, plot* révéler, dévoiler; *secret* éventer; *person* dénoncer. **to be ~d to view** s'offrir à la vue; **digging has ~d the remains of a temple** les fouilles ont mis au jour les restes d'un temple; **to ~ o.s. to** s'exposer à. ◆ **exposed** *adj country (gen)* battu par les vents; *(Mil)* découvert; *(Tech) part* apparent; *wire* à nu; *(Phot)* exposé; *(fig)* **he is in a very ~d position** il est très exposé. ◆ **exposition** *n* exposition *f.*
◆ **exposure** **1** *n* exposition *f* (*to* à); révélation *f*; dénonciation *f*; *(Phot)* pose *f*; **to threaten sb with exposure** menacer qn d'un scandale; **to die of exposure** mourir de froid ; **2** *adj (Phot)* **exposure meter** posemètre *m.*

expostulate [ɪks'pɒstjʊleɪt] **1** *vt* protester. **2** *vi*: **to ~ with sb about sth** faire des remontrances à qn au sujet de qch. ◆ **expostulation** *n* protestation *f*; remontrances *fpl.*

expound [ɪks'paʊnd] *vt theory, text* expliquer; *one's views* exposer.

express [ɪks'pres] **1** *vt* (**a**) *(gen)* exprimer; *a truth, proposition* énoncer; *wish* formuler. **to ~ o.s.** s'exprimer; **to ~ an interest in** manifester de l'intérêt pour. (**b**) *(send) letter, parcel* expédier par exprès. **2** *adj* (**a**) *instructions* exprès, formel; *intention* explicite. **with the ~ purpose of** dans le seul but de. (**b**) *(fast) letter, delivery* exprès *inv*; *coach etc* express *inv.* **~ train** rapide *m*; *(esp US)* **~ way** voie *f* express. **3** *adv* très rapidement; *post* par exprès. **4** *n (train)* rapide *m.* ◆ **expression** *n (gen)* expression *f*; *(phrase etc)* expression, tournure *f*; **set ~ion** expression consacrée. ◆ **expressionism** *n* expressionnisme *m.* ◆ **expressionist** *adj, n* expressionniste *(mf).* ◆ **expressive** *adj language, face, hands* expressif; *gestures, silence* éloquent; *look, smile* significatif. ◆ **expressively** *adv* d'une manière expressive. ◆ **expressly** *adv* expressément.

expulsion [ɪks'pʌlʃ(ə)n] *n* expulsion *f*; *(Scol etc)* renvoi *m.* **~ order** arrêté *m* d'expulsion.

expurgate ['ekspɜːgeɪt] *vt* expurger.

exquisite [ɪks'kwɪzɪt] *adj (gen)* exquis; *sensibility* raffiné; *sense of humour* subtil; *satisfaction, pleasure* vif (*f* vive); *pain* aigu (*f* -guë). ◆ **exquisitely** *adv (gen)* d'une façon exquise; *(extremely)* extrêmement; **~ly beautiful** d'une beauté exquise.

extant [eks'tænt] *adj* qui existe encore. **a few examples are still ~** quelques exemples subsistent.

extempore [ɪks'tempərɪ] *adv, adj* impromptu.
◆ **extemporize** *vti* improviser.

extend [ɪks'tend] **1** *vt* (**a**) *(stretch out) arm* étendre; *one's hand* tendre (*to sb* à qn); *(offer) help* apporter; *hospitality, friendship* offrir; *thanks, condolences, congratulations* présenter; *welcome* souhaiter; *invitation* faire, lancer; *loan* consentir. (**b**) *(prolong) street, line, visit* prolonger (*by, for* de); *(enlarge) house, property* agrandir; *research* pousser plus loin; *powers, limits, business* étendre; *insurance cover* aug-

menter le montant de; *knowledge* accroître; *frontiers* reculer; *vocabulary* enrichir; *(make demands on) worker, pupil* faire donner son maximum à. **~ed credit** un long crédit; **the ~ed family** la famille étendue; **an ~ed play record** un disque double (durée).
2 *vi [wall, estate]* s'étendre (*to, as far as* jusqu'à); *[meeting, visit]* se prolonger (*over* pendant; *for* durant).
◆ **extension 1** *n* extension *f*; prolongation *f*; agrandissement *m*; *(to road, line)* prolongement *m*; *(for table, wire, electric flex)* rallonge *f*; *(to holidays, leave)* prolongation; *(telephone) [private house]* appareil *m* supplémentaire; *[office]* poste *m*; **extension 21** poste 21; **to have an extension built on to the house** faire agrandir la maison; **come and see our extension** venez voir nos agrandissements *mpl* ; **2** *adj*: *(Elec)* **extension cable** *or* **lead** prolongateur *m;* **university extension courses** cours *mpl* publics du soir (organisés par l'Université); **extension ladder** échelle *f* coulissante. ◆ **extensive** *adj estate, forest, knowledge* vaste, étendu; *study, research* approfondi; *investments, alterations* considérable; *plans, reforms, business* de grande envergure; *use* répandu. ◆ **extensively** *adv alter* considérablement; *discuss* abondamment; *advertise* largement; *use, travel* beaucoup.

extent [ɪks'tent] *n [estate, knowledge, activities, power]* étendue *f*; *[road etc]* longueur *f*; *[damage, commitments, losses]* importance *f*; *(degree)* mesure *f*, degré *m*. **to open to its fullest ~** ouvrir entièrement; **to what ~** dans quelle mesure; **to a certain ~** jusqu'à un certain point, dans une certaine mesure; **to a large ~** en grande partie; **to a small ~** dans une faible mesure; **to such an ~ that** à tel point que; **to the ~ of doing** au point de faire.

extenuating [ɪk'stenjʊeɪtɪŋ] *adj* atténuant.

exterior [ɪks'tɪərɪəʳ] **1** *adj* extérieur (*to* à). **~ decoration** peintures *fpl* d'extérieur; **paint for ~ use** peinture *f* pour bâtiment. **2** *n* extérieur *m*. **on the ~** à l'extérieur.

exterminate [ɪks'tɜːmɪneɪt] *vt pests, group of people* exterminer; *beliefs, ideas* supprimer. ◆ **extermination** *n* extermination *f*. ◆ **exterminator** *n (US)* employé(e) *m(f)* de la désinfection.

external [eks'tɜːnl] **1** *adj surface* externe, extérieur; *wall* extérieur; *influences* du dehors; *factor, trade* extérieur. *(Pharm)* **for ~ use only** pour usage externe; **~ examiner** examinateur *m* venu de l'extérieur *(d'une autre université)*. **2** *n*: **the ~s** l'extérieur *m*, les apparences *fpl*. ◆ **externally** *adv* extérieurement.

extinct [ɪks'tɪŋ(k)t] *adj (gen)* éteint; *race, species* disparu. ◆ **extinction** *n* extinction *f*.

extinguish [ɪks'tɪŋgwɪʃ] *vt (lit, fig)* éteindre. ◆ **extinguisher** *n* extincteur *m*.

extol [ɪks'təʊl] *vt* louer avec enthousiasme.

extort [ɪks'tɔːt] *vt money, signature* extorquer (*from* à); *promise, confession, secret* arracher (*from* à). ◆ **extortion** *n* extorsion *f*. ◆ **extortionate** *adj* exorbitant.

extra ['ekstrə] **1** *adj (more)* de plus, supplémentaire; *(spare)* en trop. **an ~ chair** une chaise de plus *or* supplémentaire; **~ money** de l'argent de plus; **the ~ money/chair** l'argent/la chaise supplémentaire; **the chair is ~** *(spare)* la chaise est en trop; *(costs more)* la chaise est en supplément; *(Ftbl)* **after ~ time** après prolongation *f*; **I have had ~ work** j'ai eu plus de travail que d'habitude; **~ police/troops** des renforts *mpl* de police/de l'armée; **there will be no ~ charge** on ne vous comptera pas de supplément; **take ~ care!** faites particulièrement attention!; **~ pay** supplément *m* de salaire (*for* de); **for ~ safety** pour plus de sécurité; **postage ~** frais *mpl* de port en sus ; **I bought a few ~ tins** j'ai acheté quelques boîtes de réserve.
2 *adv* plus que d'habitude, particulièrement. **~ kind** plus gentil que d'habitude.
3 *n (perk)* à-côté *m*; *(luxury)* agrément *m*; *(in restaurant: ~ dish)* supplément *m*; *(Cine, Theat: actor)* figurant(e) *m(f)*; *(US: gasoline)* super(carburant) *m*. **singing and piano are ~s** les leçons de chant et de piano ne sont pas comprises.
◆ **extrafine** *adj* extra-fin. ◆ **extra-smart** *adj* ultra-chic * *inv*. ◆ **extra-strong** *adj person* extrêmement fort; *material* extra-solide.

extract [ɪks'trækt] **1** *vt (gen)* extraire (*from* de); *tooth* arracher (*from* à); *(fig) confession, permission, promise* arracher (*from* à); *information, meaning, moral* tirer (*from* de); *money* soutirer (*from* à). **2** ['ekstrækt] *n* extrait *m*. ◆ **extraction** *n* extraction *f (also Dentistry)*; *(descent)* origine *f*. ◆ **extractor** *adj*: **~or fan** ventilateur *m*.

extracurricular ['ekstrəkə'rɪkjʊləʳ] *adj (Scol gen)* périscolaire, en dehors du programme.

extradite ['ekstrədaɪt] *vt* extrader. ◆ **extradition** *n* extradition *f*.

extramarital ['ekstrə'mærɪtl] *adj* en dehors du mariage.

extramural ['ekstrə'mjʊər(ə)l] *adj course* hors faculté; *lecture* public.

extraneous [ɪk'streɪnɪəs] *adj issue* non pertinent.

extraordinary [ɪks'trɔːdnrɪ] *adj (gen)* extraordinaire; *quality* exceptionnel; *action, speech, behaviour* étonnant, surprenant; *insults, violence* inouï. **an ~ meeting of the shareholders** une assemblée extraordinaire des actionnaires; **I find it ~ that he hasn't replied** je trouve extraordinaire *or* inouï qu'il n'ait pas répondu; **there's nothing ~ about that** cela n'a rien d'étonnant; **it's ~ to think that...** il semble incroyable que... + *subj*; **the ~ fact is that he succeeded** ce qu'il y a d'étonnant c'est qu'il a *or* ait réussi. ◆ **extraordinarily** *adv* extraordinairement.

extrasensory ['ekstrə'sensərɪ] *adj*: **~ perception** perception extra-sensorielle.

extraspecial ['ekstrə'speʃ(ə)l] *adj (gen)* exceptionnel; *care* tout particulier; *occasion* grand.

extraterrestrial [ekstrətɪ'restrɪəl] **1** *adj* extraterrestre. **2** *n* extraterrestre *mf*.

extravagance [ɪks'trævəgəns] *n (excessive spending)* prodigalité *f*; *(wastefulness)* gaspillage *m*; *(thing bought)* folie *f*. **that hat was a great ~** ce chapeau était une vraie folie. ◆ **extravagant** *adj (wasteful) person* dépensier, prodigue; *taste* dispendieux; *(exaggerated) (gen)* extravagant; *opinions, praise, claims* exagéré; *prices* exorbitant. ◆ **extravagantly** *adv (lavishly)* avec prodigalité; *(flamboyantly)* d'une façon extravagante; **to use sth extravagantly** gaspiller qch. ◆ **extravaganza** *n* fantaisie *f*; *(show)* spectacle somptueux.

extreme [ɪks'triːm] **1** *adj (exceptional, exaggerated)* extrême; *(furthest)* extrême *(before n)*. **in ~ danger** en très grand danger; *(Pol)* **the ~ right** l'extrême droite *f*; **at the ~ end of the path** à l'extrémité du chemin; **how ~!** c'est un peu poussé! **2** *n* extrême *m*. **in the ~** à l'extrême, au plus haut degré; **to go to ~s** pousser les choses à l'extrême. ◆ **extremely** *adv* extrêmement. ◆ **extremist 1** *adj opinion* extrême; *person* extrémiste; *party* d'extrémistes ; **2** *n* extrémiste *mf*. ◆ **extremity** [ɪks'tremɪtɪ] *n (gen)* extrémité *f*; *[despair, happiness]* extrême degré *m*.

extricate ['ekstrɪkeɪt] *vt object* dégager (*from* de). *(fig)* **to ~ o.s.** se tirer (*from* de).

extrovert ['ekstrəʊ'vɜːt] **1** *adj* extraverti. **2** *n* extraverti(e) *m(f)*.

exuberance [ɪg'zuːb(ə)r(ə)ns] *n* exubérance *f*. ◆ **exuberant** *adj* exubérant. ◆ **exuberantly** *adv* avec exubérance.

exude [ɪg'zju:d] *vti (lit)* exsuder. *(fig)* **he ~d charm** le charme lui sortait par tous les pores; **he ~s confidence** il respire la confiance en soi.

exult [ɪg'zʌlt] *vi (rejoice)* se réjouir (*in* de; *over* de, à propos de), exulter; *(triumph)* jubiler. ◆ **exultant** *adj expression, shout* de triomphe; *[person]* **to be ~ant** jubiler. ◆ **exultantly** *adv* triomphalement. ◆ **exultation** *n* exultation *f*.

eye [aɪ] **1** *n* œil *m* (*pl* yeux). **girl with blue ~s, blue-~d girl** fille aux yeux bleus; **to have brown ~s** avoir les yeux bruns; **with tears in her ~s** les larmes aux yeux; **with one's ~s closed** les yeux fermés; **to have the sun in one's ~s** avoir le soleil dans les yeux; **before my very ~s** sous mes yeux; **for your ~s only** ultra-confidentiel; **as far as the ~ can see** à perte de vue; **in the ~s of** aux yeux de; **to look at a question through the ~s of an economist** envisager une question du point de vue de l'économiste; **under the ~ of** sous l'œil de; **with my own ~s** de mes propres yeux; **with an ~ to the future** en prévision de l'avenir; **with an ~ to buying** en vue d'acheter; **that's one in the ~ for him *** c'est bien fait pour lui; **to be all ~s** être tout yeux; **to be up to the** *or* **one's ~s in work** être dans le travail jusqu'au cou; **to shut one's ~s to** *sb's shortcomings* fermer les yeux sur; *evidence* se refuser à; *dangers, truth* se dissimuler; **his ~ fell on...** son regard est tombé sur...; **to get one's ~ in** ajuster son coup d'œil; **to have one's ~ on sth/sb** avoir qch/qn en vue; **to have an ~ to the main chance** ne jamais perdre de vue ses propres intérêts; **to have an ~ for sth** savoir reconnaître qch; **to keep one's ~ on the ball** fixer la balle; **to keep an ~ on sth/sb** surveiller qch/qn; **to keep an ~ on things *** avoir l'œil (à tout); **to keep one's ~s open** être vigilant, ouvrir l'œil; **to keep one's ~s open for sth** essayer de trouver qch; **he couldn't keep his ~s open *** il dormait debout; *(fig)* **with one's ~s wide open** en connaissance de cause; **to look sb straight in the ~** regarder qn dans les yeux; **to make ~s at *** faire de l'œil à *; **to see ~ to ~ with sb** partager le point de vue de qn; **I've never set ~s on him** je ne l'ai jamais vu de ma vie; **he didn't take his ~s off her** il ne l'a pas quittée des yeux; **he never uses his ~s** il ne sait pas voir; **use your ~s** tu es aveugle?

2 *vt* regarder. **he was ~ing the girls** il reluquait les filles.

◆ **eyeball** *n* globe *m* oculaire. ◆ **eyebath** *n* œillère *f (pour bains d'œil)*. ◆ **eyebrow** **1** *n* sourcil *m*; **2** *adj*: **~brow pencil** crayon *m* à sourcils; **~brow tweezers** pince *f* à épiler. ◆ **eye-catching** *adj dress, colour* qui tire l'œil; *publicity, poster* accrocheur. ◆ **eye doctor** *n* oculiste *mf*. ◆ **eyedrops** *npl* gouttes *fpl* pour les yeux. ◆ **eyeful** *n*: **he got an ~ful of mud** il a reçu de la boue plein les yeux; **she's quite an ~ful *** cette fille, c'est un régal pour l'œil. ◆ **eyelash** *n* cil *m*. ◆ **eyelet** *n* œillet *m (dans du tissu etc)*. ◆ **eyelevel** *adj* à hauteur des yeux; **~-level grill** gril *m* surélevé. ◆ **eyelid** *n* paupière *f*. ◆ **eyeliner** *n* eye-liner *m*. ◆ **eye-opener** *n* révélation *f*. ◆ **eye-patch** *n* cache *m*. ◆ **eyeshade** *n* visière *f*. ◆ **eyeshadow** *n* fard *m* à paupières. ◆ **eyesight** *n* vue *f*. ◆ **eyestrain** *n*: **to have ~strain** avoir la vue fatiguée. ◆ **eye-tooth** *n* canine *f* supérieure; *(fig)* **I'd give my ~-teeth * for that/to do that** qu'est-ce que je ne donnerais pas pour avoir ça/pour faire ça. ◆ **eyewash *** *n (fig)* fadaises *fpl*. ◆ **eyewitness** *n* témoin *m* oculaire.

eyrie ['ɪərɪ] *n* aire *f (d'aigle)*.

F, f [ef] *n* F, f *m or f*; *(Mus)* fa *m*.

fa [fɑː] *n (Mus)* fa *m*.

fable ['feɪbl] *n* fable *f*. ◆ **fabled** *adj* légendaire.

fabric ['fæbrɪk] *n (cloth)* tissu *m*, étoffe *f*; *[building, system, society]* structure *f*. ◆ **fabricate** *vt* fabriquer. ◆ **fabrication** *n* fabrication *f*.

fabulous ['fæbjʊləs] *adj (gen)* fabuleux; *(*: wonderful)* formidable *, sensationnel *. **a ~ price** * un prix fou.

façade [fə'sɑːd] *n* façade *f*.

face [feɪs] **1** *n* visage *m*, figure *f*; *(expression)* mine *f*; *[building]* façade *f*; *[clock]* cadran *m*; *[cliff]* paroi *f*; *[coin]* côté *m*; *[the earth]* surface *f*; *[document]* recto *m*; *[playing card]* face *f*, dessous *m*. **~ down(wards)** *person* face contre terre; *card* face en dessous; **~ up(wards)** *person* sur le dos; *card* retourné; **to turn sth ~ up** retourner qch à l'endroit; *(Med)* **injuries to the ~** blessures *fpl* à la face; **you can shout till you're black in the ~, he...** tu auras beau t'exténuer à crier, il...; **to change the ~ of a town** changer le visage d'une ville; **he vanished off the ~ of the earth** il a complètement disparu de la circulation; **I've got a good memory for ~s** je suis physionomiste; **he laughed in my ~** il m'a ri au nez; **he won't show his ~ here again** il ne se montrera plus ici; **he told him so to his ~** il le lui a dit tout cru; **in the ~ of** *the enemy* face à; *threat, danger* devant; *difficulty* en dépit de; **to set one's ~ against sth** se dresser contre qch; **to set one's ~ against doing** se refuser à faire; **to put a bold** *or* **brave ~ on things** faire bon visage; **to lose ~** perdre la face; **to save (one's) ~** sauver la face; **to make** *or* **pull ~s** faire des grimaces (*at* à); **to make a (disapproving) ~** faire une moue de désapprobation; **on the ~ of it** à première vue; **to have the ~ to do** * avoir le toupet * de faire. **2** *adj*: **~ card** figure *f*; **~ cream** crème *f* pour le visage; **~ cloth** *or* **flannel** gant *m* de toilette; **~ pack** masque *m* de beauté; **~ powder** poudre *f* de riz; **~ value** *[coin]* valeur *f* nominale; *[stamp, card]* valeur; *(fig)* **to take sb** *or* **sth at ~ value** se laisser tromper par les apparences.
3 *vt* (**a**) *(turn towards)* faire face à; *(also* **be facing***)* *person* être en face de; *wall etc* être face à; *[building] (be opposite)* être en face de; *(look towards)* donner sur. **problem facing me** problème devant lequel je me trouve; **facing one another** en face l'un de l'autre; **the picture facing page 16** l'illustration en regard de la page 16; **to be ~d with** *possibility, prospect* se trouver devant; *danger, defeat* être menacé par; **to be ~d with the prospect of doing** risquer d'avoir à faire; **~d with the prospect of...** devant la perspective de...; **~d with their demands** devant leurs revendications. (**b**) *(confront) enemy, danger, problem* faire face à; *(tackle)* s'attaquer à. **I can't ~ him** *(ashamed)* je n'ose pas le regarder en face; *(fed up)* je n'ai pas le courage de le voir; **to ~ the music** braver l'orage; **to ~ facts** regarder les choses en face; **to ~ the fact that...** admettre que...; **I can't ~ doing it** je n'ai pas le courage de le faire. (**c**) *(present sb with)* **you must face him with the decision/the truth** vous devez le contraindre à faire face à cette décision/à regarder la vérité en face.
4 *vi [person]* **to ~/be facing this way** se tourner/être tourné de ce côté; *(fig)* **to ~ both ways** ménager la chèvre et le chou; *[house]* **facing north** orienté au nord; **facing towards the sea** face à la mer.
◆ **face up to** *vt fus danger, difficulty* faire face à. **to ~ up to the fact that** admettre que.
◆ **faceless** *adj* anonyme. ◆ **face-lift** *n* lifting *M;* **to have a ~-lift** se faire faire un lifting; **to give a ~-lift * to** *(gen)* refaire une beauté * à; *house* ravaler. ◆ **face-off** *n (US) (Hockey)* remise *f* en jeu; *(fig)* confrontation *f*. ◆ **face-saving** *adj* qui sauve la face. ◆ **face-to-face 1** *adv* face à face ; **2** *adj*: **~-to-~ discussion** face à face *m inv*. ◆ **facial 1** *adj* facial ; **2** *n* soin *m* du visage. ◆ **facing** *n (Constr)* revêtement *m*; *(Sewing)* revers *m*.

facet ['fæsɪt] *n* facette *f*.

facetious [fə'siːʃəs] *adj person* facétieux; *remark* bouffon. ◆ **facetiously** *adv* facétieusement.

facility [fə'sɪlɪtɪ] *n* facilité *f* (*in, for doing* pour faire). **facilities** *(equipment, material)* équipements *mpl* (*for* de); *(installation)* installations *fpl*; *(means)* moyens *mpl* (*for* de); *(gen)* **facilities for** facilités *fpl* de; **recreational facilities** les facilités pour le sport et les loisirs; **the watch has a stopwatch ~** la montre a un système de chronomètre; **this ~ for the public** cette possibilité offerte au public; **there are no facilities for it** ce n'est pas équipé pour cela. ◆ **facilitate** *vt* faciliter.

facsimile [fæk'sɪmɪlɪ] *n* fac-similé *m*. **~ machine** télécopieur *m*.

fact [fækt] *n* fait *m*. **it is a ~ that** il est de fait que + *indic*; **is it a ~ that** est-il vrai que + *subj (often * indic)*; **to know (it) for a ~ that** savoir de source sûre que; **the ~s of life** *(sex etc)* les choses *fpl* de la vie; *(fig)* les réalités *fpl* de la vie; **~ and fiction** le réel et l'imaginaire; **story founded on ~** histoire basée sur des faits; **in (point of) ~, as a matter of ~** en fait; **the ~ of the matter is that...** le fait est que... ◆ **fact-finding** *adj*: **~-finding committee** commission *f* d'enquête; **they were on a ~-finding mission to the war front** ils étaient partis enquêter au front. ◆ **factual** *adj report, description* basé sur les faits; *error* de fait. ◆ **factually** *adv* en se tenant aux faits.

faction[1] ['fækʃ(ə)n] *n* faction *f*.

faction[2] ['fækʃ(ə)n] *n (TV etc)* docudrame *m*.

factor ['fæktəʳ] *n* facteur *m*. **safety ~** facteur de sécurité; **human ~** élément *m* humain.

factory ['fækt(ə)rɪ] **1** *n* usine *f*, *(gen smaller)* fabrique *f*; *[arms, china, tobacco]* manufacture *f*; *(fig)* usine. **shoe ~** usine *or* fabrique de chaussures. **2** *adj work, worker, chimney* d'usine; *inspector* du travail. **~ farming** élevage *m* industriel; **~ ship** navire-usine *m*.

factotum [fæk'təʊtəm] *n* factotum *m*.

faculty ['fæk(ə)ltɪ] *n* faculté *f*.

fad [fæd] *n (habit)* marotte *f*; *(fashion)* folie *f* (*for* de). ◆ **faddy** *adj person* qui a des marottes; *distaste* capricieux.

fade [feɪd] **1** *vi [flower]* se faner; *[colour, material]* passer; **(~ away)** *[daylight, one's faculties]* baisser; *[memory, vision]* s'effacer; *[hopes, smile]* s'évanouir; *[interest]* diminuer; *[sound]* s'affaiblir; *[person]*

dépérir. **the castle ~d from sight** le château disparut aux regards.
2 *vt*: **to ~ in/out** *(Cine, TV)* faire apparaître/ disparaître en fondu; *(Rad)* monter/couper par un fondu sonore.

faeces ['fi:si:z] *npl* fèces *fpl*.

fag [fæg] **1** *n* (‡: *nasty work*) corvée *f*; (‡: *cigarette*) sèche ‡ *f*; *(Brit Scol)* petit *m (élève au service d'un grand)*. **2** *adj*: **~ end** *(remainder)* restant *m*, reste *m*; (‡) *[cigarette]* mégot * *m*. **3** *vt* (**~ out**) éreinter.

fag(g)ot ['fægət] *n* fagot *m*.

fah [fɑ:] *n (Mus)* fa *m*.

Fahrenheit ['fær(ə)nhaɪt] *adj* Fahrenheit *inv*.

fail [feɪl] **1** *vi* (**a**) *(gen)* échouer; *[candidate]* échouer, être collé * *(in an exam* à un examen; *in Latin* en latin); *[play, show]* être un four; *[bank, business]* faire faillite. **to ~ to do** ne pas réussir à faire; **to ~ by 5 votes** échouer à 5 voix près; **to ~ in one's duty** manquer à son devoir. (**b**) *[faculty]* baisser; *[person, voice]* s'affaiblir; *[light]* baisser; *[crops]* être perdu; *[power, electricity, water supply]* manquer; *[engine]* tomber en panne; *[brakes]* lâcher.
2 *vt* (**a**) *examination* échouer à, être collé * à; *subject* échouer en; *candidate* refuser, coller *. (**b**) *(let down) [person]* décevoir, laisser tomber *; *[memory etc]* trahir. **don't ~ me!** ne me laissez pas tomber! *, je compte sur vous!; **his heart ~ed him** le cœur lui a manqué; **words ~ me!** les mots me manquent! (**c**) *(omit)* manquer, négliger *(to do* de faire). **to ~ to appear** *(Jur)* faire défaut; *(gen)* ne pas se montrer; **I ~ to see why** je ne vois pas pourquoi.
3 *n (in exam)* échec *m*. **without ~** *come, do* sans faute; *happen, befall* immanquablement.
◆ **failing 1** *n* défaut *m* ; **2** *prep* à défaut de; **~ing this** à défaut. ◆ **failsafe** *adj* à sûreté intégrée. ◆ **failure** *n (gen)* échec *m (in an exam* à un examen; *in Latin* en latin); *[bank, business]* faillite *f*; *[electricity, engine]* panne *f*; *[crops]* perte *f*; *(unsuccessful person)* raté(e) *m(f)*; **a total ~ure** un fiasco; **his ~ure to convince them** son impuissance *f* à les convaincre; **he's a ~ure as a writer** il ne vaut rien comme écrivain.

faint [feɪnt] **1** *adj breeze, smell, sound, hope, trace* léger, faible; *colour* pâle; *voice, breathing* faible; *idea, smile* vague. **I haven't the ~est idea** je n'en ai pas la moindre idée; **to make a ~ attempt at doing** essayer sans conviction de faire; **to grow ~(er)** s'affaiblir; *(Med)* **to feel ~** être pris d'un malaise; **~ with hunger** défaillant de faim. **2** *n* évanouissement *m*. **3** *vi* s'évanouir *(from* de). **to be ~ing** défaillir *(from* de). ◆ **fainthearted** *adj* pusillanime, timide. ◆ **faintly** *adv (gen)* faiblement; *write, mark* légèrement; *disappointed* légèrement; *smiling, reminiscent* vaguement. ◆ **faintness** *n* faiblesse *f*; légèreté *f*.

fair¹ [fɛəʳ] *n (gen)* foire *f*; *(fun ~)* fête *f* foraine. *(Comm)* **Book F~** Foire du livre. ◆ **fairground** *n* champ *m* de foire.

fair² [fɛəʳ] **1** *adj* (**a**) *person, decision* juste *(to sb* vis-à-vis de qn), équitable; *deal, exchange* équitable; *fight, competition, match* loyal; *profit, comment* justifié, mérité; *sample* représentatif. **it's not ~** ce n'est pas juste; **to be ~ (to him), he...** rendons-lui cette justice, il...; **as is only ~** et ce n'est que justice; **~ enough!** d'accord!; **to give sb a ~ deal** *or (US)* **a ~ shake** agir équitablement envers qn; **he was ~ game for the critics** c'était une proie rêvée pour les critiques; **by ~ means or foul** par tous les moyens; **~ play** fair-play *m*; **his ~ share of** sa part de; **~ shares for all** à chacun son dû; **it was all ~ and square** tout était très correct; **through ~ and foul** à travers toutes les épreuves. (**b**) *work, result* passable, assez bon. (**c**) *(quite large) sum* considérable; *number* respectable; *speed* bon. **he is in a ~ way to doing** il y a de bonnes chances pour qu'il fasse; **a ~ amount** * pas mal *(of* de). (**d**) *(light-coloured) hair, person etc* blond; *complexion, skin* clair. (**e**) *(fine) wind* propice, favorable; *weather, promises, words* beau. **it's set ~** le temps est au beau fixe; **the ~ sex** le beau sexe; **~ copy** *(rewritten)* copie *f* au propre; *(model answer etc)* corrigé *m*.
2 *adv*: **to play ~** jouer franc jeu; **to act ~ and square** agir loyalement; **the branch struck him ~ and square in the face** la branche l'a frappé en plein (milieu du) visage.
◆ **fair-haired** *adj* blond. ◆ **fairly** *adv* (**a**) *(justly) treat* équitablement; *obtain* honnêtement; *compare, judge* impartialement; **~ly and squarely = fair and square** ; *V* **fair² 2**; (**b**) *(reasonably)* assez; **I'm ~ly sure that...** je suis presque sûr que...; (**c**) *(utterly)* absolument; **he was ~ly beside himself with rage** il était absolument hors de lui. ◆ **fair-minded** *adj* impartial. ◆ **fairness** *n* (**a**) *[hair]* blondeur *f*; *[skin]* blancheur *f*; (**b**) justice *f*, honnêteté *f*; *[decision, judgment]* équité *f*; **in all ~ness** en toute justice; **in ~ness to him** pour être juste envers lui. ◆ **fair-sized** *adj* assez grand. ◆ **fair-skinned** *adj* à la peau claire.

fairy ['fɛərɪ] **1** *n* fée *f*; (‡: *homosexual*) pédé ‡ *m*. **2** *adj helper, gift* magique; *child, dance* des fées. **~ footsteps** pas légers de danseuse *(iro)*; *(fig)* **~ godmother** bonne fée; **~ lights** guirlande *f* électrique; **~ queen** reine *f* des fées; **~ tale** conte *m* de fées; *(untruth)* conte à dormir debout. ◆ **fairyland** *n* royaume *m* des fées.

faith [feɪθ] **1** *n (all senses)* foi *f*. **F~, Hope and Charity** la foi, l'espérance et la charité; **~ in God** la foi en Dieu; **to have ~ in sb** avoir confiance en qn; **to put one's ~ in** mettre tous ses espoirs en; **to keep ~ with sb** tenir ses promesses envers qn ; **in all good ~** en toute bonne foi; **in bad ~** de mauvaise foi. **2** *adj*: **~ healer** guérisseur *m*, -euse *f* (mystique); **~ healing** guérison *f* par la foi. ◆ **faithful 1** *adj* fidèle *(to* à) ; **2** *n* **the ~ful** *(Christians)* les fidèles *mpl*; *(Muslims)* les croyants *mpl*. ◆ **faithfully** *adv* fidèlement; **to promise ~fully that** donner sa parole que; **yours ~fully** je vous prie, Monsieur *(or* Madame *etc)* d'agréer mes salutations distinguées. ◆ **faithfulness** *n* fidélité *f (to* à). ◆ **faithless** *adj* perfide. ◆ **faithlessness** *n* perfidie *f*.

fake [feɪk] **1** *n* (**a**) *(object etc)* objet *m etc* truqué; *(picture)* faux *m*. **he's a ~** il n'est pas ce qu'il prétend être. (**b**) *(US Sport)* feinte *f*. **2** *adj* (**a**) *[picture]* **to be ~** être un *(or* des) faux. (**b**) *(also* **faked***) trial, photograph* truqué; *accounts* falsifié. **3** *vt document (counterfeit)* faire un faux de; *(alter)* falsifier; *trial, photograph* truquer; *accounts* falsifier. **to ~ illness** faire semblant d'être malade. **4** *vi* (**a**) faire semblant. (**b**) *(US Sport)* faire une feinte.

falcon ['fɔ:lkən] *n* faucon *m*.

Falkland Islands ['fɔ:lklənd'aɪləndz] *npl* Malouines *fpl*, îles *fpl* Falkland.

fall [fɔ:l] *(vb: pret* **fell**, *ptp* **fallen***)* **1** *n* (**a**) *(gen)* chute *f*; *(in price, temperature)* baisse *f (in* de); *(more drastic)* chute. *(fig)* **to be riding for a ~** courir à l'échec; **the ~ of the Bastille** la prise de la Bastille; **~ of earth** éboulement *m* de terre; **~ of rock** chute de pierres; **a heavy ~ of snow** de fortes chutes de neige; *(waterfall)* **~s** chute d'eau; **the Niagara F~s** les chutes du Niagara. (**b**) *(US: autumn)* automne *m*. **in the ~** en automne.
2 *vi* (**a**) *(gen)* tomber *(into* dans; *out of, off* de); *[temperature, price, level, voice, wind]* tomber; *(less drastically)* baisser; *[building]* s'écrouler. **to ~ flat** *[person]* tomber à plat ventre; *[event etc]* ne pas répondre à l'attente; *[scheme]* faire long feu; *[joke]* tomber à plat; **to ~ to** *or* **on one's knees** tomber à genoux; **to ~ on one's feet** retomber sur ses pieds; **to ~ over a chair** tomber en butant

contre une chaise; **he was ~ing over himself to be polite** * il se mettait en quatre pour être poli; **they were ~ing over each other to get it** * ils se battaient pour l'avoir; **to let sth** ~ laisser tomber qch; **to let ~ that** laisser entendre que; **his face fell** son visage s'est assombri; **the students ~ into 3 categories** les étudiants se divisent en 3 catégories; **the responsibility ~s on you** la responsabilité retombe sur vous; **Christmas Day ~s on a Sunday** Noël tombe un dimanche; **he fell to wondering if...** il s'est mis à se demander si...; **it ~s to me to say** il m'appartient de dire; **to ~ short of** *expectations* ne pas répondre à; *perfection* ne pas atteindre.

(**b**) *(become etc)* **to ~ asleep** s'endormir; **to ~ into bad habits** prendre de mauvaises habitudes; **to ~ into conversation with sb** entrer en conversation avec qn; *(fig)* **to ~ from grace** tomber en disgrâce; **to ~ due** venir à échéance; **to ~ heir to sth** hériter de qch; **to ~ ill** *or* **sick** tomber malade; *(lit, fig)* **to ~ into line** s'aligner; *(fig)* **to ~ into line with sb** se ranger à l'avis de qn; **to ~ in love** tomber amoureux (*with* de); **to ~ for** * *person* tomber amoureux de; *idea* s'enthousiasmer pour; *(be taken in by)* se laisser prendre à; **to ~ silent** se taire.

◆**fall about** * *vi (fig: laugh)* se tordre (de rire). ◆**fall apart** *vi* tomber en morceaux; *[plans]* se désagréger; *[deal]* tomber à l'eau; *[person] (after tragedy)* s'effondrer; *(under stress)* perdre tous ses moyens. ◆**fall away** *vi [ground]* descendre en pente; *[plaster]* s'écailler; *[supporters]* déserter. ◆**fall back** *vi (retreat)* reculer. **to ~ back on sth** avoir recours à qch; **sth to ~ back on** qch en réserve. ◆**fall behind** *vi* rester en arrière; *(in race)* se laisser distancer. **to ~ behind with** *work* prendre du retard dans; *rent* être en retard pour. ◆**fall down** *vi (gen)* tomber; *[building]* s'effondrer; *(fail)* échouer, rater son coup. **to ~ down on the job** ne pas être à la hauteur. ◆**fall in** *vi (into water)* tomber (dans l'eau); *[building]* s'affaisser; *[troops]* former les rangs. ◆**fall in with** *vt fus (meet) person* rencontrer; *(group)* se mettre à fréquenter; *(agree to) proposal, sb's view* accepter. **this fell in very well with our plans** ceci a cadré avec nos projets. ◆**fall off** *vi (lit)* tomber; *[supporters]* déserter; *[numbers]* diminuer; *[interest]* tomber. ◆**fall out** *vi (quarrel)* se brouiller (*with* avec); *(Mil)* rompre les rangs. **everything fell out as we had hoped** tout s'est passé comme nous l'avions espéré. ◆**fall over** *vi* tomber (par terre); *V* **fall 2.** ◆**fall through** *vi [plans etc]* échouer. ◆**fall (up)on** *vt fus* se jeter sur; *(Mil) enemy* fondre sur.

◆**fallen 1** *adj* tombé; *(morally)* perdu; *angel, woman* déchu; **~en leaf** feuille morte; **~en arches** affaissement *m* de la voûte plantaire ; **2** *n (Mil)* **the ~en** ceux qui sont tombés au champ d'honneur. ◆**falling** *adj*: **~ing star** étoile *f* filante. ◆**fall(ing)off** *n* réduction *f* (*in* de). ◆**fallout 1** *n* retombées *fpl* ; **2** *adj*: **~out shelter** abri *m* antiatomique.

fallacy ['fæləsɪ] *n (false belief)* erreur *f*; *(false reasoning)* faux raisonnement *m*. ◆**fallacious** *adj* trompeur.

fallible ['fæləbl] *adj* faillible. ◆**fallibility** *n* faillibilité *f*.

fallopian [fə'ləʊpɪən] *adj*: **~ tube** trompe *f* utérine.

fallow ['fæləʊ] *adj*: **to lie ~** être en jachère.

false [fɔ:ls] *adj (all senses)* faux (*f* fausse) *(before n)*. **~ alarm** fausse alerte; **a ~ step** un faux pas ; **~ start** faux départ *m*; **under ~ pretences** *(Jur)* par des moyens frauduleux; *(by lying)* sous des prétextes fallacieux; **with a ~ bottom** à double fond; **~ teeth** fausses dents *fpl*.

◆**false-hearted** *adj* fourbe. ◆**falsehood** *n (lie)* mensonge *m*; **truth and ~hood** le vrai et le faux. ◆**falsely** *adv declare* faussement; *accuse* à tort. ◆**falseness** *or* ◆**falsity** *n* fausseté *f*. ◆**falsification** *n* falsification *f*. ◆**falsify** *vt document* falsifier; *evidence* maquiller; *accounts, figures* truquer.

falsetto [fɔ:l'setəʊ] **1** *n* fausset *m*. **2** *adj* de fausset.

falter ['fɔ:ltəʳ] **1** *vi [voice, speaker]* hésiter; *(waver)* vaciller; *[steps]* chanceler; *[courage]* faiblir. **2** *vt words* bredouiller.

fame [feɪm] *n (gen)* gloire *f*, célébrité *f*, *(slightly weaker)* renommée *f*. **his ~ as a writer** sa renommée d'écrivain; **he wanted ~** il était avide de gloire; **M. Mitchell of 'Gone with the Wind' ~** M. Mitchell connue pour son livre 'Autant en emporte le vent'. ◆**famed** *adj* célèbre (*for* pour).

familiar [fə'mɪljəʳ] *adj (gen)* familier; *complaint, event, protest* habituel. **a ~ figure in the town** un personnage bien connu dans la ville; **a ~ feeling** une sensation bien connue; **his face is ~** sa tête me dit quelque chose *; *(fig)* **to be on ~ ground** être en terrain de connaissance; **to be ~ with sth** bien connaître qch; **to make o.s. ~ with** se familiariser avec; *(pej)* **he got much too ~** il s'est permis des familiarités (*with* avec).

◆**familiarity** *n [sight etc]* caractère *m* familier; *(with customs etc)* familiarité *f* (*with* avec); **familiarities** familiarités *fpl*. ◆**familiarize** *vt* familiariser (*sb with sth* qn avec qch); **to ~ize o.s. with** se familiariser avec. ◆**familiarly** *adv* familièrement.

family ['fæmɪlɪ] **1** *n (all senses)* famille *f*. **has he any ~?** *(relatives)* a-t-il de la famille?; *(children)* a-t-il des enfants?; **it runs in the ~** cela tient de famille; **he's one of the ~** il fait partie de la famille. **2** *adj jewels, likeness, name, life* de famille; *friend* de la famille. *(Admin)* **~ allowance** allocations *fpl* familiales; **~ doctor** médecin *m* de famille; **~ man** bon père *m* de famille; **~ planning clinic** centre *m* de planning familial; **~ tree** arbre *m* généalogique.

famine ['fæmɪn] *n* famine *f*.

famished ['fæmɪʃt] *adj* affamé. **I'm absolutely ~** * je meurs de faim.

famous ['feɪməs] *adj* célèbre, (bien) connu (*for* pour). *(iro)* **~ last words!** * on verra bien!; *(iro)* **that's his ~ motorbike!** voilà sa fameuse moto! ◆**famously** * *adv* fameusement *, rudement bien *.

fan¹ [fæn] **1** *n* éventail *m*; *(mechanical)* ventilateur *m*. **2** *adj (Aut)* **~ belt** courroie *f* de ventilateur; **~ heater** radiateur *m* soufflant; **~ light** imposte *f (semi-circulaire)*. **3** *vt person* éventer; *fire, quarrel* attiser. *(fig)* **to ~ the flames** jeter de l'huile sur le feu. ◆**fan out** *vi [troops, searchers]* se déployer (en éventail).

fan² [fæn] **1** *n* enthousiaste *mf*; *(Sport)* supporter *m*; *[pop star etc]* fan *mf*, admirateur *m*, -trice *f*. **he is a jazz/bridge/sports/football** *etc* **~** c'est un mordu * du jazz/bridge/sport/football *etc*; **movie fan** cinéphile *mf*; **I'm definitely not one of his ~s** je suis loin d'être un de ses admirateurs. **2** *adj*: **~ club** club *m* de fans; **his ~ mail** les lettres *fpl* de ses admirateurs.

fanatic [fə'nætɪk] *n* fanatique *mf*. ◆**fanatic(al)** *adj* fanatique. ◆**fanaticism** *n* fanatisme *m*.

fancy ['fænsɪ] **1** *n (whim)* caprice *m*, fantaisie *f*. **a passing ~** un caprice passager, une lubie; **when the ~ takes him** quand cela lui plaît; **he took a ~ to go swimming** il a eu tout à coup envie d'aller se baigner; **to take a ~ to** *person* se prendre d'affection pour; *thing* prendre goût à, se mettre à aimer; **it caught the public's ~** le public l'a tout de suite aimé; **the realm of ~** le domaine de l'imaginaire.

2 *vt* (**a**) *(imagine)* se figurer, s'imaginer; *(rather think)* croire. **I rather ~ he's gone out** je crois bien qu'il est sorti; **I ~ we've met before** j'ai l'impression que nous nous sommes déjà rencontrés;

~ **that!** * tiens!; ~ **seeing you here!** * je ne m'imaginais pas vous voir ici! (**b**) *(want)* avoir envie de; *(like)* aimer. **do you ~ going for a walk?** astu envie d'aller faire une promenade?; **I don't ~ the idea** cette idée ne me dit rien *; **he fancies himself** * il ne se prend pas pour rien *; **he fancies himself as an actor** * il ne se prend pas pour une moitié d'acteur *; **he fancies her** * il la trouve attirante.
3 *adj hat, buttons, pattern* fantaisie *inv*; *(pej) cure* fantaisiste; *price* exorbitant; *(US: extra good)* de qualité supérieure. ~ **cakes** pâtisseries *fpl*; **it was all very** ~ c'était très recherché; **with his ~ house and his ~ car...** avec sa belle maison et sa voiture grand luxe...; ~ **dress** déguisement *m*; **in ~ dress** déguisé; ~**-dress ball** bal *m* masqué; ~ **goods** nouveautés *fpl*; *(pej)* ~ **man** amant *m*, jules * *m*; *(pej)* ~ **woman** bonne amie.
◆ **fancied** *adj* imaginaire. ◆ **-fancier** *n ending in cpds, e.g.* **dog-fancier** amateur *m* de chiens. ◆ **fanciful** *adj person* capricieux; *ideas* fantasque; *story, account* imaginaire.

fanfare ['fænfɛəʳ] *n* fanfare *f (air)*.

fang [fæŋ] *n (gen)* croc *m*; *[snake]* crochet *m*.

fantastic [fæn'tæstɪk] *adj (gen)* fantastique; *idea* invraisemblable; *(*: excellent)* sensationnel *, fantastique. ◆ **fantastically** *adv* fantastiquement, extraordinairement.

fantasy ['fæntəzɪ] *n (gen)* fantaisie *f*; *(idea, wish)* idée *f* fantasque; *(Psych etc)* fantasme *m*. ◆ **fantasize** *vi (Psych etc)* se livrer à des fantasmes.

far [fɑːʳ] *comp* **farther** *or* **further**, *superl* **farthest** *or* **furthest** **1** *adv* loin. **how ~ is it to...?** combien y a-t-il jusqu'à...?; **is it ~?** est-ce loin?; **is it ~ to London?** c'est loin pour aller à Londres?; **not ~ from here** pas loin d'ici; **how ~ are you going?** jusqu'où allez-vous?; *(fig)* **how ~ have you got with your plans?** où en êtes-vous de vos projets?; **to go** ~ aller loin; **I would even go so ~ as to say that...** je dirais même que...; **that's going too** ~ cela dépasse les bornes; **now you're going too** ~ alors là vous exagérez; **he has gone too ~ to back out now** il est trop engagé pour reculer maintenant; **he was ~ gone** *(ill)* il était bien bas; *(drunk)* il était bien parti *; **so** ~ jusqu'à présent; **so ~ and no further** jusque-là mais pas plus loin; **so ~ so good** jusqu'ici ça va; ~ **be it from me to say** loin de moi l'idée de dire; **as ~ as the town** jusqu'à la ville; **we didn't go as** *or* **so ~ as the others** nous ne sommes pas allés aussi loin que les autres; **as** *or* **so ~ as I know** pour autant que je sache; **as ~ as I can** dans la mesure du possible; **as ~ as the eye can see** à perte de vue; **as ~ as that goes** pour ce qui est de cela; **as ~ as I'm concerned** en ce qui me concerne; **as ~ back as I can remember** d'aussi loin que je m'en souvienne; **as ~ back as 1945** déjà en 1945; ~ **and away the best** de très loin le meilleur; ~ **and wide**, ~ **and near** partout; ~ **above** loin au-dessus (de); *(fig)* de loin supérieur (à); ~ **away**, ~ **off** au loin; ~ **away in the distance** dans le lointain; **he wasn't ~ off** il n'était pas loin; **his birthday is not ~ off** c'est bientôt son anniversaire; ~ **beyond** bien audelà (de); ~ **from** loin de (*doing* faire); ~ **from it!** loin de là!; ~ **into** très avant dans; ~ **out at sea** au (grand) large; *(fig: wrong)* **to be ~ out** *or (US)* ~ **off** *[person]* être loin du compte; *[calculations]* être complètement erroné; **by** ~ de loin, beaucoup; **this is ~ better** ceci est beaucoup *or* bien mieux.
2 *adj country* lointain, éloigné. **the F~ East** l'Extrême-Orient *m*; **the F~ North** le Grand Nord; **the F~ West** le Far West; **it's a ~ cry from...** on est loin de...; **on the ~ side of** de l'autre côté de; **at the ~ end of** à l'autre bout de; *(Pol)* **the ~ left** l'extrême gauche *f*.
◆ **faraway** *adj country, voice* lointain; *village* éloigné; *look* perdu dans le vague; *memory* flou. ◆ **far-distant** *adj* lointain. ◆ **far-fetched** *adj idea, scheme* bizarre; *explanation* tiré par les cheveux. ◆ **far-flung** *adj* vaste. ◆ **far-off** *adj* lointain, éloigné. ◆ **far-out** * *adj (modern)* d'avant-garde; *(superb)* super *. ◆ **far-reaching** *adj* d'une grande portée. ◆ **far-sighted** *adj person* clairvoyant; *decision, measure* fait (*or* pris *etc*) avec clairvoyance.

farce [fɑːs] *n (Theat, fig)* farce *f*. **the whole thing's a ~!** tout ça, c'est vraiment grotesque. ◆ **farcical** *adj* grotesque, ridicule.

fare [fɛəʳ] **1** *n* (**a**) *(charge) (on bus, in underground)* prix *m* du ticket; *(on boat, plane, train)* prix du billet; *(in taxi)* prix de la course. **~s, please!** les places, s'il vous plaît!; **~s are going up** les transports *mpl* vont augmenter; **let me pay your** ~ laissez-moi payer pour vous; **I haven't got the** ~ je n'ai pas assez d'argent pour le billet. (**b**) *(passenger)* voyageur *m*, -euse *f*; *[taxi]* client(e) *m(f)*. (**c**) *(food)* nourriture *f*. **hospital** ~ régime *m* d'hôpital. **2** *adj [bus]* ~ **stage** section *f*. **3** *vi*: **how did you ~?** comment cela s'est-il passé?
◆ **farewell** **1** *n, excl* adieu *m*; **to bid ~well to** faire ses adieux à ; **2** *adj dinner etc* d'adieu.

farm [fɑːm] **1** *n (Agr)* ferme *f*; *(fish ~ etc)* centre *m* d'élevage. **to work on a** ~ travailler dans une ferme. **2** *adj*: ~ **labourer**, ~ **worker** ouvrier *m*, -ière *f* agricole; ~ **produce** produits *mpl* de ferme. **3** *vt* cultiver. **4** *vi* être fermier.
◆ **farm out** *vt sep work* céder en sous-traitance; *(*: hum) children* parquer * (*on sb* chez qn). ◆ **farmed** *adj fish* d'élevage. ◆ **farmer** *n* fermier *m* ; **~er's wife** fermière *f*. ◆ **farmhand** *n* ouvrier *m*, -ière *f* agricole. ◆ **farmhouse** *n* (maison *f* de) ferme *f*. ◆ **farming** **1** *n* agriculture *f*; **vegetable/fruit ~ing** culture maraîchère/fruitière; **mink ~ing** élevage *m* du vison ; **2** *adj methods* de culture ; **~ing communities** collectivités *fpl* rurales. ◆ **farmland** *n* terres *fpl* cultivées. ◆ **farmstead** *n* ferme *f*. ◆ **farmyard** *n* cour *f* de ferme.

farrier ['færɪəʳ] *n* maréchal-ferrant *m*.

fart ‡ [fɑːt] **1** *n* pet ‡ *m*. **2** *vi* péter ‡.

farther ['fɑːðəʳ] *comp of* **far** **1** *adv* plus loin. **how much ~ is it?** c'est encore à combien?; **it is ~ than I thought** c'est plus loin que je ne pensais; **have you got much ~ to go?** est-ce que vous avez encore loin à aller?; **I got no ~ with him** je ne suis arrivé à rien de plus avec lui; **nothing could be ~ from the truth** rien n'est plus éloigné de la vérité; **to get ~ and ~ away** s'éloigner de plus en plus; ~ **back** plus (loin) en arrière; **move ~ back** reculez-vous; ~ **back than 1940** avant 1940; ~ **away**, ~ **off** plus éloigné, plus loin; ~ **on**, ~ **forward** plus en avant, plus loin; *(fig)* plus avancé. **2** *adj* plus éloigné, plus lointain. **the ~ end of the room** l'autre bout de la salle.

farthest ['fɑːðɪst] *superl of* **far** **1** *adj* le plus lointain, le plus éloigné. **the ~ way** la route la plus longue. **2** *adv* le plus loin.

fascinate ['fæsɪneɪt] *vt* fasciner. ◆ **fascinated** *adj* fasciné (*by* par). ◆ **fascinating** *adj* fascinant. ◆ **fascination** *n* fascination *f*.

fascism ['fæʃɪz(ə)m] *n* fascisme *m*. ◆ **fascist** *adj, n* fasciste *(mf)*.

fashion ['fæʃ(ə)n] **1** *n* (**a**) *(manner)* façon *f*, manière *f*. **in a queer** ~ d'une manière *or* façon bizarre; **after a** ~ *finish, manage* tant bien que mal; *cook, paint* si l'on peut dire; **in the French** ~ à la française; **in his own** ~ à sa manière *or* façon. (**b**) *(latest style)* mode *f*, vogue *f*. **in** ~ à la mode, en vogue; **in the latest** ~ à la dernière mode; **out of** ~ démodé; **to set the ~ for** lancer la mode de; **it is the ~ to say** il est bien porté de dire; **it's no longer the** ~ ça ne se fait plus. (**c**) *(habit)* coutume *f*, habitude *f*. **2** *vt carving* façonner; *model* fabriquer; *dress* confectionner. **3** *adj editor, magazine* de mode. ~ **designer** modéliste *mf*, *(grander)* couturier *m*; ~ **house** maison *f* de couture; ~ **model** mannequin *m (personne)*; ~ **parade,** ~ **show** présentation *f* de collections. ◆**fashionable** *adj dress, subject* à la mode; *district, shop, hotel* chic *inv*. ◆**fashionably** *adv* à la mode.

fast[1] [fɑːst] **1** *adj* (**a**) *(speedy)* rapide. *(Aut)* **the** ~ **lane** ≃ la voie la plus à gauche; ~ **train** rapide *m*; **he's a** ~ **thinker** il a l'esprit très rapide; **he's a** ~ **worker** il va vite en besogne; **to pull a** ~ **one on sb** * rouler qn *. (**b**) *[clock etc]* **to be** ~ avancer; **my watch is 5 minutes** ~ ma montre avance de 5 minutes. (**c**) *(dissipated) woman* de mœurs légères; *life* dissolu. **one of the** ~ **set** un viveur. (**d**) *(firm) rope, knot* solide; *grip* tenace; *colour* grand teint *inv*; *friend* sûr. **to make a boat** ~ amarrer un bateau. **2** *adv* (**a**) *(quickly)* vite, rapidement. **he ran off as** ~ **as his legs could carry him** il s'est sauvé à toutes jambes; **how** ~ **can you type?** à quelle vitesse pouvez-vous taper?; **not so** ~! doucement!; **he'll do it** ~ **enough if...** il ne se fera pas prier si... (**b**) *(firmly, securely) tied* solidement. ~ **asleep** profondément endormi. ◆**fastback** *n (Brit Aut)* voiture *f* à arrière profilé. ◆**fast food** *n* prêt-à-manger. ◆**fast-selling** *adj (Comm)* à écoulement rapide.

fast[2] [fɑːst] **1** *vi (not eat)* jeûner. **2** *n* jeûne *m*.

fasten ['fɑːsn] **1** *vt (gen)* attacher (*to* à); *(with nail)* clouer (*to* à); *box, door* fermer (solidement); *seat belt, dress* attacher; *responsibility* attribuer (*on sb* à qn). **to** ~ **the blame on sb** rejeter la faute sur le dos de qn. **2** *vi (gen)* se fermer; *[dress]* s'attacher.
◆**fasten down** *vt sep blind, flap* fixer en place ; *envelope* coller. ◆**fasten on** *vt sep* fixer (en place). ◆**fasten (up)on** *vt fus excuse* saisir; *idea* se mettre en tête.
◆**fastener** *or* ◆**fastening** *n* attache *f*; *[box, door, garment]* fermeture *f*; *[bag, necklace, book]* fermoir *m*.

fastidious [fæs'tɪdɪəs] *adj* (**a**) *work, research* minutieux; *(over presentation)* méticuleux; *(over detail)* tatillon; *(easily disgusted)* délicat.

fat [fæt] **1** *n (Anat)* graisse *f*; *(on meat)* gras *m*; *(for cooking)* matière *f* grasse. **to fry in deep** ~ faire cuire à la grande friture; **the** ~**'s in the fire** le feu est aux poudres; **to live off the** ~ **of the land** vivre grassement.
2 *adj person, limb* gros (*f* grosse), gras (*f* grasse) ; *face* joufflu; *cheeks* gros; *meat, bacon* gras; *volume, cheque, salary* gros; **to get** ~ grossir, engraisser; *(fig)* **he grew** ~ **on the profits** il s'est engraissé avec les bénéfices; (*: *US)* ~ **cat** gros richard *; **a** ~ **lot of good that did!** * ça a bien avancé les choses! *(iro)*; **a** ~ **lot he knows about it!** * comme s'il en savait quelque chose!
◆**fatfree** *adj diet* sans matières grasses. ◆**fathead** * *n* imbécile *mf*, cruche * *f*. ◆**fatness** *n* embonpoint *m*. ◆**fatten** *vt* (~ **up**) *(gen)* engraisser; *geese* gaver. ◆**fattening** *adj food* qui fait grossir. ◆**fatty** *adj food* gras; *tissue* adipeux.

fatal ['feɪtl] *adj (causing death) injury, disease etc* mortel; *consequences* fatal; *(disastrous) mistake, day, event* fatal; *influence* néfaste; *consequences* désastreux; *(fateful) words, decision* fatidique. **it was absolutely** ~ **to mention that** c'était une grave erreur que de parler de cela. ◆**fatalism** *n* fatalisme *m*. ◆**fatalist** *n* fataliste *mf*. ◆**fatalistic** *adj* fataliste. ◆**fatality** *n (accident)* accident mortel; *(person)* mort *m*. ◆**fatally** *adv wounded* mortellement; ~**ly ill** condamné, perdu.

fate [feɪt] *n* (**a**) *(force)* destin *m*, sort *m*. **what** ~ **has in store for us** ce que le destin nous réserve. (**b**) *(one's lot)* sort *m*. **to leave sb to his** ~ abandonner qn à son sort. ◆**fated** *adj* destiné (*to do* à faire); *friendship, person* voué au malheur. ◆**fateful** *adj words* fatidique; *day, event, moment* fatal.

father ['fɑːðəʳ] *n (all senses)* père *m*. *(Rel)* **Our F**~ Notre Père; **from** ~ **to son** de père en fils; **there was the** ~ **and mother of a row** * il y a eu une dispute à tout casser *; **F**~ **Bennet** le (révérend) père Bennet, l'abbé Bennet; **yes, F**~ oui, mon père; **F**~ **Christmas** le père Noël; **F**~**'s Day** la Fête des Pères; ~ **confessor** directeur *m* de conscience; **Old F**~ **Time** le Temps. ◆**father-figure** *n* personne *f* qui joue le rôle du père. ◆**fatherhood** *n* paternité *f*. ◆**father-in-law** *n* beau-père *m*. ◆**fatherland** *n* patrie *f*. ◆**fatherless** *adj* orphelin de père. ◆**fatherly** *adj* paternel.

fathom ['fæðəm] **1** *n (Naut)* brasse *f* (= *1,83 m)*. **2** *vt (fig:* ~ **out**) sonder. **I just can't** ~ **it out** je n'y comprends absolument rien.

fatigue [fə'tiːg] **1** *n* fatigue *f*, épuisement *m*; *(Mil)* corvée *f*. **metal** ~ fatigue du métal. **2** *vt* fatiguer.

fatuous ['fætjʊəs] *adj* stupide. ◆**fatuity** *or* ◆**fatuousness** *n* stupidité *f*.

faucet ['fɔːsɪt] *n (US)* robinet *m*.

fault [fɔːlt] **1** *n* (**a**) *(gen)* défaut *m*; *(Tech)* défaut, anomalie *f*; *(mistake)* erreur *f*; *(Tennis)* faute *f*; *(Geol)* faille *f*. **to find** ~ **with** *thing* trouver à redire à; *person* critiquer; **I have no** ~ **to find with him** je n'ai rien à lui reprocher; **generous to a** ~ généreux à l'excès; **to be at** ~ être fautif; **my memory was at** ~ ma mémoire m'a trompé *or* m'a fait défaut. (**b**) *(responsibility)* faute *f*. **whose** ~ **is it?** qui est fautif?; **whose** ~ **is it if we're late?** à qui la faute si nous sommes en retard?; **it's not my** ~ ce n'est pas de ma faute. **2** *vt*: **to** ~ **sth/sb** trouver des défauts dans qch/chez qn.
◆**faultfind** *vi* critiquer. ◆**faultfinder** *n* mécontent(e) *m(f)*. ◆**faultfinding** **1** *adj* grincheux ; **2** *n* critiques *fpl*. ◆**faultless** *adj person, behaviour* irréprochable; *work, English* impeccable. ◆**faulty** *adj* défectueux.

fauna ['fɔːnə] *n* faune *f*.

faux pas [fəʊ'pɑː] *n* impair *m*, gaffe *f*.

favour, *(US)* **favor** ['feɪvəʳ] **1** *n* (**a**) *(act)* service *m*. **to do sb a** ~ rendre (un) service à qn; **to ask a** ~ **of sb** demander un service à qn; **as a** ~ **to Paul** pour rendre service à Paul; **do me a** ~ **and...** sois gentil et... (**b**) *(approval)* faveur *f*. **to be in** ~ *[person]* être en faveur; *[style]* être à la mode; **to be in** ~ **with sb** être bien vu de qn, être en faveur auprès de qn; **to find** ~ **with sb** *[person]* s'attirer les bonnes grâces de qn; *[suggestion]* gagner l'approbation de qn. (**c**) *(advantage)* faveur *f*. **to decide in sb's** ~ donner gain de cause à qn; **in** ~ **of sb** en faveur de qn; **that's a point in his** ~ c'est un bon point pour lui. (**d**) **to be in** ~ **of sth** être partisan de qch; **I'm not in** ~ **of doing that** je ne suis pas d'avis de faire cela. (**e**) *(partiality)* faveur *f*. **to show** ~ **to sb** montrer un *or* des préjugé(s) en faveur de qn.
2 *vt (approve) political party, scheme, suggestion* être partisan de; *undertaking* favoriser; *(prefer) person* préférer; *candidate, pupil* montrer une préférence pour; *team, horse* être pour. **he** ~**ed us with a visit** il a eu l'amabilité de nous rendre visite.
◆**favo(u)rable** *adj (gen)* favorable (*to* à); *weather, wind* propice (*for, to* à). ◆**favo(u)rably** *adv, receive, impress* favorablement; *consider* d'un œil favorable; *disposed* bien. ◆**favo(u)red** *adj* favorisé ; **the** ~**ed few** les élus; **ill-**~**ed** disgracieux. ◆**favo(u)rite** **1** *n* favori(te) *m(f)*; **that song is a great** ~**ite of mine** cette chanson est une de mes préférées; **he sang a lot of old** ~**ites** il a chanté beaucoup de vieux succès ; **2** *adj* favori (*f* -ite), préféré. ◆**favo(u)ritism** *n* favoritisme *m*.

fawn[1] [fɔːn] **1** *n* faon *m*. **2** *adj (colour)* fauve.

fawn² [fɔ:n] *vi*: **to ~ (up)on sb** *[dog]* faire fête à qn; *[person]* flatter qn servilement. ◆**fawning** *adj* flagorneur.

fax [fæks] **1** *n (machine)* télécopieur *m; (transmission)* télécopie *f* **2** *vt* envoyer par télécopie.

faze * [feɪz] *vt* déconcerter.

fear [fɪəʳ] **1** *n (fright)* crainte *f*, peur *f*; *(awe)* crainte, respect *m*. **grave ~s have arisen for...** on est dans la plus vive inquiétude en ce qui concerne...; **there are ~s that...** on craint fort que... + ne + *subj*; **have no ~** ne craignez rien; **without ~ nor favour** impartialement; **to live in ~** vivre dans la peur; **to go in ~ of one's life/of being discovered** craindre pour sa vie/ d'être découvert; **in ~ and trembling** en tremblant de peur; **for ~ of waking him** de peur de le réveiller; **for ~ (that)** de peur que + ne + *subj*; **~ of heights** vertige *m*; **to put the ~ of God into sb** * faire une peur bleue à qn; **there's not much ~ of his coming** il est peu probable qu'il vienne, il ne risque guère de venir; **there's no ~ of that!** ça ne risque pas d'arriver!; **no ~!** * pas de danger! *
2 *vt* craindre, avoir peur de; *God* craindre. **to ~ the worst** craindre le pire; **to ~ that** avoir peur que + ne + *subj*, craindre que + ne + *subj*.
3 *vi* trembler (*for* pour).
◆**fearful** *adj (frightening) spectacle, noise* effrayant, affreux; *accident* épouvantable; (*bad*) *weather* affreux; *(timid)* craintif; **it's a ~ful nuisance** c'est empoisonnant *. ◆**fearfully** *adv (timidly)* craintivement; *(very)* affreusement, terriblement. ◆**fearfulness** *n* crainte *f*, appréhension *f*. ◆**fearless** *adj* intrépide. ◆**fearlessly** *adv* intrépidement. ◆**fearlessness** *n* intrépidité *f*. ◆**fearsome** *adj opponent* redoutable; *apparition* effroyable.

feasible ['fi:zəbl] *adj (practicable) plan, suggestion* faisable, possible; *(likely) story, theory* plausible, vraisemblable. ◆**feasibility 1** *n* faisabilité *f*, possibilité *f* (*of doing* de faire) ; **2** *adj*: **feasibility study** étude *f* de faisabilité.

feast [fi:st] **1** *n* festin *m*; *(Rel)* fête *f*. **~ day** (jour *m* de) fête. **2** *vi* festoyer. **to ~ on sth** se régaler de qch. **3** *vt*: **to ~ one's eyes on** se délecter à regarder.

feat [fi:t] *n* exploit *m*, prouesse *f*. **~ of architecture** *etc* triomphe *m or* réussite *f* de l'architecture *etc*; **that was quite a ~** cela a été un exploit.

feather ['feðəʳ] **1** *n* plume *f*. *(fig)* **to make the ~s fly** mettre le feu aux poudres; **that's a ~ in his cap** c'est une réussite dont il peut être fier; **you could have knocked me over with a ~** les bras m'en sont tombés. **2** *vt*: **to ~ one's nest** faire sa pelote, s'enrichir. **3** *adj mattress etc* de plumes; *headdress* à plumes. **~ duster** plumeau *m*. ◆**feather-bed 1** *n* lit *m* de plumes ; **2** *vt* protéger. ◆**feather-brained** *adj* écervelé. ◆**featherweight** *adj, n (Boxing)* poids *(m)* plume *inv*.

feature ['fi:tʃəʳ] **1** *n* (**a**) *(part of the face)* trait *m* (du visage). (**b**) *[machine, countryside, building]* caractéristique *f*; *[person] (physical)* trait *m*; *(mental etc)* caractéristique. (**c**) *(Comm etc)* spécialité *f*. (**d**) (*~ film*) grand film, long métrage; *(Press: column)* chronique *f*. *(Press)* **~ article** article *m* de fond; **it is a regular ~ in...** cela paraît régulièrement dans... **2** *vt (give prominence to) person, event* mettre en vedette; *[film]* avoir pour vedette; *name, news* faire figurer; *(depict)* représenter; *(have as ~: machine etc)* être équipé de. **3** *vi* figurer (*in* dans). *(gen)* **this ~d prominently in...** ceci a été un trait frappant dans... ◆**featureless** *adj* anonyme.

February ['febrʊərɪ] *n* février *m*; *for phrases V* **September.**

feckless ['feklɪs] *adj* inepte.

fed [fed] *pret, ptp of* **feed.** ◆**fed up** *adj*: **to be ~ up** * en avoir assez, en avoir marre * (*doing* de faire).

federal ['fedər(ə)l] *adj* fédéral.

federate ['fedəreɪt] **1** *vi* se fédérer. **2** ['fedərɪt] *adj* fédéré. ◆**federation** *n* fédération *f*.

fedora [fə'dɔ:rə] *n (US)* chapeau mou, feutre mou.

fee [fi:] *n (gen)* prix *m* (*for* de); *[professional person]* honoraires *mpl*; *[artist etc]* cachet *m*; *[private tutor]* appointements *mpl*. *(Univ etc)* **tuition ~** frais *mpl* de scolarité; **registration ~** droits *mpl* d'inscription; **membership ~** montant *m* de la cotisation; *(Ftbl)* **(transfer) ~** prix *m* (de transfert); *(gen)* **what's his ~?** combien prend-il?; **on payment of a small ~** contre une somme modique. ◆**fee-paying** *adj*: **~-paying school** établissement *m* (d'enseignement) privé.

feeble ['fi:bl] *adj (gen)* faible; *attempt, excuse* piètre; *joke* piteux. **she's such a ~ sort of person** c'est une fille si molle. ◆**feeble-minded** *adj* imbécile. ◆**feeble-mindedness** *n* imbécillité *f*. ◆**feebleness** *n* faiblesse *f*. ◆**feebly** *adv stagger, smile* faiblement; *say, explain* sans grande conviction.

feed [fi:d] *(vb: pret, ptp* **fed)** **1** *n* (**a**) *(food)* nourriture *f*; *(portion of food)* ration *f*; *[baby] (breast-~)* tétée *f*; *(bottle)* biberon *m*. **we had a good ~** * on a bien mangé. (**b**) *(on machine)* mécanisme *m* d'alimentation. **2** *vt* (**a**) *(provide food for)* nourrir; *(give food to) child, animal, bird* donner à manger à; *army etc* ravitailler; *baby (breastfed)* allaiter; *(bottle-fed)* donner le biberon à. **to ~ sth to sb** donner qch à manger à qn. (**b**) *fire, machine, reservoir* alimenter. *(fig)* **to ~ the flames** jeter de l'huile sur le feu; **to ~ the parking meter** rajouter une pièce dans le parcmètre; **to ~ sth into a machine** introduire qch dans une machine; **to ~ data into a computer** alimenter un ordinateur en données. **3** *vi [animal]* manger, se nourrir; *[baby]* manger, *(at breast)* téter. **to ~ on** se nourrir de.
◆**feed back** *vt sep results* donner (en retour). ◆**feed in** *vt sep tape, wire* introduire (*to* dans). ◆**feed up** *vt sep animal* engraisser; *geese* gaver; *person* faire manger davantage.
◆**feedback** *n (Elec)* réaction *f*; *(gen)* feed-back *m*, réactions *fpl*. ◆**feeder** *n (bib)* bavoir *m*. ◆**feeding 1** *n* alimentation *f* ; **2** *adj*: **~ing bottle** biberon *m*; **~(ing) stuffs** nourriture *f* (pour animaux).

feel [fi:l] *(vb: pret, ptp* **felt)** **1** *n (sense of touch)* toucher *m*; *(sensation)* sensation *f*. **at the ~ of** au contact de; **to know sth by the ~ of it** reconnaître qch au toucher; **I don't like the ~ of that** je n'aime pas cette sensation; *(fig)* ça ne me dit rien de bon; **let me have a ~!** * laisse-moi toucher!; **you have to get the ~ of a new car** il faut se faire à une nouvelle voiture.
2 *vt* (**a**) *(touch)* palper, tâter. **to ~ sb's pulse** tâter le pouls à qn; **~ the envelope and see if there's anything in it** palpez l'enveloppe pour voir s'il y a qch dedans; **to ~ one's way** avancer à tâtons (*towards* pour trouver); *(fig)* **I'm still ~ing my way around** j'essaie de m'y retrouver.
(**b**) *(be aware of) blow, caress, pain* sentir; *sympathy, grief* éprouver, ressentir. **I can ~ sth pricking me** je sens qch qui me pique; **to ~ the heat/cold** craindre la chaleur/le froid; **he felt it move** il l'a senti bouger; **he felt a great sense of relief** il a éprouvé *or* ressenti un grand soulagement; **the effects will be felt later** les effets se feront sentir plus tard; **he ~s his position very much** il est très conscient de la difficulté de sa situation; **she felt the loss of her father greatly** elle a été très affectée par la mort de son père.
(**c**) *(think)* avoir l'impression, estimer. **I ~ that he ought to go** je considère *or* j'estime qu'il devrait y aller; **I ~ it in my bones that...** qch en moi me dit que...; **he felt it necessary to point out...** il a

jugé nécessaire de faire remarquer...; **if you ~ strongly about it** si cela vous semble important; **what do you ~ about this idea?** que pensez-vous de cette idée?
3 *vi* (**a**) *(physical state)* se sentir. **to ~ cold/hungry/sleepy** avoir froid/faim/sommeil; **to ~ ill** se sentir malade; **I ~ much better** je me sens beaucoup mieux; **he doesn't ~ quite himself** il ne se sent pas tout à fait dans son assiette; **I felt as if I was going to faint** j'avais l'impression que j'allais m'évanouir.
(**b**) *(mental state)* être. **I ~ sure that...** je suis sûr que...; **I ~ very bad about leaving you here** cela m'ennuie beaucoup de vous laisser ici; **how do you ~ about him?** que pensez-vous de lui?; **how do you ~ about going for a walk?** est-ce que cela vous dit d'aller vous promener?; **I ~ as if there's nothing we can do** j'ai l'impression que nous ne pouvons rien faire; **what does it ~ like to do that?** quel effet cela vous fait-il de faire cela?; **to ~ like (doing) sth** avoir envie de (faire) qch; **I don't ~ like it** je n'en ai pas envie; **I ~ for you!** comme je vous comprends!
(**c**) *[objects]* **to ~ hard** être dur au toucher; **the house ~s damp** la maison donne l'impression d'être humide; **the box ~s as if it has been mended** au toucher on dirait que la boîte a été réparée; **it felt like flying** on se serait cru en train de voler; **it ~s like rain** on dirait qu'il va pleuvoir.
(**d**) *(grope: **~ about, ~ around**) (in dark)* tâtonner; *(in pocket, drawer)* fouiller (*for sth* pour trouver qch).
◆ **feel out** * *vt sep (US) person* sonder.
◆ **feeler** *n [insect]* antenne *f*; *[octopus etc]* tentacule *m*; *(fig)* **to put out ~ers** tâter le terrain (*to discover* pour découvrir).

feeling ['fi:lɪŋ] *n* (**a**) *(physical)* sensation *f*. **I've lost all ~ in my right arm** j'ai perdu toute sensation dans le bras droit; **a cold ~** une sensation de froid. (**b**) *(impression)* sentiment *m*. **a ~ of isolation** un sentiment d'isolement; **I've a funny ~ she will succeed** j'ai comme l'impression qu'elle va réussir; **there was a general ~ that...** le sentiment général a été que... (**c**) *(emotions)* **~s** sentiments *mpl*, sensibilité *f*; **you can imagine my ~s** tu t'imagines ce que je ressens; **~s ran high about it** cela a déchaîné les passions; **his ~s were hurt** on l'avait froissé. (**d**) *(sensitivity)* émotion *f*, sensibilité *f*; *(compassion)* sympathie *f*. **a woman of great ~** une femme très sensible; **with ~** *sing* avec sentiment; *speak* avec émotion; **he doesn't show much ~ for her** il ne fait pas preuve de beaucoup de sympathie pour elle; **ill** *or* **bad ~** hostilité *f*. ◆ **feelingly** *adv* avec émotion.

feet [fi:t] *npl of* **foot.**

feign [feɪn] *vt surprise* feindre; *madness* simuler. **to ~ illness** faire semblant d'être malade. ◆ **feint** **1** *n* feinte *f* ; **2** *vi* feinter.

feisty * ['feɪstɪ] *adj (US) (lively)* fringant; *(quarrelsome)* bagarreur *.

felicitous [fɪ'lɪsɪtəs] *adj* heureux. ◆ **felicity** *n* félicité *f*.

feline ['fi:laɪn] *adj, n* félin(e) *m(f)*.

fell¹ [fel] *pret of* **fall.**

fell² [fel] *vt tree* abattre.

fell³ [fel] *n (Brit) (mountain)* montagne *f*. *(moorland)* **the ~s** la lande.

fellow ['feləʊ] **1** *n* (**a**) homme *m*, type * *m*, garçon *m*. **a nice ~** un brave garçon, un brave type *; **an old ~** un vieux; **some poor ~** un pauvre malheureux; **poor little ~** pauvre petit bonhomme; **my dear ~** mon cher; **this journalist ~** ce journaliste. (**b**) *[association, society etc]* membre *m*, associé *m*; *(Univ)* ≃ professeur *m (attaché à un collège)*; *(US Univ)* boursier *m*, -ière *f*. (**c**) *(comrade)* camarade *m*, compagnon *m*; *(equal, peer)* semblable *m*. **~s in misfortune** compagnons d'infortune.
2 *adj*: **~ citizen** concitoyen(ne) *m(f)*; **~ countryman/-woman** compatriote *mf*; **~ creature** semblable *mf*; **~ feeling** sympathie *f*; **~ men** semblables *mpl*; **~ traveller** *(lit)* compagnon *m* de voyage; *(Pol: with communists)* communisant(e) *m(f)*; *(gen)* sympathisant(e) *m(f)*; **~ worker** *(in office)* collègue *mf*; *(in factory)* camarade *mf* de travail.
◆ **fellowship** *n (comradeship)* camaraderie *f*; *(Rel etc)* communion *f*; *(organization)* association *f*; *(Rel)* confrérie *f*.

felon ['felən] *n (Jur)* criminel(le) *m(f)*. ◆ **felonious** *adj* criminel. ◆ **felony** *n* crime *m*.

felt¹ [felt] *pret, ptp of* **feel.**

felt² [felt] **1** *n* feutre *m*. **2** *adj* de feutre. **a ~ hat** un feutre. ◆ **felt-tip (pen)** *n* feutre *m (crayon)*.

female ['fi:meɪl] **1** *adj animal, plant (also Tech)* femelle; *subject, slave* du sexe féminin; *company, vote* des femmes; *sex, character, quality* féminin. **~ students** étudiantes *fpl*; **~ labour** main-d'œuvre *f* féminine; *(Theat)* **~ impersonator** travesti *m*. **2** *n (person)* femme *f*, fille *f*; *(animal, plant)* femelle *f*. *(pej)* **there was a ~ there who...** * il y avait là une espèce de bonne femme qui... * *(pej)*.

feminine ['femɪnɪn] **1** *adj* féminin. **2** *n (Gram)* féminin *m*. **in the ~** au féminin. ◆ **femininity** *n* féminité *f*. ◆ **feminism** *n* féminisme *m*. ◆ **feminist** *n* féministe *mf*.

fen [fen] *n* marais *m*, marécage *m*.

fence [fens] **1** *n* (**a**) barrière *f*, palissade *f*; *(Racing)* obstacle *m*; *(round machine)* barrière. *(fig)* **to sit on the ~** ménager la chèvre et le chou. (**b**) (*⁑: of stolen goods)* receleur *m*. **2** *vt* (**~ in**) *land* clôturer. **~d in by restrictions** entravé par des restrictions. **3** *vi (Sport)* faire de l'escrime.
◆ **fencer** *n* escrimeur *m*, -euse *f*. ◆ **fencing** **1** *n* (**a**) *(Sport)* escrime *f*; (**b**) *(material)* matériaux *mpl* pour clôture ; **2** *adj*: **fencing match** assaut *m* d'escrime.

fend [fend] *vi*: **to ~ for o.s.** se débrouiller (tout seul). ◆ **fend off** *vt sep blow* parer; *attack* détourner; *attacker* repousser; *awkward question* éluder.
◆ **fender** *n [fire]* garde-feu *m inv*; *(US Aut)* pare-chocs *m inv*; *(US Rail)* chasse-pierres *m inv*.

fennel ['fenl] *n* fenouil *m*.

ferment [fə'ment] **1** *vi* fermenter. **2** *vt* faire fermenter. **3** ['fɜ:ment] *n* ferment *m*. *(fig)* **in a ~** en effervescence. ◆ **fermentation** *n* fermentation *f*.

fern [fɜ:n] *n* fougère *f*.

ferocious [fə'rəʊʃəs] *adj* féroce. ◆ **ferociously** *adv* férocement. ◆ **ferocity** *n* férocité *f*.

ferret ['ferɪt] **1** *n* furet *m*. **2** *vi* (**~ about, ~ around**) fureter. ◆ **ferret out** *vt sep* dénicher.

ferroconcrete ['fere(ʊ)'kɒŋkri:t] *n* béton *m* armé.

ferrous ['ferəs] *adj* ferreux.

ferry ['ferɪ] **1** *n* (**a**) *(~boat) (small: for people, cars)* bac *m*; *(larger: for people, cars, trains)* ferry (-boat) *m*. **~man** passeur *m*. (**b**) *(place)* passage *m*. **2** *vt* (**~ across, ~ over**) faire passer; *(fig) people* emmener, conduire; *things* porter.

fertile ['fɜ:taɪl] *adj (gen)* fertile; *creature, plant* fertile, fécond. ◆ **fertility** **1** *n* fertilité *f*; fécondité *f* ; **2** *adj* de fertilité; **fertility drug** médicament *m* contre la stérilité. ◆ **fertilization** *n [land]* fertilisation *f*; *[egg]* fécondation *f*. ◆ **fertilize** *vt* fertiliser; féconder. ◆ **fertilizer** *n* engrais *m*.

fervent ['fɜ:v(ə)nt], **fervid** ['fɜ:vɪd] *adj* fervent.
◆ **fervour,** *(US)* **fervor** *n* ferveur *f*.

fester ['festəʳ] *vi (Med)* suppurer; *[anger]* couver.

festival ['festɪv(ə)l] *n (Rel etc)* fête *f*; *(Mus etc)* festival *m*. ◆ **festive** *adj* de fête; **the festive season** la période des fêtes; **in a festive mood** en veine de réjouissances. ◆**festivity** *n* fête *f*, réjouissances *fpl*.

festoon [fes'tu:n] *vt* festonner (*with* de).

fetch [fetʃ] *vt* (**a**) *(go and get) person, thing* aller chercher; *(bring) person* amener; *thing* apporter. **to ~ and carry for sb** faire la bonne pour qn; *(to dog)* **~ it!** rapporte! (**b**) *(sell for) money* rapporter; *price* atteindre. ◆**fetch in** *vt sep person* faire rentrer; *thing* rentrer. ◆**fetch out** *vt sep person* faire sortir; *thing* sortir. ◆**fetch up 1** *vi* se retrouver (*at* à; *in* dans). **2** *vt sep object* monter; *person* faire monter; *(vomit)* vomir.

fetching ['fetʃɪŋ] *adj* charmant.

fête [feɪt] **1** *n* fête *f*. **2** *vt* fêter.

fetid ['fetɪd] *adj* fétide, puant.

fetish ['fi:tɪʃ] *n* fétiche *m (objet de culte)*; *(Psych)* objet *m* de la fétichisation. *(fig)* **she makes a ~ of...** elle est obsédée par... ◆**fetishist** *n* fétichiste *mf*.

fetter ['fetəʳ] **1** *vt person* enchaîner; *horse, slave (also fig)* entraver. **2** *npl*: **~s** chaînes *fpl*; entraves *fpl*.

fettle ['fetl] *n*: **in fine ~** en pleine forme.

fetus ['fi:təs] *n (US)* = **foetus.**

feud [fju:d] **1** *n* querelle *f*; *(stronger)* vendetta *f*. **family ~s** querelles de famille. **2** *vi* se quereller. **to ~ with sb** être l'ennemi juré de qn.

feudal ['fju:dl] *adj* féodal. ◆**feudalism** *n* féodalité *f*.

fever ['fi:vəʳ] *n* fièvre *f*. **a bout of ~** un accès de fièvre; **high ~** forte fièvre; **the gambling ~** le démon du jeu; **a ~ of impatience** une impatience fébrile; **it reached ~ pitch** c'était à son comble. ◆**feverish** *adj* fiévreux. ◆**feverishly** *adv* fiévreusement.

few [fju:] *adj, pron* (**a**) *(not many)* peu (de). **~ books** peu de livres; **~ of them** peu d'entre eux; **~ come to see him** peu de gens viennent le voir; **he is one of the ~ people who...** c'est l'une des rares personnes qui... + *indic or subj*; **in the past ~ days** ces derniers jours; **the next ~ days** les quelques jours qui viennent; **with ~ exceptions** à de rares exceptions près; **every ~ days** tous les deux ou trois jours; **they are ~ and far between** ils sont rares; **we are very ~** nous sommes peu nombreux; **the remaining ~ minutes** les quelques minutes qui restent; **the ~ who...** les rares personnes qui...; *(the minority)* la minorité qui...; **I have as ~ books as you** j'ai aussi peu de livres que vous; **I have as ~ as you** j'en ai aussi peu que vous; **how ~ there are!** qu'il y en a peu!; **how ~ they are!** qu'ils sont peu nombreux!; **so ~** si peu (de); **too ~** trop peu (de); **there were 3 too ~** il en manquait 3.
(**b**) *(some, several)* **a ~** quelques(-uns *or* -unes); **a ~ books** quelques livres; **a ~ more** quelques-un(e)s de plus; **quite a ~ books** pas mal * de livres; **quite a ~ (people) believed him** un bon nombre de gens *or* pas mal * de gens l'ont cru; **a ~ of these people** quelques-uns de ces gens; **a ~ of us** quelques-un(e)s d'entre nous; **a good ~ of** bon nombre de; **a ~ more days** encore quelques jours.
◆**fewer** *adj, pron, comp of* **few** moins (de); **we have sold ~er this year** nous en avons moins vendu cette année; **he has ~er books than you** il a moins de livres que vous; **we are ~er than...** nous sommes moins nombreux que...; **no ~er than 37** pas moins de 37; **few came and ~er stayed** peu sont venus et encore moins sont restés. ◆**fewest** *adj, pron, superl of* **few** le moins (de); **~est in number** le moins nombreux.

fiancé(e) [fɪ'ɑ̃:ŋseɪ] *n* fiancé(e) *m(f)*.

fiasco [fɪ'æskəʊ] *n* fiasco *m*.

fib * [fɪb] **1** *n* blague * *f*, mensonge *m*. **2** *vi* raconter des blagues *, mentir. ◆**fibber** * *n* menteur *m*, -euse *f*.

fibre, *(US)* **fiber** ['faɪbəʳ] *n* fibre *f*. **(dietary) ~** fibres *fpl*, cellulose *f* végétale; **high ~ diet** alimentation *f* riche en fibres. ◆**fibreboard** *n* panneau *m* fibreux. ◆**fibrefill** *n* rembourrage *m* synthétique. ◆**fibreglass** *n* fibre *f* de verre. ◆**fibre-optic cable** *n* câble *m* en fibres optiques. ◆**fibre optics** *nsg* la fibre optique. ◆**fibre-tip (pen)** *n* stylo *m* pointe fibre. ◆**fibroid** *n (Med)* fibrome *m*. ◆**fibrositis** *n* cellulite *f*. ◆**fibrous** *adj* fibreux.

fickle ['fɪkl] *adj* inconstant, volage.

fiction ['fɪkʃ(ə)n] *n* (**a**) *(Literat)* **(works of) ~** romans *mpl*; **light ~** romans faciles à lire. (**b**) *(sth made up)* fiction *f*. **legal ~** fiction légale. (**c**) *(the unreal)* le faux. ◆**fictional** *or* ◆**fictitious** *adj* fictif.

fiddle ['fɪdl] **1** *n* (**a**) violon *m*. (**b**) *(*: cheating)* truc * *m*, combine * *f*. **it was a ~** c'était une combine *; **tax ~** fraude *f* fiscale. **2** *vi* (**a**) *(Mus)* jouer du violon. (**b**) **do stop fiddling!** tiens-toi donc tranquille!; **to ~ with a pencil** tripoter un crayon. **3** *vt* (*) *accounts, expenses claim* truquer. ◆**fiddle about, fiddle around** *vi* s'occuper vaguement, bricoler. **we just ~d about yesterday** on n'a rien fait de spécial hier. ◆**fiddler** *n* violoneux * *m*; *(*: cheat)* combinard * *m*. ◆**fiddlesticks** * *excl* quelle blague! * ◆**fiddling 1** *adj* insignifiant ; **2** *n (*: cheating etc)* combines * *fpl*. ◆**fiddly** *adj task* délicat (et agaçant); *object* embêtant * à manier.

fidelity [fɪ'delɪtɪ] *n* fidélité *f*.

fidget ['fɪdʒɪt] **1** *vi* (**~ about, ~ around**) remuer (continuellement). **stop ~ing!** reste donc tranquille!; **to ~ with sth** tripoter qch. **2** *n*: **to be a ~** ne jamais se tenir tranquille. ◆**fidgety** *adj* remuant, agité.

field [fi:ld] **1** *n (gen)* champ *m*; *(Miner)* gisement *m*; *(Aviat, Sport)* terrain *m*; *(sphere of activity)* domaine *m*. *(fig)* **a year's trial in the ~** un an d'essais sur le terrain; *(Comm)* **to be first in the ~ with sth** être le premier à lancer qch; **~ of battle** champ de bataille; *(Mil)* **to die in the ~** tomber au champ d'honneur; *(Sport)* **to take the ~** entrer en jeu; **it's outside my ~** ce n'est pas de mon domaine; **his particular ~** sa spécialité; **~ of vision** champ de vision. **2** *vt (Sport) ball* attraper; *team* faire jouer. *(fig)* **to ~ questions** répondre au pied levé (à des questions). **3** *adj (fig)* **~ day** grande occasion; **they had a ~ day** * cela a été une bonne journée pour eux; **~ glasses** jumelles *fpl*; **~ gun** canon *m* de campagne; *(US)* **~ hand** ouvrier *m*, -ière *f* agricole; **~ hospital** antenne *f* chirurgicale; **~ marshal** maréchal *m*; **~ mouse** mulot *m*; **~ sports** activités *fpl* de plein air *(chasse, pêche)*; **~ trip** sortie *f* éducative. ◆**field-test 1** *vt* soumettre aux essais sur le terrain; **2** *n* essai *m* sur le terrain. ◆**fieldwork** *n (Archeol, Geol etc)* recherches *fpl* sur le terrain; *(Sociol etc)* travail *m* avec des cas sociaux.

fiend [fi:nd] *n* démon *m*. **that child's a real ~** * cet enfant est un petit monstre; **tennis ~** mordu(e) * *m(f)* du tennis. ◆**fiendish** *adj cruelty, smile, delight, plan* diabolique; *(*: unpleasant)* abominable; **I had a ~ish time * doing...** j'ai eu un mal fou à faire... ◆**fiendishly** *adv* diaboliquement; (*) *difficult etc* abominablement.

fierce [fɪəs] *adj (gen)* féroce; *desire* ardent; *attack, wind, speech* violent; *hatred* implacable; *heat* intense; *competition, fighting, opponent, partisan* acharné. ◆**fiercely** *adv* férocement; violemment; avec acharnement. ◆**fierceness** *n* férocité *f*; violence *f*; implacabilité *f*; intensité *f*.

fiery ['faɪərɪ] *adj (lit)* ardent; *sky* rougeoyant; *person, speech* fougueux; *temper* violent. ◆**fiery-tempered** *adj* irascible.

fifteen [fɪf'ti:n] *adj, n, pron* quinze *(m) inv*. **about ~ books** une quinzaine de livres; **about ~** une quinzaine; *(Rugby)* **the French ~** le quinze de France; *for other phrases V* **six.** ◆**fifteenth** *adj, n* quinzième *(mf)*; *(fraction)* quinzième *m*.

fifth [fɪfθ] *adj, n* cinquième *(mf)*; *(fraction)* cinquième *m*; *(US) measurement* le cinquième d'un gallon (= 75 cl); *(bottle)* bouteille *f (d'alcool)*. ~ **column** cinquième colonne *f*; *for other phrases V* **sixth.**

fifty ['fɪftɪ] *adj, n, pron* cinquante *(m) inv*. **about ~ books** une cinquantaine de livres; **about ~** une cinquantaine; **to go ~-~ with sb** partager moitié-moitié avec qn; **we have a ~-~ chance of success** nous avons une chance sur deux de réussir; *for other phrases V* **sixty.** ◆ **fiftieth** *adj, n* cinquantième *(mf)*; *(fraction)* cinquantième *m*.

fig [fɪg] *n* figue *f*; *(~ tree)* figuier *m*. ~ **leaf** feuille *f* de figuier; *(on statue etc)* feuille de vigne.

fight [faɪt] *(vb: pret, ptp* **fought***)* **1** *n (between persons)* bagarre * *f*; *(Mil)* combat *m*, bataille *f*; *(Boxing)* combat; *(against disease, poverty etc)* lutte *f* (*against* contre); *(quarrel)* dispute *f*. **he put up a good ~** il s'est bien défendu; **there was no ~ left in him** il n'avait plus envie de lutter.
2 *vi [person, animal]* se battre (*with* avec; *against* contre); *[troops, countries]* se battre, combattre (*against* contre); *(fig)* lutter (*for* pour; *against* contre); *(quarrel)* se disputer (*with* avec). **the dogs were ~ing over a bone** les chiens se disputaient un os; **to ~ shy of (doing) sth** tout faire pour éviter (de faire) qch; **to ~ against sleep** lutter contre le sommeil; **to ~ for one's life** lutter pour la vie.
3 *vt person, army* se battre avec *or* contre; *fire, disease, decision, legislation* lutter contre. **to ~ a battle** livrer bataille; **to ~ a losing battle against sth** se battre en pure perte contre qch; **to ~ a duel** se battre en duel; *(Jur)* **to ~ a case** défendre une cause; *(Pol etc)* **to ~ a campaign** mener une campagne; **to ~ one's way through the crowd** se frayer un passage à travers la foule.
◆ **fight back 1** *vi (in fight)* rendre les coups; *(Mil; also in argument)* se défendre; *(after illness)* réagir; *(Sport)* se reprendre. **2** *vt sep tears* refouler; *despair* lutter contre; *doubts* vaincre. ◆ **fight down** *vt sep anxiety, doubts* vaincre; *desire* réprimer. ◆ **fight off** *vt sep (Mil) attack* repousser; *disease, sleep* lutter contre. ◆ **fight out** *vt sep*: **to ~ it out** se bagarrer * (pour régler qch).
◆ **fighter 1** *n* combattant *m*; *(Boxing)* boxeur *m*; *(fig)* lutteur *m*; *(plane)* avion *m* de chasse ; **2** *adj*: **~er pilot** pilote *m* de chasse. ◆ **fighter-bomber** *n* chasseur bombardier *m*. ◆ **fighting 1** *n (Mil)* combat *m*; *(in streets etc)* échauffourées *fpl*; *(in classroom, pub)* bagarres *fpl* ; **2** *adj person* combatif; *troops* de combat; **~ing spirit** cran * *m*; **a ~ing chance** une assez bonne chance; *(Mil)* **~ing forces** forces *fpl* armées; **~ing line** front *m*; **~ing strength** effectif *m* mobilisable.

figment ['fɪgmənt] *n*: **a ~ of the imagination** une pure invention.

figure ['fɪgəʳ] **1** *n* (**a**) chiffre *m*. **in round ~s** en chiffres ronds; **he's good at ~s** il est doué pour le calcul; **a mistake in the ~s** une erreur de calcul; **the crime/unemployment** *etc* **~s** le taux de la criminalité/du chômage *etc;* **to reach three ~s** atteindre la centaine; **a 3-~ number** un nombre *ou* un numéro de 3 chiffres; **he earns well over five ~s** il gagne bien plus de dix mille livres. (**b**) *(drawing)* figure *f*. **a ~ of eight** un huit. (**c**) *(human form)* **I saw a ~ approach** j'ai vu une forme *or* une silhouette s'approcher de moi; **she has a good ~** elle est bien faite; **remember your ~!** pense à ta ligne!; **to lose one's ~** s'épaissir; **a fine ~ of a woman** une belle femme. (**d**) *(person)* figure *f*, personnage *m*. **a ~ of fun** un guignol. (**e**) *(Literat)* figure *f*. *(fig)* **it's just a ~ of speech** ce n'est qu'une façon de parler. (**f**) *(Mus)* figure *f* mélodique. **2** *vt (imagine)* penser, s'imaginer; *(guess)* penser, supposer. **3** *vi* (**a**) *(appear)* figurer (*on a list* sur une liste); *(in play etc)* jouer un rôle. (**b**) *(*: make sense)* **that ~s** ça s'explique. ◆ **figure on** *vt fus (US) (take account of)* tenir compte de; *(count on)* compter sur; *(expect)* s'attendre (*doing* à faire). ◆ **figure out** *vt sep (understand)* arriver à comprendre; *(calculate)* calculer; *(plan)* calculer. **I can't ~ it out** ça me dépasse *. ◆ **figurative** *adj language, meaning* figuré; *(Art)* figuratif.

Fiji (Islands) ['fi:dʒi:('aɪləndz)] *n(pl)* (îles *fpl*) Fi(d)ji *fpl*.

filament ['fɪləmənt] *n* filament *m*.

filch [fɪltʃ] *vt* voler, chiper *.

file¹ [faɪl] **1** *n (tool)* lime *f*. **2** *vt* **(~ away, ~ down)** limer. **to ~ one's nails** se limer les ongles. ◆ **filings** *npl* limaille *f*.

file² [faɪl] **1** *n (folder)* dossier *m*; *(with hinges)* classeur *m*; *(for drawings: also in filing drawers)* carton *m*; *(papers)* dossier (*on sb/sth* sur qn/qch); *(Comput)* fichier *m*. **to put a document on the ~** joindre une pièce au dossier. **2** *adj (US)* **~ clerk** documentaliste *mf*. **3** *vt notes* classer; *(into ~)* joindre au dossier; *(Jur) claim, petition* déposer. *(Insurance)* **to ~ an accident claim** faire une déclaration d'accident; **to ~ a suit against sb** intenter un procès à qn. ◆ **filing 1** *n*: **to do the filing** s'occuper du classement ; **2** *adj*: **filing cabinet** classeur *m (meuble)*; **filing clerk** documentaliste *mf*.

file³ [faɪl] **1** *n* file *f*. **in Indian ~** en file indienne; **in single ~** en file. **2** *vi* marcher en file. **to ~ in/out** *etc* entrer/sortir *etc* en file; **the soldiers ~d past the general** les soldats ont défilé devant le général; **they ~d past the ticket collector** ils sont passés un à un devant le poinçonneur.

filial ['fɪlɪəl] *adj* filial.

filibuster ['fɪlɪbʌstəʳ] *n (US Pol)* obstructionniste *mf*; *(pirate)* flibustier *m*.

filigree ['fɪlɪgri:] **1** *n* filigrane *m (en métal etc)*. **2** *adj* en filigrane.

fill [fɪl] **1** *vt (gen)* remplir (*with* de); *teeth* plomber; *need* répondre à. **smoke ~ed the room** la pièce s'est remplie de fumée; **the wind ~ed the sails** le vent a gonflé les voiles; **~ed with** *admiration* rempli de; *anger, despair* en proie à; **to ~ a vacancy** *[employer]* pourvoir à un emploi; *[employee]* prendre un poste vacant; **the position is already ~ed** le poste est déjà pris; **that ~s the bill** cela fait l'affaire. **2** *vi* **(~ up)** se remplir (*with* de). **3** *n*: **to eat one's ~** manger à sa faim; **to drink one's ~** boire tout son content; **I've had my ~ of listening to her** j'en ai assez de l'écouter.
◆ **fill in 1** *vi*: **to ~ in for sb** remplacer qn (temporairement). **2** *vt sep* (**a**) *form, questionnaire* remplir; *account, report* compléter. **to ~ sb in on sth *** mettre qn au courant de qch. (**b**) *hole* boucher; *door* murer; *gaps* combler; *outline* remplir. ◆ **fill out 1** *vi [sails etc]* gonfler; *[person]* forcir. **2** *vt sep form* remplir. ◆ **fill up 1** *vi (Aut)* faire le plein d'essence; *V also* **fill 2. 2** *vt sep container, form* remplir; *hole* boucher. *(Aut)* **~ her up! *** faites le plein!
◆ **filler** *n (funnel)* entonnoir *m*; *(for cracks in wood etc)* mastic *m*. ◆ **filling 1** *n (in tooth)* plombage *m*; *(Culin)* garniture *f* ; **2** *adj food* substantiel; **~ing station** station-service *f*.

fillet ['fɪlɪt] **1** *n* filet *m*. **~ steak** tournedos *m*. **2** *vt meat* désosser; *fish* découper en filets. **~ed sole** filets *mpl* de sole.

fillip ['fɪlɪp] *n* coup *m* de fouet *(fig)*.

filly ['fɪlɪ] *n* pouliche *f*.

film [fɪlm] **1** *n (Phot)* pellicule *f*; *(Cine)* film *m*; *(for wrapping food)* scellofrais *m* ®. **to go to the ~s** aller au cinéma; **the ~ is on at...** le film passe à...; **a ~ of dust** une fine couche de poussière. **2** *vt* filmer. **3** *vi* faire un film. **4** *adj*: **~ camera** caméra *f*; **~ fan** cinéphile *mf*; **~ library** cinémathèque *f*; **~ maker** cinéaste *mf;* **~ rights** droits *mpl* d'adaptation (cinématographique); **~ script** scénario *m*; **~ set** plateau *m* de tournage ; **~ star** vedette *f* (de cinéma), star *f*; **~ studio** studio *m* (de cinéma). ◆ **filmstrip** *n* film *m* fixe. ◆ **filmy** *adj* léger, vaporeux.

Filofax ['faɪləʊ,fæks] *n* ® Filofax *m* ®.

filter ['fɪltəʳ] **1** *n* filtre *m*. **2** *adj (Aut)* ~ **lane** ≃ voie *f* de droite; *(Aut)* ~ **light** flèche *f*; ~ **paper** papier *m* filtre. **3** *vt liquids* filtrer; *air* purifier. **4** *vi (Aut)* **to** ~ **to the left** tourner à la flèche; *[people]* **to** ~ **back** *etc* revenir *etc* par petits groupes (espacés); **the news began to** ~ **in** *or* **through** on a commencé petit à petit à avoir des nouvelles. ◆ **filter-tipped** *adj* à bout filtre.

filth [fɪlθ] *n (lit)* saleté *f*, crasse *f*; *(excrement)* ordure *f*; *(fig)* saletés *fpl*. **it's sheer** ~ c'est plein de saletés *or* de grossièretés. ◆ **filthy** *adj (gen)* sale, crasseux; *habit* dégoûtant; *language* ordurier; (*) *weather etc* abominable; **she's got a** ~**y mind** elle a l'esprit mal tourné.

fin [fɪn] *n [fish, whale]* nageoire *f*; *[shark]* aileron *m*; *[aircraft]* empennage *m*; *[radiator etc]* ailette *f*; *[frogman]* palme *f*.

finagle [fɪ'neɪg(ə)l] *(US)* **1** *vi* resquiller. **2** *vt:* **to** ~ **sb out of sth** carotter qch à qn.

final ['faɪnl] **1** *adj (last)* dernier; *(conclusive)* définitif. *(Fin)* ~ **instalment** versement *m* libératoire; **the umpire's decision is** ~ la décision de l'arbitre est sans appel; **and that's** ~! un point c'est tout! **2** *n (Sport)* finale *f*. *(Univ)* **the** ~**s** les examens *mpl* de dernière année.
◆ **finale** [fɪ'nɑːlɪ] *n* finale *m*; *(fig)* **the grand** ~**e** l'apothéose *f*. ◆ **finalist** *n* finaliste *mf*. ◆ **finality** *n* irrévocabilité *f*; **with an air of** ~**ity** avec fermeté. ◆ **finalization** *n* dernière mise *f* au point; confirmation *f* définitive. ◆ **finalize** *vt text, report, arrangements, plans* mettre au point les derniers détails de; *preparations* mettre la dernière main à; *decision* confirmer de façon définitive; *date* fixer de façon définitive. ◆ **finally** *adv (lastly)* enfin, pour terminer; *(eventually)* enfin, finalement; *(once and for all)* définitivement.

finance [faɪ'næns] **1** *n* finance *f*. **Ministry of F**~ ministère *m* des Finances. **2** *vt (supply money for)* financer; *(obtain money for)* trouver des fonds pour. **3** *adj company, news, page* financier. ◆ **financial** *adj (gen)* financier; **financial year** exercice *m* financier. ◆ **financier** *n* financier *m*.

finch [fɪn(t)ʃ] *n* fringillidé *m (pinson, bouvreuil, grosbec, etc)*.

find [faɪnd] *pret, ptp* **found** **1** *vt* (**a**) *(gen)* trouver; *sth or sb lost* retrouver; *cure* découvrir. **he found himself in Paris** il s'est retrouvé à Paris; **I'll** ~ **my way about all right** je trouverai très bien mon chemin; **it found its way into my handbag** ça s'est retrouvé dans mon sac; **it found its way into his essay** ça s'est glissé dans sa dissertation; **we left everything as we found it** nous avons tout laissé tel quel; **to** ~ **that** trouver que, s'apercevoir que, constater que; **I** ~ **her very pleasant** je la trouve très agréable; **he** ~**s it difficult to...** il a du mal à...; **he** ~**s it impossible to leave** il ne peut se résoudre à partir; **he** ~**s it impossible to walk** il lui est impossible de marcher; **you won't** ~ **it easy** vous ne le trouverez pas facile; **to** ~ **some difficulty in doing** éprouver une certaine difficulté à faire; *(fig)* **to** ~ **one's feet** s'adapter; *(Jur)* **to** ~ **sb guilty** prononcer qn coupable; **the court found that...** le tribunal a conclu que... (**b**) *(supply)* fournir; *(obtain)* obtenir, trouver. **wages all found** *or (US)* **and found** salaire logé et nourri; **go and** ~ **me a needle** va me chercher une aiguille; **there are no more to be found** il n'en reste plus. **2** *vi (Jur)* se prononcer (*for* en faveur de; *against* contre). **3** *n* trouvaille *f*. ◆ **find out** **1** *vi:* **to** ~ **out about sth** *(enquire)* se renseigner sur qch; *(discover)* découvrir qch, apprendre qch. **2** *vt sep (gen)* découvrir (*that* que); *answer* trouver. **to** ~ **sb out** démasquer qn.
◆ **findings** *npl (in report)* conclusions *fpl*; *(sth found)* découvertes *fpl*.

fine[1] [faɪn] **1** *n* amende *f*, contravention *f (esp Aut)*. **I got a** ~ **for...** j'ai attrapé une contravention pour... **2** *vt* condamner à une amende, donner une contravention à. **to be** ~**d** recevoir une amende *or* une contravention (*£10* de 10 livres; *for sth* pour qch; *for doing* pour avoir fait).

fine[2] [faɪn] **1** *adj* (**a**) *(not coarse) (gen)* fin; *metal* pur; *workmanship, feelings, taste* délicat; *distinction* subtil. **not to put too** ~ **a point on it...** bref...; **he's got it down to a** ~ **art** il le fait à la perfection; ~ **art, the** ~ **arts** les beaux arts *mpl*. (**b**) *clothes, future, weather* beau *(f* belle*)*; *musician etc* excellent. **it's** ~ **for two** c'est très bien pour deux personnes; **(that's)** ~! très bien!; **it's** ~ **this afternoon** il fait beau cet après-midi; *(fig)* **one** ~ **day** un beau jour; **a** ~ **lady** une grande dame; *(excl)* ~! entendu!; *(iro)* **a** ~ **thing!** * c'est du beau!; *(iro)* **you're a** ~ **one to talk!** c'est bien à toi de le dire! **2** *adv* (**a**) *(excellently)* très bien. **you're doing** ~! tu te débrouilles bien!, ça va!; **I'm feeling** ~ je me sens très bien. (**b**) *(finely)* finement, fin; *cut, chop* menu. *(fig)* **you've cut it a bit** ~ vous avez calculé un peu juste.
◆ **fine down** **1** *vi (get thinner)* s'affiner. **2** *vt sep (reduce)* réduire; *(simplify)* simplifier.
◆ **finely** *adv written* admirablement; *dressed* magnifiquement; *adjust* délicatement; *chop* menu, fin. ◆ **fineness** *n* finesse *f*; pureté *f*; délicatesse *f*; subtilité *f*. ◆ **finery** *n* parure *f*; **in all her** ~**ry** dans ses plus beaux atours. ◆ **fine-tune** *vt production* régler avec précision. ◆ **fine-tuning** *n* réglage minutieux.

finesse [fɪ'nes] *n* finesse *f*; *(Cards)* impasse *f*.

finger ['fɪŋgəʳ] **1** *n* doigt *m*. **index** ~ index *m*; **little** ~ petit doigt; **middle** ~ médius *m*; **ring** ~ annulaire *m*; **between** ~ **and thumb** entre le pouce et l'index; *(fig)* **to put one's** ~ **on** mettre le doigt sur; **to keep one's** ~**s crossed** dire une petite prière *(fig)* (*for sb* pour qn); **his** ~**s are all thumbs** il est très maladroit de ses mains; **she can twist him round her little** ~ elle le mène par le bout du nez; **he has a** ~ **in the pie** il y est pour quelque chose; **he wouldn't lift a** ~ **to help me** il ne lèverait pas le petit doigt pour m'aider; **to pull one's** ~ **out** ⁑ faire un effort.
2 *vt* toucher; *(pej)* tripoter; *keyboard, keys* toucher; *(feel) money, silk* palper.
3 *adj*: ~ **board** touche *f (de violon etc)*; ~ **bowl** rince-doigts *m inv*; ~ **mark** trace *f* de doigt.
◆ **fingernail** *n* ongle *m (de la main)*. ◆ **fingerprint** **1** *n* empreinte *f* digitale ; **2** *vt object* relever les empreintes digitales sur; *person* prendre les empreintes digitales de ; **3** *adj*: ~**print expert** expert *m* en dactyloscopie. ◆ **fingerstall** *n* doigtier *m*. ◆ **fingertip** *n* bout *m* du doigt; **he has the whole matter at his** ~**tips** il connaît l'affaire sur le bout du doigt; **a machine with** ~**tip control** une machine d'un maniement (très) léger.

finicky ['fɪnɪkɪ] *adj person* difficile (*about sth* pour qch), pointilleux; *work, job* qui demande de la patience.

finish ['fɪnɪʃ] **1** *n* (**a**) *(end)* fin *f*; *(Sport)* arrivée *f*. *(fig)* **to be in at the** ~ assister au dénouement (d'une affaire); **to fight to the** ~ se battre jusqu'au bout. (**b**) *(appearance etc)* finitions *fpl*. **it's a solid car but the** ~ **is not good** la voiture est solide mais les finitions sont mal faites; **paint with a matt** ~ peinture *f* mate; **table with an oak** ~ table *(stained)* teintée *or (veneered)* plaquée chêne.
2 *vt (end) (gen)* finir (*doing* de faire); *work* finir, terminer, achever; *(use up) supplies, cake* finir, terminer. ~ **your soup** finis *or* mange ta soupe; **to put the** ~**ing touch to sth** mettre la dernière main à qch; **that last mile nearly** ~**ed me** * ces derniers quinze cents mètres ont failli m'achever.
3 *vi (gen)* finir; *[book, film, game, meeting]* finir, s'achever, se terminer; *[holiday, contract]* prendre fin. **the meeting was** ~**ing** la réunion tirait à sa fin; **he** ~**ed by saying that...** il a terminé en disant que...; *(Sport)* **to** ~ **first** arriver premier; *(Sport)* ~**ing line** ligne *f* d'arrivée. **I've** ~**ed with the paper**

je n'ai plus besoin du journal; **I've ~ed with politics** j'en ai fini avec la politique; **she's ~ed with him** elle a rompu avec lui.

◆ **finish off** **1** *vi* terminer, finir. **2** *vt sep work* terminer, achever; *food, meal* terminer, finir; *(kill)* achever. ◆ **finish up** **1** *vi*: **it ~ed up as...** ça a fini par être...; **he ~ed up in Rome** il s'est retrouvé à Rome. **2** *vt sep food, supplies* finir.

◆ **finished** *adj product* fini; *performance* accompli; *(done for)* fichu *; (*: tired)* à plat *.

finite ['faɪnaɪt] *adj* (**a**) fini, limité. **a ~ number** un nombre fini. (**b**) *(Gram) mood, verb* fini.

Finland ['fɪnlənd] *n* Finlande *f*. ◆ **Finn** *n* Finlandais(e) *m(f)*; *(Finnish speaker)* Finnois(e) *m(f)*. ◆ **Finnish** **1** *adj* finlandais; finnois ; **2** *n* finnois *m*.

fir [fɜːʳ] *n* sapin *m*. **~ cone** pomme *f* de pin.

fire ['faɪəʳ] **1** *n* (**a**) *(gen, also fig)* feu *m*; *(heater)* radiateur *m*; *(house-~ etc)* incendie *m*. **house on ~** maison *f* en feu *or* en flammes; **the chimney was on ~** il y avait un feu de cheminée; *(fig)* **he's playing with ~** il joue avec le feu; **forest ~** incendie de forêt; **to insure o.s. against ~** s'assurer contre l'incendie; **to set ~ to sth** mettre le feu à qch; **in front of a roaring ~** devant une belle flambée. (**b**) *(Mil)* feu *m*. **to open ~** ouvrir le feu, faire feu; **~!** feu!; **to come under ~** *(Mil)* essuyer le feu de l'ennemi; *(fig: be criticized)* être vivement critiqué.

2 *adj*: **~ alarm** avertisseur *m* d'incendie; **~ brigade,** *(US)* **~ department** (sapeurs-)pompiers *mpl*; **~ door** porte *f* anti-incendie; **~ drill** exercice *m* d'évacuation *(incendie)*; **~ engine** *(vehicle)* voiture *f* de pompiers; *(apparatus)* pompe *f* à incendie; **~ escape** *(staircase)* escalier *m* de secours; *(ladder)* échelle *f* d'incendie; **~ exit** sortie *f* de secours; **~ extinguisher** extincteur *m* (d'incendie); **~ hazard** *or* **risk** danger *m* d'incendie; **~ insurance** assurance-incendie *f*; **~ irons** garniture *f* de foyer; **~ prevention** mesures *fpl* de sécurité contre l'incendie; **~ regulations** consignes *fpl* en cas d'incendie; **~ sale** vente *f* de marchandises légèrement endommagées dans un incendie; **~ station** caserne *f* de pompiers; **it's a ~ trap** c'est une véritable souricière en cas d'incendie; **~ watcher** guetteur *m* des incendies.

3 *vt* (**a**) *(set ~ to)* mettre le feu à; *imagination etc* enflammer; *pottery* cuire. (**b**) *gun* décharger; *rocket, shot, salute* tirer (*at* sur). **to ~ a gun at sb** tirer (un coup de fusil) sur qn; **to ~ questions at sb** bombarder qn de questions. (**c**) *(*: dismiss)* renvoyer, flanquer à la porte *. **you're ~d!** vous êtes renvoyé!

4 *vi* (**a**) *(shoot)* tirer, faire feu (*at* sur); *[gun]* partir. *(fig)* **~ ahead! *, ~ away! *** vas-y, raconte! (**b**) *[engine]* tourner.

◆ **firearm** *n* arme *f* à feu. ◆ **fireball** *n (meteor)* bolide *m*; *(lightning, nuclear)* boule *f* de feu; *(fig)* personne *f* très dynamique. ◆ **firebrand** *n* brandon *m*; **he's a real ~ brand** *(energetic)* il pète le feu; *(troublesome)* c'est un brandon de discorde. ◆ **firebreak** *n* pare-feu *m inv*. ◆ **firebug** * *n* pyromane *mf*. ◆ **firecracker** *n* pétard *m*. ◆ **firedogs** *npl* chenets *mpl*. ◆ **fireguard** *n* garde-feu *m inv*. ◆ **firelight** *n*: **by ~light** à la lueur du feu. ◆ **firelighter** *n* allume-feu *m inv*. ◆ **fireman** *n* (sapeur) pompier *m*. ◆ **fireplace** *n* cheminée *f*, foyer *m*. ◆ **fireproof** *adj material, door* ignifugé; *dish* allant au feu. ◆ **fire-raiser** *n* pyromane *mf*. ◆ **fireside** *n*: **by the ~side** au coin *m* du feu; **~side chair** fauteuil *m* club. ◆ **firewood** *n* bois *m* de chauffage. ◆ **firework** *n* feu *m* d'artifice; **~works (display)** feu d'artifice. ◆ **firing** **1** *n [guns]* tir *m*; *(fight)* fusillade *f* ; **2** *adj*: **firing line** ligne *f* de tir; **firing squad** peloton *m* d'exécution.

firm¹ [fɜːm] *n (Comm)* compagnie *f*, firme *f*.

firm² [fɜːm] *adj (gen)* ferme; *faith, friendship* solide; *character, look* résolu. *(fig)* **I'm on ~ ground** je suis sûr de ce que j'avance; **as ~ as a rock** ferme comme le *or* un roc; **to be ~ with sb** être ferme avec qn; **to stand ~** tenir bon. ◆ **firm up** **1** *vi [plans]* s'affermir. **2** *vt sep* affermir. ◆ **firmly** *adv (gen)* fermement; *speak* avec fermeté. ◆ **firmness** *n* fermeté *f*; solidité *f*; résolution *f*.

first [fɜːst] **1** *adj* premier. **the ~ of May** le Premier Mai; **the twenty-~ time** la vingt et unième fois; **Charles the F~** Charles Premier, Charles Iᵉʳ; **in the ~ place** d'abord, en premier lieu; **~ thing in the morning** dès le matin; *(on waking)* dès le réveil; **~ thing tomorrow** dès demain matin; **~ things first!** les choses importantes d'abord!; **to give ~ aid** donner les premiers soins; *(fig)* **he didn't even get to ~ base *** il n'a même pas franchi le premier obstacle; **~ cousin** cousin(e) *m(f)* germain(e); **~ edition** première édition *f*, *(valuable)* édition originale; **on the ~ floor** *(Brit)* au premier (étage); *(US)* au rez-de-chaussée; *(Scol)* **~ form** ≃ sixième *f*; *(US)* **~ grade** cours *m* préparatoire; *(US)* **F~ Lady** présidente *f* des États-Unis; **~ name** prénom *m*; *(Theat etc)* **~ night** première *f*; *(Jur)* **~ offender** délinquant *m* primaire; **~ performance** *(Cine, Theat)* première *f*; *(Mus)* première audition.

2 *adv* (**a**) *(gen)* d'abord; *(at first)* au début. **~ A then B** d'abord A ensuite B, premièrement A deuxièmement B; **~ of all** tout d'abord; **~ and foremost** en tout premier lieu; **~ come ~ served** les premiers arrivés seront les premiers servis; **ladies ~!** les dames d'abord!; **I would resign ~!** je préférerais démissionner; **he arrived ~** il est arrivé le premier; **he came ~ in the exam** il a été reçu premier à l'examen; **my family comes ~** ma famille passe avant tout; **he says ~ one thing and then another** il dit tantôt ceci, tantôt cela; **~ and last** avant tout; **I must finish this ~** il faut que je termine *(subj)* ceci d'abord. (**b**) *(for the ~ time)* pour la première fois. **when did you ~ meet him?** quand est-ce que vous l'avez rencontré pour la première fois? (**c**) *(in preference)* plutôt. **I'd die ~!** plutôt mourir!

3 *n* (**a**) premier *m*, -ière *f*. **they were the ~ to come** ils sont arrivés les premiers. (**b**) **at ~** d'abord, au commencement, au début; **from ~ to last** du début jusqu'à la fin; **from the ~** dès le début. (**c**) (*~ gear*) première *f* (vitesse). **in ~** en première.

◆ **first-aid** *adj*: **~-aid classes** cours *mpl* de secourisme; **~-aid kit** trousse *f* de pharmacie; **~-aid post** poste *m* de secours. ◆ **first-class** **1** *adj (Rail etc)* de première (classe); *(excellent)* excellent, de première classe; **~-class mail** courrier *m* tarif normal; **~-class honours degree** ≃ licence *f* avec mention très bien ; **2** *adv travel* en première (classe). ◆ **first-day** *adj (Post)* **~-day cover** émission *f* du premier jour. ◆ **first-generation** *adj*: **he's a ~-generation American** il n'est américain que depuis une génération. ◆ **first-hand** *adj, adv* de première main. ◆ **firstly** *adv* premièrement. ◆ **first-named** *n* premier *m*, -ière *f*. ◆ **first-rate** *adj* excellent, formidable *.

fiscal ['fɪsk(ə)l] *adj* fiscal. **~ year** exercice *m*.

fish [fɪʃ] **1** *n, pl* **~** *or* **~es** poisson *m*. **~ and chips** du poisson frit avec des frites; *(fig)* **I've got other ~ to fry** j'ai d'autres chats à fouetter; *(fig)* **it's neither ~ nor fowl nor good red herring** ce n'est ni chair ni poisson; **he's like a ~ out of water** il est complètement dépaysé; **he's a queer ~! *** c'est un drôle de numéro! * **2** *adj*: **~ farm** centre *m* de pisciculture; **~ knife** couteau *m* à poisson; **~ paste** pâte *f* d'anchois (*or* de homard *etc*); **~ shop** poissonnerie *f*; **~ slice** pelle *f* à poisson; **~ tank** aquarium *m*. **3** *vi* pêcher. **to go ~ing** aller à la pêche; **to go salmon ~ing** aller à la pêche au saumon; **to ~ for trout** pêcher la truite; **to ~ for** *compliments* chercher; *information* tâcher d'obtenir.

4 *vt trout, salmon* pêcher; *river, pool* pêcher dans. **they ~ed a cat out of the well** ils ont repêché un chat du puits; **he ~ed a handkerchief out of his pocket** il a extirpé un mouchoir de sa poche.
◆ **fish out, fish up** *vt sep (from water)* repêcher; *(from box, drawer etc)* sortir, extirper (*from* de). ◆ **fish-and-chip shop** *n* débit *m* de fritures. ◆ **fishbone** *n* arête *f* (de poisson). ◆ **fishbowl** *n* bocal *m* à poissons. ◆ **fishcake** *n* croquette *f* de poisson. ◆ **fisherman** *n* pêcheur *m*; **he's a keen ~erman** il aime beaucoup la pêche. ◆ **fishery** *n* pêcherie *f*. ◆ **fish-fingers** *npl* (*US:* **fish-sticks**) bâtonnets *mpl* de poisson. ◆ **fish-hook** *n* hameçon *m*. ◆ **fishing 1** *n* pêche *f* ; **2** *adj*: **~ing boat** bateau *m* de pêche; **~ing fleet** flottille *f* de pêche; **~ing grounds** pêches *fpl*; **~ing line** ligne *f* de pêche; **~ing net** *(on ~ing boat)* filet *m* (de pêche); *[angler]* épuisette *f*; **~ing port** port *m* de pêche; **~ing rod** canne *f* à pêche; **~ing tackle** attirail *m* de pêche. ◆ **fishmonger** *n* poissonnier *m*, -ière *f*. ◆ **fishpond** *n* étang *m* à poissons. ◆ **fish-sticks = fish-fingers.** ◆ **fish-tail** *vi (US Aut)* chasser. ◆ **fishwife** *n*: **she talks like a ~wife** elle a un langage de poissarde. ◆ **fishy** *adj smell* de poisson ; *(*: suspect)* suspect, louche.

fission ['fɪʃ(ə)n] *n* fission *f*.

fissure ['fɪʃəʳ] *n* fissure *f*.

fist [fɪst] *n* poing *m*. **he shook his ~ at me** il m'a menacé du poing. ◆ **fistful** *n* poignée *f*. ◆ **fisticuffs** *npl* coups *mpl* de poing.

fit[1] [fɪt] **1** *adj* (**a**) *(suitable, suited) person* capable (*for* de); *time, occasion* propice; *(worthy)* digne (*for* de); *(right and proper)* convenable, correct. **~ to eat** *(palatable)* mangeable; *(not poisonous)* comestible; *(qualified etc)* **to be ~ for a job** avoir la compétence nécessaire pour faire un travail; *(after illness)* **~ for duty** en état de reprendre le travail; **he's not ~ to drive** il n'est pas capable de *or* pas en état de conduire; **I'm not ~ to be seen** je ne suis pas présentable; **~ to wear** mettable; **~ for habitation** habitable; **to see** *or* **think ~ to do** trouver *or* juger bon de faire; **as I think ~** comme bon me semblera; **he's not ~ company for my son** ce n'est pas une compagnie pour mon fils; **she goes on until she's ~ to drop** * elle continue jusqu'à ce qu'elle tombe *(subj)* de fatigue. (**b**) *(in health)* en bonne santé, en pleine forme. **to be as ~ as a fiddle** se porter comme un charme.
2 *n*: **your dress is a very good ~** votre robe est tout à fait à votre taille; **it's rather a tight ~** c'est un peu juste.
3 *vt* (**a**) *[clothes etc]* aller à. **this coat ~s you well** ce manteau est bien à votre taille; **the key doesn't ~ the lock** la clef ne va pas pour la serrure; **it ~s me like a glove** cela me va comme un gant. (**b**) *(match) description* répondre à. **it doesn't ~ the facts** cela ne concorde pas avec les faits; **the punishment should ~ the crime** la punition doit être proportionnée à l'offense. (**c**) *(gen)* mettre; *(fix)* fixer (*on sth* sur qch); *(install)* poser; *garment* ajuster (*on sb* sur qn). **to ~ a key in the lock** engager une clef dans la serrure; **to ~ 2 things together** ajuster 2 objets; **to have a new window ~ted** faire poser une nouvelle fenêtre; **car ~ted with a radio** voiture équipée d'une radio; **he has been ~ted with a new hearing aid** on lui a mis un nouvel appareil auditif. (**d**) *(make ~)* préparer (*sb for sth* qn à qch; *sb to do* qn à faire).
4 *vi [clothes]* aller, être bien ajusté; *[key, machine, part]* entrer, aller; *[facts etc]* cadrer, correspondre (*with sth* avec qch). **if the description ~s, he must be the thief** si la description est la bonne, ce doit être lui le voleur; **it all ~s now!** tout s'éclaire!
◆ **fit in 1** *vi* (**a**) *[fact]* s'accorder (*with* avec). (**b**) *[remark]* être en harmonie (*with* avec). **he left the firm because he didn't ~ in** il a quitté la compagnie parce qu'il n'arrivait pas à s'intégrer. **2** *vt sep object* faire entrer; *(fig) appointment, visitor* prendre, caser *; *plans* adapter (*with* à), faire concorder (*with* avec). ◆ **fit on** *vt sep* fixer, poser. ◆ **fit out** *vt sep (gen)* équiper; *ship* armer. ◆ **fit up** *vt sep* pourvoir (*with* de).
◆ **fitment** *n* (**a**) *(built-in furniture)* meuble *m* encastré; *[kitchen]* élément *m* (de cuisine); **the table is a ~ment** la table est encastrée; (**b**) *(for vacuum cleaner, mixer etc)* accessoire *m*; **the light ~ment** l'appareil *m* d'éclairage. ◆ **fitness** *n* (**a**) *(health)* santé *f or* forme *f* (physique); (**b**) *(suitability) [remark]* à-propos *m*; *[person]* aptitudes *fpl* (*for* pour). ◆ **fitted** *adj garment* ajusté; **~ted carpet** moquette *f*; **~ted kitchen** cuisine *f* équipée; **~ted sheet** drap-housse *m*; **to be ~ted to (do) sth** être apte à (faire) qch. ◆ **fitter** *n (Dress)* essayeur *m*, -euse *f*; *(Tech)* monteur *m*; *[carpet etc]* poseur *m*.
◆ **fitting 1** *adj* approprié (*to* à); **~ting room** cabine *f* d'essayage ; **2** *n (Dress)* essayage *m*; *(in house etc)* **~tings** installations *fpl*; **furniture and ~tings** mobilier *m* et installations. ◆ **fittingly** *adv dress* de façon appropriée; *say* avec à-propos; *happen* à propos.

fit[2] [fɪt] *n* (**a**) *(Med)* accès *m*, attaque *f*. **~ of coughing** quinte *f* de toux. (**b**) *(outburst: of anger etc)* mouvement *m*, accès *m*. **~ of crying** crise *f* de larmes; **to have** *or* **throw * a ~** avoir *or* piquer * une crise; **to be in ~s (of laughter), to get a ~ of the giggles** avoir le fou rire; **~s of enthusiasm** des accès d'enthousiasme; **in ~s and starts** par à-coups. ◆ **fitful** *adj showers* intermittent; *sleep* agité. ◆ **fitfully** *adv move, work* par à-coups; *sleep* de façon intermittente.

five [faɪv] *adj, n, pron* cinq *(m)inv*; *for phrases V* **six.**
◆ **five-and-ten-cent store** *n* bazar *m*. ◆ **fivefold 1** *adj* quintuple ; **2** *adv* au quintuple. ◆ **fiver** * *n* billet *m* de cinq livres *or (US)* de cinq dollars. ◆ **five-star** *adj*: **~-star restaurant** ≃ restaurant *m* (à) trois étoiles. ◆ **five-year** *adj*: **~-year plan** plan *m* quinquennal.

fix [fɪks] **1** *vt* (**a**) *(with nails etc)* fixer; *(with ropes etc)* attacher; *(drive in)* enfoncer; *attention* fixer (*on* sur); *hopes* mettre (*on sth* en qch); *blame* mettre (*on sb* sur le dos de qn; *on sth* sur qch); *(Phot)* fixer. **to ~ one's eyes on** fixer du regard; **to ~ sth in one's mind** graver qch dans son esprit. (**b**) *(arrange, decide) details, plans* décider; *time, price, limit* fixer. **on the date ~ed** à la date convenue. (**c**) *(deal with)* arranger; *(mend)* réparer. **I'll ~ it all** je vais tout arranger; **he ~ed it with the police before...** il s'est arrangé avec la police avant de...; **I'll soon ~ him** * je vais lui régler son compte; **to ~ one's hair** * se passer un coup de peigne; **can I ~ you a drink?** puis-je vous offrir un verre?; **I'll go and ~ us sth to eat** je vais vite nous faire qch à manger. (**d**) *(*: bribe etc) person* acheter; *match, election, trial* truquer.
2 *n* (**a**) (*) ennui *m*, embêtement * *m*. **to be in a ~** être dans le pétrin; **what a ~!** nous voilà dans le pétrin! (**b**) *(Drugs sl)* piqûre *f*. (**c**) *(Aviat, Naut)* position *f*. **to take a ~ on** déterminer la position de. (**d**) *(US: trick)* **it's a ~** * c'est une combine.
◆ **fix on 1** *vt fus* choisir. **2** *vt sep lid* fixer, attacher.
◆ **fix up 1** *vi* s'arranger (*to do* pour faire). **2** *vt sep* arranger. **let's ~ it all up now** décidons tout de suite des détails; **to ~ sb up with sth** obtenir qch pour qn; **we ~ed them up for one night** nous leur avons trouvé à coucher pour une nuit.
◆ **fixation** *n (fig)* obsession *f*; **to have a ~ation about** être obsédé par. ◆ **fixative** *n* fixatif *m*.
◆ **fixed** *adj (gen)* fixe; *smile* figé; *determination* inébranlable; **of no ~ed abode** sans domicile fixe, **~ed menu** menu *m* à prix fixe; **~ed term contract** contrat *m* à durée déterminée; **how are we ~ed for time?** * on a combien de temps?; **how are you ~ed for tonight?** qu'est-ce que vous faites ce soir?
◆ **fixedly** *adv* fixement. ◆ **fixture** *n* (**a**) *(in building*

etc) ~**tures** installations *fpl*; **sold with ~tures and fittings** vendu avec toutes les installations; *(fig)* **she's a ~ture** * elle fait partie du mobilier *; (**b**) *(Sport)* match *m* (prévu); ~**ture list** calendrier *m*.

fizz [fɪz] *vi [champagne etc]* pétiller; *[steam etc]* siffler. ◆ **fizz up** *vi* mousser. ◆ **fizzy** *adj soft drink* gazeux; *wine* mousseux.

fizzle ['fɪzl] *vi* pétiller. ◆ **fizzle out** *vi [firework]* rater; *[event, enterprise, plan]* ne rien donner; *[book]* se terminer en queue de poisson; *[enthusiasm, interest]* tomber.

flabbergast * ['flæbəgɑ:st] *vt* sidérer *.

flabby ['flæbɪ] *adj* flasque.

flag¹ [flæg] **1** *n* drapeau *m*; *(Naut)* pavillon *m*; *(for charity)* insigne *m (d'une œuvre charitable)*. ~ **of convenience** pavillon de complaisance; *(fig)* **to go down with ~s flying** mener la lutte jusqu'au bout; *(fig)* **to keep the ~ flying** maintenir les traditions. **2** *vt* pavoiser; *(~* **down***)* faire signe (de s'arrêter) à. **3** *adj*: ~ **day** journée *f* de vente d'insignes (*in aid of* pour). ◆ **flagpole** *or* ◆ **flagstaff** *n* mât *m*. ◆ **flagship** *n (Naut)* vaisseau *m* amiral; *(Comm)* produit *m* vedette.

flag² [flæg] *vi [plants etc]* dépérir; *[athlete, walker, health]* s'affaiblir; *[worker, zeal, courage etc]* se relâcher; *[conversation]* languir; *[interest]* faiblir; *[enthusiasm]* tomber.

flag³ [flæg] *n (~* **stone***)* dalle *f*.

flagon ['flægən] *n* grande bouteille *f*.

flagrant ['fleɪgr(ə)nt] *adj* flagrant.

flair [flɛəʳ] *n* flair *m*. **to have a ~ for** avoir du flair pour.

flak * [flæk] *n (criticism)* critiques *fpl* (désobligeantes). ◆ **flak-jacket** *n* gilet *m* pare-balles.

flake [fleɪk] **1** *n [snow, cereal etc]* flocon *m*; *[metal etc]* paillette *f*. **2** *vi (~* **off***) [stone, plaster etc]* s'effriter; *[paint]* s'écailler; *[skin]* peler. **3** *vt (~* **off***)* écailler. ◆ **flake out** ‡ *vi (faint)* tourner de l'œil *; *(fall asleep)* s'endormir tout d'une masse.

flamboyant [flæm'bɔɪənt] *adj* flamboyant *(also Archit)*; *person* haut en couleur.

flame [fleɪm] **1** *n* flamme *f*. **in ~s** en flammes, en feu; **to go up in ~s** s'enflammer brusquement. **2** *vi [fire]* flamber; *[passion]* brûler. **her cheeks ~d** ses joues se sont empourprées. ◆ **flame up** *vi [fire]* flamber; *[anger, angry person]* exploser. ◆ **flamethrower** *n* lance-flammes *m inv*. ◆ **flaming** *adj* ardent; *(*: furious)* furibard *; *(‡: annoying)* fichu * *(before n)*.

flamingo, *pl* ~**s** *or* ~**es** [flə'mɪŋgəʊ] flamant *m* (rose).

flammable ['flæməbl] *adj* inflammable.

flan [flæn] *n* tarte *f*.

Flanders ['flɑ:ndəz] *n* Flandre(s) *f(pl)*.

flank [flæŋk] **1** *n (gen)* flanc *m*; *(Culin)* flanchet *m*. **2** *vt* flanquer. ~**ed by 2 policemen** flanqué de 2 gendarmes.

flannel ['flænl] *n* flanelle *f*; *(face ~)* gant *m* de toilette. ◆ **flannelette** *n* pilou *m*.

flap [flæp] **1** *n [pocket, envelope]* rabat *m*; *[counter]* abattant *m*; *(*: panic)* panique *f*. **to be in a ~** être dans tous ses états. **2** *vi [wings, shutters]* battre; *[sails, garment]* claquer; *(*: be panicky)* paniquer *. **3** *vt*: **to ~ its wings** battre des ailes.

flare [flɛəʳ] **1** *n* feu *m*, signal *m* (lumineux); *(Mil)* fusée *f* éclairante; *(Aviat: for target)* bombe *f* éclairante; *(for runway)* balise *f*. **2** *adj (Aviat)* ~ **path** piste *f* balisée. **3** *vi [match]* s'enflammer; *[candle]* briller; *[sunspot]* brûler. ◆ **flare up** *vi [fire]* s'embraser; *[person, political situation]* exploser; *[anger, fighting]* éclater. ◆ **flared** *adj skirt* évasé. ◆ **flare-up** *n [fire]* flambée *f* (soudaine); *[war, quarrel, fighting]* intensification *f* soudaine; *(outburst of rage)* crise *f* de colère; *(sudden dispute)* altercation *f*.

flash [flæʃ] **1** *n* (**a**) *[flame, jewels]* éclat *m*. ~ **of lightning** éclair *m*; **in a ~** en un clin d'œil, tout d'un coup; **a ~ in the pan** un feu de paille *(fig)*; ~ **of inspiration** éclair de génie. (**b**) *(news ~)* flash *m* (d'information). (**c**) *(Phot)* flash *m*. **2** *vi [jewels]* étinceler; *[light]* clignoter; *[eyes]* lancer des éclairs. *[person, vehicle]* **to ~ past** *etc* passer *etc* comme un éclair; **the thought ~ed through his mind that...** un instant, il a pensé que... **3** *vt* (**a**) *light* projeter; *torch* diriger (*on* sur). **she ~ed him a look of contempt** elle lui a jeté un regard de mépris; *(Aut)* **to ~ one's headlights** *or (US)* **the high beams** faire un appel de phares (*at sb* à qn). (**b**) *(flaunt)* étaler. **don't ~ all that money around** n'étale pas tout cet argent comme ça. **4** *adj*: ~ **bulb** ampoule *f* de flash; ~ **card** carte *f (support visuel)*; ~ **cube** cube-flash *m*; ~ **gun** flash *m*; ~ **point** *(Chem)* point *m* d'ignition; *(fig)* point critique. ◆ **flashback** *n (Cine)* flashback *m inv*. ◆ **flasher** *n (device)* clignotant *m*. ◆ **flashing** *adj*: ~**ing light** *(or* **indicator** *etc)* clignotant *m*. ◆ **flashlight** *n (Phot)* flash *m*; *(torch)* lampe *f* de poche. ◆ **flashy** *adj person, taste* tapageur; *jewellery, car, colour* tape-à-l'œil *inv*.

flask [flɑ:sk] *n (Pharm)* fiole *f*; *(bottle)* bouteille *f*; *(for pocket)* flasque *f*; *(vacuum ~)* bouteille *f* Thermos ®.

flat¹ [flæt] **1** *adj* (**a**) *(gen)* plat; *tyre* à plat; *(Sport) race* de plat. **as ~ as a pancake** * *tyre* plat comme une galette; *surface, countryside* tout plat; **a ~ dish** un plat creux; ~ **nose** nez épaté; **to have ~ feet** avoir les pieds plats; **he was lying ~ on the floor** il était étendu à plat par terre ; **lay the book ~** pose le livre à plat; ~ **fish** poisson plat; ~ **racing,** ~ **season** plat *m*; **in a ~ spin** * dans tous ses états. (**b**) *taste, style* monotone, plat; *joke, story* qui tombe à plat; *experience* plutôt décevant; *battery* à plat; *beer etc* éventé; *(not shiny) colour* mat. **I was feeling rather ~** je me sentais sans ressort. (**c**) *(Mus) voice* faux. **B ~** si *m* bémol. (**d**) *refusal, denial* net, catégorique. **and that's ~!** * un point c'est tout! * (**e**) *(fixed)* fixe. ~ **rate of pay** salaire *m* fixe; ~ **rate** taux *m* fixe.

2 *adv say, tell, refuse* carrément; *sing* faux. ~ **broke** ‡ fauché (comme les blés) *; **in 10 seconds ~** en 10 secondes pile *; **to go ~ out** *[runner]* donner son maximum; *[person running in street]* courir comme un dératé *; *[car]* rouler à sa vitesse de pointe; **to be working ~ out** travailler d'arrache-pied; **to be ~ out** *(lying)* être étendu de tout son long; *(*: exhausted)* être à plat *; *(*: asleep)* dormir; *(‡: drunk)* être rétamé ‡.

3 *n [hand, blade]* plat *m*; *(Mus)* bémol *m*; *(US Aut)* pneu *m* crevé.

◆ **flat-bottomed** *adj* à fond plat. ◆ **flat-chested** *adj* qui n'a pas de poitrine. ◆ **flatfooted** *adj* aux pieds plats. ◆ **flatiron** *n* fer *m* à repasser. ◆ **flatly** *adv deny, refuse* catégoriquement; *say* tout net. ◆ **flatness** *n* égalité *f*, aspect *m* plat; *(dullness)* monotonie *f*. ◆ **flatten** *vt path, road* aplanir; *metal* aplatir; *town, building* raser; *[wind, storm etc] crops* coucher; **to ~ten o.s. against** s'aplatir contre. ◆ **flatten out 1** *vi [countryside, road]* s'aplanir; *[aircraft]* se redresser ; **2** *vt sep path* aplanir; *metal* aplatir; *map etc* ouvrir à plat.

flat² [flæt] *n (Brit)* appartement *m*. ◆ **flat-hunting**: **to go ~-hunting** chercher un appartement. ◆ **flatlet** *n* studio *m*. ◆ **flatmate** *n*: **my ~mate** la fille (*or* le garçon *etc*) avec qui je partage mon appartement.

flatter ['flætəʳ] *vt* flatter. ◆ **flatterer** *n* flatteur *m*, -euse *f*. ◆ **flattering** *adj person, remark* flatteur; *clothes, photograph* qui avantage. ◆ **flatteringly** *adv* flatteusement. ◆ **flattery** *n* flatterie *f*.

flatulence ['flætjʊləns] *n* flatulence *f*.

flaunt [flɔ:nt] *vt* étaler, afficher.

flautist ['flɔːtɪst] *n* flûtiste *mf.*

flavour, *(US)* **flavor** ['fleɪvəʳ] **1** *n* goût *m*, saveur *f; [ice cream]* parfum *m*. **the ~ of Paris in the twenties** l'atmosphère *f* du Paris des années vingt. **2** *vt* donner du goût à; *(with fruit, spirits)* parfumer (*with* à). **pineapple-~ed** (parfumé) à l'ananas. ◆ **flavo(u)ring** *n (in sauce etc)* assaisonnement *m*; *(in cake etc)* parfum *m*; **vanilla ~ing** essence *f* de vanille.

flaw [flɔː] *n (gen)* défaut *m*; *(in contract, procedure etc)* vice *m* de forme; *(in arrangements, plans)* inconvénient *m*. ◆ **flawed** *adj* imparfait. ◆ **flawless** *adj* parfait.

flax [flæks] *n* lin *m*. ◆ **flaxen-haired** *adj* aux cheveux de lin.

flay [fleɪ] *vt (skin)* écorcher; *(beat)* rosser; *(criticize)* éreinter.

flea [fliː] *n* puce *f*. **~ market** marché *m* aux puces; **to send sb off with a ~ in his ear** * envoyer promener * qn. ◆ **fleabite** *n* piqûre *f* de puce; *(fig)* vétille *f*. ◆ **fleabitten** *adj (lit)* infesté de puces; *(fig)* miteux. ◆ **flea collar** *n* collier *m* antipuces. ◆ **flea-pit** ⁑ *n* ciné * *m* miteux.

fleck [flek] **1** *n [colour]* moucheture *f*; *[sunlight]* petite tache *f*; *[dust]* particule *f*. **2** *vt*: **blue ~ed with white** bleu moucheté de blanc; **hair ~ed with grey** cheveux *mpl* poivre et sel.

fled [fled] *pret, ptp of* **flee.**

fledged [fledʒd] *adj (fig)* **fully-~** *doctor, architect* diplômé; **a fully-~ British citizen** un citoyen britannique à part entière. ◆ **fledg(e)ling** *n* oiselet *m*.

flee [fliː] *pret, ptp* **fled** **1** *vi* fuir (*before* devant), s'enfuir (*from* de), se réfugier (*to* auprès de). **they fled** ils se sont enfuis, ils se sont sauvés. **2** *vt town, country* s'enfuir de; *temptation, danger* fuir.

fleece [fliːs] **1** *n* toison *f*. **2** *vt (rob)* voler; *(overcharge)* estamper *. ◆ **fleece-lined** *adj* doublé de mouton. ◆ **fleecy** *adj clouds* floconneux; *blanket* laineux.

fleet¹ [fliːt] *n* flotte *f*. *(fig)* **a ~ of vehicles** un parc automobile; *(Brit)* **F~ Air Arm** aéronavale *f*.

fleet² [fliːt] *adj* (**~-footed**) au pied léger.

fleeting ['fliːtɪŋ] *adj time, memory* fugitif; *beauty, pleasure* éphémère; *moment, visit* bref.

Fleming ['flemɪŋ] *n* Flamand(e) *m(f)*. ◆ **Flemish** **1** *adj* flamand ; **2** *n (Ling)* flamand *m*; **the Flemish** les Flamands *mpl*.

flesh [fleʃ] *n* chair *f*. **~ wound** blessure *f* superficielle; **to make sb's ~ creep** donner la chair de poule à qn; **I'm only ~ and blood** je ne suis qu'un homme (*or* une femme) comme les autres; **my own ~ and blood** les miens *mpl*; **it is more than ~ and blood can stand** c'est plus que la nature humaine ne peut endurer; **in the ~** en chair et en os; **to demand one's pound of ~** exiger son dû. ◆ **fleshy** *adj* charnu.

flew [fluː] *pret of* **fly².**

flex [fleks] **1** *vt body, knees* fléchir; *muscle* faire jouer. **2** *n [lamp, iron]* fil *m*; *[telephone]* cordon *m*. ◆ **flexible** *adj* flexible; **I'm ~ible** je peux toujours m'arranger; **~ible working hours** horaire *m* mobile. ◆ **flexibility** *n* flexibilité *f*. ◆ **flex(i)time** *n* horaire *m* mobile.

flick [flɪk] **1** *n* (**a**) *(with tail, duster)* petit coup; *(with finger)* chiquenaude *f*; *(with wrist)* petit mouvement (rapide). **at the ~ of a switch** rien qu'en appuyant sur un bouton. (**b**) **the ~s** ⁑ le ciné *. **2** *adj*: **~ knife** couteau *m* à cran d'arrêt. **3** *vt* donner un petit coup à. ◆ **flick off** *vt sep dust, ash* enlever d'une chiquenaude. ◆ **flick through** *vt fus book* feuilleter.

flicker ['flɪkəʳ] **1** *vi [flames, light]* danser; *(before going out)* vaciller; *[needle on dial]* osciller; *[eyelids]* battre. **2** *n* danse *f*; vacillement *m*. **in the ~ of an eyelid** en un clin d'œil; **without a ~** sans sourciller; **a ~ of hope** une lueur d'espoir. ◆ **flickering** *adj* dansant; vacillant; battant.

flier ['flaɪəʳ] *n* aviateur *m*, -trice *f*.

flight¹ [flaɪt] **1** *n (gen)* vol *m*; *[ball]* trajectoire *f*. **in ~** en plein vol; **~ number 776 from/to Madrid** le vol numéro 776 en provenance/à destination de Madrid; **did you have a good ~?** vous avez fait bon voyage?; **a ~ of fancy** une envolée de l'imagination; **in the top ~ of scientists** parmi les scientifiques les plus marquants; **a top-~ firm** une compagnie de pointe; **~ of stairs** escalier *m*; **to climb 3 ~s** monter 3 étages; **he lives three ~s up** il habite au troisième. **2** *adj*: **~ attendant** steward *m*/hôtesse *f* de l'air; **~ bag** sac *m* avion; *(Aviat)* **~deck** poste *m* de pilotage; **~ path** trajectoire *f* (de vol); **~ recorder** enregistreur *m* de vol.

flight² [flaɪt] *n(act of fleeing)* fuite *f*. **to put to ~** mettre en fuite; **to take (to) ~** prendre la fuite.

flighty [flaɪtɪ] *adj* frivole.

flimsy [flɪmzɪ] **1** *adj* **dress** trop léger; **cloth, paper** mince; **house** peu solide; **excuse, reasoning** pauvre. **2** *n* papier *m* pelure *inv*. ◆ **flimsily** *adv*: **flimsily built** peu solide.

flinch [flɪn(t)ʃ] *vi* tressaillir. **to ~ from sth** reculer devant qch; **without ~ing** sans broncher.

fling [flɪŋ] *(vb: pret, ptp* **flung***)* **1** *n (throw)* lancer *m*. *(fig)* **to have one's ~** se payer du bon temps; **to go on a ~** aller faire la foire * *(in shops)* faire des folies; *(attempt)* **to have a ~ at doing** essayer de faire. **2** *vt stone etc* jeter, lancer (*at sb* à qn; *at sth* sur *or* contre qch); *remark, accusation* lancer (*at sb* à qn). **to ~ sb into jail** jeter qn en prison; **to ~ the window open** ouvrir toute grande la fenêtre; **to ~ one's arms round sb's neck** se jeter au cou de qn; **to ~ on/off one's coat** enfiler/enlever son manteau d'un geste brusque; **to ~ o.s. into a job** se lancer à corps perdu dans un travail. **3** *vi*: **to ~ off/out** *etc* partir/sortir *etc* brusquement. ◆ **fling away** *vt sep (throw out)* jeter; *(waste)* gaspiller. ◆ **fling out** *vt sep person* mettre à la porte; *unwanted object* jeter. ◆ **fling up** *vt sep* jeter en l'air. **to ~ one's arms up** lever les bras au ciel; **he flung up his head** il a brusquement relevé la tête.

flint [flɪnt] *n (gen)* silex *m*; *(for spark, lighter)* pierre *f* (à briquet).

flip [flɪp] **1** *adj*: **the ~ side of a record** l'autre face *f* d'un disque. **2** *vt* donner une chiquenaude à. **he ~ped the letter over to me** il m'a passé la lettre d'une chiquenaude. ◆ **flip off** *vt sep* faire tomber. ◆ **flip through** *vt fus book* feuilleter. ◆ **flipboard** *n* chevalet *m (tableau à feuilles mobiles)*. ◆ **flip-flops** *npl (sandals)* tongs *fpl* ®.

flippant ['flɪpənt] *adj* désinvolte, irrévérencieux. ◆ **flippancy** *n* désinvolture *f*, irrévérence *f*. ◆ **flippantly** *adv* avec désinvolture.

flipper ['flɪpəʳ] *n [seal etc]* nageoire *f*. *[swimmer]* **~s** palmes *fpl*.

flipping * ['flɪpɪŋ] *adj* fichu * *(before n)*.

flirt [flɜːt] **1** *vi* flirter (*with* avec). **to ~ with an idea** caresser une idée. **2** *n*: **he's a great ~** il est très flirteur. ◆ **flirtation** *n* flirt *m*. ◆ **flirtatious** *adj* flirteur.

flit [flɪt] **1** *vi [bats, butterflies etc]* voltiger. **the idea ~ted through his head** l'idée lui a traversé l'esprit; **she ~ted in and out** elle n'a fait qu'entrer et sortir. **2** *n*: **to do a moonlight ~** déménager à la cloche de bois.

float [fləʊt] **1** *n (Fishing, Plumbing)* flotteur *m*; *(cork)* bouchon *m*; *[seaplane etc]* flotteur; *(vehicle in a parade)* char *m*. **2** *vi (gen)* flotter; *[ship]* être à flot; *[bather]* faire la planche; *[vision etc]* planer. **to ~ down the river** descendre la rivière. **3** *vt boat* faire flotter; *(refloat)* remettre à flot; *(fig) idea* lancer;

currency laisser flotter; *company* fonder; *share issue* émettre; *loan* lancer.

◆**float away** *vi* partir à la dérive. ◆**float off** **1** *vi [wreck etc]* se déséchouer. **2** *vt sep* déséchouer. ◆**floating** *adj dock, rib, vote, currency* flottant; *population* instable; *assets* circulant; ~**ing voter** électeur *m*, -trice *f* indécis(e).

flock [flɒk] **1** *n [animals, geese]* troupeau *m*; *[birds]* vol *m*; *[people]* foule *f*; *(Rel)* ouailles *fpl*. **2** *vi* affluer. **to** ~ **in/out** *etc* entrer/sortir *etc* en foule; **to** ~ **round sb** s'attrouper autour de qn.

floe [fləʊ] *n* banquise *f*.

flog [flɒg] *vt* (**a**) flageller. **to** ~ **an idea to death** * rabâcher une idée; *(fig)* **to** ~ **a dead horse** perdre sa peine et son temps. (**b**) *(‡: sell)* vendre. ◆**flogging** *n* flagellation *f*; *(Jur)* fouet *m (sanction)*.

flood [flʌd] **1** *n* inondation *f*; *[river]* crue *f*; *[light]* torrent *m*; *[tears, letters]* déluge *m*; *(Bible)* déluge. ~ **damage** dégâts *mpl* des eaux; ~ **tide** marée *f* haute. **2** *vt (gen, fig)* inonder (*with* de); *carburettor* noyer. **to** ~ **the market** inonder le marché (*with* de). **3** *vi [river]* déborder; *[people]* affluer. **the crowd** ~**ed into the streets** la foule a envahi les rues.

◆**flood in** *vi [sunshine]* entrer à flots; *[people]* entrer en foule. ◆**flood out** *vt sep house* inonder. **the villagers were** ~**ed out** les inondations ont forcé les villageois à évacuer leurs maisons.

◆**floodgate** *n (fig)* **to open the** ~**gates** ouvrir les vannes (*to* à). ◆**flooding** *n* inondations *fpl*. ◆**floodlight** **1** *vt pret, ptp* **floodlit** *buildings* illuminer; *match* éclairer (aux projecteurs); *(fig)* mettre en lumière ; **2** *n (device)* projecteur *m*; *(light)* lumière *f* (des projecteurs); **to play a match under** ~**lights** jouer un match en nocturne. ◆**floodlighting** *n* illumination *f*; éclairage *m*; **let's go and see the** ~**lighting** allons voir les illuminations. ◆**floodlit** *adj* illuminé; en nocturne.

floor [flɔːʳ] **1** *n* (**a**) *(gen)* sol *m*; *(~ boards)* plancher *m*; *(for dance)* piste *f* (de danse). **stone/tiled** ~ sol dallé/carrelé; **on the** ~ par terre, sur le sol; **a question from the** ~ **of the house** une question de l'auditoire; **sea** ~ fond *m* de la mer. (**b**) *(storey)* étage *m*. **on the first** ~ *(Brit)* au premier étage; *(US)* au rez-de-chaussée. **2** *vt (knock down)* terrasser; *(baffle)* couper le sifflet à *. **he was completely** ~**ed by this** il n'a rien trouvé à répondre. **3** *adj*: ~ **covering** revêtement *m* de sol; ~ **manager** *(TV)* régisseur *m* de plateau; ~ **polish** cire *f*; ~ **polisher** cireuse *f*; ~ **show** attractions *fpl (dans un cabaret etc)*. ◆**floorboard** *n* planche *f (de plancher)*. ◆**floorcloth** *n* serpillière *f*. ◆**floorwalker** *n* chef *m* de rayon.

flop [flɒp] **1** *vi* (**a**) *(drop etc)* s'effondrer, s'affaler (*on* sur; *into* dans). (**b**) *[play]* faire un four; *[scheme etc]* être un fiasco. **2** *n* (*) *[business venture, scheme]* fiasco *m*. **he was a terrible** ~ il s'est payé un échec monumental *.

floppy ['flɒpɪ] *adj, n*: ~ **(disk)** disque *m* souple.

flora ['flɔːrə] *n* flore *f*.

floral ['flɔːr(ə)l] *adj* floral. ~ **tribute** fleurs *fpl* et couronnes *fpl*.

Florence ['flɒrəns] *n* Florence. ◆**Florentine** *adj* florentin.

florid ['flɒrɪd] *adj person, complexion* rougeaud; *literary style, architecture* tarabiscoté.

florist ['flɒrɪst] *n* fleuriste *mf*.

flotation [fləʊ'teɪʃ(ə)n] *n [shares]* émission *f*; *[company]* lancement *m* (en Bourse).

flounce [flaʊns] *vi*: **to** ~ **in/out** *etc* entrer/sortir *etc* dans un mouvement d'humeur (*or* d'indignation *etc*).

flounder[1] ['flaʊndəʳ] *n (fish)* flet *m*.

flounder[2] ['flaʊndəʳ] *vi* patauger (péniblement); *(more violently)* se débattre. *(fig)* **he** ~**ed through the rest of the speech** il a fini le discours en bredouillant.

flour [flaʊəʳ] *n* farine *f*. ~ **mill** minoterie *f*.

flourish ['flʌrɪʃ] **1** *vi [plants etc]* bien venir; *[business etc]* prospérer; *[writer, artist etc]* avoir du succès; *[literature, the arts, painting]* être en plein essor; *[person]* être en pleine forme. **2** *vt stick, book etc* brandir. **3** *n (gen)* fioriture *f*; *(under signature)* parafe *m*. **he took the lid off with a** ~ il a enlevé le couvercle avec un grand moulinet du bras; **a** ~ **of trumpets** une fanfare. ◆**flourishing** *adj business, plant* florissant; *person* d'une santé florissante.

flout [flaʊt] *vt orders, advice* passer outre à; *conventions, society* se moquer de.

flow [fləʊ] **1** *vi (gen)* couler; *[electric current, blood in veins]* circuler; *[hair etc]* flotter; *(fig: result)* découler, résulter (*from* de). *[people]* **to** ~ **in/out** entrer/sortir en foule ; *[liquid]* **to** ~ **out of** s'écouler de, sortir de; **the money keeps** ~**ing in** l'argent rentre bien; **to** ~ **past sth** passer devant qch; **to** ~ **back** refluer; **the water** ~**ed over the fields** l'eau s'est répandue dans les champs; **the river** ~**s into the sea** le fleuve se jette dans la mer; **tears were** ~**ing down her cheeks** les larmes coulaient sur ses joues. **2** *n [tide]* flux *m*; *[river]* courant *m*; *[electric current, blood in veins]* circulation *f*; *[blood from wound]* écoulement *m*; *[orders, replies, words]* flot *m*; *[music]* déroulement *m*. **3** *adj*: ~ **chart,** ~ **sheet** organigramme *m*. ◆**flowing** *adj movement* gracieux; *dress, hair* flottant; *style* coulant.

flower ['flaʊəʳ] **1** *n* fleur *f*. **in** ~ en fleurs. **2** *vi* fleurir. **to be** ~**ing** être en fleurs. **3** *adj*: ~ **arrangement** *(art)* art *m* du bouquet; *(exhibit)* composition *f* florale; ~ **bed** parterre *m*; ~ **garden** jardin *m* d'agrément; ~ **shop** boutique *f* de fleuriste; **at the** ~ **shop** chez le *or* la fleuriste; ~ **show** floralies *fpl*; *(smaller)* exposition *f* de fleurs.

◆**flowered** *adj cloth etc* à fleurs. ◆**flowering** **1** *n* floraison *f* ; **2** *adj (in ~)* en fleurs; *(which ~s) shrub etc* à fleurs. ◆**flowerpot** *n* pot *m* (à fleurs). ◆**flower-seller** *n* bouquetière *f*. ◆**flowery** *adj meadow* fleuri; *material* à fleurs; *style, essay, speech* fleuri.

flown [fləʊn] *ptp of* **fly[2]**.

flu [fluː] *n* grippe *f*.

flub * [flʌb] *(US)* **1** *vt* louper *, rater *. **2** *vi* échouer. **3** *n* ratage * *m*, erreur *f*.

fluctuate ['flʌktjʊeɪt] *vi [prices etc]* fluctuer; *[person]* varier (*between* entre). ◆**fluctuation** *n* fluctuation *f*; variation *f*.

flue [fluː] *n* conduit *m* (de cheminée). ~ **brush** hérisson *m (de ramoneur)*.

fluent ['fluːənt] *adj style* coulant. **to be a** ~ **speaker** avoir la parole facile; **he is** ~ **in Italian** il parle couramment l'italien. ◆**fluency** *n* facilité *f*, aisance *f*; **his fluency** l'aisance avec laquelle il s'exprime (*in* en). ◆**fluently** *adv speak a language* couramment; *speak, write* avec facilité.

fluff [flʌf] **1** *n (on birds, young animals)* duvet *m*; *(from material)* peluche *f*; *(dust on floors)* moutons *mpl (de poussière)*. **2** *vt* (**a**) *(~* **out***) feathers* ébouriffer; *pillows, hair* faire bouffer. (**b**) *(*: do badly) lines in play etc* rater. ◆**fluffy** *adj bird* duveteux; *hair* bouffant; *toy* en peluche; *material* pelucheux.

fluid ['fluːɪd] **1** *adj* fluide. ~ **ounce** *mesure de capacité (Brit: ≃ 0,028L; US: ≃ 0,030L)*; **my plans are still fairly** ~ je n'ai pas encore de plans très fixes. **2** *n* fluide *m (also Chem)*, liquide *m*. *(as diet)* **he's on** ~**s only** il ne peut prendre que des liquides. ◆**fluidity** *n* fluidité *f*.

fluke [fluːk] *n* coup *m* de chance. **by a (sheer)** ~ par un hasard extraordinaire.

flummox * ['flʌməks] *vt* couper le sifflet à *.

flung [flʌŋ] *pret, ptp of* **fling.**

fluorescent [flʊə'resnt] *adj lighting* fluorescent. ~ **strip** tube *m* fluorescent.

fluoride ['flʊəraɪd] *n* fluor *m*. ~ **toothpaste** dentifrice *m* au fluor. ◆ **fluoridation** *n* traitement *m* au fluor.

flurry ['flʌrɪ] *n* rafale *f*; *(fig)* agitation *f*; *[activity, excitement]* accès *m*. ◆ **flurried** *adj*: **to get flurried** s'affoler (*at* pour).

flush[1] [flʌʃ] **1** *n* (**a**) *(in sky)* lueur *f* rouge; *[blood]* flux *m*; *(blush)* rougeur *f*. *(Med)* **hot ~es** bouffées *fpl* de chaleur. (**b**) *[beauty, health, youth]* éclat *m*; *[joy]* élan *m*; *[excitement]* accès *m*. **in the first ~ of victory** dans l'ivresse *f* de la victoire. **2** *vi* rougir (*with* de). **3** *vt* nettoyer à grande eau. **to ~ the lavatory** tirer la chasse (d'eau). ◆ **flush away** *vt sep (down sink/drain)* faire partir par l'évier/par l'égout; *(down lavatory)* faire partir (en tirant la chasse d'eau). ◆ **flushed** *adj* (tout) rouge; **they were ~ed with success** le succès leur tournait la tête.

flush[2] [flʌʃ] **1** *adj* (**a**) au même niveau (*with* que), au *or* à ras (*with* de). ~ **with the ground** à ras de terre; **a door ~ with the wall** une porte dans l'alignement du mur; ~ **against** tout contre. (**b**) **to be ~ (with money)** ‡ être en fonds. **2** *vt*: **to ~ a door** rendre une porte plane.

flush[3] [flʌʃ] *vt (~* **out**) *game, birds* lever; *(fig) person* forcer à se montrer.

fluster ['flʌstəʳ] *vt* énerver, troubler. **to get ~ed** s'énerver.

flute [fluːt] *n (Mus)* flûte *f*. ◆ **flutist** *n (US)* flûtiste *mf*.

flutter ['flʌtəʳ] **1** *vi [flag, ribbon]* flotter; *[bird, moth]* voleter; *[wings]* battre; *[leaf]* tomber en tourbillonnant; *[person]* aller et venir dans une grande agitation; *[heart]* palpiter; *[pulse]* battre (faiblement). **2** *vt fan, paper* jouer de. **to ~ one's eyelashes** battre des cils (*at sb* dans la direction de qn). **3** *n (nervousness)* agitation *f*. **in a ~** tout troublé; *(gamble)* **to have a ~** * parier une petite somme (*on* sur).

flux [flʌks] *n*: **to be in a state of ~** changer sans arrêt.

fly[1] [flaɪ] **1** *n* mouche *f*. **they died like flies** ils mouraient comme des mouches; **he wouldn't hurt a ~** il ne ferait pas de mal à une mouche; *(fig)* **he's the ~ in the ointment** le gros obstacle, c'est lui; **there are no flies on him** ‡ il n'est pas né d'hier. **2** *adj*: ~ **fishing** pêche *f* à la mouche; ~ **paper** papier *m* tue-mouches; ~ **swat(ter)** tapette *f*; *(Boxing)* ~ **weight** poids *m* mouche. ◆ **fly-blown** *adj* défraîchi.

fly[2] [flaɪ] *pret* **flew**, *ptp* **flown** **1** *vi* (**a**) *(gen)* voler; *[air passenger]* voyager en avion; *[flag]* flotter. **to ~ over London** survoler Londres; **the planes flew past** *or* **over at 3 p.m.** les avions sont passés à 15 heures; **to ~ across** *or* **over the Channel** *[bird, plane, person]* survoler la Manche; *[passenger]* traverser la Manche en avion; **we flew in from Rome** nous sommes venus de Rome par avion; **to ~ away** *or* **off** s'envoler; *(fig)* **he is ~ing high** il voit grand; *(fig)* **to find that the bird has flown** trouver l'oiseau envolé.

(**b**) *[time]* passer vite; *[car, people]* filer *. *[person]* **to ~ in** *etc* entrer *etc* à toute vitesse; **I must ~!** il faut que je me sauve!; **to ~ to sb's assistance** voler au secours de qn; **to ~ into a rage, to ~ off the handle** s'emporter; **to let ~ at sb** *(in angry words)* s'en prendre violemment à qn; *(shoot)* tirer sur qn; **to let ~ a stone** jeter une pierre; **to ~ at sb/at sb's throat** sauter sur qn/à la gorge de qn; **the door flew open** la porte s'est ouverte brusquement.

(**c**) *(flee)* fuir (*before* devant), s'enfuir (*from* de), se réfugier (*to* auprès de). ~ **for your life!** fuyez!

2 *vt* (**a**) *aircraft* piloter; *person* emmener par avion; *goods* transporter par avion; *standard, admiral's flag etc* arborer. *(Naut)* **to ~ the French flag** battre pavillon français; **to ~ a kite** faire voler un cerf-volant; *(fig)* lancer un ballon d'essai *(fig)*; **to ~ the Atlantic** traverser l'Atlantique (en avion); **we will ~ you to Italy for £80** nous vous offrons le voyage d'Italie par avion pour 80 livres.

(**b**) **to ~ the country** s'enfuir du pays.

3 *n*: **flies** *(on trousers)* braguette *f*; *(Theat)* cintres *mpl*.

◆ **fly-drive** *n* formule *f* avion plus voiture. ◆ **fly half** *n* demi *m* d'ouverture. ◆ **flying** **1** *n (action)* vol *m*; *(activity)* aviation *f*; **he likes ~ing** il aime l'avion ; **2** *adj fish, machine, saucer, doctor* volant; **to take a ~ing jump** sauter avec élan; *(Sport)* **~ing start** départ *m* lancé; *(fig)* **to get off to a ~ing start** prendre un excellent départ; **~ing visit** visite *f* éclair *inv*; **~ing ambulance** avion *m* (*or* hélicoptère *m*) sanitaire; **~ing boat** hydravion *m*; **~ing buttress** arc-boutant *m*; **~ing officer** lieutenant *m* de l'armée de l'air; *(Police)* **F~ing Squad** brigade *f* volante de la police judiciaire; **~ing suit** combinaison *f*; **~ing time** heures *fpl* de vol. ◆ **flyleaf** *n* page *f* de garde. ◆ **flyover** *n (Aut)* toboggan *m*; *(Aviat: also* **flypast**) défilé *m* aérien. ◆ **flysheet** *n* feuille *f* volante. ◆ **flywheel** *n* volant *m (Tech)*.

foal [fəʊl] *n* poulain *m*.

foam [fəʊm] **1** *n (gen)* mousse *f*; *[sea, animal]* écume *f*. **2** *adj*: ~ **bath** bain *m* moussant; ~ **plastic** mousse *f* de plastique; ~ **rubber** caoutchouc *m* mousse. **3** *vi [sea]* écumer; *[soapy water]* mousser. **to ~ at the mouth** *(lit)* écumer; *(fig)* écumer de rage. ◆ **foam-backed** *adj carpet* à sous-couche de mousse.

fob [fɒb] *vt*: **to ~ sth off on sb** refiler * qch à qn; **to ~ sb off with promises** se débarrasser de qn par de belles promesses.

fo'c'sle ['fəʊksl] *n* gaillard *m* d'avant.

focus ['fəʊkəs] **1** *n, pl* **~es** *or* **foci** *(gen)* foyer *m*; *[interest]* centre *m*. *(Phot)* **in ~** au point; *(fig)* **the ~ of attention** le point de mire *(fig)*. **2** *vt instrument, camera* mettre au point (*on* sur); *light* faire converger (*on* sur); *one's efforts, attention* concentrer (*on* sur). **to ~ one's eyes on sth** fixer ses yeux sur qch. **3** *vi [light, rays]* converger (*on* sur); *[eyes, person]* accommoder. **to ~ on sth** fixer son regard sur qch; *(Phot)* faire la mise au point sur qch; **we must ~ on raising funds** il faut nous concentrer sur la collecte des fonds. ◆ **focal** *adj* focal; **focal point** *(Opt)* foyer *m*; *(fig)* point *m* central.

fodder ['fɒdəʳ] *n* fourrage *m*.

foe [fəʊ] *n* adversaire *mf*.

foetus ['fiːtəs] *n* fœtus *m*. ◆ **foetal** *adj* fœtal.

fog [fɒg] **1** *n* brouillard *m*. *(fig)* **to be in a ~** ne plus savoir où l'on en est. **2** *vt person* embrouiller; *(Phot)* voiler. **to ~ the issue** embrouiller la question. **3** *adj*: ~ **bank** banc *m* de brume; ~ **signal** *(Naut)* signal *m* de brume; *(Rail)* pétard *m*. ◆ **fogbound** *adj* bloqué par le brouillard. ◆ **foggy** *adj weather* brumeux; *day* de brouillard; *ideas* confus; **it's ~gy** il fait du brouillard; **I haven't the ~giest (idea** *or* **notion)**! * pas la moindre idée! ◆ **foghorn** *n* sirène *f* de brume; **a voice like a ~ horn** une voix tonitruante. ◆ **foglamp** *or* ◆ **foglight** *n* feu *m* de brouillard.

fogey * ['fəʊgɪ] *n*: **old ~** vieille baderne * *f*.

foible ['fɔɪbl] *n* petite manie *f*.

foil[1] [fɔɪl] *n (metal sheet)* feuille *f* de métal; *(cooking or kitchen ~)* papier *m* d'aluminium, alu * *m*; *(Fencing)* fleuret *m*. **to act as a ~ to sb/sth** mettre qn/qch en valeur.

foil[2] [fɔɪl] *vt plans, attempts* déjouer.

foist [fɔɪst] *vt*: **to ~ sth off on sb** refiler * qch à qn; **to ~ o.s. on to sb** s'imposer à qn *or (as guest)* chez qn.

fold [fəʊld] **1** *n* pli *m*. *(Geol)* **~s** plissement *m*. **2** *vt (gen)* plier. **to ~ one's arms** croiser les bras. **3** *vi [chair, table]* se (re)plier; *(*: fail) [newspaper]* cesser de paraître; *[business]* fermer; *[play]* quitter l'affiche.
◆**fold away 1** *vi [table, bed]* se (re)plier. **2** *vt sep clothes etc* plier et ranger. ◆**fold back** *vt sep* rabattre. ◆**fold over** *vt sep* replier. ◆**fold up 1** *vi (*: fail)* faire fiasco. **2** *vt sep paper etc* plier, replier.
◆**foldaway** *adj bed etc* pliant. ◆**folder** *n (file)* chemise *f*; *(with hinges)* classeur *m*; *(for drawings)* carton *m*; *(papers)* dossier *m*; *(leaflet)* dépliant *m*. ◆**folding** *adj bed etc* pliant; *door* en accordéon; **~ing seat** pliant *m*; *(Aut, Theat)* strapontin *m*.

fold [fəʊld] *suf*: **twenty~** *(adj)* par vingt; *(adv)* vingt fois.

foliage ['fəʊlɪɪdʒ] *n* feuillage *m*.

folio ['fəʊlɪəʊ] *n (sheet)* folio *m*; *(volume)* in-folio, *m*.

folk [fəʊk] **1** *npl (also* **~s***)* gens *mpl (adj f if before n)*. **good ~(s)** de braves gens, de bonnes gens; **old ~(s)** les vieux *mpl*, les vieilles gens; **hullo ~s!** * bonjour tout le monde! *; **what will ~(s) think?** qu'est-ce qu'on va penser?; *(pl: relatives)* **my ~s** * ma famille. **2** *adj dance, tale* folklorique. **~ music** *(gen)* musique *f* folklorique; *(contemporary)* folk *m*; **~ singer** *(gen)* chanteur *m*, -euse *f* de chansons folkloriques *or (contemporary)* de folk; **~ song** chanson *f* folklorique; *(modern)* chanson folk *inv*; **~ wisdom** la croyance populaire. ◆**folklore** *n* folklore *m*. ◆**folksy** * *adj story, humour* populaire; *person* bon enfant *inv*.

follow ['fɒləʊ] **1** *vt (gen)* suivre; *suspect* filer; *serial, strip cartoon* lire (régulièrement); *football team* être supporter de; *career* poursuivre. **we're being ~ed** on nous suit; **to have sb ~ed** faire filer qn; **a bodyguard ~ed the president** un garde du corps accompagnait le président; **~ed by** suivi de; **he ~ed his father into the business** il est entré dans l'affaire sur les traces de son père; **to ~ sb's advice** suivre les conseils de qn; **to ~ suit** *(Cards)* fournir *(in clubs etc* à trèfle *etc)*; *(fig)* en faire autant ; **I don't quite ~ (you)** je ne vous suis pas tout à fait.
2 *vi* (**a**) *(come after)* suivre. **as ~s** comme suit; **to ~ right behind sb, to ~ hard on sb's heels** être sur les talons de qn; *(fig)* **to ~ in sb's footsteps** marcher sur les traces de qn; **as ~s** comme suit; **his argument was as ~s** son raisonnement était le suivant; **what is there to ~?** qu'est-ce qu'il y a après? (**b**) *(result)* s'ensuivre *(that* que), découler *(from* de). **that doesn't ~** pas forcément. (**c**) *(understand)* suivre, comprendre.
◆**follow about, follow around** *vt sep* suivre (partout). ◆**follow on** *vi (come after)* suivre; *(result)* découler *(from* de). ◆**follow out, follow through** *vt sep idea, plan* poursuivre jusqu'au bout. ◆**follow up 1** *vi (Ftbl etc)* suivre l'action. **2** *vt sep* (**a**) *(benefit from) advantage, success* tirer parti de; *offer* donner suite à. (**b**) *(not lose track of) person, case* suivre. (**c**) *(reinforce) victory* asseoir; *remark* faire suivre *(with* de). **they ~ed up the broadcast with another equally good** ils ont donné à cette émission une suite qui a été tout aussi excellente.
◆**follower** *n* partisan *m*; **the ~ers of fashion** ceux qui s'intéressent à la mode. ◆**following 1** *adj* suivant; **the ~ing day** le jour suivant, le lendemain; **~ing wind** vent *m* arrière ; **2** *n (supporters)* partisans *mpl*; **a large ~ing** de nombreux partisans; **he said the ~ing** il a dit ceci; *(in documents etc)* **see the ~ing** voir ce qui suit; **3** *prep*: **~ing your letter/our meeting** comme suite à votre lettre/notre entretien. ◆**follow-through** *n (to a project)* suite *f*, continuation *f*. ◆**follow-up 1** *n (on case, file)* suivi; *(to event)* suite *f* *(to* de) ; **2** *adj*: **~-up letter** rappel *m*; *(Med)* **~-up care** soins *mpl* post-hospitaliers; **~-up survey** étude *f* complémentaire; **~-up visit** visite *f* de contrôle.

folly ['fɒlɪ] *n* folie *f*.

foment [fə(ʊ)'ment] *vt* fomenter. ◆**fomentation** *n* fomentation *f*.

fond [fɒnd] *adj* (**a**) **to be ~ of** aimer beaucoup. (**b**) *(loving) husband, friend* affectueux; *parent* (trop) bon; *look* tendre; *hope, ambition* cher; *(foolish) hope, ambition* naïf. ◆**fondly** *adv* affectueusement; tendrement; naïvement; **he ~ly believed that...** il avait la naïveté de croire que... ◆**fondness** *n (for things)* prédilection *f (for* pour); *(for people)* affection *f (for* pour).

fondle ['fɒndl] *vt* caresser.

font [fɒnt] *n* (**a**) *(Rel)* fonts *mpl* baptismaux. (**b**) *(US Typ)* fonte *f*.

food [fu:d] **1** *n* nourriture *f*; *[dogs]* pâtée *f*; *[plants]* engrais *m*. **there was no ~ in the house** il n'y avait rien à manger dans la maison; **to give sb ~** donner à manger à qn; **a new ~ for babies/pigs** *etc* un nouvel aliment pour les bébés/cochons *etc;* **~s** aliments *mpl*; **to be off one's ~** * avoir perdu l'appétit; **the ~ is very good here** on mange très bien ici; **he likes plain ~** il aime la cuisine simple; **it gave me ~ for thought** cela m'a donné à penser *or* à réfléchir. **2** *adj rationing, chain* alimentaire. **~ parcel** colis *m* de vivres; **~ poisoning** intoxication *f* alimentaire; **~ processor** robot *m* de cuisine; *(US)* **~ stamps** bons *mpl* de nourriture *(pour indigents)*; **~ supplies** vivres *mpl*; **~ value** valeur *f* nutritive. ◆**foodstuffs** *npl* denrées *fpl* alimentaires.

fool [fu:l] **1** *n* imbécile *mf*, idiot(e) *m(f)*. **don't be a ~!** ne fais pas l'idiot(e)!; **some ~ of a doctor** un imbécile de médecin; **he was a ~ not to accept** il a été idiot *or* stupide de ne pas accepter; **to play the ~** faire l'imbécile; **he's nobody's ~** il n'est pas né d'hier; **more ~ you!** * tu n'avais qu'à ne pas faire l'idiot!; **he made a ~ of himself** il s'est rendu ridicule; **to make a ~ of sb** ridiculiser qn; **I went on a ~'s errand** j'y suis allé pour rien; **to live in a ~'s paradise** planer *(fig)*. **2** *vi (~ about)* faire l'imbécile *or* l'idiot(e). **I was only ~ing** je plaisantais. **3** *vt* duper.
◆**fool about, fool around** *vi (waste time)* perdre son temps; *(play the fool)* faire l'idiot(e) *or* l'imbécile *(with* avec).
◆**foolery** *n* sottises *fpl*, bêtises *fpl*. ◆**foolhardiness** *n* témérité *f*. ◆**foolhardy** *adj* téméraire. ◆**foolish** *adj* idiot, bête; **that was very ~ish of you** ça n'a pas été très malin de votre part; *(more formally)* vous avez vraiment été imprudent; **to make sb look ~ish** rendre qn ridicule. ◆**foolishly** *adv* sottement, bêtement; **and ~ishly I believed him** et je l'ai cru comme un(e) imbécile. ◆**foolishness** *n* bêtise *f*. ◆**foolproof** *adj method* infaillible; *machinery* indétraquable.

foolscap ['fu:lskæp] *n* ≃ papier *m* ministre.

foot [fʊt] **1** *n, pl* **feet** *(gen)* pied *m*; *[dog, cat, bird]* patte *f*; *[table]* (bas) bout *m*; *[page, stairs]* bas *m*; *(measure)* pied *(= 30 cm environ)*; *(Mil)* infanterie *f*. **to be on one's feet** être debout; *(fig: after illness)* être remis sur pied; **to jump to one's feet** sauter sur ses pieds; **to go on ~** aller à pied; **to get** *or* **to rise to one's feet** se mettre debout; **it brought him to his feet** à cela, il s'est levé d'un bond; *(fig)* **to put** *or* **set sb on his feet again** *(healthwise)* remettre qn sur pied; **to keep one's feet** garder l'équilibre; **it's very wet under ~** c'est très mouillé par terre; **to trample sb/sth under ~** piétiner qn/qch; *(fig)* **to get under sb's feet** venir dans les jambes de qn; **to put one's ~ down** *(be firm)* faire acte d'autorité; *(stop sth)* y mettre le holà; *(Aut*: accelerate)* appuyer sur le champignon *; **to put**

one's ~ in it * gaffer; **to put one's best ~ forward** *(hurry)* se dépêcher; *(do one's best)* faire de son mieux; **he didn't put a ~ wrong** il n'a pas commis la moindre erreur; **to get off on the right/wrong ~** bien/mal commencer; **to get a ~ in the door** établir un premier contact; **to put one's feet up** * (s'étendre pour) se reposer un peu; **he's got one ~ in the grave** * il a un pied dans la tombe; **I've never set ~ there** je n'y ai jamais mis les pieds; **at the ~ of the page** au *or* en bas de la page; **~ soldier** fantassin *m*.

2 *vt*: **to ~ the bill** * payer (la note).

◆ **footage** *n (gen, also Cine: length)* ≃ métrage *m*; *(Cine: material)* séquences *fpl* (*about* sur). ◆ **foot-and-mouth disease** *n* fièvre *f* aphteuse. ◆ **football 1** *n* (**a**) *(sport) (Brit)* football *m*; *(US)* football américain. (**b**) *(ball)* ballon *m* (de football) ; **2** *adj ground, match, team* de football; *season* du football; **~ball coupon** fiche *f* de pari (sur les matchs de football); **~ball hooliganism** vandalisme *m (lors d'un match de football)*; **~ball league** championnat *m* de football; **F~ball League** ≃ Fédération française de football; **to do the ~ball pools** parier sur les matchs de football; *(Rail)* **~ball special** train *m* de supporters *(d'une équipe de football)*. ◆ **footballer** *n* joueur *m* de football. ◆ **footbrake** *n* frein *m* à pied. ◆ **footbridge** *n* passerelle *f*. ◆ **-footed** *adj ending in cpds*: **light-~ed** au pied léger. ◆ **footfall** *n* (bruit *m* de) pas *m*. ◆ **footgear** * *n* chaussures *fpl*. ◆ **foothills** *npl* contreforts *mpl*. ◆ **foothold** *n* prise *f* (de pied); **to gain a ~hold** prendre pied; *(fig)* *[newcomer]* se faire accepter; *[idea]* s'imposer; *[movement]* se répandre. ◆ **footing** *n* prise *f* (de pied); *(fig)* position *f*; **to miss one's ~ing** perdre pied *or* l'équilibre; **to be on a friendly ~ing with sb** avoir des relations d'amitié avec qn; **on an equal ~ing** sur un pied d'égalité; **on a war ~ing** sur le pied de guerre; **to put sth on an official ~ing** rendre qch officiel. ◆ **footlights** *npl (Theat)* rampe *f*. ◆ **footloose** *adj*: **~loose and fancy-free** libre comme l'air. ◆ **footman** *n* valet *m* de pied. ◆ **footmark** *n* empreinte *f* (de pied). ◆ **footnote** *n* note *f* en bas de la page; *(fig)* post-scriptum *m*. ◆ **footpath** *n* sentier *m*; *(by highway)* chemin *m*. ◆ **footplate 1** *n (Rail)* plate-forme *f (d'une locomotive)* ; **2** *adj*: **~plate workers** *npl*, agents *mpl* de conduite. ◆ **footprint** *n* = **footmark**. ◆ **footpump** *n* pompe *f* à pied. ◆ **footsore** *adj*: **to be ~sore** avoir mal aux pieds. ◆ **footstep** *n* (bruit *m* de) pas *m*. ◆ **footstool** *n* tabouret *m*. ◆ **footwear** *n* chaussures *fpl*.

footle * ['fu:tl] *vi*: **to ~ about** perdre son temps à des futilités. ◆ **footling** *adj* futile.

for [fɔ:ʳ] **1** *prep* (**a**) *(indicating intention, destination)* pour. **is this ~ me?** c'est pour moi?; **votes ~ women!** le droit de vote pour les femmes!; **it's time ~ dinner** c'est l'heure du dîner; **a job ~ next week** un travail à faire la semaine prochaine; **she's the wife ~ me** c'est la femme qu'il me faut; **a liking ~ work** le goût du travail; **a gift ~ languages** un don pour les langues; **he's got a genius ~ saying the wrong thing** il a le don de dire ce qu'il ne faut pas; **he left ~ Italy** il est parti pour l'Italie; **trains ~ Paris** trains *mpl* en direction de *or* à destination de Paris; **the train ~ Paris** le train pour *or* de Paris; **he swam ~ the shore** il a nagé dans la direction du rivage *or* vers le rivage; **to make ~ home** prendre la direction de la maison.
(**b**) *(indicating purpose)* pour. **what ~?** pourquoi?; **what did you do that ~?** pourquoi avez-vous fait cela?; **what's this knife ~?** à quoi sert ce couteau?; **it's not ~ cutting wood** ça n'est pas fait pour couper du bois; **it's been used ~ a hammer** ça a servi de marteau; **a room ~ studying in** une pièce réservée à l'étude; **a bag ~ carrying books in** un sac pour porter des livres; **we went there ~ our holidays** nous y sommes allés pour les vacances; **he does it ~ pleasure** il le fait pour son plaisir; **to get ready ~ a journey** se préparer pour un voyage; **fit ~ nothing** bon à rien; **a campaign ~...** une campagne pour...
(**c**) *(representing)* **D ~ Daniel** D comme Daniel; *(Parl)* **member ~ Brighton** député *m* de Brighton; **agent ~ Ford cars** concessionnaire *mf* Ford; **I'll see her ~ you** je la verrai à ta place; **what is G.B. ~?** qu'est-ce que G.B. veut dire?
(**d**) *(in exchange ~)* **I'll give you this book ~ that one** je vous échange ce livre-ci contre celui-là; **to pay 5 francs ~ a ticket** payer 5 F le billet; **I sold it ~ £2** je l'ai vendu 2 livres; **he'll do it ~ £5** il le fera pour 5 livres; **there is one French passenger ~ every 10 English** sur 11 passagers il y a un Français et 10 Anglais; **what's (the) German ~ 'dog'?** comment est-ce qu'on dit 'chien' en allemand?
(**e**) *(in favour of)* pour. **~ or against** pour ou contre; **I'm all ~ helping him** je suis tout à fait partisan de l'aider; **I'm all ~ it** * je suis tout à fait pour *.
(**f**) *(because of)* pour, en raison de. **~ this reason** pour cette raison; **~ fear of being left behind** de peur d'être oublié; **famous ~ its church** célèbre pour son église; **to shout ~ joy** hurler de joie; **to go to prison ~ theft/~ stealing** aller en prison pour vol/pour avoir volé; **~ my sake** pour moi; **to choose sb ~ his ability** choisir qn en raison de sa compétence; **if it weren't ~ him, but ~ him** sans lui.
(**g**) *(considering; with regard to)* pour. **anxious ~ sb** inquiet pour qn; **~ my part** pour ma part; **as ~ him** quant à lui; **it is warm ~ January** il fait bon pour janvier; **he's tall ~ his age** il est grand pour son âge.
(**h**) *(in spite of)* **~ all his wealth** malgré toute sa richesse, tout riche qu'il soit; **~ all that** malgré tout, néanmoins.
(**i**) *(in time)* **I have been/had been waiting ~ 2 hours** j'attends/j'attendais depuis 2 heures; **I am off ~ a few days** je pars pour quelques jours; **I shall be away ~ a month** je serai absent (pendant) un mois; **he won't be back ~ a week** il ne sera pas de retour avant huit jours; **that's enough ~ the moment** cela suffit pour le moment; **he went away ~ two weeks** il est parti (pendant) quinze jours; **I have not seen her ~ 2 years** voilà 2 ans *or* cela fait 2 ans que je ne l'ai vue.
(**j**) *(distance)* pendant. **a road lined with trees ~ 3 km** une route bordée d'arbres pendant *or* sur 3 km; **we drove ~ 50 km** nous avons conduit pendant 50 km; **nothing to be seen ~ miles** rien à voir pendant des kilomètres.
(**k**) *(with infin phrases)* pour que + *subj*. **~ this to be possible** pour que cela puisse être; **it's easy ~ him to do it** il lui est facile de le faire; **I brought it ~ you to see** je l'ai apporté pour que vous le voyiez *(subj)*; **it's not ~ me to say** ce n'est pas à moi de le dire; **it would be best ~ you to go away** le mieux serait que vous vous en alliez *(subj)*; **there is still time ~ him to come** il a encore le temps d'arriver; **their one hope is ~ him to return** leur seul espoir est qu'il revienne.
(**l**) *(phrases)* **now ~ it!** allons-y!; **you're ~ it!** * qu'est-ce que tu vas prendre! *; **oh ~ a cup of tea!** je donnerais n'importe quoi pour une tasse de thé!

2 *conj* car.

forage ['fɒrɪdʒ] *vi* fourrager (*for* pour trouver).

foray ['fɒreɪ] *n* incursion *f*.

forbad(e) [fə'bæd] *pret of* **forbid.**

forbear [fɔ:'bɛəʳ] *pret* **forbore,** *ptp* **forborne** *vi* s'abstenir (*from doing, to do* de faire). ◆ **forbearance** *n* patience *f*.

forbid [fə'bɪd] *pret* **forbad(e),** *ptp* **forbidden** *vt* défendre, interdire (*sb to do* à qn de faire). **to ~ sb alcohol** interdire l'alcool à qn; **employees are ~den to do this** il est interdit *or* défendu aux employés de faire cela; **'smoking strictly ~den'** 'défense absolue de fumer'; **God ~!** * pourvu que non!, j'espère bien que non! ◆ **forbidding** *adj building, cliff, cloud* menaçant; *person, look* sévère.

forbore [fɔː'bɔʳ], **forborne** [fɔː'bɔːn] *pret, ptp of* **forbear.**

force [fɔːs] **1** *n* (**a**) *(gen)* force *f.* ~ **of gravity** pesanteur *f*; **by sheer** ~ de vive force; **by** ~ **of** à force de; **by** ~ **of habit** par la force de l'habitude; ~ **of a blow** violence *f* d'un coup; **to resort to** ~ avoir recours à la force; **I can see the** ~ **of that** je comprends la force que cela peut avoir; **to come into** ~ entrer en vigueur; **the police were there in** ~ la police était là en force; **he is a powerful** ~ **in the party** il exerce une influence puissante dans le parti; **there are several ~s at work** plusieurs influences se font sentir. (**b**) *(body of men)* force *f. (Mil)* **the ~s** les forces armées; *(Mil)* **allied ~s** armées alliées; **police** ~ forces de police, la police; *(Comm)* **our sales** ~ (l'effectif *m* de) nos représentants *mpl* de commerce.
2 *vt* (**a**) *(constrain)* contraindre, forcer (*sb to do* qn à faire). **to be ~d to do** être contraint *or* forcé de faire. (**b**) *(impose) conditions, obedience* imposer (*on sb* à qn). **to** ~ **o.s. on sb** s'imposer à qn. (**c**) *(push, thrust)* pousser. **to** ~ **books into a box** fourrer des livres dans une caisse; **to** ~ **one's way into** entrer *or* pénétrer de force dans; **to** ~ **one's way through** se frayer un passage à travers; **to** ~ **a bill through Parliament** forcer la Chambre à voter une loi; **we ~d the secret out of him** nous lui avons arraché le secret. (**d**) *(break open) lock etc* forcer. **to** ~ **sb's hand** forcer la main à qn. (**e**) *smile, answer* forcer. **to** ~ **the pace** forcer l'allure *or* le pas. ◆ **force back** *vt sep enemy, crowd* faire reculer. **to** ~ **back one's tears** refouler ses larmes. ◆ **force down** *vt sep aircraft* forcer à atterrir. **to** ~ **food down** se forcer à manger. ◆ **force out** *vt sep* faire sortir (de force); *cork* sortir en forçant. **he ~d out a reply** il s'est forcé à répondre.
◆ **forced** *adj* forcé. ◆ **force-feed** *(pret, ptp* **-fed***) vt* nourrir de force. ◆ **forceful** *adj person* énergique; *argument* vigoureux; *influence* puissant. ◆ **forcefully** *adv* avec force, avec vigueur. ◆ **forcible** *adj (done by ~)* de *or* par force; *(powerful) language, style, argument* vigoureux; *personality* puissant. ◆ **forcibly** *adv (by ~) take, feed* de force; *(vigorously) speak, object* avec véhémence. ◆ **forcing** *adj (Bridge)* **forcing bid** annonce *f* de forcing.

forceps ['fɔːseps] *npl* forceps *m.*

ford [fɔːd] **1** *n* gué *m.* **2** *vt* passer à gué. ◆ **fordable** *adj* guéable.

fore [fɔːʳ] **1** *adj* antérieur. **2** *n* avant *m.* **to come to the** ~ *[person]* se mettre en évidence; *[evidence, fact]* être révélé; **he was well to the** ~ il a été très en évidence. **3** *excl (Golf)* gare!, attention! ◆ **forearm** *n* avant-bras *m inv.* ◆ **foreboding** *n* pressentiment *m*; **to have a ~boding that** avoir le pressentiment que. ◆ **forecast** *pret, ptp* **forecast** **1** *vt (also Met)* prévoir ; **2** *n* prévision *f*; *(Betting)* pronostic *m*; **sales ~cast** prévisions de vente; **weather ~cast** bulletin *m* météorologique, météo * *f.* ◆ **forecaster** *n (Met)* journaliste *mf* météorologique; *(Econ, Pol)* prévisionniste *mf; (Sport)* pronostiqueur *m*, -euse *f.* ◆ **forecourt** *n* avant-cour *f.* ◆ **forefathers** *npl* aïeux *mpl.* ◆ **forefinger** *n* index *m.* ◆ **forefoot** *n [horse, cow etc]* pied *m* antérieur; *[cat, dog]* patte *f* antérieure. ◆ **forefront** *n*: **in the ~front of** au premier rang de. ◆ **foregather** *vi* se réunir. ◆ **forego** *pret* **-went,** *ptp* **-gone** *vt* renoncer à; **it was a ~gone conclusion** c'était prévu d'avance. ◆ **foregoing** *adj* précédent; **the ~going** ce qui précède. ◆ **foreground** *n* premier plan; **in the ~ground** au premier plan. ◆ **forehead** *n* front *m.* ◆ **foreland** *n* cap *m.* ◆ **foreleg** *n [horse, cow]* jambe antérieure; *[dog, cat]* patte *f* de devant. ◆ **foreman,** *pl* **~men** *n* contremaître *m.* ◆ **foremost** **1** *adj* le plus en vue ; **2** *adv*: **first and ~most** tout d'abord. ◆ **forename** *n* prénom *m.* ◆ **forenoon** *n* matinée *f.* ◆ **foreplay** *n* préliminaires *mpl (stimulation érotique).* ◆ **forerunner** *n (sign)* signe avant-coureur; *(person)* précurseur *m.* ◆ **foresee** *pret* **-saw,** *ptp* **-seen** *vt* prévoir, présager. ◆ **foreseeable** *adj* prévisible. ◆ **foreshadow** *vt* laisser prévoir. ◆ **foreshore** *n (beach)* plage *f.* ◆ **foresight** *n* prévoyance *f.* ◆ **forestall** *vt competitor* devancer; *desire, eventuality, objection* anticiper. ◆ **foretaste** *n* avant-goût *m.* ◆ **foretell** *pret, ptp* **-told** *vt* prédire. ◆ **forethought** *n* prévoyance *f.* ◆ **forewarn** *vt* avertir; **~warned is ~armed** un homme averti en vaut deux. ◆ **foreword** *n* avant-propos *m inv.*

foreign ['fɒrən] *adj language, visitor* étranger; *politics, trade* extérieur; *produce, aid* de l'étranger; *travel, correspondent* à l'étranger. **F~ Ministry,** *(Brit)* **F~ Office** ministère *m* des Affaires étrangères; ~ **agent** agent *m* étranger; ~ **currency** devises *fpl* étrangères; ~ **exchange market** marché *m* des changes; **F~ Legion** Légion *f* (étrangère); ~ **relations** relations *fpl* avec l'étranger *or* l'extérieur; **the** ~ **service** le service diplomatique; **that is quite** ~ **to him** cela lui est (complètement) étranger; *(Med)* ~ **body** corps *m* étranger. ◆ **foreigner** *n* étranger *m*, -ère *f.*

forensic [fə'rensɪk] *adj medicine* légal; *evidence, laboratory* médico-légal; *expert* en médecine légale.

forest ['fɒrɪst] *n* forêt *f.* ◆ **forester** *n* forestier *m.* ◆ **forestry** *n* sylviculture *f*; **the F~ry Commission** ≃ les Eaux et Forêts *fpl.*

forever [fər'evəʳ] *adv (incessantly)* toujours, continuellement; *(for always)* (pour) toujours; *(*: a long time)* une éternité.

forfeit ['fɔːfɪt] **1** *vt* perdre. **2** *n (in game)* gage *m. (game)* **~s** gages.

forgave [fə'geɪv] *pret of* **forgive.**

forge [fɔːdʒ] **1** *vt* (**a**) *(counterfeit) signature, banknote* contrefaire; *document, picture* faire un faux de. **~d** *passport* faux. (**b**) *metal, friendship, plan* forger. **2** *vi*: **to** ~ **ahead** pousser de l'avant. **3** *n* forge *f.* ◆ **forger** *n* faussaire *mf.* ◆ **forgery** *n (action)* contrefaçon *f* (frauduleuse); *(thing ~d)* faux *m.*

forget [fə'get] *pret* **-got,** *ptp* **-gotten** **1** *vt* oublier (*to do* de faire; *that* que). **to** ~ **how to do** ne plus savoir faire, oublier comment faire; **never-to-be-forgotten** inoubliable; **she never ~s a face** elle a la mémoire des visages; **he quite forgot himself** il s'est tout à fait oublié; **let's** ~ **it!** passons l'éponge!; ~ **it** * *(when thanked)* de rien *; *(let's drop the subject)* ça n'a aucune importance; *(when pestered)* laissez tomber!; *(be realistic)* n'y comptez pas! **2** *vi* oublier. **I forgot all about it** je l'ai complètement oublié; ~ **about it!** n'y pensez plus! ◆ **forgetful** *adj (absent-minded)* distrait; *(careless)* étourdi; **he is very ~ful** il a très mauvaise mémoire; **~ful of** oublieux de. ◆ **forgetfulness** *n* manque *m* de mémoire; étourderie *f.* ◆ **forget-me-not** *n* myosotis *m.*

forgive [fə'gɪv] *pret* **forgave,** *ptp* **forgiven** *vt person, mistake* pardonner (*sb for sth* qch à qn; *sb for doing* à qn de faire). ◆ **forgivable** *adj* pardonnable. ◆ **forgiveness** *n (pardon)* pardon *m*; *(compassion)* indulgence *f.* ◆ **forgiving** *adj* indulgent.

forgot(ten) [fə'gɒt(n)] *pret (ptp) of* **forget.**

fork [fɔːk] **1** *n* fourchette *f*; *(Agr)* fourche *f*; *[roads]* embranchement *m.* **take the right** ~ prenez à droite à l'embranchement. **2** *vi [roads]* bifurquer. ~ **left for Oxford** prenez à gauche pour Oxford. ◆ **fork out** ‡ **1** *vi* casquer *, payer. **2** *vt sep money* allonger ‡, sortir.
◆ **forked** *adj* fourchu; *lightning* en zigzags. ◆ **fork-lift truck** *n* chariot *m* élévateur.

forlorn [fə'lɔːn] *adj person* triste, malheureux; *house* abandonné; *attempt* désespéré. **a ~ hope** un mince espoir.

form [fɔːm] **1** *n* (**a**) *(gen)* forme *f*. **a different ~ of life** une autre forme *or* un autre genre de vie; **the various ~s of energy** les différentes formes *or* espèces d'énergie; **a ~ of apology** une sorte d'excuse; **in the ~ of** sous forme de; **it will take the ~ of...** cela consistera en...; **the same thing in a new ~** la même chose sous un aspect nouveau; **it took various ~s** cela s'est manifesté de différentes façons; **~ and content** la forme et le fond; **to take ~** prendre forme; **it lacks ~** il n'y a aucun ordre là-dedans; **as a matter of ~** pour la forme; **it's bad ~** cela ne se fait pas; **another ~ of words** une autre tournure; **the correct ~ of address for a bishop** la manière correcte de s'adresser à un évêque; **what's the ~? *** quelle est la marche à suivre?; **on ~** en forme; **in great ~, on top ~** en pleine forme. (**b**) *(document) (gen)* formulaire *m*; *(for cheque, telegram)* formule *f*; *(for tax)* feuille *f*. **printed ~** imprimé *m*. (**c**) *(bench)* banc *m*. (**d**) *(Scol)* classe *f*. **in the sixth ~** ≃ en première.
2 *adj*: **~ master, ~ mistress** professeur *m* de classe.
3 *vt shape, character, government* former; *sentence* construire; *habit* contracter; *plan* arrêter; *impression, idea* avoir; *(constitute) council, Cabinet* composer, constituer. **he ~ed it out of a piece of wood** il l'a façonné *or* fabriqué dans un morceau de bois; **he ~ed it into a ball** il l'a roulé en boule; **to ~ an opinion** se faire une opinion; **to ~ part of** faire partie de; **those who ~ the group** les gens qui font partie du groupe; *(Mil)* **to ~ fours** se mettre par quatre; **~ a line/queue/circle** mettez-vous en ligne/file/cercle.
4 *vi* se former (*into* en). **~ up behind your teacher** mettez-vous en ligne derrière votre professeur. ◆**formation** **1** *n* formation *f*; **2** *adj*: **~ation flying** vol *m* en formation. ◆**formative** *adj* formateur.

formal ['fɔːm(ə)l] *adj person* formaliste, compassé *(pej)*; *manner, style* soigné, ampoulé *(pej)*; *language* soigné; *function, announcement* officiel; *dance, dinner* grand; *(official) acceptance, surrender* en bonne et due forme; *(specific) denial, instructions* formel; *(in form only) agreement* de forme. **he is very ~** il est très à cheval sur les convenances; **don't be so ~** pas tant de cérémonies, s'il vous plaît; **~ gardens** jardins *mpl* à la française; **~ dress** tenue *f* de cérémonie; *(evening dress)* tenue de soirée; **she has no ~ training in teaching** elle n'a reçu aucune formation pédagogique. ◆**formalism** *n* formalisme *m*. ◆**formalist** *adj, n* formaliste *(mf)*. ◆**formality** *n (convention)* formalité *f*; *(stiffness)* raideur *f*; *(ceremoniousness)* cérémonie *f*; **a mere ~ity** une simple formalité. ◆**formalize** *vt* formaliser. ◆**formally** *adv (ceremoniously)* cérémonieusement; *(officially)* officiellement; **to be ~ly invited** recevoir une invitation officielle; **~ly dressed** en tenue de cérémonie (*or* de soirée).

format ['fɔːmæt] **1** *n (size)* format *m*; *(layout)* présentation *f*. **2** *vt* (**a**) *(Comput)* formater. (**b**) *(design)* concevoir le format (*or* la présentation) de.

former ['fɔːmə^r] **1** *adj* (**a**) *(previous)* ancien *(before n)*, précédent; *life* antérieur. **the ~ mayor** l'ancien maire, le maire précédent; **a ~ mayor** un ancien maire; **my ~ husband** mon ex-mari; **in ~ days** autrefois; **he was very unlike his ~ self** il ne se ressemblait plus du tout. (**b**) *(as opp to latter)* premier. **2** *pron* celui-là, celle-là. **the ~... the latter** celui-là... celui-ci. ◆**formerly** *adv* autrefois.

Formica [fɔː'maɪkə] *n* ® Formica *m* ®.

formidable ['fɔːmɪdəbl] *adj (gen)* terrible; *person, opposition* redoutable.

formula, *pl* **~s** *or* **~ae** ['fɔːmjʊlə] *n (gen)* formule *f*; *(fig)* **a ~ for averting the strike** une formule visant à éviter la grève; *(US: for baby's feed)* lait *m* en poudre *(pour biberon)*. ◆**formulate** *vt* formuler. ◆**formulation** *n* formulation *f*.

fornicate ['fɔːnɪkeɪt] *vi* forniquer. ◆**fornication** *n* fornication *f*.

forsake [fə'seɪk] *pret* **forsook**, *ptp* **forsaken** *vt person* abandonner; *place* quitter; *habit* renoncer à. **my willpower ~s me** la volonté me fait défaut; **an old ~n farmhouse** une vieille ferme abandonnée.

forsythia [fɔː'saɪθɪə] *n* forsythia *m*.

fort [fɔːt] *n (Mil)* fort *m*.

forte ['fɔːtɪ, *(US)* fɔːt] *n*: **his ~** son fort.

forth [fɔːθ] *adv* en avant. **to set ~** se mettre en route; **to go back and ~ between** aller et venir entre; **and so ~** et ainsi de suite. ◆**forthcoming** *adj book* qui va paraître; *film* qui va sortir; *play* qui va débuter; *event* à venir, futur; **his ~coming film** son prochain film; **if help is ~coming** si on nous *etc* aide; **if funds are ~coming** si on nous *etc* donne de l'argent; **he wasn't ~coming about it** il s'est montré peu disposé à en parler. ◆**forthright** *adj answer, person* franc. ◆**forthwith** *adv* sur-le-champ.

fortify ['fɔːtɪfaɪ] *vt* fortifier (*against* contre). **have a drink to ~ you *** prenez un verre pour vous remonter. ◆**fortification** *n* fortification *f*.

fortitude ['fɔːtɪtjuːd] *n* force *f* d'âme.

fortnight ['fɔːtnaɪt] *n* quinze jours *mpl*, quinzaine *f*. **a ~'s holiday** quinze jours de vacances; **a ~ tomorrow** demain en quinze. ◆**fortnightly** **1** *adj* bimensuel ; **2** *adv* tous les quinze jours.

FORTRAN ['fɔːtræn] *n* fortran *m*.

fortress ['fɔːtrɪs] *n (prison)* forteresse *f*; *(mediaeval castle)* château *m* fort.

fortuitous [fɔː'tjuːɪtəs] *adj* fortuit. ◆**fortuitously** *adv* fortuitement.

fortune ['fɔːtʃən] *n* (**a**) *(chance)* chance *f*, fortune *f*. **the ~s of war** la fortune des armes; **by good ~** par chance; **to tell sb's ~** dire la bonne aventure à qn. (**b**) *(riches)* fortune *f*. **to make a ~** faire fortune; **to come into a ~** hériter d'une fortune; **to seek one's ~** aller chercher fortune; **a small ~ *** un argent fou *. ◆**fortunate** *adj person* heureux; *circumstances, meeting, event* propice; *[person]* **to be fortunate** avoir de la chance; **we were fortunate enough to meet him** nous avons eu la chance de le rencontrer. ◆**fortune cookie** *n (US)* beignet *m* chinois *(renfermant un horoscope ou une devise)*. ◆**fortune-teller** *n* diseur *m*, -euse *f* de bonne aventure. ◆**fortune-telling** *n* pratique *f* de dire la bonne aventure.

forty ['fɔːtɪ] *adj, n, pron* quarante *(m) inv*. **about ~ books** une quarantaine de livres; **to have ~ winks *** faire un petit somme; *for other phrases V* **sixty.** ◆**fortieth** *adj, n* quarantième *(mf)*; *(fraction)* quarantième *m*.

forward ['fɔːwəd] **1** *adv (also* **forwards***)* en avant. **to go ~** avancer; **to go straight ~** aller droit devant soi; **~!, ~ march!** en avant, marche!; **from this time ~** désormais; **he went backward(s) and ~(s) between** il allait et venait entre. **2** *adj movement* en avant; *(Aut) gears* avant *inv*; *planning* à long terme; *prices, buying* à terme; *season, child* précoce; *(pert)* effronté. **I am ~ with my work** je suis en avance dans mon travail; **this seat is too far ~** cette banquette est trop en avant; **~ line** *(Mil)* première ligne *f*; *(Sport)* ligne des avants. **3** *n (Sport)* avant *m*. **4** *vt goods* expédier; *(send on) letter, parcel* faire suivre. **please ~** faire suivre S.V.P. ◆**forwarding address** *n*: **he left no ~ing address** il est parti sans laisser d'adresse. ◆**forward-looking** *adj* tourné vers les possibilités de l'avenir.

◆ **forwardness** *n [child]* précocité *f*; *(pertness)* effronterie *f*.

fossil ['fɒsl] **1** *n* fossile *m*. **2** *adj insect* fossilisé; *fuel* fossile. ◆ **fossilized** *adj* fossilisé.

foster ['fɒstəʳ] **1** *vt child* élever *(sans obligation d'adoption)*; *friendship, development* favoriser; *idea, hope* entretenir. **2** *adj child (officially arranged)* adoptif; *(where wet-nursed)* nourricier, de lait; *father, parents, family* adoptif, nourricier; *brother, sister* adoptif, de lait. ~ **home** famille *f* adoptive, famille nourricière; ~ **mother** mère *f* adoptive, nourrice *f*.

fought [fɔːt] *pret, ptp of* **fight**.

foul [faʊl] **1** *adj food, meal, taste, person* infect; *place* immonde; *smell, breath* fétide; *water* croupi; *air* vicié; *weather, temper* sale *(before n)*; *calumny, behaviour* vil; *language* ordurier; *(unfair)* déloyal; *blow* en traître. ~ **play** *(Sport)* jeu *m* irrégulier; *(fig)* qch de louche; *(Police etc)* un acte criminel; **to fall ~ of sb** se mettre qn à dos. **2** *n (Sport)* coup *m* irrégulier; *(Boxing)* coup bas; *(Ftbl)* faute *f*. **3** *vt (pollute) air* polluer; *(clog) pipe etc* obstruer; *(collide with) ship* entrer en collision avec; *fishing line* embrouiller; *propeller* s'emmêler dans. **the dog ~ed the path** le chien a fait des saletés sur le chemin. **4** *vi [rope]* s'emmêler.
◆ **foul up** * *vt sep relationship* gâcher.
◆ **foul-mouthed** *adj* au langage ordurier.
◆ **foul-smelling** *adj* fétide.

found[1] [faʊnd] *pret, ptp of* **find**. ◆ **foundling** *n* enfant *m(f)* trouvé(e).

found[2] [faʊnd] *vt (gen)* fonder; *belief* fonder (*on* sur); *suspicions* baser (*on* sur); **~ed on fact** basé sur des faits réels. ◆ **foundation** *n* fondation *f*; *(fig)* base *f*; **to lay the ~ations of** *(lit)* poser les fondations de; *(fig)* poser les bases de; **to lay the ~ation stone** poser la première pierre; **rumour entirely without ~ation** rumeur dénuée de tout fondement. ◆ **foundation cream** *n* fond *m* de teint. ◆ **foundation stone** *n* pierre commémorative. ◆ **founder**[1] *n* fondateur *m*, -trice *f*. ◆ **founding** *adj (US)* **~ing fathers** pères *mpl* fondateurs *(qui élaborèrent la Constitution fédérale)*.

founder[2] ['faʊndəʳ] *vi [ship]* sombrer; *[horse]* s'embourber; *[plans, hopes etc]* s'écrouler.

foundry ['faʊndrɪ] *n* fonderie *f*.

fount [faʊnt] *n (spring)* source *f*; *(Typ)* fonte *f*.

fountain ['faʊntɪn] **1** *n* fontaine *f*. **drinking ~** jet *m* d'eau potable. **2** *adj*: ~ **pen** stylo *m (à encre)*.

four [fɔːʳ] **1** *adj* quatre *inv*. **to the ~ corners of the earth** aux quatre coins du monde; **it's in ~ figures** c'est dans les milliers. **2** *n* quatre *m inv*. **on all ~s** à quatre pattes; **will you make up a ~ for bridge?** voulez-vous faire le quatrième au bridge?; **3** *pron* quatre *mfpl*; *for other phrases V* **six**.
◆ **four-door** *adj (Aut)* à quatre portes. ◆ **fourfold 1** *adj* quadruple ; **2** *adv* au quadruple.
◆ **fourfooted** *adj* à quatre pattes. ◆ **four-leaf(ed) clover** *n* trèfle *m* à quatre feuilles.
◆ **four-letter word** *n* gros mot *m*, ≃ mot de cinq lettres. ◆ **fourposter** *n* lit *m* à colonnes. ◆ **fourscore** *adj, n* quatre-vingts. ◆ **foursome** *n (game)* partie *f* à quatre; **we went in a ~some** nous y sommes allés à quatre. ◆ **foursquare** *adj (square)* carré; *(firm)* ferme; *(forthright)* franc. ◆ **four-star** *adj, n*: **~-star (petrol)** super *m*. ◆ **fourteen** *adj, n, pron* quatorze *(m) inv*. ◆ **fourteenth** *adj, n* quatorzième *(mf)*; *(fraction)* quatorzième *m*. ◆ **fourth** *adj, n* quatrième *(mf)*; *(fraction)* quart *m*; **~th finger** annulaire *m*; *(Pol)* **the F~th World** le quart-monde. ◆ **fourthly** *adv* quatrièmement. ◆ **four-wheel** *adj (Aut)* **with ~-wheel drive** à quatre roues motrices.

fowl [faʊl] *n* volaille *f*. ~ **pest** peste *f* aviaire.

fox [fɒks] **1** *n* renard *m*. *(fig)* **a sly ~** un fin renard. **2** *vt (puzzle)* rendre perplexe; *(deceive)* berner. **3** *adj*: ~ **cub** renardeau *m*; ~ **terrier** fox-terrier *m*. ◆ **foxglove** *n* digitale *f* (pourprée). ◆ **fox-hunt(ing)** *n* chasse *f* au renard. ◆ **foxy** *adj* rusé, finaud.

foyer ['fɔɪeɪ] *n* foyer *m (de théâtre etc)*.

fraction ['frækʃ(ə)n] *n* fraction *f*. **a ~ of a second** une fraction de seconde. ◆ **fractionally** *adv* un tout petit peu.

fractious ['frækʃəs] *adj* grincheux.

fracture ['fræktʃəʳ] **1** *n* fracture *f*. **2** *vt* fracturer. **to ~ one's leg** se fracturer la jambe. **3** *vi* se fracturer.

fragile ['frædʒaɪl] *adj* fragile. ◆ **fragility** *n* fragilité *f*.

fragment ['frægmənt] **1** *n* fragment *m*. **~s of conversation** bribes *fpl* de conversation.
2 [fræg'ment] *vt* fragmenter. **3** *vi* se fragmenter.
◆ **fragmentary** *or* ◆ **fragmented** *adj* fragmentaire.

fragrance ['freɪgr(ə)ns] *n* parfum *m*. ◆ **fragrant** *adj* parfumé; *memory* doux.

frail [freɪl] *adj person* frêle, faible; *health, happiness, hope* fragile. ◆ **frailty** *n* faiblesse *f*; fragilité *f*.

frame [freɪm] **1** *n [person, animal]* corps *m*, charpente *f*; *[building]* charpente; *[ship]* carcasse *f*; *[car, window]* châssis *m*; *[cycle, picture, racket]* cadre *m*; *[door]* encadrement *m*; *[spectacles]* monture *f*; *(in garden)* châssis; *(Cine)* image *f*. ~ **of mind** humeur *f*; ~ **of reference** système *m* de référence. **2** *adj*: ~ **house** maison *f* à charpente de bois; ~ **rucksack** sac *m* à dos à armature. **3** *vt* (**a**) *picture* encadrer. *(fig)* **~d in** encadré par. (**b**) *(construct) idea, plan* formuler; *plot* combiner; *sentence* construire. (**c**) **to ~ sb *, to have sb ~d** monter un coup contre qn *(pour faire porter l'accusation contre lui)*; **to be ~d** être victime d'un coup monté. ◆ **frame-up** ⁑ *n* coup *m* monté. ◆ **framework** *n (V* **frame 1***)* charpente *f*; carcasse *f*; châssis *m*; encadrement *m*; *[society, novel]* structure *f*; *(fig)* **in the ~work of** dans le cadre de; **~work agreement** accord-cadre *m*.

franc [fræŋk] *n* franc *m*.

France [frɑːns] *n* France *f*. **in ~** en France.

franchise ['fræntʃaɪz] *n* (**a**) *(Pol)* droit *m* de suffrage. (**b**) *(Comm)* franchise *f*.

Franco- ['fræŋkəʊ] *pref* franco-. ◆ **Franco-British** *adj* franco-britannique. ◆ **francophile** *adj, n* francophile *(mf)*. ◆ **francophobe** *adj, n* francophobe *(mf)*.

frank[1] [fræŋk] *adj* franc (*f* franche). ◆ **frankly** *adv* franchement. ◆ **frankness** *n* franchise *f*.

frank[2] [fræŋk] *vt letter* affranchir. **~ing machine** machine *f* à affranchir.

Frankfurt ['fræŋkfɜːt] *n* Francfort.

frankfurter ['fræŋkˌfɜːtəʳ] *n (Culin)* saucisse *f* de Francfort.

frantic ['fræntɪk] *adj activity, cry* frénétique; *need, desire* effréné; *person* hors de soi, dans tous ses états. ~ **with** fou (*or* folle *f*) de; **it drives her ~** cela la rend folle. ◆ **frantically** *adv wave* frénétiquement; *rush* comme un fou (*or* une folle).

fraternal [frə'tɜːnl] *adj* fraternel. ◆ **fraternity** *n* fraternité *f*; *(US Univ) (society)* confrérie *f*. ◆ **fraternization** *n* fraternisation *f*. ◆ **fraternize** *vi* fraterniser (*with* avec).

fraud [frɔːd] *n (act)* supercherie *f*; *(financial)* escroquerie *f*; *(Jur)* fraude *f*; *(person)* imposteur *m*; *(object)* attrape-nigaud *m*. **he's a ~** c'est un imposteur; *(less serious)* il joue la comédie *; **it's a ~!** c'est de la frime! * ◆ **fraudulence** *n* caractère *m* frauduleux. ◆ **fraudulent** *adj* frauduleux; **~ulent conversion** malversation *f*.

fraught [frɔːt] *adj (tense) situation* tendu. ~ **with** *danger* plein de; *hatred, menace* chargé de; **the whole business is a bit ~ *** tout ça c'est un peu risqué *.

fray[1] [freɪ] *n*: **the** ~ le combat; *(lit, fig)* **ready for the** ~ prêt à se battre.

fray[2] [freɪ] **1** *vt cloth, garment* effilocher; *cuff, trousers* effranger; *rope* user. **tempers were getting ~ed** tout le monde commençait à s'énerver; **my nerves are quite ~ed** je suis à bout de nerfs. **2** *vi* s'effilocher; s'effranger; s'user.

frazzle * ['fræzl] *n*: **worn to a** ~ éreinté, crevé *.

freak [fri:k] **1** *n (person or animal)* phénomène *m*. ~ **of nature** accident *m* de la nature; ~ **of fortune** caprice *m* de la fortune; **he won by a** ~ il a gagné grâce à un hasard extraordinaire; **a health food** ~ * un(e) fana * des aliments naturels. **2** *adj storm, weather* anormal; *error* bizarre; *victory* inattendu; (‡) *culture, clothes* hippie *f inv*. ◆**freak out** ‡ *vi (abandon convention)* se défouler *; *(get high on drugs)* se défoncer ‡; *(drop out of society)* devenir marginal.
◆**freakish** *adj weather* anormal; *error, idea* bizarre. ◆**freaky** *adj* bizarre.

freckle ['frekl] *n* tache *f* de rousseur. ◆**freckled** *adj* plein de taches de rousseur.

free [fri:] **1** *adj* (**a**) *(at liberty)* libre (*to do* de faire). **to get** ~ se libérer; **to set** ~ libérer; **he left one end of the string** ~ il a laissé un bout de la ficelle flotter libre; ~ **from** *or* **of** sans; **to be** ~ **of sb** être débarrassé de qn; ~ **of charge** *(adj)* gratuit; *(adv)* gratuitement; ~ **of tax, tax** ~ hors taxe; **to be a** ~ **agent** avoir toute liberté d'action; ~ **and easy** décontracté; **F~ Church** église *f* non-conformiste; *(fig)* **it's a** ~ **country!** on est en république! *; ~ **enterprise** libre entreprise *f*; **in** ~ **fall** en chute libre; ~ **fight** mêlée *f* générale; **to give sb a** ~ **hand** donner carte blanche à qn (*to do* pour faire); *(Sport)* ~ **kick** coup *m* franc; *(Ind)* ~ **labour** main-d'œuvre *f* non syndiquée; ~ **love** amour *m* libre; **to give** ~ **rein to** donner libre cours à; ~ **speech** liberté *f* de parole; ~ **trade** libre-échange *m*; ~ **verse** vers *m* libre; ~ **will** libre arbitre *m*; **of his own** ~ **will** de son propre gré.
(**b**) *(costing nothing) object, ticket* gratuit. ~ **on board** franco à bord; *(Comm)* ~ **sample** échantillon gratuit; ~ **gift** prime *f*.
(**c**) *(not occupied) room, seat, hour, person* libre. **there are 2** ~ **rooms left** il reste 2 chambres de libre; **I wasn't able to get** ~ **earlier** je n'ai pas pu me libérer plus tôt; *(lit, fig)* **to have one's hands** ~ avoir les mains libres.
(**d**) *(lavish)* **to be** ~ **with one's money** dépenser son argent sans compter; **you're very** ~ **with your advice** pour donner des conseils vous êtes un peu là *; **he makes** ~ **with all my things** il ne se gêne pas pour se servir de mes affaires; **feel** ~**!** * je t'en prie!, sers-toi!
2 *adv (for nothing) get, send* gratuitement.
3 *vt (gen)* libérer; *trapped person, animal* dégager; *tangle* débrouiller; *(unblock) pipe* déboucher; *(rescue)* sauver (*from* de); *(from burden)* débarrasser (*from* de); *(from tax)* exonérer (*from* de); *(from anxiety)* libérer, délivrer (*from* de). *(lit, fig)* **to** ~ **o.s. from** se débarrasser de, se libérer de.
◆**freedom** **1** *n* liberté *f*; ~**dom of the press/of speech/of worship** liberté de la presse/de la parole/du culte; ~**dom of information** liberté d'information; ~**dom of the seas** franchise *f* des mers; ~**dom from care/responsibility** le fait d'être dégagé de tout souci/de toute responsabilité; **to give sb the** ~**dom of a city** nommer qn citoyen d'honneur d'une ville; **he gave me the** ~**dom of his house** il m'a permis de me servir comme je voulais de sa maison ; **2** *adj*: ~**dom fighter** guérillero *m*, partisan *m*. ◆**free-for-all** *n* mêlée *f* générale. ◆**freehand** *adj, adv* à main levée. ◆**freehold** *adv* en propriété libre. ◆**freelance** **1** *n* free-lance *mf inv* ; **2** *adj* indépendant, free-lance *inv* ; **3** *vi* travailler en indépendant *or* en free-lance. ◆**freely** *adv give* libéralement; *spend, grow* avec luxuriance; *speak* franchement; *act* librement. ◆**freeman** *n*: ~**man of a city** citoyen(ne) *m(f)* d'honneur d'une ville. ◆**freemason** *n* franc-maçon *m*. ◆**freemasonry** *n* franc-maçonnerie *f*. ◆**freephone** *n* numéro *m* vert. ◆**free-range** *adj*: ~**-range eggs/poultry** œufs *mpl*/poulets *mpl* de ferme. ◆**free-standing** *adj* sur pied. ◆**free-style** *adj*: ~**style swimming** nage *f* libre. ◆**free-thinker** *n* libre-penseur *m*, -euse *f*. ◆**freethinking** **1** *adj* libre-penseur ; **2** *n* libre pensée *f*. ◆**freeway** *n (US)* autoroute *f (sans péage)*. ◆**freewheel** *vi [cyclist]* être en roue libre; *[motorist]* rouler au point mort. ◆**free-wheeling** *adj person* indépendant; *discussion* libre. ◆**free-will** *adj gift, offering* volontaire.

freesia ['fri:zɪə] *n* freesia *m*.

freeze [fri:z] *pret* **froze**, *ptp* **frozen** **1** *vi (gen)* geler; *(Culin)* se congeler; *(fig)* se figer. *(Met)* **to** ~ **hard** geler dur; **I'm freezing** je suis gelé; **my hands are freezing** j'ai les mains gelées; **to** ~ **to death** mourir de froid; **the lake froze** le lac a gelé; **the lake has frozen** le lac est gelé; **he froze (in his tracks)** il est resté figé sur place; ~! pas un geste!; **to** ~ **on to sb** * se cramponner à qn. **2** *vt water etc* geler; *food* congeler; *(industrially)* surgeler; *(Econ) assets* geler; *prices, wages* bloquer. **she froze him with a look** elle lui a lancé un regard qui l'a glacé. **3** *n (Met)* gel *m*; *[credits]* gel; *[prices, wages]* blocage *m*.
◆**freeze over** *vi [lakes, rivers]* geler; *(Aut) [windscreen etc]* givrer. ◆**freeze up** **1** *vi* (**a**) = **freeze over**. (**b**) *[pipes]* geler. **2** *vt sep*: **to be frozen up** être gelé.
◆**freeze-dry** *vt* lyophiliser. ◆**freezer** *n (domestic)* congélateur *m*; *(industrial)* surgélateur *m*; *(part of fridge)* freezer *m*. ◆**freeze-up** *n (Met)* gel *m*. ◆**freezing** *adj weather, look* glacial; **I'm freezing** je suis gelé; **freezing fog** brouillard *m* givrant; **below freezing point** au-dessous de zéro (centigrade).

freight [freɪt] **1** *n (goods)* fret *m*, cargaison *f*; *(transport)* transport *m*; *(charge)* fret. **2** *vt goods* transporter. **3** *adj (Rail) car, train, yard* de marchandises. ~ **plane** avion *m* de fret. ◆**freighter** *n (Naut)* cargo *m*; *(Aviat)* avion *m* de fret. ◆**freightliner** *n* train *m* de marchandises en conteneurs.

French [fren(t)ʃ] **1** *adj* français; *lesson, teacher, dictionary* de français; *king, embassy* de France. ~ **bean** haricot *m* vert; ~ **Canadian** *(adj)* canadien français; *(n)* Canadien(ne) français(e) *m(f)*; *(Ling)* français *m* canadien; ~ **chalk** craie *f* de tailleur; ~ **door** porte-fenêtre *f*; *(Culin)* ~ **dressing** *(oil and vinegar)* vinaigrette *f*; *(US: salad cream)* crème *f* à salade; ~ **fried potatoes**, ~ **fries** frites *fpl*; *(Mus)* ~ **horn** cor *m* d'harmonie; **to take** ~ **leave** filer à l'anglaise *; ~ **loaf** baguette *f (de pain)*; ~ **pastry** pâtisserie *f*; ~ **window** porte-fenêtre *f*. **2** *n (Ling)* français *m*. **the** ~ les Français *mpl*. ◆**Frenchman** *n* Français *m*. ◆**French-speaking** *adj* qui parle français; *nation etc* francophone. ◆**French-woman** *n* Française *f*.

frenzy ['frenzɪ] *n* frénésie *f*. ~ **of delight** transport *m* de joie. ◆**frenzied** *adj person* très agité; *crowd* en délire; *joy, shouts* frénétique; *efforts* désespéré.

frequent ['fri:kwənt] **1** *adj* fréquent. **it's quite** ~ cela arrive souvent; **a** ~ **visitor to our house** un habitué de la maison. **2** [frɪ'kwent] *vt* fréquenter. ◆**frequency** **1** *n* fréquence *f* ; **2** *adj (Statistics) distribution* des fréquences; *(Electronics) modulation, band* de fréquence. ◆**frequently** *adv* fréquemment, souvent.

fresco ['freskəʊ] *n* fresque *f*.

fresh [freʃ] **1** *adj (gen: not stale)* frais (*f* fraîche); *(additional, different) supplies, horse, sheet of paper* nouveau (*f* nouvelle); *clothes* de rechange; *(lively) person* plein d'entrain; *horse* fringant; *(cheeky)* trop

libre (*with sb* envers qn). **milk ~ from the cow** lait fraîchement trait; **~ butter** *(not stale)* beurre frais; *(unsalted)* beurre sans sel; **bread ~ from the oven** pain tout frais; *(US)* **~ paint** peinture fraîche; *(fig)* **to break ~ ground** faire qch d'entièrement nouveau; **to make a ~ start** prendre un nouveau départ; **~ water** *(not salt)* eau douce; **it is still ~ in my memory** j'en ai encore le souvenir tout frais; **to go out for a breath of ~ air** sortir prendre l'air; **in the ~ air** au grand air; **let's have some ~ air!** un peu d'air!; *(Met)* **it is getting ~** il commence à faire frais; **she was as ~ as a daisy** elle était fraîche comme une rose; **don't get ~ with me!** pas d'impertinences!
2 *adv*: **~ from Scotland** nouvellement *or* fraîchement arrivé d'Écosse.
◆ **fresh-air** *adj*: **~-air fiend** * mordu(e) * *m(f)* du grand air. ◆ **freshen** *vi [wind, air]* fraîchir. ◆ **freshen up** **1** *vi (wash etc)* faire un brin de toilette ; **2** *vt sep* faire un brin de toilette à; **that will ~en you up** cela vous requinquera *. ◆ **fresher** *or* ◆ **freshman** *n* bizut(h) *m*, nouveau *m*, nouvelle *f (étudiant(e) de première année)*. ◆ **freshly** *adv* nouvellement, récemment. ◆ **freshness** *n* fraîcheur *f*. ◆ **freshwater** *adj*: **~water fish** poisson *m* d'eau douce.

fret [fret] **1** *vi* s'agiter; *[baby]* pleurer. **don't ~!** ne t'en fais pas!; **the child is ~ting for its mother** le petit pleure parce qu'il veut sa mère. **2** *n*: **to be in a ~** * se faire du mauvais sang.
◆ **fretful** *adj person* agité, énervé; *baby, child* grognon. ◆ **fretfully** *adv* avec agitation, avec énervement. ◆ **fretfulness** *n* irritabilité *f*.

fretsaw ['fretsɔː] *n* scie *f* à découper.

Freudian ['frɔɪdɪən] *adj* freudien. **~ slip** lapsus *m*.

friar ['fraɪəʳ] *n* frère *m (Rel)*.

friction ['frɪkʃ(ə)n] *n* friction *f*. *(US)* **~ tape** chatterton *m*.

Friday ['fraɪdɪ] *n* vendredi *m*; *for phrases V* **Saturday**.

fridge [frɪdʒ] *n* frigo * *m*, frigidaire *m* ®.

fried [fraɪd] *pret, ptp of* **fry²**.

friend [frend] *n* ami(e) *m(f)*; *(schoolmate, workmate etc)* camarade *mf*, copain * *m*, copine * *f*. **a ~ of mine** un de mes amis; **~s of ours** des amis (à nous); **her best ~** sa meilleure amie; **to make/be ~s with sb** devenir/être ami avec qn; *(after quarrel)* **to make ~s** faire la paix; **he made a ~ of him** il en a fait son ami; **he makes ~s easily** il se fait facilement des amis; **let's be ~s again** on fait la paix?; **we're just good ~s** nous sommes simplement bons amis; **we're all ~s here** nous sommes entre amis; *(fig)* **to have ~s at court** avoir des amis influents; **F~s of the Earth** les Amis *mpl* de la Terre; *(Rel)* **Society of F~s** Quakers *mpl*.
◆ **friendliness** *n* attitude *f* amicale. ◆ **friendly** *adj (gen)* amical; *child, dog, act* gentil; *advice* d'ami; **people here are so ~ly** les gens sont si gentils ici; **I am quite ~ly with her** je suis assez ami(e) avec elle; **on ~ly terms with** en termes amicaux avec; *(Sport)* **~ly match** match *m* amical. ◆ **friendship** *n* amitié *f*.

frieze [friːz] *n (Archit)* frise *f*.

frigate ['frɪgɪt] *n* frégate *f (Naut)*.

fright [fraɪt] *n* peur *f*. **to take ~** s'effrayer (*at* de); **to get** *or* **have a ~** avoir peur; **to give sb a ~** faire peur à qn; **she looks a ~** elle est à faire peur.
◆ **frightful** *adj (gen)* affreux; *results, weather* épouvantable, effroyable. ◆ **frightfully** *adv late, ugly, hot* affreusement; *kind, pretty* terriblement; **I am ~fully sorry** je suis absolument désolé. ◆ **frightfulness** *n [crime etc]* atrocité *f*.

frighten ['fraɪtn] *vt* faire peur à, effrayer. **it nearly ~ed him out of his wits** cela lui a fait une peur bleue; **to ~ sb into doing sth** faire faire qch à qn par intimidation; **he was ~ed into doing it** il l'a fait sous le coup de la peur; **to be ~ed of (doing) sth** avoir peur de (faire) qch; **to be ~ed to death** avoir une peur bleue. ◆ **frighten away, frighten off** *vt sep birds* effaroucher; *children etc* chasser (en leur faisant peur). ◆ **frightened** *adj* effrayé; **don't be ~ed** n'ayez pas peur. ◆ **frightening** *adj* effrayant. ◆ **frighteningly** *adv* épouvantablement.

frigid ['frɪdʒɪd] *adj (Geog, Met)* glacial; *manner, welcome* froid; *woman* frigide. ◆ **frigidity** *n* froideur *f*; frigidité *f*.

frill [frɪl] *n* volant *m*; *(smaller)* ruche *f*; *(Culin)* papillote *f*. *(fig)* **without any ~s** tout simple. ◆ **frilly** *adj dress* à fanfreluches; *(fig) speech* à fioritures.

fringe [frɪndʒ] **1** *n [rug, shawl, hair]* frange *f*; *[forest]* bord *m*, lisière *f*; *[crowd]* derniers rangs *mpl*. *(fig)* **on the ~ of society** en marge de la société; **the outer ~s** la périphérie. **2** *vt shawl etc* franger (*with* de). *(fig)* **road ~d with trees** route bordée d'arbres. **3** *adj group* marginal. **~ benefits** avantages *mpl* divers; **~ theatre** théâtre *m* expérimental.

frisk [frɪsk] **1** *vi* gambader. **2** *vt criminal, suspect* fouiller. ◆ **frisky** *adj* vif, fringant.

fritter¹ ['frɪtəʳ] *vt (~* **away***)* gaspiller.

fritter² ['frɪtəʳ] *n (Culin)* beignet *m*.

frivolous ['frɪvələs] *adj* frivole. ◆ **frivolity** *n* frivolité *f*.

frizzle ['frɪzl] *vi* grésiller. ◆ **frizzled (up)** *adj food* calciné. ◆ **frizzly** *or* ◆ **frizzy** *adj hair* crêpelé.

fro [frəʊ] *adv*: **to and ~** de long en large; **to go to and ~ between** faire la navette entre; **journeys to and ~ between London and Edinburgh** allers *mpl* et retours *mpl* entre Londres et Édimbourg.

frock [frɒk] *n* robe *f*; *[monk]* froc *m*.

frog [frɒg] *n* grenouille *f*. *(fig)* **to have a ~ in one's throat** avoir un chat dans la gorge. ◆ **frogman** *n* homme-grenouille *m*. ◆ **frog-march** *vt*: **to ~-march sb in/out** *etc* amener/sortir *etc* qn de force. ◆ **frogspawn** *n* œufs *mpl* de grenouille.

frolic ['frɒlɪk] *vi (~* **about***)* folâtrer.

from [frɒm] *prep* (**a**) *(place: starting point)* de. **~ house to house** de maison en maison; **to jump ~ a wall** sauter d'un mur; **~ London to Paris** de Londres à Paris; **where are you ~?** d'où êtes-vous *or* venez-vous?; **~ above** d'en haut; **~ above the clouds** d'au-dessus des nuages; **~ afar** de loin; **she was looking at him ~ over the wall** elle le regardait depuis l'autre côté du mur; **~ under the table** de dessous la table. (**b**) *(time: starting point)* (à partir) de, dès. **(as) ~ the 14th July** à partir du 14 juillet; **~ that day onwards** à partir de ce jour-là; **~ his childhood** dès son enfance. (**c**) *(distance)* de. **the house is 10 km ~ the coast** la maison est à 10 km de la côte. (**d**) *(origin)* de, de la part de. **a letter ~ my mother** une lettre de ma mère; **tell him ~ me** dites-lui de ma part; **an invitation ~ the Smiths** une invitation (de la part) des Smith; **film ~ the novel by...** film d'après le roman de... (**e**) *(with prices, numbers)* à partir de, depuis. **wine ~ 6 francs a bottle** vins à partir de 6 F la bouteille; **dresses ~ 150 francs** robes à partir de *or* depuis 150 F; **~ 10 to 15 people** de 10 à 15 personnes. (**f**) *(source)* **to drink ~ a brook/a glass/straight ~ the bottle** boire à un ruisseau/dans un verre/à même la bouteille; **he took it ~ the cupboard** il l'a pris dans le placard; **take the knife ~ this child!** prenez le couteau à cet enfant!; **he took/stole it ~ them** il le leur a pris/volé; **to pick sb ~ the crowd** choisir qn dans la foule; **a quotation ~ Racine** une citation tirée de Racine; **to speak ~ notes** parler avec des notes; **~ your point of view** de votre point de vue. (**g**) *(change)* de. **~ bad to worse** de mal en pis; **price increase ~ 1 F to 1.50 F** augmentation de prix de 1 F à 1,50 F. (**h**) *(cause, motive)* **to act ~ convic-**

tion agir par conviction; **to die ~ fatigue** mourir de fatigue; ~ **what I heard** d'après ce que j'ai entendu; ~ **what I can see** à ce que je vois; ~ **the look of things** à en juger par les apparences; ~ **the way he talks you would think that...** à l'entendre on penserait que...

front [frʌnt] **1** *n* (**a**) *[audience, class]* premier rang *m*; *[building]* façade *f*, devant; *[boat, train, car]* avant; *[cupboard, dress]* devant; *[book] (beginning)* début *m*; *(cover)* couverture *f*. **in ~** *be, walk, put* devant; *send, move* en avant; **in ~ of the table** devant la table; *(in car)* **in the ~** à l'avant; *(Sport)* **to be in ~** mener; **to sit in the ~ of the train/bus** s'asseoir en tête du train/à l'avant de l'autobus; **the ~ of the cupboard** *(door)* la porte du placard; *(forepart)* le devant du placard; *(fig)* **to put on a bold ~** faire bonne contenance; **it's all just a ~** tout ça n'est que façade. (**b**) *(gen, Met, Mil, Pol)* front *m*. **at the ~** au front; **on all ~s** de tous côtés; **popular ~** front populaire. (**c**) *(sea ~) (beach)* plage *f*; *(prom)* front *m* de mer. **along** *or* **on the ~** sur le front de mer.
2 *adj garden, tooth* de devant; *wheel* avant *inv*; *row, page* premier. ~ **door** *[house]* porte *f* d'entrée; *[car]* portière *f* avant; **the ~ end** l'avant *m*; *(Parl)* ~ **bench** banc *m* des ministres (*or* des membres du cabinet fantôme); *(Mil)* ~ **line(s)** front *m*; **it's merely a ~ organization** cette organisation n'est qu'une couverture; *(Press)* **on the ~ page** en première page, à la une *; *(fig)* **in the ~ rank** parmi les premiers; ~ **room** pièce *f* de devant; *(lounge)* salon *m*; *(fig)* **a ~ runner for the party leadership** un des favoris pour être leader du parti; **to have a ~ seat** *(lit)* avoir une place au premier rang; *(fig)* être aux premières loges.
3 *vi*: **to ~ on to** donner sur.
4 *vt* (**a**) **house ~ed with stone** maison *f* avec façade en pierre. (**b**) *TV show* présenter.
◆ **frontage** *n* façade *f*. ◆ **frontal** *adj (gen)* frontal; *attack* de front; *nude* de face. ◆ **front-line** *adj troops, news* du front; *countries* limitrophe d'un pays hostile. ◆ **front-page** *adj*: **~-page news** gros titres *mpl*; **it was ~-page news** cela a fait la une * des journaux. ◆ **frontwards** *adv* en avant, vers l'avant. ◆ **front-wheel** *adj*: **~-wheel drive** traction *f* avant; **~-wheel drive car** traction avant.

frontier ['frʌntɪəʳ] **1** *n* frontière *f*. **2** *adj town, zone, part* frontière *inv*; *incident* de frontière.

frontispiece ['frʌntɪspiːs] *n* frontispice *m*.

frost [frɒst] **1** *n* gel *m*; *(hoar ~)* givre *m*. **late ~s** gelées *fpl* tardives; **10° of ~** 10° au-dessous de zéro. **2** *vt (freeze)* geler; *(US: ice) cake* glacer. ◆ **frostbite** *n* gelure *f*; **to get ~bite in one's hands** avoir les mains qui gèlent. ◆ **frostbitten** *adj* gelé. ◆ **frostbound** *adj* gelé. ◆ **frosted** *adj window, windscreen* givré; *nail varnish* nacré; *(opaque) glass* dépoli. ◆ **frosting** *n (US: icing)* glaçage *m*. ◆ **frosty** *adj (gen: also fig)* glacial; *window* couvert de givre; **it is going to be ~y** il va geler.

froth [frɒθ] **1** *n* mousse *f*. **2** *vi* mousser. **the dog was ~ing at the mouth** le chien avait de l'écume à la gueule. ◆ **frothy** *adj water, beer* mousseux; *sea* écumeux; *lace, nightdress* vaporeux; *play, entertainment* léger.

frown [fraʊn] **1** *n* froncement *m* (de sourcils). **2** *vi* froncer les sourcils. **to ~ at sth/sb** regarder qch/qn en fronçant les sourcils; *(fig: also* **~ on sb/sth***)* désapprouver qch/qn.

frowsy, frowzy ['fraʊzɪ] *adj room* qui sent le renfermé; *person, clothes* négligé.

froze [frəʊz] *pret of* **freeze**.

frozen ['frəʊzn] (*ptp of* **freeze**) *adj* gelé; *food* congelé. **I am ~** je suis gelé; **my hands are ~** j'ai les mains gelées; **to be ~ stiff** être gelé jusqu'aux os; ~ **food** aliments *mpl* congelés; *(industrially ~)* aliments surgelés.

frugal ['fruːg(ə)l] *adj person* économe (*with* de); *meal* frugal. ◆ **frugality** *n* frugalité *f*. ◆ **frugally** *adv give out* parcimonieusement; *live* simplement.

fruit [fruːt] **1** *n* fruit *m*. **may I have some ~?** puis-je avoir un fruit?; **more ~ is eaten nowadays** on mange actuellement plus de fruits; ~ **is good for you** les fruits sont bons pour la santé; *(lit, fig)* **to bear ~** porter fruit; **the ~ of hard work** le fruit d'un long travail. **2** *adj basket* à fruits; *salad* de fruits; *tree* fruitier. ~ **cake** cake *m*; ~ **cup** boisson *f* aux fruits *(parfois alcoolisée)*; ~ **dish** *(for dessert)* coupelle *f* à fruits; *(large)* coupe *f* à fruits; *(for holding ~)* corbeille *f* à fruits; ~ **farm** exploitation *f or* entreprise *f* fruitière; ~ **farming** arboriculture *f* (fruitière); ~ **machine** machine *f* à sous.
◆ **fruiterer** *n* fruitier *m*, -ière *f*; **~erer's shop** fruiterie *f*. ◆ **fruitful** *adj* fécond; *(fig)* fructueux. ◆ **fruitfully** *adv (fig)* fructueusement, avec profit. ◆ **fruitfulness** *n* fécondité *f*; caractère *m* fructueux. ◆ **fruition** [fruːˈɪʃən] *n*: **to bring to ~ion** réaliser; **to come to ~ion** se réaliser. ◆ **fruitless** *adj* stérile *(fig)*. ◆ **fruity** *adj flavour* fruité; *voice* bien timbré.

frump [frʌmp] *n* bonne femme *f* mal fagotée. ◆ **frumpish** *adj* mal fagoté.

frustrate [frʌs'treɪt] *vt hopes* tromper; *attempts, plans, plot* faire échouer; *person* décevoir. ◆ **frustrated** *adj person* frustré; *effort* vain; **he feels very ~d in his present job** il se sent très insatisfait dans son poste actuel. ◆ **frustrating** *adj* déprimant, irritant. ◆ **frustration** *n (emotion)* frustration *f*; *(sth frustrating etc)* déception *f*.

fry¹ [fraɪ] *n*: **the small ~** *(unimportant people)* le menu fretin; *(children)* les gosses * *mfpl*.

fry² [fraɪ] *pret, ptp* **fried** **1** *vt* (faire) frire. **to ~ eggs** faire des œufs *mpl* sur le plat; **fried eggs** œufs sur le plat; **fried fish** poisson *m* frit. **2** *vi* frire. ◆ **frying** *n*: **a smell of ~ing** une odeur de friture; **~ing pan** poêle *f* (à frire); **to jump out of the ~ing pan into the fire** tomber de Charybde en Scylla.

fuchsia ['fjuːʃə] *n* fuchsia *m*.

fuddled ['fʌdld] *adj ideas* confus; *person (muddled)* désorienté; *(tipsy)* éméché.

fudge [fʌdʒ] **1** *n (Culin)* caramel(s) *m(pl)*. **2** *vti*: **to ~ (an issue)** esquiver un problème.

fuel [fjʊəl] **1** *n (gen)* combustible *m*; *(for engine)* carburant *m*. *(fig)* **to add ~ to the flames** jeter de l'huile sur le feu; **the statistics gave him ~ for further attacks on...** les statistiques sont venues alimenter ses attaques contre... **2** *vt furnace etc* alimenter; *ships, aircraft etc* ravitailler en carburant. **3** *vi* se ravitailler en combustible *or* en carburant. *(Aviat etc)* **a ~ling stop** une escale technique. **4** *adj bill* de chauffage. ~ **oil** mazout *m*, fuel *m*; ~ **pump** pompe *f* d'alimentation; ~ **tank** réservoir *m* à carburant; *[ship]* soute *f* à mazout.

fug * [fʌg] *n (Brit)* atmosphère *f* viciée.

fugitive ['fjuːdʒɪtɪv] *adj, n* fugitif *(m)*, -ive *(f)*.

fulfil, *(US)* **fulfill** [fʊl'fɪl] *vt task, prophecy* accomplir; *order* exécuter; *condition* remplir; *plan, ambition* réaliser; *desire, hope* répondre à; *prayer* exaucer; *promise* tenir; *one's duties* s'acquitter de. **to feel ~led** se réaliser dans la vie. ◆ **fulfilling** *adj work etc* profondément satisfaisant. ◆ **fulfil(l)ment** *n [duty, desire]* accomplissement *m*; *[prayer, wish]* exaucement *m*; *[conditions, plans]* réalisation *f*; *(satisfied feeling)* contentement *m*.

full [fʊl] **1** *adj* (**a**) *(gen)* plein (*of* de); *room, theatre* comble, plein; *hotel, bus, train* complet; *day, programme* chargé. ~ **to overflowing** plein à ras bords; **a ~ life** une vie bien remplie; **his heart was ~** il avait le cœur gros; *(Theat)* **to play to a ~ house** jouer à bureaux fermés; **we are ~ (up) for July** nous sommes complets pour juillet; **you'll work better on a ~ stomach** tu travailleras mieux après

avoir mangé; *(not hungry)* **I am ~ up!** * j'ai trop mangé!; **~ of life** débordant d'entrain; **~ of oneself/of one's own importance** imbu de soi-même/de sa propre importance; **the papers were ~ of the murder** les journaux ne parlaient que du meurtre.
(**b**) *(complete) moon, employment* plein *(before n)*. **the ~ particulars** tous les détails; **~ information** des renseignements complets; **2 ~ hours** 2 bonnes heures; **to go (at) ~ blast** * *[car etc]* aller à toute pompe *; *[radio, television]* marcher à plein; **in ~ bloom** épanoui; **to pay ~ fare** payer plein tarif; **to fall ~ length** tomber de tout son long; **~ member** membre *m* à part entière; **~ name** nom et prénom(s) *mpl*; **at ~ speed** à toute vitesse; **~ speed ahead!, ~ steam ahead!** en avant toute!; *(Gram)* **~ stop** point *m*; **I'm not going, ~ stop!** * je n'y vais pas, un point c'est tout!; **working at the factory came to a ~ stop** ça a été l'arrêt complet du travail à l'usine; **battalion at ~ strength** bataillon au grand complet; **party in ~ swing** soirée qui bat son plein; **in ~ uniform** en grande tenue.
(**c**) *lips* charnu; *face* plein, rond; *figure* rondelet; *skirt etc* large.
2 *adv*: **~ well** fort bien; **~ in the face** *hit* en plein visage; *look* droit dans les yeux; **to go ~ out** aller à toute vitesse.
3 *n*: **in ~** *write sth* en toutes lettres; *publish* intégralement; **he paid in ~** il a tout payé; **to the ~** *justify* complètement; *use* au maximum.
◆**fullback** *n (Sport)* arrière *m*. ◆**full-blooded** *adj (vigorous) person* vigoureux; *(of unmixed race)* de race pure. ◆**full-blown** *adj flower* épanoui. ◆**full-bodied** *adj wine* qui a du corps. ◆**full-dress** *adj clothes* de cérémonie; *debate* dans les règles. ◆**full-grown** *adj* adulte. ◆**full-length** *adj portrait* en pied; *film* (de) long métrage. ◆**fullness** *n*: **in the ~ness of time** *(eventually)* avec le temps; *(at predestined time)* en temps et lieu. ◆**full-scale** *adj drawing, replica* grandeur nature *inv*; *search, retreat* de grande envergure; **~-scale fighting** une bataille rangée. ◆**full-sized** *adj* grandeur nature *inv*. ◆**full-time** **1** *n (Sport)* fin *f* de match ; **2** *adj, adv* à plein temps; **it's a ~-time job looking after those children** il faut s'occuper de ces enfants 24 heures sur 24. ◆**fully** *adv (completely) satisfied* entièrement; *understand* très bien; *justify* complètement; *use* au maximum; *(at least)* au moins, bien. ◆**fully-fashioned** *adj* entièrement diminué.

fulminate ['fʌlmɪneɪt] *vi* fulminer (*against* contre).

fulsome ['fʊlsəm] *adj praise* exagéré; *manner* plein d'effusions.

fumble ['fʌmbl] *vi (**~ about, ~ around**) (in the dark)* tâtonner; *(in one's pockets)* fouiller (*for sth* pour trouver qch). **to ~ with sth** tripoter qch maladroitement.

fume [fju:m] **1** *vi* fumer; *(*: be furious)* être en rage. **2** *n*: **~s** *(gen)* émanations *fpl*; *(from factory)* fumées *fpl*.

fumigate ['fju:mɪgeɪt] *vt* désinfecter par fumigation.

fun [fʌn] **1** *n*: **to have (good** *or* **great) ~** bien s'amuser; **to be (good** *or* **great) ~** être très amusant; **what ~!** ce que c'est amusant!; **for ~, in ~** pour rire; **to do sth for the ~ of it** faire qch pour s'amuser; **to spoil sb's ~** empêcher qn de s'amuser; **to spoil the ~** jouer les trouble-fête; **to have ~ and games with sth** bien s'amuser avec qch; *(fig: trouble)* en voir de toutes les couleurs * avec qch; **there'll be ~ and games over this decision** * cette décision va faire du potin *; **to make ~ of** *or* **poke ~ at sb/sth** se moquer de qn/qch. **2** *adj* (⁑) marrant *, rigolo *. **~ fur** similifourrure; **~ run** course *f* de fond pour amateurs. ◆**funfair** *n* fête *f* foraine. ◆**fun-loving** *adj* aimant s'amuser.

function ['fʌŋ(k)ʃ(ə)n] **1** *n* (**a**) *(gen)* fonction *f*. **in his ~ as judge** en sa qualité de juge. (**b**) *(meeting)* réunion *f*; *(reception)* réception *f*; *(official ceremony)* cérémonie *f* publique. **2** *vi* fonctionner. **to ~ as** faire fonction de. ◆**functional** *adj* fonctionnel. ◆**functionary** *n* fonctionnaire *mf*.

fund [fʌnd] *n* caisse *f*, fonds *m*. **to start a ~** lancer une souscription; **~s** fonds *mpl*; **in ~s** en fonds; *(Banking)* **no ~s** défaut *m* de provision; *(fig)* **a ~ of** beaucoup de. ◆**fundraise** *vi* obtenir des contributions bénévoles (*for* pour). ◆**fundraiser** *n* collecteur *m*, -trice *f* de fonds. ◆**fundraising** *n* collecte *f* de fonds.

fundamental [ˌfʌndəˈmentl] **1** *adj* fondamental. **2** *n*: **the ~s** les principes *mpl* essentiels; **to get down to (the) ~s** en venir à l'essentiel. ◆**fundamentalism** *n* fondamentalisme *m*. ◆**fundamentalist** *n, adj* fondamentaliste *(mf)*. ◆**fundamentally** *adv* fondamentalement.

funeral ['fju:n(ə)r(ə)l] **1** *n* enterrement *m*; *(in announcement etc)* obsèques *fpl* ; *(grander)* funérailles *fpl*. **my uncle's ~** l'enterrement de mon oncle; **Churchill's ~** les funérailles de Churchill; **that's your ~!** * tant pis pour toi! **2** *adj march, oration, service* funèbre. **~ director** entrepreneur *m* des pompes funèbres; **~ home, ~ parlour** dépôt *m* mortuaire; **~ procession** cortège *m* funèbre; *(in car)* convoi *m* mortuaire. ◆**funereal** [fju:'nɪərɪəl] *adj* funèbre, lugubre.

fungus, *pl* **-gi** ['fʌŋgəs, gaɪ] *n (Bot)* champignon *m*; *(mould)* moisissure *f*; *(Med)* fongus *m*.

funicular [fju:'nɪkjʊlə^r] *adj, n* funiculaire *(m)*.

funk * [fʌŋk] **1** *n*: **to be in a blue ~** avoir la trouille ⁑. **2** *vt*: **he ~ed (doing) it** il s'est dégonflé *.

funnel ['fʌnl] *n (for pouring through)* entonnoir *m*; *[ship, engine etc]* cheminée *f*.

funny ['fʌnɪ] **1** *adj* (**a**) *(comic)* drôle, amusant. **~ story** histoire *f* drôle; **he was always trying to be ~** il cherchait toujours à faire de l'esprit; **it's not ~** ça n'a rien de drôle. (**b**) *(strange)* curieux, bizarre. **a ~ idea** une drôle d'idée; **he is ~ that way** * il est comme ça; **the meat tastes ~** la viande a un drôle de goût; **there's sth ~** *or* **some ~ business * going on** il se passe qch de louche; **I felt ~** * je me suis senti tout chose *; **it gave me a ~ feeling** ça m'a fait tout drôle; **~!** c'est drôle, c'est curieux; **~ bone** * petit juif * *m*. **2** *n (Press)* **the funnies** ⁑ les bandes dessinées. ◆**funnily** *adv (amusingly)* drôlement; *(strangely)* curieusement, bizarrement; **funnily enough,...** chose curieuse,...

fur [fɜ:^r] **1** *n* (**a**) *[animal]* poil *m*, fourrure *f*. **it will make the ~ fly** cela va faire du grabuge * ; **she was dressed in ~s** elle portait de la fourrure. (**b**) *(in kettle etc)* tartre *m*. **2** *adj*: **~ coat** manteau *m* de fourrure. ◆**furred** *adj tongue* chargé. ◆**furrier** *n* fourreur *m*. ◆**furry** *adj animal* à poil; *toy* en peluche.

furbish ['fɜ:bɪʃ] *vt (polish)* fourbir; *(smarten)* remettre à neuf.

furious ['fjʊərɪəs] *adj person* furieux (*with sb* contre qn; *at having done* d'avoir fait); *storm, sea* déchaîné; *struggle* acharné; *speed* fou. **to get ~** se mettre en rage (*with sb* contre qn); **the fun was fast and ~** la fête battait son plein. ◆**furiously** *adv* furieusement; avec acharnement; à une allure folle.

furled [fɜ:ld] *adj flag* en berne.

furlough ['fɜ:ləʊ] *n* permission *f*, congé *m*.

furnace ['fɜ:nɪs] *n (Ind)* fourneau *m*; *(for central heating etc)* chaudière *f*; *(fig: hot place)* fournaise *f*.

furnish ['fɜ:nɪʃ] *vt* (**a**) *house* meubler (*with* de). **~ed flat** *or* **apartment** appartement *m* meublé; **in ~ed rooms** en meublé. (**b**) *(supply) object, information etc* fournir, donner; *person* pourvoir (*with sth* de qch). ◆**furnishing** *n*: **~ings** mobilier *m*; **with**

~ings and fittings avec objets mobiliers divers; **~ing fabrics** tissus *mpl* d'ameublement.

furniture ['fɜ:nɪtʃəʳ] **1** *n* meubles *mpl*. **a piece of ~** un meuble; **dining-room ~** des meubles *or* du mobilier de salle à manger. **2** *adj*: **~ polish** encaustique *f*; **~ remover** déménageur *m*; **~ shop** magasin *m* d'ameublement; **~ van** camion *m* de déménagement.

furore [fjʊə'rɔ:rɪ] *n (protests)* scandale *m*; *(enthusiasm)* débordement *m* d'enthousiasme.

furrow ['fʌrəʊ] **1** *n (Agr)* sillon *m*; *(in garden etc)* rayon *m*; *(on brow)* ride *f*. **2** *vt earth* sillonner; *face, brow* rider.

further ['fɜ:ðəʳ] *comp of* **far** **1** *adv* (**a**) = **farther 1.** (**b**) *(more)* davantage, plus. **without troubling any ~** sans se tracasser davantage; **I got no ~ with him** je ne suis arrivé à rien de plus avec lui; **we heard nothing ~ from him** nous n'avons plus rien reçu de lui; **and ~ I believe...** et de plus je crois...; *(Comm)* **~ to** par suite à. **2** *adj* (**a**) = **farther 2.** (**b**) *(additional)* supplémentaire, autre. **~ education** enseignement *m* post-scolaire; **college of ~ education** centre *m* d'enseignement post-scolaire; **until ~ notice** jusqu'à nouvel ordre; **upon ~ consideration** après plus ample réflexion; **awaiting ~ details** en attendant de plus amples détails; **one or two ~ details** un ou deux autres points. **3** *vt interests, cause* servir, favoriser. ◆**furtherance** *n* avancement *m*; **in ~ance of sth** pour servir qch. ◆**furthermore** *adv* en outre, de plus. ◆**furthermost** *adj* le plus éloigné.

furthest ['fɜ:ðɪst] = **farthest.**

furtive ['fɜ:tɪv] *adj action, look* furtif; *person* sournois. ◆**furtively** *adv* furtivement.

fury ['fjʊərɪ] *n [person]* fureur *f*; *[storm, wind, struggle]* violence *f*. **to be in a ~** être en furie *or* rage; **to fly into a ~** se mettre dans une rage folle; **like ~** * comme un fou (*or* une folle).

furze [fɜ:z] *n* ajoncs *mpl*.

fuse [fju:z] **1** *vt* (**a**) *(unite) metal* fondre; *(fig)* fusionner. (**b**) *(Elec)* **to ~ the television** (*or* **the iron** *or* **the lights** *etc*) faire sauter les plombs. **2** *vi* (**a**) *[metals]* fondre; *(fig:* **~ together***)* fusionner. (**b**) *(Elec)* **the television** (*or* **the lights** *etc*) **~d** les plombs ont sauté. **3** *n* (**a**) *(Elec: wire)* plomb *m*, fusible *m*. **to blow a ~** faire sauter un plomb *or* un fusible; **there's been a ~ somewhere** il y a un plomb de sauté quelque part. (**b**) *[bomb etc]* détonateur *m*; *(Min)* cordeau *m*. **4** *adj*: **~ box** *(Élec)* boîte *f* à fusibles; *(Aut)* porte-fusibles *m*; **~ wire** fusible *m*. ◆**fused** *adj*: **~d plug** prise *f* avec fusible incorporé. ◆**fusion** *n* fusion *f*.

fuselage ['fju:zəlɑ:ʒ] *n* fuselage *m*.

fusilier [,fju:zɪ'lɪəʳ] *n* fusilier *m*.

fuss [fʌs] **1** *n* histoires * *fpl*. **a lot of ~ about very little** beaucoup de bruit pour pas grand-chose; **to make a ~** faire un tas d'histoires * (*about or over sth* pour qch); **she was right to make a ~** elle a eu raison de protester; **what a ~ to get a passport!** que d'histoires * pour obtenir un passeport!; **to make a ~ of sb** être aux petits soins pour qn. **2** *vi (excitedly)* s'agiter; *(busily)* faire l'affairé(e); *(worriedly)* se tracasser. **to ~ over sb** être aux petits soins pour qn.
◆**fuss about, fuss around** *vi* faire l'affairé.
◆**fusspot** * *n* personne *f* qui fait des histoires pour rien. ◆**fussy** *adj person* tatillon; *dress, style* tarabiscoté; **she's very ~y about what she eats** elle est très tatillonne sur ce qu'elle mange; **I'm not ~y** * *(don't mind)* ça m'est égal.

fusty ['fʌstɪ] *adj smell* de renfermé; *room* qui sent le renfermé.

futile ['fju:taɪl] *adj remark* futile, vain; *attempt* vain. ◆**futility** *n* futilité *f*.

future ['fju:tʃəʳ] **1** *n* (**a**) avenir *m*. **in (the) ~** à l'avenir; **in the near ~** dans un proche avenir; **there is a real ~ in this firm** cette firme offre de réelles possibilités d'avenir; **there's no ~ in it** * *[job etc]* cela n'a aucun avenir; *(fig: no good doing that)* ça ne servira à rien. (**b**) *(Gram)* futur *m*. **in the ~** au futur. **2** *adj life, events* futur *(before n)*, à venir; *husband* futur. **at some ~ date** à une date ultérieure; *(Gram)* **~ perfect** futur *m* antérieur; **the ~ tense** le futur. ◆**futuristic** *adj* futuriste. ◆**futurologist** *n* futurologue *mf*. ◆**futurology** *n* futurologie *f*.

fuze [fju:z] *(US)* = **fuse.**

fuzz [fʌz] *n (frizzy hair)* cheveux *mpl* crépus; *(on face)* excroissance *f (hum)*; *(light growth)* duvet *m*. *(collective: police)* **the ~** ‡ les flics ‡ *mpl*. ◆**fuzzy** *adj hair* crépu; *(Phot)* flou; *ideas* confus; *person* désorienté; *(*: tipsy)* pompette *.

G

G, g [dʒiː] *n* G, g *m*; *(Mus: note)* sol *m*; *(gravity)* g *m*. *(Med)* **G.P.** = **general practitioner;** *V* **general.** ◆ **G-string** *n (garment)* cache-sexe *m inv*.

gabardine [ˌgæbəˈdiːn] *n* gabardine *f*.

gabble [ˈgæbl] **1** *vi (indistinctly)* bredouiller; *(unintelligibly)* baragouiner *. **to ~ on about sth** parler avec volubilité de qch. **2** *vt* bredouiller.

gable [ˈgeɪbl] *n* pignon *m*.

Gabon [gəˈbɒn] *n* Gabon *m*.

gad [gæd] *vi*: **to ~ about** vadrouiller *.

gadget [ˈgædʒɪt] *n* gadget *m*; *(*: thingummy)* petit truc * *m*. ◆ **gadgetry** *n* tous les gadgets *mpl*.

Gaelic [ˈgeɪlɪk] *adj, n* gaélique *(m)*.

gaff [gæf] *n (Fishing)* gaffe *f*.

gaffe [gæf] *n* gaffe *f*, bévue *f*.

gaffer ‡ [ˈgæfəʳ] *n (old man)* vieux *m*; *(foreman)* contremaître *m*; *(boss)* patron *m*; *(US Cine)* chef-électricien *m*.

gag [gæg] **1** *n* (**a**) *(in mouth)* bâillon *m*. (**b**) *(joke)* plaisanterie *f*. **it's a ~ to raise funds** c'est un truc * comique pour ramasser de l'argent. **2** *vt (silence)* bâillonner. **3** *vi (*: joke)* plaisanter; *(*: retch)* avoir des haut-le-cœur.

gage [geɪdʒ] *(US)* = **gauge.**

gaiety [ˈgeɪɪtɪ] *n* gaieté *f*.

gaily [ˈgeɪlɪ] *adv behave, speak* gaiement; *decorate* de façon gaie. ◆ **gaily-coloured** *adj* aux couleurs vives.

gain [geɪn] **1** *n (Comm, Fin) (profit)* bénéfice *m*; *(winning)* gain *m*; *(fig)* avantage *m*; *(increase)* augmentation *f*; *(in wealth)* accroissement *m* (*in* de); *(knowledge etc)* acquisition *f* (*in* de); *(St Ex)* hausse *f*. **to do sth for ~** faire qch pour le profit; **his loss is our ~** là où il perd nous gagnons.
2 *vt* (**a**) *(gen)* gagner; *experience* acquérir; *objective* atteindre; *liberty* conquérir; *friends* se faire; *supporters* s'attirer. **to ~ ground** gagner du terrain; **to ~ popularity** gagner en popularité; **what have you ~ed by doing it?** qu'est-ce que tu as gagné à faire ça? (**b**) *(increase) (St Ex)* **these shares have ~ed 3 points** ces valeurs ont enregistré une hausse de 3 points; **to ~ speed/weight** prendre de la vitesse/du poids; **she's ~ed 3 kg** elle a pris 3 kg; **my watch has ~ed 5 minutes** ma montre a pris 5 minutes d'avance; *(Pol)* **they've ~ed 3 seats** ils ont gagné trois nouveaux sièges; **to ~ the upper hand** prendre le dessus.
3 *vi* gagner (*in* en, *by* à); *[watch]* avancer; *[runners]* prendre de l'avance (*on* sur).
◆ **gainful** *adj occupation etc* rémunérateur; *employment* rémunéré.

gainsay [ˌgeɪnˈseɪ] *pret, ptp* **gainsaid** *vt person* contredire; *fact* nier; *argument* réfuter. **there's no ~ing it** c'est indéniable.

gait [geɪt] *n* démarche *f*, façon *f* de marcher.

gaiter [ˈgeɪtəʳ] *n* guêtre *f*.

gala [ˈgɑːlə] *n* fête *f*, gala *m*; *(sports)* grand concours *m*. **~ occasion** grande occasion *f*.

galaxy [ˈgæləksɪ] *n* galaxie *f*.

gale [geɪl] **1** *n* coup *m* de vent. **it was blowing a ~** le vent soufflait très fort; **there's a ~ blowing in through that window** c'est une véritable bourrasque qui entre par cette fenêtre; **~s of laughter** grands éclats *mpl* de rire. **2** *adj*: **~ force winds** coups *mpl* de vent; **~ warning** avis *m* de coups de vent.

gall¹ [gɔːl] *n* bile *f*; *(bitterness)* fiel *m*; *(*: impertinence)* culot * *m*. ◆ **gall-bladder** *n* vésicule *f* biliaire. ◆ **gallstone** calcul *m* biliaire.

gall² [gɔːl] *vt (irritate)* irriter, exaspérer. ◆ **galling** *adj (irritating)* irritant; *(humiliating)* humiliant.

gallant [ˈgælənt] *adj* (**a**) *(brave)* brave, vaillant. (**b**) [gəˈlænt] *(attentive to women)* galant. ◆ **gallantly** *adv* bravement; [gəˈlæntlɪ] galamment. ◆ **gallantry** *n* bravoure *f*.

galleon [ˈgælɪən] *n* galion *m*.

gallery [ˈgælərɪ] *n (gen)* galerie *f*; *(for spectators, reporters)* tribune *f*; *(Theat)* dernier balcon *m*; *(US: auction room)* salle *f* des ventes. **art gallery** *(private)* galerie d'art; *(state-owned)* musée *m*; *(fig)* **to play to the ~** poser *or* parler pour la galerie.

galley [ˈgælɪ] *n* (**a**) *(ship)* galère *f*; *(ship's kitchen)* coquerie *f*. **~ slave** galérien *m*. (**b**) *(Typ)* galée *f*. **~ (proof)** placard *m*.

Gallic [ˈgælɪk] *adj (of Gaul)* gaulois; *(French)* français; *charm etc* latin. ◆ **gallicism** *n* gallicisme *m*.

gallivant [ˌgælɪˈvænt] *vi* (**~ about, ~ around**) courir le guilledou *.

gallon [ˈgælən] *n* gallon *m (Brit = 4,546 litres, US = 3,785 litres)*.

gallop [ˈgæləp] **1** *n* galop *m*. **to go for a ~** faire un temps de galop; **at full ~** *[horse]* au grand galop; *[rider]* à bride abattue. **2** *vi [horse, rider]* galoper. *(lit, fig)* **to ~ away/back** *etc* partir/revenir *etc* au galop. ◆ **galloping** *adj horse* au galop; *inflation, pneumonia* galopant.

gallows [ˈgæləʊz] *npl* gibet *m*, potence *f*.

galore [gəˈlɔːʳ] *adv* en abondance, à gogo *.

galvanize [ˈgælvənaɪz] *vt* galvaniser. *(fig)* **to ~ sb into action** galvaniser qn. ◆ **galvanic** *adj (Elec)* galvanique; *effect* galvanisant. ◆ **galvanization** *n* galvanisation *f*.

Gambia [ˈgæmbɪə] *n*: **the ~** la Gambie.

gambit [ˈgæmbɪt] *n (Chess)* gambit *m*; *(fig)* manœuvre *f*.

gamble [ˈgæmbl] **1** *n* entreprise *f* risquée. **life's a ~** la vie est un jeu de hasard; **it's a pure ~** c'est affaire de chance; **the ~ paid off** ça a payé de prendre ce risque *. **2** *vi* jouer (*on* sur, *with* avec). **to ~ on the stock exchange** jouer en Bourse; *(fig)* **to ~ on** compter sur; *(less sure)* miser sur. ◆ **gamble away** *vt sep money etc* perdre au jeu. ◆ **gambler** *n* joueur *m*, -euse *f*. ◆ **gambling 1** *n* jeu *m*; **his gambling** sa passion du jeu ; **2** *adj debts* de jeu; *losses* au jeu; **gambling den, gambling house** maison *f* de jeu, tripot *m (pej)*.

gambol [ˈgæmb(ə)l] *vi* gambader. **to ~ away** *etc* partir *etc* en gambadant.

game¹ [geɪm] **1** *n* (**a**) *(gen)* jeu *m*; *[football, cricket etc]* match *m*; *[tennis, billiards, chess]* partie *f*. **~ of cards** partie de cartes; **card ~** jeu de cartes *(belote, bridge etc)*; **to have a ~ of** faire une partie de, jouer un match de; *(Scol)* **~s** sport *m*, plein air *m*; **to be good at ~s** être sportif; **that's ~** *(Tennis)* ça fait jeu; *(Bridge)* ça fait la manche; *(Tennis)* **~, set and match** jeu, set et match; **he's off his ~** il n'est pas en forme; **to put sb off his ~** troubler qn; **this**

isn't a ~! c'est sérieux!; *(fig)* **it's a profitable ~** c'est une entreprise rentable; **the ~ is up** tout est fichu *; **to play sb's ~** entrer dans le jeu de qn; **two can play at that ~** à bon chat bon rat; **what's the ~?** * qu'est-ce qui se passe? ; **I wonder what his ~ is** je me demande ce qu'il mijote *; **to beat sb at his own ~** battre qn sur son propre terrain; **how long have you been in this ~?** * ça fait combien de temps que vous faites ça?; **the ~ isn't worth the candle** le jeu n'en vaut pas la chandelle; **to make a ~ of** se moquer de. (**b**) *(Culin, Hunting)* gibier *m*. **big ~** gros gibier.
2 *adj* (**a**) **~ birds** gibier *m* à plume; **~ laws** réglementation *f* de la chasse; *(fig)* **~ plan** plan *m* d'action; **~ reserve** réserve *f* de gros gibier; **~s master, ~s mistress** professeur *m* d'éducation physique; **~ warden** *(on reserve)* gardien *m*. (**b**) *(ready)* prêt (*to do* à faire).
3 *vi* jouer, parier.
◆ **gamekeeper** *n* garde-chasse *m*. ◆ **gamesmanship** *n*: **to be good at ~smanship** être rusé; **it's a piece of ~smanship** c'est un truc * pour gagner.

game² [geɪm] *adj* courageux, brave. **to be ~** avoir du cran *; **to be ~ for sth** *or* **to do sth** se sentir de taille à faire qch; **are you ~?** tu t'en sens capable?; **~ for anything** prêt à tout.

game³ [geɪm] *adj (lame) arm, leg* estropié. **to have a ~ leg** être estropié.

gamma ['gæmə] *n* gamma *m*. **~ rays** rayons *mpl* gamma.

gammon ['gæmən] *n (ham)* jambon *m* fumé.

gamut ['gæmət] *n* gamme *f*. **to run the ~ of** passer par toute la gamme de.

gang [gæŋ] *n [workmen]* équipe *f*; *[criminals]* bande *f*, gang *m*; *[youths, friends etc]* bande; *[prisoners]* convoi *m*. ◆ **gang together** *, **gang up** * *vi* se mettre à plusieurs (*to do* pour faire). **to ~ up on** *or* **against sb** ⁑ se mettre à plusieurs contre qn. ◆ **gangland** * *n* le milieu. ◆ **gangplank** *n* passerelle *f*. ◆ **gangster** *n* gangster *m*. ◆ **gangway** *n (gen)* passage *m*; *(Naut)* passerelle *f*; *(in bus etc)* couloir *m*; *(in theatre)* allée *f*; *(excl)* **~way!** dégagez!

Ganges ['gændʒiːz] *n* Gange *m*.

gangling ['gæŋglɪŋ] *adj* dégingandé.

ganglion, *pl* **ganglia** ['gæŋglɪən, 'gæŋglɪə] *n* ganglion *m*.

gangrene ['gæŋgriːn] *n* gangrène *f*. ◆ **gangrenous** *adj* gangreneux. **to go gangrenous** se gangrener.

gannet ['gænɪt] *n (Orn)* fou *m*.

gantry ['gæntrɪ] *n (gen)* portique *m*; *(Space)* tour *f* de lancement.

gaol [dʒeɪl] *(Brit)* = **jail.**

gap [gæp] *n (gen)* trou *m*; *(in wall, hedge)* trou, ouverture *f*; *(in print, text)* blanc *m*; *(between floorboards, curtains, teeth)* interstice *m*; *(mountain pass)* trouée *f*; *(fig)* vide *m*; *(in education)* lacune *f*; *(in time)* intervalle *m*; *(in conversation, narrative)* interruption *f*, vide. **to stop up** *or* **fill in a ~** boucher un trou, combler un vide; **a ~ in his memory** un trou de mémoire; **he left a ~ which will be hard to fill** il a laissé un vide qu'il sera difficile de combler; **to close the ~ between two points of view** rapprocher deux points de vue; **to close the ~ in the balance of payments** supprimer le déficit dans la balance des paiements; *(Comm)* **a ~ in the market** un créneau.

gape [geɪp] *vi* (**a**) *[person, seam]* bâiller; *[chasm etc]* être béant. (**b**) *(stare)* rester bouche bée (*at* devant). **to ~ at sb/sth** regarder qn/qch bouche bée. ◆ **gaping** *adj hole, chasm, wound* béant; *seam* qui bâille; *person* bouche bée *inv*.

garage ['gærɑːʒ] **1** *n* garage *m*. **2** *vt* mettre au garage. **3** *adj*: **~ mechanic** mécanicien *m*; **~ proprietor** garagiste *m*; **~ sale** vente *f* d'objets usagés (chez un particulier).

garb [gɑːb] *n* costume *m*.

garbage ['gɑːbɪdʒ] **1** *n* ordures *fpl*, détritus *mpl*; *(in kitchen)* déchets *mpl*; *(fig)* rebut *m*. **2** *adj*: **~ can** boîte *f* à ordures; **~ chute** vide-ordures *m inv*; **~ collector, ~ man** éboueur *m*; **~ disposal unit** broyeur *m* d'ordures; **~ truck** benne *f* des éboueurs.

garble ['gɑːbl] *vt story* raconter de travers; *quotation* déformer; *facts* dénaturer; *instructions* embrouiller. ◆ **garbled** *adj account, instructions* embrouillé; *text* altéré; *words, speech* incompréhensible.

garden ['gɑːdn] **1** *n* jardin *m*. **the G~ of Eden** le jardin d'Éden; **~s** *(private)* parc *m*; *(public)* jardin public; *(fig)* **to lead sb up the ~ (path)** * mener qn en bateau *; *(fig)* **everything in the ~'s lovely** tout va pour le mieux. **2** *vi* faire du jardinage. **3** *adj*: **~ centre** jardinerie *f*, pépinière *f*; **~ city** cité-jardin *f*; **~ flat** appartement *m* en rez-de-jardin; **~ hose** tuyau *m* d'arrosage; **~ tools** outils *mpl* de jardinage; **~ party** garden-party *f*; **~ produce** produits *mpl* maraîchers; **~ seat** banc *m* de jardin; **~ shears** cisaille *f* de jardinier; **just over the ~ wall from us** juste à côté de chez nous. ◆ **gardener** *n* jardinier *m*, -ière *f*. ◆ **gardening** *n* jardinage *m*.

gardenia [gɑː'diːnɪə] *n* gardénia *m*.

gargle ['gɑːgl] *vi* se gargariser.

gargoyle ['gɑːgɔɪl] *n* gargouille *f*.

garish ['gɛərɪʃ] *adj (gen)* voyant, criard; *light* cru.

garland ['gɑːlənd] *n* guirlande *f*.

garlic ['gɑːlɪk] **1** *n* ail *m*. **2** *adj*: **~ press** presse-ail *m*; **~ salt** sel *m* d'ail; **~ sausage** saucisson *m* à l'ail. ◆ **garlicky** *adj flavour, smell* d'ail; *sauce* à l'ail; *food* aillé; *breath* qui sent l'ail.

garment ['gɑːmənt] *n* vêtement *m*.

garnet ['gɑːnɪt] *n* grenat *m*.

garnish ['gɑːnɪʃ] **1** *vt* garnir (*with* de). **2** *n* garniture *f*.

garret ['gærət] *n* mansarde *f*.

garrison ['gærɪs(ə)n] **1** *n* garnison *f*. **2** *vt* placer une garnison dans; *[troops]* être en garnison dans. **3** *adj town, troops, duty* de garnison.

garrulous ['gærʊləs] *adj* loquace. ◆ **garrulity** *n* loquacité *f*. ◆ **garrulously** *adv* avec volubilité.

garter ['gɑːtəʳ] **1** *n* (**a**) *(gen)* jarretière *f*; *(for men's socks)* fixe-chaussette *m*. (**b**) *(US: from belt)* jarretelle *f*. **2** *adj (US)* **~ belt** porte-jarretelles *m inv*.

gas [gæs] **1** *n* (**a**) *(gen)* gaz *m inv*; *(anaesthetic)* anesthésique *m*. **Calor ~** ® ≃ butane *m*; **to cook by** *or* **with ~** faire la cuisine au gaz; **to turn on/off the ~** allumer/fermer le gaz; *(Med etc)* **I had ~** j'ai eu une anesthésie au masque. (**b**) *(US: gasoline)* essence *f*.
2 *vt* asphyxier; *(Mil)* gazer. **to ~ o.s.** s'asphyxier.
3 *vi* (⁑) *(talk)* parler; *(chat)* bavarder.
4 *adj industry* du gaz; *engine, oven, pipe* à gaz; *lighting, heating* au gaz. **~ bracket** applique *f* à gaz; **~ burner, ~ jet** brûleur *m* à gaz; **~ chamber** chambre *f* à gaz; **~ cooker** cuisinière *f* à gaz; *(portable)* réchaud *m* à gaz; **~ fire** appareil *m* de chauffage à gaz; **to light the ~ fire** allumer le gaz; **~ fitter** ajusteur-gazier *m*; **~ heater** appareil *m* de chauffage à gaz; *(for heating water)* chauffe-eau *m inv* (à gaz); **~ lighter** *(for cooker etc)* allume-gaz *m inv*; *(for cigarettes)* briquet *m* à gaz; **~ main** canalisation *f* de gaz; **~ meter** compteur *m* à gaz; **~ oil** gas-oil *m*; *(US Aut)* **~ pedal** accélérateur *m*; **~ permeable** perméable à l'air; **~ pipeline** gazoduc *m*; **~ ring** *(part of cooker)* brûleur *m*; *(small stove)* réchaud *m* à gaz; *(US)* **~ station** station-service *f*; **~ stove** *(portable)* réchaud *m* à gaz; *(larger)* cuisinière *f* à gaz; *(US)* **~ tank** réservoir *m* à essence; **~ tap** *(on pipe)* robinet *m* à gaz; *(on cooker)* bouton

m (de cuisinière à gaz); ~ **turbine** turbine *f* à gaz; ~ **worker** gazier *m*.

◆ **gaseous** *adj* gazeux. ◆ **gas-fired** *adj* chauffé au gaz; ~**-fired central heating** chauffage central au gaz. ◆ **gaslight** *n*: **by ~light** à la lumière du gaz. ◆ **gaslit** *adj* éclairé au gaz. ◆ **gasman** * *n*: **the ~man** l'employé *m* du gaz. ◆ **gasmask** *n* masque *m* à gaz. ◆ **gasoline** *n (US)* essence *f*. ◆ **gasometer** *n* gazomètre *m*. ◆ **gassy** *adj* gazeux. ◆ **gasworks** *npl* usine *f* à gaz.

gash [gæʃ] **1** *n (in flesh)* entaille *f*; *(on face)* balafre *f*; *(in fabric)* grande déchirure *f*. **2** *vt* entailler; balafrer; déchirer. **3** *adj* (‡) de trop, en surplus. **if that box is** ~ si vous n'avez plus besoin de cette boîte.

gasket ['gæskɪt] *n [piston]* garniture *f* de piston; *[joint]* joint *m* d'étanchéité; *[cylinder head]* joint de culasse.

gasp [gɑːsp] **1** *n* halètement *m*. **to give a ~ of surprise/fear** *etc* avoir le souffle coupé par la surprise/la peur *etc*; **to be at one's last ~** *(lit)* être à l'agonie; *(*: fig)* n'en pouvoir plus. **2** *vi (choke)* haleter; *(from astonishment)* avoir le souffle coupé. *(lit, fig)* **to make sb ~** couper le souffle à qn; **to ~ for breath** *or* **air** haleter, suffoquer. **3** *vt*: **'no!' she ~ed** 'pas possible!' souffla-t-elle. ◆ **gasp out** *vt sep plea* dire dans un souffle; *word* souffler.

gastric ['gæstrɪk] *adj* gastrique; *flu* gastro-intestinal; *ulcer* de l'estomac. ◆ **gastritis** *n* gastrite *f*. ◆ **gastroenteritis** *n* gastro-entérite *f*.

gastronome ['gæstrənəʊm] *n* gastronome *mf*. ◆ **gastronomic** *adj* gastronomique. ◆ **gastronomy** *n* gastronomie *f*.

gate [geɪt] *n* (**a**) *[castle, town]* porte *f*; *[field, level crossing]* barrière *f*; *[garden]* porte, portail *m*; *(of iron)* grille *f* (d'entrée); *(into courtyard etc)* porte cochère; *(Rail: in Underground)* portillon *m*; *[lock, sluice]* vanne *f*; *[sports ground]* entrée *f*. *(at airport)* ~ **5** porte 5. (**b**) *(Sport) (attendance)* spectateurs *mpl*; *(~ money)* recette *f*, entrées *fpl*.

◆ **gatecrash** * **1** *vi (not paying)* resquiller; **2** *vt party* s'introduire sans invitation dans; *match etc* assister sans payer à. ◆ **gatecrasher** * *n (at party etc)* intrus(e) *m(f)*; *(at match etc)* resquilleur * *m*, -euse * *f*. ◆ **gate-leg(ged)** *adj*: **~-leg(ged) table** table *f* à l'anglaise. ◆ **gatepost** *n* montant *m* (de porte); *(fig)* **between you, me and the ~post** * soit dit entre nous. ◆ **gateway** *n (to a place)* porte *f (to* de); *(to success)* porte ouverte *(to* à).

gâteau ['gætəʊ] *n* grand gâteau fourré.

gather ['gæðəʳ] **1** *vt* (**a**) (**~ together**) *people* rassembler; *objects* rassembler, ramasser. (**b**) (**~ up, ~ in**) *crops* récolter; *flowers* cueillir; *sticks, mushrooms, papers* ramasser; *taxes etc* percevoir; *contributions, information* recueillir; *skirt, hair etc* ramasser; *(Sewing) material* froncer; *dust* ramasser; *energies* rassembler. **to ~ one's thoughts** se ressaisir; **to ~ speed** prendre de la vitesse; *[feeling, movement]* **to ~ strength** se renforcer; **he ~ed his cloak around him** il a resserré sa cape contre lui; **to ~ one's brows** froncer les sourcils. (**c**) *(infer)* déduire, conclure *(from sth* de qch; *that* que); croire comprendre *(from sb* d'après ce que dit qn; *from a newspaper* d'après ce que dit le journal; *that* que). **as you will have ~ed** comme vous avez dû le deviner.

2 *vi (collect) [people]* (**~ together**) se rassembler; *[crowd]* se former; *[troops etc]* s'amasser; *[objects, dust]* s'accumuler, s'amasser; *[clouds]* s'amonceler; *[storm]* se préparer.

◆ **gather round** *vi* s'approcher.

◆ **gathering** **1** *n* assemblée *f*, réunion *f*; **family ~ing** réunion de famille ; **2** *adj force, speed* croissant; *storm* qui se prépare.

gaudy ['gɔːdɪ] *adj* voyant, criard.

gauge [geɪdʒ] **1** *n (size: of pipe, gun etc)* calibre *m*; *(Rail)* écartement *m*; *(instrument)* jauge *f*, indicateur *m*. **fuel/petrol/oil ~** jauge de carburant/d'essence/du niveau d'huile; **pressure ~** manomètre *m*; **tyre ~** indicateur de pression des pneus; **wheel ~** écartement des essieux; **it was a ~ of public feeling** cela a permis de jauger le sentiment du public. **2** *vt nut, screw, gun* calibrer; *temperature* mesurer; *oil* jauger; *wind* mesurer la vitesse de; *distance, sb's capabilities* jauger; *course of events* prévoir. **he was trying to ~ how far he should move it** il essayait d'évaluer de combien il devait le déplacer; **to ~ the right moment** calculer le bon moment.

Gaul [gɔːl] *n (country)* Gaule *f*; *(person)* Gaulois(e) *m(f)*.

gaunt [gɔːnt] *adj (very thin)* émacié; *(grim)* lugubre.

gauntlet ['gɔːntlɪt] *n* gant *m* (à crispin); *[armour]* gantelet *m*. **he had to run the ~ through the crowd** il a dû foncer à travers une foule hostile.

gauze [gɔːz] *n* gaze *f*.

gave [geɪv] *pret of* **give.**

gavel ['gævl] *n* marteau *m (de commissaire-priseur etc)*.

gawker ['gɔːkəʳ] *n* badaud *m*.

gawky ['gɔːkɪ] *adj* dégingandé, godiche.

gay [geɪ] **1** *adj* (**a**) *(gen)* gai; *company, occasion* joyeux; *laughter* enjoué. **to become ~(er)** s'égayer; **with ~ abandon** avec une belle désinvolture; **to have a ~ time** prendre du bon temps. (**b**) *(*: homosexual)* homosexuel, gay *inv*. **2** *n* homosexuel(le) *m(f)*.

gaze [geɪz] **1** *n* regard *m* (fixe). **2** *vi* regarder. **to ~ into space** regarder dans le vide; **to ~ at sth** regarder (fixement) qch.

gazette [gə'zet] *n (official publication)* journal *m* officiel; *(newspaper)* gazette *f*. ◆ **gazetteer** *n* index *m* (géographique).

gazump * [gə'zʌmp] *vi (Brit) revenir sur une promesse de vente pour accepter un prix plus élevé.*

gear [gɪəʳ] **1** *n* (**a**) *(equipment) (gen)* équipement *m*, matériel *m*; *(belongings)* affaires * *fpl*, effets *mpl* (personnels); *(clothing)* vêtements *mpl*; *(‡: modern)* fringues ‡ *fpl* à la mode. **fishing** *etc* **~** matériel *or* équipement de pêche *etc*. (**b**) *(apparatus)* mécanisme *m*, dispositif *m*. **safety ~** mécanisme de sécurité. (**c**) *(Tech)* engrenage *m*; *(Aut) (mechanism)* embrayage *m*; *(speed)* vitesse *f*. **in ~** en prise; **not in ~** au point mort; **he put the car into ~** il a mis la voiture en prise; **the car slipped out of ~** la vitesse a sauté; **to change** *or (US)* **to shift ~** changer de vitesse; **first** *or* **bottom** *or* **low ~** première vitesse; **in second ~** en seconde; **to change into third ~** passer en troisième (vitesse); **production has moved into top ~** la production a atteint sa vitesse maxima.

2 *vt* adapter *(to* à). **they were not ~ed to cope with that** ils n'étaient pas préparés pour cela; *(Econ)* **~ed to the cost of living** indexé.

◆ **gear up** * *vt sep*: **to ~ o.s. up** se préparer *(for* pour); **we're ~ed up to do it** nous sommes tout prêts à le faire.

◆ **gearbox** *n (Aut)* boîte *f* de vitesses. ◆ **gear-lever** *or* ◆ **gearshift** *(US)* *n* levier *m* de vitesse. ◆ **gearwheel** *n [bicycle]* pignon *m*.

geese [giːs] *npl of* **goose.**

gel [dʒel] **1** *n (Chem)* colloïde *m*; *(gen)* gelée *f*. **2** *vi [jelly etc]* prendre; *[plan etc]* prendre tournure.

◆ **gelatin(e)** *n* gélatine *f*.

gelding ['geldɪŋ] *n* hongre *m*.

gelignite ['dʒelɪgnaɪt] *n* gélignite *f*.

gem [dʒem] **1** *n* gemme *f*, pierre *f* précieuse. *(house, helper)* **a ~** une vraie merveille. **the ~ of the collection** le joyau de la collection; **her aunt's a real ~** * sa tante est un chou *; **I must read you**

this ~ * il faut que je te lise cette perle. ◆ **gemstone** *n* pierre *f* gemme *inv*.

Gemini ['dʒemɪniː] *npl (Astron)* les Gémeaux *mpl*.

gen * [dʒen] *(Brit) n* coordonnées * *fpl* (*on* de), renseignements *mpl* (*on* sur). **what's the ~ on this?** qu'est-ce qu'on sait là-dessus? ◆ **gen up** ‡ *vt sep*: **to ~ sb up on sth** donner à qn les coordonnées * de qch.

gender ['dʒendəʳ] *n (Gram)* genre *m*. ~ **bias** parti pris contre les femmes.

gene [dʒiːn] *n* gène *m*.

genealogy [ˌdʒiːnɪ'ælədʒɪ] *n* généalogie *f*. ◆ **genealogical** *adj* généalogique. ◆ **genealogist** *n* généalogiste *mf*.

general ['dʒen(ə)r(ə)l] **1** *adj (gen)* général; *(not in detail) view, plan, inquiry* d'ensemble. **as a ~ rule** en règle générale; **in ~ use** d'usage courant; **in the ~ direction of** grosso modo * dans la direction de; **the ~ public** le grand public; **the ~ reader** le lecteur moyen; **this type of behaviour is fairly ~** ce genre de comportement est assez répandu; **the rain has been fairly ~** il a plu un peu partout; **to give sb a ~ idea of sth** donner à qn un aperçu d'ensemble sur qch; **I've got the ~ idea** je vois la question; *(US: Post)* ~ **delivery** poste *f* restante; ~ **election** élections législatives; *(Mil)* ~ **headquarters** quartier *m* général; ~ **holiday** jour *m* férié; ~ **hospital** centre *m* hospitalier; ~ **knowledge** culture *f* générale; ~ **manager** directeur *m* général; **G~ Post Office** *(building)* poste *f* centrale; *(Med)* **to be in ~ practice** faire de la médecine générale; ~ **practitioner** *(abbr* **G.P.***)* (médecin *m*) généraliste *m*; **go to your G.P.** allez voir votre médecin traitant; ~ **secretary** secrétaire général; ~ **shop** magasin *m* qui vend de tout; *(Mil etc)* ~ **staff** état-major *m*; ~ **store** grand magasin *m*. **2** *n* (**a**) général *m*. **in ~** en général. (**b**) *(Mil)* général *m*.
◆ **generality** *n (gen pl)* généralité *f*. ◆ **generalization** *n* généralisation *f*. ◆ **generalize** *vti* généraliser. ◆ **generally** *adv (usually)* généralement, en général; *(for the most part)* dans l'ensemble; **~ly speaking** en général. ◆ **general-purpose** *adj tool, dictionary* universel.

generate ['dʒenəreɪt] **1** *vt children, hope, fear* engendrer; *electricity, heat, work* produire; *(Ling)* générer. ◆ **generating** *adj*: **generating station** centrale *f* électrique; **generating unit** groupe *m* électrogène. ◆ **generation** *n* génération *f*; **the younger generation** la jeune génération; **the generation gap** le conflit des générations. ◆ **generative** *adj (Ling)* génératif. ◆ **generator** *n (Elec)* groupe *m* électrogène.

generic [dʒɪ'nerɪk] *adj* générique.

generous ['dʒen(ə)rəs] *adj (gen)* généreux (*with* de); *supply* abondant; *meal* copieux; *spoonful* bon; *size* ample. ◆ **generosity** *n* générosité *f*. ◆ **generously** *adv give etc* généreusement; *say* avec générosité; *pardon, reprieve* avec magnanimité.

genesis ['dʒenɪsɪs] *n* genèse *f*.

genetic [dʒɪ'netɪk] *adj* génétique. ~ **code** code *m* génétique; ~ **engineering** génie *m* génétique; ~ **fingerprinting** identification *f* génétique. ◆ **geneticist** *n* généticien(ne) *m(f)*. ◆ **genetics** *nsg* génétique *f*.

Geneva [dʒɪ'niːvə] *n* Genève. **Lake ~** le lac Léman.

genial ['dʒiːnɪəl] *adj person, smile, voice* cordial; *climate* doux; *warmth* réconfortant. ◆ **geniality** *n* cordialité *f*. ◆ **genially** *adv* cordialement.

genie *pl* **genii** ['dʒiːnɪ, 'dʒiːnɪaɪ] *n (Myth)* génie *m*.

genital ['dʒenɪtl] **1** *adj* génital. **2** *npl*: **~s** organes *mpl* génitaux.

genitive ['dʒenɪtɪv] *adj, n* génitif *(m)*. **in the ~** au génitif.

genius ['dʒiːnɪəs] *n* génie *m*. **to have a ~ for (doing) sth** avoir le génie de (faire) qch.

Genoa ['dʒenəʊə] *n* Gênes.

genocide ['dʒenə(ʊ)saɪd] *n* génocide *m*.

gent [dʒent] *n (abbr of* **gentleman***) (Comm)* homme *m*; *(‡: man)* monsieur *m*. *(cloakroom)* **the ~s** * les toilettes *fpl* (pour hommes).

genteel [dʒen'tiːl] *adj* qui se veut distingué. ◆ **gentility** *n* prétention *f* à la distinction.

gentle ['dʒentl] *adj person, animal, voice, disposition* doux (*f* douce); *rebuke* gentil; *exercise, heat* modéré; *slope* doux; *breeze, sound, touch* léger; *progress* mesuré; *hint, reminder* discret. ◆ **gentleness** *n* douceur *f*. ◆ **gently** *adv (gen)* doucement; *say, smile, rebuke* gentiment; **gently does it!** doucement!; **to go gently with sth** y aller doucement avec qch.

gentleman ['dʒentlmən] **1** *n, pl* **gentlemen** monsieur *m*; *(man of breeding)* homme *m* bien élevé, gentleman *m*; *(at court etc)* gentilhomme *m*. **gentlemen!** messieurs!; **a perfect ~** un vrai gentleman; **~'s agreement** accord *m* reposant sur l'honneur. **2** *adj*: ~ **farmer** gentleman-farmer *m*. ◆ **gentlemanly** *adj* bien élevé; *voice, appearance* distingué.

gentry ['dʒentrɪ] *n* petite noblesse *f*.

genuflect ['dʒenjʊflekt] *vi* faire une génuflexion.

genuine ['dʒenjʊɪn] *adj* (**a**) *(authentic) wool, silver, jewel etc* véritable; *manuscript, antique, coin* authentique; *(Comm) goods* garanti d'origine. **I'll only buy the ~ article** *(of furniture etc)* je n'achète que de l'authentique; *(of jewellery, cheeses etc)* je n'achète que du vrai. (**b**) *(sincere) laughter* franc (*f* franche); *person, tears, emotion, belief* sincère; *simplicity* vrai. *(Comm)* ~ **buyer** acheteur sérieux. ◆ **genuinely** *adv prove, originate* authentiquement; *believe* sincèrement; *sorry, surprised, unable* vraiment.

genus *pl* **genera** ['dʒenəs, 'dʒenərə] *n (Bio)* genre *m*.

geode ['dʒiːəʊd] *n* géode *f*.

geography [dʒɪ'ɒgrəfɪ] *n (gen)* géographie *f*. **I don't know the ~ of the district** je ne connais pas la topographie de la région. ◆ **geographer** *n* géographe *mf*. ◆ **geographic(al)** *adj* géographique.

geology [dʒɪ'ɒlədʒɪ] *n* géologie *f*. ◆ **geological** *adj* géologique. ◆ **geologist** *n* géologue *mf*.

geometry [dʒɪ'ɒmɪtrɪ] *n* géométrie *f*. ◆ **geometric(al)** *adj* géométrique.

geophysics [ˌdʒiːə(ʊ)'fɪzɪks] *nsg* géophysique *f*.

geopolitical [ˌdʒiːəʊpə'lɪtɪk(ə)l] *adj* géopolitique.

Georgian ['dʒɔːdʒɪən] *adj* du temps des rois George I-IV *(1714-1830)*.

geranium [dʒɪ'reɪnɪəm] *n* géranium *m*.

gerbil ['dʒɜːbɪl] *n* gerbille *f*.

geriatric [ˌdʒerɪ'ætrɪk] **1** *adj* gériatrique. ~ **medicine** gériatrie *f*; ~ **nursing** soins *mpl* aux vieillards; ~ **social work** aide *f* sociale aux vieillards. **2** *n (Med)* malade *mf* gériatrique; *(pej)* vieillard(e) *m(f)*. ◆ **geriatrics** *nsg* gériatrie *f*.

germ [dʒɜːm] **1** *n (Bio, also fig)* germe *m*; *(Med)* microbe *m*. **2** *adj*: ~ **warfare** guerre *f* bactériologique.
◆ **germ-free** *adj* stérilisé. ◆ **germicidal** *adj* antiseptique. ◆ **germicide** *n* antiseptique *m*. ◆ **germinate** **1** *vi* germer ; **2** *vt* faire germer. ◆ **germination** *n* germination *f*. ◆ **germ-killer** *n* antiseptique *m*.

Germany ['dʒɜːm(ə)nɪ] *n* Allemagne *f*. **East/West ~** Allemagne de l'Est/de l'Ouest. ◆ **German** **1** *adj* allemand; **East-/West-German** est-/ouest-allemand; **German measles** rubéole *f*; **German sheep dog** berger *m* allemand ; **2** *n* Allemand(e) *m(f)* ; *(Ling)* allemand *m*. ◆ **Germanic** *adj* germanique.

gerontology [ˌdʒerɒn'tɒlədʒɪ] *n* gérontologie *f*. ◆ **gerontologist** *n* gérontologue *mf*.

gerund ['dʒer(ə)nd] *n* gérondif *m*.

gestalt [gə'ʃtɑːlt] *n* gestalt *f*. ~ **psychology** gestaltisme *m*.

gestate [dʒes'teɪt] *vi* être en gestation. ◆ **gestation** *n* gestation *f*.

gesticulate [dʒes'tɪkjʊleɪt] *vi* gesticuler.

gesture ['dʒestʃəʳ] **1** *n (lit, fig)* geste *m*. **they did it as a ~ of support** ils l'ont fait pour manifester leur soutien. **2** *vi*: **to ~ to sb to do** faire signe à qn de faire.

get [get] *pret, ptp* **got,** *(US) ptp* **gotten** **1** *vt* (**a**) *(obtain)* avoir, trouver; *(through effort)* se procurer, obtenir; *permission, result* obtenir (*from* de); *(buy)* acheter; *(Rad) station, (Telec) person, number* avoir; *(Scol) marks* obtenir, avoir. **to ~ sth to eat** *(find food)* trouver de quoi manger; *(eat)* manger qch; **where did you ~ that hat?** où as-tu trouvé ce chapeau?; **I don't ~ much from his lectures** je ne tire pas grand-chose de ses cours; **to ~ sth for sb** trouver qch pour *or* à qn; *(fig)* **we'll never ~ anything out of him** nous ne tirerons jamais rien de lui. (**b**) *(acquire) power, wealth* acquérir; *ideas, reputation* se faire; *salary* recevoir, toucher; *help* recevoir; *prize* gagner; *fame* connaître. *(of collection, set)* **I've still 3 to ~** il m'en manque encore 3; **it got him fame** *etc* cela lui a valu la célébrité *etc*. (**c**) *(receive) letter, present* recevoir, avoir; *surprise* avoir; *wound, punishment, shock* recevoir. **I didn't ~ much for it** je ne l'ai pas vendu cher; **to ~ 2 years in prison** attraper * 2 ans de prison; **he ~s it from his mother** il le tient de sa mère; **this room ~s all the sun** cette pièce reçoit tout le soleil. (**d**) *(catch) ball, disease* attraper; *quarry, person* attraper, prendre; *(hit) target etc* atteindre, avoir; *(seize)* prendre, saisir. **to ~ sb round the neck/by the throat** saisir *or* prendre qn au cou/à la gorge; **to ~ sb by the arm** attraper *or* saisir qn par le bras; *[pain]* **it ~s me here** cela me prend ici; **got you at last!** enfin je te tiens!; **we'll ~ them yet!** on les aura!; **he'll ~ you for that!** * qu'est-ce que tu vas prendre! *; **he's got it bad (for her)** * il en pince sérieusement pour elle ⁑; **the bullet got him in the arm** il a pris la balle dans le bras. (**e**) *(fetch) person, doctor* aller chercher, faire venir; *object* chercher, apporter. **(go and) ~ my books** allez chercher mes livres; **can I ~ you a drink?** voulez-vous boire qch? (**f**) *(have, possess)* **to have got** avoir, posséder; **I've got toothache** j'ai mal aux dents; **I have got 3 sisters** j'ai 3 sœurs; **how many have you got?** combien en avez-vous? (**g**) *(causative etc)* **to ~ sb to do sth** faire faire qch à qn, obtenir que qn fasse qch; **to ~ sth done** faire faire qch; **to ~ one's hair cut** se faire couper les cheveux; **I got him to cut my hair** je me suis fait couper les cheveux par lui; **he knows how to ~ things done!** il sait faire activer les choses!; **she got her arm broken** elle a eu le bras cassé; **to ~ sth ready** préparer qch; **to ~ sb drunk** soûler qn; **to ~ one's hands dirty** se salir les mains; **to ~ sb into trouble** attirer des ennuis à qn; **we got him on to the subject of the war** nous l'avons amené à parler de la guerre. (**h**) *(put, take)* faire parvenir. **they got him home somehow** ils l'ont ramené tant bien que mal; **how can we ~ it home?** comment faire pour le rapporter à la maison?; **to ~ sth to sb** faire parvenir qch à qn; **I'll never ~ the car through here** je n'arriverai jamais à faire passer la voiture par ici; **to ~ sth past the customs** passer qch à la douane; **he got the blood off his hand** il a fait disparaître le sang de sa main; **where does that ~ us?** où est-ce que ça nous mène? (**i**) *(understand)* comprendre, saisir. **~ it?** * tu saisis? *; **I've got it!** j'y suis!; **I don't ~ it** * je ne comprends pas, je n'y suis pas du tout; **I didn't ~ your name** je n'ai pas saisi votre nom; *(to secretary etc)* **did you ~ that last sentence?** avez-vous pris la dernière phrase? (**j**) *(*: annoy)* mettre en rogne *. **it ~s (to) me** * ça m'énerve. (**k**) *(*: thrill)* **that ~s me** ça me fait qch; *(stronger)* ça m'emballe *. **2** *vi* (**a**) *(go)* aller, se rendre (*to* à, *from* de); *(arrive)* arriver (*at* à). **how do you ~ there?** comment fait-on pour y aller?; **how did that box ~ here?** comment se fait-il que cette boîte se trouve ici?; *(fig)* **he'll ~ there** il arrivera; *(fig)* **now we're ~ting somewhere!** * enfin on avance!; *(fig)* **you won't ~ anywhere if you behave like that** tu n'arriveras à rien en te conduisant comme ça; **we won't ~ anywhere with him** nous n'arriverons à rien *or* nous perdons notre temps avec lui; **where did you ~ to?** où êtes-vous allé?; *(in book, work etc)* **where have you got to?** où en êtes-vous?; **where can he have got to?** où est-il passé?; **I got as far as speaking to him** j'ai réussi à lui parler. (**b**) *(become, be)* devenir, se faire. **to ~ old** devenir vieux, vieillir; **to ~ killed** se faire tuer; **it's ~ting late** il se fait tard; **how do people ~ like that?** * comment peut-on en arriver là?; **to ~ with it** ⁑ se mettre à la mode *or* dans le vent *; *(excl)* **~ with it!** ⁑ sois un peu dans le vent! *; **to ~ to know sb** *(begin)* commencer à connaître qn; *(know better)* arriver à mieux connaître qn; *(meet)* faire la connaissance de qn; **to ~ to like sb** se mettre à aimer qn. (**c**) *(begin)* se mettre à. **to ~ going** commencer, s'y mettre; **I got talking to him** je me suis mis à parler avec lui. (**d**) *(be allowed to)* **she never ~s to drive the car** on ne la laisse jamais conduire la voiture. **3** *(modal aux usage)* **you've got to come** il faut absolument que vous veniez; **I haven't got to leave** je ne suis pas obligé de partir; **have you got to go and see her?** est-ce que vous êtes obligé d'aller la voir?; *V also* **have 2.**

◆ **get about, get around** *vi* (**a**) *(move around)* se déplacer; *(travel)* voyager. *(after illness)* **he's ~ting about again** il est de nouveau sur pied. (**b**) *[news]* se répandre. **it has got about that...** le bruit court que...

◆ **get above** *vt fus*: **to ~ above o.s.** se prendre pour plus important qu'on n'est.

◆ **get across** **1** *vi* traverser; *(fig) [play]* passer la rampe; *[meaning, message]* passer *. **he didn't ~ across to the audience** il n'a pas réussi à établir la communication avec le public. **2** *vt sep road* traverser; *person* faire traverser; *(fig) play, song* faire passer la rampe à. *(fig)* **to ~ sth across to sb** faire comprendre qch à qn. **3** *vt fus (annoy)* **to ~ across sb** se faire mal voir de qn.

◆ **get along** *vi* (**a**) *(go)* s'en aller. **~ along with you!** * *(go away)* va-t'en!; *(stop joking)* ça va, hein! * (**b**) *(manage)* se débrouiller (*without* sans); *(progress) [work]* avancer; *[pupil]* faire des progrès. **how is he ~ting along?** *(in health)* comment va-t-il? ; *(in studies etc)* comment est-ce qu'il se débrouille? (**c**) *(be on good terms)* s'entendre bien (*with sb* avec qn).

◆ **get at** *vt fus* (**a**) *(reach) place* parvenir à; *object on shelf* atteindre; *person* accéder jusqu'à; *facts, truth* découvrir. **the dog got at the meat** le chien a touché la viande; **not easy to ~ at** *house* difficile d'accès; *person* d'un abord peu facile; **let me ~ at him!** * que je l'attrape! (**b**) *(fig)* **what are you ~ting at?** où voulez-vous en venir?; **who are you ~ting at?** à qui voulez-vous faire allusion?; **I feel got at** * je me sens visé; **she's always ~ting at her brother** elle est toujours après son frère *. (**c**) *(*: bribe)* acheter, suborner. (**d**) *(start work on) task,* *essay* se mettre à. **I want to ~ at the redecorating** je veux commencer à refaire les peintures.

◆ **get away 1** *vi* (**a**) *(leave)* s'en aller, partir; *[vehicle]* partir, démarrer. **to ~ away from** *place, work* quitter; **I couldn't ~ away any sooner** je n'ai pas pu me libérer plus tôt; **~ away (with you)! *** va-t'en!; *(stop joking)* ça va, hein! * (**b**) *(escape)* s'échapper (*from* de). **to ~ away from sb/one's environment** échapper à qn/à son environnement; **to ~ away from it all** partir se reposer loin de tout; **the thief got away with the money** le voleur est parti avec l'argent; **he got away with an apology** il en a été quitte pour une simple excuse; **you'll never ~ away with that!** on ne te laissera pas passer ça! *; **he'd ~ away with murder *** il tuerait père et mère qu'on lui pardonnerait; *(fig)* **there's no ~ting away from it** le fait est là, on ne peut rien y changer. **2** *vt sep* (**a**) faire partir. **you must ~ her away to the country** il faut que vous l'emmeniez à la campagne. (**b**) **to ~ sth away from sb** arracher qch à qn.

◆ **get back 1** *vi* (**a**) *(return)* revenir, retourner. **to ~ back (home)** rentrer chez soi; **to ~ back to bed** se recoucher; **to ~ back to work** *(after pause)* se remettre au travail; *(after illness, holiday)* retourner au travail; **let's ~ back to why** revenons à la question de savoir pourquoi. (**b**) *(move back)* reculer. **~ back!** reculez! **2** *vt sep* (**a**) *(recover) sth lent* se faire rendre; *sth lost* retrouver; *possessions* recouvrer; *strength* reprendre. (**b**) *(replace)* remettre, replacer. (**c**) *(return) object* renvoyer; *person* raccompagner.

◆ **get back at *** *vt fus (retaliate against)* rendre la monnaie de sa pièce à.

◆ **get by** *vi* (**a**) *(pass)* passer. **this work just ~s by** ce travail est tout juste passable. (**b**) *(manage)* se débrouiller (*with, on* avec). **he'll ~ by** il s'en sortira *.

◆ **get down 1** *vi* descendre (*from, off* de). **~ down!** descends!; *(lie down)* couche-toi! **2** *vt sep* (**a**) *book, plate, child* descendre (*off* de); *hat, picture* décrocher. (**b**) *(swallow)* avaler. (**c**) *(make note of)* noter. (**d**) *(*: depress)* déprimer. **he ~s me down** il me fiche le cafard *; **don't let it ~ you down!** ne vous laissez pas abattre!

◆ **get down to** *vt fus*: **to ~ down to (doing) sth** se mettre à (faire) qch; **to ~ down to work** se mettre au travail; **let's ~ down to the facts** venons-en aux faits; *(fig)* **when you ~ down to it there's...** à bien regarder les faits il y a...

◆ **get in 1** *vi* (**a**) *(enter)* (réussir à) entrer; *(reach home)* rentrer; *[sunshine, air, water]* pénétrer. **to ~ in between...** se glisser entre... (**b**) *[train, bus, plane]* arriver. (**c**) *(Parl) [member]* être élu; *[party]* accéder au pouvoir. **2** *vt sep* (**a**) *thing, harvest* rentrer; *person* faire entrer; *taxes* recouvrer. (**b**) *(plant)* planter. (**c**) *(buy, obtain) groceries, coal* acheter, faire rentrer. **to ~ in supplies** faire des provisions. (**d**) *(summon) police etc* faire venir. (**e**) *(insert)* glisser. **to ~ a word in edgeways** glisser *or* placer un mot.

◆ **get into** *vt fus* (**a**) *house, park* entrer dans, pénétrer dans; *car, train* monter dans; *club, school* être accepté dans. *(fig)* **how did I ~ into all this?** comment me suis-je fourré dans un pareil pétrin? (**b**) *clothes* mettre.

◆ **get in with** *vt fus (gain favour of)* se faire bien voir de; *(become friendly with)* se mettre à fréquenter.

◆ **get off 1** *vi* (**a**) *(from vehicle)* descendre. *(fig)* **to tell sb where to ~ off *** envoyer qn sur les roses *. (**b**) *(depart)* partir; *[car]* démarrer; *[plane]* décoller. **to ~ off to a good start** prendre un bon départ; **to ~ off (to sleep)** s'endormir. (**c**) *(escape)* s'en tirer. **to ~ off lightly** s'en tirer à bon compte; **to ~ off with a fine** en être quitte pour une amende. (**d**) *(leave work)* s'en aller; *(have free time)* se libérer. **2** *vt sep* (**a**) *(remove) clothes, stains* enlever. (**b**) *(despatch) mail, child to school* expédier. **to ~ sb off to work** faire partir qn au travail; **to ~ sb off to sleep** endormir qn. (**c**) *(save from punishment)* tirer d'affaire. (**d**) *(learn)* apprendre (*by heart* par cœur). (**e**) *boat* renflouer; *crew, passengers* débarquer. **3** *vt fus* (**a**) *bus, cycle, horse* descendre de; *chair* se lever de; *subject* s'éloigner de. (**b**) *(*: avoid etc)* se faire dispenser (*sth* de qch; *doing* de faire). **to ~ off work** se libérer.

◆ **get off with *** *vt fus*: **he got off with a blonde** il a eu la touche * avec une blonde.

◆ **get on 1** *vi* (**a**) *(on bus etc)* monter. (**b**) *(make progress)* faire des progrès. **how are you ~ting on?** comment ça marche? *; **to be ~ting on (in years)** se faire vieux; **he's ~ting on for forty** il frise la quarantaine; **time is ~ting on** il se fait tard; **~ting on for 500** près de 500. (**c**) *(succeed)* réussir, faire son chemin (*in life etc* dans la vie *etc*). (**d**) *(continue)* continuer (*with sth* qch). **~ on with it!** allez, au travail!; **this will do to be ~ting on with** ça ira pour le moment. (**e**) *(agree)* bien s'entendre (*with sb* avec qn). **2** *vt sep clothes, lid* mettre. **3** *vt fus horse, bicycle* monter sur; *bus, train* monter dans.

◆ **get on to** *vt fus* (**a**) = **get on 3.** (**b**) *(recognize) truth, person responsible* découvrir. (**c**) *(nag)* être après *. (**d**) *(get in touch with)* se mettre en rapport avec; *(speak to)* parler à; *(Telec)* téléphoner à.

◆ **get out 1** *vi* (**a**) sortir (*of* de); *(from vehicle)* descendre (*of* de). (**b**) *(escape)* s'échapper (*of* de). *(fig)* **to ~ out of** *habit* perdre; *obligation* se dérober à; *duty* se soustraire à; *difficulty* se tirer de. (**c**) *[news etc]* se répandre; *[secret]* être éventé. **2** *vt sep object* sortir; *person* faire sortir (*of* de); *plug, stain* enlever; *tooth, nail* arracher; *(fig) words* prononcer; *book* sortir; *(prepare) scheme* préparer; *list* dresser; *(solve) problem, puzzle* venir à bout de.

◆ **get over 1** *vi* traverser; *[message, meaning]* passer *. **2** *vt fus* (**a**) *(cross) river, road* traverser; *fence* passer par-dessus. (**b**) *(recover from) illness, loss* se remettre de; *surprise* revenir de; *lost lover* oublier. **I can't ~ over the fact that...** je n'en reviens pas que... + *subj*; **you'll ~ over it!** tu n'en mourras pas! (**c**) *(overcome) obstacle* surmonter; *objections, difficulties* venir à bout de. **3** *vt sep* (**a**) *person, vehicle* faire passer. (**b**) *(swallow)* avaler. (**c**) *(have done with)* en finir avec. **let's ~ it over (with)** finissons-en. (**d**) *(Theat) play* faire passer la rampe à; *song etc* faire accepter; *(gen: communicate)* faire comprendre (*to sb* à qn; *that* que).

◆ **get round 1** *vi* (**a**) = **get about.** (**b**) **to ~ round to doing sth** arriver à faire qch, trouver le temps de faire qch; **if I ~ round to it** si j'y arrive. **2** *vt fus obstacle* contourner; *difficulty, regulation* tourner. **he knows how to ~ round her** il sait la prendre; **she got round him in the end** elle a fini par l'entortiller *.

◆ **get through 1** *vi* (**a**) *[message, news]* parvenir (*to* à); *[signal, candidate]* être reçu; *[motion, bill]* passer. *[football team etc]* **to ~ through to the third round** se classer pour le troisième tour; **to ~ through to sb** *(Telec)* avoir qn, obtenir la communication avec qn; *(contact)* contacter qn; *(fig: communicate with)* se faire comprendre de qn. (**b**) *(finish)* terminer, finir. **to ~ through with sth *** en finir avec qch. **2** *vt fus* (**a**) *hole, window* passer par; *hedge* passer à travers; *crowd* se frayer un chemin à travers; *enemy lines* franchir. (**b**) *(finish) task, book, supplies* venir au bout de. **he got through a lot of work** il a abattu de la besogne; **how can I ~ through the week without you?** comment vais-je pouvoir vivre une semaine sans toi? (**c**) *(consume, use) food, supplies* consommer. **we ~ through 10 bottles/£50 a week** il nous faut 10 bouteilles/50 livres par semaine. **3** *vt sep* (**a**) *person, object* faire passer; *message* faire parvenir (*to* à). **I can't ~ it through to him that...** je n'arrive pas à lui faire comprendre que... (**b**) *bill, motion* faire adopter. *(exam)* **he got them through** ils ont été reçus grâce à lui.

◆ **get together 1** *vi* se rassembler, se réunir. **let's ~ together on Thursday** on se retrouve jeudi; **you'd better ~ together with him** vous feriez bien de le consulter. **2** *vt sep* rassembler.

◆ **get under 1** *vi (pass underneath)* passer par-dessous. **2** *vt fus fence, rope* passer sous.

◆ **get up 1** *vi* (**a**) *(rise)* se lever (*from* de). **~ up out of bed!** sors du lit! (**b**) *(on horse)* monter. **2** *vt fus tree, ladder* monter à; *hill* gravir. **3** *vt sep* (**a**) *person (on to ladder etc)* faire monter; *(from chair, bed)* faire lever; *(wake)* réveiller; *thing* monter; *sail* hisser. (**b**) *(organize) play, plot* monter; *story* fabriquer; *petition* organiser. (**c**) *(prepare, arrange) article for sale* préparer. **to ~ o.s. up as** se déguiser en; **beautifully got up** *person* très bien habillé; *book* très bien présenté. (**d**) *(study) history etc* travailler, bûcher *; *speech, lecture* préparer.

◆ **get up to** *vt fus (catch up with)* rattraper; *(reach)* arriver à. **I've got up to page 17** j'en suis à la page 17; **to ~ up to mischief** faire des bêtises; **you never know what he'll ~ up to next** on ne sait jamais ce qu'il va encore inventer.

◆ **get-at-able** * *adj* accessible. ◆ **getaway 1** *n [criminals]* fuite *f*; **to make a ~away** filer; **2** *adj*: **a ~away car** une voiture pour filer. ◆ **get-together** *n* (petite) réunion *f*. ◆ **getup** * *n (clothing)* mise *f*, tenue *f*; *(presentation)* présentation *f*. ◆ **get-well card** *n* carte *f* de vœux de bon rétablissement.

geyser ['gi:zəʳ] *n* geyser *m*; *(water-heater)* chauffe-bain *m inv*.

ghastly ['gɑ:stlɪ] *adj (pale)* blême, livide; *(horrible)* horrible, affreux.

gherkin ['gɜ:kɪn] *n (Culin)* cornichon *m*.

ghetto ['getəʊ] *n (lit, fig)* ghetto *m*. ◆ **ghetto-blaster** * *n* grosse radio-cassette *f*.

ghost [gəʊst] **1** *n* fantôme *m*, revenant *m*. *(fig)* **the ~ of a smile** un pâle sourire; **the ~ of a chance** l'ombre *f* d'une chance. **2** *vt sb else's book etc* écrire. **3** *adj film, story* de revenants; *ship, train* fantôme; *town* mort. ◆ **ghostly** *adj* spectral, fantomatique.

ghoul [gu:l] *n* goule *f*, vampire *m*. *(fig)* **he's a ~** il est morbide. ◆ **ghoulish** *adj* morbide.

giant ['dʒaɪənt] **1** *n* géant *m*. **2** *adj tree, packet* géant; *strides* de géant; *amount, task* gigantesque; *size* géant.

gibber ['dʒɪbəʳ] *vi* baragouiner *; *(with rage)* bégayer. ◆ **gibberish** *n* charabia * *m*, baragouin * *m*.

gibe [dʒaɪb] **1** *vi* (**a**) **to ~ at sb** railler qn. (**b**) *[boat]* virer lof pour lof. **2** *n* raillerie *f*.

giblets ['dʒɪblɪts] *npl* abattis *mpl (de volaille)*.

Gibraltar [dʒɪ'brɔ:ltəʳ] *n* Gibraltar *m*.

giddy ['gɪdɪ] *adj (dizzy)* pris de vertige; *height* vertigineux; *(heedless)* écervelé; *(not serious)* léger. **I feel ~** la tête me tourne; **to go ~** être pris de vertige; **to make sb ~** donner le vertige à qn. ◆ **giddiness** *n (Med)* vertige *m*; **a bout of giddiness** un vertige.

gift [gɪft] **1** *n* (**a**) cadeau *m*; *(Comm)* prime *f*. **it was a ~** on me l'a offert; *(*: fig: easy)* c'était du gâteau *; **I wouldn't have it as a ~** on m'en ferait cadeau que je n'en voudrais pas; **to make sb a ~ of sth** faire don *or* cadeau de qch à qn. (**b**) *(talent)* don *m*. **to have the ~ of the gab** * avoir la langue bien pendue. **2** *vt (esp Jur)* donner. *(fig)* **to be ~ed with patience** *etc* être doué de patience *etc*. **3** *adj (Comm)* **~ coupon** *or* **voucher** bon-prime *m*; **~ token** chèque-cadeau *m*. ◆ **gifted** *adj* doué (*for* pour, *with* de); **the ~ed child** l'enfant surdoué. ◆ **giftwrap** *vt*: **to ~wrap a package** faire un paquet-cadeau. ◆ **gift-wrapping** *n* emballage-cadeau *m*.

gig * [gɪg] *n (Theat etc)* gig *f*; *(US fig)* job *m* temporaire.

gigantic [dʒaɪ'gæntɪk] *adj* gigantesque.

giggle ['gɪgl] **1** *vi* rire (sottement), avoir le fou rire. **2** *n* petit rire sot. **to have/get the ~s** avoir/attraper le fou rire; **he did it for a ~** * il a fait ça pour rigoler. ◆ **giggly** *adj* qui pouffe de rire.

gild [gɪld] *vt* dorer. **to ~ the lily** renchérir sur la perfection.

gill[1] [gɪl] *n [mushroom]* lamelle *f*. *[fish]* **~s** ouïes *fpl*. *(fig)* **green around the ~s** * vert *(de peur etc)*.

gill[2] [dʒɪl] *n = 0,142 litre*.

gilt [gɪlt] *(ptp of* **gild***)* **1** *adj* doré. **2** *n* dorure *f*. **to take the ~ off the gingerbread** gâter le plaisir. ◆ **gilt-edged** *adj*: **~-edged securities** valeurs *fpl* de tout repos.

gimlet ['gɪmlɪt] *n* vrille *f*.

gimmick ['gɪmɪk] *n* truc * *m*, astuce *f*; *(US: trick)* truc * *m*, combine *f*. **advertising/sales ~** truc * publicitaire/promotionnel; **he put on an accent as a ~** il a pris un accent pour l'effet. ◆ **gimmickry** *n* trucs * *mpl*. ◆ **gimmicky** *adj photography* à trucs *; *presentation* à astuces.

gin [dʒɪn] *n* gin *m*. **~ and tonic** gin-tonic *m*.

ginger ['dʒɪn(d)ʒəʳ] **1** *n* gingembre *m*. *(nickname)* **G~** Poil de Carotte. **2** *adj hair* roux, rouquin *; *biscuit etc* au gingembre. **~ ale** *or* **beer** boisson *f* gazeuse au gingembre; *(esp Pol)* **~ group** groupe *m* de pression. ◆ **ginger up** * *vt sep person* secouer; *event* mettre de l'entrain dans. ◆ **gingerbread** *n* pain *m* d'épice. ◆ **gingerly** *adv* avec précaution. ◆ **gingernut** *or* ◆ **gingersnap** *n* gâteau *m* sec au gingembre.

gingham ['gɪŋəm] *n (Tex)* vichy *m*.

gipsy ['dʒɪpsɪ] **1** *n (gen)* bohémien(ne) *m(f)*; *(Spanish)* gitan(e) *m(f)*; *(Central European)* Tsigane *mf*; *(pej)* romanichel(le) *m(f)*. **2** *adj (gen)* de bohémien, de gitan; *music* des gitans, tsigane.

giraffe [dʒɪ'rɑ:f] *n* girafe *f*. **baby ~** girafeau *m*.

girder ['gɜ:dəʳ] *n* poutre *f*.

girdle ['gɜ:dl] *n (belt)* ceinture *f*; *(corset)* gaine *f*.

girl [gɜ:l] **1** *n* (jeune *or* petite) fille *f*. **a little ~** une petite fille, une fillette; **an English ~** une jeune *or* petite Anglaise; **poor little ~** pauvre petite; **the Smith ~s** les filles des Smith ; **~s' school** école *f or* lycée *m* de filles; **yes, old ~** ‡ oui, ma vieille *; **the old ~ * next door** la vieille d'à côté. **2** *adj*: **~ Friday** aide *f* de bureau; **~ scout** éclaireuse *f*, guide *f*. ◆ **girlfriend** *n [boy]* petite amie *f*; *[girl]* amie *f*, copine * *f*. ◆ **girlhood** *n* enfance *f*, jeunesse *f*. ◆ **girlie** *adj magazine* déshabillé. ◆ **girlish** *adj (of woman)* de jeune fille; *(of man, boy)* efféminé.

giro ['dʒaɪrəʊ] *n*: **bank ~ system** système *m* de virement bancaire; **National G~** ≃ Comptes Chèques Postaux, C.C.P. *mpl*.

girth [gɜ:θ] *n [tree]* circonférence *f*; *[waist etc]* tour *m* (de taille *etc*). **his (great) ~** sa corpulence.

gist [dʒɪst] *n (gen)* essentiel *m*. **give me the ~ of what he said** mettez-moi au courant de ce qu'il a dit, en deux mots.

give [gɪv] *pret* **gave,** *ptp* **given 1** *vt* (**a**) *(gen)* donner (*to* à); *(as gift)* faire cadeau *or* don de, offrir (*to* à); *honour, title* conférer (*to* à); *help, support* prêter (*to* à); *food, hospitality, meal* offrir (*to* à); *(dedicate) one's life, fortune* consacrer (*to* à); *message* remettre (*to* à); *description, particulars* donner, fournir (*to* à); *pain, pleasure* occasionner (*to* à); *punishment* infliger (*to* à). **one must ~ and take** il faut faire des concessions; **~ or take a few minutes** à quelques minutes près; **he gave as good as he got** il a rendu coup pour coup; **to ~ sb sth to eat/drink** donner à manger/boire à qn; **can you ~ him sth to do?** pouvez-vous lui trouver qch à faire?; **you've ~n me your cold** tu m'as passé ton rhume; *(Telec)* **~ me Moordown, 231** passez-moi le 231 à Moordown; **I'll ~ him something to cry about!** * je lui apprendrai à pleurer!; **I don't ~ a damn** * je m'en fiche *; **the judge gave him 5 years** le juge l'a condamné à 5 ans de prison; *(in age)* **I can ~ him 10 years** il est de 10 ans mon cadet; **how long do you ~ that marriage?** combien de temps crois-tu que ce mariage tiendra?; *[creditor]* **I can't ~ you any longer** je ne peux plus vous accorder de délai; *(agreeing)* **I'll ~ you that** je vous accorde cela; **~ me time** laissez-moi du temps; **~ me Mozart every time!** * pour moi, rien ne vaut Mozart; **to ~ sb to understand that** donner à entendre à qn que; **to ~ sb to believe sth** faire croire qch à qn; **~ him my love** faites-lui mes amitiés; **what will you ~ me for it?** combien m'en donnez-vous?; **what did you ~ for it?** combien l'avez-vous payé?; **I'd ~ anything to know** je donnerais n'importe quoi pour savoir.

(**b**) *(perform etc) jump, gesture* faire; *answer, lecture, party, performance* donner; *sigh, cry, laugh* pousser. **to ~ sb a look** lancer un regard à qn; **~ us a song** chantez-nous qch.

(**c**) *(produce, supply)* donner, rendre; *sound* rendre; *(Math etc) result* donner. **this lamp ~s a poor light** cette lampe éclaire mal; **5 times 4 ~s 20** 5 fois 4 font 20; **it ~s a total of 100** cela fait 100 en tout.

(**d**) **to ~ way** *[building, ceiling, ground]* s'affaisser; *[plaster]* s'effriter; *[cable, rope, ladder etc]* casser; *[legs]* fléchir; *[health]* s'altérer; *[person] (stand back)* s'écarter; *(yield)* céder (*to sb* devant qn; *to a demand* à une revendication; *under* sous); *(agree)* consentir; *(Aut)* céder la priorité (*to* à); *[troops]* battre en retraite. **the radio gave way to television** la radio a fait place à la télévision; *(Aut)* **'~ way'** 'cédez la priorité'.

2 *vi [road, beam etc]* céder (*to* à; *under* sous); *[cloth, elastic etc]* prêter.

◆ **give away** *vt sep* (**a**) *money, goods* donner; *prizes* distribuer; *bride* conduire à l'autel. (**b**) *(betray) names, details* révéler. **to ~ sb away** *[accomplice]* dénoncer qn; *[mistake]* trahir qn; **to ~ o.s. away** se trahir; **don't ~ anything away** ne dis rien; **to ~ the game** *or* **show away** * vendre la mèche *.

◆ **give back** *vt sep (gen)* rendre (*to* à); *property* restituer (*to* à); *echo, image* renvoyer.

◆ **give in 1** *vi (yield)* renoncer, abandonner. **to ~ in to sb** céder à qn; **I ~ in!** je renonce!; *(in guessing)* je donne ma langue au chat! * **2** *vt sep parcel, document* remettre; *essay* rendre; *one's name* donner.

◆ **give off** *vt sep heat, smell* émettre; *gas* dégager.

◆ **give on to** *vt fus [door, window]* donner sur.

◆ **give out 1** *vi [supplies]* s'épuiser; *[car, engine]* tomber en panne. **my patience is giving out** ma patience est à bout; **my patience gave out** la patience m'a manqué. **2** *vt sep* (**a**) *(distribute) books, food etc* distribuer. (**b**) *(announce) news* annoncer; *list etc* faire connaître.

◆ **give over 1** *vt sep (devote)* consacrer (*to* à); *(transfer)* affecter (*to* à). **building ~n over to offices** bâtiment affecté à des bureaux. **2** *vt fus (*: stop)* cesser (*doing* de faire). **~ over!** arrête!

◆ **give up 1** *vi* abandonner, renoncer. **don't ~ up!** tenez bon!; **I ~ up** je renonce; *(in guessing)* je donne ma langue au chat *. **2** *vt sep* (**a**) *(devote)* consacrer (*to* à). **to ~ o.s. up to sth** se livrer à qch. (**b**) *(renounce)* renoncer (*doing* à faire); *friends, interests, habit, idea* abandonner; *seat, place* céder; *job* quitter; *appointment* démissionner de; *business* se retirer de; *subscription* cesser. **he'll never ~ her up** il ne renoncera jamais à elle; **I gave it up as a bad job** j'ai laissé tomber *. (**c**) *(hand over) prisoner* livrer (*to* à); *authority* se démettre de; *keys of city etc* rendre. **to ~ o.s. up** se livrer (*to the police* à la police), se rendre. (**d**) *(abandon hope for) patient* condamner; *expected visitor* ne plus espérer voir; *problem, riddle* renoncer à résoudre. **to ~ sb up for lost** considérer qn comme perdu.

◆ **give-and-take** *n* concessions *fpl* mutuelles. ◆ **giveaway 1** *n* révélation *f* involontaire; *(Comm: free gift)* prime *f* ; **2** *adj fact, expression* révélateur; *price* dérisoire. ◆ **given** *adj time, size* donné, déterminé; **~n name** prénom *m*; **to be ~n to (doing) sth** être enclin à (faire) qch; **~n that he is...** supposé qu'il soit... ◆ **giver** *n* donateur *m*, -trice *f*.

glacé ['glæseɪ] *adj fruit* confit.

glacial ['gleɪsɪəl] *adj* glacial; *(Geol)* glaciaire.

glacier ['glæsɪə^r] *n* glacier *m*.

glad [glæd] *adj person* content, heureux (*of, about* de; *to do* de faire; *that* que + *subj*); *news* heureux; *occasion* joyeux. **I am ~ about it** cela me fait plaisir, j'en suis bien content, j'en suis ravi; **he's only too ~ to do it** il ne demande pas mieux que de le faire. ◆ **gladden** *vt person* rendre heureux; *heart, occasion* réjouir. ◆ **glad-hand** *vt (esp US)* accueillir avec effusion. ◆ **gladly** *adv (joyfully)* avec joie; *(willingly)* avec plaisir, volontiers. ◆ **gladness** *n* joie *f*.

glade [gleɪd] *n* clairière *f*.

gladiolus, *pl* **-oli** [ˌglædɪ'əʊləs, əʊlaɪ] *n* glaïeul *m*.

glamour ['glæmə^r] *n [person]* séductions *fpl*, fascination *f*; *[occasion]* éclat *m*; *[situation]* prestige *m*. **to lend ~ to sth** prêter de l'éclat à qch; **~ boy** * beau gars * *m*; **~ girl** * pin-up ‡ *f inv*. ◆ **glamorize** *vt place, event* présenter sous des couleurs séduisantes. ◆ **glamorous** *adj spectacle, life* brillant; *production* à grand spectacle; *dress, photo* splendide; *person* séduisant, fascinant; *job* prestigieux.

glance [glɑːns] **1** *n* coup *m* d'œil, regard *m*. **at a ~** d'un coup d'œil; **at first ~** à première vue; **without a backward ~** sans se retourner; *(fig)* sans plus de cérémonies. **2** *vi* (**a**) *(look)* jeter un coup d'œil (*at* sur, à), lancer un regard (*at* à). **to ~ away** détourner le regard; **he ~d over the paper** il a jeté un coup d'œil sur le journal. (**b**) **to ~ off sth** dévier sur qch; **to ~ off** dévier. ◆ **glancing** *adj blow* oblique.

gland [glænd] *n* glande *f*. ◆ **glandular** *adj* glandulaire; **~ular fever** mononucléose *f* infectieuse.

glare [glɛə^r] **1** *vi* (**a**) lancer un regard furieux (*at* à). (**b**) *[sun, lights]* briller d'un éclat éblouissant. **2** *n* (**a**) regard furieux. (**b**) *[light]* éclat éblouissant; *(Aut)* éblouissement *m*; *[publicity]* feux *mpl*.

◆ **glaring** *adj light* éblouissant; *sun* aveuglant; *colour* criard; *fact, mistake* qui crève les yeux; *injustice, lie* flagrant.

glass [glɑːs] **1** *n (substance; tumbler)* verre *m*; *(*~**ware**) verrerie *f*; *(mirror)* glace *f*; *(magnifying ~)* loupe *f*; *(telescope)* longue-vue *f*; *(barometer)* baromètre *m*. **broken ~** des éclats *mpl* de verre; **pane of ~** vitre *f*; **window ~** verre à vitre; **a ~ of wine** un verre de vin; **a wine ~** un verre à vin; **grown under ~** cultivé sous verre; **displayed under ~** exposé en vitrine; **~es** *(spectacles)* lunettes *fpl*; *(binoculars)* jumelles *fpl*. **2** *adj bottle, ornament* de verre, en verre; *slipper, eye* de verre; *industry* du verre; *door* vitré. **~ case** vitrine *f*; **to keep sth in a ~ case** garder qch sous verre; **~ fibre** fibre *f* de verre; **~ wool** laine *f* de verre. ◆ **glasscloth** *n* essuie-verres *m inv*. ◆ **glasscutter** *n (tool)* diamant *m*. ◆ **glassful** *n* (plein) verre *m*. ◆ **glasshouse** *n (for plants)* serre *f*. ◆ **glasspaper** *n* papier *m* de verre. ◆ **glassware** *n* verrerie *f*. ◆ **glassworks** *n* verrerie *f (fabrique)*. ◆ **glassy** *adj substance, eye, look* vitreux; *surface, sea* uni (comme un miroir).

glaucoma [glɔː'kəʊmə] *n* glaucome *m*.

glaze [gleɪz] **1** *vt door, window* vitrer; *picture* mettre sous verre; *pottery, tiles* vernisser; *cake, meat* glacer. **2** *n* vernis *m*; glaçage *m*. ◆ **glazed** *adj door* vitré; *pottery* vernissé; *paper, photograph* brillant; *eyes* vitreux. ◆ **glazier** *n* vitrier *m*.

gleam [gliːm] **1** *n* lueur *f (also fig)*; *[metal]* reflet *m*; *[water]* miroitement *m*. **2** *vi (gen)* luire; *[metal, shoes etc]* reluire; *[water]* miroiter. ◆ **gleaming** *adj (gen)* brillant; *(clean)* reluisant.

glean [gliːn] *vti (lit, fig)* glaner.

glee [gliː] *n* joie *f*. ~ **club** chorale *f*. ◆ **gleeful** *adj* joyeux, jubilant. ◆ **gleefully** *adv* joyeusement.

glen [glen] *n* vallon *m*.

glib [glɪb] *adj excuse, lie* désinvolte; *person* qui a la parole facile. ◆ **glibly** *adv speak* avec aisance; *reply* sans hésiter; *make excuses, lie* avec désinvolture.

glide [glaɪd] *vi* (**a**) **to** ~ **in/out** *etc (silently)* entrer/sortir *etc* sans bruit; *(gracefully)* entrer/sortir *etc* avec grâce; *[ship]* entrer/sortir *etc* comme en glissant. (**b**) *(Ski)* glisser. (**c**) *[birds, aircraft]* planer. ◆ **glider** *n (Aviat)* planeur *m*; *(US: swing)* balançoire *f*. ◆ **gliding** *n (Aviat)* vol *m* plané; *(sport)* vol *m* à voile.

glimmer ['glɪməʳ] **1** *vi (gen)* luire faiblement; *[water]* miroiter. **2** *n* faible lueur *f (also fig)*; *[water]* miroitement *m*.

glimpse [glɪm(p)s] **1** *n* aperçu *m*. **2** *vt (also* **catch a** ~ **of***)* entrevoir.

glint [glɪnt] **1** *n [light]* trait *m* de lumière; *[metal]* reflet *m*. **2** *vi* luire, briller.

glisten ['glɪsn] *vi [water]* miroiter; *[wet surface]* luire; *[metal object]* briller; *[eyes]* être brillant (*with* de).

glitter ['glɪtəʳ] **1** *vi (gen)* scintiller; *[eyes]* briller (de haine *or* de convoitise *etc*). **2** *n* scintillement *m*; *(fig)* éclat *m*. ◆ **glittering** *adj* scintillant, brillant; *(fig)* resplendissant.

gloat [gləʊt] *vi* exulter, jubiler *; *(maliciously)* se réjouir avec malveillance (*over, upon* de). **to** ~ **over** *money, possessions* jubiler * à la vue *or* à l'idée de; *beaten enemy* triompher de; *success* savourer.

globe [gləʊb] *n* globe *m*. *(Geog)* **all over the** ~ sur toute la surface du globe. ◆ **global** *adj (worldwide)* mondial; *(comprehensive)* global; **the global village** le village planétaire. ◆ **globe-trotter** *n* globe-trotter *m*. ◆ **globe-trotting** *n* voyages *mpl* à travers le monde.

globule ['glɒbjuːl] *n* globule *m*; *[water etc]* gouttelette *f*.

gloom [gluːm] *n (darkness)* ténèbres *fpl*; *(melancholy)* tristesse *f*. **to cast a** ~ **over** *event* jeter une ombre sur; *person* attrister. ◆ **gloomily** *adv* tristement, d'un air triste *or* lugubre. ◆ **gloomy** *adj person, voice, place* triste, morne; *(stronger)* lugubre; *prospects, day, thoughts, weather* sombre; **he took a** ~**y view of everything** il voyait tout en noir; **to feel** ~**y** avoir des idées noires.

glory ['glɔːrɪ] **1** *n* gloire *f (also Rel)*; *(magnificence)* splendeur *f*. **Rome at the height of its** ~ Rome à l'apogée de sa gloire; **there she was in all her** ~ * elle était là dans toute sa splendeur; **she was in her** ~ * elle était tout à fait à son affaire; ~ **be!** * Seigneur!; **the city's greatest** ~ le principal titre de gloire de la ville. **2** *vi*: **to** ~ **in sth** être très fier *(proud) or* très heureux *(glad)* de qch. **3** *adj*: ~ **hole** * capharnaüm * *m*. ◆ **glorify** *vt God* rendre gloire à; *person* exalter; **it was nothing but a glorified...** ce n'était guère que... ◆ **glorious** *adj martyr* glorieux; *person* illustre; *victory* éclatant; *clothes, view, weather etc* magnifique; **glorious deed** action *f* d'éclat.

gloss¹ [glɒs] **1** *n (shine)* lustre *m*, brillant *m*. **2** *adj paint* laqué; *paper* glacé. ~ **finish** brillant *m*; *(Phot)* glaçage *m*. ◆ **glossy** *adj fur, material* lustré; *paper* glacé; *paint* laqué; *hair, metal* brillant; *leaves* vernissé; *magazine* de luxe.

gloss² [glɒs] **1** *n (interpretation)* paraphrase *f*. **2** *vi*: **to** ~ **over sth** *(play down)* glisser sur qch; *(hide)* dissimuler qch. ◆ **glossary** *n* glossaire *m*.

glove [glʌv] **1** *n* gant *m*. *(fig)* **the** ~**s are off** j'y vais (*or* il y va *etc*) sans prendre de gants. **2** *adj*: *(Aut)* ~ **compartment** boîte *f* à gants; ~ **puppet** marionnette *f* (à gaine).

glow [gləʊ] **1** *vi [fire, metal, sky]* rougeoyer; *[cigarette end, lamp]* luire; *[colour, jewel]* rutiler; *[complexion, eyes]* rayonner; *[cheeks]* être en feu; *(fig)* brûler (*with* de). **it makes your body** ~ cela vous fouette le sang. **2** *n [coal, metal]* rougeoiement *m*, incandescence *f*; *[sun, complexion, colour]* éclat *m*; *[lamp]* lueur *f*; *[passion]* feu *m*; *[enthusiasm]* élan *m*. ◆ **glowing** *adj (V* **glow 1***)* rougeoyant; luisant; rutilant; rayonnant; *person (with health)* florissant (de santé); *(with pleasure)* radieux; *words* chaleureux; *description* enthousiaste; *(fig)* **to paint sth in** ~**ing colours** présenter qch en rose. ◆ **glowworm** *n* ver *m* luisant.

glower ['glaʊəʳ] *vi*: **to** ~ **at sb/sth** lancer à qn/qch des regards noirs. ◆ **glowering** *adj look* noir; *person* à l'air mauvais.

glucose ['gluːkəʊs] *n* glucose *m*.

glue [gluː] **1** *n* colle *f*, glu *f*. **2** *vt* coller (*to, on* à). **to** ~ **sth together** recoller qch; **to keep one's eyes** ~**d to sb/sth** * ne pas détacher les yeux de qn/qch; **he stood there** ~**d to the spot** * il était là comme s'il avait pris racine; **he was** ~**d to television** * il est resté cloué devant la télévision. ◆ **glue-sniffing** *n* intoxication *f* à la colle.

glum [glʌm] *adj* triste; *(stronger)* lugubre. ◆ **glumly** *adv walk* d'un air triste; *answer* d'un ton triste; *look* d'un regard morne.

glut [glʌt] *n* surabondance *f*, surplus *m*.

glutton ['glʌtn] *n* glouton(ne) *m(f)*. **a** ~ **for work** un bourreau de travail; **a** ~ **for punishment** un(e) masochiste *(fig)*. ◆ **gluttony** *n* gloutonnerie *f*.

glycerin(e) [ˌglɪsə'riːn] *n* glycérine *f*.

gnarled [nɑːld] *adj* noueux.

gnash [næʃ] *vt*: **to** ~ **one's teeth** grincer des dents.

gnat [næt] *n* moucheron *m*.

gnaw [nɔː] **1** *vi* ronger. **to** ~ **through** couper à force de ronger. **2** *vt* ronger. ◆ **gnawing** *adj remorse, anxiety, hunger* tenaillant; *pain* harcelant.

gnome [nəʊm] *n* gnome *m*.

go [gəʊ] *pret* **went**, *ptp* **gone** **1** *vi* (**a**) *(gen)* aller (*to* à, en; *from* de). **to** ~ **on a journey** faire un *or* partir en voyage; **to** ~ **up/down** monter/ descendre; **to** ~ **swimming** *(in general)* faire de la natation; *(on one occasion)* (aller) nager; **to** ~ **looking for sth** aller *or* partir à la recherche de qch; **we can talk as we** ~ nous pouvons parler en chemin; ~ **after him!** poursuivez-le!; **there he** ~**es!** le voilà!; **there he** ~**es again!** *(fig: he's at it again)* le voilà qui recommence!; **here** ~**es!** * allez, on y va!; **who** ~**es there?** qui va là?; *(US: in café)* **two hotdogs to** ~ deux hot-dogs à emporter; **you** ~ **first** passe devant; **you** ~ **next** à toi après; ~ **and shut the door** va fermer la porte; **she went and broke a cup** elle a trouvé le moyen de casser une tasse; **to** ~ *or* **be** ~**ing to do** aller faire; **to be just** ~**ing to do** être sur le point de faire; **the child went to his mother** l'enfant est allé vers sa mère; **to** ~ **to the doctor** aller voir le médecin; **to** ~ **to sb for sth** aller demander qch à qn; **the train** ~**es at 90 km/h** le train fait du *or* roule à 90 km/h; **we had gone only 3 km** nous n'avions fait que 3 km ; **I wouldn't** ~ **as far as to say that** je n'irais pas jusqu'à dire cela; **that's** ~**ing too far!** c'est un peu poussé!; **you've gone too far!** tu exagères! (**b**) *(depart)* partir, s'en aller; *[train]* partir; *(disappear)* disparaître; *[time]* passer; *[money]* disparaître, filer; *[strength]* manquer; *[hearing, sight etc]* baisser; *[health]* se détériorer. **his mind is ~ing** il n'a plus toute sa tête; **the coffee has all gone** il n'y a plus de café; **my voice has gone** je n'ai plus de voix; **he is gone** *(dead)* il n'est plus; **we must be ~ing** il faut partir; **gone with the wind** autant en emporte le vent; *(Sport)* ~! partez!; *(fig)* **from the word** ~ dès le départ; *(US)* **it's ~ing on 3** il va être 3 heures; **it's just gone 3 o'clock** il vient de sonner 3 heures; **it was gone 4** il était plus de 4 heures; **to let** ~ *or* **leave** ~ lâcher prise; **to let** ~ *or* **leave** ~ **of sth/sb** lâcher qch/qn; **to let o.s.** ~ se laisser aller; **they have let their garden** ~ ils ont laissé leur jardin à l'abandon; **I've let my music** ~ je n'ai pas travaillé ma musique; **we'll let it** ~ **at that** ça ira comme ça; **he/it will have to** ~ il va falloir se débarrasser de lui/se passer de cela; **'X must ~!'** 'à bas X!'; **it was ~ing cheap** cela se vendait à bas prix; **~ing, ~ing, gone!** une fois, deux fois, adjugé!; *(fig)* **7 down and 3 to** ~ 7 de faits, il n'en reste plus que 3; *(pregnant)* **6 months gone** * enceinte de 6 mois.

(**c**) *(start up)* démarrer; *(function)* marcher, fonctionner. **it ~es on petrol** ça marche *or* fonctionne à l'essence; *[machine]* **to be ~ing** être en marche; **to set** *or* **get ~ing** *machine* mettre en marche; *work, business* mettre en train; **to keep ~ing** *[person]* se maintenir en activité; *[business]* se maintenir à flot; *[machine]* continuer à marcher; **to keep the fire ~ing** entretenir le feu; **she needs it to keep her ~ing** elle en a besoin pour tenir le coup; **to keep sb ~ing in money** *etc* donner à qn ce qu'il lui faut d'argent *etc*; **to make the party** ~ animer la soirée; **to get things ~ing** faire démarrer les choses; **to make things** ~ faire marcher les choses; **to get ~ing on** *or* **with sth** se mettre à faire qch, s'attaquer à qch; **once he gets ~ing...** une fois lancé...

(**d**) *(progress)* aller, marcher. **the evening went very well** la soirée s'est très bien passée; **the project was ~ing well** le projet était en bonne voie; **how's it ~ing?** comment ça va? *; **how does the story ~?** comment c'est * cette histoire?; **the tune ~es like this** voici l'air; **let's wait and see how things** ~ attendons de voir ce qui va se passer; **as things** ~ dans l'état actuel des choses; **all will** ~ **well** tout ira bien; **all went well for him** tout a bien marché (pour lui).

(**e**) *(be, become)* devenir, se faire. *[person]* **to** ~ **unpunished** s'en tirer sans châtiment; **to** ~ **hungry** avoir faim; **to** ~ **red** rougir; **the constituency went Labour** la circonscription est passée aux travaillistes.

(**f**) *(be, accepted)* **the story ~es that...** le bruit court que...; **anything ~es** * tout est permis; **that ~es without saying** cela va sans dire; **what he says ~es** c'est lui qui commande; **that ~es for me too** *(applies to me)* cela s'applique à moi aussi; *(I agree)* je suis aussi de cet avis.

(**g**) *(break etc)* *[rope]* céder; *[fuse, lamp]* sauter; *[material]* s'user. **the skirt went at the seams** la jupe a craqué aux coutures; **this jacket has gone at the elbows** cette veste est percée aux coudes; **there ~es another button!** voilà encore un bouton de sauté!

(**h**) *(extend)* aller, s'étendre. **the garden ~es as far as the river** le jardin va *or* s'étend jusqu'à la rivière; **as far as that ~es** pour ce qui est de cela; **this book is good, as far as it ~es** c'est un bon livre, compte tenu de ses limites; **he's not bad, as boys** ~ il n'est pas trop mal, pour un garçon; **it's a fairly good garage as garages** ~ comme garage ça peut aller; **money does not** ~ **very far** l'argent ne va pas loin.

(**i**) *(be contained)* aller. **it won't** ~ **into my case** je ne peux pas le mettre dans ma valise; **4 into 12 ~es 3 times** 12 divisé par 4 égale 3; **2 won't** ~ **exactly into 11** 11 n'est pas exactement divisible par 2; **4 into 3 won't** ~ 3 divisé par 4 ne tombe pas juste; **the books** ~ **in that cupboard** les livres se mettent *or* vont dans ce placard-là.

(**j**) *[prize, reward]* aller, être donné (*to* à); *[inheritance]* passer (*to* à).

(**k**) *(be available)* **are there any jobs ~ing?** est-ce qu'on peut trouver du travail?; **is there any coffee ~ing?** est-ce qu'il y a du café?; **I'll have what's ~ing** je prendrai de ce qu'il y a.

(**l**) *(contribute)* contribuer (*to* à). **that will** ~ **to make him happy** cela contribuera à le rendre heureux; **the qualities that** ~ **to make a great man** les qualités qui font un grand homme; **the money will** ~ **towards** l'argent sera consacré à.

(**m**) *(make sound or movement)* faire; *[bell, clock]* sonner. ~ **like that with your foot** faites comme ça du pied; **to** ~ **bang** faire 'pan'; **he went 'psst'** 'psst' fit-il.

2 *vt*: **to** ~ **it alone** *(gen)* se débrouiller tout seul; *(Pol etc)* faire cavalier seul; **to** ~ **one better** faire (*or* dire) mieux (*than sb* que qn); *(Cards)* **he went 3 spades** il a annoncé 3 piques.

3 *n, pl* **~es** (**a**) *(energy)* énergie *f*, dynamisme *m*. **he is always on the** ~ il ne s'arrête jamais; **to keep sb on the** ~ ne pas laisser souffler qn; **he has 2 books on the** ~ il a 2 livres en train; **it's all ~!** * ça n'arrête pas! (**b**) *(attempt)* coup *m*, essai *m*. **to have a** ~ essayer (*at (doing) sth* de faire qch); **to have another** ~ essayer une nouvelle fois; **at one** ~ d'un seul coup; *(in games)* **it's your** ~ c'est à toi. (**c**) *(success)* **to make a** ~ **of sth** réussir qch; **no ~!** * rien à faire! (**d**) *(criticism)* **to have a** ~ **at sb** * critiquer qn.

4 *adj (fig)* **all systems are** ~ * tout est O.K.

◆ **go about 1** *vi* (**a**) circuler; *[rumour]* courir. **to** ~ **about with** *friends* fréquenter; *boyfriend etc* sortir avec. (**b**) *(Naut)* virer de bord. **2** *vt fus* (**a**) *(set to work at) task* se mettre à. **he knows how to** ~ **about it** il sait s'y prendre; **how does one** ~ **about getting seats?** comment fait-on pour avoir des places? (**b**) *(be occupied with) business* s'occuper de. **to** ~ **about one's normal work** vaquer à ses occupations habituelles.

◆ **go across** *vi, vt fus* traverser.

◆ **go after** *vt fus job, prize* essayer d'avoir.

◆ **go against** *vt fus* (**a**) *(prove hostile to) [luck, events etc]* être contraire à; *[appearance, evidence]* nuire à; *[decision]* être défavorable à. (**b**) *(oppose) public opinion* aller à l'encontre de; *sb's wishes* aller contre. **it ~es against my conscience** ma conscience s'y oppose.

◆ **go ahead** *vi*: ~ **ahead!** allez-y!; **to** ~ **ahead with a scheme** mettre un projet à exécution; **they went ahead with it** ils l'ont fait.

◆ **go along** *vi* aller, avancer. **I'll tell you as we** ~ **along** je vous le dirai en chemin; **to** ~ **along with sb** *(lit)* accompagner qn; *(fig)* être d'accord avec qn; **I check as I** ~ **along** je vérifie au fur et à mesure.

◆ **go around** *vi* = **go about 1a.**

◆ **go at** *vt fus (attack) person* attaquer; *(undertake) task* s'attaquer à.

◆ **go away** *vi* s'en aller, partir.

◆ **go back** *vi* (**a**) *(return)* revenir, retourner. **to** ~ **back to a subject** revenir sur un sujet; **to** ~ **back to the beginning** recommencer. (**b**) *(retreat)* reculer. (**c**) *[memory, family]* remonter (*to* à). (**d**) *(revert)* revenir (*to* à). (**e**) *(extend) [garden etc]* s'étendre (*to* jusqu'à). **the cave ~es back 300 metres** la grotte a 300 mètres de profondeur.

◆ **go back on** *vt fus decision, promise* revenir sur; *friend* laisser tomber.

◆ **go before** *vi* aller au devant. *(fig)* **all that has gone before** tout ce qui s'est passé avant.

◆ **go below** *vi (Naut)* descendre dans l'entrepont.

◆ **go by** **1** *vi [person, period of time]* passer. **we've let the opportunity ~ by** nous avons laissé échapper l'occasion; **as time ~es by** à mesure que le temps passe. **2** *vt fus appearances* juger d'après; *instructions* suivre. **that's nothing to ~ by** ça ne prouve rien; **I ~ by what I'm told** je me fonde sur ce qu'on me dit; **the only thing we've got to ~ by** la seule chose sur laquelle nous puissions nous baser.

◆ **go down** *vi* (**a**) *(descend)* descendre; *(fall) [person]* tomber; *[building]* s'écrouler; *(sink) [ship, person]* couler; *[sun, moon]* se coucher. **to ~ down to the country/the sea** aller à la campagne/au bord de la mer; **~ down to the bottom of the page** continuez jusqu'au bas de la page; **to ~ down to posterity** passer à la postérité; **to ~ down with flu** attraper la grippe; *(swallowed)* **it went down the wrong way** j'ai (*or* il a *etc*) avalé de travers; *(fig)* **that won't ~ down with me** ça ne prend pas avec moi; **his speech didn't ~ down well** son discours a été très mal reçu. (**b**) *(drop etc) [wind, floods, temperature, curtain]* tomber; *[tide]* descendre; *[balloon, tyre, swelling]* se dégonfler; *[amount, numbers]* diminuer; *[standards, price]* baisser. **to ~ down in value** perdre de sa valeur; **this neighbourhood has gone down** ce quartier n'est plus ce qu'il était. (**c**) *(be defeated, fail)* être battu (*to* par); *(Bridge)* chuter; *(fail examination)* échouer (*in* en).

◆ **go for** *vt fus* (**a**) *(attack) person* s'élancer sur; *(verbally)* s'en prendre à; *(in newspaper)* attaquer. *(to dog)* **~ for him!** mords-le! (**b**) *(*: admire) person, object* adorer *. **I don't ~ much for that** ça ne me dit pas grand-chose. (**c**) *(strive for)* essayer d'avoir; *(choose)* choisir. (**d**) *(fig)* **he's got a lot ~ing for him** il a beaucoup d'atouts.

◆ **go forward** *vi [person, vehicle]* avancer. **to let a suggestion ~ forward** transmettre une proposition.

◆ **go in** *vi (enter)* entrer, rentrer; *[troops]* attaquer; *[sun, moon]* se cacher (*behind* derrière). **what time does the theatre ~ in?** à quelle heure commence la pièce?

◆ **go in for** *vt fus* (**a**) *examination* se présenter à; *appointment* poser sa candidature à; *competition, race* prendre part à. (**b**) *sport, hobby, politics* faire; *style, principle, cause* adopter; *lectures* suivre; *profession* se consacrer à. **we don't ~ in for that sort of thing** nous n'aimons pas beaucoup ce genre de chose; **he's ~ing in for science** il va se spécialiser dans les sciences.

◆ **go into** *vt fus* (**a**) *(join, take up)* entrer à *or* dans. (**b**) *(embark on) explanation* se lancer dans. **let's not ~ into that now** laissons cela pour le moment; **to ~ into fits of laughter** être pris de fou rire. (**c**) *(investigate) question, problem* examiner, étudier.

◆ **go in with** *vt fus* se joindre à (*in* dans; *to do* pour faire); *(to buy sth)* se cotiser avec.

◆ **go off** **1** *vi* (**a**) *(leave)* partir, s'en aller; *(Theat)* quitter la scène. **to ~ off with sth** emporter qch; **to ~ off with sb** partir avec qn; *(off duty)* **I ~ off at 3 o'clock** je pars à trois heures. (**b**) *[alarm clock]* sonner; *[gun]* partir. **the gun didn't ~ off** le coup n'est pas parti; **the pistol went off in his hand** le pistolet lui est parti dans la main. (**c**) *(stop) [light, heating etc]* s'éteindre. (**d**) *(spoil) [meat, fish etc]* se gâter; *[milk]* tourner; *[sportsman]* perdre de sa forme; *[woman]* perdre de sa beauté. (**e**) *[feeling, effect]* passer. (**f**) *(go to sleep)* s'endormir. (**g**) *[event]* se passer. **the evening went off very well** la soirée s'est très bien passée. **2** *vt fus food etc* perdre le goût de. **I've gone off Dickens** je n'ai plus envie de lire Dickens.

◆ **go on** **1** *vi* (**a**) *[lid]* aller. **these shoes won't ~ on** je n'entre pas dans ces chaussures. (**b**) *(proceed)* poursuivre son chemin. **to ~ on to another matter** passer à une autre question; **he went on to say that...** il a dit ensuite que... (**c**) *(continue)* continuer (*with sth* qch; *doing* de *or* à faire). **~ on trying!** essaie encore!; **~ on (with you)! *** allons donc!; **you have enough to be ~ing on with** tu as de quoi faire * pour le moment; **he ~es on and on about it *** il ne finit pas d'en parler; **don't ~ on about it!** arrête! (**d**) *(happen)* se passer; *[game, argument]* être en train; *(last)* durer. **while this was ~ing on** au même moment; **what's ~ing on here?** qu'est-ce qui se passe ici? (**e**) *(pass) [time, years]* passer. **as the years went on he...** avec le passage des années, il... (**f**) *(behave)* se conduire. (**g**) *(Theat)* entrer en scène; *(Sport) [substitute]* entrer en jeu. (**h**) *(progress) [patient]* se porter; *[life, affairs]* continuer. **2** *vt fus (judge by)* se fonder sur. **what have you to ~ on?** sur quoi vous fondez-vous?; **we don't have much to ~ on** nous ne pouvons pas nous fonder sur grand-chose.

◆ **go on at** *vt fus (nag)* s'en prendre (continuellement) à.

◆ **go on for** *vt fus:* **to be ~ing on for** approcher de; **it's ~ing on for 5 o'clock** il est presque 5 heures.

◆ **go out** *vi (leave)* sortir; *(depart)* partir (*to* pour, à); *[tide]* descendre; *[sea]* se retirer; *[fashion]* se démoder; *[custom]* disparaître; *[fire, light]* s'éteindre; *(Cards etc)* terminer; *[pamphlet, circular]* être distribué (*to* à). **to ~ out of a room** quitter une pièce; **to ~ out riding** faire une sortie à cheval; **to ~ out for a meal** manger en ville (*or* chez des amis); **he ~es out a lot** il sort beaucoup; **she doesn't ~ out with him any more** elle ne sort plus avec lui; **to ~ out to work** travailler au dehors.

◆ **go over** **1** *vi* (**a**) *(cross)* **to ~ over to America** aller aux États-Unis; *(fig)* **his speech went over well** son discours a été très bien reçu. (**b**) *(change allegiance)* passer (*to* à). **to ~ over to the enemy** passer à l'ennemi. (**c**) *(be overturned) [vehicle, boat]* se retourner. **2** *vt fus* (**a**) *(examine) accounts, report* vérifier; *house* visiter; *[doctor] patient* examiner. (**b**) *(rehearse, review) lesson, rôle* revoir; *facts etc* récapituler; *events* retracer; *sb's faults, evidence* passer au crible. **to ~ over sth in one's mind** repasser qch dans son esprit; **let's ~ over it again** reprenons les faits; (**c**) *(touch up)* retoucher.

◆ **go round** *vi* (**a**) *[wheel etc]* tourner. **my head is ~ing round** j'ai la tête qui tourne. (**b**) *(make a detour)* faire un détour (*by* par). (**c**) **to ~ round to sb's house/to see sb** passer chez qn/voir qn. (**d**) *(be sufficient)* suffire (pour tout le monde). **enough food to ~ round** assez de nourriture pour tout le monde. (**e**) *(circulate) [rumour etc]* circuler.

◆ **go through** **1** *vi [law, bill]* être voté; *[business deal]* être conclu. **2** *vt fus* (**a**) *(suffer)* subir. **we've all gone through it** nous sommes tous passés par là. (**b**) *(examine) list, book* éplucher; *mail* dépouiller; *subject* examiner à fond; *clothes, wardrobe* trier; *one's pockets* fouiller dans; *(Customs)* fouiller. **to ~ through sb's pockets** faire les poches à qn *. (**c**) *(use up) money* dépenser; *a fortune* engloutir; *(wear out) garment, shoes* user. **it has already gone through 13 editions** il y en a déjà eu 13 éditions. (**d**) *(perform) lesson* réciter; *formalities* remplir; *programme, entertainment* exécuter; *course of study* suivre; *apprenticeship* faire.

◆ **go through with** *vt fus (complete) plan, crime, undertaking* exécuter. **she couldn't ~ through with it** elle n'a pas pu aller jusqu'au bout.

◆ **go together** *vi (gen)* aller bien ensemble; *[events, conditions]* aller de pair. **Ann and Peter are ~ing together** Ann et Peter sortent ensemble.

◆ **go under** *vi (sink) [ship, person]* couler; *(fail) [person]* être vaincu; *[business etc]* couler.

◆ **go up** **1** *vi* (**a**) *(rise) [price, value, temperature]* monter, être en hausse; *[curtain]* se lever. **to ~ up in price** augmenter. (**b**) *(ascend)* monter; *(to bed)* monter se coucher. (**c**) *(explode)* exploser. **2** *vt fus hill* monter.

◆ **go with** *vt fus* (**a**) *(accompany) [circumstances, event, conditions]* aller de pair avec. **the house ~es with the job** le logement va avec le poste; **to ~ with the crowd** suivre la foule. (**b**) *(suit) [colours]* s'assortir avec; *[furnishings]* être assorti à; *[behaviour, opinions]* s'accorder avec. (**c**) (**: also* ~ **steady with**) sortir avec.
◆ **go without** **1** *vi* s'en passer. **2** *vt fus* se passer de.
◆ **go-ahead** **1** *adj* dynamique ; **2** *n*: **to give sb the ~-ahead** * donner à qn le feu vert (*for* pour; *to do* pour faire). ◆ **go-between** *n* intermédiaire *mf*. ◆ **go-by** * *n*: **to give sb/sth the ~-by** * laisser tomber qn/qch. ◆ **go-getter** *n* battant(e) *m(f)*. ◆ **going** **1** *n (pace)* **that was good ~ing** ça a été rapide; **it was slow ~ing** on n'avançait pas; *(conditions)* **it's rough ~ing** *(walking)* on marche mal; *(Aut etc)* la route est mauvaise; **while the ~ing was good** au bon moment ; **2** *adj price* actuel; **the ~ing rate** le taux en vigueur; **a ~ing concern** une affaire qui marche. ◆ **going-over** *n [accounts, patient]* examen *m*; *(fig: beating-up)* passage *m* à tabac *. ◆ **goings-on** * *npl (behaviour)* activités *fpl*. ◆ **go-kart** *n* kart *m*. ◆ **go-slow (strike)** *n* grève *f* perlée.

goad [gəʊd] *vt (lit, fig)* aiguillonner. **to ~ sb into doing** talonner qn jusqu'à ce qu'il fasse.

goal [gəʊl] *n* but *m*, objectif *m*; *(Sport)* but. **to play in ~** être gardien de but; **to win by 3 ~s to 2** gagner par 3 buts à 2. ◆ **goalie** * *n* goal * *m*. ◆ **goalkeeper** *n* gardien *m* de but. ◆ **goal-kick** *n* coup *m* de pied de but. ◆ **goalmouth** *n*: **in the ~mouth** juste devant les poteaux. ◆ **goal-post** *n* poteau *m* de but.

goat [gəʊt] *n* chèvre *f*; *(he-~)* bouc *m*. **to act the ~** * faire l'andouille *; **he/it gets my ~** * il/ça me tape sur les nerfs *.

gobble ['gɒbl] *vt* (**~ down, ~ up**) engloutir. ◆ **gobbledegook** * *n* charabia * *m*.

goblet ['gɒblɪt] *n* coupe *f*; *(modern)* verre *m* à pied.

goblin ['gɒblɪn] *n* lutin *m*.

god [gɒd] *n* dieu *m (also fig)*. **G~** Dieu *m*; **G~ save the Queen** que Dieu bénisse la reine; **for G~ 's sake!** ⁑ nom d'un chien! *; **(my) G~!** ⁑ bon Dieu! ⁑; **G~ knows** * Dieu seul le sait; **G~ forbid!** * Dieu m'en garde!; **G~ willing** s'il plaît à Dieu; *(Theat)* **the ~s** * le poulailler *. ◆ **godchild** *n* filleul(e) *m(f)*. ◆ **goddamn(ed)** ⁑ *adj* foutu ⁑ *(before n)*. ◆ **goddaughter** *n* filleule *f*. ◆ **goddess** *n* déesse *f*. ◆ **godfather** *n* parrain *m*. ◆ **god-fearing** *adj* très croyant. ◆ **godforsaken** *adj place* perdu; *existence* misérable. ◆ **godhead** *n* divinité *f*. ◆ **godless** *adj* impie. ◆ **godlike** *adj* divin. ◆ **godly** *adj* pieux. ◆ **godmother** *n* marraine *f*. ◆ **godparents** *npl*: **his ~parents** son parrain et sa marraine. ◆ **godsend** *n* bénédiction *f*, don *m* du ciel (*to* pour). ◆ **godson** *n* filleul *m*.

gofer * ['gəʊfəʳ] *n (US)* coursier *m*, -ière *f*.

goggle ['gɒgl] **1** *vi* rouler de gros yeux ronds. **to ~ at sb/sth** regarder qn/qch en roulant de gros yeux ronds. **2** *npl*: **~s** *(gen)* lunettes protectrices; *[skindiver]* lunettes de plongée.

gold [gəʊld] **1** *n* or *m*. **in ~** en or; **heart of ~** cœur *m* d'or. **2** *adj watch, tooth* en or; *coin, cloth, reserves, mine* d'or; *(~-coloured)* or *inv*. **~ braid** galon *m* d'or; **~ dust** poudre *f* d'or; **~ leaf** or *m* en feuille; **~ plate** *(coating)* mince couche *f* d'or; *(dishes)* vaisselle *f* d'or; **~ rush** ruée *f* vers l'or; **~ standard** étalon-or *m*. ◆ **gold-digger** * *n* aventurière *f*. ◆ **golden** *adj hair* doré; *jewellery, voice* d'or, en or; *era* idéal; *afternoon* merveilleux; *opportunity* magnifique; *remedy* souverain; *rule, age* d'or; **~en eagle** aigle *m* royal; *(fig)* **~en handshake** gratification *f* de fin de service; **~en jubilee** fête *f* du cinquantième anniversaire; **the ~en mean** le juste milieu; **~en oldie** *(song)* vieux succès *m* de la chanson; *(film)* vieux succès de l'écran; *(Bot)* **~en rod** gerbe *f* d'or; **~en syrup** mélasse *f* raffinée; **~en wedding (anniversary)** noces *fpl* d'or. ◆ **goldfinch** *n* chardonneret *m*. ◆ **goldfish** *n* poisson *m* rouge; **~fish bowl** bocal *m* (à poissons). ◆ **gold-plated** *adj* plaqué or. ◆ **goldsmith** *n* orfèvre *m*.

golf [gɒlf] **1** *n* golf *m*. **2** *vi*: **to go ~ing** jouer au golf. **3** *adj*: **~ ball** balle *f* de golf; *(on typewriter)* boule *f*; **~ club** *(stick, place)* club *m* de golf; **~ course** terrain *m* de golf. ◆ **golfer** *n* joueur *m*, -euse *f* de golf.

gone [gɒn] *ptp of* **go**. ◆ **goner** ⁑ *n*: **to be a ~r** être fichu * *or* foutu ⁑.

gong [gɒŋ] *n* gong *m*.

gonorrhoea [,gɒnə'rɪə] *n* blennorragie *f*.

goo * [guː] *n* matière *f* gluante; *(sentimentality)* sentimentalité *f* mièvre. ◆ **gooey** * *adj substance* gluant; *cake* qui colle aux dents; *(fig)* sentimental.

good [gʊd] **1** *adj, comp* **better**, *superl* **best** (**a**) *(gen)* bon (*f* bonne); *(well-behaved) child, animal* sage; *(kind)* bon, gentil. **a ~ man** un homme bien, quelqu'un de bien; **he's a ~ man** il est bon; **to lead a ~ life** mener une vie vertueuse; **as ~ as gold** sage comme une image; **be ~!** sois sage!; **be ~ to him** soyez gentil avec lui; **that's very ~ of you** vous êtes bien aimable *or* gentil; **would you be ~ enough to tell me** seriez-vous assez aimable pour me dire; **G~ Friday** Vendredi saint; **~ sort** * brave type * *m or* fille *f*; **~ old Charles!** * ce bon vieux Charles!; **my ~ friend** mon cher ami; **my ~ man** mon brave; **very ~, sir!** très bien, monsieur!; **to do ~ works** faire de bonnes œuvres; **a ~ dress** une robe de qualité; **her ~ dress** sa belle robe; **nothing was too ~ for** rien n'était trop beau pour; *(in shop)* **I want sth ~** je veux qch de bien; **that's not ~ enough** c'est déplorable; **that's ~ enough for me** cela me suffit; **~ for you!** bravo!; **~!** très bien!; *(joke, story)* **that's a ~ one!** elle est bien bonne celle-là!; *(iro)* à d'autres! *; **he's as ~ as you** il vaut autant que vous; **it's as ~ a way as any other** c'est une façon comme une autre; **he was as ~ as his word** il a tenu sa promesse.
(**b**) *(beneficial)* bon (*for* pour). **it's ~ for you** ça te fait du bien; *(fig)* **if you know what's ~ for you** si tu as le moindre bon sens; **the shock was ~ for him** le choc lui a été salutaire; **to drink more than is ~ for one** boire plus qu'on ne le devrait; *[food]* **to stay ~** (bien) se conserver.
(**c**) *(efficient, competent)* bon (*at* en). **~ at French** bon *or* fort en français; **she's ~ with children** elle sait s'y prendre avec les enfants; **he's ~ at telling stories** il sait bien raconter les histoires; **he's not ~ enough to do it alone** il ne s'y connaît pas assez pour le faire tout seul; **he's too ~ for that** il mérite mieux que cela.
(**d**) *(agreeable)* bon; *visit, holiday* bon, agréable; *weather, day* beau (*f* belle); *news* bon, heureux. **we had a ~ time** nous nous sommes bien amusés; **I've had a ~ life** j'ai eu une belle vie; **too ~ to be true** trop beau pour être vrai; **it's ~ to be alive** il fait bon vivre; **it's ~ to be here** cela fait plaisir d'être ici; **I feel ~** je me sens bien; **I don't feel too ~ about that** * *(worried)* cela m'inquiète un peu; *(ashamed)* j'en ai un peu honte; **Robert sends his ~ wishes** Robert envoie ses amitiés; **with every ~ wish, with all ~ wishes** tous mes meilleurs vœux.
(**e**) *(in greetings)* **~ afternoon** *(early)* bonjour; *(later, on leaving)* bonsoir; **~ evening** bonsoir; **~ morning** bonjour; **~bye, ~night** *V below*.
(**f**) *(handsome) appearance* beau, joli. **~ looks** beauté *f*; **you look ~ in that, that looks ~ on you** ça vous va bien; **she's got a ~ figure** elle est bien faite; **~ legs** jambes bien faites.
(**g**) *(favourable) terms, contract, deal* avantageux; *offer* favorable, bon; *omen, chance, opportunity* bon;

marriage beau; *address* chic *inv*. **you've never had it so ~!** * vous n'avez jamais eu la vie si belle!; **he's on to a ~ thing** * il a trouvé un filon *; **to make a ~ thing out of sth** * tirer bon parti de qch; **it would be a ~ thing to ask him** il serait bon de lui demander; **it's a ~ thing I was there** heureusement que j'étais là; **that's a ~ thing!** tant mieux!; **it's too much of a ~ thing** il ne faut pas abuser des bonnes choses; **this is as ~ a time as any to do it** autant le faire maintenant.
(**h**) *(reliable, valid) car, tools, machinery* bon, sûr; *cheque* bon; *reason, excuse* bon, valable. **ticket ~ for 3 months** billet bon *or* valable 3 mois; **he's ~ for another 20 years yet** il en a encore bien pour 20 ans.
(**i**) *(considerable, not less than) mile, hour etc* bon. **a ~ deal (of), a ~ many** beaucoup (de); **a ~ way** un bon bout de chemin; **a ~ while** assez longtemps; **a ~ 8 kilometres** 8 bons kilomètres; **that was a ~ 10 years ago** il y a bien 10 ans de cela; **a ~ thrashing** une bonne correction; **to give sth a ~ clean** * nettoyer qch à fond.
(**j**) *(phrases)* **as ~ as** pour ainsi dire, pratiquement; **as ~ as new** comme neuf; **she as ~ as told me that...** elle m'a dit à peu de chose près que...; **it's as ~ as saying that...** autant dire que...; **it was as ~ as a play!** c'était une vraie comédie!; **to make ~** *(vi) (succeed)* faire son chemin; *[ex-criminal etc]* se refaire une vie; *(vt) deficit* combler; *deficiency, losses* compenser; *expenses* rembourser; *injustice, damage* réparer; *promise* tenir; *escape* réussir.
2 *adv* bien. **a ~ strong stick** un bâton bien solide; **a ~ long walk** une bonne promenade; **we had a ~ long talk** nous avons discuté bien longuement; **~ and hot** bien chaud.
3 *n* (**a**) *(virtue)* bien *m*. **to do ~** faire du bien; **she's up to no ~** * elle prépare quelque mauvais coup; **there's some ~ in him** il a du bon; **for ~ or bad** que ce soit un bien ou un mal; **he'll come to no ~** il finira mal.
(**b**) *(people)* **only the ~ die young** ce sont toujours les meilleurs *mpl* qui partent les premiers.
(**c**) *(advantage, profit)* bien *m*, avantage *m*. **the common ~** l'intérêt *m* commun; **for your own ~** pour votre bien; **for the ~ of his health** pour sa santé; **that will do you ~** cela vous fera du bien; **what ~ will that do you?** ça t'avancera à quoi?; **what's the ~?** à quoi bon?; **what's the ~ of hurrying?** à quoi bon se presser?; **a (fat) lot of ~ that will do you!** * tu seras bien avancé!; **much ~ may it do you!** grand bien vous fasse!; **we were £5 to the ~** cela nous a fait 5 livres de gagnées; **that's all to the ~!** tant mieux!; **it's no ~** ça ne sert à rien; **that's no ~** cela ne va pas; **that won't be much ~** cela ne servira pas à grand-chose; **if that is any ~ to you** si ça peut vous être utile; **it's no ~ saying that** ce n'est pas la peine de dire cela.
(**d**) *(adv phrase)* **for ~** pour de bon; **for ~ and all** une fois pour toutes.
◆ **goodbye** *excl* au revoir. ◆ **good-for-nothing** *adj, n* propre à rien *(mf)*. ◆ **good-hearted** *adj* qui a bon cœur. ◆ **good-humoured** *adj* bon enfant *inv*. ◆ **good-humouredly** *adv* avec bonhomie. ◆ **good-looker** * *n* beau garçon *m*, jolie fille *f*. ◆ **good-looking** *adj* beau, bien *inv*. ◆ **goodly** *adj* († *or liter) appearance* beau; *size* grand; *number* considérable. ◆ **good-natured** *adj person* débonnaire; *smile, laughter* bon enfant *inv*; *discussion* enjoué. ◆ **goodness** *n [person]* bonté *f*; *[thing]* (bonne) qualité *f*; **(my) ~ness!** *, **~ness gracious!** * Seigneur!; **~ness knows** * Dieu sait; **for ~ness' sake** * par pitié. ◆ **goodnight** *excl* bonsoir, bonne nuit. ◆ **goods** *npl* marchandises *fpl*, articles *mpl*; **leather/knitted ~s** articles de cuir/en tricot; **all his ~s and chattels** tous ses biens et effets *mpl*; **~s train** train *m* de marchandises; **~s yard** dépôt *m* de marchandises. ◆ **good-tempered** *adj person* qui a bon caractère; *smile, look* aimable. ◆ **good-time girl** * *n* fille *f* qui ne pense qu'à s'amuser. ◆ **goodwill** *n* bonne volonté; **to gain sb's ~will** se faire bien voir de qn; *(Pol)* **~will mission** visite *f* d'amitié; *(Comm)* **the ~will goes with the business** les incorporels *mpl* sont vendus avec le fonds de commerce. ◆ **goody** * **1** *excl* chic! * ; **2** *n (Cine)* **the ~ies and the baddies** * les bons *mpl* et les méchants *mpl*; *(Culin)* **~ies** * friandises *fpl*. ◆ **goody-goody** * *n* modèle *m* de vertu *(iro)*.

goose, *pl* **geese** [guːs, giːs] *n* oie *f*. **the ~ that lays the golden eggs** la poule aux œufs d'or; **don't be such a ~** * ne sois pas si dinde *. ◆ **gooseberry** *n* groseille *f* à maquereau; *(~berry bush)* groseiller *m*. ◆ **gooseflesh** *n or* ◆ **goosepimples** *npl or* ◆ **goosebumps** *npl* la chair de poule. ◆ **goose-step** *vi* faire le pas de l'oie.

gore [gɔːʳ] *vt [bull etc]* blesser d'un coup de corne.

gorge [gɔːdʒ] **1** *n (Anat, Geog)* gorge *f*. **it makes my ~ rise** cela me soulève le cœur. **2** *vt*: **to ~ o.s.** se gorger (*on* de).

gorgeous [ˈgɔːdʒəs] *adj* magnifique, splendide; (*) *holiday etc* sensationnel *, formidable *. **we had a ~ time** * on a passé un moment sensationnel *.

gorilla [gəˈrɪlə] *n* gorille *m*.

gormless * [ˈgɔːmlɪs] *adj* bête.

gorse [gɔːs] *n* ajoncs *mpl*. **~ bush** ajonc *m*.

gory [ˈgɔːrɪ] *adj wound, battle etc* sanglant; *person* ensanglanté. **all the ~ details** tous les détails les plus horribles.

gosh * [gɒʃ] *excl* ça alors! *

gospel [ˈgɒsp(ə)l] *n* évangile *m*. **it's the ~ truth** * c'est parole d'évangile; **~ (music)** gospel *m*; **~ song** ≃ negro-spiritual *m*.

gossip [ˈgɒsɪp] **1** *n* (**a**) *(chatter)* commérages *mpl*, potins *mpl*; *(in newspaper)* échos *mpl*. **a piece of ~** un ragot; **we had a good old ~** nous nous sommes raconté tous les potins. (**b**) *(person)* commère *f*. **he's a real ~** c'est une vraie commère. **2** *vi* bavarder; *(maliciously)* potiner, faire des commérages (*about* sur). **3** *adj (Press)* **~ column** échos *mpl*; **~ columnist** *or* **writer** échotier *m*, -ière *f*. ◆ **gossiping** **1** *adj* bavard, cancanier *(pej)* ; **2** *n* bavardage *m*, commérage *m (pej)*.

got [gɒt], *(US)* **gotten** [ˈgɒtn] *pret, ptp of* **get**.

Gothic [ˈgɒθɪk] *adj, n* gothique *(m)*.

gouge [gaʊdʒ] *vt* (**~ out**) *(with gouge)* gouger; *(with knife etc)* évider.

goulash [ˈguːlæʃ] *n* goulache *m or f*.

gourd [gʊəd] *n* gourde *f*.

gourmand [ˈgʊəmənd] *n* gourmand(e) *m(f)*.

gourmet [ˈgʊəmeɪ] *n* gourmet *m*.

gout [gaʊt] *n (Med)* goutte *f*.

govern [ˈgʌv(ə)n] **1** *vt country* gouverner; *province, city, business* administrer; *emotions etc* maîtriser; *(Tech)* régler; *(influence) events, speed* déterminer; *(Gram)* gouverner. **2** *vi (Pol)* gouverner. ◆ **governess** *n* gouvernante *f*. ◆ **governing** *adj (Pol etc)* gouvernant; *belief etc* dominant; **~ing body** conseil *m* d'administration. ◆ **government** **1** *n* gouvernement *m*; *(the State)* l'État *m*; **local ~ment** administration *f* locale; **2** *adj policy, decision, department* gouvernemental; *responsibility, loan, spending* de l'État, public. ◆ **governmental** *adj* gouvernemental. ◆ **governor** *n [state, bank]* gouverneur *m*; *[prison]* directeur *m*, -trice *f*; *[institution etc]* administrateur *m*, -trice *f*; *(Brit Scol)* ≃ membre *m* d'un conseil d'établissement *(de lycée ou d'IUT)*.

gown [gaʊn] *n* robe *f*; *(Jur, Univ)* toge *f*.

grab [græb] **1** *n* (**a**) **to make a ~ for** *or* **at sth** faire un geste vif pour saisir qch. (**b**) *(Tech)* benne *f* preneuse. **2** *vt object, opportunity* saisir ; *land* se saisir de; *seat, sb's attention* accaparer; *power* prendre. **to ~ (hold of) sb** empoigner qn; **to ~ sth from sb** arracher qch à qn; **how does that ~ you *?** est-ce que ça te dit? *

grace [greɪs] *n* grâce *f*. **by the ~ of God** par la grâce de Dieu; *(fig hum)* **to fall from ~** tomber en disgrâce; **to say ~** *(before meals)* dire le bénédicité; *(after meals)* dire les grâces; **to be in sb's good ~s** être bien vu de qn; **to do sth with good/bad ~** faire qch de bonne/mauvaise grâce; **he had the ~ to apologize** il a eu la bonne grâce de s'excuser; **his saving ~** ce qui le rachète; **a day's ~** un jour de grâce *or* de répit; **His G~** *(archbishop)* Monseigneur l'Archevêque; *(duke)* Monsieur le Duc. ◆ **graceful** *adj (gen)* gracieux; *apology* élégant. ◆ **gracefully** *adv (gen)* gracieusement; *apologize* avec élégance. ◆ **gracefulness** *n* grâce *f*.

gracious ['greɪʃəs] *adj person, smile* gracieux, bienveillant (*to* envers); *action* courtois; *God* miséricordieux (*to* envers); *house, gardens* d'une élégance raffinée. **~ living** vie élégante; **(good) ~! *** juste ciel! ◆ **graciously** *adv smile, consent* gracieusement; *agree* avec bonne grâce; *live* avec raffinement. ◆ **graciousness** *n* bienveillance *f* (*towards* envers).

gradate [grə'deɪt] **1** *vt* graduer. **2** *vi* être gradué. ◆ **gradation** *n* gradation *f*.

grade [greɪd] **1** *n* (**a**) *(in hierarchy)* catégorie *f*; *(on scale)* échelon *m*, grade *m*; *(Mil: rank)* rang *m*; *(of steel, butter, goods etc)* qualité *f*; *(size: of eggs, anthracite nuts etc)* calibre *m*; *(US: level)* niveau *m*. **the lowest ~ of skilled worker** la catégorie la plus basse des ouvriers qualifiés; **~ B milk** lait *m* de qualité B; **high-~** de première qualité; *(fig)* **to make the ~** avoir les qualités requises. (**b**) *(US) (class)* classe *f*; *(mark)* note *f*. (**c**) *(slope)* rampe *f*, pente *f*.
2 *adj (US)* **~ book** registre *m* de notes; *(US)* **~ crossing** passage *m* à niveau; *(US)* **~ school** école *f* primaire; *(US)* **~ sheet** relevé *m* des notes.
3 *vt* (**a**) *(sort into groups: gen)* classer; *(by size) apples etc* calibrer. **exercises ~d according to difficulty** exercices classés selon leur degré de difficulté. (**b**) *(make progressively easier, darker etc) exercises, colours etc* graduer. (**c**) *(US Scol: mark)* noter. ◆ **grader** *n (US Scol)* correcteur *m*. ◆ **grading** *n (gen)* classification *f*; *(by size)* calibration *f*; *(Scol etc)* notation *f*.

gradient ['greɪdɪənt] *n* rampe *f*, inclinaison *f*. **a ~ of one in ten** une inclinaison de dix pour cent.

gradual ['grædjʊəl] *adj change* graduel, progressif; *slope* doux. ◆ **gradually** *adv* graduellement, petit à petit.

graduate ['grædjʊeɪt] **1** *vt* (**a**) *jug* graduer (*in* en; *according to* selon). (**b**) *(US Scol, Univ)* conférer un diplôme à. **2** *vi* (**a**) *(Univ)* ≃ obtenir sa licence (*or* son diplôme *etc*); *(US Scol)* ≃ obtenir son baccalauréat. **he ~d as an architect** *etc* il a eu son diplôme d'architecte *etc*. (**b**) *[colours etc]* se changer graduellement (*into* en). **3** ['grædjʊɪt] *n (Univ)* ≃ licencié(e) *m(f)*, diplômé(e) *m(f)*. **4** ['grædjʊɪt] *adj (teacher)* ≃ licencié, diplômé; *studies* de troisième cycle. *(US)* **~ assistant** étudiant(e) chargé(e) de travaux dirigés. **~ course** ≃ études *fpl* de troisième cycle. ◆ **graduation** *n (Univ, also US Scol: ceremony)* remise *f* des diplômes *etc*.

graffiti [grə'fi:tɪ] *npl* graffiti *mpl*.

graft [grɑ:ft] **1** *n* (**a**) *(Agr, Med)* greffe *f*. **they did a kidney/skin ~ on him** on lui a greffé un rein/fait une greffe de la peau. (**b**) *(bribery etc)* corruption *f*; *(*: work)* dure besogne *f*. **2** *vt* greffer (*on* sur). ◆ **grafter** *n* (**a**) *(swindler)* escroc *m* ; (**b**) *(*: worker)* bourreau *m* de travail.

graham cracker ['greɪəm,krækə^r] *n (US)* biscuit *m* de farine complète.

grain [greɪn] **1** *n* (**a**) *(cereals in gen)* grain *m*, céréale *f*; *(wheat)* blé *m*. (**b**) *(single ~: of wheat, salt, sense)* grain *m*. (**c**) *(in leather; also Phot)* grain *m*; *(in wood, meat)* fibre *f*; *(in stone)* veine *f*. **with/against the ~** dans le sens de/en travers de la fibre (*or* de la veine *etc*); **it goes against the ~ for him to apologize** cela va à l'encontre de sa nature de s'excuser; **I'll do it, but it goes against the ~** je le ferai, mais pas de bon cœur. **2** *adj exports, prices, alcohol* de grain. *(US)* **~ elevator** silo *m* à céréales. ◆ **grainy** *adj (Phot)* qui a du grain; *substance* granuleux.

gram(me) [græm] *n* gramme *m*.

grammar ['græmə^r] **1** *n* grammaire *f*. **that is bad ~** cela n'est pas grammatical. **2** *adj*: **~ school** *(Brit)* ≃ lycée *m*; *(US)* ≃ cours *m* moyen. ◆ **grammarian** *n* grammairien(ne) *m(f)*. ◆ **grammatical** *adj* grammatical. ◆ **grammatically** *adv* grammaticalement.

gramophone ['græməfəʊn] **1** *n* phonographe *m*. **2** *adj needle* de phonographe. **~ record** disque *m*.

granary ['grænərɪ] *n* grenier *m (à blé etc)*.

grand [grænd] **1** *adj (gen)* grand; *person* magnifique, splendide; *character* grand, noble; *style, scenery, house* grandiose, splendide; *job, post* important; *chorus, concert* grand; *(excellent)* magnifique, formidable *. **~ duke** grand duc; **~ jury** jury *m* d'accusation; **~ opera** grand opéra; **~ piano** piano *m* à queue; **~ staircase** escalier *m* d'honneur; **~ total** résultat final; **a ~ tour** le tour complet; **the ~ old man of...** le patriarche de...; **we had a ~ time** nous nous sommes formidablement * amusés. **2** *n (US* ‡*)* mille dollars *mpl*. ◆ **grandchild** *n* petit(e)-enfant *m(f)*, petit-fils *m*, petite-fille *f*. ◆ **grandchildren** *npl* petits-enfants *mpl*. ◆ **grand(d)ad *** *or* ◆ **grand(pa)pa *** *n* grand-papa * *m*. ◆ **granddaughter** *n* petite-fille *f*. ◆ **grandeur** *n* grandeur *f*, splendeur *f*. ◆ **grandfather** *n* grand-père *m*; **~father clock** ≃ horloge *f* de parquet. ◆ **grand(ma)ma *** *n* grand-maman * *f*. ◆ **grandmaster** *n (Chess)* grand maître *m*. ◆ **grandmother** *n* grand-mère *f*. ◆ **grandparents** *npl* grands-parents *mpl*. ◆ **grandson** *n* petit-fils *m*. ◆ **grandstand** *n (Sport)* tribune *f*; *(fig)* **to have a ~stand view** être aux premières loges (*of sth* pour voir qch).

grandiose ['grændɪəʊz] *adj* grandiose.

granite ['grænɪt] *n* granit *m*.

granny * ['grænɪ] *n* grand-maman * *f*; *(~ knot)* nœud *m* de vache; **~ flat *** petite annexe *f* indépendante; **~ glasses** petites lunettes *fpl* cerclées de métal.

granola [græ'nəʊlə] *n (US)* muesli *m*.

grant [grɑ:nt] **1** *vt (gen)* accorder; *prayer* exaucer; *request* accéder à; *(admit)* admettre, reconnaître (*that* que). **~ed that this is true** en admettant que ce soit vrai; **I ~ you that** je vous l'accorde; **~ed!** d'accord!; **he takes her for ~ed** il la considère comme faisant partie du décor; **to take details/sb's agreement** *etc* **for ~ed** considérer les détails/l'accord de qn *etc* comme convenu(s) *or* certain(s); **you take too much for ~ed** vous prenez vos désirs pour des réalités. **2** *n (subsidy)* subvention *f*; *(scholarship)* bourse *f*. **he is on a ~ of £900** il a une bourse de 900 livres. ◆ **grant-aided** *adj* subventionné par l'État.

granule ['grænju:l] *n* granule *m*. ◆ **granular** *adj* granuleux. ◆ **granulated sugar** *n* sucre *m* semoule.

grape [greɪp] **1** *n* (grain *m* de) raisin *m*. **~s** du raisin, des raisins; **to harvest the ~s** vendanger. **2** *adj juice* de raisin. **~ harvest** vendange *f*.
◆ **grapefruit** *n* pamplemousse *m*. ◆ **grapevine** *n (fig)* **I hear on the ~vine that...** j'ai appris par le téléphone arabe que...

graph [grɑːf] *n* graphique *m*. ~ **paper** ≃ papier *m* millimétré. ◆ **graphic** *adj (gen)* graphique; *description* vivant; *(of sth unpleasant)* cru. ◆ **graphics** *n (sg: art of drawing)* art *m* graphique; *(pl: sketches)* représentations *fpl* graphiques; *(TV etc)* ~**ics by...** art graphique (de)...

graphology [græ'fɒlədʒɪ] *n* graphologie *f*. ◆ **graphologist** *n* graphologue *mf*.

grapple ['græpl] *vi*: **to** ~ **with** *person* lutter avec; *problem, difficult subject* se débattre avec.

grasp [grɑːsp] **1** *vt* (**a**) *(seize) object* saisir; *power, opportunity, territory* s'emparer de. *(fig)* **to** ~ **the nettle** aborder de front la difficulté. (**b**) *(understand)* saisir, comprendre. **2** *n*: **a strong** ~ une forte poigne; **to lose one's** ~ **on** *or* **of sth** lâcher qch; *(lit, fig)* **within one's** ~ à portée de la main; *(fig)* **in one's** ~ en son pouvoir; *(fig)* **within everyone's** ~ à la portée de chacun; **a good** ~ **of mathematics** une solide connaissance des mathématiques; **it is beyond my** ~ cela me dépasse. ◆ **grasping** *adj* cupide.

grass [grɑːs] **1** *n* (**a**) herbe *f*; *(lawn)* gazon *m*; *(grazing)* herbage *m*. **'keep off the** ~**'** 'défense de marcher sur le gazon'; *(fig)* **to let the** ~ **grow under one's feet** laisser traîner les choses; **to put out to** ~ *horse* mettre au vert; *(fig) person* mettre au repos; *(Agr)* **under** ~ en pré; *(Tennis)* **on** ~ sur gazon; *(Bot)* ~**es** graminées *fpl*. (**b**) *(Drugs sl: marijuana)* herbe *f (sl)*. (**c**) *(Prison sl: informer)* mouchard * *m*. **2** *adj tennis court* en gazon; ~ **cutter** grosse tondeuse *f* à gazon; *(fig)* ~ **roots** *(n)* base *f*; *(adj) candidate, movement* populaire, de la masse; ~ **snake** couleuvre *f*; *(US)* ~ **widow** divorcée *f*. **3** *vi (Prison sl)* moucharder *. **to** ~ **on sb** vendre qn. ◆ **grasshopper** *n* sauterelle *f*. ◆ **grassland** *n* herbages *mpl*. ◆ **grassy** *adj* herbeux.

grate[1] [greɪt] *n (metal part)* grille *f* de foyer; *(fireplace)* cheminée *f*. ◆ **grating**[1] *n* grille *f*.

grate[2] [greɪt] **1** *vt* (**a**) *cheese, carrot etc* râper. (**b**) *metallic object, chalk* faire grincer. **to** ~ **one's teeth** grincer des dents. **2** *vi* grincer (*on* sur). **to** ~ **on the ears** écorcher les oreilles; **it** ~**d on his nerves** cela lui tapait sur les nerfs *. ◆ **grater** *n* râpe *f*; **cheese** ~**r** râpe à fromage. ◆ **grating**[2] *adj sound* grinçant; *voice* discordant; *(annoying)* énervant.

grateful ['greɪtf(ʊ)l] *adj* reconnaissant (*to* à; *towards* envers; *for* de); *letter* plein de reconnaissance; *(fig) warmth* réconfortant. **I am most** ~ **to you** je vous suis très reconnaissant; **I should be** ~ **if you would come** je vous serais reconnaissant de venir; **with** ~ **thanks** avec mes plus sincères remerciements. ◆ **gratefully** *adv* avec reconnaissance.

gratify ['grætɪfaɪ] *vt person* faire plaisir à, être agréable à; *desire etc* satisfaire. ◆ **gratification** *n* satisfaction *f*. ◆ **gratified** *adj* content; **I was gratified to hear...** j'ai appris avec grand plaisir... ◆ **gratifying** *adj (gen)* agréable; *attentions etc* flatteur.

gratis ['grætɪs] *adv, adj* gratis *inv*.

gratitude ['grætɪtjuːd] *n* reconnaissance *f*, gratitude *f* (*towards* envers; *for* de).

gratuitous [grə'tjuːɪtəs] *adj* gratuit. ◆ **gratuitously** *adv* gratuitement. ◆ **gratuity** *n (Mil etc)* prime *f* de démobilisation; *(tip)* gratification *f*.

grave[1] [greɪv] **1** *n* tombe *f*; *(more elaborate)* tombeau *m*. **someone is walking over my** ~ * j'ai eu un frisson. ◆ **gravedigger** *n* fossoyeur *m*. ◆ **gravestone** *n* pierre *f* tombale. ◆ **graveyard** *n* cimetière *m*.

grave[2] [greɪv] *adj* (**a**) *(serious: gen)* grave, sérieux; *symptoms* grave, inquiétant. (**b**) [grɑːv] *(Ling) accent* grave. ◆ **gravely** *adv* gravement, sérieusement; *ill* gravement; *wounded* grièvement; *displeased* extrêmement. ◆ **graveness** *n* gravité *f*.

gravel ['græv(ə)l] **1** *n* gravier *m*; *(finer)* gravillon *m*. **2** *adj*: ~ **path** allée *f* de gravier; ~ **pit** carrière *f* de cailloux.

gravity ['grævɪtɪ] *n* (**a**) *(Phys)* pesanteur *f*. **the law of** ~ la loi de la pesanteur; ~ **feed** alimentation *f* par gravité. (**b**) *(seriousness)* gravité *f*, sérieux *m*. ◆ **gravitate** *vi (fig)* être attiré (*towards* vers). ◆ **gravitation** *n* gravitation *f*. ◆ **gravitational** *adj* de gravitation.

gravy ['greɪvɪ] *n* sauce au jus *m* de viande. ~ **boat** saucière *f*.

gray [greɪ] = **grey**.

graze[1] [greɪz] **1** *vi* brouter, paître. **2** *vt grass, cattle* paître; *field* pâturer (dans).

graze[2] [greɪz] **1** *vt (touch lightly)* frôler, effleurer; *(scrape) skin, hand etc* érafler. **to** ~ **one's knees** s'érafler les genoux. **2** *n* éraflure *f*.

grease [griːs] **1** *n (gen)* graisse *f*; *(Aut, Tech)* lubrifiant *m*, graisse *f*; *(dirt)* crasse *f*. **to get the** ~ **out of sth** dégraisser qch. **2** *vt* graisser. **like** ~**d lightning** * en quatrième vitesse *. ◆ **grease-gun** *n* (pistolet *m*) graisseur *m*. ◆ **greasepaint** *n* fard *m* gras; **stick of** ~**paint** crayon *m* gras. ◆ **greaseproof paper** *n* papier *m* sulfurisé. ◆ **grease-stained** *adj* graisseux. ◆ **greasiness** *n* graisse *f*; *[road etc]* surface *f* glissante. ◆ **greasy** *adj (gen)* graisseux; *hair, food, ointment* gras; *(slippery) surface, road etc* glissant; *clothes, collar* sale, crasseux; *(fig)* **a greasy character** un personnage fuyant.

great [greɪt] **1** *adj (gen)* grand; *heat, pain* fort, intense; *determination, will-power* fort; *(*: excellent) holiday, results etc* magnifique, sensationnel *. **Alexander the G**~ Alexandre le Grand; **G**~ **Britain** Grande-Bretagne *f*; **the G**~ **Lakes** les Grands Lacs; **G**~**er London** le grand Londres; **the G**~ **War** la Grande Guerre; **a** ~ **man** un grand homme; **the** ~ **masters** les grands maîtres; **a** ~ **deal (of), a** ~ **many** beaucoup (de); **to reach a** ~ **age** parvenir à un âge avancé; ~ **big** énorme; **he has a** ~ **future** il a beaucoup d'avenir; **at a** ~ **pace** à vive allure; **a** ~ **while ago** il y a bien longtemps; **you look** ~! tu as de l'allure!; **you were** ~ * tu as été magnifique! *; **it was** ~ * c'était formidable * *or* terrible *; **we had a** ~ **time** nous nous sommes rudement * bien amusés; **he's a** ~ **angler** *(keen)* il est passionné de pêche; *(expert)* c'est un pêcheur émérite; **he's** ~ * **at football** il est doué pour le football; **he's a** ~ **one * for cathedrals** il adore visiter les cathédrales; **he's a** ~ **one * for criticizing others** il ne rate pas une occasion de critiquer les autres; **he's** ~ * **on jazz** il connaît à fond le jazz; ~ **Scott! ***; grands dieux!; *(excl)* ~! formidable! **2** *n*: **the** ~ les grands *mpl*. ◆ **great-aunt** *n* grand-tante *f*. ◆ **greatcoat** *n* pardessus *m*; *(Mil)* capote *f*. ◆ **great-grandchild** *n* arrière-petit(e)-enfant *m(f)*. ◆ **great-granddaughter** *n* arrière-petite-fille *f*. ◆ **great-grandfather** *n* arrière-grand-père *m*. ◆ **great-grandmother** *n* arrière-grand-mère *f*. ◆ **great-grandson** *n* arrière-petit-fils *m*. ◆ **great-great-grandfather** *n* arrière-arrière-grand-père *m*. ◆ **great-hearted** *adj* au grand cœur. ◆ **greatly** *adv (gen) love* beaucoup; *loved* très; *superior, prefer* de beaucoup; *improve, increase, contribute* considérablement; **you're** ~**ly mistaken** vous vous trompez grandement; **it is** ~**ly to be feared** il est fort à craindre. ◆ **great-nephew** *n* petit-neveu *m*. ◆ **greatness** *n* grandeur *f*. ◆ **great-niece** *n* petite-nièce *f*. ◆ **great-uncle** *n* grand-oncle *m*.

Greece [griːs] *n* Grèce *f*. ◆ **Greek** **1** *adj* grec (*f* grecque); **Greek Orthodox Church** Église *f* orthodoxe grecque ; **2** *n* Grec(que) *m(f)*; *(Ling)* grec *m*; **ancient/modern Greek** grec classique/moderne; *(fig)* **that's (all) Greek to me** * tout ça c'est de l'hébreu pour moi *.

greed [griːd] *n*, **greediness** [ˈgriːdɪnɪs] *n (gen)* avidité *f*; *(for food)* gloutonnerie *f*. ◆ **greedily** *adv* avidement; *eat* gloutonnement; *drink* avec avidité; *eye food, lick lips* d'un air vorace. ◆ **greedy** *adj* avide (*for* de), cupide; *(for food)* vorace, glouton; **don't be ~y!** *(gen)* n'en demande pas tant!; *(at table)* ne sois pas si gourmand!

green [griːn] **1** *adj (colour)* vert; *corn* en herbe; *bacon* non fumé; *memory* vivace; *(inexperienced)* inexpérimenté; *(naïve)* naïf. ~ **bean** haricot *m* vert; *(Planning)* ~ **belt** zone *f* de verdure; ~ **card** *(Brit Aut)* carte verte; *(US: work permit)* permis *m* de travail; *(fig)* **he's got ~ fingers** *or* **a ~ thumb** il a la main verte; *(Aut; fig)* ~ **light** feu *m* vert; ~ **peas** petits pois *mpl*; ~ **pepper** poivron *m* vert; ~ **politics** le mouvement écologiste; *(Econ)* **the ~ pound** la livre verte; *(Theat)* ~ **room** foyer *m* des artistes; ~ **salad** salade *f* (verte); ~ **vegetables** légumes *mpl* verts; **to turn ~** verdir; ~ **with envy** vert de jalousie; **to make sb ~ with envy** faire pâlir qn de jalousie; *(fig)* **I'm not as ~ as I look!** * je ne suis pas si naïf que j'en ai l'air!
2 *n (colour)* vert *m*; *(grass)* pelouse *f*, gazon *m*; *(Golf)* green *m; (bowling ~) terrain gazonné pour le jeu de boules.* **village ~** ≃ place *f* (du village) *(gazonnée)*; *(Culin)* **~s** légumes *mpl* verts; *(Pol)* **the G~s** les verts.
◆ **greenback** *n (US)* billet *m* d'un dollar. ◆ **greenery** *n* verdure *f*. ◆ **greenfinch** *n* verdier *m*. ◆ **greenfly** *n* puceron *m* (des plantes). ◆ **greengage** *n* reine-claude *f*. ◆ **greengrocer** *n* marchand(e) *m(f)* de légumes; **~grocer's (shop)** fruiterie *f*. ◆ **greenhouse** *n* serre *f*; **~house effect** effet *m* de serre. ◆ **greenish** *adj* verdâtre. ◆ **greenness** *n* vert *m*; *[countryside etc]* verdure *f*; *[wood, fruit etc]* verdeur *f*. ◆ **greenstick fracture** *n* fracture *f* incomplète. ◆ **greenstuff** *n* verdure *f*.

Greenland [ˈgriːnlənd] *n* Groënland *m*.

Greenwich [ˈgrɪnɪdʒ] *n*: ~ **(mean) time** heure *f* de Greenwich.

greet [griːt] *vt person* accueillir (*with songs etc* avec des chansons *etc*), saluer; *announcement* accueillir. **he ~ed me with the news that...** il m'a accueilli en m'apprenant que... ◆ **greeting** *n* salut *m*, salutation *f*; *(welcome)* accueil *m*; **~ings** compliments *mpl*, salutations *fpl;* **Xmas ~ings** vœux *mpl* de Noël; **~ing(s) card** carte *f* de vœux; **my mother sends you her ~ings** ma mère vous envoie son bon souvenir.

gregarious [grɪˈgɛərɪəs] *adj animal, instinct* grégaire; *person* sociable.

grenade [grɪˈneɪd] *n (Mil)* grenade *f*.

grew [gruː] *pret of* **grow.**

grey [greɪ] **1** *adj* gris; *hair* gris, grisonnant; *complexion* blême; *outlook, prospect* morne. **to go ~** *(from fear etc)* blêmir; *[hair]* grisonner; ~ **skies** ciel gris *or* morne; **a ~ day** un jour gris; *(fig)* un jour triste; *(fig)* ~ **matter** * matière *f* grise, cervelle * *f*; *(fig)* **a ~ area** une zone d'incertitude (*between* entre). **2** *n (colour)* gris *m*; *(horse)* cheval gris. **3** *vi [hair]* grisonner. ◆ **greybeard** *n* vieil homme. ◆ **grey-haired** *adj* aux cheveux gris. ◆ **greyhound** *n* lévrier *m*. ◆ **greyish** *adj* grisâtre; *hair, beard* grisonnant.

grid [grɪd] *n (gen)* grille *f*; *(Culin: utensil)* gril *m*; *(Aut: on roof)* galerie *f*; *(Elec: system)* réseau *m*. *(Elec)* **the national ~** le réseau électrique national. ◆ **grid(iron)** *n (utensil)* gril *m*; *(US Sport)* terrain *m* de football.

griddle [ˈgrɪdl] *n* plaque *f* en fonte *(pour cuire)*.

grief [griːf] *n* chagrin *m*, douleur *f*. **to come to ~** *(gen)* avoir des ennuis; *[vehicle, rider, driver]* avoir un accident; *[plan, marriage etc]* tourner mal; **good ~!** * grands dieux! ◆ **grief-stricken** *adj* accablé de douleur.

grieve [griːv] **1** *vt* peiner, chagriner; *(stronger)* désoler. **it ~s us to see** nous sommes peinés de voir. **2** *vi* avoir de la peine *or* du chagrin (*at, about, over* à cause de); *(stronger)* se désoler (*at, about, over* de). **to ~ for sb/sth** pleurer qn/qch. ◆ **grievance** *n (ground for complaint)* grief *m* (*against* contre); *(complaint)* doléance *f*; *(Ind)* différend *m*, conflit *m*; **to have a grievance against sb** en vouloir à qn. ◆ **grievous** *adj pain, loss, blow* cruel; *injury, fault, wrongs* grave; *crime, offence* odieux; *news* pénible; *(Jur)* **grievous bodily harm** coups *mpl* et blessures *fpl*. ◆ **grievously** *adv* cruellement; gravement; *wounded* grièvement.

grill [grɪl] **1** *n* (**a**) *(cooking utensil)* gril *m*; *(food)* grillade *f*; *(~ room)* grill *m*. **under the ~** au gril. (**b**) *(also* **grille***)* *(grating)* grille *f*; *(Aut: radiator ~)* calandre *f*. **2** *vt* (**a**) faire griller. **~ed fish** poisson grillé. (**b**) *(*: interrogate)* faire subir un interrogatoire serré à, cuisiner *. **3** *vi* griller. **it's ~ing in here** * on grille ici *. ◆ **grilling** *n (fig)* interrogatoire *m* serré.

grim [grɪm] *adj (gen)* sinistre; *landscape, building* lugubre; *joke* macabre; *smile* sardonique; *face* sévère; *reality, necessity* dur *(before n)*; *truth* brutal; *(*: unpleasant)* désagréable. **with ~ determination** avec une volonté inflexible; **to hold on to sth like ~ death** rester cramponné à qch de toutes ses forces; **life is rather ~** * la vie n'est pas drôle; **she's feeling pretty ~** * *(ill)* elle ne se sent pas bien du tout; *(depressed)* elle n'a pas le moral *. ◆ **grimly** *adv frown, look* d'un air mécontent; *continue, hold on* inexorablement; *fight, struggle* avec acharnement; *pledge* d'un air résolu.

grimace [grɪˈmeɪs] **1** *n* grimace *f*. **2** *vi (from disgust etc)* faire la grimace; *(for fun)* faire des grimaces.

grime [graɪm] *n* crasse *f*, saleté *f*. ◆ **grimy** *adj* crasseux, sale.

grin [grɪn] **1** *vi* sourire; *(broadly)* avoir un grand sourire. **we must just ~ and bear it** il faut le prendre avec le sourire. **2** *n* (grand) sourire *m*.

grind [graɪnd] *(vb: pret, ptp* **ground***)* **1** *n* (*) boulot * *m* pénible. **the daily ~** le boulot * quotidien; **I find maths a dreadful ~** pour moi les maths sont une vraie corvée. **2** *vt corn, coffee etc* moudre; *(crush)* écraser; *(US) meat* hacher; *gems, lens* polir; *knife, blade* aiguiser (à la meule); *handle, pepper mill* tourner; *barrel organ* jouer de. **to ~ one's teeth** grincer des dents. **3** *vi* grincer. **to ~ to a halt** *[vehicle]* s'arrêter dans un grincement de freins; *[process, production]* s'arrêter progressivement.
◆ **grind down** *vt sep substance* pulvériser; *(fig: oppress)* écraser. ◆ **grind up** *vt sep* pulvériser.
◆ **grinder** *n (apparatus)* broyeur *m*; *(in kitchen)* moulin *m*; *(for knives)* affûteuse *f*. ◆ **grinding** **1** *n (sound)* grincement *m* ; **2** *adj poverty* accablant.

grip [grɪp] **1** *n* (**a**) *(handclasp)* poigne *f*; *(hold)* prise *f*, étreinte *f*. **to hold sth in a vice-like ~** tenir qch comme un étau; **to get a ~ on sth** empoigner qch; *(fig)* **to get a ~ on o.s. *, to keep a ~ on o.s.** se contrôler; **to lose one's ~** lâcher prise; *(*: grow less efficient etc)* baisser *; **he lost his ~ on the rope** il a lâché la corde; **the tyres lost their ~ on the icy road** les pneus ont perdu leur adhérence sur la chaussée gelée; **he has a good ~ of his subject** il possède bien son sujet; **to come** *or* **get to ~s with** *person* en venir aux prises avec; *problem, situation* s'attaquer à; **in the ~ of winter/a strike** paralysé par l'hiver/par une grève. (**b**) *(suitcase)* valise *f*; *(bag)* sac *m* (de voyage). **2** *vt (grasp)* saisir; *(hold)* serrer, tenir serré; *[fear etc]* saisir; *[film, story]* empoigner. **to ~ the road** *[tyres]* adhérer à la chaussée; *[car]* coller à la route. **3** *vi [wheels]* adhérer; *[vice, brakes]* mordre; *[anchor]* crocher. ◆ **gripping** *adj story, play* passionnant.

gripe [graɪp] **1** *n* (**a**) *(Med)* coliques *fpl*. (**b**) *(*: complaint)* (sujet *m* de) rogne *. **2** *vt (*: anger)*

mettre en boule *. **3** *vi* (‡: *grumble*) rouspéter * (*at* contre).
◆ **griping** **1** *adj* pain lancinant; **2** *n* (‡: *grumbling*) rouspétance * *f*.

grisly ['grɪzlɪ] *adj* macabre.

gristle ['grɪsl] *n* tendons *mpl* (*dans la viande cuite*). ◆ **gristly** *adj meat* tendineux.

grit [grɪt] **1** *n* (*sand*) sable *m*; (*gravel*) gravillon *m*; (*for fowl*) gravier *m*; (*: *courage*) cran * *m*. **a piece of ~ in the eye** une poussière dans l'œil; **he's got ~** * il a du cran *; (*US*) **~s** gruau *m* de maïs. **2** *vt* (**a**) **to ~ one's teeth** serrer les dents. (**b**) *road* sabler. ◆ **gritty** *adj path etc* couvert de gravier; *fruit* graveleux.

grizzle ['grɪzl] *vi* (*whine*) pleurnicher.

grizzled ['grɪzld] *adj* grisonnant.

grizzly ['grɪzlɪ] *n* (~ *bear*) ours *m* gris.

groan [grəʊn] **1** *n* (*of pain etc*) gémissement *m*; (*of disapproval, dismay*) grognement *m*. **2** *vi* gémir (*with* de); grogner; [*planks etc*] gémir.

grocer ['grəʊsəʳ] *n* épicier *m*. **at the ~'s (shop)** à l'épicerie, chez l'épicier. ◆ **grocery** *n* (*shop*) épicerie *f*; **~ies** (*goods*) provisions *fpl*.

groggy * ['grɒgɪ] *adj* (*weak*) faible; (*unsteady, also from blow etc*) groggy *.

grogram ['grɒgrəm] *n* gros-grain *m*.

groin [grɔɪn] *n* aine *f*.

groom [gru:m] **1** *n* (*for horses*) valet *m* d'écurie; (*bridegroom*) (futur *or* jeune) marié *m*. **2** *vt horse* panser. **the animal was ~ing itself** l'animal faisait sa toilette; **well-~ed** *person* très soigné; (*fig*) **to ~ sb for a post** former qn pour un poste. ◆ **grooming** *n* (*gen*) soins *mpl* de toilette *or* de beauté; (*appearance*) apparence *f* (impeccable); [*horse*] passage *m*; [*dog*] toilettage *m*.

groove [gru:v] *n* (*for sliding door etc*) rainure *f*; (*in column, screw*) cannelure *f*; (*in record*) sillon *m*; (*in penknife blade*) onglet *m*. **in the ~** ‡ (*up-to-date*) dans le vent *; **he's in a ~** * il est pris dans la routine.

grope [grəʊp] *vi* (**~ about, ~ around**) tâtonner, aller à l'aveuglette. **to ~ for sth** chercher qch à tâtons; **to ~ for words** chercher ses mots; **to ~ (one's way) in** *etc* entrer *etc* à tâtons.

gross [grəʊs] **1** *adj* (**a**) (*coarse*) grossier; (*fat*) obèse; *injustice* flagrant; *abuse* choquant; *negligence* grave; *ignorance* crasse. (**b**) *weight, income* brut. **~ national product** revenu *m* national brut. (**c**) (*US: disgusting*) dégueulasse ‡. **2** *n* (**a**) **in ~** (*wholesale*) en gros; (*fig*) en général. (**b**) (*pl inv: twelve dozen*) grosse *f*. **3** *vt* (*Comm etc*) faire une recette brute de. ◆ **grossly** *adv exaggerate etc* énormément; *unfair* extrêmement.

grotesque [grə(ʊ)'tesk] *adj* grotesque.

grotto ['grɒtəʊ] *n* grotte *f*.

grotty * ['grɒtɪ] *adj room, food* minable *, affreux. **he was feeling ~** il ne se sentait pas bien.

grouch * [graʊtʃ] **1** *vi* rouspéter *. **2** *n* (sujet *m* de) rogne * *f*. ◆ **grouchy** * *adj* maussade.

ground¹ [graʊnd] **1** *n* (**a**) terre *f*, sol *m*; (*US Elec*) masse *f*. **(down) on the ~** par terre, sur le sol; **above ~** en surface (*du sol*); **to fall to the ~** tomber à *or* par terre; **to get off the ~** [*plane*] décoller; [*scheme etc*] démarrer *. (**b**) (*soil*) sol *m*, terre *f*, terrain *m*. **stony ~** sol *or* terrain caillouteux. (**c**) (*area, piece of land*) terrain *m*; (*larger*) domaine *m*, terres *fpl*; (*territory*) territoire *m*; **hilly ~** pays *m* vallonné; **on French ~** en territoire français; **to hold** *or* **stand one's ~** ne pas lâcher pied; (*fig*) **to change** *or* **shift one's ~** changer son fusil d'épaule; **to gain ~** (*Mil*) gagner du terrain; [*idea etc*] faire son chemin; (*Mil, fig*) **to lose ~** perdre du terrain; (*fig*) **on dangerous ~** sur un terrain glissant; (*fig*) **to go over the same ~** reprendre les mêmes points; (*fig*) **on his own ~** sur son propre terrain; **football ~** terrain de football; (*gardens etc*) **~s** parc *m*. (**d**) (*reason*) **~s** raison *f*; **on medical ~s** pour (des) raisons médicales; **~s for divorce** motifs *mpl* de divorce; **on what ~s?** à quel titre?; **on the ~(s) of** pour raison de. (**e**) **(coffee) ~s** marc *m* (de café).
2 *vt* (**a**) *plane, pilot* interdire de voler à; (*keep on ~*) retenir au sol; (*US fig*) *student etc* consigner. (**b**) (*US Elec*) mettre une prise de terre à.
3 *adj attack, control, staff* au sol. (*Aviat*) **~ crew** équipe *f* au sol; **~ floor** rez-de-chaussée *m*; (*Mil*) **~ forces** armée *f* de terre; **~ frost** gelée *f* blanche; **at ~ level** au ras du sol; **~ rules** (*gen*) procédure *f*; **to change the ~ rules** changer les règles du jeu; (*US Elec*) **~ wire** fil *m* de terre.
◆ **grounding** *n* (**a**) [*plane*] interdiction *f* de vol; (**b**) (*in education*) connaissances *fpl* fondamentales, base *f*; **a good ~ing in French** une base solide en français. ◆ **groundless** *adj fear etc* sans fondement. ◆ **groundnut** **1** *n* arachide *f*; **2** *adj oil* d'arachide. ◆ **groundsheet** *n* tapis *m* de sol. ◆ **groundsman** *or* ◆ **groundkeeper** *n* gardien *m* de stade. ◆ **groundspeed** *n* (*Aviat*) vitesse-sol *f*. ◆ **groundswell** *n* [*sea*] lame *f* de fond; (*fig*) vague *f* de fond. ◆ **ground-to-air** *adj* sol-air *inv*. ◆ **ground-to-ground** *adj* sol-sol *inv*. ◆ **groundwork** *n* [*undertaking*] base *f*, travail *m* préparatoire; [*novel, play etc*] plan *m*.

ground² [graʊnd] (*pret, ptp of* **grind**) *adj coffee etc* moulu.

group [gru:p] **1** *n* (*gen*) groupe *m*; (*literary etc*) cercle *m*. **in ~s** par groupes. **2** *adj*: **~ dynamics** dynamique *f* de groupe(s); (*Med*) **~ practice** cabinet *m* collectif; (*Psych*) **~ therapy** psychothérapie *f* de groupe. **3** *vi* [*people*] se grouper. **4** *vt* (**~ together**) grouper. ◆ **grouping** *n* groupement *m*.

grouse¹ [graʊs] *n, pl inv* (*Orn*) grouse *f*.

grouse² * [graʊs] **1** *vi* (*grumble*) râler * (*at, about* contre). **2** *n* grief *m*.

grovel ['grɒvl] *vi* être à plat ventre (*to, before* devant). ◆ **grovelling** *adj* rampant.

grow [grəʊ] *pret* **grew**, *ptp* **grown** **1** *vi* [*plant, hair*] pousser; [*person, animal, friendship*] grandir; [*numbers, amount*] augmenter; [*club, group*] s'agrandir; [*love, influence, knowledge*] augmenter, s'accroître. **to ~ into a man** devenir un homme; **we have ~n away from each other** nous nous sommes éloignés l'un de l'autre avec les années; **to ~ to like** finir par aimer; **to ~ big(ger)** grandir; **to ~ angry** se fâcher. **2** *vt plants* cultiver, faire pousser; *one's hair etc* laisser pousser.
◆ **grow in** *vi* [*hair*] repousser. ◆ **grow into** *vt fus clothes* devenir assez grand pour mettre; *habit* acquérir (avec le temps). ◆ **grow on** *vt fus* [*habit etc*] s'imposer petit à petit à. **his paintings ~ on one** plus on voit ses tableaux plus on les apprécie. ◆ **grow out of** *vt fus clothes* devenir trop grand pour mettre; *habit* perdre (en grandissant *or* avec l'âge). ◆ **grow up** *vi* (**a**) devenir adulte. **when I ~ up** quand je serai grand; **~ up!** * ne sois pas si enfant! (**b**) [*friendship, custom*] naître.
◆ **grower** *n* cultivateur *m*, -trice *f*. ◆ **growing** *adj plant* qui pousse; *child* qui grandit; *amount, friendship, feeling* grandissant; *group* qui s'agrandit; *opinion* de plus en plus répandu; **to have a ~ing desire to do sth** avoir de plus en plus envie de faire qch; **fast-~ing** *plant* à croissance rapide; *conviction, group* croissant; **~ing pains** * (*Med*) douleurs *fpl* de croissance; [*business, project*] difficultés *fpl* de croissance. ◆ **grown** *adj* (*fully ~n*) adulte; **he's a ~n man** il est adulte. ◆ **grown-up** **1** *n* grande personne *f*; **2** *adj* de grande personne; **she's very ~n-up** elle fait très grande personne. ◆ **growth** **1** *n* (**a**) (*gen*) croissance *f*; [*numbers, amount etc*] augmentation *f* (*in* de); **the ~th of interest in...** l'intérêt croissant pour...; **a 5 days' ~th of beard** une barbe de 5 jours; **a new ~th of hair**

une nouvelle poussée de cheveux; (**b**) *(Med)* grosseur *f (on* à); **2** *adj market, industry etc* en (pleine) expansion; **~th hormone** hormone *f* de croissance; **~th rate** taux *m* de croissance.

growl [graʊl] **1** *vi* grogner *(at* contre); *[thunder]* gronder. **2** *vt* grogner. **3** *n* grognement *m.*

groyne [grɔɪn] *n* brise-lames *m inv.*

grub [grʌb] **1** *n* (**a**) *(larva)* larve *f.* (**b**) *(‡: food)* bouffe ‡ *f.* **2** *vi* (**~ about, ~ around**) fouiller *(in, among* dans; *for* pour trouver).

grubby [ˈgrʌbɪ] *adj* sale. ◆ **grubbiness** *n* saleté *f.*

grudge [grʌdʒ] **1** *vt*: **to ~ sb sth** en vouloir à qn de qch; **to ~ doing** faire à contrecœur; **she ~s paying £2** cela lui fait mal au cœur de payer 2 livres; **it's not the money I ~ but the time** ce n'est pas la dépense mais le temps que je plains. **2** *n* rancune *f.* **to bear a ~ against sb** en vouloir à qn, garder rancune à qn *(for* de). ◆ **grudging** *adj person* mesquin, peu généreux; *contribution* parcimonieux; *gift, praise etc* accordé à contrecœur; *admiration* réticent. ◆ **grudgingly** *adv* de mauvaise grâce.

gruelling [ˈgrʊəlɪŋ] *adj* exténuant.

gruesome [ˈgru:səm] *adj* horrible, épouvantable.

gruff [grʌf] *adj* bourru. ◆ **gruffly** *adv* d'un ton bourru.

grumble [ˈgrʌmbl] **1** *vi* grogner, ronchonner * *(at, about* contre), se plaindre *(about, at* de). **2** *npl* **~s** récriminations *fpl*; **without a ~** sans murmurer. ◆ **grumbling** **1** *n* récriminations *fpl* ; **2** *adj person* grincheux; *(Med)* **grumbling appendix** appendicite *f* chronique.

grumpy [ˈgrʌmpɪ] *adj* maussade, grincheux. ◆ **grumpily** *adv* d'une façon maussade.

grunt [grʌnt] **1** *vti* grogner. **2** *n* grognement *m.* **to give a ~** pousser un grognement; *(in reply)* répondre par un grognement.

Guadeloupe [ˌgwɑ:d(ə)ˈlu:p] *n* la Guadeloupe.

guarantee [ˌgær(ə)nˈti:] **1** *n* garantie *f (against* contre). **there is a year's ~ on this watch** cette montre a une garantie d'un an; **'money-back ~ with all items'** 'remboursement garanti sur tous articles'; **there's no ~ that it will happen** il n'est pas garanti que cela arrivera; **there's no ~ that it actually happened** il n'est pas certain que cela soit arrivé. **2** *adj*: **~ form** garantie *f (fiche).* **3** *vt goods etc* garantir *(against* contre; *for 2 years* pendant 2 ans); *behaviour, loan* se porter garant de. **I ~ that he will do it** je garantis *or* certifie qu'il le fera; **I can't ~ that he will come** je ne peux pas certifier qu'il viendra; **I can't ~ that he did it** je ne peux pas certifier qu'il l'ait fait. ◆ **guarantor** *n* garant(e) *m(f).*

guard [gɑ:d] **1** *n* (**a**) *(gen, also Mil, Boxing etc)* garde *f.* **to go on/come off ~** prendre/finir son tour de garde; **to be on ~** être de garde; **to keep** *or* **stand ~** monter la garde; **to keep** *or* **stand ~ on sb/sth** *V* **3** *below*; **he was taken under ~ to...** il a été emmené sous escorte à...; **to keep sb under ~** garder qn sous surveillance; **to put a ~ on sb/sth** faire surveiller qn/qch; **to be on one's ~** se tenir sur ses gardes *(against* contre); **to put sb on his ~** mettre qn en garde *(against* contre); **to catch sb off his ~** prendre qn au dépourvu. (**b**) *(Mil etc: squad)* garde *f*; *(one man)* garde *m.* **~ of honour** garde *f* d'honneur; *(on either side)* haie *f* d'honneur; **one of the old ~** un vieux de la vieille *; *(Mil)* **the G~s** les régiments *mpl* de la garde royale. (**c**) *(Brit Rail)* chef *m* de train. *(Brit Rail)* **~'s van** fourgon *m* du chef de train. (**d**) *(on machine)* dispositif *m* de sûreté; *(fire ~)* garde-feu *m inv.*

2 *adj*: **~ dog** chien *m* de garde; *(Mil)* **on ~ duty** de garde.

3 *vt (also* **keep** *or* **stand ~ on**) *(against attack)* garder *(from, against* contre); *(against theft, escape)* surveiller.

◆ **guard against** *vt fus infection etc* se protéger contre; *anger, reaction* se tenir sur ses gardes contre. **to ~ against doing** se garder de faire; **to ~ against sth happening** empêcher que qch ne se produise.

◆ **guarded** *adj remark, tone etc* circonspect. ◆ **guardedly** *adv* avec circonspection. ◆ **guardhouse** *n (Mil)* corps *m* de garde; *(for prisoners)* salle *f* de police. ◆ **guardian** *n (gen)* gardien(ne) *m(f)*; *[child]* tuteur *m*, -trice *f*; **~ian angel** ange *m* gardien. ◆ **guardrail** *n* barrière *f* de sécurité. ◆ **guardroom** *n (Mil)* corps *m* de garde. ◆ **guardsman** *n (Brit Mil)* garde *m (de la garde royale)*; *(US)* soldat *m* de la garde nationale.

Guatemala [gwɑ:tɪˈmɑ:lə] *n* Guatemala *m.*

guava [ˈgwɑ:və] *n* goyave *f.*

gudgeon [ˈgʌdʒ(ə)n] *n (fish)* goujon *m*; *(Tech)* tourillon *m.*

Guernsey [ˈgɜ:nzɪ] *n* Guernesey *m or f.*

guerrilla [gəˈrɪlə] **1** *n* guérillero *m.* **2** *adj tactics* de guérilla; *strike* sauvage. **~ group** guérilla *f (troupe)*; **~ war(fare)** guérilla *f (guerre).*

guess [ges] **1** *n* supposition *f*, conjecture *f.* **to have** *or* **make a ~** essayer de deviner *(at sth* qch); *(more formally)* hasarder une conjecture; **have a ~!** essaie de deviner!; **that was a good ~ but...** c'était une bonne intuition mais...; **it was just a lucky ~** j'ai deviné juste, c'est tout; **an educated ~** une hypothèse fondée; **at a (rough) ~** à vue de nez, grosso modo; **my ~ is that he refused** d'après moi il aura refusé; **your ~ is as good as mine!** * je n'en sais pas plus que toi!; **it's anyone's ~ * who will win** impossible de prévoir qui va gagner; **by ~ and by God *** Dieu sait comment. **2** *vt* (**a**) *answer, sb's age, name etc* deviner; *height, numbers etc* estimer, évaluer. **I ~ed him to be about 20** j'estimais qu'il avait à peu près 20 ans; **~ how heavy he is** devine combien il pèse; **I ~ed as much** je m'en doutais; **~ who! *** devine qui c'est! (**b**) *(surmise)* supposer *(that* que); *(US: believe)* croire, penser. **I ~ so** probablement; **I ~ not** je ne crois pas. **3** *vi* deviner. **to ~ right** deviner juste; **to ~ wrong** tomber à côté *; **to keep sb ~ing** laisser qn dans le doute; **to ~ at = guess 2a.** ◆ **guesstimate** *n* estimation approximative *or* à vue de nez. ◆ **guesswork** *n*: **it was sheer ~work** ce n'étaient que des conjectures *fpl*; **by ~work** en devinant, par flair.

guest [gest] **1** *n (at home)* invité(e) *m(f)*, hôte *mf*; *(at table)* convive *mf*; *(in hotel)* client(e) *m(f)*; *(in boarding house)* pensionnaire *mf.* **~ of honour** invité(e) d'honneur; **be my ~!** * fais comme chez toi! * **2** *adj speaker etc* invité; *list* des invités. **~ artist** artiste *mf* en vedette américaine; **~ room** chambre *f* d'amis. ◆ **guest house** *n* pension *f* de famille.

guffaw [gʌˈfɔ:] **1** *vi* rire bruyamment. **2** *n* gros rire *m.*

guide [gaɪd] **1** *n* (**a**) *(gen)* guide *m*; *(fig)* indication *f.* **let reason be your ~** il faut vous laisser guider par la raison; **this figure is only a ~** ce chiffre n'est qu'une indication; **as a rough ~** en gros, à peu près. (**b**) *(~ book)* guide *m (to* de); *(instructions)* manuel *m.* **beginner's ~ to sailing** manuel d'initiation à la voile. (**c**) *(girl ~)* éclaireuse *f*, guide *f.* **2** *vt*: **to be ~d by** se laisser guider par. **3** *adj*: **~ dog** chien *m* d'aveugle.

◆ **guidance** **1** *n* (**a**) conseils *mpl (about* quant à); **for your guidance** à titre d'information; (**b**) *[rocket etc]* guidage *m* ; **2** *adj system* de guidage; *(US Scol)* **guidance counselor** conseiller *m*, -ère *f* d'orientation. ◆ **guided** *adj missile etc* téléguidé; **~d tour** visite *f* guidée. ◆ **guidelines** *npl* lignes *fpl* directrices. ◆ **guiding** *adj principle* directeur; **guiding star** guide *m*; **he needs a guiding hand** il faut l'aider de temps en temps.

guild [gɪld] *n (gen)* association *f*; *(Hist)* guilde *f*.

guile [gaɪl] *n (deceit)* fourberie *f*; *(cunning)* ruse *f*. ◆ **guileless** *adj* franc (*f* franche), sincère.

guillotine [ˌgɪlə'tiːn] **1** *n* guillotine *f*; *(for paper-cutting)* massicot *m*; *(Parl)* limite *f* de temps. **2** *vt* guillotiner; massicoter.

guilt [gɪlt] *n* culpabilité *f*. **tormented by ~** torturé par un sentiment de culpabilité; *(Psych)* **~ feelings** sentiments *mpl* de culpabilité (*about sth* quant à qch; *about sb* vis-à-vis de qn). ◆ **guiltless** *adj* innocent (*of* de). ◆ **guilty** *adj* coupable (*of* de); **~y person** *or* **party** coupable *mf*; **to plead ~y/not ~y** plaider coupable/non coupable; **verdict of ~y/not ~y** verdict *m* de culpabilité/d'acquittement; **I have been ~y of that myself** j'ai moi-même commis la même erreur; **I feel very ~y about not writing to her** je suis plein de remords de ne pas lui avoir écrit.

Guinea ['gɪnɪ] *n* Guinée *f*.

guinea-pig ['gɪnɪpɪg] *n* cochon *m* d'Inde. *(fig)* **to be a ~** servir de cobaye *m* (*for sth* pour qch).

guitar [gɪ'tɑːʳ] *n* guitare *f*. ◆ **guitarist** *n* guitariste *mf*.

guise [gaɪz] *n*: **under the ~ of friendship** sous le couvert de l'amitié.

gulf [gʌlf] *n (lit, fig)* gouffre *m*; *(in ocean)* golfe *m*. **the Persian G~** le golfe Persique; **G~ States** États *mpl* du Golfe; **G~ Stream** Gulf Stream *m*.

gull [gʌl] *n* mouette *f*, goéland *m*.

gullet ['gʌlɪt] *n* gosier *m*.

gullible ['gʌlɪbl] *adj* crédule. ◆ **gullibility** *n* crédulité *f*.

gully ['gʌlɪ] *n* ravine *f*.

gulp [gʌlp] **1** *n*: **to swallow sth at one ~** avaler qch d'un seul coup; **'yes' he replied with a ~** 'oui' répondit-il la gorge serrée; **he took a ~ of milk** il a avalé une gorgée de lait. **2** *vt* **(~ down)** *food* avaler à grosses bouchées; *drink* avaler à pleine gorge. **3** *vi* essayer d'avaler. **he ~ed** *(from emotion etc)* sa gorge s'est serrée.

gum¹ [gʌm] *n (Anat)* gencive *f*. ◆ **gumboil** *n* fluxion *f* dentaire.

gum² [gʌm] **1** *n (glue)* gomme *f*, colle *f*; *(for chewing)* chewing-gum *m*; *(sweet: fruit ~)* boule *f* de gomme. **by ~!** * nom d'un chien! *; *(fig)* **to be up a ~ tree** ⁑ être dans le lac * *(fig)*. **2** *vt (put ~ on)* **(~down)** coller. **~med label** étiquette *f* gommée. ◆ **gum down** *vt sep* coller (et fermer). ◆ **gum up** ⁑ *vt sep (spoil)* abîmer, bousiller ⁑. ◆ **gumboots** *npl* bottes *fpl* de caoutchouc.

gumption * ['gʌm(p)ʃ(ə)n] *n* jugeote * *f*, bon sens *m*.

gun [gʌn] **1** *n* revolver *m*, pistolet *m*; *(rifle)* fusil *m*; *(cannon)* canon *m*. **he's got a ~!** il est armé!; **he was carrying a ~** il avait une arme (à feu); **to draw a ~ on sb** braquer une arme sur qn; **a 21-~ salute** une salve de 21 coups de canon; *(Mil)* **the ~s** les canons, l'artillerie *f*; **the big ~s** *(Mil)* les gros canons; *(*: people)* les grosses légumes ⁑; **to be going great ~s** ⁑ *[business]* marcher à pleins gaz ⁑; *[person]* être en pleine forme; **paint ~** pistolet *m* à peinture. **2** *adj (Mil)* **~ crew** peloton *m* de pièce; **~ dog** chien *m* de chasse; **~ licence** permis *m* de port d'armes. **3** *vt* **(a)** **(~ down)** abattre. **(b)** *(Aut)* **to ~ the engine** faire ronfler le moteur. **4** *vi (fig)* **to be ~ning for sb** * chercher qn, essayer d'avoir qn. ◆ **gunboat** *n* canonnière *f*. ◆ **gunfight** *n* échange *m* de coups de feu. ◆ **gunfire** *n [rifles etc]* fusillade *f*; *[cannons]* tir *m* d'artillerie. ◆ **gunman** *n* bandit *m* armé; *(Pol etc)* terroriste *m*. ◆ **gunner** *n* artilleur *m*. ◆ **gunnery** **1** *n (science etc)* tir *m* au canon; *(guns)* artillerie *f* ; **2** *adj officer* de tir. ◆ **gunpoint** *n*: **at ~point** *hold sb* sous son revolver, au bout de son fusil; *do sth, force sb* sous la menace du revolver. ◆ **gunpowder** *n* poudre *f* à canon. ◆ **gunrunner** *n* trafiquant *m* d'armes. ◆ **gunrunning** *n* trafic *m* d'armes. ◆ **gunship** *n* hélicoptère *m* de combat. ◆ **gunshot** **1** *n (sound)* coup *m* de feu ; **2** *adj*: **~shot wound** blessure *f* de balle. ◆ **gunsmith** *n* armurier *m*.

gunge * [gʌndʒ] *n* magma *m* gluant.

gung ho * ['gʌŋ 'həʊ] *adj* enthousiaste et naïf.

gunk * [gʌŋk] *n* magma *m* (infâme).

gurgle ['gɜːgl] **1** *n [water]* glouglou *m*; *[stream]* murmure *m*; *[laughter]* gloussement *m*; *[baby]* gazouillis *m*. **2** *vi* glouglouter; murmurer; glousser; gazouiller.

guru ['gʊruː] *n* gourou *m*.

gush [gʌʃ] **1** *n* flot *m*. **2** *vi* **(a)** **(~ out)** jaillir. *[water]* **to ~ in** *etc* entrer *etc* en bouillonnant. **(b)** *[person]* se répandre en compliments (*over* sur; *about* à propos de). ◆ **gushing** *adj water etc* bouillonnant; *person* trop démonstratif.

gust [gʌst] *n [wind]* coup *m* de vent, rafale *f*; *[smoke]* bouffée *f*; *[rage etc]* accès *m*. **~ of rain** averse *f*; **a ~ of laughter** un grand éclat de rire.

gusto ['gʌstəʊ] *n* enthousiasme *m*. **with ~** *say* vivement; *eat* avec grand appétit.

gut [gʌt] **1** *n (Anat)* boyau *m*, intestin *m*; *(Med: for stitching)* catgut *m*; *(Mus etc)* corde *f* de boyau. **~s** *(Anat)* boyaux; *(fig: central point)* point *m* fondamental; *(*fig: courage)* cran * *m*; **I hate his ~s** ⁑ je ne peux pas le sentir *. **2** *vt (Culin)* vider. **fire ~ted the house** le feu n'a laissé que les quatre murs de la maison. **3** *adj*: **~ feeling** sentiment *m* instinctif; **~ reaction** réaction *f* viscérale. ◆ **gutless** * *adj* qui manque de cran *. ◆ **gutsy** ⁑ *adj* qui a du punch.

gutter ['gʌtəʳ] **1** *n [roof]* gouttière *f*; *[road]* caniveau *m*. *(fig)* **language of the ~** langage *m* de corps de garde; **to rise from the ~** sortir du ruisseau *(fig)*. **2** *vi [candle]* couler; *[flame]* vaciller. **3** *adj*: **the ~ press** la presse à scandale. ◆ **guttersnipe** *n* gamin(e) *m(f)* des rues.

guttural ['gʌt(ə)r(ə)l] *adj* guttural.

guy¹ [gaɪ] **1** *n* (*) type * *m*, individu *m*. **the good/bad ~s** les bons *mpl*/les méchants *mpl;* **nice ~** type bien *; **smart** *or* **wise ~** malin *m*; **tough ~** dur * *m*. **2** *vt person* tourner en ridicule; *(Theat) part* travestir.

guy² [gaɪ] *n* **(~-rope)** corde *f* de tente.

Guyana [gaɪ'ænə] *n* Guyane *f*.

guzzle ['gʌzl] **1** *vi* s'empiffrer *. **2** *vt food* bâfrer *; *drink* siffler *.

gym [dʒɪm] **1** *n (gymnastics)* gym * *f*; *(gymnasium)* gymnase *m*; *(Scol)* salle *f* de gym *. **2** *adj*: **~ shoes** (chaussures *fpl* de) tennis *fpl*.

gymnasium [dʒɪm'neɪzɪəm] *n* gymnase *m*. ◆ **gymnast** *n* gymnaste *mf*. ◆ **gymnastic** *adj* gymnastique. ◆ **gymnastics** *n (sg: art)* gymnastique *f*; *(pl: activity)* **to do gymnastics** faire de la gymnastique.

gynaecology, *(US)* **gynecology** [ˌgaɪnɪ'kɒlədʒɪ] *n* gynécologie *f*. ◆ **gyn(a)ecological** *adj* gynécologique. ◆ **gyn(a)ecologist** *n* gynécologue *mf*.

gypsy ['dʒɪpsɪ] = **gipsy.**

gyrate [ˌdʒaɪ(ə)'reɪt] *vi* décrire des girations. ◆ **gyration** *n* giration *f*.

gyro... ['dʒaɪ(ə)rə(ʊ)] *pref* gyro... ◆ **gyrocompass** *n* gyrocompas *m*. ◆ **gyroscope** *n* gyroscope *m*. ◆ **gyrostabilizer** *n* gyrostabilisateur *m*.

H

H, h [eɪtʃ] *n* H, h *m or f*. **aspirate/silent h** h aspiré/ muet. ◆ **H-bomb** *n* bombe *f* H.

haberdasher [ˈhæbədæʃəʳ] *n (Brit)* mercier *m*, -ière *f*; *(US)* chemisier *m*, -ière *f*. ◆ **haberdashery** *n* mercerie *f*; chemiserie *f*.

habit [ˈhæbɪt] *n* (**a**) *(custom)* habitude *f*, coutume *f*. **to be in the** ~ *or* **to make a** ~ *or* **to have a** ~ **of doing** avoir l'habitude *or* la manie *(slightly pej)* de faire; **I don't make a** ~ **of it** je le fais rarement, je ne le fais pas souvent; **don't make a** ~ **of it!** et ne recommence pas!; **to get** *or* **fall into bad** ~**s** prendre *or* contracter de mauvaises habitudes; **to get into/out of the** ~ **of doing** prendre/ perdre l'habitude de faire; **to get sb into the** ~ **of doing** habituer qn à faire; **from (sheer)** ~ par (pure) habitude. (**b**) *(costume)* habit *m*. ◆ **habit-forming** *adj* qui crée une accoutumance.

habitable [ˈhæbɪtəbl] *adj* habitable. ◆ **habitat** *n* habitat *m*. ◆ **habitation** *n* habitation *f*; **fit for habitation** habitable.

habitual [həˈbɪtjʊəl] *adj (gen)* habituel; *liar, drinker etc* invétéré. ◆ **habitually** *adv* habituellement, d'habitude. ◆ **habituate** *vt* habituer (*to* à).

hacienda [ˌhæsɪˈendə] *n (US)* hacienda *f*.

hack¹ [hæk] *vt* (**a**) *(cut:* ~ **up***)* hacher, tailler. **to** ~ **sth to pieces** tailler qch en pièces. (**b**) *(strike)* frapper; *(kick)* donner des coups de pied à. ◆ **hack down** *vt sep* abattre (à coups de couteau *etc*). ◆ **hacking¹** **1** *adj*: ~**ing cough** toux *f* sèche (et opiniâtre) ; **2** *n* effraction *f* informatique. ◆ **hacker** * *n (Comput)* pirate *m* informatique. ◆ **hacksaw** *n* scie *f* à métaux.

hack² [hæk] **1** *n* (**a**) *(worn-out horse)* haridelle *f*; *(ride)* promenade *f* à cheval. **to go for a** ~ (aller) se promener à cheval. (**b**) *(~ writer)* écrivaillon *m (écrivain)*. **he was just a (literary)** ~ il ne faisait que de la littérature alimentaire. **2** *vi*: **to go** ~**ing** (aller) se promener à cheval. ◆ **hacking²** *adj*: ~**ing jacket** veste *f* de cheval. ◆ **hackwork** *n* travail *m* de nègre. ◆ **hack-writing** *n* écrits *mpl* alimentaires.

hackney [ˈhæknɪ] *adj*: ~ **carriage** voiture *f* de louage. ◆ **hackneyed** *adj subject* rebattu; *phrase* galvaudé; ~**ed expression** cliché *m*.

had [hæd] *pret, ptp of* **have.**

haddock [ˈhædək] *n* églefin *m*. **smoked** ~ haddock *m*.

haem(a)..., *(US)* **hem(a)...** [ˈhiːm(ə)] *pref* hém(a)... ◆ **h(a)ematology** *n* hématologie *f*. ◆ **h(a)emoglobin** *n* hémoglobine *f*. ◆ **h(a)emophilia** *n* hémophilie *f*. ◆ **h(a)emophiliac** *adj, n* hémophile *(mf)*. ◆ **h(a)emorrhage** **1** *n* hémorragie *f* ; **2** *vi* faire une hémorragie. ◆ **h(a)emorrhoids** *npl* hémorroïdes *fpl*.

hag [hæg] *n (ugly)* vieille sorcière *f*; *(*: nasty)* chameau * *m*. ◆ **hag-ridden** *adj* tourmenté.

haggard [ˈhægəd] *adj (careworn)* défait, abattu; *(wild)* égaré.

haggle [ˈhægl] *vi* marchander. **to** ~ **about** *or* **over sth** chicaner sur qch. ◆ **haggling** *n* marchandage *m*.

Hague [heɪg] *n*: **The** ~ La Haye.

hail¹ [heɪl] **1** *n* grêle *f (also fig: of missiles etc)*. **2** *vi* grêler. ◆ **hailstone** *n* grêlon *m*. ◆ **hailstorm** *n* averse *f* de grêle.

hail² [heɪl] **1** *vt* (**a**) *(acknowledge)* acclamer (*as* comme); *(greet)* saluer. *(excl)* ~! je vous salue!; **the H~ Mary** l'Avé Maria *m*. (**b**) *ship, taxi, person* héler. **2** *vi (Naut)* être en provenance (*from* de); *[person]* être originaire (*from* de). **where do you** ~ **from?** d'où êtes-vous? **3** *n* appel *m*. **within** ~ à portée de voix. ◆ **hail-fellow-well-met** *adj* liant, exubérant.

hair [hɛəʳ] **1** *n* (**a**) *[person]* cheveux *mpl*; *(on body)* poils *mpl*; *[animal]* pelage *m*. **he has black** ~ il a les cheveux noirs; **a man with long** ~**, a long-**~**ed man** un homme aux cheveux longs; **a fine head of** ~ une belle chevelure; **to wash one's** ~ se laver les cheveux *or* la tête; **to do one's** ~ se coiffer; **she always does my** ~ **very well** elle me coiffe toujours très bien; **her** ~ **is always very nice** elle est toujours très bien coiffée; **to have one's** ~ **done** se faire coiffer; **to get one's** ~ **cut** se faire couper les cheveux; **to make sb's** ~ **stand on end** faire dresser les cheveux sur la tête à qn; *(fig)* **to let one's** ~ **down** * se défouler *; **keep your** ~ **on!** * du calme!; **he gets in my** ~ * il me tape sur les nerfs *. (**b**) *(single* ~*)* *[head]* cheveu *m*; *[body, animal]* poil *m*. **not a** ~ **of his head was harmed** on ne lui a pas touché un cheveu; **it was hanging by a** ~ cela ne tenait qu'à un cheveu; **to remove unwanted** ~ **from one's legs** *etc* s'épiler les jambes *etc*; **he's got him by the short** ~**s** * il lui tient le couteau sur la gorge; **try a** ~ **of the dog that bit you** * reprends un petit verre pour faire passer ta gueule de bois *.

2 *adj* (**a**) *sofa, mattress etc* de crin. (**b**) ~ **appointment** rendez-vous *m* chez le coiffeur; ~ **clippers** *(npl)* tondeuse *f*; ~ **cream** brillantine *f*; ~ **gel** gel *m* coiffant; ~ **lacquer** laque *f*; ~ **oil** huile *f* capillaire; ~ **remover** crème *f* épilatoire; ~ **restorer** régénérateur *m* des cheveux; ~ **roller** rouleau *m*; ~ **set** mise *f* en plis; ~ **slide** barrette *f*; ~ **spray** laque *f* (en bombe *etc*); **a can of** ~ **spray** une bombe de laque; ~ **style** coiffure *f (arrangement des cheveux)*; ~ **stylist** coiffeur *m*, -euse *f*.

◆ **hairband** *n* bandeau *m*. ◆ **hairbreadth** *or* ◆ **hairsbreadth** *n*: **by a** ~**breadth** de justesse; **he was within a** ~**breadth of doing** il a failli faire. ◆ **hairbrush** *n* brosse *f* à cheveux. ◆ **haircut** *n*: **to have** *or* **get a** ~**cut** se faire couper les cheveux; **I like your** ~**cut** j'aime ta coupe de cheveux. ◆ **hairdo** * *n* coiffure *f*. ◆ **hairdresser** *n* coiffeur *m*, -euse *f*; ~**dresser's (shop** *or* **salon)** salon *m* de coiffure. ◆ **hairdressing** *n* coiffure *f (métier)*. ◆ **hair-drier** *n* séchoir *m* à cheveux; *(free-standing)* casque *m*. ◆ **hair-grip** *n* pince *f* à cheveux. ◆ **hairline** **1** *n* naissance *f* des cheveux; **he has a receding** ~**line** son front se dégarnit ; **2** *adj*: ~**line fracture** fêlure *f*; ~**line crack** légère fêlure. ◆ **hairnet** *n* résille *f*. ◆ **hairpiece** *n* postiche *m*. ◆ **hairpin** **1** *n* épingle *f* à cheveux ; **2** *adj*: ~**pin bend,** *(US)* ~**pin curve** virage *m* en épingle à cheveux. ◆ **hair-raising** *adj* à vous faire dresser les cheveux sur la tête. ◆ **hair-splitting** **1** *n* ergotage *m*, chicanerie *f* ; **2** *adj* ergoteur, chicanier. ◆ **hairy** *adj body, animal* velu, poilu; *scalp* chevelu;

person hirsute; *(Bot)* velu; *(*: frightening)* à vous faire dresser les cheveux sur la tête.

Haiti ['heɪtɪ] Haïti *m*.

hake [heɪk] *n* colin *m*.

hale [heɪl] *adj*: ~ **and hearty** en pleine santé.

half, *pl* **halves** [hɑ:f, hɑ:vz] **1** *n* (**a**) moitié *f*; demi(e) *m(f)*. **to cut/break in** ~ couper/casser en deux; **one** ~ **of the apple** une *or* la moitié de la pomme; **to take** ~ **of** prendre la moitié de; **two halves make a whole** deux demis font un tout; **he doesn't do things by halves** il ne fait pas les choses à moitié; **to go halves in sth with sb** se mettre de moitié avec qn pour qch; **bigger by** ~ moitié plus grand; **too clever by** ~ un peu trop malin; **and that's not the** ~ **of it!** * et ce n'est pas le mieux!; *(fig)* **to see how the other** ~ **lives** * aller voir comment vivent les autres; *(beer)* ~ **of Guinness** ≃ un bock de Guinness; *[rail ticket]* **outward/return** ~ billet *m* aller/retour. (**b**) *(Sport) (player)* demi *m*; *(part of match)* mi-temps *f*; *(Scol: term)* semestre *m*.
2 *adj* demi. **a** ~ **cup,** ~ **a cup** une demi-tasse; **two and a** ~ **hours** deux heures et demie; **two and a** ~ **kilos** deux kilos et demi; *(fig)* **in** ~ **a second** * en moins de rien; **to listen with** ~ **an ear** n'écouter que d'une oreille; **I don't like** ~ **measures** je n'aime pas faire les choses à moitié.
3 *adv* (**a**) à moitié, à demi. ~ **asleep/full/done** à moitié endormi/plein/fait; ~ **dressed/open** à demi vêtu/ouvert; ~ **French** ~ **English** mi-français mi-anglais; ~ **laughing** ~ **crying** moitié riant moitié pleurant; **he** ~ **rose to his feet** il s'est levé à demi; **I** ~ **think** je serais tenté de penser; **I** ~ **suspect that...** je soupçonne presque que...; **I'm** ~ **afraid that** j'ai un peu peur que + ne + *subj*; **not** ~ ‡ **rich** drôlement * riche; **she didn't** ~ ‡ **like it** ça lui a drôlement * plu; **not** ~! ‡ et comment! *; **it is** ~ **past three** il est trois heures et demie. (**b**) ~ **as big as** moitié moins grand que; ~ **as big again** moitié plus grand; ~ **as much as** moitié moins que; ~ **as much again** moitié plus.
◆ **half-and-half 1** *adv* moitié-moitié ; **2** *n (US) mélange mi-crème mi-lait.* ◆ **half-back** *n (Sport)* demi *m*. ◆ **half-baked** *adj (fig)* à la manque *. ◆ **half-board** *n* demi-pension *f*. ◆ **half-brother** *n* demi-frère *m*. ◆ **half-caste** *adj, n* métis(se) *m(f)*. ◆ **half-circle** *n* demi-cercle *m*. ◆ **half-day** *n* demi-journée *f*. ◆ **half-dead** *adj* à moitié mort (*with* de). ◆ **half-dozen** *or* ◆ **half-a-dozen** *n* demi-douzaine *f*. ◆ **half-fare 1** *n* demi-tarif *m* ; **2** *adv* à demi-tarif. ◆ **half-fill** *vt* remplir à moitié. ◆ **half-hearted** *adj manner, person* tiède; *attempt* sans conviction; *welcome* peu enthousiaste. ◆ **half-heartedly** *adv* avec tiédeur; sans conviction; sans enthousiasme. ◆ **halfholiday** *n* demi-journée *f* de congé. ◆ **half-hour** *or* ◆ **half-an-hour** *n* demi-heure *f*. ◆ **half-hourly** *adv, adj* toutes les demi-heures. ◆ **half-light** *n* demi-jour *m*. ◆ **half-mast** *n*: **at** ~**-mast** en berne. ◆ **half-moon** *n* demi-lune *f*; *(on fingernail)* lunule *f*. ◆ **half-open 1** *adj* entrouvert ; **2** *vt* entrouvrir. ◆ **half-pay** *n*: **on** ~**-pay** à demi-salaire; *(Mil)* en demi-solde. ◆ **halfpenny** ['heɪpnɪ] *n* demi-penny *m*; **he hasn't got a** ~**penny** il n'a pas le sou. ◆ **half-price** *n*: **at** ~**-price** à moitié prix; **the goods were reduced to** ~**-price** le prix des articles était réduit de moitié; **children admitted at** ~**-price** les enfants paient demi-tarif. ◆ **half-seas over** ‡ *adj* dans les vignes du Seigneur. ◆ **half-sister** *n* demi-sœur *f*. ◆ **half-starved** *adj* affamé. ◆ **half term (holiday)** *n* congé *m* de demi-trimestre. ◆ **half-time 1** *n (Sport, Ind)* mi-temps *f*; **2** *adv, adj* à mi-temps. ◆ **halfway** *adv, adj* à mi-chemin (*to* de; *between* entre); ~**way up** *or* **down (the hill)** à mi-côte, à mi-pente; **we're** ~**way there** nous n'avons plus que la moitié du chemin à faire; **to meet sb** ~**way** aller à la rencontre de qn; *(fig)* **I'll meet you** ~**way** coupons la poire en deux; ~**way through sth** à la moitié de qch. ◆ **halfwit** *n* idiot(e) *m(f)*. ◆ **halfwitted** *adj* idiot. ◆ **half-yearly 1** *adj* semestriel ; **2** *adv* tous les six mois.

halibut ['hælɪbət] *n* flétan *m*.

halitosis [ˌhælɪ'təʊsɪs] *n* mauvaise haleine.

hall [hɔ:l] **1** *n* (**a**) *(public room)* (grande) salle *f*. (**b**) *(mansion)* manoir *m*. *(Univ)* ~ **of residence** résidence *f* universitaire. (**c**) *(entrance way)* entrée *f*, hall *m*; *(corridor)* couloir *m*. **2** *adj*: ~ **porter** concierge *mf*. ◆ **hallmark** *n* poinçon *m*; *(fig)* marque *f*. ◆ **hallstand** *n or* ◆ **hall-tree** *(US) n* portemanteau *m*. ◆ **hallway** *n* vestibule *m*; *(corridor)* couloir *m*.

hallo [hə'ləʊ] *excl (in greeting)* bonjour!; *(Telec)* allô!; *(to attract attention)* hé!; *(in surprise)* tiens!

Hallowe'en ['hæləʊ'i:n] *n* veille *f* de la Toussaint.

hallucination [həˌlu:sɪ'neɪʃ(ə)n] *n* hallucination *f*.

halo ['heɪləʊ] *n* auréole *f*; *(Astron)* halo *m*.

halt [hɔ:lt] **1** *n* halte *f*, arrêt *m*. **5 minutes'** ~ 5 minutes d'arrêt; **to come to a** ~ s'arrêter; **to call a** ~ *(order a stop)* commander halte; *(stop)* faire halte; *(fig)* **to call a** ~ **to sth** mettre fin à qch. **2** *vi* s'arrêter. ~! halte! **3** *vt vehicle* faire arrêter; *process* interrompre. ◆ **halting** *adj* hésitant. ◆ **haltingly** *adv* de façon hésitante.

halter ['hɔ:ltəʳ] *n* licou *m*.

halve [hɑ:v] *vt apple etc* partager en deux (moitiés égales); *expense, time* réduire de moitié.

halves [hɑ:vz] *npl of* **half.**

ham [hæm] **1** *n* (**a**) jambon *m*. ~ **and eggs** œufs *mpl* au jambon. (**b**) *(Theat *: pej)* cabotin(e) * *m(f)*; *(Rad *)* radio-amateur *m*. **2** *adj sandwich* au jambon. **3** *vti (Theat *: also* ~ **it up***)* forcer son rôle. ◆ **ham-fisted** *or* ◆ **ham-handed** *adj* maladroit. ◆ **hamstring** *vt (fig)* couper ses moyens à.

Hamburg ['hæmbɜ:g] *n* Hambourg.

hamburger ['hæmˌbɜ:gəʳ] *n (gen)* hamburger *m*; *(US: also* ~ **meat***)* viande *f* hachée.

hamlet ['hæmlɪt] *n* hameau *m*.

hammer ['hæməʳ] **1** *n* marteau *m*. **the** ~ **and sickle** la faucille et le marteau; **to go at sth** ~ **and tongs** faire qch avec acharnement; **to come under the** ~ être mis aux enchères. **2** *vt* marteler; *(*: defeat)* battre à plate couture; *(criticize severely) film etc* éreinter. **to** ~ **a nail into a plank** enfoncer un clou dans une planche (à coups de marteau); **to** ~ **into shape** *metal* façonner au marteau; *plan* mettre au point; **to** ~ **an idea into sb's head** faire entrer de force une idée dans la tête de qn. **3** *vi (lit)* frapper (au marteau). *(fig)* **he was** ~**ing at the door** il frappait à la porte à coups redoublés. ◆ **hammer down** *vt sep nail* enfoncer; *plank* fixer. ◆ **hammer out** *vt sep plan, agreement* élaborer (avec difficulté).

hammock ['hæmək] *n* hamac *m*.

hamper¹ ['hæmpəʳ] *n (basket)* panier *m* d'osier.

hamper² ['hæmpəʳ] *vt (hinder)* gêner.

hamster ['hæmstəʳ] *n* hamster *m*.

hand [hænd] **1** *n* (**a**) main *f*. **on (one's)** ~**s and knees** à quatre pattes; **to have in one's** ~ *book* tenir à la main; *money* avoir dans la main; *victory* tenir entre ses mains; **give me your** ~ donne-moi la main; **to take sb's** ~ prendre la main de qn; **by the** ~ par la main; **with** *or* **in both** ~**s** à deux mains; ~**s up!** *(at gunpoint)* haut les mains!; *(in school etc)* levez la main!; ~**s off!** bas les pattes! ‡; ~**s off the sweets!** ne touche pas aux bonbons!; ~**s off our village** laissez notre village tranquille; *(lit)* ~ **over** ~ *or* **fist** main sur main; *(fig)* **he's making money** ~ **over fist** il fait des affaires d'or; **good with his** ~**s** adroit de ses mains.

(**b**) *(phrases)* **at** ~ *object* à portée de la main; *money, information* disponible; *summer, date* tout proche; **at first** ~ de première main; **by** ~ à la main; **from** ~ **to** ~ de main en main; **to live from** ~ **to mouth** vivre au jour le jour; **pistol in** ~ pistolet *m* au poing; **to put in(to) sb's** ~**s** remettre entre les mains de qn; **in good** ~**s** en bonnes mains; **I have this matter in** ~ je suis en train de m'occuper de cette affaire; **he had £6,000 in** ~ il avait 6 000 livres de disponibles; **cash in** ~ encaisse *f*; **the matter in** ~ l'affaire en question; **he had the situation well in** ~ il avait la situation bien en main; **she took the child in** ~ elle a pris l'enfant en main; **to keep o.s. well in** ~ se contrôler; **work in** ~ travail *m* en cours; **to have sth on one's** ~**s** avoir qch sur les bras; **on the right/left** ~ du côté droit/gauche; **on my right** ~ à ma droite; **on every** ~, **on all** ~**s** de tous côtés; **on the one** ~... **on the other** ~ d'une part... d'autre part; **to get sth off one's** ~**s** se débarrasser de qch; **it/she was off his** ~**s** il n'avait plus à s'en occuper/à s'occuper d'elle; **out of** ~ *(gen: instantly)* d'emblée; *condemn* sans jugement; *execute* sommairement; **to get out of** ~ *(gen)* devenir impossible; *(prices)* déraper; **to** ~ sous la main; **they are** ~ **in glove** ils s'entendent comme larrons en foire; ~ **in glove with** de mèche avec; **he never does a** ~**'s turn** il ne remue pas le petit doigt; **to eat out of sb's** ~ manger dans la main de qn; *(fig)* marcher au doigt et à l'œil; **to get one's** ~ **in** se faire la main; **to keep one's** ~**s off sth** s'empêcher de toucher à qch; **to have one's** ~**s full** avoir fort à faire (*with* avec); **to have a** ~ **in** *piece of work, decision* être pour qch dans; *crime, plot* être mêlé à; **she had a** ~ **in it** elle y était pour qch; **I will have no** ~ **in it** je ne veux rien avoir à faire là-dedans; **to take a** ~ **in (doing) sth** contribuer à (faire) qch; **to give sb a** ~ donner un coup de main à qn (*to do* pour faire); **to get/have the upper** ~ **of sb** prendre/avoir le dessus sur qn; **to put** *or* **set one's** ~ **to sth** entreprendre qch; **empty-**~**ed** les mains vides; **to win sth** ~**s down** gagner qch haut la main; **to be waited on** ~ **and foot** se faire servir comme un prince; *[horse]* **13** ~**s high** de 13 paumes.

(**c**) *(worker)* travailleur *m*, -euse *f* manuel(le), ouvrier *m*, -ière *f*. ~**s** *(Ind etc)* main-d'œuvre *f*; *(Naut)* hommes *mpl*; **all** ~**s on deck** tout le monde sur le pont; *(Naut)* **lost with all** ~**s** perdu corps et biens; **he's a great** ~ **at (doing) that** il est vraiment doué pour (faire) cela; **he's an old** ~ **at it** il n'en est pas à son coup d'essai.

(**d**) *[clock etc]* aiguille *f*.

(**e**) *(Cards)* main *f*; *(game etc)* partie *f*. **I've got a good** ~ j'ai une belle main; **we played a** ~ **of bridge** nous avons fait une partie de bridge.

2 *adj cream etc* pour les mains. ~ **towel** essuie-mains *m inv*.

3 *vt* passer, donner (*to* à). *(fig)* **you've got to** ~ **it to him** * c'est une justice à lui rendre; **it was** ~**ed to him on a plate** * ça lui a été apporté sur un plateau.

◆ **hand back** *vt sep* rendre (*to* à). ◆ **hand down** *vt sep object* passer *(de haut en bas)*; *heirloom, tradition* transmettre (*to* à). ◆ **hand in** *vt sep* remettre (*to* à). ◆ **hand on** *vt sep* transmettre (*to* à). ◆ **hand out** *vt sep* distribuer. ◆ **hand over 1** *vi (fig)* **to** ~ **over to sb** passer le relais à qn. **2** *vt sep object* remettre (*to* à); *prisoner* livrer (*to* à); *powers (transfer)* transmettre (*to* à); *(surrender)* céder (*to* à); *property, business* céder. ◆ **hand round** *vt sep bottles, papers* faire circuler; *cakes* faire passer, *[hostess]* offrir. ◆ **hand up** *vt sep* passer *(de bas en haut)*.

◆ **handbag** *n* sac *m* à main. ◆ **handball** *n* handball *m*. ◆ **handbasin** *n* lavabo *m*. ◆ **handbell** *n* sonnette *f*. ◆ **handbill** *n* prospectus *m*. ◆ **handbook** *n (instructions)* manuel *m*; *[tourist]* guide *m*; *[museum]* livret *m*. ◆ **handbrake** *n* frein *m* à main. ◆ **handclasp** *n* poignée *f* de main. ◆ **handcuff 1** *n* menotte *f* ; **2** *vt* passer les menottes à; **to be** ~**cuffed** avoir les menottes aux poignets. ◆ **hand-drier** *n* sèche-mains *m inv*. ◆ **handful** *n* poignée *f*; **in** ~**fuls** à *or* par poignées; *(fig)* **the children are a** ~**ful** * les enfants ne me laissent pas une minute de répit. ◆ **hand grenade** *n* grenade *f* (à main). ◆ **handicraft** *n (work)* artisanat *m*; *(skill)* habileté *f* manuelle; **exhibition of** ~**icrafts** exposition *f* d'objets artisanaux. ◆ **hand-in-hand** *adv* la main dans la main; *(fig)* ensemble; *(fig)* **to go** ~**-in-**~ **with** aller de pair avec. ◆ **handiwork** *n* ouvrage *m*; *(fig)* œuvre *f*. ◆ **handkerchief** ['hæŋkətʃɪf] *n* mouchoir *m*. ◆ **hand-knitted** *adj* tricoté à la main. ◆ **hand-luggage** *n* bagages *mpl* à main. ◆ **handmade** *adj* fait à la main. ◆ **hand-me-downs** * *npl* vêtements *mpl* d'occasion. ◆ **handout** *n (leaflet)* prospectus *m*; *(at meeting)* documentation *f*; *(press release)* communiqué *m*; *(money)* aumône *f*; *(aid)* aide *f*. ◆ **hand-picked** *adj* trié sur le volet. ◆ **handrail** *n [stairs etc]* rampe *f*; *[bridge, quay]* garde-fou *m*. ◆ **handsaw** *n* scie *f* à main. ◆ **handshake** *n* poignée *f* de main. ◆ **hands-off** *adj (fig: policy)* de non-intervention. ◆ **hands-on** *adj, adv (gen)* sur le tas; *(Comput)* appareil en main. ◆ **handspring** *n* saut *m* de mains. ◆ **handstand** *n*: **to do a** ~**stand** faire l'arbre droit. ◆ **hand-to-hand 1** *adv* corps à corps ; **2** *adj*: ~**-to-**~ **fighting** corps à corps *m*. ◆ **handwork** *n* = **handiwork**. ◆ **hand-woven** *adj* tissé à la main. ◆ **handwriting** *n* écriture *f*. ◆ **handwritten** *adj* manuscrit, écrit à la main.

handicap ['hændɪkæp] **1** *n* handicap *m*. **his appearance is a great** ~ son aspect physique le handicape beaucoup. **2** *vt* handicaper. ◆ **handicapped 1** *adj* handicapé; **mentally/physically** ~**ped** handicapé mentalement/physiquement ; **2** *npl*: **the** ~**ped** les handicapés *mpl*; **the mentally/ physically** ~**ped** les handicapés mentaux/physiques.

handle ['hændl] **1** *n [basket, bucket]* anse *f*; *[broom, spade, knife]* manche *m*; *[door, drawer, suitcase, tap]* poignée *f*; *[saucepan]* queue *f*; *[pump, stretcher, wheelbarrow]* bras *m*. *[car]* **(starting)** ~ manivelle *f*. **2** *vt* (**a**) *(wield) bow, weapon* manier; *(shift etc: esp Ind)* manipuler; *(touch) goods etc* toucher à; *(Sport) ball* toucher de la main. '~ **with care**' 'fragile'. (**b**) *(fig) ship, car* manœuvrer; *person, animal* manier, s'y prendre avec. **he knows how to** ~ **a gun/his son** il sait se servir d'un revolver/s'y prendre avec son fils; **he** ~**d the situation very well** il a très bien conduit l'affaire; **I'll** ~ **this** je m'en charge; **we don't** ~ **that type of product** nous ne faisons pas ce genre de produit; **we don't** ~ **that type of business** nous ne nous occupons pas de ce type d'affaires; **Orly** ~**s 5 million passengers a year** 5 millions de passagers passent par Orly chaque année; **can the port** ~ **big ships?** le port peut-il recevoir les gros bateaux?

◆ **handlebars** *npl* guidon *m*. ◆ **handler** *n (dog* ~*)* maître-chien *m*. ◆ **handling** *n [ship]* manœuvre *f*; *[car]* maniement *m*; *[goods, objects] (Ind)* manutention *f*; *(fingering)* maniement; **his handling of the matter** la façon dont il a traité l'affaire; *[person, object]* **to get some rough handling** se faire malmener.

handsome ['hænsəm] *adj (good-looking)* beau; *conduct, compliment, gift* généreux; *apology* honorable; *amount, fortune, profit* considérable. ◆ **handsomely** *adv (elegantly) construct* avec élégance; *(generously) contribute* généreusement; *apologize* avec bonne grâce; *behave* élégamment.

handy ['hændɪ] *adj* (**a**) *person* adroit (de ses mains). **to be** ~ **with sth** savoir se servir de qch. (**b**) *(at hand) tool* sous la main, prêt; *place* commode; *(nearby) shops etc* accessible. (**c**) *(convenient) tool,* *method* pratique. *(fig)* **that's ~!** ça tombe bien!; **that would come in very ~** cela tomberait bien. ◆ **handyman** *n (servant)* homme *m* à tout faire; *(do-it-yourself)* bricoleur *m*.

hang [hæŋ] *pret, ptp* **hung** **1** *vt* (**a**) *(suspend) lamp* suspendre (*on* à); *curtains, hat, picture* accrocher (*on* à); *door* monter; *clothes* pendre (*on, from* à); *wallpaper* poser; *dangling object* laisser pendre. **to ~ one's head** baisser la tête; **trees hung with lights** arbres chargés de lumières; **room hung with paintings** pièce aux murs couverts de tableaux; **to ~ fire** *[guns]* faire long feu; *[plans etc]* traîner (en longueur). (**b**) (*pret, ptp* **hanged**) *criminal* pendre (*for* pour).
2 *vi* (**a**) *[rope, dangling object]* pendre, être accroché *or* suspendu (*on, from* à); *[drapery]* pendre, tomber; *[hair]* tomber; *[picture]* être accroché (*on* à); *[criminal etc]* être pendu. **he'll ~ for it** cela lui vaudra la corde; **to ~ out of the window** *[person]* se pencher par la fenêtre; *[thing]* pendre à la fenêtre; *(fig)* **to ~ by a hair** ne tenir qu'à un cheveu. (**b**) *[fog, threat]* planer, peser (*over* sur); *[hawk]* être comme suspendu.
3 *n*: **to get the ~ * of doing sth** attraper le coup * pour faire qch.
◆ **hang about, hang around** **1** *vi [loiterer]* traîner. **to keep sb ~ing about** faire attendre qn. **2** *vt fus person* coller à; *place* hanter. ◆ **hang back** *vi (in walking etc)* hésiter à aller de l'avant; *(fig)* être réticent (*from doing* pour faire). ◆ **hang down** *vi, vt sep* pendre. ◆ **hang on** **1** *vi* (**a**) *(*: wait)* attendre. **~ on!** attendez!; *(on phone)* ne quittez pas! (**b**) *(hold out)* tenir bon, résister. (**c**) **to ~ on to sth** * *(keep hold of)* ne pas lâcher qch; *(keep)* garder qch. **2** *vt fus (depend on)* dépendre de. ◆ **hang out** **1** *vi (gen)* pendre; *(‡: live)* percher *, habiter; *(spend time)* traîner; *(*: resist)* tenir bon. **2** *vt sep streamer* suspendre (dehors); *washing* étendre (dehors); *flag* arborer. ◆ **hang together** *vi [argument, details]* se tenir; *[story]* tenir debout; *[statements]* concorder. ◆ **hang up** **1** *vi (Telec: also* **~ up on sb**) raccrocher. **2** *vt sep* accrocher (*on* à, sur). *(fig)* **he's hung up about it** * il en fait tout un complexe.
◆ **hangdog expression** *n* air *m* de chien battu. ◆ **hanger** *n (clothes ~)* cintre *m*. ◆ **hanger-on** *n* parasite *m (personne)*. ◆ **hang-glider** *n (person)* libériste *mf*; *(device)* aile *f* volante. ◆ **hang-gliding** *n*: **to go ~-gliding** pratiquer le vol libre. ◆ **hanging** **1** *n (execution)* pendaison *f* ; **2** *adj bridge* suspendu; *lamp, light* pendant. ◆ **hangman** *n* bourreau *m*. ◆ **hangover** *n*: **to have a ~over** avoir une *or* la gueule de bois ‡; **a ~over from the previous administration** un reliquat de l'administration précédente. ◆ **hang-up** * *n* complexe *m* (*about* en ce qui concerne).

hangar ['hæŋəʳ] *n (Aviat)* hangar *m*.

hank [hæŋk] *n [wool etc]* écheveau *m*.

hanker ['hæŋkəʳ] *vi*: **to ~** *or* **have a ~ing for** *or* **after** avoir envie de.

hankie * ['hæŋkɪ] *n abbr of* **handkerchief.**

hanky-panky * ['hæŋkɪ'pæŋkɪ] *n* entourloupette * *f*. **there's some ~ going on** il y a une entourloupette * là-dessous.

ha'penny ['heɪpnɪ] *n* = **halfpenny.**

haphazard [,hæp'hæzəd] *adj* (fait) au hasard; *arrangement* fortuit. ◆ **haphazardly** *adv* au hasard.

happen ['hæp(ə)n] *vi* arriver, se passer, se produire. **sth ~ed** il est arrivé *or* il s'est passé qch; **what's ~ed?** qu'est-ce qui s'est passé *or* est arrivé?; **as if nothing had ~ed** comme si de rien n'était; **whatever ~s** quoi qu'il arrive; **don't let it ~ again!** et que ça ne se reproduise pas!; **these things ~** ce sont des choses qui arrivent; **what has ~ed to him?** *(befallen)* qu'est-ce qui lui est arrivé?; *(become of)* qu'est-ce qu'il est devenu?; **a funny thing ~ed to me this morning** il m'est arrivé qch de bizarre ce matin; **how does it ~ that?** comment se fait-il que? + *subj*; **it might ~ that** il pourrait se faire que + *subj*; **it so ~s that I'm going there** il se trouve que j'y vais justement; **do you ~ to have a pen?** aurais-tu par hasard un stylo?; **if he does ~ to see her** s'il lui arrive de la voir. ◆ **happening** *n* événement *m*; *(Theat)* happening *m*. ◆ **happenstance** * *n (US)* événement *m* fortuit.

happy ['hæpɪ] *adj* heureux (*to do* de faire). **I'm not ~ about the plan** je ne suis pas très heureux de ce projet; **I'm not ~ about leaving him alone** je ne suis pas tranquille de le laisser seul; **I'll be quite ~ to do it** je le ferai volontiers; **she was quite ~ to stay there** cela ne l'ennuyait pas de rester là; **I'm ~ here reading** je suis très bien ici à lire; **it has a ~ ending** cela se termine bien; **the ~ few** les rares privilégiés *mpl*; *(US)* **~ hour** le 5 à 7; **~ birthday!** bon *or* joyeux anniversaire!; **~ Christmas!** joyeux Noël!; **~ New Year!** bonne année!; **a ~ thought** une heureuse inspiration; **a ~ medium** un moyen terme. ◆ **happily** *adv (contentedly) play, walk, talk* tranquillement; *say, smile* joyeusement; *(fortunately)* heureusement; *(felicitously) word, choose* avec bonheur; **to live happily** vivre heureux; **they lived happily (for) ever after** après cela ils vécurent toujours heureux. ◆ **happiness** *n* bonheur *m*. ◆ **happy-go-lucky** *adj person* insouciant; *arrangement* fait au petit bonheur.

harangue [hə'ræŋ] **1** *vt* haranguer (*about* à propos de). **he ~d her into doing it** il n'a eu de cesse qu'elle ne le fasse. **2** *n* harangue *f*.

harass ['hærəs] *vt (harry) troops, the enemy etc* harceler; *(worry)* tracasser; *(stronger)* harceler. ◆ **harassed** *adj* tracassé, surmené, harcelé. ◆ **harassment** *n* harcèlement *m*, surmenage *m*.

harbour, *(US)* **harbor** ['hɑːbəʳ] **1** *n* port *m*. **2** *adj*: **~ master** capitaine *m* de port. **3** *vt refugee* héberger, abriter; *criminal* receler; *suspicions, fear* entretenir. **to ~ a grudge against sb** garder rancune à qn.

hard [hɑːd] **1** *adj* (**a**) *substance* dur; *mud, snow* durci; *muscle* ferme. **~ hat** casque *m*; *(riding hat)* bombe *f*; *(Comput)* **~ copy** copie *f* papier; *(Tennis)* **~ court** court *m* en dur; *(Comput)* **~ disk** disque *m* dur; *(Aut)* **~ shoulder** accotement *m* stabilisé; **to grow ~** durcir; **a ~ nut to crack** *(problem etc)* un gros problème; *(person)* un(e) dur(e) à cuire *; **he is as ~ as nails** *(physically)* c'est un paquet de muscles; *(mentally)* il est dur. (**b**) *(difficult) problem, examination* difficile; *task* pénible, dur. **~ to understand** difficile *or* dur à comprendre; **I find it ~ to explain** j'ai du mal à l'expliquer; **I find it ~ to believe that...** j'ai du mal à croire que...+ *subj*; **~ to please** exigeant, difficile; **~ to get on with** difficile à vivre; **that is ~ to beat** on peut difficilement faire mieux; **~ of hearing** dur d'oreille. (**c**) *(severe)* dur, sévère (*on, to* avec; *towards* envers); *heart* dur, impitoyable. **he's a ~ man** il est dur, c'est un homme impitoyable; **to grow ~** s'endurcir; **~ sell** promotion *f* de vente agressive. (**d**) *(harsh) life* dur, difficile; *words, work* dur; *climate, winter* rude; *fall* mauvais; *rule, decision, treatment* sévère; *(tough) battle, fight* acharné; *match* âprement disputé; *study* assidu; *worker* dur à la tâche. **it's ~ work!** c'est dur!; **he drives a ~ bargain** il ne fait pas de cadeaux *(fig)*; **a ~ blow** un coup dur, un rude coup; *(Brit)* **~ luck! *, ~ lines! *** pas de veine! *; **it's ~ luck on him *** il n'a pas de veine *; **~ liquor** boisson *f* fortement alcoolisée; **~ drinker** gros buveur *m*; **a ~ core of offenders** un noyau irréductible de délinquants; *(Pol)* **the ~ core of the party** les inconditionnels *mpl* parmi les membres du parti; **the ~ facts** la réalité brutale; **~ feeling** amertume *f*; **no ~ feelings!** sans rancune!; **~ frost** forte gelée *f*; **it was ~ going** ça a été dur *; *(Jur)* ~ **labour** travaux *mpl* forcés; **she had a ~ time of it** elle a traversé des moments difficiles; **you'll have a ~ time of it persuading...** vous allez avoir du mal à persuader...; **these are ~ times** les temps sont durs; *(Mus)* ~ **rock** (rock *m*) hard *m*. (**e**) *(fig) light, line, colour, drug* dur; *water* calcaire; *(Fin) market* ferme. ~ **cash** espèces *fpl*; ~ **evidence** preuve(s) *f(pl)* concrète(s); ~ **news** de l'information *f* sérieuse.

2 *adv pull* fort; *hit* dur, fort; *fall down* durement; *run* à toutes jambes; *think* sérieusement; *work, study* d'arrache-pied; *drink* beaucoup. **as ~ as one can** de toutes ses forces; **it's raining ~** il pleut à verse; **it's snowing ~** il neige dru; **it's freezing ~** il gèle dur; **frozen ~** *lake* profondément gelé; *ground* durci par le gel; **to hold on ~** tenir bon *or* ferme; **to look ~ at** *person* dévisager; *thing* regarder de près; **to try ~** faire un gros effort; **to be ~ hit** être sérieusement touché; ~ **at it** * attelé à la tâche; ~ **by** tout près; **to follow ~ upon sb's heels** suivre qn de très près; **to be ~ put to it to do** avoir beaucoup de mal à faire; ~ **pressed** *(for time)* débordé; *(for money)* à court; **she took it pretty ~** elle a été très affectée; ~ **done by** * traité injustement.

◆ **hard-and-fast** *adj* inflexible; *rule* absolu. ◆ **hardback** *n* livre *m* cartonné. ◆ **hardball** *n (US)* baseball *m*. ◆ **hard-bitten** *adj* dur à cuire *. ◆ **hardboard** *n* Isorel *m* ®. ◆ **hard-boiled** *adj egg* dur; *(fig) person* dur à cuire *. ◆ **hard-core** *adj support, opposition* inconditionnel; *pornography* dur. ◆ **hard-earned** *adj money* durement gagné; *holiday* bien mérité. ◆ **harden 1** *vt (gen)* durcir; *person* endurcir; **to ~en one's heart** s'endurcir ; **2** *vi [substances]* durcir; *[voice]* se faire dur; *[prices]* être en hausse; *[market]* s'affermir. ◆ **hardened** *adj* durci; *criminal* endurci; *sinner* invétéré; **I'm ~ened to it** j'ai l'habitude. ◆ **hardening** *n* durcissement *m*. ◆ **hard-fought** *adj* âprement disputé. ◆ **hard-headed** *adj* réaliste. ◆ **hard-hearted** *adj* impitoyable, au cœur dur. ◆ **hard-liner** *n* inconditionnel(le) *m(f)*. ◆ **hardly** *adv* (**a**) *(scarcely)* à peine, ne... guère; **he can ~ly write** il sait à peine écrire; **it's ~ly his business if...** ce n'est guère son affaire si...; **you'll ~ly believe it** vous aurez de la peine à le croire; **I need ~ly point out that** je n'ai pas besoin de faire remarquer que; **I ~ly know** je n'en sais trop rien; **~ly anyone/anywhere/ever** presque personne/nulle part/jamais; **~ly!** *(not at all)* certainement pas!; *(not exactly)* pas précisément!; (**b**) *(harshly)* durement, sévèrement. ◆ **hardness** *n* dureté *f* ; fermeté *f*; difficulté *f*; sévérité *f*. ◆ **hardnosed** *adj* impitoyable, dur. ◆ **hard-of-hearing** *npl*: **the ~-of-hearing** les mal-entendants. ◆ **hardship** *n* épreuves *fpl*; *(suffering)* souffrance *f*; *(poverty)* pauvreté *f*; **there's a certain amount of ~ship involved** ce sera assez dur; **a life of ~ship** une vie pleine d'épreuves; **it's no great ~ship to go and see her** ce n'est tout de même pas une épreuve d'aller la voir; **~ships** épreuves *fpl*, privations *fpl*. ◆ **hardtop** *n (US Aut)* voiture *f* à toit de tôle amovible. ◆ **hard-up** * *adj* fauché *. ◆ **hardware 1** *n (Comm)* quincaillerie *f*; *(Mil, Police etc)* matériel *m*; *(Comput, Space)* hardware *m* ; **2** *adj*: **~ware dealer** quincaillier *m*; **~ware shop** quincaillerie *f*; *(Comput)* **~ware specialist** technicien(ne) *m(f)* du hardware. ◆ **hard-wearing** *adj* solide, résistant. ◆ **hardwood** *n* bois *m* dur. ◆ **hard-working** *adj* travailleur.

hardy ['hɑːdɪ] *adj (strong)* robuste; *(bold)* hardi; *plant* résistant (au gel); *tree* de plein vent. ◆ **hardihood** *n* hardiesse *f*. ◆ **hardiness** *n* force *f*, vigueur *f*.

hare [hɛəʳ] **1** *n* lièvre *m*. **2** *vi*: **to ~ in** * *etc* entrer *etc* en trombe. ◆ **harebell** *n* campanule *f*. ◆ **hare-brained** *adj person* écervelé; *plan* insensé. ◆ **hare-coursing** *n* chasse *f* au lièvre. ◆ **harelip** *n* bec-de-lièvre *m*.

haricot ['hærɪkəʊ] *n*: ~ **(bean)** haricot *m* blanc.

hark [hɑːk] *excl* écoutez! ◆ **hark back** *vi* revenir (*to* sur).

harm [hɑːm] **1** *n (gen)* mal *m*; *(to reputation, interests)* tort *m*. **to do sb ~** faire du mal *or* du tort à qn; **no ~ done** il n'y a pas de mal; **he means no ~** il n'a pas de mauvaises intentions; **he meant no ~ by what he said** il ne l'a pas dit méchamment; **he doesn't mean us any ~** il ne nous veut pas de mal; **you will come to no ~** il ne t'arrivera rien; **I don't see any ~ in it** je n'y vois aucun mal; **there's no ~ in it** cela ne peut pas faire de mal; **there's no ~ in doing that** il n'y a pas de mal à faire cela; **out of ~'s way** en sûreté. **2** *vt person* faire du mal *or* du tort à; *crops* endommager; *object* abîmer; *reputation* salir; *interests, a cause* causer du tort à. ◆ **harmful** *adj* nuisible (*to* à). ◆ **harmless** *adj animal, joke* inoffensif; *person* sans méchanceté; *action, game* innocent; *suggestion, conversation* anodin.

harmony ['hɑːmənɪ] *n* harmonie *f*. ◆ **harmonica** *n* harmonica *m*. ◆ **harmonics** *n (Mus: sg: science)* harmonie *f*; *(pl: overtones)* harmoniques *mpl*. ◆ **harmonious** *adj* harmonieux. ◆ **harmonium** *n* harmonium *m*. ◆ **harmonize 1** *vt* harmoniser ; **2** *vi (Mus)* chanter en harmonie; *[colours etc]* s'harmoniser (*with* avec); *[person, facts]* s'accorder (*with* avec).

harness ['hɑːnɪs] **1** *n* harnais *m*. *(fig)* **to get back into ~** reprendre le collier; *(fig)* **to die in ~** mourir à la tâche. **2** *vt horse* harnacher; *(to carriage)* atteler (*to* à); *(fig) resources etc* exploiter.

harp [hɑːp] **1** *n* harpe *f*. **2** *vi*: **to ~ on (about) sth** * rabâcher qch, revenir toujours sur qch.

harpoon [hɑː'puːn] **1** *n* harpon *m*. **2** *vt* harponner.

harpsichord ['hɑːpsɪkɔːd] *n* clavecin *m*.

harrow ['hærəʊ] *n* herse *f*. ◆ **harrowing** *adj story* poignant; *cry* déchirant; *experience* atroce.

harsh [hɑːʃ] *adj* (**a**) *punishment, person* dur (*with sb* avec *or* envers qn), sévère; *words, tone* cassant, dur; *fate* cruel; *climate* rigoureux. (**b**) *(discordant etc) sound* discordant; *voice, colour* criard; *contrast* heurté; *taste* âpre. ◆ **harshly** *adv reply (gen)* durement; *treat* sévèrement. ◆ **harshness** *n* dureté *f*; sévérité *f*; cruauté *f*; discordance *f*; aspect criard *or* heurté; âpreté *f*.

harum-scarum ['hɛərəm'skɛərəm] *adj, n* écervelé(e) *m(f)*.

harvest ['hɑːvɪst] **1** *n (gen)* moisson *f*; *[fruit]* récolte *f*; *[grapes]* vendange *f*. **2** *vt* moissonner *(also fig)*; récolter; vendanger. **3** *vi* faire la moisson. **4** *adj*: ~ **festival** fête *f* de la moisson; ~ **moon** pleine lune (de l'équinoxe d'automne); **at ~ time** à la moisson. ◆ **harvester** *n (person)* moissonneur *m*, -euse *f*; *(machine)* moissonneuse *f*.

has [hæz] *V* **have.** ◆ **has-been** * *n (person)* homme *m* fini, femme *f* finie; *(object)* vieillerie *f*.

hash [hæʃ] *n (Culin)* hachis *m*; *(US Culin) mélange de pommes de terre et de viande hachée; (* fig)* gâchis *m*. *(US Culin)* ~ **browns** pommes de terre sautées *(servies au petit déjeuner)*; **to make a ~ * of sth** saboter qch; **a ~(-up) * of old ideas** un réchauffé de vieilles idées.

hashish ['hæʃɪʃ] *n* hachisch *m*.

hassle * ['hæsl] **1** *n (squabble)* bagarre * *f*; *(fuss, trouble)* histoire * *f* (*to do* pour faire). **2** *vt* tracasser, enquiquiner *.

haste [heɪst] *n* hâte *f*. **in ~** à la hâte; **in great ~** en toute hâte; **to make ~** se hâter (*to do* de faire). ◆ **hasten** ['heɪsn] *vi (gen)* se hâter (*to do* de faire); **I ~n to add...** je m'empresse d'ajouter... ; **to ~n away** *etc* partir *etc* à la hâte. ◆ **hastily** *adv (speedily)* à la hâte; *(too speedily)* précipitamment; *(without* *thinking)* trop hâtivement; **he suggested hastily** il s'est empressé de suggérer. ◆ **hasty** *adj departure, marriage* précipité; *visit, glance, meal* hâtif; *sketch* fait à la hâte; *action, decision, words* irréfléchi; **don't be so hasty!** ne va pas si vite!

hat [hæt] **1** *n* chapeau *m*. ~ **in hand** *(lit)* chapeau bas; *(fig)* obséquieusement; *(fig)* **to take off one's** ~ **to** tirer son chapeau à; **to keep sth under one's** ~ * garder qch pour soi; **to talk through one's** ~ * dire n'importe quoi; *(fig)* **to pass round the** ~ **for sb** faire la quête pour qn; **that's old** ~**!** * c'est vieux tout ça! **2** *adj*: **to get a** ~ **trick** réussir trois coups (*or* gagner trois matchs *etc*) consécutifs. ◆ **hatcheck girl** *n (US)* dame *f* du vestiaire.

hatch[1] [hætʃ] **1** *vt chick, egg* faire éclore; *plot* ourdir, tramer; *plan* couver. **2** *vi* (~ **out**) *[chick, egg]* éclore.

hatch[2] [hætʃ] *n* (**a**) *(Naut: ~way)* écoutille *f*. *(drinks)* **down the** ~**!** ⁑ à la bonne vôtre! (**b**) *(service ~)* passe-plats *m inv*. ◆ **hatchback** *n (Aut) (two-door)* coupé *m or (four-door)* berline *f* avec hayon arrière.

hatchet ['hætʃɪt] **1** *n* hachette *f*. **2** *adj*: **to do a** ~ **job on sb** démolir qn; ~ **man** * *(killer)* tueur *m* (à gages); *(fig)* homme *m* de main. ◆ **hatchet-faced** *adj* au visage en lame de couteau.

hate [heɪt] **1** *vt person* haïr; *(weaker)* détester; *thing* détester, avoir horreur de. **to** ~ **to do** *or* **doing** détester faire, avoir horreur de faire; **he** ~**s to be** *or* **being ordered about** il a horreur qu'on lui donne *(subj)* des ordres; **I** ~ **to say so** cela m'ennuie beaucoup de devoir le dire; **I should** ~ **to keep you waiting** je ne voudrais surtout pas vous faire attendre; **I should** ~ **him to think...** je ne voudrais surtout pas qu'il pense *(subj)*... **2** *n (hatred)* haine *f*. **pet** ~ * bête *f* noire. ◆ **hateful** *adj* haïssable, détestable. ◆ **hatred** *n* haine *f*.

haughty ['hɔːtɪ] *adj* hautain, arrogant. ◆ **haughtily** *adv* avec hauteur, avec arrogance. ◆ **haughtiness** *n* hauteur *f*, arrogance *f*.

haul [hɔːl] **1** *n* (**a**) *(Aut etc: journey)* voyage *m*. *(lit, fig)* **it's a long** ~ la route est longue. (**b**) *[fishermen]* prise *f*; *[thieves]* butin *m*. **they made a good** ~ **of jewels** ils ont eu un beau butin en bijoux; *(fig)* **a good** ~ * **of presents** une bonne récolte de cadeaux.

2 *vt* (**a**) *(pull)* traîner, tirer. *(fig)* **to** ~ **sb over the coals** passer un savon * à qn. (**b**) *(transport by truck)* camionner.

◆ **haul down** *vt sep flag, sail* amener; *(gen) object* descendre *(en tirant)*. ◆ **haul in, haul out** *vt sep (from water) line, catch* amener; *drowning man* tirer (de l'eau). ◆ **haul up** *vt sep flag, sail* hisser; *(gen) object* monter *(en tirant)*.

◆ **haulage** *n (road transport)* transport *m* routier. ◆ **haulage contractor** *or* ◆ **haulier** *n* entrepreneur *m* de transports (routiers).

haunch [hɔːn(t)ʃ] *n* hanche *f*; *(Culin)* cuissot *m*. **squatting on his** ~**es** *person* accroupi; *dog* assis (sur son derrière).

haunt [hɔːnt] **1** *vt (lit, fig)* hanter. **2** *n [criminals]* repaire *m*. **one of his favourite** ~**s** un des lieux où on le trouve souvent. ◆ **haunted** *adj house* hanté; *expression* égaré; *face* hagard. ◆ **haunting 1** *adj* obsédant ; **2** *n* apparition *f*.

Havana [hə'vænə] *n* La Havane.

have [hæv] *pret, ptp* **had 1** *aux vb* avoir; être. **to** ~ **been** avoir été; **to** ~ **eaten** avoir mangé; **to** ~ **gone** être allé; **to** ~ **got up** s'être levé; **I** ~ **just seen him** je viens de le voir; **I had just seen him** je venais de le voir; **I've just come from London** j'arrive à l'instant de Londres; **you've seen her,** ~**n't you?** vous l'avez vue, n'est-ce pas?; **you** ~**n't seen her,** ~ **you?** vous ne l'avez pas vue, je suppose?; **you~ n't seen her — yes I** ~**!** vous ne l'avez pas vue — si!; **you've made a mistake — no I** ~**n't!** vous vous êtes trompé — mais non!; **you've dropped your book — so I** ~**!** vous avez laissé tomber votre livre — en effet!; ~ **you been there? if you** ~**/**~**n't...** y êtes-vous allé? si oui/non...; ~ **got** *V* **2** *and* **3** *below*.

2 *modal aux vb (be obliged)* **I** ~ **(got) to speak to you at once** je dois vous parler *or* il faut que je vous parle *(subj)* immédiatement; **I** ~**n't got to do it, I don't** ~ **to do it** je ne suis pas obligé de le faire; **do you** ~ **to make such a noise?** tu ne pourrais pas faire un peu moins de bruit?; **you didn't** ~ **to tell her!** tu n'avais pas besoin de le lui dire!; ~**n't you got to write to your mother?** est-ce que tu ne dois pas écrire à ta mère?; **if you go through Dijon you** ~**n't got to** *or* **you don't** ~ **to go to Lyons** si vous passez par Dijon vous n'avez pas besoin d'aller à Lyon; **you** ~**n't (got) to say a word about it!** * tu ne dois pas en dire un mot!; *(US)* **it's got to be** *or* **it has to be the biggest** ça doit être le plus grand.

3 *vt* (**a**) *(possess)* avoir, posséder. **she has (got) blue eyes** elle a les yeux bleus; **all I** ~ **(got)** tout ce que je possède; **I** ~**n't (got) any more** je n'en ai plus; **I've got an idea** j'ai une idée; **I** ~ **(got) no German** je ne parle pas un mot d'allemand.

(**b**) *meals etc* avoir, prendre. **he has had lunch** il a déjeuné; **to** ~ **tea with sb** prendre le thé avec qn; **what will you** ~**? — I'll** ~ **an egg** qu'est-ce que vous voulez? — je prendrai un œuf; **he had eggs for breakfast** il a mangé des œufs au petit déjeuner; **I** ~ **had some more** j'en ai repris; **he had a cigarette** il a fumé une cigarette.

(**c**) *(receive, obtain, take)* avoir, recevoir. **I had a telegram from him** j'ai reçu un télégramme de lui; **to** ~ **a child** avoir un enfant; **I** ~ **it from my sister that...** je tiens de ma sœur que...; **I must** ~ **more time** il me faut davantage de temps; **I must** ~ **them by this afternoon** il me les faut pour cet après-midi; **which one will you** ~**?** lequel voulez-vous?; **let me** ~ **your address** donnez-moi votre adresse; **I shall let you** ~ **it for 10 francs** je vous le laisse pour 10 F; **there are no newspapers to be had** on ne trouve pas de journaux.

(**d**) *(hold)* tenir. **he had (got) me by the throat/the hair** il me tenait à la gorge/par les cheveux ; **I** ~ **(got) him where I want him!** * je le tiens (à ma merci)!

(**e**) *(maintain, allow)* **he will** ~ **it that Paul is guilty** il soutient que Paul est coupable; **he won't** ~ **it that Paul is guilty** il n'admet pas que Paul soit coupable; **rumour has it that...** le bruit court que...; **as gossip has it** selon les racontars; **I won't** ~ **this nonsense/him hurt** je ne tolérerai pas cette absurdité/qu'on lui fasse du mal.

(**f**) *(causative etc)* **to** ~ **one's hair cut** se faire couper les cheveux; **I had my luggage brought up** j'ai fait monter mes bagages; ~ **it mended** faites-le réparer; **I had him clean the car** je lui ai fait nettoyer la voiture; **what would you** ~ **me say?** que voulez-vous que je dise?; **he had his car stolen** on lui a volé sa voiture.

(**g**) *(phrases)* **I had better go** je devrais partir; **you'd better not tell him that!** tu ferais mieux de ne pas lui dire ça!; **I had as soon not see him** j'aimerais autant ne pas le voir; **I had rather do it myself** j'aimerais mieux *or* je préférerais le faire moi-même; **to** ~ **a walk** faire une promenade; **to** ~ **a good time** bien s'amuser; **to** ~ **a pleasant evening** passer une bonne soirée; **he has (got) flu** il a la grippe; **I've (got) a headache** j'ai mal à la tête; **I've (got) £6 left** il me reste 6 livres; **to** ~ **(got) sth to do/to read** *etc* avoir qch à faire/à lire *etc*; **I** ~ **(got) nothing to do with it** je n'y suis pour rien; **there you** ~ **me!** ça je n'en sais rien!; **I** ~ **it!** j'y suis!, ça y est, j'ai trouvé!; **you've been had** * tu t'es fait avoir *; **I've had it** * *(in danger)* je suis

fichu *; *(US: fed up)* j'en ai marre * , j'en ai ras-le-bol *!; **I'm not having any** ⁑ ça ne prend pas *. **4** *n*: **the ~s and the ~-nots** les riches *mpl* et les pauvres *mpl*; **the ~-nots** les déshérités *mpl*.
◆ **have in** *vt sep* (**a**) *sb waiting outside* faire entrer; *doctor, employee* faire venir. **we had him in for the evening** il est venu passer la soirée chez nous. (**b**) **to ~ it in for sb** * avoir une dent contre qn. ◆ **have on** *vt sep* (**a**) *clothes* porter. **he had (got) nothing on** il était tout nu. (**b**) *(be busy)* **I've got so much on this week that...** j'ai tant à faire cette semaine que...; **I ~ got nothing on (for) this evening** je ne suis pas pris ce soir. (**c**) *(trick)* **to ~ sb on** * faire marcher * qn. ◆ **have out** *vt sep*: **to ~ a tooth out** se faire arracher une dent; **to ~ it out with sb** s'expliquer avec qn. ◆ **have up** *vt sep person* faire venir; *(from below)* faire monter. **he was had up by the headmaster** il a été appelé chez le proviseur; **to be had up by the police** être arrêté (*for doing* pour avoir fait).

haven ['heɪvn] *n (fig)* havre *m*, abri *m*.

haversack ['hævəsæk] *n* musette *f*.

havoc ['hævək] *n* ravages *mpl*. **to wreak ~ in** ravager; *(fig)* **to play ~ with** *(gen)* désorganiser complètement; *stomach* abîmer.

haw [hɔː] *n (Bot)* cenelle *f*.

Hawaii [hə'wa(ɪ)iː] (îles *fpl*) Hawaii *m*.

hawk [hɔːk] *n* faucon *m (also Pol fig)*. **to have eyes like a ~** avoir des yeux de lynx.

hawker ['hɔːkər] *n (street)* colporteur *m*; *(door-to-door)* démarcheur *m*.

hawthorn ['hɔːθɔːn] *n* aubépine *f*.

hay [heɪ] **1** *n* foin *m*. *(fig)* **to make ~ while the sun shines** profiter de l'occasion. **2** *adj*: **~ fever** rhume *m* des foins. ◆ **haycock** *n* meulon *m* (de foin). ◆ **haymaker** *n* faneur *m*, -euse *f*. ◆ **haymaking** *n* fenaison *f*. ◆ **hayrick** *or* ◆ **haystack** *n* meule *f* de foin. ◆ **haywire** * *adj*: **to go ~wire** *[person]* perdre la tête; *[plans etc]* mal tourner; *[equipment etc]* se détraquer.

hazard ['hæzəd] **1** *n (chance)* hasard *m*, chance *f*; *(risk)* risque *m*; *(stronger)* danger *m*. **natural/professional ~** risque naturel/du métier; **a nasty ~ for pedestrians** un danger pour les piétons; *(Aut)* **~ warning lights** feux *mpl* de détresse. **2** *vt life, reputation, attempt* risquer; *remark, forecast* hasarder. **to ~ a guess** risquer une hypothèse; **'I could do it' she ~ed** 'moi je pourrais le faire' se risqua-t-elle à dire. ◆ **hazardous** *adj* hasardeux.

haze [heɪz] *n* brume *f*; *[smoke etc]* vapeur *f*. *(fig)* **to be in a ~** être dans le brouillard. ◆ **hazy** *adj day, weather* brumeux; *outline, photograph* flou; *idea* vague; **to be hazy about sth** avoir une idée très vague de qch.

hazel ['heɪzl] **1** *n* noisetier *m*. **2** *adj (colour)* (couleur) noisette *inv*. ◆ **hazelnut** *n* noisette *f*.

he [hiː] *pers pron* (**a**) *(unstressed)* il. **~ has come** il est venu; **here ~ is** le voici; **~ is a doctor** il est médecin, c'est un médecin. (**b**) *(stressed)* lui. **younger than ~** plus jeune que lui; **HE didn't do it** ce n'est pas lui qui l'a fait. (**c**) *(+ rel pron)* celui. **~ who can** celui qui peut. (**d**) **it's a ~** * *(animal)* c'est un mâle; *(baby)* c'est un garçon. ◆ **he-bear** *etc n* ours *m etc* mâle. ◆ **he-man** * *n* (vrai) mâle *m*.

head [hed] **1** *n* (**a**) tête *f*. **~ of hair** chevelure *f*; **covered** *etc* **from ~ to foot** couvert *etc* de la tête aux pieds; **~ down** *(upside down)* la tête en bas; *(looking down)* la tête baissée; **~ downwards** la tête en bas; **~ first, ~ foremost** la tête la première; **my ~ aches, I've got a bad ~** j'ai mal à la tête; **to hit sb on the ~** frapper qn à la tête; **to stand on one's ~** faire le poirier; **I could do it standing on my ~** * c'est bête comme chou *; *(fig)* **he stands ~ and shoulders above everybody else** il surpasse tout le monde; **she is a ~ taller than her sister** elle dépasse sa sœur d'une tête; *[horse]* **to win by a (short) ~** gagner d'une (courte) tête; **~ over ears in debt** dans les dettes jusqu'au cou; **to turn** *or* **go ~ over heels** *(accidentally)* faire la culbute; *(on purpose)* faire une galipette; **~ over heels in love with** éperdument amoureux de; *(fig)* **to keep one's ~ above water** se maintenir à flot; **he was talking his ~ off** * il n'arrêtait pas de parler; **to sing/shout one's ~ off** * chanter/crier à tue-tête; **I'm saying that off the top of my ~** * je dis ça sans savoir exactement; **to give a horse its ~/sb his ~** lâcher la bride à un cheval/à qn; **on your ~ be it!** à vos risques et périls!; **10 francs a ~** 10 F par tête.
(**b**) *(mind, intellect)* tête *f*. **to get sth into one's ~** se mettre qch dans la tête; **to take it into one's ~ to do** se mettre en tête de faire; **it didn't enter his ~ that/to do** il ne lui est pas venu pas à l'idée que/de faire; **you never know what's going on in his ~** on ne sait jamais ce qui lui passe par la tête; **what put that idea into his ~?** qu'est-ce qui lui a mis cette idée-là dans la tête?; **I can't get it out of my ~** je ne peux pas me sortir ça de la tête; **it's gone right out of my ~** ça m'est tout à fait sorti de la tête; **that tune has been running through my ~ all day** cet air m'a trotté par la tête toute la journée; **he has a good ~ for mathematics** il a des dispositions *fpl* pour les mathématiques; **he has a good ~ for heights** il n'a jamais le vertige; **he has a good business ~** il a le sens des affaires; **he has a good ~ (on his shoulders)** il a de la tête; **he's got his ~ screwed on right** * il a la tête sur les épaules; **two ~s are better than one** deux avis valent mieux qu'un; **we put our ~s together** nous nous sommes consultés; **I can't do it in my ~** je ne peux pas faire ça de tête; **he gave orders over my ~** il a donné des ordres sans me consulter; **it's quite above my ~** cela me dépasse complètement; **to keep one's ~** garder son sang-froid; **to lose one's ~** perdre la tête; **it went to his ~** cela lui est monté à la tête; **he has gone** *or* **he is off his ~** * il a perdu la boule *; **weak** *or* **soft** * **in the ~** faible *or* simple d'esprit.
(**c**) *[flower, nail, hammer, abscess]* tête *f*; *[arrow]* pointe *f*; *[celery]* pied *m*; *[lettuce]* pomme *f*; *[bed]* chevet *m*; *[tape recorder]* tête magnétique; *[page, staircase]* haut *m*; *[river]* source *f*; *[beer]* mousse *f*; *[lake, pier]* extrémité *f*. **~ of steam** pression *f*; **at the ~ of** *(in charge of)* à la tête de; *(in front row of, at top of)* en tête de; **at the ~ of the list/the queue** en tête de liste/de file; **at the ~ of the table** au haut bout de la table; **to come to a ~** *[abscess etc]* mûrir; *[situation etc]* devenir critique; **to bring things to a ~** précipiter une crise.
(**d**) *(leader) [family, business etc]* chef *m*. *(Scol)* **the ~** le directeur, la directrice; **~ of department** *[business firm]* chef de service; *[shop]* chef de rayon; *[school, college etc]* chef de section; *(Pol)* **~ of state** chef d'État.
(**e**) *(title)* titre *m*; *(subject ~ing) (in newspaper)* rubrique *f*; *(in essay, speech, article)* tête *f* de chapitre. **this comes under the ~ of** ceci se classe sous la rubrique de.
(**f**) *[coin]* face *f*. **to toss ~s or tails** jouer à pile ou face; **~s or tails?** pile ou face?; **~s I win!** face je gagne!; **he called ~s** il a annoncé 'face'; **I can't make ~ nor tail of what he's saying** je ne comprends rien à ce qu'il dit.
2 *adj* (**a**) *typist, assistant etc* principal. **~ clerk** chef *m* de bureau; **~ gardener** jardinier *m* en chef; *(US)* **~ nurse** infirmier *m*, -ière *f* en chef; **~ office** bureau *m or* siège *m* central; **~ waiter** maître *m* d'hôtel. (**b**) **~ cold** rhume *m* de cerveau; **to have a ~ start** avoir une grosse avance (*over, on* sur).
3 *vt* (**a**) *procession, list, poll* être en tête de; *group of people* être à la tête de. (**b**) *(direct)* **he ~ed the car towards town** il a pris la direction de la ville.

(**c**) *(entitle)* intituler. ~**ed writing paper** papier *m* à en-tête. (**d**) *(Ftbl)* **to** ~ **the ball** faire une tête. **4** *vi* se diriger. **to** ~ **for** *[person, car etc]* se diriger vers; *[ship]* mettre le cap sur; **he** ~**ed up the hill** il s'est mis à monter la colline; **he was** ~**ing home** il était sur le chemin du retour; **he's** ~**ing for a disappointment** il va vers une déception; **he's** ~**ing for a fall** il court à un échec.

◆ **head off** **1** *vi* partir (for pour; *towards* vers). **he** ~**ed off on to the subject of...** il est passé à la question de... **2** *vt sep enemy* forcer à se rabattre; *person (lit)* détourner de son chemin; *(fig)* détourner (*from* de); *questions* parer.

◆ **headache** *n* mal *m* de tête; *(worse)* migraine *f*; **to have a** ~**ache** avoir mal à la tête, avoir la migraine; *(fig)* **that's his** ~**ache** c'est son problème à lui; **the whole business was a** ~**ache from beginning to end** nous n'avons connu que des ennuis avec cette affaire. ◆ **headband** *n* bandeau *m*. ◆ **headboard** *n* dosseret *m*. ◆ **headcount** *n*: **let's do a** ~**count** on va les compter. ◆ **headdress** *n (feathers etc)* coiffure *f*; *(lace)* coiffe *f*. ◆ **header** * *n (dive, fall)* plongeon *m*; (*Ftbl*) (coup *m* de) tête *f*; **to take a** ~**er into the water** piquer une tête dans l'eau. ◆ **headgear** *n* couvre-chef *m*; **I haven't any** ~**gear** je n'ai rien à me mettre sur la tête. ◆ **headhunter** *n (lit, fig)* chasseur *m* de têtes. ◆ **heading** *n (gen)* titre *m*; *(subject title)* rubrique *f*; *(chapter* ~*ing)* tête *f* de chapitre; *(printed: on document etc)* en-tête *m*; **essay divided into several** ~**ings** dissertation divisée en plusieurs têtes de chapitre. ◆ **headlamp** *or* ◆ **headlight** *n (Aut)* phare *m*. ◆ **headland** *n* promontoire *m*. ◆ **headline** **1** *n [newspaper]* manchette *f*, gros titre *m*; *(TV)* grand titre; **it's in the** ~**lines in the papers** c'est en gros titre *or* en manchette dans les journaux; **to hit the** ~**lines** * faire les gros titres ; **2** *vt* mettre en manchette. ◆ **headlong** **1** *adv fall* la tête la première; *run, rush* à toute allure ; **2** *adj fall etc* la tête la première; ~**long flight** débandade *f*; **a** ~**long dash for** une ruée générale vers. ◆ **headman** *n* chef *m*. ◆ **headmaster** *n [school]* directeur *m*; *[college]* principal *m*; *(US Scol)* directeur *m* d'école privée. ◆ **headmistress** *n (gen)* directrice *f*; *[college]* principale *f*; *(US Scol)* directrice d'école privée. ◆ **head-on** **1** *adj collision* de plein fouet; *confrontation* en face à face ; **2** *adv*: **to collide with sth** ~**-on** *(gen)* heurter qch de front; *(fig)* **to meet sb/sth** ~**-on** s'attaquer de front à qn/qch. ◆ **headphones** *npl* casque *m* (à écouteurs). ◆ **headquarters** *n (gen, Comm)* siège *m* central; *(Mil)* quartier *m* général. ◆ **headrest** *n* appui-tête *m*. ◆ **headroom** *n*: **there is not enough** ~**room** le toit n'est pas assez haut. ◆ **headscarf** *n* foulard *m*. ◆ **headset** *n* casque *m* (à écouteurs). ◆ **headsquare** *n* = ~**scarf.** ◆ **headstand** *n*: **to do a** ~**stand** faire le poirier. ◆ **headstone** *n [grave]* pierre *f* tombale. ◆ **headstrong** *adj (obstinate)* têtu; *(rash)* impétueux. ◆ **headway** *n*: **to make** ~**way** *(gen)* faire des progrès (*with* avec); *[ship]* faire route. ◆ **headwind** *n* vent *m* contraire. ◆ **heady** *adj wine, perfume* capiteux; *success, pleasure* grisant.

heal [hi:l] **1** *vi* (~ **over,** ~ **up)** *[wound]* se cicatriser. **2** *vt (gen) person* guérir (*of* de); *wound* cicatriser; *differences* régler; *troubles* apaiser. ◆ **healer** *n* guérisseur *m*, -euse *f*. ◆ **healing** **1** *n* guérison *f* ; **2** *adj ointment* cicatrisant; *hands* de guérisseur.

health [helθ] **1** *n* santé *f*. **in good/bad** ~ en bonne/ mauvaise santé; **mental** ~ santé mentale; **Ministry of H**~ ministère *m* de la Santé publique; **to drink (to) sb's** ~ boire à la santé de qn; **your** ~**!, good** ~! à votre santé! **2** *adj*: ~ **centre** ≃ centre *m* médico-social; *(Scol)* ~ **education** hygiène *f*; ~ **farm** établissement *m* de cure (de rajeunissement *etc*); ~ **foods** aliments *mpl* naturels; ~ **food shop** boutique *f* de produits diététiques; ~ **hazard** *or* **risk** risque *m* pour la santé; ~ **insurance** assurance *f* maladie; *(US Univ)* ~ **service** infirmerie *f*; **the H**~ **Service** ≃ la Sécurité sociale; **I got my specs on the H**~ **Service** * la Sécurité sociale m'a remboursé mes lunettes; **H**~ **Service doctor/nursing home** médecin/clinique conventionné(e); ~ **visitor** ≃ infirmière *f* visiteuse. ◆ **healthful** *or* ◆ **health-giving** *adj air* salubre; *exercise etc* salutaire. ◆ **healthily** *adv* sainement. ◆ **healthy** *adj person, animal, plant* en bonne santé ; *climate, air* salubre; *food, skin, surroundings* sain ; *appetite* robuste; *exercise* salutaire; *(fig) economy, interest, attitude* sain; *respect, doubts* salutaire; **to make sth** ~**y** *or* **healthier** assainir qch.

heap [hi:p] **1** *n* tas *m*, monceau *m*. ~**s of** * *money, books, jobs, people* des tas * de, des masses * de; **we've got** ~**s** * **of time** nous avons largement le temps. **2** *vt* (~ **up)** entasser, empiler (*on sth* sur qch). **to** ~ **gifts/praises** *etc* **on sb** couvrir qn de cadeaux/d'éloges *etc*; *(fig)* **to** ~ **coals of fire on sb** rendre le bien pour le mal à qn; **she** ~**ed (up) her plate with cakes** elle a empilé des gâteaux sur son assiette; *(Culin)* ~**ed spoonful** grosse cuillerée.

hear [hɪəʳ] *pret, ptp* **heard** [hɜ:d] **1** *vt* (**a**) entendre. **I can't** ~ **you** je ne vous entends pas; **I heard him say** je l'ai entendu dire; **I heard sb come in** j'ai entendu qn entrer; **he was heard to say** on l'a entendu dire; **to make o.s. heard** se faire entendre; **he likes to** ~ **himself talk** il aime s'écouter parler; **to** ~ **him (talk), you'd think he was...** à l'entendre, vous le prendriez pour... (**b**) *(learn)* entendre dire (*that* que); *news, facts* apprendre. **have you heard the rumour that...**? avez-vous entendu dire que...?; **I** ~ **you've been ill** il paraît que vous avez été malade; **I have heard it said that** j'ai entendu dire que; **I've heard tell of** j'ai entendu parler de; **have you heard the one about the Scotsman who...** tu connais l'histoire de l'Écossais qui... (**c**) *(listen to) lecture etc* assister à; *mass, law case* entendre. **to** ~ **a child's lessons** faire répéter ses leçons à un enfant; *(excl)* ~, ~! bravo! **2** *vi (gen)* entendre; *(get news)* recevoir *or* avoir des nouvelles (*from sb* de qn). **I** ~ **about him from his mother** j'ai de ses nouvelles par sa mère; **I've never heard of him** je ne le connais pas; **everyone has heard of him** tout le monde a entendu parler de lui; **he was never heard of again** on n'a jamais plus entendu parler de lui; **that's the first I've heard of it!** c'est la première fois que j'entends parler de ça!; **I won't** ~ **of you going there** je ne veux absolument pas que tu y ailles; **I wouldn't** ~ **of it!** pas question!

◆ **hear out** *vt sep* écouter jusqu'au bout.

◆ **hearer** *n* auditeur *m*, -trice *f*. ◆ **hearing** **1** *n* (**a**) *(sense)* ouïe *f*; **to have good** ~**ing** avoir l'oreille fine; **within** ~**ing (distance)** à portée de voix; **in my** ~**ing** en ma présence; (**b**) *[witness, evidence]* audition *f*; **give him a** ~**ing!** laissez-le parler!, écoutez ce qu'il a à dire!; **he was refused a** ~**ing** on a refusé de l'entendre; (**c**) *(meeting: of committee etc)* séance *f* ; **2** *adj person* qui entend (bien); ~**ing aid** appareil *m* acoustique. ◆ **hearsay** **1** *n* ouï-dire *m inv*; **from** ~**say** par ouï-dire; **it's only** ~**say** ce ne sont que des rumeurs ; **2** *adj report, account* fondé sur des ouï-dire; *evidence* sur la foi d'un tiers.

hearse [hɜ:s] *n* corbillard *m*.

heart [hɑ:t] **1** *n* (**a**) cœur *m (also fig)*. **to have a weak** ~ être cardiaque; **at** ~ au fond; **a man after my own** ~ un homme selon mon cœur; **he knew in his** ~ il savait instinctivement; **in his** ~ **(of** ~**s) he thought...** en son for intérieur il pensait...; **with all my** ~ de tout mon cœur; **from (the bottom of) one's** ~ du fond du cœur; **to take sth to** ~ prendre qch à cœur; **I hadn't the** ~ **to tell him** je n'ai pas eu le courage *or* le cœur de lui dire; **have a** ~**!** * pitié! *; **to eat/sleep to one's** ~**'s content**

manger/dormir tout son content; **it did my ~ good to see them** cela m'a réchauffé le cœur de les voir; ~ **and soul** corps et âme; **his ~ isn't in his work** il n'a pas le cœur à l'ouvrage; **to lose/take** ~ perdre/prendre courage; **to be in good** ~ avoir bon moral; **a ~ of gold/stone** un cœur d'or/de pierre; **his ~ is in the right place** il a bon cœur; **to lose one's ~ to sb** tomber amoureux de qn; **it is close to his ~** cela lui tient à cœur; **to set one's ~ on (doing) sth** vouloir à tout prix (faire) qch; **to wear one's ~ on one's sleeve** laisser voir ses sentiments; **his ~ was in his boots** il avait la mort dans l'âme; **my ~ sank** j'ai eu un coup au cœur; **she had her ~ in her mouth** son cœur battait la chamade; **to learn/know by ~** apprendre/savoir par cœur; **in the ~ of winter/the forest** au cœur de l'hiver/de la forêt; **the ~ of the matter** le fond du problème; **in the ~ of the country** en pleine campagne.
(**b**) *(Cards)* ~**s** cœur *m*; **queen of ~s** dame *f* de cœur; **have you any ~s?** avez-vous du cœur?; **he played a ~** il a joué cœur.
2 *adj disease* de cœur; *surgery* du cœur. ~ **attack** crise *f* cardiaque; *(Med)* ~ **case** cardiaque *mf*; ~ **complaint** maladie *f* de cœur; **to have a ~ condition** être cardiaque; ~ **failure** arrêt *m* du cœur; ~ **surgeon** chirurgien *m* cardiologue; ~ **transplant** greffe *f* du cœur; ~ **trouble** troubles *mpl* cardiaques.
◆ **heartache** *n* chagrin *m*. ◆ **heartbeat** *n* battement *m* de cœur. ◆ **heartbreak** *n* immense chagrin *m*. ◆ **heartbreaking** *adj sight* navrant; *appeal* déchirant. ◆ **heartbroken** *adj*: **to be ~broken** avoir un immense chagrin; *(stronger)* avoir le cœur brisé; *[child]* avoir un gros chagrin. ◆ **heartburn** *n (Med)* brûlures *fpl* d'estomac. ◆ **heartburning** *n (ill feeling)* rancœur *f*; *(regret)* regrets *mpl*. ◆ **hearten** *vt* encourager. ◆ **heartening** *adj* encourageant. ◆ **heartfelt** *adj* sincère. ◆ **heartily** *adv say, welcome* chaleureusement; *laugh, work* de tout son cœur; *eat* avec appétit; *agree* absolument; *glad, tired* extrêmement. ◆ **heartland** *n* cœur *m*, centre *n*; *(fig)* **the Tory ~land** le pays des conservateurs par excellence. ◆ **heartless** *adj person* sans cœur; *treatment* cruel. ◆ **heartlessness** *n* manque *m* de cœur; cruauté *f*. ◆ **heart-lung machine** *n* cœur-poumon *m* (artificiel). ◆ **heartrending** *adj* déchirant, qui fend le cœur. ◆ **heart-searching** *n*: **after much ~-searching he...** après s'être longuement interrogé, il... ◆ **heart-throb** * *n* idole *f*. ◆ **heart-to-heart** **1** *adj, adv* à cœur ouvert ; **2** *n*: **to have a ~-to-~** * parler à cœur ouvert. ◆ **heartwarming** *adj* qui réchauffe le cœur. ◆ **hearty** *adj welcome, approval* chaleureux; *laugh* franc; *meal* copieux; *appetite* solide; *kick, slap* bien senti; *person (healthy)* vigoureux; *(cheerful)* jovial; **to have a ~y dislike of sth** détester qch de tout son cœur.

hearth [hɑːθ] *n* foyer *m*. ~ **rug** devant *m* de foyer.

heat [hiːt] **1** *n* (**a**) *(gen, Phys)* chaleur *f*; *[fire, flames, sun]* ardeur *f*; **I can't stand** ~ je ne supporte pas la chaleur; *(Culin)* **at low** ~ à feu doux; *(Culin)* **lower the** ~ réduire la chaleur; **in the ~ of** *day, afternoon* au plus chaud de; *battle, argument* dans le feu de; *departure etc* dans l'agitation de; **in the ~ of the moment** dans le feu de l'action; **to speak with some** ~ parler avec feu; **in** *or* **on** ~ *animal* en chaleur; **we had no ~ all day** nous avons été sans chauffage toute la journée; *(fig)* **to put the ~ on sb** * faire pression sur qn. (**b**) *(Sport)* éliminatoire *f*.
2 *adj*: ~ **exchanger** échangeur *m* de chaleur; ~ **exhaustion** épuisement *m* dû à la chaleur; ~ **haze** brume *f* de chaleur; ~ **loss** perte *f* calorifique; *(Med)* ~ **rash** irritation *f* (due à la chaleur); *(Med)* ~ **treatment** thermothérapie *f*.
3 *vt* (~ **up) chauffer**; *(reheat)* réchauffer.
4 *vi* (~ **up)** *[liquids etc]* chauffer; *[room]* se réchauffer.
◆ **heated** *adj (lit)* chauffé; *(fig) argument* passionné; *words* vif; *person* échauffé; **to grow ~ed** s'échauffer. ◆ **heatedly** *adv* avec passion. ◆ **heater** *n* appareil *m* de chauffage. ◆ **heating** *n* chauffage *m*; *(for water)* chauffe-eau *m; (in car)* chauffage *m*. ◆ **heatproof** *or* ◆ **heat-resistant** *adj material* résistant à la chaleur; *dish* allant au four. ◆ **heatpump** *n* pompe *f* à chaleur. ◆ **heatstroke** *n (Med)* coup *m* de chaleur. ◆ **heatwave** *n* vague *f* de chaleur.

heath [hiːθ] *n (moorland)* lande *f*; *(plant)* bruyère *f*.

heathen ['hiːð(ə)n] *adj, n* païen(ne) *m(f)*. ◆ **heathenish** *adj (pej)* de païen.

heather ['heðə^r] *n* bruyère *f*.

heave [hiːv] **1** *vt (lift)* lever *or (pull)* tirer *or (drag)* traîner avec effort; *(throw)* lancer. **to ~ a sigh** pousser un (gros) soupir. **2** *vi* (**a**) *(pant)* haleter; *(retch)* avoir des haut-le-cœur; *(vomit)* vomir; *[sea, chest, stomach]* se soulever. (**b**) *(pret, ptp* **hove**) *[ship]* **to ~ in(to) sight** poindre (à l'horizon), paraître; **to ~ to** se mettre en panne.

heaven ['hevn] *n* ciel *m*, paradis *m*. **to go to ~** aller au ciel *or* au paradis; **in ~** au ciel, au paradis; **in the seventh ~** au septième ciel; ~ **forbid!** * surtout pas!; ~ **knows what/when** * Dieu sait quoi/ quand; ~ **knows!** * Dieu seul le sait!; **(good) ~s!** * Seigneur!; **for ~'s sake** * *(pleading)* pour l'amour du ciel *; *(protesting)* zut alors! *; **it was ~** * c'était divin; ~ **on earth** paradis sur terre; **the ~s opened** le ciel s'est mis à déverser des trombes d'eau. ◆ **heavenly** *adj* céleste; *(delightful)* divin. ◆ **heaven-sent** *adj* providentiel.

heavy ['hevɪ] **1** *adj (gen, also fig)* lourd (*with* de); *payments* important; *crop* abondant; *loss, sigh, sea, rain* gros *(before n)*; *fog, features, underlining* épais; *eyes* battu; *day* chargé; *blow* violent; *book, film* indigeste; *humour, irony* peu subtil; *population, traffic* dense; *silence* pesant; *sky* couvert; *task* pénible. ~ **(goods) vehicle** poids lourd *m*; ~ **luggage** gros bagages *mpl*; **to make heavier** alourdir; **how ~ are you?** combien pesez-vous?; *(US)* ~ **cream** crème fraîche épaisse; **to be a ~ drinker/smoker** *etc* boire/fumer *etc* beaucoup; **to be a ~ sleeper** avoir le sommeil profond; **the car is ~ on petrol** la voiture consomme beaucoup; ~ **fighting** combats *mpl* acharnés; ~ **gunfire** feu *m* nourri; **there were ~ casualties** il y a eu de nombreuses victimes *fpl*; *(Med)* ~ **cold** gros rhume *m*; *(fig)* **it's ~ going** ça n'avance pas; **with a ~ heart** le cœur gros; *(fig)* **he made ~ weather of doing it** il a fait toute une histoire * pour le faire; **the ~ work** le gros travail; *(Ind etc)* ~ **workers** travailleurs *mpl* de force; *(Mus)* ~ **metal** heavy metal.
2 *adv weigh, lie* lourd.
3 *n (*: gangster)* casseur *m*.
◆ **heavily** *adv load, tax, walk* lourdement; *underline* fortement; *sleep, sigh* profondément; *breathe* bruyamment; *move* avec difficulté; *lean* de tout son poids; *say* d'une voix accablée; *rain, snow* très fort; *drink, smoke* beaucoup; **to lose heavily** *[team]* se faire écraser; *[gambler]* perdre gros. ◆ **heavily-built** *adj* solidement bâti. ◆ **heavily-laden** *adj* (très) lourdement chargé. ◆ **heaviness** *n* pesanteur *f*, poids *m*. ◆ **heavy-duty** *adj (carpet)* résistant; *(equipment)* à usage industriel. ◆ **heavy-handed** *adj* maladroit. ◆ **heavy-hearted** *adj*: **to be ~-hearted** avoir le cœur gros. ◆ **heavyweight** **1** *n (Boxing)* poids lourd; *(*: influential person)* personne *f* de poids ; **2** *adj (Boxing)* poids lourd *inv*; *cloth* lourd.

Hebrew ['hiːbruː] **1** *adj* hébreu *(m only)*, hébraïque. **2** *n* Hébreu *m*; *(Ling)* hébreu *m*.

Hebrides ['hebrɪdiːz] *n* Hébrides *fpl*.

heckle ['hekl] **1** *vi (shout)* chahuter *(pour troubler l'orateur); (interrupt)* interrompre bruyamment. **2** *vt speaker* interrompre. ◆ **heckler** *n* perturbateur *m.* ◆ **heckling** *n* chahut *m*; interpellations *fpl.*

hectic ['hektɪk] *adj life, day (busy)* très bousculé; *(eventful)* très mouvementé; *traffic* terrible; *journey* très mouvementé. **I've had a ~ rush** ça a vraiment été une course folle.

hector ['hektəʳ] *vt* rudoyer. ◆ **hectoring** *adj* autoritaire.

hedge [hedʒ] **1** *n* haie *f.* **beech ~** haie *f* de hêtres. **2** *vi (in answering)* répondre évasivement; *(in explaining etc)* expliquer *etc* avec des détours. **3** *vt* (**a**) **~d with difficulties** entouré de difficultés; **to ~ one's bet** se couvrir *(fig).* (**b**) *(US)* **to ~ the issue** esquiver la question. ◆ **hedgehog** *n* hérisson *m.* ◆ **hedgehop** *vi (Aviat)* voler en rase-mottes. ◆ **hedgerow** *n* haie *f.*

hedonism ['hi:dənɪz(ə)m] *n* hédonisme *m.* ◆ **hedonist** *adj, n* hédoniste *(mf).*

heebie-jeebies * ['hi:bɪ'dʒi:bɪz] *npl*: **to have the ~** *(shaking)* avoir la tremblote *; *(fright, nerves)* avoir la frousse *; **it gives me the ~** *(revulsion)* ça me donne la chair de poule; *(fright)* ça me donne la frousse *.

heed [hi:d] **1** *vt* faire attention à, tenir compte de. **2** *n*: **to take ~ of, to pay ~ to** faire attention à, tenir compte de. ◆ **heedless** *adj (not thinking)* étourdi; *(not caring)* insouciant; **~less of** sans se soucier de. ◆ **heedlessly** *adv* étourdiment; avec insouciance.

heel¹ [hi:l] **1** *n* (**a**) talon *m.* **at** *or* **on sb's ~s** sur les talons de qn; **to take to one's ~s** prendre ses jambes à son cou; **to turn on one's ~** tourner les talons; *(to dog)* **~!** au pied!; **to come to ~** venir au pied; *(fig)* **to bring sb to ~** rappeler qn à l'ordre. (**b**) *(*: unpleasant person)* chameau * *m.* **2** *vt ball* talonner. *(fig)* **well-~ed** * plein de sous *. ◆ **heel-bar** *n* talon-minute *m.*

heel² [hi:l] *vi* (**~ over**) *[ship]* gîter; *[truck, structure]* pencher dangereusement.

hefty * ['heftɪ] *adj person* costaud *; *parcel* lourd; *part, piece, price* gros *(before n).*

heifer ['hefəʳ] *n* génisse *f.*

height [haɪt] *n* (**a**) *[building]* hauteur *f*; *[person]* taille *f*; *[mountain, plane]* altitude *f.* **what ~ are you?** combien mesurez-vous?; **he is 1 metre 80 in ~** il fait 1 m 80; **of average ~** de taille moyenne; **he drew himself up to his full ~** il s'est dressé de toute sa hauteur; **a building 40 metres in ~** un bâtiment de 40 mètres de haut; **~ above sea level** altitude au-dessus du niveau de la mer; *(high ground)* **the ~s** les sommets *mpl.* (**b**) *[success]* apogée *m*; *[absurdity, ill manners]* comble *m.* **at the ~ of** *storm, battle etc* au cœur de; **at the ~ of his power** au summum de sa puissance; **at the ~ of summer/the season** en plein été/pleine saison; **the ~ of fashion** la toute dernière mode; **to be at its ~** *[fair, party]* battre son plein; *[excitement etc]* être à son maximum. ◆ **heighten** *vt (gen)* intensifier; *flavour* relever.

heir [ɛəʳ] *n* héritier *m* (*to* de). **~ apparent** héritier présomptif. ◆ **heiress** *n* héritière *f.* ◆ **heirloom** *n* héritage *m*; *(picture/jewel etc)* **a family ~loom** un tableau/bijou *etc* de famille.

held [held] *pret, ptp of* **hold.**

helicopter ['helɪkɒptəʳ] **1** *n* hélicoptère *m.* **2** *adj patrol, rescue* en hélicoptère; *pilot* d'hélicoptère. ◆ **heliport** *n* héliport *m.*

helium ['hi:lɪəm] *n* hélium *m.*

hell [hel] *n* enfer *m.* **in ~** en enfer; **all ~ was let loose** ça a été infernal; **come ~ or high water** quoi qu'il arrive; **to go ~ for leather** aller à un train d'enfer; **a ~ of a noise** * un boucan du diable *; **a ~ of a lot of** * tout un tas de; **we had a ~ of a time** * *(bad)* ça n'a pas été marrant *; *(good)* ça a été du tonnerre *; **to run** *etc* **like ~** * courir *etc* comme un fou; **to give sb ~** * *(make his life a misery)* faire mener une vie infernale à qn; *(scold)* passer une engueulade ‡ à qn; **oh ~!** * flûte! *; **to ~ with it!** * la barbe! *; **go to ~!** * va te faire voir! *; **what the ~ does he want?** * qu'est-ce qu'il peut bien vouloir?; **why/where** *etc* **the ~** *... mais bon sang *, pourquoi/où est-ce que...; **~'s angel** blouson *m* noir. ◆ **hellbent** * *adj* acharné (*on doing* à faire). ◆ **hellish** *adj* diabolique; *(*: unpleasant)* infernal. ◆ **hellishly** * *adv* vachement ‡.

hello [hə'ləʊ] *excl* = **hallo.**

helm [helm] *n (Naut)* barre *f.* **to be at the ~** *(also fig)* tenir la barre. ◆ **helmsman** *n* timonier *m.*

helmet ['helmɪt] *n* casque *m.*

help [help] **1** *n* (**a**) aide *f*, secours *m. (excl)* **~!** au secours!; *(in dismay)* mon Dieu!; **thanks for your ~** merci de votre aide; **with the ~ of** *person* avec l'aide de; *tool etc* à l'aide de; **to shout for ~** appeler au secours *or* à l'aide; **to go to sb's ~** aller au secours de qn; **to be of ~ to sb** rendre service à qn; **he's a great ~ to me** il m'aide beaucoup; **she has no ~ in the house** elle n'a pas de femme de ménage; **we need more ~ in the shop** il nous faut davantage de personnel au magasin; **he's beyond ~** on ne peut plus rien pour lui ; **there's no ~ for it** il n'y a rien à faire. (**b**) *(charwoman)* femme *f* de ménage.
2 *vt* (**a**) aider (*sb to do* qn à faire; *sb with sth* qn à faire qch). **to ~ sb with his luggage** aider qn à porter ses bagages; **he got his brother to ~ him** il s'est fait aider par son frère; **that doesn't ~ much** cela ne sert pas à grand-chose; **that won't ~ you** cela ne vous servira à rien; **so ~ me God!** je le jure devant Dieu!; **this money will ~ to save the church** cet argent contribuera à sauver l'église; *(in shops etc)* **can I ~ you?** vous désirez?; **he is ~ing the police with their inquiries** il est en train de répondre aux questions de la police; **to ~ sb across/down** *etc* aider qn à traverser/à descendre *etc*; **to ~ sb on/off with his coat** aider qn à mettre/à enlever son manteau. (**b**) servir. **she ~ed him to potatoes** elle l'a servi de pommes de terre; **~ yourself** servez-vous (*to* de); **he's ~ed himself to my pencil** * il m'a piqué * mon crayon. (**c**) **I couldn't ~ laughing** je n'ai pas pu m'empêcher de rire; **it can't be ~ed** tant pis!, on n'y peut rien!; **I can't ~ it if...** je n'y peux rien si...; **not if I can ~ it!** sûrement pas!; **he won't come if I can ~ it** je vais faire tout mon possible pour l'empêcher de venir; **he can't ~ being stupid** ce n'est pas de sa faute s'il est idiot; **don't say more than you can ~** n'en dites pas plus qu'il ne faut. ◆ **help out 1** *vi* aider, donner un coup de main. **2** *vt sep (gen)* aider, donner un coup de main à; *(sb in trouble)* dépanner, tirer d'embarras. **to ~ each other out** s'entraider.
◆ **helper** *n* aide *mf*, assistant(e) *m(f).* ◆ **helpful** *adj person (willing)* obligeant; *(useful)* qui est d'un grand secours; *book, gadget, advice* utile. ◆ **helpfully** *adv* avec obligeance. ◆ **helpfulness** *n* obligeance *f.* ◆ **helping 1** *n* portion *f*; **to take a second ~ing of sth** reprendre de qch; **I've had three ~ings** j'en ai repris deux fois ; **2** *adj*: **to lend a ~ing hand** donner un coup de main (*to* à). ◆ **helpless** *adj (mentally, morally)* impuissant; *(physically)* impotent; *(powerless)* sans ressource; **she is a ~less invalid** elle est complètement impotente; **~less with laughter** malade de rire. ◆ **helplessly** *adv struggle* en vain; *try, agree* désespérément; *lie, remain* sans pouvoir bouger; *say* d'un ton d'impuissance; **to laugh ~lessly** être pris d'un fou rire. ◆ **helplessness** *n* impuissance *f*; impotence *f.*

Helsinki ['helsɪŋkɪ] *n* Helsinki.

helter-skelter ['heltə'skeltər] **1** *adv* à la débandade. **2** *n (rush)* débandade *f*; *(in fairground)* toboggan *m*.

hem [hem] **1** *n (part doubled over)* ourlet *m*; *(edge)* bord *m*. **I've let the ~ down on my skirt** j'ai rallongé ma jupe. **2** *vt* ourler. ◆ **hem in** *vt sep (physically)* cerner; *[rules etc]* entraver. **I feel ~med in** ça m'oppresse.

hem(a)... ['hi:m(ə)] *pref (esp US)* = **haem(a)...**

hemisphere ['hemɪsfɪər] *n* hémisphère *m*. **the northern/southern ~** l'hémisphère nord/sud.

hemlock ['hemlɒk] *n* ciguë *f*.

hemp [hemp] *n* chanvre *m*.

hen [hen] **1** *n* poule *f*; *(female bird)* femelle *f*. **2** *adj*: **~ bird** oiseau *m* femelle; **~ party** * réunion *f* de femmes *or* filles. ◆ **henhouse** *n* poulailler *m*. ◆ **henpecked** *adj* dominé par sa femme.

hence [hens] *adv (therefore)* d'où, de là; *(from now on)* d'ici. ◆ **henceforth** *or* ◆ **henceforward** *adv* dorénavant, désormais.

henchman ['hen(t)ʃmən] *n* acolyte *m (pej)*.

henna ['henə] *n* henné *m*.

hepatitis [ˌhepə'taɪtɪs] *n* hépatite *f*.

her [hɜ:r] **1** *pers pron* **(a)** *(direct) (unstressed)* la; *(before vowel)* l'; *(stressed)* elle. **I see ~** je la vois; **I have seen ~** je l'ai vue; **I have never seen HER** elle, je ne l'ai jamais vue. **(b)** *(indirect)* lui. **I give ~ the book** je lui donne le livre; **I'm speaking to ~** je lui parle. **(c)** *(after prep etc)* elle. **I am thinking of ~** je pense à elle; **without ~** sans elle; **if I were ~** si j'étais elle; **it's ~** c'est elle; **younger than ~** plus jeune qu'elle. **2** *poss adj* son, sa, ses. **~ book** son livre; **~ table** sa table; **~ friend** son ami(e); **~ clothes** ses vêtements.

◆ **hers** *poss pron* le sien, la sienne, les siens, les siennes; **this book is ~s** ce livre est à elle, ce livre est le sien; **a friend of ~s** un de ses amis (à elle); **is this poem ~s?** ce poème est-il d'elle?; *(pej)* **that car of ~s** sa fichue * voiture. ◆ **herself** *pers pron (reflexive: direct and indirect)* se; *(emphatic)* elle-même; *(after prep)* elle; **she has hurt ~self** elle s'est blessée; **she said to ~self** elle s'est dit; **she told me ~self** elle me l'a dit elle-même; **she kept 3 for ~self** elle s'en est réservé 3; **he asked her for a photo of ~self** il lui a demandé une photo d'elle; **(all) by ~self** toute seule; **she is not ~self** elle n'est pas dans son état normal.

herald ['her(ə)ld] **1** *n* héraut *m*. **2** *vt* annoncer. ◆ **heraldic** [he'rældɪk] *adj* héraldique. ◆ **heraldry** ['her(ə)ldrɪ] *n* héraldique *f*.

herb [hɜ:b] *n* herbe *f*. *(Culin)* **~s** fines herbes. **2** *adj*: **~ garden** jardin *m* d'herbes aromatiques; **~ tea** tisane *f*. ◆ **herbaceous** *adj* herbacé; **~aceous border** bordure *f* de plantes herbacées. ◆ **herbal** **1** *adj* d'herbes ; **2** *n* herbier *m*. ◆ **herbalist** *n* herboriste *mf*. ◆ **herbivorous** *adj* herbivore.

herd [hɜ:d] **1** *n (lit, fig)* troupeau *m*. **2** *adj*: **~ instinct** instinct *m* grégaire. **3** *vt* diriger. ◆ **herd together** **1** *vi* s'attrouper. **2** *vt sep* rassembler en troupeau.

here [hɪər] **1** *adv* **(a)** *(place)* ici. **come ~** venez ici; *(at roll call)* **~!** présent!; **~ I am** me voici; **~ is my brother** voici mon frère; **~ are the others** voici les autres; *(bringing sth)* **~ we are!** voici!; *(giving sth)* **~ you are!** tenez!; **~ come my friends** voici mes amis qui arrivent; **he's ~ at last** il est enfin arrivé; **spring is ~** c'est le printemps; **my sister ~ says...** ma sœur que voici dit...; **this man ~ saw it** cet homme-ci l'a vu; **~'s to you!** à la vôtre!; **~'s to your success!** à votre succès!; **about** *or* **around ~** par ici; **put it in ~** mettez-le ici; **come in ~ please** par ici s'il vous plaît; **over ~** ici; **it's cold up ~** il fait froid ici; **up to** *or* **down to ~** jusqu'ici; **from ~ to there** d'ici jusqu'à là-bas; **it's 10 km from ~ to Paris** il y a 10 km d'ici à Paris; **Mr Smith is not ~ just now** M. Smith n'est pas là *or* ici en ce moment; **are you there? — yes I'm ~** vous êtes là? — oui je suis là; **~ and there** par-ci par-là; **~, there and everywhere** un peu partout; *(fig)* **it's neither ~ nor there** tout cela n'a aucune importance; **~ goes!** * allons-y!; **~ and now** sur-le-champ; **the ~ and now** le présent; **~ below** ici-bas; **~ lies** ci-gît. **(b)** *(time)* alors, à ce moment-là.

2 *excl* tenez!; *(protesting)* écoutez!

◆ **hereabouts** *adv* près d'ici. ◆ **hereafter** **1** *adv* après ; **2** *n* au-delà *m*. ◆ **hereby** *adv* par la présente. ◆ **hereupon** *adv* là-dessus. ◆ **herewith** *adv*: **I am sending you ~with** je vous envoie ci-joint *or* sous ce pli.

heredity [hɪ'redɪtɪ] *n* hérédité *f*. ◆ **hereditary** *adj* héréditaire.

heresy ['herəsɪ] *n* hérésie *f*. **an act of ~** une hérésie. ◆ **heretic** *n* hérétique *mf*. ◆ **heretical** [hɪ'retɪk(ə)l] *adj* hérétique.

heritage ['herɪtɪdʒ] *n* patrimoine *m*. **our national ~** notre patrimoine national.

hermetic [hɜ:'metɪk] *adj* hermétique. ◆ **hermetically** *adv* hermétiquement; **~ally sealed** fermé hermétiquement.

hermit ['hɜ:mɪt] *n* ermite *m*.

hernia ['hɜ:nɪə] *n* hernie *f*.

hero ['hɪərəʊ] *n* héros *m*. *(US)* **~ (sandwich)** grand sandwich *m* mixte. ◆ **heroic** [hɪ'rəʊɪk] *adj* héroïque. ◆ **heroically** *adv* héroïquement. ◆ **heroics** *npl (pej) (words)* grandiloquence *f*; *(deeds)* comédie * *f*. ◆ **heroine** ['herəʊɪn] *n* héroïne *f (femme)*. ◆ **heroism** ['herəʊɪz(ə)m] *n* héroïsme *m*. ◆ **hero-worship** **1** *n* culte *m* ; **2** *vt* avoir un culte pour.

heroin ['herəʊɪn] *n* héroïne *f (drogue)*. **~ addict** héroïnomane *mf*.

heron ['herən] *n* héron *m*.

herpes ['hɜ:pi:z] *n* herpès *m*.

herring ['herɪŋ] *n* hareng *m*. ◆ **herringbone (pattern)** *n* chevrons *mpl*.

hesitate ['hezɪteɪt] *vi* hésiter (*over, about, at* sur, devant; *to do* à faire). ◆ **hesitancy** *n* hésitation *f*. ◆ **hesitant** *adj* hésitant; **to be hesitant about doing** hésiter à faire. ◆ **hesitantly** *adv* avec hésitation; *speak, suggest* d'une voix hésitante. ◆ **hesitation** *n* hésitation *f*; **I have no hesitation in saying** je n'hésite pas à dire.

hessian ['hesɪən] *n* toile *f* de jute.

heterogeneous ['hetərə(ʊ)'dʒi:nɪəs] *adj* hétérogène.

heterosexual ['hetərə(ʊ)'seksjʊəl] *adj, n* hétérosexuel(le) *m(f)*.

het up * ['het'ʌp] *adj* agité (*about* par).

hew [hju:] *pret* **hewed,** *ptp* **hewn** *or* **hewed** *vt stone* tailler; *wood* couper; *coal* abattre. **to ~ sth out of wood** *etc* tailler qch dans du bois *etc*.

hex [heks] **1** *n* sort *m*. **2** *vt* jeter un sort sur.

hexagon ['heksəgən] *n* hexagone *m*. ◆ **hexagonal** [heks'ægən(ə)l] *adj* hexagonal.

heyday ['heɪdeɪ] *n [thing]* âge *m* d'or. **in his ~** à l'apogée de sa gloire.

hi * [haɪ] *excl* hé!; *(*: greeting)* salut! *

hiatus [haɪ'eɪtəs] *n* lacune *f*; *(fig)* interruption *f*.

hibernate ['haɪbəneɪt] *vi* hiberner. ◆ **hibernation** *n* hibernation *f*.

hiccough, hiccup ['hɪkʌp] **1** *n* hoquet *m*; *(fig)* contretemps *m*. **to have ~s** avoir le hoquet. **2** *vi* hoqueter.

hide¹ [haɪd] *pret* **hid,** *ptp* **hidden** **1** *vt (gen)* cacher (*from sb* à qn); *feelings* dissimuler (*from sb* à qn). **to ~ one's face** se cacher le visage; **hidden from sight** dérobé aux regards, caché; *(fig)* **to ~ one's light under a bushel** cacher ses talents. **2** *vi* (**~ away, ~ out**) se cacher (*from sb* de qn). *(fig)* **he's**

hiding behind his boss il se réfugie derrière son patron. ◆ **hide-and-(go-)seek** *n* cache-cache *m*. ◆ **hideaway** *or* ◆ **hideout** *n* cachette *f*. ◆ **hiding**[1] **1** *n*: **to be in hiding** se tenir caché; **to go into hiding** se cacher ; **2** *adj*: **hiding place** cachette *f*.

hide[2] [haɪd] **1** *n (skin)* peau *f*; *(leather)* cuir *m*. **2** *adj chair etc* de cuir. ◆ **hidebound** *adj* borné.

hideous ['hɪdɪəs] *adj sight, person* hideux; *crime* atroce; *disappointment* terrible. ◆ **hideously** *adv* hideusement; atrocement; terriblement.

hiding[2] ['haɪdɪŋ] *n* correction *f*, raclée *f*. **to give sb a good** ~ donner une bonne correction à qn.

hierarchy ['haɪərɑːkɪ] *n* hiérarchie *f*.

hieroglyph ['haɪərəglɪf], **hieroglyphic** [,haɪərə'glɪfɪk] *n* hiéroglyphe *m*.

hi-fi ['haɪ'faɪ] *(abbr of* **high fidelity***)* **1** *n* (**a**) hifi *f inv*, haute fidélité *inv*. (**b**) *(gramophone/radio)* chaîne *f*/radio *f* hi-fi *inv*. **2** *adj* hi-fi *inv*. ~ **equipment** *or* **system** chaîne *f* (hi-fi).

higgledy-piggledy * ['hɪgldɪ'pɪgldɪ] *adv* pêle-mêle.

high [haɪ] **1** *adj* (**a**) *(gen)* haut. **building 40 metres** ~ bâtiment de 40 mètres de haut, bâtiment qui a *or* fait 40 mètres de haut; **how ~ is that tower?** quelle est la hauteur de cette tour?; **when he was so ~ *** quand il était grand comme ça; ~ **cheekbones** pommettes saillantes; *(Sport)* ~ **jump** saut *m* en hauteur; **he's for the ~ jump *** il est bon pour une engueulade ⁑; ~ **chair** chaise *f* haute *(d'enfant)*; *(fig)* **on one's ~ horse** sur ses grands chevaux; **at ~ tide** *or* **water** à marée haute.

(**b**) *frequency, latitude, tension, pressure, official* haut *(before n)*; *speed, value, respect* grand *(before n)*; *fever* fort *(before n)*; *complexion, colour* vif; *polish* brillant; *wind* violent; *salary, number, rent, price* élevé; *sound, voice* aigu; *(Mus) note* haut; *character, ideal* noble; *(Culin) game, meat* faisandé; *butter* rance; (⁑: *intoxicated)* parti *. ~ ⁑ **on drugs/hashish** défoncé ⁑ par la drogue/au hachisch; **in the ~est degree** au plus haut degré; **to buy sth at a ~ price** acheter qch cher; *(lit, fig)* **to pay a ~ price for sth** payer qch cher; **to have a ~ old time *** s'amuser follement; ~ **altar** maître-autel *m*; ~ **beam** optique *f* feux de route; **H~ Church** Haute Église *f*; **H~ Mass** grand-messe *f*; ~ **priest** grand prêtre *m*; *(fig)* **to leave sb ~ and dry** laisser qn en plan *; **to be ~ and mighty *** se donner de grands airs; *(Mil)* ~ **command** haut commandement *m*; ~ **commissioner** haut commissaire *m*; *(Jur)* ~ **court** cour *f* suprême; ~ **explosive** explosif *m* puissant; **to have ~ jinks *** se payer du bon temps *; ~ **life** grande vie *f*; ~ **noon** plein midi; ~ **point** *[show]* point *m* culminant; *[holiday]* grand moment; **the ~ season** la haute saison; ~ **school** *(Brit)* lycée *m*; *(US)* collège *m* d'enseignement secondaire; *(US)* ~ **school diploma** diplôme *m* de fin d'études secondaires; **on the ~ seas** en haute mer; ~ **society** haute société *f*; ~ **spirits** entrain *m*; **the ~ spot** *[evening, show]* le clou; *[visit, holiday]* le grand moment; **to hit the ~ spots *** faire la noce * *(dans un night-club etc)*; *(lit, fig)* **to play for ~ stakes** jouer gros jeu; ~ **street** *[village]* grand-rue *f*; *[town]* rue principale; **in ~ summer** au cœur de l'été; ~ **table** table *f* d'honneur; *(Univ)* table des professeurs; ~ **tea** repas *m* du soir, dîner *m* ~ **technology** technologie *f* de pointe; ~ **treason** haute trahison *f*.

2 *adv rise, float, be, aim* haut; *fly etc* à haute altitude. ~ **up** en haut; **~er up** plus haut; **~er and ~er** de plus en plus haut; ~ **above our heads** bien au-dessus de nos têtes; **to go as ~ as 200 francs** monter jusqu'à 200 F; **to hunt ~ and low** chercher partout; **to hold one's head up** ~ avoir la tête haute; *(fig)* **to fly** ~ voir grand, viser haut. **3** *n* (**a**) **on** ~ en haut. (**b**) *(record)* **a new** ~ un nouveau record.

◆ **highball** *n* whisky *m* à l'eau (avec de la glace). ◆ **highbrow** **1** *n* intellectuel(le) *m(f)* ; **2** *adj interests* intellectuel; *music* pour intellectuels. ◆ **high-class** *adj hotel, food* de premier ordre; *neighbourhood, flat, publicity* (de) grand standing; *person* du grand monde. ◆ **higher** **1** *adj* supérieur (*than* à) ; **2** *adv* plus haut. ◆ **high-fidelity** *adj* haute fidélité *inv*. ◆ **high-flier** *n* ambitieux *m*, -euse *f*; *(gifted)* doué(e) *m(f)*. ◆ **high-flown** *adj* ampoulé. ◆ **high-flying** *adj aircraft* volant à haute altitude; *person* ambitieux. ◆ **high-frequency** *adj* de *or* à haute fréquence. ◆ **high-grade** *adj* de haute qualité. ◆ **high-handed** *adj* tyrannique. ◆ **high-handedly** *adv* très autoritairement. ◆ **high-heeled** *adj* à hauts talons. ◆ **highjack** *etc* = **hijack** *etc*. ◆ **highlands** *npl* hautes terres *fpl; (in Scotland)* **the H~lands** les Highlands *fpl*. ◆ **high-level** *adj talks* à très haut niveau. ◆ **highlight** **1** *n (Art)* rehaut *m*; *(in hair)* reflet *m*; *(fig: evening etc)* clou *m*; *[match etc]* instant *m* le plus marquant ; **2** *vt* (**a**) mettre en lumière. (**b**) *(with pen)* mettre en lumière *(avec un surligneur lumineux)*. ◆ **highlighter** *n (pen)* surligneur *m* lumineux. ◆ **highly** *adv pleased, interesting* extrêmement; *recommended* chaudement; *pay* très bien; *season* fortement; **~ly coloured** *object* haut en couleur; *description etc* exagéré; **~ly strung** nerveux; **to speak/think ~ly of** dire/penser beaucoup de bien de. ◆ **high-minded** *adj person* de caractère élevé; *ambition* noble. ◆ **high-necked** *adj* à col haut. ◆ **highness** *n*: **Your H~ness** Votre Altesse *f*. ◆ **high-pitched** *adj* aigu. ◆ **high-powered** *adj car* très puissant; *person* très important. ◆ **high-pressure** *adj* à haute pression; *(Met)* de hautes pressions; *(fig) salesman* de choc *. ◆ **high-priced** *adj* coûteux, cher. ◆ **high-principled** *adj* qui a des principes élevés. ◆ **high-ranking official** *n* haut fonctionnaire *m*. ◆ **high-rise block** *n* tour *f* (d'habitation). ◆ **highroad** *n* grand-route *f*. ◆ **high-sounding** *adj* sonore; grandiloquent *(pej)*. ◆ **high-speed** *adj* ultra-rapide; *lens* à obturation ultra-rapide; **~-speed train** train *m* à grande vitesse, TGV *m*. ◆ **high-spirited** *adj person* plein d'entrain; *horse* fougueux. ◆ **high-tech** **1** *n (technology)* technologie *f* de pointe; *(furniture)* high-tech *m* ; **2** *adj solution* utilisant la technologie de pointe; *camera, system* ultra-perfectionné; *furniture* high-tech *inv*. ◆ **high-up** **1** *adj person, post* haut placé ; **2** *n* (*) grosse légume * *f*. ◆ **highway** *n* grande route *f*; **public ~ way, the king's** *or* **queen's ~way** la voie publique; **through the ~ways and byways of Sussex** par tous les chemins du Sussex; **the ~way code** le code de la route; *(US)* **(state) ~way patrol** police *f* de la route *or* des autoroutes. ◆ **highwayman** *n* bandit *m* de grand chemin.

hijack ['haɪdʒæk] **1** *vt* détourner *(par la force)*. **2** *n* détournement *m*. ◆ **hijacker** *n [plane]* pirate *m* (de l'air); *[coach, train, truck]* gangster *m*. ◆ **hijacking** *n* détournement *m*.

hike [haɪk] **1** *n* excursion *f* à pied; *(Mil, Sport)* marche *f* à pied. **to go on** *or* **for a** ~ faire une excursion à pied. **2** *vi* aller à pied (*to* à). **to go hiking** faire des excursions. **3** *vt (raise) price* augmenter. ◆ **hiker** *n* excursionniste *mf (à pied)*.

hilarious [hɪ'lɛərɪəs] *adj (merry)* hilare; *(funny)* désopilant. ◆ **hilarity** *n* hilarité *f*.

hill [hɪl] *n* colline *f*; *(slope)* côte *f*, pente *f*. **up ~ and down dale** par monts et par vaux; **as old as the ~s** vieux comme les chemins; **this car is not good on ~s** cette voiture ne grimpe pas bien. ◆ **hillbilly music** *n* musique *f* folk *inv*. ◆ **hillock** *n* petite colline. ◆ **hillside** *n* coteau *m*; **on the ~side** à flanc de coteau. ◆ **hilltop** *n*: **on the ~top** en haut de la colline. ◆ **hilly** *adj* accidenté.

hilt [hɪlt] *n [sword]* poignée *f*, garde *f*. **up to the ~** *be in trouble, debt, involved* jusqu'au cou; *back sb* quoiqu'il arrive; *mortgage* au maximum.

him [hɪm] *pers pron* (**a**) *(direct) (unstressed)* le; *(before vowel)* l'; *(stressed)* lui. **I see** ~ je le vois; **I have seen** ~ je l'ai vu; **I've never seen HIM** lui, je ne l'ai jamais vu. (**b**) *(indirect)* lui. **I give** ~ **the book** je lui donne le livre; **I'm speaking to** ~ je lui parle. (**c**) *(after prep etc)* lui. **I am thinking of** ~ je pense à lui; **without** ~ sans lui; **if I were** ~ si j'étais lui; **it's** ~ c'est lui; **younger than** ~ plus jeune que lui. ◆ **himself** *pers pron (reflexive: direct and indirect)* se; *(emphatic)* lui-même; *(after prep)* lui. **he has hurt** ~**self** il s'est blessé; **he said to** ~**self** il s'est dit; **he told me** ~**self** il me l'a dit lui-même; **he kept 3 for** ~**self** il s'en est réservé 3; **she asked him for a photo of** ~**self** elle lui a demandé une photo de lui; **(all) by** ~**self** tout seul; **he is not** ~**self** il n'est pas dans son état normal.

Himalayas [ˌhɪmə'leɪəz] *npl*: **the** ~ l'Himalaya *m*.

hind [haɪnd] *adj*: ~ **legs,** ~ **feet** pattes *fpl* de derrière; **she would talk the** ~ **legs off a donkey** * c'est un vrai moulin à paroles *. ◆ **hindquarters** *npl* arrière-train *m*. ◆ **hindsight** *n*: **with the benefit of** ~**sight** rétrospectivement.

hinder ['hɪndəʳ] *vt (obstruct)* gêner; *(delay)* retarder; *(prevent)* empêcher (*sb from doing* qn de faire). ◆ **hindrance** *n*: **to be a hindrance to sb/sth** gêner qn/qch.

Hindu ['hɪn'du:] **1** *adj* hindou. **2** *n* Hindou(e) *m(f)*. ◆ **Hinduism** *n* hindouisme *m*.

hinge [hɪn(d)ʒ] **1** *n [door]* gond *m*; *[box, stamp]* charnière *f*. **the door came off its** ~**s** la porte est sortie de ses gonds. **2** *vi (fig)* dépendre (*on* de). ◆ **hinged** *adj lid* à charnières; *counter flap* relevable.

hint [hɪnt] **1** *n* allusion *f*, insinuation *f (pej)*. **to drop a** ~ faire une allusion (*that* que); **he dropped me a** ~ **that** il m'a fait comprendre que; **gentle/broad** ~ allusion discrète/à peine voilée; **he knows how to take a** ~ il comprend à demi-mot; **I can take a** ~ (ça va) j'ai compris; *(in guessing etc)* **give me a** ~ donne-moi une indication; **he gave no** ~ **of his feelings** il n'a donné aucune indication sur ce qu'il ressentait; ~**s for travellers/on maintenance** conseils *mpl* aux voyageurs/d'entretien; **a** ~ **of garlic** un soupçon d'ail; **there was not the slightest** ~ **of a dispute** il n'y a pas eu l'ombre d'une dispute; **a** ~ **of sadness** un je ne sais quoi de mélancolique. **2** *vt* insinuer, suggérer (*that* que). **he** ~**ed to me that** il m'a laissé comprendre que. **3** *vi*: **to** ~ **at sth** faire (une) allusion à qch; **what are you** ~**ing at?** qu'est-ce que vous voulez dire par là?

hip¹ [hɪp] **1** *n (Anat)* hanche *f*. **with one's hands on one's** ~**s** les mains sur les hanches; **to break one's** ~ se casser le col du fémur. **2** *adj*: ~ **bath** bain *m* de siège. ~ **flask** flacon *m* plat (pour la poche), flasque *f*; ~ **joint** articulation *f* de la hanche; ~ **pocket** poche *f* revolver; ~ **size** tour *m* de hanches. ◆ **hipbone** *n* os *m* iliaque. ◆ **hipsters** *npl* pantalon *m* taille basse.

hip² [hɪp] *n (Bot)* gratte-cul *m*.

hippie * ['hɪpɪ] *adj, n* hippie *(mf)*.

hippopotamus, *pl* **-mi** [ˌhɪpə'pɒtəməs, maɪ] *n* hippopotame *m*.

hire ['haɪəʳ] **1** *n* location *f*; *(price)* prix *m* de la location. **for** ~ à louer; *(on taxi)* 'libre'; **on** ~ en location; **car** ~ location *f* de voiture. **2** *adj*: ~ **car** voiture *f* de location; ~ **purchase** achat *m* à crédit; **on** ~ **purchase** à crédit. **3** *vt* (**a**) *thing* louer; *person* engager. ~**d man** ouvrier *m* payé à l'heure; ~**d car** voiture *f* louée. (**b**) (~ **out**) donner en location.

his [hɪz] **1** *poss adj* son, sa, ses. ~ **book** son livre; ~ **table** sa table; ~ **friend** son ami(e); ~ **clothes** ses vêtements. **2** *poss pron* le sien, la sienne, les siens, les siennes. **this book is** ~ ce livre est à lui; **a friend of** ~ un de ses amis (à lui); **is this poem** ~? ce poème est-il de lui?; *(pej)* **that car of** ~ sa fichue * voiture.

hiss [hɪs] **1** *vti* siffler. **2** *n* sifflement *m*; *(Theat etc)* sifflet *m*.

history ['hɪst(ə)rɪ] *n* histoire *f*. **to make** ~, **to go down in** ~ *[person]* entrer dans l'histoire (*for* pour); *[event, day, decision]* être historique; **he has a** ~ **of psychiatric disorders** il a dans son passé des désordres psychiatriques; **medical** ~ passé *m* médical. ◆ **historian** *n* historien(ne) *m(f)*. ◆ **historic(al)** *adj* historique.

histrionic [ˌhɪstrɪ'ɒnɪk] *adj (pej)* de cabotin; *(gen)* théâtral; *talent* dramatique. ◆ **histrionics** *npl (pej)* airs *mpl* dramatiques.

hit [hɪt] *(vb: pret, ptp* **hit***)* **1** *n* (**a**) *(stroke, blow)* coup *m*; *(Baseball/Tennis etc)* coup de batte/raquette *etc*. *(fig)* **that's a** ~ **at me** c'est moi qui suis visé. (**b**) *(as opp to miss)* coup *m* réussi, beau coup. **3** ~**s and 3 misses** 3 succès *mpl* et 3 échecs *mpl;* **direct** ~ coup dans le mille. (**c**) *(song/book/film etc)* chanson *f*/livre *m*/film *m* à succès. **to make a** ~ **of sth** * réussir (pleinement) qch; **to make a** ~ **with sb** * faire une grosse impression sur qn; **to be a big** ~ avoir un énorme succès.

2 *adj song, show* à succès. ~ **parade** hit parade *m*; ~ **list** liste *f* noire.

3 *vt* (**a**) *(strike)* frapper; *(knock against)* heurter, cogner; *(collide with)* heurter, entrer en collision avec; *(reach)* atteindre; *(hurt, annoy)* affecter, toucher. **he** ~ **me!** il m'a frappé!; **his father used to** ~ **him** son père le battait; **to** ~ **sb a blow** porter un coup à qn; *(fig)* **to** ~ **a man when he's down** frapper un homme à terre; **to** ~ **one's head against sth** se cogner *or* se heurter la tête contre qch; **his head** ~ **the pavement** sa tête a donné contre le trottoir; *(fig)* **it** ~**s you in the eye** cela saute aux yeux; **he** ~ **the nail with a hammer** il a tapé sur le clou avec un marteau; *(fig)* **to** ~ **the nail on the head** mettre le doigt dessus; *(fig)* **to** ~ **the mark** atteindre son but; *(fig)* **that** ~ **home!** le coup a porté!; **to be** ~ **by a stone/bullet/bomb** recevoir une pierre/une balle/une bombe; *[plane]* **to be** ~ être touché; *(fig)* **to be** ~ **by a strike/price rise** être touché par une grève/hausse des prix; *(realization)* **then it** ~ **me** * alors j'ai réalisé * d'un seul coup!; **you've** ~ **it!** * ça y est *, tu as trouvé!; *[news, story]* **to** ~ **the papers** *or* **the front page** être à la une * des journaux; **to** ~ **the bottle** * picoler *; *(fig)* **to** ~ **the ceiling** * sortir de ses gonds; **to** ~ **the hay** ‡ se coucher; **to** ~ **the road** * *or* **the trail** * mettre les voiles *. (**b**) *(find)* trouver, tomber sur; *problems, difficulties* rencontrer; *(*: arrive at) town etc* débarquer à *or* dans. **at last we** ~ **the right road** nous sommes tombés enfin sur la bonne route.

4 *vi (collide)* se heurter, se cogner (*against* à, contre).

◆ **hit back** **1** *vi (fig)* riposter. **to** ~ **back at sb** riposter, répondre à qn. **2** *vt sep*: **to** ~ **sb back** rendre son coup à qn. ◆ **hit off** *vt sep likeness* saisir. **he** ~ **him off beautifully** il l'a imité à la perfection; **to** ~ **it off with sb** bien s'entendre avec qn. ◆ **hit out at** *vt fus* décocher un coup à; *(fig)* attaquer. ◆ **hit (up)on** *vt fus* tomber sur, trouver. ◆ **hit-and-run driver** *n* chauffard * *m* (coupable du délit de fuite). ◆ **hit-and-run raid** *n* raid *m* éclair *inv*. ◆ **hitman** tueur *m*. ◆ **hit-or-miss** **1** *adv* au petit bonheur ; **2** *adj work* fait au petit bonheur; *attitude* désinvolte.

hitch [hɪtʃ] **1** *n* anicroche *f* (*in* dans). **without a** ~ sans anicroche; **technical** ~ incident *m* technique. **2** *vt* (**a**) (~**up**) *trousers* remonter (d'une saccade). (**b**) *(fasten)* accrocher (*to* à); *carriages, horses* atteler (*to* à). **to get** ~**ed** ‡ se marier. (**c**) (*) **to** ~ **a lift to Paris** faire du stop * jusqu'à Paris; **I** ~**ed a lift to Paris with my father** je me suis fait emmener en voiture jusqu'à Paris par mon père.

3 *vi* (*) = **hitch-hike.** ◆ **hitch-hike** *vi* faire du stop * *or* de l'auto-stop (*to* jusqu'à). ◆ **hitch-hiker** *n* auto-stoppeur *m*, -euse *f*. ◆ **hitch-hiking** *n* auto-stop *m*.

hither ['hɪðəʳ] *adv* (†) ici. *(not †)* ~ **and thither** çà et là.

hive [haɪv] *n* ruche *f*. **a** ~ **of industry** une vraie ruche. ◆ **hive off** * **1** *vi* se séparer (*from* de). **2** *vt sep* séparer (*from* de).

hoard [hɔ:d] **1** *n* réserves *fpl*, provision *f*; *(treasure)* trésor *m*. **a** ~ **of food** des provisions, des réserves; **a squirrel's** ~ **of nuts** les réserves *or* provisions de noisettes d'un écureuil; **a** ~ **of money** un trésor, un magot; ~**s** * **of things** un tas * de choses. **2** *vt* (~ **up**) *food etc* amasser, mettre en réserve; *money* amasser. ◆ **hoarder** *n*: **to be a** ~**er** ne rien jeter.

hoarding ['hɔ:dɪŋ] *n (fence)* palissade *f*; *(for advertisements)* panneau *m* d'affichage.

hoarfrost ['hɔ:'frɒst] *n* givre *m*.

hoarse [hɔ:s] *adj* enroué. ◆ **hoarsely** *adv* d'une voix enrouée. ◆ **hoarseness** *n* enrouement *m*.

hoary ['hɔ:rɪ] *adj hair* blanc neigeux *inv*; *person* chenu; *(fig)* vénérable; *joke* éculé.

hoax [həʊks] **1** *n* canular *m*. **2** *vt* faire un canular à. **we were** ~**ed** on nous a eus *.

hob [hɒb] *n* plaque *f* chauffante.

hobble ['hɒbl] *vi* clopiner. **to** ~ **in/out** *etc* entrer/sortir *etc* en clopinant.

hobby ['hɒbɪ] *n* passe-temps *inv* favori, hobby *m*. ◆ **hobby-horse** *n (fig)* dada *m*; **he's off on his** ~**-horse** le voilà reparti (sur son dada). ◆ **hobbyist** *n (US)* amateur *m*.

hobnob ['hɒbnɒb] *vi* frayer (*with* avec).

hobo ['həʊbəʊ] *n (US)* vagabond *m*.

hock¹ [hɒk] *n [animal, beef]* jarret *m*.

hock² [hɒk] *n (wine)* vin *m* du Rhin.

hockey ['hɒkɪ] *n (also US* **field** ~*)* hockey *m*; *(US; also Brit* **ice-**~*)* hockey *m* sur glace.

hocus-pocus ['həʊkəs'pəʊkəs] *n (trickery)* supercherie *f*; *(talk)* charabia * *m*.

hoe [həʊ] **1** *n* houe *f*, binette *f*. **2** *vt ground* biner; *plants* sarcler.

hog [hɒg] **1** *n* cochon *m*, porc *m*. **he's a greedy** ~ c'est un vrai goinfre *; *(fig)* **to go the whole** ~ aller jusqu'au bout. **2** *vt* (*) *food* se goinfrer * de; *(take selfishly) best chair etc* accaparer. **don't** ~ **all the sweets** ne garde pas tous les bonbons pour toi.

hoi polloi [ˌhɔɪpə'lɔɪ] *n* gens *mpl* du commun.

hoist [hɔɪst] **1** *vt* hisser. **2** *n* appareil *m* de levage; *(for goods)* monte-charge *m inv*.

hold [həʊld] *(vb: pret, ptp* **held***)* **1** *n* (**a**) prise *f*. **to catch** *or* **get** ~ **of** saisir, s'emparer de; *(fig: contact)* **to get** ~ **of sb** contacter *or* joindre qn; **he caught** ~ **of her arm** il lui a saisi le bras; *(fig)* **can you get** ~ **of a piece of wire?** est-ce que tu peux trouver un morceau de fil de fer?; **to get (a)** ~ **of o.s.** se contrôler; **to have** ~ **of** tenir; **I've got a firm** ~ **on the rope** je tiens bien la corde; **to keep** ~ **of** *object* ne pas lâcher; *idea* s'accrocher à; *(fig)* **to have a** ~ **over sb** avoir prise sur qn; *(US)* **on** ~ *phone call, order* en attente; *(US)* **to put sth on** ~ mettre qch en attente; *(fig)* **no** ~**s barred** * tous les coups sont permis.
(**b**) *(Naut)* cale *f*.
2 *vt* (**a**) *(gen)* tenir; *(contain)* contenir; *(fig) audience* tenir; *sb's interest, attention* retenir; *opinion* avoir. **to** ~ **in one's hand** *book* tenir à la main; *coin* tenir dans la main; **they were** ~**ing hands** ils se tenaient par la main; **he held my arm** il me tenait le bras; **to** ~ **sb tight** *(in embrace)* serrer qn très fort; *(to prevent fall etc)* bien tenir qn; **the bottle** ~**s one litre** la bouteille contient un litre; **the room** ~**s 20 people** 20 personnes peuvent tenir dans la salle; **the ladder won't** ~ **you** l'échelle ne supportera pas ton poids; **the nails** ~ **the carpet in place** les clous maintiennent la moquette en place; **to** ~ **o.s. upright/ready** se tenir droit/prêt; **to** ~ **one's head high** porter la tête haute; *(fig)* **he was left** ~**ing the baby** * tout est retombé sur sa tête; **to** ~ **one's breath** retenir son souffle; **to** ~ **one's tongue** se taire; **to** ~ **one's own** *[invalid]* se maintenir; *(in conversation etc)* se débrouiller; *(Telec)* **to** ~ **the line** attendre; ~ **the line!** ne quittez pas!; **this car** ~**s the road well** cette voiture tient bien la route; **what the future** ~**s** ce que l'avenir nous réserve.
(**b**) *meeting, election, conversation etc* tenir; *examination* organiser; *check, count* faire. **the exhibition is always held here** l'exposition a toujours lieu ici; *(Rel)* **to** ~ **a service** célébrer un office; *[employer]* **to** ~ **an interview** recevoir des candidats.
(**c**) *(believe)* considérer, maintenir (*that* que). **to** ~ **in high esteem** tenir en haute estime; **to** ~ **sb responsible for sth** considérer qn responsable de qch; **all that he** ~**s dear** tout ce qui lui est cher.
(**d**) *(restrain) person* retenir; *(keep) object, money* garder. **to** ~ **a train** empêcher un train de partir; ~ **the letter until...** n'envoyez pas la lettre avant que... + *subj*; **the police held him for 2 days** la police l'a gardé (à vue) pendant 2 jours; **there's no** ~**ing him** il n'y a pas moyen de le retenir; ~ **it!** * arrêtez!, minute! *
(**e**) *(possess) ticket, card* avoir, posséder; *(Mil)* tenir (*against* contre); *post, position* avoir, occuper; *ticket, permit, shares* avoir, détenir; *(Sport) record* détenir. *(Parl)* **to** ~ **office** avoir *or* tenir un portefeuille; *(fig)* **to** ~ **the fort** monter la garde; *(fig)* **to** ~ **the stage** tenir le devant de la scène.
3 *vi [rope, nail etc]* tenir, être solide; *[weather]* se maintenir; *[statement, promise] (also* ~ **good***)* être valable. **to** ~ **firm** *or* **tight** *or* **fast** tenir bon *or* ferme.
◆ **hold back** **1** *vi (fig)* se retenir (*from sth* de qch; *from doing* de faire). **2** *vt sep* (**a**) *fears, emotions* maîtriser; *crowd* contenir. **to** ~ **sb back from doing** retenir qn de faire. (**b**) *(not disclose) facts, name* ne pas donner. **he was** ~**ing sth back from me** il me cachait qch. (**c**) *(US Scol) pupil* faire redoubler une classe à. ◆ **hold down** *vt sep* (**a**) *(keep on ground)* maintenir à terre; *(keep in place)* maintenir en place. **to** ~ **one's head down** tenir la tête baissée. (**b**) *job (have)* avoir, occuper; *(keep)* garder. ◆ **hold forth** *vi* pérorer (*on* sur). ◆ **hold in** *vt sep* retenir; *stomach* rentrer. *(fig)* **to** ~ **o.s. in** se retenir. ◆ **hold off** **1** *vi (fig)* **the rain has held off so far** jusqu'ici il n'a pas plu. **2** *vt sep enemy* tenir à distance; *(fig) visitor etc* faire patienter. ◆ **hold on** **1** *vi (endure)* tenir bon, tenir le coup; *(wait)* attendre. ~ **on!** attendez!; *(Telec)* ne quittez pas! **2** *vt sep lid etc* tenir en place. ◆ **hold on to** *vt fus (cling to) rope, branch* se cramponner à; *hope, idea* se raccrocher à; *(keep) object, money* garder; *used clothes etc* conserver. ~ **on to this for me** *(hold it)* tiens-moi ça; *(keep it)* garde-moi ça. ◆ **hold out** **1** *vi* (**a**) *[supplies etc]* durer. (**b**) *(endure)* tenir bon, tenir le coup. **to** ~ **out against** *enemy, attacks* tenir bon devant; *change, progress, threats* résister à; **they are** ~**ing out for more pay** ils tiennent bon pour avoir une augmentation; **you've been** ~**ing out on me!** * tu m'as caché qch! **2** *vt sep* tendre, offrir (*sth to sb* qch à qn); *one's arms* ouvrir; *(fig) hope* offrir. ◆ **hold over** *vt sep meeting etc* remettre (*until* à). ◆ **hold together** **1** *vi [objects]* tenir (ensemble); *[people]* rester unis. **2** *vt sep objects* maintenir (ensemble); *a group* maintenir l'union de. ◆ **hold up** **1** *vi [building]* tenir debout. **2** *vt sep* (**a**) *(raise)* lever, élever. ~ **up your hand** levez la main; **to** ~ **sth up to the light** élever qch à la

lumière. (**b**) *(support) roof etc* soutenir. (**c**) *(stop)* arrêter; *(delay) traffic* retarder; *person* retenir. (**d**) *[robber] bank, shop* faire un hold-up dans ; *coach, person* attaquer (à main armée). ◆ **hold with** * *vt fus*: **she doesn't ~ with people smoking** elle désapprouve que l'on fume *(subj)*.

◆ **holdall** *n* fourre-tout *m inv*. ◆ **holder** *n* (**a**) *[ticket, card, record, title, stocks]* détenteur *m*, -trice *f*; *[passport, post]* titulaire *mf*; (**b**) *(object)* support *m*; **pen ~er** porte-plume *m inv*. ◆ **holding** *n (farm)* propriété *f*, ferme *f*; *(Fin)* **~ings** *(lands)* avoirs *mpl* fonciers; *(stocks)* intérêts *mpl*; *(Fin)* **~ing company** holding *m*. ◆ **hold-up** *n (robbery)* hold-up *m inv*, attaque *f* à main armée; *(delay)* retard *m*; *(in traffic)* bouchon *m*.

hole [həʊl] *n* (**a**) *(gen)* trou *m*; *[rabbit, fox]* terrier *m*; *(in defences, dam)* brèche *f*; *(in argument etc)* faille *f*. **to wear a ~ in a garment** trouer un vêtement; *[sock etc]* **to go into ~s** se trouer; *(fig)* **it made a ~ in his savings** cela a fait un trou dans ses économies; **to be in a (nasty) ~** * avoir des ennuis, être dans l'embarras; **he got me out of a ~** * il m'a tiré d'embarras *. (**b**) *(* pej) (town)* bled * *m*; *(room, house)* bouge *m*. ◆ **hole up** *vi [animal, wanted man]* se terrer. ◆ **hole-and-corner** *adj (furtive)* furtif; *(underhand)* fait en douce *. ◆ **hole-in-the-heart** *n (Med)* communication *f* interventriculaire. ◆ **holey** *adj* plein de trous.

holiday ['hɒlɪdeɪ] **1** *n (vacation)* vacances *fpl*; *(day off)* jour *m* de congé. **on ~** en vacances, en congé ; **to take a month's ~** prendre un mois de vacances; **~s with pay** congés *mpl* payés; **school ~s** vacances scolaires. **2** *vi* passer ses vacances. **3** *adj camp, clothes, atmosphere* de vacances; *mood etc* gai, joyeux. **~ resort** villégiature *f*; **~ season** saison *f* des vacances; **~ spirit** esprit *m* de vacances; **~ traffic** circulation *f* des départs (*or* des rentrées) de vacances. ◆ **holiday-maker** *n* vacancier *m*, -ière *f*; *(in summer)* estivant(e) *m(f)*.

Holland ['hɒlənd] *n* Hollande *f*, Pays-Bas *mpl*.

holler * ['hɒləʳ] **1** *n* braillement *m*. **2** *vti* brailler.

hollow ['hɒləʊ] **1** *adj (gen)* creux; *eyes* cave; *sound (from box etc)* creux; *(from cave etc)* caverneux; *voice* caverneux; *sympathy, victory* faux; *promise* vain. **to give a ~ laugh** rire jaune. **2** *n [back, hand, tree]* creux *m*; *(in ground)* dénivellation *f*; *(valley)* cuvette *f*. **3** *vt* (**~ out**) creuser. ◆ **hollow-cheeked** *adj* aux joues creuses. ◆ **hollow-eyed** *adj* aux yeux caves.

holly ['hɒlɪ] *n* houx *m*. **~ bush** buisson *m* de houx.

hollyhock ['hɒlɪhɒk] *n* rose *f* trémière.

holocaust ['hɒləkɔːst] *n* holocauste *m*.

hologram ['hɒləˌgræm] *n* hologramme *m*.

holster ['həʊlstəʳ] *n* étui *m* de revolver.

holy ['həʊlɪ] **1** *adj place, life, poverty* saint *(after n)*; *person, oil, Bible, Communion, Trinity* saint *(before n)*; *bread, water* bénit; *ground* sacré. **the H~ Father** le Saint-Père; **the H~ Ghost** *or* **Spirit** le Saint-Esprit; **the H~ Land** la Terre Sainte; **~ orders** ordres *mpl* (majeurs); **H~ Week** la Semaine Sainte; **he's a ~ terror** * c'est un vrai démon. **2** *n*: **the ~ of holies** le Saint des Saints. ◆ **holiness** *n* sainteté *f*; **His Holiness** Sa Sainteté.

homage ['hɒmɪdʒ] *n* hommage *m*. **to pay ~ to** rendre hommage à.

home [həʊm] **1** *n* (**a**) maison *f*; *(Bot, Zool)* habitat *m*. **he left ~ in 1978** il a quitté la maison en 1978; **he was glad to see his ~ again** il était content de revoir sa maison; **it is quite near my ~** c'est tout près de chez moi; **my ~ is in London** *(live there)* j'habite Londres; *(was born there)* je suis de Londres; **~ for me is Edinburgh** c'est à Édimbourg que j'ai mes racines; **for some years he made his ~ in France** pendant quelques années il a habité en France; **refugees who made their ~ in Britain** les réfugiés qui se sont installés en Grande-Bretagne; **he is far from ~** il est loin de chez lui; **there's no place like ~** on n'est vraiment bien que chez soi; **to have a ~ of one's own** avoir un foyer *or* un chez-soi; **to give sb a ~** recueillir qn chez soi; **she made a ~ for her brothers** elle a fait un (vrai) foyer pour ses frères; **it's a ~ from ~** c'est un second chez-soi; **she has a lovely ~** elle a un joli intérieur; **he comes from a good ~** il a une famille comme il faut; **'good ~ wanted for kitten'** 'cherche foyer accueillant pour chaton'; **a broken ~** un foyer désuni; **safety in the ~** prudence à la maison; **at ~** chez soi, à la maison; *(Ftbl)* **Celtic are playing Rangers at ~** le Celtic reçoit les Rangers; *(fig)* **Mrs Smith is not at ~ to anyone** Mme Smith ne reçoit personne; **to feel at ~** se sentir à l'aise (*with sb/sth* avec qn/qch); **to make o.s. at ~** faire comme chez soi.

(**b**) pays *m* natal, patrie *f*. **at ~ and abroad** chez nous et à l'étranger; *(fig)* **let us consider sth nearer ~** considérons qch qui nous intéresse plus directement.

(**c**) *(institution)* maison *f*, institution *f*. **children's ~** maison pour enfants.

2 *adv* (**a**) chez soi, à la maison. **to go** *or* **get ~** rentrer (chez soi *or* à la maison); **I'll be ~ at 5 o'clock** je rentrerai à 5 heures; **on the journey ~** sur le chemin du retour; **to see sb ~** accompagner qn jusque chez lui; **I must write ~** il faut que j'écrive à la maison; **it's nothing to write ~ about** * ça ne casse rien *; *(fig)* **~ and dry** sauvé des eaux *(fig)*.

(**b**) *(from abroad)* **he came ~** il est rentré de l'étranger; **to send sb ~** rapatrier qn; **to go** *or* **return ~** rentrer dans son pays.

(**c**) *(right in etc) hammer, drive* à fond. *(fig)* **to bring sth ~ to sb** faire comprendre qch à qn; **the situation was brought ~ to him when...** la situation lui est apparue pleinement quand...

3 *adj atmosphere, life* de famille, familial; *troubles* de famille, domestique; *comforts* du foyer; *cooking* familial; *[doctor etc] visit* à domicile; *(Econ, Pol etc)* du pays, national; *policy, market, sales etc* intérieur; *(Sport) team etc* qui reçoit; *match* joué à domicile. **~ address** domicile *m* (permanent); *(as opp to business address)* adresse *f* personnelle; *(Baseball)* **~ base** base *f* de départ; **~ computer** ordinateur *m* familial; **the ~ country** le vieux pays; **~ economics** économie *f* domestique; *(Pol etc)* **on the ~ front** à l'intérieur; **~ help** aide *f* ménagère; **~ leave** congé *m* de longue durée; **~ loan** prêt *m* immobilier; **~ news** *(gen)* nouvelles *fpl* de chez soi; *(Pol)* nouvelles de l'intérieur; *(Brit)* **H~ Office** ≃ ministère *m* de l'Intérieur; **~ owners** ceux qui possèdent leur propre habitation; *(Naut)* **~ port** port *m* d'attache; **~ rule** autonomie *f*; **~ run** *[ship, truck]* voyage *m* de retour; *(Baseball)* coup *m* de circuit; *(Brit)* **H~ Secretary** ≃ ministre *m* de l'Intérieur; *(fig)* **to be in the ~ straight** voir la lumière au bout du tunnel; **my ~ town** *(place of birth)* ma ville natale; *(where I grew up)* la ville où j'ai grandi; **~ truths** vérités *fpl* bien senties.

4 *vi [pigeons]* revenir au colombier.

◆ **home in on, home on to** *vt fus* se diriger (automatiquement) vers *or* sur.

◆ **home-baked** *or* **-brewed** *or* **-cooked** *etc adj* fait à la maison. ◆ **homecoming** *n* retour *m* au foyer (*or* au pays). ◆ **home-grown** *adj (not foreign)* du pays; *(from own garden)* du jardin. ◆ **homeland** *n* patrie *f*. ◆ **homeless** **1** *adj* sans abri ; **2** *npl*: **the ~less** les sans-abri *mpl*. ◆ **homelike** *adj* accueillant, confortable. ◆ **home-lover** *n* casanier *m*, -ière *f*. ◆ **home-loving** *adj* casanier. ◆ **homely** *adj* (**a**) *food, person* simple; *atmosphere* confortable; (**b**) *(US: plain)* laid. ◆ **home-made** *adj* fait à la maison. ◆ **homesick** *adj* nostalgique; **to be ~sick** avoir la nostalgie (*for sth* de qch); *(abroad)* avoir le mal du pays. ◆ **homesickness** *n* nostalgie *f* (*for* de), mal *m* du pays. ◆ **homespun** *adj (fig)* simple. ◆ **homestead** *n (house etc)* propriété *f*; *(farm)* ferme *f*. ◆ **homeward** **1** *adj* du retour; **~ward journey** retour *m* ; **2** *adv (also* **~wards***)* vers la maison; **~ward bound** sur le chemin du retour. ◆ **homework** *n* devoirs *mpl* (à la maison). ◆ **homing** *adj missile* à tête chercheuse; **homing device** tête *f* chercheuse; **homing pigeon** pigeon *m* voyageur.

homicide ['hɒmɪsaɪd] *n* homicide *m*. ◆ **homicidal** *adj* homicide.

hominy grits ['hɒmɪnɪ'grɪts] *n (US)* maïs *m* concassé et bouilli.

homoeopath, *(US)* **homeopath** ['həʊmɪə(ʊ)pæθ] *n* homéopathe *mf*. ◆ **hom(o)eopathic** *adj medicine, methods* homéopathique; *doctor* homéopathe. ◆ **hom(o)eopathy** *n* homéopathie *f*.

homogeneity [ˌhɒməʊdʒə'ni:ɪtɪ] *n* homogénéité *f*. ◆ **homogeneous** [ˌhɒmə'dʒi:nɪəs] *adj* homogène. ◆ **homogenize** [hə'mɒdʒənaɪz] *vt* homogénéiser.

homonym ['hɒmənɪm] *n* homonyme *m*.

homosexual ['hɒmə(ʊ)'seksjʊəl] *adj, n* homosexuel(le) *m(f)*. ◆ **homosexuality** *n* homosexualité *f*.

Honduras [hɒn'djʊərəs] *n* Honduras *m*.

hone [həʊn] *vt* aiguiser.

honest ['ɒnɪst] *adj person, action* honnête; *opinion* sincère; *face* franc; *means, method* légitime; *money, profit* honnêtement acquis. **the ~ truth** la pure vérité; **tell me your ~ opinion of it** dites-moi sincèrement ce que vous en pensez; **to be ~ with you, I don't like it** à vous dire la vérité, je n'aime pas ça; **be ~!** parle franchement!; *(be objective)* sois objectif!; **you've not been ~ with me** tu n'as pas été franc avec moi; **an ~ day's work** une bonne journée de travail; **~ to goodness!** * ça alors! ◆ **honestly** *adv act, behave* honnêtement; **~ly, I don't care** franchement, ça m'est égal; **I didn't do it, ~ly!** je ne l'ai pas fait, je vous le jure!; **~ly?** c'est vrai?; *(exasperated)* **~ly!** ça alors! ◆ **honesty** *n* (**a**) honnêteté *f*; **in all ~y** en toute sincérité; (**b**) *(Bot)* monnaie-du-pape *f*.

honey ['hʌnɪ] *n* miel *m*. **clear/thick ~** miel liquide/solide; **yes, ~** * oui, chéri(e); **she's a ~** * elle est adorable. ◆ **honeybee** *n* abeille *f*. ◆ **honeycomb** **1** *n* rayon *m* de miel; *(Tex)* nid *m* d'abeille; *(Metal)* soufflure *f* ; **2** *adj pattern* en nid d'abeille; **3** *vt (fig)* cribler (*with* de). ◆ **honeyed** *adj words* mielleux. ◆ **honeymoon** **1** *n* lune *f* de miel ; **2** *vi* passer sa lune de miel ; **3** *adj*: **the ~moon couple** les nouveaux mariés *mpl ; (fig)* **the ~moon period** *(gen)* la lune de miel; *(Pol)* l'état de grâce. ◆ **honeysuckle** *n* chèvrefeuille *m*.

Hong Kong ['hɒŋ'kɒŋ] *n* Hong Kong.

honk [hɒŋk] *vi [car]* klaxonner; *[geese]* cacarder.

honor *etc (US)* = **honour** *etc*.

honorary ['ɒn(ə)rərɪ] *adj person* honoraire; *duties* honorifique. **~ degree** grade *m* honoris causa.

honour, *(US)* **honor** ['ɒnəʳ] **1** *n* honneur *m*. **in ~ of** en l'honneur de; **on my ~!** parole d'honneur!; **to put sb on his ~ to do** engager qn sur l'honneur à faire; **to be (in) ~ bound to do** être tenu par l'honneur de faire; **to have the ~ to do** *or* **of doing** avoir l'honneur de faire; **Your H~** Votre Honneur; **to do the ~s** faire les présentations *(entre invités)*; *(Univ)* **he got first-/second-class ~s in English** ≃ il a eu sa licence d'anglais avec mention très bien/mention bien. **2** *vt* honorer (*with* de). ◆ **hono(u)rable** *adj* honorable. ◆ **hono(u)rably** *adv* honorablement.

hooch ‡ [hu:tʃ] *n* gnôle * *f*.

hood [hʊd] *n (gen)* capuchon *m*; *(Ku Klux Klan type)* cagoule *f*; *(rain-~)* capuche *f*; *(Brit Aut)* capote *f*; *(US Aut)* capot *m*; *[pram]* capote; *(over cooker etc)* hotte *f*. ◆ **hooded** *adj* encapuchonné; *prisoner, gunman* au visage couvert. ◆ **hoodlum** *n (US)* voyou *m*. ◆ **hoodwink** *vt* tromper.

hooey ‡ ['hu:ɪ] *n* blagues * *fpl*.

hoof, *pl* **~s** *or* **hooves** [hu:f, hu:vz] sabot *m (d'animal)*.

hoo-ha * ['hu:ˌhɑ:] *n (noise)* brouhaha *m*; *(excitement)* animation *f*; *(pej: publicity)* baratin * *m*. **there was a great ~ about it** on en a fait tout un plat *.

hook [hʊk] **1** *n (gen)* crochet *m*; *(for coats)* patère *f*; *(on dress)* agrafe *f*; *(Fishing)* hameçon *m*; *(Agr)* faucille *f*; *(Boxing)* crochet. *(Sewing)* **~s and eyes** agrafes; *(fig)* **he swallowed it ~, line and sinker** * il a gobé tout ce qu'on lui a raconté; **by ~ or by crook** par tous les moyens; **to get sb off the ~** * tirer qn d'affaire. **2** *vt* accrocher (*to* à); *(Fishing)* prendre; *dress* agrafer. **she finally ~ed him** * elle a fini par lui passer la corde au cou. ◆ **hook on** **1** *vi* s'accrocher (*to* à). **2** *vt sep* accrocher (*to* à). ◆ **hook up** *vt sep dress etc* agrafer; *(*: TV etc)* faire un duplex entre. ◆ **hooked** *adj (hook-shaped)* recourbé; *(having hooks)* muni de crochets; *(*: fascinated)* accroché; *(fig)* **he's ~ed * on it** il ne peut plus s'en passer; **to get ~ed * on drugs** se droguer; **to get ~ed * on jazz** devenir enragé * de jazz; **he's really ~ed * on her** il en est fou. ◆ **hook-nosed** *adj* au nez recourbé. ◆ **hook-up** * *n (TV etc)* relais *m* temporaire. ◆ **hooky** ‡ *n*: **to play ~y** ‡ sécher les cours.

hooligan ['hu:lɪgən] *n* voyou *m*. ◆ **hooliganism** *n* vandalisme *m*.

hoop [hu:p] *n [barrel]* cercle *m*; *(toy; in circus; for skirt)* cerceau *m*; *(Croquet)* arceau *m*. *(fig)* **they put him through the ~** * ils l'ont mis sur la sellette. ◆ **hoopla** *n* jeu *m* d'anneaux.

hoot [hu:t] **1** *vi [owl]* hululer; *(Aut)* klaxonner; *[siren]* mugir; *[train]* siffler; *(jeer)* huer; *(with laughter)* s'esclaffer. **2** *n* hululement *m*; coup *m* de klaxon; mugissement *m*; sifflement *m*; huée *f*. **I don't care a ~** * je m'en fiche * éperdument; **it was a ~** ‡ c'était tordant * *or* marrant ‡. ◆ **hooter** *n [factory]* sirène *f*; *(Aut)* klaxon *m*.

hoover ['hu:vəʳ] ® **1** *n* aspirateur *m*. **2** *vt* passer l'aspirateur sur *or* dans.

hop[1] [hɒp] **1** *n (gen)* saut *m*; *[bird]* sautillement *m*; *(*: dance)* sauterie *f*; *(Aviat)* étape *f*. *(fig)* **to catch sb on the ~** prendre qn au dépourvu. **2** *vi* sauter; *(on one foot)* sauter à cloche-pied; *[bird]* sautiller. **he ~ped over to the window** il est allé à cloche-pied jusqu'à la fenêtre; *(in car etc)* **~ in!** montez!; **to ~ off, to ~ it** * ficher le camp *. ◆ **hopscotch** *n* marelle *f*.

hop[2] [hɒp] *n (also* **~s***)* houblon *m*. ◆ **hopfield** *n* houblonnière *f*. ◆ **hop-picker** *n* cueilleur *m*, -euse *f* de houblon.

hope [həʊp] **1** *n* espoir *m*. **past** *or* **beyond (all) ~** sans espoir; **to live in ~** vivre d'espoir; **in the ~ of (doing) sth** dans l'espoir de (faire) qch; **to have ~s of doing** avoir l'espoir de faire; **I haven't much ~ of succeeding** je n'ai pas beaucoup d'espoir de réussir; **there is no ~ of that** on ne peut pas y compter; **with high ~s** avec l'espoir de faire de grandes choses; **to raise sb's ~s** donner de l'espoir à qn; **you're my last ~** tu es mon dernier espoir; **what a ~! *, some ~! *** tu parles! * **2** *vti* espérer (*that* que; *to do* faire). **to ~ for success** espérer avoir du succès; **don't ~ for too much** n'en attendez pas trop; **to ~ for the best** être optimiste; **to ~ against hope** espérer en dépit de tout; **hoping to hear from you** dans l'espoir d'avoir de vos nouvelles; **I ~ so/not** j'espère que oui/non. ◆ **hopeful** **1** *adj person* plein d'espoir; *situation* qui promet; *response, sign* encourageant; *future* qui se présente bien; **we are ~ful about the results** nous attendons avec confiance les résultats; **I am ~ful that...** j'ai bon espoir que...; **I'm not too ~ful** je n'ai pas tellement d'espoir ; **2** *n*: **a young ~ful** un jeune loup *(fig)*. ◆ **hopefully** *adv* (**a**) *speak, smile* avec optimisme; *develop, progress* d'une façon encourageante; (**b**) *(esp US)* **~fully * it won't rain** on espère qu'il ne va pas pleuvoir. ◆ **hopeless** *adj person, situation, outlook* désespéré; *task* impossible; *(*: bad) work* lamentable, nul; *person* bon à rien; *liar, drunkard etc* invétéré, incorrigible; **it's ~less!** c'est désespérant; **he's a ~less * teacher** il est nul comme professeur; **I'm ~less * at maths** je suis nul en maths; **he's ~less *** c'est un cas désespéré. ◆ **hopelessly** *adv act* sans espoir; *speak* avec désespoir; *lost etc* complètement; *in love* éperdument; **~lessly naïve** *etc* d'une naïveté *etc* désespérante.

horde [hɔ:d] *n* foule *f*, horde *f (pej)*.

horizon [həˈraɪzn] *n* horizon *m (also fig)*. **on the ~** à l'horizon. ◆ **horizontal 1** *adj* horizontal ; **2** *n* horizontale *f*. ◆ **horizontally** *adv* horizontalement.

hormone [ˈhɔ:məʊn] *n* hormone *f*. **~ treatment** traitement *m* hormonal.

horn [hɔ:n] *n (gen)* corne *f*; *(Mus)* cor *m*; *(Aut)* klaxon *m*; *(Naut)* sirène *f*. **to draw in one's ~s** *(back down)* diminuer d'ardeur; *(spend less)* restreindre son train de vie. ◆ **horn-rimmed spectacles** *npl* lunettes *fpl* à monture d'écaille. ◆ **horny** *adj hands* calleux.

hornet [ˈhɔ:nɪt] *n* frelon *m*.

horoscope [ˈhɒrəskəʊp] *n* horoscope *m*.

horrible [ˈhɒrɪbl] *adj sight, murder* horrible; *holiday, weather etc* affreux, atroce. ◆ **horribly** *adv* horriblement; affreusement.

horrid [ˈhɒrɪd] *adj person* méchant; *thing* affreux.

horrify [ˈhɒrɪfaɪ] *vt* horrifier. ◆ **horrific** *adj* horrible. ◆ **horrifying** *adj* horrifiant.

horror [ˈhɒrəʳ] **1** *n* horreur *f*. **to have a ~ of (doing) sth** avoir horreur de (faire) qch; **that child is a ~ *** cet enfant est un petit monstre; **that gives me the ~s *** cela me donne le frisson. **2** *adj film, comic* d'épouvante. ◆ **horror-stricken** *adj* glacé d'horreur.

horse [hɔ:s] **1** *n* cheval *m*; *(Gymnastics)* cheval *m* d'arçons. *(fig)* **straight from the ~'s mouth** de source sûre. **2** *adj race* de chevaux; *meat* de cheval. **~ brass** médaillon *m* de cuivre (d'une martingale); **~ chestnut** marron *m* (d'Inde); *(tree)* marronnier *m* (d'Inde); *(Cine, TV)* **~ opera *** western *m* ; **~ show** *or* **trials** concours *m* hippique.
◆ **horseback** *n*: **on ~back** à cheval. ◆ **horse-box** *n (Aut)* fourgon *m* à chevaux. ◆ **horse-dealer** *n* maquignon *m*. ◆ **horse-drawn** *adj* à chevaux. ◆ **horseflesh** *n (horses)* chevaux *mpl*; *(Culin)* viande *f* de cheval. ◆ **horsefly** *n* taon *m*. ◆ **horsehair** *n* crin *m* (de cheval). ◆ **horse-laugh** *n* gros rire *m*. ◆ **horseman** *n* cavalier *m*. ◆ **horsemanship** *n (activity)* équitation *f*; *(skill)* talent *m* de cavalier. ◆ **horseplay** *n* jeu *m* de mains; chahut *m*. ◆ **horsepower** *n* puissance *f* (en chevaux). ◆ **horse-racing** *n* courses *fpl* de chevaux. ◆ **horseradish** *n* raifort *m*. ◆ **horse-sense *** *n* gros bon sens *m*. ◆ **horseshoe 1** *n* fer *m* à cheval ; **2** *adj* en fer à cheval. ◆ **horse-trader** *n (lit, fig)* maquignon *m*. ◆ **horse-trading** *n* maquignonnage *m*. ◆ **horsewhip** *vt* cravacher. ◆ **horsey *** *adj person* féru de cheval; *appearance* chevalin.

horticulture [ˈhɔ:tɪkʌltʃəʳ] *n* horticulture *f*. ◆ **horticultural** *adj* horticole. ◆ **horticulturist** *n* horticulteur *m*, -trice *f*.

hose [həʊz] **1** *n* (**a**) *(also* **~pipe***)* tuyau *m*. (**b**) *(pl: stockings)* bas *mpl*. **2** *vt (in garden)* arroser au jet; *[firemen]* arroser à la lance. **to ~ sth down** *or* **out** laver qch au jet. ◆ **hosiery** *n* bonneterie *f*.

hospice [ˈhɒspɪs] *n* hospice *m*.

hospitable [hɒsˈpɪtəbl] *adj* hospitalier. ◆ **hospitably** *adv* avec hospitalité. ◆ **hospitality** [ˌhɒspɪˈtælɪtɪ] *n* hospitalité *f*.

hospital [ˈhɒspɪtl] **1** *n* hôpital *m*. **in ~** à l'hôpital. **2** *adj treatment, staff* hospitalier; *bed etc* d'hôpital. **~ case** patient *m* hospitalisé; **the ~ doctors** les médecins *mpl* des hôpitaux; **the ~ facilities** *or* **service** le service hospitalier. ◆ **hospitalize** *vt* hospitaliser.

host¹ [həʊst] **1** *n* hôte *m*. **2** *adj plant, animal* hôte; *town etc* qui reçoit; *country* d'accueil. **3** *vt TV show* animer. ◆ **hostess** *n* hôtesse *f*; *(in night club)* entraîneuse *f*.

host² [həʊst] *n [people]* foule *f*; *[reasons]* tas * *m*.

host³ [həʊst] *n (Rel)* hostie *f*.

hostage [ˈhɒstɪdʒ] *n* otage *m*. **to take sb ~** prendre qn comme otage.

hostel [ˈhɒst(ə)l] **1** *n (gen)* foyer *m*. **(youth) ~** auberge *f* de jeunesse. **2** *vi*: **to go (youth) ~ling** passer ses vacances dans des auberges de jeunesse. ◆ **hosteller** *n* ajiste *mf*.

hostile [ˈhɒstaɪl] *adj* hostile (*to* à). ◆ **hostility** *n* hostilité *f*.

hot [hɒt] **1** *adj* (**a**) *(gen)* chaud; *sun* brûlant. **to be ~** *[person]* avoir (très *or* trop) chaud; *[thing]* être (très) chaud; *(Met)* faire (très) chaud; **this room is ~** il fait (très *or* trop) chaud dans cette pièce; **to get ~** *[person]* s'échauffer; *(in guessing)* brûler; *[thing]* chauffer; *(Met)* commencer à faire chaud; **~ spring** source *f* chaude; **in the ~ weather** pendant les chaleurs; **I can't drink ~ things** je ne peux pas boire chaud; *(fig)* **in the ~ seat** en première ligne; *(Med)* **~ flush** bouffée *f* de chaleur; *(fig)* **to be in/get into ~ water** être/se mettre dans le pétrin; **to be ~ and bothered** *(perspiring)* être en nage; *(flustered)* être dans tous ses états (*about* au sujet de); **to be/get ~ under the collar *** être/se mettre dans tous ses états (*about* au sujet de); *(fig)* **~ air *** blablabla * *m*; *(Culin)* **~ dog** hot-dog *m*; *(Telec)* **~ line** téléphone *m* rouge (*to* avec); *(fig)* **~ potato *** sujet *m* brûlant; **he dropped the idea like a ~ potato *** il a laissé tomber comme si ça lui brûlait les doigts; **~ spot *** *(trouble area)* point *m or* coin *m* névralgique; *(night club)* boîte *f* (de nuit); **to be ~ stuff *** être sensationnel *; *(US)* **~ tub** jacuzzi *m*.
(**b**) *curry, spices etc* fort; *news, report* tout frais; *struggle, dispute* acharné; *temperament, supporter* passionné. **~ jazz** hot *m*; **he's got a ~ temper** il est très colérique; *(Pol)* **a ~ war *** une guerre ouverte; **~ favourite** grand favori *m*; **~ tip** tuyau *m* sûr; **news ~ from the press** informations de dernière minute; **to make things ~ for sb *** mener la vie dure à qn; **not so ~ *** pas formidable *; **he's pretty ~ * at maths** il a la bosse * des maths; **he's pretty ~ * at football** il est très calé en football; *(stolen)* **it's ~ ⁑** ça a été volé. **2** *adv*: **to be ~ on the trail** être sur la bonne piste; **~ on sb's trail** sur les talons de qn; **he went at it ~ and strong** il n'y est pas allé de main morte *; **to give it to sb ~ and strong *** sonner les cloches à qn *.
◆ **hot up * 1** *vi [food etc]* se réchauffer; *[situation, party]* chauffer *. **2** *vt sep food* réchauffer; *evening* mettre de l'animation dans; *music* faire balancer *; *car engine* gonfler *. **a ~ted-up Mini** une Mini au moteur gonflé.
◆ **hot-air balloon** *n* ballon *m (Aviat)*. ◆ **hotbed** *n* foyer *m (de vice etc)*. ◆ **hot-blooded** *adj* passionné. ◆ **hotfoot 1** *adv* à toute vitesse ; **2** *vt*: **to ~foot it *** galoper. ◆ **hothead** *n* tête *f* brûlée. ◆ **hotheaded** *adj* impétueux. ◆ **hothouse** *n* serre *f* (chaude). ◆ **hotly** *adv* passionnément, violemment. ◆ **hotplate** *n* plaque *f* chauffante.

◆ **hotpot** *n* ragoût *m*. ◆ **hotrod** * *n (Aut)* voiture *f* gonflée *. ◆ **hotshot** *n (US)* gros bonnet *m*. ◆ **hot-tempered** *adj* colérique. ◆ **hot-water bottle** *n* bouillotte *f*.

hotchpotch ['hɒtʃpɒtʃ] *n* fatras *m*.

hotel [hə(ʊ)tel] **1** *n* hôtel *m*. **2** *adj prices, porter, room* d'hôtel. **the ~ industry** l'industrie hôtelière; **he's looking for ~ work** il cherche un travail dans l'hôtellerie; **~ workers** le personnel hôtelier. ◆ **hotelier** *or* ◆ **hotelkeeper** *n* hôtelier *m*, -ière *f*.

hound [haʊnd] **1** *n* chien *m* courant. **the ~s** la meute; **to ride to ~s** chasser à courre. **2** *vt debtor etc* traquer (*for sth* pour obtenir qch). **to ~ sb out of town** chasser qn hors de la ville; **to ~ sb down** (traquer et) capturer qn.

hour ['aʊə^r] **1** *n* heure *f*. **~ by ~** heure par heure; **80 km an ~** 80 km à l'heure; **to pay sb by the ~** payer qn à l'heure; **she is paid £2 an ~** elle est payée 2 livres (de) l'heure; *(lit, fig)* **she's been waiting for ~s** elle attend depuis des heures; **on the ~** toutes les heures à l'heure juste; **his ~ has come** son heure est venue; **in the early** *or* **small ~s (of the morning)** au petit matin; **at all ~s (of the day and night)** à toute heure (du jour et de la nuit); **at this ~** à cette heure-ci; *(fig)* **at this late ~** à ce stade avancé; **in the ~ of danger** à l'heure du danger; **to keep regular ~s** avoir une vie réglée; **to work long ~s** avoir une journée très longue; **after ~s** après l'heure de fermeture; **out of ~s** en dehors des heures d'ouverture. **2** *adj [watch etc]* **~ hand** petite aiguille *f*. ◆ **hourglass** *n* sablier *m*. ◆ **hourly** **1** *adj (every hour) bus service etc* toutes les heures; *(per hour) rate* horaire; *(incessant) fear* constant ; **2** *adv* toutes les heures; *(fig)* continuellement; **~ly paid workers** ouvriers payés à l'heure.

house [haʊs] **1** *n* (**a**) maison *f*. **at** *or* **to my ~** chez moi; *(fig)* **they got on like a ~ on fire** ils s'entendaient comme larrons en foire; **the children were playing at ~(s)** les enfants jouaient à papa et maman; **~ of cards** château *m* de cartes; *(US)* **~ of correction** maison d'arrêt; **she looks after the ~ herself** c'est elle qui s'occupe de son ménage; **she needs more help in the ~** il faudrait qu'elle soit plus aidée à la maison; **to keep ~** tenir la maison (*for sb* de qn); *(fig)* **to put one's ~ in order** mettre de l'ordre dans ses affaires. (**b**) *(Parl)* **the H~** la Chambre; **H~ of Commons/of Lords** Chambre des communes/des lords; *(US)* **H~ of Representatives** Chambre des députés; **the H~s of Parliament** le Palais de Westminster. (**c**) *(Theat etc)* salle *f*, spectateurs *mpl*. **in the front of the ~** parmi les spectateurs; **a full** *or* **good ~** une salle pleine; **to play to full ~s** jouer à guichets fermés; **'~ full'** 'complet'; **the second ~** la deuxième séance; *(fig)* **to bring the ~ down** faire crouler la salle sous les applaudissements. (**d**) *(Comm, Rel etc)* maison *f*. **the H~ of Windsor** la maison des Windsors; **banking ~** établissement *m* bancaire; **business ~** maison de commerce; **publishing ~** maison d'édition; *(fig: free)* **on the ~** aux frais de la maison.

2 *adj prices, sale* immobilier. **~ plant** plante *f* d'intérieur.

3 [haʊz] *vt [person, town council etc]* loger; *[building]* abriter. **the freezer is ~d in the basement** on garde le congélateur au sous-sol.

◆ **house agent** *n* agent *m* immobilier. ◆ **house arrest** *n*: **to put sb under ~ arrest** assigner qn à domicile. ◆ **houseboat** *n* péniche *f* (aménagée). ◆ **housebound** **1** *adj* confiné chez soi ; **2** *npl*: **the ~bound** les personnes isolées. ◆ **housebreaking** *n* cambriolage *m*. ◆ **housebroken** *adj animal* propre. ◆ **housecleaning** *n* ménage *m*. ◆ **housecoat** *n* peignoir *m*. ◆ **housefather/mother** *n* responsable *m/f* (de groupe) *(dans une institution)*. ◆ **housefly** *n* mouche *f* (commune). ◆ **houseful** *n*: **a ~ful of people** une pleine maisonnée de gens. ◆ **houseguest** *n* invité(e) *m(f)*. ◆ **household** **1** *n (persons)* (gens *mpl* de la) maison *f*; *(Admin, Econ etc)* ménage *m*; **there were 7 people in his ~hold** sa maison était composée de 7 personnes ; **2** *adj accounts, expenses, equipment* de *or* du ménage; **~hold ammonia** ammoniaque *f*; **~hold goods** *(gen)* appareils *mpl* ménagers; **~hold linen** linge *m* de maison; *(fig)* **it's a ~hold word** c'est un mot que tout le monde connaît. ◆ **householder** *n* occupant(e) *m(f)*; *(head of house)* chef *m* de famille. ◆ **househunt** *vi* chercher un appartement *or* une maison. ◆ **housekeeper** *n (in sb else's house)* gouvernante *f*; *(in institution)* économe *f*; **his wife is a good ~keeper** sa femme est bonne ménagère. ◆ **housekeeping** **1** *n (work)* ménage *m* ; **2** *adj*: **~keeping money** argent *m* du ménage. ◆ **housemaid** *n* bonne *f*. ◆ **houseman** *n (in hospital)* ≃ interne *m*. ◆ **house-painter** *n* peintre *m* en bâtiments. ◆ **house-party** *n* partie *f* de campagne. ◆ **house physician** *n* ≃ interne *mf* en médecine. ◆ **house-proud** *adj* très méticuleux.

◆ **houseroom** *n*: **I wouldn't give it ~room** je n'en voudrais pas chez moi. ◆ **house surgeon** *n* ≃ interne *mf* en chirurgie. ◆ **house-to-house** **1** *adv* porte à porte *inv* ; **2** *adj*: **to make a ~-to-~ search for sb** aller de porte en porte à la recherche de qn. ◆ **housetop** *n*: **to proclaim sth from the ~tops** crier qch sur les toits. ◆ **house-trained** *adj animal* propre. ◆ **housewarming** *n*: **to give a ~warming (party)** pendre la crémaillère. ◆ **housewife**, *pl* **~wives** *n* ménagère *f*; *(as opposed to career woman)* femme *f* au foyer. ◆ **housewifely** *adj* de ménagère. ◆ **housework** *n* (travaux *mpl* de) ménage *m*; **to do the ~work** faire le ménage.

housing ['haʊzɪŋ] **1** *n* logement *m*. **Ministry of H~** ministère *m* du Logement. **2** *adj shortage, crisis* du logement. **~ association** *association fournissant des logements;* **~ estate** *or* **scheme** *or* **project** cité *f*, lotissement *m*.

hove [həʊv] *pret, ptp of* **heave**.

hovel ['hɒv(ə)l] *n* taudis *m*.

hover ['hɒvə^r] *vi (gen)* planer (*above* au-dessus de); *[insect, small bird]* voltiger; *[person]* (**~ about, ~ around**) rôder; *[smile]* errer. **he was ~ing between life and death** il restait suspendu entre la vie et la mort. ◆ **hovercraft** *n* aéroglisseur *m*. ◆ **hoverport** *n* hoverport *m*.

how [haʊ] **1** *adv* (**a**) *(gen)* comment. **~ did you come?** comment êtes-vous venu?; **~ are you?** comment allez-vous?; **~ do you do?** *(greeting)* bonjour; *(on being introduced)* (enchanté) Monsieur *(etc)*; **to learn ~ to do sth** apprendre à faire qch; **I know ~ to do it** je sais le faire; **~ was the play?** comment avez-vous trouvé la pièce?; **~ is it that...?** comment se fait-il que...? + *subj;* **~ come?** * comment ça se fait? *; **~ come you aren't going out?** * comment ça se fait que tu ne sors pas? *; **~ about going for a walk?** si on allait se promener?; **and ~!** * et comment! * (**b**) que, comme. **~ big he is!** comme *or* qu'il est grand!, ce qu'il est grand!; **~ splendid!** c'est merveilleux!; **~ very kind of you!** c'est très aimable à vous; **~ long is the boat?** quelle est la longueur du bateau?; **~ tall is he?** combien mesure-t-il?; **~ old is he?** quel âge a-t-il?; **~ soon can you come?** quand pouvez-vous venir?; **~ much, ~ many** combien; **~ many days?** combien de jours? (**c**) *(that)* que. **she told me ~ she had seen the child lying on the ground** elle m'a raconté qu'elle avait vu l'enfant couché par terre. **2** *n*: **the ~ and the why of it** le comment et le pourquoi de cela.

◆ **however** **1** *adv*: **~ever you may do it, it will never be right** de quelque manière que vous le fassiez, ce ne sera jamais bien fait; ~**ever that may be** quoi qu'il en soit; ~**ever tall he may be** *or* **is** quelque *or* si grand qu'il soit; ~**ever little** si peu que ce soit; ~**ever did you do it?** * comment avez-vous bien pu faire ça? ; **2** *conj* pourtant, cependant, toutefois, néanmoins.

howl [haʊl] **1** *vi [person, animal]* hurler (*with pain etc* de douleur *etc*); *(cry)* pleurer; *[wind]* mugir. **to ~ with laughter** rire aux éclats. **2** *vt* hurler. **3** *n* hurlement *m*; mugissement *m*. ◆ **howler** * *n* gaffe *f*; **schoolboy ~er** perle *f* d'écolier. ◆ **howling** *adj (lit)* hurlant; **a ~ing gale** une violente tempête; ~**ing success** * succès *m* fou *.

hub [hʌb] *n* moyeu *m*; *(fig)* pivot *m*. *(Aut)* ~ **cap** enjoliveur *m*.

hubbub ['hʌbʌb] *n* brouhaha *m*.

huddle ['hʌdl] **1** *n* petit groupe *m* (compact). **to go into a ~** * se réunir en petit comité *(fig)*. **2** *vi* se blottir (les uns contre les autres); *(US: for discussion)* se réunir en petit comité. ◆ **huddle down** *vi (crouch)* se recroqueviller; *(snuggle)* se blottir. ◆ **huddle together** *vi (for warmth)* se blottir les uns contre les autres; *(for discussion)* se réunir en petit groupe. ◆ **huddled** *adj (under blanket etc)* blotti, pelotonné; ~**d over his books** penché sur ses livres.

hue[1] [hju:] *n*: **to raise a ~ and cry** crier haro (*against* sur).

hue[2] [hju:] *n (colour)* teinte *f*, nuance *f*.

huff * [hʌf] *n*: **in a ~** froissé; **to take the ~, to get into a ~** prendre la mouche. ◆ **huffily** * *adv leave* avec humeur; *say* d'un ton froissé. ◆ **huffiness** * *n* mauvaise humeur *f*. ◆ **huffy** * *adj* froissé.

hug [hʌg] **1** *vt* serrer dans ses bras, étreindre; *[bear, gorilla]* écraser entre ses bras; *[car etc] coast, kerb* serrer. **2** *n* étreinte *f*.

huge [hju:dʒ] *adj object, sum of money, helping* énorme; *house* immense, vaste; *man* énorme, gigantesque; *success* fou. ◆ **hugely** *adv* énormément; *(very)* extrêmement. ◆ **hugeness** *n* immensité *f*.

hulk [hʌlk] *n (ship)* épave *f*; *(vehicle, building etc)* carcasse *f*. **big ~ of a man** malabar * *m*. ◆ **hulking** *adj* lourdaud.

hull [hʌl] *n* coque *f*.

hullabaloo * [ˌhʌləbə'lu:] *n (noise)* raffut * *m*; *(fuss)* histoire * *f*.

hullo [hʌ'ləʊ] *excl* = **hallo**.

hum [hʌm] **1** *vi [insect, wire]* bourdonner; *[person]* fredonner; *[aeroplane, engine]* vrombir; *[wireless etc]* ronfler. *(fig)* **to make things ~** * mener les choses rondement; **things began to ~** * les choses ont commencé à s'animer. **2** *vt tune* fredonner. **3** *n* bourdonnement *m*; vrombissement *m*; ronflement *m*. ◆ **hummingbird** *n* colibri *m*.

human ['hju:mən] **1** *adj* humain. ~ **being** être *m* humain; ~ **nature** nature *f* humaine; **it's only ~ nature to want revenge** c'est humain de chercher à se venger; **he's only ~** il n'est pas un saint. **2** *n* être *m* humain; ~ **rights** droits *mpl* de l'homme. ◆ **humane** *adj person* plein d'humanité; *method* humain. ◆ **humanely** *adv* avec humanité. ◆ **humanism** *n* humanisme *m*. ◆ **humanist** *n* humaniste *mf*. ◆ **humanitarian** *adj, n* humanitaire *(mf)*. ◆ **humanity** *n* humanité *f*. ◆ **humanize** *vt* humaniser. ◆ **humanly** *adv* humainement. ◆ **humanoid** *adj, n* humanoïde *(mf)*.

humble ['hʌmbl] **1** *adj* humble. **of ~ origin** d'origine modeste; **in my ~ opinion** à mon humble avis; **to eat ~ pie** faire des excuses humiliantes. **2** *vt* humilier. ◆ **humbly** *adv* humblement.

humbug ['hʌmbʌg] *n (person)* fumiste * *mf*; *(behaviour, talk)* fumisterie * *f*.

humdinger ‡ ['hʌmdɪŋə[r]] *n* qn *or* qch de sensationnel *. **it's a ~!** c'est sensass! ‡

humdrum ['hʌmdrʌm] *adj* monotone.

humid ['hju:mɪd] *adj* humide. ◆ **humidifier** *n* humidificateur *m*. ◆ **humidity** *n* humidité *f*.

humiliate [hju:'mɪlɪeɪt] *vt* humilier. ◆ **humiliating** *adj* humiliant. ◆ **humiliation** *n* humiliation *f*.

humility [hju:'mɪlɪtɪ] *n* humilité *f*.

humour, *(US)* **humor** ['hju:mə[r]] **1** *n* (**a**) *(sense of fun)* humour *m*. **he has no sense of ~** il n'a pas le sens de l'humour. (**b**) *(temper)* humeur *f*. **to be in a good/bad ~** être de bonne/mauvaise humeur; **he is in no ~ for working** il n'est pas d'humeur à travailler. **2** *vt person* faire plaisir à; *sb's wishes* se prêter à. ◆ **humorist** *n* humoriste *mf*. ◆ **humorous** *adj book, story, writer* humoristique; *person, remark, tone* plein d'humour. ◆ **humorously** *adv* avec humour. ◆ **humo(u)rless** *adj* qui manque d'humour. ◆ **humo(u)rlessly** *adv* sans humour.

hump [hʌmp] **1** *n* bosse *f*. *(fig)* **we're over the ~** * le plus difficile est fait; **he's got the ~** ‡ il a le cafard *. **2** *vt back, shoulders* voûter; *(*: carry)* porter. ◆ **humpback** *n* bossu(e) *m(f)*. ◆ **humpbacked** *adj person* bossu; *bridge* en dos d'âne.

humus ['hju:məs] *n* humus *m*.

hunch [hʌntʃ] **1** *vt* (~ **up**) *back, shoulders* voûter. ~**ed (up) over his books** courbé sur ses livres. **2** *n* (**a**) *(hunk)* gros morceau *m*. (**b**) *(*: premonition)* intuition *f*. **to have a ~ that** avoir idée que, soupçonner que; **you should follow your ~** il faut suivre son intuition; **it's only a ~** ce n'est qu'une idée. ◆ **hunchback** *n* bossu(e) *m(f)*. ◆ **hunchbacked** *adj* bossu.

hundred ['hʌndrɪd] *adj, n* cent *(m)*. **a ~ books/chairs** cent livres/chaises; **two ~ chairs** deux cents chaises; **about a ~ books** une centaine de livres; **about a ~** une centaine; ~**s of** des centaines de; **a ~ and one** cent un; **the ~ and first** le *or* la cent unième; **it was a ~ per cent successful** cela a réussi à cent pour cent; **to live to be a ~** devenir centenaire; **they came in (their) ~s** ils sont venus par centaines. ◆ **hundredth 1** *adj* centième ; **2** *n* centième *mf*; *(fraction)* centième *m*. ◆ **hundredweight** *n (Brit, Can)* = *50,7 kg, (US)* = *45,3 kg*.

hung [hʌŋ] **1** *pret, ptp of* **hang**. **2** *adj jury, parliament* sans majorité. ~ **up** * complexé.

Hungary ['hʌŋgərɪ] *n* Hongrie *f*.

hunger ['hʌŋgə[r]] **1** *n (lit, fig)* faim *f* (*for* de). **2** *adj*: ~ **strike** grève *f* de la faim; ~ **striker** gréviste *mf* de la faim. **3** *vi* avoir faim (*for* de).

hungry ['hʌŋgrɪ] *adj*: **to be** *or* **feel ~** avoir faim; **to be very ~** avoir très faim, être affamé; **to make sb ~** donner faim à qn; **to go ~** *(starve)* souffrir de la faim; *(miss a meal)* se passer de manger; **you look ~** tu as l'air d'avoir faim; *(fig)* ~ **for** avide de. ◆ **hungrily** *adv* avidement.

hunk [hʌŋk] *n* gros morceau *m*.

hunt [hʌnt] **1** *n (gen)* chasse *f*; *(for sth or sb missing)* recherche *f* (*for* de); *(huntsmen)* chasseurs *mpl*. **tiger ~** chasse au tigre; **the ~ for the murderer** la chasse au meurtrier; **I've had a ~ for my gloves** j'ai cherché mes gants partout. **2** *vt (Sport)* chasser, faire la chasse à; *(pursue)* poursuivre; *(seek)* chercher. **we ~ed the town for that** nous avons fait * toute la ville pour trouver ça; **I've ~ed my desk for it** j'ai retourné tout mon bureau pour le trouver. **3** *vi (Sport)* chasser. **to go ~ing** aller à la chasse; **to ~ for** *game* chasser; *object, facts* rechercher (partout); **he ~ed in his pocket for his pen** il a fouillé dans sa poche pour trouver son stylo. ◆ **hunt down** *vt sep animal* forcer; *person* traquer; *object, quotation* dénicher. ◆ **hunt up** *vt sep* rechercher.

◆ **hunter** *n (Sport)* chasseur *m*; *(gen)* poursuivant *m*; *(horse)* cheval *m* de chasse.
◆ **hunter-killer submarine** *n* sous-marin *m* nucléaire d'attaque. ◆ **hunting 1** *n (Sport)* chasse *f* (à courre); **fox-~ing** chasse au renard ; **2** *adj*: **~ing lodge** pavillon *m* de chasse. ◆ **huntsman** *n* chasseur *m*.

hurdle ['hɜːdl] *n (for fences)* claie *f*; *(Sport)* haie *f*; *(fig)* obstacle *m*. *(Sport)* **the 100-metre ~s** le 100 mètres haies.

hurl [hɜːl] *vt stone* jeter *or* lancer (avec violence) (*at* contre); *abuse etc* lancer (*at* à). **they were ~ed to the ground by the blast** ils ont été précipités à terre par le souffle de l'explosion; **to ~ o.s.** se jeter; **to ~ o.s. at sb/sth** se ruer sur qn/qch; *(fig)* **to be ~ed into** être précipité dans.

hurrah [hʊ'rɑː] *n*, **hurray** [hʊ'reɪ] *n* hourra *m*. **hip, hip, ~!** hip, hip, hip, hourra!; **~ for Richard Thomas!** vive Richard Thomas!; *(US)* **last ~** *(gen)* dernière tentative *f; (Pol)* dernière campagne *f*.

hurricane ['hʌrɪkən] *n* ouragan *m*. **~ lamp** lampe-tempête *f*.

hurry ['hʌrɪ] **1** *n (haste)* hâte *f*; *(eagerness)* empressement *m*. **to be in a ~** être pressé; **to be in a ~ to do** avoir hâte de faire; **done in a ~** fait à la hâte; **I won't do that again in a ~!** * je ne suis pas près de recommencer!; **are you in a ~ for this?** vous le voulez très vite?; **what's the ~?** qu'est-ce qui presse?; **there's no ~** rien ne presse; **there's no ~ for it** ça ne presse pas.
2 *vi* se dépêcher, se presser (*to do* de faire). **do ~** dépêchez-vous; **don't ~ over that essay** prenez votre temps pour faire cette dissertation; **to ~ over a meal** manger rapidement; **to ~ in/out** *etc* entrer/sortir *etc* à la hâte *or* précipitamment; **he hurried after her** il a couru pour la rattraper.
3 *vt person* faire presser, faire se dépêcher; *piece of work* presser. **don't ~ your meal** ne mangez pas trop vite; **I don't want to ~ you** je ne veux pas vous bousculer; **you can't ~ him, he won't be hurried** vous ne le ferez pas se dépêcher; **it can't be hurried** cela exige d'être fait sans hâte; **to ~ sb in/out** *etc* faire entrer/sortir *etc* qn à la hâte; **they hurried him to a doctor** ils l'ont emmené d'urgence chez un médecin; **troops were hurried to the spot** des troupes ont été envoyées d'urgence sur place. ◆ **hurry along 1** *vi* marcher d'un pas pressé. **~ along!** pressons un peu! **2** *vt sep* = **hurry up 2.** ◆ **hurry back** *vi* se presser de revenir (*or* de retourner). ◆ **hurry on 1** *vi* continuer à la hâte. **they hurried on to the next question** ils sont vite passés à la question suivante. **2** *vt sep* = **hurry up 2.** ◆ **hurry up 1** *vi* se dépêcher, se presser. **~ up!** dépêchez-vous! **2** *vt sep person* faire se dépêcher; *work* activer.
◆ **hurried** *adj steps, departure* précipité; *remark* dit à la hâte; *reading, work* fait à la hâte; **to have a hurried meal** manger à la hâte. ◆ **hurriedly** *adv (fast)* en toute hâte; *(too fast)* précipitamment.

hurt [hɜːt] *pret, ptp* **hurt 1** *vt* (**a**) *(physically)* faire mal à, blesser. **to ~ o.s.** se faire mal, se blesser; **to ~ one's arm** se blesser au bras; **I hope I haven't ~ you** j'espère que je ne vous ai pas fait mal?; **where does it ~ you?** où avez-vous mal?; **to get ~** se faire mal. (**b**) *(mentally etc)* faire de la peine à. **sb is bound to get ~** il y a toujours qn qui écope *; **what ~ most was...** ce qui faisait le plus mal c'était...; **to ~ sb's feelings** froisser *or* blesser qn; **his feelings were ~** cela l'a froissé. (**c**) *thing, material* abîmer, endommager; *reputation, trade* nuire à. **it wouldn't ~ the grass to water it** ça ne ferait pas de mal au gazon d'être arrosé.
2 *vi* faire mal. **that ~s** ça fait mal; **my arm ~s** mon bras me fait mal; **where does it ~?** où avez-vous mal?; **it won't ~ for being left** il n'y aura pas de mal à laisser cela de côté.
3 *n (physical)* mal *m*, blessure *f*. *(fig)* **the real ~ lay in...** ce qui lui (*etc*) faisait vraiment mal c'était...
4 *adj* blessé; *(offended)* froissé, blessé.
◆ **hurtful** *adj (harmful)* nuisible (*to* à); *remark etc* blessant.

hurtle ['hɜːtl] *vi*: **to ~ along** *etc* avancer *etc* à toute vitesse *or* allure.

husband ['hʌzbənd] **1** *n* mari *m*; *(spouse)* époux *m*. **they were living as ~ and wife** ils vivaient maritalement. **2** *vt* ménager.

hush [hʌʃ] **1** *n* silence *m*, calme *m*. **~!** chut!, silence! **2** *adj*: **to pay sb ~ money *** acheter le silence de qn; *(US Culin)* **~ puppy** *espèce de beignet.* **3** *vt (silence)* faire taire; *(soothe)* calmer. ◆ **hush up** *vt sep scandal* étouffer; *fact* cacher; *person* faire taire. ◆ **hushed** *adj voice, conversation* étouffé; *silence* grand, profond. ◆ **hush-hush** * *adj* (ultra-) secret.

husk [hʌsk] *n [grain]* balle *f*; *[nut]* écale *f*.

husky ['hʌskɪ] *adj* (**a**) *(hoarse) person* enroué; *voice* rauque; *singer's voice* voilé. (**b**) *(burly)* costaud * *f inv*. ◆ **huskily** *adv* d'une voix rauque; d'une voix voilée. ◆ **huskiness** *n* enrouement *m*.

hustle ['hʌsl] **1** *vt*: **to ~ sb in/out** *etc (push)* pousser *or (hurry)* bousculer qn pour le faire entrer/sortir *etc*; **to ~ things along** faire activer les choses. **2** *vi*: **to ~ in/out** *etc* entrer/sortir *etc* à la hâte. **3** *n*: **~ and bustle** tourbillon *m* (d'activité).

hut [hʌt] *n* hutte *f*; *(shed)* cabane *f*; *(Mil)* baraquement *m*; *(in mountains)* refuge *m*.

hutch [hʌtʃ] *n* clapier *m*.

hyacinth ['haɪəsɪnθ] *n* jacinthe *f*.

hybrid ['haɪbrɪd] *adj, n* hybride *(m)*.

hydrangea [haɪ'dreɪn(d)ʒə] *n* hortensia *m*.

hydrant ['haɪdr(ə)nt] *n* prise *f* d'eau. **fire ~** bouche *f* d'incendie.

hydraulic [haɪ'drɒlɪk] *adj* hydraulique. ◆ **hydraulics** *nsg* hydraulique *f*.

hydr(o)... ['haɪdr(əʊ)] *pref* hydr(o)... ◆ **hydrochloric** *adj* chlorhydrique. ◆ **hydroelectric** *adj* hydro-électrique. ◆ **hydrofoil** *n* hydrofoil *m*. ◆ **hydrophobia** *n* hydrophobie *f*. ◆ **hydroplane** *n* hydroglisseur *m*.

hydrogen ['haɪdrɪdʒ(ə)n] *n* hydrogène *m*. **~ bomb** bombe *f* à hydrogène; **~ peroxide** eau *f* oxygénée.

hyena [haɪ'iːnə] *n* hyène *f*.

hygiene ['haɪdʒiːn] *n* hygiène *f*. ◆ **hygienic** *adj* hygiénique.

hymn [hɪm] *n* hymne *m*, cantique *m*. ◆ **hymnal** *n* ['hɪmnəl] livre *m* de cantiques.

hype * [haɪp] **1** *n [product]* campagne *f* publicitaire. **2** *vt product* lancer à grand renfort de publicité.

hyper... ['haɪpə[r]] *pref* hyper... ◆ **hypercritical** *adj* hypercritique. ◆ **hypermarket** *n* hypermarché *m*. ◆ **hypersensitive** *adj* hypersensible. ◆ **hypertension** *n* hypertension *f*.

hyphen ['haɪf(ə)n] *n* trait *m* d'union. ◆ **hyphenate** *vt* mettre un trait d'union à; **~ated word** mot *m* à trait d'union.

hypnosis [hɪp'nəʊsɪs] *n* hypnose *f*. **under ~** en état d'hypnose. ◆ **hypnotic** *adj* hypnotique. ◆ **hypnotism** *n* hypnotisme *m*. ◆ **hypnotist** *n* hypnotiseur *m*, -euse *f*. ◆ **hypnotize** *vt* hypnotiser; **to hypnotize sb into doing sth** faire faire qch à qn sous hypnose.

hypochondria [ˌhaɪpə(ʊ)'kɒndrɪə] *n* hypocondrie *f*. ◆ **hypochondriac 1** *adj* hypocondriaque ; **2** *n* malade *mf* imaginaire.

hypocrisy [hɪ'pɒkrɪsɪ] *n* hypocrisie *f*. ◆ **hypocrite** *n* hypocrite *mf*. ◆ **hypocritical** *adj* hypocrite. ◆ **hypocritically** *adv* hypocritement.

hypodermic [ˌhaɪpəˈdɜːmɪk] **1** *adj* hypodermique. **2** *n* seringue *f* hypodermique.

hypothermia [ˌhaɪpə(ʊ)ˈθɜːmɪə] *n* hypothermie *f*.

hypothesis, *pl* **-eses** [haɪˈpɒθɪsɪs, ɪsiːz] *n* hypothèse *f*. ◆ **hypothetic(al)** *adj* hypothétique. ◆ **hypothetically** *adv* hypothétiquement.

hysterectomy [ˌhɪstəˈrektəmɪ] *n* hystérectomie *f*.

hysteria [hɪsˈtɪərɪə] *n (Psych)* hystérie *f*; *(gen)* crise *f* de nerfs. ◆ **hysterical** *adj (Psych)* hystérique; *(gen) person* surexcité; *laugh, sobs* convulsif; ~ **laughter** fou rire *m*; **to become hysterical** avoir une violente crise de nerfs. ◆ **hysterically** *adv (Psych)* hystériquement; *(gen) laugh* convulsivement; *shout, argue* comme un(e) hystérique. ◆ **hysterics** *npl* violente crise *f* de nerfs; *(*: laughter)* fou rire *m*; **to have hysterics** avoir une violente crise de nerfs; *(laughing)* attraper un fou rire.

I

I¹, i [aɪ] *n (letter)* I, i *m*.

I² [aɪ] *pers pron (unstressed)* je; *(before vowel)* j'; *(stressed)* moi. **he and ~ are going to sing** lui et moi allons chanter; **I'LL do it** c'est moi qui vais le faire; **it's ~** c'est moi.

Iberian [aɪ'bɪərɪən] *adj:* **the ~ Peninsula** la péninsule ibérique.

ice [aɪs] **1** *n* (**a**) glace *f*; *(on road)* verglas *m*. **my hands are like ~** j'ai les mains glacées; *(fig)* **to be on thin ~** s'aventurer en terrain glissant; *(fig)* **to put sth on ~** mettre qch en attente; **'Cinderella on ~'** 'Cendrillon, spectacle sur glace'. (**b**) *(~ cream)* glace *f*. **raspberry ~** glace à la framboise. **2** *adj*: **~ age** période *f* glaciaire; **~ axe** piolet *m*; **~ bucket** seau *m* à glace; **~ cube** glaçon *m (cube)*; **~ floe** banquise *f*; **~ hockey** hockey *m* sur glace; **~ rink** patinoire *f*; **~ show** spectacle *m* sur glace. **3** *vt cake* glacer. **4** *vi*: **to ~ over** *or* **up** *[wings, windscreen]* givrer; *[river]* geler. ◆ **iceberg** *n* iceberg *m*. ◆ **icebox** *n (US: refrigerator)* réfrigérateur *m*, frigidaire ® *m*; *(Brit: part of refrigerator)* freezer *m*; *(insulated box)* glacière *f (also fig: of room etc)*. ◆ **icebreaker** *n (Naut)* brise-glaces *m inv*. ◆ **ice-cold** *adj drink, hands* glacé; *room, manners, person* glacial. ◆ **ice cream** *n* glace *f*. ◆ **ice-cream soda** *n* ice-cream soda *m*. ◆ **iced** *adj tea, coffee* glacé; *martini* avec des glaçons; *champagne* frappé; *melon* rafraîchi. ◆ **ice(d) lolly** *n* ≃ esquimau *m (glace)*. ◆ **ice-skate** *vi* patiner (sur glace). ◆ **ice-skating** *n* patinage *m* (sur glace). ◆ **ice-tray** *n* bac *m* à glaçons. ◆ **icily** *adv* d'un air (*or* d'un ton) glacial. ◆ **icing** *n (Culin)* glaçage *m*; **icing sugar** sucre *m* glace; **chocolate icing** glaçage au chocolat. ◆ **icy** *adj* (**a**) (**icy cold**) *wind, weather, stare* glacial; *ground, hands* glacé; (**b**) *road* verglacé.

Iceland ['aɪslənd] *n* Islande *f*.

icicle ['aɪsɪkl] *n* glaçon *m (naturel)*.

icon ['aɪkɒn] *n* icône *f*.

id [ɪd] *n (Psych)* ça *m*.

idea [aɪ'dɪə] *n* idée *f*. **brilliant ~** idée géniale; **good ~!** bonne idée!; **I can't bear the ~ (of it)** je n'ose pas y penser; **it might not be a bad ~ to wait** ce ne serait pas une mauvaise idée d'attendre; **the ~ is to sell the car to him** il s'agit de lui vendre la voiture; **it wasn't my ~!** ce n'est pas moi qui en ai eu l'idée!; **where did you get that ~?** où est-ce que tu as pris cette idée-là?; **what gave you the ~ that...?** qu'est-ce qui t'a fait penser que...?; **don't get any ~s!** * ce n'est pas la peine de t'imaginer des choses! *; **to put ~s into sb's head** mettre des idées dans la tête de qn; **according to his ~** selon sa façon de penser; **if that's your ~ of fun** si c'est ça que tu appelles t'amuser; **I've got some ~ of physics** j'ai quelques notions de physique; **I haven't the least** *or* **slightest** *or* **foggiest * ~** je n'en ai pas la moindre idée; **I have an ~ that...** j'ai idée *or* j'ai dans l'idée que...; **I had no ~ that...** j'ignorais absolument que...; **can you give me a rough** *or* **general ~ of how many you want?** pouvez-vous m'indiquer en gros combien vous en voulez?; **you're getting the ~!** * tu y es!; **I've got the general ~** * je vois à peu près (ce dont il s'agit); **that's the ~!** * c'est ça!; **what's the big ~?** * qu'est-ce que c'est que cette histoire?, ça ne va pas, non? ‡

ideal [aɪ'dɪəl] *adj, n* idéal *(m)*. ◆ **idealism** *n* idéalisme *m*. ◆ **idealist** *adj, n* idéaliste *(mf)*. ◆ **idealistic** *adj* idéaliste. ◆ **idealize** *vt* idéaliser. ◆ **ideally** *adv suited* idéalement; *placed, equipped, shaped* d'une manière idéale; **~ly the house should have...** l'idéal serait que la maison ait...

identical [aɪ'dentɪk(ə)l] *adj* identique (*to* à); *twins* vrais. ◆ **identically** *adv* identiquement.

identify [aɪ'dentɪfaɪ] **1** *vt* identifier (*as* comme étant; *with* avec, à). **2** *vi* s'identifier (*with* avec, à). ◆ **identification** **1** *n* identification *f*; *(document)* pièce *f* d'identité ; **2** *adj mark* d'identification; *papers, tag* d'identité. ◆ **identikit** *n* portrait-robot *m*. ◆ **identity** **1** *n* identité *f*; **a case of mistaken identity** une erreur d'identité ; **2** *adj card, disc, papers* d'identité; **identity parade** séance *f* d'identification (d'un suspect).

ideology [ˌaɪdɪ'ɒlədʒɪ] *n* idéologie *f*. ◆ **ideological** *adj* idéologique.

idiom ['ɪdɪəm] *n (phrase)* expression *f* idiomatique; *(language)* idiome *m*. ◆ **idiomatic** *adj* idiomatique. ◆ **idiomatically** *adv* de façon idiomatique.

idiosyncrasy [ˌɪdɪə'sɪŋkrəsɪ] *n* particularité *f*. ◆ **idiosyncratic** *adj* particulier, caractéristique.

idiot ['ɪdɪət] *n* idiot(e) *m(f)*, imbécile *mf*. ◆ **idiocy** *n* idiotie *f*. ◆ **idiotic** *adj* idiot, bête, stupide. ◆ **idiotically** *adv say, do* bêtement, stupidement; *behave* en idiot *or* en imbécile.

idle ['aɪdl] **1** *adj* (**a**) *(doing nothing)* oisif, désœuvré; *(unemployed)* en chômage; *(lazy)* paresseux; *life* oisif; *machine* au repos. **the ~ rich** l'élite oisive; **in my ~ moments** à mes moments de loisir; *(Ind)* **to make sb ~** réduire qn au chômage; **the whole factory stood ~** l'usine entière était arrêtée. (**b**) *speculation, question, threat* oiseux, vain; *promises, words* en l'air; *fears* sans fondement; *pleasures* futile. **out of ~ curiosity** par curiosité pure et simple; **~ gossip** racontars *mpl;* **it is ~ to hope that...** il est inutile d'espérer que... **2** *vi* (**a**) (**~ about, ~ around**) paresser. (**b**) *[engine]* tourner au ralenti. ◆ **idleness** *n* oisiveté *f*, désœuvrement *m*; chômage *m*; paresse *f*. ◆ **idler** *n* oisif *m*, -ive *f*, désœuvré(e) *m(f)*; paresseux *m*, -euse *f*. ◆ **idly** *adv (without working)* sans travailler; *(lazily)* paresseusement; *say, suggest* négligemment.

idol ['aɪdl] *n* idole *f*. ◆ **idolize** *vt* idolâtrer.

idyll ['ɪdɪl] *n* idylle *f*. ◆ **idyllic** *adj* idyllique.

if [ɪf] **1** *conj* (**a**) si. **I'll go ~ you come with me** j'irai si tu m'accompagnes; **~ I were you** si j'étais vous; **even ~ I knew** même si je le savais; **~ I'm not mistaken** si je ne me trompe, à moins que je ne me trompe *(subj);* **~ only I'd known!** si seulement j'avais su!; **~ necessary** s'il le faut, au besoin; **~ anything, this one is bigger** c'est plutôt celui-ci qui est le plus grand; **~ so** s'il en est ainsi; **~ not** sinon; **~ only for a moment** ne serait-ce que pour un instant; **~ it isn't Smith!** par exemple! Smith!; **~ I know HER, she'll refuse** telle que je la connais, elle refusera. (**b**) *(whenever)* si. **~ I asked him he'd help me** si je le lui demandais il m'aiderait. (**c**) *(although, admitting that)* **(even) ~ it takes me all day** même si cela doit *or* quand bien même cela devrait me prendre toute la journée; **nice weather, ~ rather cold** temps agréable, bien qu'un peu froid; **even ~ it is a good film it's rather long** c'est un bon film bien qu'il soit un peu long. (**d**) *(whether)* si. **do you know ~ they have gone?** savez-vous s'ils sont partis? (**e**) **as ~** comme (si). **he acts as ~ he were rich** il se conduit comme s'il était riche; **as ~ by chance** comme par hasard. **2** *n*: **~s and buts** les si *mpl* et les mais *mpl*; **it's a big ~** c'est un grand point d'interrogation.

igloo ['ɪgluː] *n* igloo *m*.

ignite [ɪg'naɪt] **1** *vt* mettre le feu à. **2** *vi* prendre feu. ◆ **ignition 1** *n (gen)* ignition *f*; *(Aut)* allumage *m*; **to switch on the ignition** mettre le contact ; **2** *adj*: **ignition key** clef *f* de contact; **ignition switch** contact *m*.

ignoble [ɪg'nəʊbl] *adj* ignoble.

ignominious [ˌɪgnə'mɪnɪəs] *adj* ignominieux. ◆ **ignominiously** *adv* ignominieusement. ◆ **ignominy** *n* ignominie *f*.

ignoramus [ˌɪgnə'reɪməs] *n* ignare *mf*.

ignorance ['ɪgn(ə)r(ə)ns] *n* ignorance *f* (*of a fact* d'un fait; *of geography etc* en matière de géographie *etc*). **to be in ~ of sth** ignorer qch; **to keep sb in ~ of sth** laisser ignorer qch à qn; **~ of the law is no excuse** nul n'est censé ignorer la loi; **don't show your ~!** ce n'est pas la peine d'étaler ton ignorance! ◆ **ignorant** *adj person* ignorant (*of* de); *words* qui trahit l'ignorance; **to be ignorant of sth** ignorer qch. ◆ **ignorantly** *adv* par ignorance.

ignore [ɪg'nɔːʳ] *vt remark, objection, awkward fact* ne tenir aucun compte de; *sb's behaviour* faire semblant de ne pas s'apercevoir de; *person* faire semblant de ne pas reconnaître; *invitation, letter* ne pas répondre à; *rule, prohibition* ne pas respecter; *facts* méconnaître. **I shall ~ your impertinence** je ne relèverai pas votre impertinence; **we cannot ~ this behaviour any longer** nous ne pouvons plus fermer les yeux sur ces agissements.

ill [ɪl] **1** *adj*, *comp* **worse**, *superl* **worst** (**a**) *(sick)* malade; *(less serious)* souffrant. **to be ~** être malade *or* souffrant; **to fall** *or* **be taken ~** tomber malade; **he's seriously ~ in hospital** il est à l'hôpital dans un état grave; **~ with anxiety** malade d'inquiétude. (**b**) *(bad) deed, health, omen* mauvais *(before n)*. **~ effects** conséquences *fpl* désastreuses; **~ feeling** ressentiment *m*; **no ~ feeling!** sans rancune!; **~ humour** *or* **temper** mauvaise humeur *f*; **~ luck** malchance *f*; **~ nature** méchanceté *f*; **~ will** malveillance *f*; **I bear him no ~ will** je ne lui en veux pas; **it's an ~ wind that blows nobody any good** à quelque chose malheur est bon.
2 *n* mal *m*. **to speak ~ of** dire du mal de; *(misfortunes)* **~s** malheurs *mpl*.
3 *adv nourished, prepared etc* mal. **he can ~ afford to do it** il peut difficilement se permettre de le faire; **to go ~ with sb** aller mal pour qn.
◆ **ill-advised** *adj decision, remark* peu judicieux *(V also* **advise**). ◆ **ill-bred** *adj* mal élevé. ◆ **ill-considered** *adj* irréfléchi. ◆ **ill-fated** *adj person* infortuné; *day* néfaste; *action, effort* malheureux. ◆ **ill-favoured** *adj* laid. ◆ **ill-gotten gains** *npl* biens *mpl* mal acquis. ◆ **ill-humoured** *adj* maussade. ◆ **ill-informed** *adj person* mal renseigné; *essay, speech* plein d'inexactitudes. ◆ **ill-judged** *adj* peu judicieux. ◆ **ill-mannered** *adj person* mal élevé; *behaviour* impoli. ◆ **ill-natured** *adj* désagréable. ◆ **illness** *n* maladie *f*; **to have a long ~ness** faire une longue maladie. ◆ **ill-tempered** *adj (habitually)* qui a mauvais caractère; *(on one occasion)* de mauvaise humeur. ◆ **ill-timed** *adj* inopportun, intempestif. ◆ **ill-treat** *or* ◆ **ill-use** *vt* maltraiter. ◆ **ill-treatment** *n* mauvais traitements *mpl*.

illegal [ɪ'liːg(ə)l] *adj* illégal. ◆ **illegality** *n* illégalité *f*. ◆ **illegally** *adv* illégalement.

illegible [ɪ'ledʒəbl] *adj* illisible. ◆ **illegibly** *adv* illisiblement.

illegitimate [ˌɪlɪ'dʒɪtɪmɪt] *adj action, child* illégitime; *conclusion* injustifié. ◆ **illegitimacy** *n* illégitimité *f*. ◆ **illegitimately** *adv* illégitimement.

illicit [ɪ'lɪsɪt] *adj* illicite. ◆ **illicitly** *adv* illicitement.

illiterate [ɪ'lɪt(ə)rɪt] **1** *adj person* illettré, analphabète; *letter, sentence* plein de fautes. **2** *n* illettré(e) *m(f)*, analphabète *mf*. ◆ **illiteracy** *n* analphabétisme *m*.

illogical [ɪ'lɒdʒɪk(ə)l] *adj* illogique. ◆ **illogicality** *n* illogisme *m*. ◆ **illogically** *adv* illogiquement.

illuminate [ɪ'luːmɪneɪt] *vt (gen, also fig)* éclairer; *(for special occasion or effect) building etc* illuminer; *manuscript* enluminer. **~d sign** enseigne *f* lumineuse. ◆ **illuminating** *adj* éclairant. ◆ **illumination** *n* éclairage *m*; illumination *f*; **illuminations** illuminations *fpl*.

illusion [ɪ'luːʒ(ə)n] *n* illusion *f*. **to be under the ~ that** avoir l'illusion que + *indic*; **to have no ~s** ne se faire aucune illusion (*about* sur). ◆ **illusive** *or* ◆ **illusory** *adj* illusoire.

illustrate ['ɪləstreɪt] *vt (lit, fig)* illustrer. **~d paper** *or* **journal** illustré *m*. ◆ **illustration** *n* illustration *f*; *(fig)* **by way of illustration** à titre d'exemple. ◆ **illustrative** *adj* explicatif. ◆ **illustrator** *n* illustrateur *m*, -trice *f*.

illustrious [ɪ'lʌstrɪəs] *adj* illustre. ◆ **illustriously** *adv* glorieusement.

image ['ɪmɪdʒ] *n (gen)* image *f*; *(reflection)* réflexion *f*. *(fig)* **he is the ~ of his father** c'est tout le portrait de son père; **I had a sudden (mental) ~ of her** soudain je l'ai vue en imagination; **they had quite the wrong ~ of him** ils se faisaient une idée tout à fait fausse de lui; *[politician, town etc]* **(public) ~** image *f* de marque *(fig)*; **he's got the wrong ~ for that** son image de marque ne convient guère à cela. ◆ **imagery** *n* images *fpl*.

imagine [ɪ'mædʒɪn] *vt* (**a**) *(picture to o.s.)* (s')imaginer. **~ that you were at school** imagine que tu sois à l'école; **I can't ~ myself at 60** je ne m'imagine pas du tout à 60 ans; **just ~!** tu (t')imagines!; **I can ~!** je m'en doute!; **you can ~ how I felt!** imaginez-vous ce que j'ai pu ressentir!; **you can ~ how pleased I was!** vous pensez si j'étais content!; **you can't ~ how difficult it is** vous ne pouvez pas vous imaginer *or* vous figurer combien c'est difficile; **he's always imagining things** il se fait des idées. (**b**) *(suppose, believe)* imaginer, supposer (*that* que). **don't ~ that I can help you** n'allez pas croire *or* vous imaginer que je puisse vous aider; **I didn't ~ he would come** je ne me doutais pas qu'il viendrait. ◆ **imaginable** *adj* imaginable; **the quietest person imaginable** la personne la plus silencieuse qu'on puisse imaginer. ◆ **imaginary** *adj* imaginaire. ◆ **imagination** *n* imagination *f*; **to have a vivid imagination** avoir l'imagination fertile; **he's got imagination** il a de l'imagination; **she lets her imagination run away with her** elle se laisse emporter par son imagination; **in imagination** en imagination; **it is all (your) imagination!** vous vous faites des idées!; **use your imagination!** aie donc un peu d'imagination! ◆ **imaginative** *adj* plein d'imagination. ◆ **imaginatively** *adv* avec imagination.

imam [ɪ'mɑːm] *n* imam *m*.

imbalance [ɪm'bæləns] *n* déséquilibre *m*.

imbecile ['ɪmbəsiːl] *adj, n* imbécile *(mf)*. **you ~!** espèce d'imbécile! ◆ **imbecility** *n* imbécillité *f*.

imbibe [ɪm'baɪb] *vt (drink)* boire; *(absorb: also fig)* absorber.

imitate ['ɪmɪteɪt] *vt* imiter. ◆ **imitation 1** *n* imitation *f*; **in imitation of** à l'imitation de ; **2** *adj* *jewellery etc* faux; *precious stone* artificiel; **imitation leather/marble** *etc* imitation *f* cuir/marbre *etc*. ◆ **imitative** *adj* imitatif. ◆ **imitator** *n* imitateur *m*, -trice *f*.

immaculate [ɪ'mækjʊlɪt] *adj (gen)* impeccable; *behaviour* irréprochable. **the I~ Conception** l'Immaculée Conception *f*. ◆ **immaculately** *adv dress* avec un soin impeccable; *behave* de façon irréprochable.

immaterial [ˌɪmə'tɪərɪəl] *adj* peu important. **it is ~ whether** il importe peu que + *subj*; **that's quite ~** la question n'est pas là; **that is quite ~ to me** cela m'est indifférent.

immature [ˌɪmə'tjʊəʳ] *adj fruit* qui n'est pas mûr; *animal, tree* jeune; *person* qui manque de maturité. ◆ **immaturity** *n* manque *m* de maturité.

immeasurable [ɪ'meʒ(ə)rəbl] *adj (lit)* incommensurable; *(fig)* infini. ◆ **immeasurably** *adv (fig)* infiniment.

immediate [ɪ'mi:dɪət] *adj (gen)* immédiat; *knowledge* immédiat, direct; *measures, need* immédiat, urgent. **to take ~ action** agir immédiatement (*to do* pour faire); **in the ~ future** dans un avenir immédiat; **my ~ object** mon premier but; **the ~ area** les environs immédiats. ◆ **immediacy** *n* caractère *m* immédiat. ◆ **immediately** **1** *adv (at once)* immédiatement, tout de suite; *(directly) affect, concern* directement; **~ly after** aussitôt après ; **2** *conj (gen)* dès que; **~ly I returned** dès mon retour.

immense [ɪ'mens] *adj* immense. ◆ **immensely** *adv rich* immensément, extrêmement; *enjoy o.s.* énormément. ◆ **immensity** *n* immensité *f*.

immerse [ɪ'mɜ:s] *vt* plonger (*in* dans), immerger. **~d in one's work** plongé dans son travail. ◆ **immersion** **1** *n* immersion *f* ; **2** *adj*: **immersion heater** chauffe-eau *m inv* électrique.

immigrant ['ɪmɪgr(ə)nt] *adj, n (newly arrived)* immigrant(e) *m(f)*; *(established)* immigré(e) *m(f)*. ◆ **immigrate** *vi* immigrer. ◆ **immigration** *n* immigration *f*; **to go through customs and immigration** passer la douane et le contrôle de police; **immigration authorities** service *m* de l'immigration.

imminent ['ɪmɪnənt] *adj* imminent. ◆ **imminence** *n* imminence *f*.

immobile [ɪ'məʊbaɪl] *adj* immobile. ◆ **immobility** *n* immobilité *f*. ◆ **immobilize** *vt* immobiliser.

immoderate [ɪ'mɒd(ə)rɪt] *adj* immodéré. ◆ **immoderately** *adv* immodérément.

immodest [ɪ'mɒdɪst] *adj (indecent)* immodeste; *(bumptious)* présomptueux.

immoral [ɪ'mɒr(ə)l] *adj* immoral. ◆ **immorality** *n* immoralité *f*.

immortal [ɪ'mɔ:tl] *adj, n* immortel(le) *m(f)*. ◆ **immortality** *n* immortalité *f*. ◆ **immortalize** *vt* immortaliser.

immovable [ɪ'mu:vəbl] *adj object* fixe; *courage* inébranlable; *person* insensible.

immune [ɪ'mju:n] *adj (Med)* immunisé (*from, to, against* contre). **~ response** réaction *f* immunitaire; *(fig)* **~ to inflation/criticism** à l'abri de l'inflation/de la critique; **~ from taxation** exempt d'impôts. ◆ **immunity** *n* immunité *f*. ◆ **immunization** *n* immunisation *f*. ◆ **immunize** *vt* immuniser (*against* contre).

immutable [ɪ'mju:təbl] *adj* immuable. ◆ **immutably** *adv* immuablement.

imp [ɪmp] *n* diablotin *m*; *(child)* petit(e) espiègle *m(f)*.

impact ['ɪmpækt] *n (lit, fig)* impact *m* (*on* sur). **to make an ~ on sb** faire une forte impression sur qn. ◆ **impacted** *adj tooth* inclus; *(US)* **~ed area** quartier *m* surpeuplé.

impair [ɪm'pɛəʳ] *vt abilities, faculties* diminuer; *negotiations, relations* porter atteinte à; *health* détériorer; *sight, hearing* affaiblir.

impart [ɪm'pɑ:t] *vt (make known) news, knowledge* communiquer; *(bestow)* transmettre.

impartial [ɪm'pɑ:ʃ(ə)l] *adj* impartial. ◆ **impartiality** *n* impartialité *f*. ◆ **impartially** *adv* impartialement.

impassable [ɪm'pɑ:səbl] *adj barrier, river* infranchissable; *road* impraticable.

impassioned [ɪm'pæʃnd] *adj* passionné.

impassive [ɪm'pæsɪv] *adj* impassible. ◆ **impassively** *adv* impassiblement.

impatient [ɪm'peɪʃ(ə)nt] *adj* (**a**) impatient (*to do* de faire). **to grow ~** s'impatienter. (**b**) intolérant (*of sth* à l'égard de qch; *with sb* vis-à-vis de qn). ◆ **impatience** *n* impatience *f* (*to do* de faire); intolérance *f* (*with sb* vis-à-vis de qn). ◆ **impatiently** *adv* avec impatience.

impeach [ɪm'pi:tʃ] *vt public official* mettre en accusation; *sb's character* attaquer; *motives, honesty* mettre en doute.

impeccable [ɪm'pekəbl] *adj* impeccable. ◆ **impeccably** *adv* impeccablement.

impecunious [ˌɪmpɪ'kju:nɪəs] *adj* impécunieux.

impede [ɪm'pi:d] *vt* gêner, entraver.

impediment [ɪm'pedɪmənt] *n* obstacle *m*. **speech ~** défaut *m* d'élocution.

impel [ɪm'pel] *vt (compel)* obliger, forcer (*to do* à faire); *(drive forward)* pousser.

impending [ɪm'pendɪŋ] *adj birth, arrival* imminent, prochain *(after n)*; *danger, storm* imminent, menaçant.

impenetrable [ɪm'penɪtrəbl] *adj* impénétrable.

impenitent [ɪm'penɪt(ə)nt] *adj* impénitent. ◆ **impenitently** *adv* sans repentir.

imperative [ɪm'perətɪv] **1** *adj need, voice, manner* impérieux; *order* impératif; *(Gram)* impératif. **silence is ~** le silence s'impose; **it is ~ that** il faut absolument que + *subj*. **2** *n* impératif *m*. **in the ~** à l'impératif.

imperceptible [ˌɪmpə'septəbl] *adj* imperceptible. ◆ **imperceptibly** *adv* imperceptiblement.

imperfect [ɪm'pɜ:fɪkt] **1** *adj reasoning* imparfait; *car, machine* défectueux; *(Gram)* imparfait. **2** *n* imparfait *m*. **in the ~** à l'imparfait. ◆ **imperfection** *n* imperfection *f*. ◆ **imperfectly** *adv* imparfaitement.

imperial [ɪm'pɪərɪəl] *adj (gen)* impérial; *(lordly) splendour* majestueux; *gesture* impérieux; *(Brit) weight, measure* légal. ◆ **imperialism** *n* impérialisme *m*. ◆ **imperialist** *adj, n* impérialiste *(mf)*. ◆ **imperially** *adv* impérieusement.

imperil [ɪm'perɪl] *vt* mettre en péril.

imperious [ɪm'pɪərɪəs] *adj* impérieux. ◆ **imperiously** *adv* impérieusement.

impermanent [ɪm'pɜ:mənənt] *adj* éphémère.

impermeable [ɪm'pɜ:mɪəbl] *adj* imperméable.

impersonal [ɪm'pɜ:snl] *adj* impersonnel. ◆ **impersonally** *adv* impersonnellement.

impersonate [ɪm'pɜ:səneɪt] *vt (gen)* se faire passer pour; *(Theat)* imiter. ◆ **impersonation** *n (Theat)* imitation *f*. ◆ **impersonator** *n (Theat)* imitateur *m*, -trice *f*.

impertinent [ɪm'pɜ:tɪnənt] *adj* impertinent (*to sb* envers qn). ◆ **impertinence** *n* impertinence *f*. ◆ **impertinently** *adv* avec impertinence.

imperturbable [ˌɪmpə'tɜ:bəbl] *adj* imperturbable.

impervious [ɪm'pɜ:vɪəs] *adj* imperméable; *(fig)* sourd (*to* à).

impetigo [ˌɪmpɪ'taɪgəʊ] *n* impétigo *m*.

impetuous [ɪm'petjʊəs] *adj* impétueux. ◆ **impetuosity** *n* impétuosité *f*. ◆ **impetuously** *adv* impétueusement.

impetus ['ɪmpɪtəs] *n [object]* force *f* d'impulsion; *[runner]* élan *m*; *(fig)* impulsion *f*.

impiety [ɪm'paɪətɪ] *n* impiété *f*.

impinge [ɪm'pɪn(d)ʒ] *vi*: **to ~ on sb/sth** *(gen)* affecter qn/qch; **it suddenly ~d on him** il en a brusquement pris conscience; **to ~ on sb's rights** empiéter sur les droits de qn.

impious ['ɪmpɪəs] *adj* impie.

implacable [ɪm'plækəbl] *adj* implacable (*towards* envers). ◆ **implacably** *adv* implacablement.

implant [ɪm'plɑːnt] **1** *vt* implanter (*in* dans). **2** ['ɪmplɑːnt] *n (under skin)* implant *m; (graft)* greffe *f*.

implausible [ɪm'plɔːzəbl] *adj* peu plausible.

implement ['ɪmplɪmənt] **1** *n* outil *m*, instrument *m*; *(fig)* instrument. **~s** matériel *m*, outils; *(for cooking)* ustensiles *mpl*. **2** ['ɪmplɪment] *vt contract, decision* exécuter; *promise* accomplir; *law* appliquer; *plan* réaliser; *ideas* mettre en pratique.

implicate ['ɪmplɪkeɪt] *vt* impliquer, compromettre (*in* dans). ◆ **implication**[1] *n* implication *f*.

implication[2] [ˌɪmplɪ'keɪʃ(ə)n] *n (V* **imply***)* insinuation *f*, implication *f*; **by implication** implicitement; **I know only from implication** je ne sais que d'après ce qui a été insinué; **the full implications of his words** la portée de ses paroles; **we shall have to study all the implications** il nous faudra étudier toutes les conséquences possibles.

implicit [ɪm'plɪsɪt] *adj* (**a**) *(implied) threat, acceptance* implicite (*in* dans). (**b**) *(unquestioning) belief, faith* absolu; *obedience* aveugle. ◆ **implicitly** *adv* (**a**) implicitement. (**b**) absolument; aveuglément.

implore [ɪm'plɔːʳ] *vt* implorer, supplier (*sb to do* qn de faire); *sb's help etc* implorer. ◆ **imploring** *adj* suppliant. ◆ **imploringly** *adv* d'un air *or* d'un ton suppliant.

imply [ɪm'plaɪ] *vt* (**a**) *[person]* laisser entendre; *(insinuate)* insinuer *(pej)*. **it is implied that...** il faut sous-entendre que... (**b**) *[fact, event]* suggérer, impliquer. ◆ **implied** *adj* sous-entendu.

impolite [ˌɪmpə'laɪt] *adj* impoli (*to, towards* envers). ◆ **impolitely** *adv* impoliment. ◆ **impoliteness** *n* impolitesse *f*.

imponderable [ɪm'pɒndərəbl] *adj, n* impondérable *(m)*.

import ['ɪmpɔːt] **1** *n* (**a**) *(Comm)* importation *f*. (**b**) *(meaning: gen)* sens *m*; *[document]* teneur *f*. (**c**) *(importance)* importance *f*. **2** *adj duty, licence, surcharge* d'importation. **3** [ɪm'pɔːt] *vt* importer. ◆ **importation** *n* importation *f*. ◆ **importer** *n* importateur *m*.

important [ɪm'pɔːt(ə)nt] *adj* important (*to sth* pour qch; *to sb* à qn). **it is ~ that** il est important que + *subj*; **that's not ~** ça n'a pas d'importance; **he was trying to look ~** il se donnait des airs importants. ◆ **importance** *n* importance *f*; **to be of importance** avoir de l'importance; **it is of the highest importance that...** il est de la plus haute importance que... + *subj;* **to give importance to sth** *[person]* accorder de l'importance à qch; *[event]* donner de l'importance à qch; **of no importance** sans importance; **full of his own importance** plein de lui-même. ◆ **importantly** *adv (pej) say etc* d'un air important; **but, more ~ly,...** mais, ce qui est plus important,...

importune [ˌɪmpɔː'tjuːn] *vt [questioner etc]* importuner; *[creditor]* harceler; *[prostitute etc]* racoler. ◆ **importunate** *adj* importun. ◆ **importuning** *n (Jur)* racolage *m*.

impose [ɪm'pəʊz] **1** *vt task, conditions* imposer (*on* à); *sanctions, fine* infliger (*on* à); *tax* mettre (*on* sur). **to ~ o.s. on sb** s'imposer à qn. **2** *vi*: **to ~ on sb** abuser de la gentillesse de qn. ◆ **imposing** *adj* imposant, impressionnant. ◆ **imposition** *n* imposition *f*; **it's rather an imposition on her** c'est abuser de sa gentillesse.

impossible [ɪm'pɒsəbl] **1** *adj* impossible. **it is ~ for him to leave** il lui est impossible de partir; **he made it ~ for me to accept** il m'a mis dans l'impossibilité d'accepter; **it is/is not ~ that** il est/n'est pas impossible que + *subj*. **2** *n*: **the ~** l'impossible *m*. ◆ **impossibility** *n* impossibilité *f* (*of sth* de qch; *of doing* de faire). ◆ **impossibly** *adv behave* de façon impossible; *late etc* épouvantablement; *stubborn* incroyablement; **if, impossibly, he were to succeed** si, par impossible, il réussissait; **impossibly difficult** d'une difficulté insurmontable.

impostor [ɪm'pɒstəʳ] *n* imposteur *m*. ◆ **imposture** *n* imposture *f*.

impotent ['ɪmpət(ə)nt] *adj (gen; also sexual)* impuissant; *(Med gen)* impotent. ◆ **impotence** *n* impuissance *f*; impotence *f*.

impound [ɪm'paʊnd] *vt* confisquer.

impoverished [ɪm'pɒv(ə)rɪʃt] *adj* appauvri. ◆ **impoverishment** *n* appauvrissement *m*.

impracticable [ɪm'præktɪkəbl] *adj* impraticable. ◆ **impracticability** *n* impraticabilité *f*.

impractical [ɪm'præktɪk(ə)l] *adj person* qui manque d'esprit pratique; *plan, idea* peu réaliste, pas pratique. ◆ **impracticality** *n* manque *m* de réalisme.

imprecise [ˌɪmprɪ'saɪs] *adj* imprécis.

impregnable [ɪm'pregnəbl] *adj (Mil)* imprenable; *(fig) position* inattaquable, irréfutable.

impregnate ['ɪmpregneɪt] *vt (fertilize)* féconder; *(saturate: also fig)* imprégner (*with* de).

impresario [ˌɪmpre'sɑːrɪəʊ] *n* impresario *m*.

impress [ɪm'pres] *vt* (**a**) *person* impressionner. **how did he ~ you?** quelle impression vous a-t-il faite?; **he ~ed me favourably** il m'a fait une bonne impression; **I am not ~ed** ça ne m'impressionne pas. (**b**) *seal, imprint* imprimer (*on* sur). *(fig)* **to ~ sth on sb** faire bien comprendre qch à qn; **to ~ on sb that** faire bien comprendre à qn que. ◆ **impression** *n* impression *f*; **to make an ~ion** faire de l'effet (*on sb* à qn); **the water made no ~ion on the stains** l'eau n'a fait aucun effet sur les taches; **I am under the ~ion that...** j'ai l'impression que...; **that wasn't my ~ion!** ce n'est pas l'impression que j'ai eue! ◆ **impressionable** *adj* impressionnable; *age* où l'on est impressionnable. ◆ **impressionism** *n* impressionnisme *m*. ◆ **impressionist** *adj, n* impressionniste *(mf)*. ◆ **impressionistic** *adj* impressionniste. ◆ **impressive** *adj* impressionnant. ◆ **impressively** *adv* de façon impressionnante.

imprint [ɪm'prɪnt] **1** *vt* imprimer (*on* sur). **2** ['ɪmprɪnt] *n* empreinte *f*. **published under the Collins ~** édité chez Collins.

imprison [ɪm'prɪzn] *vt* emprisonner; *[judge]* condamner à la prison. **he had been ~ed for 3 months when...** il avait été en prison 3 mois quand... ◆ **imprisonment** *n (action, state)* emprisonnement *m*; **one month's ~ment** un mois de prison.

improbable [ɪm'prɒbəbl] *adj event* improbable; *story, excuse* invraisemblable. **it is ~ that** il est improbable que + *subj*. ◆ **improbability** *n* improbabilité *f*; invraisemblance *f*.

impromptu [ɪm'prɒm(p)tjuː] *adv, adj, n* impromptu *(m)*.

improper [ɪm'prɒpəʳ] *adj (unsuitable)* déplacé; *(indecent)* indécent; *(dishonest)* malhonnête ; *(wrong)* incorrect. ◆ **improperly** *adv* d'une manière déplacée; indécemment; malhonnêtement; incorrectement. ◆ **impropriety** *n* inconvenance *f*.

improve [ɪm'pru:v] **1** *vt (gen)* améliorer; *physique* développer; *machine, invention* améliorer, perfectionner; *site* embellir; *soil, land* amender. **to ~ sb's looks** embellir qn; **that should ~ his chances of success** ceci devrait lui donner de meilleures chances de réussir; **to ~ one's mind** se cultiver; **to ~ one's French** se perfectionner en français; **to ~ the occasion** tirer parti de l'occasion. **2** *vi* s'améliorer; se développer; être amélioré, être perfectionné; s'amender. **to ~ on acquaintance** gagner à être connu; **the invalid is improving** l'état du malade s'améliore; **his maths have ~d** il a fait des progrès en maths; **business is improving** les affaires reprennent; **things are improving** les choses vont mieux; **to ~ on sth** faire mieux que qch; **to ~ on sb's offer** enchérir sur qn. ◆ **improvement** *n* amélioration *f*; développement *m*; perfectionnement *m*; embellissement *m*; amendement *m*; **there's been quite an ~ment** il y a du mieux; **to show some ~ment in French** faire quelques progrès en français; **this model is an ~ment on the previous one** ce modèle marque un progrès sur le précédent; **there is room for ~ment** cela pourrait être mieux; **to carry out ~ments to sth** apporter des améliorations à qch; **~ment grant** subvention *f* pour l'amélioration de l'habitat. ◆ **improving** *adj book etc* édifiant.

improvident [ɪm'prɒvɪd(ə)nt] *adj* imprévoyant.

improvise ['ɪmprəvaɪz] *vti* improviser. ◆ **improvisation** *n* improvisation *f*.

imprudent [ɪm'pru:d(ə)nt] *adj* imprudent. ◆ **imprudence** *n* imprudence *f*. ◆ **imprudently** *adv* imprudemment.

impudent ['ɪmpjʊd(ə)nt] *adj* impudent. ◆ **impudence** *n* impudence *f*. ◆ **impudently** *adv* impudemment.

impulse ['ɪmpʌls] **1** *n* impulsion *f*. **rash ~** coup *m* de tête; **on a sudden ~ he...** pris d'une impulsion soudaine il...; **to act on (an) ~** agir par impulsion. **2** *adj*: **~ buying** tendance *f* à faire des achats sur un coup de tête. ◆ **impulsion** *n* impulsion *f*. ◆ **impulsive** *adj movement, action* impulsif; *temperament* primesautier; *remark* irréfléchi. ◆ **impulsively** *adv* par impulsion. ◆ **impulsiveness** *n* caractère *m* impulsif.

impunity [ɪm'pju:nɪtɪ] *n*: **with ~** impunément.

impure [ɪm'pjʊə[r]] *adj* impur. ◆ **impurity** *n* impureté *f*.

impute [ɪm'pju:t] *vt* imputer (*to* à). ◆ **imputation** *n* imputation *f*.

in [ɪn] **1** *prep* (**a**) *(gen)* dans. **~ the garden** dans le *or* au jardin; **~ the country** à la campagne; **~ town** en ville; **~ here** ici; **~ there** là-dedans; **~ school** à l'école; **~ the school** dans l'école; **~ a friend's house** chez un ami; **~ the army** dans l'armée; **he's ~ the motor trade** il travaille dans l'industrie automobile.

(**b**) *(in geog names) (countries: gen, also fem US states and fem French provinces)* **in England/France** *etc* en Angleterre/France *etc;* **in Virginia/Brittany** en Virginie/Bretagne; *(countries: plurals or beginning with initial consonant)* **in Japan/the United States** au Japon/aux États-Unis; *(towns: gen, also masc islands)* **in London/Paris** *etc* à Londres/Paris *etc;* **in Cuba** à Cuba; **in Sussex** dans le Sussex.

(**c**) *(people, works)* chez, en, dans. **we find it ~ Dickens** nous le trouvons chez *or* dans Dickens; **rare ~ a child of that age** rare chez un enfant de cet âge; **he has got it ~ him to succeed** il est capable de réussir; **they've got a great leader ~ him** ils ont en lui un excellent dirigeant.

(**d**) *(time: during)* **~ 1989** en 1989; **~ the sixties** dans les années soixante; **~ the reign of** sous le règne de; **~ June** en juin, au mois de juin; **~ spring** au printemps; **~ summer/autumn/winter** en été/automne/hiver; **~ the morning** le matin, dans la matinée; **~ the mornings** le matin; **~ the daytime** pendant la journée; **~ the evening** le soir, pendant la soirée; **~ the night** la nuit, pendant la nuit; **3 o'clock ~ the afternoon** 3 heures de l'après-midi; **~ those days** à cette époque-là; **~ these days** de nos jours; **I haven't seen him ~ years** cela fait des années que je ne l'ai pas vu.

(**e**) *(time: in the space of)* en. **I did it ~ 2 hours** je l'ai fait en 2 heures, j'ai mis 2 heures à le faire.

(**f**) *(time: at the end of)* dans, au bout de. **~ a moment** dans une minute; **he will arrive ~ a week** il arrivera dans une semaine; **he returned ~ a week** il est rentré au bout d'une semaine.

(**g**) *(manner etc)* **~ a loud voice** d'une voix forte; **~ a soft voice** à voix basse; **~ a whisper** en chuchotant; **~ ink** à l'encre; **~ pencil** au crayon; **~ French** en français; **~ writing** par écrit; **to paint ~ oils** peindre à l'huile; **to stand ~ a row** être en ligne; **~ large/small quantities** en grande/petite quantité; **~ some measure** dans une certaine mesure; **~ part** en partie; **~ hundreds** par centaines; **dressed ~ white** habillé en *or* vêtu de blanc; **~ slippers** en pantoufles; **you look nice ~ that dress** tu es jolie avec cette robe.

(**h**) *(material)* en. **~ silk** en soie; **~ marble** en marbre.

(**i**) *(circumstances)* **~ the rain** sous la pluie; **~ the sun** au soleil; **~ the shade** à l'ombre; **~ darkness** dans l'obscurité; **~ the moonlight** au clair de lune; **~ all weathers** par tous les temps.

(**j**) *(state, condition)* **~ good health** en bonne santé; **~ tears** en larmes; **~ despair** au désespoir; **to be ~ a rage** être en rage; **~ good repair** en bon état; **to live ~ luxury** vivre dans le luxe; **~ private** en privé; **~ secret** en secret.

(**k**) *(ratio)* **one man ~ ten** un homme sur dix; **once ~ a hundred years** une fois tous les cent ans; **a day ~ a thousand** un jour entre mille; **15 pence ~ the pound** 15 pence par livre sterling.

(**l**) *(in respect of)* **blind ~ the left eye** aveugle de l'œil gauche; **poor ~ maths** faible en maths; **10 metres ~ height by 30 ~ length** 10 mètres de haut sur 30 de long; **5 ~ number** au nombre de 5; **~ that, he resembles his father** en cela, il ressemble à son père.

(**m**) *(after superlative)* de. **the best pupil ~ the class** le meilleur élève de la classe.

(**n**) **~ that there are 5 of them** étant donné qu'il y en a 5; **~ so** *or* **as far as** dans la mesure où; **~ all** en tout.

2 *adv*: **to be ~** *(at home, office etc)* être là; *[fire]* brûler encore; *[train]* être arrivé; *[harvest]* être rentré; *(in season) [fruit etc]* être en saison; *(in fashion) [colour, style]* être à la mode; *(in power) [political party]* être au pouvoir; *[candidate]* être élu. **there is nobody ~** il n'y a personne (à la maison); **we were asked ~** on nous a invités à entrer; *(Pol)* **to put sb ~** porter qn au pouvoir; **~ between** *(space)* entre, au milieu; *(time)* entre-temps; **we are ~ for trouble** nous allons avoir des ennuis; **he's ~ for it! *** il va en prendre pour son grade! *; **you don't know what you're ~ for! *** tu ne sais pas ce qui t'attend!; **are you ~ for the race?** est-ce que tu es inscrit pour la course?; **he's ~ for the job of...** il est candidat au poste de...; **to have it ~ for sb *** avoir une dent contre qn; **to be ~ on a plan/secret** être au courant d'un plan/d'un secret; **to be (well) ~ with sb** être bien avec qn; **day ~ day out** jour après jour.

3 *adj*: **~ tray** corbeille *f* du courrier du jour; **it's the ~ * thing to do that** c'est très dans le vent * de faire ça; **an ~ * joke** une plaisanterie qui n'est comprise que des initiés.

4 *n*: **the ~s and outs** les tenants et les aboutissants *mpl*.

◆ **in-between 1** *n*: **the ~-betweens** ceux qui sont entre les deux ; **2** *adj*: **it's ~-between** c'est entre les deux; ~-**between times** dans les intervalles. ◆ **in-fighting** *n (fig: within group etc)* querelles *fpl* internes. ◆ **in-flight** *adj* en vol. ◆ **in-group** *n* noyau *m* (fermé). ◆ **in-house** *adj publication* interne; *training* effectué sur place. ◆ **in-laws** * *npl (parents-in-law)* beaux-parents *mpl*; *(others)* belle-famille *f*. ◆ **in-patient** *n* malade *mf* hospitalisé(e). ◆ **in-service training** *n* formation *f* continue *or* en cours d'emploi.

inability [ˌɪnəˈbɪlɪtɪ] *n* incapacité *f* (*to do* de faire), impuissance *f* (*to do* à faire).

inaccessible [ˌɪnækˈsesəbl] *adj* inaccessible (*to* à). ◆ **inaccessibility** *n* inaccessibilité *f*.

inaccurate [ɪnˈækjʊrɪt] *adj (gen)* inexact; *word, expression* impropre; *story, report, translation* manquant de précision. ◆ **inaccuracy** *n* inexactitude *f*; impropriété *f*; manque *m* de précision. ◆ **inaccurately** *adv* avec inexactitude, inexactement; *multiply* incorrectement.

inactive [ɪnˈæktɪv] *adj person* inactif; *life* peu actif; *volcano* qui n'est pas en activité. ◆ **inaction** *n* inaction *f*. ◆ **inactivity** *n* inactivité *f*.

inadequate [ɪnˈædɪkwɪt] *adj (gen)* insuffisant; *piece of work* médiocre; *person* incompétent, inadéquat; *(Psych)* mal adapté (sur le plan socio-affectif). **he felt totally** ~ il ne se sentait absolument pas à la hauteur. ◆ **inadequacy** *n* insuffisance *f*; médiocrité *f*; incompétence *f*; *(Psych)* inadaptation *f* socio-affective. ◆ **inadequately** *adv* insuffisamment.

inadmissible [ˌɪnədˈmɪsəbl] *adj* inadmissible; *(Jur) evidence* irrecevable.

inadvertent [ˌɪnədˈvɜːt(ə)nt] *adj* fait (*or* dit *etc*) par inadvertance *or* par mégarde. ◆ **inadvertently** *adv* par inadvertance, par mégarde.

inadvisable [ˌɪnədˈvaɪzəbl] *adj* peu sage, à déconseiller. **it is** ~ **to...** il est déconseillé de... + *infin*. ◆ **inadvisability** *n* inopportunité *f* (*of doing* de faire).

inane [ɪˈneɪn] *adj* inepte, stupide. ◆ **inanity** *n* ineptie *f*.

inanimate [ɪnˈænɪmɪt] *adj* inanimé.

inapplicable [ɪnˈæplɪkəbl] *adj* inapplicable (*to* à).

inappropriate [ˌɪnəˈprəʊprɪɪt] *adj (gen)* inopportun; *word* impropre; *name* mal choisi. ◆ **inappropriately** *adv* inopportunément; improprement.

inarticulate [ˌɪnɑːˈtɪkjʊlɪt] *adj person* qui s'exprime avec difficulté; *speech* indistinct; *(Anat, Bot)* inarticulé. ~ **with anger** bafouillant de colère.

inartistic [ˌɪnɑːˈtɪstɪk] *adj work* peu artistique; *person* dépourvu de sens artistique. ◆ **inartistically** *adv* de façon peu artistique.

inattention [ˌɪnəˈtenʃ(ə)n] *n* manque *m* d'attention (*to* accordée à). ◆ **inattentive** *adj (not paying attention)* inattentif; *(neglectful)* peu attentionné (*towards sb* envers qn). ◆ **inattentively** *adv* sans prêter attention.

inaudible [ɪnˈɔːdəbl] *adj* inaudible. **he was** ~ on ne l'entendait pas. ◆ **inaudibly** *adv* de manière inaudible.

inaugurate [ɪˈnɔːgjʊreɪt] *vt (gen)* inaugurer; *person* investir de ses fonctions. ◆ **inaugural** *adj* inaugural; *(Univ)* **inaugural lecture** leçon *f* inaugurale. ◆ **inauguration** *n* inauguration *f*; investiture *f*.

inauspicious [ˌɪnɔːsˈpɪʃəs] *adj beginning, sign* de mauvais augure; *occasion* peu propice; *circumstances* malencontreux. ◆ **inauspiciously** *adv* d'une façon peu propice; malencontreusement.

inborn [ˌɪnˈbɔːn] *adj*, **inbred** [ˌɪnˈbred] *adj feeling* inné. **an inbred family** une famille qui a un fort degré de consanguinité.

incalculable [ɪnˈkælkjʊləbl] *adj* incalculable.

incandescent [ˌɪnkænˈdesnt] *adj* incandescent. ◆ **incandescence** *n* incandescence *f*.

incantation [ˌɪnkænˈteɪʃ(ə)n] *n* incantation *f*.

incapable [ɪnˈkeɪpəbl] *adj* incapable (*of doing* de faire). ◆ **incapability** *n* incapacité *f* (*of doing* de faire).

incapacity [ˌɪnkəˈpæsɪtɪ] *n* incapacité *f* (*to do* de faire). ◆ **incapacitate** *vt* rendre incapable (*for work etc* de travailler *etc*).

incarcerate [ɪnˈkɑːsəreɪt] *vt* incarcérer.

incarnate [ɪnˈkɑːnɪt] *adj* incarné. ◆ **incarnation** *n* incarnation *f*.

incautious [ɪnˈkɔːʃəs] *adj* imprudent.

incendiary [ɪnˈsendɪərɪ] **1** *adj* incendiaire. **2** *n (bomb)* engin *m* incendiaire.

incense[1] [ɪnˈsens] *vt* mettre en fureur. ◆ **incensed** *adj* outré (*at, by* de).

incense[2] [ˈɪnsens] *n* encens *m*.

incentive [ɪnˈsentɪv] **1** *n (no pl: reason)* motivation *f*; *(reward)* récompense *f*. **there is no** ~ **to hard work** il n'y a rien qui incite *(subj)* à travailler dur; **he has no** ~ **to do it** il n'a rien qui l'incite *(subj)* à le faire; **it gave me an** ~ cela m'a encouragé. **2** *adj*: ~ **bonus** prime *f* d'encouragement.

inception [ɪnˈsepʃ(ə)n] *n* commencement *m*.

incertitude [ɪnˈsɜːtɪtjuːd] *n* incertitude *f*.

incessant [ɪnˈsesnt] *adj* incessant. ◆ **incessantly** *adv* sans cesse, incessamment.

incest [ˈɪnsest] *n* inceste *m*. ◆ **incestuous** *adj* incestueux.

inch [ɪn(t)ʃ] **1** *n* pouce *m* (*= 2,54 cm*). **a few** ~**es** ≃ quelques centimètres; **not an** ~ **of** ≃ pas un centimètre de; **every** ~ **of the...** tout le (*or* toute la)...; **he wouldn't budge an** ~ il n'a pas voulu *(lit)* bouger *or (fig)* céder d'un pouce; **he's every** ~ **a soldier** c'est un vrai soldat; **within an** ~ **of (doing) sth** à deux doigts de (faire) qch; ~ **by** ~ petit à petit. **2** *vi*: **to** ~ **(one's way) forward/out** *etc* avancer/sortir *etc* petit à petit. ◆ **inchtape** *n* centimètre *m* (de couturière).

incidence [ˈɪnsɪd(ə)ns] *n* fréquence *f*, taux *m*. **the high** ~ **of** le taux élevé de; **the low** ~ **of** la faible fréquence de.

incident [ˈɪnsɪd(ə)nt] **1** *n (gen)* incident *m*; *(in book, play etc)* épisode *m*. **2** *adj (Police etc)* ~ **room** salle *f* d'opérations.
◆ **incidental** [ˌɪnsɪˈdentl] **1** *adj (accompanying)* accessoire; *(secondary)* d'importance secondaire; *(unplanned)* accidentel; ~**al expenses** faux frais *mpl*; ~**al music** musique *f* d'accompagnement; **2** *n*: ~**als** *(expenses)* frais *mpl* accessoires. ◆ **incidentally** *adv happen etc* accidentellement; *(by the way)* à propos, entre parenthèses.

incinerate [ɪnˈsɪnəreɪt] *vt* incinérer. ◆ **incineration** *n* incinération *f*. ◆ **incinerator** *n* incinérateur *m*.

incipient [ɪnˈsɪpɪənt] *adj* naissant, qui commence.

incise [ɪnˈsaɪz] *vt* inciser; *(Art)* graver. ◆ **incision** *n* incision *f*. ◆ **incisive** *adj (trenchant)* incisif; *(acute)* pénétrant. ◆ **incisively** *adv* d'une façon incisive *or* pénétrante. ◆ **incisor** *n* incisive *f*.

incite [ɪnˈsaɪt] *vt* pousser, inciter (*sb to sth* qn à qch; *sb to do* qn à faire). ◆ **incitement** *n* incitation *f*.

incivility [ˌɪnsɪˈvɪlɪtɪ] *n* incivilité *f*.

inclement [ɪnˈklemənt] *adj* inclément.

incline [ɪnˈklaɪn] **1** *vt (lean)* incliner, pencher. ~**d plane** plan *m* incliné; **to** ~ **sb to do** incliner qn *or* rendre qn enclin à faire; *[person]* **to be** ~**d to do** incliner à faire; **he is** ~**d to be lazy** il incline à *or* il est enclin à la paresse; **it's** ~**d to break** cela se casse facilement; **he's that way** ~**d** il a tendance à être comme ça; **if you feel** ~**d** si le cœur vous en dit; **well** ~**d towards sb** bien disposé à l'égard de qn. **2** *vi* (**a**) *(slope)* s'incliner. (**b**) *[colour, beliefs etc]* tendre (*towards* vers). **to ~ to an opinion** *etc* pencher pour une opinion *etc*. **3** ['ɪnklaɪn] *n* inclinaison *f*. ◆ **inclination** *n (all senses)* inclination *f*; **my inclination is to leave** j'incline à partir; **I have no inclination to help him** je n'ai aucune envie de l'aider.

include [ɪn'klu:d] *vt* inclure, comprendre. **it is not ~d** *(on list)* cela n'est pas inclus; *(in bill)* ce n'est pas compris *or* inclus; **everything ~d** tout compris; **does that ~ me?** est-ce que cela s'applique aussi à moi?; **the invitation ~s everybody** l'invitation s'adresse à tout le monde; **the children ~d** y compris les enfants. ◆ **including** *prep* y compris, compris, inclus; **including the kitchen** la cuisine comprise, y compris la cuisine; **including the service charge** service compris; **not including tax** taxe non comprise; **up to and including 4th May** jusqu'au 4 mai inclus. ◆ **inclusion** *n* inclusion *f*. ◆ **inclusive** *adj charge, sum* global; **from 1st to 6th May inclusive** du 1er au 6 mai inclus; **to be inclusive of** inclure, comprendre; **cost inclusive of travel** prix *m* voyage compris. ◆ **inclusively** *adv* inclusivement.

incognito [ɪn'kɒgnɪtəʊ] **1** *adv* incognito. **2** *adj*: **to remain ~** garder l'incognito.

incoherent [,ɪnkə(ʊ)'hɪər(ə)nt] *adj* incohérent. ◆ **incoherence** *n* incohérence *f*. ◆ **incoherently** *adv* d'une façon incohérente.

incombustible [,ɪnkəm'bʌstəbl] *adj* incombustible.

income ['ɪnkʌm] **1** *n (gen)* revenu *m*. **private ~** rentes *fpl*; **to live beyond/within one's ~** dépasser/ne pas dépasser son revenu. **2** *adj*: **the lowest ~ group** les économiquement faibles *mpl*; **the middle/upper ~ group** la classe à revenus moyens/élevés; **~s policy** politique *f* des revenus; **~ tax** impôt *m* sur le revenu; **~ tax return** déclaration *f* d'impôts.

incomer ['ɪn,kʌmə[r]] *n* arrivant(e) *m(f)*. ◆ **incoming** *adj crowd* qui entre; *tide* montant; *tenant, mayor* nouveau *(before n)*.

incoming ['ɪn,kʌmɪŋ] *adj people, flight* qui arrive; *tenant, president* nouveau. **~ tide** marée *f* montante.

incommunicado [,ɪnkəmjʊnɪ'kɑ:dəʊ] *adj* tenu au secret.

incomparable [ɪn'kɒmp(ə)rəbl] *adj* incomparable. ◆ **incomparably** *adv* incomparablement.

incompatible [,ɪnkəm'pætəbl] *adj* incompatible. ◆ **incompatibility** *n* incompatibilité *f*; *(in divorce)* incompatibilité d'humeur.

incompetent [ɪn'kɒmpɪt(ə)nt] *adj* incompétent. ◆ **incompetence** *or* ◆ **incompetency** *n* incompétence *f*.

incomplete [,ɪnkəm'pli:t] *adj* incomplet. ◆ **incompletely** *adv* incomplètement.

incomprehensible [ɪn,kɒmprɪ'hensəbl] *adj* incompréhensible. ◆ **incomprehensibly** *adv* de manière incompréhensible.

inconceivable [,ɪnkən'si:vəbl] *adj* inconcevable. ◆ **inconceivably** *adv*: **inconceivably stupid** d'une stupidité inconcevable.

inconclusive [,ɪnkən'klu:sɪv] *adj result, discussion* peu concluant; *evidence, argument* peu convaincant; *action* sans résultat concluant; *fighting* indécis. ◆ **inconclusively** *adv* d'une manière peu concluante *or* peu convaincante; sans résultat concluant.

incongruous [ɪn'kɒŋgrʊəs] *adj (out of place) remark, act* incongru, déplacé; *(absurd)* absurde, grotesque. ◆ **incongruity** [,ɪnkɒŋ'gru:ɪtɪ] *n* incongruité *f*; absurdité *f*.

inconsequent [ɪn'kɒnsɪkwənt] *adj* inconséquent. ◆ **inconsequential** *adj* (**a**) *(illogical)* inconséquent. (**b**) *(unimportant)* sans conséquence.

inconsiderable [,ɪnkən'sɪd(ə)rəbl] *adj* insignifiant.

inconsiderate [,ɪnkən'sɪd(ə)rɪt] *adj person* qui manque d'égards; *action, reply* inconsidéré. **you were very ~** tu as agi sans aucun égard.

inconsistent [,ɪnkən'sɪst(ə)nt] *adj speech, person* inconsistant. **~ with** incompatible avec. ◆ **inconsistency** *n* inconsistance *f*.

inconsolable [,ɪnkən'səʊləbl] *adj* inconsolable.

inconspicuous [,ɪnkən'spɪkjʊəs] *adj* qui passe inaperçu, qui ne se fait pas remarquer. **to make oneself ~** essayer de passer inaperçu. ◆ **inconspicuously** *adv behave, move* sans se faire remarquer; *dress* de façon discrète.

inconstant [ɪn'kɒnst(ə)nt] *adj* inconstant. ◆ **inconstancy** *n* inconstance *f*.

incontestable [,ɪnkən'testəbl] *adj* incontestable.

incontinent [ɪn'kɒntɪnənt] *adj* incontinent. ◆ **incontinence** *n* incontinence *f*.

incontrovertible [ɪn,kɒntrə'vɜ:təbl] *adj fact* indéniable; *argument, explanation* irréfutable; *sign, proof* irrécusable. ◆ **incontrovertibly** *adv* indéniablement.

inconvenient [,ɪnkən'vi:nɪənt] *adj time, place* mal choisi; *house, equipment* incommode, peu pratique; *visitor* gênant, importun. **if it is not ~** si cela ne vous dérange pas; **it is most ~** c'est très gênant. ◆ **inconvenience 1** *n (annoying thing)* inconvénient *m*; **to put sb to great inconvenience** causer beaucoup de dérangement à qn; **he went to a great deal of inconvenience to help me** il s'est donné beaucoup de mal pour m'aider ; **2** *vt* déranger, incommoder; *(stronger)* gêner. ◆ **inconveniently** *adv design* incommodément; *happen, arrive* à contretemps.

incorporate [ɪn'kɔ:pəreɪt] *vt (put in)* incorporer (*into* dans; *(Culin) into* à); *(include, contain)* contenir; *(Comm, Jur)* se constituer en société unique avec. **~d company** société *f* à responsabilité limitée.

incorrect [,ɪnkə'rekt] *adj wording, calculation, dress, behaviour* incorrect; *statement, opinion, report, time, text* inexact. **he is ~ in stating that...** il se trompe quand il affirme que...; **it would be ~ to say** il serait inexact de dire. ◆ **incorrectly** *adv* incorrectement; inexactement.

incorrigible [ɪn'kɒrɪdʒəbl] *adj* incorrigible.

incorruptible [,ɪnkə'rʌptəbl] *adj* incorruptible.

increase [ɪn'kri:s] **1** *vi* augmenter; *[demand, strength, supply, population, speed]* augmenter, s'accroître; *[joy, rage, effort, pain]* augmenter, s'intensifier; *[sorrow, surprise, possessions, trade]* s'accroître, augmenter; *[noise, pride]* grandir; *[business firm, institution]* s'agrandir, se développer. **to ~ in volume/weight** prendre du volume/poids; **to ~ in width** s'élargir; **to ~ in height** *[person]* grandir; *[tree]* pousser. **2** *vt* augmenter; accroître; intensifier; agrandir; développer. **to ~ (one's) speed** accélérer. **3** ['ɪnkri:s] *n* augmentation *f* (*in, of* de); accroissement *m*; intensification *f*; agrandissement *m*; développement *m*. **there has been an ~ in police activity** la police a redoublé d'activité; **an ~ in pay** une hausse de salaire, une augmentation; **to be on the ~ = to ~**, *V* **1**. ◆ **increasing** *adj* croissant. ◆ **increasingly** *adv* de plus en plus.

incredible [ɪn'kredəbl] *adj* incroyable. ◆ **incredibly** *adv* incroyablement.

incredulous [ɪn'kredjʊləs] *adj* incrédule. ◆ **incredulity** *n* incrédulité *f*. ◆ **incredulously** *adv* d'un air *or* d'un ton incrédule.

increment ['ɪnkrɪmənt] *n* augmentation *f*.

incriminate [ɪn'krɪmɪneɪt] *vt* incriminer, compromettre. ◆ **incriminating** *adj* compromettant; *(Jur: exhibits etc)* **incriminating evidence** pièces *fpl* à conviction.

incubate ['ɪnkjʊbeɪt] **1** *vt eggs, scheme* couver; *disease* incuber. **2** *vi* couver; être en incubation. ◆ **incubation 1** *n* incubation *f*; **2** *adj* d'incubation. ◆ **incubator** *n [chicks, eggs, infants]* couveuse *f*; *[bacteria, cultures]* incubateur *m*; **in an incubator** en couveuse.

inculcate ['ɪnkʌlkeɪt] *vt* inculquer (*sth into sb* qch à qn).

incumbent [ɪn'kʌmbənt] **1** *adj* (**a**) **to be ~ upon sb to do sth** incomber à qn de faire qch. (**b**) *minister, president* en exercice. **2** *n (Rel etc)* titulaire *m*. ◆ **incumbency** *n* charge *f (Rel)*.

incur [ɪn'kɜːʳ] *vt anger, blame* s'attirer, encourir; *risk* courir; *obligation, debts* contracter; *loss* subir; *expenses* encourir.

incurable [ɪn'kjʊərəbl] *adj, n* incurable *(mf)*. ◆ **incurably** *adv* incurablement.

incurious [ɪn'kjʊərɪəs] *adj* sans curiosité.

incursion [ɪn'kɜːʃ(ə)n] *n* incursion *f*.

indebted [ɪn'detɪd] *adj* redevable (*to sb for sth* à qn de qch; *to sb for doing* à qn d'avoir fait).

indecent [ɪn'diːsnt] *adj (offensive)* indécent; *(unseemly)* inconvenant. *(Jur)* ~ **assault** attentat *m* à la pudeur (*on* sur); ~ **exposure** outrage *m* public à la pudeur. ◆ **indecency** *n* indécence *f*; inconvenance *f*; *(Jur)* outrage *m* public à la pudeur. ◆ **indecently** *adv* indécemment; de façon inconvenante.

indecipherable [ˌɪndɪ'saɪf(ə)rəbl] *adj* indéchiffrable.

indecisive [ˌɪndɪ'saɪsɪv] *adj (gen)* indécis; *discussion, argument* peu concluant. ◆ **indecision** *n* indécision *f*. ◆ **indecisively** *adv* de façon indécise.

indecorous [ɪn'dekərəs] *adj* peu convenable.

indeed [ɪn'diːd] *adv* en effet, vraiment. **and ~ he did so** et en effet il l'a bien fait; **I feel, ~ I know...** je sens, et même je sais...; **I may ~ come** il se peut effectivement que je vienne; **yes ~!** mais certainement, (mais) bien sûr!; **~?** vraiment?, c'est vrai?; **very pleased ~** extrêmement content, vraiment très content; **very grateful ~** infiniment reconnaissant; **thank you very much ~** merci mille fois.

indefatigable [ˌɪndɪ'fætɪgəbl] *adj* infatigable. ◆ **indefatigably** *adv* infatigablement.

indefensible [ˌɪndɪ'fensəbl] *adj (gen)* indéfendable; *crime* injustifiable.

indefinable [ˌɪndɪ'faɪnəbl] *adj* indéfinissable.

indefinite [ɪn'defɪnɪt] *adj intentions, doubts, feelings* incertain, indéfini, vague; *answer* vague; *outline* indistinct; *size, number, duration* indéterminé; *period* indéfini, indéterminé; *plan* mal défini, peu précis; *(Gram)* indéfini. ◆ **indefinitely** *adv wait etc* indéfiniment; **postponed ~ly** remis à une date indéterminée.

indelible [ɪn'deləbl] *adj* indélébile; *(fig)* ineffaçable. ◆ **indelibly** *adv* de façon indélébile; ineffaçablement.

indelicate [ɪn'delɪkɪt] *adj (gen)* indélicat; *(tactless)* indiscret. ◆ **indelicacy** *n* indélicatesse *f*; manque *m* de discrétion.

indemnify [ɪn'demnɪfaɪ] *vt (compensate)* indemniser, dédommager (*for*, de); *(safeguard)* garantir (*against* contre). ◆ **indemnity** *n* indemnité *f*; garantie *f*.

indent [ɪn'dent] **1** *vt border* denteler; *(Typ)* mettre en retrait. **2** *vi (Comm)* **to ~ for sth** commander qch (*on sb* à qn). **3** ['ɪndent] *n (Comm)* commande *f*. ◆ **indentation** *n (hollow impression)* empreinte *f* (en creux). ◆ **indented** *adj border* dentelé; *coast* échancré; *(Typ)* en retrait. ◆ **indentures** *npl* contrat *m* d'apprentissage.

independent [ˌɪndɪ'pendənt] **1** *adj* indépendant (*of* de); *(unrelated) reports* émanant de sources différentes; *radio* libre. *(Pol)* **I~** non-inscrit; **an ~ thinker** un penseur original; **to ask for an ~ opinion** demander l'avis d'un tiers. **2** *n (Pol)* **I~** non-inscrit *m*, non-affilié *m*. ◆ **independence 1** *n* indépendance *f* (*from* par rapport à); **the country got its independence** le pays est devenu indépendant ; **2** *adj (US)* **Independence Day** fête *f* de l'Indépendance américaine *(le 4 juillet)*. ◆ **independently** *adv* de façon indépendante; **~ly of** indépendamment de.

indescribable [ˌɪndɪs'kraɪbəbl] *adj* indescriptible. ◆ **indescribably** *adv* indescriptiblement.

indestructible [ˌɪndɪs'trʌktəbl] *adj* indestructible.

indeterminate [ˌɪndɪ'tɜːm(ɪ)nɪt] *adj* indéterminé.

index ['ɪndeks] **1** *n* (**a**) *(pl* **~es***) (in book etc)* index *m*; *(in library etc)* catalogue *m* (alphabétique). *(Rel)* **to put a book on the I~** mettre un livre à l'Index. (**b**) *(pl* **indices***)* indice *m*. **cost-of-living ~** indice du coût de la vie; *(fig)* **it is an ~ of how much...** c'est un signe révélateur qui permet de se rendre compte combien... **2** *adj*: **~ card** fiche *f* ; **~ finger** index *m*. **3** *vt book* faire l'index de; *library books, information* cataloguer (alphabétiquement); *item, article* classer (*under* sous, à). ◆ **index-linked** *adj* indexé.

India ['ɪndɪə] *n* Inde *f*. ◆ **Indian 1** *n* Indien(ne) *m(f)* ; **2** *adj* indien, de l'Inde; *(Brit Hist)* des Indes; *elephant* d'Asie; *ink* de Chine; *tea* indien; **(American) ~n** indien, des Indiens (d'Amérique); **in ~n file** en file indienne; **~n Ocean** océan *m* Indien; *(fig)* **~n summer** été *m* de la Saint-Martin. ◆ **indiarubber** *n (substance)* caoutchouc *m*; *(eraser)* gomme *f (à effacer)*.

indicate ['ɪndɪkeɪt] *vt (gen)* indiquer (*that* que); *intentions* manifester. *(Aut)* **he was indicating left** il avait mis son clignotant gauche. ◆ **indication** *n* indication *f*; **there is every indication that** tout porte à croire que + *indic*; **there is no indication that** rien ne porte à croire que + *subj*; **it is some indication of** cela permet de se rendre compte de. ◆ **indicative** *adj, n* indicatif *(m)*; **to be indicative of sth/of the fact that...** montrer qch/que...; **in the indicative** à l'indicatif. ◆ **indicator** *n (gen)* indicateur *m*; *(needle on scale etc)* aiguille *f*; *(Aut)* clignotant *m*; *(plan)* **town indicator** table *f* d'orientation; *(Rail)* **arrival indicator** tableau *m* des arrivées.

indict [ɪn'daɪt] *vt* accuser (*for, on a charge of* de). ◆ **indictable** *adj*: **~able offence** délit pénal. ◆ **indictment** *n* mise *f* en accusation (*for, of* de).

Indies ['ɪndɪz] *npl* Indes *fpl*. **East ~** Indes orientales; **West ~** Antilles *fpl*.

indifferent [ɪn'dɪfr(ə)nt] *adj* indifférent (*to* à); *(mediocre)* médiocre, quelconque. ◆ **indifference** *n* indifférence *f* (*to* à; *towards* envers); médiocrité *f*. ◆ **indifferently** *adv* indifféremment; médiocrement.

indigenous [ɪn'dɪdʒɪnəs] *adj* indigène (*to* de).

indigestion [ˌɪndɪ'dʒestʃ(ə)n] *n*: **to have ~** *(acute)* avoir une indigestion; *(chronic)* avoir une mauvaise digestion. ◆ **indigestible** *adj* indigeste.

indignant [ɪn'dɪgnənt] *adj* indigné (*about* à propos de; *at sth* de *or* devant qch; *with sb* contre qn). **to grow ~** s'indigner; **to make sb ~** indigner qn. ◆ **indignantly** *adv* avec indignation. ◆ **indignation** *n* indignation *f*; **indignation meeting** * réunion *f* de protestation.

indignity [ɪn'dɪgnɪtɪ] *n* indignité *f*.

indigo ['ɪndɪgəʊ] **1** *n* indigo *m*. **2** *adj* indigo *inv*.

indirect [ˌɪndɪ'rekt] *adj (gen)* indirect; *route, means etc* détourné. ◆ **indirectly** *adv* indirectement.

indiscreet [ˌɪndɪs'kriːt] *adj* indiscret. ◆ **indiscreetly** *adv* indiscrètement. ◆ **indiscretion** *n* indiscrétion *f*.

indiscriminate [ˌɪndɪsˈkrɪmɪnɪt] *adj punishment, blows* distribué au hasard; *killings* commis au hasard; *person* manquant de discernement; *admiration* aveugle. ◆ **indiscriminately** *adv choose, kill* au hasard; *watch TV* sans aucun sens critique; *accept, admire* aveuglément.

indispensable [ˌɪndɪsˈpensəbl] *adj* indispensable (*to* à). **you're not** ~! on peut se passer de toi!

indisposed [ˌɪndɪsˈpəʊzd] *adj (unwell)* indisposé, souffrant; *(disinclined)* peu disposé (*to do* à faire). ◆ **indisposition** *n* indisposition *f*.

indisputable [ˌɪndɪsˈpjuːtəbl] *adj* incontestable. ◆ **indisputably** *adv* incontestablement.

indistinct [ˌɪndɪsˈtɪŋ(k)t] *adj object, voice, words* indistinct; *memory* vague; *noise* confus. *(on telephone)* **you're very** ~ je ne vous entends pas bien. ◆ **indistinctly** *adv* indistinctement.

indistinguishable [ˌɪndɪsˈtɪŋgwɪʃəbl] *adj* indifférenciable (*from* de); *(slight)* imperceptible.

individual [ˌɪndɪˈvɪdjʊˈəl] **1** *adj (separate) portion, attention* individuel; *(characteristic) style* original, particulier. **2** *n* individu *m*. ◆ **individualism** *n* individualisme *m*. ◆ **individualist** *n* individualiste *mf*. ◆ **individualistic** *adj* individualiste. ◆ **individuality** *n* individualité *f*. ◆ **individually** *adv* individuellement.

indivisible [ˌɪndɪˈvɪzəbl] *adj* indivisible.

Indo- [ˈɪndəʊ] *pref* indo-. ◆ **Indo-China** *n* Indochine *f*. ◆ **Indo-European** *adj, n* indo-européen *(m)*.

indoctrinate [ɪnˈdɒktrɪneɪt] *vt* endoctriner. **to** ~ **sb with sth** inculquer qch à qn. ◆ **indoctrination** *n* endoctrinement *m*.

indolent [ˈɪndələnt] *adj* indolent. ◆ **indolence** *n* indolence *f*. ◆ **indolently** *adv* indolemment.

indomitable [ɪnˈdɒmɪtəbl] *adj* indomptable.

Indonesia [ˌɪndə(ʊ)ˈniːzɪə] *n* Indonésie *f*. ◆ **Indonesian** **1** *adj* indonésien ; **2** *n* Indonésien(ne) *m(f)*.

indoor [ˈɪndɔːʳ] *adj shoes, film scene, photography* d'intérieur; *aerial* intérieur; *plant* d'appartement; *swimming pool, tennis court* couvert; *hobby, game, job* pratiqué en intérieur; *athletics* en salle. ◆ **indoors** *adv (in building)* à l'intérieur; *(at home)* à la maison; *(under cover)* à l'abri; **to go** ~**s** entrer, rentrer.

indubitable [ɪnˈdjuːbɪtəbl] *adj* indubitable. ◆ **indubitably** *adv* indubitablement.

induce [ɪnˈdjuːs] *vt (gen)* persuader (*sb to do* qn de faire); *reaction, sleep* provoquer (*in sb* chez qn). *(Med)* **to** ~ **labour** déclencher l'accouchement *(artificiellement)*. ◆ **inducement** *n (gen)* encouragement *m* (*to do* à faire); *(pej: bribe)* pot-de-vin *m*; **there is an** ~**ment/no** ~**ment to work hard** il y a qch qui incite *(indic)* /il n'y a rien qui incite *(subj)* à travailler dur; **as an added** ~**ment we are offering...** comme avantage *m* supplémentaire nous offrons...; **he received £100 as an** ~**ment** il a reçu 100 livres à titre de gratification *f*.

induct [ɪnˈdʌkt] *vt clergyman, president* installer. ◆ **induction** *n* installation *f*; *(Elec, Philos)* induction *f*; ~**ion course** stage *m* préparatoire.

indulge [ɪnˈdʌldʒ] **1** *vt person (spoil)* gâter; *(give way to)* céder à; *sb's wishes* se prêter à; *one's own desires* satisfaire; *one's own laziness* se laisser aller à. **I'll** ~ **myself and have a chocolate** je vais me faire plaisir et manger un chocolat. **2** *vi*: **to** ~ **in** *emotion etc* s'adonner à; **to** ~ **in a cigarette** se permettre une cigarette; **to** ~ **in sth to excess** abuser de qch.

indulgent [ɪnˈdʌldʒ(ə)nt] *adj* indulgent (*to* envers). ◆ **indulgence** *n* indulgence *f (also Rel)*; **his little indulgences** les petites faiblesses *fpl* qu'il se permet. ◆ **indulgently** *adv* avec indulgence.

industry [ˈɪndəstrɪ] *n* (**a**) industrie *f*. **tourist** ~ tourisme *m*, industrie touristique; **Department of I**~ ministère *m* de l'Industrie. (**b**) *(industriousness)* assiduité *f* (au travail). ◆ **industrial** *adj (gen)* industriel; *worker* de l'industrie; *disease* professionnel; *accident, medicine* du travail; *dispute* ouvrier; **industrial action** action *f* revendicative; *(strike)* (mouvement *m* de) grève *f*; **to take industrial action** se mettre en grève; *(US)* **industrial arts** enseignement *m* technique; **industrial dispute** conflit *m* social; **industrial engineering** génie *m* industriel; **industrial estate** *or (US)* **park** zone *f* industrielle; **industrial rehabilitation** réadaptation *f* fonctionnelle; **industrial tribunal** ≃ conseil *m* de prud'hommes ; **industrial unrest** agitation *f* ouvrière; **industrial waste** *or (US)* **wastes** déchets *mpl* industriels. ◆ **industrialism** *n* industrialisme *m*. ◆ **industrialist** *n* industriel *m*. ◆ **industrialization** *n* industrialisation *f*. ◆ **industrialize** *vt* industrialiser. ◆ **industrious** *adj* industrieux. ◆ **industriously** *adv* industrieusement. ◆ **industriousness** *n* assiduité *f* (au travail).

inedible [ɪnˈedɪbl] *adj (not to be eaten)* non comestible; *(not fit to be eaten)* immangeable.

ineffective [ˌɪnɪˈfektɪv] *adj*, **ineffectual** [ˌɪnɪˈfektjʊəl] *adj remedy, measures* inefficace; *attempt* vain *(before n)*; *person* incompétent. ◆ **ineffectively** *or* ◆ **ineffectually** *adv use* inefficacement; *try* vainement.

inefficient [ˌɪnɪˈfɪʃ(ə)nt] *adj (gen)* inefficace; *person* incompétent; *use* mauvais. ◆ **inefficiency** *n* inefficacité *f*; *[person]* incompétence *f*. ◆ **inefficiently** *adv* inefficacement; sans compétence; **work** ~**ly done** travail mal exécuté.

inelegant [ɪnˈelɪgənt] *adj* inélégant. ◆ **inelegantly** *adv* inélégamment.

ineligible [ɪnˈelɪdʒəbl] *adj candidate* inéligible. **to be** ~ **for sth/to do** ne pas avoir droit à qch/le droit de faire.

inept [ɪˈnept] *adj* inepte, stupide. ◆ **ineptitude** *n* ineptie *f*, stupidité *f*.

inequality [ˌɪnɪˈkwɒlɪtɪ] *n* inégalité *f*.

ineradicable [ˌɪnɪˈrædɪkəbl] *adj* indéracinable.

inert [ɪˈnɜːt] *adj* inerte. ◆ **inertia** *n* inertie *f*; *(Aut)* ~**ia reel belts** ceintures *fpl* de sécurité à enrouleurs.

inescapable [ˌɪnɪsˈkeɪpəbl] *adj* inéluctable.

inestimable [ɪnˈestɪməbl] *adj* inestimable.

inevitable [ɪnˈevɪtəbl] *adj (gen)* inévitable; *consequence, result* inévitable, fatal. **it was** ~ **that she should discover...** elle devait inévitablement *or* fatalement découvrir...; *(hum)* **his** ~ **camera** son inévitable appareil-photo. ◆ **inevitability** *n* caractère *m* inévitable. ◆ **inevitably** *adv* inévitablement, fatalement.

inexact [ˌɪnɪgˈzækt] *adj* inexact. ◆ **inexactly** *adv* inexactement.

inexcusable [ˌɪnɪksˈkjuːzəbl] *adj* inexcusable. ◆ **inexcusably** *adv* inexcusablement.

inexhaustible [ˌɪnɪgˈzɔːstəbl] *adj* inépuisable.

inexorable [ɪnˈeks(ə)rəbl] *adj* inexorable. ◆ **inexorably** *adv* inexorablement.

inexpensive [ˌɪnɪksˈpensɪv] *adj* bon marché *inv*, peu coûteux. ◆ **inexpensively** *adv buy* à bon marché; *live* à peu de frais.

inexperience [ˌɪnɪksˈpɪərɪəns] *n* inexpérience *f*. ◆ **inexperienced** *adj* inexpérimenté; **to be** ~**d in** avoir peu d'expérience en.

inexpert [ɪnˈekspɜːt] *adj* maladroit (*in* en). ◆ **inexpertly** *adv* maladroitement.

inexplicable [ˌɪnɪksˈplɪkəbl] *adj* inexplicable. ◆ **inexplicably** *adv* inexplicablement.

inexpressible [ˌɪnɪksˈpresəbl] *adj* inexprimable.

inextricable [ˌɪnɪksˈtrɪkəbl] *adj* inextricable. ◆ **inextricably** *adv* inextricablement.

infallible [ɪnˈfæləbl] *adj* infaillible. ◆ **infallibility** *n* infaillibilité *f*. ◆ **infallibly** *adv* infailliblement.

infamous ['ɪnfəməs] *adj* infâme.

infant ['ɪnfənt] **1** *n (baby)* bébé *m*; *(young child)* tout(e) petit(e) enfant *m(f)*; *(Jur)* mineur(e) *m(f)*; *(Brit Scol)* petit(e) *m(f) (de 5 à 7 ans)*. **2** *adj disease, mortality* infantile. *(Brit)* ~ **school** ≃ classes *fpl* de onzième et de dixième. ◆ **infancy** *n* toute petite enfance *f*, bas âge *m*; *(Jur)* minorité *f*; *(fig)* **still in its infancy** encore à ses débuts. ◆ **infanticide** *n* infanticide *m*. ◆ **infantile** *adj* infantile.

infantry ['ɪnf(ə)ntrɪ] *n* infanterie *f*. ◆ **infantryman** *n* fantassin *m*.

infatuated [ɪn'fætjʊeɪtəd] *adj*: ~ **with** *person* entiché de; *idea etc* engoué de; **to become** ~ **with** s'enticher de, s'engouer pour; **he was ~d** il avait la tête tournée. ◆ **infatuation** *n* entichement *m*; engouement *m* (*with* pour).

infect [ɪn'fekt] *vt* (**a**) *(Med)* infecter; *(fig) person* corrompre. **to** ~ **sb with a disease/one's enthusiasm** communiquer une maladie/son enthousiasme à qn; **~ed with leprosy** atteint de la lèpre. ◆ **infected** *adj* infecté. ◆ **infection** *n* infection *f*; **to have a slight ~ion** être légèrement souffrant. ◆ **infectious** *adj disease* infectieux; *person* contagieux; *laughter* contagieux.

infer [ɪn'fɜːʳ] *vt* déduire, inférer (*from* de; *that* que). ◆ **inference** ['ɪnf(ə)r(ə)ns] *n* déduction *f*, inférence *f*; **by ~ence** par déduction.

inferior [ɪn'fɪərɪəʳ] **1** *adj* inférieur (*to* à); *work, goods* de qualité inférieure. **he makes me feel** ~ il me donne un sentiment d'infériorité. **2** *n* inférieur(e) *m(f)*; *(in rank)* subordonné(e) *m(f)*. ◆ **inferiority** *n* infériorité *f* (*to* par rapport à); **~ity complex** complexe *m* d'infériorité.

infernal [ɪn'fɜːnl] *adj* infernal. ◆ **infernally** *adv* abominablement.

inferno [ɪn'fɜːnəʊ] *n*: **a (blazing)** ~ un brasier.

infertile [ɪn'fɜːtaɪl] *adj* infertile; *person* stérile. ◆ **infertility** *n* infertilité *f*; stérilité *f*.

infest [ɪn'fest] *vt* infester (*with* de). ◆ **infestation** *n* infestation *f*.

infidelity [ˌɪnfɪ'delɪtɪ] *n* infidélité *f*; *(Jur: in divorce)* adultère *m*.

infiltrate ['ɪnfɪltreɪt] **1** *vi* s'infiltrer (*into* dans). **2** *vt enemy lines* s'infiltrer dans; *group* noyauter; *(put in) troops* faire s'infiltrer (*into* dans). ◆ **infiltration** *n* infiltration *f*; noyautage *m*.

infinite ['ɪnf(ɪ)nɪt] *adj, n* infini *(m)*. ◆ **infinitely** *adv* infiniment. ◆ **infiniteness** *n* infinitude *f*. ◆ **infinitesimal** *adj* infinitésimal. ◆ **infinitive** *n* infinitif *m*; **in the infinitive** à l'infinitif. ◆ **infinitude** *n* infinité *f*. ◆ **infinity** *n (as opp to time and space)* infini *m*; *(infinite quantity etc)* infinité *f* (*of* de); *(infiniteness)* infinitude *f*; *(Math)* infini *m*; **to infinity** à l'infini.

infirm [ɪn'fɜːm] *adj* infirme. ◆ **infirmary** *n* hôpital *m*. ◆ **infirmity** *n* infirmité *f*.

inflame [ɪn'fleɪm] *vt (Med)* enflammer; *(fig)* attiser. ◆ **inflammable** *adj* inflammable. ◆ **inflammation** *n* inflammation *f*. ◆ **inflammatory** *adj speech etc* incendiaire.

inflate [ɪn'fleɪt] *vt tyre* gonfler (*with* de); *prices* faire monter; *bill, account* grossir. ◆ **inflatable** *adj* gonflable. ◆ **inflated** *adj tyre etc* gonflé; *lung* dilaté; *value, prices* exagéré; **an ~d sense of** une idée exagérée de. ◆ **inflation** *n (Econ)* inflation *f*. ◆ **inflationary** *adj* inflationniste.

inflect [ɪn'flekt] **1** *vt (Ling)* modifier la désinence de; *voice* moduler. **2** *vi (Ling)* prendre une désinence. ◆ **inflection** *or* ◆ **inflexion** *n (Ling: affix)* désinence *f*; *[voice]* inflexion *f*.

inflexible [ɪn'fleksəbl] *adj object* rigide; *person, attitude* inflexible, rigide. ◆ **inflexibility** *n* rigidité *f*; inflexibilité *f*.

inflict [ɪn'flɪkt] *vt* infliger (*on* à). **to** ~ **o.s. on sb** imposer sa compagnie à qn.

influence ['ɪnflʊəns] **1** *n* influence *f* (*on* sur). **under the** ~ **of** *person* sous l'influence de; *drugs* sous l'effet *m* de; *(Jur)* **driving under the** ~ **of drink** conduite *f* en état d'ivresse; **he was a bit under the** ~ * il avait bu un coup de trop *; **to use one's** ~ **with sb to get sth** user de son influence auprès de qn pour obtenir qch; **to be a good** ~ **on sb** exercer une bonne influence sur qn. **2** *vt (gen)* influencer; *attitude, decision* influencer, influer sur. **to be ~d by** *(gen)* se laisser influencer par; *[artist, writer]* être influencé par; **easily ~d** très influençable. ◆ **influential** *adj* influent; **to be influential** avoir de l'influence; **influential friends** amis *mpl* haut placés.

influenza [ˌɪnflʊ'enzə] *n* grippe *f*.

influx ['ɪnflʌks] *n [people]* afflux *m*, flot *m*; *[new ideas, attitudes]* flot, flux *m*.

inform [ɪn'fɔːm] **1** *vt* informer, avertir (*of* de), renseigner (*about* sur); *police* avertir. **to** ~ **sb of sth** informer *or* avertir qn de qch, faire part de qch à qn; **keep me ~ed** tenez-moi au courant (*of* de). **2** *vi*: **to** ~ **against sb** dénoncer qn. ◆ **informant** *n* informateur *m*, -trice *f*; *(Ling: native* **~ant***)* informateur *m*, -trice *f*. ◆ **information** **1** *n* renseignements *mpl*, information(s) *f(pl)*; **a piece of ~ation** un renseignement, une information; **to get ~ation about** se renseigner sur; **more ~ation** des renseignements plus complets, des informations plus complètes; **until more ~ation is available** jusqu'à plus ample informé; **his ~ation on the subject is astonishing** ses connaissances *fpl* en la matière sont stupéfiantes; **for your ~ation, he...** je dois vous prévenir qu'il...; **for your ~ation** à titre d'information ; **2** *adj bureau* de renseignements; *content* informationnel; *theory* de l'information; **~ation processing** informatique *f*; **~ation retrieval** recherche *f* de l'information; *(Police)* **~ation room** (salle *f*) radio *f*; **~ation service** bureau *m* de renseignements; **~ation technology** informatique *f*. ◆ **informative** *adj book, meeting* instructif; **he's not very ~ative about it** il n'en dit pas grand-chose. ◆ **informed** *adj person* informé, renseigné (*about* sur); *opinion* bien informé; *guess* bien fondé. ◆ **informer** *n* dénonciateur *m*, -trice *f*; **police ~er** indicateur *m*, -trice *f* (de police); **to turn ~er** dénoncer ses complices.

informal [ɪn'fɔːm(ə)l] *adj tone, manner, style* simple, familier; *language* de la conversation; *person* simple, qui ne fait pas de façons; *announcement, acceptance, arrangement* officieux; *instructions, invitation, meeting* dénué de caractère officiel; *welcome, visit, discussion* dénué de formalité; *dance, dinner* entre amis. **'dress ~'** 'tenue de ville'; **we had an ~ talk about it** nous en avons discuté entre nous; **it will be quite** ~ ce sera sans cérémonie *or* en toute simplicité. ◆ **informality** *n [person, manner]* simplicité *f*; *[visit, welcome etc]* simplicité, absence *f* de formalité; *[arrangement, agreement etc]* caractère *m* officieux; *[meeting]* absence *f* de cérémonie. ◆ **informally** *adv invite* sans cérémonie; *arrange, agree, meet* officieusement; *behave, speak, dress* de façon toute simple.

infra dig * ['ɪnfrə'dɪg] *adj* au-dessous de sa (*or* ma *etc*) dignité.

infrared ['ɪnfrə'red] *adj* infrarouge.

infrastructure ['ɪnfrəˌstrʌktʃəʳ] *n* infrastructure *f*.

infrequent [ɪn'friːkwənt] *adj* peu fréquent, rare. ◆ **infrequency** *n* rareté *f*. ◆ **infrequently** *adv* rarement.

infringe [ɪn'frɪn(d)ʒ] **1** *vt* contrevenir à. **2** *vi*: **to** ~ **on** empiéter sur. ◆ **infringement** *n* infraction *f* (*of* à).

infuriate [ɪn'fjʊərɪeɪt] *vt* rendre furieux, exaspérer. ◆ **infuriating** *adj* exaspérant. ◆ **infuriatingly** *adv* de façon exaspérante; **infuriatingly slow** d'une lenteur exaspérante.

infuse [ɪn'fjuːz] *vt* infuser (*into* dans); *tea, herbs* faire infuser; *(fig)* insuffler (*into* à). ◆ **infusion** *n* infusion *f*.

ingenious [ɪn'dʒiːnɪəs] *adj* ingénieux. ◆ **ingeniously** *adv* ingénieusement. ◆ **ingenuity** *n* ingéniosité *f*.

ingenuous [ɪn'dʒenjʊəs] *adj* ingénu. ◆ **ingenuousness** *n* ingénuité *f*.

inglorious [ɪn'glɔːrɪəs] *adj defeat etc* déshonorant.

ingot ['ɪŋgət] *n* lingot *m*.

ingrained ['ɪn'greɪnd] *adj habit* invétéré; *prejudice* enraciné; *hatred* tenace. ~ **dirt** crasse *f*; ~ **with dirt** encrassé.

ingratiate [ɪn'greɪʃɪeɪt] *vt*: **to ~ o.s. with sb** s'insinuer dans les bonnes grâces de qn. ◆ **ingratiating** *adj* insinuant, doucereux.

ingratitude [ɪn'grætɪtjuːd] *n* ingratitude *f*.

ingredient [ɪn'griːdɪənt] *n (Culin etc)* ingrédient *m*; *[character, success etc]* élément *m*.

ingrowing [ˌɪn'grəʊɪŋ], *(US)* **ingrown** [ˌɪn'grəʊn] *adj* incarné.

inhabit [ɪn'hæbɪt] *vt town, country* habiter; *house* habiter (dans). ◆ **inhabitable** *adj* habitable. ◆ **inhabitant** *n* habitant(e) *m(f)*. ◆ **inhabited** *adj* habité.

inhale [ɪn'heɪl] **1** *vt vapour, gas etc* inhaler; *[smoker]* avaler; *perfume* aspirer. **2** *vi [smoker]* avaler la fumée. ◆ **inhalant** *n* inhalant *m*. ◆ **inhalation** *n* inhalation *f*. ◆ **inhaler** *or* ◆ **inhalator** *n* inhalateur *m*.

inherent [ɪn'hɪər(ə)nt] *adj* inhérent (*in, to* à). ◆ **inherently** *adv difficult etc* en soi; *curious, lazy* fondamentalement.

inherit [ɪn'herɪt] *vt* hériter (de); *title* succéder à; *qualities, characteristics* tenir (*from sb* de qn). **to ~ a house** hériter (d')une maison; **to ~ a house from sb** hériter une maison de qn. ◆ **inheritance** *n (gen)* héritage *m*; **our national ~ance** notre patrimoine *m* national.

inhibit [ɪn'hɪbɪt] *vt [person] impulse, desire* dominer, maîtriser; *(Psych)* inhiber; *[situation, sb's presence]* entraver, gêner. **to ~ sb from doing** empêcher qn de faire. ◆ **inhibited** *adj* refoulé *; *(Psych)* qui a beaucoup d'inhibitions. ◆ **inhibiting** *adj* inhibant. ◆ **inhibition** *n* inhibition *f*.

inhospitable [ˌɪnhɒs'pɪtəbl] *adj* inhospitalier.

inhuman [ɪn'hjuːmən] *adj* inhumain. ◆ **inhumanity** *n* inhumanité *f*.

inimical [ɪ'nɪmɪk(ə)l] *adj (hostile)* hostile (*to* à).

inimitable [ɪ'nɪmɪtəbl] *adj* inimitable. ◆ **inimitably** *adv* d'une façon inimitable.

iniquitous [ɪ'nɪkwɪtəs] *adj* inique. ◆ **iniquitously** *adv* iniquement. ◆ **iniquity** *n* iniquité *f*.

initial [ɪ'nɪʃ(ə)l] **1** *adj* initial, premier. **in the ~ stages** au début, au commencement. **2** *n* initiale *f*. **~s** initiales *fpl*; *(as signature)* parafe *m*. **3** *vt* parafer. ◆ **initialize** *vt (Comput)* initialiser. ◆ **initially** *adv* initialement.

initiate [ɪ'nɪʃɪeɪt] **1** *vt* (**a**) *reform* promouvoir; *negotiations* amorcer; *enterprise* se lancer dans; *scheme, programme* instaurer; *fashion* lancer. *(Jur)* **to ~ proceedings against sb** intenter une action à qn. (**b**) *(Rel etc) person* initier (*into a secret* à un secret). **to ~ sb into a society** admettre qn au sein d'une société secrète. **2** [ɪ'nɪʃɪɪt] *adj, n* initié(e) *m(f)*. ◆ **initiation 1** *n* initiation *f*; admission *f* ; **2** *adj rite* d'initiation. ◆ **initiative** *n* initiative *f*; **to take the initiative** prendre l'initiative (*in doing sth* de faire qch); **on one's own initiative** de sa propre initiative; **he's got initiative** il a de l'initiative. ◆ **initiator** *n [plan etc]* auteur *m*.

inject [ɪn'dʒekt] *vt* injecter (*sth into sth* qch dans qch); *(fig)* insuffler (*into* à). **to ~ sb with sth** faire une piqûre *or* une injection de qch à qn. ◆ **injection** *n* injection *f*; *(Med)* injection, piqûre *f*.

injudicious [ˌɪndʒʊ'dɪʃ(ə)s] *adj* peu judicieux. ◆ **injudiciously** *adv* peu judicieusement.

injunction [ɪn'dʒʌŋ(k)ʃ(ə)n] *n (gen)* ordre *m*; *(court order)* ordonnance *f* (*to do* de faire). **to give sb strict ~s to do** enjoindre formellement à qn de faire.

injure ['ɪn(d)ʒə^r] *vt* (**a**) *(Med)* blesser. **to ~ one's leg** se blesser à la jambe. (**b**) *(wrong, damage) person, interests, reputation* nuire à; *(offend)* blesser, offenser. **to ~ sb's feelings** offenser qn. ◆ **injured 1** *adj (Med)* blessé; *(in accident)* accidenté; *(offended)* offensé; *(Jur)* **the ~d party** la partie lésée ; **2** *npl*: **the ~d** les blessés *mpl*. ◆ **injurious** *adj* nuisible (*to* à). ◆ **injury** *n (Med)* blessure *f*; *(wrong) (to person)* tort *m*; *(to reputation)* atteinte *f*; *(Ftbl)* **injury time** arrêts *mpl* de jeu.

injustice [ɪn'dʒʌstɪs] *n* injustice *f*. **to do sb an ~** être injuste envers qn.

ink [ɪŋk] **1** *n* encre *f*. **in ~** à l'encre. **2** *adj bottle* d'encre; *eraser* à encre. **3** *vt* encrer. **to ~ sth in** repasser qch à l'encre. ◆ **inkpad** *n* tampon *m* encreur. ◆ **inkpot** *or* ◆ **inkwell** *n* encrier *m*. ◆ **inky** *adj book, hand* taché d'encre; *pad* encré; *darkness etc* noir comme de l'encre.

inkling ['ɪŋklɪŋ] *n* petite idée *f*, soupçon *m*. **I had no ~ that...** je n'avais pas la moindre idée que...; **there was no ~ of the disaster** rien ne laissait présager le désastre.

inlaid ['ɪn'leɪd] *adj (gen)* incrusté (*with* de); *box, table* marqueté. ~ **floor** parquet *m*.

inland ['ɪnlænd] **1** *adj* (**a**) *sea, town* intérieur; *navigation* fluvial. ~ **waterways** canaux *mpl* et rivières *fpl*. (**b**) *(domestic) mail, trade* intérieur. **the ~ revenue** le fisc. **2** [ɪn'lænd] *adv* à l'intérieur. **to go ~** pénétrer dans les terres.

inlet ['ɪnlet] **1** *n* (**a**) *[sea]* bras *m* de mer; *[river]* bras de rivière. (**b**) *(Tech)* arrivée *f*; *[ventilator]* prise *f* (d'air). **2** *adj pipe* d'arrivée.

inmate ['ɪnmeɪt] *n [prison]* détenu(e) *m(f)*; *[asylum]* interné(e) *m(f)*; *[hospital]* malade *mf*.

inmost ['ɪnməʊst] *adj part* le plus profond; *thoughts, feelings* le plus secret. **one's ~ being** le fin fond de son être; **in one's ~ heart** dans le fond de son cœur.

inn [ɪn] *n (small, wayside)* auberge *f*; *(larger, wayside)* hostellerie *f*; *(in town)* hôtel *m*; *(†: tavern)* cabaret † *m*. ◆ **innkeeper** *n* aubergiste *mf*; hôtelier *m*, -ière *f*.

innards * ['ɪnədz] *npl* entrailles *fpl*.

innate [ɪ'neɪt] *adj* inné, naturel.

inner ['ɪnə^r] *adj room, court* intérieur, de dedans; *ear* interne; *shoe sole* intérieur; *emotions, thoughts* intime, secret, profond; *life* intérieur. **an ~ circle within the society** un petit cercle fermé à l'intérieur de la société; ~ **city** vieux quartiers *mpl* déshérités; ~ **city schools** établissements *mpl* scolaires des vieux quartiers pauvres; ~ **harbour** arrière-port *m*; *[tyre]* ~ **tube** chambre *f* à air. ◆ **innermost** = **inmost.**

innings ['ɪnɪŋz] *n (Cricket)* tour *m* de batte. *(fig)* **I've had a good ~** j'ai bien profité de l'existence (*or* de la situation *etc*).

innocent ['ɪnəsnt] **1** *adj* innocent (*of* de). **as ~ as a newborn babe** innocent comme l'enfant qui vient de naître; **to put on an ~ air** faire l'innocent; ~ **of any desire to...** dénué de tout désir de... **2** *n* innocent(e) *m(f)*. ◆ **innocence** *n* innocence *f*. ◆ **innocently** *adv* innocemment.

innocuous [ɪ'nɒkjʊəs] *adj* inoffensif.

innovate ['ɪnəʊ'veɪt] *vti* innover. ◆ **innovation** *n* innovation *f* (*in* en matière de); **to make inno-**

vations in apporter des innovations à. ◆ **innovator** *n* innovateur *m*, -trice *f*.

innuendo [ˌɪnjʊ'endəʊ] *n* insinuation *f* malveillante.

innumerable [ɪ'njuːm(ə)rəbl] *adj* innombrable, sans nombre. **I've told you ~ times** je te l'ai dit cent fois.

inoculate [ɪ'nɒkjʊleɪt] *vt* inoculer (*against* contre; *sb with sth* qch à qn). ◆ **inoculation** *n* inoculation *f*.

inoffensive [ˌɪnə'fensɪv] *adj* inoffensif.

inoperable [ɪn'ɒp(ə)rəbl] *adj* inopérable.

inoperative [ɪn'ɒp(ə)rətɪv] *adj* inopérant.

inopportune [ɪn'ɒpətjuːn] *adj (gen)* inopportun; *remark* déplacé. ◆ **inopportunely** *adv* inopportunément.

inordinate [ɪ'nɔːdɪnɪt] *adj sum of money, price* exorbitant; *size* démesuré; *quantity, demands* excessif; *passion* immodéré. **an ~ amount of** énormément de. ◆ **inordinately** *adv* démesurément; excessivement; immodérément.

inorganic [ˌɪnɔː'gænɪk] *adj* inorganique.

input ['ɪnpʊt] *n (Elec)* énergie *f*, puissance *f*; *(Comput) (data)* données *fpl* à traiter; *(act of inputting)* entrée *f* des données.

inquest ['ɪnkwest] *n* enquête *f* (criminelle).

inquire [ɪn'kwaɪəʳ] **1** *vi* s'informer (*about, after* de), se renseigner (*about* sur); *(ask)* demander. **to ~ for sb** demander qn; **to ~ into** *subject* faire des recherches sur; *possibilities* se renseigner sur; *(Admin, Jur)* faire une enquête sur; *truth of sth* vérifier; **'~ at the information desk'** 's'adresser aux renseignements'. **2** *vt* demander (*sth from sb* qch à qn). **he ~d how to get to the theatre** il a demandé le chemin du théâtre; **he ~d what she wanted** il a demandé ce qu'elle voulait. ◆ **inquiring** *adj attitude, mind* curieux; *look* interrogateur. ◆ **inquiringly** *adv* avec curiosité; d'un air interrogateur.

inquiry [ɪn'kwaɪərɪ] **1** *n* (**a**) *(from individual)* demande *f* de renseignements. **to make inquiries about sb/sth** se renseigner sur qn/qch (*of sb* auprès de qn); **on ~ he found that...** renseignements pris, il a découvert que...; **'all inquiries to...'** 'pour tous renseignements s'adresser à...'; *(sign)* **'Inquiries'** 'Renseignements'. (**b**) *(Admin, Jur)* enquête *f*. **committee of ~** commission *f* d'enquête; **to hold an ~ into** enquêter *or* faire une enquête sur; **a fruitful line of ~** une bonne direction dans laquelle pousser les recherches; **the police are making inquiries** la police enquête. **2** *adj*: **~ desk, ~ office** bureau *m* de renseignements.

inquisition [ˌɪnkwɪ'zɪʃ(ə)n] *n* investigation *f*. *(Rel)* **the I~** l'Inquisition *f*. ◆ **inquisitive** *adj* (trop) curieux. ◆ **inquisitively** *adv* (trop) curieusement. ◆ **inquisitiveness** *n* curiosité *f* (indiscrète).

inroad ['ɪnrəʊd] *n (Mil)* incursion *f* (*into* en, dans). *(fig)* **to make ~s into** entamer.

inrush ['ɪnˌrʌʃ] *n* irruption *f*.

insane [ɪn'seɪn] **1** *adj (Med)* aliéné; *(gen) person* fou; *desire* insensé; *project* démentiel. **to become ~** perdre la raison; **to drive sb ~** rendre qn fou; *(US)* **~ asylum** asile *m* d'aliénés. **2** *npl (Med)* **the ~** les aliénés *mpl*. ◆ **insanely** *adv laugh* comme un fou (*or* une folle); *behave* de façon insensée; *jealous* follement. ◆ **insanity** *n (Med)* aliénation *f* mentale; *(gen)* folie *f*, démence *f*.

insanitary [ɪn'sænɪt(ə)rɪ] *adj* insalubre.

insatiable [ɪn'seɪʃəbl] *adj* insatiable.

inscribe [ɪn'skraɪb] *vt (write)* inscrire (*in* dans); *(engrave)* graver (*on* sur); *(dedicate)* dédicacer (*to* à). **watch ~d with his name** montre gravée à son nom. ◆ **inscription** *n* inscription *f*; dédicace *f*.

inscrutable [ɪn'skruːtəbl] *adj* impénétrable *(fig)*.

insect ['ɪnsekt] **1** *n* insecte *m*. **2** *adj bite* d'insecte; *powder, spray* insecticide. **~ eater** insectivore *m*; **~ repellent** crème *f* (*or* bombe *f etc*) anti-insecte *inv*. ◆ **insecticide** *n* insecticide *m*.

insecure [ˌɪnsɪ'kjʊəʳ] *adj nail, rope, padlock* peu solide, qui tient mal; *structure, ladder* branlant; *lock* peu sûr; *door* qui ferme mal; *career, future* incertain; *(worried) person* anxieux; *(Psych etc)* insécurisé. ◆ **insecurity** *n* insécurité *f*.

insemination [ɪnˌsemɪ'neɪʃ(ə)n] *n* insémination *f*. **artificial ~** insémination artificielle.

insensible [ɪn'sensəbl] *adj (gen)* insensible (*of* à); *(unconscious)* sans connaissance. ◆ **insensibility** *n* insensibilité *f*. ◆ **insensibly** *adv* insensiblement.

insensitive [ɪn'sensɪtɪv] *adj* insensible (*to* à). ◆ **insensitivity** *n* insensibilité *f*.

inseparable [ɪn'sep(ə)rəbl] *adj* inséparable (*from* de). ◆ **inseparably** *adv* inséparablement.

insert [ɪn'sɜːt] **1** *vt* insérer. **2** ['ɪnsɜːt] *n (gen)* insertion *f*; *(page)* encart *m*. ◆ **insertion** *n* insertion *f*.

inshore ['ɪn'ʃɔːʳ] **1** *adj (gen)* côtier; *wind* de mer. **2** *adv fish* près de la côte; *move* vers la côte.

inside ['ɪn'saɪd] **1** *adv* (**a**) dedans, au dedans, à l'intérieur. **~ and outside** au dedans et au dehors; **come ~!** entrez (donc)!; **it is warmer ~** il fait plus chaud à l'intérieur *or* dedans. (**b**) (*‡*: *in jail*) en taule *‡*.
2 *prep* (**a**) *(of place)* à l'intérieur de, dans. **~ the house** à l'intérieur (de la maison). (**b**) *(of time)* en moins de. **~ 10 minutes** en moins de 10 minutes; **he was well ~ the record time** il avait largement battu le record.
3 *n* (**a**) intérieur *m*. **on the ~** au dedans, à l'intérieur; **on the ~ of the pavement** sur le trottoir du côté maisons; *(fig)* **I see the firm from the ~** je vois la compagnie de l'intérieur. (**b**) **your coat is ~ out** ton manteau est à l'envers; **the wind blew the umbrella ~ out** le vent a retourné le parapluie; **I turned the bag ~ out** j'ai retourné le sac entièrement; **to know ~ out** *subject* connaître à fond; *district* connaître comme sa poche. (**c**) (***: *stomach*) ventre *m*, intestins *mpl*.
4 *adj* (**a**) intérieur. **~ leg measurement** hauteur *f* de l'entrejambes; **to get ~ information** obtenir des renseignements *mpl* à la source; **'the ~ story of the plot'** 'le complot raconté par un des participants'; *(of theft etc)* **an ~ job *** un coup monté de l'intérieur. (**b**) *(Aut) wheel, headlight etc (Brit)* gauche; *(US, Europe etc)* droit. **the ~ lane** *(Brit)* la voie de gauche; *(US, Europe etc)* la voie de droite; *(Sport)* **to be on the ~ track** tenir la corde. ◆ **inside-forward** *n* intérieur *m*. ◆ **inside-left/-right** *n* intérieur *m* gauche/droit. ◆ **insider** *n (gen)* quelqu'un qui connaît les choses de l'intérieur; *(in firm)* quelqu'un qui est dans la place; *(with influence, knowledge)* initié(e) *m(f)*; **~r dealing** opérations *fpl* d'initiés.

insidious [ɪn'sɪdɪəs] *adj* insidieux. ◆ **insidiously** *adv* insidieusement.

insight ['ɪnsaɪt] *n (discernment)* pénétration *f*, perspicacité *f*; *(glimpse)* aperçu *m* (*into* de). **I gained an ~ into...** cela m'a permis de comprendre...

insignia [ɪn'sɪgnɪə] *npl* insignes *mpl*.

insignificant [ˌɪnsɪg'nɪfɪkənt] *adj* insignifiant. ◆ **insignificance** *n* insignifiance *f*.

insincere [ˌɪnsɪn'sɪəʳ] *adj* peu sincère. ◆ **insincerity** *n* manque *m* de sincérité.

insinuate [ɪn'sɪnjʊeɪt] *vt* insinuer (*into* dans; *sth to sb* qch à qn; *that* que). ◆ **insinuation** *n* insinuation *f*.

insipid [ɪn'sɪpɪd] *adj* insipide, fade.

insist [ɪn'sɪst] **1** *vi* insister (*on doing* pour faire). **he ~ed on my waiting for him** il a tenu à ce que *or* insisté pour que je l'attende; **to ~ on silence** exiger le silence; **if you ~** si vous insistez, si vous y tenez; **he ~s on the justice of his claim** il affirme *or* soutient que sa revendication est juste. **2** *vt* (**a**) insister. **I ~ that you let me help** j'insiste pour que tu me permettes d'aider. (**b**) affirmer, soutenir. **he ~s that he has seen her before** il affirme *or* soutient qu'il l'a déjà vue. ◆ **insistence** *n* insistance *f*; **at his ~ence** parce qu'il a insisté. ◆ **insistent** *adj* insistant, pressant. ◆ **insistently** *adv* avec insistance.

insole ['ɪn,səʊl] *n (removable)* semelle *f* intérieure; *[shoe]* première *f*.

insolent ['ɪns(ə)lənt] *adj* insolent (*to* envers). ◆ **insolence** *n* insolence *f*. ◆ **insolently** *adv* insolemment.

insoluble [ɪn'sɒljʊbl] *adj* insoluble.

insolvent [ɪn'sɒlv(ə)nt] *adj* insolvable; *(bankrupt)* en faillite. ◆ **insolvency** *n* insolvabilité *f*.

insomnia [ɪn'sɒmnɪə] *n* insomnie *f*. ◆ **insomniac** *adj, n* insomniaque *(mf)*.

inspect [ɪn'spekt] *vt (gen)* inspecter; *document, object* examiner; *(Customs) luggage* visiter; *ticket* contrôler; *troops etc (check)* inspecter; *(review)* passer en revue. ◆ **inspection** **1** *n* inspection *f*; examen *m*; visite *f*; contrôle *m*; revue *f* ; **2** *adj (Aut)* **~ion pit** fosse *f* à réparations. ◆ **inspector** *n [schools, police etc]* inspecteur *m*, -trice *f*; *(on bus, train)* contrôleur *m*, -euse *f*.

inspire [ɪn'spaɪəʳ] *vt* inspirer (*sth in sb, sb with sth* qch à qn). **he was ~d by her beauty to write...** inspiré par sa beauté il a écrit...; **what ~d you to offer to help?** qu'est-ce qui vous a donné l'idée de proposer votre aide?. ◆ **inspiration** *n* inspiration *f*; **to be an inspiration to sb** être une source d'inspiration pour qn. ◆ **inspired** *adj book, poet* inspiré; *moment* d'inspiration; **an ~d idea, guess** *etc* une inspiration. ◆ **inspiring** *adj book, poem* qui suscite l'inspiration; **it isn't inspiring** ça n'a rien d'inspirant.

instability [,ɪnstə'bɪlɪtɪ] *n* instabilité *f*.

install [ɪn'stɔ:l] *vt* installer. ◆ **installation** *n* installation *f*. ◆ **instalment** *or (US)* ◆ **installment** **1** *n [payment]* versement *m* partiel, acompte *m*; *[story, serial]* épisode *m*; *[book]* fascicule *m*, livraison *f*; **to pay an ~ment** verser un acompte, faire un versement partiel; **by ~ments** en plusieurs versements, par acomptes ; **2** *adj*: **~ment plan** système *m* de crédit; **to buy on the ~ment plan** acheter à tempérament.

instance ['ɪnstəns] **1** *n* exemple *m*, cas *m*. **for ~** par exemple; **in the present ~** dans le cas présent; **in many ~s** dans bien des cas; **in the first ~** en premier lieu; **as an ~ of** comme exemple de. **2** *vt (cite)* donner en exemple; *(exemplify)* illustrer.

instant ['ɪnstənt] **1** *adj obedience, relief* immédiat, instantané; *coffee* soluble; *potatoes* déshydraté; *food* à préparation rapide; *soup* en poudre. **~ camera** appareil *m* à développement instantané; **your letter of the 10th inst(ant)** votre lettre du 10 courant. **2** *n* instant *m*, moment *m*. **come here this ~** viens ici tout de suite *or* immédiatement; **in an ~** *(+ past tense)* en un instant; *(+ future tense) dans un instant;* **the ~ he heard the news** dès qu'il a appris la nouvelle. ◆ **instantaneous** *adj* instantané. ◆ **instantaneously** *adv* instantanément. ◆ **instantly** *adv* immédiatement, tout de suite.

instead [ɪn'sted] *adv* au lieu de cela. **do that ~** faites plutôt cela; **if he isn't going, I shall go ~** s'il n'y va pas, j'irai à sa place; **I went to the pictures ~** au lieu de cela je suis allé au cinéma; **~ of (doing) sth** au lieu de (faire) qch; **~ of sb** à la place de qn; **~ of him** à sa place; **this is ~ of a present** ceci tient lieu de cadeau.

instep ['ɪnstep] *n (Anat)* cou-de-pied *m*; *[shoe]* cambrure *f*.

instigate ['ɪnstɪgeɪt] *vt* inciter (*sb to do* qn à faire); *rebellion etc* fomenter. ◆ **instigation** *n*: **at his instigation** à son instigation *f*.

instil [ɪn'stɪl] *vt courage etc* insuffler (*into sb* à qn); *knowledge, principles* inculquer (*into sb* à qn); *idea, fact* faire comprendre (*into sb* à qn). **to ~ into sb that** faire pénétrer dans l'esprit de qn que.

instinct ['ɪnstɪŋ(k)t] *n* instinct *m*. **by ~** d'instinct ; **business ~** l'instinct des affaires. ◆ **instinctive** *adj* instinctif. ◆ **instinctively** *adv* instinctivement.

institute ['ɪnstɪtju:t] **1** *vt system, rules* instituer, établir; *post, organization* fonder, créer; *(Jur etc) inquiry* ouvrir; *proceedings* entamer (*against sb* contre qn). **2** *n* institut *m*.

institution [,ɪnstɪ'tju:ʃ(ə)n] *n* (**a**) *(organization, school etc)* établissement *m*; *(private)* institution *f; (mental hospital)* hôpital *m* psychiatrique. **he has been in ~s all his adult life** il a passé toute sa vie d'adulte dans des collectivités. (**b**) *(custom etc)* institution *f*. **it is too much of an ~ to abolish** c'est une telle institution qu'il serait impossible de le supprimer. ◆ **institutional** *adj reform etc* institutionnel; *(fig pej) food* d'internat; *furniture* d'hospice; **~al life** la vie réglementée d'un établissement *(social, médical ou pédagogique)*. ◆ **institutionalized** *adj* marqué par la vie en collectivité.

instruct [ɪn'strʌkt] *vt* (**a**) *(teach)* instruire. **to ~ sb in sth** instruire qn en qch, enseigner qch à qn; **to ~ sb in how to do sth** enseigner à qn comment faire qch. (**b**) *(order: also Jur)* donner des instructions à. **to ~ sb to do** ordonner à qn de faire. ◆ **instruction** **1** *n* instruction *f*; **~ions** *(Mil)* consigne *f*; *(Pharm, Tech)* indications *fpl*; **'~ions for use'** 'mode *m* d'emploi'; *(Comm, Tech)* **the ~ions are on the back of the box** le mode d'emploi est indiqué au dos de la boîte; **he gave me ~ions not to leave until...** il m'a donné des instructions selon lesquelles je ne devais pas partir avant...; **to give ~ions** donner des instructions (*for sb to do* pour que qn fasse); **driving ~ion** leçons *fpl* de conduite ; **2** *adj*: **~ion book** manuel *m* d'entretien. ◆ **instructive** *adj* instructif. ◆ **instructor** *n (gen)* professeur *m*; *(Mil)* instructeur *m*; *(Ski)* moniteur *m*; **driving ~or** moniteur *m* d'auto-école. ◆ **instructress** *n (gen)* professeur *m (femme)*; *(Ski)* monitrice *f*.

instrument ['ɪnstrʊmənt] **1** *n* instrument *m*. **2** *adj:* **instrument flying** pilotage aux instruments. **~ board** *or* **panel** tableau *m* de bord. ◆ **instrumental** *adj* (**a**) **to be ~al in (doing) sth** contribuer à (faire) qch; (**b**) *(Mus)* instrumental. ◆ **instrumentalist** *n* instrumentiste *mf*.

insubordinate [,ɪnsə'bɔ:dənɪt] *adj* insubordonné. ◆ **insubordination** *n* insubordination *f*.

insufferable [ɪn'sʌf(ə)rəbl] *adj* insupportable. ◆ **insufferably** *adv* insupportablement.

insufficient [,ɪnsə'fɪʃ(ə)nt] *adj* insuffisant. ◆ **insufficiently** *adv* insuffisamment.

insular ['ɪnsjələʳ] *adj climate* insulaire; *(fig pej) outlook* borné; *person* aux vues étroites.

insulate ['ɪnsjʊleɪt] *vt (gen, also Elec)* isoler; *(against sound)* insonoriser; *water tank* calorifuger; *person (separate)* séparer (*from* de); *(protect)* protéger (*against* de). ◆ **insulated** *adj* isolant. ◆ **insulating** *adj*: **insulating material** isolant *m*; **insulating tape** chatterton *m*. ◆ **insulation** *n* isolation *f* ; insonorisation *f*; calorifugeage *m*; *(material)* isolant *m*. ◆ **insulator** *n (device)* isolateur *m*; *(material)* isolant *m*.

insulin ['ɪnsjʊlɪn] **1** *n* insuline *f.* **2** *adj treatment* à l'insuline; *injection* d'insuline; *shock* insulinique.

insult [ɪn'sʌlt] **1** *vt* insulter. **2** ['ɪnsʌlt] *n* insulte *f.* **to hurl ~s at sb** injurier qn. ◆ **insulting** *adj* insultant, injurieux; **~ing language** paroles *fpl* injurieuses *or* insultantes. ◆ **insultingly** *adv* d'une voix *or* d'une manière insultante.

insuperable [ɪn'su:p(ə)rəbl] *adj* insurmontable.

insure [ɪn'ʃʊəʳ] *vt* (**a**) *car, house* assurer (*against* contre). **to ~ o.s.** *or* **one's life** prendre une assurance-vie; **the ~d** l'assuré(e) *m(f)*; *(fig)* **we ~d (ourselves) against possible disappointment** nous avons paré aux déceptions possibles; **in order to ~ against any delay...** pour nous (*or* les *etc*) garantir contre les délais. (**b**) *(make sure)* s'assurer (*that* que + *subj*); *(make sure of) success* assurer. **this will ~ that you...** grâce à ceci vous êtes assuré de... ◆ **insurance 1** *n (gen)* assurance *f* (*on, for sth* pour qch; *against* contre); *(cover)* garantie *f* (d'assurances), couverture *f*; *(policy)* contrat *m* d'assurance; **to take out (an) insurance against** s'assurer contre; **they've got no insurance for this** ils ne sont pas assurés pour cela; **it's an insurance against inflation** cela protège de l'inflation ; **2** *adj agent, company* d'assurances; *certificate, policy, premium* d'assurance; **insurance scheme** régime *m* d'assurances; *(Admin)* **insurance stamp** timbre *m* de contribution à la Sécurité sociale.

insurgent [ɪn'sɜ:dʒənt] *adj, n* insurgé(e) *m(f)*.

insurmountable [ˌɪnsə'maʊntəbl] *adj* insurmontable.

insurrection [ˌɪnsə'rekʃən] *n* insurrection *f.*

intact [ɪn'tækt] *adj* intact.

intake ['ɪnteɪk] **1** *n* (**a**) *[water]* adduction *f*; *[gas, air, steam]* admission *f.* (**b**) *(Scol, Univ)* admissions *fpl*; *(Mil)* contingent *m.* (**c**) *[protein, liquid etc]* consommation *f.* **food ~** *[animals]* ration *f* alimentaire; *[person]* consommation de nourriture. **2** *adj*: **~ class** cours *m* préparatoire.

intangible [ɪn'tændʒəbl] **1** *adj* intangible. **2** *n* impondérable *m.*

integral ['ɪntɪgr(ə)l] *adj* (**a**) *part* intégrant, constituant. **to be an ~ part of** faire partie intégrante de. (**b**) *(whole) payment* intégral. (**c**) **~ calculus** calcul *m* intégral.

integrate ['ɪntɪgreɪt] **1** *vt (gen)* intégrer, incorporer (*in, into* dans). **2** *vi* (**a**) *(US: racially) [school, neighbourhood etc]* pratiquer la déségrégation raciale. (**b**) *[person, religious or ethnic group etc]* s'intégrer (*into* dans). ◆ **integrated** *adj personality* bien intégré; *(US) school* où se pratique la déségrégation raciale; **~d circuit** circuit *m* intégré. ◆ **integration** *n (gen)* intégration *f*; **racial integration** déségrégation *f* raciale.

integrity [ɪn'tegrɪtɪ] *n* intégrité *f.* **man of ~** homme *m* intègre.

intellect ['ɪntɪlekt] *n* intellect *m*, intelligence *f*; *(person)* intelligence *f*, esprit *m.* ◆ **intellectual** *adj, n* intellectuel(le) *m(f)*. ◆ **intellectually** *adv* intellectuellement.

intelligence [ɪn'telɪdʒəns] **1** *n (cleverness)* intelligence *f*; *(information)* informations *fpl.* **Military I~** service *m* de renseignements de l'armée de Terre; **he's in I~** il est dans les services de renseignements. **2** *adj agent, officer, service* de renseignements. **~ quotient** quotient *m* intellectuel; **~ test** test *m* d'aptitude intellectuelle. ◆ **intelligent** *adj* intelligent. ◆ **intelligently** *adv* intelligemment. ◆ **intelligentsia** *n* intelligentsia *f.*

intelligible [ɪn'telɪdʒəbl] *adj* intelligible. ◆ **intelligibility** *n* intelligibilité *f.* ◆ **intelligibly** *adv* intelligiblement.

intemperate [ɪn'temp(ə)rɪt] *adj climate* sévère ; *haste* excessif; *rage* incontrôlé; *person* immodéré.

intend [ɪn'tend] *vt* avoir l'intention, se proposer (*to do, doing* de faire), penser (*to do* faire); *gift, remark etc* destiner (*for* à). **I ~ him to go with me** j'ai l'intention qu'il m'accompagne *(subj)*; **I fully ~ to punish him** j'ai la ferme intention de le punir; **this scheme is ~ed to help...** ce projet est destiné à aider...; **~ed for** *(gen)* destiné à, conçu pour ; **I ~ it as a present for Robert** c'est un cadeau que je destine à Robert; **I ~ed it as a compliment** dans mon esprit cela voulait être un compliment; **he ~ed no harm** il l'a fait sans mauvaise intention; **did you ~ that?** est-ce que vous avez fait cela exprès? ◆ **intended** *adj (deliberate) insult etc* intentionnel; *(planned) journey* projeté; *effect* voulu.

intense [ɪn'tens] *adj (gen)* intense; *enthusiasm, interest* énorme, vif; *person, tone* véhément; *expression (interested)* concentré; *(fervent)* exalté. ◆ **intensely** *adv live, look* intensément; *moved* profondément; *cold* extrêmement. ◆ **intensify 1** *vt* intensifier ; **2** *vi* s'intensifier. ◆ **intensity** *n* intensité *f*; véhémence *f.* ◆ **intensive** *adj (gen)* intensif; *(Med)* **intensive care unit** service *m* de réanimation; **in intensive care** en réanimation; **capital-intensive** *etc* à forte intensité de capital *etc.* ◆ **intensively** *adv* intensivement.

intent [ɪn'tent] **1** *n* intention *f*, dessein *m.* **to all ~s and purposes** en fait, pratiquement; **with good ~** dans une bonne intention; **with criminal ~** dans un but délictueux. **2** *adj* absorbé. **~ stare** regard *m* fixe; **~ on his work** absorbé par son travail; **~ on leaving** bien décidé à partir; **he was so ~ on doing it that he forgot...** dans sa préoccupation de le faire, il a oublié... ◆ **intently** *adv* avec une vive attention.

intention [in'tenʃ(ə)n] *n* intention *f.* **to have the ~ of doing** avoir l'intention de faire; **to have no ~ of doing** n'avoir aucune intention de faire; **with the ~ of doing** dans l'intention de faire. ◆ **intentional** *adj* intentionnel, voulu; **it wasn't ~al** ce n'était pas fait exprès. ◆ **intentionally** *adv (gen)* intentionnellement; *do, say* exprès.

inter [ɪn'tɜ:ʳ] *vt* enterrer. ◆ **interment** *n* enterrement *m.*

inter... ['ɪntəʳ] *pref* inter... ◆ **inter-city** *adj*: **~-city link** *or* **train** ligne *f* interurbaine. ◆ **inter-schools** *adj* interscolaire. ◆ **inter-war** *adj*: **the ~-war period** l'entre-deux-guerres *m.*

interact [ˌɪntər'ækt] *vi [substances]* avoir une action réciproque; *(Comput)* dialoguer (*with* avec). ◆ **interaction** *n* interaction *f.* ◆ **interactive** *adj (Comput, also gen)* interactif.

intercede [ˌɪntə'si:d] *vi* intercéder (*with* auprès de; *for* pour, en faveur de).

intercept [ˌɪntə'sept] *vt (Mil etc) ship, message, messenger* intercepter; *(gen) person* arrêter au passage. ◆ **interception** *n* interception *f.*

intercession [ˌɪntə'seʃ(ə)n] *n* intercession *f.*

interchange ['ɪntəˌtʃeɪndʒ] **1** *n [motorway]* échangeur *m.* **2** [ˌɪntə'tʃeɪndʒ] *vt (exchange) letters, ideas* échanger (*with sb* avec qn); *(alternate)* faire alterner (*with* avec); *(change positions of)* changer de place. ◆ **interchangeable** *adj* interchangeable.

intercom * ['ɪntəkɒm] *n* interphone *m.*

intercontinental ['ɪntəˌkɒntɪ'nentl] *adj* intercontinental.

intercourse ['ɪntəkɔ:s] *n* (**a**) relations *fpl*, rapports *mpl.* (**b**) **(sexual) ~** rapports *mpl* (sexuels); **to have ~** avoir des rapports (*with* avec).

interdenominational ['ɪntədɪˌnɒmɪ'neɪʃənl] *adj* interconfessionnel.

interdepartmental ['ɪntəˌdi:pɑ:t'mentl] *adj (within firm)* entre services; *(within ministry)* entre départements.

interdependent [ˌɪntədɪ'pendənt] *adj* interdépendant.

interdisciplinary [ˌɪntəˈdɪsɪplɪnərɪ] *adj* interdisciplinaire.

interest [ˈɪntrɪst] **1** *n* (**a**) intérêt *m*. **to take an ~ in** s'intéresser à; **to show an ~ in** manifester de l'intérêt pour; **to be of ~ to sb** intéresser qn; **of little ~** présentant peu d'intérêt; **I'm doing it for ~'s sake** je le fais parce que cela m'intéresse; **my main ~ is reading** ce qui m'intéresse le plus c'est la lecture. (**b**) *(advantage)* intérêt *m*, avantage *m*, profit *m*. **it is in your ~ to do so** il est dans votre intérêt d'agir ainsi; **you have an ~ in doing so** vous avez intérêt à agir ainsi; **to act in sb's ~(s)** agir dans l'intérêt de qn; **in the ~ of peace** dans l'intérêt de la paix. (**c**) *(share, concern)* intérêts *mpl*. **I have an ~ in a hairdressing business** j'ai des intérêts dans un salon de coiffure; **British ~s in Africa** les intérêts britanniques en Afrique; **shipping ~s** les intérêts maritimes. (**d**) *(Fin)* intérêt(s) *m(pl)*. **simple/compound ~** intérêts simples/composés; **~ on an investment** intérêts d'un placement; **at an ~ of 10%** à un taux d'intérêt de 10%.
2 *adj*: **~ rate** taux *m* d'intérêt.
3 *vt* intéresser. **to be** *or* **become ~ed in** s'intéresser à; **I am ~ed in going** ça m'intéresse d'y aller; **can I ~ you in contributing to...?** est-ce que cela vous intéresserait de contribuer à...?
◆ **interested** *adj person* intéressé; *look, attitude* d'intérêt; **the ~ed parties** les intéressés *mpl*. ◆ **interest-free** *adj* sans intérêt. ◆ **interesting** *adj* intéressant. ◆ **interestingly** *adv speak* de façon intéressante ; **~ingly enough I...** ce qui est très intéressant, c'est que je...

interface [ˈɪntəfeɪs] **1** *n (Comput, Tech)* interface *f*; *(fig)* intermédiaire *mf*. **2** *vt* connecter (*with* avec).

interfere [ˌɪntəˈfɪəʳ] *vi* s'ingérer (*in* dans), se mêler des affaires des autres. **stop interfering!** ne vous mêlez pas de mes (*or* leurs *etc*) affaires!; **he's always interfering** il se mêle toujours de tout; *[circumstances etc]* **to ~ with sb's plans** contrecarrer les projets de qn; **he never allows his hobbies to ~ with his work** il ne laisse jamais ses distractions empiéter sur son travail. ◆ **interference** *n* ingérence *f* (*in* dans); *(Rad)* parasites *mpl*. ◆ **interfering** *adj* importun, qui se mêle toujours des affaires des autres.

interferon [ˌɪntəʳˈfɪərɒn] *n* interféron *m*.

interim [ˈɪntərɪm] **1** *n* intérim *m*. **2** *adj government, arrangements* provisoire; *post, holder of post, dividend* intérimaire.

interior [ɪnˈtɪərɪəʳ] **1** *adj (gen)* intérieur. **~ decoration/decorator** décoration *f*/décorateur *m*, -trice *f* d'intérieurs. **2** *n* intérieur *m*. **Ministry of the I~** ministère *m* de l'Intérieur.

interject [ˌɪntəˈdʒekt] *vt* placer. **'yes' he ~ed** 'oui' réussit-il à placer. ◆ **interjection** *n* interjection *f*.

interloper [ˈɪntələʊpəʳ] *n* intrus(e) *m(f)*.

interlude [ˈɪntəluːd] *n* intervalle *m*; *(Theat)* intermède *m*. **musical ~** interlude *m*.

intermarry [ˈɪntəˈmærɪ] *vi*: **they do not ~** ils ne se marient pas entre eux; **they do not ~ with their neighbours** ils ne se marient pas avec leurs voisins.

intermediary [ˌɪntəˈmiːdɪərɪ] *adj, n* intermédiaire *(mf)*.

intermediate [ˌɪntəˈmiːdɪət] **1** *adj (gen)* intermédiaire; *(Scol etc)* moyen; *(Mil)* **~ range weapon** missile *m* de moyenne portée. **2** *n (US) (person)* intermédiaire *mf*; *(car)* automobile *f* de taille moyenne.

interminable [ɪnˈtɜːmɪnəbl] *adj* interminable.

intermission [ˌɪntəˈmɪʃ(ə)n] *n (in work, session)* interruption *f*; *(in hostilities)* trêve *f*; *(Cine, Theat)* entracte *m*; *(Med)* intermission *f*.

intermittent [ˌɪntəˈmɪt(ə)nt] *adj* intermittent. ◆ **intermittently** *adv* par intermittence.

intern [ɪnˈtɜːn] **1** *vt (Pol etc)* interner *(pour raisons de sécurité)*. **2** [ˈɪntɜːn] *n (US Med)* interne *mf*. ◆ **internee** *n (Pol)* interné(e) *m(f)*. ◆ **internment** *n* internement *m*.

internal [ɪnˈtɜːnl] *adj (Med, Tech)* interne; *(Ind, Pol) dispute, reorganization* intérieur, interne; *evidence* intrinsèque; *belief, conviction* intime. **~ combustion engine** moteur *m* à combustion interne *or* à explosion; **~ injuries** lésions *fpl* internes; *(Pol)* **~ quarrels** querelles intestines; *(US)* **~ revenue** fisc *m*. ◆ **internalize** *vt skill* assimiler à fond; *problem* intérioriser. ◆ **internally** *adv* intérieurement.

international [ˌɪntəˈnæʃnəl] **1** *adj* international. **2** *n (match, player)* international *m*. ◆ **internationally** *adv* internationalement, dans le monde entier.

internist [ɪnˈtɜːnɪst] *n (US Med)* ≃ spécialiste *mf* des maladies organiques.

interplay [ˈɪntəpleɪ] *n* effet *m* réciproque.

interpolate [ɪnˈtɜːpəleɪt] *vt* interpoler. ◆ **interpolation** *n* interpolation *f*.

interpose [ˌɪntəˈpəʊz] *vt* intercaler.

interpret [ɪnˈtɜːprɪt] *vti* interpréter. ◆ **interpretation** *n* interprétation *f*. ◆ **interpreter** *n* interprète *mf*.

interrelated [ˌɪntərɪˈleɪtəd] *adj* en corrélation.

interrogate [ɪnˈterəgeɪt] *vt (gen, also Comput)* interroger; *(Police)* soumettre à un interrogatoire. ◆ **interrogation** **1** *n* interrogation *f*; interrogatoire *m* ; **2** *adj* **interrogation mark** point *m* d'interrogation. ◆ **interrogative** **1** *adj* interrogateur; *(Ling)* interrogatif ; **2** *n*: **in the interrogative** à l'interrogatif *m*. ◆ **interrogatively** *adv* d'un air interrogateur; *(Ling)* interrogativement. ◆ **interrogator** *n* interrogateur *m*, -trice *f*.

interrupt [ˌɪntəˈrʌpt] *vt* interrompre. ◆ **interruption** *n* interruption *f*.

intersect [ˌɪntəˈsekt] **1** *vt* couper; *(Math)* intersecter. **2** *vi [lines, wires, roads etc]* s'entrecouper; *(Math)* s'intersecter. ◆ **intersection** *n (crossroads)* croisement *m*; *(Math)* intersection *f*.

interspersed [ˌɪntəˈspɜːsd] *adj*: **~ with...** avec, de temps en temps...

interval [ˈɪntəv(ə)l] *n* intervalle *m*; *(Scol)* récréation *f*; *(Sport)* mi-temps *f*; *(Theat)* entracte *m*; *(Mus)* intervalle. **at ~s** par intervalles; **at frequent/regular ~s** à intervalles rapprochés/réguliers; **there was an ~ for discussion** il y eut une pause pour la discussion; *(Met)* **bright ~s** belles éclaircies *fpl*.

intervene [ˌɪntəˈviːn] *vi [person]* intervenir (*in* dans); *[event, circumstances etc]* survenir, intervenir; *[time, years]* s'écouler (*between* entre). ◆ **intervening** *adj event* survenu; *period* intermédiaire; *years* qui s'écoulent entre-temps. ◆ **intervention** *n* intervention *f*; *(Econ)* **intervention price** prix *m* d'intervention.

interview [ˈɪntəvjuː] **1** *n (gen)* entrevue *f*; *(Press, Rad, TV)* interview *f*. **to call** *or* **invite sb to an ~** convoquer qn; **I had an ~ with the manager** j'ai eu une entrevue avec le directeur; **the ~s will be held next week** les entrevues auront lieu la semaine prochaine.
2 *vt* (**a**) *(for job etc)* avoir une entrevue avec. **he is being ~ed on Monday** on le convoque pour lundi. (**b**) *(Press, Rad, TV)* interviewer.
◆ **interviewer** *n (Press, Rad, TV)* interviewer *m*; *(in market research, opinion poll)* enquêteur *m*, -euse *f*; *(for job etc)* **the ~er asked me...** la personne qui me faisait passer mon entrevue m'a demandé...

intestine [ɪnˈtestɪn] *n* intestin *m*.

intimate ['ɪntɪmɪt] **1** *adj (gen)* intime; *knowledge, analysis* approfondi. **they became ~** ils sont devenus amis intimes; *(sexually)* ils ont eu des rapports intimes. **2** *n* intime *mf*. **3** ['ɪntɪmeɪt] *vt (make known officially)* annoncer, faire connaître (*that* que); *(indirectly)* laisser entendre. ◆ **intimacy** *n* (**a**) intimité *f*. (**b**) *(sexual)* rapports *mpl* intimes *or* sexuels. (**c**) **intimacies** familiarités *fpl*. ◆ **intimately** *adv know, talk* intimement; *connected* étroitement; **~ly involved in sth** mêlé de près à qch. ◆ **intimation** *n (gen)* annonce *f*; *[death]* avis *m*; *(hint, sign)* indication *f*.

intimidate [ɪn'tɪmɪdeɪt] *vt* intimider. ◆ **intimidation** *n* intimidation *f*.

into ['ɪntʊ] *prep* dans; en. **to come** *or* **go ~ a room** entrer dans une pièce; **to go ~ town** aller en ville; **to get ~ a car** monter dans une voiture *or* en voiture; **he helped her ~ the car** il l'a aidée à monter en voiture; **to change traveller's cheques ~ francs** changer des chèques de voyage contre des francs; **far ~ the night** très avant dans la nuit; **4 ~ 12 goes 3 times** 12 divisé par 4 donne 3; **the children are ~ everything** * les enfants touchent à tout; *(fig)* **she's ~** ‡ **health foods** *etc* elle donne à fond * dans les aliments naturels *etc*.

intolerable [ɪn'tɒl(ə)rəbl] *adj* intolérable (*that* que + *subj*). ◆ **intolerably** *adv* intolérablement. ◆ **intolerance** *n* intolérance *f*. ◆ **intolerant** *adj* intolérant (**of** de; *(Med) of* à). ◆ **intolerantly** *adv* avec intolérance.

intonation [ˌɪntə(ʊ)'neɪʃ(ə)n] *n (Ling)* intonation *f*.

intoxicate [ɪn'tɒksɪkeɪt] *vt (lit, fig)* enivrer. ◆ **intoxicated** *adj (lit)* ivre; *(Jur)* en état d'ivresse; *(fig)* ivre (*with* de), grisé (*with* par). ◆ **intoxication** *n* ivresse *f*.

intra... ['ɪntrə] *pref* intra... ◆ **intramuscular** *adj* intramusculaire. ◆ **intravenous** *adj* intraveineux.

intractable [ɪn'træktəbl] *adj child* intraitable ; *problem* insoluble; *illness* opiniâtre.

intransigence [ɪn'trænsɪdʒ(ə)ns] *n* intransigeance *f*. ◆ **intransigent** *adj, n* intransigeant(e) *m(f)*.

intransitive [ɪn'trænsɪtɪv] *adj, n (Gram)* intransitif *(m)*.

intrepid [ɪn'trepɪd] *adj* intrépide.

intricate ['ɪntrɪkɪt] *adj plot, problem* complexe; *mechanism, pattern, style* compliqué. ◆ **intricacy** *n* complexité *f*; complication *f*. ◆ **intricately** *adv* de façon complexe *or* compliquée.

intrigue [ɪn'tri:g] **1** *vt* intriguer. **2** *vi* intriguer (*with sb* avec qn; *to do* pour faire). **3** *n* intrigue *f*. ◆ **intriguer** *n* intrigant(e) *m(f)*. ◆ **intriguing 1** *adj* fascinant ; **2** *n* intrigues *fpl*.

intrinsic [ɪn'trɪnsɪk] *adj* intrinsèque. ◆ **intrinsically** *adv* intrinsèquement.

introduce [ˌɪntrə'dju:s] *vt* (**a**) *(bring in) reform, innovation* introduire; *subject, speaker* présenter; *practice* faire adopter, introduire; *(Rad, TV) programme* présenter; *(Parl) bill* déposer. **to ~ sb into a firm** faire entrer qn dans une compagnie. (**b**) *(make acquainted)* présenter (*to sb* à qn). **he ~d me to the delights of skiing** il m'a initié aux plaisirs du ski; **I was ~d to Shakespeare too young** on m'a fait connaître Shakespeare quand j'étais trop jeune; **who ~d them?** qui les a présentés l'un à l'autre?; **may I ~ Mr Martin?** puis-je (me permettre de) vous présenter M. Martin? (**c**) *(insert) key etc* introduire (*into* dans). ◆ **introduction** *n (gen)* introduction *f* (*into* dans; *to* à); présentation *f* (*of sb to sb* de qn à qn); **my introduction to life in London** mon premier contact avec la vie londonienne; **letter of introduction** lettre *f* de recommandation (*to sb* auprès de qn). ◆ **introductory** *adj remarks, words* préliminaire, d'introduction; *(Comm) offer* de lancement.

introspective [ˌɪntrə(ʊ)'spektɪv] *adj* introspectif. ◆ **introspection** *n* introspection *f*.

introvert ['ɪntrəʊ'vɜ:t] *adj, n* introverti(e) *m(f)*. ◆ **introversion** *n* introversion *f*.

intrude [ɪn'tru:d] *vi [person]* être importun, s'imposer; *[feeling, emotion]* se manifester. **to ~ on** *person* s'imposer à; *conversation* s'immiscer dans; **am I intruding?** est-ce que je vous gêne? ◆ **intruder** *n* intrus(e) *m(f)*. ◆ **intrusion** *n* intrusion *f* (*into* dans), imposition *f* (*on* à). ◆ **intrusive** *adj* importun, gênant; *(Ling)* **the intrusive 'r'** *le 'r' rajouté en anglais en liaison abusive.*

intuition [ˌɪntju:'ɪʃ(ə)n] *n* intuition *f*. ◆ **intuitive** *adj* intuitif. ◆ **intuitively** *adv* intuitivement.

inundate ['ɪnʌndeɪt] *vt (lit, fig)* inonder (*with* de). **~d with work** débordé (de travail); **~d with visits** inondé de visiteurs.

inure [ɪn'jʊəʳ] *vt* habituer, aguerrir (*to* à).

invade [ɪn'veɪd] *vt (Mil, gen, fig)* envahir; *privacy* violer; *sb's rights* empiéter sur. ◆ **invader** *n* envahisseur *m*, -euse *f*. ◆ **invading** *adj army, troops* d'invasion.

invalid¹ ['ɪnvəlɪd] **1** *n (sick person)* malade *mf*; *(with disability)* invalide *mf*, infirme *mf*. **2** *adj (ill)* malade; *(with disability)* invalide, infirme; *car* d'infirme; **~ chair** fauteuil *m* d'infirme. ◆ **invalid out** *vt sep (Mil)* réformer (pour blessures *or* pour raisons de santé).

invalid² [ɪn'vælɪd] *adj* non valide, non valable.

invalidate [ɪn'vælɪdeɪt] *vt (gen)* invalider; *will* rendre nul et sans effet; *contract etc* vicier.

invaluable [ɪn'vælj(ʊ)əbl] *adj* inestimable, inappréciable.

invariable [ɪn'vɛərɪəbl] *adj* invariable. ◆ **invariably** *adv* invariablement.

invasion [ɪn'veɪʒ(ə)n] *n* invasion *f*. **it is an ~ of his privacy** c'est une incursion dans sa vie privée.

invective [ɪn'vektɪv] *n* invective *f*. **stream of ~** flot *m* d'invectives.

inveigh [ɪn'veɪ] *vi* fulminer (*against* contre).

inveigle [ɪn'vi:gl] *vt* entraîner (par la ruse *etc*) (*into sth* dans qch; *into doing* à faire).

invent [ɪn'vent] *vt (lit, fig)* inventer. ◆ **invention** *n* invention *f*. ◆ **inventive** *adj* inventif. ◆ **inventiveness** *n* esprit inventif. ◆ **inventor** *n* inventeur *m*, -trice *f*.

inventory ['ɪnvəntrɪ] *n* inventaire *m*.

inverse ['ɪn'vɜ:s] *adj* inverse. **in ~ proportion** *or* **ratio** en raison inverse (*to* de). ◆ **inversely** *adv* inversement. ◆ **inversion** *n* inversion *f*; *(Mus)* renversement *m*; *[values, roles etc]* renversement.

invert [ɪn'vɜ:t] **1** *vt (gen)* inverser, intervertir; *cup, object* retourner; *process* renverser. **in ~ed commas** entre guillemets *mpl*. **2** ['ɪnvɜ:t] *n* inverti(e) *m(f)*.

invertebrate [ɪn'vɜ:tɪbrɪt] *adj, n* invertébré *(m)*.

invest [ɪn'vest] **1** *vt capital, funds* investir (*in* dans); *money* placer (*in* dans, en); *time* consacrer (*in* à); *(endow)* revêtir, investir (*sb with sth* qn de qch). **2** *vi* placer son argent (*in* en). **I've ~ed in a new car** * je me suis payé * une nouvelle voiture. ◆ **investiture** *n* investiture *f*. ◆ **investment 1** *n* investissement *m* ; **2** *adj (US)* **~ bank** banque *f* d'acceptation. ◆ **investor** *n (gen)* investisseur *m* ; *(in a company)* actionnaire *mf*.

investigate [ɪn'vestɪgeɪt] *vt question, possibilities* étudier; *motive, reason* scruter; *crime* enquêter sur. ◆ **investigation** *n [researcher]* investigation *f*; *[policeman etc]* enquête *f*; **the matter under investigation** la question à l'étude. ◆ **investigative** *adj technique* d'investigation; **investigative journalism** enquête-reportage *f*. ◆ **investigator** *n* investigateur *m*, -trice *f*; *(Police)* enquêteur *m*; **private investigator** détective *m*.

inveterate [ɪn'vet(ə)rɪt] *adj* invétéré.

invidious [ɪn'vɪdɪəs] *adj (gen)* injuste; *comparison* blessant.

invigilate [ɪn'vɪdʒɪleɪt] **1** *vi* être de surveillance (*at* à). **2** *vt examination* surveiller. ◆ **invigilator** *n* surveillant(e) *m(f) (à un examen)*.

invigorate [ɪn'vɪgəreɪt] *vt [drink, food, thought]* fortifier; *[fresh air, snack]* revigorer; *[climate, air, exercise]* donner du tonus à. ◆ **invigorating** *adj* vivifiant, tonifiant; *speech* stimulant.

invincible [ɪn'vɪnsəbl] *adj* invincible.

invisible [ɪn'vɪzəbl] *adj (gen)* invisible; *ink* sympathique. ~ **exports** exportations *fpl* invisibles. ~ **mending** stoppage *m*. ◆ **invisibility** *n* invisibilité *f*. ◆ **invisibly** *adv* invisiblement.

invite [ɪn'vaɪt] *vt person* inviter (*to do* à faire); *opinions, subscriptions etc* demander; *doubts, ridicule* appeler; *discussion* inviter à; *trouble, defeat* chercher. **to ~ sb to dinner** inviter qn à dîner; **to ~ sb in/up** *etc* inviter qn à entrer/monter *etc*. ◆ **invite out** *vt sep* inviter (à sortir). **I've been ~d out to dinner** j'ai été invité à dîner. ◆ **invite over** *vt sep* inviter (à venir). **they often ~ us over for a drink** ils nous invitent souvent à venir prendre un verre chez eux.
◆ **invitation** *n* invitation *f*; **at sb's invitation** à *or* sur l'invitation de qn; **by invitation only** sur invitation seulement; **it is an invitation to burglars** c'est une invite aux cambrioleurs. ◆ **inviting** *adj appearance, goods* attrayant; *gesture* encourageant; *meal, odour* appétissant. ◆ **invitingly** *adv describe* d'une manière attrayante; *speak* d'un ton encourageant.

invoice ['ɪnvɔɪs] **1** *n* facture *f*. **2** *vt* facturer. **3** *adj*: ~ **clerk** facturier *m*, -ière *f*.

invoke [ɪn'vəʊk] *vt* invoquer.

involuntary [ɪn'vɒlənt(ə)rɪ] *adj* involontaire. ◆ **involuntarily** *adv* involontairement.

involve [ɪn'vɒlv] *vt* (**a**) *(gen)* mêler (*in* à), entraîner (*in* dans); *(implicate, associate)* impliquer (*in* dans). **to be ~d in a quarrel** être mêlé à une querelle; **we would prefer not to ~ Robert** nous préférerions ne pas mêler Robert à l'affaire *or* ne pas impliquer Robert; **to ~ sb in expense** entraîner qn à faire des frais; **how did you come to be ~d?** comment vous êtes-vous trouvé impliqué?; **he was so ~d in politics that...** il était tellement engagé dans la politique que...; **the police became ~d** la police est intervenue; **a question of principle is ~d** c'est une question de principe qui est en jeu; **the factors ~d** les facteurs en jeu; **the person ~d** la personne en question; **to feel personally ~d** se sentir concerné; **we are all ~d** nous sommes tous concernés; **to get ~d with sb** *(gen)* se trouver mêlé aux affaires de qn; *(socially)* se trouver lié intimement à qn; *(fall in love with)* tomber amoureux de qn. (**b**) *(entail) expense, trouble* entraîner. **the job ~s living in the country** le poste nécessite qu'on réside *(subj)* à la campagne; **there's a good deal of work ~d** cela nécessite un gros travail. ◆ **involved** *adj* compliqué. ◆ **involvement** *n* (**a**) rôle *m* (*in* dans), participation *f* (*in* à); **we don't know the extent of his ~ment** nous ne savons pas dans quelle mesure il est impliqué; **his ~ment in politics** son engagement *m* dans la politique; (**b**) *(difficulty)* difficulté *f*; **financial ~ments** difficultés financières; (**c**) *[style etc]* complications *fpl*.

invulnerable [ɪn'vʌln(ə)rəbl] *adj* invulnérable. ◆ **invulnerability** *n* invulnérabilité *f*.

inward ['ɪnwəd] **1** *adj movements* vers l'intérieur; *happiness, peace* intérieur; *thoughts, conviction* intime. **2** *adv (also* **~s***)* vers l'intérieur. ◆ **inwardly** *adv* (**a**) *(in the inside)* à l'intérieur; (**b**) *(secretly) feel, think, know* en son (*or* mon *etc*) for intérieur.

iodine ['aɪədi:n] *n* iode *m*; *(Med)* teinture *f* d'iode.

ion ['aɪən] *n* ion *m*.

Ionian Sea [aɪəʊniən'si:] *n* mer *f* Ionienne.

iota [aɪ'əʊtə] *n* iota *m*; *[truth]* brin *m*; *[sense]* grain *m*.

IOU [ˌaɪəʊ'ju:] *n (abbr of* **I owe you***)* reconnaissance *f* de dette (*for* pour).

Iran [ɪ'rɑ:n] *n* Iran *m*.

Iraq [ɪ'rɑ:k] *n* Irak *m*.

irascible [ɪ'ræsɪbl] *adj* irascible. ◆ **irascibility** *n* irascibilité *f*. ◆ **irascibly** *adv* irasciblement.

irate [aɪ'reɪt] *adj* furieux.

Ireland ['aɪələnd] *n* Irlande *f*. **Northern ~** Irlande du Nord; **Republic of ~** République *f* d'Irlande. ◆ **Irish 1** *adj* irlandais; **Irish coffee** café *m* irlandais; **Irish Sea** mer *f* d'Irlande; **2** *n* (**a**) **the Irish** les Irlandais *mpl*; (**b**) *(Ling)* irlandais *m*. ◆ **Irishman** *n* Irlandais *m*. ◆ **Irishwoman** *n* Irlandaise *f*.

iris ['aɪərɪs] *n (Anat, Bot)* iris *m*.

irksome ['3:ksəm] *adj* ennuyeux.

iron ['aɪən] **1** *n (metal)* fer *m*; *(for laundry)* fer (à repasser). **scrap ~** ferraille *f*; **to strike while the ~ is hot** battre le fer pendant qu'il est chaud; **electric ~** fer électrique; *(fig)* **to have too many ~s in the fire** mener trop d'affaires de front; **I've got a lot of ~s in the fire** j'ai des quantités d'affaires en train; *(fetters)* **~s** fers *mpl*. **2** *adj tool, bridge* de *or* en fer; *(fig) determination, will, constitution* de fer. **the I~ Age** l'âge *m* de fer; **the ~ and steel industry** l'industrie *f* sidérurgique; *(Pol)* **~ curtain** rideau *m* de fer; **an ~ fist** *or* **hand in a velvet glove** une main de fer dans un gant de velours; **~ foundry** fonderie *f* de fonte; *(Med)* **~ lung** poumon *m* d'acier; **~ ore** minerai *m* de fer; **~ rations** vivres *mpl* de réserve. **3** *vt clothes etc* repasser. **4** *vi [clothes etc]* se repasser.
◆ **iron out** *vt sep creases* faire disparaître au fer; *difficulties* aplanir; *problems* faire disparaître.
◆ **ironing 1** *n* repassage *m* ; **2** *adj*: **~ing board** planche *f* à repasser. ◆ **ironmonger** *n* quincaillier *m*. ◆ **ironmongery** *n* quincaillerie *f*. ◆ **ironworks** *n* usine *f* sidérurgique.

irony ['aɪərənɪ] *n* ironie *f*. **the ~ of it is that...** ce qu'il y a d'ironique là-dedans c'est que... ◆ **ironic(al)** *adj* ironique. ◆ **ironically** *adv* ironiquement.

irradiate [ɪ'reɪdɪeɪt] *vt (illuminate)* illuminer; *(Phys)* irradier. ◆ **irradiation** *n* illumination *f*; irradiation *f*.

irrational [ɪ'ræʃənl] *adj person* qui n'est pas rationnel; *belief* déraisonnable; *behaviour* irrationnel. **she had become quite ~ about it** elle n'était plus du tout capable d'y penser rationnellement. ◆ **irrationally** *adv* déraisonnablement; irrationnellement.

irreconcilable [ɪˌrekən'saɪləbl] *adj enemies* irréconciliable; *hatred* implacable; *belief* inconciliable (*with* avec).

irredeemable [ˌɪrɪ'di:məbl] *adj person* incorrigible; *error* irréparable; *disaster* irrémédiable.

irrefutable [ˌɪrɪ'fju:təbl] *adj* irréfutable.

irregular [ɪ'regjʊlə^r] *adj (gen)* irrégulier; *surface* inégal. ◆ **irregularity** *n* irrégularité *f*.

irrelevant [ɪ'reləvənt] *adj factor, detail* sans rapport; *question, remark* hors de propos. **that's ~** cela n'a rien à voir avec la question. ◆ **irrelevance** *n* manque *m* de rapport, manque d'à-propos (*to* avec).

irreligious [ˌɪrɪ'lɪdʒəs] *adj* irréligieux.

irreparable [ɪ'rep(ə)rəbl] *adj* irréparable. ◆ **irreparably** *adv* irréparablement.

irreplaceable [ˌɪrɪ'pleɪsəbl] *adj* irremplaçable.

irrepressible [ˌɪrɪ'presəbl] *adj laughter etc* irrépressible, irrésistible. **she's quite** ~ elle est d'une vitalité débordante; *(of child)* c'est un vrai petit diable.

irreproachable [ˌɪrɪ'prəʊtʃəbl] *adj* irréprochable.

irresistible [ˌɪrɪ'zɪstəbl] *adj* irrésistible. ◆ **irresistibly** *adv* irrésistiblement.

irresolute [ɪ'rezəlu:t] *adj* irrésolu, indécis.

irrespective [ˌɪrɪ'spektɪv] *adj*: ~ **of sth** sans tenir compte de qch; ~ **of whether it's useful or not** que ce soit utile ou non.

irresponsible [ˌɪrɪs'pɒnsəbl] *adj* irréfléchi. ◆ **irresponsibly** *adv (gen)* sans penser à ses (*or* leurs *etc*) responsabilités; *(without thinking enough)* à la légère.

irretrievable [ˌɪrɪ'tri:vəbl] *adj loss, damage* irréparable; *object* introuvable.

irreverent [ɪ'rev(ə)rənt] *adj* irrévérencieux. ◆ **irreverence** *n* irrévérence *f*. ◆ **irreverently** *adv* irrévérencieusement.

irrevocable [ɪ'revəkəbl] *adj* irrévocable. ◆ **irrevocably** *adv* irrévocablement.

irrigate ['ɪrɪgeɪt] *vt* irriguer. ◆ **irrigation** *n* irrigation *f*.

irritable ['ɪrɪtəbl] *adj (cross)* irritable; *(irascible)* irascible. ◆ **irritability** *n* irritabilité *f*; irascibilité *f*. ◆ **irritably** *adv behave, nod* avec humeur; *speak* d'un ton irrité.

irritate ['ɪrɪteɪt] *vt (gen, Med)* irriter. ◆ **irritant** *adj, n* irritant *(m)*. ◆ **irritating** *adj* irritant. ◆ **irritation** *n* irritation *f*.

irruption [ɪ'rʌpʃ(ə)n] *n* irruption *f*.

Islam ['ɪzlɑ:m] *n* Islam *m*. ◆ **Islamic** *adj* islamique.

Islamabad [ɪz'lɑ:mɑ:ˌbɑ:d] *n* Islamabad.

island ['aɪlənd] **1** *n* (**a**) île *f*. (**b**) *(traffic or street ~)* refuge *m (pour piétons)*; *(on roundabout)* terre-plein *m*. **2** *adj people, community* insulaire. ◆ **islander** *n* insulaire *mf*.

isle [aɪl] *n (liter)* île *f*. ◆ **islet** *n* îlot *m*.

isolate ['aɪsəʊ'leɪt] *vt* isoler (*from* de). ◆ **isolated** *adj* isolé. ◆ **isolation 1** *n (action)* isolation *f*; *(state)* isolement *m* ; **2** *adj hospital* d'isolement; *ward* des contagieux. ◆ **isolationism** *n* isolationnisme *m*. ◆ **isolationist** *adj, n* isolationniste *(mf)*.

isotope ['aɪsəʊ'təʊp] *adj, n* isotope *(m)*.

Israel ['ɪzreɪl] *n* Israël *m*. ◆ **Israeli 1** *adj* israélien ; **2** *n* Israélien(ne) *m(f)*.

issue ['ɪʃu:] **1** *n* (**a**) *(matter, question)* question *f*, problème *m*. **he raised several new ~s** il a soulevé plusieurs points nouveaux; **the ~ is whether...** la question consiste à savoir si...; **to confuse** *or* **obscure the ~** brouiller les cartes; **to face the ~** regarder le problème en face; **to force the ~** forcer une décision; **to avoid the ~** prendre la tangente; **to make an ~ of sth** faire un problème de qch; **I don't want to make an ~ of it** je ne veux pas trop insister là-dessus; **the factors at ~** les facteurs en jeu; **the point at ~** le point controversé; **to be at ~** être en cause; **to take ~ with sb** engager une controverse avec qn; **I must take ~ with you on this** je me permets de ne pas partager votre avis làdessus. (**b**) *(outcome)* résultat *m*, issue *f*. (**c**) *(act) [goods, tickets]* distribution *f*; *[passport, document]* délivrance *f*; *[banknote, cheque, shares, stamp]* émission *f*; *[warrant, writ, summons]* lancement *m*. **these coins are a new ~** ces pièces viennent d'être émises. (**d**) *(copy) [newspaper, magazine]* numéro *m*. **back ~** vieux numéro. (**e**) *(offspring)* descendance *f*.

2 *vt book* publier; *order* donner; *goods, tickets* distribuer; *passport, document* délivrer; *banknote, cheque, shares, stamps* émettre; *proclamation* faire; *warrant, warning, writ* lancer. **to ~ a statement** faire une déclaration; **to ~ sth to sb, to ~ sb with sth** fournir qch à qn.

Istanbul [ɪstæn'bu:l] *n* Istamboul, Istanbul.

isthmus ['ɪsməs] *n* isthme *m*.

it [ɪt] *pron* (**a**) *(specific) (nominative)* il, elle; *(accusative)* le, la; *(before vowel)* l'; *(dative)* lui. **where is the book? — ~'s on the table** où est le livre? — il est sur la table; **my machine is old but ~ works** ma machine est vieille mais elle marche; **here's the pencil — give ~ to me** voici le crayon — donne-le-moi; **if you can find the watch give ~ to him** si tu trouves la montre donne-la-lui; **of ~, from ~, about ~, for ~, out of ~** *etc* en; **he's afraid of ~** il en a peur; **he didn't speak to me about ~** il ne m'en a pas parlé; *(following French verbs with 'de')* **I doubt ~** j'en doute; **in ~, to ~, at ~** *etc* y; *(meeting etc)* **he'll be at ~** il y sera; *(following French verbs with 'à')* **taste ~!** goûtez-y!; **above ~, over ~** (au-)dessus; **below ~, beneath ~, under ~** (au-)dessous, (en-)dessous.
(**b**) *(impersonal) (nominative)* il, ce, cela, ça; *(accusative)* le; *(dative)* y. **~ is raining** il pleut; **~ frightens me** cela *or* ça m'effraie; **~'s pleasant here** c'est agréable ici; **I've done it** je l'ai fait; **I've thought about it** j'y ai pensé; **~'s Wednesday 16th October** nous sommes le mercredi 16 octobre; **~'s 3 o'clock** il est 3 heures; **who is ~?** qui est-ce?; **~'s me** c'est moi; **what is ~?** qu'est-ce que c'est?; **that's ~!** *(approval, agreement)* c'est ça!; *(achievement, dismay)* ça y est!; **~'s difficult to understand** c'est difficile à comprendre; **~'s difficult to understand why** il est difficile de comprendre pourquoi; **I considered ~ pointless to protest** j'ai jugé (qu'il était) inutile de protester; **~ was your father who phoned** c'est ton père qui a téléphoné.
(**c**) *(in games)* **you're ~!** c'est toi le chat!
◆ **its 1** *poss adj* son, sa, ses ; **2** *poss pron* le sien, la sienne, les siens, les siennes. ◆ **it's = it is, it has.** ◆ **itself** *pron (emphatic)* lui-même *m*, elle-même *f*; *(reflexive)* se; **in the theatre ~self** dans le théâtre même; **the door closes by ~self** la porte se ferme automatiquement *or* toute seule.

italic [ɪ'tælɪk] **1** *adj (Typ)* italique. **2** *npl*: **~s** italique *m*. **in ~s** en italique.

Italy ['ɪtəlɪ] *n* Italie *f*. ◆ **Italian** [ɪ'tæljən] **1** *adj* italien, d'Italie ; **2** *n* (**a**) Italien(ne) *m(f)*; (**b**) *(Ling)* italien *m*.

itch [ɪtʃ] **1** *n* démangeaison *f*. *(fig)* **I've got an ~ * to travel** l'envie de voyager me démange. **2** *vi [person]* éprouver des démangeaisons. **his legs ~** ses jambes le démangent; *(fig)* **to be ~ing * to do sth** avoir une envie qui vous démange de faire qch; **I am ~ing to tell him the news** la langue me démange de lui annoncer la nouvelle. ◆ **itching** *adj*: **~ing powder** poil *m* à gratter. ◆ **itchy** *adj* qui démange; **I've got an ~y back** j'ai le dos qui me démange; *(fig)* **he's got ~y feet *** il a la bougeotte *; *(fig)* **he's got ~y fingers *** il est chapardeur *.

item ['aɪtəm] *n (on agenda, at meeting)* question *f*; *(in variety show)* numéro *m*; *(in catalogue, newspaper, shopping list; also Comm)* article *m*; *(Jur: in contract)* article; *(Book-keeping)* poste *m*. **an ~ of furniture** un meuble; **~s on the agenda** questions à l'ordre du jour; *(Rad, TV)* **the main ~ in the news** la grosse nouvelle, le fait du jour; **an important ~ in our policy** un point important de notre politique.
◆ **itemize** *vt* détailler, spécifier.

itinerary [aɪ'tɪn(ə)rərɪ] *n* itinéraire *m*. ◆ **itinerant** *adj preacher* itinérant; *actors etc* ambulant.

ivory ['aɪv(ə)rɪ] **1** *n* ivoire *m*. **2** *adj statue, figure* en ivoire, d'ivoire; *(also* **~-coloured***)* ivoire *inv*. **I~ Coast** Côte *f* d'Ivoire; *(fig)* **~ tower** tour *f* d'ivoire.

ivy ['aɪvɪ] *n* lierre *m*. *(US)* **I~ League** *(n) les huit grandes universités privées.*

J

J, j [dʒeɪ] *n* J, j *m*.

jab [dʒæb] **1** *vti* enfoncer, planter (*into* dans). **to ~ (at) sth with sth, to ~ sth into sth** enfoncer qch dans qch, planter qch dans *or* sur qch. **2** *n* coup *m (donné avec un objet pointu)*; *(*: injection)* piqûre *f*.

jabber [ˈdʒæbəʳ] **1** *vt* bafouiller, bredouiller. **2** *vi* **(~away)** *(chatter)* jacasser; *(talk unintelligibly)* baragouiner *.

jack [dʒæk] *n (Aut)* cric *m*; *(Bowling)* cochonnet *m*; *(Cards)* valet *m*. **before you could say J~ Robinson** * en moins de temps qu'il n'en faut pour le dire; **~ tar** matelot *m*; **every man ~** chacun. ◆**jack in** ‡ *vt sep* plaquer ‡. ◆**jack up** *vt sep car* soulever avec un cric; *(*: raise) prices* faire grimper. **~ed up** *car* sur le cric.
◆**jackass** *n (lit, fig)* âne *m*. ◆**jackboots** *npl* bottes *fpl* à l'écuyère. ◆**jackdaw** *n* choucas *m*. ◆**jackhammer** *n (US)* marteau-piqueur *m*. ◆**jack-in-office** * *n* gratte-papier *m inv* (qui joue à l'important). ◆**jack-in-the-box** *n* diable *m* (à ressort). ◆**jack-knife** **1** *n* couteau *m* de poche ; **2** *vi*: **the lorry ~-knifed** la remorque (du camion) s'est mise en travers. ◆**jackleg** *adj (US) carpenter* amateur; *work* louche; *structure* de fortune. ◆**jack-of-all-trades** *n* bricoleur *m*. ◆**jack plug** *n* prise *f* à fiche. ◆**jackpot** *n*: **to hit the ~pot** *[person]* gagner le gros lot; *[song, disc]* faire un malheur *.

jackal [ˈdʒækɔːl] *n* chacal *m*.

jacket [ˈdʒækɪt] *n [man]* veston *m*; *[woman]* veste *f*; *[child]* paletot *m*; *[book]* couverture *f*. **~ potatoes, potatoes baked in their ~s** pommes *fpl* de terre au four.

Jacobean [ˌdʒækəˈbiːən] *adj* de l'époque de Jacques Ier *(1603-1625)*.

jacuzzi [dʒəˈkuːzɪ] ® *n* jacuzzi ® *m*, bain *m* à jet propulsé.

jade [dʒeɪd] **1** *n* jade *m*. **2** *adj (colour)* jade *inv*. **~-green** vert jade *inv*.

jaded [ˈdʒeɪdɪd] *adj person* las (*with* de), blasé; *palate* blasé.

jagged [ˈdʒægɪd] *adj* irrégulier, déchiqueté.

jaguar [ˈdʒægjʊəʳ] *n* jaguar *m*.

jail [dʒeɪl] **1** *n* prison *f*. **in ~** en prison; **to be in ~ for 5 years** faire 5 ans de prison; **to send sb to ~/to ~ for 5 years** condamner qn à la prison/à 5 ans de prison. **2** *vt* mettre en prison (*for murder etc* pour meurtre *etc*). **~ed for life** condamné à perpétuité. ◆**jailbird** *n* récidiviste *mf*. ◆**jailbreak** *n* évasion *f* (de prison). ◆**jailbreaker** *n* évadé(e) *m(f)*. ◆**jailer** *n* geôlier *m*, -ière *f*.

jam[1] [dʒæm] **1** *n* (**a**) *[people]* foule *f*, cohue *f*; *[logs, vehicles etc]* embouteillage *m*. (**b**) **to get into a ~** * se mettre dans le pétrin; **to get sb out of a ~** * tirer qn du pétrin. **2** *vt* (**a**) *(cram) (into box, drawer, suitcase)* enfoncer, tasser (*into* dans); *(into room, vehicle)* entasser (*into* dans); *hat* enfoncer (*on* sur); *(wedge)* coincer (*between* entre). **he ~med his finger in the door** il s'est coincé le doigt dans la porte. (**b**) *(block) brake* bloquer; *door* coincer; *gun, machine* enrayer; *(Rad) station, broadcast* brouiller; *(Telec) line* encombrer; *[crowd, cars etc] street, corridor* encombrer, embouteiller. **street ~med with cars** rue embouteillée; **street ~med with people** rue noire de monde. **3** *vi* (**a**) *[crowd]* s'entasser (*into* dans). (**b**) *(V* **2b** *above)* se bloquer; se coincer; s'enrayer.
◆**jam in** *vt sep (into box etc)* serrer; *car, person* coincer. ◆**jam on** *vt sep hat* enfoncer. *(Aut)* **to ~ on the brakes** freiner à mort *.
◆**jam-full** *or* ◆**jam-packed** *adj vehicle, place* plein à craquer; *container* plein à ras bord. ◆**jamming** *n (Rad)* brouillage *m*.

jam[2] [dʒæm] **1** *n* confiture *f*. **cherry ~** confiture de cerises; *(fig)* **you want ~ on it!** * et quoi encore! **2** *adj tart* à la confiture. *(Mus)* **~ session** séance *f* de jazz improvisé. ◆**jamjar** *or* ◆**jampot** *n* pot *m* à confitures.

Jamaica [dʒəˈmeɪkə] *n* Jamaïque *f*. **in ~** à la Jamaïque. ◆**Jamaican** **1** *adj* jamaïquain ; **2** *n* Jamaïquain(e) *m(f)*.

jamb [dʒæm] *n* montant *m (de porte etc)*.

jamboree [ˌdʒæmbəˈriː] *n* festivités *fpl*.

jangle [ˈdʒæŋgl] **1** *vi [bells]* retentir; *[bracelets, chains]* cliqueter. **2** *vt* faire retentir; faire cliqueter. ◆**jangled** *adj nerves* en pelote. ◆**jangling** *adj bells* discordant; *chains* cliquetant.

janitor [ˈdʒænɪtəʳ] *n* concierge *m*.

January [ˈdʒænjʊərɪ] *n* janvier *m*; *for phrases V* **September**.

Japan [dʒəˈpæn] *n* Japon *m*. ◆**Japanese** **1** *adj* japonais ; **2** *n (person: pl inv)* Japonais(e) *m(f)*; *(Ling)* japonais *m*.

japonica [dʒəˈpɒnɪkə] *n* cognassier *m* du Japon.

jar[1] [dʒɑːʳ] **1** *n (jolt: lit, fig)* secousse *f*, choc *m*. **2** *vi (vibrate)* vibrer, trembler; *(be wrong) [note]* détonner; *[colours]* jurer (*with* avec); *[ideas, opinions]* ne pas s'accorder (*with* avec). **to ~ on sb's nerves** porter sur les nerfs à qn; **to ~ on sb's ears** écorcher les oreilles à qn. **3** *vt structure* ébranler; *person* ébranler, secouer; *(fig)* secouer. **you ~red my elbow** tu m'as cogné le coude. ◆**jarring** *adj sound* discordant; *(fig)* **to strike a ~ring note** être plutôt choquant.

jar[2] [dʒɑːʳ] *n (of earthenware)* pot *m*, jarre *f*; *(for jam etc)* pot; *(for pickles etc)* bocal *m*.

jargon [ˈdʒɑːgən] *n* jargon *m*.

jasmine [ˈdʒæzmɪn] *n* jasmin *m*.

jaundice [ˈdʒɔːndɪs] *n* jaunisse *f*. ◆**jaundiced** *adj (bitter)* amer; *(critical)* désapprobateur; **to have a ~d view of things** voir les choses en noir; **to give sb a ~d look** jeter un regard noir à qn.

jaunt [dʒɔːnt] *n* balade * *f*. **to go for a ~** aller se balader *.

jaunty [ˈdʒɔːntɪ] *adj (sprightly)* enjoué, vif; *(carefree)* désinvolte; *(swaggering)* crâneur *. ◆**jauntily** *adv* d'un pas vif; de façon désinvolte; d'un air crâneur *.

javelin [ˈdʒævlɪn] **1** *n* javelot *m*. **2** *adj (Sport)* **~ throwing** lancement *m* du javelot.

jaw [dʒɔː] *n* mâchoire *f*. **the ~s of death** l'étreinte *f* de la mort; **the ~s of hell** les portes *fpl* de l'enfer.
◆**jawbone** *n* maxillaire *m*.

jay [dʒeɪ] *n* geai *m*. ◆**jaywalker** *n* piéton *m* indiscipliné.

jazz [dʒæz] **1** *n (Mus)* jazz *m*. *(fig)* **he gave them a lot of ~ * about his marvellous job** il leur a fait tout un baratin * sur sa magnifique situation ; **...and all that ~** ⁑ ... et tout le bataclan *. **2** *adj band, music* de jazz. ◆ **jazz up** *vt sep* (**a**) *(Mus) (play)* jouer en jazz; *(arrange)* adapter pour le jazz. (**b**) (⁑) *party* mettre de l'entrain dans; *old dress etc* égayer.

jealous ['dʒeləs] *adj* jaloux (*of* de). ◆ **jealously** *adv (enviously)* jalousement; *(watchfully)* d'un œil jaloux. ◆ **jealousy** *n* jalousie *f*.

jeans [dʒi:nz] *npl* blue-jean *m*, jean *m*.

jeep [dʒi:p] *n* jeep *f*.

jeer [dʒɪəʳ] **1** *vi [individual]* railler; *[crowd]* huer. **to ~ at sb** railler qn. **2** *vt* huer. **3** *n* raillerie *f*; huée *f*. ◆ **jeering 1** *adj* railleur ; **2** *n* railleries *fpl*; huées *fpl*.

Jehovah [dʒɪ'həʊvə] *n* Jéhovah *m*.

jell [dʒel] *vi [jelly etc]* épaissir, prendre; (*) *[plan etc]* prendre tournure. ◆ **jello** ® *n (US)* gelée *f*. ◆ **jelly** *n* gelée *f*; *(US: jam)* confiture *f*; **~y baby** bonbon *m* à la gélatine en forme de bébé; **~y bean** dragée *f* à la gelée de sucre. ◆ **jellyfish** *n* méduse *f*.

jemmy ['dʒemɪ] *n* pince-monseigneur *f*.

jeopardy ['dʒepədɪ] *n* danger *m*, péril *m*. **in ~** *life* en danger; *happiness* menacé, en péril; *business* en mauvaise posture. ◆ **jeopardize** *vt* mettre en danger, compromettre.

jerk [dʒɜ:k] **1** *n (gen)* secousse *f*; *(mechanical)* à-coup *m*; *(Med)* crispation nerveuse; (⁑*pej: person*) pauvre type * *m*. **2** *vt (pull)* tirer brusquement; *(shake)* donner une secousse à. **he ~ed the book out of my hand** d'une secousse il m'a fait lâcher le livre. **3** *vi [person, muscle]* se crisper. ◆ **jerkily** *adv move* par à-coups; *speak* d'une voix saccadée. ◆ **jerky** *adj motion* saccadé; *(fig) style* heurté.

jerkin ['dʒɜ:kɪn] *n* blouson *m*; *(Hist)* justaucorps *m*.

jerry-building ['dʒerɪˌbɪldɪŋ] *n* construction *f* bon marché. ◆ **jerry-built** *adj* en carton-pâte *(fig)*.

jerry-can ['dʒerɪˌkæn] *n* jerrycan *m*.

Jersey ['dʒɜ:zɪ] *n* Jersey *f*. ◆ **jersey** *n (garment)* tricot *m*; *(material)* jersey *m*.

Jerusalem [dʒə'ru:sləm] *n* Jérusalem.

jest [dʒest] **1** *n* plaisanterie *f*. **in ~** pour rire. **2** *vi* plaisanter. ◆ **jester** *n* bouffon *m*.

Jesuit ['dʒezjʊɪt] *n* Jésuite *m*.

Jesus ['dʒi:zəs] *n* Jésus *m*. **~ Christ** Jésus-Christ.

jet[1] [dʒet] **1** *n [liquids, gas]* jet *m*; *(~ plane)* avion *m* à réaction, jet *m*; *(nozzle)* brûleur *m*; *(Aut)* gicleur *m*. **2** *adj (Aviat) travel* en jet; *engine, fighter* à réaction; *propulsion* par réaction. **~ fuel** kérosène *m*; **~ lag** (troubles *mpl* dûs au) décalage *m* horaire; **to have ~ lag** souffrir du décalage horaire; **the ~ set** * le jet set; **~ setter** membre *m* du jet set. ◆ **jet-foil** *n* hydroglisseur *m*. ◆ **jet-propelled** *adj* à réaction.

jet[2] [dʒet] *n* jais *m*. **~-black** noir comme jais.

jettison ['dʒetɪsn] *vt (gen) burden* se délester de; *(Naut)* jeter par-dessus bord; *(Aviat) bombs* larguer; *hopes* abandonner.

jetty ['dʒetɪ] *n (breakwater)* jetée *f*, digue *f*; *(landing pier)* embarcadère *m*.

Jew [dʒu:] *n* Juif *m*. **~'s harp** guimbarde *f*. ◆ **Jewess** *n* Juive *f*. ◆ **Jewish** *adj* juif. ◆ **Jewry** *n* les Juifs *mpl*.

jewel ['dʒu:əl] *n* bijou *m*, joyau *m*; *(in watch)* rubis *m*; *(fig)* bijou *m*. ◆ **jewel-case** *n* coffret *m* à bijoux. ◆ **jewelled,** *(US)* **jeweled** *adj* orné de bijoux. ◆ **jewel(l)er** *n* bijoutier *m*, joaillier *m*; **~ler's (shop)** bijouterie *f*, joaillerie *f*. ◆ **jewel(l)ery** *n* bijoux *mpl*, joyaux *mpl*; **a piece of ~lery** un bijou.

jib [dʒɪb] **1** *n (Naut)* foc *m*; *[crane]* flèche *f*. **2** *vi [person]* regimber (*at sth* devant qch), se refuser (*at doing* à faire); *[horse]* regimber.

jibe [dʒaɪb] = **gibe.**

jiffy * ['dʒɪfɪ] *n*: **wait a ~** attends une seconde; **in a ~** en moins de deux *; **J~bag** ® enveloppe *f* rembourrée.

jig [dʒɪg] *n (dance)* gigue *f*; *(Tech)* calibre *m*. ◆ **jigsaw (puzzle)** *n* puzzle *m*.

jilt [dʒɪlt] *vt* laisser tomber * *[un(e) fiancé(e)]*.

jingle ['dʒɪŋgl] **1** *n [keys etc]* tintement *m*. **advertising ~** couplet *m* publicitaire. **2** *vi* tinter. **3** *vt* faire tinter.

jingoism ['dʒɪŋgəʊɪzəm] *n* chauvinisme *m*.

jinx * [dʒɪŋks] *n* porte-poisse * *m inv*. **there's a ~ on...** on a jeté un sort à...

jitters * ['dʒɪtəz] *npl* frousse * *f*. **to have the ~** être agité. ◆ **jittery** * *adj* froussard *.

jiujitsu [dʒu:'dʒɪtsu:] *n* jiu-jitsu *m*.

jive [dʒaɪv] *n (music, dancing)* swing *m*.

job [dʒɒb] **1** *n* (**a**) *(piece of work)* travail *m*, boulot * *m*. **I have a little ~ for you** j'ai un petit travail pour vous; **he has made a good/bad ~ of it** il a fait du bon/du sale boulot *; **he's done a good ~ of work** il a fait du bon travail; **this new airliner is a lovely ~ *** ce nouvel avion c'est vraiment du beau travail *. (**b**) *(post, situation)* travail *m*, emploi *m*, boulot * *m*. **he found a ~ as a librarian** il a trouvé un poste de bibliothécaire; **to look for a ~** chercher du travail *or* un emploi; **to be out of a ~** être au chômage; **he has a very good ~** il a une belle situation; **on the ~** pendant le travail; **on-the-~ training** formation *f* sur le tas; **~s for the boys *** des planques *fpl* pour les petits copains *. (**c**) *(duty)* travail *m*, boulot * *m*. **he's only doing his ~** il ne fait que son boulot *; **he knows his ~** il connaît son affaire; **that's not his ~** ce n'est pas à lui de faire ça; **I had the ~ of telling them** c'est moi qui ai été obligé de le leur dire. (**d**) **it's a good ~ that...** c'est heureux que + *subj*; **a good ~ too!** à la bonne heure!; **it's a bad ~** c'est une sale affaire; **to give sth/sb up as a bad ~** renoncer à qch/qn en désespoir de cause; **this is just the ~ *** c'est exactement ce qu'il faut; **to have a ~ to do sth** *or* **doing sth** avoir du mal à faire qch; **it's been quite a ~ finding it** ça a été toute une affaire pour le trouver; **a put-up ~ *** un coup monté; **remember that bank ~? *** tu te rappelles le coup de la banque?
2 *adj* (**a**) *(US Ind)* **~ action** action *f* revendicative, (mouvement *m* de) grève *f*; *(Ind)* **~ analysis** analyse *f* des tâches; **~ centre** ≃ ANPE, agence *f* nationale pour l'emploi; **~ creation** création *f* d'emplois nouveaux; **~ description** description *f* de poste; **~ evaluation** qualification *f* du travail; **~ hunting** chasse *f* à l'emploi; **~ satisfaction** satisfaction *f* au travail; **~ security** garantie *f* de l'unité de l'emploi. (**b**) **~ lot** lot *m* d'articles divers.
◆ **jobber** *n (St Ex) intermédiaire qui traite directement avec l'agent de change*. ◆ **jobbing** *adj gardener* à la journée; *workman* à la tâche. ◆ **jobless 1** *adj* sans travail, au chômage ; **2** *npl*: **the ~less** les chômeurs *mpl*.

Job's comforter ['dʒəʊbz'kʌmfətəʳ] *n* piètre consolateur *m*, -trice *f*.

jockey ['dʒɒkɪ] **1** *n* jockey *m*. **2** *vi*: **to ~ about** se bousculer; **to ~ for position** manœuvrer pour se placer avantageusement. **3** *vt*: **to ~ sb into doing** manœuvrer qn pour qu'il fasse.

jockstrap ['dʒɒkstræp] *n* suspensoir *m*.

jocular ['dʒɒkjʊləʳ] *adj* jovial; *(joking)* badin.

jodhpurs ['dʒɒdpɜ:z] *npl* jodhpurs *mpl*.

jog [dʒɒg] **1** *n* (**a**) *(nudge)* légère poussée *f*; *(with elbow)* coup *m* de coude. (**b**) *(~-trot)* petit trot *m*. **2** *vt sb's elbow* pousser; *sb's memory* rafraîchir. *(fig)*

to ~ sb into action secouer qn. **3** *vi (Sport)* faire du jogging. ◆**jog along** *vi [vehicle]* aller son petit bonhomme de chemin; *(bumpily)* aller en brinquebalant; *(fig) [person]* aller cahin-caha *; *[piece of work]* aller tant bien que mal. ◆**jogger** *n* jogger *mf*. ◆**jogging** *n (Sport)* jogging *m*; **~ging shoes** chaussures *fpl* de jogging.

joggle ['dʒɒgl] *vt* secouer.

join [dʒɔɪn] **1** *vt* (**a**) *(~ together) (gen)* joindre, unir; *(link)* relier (*to* à); *broken halves* raccorder; *batteries* connecter. **to ~ battle** engager le combat (*with* avec); **to ~ hands** se donner la main; *(Mil, fig)* **to ~ forces** unir leurs forces; *(fig)* **to ~ forces (with sb) to do** s'unir (à qn) pour faire. (**b**) *club* devenir membre de; *political party* adhérer à; *university* entrer à; *procession* se joindre à; *army* s'engager dans; *one's regiment, ship* rejoindre; *religious order, business firm* entrer dans; *queue* prendre. (**c**) *person* rejoindre, retrouver. **Paul ~s me in wishing you...** Paul se joint à moi pour vous souhaiter...; **will you ~ us?** *(come with us)* voulez-vous venir avec nous?; *(be one of us)* voulez-vous être des nôtres?; *(in club, restaurant etc)* voulez-vous vous joindre à nous?; **will you ~ me in a drink?** vous prendrez un verre avec moi? (**d**) *[river, road]* rejoindre. **2** *vi (~ together; V* **1a***)* se joindre, s'unir (*with* à); *[lines]* se rencontrer; *[roads, rivers]* se rejoindre; *[club member]* devenir membre. **3** *n (in mended crockery etc)* ligne *f* de raccord; *(seam)* couture *f*. ◆**join in** **1** *vi* participer. *(in singing etc)* **~ in!** chantez *etc* avec nous! **2** *vt fus game, activity, conversation* prendre part à; *protest, shouts* joindre sa voix à; *thanks, wishes* s'associer à. ◆**join on** **1** *vi (in queue)* prendre son rang dans la queue; *[links, parts of structure]* se joindre (*to* à). **2** *vt sep* fixer; *(by tying)* attacher. ◆**join up** **1** *vi (Mil)* s'engager. **2** *vt sep (gen)* joindre; *wires etc* connecter.

◆**joiner** *n* menuisier *m*. ◆**joinery** *n* menuiserie *f*.

joint [dʒɔɪnt] **1** *n* (**a**) *(Anat)* articulation *f*. **out of ~** *shoulder* déboîté; *wrist* luxé; *(fig)* de travers; **to put out of ~** *one's shoulder* se déboîter; *one's wrist* se luxer. (**b**) *(Carpentry)* jointure *f*; articulation *f*. (**c**) *(Culin)* rôti *m*. **a cut off the ~** une tranche de rôti. (**d**) (*‡: place*) boîte * *f*. (**e**) *(Drugs sl: reefer)* joint *m (sl)*. **2** *adj decision, account* commun; *(Admin)* conjoint; *committee* mixte; *consultations* bilatéral; *effort* commun. **~ author** coauteur *m*; **~ ownership** copropriété *f*; **~ responsibility** coresponsabilité *f*. **3** *vt (Culin)* découper (aux jointures). ◆**jointed** *adj doll etc* articulé; *tent pole etc* démontable. ◆**jointly** *adv* en commun, conjointement. ◆**joint-stock company** *n* société *f* par actions.

joist [dʒɔɪst] *n* solive *f*.

joke [dʒəʊk] **1** *n* (**a**) plaisanterie *f*, blague * *f*. **for a ~** pour rire; **to make a ~ about** plaisanter sur; **he can't take a ~** il ne comprend pas la plaisanterie; **it's no ~** ce n'est pas drôle (*doing* de faire); **what a ~!** ce que c'est drôle!; **it's beyond a ~** * ça cesse d'être drôle; **the ~ is that...** le plus drôle c'est que...; **he is the ~ of the village** il est la risée du village. (**b**) *(practical ~)* tour *m*. **to play a ~ on sb** jouer un tour à qn. **2** *vi* plaisanter, blaguer *. **you're joking!** vous voulez rire!, sans blague! *; **I was only joking** ce n'était qu'une plaisanterie; **to ~ about sth** plaisanter sur qch; *(mock)* se moquer de qch.

◆**joker** *n* blagueur * *m*, -euse * *f*; (*‡: person*) type * *m*; *(Cards)* joker *m*. ◆**joking** **1** *adj tone* de plaisanterie; **2** *n* plaisanteries *fpl*, blagues * *fpl*. ◆**jokingly** *adv* en plaisantant; **it was jokingly called a luxury hotel** on l'avait baptisé, avec le plus grand sérieux, hôtel de luxe.

jolly ['dʒɒlɪ] **1** *adj (merry)* enjoué, jovial; (*: *pleasant)* agréable, amusant. **2** *adv* (*) drôlement *, rudement *. **you are ~ lucky** tu as une drôle de veine *; **you ~ well will go!** pas question que tu n'y ailles pas! ◆**jollification** * *n* réjouissances *fpl*. ◆**jollity** *n* joyeuse humeur *f*.

jolt [dʒəʊlt] **1** *vi [vehicle]* cahoter. **to ~ along** avancer en cahotant. **2** *vt (lit, fig)* secouer, cahoter. *(fig)* **to ~ sb into action** secouer qn, inciter qn à agir. **3** *n (jerk)* secousse *f*, à-coup *m*; *(fig)* choc *m*. **it gave me a ~** ça m'a fait un coup *.

Jordan ['dʒɔːdn] *n (country)* Jordanie *f*; *(river)* Jourdain *m*.

joss stick ['dʒɒsstɪk] *n* bâton *m* d'encens.

jostle ['dʒɒsl] **1** *vi* se bousculer. **he ~d against me** il m'a bousculé; **to ~ for sth** jouer des coudes pour obtenir qch. **2** *vt* bousculer.

jot [dʒɒt] **1** *n* brin *m*, iota *m*. **not a ~ of truth** pas un grain de vérité. **2** *vt* (**~ down**) *details* noter; *notes* prendre. ◆**jotter** *n (book)* cahier *m* (de brouillon); *(pad)* bloc-notes *m*. ◆**jottings** *npl* notes *fpl*.

journal ['dʒɜːnl] *n (periodical)* revue *f*; *(newspaper)* journal *m*; *(Naut)* livre *m* de bord; *(Comm)* livre de comptes; *(Jur)* compte rendu *m*; *(diary)* journal *m*. ◆**journalese** *n* jargon *m* journalistique. ◆**journalism** *n* journalisme *m*. ◆**journalist** *n* journaliste *mf*. ◆**journalistic** *adj* journalistique.

journey ['dʒɜːnɪ] **1** *n (travelling, trip)* voyage *m*; *(short, regular)* trajet *m*; *(distance covered)* trajet *m*. **a 2 days' ~** un voyage de 2 jours; **a 10 mile ~** un trajet de 10 miles; **to go on a ~** partir en voyage; **to reach one's ~'s end** arriver à destination; **the ~ from home to office** le trajet de la maison au bureau; **the return ~** le (voyage de) retour; **the ~ there and back** le voyage *or* trajet aller et retour; **a car ~** un voyage en voiture; **a long bus ~** un long trajet en autobus; **~ time** durée *f* du trajet. **2** *vi* voyager.

jovial ['dʒəʊvɪəl] *adj* jovial. ◆**joviality** *n* jovialité *f*.

joy [dʒɔɪ] *n* (**a**) joie *f*. **to my great ~** à ma grande joie; *(iro)* **I wish you ~ of it!** je vous souhaite du plaisir! (**b**) *(gen pl)* **~s** plaisirs *mpl*; **it's a ~ to hear him** c'est un vrai plaisir de l'entendre. ◆**joyful** *adj* joyeux. ◆**joyfully** *adv* joyeusement. ◆**joyous** *adj (liter)* joyeux. ◆**joyride** *n*: **to go for a ~ride** faire une virée * en voiture *(parfois volée)*. ◆**joystick** *n (Aviat, Comput)* manche *m* à balai.

jubilant ['dʒuːbɪlənt] *adj* débordant de joie. *[person]* **to be ~** jubiler. ◆**jubilation** *n* (**a**) *(emotion)* allégresse *f*, jubilation *f*; (**b**) *(celebration)* réjouissance(s) *f(pl)*.

jubilee ['dʒuːbɪliː] *n* jubilé *m*.

judge [dʒʌdʒ] **1** *n* juge *m*. **to be a good ~ of** *character* savoir juger; *wine* s'y connaître en. **2** *vt* juger. **to ~ it necessary to do** juger *or* estimer nécessaire de faire; **he ~d the moment well** il a bien su choisir son moment (*to do* pour faire). **3** *vi* juger. **to ~ for oneself** juger par soi-même; **as far as one can ~** autant qu'on puisse en juger; **judging by** *or* **from** à en juger par *or* d'après. ◆**judg(e)ment** *n* jugement *m*; **to pass ~ment** prononcer un jugement (*on* sur); *(fig)* **to give one's ~ment** donner son avis (*on* sur). ◆**judg(e)mental** *adj*: **he is very ~mental** il s'érige toujours en juge.

judicial [dʒuːˈdɪʃ(ə)l] *adj* (**a**) *(Jur) power, proceedings, inquiry* judiciaire; *murder* juridique. (**b**) *(critical) mind, faculty* critique.

judiciary [dʒuːˈdɪʃ(ɪə)rɪ] *n* magistrature *f*.

judicious [dʒuːˈdɪʃəs] *adj* judicieux. ◆**judiciously** *adv* judicieusement.

judo ['dʒuːdəʊ] *n* judo *m*.

jug [dʒʌg] *n* (**a**) *(gen)* pot *m*; *(for wine)* pichet *m*; *(for washing water)* broc *m*; *(heavy, jar-shaped)* cruche *f*. (**b**) *(prison)* **in ~ ‡** en taule ‡ *f*. ◆**jugged** *adj*: **~ged hare** civet *m* de lièvre.

juggernaut ['dʒʌgənɔːt] *n (Aut)* mastodonte *m*.

juggle ['dʒʌgl] **1** *vi* jongler (*with* avec). **2** *vt* jongler avec. ◆**juggler** *n* jongleur *m*, -euse *f*; *(conjurer)* prestidigitateur *m*, -trice *f*.

jugular ['dʒʌgjʊləʳ] *adj (Anat)* jugulaire.

juice [dʒu:s] *n [fruit, meat]* jus *m (also fig: petrol etc)*. *(Physiol)* ~**s** sucs *mpl*. ◆**juicer** *n (US)* presse-fruits *m inv* (électrique). ◆**juiciness** *n* juteux *m*. ◆**juicy** *adj fruit* juteux; *meat* moelleux; *story* savoureux.

jujitsu [dʒu:'dʒɪtsu:] *n* jiu-jitsu *m*.

jukebox ['dʒu:kbɒks] *n* juke-box *m*.

July [dʒu:'laɪ] *n* juillet *m*; *for phrases V* **September**.

jumble ['dʒʌmbl] **1** *vt* (~ **up**) *objects* mélanger; *facts, details* brouiller, embrouiller. ~**d (up)** pêle-mêle. **2** *n* (**a**) mélange *m*, fouillis *m*. (**b**) *(at ~ sale)* bric-à-brac *m*. **3** *adj*: ~ **sale** vente *f* de charité *(d'objets d'occasion)*.

jumbo ['dʒʌmbəʊ] **1** *n* (*) éléphant *m*. **2** *adj*: ~ **jet** jumbo-jet *m*.

jump [dʒʌmp] **1** *n* (**a**) saut *m*; *(of fear)* sursaut *m*. **to give a** ~ faire un saut, sauter; *(nervously)* sursauter; **at one** ~ d'un (seul) bond; **the** ~ **in prices** la hausse brutale des prix. (**b**) *(showjumping)* saut *m*; *(fence)* obstacle *m*.
2 *vi (leap)* sauter, bondir; *(nervously)* sursauter; *[prices]* faire un bond, monter en flèche. **to** ~ **up and down** sautiller; **to** ~ **in/out** *etc* entrer/sortir *etc* d'un bond; **to** ~ **off sth** sauter de qch; **to** ~ **on(to) a bus** sauter dans un autobus; **to** ~ **on(to) a bicycle** sauter sur un vélo; ~ **in!** *(into vehicle)* montez vite!; *(into swimming pool)* sautez!; *(onto truck, bus)* ~ **on!** montez vite!; **to** ~ **out of bed** sauter (à bas) du lit; **to** ~ **out of the window** sauter par la fenêtre; **to** ~ **out of a car** sauter d'une voiture; *(from car etc)* ~ **out!** sortez *or* descendez vite!; ~ **to it!** * et que ça saute! *; *(fig)* **to** ~ **at sth** sauter sur qch; *(fig)* **to** ~ **on sb** * prendre qn à partie; **to** ~ **at** *chance, offer* sauter sur; **to** ~ **to a conclusion** conclure hâtivement; **you mustn't** ~ **to conclusions** il ne faut pas tirer des conclusions trop hâtives; **to** ~ **down sb's throat** * rabrouer qn; **it almost made him** ~ **out of his skin** * ça l'a fait sauter au plafond *.
3 *vt ditch etc* sauter, franchir (d'un bond); *horse* faire sauter. *[train]* **to** ~ **the rails** dérailler; **to** ~ **the points** dérailler à l'aiguillage; *[pickup]* **to** ~ **a groove** sauter; *(Jur)* **to** ~ **bail** se soustraire à la justice (après paiement de caution); *(fig)* **to** ~ **the gun** * agir prématurément; *(Aut)* **to** ~ **the lights** passer au rouge; **to** ~ **the queue** resquiller; **to** ~ **ship** déserter le navire; **to** ~ **sb** ⁑ rouler qn *.
◆**jump about, jump around** *vi* sautiller. ◆**jump down** *vi* descendre (d'un bond). ◆**jump up** *vi* se lever d'un bond. *(to fallen child)* ~ **up now!** lève-toi!
◆**jumped-up** * *adj (pushing)* parvenu; *(conceited)* prétentieux. ◆**jumper** *n* pull(over) *m*; *(US Aut)* ~**er cables** câbles *mpl* de démarrage *(pour batterie)*. ◆**jumping rope** *n (US)* corde *f* à sauter. ◆**jump leads** *mpl (Aut)* câbles *mpl* de démarrage *(pour batterie)*. ◆**jumpy** * *adj person* nerveux.

junction ['dʒʌŋ(k)ʃ(ə)n] *n* (**a**) *(meeting place) [pipes]* raccordement *m*; *[roads]* bifurcation *f*; *[rivers]* confluent *m*; *[railway lines]* embranchement *m*. (**b**) *(crossroads)* carrefour *m*; *(station)* gare *f* de jonction.

juncture ['dʒʌŋ(k)tʃəʳ] *n (joining place)* point *m* de jonction; *(state of affairs)* conjoncture *f*. **at this** ~ à ce moment-là.

June [dʒu:n] *n* juin *m*; *for phrases V* **September**.

jungle ['dʒʌŋgl] **1** *n* jungle *f*. **2** *adj animal* de la jungle; *warfare* de jungle.

junior ['dʒu:nɪəʳ] **1** *adj (younger)* (plus) jeune, cadet; *(Sport)* ≃ cadet; *employee, officer, job* subalterne. **John Smith J**~ John Smith fils *or* junior; *(Brit)* ~ **school** école *f* primaire *(de 7 à 11 ans)*, cours moyen; *(Comm)* ~ **miss** fillette *f (de 11 à 14 ans)*; *(US)* ~ **high school** ≃ collège *m*; ~ **executive** jeune cadre *m*; *(Parl)* **J**~ **Minister** ≃ secrétaire *m* d'État; ~ **partner** associé(-adjoint) *m*. **2** *n* cadet(te) *m(f)*; *(Brit Scol)* petit(e) élève *m(f) (de 7 à 11 ans)*.

juniper ['dʒu:nɪpəʳ] *n* genévrier *m*. ~ **berries** du genièvre.

junk[1] [dʒʌŋk] **1** *n (rubbish)* bric-à-brac *m inv*; *(metal)* ferraille *f*; (*: *bad quality goods)* camelote * *f*; (⁑: *nonsense)* âneries *fpl*; *(Drugs sl)* came *f (sl)*.
2 *adj*: ~ **food** * aliments *mpl* sans valeur nutritive; ~ **heap** dépotoir *m*. ~ **mail** prospectus *mpl* adressés par la poste.
◆**junkie** *n (Drugs sl)* drogué(e) *m(f)*. ◆**junkshop** *n* boutique *f* de brocanteur.

junk[2] [dʒʌŋk] *n (boat)* jonque *f*.

junket ['dʒʌŋkɪt] *n* (**a**) *(Culin)* lait *m* caillé. (**b**) *(also* **junketing**) *(merrymaking)* bombance *f*; (*: *trip at public expense)* voyage *m* aux frais de la princesse *.

junta ['dʒʌntə] *n* junte *f*.

Jupiter ['dʒu:pɪtəʳ] *n (Myth)* Jupiter *m*; *(Astron)* Jupiter *f*.

jurisdiction [ˌdʒʊərɪs'dɪkʃ(ə)n] *n* juridiction *f*. **it comes within our** ~ c'est de notre compétence.

jury ['dʒʊərɪ] **1** *n (Jur)* jury *m*, jurés *mpl*; *[exhibition etc]* jury *m*. **to be on the** ~ faire partie du jury. **2** *adj*: ~ **box** banc *m* des jurés. ◆**juror** *n* juré *m*; **woman juror** femme *f* juré. ◆**juryman** *n* juré *m*.

just[1] [dʒʌst] *adv* (**a**) *(exactly)* juste, exactement. **it's** ~ **on 9** il est tout juste 9 heures; **it cost** ~ **on 50 francs** cela a coûté tout juste 50 F; ~ **what did he say?** qu'est-ce qu'il a dit exactement *or* au juste?; *(fig)* **come** ~ **as you are** venez comme vous êtes; ~ **as I thought, you...** c'est bien ce que je pensais, tu...; ~ **as you wish** comme vous voulez; ~ **at that moment** à ce moment-là; ~ **when everything is going so well!** juste quand tout va si bien!; **that's** ~ **it!, that's** ~ **the point!** justement!; **that's** ~ **Robert, always late** c'est bien Robert, toujours en retard; ~ **so!** exactement!; **everything was** ~ **so** * tout était bien en ordre.
(**b**) *(at this or that moment)* juste. **we're** ~ **off** nous partons; **(I'm)** ~ **coming!** j'arrive!; **we're** ~ **about to start** nous sommes sur le point de commencer; **to have** ~ **done** venir de faire; ~ **this minute,** ~ **this instant** à l'instant.
(**c**) *(almost not)* juste, de justesse. **we (only)** ~ **caught the train** c'est tout juste si nous avons eu le train; **we only** ~ **missed the train** nous avons manqué le train de très peu; **you're** ~ **in time** vous arrivez juste à temps; **I have only** ~ **enough money** j'ai tout juste assez d'argent; **he passed the exam but only** ~ il a été reçu à l'examen mais de justesse.
(**d**) *(with expressions of place)* juste. ~ **here** juste ici; ~ **over there/here** juste là/ici; ~ **by the church** juste à côté de l'église.
(**e**) *(almost)* ~ **about** à peu près, presque. **I've had** ~ **about enough!** * j'en ai par-dessus la tête! *
(**f**) *(in comparison)* ~ **as** tout aussi; **you sing** ~ **as well as I do** vous chantez tout aussi bien que moi.
(**g**) *(+ imper)* donc, un peu. ~ **taste this!** goûte un peu à ça! *; ~ **look at that!** regarde-moi ça! *; ~ **shut up!** * veux-tu te taire!; ~ **let me get my hands on him!** * que je l'attrape *(subj)* un peu! *
(**h**) *(slightly, immediately)* (un) peu, juste. ~ **over/under £10** un peu plus/moins de 10 livres; ~ **after 9 o'clock he came in** peu après 9 heures il est entré; **it's** ~ **after 9 o'clock** il est un peu plus de 9 heures; ~ **after he came** juste après son arrivée; ~ **before it rained** juste avant la pluie; **that's** ~ **over the kilo** cela fait tout juste un peu plus du kilo; **it's** ~ **to the left** c'est juste à gauche.

(**i**) *(only)* juste. ~ **a moment please** un instant s'il vous plaît; **he's ~ a lad** ce n'est qu'un gamin; **don't go yet, it's ~ 9 o'clock** ne partez pas encore, il n'est que 9 heures; **I've come ~ to see you** je suis venu exprès pour te voir; **he did it ~ for a laugh *** il l'a fait histoire de rire *; ~ **a line to let you know that...** juste un petit mot pour vous dire que...
(**j**) *(simply)* (tout) simplement, seulement. **I ~ told him to go away** je lui ai tout simplement dit de s'en aller; **you should ~ send it back** vous n'avez qu'à le renvoyer; **I would ~ like to say this** je voudrais seulement *or* simplement dire ceci; **I ~ can't imagine what's happened to him** je ne peux vraiment pas m'imaginer *or* je n'arrive pas à imaginer ce qui lui est arrivé; **we shall ~ drop in on him** nous ne ferons que passer chez lui; **it's ~ one of those things *** c'est la vie.
(**k**) *(emphatic)* absolument, tout simplement. **it's ~ fine!** c'est parfait!; **did you enjoy it? — did we ~! *** *or* **I should ~ say we did! *** cela vous a plu? — et comment! *
(**l**) *(phrases)* **it's ~ as well it's insured** heureusement que c'est assuré; **it would be ~ as well if he took it** il ferait aussi bien de le prendre; **I'm busy ~ now** je suis occupé pour l'instant; **I saw him ~ now** je l'ai vu tout à l'heure; **not ~ yet** pas tout de suite; **I'm taking my umbrella, ~ in case** je prends mon parapluie on ne sait jamais *or* à tout hasard; ~ **the same *, you...** tout de même, tu...; **I'd ~ as soon you kept quiet about it** j'aimerais autant que vous n'en disiez rien à personne.

just[2] [dʒʌst] *adj (fair: gen)* juste (*to, towards* envers, avec). **it is only ~ to point out that...** ce n'est que justice de faire remarquer que... ◆ **justice** *n* (**a**) *(Jur)* justice *f*; **to bring sb to ~ice** amener qn devant les tribunaux; *(US)* **Department of Justice** ministère *m* de la Justice; (**b**) *(fairness)* équité *f*; **in ~ice to him he..., to do him ~ice he...** pour être juste envers lui il...; **this photo doesn't do him ~ice** cette photo ne l'avantage pas; **she never does herself ~ice** elle ne se montre jamais à sa juste valeur; **to do ~ice to a meal** faire honneur à un repas; (**c**) *(judge)* juge *m*; *(US)* juge *m* de la Cour Suprême; *(Brit)* **Justice of the Peace** juge de paix. ◆ **justly** *adv* avec raison, tout à fait justement. ◆ **justness** *n [cause]* justice *f*; *[decision etc]* justesse *f*.

justify ['dʒʌstɪfaɪ] *vt* (**a**) *(gen)* justifier; *decision* prouver le bien-fondé de. **to be justified in doing** être en droit de faire; **am I justified in thinking...?** est-ce que j'ai raison de penser...? (**b**) *(Typ)* justifier. ◆ **justifiable** *adj* justifiable, légitime. ◆ **justifiably** *adv* légitimement, avec raison. ◆ **justification** *n* justification *f* (*of* de, *for* à, pour).

jut [dʒʌt] *vi* **(~ out)** *(gen)* faire saillie; *[hidden object]* dépasser; *[cliff]* avancer. **to ~ (out) over sth** surplomber qch.

jute [dʒu:t] *n* jute *m*.

juvenile ['dʒu:vənaɪl] *adj* juvénile; *(pej)* puéril; *books, court* pour enfants. ~ **delinquency** délinquance *f* juvénile; ~ **delinquent** jeune délinquant(e) *m(f)*.

juxtaposition [ˌdʒʌkstəpə'zɪʃ(ə)n] *n* juxtaposition *f*. **to be in ~** se juxtaposer.

K

K, k [keɪ] *n* K, k *m*.

kaftan [ˈkæftæn] *n* kaftan *m*.

kail, kale [keɪl] *n* chou *m* frisé.

kaleidoscope [kəˈlaɪdəskəʊp] *n* kaléidoscope *m*.

Kampala [kæmˈpɑːlə] *n* Kampala.

kangaroo [ˌkæŋgəˈruː] *n* kangourou *m*.

kaolin [ˈkeəlɪn] *n* kaolin *m*.

kapok [ˈkeɪpɒk] *n* kapok *m*.

kaput ⁑ [kəˈpʊt] *adj* fichu *, kaput ⁑ *inv*.

karate [kəˈrɑːtɪ] *n* karaté *m*; ~ **chop** coup *m* de karaté (donné avec le tranchant de la main).

kart [kɑːt] **1** *n* kart *m*. **2** *vi*: **to go ~ing** faire du karting.

kayak [ˈkaɪæk] *n* kayak *m*.

kazoo [kəˈzuː] *n* mirliton *m*.

kebab [kəˈbæb] *n* kébab *m*, brochette *f*.

kedgeree [ˌkedʒəˈriː] *n* ≃ pilaf *m* de poisson.

keel [kiːl] *n (Naut)* quille *f*. **on an even ~** *(Naut)* dans ses lignes, à égal tirant d'eau; *(fig)* stable, en équilibre. ◆ **keel over** *vi (Naut)* chavirer; *[person]* tomber dans les pommes *, s'évanouir.

keen [kiːn] *adj* (**a**) *blade, appetite* aiguisé; *point* aigu; *wind, cold* piquant; *air, interest* vif; *pleasure, desire, feeling* intense; *eye* perçant; *hearing, ear* fin; *price, competition* serré; *intelligence, judgment* pénétrant. (**b**) *(enthusiastic) person* enthousiaste, ardent. **to be as ~ as mustard** déborder d'enthousiasme; **a ~ footballer** un passionné du football; **a very ~ socialist** un socialiste passionné; **to be ~ on** *music* avoir la passion de; *idea, suggestion* être enthousiasmé par; *person* avoir un béguin pour; **to grow ~ on sth/sb** se passionner pour qch/qn; **I'm not too ~ on him** il ne me plaît pas beaucoup; **he's very ~ on Mozart/football** *etc* c'est un passionné de Mozart/du football *etc*; **he's not ~ on her coming** il ne tient pas tellement à ce qu'elle vienne; **to be ~ to do** tenir absolument à faire. ◆ **keenly** *adv* (**a**) *(enthusiastically)* avec enthousiasme; (**b**) *(acutely) interest, feel* vivement; *desire* ardemment; *observe* astucieusement; *look* d'un regard pénétrant. ◆ **keenness** *n* enthousiasme *m*.

keep [kiːp] *pret, ptp* **kept** **1** *vt* (**a**) *(gen)* garder. **you must ~ the receipt** il faut garder *or* conserver le reçu; **they ~ themselves to themselves** *[group]* ils font bande à part; *[couple]* ils se tiennent à l'écart; **to ~ sth clean** tenir *or* garder qch propre; **to ~ o.s. clean** être toujours propre; **exercise will ~ you fit** l'exercice physique vous maintiendra en forme; **the garden was well kept** le jardin était bien entretenu; **he kept them working** *or* **at it** il les a forcés à continuer de travailler; **to ~ sb waiting** faire attendre qn; **she kept him to his promise** elle l'a forcé à tenir sa promesse; **to ~ a piece of news from sb** cacher une nouvelle à qn; **~ it to yourself, ~ it under your hat** * garde-le pour toi. (**b**) *(put aside)* garder, mettre de côté. **I've kept some for him** je lui en ai gardé; **I'm ~ing some sugar just in case** j'ai du sucre en réserve à tout hasard; **~ it somewhere safe** mettez-le en lieu sûr; **you must ~ it in a cold place** il faut le garder *or* le conserver au froid. (**c**) *(detain)* garder, retenir. **to ~ sb in prison** garder qn en prison; **what kept you?** qu'est-ce qui vous a retenu? (**d**) *(own, have)* *shop, hotel, servants* avoir; *(Comm: stock)* vendre, avoir. *(Agr) animals* élever. (**e**) *accounts, diary* tenir. **to ~ a note of** noter. (**f**) *(support) family* faire vivre. **I earn enough to ~ myself** je gagne assez pour vivre; **to ~ sb in food/clothing** nourrir/habiller qn. (**g**) *(restrain)* **to ~ sb from doing** empêcher qn de faire; **~ him from school** ne l'envoyez pas à l'école. (**h**) *(fulfil) promise* tenir; *law, rule, Lent* observer; *treaty* respecter; *vow* rester fidèle à; *obligations* remplir; *feast day* célébrer; *sb's birthday* fêter. **to ~ an appointment** se rendre à un rendez-vous.

2 *vi* (**a**) *(continue)* continuer, suivre; *(remain)* rester, se tenir. **~ on this road until...** suivez cette route jusqu'à...; **to ~ (to the) left/right** garder sa gauche/droite; *(Aut)* tenir sa gauche/droite; **to ~ straight on** continuer tout droit; **to ~ to** *promise* tenir; *subject* ne pas s'écarter de; *text* serrer; **to ~ doing** continuer à faire, ne pas cesser de faire; **she ~s talking** elle n'arrête pas de parler; **I ~ hoping that...** j'espère toujours que...; **~ going!** allez-y!; **~ smiling!** gardez le sourire!; **to ~ fit** se maintenir en forme; **he ~s in good health** il est toujours en bonne santé; **to ~ still** rester *or* se tenir tranquille; **~ at it!** continuez!; **she ~s at him all the time** elle le harcèle, elle est toujours après lui; **'~ off the grass'** 'défense de marcher sur les pelouses'; **to ~ from doing** s'abstenir *or* se retenir de faire; **to ~ in with sb** * rester en bons termes avec qn; *(for one's own purposes)* cultiver qn; **to ~ to one's room/bed** garder la chambre/le lit; **they ~ to themselves** *[group]* ils font bande à part; *[couple]* ils se tiennent à l'écart. (**b**) *(in health)* aller. **how are you ~ing?** comment allez-vous?; **she's not ~ing very well** elle ne va pas très bien; **he's ~ing better** il va mieux. (**c**) *[food etc]* se garder, se conserver. **apples that ~ all winter** des pommes qui se gardent *or* se conservent tout l'hiver; **this business can ~** * cette affaire peut attendre.

3 *n* (**a**) *(food etc)* **to earn one's ~** gagner de quoi vivre; **I got £15 a week and my ~** j'ai gagné 15 livres par semaine logé et nourri; **he's not worth his ~** il ne vaut pas ce qu'on dépense pour l'entretenir. (**b**) *(Archit)* donjon *m*. (**c**) **for ~s** * pour de bon.

◆ **keep away** **1** *vi (lit)* ne pas s'approcher (*from* de). *(fig)* **to ~ away from drink** s'abstenir de boire, ne pas boire. **2** *vt sep person* empêcher de s'approcher (*from* de). ◆ **keep back** **1** *vi* rester en arrière, ne pas approcher. **2** *vt sep* (**a**) *(withhold) part of wages etc* retenir. (**b**) *(conceal) facts, names* ne pas dire, ne pas révéler; *secrets* taire. (**c**) *(make late)* retarder. (**d**) *crowd* empêcher de s'approcher. ◆ **keep down** **1** *vi* rester assis (*or* allongé *etc*). **2** *vt sep* (**a**) *(control) revolt, one's anger* réprimer, contenir; *dog* retenir, maîtriser. **you can't ~ a good man down** un homme de valeur reprendra toujours le dessus. (**b**) *spending* restreindre, limiter; *prices* empêcher de monter. (**c**) *(Scol) pupil* faire redoubler une classe à. (**d**) **the sick man can't ~ anything down** le malade ne garde rien. ◆ **keep in** *vt sep* (**a**) *anger, feelings* contenir, réprimer. (**b**) *person* empêcher de sortir; *(Scol) pupil* garder en retenue; *stomach, elbows* rentrer. ◆ **keep off** **1** *vi [person]* rester à l'écart. **~ off!** n'approchez pas!;

if the rain ~s off s'il ne pleut pas. **2** *vt sep dog, person* empêcher de s'approcher. ~ **your hands off!** ne touchez pas! ◆ **keep on 1** *vi* continuer (*to do* à faire), ne pas arrêter (*to do* de faire). **don't ~ on so!** arrête!; **she does ~ on about...** elle n'arrête pas de parler de...; ~ **on past the church till...** continuez après l'église jusqu'à...; **if you ~ on as you're doing now** si tu continues comme ça; **to ~ on at sb** harceler qn. **2** *vt sep* garder. ◆ **keep out 1** *vi* rester en dehors. **'~ out'** 'défense d'entrer'; **to ~ out of danger** rester à l'abri du danger; **to ~ out of a quarrel** ne pas se mêler à une dispute; ~ **out of this!** mêlez-vous de ce qui vous regarde! **2** *vt sep person, dog* empêcher d'entrer. **to ~ out the cold** protéger du froid. ◆ **keep together 1** *vi [people]* rester ensemble. **2** *vt sep* garder ensemble. ◆ **keep up 1** *vi* (**a**) *(continue)* continuer; *[prices]* se maintenir. (**b**) **to ~ up with sb** *(in race, walk etc)* aller aussi vite que qn; *(in work, achievement)* se maintenir au niveau de qn; *(in comprehension)* suivre qn; *(fig)* **to ~ up with the Joneses** ne pas se trouver en reste avec les voisins. (**c**) *(stay friends with)* **to ~ up with sb** rester en relations avec qn. **2** *vt sep* (**a**) *(gen)* continuer, ne pas abandonner; *correspondence* entretenir; *subscription, custom* maintenir; *one's French etc* entretenir. ~ **it up!** continuez! (**b**) *(maintain) house, paintwork, road* entretenir.
◆ **keeper** *n (gen)* gardien(ne) *m(f)*; *(in museum etc)* conservateur *m*, -trice *f*; *(game ~)* garde-chasse *m*. ◆ **keep-fit** *adj*: **~-fit classes** cours *mpl* de culture physique; **~-fit (exercises)** culture *f* physique. ◆ **keeping** *n* (**a**) *(care)* garde *f*; **to put in sb's ~ing** confier à qn; (**b**) **to be in ~ing with** s'accorder avec; **in ~ing with** en accord avec. ◆ **keepsake** *n* souvenir *m (objet)*.

keg [keg] *n* tonnelet *m*; *[fish]* caque *f*. ~ **beer** bière *f* en tonnelet.

kelp [kelp] *n* varech *m*.

ken [ken] *n*: **that is beyond my ~** je ne m'y connais pas.

kennel ['kenl] *n [dog]* niche *f*; *[hound]* chenil *m*. **to put a dog in ~s** mettre un chien dans un chenil.

Kenya ['kenjə] *n* Kénya *m*. ◆ **Kenyan 1** *adj* kényen ; **2** *n* Kényen(ne) *m(f)*.

kept [kept] *pret, ptp of* **keep**.

kerb [kɜːb] *n (Brit)* bord *m* du trottoir. **along the ~** le long du trottoir; ~ **crawler** dragueur * *m* motorisé.

kernel ['kɜːnl] *n* amande *f (de noyau)*.

kerosene ['kerəsiːn] **1** *n (aircraft fuel)* kérosène *m*; *(US: for lamps)* pétrole *m* (lampant). **2** *adj* à pétrole.

kestrel ['kestr(ə)l] *n* crécerelle *f*.

ketchup ['ketʃəp] *n* ketchup *m*.

kettle ['ketl] *n* bouilloire *f*. **the ~'s boiling** l'eau bout; **I'll just put the ~ on** je vais mettre l'eau à chauffer.

key [kiː] **1** *n* (**a**) *(gen)* clef *f or* clé *f*; *[clockwork toy etc]* remontoir *m*; *[textbook] (answers)* solutions *fpl*; *(translation)* traduction *f*; *[map]* légende *f*; *[mystery etc]* clef (*to* de). **to turn the ~** donner un tour de clef. (**b**) *[piano, typewriter etc]* touche *f*; *[wind instrument]* clef *f*. (**c**) *(Mus)* ton *m*. **to be in/off ~** être/n'être pas dans le ton; **to sing in/off ~** chanter juste/faux; **in the ~ of C** en do. **2** *adj* (**a**) *(vital)* clef *or* clé *(f inv)*. ~ **industry** industrie *f* clef; ~ **jobs** postes *mpl* clefs; ~ **man** pivot *m (fig)*. (**b**) *(Mus)* ~ **signature** armature *f*. **3** *vt (also ~* **in***)* entrer.
◆ **keyboard** *n* clavier *m*; *(in pop group)* **~boards** clavier *m*. ◆ **keyhole** *n*: **through the ~hole** par le trou de la serrure. ◆ **keynote 1** *n (Mus)* tonique *f*; *[speech etc]* note *f* dominante ; **2** *adj (Pol etc)* **~note speech** discours-programme *m*. ◆ **key ring** *n* porte-clefs *m inv*. ◆ **keystone** *n* clef *f* de voûte. ◆ **keyword** *n* mot-clé *m*.

khaki ['kɑːkɪ] *adj* kaki *inv*.

kibbutz, *pl* **kibbutzim** [kɪ'bʊts, kɪ'bʊtsɪm] *n* kibboutz *m*.

kibosh ⁑ ['kaɪbɒʃ] *n*: **to put the ~ on** ⁑ mettre le holà à.

kick [kɪk] **1** *n* (**a**) coup *m* de pied. **to give sth a ~** donner un coup de pied à *or* dans qch; **to take a ~ at** lancer un coup de pied à; **to give sb a ~ in the pants** * botter * le derrière à *or* de qn; *(fig)* **it was a ~ in the teeth** ⁑ **for her** cela a été pour elle une gifle en pleine figure; *(fig)* **he gets a ~ out of it** * il trouve ça stimulant; *(pej)* il y prend un malin plaisir; **he did it for ~s** * il l'a fait pour le plaisir. (**b**) *[gun]* recul *m*; *[starting handle]* retour *m*. **2** *vi* donner *or* lancer un coup de pied; *[baby]* gigoter *; *[horse etc]* ruer; *[gun]* reculer. **to ~ at** lancer un coup de pied à; *(fig: object to)* se rebiffer * contre; *(fig)* **to ~ over the traces** ruer dans les brancards. **3** *vt [person]* donner un coup de pied à *or* dans; *[horse etc]* lancer une ruade à. **to ~ sb downstairs** faire descendre qn à coups de pied dans le derrière; **to ~ sth away** repousser qch du pied; **to ~ a goal** marquer un but; *(fig)* **to ~ the bucket** ⁑ casser sa pipe *, mourir; **I could have ~ed myself** * je me serais flanqué * des coups; *(fig)* **to ~ one's heels** poireauter *; **to ~ the habit** *(gen)* arrêter.
◆ **kick about, kick around 1** *vi* (⁑) *[objects, person]* traîner. **2** *vt sep*: **to ~ a ball about** s'amuser avec un ballon. ◆ **kick back 1** *vi [engine]* avoir un retour de manivelle. **2** *vt sep ball etc* renvoyer (du pied). ◆ **kick down** *vt sep* démolir à coups de pied. ◆ **kick in** *vt sep door* enfoncer à coups de pied. *(fig)* **to ~ sb's teeth in** * casser la figure * à qn. ◆ **kick off** *vi (Ftbl)* donner le coup d'envoi; (*) *[meeting etc]* démarrer *. ◆ **kick out 1** *vi [horse]* ruer; *[person]* envoyer de grands coups de pied (*at* à). **2** *vt sep (*fig)* mettre à la porte. ◆ **kick up** *vt sep (fig)* **to ~ up a row** * *or* **a din** * faire du tapage; **to ~ up a fuss** * faire toute une histoire.
◆ **kick-off** *n (Ftbl etc, also fig)* coup *m* d'envoi.
◆ **kick-stand** *n* béquille *f (de moto)*. ◆ **kick-start(er)** *n* démarreur *m* au pied.

kid [kɪd] **1** *n (goat, leather)* chevreau *m*; *(*: child)* gosse * *mf*; *(*: teenager)* (petit(e)) jeune *m(f)*. **2** *adj* (**a**) (*) *brother etc* petit. (**b**) *gloves etc* de chevreau. *(fig)* **to handle with ~ gloves** *person* prendre des gants avec *; *subject* traiter avec précaution. **3** *vt* (*) **to ~ sb (on)** faire marcher qn *; **no ~ding!** sans blague! *; **don't ~ yourself!** ne te fais pas d'illusions!; **he was ~ding on that he was hurt** il essayait de faire croire qu'il était blessé. **4** *vi (*: ~* **on***)* raconter des blagues *. **I was only ~ding (on)** j'ai dit ça pour rigoler *. ◆ **kiddy** * *n* gosse * *mf*, mioche * *mf*.

kidnap ['kɪdnæp] *vt* kidnapper, enlever. ◆ **kidnapper** *n* kidnappeur *m*, -euse *f*, ravisseur *m*, -euse *f*. ◆ **kidnapping** *n* enlèvement *m*, rapt *m*.

kidney ['kɪdnɪ] **1** *n (Anat)* rein *m*; *(Culin)* rognon *m*. *(fig)* **of the same ~** du même acabit. **2** *adj disease etc* rénal; *transplant* du rein. **to be on a ~ machine** être sous rein artificiel; ~ **stone** calcul *m* du rein.
◆ **kidney-bean** *n* haricot *m* rouge. ◆ **kidney-shaped** *adj* en forme de haricot.

kill [kɪl] **1** *n (at bullfight, hunt)* mise *f* à mort. *(fig)* **to be in at the ~** assister au coup de grâce. **2** *vt* (**a**) *(gen)* tuer; *(murder)* assassiner; *[huntsman, slaughterer]* abattre. **to be ~ed in action** tomber au champ d'honneur; *(fig)* **to ~ two birds with one stone** faire d'une pierre deux coups; **it was ~ or cure** c'était un remède de cheval; *(iro)* **don't ~ yourself!** * surtout ne te surmène pas!; **this heat is ~ing me** * cette chaleur me tue; **my feet are ~ing me** * j'ai affreusement mal aux pieds; **she**

was ~ing herself (laughing) * elle était pliée en deux de rire. (**b**) *(fig) proposal, attempt* faire échouer; *paragraph etc* supprimer; *story* interdire la publication de; *rumour* mettre fin à; *feeling, hope* détruire; *flavour, smell* tuer; *sound* amortir; *engine, motor* arrêter; (*) *bottle* liquider *. **to ~ time** tuer le temps.

◆ **kill off** *vt sep* exterminer; *(fig)* éliminer.

◆ **killer** **1** *n* tueur *m*, -euse *f*; *(murderer)* assassin *m*, meurtrier *m*, -ière *f*; *(lit)* **that's a ~er** cela tue; **2** *adj disease* qui tue; *instinct* qui pousse à tuer; *(fig)* **he's got the ~er instinct** il en veut *, c'est un gagneur. **~er whale** épaulard *m*. ◆ **killing** **1** *n [person]* meurtre *m*; *[people, group]* tuerie *f*, massacre *m*; *(during disturbances etc)* **there were 3 ~ings** 3 personnes ont été tuées; *(Fin)* **to make a ~ing** réussir un beau coup (de filet); **2** *adj blow, disease* meurtrier; *(*: exhausting) work* tuant; *(*: funny)* tordant *. ◆ **killjoy** *n* rabat-joie *m inv*.

kiln [kɪln] *n* four *m (de potier)*.

Kilner ® **jar** [ˈkɪlnəˌdʒɑːʳ] *n* bocal *m* à conserves.

kilo [ˈkiːləʊ] *n* kilo *m*. ◆ **kilobyte** *n (Comput)* kilooctet *m*. ◆ **kilogram(me)** *n* kilogramme *m*. ◆ **kilometre,** *(US)* **kilometer** [ˈkɪləˌmiːtəʳ, kɪˈlɒmɪtəʳ] *n* kilomètre *m*. ◆ **kilowatt** *n* kilowatt *m*.

kilt [kɪlt] *n* kilt *m*. ◆ **kilted** *adj* en kilt.

kilter * [ˈkɪltəʳ] *n*: **out of ~** détraqué.

kin [kɪn] *n* parents *mpl*, famille *f*. **his next of ~** son parent le plus proche. ◆ **kinship** *n* parenté *f*. ◆ **kinsman** *n* parent *m*. ◆ **kinswoman** *n* parente *f*.

kind [kaɪnd] **1** *n* (**a**) *(type: gen)* genre *m*, espèce *f*, sorte *f*; *(make: of car, coffee etc)* marque *f*. **what ~ do you want?** vous en (*or* le *or* la *etc*) voulez de quelle sorte?; **what ~ of car is it?** quelle marque de voiture est-ce?; **what ~ of dog is he?** qu'est-ce que c'est comme (race de) chien?; **what ~ of man is he?** quel genre d'homme est-ce?; **he is not the ~ of man to refuse** ce n'est pas le genre d'homme à refuser; **he's not that ~ of person** ce n'est pas son genre; **he's the ~ that will cheat** il est du genre à tricher; **I know his ~!** je connais les gens de son espèce; **that's the ~ of person I am** c'est comme ça que je suis; **what ~ of people does he think we are?** pour qui nous prend-il?; **what ~ of an answer do you call that?** vous appelez ça une réponse?; **and all that ~ of thing** et autres choses du même genre, et tout ça *; **you know the ~ of thing I mean** vous voyez ce que je veux dire; **it's my ~ of film** c'est le genre de film que j'aime; **sth of the ~** qch de ce genre (-là); **nothing of the ~!** absolument pas!; *(pej)* **it was beef of a ~** c'était qch qui pouvait passer pour du bœuf; **a ~ of** une sorte *or* espèce de, un genre de; **I was ~ of * frightened that** j'avais comme peur * que + ne + *subj*; **I ~ of * thought that he would come** j'avais un peu l'idée qu'il viendrait; **he was ~ of * worried-looking** il avait l'air un peu inquiet. (**b**) *(race, species)* genre *m*, espèce *f*. **they're two of a ~** ils se ressemblent; **it's the only one of its ~** c'est unique en son genre. (**c**) **to pay/payment in ~** payer/paiement *m* en nature; *(fig)* **I shall repay you in ~** *(after good deed)* je vous le rendrai; *(after bad deed)* je vous rendrai la monnaie de votre pièce.

2 *adj person* gentil (*to sb* avec qn), bon (*to sb* envers qn), aimable. **would you be ~ enough to open the door?** voulez-vous être assez aimable *or* gentil pour ouvrir la porte?; **he was ~ enough to say** il a eu la gentillesse *or* l'amabilité de dire; **it was very ~ of you to help me** vous avez été bien aimable de m'aider; **that's very ~ of you** c'est très aimable *or* gentil de votre part; **that wasn't a very ~ thing to say** ce n'était pas très gentil de dire cela.

◆ **kind-hearted** *adj* bon, qui a bon cœur. ◆ **kind-heartedness** *n* bonté *f*, bon cœur. ◆ **kindliness** *n* bienveillance *f*, bonté *f*. ◆ **kindly** **1** *adv* (**a**) *speak, act* avec bonté, avec gentillesse; (**b**) **will you ~ly shut the door** voulez-vous avoir la bonté de fermer la porte; (**c**) **I don't take ~ly to his doing that** je n'aime pas du tout qu'il fasse cela; **she didn't take it ~ly when...** elle ne l'a pas bien pris quand... ; **2** *adj person, advice* bienveillant; *voice* plein de bonté; *letter* gentil; *treatment* plein de gentillesse. ◆ **kindness** *n* bonté *f* (*towards* pour), gentillesse *f* (*towards* envers); *(kind act)* gentillesse *f*, service *m*; **out of the ~ness of his heart** par bonté d'âme; **to do sb a ~ness** rendre service à qn; **it would be a ~ness to tell him so** ce serait lui rendre service que de le lui dire.

kindergarten [ˈkɪndəˌgɑːtn] *n* jardin *m* d'enfants.

kindle [ˈkɪndl] *vt fire* allumer; *wood, emotion* enflammer. ◆ **kindling** *n* petit bois *m*.

kindred [ˈkɪndrɪd] **1** *n* parents *mpl*, famille *f*. **2** *adj languages, tribes* apparenté. **~ spirits** âmes *fpl* sœurs; **to have a ~ feeling for sb** sympathiser avec qn.

king [kɪŋ] *n* roi *m (also Cards, Chess)*; *(Draughts)* dame *f*. **K~ David** le roi David; **an oil ~** un roi *or* un magnat du pétrole. ◆ **kingdom** *n* royaume *m*; *(Bot, Zool)* règne *m*; **the K~dom of Heaven** le royaume des cieux; **till ~dom come** * jusqu'à la fin des siècles. ◆ **kingfisher** *n* martin-pêcheur *m*. ◆ **kingly** *adj* royal, de roi. ◆ **kingpin** *n (lit)* cheville *f* ouvrière; *(fig)* caïd * *m*. ◆ **king-size(d)** *adj (Comm) cigarette* long; *packet* géant; *(gen) object, headache* de première grandeur.

kink [kɪŋk] **1** *n (in rope etc)* entortillement *m*; *(fig)* aberration *f*. **2** *vi* s'entortiller. ◆ **kinky** * *adj hair* crépu; *person* bizarre; *(unpleasantly so)* malade *(fig pej)*; *(sexually)* qui a des goûts spéciaux; *idea, dress, fashion* bizarre.

kiosk [ˈkiːɒsk] *n (gen)* kiosque *m*; *(Brit: telephone ~)* cabine *f* téléphonique.

kipper [ˈkɪpəʳ] *n* hareng *m* fumé et salé, kipper *m*.

Kirbigrip ®, **kirbygrip** [ˈkɜːbɪˌgrɪp] *n* pince *m* à cheveux.

kirk [kɜːk] *n (Scot)* église *f*.

kiss [kɪs] **1** *n* baiser *m*. *(Med)* **~ of life** bouche à bouche *m*; *(fig)* **~ of death** coup *m* fatal; *(in letter)* **love and ~es** bons baisers *mpl*. **2** *vt* embrasser, donner un baiser à. **to ~ sb's cheek** embrasser qn sur la joue; **to ~ sb's hand** baiser la main de qn; **to ~ sb good night** embrasser qn en lui souhaitant bonne nuit. **3** *vi* s'embrasser.

kit [kɪt] *n* (**a**) *(equipment: gen)* matériel *m*, équipement *m*; *(Mil)* fourniment *m*; *(tools)* outils *mpl*; *(luggage)* bagages *mpl*; *(belongings)* affaires *fpl*. **fishing ~** matériel *or* équipement de pêche; **got your football ~?** tu as tes affaires de football? (**b**) *(set of items)* trousse *f*. **repair/tool ~** trousse de réparations/à outils; **first-aid ~** trousse de premiers secours. (**c**) *(parts for assembly)* kit *m*. **sold in ~ form** vendu en kit; **model aeroplane ~** maquette *f* d'avion à assembler. ◆ **kit out, kit up** *vt sep* équiper (*with* de). ◆ **kitbag** *n* sac *m (de sportif, de marin etc)*.

kitchen [ˈkɪtʃɪn] **1** *n* cuisine *f (pièce)*. **2** *adj table, salt etc* de cuisine. **~ cabinet** buffet *m* de cuisine; **~ foil** papier *m* d'aluminium; **~ garden** potager *m*; **~ paper, ~ roll** essuie-tout *m inv;* **~ sink** évier *m*; **everything but the ~ sink** * tout sauf les murs; **~-sink * drama** théâtre *m* naturaliste; **~ soap** savon *m* de Marseille; **~ unit** élément *m* de cuisine. ◆ **kitchenette** *n* kitchenette *f*. ◆ **kitchenmaid** *n* fille *f* de cuisine. ◆ **kitchenware** *n (dishes)* vaisselle *f (de cuisine)*; *(equipment)* ustensiles *mpl* de cuisine.

kite [kaɪt] *n (bird)* milan *m*; *(toy)* cerf-volant *m*.

kith [kɪθ] *n*: ~ **and kin** amis *mpl* et parents *mpl*.

kitsch [kɪtʃ] *adj, n* kitsch *(m) inv*.

kitten ['kɪtn] *n* chaton *m*, petit chat *m*. *(fig)* **to have ~s** ⁑ piquer une crise *.

kitty ['kɪtɪ] *n* (**a**) *(Cards, also fig)* cagnotte *f*. (**b**) *(*: cat)* minet * *m*.

kiwi ['kiːwiː] *n (bird)* kiwi *m*; *(also ~* **fruit***)* kiwi *m*.

kleptomania [ˌkleptə(ʊ)'meɪnɪə] *n* kleptomanie *f*. ◆ **kleptomaniac** *adj, n* kleptomane *(mf)*.

knack [næk] *n* tour *m* de main. **to learn the ~ of doing** attraper le tour de main pour faire; **to have the ~ of doing** avoir le chic pour faire.

knapsack ['næpsæk] *n* sac *m* à dos, havresac *m*.

knave [neɪv] *n* filou *m*; *(Cards)* valet *m*.

knead [niːd] *vt bread dough* pétrir; *muscles* masser.

knee [niː] *n* genou *m*. **on one's ~s** à genoux; **to go (down) on one's ~s** s'agenouiller, se mettre à genoux (*to sb* devant qn). ◆ **kneecap** *n* rotule *f*. ◆ **knee-deep** *adj*: **the water was ~-deep** l'eau arrivait aux genoux. ◆ **knee-high** *adj* à hauteur de genou. ◆ **kneepad** *n* genouillère *f*. ◆ **knee pants** *npl (US)* bermuda(s) *m(pl)*.

kneel [niːl] *pret, ptp* **knelt** *vi (~* **down***)* s'agenouiller, se mettre à genoux.

knell [nel] *n* glas *m*. **to toll the ~** sonner le glas.

knew [njuː] *pret of* **know.**

knickers ['nɪkəz] *npl* slip *m (de femme)*.

knick-knack ['nɪknæk] *n* bibelot *m*.

knife [naɪf] **1** *n, pl* **knives** *(gen)* couteau *m*; *(pocket~)* canif *m*. **~, fork and spoon** couvert *m*; *(fig)* **he's got his ~ into me** * il a une dent contre moi; *(fig)* **it's war to the ~ between them** ils sont à couteaux tirés. **2** *vt person* donner un coup de couteau à; *(kill)* tuer à coups de couteau. **3** *adj box* à couteaux. *(fig)* **on a ~ edge** *person* sur des charbons ardents; *result* qui ne tient qu'à un fil. ◆ **knife-grinder** *n* rémouleur *m*. ◆ **knifesharpener** *n* aiguisoir *m*.

knight [naɪt] **1** *n* chevalier *m*; *(Chess)* cavalier *m*. **2** *vt (Brit)* **he was ~ed for services to industry** il a été fait chevalier pour services rendus dans l'industrie. ◆ **knighthood** *n*: **to receive a ~hood** recevoir le titre de chevalier.

knit [nɪt] *pret, ptp* **knitted** *or* **knit** **1** *vt* tricoter; *(fig: ~* **together***)* lier. **to ~ one's brows** froncer les sourcils. **2** *vi* tricoter; *[bone etc]* se souder. ◆ **knitted** *adj* en tricot. ◆ **knitting** **1** *n* tricot *m* ; **2** *adj needle, wool, machine* à tricoter. ◆ **knitwear** *n* tricots *mpl*.

knob [nɒb] *n (gen)* bouton *m (de porte, de radio etc)*; *[cane etc]* pommeau *m*. **~ of butter** noix *f* de beurre. ◆ **knobb(l)y** *adj* noueux.

knock [nɒk] **1** *n (blow)* coup *m*; *(in engine etc)* cognement *m*. **there was a ~ at the door** on a frappé (à la porte); **I heard a ~** j'ai entendu frapper; **knock, knock!** toc, toc, toc!; **I'll give you a ~ at 7 o'clock** je viendrai taper à la porte à 7 heures; **he got a ~ on the head** il a reçu un coup sur la tête; *(criticism)* **~s** * critiques *fpl*; *(fig)* **to take a ~** en prendre un coup.

2 *vt* (**a**) *(hit, strike)* frapper. **to ~ a nail into a plank** planter *or* enfoncer un clou dans une planche; **he ~ed the ball into the hedge** il a envoyé la balle dans la haie; **to ~ holes in sth** faire des trous dans qch; **to ~ the bottom out of** *box* défoncer; *argument* démolir; **to ~ sb on the head** frapper qn sur la tête; *(stun)* assommer qn; **to ~ sb to the ground** jeter qn à terre; **to ~ sb unconscious** assommer qn; **she ~ed the knife out of his hand** elle lui a fait tomber le couteau des mains; **to ~ a glass off a table** faire tomber un verre d'une table ; **to ~ spots off sb** * battre qn à plates coutures; *(astonish)* **to ~ sb sideways** * ébahir qn; **to ~ some sense into sb** ramener qn à la raison. (**b**) *(collide with)* heurter. **to ~ one's head on** *or* **against** se cogner la tête contre; **he ~ed his foot against a stone** il a donné du pied contre une pierre. (**c**) *(⁑: denigrate)* dire du mal de; *(in advertising)* faire de la contre-publicité à.

3 *vi* (**a**) *(strike)* frapper, cogner (*at* à). **he ~ed on the table** il a frappé la table, il a cogné sur la table; **his knees were ~ing** il tremblait de peur. (**b**) *(bump)* **to ~ into** se cogner *or* se heurter contre, heurter; *(*: meet)* tomber sur; **to ~ about the world** vagabonder de par le monde. (**c**) *[car engine etc]* cogner.

◆ **knock about, knock around 1** *vi (travel)* vagabonder; *[sailor]* bourlinguer. **2** *vt sep (ill-treat)* maltraiter, malmener. ◆ **knock back** *vt sep* (**a**) *(*: drink)* s'envoyer *, avaler. (**b**) *(⁑: cost)* **it ~ed me back £20** ça a fait un trou de 20 livres dans mes finances. (**c**) *(*fig: shock)* sonner *, ahurir. ◆ **knock down** *vt sep* (**a**) *object* renverser; *building etc* démolir; *tree* abattre; *door* enfoncer; *person* jeter à terre; *(Aut) pedestrian* renverser; *gatepost* faire tomber. **you could have ~ed me down with a feather!** les bras m'en sont tombés! (**b**) *price* baisser, abaisser. (**c**) *lot at auction* adjuger (*to sb* à qn). ◆ **knock in** *vt sep nail* enfoncer. ◆ **knock off** **1** *vi (*: stop work)* s'arrêter (de travailler); *[striker]* débrayer *. **2** *vt sep* (**a**) *vase from shelf etc* faire tomber. *(fig)* **to ~ off £10** baisser le prix de 10 livres. (**b**) *(*: do quickly) piece of work* expédier; *(⁑: steal)* piquer ⁑, voler; *(⁑: stop)* arrêter *(doing* de faire*)*. ◆ **knock out** *vt sep* (**a**) *nail etc* faire sortir (*of* de); *one's pipe* débourrer. (**b**) *(stun)* assommer; *(Boxing)* mettre knock-out; *(*: shock)* sonner *. (**c**) *(from competition etc)* éliminer (*of* de). ◆ **knock over** *vt sep (gen)* renverser; *(Aut) pedestrian* renverser; *gatepost* faire tomber. ◆ **knock together** **1** *vi [glasses, knees]* s'entrechoquer. **2** *vt sep* (**a**) *two objects* cogner l'un contre l'autre. (**b**) *(make hurriedly)* bricoler à la hâte. ◆ **knock up** *vt sep* (**a**) *lever* faire lever d'un coup; *sb's arm* faire voler en l'air. (**b**) *(Brit: waken)* réveiller (en frappant à la porte). (**c**) *(make hurriedly) meal* préparer en vitesse; *shed* construire à la va-vite; *furniture, toy* fabriquer en un rien de temps. (**d**) *(Brit *: exhaust) person* éreinter. (**e**) *(Brit *: make ill)* rendre malade. (**f**) *(⁑: make pregnant)* faire un gosse à *.

◆ **knockdown** *adj* (**a**) *price* imbattable; (**b**) *table, shed* démontable. ◆ **knocker** *n (door-~)* marteau *m* (de porte). ◆ **knocking** *n* coups *mpl*; *(in engine)* cognement *m*; **I can hear ~ing** j'entends frapper; *(Aut)* il y a qch qui cogne. ◆ **knocking-off time** * *n* heure *f* de la sortie. ◆ **knock-kneed** *adj*. ◆ **knock-knees** *npl*: **to be ~-kneed, to have ~-knees** avoir les genoux cagneux. ◆ **knock-on** *n*: **~-on effect** réaction *f* en chaîne. ◆ **knockout** **1** *n* (**a**) *(Boxing etc)* knock-out *m*; *(fig: success)* **to be a ~out** * être sensationnel *; (**b**) *(Sport)* compétition *f* (avec épreuves éliminatoires) ; **2** *adj*: **~out drops** * soporifique *m*. ◆ **knock-up** *n (Tennis)* **to have a ~-up** faire des balles.

knoll [nəʊl] *n* tertre *m*.

knot [nɒt] **1** *n* (**a**) nœud *m*. **to tie a ~** faire un nœud. (**b**) *(Naut)* nœud *m*. **to make 20 ~s** filer 20 nœuds. **2** *vt rope* faire un nœud à, nouer. **to ~ together** nouer. ◆ **knotty** *adj wood, hand* noueux; *problem* épineux.

know [nəʊ] *pret* **knew,** *ptp* **known** **1** *vt* (**a**) *facts, a language, dates, results* savoir (*that* que; *why* pourquoi). **to ~ a lot about** en savoir long sur; **I don't ~ much about** je ne sais pas grand-chose sur; **to get to ~ sth** apprendre qch; **to ~ how to do sth** savoir faire qch; **he ~s all the answers** il s'y connaît; *(pej)* c'est un je-sais-tout *; **to ~ the difference between** connaître la différence entre; **to ~ one's mind** savoir ce qu'on veut; **he ~s what he's talking about** il sait de quoi il parle, il connaît son sujet; **you ~ what I mean...** tu vois ce que je veux dire...; **that's worth ~ing** c'est bon à

savoir; **for all I ~** (autant) que je sache; **not that I ~ (of)** pas que je sache; **there's no ~ing what he'll do** impossible de savoir ce qu'il va faire; **what do you ~!** * eh bien!, ça alors!; **not if I ~ it!** * c'est ce qu'on va voir!; **she ~s all about sewing** elle s'y connaît *or* elle est très forte en couture; **that's all you ~!** * c'est ce que tu crois!; **I ~ nothing about it** je n'en sais rien, je ne suis pas au courant; **it soon became ~n that...** on a bientôt appris que...; **it is well ~n that...** tout le monde sait que...; **to make sth ~n to sb** faire savoir qch à qn; **he is ~n to have been there** on sait qu'il y a été; **I've ~n such things to happen** j'ai déjà vu cela se produire.
(**b**) *(be acquainted with) person, place, book, subject, plan, route* connaître. **to ~ sb by sight/by name** connaître qn de vue/de nom; **I don't ~ her to speak to** je ne la connais pas assez pour lui parler; **to get to ~ sb** *(V* **get 2b**); **to make o.s. ~n to sb** se présenter à qn; **he is ~n as...** on le connaît sous le nom de...
(**c**) *(recognize)* reconnaître (*sb by his voice* qn à sa voix). **I knew him at once** je l'ai reconnu tout de suite; **he ~s a good horse when he sees one** il sait reconnaître un bon cheval; **I wouldn't ~ it from a screwdriver** je ne sais pas le reconnaître d'un tournevis; **he doesn't ~ one end of a hammer from the other** c'est à peine s'il sait ce que c'est qu'un marteau; **you wouldn't ~ him from his brother** on le prendrait pour son frère.
2 *vi* savoir. **as far as I ~** à ma connaissance; **how should I ~?** comment voulez-vous que je le sache?; **there's no ~ing** on ne peut pas savoir; **Mummy ~s best!** maman a toujours raison!; **you ~ best** tu sais ce que tu dis; **to ~ about** *or* **of sth** savoir qch, connaître qch, avoir entendu parler de qch; **she ~s about cats** elle s'y connaît en (matière de) chats; **do you ~ about Paul?** tu es au courant pour Paul? *; **there were 5 'don't ~s'** il y avait 5 'sans opinion'; **to ~ better than to do** ne pas avoir la stupidité de faire; **you ought to have ~n better** tu aurais dû réfléchir; **they don't ~ any better** ils ne savent pas ce qu'ils font; **he says he didn't do it but I ~ better** il dit que ce n'est pas lui mais je ne suis pas assez stupide pour le croire; **to ~ of** connaître, avoir entendu parler de.
3 *n*: **to be in the ~** * être au courant.
◆ **knowable** *adj* connaissable. ◆ **know-all** * *n* je-sais-tout *mf*. ◆ **know-how** * *n* technique *f*, compétence *f*. ◆ **knowing** *adj (shrewd)* fin, malin; *(wise)* sage; *look, smile* entendu. ◆ **knowingly** *adv (consciously)* sciemment; *(in ~ing way) look, smile* d'un air entendu. ◆ **known** *adj thief etc* connu; *expert* reconnu; *fact* établi.

knowledge ['nɒlɪdʒ] *n* (**a**) *(understanding, awareness)* connaissance *f*. **to have no ~ of** ne pas savoir, ignorer; **to (the best of) my ~** à ma connaissance; **without his ~** à son insu; **to bring sth to sb's ~** signaler qch à qn; **it has come to my ~ that...** j'ai appris que...; **it's common** *or* **public ~ that...** chacun sait que... (**b**) *(learning, facts learnt)* connaissances *fpl*, savoir *m*. **my ~ of English** mes connaissances d'anglais; **he has a working ~ of Japanese** il possède les éléments *mpl* de base du japonais; **he has a thorough ~ of geography** il possède la géographie à fond. ◆ **knowledgeable** *adj person* bien informé; *report* bien documenté.

knuckle ['nʌkl] *n* articulation *f* du doigt. ◆ **knuckle under** * *vi* céder. ◆ **knuckleduster** *n* coup-de-poing *m* américain.

koala [kəʊ'ɑːlə] *n* (**~ bear**) koala *m*.

Korea [kə'rɪə] *n* Corée *f*. **North/South ~** Corée du Nord/Sud. ◆ **Korean 1** *adj* coréen; **2** *n* Coréen(ne) *m(f)*.

Koran [kɒ'rɑːn] *n* Coran *m*.

kosher ['kəʊʃə] *adj* kascher *inv*.

kowtow ['kaʊ'taʊ] *vi* se prosterner (*to sb* devant qn).

Kuala Lumpur ['kwɑːlə'lʊmpʊə] *n* Kuala Lumpur.

kudos * ['kjuːdɒs] *n* gloire *f*, lauriers *mpl*.

kumquat ['kʌmkwɒt] *n* kumquat *m*.

Kurdistan [ˌkɜːdɪ'stɑːn] *n* le Kurdistan.

Kuwait [kʊ'weɪt] *n* Koweït, Kuweit.

L

L, l [el] *n* L, l *m or f*. *(Aut)* **L-plate** plaque *f* d'apprenti conducteur.

lab * [læb] *n (abbr of* **laboratory**) labo * *m*.

label ['leɪbl] **1** *n* étiquette *f*. **record on the Deltaphone** ~ disque sorti chez Deltaphone. **2** *vt* coller une *or* des étiquette(s) sur; *(Comm) goods for sale* étiqueter; *(fig) person* étiqueter (*as* comme). **the bottle was not ~led** il n'y avait pas d'étiquette sur la bouteille; **it was ~led poison** il y avait marqué poison.

laboratory [lə'bɒrət(ə)rɪ] **1** *n* laboratoire *m*. **2** *adj assistant, equipment* de laboratoire.

labour, *(US)* **labor** ['leɪbəʳ] **1** *n* (**a**) *(hard work; task)* travail *m*. ~ **of love** travail fait par plaisir. (**b**) *(Ind: workers)* main-d'œuvre *f*, ouvriers *mpl*. **Ministry** *or (US)* **Department of L~** ministère *m* du Travail. (**c**) *(Pol)* **L~** les travaillistes *mpl*; **he votes L~** il vote travailliste. (**d**) *(Med)* travail *m*. **in** ~ en travail.
2 *adj (Ind) dispute, trouble* ouvrier; *relations* ouvriers-patronat *inv*; *(Brit Pol)* **L~** *leader, party* travailliste. ~ **camp** camp *m* de travaux forcés; **L~ Day** fête *f* du Travail; **L~ Exchange** ≃ Agence *f* nationale pour l'emploi; *(Ind)* ~ **force** *(numbers)* effectifs *mpl* en ouvriers; *(personnel)* main-d'œuvre *f*; *(US)* ~ **laws** législation *f* du travail; *(Med)* ~ **pains** douleurs *fpl* de l'accouchement; *(US)* ~ **union** syndicat *m*.
3 *vi (with effort)* travailler dur (*at* à; *to do* pour faire); *(with difficulty)* peiner (*at* sur; *to do* pour faire); *[engine, motor]* peiner; *[ship]* fatiguer. **to ~ under a delusion** être victime d'une illusion; **to ~ up a hill** *[person]* monter péniblement une côte; *[car]* peiner dans une montée.
4 *vt*: **I won't ~ the point** je n'insisterai pas lourdement sur ce point.
◆ **laborious** *adj* laborieux. ◆ **laboriously** *adv* laborieusement. ◆ **labo(u)red** *adj style* laborieux ; *breathing* pénible. ◆ **labo(u)rer** *n (gen)* ouvrier *m* ; *(on roads, building sites)* manœuvre *m*. ◆ **labo(u)r-intensive** *adj* qui nécessite l'emploi de beaucoup de main-d'œuvre. ◆ **labo(u)rite** *n (Pol)* travailliste *mf*. ◆ **labo(u)r-saving** *adj* qui allège le travail ; *(in household)* **~-saving device** appareil *m* ménager.

laburnum [lə'bɜːnəm] *n* cytise *m*.

labyrinth ['læbɪrɪnθ] *n* labyrinthe *m*.

lace [leɪs] **1** *n* (**a**) *(Tex)* dentelle *f*. (**b**) *[shoe etc]* lacet *m*. **2** *adj collar, curtains* de *or* en dentelle. **3** *vt* (**a**) (**~ up**) *shoe* lacer. (**b**) *drink* arroser (*with* de), corser. ◆ **lacemaker** *n* dentellière *f*. ◆ **lacemaking** *n* fabrication *f* de la dentelle. ◆ **lace-up shoes** *npl* chaussures *fpl* à lacets. ◆ **lacy** *adj* qui ressemble à la dentelle; **the frost made a lacy pattern** il y avait une dentelle de givre.

lacerate ['læsəreɪt] *vt* lacérer; *(fig)* fendre le cœur de. ◆ **laceration** *n (Med)* déchirure *f*.

lack [læk] **1** *n* manque *m*. **for ~ of** faute de. **2** *vt* manquer de. **3** *vi*: **to be ~ing** manquer, faire défaut; **to be ~ing in, to ~ for** manquer de.
◆ **lackadaisical** *adj* nonchalant. ◆ **lacking** * *adj (stupid)* simplet, débile *. ◆ **lacklustre,** *(US)* **lackluster** *adj* terne.

lackey ['lækɪ] *n* laquais *m*.

laconic [lə'kɒnɪk] *adj* laconique. ◆ **laconically** *adv* laconiquement.

lacquer ['lækəʳ] **1** *n (substance)* laque *f*; *(object)* laque *m*. **2** *vt wood* laquer; *hair* mettre de la laque sur.

lad [læd] *n* garçon *m*, gars * *m*. **he's only a ~** ce n'est qu'un gamin *; **to have a drink with the ~s** * boire un pot avec les copains *; **come on ~s!** allez les gars! *; **he's a bit of a ~** * il est un peu noceur *.

ladder ['lædəʳ] **1** *n* échelle *f*. *(lit, fig)* **at the top of the** ~ au sommet de l'échelle; **to have a ~ in one's stocking** avoir un bas filé. **2** *vti* filer. ◆ **ladder-proof** *adj* indémaillable.

laden ['leɪdn] *adj* chargé (*with* de). **fully ~** *truck, ship* en pleine charge.

la-di-da * ['lɑːdɪ'dɑː] *adj person* bêcheur *; *voice* maniéré.

ladle ['leɪdl] **1** *n* louche *f*. **2** *vt* (**~ out**) servir (à la louche); *(* fig) money, advice* prodiguer à foison.

lady ['leɪdɪ] **1** *n* dame *f*. **the ~ of the house** la maîtresse de maison; **Ladies and Gentlemen!** Mesdames, (Mesdemoiselles,) Messieurs!; **good morning, ladies and gentlemen** bonjour mesdames, bonjour mesdemoiselles, bonjour messieurs; **young ~** *(married)* jeune femme *f*; *(unmarried)* jeune fille *f*; **this is the ~/the young ~ who...** voilà la dame/la demoiselle qui...; **ladies' hairdresser** coiffeur *m*, -euse *f* pour dames; **~'s umbrella** parapluie *m* de dame; **he's a ladies' man** il plaît aux femmes; *(Rel)* **Our L~** Notre-Dame *f*; **Ladies** *(public lavatory)* Dames; **where is the Ladies?** * où sont les toilettes?; **L~ Smith** lady Smith; **~'s maid** femme *f* de chambre *(d'une dame)*; *(vegetable)* **~'s finger** okra *m*. **2** *adj*: **L~ Day** la fête de l'Annonciation; **~ doctor** femme *f* médecin; **~ friend** * petite amie; **L~ Mayoress** femme *f* (*or* fille *f etc*) du Lord Mayor. ◆ **ladybird** *or* ◆ **ladybug** *n* coccinelle *f*. ◆ **ladyfinger** *n (US Culin)* boudoir *m (biscuit)*. ◆ **lady-in-waiting** *n* dame *f* d'honneur. ◆ **ladykiller** *n* don Juan *m*. ◆ **ladylike** *adj person* bien élevé, distingué; *manners* distingué. ◆ **ladylove** *n* bien-aimée *f*. ◆ **ladyship** *n*: **Her/Your L~ship** Madame *f* (la comtesse *etc*).

lag¹ [læg] **1** *n*: **(time)** ~ retard *m*; *(between two events)* décalage *m*. **2** *vi*: **to ~ behind sb** traîner derrière qn; *(in achievements)* avoir du retard sur qn (*in sth* dans qch).

lag² [læg] *vt pipes* calorifuger. ◆ **lagging** *n (material)* calorifuge *m*.

lag³ [læg] *n*: **old ~** * récidiviste *mf*.

lager ['lɑːgəʳ] *n* lager *f*, ≃ bière *f* blonde.

lagoon [lə'guːn] *n* lagune *f*; *(coral)* lagon *m*.

Lagos ['leɪgɒs] *n* Lagos.

lah [lɑː] *n (Mus)* la *m*.

laid [leɪd] *pret, ptp of* **lay¹**. ◆ **laid-back** *adj* relax(e) *, décontracté.

lain [leɪn] *ptp of* **lie¹**.

lair [lɛəʳ] *n* repaire *m*.

laity ['leɪɪtɪ] *collective n*: **the ~** les laïcs *mpl*.

lake [leɪk] *n* lac *m*. **the L~ District** la région des lacs.

lama ['lɑːmə] *n* lama *m (Rel)*.

lamb [læm] **1** *n (Culin, Zool)* agneau *m*. **poor ~!** * le (*or* la) pauvre!; **he took it like a** ~ il n'a pas protesté. **2** *adj*: ~ **chop** côtelette *f* d'agneau. ◆ **lambing** *n* agnelage *m*. ◆ **lambswool** *n* laine *f* d'agneau.

lame [leɪm] **1** *adj animal, person, argument* boiteux; *excuse* faible, piètre. **to be** ~ boiter (*in one leg* d'une jambe); ~ **duck** canard *m* boiteux. **2** *vt* estropier. ◆ **lamely** *adv say etc* maladroitement. ◆ **lameness** *n (Med)* claudication *f*.

lament [lə'ment] **1** *n* lamentation *f*. **2** *vt* se lamenter sur. **(late) ~ed** regretté *(before n)*. **3** *vi* se lamenter (*for, over* sur). ◆ **lamentable** *adj* lamentable, déplorable. ◆ **lamentably** *adv* lamentablement. ◆ **lamentation** *n* lamentation *f*.

laminated ['læmɪneɪtɪd] *adj metal* laminé; *windscreen* en verre feuilleté; *book-jacket* plastifié.

lamp [læmp] **1** *n (light)* lampe *f*; *(Aut)* feu *m*; *(bulb)* ampoule *f*. **2** *adj*: ~ **standard** lampadaire *m (dans la rue)*. ◆ **lamplight** *n*: **by ~light** à la lumière de la lampe. ◆ **lamppost** *n* réverbère *m*. ◆ **lampshade** *n* abat-jour *m inv*. ◆ **lampstand** *n* pied *m* de lampe.

lance [lɑ:ns] **1** *n (weapon)* lance *f*; *(Med)* lancette *f*. **2** *vt (Med)* ouvrir. ◆ **lancet** *n (Med)* lancette *f*.

land [lænd] **1** *n* (**a**) *(gen)* terre *f*. **dry** ~ terre ferme; **on** ~ à terre; **to go by** ~ voyager par voie de terre; **over** ~ **and sea** sur terre et sur mer; **we sighted** ~ nous sommes arrivés en vue d'une terre; *(fig)* **to see how the** ~ **lies** tâter le terrain; **to live off the** ~ vivre de la terre; **to work on the** ~ travailler la terre; **he bought** ~ **in Devon** il a acheté une terre dans le Devon; **my** ~ mes terres; *(smaller)* mon terrain. (**b**) *(country, nation)* pays *m*. **throughout the** ~ dans tout le pays; ~ **of milk and honey** pays de cocagne; **to be in the** ~ **of the living** être encore de ce monde. **2** *adj breeze* de terre; *defences, forces* terrestre; *law, policy, reform* agraire; *prices* des terrains; *tax* foncier. ~ **yacht** char *m* à voile. **3** *vt cargo* décharger; *passengers* débarquer; *aircraft* poser; *fish* prendre; *blow* infliger (*on sb* à qn); *(*: obtain) job, contract* décrocher *. **to** ~ **sb in trouble** * attirer des ennuis à qn; **to** ~ **sb in debt** * mettre qn dans les dettes; **to be ~ed with sth** * *(left with)* avoir qch sur les bras; *(forced to take on)* devoir se coltiner qch *. **4** *vi* (**a**) *[aircraft etc]* atterrir, se poser; *(on sea)* amerrir; *(on ship's deck)* apponter; *[air traveller]* atterrir; *(from boat)* débarquer. (**b**) *(after fall, jump etc) [person, object, bomb]* tomber; *[gymnast]* retomber. *(lit, fig)* **to** ~ **on one's feet** retomber sur ses pieds. ◆ **land up** * *vi* finir par se retrouver. ◆ **landed** *adj* foncier; **~ed gentry** aristocratie terrienne. ◆ **landfall** *n*: **to make ~fall** accoster. ◆ **landing 1** *n* (**a**) *[aircraft etc]* atterrissage *m*; *(on sea)* amerrissage *m*; *(from ship; also Mil)* débarquement *m*; (**b**) *(between stairs)* palier *m*; *(floor)* étage *m* ; **2** *adj*: **~ing card** carte *f* de débarquement; *(Aviat)* **~ing gear** train *m* d'atterrissage; *(Fishing)* **~ing net** épuisette *f*; *(Naut)* **~ing party** détachement *m* de débarquement; **~ing stage** débarcadère *m*; *(Aviat)* **~ing strip** piste *f* d'atterrissage. ◆ **landlady** *n [flat etc]* logeuse *f*; *[boarding house etc]* patronne *f*. ◆ **landlocked** *adj* sans accès à la mer. ◆ **landlord** *n [flat etc]* propriétaire *m*, logeur *m*; *[pub, boarding house]* patron *m*. ◆ **landlubber** * *n* terrien(ne) *m(f)*. ◆ **landmark** *n* point *m* de repère; *(fig)* **to be a ~mark in** faire date dans. ◆ **landmine** *n (Mil)* mine *f* terrestre. ◆ **landowner** *n* propriétaire foncier. ◆ **landscape 1** *n* paysage *m* ; **2** *vt garden* dessiner; *dirty place etc* aménager ; **3** *adj gardener, gardening* paysagiste; **~scape painter** paysagiste *m*. ◆ **landscaping** *n* aménagements *mpl* paysagers. ◆ **landslide 1** *n (lit: also* **~slip**) glissement *m* de terrain; *(loose rocks)* éboulement *m*. *(Pol)* raz-de-marée *m* électoral ; **2** *adj (Pol etc) victory* écrasant. ◆ **land-worker** *n* ouvrier *m*, -ière *f* agricole.

lane [leɪn] *n* (**a**) *(in country)* chemin *m*; *(in town)* ruelle *f*. (**b**) *(Aut) (part of road)* voie *f*; *(line of traffic)* file *f*. **'keep in ~ '** 'ne changez pas de file'; **'get into ~ '** 'mettez-vous sur la bonne file'; **3-~ road** route *f* à 3 voies; **I'm in the wrong** ~ je suis dans la mauvaise file; ~ **closure** fermeture *f* de voie(s) de circulation. (**c**) *(for aircraft, ships, runners, swimmers)* couloir *m*. **air/shipping** ~ couloir aérien/de navigation.

language ['læŋgwɪdʒ] **1** *n (gen)* langue *f*; *(means of communication; way of expressing things)* langage *m*. **the French** ~ la langue française; **modern ~s** langues vivantes; **he studies ~s** il fait des langues; **the origin of** ~ l'origine du langage; **speaking is one aspect of** ~ la parole est l'un des aspects du langage; **scientific/legal** ~ langage scientifique/juridique; *(fig)* **they do not speak the same** ~ ils ne parlent pas le même langage; **express it in your own** ~ exprimez cela en votre propre langage; **the** ~ **of official documents** le langage des documents officiels; **bad** ~ gros mots *mpl*; **watch your ~!** surveille ton langage! **2** *adj studies* de langue(s). ~ **laboratory** laboratoire *m* de langues.

languid ['læŋgwɪd] *adj* languissant. ◆ **languidly** *adv* languissamment.

languish ['læŋgwɪʃ] *vi* se languir (*for, over* après); *(in prison)* se morfondre. ◆ **languishing** *adj* languissant.

languor ['læŋgəʳ] *n* langueur *f*. ◆ **languorous** *adj* langoureux.

lank [læŋk] *adj hair* raide et terne.

lanky ['læŋkɪ] *adj* grand et maigre.

lanolin ['lænə(ʊ)lɪn] *n* lanoline *f*.

lantern ['læntən] **1** *n* lanterne *f*. **2** *adj*: ~ **slide** plaque *f* de lanterne magique. ◆ **lantern-jawed** *adj* aux joues creuses.

Laos [laʊs] *n* Laos *m*.

lap¹ [læp] *n* genoux *mpl*. *(fig)* **in the** ~ **of the gods** entre les mains des dieux; **in the** ~ **of luxury** dans le plus grand luxe. ◆ **lapdog** *n* petit chien *m* d'appartement. ◆ **laptop** *n (Comput)* portable *m*.

lap² [læp] *n (Sport)* tour *m* de piste. **to run a** ~ faire un tour de piste; **on the 10th** ~ au 10ᵉ tour; ~ **of honour** tour d'honneur; *(fig)* **we're on the last** ~ on a fait le plus gros.

lap³ [læp] **1** *vt milk* laper. **2** *vi [waves]* clapoter. ◆ **lap up** *vt sep milk etc* laper; *(* fig) compliments* boire comme du petit-lait *.

La Paz [læ'pæz] *n* La Paz.

lapel [lə'pel] *n* revers *m (de veston etc)*. ~ **microphone** micro-cravate *m*.

Lapland ['læplænd] *n* Laponie *f*.

lapse [læps] **1** *n* (**a**) *(fault)* faute *f* légère, défaillance *f*; *(in behaviour, from diet)* écart *m*. ~ **of memory** trou *m* de mémoire; **a** ~ **into bad habits** un retour à de mauvaises habitudes. (**b**) *(passage of time)* intervalle *m*. **a** ~ **of time** un laps de temps. **2** *vi* (**a**) *(err)* faire une *or* des erreur(s) passagère(s). (**b**) *(fall gradually)* tomber, retomber (*into* dans). **to** ~ **into silence** se taire; **to** ~ **into unconsciousness** (re)perdre connaissance. (**c**) *[act, law]* devenir caduc (*f* -uque); *[contract]* expirer; *[ticket, passport, insurance policy]* se périmer; *[subscription]* prendre fin. ◆ **lapsed** *adj contract, law* caduc; *ticket, passport* périmé; *Catholic etc* qui n'est plus pratiquant.

lapwing ['læpwɪŋ] *n* vanneau *m*.

larceny ['lɑ:sənɪ] *n (Jur)* vol *m* simple.

larch [lɑ:tʃ] *n* mélèze *m*.

lard [lɑ:d] *n* saindoux *m*.

larder ['lɑ:dəʳ] *n* garde-manger *m inv*.

large [lɑ:dʒ] **1** *adj (gen)* grand; *garden, room* grand, vaste; *person, animal, slice, hand, sum, loss* gros (*f* grosse); *amount* grand, important; *family, population* nombreux; *meal* copieux. **a ~ number of them** beaucoup d'entre eux; **to grow ~(r)** grandir, s'agrandir, grossir; **to make ~r** agrandir. **2** *n*: **at ~** *(at liberty)* en liberté; *(as a whole)* en général, dans son ensemble; *(at random)* au hasard; *(US Pol) congressman* non rattaché à une circonscription électorale. **3** *adv*: **by and ~** généralement. ◆ **large-hearted** *adj* au grand cœur. ◆ **largely** *adv (to a great extent)* en grande mesure *or* partie; *(principally)* pour la plupart, surtout; *(in general)* en général. ◆ **largeness** *n* grandeur *f*; grosseur *f*; importance *f*. ◆ **large-scale** *adj drawing, map* à grande échelle; *business activities, reforms, relations* sur une grande échelle; *powers* étendu. ◆ **large-size(d)** *adj* grand.

lark¹ [lɑːk] *n* alouette *f*. ◆ **larkspur** *n* pied *m* d'alouette.

lark² * [lɑːk] *n (joke etc)* blague * *f*. **for a ~** pour rigoler *; **what a ~!** quelle rigolade! * ◆ **lark about *, lark around** * *vi* faire le petit fou (*f* la petite folle) *.

larva, *pl* **-ae** ['lɑːvə, iː] *n* larve *f (Zool)*.

larynx ['lærɪŋks] *n* larynx *m*. ◆ **laryngitis** *n* laryngite *f*.

lasagne [lə'zænjə] *n* lasagnes *fpl*.

lascivious [lə'sɪvɪəs] *adj* lascif. ◆ **lasciviously** *adv* lascivement.

laser ['leɪzəʳ] *n* laser *m*. **~ beam** rayon *m* laser *inv*; **~ printer** imprimante *f* à laser.

lash [læʃ] **1** *n* (**a**) *(thong)* lanière *f*; *(blow)* coup *m* de fouet. (**b**) *(eye~)* cil *m*. **2** *vt* (**a**) *(whip)* fouetter violemment; *(flog)* flageller. *(fig)* **to ~ o.s. into a fury** s'emporter violemment; **the rain was ~ing (against) the windows** la pluie cinglait les carreaux; **to ~ its tail** fouetter l'air de sa queue. (**b**) *(fasten)* attacher (*to* à); **(~ down)** *cargo* arrimer. **3** *vi*: **to ~ against** cingler.
◆ **lash down 1** *vi [rain]* tomber avec violence. **2** *vt sep cargo* arrimer. ◆ **lash out 1** *vi* (**a**) **to ~ out at sb** envoyer de violents coups de poing à qn; *(verbally)* se répandre en invectives contre qn. (**b**) *(*: spend)* les lâcher *, beaucoup dépenser. **2** *vt sep* (*) *money* lâcher *.
◆ **lashings** *npl*: **~ings of** * énormément de *.

lass [læs] *n (esp Scot)* jeune fille *f*.

lassitude ['læsɪtjuːd] *n* lassitude *f*.

lasso [læ'suː] **1** *n* lasso *m*. **2** *vt* prendre au lasso.

last¹ [lɑːst] **1** *adj* (**a**) *(in series)* dernier *(before n)*. **the ~ 10 pages** les 10 dernières pages; **~ but one, second ~** avant-dernier; **it's the ~ round but 3** il n'y a plus que 3 rounds après celui-ci. (**b**) *(past, most recent)* dernier *(usually after n)*. **~ night** *(evening)* hier soir; *(night)* cette nuit, la nuit dernière; **~ week/year** *etc* la semaine/l'année *etc* dernière; **~ Monday** lundi dernier; **for the ~ few days** ces derniers jours; **for the ~ 2 years** depuis 2 ans; **the day before ~** avant-hier *m*; **the night before ~** avant-hier soir; **the week before ~** l'avant-dernière semaine; **(the) ~ time I saw him** la dernière fois que je l'ai vu; **~ thing at night** juste avant de se coucher; **I'm down to my ~ pound note** il ne me reste plus qu'une seule livre; **he's the ~ person to ask** c'est la dernière personne à qui demander.
2 *adv* (**a**) *(at the end) do, arrive etc* en dernier. (**b**) *(most recently)* la dernière fois. **when I ~ saw him** la dernière fois que je l'ai vu. (**c**) *(finally)* finalement, pour terminer.
3 *n* (**a**) dernier *m*, -ière *f*. **this is the ~ of the pears** voici la dernière poire (*or* les dernières poires); **the ~ of the cider** le reste du cidre; **the ~ but one** l'avant-dernier *m*, -ière *f*; **I'd be the ~ to criticize, but...** j'ai horreur de critiquer, mais... (**b**) *(phrases)* **at (long) ~** enfin; **to the ~** jusqu'au bout; **that was the ~ I saw of him** c'est la dernière fois que je l'ai vu; **we shall never hear the ~ of this** on n'a pas fini d'en entendre parler; **I shall be glad to see the ~ of this/of him** je serai content de voir tout ceci terminé/de le voir partir.
◆ **last-ditch** *adj* ultime. ◆ **lastly** *adv* pour terminer, en dernier lieu. ◆ **last-minute** *adj* de dernière minute.

last² [lɑːst] **1** *vi [pain, film, resources etc]* durer; **(~ out)** *[person]* tenir (le coup); *[money]* suffire. **too good to ~** trop beau pour durer; **no one ~s long in this job** personne ne tient longtemps dans ce poste; **he/it didn't ~ long** il/cela n'a pas fait long feu *. **2** *vt* durer. **he won't ~ the winter (out)** il ne passera pas l'hiver; **it will ~ you 3 years/a lifetime** cela vous durera *or* vous fera 3 ans/jusqu'à la fin de vos jours. ◆ **lasting** *adj (gen)* durable; **to his ~ing shame** à sa plus grande honte.

latch [lætʃ] *n* loquet *m*. **the door is on the ~** la porte n'est pas fermée à clef. ◆ **latch on to** * *vt fus* (**a**) *person* s'accrocher à. (**b**) *(understand)* saisir.
◆ **latchkey 1** *n* clef *f* (de la porte d'entrée) ; **2** *adj*: **~ child** enfant *mf* qui rentre à la maison avant ses parents qui travaillent.

late [leɪt] **1** *adj* (**a**) *(not on time) person, train* en retard. **to be ~** *(gen)* être en retard; *(arriving)* arriver en retard; **your essay is ~** vous rendez votre dissertation en retard; **the ~ arrival of the flight** le retard du vol; **to make sb ~** mettre qn en retard; **I'm ~** je suis en retard; **I'm ~ for work** je ne serai pas au travail à l'heure; **I was ~ for work** je suis arrivé au travail en retard; **I'm 2 hours ~** j'ai 2 heures de retard; **I'm 2 hours ~ for work** j'arriverai au travail avec 2 heures de retard; **I was 2 hours ~ for work** je suis arrivé au travail avec 2 heures de retard; **to be ~ in arriving** arriver en retard; **to be ~ with payments** avoir des paiements en retard; **he's a ~ developer** *(gen)* il s'est développé sur le tard; *(academically)* il a été lent à s'épanouir. (**b**) *(last or nearly last) edition, symphony* dernier *(before n)*. **to keep ~ hours** veiller tard; **at this ~ hour** à cette heure tardive; **at this ~ stage** à ce stade avancé; **~ opening Wednesdays** nocturne tous les mercredis soirs; **Easter is ~** Pâques est tard; **in ~ October** vers la fin d'octobre; **he is in his ~ sixties** il approche des soixante-dix ans; **of ~** récemment, dernièrement. (**c**) *(former)* ancien *(before n)*. **the ~ Prime Minister** l'ancien Premier ministre. (**d**) *(dead)* **the ~ Mr Jones** feu M. Jones; **our ~ colleague** notre regretté collègue.
2 *adv* (**a**) *(not on time) arrive etc* en retard. **he arrived 10 minutes ~** il est arrivé 10 minutes en retard *or* avec 10 minutes de retard; **better ~ than never** mieux vaut tard que jamais. (**b**) *(far into day etc) get up etc* tard. **to work ~ at the office** rester tard au bureau pour travailler; **it's getting ~** il se fait tard; **~ at night** tard le soir; **~ into the night** tard dans la nuit; **~ in 1960** vers la fin de 1960, fin 1960. (**c**) *(recently)* **as ~ as 1950** en 1950 encore.
◆ **latecomer** *n* retardataire *mf*. ◆ **lately** *adv* dernièrement, récemment; **till ~ly** jusqu'à ces derniers temps. ◆ **lateness** *n [person, vehicle]* retard *m*. ◆ **late-night opening** (*or* **show** *etc*) nocturne *f*. ◆ **later 1** *adj date, meeting* ultérieur; *edition* postérieur; *stage, point* plus avancé; **a ~r train** un train plus tard; **the ~r train** le deuxième train ; **2** *adv* (**a**) *(not on time)* plus en retard; (**b**) **2 weeks ~r** 2 semaines plus tard; **~r on** plus tard; **no ~r than** pas plus tard que; **not ~r than Monday** lundi au plus tard; **see you ~r!** * à tout à l'heure! ◆ **latest 1** *adj (gen)* dernier *(before n)*; *date* dernier, limite ; **2** *adv*: **the ~st you may come** l'heure limite à laquelle vous pouvez arriver; **when is the ~st you can come?** quand pouvez-vous venir, au plus tard?; **by noon at the ~st** à midi au plus tard ; **3** *n (*: news)* **have you heard the ~st?** tu connais la dernière? *; **what's the ~st on...?** qu'y a-t-il de

nouveau sur...?; *(Rad, TV)* **for the ~st on the riots** pour les dernières informations sur les émeutes; *(joke)* **have you heard his ~st?** tu connais sa dernière? *

latent ['leɪt(ə)nt] *adj* latent.

lateral ['læt(ə)r(ə)l] *adj* latéral.

latex ['leɪteks] *n* latex *m*.

lath, *pl* **laths** [læθ, lɑːðz] *n* latte *f*.

lathe [leɪð] *n (Tech)* tour *m*.

lather ['lɑːðəʳ] **1** *n [soap]* mousse *f* (de savon). *(sweating)* **in a ~** *horse* couvert d'écume; *person* en nage. **2** *vt one's face etc* savonner. **3** *vi [soap]* mousser.

Latin ['lætɪn] **1** *adj* latin. **~-American** latino-américain, d'Amérique latine. **2** *n (Ling)* latin *m*. ◆ **Latino-American** **1** *adj* latino-américain ; **2** *n (US)* Latino-Américain(e) *m(f)*.

latitude ['lætɪtjuːd] *n* (**a**) *(Geog)* latitude *f*. **at a ~ of 48° north** à 48° de latitude Nord. (**b**) *(freedom)* latitude *f*.

latrine [lə'triːn] *n* latrines *fpl*.

latter ['lætəʳ] **1** *adj* (**a**) *(second)* deuxième, dernier *(before n)*. **the ~ proposition** cette dernière *or* la deuxième proposition. (**b**) *(later)* dernier *(before n)*, deuxième. **the ~ half** la deuxième moitié; **in the ~ part of the century** vers la fin du siècle. **2** *n*: **of the two the ~ is...** des deux celui-ci (*f* celle-ci) est... ◆ **latter-day** *adj* d'aujourd'hui. ◆ **latterly** *adv (recently)* dernièrement, récemment; *(towards the end)* sur le tard.

lattice ['lætɪs] **1** *n* treillis *m*; *(fence)* treillage *m*. **2** *adj window* treillissé.

Latvia ['lætvɪə] *n* Lettonie *f*.

laudable ['lɔːdəbl] *adj* louable.

laudatory ['lɔːdət(ə)rɪ] *adj* élogieux.

laugh [lɑːf] **1** *n* rire *m*; *(brief)* éclat *m* de rire. **with a ~** en riant; **to have the ~ over sb** l'emporter finalement sur qn; **to have a good ~ at** bien rire de; **that got a ~** cela a fait rire; **if you want a ~** si tu veux t'amuser; **what a ~!** * ça, c'est marrant *!; **just for a ~** histoire de rire *; **he's always good for a ~** * il nous fera toujours bien rire; *(US)* **~ line** *(wrinkle)* ride *f* d'expression.
2 *vi* rire (*at, about, over* de). *(fig)* **to ~ at danger** se rire du danger; **there's nothing to ~ about** *or* **at** il n'y a pas de quoi rire; **he ~ed to himself** il a ri en lui-même; **he ~ed until he cried** il riait aux larmes; **he (nearly) split his sides ~ing** il se tordait de rire; **to ~ in sb's face** rire au nez de qn; **he'll soon be ~ing on the other side of his face** il n'aura bientôt plus envie de rire; *(fig)* **to ~ up one's sleeve** rire sous cape; **it's all right for him, he's ~ing** * lui il s'en fiche *, il est tranquille.
3 *vt*: **to ~ a jolly laugh** avoir un rire jovial; **to ~ sb to scorn** tourner qn en dérision; **they ~ed him out of it** ils se sont moqués de lui jusqu'à ce qu'il renonce; **to be ~ing one's head off** * rire comme un fou.
◆ **laugh off** *vt sep accusation* écarter d'une plaisanterie. **you can't ~ this one off** cette fois tu ne t'en tireras pas par la plaisanterie.
◆ **laughable** *adj suggestion* ridicule; *amount* dérisoire. ◆ **laughing** *adj* riant, rieur; **this is no ~ing matter** il n'y a pas de quoi rire; **~ing gas** gaz *m* hilarant. ◆ **laughingly** *adv say etc* en riant; **it is ~ingly called...** l'ironie de la chose, c'est qu'on l'appelle... ◆ **laughing stock** *n* risée *f*; **to make a ~ing stock of o.s.** se couvrir de ridicule. ◆ **laughter** *n* rires *mpl*; **to roar with ~ter** rire aux éclats; *(Brit)* **~ter line** *(wrinkle)* ride *f* d'expression.

launch [lɔːn(t)ʃ] **1** *n* (**a**) *(motor ~)* vedette *f* ; *(pleasure boat)* bateau *m* de plaisance; *(boat carried by warship)* chaloupe *f*. (**b**) *(Space)* lancement *m*. **~ vehicle** fusée *f* de lancement. **2** *vt (gen; also fig)* lancer; *shore lifeboat etc* faire sortir; *ship's boat* mettre à la mer. **3** *vi (fig)* se lancer (*into, on* dans).
◆ **launch out** *vi* se lancer (*into, on* dans).
◆ **launcher** *n* lanceur *m*. ◆ **launching** **1** *n* lancement *m*; *[shore lifeboat]* sortie *f*; *[ship's boat]* mise *f* à la mer ; **2** *adj*: **~ing pad/site** rampe *f*/aire *f* de lancement.

launder ['lɔːndəʳ] *vt clothes, money* blanchir. ◆ **launderette** *or* ◆ **Laundromat** ® *(US) n* laverie *f* automatique *(à libre-service)*. ◆ **laundry** **1** *n (place)* blanchisserie *f*; *(clothes)* linge *m*; **to do the laundry** faire la lessive ; **2** *adj list* de blanchissage; *mark* de la blanchisserie; *basket* à linge.

laurel ['lɒr(ə)l] *n* laurier *m*. **to rest on one's ~s** se reposer sur ses lauriers.

lava ['lɑːvə] *n* lave *f*.

lavatory ['lævətrɪ] **1** *n* toilettes *fpl*, W.-C. *mpl*, cabinets *mpl*. **2** *adj*: **~ paper** papier *m* hygiénique; **~ seat** siège *m* des W.-C.

lavender ['lævɪndəʳ] **1** *n* lavande *f*. **2** *adj (colour)* lavande *inv*. **~ bag/water** sachet *m*/eau *f* de lavande.

lavish ['lævɪʃ] **1** *adj* (**a**) *person* prodigue (*with* de). (**b**) *expenditure* très considérable; *amount* gigantesque; *meal* plantureux; *helping, hospitality* généreux; *flat, surroundings* somptueux. **to bestow ~ praise on sb** se répandre en éloges sur qn. **2** *vt* prodiguer (*sth on sb* qch à qn). ◆ **lavishly** *adv spend* sans compter; *give* généreusement; *furnish* somptueusement. ◆ **lavishness** *n [surroundings etc]* luxe *m*; *(prodigality)* prodigalité *f*.

law [lɔː] **1** *n* (**a**) *(gen)* loi *f*. **against the ~** contraire à la loi; **the ~ of the land** la législation *or* les lois du pays; **~s of nature** lois de la nature; **~ and order** l'ordre *m* public; **forces of ~ and order** forces *fpl* de l'ordre; **by ~** conformément à la loi; **by** *or* **under French ~** selon la loi française; **above the ~** au-dessus des lois; **to have the ~ on one's side** avoir la loi pour soi; **to keep within the ~** rester dans la légalité; **there's no ~ against it** il n'y a pas de loi contre *; **to take the ~ into one's own hands** faire justice soi-même; **he's a ~ unto himself** il ne connaît d'autre loi que la sienne; **his word is ~** sa parole fait loi; **court of ~** cour *f* de justice, tribunal *m*; **to go to ~** recourir à la justice; **to take to ~** *case* porter devant les tribunaux; *person* faire un procès à; **here's the ~ arriving!** ‡ voilà les flics! * (**b**) *(science, profession)* droit *m*. **to study ~** faire son *or* du droit; *(Univ)* **Faculty of L~** faculté *f* de Droit; **civil/ criminal ~** le droit civil/criminel.
2 *adj*: **~ court** cour *f* de justice, tribunal *m*; **~ enforcement officer** représentant *m* d'un service chargé de faire respecter la loi; *(Univ)* **~ school** faculté *f* de Droit; **~ student** étudiant(e) *m(f)* en droit.
◆ **law-abiding** *adj* respectueux des lois. ◆ **lawbreaker** *n* personne *f* qui transgresse la loi. ◆ **lawful** *adj* légal. ◆ **lawfully** *adv* légalement. ◆ **lawgiver** *or* ◆ **lawmaker** *n* législateur *m*, -trice *f*. ◆ **lawless** *adj country* sans loi; *person* qui n'a foi ni loi. ◆ **lawman** *n (US)* policier *m*. ◆ **lawsuit** *n* procès *m*; **to bring a ~suit against sb** intenter un procès à qn. ◆ **lawyer** *n (gen)* homme *m* de loi, juriste *m*; *(for sales, wills etc)* notaire *m*; *(for litigation)* avocat *m*; *(in firm)* conseiller *m* juridique; **I put the matter in the hands of my ~yer** j'ai mis l'affaire entre les mains de mon avocat.

lawn[1] [lɔːn] **1** *n* pelouse *f*. **2** *adj*: **~ tennis** *(gen)* tennis *m*; *(on grass)* tennis sur gazon. ◆ **lawnmower** *n* tondeuse *f* à gazon.

lawn[2] [lɔːn] *n (Tex)* linon *m*.

lax [læks] *adj conduct* relâché; *person* négligent. ◆ **laxity** *or* ◆ **laxness** *n* relâchement *m*; négligence *f*.

laxative ['læksətɪv] *adj, n* laxatif *(m)*.

lay¹ [leɪ] *pret, ptp* **laid 1** *vt* (**a**) *(put, place, set)* mettre, poser; *(stretch out) blanket etc* étendre (*over, on* sur); *tablecloth* mettre; *bricks, carpet, cable, pipe* poser; *road* faire; *[bird] egg* pondre; *tax* mettre (*on* sur); *burden* imposer (*on sb* à qn). *(euph: buried)* **to be laid to rest** être enterré; **I wish I could ~ my hands on...** si seulement je pouvais mettre la main sur...; **to ~ a hand on sb** porter la main sur qn; **I didn't ~ a finger on him** je ne l'ai même pas touché; **the scene is laid in Paris** l'action se passe à Paris; **he was laid low with flu** la grippe l'obligeait à garder le lit; **to ~ sb open to criticism** *etc* exposer qn à la critique *etc.* (**b**) *(prepare) fire* préparer; *snare, trap* tendre (*for* à); *plans* former. **to ~ the table** mettre le couvert; **to ~ the table for 5** mettre 5 couverts. (**c**) *(wager) money* parier, miser (*on* sur). **to ~ a bet** parier (*on* sur). (**d**) *(register) accusation* porter; *(Police) information* donner. *(Jur)* **to ~ a matter before the court** saisir le tribunal d'une affaire; **he laid his case before the commission** il a porté son cas devant la commission; **to ~ the facts before sb** exposer les faits à qn; **they laid their plan before him** ils lui ont soumis leur projet. (**e**) *(suppress) ghost* exorciser; *doubt, fear* dissiper; *dust* faire tomber. **2** *vi [bird etc]* pondre.

◆ **lay alongside** *vi, vt sep (Naut)* accoster. ◆ **lay aside, lay by** *vt sep* mettre de côté. ◆ **lay down** *vt sep* (**a**) *parcel, burden* poser, déposer; *one's arms* déposer; *one's cards* étaler; *wine* mettre en cave. **to ~ down one's life for sb** sacrifier sa vie pour qn. (**b**) *rule, policy* établir; *condition, price* imposer, fixer. **he laid it down that...** il a stipulé que...; *(fig)* **to ~ down the law** faire la loi (*to sb about sth* à qn sur qch). ◆ **lay in** *vt sep goods, reserves* faire provision de. **I must ~ in some fruit** il faut que je fasse provision de fruits. ◆ **lay into** * *vt fus (attack physically)* foncer sur; *(verbally)* prendre à partie; *(scold)* passer un savon à *. ◆ **lay off 1** *vt sep workers* licencier, débaucher. **2** *vi (*: stop)* arrêter. **3** *vt fus* (*) **~ off it!** arrête!; **~ off him!** fiche-lui la paix! * ◆ **lay on** *vt sep* (**a**) *tax* mettre. (**b**) *(Brit: provide) water, gas* installer; *facilities, entertainment* fournir. **a house with water laid on** une maison qui a l'eau courante; **I'll have a car laid on for you** je tiendrai une voiture à votre disposition; **everything will be laid on** il y aura tout ce qu'il faut. (**c**) *varnish, paint* étaler. *(fig)* **he laid it on thick** * *(flattered)* il a passé de la pommade *; *(exaggerated)* il y est allé un peu fort *. ◆ **lay out** *vt sep* (**a**) *(plan, design) garden* dessiner; *house* concevoir le plan de; *essay* faire le plan de; *(Typ)* faire la mise en page de. **well-laid-out flat** appartement bien conçu. (**b**) *(get ready) clothes* sortir, préparer; *goods for sale* disposer. **to ~ out a body** faire la toilette d'un mort. (**c**) *reasons* exposer systématiquement. (**d**) *(spend) money* dépenser (*on* pour). (**e**) *(knock out)* mettre knock-out. ◆ **lay over** *vi (US)* faire une halte. ◆ **lay up** *vt sep* (**a**) *store, provisions* amasser. **to ~ up trouble for o.s.** se préparer des ennuis. (**b**) *car* remiser; *ship* désarmer. **he is laid up with flu** il est au lit avec la grippe; **you'll ~ yourself up** tu vas te retrouver au lit.

◆ **layabout** * *n* fainéant(e) *m(f)*. ◆ **lay-by** *n (Aut)* petite aire *f* de stationnement *(sur bas-côté)*. ◆ **lay-off** *n (Ind)* licenciement *m*, mise *f* en chômage technique. ◆ **layout** *n [building, town]* disposition *f*; *[essay]* plan *m*; *[advertisement, newspaper article etc]* mise *f* en page. ◆ **layover** *n (US)* halte *f*.

lay² [leɪ] *pret of* **lie¹**.

lay³ [leɪ] *adj missionary, education* laïque; *brother, sister* convers; *(fig) opinion etc* des profanes. *(fig)* **to the ~ mind** pour le profane. ◆ **layman** *n (Rel)* laïc *m*; *(fig)* profane *m*.

layer ['le(ɪ)əʳ] *n* couche *f*.

laze [leɪz] *vi* (**~ about, ~ around**) paresser, traînasser *(pej)*. ◆ **lazily** *adv* paresseusement. ◆ **laziness** *n* paresse *f*, fainéantise *f (pej)*. ◆ **lazy** *adj person* paresseux, fainéant *(pej)*; *smile* paresseux; *afternoon* de paresse; **~ Susan** *(dish)* plateau *m* tournant. ◆ **lazybones** * *n* fainéant(e) *m(f)*.

lead¹ [li:d] *(vb: pret, ptp* **led***)* **1** *n* (**a**) **to be in the ~** *(in match)* mener; *(in race, league)* être en tête; **to take the ~** *(in race)* prendre la tête; *(in match)* mener; **to have a 3-point ~** avoir 3 points d'avance; **to take the ~ in doing sth** être le premier à faire qch; **thanks to his ~** grâce à son initiative; **to follow sb's ~** suivre l'exemple de qn; **to give sb a ~** *[inventor etc]* montrer le chemin à qn *(fig)*; *[clue etc]* mettre qn sur la voie; **the police have a ~** la police tient une piste; *(Cards)* **whose ~ is it?** à qui est-ce de jouer? (**b**) *(Theat)* **to play the ~** tenir le rôle principal; **male/female ~** premier rôle masculin/féminin. (**c**) *(leash)* laisse *f*. **on a ~** tenu en laisse. (**d**) *(Elec)* fil *m*; *(extension ~)* rallonge *f*. (**e**) *(Press: ~ story)* article *m* de tête.
2 *vt* (**a**) *(conduct)* mener, conduire (*to* à); *[street]* mener. **to ~ sb in/across** *etc* faire entrer/traverser *etc* qn; **to ~ sb into a room** faire entrer qn dans une pièce; *(fig)* **he is easily led** il est très influençable; *(lit, fig)* **to ~ the way** montrer le chemin; **he led the way to the garage** il nous (*or* les *etc*) a menés jusqu'au garage; **he led the party to victory** il a mené le parti à la victoire. (**b**) *(be ~er of) procession (in charge)* être à la tête de; *(at head)* être en tête de; *government, team* être à la tête de, diriger; *expedition* être à la tête de, mener; *(Ftbl etc) league* être en tête de; *orchestra (Brit)* être le premier violon de; *(US)* diriger. *(Sport, fig)* **to ~ the field** venir *or* être en tête; **this country ~s the world in textiles** ce pays est au premier rang mondial pour les textiles. (**c**) *(Cards)* jouer. (**d**) *life, existence* mener. *(fig)* **to ~ sb a dance** faire la vie à qn *. (**e**) *(induce, bring)* amener (*sb to do* qn à faire). **I am led to the conclusion that...** je suis amené à conclure que...
3 *vi* (**a**) *(in match)* mener (*by 4 goals to 3* par 4 buts à 3); *(in race)* être en tête. **to ~ by half a length/3 points** avoir une demi-longueur/3 points d'avance. (**b**) *(go ahead)* aller devant. **you ~, I'll follow** passez devant, je vous suis. (**c**) *(Cards)* jouer. (**d**) *[street, corridor, door]* mener (*to, into* à). **the streets that ~ off the square** les rues qui partent de la place. (**e**) *(result in)* **to ~ to war** conduire à; *sb's arrest* aboutir à; *confusion* créer; *change, improvement* amener, causer; **this led to their resigning** ceci les a amenés à démissionner; **one thing led to another and we...** une chose en amenant une autre, nous...

◆ **lead away** *vt sep* emmener. ◆ **lead back** *vt sep* ramener. ◆ **lead off 1** *vi (begin)* commencer. **2** *vt sep* emmener. ◆ **lead on 1** *vi*: **~ on!** allez-y, je vous suis! **2** *vt sep* (**a**) *(tease)* taquiner, faire marcher *; *(fool)* avoir *; *(raise hopes of)* donner de faux espoirs à. (**b**) *(induce)* amener (*sb to do* qn à faire). ◆ **lead up** *vi [road, stair]* conduire (*to* à). **what's all this ~ing up to?** où est-ce qu'on veut en venir avec tout ça?

◆ **leader** *n* (**a**) *[expedition, gang, tribe]* chef *m*; *[club]* dirigeant(e) *m(f)*; *(guide)* guide *m*; *[riot, strike]* meneur *m*, -euse *f*; *(Mil)* commandant *m*; *(Pol)* dirigeant(e), leader *m*; *(Brit Parl)* **L~er of the House** chef de la majorité ministérielle à la Chambre; **he's a born ~er** il est né pour commander; **the ~er of the orchestra** *(Brit)* le premier violon; *(US)* le chef d'orchestre; **one of the ~ers in the scientific field** une des sommités du monde scientifique; (**b**) *(in race)* coureur *m* de tête; *(horse)* cheval *m* de tête; *(in league)* leader *m*; (**c**) *(Press) (Brit)* éditorial *m*; *(US)* article *m* de tête. ◆ **leadership** *n* (**a**) direction *f*; **under his ~ership** sous sa direction; **qualities of ~ership** qualités *fpl* de chef; (**b**) *(~ers)* dirigeants *mpl.* ◆ **leader-writer** *n* éditorialiste *mf.* ◆ **lead-in** *n* introduction *f*, entrée *f* en matière. ◆ **leading** *adj horse, car (in procession)* de tête; *(in race)* en tête; *(chief) person, member, politician* de (tout) premier plan, principal; *position* dominant, de premier plan; *part* prépondérant, de premier plan; *theme, idea* principal; **one of the ~ing writers** un des écrivains les plus importants; **one of the ~ing figures of the twenties** un personnage marquant des années vingt; *(Press)* **~ing article** *(Brit)* éditorial *m*; *(US)* article *m* de tête; **the ~ing lady/man** *(Cine)* la vedette féminine/masculine; *(Theat)* l'acteur/l'actrice principal(e); *(fig)* **~ing light** personnalité *f* de premier plan; **~ing question** *(Jur)* question *f* tendancieuse; *(gen)* question insidieuse. ◆ **lead time** *n* délai *m* d'exécution *or* de réalisation.

lead² [led] **1** *n (metal)* plomb *m*; *(black ~)* mine *f* de plomb; *[pencil]* mine; *[fishing line]* plomb; *(for sounding)* plomb (de sonde). **(window) ~s** plombures *fpl.* **2** *adj object* de *or* en plomb; *paint* à base de plomb. ~ **pencil** crayon *m* à mine de plomb; ~ **poisoning** saturnisme *m.* ◆ **leaded** *adj window* à tout petits carreaux; *petrol* avec plomb. ◆ **leaden** *adj colour, sky* de plomb; *(heavy)* pesant; *silence* de mort; *atmosphere* chargé. ◆ **lead-free** *adj petrol* sans addition de plomb; *paint* (garanti) sans plomb.

leaf [li:f] **1** *n, pl* **leaves** (**a**) *[plant]* feuille *f.* **in ~** en feuilles. (**b**) *[book]* feuillet *m*, page *f.* *(fig)* **you should take a ~ out of his book** vous devriez prendre exemple sur lui; *(fig)* **to turn over a new ~** changer de conduite. (**c**) *[table]* rabat *m.* **2** *vi*: **to ~ through a book** feuilleter un livre. ◆ **leaflet** **1** *n* prospectus *m*; *(Pol, Rel)* tract *m*; *(instruction sheet)* mode *m* d'emploi ; **2** *vt area* distribuer des prospectus (*or* des tracts *etc*) dans. ◆ **leafy** *adj* feuillu.

league [li:g] *n* (**a**) ligue *f.* **to form a ~ against** se liguer contre; **in ~ with** en coalition avec. (**b**) *(Ftbl etc)* championnat *m*; *(Baseball)* division *f*; *(fig)* classe *f*, catégorie *f.* *(Baseball)* **major/minor ~** première/deuxième division; *(Ftbl)* **~ championship** championnat *m*; *(Ftbl)* **~ table** classement *m* du championnat.

leak [li:k] **1** *n (gen; also of information)* fuite *f*; *(in boat)* voie *f* d'eau. **to spring a ~** *[boat]* commencer à faire eau; *[bucket, pipe]* se mettre à fuir; **security ~** fuite concernant la sécurité. **2** *vi* (**a**) *[container, roof etc]* fuir; *[ship]* faire eau; *[shoes]* prendre l'eau. (**b**) (**~ out**) *[liquid]* fuir, s'échapper; *[secret, news]* être divulgué. **it ~ed (through) on to the carpet** cela a filtré jusque sur le tapis. **3** *vt liquid* répandre; *(fig) information* divulguer (*to* à). ◆ **leakage** *n (leak)* fuite *f*; *(amount lost)* perte *f.* ◆ **leaky** *adj container* qui fuit; *roof* qui a une fuite ; *boat* qui fait eau.

lean¹ [li:n] *pret, ptp* **leaned** *or* **leant** [lent] **1** *vi* (**a**) *[wall, construction etc]* pencher. *(Pol)* **to ~ towards the left** pencher vers la gauche. (**b**) *(rest) [person]* s'appuyer (*against* contre, à; *on* sur). *[person, ladder, cycle]* **to be ~ing** être appuyé (*against* contre, à); **to ~ on sb** *(lit, fig: for support)* s'appuyer sur qn; *(*: put pressure on)* faire pression sur qn. **2** *vt ladder, cycle* appuyer (*against* contre). **to ~ one's head on sb's shoulder** reposer sa tête sur l'épaule de qn.

◆ **lean back** *vi* se pencher en arrière; *(in armchair)* se laisser aller en arrière. **to ~ back against** s'adosser contre *or* à. ◆ **lean forward** *vi* se pencher en avant. ◆ **lean out** *vi* se pencher au dehors. **to ~ out of the window** se pencher par la fenêtre. ◆ **lean over** *vi [person]* se pencher *(forward)* en avant *or (sideways)* sur le côté; *[object, tree]* pencher, être penché. *(fig)* **to ~ over backwards to help sb** * se mettre en quatre pour aider qn.

◆ **leaning** **1** *n* tendance *f* (*towards* à) ; **2** *adj* penché. ◆ **lean-to** **1** *n* appentis *m* ; **2** *adj* en appentis.

lean² [li:n] **1** *adj* maigre. **we had a ~ time** on a mangé de la vache enragée. **2** *n [meat]* maigre *m.* ◆ **leanness** *n* maigreur *f.*

leap [li:p] *(vb: pret, ptp* **leaped** *or* **leapt** [lept]*)* **1** *n* saut *m*, bond *m.* **at one ~** d'un bond; **by ~s and bounds** à pas de géant; *(fig)* **a ~ in the dark** un saut dans l'inconnu; *(fig)* **a great ~ forward** un bond en avant. **2** *adj*: **~ year** année *f* bissextile. **3** *vi* sauter, bondir. **to ~ out/in** *etc* sortir/entrer *etc* d'un bond; **he leapt into the car** il a sauté dans la voiture; **to ~ over a ditch** franchir un fossé d'un bond; **he leapt for joy** il bondit de joie; **to ~ at an offer** sauter sur une offre. **4** *vt stream, hedge* sauter (par-dessus), franchir d'un bond.

◆ **leap up** *vi (off ground)* sauter en l'air; *(to one's feet)* se lever d'un bond; *[flame]* jaillir; *[prices, etc]* faire un bond.

◆ **leapfrog** **1** *n* saute-mouton *m* ; **2** *vi*: **to ~frog over** *person* sauter à saute-mouton par-dessus; *object* franchir à saute-mouton; *(fig)* dépasser ; **3** *vt (fig)* dépasser.

learn [lɜ:n] *pret, ptp* **learned** *or* **learnt** **1** *vt* apprendre. **to ~ (how) to do sth** apprendre à faire qch; *(fig)* **he's ~t his lesson** cela lui a servi de leçon, il ne recommencera pas de sitôt; **I was sorry to ~ that...** j'ai appris avec regret que...; **that'll ~ you!** ⁑ ça t'apprendra! * **2** *vi* apprendre. **to ~ about sth** *(Scol etc)* étudier qch; *(hear of)* apprendre qch; **to ~ from experience** apprendre par l'expérience; **to ~ from one's mistakes** tirer la leçon de ses erreurs; *(iro)* **he'll ~!** un jour il comprendra! ◆ **learn off** *vt sep* apprendre par cœur. ◆ **learn up** *vt sep (gen)* apprendre; *school subject* travailler. ◆ **learned** ['lɜ:nɪd] *adj (gen)* savant; *profession* intellectuel; *(Brit Jur)* **my ~ed friend** mon éminent confrère. ◆ **learner** *n* débutant(e) *m(f)*; **to be a quick ~er** apprendre vite. ◆ **learning** *n* érudition *f*, savoir *m*; **~ing difficulties** troubles *mpl* scolaires.

lease [li:s] **1** *n (Jur: contract, duration)* bail *m.* **long ~** bail à long terme; *(fig)* **to give sb a new ~ of life** redonner de la vigueur à qn; **to take on a new ~ of** *or (US)* **on life** retrouver une nouvelle jeunesse. **2** *vt [tenant, owner]* louer à bail.

◆ **leaseback** *n* cession-bail *f.* ◆ **leasehold** **1** *n* bail *m* ; **2** *adj* loué à bail. ◆ **leaseholder** *n* preneur *m*, -euse *f*, locataire *mf.* ◆ **leasing** *n* crédit-bail *m.*

leash [li:ʃ] *n* laisse *f.* **on a ~** en laisse.

least [li:st] *superl of* **little²** **1** *adj (smallest amount of)* le moins de; *(smallest)* le *or* la moindre, le *or* la plus petit(e). **the ~ money** le moins d'argent; **the ~ thing upsets her** la moindre chose *or* la plus petite chose la contrarie; **that's the ~ of our worries** c'est le cadet de nos soucis. **2** *pron* le moins. **it's the ~ I can do** c'est la moindre des choses; **to say the ~ (of it)!** c'est le moins qu'on puisse dire!; **~ said soonest mended** moins on en dit et mieux ça vaut; **at ~ £5** au moins 5 livres; **at ~ as much as** au moins autant que; **you could at ~ have told me!** tu aurais pu au moins me le dire!; **I can at ~ try** je peux toujours essayer; **...at ~ that's what he says** ...du moins c'est ce qu'il dit; **at the very ~** au moins, au minimum; **not in the ~** pas du tout. **3** *adv* le moins. **the ~ expensive car** la voiture la moins chère; **she is ~ able to afford it** c'est elle qui peut le moins se l'offrir; **~ of all him** surtout pas lui. ◆ **leastways** * *or* ◆ **leastwise** * *adv* du moins, ou plutôt.

leather ['leðəʳ] **1** *n* cuir *m*; *(wash ~)* peau *f* de chamois. **2** *adj* de *or* en cuir. **~ goods** articles *mpl* en cuir; *(handbags etc)* maroquinerie *f.*

◆ **leatherette** *n* similicuir *m*. ◆ **leathering** *n*: **to give sb a ~ing** * tanner le cuir à qn ‡. ◆ **leathery** *adj meat, substance* coriace; *skin* parcheminé.

leave [liːv] *(vb: pret, ptp* **left***)* **1** *n* (**a**) *(consent)* permission *f*. **without so much as a by-your-~** * sans même demander la permission; **to ask ~ from sb to do** demander à qn la permission de faire. (**b**) *(holiday)* congé *m*; *(Mil)* permission *f*. **on ~** en congé, en permission; **on ~ of absence** en congé exceptionnel; *(Mil)* en permission spéciale. (**c**) **to take (one's) ~ of sb** prendre congé de qn; **have you taken ~ of your senses?** avez-vous perdu la tête?
2 *vt* (**a**) *(go away from) town* quitter, partir de; *(permanently)* quitter; *room, building* sortir de, quitter; *prison, hospital* sortir de; *person, job* quitter. **to ~ school** terminer ses études (secondaires); **he left home in 1979** il est parti de la maison en 1979; **I left home at 6 o'clock** je suis sorti de chez moi à 6 heures; **he has left this address** il n'habite plus à cette adresse; **to ~ the room** *(to lavatory)* sortir *(euph)*; **to ~ the table** se lever de table; **to ~ the track** dérailler; **the car left the road** la voiture a quitté la route. (**b**) *(deposit, put)* laisser (*with sb* à qn); *(forget)* laisser, oublier. **to ~ sb a tip** laisser un pourboire à qn; **she left him her house** elle lui a laissé *or* légué sa maison. (**c**) *(allow to remain)* laisser. **to ~ the door open** laisser la porte ouverte; **~ it where it is** laisse-le là où il est; **some things are better left unsaid** il vaut mieux passer certaines choses sous silence; **let's ~ it at that** tenons-nous-en là; **I'll ~ it to you to decide** je te laisse décider; **I'll ~ it to you** je m'en remets à vous; **~ it to me!** je m'en charge!; **I'll ~ you to it** * je vous laisse (continuer); **he was left a widower** il est devenu veuf; **to ~ sb in peace** *or* **to himself** laisser qn tranquille; **left to himself, he...** tout seul *or* laissé à lui-même, il...; **take it or ~ it** c'est à prendre ou à laisser; **3 from 6 ~s 3** 3 ôté de 6, il reste 3. (**d**) **to be left (over)** rester; **what's left?** qu'est-ce qui reste?; **there'll be none left** il n'en restera pas; **how many are (there) left?** combien est-ce qu'il en reste?; **I've no money left** il ne me reste plus d'argent; **there are 3 cakes left** il reste 3 gâteaux; **have you (got) any left?** est-ce qu'il vous en reste?; *V also* **left¹**.
3 *vi* partir, s'en aller (*for* pour).
◆ **leave about, leave around** *vt sep clothes etc* laisser traîner. ◆ **leave behind** *vt sep person, object* laisser; *opponent in race* distancer; *fellow students* dépasser. ◆ **leave in** *vt sep* laisser. ◆ **leave off 1** *vi (*: stop)* s'arrêter. **2** *vt sep* (**a**) *(*: stop)* cesser, arrêter (*doing* de faire). (**b**) *lid, clothes* ne pas mettre; *gas, heating, tap* laisser fermé; *light* laisser éteint. ◆ **leave on** *vt sep lid, clothes* ne pas enlever; *gas, heating, tap* laisser ouvert; *light* laisser allumé. ◆ **leave out** *vt sep* (**a**) *(omit) (accidentally)* oublier; *(deliberately)* exclure; *(in reading etc)* sauter. **he was feeling left out** il avait l'impression de ne pas être dans le coup. (**b**) *food, note* laisser *(for sb* à qn); *(not put back) books, toys* laisser sorti, ne pas ranger. ◆ **leave over** *vt sep* (**a**) **to be left over** rester; *V* **leave 2d.** (**b**) *(postpone)* remettre (à plus tard). ◆ **leavetaking** *n* adieux *mpl*. ◆ **leaving** *n* départ *m*. ◆ **leavings** *npl* restes *mpl*.

leaven ['levn] **1** *n* levain *m*. **2** *vt* faire lever.

Lebanon ['lebənən] *n* Liban *m*.

lecherous ['letʃərəs] *adj* lubrique.

lectern ['lektən] *n* lutrin *m*.

lecture ['lektʃəʳ] **1** *n* (**a**) conférence *f*; *(Univ etc: part of series)* cours *m* (magistral). **to give a ~** faire une conférence *or* un cours (*on* sur). (**b**) *(reproof)* sermon *m*. **to give** *or* **read sb a ~** sermonner qn. **2** *vi* faire une conférence *or* un cours (*to* à; *on* sur). *(Univ)* **he ~s in law** il est professeur de droit; **he's lecturing at the moment** il fait (son) cours en ce moment. **3** *vt (reprove)* sermonner (*sb on sth/for having done* qn pour qch/pour avoir fait). **4** *adj notes* de cours. **~ course** cours *m* magistral; **~ hall** amphithéâtre *m*; **~ room** salle *f* de conférences; **~ theatre** amphithéâtre *m*. ◆ **lecturer** *n* (**a**) *(speaker)* conférencier *m*, -ière *f*; (**b**) *(Brit Univ)* ≃ assistant(e) *m(f)*; **assistant ~r** ≃ assistant(e) *m(f)*; **senior ~r** maître assistant *m*.

led [led] *pret, ptp of* **lead¹**.

ledge [ledʒ] *n (on wall)* rebord *m*, saillie *f*; *(window ~)* rebord (de la fenêtre); *(on mountain)* saillie.

ledger ['ledʒəʳ] *n* grand livre *m (Comptabilité)*.

lee [liː] **1** *n* côté *m* sous le vent. **in the ~ of** à l'abri de. **2** *adj* sous le vent.
◆ **leeward 1** *adj, adv* sous le vent ; **2** *n* côté *m* sous le vent; **to ~ward** sous le vent. ◆ **leeway** *n (Naut)* dérive *f*; *(fig)* **that gives him a certain ~way** cela lui donne une certaine liberté d'action; **a lot of ~way to make up** beaucoup de retard à rattraper.

leech [liːtʃ] *n* sangsue *f*.

leek [liːk] *n* poireau *m*.

leer [lɪəʳ] **1** *vi* lorgner. **to ~ at sb** lorgner qn. **2** *n (evil)* regard *m* mauvais; *(lustful)* regard concupiscent.

left¹ [left] *pret, ptp of* **leave.** ◆ **left-luggage** *n* bagages *mpl* en consigne; *(office)* consigne *f*. ◆ **left-luggage locker** *n* casier *m* à consigne automatique. ◆ **left-overs** *npl* restes *mpl*.

left² [left] **1** *adj (not right)* gauche. **2** *adv* à gauche. **3** *n* (**a**) gauche *f*. **on your ~** à *or* sur votre gauche; **on the ~** *be, stand, see* sur la gauche, à gauche; *drive* à gauche; **the door on the ~** la porte de gauche; **the street on the ~** la rue à gauche; *(Aut)* **to keep to the ~** tenir sa gauche; **to the ~** vers la gauche; *(Pol)* **the L~** la gauche. (**b**) *(Boxing: punch)* gauche *m*. ◆ **left-hand** *adj door, page* de gauche; **~-hand drive** conduite *f* à gauche; **on the ~-hand side** à gauche. ◆ **left-handed** *adj person* gaucher; *screw* fileté à gauche; *scissors* pour gaucher; *(fig) compliment* ambigu. ◆ **left-hander** *n (person)* gaucher *m*, -ère *f*. ◆ **leftist** *adj (Pol)* de gauche. ◆ **left-wing** *adj newspaper, view* de gauche; **he's ~-wing** il est à gauche.

leg [leg] **1** *n [person, horse]* jambe *f*; *[other animal, bird, insect]* patte *f*; *(Culin) [lamb]* gigot *m*; *[pork, chicken, frog]* cuisse *f*; *[table etc]* pied *m*; *[trousers, stocking etc]* jambe; *(stage) [journey]* étape *f*; *(in relay)* relais *m*. **my ~s won't carry me any further!** je ne tiens plus sur mes jambes!; **to be on one's last ~s** *[person, company]* être à bout de ressources; *[machine etc]* être sur le point de rendre l'âme *; **to give sb a ~ up** faire la courte échelle à qn; *(* fig)* donner un coup de pouce à qn; **he hasn't got a ~ to stand on** il n'a aucun argument valable; *(fig)* **to pull sb's ~** *(hoax)* faire marcher qn *; *(tease)* taquiner qn. **2** *adj muscle* de la jambe. **~ bone** tibia *m*. **3** *vt*: **to ~ it** * *(run)* cavaler ‡; *(flee)* se barrer ‡; *(walk)* aller à pied, faire le chemin à pied. ◆ **-legged** *adj ending*: **four-~ged** à quatre pattes ; **bare-~ged** aux jambes nues. ◆ **leggings** *npl* jambières *fpl*; *(for baby)* culotte *f* (longue). ◆ **leg-pull** * *n* canular *m*. ◆ **leg-pulling** * *n (hoaxes)* canulars *mpl*; *(teasing)* taquineries *fpl*. ◆ **legroom** *n* place *f* pour les jambes. ◆ **legwarmers** *npl* jambières *fpl*. ◆ **legwork** * *n* les déplacements *mpl*.

legacy ['legəsɪ] *n (Jur, also fig)* legs *m*. **to leave a ~ to sb** faire un legs à qn.

legal ['liːg(ə)l] *adj* (**a**) *(lawful) act, status, right* légal; *requirements* légitime. **~ currency** monnaie légale; **it's not ~ currency** cela n'a pas cours; **~ document** titre *m* authentique. (**b**) *(concerning the law) error, advice* judiciaire; *affairs, question* juridique. **to take ~ action against** intenter un procès à *or* contre; **to take ~ advice** consulter un juriste *or* un avocat; **~ adviser** conseiller *m*, -ère *f* juridique; *(Brit)* ~

aid assistance *f* judiciaire; ~ **costs** frais *mpl* de justice; ~ **department** service *m* du contentieux; **a** ~ **offence** une infraction à la loi; ~ **proceedings** procès *m*, poursuites *fpl*; **the** ~ **profession** les hommes *mpl* de loi. ◆ **legality** *n* légalité *f*. ◆ **legalization** *n* légalisation *f*. ◆ **legalize** *vt* légaliser. ◆ **legally** *adv* légalement; **to be** ~**ly binding** lier.

legation [lɪ'geɪʃ(ə)n] *n* légation *f*.

legend ['ledʒ(ə)nd] *n* légende *f*. ◆ **legendary** *adj* légendaire.

legible ['ledʒəbl] *adj* lisible. ◆ **legibility** *n* lisibilité *f*. ◆ **legibly** *adv* lisiblement.

legion ['li:dʒ(ə)n] *n* légion *f*. ◆ **legionary 1** *n* légionnaire *m* ; **2** *adj* de la légion.

legionnaire [,li:dʒə'nɛəʳ] *n* légionnaire *m*. *(Med)* ~**'s disease** maladie *f* du légionnaire.

legislate ['ledʒɪsleɪt] *vi* faire des lois, légiférer. ◆ **legislation** *n* législation *f*; **a piece of legislation** une loi; **to introduce legislation** faire des lois. ◆ **legislative** *adj* législatif. ◆ **legislator** *n* législateur *m*, -trice *f*. ◆ **legislature** *n* corps *m* législatif.

legitimate [lɪ'dʒɪtɪmɪt] *adj (Jur etc)* légitime; *argument, cause, excuse* bon, valable; *complaint* légitime; *reasoning, conclusion* logique. **the** ~ **theatre** le théâtre littéraire. ◆ **legitimacy** *n* légitimité *f*. ◆ **legitimately** *adv*: **one might** ~**ly think** on serait en droit de penser. ◆ **legitimize** *vt* légitimer.

leisure ['leʒəʳ] **1** *n* loisir *m*, temps *m* libre. *(hum)* **a lady of** ~ une rentière *(fig hum)*; **a life of** ~ une vie pleine de loisirs; **do it at your** ~ faites-le quand vous en aurez le temps; **think about it at** ~ réfléchissez-y à tête reposée. **2** *adj*: **in my** ~ **moments** à mes moments de loisir; ~ **time** loisir *m*, temps *m* libre. ◆ **leisured** *adj* qui a beaucoup de loisirs; *classes* oisif. ◆ **leisurely** *adj pace, movement* lent, tranquille; *person* placide; *journey, stroll* fait sans se presser; *occupation* peu fatigant; **in a** ~**ly way** *walk* sans se presser; *work* sans faire de gros efforts.

lemon ['lemən] **1** *n (fruit, colour)* citron *m*; *(tree)* citronnier *m*. **2** *adj (colour)* citron *inv*. ~ **cheese** *or* **curd** ≃ crème *f* de citron; ~ **drink** *or* **squash** citronnade *f*; *(fresh lemon)* citron pressé; ~ **juice** jus *m* de citron; ~ **sole** limande-sole *f*; ~ **squeezer** presse-citron *m inv*; ~ **tea** thé *m* au citron; ~ **yellow** jaune citron *inv*. ◆ **lemonade** *n* limonade *f*; *(still)* citronnade *f*.

lemur ['li:məʳ] *n* maki *m*.

lend [lend] *pret, ptp* **lent** *vt (gen)* prêter (*to sb* à qn); *(fig) importance, one's name* prêter (*to* à); *mystery, dignity, authority* conférer (*to* à). **to** ~ **an ear** écouter, prêter l'oreille; **to** ~ **o.s. to sth** se prêter à qch. ◆ **lender** *n* prêteur *m*, -euse *f*. ◆ **lending 1** *n* prêt *m* ; **2** *adj library* de prêt; ~**ing rate** taux *m* de prêt.

length [leŋθ] *n* (**a**) *(gen)* longueur *f*; *(duration)* durée *f*. **it was 6 metres in** ~ cela avait 6 mètres de long; **what is the** ~ **of the field?** quelle est la longueur du champ?; **along the whole** ~ **of** sur toute la longueur de; **what** ~ **of cloth did you buy?** quel métrage de tissu as-tu acheté?; *(fig)* **over the** ~ **and breadth of England** dans toute l'Angleterre; **to fall full** ~ tomber de tout son long; **what** ~ **is the film?** quelle est la durée du film?; ~ **of life** durée de vie; ~ **of time** temps *m*; *(Admin)* ~ **of service** ancienneté *f*; **4,000 words in** ~ de 4 000 mots; **at** ~ *(at last)* enfin, à la fin; **at (great)** ~ *(in many words)* fort longuement; *(in detail)* dans le détail; **to go to the** ~ **of doing** aller jusqu'à faire; **to go to great** ~**s to do** se donner beaucoup de mal pour faire; **to go to any** ~**(s) to do** ne reculer devant rien pour faire; **to win by a** ~ gagner d'une longueur; **he was 3 car** ~**s behind me** il était à 3 longueurs de voiture derrière moi. (**b**) *(section: gen)* morceau *m*, bout *m*; *[wallpaper]* lé *m*; *[dress material]* métrage *m*, hauteur *f*; *[tubing, track]* tronçon *m*. **skirt** ~ hauteur de jupe. ◆ **lengthen 1** *vt object* rallonger; *visit, life* prolonger; *vowel* allonger ; **2** *vi* rallonger; se prolonger; s'allonger; *[days, nights]* rallonger. ◆ **lengthily** *adv* longuement. ◆ **lengthways** *or* ◆ **lengthwise 1** *adv* dans le sens de la longueur ; **2** *adj* en longueur. ◆ **lengthy** *adj* (très) long; *(tedious)* interminable.

lenient ['li:nɪənt] *adj judge, parent* indulgent (*to* envers, pour); *government* clément (*to* envers). ◆ **lenience** *or* ◆ **leniency** *n* indulgence *f*; clémence *f*. ◆ **leniently** *adv* avec indulgence; avec clémence.

lens [lenz] **1** *n (for magnifying)* lentille *f*; *[camera]* objectif *m*; *[spectacles]* verre *m*; *[eye]* cristallin *m*. **2** *adj*: ~ **cap** bouchon *m* d'objectif; ~ **holder** porte-objectif *m inv*; ~ **hood** parasoleil *m*.

lent [lent] *pret, ptp of* **lend.**

Lent [lent] *n* Carême *m*. **I gave it up for** ~ j'y ai renoncé pour le Carême.

lentil ['lentl] *n* lentille *f*. ~ **soup** soupe *f* aux lentilles.

Leo ['li:əʊ] *n (Astron)* le Lion.

leopard ['lepəd] *n* léopard *m*. **the** ~ **cannot change its spots** on ne peut pas changer sa nature. ◆ **leopardess** *n* léopard *m* femelle.

leotard ['li:ətɑ:d] *n* collant *m (de danseur etc)*.

leper ['lepəʳ] *n* lépreux *m*, -euse *f (also fig)*. ~ **colony** léproserie *f*. ◆ **leprosy** *n* lèpre *f*. ◆ **leprous** *adj* lépreux.

lesbian ['lezbɪən] **1** *adj* lesbien. **2** *n* lesbienne *f*. ◆ **lesbianism** *n* lesbianisme *m*.

lesion ['li:ʒ(ə)n] *n (Med)* lésion *f*.

Lesotho [lɪ'su:tu:] *n* Lesotho *m*.

less [les] *comp of* **little²** **1** *adj, pron* moins (de). ~ **butter** moins de beurre; **I have** ~ **than you** j'en ai moins que vous; **even** ~ encore moins; **much** ~ **milk** beaucoup moins de lait; **a little** ~ **cream** un peu moins de crème; ~ **and** ~ de moins en moins; ~ **than that** moins que cela; **it costs** ~ **than** cela coûte moins cher que; ~ **than half the audience** moins de la moitié de l'assistance; **he couldn't have done** ~ il n'aurait pas pu faire moins; **of** ~ **importance** de moins d'importance; **I have** ~ **time for reading** j'ai moins de temps pour lire; **it is** ~ **than perfect** on ne peut pas dire que ce soit parfait; ~ **than a month/a kilo** moins d'un mois/d'un kilo; ~ **than you think** moins que vous ne croyez; **can't you let me have it for** ~**?** vous ne pouvez pas me le laisser à moins?; **no** ~ **a person than** rien moins que; **he's bought a car, no** ~ * il s'est payé une voiture, s'il vous plaît *; **no** ~ **than 4 months' holiday** au moins 4 mois de vacances; **the** ~ **said about it the better** mieux vaut ne pas en parler; **the** ~ **you buy the** ~ **you spend** moins vous achetez moins vous dépensez; **he's nothing** ~ **than a thief** il n'est rien moins qu'un voleur; **nothing** ~ **than a bomb would move them** il faudrait au moins une bombe pour les faire bouger; **it's nothing** ~ **than disgraceful** le moins qu'on puisse dire, c'est que c'est une honte.
2 *adv* moins. **you must eat** ~ vous devez moins manger; **to grow** ~ diminuer; ~ **and** ~ de moins en moins; ~ **often** moins souvent; ~ **expensive than you think** moins cher que vous ne croyez; **the** ~ **you say about it the better** le moins vous en parlerez et mieux ça vaudra; **he was none the** ~ **pleased to see me** il n'en était pas moins content de me voir.
3 *prep* moins. ~ **10%** moins 10%.
◆ **lessen 1** *vt (gen)* diminuer; *cost* réduire; *anxiety, pain, effect, shock* atténuer; *(Pol) tension* relâcher ; **2** *vi* diminuer; s'atténuer; se relâcher. ◆ **less-**

ening *n* diminution *f*. ◆ **lesser** *adj* moindre; **to a ~er degree** *or* **extent** à un moindre degré; **the ~er of** le *or* la moindre de.

...less [lɪs] *adj ending*: **hatless** sans chapeau; **childless** sans enfants.

lessee [le'si:] *n* preneur *m*, -euse *f* (à bail).

lesson ['lesn] *n* leçon *f* *(also fig)*. **a French ~** une leçon de français; **to take/give ~s in** prendre/donner des leçons de; **we have ~s from 9 to midday** nous avons classe *or* cours de 9 heures à midi; **let that be a ~ to you!** que cela vous serve de leçon!; *(US Scol)* **~ plans** dossier *m* pédagogique.

lest [lest] *conj* de peur *or* de crainte de + *infin*; de peur *or* de crainte que (+ ne) + *subj*.

let [let] *pret, ptp* **let** *vt* (**a**) laisser (*sb do* qn faire), permettre (*sb do* à qn de faire, que qn fasse). **he wouldn't ~ us** il n'a pas voulu, il ne nous a pas permis; **to ~ sb into the house/into a secret** faire entrer qn dans la maison/dans un secret; **to ~ sb/sth past** *or* **through** laisser passer qn/qch; *(fig)* **to ~ sb off (doing) sth** dispenser qn de (faire) qch; **don't ~ me forget** rappelle-moi; **don't ~ the fire go out** ne laisse pas s'éteindre le feu; **~ me have a look** laissez-moi regarder, faites voir; **when can you ~ me have it?** quand est-ce que je pourrai l'avoir?; **~ him have it** donnez-le-lui; **~ him be!** laisse-le tranquille!; **just you ~ me catch you stealing again** * que je t'y prenne encore à voler; **I ~ myself be persuaded** je me suis laissé convaincre ; **to ~ a window into a wall** percer une fenêtre dans un mur; **~ alone** *(used as conj)* *V* **alone**. (**b**) *(in verb forms)* **~ us** *or* **~'s go** allons; **~'s sit down** asseyons-nous; **~ me think** laissez-moi réfléchir; **don't ~ me keep you** que je ne vous retienne pas; **~ him come himself** qu'il vienne lui-même; **~ that be a warning to you** que cela vous serve d'avertissement; **just ~ them try!** qu'ils essaient *(subj)* un peu!; **~ x equal 2** soit x égal à 2. (**c**) *(hire out)* *house etc* louer, mettre en location. **'to ~'** 'à louer'.

◆ **let away** *vt sep (allow to leave)* laisser partir. *(fig)* **you can't ~ him away with that!** tu ne peux pas le laisser s'en tirer comme ça! ◆ **let down** *vt sep* (**a**) *window* baisser; *dress* rallonger; *hem* lâcher; *tyre* dégonfler; *(on rope etc) person, object* descendre. *(fig)* **he ~ me down gently** *(about bad news)* il m'a traité avec ménagement; *(in punishing etc)* il n'a pas été trop sévère avec moi. (**b**) *(fail)* **to ~ sb down** *(gen)* décevoir qn; *[car, watch]* jouer des tours à qn; **don't ~ us down** nous comptons sur vous; **the weather ~ us down** le beau temps n'a pas été de la partie. ◆ **let in** **1** *vi [shoes, tent]* prendre l'eau; *[roof]* laisser entrer la pluie. **2** *vt sep person, cat* faire entrer, laisser entrer; *light, rain* laisser entrer. **can you ~ him in?** pouvez-vous lui ouvrir?; **he ~ himself in with a key** il est entré avec une clef; *(fig)* **to ~ sb in for (doing) sth** entraîner qn à (faire) qch; **you don't know what you're ~ting yourself in for** tu ne sais pas à quoi tu t'engages; **to ~ sb in on sth** mettre qn au courant de qch. ◆ **let off** *vt sep* (**a**) *(explode etc) bomb* faire éclater; *firework, firearm* faire partir. (**b**) *(release) gas etc* dégager, lâcher. (**c**) *(allow to leave) pupils etc* laisser partir. **if you don't want to do it, I'll ~ you off** si tu ne veux pas le faire, je t'en dispense. (**d**) *(not punish)* ne pas punir, faire grâce à. **he ~ me off with a warning** il m'a seulement donné un avertissement; **to ~ sb off lightly** laisser qn s'en tirer à bon compte. (**e**) *rooms etc* louer. ◆ **let on** * **1** *vi (acknowledge)* dire. **I won't ~ on** je ne dirai rien, je garderai ça pour moi. **2** *vt sep (acknowledge)* dire, aller raconter (*that* que); *(pretend)* prétendre, raconter (*that* que). ◆ **let out** *vt sep* (**a**) *person, cat* faire *or* laisser sortir; *prisoner* relâcher; *sheep, cattle* faire sortir (*of* de); *caged bird* lâcher; *water* vider; *fire, candle* laisser s'éteindre; *secret, news* laisser échapper, révéler. **I'll ~ you out** je vais vous ouvrir la porte; **to ~ o.s. out** sortir; **can you ~ yourself out?** vous m'excuserez de ne pas vous reconduire?; **to ~ the air out of a tyre** dégonfler un pneu; **his alibi ~s him out** son alibi le met hors de cause. (**b**) *shout, cry* laisser échapper; *laugh* avoir. (**c**) *dress* élargir; *seam* lâcher; *belt* desserrer. (**d**) *house etc* louer. ◆ **let up** **1** *vi [rain]* diminuer; *[cold weather]* s'adoucir; *[worker, talker]* s'arrêter (un moment). **2** *vt sep (allow to rise)* **to ~ sb up** permettre à qn de se lever.

◆ **let-down** * *n* déception *f*. ◆ **let-out** *n* échappatoire *m*. ◆ **letting** *n [house etc]* location *f*. ◆ **let-up** * *n (decrease)* diminution *f*; *(stop)* arrêt *m*; *(respite)* répit *m*.

lethal ['li:θ(ə)l] *adj poison, blow* mortel; *effect* fatal; *weapon* meurtrier. **this coffee's ~!** * ce café est atroce! *

lethargy ['leθədʒɪ] *n* léthargie *f*. ◆ **lethargic** [le'θɑ:dʒɪk] *adj* léthargique.

letter ['letəʳ] **1** *n* (**a**) *(of alphabet)* lettre *f*. **the ~ L** la lettre L; **in ~s** en lettres; **he's got a lot of ~s after his name** * il a des tas * de diplômes *(or* de décorations *etc)*; *(fig)* **the ~ of the law** la lettre de la loi; **to follow sth to the ~** suivre qch à la lettre. (**b**) *(written communication)* lettre *f*. **were there any ~s for me?** y avait-il du courrier *or* des lettres pour moi?; **he was invited by ~** il a reçu une invitation écrite; **~ of introduction** lettre de recommandation. (**c**) *(learning)* **man of ~s** homme *m* de lettres. **2** *vt (put ~ on)* inscrire des lettres sur; *(engrave)* graver (des lettres sur). ◆ **letter-bomb** *n* lettre *f* piégée. ◆ **letterbox** *n* boîte *f* à lettres. ◆ **letter-card** *n* carte-lettre *f*. ◆ **letter-head** *n* en-tête *m*. ◆ **lettering** *n (engraving)* gravure *f*; *(letters)* caractères *mpl*. ◆ **letter-opener** *n* coupe-papier *m inv*. ◆ **letter paper** *n* papier *m* à lettres. ◆ **letter-perfect** *adj*: **to be ~-perfect in sth** savoir qch sur le bout du doigt. ◆ **letterpress** *n (method)* typographie *f*; *(text)* texte *m* imprimé. ◆ **letter-writer** *n* correspondant(e) *m(f)*.

lettuce ['letɪs] *n* laitue *f*; *(Culin)* laitue, salade *f*.

leuk(a)emia [lu:'ki:mɪə] *n* leucémie *f*.

level ['levl] **1** *n* (**a**) niveau *m*. **at roof ~** au niveau du toit; **to find one's own ~** trouver son niveau; **he came down to their ~** il s'est mis à leur niveau; **it is on a ~ with** *(lit)* c'est du niveau de, c'est à la hauteur de; *(fig)* ça vaut bien; **top-~ talks** conférence *f* au niveau le plus élevé; **at departmental/ministerial ~** à l'échelon départemental/ministériel. (**b**) *(Aut, Rail)* palier *m*. **speed on the ~** vitesse *f* en palier; *(fig)* **is this on the ~?** * est-ce qu'il joue franc jeu? (**c**) *(spirit ~)* niveau *m* à bulle d'air. (**d**) *(flat place)* terrain *m* plat.

2 *adj* (**a**) *(flat) surface, ground* plat, uni; *tray* horizontal. *(Brit Rail)* **~ crossing** passage *m* à niveau; **a ~ spoonful** une cuillerée rase; **to do one's ~ best** * faire tout son possible (*to do* pour faire). (**b**) *(equal) contestants* à égalité. **to be ~ with** *(in race)* être à la même hauteur que; *(in league)* être à égalité avec; *(in studies, achievements)* être au même niveau que; *(in salary, rank)* être au même échelon que; **to draw ~ with** arriver à la même hauteur *etc* que; **~ with the ground** au niveau du sol. (**c**) *(steady) voice, tones* calme, assuré; *judgment* sain. **to keep a ~ head** garder tout son sang-froid. (**d**) *(US *: honest)* honnête, régulier.

3 *vt* (**a**) *(make level) site, ground* niveler, aplanir; *quantities* répartir également; *(demolish) building, town* raser. (**b**) *(aim) blow* allonger (*at sb* à qn); *gun* braquer (*at sb* sur qn); *accusation* lancer (*at sb* contre qn).

4 *vi* (**a**) (**~ off**) *[curve on graph, prices etc]* se stabiliser; *[aircraft]* amorcer le vol en palier. (**b**) *(US)* **to ~ with sb** * être franc avec qn. ◆ **levelheaded** *adj* équilibré. ◆ **levelling** *adj effect, process* de nivellement.

lever ['li:vəʳ] **1** *n (lit, fig)* levier *m*. **2** *vt*: **to ~ sth out/up** extraire/soulever qch au moyen d'un levier. ◆ **leverage** *n* force *f* (de levier); *(fig: influence)* influence *f* (*on or with sb* sur qn).

levity ['levɪtɪ] *n* manque *m* de sérieux.

levy ['levɪ] **1** *n (gen)* prélèvement *m* (*on* sur); *(act, amount)* taxation *f*; *(tax)* impôt *m*, taxe *f*. **2** *vt* (**a**) *(impose) tax* prélever, mettre (*on sth* sur qch); *fine* imposer (*on sb* à qn). (**b**) *(collect) contributions* percevoir.

lewd [lu:d] *adj* lubrique. ◆ **lewdness** *n* lubricité *f*.

lexical ['leksɪk(ə)l] *adj* lexical.

lexicography [ˌleksɪ'kɒgrəfɪ] *n* lexicographie *f*. ◆ **lexicographer** *n* lexicographe *mf*.

lexicology [ˌleksɪ'kɒlədʒɪ] *n* lexicologie *f*. ◆ **lexicologist** *n* lexicologue *mf*.

lexicon ['leksɪk(ə)n] *n* lexique *m*.

liable ['laɪəbl] *adj* (**a**) *(likely)* **to be ~ to do** *(gen)* risquer de faire; *(more formally)* être susceptible de faire; **it's ~ to explode** cela risque d'exploser; **he's ~ to refuse** il est possible qu'il refuse *(subj)*; **we are ~ to get shot at** on risque de se faire tirer dessus; **it's ~ to be hot** il se peut qu'il fasse très chaud. (**b**) *(subject to) person* passible (*to* de), sujet (*to* à); *thing* assujetti (*to* à). **~ for military service** astreint au service militaire. (**c**) *(responsible)* (civilement) responsable (*for* de). ◆ **liability** *n (for accident etc)* responsabilité *f* (*for* de); *(handicap)* handicap *m*; *(person)* poids *m* mort; **liabilities** *(debts)* engagements *mpl*; *(Bookkeeping)* passif *m*.

liaison [li:'eɪzɒn] **1** *n* liaison *f*. **2** *adj committee, officer* de liaison.

liar ['laɪəʳ] *n* menteur *m*, -euse *f*.

lib ‡ [lɪb] *n abbr of* **liberation.**

libel ['laɪb(ə)l] **1** *n* diffamation *f* (par écrit). **2** *adj laws* contre la diffamation. **~ proceedings** *or* **suit** procès *m* en diffamation. **3** *vt (Jur)* diffamer (par écrit); *(gen)* calomnier, médire de. ◆ **libellous,** *(US)* **libelous** *adj* diffamatoire.

liberal ['lɪb(ə)r(ə)l] **1** *adj (all senses)* libéral (*with* de). **2** *n (Pol)* **L~** libéral(e) *m(f)*. ◆ **liberalism** *n* libéralisme *m*. ◆ **liberality** *n (broad-mindedness)* libéralisme *m*; *(generosity)* libéralité *f*. ◆ **liberally** *adv* libéralement.

liberate ['lɪbəreɪt] *vt* libérer. ◆ **liberated** *adj* libéré. ◆ **liberation** *n* libération *f*. ◆ **liberator** *n* libérateur *m*, -trice *f*.

Liberia [laɪ'bɪərɪə] *n* Libéria *m*, Liberia *m*.

liberty ['lɪbətɪ] *n* liberté *f*. **at ~** *(not detained)* en liberté; *(not busy)* libre; **at ~ to choose** libre de choisir; **~ of the press** liberté de la presse; **to take liberties** se permettre des libertés (*with* avec); **to take the ~ of doing** se permettre de faire; *(Dress)* **~ bodice** chemise *f* américaine.

libido [lɪ'bi:dəʊ] *n* libido *f*.

Libra ['li:brə] *n (Astron)* la Balance.

library ['laɪbrərɪ] **1** *n* bibliothèque *f*. **2** *adj book* de bibliothèque. *(Comput)* **~ software** logiciel-bibliothèque *m*; **~ ticket** carte *f* de lecteur. ◆ **librarian** *n* bibliothécaire *mf*. ◆ **librarianship** *n* bibliothéconomie *f*.

libretto [lɪ'bretəʊ] *n* libretto *m*, livret *m*. ◆ **librettist** *n* librettiste *mf*.

Libya ['lɪbɪə] *n* Libye *f*.

lice [laɪs] *npl of* **louse.**

licence ['laɪs(ə)ns] **1** *n* (**a**) *(permit)* autorisation *f*, permis *m*; *(for manufacturing, trading)* licence *f*; *(Aut) (for driver)* permis; *(for car)* vignette *f*; *(for radio, TV set)* redevance *f*. **driving/export ~** permis de conduire/d'exporter; **pilot's ~** brevet *m* de pilote; **married by special ~** marié avec dispense de bans; **to manufacture under ~** fabriquer sous licence. (**b**) *(freedom)* liberté *f*. **poetic ~** licence *f* poétique. **2** *adj [car]* **~ plate/number** plaque *f*/numéro *m* minéralogique *or* d'immatriculation. ◆ **licentious** *adj* licencieux.

license ['laɪs(ə)ns] **1** *n (US)* = **licence. 2** *vt* (**a**) *(give licence to)* donner une licence à; *car [licensing authority]* délivrer la vignette de; *[owner]* acheter la vignette de *or* pour. **to be ~d to sell tobacco** détenir une licence de bureau de tabac; **on ~d premises** dans un établissement ayant une licence de débit de boissons. (**b**) *(allow)* autoriser (*sb to do* qn à faire). ◆ **licensee** *n [pub]* patron(ne) *m(f)*.

lick [lɪk] **1** *n* (**a**) coup *m* de langue. **to give o.s. a ~ and a promise** * faire un petit brin de toilette; **a ~ of paint** un petit coup de peinture. (**b**) *(speed)* **at full ~** * en quatrième vitesse *. **2** *vt* (**a**) *(gen)* lécher. **to ~ one's lips** se lécher les lèvres; *(fig)* se frotter les mains *(fig)*; **to ~ sth clean/off** *etc* nettoyer/enlever *etc* qch à coups de langue; *(fig)* **to ~ sb's boots** jouer les lèche-bottes * envers qn; *(fig)* **to ~ one's wounds** panser ses blessures *(fig)*. (**b**) (*) *(defeat)* battre à plates coutures; *(outdo)* battre; *(thrash)* rosser. ◆ **licking** * *n (whipping)* rossée * *f*; *(defeat)* déculottée ‡ *f*.

lickety-split ['lɪkɪtɪ'splɪt] *adv (US)* à fond de train.

lid [lɪd] *n (gen)* couvercle *m*; *(eye~)* paupière *f*. *(fig)* **to take the ~ off sth** étaler qch au grand jour; **that puts the ~ on it!** ça, c'est un comble!; *(US: act against sth)* **to put the ~ on sth** * prendre des mesures contre qch.

lido ['li:dəʊ] *n (resort)* complexe *m* balnéaire; *(swimming pool)* piscine *f (en plein air)*.

lie¹ [laɪ] *pret* **lay,** *ptp* **lain** *vi* (**a**) *[person etc]* (**~ down**) s'allonger, s'étendre, se coucher; **(be lying)** être allongé *or* étendu *or* couché; *[dead body] (at funeral etc)* reposer; *(in grave etc)* être enterré. **he was lying on the floor** *(unable to move)* il était étendu *or* il gisait par terre; **she lay in bed until 10 o'clock** elle est restée au lit jusqu'à 10 heures; **she was lying in bed reading** elle lisait au lit; **he lay dead** il était étendu mort; **he was lying still** il était étendu immobile; **~ still!** ne bouge pas!; **his body was lying on the ground** son corps gisait sur le sol; *(on tombstone)* **here ~s** ci-gît; *(fig)* **to ~ low** ne pas se faire remarquer; *(hide)* se cacher.

(**b**) *(be) [object]* être; *[place, road]* se trouver, être; *[land, sea etc]* s'étendre; *(remain)* rester, être. **the book lay on the table** le livre était sur la table; **the book lay unopened all day** le livre est resté fermé toute la journée; **to ~ at anchor** être à l'ancre; **the snow lay thick on the ground** il y avait une épaisse couche de neige sur le sol; **the snow will not ~** la neige ne tiendra pas; **to ~ heavy on** peser sur; **the valley lay before us** la vallée s'étendait devant nous; **the years that ~ before us** les années qui sont devant nous; **the difference ~s in the fact that...** la différence vient de ce que...; **the real remedy ~s in...** le vrai remède se trouve dans...

◆ **lie about, lie around** *vi [clothes, books]* traîner; *[person]* traînasser *. ◆ **lie back** *vi* se renverser (en arrière). *(fig)* **~ back and enjoy yourself!** laisse-toi donc vivre! ◆ **lie down** *vi* s'allonger, s'étendre. **to be lying down** être allongé; *(to dog)* **~ down!** couché!; *(fig)* **to take sth lying down** accepter qch sans protester. ◆ **lie in** *vi (stay in bed)* faire la grasse matinée. ◆ **lie up** *vi (stay in bed)* garder le lit; *(hide)* se cacher.

◆ **lie-down** * *n*: **to have a ~-down** s'allonger, s'étendre. ◆ **lie-in** * *n*: **to have a ~-in** faire la grasse matinée.

lie² [laɪ] *(vb: pret, ptp* **lied***)* **1** *n* mensonge *m*. **to tell ~s** mentir, dire des mensonges; **to give the ~ to** démentir. **2** *vi* mentir. **3** *vt*: **to ~ one's way out of it** essayer de s'en sortir par des mensonges. **4** *adj*: **~ detector** détecteur *m* de mensonges.

Liechtenstein ['lɪktənstaɪn] *n* Liechtenstein *m*.

lieu [lu:] *n*: **in ~ of** au lieu de.

lieutenant [lef'tenənt, *(US)* lu:'tenənt] *n (Brit: in army)* lieutenant *m*; *(Brit, US: in navy)* [lə'tenənt, *(US)* lu:'tenənt] lieutenant de vaisseau; *(fig)* second *m*; *(US Army)* **first ~** lieutenant *m*. ◆ **lieutenant colonel** *n* lieutenant-colonel *m*. ◆ **lieutenant general** *n* général *m* de corps d'armée; *(US Air Force)* général *m* de corps aérien.

life [laɪf] **1** *n, pl* **lives** (**a**) *(gen)* vie *f*. **animal and plant ~** vie animale et végétale; **bird ~** les oiseaux *mpl*; **insect ~** les insectes *mpl*; **a matter of ~ and death** une question de vie ou de mort; **to bring sb back to ~** ranimer qn; **to come to ~** *[person]* reprendre conscience; *[town etc]* s'éveiller *(fig)*.
(**b**) *(existence)* vie *f*; *[car, government, battery etc]* durée *f*. **he lived in France all his ~** il a vécu toute sa vie en France; **for the rest of his ~** pour le restant de ses jours; **to be sent to prison for ~, to get ~** * être condamné à la prison à vie; **he's doing ~** * il tire une condamnation à perpétuité; **it will last you all your ~** cela vous durera toute votre vie; **never in all my ~** jamais de ma vie; **in later ~** plus tard (dans la vie); **late in ~** sur le tard; **~ isn't worth living** la vie ne vaut pas la peine d'être vécue; **tired of ~** las de vivre; **to take one's (own) ~** se donner la mort; **to take one's ~ in one's hands** jouer sa vie; **town ~** la vie à la ville; **it's a good ~** c'est la belle vie; **to lead a quiet ~** mener une vie tranquille; **portrait taken from ~** portrait d'après nature; **it was Paul to the ~** c'était Paul tout craché *; **I couldn't for the ~ of me** * je ne pouvais absolument pas; **how's ~?** * comment ça va? *; **that's ~!** c'est la vie!; **this is the ~!** * voilà comment je comprends la vie!; **not on your ~!** * jamais de la vie!
(**c**) *(liveliness)* vie *f*. **full of ~** plein de vie; **he's the ~ and soul of the party** c'est un boute-en-train; **it put new ~ into me** ça m'a fait revivre; **there isn't much ~ in our village** notre village est plutôt mort.
2 *adj president, member* à vie. **~ cycle** cycle *m* de (la) vie; **~ expectancy** espérance *f* de vie; **the ~ force** la force vitale; **~ imprisonment** prison *f* à vie; **~ insurance** assurance-vie *f*; **~ peer/peerage** pair *m*/pairie *f* à vie; *(US)* **~ preserver** gilet *m* de sauvetage; **~ raft** radeau *m* de sauvetage; **the ~ sciences** les sciences *fpl* de la vie; **~ sentence** condamnation *f* à perpétuité; **~ span** durée *f or* espérance *f* de vie; **~ story** biographie *f*; **~ style** style *m* de vie; **~ support system** *(in space)* équipement *m* de vie; *(Med)* **on a ~ support system** sous assistance respiratoire.
◆ **life-and-death** *adj*: **~-and-death struggle** lutte *f* désespérée. ◆ **lifebelt** *n* bouée *f* de sauvetage. ◆ **lifeblood** *n* élément *m* vital. ◆ **lifeboat** *n (shore)* canot *m* de sauvetage; *(from ship)* chaloupe *f* de sauvetage. ◆ **lifebuoy** *n* bouée *f* de sauvetage. ◆ **life-giving** *adj* vivifiant. ◆ **lifeguard** *n (on beach)* surveillant *m* de plage *or* de baignade. ◆ **life-jacket** *or* ◆ **life-vest** *n* gilet *m* de sauvetage. ◆ **lifeless** *adj body, matter* inanimé; *(fig) style* sans vigueur. ◆ **lifelessness** *n (fig)* manque *m* de vigueur. ◆ **lifelike** *adj* qui semble vivant *or* vrai. ◆ **lifeline** *n (on ship)* main *f* courante; *(for diver)* corde *f* de sécurité; *(fig)* **it was his ~line** c'était vital pour lui. ◆ **lifelong** *adj ambition* de toute ma (*or* sa *etc*) vie; *friend, friendship* de toujours; *task* de toute une vie. ◆ **life-saver** *n (person)* surveillant(e) *m(f)* de baignade; *(fig)* **that money was a ~-saver** cet argent m'a (*or* lui a *etc*) sauvé la vie. ◆ **life-saving** **1** *n (rescuing)* sauvetage *m*; *(first aid)* secourisme *m* ; **2** *adj* de sauvetage. ◆ **life-sized** *adj* grandeur nature *inv*. ◆ **lifetime** *n* vie *f*; **not in my ~time** pas de mon vivant; **once in a ~time** une fois dans la vie; **the work of a ~time** l'œuvre de toute une vie; **it seemed a ~time** cela a semblé une éternité. ◆ **lifework** *n* œuvre *f* de toute une (*or* ma *etc*) vie.

lift [lɪft] **1** *n* (**a**) *(Brit) (elevator)* ascenseur *m*; *(for goods)* monte-charge *m inv*. (**b**) **can I give you a ~?** est-ce que je peux vous déposer quelque part?; **I gave him a ~ to Paris** je l'ai emmené (en voiture) jusqu'à Paris; **he was hoping for a ~** il espérait être pris en stop. (**c**) **to give sb/sth a ~ up** soulever qn/qch; *(fig)* **to give sb a ~** remonter le moral à *or* de qn.
2 *vt (gen)* lever, soulever; *(fig) restrictions* supprimer, abolir; *ban, blockade, siege* lever; *(*: steal)* chiper *; *quotation, idea* prendre, voler (*from sb* à qn). **to ~ sth into the air** lever qch en l'air; **to ~ sb/sth onto a table** soulever qn/qch pour le poser sur une table; **to ~ sb over a wall** faire passer qn par-dessus un mur; **he didn't ~ a finger to help** il n'a pas levé le petit doigt pour aider.
3 *vi [lid etc]* se soulever; *[fog]* se lever.
◆ **lift down** *vt sep* descendre (*from* de). ◆ **lift off** **1** *vi (Space)* décoller. **2** *vt sep lid* enlever; *child* descendre. ◆ **lift out** *vt sep object* sortir; *troops* évacuer par avion (*or* hélicoptère). ◆ **lift up** **1** *vi [drawbridge etc]* se soulever. **2** *vt sep object, person* soulever; *one's eyes, head* lever. ◆ **liftboy** *or* ◆ **liftman** *n (Brit)* liftier *m*. ◆ **liftgate** *n (Aut: esp US)* hayon *m*. ◆ **lift-off** *n (Space)* décollage *m*.

light[1] [laɪt] *(vb: pret, ptp* **lit** *or* **lighted***)* **1** *n* (**a**) *(gen)* lumière *f*. **electric ~** éclairage *m or* lumière électrique; **to put on the ~** allumer; **to put off the ~** éteindre; **there were ~s on in the room** il y avait de la lumière dans la pièce; **~s out** extinction *f* des feux; **by the ~ of** à la lumière de; **at first ~** au point du jour; **the ~ was beginning to fail** le jour commençait à baisser; **she was sitting with her back to the ~** elle tournait le dos à la lumière; **to stand sth in the ~** mettre qch à la lumière; **you're holding it against the ~** vous le tenez à contre-jour; **you're in my ~** tu me fais de l'ombre; **the ~ isn't good enough** il n'y a pas assez de lumière; *(Art, Phot)* **~ and shade** les clairs *mpl* et les ombres *fpl*; *(fig: understand)* **to see the ~** * comprendre. (**b**) *(fig)* **to bring to ~** mettre en lumière, révéler; **to come to ~** être découvert; **to throw some ~ on sth** éclaircir qch; **it revealed him in a new ~** cela l'a montré sous un jour nouveau; **in the ~ of what you say** tenant compte de ce que vous dites; *(fig)* **according to his ~s** d'après sa façon de voir les choses. (**c**) *(lamp etc)* lampe *f*. **desk/reading** *etc* **~** lampe de bureau/de lecture *etc*. (**d**) *(Aut) [motor vehicle] (gen)* feu *m*; *(headlamp)* phare *m*; *[cycle]* feu. (**e**) *(traffic ~s)* **the ~s** *(gen)* les feux *mpl (de circulation)*. **the ~s were at red** le feu était (au) rouge. (**f**) *(for cigarette etc)* **have you got a ~?** avez-vous du feu?; **to put a ~ to sth, to set ~ to sth** mettre le feu à qch.
2 *adj* (**a**) *evening, room* clair. **while it's ~** pendant qu'il fait jour. (**b**) *hair* blond; *colour, complexion, skin* clair. **~ green** vert clair *inv*. (**c**) **~ bulb** ampoule *f*, lampe *f*; *(Phot)* **~ meter** photomètre *m*; *(Comput)* **~ pen** photostyle *m*, crayon *m* optique; **~ wave** onde *f* lumineuse.
3 *vt* (**a**) *candle, cigarette, gas* allumer; *match* frotter. **he lit the fire** il a allumé le feu; **he lit a fire** il a fait du feu. (**b**) *room* éclairer. **lit by electricity** éclairé à l'électricité; **this will ~ your way** ceci vous éclairera le chemin.
4 *vi [match]* s'allumer; *[coal, wood]* prendre (feu).
◆ **light up** **1** *vi [lamp]* s'allumer; *[eyes, face]* s'éclairer; *(*: smoke)* allumer une cigarette (*or* une pipe *etc*). **2** *vt sep [lighting, sun] room* éclairer.
◆ **light-coloured** *adj* clair, de couleur claire.
◆ **lighten**[1] **1** *vt darkness, face* éclairer; *colour, hair* éclaircir ; **2** *vi* s'éclairer; s'éclaircir. ◆ **lighter** **1** *n (cigarette ~)* briquet *m* ; **2** *adj*: **~er fuel** gaz *m* à briquet. ◆ **light-haired** *adj* blond. ◆ **lighthouse** *n* phare *m (sur la côte etc)*. ◆ **lighting** **1**

n (Elec etc) éclairage *m; (Theat)* éclairages ; **2** *adj:* **~ing engineer** éclairagiste *m;* **~ing-up time** heure *f* de l'éclairage des véhicules. ◆ **lightness**[1] *n (brightness)* clarté *f.* ◆ **lightship** *n* bateau-phare *m.* ◆ **light-year** *n* année-lumière *f.*

light[2] [laɪt] **1** *adj (gen: lit, fig)* léger; *rain* fin. **as ~ as a feather** léger comme une plume; **to be ~ on one's feet** *(gen)* avoir le pas léger; **to be a ~ sleeper** avoir le sommeil léger; **~ ale** bière *f* blonde légère; *(US)* **~ beer** bière *f* basses calories; **~ industry** industrie *f* légère; **~ opera** opérette *f;* **~ reading** lecture *f* distrayante; **~ verse** poésie *f* légère; **with a ~ heart** le cœur léger; **'woman wanted for ~ work'** 'on demande employée de maison pour travaux légers'; **to make ~ work of sth** faire qch sans difficulté; **to make ~ of sth** prendre qch à la légère. **2** *adv travel* avec peu de bagages. **3** *npl (meat)* **~s** mou *m (abats).* ◆ **lighten**[2] *vt* alléger. ◆ **light-fingered** *adj* chapardeur. ◆ **light-headed** *adj (dizzy, foolish)* étourdi; *(excited)* exalté. ◆ **light-hearted** *adj person* gai; *laugh, atmosphere* joyeux, gai; *discussion* enjoué. ◆ **lightly** *adv (gen)* légèrement; **to sleep ~ly** avoir le sommeil léger; **to get off ~ly** s'en tirer à bon compte. ◆ **lightness**[2] *n (in weight)* légèreté *f.* ◆ **lightweight** *adj (lit, fig)* léger.

lightning ['laɪtnɪŋ] **1** *n* éclair *m,* foudre *f.* **we saw ~** nous avons vu un éclair *or* des éclairs; **a lot of ~** beaucoup d'éclairs; **a flash of ~** un éclair; **struck by ~** frappé par la foudre; **like ~ *** avec la vitesse de l'éclair. **2** *adj attack* foudroyant; *strike* surprise *inv; visit* éclair *inv.* **~ conductor,** *(US)* **~ rod** paratonnerre *m.*

like[1] [laɪk] **1** *adj* semblable, du même genre. **to be as ~ as two peas** se ressembler comme deux gouttes d'eau.

2 *prep* (**a**) comme, en. **he behaved ~ a fool** il s'est conduit comme un imbécile *or* en imbécile; **it wasn't ~ that at all** ce n'était pas du tout comme ça; **it was ~ this, I'd just got home...** voilà, je venais de rentrer... (**b**) *(resembling)* comme, pareil à. **to be ~ sb/sth** ressembler à qn/qch; **a house ~ mine** une maison pareille à *or* comme la mienne; **an idiot ~ you** un imbécile comme vous; **~ father, ~ son** tel père, tel fils; **I found one ~ it** j'en ai trouvé un pareil; **I never saw anything ~ it!** je n'ai jamais rien vu de pareil!; **that's just ~ him!** c'est bien de lui!; **it's not ~ him to be late** ça n'est pas son genre d'être en retard; **sth ~ that** qch comme ça *; **I was thinking of giving her sth ~ a necklace** je pensais lui offrir un collier ou qch dans ce genre-là; **that's sth ~ a steak! *** voilà ce que j'appelle un bifteck!; **that's more ~ it!** voilà qui est mieux!; **that's nothing ~ it!** ça n'est pas du tout ça!; **there's nothing ~ real silk** rien ne vaut la soie véritable; **what's he ~?** comment est-il?; **what's the film ~?** comment as-tu trouvé le film?; **what's the weather ~?** quel temps fait-il? (**c**) *(such as)* comme, tel que, par exemple. **the basic necessities of life, ~ food and drink** les éléments indispensables à la vie, tels que *or* comme la nourriture et la boisson.

3 *adv:* **it's nothing ~ as good as...** c'est loin d'être aussi bon que...; **more ~ 30 than 25** plutôt 30 que 25; **~ enough, as ~ as not, very ~** probablement.

4 *conj (*: as)* comme. **he did it ~ I did** il l'a fait comme moi.

5 *n:* **did you ever see the ~ of it?** a-t-on jamais vu chose pareille?; **oranges, lemons and the ~** *or* **and such ~** des oranges, des citrons et autres fruits de ce genre; **the ~ of which we'll never see again** comme on n'en reverra plus jamais; **his ~** son pareil; **the ~s of him *** des gens comme lui.

◆ **like-minded** *adj* de même opinion. ◆ **liken** *vt* comparer (*to* à). ◆ **likeness** *n* (**a**) *(resemblance)* ressemblance *f* (*to* avec; *between* entre); **a family ~ness** un air de famille marqué; **it is a good ~ness** c'est très ressemblant; (**b**) *(appearance)* forme *f;* **in the ~ness of** sous la forme de. ◆ **likewise** *adv (similarly)* de même; *(also)* aussi; *(moreover)* de plus; **to do ~wise** en faire autant.

like[2] [laɪk] **1** *vt* (**a**) *person, thing, activity* aimer (bien). **I ~ him** *(of relative, friend)* je l'aime bien; *(of acquaintance, colleague etc)* il me plaît; **I ~ that hat** j'aime bien ce chapeau, ce chapeau me plaît; **which do you ~ best?** lequel préfères-tu?; **this plant doesn't ~ sunlight** cette plante ne se plaît pas à la lumière du soleil; **to ~ doing** *or* **to do sth** aimer (bien) faire qch; **I ~ people to be punctual** j'aime (bien) que les gens soient à l'heure; *(iro)* **well, I ~ that! *** ah ça, par exemple!; **how do you ~ him?** comment le trouvez-vous?; **how do you ~ it here?** vous vous plaisez ici?; **whether he ~s it or not** que cela lui plaise ou non.

(**b**) *(want)* aimer (bien), vouloir (*to do* faire, *sb to do* que qn fasse). **I should ~ to go home** j'aimerais (bien) *or* je voudrais (bien) rentrer chez moi ; **I didn't ~ to disturb you** je ne voulais pas vous déranger; **I thought of asking him but I didn't ~ to** j'ai bien pensé à le lui demander mais je n'ai pas osé; **would you ~ a drink?** voulez-vous boire qch?; **I would ~ you to speak to him** je voudrais que tu lui parles *(subj);* **how would you ~ to go to Paris?** est-ce que cela te plairait d'aller à Paris?; **I can do it when I ~** je peux le faire quand je veux; **whenever you ~** quand vous voudrez; **you can do as you ~** vous pouvez faire comme vous voulez; **if you ~** si vous voulez; **she can do what she ~s with him** elle fait tout ce qu'elle veut de lui.

2 *n:* **~s** goûts *mpl,* préférences *fpl;* **all my ~s and dislikes** tout ce que j'aime et tout ce que je n'aime pas.

◆ **likeable** *adj* sympathique, agréable. ◆ **liking** *n (for person)* sympathie *f (for* pour); *(for thing)* goût *m (for* pour); **to take a liking to sb** se prendre d'amitié pour qn; **to take a liking to (doing) sth** se mettre à aimer (faire) qch; **to have a liking for sb/sth** aimer bien qn/qch; **to your liking** à votre goût.

likely ['laɪklɪ] **1** *adj* (**a**) *happening, outcome* probable; *explanation, excuse* plausible. **which is the likeliest time to find him at home?** à quelle heure a-t-on le plus de chances de le trouver chez lui?; **a ~ place for mushrooms** un bon endroit pour les champignons; **the likeliest place** le meilleur endroit; *(iro)* **a ~ story!** comme si j'allais croire ça!; **the most ~ candidates** les candidats qui ont le plus de chances de réussir; **it is ~ that** il est probable que + *fut indic,* il y a des chances pour que + *subj;* **it is not ~ that** il est peu probable que + *subj,* il y a peu de chances que + *subj;* **it is very ~ that** il y a de grandes chances que + *subj* ; **it's hardly ~ that** il n'est guère probable que + *subj;* **is it ~ that he would forget?** risque-t-il d'oublier? (**b**) *(probable: gen)* **he/it is ~ to...** il est bien possible qu'il/que cela... + *subj; (of person: good outcome)* **to be ~ to win** avoir de fortes chances de gagner; *(bad outcome)* **to be ~ to refuse** risquer de refuser; **it is ~ to improve** il y a de fortes chances que cela s'améliore *(subj);* **it is ~ to break** cela risque de se casser; **she is ~ to arrive at any time** elle va probablement arriver *or* elle risque d'arriver d'une minute à l'autre; **she is not ~ to come** il est peu probable *or* il y a peu de chances qu'elle vienne; **the man most ~ to succeed** l'homme qui a le plus de chances de réussir.

2 *adv* probablement. **very** *or* **most ~** très probablement; **as ~ as not** sûrement, probablement; **are you going? — not ~!** tu y vas? — pas de danger! *; **I expect he'll let me off with a warning —** *(iro)* **not ~!** je pense qu'il me laissera m'en tirer avec un avertissement — tu crois ça!

◆ **likelihood** *n* probabilité *f*, chance *f*; **there is little likelihood of his coming** *or* **that he will come** il y a peu de chances *or* il est peu probable qu'il vienne; **there is a strong likelihood of his coming** *or* **that he will come** il y a de fortes chances pour qu'il vienne, il est très probable qu'il viendra; **there is no likelihood of that** cela ne risque pas d'arriver; **in all likelihood** selon toute probabilité.

lilac ['laɪlək] **1** *n* lilas *m*. **2** *adj (colour)* lilas *inv*.

Lilo ['laɪˌləʊ] *n* ® matelas *m* pneumatique.

lilt [lɪlt] *n [song]* rythme *m*; *[voice]* cadence *f*.

lily ['lɪlɪ] *n* lis *m*. ~ **of the valley** muguet *m*.

Lima ['liːmə] *n* Lima.

limb [lɪm] *n (gen)* membre *m*; *[tree]* grosse branche *f*. **to tear** ~ **from** ~ mettre en pièces; *(fig)* **out on a** ~ *(isolated)* isolé; *(vulnerable)* dans une situation délicate.

limber ['lɪmbəʳ] *adj* souple. ◆ **limber up** *vi (Sport etc)* faire des exercices d'assouplissement.

lime¹ [laɪm] *n (Chem)* chaux *f*. ◆ **limestone** *n* pierre *f* à chaux.

lime² [laɪm] *n* citron *m* vert.

lime³ [laɪm] *n (tree)* tilleul *m*.

limelight ['laɪmlaɪt] *n*: **in the** ~ *(Theat)* sous les feux de la rampe; *(fig)* en vedette.

limerick ['lɪmərɪk] *n* petit poème *m* humoristique.

limit ['lɪmɪt] **1** *n (gen)* limite *f*; *(restriction on amount, number etc)* limitation *f*. **it is true within** ~**s** c'est vrai dans une certaine limite *or* mesure; **weight/ speed** ~ limitation de poids/de vitesse; *(US)* **off** ~**s** d'accès interdit; **there is a** ~ **to my patience** ma patience a des limites *or* des bornes; **there are** ~**s!** * il y a une limite à tout!; **there is no** ~ **on the amount** la quantité n'est pas limitée; **there is a** ~ **to what one can do** il y a une limite à ce qu'on peut faire; **that's the** ~**!** * ça dépasse les bornes!
2 *vt* limiter (*to* à). **to** ~ **o.s. to (doing) sth** se borner à (faire) qch; **to** ~ **o.s. to 10 cigarettes** se limiter à 10 cigarettes; **that plant is** ~**ed to Spain** cette plante ne se trouve qu'en Espagne; **our reorganization plans are** ~**ed to Africa** nos projets de réorganisation se limitent à l'Afrique.
◆ **limitation** *n* limitation *f*, restriction *f*; **he has/ knows his** ~**ations** il a/connaît ses limites. ◆ **limited** *adj (gen)* restreint, limité; *edition* à tirage limité; *(pej) intelligence, person* borné; **to a** ~**ed extent** jusqu'à un certain point; **we are** ~**ed in what we can do** nous sommes limités dans ce que nous pouvons faire; **Smith and Sons L**~**ed** *(abbr* **Ltd***)* ≃ Smith et fils, Société anonyme *(abbr* S.A.*)*; ~**ed (liability) company** société *f* à responsabilité limitée. ◆ **limiting** *adj* restrictif. ◆ **limitless** *adj* illimité.

limo * ['lɪməʊ] *n (US)*, **limousine** *n* limousine *f*.

limp¹ [lɪmp] *adj (gen)* mou (*f* molle); *person* ramolli; *flesh, skin, body* flasque; *dress, hat* avachi. *[book]* ~ **cover(s)** reliure *f* souple; **let your arm go** ~ décontractez votre bras. ◆ **limply** *adv* mollement. ◆ **limpness** *n* mollesse *f*.

limp² [lɪmp] **1** *vi* boiter. **to** ~ **in/out** *etc* entrer/ sortir *etc* en boitant; **the plane** ~**ed home** l'avion a regagné sa base tant bien que mal. **2** *n* claudication *f*. **to have a** ~ boiter.

limpet ['lɪmpɪt] *n* patelle *f*. **to stick to sth like a** ~ s'accrocher à qch comme une moule au rocher.

limpid ['lɪmpɪd] *adj (lit, fig)* limpide.

line¹ [laɪn] **1** *n* (**a**) *(mark: gen)* ligne *f*; *(pen stroke)* trait *m*; *(wrinkle)* ride *f*; *(boundary)* frontière *f*. **to draw a** ~ **under sth** tirer un trait sous qch; **to put a** ~ **through sth** barrer qch; *(descent)* **in direct** ~ **from** en droite ligne de; **he comes from a long** ~ **of artists** il vient d'une longue lignée d'artistes; *(Bridge)* **above/below the** ~ en points d'honneur/ de marche.
(**b**) *(rope)* corde *f*; *(wire)* fil *m*; *(Fishing)* ligne *f*; *(diver's; clothes* ~*)* corde. **a** ~ **of washing** du linge étendu sur une corde.
(**c**) *(pipe)* tuyau *m*; *(larger, for oil, gas etc)* pipeline *m*; *(Elec: cable)* ligne *f*. *(Comput)* **on** ~ en ligne (*to* avec).
(**d**) *(Telec)* ligne *f*. **the** ~**'s gone dead** *(cut off)* on nous a coupés; (*no dialling tone*) il n'y a plus de tonalité; **Mr Smith is on the** ~ (c'est) M. Smith au téléphone; **he's on the** ~ **to the manager** il téléphone au directeur.
(**e**) *[print, writing]* ligne *f*; *[poem]* vers *m*; *(*: letter)* mot *m*. *(fig)* **to read between the** ~**s** lire entre les lignes; *(in dictation)* **new** ~ à la ligne; **one of the best** ~**s in 'Hamlet'** l'un des meilleurs vers de 'Hamlet'; *(Theat)* **to learn one's** ~**s** apprendre son texte; **drop me a** ~ envoyez-moi un mot.
(**f**) *(row) [trees, parked cars]* rangée *f*; *[traffic etc]* file *f*; *[hills]* chaîne *f*; *[people] (side by side)* rang *m*, rangée; *(behind one another)* file; *(esp US: queue)* queue *f*. *(US)* **to stand in** ~ faire la queue; **they were standing in a** ~ ils étaient alignés; **he got into** ~ *(beside others)* il s'est mis dans le rang; *(behind others)* il s'est mis dans la file; *(fig)* **to bring sb into** ~ mettre qn au pas; *(fig)* **to come** *or* **fall into** ~ se conformer (*with sth* à qch), tomber d'accord (*with sb* avec qn); *(fig)* **he stepped out of** ~ il a refusé de se conformer; *(fig)* **all along the** ~ sur toute la ligne.
(**g**) *(direction)* ligne *f*, direction *f*. ~ **of fire** ligne de tir; **right in the** ~ **of fire** en plein champ de tir; **to take the** ~ **of least resistance** choisir la solution de facilité; **in the** ~ **of duty** dans l'exercice de ses fonctions; ~ **of attack** *(Mil)* plan *m* d'attaque; *(fig)* plan d'action; ~ **of research** ligne de recherches; **what's your** ~ **of business?** que faites-vous (dans la vie)?; **it's not my** ~ *(not my speciality)* ce n'est pas dans mes cordes; *(not to my taste)* ce n'est pas mon genre; **to take a strong** ~ **on** adopter une attitude ferme sur; **in** ~ **with** en accord avec, conforme à; **he's in** ~ **for the job** on pense à lui pour le poste; **we are all thinking along the same** ~**s** nous pensons tous de la même façon; **your essay is more or less along the same** ~**s** votre dissertation suit plus ou moins le même plan; **sth along those** ~**s** qch dans ce genre-là; **on the right** ~**s** sur la bonne voie.
(**h**) (*) *(information)* renseignement *m* (*on sth* sur qch); *(clue)* tuyau * *m* (*on sth* pour qch). **we've got a** ~ **on where he's gone to** nous croyons savoir où il est allé.
(**i**) *(shipping company)* compagnie *f*; *(route)* ligne *f*; *(Rail; also Underground)* ligne; *(track)* voie *f*. **the Brighton** ~ la ligne de Brighton; **the** ~ **was blocked** la voie était bloquée.
(**j**) *(Mil)* ligne *f*. *(Mil, fig)* **in the front** ~ en première ligne; **behind the enemy** ~**s** derrière les lignes ennemies; ~ **of battle** ligne de combat.
(**k**) *(Comm)* article *m*. **a new** ~ une nouveauté.
2 *adj*: ~ **drawing** dessin *m* (au trait).
3 *vt paper* régler.
◆ **line up 1** *vi (stand in row)* s'aligner; *(in queue)* faire la queue. **2** *vt sep people, objects* aligner. **we must** ~ **up a chairman** il faut que nous trouvions *(subj)* un président; **have you got sb** ~**d up?** avez-vous qn en vue?; **I wonder what he's got** ~**d up for us** je me demande ce qu'il nous prépare.
◆ **lined¹** *adj paper* réglé; *face* ridé. ◆ **linesman** *n (Tennis)* juge *m* de ligne; *(Ftbl)* juge de touche.
◆ **line-up** *n (row: of people etc)* file *f*; *(Ftbl etc)* (composition *f* de l')équipe *f*; *(Pol: of powers, countries)* front *m*; *(fig: Pol etc)* **the new** ~**-up** la nouvelle composition du Parlement (*or* du Congrès *etc*).

line² [laɪn] *vt clothes* doubler (*with* de); *(Tech)* revêtir. *(fig)* **to** ~ **one's pockets** se garnir *or* se remplir les poches; **streets** ~**d with trees/people** rues bordées d'arbres/d'une haie de spectateurs; **crowds**

~d the route une foule faisait la haie tout le long du parcours; **walls ~d with books** murs couverts de livres. ◆ **lined²** *adj* doublé. ◆ **lining** *n* doublure *f*; *(Tech)* revêtement *m*; *[brakes]* garniture *f*.

linen ['lɪnɪn] **1** *n (material)* (toile *f* de) lin *m*; *(sheets, tablecloths, underwear)* linge *m*. **dirty ~** linge sale. **2** *adj sheet* de fil; *suit, thread* de lin; *cupboard* à linge. **~ basket** panier *m* à linge.

liner ['laɪnəʳ] *n* (**a**) *(ship)* paquebot *m* (de grande ligne); *(plane)* avion *m* (de ligne). (**b**) **dustbin ~** sac *m* à poubelle.

ling¹ [lɪŋ] *n (Bot)* brande *f*.

ling² [lɪŋ] *n (sea fish)* morue *f* longue; *(freshwater fish)* lotte *f* de rivière.

linger ['lɪŋgəʳ] *vi [person] (wait)* s'attarder; *(take one's time)* prendre son temps; *(dawdle)* traîner; *[smell, pain, tradition, memory]* persister; *[doubt]* subsister. **after the accident he ~ed (on) for several months** après l'accident il a traîné quelques mois avant de mourir; **he always ~s behind everyone else** il est toujours à la traîne; **to ~ over a meal** manger sans se presser; **to ~ on a subject** s'attarder sur un sujet. ◆ **lingering** *adj look* insistant; *doubt* qui subsiste (encore); *hope* faible; *death* lent.

lingerie ['lænʒəriː] *n* lingerie *f*.

lingo * ['lɪŋgəʊ] *n (pej) (foreign language etc)* baragouin *m*; *(jargon)* jargon *m (pej)*.

lingua franca ['lɪŋgwə'fræŋkə] *n* langue *f* véhiculaire.

linguist ['lɪŋgwɪst] *n* linguiste *mf*. **I'm no ~** je ne suis pas doué pour les langues. ◆ **linguistic** *adj* linguistique. ◆ **linguistics 1** *nsg* linguistique *f*; **2** *adj (gen)* de linguistique; *student* en linguistique.

liniment ['lɪnɪmənt] *n* liniment *m*.

link [lɪŋk] **1** *n [chain]* maillon *m*; *(connection)* lien *m*. **rail ~** liaison *f* ferroviaire; **there must be a ~ between...** il doit y avoir un lien *or* un rapport entre...; **he broke off all ~s with them** il a cessé toutes relations avec eux. **2** *vt* (**a**) *(connect)* relier; *(fig)* lier. **~ed by rail** relié par chemin de fer; *(fig)* **closely ~ed to** étroitement lié à. (**b**) *(join: ~* **together***)* lier. **to ~ arms** se donner le bras. ◆ **link up 1** *vi [persons, roads]* se rejoindre; *[firms, organizations etc]* s'associer; *[spacecraft]* opérer l'arrimage. **to ~ up with sb** rejoindre qn. **2** *vt sep (Rad, Telec, TV)* assurer la liaison entre. ◆ **linkman** *n (TV, Rad)* présentateur-réalisateur *m*. ◆ **link-up** *n (gen)* lien *m*; *(Rad, TV: connection)* liaison *f*; *(Rad, TV: programme)* émission *f* duplex; *(Space)* jonction *f*.

linoleum [lɪ'nəʊlɪəm] *n* linoléum *m*, lino *m*.

linseed ['lɪnsiːd] *n*: **~ oil** huile *f* de lin.

lint [lɪnt] *n* (**a**) *(Med)* tissu *m* ouaté. **piece of ~** compresse *f*. (**b**) *(US: fluff)* peluches *fpl*.

lintel ['lɪntl] *n* linteau *m*.

lion ['laɪən] **1** *n* lion *m*; *(fig: person)* célébrité *f*. *(fig)* **to take the ~'s share** se tailler la part du lion; *(fig)* **to put one's head in the ~'s mouth** se jeter dans la gueule du loup. **2** *adj*: **~ cub** lionceau *m*. ◆ **lioness** *n* lionne *f*. ◆ **lion-hearted** *adj* d'un courage de lion. ◆ **lionize** *vt* fêter comme une célébrité. ◆ **lion-tamer** *n* dompteur *m*, -euse *f* de lions.

lip [lɪp] **1** *n (Anat) (gen)* lèvre *f*; *[dog]* babine *f*; *[jug]* bec *m*; *[cup]* rebord *m*; *[crater, wound]* bord *m*; *(*: insolence)* culot * *m*. **2** *adj*: **he pays ~ service to socialism but...** il prétend être socialiste mais...; **that was merely ~ service on his part** il ne l'a dit que pour la forme. ◆ **lipread** *vti* lire sur les lèvres. ◆ **lip-reading** *n* lecture *f* sur les lèvres. ◆ **lipstick** *n* rouge *m* à lèvres.

liquefy ['lɪkwɪfaɪ] **1** *vt* liquéfier. **2** *vi* se liquéfier. ◆ **liquefaction** *n* liquéfaction *f*.

liqueur [lɪ'kjʊəʳ] *n* liqueur *f*.

liquid ['lɪkwɪd] **1** *adj substance, diet* liquide; *container* pour les liquides; *eyes, voice* limpide. *(Pharm)* **~ paraffin** huile *f* de paraffine; **~ petroleum gas** gaz *m* de pétrole liquéfié; **~ crystal display** affichage *m* à cristaux liquides; *(Fin)* **~ assets** liquidités *fpl*. **2** *n (fluid)* liquide *m*. ◆ **liquidate** *vt* liquider. ◆ **liquidation** *n* liquidation *f*; **to go into ~ation** déposer son bilan. ◆ **liquidize** *vt* liquéfier; *(Culin)* passer au mixeur. ◆ **liquidizer** *n (Culin)* mixeur *m*.

liquor ['lɪkəʳ] *n (alcohol)* spiritueux *m*; *(Culin)* liquide *m*. *(US)* **~ store** marchand *m* de vins et spiritueux.

liquorice ['lɪkərɪs] *n (plant)* réglisse *f*; *(sweet)* réglisse *m*.

lira, *pl* **lire** ['lɪərə, 'lɪərɪ] *n* lire *f*.

Lisbon ['lɪzbən] *n* Lisbonne.

lisp [lɪsp] **1** *vi* zézayer. **2** *vt* dire en zézayant. **3** *n* zézaiement *m*. **with a ~** en zézayant.

list¹ [lɪst] **1** *n* liste *f*; *(Comm)* catalogue *m*. **at the top/bottom of the ~** en tête/en fin de liste. **2** *adj*: **~ price** prix *m* de catalogue. **3** *vt (make ~ of)* faire *or* dresser la liste de; *(produce list of, also Comput)* lister; *(enumerate)* énumérer; *(classify)* classer. **your name isn't ~ed** votre nom n'est pas inscrit (sur la liste); **~ed building** monument *m* classé. ◆ **listing** *n (gen, Comput)* listage *m*.

list² [lɪst] *vi [ship]* gîter (*20°* de 20°).

listen ['lɪsn] *vi* écouter. **to ~ to sb/sth** écouter qn/qch; *(Rad)* **to ~ in** être à l'écoute; **to ~ for** *voice* guetter; *footsteps* guetter le bruit de; **to ~ to reason** entendre raison. ◆ **listener** *n (to speaker, radio etc)* auditeur *m*, -trice *f*; **she's a good ~er** elle sait écouter (avec patience et sympathie).

listeria [lɪs'tɪərɪə] *n (bacteria)* listeria *f; (illness)* listériose *f*.

listless ['lɪstlɪs] *adj (gen)* indolent, sans énergie; *(uninterested)* indifférent. ◆ **listlessly** *adv* avec indolence, sans énergie; avec indifférence. ◆ **listlessness** *n* indolence *f*, manque *m* d'énergie; indifférence *f*.

lit [lɪt] *pret, ptp of* **light¹**.

litany ['lɪtənɪ] *n* litanie *f*.

liter ['liːtəʳ] *n (US)* = **litre.**

literacy ['lɪt(ə)rəsɪ] **1** *n* fait *m* de savoir lire et écrire. **2** *adj*: **~ campaign** campagne *f* d'alphabétisation.

literal ['lɪt(ə)r(ə)l] *adj translation* littéral; *interpretation* au pied de la lettre; *meaning* littéral, propre; *person (also* **~-minded***)* prosaïque. ◆ **literally** *adv (gen)* littéralement; *interpret* au pied de la lettre.

literary ['lɪt(ə)rərɪ] *adj (gen)* littéraire. **a ~ man** un homme de lettres.

literate ['lɪt(ə)rɪt] *adj* qui sait lire et écrire.

literature ['lɪt(ə)rɪtʃəʳ] *n* littérature *f*; *(brochures etc)* documentation *f*.

lithe [laɪð] *adj person* agile; *body* souple.

lithograph ['lɪθəʊ'grɑːf] *n* lithographie *f (estampe)*. ◆ **lithographer** *n* lithographe *mf*. ◆ **lithography** *n* lithographie *f (procédé)*.

Lithuania [lɪθjuː'eɪn(ɪ)ə] *n* Lituanie *f*.

litigation [ˌlɪtɪ'geɪʃ(ə)n] *n* litige *m*.

litmus ['lɪtməs] *n*: **~ paper** papier *m* de tournesol; **~ test** *(lit)* réaction *f* au (papier de) tournesol; *(fig)* test *m* décisif.

litre ['liːtəʳ] *n* litre *m*.

litter ['lɪtəʳ] **1** *n* (**a**) *(rubbish)* détritus *mpl*; *(dirtier)* ordures *fpl*; *(papers)* vieux papiers *mpl*. **to leave ~** jeter des détritus *or* des papiers; **a ~ of books** un fouillis de livres. (**b**) *[puppies etc]* portée *f*. (**c**) *(bed)* litière *f*; *(cat ~)* litière *f (pour chats)*. **2** *vt [person] countryside* laisser des détritus dans; *[rubbish, papers] street, floor etc* joncher; *desk* couvrir. **there were books ~ed about the room** il y avait des livres qui traînaient dans toute la pièce.

◆ **litter basket** *or* ◆ **litter bin** *n* boîte *f* à ordures. ◆ **litterbug** *or* ◆ **litter-lout** *n personne qui jette des détritus par terre.*

little[1] ['lɪtl] *adj (gen)* petit; *stick, piece of string* petit, court; *period, holiday, visit* court, petit; *voice, noise* petit, faible; *smell* petit, léger; *(small-scale) shopkeeper* petit. ~ **finger** petit doigt; **a tiny ~ baby** un tout petit bébé; **poor ~ thing!** pauvre petit(e)! ◆ **littleness** *n* petitesse *f.*

little[2] ['lɪtl] *comp* **less,** *superl* **least 1** *adj, pron* peu (de). ~ **money** peu d'argent; **he reads** ~ il lit peu, il ne lit guère; **he did ~ to help** il n'a pas fait grand-chose pour aider; **he did very** ~ il a fait très peu de chose; **there was ~ one could do** il n'y avait pas grand-chose à faire; **that has very ~ to do with it!** ça n'a pas grand-chose à voir (avec ça)!; ~ **or nothing** rien ou presque rien; **to make ~ of sth** *(belittle)* rabaisser qch; *(fail to understand)* ne pas comprendre grand-chose à qch; **as ~ as possible** le moins possible; **you could pay as ~ as 20 francs for that** vous pourriez ne payer que 20 F pour cela; **very** ~ très peu (de); **so** ~ si peu (de); **too** ~ trop peu (de); **a** ~ un peu (de); **the** ~ le peu (de); **a ~ milk** un peu de lait; **give me a** ~ donne-m'en un peu; ~ **by** ~ petit à petit, peu à peu; **what ~ I could** le peu que j'ai pu; **for a ~ (time** *or* **while)** un petit moment. **2** *adv* (**a**) *(slightly)* **a** ~ un peu; **a ~ big** un peu grand; **he was not a ~ surprised** il n'a pas été peu surpris; **a ~ more/less cream** un peu plus/moins de crème; **a ~ more** encore un peu. (**b**) *(not much)* **it's ~ better** ça n'est guère mieux; ~ **more than a month ago** il y a à peine plus d'un mois; ~ **did he know that...** il était bien loin de se douter que...; ~ **do you know!** si seulement vous saviez!; ~**-known** peu connu; **I like him as ~ as you do** je ne l'aime guère plus que vous; **as ~ as before** aussi peu qu'auparavant. (**c**) *(rarely) happen* rarement, peu souvent.

liturgy ['lɪtədʒɪ] *n* liturgie *f.*

live[1] [lɪv] **1** *vi* (**a**) *(exist)* vivre. **he was still living when...** il était encore en vie quand...; **as long as I** ~ tant que je vivrai; **to ~ to be 90** vivre jusqu'à 90 ans; **she'll never ~ to see it** elle ne vivra pas assez longtemps pour le voir; **she has only 6 months to** ~ il ne lui reste plus que 6 mois à vivre; **long ~ the King!** vive le roi!; **the doctor said she would** ~ le docteur a dit qu'elle s'en sortirait; *(iro)* **you'll ~!** * tu n'en mourras pas!; **she has ~d through two wars** elle a vu deux guerres; **the difficult years he has ~d through** les années difficiles qu'il a vécues; **he can't ~ through the winter** il ne passera pas l'hiver; **to ~ well** *or* **like a lord** vivre sur un grand pied; **they ~d happily ever after** après cela ils vécurent toujours heureux; *(in fairy tales)* ils furent heureux et ils eurent beaucoup d'enfants; **to ~ by journalism** gagner sa vie comme journaliste; **she ~s for her children/for the day when...** elle ne vit que pour ses enfants/pour le jour où...; **I've got nothing left to ~ for** je n'ai plus de raison de vivre; **you must learn to ~ with it** il faut que tu t'y fasses; **he will have to ~ with that awful memory** il lui faudra vivre avec cet horrible souvenir; ~ **and let** ~ il faut se montrer tolérant; **(we) ~ and learn** on apprend à tout âge. (**b**) *(reside)* vivre, habiter. **to ~ in London** habiter (à) *or* vivre à Londres; **to ~ in a flat** habiter un appartement; **where do you ~?** où habitez-vous?; **she ~s in the rue de la Paix** elle habite rue de la Paix; **this house isn't fit to ~ in** cette maison n'est pas habitable; **he's not an easy person to ~ with** il n'est pas facile à vivre; **he ~s with his mother** il vit *or* habite avec sa mère; *(in her house)* il vit chez sa mère; **he's living with Anne** *(as man and wife)* il vit avec Anne.
2 *vt*: **to ~ a healthy life** mener une vie saine; **to ~ a life of luxury** vivre dans le luxe; **to ~ one's faith** vivre pleinement sa foi; *(Theat, fig)* **to ~ the part** entrer dans la peau du personnage.
◆ **live down** *vt sep disgrace* faire oublier (avec le temps). ◆ **live in** *vi [servant]* être logé et nourri; *[student, doctor]* être interne. ◆ **live off** *vt fus rice etc* vivre de; *one's parents* vivre aux dépens de. **to ~ off the land** vivre du pays. ◆ **live on 1** *vi* survivre. **2** *vt fus rice, one's salary* vivre de. **you can't ~ on air** * on ne vit pas de l'air du temps; **to ~ on £3,000 a year** vivre avec 3 000 livres par an; **just enough to ~ on** juste de quoi vivre; **what does he ~ on?** de quoi est-ce qu'il vit? ◆ **live out** *vi [servant]* ne pas être logé; *[student, doctor]* être externe. ◆ **live together** *vi* vivre ensemble. ◆ **live up** *vt sep*: **to ~ it up** * *(in luxury)* mener la grand vie; *(have fun)* mener une vie de bâton de chaise. ◆ **live up to** *vt fus one's principles* vivre en accord avec; *one's promises* être fidèle à; *sb's hopes, a challenge* se montrer à la hauteur de; *praise, reputation* se montrer digne de. **it didn't ~ up to expectations** cela n'a pas été ce qu'on avait espéré. ◆ **livable** *adj climate, life* supportable; *house* habitable; **he is not livable-with** * il est invivable *. ◆ **live-in** *adj housekeeper* à demeure; ~**-in lover** petit(e) ami(e) *m(f)* avec qui on vit; ~**-in partner** concubin(e) *m(f)*. ◆ **livelihood** *n* moyens *mpl* d'existence, gagne-pain *m inv*; **their principal ~lihood is...** leur principale source de revenu est... ◆ **livelong** *adj*: **all the ~long day** toute la journée.

live[2] [laɪv] **1** *adj* (**a**) *person etc (alive)* vivant; *(lively)* dynamique; *issue, problem* brûlant; *broadcast* en direct. ~ **bait** vif *m (appât)*; **a real ~ spaceman** un astronaute en chair et en os; **performed before a ~ audience** joué en public. (**b**) *coal* ardent; *ammunition, shell, cartridge* de combat; *(unexploded)* non explosé. *(Elec)* **that's ~!** c'est branché!; ~ **rail** rail *m* conducteur; ~ **wire** fil *m* sous tension; *(fig)* **he's a ~ wire** * il a un dynamisme fou; **the drier was** ~ le séchoir était mal isolé (et dangereux). **2** *adv broadcast* en direct. ◆ **livestock** *n* bétail *m.*

lively ['laɪvlɪ] *adj person, character, party, discussion* plein d'entrain, animé; *imagination, interest, colour, speed* vif; *description, account, style* vivant; *expression, example, argument* frappant, vigoureux; *campaign* vigoureux; *tune* entraînant, gai; *evening, week* mouvementé. **things are getting** ~ ça commence à s'animer; *(pej)* ça commence à barder *. ◆ **liveliness** *n* entrain *m*; animation *f*; vivacité *f*; vigueur *f*; gaieté *f.* ◆ **liven up 1** *vt sep person, room* égayer; *evening, discussion etc* animer ; **2** *vi* s'animer.

liver ['lɪvəʳ] **1** *n* foie *m.* **2** *adj disease, pâté* de foie; *sausage* au pâté de foie. ◆ **liverish** * *adj (bilious)* qui a mal au foie.

livery ['lɪvərɪ] **1** *n* livrée *f.* **2** *adj*: ~ **stable** écurie *f* (de louage *etc*).

livid ['lɪvɪd] *adj* (**a**) *(in colour) complexion* livide; *sky* de plomb. (**b**) *(furious)* furieux, furibond.

living ['lɪvɪŋ] **1** *adj* (**a**) *(alive: gen)* vivant; *person* vivant, en vie. ~ **or dead** mort ou vif; **the greatest ~ pianist** le plus grand pianiste actuellement vivant; **there wasn't a ~ soul** il n'y avait pas âme qui vive; **a ~ skeleton** un cadavre ambulant; **within ~ memory** de mémoire d'homme. (**b**) *conditions* de vie. ~ **expenses** frais *mpl* de subsistance; ~ **quarters** logement *m*; ~ **room** salle *f* de séjour; ~ **space** espace *m* vital; ~ **standards** niveau *m* de vie; **a ~ wage** un salaire permettant de vivre décemment. **2** *n* vie *f.* **to earn** *or* **make a** ~ gagner sa vie; **to work for a** ~ travailler pour vivre; **gracious** ~ vie élégante; *(pl: people)* **the** ~ les vivants *mpl.*

lizard ['lɪzəd] **1** *n* lézard *m.* **2** *adj bag etc* en lézard.

llama ['lɑːmə] *n* lama *m (Zool).*

load [ləʊd] **1** *n* (**a**) *(gen, Constr, Elec, Tech)* charge *f*; *[lorry]* chargement *m*; *[ship]* cargaison *f*; *(weight, pressure)* poids *m*; *(fig) (burden)* fardeau *m*, charge; *(mental strain)* poids. **to take a ~ off sb's mind** débarrasser qn de ce qui lui pèse *(fig)*; **that's a ~ off my mind!** quel soulagement! (**b**) *(fig)* **a ~ of ***, **~s of *** des tas de *, énormément de, des masses de *; **we've got ~s of time *** on a largement le temps.
2 *vt (gen: often ~* **down** *or* **up**) charger (*with* de); *(Comput)* charger. **she was ~ed (down) with shopping** elle pliait sous le poids de ses achats; **pockets ~ed with sweets** poches bourrées de bonbons; **to ~ sb (down) with gifts** couvrir qn de cadeaux; **~ed with cares/sorrow** accablé de soucis/chagrin; *[ship etc]* **to ~ coal** *etc* charger du charbon *etc*.
3 *vi* (**~ up**) *[lorry]* charger, prendre un chargement; *[ship]* embarquer une cargaison; *[camera, gun]* se charger.
◆ **loaded** *adj* (**a**) *(gen)* chargé; *dice* pipé; *cane* plombé; *word, question* insidieux; *(fig)* **the dice were ~ed against him** les cartes étaient truquées à son désavantage; (**b**) *(‡: rich)* bourré de fric ‡. ◆ **loader** *n* chargeur *m*. ◆ **loading 1** *n* chargement *m*; **2** *adj*: **~ing bay** aire *f* de chargement.

loaf[1], *pl* **loaves** [ləʊf, ləʊvz] *n* (**a**) *(~ of bread)* pain *m*. **half a ~ is better than no bread** mieux vaut peu que pas du tout. (**b**) **sugar ~** pain *m* de sucre.

loaf[2] [ləʊf] *vi* (**~ about** *or* **~ around**) traînasser.

loam [ləʊm] *n* terreau *m*.

loan [ləʊn] **1** *n (lent)* prêt *m*; *(borrowed)* emprunt *m*. **on ~** *object* prêté (*from* par; *to* à); *employee* détaché (*from* de; *to* à); *library book* sorti; **I have it on ~** je l'ai emprunté; **to ask for the ~ of sth** demander à emprunter qch; **to give sb the ~ of sth** prêter qch à qn. **2** *vt* prêter (*to* à). **3** *adj capital, word* d'emprunt.

loath [ləʊθ] *adj*: **to be ~ to do** ne pas être disposé à faire; *(stronger)* répugner à faire.

loathe [ləʊð] *vt* détester (*doing* faire; *sb's doing* que qn fasse). ◆ **loathing** *n* dégoût *m*. ◆ **loathsome** *adj* détestable, répugnant.

lobby ['lɒbɪ] **1** *n* (**a**) vestibule *m*. (**b**) *(Parl) (for public)* ≃ salle *f* des pas perdus; *(division ~)* vestibule *(où l'on vote)*; *(pressure group)* groupe *m* de pression, lobby *m*. **2** *adj*: **~ correspondent** journaliste *mf* parlementaire. **3** *vt (Parl, also gen)* faire pression sur; *(esp US) cause* faire pression en faveur de. **4** *vi (Pol)* faire pression (*for sth* pour obtenir qch).

lobe [ləʊb] *n* lobe *m*.

lobster ['lɒbstəʳ] *n* homard *m*. **~ pot** casier *m* à homards.

local ['ləʊk(ə)l] **1** *adj (gen)* local; *shops, library* du *or* de quartier; *wine, speciality* du pays, local; *pain* localisé. **~ anaesthetic** anesthésie *f* locale; *(Telec)* **a ~ call** une communication urbaine; **what is the ~ situation?** quelle est la situation *(here)* ici? *or (there)* là-bas?; **he's a ~ man** il est du pays *or* du coin *; **the ~ doctor** le médecin du quartier (*or* du village *etc*); **~ colour** couleur *f* locale; **~ authority** *(n)* autorité *f* (locale); *(adj)* des autorités locales; **~ education authority** ≃ office *m* régional de l'enseignement; **~ government** administration *f* locale; **~ government elections** élections *fpl* municipales; **~ government officer** *or* **official** administrateur *m* local, ≃ fonctionnaire *mf*. **2** *n* (**a**) *(*: person)* personne *f* du pays. **the ~s** les gens *mpl* du pays. (**b**) *(Brit *: pub)* café *m* du coin.
◆ **locality** *n (neighbourhood)* environs *mpl*; *(district)* région *f*; *(place, position)* lieu *m*, endroit *m*. ◆ **localize** *vt* localiser. ◆ **locally** *adv (in certain areas; not centrally)* localement; *(nearby)* dans les environs; *(near here)* par ici; *(out there)* là-bas; **showers ~ly** temps localement pluvieux; **~ly appointed staff** personnel recruté localement.

locate [lə(ʊ)'keɪt] *vt* (**a**) *(find) place, person, object* repérer, trouver; *noise, leak, cause* localiser. (**b**) *(situate) factory, school etc* situer. **to be ~d** être situé, se trouver; *(US: live)* être installé. ◆ **location** *n* emplacement *m*; *(Cine)* **on location** en extérieur.

loch [lɒx] *n (Scot)* lac *m*, loch *m*.

lock[1] [lɒk] **1** *n* (**a**) *(gen)* serrure *f*; *(on steering wheel)* antivol *m*. **under ~ and key** *possessions* sous clef; *prisoner* sous les verrous; *(fig)* **~, stock and barrel** en bloc. (**b**) *[canal]* écluse *f*. (**c**) *(Aut: turning)* rayon *m* de braquage. **2** *vt door, suitcase, safe* fermer à clef; *person* enfermer (*in* dans); *mechanism* bloquer. **behind ~ed doors** à huis clos; **~ed in her arms** serré dans ses bras; **~ed in a close embrace** unis dans une étreinte passionnée; **~ed in combat** aux prises. **3** *vi [door]* fermer à clef; *[wheel, steering wheel]* se bloquer. *(Space)* **to ~ on to sth** s'arrimer à qch.
◆ **lock away** *vt sep object* mettre sous clef; *criminal* mettre sous les verrous; *mental patient etc* enfermer. ◆ **lock in** *vt sep* enfermer (à l'intérieur). ◆ **lock out** *vt sep (deliberately)* mettre à la porte; *(by mistake)* enfermer dehors; *(Ind) workers* lockouter. **to ~ o.s. out of one's car** fermer la voiture en laissant les clefs à l'intérieur. ◆ **lock up 1** *vi* tout fermer (à clef). **2** *vt sep object* mettre sous clef; *house* fermer (à clef); *criminal* mettre sous les verrous; *mental patient etc* enfermer; *funds* bloquer (*in* dans).
◆ **locker** *n* casier *m*, petit placard. ◆ **locker-room 1** *n* vestiaire *m* ; **2** *adj joke* de corps de garde. ◆ **locking 1** *adj* verrouillable; *(Aut)* **~ petrol cap** bouchon *m* anti-vol *(pour réservoir)* ; **2** *n* verrouillage *m*. ◆ **lockjaw** *n* tétanos *m*. ◆ **lock keeper** *n* éclusier *m*, -ière *f*. ◆ **lockout** *n (Ind)* lock-out *m inv*. ◆ **locksmith** *n* serrurier *m*. ◆ **lock-up** *n (garage)* box *m*; *(shop)* boutique *f (sans logement)*; *(prison)* prison *f*; *(cell)* cellule *f* (provisoire).

lock[2] [lɒk] *n [hair]* mèche *f*. **~s** chevelure *f*.

locket ['lɒkɪt] *n* médaillon *m (bijou)*.

locomotion [ˌləʊkə'məʊʃ(ə)n] *n* locomotion *f*. ◆ **locomotive 1** *n (Rail)* locomotive *f* ; **2** *adj* locomotif.

locum ['ləʊkəm] *n* suppléant(e) *m(f) (de médecin etc)*.

locust ['ləʊkəst] *n* sauterelle *f*.

lodge [lɒdʒ] **1** *n (house)* pavillon *m* de gardien; *(porter's rooms)* loge *f*; *(Freemasonry)* loge. **2** *vt person, bullet* loger; *money* déposer; *statement, report* présenter (*with sb* à qn). *(Jur)* **to ~ an appeal** se pourvoir en cassation. **3** *vi [person]* être logé (*with* chez); *[bullet]* se loger. ◆ **lodger** *n (room only)* locataire *mf*; *(with meals)* pensionnaire *mf*; **to take (in) ~rs** louer des chambres; *(with meals)* prendre des pensionnaires.

lodging ['lɒdʒɪŋ] **1** *n* (**a**) *(accommodation)* logement *m*. **they gave us a night's ~** ils nous ont logés une nuit. (**b**) **~s** *(room)* chambre *f*; *(flatlet)* logement *m*; **he's in ~s** il vit en meublé; **to look for ~s** chercher une chambre meublée (*or* un logement meublé); *(with meals)* chercher à prendre pension. **2** *adj*: **~ house** pension *f*.

loft [lɒft] **1** *n* grenier *m*. **2** *vt (into air)* lancer très haut.

lofty ['lɒftɪ] *adj mountain* très haut; *feelings, aims* élevé; *(haughty)* hautain. ◆ **loftily** *adv* avec hauteur.

log[1] [lɒg] **1** *n* (**a**) *(tree trunk)* rondin *m*; *(for fire)* bûche *f*. **he lay like a ~** il ne bougeait pas plus qu'une souche. (**b**) *(~book) (Naut)* livre *m* de bord; *(Aviat)* carnet *m* de vol; *[lorry driver etc]* carnet de route; *(gen)* registre *m*. **2** *adj*: **~ cabin**

cabane *f* en rondins; ~ **fire** feu *m* de bois. **3** *vt* (**a**) *(record) (gen)* noter, consigner; *(Naut)* inscrire au livre de bord; *(Aviat)* inscrire sur le carnet de vol. (**b**) (~ **up**) *distance, speed etc* faire. **to ~ 50 mph** faire 80 km/h. ◆ **logbook** *n (Aut)* carte *f* grise *(V also* **log¹ 1b***)*. ◆ **log in** *vi (also* ~ **on***) (Comput)* entrer. ◆ **log out** *vi (also* ~ **off***) (Comput)* sortir.

log² [lɒg] *n (abbr of* **logarithm***)* log * *m*.

logarithm ['lɒgərɪθ(ə)m] *n* logarithme *m*.

loggerheads ['lɒgəhedz] *npl*: **at** ~ en désaccord complet (*with* avec).

logic ['lɒdʒɪk] *n* logique *f*. ◆ **logical** *adj* logique. ◆ **logically** *adv* logiquement. ◆ **logician** *n* logicien(ne) *m(f)*. ◆ **logistics** *n* logistique *f*.

logo ['ləʊgəʊ] *n* logo *m*.

loin [lɔɪn] **1** *n* (**a**) ~**s** reins *mpl*. (**b**) *(Culin) (gen)* filet *m*; *[veal, venison]* longe *f*; *[beef]* aloyau *m*. **2** *adj*: ~ **chop** côte *f* première; ~ **cloth** pagne *m*.

loiter ['lɔɪtəʳ] *vi* traîner; *(Police etc)* traîner d'une manière suspecte.

loll [lɒl] *vi [head, tongue]* pendre. ◆ **loll about, loll around** *vi* fainéanter. ◆ **loll back** *vi [person]* se prélasser.

lollipop ['lɒlɪpɒp] *n* sucette *f (bonbon)*.

lolly ['lɒlɪ] *n* (**a**) = **lollipop**. (**b**) (‡: *money)* fric ‡ *m*.

London ['lʌndən] **1** *n* Londres *m*. **2** *adj (gen)* londonien; *people* de Londres. ◆ **Londoner** *n* Londonien(ne) *m(f)*.

lone [ləʊn] *adj person* solitaire; *village, house* isolé; *(unique)* unique. *(fig)* **to play a ~ hand** mener une action solitaire; *(fig)* ~ **wolf** solitaire *mf*.

lonely ['ləʊnlɪ], **lonesome** ['ləʊnsəm] *adj (gen)* solitaire; *person* seul, solitaire. **to feel** ~ se sentir seul; **a small ~ figure** une petite silhouette seule *or* solitaire; ~ **hearts' club** club *m* de rencontres (pour personnes seules). ◆ **loneliness** *or* ◆ **lonesomeness** *n [person, life]* solitude *f*; *[house, road] (position)* isolement *m*; *(atmosphere)* solitude.

long¹ [lɒŋ] **1** *adj* (**a**) *(in size)* long (*f* longue). **how ~ is the field?** quelle est la longueur du champ?; **10 metres** ~ (long) de 10 mètres; **to get ~er** rallonger; **to pull a ~ face** faire une grimace; ~ **division** division écrite complète; *(Sport)* ~ **jump** saut *m* en longueur; *(fig)* **it's a ~ shot** *or* **chance** c'est très risqué; *(Rad)* **on the ~ wave** sur (les) grandes ondes. (**b**) *(in time)* long. **6 months** ~ qui dure 6 mois, de 6 mois; **a ~ time** longtemps; **at ~ last** enfin; **he wasn't ~ in coming** il n'a pas mis longtemps pour venir; **how ~ are the holidays?** les vacances durent combien de temps?; **to take a ~ look at** regarder longuement; *(fig)* regarder bien en face; **a ~ drink of water** une grande gorgée d'eau; **a ~ drink** un long drink; *(fig)* **in the ~ run** à la longue, en fin de compte; **it will be a ~ job** cela demandera du temps; **to have a ~ memory** avoir de la mémoire; **to be ~ on sth** * être doué pour qch, avoir beaucoup de qch.

2 *adv* (**a**) depuis longtemps. **it has ~ been used in industry** c'est employé depuis longtemps dans l'industrie; ~**-awaited** (si) longtemps attendu. (**b**) *(a ~ time)* longtemps. ~ **ago** il y a longtemps; **how ~ ago?** il y a combien de temps?; **as ~ ago as 1930** déjà en 1930; ~ **before** longtemps avant (que + *subj*); ~ **before now** il y a longtemps; **not ~ before** peu de temps avant (que + *subj*); ~ **since dead** mort depuis longtemps; **how ~ is it since you saw him?** cela fait combien de temps que tu ne l'as pas vu?; **have you been waiting ~?** il y a longtemps que vous attendez?; **I only had ~ enough to buy a paper** je n'ai eu que le temps d'acheter un journal; **wait a little ~er** attendez encore un peu; **will you be ~?** tu en as pour longtemps?; **don't be** ~ dépêche-toi; **how ~?** combien de temps?; **as ~ as I live** tant que je vivrai; **before** ~ *(+ future)* dans peu de temps; *(+ past)* peu de temps après; **for** ~ pour longtemps; **at (the) ~est** au plus. (**c**) **all night** ~ toute la nuit; **so ~ as, as ~ as** pourvu que + *subj*; **so ~!** * à bientôt!, salut! *; **he is no ~er living there** il n'habite plus là.

3 *n*: **the ~ and the short of it is that...** le fin mot de l'histoire, c'est que...

◆ **long-distance** *adj race, runner* de fond; *(Telec) call* interurbain; *flight* sur long parcours. ◆ **long-drawn-out** *adj* qui traîne, interminable. ◆ **long-forgotten** *adj* oublié depuis longtemps. ◆ **long-haired** *adj person* aux cheveux longs; *animal* à longs poils. ◆ **longhand** *adj* en écriture normale. ◆ **long johns** * *npl* caleçon *m* long. ◆ **long-legged** *adj person, horse* aux jambes longues; *other animal* à longues pattes. ◆ **long-lived** *adj* d'une grande longévité. ◆ **long-lost** *adj* perdu depuis longtemps. ◆ **long-playing** *adj*: ~**-playing record** 33 tours *m inv*. ◆ **long-range** *adj gun* à longue portée; *plane (Mil)* à grand rayon d'action; *(civil)* long-courrier; *weather forecast* à long terme. ◆ **long-shoreman** *n* débardeur *m*. ◆ **long-sighted** *adj (lit)* hypermétrope; *(in old age)* presbyte; *(fig) person* prévoyant, qui voit loin; *decision* pris avec prévoyance. ◆ **long-sleeved** *adj* à manches longues. ◆ **long-standing** *adj* de longue date. ◆ **long-suffering** *adj* très patient. ◆ **long-term** *adj* à long terme. ◆ **longways** *adv* en longueur, en long; ~**ways on** dans le sens de la longueur. ◆ **long-winded** *adj person* intarissable; *speech* interminable.

long² [lɒŋ] *vi* avoir très envie (*to do* de faire; *for sth* de qch; *for sb to do* que qn fasse); **to ~ for sb** se languir de qn.

◆ **longing** **1** *n (urge)* désir *m* (*to do* de faire; *for sth* de qch; *for sb* de voir qn); *(nostalgia)* nostalgie *f*; *(for food)* envie *f* ; **2** *adj look* plein de désir *or* de nostalgie *or* d'envie. ◆ **longingly** *adv* avec désir *or* nostalgie.

longitude ['lɒŋgɪtju:d] *n* longitude *f*.

loo * [lu:] *n (Brit)* cabinets *mpl*, petit coin * *m*. **in the** ~ au petit coin *, aux cabinets.

look [lʊk] **1** *n* (**a**) regard *m*, coup *m* d'œil. **to have** *or* **take a ~ at sth** regarder qch, jeter un coup d'œil à qch; *(in order to repair it etc)* s'occuper de qch; **to take a good ~ at sth** (bien) examiner qch; **to take a good ~ at sb** (bien) observer qn; **let me have a** ~ faites voir; **to have a ~ round the house** faire un tour dans la maison; **I just want to have a ~ round** *(in town)* je veux simplement faire un tour; *(in shop)* je ne fais que regarder; *(in house etc)* je veux simplement jeter un coup d'œil; **with a nasty ~ in his eye** avec un regard méchant; **we got some very odd ~s** les gens nous regardaient d'un drôle d'air; **if ~s could kill * I'd be dead** il (*or* elle *etc*) m'a fusillé *or* foudroyé du regard; **to have a ~ for sth** chercher qch.

(**b**) *(appearance etc)* air *m*, allure *f*. **she has a ~ of her mother about her** elle a qch de sa mère; **there was a sad ~ about him** il avait l'air plutôt triste; **I like the ~ of her** je lui trouve l'air sympathique; **I don't like the ~ of him** je n'aime pas son allure *or* son air; **I don't like the ~ of this** ça ne me plaît pas du tout; **you can't go by ~s** on ne peut pas se fier aux apparences; **by the ~ of him** à le voir; **by the ~(s) of it, by the ~(s) of things** * de toute apparence; **(good) ~s** beauté *f*; **she has kept her ~s** elle est restée belle; *(Fashion)* **the leather** ~ la mode du cuir.

2 *vi* (**a**) *(see, glance)* regarder. **to ~ at** *person, object* regarder; *situation, problem* considérer; **just ~ at you!** regarde de quoi tu as l'air!; **to ~ at him you would never think that...** à le voir on ne penserait jamais que...; **it isn't much to ~ at** ça ne paie pas de mine; **that's one way of ~ing at it** c'est une façon de voir les choses; **I wouldn't ~ at the job**

je n'accepterais ce poste pour rien au monde; **will you ~ at the carburettor?** pourriez-vous vérifier le carburateur?; **I'll ~ at it tomorrow** je m'en occuperai demain; **to ~ for sth/sb** chercher qch/qn; **to ~ into** *complaint, matter, possibility* examiner; **I shall ~ into it** je vais me renseigner là-dessus; **I ~ on him as...** je le considère comme...; **~ and see if...** regarde voir si...; **let me ~** laisse-moi voir; **~ who's here!** regarde qui est là!; **~ here,...** écoutez,...; *(protesting)* **~ here!** enfin voyons!; **to ~ the other way** regarder ailleurs; *(fig)* fermer les yeux *(fig)*; **~ before you leap** il ne faut pas se lancer à l'aveuglette; **to ~ ahead** *(in front)* regarder devant soi; *(to future)* considérer l'avenir; **to ~ down the list** parcourir la liste; **she ~ed into his eyes** elle a plongé son regard dans le sien; **the house ~s on to the main street** la maison donne sur la grand-rue; **you should have ~ed more carefully** tu aurais dû chercher plus soigneusement *or* mieux regarder.
(**b**) sembler, avoir l'air. **she ~s (as if she's) tired** elle semble *or* elle a l'air fatiguée; **how pretty you ~!** que vous êtes jolie!; **you ~** *or* **you're ~ing well** vous avez bonne mine; **he doesn't ~ himself, he doesn't ~ very great** * il n'a pas l'air bien; **he ~s about 40/1 metre 80** il a l'air d'avoir 40 ans/de faire 1 mètre 80; **she ~s her age** elle fait son âge; **she's tired and she ~s it** elle est fatiguée et ça se voit; **you must ~ your best** il faut que tu sois à ton avantage; **they made me ~ a fool** *or* **foolish** ils m'ont fait paraître ridicule; *(fig)* **to make sb ~ small** rabaisser qn; *(fig)* **it made me ~ small** j'ai eu l'air fin! * *(iro)*; *(fig)* **he just does it to ~ big** il fait cela uniquement pour se donner de l'importance; **ugly-~ing** laid; *(fig)* **to ~ the part** avoir le physique de l'emploi; **don't ~ like that!** ne faites pas cette tête-là!; **try to ~ as if you're glad to see them** essaie d'avoir l'air content de les voir; **~ sharp about it!** * dépêche-toi!; **he ~s good in uniform** l'uniforme lui va bien; **it makes her ~ old** cela la vieillit; **how did she ~?** *(health)* est-ce qu'elle avait bonne mine?; *(on hearing news etc)* quelle tête faisait-elle?; **how do I ~?** est-ce que ça va?; **that ~s good** *[food]* ça a l'air bon; *[picture etc]* ça fait très bien; *[plan, book]* ça a l'air intéressant; **it ~s good on paper** c'est très bien en théorie; **it doesn't ~ right** il y a qch qui ne va pas; **it ~s all right to me** je trouve que ça va; **how does it ~ to you?** ça va à votre avis?; **it ~s promising** c'est prometteur; **it will ~ bad** cela fera mauvais effet.
(**c**) **it ~s as if it's going to snow** on dirait qu'il va neiger; **it ~s as if he isn't coming** il n'a pas l'air de venir; **it ~s to me as if he isn't coming** j'ai l'impression qu'il ne va pas venir; **what does it/he ~ like?** comment est-ce/est-il?; **he ~s like his brother** il ressemble à son frère; **he ~s like a soldier** il a l'air d'un soldat; **it ~s like salt** ça a l'air d'être du sel; **it ~s like rain** on dirait qu'il va pleuvoir; **it certainly ~s like it** c'est bien probable; **the evening ~ed like being interesting** la soirée promettait d'être intéressante.
3 *vt* regarder. **she ~ed him full in the face/straight in the eye** elle l'a regardé bien en face/droit dans les yeux; **to ~ sb up and down** regarder qn de haut en bas; **~ where you're going!** regarde où tu vas!
◆ **look about, look around** *vi* regarder autour de soi. **to ~ about for sth** chercher qch des yeux. ◆ **look after** *vt fus (gen)* s'occuper de; *possessions* faire attention à; *one's car* entretenir; *one's interests* protéger. **she doesn't ~ after herself very well** elle néglige sa santé; **~ after yourself!** * fais bien attention à toi! *; **she's old enough to ~ after herself** elle est assez grande pour se défendre * toute seule; *(take responsibility for)* **to ~ after sth for sb** garder qch pour qn. ◆ **look away** *vi* détourner les yeux (*from* de). ◆ **look back** *vi* regarder derrière soi; *(remember)* regarder en arrière. **to ~ back at sth/sb** se retourner pour regarder qch/qn; **to ~ back on** revoir en esprit, penser à; **we can ~ back on 20 years of...** nous avons derrière nous 20 ans de...; **after that he never ~ed back** * après, ça n'a fait qu'aller de mieux en mieux. ◆ **look down** *vi* baisser les yeux; *(from height)* regarder en bas. **to ~ down at sb/sth** regarder qn/qch d'en haut; *(fig)* **to ~ down on sb/sth** mépriser qn/qch. ◆ **look forward to** *vt fus* attendre avec impatience. **I'm ~ing forward to seeing you** j'attends avec impatience le plaisir de vous voir; *(in letter)* **~ing forward to hearing from you** en espérant avoir bientôt une lettre de vous, dans l'attente de votre réponse; **are you ~ing forward to it?** est-ce que vous êtes content à cette perspective?; **I'm so ~ing forward to it** je m'en réjouis à l'avance. ◆ **look in** *vi* (**a**) *(~ inside)* regarder à l'intérieur; *(visit)* passer. **to ~ in on sb** passer voir qn; **the doctor will ~ in again** le docteur repassera. (**b**) *(*: watch television)* regarder la télévision. ◆ **look on** *vi* regarder. **he wrote the letter while I ~ed on** il a écrit la lettre tandis que je le regardais faire. ◆ **look out 1** *vi* (**a**) *(outside)* regarder dehors. **to ~ out of the window** regarder par la fenêtre; *(fig)* **to ~ out for sb** *(seek)* chercher qn; *(watch for)* guetter qn. (**b**) *(take care)* faire attention, prendre garde. **~ out!** attention!; **~ out for ice on the road** (faites) attention au verglas, méfiez-vous du verglas. **2** *vt sep* chercher et trouver. **I shall ~ out some old magazines** je vais essayer de trouver quelques vieux magazines. ◆ **look over** *vt sep essay* jeter un coup d'œil à; *book* parcourir; *town, building* visiter; *person (quickly)* jeter un coup d'œil à; *(slowly)* regarder de la tête aux pieds. ◆ **look round 1** *vi* (**a**) regarder (autour de soi); *(in shop)* regarder. **to ~ round for sth** chercher qch. (**b**) *(~ back)* regarder derrière soi. **to ~ round to see sth** se retourner pour voir qch; **don't ~ round!** ne vous retournez pas! **2** *vt fus town, factory* visiter, faire le tour de. ◆ **look through** *vt fus papers, book* examiner; *(briefly)* parcourir; *(revise)* revoir. ◆ **look to** *vt fus (look after) children* s'occuper de; *(rely on)* compter sur (*for sth* pour qch). **I ~ to you for help** je compte sur votre aide; **I always ~ to my mother for advice** quand j'ai besoin d'un conseil je me tourne vers ma mère. ◆ **look up 1** *vi* (**a**) regarder en haut; *(from reading etc)* lever les yeux. *(fig)* **to ~ up to sb** respecter qn. (**b**) *(improve) [prospects]* s'améliorer; *[business]* reprendre; *[weather]* se lever; *[shares, sales]* remonter. **things are ~ing up** ça a l'air d'aller mieux (*for sb* pour qn). **2** *vt sep* (**a**) *(visit) person* passer voir. (**b**) *(in dictionary)* chercher (*in* dans). **3** *vt fus reference book* consulter.
◆ **look-alike** *n*: **a Churchill ~-alike** un sosie de Churchill. ◆ **looker-on** *n* spectateur *m*, -trice *f*. ◆ **look-in** * *n*: **they didn't have** *or* **get a ~-in** ils n'ont jamais eu la moindre chance. ◆ **looking-glass** *n* miroir *m*. ◆ **look-out 1** *n* (**a**) **to keep a ~-out, to be on the ~-out** guetter (*for sb/sth* qn/qch); **to be on the ~-out for danger** être sur ses gardes à cause d'un danger éventuel; (**b**) *(observer) (gen)* guetteur *m*; *(Mil)* homme *m* de guet; *(Naut)* homme de veille; (**c**) *(~-out post) (gen, Mil)* poste *m* de guet; *(Naut)* vigie *f*; (**d**) **it's a poor ~-out for...** ça s'annonce mal pour...; **that's your ~-out!** cela vous regarde!, c'est votre affaire! ; **2** *adj tower* d'observation.

loom[1] [lu:m] *vi* **(~ up)** *[building, mountain]* apparaître indistinctement; *[figure, ship]* surgir; *[disaster]* menacer; *[event]* être imminent.

loom[2] [lu:m] *n (Tex)* métier *m* à tisser.

loony * ['lu:nɪ] *adj* timbré, cinglé.

loop [lu:p] **1** *n (gen)* boucle *f (de ficelle etc)*; *(Elec)* circuit *m* fermé; *(by motorway etc)* bretelle *f*;

(curtain fastener) embrasse *f*; *(contraceptive)* stérilet *m*. **2** *vt string etc* faire une boucle à. **to ~ a rope round a post** passer une corde autour d'un poteau; *(Aviat)* **to ~ the loop** boucler la boucle; **to ~ back a curtain** relever un rideau avec une embrasse. ◆ **loophole** *n (in argument, regulations)* point *m* faible; **to find a ~hole** trouver une échappatoire.

loose [luːs] **1** *adj* (**a**) *knot, shoelace* qui se défait; *screw* desserré; *brick, tooth* qui branle; *page from book* détaché; *hair* dénoué; *animal etc* en liberté. **to be working ~** se défaire, se desserrer, branler, se détacher, se dénouer; *[animal etc]* **to get ~** s'échapper; **to let** *or* **set** *or* **turn ~** lâcher; **a ~ sheet of paper** une feuille volante; *[horse]* **~ box** fourgon *m* à chevaux; *(on roadway)* **~ chippings** gravillons *mpl*; *(Elec)* **~ connection** mauvais contact *m*; *[furniture]* **~ covers** housses *fpl*; **~ end of a rope** bout *m* pendant d'une corde; **to be at a ~ end** ne pas trop savoir quoi faire; *(fig)* **to tie up ~ ends** régler les détails qui restent. (**b**) *(not packed) biscuits, carrots etc* en vrac; *butter, cheese* au poids. **just put them ~ into the basket** mettez-les à même dans le panier. (**c**) *coat, dress (not close-fitting)* vague, ample; *(not tight enough)* lâche, large; *skin* flasque; *collar* lâche. (**d**) *soil* meuble; *(fig) association, link* vague; *discipline, style* relâché; *reasoning, thinking* confus, imprécis; *translation* assez libre. **a ~ weave** un tissu lâche; **~ bowels** intestins relâchés. (**e**) *(pej) woman* facile; *morals* relâché. **~ living** vie *f* dissolue.

2 *vt* (**a**) *(undo)* défaire; *(untie)* délier; *screw etc* desserrer; *(free) animal* lâcher; *prisoner* relâcher. **to ~ a boat (from its moorings)** larguer les amarres; **they ~d the dogs on him** ils ont lâché les chiens après lui. (**b**) (**~ off**) *gun* décharger (*on or at sb* sur qn); *arrow* tirer (*on or at sb* sur qn); *abuse* lâcher (*on sb* sur qn).

◆ **loose-fitting** *adj* ample. ◆ **loose-leaf(ed)** *adj* à feuilles volantes; **~-leaf binder** classeur *m (dossier)*. ◆ **loose-limbed** *adj* agile. ◆ **loosely** *adv attach, tie, hold* sans serrer; *be fixed, weave* lâchement; *associate* vaguement; *translate* assez librement; *use word* de façon plutôt impropre. ◆ **loosen** **1** *vt (slacken) screw, belt, knot* desserrer; *rope, one's grip* relâcher; *(untie)* défaire; *tongue* délier; *soil* rendre meuble; *bowels* relâcher ; **2** *vi [fastening]* se défaire; *[screw]* se desserrer; *[knot] (slacken)* se desserrer; *(come undone)* se défaire; *[rope]* se détendre; **to ~n up** *(limber up)* faire des exercices d'assouplissement; *(be less shy)* se dégeler. ◆ **looseness** *n [knot]* desserrement *m*; *[screw, tooth]* jeu *m*; *[rope]* relâchement *m*; *[clothes]* ampleur *f*; *[translation]* imprécision *f*; *[behaviour]* relâchement.

loot [luːt] **1** *n* butin *m*. **2** *vt* piller. **3** *vi*: **to go ~ing** se livrer au pillage. ◆ **looter** *n* pillard *m*. ◆ **looting** *n* pillage *m*.

lop [lɒp] *vt tree* tailler; *branch* couper. ◆ **lop off** *vt sep* couper. ◆ **lop-eared** *adj* aux oreilles pendantes. ◆ **lop-sided** *adj (not straight)* de travers; *(asymmetric)* disproportionné.

lope [ləʊp] *vi*: **to ~ along/in** *etc* avancer/entrer *etc* en bondissant.

loquacious [ləˈkweɪʃəs] *adj* loquace. ◆ **loquacity** *n* loquacité *f*.

lord [lɔːd] **1** *n* seigneur *m*. **~ of the manor** châtelain *m*; **~ and master** seigneur et maître; **L~ (John) Smith** lord (John) Smith; **the House of L~s** la Chambre des Lords; **my L~** Monsieur le baron (*or* comte *etc*); *(to judge)* Monsieur le Juge; *(to bishop)* Monseigneur; *(Rel)* **Our L~** Notre Seigneur; **the L~'s supper** la sainte Cène; **the L~'s prayer** le Notre-Père; **good L~!** * Seigneur!; **oh L~!** * zut! * **2** *vt*: **to ~ it over sb** * traiter qn de haut. ◆ **lordliness** *n* noblesse *f*; *(pej)* hauteur *f*. ◆ **lordly** *adj (dignified)* noble, de grand seigneur; *(arrogant)* hautain. ◆ **lordship** *n* autorité *f* (*over* sur); **Your L~ship** Monsieur le comte (*or* le baron *etc*); *(to judge)* Monsieur le Juge; *(to bishop)* Monseigneur.

lore [lɔːʳ] *n* traditions *fpl*. **bird/wood** *etc* **~** connaissance *f* des oiseaux/de la vie dans les forêts *etc*.

lorry [ˈlɒrɪ] *(Brit)* **1** *n* camion *m*. **2** *adj*: **~ driver** camionneur *m*; *(long-distance)* routier *m*; **~ load** chargement *m*.

lose [luːz] *pret, ptp* **lost** **1** *vt* (**a**) *(gen)* perdre. **he got lost** il s'est perdu *or* égaré; **the key got lost** on a perdu *or* égaré la clef; **get lost!** ⁑ va te faire voir! *; **I lost my father when I was 10** j'ai perdu mon père à l'âge de 10 ans; **you've nothing to ~** tu n'as rien à perdre, tu ne risques rien (*by doing* à faire); **to ~ one's life** périr, perdre la vie; **two posts have been lost** il y a eu deux suppressions *fpl* d'emploi; **100 men** *or* **lives were lost** 100 hommes ont péri, on a perdu 100 hommes; **20 lives were lost** 20 personnes ont péri; **there were no lives lost** il n'y a eu aucun mort *or* aucune victime; **to be lost at sea** périr en mer; **I lost his last sentence** je n'ai pas entendu sa dernière phrase; **to ~ one's breath** perdre haleine; **to have lost one's breath** être hors d'haleine; *(Aut)* **he's lost his licence** on lui a retiré son permis de conduire; **to ~ one's way** perdre son chemin, se perdre; **we mustn't ~ any time** il ne faut pas perdre de temps; **to ~ no time in doing sth** faire qch au plus vite; **there's not a minute to ~** il n'y a pas une minute à perdre; **he managed to ~ the detective who was following him** il a réussi à semer le détective qui le suivait; *(after explanation etc)* **you've lost me there** * je ne vous suis plus. (**b**) *(cause loss of)* faire perdre. **that will ~ you your job** cela va vous faire perdre votre place. (**c**) *[clock etc]* **to ~ 10 minutes a day** retarder de 10 minutes par jour.

2 *vi* (**a**) *[player, team]* perdre. **to ~ to sb** se faire battre par qn; **they lost 6-1** ils ont perdu *or* ils se sont fait battre 6-1; *(fig)* **he lost (out) on the deal** il a été perdant dans l'affaire; **you can't ~** * tu ne risques rien; *(fig)* **it ~s in translation** cela perd à la traduction. (**b**) *[watch, clock]* retarder.

◆ **loser** *n* perdant(e) *m(f)*; **good/bad ~r** bon/mauvais joueur, bonne/mauvaise joueuse; **to come off the ~r** être perdant; **he's a born ~r** il n'a jamais de veine *. ◆ **losing** *adj team, number* perdant; *business, concern* mauvais; **on a losing streak** * en période de déveine *; *(fig)* **a losing battle** une bataille perdue d'avance.

loss [lɒs] *n* (**a**) perte *f*. **without ~ of life** sans qu'il y ait de victimes; *(Mil)* **heavy ~es** pertes sévères; *(Pol)* **Labour ~es** les sièges perdus par les travaillistes; **to sell at a ~** vendre à perte; *(Comm)* **~ leader** article *m* pilote *(vendu à perte pour attirer les clients)*; **he's no great ~** * ce n'est pas une grosse perte. (**b**) **to be at a ~** être perplexe; **at a ~ to explain** incapable d'expliquer; **we are at a ~ to know** nous ne savons absolument pas; **to be at a ~ for words** chercher ses mots.

lost [lɒst] *(pret, ptp of* **lose***) adj cause, opportunity* perdu; *(fig) (bewildered)* perdu, désorienté; *(uncomprehending)* perdu, perplexe; *(absorbed)* perdu (*in* dans), absorbé (*in* par). **several ~ children** plusieurs enfants qui s'étaient perdus; **a ~ soul** une âme en peine; **the ~ sheep** la brebis égarée; **to make up for ~ time** rattraper le temps perdu; **~ property**, *(US)* **~ and found** objets *mpl* trouvés; **~ property office**, **~-and-found department** bureau *m* des objets trouvés; **he looked quite ~** il avait l'air complètement désorienté; **to give sb/sth up for ~** considérer qn/qch comme perdu; **my advice/the remark was ~ on him** il n'a pas écouté mes conseils/pas compris la remarque; **~ in thought** perdu dans ses pensées.

lot [lɒt] *n* (**a**) *(destiny)* sort *m*. **the common ~** le sort commun; **it was not his ~ to make a fortune** il n'était pas destiné à faire fortune; **it fell to my ~ to do it** il m'est revenu de le faire; **to throw in one's ~ with sb** partager le sort de qn. (**b**) *(random selection)* **by ~** par tirage au sort; **to draw ~s (for sth)** tirer (qch) au sort. (**c**) *(at auctions; also batch: of people, goods)* lot *m*. **he's a bad ~ *** il ne vaut pas cher *. (**d**) *(land)* lot *m* (de terrain), parcelle *f*. **building ~** lotissement *m*; **parking ~** parking *m*. (**e**) **the ~** *(everything)* (le) tout; *(everyone)* tous *mpl*, toutes *fpl*; **that's the ~** c'est tout; **take the ~** prends tout ce qu'il y a, prends le tout; **the ~ of you** vous tous; **the whole ~ of them went off** ils sont tous partis. (**f**) *(large amount)* beaucoup. **a ~ of, ~s of** beaucoup de; **what a ~ of people!** que de monde! *or* de gens!; **what a ~!** quelle quantité!; **there wasn't a ~ we could do** nous ne pouvions pas faire grand-chose; **I'd give a ~ to know...** je donnerais cher pour savoir...; **quite a ~ of** pas mal de; **such a ~ of** tellement de, tant de; **an awful ~ of *** énormément * de; **a ~ better** beaucoup *or* bien mieux; **we don't go out a ~** nous ne sortons pas beaucoup *or* pas souvent; **thanks a ~! *** merci beaucoup!; *(iro)* **a ~** *or* **a fat lot you care! *** comme si ça te faisait qch!

lotion ['ləʊʃ(ə)n] *n* lotion *f*.

lottery ['lɒtərɪ] *n* loterie *f*.

loud [laʊd] **1** *adj voice* fort, sonore; *laugh* grand, bruyant; *noise, cry* sonore, grand; *music* bruyant; *thunder* fracassant; *applause* vif (*f* vive); *protests* vigoureux; *behaviour* tapageur; *colour, clothes* voyant. **the radio is too ~** la radio joue trop fort; *(Mus)* **~ pedal** pédale *f* forte. **2** *adv speak etc* fort, haut. **out ~** tout haut. ◆ **loudhailer** *n (Brit)* mégaphone *m*. ◆ **loudly** *adv shout, speak* fort; *proclaim* vigoureusement; *knock, laugh* bruyamment. ◆ **loud-mouthed** *adj* braillard, fort en gueule ⁑. ◆ **loudness** *n [voice, music etc]* force *f*; *[applause]* bruit *m*; *[protests]* vigueur *f*. ◆ **loudspeaker** *n* haut-parleur *m*; *[stereo]* baffle *m*.

lounge [laʊn(d)ʒ] **1** *n* salon *m (d'une maison, d'un hôtel etc)*. **2** *adj*: *(US)* **~ jacket** veste *f* d'intérieur; **~ suit** complet(-veston) *m*; *(US)* pyjama d'intérieur *(de femme)*; *(on invitation)* 'tenue de ville'. **3** *vi (on bed etc)* se prélasser; *(stroll)* flâner; *(also* **~ about**: *idle)* paresser, être oisif. ◆ **lounger** *n (sun-bed)* lit *m* de plage.

louse, *pl* **lice** [laʊs, laɪs] *n (insect)* pou *m*; *(⁑: person)* salaud ⁑ *m*. ◆ **louse up** ⁑ *vt sep deal, event* bousiller *. ◆ **lousy** *adj (lit)* pouilleux; *(⁑: terrible)* infect; **he's a lousy teacher** il est nul comme prof *; **a lousy trick** un tour de cochon *; **I feel lousy** je suis mal fichu *.

lout [laʊt] *n* rustre *m*. ◆ **loutish** *adj* de rustre.

love [lʌv] **1** *n* (**a**) amour *m* (*of* de, pour; *for* pour). **to be/fall in ~** être/tomber amoureux (*with* de); **they are in ~** ils s'aiment; **~ at first sight** le coup de foudre; **to make ~** faire l'amour (*with* avec; *to* à); **there's no ~ lost between them** ils ne peuvent pas se sentir *; **for the ~ of God** pour l'amour de Dieu; *(*: indignantly: also* **for the ~ of Mike ***)* pour l'amour du Ciel; **to marry for ~** faire un mariage d'amour; **for ~ of** par amour pour; **not for ~ nor money** *do* pour rien au monde; *sell* à aucun prix; **give her my ~** dis-lui bien des choses de ma part; *(stronger)* embrasse-la pour moi; **he sends you his ~** il t'envoie bien des choses; *(stronger)* il t'embrasse; *(in letter)* **~ from Jim** affectueusement, Jim; *(stronger)* bons baisers, Jim; **yes (my) ~** oui mon amour; **the theatre was her great ~** le théâtre était sa grande passion; **he studies history for the ~ of it** il étudie l'histoire pour son plaisir. (**b**) *(Tennis etc)* rien *m*, zéro *m*. **~ 30** rien à 30, zéro 30.

2 *vt* (**a**) *spouse, child* aimer; *relative, friend* aimer (beaucoup). **he didn't just like her, he LOVED her** il ne l'aimait pas d'amitié, mais d'amour; **she ~d him dearly** elle l'aimait tendrement. (**b**) *food, activity, place* aimer (beaucoup); *(stronger)* adorer. **to ~ to do** *or* **doing sth** aimer (beaucoup) *or* adorer faire qch; **I'd ~ to come** je serais ravi de venir; **I'd ~ to!** cela me ferait très plaisir!

3 *adj letter, song, story, scene* d'amour. **~ affair** liaison *f* (amoureuse); **how's your ~ life these days? *** comment vont les amours?; **~ match** mariage *m* d'amour.

◆ **lovable** *adj person* très sympathique; *child, animal* adorable. ◆ **loveless** *adj* sans amour. ◆ **lovemaking** *n* amour *m (acte sexuel)*. ◆ **lover** *n* (**a**) amant *m*; *(romantic)* amoureux *m*; **~rs' vows** promesses *fpl* d'amoureux; **they are ~rs** ils ont une liaison; (**b**) **theatre ~r** amateur *m* de théâtre; **a ~r of Brahms** un(e) fervent(e) de Brahms. ◆ **lovesick** *adj* qui languit d'amour. ◆ **lovey-dovey *** *adj (hum)* (trop) tendre. ◆ **loving** *adj (gen)* affectueux; *(tender)* tendre; *wife, son* aimant; **money-loving** qui aime l'argent. ◆ **lovingly** *adv* affectueusement; tendrement; *(stronger)* avec amour.

lovely ['lʌvlɪ] *adj (pretty: gen)* (très) joli, ravissant; *baby* mignon, joli; *(pleasant: gen)* charmant; *meal, evening, party, voice* très agréable; *night, sunshine, weather* beau; *holiday* excellent; *idea, suggestion* merveilleux; *smell, food* bon. **we had a ~ time** nous nous sommes bien amusés; **it's been ~ seeing you** j'ai été vraiment content de vous voir; **~ and cool** *etc* délicieusement frais *etc*. ◆ **loveliness** *n* beauté *f*, charme *m*.

low¹ [ləʊ] **1** *adj (gen)* bas (*f* basse); *density, groan, income, intelligence* faible; *murmur* étouffé; *stock, supply* presque épuisé; *speed* petit, faible; *standard* bas, faible; *quality* inférieur; *person (feeble)* faible, affaibli; *(depressed)* déprimé; *(Bio, Zool: primitive)* inférieur; *(pej) taste* mauvais; *café etc* de bas étage; *(shameful) behaviour* ignoble. *[person, object, sum]* **to be ~ down** être (bien) bas *inv*; **~er down the hill** plus bas sur la colline; **the L~ Countries** les Pays-Bas; **fog on ~ ground** brouillard *m* à basse altitude; **town on ~ ground** ville bâtie dans une dépression; **at ~ tide** *or* **water** à marée basse; **in a ~ voice** à voix basse; *(fig: of sb's career)* **the ~ point** le nadir; *(of radio etc)* **it's a bit ~** ça n'est pas assez fort, c'est trop bas; *(Cards)* **a ~ diamond** un petit carreau; *(Aut)* **in ~ gear** en première ou seconde vitesse; *(Culin)* **at a ~ heat** à feu doux; **to become** *or* **get ~er** baisser; **L~ Church** Basse Église *(Anglicane)*; **~ flying** vol(s) *m (pl)* à basse altitude; **L~ Latin** bas latin; **L~ Sunday** dimanche *m* de Quasimodo; **~er** *deck, jaw* inférieur; *(Typ)* **~er case** bas *m* de casse; **~er middle class** *(n)* petite bourgeoisie; *(adj)* petit bourgeois; **the ~er classes** *(socially)* les classes inférieures; *(Scol)* **the ~er school** le premier cycle; **the ~er income groups** les économiquement faibles *mpl*; *(Parl)* **the L~er House** la Chambre basse; **the ~er paid** la tranche inférieure des salariés *or* du salariat; **they were ~ on water** ils étaient à court d'eau; **I'm ~ on funds** je suis à court (d'argent); **to be in ~ spirits, to feel ~** être déprimé, ne pas avoir le moral *; **~ forms of life** les formes de vie inférieures *or* les moins évoluées; **the ~est of the ~** le dernier des derniers; **a ~ trick** un sale tour *.

2 *adv aim, sing* bas; *fly* bas; *(of plane)* à basse altitude; *bow, fall, sink* bien bas. *(Elec)* **to turn sth down ~** baisser qch; **supplies are running ~** les provisions baissent; *(Cards)* **to play ~** jouer une basse carte.

3 *n* (**a**) *(Met)* dépression *f*. (**b**) *(low point)* niveau bas, point bas. **to reach a new ~** atteindre son niveau le plus bas.

◆ **lowbrow** **1** *n* personne *f* sans prétentions intellectuelles ; **2** *adj* sans prétentions intellectuelles. ◆ **low-budget** *adj film, project* à petit budget; *car* pour les petits budgets. ◆ **low-calorie** *adj* à basses calories. ◆ **low-cost** *adj* bon marché *inv*; ~**-cost housing** habitations *fpl* à loyer modéré, H.L.M. *mpl.* ◆ **low-cut** *adj* décolleté. ◆ **low-down** **1** *adj (mean)* méprisable; *(spiteful)* mesquin ; **2** *n*: **to give sb the ~-down on** * mettre qn au courant de. ◆ **lower** **1** *vt (gen)* baisser; *sail, flag* abaisser; *boat, lifeboat* mettre à la mer; *sb/sth on a rope* descendre; *sb's resistance* diminuer; **to ~er one's guard** *(Boxing)* baisser sa garde; *(fig)* ne plus être sur ses gardes; **to ~er sb's morale** démoraliser qn; **~er your voice!** (parle) moins fort!; **to ~er o.s. to do sth** s'abaisser à faire qch ; **2** *vi (lit)* baisser. ◆ **lower-class** *adj* de la classe inférieure. ◆ **lowering**[1] **1** *n [window, flag, temperature]* abaissement *m*; *[boat]* mise *f* à la mer; *[price, pressure]* baisse *f* ; **2** *adj* abaissant, dégradant. ◆ **low-fat** *adj* maigre. ◆ **low-flying** *adj* volant à basse altitude. ◆ **low-grade** *adj* de qualité *or* de catégorie inférieure. ◆ **low-heeled** *adj* à talons plats. ◆ **low-key** *adj* modéré; *operation* très discret; **to keep sth ~-key** faire qch de façon discrète. ◆ **lowland** *n* plaine *f*; **the L~lands of Scotland** les Basses-Terres *fpl* d'Écosse. ◆ **low-level** *adj* bas; *(fig) job* subalterne. ◆ **lowliness** *n* humilité *f*. ◆ **lowly** *adj (humble)* humble; *(low-born)* d'origine modeste. ◆ **low-lying** *adj* à basse altitude. ◆ **low-necked** *adj* décolleté. ◆ **lowness** *n (in height)* manque *m* de hauteur; *[price, wages]* modicité *f*; *[temperature]* peu *m* d'élévation. ◆ **low-paid** *adj* mal payé; **the ~-paid workers** les petits salaires. ◆ **low-priced** *adj* à bas prix, bon marché *inv*. ◆ **low-profile** *adj* = **low-key.** ◆ **low-rise** *adj (Archit)* de hauteur limitée, bas. ◆ **low-spirited** *adj* déprimé, démoralisé.

low[2] [ləʊ] *vi [cattle]* meugler. ◆ **lowing** *n* meuglement *m*.

lowering[2] ['laʊərɪŋ] *adj* sombre, menaçant.

lox [lɒks] *n (US)* saumon *m* fumé.

loyal ['lɔɪ(ə)l] *adj* loyal *(to sb* envers qn), fidèle *(to sb* à qn). *(Brit)* **the ~ toast** le toast porté au souverain. ◆ **loyalist** *adj, n* loyaliste *(mf)*. ◆ **loyally** *adv* fidèlement, loyalement. ◆ **loyalty** *n* loyauté *f*, fidélité *f*.

lozenge ['lɒzɪn(d)ʒ] *n (Med)* pastille *f*; *(Her, Math)* losange *m*.

lubricate ['lu:brɪkeɪt] *vt* lubrifier; *(Aut)* graisser. **lubricating oil** huile *f* (de graissage). ◆ **lubricant** *adj, n* lubrifiant *(m)*. ◆ **lubrication** *n* lubrification *f*; *(Aut)* graissage *m*. ◆ **lubricator** *n* graisseur *m*.

lucid ['lu:sɪd] *adj* lucide. ◆ **lucidity** *n* lucidité *f*. ◆ **lucidly** *adv* lucidement.

luck [lʌk] *n* (**a**) *(chance, fortune)* chance *f*, hasard *m*. **good ~** (bonne) chance, veine * *f*; **bad ~** malchance *f*, déveine * *f*; **to bring sb good/bad ~** porter bonheur/malheur à qn; **good ~!** bonne chance!; **bad** *or* **hard ~!** pas de chance!; **better ~ next time!** ça ira mieux la prochaine fois!; **yes, worse ~** oui, malheureusement; **as ~ would have it** comme par hasard; *(fig)* **it's the ~ of the draw** c'est une question de chance; **it's good/bad ~ to see a black cat** cela porte bonheur/malheur de voir un chat noir; **to be down on one's ~** être dans une mauvaise passe. (**b**) *(good fortune)* (bonne) chance *f*, veine * *f*. **you're in ~, your ~'s in** tu as de la chance *or* de la veine *; **that's a bit of ~!** quelle chance!, quelle veine! *; **he had the ~ to meet her in the street** il a eu la chance de la rencontrer dans la rue; **no such ~!** * ç'aurait été trop beau!; **with any ~...** avec un peu de chance...; *(iro)* **and the best of ~!** * je vous *(or* leur *etc)* souhaite bien du plaisir! * *(iro)*; **he's got the ~ of the devil** * il a une veine de pendu *.

◆ **luckily** *adv* heureusement, par bonheur. ◆ **luckless** *adj person* malchanceux; *action* malencontreux. ◆ **lucky** *adj person* qui a de la chance; *day* de chance, de veine *; *shot, guess, coincidence* heureux; *horseshoe, charm* porte-bonheur *inv*; **you are ~y to be alive** tu as de la chance de t'en sortir vivant; **he was ~y enough to get a seat** il a eu la chance *or* la veine * de trouver une place; **you ~y thing!** veinard(e)! *; **it was ~y for him that...** heureusement pour lui que...; **how ~y!** quelle chance!; **to have a ~y break** * avoir un coup de veine *; **~y dip** pêche *f* miraculeuse; *(fig)* loterie *f*; **~y number** chiffre *m* porte-bonheur.

lucrative ['lu:krətɪv] *adj* lucratif.

ludicrous ['lu:dɪkrəs] *adj* ridicule. ◆ **ludicrously** *adv* ridiculement.

ludo ['lu:dəʊ] *n* jeu *m* des petits chevaux.

lug [lʌg] *vt* traîner, tirer.

luggage ['lʌgɪdʒ] **1** *n* bagages *mpl*. **~ in advance** bagages non accompagnés. **2** *adj (Brit Aut)* **~ boot** coffre *m*; **~ label** étiquette *f* à bagages; **~ locker** (casier *m* de) consigne *f* automatique; **~ rack** *(Rail)* porte-bagages *m inv*, filet *m*; *(Aut)* galerie *f*; **~ van** fourgon *m* (à bagages).

lugubrious [lu:'gu:brɪəs] *adj* lugubre. ◆ **lugubriously** *adv* lugubrement.

lukewarm ['lu:kwɔ:m] *adj* tiède.

lull [lʌl] **1** *n (gen)* arrêt *m*; *[storm]* accalmie *f*; *(in work etc)* moment *m* de calme. **2** *vt* apaiser, calmer. **to ~ a child to sleep** endormir un enfant en le berçant *etc*; *(fig)* **to be ~ed into a false sense of security** s'endormir dans une fausse sécurité. ◆ **lullaby** *n* berceuse *f*.

lumbago [lʌm'beɪgəʊ] *n* lumbago *m*.

lumber[1] ['lʌmbə^r] **1** *n (wood)* bois *m* de charpente; *(junk)* bric-à-brac *m inv*. **2** *vt* (**a**) *room* encombrer. (**b**) *(US Forestry) (fell)* abattre; *(saw up)* débiter. (**c**) *(Brit *: burden)* **to ~ sb with sth** coller * qch à qn. ◆ **lumberjack** *n* bûcheron *m*. ◆ **lumberjacket** *n* blouson *m*. ◆ **lumber-room** *n* débarras *m*. ◆ **lumber yard** *n* chantier *m* de scierie.

lumber[2] ['lʌmbə^r] *vi* **(~ about, ~ along)** *(gen)* marcher pesamment; *[vehicle]* rouler pesamment. ◆ **lumbering** *adj* lourd, pesant.

luminous ['lu:mɪnəs] *adj* lumineux.

lump[1] [lʌmp] **1** *n (gen)* morceau *m*; *(larger)* gros morceau; *[clay, earth]* motte *f*; *(in sauce etc)* grumeau *m*; *(* pej: person)* lourdaud(e) *m(f)*; *(Med)* grosseur *f* *(on* à). *(fig)* **to have a ~ in one's throat** avoir la gorge serrée. **2** *adj*: **~ sugar** sucre *m* en morceaux; **~ sum** somme *f* globale *or* forfaitaire; *(payment)* paiement *m* unique. ◆ **lump together** *vt sep (gen)* réunir; *(fig) people, cases* mettre dans la même catégorie. ◆ **lumpy** *adj gravy* grumeleux; *bed* défoncé.

lump[2] * [lʌmp] *vt (endure)* **you'll just have to ~ it** il faut bien que tu acceptes *(subj)* sans rien dire.

lunacy ['lu:nəsɪ] *n* aliénation *f* mentale, folie *f*; *(fig)* folie. **that's sheer ~!** c'est de la pure folie! ◆ **lunatic** **1** *n (Med)* fou *m*, folle *f*; *(Jur)* dément(e) *m(f)*; *(fig)* fou, folle ; **2** *adj person* fou *(f* folle), dément; *idea, action (crazy)* absurde; *(stupid)* idiot; **lunatic asylum** asile *m* d'aliénés; **the lunatic fringe** les enragés * *mpl*.

lunar ['lu:nə^r] *adj (gen)* lunaire; *eclipse* de la lune. **~ landing** alunissage *m*.

lunch [lʌntʃ] **1** *n* déjeuner *m*. **to have ~** déjeuner; **come to** *or* **for ~ on Sunday** venez déjeuner dimanche. **2** *vi* déjeuner *(on, off* de). **3** *vt* offrir un déjeuner à. **4** *adj:* **~ break** heure *f* du déjeuner; **his ~ hour** l'heure *f* de son déjeuner. ◆ **lunchtime** *n* heure *f* de *or* du déjeuner.

luncheon ['lʌntʃən] **1** *n* déjeuner *m*. **2** *adj:* **~ meat** ≃ mortadelle *f*; **~ voucher** ticket-repas *m*.

lung [lʌŋ] **1** *n* poumon *m*. *(fig)* **at the top of one's ~s** à pleins poumons. **2** *adj disease* pulmonaire. **~ cancer** cancer *m* du poumon.

lunge [lʌndʒ] **1** *n* brusque mouvement *m* en avant. **2** *vi* (**~ forward**) faire un mouvement brusque en avant; **to ~ at sb** envoyer un coup à qn.

lurch[1] [lɜːtʃ] **1** *n [car, ship]* embardée *f*. **2** *vi [person]* tituber; *[car, ship]* faire une embardée. *[person]* **to ~ in** *etc* entrer *etc* en titubant.

lurch[2] [lɜːtʃ] *n*: **to leave sb in the ~** faire faux bond à qn.

lure [ljʊəʳ] **1** *n (charm: of sea etc)* attrait *m*; *(false attraction)* leurre *m*. **2** *vt* attirer (par la ruse). **to ~ sb into a trap** attirer qn dans un piège; **to ~ sb in** *etc* persuader qn par la ruse d'entrer *etc*.

lurex ['lʊəreks] *n* lurex *m*.

lurid ['ljʊərɪd] *adj* (**a**) *détails* atroce; *account, tale (gruesome)* terrifiant; *(sensational)* à sensation; *description* saisissant. (**b**) *colour* criard; *sky, sunset* empourpré.

lurk [lɜːk] *vi [person] (hide)* se cacher, se tapir; *(creep about)* rôder; *[danger]* menacer; *[doubt]* persister. ◆ **lurking** *adj fear etc* vague.

luscious ['lʌʃəs] *adj* succulent.

lush [lʌʃ] *adj vegetation* luxuriant; *pasture* riche; (*) *house etc* luxueux.

lust [lʌst] *n (gen)* désir *m (sexuel)*; *(for power etc)* soif *f* (*for* de).

lustre, *(US)* **luster** ['lʌstəʳ] *n* lustre *m*.

lusty ['lʌstɪ] *adj* vigoureux.

lute [luːt] *n* luth *m*.

Luxembourg ['lʌksəmbɜːg] *n* Luxembourg *m*.

luxuriant [lʌg'zjʊərɪənt] *adj (gen)* luxuriant; *beard* exubérant; *soil* riche. ◆ **luxuriance** *n* luxuriance *f*; exubérance *f*; richesse *f*. ◆ **luxuriate** *vi* s'abandonner avec délices (*in* à).

luxury ['lʌkʃərɪ] **1** *n* luxe *m*. **it's quite a ~ for me to do that** c'est du luxe pour moi que de faire ça. **2** *adj goods* de luxe; *flat, hotel* de grand luxe. ◆ **luxurious** *adj hotel, surroundings* luxueux, somptueux; *tastes* de luxe. ◆ **luxuriously** *adv furnish* luxueusement; *live* dans le luxe; *yawn, stretch* voluptueusement.

lychee [ˌlaɪ'tʃiː] *n* litchi *m*, letchi *m*.

lying ['laɪɪŋ] **1** *n* mensonge(s) *m(pl)*. **2** *adj person* menteur; *statement, story* mensonger, faux (*f* fausse).

lymphatic [lɪm'fætɪk] *adj* lymphatique.

lynch [lɪn(t)ʃ] *vt (lit, fig)* lyncher. ◆ **lynching** *n* lynchage *m*.

lynx [lɪŋks] *n* lynx *m inv*.

Lyons ['laɪənz] *n* Lyon.

lyre ['laɪəʳ] *n* lyre *f*. **~ bird** oiseau-lyre *m*.

lyric ['lɪrɪk] **1** *n (poem)* poème *m* lyrique. *(words of song)* **~s** paroles *fpl*. **2** *adj poem, poet* lyrique. ◆ **lyrical** *adj* lyrique *(also fig)*. ◆ **lyrically** *adv* avec lyrisme. ◆ **lyricism** *n* lyrisme *m*. ◆ **lyric-writer** *n* parolier *m*, -ière *f*.

M

M, m [em] *n (letter)* M, m *m or f.* *(abbr of* **motorway***)* **on the M6** ≃ sur l'A6.

ma'am [mæm] *n abbr of* **madam (a).**

mac * [mæk] *n (Brit:* **mackintosh***)* imper * *m.*

macadam [mə'kædəm] *n* macadam *m.* ◆ **macadamize** *vt* macadamiser.

macaroni [ˌmækə'rəʊnɪ] *n* macaroni *m.* ~ **cheese** macaroni au gratin.

macaroon [ˌmækə'ru:n] *n* macaron *m.*

macaw [mə'kɔ:] *n* ara *m.*

mace¹ [meɪs] *n (spice)* macis *m.*

mace² [meɪs] *n (weapon)* massue *f*; *(ceremonial)* masse *f.* ~ **bearer** massier *m.*

macerate ['mæsəreɪt] *vti* macérer.

Mach [mæk] *n*: **at** ~ **2** à Mach 2.

machete [mə'tʃeɪtɪ] *n* machette *f.*

machine [mə'ʃi:n] **1** *n (gen, also fig)* machine *f*; *(plane)* appareil *m.* **adding** *etc* ~ machine à calculer *etc*; **the** ~ **of government** la machine politique; *(US Pol)* **the democratic** ~ la machine administrative du parti démocrate. **2** *vt (Tech)* usiner; *(Sewing)* piquer à la machine. ◆ **machine code** *n (Comput)* code *m* machine. ◆ **machine-gun** **1** *n* mitrailleuse *f* ; **2** *vt* mitrailler. ◆ **machine-gunner** *n* mitrailleur *m.* ◆ **machine language** *n (Comput)* langage-machine *m.* ◆ **machine-made** *adj* fait à la machine. ◆ **machine operator** *n* opérateur *m*, -trice *f.* ◆ **machinery** *n (machines)* machines *fpl*; *(parts)* mécanisme *m*, rouages *mpl*; **a piece of ~ry** un mécanisme; **the ~ry of government** les rouages de l'État. ◆ **machine-shop** *n* atelier *m* d'usinage. ◆ **machine-stitch** *vt* piquer à la machine. ◆ **machine-tool** *n* machine-outil *f.* ◆ **machinist** *n* machiniste *mf; (on sewing, knitting machines)* mécanicien(ne) *m(f).*

machismo [mæ'kɪzməʊ] *n* machisme *m.*

macho ['mætʃəʊ] **1** *adj* macho *inv.* **2** *n* macho *m.*

mackerel ['mækr(ə)l] *n, pl inv* maquereau *m.*

mackintosh ['mækɪntɒʃ] *n* imperméable *m.*

macrame [mə'krɑ:mɪ] *m* macramé *m.*

macrobiotic [ˌmækrəʊbaɪ'ɒtɪk] *adj* macrobiotique. ◆ **macrobiotics** *n* macrobiotique *f.*

mad [mæd] *adj person* fou (*f* folle), cinglé *; *bull* furieux; *dog* enragé; *(rash) person* fou; *hope, plan* insensé; *race, gallop* effréné; *(*: angry)* furieux (*at, with sb* contre qn). **to go** ~ devenir fou; **to drive sb** ~ *(gen)* rendre qn fou; *(exasperate)* exaspérer qn; *(anger)* mettre qn en fureur; **as** ~ **as a hatter** *or* **a March hare** complètement fou; **stark raving** *or* **staring** ~ fou à lier; ~ **with grief** fou de douleur; **you're** ~ **to think of it!** tu es fou d'y songer!; **are you** ~**?** ça ne va pas? * *(iro)*; *(adv phrase)* **like** ~ * comme un fou (*or* une folle); **I'm in a** ~ **rush** c'est une vraie course contre la montre; **to get** ~ **at sb** * s'emporter contre qn; **hopping** *or* **spitting** ~ * fou furieux; ~ **(keen) * about** *or* **on** fou de, mordu de *; **I'm not** ~ **about it** * ça ne m'emballe pas *. ◆ **madden** *vt* rendre fou; *(infuriate)* exaspérer. ◆ **maddening** *adj* exaspérant. ◆ **maddeningly** *adv* à un degré exaspérant, à vous rendre fou ; **~deningly slow** d'une lenteur exaspérante. ◆ **madhouse** *n* maison *f* de fous. ◆ **madly** *adv behave* comme un fou; *interest, excite* follement; *love sb* à la folie; **~ly keen on** fou *or* passionné de ; **I ~ly offered to help her** j'ai eu la folie de lui offrir mon aide. ◆ **madman** *n* fou *m*, aliéné *m.* ◆ **madness** *n* folie *f.* ◆ **madwoman** *n* folle *f*, aliénée *f.*

Madagascar [ˌmædə'gæskəʳ] *n* Madagascar *f.* **in** ~ à Madagascar.

madam ['mædəm] *n* (**a**) madame *f*; *(unmarried)* mademoiselle *f.* *(in letters)* **Dear M~** Madame (*or* Mademoiselle); **M~ Chairman** Madame la Présidente. (**b**) **a little** ~ une petite pimbêche.

made [meɪd] *pret, ptp of* **make**. ◆ **made-to-measure** *adj* fait sur mesure. ◆ **made-to-order** *adj* fait sur commande. ◆ **made-up** *adj story* inventé, factice; *(pej)* faux (*f* fausse); *face, person* maquillé; *eyes, nails* fait.

Madeira [mə'dɪərə] *n (Geog)* Madère *f*; *(wine)* madère *m.*

Madonna [mə'dɒnə] *n* madone *f.*

Madrid [mə'drɪd] *n* Madrid.

mafia ['mæfɪə] *n* maffia *f.*

magazine [ˌmægə'zi:n] *n (Press: abbr* **mag** ***)* revue *f*, magazine *m*; *(Rad, TV: ~ programme)* magazine; *(Mil: store)* magasin *m*; *(in gun) (compartment)* magasin *m; (cartridges)* chargeur *m; (in slide projector)* magasin.

maggot ['mægət] *n* ver *m*, asticot *m.* ◆ **maggoty** *adj* véreux.

magic ['mædʒɪk] **1** *n* magie *f.* **like** ~ comme par enchantement; **it's** ~**!** * c'est génial *. **2** *adj* magique; *(fig)* merveilleux; *beauty* enchanteur (*f* -teresse). ~ **lantern** lanterne *f* magique; ~ **spell** sortilège *m*; **to say the** ~ **word** prononcer la formule magique. ◆ **magical** *adj* magique. ◆ **magically** *adv* magiquement. ◆ **magician** [mə'dʒɪʃ(ə)n] *n* magicien(ne) *m(f)*; *(Theat etc)* illusionniste *mf.*

magistrate ['mædʒɪstreɪt] *n* magistrat *m.*

magnanimous [mæg'nænɪməs] *adj* magnanime. ◆ **magnanimity** *n* magnanimité *f.* ◆ **magnanimously** *adv* magnanimement.

magnate ['mægneɪt] *n* magnat *m.* **industrial** ~ magnat de l'industrie.

magnesia [mæg'ni:ʃə] *n* magnésie *f.*

magnesium [mæg'ni:zɪəm] *n* magnésium *m.*

magnet ['mægnɪt] *n* aimant *m.* ◆ **magnetic** *adj* magnétique; **~ic tape** *(Comput)* bande *f* magnétique. ◆ **magnetically** *adv* magnétiquement. ◆ **magnetism** *n* magnétisme *m.* ◆ **magnetize** *vt* magnétiser. ◆ **magneto** *n* magnéto *f.*

magnificent [mæg'nɪfɪs(ə)nt] *adj* magnifique, splendide; *(sumptuous)* somptueux. ◆ **magnificence** *n* magnificence *f*, splendeur *f*; somptuosité *f.* ◆ **magnificently** *adv* magnifiquement.

magnify ['mægnɪfaɪ] *vt image* grossir; *sound* amplifier; *incident etc* exagérer. **~ing glass** loupe *f.* ◆ **magnification** *n* grossissement *m*; amplification *f.*

magnitude ['mægnɪtju:d] *n (gen)* grandeur *f*; *(Astron)* magnitude *f.*

magnolia [mæg'nəʊlɪə] *n* magnolia *m.*

magnum ['mægnəm] *n* magnum *m.*

magpie ['mægpaɪ] *n* pie *f.*

mahjong [ˌmɑ:'dʒɒŋ] *n* ma(h)jong *m.*

mahogany [mə'hɒgənɪ] **1** *n* acajou *m*. **2** *adj (made of ~)* en acajou; *(~-coloured)* acajou *inv*.

Mahomet [mə'hɒmɪt] *n* Mahomet *m*. ◆ **Mahometan** **1** *adj* mahométan; **2** *n* Mahométan(e) *m(f)*.

maid [meɪd] *n* (**a**) *(servant)* bonne *f*. (**b**) *(pej)* **old ~** vieille fille; *(Hist)* **the M~ (of Orleans)** la Pucelle (d'Orléans). ◆ **maid-of-all-work** *n* bonne *f* à tout faire. ◆ **maid-of-honour** *n* demoiselle *f* d'honneur.

maiden ['meɪdn] **1** *n (liter)* jeune fille *f*. **2** *adj* (**a**) **~ aunt** tante *f* célibataire; **~ lady** demoiselle *f*; **~ name** nom *m* de jeune fille. (**b**) *flight, voyage* premier *(before n)*, inaugural. *(Parl)* **~ speech** premier discours *(d'un député etc)*. ◆ **maidenhair (fern)** *n* capillaire *m (Bot)*.

mail [meɪl] **1** *n* poste *f*; *(letters)* courrier *m*. **by ~** par la poste; **here's your ~** voici votre courrier. **2** *vt* poster. **3** *adj (US Rail)* **~ car** wagon-poste *m*; *(US)* **~ carrier** facteur *m*, préposé(e) *m(f)*; **~ clerk** préposé(e) *m(f)* au courrier; **~ shot** publipostage *m; (US)* **~ slot** entrée *f* des lettres; **~ train** train-poste *m*; *(Brit)* **~ van** *(Aut)* voiture *f or* fourgon *m* des postes; *(Rail)* wagon-poste *m*. ◆ **mailbag** *n* sac postal. ◆ **mailbomb** *n* colis *m* piégé. ◆ **mailbox** *n (US)* boîte *f* aux lettres. ◆ **mailing** *n* publipostage *m;* **~ing list** liste *f* d'adresses. ◆ **mailman** *n (US)* facteur *m*, préposé *m*. ◆ **mail-order** **1** *n* vente *m or* achat *m* par correspondance ; **2** *adj*: **~-order firm** maison *f* de vente par correspondance.

maim [meɪm] *vt* estropier, mutiler.

main [meɪn] **1** *adj feature, objective* principal, essentiel; *door, deck, shop* principal; *pipe, beam* maître (*f* maîtresse). **the ~ body of the army/the crowd** le gros de l'armée/de la foule; **one of his ~ ideas** l'une de ses idées principales; **my ~ idea was...** mon idée directrice était...; **the ~ thing is to...** l'essentiel est de...; **the ~ thing to remember is...** ce qu'il ne faut surtout pas oublier c'est...; *(Aut etc)* **~ bearing** palier *m*; *(Culin)* **~ course** plat *m* de résistance; *(Rail)* **~ line** grande ligne *f*; **a ~ road** une grande route, une route à grande circulation; **the ~ road** la grand-route; **~ street** grand-rue *f*, rue principale.
2 *n* (**a**) *(principal pipe, wire)* canalisation *f or* conduite *f* maîtresse. **electricity ~** conducteur principal; **gas ~** *(in street)* conduite principale; *(house)* conduite de gaz; **~ (sewer)** égout *m* collecteur; **water ~** *(in street or house)* conduite d'eau de la ville; **water from the ~s** eau *f* de la ville; *(Elec)* **connected to the ~s** branché sur le secteur; **it works by battery or from the ~s** cela marche sur piles ou sur le secteur; **to turn off at the ~(s)** couper au compteur. (**b**) **in the ~** dans l'ensemble.
◆ **mainframe (computer)** *n (central computer)* unité *f* centrale; *(large computer)* gros ordinateur *m*. ◆ **mainland** *n* continent *m (opposé à une île)*; **the ~land of Greece** la Grèce continentale. ◆ **mainline *** **1** *vi* se shooter ; **2** *vt* **to ~line heroin** se shooter à l'héroïne. ◆ **mainly** *adv* principalement; *(especially)* surtout. ◆ **mainmast** *n* grand mât *m*. ◆ **mainsail** *n* grand-voile *f*. ◆ **mainspring** *n [clock etc]* ressort *m* principal; *(fig)* mobile *m* principal. ◆ **mainstay** *n (fig)* pilier *m*, soutien *m*. ◆ **mainstream** **1** *n [politics etc]* courant *m* dominant; **2** *adj* dans la ligne du courant dominant.

maintain [meɪn'teɪn] *vt* (**a**) *(continue: gen)* maintenir; *silence* garder; *radio silence* maintenir; *friendship, correspondence* entretenir; *attitude, advantage* conserver; *cause, rights, one's strength* soutenir. **the improvement is ~ed** l'amélioration se maintient. (**b**) *(support) army, family* entretenir. (**c**) *(keep in repair) road, building, machine* entretenir. (**d**) *(assert)* soutenir, maintenir (*that* que).
◆ **maintenance** **1** *n (gen)* maintien *m*; *[army, family, road]* entretien *m*; *(after divorce)* pension *f* alimentaire ; **2** *adj crew, costs* d'entretien; **maintenance allowance** *or* **grant** *[student]* bourse *f* (d'études); *[worker away from home]* indemnité *f* pour frais de déplacement; *(Jur)* **maintenance order** obligation *f* alimentaire.

maisonette [ˌmeɪzə'net] *n* duplex *m*.

maize [meɪz] *n* maïs *m*.

majesty ['mædʒɪstɪ] *n* majesté *f*. **His M~ the King** Sa Majesté le Roi. ◆ **majestic** *adj* majestueux. ◆ **majestically** *adv* majestueusement.

major ['meɪdʒəʳ] **1** *adj* majeur. *(Mus)* **~ key** ton *m* majeur; **in the ~ key** en majeur; **the ~ part** la majeure partie; **for the ~ part** en grande partie; **~ repairs** grosses réparations *fpl;* **~ road** route *f* à priorité; *(Cards)* **~ suit** majeure *f*. **2** *n* (**a**) *(Mil)* commandant *m*. (**b**) *(Jur)* majeur(e) *m(f)*. (**c**) *(US Univ)* matière *f* principale. **3** *vi (US Univ)* se spécialiser (*in* en). ◆ **major-general** *n (Mil)* général *m* de division; *(US Air Force)* général de division aérienne. ◆ **majority** **1** *n (all senses)* majorité *f*; **to be in the ~ity** être en majorité; **elected by a ~ity of 9** élu avec une majorité de 9 voix; **the ~ity of people** la plupart des gens ; **2** *adj government, verdict* majoritaire.

Majorca [mə'jɔːkə] *n* Majorque *f*. **in ~** à Majorque.

make [meɪk] *pret, ptp* **made** **1** *vt* (**a**) *(gen)* faire; *(Comm)* faire, fabriquer; *building* construire; *points, score* marquer. **God made Man** Dieu a créé l'homme; **made in France** fabriqué en France; *(on label)* 'made in France'; **made of gold** en or; *(fig)* **to show what one is made of** donner sa mesure; **as clever as they ~'em *** malin comme pas un *; **this business has made him** cette affaire a fait son succès; **that film made her** ce film l'a consacrée; **he was made for life** son avenir était assuré; **to ~ or break sb** assurer ou briser la carrière de qn; **that made my day! *** ça a transformé ma journée!
(**b**) *(cause to be)* faire; *(+ adj)* rendre. **to ~ sb sad** rendre qn triste; **to ~ o.s. ill** *etc* se rendre malade *etc*; **to ~ o.s. understood** se faire comprendre; **to ~ yellow** jaunir; **to ~ sb king** faire qn roi; **he made him his assistant** il en a fait son assistant; **to ~ sth into sth else** transformer qch en qch d'autre; **let's ~ it £3** si on disait 3 livres.
(**c**) *(force)* faire; *(stronger)* obliger, forcer. **to ~ sb do sth** faire faire qch à qn, obliger *or* forcer qn à faire qch; **to ~ sb wait** faire attendre qn; **I don't know what ~s him do it** je ne sais pas ce qui le pousse à le faire; **you can't ~ me!** tu ne peux pas m'y forcer!; **to ~ believe** faire semblant (*that one is* d'être); **to ~ do with sth/sb** *(be satisfied)* s'arranger de qch/qn; *(manage)* se débrouiller avec qch/qn; *(fig)* **to ~ do and mend** se débrouiller avec ce qu'on a.
(**d**) *(earn etc) money [person]* gagner, *[business deal etc]* rapporter; *profits* faire. **he made £500 on it, it made him £500** cela lui a rapporté 500 livres.
(**e**) *(equal; constitute)* faire. **2 and 2 ~ 4** 2 et 2 font 4; **that ~s 20** ça fait 20; *(in shop etc)* **how much does that ~?** combien ça fait?; **these books ~ a set** ces livres forment une collection; **it ~s pleasant reading** c'est agréable à lire; **they ~ a handsome pair** ils forment un beau couple; **he made a good husband** il s'est montré bon mari; **she made him a good wife** elle a été une bonne épouse pour lui; **he'll ~ a good footballer** il fera un bon joueur de football.
(**f**) *(reach) destination* arriver à; *(catch) train etc* attraper, avoir. **will we ~ (it to) Paris before lunch?** est-ce que nous arriverons à Paris avant le déjeuner?; **to ~ port** arriver au port; **he made (it into) the first team** il a réussi à être sélectionné dans la première équipe; **to ~ it** *(arrive)* arriver;

(achieve sth) parvenir à qch; *(succeed)* réussir, y arriver; **can you ~ it by 3 o'clock?** est-ce que tu peux y être pour 3 heures?; *(Naut)* **to ~ 10 knots** filer 10 nœuds.
(**g**) *(reckon; believe)* **what time do you ~ it?** quelle heure as-tu?; **I ~ it 100 km from here to Paris** selon moi *or* d'après moi il y a 100 km d'ici à Paris; **what do you ~ of him/of it?** qu'est-ce que tu penses de lui/tu en penses?; **I can't ~ anything of it** je n'y comprends rien.
(**h**) *cards* battre; *trick* faire.
2 *vi* (**a**) **to ~ as if to do** faire mine de faire.
(**b**) *(go)* aller, se diriger (*for, towards* vers); *[ship]* faire route (*for* pour). **they made after him** ils se sont mis à sa poursuite; **to ~ for home** rentrer, prendre le chemin du retour; *(fig)* **to ~ for sth** *(result in)* tendre à qch; *(contribute to)* contribuer à qch; *(conduce to)* être favorable à qch.
3 *n* (**a**) *(Comm) (brand)* marque *f*; *(manufacture)* fabrication *f*. **French ~ of car** marque française de voiture; **these are our own ~** ceux-ci sont fabriqués par nous. (**b**) **he's on the ~** * *(wants success)* c'est le succès qui l'intéresse; *(wants money)* il cherche à se remplir les poches.
◆**make away** *vi* = **make off.**
◆**make away with** *vt fus (kill)* supprimer, tuer.
◆**make off** *vi* se sauver, filer *. **to ~ off with sth** filer avec qch.
◆**make out 1** *vi (*: get on)* se débrouiller. **2** *vt sep* (**a**) *(draw up) list, account* faire, dresser; *bill, will* faire; *cheque* faire (*to* à l'ordre de). (**b**) *(distinguish) object, person* distinguer; *(decipher) handwriting* déchiffrer; *(understand) sb's motives* comprendre. **I can't ~ it out at all** je n'y comprends rien; **how do you ~ that out?** qu'est-ce qui vous fait penser cela? (**c**) *(claim)* prétendre (*that* que); *(imply)* faire paraître. **it ~s her out to be naïve** cela la fait passer pour naïve.
◆**make over** *vt sep* (**a**) *(assign) money, land* céder (*to* à). (**b**) *(remake) garment* refaire.
◆**make up 1** *vi* (**a**) *(~ friends again)* se réconcilier. (**b**) *(apply cosmetics)* se maquiller. **2** *vt sep* (**a**) *(invent) story* inventer. (**b**) *(put together) packet, parcel, list, bed* faire; *medicine, solution* préparer; *prescription* exécuter. **to ~ sth up into a bundle** faire un paquet de qch. (**c**) *(complete etc) loss, deficit* combler; *quantity, total* compléter; *lost time* rattraper; *lost ground* regagner. **he made it up to £100** il a complété les 100 livres; **to ~ it up to sb for sth** dédommager qn de qch. (**d**) *(settle) dispute* mettre fin à. **to ~ it up** se réconcilier; **let's ~ it up** faisons la paix. (**e**) *(cosmetics)* maquiller. (**f**) *(form) a whole etc* former. **group made up of** groupe fait *or* formé *or* composé de.
◆**make up for** *vt fus loss, injury* compenser; *lost time* rattraper; *trouble caused* se faire pardonner; *mistake* se rattraper pour.
◆**make up on** *vt fus (catch up with)* rattraper.
◆**make up to** * *vt fus (curry favour with)* essayer de se faire bien voir par.
◆**make-believe** *n*: **the land of ~-believe** le pays des chimères; **it's just ~-believe** *(activity)* c'est pour faire semblant; *(pej: story)* c'est de l'invention pure. ◆**maker** *n (Comm)* fabricant *m*; *(Rel)* **our M~r** le Créateur. ◆**makeshift 1** *n* expédient *m* ; **2** *adj* de fortune. ◆**make-up 1** *n* (**a**) *(nature etc) [object, group etc]* constitution *f*; *[person]* caractère *m*; (**b**) *(cosmetics)* maquillage *m* ; **2** *adj*: **~-up artist** maquilleur *m*, -euse *f*; **~-up bag** trousse *f* de maquillage; *(US Scol)* **~-up class** cours *m* de rattrapage; **~-up remover** démaquillant *m*. ◆**making** *n* (**a**) *(Comm, gen)* fabrication *f*; *[dress, food]* confection *f*; **in the making** en formation; **still in the making** encore en cours de développement; **history in the making** l'histoire en train de se faire; **war in the making** la guerre qui se prépare; **troubles of his own making** des ennuis qu'il a provoqués lui-même; **it was the making of him/her** cela en a fait un homme/une femme; (**b**) **the makings of a library** ce qu'il faut pour faire une bibliothèque; **he has the makings of a footballer** il a l'étoffe d'un joueur de football.

maladjusted [ˌmæləˈdʒʌstɪd] *adj (Psych)* inadapté.
maladroit [ˌmæləˈdrɔɪt] *adj* maladroit.
malady [ˈmælədɪ] *n* maladie *f*, mal *m*.
malaria [məˈlɛərɪə] *n* malaria *f*.
Malawi [məˈlɑːwɪ] *n* Malawi *m*.
Malaya [məˈleɪə] *n* Malaisie *f*. ◆**Malay(an) 1** *adj* malais; **2** *n* Malais(e) *m(f)*.
male [meɪl] **1** *adj (gen)* mâle; *sex* masculin; *clothes* d'homme. **~ chauvinist pig** sale phallocrate ‡ *m*. **2** *n* mâle *m*.
malevolent [məˈlevələnt] *adj* malveillant. ◆**malevolence** *n* malveillance *f*. ◆**malevolently** *adv* avec malveillance.
malformation [ˌmælfɔːˈmeɪʃ(ə)n] *n* malformation *f*.
malfunction [ˌmælˈfʌŋkʃ(ə)n] **1** *n* mauvais fonctionnement *m*. **2** *vi* mal fonctionner.
malice [ˈmælɪs] *n* méchanceté *f*; *(stronger)* malveillance *f*. **to bear sb ~** vouloir du mal à qn; *(Jur)* **~ aforethought** préméditation *f*. ◆**malicious** *adj* méchant; malveillant; *(Jur) damage* causé avec intention de nuire. ◆**maliciously** *adv* avec méchanceté; avec malveillance.
malign [məˈlaɪn] **1** *adj* pernicieux, nuisible. **2** *vt* calomnier. ◆**malignancy** [məˈlɪgnənsɪ] *n [look, intention]* malveillance *f*; *[action, effect]* malfaisance *f*; *(Med)* malignité *f*. ◆**malignant** *adj* malveillant; malfaisant; *(Med)* malin (*f* -igne).
malinger [məˈlɪŋgəʳ] *vi* faire le (*or* la) malade. ◆**malingerer** *n* faux (*or* fausse) malade *m(f)*.
mall [mɔːl] *n (US) (street)* rue *f* piétonnière; *(also* **shopping ~***)* centre *m* commercial.
mallard [ˈmæləd] *n* canard *m* sauvage.
malleable [ˈmælɪəbl] *adj* malléable.
mallet [ˈmælɪt] *n (all senses)* maillet *m*.
malnutrition [ˌmælnjʊˈtrɪʃ(ə)n] *n* sous-alimentation *f*.
malt [mɔːlt] **1** *n* malt *m*. **2** *adj vinegar* de malt. **~ed milk** lait malté; *(US)* **~ liquor** bière *f*; **~ whisky** whisky *m* pur malt.
Malta [ˈmɔːltə] *n* Malte *f*. **in ~** à Malte.
maltreat [ˌmælˈtriːt] *vt* maltraiter. ◆**maltreatment** *n* mauvais traitement *m*.
mam(m)a [məˈmɑː] *n* maman *f*.
mammal [ˈmæm(ə)l] *n* mammifère *m*.
mammoth [ˈmæməθ] **1** *n* mammouth *m*. **2** *adj* monstre.
man [mæn] **1** *n, pl* **men** *(gen)* homme *m*; *(servant)* valet *m*; *(in factory etc)* ouvrier *m*; *(in office, shop etc)* employé *m*; *(Mil)* homme (de troupe), soldat *m*; *(Naut)* homme (d'équipage), matelot *m*; *(Sport: player)* joueur *m*; *(husband)* homme, type * *m*; *(Chess)* pièce *f*; *(Draughts)* pion *m*. **an old ~** un vieillard; **a blind ~** un aveugle; **that ~ Smith** ce Smith; **men's room** toilettes *fpl* pour hommes; **as one ~** comme un seul homme; **they're communists to a ~** ils sont tous communistes sans exception; **to the last ~** jusqu'au dernier; **every ~ jack of them** tous autant qu'ils sont; **~ and wife** mari et femme; **to live as ~ and wife** vivre maritalement; **he was ~ enough to apologize** il a eu le courage de s'excuser; **he's a Leeds ~** il est *or* vient de Leeds; **he's not the ~ to fail** il n'est pas homme à échouer; **the ~ for the job** l'homme qu'il faut pour ce travail; **a medical ~** un docteur; **the ~ in the street** l'homme de la rue; **~ of the world** homme d'expérience; **~ about town** homme du monde; **the ice-cream ~** le marchand de glaces; *(humanity)* **M~** l'homme; **men say that...** on dit

que...; **any ~ would have...** n'importe qui aurait...; **hurry up, ~! *** *(to friend etc)* dépêche-toi mon vieux! *; **my little** ~ mon grand; **good ~!** bravo!

2 *vt* (**a**) *(provide staff for)* assurer une permanence à; *(work at)* être de service à. **the telephone is ~ned 12 hours a day** il y a une permanence au téléphone 12 heures par jour. (**b**) *(Mil)* **to ~ a ship** *(gen)* équiper un navire en personnel; **the ship was ~ned by Chinese** l'équipage était composé de Chinois; **the troops who ~ned the look-out posts** les troupes qui étaient de service aux postes d'observation; **the soldiers ~ning the fortress** les soldats qui étaient en garnison dans la forteresse.

◆ **man-eating** *adj animal* mangeur d'hommes; *tribe etc* anthropophage. ◆ **manful** *adj* vaillant. ◆ **manfully** *adv* vaillamment. ◆ **manhandle** *vt (treat roughly)* malmener; *(move by hand) goods etc* manutentionner. ◆ **manhole** *n* regard *m* (d'égout) ; **~hole cover** plaque *f* d'égout. ◆ **manhood** *n* (**a**) *(age, state)* âge *m* d'homme; **during his early ~hood** quand il était jeune homme; (**b**) *(manliness)* virilité *f*; (**c**) *(collect n)* **Scotland's ~hood** tous les hommes d'Écosse. ◆ **man-hour** *n (Ind)* heure *f* de main-d'œuvre. ◆ **manhunt** *n* chasse *f* à l'homme. ◆ **mankind** *n* l'homme *m*, le genre humain. ◆ **manlike** *adj form, figure* à l'aspect humain; *qualities* humain. ◆ **manliness** *n* virilité *f*. ◆ **manly** *adj* viril. ◆ **man-made** *adj fibre* synthétique; *lake* artificiel. ◆ **mannish** *adj* masculin, hommasse *(pej)*. ◆ **manpower** *n (gen, Ind)* main-d'œuvre *f*; *(Mil)* effectifs *mpl*. ◆ **manservant** *n* valet *m* de chambre. ◆ **man-sized** *adj (fig)* grand, de taille. ◆ **manslaughter** *n (Jur)* homicide *m* involontaire. ◆ **man-to-man** *adj, adv* d'homme à homme. ◆ **mantrap** *n* piège *m* à hommes.

manacle ['mænəkl] *n* menotte *f (de prisonnier)*.

manage ['mænɪdʒ] **1** *vt* (**a**) *(direct: gen, Comm)* gérer; *institution, organization* diriger; *farm* exploiter; *(pej) election etc* truquer. (**b**) *(deal with) boat, vehicle* manœuvrer; *tool* manier; *animal, person* savoir s'y prendre avec. **you ~d the situation very well** tu t'en es très bien tiré. (**c**) *(succeed, contrive)* réussir, arriver *(to do* à faire). **how did you ~ not to spill it?** comment as-tu fait pour ne pas le renverser?; *(iro)* **he ~d to annoy them** il a trouvé le moyen de les mécontenter; **I can't ~ it** je ne peux pas; **I can ~ 10 francs** je peux y mettre 10 F; **can you ~ the suitcases?** pouvez-vous porter les valises?; **can you ~ 8 o'clock?** 8 heures, ça vous convient? **2** *vi* (**a**) *(succeed)* **can you ~?** tu y arrives?; **I can ~** ça va; **to ~ without sth/sb** se passer de qch/qn. (**b**) *(financially)* se débrouiller *(on* avec).

◆ **manageable** *adj vehicle, boat* facile à manœuvrer; *person, animal* docile; *size, proportions* maniable; *hair* souple. ◆ **management** **1** *n* (**a**) *(act: V* **manage 1a***)* gestion *f*; direction *f*; exploitation *f*; **'under new ~ment'** 'changement de direction'; (**b**) *(people) [business, firm]* cadres *mpl*, direction *f*; *[hotel, shop, theatre]* direction; **the ~ment and the workers** les cadres et les ouvriers; **~ment and unions** les partenaires *mpl* sociaux; **2** *adj committee* de direction; **~ment consultant** conseiller *m* de gestion; **~ment trainee** cadre *m* stagiaire. ◆ **manager** *n (gen)* directeur *m*; *[restaurant, shop]* gérant *m*; *[farm]* exploitant *m*; *[actor, singer, boxer etc]* manager *m*; **sales ~r** directeur commercial. ◆ **manageress** *n [hotel, shop]* gérante *f*; *[theatre]* directrice *f*. ◆ **managerial** *adj* directorial; **the ~rial class** les cadres *mpl*. ◆ **managing** *adj* (**a**) **managing director** directeur général, ≃ P.-D.G. *m*; (**b**) *(bossy)* autoritaire.

mandarin ['mændərɪn] *n* (**a**) *(person)* mandarin *m*. (**b**) ~ **(orange)** mandarine *f*.

mandate ['mændeɪt] *n* mandat *m* *(to do* de faire). ◆ **mandatory** *adj* obligatoire.

mandolin(e) ['mændəlɪn] *n* mandoline *f*.

mane [meɪn] *n* crinière *f*.

maneuver [mə'nu:vər] *etc (US)* = **manœuvre** *etc*.

manganese [ˌmæŋgə'ni:z] *n* manganèse *m*.

mange [meɪn(d)ʒ] *n* gale *f*.

manger ['meɪn(d)ʒər] *n* mangeoire *f*; *(Rel)* crèche *f*.

mangle[1] ['mæŋgl] **1** *n (wringer)* essoreuse *f (à rouleaux)*. **2** *vt* essorer.

mangle[2] ['mæŋgl] *vt (mutilate) object, body* déchirer; *text* mutiler; *quotation, message* estropier.

mango ['mæŋgəʊ] *n (fruit)* mangue *f*; *(tree)* manguier *m*. ~ **chutney** condiment *m* à la mangue.

mania ['meɪnɪə] *n* manie *f*. **persecution** ~ manie de la persécution; **to have a ~ for (doing) sth *** avoir la manie de (faire) qch. ◆ **maniac** **1** *n (Psych)* maniaque *mf*; *(*: fig)* fou *m* (folle *f*) à lier; **football ~c *** mordu * *m* du football ; **2** *adj* maniaque; fou. ◆ **manic** *adj (Psych)* maniaque; **manic depression** cyclothymie *f*. ◆ **manic-depressive** *adj, n* cyclothymique *(mf)*.

manicure ['mænɪˌkjʊər] **1** *n* soin *m* des mains. **2** *vt nails* (se) faire. ◆ **manicurist** *n* manucure *mf*.

manifest ['mænɪfest] **1** *adj* manifeste. **2** *vt* manifester. **3** *n* manifeste *m (Aviat, Naut)*. ◆ **manifestation** *n* manifestation *f*. ◆ **manifestly** *adv* manifestement. ◆ **manifesto** *n* manifeste *m (Pol etc)*.

manifold ['mænɪfəʊld] **1** *adj (varied)* divers; *(numerous)* multiple; *wisdom* infini. **2** *n (Aut etc)* **exhaust** ~ tubulure *f* d'échappement.

Manila [mə'nɪlə] *n* Manille, Manila.

manipulate [mə'nɪpjʊleɪt] *vt tool etc* manipuler; *vehicle, person* manœuvrer; *(pej) facts, figures* tripoter *. **to ~ a situation** exploiter une situation à son avantage. ◆ **manipulation** *n* manipulation *f*; manœuvre *f*; *(pej)* tripotage * *m*.

manna ['mænə] *n* manne *f*.

mannequin ['mænɪkɪn] *n* mannequin *m*.

manner ['mænər] *n* (**a**) *(mode, way)* manière *f*, façon *f*. **the ~ in which he did it** la manière *or* façon dont il l'a fait; **in such a ~ that** de telle sorte que + *indic (actual result) or* + *subj (intended result)*; **in this** ~ de cette manière *or* façon; **in a ~ of speaking** pour ainsi dire; **it's a ~ of speaking** c'est une façon de parler; ~ **of payment** mode *m* de paiement; **(as) to the ~ born** comme s'il *(or* elle *etc)* avait cela dans le sang. (**b**) *(attitude)* attitude *f (to sb* envers qn), comportement *m*. (**c**) *(social)* **~s** manières *fpl*; **it's good/bad ~s** cela se fait/ne se fait pas *(to do* de faire); **road ~s** politesse *f* au volant; **comedy of ~s** comédie *f* de mœurs. (**d**) *(type)* sorte *f*, genre *m*. **all ~ of** toutes sortes de.

◆ **mannered** *adj* maniéré. ◆ **mannerism** *n* (**a**) *(habit)* trait *m* particulier; *(pej)* tic *m*; (**b**) *(Art etc)* maniérisme *m*. ◆ **mannerly** *adj* poli, bien élevé.

man(n)ikin ['mænɪkɪn] *n* (**a**) *(dwarf etc)* nabot *m*. (**b**) *(dummy)* mannequin *m (objet)*.

manœuvre [mə'nu:vər] **1** *n* manœuvre *f*. *(Mil etc)* **on ~s** en manœuvres. **2** *vt (all senses)* manœuvrer *(sth into position* qch pour le mettre en position; *sb into doing* qn pour qu'il fasse). **to ~ sth through** *etc* faire traverser *etc* qch en manœuvrant. **3** *vi* manœuvrer. ◆ **manœuvrability** *n* manœuvrabilité *f*. ◆ **manœuvrable** *adj* facile à manœuvrer.

manor ['mænər] *n* (~ **house)** manoir *m*.

mansion ['mænʃ(ə)n] *n (in town)* hôtel *m* particulier; *(in country)* château *m*, manoir *m*.

mantel ['mæntl] *n* (**~piece, ~shelf)** (tablette *f* de) cheminée *f*.

mantle ['mæntl] *n* (†: *garment)* cape *f*; *[gas lamp]* manchon *m*. ~ **of snow** manteau *m* de neige.

manual ['mænjʊəl] **1** *adj* manuel. ~ **worker** travailleur manuel. **2** *n (book)* manuel *m*; *[organ]* clavier *m*. ◆ **manually** *adv* à la main.

manufacture [ˌmænjʊ'fæktʃə^r] **1** *n (gen)* fabrication *f*; *[clothes]* confection *f*. **2** *vt* fabriquer *(also fig)*; confectionner. ~**d goods** produits manufacturés. ◆ **manufacturing 1** *n* fabrication *f* ; **2** *adj town* industriel; *industry* de fabrication manufacturière. ◆ **manufacturer** *n* fabricant *m*.

manure [mə'njʊə^r] **1** *n* fumier *m*; *(artificial)* engrais *m*. **liquid** ~ *(organic)* purin *m*, lisier *m; (artificial)* engrais *m* liquide. **2** *adj*: ~ **heap** tas *m* de fumier. **3** *vt* fumer; répandre des engrais sur.

manuscript ['mænjʊskrɪpt] *adj, n* manuscrit *(m)*.

Manx [mæŋks] **1** *adj* de l'île de Man. **2** *n (Ling)* mannois *m*.

many ['menɪ] *adj, pron: comp* **more,** *superl* **most** (**a**) beaucoup (de), un grand nombre (de). ~ **books** beaucoup de livres, un grand nombre de livres, de nombreux livres; **very** ~ un très grand nombre (de); ~ **of them/of those books** un grand nombre d'entre eux/de ces livres; **a good** ~ **of** un bon nombre de; ~ **came** beaucoup sont venus; ~ **times** bien des fois; ~ **years** bien des années, longtemps; **of** ~ **kinds** de toutes sortes; **a good** *or* **great** ~ **things** pas mal de choses *; **in** ~ **cases** dans bien des cas; ~ **a man would be...** il y en a plus d'un qui serait...; ~ **happy returns (of the day)!** bon *or* joyeux anniversaire!
(**b**) *(in phrases)* **as** ~ **as** autant que; **as** ~ **books as** autant de livres que; **as** ~ **as 100 people** jusqu'à 100 personnes; **how** ~**?** combien?; **how** ~ **people?** combien de gens?; **how** ~ **there are!** qu'ils sont nombreux!; **however** ~ **books you have** quel que soit le nombre de livres que vous ayez; **so** ~ tant *(that* que); **so** ~ **dresses** tant de robes; **ever so** ~ **times** je ne sais combien de fois; **too** ~ trop; **too** ~ **cakes** trop de gâteaux; **3 too** ~ 3 de trop; *(fig)* **he's had one too** ~ * il a bu un coup de trop; **there are too** ~ **of you** vous êtes trop nombreux. ◆ **many-coloured** *adj* multicolore. ◆ **many-sided** *adj object* qui a de nombreux côtés; *(fig) person* aux intérêts (*or* talents) variés; *problem* complexe.

map [mæp] **1** *n (gen)* carte *f*; *[town, railway]* plan *m*. *(fig)* **this will put Moordown on the** ~ cela fera connaître Moordown; *(fig)* **wiped off the** ~ rayé de la carte; *(fig)* **off the** ~ * à l'autre bout du monde, perdu. **2** *vt* faire la carte *or* le plan de; *route* tracer. ◆ **map out** *vt sep route* tracer; *book* établir les grandes lignes de; *one's time, career* organiser; *plan* élaborer. ◆ **mapmaker** *n* cartographe *m*. ◆ **mapmaking** *n* cartographie *f*. ◆ **mapping pen** *n* plume *f* à dessin.

maple ['meɪpl] **1** *n* érable *m*. **2** *adj* d'érable.

mar [mɑː^r] *vt* gâter. **to make or** ~ **sth** assurer le succès ou l'échec de qch.

maraschino [ˌmærəs'kiːnəʊ] *n* marasquin *m*.

marathon ['mærəθ(ə)n] **1** *n* marathon *m*. **2** *adj meeting etc* marathon *inv*; *(Sport) runner* de marathon.

maraud [mə'rɔːd] *vi* marauder. **to go** ~**ing** aller à la maraude. ◆ **marauder** *n* maraudeur *m*, -euse *f*. ◆ **marauding** *adj* maraudeur.

marble ['mɑːbl] **1** *n* (**a**) *(substance, sculpture etc)* marbre *m*. (**b**) *(toy)* bille *f*. **to play** ~**s** jouer aux billes. **2** *adj staircase* de *or* en marbre; *industry* marbrier. ~ **quarry** marbrière *f*.

March [mɑːtʃ] *n* mars *m*; *for phrases V* **September.**

march [mɑːtʃ] **1** *n (gen)* marche *f*; *(demonstration)* défilé *m*. **on the** ~ en marche; **quick/slow** ~ marche rapide/lente; **a day's** ~ une journée de marche. **2** *vi (Mil etc)* marcher au pas; *(demonstrate)* manifester. **to** ~ **into battle** marcher au combat; **to** ~ **past** défiler; **to** ~ **past sb** défiler devant qn; ~! marche!; **to** ~ **in** *etc (Mil)* entrer *etc* (au pas); *(gen)* entrer *etc (briskly)* d'un pas énergique *or (angrily)* d'un air furieux; **he** ~**ed up to me** il s'est approché de moi d'un air décidé; **to** ~ **up and down the room** faire les cent pas dans la pièce. **3** *vt (Mil)* faire marcher (au pas). *(gen)* **to** ~ **sb in** *etc* faire entrer *etc* qn tambour battant; **to** ~ **sb off to prison** embarquer qn en prison *. ◆ **marcher** *n* manifestant(e) *m(f)*. ◆ **marching** *adj song* de route; *(US)* ~**ing band** orchestre *m* d'école (avec majorettes); ~**ing orders** feuille *f* de route; *(fig)* **to give sb his** ~**ing orders** * flanquer * qn à la porte. ◆ **march-past** *n* défilé *m (Mil etc)*.

marchioness ['mɑːʃ(ə)nɪs] *n* marquise *f (title)*.

mare [mɛə^r] *n* jument *f*.

margarine [ˌmɑːdʒə'riːn] *n (abbr* **marge** *) margarine *f*.

margin ['mɑːdʒɪn] *n (gen, also fig)* marge *f*; *[wood]* lisière *f*. **notes in the** ~ notes en marge; **do not write in the** ~ n'écrivez pas dans la marge; *(fig)* **to win by a wide/narrow** ~ gagner de loin/de peu; **elected by a narrow** ~ élu avec peu de voix de majorité. ◆ **marginal** *adj (gen)* marginal; *ability* très moyen; *importance* secondaire; *case* limite; *existence* précaire; *land* de faible rendement; *(Parl)* ~**al seat** siège *m* disputé. ◆ **marginally** *adv* très légèrement.

marguerite [ˌmɑːgə'riːt] *n* marguerite *f*.

marigold ['mærɪgəʊld] *n (Bot)* souci *m*.

marijuana [ˌmærɪ'hwɑːnə] *n* marijuana *f*.

marina [mə'riːnə] *n* marina *f*.

marinade [ˌmærɪ'neɪd] *n* marinade *f*. ◆ **marinate** *vt* mariner.

marine [mə'riːn] **1** *adj plant, animal, life* marin; *products* de mer; *forces, insurance* maritime. ~ **engineering** génie *m* maritime. **2** *n* (**a**) **mercantile** *or* **merchant** ~ marine *f* marchande. (**b**) *(Mil)* fusilier *m* marin; *(US)* marine *m* (américain). *(fig)* **tell that to the** ~**s!** * à d'autres! ◆ **mariner** ['mærɪnə^r] *n (liter)* marin *m*; ~**r's compass** boussole *f*.

marionette [ˌmærɪə'net] *n* marionnette *f*.

marital ['mærɪtl] *adj problems* matrimonial; *happiness, relations* conjugal. *(Admin)* ~ **status** situation, *f* de famille.

maritime ['mærɪtaɪm] *adj* maritime.

marjoram ['mɑːdʒ(ə)rəm] *n* marjolaine *f*.

mark[1] [mɑːk] *n (currency)* mark *m*.

mark[2] [mɑːk] **1** *n* (**a**) *(gen)* marque *f*. **to make a** ~ **on** marquer; **the** ~**s of his shoes in...** l'empreinte *f* de ses souliers dans...; **without a** ~ **on his body** sans trace *f* de coups sur le corps; *(fig)* **to make one's** ~ **as** se faire un nom en tant que; **to leave one's** ~ **on sth** laisser son empreinte sur qch; **the** ~ **of a good teacher** le signe d'un bon professeur; **the** ~ **of genius** la marque du génie; **as a** ~ **of my gratitude** en témoignage de ma gratitude; **punctuation** ~ signe *m* de ponctuation; **finger** ~ trace *f* de doigt. (**b**) *(Scol)* note *f*. **good/bad** ~ bonne/mauvaise note (*in* en); **to fail by 2** ~**s** échouer à 2 points; *(fig)* **I give him full** ~**s for helping** je lui donne un bon point pour son aide; **there are no** ~**s for guessing his name** il n'y a pas besoin d'être un génie pour savoir de qui on parle. (**c**) *(Sport etc: target)* but *m*, cible *f*. *(fig)* **to hit the** ~ mettre le doigt dessus *; *(fig)* **to miss** *or* **be wide of the** ~ être loin de la vérité. (**d**) *(Sport)* ligne *f* de départ. **on your** ~**s! get set! go!** à vos marques! prêts! partez!; *(lit, fig)* **to get off the** ~ démarrer; *(fig)* **to be quick off the** ~ ne pas perdre de temps (*in doing* pour faire); **up to the** ~ *(in health)* en forme; *(in efficiency etc) person* à la hauteur; *work* satisfaisant; **to come up to the** ~ répondre à l'attente. (**e**) *(Tech)* **M**~ série *f*; **Concorde M**~ **1** Concorde première série.

2 *vt* (**a**) *(make a ~ on)* marquer; *(stain)* tacher, marquer. (**b**) *(indicate) price, score* marquer; *change, improvement* indiquer. **X ~s the spot** l'endroit est marqué d'une croix; **in order to ~ the occasion** pour marquer l'occasion; **to ~ time** *(Mil)* marquer le pas; *(fig)* faire du sur-place; *(by choice: before doing sth)* attendre son heure. (**c**) *exam* corriger. **to ~ sth right/wrong** marquer qch juste/faux. (**d**) *(note)* noter; *(Sport) opposing player* marquer. **~ my words** écoutez-moi bien.
3 *vi*: **this material ~s easily** tout marque ce tissu; **this material will not ~** rien ne se voit sur ce tissu.
◆ **mark down** *vt sep* (**a**) *(write down)* inscrire, noter. (**b**) *(reduce) price* baisser; *goods* démarquer. (**c**) *(single out)* désigner (*for* pour).
◆ **mark off** *vt sep* (**a**) *(separate)* séparer, distinguer (*from* de). (**b**) *(tick off) names* cocher.
◆ **mark out** *vt sep* (**a**) *zone etc* délimiter; *field* borner; *tennis court* tracer les lignes de. (**b**) *(single out)* désigner (*for* pour). **it ~ed him out from the others** cela le distinguait des autres.
◆ **mark up** *vt sep* (**a**) *(write up) price, score* marquer. (**b**) *(increase) price* augmenter; *goods* majorer le prix de. **to be ~ed up** augmenter.
◆ **marked** *adj difference, accent, bias* marqué; *improvement, increase* sensible; **a ~ed man** un homme marqué. ◆ **markedly** *adv differ* d'une façon marquée; *improve* sensiblement. ◆ **marker** *n* (**a**) *(pen)* marqueur *m* indélébile; *(tool: for laundry etc)* marquoir *m*; (**b**) *(flag, stake)* marque *f*, jalon *m*; *(light etc)* balise *f*; (**c**) *(bookmark)* signet *m*; (**d**) *(Sport: person)* marqueur *m*, -euse *f*; (**e**) *(Scol)* correcteur *m*. ◆ **marking** **1** *n* (**a**) *(Scol)* correction *f* (de copies); *(giving marks)* notation *f*; (**b**) *(on animal etc)* marques *fpl*; *(on road)* signalisation *f* horizontale ; **2** *adj*: **~ing ink** encre *f* à marquer. ◆ **marksman** *n* tireur *m* d'élite. ◆ **marksmanship** *n* adresse *f* au tir. ◆ **mark-up** *n (profit)* marge *f* bénéficiaire; *(increase)* hausse *f*.

market ['mɑːkɪt] **1** *n* marché *m*. **to go to ~** aller au marché; **the wholesale ~** le marché de gros; **cattle ~** marché *or* foire *f* aux bestiaux; **the ~ in sugar** le marché du sucre; *(St Ex)* **the ~ is rising** les cours *mpl* sont en hausse; **to have a good ~ for sth** avoir une grosse demande pour qch; **there is a ready ~ for small cars** les petites voitures se vendent bien; **this appeals to the French ~** cela se vend bien en France; **to be in the ~ for sth** être acheteur de qch; **on the ~** sur le marché; **on the open ~** en vente libre. **2** *adj day, analysis* de marché; *square, trends* du marché; *value, price* marchand. **~ economy** économie *f* de marché; **~ garden** jardin *m* maraîcher; **~ gardener** maraîcher *m*, -ère *f*; **~ gardening** culture *f* maraîchère; *(Econ)* **in the ~ place** sur le marché; *(St Ex)* **~ prices** cours *m* du marché; **~ research** étude *f* de marché (*in* de); **~ value** valeur *f* marchande, valeur du marché. **3** *vt (sell)* vendre; *(launch)* lancer sur le marché; *(find outlet for)* trouver un débouché pour. ◆ **marketable** *adj* vendable. ◆ **marketing** *n* marketing *m*.

marmalade ['mɑːməleɪd] *n* confiture *f* d'oranges. **~ orange** orange *f* amère.

marmoset ['mɑːmə(ʊ)zet] *n* ouistiti *m*.

marmot ['mɑːmət] *n* marmotte *f*.

maroon[1] [mə'ruːn] *adj (colour)* bordeaux *inv*.

maroon[2] [mə'ruːn] *vt*: **~ed** *(on island)* abandonné; *(by sea, traffic, strike etc)* bloqué (*by* par).

marquee [mɑː'kiː] *n* grande tente *f*.

marquess, marquis ['mɑːkwɪs] *n* marquis *m*.

marriage ['mærɪdʒ] **1** *n* mariage *m*. **by ~** par alliance. **2** *adj bed* conjugal; *vows* de mariage. **~ bureau** agence *f* matrimoniale; **~ certificate** extrait *m* d'acte de mariage; **~ guidance counsellor** conseiller *m*, -ère *f* conjugal(e); **~ licence** ≃ certificat *m* de publication des bans. ◆ **marriageable** *adj*: **of ~able age** en âge de se marier.

marrow ['mærəʊ] *n* (**a**) *[bone]* moelle *f*. **~ bone** os *m* à moelle; **chilled to the ~** gelé jusqu'à la moelle des os. (**b**) *(vegetable)* courge *f*. **baby ~** courgette *f*.

marry ['mærɪ] **1** *vt (take in marriage)* épouser, se marier avec; *[priest, parent]* marier. **will you ~ me?** voulez-vous m'épouser?; **to get** *or* **be married** se marier. **2** *vi* se marier. **to ~ into a family** s'allier à une famille par le mariage; **to ~ beneath o.s.** se mésallier; **to ~ again** se remarier. ◆ **married** *adj person* marié; *name* de femme mariée; *life, love* conjugal; *(Mil)* **married quarters** appartements *mpl* pour familles.

Mars [mɑːz] *n (Astron)* Mars *f*; *(Myth)* Mars *m*.

Marseilles [mɑː'seɪlz] *n* Marseille.

marsh [mɑːʃ] *n (also ~land)* marais *m*, marécage *m*. ◆ **marshmallow** *n* guimauve *f*. ◆ **marsh marigold** *n* souci *m* d'eau. ◆ **marshy** *adj* marécageux.

marshal ['mɑːʃ(ə)l] **1** *n (Mil etc)* maréchal *m*; *(at demonstration, meeting etc)* membre *m* du service d'ordre. **2** *vt troops* rassembler; *crowd* faire entrer *etc* en bon ordre; *wagons* trier; *(fig) facts, one's wits* rassembler. ◆ **marshalling yard** *n* gare *f* de triage.

marsupial [mɑː'suːpɪəl] *adj, n* marsupial *(m)*.

marten ['mɑːtɪn] *n* martre *f*.

martial ['mɑːʃ(ə)l] *adj* martial. **~ arts** arts *mpl* martiaux; **~ law** loi martiale.

Martian ['mɑːʃɪən] *n* Martien(ne) *m(f)*.

martin ['mɑːtɪn] *n (house ~)* hirondelle *f* (de fenêtre).

martinet [ˌmɑːtɪ'net] *n*: **to be a ~** être impitoyable en matière de discipline.

martyr ['mɑːtəʳ] *n* martyr(e) *m(f)*. **he is a ~ to migraine** ses migraines lui font souffrir le martyre. ◆ **martyrdom** *n* martyre *m*.

marvel ['mɑːv(ə)l] **1** *n [nature, patience]* merveille *f*; *[science, skill]* prodige *m*. **it will be a ~ if...** ce sera (un) miracle si...; **it's a ~ to me how...** je ne sais vraiment pas comment...; **it's a ~ to me that** cela me paraît un miracle que + *subj*, je n'en reviens pas que + *subj*; **it's a ~ that** c'est un miracle que + *subj*. **2** *vi* s'émerveiller, s'étonner (*at* de; *that* de ce que + *indic or subj*). ◆ **marvellous,** *(US)* **marvelous** *adj* merveilleux. ◆ **marvel(l)ously** *adv* merveilleusement.

Marxism ['mɑːksɪz(ə)m] *n* marxisme *m*. ◆ **Marxist** *adj, n* marxiste *(mf)*.

marzipan [ˌmɑːzɪ'pæn] *n* pâte *f* d'amandes.

mascara [mæs'kɑːrə] *n* mascara *m*.

mascot ['mæskət] *n* mascotte *f*.

masculine ['mæskjʊlɪn] *adj, n* masculin *(m)*. ◆ **masculinity** *n* masculinité *f*.

mash [mæʃ] **1** *n (also* **~ed potatoes***)* purée *f* (de pommes de terre). **2** *vt* (**~ up**) *(Culin)* faire une purée de; *(gen, Tech)* écraser.

mask [mɑːsk] **1** *n* masque *m*. **2** *vt* masquer. ◆ **masking tape** *n* papier-cache *m* adhésif.

masochism ['mæsə(ʊ)kɪz(ə)m] *n* masochisme *m*. ◆ **masochist** *n* masochiste *mf*. ◆ **masochistic** *adj* masochiste.

mason ['meɪsn] *n* maçon *m*; *(free ~)* franc-maçon *m*. *(US)* **M~ jar** bocal *m* à conserves (étanche). ◆ **masonic** [mə'sɒnɪk] *adj* franc-maçonnique. ◆ **masonry** *n* maçonnerie *f*; franc-maçonnerie *f*.

Masonite ® ['meɪsənaɪt] *n* aggloméré *m*.

masquerade [ˌmæskə'reɪd] **1** *n* mascarade. **2** *vi*: **to ~ as** se faire passer pour.

mass[1] [mæs] **1** *n* masse *f*. **in the ~** dans l'ensemble; **he was a ~ of bruises** il était couvert de bleus;

~es of * des masses de *, des tas de *; *(people)* **the ~(es)** la masse, les masses populaires; **Shakespeare for the ~es** Shakespeare à l'usage des masses. **2** *adj culture* de masse; *psychology, education* des masses; *support, destruction* massif, généralisé; *rally* monstre; *resignations* en masse; *demonstration* en masse, massif; *funeral, protest, hysteria* collectif. ~ **grave** fosse *f* commune; ~ **media** mass-media *mpl*; ~ **meeting** grand rassemblement *m*; ~ **murders** tueries *fpl*; ~ **murderer** boucher *m*. **3** *vt troops etc* masser. **4** *vi [people]* se masser; *[clouds]* s'amonceler. ◆ **mass-produce** *vt* fabriquer en série. ◆ **mass production** *n* production *f or* fabrication *f* en série.

mass² [mæs] *n (Rel)* messe *f*. **to say** ~ dire la messe; **to go to** ~ aller à la messe.

massacre ['mæsəkəʳ] **1** *n* massacre *m*. **2** *vt* massacrer.

massage ['mæsɑːʒ] **1** *n* massage *m*. ~ **parlour** institut *m* de massage (spécialisé). **2** *vt* masser. ◆ **masseur** *n* masseur *m*. ◆ **masseuse** *n* masseuse *f*.

massive ['mæsɪv] *adj* massif.

mast [mɑːst] *n [ship, flag]* mât *m*; *[radio]* pylône *m*. **to sail before the** ~ servir comme simple matelot.

master ['mɑːstəʳ] **1** *n* (**a**) *(gen)* maître *m*. **the ~ of the house** le maître de maison; ~ **in one's own house** maître chez soi; **I am the ~ now** c'est moi qui commande maintenant; *(fig)* **he has met his ~** il a trouvé son maître; **to be ~ of the situation** être maître de la situation; ~ **of ceremonies** maître des cérémonies; *(TV etc)* animateur *m*; *(Univ)* **M~ of Arts/Science** *etc* titulaire *mf* d'une maîtrise ès lettres/sciences *etc*; **a ~'s degree** une maîtrise. (**b**) *(teacher)* professeur *m*. **music** ~ professeur de musique. (**c**) *[ship]* capitaine *m*; *[liner]* (capitaine) commandant *m*; *[fishing boat]* patron *m*. (**d**) **M~ John Smith** Monsieur John Smith *(jeune garçon)*.

2 *adj beam, card* maître (*f* maîtresse); *control, switch, bedroom* principal. ~ **baker/butcher** *etc* maître boulanger/boucher *etc*; ~ **builder** entrepreneur *m* (de bâtiments); ~ **class** cours *m* de grand maître; ~ **hand** *(skill)* main *f* de maître; **to be a ~ hand at (doing) sth** être maître dans l'art de (faire) qch; ~ **key** passe-partout *m inv*; ~ **mariner** *(foreign-going)* ≃ capitaine *m* au long cours; *(home trade)* ≃ capitaine de la marine marchande; ~ **plan** plan *m* directeur; **the ~ race** la race supérieure; *(US)* ~ **sergeant** adjudant *m*; *(US Aviat)* sergent-chef *m*; ~ **stroke** coup *m* de maître.

3 *vt* (**a**) *person, animal, emotion* maîtriser; *difficulty* venir à bout de. (**b**) *(understand) theory* saisir; *(learn) language, skill* apprendre. **to have ~ed sth** posséder qch à fond; **he'll never ~ the violin** il ne saura jamais bien jouer du violon.

◆ **masterful** *adj* dominateur, autoritaire. ◆ **masterfully** *adv act, decide* en maître, avec autorité; *speak, announce* sur un ton d'autorité. ◆ **masterly** *adj* magistral; **in a ~ly way** magistralement. ◆ **mastermind** **1** *n (genius)* intelligence *f* supérieure; *[plan, crime etc]* cerveau *m* ; **2** *vt operation etc* diriger, organiser. ◆ **masterpiece** *n* chef-d'œuvre *m*. ◆ **mastery** *n [subject, musical instrument]* connaissance *f* approfondie (*of* de); *(skill)* maîtrise *f*; *(of the seas etc)* maîtrise *m*; *(over opponent etc)* supériorité *f* (*over* sur).

mastic ['mæstɪk] *n* mastic *m*.

masticate ['mæstɪkeɪt] *vti* mastiquer.

mastiff ['mæstɪf] *n* mastiff *m*.

mastoid ['mæstɔɪd] **1** *adj* mastoïde. **2** *n* (*) mastoïdite *f*. ◆ **mastoiditis** *n* mastoïdite *f*.

masturbate ['mæstəbeɪt] **1** *vi* se masturber. **2** *vt* masturber. ◆ **masturbation** *n* masturbation *f*.

mat [mæt] *n* (**a**) *(on floor)* (petit) tapis *m*; *(of straw etc)* natte *f*; *(at door)* paillasson *m*. (**b**) *(on table etc)* *(heat-resistant)* dessous-de-plat *m inv*; *(decorative)* set *m* (de table); *(embroidered linen)* napperon *m*. ◆ **matted** *adj hair* emmêlé; *sweater* feutré. ◆ **matting** *n* tapis *m* de corde *etc*.

match¹ [mætʃ] *n* allumette *f*. **box/book of ~es** boîte *f*/pochette *f* d'allumettes; **to put a ~ to** mettre le feu à. ◆ **matchbox** *n* boîte *f* à allumettes. ◆ **matchstick** *n* allumette *f*. ◆ **matchwood** *n*: **to smash to ~wood** réduire en miettes.

match² [mætʃ] **1** *n* (**a**) *(Sport)* match *m*; *(game)* partie *f*. **to play a ~ against sb** disputer un match contre qn; ~ **abandoned** match suspendu. (**b**) *(equal)* égal(e) *m(f)*. **to meet one's ~** trouver à qui parler (*in sb* avec qn); **he's a ~ for anybody** il est de taille à faire face à n'importe qui; **he was more than a ~ for Paul** Paul n'était pas à sa mesure. (**c**) *[colours etc]* **to be a good ~** aller bien ensemble. (**d**) *(marriage)* mariage *m*. **2** *vt* (**a**) *(equal: ~ **up to**) [person]* égaler; *[piece of work]* égaler, valoir. **it didn't ~ our hopes** cela a déçu nos espérances. (**b**) **to ~ sb's offer/proposal** faire une offre/une proposition équivalente à celle de qn; **to ~ sb's price** offrir le même prix que qn. (**c**) *[clothes, colours etc]* aller bien avec. **his looks ~ his character** son physique s'accorde avec sa personnalité. (**d**) *(find similar to: ~ **up**) cups etc* assortir. **can you ~ (up) this material?** avez-vous du tissu assorti à celui-ci?; **to ~ sb against sb** opposer qn à qn; **they are well ~ed** *[opponents]* ils sont de force égale; *[married couple etc]* ils sont bien assortis. **3** *vi [colours, materials]* être bien assortis. **with a ~ing skirt** avec une jupe assortie. ◆ **matchless** *adj* sans égal. ◆ **matchmake** *vi*: **she's always matchmaking** elle veut toujours marier les gens. ◆ **matchmaker** *n* marieur *m*, -euse *f*.

mate¹ [meɪt] **1** *n* (**a**) *(at work)* camarade *mf* (de travail); *(*: friend)* copain * *m*, copine * *f*. **hey, ~!** ⁑ eh mon vieux! * (**b**) *(assistant)* aide *mf*. **plumber's ~** aide-plombier *m*. (**c**) *(animal)* mâle *m*, femelle *f*. (**d**) *(Merchant Navy)* ≃ second *m*. **2** *vt* accoupler (*with* à). **3** *vi* s'accoupler (*with* à, avec). ◆ **mating** **1** *n* accouplement *m* ; **2** *adj call* du mâle; *season* des amours.

mate² [meɪt] *(Chess)* **1** *n* mat *m*. **2** *vt* mettre échec et mat.

material [mə'tɪərɪəl] **1** *adj* (**a**) *success, object, needs* matériel. (**b**) *(important)* essentiel; *(relevant)* qui importe (*to* à); *(Jur) fact, evidence* pertinent; *witness* direct. **2** *n* (**a**) *(substance)* substance *f*, matière *f*; *(cloth etc)* tissu *m*, étoffe *f*. **dress ~** tissu pour robes; (**b**) *(Ind: used in production)* matériau *m*. **building ~s** matériaux de construction. (**c**) *(things needed) (gen)* matériel. **his writing ~s** son matériel nécessaire pour écrire; **reading ~** de la lecture. (**d**) *(facts, data)* matériaux *mpl*. **background ~** documentation *f* d'appui. (**e**) *(work done)* **all his ~ is original** tout ce qu'il écrit (*or* chante *etc*) est original; **publicity ~** matériel *m* promotionnel; **teaching ~s** matériel pédagogique. (**f**) *(fig)* **he is officer ~** il a l'étoffe d'un officier. ◆ **materialism** *n* matérialisme *m*. ◆ **materialist** *adj, n* matérialiste *(mf)*. ◆ **materialistic** *adj* matérialiste. ◆ **materialize** *vi (gen)* se matérialiser; *[idea]* prendre forme; **at last the bus ~ized *** le bus est enfin arrivé. ◆ **materially** *adv (V **1** above)* matériellement; essentiellement.

maternity [mə'tɜːnɪtɪ] **1** *n* maternité *f*. **2** *adj clothes* de grossesse. ~ **allowance,** ~ **benefit** ≃ allocation *f* de maternité; ~ **home** *or* **hospital** maternité *f*; ~ **leave** congé *m* de maternité; ~ **ward** (service *m* de) maternité *f*. ◆ **maternal** *adj* maternel.

mathematics [ˌmæθ(ə)'mætɪks] *n (abbr* **maths *,** *(US)* **math ***) mathématiques *fpl*, math(s) * *fpl*. ◆ **mathematical** *adj process etc* mathématique; **I'm not mathematical** je n'ai pas le sens des mathématiques. ◆ **mathematically** *adv* mathématiquement. ◆ **mathematician** *n* mathématicien(ne) *m(f)*.

matinée ['mætɪneɪ] *n* matinée *f (Theat)*.

matriarch ['meɪtrɪɑːk] *n* femme *f* chef de famille. ◆ **matriarchal** *adj* matriarcal. ◆ **matriarchy** *n* matriarcat *m*.

matricide ['meɪtrɪsaɪd] *n* matricide *m*.

matriculate [mə'trɪkjʊleɪt] *vi* s'inscrire. ◆ **matriculation** *n* inscription *f*.

matrimony ['mætrɪm(ə)nɪ] *n* mariage *m*. ◆ **matrimonial** *adj* matrimonial.

matrix ['meɪtrɪks] *n* matrice *f*.

matron ['meɪtr(ə)n] *n (gen)* matrone *f*; *[hospital]* infirmière *f* en chef; *(in school)* infirmière; *[old people's home etc]* directrice *f*. ◆ **matronly** *adj person* très digne, matrone *(pej)*. ◆ **matron-of-honour** *n* dame *f* d'honneur.

matt [mæt] *adj* mat.

matter ['mætəʳ] **1** *n* (**a**) *(physical substance: gen, Philos, Phys etc)* matière *f*; *(Med: pus)* pus *m*. **colouring** ~ substance *f* colorante; **reading** ~ de quoi lire; **advertising** ~ publicité *f*. (**b**) *(content)* fond *m*. ~ **and form** le fond et la forme. (**c**) *(affair, concern)* affaire *f*, question *f*. **the** ~ **in hand** l'affaire en question; **business** ~**s** (questions d')affaires *fpl*; **there's the** ~ **of my expenses** il y a la question de mes frais; **that's quite another** ~ ça, c'est une autre affaire; **that will only make** ~**s worse** cela ne fera qu'aggraver la situation; **in this** ~ à cet égard; **the** ~ **is closed** l'affaire est close; **a** ~ **of great concern to us** une source de profonde inquiétude pour nous; **it's not a laughing** ~ il n'y a pas de quoi rire; **there's the small** ~ **of that £200** il y a la petite question des 200 livres; **it will be no easy** ~ cela ne sera pas facile; **in the** ~ **of** en ce qui concerne; **as** ~**s stand** dans l'état actuel des choses; **for that** ~ d'ailleurs; **as a** ~ **of course** tout naturellement; **as a** ~ **of fact** en réalité, en fait; **in a** ~ **of 10 minutes** en l'espace de 10 minutes. (**d**) *(importance)* **no** ~! peu importe!; **no** ~ **how** par n'importe quel moyen; **no** ~ **when he comes** quelle que soit l'heure (*or* la date) de son arrivée; **no** ~ **how big it is** si grand qu'il soit; **no** ~ **what he says** quoi qu'il dise; **no** ~ **where/who** où/qui que ce soit. (**e**) *(difficulty, problem)* **what's the** ~? qu'est-ce qu'il y a?; **what's the** ~ **with him?** qu'est-ce qu'il a?; **what's the** ~ **with my hat?** qu'est-ce qu'il a, mon chapeau? *; **what's the** ~ **with trying to help him?** quelle objection y a-t-il à ce qu'on l'aide *(subj)*?; **there's sth the** ~ **with my arm** j'ai qch au bras; **there's sth the** ~ **with the engine** il y a qch qui ne va pas dans le moteur; **as if nothing was the** ~ comme si de rien n'était; **nothing's the** ~ * il n'y a rien; **there's nothing the** ~ **with me!** moi, je vais tout à fait bien!; **there's nothing the** ~ **with that idea** il n'y a rien à redire à cette idée.

2 *vi* importer (*to* à). **the place doesn't** ~ l'endroit n'a pas d'importance; **it doesn't** ~ cela ne fait rien (*whether* si); **it doesn't** ~ **who/where** *etc* peu importe qui/où *etc*; **what does it** ~ **(to you)?** qu'est-ce que cela peut bien (vous) faire?; **why should it** ~ **to me?** pourquoi est-ce que cela me ferait qch?

◆ **matter-of-fact** *adj tone, voice* neutre; *style* prosaïque; *attitude, person* terre à terre; *assessment, account* qui se limite aux faits; **in a very matter-of-fact way** sans avoir l'air de rien.

mat(t)ins ['mætɪnz] *n* matines *fpl*.

mattress ['mætrɪs] *n* matelas *m*. ~ **cover** *(gen)* protège-matelas *m*; *(waterproof)* alèse *f*.

mature [mə'tjʊəʳ] **1** *adj* mûr. **he's much more** ~ il a beaucoup mûri. **2** *vi [person]* mûrir; *[wine, cheese]* se faire. ◆ **maturity** *n* maturité *f*.

maudlin ['mɔːdlɪn] *adj* larmoyant.

maul [mɔːl] *vt [tiger etc]* lacérer; *(to death)* déchiqueter; *[person]* malmener *(also fig)*.

Maundy ['mɔːndɪ] *n*: ~ **Thursday** le jeudi saint.

Mauritania [ˌmɔːrɪ'teɪnɪə] *n* Mauritanie *f*.

mausoleum [ˌmɔːsə'lɪəm] *n* mausolée *m*.

mauve [məʊv] *adj* mauve.

maverick ['mæv(ə)rɪk] *n* dissident(e) *m(f)*, franc-tireur *m (fig)*.

mawkish ['mɔːkɪʃ] *adj* d'une sentimentalité excessive.

maxi * ['mæksɪ] *n*: ~ **single record** disque *m* double durée.

maxim ['mæksɪm] *n* maxime *f*.

maximum ['mæksɪməm] **1** *n, pl* **-ima** maximum *m*. **2** *adj* maximum *(f inv or* maxima). ~ **prices** prix *mpl* maximums *or* maxima; *(Aut etc)* ~ **speed** *(highest permitted)* vitesse *f* limite *or* maximum; *(highest possible)* vitesse maximale; ~ **temperatures** températures maximales. ◆ **maximize** *vt* porter au maximum.

may[1] [meɪ] *modal aux vb (pret and cond* **might***)* (**a**) *(possibility)* **he** ~ **arrive** il va peut-être arriver, il peut arriver; **he might arrive** il pourrait arriver; **you** ~ **be making a big mistake** tu fais peut-être une grosse erreur; **I might have left it behind** je l'ai peut-être bien oublié; **you might have killed me!** tu aurais pu me tuer!; **as soon as** ~ **be** aussitôt que possible; **be that as it** ~ quoi qu'il en soit; **one might well ask whether...** on est en droit de demander si...; **what might your name be?** comment vous appelez-vous? (**b**) *(permission)* ~ **I have a word with you? — you** ~ puis-je vous parler un instant? — oui, bien sûr; **might I see it?** est-ce que je pourrais le voir?; **might I suggest that...?** puis-je me permettre de suggérer que...?; ~ **I sit here?** vous permettez que je m'assoie ici?; ~ **I?** vous permettez?; **if I** ~ **say so** si je puis me permettre; **he said I might leave** il a dit que je pouvais partir. (**c**) *(suggestion: 'might' only)* **you might try writing to him** tu pourrais toujours lui écrire; **you might have told me that!** tu aurais (tout de même) pu me le dire! (**d**) *(phrases)* **one might as well say £5** autant dire 5 livres; **I** ~ *or* **might as well tell you all about it** je ferais aussi bien de tout vous dire; **you may** *or* **might as well leave now as wait** vous feriez aussi bien de partir tout de suite plutôt que d'attendre; **they might just as well not have gone** ils auraient tout aussi bien pu ne pas y aller; **she blushed, as well she might!** elle a rougi, et pour cause!; ~ **God bless you!** que Dieu vous bénisse!

may[2] [meɪ] **1** *n* (**a**) *(month)* **M**~ mai *m*; *for phrases V* **September.** (**b**) *(hawthorn)* aubépine *f*. **2** *adj*: **M**~ **Day** le Premier Mai *(fête du Travail)*. ◆ **mayday** *n (Aviat, Naut)* S.O.S. *m*. ◆ **mayfly** *n* éphémère *m*. ◆ **maypole** *n* ≃ arbre *m* de mai.

maybe ['meɪbiː] *adv* peut-être. ~ **he'll be there** peut-être sera-t-il là, peut-être qu'il sera là, il sera peut-être là.

mayonnaise [ˌme(ɪə)'neɪz] *n* mayonnaise *f*.

mayor [mɛəʳ] *n* maire *m*. **Lord M**~ *titre du maire des principales villes*. ◆ **mayoress** *n* femme *f* du maire.

maze [meɪz] *n* labyrinthe *m*, dédale *m*.

me [miː] *pers pron* (**a**) *(direct) (unstressed)* me; *(before vowel)* m'; *(stressed)* moi. **he can see** ~ il me voit; **he saw** ~ il m'a vu; **you saw ME!** vous m'avez vu, moi! (**b**) *(indirect)* me, moi; *(before vowel)* m'. **he gave** ~ **the book** il me donna *or* m'a donné le livre; **give it to** ~ donnez-le-moi; **he was speaking to** ~ il me parlait. (**c**) *(after prep etc)* moi. **without** ~ sans moi; **it's** ~ c'est moi; **smaller than** ~ plus petit que moi; **poor (little)** ~! * pauvre de moi!; **dear** ~! * mon Dieu!

meadow ['medəʊ] *n* pré *m*, prairie *f*. ◆ **meadowsweet** *n* reine *f* des prés.

meagre, *(US)* **meager** ['mi:gəʳ] *adj* maigre *(before n)*.

meal[1] [mi:l] **1** *n* repas *m*. **to have a ~** manger; **to have a good ~** bien manger; **that was a lovely ~!** nous avons très bien déjeuné (*or* dîné); **midday ~** déjeuner *m; evening* **~** dîner *m; (fig)* **to make a ~ of sth** * faire toute une histoire de qch *. **2** *adj*: **~ ticket** *(lit)* ticket-repas *m*; *(* fig: job, person etc)* gagne-pain *m inv*. ◆ **mealtime** *n* heure *f* du repas; **at ~ times** aux heures des repas.

meal[2] [mi:l] *n (flour etc)* farine *f (d'avoine etc)*. ◆ **mealies** *npl* maïs *m*. ◆ **mealy** *adj* farineux. ◆ **mealy-mouthed** *adj:* **to be ~y-mouthed** ne pas s'exprimer franchement.

mean[1] [mi:n] *pret, ptp* **meant** [ment] *vt* (**a**) vouloir dire, signifier; *(imply)* vouloir dire. **'homely' ~s something different in America** 'homely' a un sens différent en Amérique; **what do you ~ by that?** que voulez-vous dire par là?; **you don't really ~ that** vous ne parlez pas sérieusement; **I always ~ what I say** je pense toujours ce que je dis; **the name ~s nothing to me** ce nom ne me dit rien; **the play didn't ~ a thing to her** la pièce n'avait aucun sens pour elle; **this ~s war** c'est la guerre à coup sûr; **it will ~ a lot of expense** cela entraînera beaucoup de dépenses; **catching the train ~s getting up early** pour avoir ce train il faut se lever tôt; **a pound ~s a lot to him** une livre représente une grosse somme pour lui; **holidays don't ~ much to me** les vacances comptent peu pour moi; **don't I ~ anything to you at all?** je ne suis donc rien pour toi?
(**b**) *(intend)* avoir l'intention (*to do* de faire), compter, vouloir (*to do* faire); *gift etc* destiner (*for* à); *remark* adresser (*for* à). **I didn't ~ to break it** je n'ai pas fait exprès de le casser; **I ~ to succeed** j'ai bien l'intention de réussir; **I ~ you** *or (US)* **I ~ for you to leave** je veux que vous partiez *(subj);* **he said it as if he meant it** il a dit cela sans avoir l'air de plaisanter; **I meant it as a joke** j'ai dit (*or* fait) cela pour rire; **to be meant to do** être censé faire; **she ~s well** elle est pleine de bonnes intentions; **he ~s trouble** il cherche la bagarre; **it ~s trouble** ça nous annonce des ennuis; **do you ~ me?** *(are you speaking to me)* c'est à moi que vous parlez?; *(about me)* c'est de moi que vous parlez? ◆ **meaning 1** *n [word]* sens *m*; *[phrase, action]* signification *f*; **with a double ~ing** à double sens; **literal ~ing** sens propre *or* littéral; **what is the ~ing of this word?** que signifie ce mot?; *(in anger etc)* **what is the ~ing of this?** qu'est-ce que cela signifie?; **you haven't got my ~ing** vous m'avez mal compris ; **2** *adj* significatif, éloquent. ◆ **meaningful** *adj* significatif, éloquent; *(talks)* positif. ◆ **meaningless** *adj word, action* dénué de sens; *waste, suffering* insensé.

mean[2] [mi:n] **1** *n* (**a**) *(middle term)* milieu *m*; *(Math)* moyenne *f*. **the golden** *or* **happy ~** le juste milieu. (**b**) *(way)* **~s** moyen *m*; **to find the ~s to do** *or* **of doing** trouver le moyen de faire; **to find a ~s of doing** trouver moyen de faire; **there's no ~s of getting in** il n'y a pas moyen d'y entrer; **the ~s to an end** le moyen d'arriver à ses fins; **by ~ s of** *tool etc* au moyen de; *person* par l'entremise de; *hard work etc* à force de; **come in by all ~ s!** je vous en prie, entrez!; **by all ~s!** mais certainement!; **by all manner of ~s** par tous les moyens; **by any (manner of) ~s** n'importe comment; **by no ~s** nullement, pas du tout; **by some ~s or other** d'une façon ou d'une autre; **by this ~s** de cette façon. (**c**) *(wealth etc)* **~s** moyens *mpl*; **to live within/beyond one's ~s** vivre selon ses moyens/au-dessus de ses moyens; **private ~s** fortune *f* personnelle; **slender ~s** ressources *fpl* très modestes. **2** *adj distance, temperature* moyen. ◆ **means test** *n* examen *m* des ressources *(d'une personne qui demande une aide pécuniaire)*. ◆ **means-test** *vt* examiner les ressources de *(avant d'accorder certaines prestations sociales)*. ◆ **meantime** *or* ◆ **meanwhile** *adv (also* **in the ~time** *or* **~while***)* en attendant, pendant ce temps.

mean[3] [mi:n] *adj* (**a**) *(stingy)* avare (*with* de), radin *. (**b**) *(unkind)* mesquin, méchant. **a ~ trick** un sale tour; **you ~ thing!** * chameau! *; **you were ~ to me** tu n'as vraiment pas été chic * avec moi; **to feel ~ about sth** * avoir un peu honte de qch. (**c**) *(US*: vicious) animal etc* méchant; *person* salaud ‡. (**d**) *(poor) appearance* misérable. **the ~est citizen** le dernier des citoyens. ◆ **meanness** *n* avarice *f*; mesquinerie *f*, méchanceté *f*; aspect *m* misérable.

meander [mɪ'ændəʳ] **1** *vi [river]* faire des méandres. *[person]* **to ~ in** *etc* entrer *etc* sans se presser. **2** *n* méandre *m*.

measles ['mi:zlz] *n* rougeole *f*.

measly * ['mi:zlɪ] *adj* misérable *(before n)*, minable.

measure ['meʒəʳ] **1** *n* (**a**) *(gen)* mesure *f*. **to give good** *or* **full ~** faire bonne mesure; *(fig)* **for good ~** pour faire bonne mesure; **made to ~** fait sur mesure; **a pint ~** une mesure d'un demi-litre; *(fig)* **I've got his ~** je sais ce qu'il vaut; **happiness beyond ~** bonheur sans bornes; **a ~ of success** un certain succès; **in some/large ~** dans une certaine/large mesure. (**b**) *(for measuring) (ruler)* règle *f; (folding)* mètre *m* pliant; *(tape)* mètre à ruban; *(jug/glass)* pot *m*/verre *m* gradué; *(post)* toise *f*. (**c**) *(step)* mesure *f*. **strong/drastic ~s** mesures énergiques/draconiennes. **2** *vt* mesurer *(also fig)*. **to ~ off** *or* **out** *or* **up** mesurer; **to be ~d for a dress** faire prendre ses mesures pour une robe; **what does it ~?** quelles sont ses dimensions?; **the carpet ~s 3 metres by 2 metres across** le tapis fait *or* mesure 3 mètres sur 2 mètres de large; *(fall)* **to ~ one's length** tomber de tout son long. **3** *vi*: **to ~ up to** être à la hauteur de. ◆ **measured** *adj (gen)* mesuré; *(Sport etc)* **over a ~d kilometre** sur un kilomètre exactement. ◆ **measureless** *adj* incommensurable. ◆ **measurements** *npl* mesures *fpl*. ◆ **measuring** *adj*: **measuring device** appareil *m* de mesure *or* de contrôle; **measuring jug** pot *m* gradué; **measuring rod** règle *f*; **measuring tape** mètre *m* à ruban.

meat [mi:t] **1** *n* viande *f*. **~ and drink** de quoi manger et boire; *(fig)* **this is ~ and drink to them** c'est une aubaine pour eux; **one man's ~ is another man's poison** ce qui guérit l'un tue l'autre; **there's not much ~ in his book** son livre n'a pas beaucoup de substance. **2** *adj*: **~ diet** régime *m* carné; **~ extract** concentré *m* de viande; **~ pie** pâté *m* en croûte. ◆ **meatball** *n* boulette *f* de viande. ◆ **meat-eater** *n (animal)* carnivore *m*; **he's a big ~-eater** c'est un gros mangeur de viande. ◆ **meat-eating** *adj* carnivore. ◆ **meaty** *adj flavour* de viande; *(fig) book* étoffé.

Mecca ['mekə] *n* la Mecque. *(fig)* **a ~** la Mecque (*for* de).

mechanic [mɪ'kænɪk] *n* mécanicien *m*. **motor ~** mécanicien garagiste *or* auto. ◆ **mechanical** *adj (lit)* mécanique; *(fig) action, reply* machinal, automatique; **~al engineer** ingénieur *m* mécanicien; **~al engineering** génie *m* mécanique. ◆ **mechanically** *adv* mécaniquement; *(fig)* machinalement. ◆ **mechanics** *n* (**a**) *(sg: science)* mécanique *f*; (**b**) *(pl) (lit)* mécanisme *m*; *(fig)* **the ~s of running an office** le processus de la gestion d'un bureau. ◆ **mechanism** *n* mécanisme *m*. ◆ **mechanistic** *adj* mécaniste. ◆ **mechanization** *n* mécanisation *f*. ◆ **mechanize** *vt process, industry* mécaniser; *army, troops* motoriser.

medal ['medl] *n* médaille *f*. **swimming ~** médaille de natation. ◆ **medallion** *n* médaillon *m*.

◆ **medallist,** *(US)* **medalist** *n* médaillé(e) *m(f)*; **gold/silver ~(l)ist** médaillé d'or/d'argent.

meddle ['medl] *vi* (**a**) *(interfere)* se mêler (*in* de). **stop meddling!** cesse de te mêler de ce qui ne te regarde pas! (**b**) *(tamper)* toucher (*with* à). ◆ **meddler** *n (busybody)* mouche *f* du coche; *(touching things)* touche-à-tout *m inv*. ◆ **meddlesome** *or* ◆ **meddling** *adj (interfering)* qui fourre son nez partout; *(touching)* qui touche à tout.

media ['mi:dɪə] **1** *npl of* **medium** *(souvent employé au sg) (gen: Press, Rad, TV)* média *mpl*. *(journalists)* **the ~ were waiting for him at the airport** * les journalistes et les photographes l'attendaient à l'aéroport. **2** *adj attention, coverage* des média; *event* médiatique. **~ man** *(Press, Rad, TV)* reporter *m*; *(Publicity)* agent *m* publicitaire; *(Univ)* **~ studies** études *fpl* des média.

mediaeval [,medɪ'i:v(ə)l] *adj* médiéval, du moyen âge; *streets, charm* moyenâgeux *(also pej)*.

mediate ['mi:dɪeɪt] **1** *vi* servir d'intermédiaire (*between* entre; *in* dans). **2** *vt settlement* obtenir par médiation. ◆ **mediating** *adj* médiateur. ◆ **mediation** *n* médiation *f*. ◆ **mediator** *n* médiateur *m*, -trice *f*.

medical ['medɪk(ə)l] *adj (gen)* médical; *studies, faculty* de médecine; *student* en médecine. **~ board** commission *f* médicale; *(Mil)* conseil *m* de révision; **~ examination** examen *m* médical; *(at work etc)* visite *f* médicale; **~ insurance** assurance *f* maladie; **~ officer** *(Ind)* médecin *m* du travail; *(Mil)* médecin-major *m* (*or* -colonel *etc*); *[town, country]* directeur *m* de la santé publique; **~ practitioner** généraliste *mf*; **the ~ profession** *(doctors etc)* le corps médical. ◆ **medically** *adv* médicalement; **to be ~ly examined** subir un examen médical.

Medicare ['medɪkɛə^r] *n (US)* assistance *f* médicale aux personnes âgées.

medicated ['medɪkeɪtɪd] *adj* médical. ◆ **medication** *n* médication *f*.

medicine ['meds(ɪ)n, 'medɪs(ɪ)n] **1** *n* (**a**) *(science)* médecine *f*. **to study ~** faire des études de médecine; **Doctor of M~** docteur *m* en médecine. (**b**) *(drug etc)* médicament *m*. **to take one's ~** prendre son médicament; *(fig)* avaler la pilule; *(fig)* **to give sb a taste of his own ~** rendre à qn la monnaie de sa pièce. **2** *adj*: **~ box** *or* **chest** pharmacie *f* (portative); **~ cabinet** *or* **chest** *or* **cupboard** armoire *f* à pharmacie; **~ man** sorcier *m*. ◆ **medicinal** [me'dɪsɪnl] *adj* médicinal.

medieval [,medɪ'i:v(ə)l] = **mediaeval.**

mediocre [,mi:dɪ'əʊkə^r] *adj* médiocre. ◆ **mediocrity** *n* médiocrité *f*.

meditate ['medɪteɪt] *vti* méditer (*sth* qch; *doing* de faire; *on, about* sur). ◆ **meditation** *n* méditation *f*. ◆ **meditative** *adj* méditatif. ◆ **meditatively** *adv* d'un air méditatif.

Mediterranean [,medɪtə'reɪnɪən] *adj* méditerranéen. **the ~ (Sea)** la (mer) Méditerranée.

medium ['mi:dɪəm] **1** *n, pl* **media** (**a**) *(Bio, Chem, gen)* milieu *m*; *(Phys etc)* véhicule *m*; *(fig)* moyen *m*, véhicule *m*. *(fig)* **through the ~ of the press** par voie de presse; **advertising ~** organe *m* de publicité; **artist's ~** moyens *mpl* d'expression d'un artiste; **television is the best ~ for this** c'est la télévision qui est le meilleur véhicule pour cela. (**b**) **the happy ~** le juste milieu. (**c**) *(pl* **-s**: *Spiritualism)* médium *m*. **2** *adj* moyen. *(Culin)* **a ~ (rare) steak** un steak à point; *(Rad)* **on the ~ wavelength** sur les ondes moyennes. ◆ **medium-dry** *adj wine* demi-sec. ◆ **medium-sized** *adj* de grandeur *or* de taille moyenne.

medley ['medlɪ] *n* mélange *m*; *(Mus)* pot-pourri *m*.

meek [mi:k] *adj* doux, humble. **~ and mild** doux comme un agneau. ◆ **meekly** *adv* avec douceur, humblement. ◆ **meekness** *n* douceur *f*, humilité *f*.

meet [mi:t] *pret, ptp* **met** **1** *vt* (**a**) *(gen)* rencontrer; *sb coming in opposite direction* croiser; *(by arrangement)* retrouver, rejoindre; *(go to ~)* aller *or* venir chercher. **to arrange to ~ sb at 3 o'clock** donner rendez-vous à qn pour 3 heures; **I am being met** on doit venir me chercher *or* m'attendre; **the car will ~ the train** la voiture sera là à l'arrivée du train; **he went out to ~ them** il est allé à leur rencontre. (**b**) *(get to know)* rencontrer, faire la connaissance de. **~ Mr Jones** je vous présente M. Jones; **pleased to ~ you** enchanté (de faire votre connaissance). (**c**) *(encounter) team, obstacle* rencontrer; *(face) enemy, danger* affronter; *(in duel)* se battre avec. **to ~ one's death** *or* **end** trouver la mort. (**d**) *(satisfy etc) expenses, bill* régler, payer; *deficit* combler; *demand* satisfaire à; *need* répondre à; *order* satisfaire; *condition* remplir; *charge, objection* réfuter. **this will ~ the case** ceci fera l'affaire. (**e**) **it met his ears** cela a frappé ses oreilles; **the sight which met my eye(s)** le spectacle qui s'est offert à mes yeux; **I dared not ~ her eye** je n'osais pas la regarder en face; **there's more to this than ~s the eye** c'est moins simple que cela n'en a l'air. **2** *vi* (**a**) *[people] (by chance)* se rencontrer; *(by arrangement)* se retrouver, se rejoindre; *(more than once)* se voir; *(get to know each other)* se rencontrer, faire connaissance. **to ~ again** se revoir; **until we ~ again!** à la prochaine fois!; **have you met before?** vous vous connaissez déjà?; **they arranged to ~ at 10 o'clock** ils se sont donné rendez-vous pour 10 heures. (**b**) *[committee, Parliament]* se réunir. **the class ~s in the art room** le cours a lieu dans la salle de dessin. (**c**) *[armies, teams, rivers]* se rencontrer.

3 *n (Hunting)* rendez-vous *m* (de chasse); *(US Sport etc)* meeting *m*.

◆ **meet up** *vi (by chance)* se rencontrer; *(by arrangement)* se retrouver. **to ~ up with sb** rencontrer *or* retrouver qn.

◆ **meet with** *vt fus* (**a**) *difficulties, resistance* rencontrer; *refusal, losses, storm* essuyer; *welcome* recevoir. **he met with an accident** il lui est arrivé un accident; **we met with kindness** on nous a traités avec gentillesse. (**b**) *(esp US)* = **meet 1a.**

◆ **meeting** **1** *n* (**a**) *[group of people, club, political party]* réunion *f*, *(formal)* assemblée *f*; *(business ~)* séance *f or* réunion de travail; *(Pol, Sport: rally)* meeting *m*; **to call a ~ing of shareholders** convoquer les actionnaires; **to call a ~ing to discuss sth** convoquer une réunion (*or* une assemblée *etc*) pour débattre qch; **he's in a ~ing** il est en conférence; (**b**) *(between individuals)* rencontre *f*; *(arranged)* rendez-vous *m*; *(formal)* entrevue *f*; (**c**) *(Quakers)* culte *m* ; **2** *adj*: **~ing place** lieu *m* de réunion.

mega... ['megə] *pref* méga... ◆ **megabyte** *n (Comput)* mégaoctet *m*, Mo *m*. ◆ **megacycle** *n* mégacycle *m*. ◆ **megalith** *n* mégalithe *m*. ◆ **megaton** *n* mégatonne *f*.

megalomania [,megələ(ʊ)'meɪnɪə] *n* mégalomanie *f*. ◆ **megalomaniac** *adj, n* mégalomane *(mf)*.

megaphone ['megəfəʊn] *n* porte-voix *m inv*.

melamine ['meləmi:n] *n* mélamine *f*.

melancholy ['melənk(ə)lɪ] **1** *n* mélancolie *f*. **2** *adj person* mélancolique; *thing* triste. ◆ **melancholia** *n* mélancolie *f (Med)*. ◆ **melancholic** *adj* mélancolique. ◆ **melancholically** *adv* mélancoliquement.

mellow ['meləʊ] **1** *adj fruit* bien mûr; *wine, voice* moelleux; *colour, light* velouté; *building* patiné; *person* mûri (et tranquille). **to grow ~** mûrir, s'adoucir. **2** *vi* mûrir; devenir moelleux; se velouter;

se patiner; *[person, character]* s'adoucir. **3** *vt*: **the years have ~ed him** il s'est adouci avec les années.

melodrama ['melə(ʊ)ˌdrɑːmə] *n* mélodrame *m*. ◆ **melodramatic** *adj* mélodramatique. ◆ **melodramatically** *adv* d'un air mélodramatique.

melody ['melədɪ] *n* mélodie *f*. ◆ **melodious** *adj* mélodieux. ◆ **melodiously** *adv* mélodieusement.

melon ['melən] *n* melon *m*.

melt [melt] **1** *vi* (**a**) *(gen)* fondre. **to ~ in the mouth** fondre dans la bouche; *(fig)* **she looks as if butter wouldn't ~ in her mouth** on lui donnerait le bon Dieu sans confession *; *(be too hot)* **to be ~ing** * être en nage. (**b**) *[colours, sounds]* se fondre (*into* dans); *[anger]* tomber; *[resolution, determination]* fléchir. **to ~ into tears** fondre en larmes; **he ~ed into the crowd** il s'est fondu dans la foule. **2** *vt (gen)* fondre; *sb's heart* attendrir.
◆ **melt away** *vi [ice, savings]* fondre; *[anger, fog]* se dissiper; *[confidence]* disparaître; *[crowd]* se disperser; *[person]* se volatiliser. ◆ **melt down** *vt sep* fondre; *scrap* remettre à la fonte.
◆ **meltdown** *n* fusion *f* (du cœur d'un réacteur nucléaire). ◆ **melting** **1** *adj snow* fondant; *voice, look* attendri; *words* attendrissant; **~ing point** point *m* de fusion; *(fig)* **a ~ing pot of many nationalities** le creuset de bien des nationalités; **it's back in the ~ing pot** c'est remis en question; **it's still all in the ~ing pot** c'est encore au stade des discussions ; **2** *n [snow]* fonte *f*; *[metal]* fusion *f*.

member ['membəʳ] **1** *n (gen)* membre *m*; *[club, party]* adhérent(e) *m(f)* (*of* à), membre (*of* de). *(notice)* '**~s only**' 'réservé aux adhérents'; **they treated her like a ~ of the family** ils l'ont traitée comme si elle faisait partie de la famille; **M~ of Parliament** ≃ député *m* (*for* de); **~ of the public** simple particulier *m* (*f* -ère); **a ~ of the staff** *(gen)* un(e) employé(e); *(Scol, Univ)* **a ~ of staff** un professeur. **2** *adj*: **~ nations** les États *mpl* membres.
◆ **membership** **1** *n (gen)* adhésion *f* (*of* à); **a ~ship of over 800** plus de 800 membres ; **2** *adj card* d'adhérent, de membre; **~ship fee** cotisation *f*.

membrane ['membreɪn] *n* membrane *f*.

memento [mə'mentəʊ] *n* souvenir *m (objet etc)*. **as a ~ of** en souvenir de.

memo ['meməʊ] *n (abbr of* **memorandum***)* note *f* (de service). ◆ **memo pad** *n* bloc-notes *m*.

memoir ['memwɑːʳ] *n* mémoire *m* (*on* sur); *(biography)* notice *f* biographique. **~s** *(autobiographical)* mémoires; *[learned society]* actes *mpl*.

memory ['memərɪ] *n* (**a**) *(gen, Comput)* mémoire *f*. **to have a good/bad ~** avoir bonne/mauvaise mémoire; **a ~ for faces** la mémoire des visages; **from ~** de mémoire; **loss of ~** perte *f* de mémoire; *(Med)* amnésie *f*; *(Comput)* **~ capacity** capacité *f* de mémoire; *(Comput)* **~ chip** puce *f* mémoire. (**b**) *(recollection)* souvenir *m*. **childhood memories** souvenirs d'enfance; **in ~ of** en souvenir de; **sacred to the ~ of** à la mémoire de; **of blessed ~** de glorieuse mémoire. ◆ **memorable** *adj* mémorable. ◆ **memorandum,** *pl* **-anda** *n (gen)* mémorandum *m*; *(informal letter etc)* note *f* (de service). ◆ **memorial** **1** *adj* commémoratif; *(US)* **Memorial Day** le jour des morts au champ d'honneur; *(US)* **memorial park** cimetière *m*; **memorial service** ≃ messe *f* de souvenir ; **2** *n* monument *m* (*to* à); **war memorial** monument *m* aux morts; **this scholarship is a memorial to...** cette bourse est en mémoire de... ◆ **memorize** *vt facts, figures* retenir; *poem* apprendre par cœur.

men [men] *npl of* **man.** ◆ **menfolk** * *npl* hommes *mpl*. ◆ **menswear** *n (Comm) (clothing)* habillement *m* masculin; *(dept)* rayon *m* hommes.

menace ['menɪs] **1** *n* menace *f*; *(fig: sth or sb annoying)* plaie * *f*. **a public ~** un danger public. **2** *vt* menacer. ◆ **menacing** *adj* menaçant. ◆ **menacingly** *adv* d'un air *or* d'un ton menaçant.

mend [mend] **1** *vt clothes* raccommoder; *other object* réparer; *mistake etc* corriger, rectifier. **to ~ matters** arranger les choses; **to ~ one's ways** *or* **manners** s'amender. **2** *vi (darn etc)* faire le raccommodage. **3** *n*: **to be on the ~** *(gen)* s'améliorer; *[invalid]* aller mieux. ◆ **mending** *n (act)* raccommodage *m*; *(clothes)* vêtements *mpl* à raccommoder.

menial ['miːnɪəl] *adj person* servile; *task* inférieur; *position* subalterne.

meningitis [ˌmenɪn'dʒaɪtɪs] *n* méningite *f*.

menopause ['menə(ʊ)pɔːz] *n* ménopause *f*. ◆ **menopausal** *adj symptom* dû à la ménopause; *woman* à la ménopause.

menstruate ['menstrʊeɪt] *vi* avoir ses règles. ◆ **menstruation** *n* menstruation *f*.

mental ['mentl] *adj (gen)* mental; *ability, process* mental, intellectuel; *calculation* mental, de tête; *prayer* intérieur; *treatment* psychiatrique; *(*: mad)* timbré *. **~ arithmetic** calcul *m* mental; **~ defective** débile *mf* mental(e); **~ deficiency** débilité *f* mentale; **~ home** *or* **hospital** *or* **institution** hôpital *m* psychiatrique; **~ illness** maladie mentale; **~ patient** malade *mf* mental(e); **~ powers** facultés *fpl* intellectuelles; **~ strain** *(tension)* tension *f* nerveuse; *(overwork)* surmenage *m* intellectuel; **he made a ~ note to do it** il a pris note mentalement de le faire; **~ reservations** doutes *mpl* (*about* sur).
◆ **mentality** *n* mentalité *f*. ◆ **mentally** *adv calculate* mentalement; **~ly defective** mentalement déficient; **~ly handicapped** handicapé mental; **she is ~ly handicapped** c'est une handicapée mentale; **~ly ill** atteint de maladie mentale; **~ly retarded** (mentalement) arriéré.

menthol ['menθɒl] **1** *n* menthol *m*. **2** *adj* mentholé.

mention ['menʃ(ə)n] **1** *vt (gen)* mentionner (*sth to sb* qch à qn; *that* que); *(quote) figures, names, dates* citer. **I'll ~ it to him** je lui en toucherai un mot, je le lui signalerai; **to ~ sb in one's will** coucher qn sur son testament; **he didn't ~ the accident** il n'a pas parlé de *or* fait mention de l'accident; **just ~ my name** dites que c'est de ma part; **too numerous to ~** trop nombreux pour qu'on les mentionne *(subj)*; **don't ~ it!** il n'y a pas de quoi!; **I need hardly ~ that...** il va sans dire que...; **not to ~, without ~ing** sans compter; **it is not worth ~ing** cela ne vaut pas la peine d'en parler; **nothing worth ~ing** pour ainsi dire rien. **2** *n (gen)* mention *f*. **it got a ~ * in the news** on en a parlé aux informations.

menu ['menjuː] *n (gen, Comput)* menu *m*; *(printed)* menu, carte *f*.

mercenary ['mɜːsɪn(ə)rɪ] *adj, n* mercenaire *(m)*.

merchandise ['mɜːtʃ(ə)ndaɪz] *n* marchandises *fpl*. ◆ **merchandizing** *n* merchandising *m*.

merchant ['mɜːtʃ(ə)nt] **1** *n (trader)* négociant *m*; *(shopkeeper)* commerçant *m*. **builders'** *etc* **~** fournisseur *m* en matériaux de construction *etc;* **wine ~** marchand *m* de vins; *(large-scale)* négociant en vins. **2** *adj bank, ship* de commerce. *(US)* **~ marine,** *(Brit)* **~ navy** marine marchande; **~ seaman** marin *m* de la marine marchande.

mercury ['mɜːkjʊrɪ] *n* mercure *m*. **M~** *(Astron, Myth)* Mercure *m*.

mercy ['mɜːsɪ] **1** *n* pitié *f*, indulgence *f*; *(Rel)* miséricorde *f*. **without ~** sans pitié; **for ~'s sake** par pitié; **no ~ was shown to them** on les a traités sans merci; **to have ~ on** avoir pitié de; **to beg for ~** demander grâce; **to show ~ towards** *or* **to sb** montrer de l'indulgence pour *or* envers qn; **to throw o.s. on sb's ~** s'en remettre à la merci de qn; **at the ~ of** à la merci de; **to leave to the**

tender ~ of abandonner aux bons soins de *(iro)*; **thankful for small mercies** reconnaissant du peu qui s'offre; **it's a ~ that** heureusement que + *indic*. **2** *adj flight* de secours. ~ **killing** euthanasie *f*. ◆ **merciful** *adj* miséricordieux (*to* pour); **a merciful release** une véritable délivrance. ◆ **mercifully** *adv* miséricordieusement; *(*: fortunately)* par bonheur. ◆ **merciless** *adj* impitoyable. ◆ **mercilessly** *adv* impitoyablement.

mere [mɪəʳ] *adj formality* simple; *thought etc* seul *(before n)*; *chance, spite, coincidence* pur *(before n)*. **he's a ~ child** ce n'est qu'un enfant; **a ~ clerk** un simple employé de bureau; **the ~ sight of him** sa seule vue; **a ~ nothing** une vétille. ◆ **merely** *adv want, say* simplement, seulement; **he ~ly nodded** il se contenta de faire un signe de tête; **I did it ~ly to please her** je ne l'ai fait que pour lui faire plaisir; **it's ~ly a formality** ce n'est qu'une formalité.

merge [mɜːdʒ] **1** *vi [colours, shapes, sounds]* se mêler (*into, with* à); *[roads]* se rejoindre (*with* avec); *[river]* confluer (*with* avec); *[states]* s'unir (*with* à); *[companies]* fusionner (*with* avec). **2** *vt (Comm, Fin, also Comput)* fusionner. ◆ **merger** *n* fusion *f*.

meringue [mə'ræŋ] *n* meringue *f*.

merino [mə'riːnəʊ] *n* mérinos *m*.

merit ['merɪt] **1** *n* mérite *m*. **to decide a case on its ~s** décider d'un cas en toute objectivité; **they went into the ~s of the new plan** ils ont discuté le pour et le contre du nouveau projet. **2** *adj*: ~ **list** tableau *m* d'honneur. **3** *vt* mériter. ◆ **meritocracy** *n* méritocratie *f*.

mermaid ['mɜːmeɪd] *n* sirène *f (Myth)*.

merry ['merɪ] *adj* joyeux, gai; *(*: tipsy)* éméché. **M~ Christmas** Joyeux Noël; **M~ England** l'Angleterre du bon vieux temps. ◆ **merrily** *adv* joyeusement, gaiement. ◆ **merriment** *n* gaieté *f*, joie *f*; *(laughter)* hilarité *f*. ◆ **merry-go-round** *n (in fairground)* manège *m (de foire etc)*; *(fig)* tourbillon *m*. ◆ **merrymaker** *n* fêtard *m*. ◆ **merrymaking** *n* réjouissances *fpl*.

mesa ['meɪzə] *n (US)* mesa *f*, plateau *m*.

mesh [meʃ] **1** *n* (**a**) *[net etc]* maille *f*. **netting with 5-cm ~** filet *m* à mailles de 5 cm; **the ~ of lies/of intrigue** le réseau de mensonges/d'intrigues. (**b**) *(fabric)* tissu *m* à mailles. **nylon ~** tulle *m* de nylon; **wire ~** grillage *m*. (**c**) *[gears etc]* engrenage *m*. **in ~** en prise. **2** *adj stockings (net)* filet *inv*; *(nonrun)* indémaillable. ~ **bag** filet *m* (à provisions). **3** *vi [wheels]* s'engrener; *[plans]* concorder.

mesmerize ['mezməraɪz] *vt* hypnotiser; *[snake]* fasciner. *(fig)* **I was ~d** je ne pouvais pas détourner mon regard.

mess [mes] **1** *n* (**a**) *(confusion of objects)* désordre *m*, fouillis *m*; *(dirt)* saleté *f*; *(muddle)* gâchis *m*. **to make a ~** faire du désordre (*or* mettre de la saleté) partout; **the cat has made a ~** le chat a fait des saletés; **get this ~ cleared up!** *(tidy)* range *or (clean)* nettoie tout ça!; *[object, room]* **to be (in) a ~** être en désordre (*or* très sale); **to be (in) a terrible ~** être dans un état épouvantable; **you look a ~** tu n'es pas présentable; **to make a ~ of** *(dirty)* salir; *(tear)* déchirer; *(wreck)* saccager; *essay, career, one's life* gâcher; **to make a ~ of things** * tout bousiller *, tout gâcher; *[person]* **to be/get (o.s.) in a ~** * être/se mettre dans de beaux draps; **to get sb/get o.s. out of a ~** sortir qn/se sortir d'un mauvais pas. (**b**) *(Mil)* mess *m*; *(Naut)* carré *m*. **2** *vt* salir, souiller. **3** *vi* manger (*with* avec).
◆ **mess about** *, **mess around** * **1** *vi (in water, mud)* patauger; *(waste time)* perdre son temps; *(dawdle)* lambiner *; *(hang about)* traîner. **what were you doing? — just ~ing about** que faisais-tu? — rien de particulier; **to ~ about** *or* **around with** *object* tripoter; *person* s'amuser avec; *(sexually)* peloter *. **2** *vt sep person* embêter *; *arrangements* chambouler *. ◆ **mess up** *vt sep clothes* salir; *room* mettre en désordre; *hair* ébouriffer; *situation, plans, life etc* gâcher.
◆ **mess-up** * *n* gâchis *m*. ◆ **messy** *adj (dirty)* sale; *(untidy) room* en désordre; *piece of work* pas assez soigné; *text, page* sale; *job* salissant; *situation* compliqué.

message ['mesɪdʒ] *n* message *m*. **telephone ~** message téléphonique; **to leave a ~** laisser un mot (*for sb* à qn); **would you give him this ~?** voudriez-vous lui faire cette commission?; *(fig)* **to get the ~** * comprendre, piger ⁑. ◆ **messaging** *n (Comput)* messagerie *f*. ◆ **messenger** **1** *n* messager *m*, -ère *f*; *(in office etc)* coursier *m* ; **2** *adj*: **messenger boy** garçon *m* de courses.

Messiah [mɪ'saɪə] *n* Messie *m*.

Messrs ['mesəz] *npl* messieurs *mpl (abbr* MM.*)*.

met¹ [met] *pret, ptp of* **meet.**

met² [met] *adj (abbr of* **meteorological***)* **the M~ Office** ≃ l'O.N.M. *m*; ~ **report** bulletin *m* de la météo *.

metabolism [me'tæbəlɪz(ə)m] *n* métabolisme *m*.

metal ['metl] **1** *n* métal *m*. **road ~** empierrement *m*. **2** *adj* en *or* de métal. ~ **detector** détecteur *m* de métaux; ~ **polish** produit *m* d'entretien (pour métaux). **3** *vt road* empierrer. ◆ **metallic** *adj* métallique. ◆ **metallurgist** *n* métallurgiste *m*. ◆ **metallurgy** *n* métallurgie *f*. ◆ **metalwork** *n (articles)* ferronnerie *f*; *(craft)* travail *m* des métaux. ◆ **metalworker** *n (Ind)* ouvrier *m* métallurgiste.

metamorphosis [ˌmetə'mɔːfəsɪs] *n* métamorphose *f*. ◆ **metamorphose** *vi* se métamorphoser (*into* en).

metaphor ['metəfəʳ] *n* métaphore *f*. ◆ **metaphorical** *adj* métaphorique.

metaphysics [ˌmetə'fɪzɪks] *nsg* métaphysique *f*. ◆ **metaphysical** *adj* métaphysique.

mete [miːt] *vt*: **to ~ out** *punishment* infliger; *reward* décerner; *justice* rendre.

meteor ['miːtɪəʳ] *n* météore *m*. ◆ **meteoric** *adj* météorique; *(fig)* fulgurant; **~ic rise** montée *f* en flèche. ◆ **meteorite** *n* météorite *m or f*.

meteorology [ˌmiːtɪə'rɒlədʒɪ] *n* météorologie *f*. ◆ **meteorological** *adj* météorologique. ◆ **meteorologist** *n* météorologue *mf*.

meter ['miːtəʳ] **1** *n* (**a**) *(gen)* compteur *m*; *(parking ~)* parcmètre *m*. **electricity/gas/water ~** compteur d'électricité/à gaz/à eau. (**b**) *(US)* = **metre.** **2** *adj (US Aut)* ~ **maid** contractuelle *f*; ~ **reader** releveur *m* de compteurs.

methadone ['meθəˌdəʊn] *n* méthadone *f*.

methane ['miːθeɪn] *n* méthane *m*.

method ['meθəd] *n* (**a**) *(gen)* méthode *f*. **there's ~ in his madness** sa folie ne manque pas d'une certaine logique. (**b**) *(manner)* méthode *f*, façon *f*. **his ~ of working** sa méthode de travail, sa façon de travailler. ◆ **methodical** *adj* méthodique. ◆ **Methodism** *n* méthodisme *m*. ◆ **Methodist** *adj, n* méthodiste *(mf)*. ◆ **methodology** *n* méthodologie *f*.

meths * [meθs] *n abbr of* **methylated spirit(s).**

methyl ['meθɪl] *n* méthyle *m*. ◆ **methylated spirit(s)** *n* alcool *m* à brûler.

meticulous [mɪ'tɪkjʊləs] *adj* méticuleux. ◆ **meticulously** *adv* méticuleusement.

métier ['meɪtɪeɪ] *n (trade etc)* métier *m*; *(one's particular work etc)* partie *f*, rayon * *m*; *(strong point)* point *m* fort.

metre ['miːtəʳ] *n (all senses)* mètre *m*. ◆ **metric** *adj* métrique; **to go metric** * adopter le système métrique. ◆ **metrication** *n* conversion *f* au système métrique.

metronome ['metrənəʊm] *n* métronome *m*.

metropolis [mɪ'trɒpəlɪs] *n* métropole *f (ville)*. ◆ **metropolitan** *adj* métropolitain.

mettle ['metl] *n* fougue *f*. **on one's** ~ prêt à donner le meilleur de soi-même; **to show one's** ~ montrer ce dont on est capable.

mew [mju:] **1** *n* miaulement *m*. **2** *vi* miauler.

mews [mju:z] *(Brit) nsg or pl* ruelle *f*. ~ **flat** petit appartement *m* assez chic.

Mexico ['meksɪkəʊ] *n* Mexique *m*. ~ **City** Mexico. ◆ **Mexican** **1** *adj* mexicain ; **2** *n* Mexicain(e) *m(f)*.

mezzanine ['mezəni:n] *n* mezzanine *f*.

mezzo-soprano [ˌmetsəʊsə'prɑ:nəʊ] *n (voice)* mezzo-soprano *m*; *(singer)* mezzo(-soprano) *f*.

mi [mi:] *n (Mus)* mi *m*.

miaow [mi:'aʊ] **1** *n* miaou *m*. **2** *vi* miauler.

mica ['maɪkə] *n* mica *m*.

mice [maɪs] *npl of* **mouse**.

Michaelmas ['mɪklməs] **1** *n* la Saint-Michel. **2** *adj*: ~ **daisy** aster *m* d'automne.

mickey * ['mɪkɪ] *n*: **to take the** ~ **out of sb** ‡ se payer la tête de qn *. ◆ **mickey-mouse** * *adj pej car, degree* à la noix; *job* pas sérieux.

micro ['maɪkrəʊ] *n* micro-ordinateur *m*.

micro... ['maɪkrə(ʊ)] *pref* micro-. ◆ **microbiology** *n* microbiologie *f*. ◆ **microchip** *n* microplaquette *f*. ◆ **microcircuit** *n* microcircuit *m*. ◆ **microclimate** *n* microclimat *m*. ◆ **microcomputer** *n* micro-ordinateur *m*. ◆ **microdot** *n* micro-image-point *m*. ◆ **microelectronic** *adj* micro-électronique. ◆ **microelectronics** *nsg* micro-électronique *f*. ◆ **microfilm** **1** *n* microfilm *m* ; **2** *vt* microfilmer. ◆ **microgroove** *n* microsillon *m*. ◆ **microlight** *n (Aviat)* ULM *m*, ultra-léger-motorisé *m*. ◆ **micromesh** *adj stockings* super-fin. ◆ **micrometer** *n* micromètre *m*. ◆ **micron** *n* micron *m*. ◆ **microorganism** *n* micro-organisme *m*. ◆ **microprocessor** *n* microprocesseur *m*. ◆ **microreader** *n* microlecteur *m*. ◆ **microstructure** *n* microstructure *f*. ◆ **microsurgery** *n* microchirurgie *f*. ◆ **microwave** *n* micro-onde *f*. ~**wave (oven)** four *m* à micro-ondes.

microbe ['maɪkrəʊb] *n* microbe *m*.

microcosm ['maɪkrə(ʊ)kɒz(ə)m] *n* microcosme *m*.

microphone ['maɪkrəfəʊn] *n* microphone *m*.

microscope ['maɪkrəskəʊp] *n* microscope *m*. **under the** ~ au microscope. ◆ **microscopic** *adj* microscopique.

mid [mɪd] *adj*: **in** ~ **May** à la mi-mai, au milieu de mai; **in** ~ **morning** au milieu de la matinée; **in** ~ **air** *(lit)* en plein ciel; *(fig) leave sth etc* en suspens; **in** ~ **course** à mi-course; **in** ~ **Atlantic** au milieu de l'Atlantique; ~**-Victorian** du milieu de l'époque victorienne. ◆ **midday** **1** *n* midi *m*; **at** ~**day** à midi ; **2** *adj sun* de midi. ◆ **midfield** *n (Ftbl)* milieu *m* de terrain. ◆ **midland** **1** *n*: **the Midlands** les comtés *mpl* du centre de l'Angleterre ; **2** *adj* du centre (du pays); *region* central. ◆ **midlife** *adj* de la quarantaine. ◆ **midnight** **1** *n* minuit *m*; **at** ~**night** à minuit ; **2** *adj* de minuit; **to burn the** ~**night oil** travailler (*or* lire *etc*) fort avant dans la nuit. ◆ **midriff** *n (diaphragm)* diaphragme *m*; *(stomach)* estomac *m*. ◆ **midshipman** *n* midshipman *m*. ◆ **midst** *n*: **in the** ~**st of** *(in the middle of)* au milieu de; *(surrounded by)* entouré de; *(among)* parmi; *(during)* pendant; **in our** ~**st** parmi nous. ◆ **midstream** *n*: **in** ~**stream** au milieu du courant. ◆ **midsummer** **1** *n (height of summer)* milieu *m* de l'été; *(solstice)* solstice *m* d'été; **at** ~**summer** à la Saint-Jean ; **2** *adj* de plein été; **Midsummer Day** la Saint-Jean. ◆ **midterm** *n (holiday)* ≃ vacances *fpl* de la Toussaint (*or* de février *or* de Pentecôte). ◆ **midway** *adj, adv* à mi-chemin. ◆ **midweek** **1** *adv* vers le *or* au milieu de la semaine ; **2** *adj* de milieu de semaine. ◆ **Midwest** *n (US)* Midwest *m*. ◆ **midwinter** **1** *n (heart of winter)* milieu *m* de l'hiver; *(solstice)* solstice *m* d'hiver; **in** ~**winter** en plein hiver ; **2** *adj* de plein hiver.

middle ['mɪdl] **1** *adj chair, period etc* du milieu; *size, quality* moyen. *(fig)* **to take the** ~ **course** choisir le moyen terme; **during his** ~ **age** quand il n'était déjà plus jeune; **he fears** ~ **age** il a peur de la cinquantaine; **the M~ Ages** le moyen âge; **M~ America** l'Amérique moyenne; *(Mus)* ~ **C** do *m* du milieu du piano; **the** ~ **classes** les classes moyennes, la bourgeoisie; **in the** ~ **distance** *(Art etc)* au second plan; *(gen)* à mi-distance; **M~ East** Moyen-Orient *m*; ~ **finger** médius *m*, majeur *m*; ~ **management** cadres *mpl* moyens; ~ **manager** cadre *m* moyen; ~ **name** deuxième nom *m*; ~ **school** ≃ *(Brit Admin)* cours *m* moyen; *(US)* **M~ West** Middle West *m*. **2** *n* (**a**) milieu *m*. **in the** ~ **of** au milieu de; **right in the** ~ au beau milieu; **it's in the** ~ **of nowhere** * c'est en plein bled *; **a village in the** ~ **of nowhere** * un petit trou perdu *; **I was in the** ~ **of my work** j'étais en plein travail; **I'm in the** ~ **of reading it** je suis justement en train de le lire. (**b**) (*: *waist*) taille *f*. ◆ **middle-aged** *adj* d'un certain âge. ◆ **middle-class** *adj* bourgeois, des classes moyennes. ◆ **middleman** *n* intermédiaire *m*. ◆ **middle-of-the-road** *adj politics* modéré; *solution* du juste milieu; *music* neutre. ◆ **middle-sized** *adj tree, building* de grandeur moyenne; *parcel* de grosseur moyenne; *person* de taille moyenne. ◆ **middleweight** *n* poids *m* moyen. ◆ **middling** *adj* moyen.

midge [mɪdʒ] *n* moucheron *m*.

midget ['mɪdʒɪt] **1** *n* nain(e) *m(f)*. **2** *adj* minuscule.

midwife ['mɪdwaɪf] *n* sage-femme *f*. ◆ **midwifery** ['mɪdwɪf(ə)rɪ] *n* obstétrique *f*.

might[1] [maɪt] *modal aux vb V* **may[1]**. ◆ **might-have-been** *n (thing)* ce qui aurait pu être; *(person)* raté(e) *m(f)*.

might[2] [maɪt] *n* force(s) *f(pl)*. **with** ~ **and main, with all one's** ~ de toutes ses forces.

mighty ['maɪtɪ] **1** *adj (gen)* puissant; *achievement* formidable; *ocean* vaste; (*: *very big) row, rage* sacré * *(before n)*. **2** *adv* (*) rudement *.

migraine ['mi:greɪn] *n* migraine *f*.

migrate [maɪ'greɪt] *vi* migrer. ◆ **migrant** **1** *adj bird* migrateur; *worker* migrant ; **2** *n (Agr)* saisonnier *m*. ◆ **migration** *n* migration *f*.

mike * [maɪk] *n (microphone)* micro *m*.

Milan [mɪ'læn] *n* Milan.

mild [maɪld] *adj (gen)* doux (*f* douce); *reproach, punishment, beer, sedative* léger; *exercise, effect* modéré; *sauce* peu épicé; *curry* pas trop fort; *illness* bénin. **it's** ~ **today** il fait doux aujourd'hui; **a** ~ **form of polio** la poliomyélite sous une forme bénigne. ◆ **mildly** *adv (gently)* doucement; *(slightly)* légèrement; **to put it** ~**ly** *... pour ne pas dire plus...; **that's putting it** ~**ly** * c'est le moins qu'on puisse dire. ◆ **mildness** *n* douceur *f*; légèreté *f*.

mildew ['mɪldju:] *n (gen)* moisissure *f*; *(on plants)* rouille *f*; *(on vine)* mildiou *m*. ◆ **mildewed** *adj* moisi; piqué de rouille; mildiousé.

mile [maɪl] *n* mile *m or* mille *m (= 1 609,33 m)*. **20** ~**s per gallon** ≃ 14 litres aux cent; ~**s and** ~**s** ≃ des kilomètres et des kilomètres; *(fig)* **not a hundred** ~**s from here** sans aller chercher bien loin; ~**s away** à cent lieues d'ici (*or* de là); **you could see it a** ~ **off** ça se voyait d'une lieue; ~**s** * **bigger than** bien plus grand que. ◆ **mileage** **1** *n (Aut etc) (distance covered)* ≃ kilométrage *m*; *(distance per gallon etc)* ≃ consommation *f* aux cent; **the car had a low** ~**age** ≃ la voiture avait peu de kilomètres; *(fig)* **there's some** ~**age in it** on peut en tirer quelque chose ; **2** *adj*: ~**age allowance** ≃

indemnité *f* kilométrique. ◆ **mil(e)ometer** *n* ≃ compteur *m* kilométrique. ◆ **milepost** *or* ◆ **milestone** *n* borne *f* (milliaire), ≃ borne kilométrique; *(in career etc)* jalon *m (fig)*.

milieu ['miːljɜː] *n* milieu *m* (social).

militant ['mɪlɪt(ə)nt] *adj, n* militant(e) *m(f)*. ◆ **militarism** *n* militarisme *m*. ◆ **militarist(ic)** *adj* militariste. ◆ **military** **1** *adj (gen)* militaire; *service* militaire, national ; **2** *npl*: **the military** l'armée *f*. ◆ **militate** *vi* militer (*against* contre). ◆ **militia** *collective n* milices *fpl*; *(US)* **the militia** la réserve (territoriale).

milk [mɪlk] **1** *n* lait *m*. **coconut** ~ lait de coco; ~ **of magnesia** lait de magnésie; **a land flowing with ~ and honey** un pays de cocagne; *(hum)* **he came home with the** ~ * il est rentré à l'aube. **2** *vt cow* traire; *(fig) person* exploiter; *strength* saper. **3** *adj product* laitier; *chocolate* au lait; *diet* lacté; *tooth* de lait. ~ **bar** milk-bar *m*; ~ **churn** bidon *m* à lait; ~ **float** voiture *f* de laitier; ~ **jug** pot *m* à lait; ~ **pan** petite casserole *f* pour le lait; ~ **powder** lait en poudre; ~ **pudding** entremets *m* au lait; ~ **shake** milk-shake *m*. ◆ **milk-and-water** *adj* insipide. ◆ **milking** **1** *n* traite *f*; **2** *adj*: ~**ing machine** trayeuse *f* (mécanique). ◆ **milkman** *n* laitier *m*. ◆ **milksop** * *n* chiffe *f* molle * *(fig)*. ◆ **milky** *adj diet, product* lacté; *coffee, tea* au lait; *drink* à base de lait; *(fig: in colour etc)* laiteux; **M~y Way** Voie *f* lactée.

mill [mɪl] **1** *n* (**a**) *(gen)* moulin *m*; *(Ind: for grain)* minoterie *f*. **wind** ~ moulin à vent; **pepper-**~ moulin à poivre; *(fig)* **to go through the** ~ en voir de dures *; **to put sb through the** ~ en faire voir de dures à qn *. (**b**) *(factory)* usine *f*, fabrique *f*. **steel** ~ aciérie *f*; **paper** ~ usine *f* de papeterie; **cotton** ~ filature *f* de coton. **2** *adj* (**a**) ~ **race** bief *m* de moulin; ~ **stream** courant *m* du bief; ~ **wheel** roue *f* d'un moulin. (**b**) ~ **girl** ouvrière *f* des filatures; ~ **owner** industriel *m* du textile. **3** *vt flour, coffee, pepper* moudre; *screw, nut* moleter. *[coin]* ~**ed edge** crénelage *m*. **4** *vi* (~ **about** *or* **around**) *[crowd etc]* grouiller. ◆ **miller** *n* meunier *m*; *(Ind: large-scale)* minotier *m*. ◆ **millhand** *or* ◆ **millworker** *n* ouvrier *m* des filatures. ◆ **milling** *adj crowd* grouillant. ◆ **millpond** *n*: **sea like a ~pond** mer *f* d'huile. ◆ **millstone** *n* meule *f*; *(fig)* **a ~stone round his neck** un boulet qu'il traîne avec lui.

millennium [mɪ'lenɪəm] *n* millénaire *m*; *(Rel, also fig)* millénium *m*.

millet ['mɪlɪt] *n* millet *m*.

milli... ['mɪlɪ] *pref* milli... ◆ **millibar** *n* millibar *m*. ◆ **milligram(me)** *n* milligramme *m*. ◆ **millimetre,** *(US)* **millimeter** *n* millimètre *m*.

milliner ['mɪlɪnəʳ] *n* modiste *f*. ◆ **millinery** *n* modes *fpl (chapeaux)*.

million ['mɪljən] *n* million *m*. **a ~ men** un million d'hommes; **he's one in a** ~ * c'est la crème des hommes; *(fig)* ~**s of** * des milliers de; **thanks a** ~! * merci mille fois!; *(US)* **to feel like a ~ dollars** * se sentir dans une forme époustouflante *. ◆ **millionaire** *n* millionnaire *m*, ≃ milliardaire *m*. ◆ **millionth** *adj, n* millionième *(mf)*; *(fraction)* millionième *m*.

millipede ['mɪlɪpiːd] *n* mille-pattes *m inv*.

mime [maɪm] **1** *n (Theat) (skill, classical play)* mime *m*; *(modern play)* mimodrame *m*; *(fig: gestures etc)* mimique *f*. **2** *vti* mimer.

mimic ['mɪmɪk] **1** *n* imitateur *m*, -trice *f*. **2** *vt* imiter. ◆ **mimicry** *n* imitation *f*.

mimosa [mɪ'məʊzə] *n* mimosa *m*.

mince [mɪns] **1** *n (Culin)* bifteck *m* haché. **2** *adj*: ~ **pie** tartelette *f* de Noël (au mincemeat). **3** *vt (Culin:* ~ **up***)* hacher. *(fig)* **to ~ matters** *or* **one's words** mâcher ses mots. **4** *vi (in talking)* parler du bout des lèvres; *(in walking)* marcher à petits pas maniérés. ◆ **mincemeat** *n* hachis *m* de fruits secs; *(fig)* **to make ~meat of** pulvériser *(fig)*. ◆ **mincer** *n* hachoir *m (appareil)*. ◆ **mincing** *adj* affecté, minaudier.

mind [maɪnd] **1** *n* (**a**) *(gen)* esprit *m*; *(sanity)* raison *f*; *(memory)* mémoire *f*; *(opinion)* avis *m*. **in one's ~'s eye** en imagination; **his ~ is going** il n'a plus tout à fait sa tête; **his ~ went blank** ça a été le vide complet dans sa tête; **I'm not clear in my own ~ about it** je ne sais pas qu'en penser moi-même; **to be easy in one's** ~ avoir l'esprit tranquille; **one of the great ~s of the century** un des grands cerveaux du siècle; **it was a case of ~ over matter** c'était la victoire de l'esprit sur la matière; **to be out of one's** ~ ne plus avoir toute sa raison *or* sa tête; **you must be out of your** ~! * tu as perdu la tête!; **he went out of his** ~ il a perdu la tête. (**b**) *(phrases)* **with one** ~ comme un seul homme; **of one** ~ du même avis; **to be in two ~s about (doing) sth** se tâter pour ce qui est de (faire) qch; **I was of the same ~ as my brother** j'étais du même avis que mon frère, je partageais l'opinion de mon frère; **to my** ~ à mon avis; **nothing is further from my ~ than doing that** loin de moi la pensée de faire cela; **ecology-~ed** très sensibilisé sur l'écologie; **an industrially-~ed nation** une nation orientée vers l'industrie; **to bear** *or* **keep sth in** ~ *(take account of)* tenir compte de qch; *(remember)* penser à qch, ne pas oublier qch; **to bring** *or* **call to** ~ rappeler; **you must get it into your ~ that...** tu dois te mettre dans la tête que...; **I can't get it out of my** ~ je ne peux m'empêcher d'y penser; **to give one's ~ to sth, to keep one's ~ on sth** se concentrer sur qch; **to give sb a piece of one's** ~ * dire ses quatre vérités à qn; **it went right** *or* **clean** * **out of my** ~ cela m'est complètement sorti de la tête *; **if you have a ~ to** si vous le voulez vraiment; **to have (it) in ~ to do** avoir dans l'idée de faire; **I've a good ~ to do it** * j'ai bien envie de le faire; **I've half a ~ to do it** * j'ai presque envie de le faire; **to have in** ~ *thing* avoir dans l'idée; *person* avoir en vue; **to have sth on one's** ~ avoir l'esprit préoccupé de qch; **what's on your** ~? qu'est-ce qui vous préoccupe?; **to know one's own** ~ savoir ce que l'on veut; **to let one's ~ run on sth** se laisser aller à penser à qch; **to let one's ~ wander** laisser flotter son attention; **to make up one's ~ about sth/to do** prendre une décision à propos de qch/la décision de faire; **that puts me in ~ of...** cela me rappelle...; **to put sth out of one's** ~ oublier qch; **to put** *or* **set one's ~ to sth** s'appliquer à qch; **to set one's ~ on (doing) sth** vouloir fermement (faire) qch; **to set sb's ~ at rest** rassurer qn; **this will take her ~ off it** cela lui changera les idées; **the noise takes my ~ off my work** le bruit m'empêche de me concentrer sur mon travail.

2 *vt* (**a**) *(pay attention to)* faire attention à; *(beware of)* prendre garde à. **never** ~! *(don't worry)* ne t'en fais pas!; *(it makes no odds)* ça ne fait rien!; *(iro)* **don't ~ me!** * ne vous gênez surtout pas pour moi! * *(iro)*; **never ~ the expense!** tant pis pour le prix!; ~ **your language!** surveille ton langage!; ~ **what you're doing!** attention à ce que tu fais!; ~ **the step!** attention à la marche!; ~ **you don't fall** prenez garde de ne pas tomber; ~ **you tell her** n'oublie pas de le lui dire; ~ **you *, I...** remarquez, je... (**b**) *(object to)* **do you ~ if I take this book? — I don't** ~ cela ne vous ennuie pas que je prenne ce livre? — je vous en prie!; **which? — I don't** ~ lequel? — ça m'est égal; **if you don't** ~ si cela ne vous fait rien; **did she ~ (it) when he got married?** a-t-elle été malheureuse quand il s'est marié?; **I don't ~ going with you** je veux bien vous accompagner; **I don't ~ the cold** le froid ne me gêne pas; **would you ~ doing that?** cela

vous ennuierait de faire cela?; *(abruptly)* je vous prie de faire cela; **do you ~ the noise?** le bruit vous gêne-t-il?; **I don't ~ what people say** je me moque du qu'en-dira-t-on; **I wouldn't ~ a cup of coffee** je prendrais bien une tasse de café. (**c**) *(take charge of) children, animals, shop* garder.
◆ **mind out** * **1** *vi* faire attention. ~ **out!** attention!
◆ **mind-bending** *. ◆ **mind-blowing** * *adj drug* hallucinogène; *experience* hallucinant. ◆ **mind-boggling** * *adj* ahurissant. ◆ **minded** *adj* disposé (*to do* à faire). ◆ **minder** *n (of child etc)* gardienne *f*. ◆ **mindful** *adj*: **~ful of** attentif à. ◆ **mindless** *adj* stupide, idiot. ◆ **mindreader** *n*: **he's a ~reader!** il lit dans la pensée des gens!

mine[1] [maɪn] *poss pron* le mien, la mienne, les mien(ne)s. **this pencil is** ~ ce crayon est le mien *or* à moi; **a friend of** ~ un de mes amis.

mine[2] [maɪn] **1** *n* (**a**) *(Min)* mine *f*. **coal** ~ mine de charbon; **to go down the ~s** travailler à la mine; *(fig)* **a ~ of information** une véritable mine de renseignements. (**b**) *(Mil, Naut etc)* mine *f*. **to lay a** ~ poser une mine. **2** *vt* (**a**) *(Min) coal, ore* extraire. (**b**) *(Mil etc) sea* miner. **3** *vi* exploiter un gisement. **to ~ for coal** exploiter une mine (de charbon). **4** *adj*: ~ **detector** détecteur *m* de mines; ~ **disposal** déminage *m*.
◆ **minefield** *n* champ *m* de mines; *(fig)* **a legal ~field** un sac d'embrouilles * juridiques. ◆ **minelayer** *n* mouilleur *m* de mines. ◆ **minelaying** *n* mouillage *m* de mines. ◆ **miner** *n* mineur *m*. ◆ **mineshaft** *n* puits *m* de mine. ◆ **minesweeper** *n* dragueur *m* de mines. ◆ **minesweeping** *n* dragage *m* de mines. ◆ **mining 1** *n* (**a**) *(Min)* exploitation *f* minière; (**b**) *(Mil, Naut)* mouillage *m* de mines; **2** *adj area, village, industry* minier; *engineer* des mines; *family* de mineurs.

mineral ['mɪn(ə)rəl] **1** *n* minéral *m*. *(soft drinks)* **~s** boissons *fpl* gazeuses. **2** *adj* minéral. ~ **water** *(natural)* eau *f* minérale; *(soft drink)* boisson *f* gazeuse. ◆ **mineralogist** *n* minéralogiste *mf*. ◆ **mineralogy** *n* minéralogie *f*.

minestrone [ˌmɪnɪ'strəʊnɪ] *n* minestrone *m*.

mingle ['mɪŋgl] **1** *vt* mêler (*with* à). **2** *vi (gen)* se mêler (*with* à); *(consort)* frayer (*with* avec).

mingy * ['mɪndʒɪ] *adj person* radin *; *share* misérable.

mini ['mɪnɪ] **1** *n (fashion)* mini *m*; *(~ skirt)* mini (-jupe) *f*; *(car)* mini *f* ®. **2** *pref* mini-. **he's a kind of ~-dictator** c'est une sorte de mini-dictateur.
◆ **minibus** *n* minibus *m*. ◆ **minicab** *n* taxi *m (qu'il faut appeler par téléphone)*. ◆ **minicar** *n* toute petite voiture *f*. ◆ **minicomputer** *n* mini-ordinateur *m*. ◆ **minimarket** *or* ◆ **minimart** *n* minilibre-service *m*. ◆ **miniskirt** *n* minijupe *f*.

miniature ['mɪnɪtʃə'] **1** *n* miniature *f*. **in** ~ en miniature. **2** *adj (gen)* (en) miniature; *(tiny)* minuscule; *camera* de petit format; *poodle* nain; *railway* miniature; *submarine* de poche. ~ **bottle** mini-bouteille *f*; ~ **model** maquette *f*. ◆ **miniaturize** *vt* miniaturiser.

minimum ['mɪnɪməm] **1** *n* minimum *m*. **to reduce to a** ~ réduire au minimum; **to keep sth to a** ~ limiter qch autant que possible. **2** *adj* minimum (*f inv or* -ima). *(Econ)* ~ **lending rate** taux *m* de crédit minimum; ~ **wage** salaire *m* minimum, ≃ SMIC * *m*. ◆ **minimal** *adj* minimal. ◆ **minimize** *vt (reduce)* réduire au minimum; *(when assessing)* minimiser.

minister ['mɪnɪstə'] **1** *n (gen)* ministre *m*; *(Rel)* pasteur *m*. **M~ of State** ≃ secrétaire *m* d'État; **M~ of Health** ministre de la Santé. **2** *vi*: **to ~ to** *needs* pourvoir à; *person* donner ses soins à. ◆ **ministerial** *adj decision, crisis* ministériel; *benches* des ministres. ◆ **ministrations** *npl* soins *mpl*. ◆ **ministry** *n* (**a**) *(Pol etc)* ministère *m*; **Ministry of Health** ministère de la Santé; (**b**) *(Rel)* **the ministry** le (saint) ministère; **to go into the ministry** devenir pasteur.

mink [mɪŋk] **1** *n* vison *m*. **2** *adj* de vison.

minnow ['mɪnəʊ] *n* vairon *m*; *(any small fish)* fretin *m*; *(fig: person)* menu fretin *m*.

minor ['maɪnə'] **1** *adj (gen, Jur, Mus etc)* mineur; *detail, role, expenses, repairs* petit; *importance, interest* secondaire. *(Mus)* **G** ~ sol mineur; *(Mus)* ~ **key** ton *m* mineur; **in the ~ key** en mineur; ~ **offence** ≃ contravention *f* de simple police; *(Med)* ~ **operation** opération *f* bénigne; *(Cards)* ~ **suit** (couleur *f*) mineure *f*. **2** *n* (**a**) *(Jur)* mineur(e) *m(f)*. (**b**) *(US Univ)* matière *f* secondaire.
◆ **minority** [maɪ'nɒrɪtɪ] **1** *n* minorité *f*; **in the ~ity** en minorité ; **2** *adj (gen)* minoritaire; *report* soumis par un groupe minoritaire.

Minorca [mɪ'nɔːkə] *n* Minorque *f*. **in** ~ à Minorque.

minstrel ['mɪnstr(ə)l] *n* ménestrel *m*.

mint[1] [mɪnt] **1** *n* (hôtel *m* de la) Monnaie *f*; *(fig: big sum)* des sommes *fpl* folles. **to make a ~ of money** faire des affaires d'or. **2** *adj*: **in ~ condition** à l'état de neuf. **3** *vt coins* battre; *gold* monnayer (*into* pour obtenir); *(fig) word* inventer. *(fig)* **he ~s money** il fait des affaires d'or.

mint[2] [mɪnt] **1** *n (plant)* menthe *f*; *(sweet)* bonbon *m* à la menthe. **2** *adj* à la menthe. ~ **sauce** menthe *f* au vinaigre.

minus ['maɪnəs] **1** *prep (Math etc)* moins; *(*: without)* sans. **2** *adj*: ~ **quantity** *(Math)* quantité *f* négative; *(*: fig)* quantité négligeable; ~ **sign** moins *m*.

minute[1] ['mɪnɪt] **1** *n* (**a**) *(of time)* minute *f*. **it is 20 ~s past 2** il est 2 heures 20 (minutes); **at 4 o'clock to the** ~ à 4 heures pile; **we got the train without a ~ to spare** une minute de plus et nous manquions le train; **I'll do it in a** ~ je le ferai dans une minute; **the ~ he comes** dès qu'il arrivera; **do it this ~!** fais-le à la minute!; **he went out this** ~ il vient tout juste de sortir; **any ~ now** d'une minute à l'autre; **I shan't be a** ~ j'en ai pour deux secondes; **it won't take five ~s** ce sera fait en un rien de temps; **wait a** ~ attendez une minute *or* un instant; *(indignantly)* minute!; **up to the** ~ *equipment* dernier modèle *inv*; *fashion* dernier cri *inv*; *news* de dernière heure. (**b**) *(Geog, Math)* minute *f*. (**c**) *(memorandum)* note *f*. *[meeting]* **~s** procès-verbal *m*; **to take the ~s** rédiger le procès-verbal. **2** *adj* (**a**) ~ **hand** grande aiguille *f*; ~ **steak** entrecôte *f* minute. (**b**) ~ **book** registre *m* des délibérations. **3** *vt fact, detail* prendre note de.

minute[2] [maɪ'njuːt] *adj (gen)* minuscule; *change, differences* minime, infime; *examination, description* minutieux. **in ~ detail** dans les moindres détails.
◆ **minutely** *adv examine etc* minutieusement; *change* très peu; **~ly resembling...** ayant très vaguement l'apparence de... ◆ **minutiae** *npl* menus détails *mpl*.

miracle ['mɪrəkl] **1** *n* miracle *m (also fig)*. **by a** *or* **some** ~ par miracle; **it is a ~ that** c'est miracle que + *subj;* **it will be a ~ if** ce sera un miracle si. **2** *adj*: ~ **cure** *or* **drug** remède-miracle *m*; ~ **play** miracle *m (Theat)*. ◆ **miraculous** *adj* miraculeux. ◆ **miraculously** *adv* miraculeusement.

mirage ['mɪrɑːʒ] *n* mirage *m*.

mirror ['mɪrə'] **1** *n (gen)* miroir *m*, glace *f*; *(Aut)* rétroviseur *m*. **hand** ~ glace à main; **pocket** ~ miroir de poche. **2** *adj* ~ **image** image *f* inversée. **3** *vt* refléter. **to be ~ed in** se refléter dans.

mirth [mɜːθ] *n* hilarité *f*, rires *mpl*.

misadventure [ˌmɪsəd'ventʃə'] *n* mésaventure *f*, *(less serious)* contretemps *m*. *(Jur)* **death by** ~ mort *f* accidentelle.

misanthropy [mɪ'zænθrəpɪ] *n* misanthropie *f*.
◆ **misanthropic** *adj person* misanthrope; *mood*

misanthropique. ◆ **misanthropist** *n* misanthrope *mf*.

misapply ['mɪsə'plaɪ] *vt (gen)* mal employer; *funds* détourner.

misapprehension ['mɪsˌæprɪ'henʃ(ə)n] *n* malentendu *m*, méprise *f*. **he's (labouring) under a ~** il se trompe.

misappropriate ['mɪsə'prəʊprɪeɪt] *vt* détourner. ◆ **misappropriation** *n* détournement *m*.

misbehave ['mɪsbɪ'heɪv] *vi (gen)* se conduire mal; *[child]* ne pas être sage. ◆ **misbehaviour,** *(US)* **misbehavior** *n* mauvaise conduite *f*.

miscalculate ['mɪs'kælkjʊleɪt] **1** *vt* mal calculer. **2** *vi (fig)* se tromper. ◆ **miscalculation** *n* erreur *f* de calcul.

miscarry [ˌmɪs'kærɪ] *vi* (**a**) *[plan]* échouer, avorter. (**b**) *(Med)* faire une fausse couche. ◆ **miscarriage** *n* (**a**) *[plan]* échec *m*; **miscarriage of justice** erreur *f* judiciaire; (**b**) *(Med)* fausse couche.

miscast ['mɪs'kɑːst] *adj*: **he was ~** on n'aurait jamais dû lui donner ce rôle.

miscellaneous [ˌmɪsɪ'leɪnɪəs] *adj* divers. **~ expenses** frais *mpl* divers. ◆ **miscellany** [mɪ'selənɪ] *n [objects etc]* collection *f*; *(Literat)* recueil *m*; *(Rad, TV)* sélection *f*.

mischance [ˌmɪs'tʃɑːns] *n*: **by (a) ~** par malheur.

mischief ['mɪstʃɪf] *n* (**a**) *(roguishness)* espièglerie *f*; *(naughtiness)* sottises *fpl*; *(maliciousness)* méchanceté *f*. **he's up to (some) ~** *[child]* il prépare une sottise; *[adult] (in fun)* il prépare une farce quelconque; *(from malice)* il médite un mauvais coup; **to get into ~** faire des sottises; **to keep sb out of ~** empêcher qn de faire des sottises; **full of ~** espiègle; **bubbling over with ~** pétillant de malice; **to make ~** créer des ennuis (*for sb* à qn); **to make ~ between** semer la discorde entre; **to do o.s. a ~** se faire mal. (**b**) *(*: child)* polisson(ne) *m(f)*. ◆ **mischief-maker** *n* semeur *m*, -euse *f* de discorde; *(esp gossip)* mauvaise langue *f*. ◆ **mischievous** *adj (playful, naughty)* espiègle; *(harmful)* malveillant. ◆ **mischievously** *adv* par espièglerie; avec malveillance. ◆ **mischievousness** *n (roguishness)* espièglerie *f*; *(naughtiness)* polissonnerie *f*; *(maliciousness)* méchanceté *f*.

misconceived [ˌmɪskən'siːvd] *adj* peu judicieux.

misconception ['mɪskən'sepʃ(ə)n] *n (wrong idea/ opinion)* idée/opinion *f* fausse; *(misunderstanding)* malentendu *m*.

misconduct [ˌmɪs'kɒndʌkt] *n* inconduite *f*; *(sexual)* adultère *m*.

misconstrue ['mɪskən'struː] *vt* mal interpréter. ◆ **misconstruction** *n* fausse interprétation *f*.

miscount ['mɪs'kaʊnt] **1** *n (gen)* mécompte *m*; *(during election)* erreur *f* dans le compte. **2** *vti* mal compter.

misdeal ['mɪs'diːl] *(vb: pret, ptp* **-dealt** [-delt]*)* *(Cards)* **1** *n* maldonne *f*. **2** *vi* faire maldonne.

misdeed ['mɪs'diːd] *n* méfait *m*.

misdemeanour, *(US)* **misdemeanor** [ˌmɪsdɪ'miːnəʳ] *n* incartade *f*; *(Jur)* infraction *f*; *(US Jur)* délit *m*.

misdirect ['mɪsdɪ'rekt] *vt letter etc* mal adresser; *person* mal renseigner; *operation* mener mal; *(Jur) jury* mal instruire.

miser ['maɪzəʳ] *n* avare *mf*. ◆ **miserliness** *n* avarice *f*. ◆ **miserly** *adj* avare.

miserable ['mɪz(ə)r(ə)bl] *adj* (**a**) *(unhappy)* malheureux, triste; *(deplorable) sight, failure* pitoyable, lamentable. **to feel ~** avoir le cafard *; *(physically)* être mal fichu *; **to make sb ~** *(depress)* déprimer qn; *(hurt)* peiner qn; **don't look so ~!** ne fais pas cette tête d'enterrement! (**b**) *(filthy, wretched)* misérable, minable. (**c**) *(*: unpleasant) weather etc* maussade; *(stronger)* sale * *(before n)*. (**d**) *(contemptible) meal, gift* piteux; *amount, offer* dérisoire; *salary* de misère. **a ~ 50 francs** la misérable somme de 50 F. ◆ **miserably** *adv smile, answer* pitoyablement; *fail* lamentablement; *live, pay* misérablement.

misery ['mɪzərɪ] *n (unhappiness)* tristesse *f*; *(suffering)* souffrances *fpl*; *(wretchedness)* misère *f*. **a life of ~** une vie de misère; **to make sb's life a ~** *[person]* mener la vie dure à qn; *[arthritis]* gâcher la vie de qn; **to put an animal out of its ~** achever un animal; **put him out of his ~ * and tell him** abrégez son supplice et dites-le-lui; **what a ~ you are!** ce que tu peux être grincheux!

misfire ['mɪs'faɪəʳ] *vi [gun, plan]* faire long feu; *[joke]* foirer *; *[car engine]* avoir des ratés.

misfit ['mɪsfɪt] *n (person)* inadapté(e) *m(f)*.

misfortune [mɪs'fɔːtʃ(ə)n] *n (single event)* malheur *m*; *(bad luck)* malchance *f*. **it is his ~ that he is deaf, he has the ~ to be deaf** pour son malheur il est sourd; **that's YOUR ~!** tant pis pour toi!

misgiving [mɪs'gɪvɪŋ] *n* appréhension *f*. **not without ~(s)** non sans appréhension; **to have ~s about** avoir des doutes *mpl* quant à.

misgovern ['mɪs'gʌvən] *vti* mal gouverner.

misguided ['mɪs'gaɪdɪd] *adj person* abusé; *attempt* malencontreux; *decision, action* peu judicieux. ◆ **misguidedly** *adv* malencontreusement; peu judicieusement.

mishandle ['mɪs'hændl] *vt object* manipuler sans précaution; *person* s'y prendre mal avec; *problem* traiter mal. **he ~d the whole situation** il a été tout à fait maladroit.

mishap ['mɪshæp] *n* mésaventure *f*. **without ~** sans encombre.

mishear ['mɪs'hɪəʳ] *pret, ptp* **-heard** [-hɜːd] *vt* mal entendre.

mishmash * ['mɪʃmæʃ] *n* méli-mélo * *m*.

misinform ['mɪsɪn'fɔːm] *vt* mal renseigner.

misinterpret ['mɪsɪn'tɜːprɪt] *vt* mal interpréter. ◆ **misinterpretation** *n* interprétation *f* erronée (*of* de); *(in translation)* contresens *m*; **open to ~ation** qui prête à contresens.

misjudge ['mɪs'dʒʌdʒ] *vt amount, time* mal évaluer; *(underestimate)* sous-estimer; *person* se méprendre sur le compte de.

mislay [ˌmɪs'leɪ] *pret, ptp* **mislaid** *vt* égarer.

mislead [ˌmɪs'liːd] *pret, ptp* **misled** *vt* tromper. ◆ **misleading** *adj* trompeur.

mismanage ['mɪs'mænɪdʒ] *vt business* mal gérer; *organization* mal administrer. ◆ **mismanagement** *n* mauvaise administration *f*.

misname ['mɪs'neɪm] *vt* mal nommer.

misnomer ['mɪs'nəʊməʳ] *n* nom *m* mal approprié.

misogynist [mɪ'sɒdʒɪnɪst] *n* misogyne *mf*.

misplace ['mɪs'pleɪs] *vt word, trust* mal placer; *(lose)* égarer. ◆ **misplaced** *adj* déplacé.

misprint ['mɪsprɪnt] *n* faute *f* d'impression, coquille *f*.

mispronounce ['mɪsprə'naʊns] *vt* prononcer de travers. ◆ **mispronunciation** *n* faute(s) *f(pl)* de prononciation.

misquote ['mɪs'kwəʊt] *vt* citer inexactement. **he was ~d as having said...** on lui a incorrectement fait dire que... ◆ **misquotation** *n* citation *f* inexacte.

misread ['mɪs'riːd] *pret, ptp* **misread** ['mɪs'red] *vt* mal lire; *(misinterpret)* mal interpréter.

misrepresent ['mɪsˌreprɪ'zent] *vt facts* dénaturer; *person* donner une impression incorrecte de.

miss[1] [mɪs] **1** *n (shot etc)* coup *m* manqué *or* raté. *(lit, fig)* **that was a near ~** il s'en est fallu de peu *or* d'un cheveu; *(fig)* **to have a near ~** l'échapper belle; **to give sth a ~ *** *(job etc)* ne pas faire qch;

(concert etc) ne pas aller à qch; **I'll give the wine a ~** je me passerai de vin; **give it a ~!** * arrête! **2** *vt* (**a**) *(gen) train, target, deadline etc* manquer, rater; *thing looked out for, solution* ne pas trouver; *remark (not hear)* ne pas entendre; *(not understand)* ne pas comprendre; *(omit) meal, page, day* sauter; *class* manquer; *(deliberately)* sécher *. **it just ~ed me** ça m'a manqué de justesse; **the plane just ~ed the tower** l'avion a failli toucher la tour; *(iro)* **you haven't ~ed much!** vous n'avez pas manqué grand-chose!; *(fig)* **to ~ the boat** * *or* **the bus** * manquer le coche *; **to ~ one's footing** glisser; **she doesn't ~ a trick** * rien ne lui échappe; **to ~ one's way** perdre son chemin; **you can't ~ our house** vous trouverez tout de suite notre maison; **don't ~ the Louvre** ne manquez pas d'aller au Louvre; **we shall ~ Bourges** nous ne verrons pas Bourges; **you've ~ed the whole point!** vous n'avez rien compris!; (**b**) *(avoid) accident, bad weather* échapper à. **he narrowly ~ed being killed** il a manqué se faire tuer. (**c**) *(long for) person* regretter l'absence de. **I do ~ Paris/him** Paris/il me manque beaucoup; **we ~ you very much** tu nous manques beaucoup, nous regrettons beaucoup ton absence; **he won't be ~ed** personne ne le regrettera. (**d**) *(notice loss of) money, valuables* remarquer l'absence *or* la disparition de. **I suddenly ~ed my wallet** tout d'un coup je me suis aperçu que je n'avais plus mon portefeuille; **I shan't ~ it** ça ne me fera pas défaut.
3 *vi* (**a**) *[shot, person]* manquer, rater. **you can't ~!** vous ne pouvez pas ne pas réussir!; **he never ~es** il ne manque jamais son coup. (**b**) **to be ~ing** avoir disparu; **there is one plate ~ing** il manque une assiette; **one of our aircraft is ~ing** un de nos avions n'est pas rentré.

◆ **miss out** *vt sep (accidentally)* sauter, oublier; *(on purpose) course at meal* ne pas prendre; *name on list, person* omettre; *word, line of verse, page* sauter; *lecture, museum* ne pas aller à. ◆ **miss out on** * *vt fus opportunity, bargain* laisser passer, louper *. **he ~ed out on the deal** il n'a pas obtenu tout ce qu'il aurait pu de l'affaire.

◆ **missing** *adj person* absent, disparu; *(Mil)* disparu; *object (lost)* perdu; *(left out)* manquant; *word* qui manque; *(Police etc)* **~ing person** personne *f* absente; **the ~ing students** les étudiants dont on est sans nouvelles; *(fig)* **the ~ing link** le chaînon manquant; *(Mil)* **reported ~ing** porté disparu.

miss² [mɪs] *n* mademoiselle *f*. **M~ Smith** Mademoiselle Smith, Mˡˡᵉ Smith; *(in letter)* **Dear M~ Smith** Chère Mademoiselle; **yes M~ Smith** oui mademoiselle; **M~ France 1982** Miss France 1982; **the modern ~** la jeune fille moderne.

missal ['mɪs(ə)l] *n* missel *m*.

misshapen [mɪs'ʃeɪp(ə)n] *adj* difforme.

missile ['mɪsaɪl] **1** *n (gen)* projectile *m*; *(Mil)* missile *m*. **2** *adj*: **~ base** base *f* de missiles; **~ launcher** lance-missiles *m inv*.

mission ['mɪʃ(ə)n] **1** *n (all senses)* mission *f*. **trade ~** mission de commerce; **on a ~ to sb** en mission auprès de qn; **his ~ in life is to help others** il s'est donné pour mission d'aider autrui. **2** *adj (Space etc)* **~ control** centre *m* de contrôle. ◆ **missionary** **1** *n* missionnaire *mf* ; **2** *adj* de missionnaire(s).

misspell ['mɪs'spel] *pret, ptp* **misspelt** *vt* mal orthographier. ◆ **misspelling** *n* faute *f* d'orthographe.

mist [mɪst] **1** *n* brume *f*; *(on glass)* buée *f*; *[perfume]* nuage *m*; *[ignorance, tears]* voile *m*. **lost in the ~s of time** perdu dans la nuit des temps. **2** *vi* (**~ over, ~ up**) *[scene, landscape]* se couvrir de brume; *[mirror, eyes]* s'embuer. ◆ **misty** *adj weather* brumeux; *mirror, eyes* embué; *outline, recollection* flou.

mistake [mɪs'teɪk] *(vb: pret* **mistook,** *ptp* **mistaken***)* **1** *n* erreur *f*, faute *f*; *(misunderstanding)* méprise *f*. **to make a ~ in a dictation/problem** faire une faute dans une dictée/une erreur dans un problème; **I made a ~ about the book/about him** je me suis trompé sur le livre/sur son compte; **I made a ~ about** *or* **over the road to take/about** *or* **over the dates** je me suis trompé de route/de dates; **make no ~ about it** ne vous y trompez pas; **you're making a big ~** tu fais une grave erreur; **to make the ~ of doing** avoir le tort de faire; **by ~** par erreur; *(carelessly)* par mégarde; **there must be some ~** il doit y avoir erreur; **there must be no ~ about it** qu'on ne s'y trompe pas; **he's wrong and no ~** décidément il a tort; **my ~!** c'est de ma faute! **2** *vt meaning* mal comprendre; *intentions* se méprendre sur; *time, road* se tromper de; *sb's voice* ne pas reconnaître. **to ~ A for B** prendre A pour B. ◆ **mistaken** *adj idea, opinion, conclusion* erroné; *generosity* mal placé; **in the ~n belief that...** croyant à tort que...; *[person]* **to be ~n** se tromper (*about* sur); **if I'm not ~n** si je ne me trompe. ◆ **mistakenly** *adv* par erreur; *(carelessly)* par mégarde.

mistime ['mɪs'taɪm] *vt (do etc at unsuitable time)* faire *etc* à contretemps. **he ~d it** il a choisi le mauvais moment.

mistletoe ['mɪsltəʊ] *n* gui *m*.

mistranslate ['mɪstrænz'leɪt] *vt* mal traduire. ◆ **mistranslation** *n* contresens *m*.

mistress ['mɪstrɪs] *n (gen)* maîtresse *f*; *(teacher)* professeur *m*. **English ~** professeur d'anglais.

mistrust ['mɪs'trʌst] **1** *n* méfiance *f* (*of* à l'égard de). **2** *vt person, motives* se méfier de; *one's own abilities* douter de. ◆ **mistrustful** *adj* méfiant. ◆ **mistrustfully** *adv* avec méfiance.

misunderstand ['mɪsʌndə'stænd] *pret, ptp* **-stood** *vt* mal comprendre. ◆ **misunderstanding** *n* méprise *f*; *(disagreement)* malentendu *m*. ◆ **misunderstood** *adj person* incompris.

misuse ['mɪs'ju:z] **1** *vt power, authority* abuser de; *word, tool* employer incorrectement; *money, resources, energies, one's time* mal employer; *funds* détourner. **2** ['mɪs'ju:s] *n* abus *m*; emploi *m* incorrect; mauvais emploi; détournement *m*.

mite [maɪt] *n* (**a**) *(small amount) [good sense etc]* grain *m*; *[truth]* parcelle *f*. **a ~ of consolation** une toute petite consolation; **the widow's ~** le denier de la veuve. (**b**) *(small child)* petit(e) *m(f)*. **poor little ~** le pauvre petit. (**c**) *(Zool)* mite *f*. **cheese ~** mite de fromage.

mitigate ['mɪtɪgeɪt] *vt* atténuer. **mitigating circumstances** circonstances *fpl* atténuantes. ◆ **mitigation** *n* atténuation *f*.

mitre, *(US)* **miter** ['maɪtəʳ] *n (Rel)* mitre *f*; *(Carpentry)* onglet *m*.

mitt [mɪt] *n (also* **mitten***) (cut-off fingers)* mitaine *f*; *(no separate fingers)* moufle *f*; *(Baseball)* gant *m*.

mix [mɪks] **1** *n* mélange *f*. **cake ~** préparation *f* pour gâteau. **2** *vt liquids, ingredients, colours* mélanger (*with* avec); *small objects* mêler, mélanger (*with* à); *metals* allier; *cement, mortar* malaxer; *cake, sauce, cocktails* préparer; *salad* retourner. **to ~ to a smooth paste** battre pour obtenir une pâte homogène; **to ~ business with pleasure** combiner les affaires et le plaisir; **to ~ one's metaphors** faire des métaphores incohérentes. **3** *vi* se mélanger; se mêler; s'allier. **he ~es with all kinds of people** il fréquente toutes sortes de gens; **he doesn't ~ well** il est peu sociable; **they just don't ~** *[patterns]* ils ne vont pas ensemble; *[people]* ils n'ont rien en commun.

◆ **mix in** *vt sep eggs etc* incorporer (*with* à). ◆ **mix together** *vt sep* mélanger. ◆ **mix up** *vt sep* (**a**) *(prepare) drink, medicine* mélanger, préparer. (**b**) *(in disorder) documents, garments* mêler, mélanger. (**c**) *(confuse) two objects, two people* confondre (*with* avec). (**d**) **to be/get ~ed up in an affair** être/se trouver mêlé à une affaire; **don't get ~ed up in it!**

restez à l'écart!; **he has got ~ed up with a lot of criminals** il s'est mis à fréquenter des malfaiteurs. (**e**) *(muddle) person* embrouiller. **to be ~ed up** *[person]* être déboussolé *; *[account, facts]* être embrouillé; **I am all ~ed up about it** je ne sais plus où j'en suis.
◆ **mixed** *adj marriage, school, economy* mixte; *biscuits, nuts* assortis; *weather* variable; *metaphor* incohérent; *motives* complexe; *feelings* contradictoires; *reception* mitigé; *(fig)* **it's a ~ed bag** * il y a un peu de tout; **it's a ~ed blessing** c'est une bonne chose qui a son mauvais côté; **man/woman of ~ed blood** un/une sang-mêlé; **in ~ed company** en présence d'hommes et de femmes; *(Tennis)* **~ed doubles** double *m* mixte; **~ed farming** polyculture *f*.
◆ **mixed-ability** *adj group, teaching* sans groupes de niveaux. ◆ **mixed-up** *adj person* déboussolé *; *account* embrouillé. ◆ **mixer** **1** *n* (**a**) *(Culin)* mixeur *m*; *[mortar etc]* malaxeur *m*; *[industrial liquids]* agitateur *m*; **cement ~er** bétonnière *f*; (**b**) **he's a good ~er** il est très sociable *or* liant; (**c**) *(US: social gathering)* soirée-rencontre *f*; (**d**) *(drink)* boisson *f* gazeuse ; **2** *adj*: **~er tap** mélangeur *m*.
◆ **mixing** **1** *n (V* **mix 2***)* mélange *m*; alliage *m*; malaxage *m*; préparation *f* ; **2** *adj*: **~ing bowl** jatte *f*. ◆ **mixture** *n* mélange *m*; *(Med)* préparation *f*, mixture *f*; *(fig)* **it's just the ~ture as before** il n'y a rien de nouveau. ◆ **mix-up** *n* confusion *f* (*over* en ce qui concerne).

moan [məʊn] **1** *n (gen)* gémissement *m*; *(*: complaint)* plainte *f*. **2** *vi (gen)* gémir; *(*: complain)* se plaindre, rouspéter *. **3** *vt* dire en gémissant.

moat [məʊt] *n* fossés *mpl*.

mob [mɒb] **1** *n [people]* foule *f*, masse *f*; *(disorderly)* cohue *f*; *(rioting)* émeutiers *mpl*; *(pej)* populace *f*; *[criminals, bandits etc]* gang *m*; *(*: group)* bande *f*. **2** *adj*: **~ rule** la loi de la populace. **3** *vt person* assaillir; *place* assiéger.

mobile ['məʊbaɪl] **1** *adj* mobile. *(fig)* **I'm not ~ this week** * je ne suis pas motorisé * cette semaine; **~ canteen** (cuisine) roulante *f*; **~ home** grande caravane *f (utilisée comme domicile)*; **~ library** bibliobus *m*; *(Rad, TV)* **~ studio** car *m* de reportage. **2** *n (Art)* mobile *m*. ◆ **mobility** *n* mobilité *f*. ◆ **mobilization** *n* mobilisation *f*. ◆ **mobilize** *vti* mobiliser.

mock [mɒk] **1** *vt (ridicule)* ridiculiser; *(scoff at)* se moquer de. **2** *vi* se moquer (*at* de). **3** *adj leather etc* imitation *inv (before n)*, faux *(before n)*; *anger* feint. **a ~ battle/trial** un simulacre de bataille/de procès; **~ exam** examen blanc; **~ turtle soup** consommé *m* à la tête de veau.
◆ **mock up** *vt sep* faire la maquette de.
◆ **mocker** *n* moqueur *m*, -euse *f*. ◆ **mockery** *n (gen)* moquerie *f*; *(of justice etc)* parodie *f*; **to make a ~ery of** tourner en dérision. ◆ **mocking** **1** *n* moquerie *f* ; **2** *adj* moqueur; *(malicious)* narquois.
◆ **mockingbird** *n* moqueur *m (oiseau)*. ◆ **mockingly** *adv* d'un ton *or* d'un air moqueur.
◆ **mock-up** *n* maquette *f*.

mod * [mɒd] *(abbr of* **modern***) adj*: **~ cons** *V* **modern 1**.

mode [məʊd] *n (Comput, Ling, Mus etc)* mode *m*; *(Fashion)* mode *f*. ◆ **modal** *adj* modal.

model ['mɒdl] **1** *n (gen, also fig)* modèle *m*; *(small-scale)* modèle réduit; *(Archit, Tech, Town Planning etc)* maquette *f*; *(artist's ~)* modèle; *(fashion ~)* mannequin *m*. **to take sb/sth as one's ~** prendre modèle sur qn/qch; *(Comm)* **a 1978 ~** un modèle 1978; *(Aut)* **sports ~** modèle sport; **factory ~** modèle de fabrique; **male ~** mannequin masculin. **2** *adj (gen) prison, school, behaviour* modèle; *(small-scale) plane, car* modèle réduit *inv*; *railway, village* en miniature. **~ factory** usine-pilote *f*. **3** *vt (gen)* modeler (*in* en; *on* sur); *garment* présenter. **to ~ o.s. on sb** prendre modèle sur qn. **4** *vi (Art etc)* poser (*for* pour); *(Fashion)* être mannequin (*for sb* chez qn).
◆ **modelling,** *(US)* **modeling** **1** *n (Sculp etc)* modelage *m* ; **2** *adj*: **~(l)ing clay** pâte *f* à modeler.

modem ['məʊdem] *n (Comput)* modem *m*.

moderate ['mɒdərɪt] **1** *adj (gen)* modéré; *climate* tempéré; *language, terms* mesuré; *result* passable. **2** *n (esp Pol)* modéré(e) *m(f)*. **3** ['mɒdəreɪt] *vt* modérer. **4** *vi* se modérer. ◆ **moderately** *adv act* avec modération; *successful* modérément; *pleased* plus ou moins; **~ly priced** d'un prix raisonnable. ◆ **moderation** *n* modération *f*; **in moderation** *eat, drink* modérément; **it's all right in moderation** ça ne fait pas de mal à petites doses.

modern ['mɒd(ə)n] **1** *adj* moderne. **all ~ conveniences** *(abbr* **mod cons***)* tout le confort (moderne); **~ languages** langues *fpl* vivantes. **2** *n (person)* moderne *mf*. ◆ **modernity** *n* modernité *f*. ◆ **modernization** *n* modernisation *f*.
◆ **modernize** *vt* moderniser.

modest ['mɒdɪst] *adj (all senses)* modeste. **to be ~ about** ne pas se faire gloire de. ◆ **modestly** *adv* modestement. ◆ **modesty** *n* modestie *f*; **with all due ~y** en toute modestie.

modicum ['mɒdɪkəm] *n*: **a ~ of** un minimum de.

modify ['mɒdɪfaɪ] *vt (change)* modifier *(also Gram)*; *(make less strong) demands* modérer. ◆ **modification** *n* modification *f* (*to, in* à). ◆ **modifier** *n* modificateur *m*; *(Gram)* modificatif *m*.

modulate ['mɒdjʊleɪt] *vt* moduler. ◆ **modulation** *n* modulation *f*.

module ['mɒdju:l] *n* module *m*.

mogul ['məʊgəl] *n* **1** *adj*: **M~** des Mog(h)ols. **2** *n* (**a**) **M~** Mog(h)ol *m*. (**b**) *(fig: powerful person)* nabab *m*.

mohair ['məʊhɛəʳ] **1** *n* mohair *m*. **2** *adj* en *or* de mohair.

Mohammed [məʊ'hæmɪd] *n* Mahomet *m*.
◆ **Mohammedan** **1** *adj* mahométan, musulman ; **2** *n* Mahométan(e) *m(f)*.

moist [mɔɪst] *adj hand, atmosphere* moite; *climate, wind, surface, eyes* humide; *cake* moelleux. ◆ **moisten** *vt* mouiller légèrement; **to ~en one's lips** s'humecter les lèvres. ◆ **moistness** *n* moiteur *f*; humidité *f*. ◆ **moisture** *n (gen)* humidité *f*; *(on glass etc)* buée *f*. ◆ **moisturize** *vt air, humidifier; skin* hydrater. ◆ **moisturizer** *n (for skin)* lait *m* hydratant.

molar ['məʊləʳ] *adj, n* molaire *(f)*.

molasses [mə(ʊ)'læsɪz] *n* mélasse *f*.

mold [məʊld] *etc (US)* = **mould** *etc*.

mole[1] [məʊl] *n* taupe *f (also fig: spy)*. ◆ **molehill** *n* taupinière *f*. ◆ **moleskin** *n* (peau *f* de) taupe *f*; *(Tex)* velours *m* de coton.

mole[2] [məʊl] *n (on skin)* grain *m* de beauté.

molecule ['mɒlɪkju:l] *n* molécule *f*.

molest [mə(ʊ)'lest] *vt (trouble)* importuner; *(harm)* molester; *(Jur: sexually)* attenter à la pudeur de; *[dog]* s'attaquer à.

mollify ['mɒlɪfaɪ] *vt* apaiser, calmer.

mollusc, *(US)* **mollusk** ['mɒləsk] *n* mollusque *m*.

mollycoddle ['mɒlɪkɒdl] *vt* chouchouter *.

molten ['məʊlt(ə)n] *adj* en fusion.

mom * [mɒm] *n (US)* maman *f*.

moment ['məʊmənt] *n* (**a**) moment *m*, instant *m*. **man of the ~** homme *m* du moment; **the ~ of truth** la minute de vérité; **just a ~!, one ~!, half a ~!** * un instant!; *(objecting to sth)* minute!; **I shan't be a ~** j'en ai pour un instant; **a ~ ago** il y a un instant; **the ~ he arrives** dès qu'il arrivera; **I've just this ~ heard of it** je viens de l'apprendre à l'instant (même); **it won't take a ~** c'est l'affaire d'un instant; **at the (present) ~, at this ~ in time** en ce moment; **at any ~** d'un moment *or* instant à l'autre; **at the right/last** ~ au bon/dernier moment; **for a** ~ un instant; **not for a** ~**!** jamais de la vie!; **from the** ~ **I saw him** dès l'instant où je l'ai vu; **I'll come in a** ~ j'arrive dans un instant; **it was all over in a** ~ tout s'est passé en un instant; ~ **of truth** l'heure *f* de vérité; **I have my** (*or* **he has his** *etc*) ~**s** * il m'arrive (or il lui arrive *etc*) de faire des étincelles *. (**b**) *(importance)* importance *f*. ◆ **momentarily** *adv* momentanément. ◆ **momentary** *adj* momentané. ◆ **momentous** *adj* très important. ◆ **momentum** *n (Phys etc)* moment *m*; *(fig)* élan *m*, vitesse *f* (acquise); **to gather** ~**um** *[vehicle]* prendre de la vitesse; *[protests, campaign etc]* gagner du terrain; *(lit, fig)* **to lose** ~**um** être en perte de vitesse.

Monaco ['mɒnəkəʊ] *n* Monaco *m*. ◆ **Monegasque 1** *adj* monégasque ; **2** *n* Monégasque *mf*.

monarch ['mɒnək] *n* monarque *m*. ◆ **monarchism** *n* monarchisme *m*. ◆ **monarchist** *adj, n* monarchiste *(mf)*. ◆ **monarchy** *n* monarchie *f*.

monastery ['mɒnəst(ə)rɪ] *n* monastère *m*. ◆ **monastic** *adj* monastique. ◆ **monasticism** *n* monachisme *m*.

Monday ['mʌndɪ] *n* lundi *m*; *for phrases V* **Saturday**.

monetary ['mʌnɪt(ə)rɪ] *adj* monétaire. ◆ **monetarism** *n* politique *f* monétaire.

money ['mʌnɪ] **1** *n* argent *m*. **French** ~ argent français; **paper** ~ papier-monnaie *m*; ~ **for jam** * *or* **for old rope** * de l'argent vite gagné; **to make** ~ *[person]* gagner de l'argent; *[business etc]* rapporter; **how did he make his** ~**?** comment est-ce qu'il a fait fortune?; **he's earning good** ~ il gagne bien sa vie; **I paid good** ~ **for it** ça m'a coûté de l'argent; **he's earning big** ~ il gagne gros; **that's big** ~ c'est une grosse somme; **when do I get my** ~**?** quand est-ce que j'aurai mon argent?; **to get one's** ~**'s worth** en avoir pour son argent; **to get one's** ~ **back** *(refund)* être remboursé; *(with difficulty)* récupérer son argent; **to put** ~ **into sth** placer son argent dans qch; **is there** ~ **in it?** est-ce qu'il y a qch à gagner?; **it's a bargain for the** ~ à ce prix-là, c'est une occasion; *(fig)* **for my** ~ à mon avis; **he's made of** ~ *, **he has pots of** ~ * il roule sur l'or *; **he's got** ~ **to burn** il a de l'argent à ne savoir qu'en faire; **we're in the** ~**!** * nous roulons sur l'or *; ~ **doesn't grow on trees** l'argent ne tombe pas du ciel. **2** *adj difficulties, questions* d'argent, financier. ~ **order** mandat-poste *m*; ~ **supply** masse *f* monétaire. ◆ **moneybox** *n* tirelire *f*. ◆ **moneyed** *adj* riche. ◆ **moneygrubbing 1** *n* rapacité *f* ; **2** *adj* rapace. ◆ **moneylender** *n* prêteur *m* sur gages. ◆ **moneylending** *n* prêt *m* à intérêt. ◆ **moneymaker** *n* affaire *f* lucrative. ◆ **moneymaking 1** *n* acquisition *f* d'argent ; **2** *adj* qui rapporte. ◆ **moneyman** * *n* financier *m*.

mongol ['mɒŋgəl] *n (Med)* mongolien(ne) *m(f)*.

Mongolia [mɒŋ'gəʊlɪə] *n* Mongolie *f*. ◆ **Mongol**, ◆ **Mongolian 1** *adj* mongol ; **2** *n* Mongol(e) *m(f)*.

mongoose ['mɒŋgu:s] *n* mangouste *f*.

mongrel ['mʌŋgr(ə)l] *n* (chien *m*) bâtard *m*.

monitor ['mɒnɪtə^r] **1** *n (Rad: person)* rédacteur *m*, -trice *f* d'un service d'écoute; *(Med, Tech, TV: device)* moniteur *m*; *(Scol)* ≃ chef *m* de classe. **2** *vt (Rad) broadcast* être à l'écoute de; *pupil, work, machine, system* contrôler (les performances de); *progress* contrôler; *discussion, group* assister à (à titre de conseiller). **to** ~ **the situation** surveiller l'évolution des choses. ◆ **monitoring** *n (Med, Tech)* monitorage *m*.

monk [mʌŋk] *n* moine *m*, religieux *m*. ◆ **monkish** *adj* de moine.

monkey ['mʌŋkɪ] **1** *n* singe *m*. **female** ~ guenon *f*; *(child)* **little** ~ petit(e) polisson(ne) *m(f)*. **2** *adj*: ~ **business** * *or* **tricks** * *(dishonest)* qch de louche; *(mischievous)* singeries *fpl*; **no** ~ **business now!** * pas de blagues! *; ~ **nut** cacahuète *f*; *(tree)* ~ **puzzle** araucaria *m*; ~ **wrench** clef *f* anglaise *or* à molette. ◆ **monkey about** *, **monkey around** * *vi (waste time)* perdre son temps; *(play the fool)* faire l'imbécile. **to** ~ **about with sth** tripoter qch.

mono ['mɒnəʊ] **1** *adj (abbr of* **monophonic**) *mono* * *inv*. **2** *n*: **in** ~ en monophonie. **3** *pref* mono...

monochrome ['mɒnəkrəʊm] *n* camaïeu *m*; *(Phot, TV)* noir et blanc *m*.

monocle ['mɒnəkl] *n* monocle *m*.

monogamy [mɒ'nɒgəmɪ] *n* monogamie *f*. ◆ **monogamous** *adj* monogame.

monogram ['mɒnəgræm] *n* monogramme *m*.

monograph ['mɒnəgræf] *n* monographie *f*.

monolith ['mɒnə(ʊ)lɪθ] *n* monolithe *m*.

monologue ['mɒnəlɒg] *n* monologue *m*.

monomania [,mɒnə(ʊ)'meɪnɪə] *n* monomanie *f*. ◆ **monomaniac** *n* monomane *mf*.

monoplane ['mɒnə(ʊ)pleɪn] *n* monoplan *m*.

monopoly [mə'nɒpəlɪ] *n* monopole *m* (*of, in* de). ◆ **monopolize** *vt* monopoliser.

monorail ['mɒnə(ʊ)reɪl] *n* monorail *m*.

monosyllable ['mɒnə'sɪləbl] *n* monosyllabe *m*. ◆ **monosyllabic** ['mɒnə(ʊ)sɪ'læbɪk] *adj word* monosyllabe; *reply* monosyllabique.

monotone ['mɒnətəʊn] *n*: **in a** ~ sur un ton monocorde. ◆ **monotonous** [mə'nɒtənəs] *adj* monotone. ◆ **monotony** *n* monotonie *f*.

monsoon [mɒn'su:n] *n* mousson *f*.

monster ['mɒnstə^r] *n, adj* monstre *(m)*. ◆ **monstrosity** *n* monstruosité *f*. ◆ **monstrous** *adj (huge)* colossal; *(dreadful)* monstrueux. ◆ **monstrously** *adv* monstrueusement.

month [mʌnθ] *n* mois *m*. **in the** ~ **of May** au mois de mai, en mai; **paid by the** ~ payé au mois; **every** ~ *happen* tous les mois; *pay* mensuellement; **which day of the** ~ **is it?** le combien sommes-nous?; **he'll never do it in a** ~ **of Sundays** * il le fera la semaine des quatre jeudis *. ◆ **monthly 1** *adj (gen)* mensuel; ~**ly instalment** *or* **payment** mensualité *f*; ~ **ticket** carte *f* (d'abonnement) mensuelle ; **2** *n (Press)* revue *f* mensuelle ; **3** *adv pay* mensuellement; *happen* tous les mois.

monument ['mɒnjʊmənt] *n* monument *m* (*to* à). ◆ **monumental** *adj* monumental; ~**al mason** marbrier *m*.

moo [mu:] **1** *n* meuglement *m*. **2** *vi* meugler.

mooch ⁑ [mu:tʃ] *vi*: **to** ~ **about** *or* **around** traînasser; **to** ~ **in** *etc* entrer *etc* en traînant.

mood [mu:d] **1** *n (gen)* humeur *f*; *(Gram, Mus)* mode *m*. **in a good/bad** ~ de bonne/mauvaise humeur; **in an ugly** ~ *(angry)* d'une humeur massacrante; *(threatening)* menaçant; **I'm in the** ~ **for dancing** j'ai envie de danser; **I'm in no** ~ **to listen to him** je ne suis pas d'humeur à l'écouter; **when he's in the** ~ quand ça lui chante *; **I'm not in the** ~ ça ne me dit rien; **he's in one of his** ~**s** il est encore mal luné *; **she has** ~**s** elle a des sautes *fpl* d'humeur; **the** ~ **of the meeting** l'état *m* d'esprit de l'assemblée. **2** *adj*: ~ **music** musique *f* d'ambiance. ◆ **moodily** *adv (bad-temperedly)* d'un air *etc* maussade; *(gloomily)* d'un air morose. ◆ **moodiness** *n (V* **moody***)* humeur *f* changeante *or* maussade. ◆ **moody** *adj (variable)* d'humeur changeante; *(sulky)* maussade.

moon [mu:n] **1** *n* lune *f*. **full/new** ~ pleine/nouvelle lune; **there was no** ~ c'était une nuit sans lune; **there was a** ~ il y avait clair de lune; **by the light**

of the ~ à la clarté de la lune; **the man in the ~** l'homme (que l'on voit) dans la lune; *(fig)* **to ask** *or* **cry for the ~** demander la lune; **to be over the ~** * être ravi (*about* de). **2** *adj*: ~ **landing** alunissage *m*; ~ **shot** tir *m* lunaire.

◆ **moon about, moon around** *vi* musarder en rêvassant.

◆ **moonbeam** *n* rayon *m* de lune. ◆ **moonboots** *npl* après-ski(s) *mpl*. ◆ **moonlight** **1** *n* clair *m* de lune; **by ~light** au clair de (la) lune ; **2** *adj walk* au clair de lune; *night* de lune; *(fig)* **to do a ~light flit** déménager à la cloche de bois ; **3** *vi* (*: *work)* travailler au noir. ◆ **moonlighting** * *n* travail *m* au noir. ◆ **moonlit** *adj* éclairé par la lune; **~lit night** nuit *f* de lune. ◆ **moonrise** *n* lever *m* de (la) lune. ◆ **moonshine** * *n* *(nonsense)* balivernes *fpl*. ◆ **moonstone** *n* pierre *f* de lune. ◆ **moonstruck** *adj* dans la lune *(fig)*.

moor[1] [mʊəʳ] *n* lande *f*. ◆ **moorhen** *n* poule *f* d'eau. ◆ **moorland** *n* lande *f*.

moor[2] [mʊəʳ] **1** *vt ship* amarrer. **2** *vi* mouiller. ◆ **mooring** *n (place)* mouillage *m*; **at her ~ings** sur ses amarres *fpl*.

moose [mu:s] *n (Zool)* élan *m*; *(Canada)* orignal *m*.

moot [mu:t] **1** *adj*: **it's a ~ point** c'est discutable. **2** *vt*: **it has been ~ed that** on a suggéré que.

mop [mɒp] **1** *n (for floor)* balai *m* laveur; *(for dishes)* lavette *f* (à vaisselle). ~ **of hair** tignasse *f*; ~ **of curls** toison *f* bouclée. **2** *vt floor, surface* essuyer. **to ~ one's brow** s'éponger le front. ◆ **mop up** *vt sep liquid* éponger; *surface* essuyer; *(Mil) remnants* éliminer. ◆ **mopping-up** *or (US)* ◆ **mop-up operations** *npl (Mil)* nettoyage *m*.

mope [məʊp] *vi* se morfondre (*about* en pensant à). **to ~ about** *or* **around** passer son temps à se morfondre.

moped ['məʊped] *n* vélomoteur *m*.

moral ['mɒr(ə)l] **1** *adj* moral. **to have a ~ obligation to do** être dans l'obligation morale de faire; ~ **support** soutien *m* moral; ~ **philosophy** la morale, l'éthique *f*; **to raise ~ standards** relever les mœurs. **2** *n* (**a**) *[story]* morale *f*. **to point the ~** faire ressortir la morale. (**b**) *[person, act, attitude]* **~s** moralité *f*.

◆ **morale** [mɒ'rɑ:l] *n* moral *m*; **to raise sb's ~e** remonter le moral à qn. ◆ **moralist** *n* moraliste *mf*. ◆ **morality** *n* moralité *f*. ◆ **moralize** *vi* moraliser (*about* sur). ◆ **moralizing** **1** *adj* moralisateur ; **2** *n* leçons *fpl* de morale. ◆ **morally** *adv act* moralement; **~ly wrong** immoral.

morass [mə'ræs] *n* marécage *m*. *(fig)* **a ~ of problems/paperwork** des problèmes/des papiers à n'en plus finir.

morbid ['mɔ:bɪd] *adj (gen)* morbide; *fear* maladif. ◆ **morbidly** *adv imagine* d'une façon morbide; *obsessed, curious* morbidement.

more [mɔ:ʳ] *comp of* **many, much** **1** *adj, pron (greater in number etc)* plus (de), davantage (de) ; *(additional)* encore (de); *(other)* d'autres. ~ **money/books than** plus d'argent/de livres que; **he's got ~ than you** il en a plus que toi; ~ **people than we expected** plus de gens que prévu *or* que nous ne l'escomptions; **many came but ~ stayed away** beaucoup de gens sont venus mais davantage *or* un plus grand nombre se sont abstenus; **many ~, a lot ~** beaucoup plus (de); **a few ~ books** encore quelques livres, quelques livres de plus; **a little ~** un peu plus (de); **some ~ meat** encore de la viande, un peu plus de viande; **there's no ~ meat** il n'y a plus de viande; **is there (any) ~ wine?** y a-t-il encore du vin?; **has she any ~ children?** a-t-elle d'autres enfants?; **no ~ shouting!** arrêtez de crier!; **I've got no ~, I haven't any ~** je n'en ai plus, il ne m'en reste plus; **he can't afford ~ than a small house** il ne peut se payer qu'une petite maison; **have you heard any ~ about him?** avez-vous d'autres nouvelles de lui?; **one pound is ~ than 50p** une livre est plus que 50 pence; ~ **than a kilo** plus d'un kilo; ~ **than enough** plus que suffisant; **I've got ~ like these** j'en ai d'autres comme ça; *(fig)* **you couldn't ask for ~** on ne peut guère en demander plus; **the ~ the merrier** plus on est de fous, plus on rit; **and what's ~...** et qui plus est...; **nothing ~** rien de plus; **sth ~** qch d'autre *or* de plus.

2 *adv (gen)* plus; *exercise, sleep* plus (*than* que), davantage. ~ **difficult** plus difficile; ~ **easily** plus facilement; ~ **and ~** de plus en plus; **he's no ~ a duke than I am** il n'est pas plus duc que moi; ~ **or less** plus ou moins; **neither ~ nor less** ni plus ni moins (*than* que); **it will ~ than cover the cost** cela couvrira largement les frais; **no ~ can** *(or do etc)* **I** ni moi non plus; **the ~ I think of it the ~ ashamed I feel** plus j'y pense, plus j'ai honte; **the ~ fool you to go!** tu es d'autant plus idiot d'y aller!; **(all) the ~ so as...** d'autant plus que...; **no ~, not any ~** ne... plus; **I won't do it any ~** je ne le ferai plus; **once ~** une fois de plus, encore une fois.

moreover [mɔ:'rəʊvəʳ] *adv (further)* de plus, en outre; *(besides)* d'ailleurs, du reste.

morgue [mɔ:g] *n* morgue *f*.

moribund ['mɒrɪbʌnd] *adj* moribond.

morning ['mɔ:nɪŋ] **1** *n (date, part of day)* matin *m*; *(expressing duration)* matinée *f*. **good ~** *(hallo)* bonjour; *(goodbye)* au revoir; **in the ~** le matin, dans la matinée; *(tomorrow)* demain matin; **I work in the ~(s)** je travaille le matin; **a ~'s work** une matinée de travail; **I have a ~ off every week** j'ai une matinée de libre par semaine; **all (the) ~** toute la matinée; **on the ~ of January 23rd** le 23 janvier au matin; **what a beautiful ~!** quelle belle matinée!; **7 o'clock in the ~** 7 heures du matin; **this ~** ce matin; **yesterday ~** hier matin; **one summer ~** par un matin d'été. **2** *adj walk, swim* matinal, du matin; *paper* du matin. ~ **dress** habit *m*; ~ **prayer** *or* **service** office *m* du matin; ~ **sickness** nausées *fpl* matinales.

Morocco [mə'rɒkəʊ] *n* Maroc *m*.

moron ['mɔ:rɒn] *n (gen)* idiot(e) *m(f)*, crétin(e) *m(f)*; *(Med)* débile léger *m*, débile légère *f*. ◆ **moronic** [mə'rɒnɪk] *adj* crétin.

morose [mə'rəʊs] *adj* morose. ◆ **morosely** *adv* d'un air *etc* morose.

morphia ['mɔ:fɪə], **morphine** ['mɔ:fi:n] *n* morphine *f*. ~ **addict** morphinomane *mf*.

morphology [mɔ:'fɒlədʒɪ] *n* morphologie *f*.

Morse [mɔ:s] **1** *n* (~ **code**) morse *m*. **2** *adj alphabet* morse; *signals* en morse.

morsel ['mɔ:sl] *n* (petit) morceau *m*; *[food]* bouchée *f*.

mortal ['mɔ:tl] **1** *adj (gen)* mortel; *combat* à mort. **2** *n* mortel(le) *m(f)*. ◆ **mortality** *n* mortalité *f*. ◆ **mortally** *adv* mortellement.

mortar ['mɔ:təʳ] *n* mortier *m*.

mortgage ['mɔ:gɪdʒ] **1** *n (in house buying)* emprunt-logement *m*; *(second loan)* hypothèque *f*. **to take out a ~** obtenir un emprunt-logement (*on, for* pour), prendre une hypothèque; **to pay off a ~** rembourser un emprunt-logement, purger une hypothèque. **2** *vt* hypothéquer *(also fig)*.

mortice, mortise ['mɔ:tɪs] *n* mortaise *f*. ~ **lock** serrure *f* encastrée.

mortician [mɔ:'tɪʃən] *n (US)* entrepreneur *m* de pompes funèbres.

mortify ['mɔ:tɪfaɪ] *vt* mortifier. ◆ **mortification** *n* mortification *f (also Rel)*; humiliation *f*. ◆ **mortifying** *adj* mortifiant.

mortuary ['mɔ:tjʊərɪ] *n* morgue *f*.

mosaic [mə(ʊ)'zeɪɪk] *n, adj* mosaïque *(f)*.

Moslem ['mɒzləm] = **Muslim.**

mosque [mɒsk] *n* mosquée *f.*

mosquito [mɒs'kiːtəʊ] *n* moustique *m.* ~ **net** moustiquaire *f.*

moss [mɒs] *n* mousse *f (Bot).* ◆ **mossy** *adj* moussu.

most [məʊst] *superl of* **many, much 1** *adj, pron* (**a**) *(gen)* le plus (de), la plus grande quantité (de), le plus grand nombre (de). **(the)** ~ **money/ records** le plus d'argent/de disques; **who has got (the)** ~**?** qui en a le plus?; **at (the)** ~ au maximum, tout au plus; **to make the** ~ **of** *one's time* bien employer; *respite, opportunity, sunshine, sb's absence* profiter au maximum de; *talents, money* tirer le meilleur parti de; *resources* utiliser au mieux; **make the** ~ **of it!** profitez-en bien! (**b**) *(largest part)* la plus grande partie (de); *(greatest number)* la majorité (de), la plupart (de). ~ **(of the) people/ books** *etc* la plupart *or* la majorité des gens/des livres *etc*; ~ **of the money** la plus grande partie de l'argent, presque tout l'argent; ~ **of it** presque tout; ~ **of them** la plupart d'entre eux; ~ **of the day** la plus grande partie de la journée; ~ **of the time** la plupart du temps; **for the** ~ **part** pour la plupart, en général; **in** ~ **cases** dans la plupart des cas.
2 *adv* (**a**) *work etc* le plus. **the** ~ **intelligent** le plus intelligent (*of, in* de); ~ **easily** le plus facilement. (**b**) *(very)* bien, très. ~ **likely** très probablement.
◆ **mostly** *adv (chiefly)* surtout; *(almost all)* pour la plupart; *(most often)* le plus souvent, la plupart du temps.

motel [məʊ'tel] *n* motel *m.*

moth [mɒθ] *n* papillon *m* de nuit; *(in clothes)* mite *f.* ◆ **mothball** *n* boule *f* de naphtaline. ◆ **moth-eaten** *adj* mangé aux mites. ◆ **mothproof 1** *adj* traité à l'antimite ; **2** *vt* traiter à l'antimite.

mother ['mʌðə^r^] **1** *n* mère *f.* ~**'s help** aide *f* familiale; **M**~**'s Day** la fête des Mères; **M**~ **Nature** Dame Nature *f*; **M**~ **Superior** Mère supérieure. **2** *vt (fig)* être une vraie mère pour. **3** *adj*: ~ **country** mère patrie *f*; ~ **love** amour maternel; ~ **tongue** langue *f* maternelle.
◆ **mothercraft** *n* puériculture *f.* ◆ **motherhood** *n* maternité *f.* ◆ **mother-in-law** *n* belle-mère *f.* ◆ **motherland** *n* patrie *f.* ◆ **motherly** *adj* maternel. ◆ **mother-of-pearl** *n* nacre *f* (de perle). ◆ **mother-to-be** *n* future maman *f.*

motion ['məʊʃ(ə)n] **1** *n* (**a**) *(gen)* mouvement *m*, marche *f.* **to set in** ~ *machine, vehicle* mettre en marche; *process etc* mettre en branle; *(fig)* **to go through the** ~**s of doing sth** *(mechanically)* faire qch machinalement; *(insincerely)* faire semblant de faire qch. (**b**) *(at meeting etc)* motion *f*; *(Parl)* proposition *f.* (**c**) *(bowel* ~*)* selles *fpl.* **2** *adj*: ~ **picture** film *m*; ~**-picture industry** (industrie *f* du) cinéma *m*; ~ **sickness** mal *m* de la route (*or* de mer *etc*). **3** *vti*: **to** ~ **(to) sb to do** faire signe à qn de faire.
◆ **motionless** *adj* immobile.

motive ['məʊtɪv] *n (gen)* motif *m*; *(Jur)* mobile *m* (*for, of* de). **from the best** ~**s** avec les meilleures intentions, avec les motifs les plus louables; **his** ~ **for saying that** la raison pour laquelle il a dit cela.
◆ **motivate** *vt act, decision* motiver; *person* pousser (*to do* à faire). ◆ **motivation** *n* motivation *f.*

motley ['mɒtlɪ] *adj (mixed)* hétéroclite; *(manycoloured)* bariolé.

motocross ['məʊtə,krɒs] *n* motocross *m.*

motor ['məʊtə^r^] **1** *n (engine)* moteur *m*; *(car)* voiture *f*, auto(mobile) *f.* **2** *adj* (**a**) *muscle* moteur. (**b**) *(Aut) industry* de l'automobile; *accident* de voiture, d'auto. *(US)* ~ **home** camping-car *m*; ~ **mechanic** mécanicien *m* garagiste; ~ **scooter** scooter *m*; ~ **mower** tondeuse *f* (à gazon) à moteur; **the M**~ **Show** le Salon de l'Automobile; ~ **vehicle** véhicule *m* automobile. **3** *vi*: **to go** ~**ing** faire de l'auto.
◆ **motorbike** * *n* moto * *f.* ◆ **motorboat** *n* canot *m* automobile. ◆ **motorcade** *n (US)* cortège *m* d'automobiles. ◆ **motorcar** *n* auto(mobile) *f*, voiture *f.* ◆ **motorcycle** *n* motocyclette *f.* ◆ **motorcycling** *n* motocyclisme *m.* ◆ **motorcyclist** *n* motocycliste *mf.* ◆ **motoring 1** *n* conduite *f* automobile ; **2** *adj accident* de voiture; *holiday* en voiture; **the** ~**ing public** les automobilistes *mpl.* ◆ **motorist** *n* automobiliste *mf.* ◆ **motorization** *n* motorisation *f.* ◆ **motorize** *vt* motoriser. ◆ **motorman** *n (US)* conducteur *m (d'un train etc électrique).* ◆ **motor-racing** *n* course *f* automobile. ◆ **motorway** *n* autoroute *f.*

Motown ['məʊtaʊn] *n (Mus)* Motown *m.*

MOT test [eməʊ'tiːtest] *n contrôle périodique obligatoire des véhicules.*

mottled ['mɒtld] *adj* tacheté; *complexion* brouillé.

motto ['mɒtəʊ] *n* devise *f.*

mould[1] [məʊld] **1** *n (Art, Culin, Tech etc)* moule *m.* **2** *vt clay* mouler; *figure* modeler (*in, out of* en); *(fig) character, opinion* former. ◆ **moulding** *n (Archit etc)* moulure *f*; *(Aut)* baguette *f.*

mould[2] [məʊld] *n (fungus)* moisissure *f.* ◆ **moulder** *vi [cheese]* moisir; *[building]* tomber en poussière.
◆ **mouldy** *adj* moisi; *(* fig: unpleasant)* minable *; **to go** ~**y** moisir; **to smell** ~**y** sentir le moisi.

moult, *(US)* **molt** [məʊlt] *vi [snake, bird]* muer; *[dog, cat]* perdre ses poils.

mound [maʊnd] *n* (**a**) *[earth]* tertre *m*; *(Archeol)* tertre artificiel; *(burial* ~*)* tumulus *m.* (**b**) *(pile)* tas *m.*

mount[1] [maʊnt] *n (liter)* mont *m*, montagne *f.* **M**~ **Everest** le mont Everest.

mount[2] [maʊnt] **1** *n* (**a**) *(horse)* monture *f.* (**b**) *(support) [machine]* support *m*; *[lens, specimen]* monture *f*; *[transparency]* cadre *m* (en carton *etc*). **2** *vt* (**a**) *(gen)* monter sur; *(climb) hill, stairs* monter. (**b**) *machine, picture, jewel* monter (*on, in* sur). (**c**) *play, demonstration, plot* monter. *(Mil)* **to** ~ **guard** monter la garde (*on* sur; *over* auprès de). **3** *vi [prices etc]* monter. **it all** ~**s up** tout cela finit par chiffrer. ◆ **mounted** *adj* monté, à cheval.

mountain ['maʊntɪn] **1** *n* montagne *f.* **to go to/ live in the** ~**s** aller à/habiter la montagne; **to make a** ~ **out of a molehill** se faire une montagne d'un rien; *(Econ)* **butter** ~ montagne de beurre; **a** ~ **of work** un travail fou. **2** *adj tribe, people* montagnard; *animal, plant* de(s) montagne(s); *air* de la montagne; *path, scenery, shoes, chalet* de montagne. ~ **cat** *or* **lion** puma *m*; ~ **climber** alpiniste *mf*; ~ **range** chaîne *f* de montagnes; ~ **top** sommet *m* de la (*or* d'une) montagne, cime *f.*
◆ **mountaineer 1** *n* alpiniste *mf* ; **2** *vi* faire de l'alpinisme. ◆ **mountaineering** *n* alpinisme *m.* ◆ **mountainous** *adj country* montagneux; *(fig)* gigantesque. ◆ **mountainside** *n*: **to go up/down the** ~**side** monter/descendre le flanc de la montagne.

mourn [mɔːn] **1** *vi* pleurer. **to** ~ **for sb** pleurer (la mort de) qn. **2** *vt* pleurer.
◆ **mourner** *n*: **the** ~**ers** le cortège funèbre. ◆ **mournful** *adj person* mélancolique, triste; *thing* lugubre. ◆ **mournfully** *adv* mélancoliquement; lugubrement. ◆ **mournfulness** *n* tristesse *f*; aspect *m* lugubre. ◆ **mourning** *n* deuil *m*; *(clothes)* vêtements *mpl* de deuil; **in** ~**ing** en deuil (*for sb* de qn).

mouse, *pl* **mice** [maʊs, maɪs] *n (Zool, Comput)* souris *f.* ◆ **mousehole** *n* trou *m* de souris. ◆ **mousetrap** *n* souricière *f.* ◆ **mousy** *adj person* timide, effacé; *hair* châtain clair *inv* (sans éclat).

moussaka [mʊ'sɑːkə] *n* moussaka *f.*

mousse [muːs] *n* mousse *f.*

moustache [məs'tɑːʃ] *n* moustache(s) *f(pl)*. **man with a ~** homme à moustache.

mouth [maʊθ] **1** *n (gen)* bouche *f*; *[dog, cat, lion etc]* gueule *f*; *[river]* embouchure *f*; *[bag]* ouverture *f*; *[hole, cave, harbour etc]* entrée *f*; *[volcano, gun]* bouche *f*. **with one's ~ wide open** bouche bée; **he kept his ~ shut about it** il n'en a parlé à personne; **shut your ~!** ‡ ferme-la! ‡; **you've got a big ~!** ‡ tu ne pouvais pas la fermer! ‡; **it makes my ~ water** cela me fait venir l'eau à la bouche. **2** [maʊð] *vt (gen)* dire silencieusement; *(moving lips)* faire semblant de prononcer (*or* chanter *etc*). ◆ **mouthful** *n [food]* bouchée *f*; *[drink]* gorgée *f*. ◆ **mouth organ** *n* harmonica *m*. ◆ **mouthpiece** *n [musical instrument]* bec *m*; *[telephone]* microphone *m*; *(spokesman)* porte-parole *m inv*. ◆ **mouth-to-mouth (resuscitation)** *n* bouche à bouche *m inv*. ◆ **mouthwash** *n* eau *f* dentifrice; *(for gargling)* gargarisme *m*. ◆ **mouth-watering** *adj* appétissant.

move [muːv] **1** *n* (**a**) mouvement *m*. **to be on the ~** être en marche; **to be always on the ~** *[gipsies etc]* se déplacer continuellement; *[military personnel etc]* être toujours en déplacement; *[child, animal]* ne jamais rester en place; *(*: be busy)* ne jamais arrêter; **to make a ~** *(leave)* partir; *(act)* agir; **he made a ~ towards the door** il a esquissé un mouvement vers la porte; **get a ~ on!** * remuetoi! * (**b**) *(change of house)* déménagement *m*; *(change of job)* changement *m* d'emploi. **it's time he had a ~** il a besoin de changer d'horizon. (**c**) *(Chess, Draughts etc: turn)* tour *m*; *(fig)* manœuvre *f*. **knight's ~** marche *f* du cavalier; **a silly ~** *(in game)* un coup stupide; *(fig)* une manœuvre stupide; **it's your ~** c'est à vous de jouer; *(fig)* **he knows every ~ in the game** il connaît toutes les astuces; *(fig)* **one false ~ and...** un faux pas et...; **his first ~ after the election** son premier acte après son élection; **what's the next ~?** et maintenant qu'est-ce qu'on fait?; **to make the first ~** faire les premiers pas; **there was a ~ to defeat the proposal** il y a eu une tentative pour faire échec à la proposition.

2 *vt* (**a**) *(change position of) object* changer de place, déplacer; *limbs* remuer; *troops, animals* transporter; *chessman* jouer; *employee (to another town)* muter (*to* à); *(to another job)* affecter (*to* à). **~ your chair nearer the fire** approchez votre chaise du feu; **they ~d the crowd off the grass** ils ont fait partir la foule de sur la pelouse; **to ~ house** déménager; **to ~ one's job** changer d'emploi; **his firm want to ~ him** son entreprise veut l'envoyer ailleurs; **to ~ heaven and earth to do sth** remuer ciel et terre pour faire qch; **he didn't ~ a muscle** *(flinch)* il n'a pas bronché; **the wind ~s the leaves** le vent agite les feuilles. (**b**) *(fig)* inciter (*sb to do* qn à faire). **I am ~d to ask** je suis incité à demander; **if the spirit ~s me** si le cœur m'en dit. (**c**) **this did not ~ him** ceci n'a pas réussi à l'ébranler *or (emotionally)* l'émouvoir; **she's easily ~d** elle s'émeut facilement; **to ~ sb to tears** émouvoir qn jusqu'aux larmes; **to ~ to anger** mettre en colère; **to ~ to pity** attendrir. (**d**) *resolution etc* proposer (*that* que + *subj*).

3 *vi* (**a**) *(stir)* bouger; *(go)* aller, se déplacer; *[clouds]* passer. *[vehicle]* **to be moving** être en marche; **don't ~!** ne bougez pas!; **he ~d slowly towards the door** il s'est dirigé lentement vers la porte; **let's ~ into the garden** passons dans le jardin; **she ~s well** elle a une démarche aisée; **they ~d across the lawn** ils ont traversé la pelouse; **keep moving** *(to keep warm etc)* ne restez pas sans bouger; *(pass along etc)* circulez; **he ~d into another class** il est passé dans une autre classe; **to ~ freely** *[piece of machinery]* jouer librement; *[people, cars]* circuler aisément; *[traffic]* être fluide; **to keep the traffic moving** assurer la circulation ininterrompue des véhicules; **you can't ~ for books** on ne peut plus se retourner tellement il y a de livres; *(depart)* **it's time we were moving** il est temps que nous partions *(subj)*; **things are moving at last!** enfin ça avance!; **he got things moving** avec lui ça a bien démarré. (**b**) *(~ house)* déménager; *(move office etc)* être transféré. **to ~ to the country** aller habiter la campagne. (**c**) *(act)* agir. **the government won't ~ until...** le gouvernement ne fera rien tant que...; **to ~ first** prendre l'initiative. (**d**) *(in games) [player]* jouer; *[chesspiece]* marcher. **it's you to ~** c'est votre tour de jouer.

◆ **move about, move around 1** *vi (fidget)* remuer; *(walk about)* se déplacer; *(travel)* voyager. **2** *vt sep* déplacer.

◆ **move along 1** *vi (gen)* avancer; *(on bench etc)* se pousser. **2** *vt sep* faire avancer.

◆ **move away 1** *vi (gen)* s'éloigner (*from* de); *(move house)* déménager. **2** *vt sep* éloigner (*from* de).

◆ **move back 1** *vi (gen)* reculer; *(to original position)* retourner, revenir. **2** *vt sep crowd* faire reculer; *troops* replier; *object* reculer; *(to original position) person* faire revenir *or* retourner; *object* remettre.

◆ **move down 1** *vi* descendre. **2** *vt sep person* faire descendre; *object* descendre.

◆ **move forward 1** *vi (gen)* avancer; *[troops]* se porter en avant. **2** *vt sep person, vehicle* faire avancer; *troops* porter en avant; *object* avancer.

◆ **move in 1** *vi* (**a**) *[police etc]* avancer (*on* sur); intervenir. (**b**) *(to a house)* emménager; *(* fig: try for control)* essayer de se tailler une place. **2** *vt sep person* faire entrer; *furniture etc* rentrer; *(on removal day)* installer.

◆ **move off 1** *vi (gen)* partir; *[car]* démarrer. **2** *vt sep object* enlever.

◆ **move on 1** *vi [person, vehicle]* avancer; *(after stopping)* se remettre en route; *(fig: in story etc)* passer (*to* à). **2** *vt sep crowd* faire circuler; *hands of clock* avancer.

◆ **move out 1** *vi* déménager (*of* de). **2** *vt sep person, animal* faire sortir; *troops* retirer; *object* sortir; *(on removal day)* déménager.

◆ **move over 1** *vi* se pousser. **2** *vt sep* pousser.

◆ **move up 1** *vi (gen)* monter; *[employee]* avoir de l'avancement; *(Sport: in league)* avancer. **2** *vt sep person* faire monter; *object* monter; *(promote) employee* donner de l'avancement à.

◆ **movable** *adj* mobile. ◆ **movement** *n (gen)* mouvement *m*; **~ments** *[suspect]* allées et venues *fpl*. ◆ **movie** * **1** *n* film *m (de cinéma)*; **to go to the movies** aller au cinéma *or* au ciné *; **2** *adj industry, star* du cinéma; **movie camera** caméra *f*. ◆ **moviegoer** *n* amateur *m* de cinéma. ◆ **movie house** *or* **theater** *(US) n* (salle *f* de) cinéma *m*. ◆ **movieland** *n* le (monde du) cinéma. ◆ **movie maker** *n* cinéaste *mf*. ◆ **moving** *adj* (**a**) *vehicle* en marche; *object, crowd* en mouvement; *pavement, staircase* roulant; *power* moteur; *machine-part* mobile; **the moving spirit in the whole affair** l'âme *f* de toute l'affaire; **moving target** cible *f* mouvante; **moving walkway** trottoir *m* roulant; (**b**) *(touching) sight* émouvant. ◆ **movingly** *adv* d'une manière émouvante.

mow [məʊ] *pret* **mowed,** *ptp* **mowed** *or* **mown** *vt corn* faucher; *lawn* tondre. **to ~ sb down** faucher qn. ◆ **mower** *n (Agr)* faucheuse *f*; *(lawn ~)* tondeuse *f* (à gazon).

Mozambique [məʊzæm'biːk] *n* Mozambique *m*.

Mr ['mɪstəʳ] *n* monsieur *m*. **~ Smith** Monsieur Smith, M. Smith; **yes ~ Smith** oui monsieur; **~ Chairman** monsieur le président.

Mrs ['mɪsɪz] *n* madame *f*. **~ Smith** Madame Smith, Mme Smith; **yes, ~ Smith** oui, madame.

Ms [mɪz, məz] *n titre évitant la distinction entre madame et mademoiselle.*

much [mʌtʃ] *comp* **more,** *superl* **most** **1** *adj, pron* (**a**) beaucoup (de). ~ **money** beaucoup d'argent; **have you got** ~? est-ce que vous en avez beaucoup?; **does it cost** ~? est-ce que ça coûte cher?; ~ **of the town** une bonne partie de la ville; **he hadn't** ~ **to say** il n'avait pas grand-chose à dire; **we don't see** ~ **of each other** nous ne nous voyons pas souvent; **it isn't up to** ~ * ça ne vaut pas grand-chose; **he's not** ~ **to look at** il ne paie pas de mine; **he is not** ~ **of a writer** il n'est pas extraordinaire comme écrivain; **it wasn't** ~ **of an evening** ce n'était pas une très bonne soirée; **I don't think** ~ **of that** à mon avis ça ne vaut pas grand-chose; **there wasn't** ~ **in it** *(in choice)* c'était kif-kif *; *(in race etc)* il a gagné de justesse; **to make** ~ **of sb/sth** faire grand cas de qn/qch; **I couldn't make** ~ **of what he was saying** je n'ai pas bien compris ce qu'il disait; **they're** ~ **of a muchness** c'est blanc bonnet et bonnet blanc; *(fig)* **it's a bit** ~! * c'est un peu fort! (**b**) *(phrases)* **as** ~ **as** autant que; **as** ~ **time as** autant de temps que; **as** ~ **again** encore autant; **twice as** ~ deux fois autant *or* plus (de); **it's as** ~ **as he can do to stand up** c'est tout juste s'il peut se lever; **you could pay as** ~ **as 20 francs** vous pourriez payer jusqu'à 20 F; **as** ~ **as to say** comme pour dire; **how** ~? combien (de)?; **however** ~ **you protest, he...** vous avez beau protester, il...; **so** ~ tant (de); **so** ~ **that** tellement *or* tant que...; **without so** ~ **as a word** sans même dire un mot; **so** ~ **for that!** *(resignedly)* tant pis!; *(and now for the next)* et d'une! *; **so** ~ **for his promises** voilà ce que valaient ses promesses; **this** *or* **that** ~ **bread** ça de pain; **I know this** ~ je sais tout au moins ceci; **this** ~ **is true** il y a ceci de vrai; **too** ~ trop (de); **I've eaten too** ~ j'ai trop mangé; **that's too** ~ **, that's a bit** ~ c'est trop; *(fig)* c'est trop fort; **this work is too** ~ **for me** ce travail est trop fatigant pour moi.
2 *adv* beaucoup. **thank you very** ~ merci beaucoup, merci bien; **it doesn't** ~ **matter** cela n'a pas beaucoup d'importance; ~ **bigger** beaucoup plus grand; ~ **the cleverest** de beaucoup *or* de loin le plus intelligent; **as** ~ **as** autant que; **as** ~ **as ever** toujours autant; **I don't like it as** ~ **as all that** je ne l'aime pas tant que ça; **not so** ~ **a question of money as of staff** pas tant un problème d'argent que de personnel; **so** ~ **that** tellement *or* tant que; **so** ~ **so that** à tel point que; **too** ~ trop; **I don't know him,** ~ **less his father** lui, je ne le connais pas, et son père encore moins; **(very** *or* **pretty)** ~ **the same** presque le même (*as* que); ~ **as I would like to go** bien que je désire *(subj)* beaucoup y aller; ~ **to my amazement** à ma grande stupéfaction.

mucilage ['mju:sɪlɪdʒ] *n* mucilage *m.*

muck [mʌk] *n (manure)* fumier *m*; *(mud)* boue *f*; *(dirt)* saletés *fpl*; *(fig: scandal)* scandale *m; (rubbish)* cochonneries *fpl.* **dog** ~ crotte *f* de chien. ◆ **muck about** *, **muck around** * **1** *vi (aimlessly)* traîner, perdre son temps; *(play the fool)* faire l'imbécile. **to** ~ **about with sth** tripoter qch. **2** *vt sep person* créer des complications à. ◆ **muck out** *vt sep stable* nettoyer. ◆ **muck up** ‡ *vt sep (ruin) plans, life* gâcher; *car, machine* bousiller *; *(dirty) room, clothes* salir.
◆ **muckiness** *n* saleté *f.* ◆ **muckraking** *n* mise *f* au jour de scandales. ◆ **muck-up** ‡ *n* gâchis *m.* ◆ **mucky** *adj (muddy)* boueux; *(filthy)* sale.

mucus ['mju:kəs] *n* mucus *m.*

mud [mʌd] **1** *n (gen)* boue *f*; *(in river, sea)* vase *f.* **stuck in the** ~ embourbé; *(fig)* **to throw** ~ **at sb** couvrir qn de boue; **my name is** ~ * **here** je suis très mal vu ici. **2** *adj (Aut)* ~ **flap** pare-boue *m inv*; ~ **flat** laisse *f* de vase; ~ **hut** hutte *f* de terre; ~ **pie** pâté *m* (de terre). ◆ **mudbank** *n* banc *m* de vase. ◆ **muddy** *adj road, water* boueux; *clothes, hands* couvert de boue; *liquid* trouble; *complexion* terreux. ◆ **mudguard** *n* garde-boue *m inv.* ◆ **mudpack** *n* masque *m* de beauté.

muddle ['mʌdl] **1** *n (disorder)* désordre *m*, pagaille *f*; *(perplexity, mix-up)* confusion *f.* **to be in a** ~ *[room, books]* être en désordre; *[person]* ne plus s'y retrouver (*over sth* dans qch); *[ideas]* être embrouillé *or* confus; *[plans, arrangements]* être confus; **to get into a** ~ *(confused)* s'embrouiller (*over* dans); **there's been a** ~ **over the seats** il y a eu confusion en ce qui concerne les places. **2** *vt* (~**up**) confondre (*A with B* A avec B); *person, story, details* embrouiller. **to get** ~**d (up)** s'embrouiller; **to be** ~**d (up)** être embrouillé. ◆ **muddle along, muddle on** *vi* continuer tant bien que mal. ◆ **muddle through** *vi* s'en sortir tant bien que mal. ◆ **muddle-headed** *adj person* brouillon; *plan* confus. ◆ **muddler** *n* esprit *m* brouillon *(personne).* ◆ **muddle-up** *n* confusion *f.*

muesli ['mju:zlɪ] *n* muesli *m.*

muff [mʌf] **1** *n* manchon *m.* **2** *vt*: **to** ~ **it** * rater son coup.

muffle ['mʌfl] *vt* (**a**) *sound* assourdir. (**b**) (~ **up**: *wrap up)* emmitoufler. ◆ **muffled** *adj sound, voice* sourd. ◆ **muffler** *n (scarf)* cache-nez *m inv*; *(US Aut)* silencieux *m.*

mufti ['mʌftɪ] *n*: **in** ~ en civil.

mug [mʌg] **1** *n* (**a**) chope *f*; *(of metal)* gobelet *m.* (**b**) *(* ‡: *fool)* nigaud(e) *m(f)*, andouille ‡ *f.* **what a** ~! quelle andouille ‡!; **it's a** ~**'s game** * on se fait toujours avoir *. **2** *vt (assault)* agresser. ◆ **mug up** ‡ *vt sep* bûcher *, étudier. ◆ **mugger** *n* agresseur *m.* ◆ **mugging** *n* agression *f.*

muggy ['mʌgɪ] *adj room* qui sent le renfermé; *climate* mou. **it's** ~ il fait lourd.

mulatto [mju:'lætəʊ] *n* mulâtre(sse) *m(f).*

mulberry ['mʌlb(ə)rɪ] *n* mûre *f*; *(tree)* mûrier *m.*

mule [mju:l] *n* mulet *m*; *(female)* mule *f.* **stubborn as a** ~ têtu comme une mule. ◆ **mulish** *adj* têtu.

mull [mʌl] *vt wine* chauffer et épicer. ~**ed wine** vin *m* chaud. ◆ **mull over** *vt sep* ruminer *(fig).*

mullet ['mʌlɪt] *n*: **grey** ~ mulet *m*; **red** ~ rouget *m.*

mulligatawny [ˌmʌlɪgə'tɔ:nɪ] *n* potage *m* au curry.

multi... ['mʌltɪ] *pref* multi...; *(often translated by 'plusieurs') e.g.* ~**-person vehicle** véhicule *m* pour plusieurs personnes. ◆ **multichannel** *adj TV* à canaux multiples. ◆ **multicoloured** *adj* multicolore. ◆ **multicultural** *adj* multiculturel. ◆ **multifunction** *adj* multifonctionnel. ◆ **multimillionaire** *n* ≃ multimilliardaire *mf.* ◆ **multinational** **1** *adj* multinational ; **2** *n* multinationale *f.* ◆ **multipack** *n* pack *m.* ◆ **multi-party** *adj (Pol)* pluripartite. ◆ **multipurpose** *adj* multiusages *inv.* ◆ **multiracial** *adj* multiracial. ◆ **multistorey(ed)** *adj* à étages.

multiple ['mʌltɪpl] **1** *n* multiple *m.* **2** *adj* multiple. ~ **crash** carambolage *m;* ~ **sclerosis** sclérose *f* en plaques; ~ **store** grand magasin *m* à succursales multiples. ◆ **multiple-choice** *adj* à choix multiples. ◆ **multiplication** *n* multiplication *f.* ◆ **multiply** **1** *vt* multiplier (*by* par) ; **2** *vi* se multiplier.

multitude ['mʌltɪtju:d] *n* multitude *f.*

mum[1] * [mʌm] *n (mother)* maman *f.*

mum[2] [mʌm] *adj*: **to keep** ~ **(about sth)** ne pas souffler mot (de qch); ~**'s the word!** motus!

mumble ['mʌmbl] *vti* marmotter.

mumbo jumbo [ˌmʌmbəʊ'dʒʌmbəʊ] *n (nonsense)* charabia * *m*; *(pretentious word)* jargon *m* obscur.

mummy[1] ['mʌmɪ] *n (embalmed)* momie *f.* ◆ **mummify** *vt* momifier.

mummy[2] * ['mʌmɪ] *n (mother)* maman *f*. ~**'s boy** fils *m* à sa mère.

mumps [mʌmps] *nsg* oreillons *mpl*.

munch [mʌn(t)ʃ] *vti (gen)* croquer; *(chew)* mastiquer.

mundane [ˌmʌn'deɪn] *adj (humdrum)* banal; *(worldly)* de ce monde.

Munich ['mju:nɪk] *n* Munich.

municipal [mju:'nɪsɪp(ə)l] *adj* municipal. ◆ **municipality** *n* municipalité *f*.

munificence [mju:'nɪfɪsns] *n* munificence *f*. ◆ **munificent** *adj* munificent.

munitions [mju:'nɪʃ(ə)nz] **1** *npl* munitions *fpl*. **2** *adj*: ~ **dump** entrepôt *m* de munitions.

mural ['mjʊər(ə)l] **1** *adj* mural. **2** *n* peinture *f* murale.

murder ['mɜ:dəʳ] **1** *n* meurtre *m*; *(premeditated)* assassinat *m*. *(fig)* **he was shouting blue** ~ * il criait comme un putois; **they get away with** ~ * ils peuvent faire n'importe quoi impunément; **it's** ~ * c'est infernal; **the roads were** ~ * les routes étaient un cauchemar. **2** *adj*: ~ **case** *(Jur)* procès *m* en homicide; *(Police)* affaire *f* d'homicide; ~ **trial** ≃ procès capital; **the** ~ **weapon** l'arme *f* du meurtre. **3** *vt person* assassiner; *(fig) song* massacrer; *opponent* écraser. **the** ~**ed man** la victime. ◆ **murderer** *n* meurtrier *m*, assassin *m*. ◆ **murderess** *n* meurtrière *f*. ◆ **murderous** *adj* meurtrier.

murky ['mɜ:kɪ] *adj (gen)* obscur; *darkness* épais; *water, sb's past* trouble.

murmur ['mɜ:məʳ] **1** *n* murmure *m*; *[bees, traffic, voices]* bourdonnement *m*. **without a** ~ sans murmure; *(Med)* **a heart** ~ un souffle au cœur. **2** *vti* murmurer; bourdonner.

muscle ['mʌsl] *n* (**a**) *(Anat)* muscle *m*. (**b**) *(fig: power)* pouvoir *m* effectif, impact *m*. ◆ **muscle in** * *vi* intervenir. **to** ~ **in on** essayer de s'imposer dans. ◆ **muscular** *adj person, arm* musclé; *tissue, disease* musculaire; **muscular dystrophy** dystrophie *f* musculaire.

muse [mju:z] **1** *vi* songer (*on, about, over* à). **2** *n* muse *f*. ◆ **musing** **1** *adj* songeur ; **2** *n* songerie *f*.

museum [mju:'zɪəm] *n* musée *m*.

mushroom ['mʌʃrʊm] **1** *n* champignon *m* (comestible). **2** *adj soup, omelette* aux champignons; *flavour* de champignons; *(colour)* beige rosé *inv*; *(fig) town* champignon *inv*; *growth* soudain. ~ **cloud** champignon *m* atomique. **3** *vi* (**a**) *(grow)* pousser comme un champignon. (**b**) **to go** ~**ing** aller aux champignons.

mushy ['mʌʃɪ] *adj food* en bouillie; *fruit* blet. ~ **peas** purée *f* de pois.

music ['mju:zɪk] **1** *n* musique *f*. **to set to** ~ mettre en musique; *(fig)* **it was** ~ **to his ears** c'était doux à son oreille. **2** *adj teacher, lesson* de musique; *critic* musical. ~ **case** porte-musique *m inv*; ~ **centre** chaîne *f* compacte stéréo; ~ **festival** festival *m*; ~ **hall** music-hall *m*; ~ **lover** mélomane *mf*. ◆ **musical** **1** *adj (gen)* musical; *person, family* musicien; ~**al box** boîte *f* à musique; ~**al instrument** instrument *m* de musique ; **2** *n (Cine, Theat)* comédie *f* musicale. ◆ **musically** *adv* musicalement. ◆ **musician** *n* musicien(ne) *m(f)*. ◆ **musicianship** *n* sens *m* de la musique. ◆ **musicologist** *n* musicologue *mf*. ◆ **musicology** *n* musicologie *f*.

musk [mʌsk] *n* musc *m*. ◆ **muskrat** *n* rat *m* musqué.

musket ['mʌskɪt] *n* mousquet *m*.

Muslim ['mʊslɪm] *adj, n* musulman(e) *m(f)*.

muslin ['mʌzlɪn] *n* mousseline *f (Tex)*.

musquash ['mʌskwɒʃ] *n* rat *m* musqué.

mussel ['mʌsl] *n* moule *f*.

must [mʌst] **1** *modal aux vb* (**a**) *(obligation)* **you** ~ **leave** vous devez partir, il faut que vous partiez *(subj)*; *(on notice)* **'the windows** ~ **not be opened'** 'défense d'ouvrir les fenêtres'; **you** ~**n't touch it** il ne faut pas *or* tu ne dois pas y toucher; **sit down if you** ~ asseyez-vous si c'est indispensable; **I** ~ **say** franchement; *(iro)* ça alors! * (**b**) *(certainty)* **he** ~ **be wrong** il doit se tromper, il se trompe certainement; **is he mad? — he** ~ **be!** est-ce qu'il est fou? — sûrement!; **I** ~ **have made a mistake** j'ai dû me tromper. **2** *n*: **this book is a** ~ * c'est un livre qu'il faut absolument avoir *or* lire; **a car is a** ~ * une voiture est absolument indispensable.

mustache ['mʌstæʃ] *(US)* = **moustache.**

mustard ['mʌstəd] *n (Bot, Culin)* moutarde *f*. ~ **pot** moutardier *m*.

muster ['mʌstəʳ] **1** *n (gathering)* assemblée *f*; *(Mil, Naut:* ~ **roll***)* rassemblement *m*; *(roll-call)* appel *m*. *(fig)* **to pass** ~ être acceptable. **2** *vt number, sum, helpers* réunir; **(**~ **up)** *strength, energy* rassembler. **he** ~**ed (up) the courage to say so** il a pris son courage à deux mains pour le dire; **I couldn't** ~ **(up) enough energy to protest** je n'ai pas eu l'énergie de protester. **3** *vi [people]* se réunir, se rassembler.

musty ['mʌstɪ] *adj taste, smell* de moisi; *room* qui sent le moisi; *ideas* vieux jeu *inv*. **to grow** ~ moisir; **to smell** ~ avoir une odeur de moisi. ◆ **mustiness** *n* moisi *m*.

mutate [mju:'teɪt] *vi* subir une mutation. ◆ **mutant** *adj, n* mutant *(m)*. ◆ **mutation** *n* mutation *f*.

mute [mju:t] **1** *adj* muet. **2** *n (Med)* muet(te) *m(f)*; *(Mus)* sourdine *f*. ◆ **muted** *adj voice, sound* assourdi; *colour* sourd; *(Mus)* en sourdine; *criticism, protest* voilé.

mutilate ['mju:tɪleɪt] *vt* mutiler. ◆ **mutilation** *n* mutilation *f*.

mutiny ['mju:tɪnɪ] **1** *n* mutinerie *f*; *(fig)* révolte *f*. **2** *vi* se mutiner; se révolter. ◆ **mutineer** *n* mutiné *m*, mutin *m*. ◆ **mutinous** *adj* mutiné; *(fig) attitude* rebelle; *look* plein de rébellion.

mutter ['mʌtəʳ] **1** *n* marmonnement *m*; *(grumbling)* grommellement *m*. **2** *vt* marmonner. **3** *vi* marmonner; *(grumble)* grommeler; *[thunder]* gronder.

mutton ['mʌtn] *n* mouton *m (Culin)*. **leg of** ~ gigot *m*.

mutual ['mju:tjʊəl] *adj affection, help* mutuel; *(common) friend, cousin* commun. **the feeling is** ~ c'est réciproque. ◆ **mutually** *adv* mutuellement.

Muzak ['mju:zæk] *n* ® musique *f* enregistrée.

muzzle ['mʌzl] **1** *n [dog, fox etc]* museau *m*; *[gun]* bouche *f*; *(anti-biting device: also fig)* muselière *f*. **2** *vt* museler *(also fig)*.

muzzy ['mʌzɪ] *adj ideas* confus; *outline* flou. **this cold makes me feel** ~ ce rhume m'abrutit.

my [maɪ] *poss adj* mon, ma, mes. ~ **book** mon livre; ~ **table** ma table; ~ **friend** mon ami(e); ~ **clothes** mes vêtements; **I've broken** ~ **leg** je me suis cassé la jambe. ◆ **myself** *pers pron (reflexive: direct and indirect)* me; *(emphatic)* moi-même; *(after prep)* moi; **I've hurt** ~**self** je me suis blessé; **all by** ~**self** tout seul; **I'm not** ~**self** je ne suis pas dans mon état normal.

myopic [maɪ'ɒpɪk] *adj* myope.

myrtle ['mɜ:tl] *n* myrte *m*.

mystery ['mɪst(ə)rɪ] **1** *n* mystère *m*; *(book:* ~ *story)* roman *m* à suspense. **there's no** ~ **about it** ça n'a rien de mystérieux; **it's a** ~ **to me how...** je n'arrive pas à comprendre comment...; **to make a great** ~ **of sth** faire grand mystère de qch. **2** *adj ship, man* mystérieux. ◆ **mysterious** *adj* mystérieux. ◆ **mysteriously** *adv* mystérieusement.

◆ **mystification** *n (act)* mystification *f*; *(feeling)* perplexité *f*. ◆ **mystify** *vt* mystifier; *(accidentally)* rendre perplexe.

mystic ['mɪstɪk] *adj, n* mystique *(mf)*. ◆ **mystical** *adj* mystique. ◆ **mysticism** *n* mysticisme *m*. ◆ **mystique** *n* mystique *f*.

myth [mɪθ] *n* mythe *m*. ◆ **mythical** *adj* mythique. ◆ **mythological** *adj* mythologique. ◆ **mythology** *n* mythologie *f*.

myxomatosis [ˌmɪksə(ʊ)mə'təʊsɪs] *n* myxomatose *f*.

N

N, n [en] *n (letter)* N, n *m*. **to the nth power** *or* **degree** à la puissance n; **for the nth time** * pour la énième fois.

nab * [næb] *vt wrongdoer* pincer *, attraper; *sb to speak to* coincer *; *chair* accaparer.

nadir ['neɪdɪəʳ] *n (Astron)* nadir *m*; *(fig)* point *m* le plus bas.

nag¹ [næg] *n* canasson * *m*, mauvais cheval *m*.

nag² [næg] **1** *vti* (~ **at**) être toujours après *; *[doubt etc]* harceler; *[conscience]* travailler. **to ~ sb to do/ into doing** harceler qn pour qu'il fasse/ jusqu'à ce qu'il fasse. **2** *n*: **he's a dreadful ~** * *(scolding)* il n'arrête pas de faire des remarques; *(pestering)* il n'arrête pas de nous (*or* le *etc*) harceler. ◆ **nagging 1** *adj person* qui n'arrête pas de faire des remarques; *pain, doubt* tenace ; **2** *n* remarques *fpl* continuelles, criailleries *fpl*.

nail [neɪl] **1** *n (Anat)* ongle *m*; *(Tech)* clou *m*. *(fig)* **to pay on the ~** payer rubis sur l'ongle. **2** *adj*: **~ polish** *or* **varnish** vernis *m* à ongles; **~ polish remover** dissolvant *m*; **~ scissors** ciseaux *mpl* à ongles. **3** *vt* clouer; *(fig) wrongdoer* pincer *, attraper; *lie* démasquer; *rumour* démentir. **to ~ the lid on a crate** clouer le couvercle d'une caisse; *(fig)* **to be ~ed to the spot** rester cloué sur place; **~ed shoes** chaussures cloutées.

◆ **nail down** *vt sep lid* clouer; *(fig) hesitating person* obtenir une décision de. ◆ **nail up** *vt sep picture etc* fixer par des clous; *door, window* condamner *(en clouant)*; *box, crate* clouer.

◆ **nailbiting** *n* habitude *f* de se ronger les ongles. ◆ **nailbrush** *n* brosse *f* à ongles. ◆ **nailfile** *n* lime *f* à ongles.

Nairobi [naɪ'rəʊbɪ] *n* Nairobi.

naïve [naɪ'iːv] *adj* naïf. ◆ **naïvely** *adv* naïvement. ◆ **naïveté** *or* ◆ **naïvety** *n* naïveté *f*.

naked ['neɪkɪd] *adj person* (tout) nu; *flame, sword* nu; *facts* brut; *truth* tout nu. **to the ~ eye** à l'œil nu. ◆ **nakedness** *n* nudité *f*.

namby-pamby * ['næmbɪ'pæmbɪ] **1** *n* gnangnan * *mf*. **2** *adj* gnangnan * *inv*.

name [neɪm] **1** *n* nom *m*; *(reputation)* réputation *f*. **what's your ~?** comment vous appelez-vous?; **my ~ is Robert** je m'appelle Robert; **to take sb's ~ and address** prendre les nom et adresse de qn; *(Ftbl etc)* **to have one's ~ taken** recevoir un avertissement; **by the ~ of Smith** du nom de Smith; **by** *or* **under another ~** sous un autre nom; **to go by** *or* **under the ~ of** se faire appeler; **I know him only by ~** je ne le connais que de nom; **he knows them all by ~** il les connaît tous par leur nom; **in ~ only** *(adv) reign, exist* de nom seulement; *(adj) marriage etc* nominal; **to refer to sb by ~** désigner qn par son nom; **naming** *or* **mentioning no ~s** pour ne nommer personne; **to put one's ~ down for** *job* poser sa candidature à; *competition, class* s'inscrire à; *car, ticket etc* faire une demande pour avoir; *(fig)* **that's the ~ of the game** *(what matters)* c'est ce qui compte; **to call sb ~s** traiter qn de tous les noms; **in God's ~** au nom de Dieu; **in the king's ~** de par le roi; **I haven't a penny to my ~** * je n'ai pas le sou; **one of the big ~s in show business** un des grands noms du monde du spectacle; **he has a ~ for honesty** il a la réputation d'être honnête; **to protect one's (good) ~** protéger sa réputation; **to get a bad ~** se faire une mauvaise réputation; **it made his ~** cela l'a rendu célèbre; **to make one's ~** se faire un nom (*as* en tant que).

2 *vt* (**a**) *child, puppy* appeler; *ship* baptiser; *star, new product* donner un nom à. **a person ~d Smith** un(e) nommé(e) Smith; **to ~ a child after sb** donner à un enfant le nom de qn. (**b**) *(give ~ of; designate)* nommer; *(fix) date, price* fixer. **he was ~d as chairman/as the thief/as a witness** il a été nommé président/désigné comme étant le voleur/cité comme témoin; **my collaborators are ~d in the preface** mes collaborateurs sont mentionnés dans l'avant-propos; *(wedding)* **to ~ the day** fixer la date du mariage; **you ~ it, they have it** * tout ce que vous pouvez imaginer, ils l'ont!

◆ **name day** *n* fête *f (d'une personne)*. ◆ **name-dropping** *n*: **there was a lot of ~-dropping * in his speech** son discours était truffé de noms de gens en vue. ◆ **nameless** *adj person (unknown)* sans nom ; *(anonymous)* anonyme; *fear* indéfinissable; *vice* innommable; **a certain person who shall be ~less** une certaine personne que je ne nommerai pas. ◆ **namely** *adv* à savoir, c'est-à-dire. ◆ **name part** *n (Theat)* rôle *m* titulaire. ◆ **nameplate** *n (on door etc)* plaque *f*; *(on goods)* plaque du fabricant. ◆ **namesake** *n* homonyme *m (personne)*. ◆ **name tape** *n* (ruban *m* de) noms *mpl* tissés.

nan * [næn], **nana** * ['nænə] *n* mamie *f*, mémé *f*.

nanny ['nænɪ] *n* nurse *f*. ◆ **nanny-goat** *n* chèvre *f*.

nap [næp] **1** *n (sleep)* petit somme *m*. **afternoon ~** sieste *f*; **to have** *or* **take a ~** faire un petit somme (*or* la sieste). **2** *vi* sommeiller. *(fig)* **to catch sb ~ping** prendre qn au dépourvu *(unawares) or* en défaut *(in error etc)*.

napalm ['neɪpɑːm] **1** *n* napalm *m*. **2** *adj bomb, bombing* au napalm.

nape [neɪp] *n* nuque *f*.

napkin ['næpkɪn] *n* (**a**) *(table ~)* serviette *f* (de table). **~ ring** rond *m* de serviette. (**b**) *(Brit: also* **nappy***)* couche *f (de bébé)*. **to have nappy rash** avoir les fesses rouges.

Naples ['neɪplz] *n* Naples.

narcissus, *pl* **-issi** [nɑː'sɪsəs, -ɪsaɪ] *n* narcisse *m*. ◆ **narcissistic** *adj* narcissique.

narcotic [nɑː'kɒtɪk] *adj, n* narcotique *(m)*.

narrate [nə'reɪt] *vt* raconter. ◆ **narration** *n* narration *f*. ◆ **narrative 1** *n* récit *m* ; **2** *adj* narratif. ◆ **narrator** *n* narrateur *m*, -trice *f*.

narrow ['nærəʊ] **1** *adj (gen)* étroit; *garment* étriqué; *outlook, mind* étroit, borné; *person* aux vues étroites; *meaning* restreint; *scrutiny* serré; *means, resources, income, existence* limité; *majority* faible; *advantage* petit; *victory* remporté de justesse. **to have a ~ escape** s'en tirer de justesse, l'échapper belle; **~ boat** péniche *f*. **2** *vi [road, valley]* se rétrécir; *[majority]* s'amenuiser. **his eyes ~ed** il a plissé les yeux; **to ~ down to** *[search, choice]* se limiter à; *[problem, question]* se ramener à. **3** *vt* (**~ down**) *road* rétrécir; *meaning* préciser; *choice* restreindre. *(fig)* **to ~ the field (down)** restreindre le champ; **with ~ed eyes** en plissant les yeux *(de méfiance etc)*.

◆ **narrowly** *adv* (**a**) *(by a small margin) miss etc* de justesse; **he ~ly escaped being killed** il a bien failli être tué; (**b**) *(strictly) interpret rules etc* strictement; (**c**) *(closely) examine* de près, minutieusement. ◆ **narrow-minded** *adj person* aux vues étroites; *ideas, outlook* étroit. ◆ **narrow-mindedness** *n* étroitesse *f* d'esprit. ◆ **narrowness** *n* étroitesse *f*.

nasal ['neɪz(ə)l] *adj (Anat, Ling)* nasal; *accent* nasillard. **to speak in a ~ voice** parler du nez. ◆ **nasalize** *vt* nasaliser.

nasturtium [nəs'tɜːʃ(ə)m] *n* capucine *f*.

nasty ['nɑːstɪ] *adj person, temper* désagréable (*to* envers, avec); *(stronger)* mauvais; *moment, experience* désagréable; *(stronger)* pénible; *taste, smell, trick* mauvais; *cold, weather, accident, job* sale *(before n)*; *remark* méchant; *wound, bend in road* dangereux; *(obscene) book, film* obscène. **to taste/smell ~** avoir un mauvais goût/une mauvaise odeur; **a ~ piece of work** * *(action)* un sale coup *; *(person)* un sale type *, une sale bonne femme; **he had a ~ time of it** *(short spell)* il a passé un mauvais quart d'heure; *(longer period)* il a passé de mauvais moments; *(fig)* **what a ~ mess!** quel gâchis épouvantable!; **to have a ~ mind** avoir l'esprit mal tourné; **to have a ~ look in one's eye** avoir l'œil mauvais; **events took a ~ turn** la situation a très mal tourné. ◆ **nastily** *adv (unpleasantly)* désagréablement; *(spitefully)* méchamment. ◆ **nastiness** *n* caractère *m* désagréable; méchanceté *f*.

nation ['neɪʃ(ə)n] *n (gen)* nation *f*. **people of all ~s** des gens de toutes les nationalités. ◆ **national** **1** *adj* national; **~al anthem** hymne *m* national; **~al debt** dette *f* publique; **~al dress** costume *m* national; *(Brit)* **N~al Health Service, N~al Insurance** ≃ Sécurité *f* sociale; **~al holiday** fête *f* nationale; *(Mil)* **~al service** service *m* militaire; *(Brit)* **N~al Trust** ≃ Caisse *f* nationale des monuments historiques et des sites; **on a ~al scale** à l'échelon national; **~al strike of miners** grève *f* des mineurs touchant l'ensemble du pays; *(Press)* **the ~al and local papers** la grande presse et la presse locale ; **2** *n (person)* ressortissant(e) *m(f)*. ◆ **nationalism** *n* nationalisme *m*. ◆ **nationalist** *adj, n* nationaliste *(mf)*. ◆ **nationality** *n* nationalité *f*. ◆ **nationalization** *n* nationalisation *f*. ◆ **nationalize** *vt* nationaliser. ◆ **nationally** *adv consider, matter* du point de vue national; *broadcast* dans le pays tout entier; *be known, be felt, apply* dans tout le pays. ◆ **nation-wide** *adj strike, protest* touchant l'ensemble du pays; **there was a ~-wide search for them** on les recherchait à travers tout le pays.

native ['neɪtɪv] **1** *adj* (**a**) *country, town* natal; *language* maternel. **~ land** pays *m* natal, patrie *f*; *(US fig)* **~ son** enfant *m* du pays. (**b**) *(innate) ability* inné. (**c**) *(indigenous) plant, animal* indigène; *product, resources* naturel, du pays. **~ to** originaire de; **French ~ speaker** personne *f* dont la langue maternelle est le français. (**d**) *(of the ~s) customs, costume, matters, rights* du pays; *labour, quarter* indigène. *(US)* **~ American** Indien(ne) *m(f)* d'Amérique.

2 *n* autochtone *mf*; *(esp of colony)* indigène *mf*. **a ~ of France** un(e) Français(e) de naissance; **she speaks French like a ~** elle parle français comme si c'était sa langue maternelle; *[person, animal, plant]* **to be a ~ of** être originaire de. ◆ **nativity** *n* nativité *f*; **nativity play** mystère *m* de la Nativité.

natter * ['nætəʳ] **1** *vi* bavarder. **2** *n* causette * *f*.

natty * ['nætɪ] *adj (neat)* chic *inv*; *(handy)* astucieux.

natural ['nætʃr(ə)l] **1** *adj (gen)* naturel. **it is ~ for you to think** *or* **that you should think** il est naturel *or* normal que vous pensiez *(subj)*; **~ childbirth** accouchement *m* sans douleur; *(Jur)* **death from ~ causes** mort *f* naturelle; **to die a ~ death** mourir de sa belle mort; **~ philosophy** physique *f*; *(Mus)* **B ~** si *m* bécarre; **he's a ~ painter** c'est un peintre né; **~ resources** ressources *fpl* naturelles; **to reduce staff by ~ wastage** réduire le personnel par départs naturels. **2** *n* (**a**) *(Mus: sign)* bécarre *m*. (**b**) **he's a ~!** * il est comme un poisson dans l'eau!

◆ **naturalism** *n* naturalisme *m*. ◆ **naturalist** *adj, n* naturaliste *(mf)*. ◆ **naturalization** *n* naturalisation *f*. ◆ **naturalize** *vt*: **to be ~ized** se faire naturaliser. ◆ **naturally** *adv* (**a**) *(of course; as is normal)* naturellement; **~ly not!** bien sûr que non!; (**b**) *(by nature)* de nature; **~ly lazy** paresseux de nature; **her hair is ~ly curly** elle frise naturellement; **it comes ~ly to him to do this** il fait cela tout naturellement; (**c**) *(unaffectedly) behave* avec naturel, sans affectation.

nature ['neɪtʃəʳ] **1** *n* (**a**) nature *f*. **the laws of ~** les lois *fpl* de la nature; **to paint from ~** peindre d'après nature; **against ~** contre nature. (**b**) *(character etc)* nature *f*, naturel *m*. **by ~** de nature; **good ~** bon caractère; **he has a nice ~** il a un naturel *or* un caractère facile; **it is not in his ~ to lie** il n'est pas dans sa nature de mentir; **jealous- ~d** jaloux de nature, d'un naturel jaloux. (**c**) *(essential quality; type)* nature *f*. **it is in the ~ of things** c'est dans la nature des choses; **in the ~ of this case it is clear that** vu la nature de ce cas il est clair que; **things of this ~** les choses de cette nature *or* de ce genre; **sth in the ~ of an apology** une sorte d'excuse. **2** *adj*: **~ conservancy** protection *f* de la nature; **~ cure** naturisme *m (Med)*; **~ lover** amoureux *m*, -euse *f* de la nature; **~ reserve** réserve naturelle; **~ study** histoire naturelle; *(Scol)* sciences naturelles; **~ trail** itinéraire *m* aménagé pour amateurs de la nature. ◆ **naturism** *n* naturisme *m*, nudisme *m*. ◆ **naturist** *n* naturiste *mf*, nudiste *mf*.

naught [nɔːt] *n* (**a**) *(Math)* zéro *m*. **~s and crosses** ≃ (jeu *m* du) morpion *m*. (**b**) *(† or liter: nothing)* rien *m*.

naughty ['nɔːtɪ] *adj child etc* vilain, pas sage; *joke, story* grivois. **~ word** vilain mot. ◆ **naughtily** *adv say* avec malice; **to behave naughtily** être vilain. ◆ **naughtiness** *n* mauvaise conduite *f*; **a piece of naughtiness** une désobéissance.

nausea ['nɔːsɪə] *n* nausée *f*; *(fig)* écœurement *m*. ◆ **nauseate** *vt (Med, fig)* écœurer. ◆ **nauseating** *adj* écœurant. ◆ **nauseatingly** *adv* d'une façon écœurante.

nautical ['nɔːtɪk(ə)l] *adj* nautique.

naval ['neɪv(ə)l] *adj battle, strength, base, college* naval; *affairs, matters* de la marine; *officer* de marine; *hospital, barracks, stores* maritime. **~ architect** ingénieur *m* des constructions navales; **~ aviation** aéronavale *f*; **~ forces** marine *f* de guerre; **one of the ~ powers** l'une des puissances maritimes.

nave [neɪv] *n [church]* nef *f*.

navel ['neɪv(ə)l] *n* nombril *m*. **~ orange** orange *f* navel.

navigate ['nævɪgeɪt] **1** *vi* naviguer. **2** *vt ship* diriger; *seas* naviguer sur. ◆ **navigable** *adj river* navigable. ◆ **navigation** *n* navigation *f*. ◆ **navigator** *n* navigateur *m*.

navvy ['nævɪ] *n (Brit)* terrassier *m*.

navy ['neɪvɪ] **1** *n* marine *f* (de guerre). *(Brit)* **Royal N~** marine nationale; **merchant ~** marine marchande; *(US)* **Department of the N~** ministère *m* de la Marine. **2** *adj* (**~-blue**) bleu marine *inv*.

Nazi ['nɑːtsɪ] **1** *n* Nazi(e) *m(f)*. **2** *adj* nazi. ◆ **Nazism** *n* nazisme *m*.

near [nɪəʳ] **1** *adv* (**a**) près (*to* de). **~ at hand** *object* tout près; *event* tout proche; *place* dans le voisinage; **to draw** *or* **come ~** s'approcher (*to* de); *[Christmas, exams]* approcher; **to come ~er** s'approcher davantage; **to come ~ to doing** faillir faire; **to bring sth ~er** rapprocher qch; **~ to where** près de l'endroit où; **~ to tears** au bord des larmes. (**b**) *(nearly)* presque. **nowhere ~ full** loin d'être plein; **as ~ as I can judge** autant que je puisse juger; **that's ~ enough** * ça pourra aller; **60 people, ~ enough** * 60 personnes, à peu près; **as ~ as dammit** * ou c'est tout comme *.

2 *prep* près de. **~ here/there** près d'ici/de là; **he was standing ~ the table** il se tenait près de *or* auprès de la table; **don't come ~ me** ne vous approchez pas de moi; **~ the end of the book** vers la fin du livre; **her birthday is ~ mine** son anniversaire est proche du mien; **he won't go ~ anything illegal** il ne se risquera jamais à faire quoi que ce soit d'illégal; **~ tears** au bord des larmes; **~ death** sur le point de mourir; **the sun was ~ setting** le soleil était près de se coucher; **he was very ~ refusing** il était sur le point de refuser; **the same thing or ~ it** la même chose ou presque *or* ou à peu près; **it's as ~ snowing as makes no difference** il neige ou peu s'en faut; **nobody comes anywhere ~ him at swimming** personne ne lui arrive à la cheville en natation; *(fig)* **that's ~er it** voilà qui est mieux.

3 *adj* (**a**) *(close: gen)* proche. **these glasses make things look ~er** ces lunettes rapprochent les objets; **the N~ East** le Proche-Orient; *(Math)* **to the ~est decimal place** à la plus proche décimale près; **to the ~est pound** à une livre près; **the ~est way** la route la plus directe; **in the ~ future** dans un proche avenir. (**b**) *relative, relationship* proche; *friend, friendship* intime; *guess* près de la vérité; *resemblance* assez exact; *portrait* ressemblant; *race, contest, result* serré. **my ~est and dearest** * mes proches *mpl*; **the ~est equivalent** ce qui s'en rapproche le plus; *(Aviat)* **a ~ miss** une quasi-collision; *(fig)* **that was a ~ thing** * il s'en est fallu de peu; **that's the ~est thing to a compliment** c'est presque un compliment.

4 *vt place* approcher de; *event, date* être près de. **to be ~ing one's goal** toucher au but; **my book is ~ing completion** mon livre est presque achevé.

◆ **nearby** **1** *adv* près, tout près ; **2** *adj* proche, avoisinant. ◆ **nearly** *adv (gen)* presque; **he ~ly laughed** il a failli rire; **she was ~ly crying** elle était sur le point de pleurer; **not ~ly** loin de; **she is not ~ly so old as you** elle est loin d'être aussi âgée que vous; **that's not ~ly enough** c'est loin d'être suffisant. ◆ **nearness** *n* proximité *f*. ◆ **nearside** *n (Aut) (in Britain)* côté *m* gauche; *(in France, US etc)* côté droit. ◆ **near-sighted** *adj* myope. ◆ **near-sightedness** *n* myopie *f*.

neat [niːt] *adj* (**a**) *(gen)* net (*f* nette), soigné; *room, handwriting* net; *work* soigné; *desk* bien rangé; *ankles, legs* fin; *phrase, style, solution* élégant; *plan* habile. **~ as a new pin** propre comme un sou neuf; **he is a ~ worker** il est soigneux dans son travail; **she has a ~ figure** elle est bien faite; **a ~ little car** une jolie petite voiture; **to make a ~ job of sth** bien faire qch. (**b**) *(undiluted) spirits* pur, sec. **I'll take it ~** je le prendrai sec.

◆ **neaten** *vt dress* ajuster; *desk* ranger. ◆ **neatly** *adv* (**a**) *(tidily) fold, wrap, dress* avec soin; *write* proprement; (**b**) *(skilfully) avoid, manage* habilement; **~ly put** joliment dit. ◆ **neatness** *n (tidiness)* netteté *f*; *(skilfulness)* habileté *f*, adresse *f*.

nebula, *pl* **-ae** ['nebjʊlə, iː] *n* nébuleuse *f*. ◆ **nebulous** *adj (Astron)* nébuleux; *(fig)* nébuleux, vague, flou.

necessary ['nesɪs(ə)rɪ] **1** *adj (gen)* nécessaire (*to, for* à); *result* inévitable. **it is ~ to do** il faut faire, il est nécessaire de faire; **it is ~ for him to be there** il faut qu'il soit là, il est nécessaire qu'il soit là; **it is ~ that...** il faut que... + *subj*, il est nécessaire que... + *subj;* **if ~** s'il le faut; **to do what is ~** faire le nécessaire (*for* pour); **to make it ~ for sb to do** mettre qn dans la nécessité de faire; **more than is ~** plus qu'il n'en faut; **to do no more than is ~** ne faire que le nécessaire; **all the ~ qualifications** toutes les qualités requises (*for* pour).

2 *n*: **to do the ~** * faire le nécessaire.

◆ **necessarily** *adv (gen)* nécessairement, forcément; *lead to, result in* inévitablement. ◆ **necessitate** *vt* nécessiter. ◆ **necessity** *n (gen)* nécessité *f* (*of doing, to do* de faire); **from** *or* **out of necessity** par nécessité; **of necessity** nécessairement; **case of absolute necessity** cas *m* de force majeure; **there is no necessity for you to do that** vous n'avez pas besoin de faire cela; **in case of necessity** en cas de besoin; **is there any necessity?** est-ce nécessaire?; **the bare necessities of life** les choses *fpl* nécessaires à la vie; **it's a necessity** c'est une chose indispensable.

neck [nek] **1** *n* (**a**) cou *m*; *[horse, garment]* encolure *f*; *[bottle, vase]* col *m*. **to have a sore ~** avoir mal au cou; **to fling one's arms round sb's ~** se jeter au cou de qn; **to be ~ and ~** être à égalité; **to be up to one's ~ in work** avoir du travail par-dessus la tête; **up to one's ~ in a crime** totalement impliqué dans un crime; *(fig)* **he got it in the ~** * il en a pris pour son grade *; **to stick one's ~ out** * se mouiller ‡, prendre des risques; **I don't want him round my ~** * je ne veux pas l'avoir sur le dos; **it's ~ or nothing** * il faut jouer le tout pour le tout; **in your ~ of the woods** * dans vos parages; **~ of mutton** collet *m* de mouton; *(Culin)* **best end of ~** côtelettes *fpl* premières; *[dress]* **high ~** col *m* montant; **square ~** encolure *f* carrée; **dress with a low ~, low-~ed dress** robe décolletée; **shirt with a 38 cm ~** chemise qui fait 38 cm d'encolure. (**b**) *(Brit* ‡*: impertinence)* culot * *m*. **2** *vi* (*) se peloter *. **to ~ with sb** * peloter * qn.

◆ **necking** * *n* pelotage * *m*. ◆ **necklace** *n* collier *m*; *(long)* sautoir *m*; **pearl ~lace** collier de perles. ◆ **neckline** *n* encolure *f*. ◆ **necktie** *n* cravate *f*.

nectar ['nektəʳ] *n* nectar *m*.

nectarine ['nekt(ə)rɪn] *n* brugnon *m*.

need [niːd] **1** *n* besoin *m*. **if ~ be** si besoin est, s'il le faut; **there's no ~ to hurry** on n'a pas besoin de se presser; **no ~ to tell him** pas besoin de lui dire; **there's no ~ for you to come** vous n'êtes pas obligé de venir; **there is much ~ of food** il y a un grand besoin de vivres; **to have ~ of, to be in ~ of** avoir besoin de; **to be badly** *or* **greatly in ~ of** avoir grand besoin de; **to be in ~** être dans le besoin; **in times of ~** aux heures *fpl* difficiles; **to supply sb's ~s** subvenir aux besoins de qn; **his ~s are few** il a peu de besoins; **the greatest ~s of industry** ce dont l'industrie a le plus besoin.

2 *pret, ptp* **needed** *vt (gen)* avoir besoin de. **I ~ money** j'ai besoin d'argent, il me faut de l'argent; **I ~ it** j'en ai besoin, il me le faut; **all that you ~** tout ce qu'il vous faut; **it's just what I ~ed** c'est tout à fait ce qu'il me fallait; **a visa is ~ed** il faut un visa; **a much-~ed holiday** des vacances dont on a (*or* j'ai *etc*) grand besoin; **it** *or* **he doesn't ~ me to tell him** il n'a pas besoin que je le lui dise; **she ~s watching** *or* **to be watched** elle a besoin d'être surveillée; **he ~s to have everything explained to him** il faut tout lui expliquer; **you only ~ed to ask** tu n'avais qu'à demander; **this book ~s careful reading** ce livre doit être lu attentivement; **the situation ~s detailed consideration** la situation doit être considérée *or* exige qu'on la considère *(subj)* dans le détail.

3 *modal auxiliary vb (ne s'emploie qu'à la forme interrogative, négative et avec 'hardly', 'scarcely' etc)* **~ he go?** a-t-il besoin *or* est-il obligé d'y aller?, faut-il qu'il y aille?, est-ce qu'il doit vraiment y aller?; **you ~n't wait** vous n'avez pas besoin *or* vous n'êtes pas obligé d'attendre; **you ~n't bother/have bothered to write** ce n'est/n'était pas la peine d'écrire; **~ we go into all this now?** faut-il discuter de tout cela maintenant?; **I ~ hardly say that...**

je n'ai guère besoin de dire que...; **no one ~ go** *or* **~s to go hungry** personne n'est condamné à avoir faim; **~ that be true?** est-ce nécessairement vrai?; **it ~ not follow that...** il ne s'ensuit pas nécessairement que... + *subj.*

◆ **needful 1** *adj* nécessaire ; **2** *n*: **to do the ~ful** * faire ce qu'il faut. ◆ **neediness** *n* dénuement *m*, nécessité *f*. ◆ **needless** *adj* inutile; **~less to say it began to rain** inutile de dire que la pluie s'est mise à tomber. ◆ **needlessly** *adv* inutilement. ◆ **needs** *adv (ne s'emploie qu'avec 'must')* **I must ~s leave** il me faut absolument partir; **if ~s must** s'il le faut absolument. ◆ **needy** *adj* nécessiteux; **in ~y circumstances** dans le besoin.

needle ['ni:dl] **1** *n (gen)* aiguille *f*; *[record-player]* saphir *m*. **knitting ~** aiguille à tricoter; *(fig)* **to look for a ~ in a haystack** chercher une aiguille dans une botte de foin. **2** *vt* (*) *(annoy)* agacer; *(sting)* piquer au vif; *(nag)* harceler. **she was ~d * into replying** touchée au vif elle a répondu. ◆ **needle case** *n* porte-aiguilles *m inv*. ◆ **needlecord** *n* velours *m* mille-raies. ◆ **needlepoint** *n* tapisserie *f* à l'aiguille. ◆ **needlework** *n (gen)* travaux *mpl* d'aiguille; *(Scol: subject)* couture *f*; *(work)* ouvrage *m*.

ne'er [nɛəʳ] *adv (liter)* = **never.** ◆ **ne'er-do-well** *n* propre *mf* à rien.

negative ['negətɪv] **1** *adj* négatif. **2** *n* (**a**) *(answer)* réponse *f* négative. **in the ~** *(adj) be* négatif; *(adv) answer* négativement. (**b**) *(Gram)* négation *f*. **put into the ~** mettez à la forme négative. (**c**) *(Phot, Elec)* négatif *m*. ◆ **negation** *n* négation *f*. ◆ **negatively** *adv* négativement.

neglect [nɪ'glekt] **1** *vt (gen)* négliger (*to do* de faire); *animal, invalid* ne pas s'occuper de, négliger; *one's wife, one's friends* délaisser, négliger; *garden, house, car, machinery* ne pas s'occuper de; *rule, law, advice* ne tenir aucun compte de; *business, work, hobby* se désintéresser de, négliger; *opportunity* laisser échapper, négliger; *promise, duty, obligation* manquer à.

2 *n (gen)* manque *m* de soins (*of sb* envers qn); *[duty, obligation]* manquement *m* (*of* à); *[work]* manque d'intérêt (*of* pour). **~ of one's appearance** manque de soins apportés à son apparence; **his ~ of his car** *etc* le fait qu'il ne s'occupe pas de sa voiture *etc*; **in a state of ~** mal tenu; **it happened through ~** c'est dû à la négligence.

◆ **neglected** *adj appearance* négligé, peu soigné; *person* abandonné, délaissé; *house, garden* mal tenu. ◆ **neglectful** *adj* négligent; **to be ~ful of sb/sth** négliger qn/qch. ◆ **neglectfully** *adv* avec négligence.

negligence ['neglɪdʒ(ə)ns] *n* négligence *f*. ◆ **negligent** *adj* négligent. ◆ **negligently** *adv* (**a**) *(offhandedly)* négligemment; (**b**) *(carelessly) omit* par négligence; *behave* avec négligence. ◆ **negligible** *adj* négligeable.

negotiate [nɪ'gəʊʃɪeɪt] **1** *vt* (**a**) *sale, loan, bill* négocier. (**b**) *obstacle, hill* franchir; *river (sail on)* naviguer; *(cross)* franchir; *bend in road* prendre; *difficulty* surmonter. **2** *vi* négocier (*with sb for sth* avec qn pour obtenir qch). ◆ **negotiable** *adj* (**a**) *(Fin)* négociable; (**b**) *obstacle* franchissable; *river* navigable; *road* praticable. ◆ **negotiation** *n* négociation *f*. ◆ **negotiator** *n* négociateur *m*, -trice *f*.

Negro ['ni:grəʊ] **1** *adj* noir. **2** *n* Noir *m*. ◆ **Negress** *n* Noire *f*. ◆ **negroid** *adj* négroïde.

neigh [neɪ] **1** *vi* hennir. **2** *n* hennissement *m*.

neighbour, *(US)* **neighbor** ['neɪbəʳ] *n* voisin(e) *m(f)*; *(Bible etc)* prochain(e) *m(f)*. ◆ **neighbo(u)rhood 1** *n (gen)* voisinage *m*; **all the children of the ~hood** tous les enfants du voisinage *or* du quartier; **it's not a nice ~hood** ce n'est pas un quartier bien; **in the ~hood of the church** aux alentours *or* dans le voisinage de l'église; **in the ~hood of the crime** dans les parages *mpl* du crime; **in the ~hood of £100** dans les 100 livres ; **2** *adj chemist etc* du *or* de quartier. ◆ **neighbo(u)ring** *adj* avoisinant, voisin. ◆ **neighbo(u)rly** *adj person* bon voisin, obligeant; *feelings, action* de bon voisin; *relations* de bon voisinage.

neither ['naɪðəʳ] **1** *adv* ni. **~... nor** ni... ni (+ ne *before vb*); **~ you nor I know** ni vous ni moi ne le savons; **he can ~ read nor write** il ne sait ni lire ni écrire; *(fig)* **that's ~ here nor there** cela n'a rien à voir. **2** *conj*: **if you don't go, ~ shall I** si tu n'y vas pas, je n'irai pas non plus; **~ am I** (*or* **do I** *etc*) moi non plus, ni moi. **3** *adj*: **~ story is true** ni l'une ni l'autre des deux histoires n'est vraie; **in ~ case** ni dans un cas ni dans l'autre. **4** *pron* ni l'un(e) ni l'autre (+ ne *before vb*). **~ of them knows** ni l'un ni l'autre ne le sait, ils ne le savent ni l'un ni l'autre.

neo... ['ni:əʊ] *pref* néo-. **~classical** néo-classique; **~fascist** *(adj, n)* néo-fasciste *(mf)*; **~natal** *adj* néonatal; **~nazi** *(adj, n)* néo-nazi(e) *m(f)*.

neolithic [,ni:əʊ'lɪθɪk] *adj* néolithique.

neologism [nɪ'ɒlədʒɪz(ə)m] *n* néologisme *m*.

neon ['ni:ɒn] **1** *n* (gaz *m)* néon *m*. **2** *adj* au néon. **~ sign** enseigne *f* au néon.

Nepal [nɪ'pɔ:l] *n* Népal *m*.

nephew ['nevju:, 'nefju:] *n* neveu *m*.

nephritis [ne'fraɪtɪs] *n* néphrite *f*.

nerve [nɜ:v] **1** *n* (**a**) nerf *m*; *(Bot)* nervure *f*. **her ~s are bad** elle est très nerveuse; *(before performance)* **to have an attack of ~s** avoir le trac *; **it's only ~s** c'est de la nervosité; **to be a bundle of ~s** être un paquet de nerfs; **he was in a state of ~s, his ~s were on edge** il était sur les nerfs; **he gets on my ~s** il me tape sur les nerfs *; **to have ~s of steel** avoir les nerfs solides; **war of ~s** guerre *f* des nerfs.

(**b**) *(courage)* courage *m*; *(calm)* sang-froid *m*; *(self-confidence)* assurance *f*, confiance *f* en soi (-même); *(*: cheek)* culot * *m*. **to keep/lose one's ~** conserver/perdre son sang-froid; **he lost his ~, his ~ failed him** il n'a jamais retrouvé sa confiance en lui-même; **I haven't the ~ to do that** je n'ai pas le courage *or (cheek)* le culot * de faire ça; **you've got a ~!** * tu as du culot! *

2 *vt*: **to ~ sb to do** donner à qn le courage de faire; **to ~ o.s. to do** s'armer de courage pour faire.

3 *adj cell* nerveux; *gas* neuroplégique. **~ centre** *(Anat)* centre *m* nerveux; *(fig)* centre d'opérations; **~ specialist** neurologue *mf*.

◆ **nerve-racking** *adj* angoissant. ◆ **nerviness** * *n (Brit)* nervosité *f*; *(US)* culot * *m*. ◆ **nervy** * *adj* (**a**) *(Brit: tense)* énervé; (**b**) *(US: cheeky)* qui a du culot *.

nervous ['nɜ:vəs] *adj (Anat, Med)* nerveux; *(tense)* nerveux; *(apprehensive)* inquiet; *(self-conscious)* intimidé. **to have a ~ breakdown** faire une dépression nerveuse; **~ energy** vitalité *f*; **~ exhaustion** fatigue *f* nerveuse; *(serious)* surmenage *m* mental; **in a ~ state** très agité; **to feel ~** se sentir mal à l'aise; *(before performance etc)* avoir le trac *; **he makes me ~** *(fearful)* il m'intimide; *(tense)* il m'énerve; *(unsure of myself)* il me fait perdre mes moyens; **I'm rather ~ about diving** j'ai un peu peur de plonger; **he's a ~ wreck** * il est à bout de nerfs. ◆ **nervously** *adv (tensely)* nerveusement; *(apprehensively)* avec inquiétude. ◆ **nervousness** *n* nervosité *f*; *(apprehension)* inquiétude *f*; *(before performance)* trac * *m*.

nest [nest] **1** *n* nid *m*. **2** *vi* faire son nid. **3** *adj (fig)* **~ egg** pécule *m*.

nestle ['nesl] *vi [person]* se blottir (*up to, against* contre); *[house etc]* se nicher. **to ~ down in bed** se pelotonner dans son lit; **a house nestling**

among the trees une maison nichée parmi les arbres.

nestling ['nestlɪŋ, 'neslɪŋ] *n* oisillon *m*.

net[1] [net] **1** *n* (**a**) *(gen)* filet *m*. **hair** ~ résille *f*. (**b**) *(Tex)* voile *m*. **2** *vt fish, game* prendre au filet. **3** *adj*: ~ **curtains** voilage *m*; *(half length)* brise-bise *m inv*. ◆ **netball** *n* netball *m*. ◆ **netting** *n (nets)* filets *mpl*; *(mesh)* mailles *fpl*; *(Tex)* voile *m (pour rideaux)*; *(wire ~ting)* treillis *m* (métallique). ◆ **network** *n (gen, Elec, Comput)* réseau *m*; *(Rad)* station *f*; *(fig) [streets, veins]* lacis *m*; *[spies, salesmen]* réseau; *(TV: esp US)* **the ~works** les chaînes *fpl*. ◆ **networking** *n (Comput)* gestion *f* de réseau.

net[2], **nett** [net] *adj price, weight* net. **the price is £15** ~ le prix est de 15 livres net.

Netherlands ['neðələndz] *npl* Pays-Bas *mpl*.

nettle ['netl] **1** *n* ortie *f*. *(fig)* **to grasp the** ~ prendre le taureau par les cornes. **2** *vt* agacer. **he was ~d into replying** agacé, il a répondu. **3** *adj*: ~ **sting** piqûre *f* d'ortie. ◆ **nettlerash** *n* urticaire *f*.

neuralgia [njʊə'rældʒə] *n* névralgie *f*.

neuritis [njʊə'raɪtɪs] *n* névrite *f*.

neuro... ['njʊərə(ʊ)] *pref* neuro..., névro... ◆ **neurosurgeon** *n* neurochirurgien(ne) *m(f)*. ◆ **neurosurgery** *n* neurochirurgie *f*.

neurology [njʊə'rɒlədʒɪ] *n* neurologie *f*. ◆ **neurological** *adj* neurologique. ◆ **neurologist** *n* neurologue *mf*.

neurosis, *pl* **-oses** [njʊə'rəʊsɪs, si:z] *n* névrose *f*. ◆ **neurotic** **1** *adj person* névrosé; *disease* névrotique; *(fig)* **she's getting quite neurotic about it** elle en fait une véritable maladie, ça devient une obsession chez elle ; **2** *n* névrosé(e) *m(f)*.

neuter ['nju:tə^r] **1** *adj* neutre. **2** *n (Gram)* neutre *m*. **in the** ~ au neutre. **3** *vt cat etc* châtrer.

neutral ['nju:tr(ə)l] **1** *adj* neutre. **2** *n (Aut)* point *m* mort. **in** ~ au point mort. ◆ **neutralist** *adj, n* neutraliste *(mf)*. ◆ **neutrality** *n* neutralité *f*. ◆ **neutralize** *vt* neutraliser.

neutron ['nju:trɒn] *n* neutron *m*. ~ **bomb** bombe *f* à neutrons.

never ['nevə^r] *adv* ne... jamais. **I** ~ **eat it** je n'en mange jamais; **I have** ~ **seen him** je ne l'ai jamais vu; ~ **before had there been such a disaster** jamais on n'avait connu tel désastre; ~ **again!** plus jamais!; **I have** ~ **yet been able to** je n'ai encore jamais pu; **that will** ~ **do!** c'est inadmissible!; **he** ~ **said a word** il n'a pas dit le moindre mot; **you've** ~ **left it behind!** ne me dites pas que vous l'avez oublié!; ~! ça n'est pas vrai!; **well I** ~ **(did)!** * ça par exemple!; ~ **mind** ça ne fait rien. ◆ **never-ending** *adj* sans fin. ◆ **never-never** **1** *n*: **to buy on the never-never** * acheter à crédit ; **2** *adj*: **never-never land** pays *m* de cocagne. ◆ **nevertheless** *adv* néanmoins, (et) pourtant, quand même. ◆ **never-to-be-forgotten** *adj* inoubliable, qu'on n'oubliera jamais.

new [nju:] *adj* nouveau (*usually before n: before vowel* nouvel, *f* nouvelle); *(brand-new)* neuf (*f* neuve); *(different)* nouveau, autre; *bread, milk, cheese* frais; *wine* nouveau. **I've got a** ~ **car** *(different)* j'ai une nouvelle *or* une autre voiture; *(brand-new)* j'ai une voiture neuve; **he has written a** ~ **book** il a écrit un nouveau livre; ~ **potatoes** pommes de terre nouvelles; **the** ~ **moon** la nouvelle lune; **N~ Testament** Nouveau Testament; **the N~ World** le Nouveau Monde; **dressed in** ~ **clothes** habillé de neuf; **as good as** ~ comme neuf, à l'état de neuf; **this idea is not** ~ ce n'est pas une idée nouvelle *or* neuve; **the** ~ **nations** les pays neufs; **a** ~ **town** une ville nouvelle; **this sort of work is** ~ **to me** ce genre de travail est qch de nouveau pour moi; **I'm** ~ **to this kind of work** je n'ai jamais fait ce genre de travail; **he's** ~ **to the trade** il est nouveau dans le métier; **he's quite** ~ **to the town** il est tout nouvellement arrivé dans la ville; ~ **recruit** nouvelle recrue *f*, bleu * *m*; **the** ~ **students** *or* **pupils** les nouveaux *mpl*, les nouvelles *fpl*; **the** ~ **diplomacy** la diplomatie moderne; **the** ~ **rich** les nouveaux riches *mpl*; **bring me a** ~ **glass** apportez-moi un autre verre; **that's a** ~ **one on me!** * on en apprend tous les jours!; **what's ~?** * quoi de neuf?

◆ **newborn** *adj* nouveau-né(e) *m(f)*. ◆ **New Caledonia** *n* Nouvelle-Calédonie *f*. ◆ **newcomer** *n* nouveau venu *m*, nouvelle venue *f*. ◆ **New Delhi** *n* New Delhi. ◆ **New England** *n* Nouvelle-Angleterre *f*. ◆ **new-fangled** *adj* nouveau genre *inv*. ◆ **Newfoundland** *n* Terre-Neuve *f*. ◆ **New Guinea** *n* Nouvelle-Guinée *f*. ◆ **new-laid** *adj egg* tout frais. ◆ **new-look** *adj* new-look *inv*. ◆ **newly** *adv* nouvellement, récemment; **~ly made** neuf. ◆ **newly-weds** *npl* jeunes mariés *mpl*. ◆ **newness** *n [fashion, ideas etc]* nouveauté *f*; *[clothes etc]* état *m* de neuf. ◆ **New Orleans** *n* Nouvelle-Orléans *f*. ◆ **New Year** **1** *n* nouvel an *m*, nouvelle année *f*; **to bring in** *or* **see in the N~ Year** faire le réveillon (de la Saint-Sylvestre *or* du jour de l'an); **Happy N~ Year!** bonne année!; **to wish sb a happy N~ Year** souhaiter une *or* la bonne année à qn; **N~ Year's Day** jour *m* *or* premier *m* de l'an; **N~ Year's Eve** la Saint-Sylvestre. **2** *adj resolution* de nouvel an. ◆ **New York** *n* New York. ◆ **New Zealand** **1** *n* Nouvelle-Zélande *f* ; **2** *adj* néo-zélandais. ◆ **New Zealander** *n* Néo-Zélandais(e) *m(f)*.

news [nju:z] **1** *n* (**a**) nouvelles *fpl*. **a piece** *or* **an item of** ~ *(gen)* une nouvelle; *(Press)* une information; **have you heard the ~?** vous connaissez la nouvelle?; **have you heard the** ~ **about Paul?** vous savez ce qui est arrivé à Paul?; **have you any** ~ **of him?** avez-vous de ses nouvelles?; **what's your ~?** quoi de neuf?; **is there any ~?** y a-t-il du nouveau?; **I've got** ~ **for you!** j'ai du nouveau à vous annoncer!; **this is** ~ **to me!** première nouvelle! *; **good** ~ bonnes nouvelles; **when the** ~ **broke** quand on a su la nouvelle; **to make** ~ faire parler de soi; *(fig)* **he's in the** ~ **again** le voilà qui refait parler de lui. (**b**) *(Press, Rad, TV)* informations *fpl*; *(Cine, TV)* actualités *fpl*. **financial/sporting** *etc* ~ chronique *f* financière/sportive *etc*. **2** *adj*: ~ **agency** agence *f* de presse; *(US: Rad, TV)* ~ **analyst** commentateur *m*; ~ **bulletin** *(Rad)* bulletin *m* d'informations; *(TV)* actualités *fpl* télévisées; ~ **conference** conférence *f* de presse; ~ **desk** service *m* des informations; ~ **editor** rédacteur *m*; ~ **flash** flash *m* d'information; ~ **headlines** titres *mpl* de l'actualité; ~ **photographer** reporter *m* photographe; ~ **pictures** reportage *m* photographique; ~ **service** agence *f* de presse; ~ **sheet** feuille *f* d'informations; ~ **stand** kiosque *m* (à journaux); ~ **theatre** cinéma *m* d'actualités; **to have** ~ **value** présenter un intérêt pour le public. ◆ **newsagent** *(Brit)* *or* ◆ **newsdealer** *(US)* *n* marchand(e) *m(f)* de journaux. ◆ **newsboy** *n* vendeur *m* de journaux. ◆ **newscast** *n (Rad)* (bulletin *m* d')informations *fpl*; *(TV)* actualités *fpl* (télévisées). ◆ **newscaster** *n* présentateur *m*, -trice *f*. ◆ **newsclip** *n (US Press)* coupure *f* de journal. ◆ **newsletter** *n* bulletin *m (de société, de compagnie etc)*. ◆ **newsmaker** *n (US) (event)* sujet *m* d'actualité; *(person)* vedette *f* de l'actualité. ◆ **newsman** *n* journaliste *m*. ◆ **newspaper** *n* journal *m*; **~paper office** bureaux *mpl* de la rédaction. ◆ **newspaperman** *n* journaliste *m*. ◆ **newsprint** *n* papier *m* journal. ◆ **newsreader** *n* présentateur *m*, -trice *f*. ◆ **newsreel** *n* actualités *fpl* filmées. ◆ **newsroom** *n (Press)* salle *f* de rédaction; *(Rad, TV)* studio *m*. ◆ **newsworthy** *adj* qui vaut la peine d'être publié. ◆ **newsy** * *adj* plein de nouvelles.

newt [nju:t] *n* triton *m*.

next [nekst] **1** *adj (immediately adjoining) house, room, street* d'à côté, voisin; *(immediately following) bus stop, turning (in future)* prochain; *(in past)* suivant; *page, case* suivant. **get off at the ~ stop** descendez au prochain arrêt; **he got off at the ~ stop** il est descendu à l'arrêt suivant; **~ week** la semaine prochaine; **the ~ week** la semaine suivante *or* d'après; **this time ~ week** d'ici huit jours; **the ~ day** le lendemain, le jour suivant; **I will finish this in the ~ 5 days** je finirai ceci dans les 5 jours qui viennent; **the ~ morning** le lendemain matin; **(the) ~ time I see him** la prochaine fois que je le verrai; **the ~ time I saw him** la première fois que je l'ai revu; **the ~ moment** l'instant d'après; **from one moment to the ~** d'un moment à l'autre; **the year after ~** dans deux ans; **who's ~?** à qui le tour?; **you're ~** c'est votre tour, c'est à vous; **I was ~ to speak** ce fut ensuite à mon tour de parler; **the very ~ person I see** la première personne que je verrai; **the ~ thing to do** *(firstly)* la première chose à faire; *(next after this)* ce qu'il faut faire ensuite; **the ~ size** la taille au-dessus.
2 *adv* ensuite, après. **~ we had lunch** ensuite *or* après nous avons déjeuné; **what shall we do ~?** qu'allons-nous faire maintenant?; **when ~ you come to see us** la prochaine fois que vous viendrez nous voir; **when I ~ saw him** quand je l'ai revu (la fois suivante); **what ~?** et puis quoi encore?; **the ~ best thing would be** à défaut le mieux serait; **who's the ~ tallest?** qui est le plus grand après?; **~ to** *(beside)* auprès de, à côté de; *(almost)* presque; **wool ~ to the skin** de la laine à même la peau; **the ~ to last** l'avant-dernier; **~ to nothing** presque rien; **I got it for ~ to nothing** je l'ai payé trois fois rien.
3 *prep (Brit: beside)* à côté de, auprès de.
4 *n* prochain(e) *m(f)*. **the ~ to speak is Paul** c'est Paul qui parle ensuite; **to be continued in our ~** suite au prochain numéro.
◆ **next door** **1** *n* la maison d'à côté; **from ~ door** d'à côté ; **2** *adv*: **~ door to us** à côté de chez nous; **the boy ~ door** le garçon d'à côté ; **3** *adj*: **~-door house** maison *f* d'à côté; **~-door neighbour** voisin(e) *m(f)* d'à côté. ◆ **next-of-kin** *n (relative)* parent *m* le plus proche; *(family)* famille *f* proche.

nib [nɪb] *n [pen]* (bec *m* de) plume *f*.

nibble ['nɪbl] *vti* grignoter; *[sheep, goats etc]* brouter; *[fish]* mordre, mordiller. *(fig)* **to ~ (at) an offer** se montrer tenté par une offre.

Nicaragua [nɪkə'rægjʊə] *n* Nicaragua *m*. ◆ **Nicaraguan** **1** *adj* nicaraguayen ; **2** *n* Nicaraguayen(ne) *m(f)*.

nice [naɪs] *adj* (**a**) *(gen: pleasant)* agréable; *person* gentil, sympathique; *meal, smell, taste* bon, agréable; *(pretty)* joli. **how ~ you look!** vous êtes vraiment bien!; **be ~ to him** soyez gentil *or* aimable avec lui; **they had a ~ time** ils se sont bien amusés; **how ~ of you to...** comme c'est gentil *or* aimable à vous de...; **it's ~ here** on est bien ici; *(fig: iro)* **you're in a ~ mess** vous voilà dans de beaux draps; *(iro)* **that's a ~ way to talk!** c'est du joli ce que vous dites là!; **~ and warm** bien chaud; **~ and easy** très facile; **he gets ~ long holidays** ce qui est bien c'est qu'il a de longues vacances. (**b**) *(respectable, refined)* convenable, comme il faut. **they are not very ~ people** ce ne sont pas des gens très convenables *or* très comme il faut *or* très bien; **that's not very ~** ce n'est pas très convenable, ce n'est pas beau *. (**c**) *(hard to please) person* difficile (*about* pour); *(subtle) distinction* délicat, subtil. ◆ **nice-looking** *adj* joli, beau. ◆ **nicely** *adv (kindly)* gentiment; *(pleasantly)* agréablement; *(prettily)* joliment; *(well)* bien; *(carefully)* minutieusement; *(exactly)* exactement; **that will do ~ly** cela fera très bien l'affaire. ◆ **niceness** *n [person]* gentillesse *f*; *[place, thing]* caractère *m* agréable. ◆ **nicety** *n [judgment]* précision *f*; **to a ~ty** à la perfection; **~ties** finesses *fpl*.

niche [ni:ʃ] *n (Archit)* niche *f*. *(fig)* **to find one's ~** trouver sa voie.

nick [nɪk] **1** *n* (**a**) *(in blade, dish)* ébréchure *f*; *(on skin, in wood)* entaille *f*. *(fig)* **in the ~ of time** juste à temps. (**b**) (‡: *prison)* taule ‡ *f*. **in the ~** en taule ‡. (**c**) **in good ~** ‡ en bonne condition. **2** *vt* (**a**) ébrécher; entailler. (**b**) (‡: *arrest)* pincer *, arrêter. **to get ~ed** ‡ se faire pincer *. (**c**) (‡: *steal)* piquer ‡, voler. (**d**) *(US)* **how much did they ~ you for that suit?** ‡ tu t'es fait avoir * de combien pour ce costume?

nickel ['nɪkl] *n (metal)* nickel *m*; *(Can, US: coin)* pièce *f* de cinq cents. ◆ **nickel-plated** *adj* nickelé.

nickname ['nɪkneɪm] **1** *n* surnom *m*; *(humorous; malicious)* sobriquet *m*. **2** *vt*: **to ~ sb sth** surnommer qn qch; donner à qn le sobriquet de qch.

Nicosia [nɪkə'si:ə] *n* Nicosie.

nicotine ['nɪkəti:n] **1** *n* nicotine *f*. **2** *adj*: **~ poisoning** nicotinisme *m*. ◆ **nicotine-stained** *adj* jauni de nicotine.

niece [ni:s] *n* nièce *f*.

nifty ‡ ['nɪftɪ] *adj car, jacket* très chic *inv*; *tool, gadget* astucieux; *blow, action* habile; *(US: great)* formidable. **that was a ~ piece of work** ça a été vite fait.

Niger ['naɪdʒəʳ] *n (country, river)* Niger *m*.

Nigeria [naɪ'dʒɪərɪə] *n* Nigeria *m*. ◆ **Nigerian** **1** *adj* nigérian ; **2** *n* Nigérian(e) *m(f)*.

niggardly ['nɪgədlɪ] *adj person* pingre; *amount, portion* mesquin.

niggle ['nɪgl] **1** *vi (go into detail)* couper les cheveux en quatre; *(find fault)* toujours trouver à redire. **2** *vt (gen)* agacer; *[conscience]* travailler. ◆ **niggling** **1** *adj person* tatillon; *details* insignifiant; *doubt, pain* persistant ; **2** *n* chicanerie *f*.

night [naɪt] **1** *n* nuit *f*. **at ~, in the ~** la nuit; **by ~, in the ~** de nuit; **last ~** la nuit dernière, cette nuit; *(evening)* hier soir; **tomorrow ~** demain soir; **the ~ before** la veille au soir; **the ~ before last** avant-hier soir; **in the ~, during the ~** pendant la nuit; **Monday ~** lundi soir, la nuit de lundi à mardi; **6 o'clock at ~** 6 heures du soir; **to spend the ~** passer la nuit; **to have a good/bad ~** bien/mal dormir; **~ and day** nuit et jour; **to sit up all ~ talking** passer la nuit entière à bavarder; **to have a ~ out** sortir le soir; **the maid's ~ out** le soir de sortie de la bonne; **let's make a ~ of it** il est trop tôt pour aller se coucher; **he's working ~s** il est de nuit; **I've had too many late ~s** je me suis couché tard trop souvent; **a ~'s sleep** une bonne nuit de sommeil; **a ~'s lodging** un toit pour la nuit; **~ is falling** le soir tombe; *(Theat)* **the last 3 ~s of** les 3 dernières représentations de; **Mozart ~** soirée *f* Mozart. **2** *adj clothes, work, flight, nurse* de nuit. *(US)* **~ letter** télégramme-lettre *m* de nuit; *(fig)* **~ owl** couche-tard *mf*; **~ porter** gardien *m* de nuit; **~ school** cours *mpl* du soir; **~ storage heater/heating** radiateur *m*/chauffage *m* par accumulation; **~ safe** coffre *m* de nuit; *(US Police)* **~ stick** matraque *f* (d'agent de police); **~ watchman** veilleur *m or* gardien *m* de nuit. ◆ **nightcap** *n* bonnet *m* de nuit; *(drink)* **would you like a ~cap?** voulez-vous boire qch avant de vous coucher? ◆ **nightclub** *n* boîte *f* de nuit. ◆ **nightdress** *or* ◆ **nightgown** *or* ◆ **nightie** * *n* chemise *f* de nuit *(de femme)*. ◆ **nightfall** *n*: **at ~fall** à la nuit tombante. ◆ **nightingale** *n* rossignol *m*. ◆ **nightlife** *n* activités *fpl* nocturnes. ◆ **nightlight** *n (child's)* veilleuse *f*. ◆ **nightly** **1** *adj* de tous les soirs, de toutes les nuits ; **2** *adv* tous les soirs, chaque nuit; **twice ~ly** deux fois par soir *or* nuit. ◆ **nightmare** *n* cauchemar *m*. ◆ **nightmarish** *adj* de cauchemar. ◆ **nightshade** *n*: **deadly ~shade** belladone *f*. ◆ **nightshift** *n (workers)* équipe *f* de nuit; *(work)* poste *m* de nuit; **on ~shift** de nuit. ◆ **nightshirt** *n* chemise *f* de nuit *(d'homme)*. ◆ **night-time** *n* nuit *f*; **at ~-time** la nuit; **in the ~-time** pendant la nuit. ◆ **nightwear** *n* vêtements *mpl* de nuit.

nil [nɪl] *n* rien *m*; *(in form-filling)* néant *m*; *(Sport)* zéro *m*.

Nile [naɪl] *n* Nil *m*.

nimble ['nɪmbl] *adj person, fingers* agile; *old person* alerte; *mind* vif, prompt. ◆ **nimble-fingered/-footed** *adj* aux doigts/pieds agiles. ◆ **nimbleness** *n* agilité *f*; vivacité *f*. ◆ **nimble-witted** *adj* à l'esprit vif. ◆ **nimbly** *adv* agilement.

nincompoop * ['nɪŋkəmpu:p] *n* idiot(e) *m(f)*, gourde * *f*.

nine [naɪn] **1** *adj* neuf *inv*. **~ times out of ten** neuf fois sur dix; *(fig)* **he's got ~ lives** il a l'âme chevillée au corps; **a ~ days' wonder** la merveille d'un jour; **a ~-hole golf course** un parcours de neuf trous. **2** *n* neuf *m inv*. **dressed up to the ~s** sur son trente et un; *for other phrases V* **six**.
◆ **ninepins** *npl* (jeu *m* de) quilles *fpl*; **to go down like ~pins** tomber comme des mouches. ◆ **nineteen** **1** *adj* dix-neuf *inv* ; **2** *n* dix-neuf *m inv*; **to talk ~teen to the dozen** * être un vrai moulin à paroles. ◆ **nineteenth** *adj, n* dix-neuvième *(mf)*; *(fraction)* dix-neuvième *m*. ◆ **ninetieth** *adj, n* quatre-vingt-dixième *(mf)*; *(fraction)* quatre-vingt-dixième *m*. ◆ **nine-to-five** *adj job* de bureau routinier. ◆ **ninety** *adj, n* quatre-vingt-dix *(m) inv*; **to be in one's ~ties** avoir plus de quatre-vingt-dix ans. ◆ **ninth** *adj, n* neuvième *(mf)*; *(fraction)* neuvième *m*.

nip[1] [nɪp] **1** *n (pinch)* pinçon *m*; *(bite)* morsure *f*. **there's a ~ in the air** l'air est piquant. **2** *vt (pinch)* pincer; *(bite)* donner un (petit) coup de dent à; *[cold] face etc* piquer; *plants* brûler. *(fig)* **to ~ in the bud** écraser dans l'œuf. **3** *vi*: **to ~ * up/out** *etc* monter/sortir *etc* en courant; **he ~ped into the café** il a fait un saut au café; **I've just ~ped in for a minute** je ne fais qu'entrer et sortir. ◆ **nippy** * *adj* (**a**) *(spry)* alerte, preste; **be ~py about it!** fais vite!; (**b**) *wind* piquant, coupant; **it's ~py** l'air est piquant; (**c**) *flavour* fort, piquant.

nip[2] [nɪp] *n (drink)* goutte *f*, petit verre *m*.

nipple ['nɪpl] *n (Anat)* bout *m* de sein; *[baby's bottle]* tétine *f*.

nirvana [nɪə'vɑ:nə] *n* nirvâna *m*.

nit [nɪt] *n* (**a**) *[louse]* lente *f*. (**b**) *(‡: fool)* crétin(e) * *m(f)*. ◆ **nit-pick** * *vi* être tatillon. ◆ **nitty-gritty** * *n*: **to get down to the ~ty-gritty** en venir aux choses sérieuses. ◆ **nitwit** * *n* nigaud(e) * *m(f)*.

nitrogen ['naɪtrədʒən] *n* azote *m*. ◆ **nitric** *adj* nitrique, azotique. ◆ **nitroglycerin(e)** *n* nitroglycérine *f*. ◆ **nitrous** *adj* nitreux, azoteux.

no [nəʊ] **1** *particle, n* non *(m inv)*. **I won't take ~ for an answer** il n'est pas question de me dire non.
2 *adj (not any)* pas de, aucun, nul (*f* nulle) *(all used with 'ne')*. **she had ~ coat** elle n'avait pas de manteau; **I have ~ idea** je n'ai aucune idée; **I have ~ more money** je n'ai plus d'argent; **~ two men would agree** il n'y a pas deux hommes qui seraient d'accord; **~ other man** nul autre, personne d'autre; **~ sensible man** aucun homme de bon sens; **it's of ~ interest** c'est sans intérêt; **~ go!** * pas moyen!; **~ two are alike** il n'y en a pas deux qui se ressemblent; **he's ~ friend of mine** il n'est pas de mes amis; **he's ~ genius** il n'a rien d'un génie; **this is ~ place for children** ce n'est pas un endroit pour les enfants; **it's ~ small matter** ce n'est pas une petite affaire; **there's ~ such thing** cela n'existe pas; **~ smoking** défense de fumer; **~ parking** stationnement *m* interdit; **~ surrender!** on ne se rend pas!; **there's ~ saying what he'll do** il est impossible de dire ce qu'il fera; **there's ~ pleasing him** quoi qu'on fasse il n'est jamais satisfait.
3 *adv*: **I can go ~ farther** je ne peux pas aller plus loin; **I can bear it ~ longer** *or* **~ more** je ne peux plus le supporter; **~ less than 4** pas moins de 4; **she came herself, ~ less!** elle est venue en personne, voyez-vous ça! *(iro)*.
◆ **nobody** *V below*. ◆ **no-claim(s) bonus** *n* bonification *f* pour non-sinistre. ◆ **no-go area** *n* zone *f* interdite *(à la police et à l'armée)*. ◆ **no-good** * *adj, n* propre *(mf)* à rien. ◆ **nohow** * *adv* en aucune façon. ◆ **no-man's-land** *n* no man's land *m*. ◆ **no-nonsense** *adj* plein de bon sens. ◆ **no one = nobody 1.** ◆ **nothin** *V below*. ◆ **noway(s)** *or* ◆ **nowise** *adv* en aucune façon. ◆ **nowhere** *adv* nulle part (+ ne *before vb*); **he went ~where** il n'est allé nulle part; **~where in Europe** nulle part en Europe; **it's ~where you know** ce n'est pas un endroit que tu connais; **~where else** nulle part ailleurs; **~where to be found** introuvable; **she is ~where to be seen** on ne la voit nulle part; **they appeared from ~where** ils sont apparus comme par miracle; *(fig)* **that will get you ~where** ça ne te servira à rien; **we're getting ~where** * ça ne nous mène strictement à rien; **~where near** *(gen)* loin de; **she is ~where near as clever as he is** elle est loin d'être aussi intelligente que lui; **you're ~where near it!** tu n'y es pas du tout!

nobble * ['nɒbl] *vt (Brit)* (**a**) *(bribe) person* acheter, soudoyer. (**b**) *(Racing) horse, dog* droguer *(pour l'empêcher de gagner)*. (**c**) *(catch) wrongdoer* pincer *, arrêter; *sb to speak to* coincer.

noble ['nəʊbl] **1** *adj (gen)* noble; *(*: unselfish)* magnanime. **2** *n* noble *m*. ◆ **nobility** *n* noblesse *f*. ◆ **nobleman** noble *m*. ◆ **nobly** *adv (aristocratically)* noblement; *(magnificently) proportioned* majestueusement; *(*: selflessly)* généreusement.

nobody ['nəʊb(ə)dɪ] **1** *pron* personne, nul (+ ne *before vb*). **I saw ~** je n'ai vu personne; **~ knows** personne *or* nul ne le sait; **who saw him? — ~** qui l'a vu? — personne. **2** *n*: **he's a ~** c'est un rien du tout; **when he was ~** alors qu'il était encore inconnu.

nocturnal [nɒk'tɜ:nl] *adj* nocturne.

nod [nɒd] **1** *n* signe *m* de la tête. **to give sb a ~** faire un signe de (la) tête à qn; *(answering yes)* faire signe que oui à qn. **2** *vi* (**a**) *(also* **~ one's head***)* faire un signe de la tête; *(as sign of assent)* faire signe que oui, faire un signe de tête affirmatif. **to ~ to sb** faire un signe de tête à qn; *(in greeting)* saluer qn d'un signe de tête; *(meaning 'yes')* il m'a fait signe que oui de la tête; **he ~ded to me to go** de la tête il m'a fait signe de m'en aller; **we have a ~ding acquaintance** nous nous connaissons vaguement. (**b**) *(doze)* somnoler. (**c**) *[flowers etc]* se balancer. ◆ **nod off** *vi* s'endormir.

node [nəʊd] *n* nœud *m*.

noise [nɔɪz] *n (sound)* bruit m; *(din)* bruit, tapage *m*; *(Rad, TV)* parasites *mpl*; *(Telec)* friture *f*. **I heard a small ~** j'ai entendu un petit bruit; **~s in the ears** bourdonnements *mpl* d'oreilles; **a hammering ~** un martèlement; **the ~ of the traffic** le bruit *or* le vacarme de la circulation; **I hate ~** j'ai horreur du bruit; **~ pollution** les nuisances *fpl* sonores; *(lit, fig)* **to make a ~** faire du bruit *or* du tapage; *(fig)* **she made ~s * about wanting to go home** elle a marmonné qu'elle voulait rentrer; *(person)* **a big ~ *** une huile *. ◆ **noiseless** *adj* silencieux. ◆ **noiselessly** *adv* sans bruit, silencieusement. ◆ **noisily** *adv* bruyamment. ◆ **noisy** *adj (gen)* bruyant; *(boisterous)* bruyant, tapageur; **to be noisy** faire du bruit *or* du tapage.

nomad ['nəʊmæd] *n* nomade *mf*. ◆ **nomadic** *adj* nomade.

nom de plume ['nɒmdə'plu:m] *n (Literat)* pseudonyme *m*.

nominal ['nɒmɪnl] *adj (gen)* nominal; *rule* de nom seulement; *rent* insignifiant. ◆ **nominally** *adv* nominalement.

nominate ['nɒmɪneɪt] *vt (appoint)* nommer (*sb to a post* qn à un poste), désigner; *(propose)* proposer, présenter (*sb for sth* qn comme candidat à qch). ◆ **nomination** *n* nomination *f* (*to* à), proposition *f* de candidat. ◆ **nominative** *adj, n (Gram)* nominatif *m*. ◆ **nominee** *n* personne *f* nommée, candidat(e) *m(f)* agréé(e).

non- [nɒn] *pref* non-, *e.g.* ~**-strikers** non-grévistes. ◆ **non-agression** *n* non-agression *f*. ◆ **non-alcoholic** *adj* non alcoolisé, sans alcool. ◆ **non-aligned** *adj* non-aligné. ◆ **non-arrival** *n* non-arrivée *f*. ◆ **non-believer** *n* incroyant(e) *m(f)*. ◆ **non-Catholic** *adj, n* non-catholique *(mf)*. ◆ **non-combatant** *adj, n* non-combattant *(m)*. ◆ **non-combustible** *adj* non-combustible. ◆ **non-commissioned officer** *n* sous-officier *m*. ◆ **non-commital** *adj* évasif. ◆ **non-communication** *n* manque *m* de communication. ◆ **non-conformist** *adj, n* non-conformiste *(mf)*. ◆ **non-contributory** *adj* sans cotisations. ◆ **noncooperation** *n* refus *m* de coopération. ◆ **nondrinker** *n* personne *f* qui ne boit jamais d'alcool. ◆ **non-essentials** *npl* accessoires *mpl*. ◆ **non-event** *n*: **the meeting was a ~-event** * la réunion n'a jamais démarré. ◆ **non-existence** *n* non-existence *f*. ◆ **non-existent** *adj* inexistant. ◆ **non-fattening** *adj* qui ne fait pas grossir. ◆ **non-fiction** *n* littérature *f* non romanesque. ◆ **non-greasy** *adj* qui ne graisse pas. ◆ **non-inflammable** *adj* ininflammable. ◆ **non-interference** *n* non-intervention *f*. ◆ **non-intervention** *n* non-intervention *f*. ◆ **non-involvement** *n* non-engagement *m*. ◆ **non-iron** *adj* qui ne nécessite aucun repassage. ◆ **non-member** *n* personne *f* étrangère (au club *etc*) ; **open to ~-members** ouvert au public. ◆ **non-party** *adj vote, decision* indépendant (de tout parti politique). ◆ **non-payment** *n* non-paiement *m*. ◆ **non-poisonous** *adj snake* non venimeux; *plant* non vénéneux; *mixture* non toxique. ◆ **non-political** *adj* apolitique. ◆ **non-professional** *adj, n* amateur *(mf)*. ◆ **non-profitmaking** *or* ◆ **non-profit** *(US) adj* sans but lucratif. ◆ **non-resident** **1** *adj person* non résidant ; **2** *n* non-résident(e) *m(f)*; *(in hotel)* client(e) *m(f)* de passage. ◆ **non-returnable** *adj* non consigné. ◆ **non-run** *adj* indémaillable. ◆ **non-sectarian** *adj* non confessionnel. ◆ **non sequitur** *n*: **it's a ~ sequitur** c'est illogique. ◆ **non-shrink** *adj* irrétrécissable. ◆ **non-skid** *adj* antidérapant. ◆ **non-slip** *adj* antidérapant. ◆ **non-smoker** *n* non-fumeur *m*, personne *f* qui ne fume pas. ◆ **non-starter** *n (fig)* **to be a ~-starter** * ne rien valoir. ◆ **non-stick** *adj saucepan* qui n'attache pas, Téfal *inv* ®. ◆ **non-stop** **1** *adj (gen)* sans arrêt; *train, flight* direct ; **2** *adv talk* sans arrêt; *(Aviat)* sans escale. ◆ **non-taxable** *adj* non-imposable. ◆ **non-union** *adj workers, labour* non syndiqué. ◆ **nonviolence** *n* non-violence *f*. ◆ **nonviolent** *adj* non-violent. ◆ **non-white** **1** *n* personne *f* de couleur ; **2** *adj* de couleur.

nonchalant ['nɒnʃ(ə)lənt] *adj* nonchalant. ◆ **nonchalance** *n* nonchalance *f*. ◆ **nonchalantly** *adv* nonchalamment.

noncommittal ['nɒnkə'mɪtl] *adj person* réservé; *statement* qui n'engage à rien; *answer* diplomatique.

nondescript ['nɒndɪskrɪpt] *adj colour* indéfinissable; *person* quelconque.

none [nʌn] **1** *pron* (**a**) *(thing)* aucun(e) *m(f)* (+ ne *before vb*); *(form-filling)* néant *m*. ~ **of the books** aucun livre, aucun des livres; ~ **of this** rien de ceci; ~ **of that!** pas de ça!; **he would have ~ of it** il ne voulait rien savoir; ~ **at all** rien, pas du tout; *(not a single one)* pas un(e) seul(e); ~ **of this money** pas un centime de cet argent; ~ **of this milk** pas une goutte de ce lait; **there's ~ left** il n'en reste plus. (**b**) *(person)* personne, aucun(e) *m(f)* (+ ne). ~ **of them** aucun d'entre eux; ~ **but you can do it** vous seul êtes capable de le faire; **I know, ~ better, that...** je sais mieux que personne que...; **their guest was ~ other than...** leur invité n'était autre que...
2 *adv*: **he's ~ the worse for it** il ne s'en porte pas plus mal; **I'm ~ the worse for having eaten it** je ne me ressens pas de l'avoir mangé; **I like him ~ the worse for it** je ne l'en aime pas moins pour cela; **he was ~ the wiser** il n'était pas plus avancé; **it's ~ too warm** il ne fait pas tellement chaud; **and ~ too soon either!** et ce n'est pas trop tôt! ◆ **nonetheless = nevertheless.**

nonentity [nɒ'nentɪtɪ] *n* personne *f* insignifiante, nullité *f*.

nonplus ['nɒn'plʌs] *vt* déconcerter, dérouter.

nonsense ['nɒns(ə)ns] **1** *n* absurdités *fpl*, sottises *fpl*, idioties *fpl*. **to talk ~** dire *or* débiter des absurdités; **that's a piece of ~!** c'est une absurdité *or* sottise *or* idiotie!; **~!** ne dis pas de sottises *or* d'idioties!; **it is ~ to say** il est absurde *or* idiot de dire; **he will stand no ~** il ne se laissera pas faire (*from* par; *about* en ce qui concerne); **no ~!** pas d'histoires! *; **there's no ~ about him** c'est un homme très carré; **to make (a) ~ of sth** rendre qch complètement ridicule. **2** *adj*: ~ **verse** vers *mpl* amphigouriques. ◆ **nonsensical** *adj* absurde.

noodles ['nu:dlz] *npl* nouilles *fpl*.

nook [nʊk] *n* coin *m*. **~s and crannies** coins et recoins.

noon [nu:n] *n* midi *m*. **at ~** à midi.

noose [nu:s] *n* nœud *m* coulant; *(as trap)* collet *m*; *[cowboy]* lasso *m*; *[hangman]* corde *f*. *(fig)* **to put one's head in the ~** se jeter dans la gueule du loup.

nor [nɔ:ʳ] *conj* (**a**) *(following 'neither')* ni. **neither you ~ I can do it** ni vous ni moi (nous) ne pouvons le faire; **she neither eats ~ drinks** elle ne mange ni ne boit. (**b**) *(= and not)* **I don't know, ~ do I care** je ne sais pas et d'ailleurs je m'en moque; **~ do I** *(or* **can I** *etc)* ni moi non plus.

norm [nɔ:m] *n* norme *f*. ◆ **normal** **1** *adj* normal; **it was quite ~al for him to object** il était tout à fait normal *or* naturel qu'il fasse des objections; **it's quite a ~al thing for children to fight** c'est une chose très normale que les enfants se battent *(subj)* ; **2** *n* normale *f*; **below ~al** au-dessous de la normale. ◆ **normalcy** *or* ◆ **normality** *n* normalité *f*. ◆ **normalize** *vt* normaliser, régulariser. ◆ **normally** *adv* normalement.

Norman ['nɔ:mən] **1** *adj* normand; *(Archit)* roman. **2** *n* Normand(e) *m(f)*. ◆ **Normandy** *n* Normandie *f*.

Norse [nɔ:s] *n (Ling)* norrois *m*.

north [nɔ:θ] **1** *n* nord *m*. **(to the) ~ of** au nord de; *[wind]* **to veer to the ~, to go into the ~** tourner au nord; **the wind is in the ~** le vent est au nord; **to live in the ~** habiter dans le nord; **in the ~ of** dans le nord de; *(US Hist)* **the N~** les États *mpl* du nord.
2 *adj (gen)* nord *inv*; *coast, door* nord, septentrional; *wind* du nord. **in the N~ Atlantic** dans l'Atlantique *m* Nord; **N~ Africa** Afrique *f* du Nord; **N~ African** *(adj)* nord-africain; *(n)* Nord-Africain(e) *m(f)*; **N~ America** Amérique *f* du Nord; **N~ American** *(adj)* nord-américain; *(n)* Nord-Américain(e) *m(f)*; **N~ Sea** mer *f* du Nord; **N~ Sea oil** pétrole *m* de la mer du Nord; ~ **Star** étoile *f* polaire.

3 *adv* au nord, vers le nord. **the town lies ~ of the border** la ville est située au nord de la frontière; **we drove ~ for 100 km** nous avons roulé pendant 100 km en direction du nord; **to sail due ~** aller droit vers le nord, avoir le cap au nord *(Naut)*. ◆ **northbound** *adj traffic* en direction du nord; *carriageway* nord *inv*. ◆ **north-country** *adj* du Nord (de l'Angleterre). ◆ **north-east 1** *adj, n* nord-est *(m) inv* ; **2** *adv* vers le nord-est. ◆ **north-eastern** *adj* nord-est *inv*. ◆ **northerly** *adj wind* du nord; *situation, aspect* au nord; **in a ~erly direction** vers le nord. ◆ **northern** *adj region* nord *inv*, du nord; *wall, side* exposé au nord; *coast* nord, septentrional; **in ~ern Spain** dans le nord de l'Espagne; **~ern lights** aurore *f* boréale. ◆ **northerner** *n* homme *m or* femme *f* du Nord; *(US Hist)* Nordiste *mf*. ◆ **northernmost** *adj* le plus au nord. ◆ **north-north-east 1** *adj, n* nord-nord-est *(m) inv* ; **2** *adv* vers le nord-nord-est. ◆ **northward 1** *adj* au nord ; **2** *adv (also* **~wards)** vers le nord. ◆ **north-west 1** *adj, n* nord-ouest *(m) inv* ; **2** *adv* vers le nord-ouest. ◆ **north-western** *adj* nord-ouest *inv*.

Norway ['nɔːweɪ] *n* Norvège *f*. ◆ **Norwegian 1** *adj* norvégien ; **2** *n* Norvégien(ne) *m(f)*; *(Ling)* norvégien *m*.

nose [nəʊz] **1** *n* nez *m*. **his ~ was bleeding** il saignait du nez; **to speak through one's ~** parler du nez; **red-~d** au nez rouge; *(fig)* **right under his ~** juste sous son nez; **his ~ is out of joint** il est dépité; **to lead sb by the ~** mener qn par le bout du nez; **to look down one's ~ at sb/sth** faire le nez à qn/devant qch; **to turn up one's ~** faire le dégoûté (*at* devant); **to keep one's ~ to the grindstone** travailler sans répit; **to poke** *or* **stick one's ~ into sth** mettre son nez dans qch; **to have a (good) ~ for...** avoir du flair pour...; **a line of cars ~ to tail** une file de voitures pare-chocs contre pare-chocs. **2** *adj*: **~ drops** gouttes *fpl* pour le nez; **to have a ~ job** * se faire rectifier le nez.

◆ **nose about, nose around** *vi* fouiller, fureter.

◆ **nose out** *vt sep [dog]* flairer; *(fig) secret* découvrir; *person* dénicher.

◆ **nosebag** *n* musette *f* mangeoire. ◆ **nosebleed** *n* saignement *m* de nez; **to have a ~bleed** saigner du nez. ◆ **nose-dive** *(Aviat)* **1** *n* piqué *m* ; **2** *vi* descendre en piqué. ◆ **nosegay** *n* petit bouquet *m*. ◆ **nose-to-tail** *adv* pare-chocs contre pare-chocs. ◆ **nos(e)y** * *adj* curieux; **don't be so ~y** mêlezvous de ce qui vous regarde!; **N~y Parker** fouinard(e)* *m(f)*.

nostalgia [nɒs'tældʒɪə] *n* nostalgie *f*. ◆ **nostalgic** *adj* nostalgique.

nostril ['nɒstr(ə)l] *n* narine *f*; *[horse]* naseau *m*.

not [nɒt] *adv* ne... pas. **he is ~ here** il n'est pas ici; **he hasn't come** il n'est pas venu; **he won't stay** il ne restera pas; **he told me ~ to come** il m'a dit de ne pas venir; **~ to mention...** pour ne pas parler de...; **I hope ~** j'espère que non; **whether he comes or ~** qu'il vienne ou non; **~ at all** pas du tout; *(after thanks)* il n'y a pas de quoi; **~ in the least** pas du tout, nullement; **~ that I know of** pas que je sache; **why ~?** pourquoi pas?; **~ a few...** bien des...; **~ without reason** et pour cause; **~ I!** moi pas!, pas moi!; **~ one book** pas un livre; **~ yet** pas encore; **~ guilty** non coupable.

notable ['nəʊtəbl] **1** *adj (gen)* notable. **it is ~ that** ... il est remarquable que... + *subj*. **2** *n* notable *m*. ◆ **notably** *adv (in particular)* notamment; *(outstandingly)* notablement.

notary ['nəʊtərɪ] *n* **(~ public)** notaire *m*.

notation [nəʊ'teɪʃ(ə)n] *n* notation *f*.

notch [nɒtʃ] **1** *n (in wood, stick)* encoche *f*; *(in belt)* cran *m*; *(in wheel, saw, board)* dent *f*; *(in blade)* ébréchure *f*; *(Sewing)* cran. **2** *vt stick etc* encocher; *blade* ébrécher; *seam* cranter. ◆ **notch up** *vt sep score etc* marquer. ◆ **notchback** *n (US: car)* trois-volumes *f*, voiture *f* avec coffre à bagages.

note [nəʊt] **1** *n* **(a)** *(gen, Diplomacy, Liter etc)* note *f*. **to take** *or* **make a ~ of sth** prendre note de qch; *(fig)* **I must make a ~ to buy some more** il faut que je me souvienne d'en racheter; **to take** *or* **make ~s** prendre des notes; **lecture ~s** notes de cours. **(b)** *(informal letter)* mot *m*. *(to secretary)* **take a ~ to Mr...** je vais vous dicter un mot pour M. ...; **just a quick ~ to tell you...** un petit mot à la hâte pour vous dire... **(c)** *(Mus)* note *f*; *[piano]* touche *f*; *[bird]* note. **to play (or sing) a false ~** faire une fausse note; *(fig)* **his speech struck the right/ wrong ~** son discours était bien dans la note/n'était pas dans la note; **with a ~ of anxiety in his voice** avec une note d'anxiété dans la voix; **a ~ of desperation** un accent de désespoir; **a ~ of warning** un avertissement discret. **(d)** *(Comm, Banking)* billet *m*. **bank ~** billet de banque; **one-pound ~** billet d'une livre. **(e)** *(of person)* **of ~** éminent, de marque; **nothing of ~** rien d'important. **(f)** *(notice)* **to take ~ of** prendre note de; **worthy of ~** digne d'attention.

2 *vt (take ~ of)* noter (*that* que), prendre note de; *(notice)* remarquer, constater; **(~ down)** noter, inscrire.

◆ **notebook** *n* carnet *m*; *(Scol)* cahier *m*; *[stenographer]* bloc-notes *m*. ◆ **note-case** *n* porte-feuille *m*. ◆ **noted** *adj* (bien) connu (*for* pour), célèbre. ◆ **notepad** *n* bloc-notes *m*. ◆ **notepaper** *n* papier *m* à lettres. ◆ **noteworthy** *adj* notable.

nothing ['nʌθɪŋ] **1** *n* rien *m* (+ ne *before vb*); *(numeral)* zéro *m*. **I saw ~** je n'ai rien vu; **~ happened** il ne s'est rien passé; **to eat ~** ne rien manger; **~ to eat** rien à manger; **there is ~ that pleases him** il n'y a rien qui lui plaise; **~ new** rien de nouveau; **~ on earth** rien au monde; **you look like ~ on earth** * tu as l'air de je ne sais quoi; **as if ~ had happened** comme si de rien n'était; **fit for ~** propre à rien; **to say ~ of...** sans parler de...; **I can do ~ about it** je n'y peux rien; **he is ~ if not polite** il est avant tout poli; **for ~** *(in vain)* en vain; *(without payment)* gratuitement; *(for no reason)* sans raison; *(hum)* **I'm not Scottish for ~** * je ne suis pas écossais pour rien; **it's ~** ce n'est rien; **that is ~ to you** *(easy for you)* pour vous ce n'est rien; *(not your business)* cela ne vous regarde pas; **she means ~ to him** elle n'est rien pour lui; **it's ~ to me whether he comes or not** il m'est indifférent qu'il vienne ou non; **she is ~ to** *or* **~ compared with her sister** elle ne vaut pas sa sœur; **I can make ~ of it** je n'y comprends rien; **to have ~ on** *(be naked)* être nu; **I have ~ on for this evening** je n'ai rien de prévu ce soir; **there's ~ in it** *(not interesting)* c'est sans intérêt; *(not true)* ce n'est absolument pas vrai; *(almost the same)* c'est du pareil au même *; **there's ~ in it for us** nous n'avons rien à y gagner; **there's ~ to it** * c'est facile comme tout *; **there's ~ like exercise for keeping one fit** il n'y a rien de tel que l'exercice pour garder la forme; **to come to ~** ne rien donner; **~ much** pas grand-chose; **~ but** rien que; **he does ~ but eat** il ne fait que manger; **I get ~ but complaints** je n'entends que des plaintes; **there's ~ for it but to go** il ne nous reste qu'à partir; **~ less than** rien moins que; **~ more** rien de plus; **~ else** *(no other thing)* rien d'autre; *(nothing further)* rien de plus; **there's ~ else for it** c'est inévitable; **that has ~ to do with us** nous n'avons rien à voir là-dedans; **I've got ~ to do with it** je n'y suis pour rien; **have ~ to do with it!** ne vous en mêlez pas!; **that has ~ to do with it** cela n'a rien à voir; **there is ~ to laugh at** il n'y a pas de quoi rire; **I have ~ against him** je n'ai rien contre lui; **there was ~ doing * at the club** il ne se passait rien d'intéressant au club; **~ doing!** * pas question!; **it's a**

mere ~ compared with ça n'est rien en comparaison de; **he's just a ~** c'est une nullité.
2 *adv* nullement, pas du tout. **it was ~ like as big as** c'était loin d'être aussi grand que.
◆ **nothingness** *n* néant *m*.

notice ['nəʊtɪs] **1** *n* (**a**) *(warning)* avis *m*, notification *f*; *(period)* délai *m*. **advance** *or* **previous ~** préavis *m*; **a week's ~** une semaine de préavis; **to give ~ to** *(to tenant)* donner congé à; *(to landlord etc)* donner un préavis de départ à; **to give sb ~** *(Admin etc: inform)* aviser qn (*to do* de faire; *that* que); *(sack) (employee)* licencier qn *(servant etc)* congédier qn; **to give ~** *[professional or office worker]* donner sa démission; *[servant]* donner ses huit jours; **to give ~ of sth** annoncer qch; **to give sb ~ of sth** prévenir qn de qch; **give me a week's ~ if you want to do...** prévenez-moi une semaine à l'avance si vous voulez faire...; **until further ~** jusqu'à nouvel ordre; **at very short ~** *leave* dans les plus brefs délais; *inform* très peu de temps à l'avance; **at a moment's ~** sur-le-champ; **at 3 days' ~** dans un délai de 3 jours.
(**b**) *(announcement)* avis *m*, annonce *f*; *(poster)* affiche *f*; *(sign)* pancarte *f*. **public ~** avis au public; **to put a ~ in the paper** mettre une annonce *or* un entrefilet dans le journal; *(Press)* **death** *etc* **~** annonce de décès *etc*.
(**c**) *(review: play)* compte rendu *m*, critique *f*.
(**d**) **to take ~ of sb/sth** tenir compte de qn/qch, faire attention à qn/qch; **to take no ~ of sb/sth** ne tenir aucun compte de qn/qch, ne pas faire attention à qn/qch; **take no ~!** ne faites pas attention!; **it has attracted a lot of ~** cela a suscité un grand intérêt; **it escaped his ~ that...** il n'a pas remarqué que...; **to avoid ~** passer inaperçu; **it came to his ~ that...** il s'est aperçu que...; **it has been brought to my ~ that...** il a été porté à ma connaissance que...; **beneath my ~** indigne de mon attention.
2 *vt (perceive)* remarquer, s'apercevoir de; *(heed)* faire attention à. **I ~d a tear in his coat** j'ai remarqué un accroc dans son manteau; **when he ~d me** quand il s'est aperçu que j'étais là; **I'm afraid I didn't ~** malheureusement je n'ai pas remarqué; **I ~ you have a new dress** je vois que vous avez une nouvelle robe.
3 *adj*: **~ board** panneau *m* d'affichage.
◆ **noticeable** *adj (perceptible)* perceptible; *(obvious)* évident, net; **it isn't really ~able** ça ne se voit pas vraiment. ◆ **noticeably** *adv* perceptiblement; nettement.

notify ['nəʊtɪfaɪ] *vt*: **to ~ sth to sb** signaler *or* notifier qch à qn; **to ~ sb of sth** aviser qn de qch. ◆ **notification** *n* annonce *f*, notification *f*; *(announcement)* annonce; *(to authorities)* déclaration *f*.

notion ['nəʊʃ(ə)n] *n* (**a**) idée *f*. **he somehow got hold of the ~ that she...** il s'est mis en tête l'idée qu'elle...; **according to his ~** selon sa façon de penser; **if that's your ~ of fun...** si c'est ça que tu appelles t'amuser...; **I've got some ~ of physics** j'ai quelques notions de physique; **to have no ~ of time** ne pas avoir la notion du temps; **I haven't the least** *or* **slightest** *or* **foggiest * ~** je n'en ai pas la moindre idée; **I have a ~ that** j'ai dans l'idée que; **I had no ~ that** j'ignorais absolument que; **can you give me a rough ~ of how many?** pouvez-vous m'indiquer en gros combien? (**b**) *(US: ribbons etc)* **~s** mercerie *f (articles)*.

notorious [nə(ʊ)'tɔːrɪəs] *adj event, act* d'une triste notoriété; *crime* notoire, célèbre; *person, case* tristement célèbre; *liar, thief, criminal* notoire; *place* mal famé. **~ for his dishonesty** d'une malhonnêteté notoire; **it is ~ that...** il est de notoriété publique que... ◆ **notoriety** *n* notoriété *f*. ◆ **notoriously** *adv* notoirement.

notwithstanding [,nɒtwɪθ'stændɪŋ] **1** *prep* malgré, en dépit de. **2** *adv* néanmoins, malgré tout. **3** *conj*: **~ that** quoique + *subj*, bien que + *subj*.

nought [nɔːt] *n* = **naught.**

noun [naʊn] *n* nom *m*, substantif *m*.

nourish ['nʌrɪʃ] *vt* nourrir (*with* de). ◆ **nourishing** *adj* nourrissant. ◆ **nourishment** *n* nourriture *f*, aliments *mpl*; **to take ~ment** s'alimenter.

Nova Scotia ['nəʊvə'skəʊʃə] *n* Nouvelle-Écosse *f*.

novel ['nɒv(ə)l] **1** *n (Literat)* roman *m*. **2** *adj* nouveau *(after n)*, original. ◆ **novelette** *n* nouvelle *f*; *(love story)* roman *m* à l'eau de rose. ◆ **novelist** *n* romancier *m*, -ière *f*. ◆ **novelty** *n* nouveauté *f*; *(idea, thing)* innovation *f*; *(Comm)* article *m* de nouveauté.

November [nə(ʊ)'vembəʳ] *n* novembre *m*; *for phrases V* **September.**

novice ['nɒvɪs] *n* novice *mf* (*at* en).

now [naʊ] **1** *adv* (**a**) *(gen)* maintenant; *(these days)* actuellement, en ce moment; *(at that time)* alors. **right ~** en ce moment, à l'instant même; **~ is the time to do it** c'est le moment de le faire; **~ is the best time to go** c'est maintenant le meilleur moment pour y aller; **I saw him come in just ~** je l'ai vu arriver à l'instant; **they won't be long ~** ils ne vont plus tarder; **here and ~** sur-le-champ; **~ and again, (every) ~ and then** de temps en temps, par moments; **it's ~ or never!** c'est le moment ou jamais!
(**b**) *(with prep)* **you should have done that before ~** vous auriez dû l'avoir déjà fait; **long before ~** il y a longtemps déjà; **between ~ and next Tuesday** d'ici (à) mardi prochain; **they should have arrived by ~** ils devraient être déjà arrivés; **haven't you finished by ~?** vous n'avez toujours pas fini?; **that will do for ~** ça ira pour le moment; **from ~ on(wards)** à partir de maintenant; **in 3 weeks from ~** d'ici (à) 3 semaines; **from ~ until then** d'ici là; **until ~, up to ~** jusqu'à présent; **~ here, ~ there** tantôt par ici, tantôt par là; **~ (then)!** bon!, alors!; *(remonstrating)* allons!; **well, ~!** eh bien!; **~, they had been looking for him** or, ils l'avaient cherché.
2 *conj*: **~ (that)** maintenant que, à présent que.
◆ **nowadays** *adv* aujourd'hui, actuellement.

nowt [naʊt] *n (Brit dial)* = **nothing.**

noxious ['nɒkʃəs] *adj* nocif.

nozzle ['nɒzl] *n [hose, flamethrower]* ajutage *m*; *[syringe]* canule *f*; *[bellows]* bec *m*; *[vacuum cleaner]* suceur *m*; *(for icing)* douille *f*.

nuclear ['njuːklɪəʳ] *adj (gen)* nucléaire. **~ physicist** physicien(ne) *m(f)* atomiste; **~ physics** physique *f* nucléaire; **~ powers** puissances *fpl* nucléaires; **~ processing plant** usine *f* de retraitement des déchets nucléaires; **~ scientist** (savant *m*) atomiste *m*. ◆ **nuclear-powered** *adj* nucléaire.

nucleus, *pl* **-ei** ['njuːklɪəs, aɪ] *n (Astron, Phys)* noyau *m*; *(Bio)* nucléus *m*; *(fig)* éléments *mpl* de base.

nude [njuːd] **1** *adj* nu. **2** *n (Art)* nu *m*. **in the ~** nu. ◆ **nudism** *n* nudisme *m*. ◆ **nudist** *adj, n* nudiste *(mf)*; **nudist camp** camp *m* de nudistes. ◆ **nudity** *n* nudité *f*.

nudge [nʌdʒ] **1** *vt* pousser du coude. **2** *n* coup *m* de coude.

nugget ['nʌgɪt] *n* pépite *f*.

nuisance ['njuːsns] *n (thing, event)* ennui *m*, embêtement * *m*; *(person)* peste *f*, fléau *m*. **it's a ~** c'est ennuyeux *or* embêtant * (*that* que + *subj; doing* de devoir faire); **it/he is a ~** ça/il m'embête *; **what a ~!** quelle barbe! *; **you're being a ~** tu nous embêtes *; **to make a ~ of o.s.** embêter le monde *; **a public ~ *** une calamité publique *.

nuke * [nju:k] *vt (attack) city* lancer une bombe atomique sur; *enemy* lancer une attaque nucléaire contre; *(destroy)* détruire à l'arme atomique.

null [nʌl] *adj (Jur)* ~ **and void** nul et non avenu. ◆ **nullify** *vt* infirmer, invalider. ◆ **nullity** *n* nullité *f*.

numb [nʌm] *adj* engourdi (*with* par); *(fig)* paralysé (*with fright etc* par la peur *etc*). ◆ **numbness** *n* engourdissement *m*. ◆ **numbskull** *n* imbécile *mf*.

number ['nʌmbəʳ] **1** *n* (**a**) *(gen)* nombre *m; (actual figure: when written etc)* chiffre *m; (gen, Gram etc)* nombre. **even/odd** ~ nombre pair/impair; **in round ~s** en chiffres ronds. (**b**) *(quantity, amount)* nombre *m*, quantité *f*. **a ~ of people** un certain nombre de gens, plusieurs personnes; **a large ~ of** *people, mistakes, cases* un grand nombre de; *things* une grande quantité de; **on a ~ of occasions** à plusieurs occasions; **a fair** ~ un assez grand nombre; **in equal ~s** en nombre égal; **~s being equal** à nombre égal; **10 in** ~ au nombre de 10; **in small/large ~s** en petit/grand nombre; **times without** ~ à maintes reprises; **any ~ can play** le nombre de joueurs est illimité; **the power of ~s** le pouvoir du nombre; **by force of ~s, by sheer ~s** par la force du nombre; **one of their** ~ un d'entre eux. (**c**) *[house, page etc]* numéro *m*. *(Telec)* **wrong** ~ faux numéro; **at ~ 4** au (numéro) 4; **reference** ~ numéro de référence; *(Aut, Mil)* **registration** ~ numéro d'immatriculation; *(fig)* **I've got his ~!** * je le connais, lui!; **his ~'s up** * il est fichu *; **the ~ one player** le meilleur joueur; **he's the ~ one there** c'est lui qui dirige tout là-dedans; **he's my ~ two** * il est mon second. (**d**) *[goods, clothes, car]* modèle *m*; *[newspaper]* numéro *m*. **the January** ~ le numéro de janvier. (**e**) *[music hall, circus]* numéro *m*; *[pianist, dance band]* morceau *m*; *[singer]* chanson *f*; *[dancer]* danse *f*.
2 *adj*: *(Aut)* ~ **plate** plaque *f* d'immatriculation *or* minéralogique.
3 *vt* (**a**) *(give a number to)* numéroter. **they are not ~ed** ils n'ont pas de numéro; *(fig)* **his days were ~ed** ses jours étaient comptés. (**b**) *(include, amount to)* compter (*among* parmi).
4 *vi* (~ **off**) se numéroter (*from* en partant de).
◆ **numbering** *n [houses etc]* numérotage *m*.
◆ **numberless** *adj* innombrable, sans nombre.

numeral ['nju:m(ə)r(ə)l] *n* chiffre *m*, nombre *m*.

numerate ['nju:m(ə)rɪt] *adj*: **to be** ~ savoir compter. ◆ **numeracy** *n* notions *fpl* de calcul.

numerical [nju:'merɪk(ə)l] *adj* numérique. **in ~ order** dans l'ordre numérique. ◆ **numerically** *adv* numériquement.

numerous ['nju:m(ə)rəs] *adj* nombreux.

numismatics [ˌnju:mɪz'mætɪks] *nsg* numismatique *f*. ◆ **numismatist** *n* numismate *mf*.

nun [nʌn] *n* religieuse *f*, bonne sœur * *f*.

nuptial ['nʌpʃ(ə)l] *adj* nuptial.

nurse [nɜ:s] **1** *n* (**a**) infirmière *f*. *(US)* **~'s aide** aide-soignant(e) *m(f)*. (**b**) *(children's ~)* nurse *f*, bonne *f* d'enfants. **2** *vt (Med)* soigner; *(suckle)* allaiter; *(cradle in arms)* bercer (dans ses bras); *hope, wrath* nourrir; *horse, car engine* ménager. **she ~d him back to health** il a guéri grâce à ses soins; **to ~ a constituency** soigner les électeurs. ◆ **nursemaid** *n* bonne *f* d'enfants. ◆ **nursing 1** *adj* (**a**) *mother* qui allaite; (**b**) *[hospital]* **the nursing staff** le personnel soignant *or* infirmier; **nursing auxiliary** aide *f* soignante; **nursing home** clinique *f*; **nursing studies** études *fpl* d'infirmière; **2** *n (care of invalids)* soins *mpl*; *(profession of nurse)* profession *f* d'infirmière; **she's going in for nursing** elle va être infirmière.

nursery ['nɜ:s(ə)rɪ] **1** *n (room)* nursery *f*, chambre *f* d'enfants; *(institution)* pouponnière *f*; *(Agr)* pépinière *f*. **2** *adj*: ~ **education** enseignement *m* de la maternelle; ~ **nurse** puéricultrice *f*; ~ **rhyme** comptine *f*; ~ **school** *(state-run)* école *f* maternelle; *(private)* jardin *m* d'enfants; *(Ski)* ~ **slopes** pentes *fpl* pour débutants. ◆ **nurseryman** *n* pépiniériste *m*.

nut [nʌt] **1** *n* (**a**) *(Bot) terme générique pour fruits à écale (no generic term in French)*. **a bag of mixed ~s** un sachet de noisettes, cacahuètes, amandes *etc* panachées; **~s and raisins** mendiants *mpl*; *(fig)* **he's a tough** ~ c'est un dur à cuire *; **a hard ~ to crack** *(problem)* un problème difficile à résoudre; **he can't paint for ~s** ‡ il peint comme un pied ‡. (**b**) *(Tech)* écrou *m*. *(fig)* **the ~s and bolts of...** les détails *mpl* pratiques de... (**c**) (‡: *mad person, also* **nutcase** ‡) fou *m*, folle *f*, cinglé(e) * *m(f)*. **2** *excl*: **~s!** * des clous! ‡ **3** *adj chocolate* aux amandes (*or* noisettes *etc*); *cutlet* à base de cacahuètes (*or* noisettes *etc*) hachées. ◆ **nutcracker(s)** *npl* casse-noix *m inv*, casse-noisettes *m inv*. ◆ **nuthouse** ‡ *n* maison *f* de fous. ◆ **nutmeg** *n (nut)* (noix *f*) muscade *f*; *(tree)* muscadier *m*. ◆ **nuts** ‡ *adj* dingue ‡, fou (*about* de); **to go ~s** * perdre la boule ‡. ◆ **nutshell** *n* coquille *f* de noix *or* noisette *etc*; *(fig)* **(to put) in a ~shell** (résumer) en un mot. ◆ **nutty** *adj* (**a**) *chocolate etc* aux noisettes *(etc)*; *flavour* au goût de noisette *etc*; (**b**) (‡: *mad*) = **nuts**.

nutrient ['nju:trɪənt] **1** *adj* nutritif. **2** *n* élément *m* nutritif. ◆ **nutrition** *n* nutrition *f*, alimentation *f*. ◆ **nutritional** *adj* alimentaire. ◆ **nutritionist** *n* nutritionniste *mf*. ◆ **nutritious** *or* ◆ **nutritive** *adj* nutritif.

nuzzle ['nʌzl] *vi*: **to ~ up/into** fourrer son nez contre/dans.

nylon ['naɪlɒn] **1** *n* nylon *m*. **2** *adj* de *or* en nylon. ~ **stockings, ~s** bas *mpl* nylon.

nymph [nɪmf] *n* nymphe *f*.

nymphomania [ˌnɪmfə(ʊ)'meɪnɪə] *n* nymphomanie *f*. ◆ **nymphomaniac** *adj, n* nymphomane *(f)*.

O, o [əʊ] *n (letter)* O, o *m*; *(number: Telec etc)* zéro *m*.

oaf [əʊf] *n (awkward)* balourd(e) * *m(f)*; *(badmannered)* mufle *m*. ◆ **oafish** *adj person* mufle; *behaviour* de mufle.

oak [əʊk] **1** *n* chêne *m*. **2** *adj (made of ~)* de *or* en chêne. ~ **apple** galle *f* du chêne. ◆ **oakwood** *n (forest)* bois *m* de chênes.

oakum ['əʊkəm] *n* étoupe *f*.

oar [ɔːʳ] *n* aviron *m*, rame *f*. *(fig)* **he always puts his ~ in** il faut toujours qu'il y mette son grain de sel. ◆ **oarlock** *n* tolet *m*. ◆ **oarsman** *n* rameur *m*; *(Naut, also Sport)* nageur *m*.

oasis, *pl* **oases** [əʊ'eɪsɪs, əʊ'eɪsiːz] *n* oasis *f*.

oat [əʊt] **1** *n*: ~**s** avoine *f*. ◆ **oatcake** *n* biscuit *m* d'avoine. ◆ **oatmeal** **1** *n (cereal)* flocons *mpl* d'avoine; *(US: porridge)* bouillie *f* d'avoine ; **2** *adj (colour)* beige.

oath [əʊθ] *n* (**a**) *(Jur etc)* serment *m*. **to take the ~** prêter serment; **to swear an ~** *or* **on one's ~** jurer (*to do* de faire; *that* que); **on** *or* **under ~** sous serment; *witness* assermenté; **to put sb on ~** faire prêter serment à qn; **to put sb on** *or* **under ~ to do sth** faire promettre à qn sous serment de faire qch; **on my ~!** je vous le jure! (**b**) *(bad language)* juron *m*.

obdurate ['ɒbdjʊrɪt] *adj (stubborn)* obstiné; *(unyielding)* inflexible; *(unrepentant)* impénitent. ◆ **obduracy** *n* obstination *f*; inflexibilité *f*; impénitence.

obedient [ə'biːdɪənt] *adj* obéissant (*to sb* envers qn; *to sth* à qch). ◆ **obedience** *n* obéissance *f* (*to* à); *(Rel)* obédience *f* (*to* à); **in obedience to sth** conformément à qch. ◆ **obediently** *adv* docilement; *smile* d'un air soumis.

obelisk ['ɒbɪlɪsk] *n* obélisque *m*.

obese [ə(ʊ)'biːs] *adj* obèse. ◆ **obesity** *n* obésité *f*.

obey [ə'beɪ] **1** *vt (gen)* obéir à; *instructions* se conformer à. **the machine ~s the controls** la machine répond aux commandes. **2** *vi* obéir.

obituary [ə'bɪtjʊərɪ] *n*: ~ **(notice)** nécrologie *f*; ~ **column** nécrologie *(rubrique)*.

object ['ɒbdʒɪkt] **1** *n* (**a**) *(gen)* objet *m*. *(pej)* **what an ~ she looks!** * de quoi est-ce qu'elle a l'air! * (**b**) *(Gram)* complément *m* (d'objet). (**c**) *(aim)* but *m*, objectif *m*. **with this ~ in view** *or* **in mind** dans ce but, à cette fin; **with the ~ of doing** dans le but de faire; **what ~ is there in doing that?** à quoi bon faire cela?; **'distance no ~'** 'toutes distances'. **2** *adj*: *(fig)* ~ **lesson** démonstration *f* (*in* de).
3 [əb'dʒekt] *vi* élever une objection (*to* contre), trouver à redire. **I ~!** je proteste! (*to* contre); **if you don't ~** si vous n'y voyez pas d'objection; **he didn't ~ when...** il n'a élevé aucune objection quand...; **he ~s to her behaviour/her drinking** il désapprouve sa conduite/qu'elle boive; **do you ~ to my smoking?** est-ce que cela vous gêne si je fume?; **I don't ~ to helping you** je veux bien vous aider; **to ~ to sb** soulever des objections contre qn; **I wouldn't ~ to a bite to eat** * je mangerais bien un morceau.
4 [əb'dʒekt] *vt* objecter (*that* que).
◆ **objection** *n* objection *f*; *(drawback)* inconvénient *m*, obstacle *m*; **to have an ~ion to = to object to** *(V* **3** *above)*; **to make** *or* **raise an ~ion** soulever *or* élever une objection (*to* contre). ◆ **objectionable** *adj person, behaviour, smell* extrêmement désagréable; *remark, language* choquant. ◆ **objective** **1** *adj* (**a**) *(impartial)* objectif (*about* en ce qui concerne); (**b**) *(Gram) case* accusatif; *pronoun* complément d'objet ; **2** *n* objectif *m*; *(Gram)* accusatif *m*. ◆ **objectively** *adv* objectivement. ◆ **objectivity** *n* objectivité *f*. ◆ **objector** *n*: **the ~ors to...** ceux qui s'opposent à...

obligation [ˌɒblɪ'geɪʃ(ə)n] *n* obligation *f*. **to be/put sb under an ~ to do** être/mettre qn dans l'obligation de faire; **I'm under no ~ to do it** rien ne m'oblige à le faire; **'without ~'** 'sans engagement'; **to meet/fail to meet one's ~s** satisfaire à/manquer à ses obligations; **to be under an ~ to sb for sth** devoir de la reconnaissance à qn pour qch. ◆ **obligatory** [ɒ'blɪgət(ə)rɪ] *adj* obligatoire ; *(imposed by custom)* de rigueur; **to make it obligatory for sb to do** imposer à qn l'obligation de faire.

oblige [ə'blaɪdʒ] *vt* (**a**) *(compel)* obliger (*sb to do* qn à faire). **to be ~d to do** être obligé de faire, devoir faire. (**b**) *(do a favour to)* rendre service à, obliger. **anything to ~!** * toujours prêt à rendre service!; **to be ~d to sb for sth** être reconnaissant à qn de qch; **I am much ~d to you** je vous remercie infiniment. ◆ **obliging** *adj* obligeant; **it is very obliging of them** c'est très aimable de leur part. ◆ **obligingly** *adv* obligeamment, aimablement; **the books which you obligingly gave me** les livres que vous avez eu l'obligeance *or* l'amabilité de me donner.

oblique [ə'bliːk] **1** *adj (gen)* oblique; *allusion, route, method* indirect. **2** *n (Typ)* oblique *f*. ◆ **obliquely** *adv* obliquement; *(fig)* indirectement.

obliterate [ə'blɪtəreɪt] *vt (gen)* effacer; *stamp* oblitérer. ◆ **obliteration** *n* effacement *m*; oblitération *f*.

oblivion [ə'blɪvɪən] *n* oubli *m*. ◆ **oblivious** *adj (forgetful)* oublieux (*to, of* de); *(unaware)* inconscient (*to, of* de).

oblong ['ɒblɒŋ] **1** *adj* oblong. ~ **dish** plat *m* rectangulaire. **2** *n* rectangle *m*.

obnoxious [əb'nɒkʃəs] *adj person, behaviour* odieux; *smell* infect.

oboe ['əʊbəʊ] *n* hautbois *m*.

obscene [əb'siːn] *adj* obscène. ◆ **obscenely** *adv* d'une manière obscène. ◆ **obscenity** *n* obscénité *f*.

obscure [əb'skjʊəʳ] **1** *adj (gen)* obscur; *feeling, memory* vague. **2** *vt (darken)* obscurcir; *(hide) sun, view* cacher; *argument, idea* embrouiller. **to ~ the issue** embrouiller la question. ◆ **obscurely** *adv* obscurément. ◆ **obscurity** *n* obscurité *f*.

obsequies ['ɒbsɪkwɪz] *npl* obsèques *fpl*.

obsequious [əb'siːkwɪəs] *adj* obséquieux (*to* devant). ◆ **obsequiously** *adv* obséquieusement.

observance [əb'zɜːv(ə)ns] *n* (**a**) *(act of observing) [rule]* observation *f*; *[rite, custom, Sabbath]* observance *f*. (**b**) *(custom etc)* observance *f*. **religious ~s** observances religieuses. ◆ **observant** *adj* observateur.

observation [ˌɒbzəˈveɪʃ(ə)n] **1** *n* (**a**) *(gen, Med)* observation *f*; *(Police, Mil etc)* surveillance *f*. **to keep under ~** *patient* garder en observation; *suspect, place* surveiller; **powers of ~** facultés *fpl* d'observation. (**b**) *(remark)* observation *f*, remarque *f*. **2** *adj balloon, post* d'observation. *(US Rail)* **~ car** voiture *f* panoramique; **~ tower** mirador *m*. ◆ **observatory** *n* observatoire *m*.

observe [əbˈzɜːv] *vt* (**a**) *(obey, note, study)* observer; *anniversary* célébrer. (**b**) *(remark)* faire remarquer, faire observer (*that* que). ◆ **observer** *n (gen)* observateur *m*, -trice *f*; *(analyst)* spécialiste *mf*.

obsess [əbˈses] *vt* obséder, hanter. ◆ **obsession** *n (gen)* obsession *f* (*with* de); *(of sth unpleasant)* hantise *f* (*with* de); **sport is an ~ion with him** le sport c'est son idée fixe, le sport tient de l'obsession chez lui; **his ~ion with her** la manière dont elle l'obsède; **his ~ion with death** son obsession *or* sa hantise de la mort. ◆ **obsessive** *adj* obsessionnel. ◆ **obsessively** *adv* d'une manière obsédante; *(Psych)* obsessionnellement.

obsolete [ˈɒbsəliːt] *adj attitude, idea, process* dépassé, démodé; *passport, ticket* périmé; *goods, machine* vieux; *law* caduc; *word* obsolète, vieilli; *(Bio)* atrophié. **to become ~** tomber en désuétude. ◆ **obsolescence** *n [goods, words]* vieillissement *m*; *[machinery]* obsolescence *f*; **planned** *or* **built-in obsolescence** obsolescence calculée. ◆ **obsolescent** *adj machinery* obsolescent; *word* vieilli; *goods* vieux.

obstacle [ˈɒbstəkl] **1** *n* obstacle *m*. **to be an ~ to, to put an ~ in the way of** faire obstacle à. **2** *adj race* d'obstacles; *(Mil)* **~ course** parcours *m* du combattant.

obstetrics [ɒbˈstetrɪks] *nsg* obstétrique *f*. ◆ **obstetric(al)** *adj techniques etc* obstétrical; *clinic* obstétrique. ◆ **obstetrician** *n* médecin *m* accoucheur.

obstinate [ˈɒbstɪnɪt] *adj (gen)* obstiné (*in doing* à faire; *about* sur); *pain, illness* persistant; *fever* rebelle. **as ~ as a mule** têtu comme une mule. ◆ **obstinacy** *n* obstination *f* (*in doing* à faire). ◆ **obstinately** *adv* obstinément; **he tried ~ly to do it** il s'est obstiné à le faire.

obstreperous [əbˈstrep(ə)rəs] *adj (noisy)* tapageur; *(unruly)* chahuteur; *(rebellious)* rouspéteur *. ◆ **obstreperously** *adv* tapageusement; en rouspétant *.

obstruct [əbˈstrʌkt] *vt (block) road* encombrer (*with* de), boucher (*with* avec); *pipe, view* boucher (*with* avec, *by* par); *artery* obstruer; *traffic* bloquer; *(hinder)* entraver; *(Sport)* faire obstruction à. ◆ **obstruction** *n (sth which obstructs)* obstacle *m*; *(to pipe)* bouchon *m*; *(to artery)* caillot *m*; *(Sport)* obstruction *f*; *(in road etc)* **to cause an ~ion** *(gen)* encombrer la voie publique; *(Aut)* bloquer la circulation. ◆ **obstructionist** *adj* obstructionniste. ◆ **obstructive** *adj* obstructionniste; **you're being ~ive** vous ne pensez qu'à mettre des bâtons dans les roues.

obtain [əbˈteɪn] *vt (gen)* obtenir; *goods* se procurer; *(for sb else)* procurer (*for sb* à qn). *(Comm)* **it may be ~ed from...** on peut se le procurer chez... ◆ **obtainable** *adj*: **where is that ~able?** où peut-on se le procurer?

obtrude [əbˈtruːd] **1** *vt* imposer (*on* à). **2** *vi* s'imposer. ◆ **obtrusion** *n* intrusion *f*. ◆ **obtrusive** *adj person* importun; *opinions* ostentatoire; *smell* pénétrant; *building etc* trop en évidence. ◆ **obtrusively** *adv* importunément.

obtuse [əbˈtjuːs] *adj* obtus. ◆ **obtuseness** *n* stupidité *f*.

obverse [ˈɒbvɜːs] *n [coin]* face *f*; *[statement]* contrepartie *f*.

obviate [ˈɒbvɪeɪt] *vt* obvier à.

obvious [ˈɒbvɪəs] *adj* évident, manifeste. **it's ~ that** il est évident *or* manifeste que, il est de toute évidence que; **the ~ thing to do is to leave** la chose à faire c'est évidemment de partir; **that's the ~ one** c'est bien évidemment celui-là; **~ statement** truisme *m*; **we must not be too ~ about it** il va falloir ne pas trop montrer notre jeu. ◆ **obviously** *adv (of course)* évidemment; *(clearly)* manifestement; **he was ~ly not drunk** il était évident qu'il n'était pas ivre; **he was not ~ly drunk** il n'était pas visiblement ivre; **~ly!** bien sûr!, évidemment!

occasion [əˈkeɪʒ(ə)n] **1** *n* (**a**) occasion *f*, circonstance *f*. **on the ~ of** à l'occasion de; **on the first ~ that...** la première fois que...; **on that ~** à cette occasion, cette fois-là; **on several ~s** à plusieurs occasions; **on rare ~s** en de rares occasions; **on great ~s** dans les grandes occasions; **on ~** à l'occasion; **should the ~ arise** le cas échéant; **this would be a good ~ to try it out** c'est l'occasion tout indiquée pour l'essayer; **to rise to the ~** se montrer à la hauteur de la situation; **there was no ~ for it** ce n'était pas nécessaire; **you had no ~ to say that** vous n'aviez aucune raison de dire cela; **I had ~ to say** j'ai eu l'occasion de dire. (**b**) *(event)* événement *m*. **a big ~** un grand événement; **it was quite an ~** cela n'a pas été un petit événement.
2 *vt* occasionner, causer.
◆ **occasional** *adj event* qui a lieu de temps en temps; *visits* espacés; *rain, showers* intermittent; **we have an ~al visitor** il nous arrive d'avoir qn de temps en temps; **they had passed an ~al car** ils avaient croisé quelques rares voitures; **~al table** guéridon *m*. ◆ **occasionally** *adv* de temps en temps, quelquefois; **very ~ally** très peu souvent.

occident [ˈɒksɪd(ə)nt] *n (liter)* occident *m*. ◆ **occidental** *adj* occidental.

occult [ɒˈkʌlt] **1** *adj* occulte. **2** *n* surnaturel *m*.

occupant [ˈɒkjʊpənt] *n (gen)* occupant(e) *m(f)*; *(tenant)* locataire *mf*; *[job, post]* titulaire *mf*.

occupation [ˌɒkjʊˈpeɪʃ(ə)n] **1** *n* (**a**) *(gen, Mil)* occupation *f*. **house ready for ~** maison prête à être habitée; **in ~** installé; **army of ~** armée *f* d'occupation; **under military ~** sous occupation militaire. (**b**) *(trade)* métier *m*; *(profession)* profession *f*; *(work)* emploi *m*, travail *m*; *(activity, pastime)* occupation *f*. **he is a plumber by ~** il est plombier de son métier. **2** *adj troops* d'occupation. ◆ **occupational** *adj disease* du travail; *hazard* du métier; **~al therapist** ergothérapeute *mf*; **~al therapy** ergothérapie *f*.

occupy [ˈɒkjʊpaɪ] *vt* occuper. **occupied in** *or* **with doing** occupé à faire; **to ~ o.s.** *or* **one's time** s'occuper (*with or by doing* à faire); **to keep one's mind occupied** s'occuper l'esprit. ◆ **occupier** *n (gen)* occupant(e) *m(f)*; *(tenant)* locataire *mf*.

occur [əˈkɜːʳ] *vi* (**a**) *[event]* avoir lieu, arriver; *[word, error, plant, disease]* se rencontrer, se trouver; *[difficulty, opportunity]* se présenter; *[change]* s'opérer. **don't let it ~ again!** que cela ne se reproduise plus!; **if a vacancy ~s** en cas de poste vacant; **should the case ~** le cas échéant. (**b**) **it ~s to me that...** il me vient à l'esprit que...; **it didn't ~ to him to refuse** il n'a pas eu l'idée de refuser; **an idea ~red to me** une idée m'est venue; **it ~red to me that we could...** j'ai pensé *or* je me suis dit que nous pourrions... ◆ **occurrence** *n* événement *m*; **an everyday ~rence** un fait journalier; **this is a common ~rence** ceci arrive souvent.

ocean [ˈəʊʃ(ə)n] **1** *n* océan *m*. **~s of** * énormément de. **2** *adj climate, region* océanique; *cruise* sur l'océan. **~ bed** fond *m* sous-marin. ◆ **ocean-going** *adj* de haute mer. ◆ **oceanic** [ˌəʊʃɪˈænɪk] *adj* océanique. ◆ **oceanography** *n* océanographie *f*.

ocelot ['əʊsɪlɒt] *n* ocelot *m.*

ochre, *(US)* **ocher** ['əʊkəʳ] *n* ocre *f.*

o'clock [ə'klɒk] *adv*: **it is one** ~ il est une heure; **what** ~ **is it?** quelle heure est-il?; **at 5** ~ à 5 heures; **at twelve** ~ *(midday)* à midi; *(midnight)* à minuit.

octagon ['ɒktəgən] *n* octogone *m.* ◆ **octagonal** *adj* octogonal.

octane ['ɒkteɪn] *n* octane *m.* **high-**~ **petrol** carburant *m* à indice d'octane élevé.

octave ['ɒktɪv] *n (Mus, Rel)* octave *f*; *(Poetry)* huitain *m.*

octavo [ɒk'teɪvəʊ] *n* in-octavo *m.*

octet [ɒk'tet] *n* octuor *m.*

October [ɒk'təʊbəʳ] *n* octobre *m*; *for phrases V* **September.**

octogenarian [,ɒktəʊdʒɪ'nɛərɪən] *adj, n* octogénaire *(mf).*

octopus ['ɒktəpəs] *n* pieuvre *f.*

oculist ['ɒkjʊlɪst] *n* oculiste *mf.*

odd [ɒd] *adj* (**a**) *(strange)* bizarre, étrange, curieux. **how** ~ **that...** comme c'est curieux que + *subj;* **what an** ~ **thing for him to do!** c'est curieux *or* bizarre qu'il ait fait cela!; **he says some very** ~ **things** il dit de drôles de choses. (**b**) *(Math) number* impair. (**c**) *(extra, left over)* qui reste(nt); *(from pair) shoe, sock* dépareillé; *(from set)* dépareillé. **£5 and some** ~ **pennies** 5 livres et quelques pennies; **a few** ~ **hats** deux ou trois chapeaux; **to be the** ~ **one over** être en surnombre; **the** ~ **man out, the** ~ **one out** l'exception *f*; **60-**~ 60 et quelques. (**d**) *(occasional)* **in** ~ **moments he...** à ses moments perdus il...; **at** ~ **times** de temps en temps; **any** ~ **piece of wood** un morceau de bois quelconque; ~ **jobs** menus travaux *mpl*; **to do** ~ **jobs about the house** *(gen)* faire de menus travaux domestiques; *(do-it-yourself)* bricoler dans la maison; **I've got one or two** ~ **jobs for you to do** j'ai deux ou trois choses à te faire faire; **he has written the** ~ **article** il a écrit un ou deux articles; **I get the** ~ **letter from him** de temps en temps je reçois une lettre de lui. ◆ **oddball** ⁑ *adj, n* excentrique *(mf).* ◆ **oddity** *n* (**a**) *(also* **oddness***)* étrangeté *f*, bizarrerie *f*; (**b**) *(person/thing etc)* personne *f*/chose *f etc* étrange *or* bizarre. ◆ **odd-job man** *n* homme *m* à tout faire. ◆ **oddly** *adv* bizarrement, curieusement; ~**ly enough she was at home** chose curieuse elle était chez elle; **she was** ~**ly attractive** elle avait un charme insolite. ◆ **oddment** *n (Comm)* fin *f* de série; *[cloth]* coupon *m.*

odds [ɒdz] **1** *npl* (**a**) *(Betting)* cote *f* (*of 5 to 1* de 5 contre 1). **short/long** ~ faible/forte cote; *(fig)* **the** ~ **are against his coming/that he will come** il y a peu de chances/de fortes chances qu'il vienne; **to fight against heavy** ~ lutter contre des forces supérieures; **he succeeded against all the** ~ il a réussi alors que tout était contre lui; **by all the** ~ d'après ce que l'on sait; **it makes no** ~ cela n'a pas d'importance, ça m'est égal; **what's the** ~**?** * qu'est-ce que ça peut bien faire? (**b**) **to be at** ~ être en désaccord (*with sb over sth* avec qn sur qch). (**c**) ~ **and ends** *(gen)* des petites choses qui restent; *[cloth]* bouts *mpl*; *[food]* restes *mpl.*

ode [əʊd] *n* ode *f* (*to* à, *on* sur).

odious ['əʊdɪəs] *adj* odieux. ◆ **odium** *n* réprobation *f* générale.

odometer [ɒ'dɒmɪtəʳ] *n (US)* odomètre *m.*

odour, *(US)* **odor** ['əʊdəʳ] *n* odeur *f. (fig)* **to be in good/bad** ~ **with sb** être bien/mal vu de qn. ◆ **odo(u)rless** *adj* inodore.

odyssey ['ɒdɪsɪ] *n* odyssée *f.*

oecology [ɪ'kɒlədʒɪ] *etc* = **ecology** *etc.*

oestrogen ['iːstrə(ʊ)dʒ(ə)n] *n* œstrogène *m.*

of [ɒv, əv] *prep* (**a**) *(gen)* de. **the wife** ~ **the doctor** la femme du médecin; **a friend** ~ **ours** un de nos amis; **that funny nose** ~ **hers** son drôle de nez; **there were 6** ~ **us** nous étions 6; **he asked the six** ~ **us to lunch** il nous a invités tous les six à déjeuner; ~ **the ten only one was...** sur les dix un seul était...; **he is not one** ~ **us** il n'est pas des nôtres; **the 2nd** ~ **June** le 2 juin; **today** ~ **all days** ce jour entre tous; *(US)* **a quarter** ~ **6** 6 heures moins le quart; **girl** ~ **10** petite fille de 10 ans; **question** ~ **no importance** question sans importance; **town** ~ **narrow streets** ville aux rues étroites; **that idiot** ~ **a doctor** cet imbécile de docteur; **it was horrid** ~ **him to say so** c'était méchant de sa part (que) de dire cela. (**b**) *(concerning)* de. **what do you think** ~ **him?** que pensez-vous de lui?; **what** ~ **it?** et alors? (**c**) *(origin, cause)* de. ~ **noble birth** de naissance noble; **to die** ~ **hunger** mourir de faim; **dress (made)** ~ **wool** robe en *or* de laine.

off [ɒf] **1** *adv* (**a**) *(distance)* **5 km** ~ à 5 km; **my holiday is a week** ~ je serai en vacances dans une semaine; *(Theat)* **voices** ~ voix *fpl* dans les coulisses. (**b**) *(departure)* **to be** ~ partir, s'en aller; ~ **you go!** va-t'en!, sauve-toi! *; *(Sport)* **they're** ~**!** et les voilà partis!; **where are you** ~ **to?** où allez-vous?; **we're** ~ **to France today** nous partons pour la France aujourd'hui; **he's** ~ **fishing** *(going)* il va à la pêche; *(gone)* il est à la pêche. (**c**) *(absence)* **to take a day** ~ prendre un jour de congé; **I've got this afternoon** ~ j'ai congé cet après-midi; (**d**) *(removal)* **he had his coat** ~ il avait enlevé son manteau; **with his hat** ~ sans chapeau; ~ **with those socks!** enlève tes chaussettes!; **the lid was** ~ on avait enlevé le couvercle; **the handle is** ~ la poignée s'est détachée; **there are 2 buttons** ~ il manque 2 boutons; **I'll give you 5%** ~ je vais vous faire une remise de 5%. (**e**) *(phrases)* ~ **and on, on and** ~ de temps à autre; **right** ~ *, **straight** ~ * tout de suite.

2 *prep* (**a**) *(gen)* de. **he fell/jumped** ~ **the wall** il est tombé/a sauté du mur; **he took the book** ~ **the table** il a pris le livre sur la table; **there are buttons** ~ **my coat** il manque des boutons à mon manteau; **the lid was** ~ **the tin** on avait ôté le couvercle de la boîte; **they eat** ~ **chipped plates** ils mangent dans des assiettes ébréchées; **they dined** ~ **a chicken** ils ont dîné d'un poulet; **a slice** ~ **the cake** une tranche du gâteau; **sth** ~ **the price** une remise (sur le prix). (**b**) *(distant from)* éloigné de. *(Naut)* ~ **Portland Bill** au large de Portland Bill; **a yard** ~ **me** à un mètre de moi; **height** ~ **the ground** hauteur *f* à partir du sol; **street (leading)** ~ **the square** rue qui part de la place; **house** ~ **the main road** maison à l'écart de la grand-route; **I'm** ~ *or* **I've gone** ~ **sausages** * je n'aime plus les saucisses.

3 *adj* (**a**) *(absence)* **he's** ~ **on Tuesdays** il n'est pas là le mardi; **she's** ~ **at 4 o'clock** elle est libre à 4 heures; **to be** ~ **sick** être absent pour cause de maladie; **he's been** ~ **for 3 weeks** cela fait 3 semaines qu'il est absent. (**b**) *(not functioning)* **to be** ~ *[brakes]* être desserré; *[machine, television, light]* être éteint; *[engine, gas at main, electricity, water]* être coupé; *[tap, gas-tap]* être fermé. (**c**) **the play is** ~ *(cancelled)* la pièce est annulée; *(no longer running)* la pièce a quitté l'affiche; **their engagement is** ~ ils ont rompu leurs fiançailles; *(in restaurant)* **the cutlets are** ~ il n'y a plus de côtelettes. (**d**) *(stale etc)* **to be** ~ *[meat]* être mauvais *or* avancé; *[milk]* être tourné; *[butter]* être rance; *(fig)* **that's a bit** ~**!** * c'est un peu exagéré! *; **he was having an** ~ **day** * il n'était pas en forme ce jour-là. (**e**) **on the** ~ **chance** à tout hasard; **on the** ~ **chance of seeing her** *or* **that I could see her** au cas où je pourrais la voir.

◆ **offbeat** *adj (fig)* excentrique, original. ◆ **off-centre** *adj* décentré; *construction* en porte-à-faux.

◆ **off-campus** *adj (US)* en dehors du campus. ◆ **off-colour** *adj person* mal fichu *; (*) *story* osé. ◆ **offhand 1** *adj (also* **offhanded***) (casual)* désinvolte, sans-gêne *inv*; *(curt)* brusque ; **2** *adv*: **I can't just say ~hand** je ne peux pas vous le dire à l'improviste *or* comme ça *. ◆ **offhandedly** *adv* avec désinvolture, avec sans-gêne; avec brusquerie. ◆ **offhandedness** *n* désinvolture *f*, sans-gêne *m*; brusquerie *f*. ◆ **offing** *n*: **in the ~ing** en perspective. ◆ **off-key** *adj, adv (Mus)* faux. ◆ **off-licence** *n (Brit)* magasin *m* de vins et de spiritueux. ◆ **off-limits** *adj (US Mil)* interdit (au personnel militaire). ◆ **off-line** *adj (Comput)* autonome. ◆ **off-load** *vt goods, passengers* débarquer; *task* passer (*onto sb* à qn). ◆ **off-peak** *adj hours* creux; *traffic* aux heures creuses; *tariff* réduit; *ticket* au tarif réduit heures creuses; *heating* par accumulation. ◆ **off-putting** * *adj task* rebutant; *food* peu ragoûtant; *person, manner, welcome* peu engageant. ◆ **off-season** *n* morte-saison *f*. ◆ **offset** *(vb: pret, ptp* **offset***)* **1** *n (Typ)* **~set printing** offset *m* ; **2** *vt* compenser. ◆ **offshoot** *n (Bot)* rejeton *m*; *[organization]* ramification *f*; *[discussion, action etc]* conséquence *f*. ◆ **offshore** *adj breeze* de terre; *island* proche du littoral; *waters, fishing* côtier; *drilling* en mer. ◆ **offside 1** *n (Aut) (in Britain)* côté *m* droit; *(in France, US etc)* côté gauche ; **2** *adj* de droite; de gauche; *(Sport)* hors jeu. ◆ **offspring** *n (pl inv)* progéniture *f*. ◆ **offstage** *adj, adv* dans les coulisses. ◆ **off-the-cuff** *adj* impromptu. ◆ **off-the-peg,** *(US)* **off-the-rack** *adj* prêt-à-porter. ◆ **off-the-record** *adj (unofficial)* sans caractère officiel; *(secret)* confidentiel. ◆ **off-the-shelf** *adj goods* immédiatement disponible. ◆ **off-the-wall** * *adj (US)* bizarre, dingue *. ◆ **off-white** *adj* blanc cassé *inv*.

offal ['ɒf(ə)l] *n* abats *mpl*.

offence, *(US)* **offense** [ə'fens] *n* (**a**) *(Jur)* délit *m* (*against* contre); *(Rel etc)* offense *f*. *(Jur etc)* **it is an ~ to do that** il est contraire à la loi de faire cela; **capital ~** crime *m* capital. (**b**) **to give ~ to sb** offenser qn; **to take ~** se vexer, s'offenser (*at* de).

offend [ə'fend] **1** *vt person* blesser, offenser; *ears, eyes, reason* choquer. **to be ~ed (at)** se vexer (de), s'offenser (de). **2** *vi*: **to ~ against** *law, rule* enfreindre; *good taste, common sense* être une insulte à.

◆ **offender** *n (lawbreaker)* délinquant(e) *m(f)*; *(against traffic regulations etc)* contrevenant(e) *m(f)*; *(Jur)* **first ~er** délinquant(e) primaire. ◆ **offending** *adj word, object* incriminé. ◆ **offensive 1** *adj* (**a**) *(shocking)* offensant, choquant; *(disgusting)* repoussant; *(insulting)* injurieux; **to be offensive to sb** insulter qn; (**b**) *tactics, weapon* offensif ; **2** *n (Mil)* offensive *f*; **to be on the offensive** avoir pris l'offensive. ◆ **offensively** *adv behave* d'une manière offensante *or* choquante; *say* d'une manière injurieuse.

offer ['ɒfəʳ] **1** *n (gen)* offre *f* (*of* de; *for* pour; *to do* de faire). **~ of marriage** demande *f* en mariage; **to make sb an ~ for sth** faire une offre à qn pour qch; *(in advertisement)* **£5 or near(est) ~** 5 livres à débattre; *(Comm)* **on ~** en promotion. **2** *vt job, gift, prayers, apology, opportunity* offrir (*to* à); *help, object, money* proposer (*to* à); *remark, opinion* émettre. **to ~ to do** offrir *or* proposer de faire. ◆ **offering** *n* offrande *f*. ◆ **offertory** *n (part of service)* offertoire *m*; *(collection)* quête *f*.

office ['ɒfɪs] **1** *n* (**a**) *(place)* bureau *m*; *[lawyer]* étude *f*; *[doctor]* cabinet *m*. **our London ~** notre bureau *or* notre section *f* de Londres; *[house etc]* **'usual ~s'** 'cuisine, sanitaires'. (**b**) *(function)* fonction *f*; *(duty)* fonctions, devoir *m*. **to be in ~, to hold ~** *[mayor, chairman]* être en fonctions; *[minister]* avoir un portefeuille; *[political party]* être au pouvoir; **public ~** fonctions officielles; **through his good ~s** par ses bons offices *mpl*; **through the ~s of** par l'entremise de. (**c**) *(Rel)* office *m*. **2** *adj staff, furniture, work* de bureau. **~ automation** bureautique *f*; *[club, society]* **~ bearer** membre *m* du comité directeur; **~ block** immeuble *m* de bureaux; **~ boy** garçon *m* de bureau; **~ hours** heures *fpl* de bureau. ◆ **office-worker** *n* employé(e) *m(f)* de bureau.

officer ['ɒfɪsəʳ] *n* (**a**) *(Aviat, Mil, Naut)* officier *m*. **~s' mess** mess *m*. (**b**) *[local government]* fonctionnaire *m*; *[organization, club]* membre *m* du comité directeur. **police ~** policier *m*.

official [ə'fɪʃ(ə)l] **1** *adj (gen)* officiel; *language, style* administratif; *uniform* réglementaire. **2** *n (gen, Sport etc)* officiel *m*; *[civil service, local government]* fonctionnaire *mf*; *[railways, post office etc]* employé(e) *m(f)*. ◆ **officialdom** *n* bureaucratie *f*. ◆ **officialese** *n* jargon *m* administratif. ◆ **officially** *adv* officiellement. ◆ **officiate** *vi (Rel)* officier; *(gen)* **to officiate as** remplir les fonctions de.

officious [ə'fɪʃ(ə)s] *adj* trop empressé. ◆ **officiously** *adv* avec un empressement excessif. ◆ **officiousness** *n* excès *m* d'empressement.

often ['ɒf(ə)n] *adv* souvent, fréquemment. **as ~ as not, more ~ than not** le plus souvent; **every so ~** *(in time)* de temps en temps; *(in spacing, distance etc)* çà et là; **once too ~** une fois de trop; **it cannot be said too ~ that...** on ne répétera jamais assez que...; **how ~ have you seen her?** combien de fois l'avez-vous vue?; **how ~ do the boats leave?** les bateaux partent tous les combien?

ogle ['əʊgl] *vt* lorgner *.

ogre ['əʊgəʳ] *n* ogre *m*.

oh [əʊ] *excl* oh!; *(cry of pain)* aïe!

oil [ɔɪl] **1** *n* (**a**) *(Geol, Comm, Ind etc)* pétrole *m*. *(fig)* **to pour ~ on troubled waters** ramener le calme. (**b**) *(Art, Aut, Culin etc)* huile *f*. **fried in ~** frit à l'huile; **~ and vinegar (dressing)** vinaigrette *f*; **painted in ~s** peint à l'huile.

2 *vt* graisser, lubrifier. *(fig)* **to ~ the wheels** mettre de l'huile dans les rouages.

3 *adj industry, shares* pétrolier; *magnate etc* du pétrole; *lamp, stove* à pétrole; *(Aut) level, pressure* d'huile; *(Aut)* **~ change** vidange *f*; *(Aut)* **~ filter** filtre *m* à huile; **~ gauge** jauge *f* de niveau d'huile; *(Art)* **~ paint** couleur *f* à l'huile; **~ painting** peinture *f* à l'huile; **she's no ~ painting** * ce n'est vraiment pas une beauté; **~ pollution** pollution *f* aux hydrocarbures; **~ producers** pays *mpl* producteurs de pétrole; **~ rig** *(land)* derrick *m*; *(sea)* plateforme *f* pétrolière; **~ slick** nappe *f* de pétrole; *(on beach)* marée *f* noire; **~ storage tank** *(for central heating)* cuve *f* à mazout; **~ tanker** *(ship)* pétrolier *m*; *(truck)* camion-citerne *m* (à pétrole); **~ well** puits *m* de pétrole.

◆ **oil-burning** *adj lamp* à pétrole; *stove (paraffin)* à pétrole; *(fuel oil)* à mazout. ◆ **oilcan** *n (for lubricating)* burette *f* à huile; *(for storage)* bidon *m* à huile. ◆ **oilcloth** *n* toile *f* cirée. ◆ **oilfield** *n* gisement *m or* champ *m* pétrolifère. ◆ **oil-fired** *adj boiler* à mazout; *central heating* au mazout. ◆ **oiliness** *n (V* **oily** *below)* aspect *m* huileux *or* graisseux *or (Culin)* gras; onction *f*. ◆ **oilpan** *n (US Aut)* carter *m*. ◆ **oilskins** *npl* ciré *m*. ◆ **oily** *adj liquid, consistency* huileux; *stain* d'huile; *rag, clothes, hands* graisseux; *cooking, food* gras; *(fig pej) manners, tone* onctueux.

ointment ['ɔɪntmənt] *n* onguent *m*, pommade *f*.

O.K. * ['əʊ'keɪ] *(vb: pret, ptp* **O.K.'d***)* **1** *excl* d'accord!, O.K.! *(don't fuss)* **O.K., O.K.!** ça va, ça va! **2** *adj (good)* très bien; *(not bad)* pas mal. **is it ~ with you if I come too?** ça ne vous ennuie pas que je vous accompagne? *(subj)*; **I'm coming too, ~?** je viens aussi, d'accord?; **I'm ~** ça va; **the car is ~** la voiture est *(undamaged)* intacte *or (repaired* *etc)* en bon état; **everything's ~** tout va bien. **3** *vt* approuver.

okapi [əʊ'kɑːpɪ] *n* okapi *m*.

old [əʊld] **1** *adj* (**a**) *(gen)* vieux *(before vowel etc* vieil, *f* vieille*)*. **an ~ man** un vieil homme, un vieillard; *(pej)* **he's a real ~ woman** il a des manies de petite vieille; **~ people, ~ folk** personnes *fpl* âgées, vieux *mpl*; **~ people's home, ~ folks' home** hospice *m* de vieillards; *(private)* maison *f* de retraite; **~ for his years** mûr pour son âge; **to grow** *or* **get ~(er)** vieillir, se faire vieux; **in his ~ age** sur ses vieux jours; **the ~ country** la mère patrie; **Old English** vieil anglais; **~ maid** vieille fille *f*; *(Art)* **~ master** *(artist)* grand peintre *m*; *(painting)* tableau *m* de maître; **the Old World** l'ancien monde *m*; **an ~ chair** une vieille chaise; *(valuable)* une chaise ancienne; **~ wine** vin *m* vieux; **that's an ~ one!** ce n'est pas nouveau!; **as ~ as the hills** vieux comme les chemins; **the ~ part of Nice** le vieux Nice; **~ friends** de vieux amis; **any ~ how/where *** *etc* n'importe comment/où *etc*; **any ~ thing *** n'importe quoi; **we had a great ~ time *** on s'est vraiment bien amusé; *(fig)* **it's the same ~ story *** c'est toujours la même histoire; **~ Paul here *** ce bon vieux Paul; **a good ~ dog** un brave chien; **you ~ scoundrel!** sacré vieux! *; **I say, ~ man** *or* **~ fellow** dites donc mon vieux *.
(**b**) **how ~ are you?** quel âge avez-vous?; **he is 10 years ~** il a 10 ans; **at 10 years ~** à (l'âge de) 10 ans; **a 6-year-~ boy** un garçon de 6 ans; **~ enough to dress himself** assez grand pour s'habiller tout seul; **~ enough to vote** en âge de voter; **you're ~ enough to know better!** à ton âge tu devrais avoir plus de bon sens!; **too ~ for that sort of work** trop âgé pour ce genre de travail; *(to child)* **when you're ~er** quand tu seras plus grand; **if I were ~er** si j'étais plus âgé; **if I were 10 years ~er** si j'avais 10 ans de plus; **~er than you** plus âgé que toi; **he's 6 years ~er than you** il a 6 ans de plus que toi; **~er brother** frère aîné; **the ~er generation** la génération antérieure.
(**c**) *(former) school, mayor, home* ancien *(before n)*. **~ boy** ancien élève; **in the ~ days** dans le temps, autrefois; **the good ~ days** le bon vieux temps; **this is the ~ way of doing it** on s'y prenait comme cela autrefois; **~ soldier** vétéran *m*.
2 *n* (**a**) **the ~** les vieux *mpl*, les vieillards *mpl*, les vieilles gens *mpl*.
(**b**) **(in days) of ~** autrefois, jadis; **the men of ~** les hommes de jadis; **I know him of ~** je le connais depuis longtemps.
◆ **old-age** *adj*: **~-age pension** pension *f* vieillesse *(de la Sécurité sociale)*; **~-age pensioner** retraité(e) *m(f)*. ◆ **olden** *adj*: **in ~en times** *or* **days** jadis. ◆ **old-established** *adj* ancien *(after n)*. ◆ **old-fashioned** *adj (old)* d'autrefois; *(out-of-date)* démodé; *person, attitude* vieux jeu *inv*; *(fig)* **to give sb/sth an ~fashioned look *** regarder qn/qch de travers. ◆ **old-style** *adj* à l'ancienne (mode). ◆ **old-time** *adj* du temps jadis; *dancing* d'autrefois. ◆ **old-timer *** *n* vieillard *m*, ancien *m*. ◆ **old wives' tale** *n* conte *m* de bonne femme. ◆ **old-womanish** *adj* qui a des manies de petite vieille. ◆ **old-world** *adj place* très vieux et pittoresque; *charm, style* suranné.

oleaginous [ˌəʊlɪ'ædʒɪnəs] *adj* oléagineux.

oleander [ˌəʊlɪ'ændəʳ] *n* laurier-rose *m*.

oligarchy ['ɒlɪgɑːkɪ] *n* oligarchie *f*.

olive ['ɒlɪv] **1** *n* olive *f*; *(~ tree)* olivier *m*. *(fig)* **to hold out the ~ branch** se présenter le rameau d'olivier à la main. **2** *adj* (**a**) *skin* olivâtre. **~ oil** huile *f* d'olive. (**b**) *(also* **olive-green***)* vert olive *inv*.

Olympic [ə(ʊ)'lɪmpɪk] *adj* olympique. **~ Games, ~s** Jeux *mpl* olympiques.

Oman [əʊ'mɑːn] *n* Oman *m*.

ombudsman ['ɒmbʊdzmən] *n* médiateur *m (Admin)*.

omelet(te) ['ɒmlɪt] *n* omelette *f*.

omen ['əʊmən] *n* présage *m*, augure *m*. **it is a good ~ that...** il est de bon augure que... + *subj*. ◆ **ominous** *adj event* de mauvais augure; *look, cloud, voice* menaçant; *sound, sign* alarmant. ◆ **ominously** *adv* d'une façon menaçante *or* alarmante; **he was ominously silent** son silence ne présageait rien de bon.

omit [ə(ʊ)'mɪt] *vt (accidentally)* omettre (*to do* de faire); *(deliberately)* omettre, négliger (*to do* de faire). ◆ **omission** *n* omission *f*.

omni... ['ɒmnɪ] *pref* omni...

omnibus ['ɒmnɪbəs] *n (†: bus)* omnibus † *m*; *(book)* recueil *m*.

omnipotent [ɒm'nɪpət(ə)nt] *adj* omnipotent. ◆ **omnipotence** *n* omnipotence *f*.

omnivorous [ɒm'nɪv(ə)rəs] *adj* omnivore; *reader* insatiable.

on [ɒn] **1** *prep* (**a**) *(position, direction)* sur, à. **~ the table** sur la table; **with a coat ~ his arm** un manteau sur le bras; **with a ring ~ her finger** une bague au doigt; **the ring ~ her finger** la bague qu'elle avait au doigt; **I have no money ~ me** je n'ai pas d'argent sur moi; **he turned his back ~ us** il nous a tourné le dos; **~ the right** à droite; **~ the blackboard/ceiling** au tableau/plafond; **he hung his hat ~ the nail** il a suspendu son chapeau au clou; **house ~ the main road** maison sur la grand-route.
(**b**) *(fig)* **~ the/his violin** au/sur son violon; **with Louis Armstrong ~ the trumpet** avec Louis Armstrong à la trompette; **he swore it ~ the Bible** il l'a juré sur la Bible; **an attack ~ the government** une attaque contre le gouvernement; **it works ~ oil** cela marche au mazout; **~ the radio** à la radio; **~ the BBC** *(TV)* sur la B.B.C.; *(Rad)* à la B.B.C.; *(Rad)* **~ France-Inter** sur France-Inter; **I'm ~ £6,000 a year** je gagne 6 000 livres par an; **a student ~ a grant** un boursier; **he's ~ a course** il suit un cours; **to be ~ the team/committee** faire partie de l'équipe/du comité; **to be ~ pills** prendre des pilules; **to be ~ drugs** se droguer; **he's ~ heroin** il se drogue à l'héroïne; **I'm back ~ cigarettes** je me suis remis à fumer; **we're ~ irregular verbs** nous en sommes aux verbes irréguliers; **let's have a drink ~ it** on va boire un coup * pour fêter ça; **prices are up ~ last year's** les prix sont en hausse par rapport à ceux de l'année dernière; **this round's ~ me** c'est ma tournée; **have it ~ me** je vous le paie; **~ the train/plane** *etc* dans le train/l'avion *etc*.
(**c**) *(time)* **~ Sunday** dimanche; **~ Sundays** le dimanche; **~ December 1st** le 1er décembre; **~ the evening of December 3rd** le 3 décembre au soir; **~ or about the 20th** vers le 20; **~ and after the 20th** à partir du 20; **~ Easter Day** le jour de Pâques; **it's just ~ 5 o'clock** il va être 5 heures; **~ my arrival** à mon arrivée; **~ my refusal to go away** lorsque j'ai refusé de partir; **~ hearing this** en entendant cela.
(**d**) *(about, concerning)* sur, de. **he lectures ~ Dante** il fait un cours sur Dante; **a book ~ grammar** un livre de grammaire; **an essay ~...** une dissertation sur...; **he spoke ~ oil** il a parlé du pétrole; **have you heard him ~ V.A.T.?** vous l'avez entendu parler de la T.V.A.?; **Jones ~ Marx** ce que Jones a écrit sur Marx; **I'm ~ a new project** je travaille à un nouveau projet; **away ~ an errand** parti faire une course; **while we're ~ the subject** pendant que nous y sommes.
2 *adv* (**a**) *(covering)* **he had his coat ~** il avait mis son manteau; **~ with your pyjamas!** allez, mets ton pyjama!; **she had nothing ~** elle était toute nue; **what had he got ~?** qu'est-ce qu'il portait?; **the lid is ~** le couvercle est mis.

(**b**) *(forward)* **from that time** ~ à partir de ce moment-là; **it's getting ~ for 2 o'clock** il n'est pas loin de 2 heures; **well ~ in May** bien avant dans le mois de mai; **it was well ~ into May** mai était déjà bien avancé.
(**c**) *(continuation)* **go ~ with your work** continuez votre travail; **and so ~** et ainsi de suite; **they talked ~ and ~** ils ont parlé sans discontinuer *or* sans arrêt.
(**d**) *(phrases)* **he is always ~ at me *** il est toujours après moi *; **to get ~ to sb** se mettre en rapport avec qn (*about sth* à propos de qch); **I'm ~ to something** je suis sur une piste intéressante; **the police are ~ to him** la police est sur sa piste; **she's ~ to the fact that...** elle sait que...
3 *adj (functioning etc)* **to be ~** *[machine, engine]* être en marche; *[light]* être allumé; *[TV, radio]* être allumé, marcher; *[tap]* être ouvert; *[brake]* être serré; *[meeting, programme etc]* être en cours; **while the meeting was ~** pendant la réunion; **the show is ~ already** le spectacle a déjà commencé; **the play is still ~** la pièce se joue toujours; **what's ~ at the cinema?** qu'est-ce qu'on donne au cinéma?; *(Rad, TV)* **what's ~?** qu'y a-t-il à la radio/à la télé?; *(Rad, TV)* **X is ~ tonight** il y a X ce soir; **you're ~ now!** c'est à vous maintenant!; **we are going out, are you ~? *** nous sortons, vous venez?; **you're ~! *** tope là!; **it's not ~ *** *(refusing)* pas question!; *(not done)* cela ne se fait pas.
◆ **on-campus** *adj (US)* sur le campus. ◆ **oncoming** *adj car* venant en sens inverse. ◆ **ongoing** *adj project* en cours. ◆ **on-line** *adj (Comput)* en ligne. ◆ **onlooker** *n* spectateur *m*, -trice *f*. ◆ **onrush** *n [people]* ruée *f*; *[water]* torrent *m*. ◆ **onset** *n (start)* début *m*; *(approach)* approche *f*. ◆ **onshore** *adj wind* de mer. ◆ **onslaught** *n* attaque *f*. ◆ **onto** *prep* = **on to.** ◆ **onward 1** *adv* (*also* **onwards**) en avant; **from this time ~ward(s)** désormais; **from today ~ward(s)** à partir d'aujourd'hui ; **2** *adj* en avant.

once [wʌns] **1** *adv* (**a**) *(on one occasion)* une fois. **~ only** une seule fois; **~ before** une fois déjà; **~ when I was young** un jour quand j'étais jeune; **~ again, ~ more** encore une fois; **~ and for all** une fois pour toutes; **~ a week** une fois par semaine; **~ in a while, ~ in a way** de temps en temps; **more than ~** plus d'une fois; **~ or twice** une fois ou deux; **for ~** pour une fois; **just this ~** juste pour cette fois-ci; **not ~, never ~** pas une seule fois; **if ~ you...** si jamais vous...; **~ a journalist always a journalist** qui a été journaliste le reste toute sa vie. (**b**) *(formerly)* jadis, autrefois. **~ upon a time there was** il y avait une fois, il était une fois; **~ powerful** jadis *or* autrefois puissant. (**c**) **at ~** *(immediately)* tout de suite; *(simultaneously)* à la fois; **all at ~** *(suddenly)* tout à coup, soudain. **2** *conj* une fois que. **~ she'd seen him she...** une fois qu'elle l'eut vu *or* après l'avoir vu * elle... ◆ **once-over *** *n*: **to give sth the ~-over** vérifier qch très rapidement.

one [wʌn] **1** *adj* (**a**) un(e). **~ hundred and twenty** cent vingt; **twenty-~ apples** vingt et une pommes; **that's ~ way of doing it** c'est une façon de le faire; **she is ~ (year old)** elle a un an; **it's ~ o'clock** il est une heure; **for ~ thing...** d'abord...; **with ~ voice** d'une seule voix; **~ day** un jour; **~ Sunday morning** un dimanche matin; **~ hot summer afternoon** par un chaud après-midi d'été. (**b**) *(sole)* un(e) seul(e). **there is ~ man who** il y a un seul homme qui + *subj;* **the ~ man who** le seul qui + *subj;* **~ and only** seul et unique; *(Comm)* **'~ size'** 'taille unique'. (**c**) *(same)* (le) même. **in the ~ car** dans la même voiture; **~ and the same person** une seule et même personne; **~ and the same thing** exactement la même chose. **2** *n* un(e) *m(f)*. **twenty-~** vingt et un(e); **~ hundred and ~** cent un(e); **there are three ~s in her phone number** il y a trois uns dans son numéro de téléphone; **~ of them** *(people)* l'un d'eux, l'une d'elles; *(things)* (l')un, (l')une; **chapter ~** chapitre un; **I for ~ don't believe it** pour ma part je ne le crois pas; **who doesn't agree? — I for ~!** qui n'est pas d'accord? — moi pour commencer! ; **~ by ~** un à un; **in ~s and twos** *arrive* par petits groupes; *get, send* quelques-uns à la fois; **~ after the other** l'un après l'autre; **~ and all** tous sans exception; **it's all ~** c'est tout un; **it's all ~ to me** cela m'est égal; **to be ~ up *** avoir l'avantage (*on sb* sur qn); **to go ~ better than sb** faire mieux que qn.
3 *pron* (**a**) *(indefinite)* un(e) *m(f)*. **would you like ~?** en voulez-vous un?; **have you got ~?** en avez-vous un?; **the question is ~ of money** c'est une question d'argent; **~ of my best friends** un de mes meilleurs amis; **he's ~ of us** il est des nôtres; **you can't have ~ without the other** on ne peut avoir l'un sans l'autre. (**b**) *(specific)* **this ~** celui-ci, celle-ci; **that ~** celui-là, celle-là; **the ~ who** *or* **that** *or* **which** celui qui, celle qui; **the ~ on the floor** celui *or* celle qui est par terre; **he's the ~ with brown hair** c'est celui qui a les cheveux bruns; **which ~?** lequel?, laquelle?; **I want the red ~** je veux le rouge; **you've taken the wrong ~** vous n'avez pas pris le bon; **that's a difficult ~!** ça c'est difficile!; **the little ~s** les petits; **my dearest ~** mon chéri, ma chérie; **he's a clever ~** c'est un malin; **for ~ who claims to know the language, he...** pour quelqu'un qui prétend connaître la langue, il...; **he's not ~ to do that sort of thing** il n'est pas de ceux qui font cela; **he's a great ~ * for chess** c'est un mordu * des échecs. (**c**) **~ another = each other** ; *V* **each 2b.** (**d**) *(impersonal) (subject)* on; *(object)* vous. **~ must remember** on doit *or* il faut se souvenir; **it tires ~ too much** cela vous fatigue trop; **~ likes to see ~'s friends happy** on aime que ses amis soient heureux.
◆ **one-armed** *adj* manchot; **~-armed bandit *** machine *f* à sous *(jeu)*. ◆ **one-eyed** *adj* borgne. ◆ **one-horse town *** *n* bled * *m*, trou * *m*. ◆ **one-legged** *adj* unijambiste. ◆ **one-man** *adj job* fait *or* à faire par un seul homme; *business* que fait marcher un seul homme; *exhibition etc* consacré à un seul artiste; *woman etc* qui n'aime qu'un seul homme; *(Mus: person)* **~-man band** homme-orchestre *m*; *(fig)* **it's a ~-man band *** un seul homme fait marcher toute l'affaire; *(variety)* **~-man show** one-man show *m*. ◆ **one-night stand** *n (Theat)* représentation *f* unique; *(sex)* amour *m* de rencontre. ◆ **one-off *** *or* ◆ **one-shot *** *(US) adj object* unique; *event* exceptionnel. ◆ **one-one** *adj (US)* univoque. ◆ **one-parent family** *n* famille *f* monoparentale. ◆ **one-room(ed)** *adj* d'une pièce. ◆ **oneself** *pron* se, soi-même; *(after prep)* soi(-même); *(emphatic)* soi-même; **to hurt ~self** se blesser; **to dress ~self** s'habiller; **to speak to ~self** se parler à soi-même; **to be sure of ~self** être sûr de soi; **one must do it ~self** il faut le faire soi-même; **(all) by ~self** (tout) seul. ◆ **one-sided** *adj decision* unilatéral; *contest, game* inégal; *judgment, account* partial; *contract* inéquitable. ◆ **one-time** *adj* ancien *(before n)*. ◆ **one-to-one** *adj relationship* univoque; *discussion* en tête-à-tête. ◆ **one-track** *adj*: **to have a ~-track mind *** n'avoir qu'une idée en tête. ◆ **one-upmanship *** *n (hum)* art *m* de faire mieux que les autres. ◆ **one-way** *adj street* à sens unique; *traffic* en sens unique; *ticket* simple; *emotion etc* non partagé.

onerous ['ɒnərəs] *adj task* pénible; *responsibility* lourd.

onion ['ʌnjən] **1** *n* oignon *m*. **2** *adj soup* à l'oignon; *skin* d'oignon; *stew* aux oignons. ◆ **onion-shaped** *adj* bulbeux.

only ['əʊnlɪ] **1** *adj* seul. **the ~ book that remains** le seul livre qui reste *(subj);* **~ child** enfant *mf*

unique; **you're the ~ one to think of that** vous êtes le seul à y avoir pensé; **it's the ~ one left** c'est le seul qui reste *(subj)*; **the ~ thing is that it's too late** seulement il est trop tard; **that's the ~ way to do it** c'est la seule façon de le faire.
2 *adv* seulement, simplement, ne... (plus) que. **~ Paul can wait** il n'y a que Paul qui puisse attendre; **he can ~ wait** il ne peut qu'attendre; **I can ~ say that...** tout ce que je peux dire c'est que...; **it's ~ that I thought...** simplement, je pensais...; **I will ~ say that...** je dirai simplement que...; **it will ~ take a minute** ça ne prendra qu'une minute; **I'm ~ the secretary** je ne suis que le secrétaire; **a ticket for one person ~** un billet pour une seule personne; **'ladies ~'** 'réservé aux dames'; **I ~ looked at it** je n'ai fait que le regarder; **you've ~ to ask** vous n'avez qu'à demander; **~ to think of it** rien que d'y penser; **it's ~ too true** ce n'est que trop vrai; **not ~ A but also B** non seulement A mais aussi B; **~ yesterday** pas plus tard qu'hier; **he has ~ just arrived** il vient tout juste d'arriver; **I caught the train but ~ just** j'ai eu le train mais de justesse; **if ~** si seulement.
3 *conj* seulement, mais. **I would buy it, ~ it's too dear** je l'achèterais bien, seulement *or* mais il est trop cher.

onomatopoeia [ˌɒnə(ʊ)mætə(ʊ)'piːə] *n* onomatopée *f*.

onus ['əʊnəs] *n (no pl)* **the ~ is on him** c'est sa responsabilité (*to do* de faire).

onyx ['ɒnɪks] *n* onyx *m*.

ooze [uːz] **1** *n* vase *f*. **2** *vi [water, pus, walls]* suinter; *[resin, gum]* exsuder. **3** *vt*: **his wounds ~d pus** le pus suintait de ses blessures; *(fig pej)* **she was oozing charm** le charme lui sortait par tous les pores.
◆ **ooze away** *vi*: **his strength** *etc* **was oozing away** ses forces *etc* l'abandonnaient.

opal ['əʊp(ə)l] *n* opale *f*.

opaque [ə(ʊ)'peɪk] *adj* opaque.

open ['əʊp(ə)n] **1** *adj* (**a**) *(gen)* ouvert. **wide ~** grand ouvert; **half-~, slightly ~** entrouvert; **to welcome with ~ arms** *person* accueillir à bras ouverts; *news* accueillir avec joie; **our grocer is ~ on Mondays** notre épicier ouvre *or* est ouvert le lundi; *(fig)* **to keep ~ house** tenir table ouverte; *(Brit)* **~ day** journée *f* du public.
(**b**) *(fig) boat, letter, cheque, city* ouvert; *river (not obstructed)* ouvert à la navigation; *(not frozen)* non gelé; *road, corridor* dégagé; *pipe* ouvert, non bouché; *car* décapoté; *sewer* à ciel ouvert; *prison* à régime libéral; *(Med) bowels* relâché; *pores* dilaté. **road ~ to traffic** route ouverte à la circulation; **the way to Paris lay ~** la route de Paris était libre; **the ~ road** la grand-route; **the ~ air** le plein air; **in the ~ air** *(gen)* en plein air; *sleep* à la belle étoile; **in ~ country** en rase campagne; **patch of ~ ground** *(between trees)* clairière *f*; *(in town)* terrain *m* vague; **the ~ sea** la haute mer, le large; **~ space** espace *m* libre; **~ to the elements/to attack** exposé aux éléments/à l'attaque; **~ sandwich** canapé *m* (froid); **~ to persuasion** ouvert à la persuasion; **I'm ~ to advice** je me laisserais volontiers conseiller; **I'm ~ to correction, but...** dites-moi si je me trompe, mais...; **~ to improvement** que l'on peut améliorer; **it is ~ to doubt whether...** on peut douter que... + *subj*.
(**c**) *market, meeting, trial* public; *competition, scholarship* ouvert à tous. **the course is not ~ to schoolchildren** ce cours n'est pas ouvert aux lycéens ; **several choices were ~ to them** plusieurs choix s'offraient à eux; **this post is still ~** ce poste est encore vacant; *(Jur)* **in ~ court** en audience publique; **~ day** journée *f* portes ouvertes au public; *(Sport)* **~ season** saison *f* de la chasse; **the O~ University** ≃ le Centre d'enseignement par correspondance.
(**d**) *(frank, not hidden) person, face* ouvert, franc; *enemy* déclaré; *admiration, envy* manifeste; *attempt* non dissimulé; *scandal* public. **in ~ revolt** en rébellion ouverte (*against* contre); **it's an ~ secret that** ce n'est un secret pour personne que.
(**e**) *(undecided) question* non résolu, non tranché. **the race was still wide ~** l'issue de la course était encore indécise; **it's an ~ question whether...** on ne sait pas si...; **to leave ~** *matter* laisser en suspens; *date* ne pas préciser; **to have an ~ mind on sth** ne pas avoir formé d'opinion sur qch; *(Jur)* **~ verdict** *(not stating cause of death)* verdict *m* de décès avec causes indéterminées; *(where guilty party unknown)* verdict sans désignation de coupable; **~ ticket** billet *m* open.
2 *n*: **out in the ~** *(out of doors)* dehors, en plein air; *sleep* à la belle étoile; *(in the country)* au grand air; **to come out into the ~** *(lit)* sortir au grand jour; *(fig) [secret, plans]* se faire jour; *[person]* parler franchement (*about* de); **to bring out into the ~** divulguer.
3 *vt (gen: lit, fig)* ouvrir; *bowels* relâcher; *pores* dilater; *legs* écarter; *hole* percer; *conversation, negotiations* engager. **to ~ wide** ouvrir tout grand; **to ~ slightly** entrouvrir; **to ~ again** rouvrir; *(lit, fig)* **he didn't ~ his mouth** il n'a pas ouvert la bouche; **to ~ Parliament** ouvrir la session parlementaire; *(Mil)* **to ~ fire** ouvrir le feu (*on* sur).
4 *vi* (**a**) *(gen)* s'ouvrir; *[shop, museum, bank etc]* ouvrir. **this door never ~s** cette porte n'ouvre jamais; **the door ~ed** la porte s'est ouverte; **to ~ slightly** s'entrouvrir; **to ~ again** se rouvrir; *[door, room]* **to ~ on to** *or* **into** donner sur. (**b**) *(begin) [class, debate, meeting, play, book]* s'ouvrir, commencer (*with* par); *[speaker]* commencer (*with* par); *(Bridge)* ouvrir (*with* de). *(Theat)* **the play ~s next week** la première a lieu la semaine prochaine.
◆ **open out 1** *vi [flower, person]* s'ouvrir; *[passage, tunnel, street]* s'élargir. **to ~ out on to** déboucher sur. **2** *vt sep* ouvrir.
◆ **open up 1** *vi* (**a**) *[flower, shop, career, opportunity]* s'ouvrir (*fig: to sb* à qn; *about sth* de qch). (**b**) *(start shooting)* ouvrir le feu. **2** *vt sep (gen)* ouvrir; *jungle* rendre accessible; *blocked road* dégager; *prospects, possibility* découvrir, révéler; *horizons, career* ouvrir.
◆ **open-air** *adj games, activities* de plein air; *swimming pool, market, meeting* en plein air; *theatre* de verdure. ◆ **open-and-shut case** *n* cas *m* incontestable. ◆ **opencast mining** *n* exploitation *f* à ciel ouvert. ◆ **open-ended** *or* ◆ **open-end** *(US) adj tube* à deux ouvertures; *discussion, meeting* sans limite de durée; *offer* flexible. ◆ **opener** *n (for bottles)* ouvre-bouteilles *m inv*; *(for tins)* ouvre-boîtes *m inv*; *(Theat: act)* lever *m* de rideau. ◆ **open-handed** *adj* généreux. ◆ **open-hearted** *adj* franc, sincère. ◆ **open-heart surgery** *n* chirurgie *f* à cœur ouvert. ◆ **opening 1** *n* (**a**) *(gen)* ouverture *f*; *(in wall)* brèche *f*; *(in trees, forest, clouds)* trouée *f*; *(in roof)* percée *f*; (**b**) *(beginning)* ouverture *f*; (**c**) *(opportunity)* occasion *f* (*to do* de faire); *(trade outlet)* débouché *m* (*for* pour); *(work: gen)* débouché *m; (specific job)* poste *m;* **to give one's opponent an ~ing** prêter le flanc à son adversaire ; **2** *adj ceremony, speech* d'inauguration; *remark* préliminaire; *(St Ex) price* d'ouverture; *(Theat)* **~ing night** première *f*; *(Brit)* **~ing time** l'heure *f* d'ouverture *(des pubs)*. ◆ **openly** *adv (frankly)* ouvertement; *(publicly)* publiquement. ◆ **open-minded** *adj* à l'esprit ouvert. ◆ **open-mouthed** *adj, adv* bouche bée. ◆ **open-necked** *adj* à col ouvert, échancré. ◆ **openness** *n (candour)* franchise *f*. ◆ **open-plan** *adj office* paysagé.

opera ['ɒp(ə)rə] **1** *n* opéra *m*. **2** *adj*: ~ **glasses** jumelles *fpl* de théâtre; ~ **house** (théâtre *m* de l')opéra *m*; ~ **singer** chanteur *m*, -euse *f* d'opéra. ◆ **opera-goer** *or* ◆ **opera-lover** *n* amateur *m* d'opéra. ◆ **operatic** *adj* d'opéra. ◆ **operetta** *n* opérette *f*.

operate ['ɒpəreɪt] **1** *vi (gen)* opérer; *(Med)* opérer (*on sb* qn; *for sth* de qch); *[drug, propaganda]* opérer (*on* sur); *[machine, vehicle]* marcher, fonctionner (*by electricity etc* à l'électricité *etc*); *[system, sb's mind]* fonctionner; *[factors]* jouer (*to produce* pour produire). **he was ~d on for appendicitis** il a été opéré de l'appendicite; **to ~ on sb's eyes** opérer qn des yeux.
2 *vt* (**a**) *[person] machine, telephone, brakes etc* faire marcher, faire fonctionner; *[switch]* actionner. **a machine ~d by electricity** une machine qui marche à l'électricité. (**b**) *business, factory* diriger; *coalmine, oil well* exploiter; *system, changes* opérer; *swindle* réaliser.
◆ **operable** *adj* opérable. ◆ **operating** *adj* (**a**) *(Comm) costs* d'exploitation; (**b**) *(Med) table* d'opération; **operating theatre** salle *f* d'opération. ◆ **operation** *n* (**a**) *(gen, Med, Mil etc)* opération *f*; **to have an operation** se faire opérer; **a lung operation** une opération au poumon; **to perform an operation on sb** opérer qn; *(Mil, Police)* **operations room** centre *m* d'opérations; (**b**) *(act of operating)* **to be in operation** *[machine]* être en service; *[business etc]* fonctionner; *[mine etc]* être en exploitation; *[law, system]* être en vigueur; **to come into operation** entrer en service (*or* en vigueur *etc*); **to put into operation** mettre en service *etc*. ◆ **operational** *adj* opérationnel. ◆ **operative** **1** *adj law, measure, system* en vigueur; **the operative word** le mot clef ; **2** *n (worker)* ouvrier *m*, -ière *f*; *(machine operator)* opérateur *m*, -trice *f*; *(US Pol)* membre *m* de l'état-major *(d'un candidat)*; **the steel operatives** la main-d'œuvre des aciéries. ◆ **operator** *n (gen)* opérateur *m*, -trice *f*; *[telephones]* téléphoniste *mf*; **radio operator** radio *m*; **tour operator** organisateur *m*, -trice *f* de voyages.

ophthalmia [ɒf'θælmɪə] *n* ophtalmie *f*. ◆ **ophthalmic** *adj surgeon* ophtalmologique.

opiate ['əʊpɪɪt] *n* opiat *m*.

opinion [ə'pɪnjən] **1** *n (point of view)* opinion *f*, avis *m*; *[lawyer, doctor]* avis; *(belief)* opinion. **in my ~** à mon avis, d'après moi; **in the ~ of** d'après, selon; **public ~** l'opinion publique; **it's a matter of ~ whether...** c'est une affaire d'opinion pour ce qui est de savoir si...; **I'm of your ~** je suis de votre avis *or* opinion; **to be of the ~ that** être d'avis que, estimer que; **political ~s** opinions politiques; **to have a high/low ~ of** avoir/ne pas avoir bonne opinion de; **what is your ~ of this book?** que pensez-vous de ce livre?; *(Med)* **to take a second ~** prendre l'avis d'un autre médecin. **2** *adj*: ~ **poll** sondage *m* d'opinion. ◆ **opinionated** *adj* dogmatique.

opium ['əʊpɪəm] *n* opium *m*. ~ **addict** opiomane *mf*.

opossum [ə'pɒsəm] *n* opossum *m*.

opponent [ə'pəʊnənt] *n (gen)* adversaire *mf*; *(in discussion, debate)* antagoniste *mf*. **he has always been an ~ of...** il a toujours été contre...

opportune ['ɒpətju:n] *adj* opportun. ◆ **opportunely** *adv* opportunément. ◆ **opportuneness** *n* opportunité *f*. ◆ **opportunism** *n* opportunisme *m*. ◆ **opportunist** *adj, n* opportuniste *(mf)*.

opportunity [,ɒpə'tju:nɪtɪ] *n* occasion *f*. **to have the** *or* **an ~ to do** *or* **of doing** avoir l'occasion de faire; **to take the ~ of doing** *or* **to do** profiter de l'occasion pour faire; **at the earliest ~** à la première occasion; **when the ~ occurs** à l'occasion; **if you get the ~** si vous en avez l'occasion; **equality of ~** égalité *f* de chances; **to make the most of one's opportunities** profiter pleinement de ses chances; **this job offers great opportunities** ce poste offre d'excellentes perspectives *fpl* d'avenir.

oppose [ə'pəʊz] *vt (gen)* s'opposer à; *motion, resolution (Pol)* faire opposition à; *(in debate)* parler contre. **he ~s our coming** il s'oppose à ce que nous venions *(subj)*. ◆ **opposed** *adj* opposé, hostile (*to* à); **I'm ~d to your doing that** je m'oppose à ce que vous fassiez cela; **as ~d to** par opposition à; **as ~d to that,...** par contre,... ◆ **opposing** *adj army* opposé.

opposite ['ɒpəzɪt] **1** *adj house etc* d'en face; *side, end, direction, point of view* opposé. **'see map on ~ page'** 'voir plan ci-contre'; **the ~ sex** l'autre sexe *m*; **his ~ number** son homologue *mf*. **2** *adv* (d')en face. ~ **to** en face de; **the house ~** la maison d'en face; **the house is directly ~** la maison est directement en face. **3** *prep* en face de. ~ **one another** en vis-à-vis; **they live ~ us** ils habitent en face de chez nous; *(Theat etc)* **to play ~ sb** partager la vedette avec qn. **4** *n* contraire *m*, opposé *m*. **quite the ~!** au contraire!; **he told me just the ~** il m'a dit exactement le contraire.

opposition [,ɒpə'zɪʃ(ə)n] **1** *n* opposition *f* (*to* à). **in ~ to** en opposition avec; *(Pol)* **the ~** l'opposition; **the party in ~** le parti de l'opposition; *(Pol)* **to be in ~** être dans l'opposition; **the ~** * *(Sport, Pol)* l'adversaire *m*; *(Comm)* la concurrence; **they put up considerable ~** ils opposèrent une vive résistance. **2** *adj (Pol)* de l'opposition.

oppress [ə'pres] *vt (Mil, Pol etc)* opprimer; *[anxiety, heat etc]* oppresser. ◆ **oppression** *n* oppression *f*. ◆ **oppressive** *adj (Mil, Pol etc)* oppressif; *anxiety, heat* accablant; *weather* lourd. ◆ **oppressively** *adv (Mil, Pol etc)* tyranniquement; **it was ~ively hot** il faisait une chaleur accablante. ◆ **oppressor** *n* oppresseur *m*.

opprobrium [ə'prəʊbrɪəm] *n* opprobre *m*.

opt [ɒpt] *vi*: **to ~ for sth** opter pour qch *(also Jur)*; **to ~ to do** choisir de faire. ◆ **opt in** * *vi* choisir de participer (*to* à). ◆ **opt out** * *vi* choisir de ne pas participer (*of* à), se récuser. **to ~ out of doing** choisir de ne pas faire.

optical ['ɒptɪk(ə)l] *adj glass, lens, disk* optique; *instrument, illusion* d'optique. ~ **character recognition/reader** lecture *f* /lecteur *m* optique. ◆ **optician** *n* opticien(ne) *m(f)*. ◆ **optics** *nsg* optique *f*.

optimism ['ɒptɪmɪz(ə)m] *n* optimisme *m*. ◆ **optimist** *n* optimiste *mf*. ◆ **optimistic** *adj* optimiste. ◆ **optimistically** *adv* avec optimisme. ◆ **optimize** *vt* optimiser.

optimum ['ɒptɪməm] *adj* optimum.

option ['ɒpʃ(ə)n] *n* option *f* (*on* sur); *(Scol)* matière *f* à option. *(Jur)* **6 months with the ~ of a fine** 6 mois avec substitution d'amende; **I have no ~** je n'ai pas le choix; **he had no ~ but to come** il n'a pas pu faire autrement que de venir; **you have the ~ of remaining here** vous pouvez rester ici si vous voulez; *(fig)* **he kept his ~s open** il n'a pas voulu s'engager. ◆ **optional** *adj (gen, Scol etc)* facultatif; *(Comm)* **~al extras** accessoires *mpl* en option.

opulent ['ɒpjʊlənt] *adj* opulent. ◆ **opulence** *n* opulence *f*. ◆ **opulently** *adv* avec opulence.

or [ɔ:ʳ] *conj* ou; *(with neg)* ni. ~ **else** ou bien; **do it ~ else!** * fais-le, sinon! *; **without tears ~ sighs** sans larmes ni soupirs; **he could not read ~ write** il ne savait ni lire ni écrire; **an hour ~ so** environ une heure.

oracle ['ɒrəkl] *n* oracle *m*.

oral ['ɔ:r(ə)l] **1** *adj* oral. **2** *n* oral *m*, épreuve *f* orale. ◆ **orally** *adv* oralement; *(Pharm)* par voie orale.

orange ['ɒrɪn(d)ʒ] **1** *n (fruit)* orange *f*; *(~-tree)* oranger *m*; *(colour)* orange *m*. **2** *adj (colour)* orange *inv*; *drink, flavour* d'orange; *liqueur* à l'orange. ~ **blossom** fleur(s) *f(pl)* d'oranger; ~ **marmalade** confiture *f* d'oranges; ~ **stick** bâtonnet m *(pour manucure etc)*. ◆ **orangeade** *n* orangeade *f*.

orang-outang [ɔːˌræŋuː'tæŋ], **orang-utan** [ɔːˌræŋuː'tæn] *n* orang-outang *m*.

oration [ɔː'reɪʃ(ə)n] *n* discours *m* solennel. **funeral** ~ oraison *f* funèbre. ◆ **orator** ['ɒrətəʳ] *n* orateur *m*, -trice *f*. ◆ **oratorical** *adj* oratoire. ◆ **oratorio** *n* oratorio *m*. ◆ **oratory** *n (art)* art *m* oratoire; *(what is said)* éloquence *f*; **piece of oratory** discours *m*.

orbit ['ɔːbɪt] **1** *n* orbite *f*. **in(to)** ~ en orbite (*around* autour de); *(fig)* **that doesn't come within my** ~ ceci n'est pas de mon domaine; **the American** ~ la sphère d'influence américaine. **2** *vti* orbiter.

orchard ['ɔːtʃəd] *n* verger *m*. **apple** ~ verger de pommiers.

orchestra ['ɔːkɪstrə] *n* orchestre *m*; *(US Theat)* (fauteuils *mpl* d') orchestre *m*. ◆ **orchestral** [ɔː'kestr(ə)l] *adj music* orchestral; *concert* symphonique. ◆ **orchestrate** *vt* orchestrer. ◆ **orchestration** *n* orchestration *f*.

orchid ['ɔːkɪd] *n* orchidée *f*. **wild** ~ orchis *m*.

ordain [ɔː'deɪn] *vt* (**a**) décréter (*that* que). *(fig)* **it was ~ed that** le destin a voulu que + *subj*. (**b**) *(Rel)* ordonner (*sb priest* qn prêtre).

ordeal [ɔː'diːl] *n* (terrible) épreuve *f*. **it was a real ~ for him** cela le mettait au supplice.

order ['ɔːdəʳ] **1** *n* (**a**) *(sequence)* ordre *m*. **word** ~ ordre des mots; **what ~ should these cards be in?** dans quel ordre ces cartes devraient-elles être?; **in ~ of merit/appearance** par ordre de mérite/d'entrée en scène; **the cards were out of** ~ les cartes n'étaient pas en ordre; **to put in(to)** ~ mettre en ordre; **in the ~ of things** dans l'ordre des choses; **the old ~ is changing** l'ancien état de choses change. (**b**) *(good ~)* ordre *m*. **in** ~ *room etc* en ordre; *passport, documents* en règle; **to be in** ~ *[request]* être dans les règles; **to put in** ~ mettre en ordre; *(US)* **in short** ~ tout de suite; **out of ~, not in working** *or* **running** ~ *machine* en panne, détraqué; *(Telec) line* en dérangement; **to be in running** *or* **working** ~ marcher bien. (**c**) **in ~ to do** pour faire, afin de faire; **in ~ that** afin que + *subj*, pour que + *subj*. (**d**) *(correct procedure)* ordre *m*. *(Parl)* **order, order!** à l'ordre!; **to call sb to** ~ rappeler qn à l'ordre; **on a point of** ~ sur une question de forme *or* de procédure; **is it in ~ to do that?** est-il permis de faire cela?; **his request is quite in** ~ sa demande est tout à fait normale. (**e**) *(peace, control)* ordre *m*. **to keep** ~ *[police etc]* maintenir l'ordre; *[teacher]* faire régner la discipline; **to keep sb in** ~ tenir qn. (**f**) *(Bio)* ordre *m*; *(social class)* classe *f*. *(fig)* **of a high** ~ de premier ordre; **of the ~ of 500** de l'ordre de 500; **Benedictine O~** ordre des bénédictins; **(holy) ~s** ordres *mpl* (majeurs); **to be in/take ~s** être/entrer dans les ordres. (**g**) *(command)* ordre *m*, consigne *f (Mil)*. **to give sb ~s to do sth** ordonner à qn de faire qch; **I don't take ~s from you!** je ne suis pas à vos ordres!; **on the ~s of** sur l'ordre de; **by ~ of** par ordre de; **to be under ~s to do** avoir reçu l'ordre de faire; *(fig)* **strikes were the ~ of the day** les grèves étaient à l'ordre du jour; *(Jur)* ~ **of the Court** injonction *f* de la cour; **deportation** ~ arrêté *m* d'expulsion. (**h**) *(Comm)* commande *f*. **made to** ~ fait sur commande; **to place an ~ with sb (for sth)** passer une commande (de qch) à qn; **they are on** ~ ils sont commandés; *(Comm, fig)* **to** ~ sur commande; ~ **to view** permis *m* de visiter; **money** ~ mandat *m*; *(Banking)* **to the ~ of** à l'ordre de.
2 *adj*: ~ **book** carnet *m* de commandes; ~ **form** bon *m* de commande.
3 *vt* (**a**) *(command)* ordonner (*sb to do* à qn de faire; *that* que + *subj*). **he was ~ed to be quiet** on lui a ordonné de se taire; **to ~ sb in/up** *etc* ordonner à qn d'entrer/de monter *etc*. (**b**) *goods, meal* commander; *taxi* faire venir. (**c**) *(put in ~) one's affairs etc* régler.
4 *vi (in restaurant etc)* passer sa commande.
◆ **order about, order around** *vt sep* commander.
◆ **orderliness** *n* (habitudes *fpl* d')ordre *m*.
◆ **orderly 1** *adj room* en ordre; *mind* méthodique; *life* réglé; *person* qui a de l'ordre; *crowd* discipliné; **in an ~ly way** avec ordre ; **2** *n (Mil)* planton *m*; *(Med)* garçon *m* de salle; **~ly room** salle *f* de rapport.

ordinal ['ɔːdɪnl] *adj, n* ordinal *(m)*.

ordinance ['ɔːdɪnəns] *n* ordonnance *f (Admin)*.

ordinary ['ɔːdnrɪ] **1** *adj* (**a**) *(usual)* ordinaire *(also pej)*, habituel. **in the ~ way** en temps normal; **for all ~ purposes** pour l'usage courant. (**b**) *(average) intelligence, reader etc* moyen. **just an ~ fellow** un homme comme les autres. **2** *n*: **out of the** ~ qui sort de l'ordinaire. ◆ **ordinarily** *adv* ordinairement.

ordination [ˌɔːdɪ'neɪʃ(ə)n] *n* ordination *f*.

ordnance ['ɔːdnəns] *(Mil)* **1** *n* artillerie *f*. **2** *adj*: **O~ Corps** Service *m* du matériel; *(Brit)* **O~ Survey map** ≃ carte *f* d'État-Major.

ore [ɔːʳ] *n* minerai *m*. **iron** ~ minerai de fer.

oregano [ˌɒrɪ'gɑːnəʊ] *n* origan *m*.

organ ['ɔːgən] **1** *n (Anat, also fig, Press etc)* organe *m*; *(Mus)* orgue *m*, orgues *fpl*. **2** *adj*: ~ **grinder** joueur *m*, -euse *f* d'orgue de Barbarie; ~ **loft** tribune *f* d'orgue. ◆ **organic** *adj (gen, Bio etc)* organique; *part* fondamental; *being* organisé; *food* naturel; *vegetables, farming* biologique; **~ic whole** tout *m* systématique. ◆ **organically** *adv* organiquement; *(basically)* foncièrement. ◆ **organism** *n* organisme *m (Bio)*. ◆ **organist** *n* organiste *mf*.

organize ['ɔːgənaɪz] *vt* organiser. **to get ~d** s'organiser. ◆ **organization** *n* (**a**) organisation *f*; **charitable organization** œuvre *f* charitable; (**b**) organisation *f*; **his work lacks organization** son travail manque d'organisation. ◆ **organizational** *adj (gen)* organisationnel. ◆ **organized** *adj (gen)* organisé; **~d crime** le grand banditisme *m*; **~d labour** main-d'œuvre syndiquée. ◆ **organizer** *n* organisateur *m*, -trice *f*; *(for holding things)* vide-poches *m*. ◆ **organizing** *adj committee* chargé de l'organisation; *(bossy)* qui n'arrête pas de dire aux autres ce qu'ils doivent faire.

orgasm ['ɔːgæz(ə)m] *n* orgasme *m*.

orgy ['ɔːdʒɪ] *n (lit, fig)* orgie *f*.

orient ['ɔːrɪənt] *n* orient *m*. ◆ **oriental 1** *adj* oriental ; **2** *n*: **O~** Oriental(e) *m(f)*. ◆ **orientate** *vt* orienter. ◆ **orientation** *n* orientation *f*. ◆ **oriented** *adj (giving priority to)* axé sur; *(specially for needs of)* conçu pour, adapté aux besoins de; **user-/pupil-/** *etc* ~ adapté aux besoins de *or* spécialement conçu pour l'usager/l'élève *etc*. ◆ **orienteering** *n (Sport)* exercice *m* d'orientation sur le terrain.

origami [ˌɒrɪ'gɑːmɪ] *n* (art *m* du) pliage *m*.

origin ['ɒrɪdʒɪn] *n* origine *f*. ◆ **original 1** *adj* (**a**) *(first) sin, inhabitant, purpose, meaning* originel; (**b**) *(not copied etc) painting, idea, writer* original; *(unconventional) character, person* original, excentrique ; **2** *n [painting etc]* original *m*; **to read Dante in the ~al** lire Dante dans l'original. ◆ **originality** *n* originalité *f*. ◆ **originally** *adv* (**a**) *(in the beginning)* à l'origine; *(at first)* originellement; (**b**) *(not copying)* originalement. ◆ **originate 1** *vt [person]* être l'auteur de; *[event, effect]* donner naissance à ; **2** *vi [person]* être originaire (*from* de); *[stream, custom]* prendre naissance (*in* dans); *[goods]* provenir (*from* de); *[suggestion, idea]* émaner (*from* de). ◆ **originator** *n* auteur *m*.

Orkneys ['ɔːknɪz] *npl* Orcades *fpl*.

orlon ['ɔːlɒn] ® **1** *n* orlon *m* ®. **2** *adj* en orlon.

ornament ['ɔːnəmənt] **1** *n (gen)* ornement *m*; *(object)* bibelot *m*. **2** *vt style, dress* orner (*with* de); *room, building, ceiling* ornementer (*with* de). ◆ **ornamental** *adj (gen)* ornemental; *garden, lake* d'agrément. ◆ **ornamentation** *n* ornementation *f*.

ornate [ɔː'neɪt] *adj* très orné.

ornithology [ˌɔːnɪ'θɒlədʒɪ] *n* ornithologie *f*. ◆ **ornithological** *adj* ornithologique. ◆ **ornithologist** *n* ornithologue *mf*.

orphan ['ɔːf(ə)n] **1** *adj, n* orphelin(e) *m(f)*. **2** *vt*: **to be ~ed** devenir orphelin(e). ◆ **orphanage** *n* orphelinat *m*.

orthodontics [ˌɔːθə(ʊ)'dɒntɪks] *nsg* orthodontie *f*.

orthodox ['ɔːθədɒks] *adj* orthodoxe. ◆ **orthodoxy** *n* orthodoxie *f*.

orthography [ɔː'θɒgrəfɪ] *n* orthographe *f*.

orthopaedic, *(US)* **orthopedic** [ˌɔːθə(ʊ)'piːdɪk] *adj surgery etc* orthopédique; *bed* très ferme. **~ surgeon** chirurgien(ne) *m(f)* orthopédiste. ◆ **orthop(a)edics** *nsg* orthopédie *f*. ◆ **orthop(a)edist** *n* orthopédiste *mf*.

oscillate ['ɒsɪleɪt] **1** *vi* osciller. **2** *vt* faire osciller. ◆ **oscillation** *n* oscillation *f*.

Oslo ['ɒzləʊ] *n* Oslo.

osprey ['ɒspreɪ] *n* orfraie *f*.

ossify ['ɒsɪfaɪ] *vi* s'ossifier. ◆ **ossification** *n* ossification *f*.

ostensible [ɒs'tensəbl] *adj* prétendu, apparent. ◆ **ostensibly** *adv*: **he was ostensibly a student** il était soi-disant étudiant; **he went out, ostensibly to telephone** il est sorti sous prétexte de téléphoner.

ostentatious [ˌɒsten'teɪʃəs] *adj surroundings, person* prétentieux; *dislike, attempt* exagéré, ostentatoire. ◆ **ostentation** *n* ostentation *f*. ◆ **ostentatiously** *adv (gen)* avec ostentation.

osteo... ['ɒstɪəʊ] *pref* ostéo... ◆ **osteoarthritis** *n* ostéoarthrite *f*. ◆ **osteopath** *n* ostéopathe *mf*. ◆ **osteopathy** *n* ostéopathie *f*.

ostracize ['ɒstrəsaɪz] *vt* frapper d'ostracisme. ◆ **ostracism** *n* ostracisme *m*.

ostrich ['ɒstrɪtʃ] *n* autruche *f*.

other ['ʌðəʳ] **1** *adj* autre. **the ~ one** l'autre *mf*; **the ~ 5** les 5 autres; **~ people have done it** d'autres l'ont fait; **~ people's property** la propriété d'autrui; **the ~ day** l'autre jour; **some ~ day** un autre jour; **~ than** autre que; **someone or ~ said** je ne sais qui a dit; **some writer or ~** je ne sais quel écrivain; **some fool or ~** un idiot quelconque.
2 *pron* autre *mf*. **some ~s** d'autres; **several ~s** plusieurs autres; **one after the ~** l'un après l'autre; **some... ~s...** les uns... les autres...; **one or ~ of them will come** il y en aura bien un qui viendra; **that man of all ~s** cet homme entre tous; **you and no ~** vous et personne d'autre; **no ~ than** nul autre que.
3 *adv* autrement (*than* que). **I couldn't do ~ than come** je ne pouvais faire autrement que de venir; **no one ~ than** nul autre que.
◆ **otherwise** **1** *adv (in another way)* autrement; *(in other respects)* autrement, à part cela; **it cannot be ~wise** il ne peut en être autrement; **he was ~wise engaged** il était occupé à autre chose; **except where ~wise stated** sauf indication contraire; **should it be ~wise** dans le cas contraire; **an ~wise excellent essay** une dissertation par ailleurs excellente ; **2** *conj* autrement, sinon.

otter ['ɒtəʳ] *n* loutre *f*.

ouch [aʊtʃ] *excl* aïe!

ought¹ [ɔːt] *pret* **ought** *modal aux vb* **I ~ to do it** je devrais le faire, il faudrait que je le fasse; **I ~ to have done it** j'aurais dû le faire; **he thought he ~ to tell you** il a pensé qu'il devait vous le dire; **if they behave as they ~** s'ils se conduisent comme ils le doivent.

ought² [ɔːt] *n* = **aught.**

ounce [aʊns] *n* once *f (= 28,35 grammes)*.

our ['aʊəʳ] *poss adj* notre, *pl* nos. ◆ **ours** *poss pron* le nôtre, la nôtre, les nôtres; **this car is ~s** cette voiture est à nous *or* nous appartient *or* est la nôtre; **a friend of ~s** un de nos amis (à nous), un ami à nous *. ◆ **ourselves** *pers pron (reflexive: direct and indirect)* nous; *(emphatic)* nous-mêmes; *(after prep)* nous; **we've hurt ~selves** nous nous sommes blessés; **we said to ~selves** nous nous sommes dit, on s'est dit *; **we saw it ~selves** nous l'avons vu nous-mêmes; **we were talking amongst ~selves** nous discutions entre nous; **(all) by ~selves** tout seuls, toutes seules.

oust [aʊst] *vt* évincer (*from* de), supplanter (*sb as* qn comme).

out [aʊt] **1** *adv* **(a)** *(outside; not here etc)* dehors. **he's ~ in the garden** il est dans le jardin; **Paul is ~** Paul est sorti *or* n'est pas là; **he's ~ fishing** il est parti à la pêche; **to be ~ and about again** être de nouveau sur pied; **you should be ~ and about!** ne restez donc pas enfermé!; **to go** *or* **get ~** sortir; **to lunch ~** déjeuner dehors; **to have a day ~** sortir pour la journée; **it's her evening ~** c'est sa soirée de sortie; **let's have a night ~** si on sortait?; **~ there** là-bas; **~ here** ici; **when he was ~ in Iran** lorsqu'il était en Iran; **the voyage ~** l'aller *m*; **the boat was 10 km ~** le bateau était à 10 km du rivage; **5 days ~ from Liverpool** à 5 jours de Liverpool; *(Sport)* **the ball is ~** le ballon est sorti; *(Tennis)* **'out!'** 'dehors!'; **~ loud** tout haut; **~ with it!** vas-y, parle!
(b) *(fig)* **to be ~** *[person] (unconscious)* être sans connaissance; *(out of game etc)* être éliminé; *(on strike)* être en grève; *(out of fashion)* être démodé; *(have appeared etc) [roses etc]* être épanoui; *[trees]* être vert; *(in blossom)* être en fleurs; *[stars]* briller; *[moon, sun]* être levé; *[secret, news]* être révélé; *[book]* être publié; *[tide]* être bas; *(extinguished) [light, fire, gas]* être éteint; **the socialists are ~** les socialistes ne sont plus au pouvoir; **before the month was ~** avant la fin du mois; *(wrong)* **he was ~ in his calculations, his calculations were ~** il s'est trompé dans ses calculs (*by 20 cm* de 20 cm); **you're not far ~** tu ne te trompes pas de beaucoup; **my watch is 10 minutes ~** ma montre *(fast)* avance *or (slow)* retarde de 10 minutes; *(want)* **to be ~ for sth** vouloir à tout prix qch; **to be ~ to do sth** être résolu à faire qch; **they were ~ to get him** ils avaient résolu sa perte; **to be all ~** * être éreinté; **the car was going all ~** *or* **flat ~** la voiture fonçait à toute vitesse; *(unequivocally)* **right ~, straight ~** franchement; **it's the best car ~** * c'est la meilleure voiture qu'il y ait; **~ and away the youngest** de loin le plus jeune.
2 out of *prep* **(a)** *(outside)* en dehors de, hors de. **to go** *or* **come ~ of the room** sortir de la pièce; **let's get ~ of here!** ne restons pas ici!, partons!; **~ of the window** par la fenêtre; **~ of the way!** écartez-vous!; **you're well ~ of it** c'est aussi bien que vous ne soyez pas dans le coup *; **to feel ~ of it** ne pas se sentir dans le coup *. **(b)** *(cause, motive)* par. **~ of curiosity** par curiosité. **(c)** *(origin, source)* de; dans. **one chapter ~ of a novel** un chapitre d'un roman; **a box made ~ of onyx** une boîte en onyx; **he made the table ~ of a crate** il a fait

la table avec une caisse; **carved ~ of wood** sculpté dans le bois; **to eat/drink ~ of sth** manger/ boire dans qch; **to take sth ~ of a drawer** prendre qch dans un tiroir; **he copied the poem ~ of a book** il a copié le poème dans un livre; **it was like sth ~ of a nightmare** on aurait dit un cauchemar. (**d**) *(from among)* sur. **in 9 cases ~ of 10** dans 9 cas sur 10; **one ~ of 5 smokers** un fumeur sur 5. (**e**) *(without)* sans. **to be ~ of money** être sans argent, ne plus avoir d'argent.

3 *n (*) (pretext)* excuse *f*, échappatoire *f; (solution)* solution *f*.

4 *adj:* ~ **tray** corbeille *f* du courrier à expédier. ◆ **out-and-out** *adj fool, liar, crook* fieffé; *revolutionary, believer* à tout crin; *defeat, victory* total. ◆ **outback** *n (Austr)* intérieur *m* du pays. ◆ **outbid** *pret* **outbid**, *ptp* **outbidden** *vt* enchérir sur. ◆ **outboard** *adj, n* hors-bord *(m) inv*. ◆ **outbreak** *n [war, fighting, disease, epidemic etc]* début *m*; *[violence, spots]* éruption *f*; *[emotion, anger, fever]* accès *m*; *[demonstrations]* vague *f*; **at the ~break of war** lorsque la guerre a éclaté. ◆ **outbuildings** *npl* dépendances *fpl*. ◆ **outburst** *n* explosion *f*; *(angry ~)* crise *f* de colère. ◆ **outcast** *n* proscrit(e) *m(f)*; *(socially)* paria *m*. ◆ **outcome** *n* issue *f*, résultat *m*. ◆ **outcrop** *n (Geol)* affleurement *m*. ◆ **outcry** *n* protestations *fpl*; **to raise an ~cry about sth** ameuter l'opinion sur qch. ◆ **outdated** *adj (gen)* démodé; *word, custom* vieilli. ◆ **outdistance** *vt* distancer. ◆ **outdo** *pret* **outdid**, *ptp* **outdone** *vt* l'emporter sur (*sb in sth* qn en qch); **he was not to be ~done** il refusait de s'avouer vaincu. ◆ **outdoor** *adj activity, games* de plein air; *swimming pool* à ciel ouvert; *clothes* chaud, imperméable; *life* au grand air; **~door centre** centre *m* aéré. ◆ **outdoors** **1** *adv stay, play* dehors; *live* au grand air; *sleep* à la belle étoile ; **2** *n*: **the great ~doors** le grand air. ◆ **outer** *adj door, wrapping* extérieur; *garments* de dessus; *space* cosmique; **the ~er suburbs** la grande banlieue. ◆ **outermost** *adj* le plus à l'extérieur. ◆ **outfit** *etc V below.* ◆ **outfront *** *adj (US: frank)* ouvert, droit. ◆ **outgoing** *adj tenant, president* sortant; *train, boat, plane, mail* en partance; *tide* descendant; *(fig) person, personality* ouvert. ◆ **outgoings** *npl* dépenses *fpl*. ◆ **outgrow** *pret* **outgrew**, *ptp* **outgrown** *vt clothes* devenir trop grand pour; *hobby* ne plus s'intéresser à (en grandissant); *habit* perdre en prenant de l'âge. ◆ **outhouse** *n* appentis *m*; *(US)* cabinets *mpl* extérieurs. ◆ **outing** *n* sortie *f*, excursion *f*. ◆ **outlandish** *adj* exotique; *(pej)* bizarre. ◆ **outlast** *vt* survivre à. ◆ **outlaw** **1** *n* hors-la-loi *m inv* ; **2** *vt person* mettre hors la loi; *activity, organization* proscrire. ◆ **outlay** *n* frais *mpl*, dépenses *fpl*. ◆ **outlet** **1** *n (for water etc)* sortie *f*; *(US Elec)* prise *f* de courant; *[lake]* déversoir *m*; *[river, stream]* embouchure *f*; *[tunnel]* sortie; *(for manufactured goods, talents etc)* débouché *m*; *(for energy, emotions)* exutoire *m* (*for* à); **2** *adj pipe, valve* d'échappement. ◆ **outline** *V below.* ◆ **outlive** *vt* survivre à (*by* de). ◆ **outlook** *n (view)* vue *f* (*on, over* sur); *(fig: prospect)* perspective *f* (d'avenir); *(point of view)* attitude *f* (*on* à l'égard de), point *m* de vue (*on* sur); **the ~look for June is wet** on annonce de la pluie pour juin; **the ~look is rather rosy *** les choses s'annoncent assez bien (*for* pour). ◆ **outlying** *adj (peripheral)* périphérique; *(remote)* écarté. ◆ **outmoded = outdated.** ◆ **outnumber** *vt* surpasser en nombre. ◆ **out-of-date** *adj passport, ticket* périmé; *custom* désuet; *clothes, theory, concept* démodé; *word* vieilli. ◆ **out-of-doors** *adv* = **outdoors 1.** ◆ **out-of-pocket expenses** *npl* débours *mpl*. ◆ **out-of-the-way** *adj place* écarté, perdu; *(unusual)* insolite. ◆ **outpace** *vt* distancer. ◆ **outpatient** *n* malade *mf* en consultation externe; **~patients department** service *m* (hospitalier) de consultation externe. ◆ **outpost** *n* avant-poste *m*; *[organization]* antenne *f*. ◆ **output** **1** *n (gen)* production *f*; *[land, machine, factory worker]* rendement *m*; *(Comput)* sortie *f*; *(Elec)* puissance *f* fournie ; **2** *vi (Comput)* sortir. ◆ **outrage** *V below.* ◆ **outrider** *n* motocycliste *m*, motard * *m (d'une escorte)*. ◆ **outright** **1** *adv kill* sur le coup; *win, own* complètement; *buy* comptant; *reject, refuse, deny* catégoriquement; *(forthrightly) say* carrément ; **2** *adj win* complet, total; *selfishness* pur; *denial etc* catégorique; *supporter* inconditionnel; *winner* incontesté. ◆ **outrun** *pret* **outran**, *ptp* **outrun** *vt* distancer. ◆ **outset** *n* début *m*. ◆ **outshine** *pret, ptp* **outshone** *vt* éclipser. ◆ **outside** *V below.* ◆ **outsize** *adj (gen)* énorme; *clothes* grande taille *inv*; *shop* spécialisé dans les grandes tailles. ◆ **outskirts** *npl [town]* faubourgs *mpl*, banlieue *f*; *[forest]* lisière *f*. ◆ **outspoken** *adj* franc. ◆ **outspokenly** *adv* franchement, carrément. ◆ **outspokenness** *n* franchise *f*. ◆ **outstanding** *adj* (**a**) *(exceptional)* remarquable, exceptionnel; *detail, event* marquant; *feature* dominant; (**b**) *(unfinished etc) business* en suspens; *account, debt* impayé; *interest* à échoir; *problem* non résolu; **the work is still ~standing** ce travail reste à faire. ◆ **outstandingly** *adv* remarquablement, exceptionnellement. ◆ **outstay** *vt*: **to ~stay sb** rester plus longtemps que qn; **to ~stay one's welcome** abuser de l'hospitalité de qn. ◆ **outstretched** *adj body, leg* étendu; *arm* tendu; *wings* déployé. ◆ **outstrip** *vt* devancer. ◆ **outward** **1** *adv (also* **~wards***)* vers l'extérieur; *(Naut)* **~ward bound** en partance (*for* pour, *from* de) ; **2** *adj movement* vers l'extérieur; *ship, freight* en partance; *appearance etc* extérieur; **~ward journey** aller *m*; **with an ~ward show of pleasure** en faisant mine d'être ravi. ◆ **outwardly** *adv* extérieurement, du dehors; *(apparently)* en apparence. ◆ **outweigh** *vt* l'emporter sur. ◆ **outwit** *vt* se montrer plus malin que. ◆ **outworn** *adj clothes* usé; *custom, doctrine, idea* périmé.

outfit ['aʊtfɪt] *n* (**a**) *(clothes and equipment)* équipement *m*; *(tools)* matériel *m*. **a Red Indian ~** une panoplie d'Indien; **puncture repair ~** trousse *f* de réparation (de pneus). (**b**) *(set of clothes)* tenue *f*. **skiing ~** tenue *f* de ski. (**c**) *(*: organization etc)* équipe * *f*. **he's not in our ~** il n'est pas un des nôtres.

◆ **outfitter** *n*: **gents' ~ter** spécialiste *mf* de confection pour hommes; **sports ~ter's** maison *f* d'articles de sport.

outline ['aʊtlaɪn] **1** *n [object]* contour *m*; *[building, tree, face]* profil *m*; *(shorthand)* sténogramme *m*; *(plan)* plan *m; (less exact)* esquisse *f*. *(main features)* **~s** grandes lignes *fpl*; **rough ~ of an article** canevas *m* d'un article; **to give the broad ~s of sth** esquisser qch à grands traits. **2** *vt theory, plan, idea* exposer les grandes lignes de; *book, event* faire un bref compte rendu de; *facts, details* passer brièvement en revue; *situation* donner un aperçu de.

outrage ['aʊtreɪdʒ] **1** *n (act)* atrocité *f*; *(during riot etc)* acte *m* de violence; *(emotion)* intense indignation *f*. **it's an ~ against humanity** c'est un crime contre l'humanité; **an ~ against justice** un outrage à la justice; **bomb ~** attentat *m* à la bombe; **it's an ~!** c'est un scandale! **2** *vt* [aʊt'reɪdʒ] *sb's feelings* outrager. **to be ~d by sth** trouver qch monstrueux. ◆ **outrageous** *adj crime, suffering, action* atroce, monstrueux; *remark* outrageant; *sense of humour* scabreux; *price* exorbitant; *hat, fashion* extravagant; **it's ~ous that...** il est scandaleux que... + *subj*. ◆ **outrageously** *adv suffer* atrocement; *behave, speak, lie* outrageusement; *dress* de manière grotesque; *expensive* atrocement.

outside [ˌaʊt'saɪd] **1** *adv* (au) dehors, à l'extérieur. **go and play ~** va jouer dehors; **the box was clean ~** la boîte était propre à l'extérieur; **to go ~** sortir.

2 *prep* (**a**) *(lit)* à l'extérieur de, hors de. ~ **the house** dehors, à l'extérieur de la maison, hors de la maison; ~ **the door** à la porte; **don't go** ~ **the garden** ne sors pas du jardin; ~ **the harbour** au large du port. (**b**) *(fig)* en dehors de. ~ **the festival proper** en dehors du vrai festival; **it's** ~ **the normal range** ceci sort de la gamme normale. **3** *n* extérieur *m (also fig)*, dehors *m*. ~ **in = inside out** *(V* **inside***)*; *(fig)* **judging from the** ~ à en juger par les apparences; **he passed the car on the** ~ il a doublé la voiture *(Brit)* sur la droite *or (US, Europe etc)* sur la gauche; **at the very** ~ tout au plus, au maximum.
4 *adj* extérieur *(also fig)*; *(maximum)* maximum. *(in plane etc)* **an** ~ **seat** une place côté couloir; *(Aut)* **the** ~ **lane** *(Brit)* la voie de droite; *(US, Europe etc)* la voie de gauche; *(Rad, TV)* ~ **broadcast** émission *f* réalisée à l'extérieur; *(Telec)* ~ **line** ligne *f* extérieure; ~ **interests** passe-temps *mpl inv;* **to get an** ~ **opinion** demander l'avis d'une personne indépendante; *(fig)* **an** ~ **chance** une très faible chance.
◆ **outside-left/-right** *n* ailier *m* gauche/droit. ◆ **outsider** *n (stranger)* étranger *m*, -ère *f*; *(horse or person unlikely to win)* outsider *m*.

oval ['əʊv(ə)l] *adj, n* ovale *(m)*.

ovary ['əʊvərɪ] *n* ovaire *m*.

ovation [ə(ʊ)'veɪʃ(ə)n] *n* ovation *f*.

oven ['ʌvn] **1** *n* four *m*. *(Culin)* **in the** ~ au four; **in a hot/cool** ~ à four chaud/doux; **it is like an** ~ c'est une fournaise. **2** *adj*: ~ **glove** gant *m* isolant. ◆ **ovenproof** *adj* allant au four. ◆ **oven-ready** *adj* prêt à cuire. ◆ **ovenware** *n* plats *mpl* allant au four.

over ['əʊvə^r] **1** *adv* (**a**) *(above)* (par-)dessus. **children of 8 and** ~ enfants à partir de 8 ans. (**b**) *(across)* ~ **here** ici; ~ **there** là-bas; **he has gone** ~ **to Belgium** il est parti en Belgique; **they're** ~ **from Canada** ils arrivent du Canada; **he drove us** ~ **to the other side of town** il nous a conduits de l'autre côté de la ville; *(Telec etc)* ~ **to you!** à vous!; **he went** ~ **to his mother's** il est passé chez sa mère; **let's ask Paul** ~ si on invitait Paul à venir nous voir?; **I'll be** ~ **at 7 o'clock** je passerai à 7 heures; **they were** ~ **for the day** ils sont venus passer la journée; *(fig)* **he went** ~ **to the enemy** il est passé à l'ennemi; *(fig)* **I've gone** ~ **to a new brand of coffee** j'ai changé de marque de café; ~ **against the wall** là-bas contre le mur. (**c**) **all** ~ partout; **the world** ~ dans le monde entier; **covered all** ~ **with dust** tout couvert de poussière; **embroidered all** ~ tout brodé; **he was trembling all** ~ il tremblait de tous ses membres; *(fig)* **that's him all** ~! c'est bien de lui! (**d**) *(down etc)* **he hit her and** ~ **she went** il l'a frappée et elle a basculé; **he turned the watch** ~ **and** ~ il a retourné la montre dans tous les sens. (**e**) *(again)* encore (une fois). ~ **and** ~ **(again)** à maintes reprises; **5 times** ~ 5 fois de suite; **start all** ~ **again** recommencez au début. (**f**) *(finished)* fini. **the rain is** ~ la pluie s'est arrêtée; **the danger was** ~ le danger était passé; **it was just** ~ cela venait de finir *or* de se terminer; ~ **and done with** tout à fait fini. (**g**) *(too)* trop, très. **she's not** ~ **strong** elle n'est pas trop *or* tellement solide. (**h**) *(remaining)* en plus. **if there is any meat (left)** ~ s'il reste de la viande; **there are 3** ~ il en reste 3; **6 metres and a bit** ~ un peu plus de 6 mètres.
2 *prep* (**a**) *(on top of)* sur, par-dessus. **he spread the blanket** ~ **the bed** il a étendu la couverture sur le lit; **I spilled coffee** ~ **it** j'ai renversé du café dessus; **she put on a cardigan** ~ **her blouse** elle a mis un gilet par-dessus son corsage. (**b**) *(above)* au-dessus de. **a lamp** ~ **the table** une lampe au-dessus de la table. (**c**) *(across)* par-dessus; de l'autre côté de. **the house** ~ **the road** la maison d'en face; **there is a café** ~ **the road** il y a un café en face; **the bridge** ~ **the river** le pont qui traverse la rivière; **it's just** ~ **the river** c'est juste de l'autre côté de la rivière; **tourists from** ~ **the Atlantic** touristes *mpl* d'outre-Atlantique; **to look** ~ **the wall/sb's shoulder** regarder par-dessus le mur/l'épaule de qn; **to jump** ~ **a wall** sauter un mur; ~ **the border** au-delà de la frontière. (**d**) *(fig) (during)* au cours de, pendant; *(near)* près de. ~ **Friday** jusqu'à vendredi soir; ~ **a period of** sur une période de; **sitting** ~ **the fire** assis tout près du feu; ~ **a cup of coffee** (tout) en buvant une tasse de café; ~ **the phone** au téléphone; ~ **the radio** à la radio; **how long will you be** ~ **it?** combien de temps cela te prendra-t-il?; **what came** ~ **you?** qu'est-ce qui t'a pris?; **they fell out** ~ **money** ils se sont brouillés pour une question d'argent; **an increase** ~ une augmentation par rapport à; ~ **and above what...** sans compter ce que...; **but** ~ **and above that...** mais en outre *or* par-dessus le marché... (**e**) *(everywhere in)* **all** ~ **France** partout en France; **all** ~ **the world** dans le monde entier. (**f**) *(more than)* plus de, au-dessus de. ~ **3 hours** plus de 3 heures; **she is** ~ **sixty** elle a plus de soixante ans; **women** ~ **21** les femmes (âgées) de plus de 21 ans; **all numbers** ~ **20** tous les chiffres au-dessus de 20.
3 *pref e.g.* **overabundant** surabondant; **overcautious** trop prudent, prudent à l'excès; **overcautiousness** excès *m* de prudence.
◆ **overact** *vi* charger son rôle. ◆ **overactive** *adj* trop actif. ◆ **overall 1** *adv survey* en général; *measure, decorate* d'un bout à l'autre ; **2** *adj study, survey* d'ensemble; *width, length* total; *(Aut)* ~**all measurements** encombrement *m*; *(Sport)* ~**all placings** le classement général ; **3** *n* blouse *f (de travail)*; *(Ind etc)* ~**s** bleus *mpl* (de travail). ◆ **overanxious** *adj* trop anxieux. ◆ **overawe** *vt* impressionner. ◆ **overbalance 1** *vi* basculer ; **2** *vt* faire basculer. ◆ **overbearing** *adj* autoritaire. ◆ **overboard** *adv* par-dessus bord; **man** ~**board!** un homme à la mer!; *(fig)* **to go** ~**board for sth** s'emballer * pour qch. ◆ **overbook** *vi [hotel]* surréserver. ◆ **overbooking** *n* surréservation *f*. ◆ **overburden** *vt* surcharger (*with* de). ◆ **overcast** *adj* couvert. ◆ **overcharge 1** *vt* (**a**) **to** ~**charge sb for sth** faire payer qch trop cher à qn; (**b**) *(Elec)* surcharger ; **2** *vi* demander un prix excessif. ◆ **overcoat** *n* manteau *m*; *[soldier]* capote *f*; *[sailor]* caban *m*. ◆ **overcome** *pret* **overcame**, *ptp* **overcome** *vt enemy, opposition* triompher de; *temptation, obstacle* surmonter; *one's rage etc* maîtriser; **we shall** ~**come!** nous vaincrons!; **to be** ~**come by** succomber à; ~**come with fear** paralysé par la peur; **she was quite** ~**come** elle était saisie. ◆ **overconfidence** *n* suffisance *f*, présomption *f*. ◆ **overconfident** *adj* suffisant, présomptueux. ◆ **overcook** *vt* faire trop cuire. ◆ **overcrowded** *adj room, bus* bondé; *house, town* surpeuplé; *class* surchargé. ◆ **overcrowding** *n (in housing, town)* surpeuplement *m*; *(in classroom)* effectifs *mpl* surchargés; *(in bus etc)* encombrement *m*. ◆ **overdo** *pret* **overdid**, *ptp* **overdone** *vt (exaggerate)* exagérer; *(overcook)* faire trop cuire; **don't** ~**do the smoking** ne fume pas trop; **to** ~**do it, to** ~**do things** *(exaggerate)* exagérer; *(work etc too hard)* s'éreinter, se surmener. ◆ **overdone** *adj* exagéré; *(overcooked)* trop cuit. ◆ **overdose** *n* surdose *f*; **to take an** ~**dose** * prendre une surdose de sédatifs (*or* barbituriques *etc*). ◆ **overdraft** *n (Fin)* découvert *m*; **I've got an** ~**draft** mon compte est à découvert. ◆ **overdraw** *pret* **overdrew**, *ptp* **overdrawn** *vt (Fin)* mettre à découvert. ◆ **overdrawn** *adj* à découvert. ◆ **overdress 1** *n* robe-chasuble *f*; **2** *vi* s'habiller avec trop de recherche. ◆ **overdrive** *n (Aut)* (vitesse *f*) surmultipliée *f*. ◆ **overdue** *adj train, bus* en retard; *reform* qui tarde (à être réalisé); *acknowledgement, apology* tardif; *account*

impayé; **the plane is 20 minutes ~due** l'avion a 20 minutes de retard; **that change is long ~due** ce changement se fait attendre depuis longtemps. ◆ **overeat** *pret* **overate,** *ptp* **overeaten** *vi* trop manger. ◆ **overeating** *n* excès *mpl* de table. ◆ **overemphasize** *vt* donner trop d'importance à. ◆ **overestimate** *vt* surestimer. ◆ **overexcited** *adj* surexcité. ◆ **overexert** *vt*: **to ~exert o.s.** se surmener. ◆ **overexertion** *n* surmenage *m*. ◆ **overexpose** *vt* surexposer. ◆ **overfeed** *pret, ptp* **overfed** *vt* suralimenter. ◆ **overfeeding** *n* suralimentation *f*. ◆ **overflow 1** *n (outlet)* trop-plein *m*; *[reservoir etc]* déversoir *m*; *(excess people, objects)* excédent *m*; **2** *vt* déborder de ; **3** *vi* déborder (*with* de); **to fill/full to ~flowing** remplir/plein à ras bords ; **4** *adj pipe* d'écoulement. ◆ **overfly** *pret* **overflew,** *ptp* **overflown** *vt* survoler. ◆ **overgrown** *adj path* envahi par l'herbe; **~grown with** recouvert de. ◆ **overhang** *pret, ptp* **overhung 1** *vt* surplomber ; **2** *n* surplomb *m*. ◆ **overhanging** *adj* en surplomb. ◆ **overhaul 1** *n [vehicle, machine]* révision *f*; *[ship]* radoub *m*; *[system]* refonte *f* ; **2** *vt* (**a**) *(check)* réviser; radouber; refondre; (**b**) *(catch up with)* rattraper. ◆ **overhead 1** *adv* au-dessus; *(in the sky)* dans le ciel ; **2** *adj cables, railway* aérien; *lighting* vertical; **~head projector** rétroprojecteur *m; (Aut)* **~head valve** soupape *f* en tête ; **3** *n (US)* **~head,** *(Brit)* **~heads** frais *mpl* généraux. ◆ **overhear** *pret, ptp* **overheard** *vt* entendre *(souvent par hasard)*. ◆ **overheat 1** *vt* surchauffer ; **2** *vi [engine]* chauffer. ◆ **overheated** *adj room* surchauffé; *brakes, engine* qui chauffe. ◆ **overjoyed** *adj* ravi, enchanté (*at, by* de; *to do* de faire; *that* que + *subj*). ◆ **overkill** *n (Mil)* (capacité *f* de) surextermination *f*; *(fig)* **that was a massive ~kill** * c'était bien plus qu'il n'en fallait! ◆ **overladen** *adj* surchargé. ◆ **overland** *adj, adv* par voie de terre. ◆ **overlap 1** *n* chevauchement *m* ; **2** *vi* se chevaucher. ◆ **overlay 1** *vt* recouvrir (*with* de) ; **2** *n* revêtement *m*. ◆ **overleaf** *adv* au verso. ◆ **overload 1** *n* surcharge *f* ; **2** *vt circuit, truck* surcharger (*with* de); *engine* surmener. ◆ **overlook** *vt* (**a**) *[house etc]* donner sur; **our garden is not ~looked** les voisins n'ont pas vue sur notre jardin; (**b**) *(miss)* oublier; (**c**) *(ignore)* fermer les yeux sur. ◆ **overlord** *n (gen)* chef *m* suprême; *(Hist)* suzerain *m*. ◆ **overmanning** *n* sureffectifs *mpl*. ◆ **overmuch 1** *adv* trop ; **2** *adj* trop de. ◆ **overnight 1** *adv (during the night)* (pendant) la nuit; *(until next day)* jusqu'à demain *or* au lendemain; *(suddenly)* du jour au lendemain ; **2** *adj stay* d'une nuit; *journey* de nuit; *(fig) change* soudain; **~night bag** nécessaire *m* de voyage. ◆ **overpass** *n (Aut)* pont *m* autoroutier; *(at flyover)* autopont *m*. ◆ **overpay** *pret, ptp* **overpaid** *vt* trop payer; **he was ~paid by £5** on lui a payé 5 livres de trop. ◆ **overpayment** *n* surpaye *f*. ◆ **overpopulated** *adj* surpeuplé. ◆ **overpopulation** *n* surpopulation *f* (*in* dans). ◆ **overpower** *vt (subdue physically)* maîtriser; *(defeat)* vaincre; *(fig)* accabler. ◆ **overpowering** *adj strength, desire* irrésistible; *smell, heat* suffocant. ◆ **overpriced** *adj* excessivement cher. ◆ **overrate** *vt* surestimer, faire trop grand cas de. ◆ **overrated** *adj* surfait. ◆ **overreach** *vt*: **to ~reach o.s.** vouloir trop entreprendre. ◆ **overreact** *vi* réagir de manière excessive. ◆ **override** *pret* **overrode,** *ptp* **overridden** *vt law* fouler aux pieds; *decision* annuler; *objections, order, wishes* passer outre à; *person* passer outre aux opinions de; **this fact ~rides all others** ce fait l'emporte sur tous les autres. ◆ **overrider** *n (Aut)* tampon *m* (de pare-choc). ◆ **overriding** *adj importance* primordial; *factor, item* prépondérant. ◆ **overrule** *vt judgment, decision* annuler; *claim, objection* rejeter; **he was ~ruled by the chairman** la décision du président a prévalu contre lui. ◆ **overrun** *pret* **overran,** *ptp* **overrun 1** *vt [rats, weeds]* envahir; *[troops]* occuper ; **2** *vi [programme]* dépasser l'heure prévue (*by* de). ◆ **overseas 1** *adv* outre-mer; *(abroad)* à l'étranger; **2** *adj colony, market* d'outre-mer; *trade* extérieur; *visitor* (venu) d'outre-mer, étranger; *aid* aux pays étrangers; **Ministry of O~seas Development** ≃ ministère *m* de la Coopération. ◆ **oversee** *pret* **oversaw,** *ptp* **overseen** *vt* surveiller. ◆ **overseer** *n (foreman)* contremaître *m*; *[prisoners, slaves]* surveillant *m*. ◆ **overshadow** *vt [clouds]* obscurcir; *(fig)* éclipser. ◆ **overshoot** *pret, ptp* **overshot** *vt* dépasser. ◆ **oversight** *n* omission *f*, oubli *m*; **by** *or* **through an ~sight** par inadvertance. ◆ **oversimplification** *n* simplification *f* excessive. ◆ **oversimplify** *vt* simplifier à l'extrême. ◆ **oversize(d)** *adj (gen)* trop grand; *class* surchargé; *family* trop nombreux. ◆ **oversleep** *pret, ptp* **overslept** *vi* dormir trop longtemps. ◆ **overspend** *pret, ptp* **overspent** *vt* dépenser au-dessus *or* au-delà de. ◆ **overspill** *n* excédent *m* de population; **an ~spill town** une ville-satellite. ◆ **overstep** *vt* outrepasser; **to ~step the mark** dépasser la mesure. ◆ **overtake** *pret* **overtook,** *ptp* **overtaken** *vt (catch up)* rattraper; *(pass) car* doubler; *competitor* dépasser; *[storm, night]* surprendre; *[fate]* frapper ; **~taken by events** dépassé par les événements. ◆ **overtax** *vt (Fin)* surimposer; *(fig) sb's strength, patience* abuser de; *person* surmener. ◆ **overthrow** *pret* **overthrew,** *ptp* **overthrown 1** *vt enemy, country* vaincre (définitivement); *dictator, government* renverser ; **2** *n* défaite *f*; renversement *m*. ◆ **overtime** *n* (**a**) *(work, pay)* heures *fpl* supplémentaires; **to work ~time** faire des heures supplémentaires; *(fig)* mettre les bouchées doubles (*to do* pour faire); (**b**) *(US Sport)* prolongation *f*. ◆ **overtone** *n [hostility, anger]* accent *m*; **political ~tones** sous-entendus *mpl* politiques. ◆ **overturn 1** *vt (gen)* renverser; *boat* faire chavirer ; **2** *vi* se renverser; *[car, plane, railway coach]* se retourner; *[boat]* chavirer. ◆ **overuse** *vt* abuser de. ◆ **overvalue** *vt* surestimer. ◆ **overview** *n* vue *f* d'ensemble. ◆ **overweight** *adj*: **to be ~weight** *[person]* être trop gros; *[suitcase etc]* être en excès du poids réglementaire; **to be 5 kilos ~weight** peser 5 kilos de trop. ◆ **overwhelm** *vt [flood, avalanche]* engloutir; *[beauty etc]* bouleverser; *enemy, opponent* écraser; *[emotions, misfortunes, shame]* accabler; *[praise, kindness]* rendre confus; **to ~whelm sb with questions** accabler qn dequestions; **~whelmed by his kindness** tout confus de sa bonté; **~whelmed** *(happy)* au comble de la joie; *(sad)* accablé (par la douleur); **~whelmed with work/offers** débordé de travail/submergé d'offres. ◆ **overwhelming** *adj victory, majority, defeat* écrasant; *desire, power, pressure* irrésistible; *misfortune, sorrow, heat* accablant; *welcome* extrêmement chaleureux. ◆ **overwhelmingly** *adv win, defeat* d'une manière écrasante; *vote, accept* en masse. ◆ **overwork 1** *n* surmenage *m* ; **2** *vt* surmener ; **3** *vi* se surmener. ◆ **overwrought** *adj* excédé.

overt [ə(ʊ)'vɜːt] *adj* déclaré, non déguisé. ◆ **overtly** *adv* ouvertement.

overture ['əʊvətʃʊə] *n (Mus, fig)* ouverture *f*.

ovulate ['ɒvjʊleɪt] *vi* produire des ovules, ovuler. ◆ **ovulation** *n* ovulation *f*. ◆ **ovum,** *pl* **ova** *n* ovule *m*.

owe [əʊ] *vt (gen)* devoir (*to* à). **to ~ sb a grudge** garder rancune à qn (*for* de); **you ~ it to yourself to make a success of it** vous vous devez de réussir. ◆ **owing 1** *adj* dû; **the amount owing on...** ce qui reste dû sur...; **the money still owing to me** la somme qu'on me doit encore ; **2 owing to** *prep* par suite de, en raison de.

owl [aʊl] *n* hibou *m*. ◆ **owlish** *adj* de hibou. ◆ **owlishly** *adv* comme un hibou.

own [əʊn] **1** *adj* propre *(before n)*. **his (very) ~ car** sa propre voiture, sa voiture à lui; **with my ~**

eyes de mes propres yeux; **it's all my ~ work!** c'est moi qui ai tout fait moi-même!; **he does his ~ cooking** il fait sa cuisine lui-même; **the house has its ~ garage** la maison a son garage particulier; **my ~ one** mon chéri, ma chérie; *(Ftbl)* **~ goal** auto-goal *m.*

2 *pron* (**a**) **that's my ~** c'est à moi, c'est le mien; **those are his ~** ceux-là sont à lui, ceux-là sont les siens; **my time is my ~** je suis libre de mon temps; **it's all my ~** c'est tout à moi; **a charm all its ~** *or* **of its ~** un charme qui lui est propre; **for reasons of his ~** pour des raisons personnelles; **a copy of your ~** votre propre exemplaire; **a house of your very ~** une maison bien à vous *or* à vous tout seul; **I have money of my ~** j'ai de l'argent à moi. (**b**) *(phrases)* **(all) on one's ~** tout seul; **to see sb on his ~** voir qn seul à seul; *(fig)* **you're on your ~ now!** à toi de jouer!; **he's got nothing to call his ~** il n'a rien à lui; **to come into one's ~** réaliser sa destinée; **to get one's ~ back** prendre sa revanche (*on sb for sth* sur qn de qch).

3 *vt* (**a**) *(possess) object, vehicle* posséder; *house, newspaper, company* être le (*or* la) propriétaire de. **who ~s this?** à qui est-ce que cela appartient?; **he looks as if he ~s the place *** on dirait qu'il est chez lui. (**b**) *(acknowledge)* avouer, reconnaître (*that* que).

4 *vi*: **to ~ to** *mistake* reconnaître avoir commis; *debts* reconnaître avoir. **he ~ed to having done it** il a avoué l'avoir fait.

◆ **own up** *vi* avouer. **to ~ up to (doing) sth** admettre (avoir fait) qch.

◆ **owner** *n* propriétaire *mf*; **who is the ~er of this book?** à qui appartient ce livre?; **all dog ~ers** tous ceux qui ont un chien; **at ~ers risk** aux risques du client. ◆ **owner-driver** *n* conducteur *m* propriétaire. ◆ **owner-occupied** *adj* occupé par son propriétaire. ◆ **owner-occupier** *n* occupant *m* propriétaire. ◆ **ownership** *n* possession *f*; *(Comm)* **'under new ~ership'** 'changement de propriétaire'.

ox, *pl* **oxen** [ɒks, 'ɒksən] *n* bœuf *m.* ◆ **oxcart** *n* char *m* à bœufs. ◆ **ox-eye daisy** *n* marguerite *f.* ◆ **oxtail soup** *n* soupe *f* à la queue de bœuf.

oxide ['ɒksaɪd] *n* oxyde *m.* ◆ **oxidize** **1** *vt* oxyder ; **2** *vi* s'oxyder.

oxyacetylene ['ɒksɪə'setɪliːn] *adj*: **~ burner** chalumeau *m* oxyacétylénique.

oxygen ['ɒksɪdʒ(ə)n] **1** *n* oxygène *m.* **2** *adj cylinder* d'oxygène; *mask, tent* à oxygène.

oyster ['ɔɪstəʳ] *n* huître *f.* **the world is his ~** le monde est à lui; **~ bed** banc *m* d'huîtres. **~ shell** coquille *f* d'huître.

ozone ['əʊzəʊn] *n* ozone *m.* **~ layer** couche *f* d'ozone. ◆ **ozone-friendly** *adj* qui ne détruit pas l'ozone.

P

P, p [piː] *n* (**a**) *(letter)* P, p *m.* **to mind one's Ps and Qs** * se surveiller. (**b**) **1 p** un (nouveau) penny; **2 p** deux (nouveaux) pence.

pa * [pɑː] *n* papa *m.*

pace [peɪs] **1** *n* (**a**) *(measure)* pas *m.* **20 ~s away** à 20 pas; *(fig)* **to put sb through his ~s** mettre qn à l'épreuve. (**b**) *(speed)* pas *m*, allure *f.* **at a good ~** d'un bon pas, à vive allure; **at a slow ~** à pas lents, à petite allure; **at a walking ~** au pas; **to set the ~** *(Sport)* donner l'allure; *(fig)* donner le ton; **to keep ~ with** aller à la même allure que; *(fig)* marcher de pair avec. **2** *vi*: **to ~ up and down** faire les cent pas. **3** *vt* (**a**) *room, street* arpenter. **to ~ sth out** mesurer qch au pas. (**b**) *(Sport) runner* régler l'allure de. ◆ **pacemaker** *n (Med)* stimulateur *m* cardiaque.

pacify [ˈpæsɪfaɪ] *vt person, fears* apaiser; *country, creditors* pacifier. ◆ **pacific** *adj* pacifique; **the Pacific (Ocean)** le Pacifique, l'océan *m* Pacifique. ◆ **pacification** *n* apaisement *m*; pacification *f.* ◆ **pacifier** *n (dummy-teat)* tétine *f*; *(person)* pacificateur *m*, -trice *f.* ◆ **pacifism** *n* pacifisme *m.* ◆ **pacifist** *adj, n* pacifiste *(mf).*

pack [pæk] **1** *n* (**a**) *[goods, cotton]* balle *f*; *[pedlar]* ballot *m*; *[~ animal]* bât *m*; *(Mil)* sac *m* (d'ordonnance); *(Comm)* paquet *m*. *(US)* **~ of cigarettes** paquet de cigarettes. (**b**) *(group) [hounds]* meute *f*; *[wolves, thieves]* bande *f.* **~ of lies** tissu *m* de mensonges. (**c**) *[cards]* jeu *m.* (**d**) *(Rugby)* pack *m.* (**e**) *(Med)* **cold/wet ~** compresse *f* froide/humide.

2 *vt* (**a**) *(put into box etc) objects, goods* emballer. *(Comm)* **~ed in dozens** en paquets de douze; **~ed lunch** repas froid; **~ed in straw** enveloppé dans de la paille. (**b**) *(fill tightly) box, suitcase* remplir (*with* de); *room, vehicle, memory* bourrer (*with* de). **to ~ one's case** faire sa valise; **to ~ one's bags** faire ses bagages *or* ses valises; *(fig)* plier bagage; **they ~ed the hall** ils se pressaient dans la salle. (**c**) *(crush together) earth, objects* tasser (*into* dans); *people* entasser (*into* dans). **~ed like sardines** serrés comme des sardines.

3 *vi* (**a**) *(do one's luggage)* faire sa valise *or* ses bagages. (**b**) *[people]* se presser, s'entasser (*into* dans).

◆ **pack away** *vt sep* ranger. ◆ **pack in** ⁑ **1** *vi (break down) [car, watch etc]* tomber en panne. **2** *vt sep (stop)* laisser tomber *. ◆ **pack off** * *vt sep* envoyer promener *. **to ~ sb off to** expédier * qn à. ◆ **pack up 1** *vi* (**a**) *(do one's luggage)* faire sa valise. (**b**) (*) *(give up)* plier bagage; *[watch, machine]* tomber en panne. **2** *vt sep* (**a**) *clothes, belongings* mettre dans une valise; *object, book* emballer. (**b**) *(⁑: give up) work, school* laisser tomber *.

◆ **package 1** *n* (**a**) *(parcel)* paquet *m*, colis *m*; (**b**) *(fig) (items for sale)* marché *m* global; *(contract)* contrat *m* global; *(purchase)* achat *m* forfaitaire; *(Comput)* progiciel; **~age (tour)** voyage *m* organisé; **~age of measures** ensemble *m* de mesures ; **2** *adj tour, holiday* organisé; **~age deal** marché *m* global ; **3** *vt (Comm)* emballer. ◆ **packaging** *n (materials)* emballage *m.* ◆ **packed** *adj room, vehicle* bondé; **~ed out** *theatre* comble; **I'm ~ed** j'ai fait mes valises. ◆ **packer** *n (person)* emballeur *m*, -euse *f*; *(device)* emballeuse *f.* ◆ **packet** *n (gen)* paquet *m*; *[needles, sweets]* sachet *m*; **to cost a ~et** * coûter les yeux de la tête. ◆ **packhorse** *n* cheval *m* de charge. ◆ **packing 1** *n* (**a**) **to do one's ~ing** faire sa valise; (**b**) *(material, Comm)* emballage *m* ; **2** *adj*: **~ing case** caisse *f* d'emballage.

pact [pækt] *n* pacte *m*, traité *m.*

pad [pæd] **1** *n* (**a**) *(to prevent friction, damage)* coussinet *m*; *(Tech)* tampon *m* (amortisseur); *(Ftbl)* protège-cheville *m inv*; *(Hockey etc)* jambière *f*; *(for inking)* tampon encreur. (**b**) *(writing ~)* bloc *m* (de papier à lettres); *(note ~)* bloc-notes *m.* (**c**) *[rabbit]* patte *f*; *[cat, dog]* coussin *m* charnu. (**d**) *(launching ~)* rampe *f* (de lancement). (**e**) (*: *sanitary towel)* serviette *f* hygiénique. **2** *vi*: **to ~ along/up** *etc* marcher/monter *etc* à pas feutrés. **3** *vt cushion, shoulders* rembourrer; *clothing* matelasser; *furniture, door* capitonner; *meal* rendre plus copieux. **to ~ out** *speech* délayer; **~ded cell** cabanon *m*; **~ded envelope** *or* **bag** enveloppe matelassée. ◆ **padding** *n* rembourrage *m*; *(in book etc)* délayage *m.*

paddle [ˈpædl] **1** *n [canoe]* pagaie *f*; *(US: Table Tennis)* raquette *f* de ping-pong. **2** *adj*: **~ steamer** bateau *m* à roues; **paddling pool** pataugeoire *f.* **3** *vt*: **to ~ a canoe** pagayer. **4** *vi* (**a**) *(walk)* barboter. (**b**) *(in canoe)* pagayer. **to ~ up/down the river** remonter/descendre la rivière en pagayant.

paddock [ˈpædək] *n* enclos *m (pour chevaux)*; *(Racing)* paddock *m.*

paddy [ˈpædɪ] *n*: **~ field** rizière *f.*

padlock [ˈpædlɒk] **1** *n [door, chain]* cadenas *m*; *[cycle]* antivol *m.* **2** *vt* cadenasser; mettre un antivol à.

padre [ˈpɑːdrɪ] *n (Mil, Naut etc)* aumônier *m.*

paediatric, *(US)* **pediatric** [ˌpiːdɪˈætrɪk] *adj department* de pédiatrie; *illness, medicine, surgery* infantile. ◆ **p(a)ediatrician** *n* pédiatre *mf.* ◆ **p(a)ediatrics** *nsg* pédiatrie *f.*

pagan [ˈpeɪgən] *adj, n (lit, fig)* païen(ne) *m(f).*

page¹ [peɪdʒ] *n* page *f.* **on ~ 10** (à la) page 10; **continued on ~ 20** suite page 20.

page² [peɪdʒ] **1** *n (also* **~ boy***) (in hotel)* groom *m*; *(at court)* page *m*; *(US Congress)* jeune huissier *m.* **2** *vt client* faire appeler; *(out loud)* appeler.

pageant [ˈpædʒ(ə)nt] *n* spectacle *m* historique. ◆ **pageantry** *n* apparat *m.*

paid [peɪd] *(pret, ptp of* **pay***) adj staff* rémunéré; *gunman etc* à gages. ◆ **paid-up** *adj member* qui a payé sa cotisation.

pail [peɪl] *n* seau *m.*

pain [peɪn] **1** *n* (**a**) *(physical)* douleur *f*; *(mental)* peine *f*; *(stronger)* douleur. **to be in (great) ~** souffrir (beaucoup); **to cause ~ to** *(physically)* faire mal à; *(mentally)* faire de la peine à; **I have a ~ in my shoulder** j'ai mal à l'épaule; **to give sb a ~ in the neck** * enquiquiner qn *; **he's a ~ (in the neck)** * il est casse-pieds *. (**b**) *(trouble)* **~s** peine *f*; **to take ~s to do sth** faire qch très soigneusement; **to take ~s over sth** se donner beaucoup de mal pour qch; **to spare no ~s** ne pas ménager ses efforts (*to do* pour faire). (**c**) **on ~ of death** sous peine de mort. **2** *vt* faire de la peine à; *(stronger)* faire souffrir. ◆ **pained** *adj* peiné. ◆ **painful** *adj wound* douloureux; *sight, task, duty* pénible; **my hand is ~ful**

j'ai mal à la main; **it is ~ful to see her** elle fait peine à voir. ◆ **painfully** *adv throb* douloureusement; *walk* péniblement; (*) *thin* terriblement *; **it was ~fully clear that...** il n'était que trop évident que... ◆ **painkiller** *n* calmant *m*. ◆ **painless** *adj operation* indolore; *extraction, childbirth* sans douleur; *(fig) experience* bénin; *exam* pas trop méchant *. ◆ **painlessly** *adv* sans douleur. ◆ **painstaking** *adj work* soigné; *person* appliqué, soigneux. ◆ **painstakingly** *adv* avec soin.

paint [peɪnt] **1** *n* peinture *f*. **~s** couleurs *fpl*; **box of ~s** boîte *f* de couleurs. **2** *vt (gen, Art)* peindre; *(Med)* badigeonner. **to ~ a wall red** peindre un mur en rouge; **to ~ one's nails** se vernir les ongles; *(fig)* **to ~ the town red** faire la bringue *. **3** *vi* peindre. ◆ **paintbox** *n* boîte *f* de couleurs. ◆ **paintbrush** *n* pinceau *m*. ◆ **painter**[1] *n (Art)* peintre *m*; **portrait ~er** portraitiste *mf*; **~er and decorator** peintre décorateur. ◆ **painting** *n* (**a**) *(activity) (Art)* peinture *f*; *[buildings]* décoration *f*; (**b**) *(picture)* tableau *m*, toile *f*. ◆ **paintpot** *n* pot *m* de peinture. ◆ **paint-remover** *n* décapant *m* (pour peinture). ◆ **paint-spray** *n* pulvérisateur *m* (de peinture); *(aerosol)* bombe *f* de peinture. ◆ **paint-stripper** *n (chemical)* décapant *m*; *(tool)* racloir *m*. ◆ **paintwork** *n* peintures *fpl*.

painter[2] ['peɪntəʳ] *n (Naut)* amarre *f*.

pair [pɛəʳ] *n* paire *f*; *(man and wife)* couple *m*. **a ~ of trousers** un pantalon; **a ~ of scissors** une paire de ciseaux; **in ~s** à *or* par deux; **the happy ~** l'heureux couple. ◆ **pair off** *vi [people]* s'arranger deux par deux.

pajamas [pə'dʒɑːməz] *npl (US)* pyjama *m*.

Pakistan [ˌpɑːkɪs'tɑːn] *n* Pakistan *m*. ◆ **Pakistani** **1** *adj* pakistanais ; **2** *n* Pakistanais(e) *m(f)*.

pal * [pæl] *n* copain * *m*, copine * *f*.

palace ['pælɪs] *n* palais *m (bâtiment)*.

palate ['pælɪt] *n (Anat, fig)* palais *m*. ◆ **palatable** *adj food* agréable au goût; *fact etc* acceptable.

palatial [pə'leɪʃ(ə)l] *adj* grandiose, magnifique.

palaver * [pə'lɑːvəʳ] *n (talk)* palabres *mpl or fpl*; *(fuss)* histoires * *fpl*, affaire *f*.

pale [peɪl] **1** *adj face, person (naturally)* pâle; *(from sickness, fear)* blême; *colour* pâle. **to grow ~** pâlir; **~ blue eyes** yeux *mpl* bleu pâle. **2** *vi [person]* pâlir, devenir blême. **to ~ into insignificance** perdre toute importance (*beside* comparé à). ◆ **paleness** *n* pâleur *f*.

Palestine ['pælɪstaɪn] *n* Palestine *f*. ◆ **Palestinian** **1** *adj* palestinien ; **2** *n* Palestinien(ne) *m(f)*.

palette ['pælɪt] *n* palette *f*.

palimony ['pælɪmənɪ] *n* pension *f* alimentaire versée à celle (*or* celui) avec qui on vivait maritalement.

paling ['peɪlɪŋ] *n (fence)* palissade *f*.

pall[1] [pɔːl] *vi* perdre son charme (*on sb* pour qn). **it never ~s on you** on ne s'en lasse jamais.

pall[2] [pɔːl] *n* drap *m* mortuaire; *[smoke]* voile *m*.

pallet ['pælɪt] *n (for goods)* palette *f*.

palladium [pə'leɪdɪəm] *n* palladium *m*.

palliate ['pælɪeɪt] *vt* pallier. ◆ **palliative** *adj, n* palliatif *(m)*.

pallid ['pælɪd] *adj* blême, blafard. ◆ **pallor** *n* pâleur *f*.

palm[1] [pɑːm] **1** *n [hand]* paume *f*. *(fig)* **to have sb in the ~ of one's hand** faire de qn ce qu'on veut; *(fig)* **to grease sb's ~** graisser la patte * à qn. **2** *vt* escamoter. ◆ **palm off** *vt sep* refiler * (*on, onto* à). ◆ **palmist** *n* chiromancien(ne) *m(f)*. ◆ **palmistry** *n* chiromancie *f*.

palm[2] [pɑːm] **1** *n (tree)* palmier *m*; *(branch)* palme *f*; *(Rel)* rameau *m*. **2** *adj*: **P~ Sunday** dimanche *m* des Rameaux.

palpable ['pælpəbl] *adj* palpable; *error* manifeste. ◆ **palpably** *adv* manifestement.

palpitate ['pælpɪteɪt] *vi* palpiter. ◆ **palpitation** *n* palpitation *f*.

paltry ['pɔːltrɪ] *adj* dérisoire.

pamper ['pæmpəʳ] *vt* dorloter, choyer.

pamphlet ['pæmflɪt] *n* brochure *f*.

pan[1] [pæn] **1** *n* (**a**) *(Culin)* casserole *f*, poêlon *m*. **frying ~** poêle *f*; **roasting ~** plat *m* à rôtir. (**b**) *[scales]* plateau *m*; *[lavatory]* cuvette *f*. **2** *adj*: **~ scrubber** tampon *m* à récurer. **3** *vt* (*: *criticize harshly) film, book* éreinter. ◆ **pan out** ⁑ *vi* tourner, se passer; *(turn out well)* réussir. ◆ **pan-fry** *vt (US)* faire sauter.

pan[2] [pæn] *vti*: **to ~ (the camera)** panoramiquer.

pan... [pæn] *pref* pan... ◆ **Pan-African** *adj* panafricain. ◆ **Pan-American** *adj* panaméricain. ◆ **Pan-Asian** *adj* panasiatique.

Panama ['pænəmɑː] *n* Panama *m*. **~ Canal** canal *m* de Panama.

pancake ['pænkeɪk] **1** *n* crêpe *f*. **as flat as a ~** plat comme une galette. **2** *adj*: **P~ Tuesday** Mardi gras.

panchromatic [ˌpænkrə(ʊ)'mætɪk] *adj* panchromatique.

pancreas ['pæŋkrɪəs] *n* pancréas *m*.

panda ['pændə] *n* panda *m*. **~ car** ≃ voiture *f* pie *inv (de la police)*.

pandemonium [ˌpændɪ'məʊnɪəm] *n* tohu-bohu *m*.

pander ['pændəʳ] *vi*: **to ~ to** *person* se prêter aux exigences de; *whims* se plier à; *tastes* flatter bassement.

pane [peɪn] *n* vitre *f*, carreau *m*.

panel ['pænl] **1** *n* (**a**) *[door, wall]* panneau *m*; *[ceiling]* caisson *m*; *[dress]* pan *m*. **instrument ~** tableau *m* de bord. (**b**) *(Jur, Admin etc) (jury)* jury *m*; *(Rad, TV etc) (gen)* invités *mpl*; *(for game)* jury *m*; *(committee)* comité *m*. *(Brit)* **to be on a doctor's ~** être inscrit sur le registre d'un médecin conventionné. **2** *adj*: **~ beater** tôlier *m*; **~ discussion** réunion-débat *f*; *(Rad/TV)* **~ game** jeu *m* radiophonique/télévisé; *(US)* **~ truck** camionnette *f*. **3** *vt* lambrisser. **~led door** porte *f* à panneaux; **oak-~led** lambrissé de chêne. ◆ **panelling,** *(US)* **paneling** *n* panneaux *mpl*, lambris *m*. ◆ **panellist,** *(US)* **panelist** *n (Rad, TV)* invité(e) *m(f)*; membre *m* d'un jury.

pang [pæŋ] *n (gen)* pincement *m* de cœur. **~s** *[death]* affres *fpl*; *[conscience]* remords *mpl*; **he saw her go without a ~** il l'a vue partir sans regret; **to feel the ~s of hunger** ressentir des tiraillements d'estomac.

panic ['pænɪk] **1** *n* panique *f*, affolement *m*. **to throw into a ~** *crowd* semer la panique dans; *person* affoler, paniquer *; **to get into a ~** s'affoler, paniquer *. **2** *adj fear* panique; *decision* de panique. **~ buying** approvisionnements *mpl* sauvages; **it was ~ stations** ⁑ ça a été la panique générale *. **3** *vi* s'affoler, être pris de panique. **don't ~!** * pas d'affolement! ◆ **panicky** *adj report, newspaper* alarmiste; *decision, action* de panique; *person* paniquard *. ◆ **panic-stricken** *adj* affolé.

pannier ['pænɪəʳ] *n (gen)* panier *m*; *[motorcycle etc]* sacoche *f*.

panorama [ˌpænə'rɑːmə] *n* panorama *m*. ◆ **panoramic** *adj* panoramique.

pansy ['pænzɪ] *n (Bot)* pensée *f*; (⁑ *pej*) tante ⁑ *f*.

pant [pænt] **1** *vi* haleter. **to ~ for breath** chercher à reprendre son souffle; **he ~ed up the hill** il a grimpé la colline en haletant. **2** *vt* dire en haletant.

pantechnicon [pæn'teknɪkən] *n* grand camion *m* de déménagement.

pantheism ['pænθiːɪz(ə)m] *n* panthéisme *m*.

panther ['pænθəʳ] *n* panthère *f.*

pantomime ['pæntəmaɪm] *n (Xmas show: Brit)* spectacle *m* de Noël *(tiré d'un conte de fée); (mime)* pantomime *f; (pej: fuss)* comédie *f (fig pej).* **in** ~ en mimant.

pantry ['pæntrɪ] *n* garde-manger *m inv.*

pants [pænts] *npl (underwear)* slip *m; (trousers)* pantalon *m.* **to catch sb with his** ~ **down** ‡ prendre qn au dépourvu. ◆ **pantsuit** *n* tailleur-pantalon *m.*

panty ['pæntɪ] *adj:* ~ **girdle** gaine-culotte *f* . ◆ **pantihose** *npl* collant *m.*

papacy ['peɪpəsɪ] *n* papauté *f.* ◆ **papal** *adj* papal; *bull, legate* du Pape.

paper ['peɪpəʳ] **1** *n* (**a**) papier *m; (wall ~)* papier peint. **a piece of** ~ *(odd bit)* un bout de papier; *(sheet)* une feuille de papier; *(document etc)* un papier; **identity ~s** papiers d'identité; **old** ~ paperasses *fpl*; **to put sth down on** ~ mettre qch par écrit; **it's a good plan on** ~ c'est un bon plan sur le papier. (**b**) *(newspaper)* journal *m.* **to write for the ~s** faire du journalisme; **in the** ~ dans le journal. (**c**) *(exam questions)* épreuve *f* (écrite); *(written answers)* copie *f.* (**d**) *(scholarly work)* article *m; (at seminar)* exposé *m; (at conference)* communication *f.*

2 *adj doll, towel, handkerchief, napkin* en papier, de papier; *plates, cups* en carton; *industry* du papier; *profit etc* théorique. ~ **bag** sac *m* en papier; *(small)* pochette *f;* ~ **chase** rallye-papier *m;* ~ **clip** trombone *m;* ~ **knife** coupe-papier *m inv;* ~ **mill** (usine *f* de) papeterie *f;* ~ **money** papier-monnaie *m;* ~ **shop** * marchand *m* de journaux; ~ **work** paperasserie *f (pej).*

3 *vt room* tapisser. *(fig)* **to** ~ **over the cracks** arranger les choses.

◆ **paperback** **1** *n* livre *m* de poche ; **2** *adj* de poche. ◆ **paperboy** *n (delivering)* livreur *m* de journaux; *(selling)* vendeur *m* de journaux. ◆ **paperweight** *n* presse-papiers *m inv.*

paprika ['pæprɪkə] *n* paprika *m.*

par [pɑːʳ] *n:* **to be on a** ~ **with** aller de pair avec; **to feel below** ~ ne pas se sentir en forme.

parable ['pærəbl] *n* parabole *f.*

paracetamol [pærə'siːtəmɒl] *n* paracétamol *m.*

parachute ['pærəʃuːt] **1** *n* parachute *m.* **2** *adj jump* en parachute; *regiment* de parachutistes. ~ **drop,** ~ **landing** parachutage *m.* **3** *vi* descendre en parachute. **4** *vt* parachuter. ◆ **parachutist** *n* parachutiste *mf.*

parade [pə'reɪd] **1** *n (procession)* défilé *m; (ceremony)* parade *f,* revue *f.* **to be on** ~ défiler; ~ **ground** terrain *m* de manœuvres; **fashion** ~ présentation *f* de collections; **mannequin** ~ défilé *m* de mannequins. **2** *vt one's wealth* faire étalage de. **3** *vi* défiler. *(fig)* **to** ~ * **about** *or* **around** se balader *.

paradise ['pærədaɪs] *n* paradis *m.* **bird of** ~ oiseau *m* de paradis.

paradox ['pærədɒks] *n* paradoxe *m.* ◆ **paradoxical** *adj* paradoxal. ◆ **paradoxically** *adv* paradoxalement.

paraffin ['pærəfɪn] **1** *n (Chem)* paraffine *f; (fuel)* pétrole *m.* **liquid** ~ huile *f* de paraffine. **2** *adj lamp* à pétrole.

paragon ['pærəgən] *n* modèle *m* (de vertu).

paragraph ['pærəgrɑːf] *n* (**a**) paragraphe *m,* alinéa *m.* **'new** ~**'** 'à la ligne'; **to begin a new** ~ aller à la ligne. (**b**) *(newspaper item)* entrefilet *m.*

Paraguay ['pærəgwaɪ] *n* Paraguay *m.* ◆ **Paraguayan** **1** *adj* paraguayen ; **2** *n* Paraguayen(ne) *m(f).*

parallel ['pærəlel] **1** *adj* parallèle (*with, to* à). **to run** ~ **to** être parallèle à. **2** *n (Geog)* parallèle *m; (Math)* (ligne *f*) parallèle *f. (fig)* **to draw a** ~ **between** établir un parallèle entre. ◆ **parallelogram** *n* parallélogramme *m.*

paralysis [pə'ræləsɪs] *n* paralysie *f.* ◆ **paralytic** [,pærə'lɪtɪk] *adj (Med)* paralytique; *(‡: drunk)* ivre mort. ◆ **paralyze** ['pærəlaɪz] *vt (Med, fig)* paralyser; **his arm is paralyzed** il est paralysé du bras; **paralyzed with fear** paralysé de peur.

paramedic [,pærə'medɪk] *n* auxiliaire *mf* médical(e).

parameter [pə'ræmɪtəʳ] *n (Math)* paramètre *m. (fig)* **the ~s of the event** les données *fpl* de l'événement; **the ~s of their policy** les grandes lignes de leur politique.

paramilitary [,pærə'mɪlɪt(ə)rɪ] **1** *adj* paramilitaire. **2** *n* membre *m* d'une force paramilitaire.

paramount ['pærəmaʊnt] *adj chief* souverain; *importance* suprême *(before n).*

paranoia [,pærə'nɔɪə] *n* paranoïa *f.* ◆ **paranoiac** *adj, n* paranoïaque *(mf).* ◆ **paranoid** *adj* paranoïde.

paranormal [,pærə'nɔːm(ə)l] *adj* paranormal.

parapet ['pærəpɪt] *n* parapet *m.*

paraphernalia [,pærəfə'neɪlɪə] *npl* attirail *m.*

paraphrase ['pærəfreɪz] **1** *n* paraphrase *f.* **2** *vt* paraphraser.

paraplegia [,pærə'pliːdʒə] *n* paraplégie *f.* ◆ **paraplegic** *adj, n* paraplégique *(mf).*

parasite ['pærəsaɪt] *n* parasite *m.* ◆ **parasitic(al)** *adj* parasite (*on* de).

parasol [,pærə'sɒl] *n* ombrelle *f; (over table etc)* parasol *m.*

paratrooper ['pærətruːpəʳ] *n* parachutiste *m (Mil).* ◆ **paratroops** *npl* parachutistes *mpl.*

parboil ['pɑːbɔɪl] *vt* faire bouillir à demi.

parcel ['pɑːsl] **1** *n* colis *m,* paquet *m; [land]* parcelle *f; [shares]* paquet; *[lies, liars etc]* tas * *m.* **2** *adj:* ~ **bomb** paquet *m* piégé; ~ **office** bureau *m* de messageries; **by** ~ **post** par colis postal. **3** *vt* (~ **up)** empaqueter. ◆ **parcel out** *vt sep* distribuer; *(share)* partager; *land* lotir.

parched [pɑːtʃt] *adj crops, land* desséché, brûlé. *[person]* **to be** ~ mourir de soif.

parchment ['pɑːtʃmənt] *n* parchemin *m.*

pardon ['pɑːdn] **1** *n* pardon *m; (Rel)* indulgence *f; (Jur: free ~)* grâce *f.* **general** ~ amnistie *f.* **2** *vt* pardonner (*sb for sth* qch à qn; *sb for doing* à qn d'avoir fait); *(Jur)* gracier; amnistier. **3** *excl (apologizing)* pardon!; *(not hearing)* comment? ◆ **pardonable** *adj* pardonnable. ◆ **pardonably** *adv* de façon bien pardonnable.

pare [pɛəʳ] *vt fruit* peler; *nails* rogner; (~ **down)** *expenses* réduire. ◆ **parer** *n* épluche-légumes *m inv.*

parent ['pɛərənt] **1** *n* père *m or* mère *f.* **his ~s** ses parents *mpl.* **2** *adj:* **the** ~ **animals** *(or* **birds** *etc)* les parents *mpl*; *(Comm, Fin)* ~ **company** maison *f* mère. ◆ **parentage** *n* naissance *f,* origine *f;* **of unknown ~age** de parents inconnus. ◆ **parental** [pə'rentl] *adj* parental. ◆ **parenthood** *n* paternité *f or* maternité *f.* ◆ **parent-teacher association** *n* association *f* des parents d'élèves et des professeurs.

parenthesis, *pl* **-eses** [pə'renθɪsɪs, ɪsiːz] *n* parenthèse *f.* **in** ~ entre parenthèses. ◆ **parenthetic(al)** *adj* entre parenthèses. ◆ **parenthetically** *adv* entre parenthèses.

Paris ['pærɪs] *n* Paris. ◆ **Parisian** **1** *adj* parisien ; **2** *n* Parisien(ne) *m(f).*

parish ['pærɪʃ] **1** *n (Rel)* paroisse *f; (civil)* commune *f.* **2** *adj church* paroissial; *hall* paroissial, municipal. ◆ **parishioner** *n* paroissien(ne) *m(f).*

parity ['pærɪtɪ] *n* parité *f.*

park [pɑːk] **1** *n (gen)* parc *m; (public)* jardin *m* public, parc. **2** *adj:* ~ **keeper** gardien *m* de parc.

3 *vt* garer, parquer. **4** *vi* se garer, stationner *(Admin)*. **I've ~ed** *or* **I'm ~ed by the church** je suis garé près de l'église. ◆ **parking 1** *n* stationnement *m*; **'~ing'** 'stationnement autorisé'; **'no ~ing'** 'stationnement interdit'; **~ing is difficult** il est difficile de trouver à se garer ; **2** *adj*: **~ing attendant** gardien *m* de parking; **~ing bay** lieu *m* de stationnement (autorisé); **~ing lights** feux *mpl* de position; **~ing lot** parking *m*; **~ing meter** parcmètre *m*; **~ing place** *(marked out)* créneau *m* de stationnement; **I couldn't find a ~ing place** je n'ai pas pu trouver à me garer; **~ing ticket** P.-V. * *m*, procès-verbal *m*. ◆ **parkland** *n* bois *mpl*. ◆ **parkway** *n (US)* avenue *f*.

parka ['pɑ:kə] *n* parka *m*.

Parkinson's disease ['pɑ:kɪnsənsdɪ'zɪ:z] *n* maladie de Parkinson.

parliament ['pɑ:ləmənt] *n* parlement *m*. **to go into P~** se faire élire député; **member of P~** ≃ député *m* (*for* de); *V* **house**. ◆ **parliamentarian** *adj, n* parlementaire *(mf)*. ◆ **parliamentary** *adj (gen)* parlementaire; *election* législatif; *(Brit)* **P~ary Secretary** ≃ chef *m* de Cabinet (*to* de).

parlour, *(US)* **parlor** ['pɑ:ləʳ] **1** *n* (petit) salon *m*. **2** *adj*: **~ game** jeu *m* de société.

parmesan [ˌpɑ:mɪ'zæn] *n* parmesan *m*.

parochial [pə'rəʊkɪəl] *adj (Rel)* paroissial; *(fig pej)* de clocher.

parody ['pærədɪ] **1** *n* parodie *f*. **2** *vt* parodier.

parole [pə'rəʊl] **1** *n*: **on ~** *(Mil)* sur parole; *(Jur)* en liberté conditionnelle. **2** *vt* mettre en liberté conditionnelle.

paroxysm ['pærəksɪz(ə)m] *n (Med)* paroxysme *m*; *[grief, pain]* paroxysme; *[anger]* accès *m*; *[delight]* transport *m*; *[tears, laughter]* crise *f*.

parquet ['pɑ:keɪ] *n* (**~ flooring**) parquet *m*.

parrot ['pærət] *n* perroquet *m*. **~ fashion** *(adv phr)* comme un perroquet.

parry ['pærɪ] *vt blow* parer; *question* éluder.

parsimony ['pɑ:sɪmənɪ] *n* parcimonie *f*. ◆ **parsimonious** *adj* parcimonieux. ◆ **parsimoniously** *adv* parcimonieusement.

parsley ['pɑ:slɪ] *n* persil *m*. **~ sauce** sauce *f* persillée.

parsnip ['pɑ:snɪp] *n* panais *m*.

parson ['pɑ:sn] *n (C of E etc)* pasteur *m*; *(gen)* ecclésiastique *m*. *(Culin)* **~'s nose** croupion *m*. ◆ **parsonage** *n* presbytère *m*.

part [pɑ:t] **1** *n* (**a**) *(section etc: gen)* partie *f*; *(Tech)* pièce *f*. **spare ~** pièce détachée; **in ~(s)** en partie; **for the most ~** dans l'ensemble; **to be ~ (and parcel) of** faire partie (intégrante) de; **the hundredth ~** le centième; **a man of ~s** un homme très doué; **the funny ~ of it is that...** le plus drôle dans l'histoire c'est que...; **in ~ two of the book** dans la deuxième partie du livre; **four-~ serial** feuilleton *m* à quatre épisodes; *(Culin)* **three ~s water to one ~ milk** trois mesures d'eau pour une mesure de lait; *[verb]* **principal ~s** temps *mpl* principaux; **what ~ of speech is it?** à quelle catégorie grammaticale est-ce que cela appartient?; **the violin ~** la partie de violon; **two-~ song** chant *m* à deux voix; **in these ~s** dans cette région; **in this ~ of the world** par ici; **in foreign ~s** à l'étranger. (**b**) *(share: also Theat etc)* rôle *m*. **he had a large ~ in the organization of...** il a joué un grand rôle dans l'organisation de...; **she had some ~ in it** elle y était pour qch; **to take ~ in** participer à; **I want no ~ in it** je ne veux pas m'en mêler. (**c**) *(side)* parti *m*; *(behalf)* part *f*. **to take sb's ~** prendre parti pour qn; **for my ~** pour ma part, quant à moi; **on the ~ of** de la part de; **to take sth in good ~** prendre qch du bon côté. (**d**) *(US) [hair]* raie *f*.
2 *adj*: **~ exchange** reprise *f* en compte; **to take sth in ~ exchange** reprendre qch en compte; **~ owner** copropriétaire *mf*; **~ payment** règlement *m* partiel; **~ song** chant *m* à plusieurs voix.
3 *adv* en partie. **~ French** en partie français.
4 *vt* (**a**) *crowd* ouvrir un passage dans; *boxers, fighters* séparer. **they were ~ed during the war** la guerre les a séparés. (**b**) **to ~ one's hair** se faire une raie; **his hair was ~ed at the side** il portait une raie sur le côté. (**c**) **to ~ company with** *(leave)* fausser compagnie à; *(disagree with)* ne plus être d'accord avec.
5 *vi [crowd]* s'ouvrir; *[boxers etc]* se séparer; *[friends]* se quitter; *[couple]* se séparer; *[rope]* se rompre. **to ~ from** se séparer de; **to ~ with** *money* débourser; *possessions* se défaire de; *employee* se séparer de.
◆ **parting 1** *n* séparation *f*; *[waters]* partage *m*; *[hair]* raie *f*; *(lit, fig)* **the ~ing of the ways** la croisée des chemins ; **2** *adj gift, words* d'adieu; *(fig)* **~ing shot** flèche *f* du Parthe. ◆ **partly** *adv* en partie. ◆ **part-time** *adj, adv* à temps partiel; *(half-time)* à mi-temps. ◆ **part-timer** *n* employé(e) *m(f)* à temps partiel.

partake [pɑ:'teɪk] *pret* **partook,** *ptp* **partaken** *vi*: **to ~ of** *meal* prendre.

partial ['pɑ:ʃ(ə)l] *adj* (**a**) *(in part)* partiel. (**b**) *(biased)* partial (*towards* envers), injuste. *(*: like)* **to be ~ to** avoir un faible pour. ◆ **partiality** *n (bias)* partialité *f* (*for* pour; *towards* envers); *(liking)* penchant *m* (*for* pour). ◆ **partially** *adv* (**a**) *(partly)* en partie; **the ~ly-sighted** les mal-voyants *mpl*; (**b**) *(with bias)* avec partialité.

participate [pɑ:'tɪsɪpeɪt] *vi* participer (*in* à). ◆ **participant** *n* participant(e) *m(f)* (*in* à). ◆ **participation** *n* participation *f* (*in* à).

participle ['pɑ:tɪsɪpl] *n* participe *m*. **past/present ~** participe passé/présent.

particle ['pɑ:tɪkl] *n (gen, Ling, Phys)* particule *f*; *[dust, truth, sense]* grain *m*. **~ physics** physique *f* des particules élémentaires.

particular [pə'tɪkjʊləʳ] **1** *adj* (**a**) *(distinct, special)* particulier; *(personal)* personnel. **in this ~ case** dans ce cas particulier; **for no ~ reason** sans raison précise; **that ~ brand** cette marque-là (et non pas une autre); **her ~ choice/type of humour** son choix/humour personnel; **her ~ bed** son lit à elle; **nothing ~** rien de particulier *or* de spécial; **he took ~ care over it** il y a mis un soin particulier; **to pay ~ attention to sth** faire bien attention à qch; **a ~ friend of his** un de ses meilleurs amis. (**b**) *(fussy etc)* méticuleux, difficile. **she is ~ about whom she goes out with** elle ne sort pas avec n'importe qui; **~ about his food** difficile pour la nourriture; **I'm not ~** cela m'est égal.
2 *n* (**a**) **in ~** en particulier; **nothing in ~** rien en *or* de particulier. (**b**) *(detail)* **in every ~** en tout point; **he is wrong in one ~** il se trompe sur un point; **~s** *(information)* détails *mpl*, renseignements *mpl*; *(description)* description *f*; *[person]* signalement *m*; *(name, address)* nom *m* et adresse *f*; **full ~s** tous les renseignements; **for further ~s apply to...** pour plus amples renseignements s'adresser à...
◆ **particularity** *n* particularité *f*. ◆ **particularize** *vt* spécifier, préciser. ◆ **particularly** *adv (in ~)* en particulier, spécialement; *(notably)* notamment, particulièrement; *(very carefully)* méticuleusement.

partisan [ˌpɑ:tɪ'zæn] *n* partisan *m*.

partition [pɑ:'tɪʃ(ə)n] **1** *n* (**a**) cloison *f*. **glass ~** cloison vitrée. (**b**) *(dividing) [country]* partition *f*; *[lands]* morcellement *m*. **2** *vt country* partager; *lands* morceler; (**~ off**) *room* cloisonner.

partitive ['pɑ:tɪtɪv] *adj, n* partitif *(m)*.

partner ['pɑ:tnəʳ] *n (gen)* partenaire *mf; (Comm, Jur, Med etc)* associé(e) *m(f)*; *(Sport)* partenaire *mf*; *(co-driver)* coéquipier *m*, -ière *f*; *(Dancing)* cavalier *m*,

-ière *f*; *(in marriage)* époux *m*, épouse *f*; *(cohabiting)* concubin(e) *m(f)*. **senior/junior** ~ associé principal/adjoint; ~**s in crime** complices *mpl* dans le crime. ◆ **partnership** *n* association *f*; **to be in** ~**ship** être en association (*with* avec), être associé (*with* à); **to go into** ~**ship** s'associer (*with* avec); **to take sb into** ~**ship** prendre qn comme associé.

partridge ['pɑːtrɪdʒ] *n* perdrix *f*; *(Culin)* perdreau *m*.

party ['pɑːtɪ] **1** *n* (**a**) *(Pol etc)* parti *m*. (**b**) *(group)* *[travellers]* groupe *m*; *[workmen]* équipe *f*; *(Mil)* détachement *m*. (**c**) *(Jur etc)* partie *f*. **third** ~ tierce personne *f*, tiers *m*; **innocent** ~ innocent(e) *m(f)*; **to be (a)** ~ **to** être mêlé à; *(Jur)* être complice de. (**d**) *(celebration)* réception *f*. **to give a** ~ inviter des amis, donner une surprise-partie; *(more formally)* donner une soirée, recevoir; **birthday** ~ fête *f* d'anniversaire; **dinner** ~ dîner *m*; **evening** ~ soirée *f*; **private** ~ réunion *f* intime; **tea** ~ thé *m*. **2** *adj politics, leader* de parti, du parti; *disputes* de partis. ~ **dress** robe *f* habillée; ~ **line** *(Pol)* ligne *f* du parti; *(Telec)* ligne commune à deux abonnés; *(Rad, TV)* ~ **political broadcast** *émission réservée à un parti politique*, ≃ 'tribune *f* libre'; ~ **political question** question *f* qui relève de la ligne du parti; ~ **spirit** *(Pol)* esprit *m* de parti; *(*: gaiety)* entrain *m*; ~ **wall** mur *m* mitoyen. **3** *vi (* US: go out)* sortir, aller danser; *(go to parties)* courir les réceptions. ◆ **party-goer** *n (frequent)* habitué(e) *m(f)* des réceptions; *(guest)* invité(e) *m(f)*.

pass [pɑːs] **1** *n* (**a**) *(permit)* *[journalist, worker etc]* laissez-passer *m inv*; *(Rail etc)* carte *f* d'abonnement; *(Theat)* billet *m* de faveur; *(Naut)* lettre *f* de mer; *(safe conduct)* sauf-conduit *m*. (**b**) *(in mountains)* col *m*, défilé *m*. (**c**) *(in exam)* moyenne *f*. **to get a** ~ **in history** avoir la moyenne en histoire. (**d**) **this is a pretty** ~! voilà à quoi on en est arrivé!; **things have reached such a** ~ **that...** les choses en sont arrivées à un tel point que... (**e**) *(Ftbl etc)* passe *f*. *(fig)* **to make a** ~ * **at a woman** faire du plat * à une femme.

2 *adj*: ~ **degree** licence *f* libre.

3 *vi* (**a**) *(come, go)* passer (*through* par); *[procession]* défiler; *(Aut: overtake)* doubler. **to** ~ **down the street** descendre la rue; **to** ~ **into oblivion** tomber dans l'oubli; **to** ~ **out of sight** disparaître; **letters** ~**ed between them** ils ont échangé des lettres. (**b**) *(be accepted)* *[coins]* avoir cours; *[behaviour]* convenir, être acceptable; *[project]* passer. **to** ~ **under the name of** être connu sous le nom de; **what** ~**es for a hat these days** ce qui de nos jours passe pour un chapeau; **he tried to** ~ **for a doctor** il a essayé de se faire passer pour un docteur; **she would** ~ **for 20** on lui donnerait 20 ans; **will this do? — oh it'll** ~ est-ce que ceci convient? — oh, ça peut aller; **he let it** ~ il l'a laissé passer; **he couldn't let it** ~ il ne pouvait pas laisser passer ça comme ça; **the estate** ~**ed to my brother** la propriété est revenue à mon frère. (**c**) *[time, afternoon etc]* passer. **how time** ~**es!** que le temps passe vite! (**d**) (~ **away**) *[memory, opportunity]* s'effacer, disparaître; *[pain]* passer. (**e**) *(in exam)* être reçu (*in* en). (**f**) *(take place)* se passer, avoir lieu. **all that** ~**ed between them** tout ce qui s'est passé entre eux; *(liter)* **it came to** ~ **that** il advint que. (**g**) *(Cards)* passer; *(Ftbl etc)* faire une passe.

4 *vt* (**a**) *(go past) building* passer devant; *person* croiser, rencontrer; *barrier, frontier, customs* passer; *(overtake) (gen, Sport)* dépasser; *(Aut)* doubler. **when you have** ~**ed the town hall** quand vous serez passé devant *or* quand vous aurez dépassé la mairie; **to** ~ **comprehension** dépasser l'entendement; **to** ~ **belief** être incroyable; **the film** ~**ed the censors** le film a reçu le visa de la censure. (**b**) *exam* être reçu à, réussir; *candidate* recevoir; *(Parl) bill* voter. **the censors have/haven't** ~**ed the film** le film a été autorisé/interdit par la censure; *(Scol, Univ)* **they didn't** ~ **him** ils l'ont refusé; **the doctor** ~**ed him fit for work** le docteur l'a déclaré en état de reprendre le travail; *(Typ)* **to** ~ **the proofs (for press)** donner le bon à tirer. (**c**) *time* passer. **to** ~ **the evening reading** passer la soirée à lire. (**d**) *(hand over)* (faire) passer; *(move)* passer; *(Sport) ball* passer; *forged money, stolen goods* écouler. ~ **me the box** passez-moi la boîte; **the telegram was** ~**ed round the room** on a fait passer le télégramme dans la salle; **to** ~ **sth down the line** faire passer qch (de main en main); **to** ~ **a rope through a ring** passer une corde dans un anneau; **to** ~ **blood** avoir du sang dans les urines; **to** ~ **a stone** évacuer un calcul; **to** ~ **water** uriner. (**e**) *(utter) comment* faire; *opinion* émettre. **to** ~ **remarks about** faire des observations sur; **to** ~ **judgment** prononcer un jugement (*on* sur); *(Jur)* **to** ~ **sentence** prononcer une condamnation (*on sb* contre qn).

◆ **pass along 1** *vi* passer. **2** *vt sep* faire passer. ◆ **pass away** *vi (die)* mourir, s'éteindre; *[memory etc]* disparaître. ◆ **pass back** *vt sep* rendre. ◆ **pass by 1** *vi* passer (à côté); *[procession]* défiler. **2** *vt sep* négliger, ignorer. **life has** ~**ed me by** je n'ai pas vraiment vécu. ◆ **pass down 1** *vi [inheritance etc]* être transmis (*to* à). **2** *vt sep* transmettre. ◆ **pass off 1** *vi* (**a**) *[faintness etc]* passer. (**b**) *[event]* se passer. **everything** ~**ed off smoothly** tout s'est passé sans accroc. **2** *vt sep* (**a**) faire passer. **to** ~ **o.s. off as** se faire passer pour. (**b**) **to** ~ **sth off on sb** repasser qch à qn. ◆ **pass on 1** *vi* (**a**) *(die)* s'éteindre, mourir. (**b**) *(continue one's way)* passer son chemin. **to** ~ **on to a new subject** passer à un nouveau sujet. **2** *vt sep (hand on) object* faire passer (*to* à); *old clothes* repasser (*to sb* à qn); *news* faire circuler; *message* transmettre. **you've** ~**ed your cold on to me** tu m'as passé ton rhume; **to** ~ **on a tax to the consumer** répercuter un impôt sur le consommateur. ◆ **pass out 1** *vi* (**a**) *(faint)* s'évanouir; *(from drink)* tomber ivre mort; *(fall asleep)* s'endormir comme une masse. (**b**) *(US)* **to** ~ **out of high school** terminer ses études secondaires. **2** *vt sep leaflets etc* distribuer. ◆ **pass over** *vt sep*: **to** ~ **over Paul in favour of Robert** préférer Robert à Paul. ◆ **pass round** *vt sep bottle* faire passer; *sweets, leaflets* distribuer. *(fig)* **to** ~ **round the hat** faire la quête. ◆ **pass through 1** *vi* passer. **2** *vt fus hardships* subir, endurer; *town, country* traverser. ◆ **pass up** *vt sep (lit)* passer; *(*: forego) opportunity* laisser passer.

◆ **passable** *adj* (**a**) *(tolerable)* passable; (**b**) *road* praticable; *river* franchissable. ◆ **passably** *adv* passablement, assez. ◆ **passage** *n* (**a**) *(passing)* passage *m*; *[bill, law]* adoption *f*; **with the** ~**age of time** avec le temps; (**b**) *(Naut)* traversée *f*; (**c**) *(way through)* passage *m*; *(corridor)* couloir *m*; (**d**) *[music, text]* passage *m*. ◆ **passageway** *n* passage *m*. ◆ **passbook** *n* livret *m* (bancaire). ◆ **passer-by** *n* passant(e) *m(f)*. ◆ **passing 1** *adj person, car* qui passe; *remark* en passant; *happiness, guest* passager; *desire* fugitif; ~**ing place** aire *f* de croisement ; **2** *n (Aut)* dépassement *m*; *(death)* mort *f*; **with the** ~**ing of time** avec le temps; **in** ~**ing** en passant. ◆ **passing-out parade** *n* défilé *m* de promotion. ◆ **passkey** *n* passe-partout *m inv*. ◆ **passmark** *n* moyenne *f*. ◆ **Passover** *n* pâque *f* des Juifs. ◆ **passport** *n* passeport *m*; *(fig)* ~**port to** clef *f* de. ◆ **password** *n* mot *m* de passe.

passé ['pæseɪ] *adj* vieux jeu *inv*.

passenger ['pæs(ɪ)n(d)ʒəʳ] **1** *n (in train)* voyageur *m*, -euse *f*; *(in boat, plane, car)* passager *m*, -ère *f*; *(fig pej)* poids *m* mort. **2** *adj coach, train* de voyageurs; *(Aviat) list* des passagers. *(Aut)* ~ **seat** siège *m* du passager.

passion ['pæʃ(ə)n] **1** *n* passion *f*; *(anger)* emportement *m*. **to have a** ~ **for music** avoir la passion de la musique; **to be in a ~** être furieux. **2** *adj (Rel)* **P~ play/Sunday** *etc* mystère *m*/dimanche *m etc* de la Passion. ◆ **passionate** *adj (gen)* passionné; *speech* véhément. ◆ **passionately** *adv* passionnément; **to be ~ately fond of** adorer. ◆ **passionflower** *n* passiflore *f*.

passive ['pæsɪv] **1** *adj (all senses)* passif. **~ smoking** tabagisme *m* passif. **2** *n* passif *m*. **in the ~** au passif. ◆ **passively** *adv* passivement; *(Gram)* au passif. ◆ **passiveness** *or* ◆ **passivity** *n* passivité *f*.

past [pɑːst] **1** *n* passé *m*. **in the ~** autrefois, dans le passé; *(Gram)* au passé; **it's a thing of the ~** cela n'existe plus, c'est fini.
2 *adj* passé. **for some time ~** depuis quelque temps; **in times ~** autrefois; **the ~ week** la semaine dernière *or* passée; **the ~ few days** ces derniers jours; **all that is ~** tout cela c'est du passé; **~ president** ancien président; **to be a ~ master at doing sth** avoir l'art de faire qch; *(Gram)* **in the ~ tense** au passé.
3 *prep* (**a**) *(in time)* plus de. **it is ~ 11 o'clock** il est plus de 11 heures, il est 11 heures passées; *(Brit)* **half ~ 3** 3 heures et demie; **quarter ~ 3** 3 heures et quart; **at 20 ~ 3** à 3 heures 20; *(Brit)* **the train goes at 5 ~ *** le train part à 5 *; **she is ~ 60** elle a plus de 60 ans, elle a 60 ans passés. (**b**) *(beyond)* plus loin que. **just ~ the post office** un peu plus loin que la poste, juste après la poste. (**c**) *(in front of)* devant. **he goes ~ the house** il passe devant la maison. (**d**) *(beyond limits of)* au-delà de. **~ endurance** insupportable; **~ all belief** incroyable; **I'm ~ caring** je ne m'en fais plus; **he is ~ work** il n'est plus en état de travailler; **he's a bit ~ it *** il n'est plus dans la course *; **that cake is ~ its best** ce gâteau n'est plus si bon; **I wouldn't put it ~ her to have done it** cela ne m'étonnerait pas d'elle qu'elle l'ait fait.
4 *adv* auprès, devant. **to go** *or* **walk ~** passer.

pasta ['pæstə] *n (Culin)* pâtes *fpl*.

paste [peɪst] **1** *n* (**a**) *(gen, also Culin)* pâte *f*; *[meat etc]* pâté *m*. **almond ~** pâte d'amandes; **liver ~** pâté de foie; **tomato ~** concentré *m* de tomate; **tooth ~** dentifrice *m*. (**b**) *(glue)* colle *f* (de pâte). **2** *adj jewellery* en strass. **3** *vt* coller; *wallpaper* enduire de colle.
◆ **paste up** *vt sep notice, list* afficher; *photos* coller. ◆ **pasteboard** *n* carton *m*. ◆ **paste-up** *n* collage *m*. ◆ **pasting** ⁑ *n (thrashing)* rossée * *f*; **to give sb a pasting** flanquer une rossée à qn *. ◆ **pasty** ['peɪstɪ] **1** *adj* pâteux; *(pej) face, complexion* terreux ; **2** ['pæstɪ] *n (Culin)* petit pâté *m*.

pastel ['pæstəl] **1** *n* pastel *m*. **2** *adj* pastel *inv*.

pasteurize ['pæstəraɪz] *vt* pasteuriser.

pastille ['pæstɪl] *n* pastille *f*.

pastime ['pɑːstaɪm] *n* passe-temps *m inv*.

pastor ['pɑːstəʳ] *n* pasteur *m*. ◆ **pastoral** *adj (gen)* pastoral. *(Educ)* **~al care system** tutorat *m*.

pastry ['peɪstrɪ] *n* (**a**) pâte *f*. (**b**) *(cake)* pâtisserie *f*. ◆ **pastrycase** *n* croûte *f*. ◆ **pastrycook** *n* pâtissier *m*, -ière *f*.

pasture ['pɑːstʃəʳ] *n* pâturage *m*.

pat¹ [pæt] **1** *vt* tapoter; *animal* caresser. **2** *n* (**a**) petite tape *f*; *(on animal)* caresse *f*. **to give o.s. a ~ on the back** s'applaudir. (**b**) **~ of butter** noix *f* de beurre.

pat² [pæt] **1** *adv*: **to answer ~** avoir une réponse toute prête. **2** *adj answer, explanation* tout prêt.

patch [pætʃ] **1** *n* (**a**) *(for clothes)* pièce *f*; *(for tube, airbed)* rustine *f*; *(over eye)* cache *m*; *(Comput)* correction *f*. **he isn't a ~ on his brother *** il n'arrive pas à la cheville de son frère. (**b**) *(small area) [colour]* tache *f*; *[sky]* morceau *m*; *[land]* parcelle *f*; *[policeman]* secteur *m*; *[vegetables]* carré *m*; *[ice]* plaque *f*; *[mist]* nappe *f*; *[water]* flaque *f*. **a damp ~** une tache d'humidité; *(fig)* **to strike a bad ~** être dans la déveine *; **bad ~es** moments *mpl* difficiles. **2** *vt clothes* rapiécer; *tyre* réparer. **3** *adj (Med)* **~ test** test *m* cutané. ◆ **patch up** *vt sep clothes* rapiécer; *machine, injured person* rafistoler *; (*) *marriage* replâtrer *. **to ~ up a quarrel** se raccommoder. ◆ **patchwork** *n* patchwork *m*. ◆ **patchy** *adj* inégal.

patent ['peɪt(ə)nt] **1** *adj* (**a**) *(obvious)* manifeste, patent. (**b**) *invention* breveté. **~ medicine** spécialité *f* pharmaceutique; **~ leather** cuir *m* verni. **2** *n* brevet *m* d'invention. **3** *vt* faire breveter. ◆ **patently** *adv* manifestement.

paternity [pə'tɜːnɪtɪ] *n* paternité *f*. *(Jur)* **~ order** reconnaissance *f* de paternité judiciaire. ◆ **paternal** *adj* paternel. ◆ **paternalist(ic)** *adj* paternaliste. ◆ **paternally** *adv* paternellement.

path [pɑːθ] *n* (**a**) *(gen)* sentier *m*, chemin *m*; *(in garden)* allée *f*; *(fig)* sentier. (**b**) *[river]* cours *m*; *[sun]* route *f*; *[missile, planet]* trajectoire *f*. ◆ **pathway** *n* sentier *m*.

pathetic [pə'θetɪk] *adj (gen)* pitoyable *(also fig pej)*; *attempt* désespéré. **it was ~ to see it** cela faisait peine à voir. ◆ **pathetically** *adv* pitoyablement ; **~ally thin** d'une maigreur pitoyable; **she was ~ally glad** son plaisir vous serrait le cœur.

pathology [pə'θɒlədʒɪ] *n* pathologie *f*. ◆ **pathological** *adj* pathologique. ◆ **pathologist** *n* pathologiste *mf*.

pathos ['peɪθɒs] *n* pathétique *m*.

patience ['peɪʃ(ə)ns] *n* (**a**) patience *f*. **to have ~** être patient; *(on one occasion)* prendre patience, patienter; **to lose ~** s'impatienter (*with sb* contre qn); **I have no ~ with these people** ces gens m'exaspèrent. (**b**) *(Cards)* réussite *f*. **to play ~** faire des réussites. ◆ **patient** **1** *adj* patient ; **2** *n (Med)* patient(e) *m(f)*; *(in hospital)* malade *mf*. ◆ **patiently** *adv* patiemment.

patriarch ['peɪtrɪɑːk] *n* patriarche *m*.

patriot ['peɪtrɪət] *n* patriote *mf*. ◆ **patriotic** *adj deed, speech* patriotique; *person* patriote. ◆ **patriotically** *adv* patriotiquement. ◆ **patriotism** *n* patriotisme *m*.

patrol [pə'trəʊl] **1** *n* patrouille *f*. **to be on ~** être de patrouille. **2** *adj vehicle* de patrouille. **~ car** voiture *f* de police; **~ leader** chef *m* de patrouille; *(US)* **~ wagon** voiture *f* cellulaire. **3** *vt district* patrouiller dans. **4** *vi* patrouiller. *(fig)* **to ~ up and down** faire les cent pas. ◆ **patrolman** *n* (**a**) *(US)* agent *m* de police; (**b**) *(Aut)* agent *m* de la sécurité routière.

patron ['peɪtr(ə)n] *n* (**a**) *[artist]* protecteur *m*, -trice *f*; *[a charity]* patron(ne) *m(f)*. **~ saint** saint(e) patron(ne) *m(f)*. (**b**) *[hotel, shop]* client(e) *m(f)*; *[theatre]* habitué(e) *m(f)*. ◆ **patronage** *n [artist etc]* patronage *m*; *(US Pol)* nomination *f* d'amis politiques à des postes de responsabilité. ◆ **patronize** *vt* (**a**) *(pej)* traiter avec condescendance; (**b**) *shop* donner sa clientèle à; *cinema* fréquenter. ◆ **patronizingly** *adv* d'un air condescendant.

patter¹ ['pætəʳ] *n (talk)* baratin * *m*.

patter² ['pætəʳ] **1** *n [rain etc]* crépitement *m*. **a ~ of footsteps** un petit bruit de pas pressés. **2** *vi [footsteps, person]* trottiner; *[rain, hail]* crépiter (*on* contre).

pattern ['pætən] **1** *n* (**a**) *(design: on wallpaper etc)* dessin(s) *m(pl)*, motif *m*. **the ~ on a tyre** les sculptures *fpl* d'un pneu. (**b**) *(Sewing etc: paper ~)* patron *m*; *(Knitting etc)* modèle *m*. (**c**) *(style)* modèle *m*, style *m*. (**d**) *(fig)* modèle *m*. **it followed the usual ~** cela s'est passé selon la formule habituelle; **behaviour ~s of teenagers** les types *mpl* de comportement chez les adolescents. (**e**) *(sample of material etc)* échantillon *m*. **2** *adj*: **~ book** *[material, wallpaper etc]* album *m* d'échantillons; *(Sewing)* catalogue *m or* album *m* de modes. **3** *vt* modeler (*on* sur). ◆ **patterned** *adj* à motifs.

paunch [pɔːn(t)ʃ] *n* panse *f*.

pauper ['pɔːpəʳ] *n* indigent(e) *m(f)*.

pause [pɔːz] **1** *n (gen)* pause *f*, arrêt *m*; *(Mus)* repos *m*. **a ~ in the conversation** un petit silence. **2** *vi (stop)* faire une pause, s'arrêter un instant; *(hesitate)* hésiter; *(linger)* s'arrêter (*on* sur). **to ~ for breath** s'arrêter pour reprendre haleine.

pave [peɪv] *vt* paver. **~d with gold** pavé d'or; *(fig)* **to ~ the way** préparer le chemin (*for* pour). ◆ **pavement** *n* (**a**) *(Brit)* trottoir *m*; (**b**) *(US)* chaussée *f*. ◆ **paving** *n (stones)* pavés *mpl*; *(flagstones)* dalles *fpl*; *(tiles)* carreaux *mpl*. ◆ **paving stone** *n* pavé *m*.

pavilion [pə'vɪlɪən] *n* pavillon *m*.

paw [pɔː] **1** *n* patte *f*. **2** *vt* (**a**) *[animal]* donner un coup de patte à. *[horse]* **to ~ the ground** piaffer. (**b**) *(sexually)* **to ~ sb** * tripoter * qn.

pawn[1] [pɔːn] *n (Chess)* pion *m*. *(fig)* **to be sb's ~** se laisser manœuvrer par qn.

pawn[2] [pɔːn] **1** *vt* mettre en gage. **2** *n*: **in ~** en gage. ◆ **pawnbroker** *n* prêteur *m*, -euse *f* sur gages. ◆ **pawnshop** *n* bureau *m* de prêteur sur gages.

pawpaw ['pɔːpɔː] *n* papaye *f*.

pay [peɪ] *(vb: pret, ptp* **paid***)* **1** *n (gen)* salaire *m*; *[manual worker]* paie *f or* paye *f*; *(Mil, Naut)* solde *f*, paie. **in the ~ of** à la solde de; **the ~'s not very good** ce n'est pas très bien payé; **holidays with ~** congés *mpl* payés.

2 *adj dispute* salarial. **~ cheque,** *(US)* **~ check** salaire *m*. **~ day** jour *m* de paie; **~ desk** caisse *f*; **~ increase** *or* **rise** augmentation *f* de salaire; **~ packet,** *(US)* **~ envelope** enveloppe *f* de paie; *(fig)* paie *f*; **~ phone,** *(US)* **~ station** cabine *f* téléphonique; **~ TV** télé-banque *f*.

3 *vt* (**a**) *money, person* payer (*to do* à faire; *for doing* pour faire); *tradesman, bill, fee* payer, régler; *deposit* verser; *debt* régler; *loan* rembourser; *interest* rapporter; *dividend* distribuer. **to ~ sb £10** payer 10 livres à qn; **he paid them for the book** il leur a payé le livre; **he paid me £2 for the ticket** il m'a payé le billet 2 livres; **he paid £2 for the ticket** il a payé le billet 2 livres; **he paid a lot for his suit** il a payé son costume très cher; **we're not paid for that** on n'est pas payé pour cela; **that's what you're paid for** c'est pour cela qu'on vous paie; **they ~ good wages** ils paient bien; **I get paid on Fridays** je touche ma paie le vendredi; **to ~ money into an account** verser de l'argent à un compte; *(fig)* **to ~ the penalty** subir les conséquences; **to ~ the price of** payer le prix de; **this paid dividends** ceci a porté ses fruits; **it's ~ing its way** ça couvre ses frais; **he likes to ~ his way** il aime payer sa part; **to put paid to** *plans* mettre par terre; *person* régler son compte à; **it will ~ you to be nice to him** vous gagnerez à *or* vous avez intérêt à être aimable avec lui; **it won't ~ him to tell the truth** il ne gagnera rien à dire la vérité. (**b**) *attention, compliments* faire; *homage* rendre; *V* **visit.**

4 *vi* payer. *(lit, fig)* **to ~ for sth** payer qch; *(fig)* **he paid dearly for it** il l'a payé cher *(fig)*; **we'll have to ~ through the nose for it** * cela va nous coûter les yeux de la tête *; **'~ as you earn' system (P.A.Y.E.)** système *m* fiscal de prélèvement à la source; **does it ~?** est-ce que ça paie?, c'est rentable?; **this business doesn't ~** cette affaire n'est pas rentable; **it ~s to advertise** la publicité rapporte; **it doesn't ~ to tell lies** cela ne sert à rien de mentir; **crime doesn't ~** le crime ne paie pas. ◆ **pay back** *vt sep* (**a**) *stolen money* restituer; *loan, person* rembourser. **to ~ sb back sth** rembourser qch à qn. (**b**) *(get even with)* **to ~ sb back for doing sth** faire payer à qn qch qu'il a fait; **I'll ~ you back for that!** je vous le revaudrai! ◆ **pay down** *vt sep (as deposit)* verser un acompte de. ◆ **pay in** *vt sep (at bank etc)* verser (*to* à). ◆ **pay off 1** *vi [trick, scheme]* être payant; *[decision]* être valable; *[patience]* être récompensé. **2** *vt sep* (**a**) *debts* régler; *creditor* rembourser. **to ~ off a grudge** régler un vieux compte. (**b**) *(discharge) worker, staff* licencier; *servant* congédier; *crew* débarquer. ◆ **pay out** *vt sep* (**a**) *rope* laisser filer. (**b**) *money (spend)* dépenser; *[cashier etc]* payer. (**c**) = **pay back (b).** ◆ **pay up 1** *vi* payer. **2** *vt sep amount* payer; *debts* régler.

◆ **payable** *adj* payable (*in* dans; *over* en); **to make a cheque ~able to sb** faire un chèque à l'ordre de qn. ◆ **payee** *n* bénéficiaire *mf*. ◆ **paying** *adj business, scheme* rentable; **~ing guest** pensionnaire *mf*, hôte *m* payant. ◆ **pay-in slip** *n (Banking)* bordereau *m* de versement. ◆ **paymaster** *n (Mil)* trésorier *m*. ◆ **payment** *n (gen)* paiement *m*; *[deposit, cheque]* versement *m*; *[bill, fee]* règlement *m*; *[debt, loan]* remboursement *m*; *(reward)* récompense *f*; **on ~ment of £50** moyennant la somme de 50 livres; **in ~ment for** *goods* en règlement de; *sum owed* en remboursement de; *work, help* en paiement de; *sb's trouble, efforts* en récompense de; **method of ~ment** mode *m* de règlement; **without ~ment** à titre gracieux; **~ment in kind** paiement en nature; **~ment in full** règlement complet; **~ment by instalments** paiement à tempérament; **in monthly ~ments of £10** payable en versements de 10 livres par mois. ◆ **payoff** * *n* remboursement *m*; *(reward)* récompense *f*; *(outcome)* résultat *m* final; *(climax)* comble *m*. ◆ **payroll** *n (list)* registre *m* du personnel; *(money)* paie *f* (de tout le personnel); *(employees)* personnel *m*; **to be on a firm's ~roll** être employé par une société. ◆ **payslip** *n* feuille *f or* bulletin *m* de paie.

pea [piː] **1** *n* pois *m*. **(green) ~s** (petits) pois; *(fig)* **they are as like as two ~s** ils se ressemblent comme deux gouttes d'eau. **2** *adj*: **~ soup** soupe *f* aux pois. ◆ **peagreen** *adj* vert pomme *inv*. ◆ **peashooter** *n* sarbacane *f*.

peace [piːs] **1** *n (not war)* paix *f*; *(calm)* paix, tranquillité *f*. **at** *or* **in ~** en paix; **at ~ with** en paix avec; **to make ~** faire la paix; *(fig)* **to make one's ~ with** se réconcilier avec; **~ of mind** tranquillité d'esprit; **to disturb sb's ~ of mind** troubler l'esprit de qn; **leave him in ~, give him some ~** laisse-le tranquille, fiche-lui la paix *; **anything for ~ and quiet** n'importe quoi pour avoir la paix; *(Jur)* **to disturb the ~** troubler l'ordre public; **to keep the ~** *[citizen]* ne pas troubler l'ordre public; *[police]* veiller à l'ordre public; *(fig: stop disagreement)* maintenir la paix.

2 *adj campaign, march* pour la paix. **~ conference** conférence *f* pour la paix; **~ initiative** initiative *f* de paix; **P~ Movement** Mouvement *m* pour la paix; *(fig)* **~ offering** cadeau *m* de réconciliation; **~ talks** pourparlers *mpl* de paix; **~ treaty** traité *m* de paix.

◆ **peaceable** *adj (calm)* paisible, pacifique. ◆ **peaceably** *adv* paisiblement, pacifiquement. ◆ **peaceful** *adj reign, period, person* paisible; *life, place, sleep* paisible, tranquille; *meeting* calme; *demonstration* non-violent; *coexistence* pacifique; **the ~ful uses of atomic energy** l'utilisation pacifique de l'énergie nucléaire. ◆ **peacefully** *adv demonstrate, reign* paisiblement; *work, lie, sleep* paisiblement, tranquillement. ◆ **peacefulness** *n* paix *f*, tranquillité *f*. ◆ **peace-keeping** *adj force* de maintien de la paix; *operation, policy* de pacification. ◆ **peace-loving** *adj* pacifique. ◆ **peacemaker** *n* pacificateur *m*, -trice *f*. ◆ **peacetime** *n*: **in ~time** en temps de paix.

peach [piːtʃ] **1** *n* pêche *f*; *(tree)* pêcher *m*. **2** *adj (colour)* pêche *inv*.

peacock ['pi:kɒk] *n* paon *m*. ~ **blue** bleu paon *inv*. ◆ **peahen** *n* paonne *f*.

peak [pi:k] **1** *n [mountain]* cime *f*, sommet *m*; *(mountain itself)* pic *m*; *[roof etc]* faîte *m*; *[cap]* visière *f*; *(on graph)* sommet; *(fig) [career, power]* apogée *m*. **at its** ~ *fame, career, empire* à son apogée; *demand, traffic* à son maximum; *business* à son point culminant; *discontent* à son comble. **2** *adj demand, production* maximum; *hours* d'affluence; *period* de pointe; *traffic* aux heures d'affluence. **a** ~ **experience** une expérience de l'ineffable. **3** *vi [sales, demand]* atteindre un niveau maximum. ◆ **peaky** *adj* fatigué, qui n'a pas l'air très en forme *.

peal [pi:l] **1** *n [thunder]* coup *m*. ~ **of bells** carillon *m*; ~ **of laughter** éclat *m* de rire. **2** *vi* (~ **out**) *[bells]* carillonner; *[thunder]* gronder; *[organ]* retentir; *[laughter]* éclater. **3** *vt bells* sonner (à toute volée).

peanut ['pi:nʌt] **1** *n (nut)* cacahuète *f*; *(plant)* arachide *f*. *(fig)* **it's just** ~**s** ‡ c'est une bagatelle. **2** *adj*: ~ **butter** beurre *m* de cacahuètes; ~ **oil** huile *f* d'arachide.

pear [pɛəʳ] *n* poire *f*; *(tree)* poirier *m*. ◆ **pear-shaped** *adj* en forme de poire.

pearl [pɜ:l] **1** *n* perle *f*. **mother of** ~ nacre *f*; **real/cultured** ~**s** perles fines/de culture; *(fig)* ~**s of wisdom** trésors *mpl* de sagesse; *(fig)* **to cast** ~**s before swine** jeter des perles aux pourceaux. **2** *adj necklace* de perles; *button* de nacre. ~ **barley** orge *m* perlé; ~ **diver** pêcheur *m*, -euse *f* de perles. ◆ **pearly** *adj* nacré; *(hum)* **the P~y Gates** les portes *fpl* du Paradis.

peasant ['pez(ə)nt] *adj, n* paysan(ne) *m(f)*.

peat [pi:t] *n* tourbe *f*. ◆ **peaty** *adj* tourbeux.

pebble ['pebl] *n* caillou *m*; *(on beach)* galet *m*. *(fig)* **he's not the only** ~ **on the beach** il n'y a pas que lui. ◆ **pebbledash** *n* crépi *m* moucheté. ◆ **pebbly** *adj road* caillouteux; *beach* de galets.

pecan [pɪ'kæn] *n* pacane *f*; *(tree)* pacanier *m*.

peck [pek] **1** *n* coup *m* de bec; *(hasty kiss)* bise * *f*. **2** *vt object, ground* becqueter; *food* picorer; *person, attacker* donner un coup de bec à; *hole* faire à coups de bec. **3** *vi [bird]* **to** ~ **at** picorer; *[person]* **to** ~ **at one's food** manger du bout des dents. ◆ **pecking order** *n* hiérarchie *f*. ◆ **peckish** * *adj*: **to be** ~**ish** avoir un peu faim.

peculiar [pɪ'kju:lɪəʳ] *adj* (**a**) *(particular) importance, qualities* particulier. **its (own)** ~ **dialect** son dialecte particulier, son propre dialecte; ~ **to** particulier à, propre à. (**b**) *(odd)* bizarre, curieux, étrange. ◆ **peculiarity** *n* (**a**) *(distinctive feature)* particularité *f*; (**b**) *(oddity)* bizarrerie *f*. ◆ **peculiarly** *adv (specially)* particulièrement; *(oddly)* étrangement.

pecuniary [pɪ'kju:nɪərɪ] *adj* pécuniaire. ~ **difficulties** ennuis *mpl* d'argent.

pedagogic(al) [,pedə'gɒdʒɪk(əl)] *adj* pédagogique.

pedal ['pedl] **1** *n* pédale *f*. **2** *vi* pédaler. **he** ~**led through the town** il a traversé la ville (à bicyclette). ◆ **pedalbin** *n* poubelle *f* à pédale. ◆ **pedalboat** *n* pédalo *m*. ◆ **pedalcar** *n* voiture *f* à pédales. ◆ **pedalo** *n* pedalo *m*.

pedant ['pedənt] *n* pédant(e) *m(f)*. ◆ **pedantic** *adj* pédant. ◆ **pedantically** *adv* avec pédantisme. ◆ **pedantry** *n* pédantisme *m*.

peddle ['pedl] *vt goods, gossip* colporter; *drugs* faire le trafic de. ◆ **peddler** *or* ◆ **pedlar** *n (door to door)* colporteur *m*; *(in street)* camelot *m*; *[drugs]* revendeur *m*, -euse *f*.

pederast ['pedəræst] *n* pédéraste *m*. ◆ **pederasty** *n* pédérastie *f*.

pedestal ['pedɪstl] *n* piédestal *m (also fig)*.

pedestrian [pɪ'destrɪən] **1** *n* piéton *m*. **2** *adj* (**a**) *(fig)* prosaïque, plat. (**b**) ~ **crossing** passage *m* pour piétons, passage clouté; ~ **precinct** zone *f* piétonnière.

pediatric *etc (US)* = **paediatric** *etc*.

pedicure ['pedɪkjʊəʳ] *n* soins *mpl* des pieds.

pedigree ['pedɪgri:] **1** *n [animal]* pedigree *m*; *[person] (lineage)* ascendance *f*, lignée *f*; *(family tree)* arbre *m* généalogique. **2** *adj animal* de (pure) race.

pedometer [pɪ'dɒmɪtəʳ] *n* podomètre *m*.

pee ‡ [pi:] *vi* faire pipi *, pisser ‡.

peek [pi:k] *n, vi*: **to (take a)** ~ **at** jeter un coup d'œil (furtif) à *or* sur.

peel [pi:l] **1** *n [apple, potato]* épluchure *f*; *[orange]* écorce *f*; *(Culin, also in drink)* zeste *m*. **candied** ~ écorce confite. **2** *vt fruit, potato* éplucher; *stick* écorcer; *shrimps* décortiquer. **to keep one's eyes** ~**ed** ‡ ouvrir l'œil * (*for* pour trouver). **3** *vi [paint]* s'écailler; *[skin]* peler.
◆ **peel away 1** *vi [skin]* peler; *[paint]* s'écailler; *[wallpaper]* se décoller. **2** *vt sep rind* peler; *film, covering* décoller. ◆ **peel back** *vt sep film, covering* décoller. ◆ **peel off 1** *vi* (**a**) = **peel away 1.** (**b**) *[plane]* s'écarter de la formation. **2** *vt sep* (**a**) = **peel away 2.** (**b**) *clothes* enlever.
◆ **peeler** *n* (couteau-)éplucheur *m*. ◆ **peeling 1** *adj wallpaper* qui se décolle ; **2** *npl*: ~**ings** épluchures *fpl*.

peep [pi:p] **1** *n* (petit) coup *m* d'œil. **to have** *or* **take a** ~ **at sth** jeter un (petit) coup d'œil à *or* sur qch. **2** *vi* jeter un (petit) coup d'œil (*at* à, sur; *into* dans; *over* par-dessus). **he was** ~**ing at us from...** il nous regardait furtivement *or* à la dérobée de... ◆ **peephole** *n (gen)* trou *m* (pour épier); *(in door)* œil *m* de porte. ◆ **Peeping Tom** *n* voyeur *m*.

peer[1] [pɪəʳ] *vi*: **to** ~ **at** regarder.

peer[2] [pɪəʳ] *n (social equal)* pair *m*; (~ **of the realm**) pair *m* (du royaume). ~ **group** pairs *mpl*. ◆ **peerage** *n* pairie *f*; **to be given a** ~**age** être anobli. ◆ **peeress** *n* pairesse *f*. ◆ **peerless** *adj* sans pareil.

peevish ['pi:vɪʃ] *adj* maussade; *child* de mauvaise humeur. ◆ **peeved** ‡ *adj* fâché, en rogne *. ◆ **peevishly** *adv* maussadement; avec (mauvaise) humeur.

peewee * ['pi:wi:] *(US)* **1** *adj* minuscule. **2** *n (child)* petit bout *m* de chou *.

peewit ['pi:wɪt] *n* vanneau *m*.

peg [peg] **1** *n (wooden)* cheville *f*; *(metal)* fiche *f*; *(for coat, hat)* patère *f*; *(tent* ~*)* piquet *m*; *(clothes* ~*)* pince *f* à linge. **I bought this off the** ~ c'est du prêt-à-porter, j'ai acheté ça tout fait; **to take sb down a** ~ **(or two)** rabattre le caquet à qn; *(fig)* **a** ~ **to hang a complaint on** un prétexte pour se plaindre. **2** *vt (Tech)* cheviller; *prices, wages* bloquer. **to** ~ **clothes (out) on the line** étendre du linge sur la corde (à l'aide de pinces). ◆ **peg down** *vt sep tent* fixer avec des piquets. *(fig)* **to** ~ **sb down to doing** réussir à décider qn à faire. ◆ **peg out** ‡ *vi (die)* claquer ‡, mourir.

pejorative [pɪ'dʒɒrɪtɪv] *adj* péjoratif.

Peking [pi:'kɪŋ] *n* Pékin.

pekin(g)ese [,pi:kɪ'ni:z] *n* pékinois *m (chien)*.

pelargonium [,pelə'gəʊnɪəm] *n* pélargonium *m*.

pelican ['pelɪkən] *n* pélican *m*. *(Aut)* ~ **crossing** feu *m* à commande manuelle.

pellet ['pelɪt] *n [paper, bread]* boulette *f*; *(for gun)* plomb *m*; *(Med)* pilule *f*; *[chemicals]* pastille *f*.

pelmet ['pelmɪt] *n (wooden)* lambrequin *m*; *(cloth)* cantonnière *f*.

pelota [pɪ'ləʊtə] *n* pelote *f* basque.

pelt [pelt] **1** *vt* bombarder, cribler (*with* de). **2** *vi* (**a**) **the rain is** *or* **it's** ~**ing (down)** * il tombe des cordes *; ~**ing rain** pluie *f* battante. (**b**) *(*: run)* **to** ~ **across** *etc* traverser *etc* à fond de train.

pelvis ['pelvɪs] *n* bassin *m*, pelvis *m*.

pen[1] [pen] **1** *n* plume *f*; *(ball-point)* stylo *m* à bille ; *(felt-tip)* feutre *m*; *(fountain ~)* stylo. **to put ~ to paper** écrire; **to put one's ~ through sth** barrer qch. **2** *adj*: **~ name** pseudonyme *m* (littéraire); **~ nib** bec *m* de plume. **3** *vt letter* écrire; *article* rédiger. ◆ **pen-and-ink drawing** *n* dessin *m* à la plume. ◆ **penfriend** *n* correspondant(e) *m(f)*. ◆ **penknife** *n* canif *m*.

pen[2] [pen] **1** *n [animals]* parc *m*, enclos *m*; *(play ~)* parc (d'enfant); *(submarine ~)* abri *m* de sous-marins. **2** *vt* (**~ in, ~ up**) *animals* parquer; *people* enfermer.

penal ['pi:nl] *adj law, clause, code* pénal; *offence* punissable; *colony* pénitentiaire. *(Jur)* **~ servitude** travaux *mpl* forcés. ◆ **penalize** *vt* (**a**) *(punish; also Sport)* pénaliser (*for* pour); (**b**) *(handicap)* handicaper; **the strike ~izes those who...** la grève touche les gens qui...

penalty ['pen(ə)ltɪ] **1** *n (punishment: gen)* pénalité *f* (*for* pour); *(Sport)* pénalisation *f*; *(Ftbl etc)* penalty *m*. **on ~ of** sous peine de; **the ~ for not doing this is...** si on ne fait pas cela la pénalité est...; *(fig)* **to pay the ~** subir les conséquences; *(in games)* **a 5-point ~ for** une pénalisation de 5 points pour. **2** *adj (Ftbl)* **~ area** surface *f* de réparation; **~ goal** but *m* sur pénalité; **~ kick** coup *m* de pied de pénalité.

penance ['penəns] *n* pénitence *f*. **to do ~ for** faire pénitence pour.

pence [pens] *npl of* **penny.**

pencil ['pensl] **1** *n* crayon *m*. **in ~** au crayon. **2** *adj note, drawing, mark* au crayon. **3** *vt* écrire au crayon, crayonner. ◆ **pencil in** *vt sep note* écrire au crayon; *(fig: note provisionally)* marquer comme possibilité. ◆ **pencil-case** *n* trousse *f* (d'écolier). ◆ **pencil-sharpener** *n* taille-crayon *m*.

pending ['pendɪŋ] **1** *adj business, question* pendant, en suspens; *(Jur) case* pendant, en instance. **2** *prep (until)* en attendant.

pendulum ['pendjʊləm] *n (gen)* pendule *m*; *[clock]* balancier *m*.

penetrate ['penɪtreɪt] *vti (also ~* **into***)* pénétrer (dans); *[bullet, knife]* pénétrer; *[sound]* pénétrer dans; *[person, vehicle] forest* pénétrer dans; *enemy territory* pénétrer en; *business firm, political party* s'infiltrer dans; *plans, mystery* pénétrer. **to ~ through** traverser. ◆ **penetrable** *adj* pénétrable. ◆ **penetrating** *adj* pénétrant. ◆ **penetratingly** *adv* avec pénétration. ◆ **penetration** *n* pénétration *f*.

penguin ['peŋgwɪn] *n* pingouin *m*; *(in Antarctic)* manchot *m*.

penicillin [,penɪ'sɪlɪn] *n* pénicilline *f*.

peninsula [pɪ'nɪnsjʊlə] *n* péninsule *f*.

penis ['pi:nɪs] *n* pénis *m*.

penitent ['penɪt(ə)nt] *adj* pénitent. ◆ **penitence** *n* pénitence *f*. ◆ **penitentiary** *n (US)* prison *f*. ◆ **penitently** *adv* d'un air contrit.

penny, *pl* **pence** *(valeur)*, **pennies** *(pièces)* ['penɪ, pens] *n* penny *m*. **one old/new ~** un ancien/un nouveau penny; *(fig)* **he is not a ~ the wiser** il n'est pas plus avancé *; **he hasn't a ~ to his name** il n'a pas le sou; **a ~ for your thoughts!** à quoi pensez-vous?; **the ~ has dropped!** * il a (*or* j'ai *etc*) enfin pigé! ⁑; *(fig)* **he keeps turning up like a bad ~** pas moyen de se débarrasser de lui; **in for a ~ in for a pound** (au point où on en est) autant faire les choses jusqu'au bout. ◆ **penniless** *adj* sans le sou. ◆ **penny-pinching** **1** *n* économies *fpl* de bouts de chandelle; **2** *adj person* qui fait des économies de bouts de chandelle.

pension ['penʃ(ə)n] **1** *n (state payment)* pension *f*; *(from company etc)* retraite *f*; *(to servant etc)* pension. **old age ~** pension vieillesse (de la Sécurité sociale); **retirement ~** (pension de) retraite. **2** *adj*: **~ fund** fonds *m* vieillesse; **~ scheme** caisse *f* de retraite. ◆ **pension off** *vt sep* mettre à la retraite. ◆ **pensionable** *adj post* qui donne droit à une pension; *age* de la retraite. ◆ **pensioner** *n* retraité(e) *m(f)*.

pensive ['pensɪv] *adj* pensif, songeur. ◆ **pensively** *adv* pensivement.

pentagon ['pentəgən] *n* pentagone *m*. ◆ **pentagonal** *adj* pentagonal.

pentathlon [pen'tæθlən] *n* pentathlon *m*.

Pentecost ['pentɪkɒst] *n* la Pentecôte. ◆ **Pentecostalism** *m* Pentecôtisme *m*. ◆ **Pentecostalist** **1** *n* Pentecôtiste *mf* ; **2** *adj* pentecôtiste.

penthouse ['penthaʊs] *n (~* **flat** *or* **apartment***)* appartement *m* de grand standing *(construit sur le toit d'un immeuble)*.

pent-up ['pent'ʌp] *adj emotions, energy* refoulé; *person* tendu.

penultimate [pɪ'nʌltɪmɪt] *adj, n* pénultième *(mf)*.

penury ['penjʊrɪ] *n* indigence *f*. ◆ **penurious** *adj* indigent.

peony (rose) ['pɪənɪ('rəʊz)] *n* pivoine *f*.

people ['pi:pl] **1** *n* (**a**) *(pl: persons)* gens *mpl (adj fem if before n)* personnes *fpl*. **old ~** les personnes âgées, les vieilles gens, les vieux *mpl*; **young ~** les jeunes gens *mpl*, les jeunes *mpl*; **clever ~** les gens intelligents; **a lot of ~** beaucoup de gens *or* de monde; **what a lot of ~!** que de monde!; **several ~ said...** plusieurs personnes ont dit...; **how many ~?** combien de personnes?; **several English ~** plusieurs Anglais; **what do you ~ think?** qu'est-ce que vous en pensez, vous autres? (**b**) *(pl: in general)* on, les gens. **~ say...** on dit..., les gens disent...; **don't tell ~ that** il ne faut pas dire ça aux gens. (**c**) *(pl: inhabitants) [a country]* peuple *m*; *[district, town]* habitants *mpl*. **country ~** les gens de la campagne, les populations rurales; **town ~** les habitants des villes, les citadins *mpl*; **the French ~** les Français, le peuple français. (**d**) *(pl) (Pol: citizens)* peuple *m*; *(general public)* public *m*. **government by the ~** gouvernement *m* par le peuple; **the king and his ~** le roi et son peuple; **the ~ at large** le grand public; **man of the ~** homme *m* du peuple. (**e**) *(sg: nation etc)* peuple *m*, nation *f*. (**f**) *(pl*: family)* famille *f*, parents *mpl*. **I am writing to my ~** * j'écris à ma famille. **2** *vt* peupler (*with* de).

pep * [pep] **1** *n* entrain *m*, dynamisme *m*. **2** *adj*: **~ pill** excitant *m*; **~ talk** petit laïus * *m* d'encouragement. ◆ **pep up** * *vt sep person* ragaillardir; *party, conversation* animer; *drink, plot* corser. ◆ **peppy** *adj (US) person (energetic)* énergique; *(lively)* plein d'entrain; *car* nerveux.

pepper ['pepəʳ] **1** *n* (**a**) *(spice)* poivre *m*. **white/black ~** poivre blanc/gris. (**b**) *(vegetable)* poivron *m*. **red/green ~** poivron rouge/vert. **2** *vt* poivrer. ◆ **pepper-and-salt** *adj* poivre et sel *inv*. ◆ **peppercorn** *n* grain *m* de poivre. ◆ **peppermint** **1** *n (sweet)* pastille *f* de menthe ; **2** *adj* à la menthe. ◆ **pepperpot** *n* poivrière *f*. ◆ **peppery** *adj food* poivré; *person* irascible.

peptic ['peptɪk] *adj*: **~ ulcer** ulcère *m* à l'estomac.

per [pɜ:ʳ] *prep* par. **~ annum** par an; **~ capita** par personne; **~ cent** pour cent; **~ day** par jour; **~ head** par tête, par personne; **100 km ~ hour** 100 km à l'heure; **she is paid 15 francs ~ hour** on la paie 15 F (de) l'heure; **3 francs ~ kilo** 3 F le kilo; **4 hours ~ person** 4 heures par personne. ◆ **percentage** *n* pourcentage *m*.

perceive [pə'si:v] *vt sound, meaning* percevoir; *(notice)* remarquer (*that* que); *object, person* apercevoir, remarquer. ◆ **perceptible** *adj* perceptible. ◆ **perceptibly** *adv* sensiblement. ◆ **perception** *n* perception *f*. ◆ **perceptive** *adj analysis, person* pénétrant, perspicace.

perch[1] [pɜ:tʃ] *n (fish)* perche *f*.

perch² [pɜːtʃ] **1** *n* perchoir *m*. **2** *vi [bird, person]* se percher. **3** *vt* percher, jucher.

percolate [ˈpɜːkəleɪt] **1** *vt coffee* passer. **~d coffee** café fait dans une cafetière à pression. **2** *vi* passer (*through* par); *[news]* filtrer. ◆ **percolator** *n* cafetière *f* à pression.

percussion [pəˈkʌʃ(ə)n] **1** *n* percussion *f*. **2** *adj (Mus)* instrument à *or* de percussion.

peregrine [ˈperɪgrɪn] *adj*: **~ falcon** faucon *m* pèlerin.

peremptory [pəˈrempt(ə)rɪ] *adj* péremptoire. ◆ **peremptorily** *adv* péremptoirement.

perennial [pəˈrenɪəl] **1** *adj (gen)* perpétuel; *plant* vivace. **2** *n* plante *f* vivace. ◆ **perennially** *adv* perpétuellement.

perfect [ˈpɜːfɪkt] **1** *adj* (**a**) *(gen)* parfait. **the ~ moment to speak to him about it** le moment idéal pour lui en parler; *(Mus)* **~ pitch** l'oreille *f* absolue; *(Gram)* **~ tense** parfait *m*. (**b**) *(emphatic) idiot etc* véritable. **he's a ~ stranger to me** je ne le connais absolument pas. **2** *n (Gram)* parfait *m*. **in the ~** au parfait. **3** [pəˈfekt] *vt work* achever, parfaire; *technique* mettre au point. **to ~ one's French** parfaire ses connaissances de français. ◆ **perfection** *n* perfection *f*. ◆ **perfectionist** *adj, n* perfectionniste *(mf)*. ◆ **perfectly** *adv* parfaitement.

perfidy [ˈpɜːfɪdɪ] *n* perfidie *f*. ◆ **perfidious** *adj* perfide. ◆ **perfidiously** *adv* perfidement.

perforate [ˈpɜːfəreɪt] *vt* perforer. **~d line** pointillé *m*. ◆ **perforation** *n* perforation *f*.

perform [pəˈfɔːm] **1** *vt* (**a**) *task* exécuter, accomplir; *function* remplir; *duty, miracle* accomplir; *rite* célébrer. **to ~ an operation** *(gen)* exécuter une opération; *(Med)* pratiquer une opération. (**b**) *(Theat etc) play, ballet, opera* donner; *symphony* jouer; *solo, acrobatics* exécuter. **2** *vi* (**a**) *[company etc]* donner une *or* des représentation(s); *[actor]* jouer; *[singer]* chanter; *[dancer]* danser; *[acrobat, trained animal]* exécuter un *or* des numéro(s). **to ~ on the violin** jouer du violon; **~ing arts** arts *mpl* du spectacle; **~ing seals** *etc* phoques *etc* savants. (**b**) *[machine, vehicle]* marcher, fonctionner. (**c**) *(Econ)* **to ~ well/badly** *[the economy, business]* avoir de bons/mauvais résultats; *[industry, factory]* avoir de bonnes/mauvaises performances. ◆ **performance** *n* (**a**) *(presentation) [play, opera, ballet, circus]* représentation *f*; *[film, concert]* séance *f*; *(fig: fuss)* **what a ~ance!** quelle affaire!, quelle histoire! *; (**b**) *[actor, musician, dancer etc]* interprétation *f*; *[acrobat]* numéro *m*; *[racehorse, athlete, team etc]* performance *f*; *(Scol)* performances *fpl; [the economy, business]* résultats *mpl; [industry, factory]* performances; (**c**) *[machine]* fonctionnement *m*; *[vehicle]* performance *f*. ◆ **performer** *n* artiste *mf*.

perfume [ˈpɜːfjuːm] **1** *n* parfum *m*. **2** [pəˈfjuːm] *vt* parfumer. ◆ **perfumery** *n* parfumerie *f*.

perfunctory [pəˈfʌŋ(k)t(ə)rɪ] *adj* négligent, pour la forme. ◆ **perfunctorily** *adv bow, greet, perform* négligemment; *answer, agree* sans conviction.

perhaps [pəˈhæps, præps] *adv* peut-être. **~ so/not** peut-être que oui/que non; **~ he will come** peut-être viendra-t-il, il viendra peut-être, peut-être qu'il viendra.

peril [ˈperɪl] *n* péril *m*, danger *m*. **in ~ of** en danger de; **at your ~** à vos risques et périls. ◆ **perilous** *adj* périlleux. ◆ **perilously** *adv* périlleusement; **they were ~ously near disaster** ils frôlaient la catastrophe.

perimeter [pəˈrɪmɪtəʳ] *n* périmètre *m*.

perineum [ˌperɪˈniːəm] *n* périnée *m*.

period [ˈpɪərɪəd] **1** *n* (**a**) *(length of time)* période *f*; *(stage: in career, development etc)* époque *f*, moment *m*. **the classical ~** la période classique; **furniture of the ~** meubles de l'époque; **the post-war ~** (la période de) l'après-guerre *m*; **at that ~ in** *or* **of his life** à cette époque *or* à ce moment de sa vie; **the holiday ~** la période des vacances; *(Met)* **rainy ~s** périodes de pluie; **in the ~ of a year** en l'espace d'une année; **within a 3-month ~** dans un délai de 3 mois. (**b**) *(Scol)* cours *m*, leçon *f*. (**c**) *(full stop)* point *m*. (**d**) *(menstruation)* règles *fpl*. **2** *adj costume* de l'époque; *furniture* d'époque. *(fig)* **~ piece** curiosité *f*. ◆ **periodic** *adj* périodique. ◆ **periodical** *adj, n* périodique *(m)*. ◆ **periodically** *adv* périodiquement.

peripatetic [ˌperɪpəˈtetɪk] *adj* ambulant; *teacher* qui dessert plusieurs établissements.

periphery [pəˈrɪfərɪ] *n* périphérie *f*. ◆ **peripheral** *adj, n* périphérique *(m)*.

periscope [ˈperɪskəʊp] *n* périscope *m*.

perish [ˈperɪʃ] *vi (die)* périr, mourir; *[rubber, foods etc]* se détériorer. ◆ **perishable 1** *adj* périssable ; **2** *n*: **~ables** denrées *fpl* périssables. ◆ **perished** * *adj* frigorifié *. ◆ **perishing** *adj*: **it's ~ing** * il fait très froid.

peritonitis [ˌperɪtəˈnaɪtɪs] *n* péritonite *f*.

periwinkle [ˈperɪˌwɪŋkl] *n (Bot)* pervenche *f*; *(Zool)* bigorneau *m*.

perjure [ˈpɜːdʒəʳ] *vt*: **to ~ o.s.** se parjurer; *(Jur)* faire un faux serment; *(Jur)* **~d evidence** faux serment. ◆ **perjury** *n* parjure *m*; *(Jur)* faux serment; **to commit perjury** se parjurer; *(Jur)* faire un faux serment.

perk [pɜːk] **1** *vi*: **to ~ up** *(cheer up)* se ragaillardir; *(show interest)* s'animer. **2** *vt* ragaillardir. *(lit, fig)* **to ~ one's ears up** dresser l'oreille. ◆ **perkily** *adv (gaily)* d'un air guilleret; *(in lively manner)* avec entrain; *(cheekily)* avec effronterie. ◆ **perky** *adj* guilleret; plein d'entrain; effronté.

perks * [pɜːks] *npl* petits bénéfices *mpl*.

perm [pɜːm] **1** *n (abbr of* **permanent wave***)* permanente *f*. **2** *vt*: **to ~ sb's hair** faire une permanente à qn; **to have one's hair ~ed** se faire faire une permanente.

permafrost [ˈpɜːməfrɒst] *n* permafrost *m*.

permanent [ˈpɜːmənənt] *adj (gen)* permanent. **I'm not ~ here** je ne suis pas ici à titre définitif; **~ address** adresse *f* fixe; *(Brit)* **P~ Undersecretary** ≃ secrétaire *m* général (de ministère); **~ wave** permanente *f*; *(Rail)* **~ way** voie *f* ferrée. ◆ **permanence** *n* permanence *f*. ◆ **permanency** *n (job)* emploi *m* permanent. ◆ **permanently** *adv remain* en permanence, de façon permanente; *appoint* à titre définitif. ◆ **permanent-press** *adj trousers* à pli permanent; *skirt* à plissé permanent.

permeate [ˈpɜːmɪeɪt] **1** *vt* filtrer à travers; *(fig)* se répandre dans *or* parmi. *(lit, fig)* **~d with** imprégné de. **2** *vi* s'infiltrer; *(fig)* se répandre.

permission [pəˈmɪʃ(ə)n] *n* permission *f*; *(official)* autorisation *f*. **to give sb ~ to do** permettre à qn de faire, autoriser qn à faire. ◆ **permissible** *adj action* permis (*to do* de faire); *attitude etc* acceptable (*to do* de faire). ◆ **permissive** *adj person, society* permissif.

permit [ˈpɜːmɪt] **1** *n (gen)* autorisation *f* (écrite); *(for specific activity)* permis *m*; *(entrance pass)* laissez-passer *m inv*; *(for goods at Customs)* passavant *m*. **building/fishing/residence ~** permis de construire/de pêche/de séjour. **2** [pəˈmɪt] *vt* permettre (*sb to do* à qn de faire); *(more formally)* autoriser (*sb to do* qn à faire). **he was ~ted to...** on lui a permis de..., on l'a autorisé à...; **to ~ sth to happen** permettre que qch se produise, laisser qch se produire. **3** [pəˈmɪt] *vi*: **to ~ of sth** permettre qch.

pernicious [pəˈnɪʃ(ə)s] *adj* nuisible; *(Med)* pernicieux.

pernickety * [pəˈnɪkɪtɪ] *adj* difficile (*about* pour), pointilleux; *job* minutieux.

peroxide [pəˈrɒksaɪd] *n* peroxyde *m*.

perpendicular [ˌpɜːp(ə)nˈdɪkjʊləʳ] **1** *adj (gen)* perpendiculaire (*to* à); *cliff, slope* à pic. **2** *n* perpendiculaire *f*. ◆ **perpendicularly** *adv* perpendiculairement.

perpetrate [ˈpɜːpɪtreɪt] *vt (gen)* faire; *crime* perpétrer. ◆ **perpetrator** *n* auteur *m (d'un crime)*.

perpetual [pəˈpetjʊəl] *adj (gen)* perpétuel. **he's a ~ nuisance** il ne cesse d'enquiquiner * le monde. ◆ **perpetually** *adv* perpétuellement. ◆ **perpetuate** *vt* perpétuer. ◆ **perpetuity** *n*: **in perpetuity** à perpétuité.

perplex [pəˈpleks] *vt* rendre perplexe. **I was ~ed by it** cela m'a rendu perplexe. ◆ **perplexed** *adj* perplexe. ◆ **perplexedly** *adv* d'un air perplexe. ◆ **perplexing** *adj* embarrassant, confus. ◆ **perplexity** *n* embarras *m*, perplexité *f*.

perquisite [ˈpɜːkwɪzɪt] *n* à-côté *m*.

persecute [ˈpɜːsɪkjuːt] *vt* persécuter (*for* pour). ◆ **persecution** *n* persécution *f*; **persecution mania** folie *f* de la persécution. ◆ **persecutor** *n* persécuteur *m*, -trice *f*.

persevere [ˌpɜːsɪˈvɪəʳ] *vi* persévérer (*in sth* dans qch), persister (*in sth* dans qch; *at doing sth* à faire qch). ◆ **perseverance** *n* persévérance *f*, ténacité *f*. ◆ **persevering** *adj* persévérant.

Persia [ˈpɜːʃə] *n* Perse *f*. ◆ **Persian** **1** *adj (Antiq)* perse; *(Hist)* persan; *carpet* de Perse; *cat* persan; **~n Gulf** golfe *m* Persique ; **2** *n* Persan(e) *m(f)*; *(Hist)* Perse *mf*; *(Ling)* persan *m*.

persist [pəˈsɪst] *vi* persister (*in sth* dans qch; *in doing* à faire). ◆ **persistence** *n* persistance *f*. ◆ **persistent** *adj (persevering)* persévérant; *(obstinate)* obstiné; *smell, pain, cough* persistant; *warnings, noise* continuel; *(Jur)* **~ent offender** multi-récidiviste *mf*. ◆ **persistently** *adv (consistently)* constamment; *(obstinately)* obstinément.

person [ˈpɜːsn] *n* personne *f*. **in ~** en personne; **in the ~ of** dans *or* en la personne de; *(Telec)* **a ~ to ~ call** une communication avec préavis; **he had a knife on his ~** il avait un couteau sur lui; *(Gram)* **in the first ~ singular** à la première personne du singulier. ◆ **personable** *adj* qui présente bien. ◆ **personage** *n* personnage *m*.

personal [ˈpɜːsnl] **1** *adj (gen, also Gram)* personnel; *liberty, rights etc* individuel; *habits, hygiene* intime; *application* fait en personne; *remark, question* indiscret. **~ assistant** secrétaire *mf* particulier (-ière); **~ computer** ordinateur *m* individuel; **~ details** coordonnées * *fpl;* **I have no ~ knowledge of this** personnellement je ne sais rien à ce sujet; **a letter marked '~'** une lettre marquée 'personnel'; **the argument grew ~** la discussion a pris un tour personnel; **don't let's get ~!** abstenons-nous de remarques désobligeantes!; **his ~ appearance** son apparence personnelle; **to make a ~ appearance** apparaître en personne; *(Brit Telec)* **~ call** *(person-to-person)* communication *f* avec préavis; *(private)* communication privée; *(Press)* **~ column** annonces *fpl* personnelles; **as a ~ favour to him** pour lui rendre service; **~ friend** ami(e) *m(f)* intime; **his ~ life** sa vie privée; **to give sth the ~ touch** ajouter une note personnelle à qch. **2** *n (US Press) (article)* entrefilet *m* mondain; *(ad)* petite annonce *f* personnelle.
◆ **personality** **1** *n (gen)* personnalité *f*; *(celebrity)* personnalité, personnage *m* connu; **a television ~ity** une vedette de la télévision; **let's keep ~ities out of this** abstenons-nous de remarques désobligeantes ; **2** *adj problem, test* de personnalité. ◆ **personalize** *vt* personnaliser. ◆ **personally** *adv (in person)* en personne; *(for my part)* personnellement, pour ma part; **~ly responsible** personnellement responsable; **don't take it ~ly!** ne croyez pas que vous soyez personnellement visé!; **I like him ~ly but not as an employer** je l'aime en tant que personne mais pas en tant que patron.

personify [pɜːˈsɒnɪfaɪ] *vt* personnifier. ◆ **personification** *n* personnification *f*.

personnel [ˌpɜːsəˈnel] **1** *n* personnel *m*. **2** *adj*: **~ department** service *m* du personnel; **~ management** direction *f* du personnel; **~ manager** chef *m* du personnel; **~ officer** responsable *mf* du personnel.

perspective [pəˈspektɪv] *n (gen, Archit, Art, Surv)* perspective *f*. *(fig)* **let's get this into ~** ne perdons pas le sens des proportions.

perspex [ˈpɜːspeks] *n* ® plexiglas *m* ®.

perspicacious [ˌpɜːspɪˈkeɪʃəs] *adj person* perspicace; *analysis* pénétrant. ◆ **perspicacity** *n* perspicacité *f*.

perspire [pəsˈpaɪəʳ] *vi* transpirer. ◆ **perspiration** *n* transpiration *f*; **bathed in perspiration** en nage.

persuade [pəˈsweɪd] *vt* persuader (*sb of sth* qn de qch; *sb that* qn que; *sb to do* qn de faire). **they ~d me not to** on m'en a dissuadé. ◆ **persuasion** *n (gen)* persuasion *f*; *(Rel)* religion *f*, confession *f*. ◆ **persuasive** *adj person* persuasif; *argument* convaincant. ◆ **persuasively** *adv* d'une manière persuasive. ◆ **persuasiveness** *n* pouvoir *m* de persuasion.

pert [pɜːt] *adj* coquin, hardi. ◆ **pertly** *adv* coquinement, hardiment. ◆ **pertness** *n* hardiesse *f*.

pertinacious [ˌpɜːtɪˈneɪʃ(ə)s] *adj* entêté. ◆ **pertinaciously** *adv* avec entêtement. ◆ **pertinacity** *n* entêtement *m*.

pertinent [ˈpɜːtɪnənt] *adj* pertinent. **~ to** qui a rapport à. ◆ **pertinently** *adv* pertinemment.

perturb [pəˈtɜːb] *vt* perturber. **I was ~ed to hear that...** j'ai appris avec inquiétude que... ◆ **perturbation** *n* perturbation *f*. ◆ **perturbing** *adj* troublant, inquiétant.

Peru [pəˈruː] *n* Pérou *m*. ◆ **Peruvian** **1** *adj* péruvien ; **2** *n* Péruvien(ne) *m(f)*.

peruse [pəˈruːz] *vt* lire. ◆ **perusal** *n* lecture *f*.

pervade [pɜːˈveɪd] *vt [smell]* se répandre dans; *[influence, ideas]* pénétrer dans; *[gloom]* envahir; *[feeling, atmosphere]* se retrouver partout dans. ◆ **pervasive** *adj smell, ideas* pénétrant; *gloom* envahissant; *influence* qui se fait sentir un peu partout.

perverse [pəˈvɜːs] *adj (wicked)* mauvais, pervers; *(contrary)* contrariant; *desire* pervers. ◆ **perversely** *adv (wickedly)* par pure méchanceté, avec perversité; *(contrarily)* par esprit de contradiction. ◆ **perversion** *n (gen, Med, Psych)* perversion *f; [justice, truth]* travestissement *m*. ◆ **perversity** *or* ◆ **perverseness** *n (wickedness)* méchanceté *f*, perversité *f*; *(contrariness)* caractère *m* contrariant, esprit *m* de contradiction. ◆ **pervert** **1** *vt* pervertir ; **2** [ˈpɜːvɜːt] *n* perverti(e) *m(f)* sexuel(le).

peso [ˈpeɪsəʊ] *n (money)* peso *m*.

pessary [ˈpesərɪ] *n* pessaire *m*.

pessimism [ˈpesɪmɪz(ə)m] *n* pessimisme *m*. ◆ **pessimist** *n* pessimiste *mf*. ◆ **pessimistic** *adj* pessimiste (*about* au sujet de, sur). ◆ **pessimistically** *adv* avec pessimisme.

pest [pest] **1** *n (insect/animal)* insecte *m*/animal *m* nuisible; *(person)* casse-pieds * *mf inv*. **it's a ~ having to go** quelle barbe * d'avoir à y aller. **2** *adj*: **~ control officer** agent *m* préposé à la lutte antiparasitaire. ◆ **pesticide** *n* pesticide *m*. ◆ **pestilence** *n* peste *f*. ◆ **pestilent** *or* ◆ **pestilential** *adj (exasperating)* sacré * *(before n)*.

pester [ˈpestəʳ] *vt* harceler (*sb to do* qn pour qu'il fasse; *sb with questions* qn de questions), casser les pieds à *. **she has been ~ing me for an answer** elle n'arrête pas de me réclamer une réponse; **stop ~ing me** fiche-moi la paix * (*about* avec).

pestle ['pesl] *n* pilon *m*.

pet [pet] **1** *n* (**a**) *(animal)* animal *m* familier. **he hasn't got any ~s** il n'a pas d'animaux chez lui; **she keeps a goldfish as a ~** en fait d'animal elle a un poisson rouge; **'no ~s allowed'** 'les animaux sont interdits'. (**b**) *(*: favourite)* chouchou(te) * *m(f)*. **be a ~ *** sois un chou *; **come here ~ *** viens ici mon chou *. **2** *adj* (**a**) *lion, snake* apprivoisé. **he's got a ~ rabbit** il a un lapin; **~ shop** boutique *f* d'animaux. (**b**) *(fig)* **~ aversion *** bête *f* noire; **~ name** petit nom *m* (d'amitié); **~ subject** marotte *f*, dada * *m*. **3** *vt (indulge)* chouchouter *; *(fondle)* câliner. **4** *vi (*: sexually)* se peloter *. ◆ **petting *** *n* pelotage * *m*.

petal ['petl] *n* pétale *m*.

peter ['pi:təʳ] *vi*: **to ~ out** *[supplies]* s'épuiser; *[stream, conversation]* tarir; *[plans]* tomber à l'eau; *[book]* tourner court; *[fire]* mourir; *[road]* se perdre.

petite [pə'ti:t] *adj* menu *(dit d'une femme)*.

petition [pə'tɪʃ(ə)n] **1** *n (list of signatures)* pétition *f* (*for* en faveur de; *against* contre); *(prayer)* prière *f*; *(request, also Jur)* requête *f*. **2** *vt person* adresser une pétition à (*for sth* pour demander qch). **3** *vi (Jur)* **to ~ for divorce** faire une demande en divorce.

petrify ['petrɪfaɪ] *vt* pétrifier; *(fig)* pétrifier de peur. ◆ **petrified** *adj* pétrifié; pétrifié de peur.

petrochemical [ˌpetrə(ʊ)'kemɪkəl] **1** *n* produit *m* pétrochimique. **2** *adj* pétrochimique.

petrol ['petr(ə)l] *(Brit)* **1** *n* essence *f*. **high-octane ~** supercarburant *m*; **to be heavy on ~** consommer beaucoup; **we've run out of ~** nous sommes en panne d'essence. **2** *adj engine* à essence; *rationing* d'essence. **~ bomb** cocktail *m* Molotov; **~ can** bidon *m* à essence; **~ cap** bouchon *m* de réservoir (d'essence); **~ gauge** jauge *f* d'essence; **~ pump** *(at garage)* pompe *f* d'essence; **~ station** station-service *f*; **~ tank** réservoir *m* (d'essence). ◆ **petroleum** *n* pétrole *m*; **~eum jelly** vaseline *f*.

petticoat ['petɪkəʊt] *n (skirt)* jupon *m*; *(slip)* combinaison *f*.

petty ['petɪ] *adj farmer, official* petit; *(trivial) detail, complaint* insignifiant, sans importance; *(pettyminded)* mesquin. **~ cash** caisse *f* de dépenses courantes; **~ criminal** petit malfaiteur *m*; *(Naut)* **~ officer** second maître *m*. ◆ **pettifogging** *adj details* insignifiant; *objections* chicanier. ◆ **pettily** *adv* avec mesquinerie. ◆ **pettiness** *n* insignifiance *f*; mesquinerie *f*.

petulant ['petjʊlənt] *adj* irritable. ◆ **petulance** *n* irritabilité *f*. ◆ **petulantly** *adv* avec mauvaise humeur.

pew [pju:] *n* banc *m* (d'église). **take a ~** ‡ assieds-toi.

pewter ['pju:təʳ] *n* étain *m*.

phantom ['fæntəm] *n, adj* fantôme *(m)*.

pharmacy ['fɑ:məsɪ] *n* pharmacie *f*. ◆ **pharmaceutical** *adj* pharmaceutique. ◆ **pharmacist** *n* pharmacien(ne) *m(f)*. ◆ **pharmacology** *n* pharmacologie *f*.

phase [feɪz] **1** *n (gen)* phase *f*. **it's just a ~ he's going through** ce n'est qu'une période difficile, ça lui passera. **2** *vt operation* faire progressivement; *execution of plan* procéder par étapes à. **a ~d withdrawal of troops** un retrait progressif des troupes. ◆ **phase in** *vt sep* introduire progressivement. ◆ **phase out** *vt sep machinery* retirer progressivement; *jobs* supprimer graduellement.

pheasant ['feznt] *n* faisan *m*.

phenobarbitone ['fi:nəʊ'bɑ:bɪtəʊn] *n* phénobarbital *m*.

phenomenon, *pl* **-ena** [fɪ'nɒmɪnən, ɪnə] *n* phénomène *m*. ◆ **phenomenal** *adj* phénoménal. ◆ **phenomenally** *adv* phénoménalement.

philander [fɪ'lændəʳ] *vi* courir après les femmes. ◆ **philanderer** *n* coureur *m* (de jupons).

philanthropy [fɪ'lænθrəpɪ] *n* philanthropie *f*. ◆ **philanthropic** *adj* philanthropique. ◆ **philanthropist** *n* philanthrope *mf*.

philately [fɪ'lætəlɪ] *n* philatélie *f*. ◆ **philatelist** *n* philatéliste *mf*.

philharmonic [ˌfɪlɑ:'mɒnɪk] *adj* philharmonique.

Philippines ['fɪlɪpi:nz] *npl*: **the ~** les Philippines *fpl*.

Phillips ['fɪlɪps] *n* ® **~ screw/screwdriver** vis *f*/ tournevis *m* cruciforme.

philology [fɪ'lɒlədʒɪ] *n* philologie *f*. ◆ **philological** *adj* philologique. ◆ **philologist** *n* philologue *mf*.

philosophy [fɪ'lɒsəfɪ] *n* philosophie *f*. **his ~ of life** sa philosophie, sa conception de la vie. ◆ **philosopher** *n* philosophe *mf*. ◆ **philosophic(al)** *adj* philosophique; *(fig: resigned)* philosophe, résigné. ◆ **philosophically** *adv* philosophiquement. ◆ **philosophize** *vi* philosopher (*about, on* sur).

phlebitis [flɪ'baɪtɪs] *n* phlébite *f*.

phlegm [flem] *n* flegme *m*. ◆ **phlegmatic** [fleg'mætɪk] *adj* flegmatique. ◆ **phlegmatically** *adv* flegmatiquement.

phobia ['fəʊbɪə] *n* phobie *f*. ◆ **phobic** *adj, n* phobique *(mf)*.

phone [fəʊn] *n, vti abbr of* **telephone. ~ card** télécarte *f*. ◆ **phone-in (programme)** *n* programme *m* à ligne ouverte.

phoneme ['fəʊni:m] *n* phonème *m*.

phonetic [fə(ʊ)'netɪk] *adj* phonétique. ◆ **phonetician** *n* phonéticien(ne) *m(f)*. ◆ **phonetics** *nsg* phonétique *f*.

phoney * ['fəʊnɪ] **1** *adj name* faux; *jewels* en toc *; *emotion* factice, simulé; *firm, company* bidon * *inv*. **he's ~** c'est un fumiste; **it sounds ~** cela a l'air d'être de la blague *. **2** *n (person)* poseur *m*, faux jeton * *m*.

phonograph ['fəʊnəgrɑ:f] *n* électrophone *m*.

phonology [fəʊ'nɒlədʒɪ] *n* phonologie *f*. ◆ **phonological** *adj* phonologique.

phosphate ['fɒsfeɪt] *n* phosphate *m*.

phosphorus ['fɒsf(ə)rəs] *n* phosphore *m*. ◆ **phosphorescence** *n* phosphorescence *f*. ◆ **phosphorescent** *adj* phosphorescent.

photo ['fəʊtəʊ] **1** *n (abbr of* **photograph***)* photo *f*. **2** *pref* photo... ◆ **photocall** *n* séance *f* de photos pour la presse. ◆ **photocopier** *n* photocopieur *m*. ◆ **photocopy** **1** *n* photocopie *f*; **2** *vt* photocopier. ◆ **photocopying** *n* photocopie *f*. ◆ **photoelectric** *adj*: **~ cell** cellule *f* photoélectrique. ◆ **photo finish** *n* photo-finish *f*. ◆ **photofit** *adj, n*: **P~fit (picture)** portrait-robot *m*. ◆ **photogenic** *adj* photogénique. ◆ **photograph** **1** *n* photographie *f*; **to take a ~ (graph) of sb/sth** prendre une photo de qn/qch, prendre qn/qch en photo; **in** *or* **on this ~(graph)** sur cette photo ; **2** *adj*: **~(graph) album** album *m* de photos ; **3** *vt* photographier, prendre en photo. ◆ **photographer** [fə'tɒgrəfəʳ] *n* photographe *mf*; **press ~grapher** reporter *m* photographe; **street ~grapher** photostoppeur *m*; **he's a keen ~grapher** il est passionné de photo. ◆ **photographic** *adj* photographique. ◆ **photographically** *adv* photographiquement. ◆ **photography** [fə'tɒgrəfɪ] *n* photographie *f*. ◆ **photosensor** *n* dispositif *m* photosensible. ◆ **photostat** = **photocopy.**

phrase [freɪz] **1** *n* (**a**) *(saying)* expression *f*; *(Ling: gen)* locution *f*. *(Ling)* **verb ~** syntagme *m* verbal. (**b**) *(Mus)* phrase *f*. **2** *vt* (**a**) *thought* exprimer; *letter* rédiger. (**b**) *(Mus)* phraser. ◆ **phrasal verb** *n* verbe *m* à particule. ◆ **phrasebook** *n* recueil *m* d'expressions. ◆ **phraseology** [ˌfreɪzɪ'ɒlədʒɪ] *n* phraséologie *f*. ◆ **phrasing** *n (Mus)* phrasé *m*.

physical ['fɪzɪk(ə)l] *adj (gen)* physique; *world, object* matériel. ~ **education** éducation *f* physique; ~ **examination** examen médical; ~ **exercises,** ~ **training,** *(Brit)* ~ **jerks** * gymnastique *f*; *(US)* ~ **therapist** kinésithérapeute *mf;* **it's a** ~ **impossibility for him to do it** il lui est matériellement impossible de le faire. ◆ **physically** *adv* physiquement; **he is** ~**ly handicapped** c'est un handicapé physique. ◆ **physician** *n* médecin *m*. ◆ **physicist** *n* physicien(ne) *m(f)*. ◆ **physics** *nsg* physique *f*.

physiognomy [ˌfɪzɪ'ɒnəmɪ] *n* physionomie *f*.

physiology [ˌfɪzɪ'ɒlədʒɪ] *n* physiologie *f*. ◆ **physiological** *adj* physiologique. ◆ **physiologist** *n* physiologiste *mf*.

physiotherapy [ˌfɪzɪə'θerəpɪ] *n* kinésithérapie *f*. ◆ **physiotherapist** *n* kinésithérapeute *mf*.

physique [fɪ'zi:k] *n (health etc)* constitution *f*; *(appearance)* physique *m*.

piano ['pjɑ:nəʊ] **1** *n* piano *m*. **grand** ~ piano à queue. **2** *adj lesson, teacher* de piano. ~ **duet** morceau *m* pour quatre mains; ~ **stool** tabouret *m*; ~ **tuner** accordeur *m* (de piano). ◆ **pianist** *n* pianiste *mf*. ◆ **piano accordion** *n* accordéon *m* à clavier. ◆ **pianola** *n* ® piano *m* mécanique.

pick [pɪk] **1** *n* (**a**) *(~axe)* pioche *f*, pic *m; (ice ~)* piolet *m*. (**b**) *(choice)* choix *m*. **to take one's** ~ faire son choix; **the** ~ **of the bunch** le meilleur de tous. **2** *vt* (**a**) *(choose)* choisir; *(Sport) sides* former, sélectionner. **to** ~ **a winner** choisir le gagnant; *(fig)* tirer le bon numéro (*in sb* avec qn); **to** ~ **one's way through** avancer avec précaution à travers; **to** ~ **a quarrel** provoquer une querelle (*with* à); **to** ~ **a fight** chercher la bagarre * (*with* avec). (**b**) *(gather) fruit, flower* cueillir. (**c**) *spot, scab* gratter. **to** ~ **one's nose** se mettre les doigts dans le nez; **to** ~ **the bones of a chicken** sucer les os d'un poulet; **to** ~ **one's teeth** se curer les dents; *(fig)* **to** ~ **holes in** relever les défauts de; **to** ~ **sb's brains** faire appel aux lumières de qn; **to** ~ **a lock** crocheter une serrure; **to** ~ **pockets** pratiquer le vol à la tire; **I've had my pocket** ~**ed** on m'a fait les poches. **3** *vi*: **to** ~ **and choose** prendre son temps pour choisir; **to** ~ **at one's food** manger du bout des dents; **don't** ~ **at that spot** ne gratte pas ce bouton.
◆ **pick off** *vt sep* (**a**) *paint* gratter; *flower, leaf* cueillir. (**b**) *(shoot)* abattre *(après avoir visé soigneusement)*. ◆ **pick on** *vt fus* (**a**) *(*: harass)* harceler, être toujours sur le dos de *. (**b**) *(single out)* choisir, désigner; *(for punishment)* s'en prendre à. ◆ **pick out** *vt sep* (**a**) *(choose)* choisir. (**b**) *(distinguish) object, acquaintance, place etc* distinguer; *(in identification parade)* identifier; *(on photo)* reconnaître. (**c**) *tune on piano* retrouver. ◆ **pick over** *vt sep fruit, goods* trier, examiner. ◆ **pick up 1** *vi* (**a**) *(improve: gen)* s'améliorer; *[prices, wages]* remonter; *[invalid]* se rétablir; *[trade]* reprendre. (**b**) *(*: continue)* continuer, reprendre. **we** ~**ed up where we'd left off** nous avons repris le travail *(etc)* où nous l'avions laissé. **2** *vt sep* (**a**) *(lift) sth dropped* ramasser; *sb fallen* relever; *child, dog* prendre dans ses bras; *telephone* décrocher; *(rescue) survivors* recueillir; *(from sea)* repêcher; *(arrest)* arrêter; *(fig) points, marks* gagner; *sb's error* relever. **to** ~ **up speed** prendre de la vitesse; *(fig)* **we** ~**ed up a rabbit in the headlights** nous avons aperçu un lapin dans la lumière des phares; **the cameras/ lights** ~**ed him up** il est entré dans le champ des caméras/ lumières; **to** ~ **sb up for having made a mistake** reprendre qn pour une faute; *(fig)* **to** ~ **up the bill** * payer, casquer *. (**b**) *(collect) object, goods, passenger* passer prendre. *(fig)* **he** ~**ed up a girl at the cinema** il a ramassé une fille au cinéma. (**c**) *(acquire)* découvrir; *sale bargain* tomber sur, trouver; *accent, habit* prendre; *information* avoir; *(learn)* apprendre. **you'll soon** ~ **it up again** vous vous y remettrez vite. (**d**) *(Rad, Telec) station, message* capter.
◆ **pickaback** *n*: **to give sb a** ~**aback** porter qn sur son dos. ◆ **pickaxe,** *(US)* **pickax** *n* pic *m*, pioche *f*. ◆ **picked** *adj (hand-~ed) objects* sélectionné; *men* trié sur le volet. ◆ **picker** *n*: **apple-**~**er** cueilleur *m*, -euse *f* de pommes. ◆ **pickings** *npl*: **there are rich** ~**ings** ça peut rapporter gros. ◆ **pick-me-up** * *n* remontant *m*. ◆ **pickpocket** *n* pickpocket *m*. ◆ **pick-up** *n* (**a**) *[record-player]* pick-up *m inv*, lecteur *m*; (**b**) *(~up truck)* camionnette *f* (découverte); (**c**) *(*: casual lover)* partenaire *mf* de rencontre. ◆ **picky** *adj (US)* difficile (à satisfaire).

picket ['pɪkɪt] **1** *n (gen)* piquet *m*; *(Ind)* piquet de grève; *(Mil) (sentry)* sentinelle *f*; *(group)* détachement *m* (de soldats). **2** *adj (Ind)* **to be on** ~ **duty** faire partie d'un piquet de grève; ~ **line** cordon *m* de piquet de grève. **3** *vt [strikers]* mettre un piquet de grève aux portes de; *[demonstrators]* former un cordon devant.

pickle ['pɪkl] **1** *n*: ~**(s)** pickles *mpl*; *(fig)* **to be in a (pretty)** ~ * être dans le pétrin. **2** *vt* conserver dans du vinaigre.

picnic ['pɪknɪk] *(vb: pret, ptp* **picnicked***)* **1** *n* pique-nique *m*. *(fig)* **it's no** ~ * ça n'est pas une partie de plaisir *; ~ **basket** panier *m* à pique-nique; *(US)* ~ **ham** ≃ jambonneau *m*. **2** *vi* pique-niquer, faire un pique-nique. ◆ **picnicker** *n* pique-niqueur *m*, -euse *f*.

pictorial [pɪk'tɔ:rɪəl] **1** *adj magazine* illustré; *record* en images; *masterpiece* de peinture. **2** *n* illustré *m*. ◆ **pictorially** *adv* au moyen d'images.

picture ['pɪktʃə^r] **1** *n* (**a**) *(gen)* image *f*; *(illustration)* image, illustration *f*; *(painting)* tableau *m*; *(portrait)* portrait *m*. **I took a** ~ **of him** j'ai pris une photo de lui; *(TV)* **we have the sound but no** ~ nous avons le son mais pas l'image; **to paint a** ~ faire un tableau; **to draw a** ~ faire un dessin; **to paint/ draw a** ~ **of sth** peindre/dessiner qch; *(fig)* **the garden is a** ~ **in June** le jardin est ravissant en juin; **he looks the** ~ **of health** il respire la santé; *(fig)* **the other side of the** ~ le revers de la médaille; **his face was a** ~**!** * si vous aviez vu sa tête! * (**b**) *(Cine)* film *m*. **they made a** ~ **about it** on en a fait un film; **to go to the** ~**s** aller au cinéma. (**c**) *(description)* tableau *m*, image *f*; *(mental image)* image. **to give sb a** ~ **of sth** décrire qch à qn; **he painted a black** ~ **of...** il nous a peint un sombre tableau de...; **I have a clear** ~ **of him** *(remembering)* je le revois clairement; *(imagining)* je me le représente très bien; **the general** ~ le tableau général de la situation; **do you get the** ~**?** * tu vois le tableau? *; **to put sb in the** ~ mettre qn au courant. **2** *adj*: ~ **book** livre *m* d'images; ~ **frame** cadre *m*; ~ **gallery** *(public)* musée *m* (de peinture); *(private)* galerie *f* (de peinture); ~ **postcard** carte *f* postale (illustrée); ~ **window** fenêtre *f* panoramique. **3** *vt* se représenter; *(remembering)* revoir. ◆ **picture-framer** *n* encadreur *m*. ◆ **picturegoer** *n* amateur *m* de cinéma. ◆ **picturesque** *adj* pittoresque.

pie [paɪ] *n [fruit, fish, meat with gravy etc]* tourte *f*; *[compact filling]* pâté *m* en croûte. **apple** ~ tourte aux pommes; **pork** ~ pâté de porc en croûte. ◆ **pie chart** *n* graphique *m* circulaire, camembert * *m*. ◆ **piecrust** *n* croûte *f* de pâté. ◆ **pie dish** *n* terrine *f*. ◆ **pie-eyed** ‡ *adj* parti *, soûl.

piebald ['paɪbɔ:ld] *adj* pie *inv*.

piece [pi:s] *n (gen)* morceau *m*; *(smaller)* bout *m*; *[ribbon, string]* bout; *(Comm, Ind, Chess, jigsaw)* pièce *f*; *(Draughts)* pion *m*. **a** ~ **of land** *(for agriculture)* une parcelle de terre; *(for building)* un lotissement; **a** ~ **of advice** un conseil; **a** ~ **of care-**

lessness de la négligence; **by a ~ of luck** par un coup de chance; **a ~ of music** un morceau de musique; **piano ~** morceau pour piano; **a ~ of poetry** un poème; **a good ~ of work** du bon travail; **a ~ out of 'Ivanhoe'** un passage d''Ivanhoé'; **made in one ~** fait d'une seule pièce; **in one ~** *object* intact; (*) *person* indemne, entier *; **a 5-franc ~** une pièce de 5 F; **a 30-~ tea set** un service à thé de 30 pièces; *(Mus)* **10-~ band** orchestre *m* de 10 exécutants; **3 ~s of luggage** 3 valises *fpl* (*or* sacs *mpl* etc); **~ by ~** pièce à pièce, morceau par morceau; **in ~s** *(broken)* en morceaux; *(not yet assembled)* en pièces détachées; **to come to ~s** *(break)* partir en morceaux; *(dismantle)* se démonter; **to take sth to ~s** démonter qch; **to go to ~s** * *(collapse)* s'effondrer; *(lose one's grip)* lâcher pied *(fig)*; **to cut sth to ~s** couper qch en morceaux *or* pièces; **to smash sth to ~s** briser qch en mille morceaux.

◆ **piece together** *vt sep broken object, facts* rassembler; *jigsaw* assembler; *events* reconstituer.

◆ **piecemeal** **1** *adv* petit à petit ; **2** *adj (gen)* fait (*or* raconté *etc*) petit à petit; *essay, argument* qui manque de rigueur. ◆ **piecework** *n* travail *m* à la pièce. ◆ **pieceworker** *n* ouvrier *m*, -ière *f* payé(e) à la pièce.

pier [pɪəʳ] *n (with amusements etc)* jetée *f (promenade)*; *(landing stage)* embarcadère *m*.

pierce [pɪəs] *vt (gen)* percer; *[cold, wind, arrow, bullet]* transpercer. **to have one's ears ~d** se faire percer les oreilles. ◆ **piercing** *adj sound, voice, look* perçant; *cold, wind* glacial.

piety ['paɪətɪ] *n* piété *f*.

pig [pɪg] **1** *n* (**a**) cochon *m*, porc *m*. *(fig)* **to buy a ~ in a poke** acheter chat en poche; **to make a ~ of o.s.** manger comme un goinfre; **you ~!** * *(mean)* espèce de chameau! *; *(dirty)* espèce de cochon! *; *(greedy)* espèce de goinfre! (**b**) *(US Ftbl)* ballon *m (de football américain)*. **2** *adj breeding, industry* porcin. ◆ **piggery** *n* porcherie *f*. ◆ **piggyback** **1** *adv, adj* sur le dos ; **2** *n:* **to give sb a ~gyback** porter qn sur son dos. ◆ **pigheaded** *adj* entêté. ◆ **pigheadedly** *adv* avec entêtement. ◆ **pigheadedness** *n* entêtement *m*. ◆ **piglet** *n* petit cochon *m*. ◆ **pigman** *n* porcher *m*. ◆ **pigskin** **1** *n* peau *f* de porc ; **2** *adj* en peau de porc. ◆ **pigsty** *n* porcherie *f*. ◆ **pigtail** *n [hair]* natte *f*.

pigeon ['pɪdʒən] *n* pigeon *m (also Culin)*. **wood-~** ramier *m*; *(fig)* **that's your ~** * c'est toi que ça regarde, c'est tes oignons *; **by ~ post** par pigeon voyageur. ◆ **pigeon-chested** *adj* à la poitrine bombée. ◆ **pigeon-fancier** *n* colombophile *mf*. ◆ **pigeonhole** **1** *n* casier *m* ; **2** *vt* classer (*as* comme). ◆ **pigeon-loft** *n* pigeonnier *m*. ◆ **pigeon-toed** *adj*: **to be ~-toed** avoir les pieds tournés en dedans.

pigment ['pɪgmənt] *n* pigment *m*. ◆ **pigmentation** *n* pigmentation *f*.

pike [paɪk] *n (fish)* brochet *m*.

pilchard ['pɪltʃəd] *n* pilchard *m*.

pile¹ [paɪl] *n (Constr etc)* pieu *m* de fondation; *(in water)* pilotis *m*; *[bridge]* pile *f*. **~ driver** sonnette *f*.

pile² [paɪl] **1** *n* (**a**) *(heap)* pile *f*; *(less tidy)* tas *m*. **in a ~** en pile, en tas; **atomic ~** pile atomique; *(fig)* **to make one's ~** * faire fortune; **~s of** *, **a ~ of** * *butter, honey* des masses de *; *cars, flowers* un tas de *. (**b**) *(Med)* **~s** hémorroïdes *fpl*. **2** *vt (stack)* empiler; *(heap)* entasser. **~d (high) with books** couvert de piles de livres; **I ~d * the children into the car** j'ai entassé les enfants dans la voiture. **3** *vi* (*) *[people]* s'entasser, s'empiler (*into* dans). **to ~ in** * s'entasser, s'empiler; **to ~ on/off** * *etc* monter/descendre *etc* en se bousculant.

◆ **pile on** *vt sep*: **to ~ it on** * exagérer, en rajouter; **to ~ on the agony** * dramatiser, faire du mélo *. ◆ **pile up** **1** *vi [snow etc]* s'amonceler; *[reasons, proof, work, business]* s'accumuler. **2** *vt sep* (**a**) *objects (stack)* empiler; *(heap)* entasser; *evidence, reasons* accumuler. (**b**) (*: *crash) car* bousiller *.

◆ **pile-up** * *n (Aut)* carambolage *m*.

pile³ [paɪl] *n [cloth, carpet]* poils *mpl*.

pilfer ['pɪlfəʳ] **1** *vt* chaparder *. **2** *vi* se livrer au chapardage *. ◆ **pilferer** *n* chapardeur * *m*, -euse * *f*. ◆ **pilfering** *n* chapardage * *m*.

pilgrim ['pɪlgrɪm] *n* pèlerin *m*. ◆ **pilgrimage** *n* pèlerinage *m*; **to go on a ~age** faire un pèlerinage.

pill [pɪl] *n* pilule *f*. *(fig)* **to sweeten the ~** dorer la pilule (*for sb* à qn); **to be on the ~** prendre la pilule.

pillage ['pɪlɪdʒ] **1** *n* pillage *m*. **2** *vt* piller. **3** *vi* se livrer au pillage.

pillar ['pɪləʳ] *n (gen)* pilier *m*; *[fire, smoke]* colonne *f*. **he was pushed around from ~ to post** on se le renvoyait de l'un à l'autre; **~ of salt** statue *f* de sel; **~ of the Church** pilier de l'Église; **he was a ~ of strength** il a vraiment été d'un grand soutien.

◆ **pillar-box** *n (Brit)* boîte *f* aux *or* à lettres; **~-box red** rouge sang *inv*.

pillion ['pɪljən] **1** *n* siège *m* arrière *(d'une moto etc)*. **~ passenger** passager *m* de derrière. **2** *adv*: **to ride ~** monter derrière.

pillow ['pɪləʊ] *n* oreiller *m*. ◆ **pillowcase** *or* ◆ **pillowslip** *n* taie *f* d'oreiller.

pilot ['paɪlət] **1** *n* pilote *m*. **2** *adj* -pilote. **~ scheme** projet *m* d'essai, projet-pilote *m*; **~ film** film-pilote *m*; **~ light** veilleuse *f (de cuisinière etc)*. **3** *vt (Aviat, Naut)* piloter; *(gen: guide)* guider, diriger.

pimento [pɪ'mentəʊ] *n* piment *m*.

pimp [pɪmp] *n* souteneur *m*.

pimple ['pɪmpl] *n* bouton *m (Med)*. ◆ **pimply** *adj* boutonneux.

pin [pɪn] **1** *n* (**a**) *(gen)* épingle *f*; *(safety ~)* épingle de sûreté *or* de nourrice; *(drawing ~)* punaise *f*. **as neat as a new ~** *room* impeccable; *person* tiré à quatre épingles; **you could have heard a ~ drop** on aurait entendu voler une mouche; **to have ~s and needles** avoir des fourmis (*in* dans); **for two ~s * I'd smack his face** pour un peu je le giflerais. (**b**) *[machine, device, hand-grenade]* goupille *f*; *(Elec)* fiche *f*; *(Med: in limb)* broche *f*; *(Bowling)* quille *f*. *(Elec)* **3-~ plug** prise *f* à 3 fiches. **2** *adj*: **~ money** argent *m* de poche. **3** *vt (gen)* épingler (*to* à; *onto* sur); *papers* attacher avec une épingle (*or* une punaise *etc*); *(Tech)* goupiller. **to ~ sb's arms to his sides** lier les bras de qn contre son corps; **to ~ sb against a wall** clouer qn à un mur; **to ~ one's hopes on sth** mettre tous ses espoirs dans qch; **to ~ a crime on sb** * mettre un crime sur le dos de qn.

◆ **pin down** *vt sep* fixer (avec une épingle *etc*); *[fallen tree] person* coincer; *(Mil) troops* bloquer. *(fig)* **to ~ sb down to a promise** obliger qn à tenir sa promesse; **I can't ~ him down** je n'arrive pas à le coincer * *(fig)*; **to ~ sb down to doing** décider qn à faire; **there's sth wrong but I can't ~ it down** il y a qch qui ne va pas mais je n'arrive pas à mettre le doigt dessus. ◆ **pin on** *vt sep* épingler. ◆ **pin up** *vt sep notice* afficher; *hem* épingler; *hair* relever avec des épingles.

◆ **pinball** *n* flipper *m*. ◆ **pincushion** *n* pelote *f* à épingles. ◆ **pinpoint** *vt place* localiser avec précision; *problem* mettre le doigt sur. ◆ **pinprick** *n* piqûre *f* d'épingle; *(fig: annoyance)* coup *m* d'épingle. ◆ **pinstripe suit** *n* costume *m* rayé. ◆ **pinup (girl)** * *n* pin-up *f inv*.

pinafore ['pɪnəfɔːʳ] *n (apron)* tablier *m*; *(overall)* blouse *f (de travail)*. **~ dress** robe-chasuble *f*.

pincers ['pɪnsəz] *npl* tenailles *fpl*.

pinch [pɪn(t)ʃ] **1** *n* (**a**) *(action)* pincement *m*; *(mark)* pinçon *m*. **to give sb a ~** pincer qn; *(fig)* **to feel the ~** commencer à être serré *or* à être à court; *(fig)* **at a ~**, *(US)* **in a ~** à la rigueur; **when it comes to the ~** au moment critique. (**b**) *[salt]* pincée *f*; *[snuff]* prise *f*. *(fig)* **to take sth with a ~ of salt** ne pas prendre qch pour argent comptant. **2** *vt* (**a**) *(gen)* pincer; *[shoes]* serrer; *bud* épincer. (**b**) (*: *steal)* piquer *, voler (*from sb* à qn). (**c**) (‡: *arrest)* pincer *, arrêter. **3** *vi [shoe]* serrer. *(fig)* **to ~ and scrape** économiser sur tout. ◆ **pinched** *adj* (**a**) *(drawn)* qui a les traits tirés; **~ed with cold** transi de froid; (**b**) **~ed for money** à court d'argent; **~ed for space** à l'étroit.

pine[1] [paɪn] **1** *n (~ tree)* pin *m*. **2** *adj*: **~ kernel** *or* **nut** pigne *f*; **~ needle** aiguille *f* de pin. ◆ **pinecone** *n* pomme *f* de pin. ◆ **pinewood** *n (grove)* pinède *f*; *(material)* (bois *m* de) pin *m*.

pine[2] [paɪn] *vi*: **to ~ for** *sth* désirer ardemment; *sb* s'ennuyer de; **to ~ away** languir.

pineapple ['paɪn,æpl] *n* ananas *m*.

ping [pɪŋ] **1** *n* bruit *m* métallique; *[bell, clock]* tintement *m*. **2** *vi* faire un bruit métallique; tinter. ◆ **ping-pong** *n* ping-pong *m*.

pinion ['pɪnjən] *n (Tech)* pignon *m*.

pink[1] [pɪŋk] **1** *n* (**a**) *(colour)* rose *m*. *(fig)* **to be in the ~** * se porter comme un charme. (**b**) *(Bot)* mignardise *f*. **2** *adj (gen)* rose; *(Pol)* gauchisant. *(US)* **~ slip** * lettre *f* de licenciement; **to turn ~** *[thing]* rosir; *[person]* rougir. ◆ **pinkish** *adj* rosâtre, rosé.

pink[2] [pɪŋk] *vt (Sewing)* denteler. ◆ **pinking shears** *npl* ciseaux *mpl* à denteler.

pinkie * ['pɪŋkɪ] *n* petit doigt *m*.

pinnacle ['pɪnəkl] *n (Archit)* pinacle *m*; *[mountain]* cime *f*; *(fig)* apogée *m*.

pinochle ['pi:nʌk(ə)l] *n (US)* (sorte *f* de) belote *f*.

pint [paɪnt] *n* pinte *f*, ≃ demi-litre *m (Brit = 0,57 litre; US = 0,47 litre)*. **a ~ of beer** ≃ un demi (de bière). ◆ **pinta** * *n abbr of* **pint of milk**. ◆ **pint-size(d)** *adj* tout petit.

pioneer [,paɪə'nɪə^r] **1** *n* pionnier *m*. **2** *vt*: **to ~ sth** être l'un des premiers à faire qch. **3** *adj research etc* complètement nouveau. ◆ **pioneering** *adj work, study* complètement nouveau.

pious ['paɪəs] *adj* pieux; *(iro) hope* légitime. ◆ **piously** *adv* pieusement.

pip [pɪp] **1** *n [fruit]* pépin *m*; *[card, dice]* point *m*; *(Radar)* spot *m*; *(Brit Mil *: on uniform)* ≃ galon *m*. *(Telec: sound)* **~s** bip-bip *m*; *(fig)* **he gives me the ~** ‡ il me hérisse le poil *. **2** *vt*: **to be ~ped at the post** * se faire coiffer au poteau.

pipe [paɪp] **1** *n* (**a**) *(for water, gas)* tuyau *m*, conduite *f*; *(smaller)* tube *m*. (**b**) *(Mus: instrument)* pipeau *m*; *[organ]* tuyau *m*. **(bag) ~s** cornemuse *f*. (**c**) pipe *f*. **he smokes a ~** il fume la pipe; **~ of peace** calumet *m* de la paix; **put that in your ~ and smoke it!** * si ça ne te plaît pas c'est le même prix! * **2** *adj tobacco* à pipe. **~ cleaner** cure-pipe *m*; *(fig)* **~ dream** château *m* en Espagne *(fig)*. **3** *vt* (**a**) *oil, water (by ~line)* transporter (*or* amener *etc*) par tuyau *or* conduite *etc*; *(through tube, hose etc)* verser (*into* dans). **to ~ icing on a cake** décorer un gâteau de fondant (à la douille); **~d music** musique *f* de fond enregistrée. (**b**) *(Naut)* **to ~ sb aboard** *etc* saluer l'arrivée *etc* de qn (au son du sifflet). (**c**) *(Sewing)* passepoiler (*with* de). (**d**) *(say)* dire d'une voix flûtée.
◆ **pipe down** ‡ *vi* mettre la sourdine *, se taire.
◆ **pipe up** * *vi* se faire entendre.
◆ **pipeline** *n (gen)* pipe-line *m*; *[oil]* oléoduc *m*; *[natural gas]* gazoduc *m*; *(fig)* **it's in the ~line** ça va venir, on s'en occupe. ◆ **piper** *n (bagpiper)* cornemuseur *m*. ◆ **piping** **1** *n (pipes)* tuyauterie *f*; *(Sewing)* passepoil *m*; **2** *adj voice* flûté ; **3** *adv*: **piping hot** tout bouillant.

pippin ['pɪpɪn] *n* (pomme *f*) reinette *f*.

piquant ['pi:kənt] *adj* piquant. ◆ **piquancy** *n (flavour)* goût *m* piquant; *[story]* piquant *m*.

pique [pi:k] **1** *vt* dépiter. **2** *n* dépit *m*.

pirate ['paɪərɪt] **1** *n* pirate *m*; *(Comm: gen)* contrefacteur *m*; *(in publishing)* démarqueur *m*. **2** *adj ship* de pirates; *radio* pirate. **3** *vt book, film* pirater; *product* contrefaire; *invention, idea* s'approprier. ◆ **piracy** *n* piraterie *f*. ◆ **pirated** *adj (Comm)* contrefait; *edition* pirate.

Pisces ['paɪsi:z] *n (Astron)* les Poissons *mpl*.

piss ‡ [pɪs] *vi* pisser ‡.

pistachio [pɪs'tɑ:ʃɪəʊ] *n* pistache *f*.

pistol ['pɪstl] **1** *n* pistolet *m*. **2** *adj*: **at ~ point** sous la menace du pistolet; **~ shot** coup *m* de pistolet. ◆ **pistol-whip** *vt* frapper avec un pistolet au visage.

piston ['pɪstən] **1** *n* piston *m (lit)*. **2** *adj engine* à pistons. *(US)* **~ pin** goupille *f*; **~ ring** segment *m* (de pistons); **~ rod** tige *f* de piston.

pit[1] [pɪt] **1** *n* (**a**) *(large hole)* trou *m*; *(on moon etc)* cratère *m*; *(coal ~)* mine *f*, puits *m* de mine; *(as game trap, in garage etc)* fosse *f*; *(quarry)* carrière *f*; *(in motor racing)* stand *m*. **chalk ~** carrière à chaux; **he works in the ~s** il travaille à la mine; **in the ~ of his stomach/back** au creux de l'estomac/des reins. (**b**) *(Brit Theat)* (fauteuils *mpl* d')orchestre *m*. **2** *adj*: **~ pony** cheval *m* de mine; **~ worker** mineur *m* de fond. **3** *vt* (**a**) opposer (*sb against sb* qn à qn). **to ~ o.s.** *or* **one's wits against sb** se mesurer avec qn. (**b**) *(mark) metal* piqueter; *skin* grêler. ◆ **pithead** *n (Min)* carreau *m* de la mine.

pit[2] [pɪt] **1** *n (fruit-stone)* noyau *m*. **2** *vt* dénoyauter.

pitapat ['pɪtə'pæt] *adv*: **to go ~** *[feet]* trottiner; *[heart]* palpiter; *[rain]* crépiter.

pitch[1] [pɪtʃ] **1** *n* (**a**) *(degree)* degré *m*, point *m*; *[voice]* hauteur *f*; *(Mus)* ton *m*, diapason *m*. *(fig)* **at its (highest) ~** à son comble; **things have reached such a ~ that...** les choses en sont arrivées à un point tel que... (**b**) *(Sport)* terrain *m*. **football** *etc* **~** terrain de football *etc*. (**c**) *(sales talk)* boniment *m*. **2** *vt* (**a**) *(throw) ball* lancer; *object* jeter, lancer. (**b**) *(Mus) note* donner. **to ~ the voice higher/lower** hausser/baisser le ton de la voix; **this song is ~ed too low** cette chanson est dans un ton trop bas; **the speech must be ~ed at the right level for the audience** le ton du discours doit être adapté au public. (**c**) *(set up) tent* dresser; *camp* établir.
3 *vi* (**a**) *(fall)* tomber; *(be jerked)* être projeté. **the ship ~ed (and tossed)** le navire tanguait. (**b**) *(Baseball)* lancer la balle.
◆ **pitch in** * *vi* s'attaquer au boulot *. ◆ **pitch into** * *vt fus (attack, abuse)* tomber sur; *(start) meal, work* s'attaquer à.
◆ **pitched** *adj*: **~ed battle** *(Mil)* bataille *f* rangée; *(fig)* véritable bataille. ◆ **pitchfork** **1** *n* fourche *f* à foin; **2** *vt*: **to be ~forked into doing sth** être forcé de faire qch immédiatement. ◆ **pitchman** * *(US) (on street)* camelot *m*; *(TV)* présentateur *m* de produits.

pitch[2] [pɪtʃ] *n (tar)* poix *f*. ◆ **pitch-black** *adj* (**a**) noir comme poix; (**b**) *(also* **pitch-dark)** **it's ~-black** *or* **~-dark** il fait noir comme dans un four. ◆ **pitch-pine** *n* pitchpin *m*.

pitcher ['pɪtʃə^r] *n* cruche *f*; *(bigger)* broc *m*.

pitfall ['pɪtfɔ:l] *n* piège *m*.

pith [pɪθ] *n [bone, plant]* moelle *f*; *[orange]* peau *f* blanche; *(fig: essence)* essence *f*. ◆ **pithy** *adj (forceful)* vigoureux; *(terse)* concis; *(pointed)* piquant.

piton ['pi:tɒn] *n* piton *m*.

pitta ['p(ɪ)tə] *adj*: **~ bread** pain *m* grec.

pittance ['pɪt(ə)ns] *n* somme *f* dérisoire; *(income)* maigre revenu *m*; *(wage)* salaire *m* de misère.

pity ['pɪtɪ] **1** *n* (**a**) pitié *f*, compassion *f*. **for ~'s sake** de grâce; **to have** *or* **take ~ on sb** avoir pitié de qn; **to feel ~ for sb** avoir pitié de qn. (**b**) *(misfortune)* dommage *m*. **it is a (great) ~** c'est (bien) dommage; **it's a ~ that** il est dommage que + *subj*; **what a ~!** quel dommage!; **(the) more's the ~!** c'est d'autant plus dommage!; **the ~ of it is that...** le plus malheureux c'est que... **2** *vt* plaindre, avoir pitié de. ◆ **piteous** *adj* pitoyable. ◆ **piteously** *adv* pitoyablement. ◆ **pitiable** *adj hovel, situation* pitoyable; *appearance, attempt* piteux. ◆ **pitiful** *adj* pitoyable; *(pej) efforts, cowardice* lamentable. ◆ **pitifully** *adv (gen)* pitoyablement; *thin etc* à faire pitié; *(pej)* lamentablement. ◆ **pitiless** *adj* impitoyable. ◆ **pitilessly** *adv* impitoyablement. ◆ **pitying** *adj* compatissant. ◆ **pityingly** *adv* avec pitié.

pivot ['pɪvət] **1** *n (Mil, Tech, fig)* pivot *m*. **2** *vt* faire pivoter. **3** *vi (Tech)* pivoter; *[person]* tourner.

pizza ['piːtsə] *n* pizza *f*. ◆ **pizzeria** *n* pizzeria *f*.

piz(z)azz [pɪ'zæz] *n (gen)* énergie *f*, vigueur *f*; *(in car)* allure *f*; *(pej)* tape-à-l'œil *m*.

placard ['plækɑːd] **1** *n* affiche *f*, placard *m*; *(at demo)* pancarte *f*. **2** *vt wall* placarder; *announcement* afficher.

placate [plə'keɪt] *vt* calmer, apaiser.

place [pleɪs] **1** *n* (**a**) *(gen)* endroit *m* ; *(more formally)* lieu *m*. **to take ~** avoir lieu; **this is the ~** c'est ici, voici l'endroit; *(US)* **no ~ *, not any ~ *** (ne...) nulle part; *(US)* **some ~ *** quelque part; **this is no ~ for children** cela n'est pas un endroit convenable pour des enfants; **this isn't the ~ to start an argument** nous ne pouvons pas commencer à discuter ici; **from ~ to ~** d'un endroit à l'autre, de lieu en lieu; **he went from ~ to ~ looking for her** il l'a cherchée de ville en ville *(etc)*; **all over the ~** partout; **to find/lose one's ~ in a book** trouver/perdre sa page dans un livre; **to keep/lose one's ~ in the queue** garder/perdre sa place dans la queue; **to laugh at the right ~** rire au bon endroit *or* moment; **to go ~s *** *(travel)* voyager; *(make good)* faire son chemin; *(make progress)* obtenir des résultats; **~ of amusement/birth/work** lieu de distractions/de naissance/de travail; **~ of worship** lieu de culte; **the time and ~ of the crime** l'heure et le lieu du crime; **it's a small ~** *(village)* c'est un petit village; *(house)* c'est une petite maison; **the town is such a big ~ now that...** la ville s'est tellement agrandie *or* étendue que...; **he needs a bigger ~** il lui faut qch de plus grand; **at Paul's ~ *** chez Paul. (**b**) *(in street names etc)* **Washington P~** rue de Washington; **market ~** place *f* du marché. (**c**) *(seat)* place *f*; *(at table)* place, couvert *m*. (**d**) *(position, situation etc)* place *f*; *[star, planet]* position *f*. **in ~ of** à la place de, au lieu de; **to take the ~ of sb/sth** remplacer qn/qch; **out of ~** *object, remark* déplacé; **I feel rather out of ~** je ne me sens pas à ma place; **in his** *(or* **its** *etc)* **~** à sa place; *(fig)* **to put sb in his ~** remettre qn à sa place; **(if I were) in your ~...** (si j'étais) à votre place...; **it's not your ~ to criticize** ce n'est pas à vous de critiquer; **to give ~ to** céder la place à. (**e**) *(job, vacancy)* place *f*, poste *m*; *(in school etc)* place. **I have got a ~ on the sociology course** j'ai été admis à faire sociologie. (**f**) *(in series, rank)* **in the first ~** en premier lieu, premièrement; **in the second ~** en second lieu, deuxièmement; **in the next ~** ensuite; **in the last ~** enfin; **to 5 decimal ~s** jusqu'à la 5e décimale; **he took second ~ in the race** il a été second dans la course; *(Ftbl etc)* **the team was in third ~** l'équipe était placée troisième; **he took second ~ in history/in the history exam** il a été deuxième en histoire/à l'examen d'histoire; **people in high ~s** les gens haut placés.

2 *adj*: **~ card** carte *f* marque-place; **~ mat** set *m* (de table); **~ name** nom *m* de lieu; **~ setting** couvert *m*.

3 *vt* (**a**) *(put: gen)* placer, mettre. **she ~d the matter in the hands of her solicitor** elle a remis l'affaire entre les mains de son avocat. (**b**) *(situate)* placer, situer. **awkwardly ~d** *shop, house* mal situé *or* placé; *(fig) person* dans une situation assez délicate; **well ~d to decide** bien placé pour décider. (**c**) *(in exam, race)* placer. **he was ~d first in French/in the race** il s'est placé premier en français/dans la course. (**d**) *(find ~ for) object, goods, employee, money* placer; *(Comm) order* passer *(with sb* à qn); *bet* placer *(with sb* chez qn); *contract* passer *(with sb* avec qn). **to ~ a book with a publisher** faire accepter un livre par un éditeur. (**e**) *(remember; identify) person* se rappeler; *face* reconnaître; *accent* situer.

◆ **placement** *n (Fin)* placement *m*; *(during studies)* stage *m*. ◆ **placing** *n [money, funds]* placement *m*; *[ball, players]* position *f*.

placid ['plæsɪd] *adj* placide, calme. ◆ **placidity** *n* placidité *f*. ◆ **placidly** *adv* avec placidité.

plagiarism ['pleɪdʒjərɪz(ə)m] *n* plagiat *m*. ◆ **plagiarist** *n* plagiaire *mf*. ◆ **plagiarize** *vt* plagier.

plague [pleɪg] **1** *n (Med)* peste *f*; *(fig) (nuisance)* fléau *m*; *(person)* plaie *f*. **to avoid like the ~** fuir comme la peste. **2** *vt* tourmenter, harceler. **to ~ sb with questions** harceler qn de questions.

plaice [pleɪs] *n* plie *f*.

plaid [plæd] *n* tissu *m* écossais.

plain [pleɪn] **1** *adj* (**a**) *(obvious)* clair, évident *(that* que); *path etc* clairement tracé *or* marqué. **it must be ~ to everyone that...** il est clair pour tout le monde que...; **as ~ as a pikestaff** *or* **as the nose on your face *** clair comme le jour; **a ~ case of jealousy** un cas manifeste *or* évident de jalousie; **he made his feelings ~** il n'a pas caché ce qu'il ressentait; **to make sth ~ to sb** faire comprendre qch à qn. (**b**) *(unambiguous) statement, meaning* clair; *answer* direct, sans ambages; *person* franc. **~ talk** propos *mpl* sans équivoque; **to be a ~ speaker, to like ~ speaking** aimer la franchise; **to use ~ language** appeler les choses par leur nom; **in ~ words, in ~ English** très clairement; **~ dealings** procédés *mpl* honnêtes; **the ~ truth of the matter is (that)...** à dire vrai...; **do I make myself ~?** est-ce que je me fais bien comprendre? (**c**) *(utter)* (tout) pur. **it's ~ madness** c'est pure folie, c'est de la folie toute pure. (**d**) *(simple, unadorned) dress, food* simple; *(in one colour) fabric* uni. *(unlined)* **~ paper** papier uni; **I'm a ~ man** je suis un homme tout simple; **they used to be called ~ Smith** ils s'appelaient Smith tout court; *(Knitting)* **~ stitch** maille *f* à l'endroit; **in ~ clothes** *(not uniform)* en civil; **~ chocolate** chocolat *m* à croquer; **~ flour** farine *f* (sans levure); **to send under ~ cover** envoyer sous pli discret. (**e**) *(not pretty)* quelconque, ordinaire *(pej)*.

2 *adv* (**a**) *(unambiguously)* franchement, carrément. **I can't put it ~er than this** je ne peux pas m'exprimer plus clairement que cela. (**b**) *(in truth)* tout bonnement. **she's just ~ shy** elle est tout bonnement timide.

3 *n* plaine *f*.

◆ **plain-clothes policeman** *n* policier *m* en civil. ◆ **plainly** *adv (obviously)* clairement, manifestement; *(unambiguously) speak* carrément, sans détours; *remember, see, explain* clairement; *(simply) dress* simplement. ◆ **plainness** *n (simplicity)* simplicité *f*; *(lack of beauty)* manque *m* de beauté. ◆ **plainsong** *n* plain-chant *m*. ◆ **plain-spoken** *adj* qui a son franc-parler.

plaintiff ['pleɪntɪf] *n (Jur)* plaignant(e) *m(f)*.

plaintive ['pleɪntɪv] *adj voice* plaintif. ◆ **plaintively** *adv* plaintivement.

plait [plæt] **1** *n* natte *f*. **2** *vt* natter.

plan [plæn] **1** *n* (**a**) *(drawing, map)* plan *m*. (**b**) *(project)* plan *m*, projet *m*. ~ **of campaign** plan de campagne; **five-year** ~ plan quinquennal; **development** ~ projet de développement; **to draw up a** ~ dresser un plan; **everything is going according to** ~ tout se passe comme prévu; **to make ~s** faire des projets; **to change one's ~s** prendre d'autres dispositions; **the best** ~ **would be to leave** le mieux serait de partir; **the** ~ **is to come back here** notre idée est de revenir ici; **have you got any ~s for tonight?** est-ce que vous avez prévu qch pour ce soir?
2 *vt* (**a**) *(Econ etc) project, enterprise (devise and work out)* élaborer, préparer; *(devise and schedule)* planifier. (**b**) *house, estate, garden etc* dresser les plans de; *programme, holiday, journey, campaign, crime, attack* organiser; *research, industry, economy* planifier; *essay* faire le plan de. **well-~ned house** maison bien conçue; **that wasn't ~ned** cela n'était pas prévu; **as ~ned** comme prévu; **to** ~ **one's family** pratiquer le contrôle des naissances dans son foyer; **~ned parenthood** contrôle des naissances; **the murder was ~ned** le meurtre était prémédité. (**c**) *(intend) visit, holiday* projeter. **to** ~ **to do** avoir l'intention de faire.
3 *vi* faire des projets (*for sth* pour qch). *(fig: expect)* **we didn't** ~ **for so many visitors** nous n'avions pas prévu tant de visiteurs. ◆ **planner** *n (Econ)* planificateur *m*, -trice *f*; **town ~ner** urbaniste *mf*. ◆ **planning 1** *n (gen) (Econ etc: V* **plan 2a***)* élaboration *f*; planification *f*; *(gen)* organisation *f*; **2** *adj*: **~ning committee** service *m* de planning; **~ning permission** permis *m* de construire.

plane¹ [pleɪn] *n (abbr of* **aeroplane, airplane***)* avion *m*.

plane² [pleɪn] **1** *n (tool)* rabot *m*. **2** *vt* raboter.

plane³ [pleɪn] *n (tree)* platane *m*.

plane⁴ [pleɪn] *n (Art, Math etc)* plan *m*.

plane⁵ [pleɪn] *vi [bird, glider, boat]* planer; *[car]* faire de l'aquaplanage.

planet ['plænɪt] *n* planète *f*. ◆ **planetarium** *n* planétarium *m*.

plank [plæŋk] *n* planche *f*.

plankton ['plæŋktən] *n* plancton *m*.

plant [plɑ:nt] **1** *n* (**a**) *(Bot)* plante *f*. (**b**) *(machinery etc)* matériel *m*, équipement *m*; *(fixed)* installation *f*; *(buildings)* bâtiments *mpl*; *(factory)* usine *f*. **2** *adj*: **the** ~ **kingdom** le règne végétal; ~ **life** flore *f*; ~ **pot** pot *m* (de fleurs). **3** *vt seeds, flag, object, kiss* planter; *field* planter (*with* en); *colonists etc* établir; *idea* implanter (*in sb's head* dans la tête de qn). *(fig)* **to** ~ * **a revolver on sb** cacher un revolver sur qn (pour le faire incriminer). ◆ **plant out** *vt sep* seedlings repiquer. ◆ **plantation** *n* plantation *f*. ◆ **planter** *n* planteur *m*.

plaque [plæk] *n* plaque *f*; *(dental ~)* plaque *f* dentaire.

plaster ['plɑ:stəʳ] **1** *n* (**a**) *(Constr)* plâtre *m*. (**b**) *(Med: for broken bones)* plâtre *m*. ~ **of Paris** plâtre de moulage; **he had his leg in** ~ il avait la jambe dans le plâtre; **sticking** ~ sparadrap *m*; **a (piece of)** ~ un pansement adhésif. **2** *adj mould etc* de *or* en plâtre. ~ **cast** *(Med)* plâtre *m*; *(Sculp)* moule *m* (en plâtre). **3** *vt* plâtrer; *(fig: cover)* couvrir (*with* de). **to** ~ **mud on sth** couvrir qch de boue; **~ed with** couvert de. ◆ **plasterboard** *n* carreau *m* de plâtre. ◆ **plastered** ‡ *adj (drunk)* beurré ‡, soûl. ◆ **plasterer** *n* plâtrier *m*.

plastic ['plæstɪk] **1** *n* matière *f* plastique, plastique *m*. **~s** matières plastiques. **2** *adj object* en *or* de (matière) plastique; *art, substance* plastique; *(*: fig, pej)* synthétique. ~ **bag** sac *m* en plastique; ~ **bullet** balle *f* de plastique; ~ **explosive** plastic *m*; **~(s) industry** industrie *f* plastique; ~ **surgeon** spécialiste *mf* de chirurgie esthétique; ~ **surgery** chirurgie *f* esthétique. ◆ **plasticine** *n* ® pâte *f* à modeler.

plate [pleɪt] **1** *n* (**a**) assiette *f*; *(platter)* plat *m*; *(for church collection)* plateau *m* de quête. *(fig)* **he was handed it on a** ~ on lui a apporté ça sur un plateau d'argent; *(fig)* **to have a lot on one's** ~ * avoir un travail fou. (**b**) **gold/silver** ~ *(objects)* vaisselle *f* d'or/d'argent. (**c**) *(flat metal)* plaque *f*; *(metal coating)* plaquage *m*; *(coated metal)* plaqué *m*. (**d**) *(Phot, Tech, also on door, battery)* plaque *f*; *(Aut: number ~)* plaque d'immatriculation; *(on cooker: hot ~)* plaque chauffante; *(book illustration)* gravure *f*; *(dental ~)* dentier *m*. **2** *vt (with metal)* plaquer; *(with gold/silver etc)* dorer/argenter *etc*. ◆ **plateful** *n* assiettée *f*, assiette *f*. ◆ **plate-glass 1** *n* verre *m* à vitre très épais ; **2** *adj*: **~-glass window** baie *f* vitrée. ◆ **platelayer** *n (Rail)* poseur *m* de rails. ◆ **plate-rack** *n* égouttoir *m*. ◆ **plate-warmer** *n* chauffe-assiettes *m inv*.

plateau ['plætəʊ] *n* plateau *m (Geog)*.

platform ['plætfɔ:m] **1** *n (on bus, scales, in scaffolding etc)* plate-forme *f*; *(for band, in hall)* estrade *f*; *(Rail)* quai *m*. **he was on the** ~ **at the meeting** il était sur l'estrade *or* il était à la tribune lors de la réunion. **2** *adj*: **the** ~ **party** la tribune; ~ **scales** (balance *f* à) bascule *f*; ~ **soles** semelles *fpl* compensées; ~ **ticket** billet *m* de quai.

platinum ['plætɪnəm] *n* platine *m*. ~ **blond(e)** *(adj)* platiné.

platitude ['plætɪtju:d] *n* platitude *f*.

platonic [plə'tɒnɪk] *adj* platonique.

platoon [plə'tu:n] *n (Mil)* section *f*.

platter ['plætəʳ] *n* plat *m*.

plausible ['plɔ:zəbl] *adj argument* plausible; *person* convaincant. ◆ **plausibility** *n* plausibilité *f*. ◆ **plausibly** *adv* plausiblement.

play [pleɪ] **1** *n* (**a**) *(amusement)* jeu *m*. **the children were at** ~ les enfants jouaient *or* s'amusaient; **to say sth in** ~ dire qch par jeu; **a** ~ **on words** un jeu de mots; *(Sport)* **there was some good** ~ **in the second half** il y a eu du beau jeu à la deuxième mi-temps; **in/out of** ~ *ball* en/hors jeu; ~ **starts at 11 o'clock** le match commence à 11 heures; *(fig)* **to make a** ~ **for sth** tout faire pour avoir qch; **to bring** *or* **call sth into** ~ faire entrer qch en jeu; **to make great** ~ **with sth** faire grand cas de qch. (**b**) *(Tech etc)* jeu *m*. **too much** ~ **in the clutch** trop de jeu dans l'embrayage; *(fig)* **to give full** *or* **free** ~ **to** donner libre cours à. (**c**) *(Theat)* pièce *f* (de théâtre). **to go to (see) a** ~ aller au théâtre; **radio** ~ pièce radiophonique; **television** ~ dramatique *f*.
2 *vt* (**a**) *game, cards* jouer à; *card, chesspiece* jouer; *opponent, opposing team* jouer contre; *match* disputer (*against* avec). **England will be ~ing Smith in the team** l'Angleterre a sélectionné Smith pour l'équipe; **the match will be ~ed on Saturday** le match aura lieu samedi; **to** ~ **the game, to** ~ **fair** *(Sport etc)* jouer franc jeu; *(fig)* jouer le jeu; **don't** ~ **games with me!** ne vous moquez pas de moi!; **to** ~ **soldiers** jouer aux soldats; **he ~ed the ball into the net** il a mis la balle dans le filet; *(fig)* **to** ~ **ball** * coopérer (*with sb* avec qn); *(Cards)* **to** ~ **hearts** jouer cœur; **to** ~ **one's ace** jouer son as; *(fig)* jouer sa carte maîtresse; *(fig)* **to** ~ **one's cards well** *or* **right** bien jouer son jeu; **to** ~ **a fish** fatiguer un poisson; *(St Ex)* **to** ~ **the market** jouer à la Bourse; *(fig)* **to** ~ **the field** * jouer sur plusieurs tableaux; *(fig)* **to** ~ **it cool** * garder son sang-froid; **to** ~ **a joke** *or* **trick on sb** jouer un tour à qn. (**b**) *(Theat etc)* jouer. **let's** ~ **it for laughs** * jouons-le en farce; *(lit, fig)* **to** ~ **one's part well** bien jouer; *(fig)* **he was only ~ing a part** il jouait la comédie; *(fig)* **to** ~ **a part in sth** contribuer à qch; *(fig)* **he ~ed no part in it** il n'y était pour rien;

to ~ **the fool** faire l'imbécile. (**c**) *(Mus etc) instrument* jouer de; *note, tune, concerto* jouer; *record* passer; *radio* faire marcher. **they were ~ing Beethoven** ils jouaient du Beethoven. (**d**) *hose, searchlight* diriger (*on* sur).

3 *vi* (**a**) *(gen)* jouer; *[lambs etc]* folâtrer; *[light, fountain]* jouer (*on* sur). **to ~ at chess** jouer aux échecs; **to ~ with sth** jouer avec qch; *(fiddle with it)* tripoter qch; **he just ~s at being a soldier** il ne prend pas au sérieux son métier de soldat; **to ~ at soldiers** jouer aux soldats; **to ~ for money/matches** jouer de l'argent/des allumettes; *(lit, fig)* **to ~ for high stakes** jouer gros jeu; *(fig)* **to ~ with fire** jouer avec le feu; *(fig)* **to ~ for time** essayer de gagner du temps; **to ~ hard to get** * se faire désirer; **to ~ fast and loose with sb** traiter qn à la légère; **to ~ into sb's hands** faire le jeu de qn; **he's just ~ing with you** il vous fait marcher; **to ~ with an idea** caresser une idée. (**b**) *(Mus)* jouer; *[radio]* marcher. **to ~ on the piano** jouer du piano. (**c**) *(Theat etc)* jouer. *(fig)* **to ~ dead** faire le mort.
◆ **play about, play around** *vi [children etc]* jouer, s'amuser. **to ~ about** *or* **around with sth** *(fiddle with it)* tripoter qch. ◆ **play along 1** *vi (fig)* **to ~ along with sb** entrer dans le jeu de qn. **2** *vt sep (fig)* **to ~ sb along** tenir qn en haleine. ◆ **play back** *vt sep tape* (ré)écouter, repasser. ◆ **play down** *vt sep effect* minimiser; *situation* dédramatiser. ◆ **play off** *vt sep* (**a**) *(fig)* **to ~ off A against B** monter A contre B (pour en tirer profit). (**b**) *(Sport)* **to ~ a match off** jouer la belle. ◆ **play on** *vt fus sb's credulity, good nature* jouer sur. **to ~ on sb's nerves** agacer qn. ◆ **play out** *vt sep*: **to be ~ed out** * *[person]* être éreinté *; *[argument]* être périmé. ◆ **play over, play through** *vt sep music* jouer. ◆ **play up 1** *vi* (**a**) *(*: give trouble) [engine, child]* faire des siennes. **his leg is ~ing up** sa jambe le tracasse. (**b**) *(curry favour with)* **to ~ up to sb** chercher à se faire bien voir de qn. **2** *vt sep*: **his leg is ~ing him up** sa jambe le tracasse; **that boy ~s his father up** ce garçon en fait voir à son père. ◆ **playact** *vi* jouer la comédie *(fig)*. ◆ **playacting** *n* comédie *f (fig)*. ◆ **playback** *n* lecture *f*. ◆ **playbill** *n* affiche *f* (de théâtre). ◆ **playboy** *n* playboy *m*. ◆ **play-by-play** *adj account (Sport)* suivi; *(fig)* circonstancié. ◆ **player** *n* (**a**) *(Sport)* joueur *m*, -euse *f*; **football ~er** joueur de football; (**b**) *(Theat)* acteur *m*, -trice *f*; (**c**) *(Mus)* musicien(ne) *m(f)*; **flute ~er** joueur *m*, -euse *f* de flûte. ◆ **playful** *adj* espiègle. ◆ **playfully** *adv* avec espièglerie. ◆ **playfulness** *n* espièglerie *f*. ◆ **playgoer** *n* amateur *m* de théâtre. ◆ **playground** *n* cour *f* de récréation. ◆ **playgroup** *or* ◆ **playschool** *n* ≈ garderie *f*. ◆ **playhouse** *n (Theat)* théâtre *m*; *(for children)* maison *f* (pliante). ◆ **playing 1** *n*: **some fine ~ing** *(Sport)* du beau jeu; *(Mus)* des passages bien joués ; **2** *adj*: **~ing card** carte *f* à jouer; **~ing field** terrain *m* de jeu *or* de sport. ◆ **playmate** *or* ◆ **playfellow** *n* petit(e) camarade *m(f)*. ◆ **play-off** *n (Sport) (after a tie)* belle *f*; *(US: final)* finale *f* de championnat. ◆ **playpen** *n* parc *m* (pour petits enfants). ◆ **play-reading** *n* lecture *f* d'une pièce (de théâtre). ◆ **playroom** *n* salle *f* de jeux *(pour enfants)*. ◆ **plaything** *n (lit, fig)* jouet *m*. ◆ **playtime** *n (Scol)* récréation *f*. ◆ **playwright** *n* auteur *m* dramatique.

plaza ['plɑːzə] *n (US) (square)* (grand-)place *f*; *(motorway services)* aire *f* de service; *(toll)* péage *m* (d'autoroute); *(parking area)* aire *f* de stationnement.

plea [pliː] *n* (**a**) *(excuse)* excuse *f*; *(claim)* allégation *f*; *(entreaty)* appel *m* (*for* à). (**b**) *(Jur) (statement)* argument *m*; *(defence)* défense *f*. **to put forward a ~ of self-defence** plaider la légitime défense; **~ bargaining** *négociations entre le juge et l'avocat de la défense pour réduire la gravité des charges.*

plead [pliːd] *pret, ptp* **pleaded** *or (*: esp US)* **pled 1** *vi* (**a**) **to ~ with sb to do** supplier *or* implorer qn de faire; **to ~ for sth** *(beg for)* implorer qch; *(make speech in favour of)* plaider pour qch; **he ~ed for help** il a imploré *or* supplié qu'on l'aide *(subj)*. (**b**) *(Jur)* plaider (*for* pour, en faveur de; *against* contre). **to ~ guilty/not guilty** plaider coupable/non coupable. **2** *vt* (**a**) *(Jur etc: argue)* plaider. *(Jur)* **to ~ sb's case,** *(fig)* **to ~ sb's cause** plaider la cause de qn. (**b**) *(give as excuse) ignorance etc* alléguer, invoquer; *(Jur) insanity etc* plaider. ◆ **pleading 1** *n* prières *fpl* (*for sb* en faveur de qn) ; **2** *adj* suppliant. ◆ **pleadingly** *adv* d'un air suppliant.

pleasant ['pleznt] *adj person (attractive)* sympathique, charmant; *(polite)* aimable. **to have a ~ time** passer un bon moment; **it's very ~ here** on est bien ici. ◆ **pleasantly** *adv (gen)* agréablement; *behave, smile, answer* aimablement. ◆ **pleasantness** *n [person, manner]* amabilité *f*; *[place, house]* charme *m*. ◆ **pleasantry** *n (joke)* plaisanterie *f*; *(polite remarks)* **~ries** propos *mpl* aimables.

please [pliːz] **1** *adv* s'il vous plaît, s'il te plaît. **yes ~** oui s'il vous plaît; **come in ~** entrez, je vous prie; *(more formally)* veuillez entrer; *(notice)* **~ do not smoke** prière de ne pas fumer; **~ do!** je vous en prie!, mais bien sûr!; **~ don't!** ne faites pas ça s'il vous plaît!

2 *vi* (**a**) *(think fit)* **do as you ~!** faites comme vous voulez *or* comme bon vous semble; **as you ~!** comme vous voulez!; **as many as you ~** autant qu'il vous plaira. (**b**) *[gift etc]* plaire, faire plaisir. **our aim is to ~** nous ne cherchons qu'à satisfaire; **anxious to ~** désireux de plaire.

3 *vt* (**a**) *(give pleasure to)* plaire à, faire plaisir à; *(satisfy)* satisfaire, contenter. **I did it just to ~ you** je ne l'ai fait que pour te faire plaisir; **that will ~ him** ça va lui faire plaisir, il va être content; **easy/hard to ~** facile/difficile à satisfaire; **there's no pleasing him** il n'y a jamais moyen de le contenter *or* de le satisfaire. (**b**) **to ~ o.s.** faire comme on veut; **~ yourself!** comme vous voulez!; **you must ~ yourself whether...** c'est à vous de décider si...
◆ **pleased** *adj* content (*with* de; *to do* de faire; *that* que + *subj*); **as ~d as Punch** heureux comme tout; **~d to meet you!** * enchanté!; **we are ~d to inform you that...** nous avons le plaisir de vous informer que... ◆ **pleasing** *adj personality* sympathique; *sight, news* qui fait plaisir, agréable. ◆ **pleasingly** *adv* agréablement.

pleasure ['pleʒəʳ] **1** *n* (**a**) plaisir *m*. **with ~** *(willingly)* avec plaisir, volontiers; **it's a ~!** je vous en prie!; **it's a ~ to see you** quel plaisir de vous voir!; **it gave me much ~ to hear that...** cela m'a fait grand plaisir d'apprendre que...; **to find/take great ~ in (doing) sth** trouver/prendre beaucoup de plaisir à (faire) qch; **a life of ~** une vie de plaisirs. (**b**) **at ~** à volonté; **at your ~** à votre gré; *(Comm)* **we await your ~** nous attendons votre décision. **2** *adj*: **~ boat** bateau *m* de plaisance; **~ cruise** croisière *f*; *(short)* promenade *f* en bateau. ◆ **pleasurable** *adj* (très) agréable. ◆ **pleasurably** *adv* (très) agréablement.

pleat [pliːt] **1** *n* pli *m*. **2** *vt* plisser.

plebeian [plɪ'biːən] *adj, n* plébéien(ne) *m(f)*.

plebiscite ['plebɪsɪt] *n* plébiscite *m*. **to hold a ~** faire un plébiscite.

pledge [pledʒ] **1** *n* (**a**) *(security, token)* gage *m*. (**b**) *(promise)* engagement *m* (*to do* de faire); *(agreement)* pacte *m*. **to be under a ~ of secrecy** avoir promis de garder le secret; *(fig)* **to sign the ~** faire vœu de tempérance. **2** *vt* (**a**) *(pawn)* mettre en gage. (**b**) *(promise)* promettre (*sth* qch; *to do* de faire); *(vow)* faire vœu (*to do* de faire). **to ~ sb to secrecy** faire promettre le secret à qn. (**c**) *(toast)* boire à la santé de.

plenary ['pli:n(ə)rɪ] *adj power* absolu; *assembly* plénier. **in ~ session** en séance plénière.

plenipotentiary [ˌplenɪpə'tenʃ(ə)rɪ] *adj* plénipotentiaire.

plenty ['plentɪ] *n* (**a**) abondance *f.* **in ~** *grow* en abondance; *live* dans l'abondance; **land of ~** pays *m* de cocagne. (**b**) **~ of** *(lots of)* beaucoup de; *(enough)* bien assez de; **I've got ~** j'en ai bien assez; **he's got ~ of friends** il a beaucoup d'amis; **10 is ~** 10 suffisent (largement *or* amplement); **that's ~** ça suffit (amplement). ◆ **plenteous** *or* ◆ **plentiful** *adj harvest, food* abondant; *meal, amount* copieux; **eggs are plentiful** il y a une abondance d'œufs.

pleurisy ['plʊərɪsɪ] *n* pleurésie *f.*

pliable ['plaɪəbl] *adj substance* flexible; *person* docile. ◆ **pliability** *n* flexibilité *f*; docilité *f.*

pliers ['plaɪəz] *npl*: **(pair of) ~** pince(s) *f(pl)*, tenailles *fpl.*

plight [plaɪt] *n* triste situation *f.* **the country's economic ~** les difficultés *fpl* économiques du pays.

plimsoll ['plɪmsəl] *n (Brit)* (chaussure *f* de) tennis *f.*

plink [plɪŋk] *vi (sound)* tinter.

plinth [plɪnθ] *n* plinthe *f.*

plod [plɒd] *vi*: **to ~ in/out** *etc* entrer/sortir *etc* d'un pas lent *or* lourd; *(fig)* **we must ~ on** il faut persévérer; *(fig)* **he was ~ding through his maths** il faisait méthodiquement son devoir de maths. ◆ **plodder** *n* bûcheur * *m*, -euse * *f.* ◆ **plodding** *adj step* pesant; *worker* bûcheur *.

plonk [plɒŋk] **1** *n (*: cheap wine)* vin *m* ordinaire. **2** *adv*: **~ in the middle of** au beau milieu de. **3** *vt* **(~ down)** poser (bruyamment). **to ~ o.s. down** se laisser tomber.

plop [plɒp] **1** *n* plouf *m.* **2** *vi [stone]* faire plouf; *[raindrops]* faire flic flac.

plosive ['pləʊsɪv] *(Ling)* **1** *adj* explosif. **2** *n* consonne *f* explosive.

plot [plɒt] **1** *n* (**a**) *(ground)* terrain *m*, lotissement *m.* **~ of grass** gazon *m*; **building ~** terrain à bâtir; **the vegetable ~** le carré des légumes. (**b**) *(conspiracy)* complot *m* (*against* contre; *to do* pour faire). (**c**) *(Literat, Theat)* intrigue *f.* *(fig)* **the ~ thickens** l'affaire se corse. **2** *vt* (**a**) **(~ out)** *course, route* déterminer; *graph, curve* tracer point par point; *boundary, piece of land* relever. *(Naut)* **to ~ one's position on the map** pointer la carte. (**b**) *(conspire) sb's death etc* comploter (*to do* de faire). ◆ **plotter** *n* conspirateur *m*, -trice *f*; *(Comput)* traceur *m* (de courbes). ◆ **plotting** *n* complots *mpl.*

plough [plaʊ] **1** *n* charrue *f.* **2** *vt field* labourer; *furrow* creuser. **3** *vi* (**a**) *(Agr)* labourer. (**b**) *(fig)* **to ~ (one's way) through the mud** avancer péniblement dans la boue; **the car ~ed through the fence** la voiture a défoncé la barrière; **to ~ through a book** lire un livre méthodiquement. ◆ **plough back** *vt sep profits* réinvestir (*into* dans). ◆ **plough up** *vt sep (lit, fig)* labourer. ◆ **ploughing** *n* labour *m*; *[field etc]* labourage *m*; *(fig)* **the ~ing back of profits** le réinvestissement des bénéfices. ◆ **ploughman** *n* laboureur *m*; **~man's (lunch)** ≃ sandwich *m (au fromage).*

plover ['plʌvəʳ] *n* pluvier *m.*

plow [plaʊ] *(US)* = **plough.**

ploy * [plɔɪ] *n* stratagème *m* (*to do* pour faire).

pluck [plʌk] **1** *n (courage)* courage *m*, cran * *m.* **2** *vt fruit, flower* cueillir; *(Mus) strings* pincer; *guitar* pincer les cordes de; *(Culin) bird* plumer. **to ~ one's eyebrows** s'épiler les sourcils. **3** *vi*: **to ~ at sb's sleeve** tirer qn doucement par la manche. ◆ **pluck off, pluck out** *vt sep feathers* arracher; *(gen)* enlever. ◆ **pluck up** *vt sep*: **he ~ed up (the) courage to tell her** il a pris son courage à deux mains et le lui a dit. ◆ **pluckily** *adv* avec cran *, courageusement. ◆ **plucky** *adj* courageux, qui a du cran *.

plug [plʌg] **1** *n* (**a**) *[bath, basin, barrel]* bonde *f*; *(to stop a leak)* tampon *m*; *(stopper)* bouchon *m*; *[volcano]* culot *m.* *(in lavatory)* **to pull the ~** tirer la chasse d'eau. (**b**) *(Elec)* prise *f* (de courant); *[switchboard]* fiche *f*; *(Aut: sparking ~)* bougie *f.* (**c**) *(*: publicity)* publicité *f* (indirecte). **to give sth/sb a ~** * donner un coup de pouce (publicitaire) à qch/qn. (**d**) *(US: tobacco) (smoking)* carotte *f*; *(chewing)* chique *f.* **2** *vt* (**a**) **(~ up)** *hole, jar* boucher; *leak* colmater; *tooth* obturer (*with* avec). (**b**) *(*: publicize)* faire de la publicité pour. ◆ **plug away** * *vi* travailler méthodiquement (*at sth* pour faire qch). **he was ~ging away at his maths** il bûchait * ses maths. ◆ **plug in** *(Elec)* **1** *vi* se brancher. **2** *vt sep* brancher. ◆ **plughole** *n* vidange *f*; **it went down the ~hole** c'est tombé dans le trou (du lavabo *etc*).

plum [plʌm] **1** *n* prune *f*; *(tree)* prunier *m.* *(choice thing)* **the** *or* **a ~** * le meilleur. **2** *adj* (**a**) *(~-coloured)* prune *inv.* (**b**) *(*: best)* **the ~ job** le meilleur travail; **a ~ job** un boulot * en or. ◆ **plum pudding** *n* (plum-)pudding *m.*

plumb [plʌm] **1** *n* plomb *m.* **2** *adj* vertical, d'aplomb. **3** *adv* en plein. **~ in the middle of** en plein milieu de. **4** *vt* (**a**) sonder. **to ~ the depths** *(lit)* sonder les profondeurs; *(fig)* toucher le fond du désespoir. (**b**) **to ~ in a machine** faire le raccordement d'une machine.

◆ **plumber** *n* plombier *m*; *(US)* **~er's helper** (débouchoir *m* à) ventouse *f.* ◆ **plumbing** *n* plomberie *f.* ◆ **plumbline** *n* fil *m* à plomb; *(Naut)* sonde *f.*

plume [plu:m] *n* plumet *m*; *(larger)* panache *m (also of smoke).*

plummet ['plʌmɪt] *vi [aircraft, bird]* descendre à pic; *[temperature, prices, sales]* baisser brusquement; *[spirits, morale]* tomber à zéro.

plump¹ [plʌmp] **1** *adj person* rondelet; *child, hand, arm* potelé; *cheek, face, cushion* rebondi; *chicken* dodu. **2** *vt* **(~ up)** *pillow* tapoter. ◆ **plumpness** *n [person]* rondeur *f.*

plump² [plʌmp] **1** *vt* **(~ down)** flanquer *. **2** *adv* en plein, exactement. **~ in the middle of** en plein milieu de. ◆ **plump down** *vi (also* **~ o.s. down***)* s'affaler. ◆ **plump for** *vt fus* se décider pour.

plunder ['plʌndəʳ] **1** *n (act)* pillage *m*; *(loot)* butin *m.* **2** *vt* piller. ◆ **plunderer** *n* pillard *m.* ◆ **plundering** **1** *n* pillage *m* ; **2** *adj* pillard.

plunge [plʌn(d)ʒ] **1** *n (gen)* plongeon *m*; *(steep fall)* chute *f*; *(rash investment)* spéculation *f* hasardeuse (*on* sur). *(fig)* **to take the ~** se jeter à l'eau, sauter le pas. **2** *vt* plonger (*into* dans). **3** *vi* (**a**) *(dive: gen)* plonger (*into* dans; *from* de); *[ship]* piquer de l'avant; *(fig) [person]* se lancer (*into* dans). (**b**) *(fall: gen) [person]* tomber (*from* de). **the plane ~d to the ground/into the sea** l'avion s'est écrasé au sol/abîmé dans la mer. (**c**) *(rush)* **to ~ in/out** *etc* entrer/sortir *etc* précipitamment. ◆ **plunger** *n (for blocked pipe)* (débouchoir *m* à) ventouse *f.*

pluperfect ['plu:'pɜ:fɪkt] *n* plus-que-parfait *m.*

plural ['plʊər(ə)l] **1** *adj form* pluriel, du pluriel; *verb, noun* au pluriel. **2** *n (Gram)* pluriel *m.* **in the ~** au pluriel.

plus [plʌs] **1** *prep* plus. **2** *adj (Elec, Math)* positif. *(fig)* **a ~ factor** un atout; **10-~ hours** plus de 10 heures. **3** *n (Math)* (signe *m*) plus *m*; *(fig: advantage)* atout *m.* *(of situation)* **the ~es** les côtés positifs.

plush [plʌʃ] **1** *n (Tex)* peluche *f.* **2** *adj* (*) *hotel etc* somptueux.

Pluto ['plu:təʊ] *n (Astron)* Pluton *f*; *(Myth)* Pluton *m.*

plutocracy [ˌplu:'tɒkrəsɪ] *n* ploutocratie *f.* ◆ **plutocrat** *n* ploutocrate *m.*

plutonium [plu:'təʊnɪəm] *n* plutonium *m*.

ply¹ [plaɪ] *n*: **three-~ wool** laine *f* trois fils. ◆ **plywood** *n* contre-plaqué *m*.

ply² [plaɪ] **1** *vt needle, tool, oar* manier; *river* naviguer sur. **to ~ one's trade** exercer son métier (*as* de); **to ~ sb with questions** presser qn de questions; **he plied them with drink** il ne cessait de remplir leur verre. **2** *vi*: **to ~ between** faire la navette entre; **to ~ for hire** faire un service de taxi.

pneumatic [nju:'mætɪk] *adj* pneumatique. **~ drill** marteau-piqueur *m*.

pneumonia [nju:'məʊnɪə] *n (Med)* pneumonie *f*.

poach¹ [pəʊtʃ] *vt (Culin)* pocher. **~ed eggs** œufs *mpl* pochés. ◆ **poacher¹** *n* pocheuse *f*.

poach² [pəʊtʃ] *vti* braconner. **to ~ for salmon** braconner du saumon; *(fig)* **to ~ on sb's preserves** braconner sur les terres de qn. ◆ **poacher²** *n* braconnier *m*. ◆ **poaching** *n* braconnage *m*.

pocket ['pɒkɪt] **1** *n* poche *f*. **with his hands in his ~s** les mains dans les poches; **to go through sb's ~s** faire les poches à qn; *(fig)* **to put one's hand in one's ~** débourser; **it put £100 in his ~** cela lui a rapporté 100 livres; **to have sb/sth in one's ~** avoir qn/qch dans sa poche; **to line one's ~s** se remplir les poches; **to be out of ~** en être de sa poche; **I was £5 in/out of ~** j'avais fait un bénéfice/essuyé une perte de 5 livres; **air ~** trou *m* d'air; **~ of gas/resistance** poche de gaz/de résistance. **2** *adj flask, edition* de poche. **~ calculator** calculette *f*. **3** *vt* empocher *(also fig: gain, steal)*; *(fig) one's pride* mettre dans sa poche. ◆ **pocketbook** *n (wallet)* portefeuille *m*; *(notebook)* calepin *m*; *(US: book)* livre *m* de poche. ◆ **pocketful** *n* poche *f* pleine. ◆ **pocket-handkerchief** **1** *n* mouchoir *m* de poche ; **2** *adj* grand comme un mouchoir de poche. ◆ **pocket-knife** *n* canif *m*. ◆ **pocket-money** *n* argent *m* de poche. ◆ **pocket-size(d)** *adj (fig)* tout petit.

pock-marked ['pɒkma:kt] *adj face* grêlé; *surface* criblé de petits trous.

pod [pɒd] *n [bean, pea etc]* cosse *f*.

podgy * ['pɒdʒɪ] *adj* rondelet.

podiatry [pɒ'di:ətrɪ] *n (US)* soins *mpl* du pied. ◆ **podiatrist** *n* pédicure *mf*.

poem ['pəʊɪm] *n* poème *m*. ◆ **poet** *n* poète *m*. ◆ **poetess** *n* poétesse *f*. ◆ **poetic** *adj* poétique; **it's poetic justice** il y a une justice immanente. ◆ **poetically** *adv* poétiquement. ◆ **poetry** *n* poésie *f*; **to write poetry** écrire des poèmes. ◆ **poetry-reading** *n* lecture *f* de poèmes.

poignant ['pɔɪnjənt] *adj* poignant. ◆ **poignancy** *n* caractère *m* poignant. ◆ **poignantly** *adv* d'une manière poignante.

point [pɔɪnt] **1** *n* (**a**) *[pencil, knife etc]* pointe *f*; *(Geog)* pointe, cap *m*. **with a sharp ~** très pointu; *(fig)* **not to put too fine a ~ on it** pour dire les choses comme elles sont; **star with 5 ~s** étoile à 5 branches *fpl*; *(Ballet)* **to be on ~s** faire des pointes; **at the ~ of a sword/revolver** à la pointe de l'épée/sous la menace du revolver.
(**b**) *(dot: gen)* point *m*; *(decimal ~)* virgule *f* (décimale). **3 ~ 6 (3.6)** 3 virgule 6 (3,6); *(Geom)* **~ A** le point A.
(**c**) *(on scale, in space, in time)* point *m*. **from that ~ onwards** *(in space)* à partir de là; *(in time)* à partir de ce moment-là; **at this** *or* **that ~** *(in space)* à cet endroit-là; *(in time)* à ce moment-là; **at this ~ in time** en ce moment; **~ of the compass** aire *f* de vent; **from all ~s (of the compass)** de tous côtés; **the train stops at Slough, and all ~s west** le train s'arrête à Slough et dans toutes les gares à l'ouest de Slough; **~ of departure/entry** point de départ/d'arrivée; **~ of sale** point *m* de vente; **from that ~ of view** de ce point de vue; **at that ~ in the road** à cet endroit de la route; *(Brit Elec)* **wall** *or* **power ~** prise *f* de courant *(femelle)*; **boiling/freezing ~** point d'ébullition/de congélation; **full to bursting ~** plein à craquer; **to be on the ~ of doing** être sur le point de faire; **the ~ of no return** le point de non-retour; *(fig)* **up to a ~** jusqu'à un certain point; **when it comes to the ~** en fin de compte; **when it came to the ~ of paying** quand le moment de payer est arrivé; **severe to the ~ of cruelty** sévère au point d'être cruel.
(**d**) *(counting unit: Scol, Sport, St Ex, Typ; also on scale)* point *m*; *(on thermometer)* degré *m*. *(Boxing)* **on ~s** aux points; **to go up 2 ~s** augmenter de 2 points.
(**e**) *(subject, item)* point *m*. **the ~ at issue** la question qui nous (*or* les *etc*) concerne; **~ of interest** point intéressant; **just as a ~ of interest, did you...?** à titre d'information, est-ce que vous...?; **12-~ plan** plan *m* en 12 points; **a ~ of detail/law/honour** *etc* un point de détail/de droit/d'honneur *etc*; **on a ~ of principle** sur une question de principe; **in ~ of fact** en fait, à vrai dire; **~ by ~** point par point; **to make a ~** faire une remarque; **to make the ~ that** faire remarquer que; **you've made your ~!** *(had your say)* vous avez dit ce que vous aviez à dire!; *(convinced me)* vous m'avez convaincu!; **I take your ~** je vois où vous voulez en venir; **~ taken!, you have a ~ there!** c'est juste! ; **to win one's ~** avoir gain de cause; **he gave me a few ~s on what to do** il m'a donné quelques conseils sur ce que je devais faire.
(**f**) *(important part, main idea etc) [argument etc]* point *m* essentiel; *[joke etc]* astuce *f*; *(meaning, purpose)* intérêt *m*, sens *m*; *(relevance)* pertinence *f*. **there's no ~ in waiting** cela ne sert à rien d'attendre; **what's the ~ of** *or* **in waiting?** à quoi bon attendre?; **I don't see any ~ in doing that** je ne vois aucun intérêt à faire cela; **the ~ is that...** le fait est que..., c'est que...; **the whole ~ was...** tout l'intérêt était...; **that's the (whole) ~!** justement!; **that's not the ~** il ne s'agit pas de cela; **beside the ~** à côté de la question; **off the ~** hors de propos; **very much to the ~** très pertinent; **the ~ of this story is that...** là où je veux en venir avec cette histoire, c'est que...; **a long story that seemed to have no ~ at all** une longue histoire qui ne rimait à rien; **I missed the ~ of that joke** je n'ai pas compris l'astuce; **you've missed the whole ~!** vous n'avez rien compris!; **to see** *or* **get the ~** comprendre, saisir; **to come to the ~** en venir au fait; **let's get back to the ~** revenons à ce qui nous préoccupe; **to keep** *or* **stick to the ~** rester dans le sujet; **to make a ~ of doing** ne pas manquer de faire.
(**g**) *(characteristic)* **good ~s** qualités *fpl*; **bad ~s** défauts *mpl*; **his strong ~** son fort; **he has his ~s** il a certaines qualités; **the ~s to look for when buying...** les détails *mpl* qu'il faut prendre en considération lors de l'achat de...
(**h**) *(Rail)* **~s** aiguilles *fpl*.
2 *adj (Police etc)* **to be on ~ duty** diriger la circulation.
3 *vt* (**a**) *(direct) telescope, hosepipe etc* pointer, diriger (*on* sur); *gun* braquer (*at* sur). **he ~ed his finger at me** il m'a montré du doigt. (**b**) *(mark, show)* montrer, indiquer. *(fig)* **it ~s the way to...** cela montre la voie pour...; *(fig)* **to ~ the moral** souligner la morale. (**c**) *(Constr) wall* jointoyer (*with* de).
4 *vi* (**a**) **to ~ at sth/sb** montrer qch/qn du doigt; *(fig)* **I want to ~ to one or two facts** je veux attirer votre attention sur un ou deux faits; **all the evidence ~s to him** *or* **to his guilt** tous les témoignages l'accusent; **it all ~s to the fact that...** tout laisse à penser que...; **everything ~s that way** tout nous amène à cette conclusion. (**b**) *[signpost]* indiquer la direction (*towards* de); *[gun]* être braqué (*at* sur); *[vehicle etc]* être tourné (*towards* vers). *[needle, clock-hand]* **to be ~ing to sth** indiquer qch. ◆ **point**

out *vt sep* (**a**) *(show)* montrer, indiquer (*to sb* à qn). (**b**) *(mention)* faire remarquer (*that* que). **to ~ sth out to sb** signaler qch à qn; **I should ~ out that...** je dois vous dire que... ◆ **point up** *vt sep* mettre en évidence.

◆ **point-blank 1** *adj shot* à bout portant; *refusal* catégorique; *request* de but en blanc; **at ~-blank range** à bout portant ; **2** *adv* à bout portant; catégoriquement; de but en blanc. ◆ **point-by-point** *adj account etc* méthodique. ◆ **pointed** *adj (gen)* pointu; *beard* en pointe; *arch* en ogive; *remark* lourd de sens. ◆ **pointedly** *adv reply* d'une manière significative; *say* d'un ton plein de sous-entendus. ◆ **pointer** *n* (**a**) *(stick)* baguette *f*; *(on scale) (indicator)* index *m*; *(needle)* aiguille *f*; *(on screen: arrow)* flèche *f* lumineuse; *(clue, indication)* indice *m* (*to* de); *(piece of advice)* conseil *m* (*on* sur); *(fig)* **this is a ~er to...** ceci laisse entrevoir...; (**b**) *(dog)* chien *m* d'arrêt. ◆ **pointing** *n (Constr)* jointoiement *m.* ◆ **pointless** *adj attempt, task, suffering* inutile, vain; *existence* dénué de sens; *murder* gratuit; *explanation, joke, story* qui ne rime à rien; **it is ~less to complain** il ne sert à rien de se plaindre. ◆ **pointlessly** *adv try, work, suffer* inutilement; *kill* sans raison. ◆ **pointlessness** *n [task]* inutilité *f*; *[murder]* gratuité *f.*

poise [pɔɪz] **1** *n (balance)* équilibre *m*; *(carriage)* maintien *m*; *(self-confidence)* assurance *f*; *(grace)* grâce *f.* **2** *vt (balance)* mettre en équilibre; *(hold balanced)* tenir en équilibre. **to be ~d** *(balanced)* être en équilibre; *(held, hanging, hovering)* être suspendu (en l'air); **~d ready to attack** tout prêt à attaquer; *(fig)* **~d on the brink of success** au bord de la réussite.

poison ['pɔɪzn] **1** *n (lit, fig)* poison *m*; *[snake]* venin *m.* **to take ~** s'empoisonner; **to die of ~** mourir empoisonné; **they hate each other like ~** ils ne peuvent pas se sentir *. **2** *adj gas* toxique. **~ ivy** sumac *m* vénéneux. **3** *vt (gen)* empoisonner. **a ~ed foot** un pied infecté; **it's ~ing his system** cela l'intoxique; **to ~ sb's mind** *(corrupt)* corrompre qn; *(instil doubts)* faire douter qn (*against sb* de qn). ◆ **poisoner** *n* empoisonneur *m*, -euse *f (lit).* ◆ **poisoning** *n (V* **poison 3***)* empoisonnement *m*; intoxication *f*; **to die of ~ing** mourir empoisonné; **arsenic ~ing** empoisonnement à l'arsenic. ◆ **poisonous** *adj snake* venimeux; *plant* vénéneux; *gas, fumes, substance* toxique; *(fig) rumours, doctrine* pernicieux; (*) *person* ignoble; (*) *coffee etc* infect.

poke [pəʊk] **1** *n (push)* poussée *f*; *(jab)* petit coup *m (de coude etc)*; *(US *: punch)* coup de poing. **I got a ~ in the eye from his umbrella** j'ai reçu son parapluie dans l'œil. **2** *vt (with elbow, finger, stick etc)* donner un coup de coude (*or* avec le doigt *or* de canne) à; *(US *: punch)* donner un coup de poing à; *(thrust) stick, finger etc* enfoncer (*into* dans; *through* à travers); *rag etc* fourrer (*into* dans); *fire* tisonner. **he ~d me with his umbrella** il m'a donné un petit coup de parapluie; **he ~d his finger in her eye** il lui a mis le doigt dans l'œil; **he ~d me in the ribs** il m'a enfoncé son coude (*or* son doigt *etc*) dans les côtes; **to ~ one's head out of the window** passer la tête par la fenêtre; *(fig)* **to ~ one's nose into sth** * fourrer le nez dans qch. **3** *vi* (**a**) (**~ out**) sortir, dépasser (*from, through* de). (**b**) **to ~ about** *or* **around in sth** fourrager *or* fouiner *(pej)* dans qch. ◆ **poker¹** *n* tisonnier *m.* ◆ **pokerwork** *n* pyrogravure *f.*

poker² ['pəʊkəʳ] *n (Cards)* poker *m.* ◆ **poker-faced** *adj* au visage impassible.

poky ['pəʊkɪ] *adj (pej)* exigu et sombre.

Poland ['pəʊlənd] *n* Pologne *f.* ◆ **Pole** *n* Polonais(e) *m(f).* ◆ **Polish 1** *adj* polonais ; **2** *n (Ling)* polonais *m.*

polar ['pəʊləʳ] *adj (Elec, Geog)* polaire. **~ bear** ours *m* blanc. ◆ **polarity** *n* polarité *f.* ◆ **polarization** *n* polarisation *f.* ◆ **polarize** *vt (lit, fig)* polariser. ◆ **Polaroid** ® *n (also* **P~oid camera***)* (appareil *m*) Polaroïd *m; (also* **P~oid print***)* photo *f* Polaroïd.

pole¹ [pəʊl] **1** *n (gen)* perche *f*; *(telegraph ~ ; in fences etc)* poteau *m*; *(flag ~; tent ~)* mât *m*; *(curtain ~)* tringle *f*; *(rod; also for vaulting, punting)* perche. *(fig)* **up the ~** * *(mad)* qui déraille *; *(mistaken)* qui se fiche dedans *. **2** *adj*: **~ vault(ing)** saut *m* à la perche. ◆ **poleax(e)** *vt person* terrasser.

pole² [pəʊl] **1** *n (Elec, Geog)* pôle *m.* **North/South P~** pôle Nord/Sud; **from ~ to ~** d'un pôle à l'autre; *(fig)* **they are ~s apart** ils sont aux antipodes (l'un de l'autre). **2** *adj*: **~ star** étoile *f* polaire.

polemic [pɒ'lemɪk] *n* polémique *f.*

police [pə'li:s] **1** *n (organization)* ≃ police *f (gen in towns)*, gendarmerie *f (throughout France).* **the ~** la police, les gendarmes *mpl*; **to join the ~** entrer dans la police; **river/railway ~** police fluviale/des chemins de fer; **the ~ are on his track** la police est sur sa piste. **2** *adj escort, vehicle, protection, inquiry* de la police *or* de la gendarmerie. **~ car** voiture *f* de police *or* de la gendarmerie; *(Brit)* **~ constable** ≃ agent *m* de police, gendarme *m*; **~ dog** *(gen)* chien policier; *(US: alsatian)* berger *m* allemand; **the ~ force** la police, les gendarmes *mpl*; **~ inspector** ≃ inspecteur *m* de police; **~ officer** agent *m* (de police), gendarme *m*; **to have a ~ record** avoir un casier judiciaire; **~ state** état *m* policier; **~ station** commissariat *m* de police, gendarmerie *f*; **~ superintendent** commissaire *m* de police. **3** *vt [vigilantes, volunteers etc] district, road, football match etc* faire la police dans (*or* à, sur *etc*); *(Mil) frontier, territory* contrôler; *(fig) agreements, controls* veiller à l'application de; *prices etc* contrôler. ◆ **policeman** *n* agent *m* (de police), gendarme *m.* ◆ **policewoman** *n* femme *f* agent.

policy¹ ['pɒlɪsɪ] **1** *n (gen)* politique *f.* **the government's policies** la politique du gouvernement; **what is company ~?** quelle est la ligne suivie par la compagnie?; **to follow a ~ of doing sth** faire qch systématiquement; **it's a matter of ~** c'est une question de principe; **it has always been our ~ to do that** nous avons toujours eu pour règle de faire cela; **it would be good/bad ~ to do that** ce serait une bonne/mauvaise politique que de faire cela; **it would not be ~ to refuse** il ne serait pas politique de refuser. **2** *adj decision, matter, statement* de principe; *discussion* de politique générale.

policy² ['pɒlɪsɪ] *n (Insurance)* police *f* (d'assurance). **to take out a ~** souscrire à une police d'assurance; **~ holder** assuré(e) *m(f)*; **~ maker** *(in organization)* décideur *m; (in party)* responsable *m* politique.

polio ['pəʊlɪəʊ] *n* polio *f.* **~ victim** polio *mf.*

poliomyelitis ['pəʊlɪəʊmaɪə'laɪtɪs] *n* poliomyélite *f.*

polish ['pɒlɪʃ] **1** *n* (**a**) *(for shoes)* cirage *m*; *(for floor, furniture)* cire *f*; *(for nails)* vernis *m* (à ongles). **metal ~** produit *m* d'entretien pour les métaux; **to give sth a ~, to put a ~ on sth** faire briller qch; **my shoes need a ~** mes chaussures ont besoin d'être cirées. (**b**) *(fig) [person]* raffinement *m*; *[style, work, performance]* élégance *f.* **2** *vt* (**~ up**) *stones, glass* polir; *shoes, floor, furniture* cirer; *car, pans, metal* astiquer; *one's French etc* perfectionner. ◆ **polish off** *vt sep food, drink* finir; *work, correspondence* expédier.

◆ **polished** *adj surface, stone, glass* poli; *floor, shoes* ciré; *silver, ornaments* brillant; *(fig) person* qui a de l'éducation; *manners* raffiné; *style* poli; *performer* accompli; *performance* impeccable. ◆ **polisher** *n (machine)* polissoir *m*; *(for floors)* cireuse *f.*

polite [pə'laɪt] *adj* poli (*to sb* avec qn). **be ~ about his car!** ne dis pas de mal de sa voiture!; **in ~ society** dans la bonne société. ◆ **politely** *adv* poliment. ◆ **politeness** *n* politesse *f.*

politic ['pɒlɪtɪk] *adj* politique, diplomatique. ◆ **political** *adj* politique; **~al analyst** politologue *mf*; **to ask for ~al asylum** demander l'asile politique. ◆ **politically** *adv* politiquement. ◆ **politician** *n* homme *m* politique, femme *f* politique, politicien(ne) *m(f) (pej)*. ◆ **politicize** *vt* politiser. ◆ **politicking** *n* politique *f* politicienne. ◆ **politics** *nsg (gen)* politique *f*; *(Univ: study)* sciences *fpl* politiques; **to talk ~s** parler politique; **to go into ~s** se lancer dans la politique.

poll [pəʊl] **1** *n* (**a**) *(general vote)* vote *m*; *(at election)* scrutin *m*; *(election)* élection *f*. **to take a ~ on sth** procéder à un vote sur qch; **to go to the ~s** aller aux urnes; **a defeat at the ~s** une défaite aux élections; **there was an 84% turnout at the ~s** la participation électorale était de 84% ; **he got 20% of the ~** il a obtenu 20% des suffrages exprimés. (**b**) *(survey)* sondage *m*. **opinion ~** sondage d'opinion; **to take a ~** sonder l'opinion (*of* de); **the Gallup ~** le sondage Gallup. **2** *vt votes* obtenir; *people* sonder l'opinion de. ◆ **polling 1** *n* élections *fpl*; **2** *adj day* des élections; **~ing booth** isoloir *m*; *(US)* polling place; *(Brit)* **~ing station** bureau *m* de vote.

pollen ['pɒlən] *n* pollen *m*. ◆ **pollinate** *vt* féconder.

pollute [pə'lu:t] *vt* polluer; *(fig)* contaminer. ◆ **pollutant** *n* polluant *m*. ◆ **pollution** *n* pollution *f*; contamination *f*.

Pollyanna [pɒlɪ'ænə] *n (US)* optimiste *m(f)* béat(e).

polo ['pəʊləʊ] *n (Sport, shirt)* polo *m*. ◆ **polonecked** *adj* à col roulé.

poltergeist ['pɔ:ltəgaɪst] *n* esprit *m* frappeur.

poly... ['pɒlɪ] *pref* poly... ◆ **polyandry** *n* polyandrie *f*. ◆ **polyanthus** *n* primevère *f (multiflore)*. ◆ **poly-cotton** *n* coton *m* polyester. ◆ **polyester** *n* polyester *m*. ◆ **polyethylene** *n (US)* polyéthylène *m*. ◆ **polygamy** *n* polygamie *f*. ◆ **polyglot** *adj, n* polyglotte *(mf)*. ◆ **polygon** *n* polygone *m*. ◆ **polygonal** *adj* polygonal. ◆ **polymer** *n* polymère *m*. ◆ **polyphonic** *adj* polyphonique. ◆ **polyphony** *n* polyphonie *f*. ◆ **polystyrene** *n* polystyrène *m*; **~styrene cement** colle *f* polystyrène; **~styrene chips** billes *fpl* de polystyrène. ◆ **polysyllabic** *adj* polysyllabe. ◆ **polysyllable** *n* polysyllabe *m*. ◆ **polytechnic** *n (Brit)* ≃ IUT *m*, Institut *m* universitaire de technologie. ◆ **polythene** *n (Brit)* polyéthylène *m*; **~thene bag** sac *m* en plastique. ◆ **polyunsaturated** *adj* polyinsaturé. ◆ **polyurethane** *n* polyuréthane *m*.

Polynesia [,pɒlɪ'ni:zɪə] *n* Polynésie *f*. ◆ **Polynesian 1** *adj* polynésien ; **2** *n* Polynésien(ne) *m(f)*.

polyp ['pɒlɪp] *n* polype *m*.

pomegranate ['pɒmə,grænɪt] *n* grenade *f (fruit)*.

pommy ‡ ['pɒmɪ] *(Australia pej)* **1** *n* Anglais(e) *m(f)*. **2** *adj* anglais.

pomp [pɒmp] *n* pompe *f*, faste *m*. **~ and circumstance** grand apparat *m*.

pompous ['pɒmpəs] *adj (pej)* pompeux. ◆ **pomposity** *n* manières *fpl* pompeuses. ◆ **pompously** *adv* pompeusement.

poncho ['pɒntʃəʊ] *n* poncho *m*.

pond [pɒnd] *n* étang *m*; *(stagnant)* mare *f*; *(artificial)* bassin *m*.

ponder ['pɒndəʳ] **1** *vt* considérer, réfléchir à *or* sur. **2** *vi* réfléchir (*over, on* à, sur).

ponderous ['pɒnd(ə)rəs] *adj (gen)* pesant; *style, joke* lourd. ◆ **ponderously** *adv* pesamment.

pong ‡ [pɒŋ] **1** *n* puanteur *f*. **2** *vi* puer.

pontiff ['pɒntɪf] *n* pontife *m*; *(pope)* souverain pontife *m*. ◆ **pontifical** *adj* pontifical. ◆ **pontificate** *vi* pontifier (*about* au sujet de, sur).

pontoon [pɒn'tu:n] *n* ponton *m*; *(Cards)* vingt-et-un *m*.

pony ['pəʊnɪ] **1** *n* poney *m*. **2** *adj*: **hair in a ~tail** cheveux *mpl* en queue de cheval. ◆ **pony trekking** *n*: **to go ~ trekking** faire une randonnée *f* à cheval.

poodle ['pu:dl] *n* caniche *m*.

poof ‡ [pʊf] *n (pej)* tante ‡ *f*, tapette ‡ *f*.

pooh-pooh [pu:'pu:] *vt* faire fi de.

pool [pu:l] **1** *n* (**a**) *[water, rain]* flaque *f*; *[blood]* mare *f*; *[light]* rond *m*; *(pond)* étang *m*; *(artificial)* bassin *m*; *(in river)* plan *m* d'eau; *(water hole)* point *m* d'eau; *(swimming ~)* piscine *f*. (**b**) *(money: gen, also Cards)* cagnotte *f*; *(common supply: gen)* fonds *m* commun (*of* de); *[cars]* parc *m*; *[ideas, experience, ability]* réservoir *m*; *[advisers, experts]* équipe *f*; *(Comm, Econ: consortium)* pool *m*. **typing ~** pool de dactylos; **genetic ~** pool *m* génétique. (**c**) **to win sth on the (football) ~s** gagner qch en pariant sur les matchs de football. (**d**) *(US: billiards)* billard *m* américain. **2** *vt money, resources, objects* mettre en commun; *knowledge, efforts* unir. ◆ **poolroom** *n* salle *f* de billard.

poor [pʊəʳ] **1** *adj (gen)* pauvre; *(inferior)* médiocre; *light, sight* faible; *effort* insuffisant; *memory, health* mauvais; *soil* pauvre; *loser etc* mauvais. **as ~ as a church mouse** pauvre comme Job; **to become ~er** s'appauvrir; *(lacking)* **~ in** pauvre en; **~ things *, they look cold** les pauvres, ils ont l'air d'avoir froid; **you ~ thing! *** mon pauvre!, ma pauvre!; **it's a ~ thing when...** c'est malheureux que... + *subj*; **it was a ~ evening** la soirée n'était pas une réussite; **to be ~ at (doing) sth** ne pas être doué pour (faire) qch; **he is a ~ traveller** il supporte mal les voyages. **2** *n*: **the ~** les pauvres *mpl*.
◆ **poorly 1** *adj* souffrant ; **2** *adv live, dress* pauvrement; *work, write, explain* médiocrement, mal; *lit, paid* mal. ◆ **poorness** *n* pauvreté *f*; médiocrité *f*.

pop¹ [pɒp] **1** *n* (**a**) *[cork etc]* pan *m*. **~!** pan!; **to go ~** faire pan. (**b**) *(*: drink)* boisson *f* gazeuse. **2** *vt* (**a**) *balloon* crever; *cork, press stud* faire sauter. (**b**) *(put: gen)* mettre. **to ~ one's head round the door** passer brusquement la tête par la porte; *(fig)* **to ~ the question** faire sa demande (en mariage); *(Drugs sl)* **to ~ pills** se droguer (avec des comprimés). **3** *vi* (**a**) *[balloon]* crever; *[cork, press stud etc]* sauter; *[corn]* éclater; *[ears]* se déboucher. **his eyes were ~ping out of his head** les yeux lui sortaient de la tête. (**b**) *(go)* **to ~ over** (*or* **round** *or* **across** *or* **out)** faire un saut (*to* à *etc*); **he ~ped into a café** il est entré en vitesse dans un café. ◆ **pop in** *vi* entrer en passant. ◆ **pop off** *vi (leave)* partir; *(‡: die)* claquer *, mourir. ◆ **pop up** *vi [person]* surgir.
◆ **popcorn** *n* pop-corn *m*. ◆ **popeyed** *adj* aux yeux écarquillés. ◆ **popgun** *n* pistolet *m* à bouchon. ◆ **popper** *n (press stud)* pression *f*.

pop² [pɒp] (*abbr of* **popular**) **1** *adj song, singer, art* pop *inv*. **2** *n* (musique *f*) pop *m*. **it's top of the ~s** c'est en tête du hit-parade.

pop³ * [pɒp] *n (esp US)* papa *m*.

pope [pəʊp] *n* pape *m*. **P~ Paul** le pape Paul. ◆ **popery** *n* papisme *m*. ◆ **popish** *adj* papiste.

poplar ['pɒpləʳ] *n* peuplier *m*.

poplin ['pɒplɪn] *n* popeline *f*.

poppadum ['pɒpədəm] *n* poppadum *m*.

poppet * ['pɒpɪt] *n*: **yes, ~** oui, mon petit chou; **she's a ~** c'est un amour.

poppy ['pɒpɪ] **1** *n* pavot *m*; *(growing wild)* coquelicot *m*. **2** *adj*: **P~ Day** anniversaire *m* de l'armistice; **~ seed** graine *f* de pavot. ◆ **poppycock** * *n* balivernes *fpl*.

Popsicle ['pɒpsɪkl] *n* ® *(US)* glace *f* à l'eau *(tenue par deux bâtonnets)*.

populace ['pɒpjʊlɪs] *n* peuple *m*, foule *f*.

popular ['pɒpjʊləʳ] *adj* (**a**) *(well-liked)* populaire; *(fashionable)* à la mode. **he is ~ with his colleagues** ses collègues l'aiment beaucoup; **he is ~ with the girls** il a du succès auprès des filles; **I'm not very ~ with the boss** * je ne suis pas très bien vu du patron. (**b**) *(for, by the people: gen, Pol)* populaire; *lecture, journal* de vulgarisation. **by ~ request** à la demande générale. ◆ **popularity** *n* popularité *f* (*with* auprès de; *among* parmi). ◆ **popularize** *vt music, fashion, product* rendre populaire; *science, ideas* vulgariser. ◆ **popularizer** *n* vulgarisateur *m*, -trice *f*. ◆ **popularly** *adv* communément.

populate ['pɒpjʊleɪt] *vt* peupler. ◆ **population** **1** *n* population *f* ; **2** *adj increase, explosion* démographique.

porcelain ['pɔːs(ə)lɪn] *n* porcelaine *f*. **a piece of ~** une porcelaine.

porch [pɔːtʃ] *n* porche *m*. **sun ~** véranda *f*.

porcupine ['pɔːkjʊpaɪn] *n* porc-épic *m*.

pore¹ [pɔːʳ] *n (Anat)* pore *m*.

pore² [pɔːʳ] *vi*: **to ~ over** *book* être absorbé dans; *letter, map* étudier de près; *problem* méditer longuement.

pork [pɔːk] *(Culin)* **1** *n* porc *m*. **2** *adj chop etc* de porc. *(US Pol)* **~ barrel** * travaux *mpl* publics entrepris à des fins électorales; **~ butcher** ≃ charcutier *m*; **~ pie** ≃ pâté *m* de porc en croûte.

pornography [pɔː'nɒgrəfɪ] *n* pornographie *f*. ◆ **porn** * *n* porno * *m or f*; **soft/hard porn** pornographie douce/dure; **porn shop** boutique *f* pornographique. ◆ **pornographic** *adj* pornographique.

porous ['pɔːrəs] *adj* poreux, perméable.

porpoise ['pɔːpəs] *n* marsouin *m (Zool)*.

porridge ['pɒrɪdʒ] *n* porridge *m*. **~ oats** flocons *mpl* d'avoine.

port¹ [pɔːt] **1** *n* port *m*. **~ of call** (port d')escale *f*; **naval/fishing ~** port militaire/de pêche; **to come into ~** entrer dans le port; **to leave ~** appareiller; *(fig)* **any ~ in a storm** nécessité n'a pas de loi. **2** *adj facilities, authorities* portuaire.

port² [pɔːt] *(Naut: left)* **1** *n* bâbord *m*. **2** *adj* de bâbord.

port³ [pɔːt] *n (wine)* porto *m*.

portable ['pɔːtəbl] **1** *adj* portatif. **2** *n* modèle *m* portatif.

Portakabin ['pɔːtəkæbɪn] *n (gen)* bâtiment *m* préfabriqué.

porter ['pɔːtəʳ] *n (for luggage)* porteur *m*; *(US: on train)* employé(e) *m(f)* des wagons-lits; *(doorkeeper)* concierge *mf*; *[public building]* gardien(ne) *m(f)*. ◆ **porterhouse (steak)** *n* ≃ chateaubriand *m*.

portfolio [pɔːt'fəʊlɪəʊ] *n* portefeuille *m (Admin)*.

porthole ['pɔːthəʊl] *n* hublot *m*.

portion ['pɔːʃ(ə)n] *n (gen)* portion *f*; *[train, ticket etc]* partie *f*.

portly ['pɔːtlɪ] *adj* corpulent.

portmanteau [pɔːt'mæntəʊ] *n* grosse valise *f*. **~ word** mot-valise *m*.

portrait ['pɔːtrɪt] **1** *n* portrait *m*. **2** *adj gallery* de portraits. **~ painter** portraitiste *mf*. ◆ **portray** [pɔː'treɪ] *vt [painter]* peindre, faire le portrait de ; *[painting]* représenter; **he portrayed him as...** *[painter]* il l'a peint sous les traits de...; *[writer, actor]* il en a fait...

Portugal ['pɔːtjʊg(ə)l] *n* Portugal *m*. ◆ **Portuguese** **1** *adj* portugais ; **2** *n (person: pl inv)* Portugais(e) *m(f)*; *(language)* portugais *m*.

pose [pəʊz] **1** *n* pose *f*. **to strike a ~** poser (pour la galerie); **it's only a ~** c'est de la pose. **2** *vi (Art etc)* poser (*for* pour; *as* en); *(fig: attitudinize)* poser. **to ~ as a doctor** se faire passer pour un docteur. **3** *vt* (**a**) *artist's model* faire prendre une pose à; *person* faire poser. (**b**) *problem, question* poser; *difficulties* créer. ◆ **poser** *n* question *f* difficile. ◆ **poseur** *n* poseur *m*, -euse *f*.

posh * [pɒʃ] **1** *adj (gen)* chic *inv*; *accent* distingué. **2** *adv*: **to talk ~** parler comme les gens bien. ◆ **posh up** ‡ *vt sep house* embellir; *(clean up)* briquer; *child* pomponner, bichonner. **to ~ o.s. up** se pomponner; **he was all ~ed up** il était sur son trente et un, il était bien sapé ‡.

posit ['pɒzɪt] *vt* énoncer, poser en principe.

position [pə'zɪʃ(ə)n] **1** *n (gen)* position *f*; *[house, shop, town, gun]* emplacement *m*; *(circumstances, also job)* situation *f*. **in(to) ~** en place, en position; **to change the ~ of sth** changer qch de place; **to take up (one's) ~** prendre position; *(Sport)* **what ~ do you play in?** à quelle place jouez-vous?; *(lit, fig)* **to jockey** *or* **manoeuvre for ~** manœuvrer pour se placer avantageusement; **in a horizontal ~** en position horizontale; **in an uncomfortable ~** dans une position incommode; **he finished in 3rd ~** il est arrivé en 3ᵉ position *or* place; **his ~ in the government** son poste *or* sa fonction dans le gouvernement; **a ~ of trust** un poste de confiance; **to be in a ~ to do sth** être en mesure de faire qch; **to be in a good ~ to do sth** être bien placé pour faire qch; **put yourself in my ~** mettez-vous à ma place; **a man in his ~** un homme dans sa situation; **the economic ~** la situation économique, la conjoncture; **in an awkward ~** dans une situation délicate; **you must make your ~ clear** vous devez dire franchement quelle est votre position (*on* sur).
2 *vt* (**a**) *(adjust angle of) light etc* mettre en position. (**b**) *(put in place: gen)* placer; *army, ship* mettre en position. **to ~ o.s.** se mettre, se placer.

positive ['pɒzɪtɪv] *adj* (**a**) *(gen)* positif; *(affirmative)* affirmatif; *(constructive) help* concret; *attitude, criticism* positif. (**b**) *(definite) order* formel; *fact, proof* indéniable; *change, increase, improvement* réel, tangible; *contribution* effectif. **it's a ~ miracle** * c'est un vrai miracle; **he's a ~ genius** * c'est un véritable génie; **~ discrimination** mesures *fpl* anti-discriminatoires en faveur des minorités. (**c**) *(certain) person* sûr, certain (*about, on, of* de); *tone* assuré. **I'm quite ~** j'en suis sûr *or* certain. ◆ **positively** *adv (indisputably)* indéniablement; *(categorically)* formellement; *(affirmatively)* affirmativement; *(with certainty)* de façon certaine; *(emphatically)* positivement; *(absolutely)* complètement; **to think ~ly** penser de façon constructive.

possess [pə'zes] *vt* posséder. **like one ~ed** comme un possédé; **what can have ~ed him to say that?** qu'est-ce qui l'a pris de dire ça? ◆ **possession** *n* possession *f*; **in ~ion of** en possession de; **to have in one's ~ion** avoir en sa possession; **to get ~ion of** acquérir, obtenir; *(improperly)* s'emparer de; **to come into sb's ~ion** tomber en la possession de qn; **the information in my ~ion** les renseignements dont je dispose; **to take ~ion of** prendre possession de, *(improperly)* s'approprier; *(confiscate)* confisquer; *(Jur)* **to be in ~ion** occuper les lieux; **a house with vacant ~ion** une maison avec jouissance immédiate. ◆ **possessive** **1** *adj* possessif (*with sb* à l'égard de qn); **to be ~ive about sth** ne pas vouloir partager qch; **an over-~ive mother** une mère abusive ; **2** *n (Gram)* possessif *m*; **in the ~ive** au possessif. ◆ **possessively** *adv* d'une façon possessive. ◆ **possessiveness** *n* possessivité *f*. ◆ **possessor** *n* possesseur *m*; **the proud ~or of** l'heureux propriétaire *m* de.

possibility [,pɒsə'bɪlɪtɪ] *n (gen)* possibilité *f*. **some ~/not much ~ of success** quelques chances/peu de chances de succès; **there is some/no ~ that** il est/n'est pas possible que + *subj*; **it's a distinct ~** c'est bien possible; **he is a ~ for the job** c'est un candidat possible; **the job has real possibilities** c'est un emploi qui offre toutes sortes de possibilités; *(of idea etc)* **it's got possibilities** c'est possible, c'est à voir.

possible ['pɒsəbl] **1** *adj* possible. **it is ~ that** il se peut que + *subj*, il est possible que + *subj*; **it's ~ to do so** il est possible de le faire; **it is ~ for him to leave** il lui est possible de partir; **if ~** si possible; **as far as ~** dans la mesure du possible; **as much as ~** autant que possible; **he did as much as ~** il a fait tout ce qu'il pouvait; **the best ~ result** le meilleur résultat possible; **one ~ result** un résultat possible *or* éventuel; **what ~ interest can you have in it?** qu'est-ce qui peut bien vous intéresser là-dedans?; **a ~ candidate** un candidat possible *or* acceptable. **2** *n*: **a list of ~s for the job** une liste de personnes susceptibles d'être retenues pour ce poste; **he's a ~ for the match** c'est un joueur possible pour le match. ◆ **possibly** *adv* (**a**) *(with 'can' etc)* **as often as I possibly can** aussi souvent qu'il m'est matériellement possible de le faire; **all he possibly can** *or* **could do** tout son possible (*to help etc* pour aider *etc*); **if I possibly can** si cela m'est possible; **I cannot possibly come** il m'est absolument impossible de venir; (**b**) *(perhaps)* peut-être.

post¹ [pəʊst] **1** *n (gen)* poteau *m*; *(door~ etc)* montant *m*. *(Sport)* **starting/winning ~** poteau de départ/d'arrivée; **to be beaten at the ~** être battu sur le poteau. **2** *vt* (**a**) (**~ up**) *notice, list* afficher. (**b**) *(announce)* annoncer. *(Mil etc)* **to ~ sth/sb missing** porter qch/qn disparu. ◆ **poster** *n* affiche *f*; *(decorative)* poster *m*; **~er paint** gouache *f*.

post² [pəʊst] **1** *n* (**a**) *(Mil, gen)* poste *m*. **at one's ~** à son poste; *(bugle call)* **last ~** extinction *f* des feux; *(at funerals)* sonnerie *f* aux morts. (**b**) *(trading ~)* comptoir *m*. (**c**) *(job)* poste *m*. **a ~ as a manager** un poste de directeur. **2** *vt* (**a**) *sentry, guard* poster. (**b**) *(send) person* affecter (*to* à). (**c**) *(US)* **to ~ bail** déposer une caution.

post³ [pəʊst] **1** *n* poste *f*; *(letters)* courrier *m*. **by ~** par la poste; **by return of ~** par retour du courrier; **first-/second-class ~** ≃ tarif *m* normal/ réduit; **to put sth in the ~** poster qch; **it's in the ~** c'est déjà posté; **it went first ~ this morning** c'est parti ce matin par le premier courrier; **to catch/miss the ~** avoir/manquer la levée; **take this to the ~** portez ceci à la poste; **has the ~ come yet?** est-ce que le courrier est arrivé?; *(cost)* **~ and packing** frais *mpl* de port et d'emballage; **Ministry of P~s and Telecommunications** ministère *m* des Postes et Télécommunications. **2** *vt* (**a**) *(send)* envoyer par la poste; *(put in mailbox)* mettre à la poste, poster. **to ~ sth on** faire suivre qch. (**b**) *(fig)* **to keep sb ~ed** tenir qn au courant. ◆ **postage** *n* tarifs *mpl* postaux (*to* pour); *(in account)* **'~ age: £2'** 'frais *mpl* de port: 2 livres'; **~age due 20p** surtaxe *f* 20 pence; *(US)* **~age meter** machine *f* à affranchir. ◆ **postal** *adj district, code, charges* postal; *application* par la poste; *vote* par correspondance; *strike* des employés des postes; **~al order** mandat *m* (postal) (*for 10 francs* de 10 F); **~al worker** employé(e) *m(f)* des postes. ◆ **postbag** *n* sac *m* postal. ◆ **postbox** *n* boîte *f* aux lettres. ◆ **postcard** *n* carte *f* postale. ◆ **postcode** *n* code *m* postal. ◆ **poste restante** *n* poste *f* restante. ◆ **post-free** *adv* franco de port. ◆ **posthaste** *adv* le plus vite possible. ◆ **postmark** **1** *n* cachet *m* de la poste; **letter with a French ~mark** lettre timbrée de France ; **2** *vt* tamponner, timbrer; **it is ~marked Paris** il y a 'Paris' sur le cachet. ◆ **postmaster** *n* receveur *m* des postes; *(Brit)* **P~master General** ministre *m* des Postes et Télécommunications. ◆ **postmistress** *n* receveuse *f* des postes. ◆ **post office** **1** *n (place)* (bureau *m* de) poste *f*; *(organization)* service *m* des postes; **he works in the ~ office** il est employé des postes; **the main ~ office** la grande poste ; **2** *adj*: **P~ Office Box** (*abbr* **P.O. Box**) **24** boîte *f* postale nº 24 (*abbr* B.P. 24); *(US)* **P~ Office Department** ministère *m* des Postes et Télécommunications; **P~ Office Savings Bank** ≃ Caisse *f* d'Épargne.

post- [pəʊst] *pref* post-. **~-1950** *(adj)* postérieur à 1950, d'après 1950; *(adv)* après 1950. ◆ **postdate** *vt* postdater. ◆ **postgraduate** **1** *adj studies, grant* ≃ de troisième cycle (universitaire); *diploma* décerné après la licence ; **2** *n* ≃ étudiant(e) *m(f)* de 3ᵉ cycle. ◆ **post-impressionism** *n* post-impressionnisme *m*. ◆ **post-mortem** *n* autopsie *f* (*on* de). ◆ **postnatal** *adj* post-natal. ◆ **postwar** *adj* de l'après-guerre; **the ~war period** l'après-guerre *m*.

posterior [pɒs'tɪərɪəʳ] *adj* postérieur (*to* à). ◆ **posterity** *n* postérité *f*.

posthumous ['pɒstjʊməs] *adj* posthume. ◆ **posthumously** *adv (gen)* après sa *(etc)* mort; *award* à titre posthume.

postpone [pəʊs(t)'pəʊn] *vt* remettre (*for* de, *until* à); renvoyer (à plus tard). ◆ **postponement** *n* renvoi *m* (à plus tard).

postscript ['pəusskrɪpt] *n* post-scriptum *m inv*.

postulate ['pɒstjʊleɪt] *vt* poser comme principe; *(Philos)* postuler.

posture ['pɒstʃəʳ] **1** *n* posture *f*. **2** *vi (pej)* poser. ◆ **posturing** *n* pose *f*, affectation *f*.

posy ['pəʊzɪ] *n* petit bouquet *m* (de fleurs).

pot [pɒt] **1** *n* (**a**) *(for flowers, jam etc)* pot *m*; *(piece of pottery)* poterie *f*; *(for cooking)* marmite *f*; *(saucepan)* casserole *f*; *(tea ~)* théière *f*; *(coffee ~)* cafetière *f*; *(chamber ~)* pot (de chambre). **jam ~** pot à confiture; **~ of jam** pot de confiture; **~s and pans** casseroles; *(fig)* **~s of** * des tas * de; **to have ~s of money** * avoir un argent fou *; **to go to ~** * *[person]* se laisser complètement aller; *[business]* aller à la dérive; *[plans]* aller à vau-l'eau. (**b**) *(*: marijuana)* marie-jeanne * *f*. **2** *adj*: *(US)* **~ cheese** ≃ fromage blanc égoutté; **~ roast** rôti *m* braisé. **3** *vt* (**a**) *plant, jam* mettre en pot. **~ted meat** ≃ rillettes *fpl* de viande; **~ted plant** plante *f* verte; *(fig)* **a ~ted version of** un abrégé de. (**b**) *(*: shoot) pheasant etc* descendre *. (**c**) (*) *baby* mettre sur le pot. **4** *vi* (**a**) *(make pottery)* faire de la poterie. (**b**) *(shoot)* **to ~ at sth** tirer qch. ◆ **potbellied** *adj (from overeating)* bedonnant *; *(from malnutrition)* au ventre ballonné. ◆ **potbound** *adj plant* (trop) à l'étroit dans son pot. ◆ **potherbs** *npl* herbes *fpl* potagères. ◆ **pothole** *n (in road)* fondrière *f*; *(underground)* caverne *f*; *(larger)* gouffre *m*. ◆ **potholer** *n* spéléologue *mf*. ◆ **potholing** *n* spéléologie *f*; **to go ~holing** faire de la spéléologie. ◆ **potluck** *n*: **to take ~luck** *(for food)* manger à la fortune du pot; *(for other things)* courir le risque. ◆ **pot-scourer** *or* ◆ **pot-scrubber** *n* tampon *m* à récurer. ◆ **potsherd** *n* tesson *m* (de poterie). ◆ **potshot** *n*: **to take a ~shot at sth** tirer qch à vue de nez.

potash ['pɒtæʃ] *n* potasse *f*.

potassium [pə'tæsɪəm] *n* potassium *m*.

potato [pə'teɪtəʊ] **1** *n*, *pl* **~es** pomme *f* de terre. **sweet ~** patate *f* douce. **2** *adj field, salad* de pommes de terre. *(US)* **~ chips**, *(Brit)* **~ crisps** pommes *fpl* chips. ◆ **potato-peeler** *n* éplucheé-légumes *m inv*.

potent ['pəʊt(ə)nt] *adj (gen)* puissant; *drink* fort. ◆ **potency** *n* puissance *f*; *[drink]* forte teneur *f* en alcool.

potential [pə(ʊ)'tenʃ(ə)l] **1** *adj (gen)* potentiel; *sales, uses* possible, éventuel. **a ~ prime minister**

un premier ministre en puissance. **2** *n (Elec, Math, Mil etc)* potentiel *m*; *(fig: possibilities)* possibilités *fpl*. **to have** ~ *(gen)* être prometteur; *[building, land]* avoir toutes sortes de possibilités; **to have the** ~ **to do** être tout à fait capable de faire; **to have great** ~ être très prometteur; **he hasn't yet realized his full** ~ il n'a pas encore donné toute sa mesure. ◆ **potentially** *adv* potentiellement.

potpourri [pəʊ'pʊrɪ] *n [flowers]* fleurs *fpl* séchées; *(fig, Mus)* pot-pourri *m*.

potter[1] ['pɒtəʳ] *vi* mener sa petite vie tranquille, bricoler *. **to** ~ **(about) round the house** faire des petits travaux dans la maison; **to** ~ **round the shops** faire les magasins sans se presser.

potter[2] ['pɒtəʳ] *n* potier *m*. ~**'s wheel** tour *m* de potier. ◆ **pottery 1** *n (craft, place)* poterie *f*; *(objects)* poteries; **a piece of** ~**y** une poterie ; **2** *adj jug, dish* de *or* en terre.

potty[1] * ['pɒtɪ] *n* pot *m* (de bébé). ◆ **potty-trained** *adj* propre.

potty[2] * ['pɒtɪ] *adj person* toqué * (*about* de); *idea* farfelu.

pouch [paʊtʃ] *n* petit sac *m*; *(for money)* bourse *f*; *(for tobacco)* blague *f*; *(US Diplomacy)* valise *f* (diplomatique); *(Anat, Zool)* poche *f*.

pouf(fe) [pu:f] *n* (**a**) *(seat)* pouf *m*. (**b**) (*) = **poof**.

poultice ['pəʊltɪs] *n* cataplasme *m*.

poultry ['pəʊltrɪ] **1** *n* volaille *f*, volailles. **2** *adj*: ~ **dealer** marchand *m* de volailles; ~ **farm** élevage *m* de volailles; ~ **farmer** éleveur *m*, -euse *f* de volailles; ~ **farming** élevage *m* de volailles. ◆ **poulterer** *n* marchand *m* de volailles.

pounce [paʊns] **1** *n* bond *m*, attaque *f* subite. **2** *vi* bondir, sauter (*on* sur). *(fig)* **to** ~ **on** *object* se précipiter sur; *suggestion* sauter sur.

pound[1] [paʊnd] *n* (**a**) *(weight)* livre *f (= 453,6 grammes)*. **sold by the** ~ vendu à la livre; **80p a** ~ 80 pence la livre. (**b**) *(money)* livre *f*. ~ **sterling** livre sterling *(inv)*; ~ **note** billet *m* d'une livre.

pound[2] [paʊnd] **1** *vt drugs, spices, nuts* piler; *meat* attendrir; *dough* battre; *earth, paving slabs* pilonner; *rocks* concasser; *[guns, bombs]* pilonner; *[sea]* battre sans arrêt contre; *[person] door etc* marteler; *typewriter, piano* taper sur; *person* bourrer de coups. **to** ~ **the beat** *[policeman]* faire sa ronde; **to** ~ **sth to a pulp** réduire qch en bouillie. **2** *vi* (**a**) *[heart]* battre fort; *[drums]* battre; *[sea, waves]* battre (*on, against* contre). *[person]* **to** ~ **on** *door* marteler; *table* frapper (du poing) sur; *piano etc* taper sur. (**b**) **to** ~ **in** *etc* entrer *etc (heavily)* en martelant le plancher *or (at a run)* en courant bruyamment. ◆ **pounding** *n*: **to take a** ~**ing** *[boat]* être battu par les vagues; *[bombed etc city]* être pilonné; *[team]* se faire battre à plate couture.

pound[3] [paʊnd] *n (for dogs, cars)* fourrière *f*.

pour [pɔ:ʳ] **1** *vt liquid* verser. **to** ~ **water away** *or* **off** vider de l'eau; **he** ~**ed me a drink** il m'a versé *or* servi à boire; *(fig)* **to** ~ **money into a scheme** investir énormément d'argent dans un projet. **2** *vi* (**a**) *[water, blood etc]* ruisseler (*from* de). **to come** ~**ing in** *[water, sunshine]* entrer à flots; *[letters]* arriver en avalanche; *[people, cars]* arriver en masse; **smoke was** ~**ing from the chimney** des nuages de fumée s'échappaient de la cheminée; *(fig)* **goods are** ~**ing out of the factories** les usines déversent des quantités de marchandises. (**b**) **it is** ~**ing (with rain)** il pleut à torrents. ◆ **pour out** *vt sep drinks* verser, servir (*for sb* à qn); *dregs, unwanted liquid* vider; *(fig) anger, emotion* donner libre cours à; *troubles* épancher; *complaint* déverser; *story* raconter d'un seul jet. ◆ **pouring** *adj sauce etc* liquide; *rain* torrentiel; **a** ~**ing wet day** une journée de pluie torrentielle.

pout [paʊt] **1** *n* moue *f*. **2** *vi* faire la moue.

poverty ['pɒvətɪ] *n (gen)* pauvreté *f*. **to live in** ~ vivre dans le besoin; **extreme** ~ misère *f*; ~ **of resources** manque *m* de ressources; **below the** ~ **line** *or* **level** en dessous du seuil de pauvreté; **the** ~ **trap** *(Brit)* le dilemme du plafond des ressources. ◆ **poverty-stricken** *adj person, family* dans la misère; *district, conditions* misérable; *(hum: hard up)* fauché *.

powder ['paʊdəʳ] **1** *n* poudre *f*. **2** *adj*: ~ **compact** poudrier *m*; ~ **puff** houppette *f*; ~ **room** toilettes *fpl* (pour dames). **3** *vt* (**a**) *chalk, rocks* pulvériser. ~**ed milk** lait *m* en poudre; *(US)* ~**ed sugar** sucre *m* glace. (**b**) *face, body* poudrer. **to** ~ **one's nose** se mettre de la poudre; *(* fig: go to lavatory)* ≃ se refaire une beauté. ◆ **powdery** *adj substance, snow* poudreux; *surface* couvert de poudre.

power ['paʊəʳ] **1** *n* (**a**) *(ability, capacity)* pouvoir *m*, capacité *f*; *(faculty)* faculté *f*. **it is not within my** ~ **to help you** il n'est pas en mon pouvoir de vous aider; **he did everything in his** ~ **to help us** il a fait tout ce qui était en son pouvoir pour nous aider; **mental** ~**s** facultés mentales; **the** ~ **of movement** la faculté de se mouvoir; **he lost the** ~ **of speech** il a perdu la parole; ~**s of persuasion** pouvoir de persuasion; ~**s of resistance** capacité de résistance; ~**s of imagination** faculté d'imagination.

(**b**) *(force) [person, blow, sun, explosion]* puissance *f*, force *f*; *[engine, telescope etc]* puissance; *(energy)* énergie *f*. **it works by nuclear** ~ ça fonctionne à l'énergie nucléaire; *(Elec)* **they cut off the** ~ ils ont coupé le courant; *(Elec)* **consumption of** ~ consommation *f* d'électricité; **engines at half** ~ moteurs à mi-régime; **the ship returned under her own** ~ le navire est rentré par ses propres moyens; **sea/air** ~ puissance navale/aérienne.

(**c**) *(authority)* pouvoir *m (also Pol)*, autorité *f*. **student** ~ le pouvoir des étudiants; **that is beyond my** ~**(s)** ceci ne relève pas de ma compétence; **at the height of his** ~ à l'apogée de son pouvoir; **the** ~ **of veto** le droit de veto; *(Jur)* **the** ~ **of attorney** la procuration; *(Pol)* **in** ~ au pouvoir; **to come to** ~ accéder au pouvoir; **to have** ~ **over sb** avoir autorité sur qn; **to have sb in one's** ~ avoir qn en son pouvoir; **to fall into sb's** ~ tomber au pouvoir de qn; **they are the real** ~ ce sont eux qui détiennent le pouvoir réel; *(fig)* **the** ~ **behind the throne** celui (*or* celle) qui tire les ficelles; **a** ~ **in the land** un homme très puissant; **the** ~**s of darkness/evil** les forces *fpl* des ténèbres/du mal; **the** ~**s that be** les autorités constituées; **the world** ~**s** les puissances mondiales; **it did me a** ~ **of good** * ça m'a fait un bien immense.

(**d**) *(Math)* puissance *f*. **5 to the** ~ **of 3** 5 puissance 3.

2 *adj* (**a**) *saw, loom, lathe* mécanique; *(Aut) brakes, steering* assisté. (**b**) *(Elec) cable* électrique; *line* à haute tension. ~ **cut** coupure *f* de courant; ~ **pack** bloc *m* d'alimentation (électrique); ~ **plant** *(building)* centrale *f* (électrique); *(in vehicle)* groupe *m* moteur; ~ **point** prise *f* de courant; ~ **station** centrale *f* (électrique *or* nucléaire). ~ **workers** travailleurs *mpl* des centrales. (**c**) ~ **base** base *f* politique; ~ **broker** éminence *f* grise; **they are engaged in** ~ **politics** ils manœuvrent pour s'assurer une place prépondérante; ~ **structure** répartition *f* des pouvoirs.

3 *vt* faire fonctionner; *(propel)* propulser. ~**ed by nuclear energy, nuclear-**~**ed** qui fonctionne à l'énergie nucléaire; ~**ed by jet engines** propulsé par des moteurs à réaction.

◆ **power-assisted** *adj* assisté. ◆ **powerboat** *n* hors-bord *m inv*. ◆ **power-driven** *adj* à moteur; *(Elec)* électrique. ◆ **powerful** *adj* puissant. ◆ **powerfully** *adv hit, strike* avec force; *affect* fortement; *write etc* puissamment; **to be** ~**fully built** avoir une carrure puissante. ◆ **powerhouse** *n*

(Elec) centrale *f* électrique; *(fig)* personne *f etc* très dynamique; **a ~house of new ideas** une mine d'idées nouvelles. ◆ **powerless** *adj* impuissant (*to do* à faire). ◆ **powerlessly** *adv* impuissamment. ◆ **power-sharing** *n (Pol)* partage *m* du pouvoir.

practicable ['præktɪkəbl] *adj* praticable. ◆ **practicability** *n [road, path]* praticabilité *f*; *[scheme, suggestion]* possibilité *f* de réalisation.

practical ['præktɪk(ə)l] **1** *adj (gen)* pratique. **~ joke** farce *f*; **for all ~ purposes** en réalité; **he's very ~** il a beaucoup de sens pratique. **2** *n (exam)* épreuve *f* pratique. ◆ **practicality** *n [person]* sens *m* pratique; *[scheme, suggestion]* aspect *m* pratique; **~ities** détails *mpl* pratiques. ◆ **practically** *adv (in a practical way)* d'une manière pratique; *say, suggest* d'une manière pragmatique; *(in practice)* dans la pratique; *(almost)* pratiquement.

practice ['præktɪs] **1** *n* (**a**) *(habits, usage)* pratique *f*, usage *m*. **to make a ~ of doing** avoir l'habitude de faire; **it's common ~** c'est courant. (**b**) *(exercise, training)* entraînement *m*; *(rehearsal)* répétition *f*. **target ~** exercices *mpl* de tir; **he does 6 hours' piano ~ a day** il fait 6 heures de piano par jour; **out of ~** rouillé *(fig)*; **~ makes perfect** c'est en forgeant qu'on devient forgeron. (**c**) *(as opp to theory)* pratique *f*. **in(to) ~** en pratique. (**d**) *[doctor, lawyer]* **to be in ~** exercer; **to go into ~ as a doctor** s'établir docteur; **he has a large ~** il a un cabinet important. **2** *adj flight, run* d'entraînement. **~ exam** examen blanc. **3** *vti (US)* = **practise.**

practise ['præktɪs] **1** *vt* (**a**) *(put into practice) charity, one's religion* pratiquer; *method* employer. **to ~ medicine/law** exercer la profession de médecin/d'avocat; **to ~ what one preaches** mettre en pratique ce que l'on prêche. (**b**) *(exercise)* s'entraîner, s'exercer (*doing* à faire); *sport* s'entraîner à; *violin etc* s'exercer à; *song, recitation* travailler; *(Mus) scales* faire. **I'm practising my German on him** je m'exerce à parler allemand avec lui.
2 *vi* (**a**) *(Mus)* s'exercer; *(Sport)* s'entraîner; *[beginner]* faire des exercices. **he ~s for 2 hours every day** il fait 2 heures d'entraînement (*or* d'exercices) par jour. (**b**) *[doctor, lawyer]* exercer.
◆ **practised, (US) practiced** *adj teacher, nurse, soldier* expérimenté; *eye, ear* exercé; *movement* expert. ◆ **practising, (US) practicing** *adj doctor* exerçant; *lawyer* en exercice; *Catholic, Buddhist* pratiquant; *homosexual etc* actif. ◆ **practitioner** *n (of an art)* praticien *m*, -ienne *f*; *(Med)* médecin *m*.

pragmatic [præg'mætɪk] *adj* pragmatique.

Prague [prɑ:g] *n* Prague.

prairie ['prɛərɪ] *n* plaine *f* (herbeuse). *(US)* **the ~(s)** la Grande Prairie.

praise [preɪz] **1** *n* éloge *m*. **in ~ of** à la louange de; **to speak (or write etc) in ~ of sb/sth** faire l'éloge de qn/qch; **I have nothing but ~ for what he has done** je ne peux que le louer de ce qu'il a fait; **a hymn of ~** un cantique; **~ be to God!** Dieu soit loué!; **~ be! *** Dieu merci! **2** *vt* louer (*sb for sth/for doing* qn de qch/d'avoir fait). **to ~ sb to the skies** porter qn aux nues. ◆ **praiseworthy** *adj* digne d'éloges.

pram [præm] *n (Brit)* voiture *f* d'enfant.

prance [prɑ:ns] *vi [horse, dancer etc]* caracoler. **to ~ in/out** *etc* entrer/sortir *etc (arrogantly)* en se pavanant *or (gaily)* gaiement.

prank [præŋk] *n (escapade)* frasque *f*; *(joke)* farce *f*, tour *m*. **a childish ~** une gaminerie; **to play a ~ on sb** jouer un tour à qn.

prattle ['prætl] *vi* babiller; *[several people]* papoter.

prawn [prɔ:n] *n* crevette *f* rose, bouquet *m*. **~ cocktail** salade *f* de crevettes.

pray [preɪ] **1** *vi* prier (*for sb* pour qn). **they ~ed to God to help them** ils prièrent Dieu de les secourir; **he ~ed for forgiveness/to die** il pria Dieu de lui pardonner/de le laisser mourir; **we're ~ing for fine weather** nous faisons des prières pour qu'il fasse beau; **he's past ~ing for *** c'est un cas désespéré. **2** *vt* prier (*sb to do* qn de faire; *that* que + *subj*). ◆ **prayer 1** *n* prière *f*; **to say one's ~ers** faire sa prière; *(as service)* **~ers** office *m* ; **2** *adj*: **~er beads** chapelet *m;* **~er book** livre *m* de messe; **the P~er Book** le rituel de l'Église anglicane; **~er mat** tapis *m* de prière; **~er meeting** réunion *f* de prière.

pre- [pri:] *pref* pré-. **~-1950** *(adj)* antérieur à 1950, d'avant 1950; *(adv)* avant 1950. ◆ **prearrange** *vt* fixer à l'avance. ◆ **precool** *vt* refroidir d'avance. ◆ **pre-establish** *vt* préétablir. ◆ **prefaded** *adj jeans* délavé.

preach [pri:tʃ] **1** *vi* prêcher. **to ~ to sb** prêcher qn; *(fig)* **to ~ to the converted** prêcher un converti. **2** *vt (gen)* prêcher; *sermon* faire. ◆ **preacher** *n* prédicateur *m*; *(US: clergyman)* pasteur *m*.

preamble [pri:'æmbl] *n* préambule *m*.

precarious [prɪ'kɛərɪəs] *adj* précaire. ◆ **precariously** *adv* précairement.

precast ['pri:'kɑ:st] *adj*: **~ concrete** béton *m* précoulé.

precaution [prɪ'kɔ:ʃ(ə)n] *n* précaution *f* (*against* contre). **as a ~** par précaution; **to take ~s** prendre ses précautions; **to take the ~ of doing** prendre la précaution de faire. ◆ **precautionary** *adj measure* de précaution.

precede [prɪ'si:d] *vt (in space, time)* précéder ; *(in rank)* avoir la préséance sur. ◆ **precedence** ['presɪd(ə)ns] *n (in rank)* préséance *f*; *(in importance)* priorité *f*; **to take precedence over** *person* avoir la préséance sur; *event, problem, need* avoir la priorité sur. ◆ **precedent** *n* précédent *m*; **to form** *or* **create a precedent** constituer un précédent. ◆ **preceding** *adj* précédent.

precept ['pri:sept] *n* précepte *m*.

precinct ['pri:sɪŋ(k)'t] *n* (**a**) *(round cathedral etc)* enceinte *f*. *(neighbourhood)* **~s** alentours *mpl*; *(fig)* **within the ~s of** dans les limites de. (**b**) *(US: Police, Pol)* circonscription *f*. **~ captain** *(Pol)* responsable *mf* politique de quartier; *(Police)* ≃ commissaire *m* (de police) de quartier.

precious ['preʃəs] **1** *adj* précieux. **~ stone** pierre *f* précieuse; **(my) ~!** mon trésor!; *(iro)* **your ~ son *** ton fils chéri *(iro)*. **2** *adv* (*) **~ few, ~ little** très peu.

precipice ['presɪpɪs] *n* à-pic *m inv*. **to fall over a ~** tomber dans un précipice.

precipitate [prɪ'sɪpɪteɪt] **1** *vt (gen, Chem)* précipiter; *(Met)* condenser. **2** *adj* hâtif. ◆ **precipitately** *adv* précipitamment.

precipitous [prɪ'sɪpɪtəs] *adj* (**a**) *slope* escarpé, à pic. (**b**) *(hasty)* hâtif. ◆ **precipitously** *adv* à pic.

précis ['preɪsi:] *n* résumé *m*.

precise [prɪ'saɪs] *adj* (**a**) *(gen)* précis; *measurement, meaning, account* exact, précis. **there were 8 to be ~** il y en avait 8 pour être exact *or* précis; **that ~ book** ce livre même; **at that ~ moment** à ce moment précis. (**b**) *(meticulous) movement* précis; *person, manner* minutieux; *(pej: over-~)* pointilleux. **in that ~ voice of hers** de sa façon de parler si nette. ◆ **precisely** *adv explain* avec précision; *(exactly)* précisément; **at 10 o'clock ~ly** à 10 heures précises; **what ~ly does he do for a living?** que fait-il au juste pour gagner sa vie? ◆ **precision 1** *n* précision *f*; exactitude *f*; minutie *f*; **2** *adj instrument, bombing* de précision. ◆ **precision-made** *adj* de haute précision.

preclude [prɪ'klu:d] *vt doubt* écarter; *misunderstanding* prévenir; *possibility* exclure. **to be ~d from doing** être dans l'impossibilité de faire; **that**

~s his leaving cela le met dans l'impossibilité de partir.

precocious [prɪ'kəʊʃəs] *adj* précoce. ◆ **precociously** *adv* précocement. ◆ **precociousness** *or* ◆ **precocity** *n* précocité *f*.

preconceived ['pri:kən'si:vd] *adj* préconçu. ◆ **preconception** *n* préconception *f*.

precondition ['pri:kən'dɪʃ(ə)n] *n* condition *f* requise.

precook [pri:'kʊk] *vt* faire cuire à l'avance. ◆ **precooked** *adj* précuit.

precursor [pri:'kɜ:səʳ] *n (person, thing)* précurseur *m*; *(event)* signe *m* avant-coureur.

predate ['pri:'deɪt] *vt (put earlier date on)* antidater; *(come before in time)* précéder.

predator ['predətəʳ] *n* prédateur *m*. ◆ **predatory** *adj animal etc* prédateur; *habits* de prédateur; *person* rapace; *armies* pillard; *look* vorace.

predecease ['pri:dɪ'si:s] *vt* prédécéder.

predecessor ['pri:dɪsesəʳ] *n* prédécesseur *m*.

predestine [pri:'destɪn] *vt* prédestiner (*to* à; *to do* à faire). ◆ **predestination** *n* prédestination *f*.

predetermine ['pri:dɪ'tɜ:mɪn] *vt* déterminer d'avance; *(Philos, Rel)* prédéterminer.

predicament [prɪ'dɪkəmənt] *n* situation *f* difficile *or* fâcheuse. **I'm in a real** ~ *(puzzled)* je ne sais vraiment pas que faire; *(in a fix)* me voilà dans de beaux draps.

predicative [prɪ'dɪkətɪv] *adj (Gram)* prédicatif. ◆ **predicatively** *adv* en tant que prédicat.

predict [prɪ'dɪkt] *vt* prédire. ◆ **predictable** *adj* prévisible. ◆ **predictably** *adv behave etc* d'une manière prévisible; **~ably, he did not appear** comme on pouvait le prévoir, il ne s'est pas montré. ◆ **prediction** *n* prédiction *f*.

predigested [,pri:daɪ'dʒestɪd] *adj* prédigéré.

predilection [,pri:dɪ'lekʃ(ə)n] *n* prédilection *f* (*for* pour).

predispose ['pri:dɪs'pəʊz] *vt* prédisposer (*to sth* à qch; *to do* à faire). ◆ **predisposition** *n* prédisposition *f*.

predominate [prɪ'dɒmɪneɪt] *vi* prédominer (*over* sur). ◆ **predominance** *n* prédominance *f*. ◆ **predominant** *adj* prédominant. ◆ **predominantly** *adv* surtout.

pre-eminent [pri:'emɪnənt] *adj* prééminent. ◆ **pre-eminence** *n* prééminence *f*. ◆ **pre-eminently** *adv* avant tout.

pre-empt [pri:'empt] *vt decision, action* anticiper, devancer; *sb's statement* empiéter sur. ◆ **pre-emptive** *adj attack* préventif.

preen [pri:n] *vt [bird]* lisser. *(fig)* **to ~ o.s.** *(before mirror etc)* se pomponner; *(be proud)* s'enorgueillir (*on* de).

prefabricate [,pri:'fæbrɪkeɪt] *vt* préfabriquer. ◆ **prefab** * *n* maison *etc* préfabriquée.

preface ['prefɪs] *n (to book)* préface *f*; *(to speech)* introduction *f*.

prefect ['pri:fekt] *n (French Admin)* préfet *m*; *(Brit Scol) élève des grandes classes chargé(e) de la discipline*. ◆ **prefecture** *n* préfecture *f*.

prefer [prɪ'fɜ:ʳ] *vt* (**a**) préférer, aimer mieux (*doing, to do* faire). **to ~ A to B** préférer A à B, aimer mieux A que B; **I ~ taking the train to going by car** je préfère prendre le train que d'aller en voiture; **I ~ you to leave** je préfère que vous partiez *(subj)*; **I much ~** je préfère de beaucoup. (**b**) *(Jur) charge* porter; *action* intenter; *complaint* déposer. ◆ **preferable** ['pref(ə)rəbl] *adj* préférable (*to sth* à qch). ◆ **preferably** *adv* de préférence. ◆ **preference 1** *n (liking)* préférence *f* (*for* pour); *(priority)* priorité *f* (*over* sur); **in ~ence to sth/to doing** plutôt que qch/que de faire ; **2** *adj*: **~ence shares** actions *fpl* privilégiées. ◆ **preferential** *adj* préférentiel.

prefix ['pri:fɪks] **1** *n* préfixe *m*. **2** *vt* préfixer.

pregnant ['pregnənt] *adj woman* enceinte; *animal* pleine; *(fig) silence* lourd de sens. **3 months ~** enceinte de 3 mois; *(fig)* **~ with** gros de. ◆ **pregnancy** *n [woman]* grossesse *f*.

prehistory ['pri:'hɪst(ə)rɪ] *n* préhistoire *f*. ◆ **prehistoric** *adj* préhistorique.

prejudge ['pri:'dʒʌdʒ] *vt question* préjuger de; *person* juger d'avance.

prejudice ['predʒʊdɪs] **1** *n* (**a**) préjugé *m*; *(collective n)* préjugés. **racial ~** préjugés raciaux; **to have a ~ against** avoir un préjugé contre. (**b**) *(Jur)* préjudice *m*. **without ~** sans préjudice (*to* de). **2** *vt* (**a**) *person* prévenir (*against* contre). (**b**) *(also Jur) claim, chance* porter préjudice à. ◆ **prejudiced** *adj person* plein de préjugés; *idea* préconçu; **to be ~d against/in favour of** avoir un préjugé contre/en faveur de. ◆ **prejudicial** *adj* préjudiciable (*to* à).

prelate ['prelɪt] *n* prélat *m*.

preliminary [prɪ'lɪmɪn(ə)rɪ] *adj, n* préliminaire *(m)*.

prelude ['prelju:d] *n* prélude *m* (*to* de).

premarital ['pri:'mærɪtl] *adj* avant le mariage.

premature ['premətʃʊəʳ] *adj (gen)* prématuré. **you are a little ~** vous anticipez un peu. ◆ **prematurely** *adv (gen)* prématurément; *be born* avant terme.

premeditate [pri:'medɪteɪt] *vt* préméditer. ◆ **premeditation** *n* préméditation *f*.

premenstrual ['pri:'menstrʊəl] *adj*: **~ tension** syndrome *m* prémenstruel.

premier ['premɪəʳ] **1** *adj* premier, primordial. **2** *n (Pol)* Premier ministre *m*.

première ['premɪɛəʳ] *n* première *f (Theat)*.

premise ['premɪs] *n* (**a**) *(hypothesis)* prémisse *f*. (**b**) *(property)* **~s** locaux *mpl*; **business ~s** locaux commerciaux; **on/off the ~s** sur les/hors des lieux; **to see sb off the ~s** escorter qn jusqu'à sa sortie des lieux.

premium ['pri:mɪəm] **1** *n* (**a**) *prime f*. **to be at a ~** faire prime; **to put a ~ on** *[person]* faire grand cas de; *[situation, event]* donner beaucoup d'importance à. (**b**) *(US: gasoline)* super (carburant) *m*. **2** *adj*: **~ bond** bon *m* à lots.

premonition [,pri:mə'nɪʃ(ə)n] *n* pressentiment *m*.

prenatal ['pri:'neɪtl] *adj* prénatal.

preoccupy [pri:'ɒkjʊpaɪ] *vt* préoccuper. ◆ **preoccupation** *n (gen)* préoccupation *f*; **his preoccupation with money** son obsession *f* de l'argent.

prep * [prep] *(Scol) abbr of* **preparation, preparatory.**

prepack(age) ['pri:'pæk(ɪdʒ)] *vt (Comm)* préconditionner.

prepaid ['pri:'peɪd] *adj* payé d'avance; *reply, carriage* payé.

prepare [prɪ'pɛəʳ] **1** *vt* préparer (*sth for sb* qch à qn; *sth for sth* qch pour qch; *sb for a shock/exam/piece of news* qn à un choc/un examen/une nouvelle; *sb for an operation* qn pour une opération). **to ~ the way/ground for sth** préparer la voie/le terrain pour qch.

2 *vi*: **to ~ for** *(make arrangements) journey, sb's arrival, event* faire des préparatifs pour; *(~ o.s. for) flood, meeting* se préparer pour; *war* se préparer à; *examination* préparer; **to ~ to do sth** se préparer à faire qch. ◆ **preparation** *n* (**a**) préparation *f*; **preparations** préparatifs *mpl* (*for* de); **in preparation** en préparation; **in preparation for** en vue de; (**b**) *(Scol)* devoirs *mpl*. ◆ **preparatory** *adj work* préparatoire; *measure, step* préliminaire; **preparatory school** *(Brit)* école *f* primaire privée; *(US)* lycée *m* privé; **preparatory to sth/to doing** avant qch/de faire. ◆ **prepared** *adj person, army, country* prêt; *statement, answer* préparé à l'avance; *(Culin) sauce, soup* tout prêt; **be ~d for bad news** préparez-vous à une mauvaise nouvelle; **I am ~d for anything** *(can cope)* j'ai tout prévu; *(won't be surprised)* je m'attends à tout; **to be ~d to do sth** être prêt à faire qch. ◆ **preparedness** *n* état *m* de préparation.

preponderance [prɪ'pɒnd(ə)r(ə)ns] *n (in numbers)* supériorité *f* numérique; *(in influence, weight)* prépondérance *f*. ◆ **preponderant** *adj* prépondérant. ◆ **preponderantly** *adv* surtout.

preposition ['prepə'zɪʃ(ə)n] *n* préposition *f*.

prepossessing [,priːpə'zesɪŋ] *adj appearance* avenant. **he is very** ~ il fait très bonne impression; **a very** ~ **young man** un jeune homme très bien *.

preposterous [prɪ'pɒst(ə)rəs] *adj* ridicule. ◆ **preposterously** *adv* ridiculement.

preppy ['prepɪ] *(US)* **1** *adj* bon chic bon genre. **2** *n* étudiant(e) *m(f)* d'une boîte * privée.

preprogrammed [priː'prəʊgræmd] *adj* programmé à l'avance.

prerecord ['priːrɪ'kɔːd] *vt song, programme* enregistrer à l'avance. **a ~ed broadcast** une émission en différé.

prerequisite ['priː'rekwɪzɪt] *n* condition *f* préalable.

prerogative [prɪ'rɒgətɪv] *n* prérogative *f*.

Presbyterian [,prezbɪ'tɪərɪən] *adj, n* presbytérien(ne) *m(f)*.

preschool ['priː'skuːl] *adj years* préscolaire; *child* d'âge préscolaire. ~ **playgroup** ≃ garderie *f*.

prescribe [prɪs'kraɪb] *vt (gen, Med)* prescrire *(sth for sb* qch pour qn). ◆ **prescribed** *adj (gen, Jur, Med)* prescrit; **~d books** œuvres *fpl* inscrites au programme. ◆ **prescription** **1** *n (Med)* ordonnance *f*; **to make out a prescription for sb** faire une ordonnance pour qn; **to make up** *or (US)* **fill a prescription** exécuter une ordonnance; **it's on prescription only** on ne peut l'obtenir que sur ordonnance ; **2** *adj (Brit Med)* **prescription charges** *somme fixe à payer lors de l'exécution de l'ordonnance.*

present ['preznt] **1** *adj* (**a**) *(there; in existence)* présent. **to be ~ at sth** être présent à qch, assister à qch; **who was ~?** qui était là?; **is there a doctor ~?** y a-t-il un docteur ici? (**b**) *(existing now: also Gram) year, circumstances* présent. **her ~ husband** son mari actuel; **at the ~ day** *or* **time** actuellement, à présent; *(Gram)* ~ **perfect** passé *m* composé.

2 *n* (**a**) *(~ time)* présent *m*. **up to the ~** jusqu'à présent; **for the ~** pour le moment; **at ~** actuellement, à présent, en ce moment; **as things are at ~** dans l'état actuel des choses; *(Gram)* **in the ~** au présent. (**b**) *(gift)* cadeau *m*. **she gave me the book as a ~** elle m'a offert le livre; **to make sb a ~ of sth** faire cadeau de qch à qn.

3 [prɪ'zent] *vt* (**a**) *(hand over etc: gen)* présenter *(to* à); *proof, evidence* fournir; *(Jur etc) case* exposer. **to ~ sb with sth, to ~ sth to sb** *(give as gift)* offrir qch à qn, faire cadeau de qch à qn; *(hand over) prize, medal* remettre qch à qn; **we were ~ed with a fait accompli** nous nous sommes trouvés devant un fait accompli; *(Mil)* **to ~ arms** présenter les armes; **to ~ o.s. at the desk/for an interview** se présenter au bureau/à une entrevue. (**b**) *(offer) problem, difficulties, features* présenter; *opportunity* donner. **it ~ed an easy target** cela offrait une cible facile. (**c**) *play, concert* donner; *film, (Rad, TV) play, programme* donner, passer; *(act as presenter of)* présenter. (**d**) *(introduce)* présenter *(sb to sb* qn à qn). **may I ~...?** permettez moi de vous présenter... ◆ **presence** *n* présence *f*; **presence of mind** présence d'esprit; **in the presence of** en présence de; **police presence** présence policière; **he certainly made his presence felt** * sa présence n'est vraiment pas passée inaperçue. ◆ **presentable** [prɪ'zentəbl] *adj* présentable. ◆ **presentation** [,prezən'teɪʃ(ə)n] *n* (**a**) *(gen)* présentation *f*; **on ~ation of** *ticket etc* sur présentation de; (**b**) *(gift)* cadeau *m*; *(ceremony)* ≃ vin *m* d'honneur; **who made the ~ation?** qui a remis le cadeau *(or* la médaille *etc*)?; (**c**) *(Univ etc)* exposé *m* oral. ◆ **present-day** *adj* actuel, d'aujourd'hui. ◆ **presenter** [prɪ'zentəʳ] *n (Rad, TV)* présentateur *m*, -trice *f*. ◆ **presently** *adv (in a little while)* tout à l'heure; *(+ vb in past)* au bout d'un certain temps; *(esp US: now)* à présent.

presentiment [prɪ'zentɪmənt] *n* pressentiment *m*.

preserve [prɪ'zɜːv] **1** *vt* (**a**) *(keep, maintain) building, traditions* conserver; *leather, wood* entretenir; *memory, dignity, sense of humour, reputation, silence* garder; *peace* maintenir. **well-~d** en bon état de conservation; *(hum) person* bien conservé (pour son âge). (**b**) *(from harm etc)* préserver *(from* de). ~ **me from that!** * le ciel m'en préserve! (**c**) *(Culin) fruit etc* conserver, mettre en conserve. **~d** en conserve. **2** *n* (**a**) **~s** *(jam)* confiture *f*; *(bottled fruit/vegetables)* fruits *mpl*/légumes *mpl* en conserve. (**b**) **that's his ~** c'est son domaine particulier. ◆ **preservation** *n* conservation *f*; *(from harm)* préservation *f*; **to put a preservation order on a building** classer un édifice. ◆ **preservationist** *n* défenseur *m* de l'environnement. ◆ **preservative** *n (Culin)* agent *m* de conservation.

preset ['priː'set] *vt pret, ptp* **preset** réglé à l'avance.

preshrunk ['priː'ʃrʌŋk] *adj* irrétrécissable.

preside [prɪ'zaɪd] *vi* présider. **to ~ at** *or* **over sth** présider qch.

president ['prezɪd(ə)nt] *n (Pol etc)* président *m*; *(US Comm)* président-directeur général, P.D.G. *m*. ◆ **presidency** *n* présidence *f*. ◆ **presidential** *adj (gen)* présidentiel; *staff* du Président.

press [pres] **1** *n (apparatus, machine: gen)* presse *f*; *(for wine, olives, cheese etc)* pressoir *m*; *(newspapers collectively)* presse. **in the ~** *(being printed)* sous presse; *(in the papers)* dans la presse; **to go to ~** être mis sous presse; **the national ~** la grande presse; **a member of the ~** un(e) journaliste; **to get a good/bad ~** avoir bonne/mauvaise presse. **2** *adj campaign, card, agency etc* de presse. ~ **agent** agent *m* de publicité; ~ **attaché** attaché(e) *m(f)* de presse; ~ **box**, *(Parl)* ~ **gallery** tribune *f* de la presse; ~ **conference** conférence *f* de presse; ~ **cutting** coupure *f* de presse; **~-cutting agency** argus *m* de la presse; ~ **photographer** reporter *m* photographe; ~ **release** communiqué *m* de presse; ~ **report** reportage *m*; *(US)* ~ **secretary** porte-parole *m*. **3** *vt* (**a**) *(push) button, switch, trigger* appuyer sur; *(squeeze etc) grapes, lemons, flowers, sb's hand* presser. **he ~ed them together** il les a pressés les uns contre les autres; **he ~ed his nose against the window** il a collé son nez à la fenêtre; **he ~ed her to him** il l'a serrée contre lui. (**b**) *clothes etc* repasser, donner un coup de fer à. (**c**) *(fig) attack, advantage* pousser; *claim, demand* renouveler; *opponent* presser; *[creditor]* poursuivre. **to ~ sb for an answer** presser qn de répondre; **to ~ a gift on sb** presser qn d'accepter un cadeau; **to ~ sb to do sth** presser qn de faire qch; **to ~ sb into doing sth** forcer qn à faire qch; **we were ~ed into service** nous avons été obligés d'offrir nos services; *(Jur)* **to ~ charges against sb** engager des poursuites contre qn; **I shan't ~ the point** je n'insisterai pas. **4** *vi [person]* appuyer *(on* sur); *[weight, burden]* faire pression *(on* sur); *[debts, troubles]* peser *(on sb* à qn). **time ~es!** le temps presse!; *(fig)* **to ~ for sth/for sth to be done** faire pression pour obtenir qch/pour que qch soit fait; **he ~ed through the crowd** il s'est frayé un chemin dans la foule; **they ~ed round his car** ils se pressaient autour de sa voiture.

◆**press down** **1** *vi* appuyer (*on* sur). **2** *vt sep* appuyer sur. ◆**press on** *vi (in work, journey etc)* continuer. *(fig)* **to ~ on with sth** continuer (à faire) qch.

◆**press-button** *n* bouton(-pression) *m.* ◆**pressed** *adj (very busy)* débordé (de travail); **to be ~ed for sth** être à court de qch, manquer de qch. ◆**press-gang** *vt*: **to ~-gang sb into doing sth** forcer la main à qn pour qu'il fasse qch. ◆**pressing** **1** *adj business, problem* urgent; *danger, invitation* pressant; **he was very ~ing** il a beaucoup insisté ; **2** *n [clothes]* repassage *m.* ◆**pressman** *n* journaliste *m.* ◆**press stud** *n* pression *f.* ◆**press-up** *n* traction *f.*

pressure ['preʃəʳ] **1** *n* pression *f.* **water ~** pression de l'eau; **a ~ of 2 kg to the square cm** une pression de 2 kg par cm²; **blood ~** pression artérielle; **high-/low-~** *(adj: Tech)* à pression haute/basse; *(Tech)* **at full ~** à pression maxima; **because of parental ~** à cause de la pression des parents; **to put ~ on sth/sb** faire pression sur qch/qn (*to do* pour qu'il fasse); **they're putting the ~ on now** ils nous *(etc)* talonnent maintenant; **under ~ from his staff** sous la pression de son personnel; **to use ~ to obtain sth** user de contrainte pour obtenir qch; **the ~ of these events** la tension créée par ces événements; **~ of work prevented him from going** il n'a pas pu y aller parce qu'il avait trop de travail; **he is under a lot of ~** il est sous pression. **2** *adj spacesuit, cabin* pressurisé. **~ group** groupe *m* de pression. **3** *vt*: **to ~ * sb to do** faire pression sur qn pour qu'il fasse; **to ~ sb * into doing** forcer qn à faire. ◆**pressure cooker** *n* cocotte-minute *f* ®. ◆**pressure gauge** *n* manomètre *m.* ◆**pressurization** *n* pressurisation *f.* ◆**pressurize** *vt* (**a**) *cabin, spacesuit* pressuriser; (**b**) *(* fig)* = **pressure 3.**

prestige [pres'ti:ʒ] **1** *n* prestige *m.* **2** *adj* de prestige. ◆**prestigious** *adj* prestigieux.

presume [prɪ'zju:m] **1** *vt (suppose)* présumer (*that* que); *(take liberty)* se permettre (*to do* de faire). **2** *vi* prendre des libertés. **to ~ (up)on** abuser de. ◆**presumably** *adv*: **you are presumably his son** je suppose *or* présume que vous êtes son fils. ◆**presumption** *n* (**a**) *(supposition)* présomption *f*; **there is a strong presumption that** tout laisse à présumer que; (**b**) *(presumptuousness)* présomption *f*, audace *f.* ◆**presumptuous** *adj* présomptueux. ◆**presumptuously** *adv* présomptueusement.

presuppose [ˌpri:sə'pəʊz] *vt* présupposer. ◆**presupposition** *n* présupposition *f.*

pretax [ˌpri:'tæks] *adj* avant impôts.

pretence, *(US)* **pretense** [prɪ'tens] *n (pretext)* prétexte *m*; *(claim)* prétention *f*; *(affectation)* prétention. **under** *or* **on the ~ of (doing) sth** sous prétexte de (faire) qch; **to make a ~ of doing** faire semblant de faire; **it's all (a) ~** tout cela est pure comédie; **his ~ of sympathy** sa feinte sympathie.

pretend [prɪ'tend] **1** *vt* (**a**) *(feign)* faire semblant (*to do* de faire; *that* que); *ignorance, illness* feindre. **let's ~ we're soldiers** jouons aux soldats; *(pej)* **he was ~ing to be a doctor** il se faisait passer pour un docteur. (**b**) *(claim)* prétendre (*that* que; *to do* de faire). **2** *vi (feign)* faire semblant. **I was only ~ing!** je plaisantais!; **let's stop ~ing!** assez joué la comédie! **3** *adj* (*) *money, house etc* pour rire *. ◆**pretended** *adj* prétendu. ◆**pretender** *n* prétendant(e) *m(f)* (*to the throne* au trône). ◆**pretension** *n* prétention *f* (*to* à). ◆**pretentious** *adj* prétentieux. ◆**pretentiously** *adv* prétentieusement. ◆**pretentiousness** *n* prétention *f.*

preterite ['pret(ə)rɪt] *n* prétérit *m*, passé *m* simple.

pretext ['pri:tekst] *n* prétexte *m* (*to do* pour faire). **under** *or* **on the ~ of (doing) sth** sous prétexte de (faire) qch.

pretty ['prɪtɪ] **1** *adj (gen)* joli *(before n).* **as ~ as a picture** *person* joli à croquer; *garden etc* ravissant; **it wasn't a ~ sight** ce n'était pas beau à voir; *(to parrot)* **~ polly!** bonjour Jacquot!; **it will cost a ~ penny** cela coûtera une jolie somme. **2** *adv* assez. **~ well** *(not badly)* pas mal; *(also* **~ nearly**: *almost)* presque, pratiquement; **~ much the same thing** pratiquement la même chose. ◆**prettily** *adv* joliment. ◆**pretty-pretty** * *adj* un peu trop joli.

pretzel ['pretsl] *n* bretzel *m.*

prevail [prɪ'veɪl] *vi* (**a**) *(win)* prévaloir (*against* contre; *over* sur). (**b**) *(be in force etc) [conditions, attitude, fashion, wind]* prédominer; *[style]* être en vogue. **the situation which now ~s** la situation actuelle. (**c**) **to ~ (up)on sb to do** persuader qn de faire. ◆**prevailing** *adj wind* dominant; *belief, attitude* courant; *conditions, situation, customs, fashion (today)* actuel; *(at that time)* à l'époque; *style, taste (today)* actuel; *(at that time)* de l'époque.

prevalent ['prevələnt] *adj belief, attitude* courant; *illness* répandu; *conditions, situation, customs (today)* actuel; *(at that time)* à l'époque; *style, taste (today)* actuel; *(at that time)* de l'époque **it is very ~** cela se voit partout. ◆**prevalence** *n [illness, belief, attitude]* fréquence *f*; *[conditions, situation, customs]* caractère *m* généralisé; *[style]* vogue *f.*

prevaricate [prɪ'værɪkeɪt] *vi* user de faux-fuyants. ◆**prevarication** *n* faux-fuyant(s) *m(pl).*

prevent [prɪ'vent] *vt (gen)* empêcher (*sb from doing, sb's doing* qn de faire); *illness* prévenir; *accident, fire, war* éviter. ◆**preventable** *adj* évitable. ◆**preventative** *adj* préventif. ◆**prevention** *n* prévention *f*; **Society for the P~ion of Cruelty to...** Société protectrice des... ◆**preventive** *adj* préventif.

preview ['pri:vju:] *n [film, exhibition]* avant-première *f.* *(fig)* **to give sb a ~ of sth** donner à qn un aperçu de qch.

previous ['pri:vɪəs] **1** *adj* précédent, antérieur. **the ~ letter** la lettre précédente; **a ~ letter** une lettre précédente *or* antérieure; **the ~ day** la veille; **the ~ evening** la veille au soir; **in a ~ life** dans une vie antérieure; **~ to** antérieur à; **have you made any ~ applications?** avez-vous déjà fait des demandes?; **I have a ~ engagement** je suis déjà pris; *(Comm)* **~ experience** expérience préalable; *(Jur)* **to have no ~ convictions** avoir un casier judiciaire vierge; **he has 3 ~ convictions** il a déjà 3 condamnations. **2** *adv*: **~ to** avant. ◆**previously** *adv (before)* précédemment, auparavant; *(in the past)* dans le temps; *(already)* déjà.

prewar ['pri:'wɔ:ʳ] *adj* d'avant-guerre.

prey [preɪ] **1** *n (lit, fig)* proie *f.* **bird of ~** oiseau *m* de proie; *(fig)* **to be a ~ to** être en proie à *(fig)*; **to fall a ~ to** devenir la victime de. **2** *vi*: **to ~ on** *[animal etc]* faire sa proie de; *[person]* s'attaquer à; *[fear, anxiety]* ronger, miner; **sth is ~ing on her mind** il y a qch qui la travaille *.

price [praɪs] **1** *n (gen, also fig)* prix *m*; *(estimate)* devis *m*; *(Betting)* cote *f*; *(St Ex)* cours *m.* **to go up in ~** augmenter; **to go down in ~** baisser; **what is the ~ of this book?** combien coûte *or* vaut ce livre?; **to put a ~ on sth** fixer le prix de qch; *(estimate value)* évaluer qch; *(fig)* **he puts a high ~ on** il attache beaucoup de valeur à; *(liter)* **beyond ~** sans prix; **we pay top ~s for gold** nous achetons l'or au prix fort; **high-~d** coûteux, cher; **he got a good ~ for it** il l'a vendu cher; *(fig)* **to pay a high ~ for sth** payer qch chèrement; *(fig)* **it's a small ~ to pay for it** c'est consentir un bien petit sacrifice pour l'avoir; **every man has his ~** tout homme est corruptible à condition d'y mettre le prix; **I wouldn't do it at any ~** je ne le ferais à aucun prix; **peace at any ~** la paix à tout prix; *(fig)* **not at any ~!** pour rien au monde!; *(fig)* **at what a ~!** à quel prix!; **he'll do it for a ~** il le fera si on y met le prix; *(St Ex)* **market ~** cours *m* du marché; **to put a ~ on sb's head** mettre à prix la tête de qn; *(fig)* **what ~ * all his promises now?** que valent toutes ses promesses maintenant? **2** *adj control, index, war, reduction, rise* des prix. **~ cut** réduction *f*, rabais *m*; **~ cutting** réductions *fpl* de prix; **~ fixing** *(by government)* contrôle *m* des prix; *(pej: by firms: also* **~ rigging**) alignement *m* des prix; **~ freeze** blocage *m* des prix; **to put a ~ limit on sth** fixer le prix maximum de qch; **~ list** tarif *m*; **~ range** gamme *f* de prix; **within**

my ~ range dans mes prix; **~s and incomes policy** politique *f* des prix et des revenus; **~ tag** *or* **ticket** étiquette *f*.

3 *vt* *(fix ~ of)* fixer le prix de; *(mark ~ on)* marquer le prix de; *(ask ~ of)* demander le prix de; *(fig: estimate value of)* évaluer. **it is ~d at £10** ça coûte 10 livres; **to ~ sth down/up** baisser/ augmenter le prix de qch; **to ~ one's goods out of the market** perdre un marché à vouloir demander des prix trop élevés.

◆ **priceless** *adj (gen)* inestimable, sans prix; *(*: amusing)* impayable *. ◆ **pricey** * *adj* coûteux, cher.

prick [prɪk] **1** *n (act, sensation, mark)* piqûre *f*. *(fig)* **~s of conscience** aiguillons *mpl* de la conscience. **2** *vt* (**a**) *(gen)* piquer; *balloon, blister* crever. **she ~ed her finger** elle s'est piqué le doigt (*with* avec); **to ~ a hole in sth** faire un trou d'épingle *(etc)* dans qch; *(fig)* **his conscience ~ed him** il n'avait pas la conscience tranquille. (**b**) **to ~ (up) one's ears** *[animal]* dresser les oreilles; *[person]* *(fig)* dresser l'oreille. **3** *vi (gen)* piquer. **my eyes are ~ing** les yeux me cuisent. ◆ **prick out** *vt sep seedlings* repiquer.

pricking ['prɪkɪŋ] *n* picotement *m*, sensation cuisante. *(fig)* **~s of conscience** remords *m(pl)*.

prickle ['prɪkl] **1** *n* (**a**) *[plant]* épine *f*; *[hedgehog etc]* piquant *m*. (**b**) *(sensation)* picotement *m*. **2** *vt* piquer. **3** *vi* picoter. ◆ **prickly** *adj plant* épineux; *animal* armé de piquants; *beard* qui pique; *(fig) person* irritable; *subject* épineux. **prickly heat** fièvre *f* miliaire; **prickly pear** figue *f* de Barbarie.

pride [praɪd] **1** *n* (**a**) *(self-respect)* amour-propre *m*; *(satisfaction)* fierté *f*; *(arrogance)* orgueil *m*. **his ~ was hurt** il était blessé dans son amour-propre; **he has too much ~ to ask for help** il est trop fier pour demander de l'aide; **she has no ~** elle n'a pas d'amour-propre; **false ~** vanité *f*; **it is a great source of ~ to her** elle en est très fière; **her ~ in her family** la fierté qu'elle tire de sa famille; **he spoke of them with ~** il a parlé d'eux avec fierté; **to take (a) ~ in** *children, achievements* être très fier de; *house, car etc* prendre grand soin de; **to take (a) ~ in doing** mettre sa fierté à faire; **to have ~ of place** avoir la place d'honneur; **she is her father's ~ and joy** elle est la fierté de son père. (**b**) *[lions]* troupe *f*. **2** *vt*: **to ~ o.s. on (doing) sth** être fier de (faire) qch.

priest [pri:st] *n (gen)* prêtre *m*; *(Catholic parish ~)* curé *m*. ◆ **priestess** *n* prêtresse *f*. ◆ **priesthood** *n*: **to enter the ~hood** se faire prêtre. ◆ **priestly** *adj* sacerdotal.

prig [prɪg] *n* pharisien(ne) *m(f)*. **what a ~ she is!** ce qu'elle peut se prendre au sérieux!; **don't be such a ~!** ne fais pas le petit saint! (*or* la petite sainte!). ◆ **priggish** *adj* suffisant. ◆ **priggishness** *n* suffisance *f*.

prim [prɪm] *adj (prudish: also ~* **and proper***)* collet monté *inv*, guindé; *(demure) person, dress* très convenable; *manner, smile, look* guindé; *house, garden* trop coquet. ◆ **primly** *adv* d'une manière guindée; *(demurely)* d'un petit air sage. ◆ **primness** *n [person]* air *m* collet monté; façons *fpl* très convenables.

prima facie ['praɪmə'feɪʃɪ] **1** *adv* à première vue. **2** *adj* légitime (à première vue). **to have a ~ case** *(Jur)* avoir une affaire recevable; *(gen)* avoir raison à première vue.

primal ['praɪm(ə)l] *adj* primordial.

primary ['praɪm(ə)rɪ] **1** *adj* (**a**) *(gen: first)* primaire. **~ education/school** enseignement *m*/école *f* primaire; **~ (school)teacher** instituteur *m*, -trice *f*. (**b**) *(basic)* principal; *colour* fondamental; *importance* primordial; *meaning of word* primitif. **2** *n (US Pol)* primaire *f*. ◆ **primarily** *adv (chiefly)* principalement; *(originally)* primitivement.

primate ['praɪmɪt] *n* (**a**) *(Rel)* primat *m*. (**b**) ['praɪmeɪt] *(Zool)* primate *m*.

prime [praɪm] **1** *adj* (**a**) *(first)* premier; *(chief, principal) cause, reason* principal, primordial, fondamental; *concern, aim* principal, premier *(before n)*. **P~ Minister** Premier ministre *m*. (**b**) *(excellent) meat* de premier choix; *quality* premier *(before n)*. **in ~ condition** en parfaite condition; **a ~ example of** un excellent exemple de. (**c**) *(Math)* premier. **2** *n*: **in the ~ of life, in one's ~** dans la fleur de l'âge; *[empire, civilisation etc]* **in its ~** à son apogée; **he is past his ~** il est sur le retour *. **3** *vt gun, pump* amorcer; *surface for painting* apprêter; *(fig: instruct) person* mettre au courant. **they ~d him about what he should say** ils lui ont bien fait répéter ce qu'il avait à dire; **she arrived well ~d** elle est arrivée tout à fait préparée. ◆ **primer** *n (textbook)* livre *m* élémentaire; *(paint)* apprêt *m*.

primeval [praɪ'mi:v(ə)l] *adj* primordial; *forest* vierge.

primitive ['prɪmɪtɪv] *adj, n* primitif *(m)*.

primordial [praɪ'mɔ:dɪəl] *adj* primordial.

primrose ['prɪmrəʊz] **1** *n* primevère *f* (jaune). **2** *adj* (**~ yellow**) primevère *inv*.

primula ['prɪmjʊlə] *n* primevère *f*.

prince [prɪns] *n* prince *m*. **P~ Charles** le prince Charles; **the P~ of Wales** le prince de Galles; **~ consort/regent** prince consort/régent. ◆ **princely** *adj* princier. ◆ **princess** *n* princesse *f*.

principal ['prɪnsɪp(ə)l] **1** *adj (gen)* principal. **the ~ horn in the orchestra** le premier cor dans l'orchestre; **~ parts of a verb** temps *mpl* primitifs d'un verbe. **2** *n* (**a**) *[school, institution etc]* directeur *m*, -trice *f*; *[lycée]* proviseur *m*, directrice *f*; *[college]* principal(e) *m(f)*; *(in orchestra)* chef *m* de pupitre; *(Theat)* vedette *f*. (**b**) *(Fin)* **~ and interest** principal *m or* capital *m* et intérêts *mpl*. ◆ **principality** *n* principauté *f*. ◆ **principally** *adv* principalement.

principle ['prɪnsəpl] *n* principe *m*. **to go back to first ~s** remonter jusqu'au principe; **in ~** en principe; **on ~, as a matter of ~** par principe; **I make it a ~ never to do that, it's against my ~s to do that** j'ai pour principe de ne jamais faire cela; **that would be totally against my ~s** cela irait à l'encontre de tous mes principes; **a man of ~(s)** un homme qui a des principes; **on the same ~** sur *or* selon le même principe.

print [prɪnt] **1** *n* (**a**) *(mark) [foot, tyre etc]* empreinte *f*. **finger~** empreinte digitale; **a thumb ~** l'empreinte d'un pouce; *(Police etc)* **to take sb's ~s** prendre les empreintes de qn. (**b**) *(Typ) (actual letters)* caractères *mpl*; *(~ed material)* texte *m* imprimé. **in small/large ~** en petits/gros caractères; **the book is out of ~/in ~** le livre est épuisé/ disponible; **he wants to see himself in ~** il veut se faire imprimer. (**c**) *(Art)* gravure *f*; *(Phot)* épreuve *f*; *(Tex)* imprimé *m*; *(~ed dress)* robe *f* imprimée. *(Phot)* **to make a ~ from a negative** tirer une épreuve d'un cliché.

2 *adj dress etc* (en) imprimé. **~ journalism** journalisme *m* de la presse écrite.

3 *vt (Typ, Tex, fig)* imprimer; *(Phot)* tirer; *(write in block letters)* écrire en caractères d'imprimerie. **~ed in England** imprimé en Angleterre; **it is being ~ed** c'est sous presse; **he has had several books ~ed** il a publié plusieurs livres; *(fig)* **~ed in sb's memory** gravé dans la mémoire.

4 *vi [machine]* imprimer. *(Phot)* **this negative won't ~** ce cliché ne donnera rien.

◆ **print out** *vt sep (Comput)* imprimer.

◆ **printable** *adj* imprimable; *(hum)* **it's just not ~able** on ne peut vraiment pas le répéter.

◆ **printed** *adj (gen)* imprimé; *writing paper* à en-tête; **~ed matter** *or* **papers** imprimés *mpl*; **the ~ed word** la chose imprimée. ◆ **printer** *n* imprimeur *m*; *(Comput)* imprimante *f*; **~er's error** faute *f* d'impression, coquille *f*; **~er's ink** encre *f* d'imprimerie. ◆ **printing** **1** *n* impression *f*; *(Phot)* tirage *m*; *(block writing)* écriture *f* en caractères d'imprimerie; **2** *adj*: **~ing press** presse *f* typographique; ~**ing works** imprimerie *f (atelier)*. ◆ **print-out** *n (Comput)* listage *m*.

prior¹ ['praɪəʳ] **1** *adj* antérieur (*to* à). **without ~ notice** sans préavis; **to have a ~ claim to sth** avoir droit à qch par priorité. **2** *adv*: ~ **to** antérieurement à, avant. ◆ **priority** *n* priorité *f*; **to have** *or* **take ~ity over** avoir la priorité sur; **to give first** *or* **top ~ity to sth** donner la priorité absolue à qch; **you must get your ~ities right** vous devez décider de ce qui compte le plus pour vous.

prior² ['praɪəʳ] *n (Rel)* prieur *m*. ◆ **prioress** *n* prieure *f*. ◆ **priory** *n* prieuré *m*.

prise [praɪz] *vt (Brit)* **to ~ open a box** ouvrir une boîte en faisant levier, forcer une boîte; **to ~ the lid off a box** forcer le couvercle d'une boîte.

prism ['prɪz(ə)m] *n* prisme *m*. ◆ **prismatic** *adj* prismatique.

prison ['prɪzn] **1** *n* prison *f*. **in ~** en prison; **to be/put sb in ~** être/mettre qn en prison; **to send sb to ~** condamner qn à la prison; **to send sb to ~ for 5 years** condamner qn à 5 ans de prison; **he was in ~ for 5 years** il a fait 5 ans de prison. **2** *adj food, conditions* dans la *or* les prison(s), pénitentiaire; *system, colony* pénitentiaire. ~ **camp** camp *m* de prisonniers; ~ **officer** gardien(ne) *m(f)* *or* surveillant(e) *m(f)* de prison. ◆ **prisoner** *n* *(gen)* prisonnier *m*, -ière *f*; *(in jail)* détenu(e) *m(f)*, prisonnier *m*, -ière *f*; ~**er of conscience** détenu(e) politique *(pour délit d'opinion)*; ~**er of war** prisonnier de guerre; *(Jur)* ~**er at the bar** accusé(e) *m(f)*, inculpé(e) *m(f)*; **the enemy took him ~er** il a été fait prisonnier par l'ennemi.

privacy ['prɪvəsɪ] *n* intimité *f*, solitude *f*. **his desire for ~** son désir d'être seul; *[public figure etc]* son désir de préserver sa vie privée; **there is no ~ in these flats** on ne peut avoir aucune vie privée dans ces appartements; **he told me in strictest ~** il me l'a dit dans le plus grand secret; **in the ~ of his own home** dans l'intimité *f* de son foyer.

private ['praɪvɪt] **1** *adj* (**a**) *(not public) conversation, meeting, land, road* privé; *(confidential) letter* confidentiel, de caractère privé; *agreement* officieux; *funeral* qui a lieu dans l'intimité. **'private'** *(on door etc)* 'privé'; *(on envelope)* 'personnel'; *(Admin, Jur)* ~ **hearing** audience *f* à huis clos; **I have ~ information that...** je sais de source privée que...; **in (his) ~ life** dans sa vie privée; **he's a very ~ person** *(gen)* c'est un homme très secret; *(Theat etc)* ~ **performance** représentation *f* privée; ~ **place** coin *m* retiré; ~ **soldier** (simple) soldat *m*; *(Art etc)* ~ **view** vernissage *m*.
(**b**) *(for one person) house, car, lesson, secretary* particulier; *(personal) bank account, advantage, joke, reasons* personnel. **a ~ income, ~ means** une fortune personnelle; **it is my ~ opinion that...** pour ma part je pense que...; *(Anat)* ~ **parts** parties *fpl* génitales; ~ **pupil** élève *mf* en leçons particulières; ~ **teacher, ~ tutor** *(for full education)* précepteur *m*, institutrice *f*; *(for one subject)* répétiteur *m*, -trice *f* (*for* en); ~ **tuition** leçons *fpl* particulières.
(**c**) *(not official or state-controlled etc) company, institution, army, school* privé; *doctor, nursing home* privé, non conventionné. *(Econ)* ~ **enterprise** entreprise *f* privée; *(Econ, Ind)* **the ~ sector** le secteur privé; *(esp Brit Med)* **to be a ~ patient** ≃ ne pas être remboursé par la Sécurité sociale; **to be in ~ practice** ≃ être médecin non conventionné; *(esp Brit Med)* ~ **treatment** ≃ traitement *m* non remboursé par la Sécurité sociale; ~ **detective, ~ investigator, ~ eye** * détective *m* privé; **a ~ citizen** un simple citoyen; *(Parl)* ~ **member** simple député *m*.
2 *n* (**a**) *(Mil)* (simple) soldat *m*. (**b**) **in ~ = privately (a)** *and* **(b)**.
◆ **privately** *adv* (**a**) *(secretly, personally)* dans son for intérieur; (**b**) *(not publicly)* en privé; (**c**) *(unofficially) write, apply* à titre personnel. ◆ **privatization** *n* privatisation *f*. ◆ **privatize** *vt* privatiser.

privation [praɪ'veɪʃ(ə)n] *n* privation *f*.

privet ['prɪvɪt] *n* troène *m*. ~ **hedge** haie *f* de troènes.

privilege ['prɪvɪlɪdʒ] **1** *n* privilège *m*; *(Parl etc)* prérogative *f*. **to have the ~ of doing** avoir le privilège de faire; **I hate ~** je déteste les privilèges. **2** *vt* *(passive only)* **to be ~d to do** avoir le privilège de faire. ◆ **privileged** *adj (gen)* privilégié; *information* confidentiel; **a ~d few** quelques privilégiés *mpl*; **the ~d few** la minorité privilégiée.

privy ['prɪvɪ] **1** *adj*: **P~ Council/Councillor** conseil *m*/conseiller *m* privé. **2** *n* cabinets *mpl*, W.-C. *mpl*.

prize¹ [praɪz] **1** *n (gen)* prix *m*; *(in lottery)* lot *m*. **to win first ~** *(Scol etc)* remporter le premier prix (*in* de); *(in lottery)* gagner le gros lot; **the Nobel P~** le prix Nobel. **2** *adj novel, entry* primé. **a ~ sheep** un mouton primé; **his ~ sheep** son meilleur mouton; **a ~ example of** un parfait exemple de; **a ~ idiot** * un(e) idiot(e) de premier ordre; ~ **draw** tombola *f*; ~ **fighter** boxeur *m* professionnel; ~ **fighting** boxe *f* professionnelle; ~ **list** palmarès *m*; ~ **money** argent *m* du prix; *(Boxing)* ~ **ring** ring *m*. **3** *vt* faire grand cas de, priser. ~**d possession** bien *m* très précieux. ◆ **prize-giving** *n (Scol etc)* distribution *f* des prix. ◆ **prizewinner** *n (Scol, gen)* lauréat(e) *m(f)*; *(in lottery)* gagnant(e) *m(f)*. ◆ **prizewinning** *adj essay, novel, entry etc* primé; *ticket* gagnant.

prize² [praɪz] *vt* = **prise.**

pro¹ [prəʊ] **1** *pref (in favour of)* pro...; ~**abortionist** partisan(e) *m(f)* de l'interruption volontaire de grossesse; ~**-French** profrançais; **he was ~-Hitler** il était partisan d'Hitler. **2** *n*: **the ~s and the cons** le pour et le contre.

pro² * [prəʊ] *n (abbr of* **professional***)* pro *mf*.

probable ['prɒb(ə)bl] *adj* (**a**) *(likely) reason, success* probable. **it is ~ that** il est probable que + *indic*; **it is hardly ~ that** il est peu probable que + *subj*. (**b**) *(credible) explanation etc* vraisemblable.
◆ **probability** *n* probabilité *f*; **in all probability** selon toute probabilité. ◆ **probably** *adv* probablement, selon toute probabilité.

probate ['prəʊbɪt] *n (Jur)* homologation *f* (d'un testament).

probation [prə'beɪʃ(ə)n] **1** *n*: **to be on ~** *(Jur)* ≃ être en sursis avec mise à l'épreuve; *[minors]* être en liberté surveillée; *(gen: in employment etc)* être engagé à l'essai; *(Rel)* être novice; *(Jur)* **to put sb on ~** mettre qn en sursis avec mise à l'épreuve *etc*. **2** *adj (Jur)* ~ **officer** agent *m* de probation; *(for minors)* ≃ délégué(e) *m(f)* à la liberté surveillée. ◆ **probationary** *adj (gen)* d'essai. ◆ **probationer** *n (gen)* employé(e) *m(f)* engagé(e) à l'essai; *(Rel)* novice *mf*.

probe [prəʊb] **1** *n (gen, Med, Space)* sonde *f*; *(investigation)* enquête *f* (*into* sur), investigation *f* (*into* de). **2** *vt hole, crack* explorer, examiner; *(Med)* sonder; *(Space)* explorer; *(also ~* **into***) sb's subconscious, past* sonder, explorer; *causes, crime, mystery* chercher à éclaircir. ◆ **probing** *adj question, study* pénétrant; *interrogation* serré; *look* inquisiteur.

probity ['prəʊbɪtɪ] *n* probité *f*.

problem ['prɒbləm] **1** *n* problème *m (also Math)*. **the housing ~** le problème du logement; **he is a great ~ to his mother** il pose de gros problèmes à sa mère; **we've got ~s with the car** nous avons des ennuis *mpl* avec la voiture; **drink ~s** des tendances *fpl* à l'alcoolisme; **it's not my ~** ça ne me concerne pas; **that's no ~ to him** ça ne lui pose pas de problème; **that's no ~!** pas de problème!; **what's the ~?** qu'est-ce qui ne va pas?; **I had no**

~ **in getting the money** je n'ai eu aucun mal à obtenir l'argent. **2** *adj situation* difficile; *child* caractériel; *family* qui pose des problèmes; *novel, play* à thèse. ~ **cases** des cas sociaux; *(Press)* ~ **page** courrier *m* du cœur. ◆ **problematic(al)** *adj* problématique; **it is ~atical whether...** il n'est pas du tout certain que... + *subj.*

procedure [prəˈsiːdʒəʳ] *n* procédure *f.* **the correct ~ is to...** pour suivre la procédure normale, il faut...; **what's the ~?** comment doit-on procéder?, qu'est-ce qu'il faut faire?

proceed [prəˈsiːd] *vi (go)* aller, avancer; *(continue)* continuer. **you must ~ cautiously** il faut avancer *or (fig: act)* procéder avec prudence; **let us ~ to the next item** passons à la question suivante; **I am not sure how to ~** je ne sais pas très bien comment m'y prendre; **to ~ to do sth** se mettre à faire qch; **to ~ with sth** continuer *or* poursuivre qch; **it is all ~ing according to plan** tout se passe *or* se déroule ainsi que prévu; *(originate)* **to ~ from** provenir de; *(Jur)* **to ~ against sb** engager des poursuites contre qn. ◆ **proceeding** *n (course of action)* façon *f or* manière *f* d'agir. ◆ **proceedings** *npl (ceremony)* cérémonie *f*; *(meeting)* séance *f*; *(discussions)* débats *mpl* ; *(records: of learned society)* actes *mpl*; *(measures)* mesures *fpl*; *(Jur: legal ~ings)* procès *m*; **to take ~ings** *(gen)* prendre des mesures *(in order to do* pour faire); *(Jur)* intenter un procès *(against sb* à qn). ◆ **proceeds** [ˈprəʊsiːdz] *npl* somme *f* recueillie.

process[1] [ˈprəʊses] **1** *n* (**a**) *(Chem, Biol etc)* processus *m; (fig, Admin etc)* procédure *f.* **the ~ of growing up** le processus de la croissance; **a natural/chemical ~** un processus naturel/chimique; **it's a slow** *or* **long ~** *(Chem etc)* c'est un processus lent; *(fig)* ça prend du temps; **he supervised the whole ~** il a supervisé l'opération *f* du début à la fin; **in the ~ of cleaning the picture, they...** pendant qu'ils nettoyaient le tableau ils...; **to be in ~** être en cours *(of sth* de qch); **in (the) ~ of doing** en train de faire. (**b**) *(specific method)* procédé *m*, méthode *f.* **the Bessemer ~** le procédé Bessemer; **a ~ for doing sth** un procédé *or* une méthode pour faire qch. (**c**) *(Jur) (action)* procès *m*; *(summons)* citation *f.*
2 *vt (Ind) raw materials, food, computer data* traiter; *(Phot) film* développer; *(Admin etc) an application, papers* s'occuper de. **~ed cheese** fromage *m* fondu. ◆ **processing** *n* traitement *m*; développement *m*; **food ~ing** préparation *f* des aliments; **data ~ing** informatique *f.*

process[2] [prəˈses] *vi (go in procession)* défiler; *(Rel)* aller en procession. ◆ **procession** *n [people, cars]* défilé *m*; *(Rel)* procession *f.*

proclaim [prəˈkleɪm] *vt (gen)* proclamer *(that* que; *sb king etc* qn roi *etc*); *peace, one's love* déclarer; *edict* promulguer; *(fig: show)* révéler. ◆ **proclamation** *n* proclamation *f.*

procrastinate [prə(ʊ)ˈkræstɪneɪt] *vi* faire traîner les choses. ◆ **procrastination** *n* procrastination *f.*

procreate [ˈprəʊkrɪeɪt] *vt* procréer. ◆ **procreation** *n* procréation *f.*

procure [prəˈkjʊəʳ] **1** *vt (for o.s.)* se procurer, obtenir; *(for sb else)* obtenir; *(Jur) prostitute etc* procurer. **to ~ sth for sb, to ~ sb sth** procurer qch à qn, faire obtenir qch à qn. **2** *vi (Jur)* faire du proxénétisme. ◆ **procurer** *n (Jur)* proxénète *m.* ◆ **procuring** *n [goods, objects]* obtention *f*; *(Jur)* proxénétisme *m.*

prod [prɒd] **1** *n (push)* poussée *f*; *(jab)* (petit) coup *m (de canne, avec le doigt etc).* **to give sb a ~** pousser qn doucement (du doigt *or* avec la pointe d'un bâton *etc*); *(fig)* pousser *or* stimuler qn. **2** *vt* pousser doucement (du doigt *or* avec la pointe d'un bâton *etc*). **he ~ded the map with his finger** il a planté son doigt sur la carte; **to ~ sb into doing sth** pousser qn à faire qch; *(fig)* **he needs ~ding** il a besoin d'être stimulé.

prodigal [ˈprɒdɪgəl] *adj* prodigue.

prodigy [ˈprɒdɪdʒɪ] *n* prodige *m*, merveille *f.* **child ~** enfant *mf* prodige. ◆ **prodigious** *adj* prodigieux. ◆ **prodigiously** *adv* prodigieusement.

produce [prəˈdjuːs] **1** *vt* (**a**) *(make: gen)* produire; *magazine* éditer; *book (write)* écrire; *(publish)* publier; *(Fin) interest, profit* rapporter; *(give birth to)* donner naissance à. **he has ~d a new pop record** il a sorti un nouveau disque pop; **oil-producing countries** pays *mpl* producteurs de pétrole. (**b**) *(bring, show) gift, documents, gun* sortir *(from* de), produire; *witness* produire; *proof* fournir. **I can't ~ £100!** je ne peux pas trouver 100 livres! (**c**) *(cause: gen)* provoquer, causer; *results, impression* produire, donner; *pleasure, interest* susciter; *(Elec) current* engendrer; *spark* faire jaillir. (**d**) *(Theat)* mettre en scène; *(Cine)* produire; *(Rad) play* mettre en ondes; *(Rad, TV) programme* réaliser; *(TV) play, film* mettre en scène.
2 [ˈprɒdjuːs] *n* produits *mpl (d'alimentation).*
◆ **producer** *n (V* **produce 1a** *and* **1d***)* producteur *m*, -trice *f*; metteur *m* en scène; metteur en ondes; réalisateur *m.*

product [ˈprɒdʌkt] *n* produit *m*; *(fig)* résultat *m.* ~ **liability** responsabilité *f* du fabricant. ◆ **production 1** *n* (**a**) *(Ind)* production *f*; **to put sth into ~ion** entreprendre la production de qch; **to take sth out of ~ion** retirer qch de la production; **the factory is in full ~ion** l'usine tourne à plein rendement; **car ~ion has risen** la production automobile a augmenté; (**b**) *(showing)* présentation *f*; **on ~ion of this ticket** sur présentation de ce billet; (**c**) *(V* **produce 1d***)* mise *f* en scène; production *f*; mise *f* en ondes; réalisation *f*; (**d**) *(work produced) (Theat)* pièce *f*; *(Cine, Rad, TV)* production *f* ; **2** *adj (Ind)* **~ion line** chaîne *f* de fabrication; **~ion manager** directeur *m* de la production. ◆ **productive** *adj land, imagination* fertile; *meeting, work* fructueux; *employment, labour* productif; *(Ling)* productif; **I've had a very ~ive day** j'ai bien travaillé aujourd'hui. ◆ **productivity 1** *n (Econ, Ind)* productivité *f* ; **2** *adj fall, increase* de productivité; **~ivity agreement** accord *m* de productivité; **~ivity bonus** prime *f* à la productivité.

profane [prəˈfeɪn] **1** *adj (secular)* profane; *(pej) language etc* impie. **2** *vt* profaner. ◆ **profanity** *n (oath)* juron *m.*

profess [prəˈfes] *vt (gen)* professer. **he ~ed himself satisfied** il s'est déclaré satisfait; **I don't ~ to be an expert** je ne prétends pas être expert en la matière. ◆ **professed** *adj atheist etc* déclaré; *(Rel) monk, nun* profès *(f* -esse).

profession [prəˈfeʃ(ə)n] *n (all senses: gen)* profession *f.* **the ~s** les professions libérales; **by ~** de son *(or* mon *etc)* métier; **the medical ~** *(calling)* la profession de médecin; *(doctors collectively)* les médecins *mpl*; ~ **of faith** profession de foi. ◆ **professional 1** *adj (gen)* professionnel; *diplomat, soldier* de carrière; *play, piece of work* de haute qualité; **~al people** les membres *mpl* des professions libérales; **to take ~al advice** *(medical/legal)* consulter un médecin/un avocat; *(on practical problem)* consulter un professionnel; *(Sport)* **to turn ~al** passer professionnel; **to have a very ~al attitude to sth** prendre qch très au sérieux; **it is well up to ~al standards** c'est d'un niveau de professionnel ; **2** *n (all senses)* professionnel(le) *m(f).* ◆ **professionally** *adv (gen)* professionnellement; *(Sport) play* en professionnel; **I never met him ~ally** je n'ai jamais eu de rapports de travail avec lui; **~ally qualified** diplômé; **have you ever sung ~ally?** avez-vous jamais été chanteur professionnel?

professor [prəˈfesəʳ] *n (Univ: Brit, US)* professeur *m* (titulaire d'une chaire); *(US: teacher)* professeur. ◆ **professorial** *adj* professoral.

proffer [ˈprɒfəʳ] *vt object, hand* tendre; *remark* faire; *thanks, apologies* présenter.

proficient [prəˈfɪʃ(ə)nt] *adj* très compétent (*in* en). ◆ **proficiency** *n* grande compétence *f*.

profile [ˈprəʊfaɪl] **1** *n (gen)* profil *m*; *(fig) [person]* portrait *m*; *[situation etc]* esquisse *f*. **in** ~ de profil; *(fig)* **to keep a low** ~ essayer de ne pas trop se faire remarquer. **2** *vt (show in ~)* profiler; *(fig: describe)* établir le profil de.

profit [ˈprɒfɪt] **1** *n (Comm)* profit *m*, bénéfice *m*; *(fig)* profit. ~ **and loss** profits et pertes; **gross/net** ~ bénéfice brut/net; **to make a** ~ faire un bénéfice (*of* de; *on* sur); **to sell sth at a** ~ vendre qch à profit; **to yield a** ~ rapporter un bénéfice. **2** *adj*: ~ **margin** marge *f* bénéficiaire. **3** *vi*: **to** ~ **by** *or* **from sth** tirer profit de qch. ◆ **profitability** *n* rentabilité *f*. ◆ **profitable** *adj (Comm etc)* rentable; *(fig) scheme, agreement* avantageux; *meeting, visit* profitable. ◆ **profitably** *adv sell* à profit; *deal* avec profit; *(fig)* avec profit, avec fruit. ◆ **profiteer** *(pej)* **1** *n* profiteur *m (pej)* ; **2** *vi* faire des bénéfices excessifs. ◆ **profitless** *adj* sans profit. ◆ **profit-making** *adj* à but lucratif; **non-~-making** à but non lucratif. ◆ **profit-sharing** *n* participation *f* aux bénéfices.

profligate [ˈprɒflɪgɪt] *adj (debauched)* débauché; *(extravagant)* extrêmement prodigue. ◆ **profligacy** *n* débauche *f*; extrême prodigalité *f*.

profound [prəˈfaʊnd] *adj* profond. ◆ **profoundly** *adv* profondément. ◆ **profundity** *n* profondeur *f*.

profuse [prəˈfjuːs] *adj vegetation, bleeding* abondant; *thanks, praise, apologies* profus. ◆ **profusely** *adv bleed, sweat* abondamment; *thank, praise* avec effusion; **to apologize ~ly** se confondre en excuses. ◆ **profusion** *n* profusion *f*; **in profusion** à profusion.

progeny [ˈprɒdʒɪnɪ] *n* progéniture *f*. ◆ **progenitor** *n (lit)* ancêtre *m*; *(fig)* auteur *m*.

prognosis, *pl* **-oses** [prɒgˈnəʊsɪs, əʊsiːz] *n* pronostic *m*. ◆ **prognosticate** *vt* pronostiquer. ◆ **prognostication** *n* pronostic *m*.

program [ˈprəʊgræm] **1** *n* (**a**) *(Comput)* programme *m*. (**b**) *(US)* programme. **2** *adj (Comput)* du *or* d'un programme. **3** *vi* établir un (*or* des) programme(s). **4** *vt (Comput etc)* programmer (*sth to do* qch de façon à faire). ◆ **programmable** *adj* programmable.

programme [ˈprəʊgræm] **1** *n (most senses)* programme *m*; *(Rad, TV: broadcast)* émission *f* (*on* sur; *about* au sujet de); *(Rad: station)* poste *m*; *(TV: station)* chaîne *f*; *[course etc]* emploi *m* du temps. *(fig)* **what's the ~ for today? *** qu'est-ce qu'on fait aujourd'hui?; **on the** ~ au programme; **on the other** ~ *(TV)* sur l'autre chaîne; *(Rad)* sur l'autre poste. **2** *adj (Rad, TV)* ~ **editor** éditorialiste *mf*; *(Theat)* ~ **seller** vendeur *m*, -euse *f* de programmes. **3** *vt (gen, Tech, fig)* programmer (*to do* pour faire). **the meeting was ~d to start at 7** le début de la réunion était prévu pour 19 heures. ◆ **programmer** *n (computer ~)* programmeur *m*, -euse *f*; *(device)* programmateur *m*. ◆ **programming** *n* programmation *f*.

progress [ˈprəʊgres] **1** *n (gen)* progrès *m(pl)*. **in the name of** ~ au nom du progrès; **to make** ~ *(gen)* faire des progrès; *(walk etc forward)* avancer; **the patient is making** ~ l'état *m* (de santé) du malade s'améliore; **the** ~ **of events** le cours des événements; **the meeting is in** ~ la réunion est en cours.

2 *adj*: ~ **report** *(gen)* compte rendu *m*; *(Med)* bulletin *m* de santé; *(Admin etc)* état *m* périodique; *(Scol)* bulletin scolaire.

3 *vi* [prəˈgres] *(lit, fig)* aller, avancer (*towards* vers); *[student etc]* faire des progrès; *[patient]* aller mieux; *[investigations, studies etc]* progresser. **as the game ~ed** à mesure que la partie se déroulait.

◆ **progression** *n* progression *f*. ◆ **progressive** **1** *adj (gradually increasing) disease, improvement* progressif; *(forward-looking) idea, party, person* progressiste; *age* de progrès ; **2** *n (Pol etc)* progressiste *mf*. ◆ **progressively** *adv* progressivement, petit à petit.

prohibit [prəˈhɪbɪt] *vt (forbid)* interdire, défendre (*sb from doing* à qn de faire); *(prevent)* empêcher (*sb from doing* qn de faire); *(Admin, Jur etc) weapons, drugs, swearing* prohiber. **smoking ~ed** défense de fumer, il est interdit *or* défendu de fumer; **pedestrians are ~ed from using this bridge** il est interdit aux piétons d'utiliser ce pont. ◆ **prohibition** *n* interdiction *f*, défense *f*; prohibition *f (also against alcohol)*. ◆ **prohibitive** *adj* prohibitif.

project [ˈprɒdʒekt] **1** *n* (**a**) *(plan, scheme)* projet *m*, plan *m* (*to do, for doing* pour faire); *(undertaking)* opération *f*, entreprise *f*; *(construction work)* grands travaux *mpl; (study)* étude *f* (*on* de); *(Scol)* dossier *m* (*on* sur). (**b**) *(US: housing ~)* cité *f*, lotissement *m*. **2** [prəˈdʒekt] *vt (all senses)* projeter. **~ed sales/revenue** projection *f* de ventes/de recettes. **3** *vi* faire saillie. **to** ~ **over** surplomber; **to** ~ **into** s'avancer dans; *(Psych)* **how does he ~?** quelle image de lui-même projette-t-il? ◆ **projecting** *adj construction, part, knob* saillant; *tooth* qui avance. ◆ **projection** **1** *n* (**a**) projection *f*; (**b**) *(overhang)* saillie *f* ; **2** *adj (Cine)* **~ion booth, ~ion room** cabine *f* de projection. ◆ **projectionist** *n* projectionniste *mf*. ◆ **projector** *n* projecteur *m*.

prolapse [ˈprəʊlæps] *n* descente *f* d'organe.

proletarian [ˌprəʊləˈtɛərɪən] **1** *n (abbr* **prole** *)* prolétaire *mf (abbr* prolo *)*. **2** *adj class, party* prolétarien; *life, mentality* de prolétaire. ◆ **proletariat** *n* prolétariat *m*.

proliferate [prəˈlɪfəreɪt] *vi* proliférer. ◆ **proliferation** *n* prolifération *f*. ◆ **prolific** *adj* prolifique.

prologue [ˈprəʊlɒg] *n* prologue *m* (*Literat: to* de; *fig: to* à).

prolong [prəˈlɒŋ] *vt* prolonger. ◆ **prolongation** *n (in space)* prolongement *m*; *(in time)* prolongation *f*. ◆ **prolonged** *adj* long, de longue durée.

prom * [prɒm] *n* (**a**) *abbr of* **promenade.** (**b**) *(Brit)* = **promenade concert.**

promenade [ˌprɒmɪˈnɑːd] **1** *n* promenade *f*. **2** *adj (Brit)* ~ **concert** *concert donné dans une salle à promenoir; (Naut)* ~ **deck** pont *m* promenade. **3** *vi (walk)* se promener. **4** *vt* promener. ◆ **promenader** * *n* auditeur *m*, -trice *f* d'un 'promenade concert'.

prominent [ˈprɒmɪnənt] *adj ridge, structure, nose* proéminent; *cheekbones* saillant; *tooth* qui avance; *(striking)* frappant; *(outstanding) person* important, très en vue. **to be** ~ **in** jouer un rôle important dans; **in a** ~ **position** bien en vue. ◆ **prominence** *n* proéminence *f*; aspect saillant *or* frappant; importance *f*. ◆ **prominently** *adv display, place, set* bien en vue; **his name figured ~ly in the case** on a beaucoup entendu parler de lui dans l'affaire.

promiscuous [prəˈmɪskjʊəs] *adj (sexually) person* de mœurs faciles; *conduct* léger, libre. ◆ **promiscuity** *or* ◆ **promiscuousness** *n* promiscuité *f* sexuelle. ◆ **promiscuously** *adv* immoralement.

promise [ˈprɒmɪs] **1** *n* promesse *f*. **to make sb a** ~ faire une promesse à qn (*to do* de faire); **is it a ~?** c'est promis?; **to keep one's** ~ tenir sa promesse; **a young man of** ~ un jeune homme qui promet; **it holds out a** ~ **of peace** cela fait espérer la paix. **2** *vt* promettre (*sth to sb* qch à qn; *sb to do* à qn de faire; *that* que). **I ~!** je vous le promets!; *(after statement)* je vous assure!; **I can't**

~ je ne vous promets rien; *(fig)* **to ~ sb the earth** *or* **the moon** promettre la lune à qn; **to ~ o.s. (to do) sth** se promettre (de faire) qch. **3** *vi (fig)* **to ~ well** *[person]* promettre; *[situation, first book, event]* être prometteur; *[crop, business]* s'annoncer bien. ◆ **promising** *adj situation, event* prometteur; *person* qui promet; **the future is promising** l'avenir s'annonce bien; **that's promising** c'est prometteur; *(iro)* ça promet! ◆ **promisingly** *adv* d'une façon prometteuse.

promontory ['prɒməntrɪ] *n* promontoire *m.*

promote [prə'məʊt] *vt* (**a**) *person* promouvoir (*to* au poste de, *(Mil)* au rang de). *(Ftbl etc)* **to be ~d to the first division** monter en première division. (**b**) *(encourage) cause, plan, sales, product* promouvoir; *trade* développer; *(Comm) firm, campaign* lancer. ◆ **promoter** *n [sport]* organisateur *m*, -trice *f*; *[product]* promoteur *m* de vente; *[business, company]* fondateur *m*, -trice *f.* ◆ **promotion** *n* promotion *f*; **to get promotion** obtenir de l'avancement, être promu.

prompt [prɒmpt] **1** *adj (speedy) action* rapide, prompt; *delivery, reply, payment, service* rapide; *(punctual)* ponctuel. **to be ~ to do** faire avec promptitude. **2** *adv*: **at 6 o'clock ~** à 6 heures exactement. **3** *vt* (**a**) *person* pousser, inciter (*sb to do* qn à faire); *reaction* provoquer, entraîner. **~ed by a desire to see...** poussé par un désir de voir...; **regret ~ed by the sight of...** regret provoqué par la vue de... (**b**) *(Theat)* souffler. **4** *n (Comput)* guidage *m.* ◆ **prompter** *n (Theat)* souffleur *m*, -euse *f.* ◆ **prompting** *n*: **at my ~ing** à mon instigation; **without (any) ~ing** de son propre chef. ◆ **promptly** *adv* rapidement, promptement; ponctuellement. ◆ **promptness** *n* promptitude *f*; ponctualité *f.*

prone [prəʊn] *adj* (**a**) *(face down)* étendu face contre terre. (**b**) *(liable)* enclin (*to sth* à qch, *to do* à faire).

prong [prɒŋ] *n [fork]* dent *f.* **three-~ed** *fork* à trois dents; *attack, advance* sur trois fronts.

pronoun ['prəʊnaʊn] *n* pronom *m.*

pronounce [prə'naʊns] **1** *vt* (**a**) *word etc* prononcer. **how is it ~d?** comment ça se prononce? (**b**) prononcer (*that* que). *(Jur)* **to ~ sentence** prononcer la sentence; **they ~d him unfit to drive** ils l'ont déclaré inapte à la conduite; **to ~ o.s. in favour of** se prononcer *or* se déclarer en faveur de. **2** *vi* se prononcer (*on* sur); *(Jur)* prononcer (*for* en faveur de, *against* contre). ◆ **pronounceable** *adj* prononçable. ◆ **pronounced** *adj* prononcé, marqué. ◆ **pronouncement** *n* déclaration *f.* ◆ **pronunciation** *n* prononciation *f.*

pronto * ['prɒntəʊ] *adv* illico *.

proof [pru:f] **1** *n* (**a**) *(gen, Jur, Math etc)* preuve *f.* **~ of identity** pièce(s) *f(pl)* d'identité; **as (a) ~ of, in ~ of** pour preuve de; **I've got ~ that he did it** j'ai la preuve qu'il l'a fait; *(fig)* **to show ~ of** faire preuve de. (**b**) **to put sth to the ~** mettre qch à l'épreuve. (**c**) *(Typ, Phot)* épreuve *f.* (**d**) **this whisky is 70°** ~ ≃ ce whisky titre 40° d'alcool. **2** *adj*: **~ against** *bullets, time, wear* à l'épreuve de; *temptation, suggestion* insensible à. **3** *vt anorak, tent* imperméabiliser. ◆ **proofread** *vt* corriger les épreuves de. ◆ **proofreader** *n* correcteur *m*, -trice *f* d'épreuves.

prop[1] [prɒp] **1** *n* support *m*; *(for wall; in tunnel etc)* étai *m*; *(for clothes-line)* perche *f*; *(fig)* soutien *m* (*to, for* de). **2** *vt* (**~ up**) *(lean) ladder, cycle* appuyer (*against* contre); *(support) tunnel, wall* étayer; *clothes-line, lid* caler; *(fig) régime* maintenir; *business, company* renflouer; *organization* soutenir; *(Fin) the pound* venir au secours de. **to ~ o.s. (up) against** se caler contre.

prop[2] * [prɒp] *n (Theat) abbr of* **property 1c.**

propaganda [,prɒpə'gændə] *n* propagande *f.*

propagate ['prɒpəgeɪt] **1** *vt* propager. **2** *vi* se propager. ◆ **propagation** *n* propagation *f.*

propel [prə'pel] *vt vehicle etc* propulser; *person* pousser (*into* dans). **to ~ sth/sb along** faire avancer qch/qn (en le poussant). ◆ **propellant** *n [rocket]* combustible *m.* ◆ **propeller** *n* hélice *f.* ◆ **propelling pencil** *n* porte-mine *m inv.*

propensity [prə'pensɪtɪ] *n* propension *f* (*to, towards, for* à; *to do, for doing* à faire).

proper ['prɒpə[r]] **1** *adj* (**a**) *(appropriate, suitable, correct) clothes* indiqué, convenable; *tool, answer* bon, qui convient; *spelling, order* correct; *method, treatment* indiqué, correct. **in the ~ way** comme il faut; *(Admin)* dans les règles; **in the ~ meaning** *or* **sense of the word** au sens propre du mot; **at the ~ time** à la bonne heure, à l'heure dite; *(Admin etc)* **to go through the ~ channels** passer par la filière officielle; **to make a ~ job of sth** bien réussir qch *(also iro)*; **to do the ~ thing by sb** bien agir envers qn; *(Gram)* **~ noun** nom *m* propre; **if you think it ~ to do so** si vous jugez bon de faire ainsi; *(Philos, Chem etc)* **~ to** propre à. (**b**) *(seemly) person* comme il faut; *book, behaviour* convenable, correct. **it isn't ~ to do that** cela ne se fait pas. (**c**) *(authentic)* véritable. **he's not a ~ electrician** ce n'est pas un véritable électricien; **outside Paris ~** en dehors de Paris proprement dit; **he's a ~ fool** c'est un imbécile fini; **I felt a ~ idiot** je me suis senti vraiment idiot; **he's a ~ gentleman** c'est un monsieur très comme il faut; **he made a ~ mess of it** il (en) a fait un beau gâchis.

2 *adv* (⁑) *talk* comme il faut; *(very)* vraiment, très.

◆ **properly** *adv* (**a**) *(appropriately, correctly) dress* convenablement; *use* correctement, comme il faut; *speak, spell* correctement; **~ly speaking** à proprement parler; **he very ~ly refused** il a refusé et avec raison; (**b**) *(in seemly way) behave, dress* convenablement, comme il faut; *speak* bien; (**c**) *(*: completely)* vraiment.

property ['prɒpətɪ] **1** *n* (**a**) *(possessions)* propriété *f*, biens *mpl; (estate)* propriété *f; (lands)* terres *fpl*; *(buildings)* biens *mpl* immobiliers; *(house)* propriété *f. (Jur)* **personal ~** biens personnels; **is this your ~?** cela vous appartient?; **a man of ~** un homme qui a des biens. (**b**) *(Chem etc)* propriété *f.* (**c**) *(Theat)* accessoire *m.* **2** *adj* (**a**) *owner, tax* foncier; *market* immobilier. **~ developer** promoteur *m* (de construction). (**b**) *(Theat)* **~ man/ mistress** accessoiriste *m/f.* ◆ **propertied** *adj* possédant.

prophecy ['prɒfɪsɪ] *n* prophétie *f.* ◆ **prophesy** ['prɒfɪsaɪ] **1** *vt* prédire (*that* que). **2** *vi* prophétiser. ◆ **prophet** *n* prophète *m.* ◆ **prophetess** *n* prophétesse *f.* ◆ **prophetic(al)** *adj* prophétique. ◆ **prophetically** *adv* prophétiquement.

propitiate [prə'pɪʃɪeɪt] *vt* se concilier. ◆ **propitiation** *n* propitiation *f.*

propitious [prə'pɪʃəs] *adj* propice. ◆ **propitiously** *adv* d'une manière propice.

proponent [prə'pəʊnənt] *n* partisan(e) *m(f).*

proportion [prə'pɔ:ʃ(ə)n] **1** *n* (**a**) *(ratio)* proportion *f* (*of sth to sth* de qch par rapport à qch). **the ~ of blacks to whites** la proportion *or* le pourcentage des noirs par rapport aux blancs; **in perfect ~** parfaitement proportionné; **in ~ as** à mesure que; **in ~ to** en proportion de; **to be in ~ to** être proportionné à; **out of ~ to** hors de proportion avec, disproportionné par rapport à; **it's out of ~** *[drawing]* c'est mal proportionné; *(fig)* c'est hors de proportion; *(lit, fig)* **he has no sense of ~** il n'a pas le sens des proportions. (**b**) *(size)* **~s** proportions *fpl.* (**c**) *(part)* part *f*, partie *f.* **in equal ~s** à parts égales; **a certain ~ of the staff** une certaine partie du personnel. **2** *vt* proportionner (*to* à). **well-~ed** bien proportionné.

◆ **proportional** *or* ◆ **proportionate** *adj* proportionnel (*to* à); **~al representation** représentation *f* proportionnelle. ◆ **proportionally** *adv* proportionnellement.

propose [prə'pəʊz] **1** *vt* (**a**) *(suggest)* proposer (*sth to sb* qch à qn; *doing* de faire; *that* que + *subj; sb for sth* qn pour qch). **to ~ a toast to sb** porter un toast à la santé de qn; **to ~ marriage to sb** demander qn en mariage. (**b**) *(have in mind)* **to ~ to do** *or* **doing** se proposer de faire. **2** *vi (offer marriage)* faire une demande en mariage (*to sb* à qn). ◆ **proposal** *n* (**a**) *(offer)* proposition *f*; *(of marriage)* demande *f* en mariage; (**b**) *(plan)* projet *m*, plan *m* (*for sth* de *or* pour qch; *to do* pour faire); *(suggestion)* proposition *f* (*to do* de faire). ◆ **proposer** *n (Admin, Parl etc)* auteur *m* de la proposition. ◆ **proposition** **1** *n (gen)* proposition *f*; *(fig)* **that's quite another proposition** ça c'est une tout autre affaire; **the journey alone is quite a proposition** rien que le voyage n'est pas une petite affaire; **to be a tough proposition** être ardu; *[person]* être coriace ; **2** *vt* faire des propositions (malhonnêtes) à.

propound [prə'paʊnd] *vt theory, idea* proposer, soumettre; *problem* poser; *programme* exposer.

proprietor [prə'praɪətəʳ] *n* propriétaire *m*. ◆ **proprietary** *adj (Comm) article* de marque déposée; **proprietary brand** (produit *m* de) marque *f* déposée; **proprietary medicine** spécialité *f* pharmaceutique; **proprietary name** marque *f* déposée. ◆ **proprietress** *n* propriétaire *f*.

propriety [prə'praɪətɪ] *n* (**a**) *(decency)* bienséance *f*, convenance *f*. **to observe the proprieties** respecter les bienséances *or* les convenances. (**b**) *(appropriateness etc) [behaviour, step, phrase]* justesse *f*.

propulsion [prə'pʌlʃ(ə)n] *n* propulsion *f*.

prosaic [prə(ʊ)'zeɪɪk] *adj* prosaïque. ◆ **prosaically** *adv* prosaïquement.

proscribe [prə(ʊ)s'kraɪb] *vt* proscrire. ◆ **proscription** *n* proscription *f*.

prose [prəʊz] **1** *n* (**a**) prose *f*. **in ~** en prose. (**b**) *(Scol etc: ~* **translation***)* thème *m*. **2** *adj*: **~ writer** prosateur *m*.

prosecute ['prɒsɪkju:t] *vt* (**a**) *(Jur etc)* poursuivre (en justice) (*for doing sth* pour qch). (**b**) *(further) enquiry* poursuivre. ◆ **prosecution** *n (Jur) (act, proceedings)* poursuites *fpl* judiciaires; **the prosecution** ≃ le ministère public; **witness for the prosecution** témoin *m* à charge. ◆ **prosecutor** *n* **(public prosecutor)** ≃ procureur *m* (de la République).

prosody ['prɒsədɪ] *n* prosodie *f*.

prospect ['prɒspekt] **1** *n (gen)* perspective *f* (*of, from* de); *(future)* (perspectives d')avenir *m*; *(hope)* espoir *m* (*of sth* de qch; *of doing* de faire). **this ~ cheered him up** cette perspective l'a réjoui; **to have sth in ~** avoir qch en perspective *or* en vue; **there is little ~ of his coming** il y a peu de chances qu'il vienne; **he has little ~ of succeeding** il a peu de chances de réussir; **there is no ~ of that** rien ne laisse prévoir cela; **there is every ~ of success/of succeeding** tout laisse prévoir le succès/qu'on réussira; **the ~s for the harvest are good** la récolte s'annonce bien; **what are his ~s?** quelles sont ses perspectives d'avenir?; **'good ~s of promotion'** 'situation *f* d'avenir'; **it offered the ~ of** cela offrait la possibilité de; **he is a good ~ for the team** c'est un bon espoir pour l'équipe; **to seem quite a good ~** sembler prometteur.
2 [prəs'pekt] *vti* prospecter (*for* pour trouver). ◆ **prospecting** *n (Min etc)* prospection *f*. ◆ **prospective** *adj son-in-law, home, legislation* futur *(before n)*; *journey* en perspective; *customer* possible. ◆ **prospector** *n* prospecteur *m*, -trice *f*; **gold ~or** chercheur *m* d'or. ◆ **prospectus** *n* prospectus *m*.

prosper ['prɒspəʳ] *vi* prospérer. ◆ **prosperity** *n* prospérité *f*. ◆ **prosperous** *adj* prospère.

prostate ['prɒsteɪt] *n (~* **gland***)* prostate *f*.

prostitute ['prɒstɪtju:t] **1** *n* prostituée *f*. **male ~** prostitué *m*. **2** *vt* prostituer. ◆ **prostitution** *n* prostitution *f*.

prostrate ['prɒstreɪt] **1** *adj* à plat ventre; *(in respect, submission)* prosterné; *(exhausted)* prostré. **2** [prɒs'treɪt] *vt*: **to ~ o.s.** se prosterner; **the news ~d him** la nouvelle l'a accablé. ◆ **prostration** *n (Med)* prostration *f*.

protagonist [prə(ʊ)'tægənɪst] *n* protagoniste *m*.

protect [prə'tekt] *vt (gen)* protéger (*from* de; *against* contre); *interests, rights* sauvegarder. ◆ **protection** **1** *n* protection *f* (*against* contre); sauvegarde *f*; **under his ~ion** sous sa protection ; **2** *adj*: **to pay ~ion money** verser de l'argent à un racketteur; **~ion racket** racket *m*. ◆ **protectionism** *n (Econ)* protectionnisme *m*; *(US Ecol)* défense *f* de l'environnement. ◆ **protectionist** **1** *adj (Econ)* protectionniste; *(US Ecol)* pour la défense de l'environnement ; **2** *n (Econ)* protectionniste; *(US Ecol)* défenseur *m* de l'environnement. ◆ **protective** *adj (gen)* protecteur; *clothing, covering* de protection. ◆ **protectively** *adv* d'un geste (*or* ton *etc*) protecteur. ◆ **protector** *n* protecteur *m*. ◆ **protectorate** *n* protectorat *m*.

protein ['prəʊti:n] *n* protéine *f*.

protest ['prəʊtest] **1** *n* protestation *f* (*against* contre; *about* à propos de); *(Pol)* contestation *f*. **to do sth under ~** faire qch en protestant. **2** *adj meeting* de protestation. **~ march** *or* **demonstration** manifestation *f*. **3** [prə'test] *vt* (**a**) protester (*that* que); *one's innocence, loyalty* protester de; (**b**) *(US)* protester contre. **4** [prə'test] *vi* protester (*against* contre; *about* à propos de; *to sb* auprès de qn). ◆ **Protestant** ['prɒtɪstənt] *adj, n* protestant(e) *m(f)*. ◆ **Protestantism** *n* protestantisme *m*. ◆ **protestation** *n* protestation *f*. ◆ **protester** *n* protestataire *mf*; *(on march, in demonstration)* manifestant(e) *m(f)*.

protocol ['prəʊtəkɒl] *n* protocole *m*.

prototype ['prəʊtəʊ'taɪp] *n* prototype *m*.

protract [prə'trækt] *vt* prolonger, faire traîner. ◆ **protracted** *adj* prolongé.

protrude [prə'tru:d] *vi [stick, gutter, rock, shelf]* dépasser; *[teeth]* avancer; *[eyes]* être globuleux. ◆ **protruding** *adj* qui dépasse; qui avance; globuleux.

protuberant [prə'tju:b(ə)r(ə)nt] *adj* protubérant. ◆ **protuberance** *n* protubérance *f*.

proud [praʊd] *adj* (**a**) *person* fier (*of* de; *that* que, + *subj; to do* de faire); *(arrogant)* fier, orgueilleux. **that's nothing to be ~ of!** il n'y a pas de quoi être fier!; **as ~ as a peacock** fier comme Artaban; *(pej)* vaniteux comme un paon; **to do o.s. ~ *** ne se priver de rien; **to do sb ~ *** *(entertain)* se mettre en frais pour qn. (**b**) *(splendid) ship* majestueux. ◆ **proudly** *adv* fièrement; *(arrogantly)* orgueilleusement; *(splendidly)* majestueusement.

prove [pru:v] **1** *vt* (**a**) *(gen)* prouver (*that* que). **you can't ~ anything against me** vous n'avez aucune preuve contre moi; **he was ~d right** il s'est avéré qu'il avait raison. (**b**) *will* homologuer. **to ~ o.s.** faire ses preuves. **2** *vi*: **he/it ~d to be...** on s'est rendu compte plus tard qu'il était/que c'était...; **he ~d (to be) incapable of helping us** il s'est révélé incapable de nous aider; **it ~d useful** cela a été utile; **if it ~s otherwise** s'il en est autrement.

Provence [prɒ'vɑ̃:(n)s] *n* Provence *f*. ◆ **Provençal** *adj, n* provençal *(m)*.

proverb ['prɒvɜ:b] *n* proverbe *m*. ◆ **proverbial** *adj* proverbial. ◆ **proverbially** *adv* proverbialement.

provide [prə'vaɪd] **1** *vt* (**a**) *(supply)* fournir (*sb with sth, sth for sb* qch à *or* pour qn); *(equip)* pourvoir (*sb with sth* qn de qch; *sth with sth* qch à qch). **to**

~ **o.s. with sth** se munir de qch; **the field ~s plenty of space for a car park** le champ offre suffisamment d'espace pour un parc à autos; **~d with** pourvu de. (**b**) *[legislation etc]* stipuler, prévoir (*that* que). **2** *vi (financially)* **to ~ for sb** pourvoir aux besoins de qn; *(in the future)* assurer l'avenir de qn; **the Lord will ~** Dieu y pourvoira; *(make arrangements)* **to ~ for sth** prévoir qch. ◆ **provided** *or* ◆ **providing** *conj* pourvu que + *subj*, à condition de + *infin.*

providence ['prɒvɪd(ə)ns] *n* providence *f.* ◆ **providential** *adj* providentiel. ◆ **providentially** *adv* providentiellement.

province ['prɒvɪns] *n* province *f.* **the ~s** *(collectively)* la province; **in the ~s** en province; *(fig)* **that is not (within) my ~** cela n'est pas de mon domaine. ◆ **provincial** *adj, n* provincial(e) *m(f).*

provision [prə'vɪʒ(ə)n] **1** *n* (**a**) *(supply)* provision *f.* **to lay in a ~ of** faire provision de; *(food etc)* **~s** provisions *fpl*; **to get in** *or* **lay in ~s** faire des provisions; **the ~ of housing** le logement; **~ of food to the soldiers** approvisionnement *m* des soldats en nourriture; **to make ~ for** *one's family etc* assurer l'avenir de; *journey, siege* prendre des dispositions pour. (**b**) *[legislation etc]* disposition *f*, clause *f.* **~ to the contrary** clause contraire; **there is no ~ for this in the rules** le règlement ne prévoit pas cela. (**c**) *(funding)* financement *m.*
2 *adj*: **~ merchant** marchand *m* de comestibles.
3 *vt* approvisionner.
◆ **provisional** *adj government, licence* provisoire; *arrangement, acceptance* à titre conditionnel; *(Admin) appointment* à titre provisoire; *(Jur)* provisionnel. ◆ **provisionally** *adv agree* à titre conditionnel; *appoint* à titre provisoire. ◆ **proviso** *n* condition *f*; *(Jur)* clause *f* restrictive; **with the proviso that** à condition que + *subj.*

provoke [prə'vəʊk] *vt* provoquer (*sb to sth* qn à faire qch; *sb to do or into doing* qn à faire). ◆ **provocation** *n* provocation *f*; **under provocation** en réponse à une provocation. ◆ **provocative** *adj (gen)* provocant; *(thought-provoking) book, title, talk* qui donne à penser. ◆ **provocatively** *adv* d'un air *or* d'un ton provocant. ◆ **provoking** *adj* agaçant.

provost ['prɒvəst] *n (Brit Univ)* principal *m*; *(US Univ)* ≃ doyen *m*; *(Scot: mayor)* maire *m*; *(Rel)* doyen *m.*

prow [praʊ] *n* proue *f.*

prowess ['praʊɪs] *n* prouesse *f.*

prowl [praʊl] *vi* (**~ about, ~ around**) rôder. ◆ **prowler** *n* rôdeur *m*, -euse *f.*

proximity [prɒk'sɪmɪtɪ] *n* proximité *f.* **in ~ to** à proximité de.

proxy ['prɒksɪ] *n (power)* procuration *f*; *(person)* mandataire *mf.* **by ~** par procuration.

prude [pru:d] *n* prude *f*, bégueule *f.* ◆ **prudery** *n* pruderie *f.* ◆ **prudish** *adj* prude.

prudent ['pru:dənt] *adj* prudent. ◆ **prudence** *n* prudence *f.* ◆ **prudently** *adv* prudemment.

prune[1] [pru:n] *n (fruit)* pruneau *m.*

prune[2] [pru:n] *vt tree* tailler; (**~ down**) *article, essay* faire des coupures dans. ◆ **pruning** **1** *n* taille *f*; **2** *adj*: **pruning knife** serpette *f.*

prurient ['prʊərɪənt] *adj* lascif. ◆ **prurience** *n* lascivité *f.*

Prussia ['prʌʃə] *n* Prusse *f.* ◆ **Prussian** **1** *adj* prussien; **2** *n* Prussien(ne) *m(f).*

pry[1] [praɪ] *vi* s'occuper de ce qui ne vous regarde pas. **to ~ into sb's desk** fureter dans le bureau de qn; **to ~ into a secret** chercher à découvrir un secret. ◆ **prying** *adj* fureteur, indiscret.

pry[2] [praɪ] *vt (US)* = **prise.**

psalm [sɑ:m] *n* psaume *m.* ◆ **psalmist** *n* psalmiste *m.*

pseudo- ['sju:dəʊ] *pref* pseudo-. **~autobiography** pseudo-autobiographie *f*; **~apologetically** sous couleur de s'excuser. ◆ **pseud** ‡ *n* bêcheur * *m*, -euse * *f.* ◆ **pseudo** * *adj* insincère, faux.

pseudonym ['sju:dənɪm] *n* pseudonyme *m.*

psoriasis [sɒ'raɪəsɪs] *n* psoriasis *m.*

psych * [saɪk] *vt* (**a**) *(guess) reaction* deviner, prévoir. (**b**) *(make uneasy: also* **~ out**) intimider. (**c**) *(prepare: also* **~ up**) préparer mentalement. **he was all ~ed up** il était gonflé à bloc.

psyche ['saɪkɪ] *n* psychisme *m*, psyché *f.*

psychedelic [,saɪkɪ'delɪk] *adj* psychédélique.

psychiatry [saɪ'kaɪətrɪ] *n* psychiatrie *f.* ◆ **psychiatric** *adj hospital, treatment, medicine* psychiatrique; *disease* mental. ◆ **psychiatrist** *n* psychiatre *mf.*

psychic(al) ['saɪkɪk(əl)] *adj* (**a**) *(supernatural) phenomenon, research* métapsychique; *(telepathic)* télépathe. **I'm not ~** * je ne suis pas devin. (**b**) *(Psych)* psychique.

psychoanalysis [,saɪkəʊə'nælɪsɪs] *n* psychanalyse *f.* ◆ **psychoanalyst** *n* psychanalyste *mf.* ◆ **psychoanalytic(al)** *adj* psychanalytique. ◆ **psychoanalyze** *vt* psychanalyser.

psychology [saɪ'kɒlədʒɪ] *n* psychologie *f.* ◆ **psychological** *adj* psychologique. ◆ **psychologically** *adv* psychologiquement. ◆ **psychologist** *n* psychologue *mf.*

psychopath ['saɪkəʊpæθ] *n* psychopathe *mf.* ◆ **psychopathic** *adj person* psychopathe; *condition* psychopathique.

psychosis, *pl* **-oses** [saɪ'kəʊsɪs, əʊsi:z] *n* psychose *f.* ◆ **psychotic** *adj, n* psychotique *(mf).*

psychosomatic ['saɪkəʊ'sə(ʊ)'mætɪk] *adj* psychosomatique.

psychotherapy ['saɪkə(ʊ)'θerəpɪ] *n* psychothérapie *f.* ◆ **psychotherapist** *n* psychothérapeute *mf.*

ptomaine ['təʊmeɪn] *n* ptomaïne *f.* **~ poisoning** intoxication *f* alimentaire.

pub [pʌb] *(Brit abbr of* **public house***)* *n* pub *m*, ≃ bistrot * *m.* **to go on a ~ crawl** * faire la tournée des bistrots *or* des pubs.

puberty ['pju:bətɪ] *n* puberté *f.*

pubis ['pju:bɪs] *n* pubis *m.* ◆ **pubic** *adj*: **pubic hair** poils *mpl* du pubis.

public ['pʌblɪk] **1** *adj (gen)* public (*f* -ique); *(Econ: ~ly owned) company* nationalisé. **to make sth ~** rendre qch public, porter qch à la connaissance du public; *(of copyright)* **in the ~ domain** dans le domaine public; *(Econ, Ind)* **the ~ sector** le secteur public; **his ~ support of the communists** son appui déclaré aux communistes; **2 ~ rooms and 3 bedrooms** 5 pièces dont 3 chambres; **~ address system** (système *m* de) sonorisation *f*; **to be in the ~ eye** être très en vue; **he's a ~ figure, he's in ~ life** c'est un homme public; **~ holiday** fête *f* légale; *(Brit)* **~ house** pub *m*, ≃ café *m*, bistrot *m*; *(US)* **~ housing** logements *mpl* sociaux; **~ lavatory** toilettes *fpl*, W.-C. *mpl*; **~ library** bibliothèque *f* municipale; **~ limited company** ≃ société *f* à responsabilité limitée; **~ opinion** opinion *f* publique; *(Pol Econ)* **~ ownership** étatisation *f*; **~ relations** relations *fpl* publiques, public-relations * *fpl*; **~ relations officer** public-relations * *mf*; **~ school** *(Brit)* collège *m* secondaire privé; *(US)* école *f* publique; **~ servant** fonctionnaire *mf*; **~ service** service *m* public; *(US)* **~ service** corporation service public non étatisé; **he is a good ~ speaker** il parle bien en public; **~ speaking** art *m* oratoire; **~ spirit** civisme *m*; *(US)* **~ television** télévision *f* éducative (non commerciale); **~ transport** transports *mpl* en commun.
2 *n* public *m.* **in ~** en public; **the reading/sporting ~** les amateurs *mpl* de lecture/de sport; **he**

couldn't disappoint his ~ il ne pouvait pas décevoir son public. ◆**publican** *n* patron(ne) *m(f)* de bistrot. ◆**publicly** *adv* publiquement, en public; *(Econ)* ~**ly-owned** nationalisé. ◆**public-spirited** *adj* qui fait preuve de civisme.

publication [ˌpʌblɪ'keɪʃ(ə)n] *n* publication *f*. **this is not for** ~ ceci doit rester entre nous.

publicity [pʌb'lɪsɪtɪ] **1** *n* publicité *f*. **adverse** ~ contre-publicité *f*. **2** *adj agency, agent* de publicité. ◆**publicize** *vt* (**a**) *(make public)* rendre public, publier; **well-publicized** dont on parle beaucoup; **I don't publicize the fact, but...** je ne le crie pas sur les toits, mais...; (**b**) *(advertise)* faire de la publicité pour.

publish ['pʌblɪʃ] *vt news, banns, book* publier; *author* éditer. **'just ~ed'** 'vient de paraître'. ◆**publisher** *n* éditeur *m*, -trice *f*. ◆**publishing** *n [book etc]* publication *f*; **he's in ~ing** il travaille dans l'édition; **~ing house** maison *f* d'édition.

pucker ['pʌkəʳ] **1** *vi* (~ **up**) *[face]* se plisser; *(Sewing)* goder. **2** *vt (Sewing)* faire goder.

pudding ['pʊdɪŋ] **1** *n (dessert)* dessert *m*; *(steamed ~, meat ~)* pudding *m*. *(sausage)* **black/white** ~ boudin *m* noir/blanc. **2** *adj*: ~ **basin** jatte *f*; ~ **rice** riz *m* à grains ronds.

puddle ['pʌdl] *n* flaque *f* d'eau.

puerile ['pjʊəraɪl] *adj* puéril.

Puerto Rico ['pwɜːtəʊ'riːkəʊ] *n* Porto Rico *f*.

puff [pʌf] **1** *n* (**a**) *[air, wind, smoke]* bouffée *f*; *(from mouth)* souffle *m*; *(sound of engine)* teuf-teuf *m*. **he took a** ~ **at his cigarette** il a tiré une bouffée de sa cigarette. (**b**) *(powder ~)* houppe *f*; *(small)* houppette *f*. *(cake)* **jam** ~ feuilleté *m* à la confiture. (**c**) *(*: Press, Rad, TV advertisement)* réclame *f*. **he gave the record a** ~ il a fait de la réclame *or* du boniment pour le disque. **2** *adj*: ~ **pastry**, *(US)* ~ **paste** pâte *f* feuilletée; ~**(ed) sleeves** manches *fpl* bouffantes. **3** *vi (blow)* souffler; *(pant)* haleter; *[wind]* souffler. **he was ~ing and panting** il soufflait comme un phoque; **to** ~ **(away) at one's pipe** tirer des bouffées de sa pipe. **4** *vt* (**a**) **to** ~ **(out) smoke** envoyer des bouffées de fumée. (**b**) *(also* ~ **out**) *sails, cheeks, chest* gonfler. **his eyes are ~ed up** il a les yeux gonflés *or* bouffis. (**c**) **to be ~ed (out)** * être à bout de souffle. (**d**) *(praise: also* ~ **up**) porter aux nues. ◆**puffball** *n* vesse-de-loup *f*. ◆**puffiness** *n* gonflement *m*, bouffissure *f*. ◆**puffy** *adj* gonflé, bouffi.

puffin ['pʌfɪn] *n* macareux *m*.

pug [pʌg] *n* carlin *m*. ◆**pug-nosed** *adj* au nez rond retroussé.

pugilism ['pjuːdʒɪlɪz(ə)m] *n* boxe *f*. ◆**pugilist** *n* pugiliste *m*.

pugnacious [pʌg'neɪʃəs] *adj* batailleur. ◆**pugnaciously** *adv* avec pugnacité. ◆**pugnacity** *n* pugnacité *f*.

puke ‡ [pjuːk] *vi* vomir, dégobiller ‡.

pukka * ['pʌkə] *adj (genuine)* véritable; *(excellent)* de premier ordre; *(socially superior)* snob *inv*.

pull [pʊl] **1** *n* (**a**) *(act, effect)* traction *f*; *[moon, magnet, the sea, sb's personality]* attraction *f*; *[current, family ties etc]* force *f*. **to give sth a** ~ tirer sur qch; **one more ~!** encore un coup!; **I felt a** ~ **at my sleeve** j'ai senti qn qui tirait ma manche; **it was a long** ~ **up the hill** la montée était longue (et raide); *(fig)* **to have some** ~ **with sb** avoir de l'influence auprès de qn. (**b**) **he took a** ~ **at the bottle** il a bu une gorgée à même la bouteille; **he took a** ~ **at his pipe** il a tiré sur sa pipe. (**c**) *(handle)* poignée *f*; *(cord)* cordon *m*.

2 *vt* (**a**) *(draw) cart, caravan, curtains* tirer. **to** ~ **a door shut** tirer une porte derrière soi; **to** ~ **a door open** ouvrir une porte en la tirant; ~ **your chair closer to the table** approchez votre chaise de la table; **he ~ed the box over to the window** il a traîné la caisse jusqu'à la fenêtre; **he ~ed her towards him** il l'a attirée vers lui. (**b**) *(tug) bell, rope* tirer; *trigger* presser; *oars* manier. **to** ~ **to pieces** *or* **to bits** *toy, box etc* mettre en pièces, démolir; *(fig) argument, scheme* démolir; *play, film, person* éreinter; **to** ~ **sb's hair** tirer les cheveux à qn; *(fig)* **to** ~ **sb's leg** faire marcher qn *; **he didn't** ~ **any punches** il n'y est pas allé de main morte; *(fig)* **to** ~ **strings** se faire pistonner *; **to** ~ **strings for sb** exercer son influence pour aider qn, pistonner * qn; *(fig)* **to** ~ **one's weight** faire sa part du travail. (**c**) *(draw out) tooth, weeds* arracher; *cork, stopper* enlever; *gun, knife* sortir; *flowers* cueillir; *beer* tirer; *(Culin) chicken* vider. **he ~ed a gun on me** il a soudain braqué un revolver sur moi. (**d**) *(strain, tear) thread* tirer; *muscle, tendon* se déchirer. (**e**) *(fig: make, do) bank raid, burglary* effectuer. **to** ~ **a fast one on sb** * rouler qn *, avoir qn *.

3 *vi* (**a**) *(tug)* tirer (*at, on* sur). **he ~ed at her sleeve** il l'a tirée par la manche; **the car is ~ing to the left** la voiture tire à gauche. (**b**) *(move)* **the coach ~ed slowly up the hill** le car a gravi lentement la colline; **the train ~ed into/out of the station** le train est entré en gare/est sorti de la gare; **he ~ed clear of the traffic** il a laissé le gros de la circulation derrière lui; **he ~ed away from the kerb** il s'est éloigné du trottoir; **the car isn't ~ing very well** la voiture manque de reprises. (**c**) *(row)* ramer (*for* vers).

◆**pull about, pull around** *vt sep* (**a**) *wheeled object etc* tirer derrière soi. (**b**) *(handle roughly) watch, ornament etc* tirailler; *person* malmener. ◆**pull along** *vt sep wheeled object etc* tirer derrière soi. **to** ~ **o.s. along** se traîner. ◆**pull ahead** *vi (in race etc)* prendre la tête. ◆**pull apart** *vt sep* (**a**) *(pull to pieces)* démonter; *(break)* mettre en pièces. (**b**) *(separate)* séparer. ◆**pull away 1** *vi [vehicle, ship, train]* démarrer. **2** *vt sep object* arracher (*from sb* à qn, des mains de qn). **he ~ed the child away from the fire** il a écarté l'enfant du feu. ◆**pull back 1** *vi (withdraw)* se retirer. **2** *vt sep object* retirer (*from* de); *person* tirer en arrière (*from* loin de); *(Mil)* retirer; *curtains* ouvrir; *lever* tirer (sur). ◆**pull down** *vt sep* (**a**) *blind* baisser, descendre; *one's skirt, hat* tirer; *one's opponent* mettre à terre; *object from shelf etc* faire tomber (*from* de). **his illness has ~ed him down** la maladie l'a affaibli. (**b**) *(demolish) building* démolir, abattre. ◆**pull in 1** *vi (Aut etc: arrive)* arriver; *[train]* entrer en gare; *(enter)* entrer; *(stop)* s'arrêter. **2** *vt sep* (**a**) *rope, fishing line* ramener; *person (into room, car)* faire entrer; *(into pool etc)* faire piquer une tête dans l'eau à. (**b**) *(restrain) horse* retenir. (**c**) *(*: earn) [person]* gagner; *[business, shop etc]* rapporter. ◆**pull off** *vt sep* (**a**) *(remove) handle, gloves, coat* enlever. (**b**) *(fig) plan, aim* réaliser; *deal* mener à bien; *attack, hoax* réussir. **he didn't** ~ **it off** il n'a pas réussi son coup. ◆**pull on** *vt sep* mettre. ◆**pull out 1** *vi* (**a**) *(leave) [train, car, ship]* démarrer; *(withdraw: lit, fig)* se retirer (*of* de). *(Aviat)* **to** ~ **out of a dive** se redresser. (**b**) *(Aut)* déboîter. **he ~ed out to overtake the truck** il a déboîté pour doubler le camion. **2** *vt sep* (**a**) *(extract) (gen)* arracher; *splinter, cork* enlever; *gun, knife, cigarette lighter, person* sortir, tirer (*of* de). (**b**) *(withdraw) troops, police etc* retirer (*of* de). ◆**pull over 1** *vi (Aut)* **to** ~ **over (to one side)** se ranger sur le côté. **2** *vt sep* (**a**) *box* traîner (*to* jusqu'à); *person* entraîner (*to* vers). (**b**) *(topple)* faire tomber. ◆**pull round 1** *vi [unconscious person]* revenir à soi; *[sick person]* se rétablir. **2** *vt sep chair, person etc* faire pivoter; *unconscious person* ranimer; *sick person* tirer de là. ◆**pull through 1** *vi (from illness, difficulties)* s'en tirer. **2** *vt sep rope etc* faire passer; *(fig) person (from illness, difficulties)* tirer de là. ◆**pull together** *vt sep*: *(fig)* **to** ~ **o.s. together** se ressaisir; ~ **yourself**

together! ressaisis-toi!, ne te laisse pas aller! ◆ **pull up 1** *vi (stop)* s'arrêter (net). **2** *vt sep* (**a**) *object* remonter; *(haul up)* hisser; *stockings* tirer. (**b**) *weed, tree* arracher. *(fig)* **to ~ up one's roots** se déraciner *(fig)*. (**c**) *(halt) vehicle, horse* arrêter; *(scold)* réprimander.
◆ **pull-in** *n (Brit) (lay-by)* parking *m*; *(café)* café *m* au bord de la route. ◆ **pull-off** *n (US)* parking *m*. ◆ **pull-out 1** *n (magazine section)* supplément *m* détachable; *[troops]* retrait *m* ; **2** *adj pages* détachable; *table leaf* rétractable. ◆ **pullover** *n* pull *m*, pullover *m*. ◆ **pull-ring** *n (on can)* anneau *m*.

pullet ['pʊlɪt] *n* jeune poule *f*.

pulley ['pʊlɪ] *n* poulie *f*.

Pullman ['pʊlmən] *n* (**~ car**) pullman *m*, voiture-salon *f*.

pulp [pʌlp] **1** *n (part of fruit)* pulpe *f*; *(for paper)* pâte *f* à papier. **crushed to a ~** complètement écrasé. **2** *adj magazine, book* à sensation. **3** *vt* réduire en pulpe *or* en pâte; *book* mettre au pilon.

pulpit ['pʊlpɪt] *n* chaire *f (Rel)*.

pulsate [pʌl'seɪt] *vi (gen)* émettre des pulsations; *[heart, blood]* battre; *[music]* vibrer. ◆ **pulsating** *adj heart (also fig)* palpitant; *music* vibrant. ◆ **pulsation** *n* pulsation *f*.

pulse¹ [pʌls] *n (Med)* pouls *m*; *(Elec, Phys, Rad)* pulsation *f*; *[radar]* impulsion *f*. **to take sb's ~** prendre le pouls de qn.

pulse² [pʌls] *n (Culin)* légume *m* sec.

pulverize ['pʌlvəraɪz] *vt* pulvériser.

puma ['pju:mə] *n* puma *m*.

pumice ['pʌmɪs] *n* (**~ stone**) pierre *f* ponce.

pummel ['pʌml] *vt* bourrer *or* rouer de coups; *(in massage)* pétrir. ◆ **pummelling** *n* volée *f* de coups; pétrissage *m*.

pump [pʌmp] **1** *n* pompe *f*. **bicycle ~** pompe à bicyclette; **petrol ~** pompe d'essence; *[petrol]* **a rise in ~ prices** une hausse à la pompe.
2 *adj*: **~ attendant** pompiste *mf*; **~ house, ~ing station** station *f* de pompage; **~ room** buvette *f (de station thermale)*.
3 *vt* (**a**) **to ~ sth out of sth** pomper qch de qch; **to ~ sth into sth** *(foam into walls etc)* injecter *or (oil into pipeline etc)* faire passer qch dans qch (au moyen d'une pompe); **to ~ water into sth** pomper de l'eau dans qch; **to ~ air into a tyre** gonfler un pneu (avec une pompe); **the water is ~ed up to the house** l'eau est amenée jusqu'à la maison au moyen d'une pompe; **they ~ed the tank dry** ils ont vidé le réservoir (à la pompe); **the heart ~s the blood** le cœur fait circuler le sang; *(fig)* **to ~ money into sth** injecter de plus en plus d'argent dans qch; *(fig: question)* **to ~ sb for sth** essayer de soutirer qch à qn. (**b**) *handle etc* lever et abaisser vigoureusement.
◆ **pump in** *vt sep* injecter *or* faire passer (à l'aide d'une pompe). ◆ **pump out** *vt sep* pomper. ◆ **pump up** *vt sep tyre* gonfler.

pumpkin ['pʌm(p)kɪn] *n* citrouille *f*; *(bigger)* potiron *m*. **~ pie** tarte *f* au potiron.

pun [pʌn] *n* calembour *m*, jeu *m* de mots.

Punch [pʌn(t)ʃ] *n* Polichinelle *m*. **~ and Judy Show** (théâtre *m* de) guignol *m*.

punch¹ [pʌn(t)ʃ] **1** *n* (**a**) *(blow)* coup *m* de poing ; *[boxer]* punch *m*; *(fig: drive) [publicity, statement]* force *f*; *[person]* punch * *m*. (**b**) *(tool) (for tickets)* poinçonneuse *f*; *(for holes in paper)* perforateur *m*; *(for metal)* emporte-pièce *m inv*; *(for nails)* chasse-clou *m*. **2** *vt* (**a**) *(with fist) person* donner un coup de poing à; *ball, door* frapper d'un coup de poing. **to ~ sb's nose** donner un coup de poing sur le nez à qn. (**b**) poinçonner; perforer; découper à l'emporte-pièce; enfoncer (au chasse-clou). **to ~ a hole in sth** faire un trou dans qch; *(Ind)* **to ~ one's card** pointer. ◆ **punchball** *or* ◆ **punching bag** *(US)* *n* sac *m* de sable. ◆ **punch(ed) card** *n* carte *f* perforée. ◆ **punch-drunk** *adj* abruti. ◆ **punch-line** *n [joke]* conclusion *f* (comique); *[speech]* trait *m* final. ◆ **punch-up** * *n* bagarre * *f*.

punch² [pʌn(t)ʃ] *n (drink)* punch *m*. **~ bowl** bol *m* à punch.

punctilious [pʌŋ(k)'tɪlɪəs] *adj* pointilleux. ◆ **punctiliously** *adv* de façon pointilleuse.

punctual ['pʌŋ(k)tjʊəl] *adj person for appointment, train* à l'heure; *employee, payment* ponctuel. ◆ **punctuality** *n* exactitude *f*. ◆ **punctually** *adv arrive* à l'heure; **~ly at 7** à 7 heures précises.

punctuate ['pʌŋ(k)tjʊeɪt] *vt* ponctuer (*with* de). ◆ **punctuation** *n* ponctuation *f*; **punctuation mark** signe *m* de ponctuation.

puncture ['pʌŋ(k)tʃəʳ] **1** *n (in tyre)* crevaison *f*; *(in skin, paper etc)* piqûre *f*. *(Aut etc)* **I've got a ~** j'ai crevé. **2** *adj*: **~ repair kit** trousse *f* de secours pour crevaisons. **3** *vt* crever; piquer. **4** *vi [tyre etc]* crever.

pundit ['pʌndɪt] *n* expert *m*, pontife *m*.

pungent ['pʌndʒ(ə)nt] *adj smell, taste* âcre; *sauce* piquant; *remark* mordant. ◆ **pungency** *n* âcreté *f*; goût *m* piquant; mordant *m*. ◆ **pungently** *adv remark* d'un ton mordant.

punish ['pʌnɪʃ] *vt (gen)* punir (*for sth* de qch; *for doing* pour avoir fait); *(fig) opponent, boxer* malmener; *engine* fatiguer; *roast beef* faire honneur à. **he was ~ed by having to clean it up** pour le punir on le lui a fait nettoyer. ◆ **punishable** *adj offence* punissable; **~able by death** passible de la peine de mort. ◆ **punishing 1** *n* punition *f* ; **2** *adj (fig: exhausting)* exténuant. ◆ **punishment** *n* punition *f* ; *(solemn)* châtiment *m*; **as a ~ment** en punition (*for* de); **capital ~ment** peine *f* capitale; **to take one's ~ment** subir sa punition; **to make the ~ment fit the crime** adapter le châtiment au crime; *(fig)* **to take a lot of ~ment** *[boxer, fighter]* encaisser *; *[opposing team]* se faire malmener.

punk [pʌŋk] *n (nonsense)* foutaises ‡ *fpl*; *(esp US ‡: ruffian)* sale * petit voyou *m*. **~ (rock)** le punk rock; **~ (rocker)** punk *m*.

punt¹ [pʌnt] **1** *n (boat)* bachot *m* à fond plat. **2** *vt boat* faire avancer à la perche. **3** *vi*: **to go ~ing** faire un tour sur la rivière.

punt² [pʌnt] *vi (bet)* parier. ◆ **punter** *n* parieur *m*, -ieuse *f*.

puny ['pju:nɪ] *adj person, animal* chétif; *effort* piteux.

pup [pʌp] *n* jeune chien(ne) *m(f)*. *(fig)* **he's an insolent young ~** c'est un petit morveux *. ◆ **puppy 1** *n* = **pup** ; **2** *adj*: **~py fat** rondeurs *fpl* d'adolescent(e); **~py love** premier amour *m (d'adolescent)*.

pupil¹ ['pju:pl] **1** *n (Scol etc)* élève *mf*. **2** *adj*: **~ power** pouvoir *m* des lycéens; **~ teacher** professeur *m* stagiaire.

pupil² ['pju:pl] *n [eye]* pupille *f*.

puppet ['pʌpɪt] **1** *n* marionnette *f*. **2** *adj theatre, play* de marionnettes; *(fig) state, leader* fantoche. **~ show** (spectacle *m* de) marionnettes *fpl*. ◆ **puppeteer** *n* marionnettiste *mf*.

purchase ['pɜ:tʃɪs] **1** *n* (**a**) *(Comm etc)* achat *m*. (**b**) *(grip, hold)* prise *f*. **to get a ~ on** avoir une prise sur. **2** *adj*: **~ price** prix *m* d'achat; **~ tax** taxe *f* à l'achat. **3** *vt* acheter (*sth from sb* qch à qn; *sth for sb* qch pour *or* à qn). ◆ **purchaser** *n* acheteur *m*, -euse *f*. ◆ **purchasing power** *n* pouvoir *m* d'achat.

pure [pjʊəʳ] *adj* pur. **as ~ as the driven snow** innocent comme l'enfant qui vient de naître; **~ in heart** au cœur pur; **~ science** science pure; **a ~ wool suit** un complet pure laine; **~ and simple** pur et simple; **it was a ~ accident** c'était un pur accident; **it was ~ chance/madness** c'était un pur hasard/de la pure folie. ◆ **purebred** **1** *adj* de race ; **2** *n* animal *m* de race; *(horse)* pur-sang *m inv*. ◆ **pure-hearted** *adj* (au cœur) pur. ◆ **purely** *adv* purement; **~ly and simply** purement et simplement. ◆ **pure-minded** *adj* pur d'esprit. ◆ **pureness** *n* pureté *f*.

purgative ['pɜːgətɪv] *adj, n* purgatif *(m)*.

purgatory ['pɜːgət(ə)rɪ] *n* purgatoire *m*. *(fig)* **it was ~** c'était un vrai purgatoire.

purge [pɜːdʒ] **1** *n (gen, Med, Pol)* purge *f*. **2** *vt* (**a**) *(gen, Med, Pol)* purger (*of* de); *traitors* éliminer. (**b**) *(Jur) person* disculper (*of* de); *accusation* se disculper de; *offence* purger.

purify ['pjʊərɪfaɪ] *vt* purifier. ◆ **purification** *n [water, metal etc]* épuration *f*; *[person]* purification *f*. ◆ **purifier** *n* purificateur *m*.

purist ['pjʊərɪst] *adj, n* puriste *(mf)*.

puritan ['pjʊərɪt(ə)n] *adj, n* puritain(e) *m(f)*. ◆ **puritanical** *adj* puritain. ◆ **puritanism** *n* puritanisme *m*.

purity ['pjʊərɪtɪ] *n* pureté *f*.

purl [pɜːl] **1** *adj* à l'envers. **2** *vt* tricoter à l'envers.

purloin [pɜː'lɔɪn] *vt* dérober.

purple ['pɜːpl] **1** *adj* violet, pourpre. **to go ~ in the face** devenir cramoisi. *(fig)* **~ passages** morceaux *mpl* de bravoure. **2** *n (colour)* violet *m*, pourpre *m*. *(Rel)* **the ~** la pourpre.

purport ['pɜːpət] **1** *n* signification *f*, portée *f*. **2** [pɜː'pɔːt] *vt*: **to ~ to be** prétendre être.

purpose ['pɜːpəs] *n (aim, intention)* but *m*, objet *m*; *(use)* usage *m*, utilité *f*. **a ~ in life** un but *or* un objectif dans la vie; **a film with a ~** un film qui contient un message; **with the ~ of doing** dans le but *or* l'intention de faire; **for this ~** dans ce but; **sense of ~** résolution *f*; **for my ~s** pour ce que je veux faire; **for the ~s of the meeting** pour les besoins de cette réunion; **on ~** exprès, délibérément; **on ~ to annoy me** exprès pour me contrarier; **to no ~** en vain; **to no ~ at all** en pure perte; **to some ~, to good ~** utilement; **to the ~** à propos; **not to the ~** hors de propos. ◆ **purpose-built** *adj* fonctionnalisé. ◆ **purposeful** *adj (determined)* résolu; *(intentional)* réfléchi. ◆ **purposefully** *adv* délibérément. ◆ **purposely** *adv* exprès, délibérément.

purr [pɜː[r]] **1** *vi [cat]* ronronner. **2** *n* ronronnement *m*.

purse [pɜːs] **1** *n (for coins)* porte-monnaie *m inv*, bourse *f*; *(wallet)* portefeuille *m*; *(US: handbag)* sac *m* à main; *(esp Sport: prize)* prix *m*. *(fig)* **beyond my ~** au-delà de mes moyens. **2** *adj (fig)* **to hold/tighten the ~ strings** tenir/serrer les cordons de la bourse. **3** *vt*: **to ~ (up) one's lips** pincer les lèvres. ◆ **purser** *n (Naut)* commissaire *m* du bord.

pursue [pə'sjuː] *vt* (**a**) *(chase: gen)* poursuivre; *pleasure, fame* rechercher; *[misfortune etc]* suivre. (**b**) *(carry on) studies, career, plan, inquiry* poursuivre; *course of action* suivre. ◆ **pursuer** *n* poursuivant(e) *m(f)*.

pursuit [pə'sjuːt] *n* (**a**) *(chase)* poursuite *f*; *(fig: of pleasure, happiness)* recherche *f*. **to go in ~ of sb/sth** se mettre à la poursuite de qn/qch; **with two policemen in hot ~** avec deux agents à ses (*or* mes *etc*) trousses. (**b**) *(occupation)* occupation *f*; *(work)* travail *m*.

purveyor [pɜː've(ɪ)ə[r]] *n (Comm etc)* fournisseur *m*, -euse *f* (*of sth* en qch; *to sb* de qn).

pus [pʌs] *n* pus *m*.

push [pʊʃ] **1** *n* (**a**) *(shove)* poussée *f*. **to give sb/sth a ~** pousser qn/qch; *(Brit fig)* **to give sb the ~** ‡ *[employer]* flanquer qn à la porte *; *[boyfriend etc]* laisser tomber qn *. (**b**) *(Mil: advance)* poussée *f*; *(fig) (effort)* gros effort *m*; *(campaign)* campagne *f*. **at a ~** * au besoin, à la rigueur; **when it comes to the ~** * au moment critique. (**c**) *(*: drive, energy)* dynamisme *m*, initiative *f*.

2 *vt* (**a**) *(shove, prod)* pousser (*into* dans; *off* de); *(press) knob, button* appuyer sur; *stick, finger etc* enfoncer (*into* dans, *between* entre); *rag etc* fourrer (*into* dans). **to ~ sb in/out** *etc* faire entrer/sortir *etc* qn en le poussant; **he ~ed him down the stairs** il l'a poussé et l'a fait tomber dans l'escalier; **they ~ed the car off the road** ils ont poussé la voiture sur le bas-côté; **he ~ed his head through the window** il a passé la tête par la fenêtre; **he ~ed the book into my hand** il m'a fourré * le livre dans la main; **to ~ a door open** ouvrir une porte en poussant; **to ~ one's way through a crowd** se frayer un chemin dans la foule; *(fig)* **it ~ed the matter right out of my mind** cela m'a fait complètement oublier l'affaire; **he's ~ing * 60** il doit friser la soixantaine.

(**b**) *(fig: press, advance) advantage* poursuivre; *claim* présenter avec insistance; *one's views* mettre en avant; *plan, solution* préconiser, recommander; *product* pousser la vente de; *candidate etc* soutenir. **to ~ home an attack** pousser à fond une attaque; **to ~ the export side** donner priorité aux exportations; **to ~ drugs** revendre de la drogue; **don't ~ your luck *** vas-y doucement!; **he's ~ing his luck *** il y va un peu fort.

(**c**) *(put pressure on)* pousser; *(force)* forcer, obliger; *(harass)* harceler. **to ~ sb for payment** presser qn à payer; **he ~es himself too hard** il exige trop de lui-même; **don't ~ him too hard** *or* **too far** ne soyez pas trop dur envers lui; **to ~ sb to do** pousser qn à faire; **to ~ sb into doing** forcer qn à faire; **to be ~ed * for time/money/boxes** être à court de temps/d'argent/de boîtes; **I'm really ~ed * today** je suis vraiment bousculé aujourd'hui; **that's ~ing it a bit! *** *(indignantly)* c'est un peu fort!; *(not much room)* c'est un peu juste!

3 *vi* (**a**) pousser. **'push'** *(on door)* 'poussez'; *(on bell)* 'sonnez'; *(fig)* **he ~es too much** il se met trop en avant; *(fig)* **to ~ for better conditions** faire pression pour obtenir de meilleures conditions. (**b**) **they ~ed into the room** ils sont entrés dans la pièce en se frayant un passage; **he ~ed past me** il a réussi à passer en me bousculant; **she ~ed through the crowd** elle s'est frayé un chemin dans la foule.

◆ **push about, push around** *vt sep* (**a**) *cart, toy* pousser de-ci de-là. (**b**) *(*: bully)* marcher sur les pieds à *(fig)*.

◆ **push aside** *vt sep* écarter (brusquement).

◆ **push away** *vt sep* repousser.

◆ **push back** *vt sep cover, blankets, lock of hair* rejeter; *curtains* ouvrir; *crowd, enemy* faire reculer; *(fig) desire* réprimer.

◆ **push down 1** *vi* appuyer (*on* sur). **2** *vt sep switch, lever* abaisser; *knob, button* appuyer sur; *pin, stick* enfoncer; *(knock over) fence, barrier, person* renverser. **he ~ed the books down into the box** il a entassé les livres dans la caisse.

◆ **push forward 1** *vi* avancer (en poussant). **2** *vt sep person, box etc* pousser en avant. **he ~ed himself forward** il s'est avancé; *(fig)* il s'est mis en avant.

◆ **push in 1** *vi (into room)* s'introduire de force; *(into discussion etc)* intervenir. **2** *vt sep* (**a**) *stick, pin, finger* enfoncer; *rag* fourrer dedans; *knob, button* appuyer sur; *person* faire entrer (en poussant); *(into water)* pousser dedans. (**b**) *(break) door, sides of box* enfoncer.

◆ **push off 1** *vi* (**a**) *(Naut)* pousser au large. (**b**) *(*: leave)* filer *, partir. **2** *vt sep* (**a**) *top, lid* enlever en poussant; *vase from shelf etc* faire tomber (*from* de); *person from cliff etc* pousser (*from* de, du haut de). (**b**) *(Naut)* déborder.

◆**push on 1** *vi (in journey)* pousser (*to* jusqu'à); *(in work)* continuer. **2** *vt sep* pousser, inciter (*sb to do* qn à faire).

◆**push out** *vt sep* (**a**) *person, object* pousser dehors; *boat* pousser au large; *stopper* faire sortir (en poussant); *(fig) employee* se débarrasser de. (**b**) *roots, shoots* produire.

◆**push over** *vt sep* (**a**) *object* pousser (*to sb* vers qn); *(over cliff etc)* pousser. (**b**) *(topple) chair, person* renverser.

◆**push through 1** *vi* se frayer un chemin. **2** *vt sep stick, hand etc* enfoncer; *(fig) deal, business* conclure à la hâte; *decision* faire accepter à la hâte; *(Parl) bill* réussir à faire voter.

◆**push to** *vt sep door* pousser (pour fermer).

◆**push up** *vt sep lever, switch, spectacles* relever; *(fig) (gen)* augmenter; *sb's temperature, blood pressure, total* faire monter.

◆**push-bike** * *n* vélo *m*. ◆**push-button** *adj machine* à commande automatique; **~-button controls** commande *f* automatique; **~-button warfare** guerre *f* presse-bouton. ◆**push-chair** *n* poussette *f (pour enfant)*. ◆**pusher** *n* (**a**) *(pej)* arriviste *mf*; (**b**) *[drugs]* revendeur *m*, -euse *f*. ◆**pushful** * *or* ◆**pushy** * *adj* qui se met trop en avant. ◆**pushing** *adj person* dynamique, entreprenant; *(pej)* arriviste, qui se met trop en avant. ◆**push-over** * *n*: **it was a ~over** c'était un jeu d'enfant. ◆**push-up** *n* traction *f (Sport)*.

pusillanimous [ˌpjuːsɪˈlænɪməs] *adj* pusillanime.

puss * [pʊs], **pussy** * [ˈpʊsɪ] *n* minet *m*, -ette *f*. ◆**pussycat** *n* minou *m*; *(US)* **hi, ~ycat** bonjour mon ange!

put [pʊt] *pret, ptp* **put 1** *vt* (**a**) *(gen)* mettre; *(place)* placer; *(lay down)* poser; *energy, time* consacrer (*into* à); *money, savings* placer (*into* dans); *advertisement in paper* passer (*in* dans); *signature* apposer (*on, to* à); *mark* faire (*on* sur, à). **he ~ some more coal on the fire** il a remis du charbon sur le feu; **to ~ one's arms round sb** prendre qn dans ses bras; **he ~ his head through the window** il a passé la tête par la fenêtre; **he ~ his hand over his mouth** il s'est mis la main devant la bouche; **he ~ me on the train** il m'a mis *or* accompagné au train; **he ~ me into a non-smoker** il m'a trouvé une place dans un compartiment non-fumeurs; **to ~ sb off a train** *etc* débarquer qn d'un train *etc*; **to ~ sb on to/off a committee** nommer qn à/renvoyer qn d'un comité; **to ~ one's confidence in** placer sa confiance en; **you get out of life what you ~ into it** on ne retire de la vie que ce qu'on y met soi-même; **he has ~ a lot into his marriage** il a fait beaucoup d'efforts pour que son mariage soit une réussite; **he ~ £10 on Black Beauty** il a parié *or* misé 10 livres sur Black Beauty ; **I shouldn't ~ him among the greatest poets** je ne le place pas parmi les plus grands poètes.

(**b**) *(thrust; direct) pointed object* enfoncer (*into* dans). **to ~ one's fist through a window** passer le poing à travers une vitre; **I ~ a bullet through his head** je lui ai tiré une balle dans la tête; *(Sport)* **to ~ the shot** *or* **the weight** lancer le poids.

(**c**) *(cause to be)* **to ~ sb in a good/bad mood** mettre qn de bonne/mauvaise humeur; **to ~ sb on a diet** mettre qn au régime; **to ~ sb to some trouble** déranger qn; **they ~ him to digging the garden** ils lui ont fait bêcher le jardin; **I ~ him to work at once** je l'ai mis au travail aussitôt; **they had to ~ 4 men on to this job** ils ont dû employer 4 hommes à ce travail.

(**d**) *(with preposition)* **to ~ one across** *or* **over on sb** * faire marcher * qn; **to ~ sb against sb** monter qn contre qn; **to ~ sb off his food** couper l'appétit à qn; **it almost ~ me off opera for good** cela a failli me dégoûter de l'opéra pour toujours; **to ~ sb off doing** ôter à qn l'envie de faire; **to ~ sb off his work** distraire qn de son travail; **to ~ sb through an examination** faire subir un examen à qn; **they really ~ him through it** * ils lui en ont fait voir de dures *.

(**e**) *(express)* dire, exprimer (*to sb* à qn). **can you ~ it another way?** pouvez-vous vous exprimer autrement?; **to ~ it bluntly** pour parler franc; **as he would ~ it** selon son expression; **as Shakespeare ~s it** comme le dit Shakespeare; **I don't know how to ~ it** je ne sais pas comment le dire; **how shall I ~ it?** comment dire?; **to ~ an expression into French** mettre une expression en français; **how would you ~ it in French?** comment le dirais-tu en français?; **to ~ into verse** mettre en vers.

(**f**) *(expound) case, problem* exposer; *proposal, resolution, arguments* présenter; *question* poser. **I ~ it to you that...** n'est-il pas vrai que...?; **it was ~ to me that** on m'a fait clairement comprendre que.

(**g**) *(estimate)* estimer, évaluer (*at* à). **what would you ~ it at?** à combien l'estimez-vous? *or* l'évaluez-vous?; **I'd ~ her age at 50** je lui donnerais 50 ans.

2 *vi (Naut)* **to ~ into port** faire escale, entrer au port; **to ~ into Southampton** entrer au port de Southampton; **to ~ to sea** appareiller, lever l'ancre.

◆**put about 1** *vi (Naut)* virer de bord. **2** *vt sep (rumour: also* **~ around***)* **he ~ it about** *or* **he ~ about the rumour that...** il a fait courir le bruit que...

◆**put across** *vt sep* (**a**) *(communicate) ideas, intentions* faire comprendre, communiquer (*to sb* à qn); *(Comm) new product* faire accepter (*to sb* à qn). **to ~ sth across to sb** faire comprendre qch à qn; **he can't ~ himself across** il n'arrive pas à se mettre en valeur. (**b**) **to ~ one** *or* **it across on sb** * faire marcher * qn.

◆**put aside** *vt sep* (**a**) *(lay down) one's book etc* poser; *(save)* mettre de côté. *(Comm)* **I have had it ~ aside for you** je vous l'ai fait mettre de côté. (**b**) *(fig) doubts, idea, hope* écarter.

◆**put away** *vt sep* (**a**) = **put aside.** (**b**) *clothes, toys, books* ranger; *car* rentrer. (**c**) *(confine) (in prison)* mettre en prison; *(in mental hospital)* (faire) enfermer. (**d**) *(*: consume) food* engloutir; *drink* siffler *. (**e**) = **put down 2h.**

◆**put back 1** *vi (Naut)* rentrer (*to* à). **2** *vt sep* (**a**) *(replace)* remettre (à sa place). (**b**) *(retard) development, progress* retarder; *project* retarder la réalisation de; *clock* retarder (*by* de); *clock hands* remettre en arrière. **this will ~ us back 10 years** cela nous ramènera où nous en étions il y a 10 ans; *(fig)* **you can't ~ the clock back** ce qui est fait est fait. (**c**) *(postpone)* remettre (*to* à).

◆**put by** *vt sep* = **put aside (a).**

◆**put down 1** *vi [aircraft]* se poser. **2** *vt sep* (**a**) *(gen)* poser; *(Aut) passenger* déposer; *umbrella* fermer; *wine* mettre en cave. *(fig)* **I couldn't ~ that book down** je ne pouvais pas m'arracher à ce livre. (**b**) *(pay) deposit, money* verser (*on* pour). (**c**) *(suppress) revolt* réprimer; *custom, practice* supprimer. (**d**) *(snub)* rabrouer; *(humiliate)* humilier. (**e**) *(record)* noter, inscrire. **to ~ sth down on paper** mettre qch par écrit; *(Comm)* **~ it down on my account** mettez-le sur mon compte; **I have ~ you down as a teacher/for £10** je vous ai inscrit comme professeur/pour 10 livres. (**f**) *(attribute)* attribuer (*sth to sth* qch à qch). (**g**) *(assess)* **I had ~ him down as a complete fool** je l'avais pris pour *or* je le considérais comme un parfait imbécile; **I'd ~ her down as about forty** je lui donnerais environ quarante ans. (**h**) *(euph: kill) dog, cat* faire piquer; *horse* abattre.

◆**put forth** *vt sep (liter) leaves* produire; *arm* tendre; *idea* avancer.

◆**put forward** *vt sep* (**a**) *(propose) theory, argument* avancer; *opinion* exprimer; *plan, person* proposer (*as* comme; *for* pour). **he ~ himself forward for the job** il a posé sa candidature au poste. (**b**) *(advance) meeting, starting time* avancer (*by* de; *to, until* à).

◆ **put in 1** *vi (Naut)* faire escale (*at* à). **2** *vt sep* (**a**) *(into box, drawer, room etc)* mettre dedans; *seeds* planter. *(packing)* **have you ~ in your shirts?** est-ce que tu as pris tes chemises? (**b**) *(insert) word, remark* ajouter; *(include: in letter, publication)* inclure. **have you ~ in why...?** est-ce que vous avez expliqué pourquoi...? (**c**) *(enter) document, claim* présenter; *application* faire; *one's name* avancer; *protest* élever. *(Jur)* **to ~ in a plea** plaider; **to ~ sb in for an exam** présenter qn à un examen; **to ~ sb in for a job/promotion** proposer qn pour un poste/pour de l'avancement. (**d**) *(esp Pol: elect) party, person* élire. (**e**) *time* passer (*on sth* à qch; *on doing* à faire). **we have an hour to ~ in before...** nous avons une heure à perdre avant...; **he has ~ in a full day's work** il a fait sa journée; *(fig)* il a bien travaillé; **can you ~ in a few hours at the weekend?** pourrais-tu travailler quelques heures pendant le week-end?; **she ~s in an hour a day at the piano** elle fait une heure de piano par jour.

◆ **put in for** *vt fus job* poser sa candidature pour *or* à; *promotion, social benefits* faire une demande de.

◆ **put off 1** *vi (Naut)* démarrer (*from* de). **2** *vt sep* (**a**) *(postpone) departure, appointment, decision* repousser, remettre à plus tard; *visitor* renvoyer à plus tard. **to ~ off doing sth** remettre qch (*for* de; *until* jusqu'à); *(fig)* **he ~ her off with vague promises** il l'a dissuadée avec de vagues promesses; **he is not easily ~ off** il ne se laisse pas facilement démonter; **he ~s me off when he laughs like that** cela me déconcerte quand il rit de cette façon; **the colour ~ me off** la couleur m'a plutôt dégoûté. (**b**) *coat, hat etc* enlever; *passenger* déposer. (**c**) *(extinguish etc) light, gas* éteindre; *radio, TV, heater* fermer.

◆ **put on** *vt sep* (**a**) *garment, glasses* mettre. (**b**) *(add, increase) pressure, speed* augmenter. **to ~ on weight** grossir, prendre du poids. (**c**) *(assume) indignation* affecter, simuler; *air, accent* prendre; *(*: deceive) person* faire marcher *. **he's just ~ting it on** il fait seulement semblant; **you're ~ting me on!** * tu me fais marcher! * (**d**) *concert, play, show* organiser; *film* projeter; *extra train, bus etc* mettre en service. *(Telec)* **~ me on to Mr Brown** passez-moi M. Brown. (**e**) *light, gas* allumer; *radio, TV, heater* ouvrir. **~ the kettle on** mets l'eau à chauffer; **I'll just ~ the soup on** je vais juste mettre la soupe à cuire; **to ~ the brakes on** freiner. (**f**) *(advance) clock* avancer (*by* de). (**g**) *(wager)* parier. (**h**) *(inform, indicate)* indiquer. **they ~ the police on to him** ils l'ont signalé à la police; **can you ~ me on to a good dentist?** pourriez-vous m'indiquer un bon dentiste?; **Paul ~ us on to you** c'est Paul qui nous envoie; **what ~ you on to it?** qu'est-ce qui vous y a fait penser?

◆ **put out 1** *vi*: **to ~ out to sea/from Dieppe** quitter le port/Dieppe. **2** *vt sep* (**a**) *(~ outside) chair etc* sortir, mettre dehors; *(get rid of) rubbish* sortir; *(expel) person, country, organization* expulser (*of* de); *the cat* faire sortir. *(fig)* **to ~ sth out of one's head** ne plus penser à qch. (**b**) *(Naut) boat* mettre à la mer. (**c**) *(stretch out, extend) arm, leg* étendre; *foot* avancer; *tongue* tirer (*at sb* à qn); *leaves* produire. **to ~ out one's hand** tendre la main; *[car driver, traffic policeman]* tendre le bras; **to ~ one's head out of the window** passer la tête par la fenêtre. (**d**) *(lay out in order) (gen)* sortir; *papers, cards* étaler; *chessmen etc* disposer. (**e**) *(extinguish) light, flames, cigarette* éteindre; *heater* fermer. (**f**) *(disconcert)* déconcerter (*by, about* par); *(vex)* contrarier, ennuyer (*by, about* par); *(inconvenience)* déranger. **she ~ herself out for us** elle s'est donné beaucoup de mal pour nous. (**g**) *(issue) news* annoncer; *report, regulations, book* publier; *rumour* faire courir; *appeal, warning* lancer; *announcement, statement* publier; *propaganda* faire. (**h**) *(spend)* dépenser (*on* pour). (**i**) *(Comm) repairs, small jobs* donner au dehors; *(Ind: subcontract)* donner à des sous-traitants. (**j**) *(exert) one's strength, tact* déployer, user de. (**k**) *(dislocate) shoulder, back* démettre.

◆ **put over** *vt sep* = **put across.**

◆ **put through** *vt sep* (**a**) *(make, complete) deal* conclure, mener à bien; *decision* prendre; *proposal* faire accepter. (**b**) *(Telec: connect) call* passer. **I'm ~ting you through now** je vous mets en communication, vous êtes en ligne; **~ me through to Mr Smith** passez-moi M. Smith.

◆ **put together** *vt sep* (**a**) *(lit)* mettre ensemble, placer l'un à côté de l'autre. **he's worth more than the rest of the family ~ together** à lui tout seul il vaut largement le reste de la famille. (**b**) *(assemble) table, radio* monter; *jigsaw* assembler; *book, story, account* composer; *(piece together) facts, what happened* reconstituer; *(mend)* réparer. **she ~ together an excellent supper** elle a improvisé un délicieux dîner; **to ~ together an application** constituer un dossier.

◆ **put up 1** *vi* (**a**) *(lodge)* descendre (*at* dans); *(for one night)* passer la nuit (*at* à). (**b**) *(offer o.s.)* se porter candidat(e) (*for* à). **2** *vt sep* (**a**) *(raise) hand* lever; *flag, sail* hisser; *tent, fence, ladder* dresser; *collar, window* remonter; *umbrella* ouvrir; *notice, picture* mettre (*on* sur); *missile, rocket* lancer; *building, bridge* construire. **~ them up!** * *(in robbery etc)* haut les mains!; *(challenge to fight)* défends-toi! (**b**) *(increase) (gen)* augmenter; *temperature, blood pressure, total* faire monter. (**c**) *(offer) proposal, idea* présenter, soumettre; *plea, resistance* offrir; *(nominate) person* proposer comme candidat (*for* à; *as* comme). **to ~ sth up for sale/auction** mettre qch en vente/aux enchères; **he was ~ up by his local branch** il a été présenté comme candidat par sa section locale; **to ~ sb up for a club** proposer qn comme membre d'un club. (**d**) *(provide) money, funds* fournir (*for* pour); *reward* offrir. **how much can you ~ up?** combien pouvez-vous (y) mettre? (**e**) *(prepare) picnic, sandwiches, prescription* préparer; *(Comm) order* exécuter. (**f**) *(lodge)* loger. (**g**) *(incite)* **to ~ sb up to doing** pousser qn à faire. (**h**) *(inform about)* **to ~ sb up to sth** mettre qn au courant de qch.

◆ **put upon** *vt fus*: **to ~ upon sb** en imposer à qn; **I won't be ~ upon any more!** je ne vais plus me laisser marcher sur les pieds!

◆ **put up with** *vt fus* supporter, encaisser *. **he has a lot to ~ up with** il a beaucoup de problèmes.

◆ **put-down** * *n (denigrating)* dénigrement *m*; *(snub)* rebuffade *f*. ◆ **put-up job** * *n* coup *m* monté. ◆ **put-you-up** *n* canapé-lit *m*.

putrefy ['pju:trɪfaɪ] **1** *vt* putréfier. **2** *vi* se putréfier. ◆ **putrefaction** *n* putréfaction *f*.

putrid ['pju:trɪd] *adj* putride; *(* fig)* dégoûtant.

putsch [pʊtʃ] *n* putsch *m*, coup *m* d'État.

putt [pʌt] *(Golf)* **1** *n* putt *m*. **2** *vti* putter. ◆ **putting** *n* putting *m*. ◆ **putting green** *n* green *m*.

putty ['pʌtɪ] *n* mastic *m (ciment)*.

puzzle ['pʌzl] **1** *n* (**a**) *(mystery)* énigme *f*, mystère *m*. **he is a real ~ to me** c'est une énigme vivante pour moi; **it is a ~ to me how...** je n'arriverai jamais à comprendre comment... (**b**) *(game)* casse-tête *m inv*; *(word game)* rébus *m*; *(cross-word)* mots *mpl* croisés; *(jigsaw)* puzzle *m*; *(riddle)* devinette *f*. **2** *vt* laisser perplexe. **I am ~d to know why** je n'arrive pas à comprendre pourquoi; **he was ~d about what to say** il ne savait pas quoi dire. **3** *vi*: **to ~ over** *or* **about** *problem, mystery* essayer de résoudre; *sb's actions, intentions* essayer de comprendre; **I'm still puzzling over why...** j'en suis encore à me demander pourquoi...

◆ **puzzle out** *vt sep problem* résoudre; *mystery* éclaircir; *writing* déchiffrer; *answer, solution* trouver; *sb's actions, attitude* comprendre. **I'm trying to ~ out why** j'essaie de comprendre pourquoi. ◆ **puzzled** *adj* perplexe. ◆ **puzzlement** *n* perplexité *f.* ◆ **puzzler** *n (gen)* énigme *f; (problem)* casse-tête *m inv.* ◆ **puzzling** *adj* incompréhensible.

pygmy [ˈpɪgmɪ] **1** *n* pygmée *m.* **2** *adj* pygmée *(f inv).*

pyjamas [pɪˈdʒɑːməz] *npl (Brit)* pyjama *m.* **in (one's) ~** en pyjama.

pylon [ˈpaɪlən] *n* pylône *m.*

pyramid [ˈpɪrəmɪd] *n* pyramide *f.*

pyre [ˈpaɪə^r] *n* bûcher *m* funéraire.

Pyrenees [pɪrəˈniːz] *npl* Pyrénées *fpl.*

Pyrex [ˈpaɪreks] *n* ® pyrex *m* ®.

pyro... [ˈpaɪərəʊ] *pref* pyro... ◆ **pyromaniac** *n* pyromane *mf.* ◆ **pyrotechnic** *adj* pyrotechnique.

python [ˈpaɪθən] *n* python *m.*

Q

Q, q [kjuː] *n (letter)* Q, q *m*. **on the q.t.** * en douce *.

Qatar [kæ'tɑːʳ] *n* Qatar *m*.

quack¹ [kwæk] **1** *n* coin-coin *m*. **2** *vi* faire coin-coin.

quack² [kwæk] **1** *n (pej)* charlatan *m*; (*‡: doctor*) toubib * *m*. **2** *adj* de charlatan.

quad [kwɒd] *n abbr of* **quadruplet** *and* **quadrangle b.**

quadrangle ['kwɒdræŋgl] *n* (**a**) *(Math)* quadrilatère *m*. (**b**) *(courtyard)* cour *f (d'un collège etc)*.

quadraphonic ['kwɒdrə'fɒnɪk] *adj* quadriphonique. **in ~ sound** en quadriphonie.

quadratic [kwɒ'drætɪk] *adj* du second degré.

quadrilateral [ˌkwɒdrɪ'læt(ə)r(ə)l] *adj, n* quadrilatère *(m)*.

quadriplegia ['kwɒdrɪ'pliːdʒɪə] *n* tétraplégie *f*. ◆ **quadriplegic** *adj, n* tétraplégique *(mf)*.

quadruped ['kwɒdrʊped] *adj, n* quadrupède *(m)*.

quadruple ['kwɒdrʊpl] **1** *adj, n* quadruple *(m)*. **2** ['kwɒ'druːpl] *vti* quadrupler. ◆ **quadruplet** *n* quadruplé(e) *m(f)*.

quagmire ['kwægmaɪəʳ] *n* bourbier *m*.

quail¹ [kweɪl] *vi (flinch)* perdre courage.

quail² [kweɪl] *n (bird)* caille *f*.

quaint [kweɪnt] *adj (odd)* bizarre, original; *(picturesque)* pittoresque; *(old-fashioned etc)* au charme vieillot. ◆ **quaintly** *adv* d'une manière originale *or* pittoresque.

quake [kweɪk] **1** *vi* trembler (*with* de). **2** *n (earth-~)* tremblement *m* de terre.

Quaker [kweɪkəʳ] *n* quaker(esse) *m(f)*.

qualification [ˌkwɒlɪfɪ'keɪʃ(ə)n] *n* (**a**) **~s** *(gen)* conditions *fpl* requises; *(degrees etc)* titres *mpl*, diplômes *mpl*; *(for a trade etc)* qualifications *fpl* professionnelles; **what are your ~s?** *(skill, degrees, experience etc)* quelle est votre formation?; *(paper ~s)* qu'est-ce que vous avez comme diplômes?; **teaching ~s** les diplômes requis pour enseigner. (**b**) *(limitation)* réserve *f*, restriction *f*. **to accept with/without ~s** accepter avec des/sans réserves.

qualify ['kwɒlɪfaɪ] **1** *vt* (**a**) *(make competent)* qualifier (*to do* pour faire); *(Admin)* donner qualité à (*for* pour; *to do* pour faire). (**b**) *(modify) attitude, praise* mitiger; *approval, support* mettre des réserves à; *statement, opinion* nuancer. (**c**) *(Gram)* qualifier. **2** *vi* obtenir son diplôme (*or* son brevet *etc*); *(Sport)* se qualifier (*for* pour). **to ~ as an engineer** obtenir son diplôme d'ingénieur; **to ~ for a job** obtenir les diplômes nécessaires pour un poste; **does he ~?** est-ce qu'il remplit les conditions requises?; *(fig)* **he hardly qualifies as a poet** il ne mérite pas vraiment le nom de poète. ◆ **qualified** *adj* (**a**) *(gen)* qualifié (*for* pour; *to do* pour faire); *engineer, doctor, teacher* diplômé; **he was not qualified for this job** il ne remplissait pas les conditions requises pour ce poste; **to be qualified to do** *(gen)* être qualifié pour faire, avoir les diplômes requis pour faire; *(Admin: officially)* avoir qualité pour faire; **they are not qualified to vote** ils ne sont pas habilités à voter; (**b**) *(modified) praise* mitigé; *support, acceptance* conditionnel; *success* modéré. ◆ **qualifier** *n (Gram)* qualificatif. ◆ **qualifying** *adj mark* de passage; *examination* d'entrée; *score* qui permet de se qualifier.

quality ['kwɒlɪtɪ] **1** *n* qualité *f*. **of the best ~** de première qualité; **of good/poor ~** de bonne/de mauvaise qualité. **2** *adj product* de qualité; *news-paper* sérieux.

qualm [kwɑːm] *n (scruple)* scrupule *m*; *(misgiving)* inquiétude *f* (*about* sur). **to have ~s about doing** avoir des scrupules à faire.

quandary ['kwɒnd(ə)rɪ] *n*: **to be in a ~** être dans l'embarras *or* dans un dilemme; **to be in a ~ about what to do** être bien embarrassé de savoir quoi faire.

quango ['kwæŋgəʊ] *n* organisme *m* (autonome) d'État.

quantity ['kwɒntɪtɪ] **1** *n* quantité *f*. **in ~** en grande quantité. **2** *adj*: **~ surveying** métrage *m*; **~ surveyor** métreur *m* (vérificateur).

quantum ['kwɒntəm] **1** *n, pl* **quanta** quantum *m*. **2** *adj mechanics, number* quantique. **~ theory** théorie *f* des quanta.

quarantine ['kwɒr(ə)ntiːn] **1** *n* quarantaine *f*. **in ~** en quarantaine. **2** *vt* mettre en quarantaine.

quarrel ['kwɒr(ə)l] **1** *n* querelle *f*, dispute *f*; *(breach)* brouille *f*. **to have a ~ with** se disputer *or* se quereller avec; **to pick a ~ with sb** chercher querelle à qn; **I have no ~ with you** je n'ai rien contre vous. **2** *vi* se disputer, se quereller (*with sb* avec qn; *about, over* à propos de); *(break off)* se brouiller (*with sb* avec qn). *(fig)* **I cannot ~ with that** je n'ai rien à redire à cela. ◆ **quarrelling,** *(US)* **quarreling** *n* disputes *fpl*, querelles *fpl*. ◆ **quarrelsome** *adj* querelleur.

quarry¹ ['kwɒrɪ] **1** *n* carrière *f (mine)*. **2** *vt stone* extraire; *hillside* exploiter. **3** *vi*: **to ~ for marble** exploiter une carrière de marbre. ◆ **quarryman** *n* (ouvrier *m*) carrier *m*. ◆ **quarry-tiled** *adj* carrelé.

quarry² ['kwɒrɪ] *n (animal, bird etc)* proie *f*; *(Hunting)* gibier *m*; *(person)* personne *f* pourchassée.

quart [kwɔːt] *n* ≃ litre *m (Brit = 1,136 litres; US = 0,946 litre)*.

quarter ['kwɔːtəʳ] **1** *n* (**a**) *(fourth part) (gen)* quart *m*; *[object, apple, beef, moon]* quartier *m*; *[year]* trimestre *m*. **to divide sth into ~s** diviser qch en quatre *or* en quartiers; **a ~ (of a pound) of tea** un quart (de livre) de thé; **a ~ as big as** quatre fois moins grand que; **a ~ of an hour** un quart d'heure; **a ~ to 7,** *(US)* **a ~ of 7** 7 heures moins le quart; **a ~ past 6,** *(US)* **a ~ after 6** 6 heures un *or* et quart; **a ~'s rent** un terme (de loyer). (**b**) *(US, Can: money)* quart *m* de dollar, 25 cents. (**c**) *(direction)* direction *f*, côté *m*; *(compass point)* point *m* cardinal. *(Naut)* **on the port ~** par la hanche de bâbord; **from all ~s** de toutes parts; **you must report that to the proper ~** vous devez signaler cela à qui de droit; **in responsible ~s** dans les milieux autorisés. (**d**) *(part of town)* quartier *m*. (**e**) *(lodgings)* **~s** résidence *f*; *(Mil)* quartiers *mpl* ; *(temporary)* cantonnement *m*.
2 *vt* (**a**) *(divide into four)* diviser en quatre, diviser en quartiers. (**b**) *(lodge) troops* caserner; *(temporarily)* cantonner; *(gen)* loger (*on* chez).
3 *adj* d'un quart. **a ~ share in sth** un quart de qch.
◆ **quarterback** *(US)* **1** *n (Ftbl)* stratège *m (souvent en position d'arrière)*. **2** *vt* (**a**) *(Ftbl)* diriger la stra-

tégie de. (**b**) *(fig)* gérer. ◆**quarter-deck** *n (Naut)* plage *f* arrière. ◆**quarter-final** *n* quart *m* de finale. ◆**quarterly** **1** *adj* trimestriel; **2** *n (periodical)* publication *f* trimestrielle. ◆**quartermaster** *n* (**a**) *(Mil)* intendant *m* militaire de troisième classe ; (**b**) *(Naut)* maître *m* de manœuvre.

quartet(te) [kwɔːˈtet] *n (gen; also classical music)* quatuor *m*; *(jazz)* quartette *m*.

quarto [ˈkwɔːtəʊ] *n, adj* in-quarto *(m) inv.*

quartz [ˈkwɔːts] **1** *n* quartz *m*. **2** *adj* de *or* en quartz; *clock* à quartz. ~ **crystal** cristal *m* de quartz.

quash [kwɒʃ] *vt verdict* casser; *rebellion* réprimer; *proposal* rejeter.

quasi- [ˈkwɑːzɪ] *pref* quasi- *(+ n)*, quasi *(+ adj)*. ~**marriage** quasi-mariage *m*; ~**revolutionary** quasi révolutionnaire.

quaver [ˈkweɪvəʳ] **1** *n (Mus: note)* croche *f*. **2** *vti (tremble)* chevroter. ◆**quavering** **1** *adj voice* chevrotant ; **2** *n* chevrotement *m*.

quay [kiː] *n* quai *m*. **at the** ~ **side** à quai.

queasy [ˈkwiːzɪ] *adj*: **to feel** ~ avoir mal au cœur, avoir envie de vomir. ◆**queasiness** *n* nausée *f*.

Quebec [kwɪˈbek] **1** *n* Québec *m*. **2** *adj* québécois.

queen [kwiːn] **1** *n* (**a**) reine *f*; *(Chess, Cards)* dame *f*. **Q**~ **Elizabeth** la reine Élisabeth; **Q**~ **Mother** reine mère; ~ **bee** reine des abeilles. (**b**) (‡ *pej: homosexual)* pédé ‡ *m (pej)*. **2** *vt* (*) **to** ~ **it** prendre des airs d'impératrice (*over sb* avec qn). ◆**queenly** *adj* de reine.

queer [kwɪəʳ] **1** *adj* (**a**) *(odd)* étrange, bizarre, drôle de *(before n)*. *(pej)* **a** ~ **customer** un drôle de type *; ~ **in the head** * toqué *; **to be in Q**~ **Street** * se trouver dans une mauvaise passe. (**b**) *(suspicious)* louche, suspect. **there's sth** ~ **going on** il se passe qch de louche. (**c**) (*: *unwell)* mal fichu *. **to feel** ~ être pris d'un malaise. (**d**) (*: *homosexual)* homosexuel. **he's** ~ * c'est un pédé ‡. **2** *n* (*: *homosexual) (male)* pédé ‡ *m*; *(female)* lesbienne *f*. **3** *vt*: **to** ~ **sb's pitch** couper l'herbe sous le pied à *or* de qn. ◆**queerly** *adv* étrangement, bizarrement. ◆**queerness** *n* étrangeté *f*, bizarrerie *f*.

quell [kwel] *vt (gen)* réprimer; *cheeky etc person* faire rentrer sous terre.

quench [kwen(t)ʃ] *vt flames* éteindre. **to** ~ **one's thirst** se désaltérer.

querulous [ˈkwerʊləs] *adj* ronchonneur *, bougon. ◆**querulously** *adv* d'un ton bougon.

query [ˈkwɪərɪ] **1** *n* (**a**) *(question)* question *f*; *(doubt)* doute *m* (*about* sur). **this raises a** ~ **about the scheme** cela met le projet en question. (**b**) *(question mark)* point *m* d'interrogation. **2** *vt* mettre en question.

quest [kwest] *n* quête *f* (*for* de). **in** ~ **of** en quête de.

question [ˈkwestʃ(ə)n] **1** *n* (**a**) question *f*. **to ask sb a** ~, **to put a** ~ **to sb** poser une question à qn. (**b**) *(doubt)* doute *m*. **without** ~ sans aucun doute; **there is no** ~ **about it** cela ne fait aucun doute; **to call sth into** ~ mettre qch en doute. (**c**) *(matter)* question *f*, affaire *f*. **that's the** ~! c'est là toute la question!; **that's not the** ~ là n'est pas la question; **that's another** ~ ça, c'est une autre affaire; **the person in** ~ la personne en question; **there's some/no** ~ **of closing the shop** il est/il n'est pas question de fermer le magasin; **there's no** ~ **of that, that is out of the** ~ il n'en est pas question; **the** ~ **is how many** la question, c'est de savoir combien; **the** ~ **is to decide...** il s'agit de décider...; **it's a** ~ **of what you want to do** tout dépend de ce que tu veux faire; **it's an open** ~ personne ne sait (*whether* si).
2 *adj*: ~ **mark** point *m* d'interrogation; *(Parl)* ~ **time** heure *f* réservée aux questions orales.
3 *vt* (**a**) *person* interroger, questionner (*on* sur; *about* au sujet de, à propos de). (**b**) *motive, account* mettre en doute *or* en question; *claim* contester. **to** ~ **whether** douter que + *subj*.
◆**questionable** *adj* discutable; *(pej)* douteux. ◆**questioner** *n* personne *f* qui pose des questions. ◆**questioning** **1** *adj* interrogateur, questionneur ; **2** *n* interrogation *f*. ◆**questionmaster** *n* meneur *m* de jeu; *(Rad, TV)* animateur *m*. ◆**questionnaire** *n* questionnaire *m*.

queue [kjuː] *(Brit)* **1** *n [people]* queue *f*, file *f* (d'attente); *[cars]* file. **to stand in a** ~, **to form a** ~ faire la queue; **the theatre** ~ les personnes qui font (*or* faisaient *etc*) la queue au théâtre; **ticket** ~ queue devant les guichets. **2** *vi* (~ **up**) *[people, cars]* faire la queue.

quibble [ˈkwɪbl] **1** *n* chicane *f*, ergotage *m*. **2** *vi* chicaner (*over* sur).

quick [kwɪk] **1** *adj* (**a**) *(rapid) train, route, method* rapide; *recovery, answer* prompt. **be** ~! dépêche-toi!, fais vite!; **try to be** ~**er** essaie de faire plus vite; *(Mil)* ~ **march!** en avant, marche!; **we had a** ~ **meal** nous avons mangé en vitesse; **to have a** ~ **one** * prendre un pot * en vitesse; **it's** ~**er by train** c'est plus rapide *or* ça va plus vite par le train. (**b**) *(lively) mind, child* vif, éveillé. **he's too** ~ **for me** il va trop vite pour moi; **he was** ~ **to see that...** il a tout de suite vu que...; **to be** ~ **to take offence** être prompt à s'offenser; **to have a** ~ **temper** s'emporter facilement; **he is** ~ **at figures** il calcule vite.
2 *n (fig)* **to cut sb to the** ~ piquer qn au vif; **the** ~ **and the dead** les vivants *mpl* et les morts *mpl*.
3 *adv* vite. **as** ~ **as lightning** *or* **as a flash** avec la rapidité de l'éclair.
◆**quick-acting** *adj drug* qui agit rapidement. ◆**quicken** **1** *vt* accélérer, hâter; *(fig) feelings* stimuler; **to** ~**en one's pace** accélérer son allure ; **2** *vi*: **the pace** ~**ened** l'allure s'est accélérée. ◆**quick-freeze,** *pret* **quick-froze,** *ptp* **quick-frozen** *vt* surgeler. ◆**quickie** * *n* chose faite en vitesse; *(drink)* pot * pris en vitesse; *(question)* question *f* éclair *inv*. ◆**quicklime** *n* chaux *f* vive. ◆**quickly** *adv (fast)* vite, rapidement; *(without delay)* promptement, sans tarder. ◆**quickness** *n* vitesse *f*, rapidité *f*; promptitude *f*; *[mind]* vivacité *f*. ◆**quicksands** *npl* sables *mpl* mouvants. ◆**quickset hedge** *n* haie *f* vive. ◆**quicksilver** *n* vif-argent *m*, mercure *m*. ◆**quickstep** *n* fox-trot *m*. ◆**quick-tempered** *adj* prompt à s'emporter. ◆**quick-witted** *adj* à l'esprit vif.

quid ‡ [kwɪd] *n (pl inv: Brit)* livre *f (sterling)*.

quiescence [kwaɪˈesns] *n* calme *m*. ◆**quiescent** *adj* passif, calme.

quiet [ˈkwaɪət] **1** *adj* (**a**) *(silent, still: gen)* tranquille, calme. **you're very** ~ tu ne dis pas grand-chose; **be** ~!, **keep** ~! taisez-vous!; **isn't it** ~! que c'est calme *or* tranquille!; **it was** ~ **as the grave** il y avait un silence de mort; **try to be a little** ~**er** essayez de ne pas faire autant de bruit; **to keep** *or* **stay** ~ *(still)* se tenir *or* rester tranquille; *(silent)* garder le silence; **to keep sb** ~ *(still)* faire tenir qn tranquille; *(silent)* faire taire qn. (**b**) *(not loud) music* doux; *voice, tone* bas; *footstep, sound* léger; *cough, laugh* petit. **keep the radio** ~ baisse le volume (de la radio). (**c**) *(subdued) person* doux; *dog, horse* docile; *dress, colour* discret. **she's a very** ~ **girl** elle n'est pas expansive. (**d**) *(peaceful, calm)* calme, paisible, tranquille. **he had a** ~ **sleep** il a dormi tranquillement; *(Mil etc)* **all** ~ rien de nouveau; **a** ~ **life** une vie tranquille; **this town is too** ~ cette ville manque d'animation; **business is** ~ les affaires sont calmes; ~ **mind** esprit *m* tranquille. (**e**) *(secret) envy* caché; *irony, humour* discret; *(private) evening, dinner* intime. **they had a** ~ **wedding** ils se sont mariés dans l'intimité; **I'll have a** ~ **word with her** je vais lui glisser un

mot à l'oreille; **they had a ~ laugh over it** ils en ont ri doucement; **he kept the whole thing ~** il n'en a pas parlé.
2 *n (silence)* silence *m*; *(peace)* calme *m*, tranquillité *f*. (*) **on the ~** *do* en cachette, en douce *; *tell* en confidence.
3 *vt* = **quieten 1.**
◆ **quieten 1** *vt (gen)* calmer; *conscience* tranquilliser ; **2** *vi* (**~en down**) se calmer; *(after unruly youth)* se ranger. ◆ **quietly** *adv (silently)* silencieusement, sans (faire de) bruit; *(not loudly) speak, sing* doucement; *(gently)* doucement, calmement; *(without fuss)* simplement; *(secretly)* en cachette, en douce *; *marry* dans la plus stricte intimité. ◆ **quietness** *n (silence)* silence *m*; *(stillness, peacefulness)* calme *m*, tranquillité *f*; *(gentleness)* douceur *f*.

quill [kwɪl] *n (feather)* penne *f*; *(also* **~-pen***)* plume *f* d'oie; *[porcupine etc]* piquant *m*.

quilt [kwɪlt] **1** *n* édredon *m* (piqué). **continental ~** couette *f*. **2** *vt eiderdown, cover* ouater et piquer; *dressing gown* matelasser; *furniture* capitonner.

quin [kwɪn] *n abbr of* **quintuplet.**

quince [kwɪns] *n* coing *m*; *(tree)* cognassier *m*.

quinine [kwɪ'ni:n] *n* quinine *f*.

quintessence [kwɪn'tesns] *n* quintessence *f*.

quintet(te) [kwɪn'tet] *n* quintette *m*.

quintuple ['kwɪntjʊpl] **1** *adj, n* quintuple *(m)*. **2** ['kwɪn'tju:pl] *vti* quintupler. ◆ **quintuplet** *n* quintuplé(e) *m(f)*.

quip [kwɪp] *n* mot *m* piquant.

quire ['kwaɪəʳ] *n* ≃ main *f (de papier)*.

quirk [kw3:k] *n* bizarrerie *f*. **by a ~ of fate** par un caprice du destin. ◆ **quirky** *adj* capricieux; *(strange)* étrange.

quit [kwɪt] *pret, ptp* **quit** *or* **quitted 1** *vt place, activity* quitter; *(esp US: stop)* arrêter *(doing* de faire). **to ~ hold** lâcher prise; **to ~ hold of sth** lâcher qch; **~ fooling!** arrête de faire l'idiot! **2** *vi (give up: in game etc)* se rendre; *(accept defeat)* abandonner la partie; *(resign)* démissionner. **3** *adj*: **~ of** débarrassé de.

quite [kwaɪt] *adv* (**a**) *(entirely)* tout à fait, complètement, entièrement. **~ (so)!** exactement!; **I ~ understand** je comprends très bien; **I ~ believe it** je le crois volontiers; **I don't ~ know** je ne sais pas trop; **that's ~ enough!** ça suffit comme ça!; **it wasn't ~ what I wanted** ce n'était pas tout à fait *or* exactement ce que je voulais; **that's ~ another matter** c'est une tout autre affaire; **he was ~ right** il avait bien raison *or* tout à fait raison; **~ new** tout (à fait) neuf; **~ alone** tout seul; **she was ~ a beauty** c'était une véritable beauté. (**b**) *(to some degree)* assez. **~ a long time** assez longtemps; **~ a few people** un assez grand nombre de gens; **~ good** pas mal du tout; **~ a good singer** un assez bon chanteur; **I ~ like it** j'aime assez ça.

Quito ['ki:təʊ] *n* Quito.

quits [kwɪts] *adj* quitte *(with sb* envers qn). **let's call it ~** restons-en là.

quiver¹ ['kwɪvəʳ] *vi [person, voice]* frémir, trembler *(with* de); *[eyelids]* battre.

quiver² ['kwɪvəʳ] *n (for arrows)* carquois *m*.

quixotic [kwɪk'sɒtɪk] *adj person* chevaleresque; *(visionary)* chimérique; *plan, feeling* donquichottesque. ◆ **quixotically** *adv* sans penser à soi.

quiz [kwɪz] **1** *n* (**a**) *(Rad/TV)* jeu-concours *m* (radiophonique/télévisé); *(in magazine etc)* série *f* de questions. (**b**) *(US Scol)* interrogation *f* rapide *(orale ou écrite)*. **2** *vt* (**a**) **to ~ sb** presser qn de questions *(about* au sujet de). (**b**) *(US Scol)* interroger rapidement. ◆ **quizmaster** *n* meneur *m* de jeu; *(Rad, TV)* animateur *m*. ◆ **quizzical** *adj* narquois. ◆ **quizzically** *adv* d'un air narquois.

quoit [kwɔɪt] *n* palet *m*. **to play ~s** jouer au palet.

quorum ['kwɔ:rəm] *n* quorum *m*. **to have a ~** atteindre le quorum.

quota ['kwəʊtə] *n (share)* quote-part *f*; *(permitted amount) [imports, immigrants]* quota *m*.

quote [kwəʊt] **1** *vt* (**a**) *author, poem, fact* citer; *reference number etc* rappeler. **don't ~ me** ne dites pas que c'est moi qui vous l'ai dit; **he was ~d as saying that...** il aurait dit que...; **~... unquote** *(in dictation)* ouvrez les guillemets... fermez les guillemets; *(in report, lecture etc)* je cite..., fin de citation. (**b**) *price (Comm)* indiquer, proposer; *(St Ex)* coter *(at* à). **2** *vi* (**a**) faire des citations. **to ~ from** citer. (**b**) *(Comm)* **to ~ for** établir un devis pour. **3** *n* (**a**) = **quotation 1.** (**b**) *(press statement)* déclaration *f*. (**c**) **he said, ~'I will never do it'** il a dit, *(in dictation)* ouvrez les guillemets *or (in lecture, report etc)* je cite 'je ne le ferai jamais'; **~s** = **quotation marks.** ◆ **quotable** *adj (authorized)* que l'on peut *(or* puisse) citer; *(worth quoting)* digne d'être cité. ◆ **quotation 1** *n* (**a**) citation *f (from* de); (**b**) *(Comm: estimate)* devis *m* ; **2** *adj*: **in quotation marks** entre guillemets *mpl*.

quotient ['kwəʊʃ(ə)nt] *n* quotient *m*.

R

R, r [ɑːʳ] *n (letter)* R, r *m*. **the three R's** la lecture, l'écriture *f* et l'arithmétique *f*.

Rabat [rəˈbɑːt] *n* Rabat.

rabbi [ˈræbaɪ] *n* rabbin *m*.

rabbit [ˈræbɪt] **1** *n* lapin *m*. **doe ~** lapine *f*. **2** *vi* (**a**) **to go ~ing** chasser le lapin. (**b**) * *(also* **~ on**) ne pas cesser de parler. **3** *adj*: **~ hole** terrier *m* (de lapin); **~ hutch** clapier *m*.

rabble [ˈræbl] *n* cohue *f*, foule *f* (confuse). *(pej)* **the ~** la populace.

rabid [ˈræbɪd] *adj (fanatical)* fanatique; *(furious)* forcené; *hate* farouche; *(Vet)* enragé.

rabies [ˈreɪbiːz] **1** *n* rage *f (Med)*. **2** *adj* (*) *injection* contre la rage.

rac(c)oon [rəˈkuːn] *n* raton *m* laveur.

race¹ [reɪs] **1** *n (Sport etc)* course *f*. **the 100 metres ~** la course sur 100 mètres, le 100 mètres; **cycle/horse ~** course cycliste/de chevaux; **~ against time** course contre la montre. **2** *vt* (**a**) *person* faire une course avec. **I'll ~ you to school!** à qui arrivera le premier à l'école! (**b**) *horse* faire courir. **the champion ~s Ferraris** le champion court sur Ferrari; *(Aut)* **to ~ the engine** emballer le moteur. **3** *vi* (**a**) **to ~ against sb** faire la course avec qn; *(fig)* **to ~ against time** courir contre la montre. (**b**) *(rush)* courir à toute allure. **to ~ in/across** *etc* entrer/traverser *etc* à toute allure. (**c**) *[engine]* s'emballer; *[propeller]* s'affoler; *[pulse]* être très rapide. ◆**racecourse** *n* champ *m* de courses, hippodrome *m*. ◆**racegoer** *n* turfiste *mf*. ◆**racehorse** *n* cheval *m* de course. ◆**racetrack,** *(US)* **raceway** *n (gen)* piste *f*. ◆**racing** **1** *n* courses *fpl*; **horse/motor racing** courses de chevaux/d'automobiles ; **2** *adj stables, cycle, car* de course; **racing driver** pilote *m* de course; **racing pigeon** pigeon *m* voyageur de compétition.

race² [reɪs] **1** *n* race *f*. **the human ~** la race *or* l'espèce humaine. **2** *adj hatred, prejudice* racial. **~ relations** relations *fpl* inter-raciales; **~ riot** émeute(s) *f(pl)* raciale(s). ◆**racial** *adj* racial. ◆**racialism** *n* racisme *m*. ◆**racialist** *or* ◆**racist** *adj, n* raciste *(mf)*. ◆**racism** *n* racisme *m*.

rack¹ [ræk] *n (for bottles, documents, files)* casier *m*; *(for luggage)* porte-bagages *m inv*; *(for dishes)* égouttoir *m*; *(for hanging tools/ties etc)* porte-outils/-cravates *etc m*; *(for vegetables)* bac(s) *m(pl)* à légumes; *(for fodder, rifles, pipes)* râtelier *m*. *(US)* **off the ~** en confection.

rack² [ræk] **1** *n* (**a**) *(torture)* chevalet *m*. (**b**) *(Tech)* **~ and pinion** crémaillère *f*. **2** *vt [pain]* torturer. *(fig)* **~ed by remorse** tenaillé par le remords; **to ~ one's brains** se creuser la tête.

rack³ [ræk] *n*: **to go to ~ and ruin** *[building]* tomber en ruine; *[business, economy]* aller à vau-l'eau; *[person, country]* aller à la ruine.

racket¹, racquet [ˈrækɪt] *n* raquette *f*.

racket² [ˈrækɪt] *n* (**a**) *(noise) [people]* tapage *m*, raffut * *m*; *[machine]* vacarme *m*. **to make a ~** faire du raffut * *or* du vacarme. (**b**) *(organized crime)* racket *m*; *(dishonest scheme)* escroquerie *f*. **the drug/stolen car ~** * le trafic de la drogue/des voitures volées; **they're on to quite a ~** * ils ont trouvé une jolie combine *; **it was a dreadful ~** * c'était du vol manifeste!; **he's in on the ~** * il est dans le coup *. ◆**racketeer** *n* racketteur *m*. ◆**racketeering** *n* racket *m*.

racy [ˈreɪsɪ] *adj speech, style* plein de verve.

radar [ˈreɪdɑːʳ] **1** *n* radar *m*. **by ~** au radar. **2** *adj screen, station* radar *inv*. **~ operator** radariste *mf*; *(Aut Police)* **~ trap** piège *m* radar.

raddled [ˈrædld] *adj* aux traits accusés.

radial [ˈreɪdɪəl] *adj*: **~ tyre,** *(US)* **~-ply tire** pneu *m* à carcasse radiale.

radiate [ˈreɪdɪeɪt] **1** *vi (gen)* rayonner (*from* de); *(Phys)* irradier. **2** *vt heat* émettre, dégager; *(fig) happiness* rayonner de; *enthusiasm* respirer. ◆**radiance** *n* éclat *m*, rayonnement *m*. ◆**radiant** *adj (gen)* rayonnant (*with* de); *colour* éclatant; *heat* radiant; *heater* à foyer rayonnant; *heating* direct. ◆**radiantly** *adv smile* d'un air radieux; **to be radiantly happy** rayonner de joie. ◆**radiation** **1** *n [heat etc]* rayonnement *m*; *(radioactivity)* radiation *f* ; **2** *adj*: **radiation sickness** mal *m* des rayons; *(Med)* **radiation treatment** * radiothérapie *f*. ◆**radiator** **1** *n* radiateur *m* ; **2** *adj (Aut)* **radiator cap** bouchon *m* de radiateur; **radiator grill** calandre *f*.

radical [ˈrædɪk(ə)l] *adj, n* radical *(m)*. ◆**radically** *adv* radicalement.

radio [ˈreɪdɪəʊ] **1** *n* (**a**) (**~ set**) poste *m* (de radio), radio *f*. **on the ~** à la radio. (**b**) *(Telec)* radio *f*, radiotélégraphie *f*. **by ~** par radio. **2** *vt person* appeler par radio; *one's position* signaler par radio; *message* envoyer par radio. **3** *vi*: **to ~ for help** appeler au secours par radio. **4** *adj beam, silence* radio *inv*; *programme, broadcast* de radio, radiophonique. **~ announcer** speaker(ine) *m(f)*; **~ beacon** radiophare *m*; **~ car** voiture-radio *f*; **~ communication** contact *m* radio *inv*; **~ link** liaison *f* radio *inv*; **~ operator** opérateur *m* (radio), radio *m*; **~ programme** émission *f* (de radio); **~ station** station *f* de radio; **~ telescope** radiotélescope *m*; **~ wave** onde *f* hertzienne; **~ valve** valve *f*. ◆**radioactive** *adj* radioactif. ◆**radioactivity** *n* radioactivité *f*. ◆**radiocab** *n* radio-taxi *m*. ◆**radio-controlled** *adj* téléguidé. ◆**radiogram** *n (message)* radiogramme *m*; *(apparatus)* combiné *m*. ◆**radiographer** *n* radiologue *mf (technicien)*. ◆**radiography** *n* radiographie *f*. ◆**radiologist** *n* radiologue *mf (médecin)*. ◆**radiology** *n* radiologie *f*. ◆**radiotaxi** *n* radio-taxi *m*. ◆**radiotelephone** *n* radiotéléphone *m*. ◆**radiotherapy** *n* radiothérapie *f*.

radish [ˈrædɪʃ] *n* radis *m*.

radium [ˈreɪdɪəm] *n* radium *m*.

radius, *pl* **radii** [ˈreɪdɪəs, ˈreɪdɪaɪ] *n* rayon *m (also Math)*. **within a ~ of** dans un rayon de.

radon [ˈreɪdɒn] *n* radon *m*.

raffia [ˈræfɪə] *n* raphia *m*.

raffle [ˈræfl] **1** *n* tombola *f*. **~ ticket** billet *m* de tombola. **2** *vt* mettre en tombola.

raft [rɑːft] *n* radeau *m*.

rafter [ˈrɑːftəʳ] *n (Archit)* chevron *m*.

rag¹ [ræg] **1** *n* (**a**) lambeau *m*; *(for wiping etc)* chiffon *m*. **~s** *(for paper-making)* chiffons; *(old clothes)* haillons *mpl*; **in ~s** en lambeaux; **dressed in ~s** vêtu de haillons; **in ~s and tatters** tout en loques; **to feel like a wet ~** * se sentir complètement vidé *.

(**b**) *(* pej: newspaper)* torchon * *m (journal)*. **2** *adj doll* de chiffon; **the ~ trade** * la confection.
◆ **rag-and-bone-man** *n* chiffonnier *m*. ◆ **rag-bag** *n* sac *m* à chiffons; *(fig)* ramassis *m*. ◆ **ragged** ['rægɪd] *adj clothes* en lambeaux; *person* en haillons; *cuff* effiloché. ◆ **ragman** *or* ◆ **ragpicker** *n* chiffonnier *m*. ◆ **ragtop** *n (US)* décapotable *f*.

rag² * [ræg] **1** *n (joke)* farce *f*, blague * *f*. **2** *vt (tease)* taquiner; *(trick)* faire une blague * à.

rage [reɪdʒ] **1** *n* rage *f*, fureur *f*. **in a ~** en rage, en fureur; **to fly into a ~** se mettre en rage; *(fig)* **to be (all) the ~** faire fureur. **2** *vi [person]* être furieux (*against* contre); *[battle]* faire rage; *[sea]* être en furie; *[storm, wind]* se déchaîner. ◆ **raging** *adj person* furieux; *thirst* ardent; *pain* atroce; *fever* violent; *sea* en furie; *wind, storm* déchaîné; **in a raging temper** dans une rage folle; **raging toothache** rage *f* de dents.

raid [reɪd] **1** *n (Mil)* raid *m*; *(by police)* rafle *f*; *(by bandits)* razzia *f*; *(by thieves)* hold-up *m inv*. **air ~** bombardement *m* aérien; **bank ~** hold-up d'une banque. **2** *vt* faire un raid *or* une rafle dans; razzier; faire un hold-up à; bombarder; *(fig) cash-box* puiser dans; *larder, orchard* dévaliser. ◆ **raider** *n (bandit)* pillard *m*; *(criminal)* brigand *m*; *(ship)* raider *m*; *(plane)* bombardier *m*; *(Mil)* **the ~ers** le commando.

rail [reɪl] **1** *n* (**a**) *(bar) [bridge, boat]* rambarde *f*; *[balcony, terrace]* balustrade *f*; *(banister)* rampe *f*; *(for curtains, spotlights etc)* tringle *f*; *(towel ~)* porte-serviettes *m inv*. *(fence)* **~s** grille *f*. (**b**) *(for train, tram)* rail *m*. **by ~** *travel* en train; *send* par chemin de fer; **to go off the ~s** *[train etc]* dérailler; *[person] (err)* s'écarter du droit chemin; *(be confused)* être déboussolé *. **2** *adj strike* des employés de chemin de fer; *traffic* ferroviaire. **~ workers** employés *mpl* du chemin de fer. ◆ **railcard** *n* carte *f* de chemin de fer (≃ carte SNCF). ◆ **railing** *n* (**a**) *(V* **rail 1a***)* rambarde *f*; balustrade *f*; rampe *f*; (**b**) *(part of fence)* barreau *m*; *(fence: also* **~ings***)* grille *f*. ◆ **railroad 1** *n (US)* = **railway** ; **2** *vt (fig)* **to ~road sb into doing sth** * forcer qn à faire qch sans qu'il ait le temps de réfléchir.

railway ['reɪlweɪ] **1** *n (system)* chemin *m* de fer; *(track)* voie *f* ferrée; *(US: for trams)* rails *mpl*. **2** *adj bridge, ticket* de chemin de fer. **~ guide** indicateur *m* des chemins de fer; **~ line** ligne *f* de chemin de fer; *(track)* voie ferrée; **~ network** réseau *m* ferroviaire; **~ station** gare *f*; **~ timetable** horaire *m* des chemins de fer. ◆ **railwayman** *n* cheminot *m*.

rain [reɪn] **1** *n* pluie *f*. **it looks like ~** le temps est à la pluie; **in the ~** sous la pluie; **heavy/light ~** pluie battante/fine; **the ~s** la saison des pluies; **~ forest** forêt *f* tropicale humide; **~ hood** capuche *f*. **2** *vi* pleuvoir *(also fig)*. **it is ~ing** il pleut; **it is ~ing heavily, it's ~ing cats and dogs** il pleut à torrents, il tombe des cordes *. ◆ **rainbow** *n* arc-en-ciel *m*. ◆ **raincheck** *n*: **I'll take a ~check** * ce n'est que partie remise. ◆ **raincoat** *n* imperméable *m*. ◆ **raindrop** *n* goutte *f* de pluie. ◆ **rainfall** *n (shower)* chute *f* de pluie; *(amount)* hauteur *f* des précipitations. ◆ **rainproof 1** *adj* imperméable; **2** *vt* imperméabiliser. ◆ **rainstorm** *n* pluie *f* torrentielle. ◆ **rainwater** *n* eau *f* de pluie. ◆ **rainy** *adj* pluvieux; *season* des pluies; *(fig)* **to put sth away for a ~y day** mettre de l'argent de côté.

raise [reɪz] **1** *vt* (**a**) *(lift: gen)* lever; *object, weight* lever, soulever; *building, level* élever; *sunken ship* renflouer; *dust* soulever; *(fig: to power, in rank)* élever. *(fig)* **he didn't ~ an eyebrow** il n'a pas sourcillé; **to ~ one's hat to sb** donner un coup de chapeau à qn, *(fig)* tirer son chapeau à qn *; **to ~ one's hand to sb** lever la main sur qn; **to ~ sb from the dead** ressusciter qn (d'entre les morts); **to ~ one's voice** élever la voix; **to ~ sb's spirits** remonter le moral de qn; **to ~ sb's hopes** donner à espérer à qn. (**b**) *(increase) salary, price* augmenter; *standard* élever; *age limit* reculer; *temperature* faire monter. (**c**) *(erect) monument* élever; *building* construire. (**d**) *(produce) ghosts* faire apparaître; *question, problems, difficulties* soulever; *objection, protest* élever; *suspicions* faire naître; *blister* provoquer. **to ~ a laugh** faire rire; **to ~ a smile** *(oneself)* ébaucher un sourire; *(in others)* faire sourire; **to ~ Cain** * *or* **hell** ‡ *or* **the roof** * *(noise)* faire du boucan ‡; *(fuss)* faire une scène de tous les diables *. (**e**) *(grow, breed) animals, children* élever; *crops* cultiver. (**f**) *(get together) army, taxes* lever; *money* se procurer; *funds (gen)* réunir. **to ~ a loan** emprunter; **to ~ money on sth** emprunter de l'argent sur qch; **I can't ~ the £500** je n'arrive pas à me procurer les 500 livres. (**g**) *(end) siege, embargo* lever. (**h**) *(contact)* **to ~ sb on the radio** entrer en contact avec qn par radio. **2** *n (US, also Brit *: payrise)* augmentation *f* (de salaire). ◆ **raise up** *vt sep* lever, soulever. **to ~ o.s. up** se soulever.

rake¹ [reɪk] **1** *n* râteau *m*. **2** *vt garden* ratisser; *hay* râteler; *fire* tisonner; *(fig: with gun)* balayer. **3** *vi (fig: search)* **to ~ through** fouiller dans.
◆ **rake in** * *vt sep money* amasser. ◆ **rake off** *vt sep stones etc* enlever à l'aide d'un râteau. ◆ **rake out** *vt sep fire* éteindre en faisant tomber la braise.
◆ **rake up** *vt sep leaves* ramasser avec un râteau; *(fig) grievance* rappeler; *the past* revenir sur; *sb's past* fouiller dans.
◆ **rake-off** * *n* profit *m (souvent illégal)*.

rake² † [reɪk] *n (person)* roué † *m*, débauché *m*.
◆ **rakish** *adj person* débauché; *appearance* cavalier; **hat at a rakish angle** chapeau campé sur le coin de l'œil.

rally ['rælɪ] **1** *n [troops]* ralliement *m*; *[people]* rassemblement *m*; *(Pol)* rassemblement, meeting *m*; *(Aut)* rallye *m*; *(Tennis)* échange *m*. **peace ~** rassemblement en faveur de la paix. **2** *vt troops, supporters* rallier. **3** *vi [troops, people]* se rallier (*also fig: to* à); *[sick person]* reprendre le dessus. **~ing point** point *m* de ralliement; *(St Ex)* **the market rallied** les cours ont repris. ◆ **rally round** *vi (fig)* venir en aide.

ram [ræm] **1** *n* bélier *m (also Astron)*. **2** *vt* (**a**) *(push down)* enfoncer; *(pack down)* tasser (*into* dans). **his hat ~med down over his ears** le chapeau enfoncé jusqu'aux oreilles; *(fig)* **to ~ sth down sb's throat** rebattre les oreilles à qn de qch; **to ~ sth into sb's head** enfoncer qch dans le crâne de qn. (**b**) *(crash into) (Naut)* heurter de l'avant; *(in battle)* éperonner; *(Aut) another vehicle* emboutir; *post, tree* percuter (contre).

ramble ['ræmbl] **1** *n* randonnée *f*. **2** *vi (wander about)* se promener au hasard; *(go on hike)* faire une randonnée; *(pej: in speech:* **~ on***)* parler pour ne rien dire; *[old person]* radoter. ◆ **rambler** *n* (**a**) *(person)* excursionniste *mf*; (**b**) *(rose)* rosier *m* grimpant. ◆ **rambling** *adj speech, writing* décousu; *person* qui radote; *town* construit au hasard; *house* plein de coins et de recoins; *plant* grimpant.

ramify ['ræmɪfaɪ] **1** *vt* ramifier. **2** *vi* se ramifier.
◆ **ramification** *n* ramification *f*.

ramp [ræmp] *n (slope)* rampe *f*; *(on road: for speed control)* casse-vitesse *m*; *(in garage etc)* pont *m* de graissage. *(Aviat)* **(boarding) ~** passerelle *f*; *(Aut: sign)* **'ramp'** 'dénivellation'.

rampage [ræm'peɪdʒ] **1** *n*: **to go on the ~** se déchaîner. **2** *vi* (**~ about, ~ around**) se déchaîner.

rampant ['ræmpənt] *adj (fig)* **to be ~** sévir.

rampart ['ræmpɑːt] *n* rempart *m*.

ramshackle ['ræm,ʃækl] *adj building* délabré; *table* branlant; *machine* déglingué *.

ran [ræn] *pret of* **run**.

ranch [rɑ:n(t)ʃ] *n* ranch *m*.

rancid ['rænsɪd] *adj* rance. **to smell** ~ sentir le rance.

rancour, *(US)* **rancor** ['ræŋkəʳ] *n* rancœur *f*. ◆ **rancorous** *adj* plein de rancœur.

random ['rændəm] **1** *n*: **at** ~ au hasard; *(stronger)* à l'aveuglette. **2** *adj choice* fait au hasard; *bullet* perdu; *sample* prélevé au hasard. *(Comput)* ~ **access memory** *(abbr* **RAM***)* mémoire *f* vive.

rang [ræŋ] *pret of* **ring²**.

range [reɪn(d)ʒ] **1** *n* (**a**) *(scope, distance covered) [telescope, gun, missile]* portée *f*; *[plane, ship]* rayon *m* d'action. **at a** ~ **of** à une distance de; **at long** ~ à longue portée; *(Mil)* **to find the** ~ régler son tir; **out of** ~ hors de portée; **within (firing)** ~ à portée de tir; ~ **of vision** champ *m* visuel. (**b**) *(extent between limits) [temperature]* variations *fpl*; *[prices, salaries, values]* échelle *f*; *[musical instrument, voice]* étendue *f*; *(selection) [colours, feelings, speeds]* gamme *f*; *[patterns, goods]* choix *m*. **a wide** ~ **of subjects** un grand choix de sujets. (**c**) *(domain, sphere) [activity]* champ *m*, rayon *m*; *[influence]* sphère *f*; *[knowledge]* étendue *f*. (**d**) *(row)* rangée *f*, rang *m*; *[mountains]* chaîne *f*. (**e**) *(US: grazing land)* prairie *f*. (**f**) *(shooting* ~*)* *(Mil)* champ *m* de tir; *(at fair)* stand *m* (de tir). (**g**) *(cooking stove)* fourneau *m* de cuisine. **2** *vt objects* ranger; *troops* aligner. **3** *vi* (**a**) *(extend) [discussion, search]* s'étendre *(from... to* de... à; *over* sur); *[numbers, opinions]* aller *(from... to* de... à); *[results, temperatures]* varier *(from... to* entre... et). *(fig)* **researches ranging over a wide field** recherches qui embrassent un large domaine. (**b**) *(roam)* **to** ~ **over** parcourir. (**c**) *[guns, missiles, shells]* **to** ~ **over** avoir une portée de. ◆ **rangefinder** *n* télémètre *m*. ◆ **ranger** *n [forest etc]* garde *m* forestier; *(US: mounted patrolman)* gendarme *m* à cheval.

Rangoon [ræŋ'gu:n] *n* Rangoon.

rank¹ [ræŋk] **1** *n* (**a**) *(row)* rang *m*. **taxi** ~ station *f* de taxis. (**b**) *(Mil)* rang *m*. **to break** ~**s** rompre les rangs; **the** ~**s,** *(Brit)* **other** ~**s** les sous-officiers *mpl* et hommes *mpl* de troupe; **the** ~ **and file** *(Mil)* les hommes de troupe; *(fig)* la masse; *[political party]* la base; **to rise from the** ~**s** sortir du rang; **to reduce to the** ~**s** casser. (**c**) *(social etc position)* rang *m*; *(Mil: grade)* grade *m*. **the** ~ **of general** le grade de général; **people of all** ~**s** des gens de toutes conditions; **a person of** ~ une personne de haut rang. **2** *vt* classer, ranger *(among* parmi). **3** *vi* compter *(among* parmi). **to** ~ **above/below sb** être supérieur/inférieur à qn.

rank² [ræŋk] *adj* (**a**) *plants* exubérant. (**b**) *smell, drains* fétide; *fats* rance; *person* répugnant. (**c**) *disgrace* absolu; *traitor, insolence* véritable; *injustice, lie* flagrant; *liar* fieffé *(before n)*; *beginner, outsider* parfait *(before n)*.

rankle ['ræŋkl] *vi*: **to** ~ **with sb** rester sur le cœur à qn.

ransack ['rænsæk] *vt town* mettre à sac; *room, drawer* fouiller (à fond) *(for* pour trouver).

ransom ['rænsəm] **1** *n* rançon *f*. **to hold sb to** ~ mettre qn à rançon; ~ **demand** demande *f* de rançon. **2** *vt* racheter.

rant [rænt] *vi* tempêter *(at sb* contre qn).

rap [ræp] **1** *n (noise)* petits coups *mpl* secs; *(blow)* tape *f*; *(US* ‡*: charge)* inculpation *f*. **there was a** ~ **at the door** on a frappé bruyamment à la porte; **to take the** ~ * payer les pots cassés. **2** *vt* (**a**) **to** ~ **sb over the knuckles** donner sur les doigts de qn. (**b**) (~ **out**) *words* dire brusquement; *order, retort* lancer. **3** *vi* frapper *(at* à), donner de petits coups secs *(on* sur). ◆ **rapping** *n* coups *mpl* secs et durs.

rapacious [rə'peɪʃəs] *adj* rapace. ◆ **rapaciously** *adv* avec rapacité. ◆ **rapacity** *n* rapacité *f*.

rape [reɪp] **1** *n* viol *m*. **2** *vt* violer. ◆ **rapist** *n* violeur *m*, auteur *m* d'un viol.

rapid ['ræpɪd] **1** *adj* rapide. *(US)* ~ **transit** métro *m*. **2** *npl (Geog)* ~**s** rapides *mpl*. ◆ **rapidity** *n* rapidité *f*. ◆ **rapidly** *adv* rapidement.

rapier ['reɪpɪəʳ] *n* rapière *f*.

rapt [ræpt] *adj attention* profond; *smile* ravi.

rapture ['ræptʃəʳ] *n* ravissement *m*, extase *f*. **to be in** ~**s over** *object* être ravi de; *person* être en extase devant; **to go into** ~**s over** s'extasier sur. ◆ **rapturous** *adj smile* de ravissement; *welcome* chaleureux; *applause* frénétique. ◆ **rapturously** *adv* avec ravissement; avec frénésie.

rare [rɛəʳ] *adj (gen)* rare; *atmosphere* raréfié; *meat* saignant. **it is** ~ **for her to come** il est rare qu'elle vienne; **to grow** ~**(r)** *[plants, atmosphere]* se raréfier; *[visits]* devenir plus rares; **we had a** ~ **old time** * nous nous sommes drôlement * bien amusés; **a very** ~ **steak** un bifteck bleu. ◆ **rarebit** *n*: **Welsh** ~**bit** toast *m* au fromage fondu. ◆ **rarefied** ['rɛərɪfaɪd] *adj atmosphere* raréfié; *(fig)* trop raffiné. ◆ **rarely** *adv* rarement. ◆ **rareness** *or* ◆ **rarity** *n* rareté *f*.

raring ['rɛərɪŋ] *adj*: **to be** ~ **to go** être très impatient de commencer.

rascal ['rɑ:sk(ə)l] *n (scoundrel)* vaurien *m*; *(scamp)* polisson(ne) *m(f)*. ◆ **rascally** *adj person* retors; *trick* vilain *(before n)*.

rash¹ [ræʃ] *n (Med: gen)* rougeurs *fpl*; *(from food etc)* urticaire *f*; *(in measles etc)* éruption *f*. **to come out in a** ~ avoir une éruption *etc*.

rash² [ræʃ] *adj person* imprudent; *words* irréfléchi. ◆ **rashly** *adv* imprudemment; sans réfléchir. ◆ **rashness** *n* imprudence *f*.

rasher ['ræʃəʳ] *n* (mince) tranche *f* (de lard).

rasp [rɑ:sp] **1** *n (tool)* râpe *f*; *(noise)* grincement *m*. **2** *vt* (**a**) *(Tech)* râper. (**b**) *(speak)* dire d'une voix grinçante. **3** *vi* grincer. ◆ **rasping** *adj* grinçant.

raspberry ['rɑ:zb(ə)rɪ] **1** *n* framboise *f*; *(bush)* framboisier *m*. *(fig)* **to blow a** ~ * faire un bruit de dérision. **2** *adj ice cream* (à la) framboise *inv*; *jam* de framboise.

Rastafarian [ˌræstə'fɛərɪən] *n, adj* rastafari *(mf) inv*.

rat [ræt] **1** *n* rat *m*. **he's a (dirty)** ~ * c'est un salaud ‡. **2** *adj*: ~ **poison** mort-aux-rats *f*; ~ **race** foire *f* d'empoigne. **3** *vi*: **to** ~ **on sb** * *(desert)* lâcher * qn; *(inform on)* moucharder * qn. ◆ **ratcatcher** *n* chasseur *m* de rats. ◆ **rat-trap** *n* ratière *f*.

ratchet ['rætʃɪt] *n* cliquet *m*. ~ **wheel** roue *f* à rochet.

rate [reɪt] **1** *n* (**a**) *(ratio, proportion)* taux *m*, proportion *f*; *(speed)* vitesse *f*, allure *f*. **birth/death** ~ (taux de) la natalité/la mortalité; **the failure** ~ le pourcentage d'échecs; ~ **of consumption** taux de consommation; *(Elec, Water)* ~ **of flow** débit *m* moyen; **at the** ~ **of** *(amount etc)* à raison de; *(speed)* à une vitesse de; *(Med)* **pulse** ~ fréquence *f* des pulsations; **at a great** ~, **at a** ~ **of knots** * à toute allure; **if you continue at this** ~ si vous continuez à ce train-là; **at his** ~ **of working** au rythme auquel il travaille; *(fig)* **at any** ~ en tout cas, de toute façon; **at that** ~ dans ce cas. (**b**) *(Comm, Fin)* taux *m*, tarif *m*. ~ **of exchange/interest/pay** taux du change/d'intérêt/de rémunération; **postage/advertising** ~**s** tarifs postaux/de publicité; **insurance** ~**s** primes *fpl* d'assurance; **reduced** ~ tarif réduit. (**c**) *(municipal tax)* ~**s** impôts *mpl* locaux; ~**s and taxes** impôts et contributions; **a penny on/off the** ~**s** une augmentation/réduction d'un pour cent des impôts locaux.

2 *vt* (**a**) *(estimate worth of, appraise)* évaluer *(at* à); *(fig: consider)* considérer *(as* comme), compter *(among* parmi). **to** ~ **sb/sth highly** faire grand cas

de qn/qch; **how does he ~ that film?** que pense-t-il de ce film? (**b**) **house ~d at £100 per annum** ≃ maison *f* dont la valeur locative imposable est de 100 livres par an. (**c**) *(deserve)* mériter.
3 *vi (be classed)* être classé (*as* comme).
◆ **rateable** *adj*: **~able value** valeur *f* locative imposable. ◆ **ratepayer** *n* contribuable *mf (impôts locaux)*. ◆ **rating** *n* (**a**) *(assessment)* estimation *f*, évaluation *f*; (**b**) *(Naut)* **the ratings** les matelots et gradés *mpl*; (**c**) *(TV)* **the ~s** l'indice *m* d'écoute.

rather ['rɑːðəʳ] *adv* (**a**) *(for preference)* plutôt. **~ than wait, he...** plutôt que d'attendre, il...; **I would ~ have the blue dress** je préférerais *or* j'aimerais mieux la robe bleue; **I would much ~...** je préférerais de beaucoup..., j'aimerais mieux...; **I would ~ do that than wait for him** je préférerais faire ça plutôt que de l'attendre; **I would ~ you came** je préférerais que vous veniez *(subj)*; **I'd ~ not** j'aime mieux pas *; **I'd ~ not go** j'aimerais mieux ne pas y aller. (**b**) *(more accurately)* plus exactement, plutôt. (**c**) *(to a considerable degree)* plutôt; *(to some extent)* un peu; *(somewhat)* quelque peu; *(fairly)* assez; *(slightly)* légèrement. **he's ~ clever** il est plutôt intelligent; **it's ~ more difficult than you think** c'est un peu plus difficile que vous ne croyez; **his book is ~ good** son livre n'est pas mauvais du tout; **that costs ~ a lot** cela coûte assez cher; **I ~ think that** je crois bien que; *(excl)* **~!** * et comment! *

ratify ['rætɪfaɪ] *vt* ratifier. ◆ **ratification** *n* ratification *f*.

ratio ['reɪʃɪəʊ] *n* proportion *f*, raison *f*. **in the ~ of 100 to 1** dans la proportion de 100 contre 1; **inverse ~** raison inverse.

ration ['ræʃ(ə)n] **1** *n (allowance: of food, goods etc)* ration *f*. *(food)* **~s** vivres *mpl*. **2** *adj*: **~ book** carte *f* de rationnement. **3** *vt thing, person* rationner. **he was ~ed to 1 kg** sa ration était 1 kg. ◆ **rationing** *n* rationnement *m*.

rational ['ræʃənl] *adj creature* doué de raison; *(Med: lucid)* lucide; *faculty* rationnel; *action, argument, person* raisonnable; *explanation, solution* logique, rationnel. ◆ **rationalization** *n* rationalisation *f*. ◆ **rationalize** **1** *vt* (**a**) *event, conduct etc* justifier (après coup); (**b**) *(organize efficiently) industry, production* rationaliser; **2** *vi* chercher une justification (après coup). ◆ **rationally** *adv* raisonnablement, rationnellement.

rattan [ræ'tæn] *n* rotin *m*.

rattle ['rætl] **1** *n* (**a**) *(sound) [vehicle]* bruit *m* (de ferraille); *[chains, bottles, dice, typewriter]* cliquetis *m*; *[hailstones, bullets]* crépitement *m*; *[rattlesnake]* sonnettes *fpl*. **death ~** râle *m*. (**b**) *(baby's) (gen)* hochet *m*; *(on pram)* boulier *m* de bébé; *[sports fan]* crécelle *f*. **2** *vi [box, object]* faire du bruit; *[articles in box]* s'entrechoquer; *[vehicle]* faire un bruit de ferraille; *[bullets, hailstones]* crépiter; *[machinery]* cliqueter; *[window]* trembler. *[vehicle]* **to ~ along** rouler dans un bruit de ferraille. **3** *vt* (**a**) *box, dice* agiter; *bottles, cans* faire s'entrechoquer; *keys* faire cliqueter. (**b**) *(*: worry)* troubler. **to get ~d** perdre son sang-froid. ◆ **rattle off** *vt sep poem* débiter à toute allure. ◆ **rattle on** *vi* parler sans arrêt (*about sth* de qch). ◆ **rattlesnake** *n* serpent *m* à sonnettes.

ratty * ['rætɪ] *adj* en rogne *.

raucous ['rɔːkəs] *adj* rauque. ◆ **raucously** *adv* d'une voix rauque.

ravage ['rævɪdʒ] **1** *n* ravage *m*. **2** *vt* ravager.

rave [reɪv] **1** *vi (be delirious)* délirer; *(talk wildly)* divaguer; *(furiously)* tempêter (*at, against* contre); *(enthusiastically)* s'extasier (*about, over* sur). **2** *adj*: **~ review** * critique *f* dithyrambique. ◆ **raving** *adj* délirant; **raving mad** fou furieux (*f* folle furieuse). ◆ **ravings** *npl* délire *m*.

raven ['reɪvn] *n* corbeau *m*. ◆ **raven-haired** *adj* aux cheveux de jais.

ravenous ['rævənəs] *adj animal, appetite* vorace; *person* affamé; *hunger* dévorant. **I'm ~** * j'ai une faim de loup. ◆ **ravenously** *adv* voracement.

ravine [rə'viːn] *n* ravin *m*.

ravioli [ˌrævɪ'əʊlɪ] *n* ravioli *mpl*.

ravish ['rævɪʃ] *vt* ravir. ◆ **ravishing** *adj* ravissant; **~ing beauty** beauté *f* enchanteresse. ◆ **ravishingly** *adv*: **she is ~ingly beautiful** elle est belle à ravir.

raw [rɔː] **1** *adj* (**a**) *food, colour* cru; *cloth, leather* écru; *ore, sugar* brut; *spirit, alcohol* pur; *data* brut. **to give sb a ~ deal** * faire un sale coup à qn *; **to get a ~ deal** * être traité fort mal; **~ material(s)** matières *fpl* premières. (**b**) *(inexperienced)* inexpérimenté; *(uncouth)* mal dégrossi. **~ recruit** bleu * *m*. (**c**) *(sore)* irrité; *skin* écorché; *wound, nerves* à vif. *[cloth etc]* **~ edge** bord *m* coupé. (**d**) *climate, wind* âpre; *air* vif. **2** *n*: **to get sb on the ~** toucher qn au vif; **nature in the ~** la nature telle qu'elle est. ◆ **rawboned** *adj* décharné. ◆ **rawness** *n* (**a**) *(lack of experience)* inexpérience *f*; (**b**) *(on skin)* irritation *f*; (**c**) *[climate]* froid *m* humide; *[wind]* âpreté *f*.

Rawalpindi [rɔːl'pɪndɪ] *n* Rawalpindi.

Rawlplug ['rɔːlplʌg] ® *n* cheville *f (Menuiserie)*.

ray¹ [reɪ] *n* rayon *m*; *(of hope)* lueur *f*.

ray² [reɪ] *n (fish)* raie *f*.

rayon ['reɪɒn] *n (Tex)* rayonne *f*.

raze [reɪz] *vt* (**~ to the ground**) raser.

razor ['reɪzəʳ] **1** *n* rasoir *m*. **2** *adj*: **~ blade** lame *f* de rasoir. ◆ **razor-sharp** *adj knife etc* tranchant comme un rasoir; *(fig) person, mind* très vif; *wit* acéré.

razzmatazz * ['ræzmə'tæz] *n* tape-à-l'œil * *m*.

re¹ [reɪ] *n (Mus)* ré *m*.

re² [riː] *prep (referring to)* au sujet de.

re... [riː] *pref (before consonant)* re..., ré...; *(before vowel)* r..., ré... **to ~do** refaire; **to ~heat** réchauffer; **to ~open** rouvrir; **to ~-elect** réélire.

reach [riːtʃ] **1** *n* (**a**) portée *f*. **within ~** à portée; **out of ~** hors de portée; **within sb's ~** à (la) portée de qn; **within easy ~** *or* **within my ~** à portée de main, sous la main; **not within easy ~** difficilement accessible; **within easy ~ of the sea** à proximité de la mer; **beyond the ~ of the law** à l'abri de la justice; **this subject is beyond his ~** ce sujet le dépasse. (**b**) *(esp Boxing)* allonge *f*. (**c**) *[river]* étendue *f*; *[canal]* bief *m*.
2 *vt* (**a**) *(get as far as) place* atteindre, arriver à; *age, goal, limit* atteindre; *agreement, conclusion, page* arriver à. **when we ~ed him** quand nous sommes arrivés auprès de lui; **the letter ~ed him** la lettre lui est parvenue; **the news ~ed us too late** nous avons appris la nouvelle trop tard; **you can ~ me at my hotel** vous pouvez me joindre à mon hôtel. (**b**) *(get and give)* passer. **~ me (over) that book** passez-moi ce livre.
3 *vi* (**a**) *[territory etc]* s'étendre; *[voice, sound]* porter (*to* jusqu'à). (**b**) *(stretch out hand:* **~ across, ~ out, ~ over)** étendre le bras (*for sth* pour prendre qch; *to grasp etc* pour saisir *etc*).

react [riː'ækt] *vi* réagir (*against* contre; *on* sur; *to* à). ◆ **reaction** *n (all senses)* réaction *f*. ◆ **reactionary** *adj, n* réactionnaire *(mf)*. ◆ **reactor** *n* réacteur *m*.

read [riːd] *pret, ptp* **read** [red] **1** *vt* (**a**) *(gen)* lire ; *meter* relever; *proofs* corriger. **I brought you sth to ~** je vous ai apporté de la lecture; **to be well-read** être très cultivé; *(fig)* **to ~ sb a lesson** * faire la leçon à qn; **to take sth as read** *(as self-evident)* considérer qch comme allant de soi; *(as agreed)* considérer qch comme convenu; *(Admin)* **to take the minutes as read** passer à l'ordre du jour; **to**

~ **sb's hand** lire les lignes de la main à qn; *(fig)* **these words can be read in several ways** ces mots peuvent s'interpréter de plusieurs façons; **to ~ between the lines** lire entre les lignes; **to ~ sb's mind** *or* **thoughts** lire la pensée de qn; **I can ~ him like a book** je sais toujours ce qu'il pense; **we mustn't ~ too much into this** nous ne devons pas y attacher trop d'importance; *(Telec)* **do you ~ me?** est-ce que vous me recevez? (**b**) *(Univ: study)* étudier, faire. **to ~ medicine/English** faire des études de médecine/d'anglais. (**c**) *[instruments]* marquer, indiquer. **2** *vi* lire. **he likes ~ing** il aime lire, il aime la lecture; **to ~ to sb** faire la lecture à qn; **I read about it in the paper** je l'ai lu dans le journal; **I've read about him** j'ai lu qch à son sujet. **3** *n*: **she enjoys a good ~ *** elle aime bien la lecture, elle aime bouquiner *; **to have a quiet ~ *** bouquiner * tranquillement.

◆ **read back** *vt sep* relire. ◆ **read off** *vt sep* (**a**) *(without pause)* lire d'un trait; *(at sight)* lire à livre ouvert. (**b**) *instrument readings* relever. ◆ **read out** *vt sep* lire à haute voix; *(Comput)* afficher. ◆ **read over** *vt sep* relire. ◆ **read through** *vt sep (rapidly)* parcourir; *(thoroughly)* lire d'un bout à l'autre. ◆ **read up** *vt sep*, **read up on** *vt fus* étudier, potasser *.

◆ **readable** *adj handwriting* lisible; *book* facile à lire. ◆ **reader** *n* (**a**) lecteur *m*, -trice *f*; **publisher's ~er** lecteur, -trice dans une maison d'édition; **he's a great ~er** il aime beaucoup lire; (**b**) *(Brit Univ)* ≃ chargé(e) *m(f)* d'enseignement; (**c**) *(reading book)* livre *m* de lecture; *(anthology)* recueil *m* de textes. ◆ **readership** *n [newspaper]* nombre *m* de lecteurs. ◆ **reading 1** *n* (**a**) *(gen)* lecture *f*; *[proofs]* correction *f*; **she likes ~ing** elle aime bien lire *or* la lecture; **it makes very interesting ~ing** c'est très intéressant (à lire); **I'd prefer some light ~ing** je préférerais un livre d'une lecture facile; (**b**) *(recital: of play, poems)* (séance *f* de) lecture *f*; (**c**) *(interpretation)* interprétation *f*; (**d**) *(variant)* variante *f*; (**e**) **to take a ~ing** *(from instrument)* lire un instrument; *(from meter)* relever un compteur; **the ~ing is...** l'instrument indique... ; **2** *adj book* de lecture; *glasses* pour lire; **to have a ~ing knowledge of Spanish** savoir lire l'espagnol; **~ing lamp** lampe *f* de bureau; **~ing list** bibliographie *f*; **~ing matter** choses *fpl* à lire; **~ing room** salle *f* de lecture. ◆ **read-only-memory** *n (abbr* **ROM**) *(Comput)* mémoire *f* morte. ◆ **read-out** *n (Comput)* affichage *m*.

readdress ['ri:ə'dres] *vt letter etc* faire suivre.

readjust ['ri:ə'dʒʌst] **1** *vt* rajuster. **2** *vi* se réadapter (*to* à).

ready ['redɪ] **1** *adj* (**a**) *(gen)* prêt. **'dinner's ~!'** 'à table!'; **everything is ~ for his visit** tout est prêt pour sa visite; **~ for anything** prêt à toute éventualité; **~ to use** *or* **for use** prêt à l'usage; **to be ~ to do** être prêt à faire; **to get ~ to do** se préparer à faire; **to be ~ with an excuse** avoir une excuse toute prête; **to get sth ~** préparer qch; *(Sport)* **~, steady, go!** prêts? 1-2-3 partez!; **I'm ~ for him!** je l'attends de pied ferme!; **get ~ for it!** tenez-vous prêt!, *(before momentous news etc)* tenez-vous bien!; *(Publishing)* **'now ~ '** 'vient de paraître'; **~ money** (argent *m*) liquide *m*; **~ reckoner** barème *m*; **he is ~ to help** il est prêt à rendre service; **I am quite ~ to see him** je suis tout à fait disposé à le voir; **he was ~ to cry** il était sur le point de pleurer. (**b**) *(prompt) reply, wit* prompt. **to have a ~ tongue** avoir la langue déliée; **to have a ~ sale** se vendre facilement. **2** *n*: **at the ~** *(Mil)* prêt à faire feu; *(fig)* tout prêt. **3** *adv (in cpds)* **~-cooked/-furnished** *etc* tout cuit/meublé *etc (d'avance)*.

◆ **readily** *adv (willingly)* volontiers; *(easily)* facilement. ◆ **readiness** *n* empressement *m* (*to do* à faire); **in readiness for** prêt pour. ◆ **ready-made** *adj curtains* tout fait; *clothes* de confection; *solution, answer* tout prêt. ◆ **ready-mix** *n* préparation *f* instantanée *(pour gâteaux etc)*. ◆ **ready-to-serve** *adj* prêt à servir. ◆ **ready-to-wear** *adj* prêt à porter.

real [rɪəl] **1** *adj* véritable, vrai *(both before n)*, réel; *reason, jewels* vrai *(before n)*, véritable; *flowers, silk* naturel; *(Philos)* réel. **in ~ life, in ~ terms** dans la réalité; **he is the ~ boss** c'est lui le véritable patron; **he has no ~ power** il n'a pas de pouvoir effectif; **when you've tasted the ~ thing, this whisky...** quand tu as (*or* auras) goûté du vrai whisky, celui-ci...; **it's the ~ thing *** c'est du vrai de vrai *. **2** *adv* (*‡: very)* rudement *. **3** *n*: **for ~ *** pour de vrai *. ◆ **real estate** *n (US)* immobilier *m*; **~-estate office** agence *f* immobilière. ◆ **realism** *n* réalisme *m*. ◆ **realist** *adj, n* réaliste *(mf)*. ◆ **realistic** *adj* réaliste. ◆ **realistically** *adv* avec réalisme, d'une façon réaliste. ◆ **reality** [ri:'ælɪtɪ] *n* réalité *f*; **in ~ity** en réalité. ◆ **really** *adv* vraiment. ◆ **real time** *n (Comput)* temps *m* réel.

realize ['rɪəlaɪz] *vt* (**a**) *(become aware of)* se rendre compte de, prendre conscience de; *(understand)* comprendre. **the committee ~s the gravity of the situation** le comité se rend compte de *or* a pris conscience de la gravité de la situation; **he had not fully ~d that she was dead** il n'avait pas vraiment réalisé qu'elle était morte; **I ~d it was raining** je me suis rendu compte qu'il pleuvait, j'ai réalisé * qu'il pleuvait; **I made her ~ that I was right** je lui ai bien fait comprendre que j'avais raison; **I ~ that...** je me rends compte du fait que..., je sais bien que...; **I ~d how/why** j'ai compris comment/pourquoi. (**b**) *hope, plan, assets* réaliser; *price* atteindre; *interest* rapporter. **how much did it ~?** combien est-ce que cela vous a rapporté? ◆ **realization** *n [assets, hope]* réalisation *f*; *(awareness)* prise *f* de conscience, découverte *f* soudaine (*that* que).

realm [relm] *n* royaume *m*; *(fig)* domaine *m*.

realtor ['rɪəltɔ:ʳ] *n (US)* agent *m* immobilier.

ream [ri:m] *n* ≃ rame *f (de papier)*. *(fig)* **~s *** des volumes *mpl*.

reap [ri:p] *vt* moissonner, faucher; *(fig) profit* récolter, tirer. ◆ **reaper** *n (person)* moissonneur *m*, -euse *f*; *(machine)* moissonneuse *f*; **~er and binder** moissonneuse-lieuse *f*.

reappear ['ri:ə'pɪəʳ] *vi* réapparaître, reparaître. ◆ **reappearance** *n* réapparition *f*.

reappraisal ['ri:ə'preɪz(ə)l] *n* réévaluation *f*.

rear¹ [rɪəʳ] **1** *n* (**a**) *(back part)* arrière *m*, derrière *m*; *(*: buttocks)* derrière *. **in** *or* **at the ~** à l'arrière; **from the ~** de derrière. (**b**) *(Mil)* arrière-garde *f*; *[squad]* dernier rang *m*; *[column]* queue *f*. **to bring up the ~** fermer la marche. **2** *adj (gen)* de derrière; *(Aut) door, window etc* arrière *inv*. **~ admiral** vice-amiral *m*. ◆ **rearguard** *n (Mil)* arrière-garde *f*; **~guard action** combat *m* d'arrière-garde. ◆ **rearmost** *adj* dernier. ◆ **rear-view mirror** *n* rétroviseur *m*.

rear² [rɪəʳ] **1** *vt* (**a**) *animals, family* élever; *plants* cultiver. (**b**) *a ladder, one's head* dresser. **violence ~s its ugly head** la violence fait son apparition dans toute son horreur. (**c**) *monument* dresser, ériger. **2** *vi* (**~ up**) *[animal]* se cabrer; *[snake]* se dresser.

rearm [,ri:'ɑ:m] *vti* réarmer. ◆ **rearmament** *n* réarmement *m*.

rearrange ['ri:ə'reɪn(d)ʒ] *vt* réarranger. ◆ **rearrangement** *n* nouvel arrangement *m*.

reason ['ri:zn] **1** *n* (**a**) *(cause: gen)* raison *f (for sth* de qch; *why* pour, laquelle). **my ~ for going** la raison pour laquelle je pars; **the ~ why** (le) pourquoi; **I have (good** *or* **every) ~ to believe that...** j'ai (tout) lieu de croire que...; **for no ~** sans raison; **for some ~ or another** pour une raison ou pour une autre; **for ~s best known to himself** pour des raisons qu'il est seul à connaître; **all the more ~ for doing** *or* **to do** raison de plus pour faire; **with ~** avec juste raison; **by ~ of** en raison de. (**b**) *(mental faculty, common sense)* raison *f.* **to lose one's ~** perdre la raison; **it stands to ~ that** il va sans dire que; **anything within ~** tout ce qui est raisonnablement possible. **2** *vi* raisonner (*with sb* qn). **3** *vt (work out)* calculer; *(argue)* soutenir (*that* que). ◆ **reasonable** *adj (gen)* raisonnable; *offer, essay, results* honnête, correct; *(Jur) doubt* bien fondé; *chance, amount, hope* certain *(before n)*. ◆ **reasonableness** *n* caractère *m* raisonnable. ◆ **reasonably** *adv* raisonnablement; **one can ~ably think that...** il est raisonnable de penser que...; **~ably priced** à un prix raisonnable. ◆ **reasoned** *adj* raisonné. ◆ **reasoning** *n* raisonnement *m.*

reassemble [ˌriːəˈsembl] **1** *vt tool, machine* remonter. **2** *vi [people]* se rassembler. **school ~s tomorrow** c'est la rentrée demain.

reassure [ˌriːəˈʃʊəʳ] *vt* rassurer. ◆ **reassurance** *n (emotional)* réconfort *m; (factual)* assurance *f.* ◆ **reassuring** *adj* rassurant.

reawaken [ˈriːəˈweɪk(ə)n] **1** *vt* réveiller de nouveau. **2** *vi* se réveiller de nouveau.

rebate [ˈriːbeɪt] *n (discount)* rabais *m*; *(money back)* remboursement *m; (on tax)* dégrèvement *m; (on rent)* réduction *f.*

rebel [ˈrebl] **1** *adj, n* rebelle *(mf)*. **2** [rɪˈbel] *vi* se rebeller (*against* contre). ◆ **rebellion** *n* rébellion *f.* ◆ **rebellious** *adj* rebelle. ◆ **rebelliousness** *n* esprit *m* de rébellion.

rebirth [ˈriːˈbɜːθ] *n* renaissance *f.*

rebound [rɪˈbaʊnd] **1** *vi* rebondir. **2** [ˈriːbaʊnd] *n [ball]* rebond *m*; *[bullet]* ricochet *m.*

rebuff [rɪˈbʌf] **1** *n* rebuffade *f.* **2** *vt* repousser.

rebuild [ˌriːˈbɪld] *pret, ptp* **rebuilt** *vt* rebâtir.

rebuke [rɪˈbjuːk] **1** *n* reproche *m.* **2** *vt* faire des reproches à. **to ~ sb for sth/sb for doing** reprocher qch à qn/à qn d'avoir fait.

rebut [rɪˈbʌt] *vt* réfuter. ◆ **rebuttal** *n* réfutation *f.*

recalcitrant [rɪˈkælsɪtr(ə)nt] *adj* récalcitrant.

recall [rɪˈkɔːl] **1** *vt* (**a**) *(call back: gen)* rappeler; *(Fin) capital* faire rentrer; *Parliament* convoquer en session extraordinaire. (**b**) *(remember)* se rappeler (*doing* avoir fait; *that* que). **2** *n* rappel *m (also Mil)*. **beyond ~** *(adv)* irrévocablement.

recant [rɪˈkænt] *vi* se rétracter; *(Rel)* abjurer.

recap¹ * [ˈriːkæp] **1** *n abbr of* **recapitulation. 2** [riːˈkæp] *vti abbr of* **recapitulate: to ~...** en résumé...

recap² [ˈriːkæp] *(US)* **1** *n (tyre)* pneu *m* rechapé. **2** *vt* rechaper.

recapitulate [ˌriːkəˈpɪtjʊleɪt] *vti* récapituler. ◆ **recapitulation** *n* récapitulation *f.*

recapture [ˈriːˈkæptʃəʳ] **1** *vt animal, escapee* reprendre; *atmosphere* retrouver, *[book etc]* recréer. **2** *n [territory]* reprise *f*; *[escapee]* arrestation *f*; *[animal]* capture *f.*

recast [ˈriːˈkɑːst] *vt play* changer la distribution de.

recede [rɪˈsiːd] *vi (gen)* s'éloigner; *[tide]* descendre; *[chin]* être fuyant; *[hopes]* s'estomper. **his hair is receding** son front se dégarnit. ◆ **receding** *adj chin, forehead* fuyant; **receding hairline** front dégarni.

receipt [rɪˈsiːt] **1** *n* (**a**) *(for payment)* reçu *m*, quittance *f* (*for* de); *(for parcel, letter)* accusé *m* de réception. (**b**) *(esp Comm)* réception *f.* **to acknowledge ~ of** accuser réception de; **on ~ of** dès réception de; **I am in ~ of...** j'ai reçu... (**c**) *(money taken)* **~s** recettes *fpl.* **2** *adj*: **~ book** livre *m* de quittances. **3** *vt bill* acquitter.

receive [rɪˈsiːv] *vt (gen)* recevoir; *money, salary* recevoir, toucher; *refusal, setback* essuyer; *(Rad, TV) transmissions* capter, recevoir; *(Jur) stolen goods* receler. *(Jur)* **to ~ (a sentence of) 2 years' imprisonment** être condamné à 2 ans de prison; *(Comm)* **~d with thanks** pour acquit; **his suggestion was well ~d** sa suggestion a reçu un accueil favorable. ◆ **received** *adj opinion* reçu; *(Ling)* **~d pronunciation** prononciation *f* standard (de l'anglais). ◆ **receiver** *n* (**a**) *(gen)* personne *f* qui reçoit qch; *[letter]* destinataire *mf*; *[goods]* réceptionnaire *mf*; *[stolen property]* receleur *m*, -euse *f*; *(in bankruptcy)* administrateur *m* judiciaire (en matière de faillite); (**b**) *[telephone]* combiné *m*; **to lift the ~r** décrocher; **to replace the ~r** raccrocher. ◆ **receiving** *n [stolen goods]* recel *m.*

recent [ˈriːsnt] *adj (gen)* récent; *development* nouveau; *acquaintance etc* de fraîche date. **in ~ years** ces dernières années. ◆ **recently** *adv* récemment; **as ~ly as** pas plus tard que; **until quite ~ly** jusqu'à ces derniers temps.

receptacle [rɪˈseptəkl] *n* récipient *m.*

reception [rɪˈsepʃ(ə)n] **1** *n (all senses)* réception *f.* **to get a favourable ~** être bien accueilli; **to give sb a warm ~** faire un accueil chaleureux à qn. **2** *adj*: **~ centre** centre *m* d'accueil; **~ desk** (bureau *m* de) réception *f;* **~ room** *(in home)* salon *m.* ◆ **receptionist** *n* réceptionniste *mf.*

receptive [rɪˈseptɪv] *adj* réceptif (*to* à). ◆ **receptivity** *n* réceptivité *f.*

recess [rɪˈses] **1** *n* (**a**) *(cessation of business) (Jur, Parl)* vacances *fpl*; *(US Jur: short break)* suspension *f* d'audience; *(Scol, esp US)* récréation *f.* (**b**) *(alcove)* renfoncement *m*; *[bed]* alcôve *f*; *[door, window]* embrasure *f*; *[statue]* niche *f.* **2** *vi (US Jur, Parl)* être en vacances. ◆ **recession** *n (Econ)* récession *f.*

recessive [rɪˈsesɪv] *adj* rétrograde; *(Genetics)* récessif.

recharge [ˈriːˈtʃɑːdʒ] *vt battery, gun* recharger. ◆ **rechargeable** *adj* rechargeable.

recidivism [rɪˈsɪdɪvɪz(ə)m] *n* récidive *f.* ◆ **recidivist** *adj, n* récidiviste *(mf)*.

recipe [ˈresɪpɪ] *n (Culin)* recette *f* (*for* de).

recipient [rɪˈsɪpɪənt] *n [letter]* destinataire *mf*; *[cheque]* bénéficiaire *mf*; *[award]* récipiendaire *mf*; *(Jur)* donataire *mf.*

reciprocate [rɪˈsɪprəkeɪt] **1** *vt (gen)* donner *or* offrir en retour; *smile* rendre; *kindness* retourner. **2** *vi* en faire autant. ◆ **reciprocal** *adj* réciproque. ◆ **reciprocally** *adv* réciproquement. ◆ **reciprocity** *n* réciprocité *f.*

recite [rɪˈsaɪt] **1** *vt poetry* réciter; *facts, details* énumérer. **2** *vi* réciter. ◆ **recital** *n* (**a**) *[poetry, music]* récital *m*; (**b**) *(account)* récit *m*; *[details]* énumération *f.* ◆ **recitation** *n* récitation *f.* ◆ **recitative** *n* récitatif *m.*

reckless [ˈreklɪs] *adj (gen)* imprudent; *person* insouciant; *(stronger)* imprudent; *(Aut) driving, driver* imprudent. ◆ **recklessly** *adv* avec insouciance; imprudemment. ◆ **recklessness** *n* insouciance *f*; imprudence *f.*

reckon [ˈrek(ə)n] **1** *vt (calculate) time, numbers, points* compter; *cost, surface* calculer; *(judge)* considérer (*sb to be* qn comme étant), compter (*among* parmi); *(*: think)* penser, croire; *(estimate)* estimer (*that* que). **about thirty, I ~** une trentaine, à mon avis. **2** *vi* compter, calculer; *(fig)* compter (*on* sur; *with* avec; *without sb* sans qn). **I wasn't ~ing on having to do that** je ne m'attendais pas à devoir faire ça; **a person to be ~ed with** une personne avec laquelle il faut compter; **he ~ed without the fact that...** il n'avait pas tenu compte du fait que... ◆ **reckon up** *vt sep (gen)* calculer; *(add)* ajouter, additionner. ◆ **reckoning** *n* compte *m*, calcul *m*; **to be out in one's ~ing** s'être trompé dans ses calculs; **on the day of ~ing** le jour où il faudra rendre des comptes; **to the best of my ~ing** pour autant que je puisse en juger.

reclaim [rɪ'kleɪm] *vt land (gen)* reconquérir; *(from forest)* défricher; *(from sea)* assécher; *(Ind) (by-product)* récupérer; *(demand back)* réclamer *(from sb* à qn).

recline [rɪ'klaɪn] *vi [person]* être étendu *or* allongé. **the seat ~s** le dossier est réglable. ◆ **reclining** *adj seat* à dossier réglable.

recluse [rɪ'klu:s] *n* reclus(e) *m(f)*.

recognition [ˌrekəg'nɪʃ(ə)n] *n* reconnaissance *f*. **in ~ of** en reconnaissance de; **to gain ~** être reconnu; **to change/change sth beyond all ~** devenir/rendre qch méconnaissable; **to improve out of (all) ~** s'améliorer jusqu'à en être méconnaissable.

recognize ['rekəgnaɪz] *vt (all senses)* reconnaître *(by* à; *as* comme étant; *that* que). ◆ **recognizable** *adj* reconnaissable. ◆ **recognized** *adj* reconnu.

recoil [rɪ'kɔɪl] **1** *vi [person]* reculer *(from* devant; *in disgust* de dégoût); *[gun]* reculer; *(fig) [actions etc]* retomber *(on* sur). **to ~ from doing** se refuser à faire. **2** *n [gun]* recul *m*; *(fig)* dégoût *m*.

recollect [ˌrekə'lekt] **1** *vt* se rappeler, se souvenir de. **2** *vi* se souvenir. ◆ **recollection** *n* souvenir *m*; **to the best of my ~ion** autant que je m'en souvienne.

recommend [ˌrekə'mend] *vt* (**a**) recommander *(sb/sth for* qn/qch pour; *sb as* qn comme; *sb to do* à qn de faire). **it is/is not to be ~ed** c'est à conseiller/à déconseiller; **she has a lot to ~ her** elle a beaucoup de qualités en sa faveur. (**b**) *(commit) child, one's soul* confier *(to* à). ◆ **recommendation** *n* recommandation *f*.

recompense ['rekəmpens] **1** *n* récompense *f*; *(Jur: for damage)* dédommagement *m*. **2** *vt* récompenser *(for* de); *(Jur)* dédommager.

reconcile ['rekənsaɪl] *vt person* réconcilier *(to* avec); *two facts or ideas* concilier. *[people]* **to become ~d** se réconcilier; **to ~ o.s. to sth** se résigner à qch; **what ~d him to it was...** ce qui le lui a fait accepter, c'était... ◆ **reconcilable** *adj* conciliable *(with* avec). ◆ **reconciliation** *n* réconciliation *f*.

recondition ['ri:kən'dɪʃ(ə)n] *vt (gen)* remettre à neuf; *engine, machine* réviser.

reconnaissance [rɪ'kɒnɪs(ə)ns] **1** *n (Aviat, Mil)* reconnaissance *f*. **2** *adj patrol* de reconnaissance.

reconnoitre, *(US)* **reconnoiter** [ˌrekə'nɔɪtəʳ] *(Mil)* **1** *vt* reconnaître. **2** *vi* faire une reconnaissance.

reconsider ['ri:kən'sɪdəʳ] *vt* reconsidérer. ◆ **reconsideration** *n* remise *f* en cause.

reconstruct ['ri:kən'strʌkt] *vt building* reconstruire; *crime* reconstituer. ◆ **reconstruction** *n* reconstruction *f*; reconstitution *f*.

record [rɪ'kɔ:d] **1** *vt* (**a**) *(register)* rapporter *(that* que); *population* recenser; *protest, disapproval* prendre acte de; *event etc* noter, *(describe)* décrire; *[thermometer etc]* enregistrer, marquer. **to ~ the proceedings** tenir le procès-verbal; **to ~ one's vote** voter; **the author ~s that...** l'auteur rapporte que... (**b**) *speech, music* enregistrer *(on tape* sur bande).

2 ['rekɔ:d] *n* (**a**) *(report)* rapport *m*; *(minutes: of meeting)* procès-verbal *m*; *(of act, decision)* minute *f*; *(Jur)* enregistrement *m*; *(historical report)* document *m*. **~ of attendance** registre *m* des présences; **the society's ~s** les actes *mpl* de la société; **public ~s** archives *fpl*; **to make** *or* **keep a ~ of sth, to put sth on ~** noter *or* consigner qch; *(fig)* **it is on ~ that...** il est établi que...; **there is no similar example on ~** aucun exemple semblable n'est attesté; **to go on ~ as saying that...** déclarer publiquement que...; **there is no ~ of his having said** il n'est noté *or* consigné nulle part qu'il ait dit; **to set the ~ straight** dissiper toute confusion possible; *(fig)* **for the ~** il faut noter que; **strictly off the ~ *** à titre purement confidentiel *or* officieux. (**b**) *(case history)* dossier *m*; *(card)* fiche *f*. **police ~** casier *m* judiciaire; **~ of previous convictions** dossier *(d'un prévenu)*; *(Police)* **he's got a clean ~, he hasn't got a ~ *** il a un casier judiciaire vierge; **France's splendid ~** les succès glorieux de la France; **his past ~** sa conduite passée; *(Scol)* **his attendance ~ is bad** il a été souvent absent; **a good ~ at school** un bon dossier scolaire; **his war ~** son passé militaire; **a good safety ~** une bonne tradition de sécurité. (**c**) *(gramophone ~)* disque *m*. **to make** *or* **cut a ~** graver un disque. (**d**) *(Sport, fig)* record *m*. **to beat** *or* **break the ~** battre le record; **to hold the ~** détenir le record; **long-jump ~** record du saut en longueur.

3 *adj* (**a**) *amount, result* record *inv*. *(Sport)* **~ holder** détenteur *m*, -trice *f* du record; **to do sth in ~ time** faire qch en un temps record. (**b**) *(Mus etc) programme, album* de disques. **~ changer** changeur *m* de disques automatique; **~ dealer** disquaire *mf*; **~ library** discothèque *f (collection)*; **~ player** électrophone *m*; **~ token** chèque-disque *m*. (**c**) **~ card** fiche *f*.

◆ **record-breaking** *adj* qui bat tous les records. ◆ **recorded** *adj* (**a**) *music* enregistré; *(Rad) programme* enregistré à l'avance; (**b**) *fact, occurrence* attesté, noté; *(Brit Post)* **by ~ed delivery** ≃ avec avis de réception. ◆ **recorder** *n* (**a**) *(tape ~er)* magnétophone *m*; (**b**) *(Jur)* ≃ juge *m* suppléant; (**c**) *(Mus)* flûte *f* à bec. ◆ **recording** **1** *n [sound, facts]* enregistrement *m*; *(Rad)* **'this programme is a ~ing'** 'ce programme est enregistré'; **2** *adj artist* qui enregistre; *apparatus* enregistreur; *session, studio* d'enregistrement; *(Rad, TV)* **~ing van** car *m* de reportage.

recount [rɪ'kaʊnt] *vt (relate)* raconter.

re-count [ˌri:'kaʊnt] **1** *vt* recompter. **2** ['ri:kaʊnt] *n [votes]* deuxième dépouillement *m* du scrutin.

recoup [rɪ'ku:p] *vt* récupérer *(ses pertes)*.

recourse [rɪ'kɔ:s] *n* recours *m (to* à).

recover [rɪ'kʌvəʳ] **1** *vt sth lost, appetite, reason, balance* retrouver; *property* reprendre *(from sb* à qn), récupérer; *lost territory* reconquérir; *sth floating* repêcher; *space capsule, wreck, (Ind etc) materials* récupérer; *debt, expenses, sight, health* recouvrer; *one's breath, strength, consciousness* reprendre; *(Jur) damages* obtenir. **to ~ land from the sea** conquérir du terrain sur la mer; *(fig)* **to ~ lost ground** se rattraper; **to ~ o.s.** *or* **one's composure** se ressaisir; **to ~ one's losses** récupérer ses pertes.

2 *vi (after accident, illness)* se rétablir *(from* de); *(regain consciousness)* reprendre connaissance; *[the economy, the dollar]* se redresser; *[stock market]* reprendre; *[shares]* remonter. **she is** *or* **has ~ed** elle est rétablie.

◆ **recovery** *n* (**a**) *(V* **recover 1***)*récupération *f*; reconquête *f*; recouvrement *m*; obtention *f*; (**b**) *(V* **recover 2***)* rétablissement *m*; redressement *m*; reprise *f*; remontée *f*; *(Med)* **on the way to ~y** en voie de guérison; *(Sport)* **to make a ~y** se ressaisir; **~y operation** opération *f* de sauvetage; *(Med)* **~y room** salle *f* de réanimation.

re-cover [ˌri:'kʌvəʳ] *vt chair etc* recouvrir.

recreation [ˌrekrɪ'eɪʃ(ə)n] **1** *n* récréation *f*. **2** *adj*: **~ ground** terrain *m* de jeux; **~ room** salle *f* de récréation. ◆ **recreational** *adj* de récréation.

recrimination [rɪˌkrɪmɪ'neɪʃ(ə)n] *n* récrimination *f*.

recruit [rɪ'kru:t] **1** *n* recrue *f*. **2** *vt* recruter. **to ~ sb to help** embaucher * qn pour aider. ◆ **recruiting** *or* ◆ **recruitment** *n* recrutement *m*.

rectangle ['rekˌtæŋgl] *n* rectangle *m*. ◆ **rectangular** *adj* rectangulaire.

rectify ['rektɪfaɪ] *vt* rectifier; *omission* réparer.

rectitude ['rektɪtju:d] *n* rectitude *f*.

rector ['rektəʳ] *n (Rel)* pasteur *m (anglican)*; *[school]* proviseur *m* (de lycée); *(Univ)* président *m* élu. ◆ **rectory** *n* presbytère *m (anglican)*.

rectum ['rektəm] *n* rectum *m*.

recumbent [rɪ'kʌmbənt] *adj* étendu, couché.

recuperate [rɪ'ku:p(ə)reɪt] **1** *vi (Med)* se rétablir. **2** *vt object, losses* récupérer. ◆ **recuperation** *n (Med)* rétablissement *m*; *[materials etc]* récupération *f*. ◆ **recuperative** *adj powers* de récupération.

recur [rɪ'kɜ:ʳ] *vi [error, event]* se reproduire, se répéter; *[theme]* se retrouver, réapparaître; *[illness]* réapparaître; *[opportunity, problem]* se représenter. ◆ **recurrence** *n* répétition *f*; réapparition *f*; **a ~rence of the illness** une rechute. ◆ **recurrent** *adj* fréquent, qui revient souvent. ◆ **recurring** *adj* (**a**) *(Math)* périodique. (**b**) *complaints* régulier; *illness* chronique.

recycle [ˌri:'saɪkl] *vt* recycler, récupérer.

red [red] **1** *adj (gen, also Pol)* rouge; *hair* roux (*f* rousse). **~ as a beetroot** rouge comme une tomate; **~ in the face** tout rouge; *(fig)* rouge de confusion; **to go** *or* **turn ~** rougir; **to see ~** voir rouge; **like a ~ rag to a bull** comme le rouge pour les taureaux; *(fig)* **to roll out the ~ carpet for sb** recevoir qn en grande pompe; **~ light** feu *m* rouge; *(Aut)* **to go through the ~ light** brûler un feu rouge; *(fig)* **to see the ~ light** * se rendre compte du danger; **R~ Cross** Croix-Rouge *f*; **~ deer** cerf *m* commun; **that's a ~ herring** c'est pour brouiller les pistes; **R~ Indian** Peau-Rouge *mf*; **Red Sea** mer *f* Rouge; *(fig)* **~ tape** paperasserie *f*, bureaucratie *f* tatillonne.
2 *n (colour)* rouge *m*; *(Pol: person)* rouge *mf*. *(fig)* **to be in the ~** * *[individual]* être à découvert; *[company]* être en déficit.
◆ **red-blooded** *adj* vigoureux. ◆ **red-brick university** *n (Brit)* université *f* de l'ère industrielle. ◆ **redcurrant** *n* groseille *f* (rouge). ◆ **redden** **1** *vt* rendre rouge ; **2** *vi [person]* rougir; *[foliage]* roussir. ◆ **reddish** *adj* rougeâtre; *hair* qui tire sur le roux. ◆ **red-eyed** *adj* aux yeux rouges. ◆ **red-faced** *adj* rougeaud; *(fig)* rouge de confusion. ◆ **red-haired** *or* ◆ **red-headed** *adj* roux. ◆ **red-handed** *adj*: **to be caught ~-handed** être pris en flagrant délit. ◆ **redhead** *n* roux *m*, rousse *f*. ◆ **red-hot** *adj* brûlant; *news* tout chaud. ◆ **red-letter day** *n* jour *m* mémorable. ◆ **red-light district** *n* quartier *m* réservé *(prostitution)*. ◆ **redneck** * *n* péquenaud *m*. ◆ **redness** *n* rougeur *f*; *[hair]* rousseur *f*. ◆ **redskin** *n* Peau-Rouge *mf*. ◆ **redwood** *n* séquoia *m*.

redeem [rɪ'di:m] *vt (buy back)* racheter; (*from pawn*) dégager; *(Fin) debt* amortir; *mortgage* purger; *(Comm) coupon* échanger; *promise* tenir; *obligation* s'acquitter de; *sinner, failing* racheter; *fault* réparer. **to ~ o.s.** se racheter. ◆ **Redeemer** *n* Rédempteur *m*. ◆ **redeeming** *adj quality* qui rachète les défauts; **only ~ing feature** seul bon côté. ◆ **redemption** *n (Rel)* rédemption *f*.

redeploy ['rɪ:dɪ'plɔɪ] *vt personnel* redéployer.

redirect [ˌri:daɪ'rekt] *vt letter* faire suivre.

redouble [ri:'dʌbl] *vt* redoubler; *(Bridge)* surcontrer.

redoubtable [rɪ'daʊtəbl] *adj* redoutable.

redound [rɪ'daʊnd] *vi* retomber (*upon* sur). **to ~ to sb's credit** être tout à l'honneur de qn.

redress [rɪ'dres] **1** *vt* redresser. **2** *n* réparation *f*.

reduce [rɪ'dju:s] **1** *vt (gen)* réduire (*to/by a certain quantity* à une/d'une certaine quantité), diminuer; *drawing, expenses* réduire; *price* baisser; *speed, voltage, tax* diminuer; *(Med) swelling* résorber; *temperature* faire descendre; *(Culin) sauce* faire réduire. *(Mil)* **to ~ to the ranks** casser; **to ~ sth to pieces/to ashes** réduire qch en morceaux/en cendres; **to ~ sb to silence/despair** réduire qn au silence/au désespoir; **~d to nothing** réduit à zéro; **he's ~d to a skeleton** il n'est plus qu'un squelette ambulant; **to be ~d to doing** être réduit *or* contraint à faire; **to ~ sb to tears** faire pleurer qn. **2** *vi (slim)* maigrir. **to be reducing** être au régime. ◆ **reduced** *adj* réduit; *sale goods* soldé; **to buy at a ~d price** *ticket* acheter à prix réduit; *goods* acheter au rabais; *(Comm)* **~d goods** soldes *mpl*; **in ~d circumstances** dans la gêne. ◆ **reduction** [rɪ'dʌkʃ(ə)n] *n* réduction *f*; diminution *f*; baisse *f*; *(Comm)* **to make a reduction on sth** faire un rabais sur qch; **to sell at a reduction** *ticket* vendre à prix réduit; *goods* vendre au rabais; **reduction for cash** escompte *m* au comptant.

redundant [rɪ'dʌnd(ə)nt] *adj (gen)* superflu; *(Literat etc)* redondant; *helper, worker* en surnombre. *(Ind)* **to be made ~, to become ~** être licencié (pour raisons économiques). ◆ **redundancy** **1** *n (Ind)* licenciement *m* (pour raisons économiques); **there is a lot of redundancy** il y a beaucoup de licenciements; excès *m*, superfluité *f*; *(Literat)* redondance *f* ; **2** *adj*: **redundancy payment** indemnité *f* de licenciement.

reed [ri:d] **1** *n (Bot)* roseau *m*; *[wind instrument]* anche *f*; *(liter: pipe)* pipeau *m*. *(Mus)* **the ~s** les instruments *mpl* à anche. **2** *adj basket etc* de *or* en roseau(x). ◆ **reedy** *adj instrument, sound* aigu (*f* -guë); *voice* flûté.

reef[1] [ri:f] *n* (**a**) récif *m*; *(fig)* écueil *m*. (**b**) *(Min)* filon *m*.

reef[2] [ri:f] **1** *n (Naut)* ris *m*. **2** *vt* prendre un ris dans. **3** *adj*: **~ knot** nœud *m* plat. ◆ **reefer** *n* (**a**) *(jacket)* caban *m*; (**b**) (‡) joint ‡ *m (de marijuana)*.

reek [ri:k] *vi*: **to ~ of sth** puer *or* empester qch.

reel [ri:l] **1** *n* (**a**) *(gen)* bobine *f*; *(Fishing)* moulinet *m*; *(Cine) [film]* bande *f*. (**b**) *(dance)* reel *m (danse écossaise)*. **2** *vi* chanceler, vaciller; *[drunken man]* tituber. **to ~ back from** s'écarter en chancelant de; *(fig)* **my head is ~ing** la tête me tourne; **I ~ed at the very thought** cette pensée m'a donné le vertige. ◆ **reel in** *vt sep* ramener. ◆ **reel off** *vt sep verses, list* débiter.

re-elect [ˌri:ɪ'lekt] *vt* réélire. ◆ **re-election** *n*: **to stand** *or* **run for re-election** se représenter.

re-enact ['ri:ɪ'nækt] *vt scene, crime* reconstituer.

re-enter [ˌri:'entəʳ] **1** *vi* (**a**) rentrer. (**b**) **to ~ for an exam** se représenter à un examen. **2** *vt* rentrer dans. ◆ **re-entry** *n* rentrée *f*.

re-examine ['ri:ɪg'zæmɪn] *vt* examiner de nouveau; *(Jur) witness* interroger de nouveau.

ref ‡ [ref] *n (Sport: abbr of* **referee***)* arbitre *m*.

refectory [rɪ'fekt(ə)rɪ] *n* réfectoire *m*.

refer [rɪ'fɜ:ʳ] **1** *vt (gen)* soumettre (*to* à). **it was ~red to us for (a) decision** on nous a demandé de prendre une décision là-dessus; **I ~red him to the manager** je lui ai dit de s'adresser au gérant; *[doctor]* **to ~ sb to a specialist** adresser qn à un spécialiste; **to ~ sb to the article on...** renvoyer qn à l'article sur...; **to ~ a cheque to drawer** refuser d'honorer un chèque.
2 *vi* (**a**) *(allude) (directly)* parler (*to* de); *(indirectly)* faire allusion (*to* à). **we shall not ~ to it again** nous n'en reparlerons pas; **he ~red to her as...** il l'a appelée...; *(Comm)* **~ring to your letter** comme suite *or* en réponse à votre lettre. (**b**) *(apply)* s'appliquer (*to* à). **does that ~ to me?** est-ce que cela s'applique à moi? (**c**) *(consult)* **to ~ to sb/sth** consulter qn/qch.
◆ **reference** ['refr(ə)ns] **1** *n* (**a**) *(allusion) (direct)* mention *f* (*to* de); *(indirect)* allusion *f* (*to* à); *(connection)* rapport *m* (*to* avec); **this has no ~ence to...** cela n'a aucun rapport avec...; **with ~ence to** en ce qui concerne; *(Comm)* comme suite à;

without ~ence to sans tenir compte de; (**b**) *(testimonial)* **~ence(s)** références *fpl*; **to give sb a good ~ence** fournir de bonnes références à qn; **to give a ~ence for sb** fournir des renseignements sur qn; **to give sb as a ~ence** donner qn en référence; (**c**) *(in book, on letter)* référence *f*; *(on map)* coordonnées *fpl* ; **2** *adj number, point* de référence; **~ence book** ouvrage *m* de référence *or* à consulter; **~ence library** bibliothèque *f* d'ouvrages à consulter.

referee [ˌrefəˈriː] **1** *n* (**a**) *(Sport, fig)* arbitre *m*. (**b**) **to be ~ for sb** fournir des références à qn; **to give sb as a ~** donner qn en référence. **2** *vt* arbitrer. **3** *vi* être arbitre.

referendum, *pl* **referenda** [ˌrefəˈrendəm, ˌrefəˈrendə] *n*: **to hold a ~** organiser un référendum.

refill [ˌriːˈfɪl] **1** *vt (gen)* remplir à nouveau; *pen, lighter* recharger. **2** [ˈriːfɪl] *n (gen)* recharge *f*; *(cartridge)* cartouche *f*; *[propelling pencil]* mine *f* de rechange; *[notebook]* feuilles *fpl* de rechange.

refine [rɪˈfaɪn] **1** *vt ore, taste* affiner; *oil, sugar* raffiner; *machine, technique* perfectionner. **2** *vi* s'affiner. **to ~ upon sth** raffiner sur qch. ◆ **refined** *adj (gen)* raffiné; *ore* affiné. ◆ **refinement** *n* (**a**) *[person, language]* raffinement *m*; (**b**) *(in machine)* perfectionnement *m* (*in* de). ◆ **refiner** *n* raffineur *m*. ◆ **refinery** *n* raffinerie *f*; **oil ~ry** raffinerie de pétrole.

refit [ˌriːˈfɪt] **1** *vt (Naut)* remettre en état. **2** [ˈriːfɪt] *n* remise *f* en état.

reflate [ˌriːˈfleɪt] *vt (Econ)* relancer. ◆ **reflation** *n* relance *f*. ◆ **reflationary** *adj* de relance.

reflect [rɪˈflekt] **1** *vt* (**a**) *heat, sound* renvoyer; *light, image* refléter; *[mirror]* réfléchir; *(fig: show)* refléter; *credit, discredit* faire rejaillir (*on* sur). **the moon is ~ed in the lake** la lune se reflète dans le lac; **I saw him ~ed in the mirror** j'ai vu son image dans le miroir *or* réfléchie par le miroir; **this is ~ed in his report** son rapport reflète cela. (**b**) *(think)* se dire, penser (*that* que). **2** *vi* (**a**) *(meditate)* réfléchir, méditer (*on* sur). (**b**) *(discredit)* **to ~ (up)on** *person* faire tort à; *reputation* nuire à; *motives, reasons* discréditer. ◆ **reflection** *n* (**a**) *(act)* réflexion *f*; *(in mirror etc)* reflet *m*; (**b**) *(thought)* réflexion *f* (*on* sur); **on ~ion** réflexion faite ; **~ions** pensées *fpl*, réflexions *fpl* (*on, upon* sur); (**c**) *(adverse criticism)* réflexion désobligeante (*on* sur); *(on sb's honour)* atteinte *f* (*on* à); **to be a ~ion on sb/sth** discréditer qn/qch. ◆ **reflector** *n* réflecteur *m*.

reflex [ˈriːfleks] **1** *n* réflexe *m*. **2** *adj (gen)* réflexe; *(Math) angle* rentrant. **~ camera** (appareil *m*) reflex *m*.

reflexion [rɪˈflekʃ(ə)n] *n* = **reflection.**

reflexive [rɪˈfleksɪv] **1** *adj* réfléchi. **2** *n* verbe *m* réfléchi.

refloat [ˌriːˈfləʊt] *vt* renflouer.

reform [rɪˈfɔːm] **1** *n* réforme *f*. **2** *adj measures* de réforme. **R~ Judaism** judaïsme *m* non orthodoxe. **3** *vt* réformer. **4** *vi [person]* s'amender. ◆ **reformation** *n* réforme *f*. ◆ **reformed** *adj (gen)* réformé; *behaviour, person* amendé. ◆ **reformer** *n* réformateur *m*, -trice *f*.

refrain¹ [rɪˈfreɪn] *vi* s'abstenir (*from sth* de qch; *from doing* de faire). **I couldn't ~ from laughing** je n'ai pas pu m'empêcher de rire.

refrain² [rɪˈfreɪn] *n (Mus etc)* refrain *m*.

refresh [rɪˈfreʃ] *vt [drink, bath]* rafraîchir; *[food, sleep]* redonner des forces à; *(fig) memory* rafraîchir. ◆ **refresher** *adj course* de recyclage. ◆ **refreshing** *adj fruit, drink* rafraîchissant; *sleep* réparateur (*f* -trice); *sight, news* réconfortant; *change* agréable; *idea, approach, point of view* nouveau. ◆ **refreshment** **1** *n*: **~ments** rafraîchissements *mpl* ; **2** *adj*: **~ment bar** buvette *f*; *(Rail)* **~ment room** buffet *m*.

refrigerate [rɪˈfrɪdʒəreɪt] *vt* réfrigérer. ◆ **refrigeration** *n* réfrigération *f*. ◆ **refrigerator** *n* réfrigérateur *m*, frigidaire *m* ®.

refuel [ˈriːˈfjʊəl] **1** *vi* se ravitailler en carburant. **2** *vt* ravitailler. ◆ **refuelling** *n* ravitaillement *m* en carburant; *(Aviat)* **~ling stop** escale *f* technique.

refuge [ˈrefjuːdʒ] *n (lit, fig)* refuge *m* (*from* contre). **place of ~** asile *m*; *(lit, fig)* **to take ~ in** se réfugier dans. ◆ **refugee** **1** *n* réfugié(e) *m(f)*; **2** *adj camp* de réfugiés.

refund [rɪˈfʌnd] **1** *vt cost, postage* rembourser (*to sb* à qn). **to ~ sb's expenses** rembourser qn de ses frais. **2** [ˈriːfʌnd] *n* remboursement *m*. **to get a ~** se faire rembourser.

refurbish [ˌriːˈfɜːbɪʃ] *vt* remettre à neuf.

refuse¹ [rɪˈfjuːz] **1** *vt* refuser (*sb sth* qch à qn; *to do* de faire), se refuser (*to do* à faire); *offer, candidate* refuser; *request, marriage proposal, suitor* rejeter. **they were ~d permission to do** on leur a refusé la permission de faire. **2** *vi* refuser. ◆ **refusal** *n* refus *m* (*to do* de faire); **to give sb first refusal of sth** accorder à qn l'option sur qch.

refuse² [ˈrefjuːs] **1** *n* détritus *mpl*, ordures *fpl*; *(industrial or food waste)* déchets *mpl*. **household ~** ordures ménagères; **garden ~** détritus de jardin. **2** *adj*: **~ bin** poubelle *f*, boîte *f* à ordures; **~ collection** ramassage *m* d'ordures; **~ collector** éboueur *m*; **~ disposal** traitement *m* des ordures; **~ disposal service** service *m* de voirie; **~ dump** *(public)* décharge *f* (publique); **~ lorry** voiture *f* d'éboueurs.

refute [rɪˈfjuːt] *vt* réfuter. ◆ **refutation** *n* réfutation *f*.

regain [rɪˈgeɪn] *vt (gen)* regagner; *health, one's sight* recouvrer; *territory* reconquérir. **to ~ consciousness** reprendre connaissance; **to ~ possession** rentrer en possession (*of* de).

regal [ˈriːg(ə)l] *adj* royal; *(fig)* majestueux.

regale [rɪˈgeɪl] *vt* régaler (*sb with sth* qn de qch).

regard [rɪˈgɑːd] **1** *vt* (**a**) *(consider)* considérer, regarder (*as* comme). **we ~ it as worth doing** à notre avis ça vaut la peine de le faire. (**b**) *(concern)* concerner, regarder. **as ~s...** pour *or* en ce qui concerne... **2** *n* (**a**) *(concern)* **to have** *or* **show little ~ for** faire peu de cas de; **to have** *or* **show no ~ for** ne faire aucun cas de; **without ~ to** *or* **for** sans égard pour; **out of ~ for** par égard pour; **in this ~** à cet égard; **with** *or* **in ~ to** relativement à. (**b**) *(esteem)* estime *f*. **to have a great ~ for sb** avoir beaucoup d'estime pour qn. (**c**) *(in messages)* **give him my ~s** transmettez-lui mon bon souvenir; **Paul sends his (kind) ~s** Paul vous envoie son bon souvenir; *(as letter-ending)* **(kindest) ~s** meilleurs souvenirs.
◆ **regarding** *prep* relativement à. ◆ **regardless** **1** *adj*: **~less of** *sb's feelings, fate* indifférent à; *future, danger* insouciant de; *consequences, cost* sans se soucier de; *rank* sans distinction de ; **2** *adv*: **he did it ~less** * il l'a fait quand même.

regatta [rɪˈgætə] *n* régates *fpl*.

regenerate [rɪˈdʒenəreɪt] **1** *vt* régénérer. **2** *vi* se régénérer. ◆ **regeneration** *n* régénération *f*.

regent [ˈriːdʒ(ə)nt] *n* régent(e) *m(f)*. **prince ~** prince *m* régent. ◆ **regency** **1** *n* régence *f* ; **2** *adj*: **Regency** Régence *inv*.

reggae [ˈregeɪ] *n* reggae *m*.

régime [reɪˈʒiːm] *n* régime *m (politique etc)*.

regiment [ˈredʒɪmənt] *n* régiment *m*. ◆ **regimental** *adj* du régiment. ◆ **regimentation** *n (pej)* discipline *f* excessive. ◆ **regimented** *adj* enrégimenté.

region ['ri:dʒ(ə)n] *n (all senses)* région *f.* *(fig)* **in the ~ of** environ, aux alentours de. ◆ **regional** *adj* régional; *(Brit Admin)* **~al development** ≃ aménagement *m* du territoire.

register ['redʒɪstəʳ] **1** *n* (**a**) *(gen)* registre *m*; *(of members etc)* liste *f.* **electoral ~** liste électorale; **~ of births, marriages and deaths** registre d'état civil. (**b**) *(Tech)* compteur *m.* **cash ~** caisse *f* (enregistreuse).
2 *vt* (**a**) *(record) fact, figure* enregistrer; *birth, death* déclarer; *vehicle* (faire) immatriculer; *trademark* déposer; *one's disappointment etc* exprimer. **~ed as disabled** officiellement reconnu comme handicapé; **to ~ a protest** protester. (**b**) *(take note of) fact* enregistrer; *(*: realize)* réaliser * (*that* que), se rendre compte de. (**c**) *(indicate) speed, quantity* enregistrer, indiquer. **he ~ed no emotion** il n'a pas paru ému. (**d**) *(Post) letter* recommander; *(Rail) luggage* faire enregistrer (*to* jusqu'à).
3 *vi* (**a**) *(gen)* s'inscrire; *(in hotel)* signer le registre. **to ~ with a doctor** se faire inscrire comme patient chez un médecin; **to ~ with the police** se déclarer à la police; **to ~ for military service** se faire recenser; **to ~ for a course** s'inscrire à un cours. (**b**) *(*: be understood)* être compris, pénétrer. **it hasn't ~ed (with him)** cela n'a pas encore pénétré, il n'a pas saisi.
◆ **registered** *adj* (**a**) *student, voter* inscrit; *vehicle* immatriculé; *name, trademark* déposé; *nursing home, charity* reconnu par les autorités; *(US)* **~ed nurse** infirmière *f* diplômée d'État; (**b**) *letter* recommandé; *luggage* enregistré; **by ~ed post** par envoi recommandé. ◆ **registrar** *n (Admin)* officier *m* de l'état civil; *(Jur: in court)* greffier *m*; *(Univ) (Brit)* secrétaire *m* (général); *(US)* chef *m* du service des inscriptions; *(Med)* chef *m* de clinique. ◆ **registration 1** *n* enregistrement *m*; déclaration *f*; inscription *f*; *[letter]* recommandation *f*; *[luggage]* enregistrement; *(Scol)* **during registration (period)** ≃ pendant l'appel *m* ; **2** *adj*: **registration fee** *(Post)* taxe *f* de recommandation; *(Univ)* droits *mpl* d'inscription; *(Aut)* **registration number** numéro *m* d'immatriculation; **car (with) registration number X** voiture immatriculée X; **a T-registration car** *immatriculation indiquant l'année de fabrication d'une voiture.* ◆ **registry office** *n (Brit)* bureau *m* de l'état civil; **to get married in a registry office** se marier civilement *or* à la mairie.

regress [rɪ'gres] *vi* régresser (*to* à). ◆ **regression** *n* régression *f.*

regret [rɪ'gret] **1** *vt* regretter (*doing, to do* de faire; *that* que + *subj*). **he is very ill, I ~ to say** il est très malade, hélas; **we ~ to hear that...** nous sommes désolés d'apprendre que...; **it is to be ~ted that...** il est regrettable que... + *subj.* **2** *n* regret *m* (*for* de). **much to my ~** à mon grand regret; **I have no ~s** je ne regrette rien. ◆ **regretful** *adj person* plein de regrets; *look* de regret. ◆ **regretfully** *adv (sadly)* avec regret; *(unwillingly)* à regret. ◆ **regrettable** *adj* regrettable (*that* que + *subj*). ◆ **regrettably** *adv late, poor* fâcheusement; **~tably, he...** malheureusement, il...

regroup [,ri:'gru:p] *vi* se regrouper.

regular ['regjʊləʳ] **1** *adj* (**a**) *(gen) pulse, shape, verb, employment, reminders* régulier. **at ~ intervals** à intervalles réguliers; **a ~ bus service to town** un service régulier d'autobus allant en ville; **he is as ~ as clockwork** il est très ponctuel; **visits as ~ as clockwork** visites très régulières. (**b**) *(in order) action, procedure* régulier, en règle; *(habitual)* habituel; *(Comm) size* standard *inv*; *price* normal; *listener, reader* fidèle; *staff* permanent; *(not conscript) soldier, army, police* de métier; *officer* de carrière; *(not territorial)* d'active. **his ~ time for getting up** l'heure à laquelle il se lève habituellement; **it is quite ~ to do so** il est tout à fait régulier de faire cela; **a ~ idiot** un véritable imbécile; *(US)* **~ guy** * chic type * *m.* **2** *n (Mil)* soldat *m* de métier; *(habitual customer etc)* habitué(e) *m(f)*; *(US: gas)* essence *f* (ordinaire). *(Rad, TV)* **he's one of the ~s on that programme** il participe régulièrement à ce programme. ◆ **regularity** *n* régularité *f.* ◆ **regularize** *vt* régulariser. ◆ **regularly** *adv* régulièrement. ◆ **regulate** *vt* régler (*by* sur). ◆ **regulation 1** *n* règlement *m* ; **2** *adj* réglementaire. ◆ **regulator** *n* régulateur *m.*

rehabilitate [,ri:ə'bɪlɪteɪt] *vt the disabled (to everyday life)* rééduquer; *(to work)* réadapter; *refugees* réadapter; *demobilized troops* réintégrer (dans la vie civile); *ex-prisoner* réinsérer; *alcoholic* rééduquer; *disgraced person* réhabiliter. ◆ **rehabilitation** *n* rééducation *f*; réadaptation *f*; réintégration *f* (dans la vie civile); réinsertion *f*; rééducation *f*; réhabilitation *f*; *(Admin)* **rehabilitation centre** centre *m* de rééducation (professionnelle).

rehash [,ri:'hæʃ] **1** *vt literary material etc* remanier. **2** ['ri:hæʃ] *n* réchauffé *m.*

rehearse [rɪ'hɜ:s] *vt (Theat)* répéter; *what one is going to say* préparer; *facts, grievances* énumérer. ◆ **rehearsal** *n* répétition *f*; **dress rehearsal** (répétition) générale *f*; **this play is in rehearsal** on répète cette pièce.

rehouse [,ri:'haʊz] *vt* reloger.

reign [reɪn] **1** *n* règne *m.* **in the ~ of** sous le règne de; *(fig)* **~ of terror** régime *m* de terreur. **2** *vi (lit, fig)* régner. **to ~ supreme** *[champion etc]* être sans rival; *[justice, peace]* régner en souverain(e). ◆ **reigning** *adj monarch* régnant; *king, champion* actuel.

reimburse [,ri:ɪm'bɜ:s] *vt* rembourser (*sb for sth* qn de qch). ◆ **reimbursement** *n* remboursement *m.*

rein [reɪn] *n (gen)* rêne *f*; *[horse in harness]* guide *f.* *(lit, fig)* **to hold the ~s** tenir les rênes; *(fig)* **to keep a tight ~ on** surveiller étroitement; **to give free ~ to** lâcher la bride à. ◆ **rein in** *vt sep* serrer la bride à.

reincarnation ['ri:ɪnkɑ:'neɪʃ(ə)n] *n* réincarnation *f.*

reindeer ['reɪndɪəʳ] *n, pl inv* renne *m.*

reinforce [,ri:ɪn'fɔ:s] *vt army, structure, wall* renforcer; *one's demands etc* appuyer. **~d concrete** béton *m* armé. ◆ **reinforcement 1** *n (action)* renforcement *m*; *(thing)* armature *f*; *(Mil, fig)* **~ments** renforts *mpl* ; **2** *adj troops* de renfort.

reinstate ['ri:ɪn'steɪt] *vt* rétablir (*in* dans). ◆ **reinstatement** *n* rétablissement *m.*

reissue [,ri:'ɪʃju:] *vt book* rééditer; *film* ressortir.

reiterate [ri:'ɪtəreɪt] *vt* réitérer. ◆ **reiteration** *n* réitération *f.*

reject [rɪ'dʒekt] **1** *vt (gen)* rejeter; *damaged goods etc [customer, shopkeeper]* refuser; *[producer]* mettre au rebut; *candidate, manuscript* refuser; *(Med) [body]* rejeter. **2** ['ri:dʒekt] *n (Comm)* article *m* de rebut. **3** ['ri:dʒekt] *adj goods* de rebut. **~ shop** magasin *m* de deuxième choix. ◆ **rejection 1** *n* rejet *m*; refus *m* ; **2** *adj*: **~ion slip** lettre *f* de refus.

rejig * [ri:'dʒɪg] , *(US)* **rejigger** * [ri:'dʒɪgəʳ] *vt* réorganiser, réarranger.

rejoice [rɪ'dʒɔɪs] *vi* se réjouir, être enchanté (*at, over* de). **to ~ in sth** jouir de qch, posséder qch. ◆ **rejoicing** *n* réjouissances *fpl.*

rejoin¹ [,ri:'dʒɔɪn] *vt (gen)* rejoindre. **to ~ ship** rallier le bord.

rejoin² [rɪ'dʒɔɪn] *vi (reply)* répliquer. ◆ **rejoinder** *n* réplique *f.*

rejuvenate [rɪ'dʒu:vɪneɪt] *vti* rajeunir.

rekindle [,ri:'kɪndl] *vt fire* rallumer; *enthusiasm* raviver.

relapse [rɪ'læps] **1** *n* rechute *f*. **to have a ~** faire une rechute. **2** *vi (gen)* retomber (*into* dans) ; *[invalid]* rechuter.

relate [rɪ'leɪt] **1** *vt* (**a**) *(recount) story* raconter, relater; *details* rapporter. **strange to ~...** chose curieuse (à dire)... (**b**) *(link)* rattacher (*sth to sth* qch à qch); *two facts etc* établir un rapport entre. **to ~ the cause to the effect** établir un rapport de cause à effet. **2** *vi* se rapporter (*to* à). ◆ **related** *adj (in family)* parent (*to* de); *(connected) ideas, subjects* liés, connexes; *substances, languages* apparentés; *[person]* **to be closely/distantly ~d** être proche parent/parent éloigné; *[fact]* **to be ~d to sth** avoir rapport à qch; **health-~d problems** problèmes liés à la santé. ◆ **relating to** *prep* relatif à.

relation [rɪ'leɪʃ(ə)n] *n* (**a**) *(relationship)* rapport *m*, relation *f*. **to bear a ~ to** avoir rapport à; **in ~ to** relativement à; **to have business ~s with** être en rapports *or* relations d'affaires avec; **diplomatic/international ~s** relations diplomatiques/internationales; **sexual ~s** rapports sexuels. (**b**) *(family: person)* parent(e) *m(f)*; *(kinship)* parenté *f*. **to be a ~ of sb's, to be some ~ to sb** avoir des liens de parenté avec qn. ◆ **relationship** *n* (**a**) *(family ties)* liens *mpl* de parenté; **what is your ~ship to him?** quels sont vos liens de parenté avec lui?; (**b**) *(connection: between 2 things)* rapport *m* (*between* entre); *(with sb)* relations *fpl*; *(personal ties)* rapports; **to see a ~ship between** voir un rapport *or* un lien entre; **friendly/business ~ship** relations d'amitié/d'affaires; **to have a ~ship with sb** *(gen)* avoir des relations avec qn; *(sexual)* avoir une liaison avec qn; **he has a good ~ship with his clients** il est en bons rapports avec ses clients; **they have a good ~ship** ils s'entendent bien.

relative ['relətɪv] **1** *adj (gen)* relatif (*to* à). **the ~ merits of A and B** les mérites respectifs de A et de B. **2** *n (person)* parent(e) *m(f)*; *(Gram)* relatif *m*. ◆ **relatively** *adv* relativement; respectivement; *(fairly, rather)* assez. ◆ **relativity** *n* relativité *f*.

relax [rɪ'læks] **1** *vt (gen)* relâcher; *muscles* décontracter; *restrictions* modérer; *measures* assouplir; *person, one's mind* détendre. **2** *vi [sb's hold]* se relâcher; *(rest)* se détendre. *(calm down)* **~!** * du calme! ◆ **relaxation** [ˌriːlæk'seɪʃ(ə)n] *n* détente *f*. ◆ **relaxed** *adj (gen)* relâché; *person, voice* détendu; *(Med)* **~ed throat** gorge *f* irritée *or* enflammée. ◆ **relaxing** *adj climate* reposant, amollissant *(pej)*; *atmosphere, activity* qui procure de la détente.

relay ['riːleɪ] **1** *n (gen)* relais *m*. **in ~s** par relais; **~ race** course *f* de relais. **2** *vt* relayer. **to ~ each other** se relayer.

release [rɪ'liːs] **1** *n* (**a**) *(gen)* libération *f*; *(from Customs)* congé *m*. **on his ~ from prison he...** dès sa sortie de prison, il... (**b**) *[news]* autorisation *f* de publier; *[film, book, record]* sortie *f*. **this film is now on general ~** ce film n'est plus en exclusivité. (**c**) *(record/film etc)* **new ~** nouveau disque/film *etc*; **his latest ~** son dernier disque *etc*. **2** *vt* (**a**) *(set free) (gen)* libérer (*from* de); *(Jur)* remettre en liberté; *(from wreckage)* dégager (*from* de); *(from promise, vow)* relever (*from* de). **his employer agreed to ~ him** son patron lui a permis de cesser son travail; *(temporarily)* son patron a accepté de le rendre disponible. (**b**) *(let go) object, pigeon* lâcher; *bomb* larguer; *gas* dégager. **to ~ one's hold of** *or* **one's grip on sth** lâcher qch. (**c**) *(issue) book, record, film* sortir; *goods* mettre en vente; *news* autoriser la publication de; *statement* publier. (**d**) *clasp, catch* faire jouer; *(Phot) shutter* déclencher; *handbrake* desserrer.

relegate ['relɪgeɪt] *vt* reléguer (*to* à; *Sport: to* en). ◆ **relegation** *n* relégation *f*.

relent [rɪ'lent] *vi* se laisser fléchir; *(change one's mind)* changer d'avis. ◆ **relentless** *adj* implacable. ◆ **relentlessly** *adv* implacablement.

relevant ['reləvənt] *adj remark, fact* pertinent (*to* à); *regulation, reference* approprié (*to* à); *information, course* utile. **to be ~ to sth** avoir rapport à qch; **that is not ~** c'est sans rapport.

reliable [rɪ'laɪəbl] *adj person, employee* sérieux, sur qui l'on peut compter; *firm, company* sérieux; *machine* solide; *memory, description* bon, auquel on peut se fier. **a ~ source of information** une source sûre. ◆ **reliability** *n [person, character]* sérieux *m*; *[device, machine]* solidité *f*. ◆ **reliably** *adv work* sérieusement; *informed* de source sûre.

reliant [rɪ'laɪənt] *adj (trusting)* confiant (*on* en); *(dependent)* dépendant (*on* de). ◆ **reliance** *n* confiance *f*; dépendance *f*.

relic ['relɪk] *n* relique *f (also Rel)*. **~s** restes *mpl*; *(fig: of the past)* vestiges *mpl*.

relief [rɪ'liːf] **1** *n* (**a**) *(from pain, anxiety)* soulagement *m* (*from* à). **to my ~** à mon grand soulagement; **that's a ~!** j'aime mieux ça!; **it was a ~ to find it** j'ai été soulagé de le retrouver. (**b**) *(assistance)* secours *m*. **to go to the ~ of** aller au secours de. (**c**) *(US Admin)* aides *fpl* sociales. **to be on ~** bénéficier d'aides sociales. (**d**) *(Mil) [town]* délivrance *f*. (**e**) *(tax ~)* dégrèvement *m*. (**f**) *(Art, Geog)* relief *m*. **to throw sth into ~** mettre qch en relief. **2** *adj* (**a**) *coach, typist* supplémentaire; *fund, work, organization, troops* de secours; *valve* de sûreté. **~ road** route *f* de délestage; **~ supplies** secours *mpl*. (**b**) *map* en relief.

relieve [rɪ'liːv] *vt* (**a**) *person, anxiety, pain* soulager; *fear, boredom* dissiper; *poverty, situation* remédier à. **to be ~d to learn** être soulagé d'apprendre; **to ~ sb of his coat** débarrasser qn de son manteau; **to ~ sb of a duty** décharger qn d'une obligation; *(Mil)* **to ~ sb of a command** relever qn de ses fonctions; **to ~ sb's mind** tranquilliser qn; **he ~d his feelings** il a déchargé sa colère; **to ~ congestion in sth** décongestionner qch; *(go to lavatory)* **to ~ o.s.** faire ses besoins *. (**b**) *(help)* secourir, aider; *(take over from)* relayer; *(Mil) guard* relever; *town* délivrer.

religion [rɪ'lɪdʒ(ə)n] *n (gen)* religion *f*. **the Christian ~** la religion chrétienne; **a new ~** un nouveau culte; **it's against my ~** c'est contraire à ma religion (*to do* de faire); **to get ~** * devenir bigot.

religious [rɪ'lɪdʒəs] **1** *adj (gen)* religieux *(also fig)*; *person* pieux *(also pej)*, croyant; *book* de piété; *wars* de religion. **2** *n* religieux *m*, -ieuse *f*. ◆ **religiously** *adv* religieusement.

relinquish [rɪ'lɪŋkwɪʃ] *vt object* lâcher; *(give up: gen)* abandonner; *plan, right* renoncer à (*to sb* en faveur de qn); *habit* renoncer à. **to ~ one's hold on sth** lâcher qch.

reliquary ['relɪkwərɪ] *n* reliquaire *m*.

relish ['relɪʃ] **1** *n* goût *m* (*for* pour). **with great ~** *do sth* avec délectation; *eat* de bon appétit; *(fig)* **it had lost all ~** cela avait perdu tout attrait. **2** *vt food, wine* savourer. **to ~ doing** se délecter à faire; **I don't ~ the thought** l'idée ne me dit rien.

relocate [ˌriːləʊ'keɪt] **1** *vt* installer ailleurs. **2** *vi* déménager, s'installer ailleurs.

reluctant [rɪ'lʌktənt] *adj person* peu disposé (*to do* à faire), peu enthousiaste; *action* fait *etc* à contrecœur; *consent, praise* accordé à contrecœur. ◆ **reluctance** *n* répugnance *f* (*to do* à faire). ◆ **reluctantly** *adv* à contrecœur, sans enthousiasme.

rely [rɪ'laɪ] *vi*: **to ~ (up)on sb/sth** compter sur qn/qch; **to ~ on sb's doing sth** compter sur le fait que qn fera qch; **I ~ on him for my income** je dépends de lui pour mes revenus; **you can ~ on**

me not to say anything about it vous pouvez compter sur moi pour ne pas en parler.

remain [rɪ'meɪn] *vi* rester. **nothing ~s to be said** il ne reste plus rien à dire; **it ~s to be seen whether...** reste à savoir si...; **that ~s to be seen** c'est ce que nous verrons; **the fact ~s that** il n'en est pas moins vrai que; **to ~ faithful** demeurer *or* rester fidèle; **to ~ behind** rester; **to ~ silent** garder le silence; **it ~s unsolved** ce n'est toujours pas résolu; *(in letters)* **I ~ , yours faithfully** je vous prie d'agréer l'expression de mes sentiments distingués. ◆ **remainder** *n (thing or things left over)* reste *m (also Math)*; *(people)* autres *mfpl*; **~ders** *(Comm) (books etc)* invendus *mpl* soldés; *(other articles)* fins *fpl* de série. ◆ **remaining** *adj* qui reste; **I have one ~ing** il n'en reste qu'un; **the ~ing cakes** le reste des gâteaux, les gâteaux qui restent. ◆ **remains** *npl (gen)* restes *mpl*; *[fortune, army]* débris *mpl*.

remake ['ri:meɪk] *n (Cine)* remake *m*.

remand [rɪ'mɑ:nd] **1** *vt (Jur)* renvoyer (*to* à). **to ~ in custody** mettre en détention préventive; **to ~ on bail** laisser en liberté provisoire (sous caution). **2** *n*: **on ~** en détention préventive; **~ home** ≃ maison *f* d'arrêt.

remark [rɪ'mɑ:k] **1** *n* remarque *f*, réflexion *f*. **worthy of ~** digne d'attention. **2** *vt* (**a**) *(say)* (faire) remarquer. (**b**) *(notice)* remarquer, observer. **3** *vi* faire des remarques (*on* sur). ◆ **remarkable** *adj* remarquable (*for* par). ◆ **remarkably** *adv* remarquablement.

remarry ['ri:'mærɪ] *vi* se remarier.

remedy ['remədɪ] **1** *n* remède *m* (*for* contre). **2** *vt* remédier à. ◆ **remedial** [rɪ'mi:dɪəl] *adj action* réparateur; *measures* de redressement; *(Med) treatment* curatif; *class* de rattrapage; **remedial exercises** gymnastique *f* corrective.

remember [rɪ'membəʳ] *vt (gen)* se souvenir de, se rappeler; *(commemorate) a battle, the fallen* commémorer. **to ~ that** se rappeler que; **I ~ doing it** je me rappelle l'avoir fait; **I ~ed to do it** j'ai pensé à le faire; **that's worth ~ing** c'est bon à savoir; **I can't ~ everything** je ne peux pas penser à tout; **I ~ when...** je me souviens de l'époque où...; **I can't ~** je ne sais plus, je ne me souviens pas; **as far as I ~** autant qu'il m'en souvienne; **if I ~ right(ly)** si j'ai bonne mémoire; **don't you ~ me?** *(face to face)* vous ne me reconnaissez pas?; *(phone)* vous ne vous souvenez pas de moi?; **I don't ~ a thing about it** je ne me souviens de rien; **let us ~ that...** n'oublions pas que...; **sth to ~ him by** un souvenir de lui; **to ~ o.s.** se reprendre; **to ~ sb in one's prayers** ne pas oublier qn dans ses prières; **~ me to your mother** rappelez-moi au bon souvenir de votre mère. ◆ **remembrance** *n* souvenir *m*; **Remembrance Day** l'Armistice *m*, le 11 Novembre; **in remembrance of** en souvenir de.

remind [rɪ'maɪnd] *vt* rappeler (*sb of sth* qch à qn, *sb that* à qn que). **you are ~ed that...** nous vous rappelons que...; **to ~ sb to do** faire penser à qn à faire; **she ~ed him of his mother** elle lui rappelait sa mère; **that ~s me!** à propos! ◆ **reminder** *n (note etc)* pense-bête *m*; *(Comm: letter)* lettre *f* de rappel; **as a ~er that** pour (vous *etc*) rappeler que; **to be a ~er of sth/sb** rappeler qch/qn.

reminisce [ˌremɪ'nɪs] *vi* raconter ses souvenirs (*about* de). ◆ **reminiscence** *n* réminiscence *f*. ◆ **reminiscent** *adj*: **reminiscent of** qui rappelle, qui fait penser à. ◆ **reminiscently** *adv smile* à ce souvenir; **to talk reminiscently of** évoquer des souvenirs de.

remiss [rɪ'mɪs] *adj* négligent. **he was ~ in not doing it** c'est négligent de sa part de ne pas l'avoir fait.

remission [rɪ'mɪʃ(ə)n] *n (gen, Med, Rel)* rémission *f*; *(Jur)* remise *f* (*for* pour).

remit [rɪ'mɪt] *vt* (**a**) *sins* pardonner; *fee, penalty* remettre. (**b**) *(send) money* envoyer. (**c**) *(Jur) case* renvoyer. ◆ **remittal** *n (Jur)* renvoi *m*. ◆ **remittance** *n (of money) (gen)* versement *m*; *(Banking etc)* remise *f* de fonds; *(payment)* paiement *m*, règlement *m*; **enclose your ~tance** joignez votre règlement.

remnant ['remnənt] **1** *n (gen)* reste *m*, restant *m*; *[cloth]* coupon *m*; *[custom, splendour]* vestige *m*; *[food, fortune, army]* débris *mpl*. *(Comm)* **~s** soldes *mpl* (de fins de série). **2** *adj*: **~ sale** soldes *mpl* (de coupons).

remonstrate ['remənstreɪt] *vti* protester (*against* contre; *that* que). **to ~ with sb about sth** faire des remontrances à qn au sujet de qch. ◆ **remonstrance** *n (protest)* protestation *f*; *(reproof)* remontrance *f*.

remorse [rɪ'mɔ:s] *n* remords *m* (*at* de; *for* pour). **a feeling of ~** un remords; **without ~** sans pitié. ◆ **remorseful** *adj* plein de remords. ◆ **remorsefully** *adv* avec remords. ◆ **remorseless** *adj* dénué de remords; *(fig)* implacable. ◆ **remorselessly** *adv* sans remords; implacablement.

remote [rɪ'məʊt] *adj* (**a**) *place (distant)* lointain, éloigné; *(isolated)* isolé; *time* lointain; *ancestor, relative* éloigné; *person* distant. **~ control** télécommande *f*; **in the ~st parts of Africa** au fin fond de l'Afrique; **~ from a main road** loin d'une grande route; **~ from the subject in hand** éloigné de la question. (**b**) *(slight) resemblance* vague; *possibility* petit. **not the ~st idea/hope** pas la moindre idée/le moindre espoir; **there is a ~ possibility that** il y a une petite chance que + *subj*. ◆ **remote-controlled** *adj* télécommandé. ◆ **remotely** *adv (slightly)* vaguement; **~ly possible** tout juste possible; **not ~ly interested** absolument pas intéressé. ◆ **remoteness** *n (in space)* éloignement *m*, isolement *m*; *(in time)* éloignement; *[person]* attitude *f* distante.

remould ['ri:məʊld] *n (tyre)* pneu *m* rechapé.

remove [rɪ'mu:v] **1** *vt (gen, also Med)* enlever (*from* de); *[removers]* déménager; *stain, graffiti* enlever, faire partir; *word, item on list* rayer; *threat, abuse* supprimer; *objection* réfuter; *difficulty, problem* résoudre; *obstacle, doubt* écarter; *suspicion, fear* dissiper; *official* déplacer. **he was ~d to the cells** on l'a emmené en cellule; **to ~ a child from school** retirer un enfant de l'école; **to ~ sb's name** rayer qn (*from* de); **to ~ one's make-up** se démaquiller; *(fig)* **far ~d from** loin de; **cousin once ~d** cousin(e) *m(f)* au deuxième degré. **2** *vi* déménager (*from* de). **to ~ to London** aller s'installer à Londres. **3** *n (fig)* **only a few ~s from** tout proche de; **it's a far ~ from...** c'est loin d'être...

◆ **removable** *adj (detachable) part, piece* amovible, détachable. ◆ **removal** **1** *n* enlèvement *m*; déménagement *m*; suppression *f*; *[pain]* soulagement *m*; *(Surgery)* ablation *f* ; **2** *adj allowance, expenses* de déménagement; **removal man** déménageur *m*; **removal van** camion *m* de déménagement. ◆ **remover** *n* (**a**) *(removal man)* déménageur *m* ; (**b**) *[varnish]* dissolvant *m*; *[stains]* détachant *m* ; *[paint]* décapant *m*; **make-up ~r** démaquillant *m*.

remunerate [rɪ'mju:nəreɪt] *vt* rémunérer. ◆ **remuneration** *n* rémunération *f* (*for* de). ◆ **remunerative** *adj* rémunérateur.

renaissance [rɪ'neɪsɑ̃:ns] **1** *n* renaissance *f*. **2** *adj*: **R~** *art, scholar* de la Renaissance; *style, palace* Renaissance *inv*.

renal ['ri:nl] *adj* rénal.

render ['rendəʳ] *vt* (**a**) *service, homage* rendre; *assistance* prêter; *account* présenter. **to account ~ed £10** facture de rappel — 10 livres. (**b**) *music* interpréter; *text* traduire (*into* en). (**c**) *(make)* rendre. **it ~ed him helpless** cela l'a rendu infirme. (**d**) *(Culin) fat* faire fondre. (**e**) *(Constr)* plâtrer. ◆ **rendering** *n [music]* interprétation *f*; *(translation)* traduction *f* (*into* en).

rendez-vous ['rɒndɪvu:] **1** *n, pl inv* rendez-vous *m*. **2** *vi* se retrouver. **to ~ with sb** rejoindre qn.

renew [rɪ'nju:] *vt (gen)* renouveler; *negotiations, discussions, strength* reprendre. **to ~ one's acquaintance with sb** renouer connaissance avec qn. ◆ **renewable** *adj* renouvelable. ◆ **renewal** *n* renouvellement *m*; reprise *f*; *[strength]* regain *m*; **~al of subscription** réabonnement *m*. ◆ **renewed** *adj* accru. **with ~ed vigour** avec une force accrue.

renounce [rɪ'naʊns] *vt (gen)* renoncer, à; *religion* abjurer; *treaty* dénoncer; *cause* renier.

renovate ['renəʊveɪt] *vt clothes, house* remettre à neuf; *building, painting* restaurer. ◆ **renovation** *n* remise *f* à neuf; restauration *f*.

renown [rɪ'naʊn] *n* renommée *f*. ◆ **renowned** *adj thing* renommé (*for* pour); *person* célèbre (*for* pour).

rent [rent] **1** *n* loyer *m*. *(US)* **for ~** à louer; **quarter's ~** terme *m*. **2** *adj*: **~ collector** receveur *m* de loyers; **~ rebate** dégrèvement *m* de loyer. **3** *vt* (**a**) *(take for ~)* louer, prendre en location. **we don't own it, only ~ it** nous ne sommes pas propriétaires, mais locataires seulement. (**b**) *(also* **~ out***)* louer, donner en location. ◆ **rent-a-car** *adj firm* de location de voitures. ◆ **rent-a-crowd** *n (gen)* agitateurs *mpl* professionnels; *(supporters)* claque *f*. ◆ **rental** *n [house, land]* loyer *m*; *[television etc]* (prix *m* de) location *f*; *[telephone]* abonnement *m*. ◆ **rent-free** **1** *adj accommodation* exempt de loyer ; **2** *adv live* sans payer de loyer.

renunciation [rɪˌnʌnsɪ'eɪʃ(ə)n] *n (V* **renounce***)* renonciation *f* (*of* à); abjuration *f*; dénonciation *f*; reniement *m*.

reopen [ˌri:'əʊp(ə)n] **1** *vt (gen)* rouvrir; *fight, battle, hostilities* reprendre. **2** *vi (gen)* rouvrir; *[wound]* se rouvrir. ◆ **reopening** *n* réouverture *f*.

reorganize ['ri:'ɔ:gənaɪz] **1** *vt* réorganiser. **2** *vi* se réorganiser. ◆ **reorganization** *n* réorganisation *f*.

rep * [rep] *n abbr of* **repertory company** *and (Comm)* **representative.**

repair [rɪ'pɛəʳ] **1** *vt* réparer. **2** *n (gen)* réparation *f*; *[roof, road]* réfection *f*. **under ~** en réparation; **damaged beyond ~** irréparable; **closed for ~s** fermé pour cause de travaux; **'road ~s'** 'chantier'; **in good/bad ~** en bon/mauvais état; **to keep in good ~** entretenir. **3** *adj*: **~ kit** *or* **outfit** trousse *f* de réparation; **~ shop** atelier *m* de réparations. ◆ **repairable** *or* ◆ **reparable** ['rep(ə)rəbl] *adj* réparable. ◆ **repairer** *n* réparateur *m*, -trice *f*; *[shoes]* cordonnier *m*. ◆ **reparation** *n* réparation *f*; **to make reparations for** réparer *(une injure etc)*.

repartee [ˌrepɑ:'ti:] *n* repartie *f*, réplique *f*.

repatriate [ri:'pætrɪeɪt] *vt* rapatrier. ◆ **repatriation** *n* rapatriement *m*.

repay [ri:'peɪ] *pret, ptp* **repaid** *vt money* rendre, rembourser; *lender* rembourser; *debt, obligation* s'acquitter de; *sb's kindness* payer de retour; *helper* récompenser (*for* de). ◆ **repayable** *adj* remboursable. ◆ **repayment** *n [money]* remboursement *m*.

repeal [rɪ'pi:l] **1** *vt law* abroger; *sentence* annuler. **2** *n* abrogation *f*; annulation *f*.

repeat [rɪ'pi:t] **1** *vt (gen)* répéter; *demand, promise* réitérer; *efforts* renouveler; *(Mus)* reprendre; *(recite) poem etc* réciter (par cœur); *(Scol) class* redoubler. *(Comm)* **this offer will never be ~ed** c'est une offre exceptionnelle; **to ~ o.s.** se répéter. **2** *n* répétition *f*; *(Mus)* reprise *f*; *(Rad, TV)* rediffusion *f*. **3** *adj (Comm) order* renouvelé. *(fig)* **a ~ performance** exactement la même chose. ◆ **repeated** *adj requests, criticism* répété; *efforts* renouvelé. ◆ **repeatedly** *adv* à maintes reprises, très souvent; **I have ~edly told you** je ne cesse de vous répéter; **he had ~edly proclaimed...** il n'avait pas cessé de proclamer...

repel [rɪ'pel] *vt* repousser; *(fig: disgust)* dégoûter. ◆ **repellent** *adj* (**a**) *(disgusting)* repoussant, répugnant; (**b**) **water-~lent** imperméabilisateur.

repent [rɪ'pent] **1** *vi* se repentir (*of* de). **2** *vt* se repentir de. ◆ **repentance** *n* repentir *m*. ◆ **repentant** *adj* repentant.

repercussion [ˌri:pə'kʌʃ(ə)n] *n* répercussion *f* (*on* sur).

repertory ['repət(ə)rɪ] **1** *n (Theat, fig: also* **repertoire***)* répertoire *m*. **~ (theatre)** théâtre *m* de répertoire; **to act in ~** faire partie d'une troupe de répertoire. **2** *adj*: **~ company** troupe *f* de répertoire.

repetition [ˌrepɪ'tɪʃ(ə)n] *n* répétition *f*. ◆ **repetitive** [rɪ'petɪtɪv] *adj person* rabâcheur; *writing* plein de redites; *work* monotone.

replace [rɪ'pleɪs] *vt* (**a**) *(put back)* remettre (à sa place), ranger. *(Telec)* **to ~ the receiver** raccrocher. (**b**) *(be or provide substitute for)* remplacer (*by, with* par). ◆ **replaceable** *adj* remplaçable. ◆ **replacement** **1** *n (person)* remplaçant(e) *m(f)*; *(product)* produit *m* de remplacement ; **2** *adj engine, part* de rechange.

replenish [rɪ'plenɪʃ] *vt* remplir de nouveau (*with* de). **to ~ one's supplies of sth** se réapprovisionner en qch. ◆ **replenishment** *n* remplissage *m*.

replete [rɪ'pli:t] *adj* rempli (*with* de); *(well-fed)* rassasié. ◆ **repletion** *n* satiété *f*.

replica ['replɪkə] *n (gen)* copie *f* exacte; *[painting]* réplique *f*; *[document, book]* fac-similé *m*. ◆ **replicate** **1** *vt* reproduire. **2** *vi (Biol)* se reproduire. ◆ **replication** *n* reproduction *f*.

reply [rɪ'plaɪ] **1** *n* réponse *f*; *(quick)* réplique *f*. **in ~** en réponse (*to* à). **2** *vti* répondre; *(quickly)* répliquer. **3** *adj (Post)* **~ coupon** coupon-réponse *m*. ◆ **reply-paid** *adj* avec réponse payée.

report [rɪ'pɔ:t] **1** *n* (**a**) *(gen)* rapport *m*; *[speech, debate, meeting]* compte rendu *m*; *(Scol)* bulletin *m* scolaire; *(Press, Rad, TV)* reportage *m*; *(at regular intervals: on weather, sales etc)* bulletin; *(rumour)* rumeur *f*. **Government ~** rapport d'enquête parlementaire (*on* sur); *(Comm)* **annual/chairman's ~** rapport annuel/présidentiel; **to make** *or* **do a ~ on** faire un rapport sur; *(Press, Rad, TV)* faire un reportage sur; *(rumour)* **there is a ~ that...** on dit que...; **I have heard a ~ that...** j'ai entendu dire que... (**b**) *(explosion)* détonation *f*; *[gun]* coup *m* de fusil *etc*.

2 *vt* (**a**) *(state)* annoncer (*that* que); *facts, figures* annoncer, rapporter; *(give account of)* rendre compte de; *[newspaper, TV programme]* signaler; *speech* faire le compte rendu de. **to ~ one's findings** présenter ses conclusions; **to ~ progress** faire un exposé de l'état de la situation; **he is ~ed as having said** il aurait dit; **a prisoner is ~ed to have escaped** un détenu se serait évadé; *(Gram)* **~ed speech** style *or* discours indirect; **our correspondent ~s from Rome that...** notre correspondant à Rome nous apprend que...; **it is ~ed from Paris that...** on annonce à Paris que... (**b**) *(notify) accident, crime, one's position* signaler (*to* à); *criminal, culprit* signaler (*sb for sth* qn pour qch), dénoncer (*to* à) *(often pej)*. **to ~ sb sick** signaler que qn est malade; **~ed missing** porté disparu; **nothing to ~** rien à signaler.

3 *vi* (**a**) se présenter (*to sb* chez qn). **to ~ for duty** se présenter au travail; *(Mil)* **to ~ to one's unit** rallier son unité; **to ~ sick** se faire porter malade; *(Admin)* **he ~s to the manager** il est sous les ordres (directs) du directeur. (**b**) *(give a ~)* faire un rap-

port (*on* sur); *(Press, Rad, TV)* faire un reportage (*on* sur).
◆ **report back** *vi* (**a**) *(return) (Mil etc)* rentrer au quartier; *(gen)* être de retour. (**b**) *(make report)* présenter son rapport (*to* à).
◆ **reportedly** *adv*: **he had ~edly seen her** il l'aurait vue. ◆ **reporter** *n (Press)* journaliste *mf*; *(Rad, TV)* reporter *m*.

repose [rɪ'pəʊz] **1** *n (rest, peace)* repos *m*; *(sleep)* sommeil *m*. **in ~** au repos. **2** *vi* se reposer; *[dead]* reposer. ◆ **repository** *n (safe place)* dépôt *m*; *(warehouse)* entrepôt *m*; *[facts etc]* mine *f*.

reprehend [ˌreprɪ'hend] *vt* réprimander. ◆ **reprehensible** *adj* répréhensible. ◆ **reprehensibly** *adv* de façon répréhensible.

represent [ˌreprɪ'zent] *vt (all senses)* représenter (*as* comme, comme étant). **many countries were ~ed at the ceremony** de nombreux pays s'étaient fait représenter à la cérémonie; **I ~ Mrs Wolff** je viens de la part de Mme Wolff. ◆ **representation** *n (gen)* représentation *f*; *(protest)* **to make ~ations to** faire une démarche auprès de. ◆ **representative 1** *adj* représentatif (*of* de) ; **2** *n* représentant(e) *m(f)*; *(Comm)* représentant (de commerce); *(US Pol)* **R~** député *m*.

repress [rɪ'pres] *vt (gen)* réprimer; *(Psych)* refouler. ◆ **repressed** *adj* réprimé; refoulé. ◆ **repression** *n* répression *f*; refoulement *m*. ◆ **repressive** *adj attitude, government* répressif; *measures* de répression.

reprieve [rɪ'priːv] **1** *n (Jur)* commutation *f* de la peine capitale; *(delay: also gen)* sursis *m*. **2** *vt (Jur)* accorder une commutation de la peine capitale à; *(delay)* surseoir à l'exécution de. *[building etc]* **to be ~d** bénéficier d'un sursis.

reprimand ['reprɪmɑːnd] **1** *n* réprimande *f*. **2** *vt* réprimander.

reprint [ˌriː'prɪnt] **1** *vt* réimprimer. **it is being ~ed** c'est en réimpression. **2** *vi* être en réimpression. **3** ['riːprɪnt] *n* réimpression *f*.

reprisal [rɪ'praɪz(ə)l] *n*: **~s** représailles *fpl*; **to take ~s** user de représailles; **as a ~ for** en représailles de.

reproach [rɪ'prəʊtʃ] **1** *n* reproche *m*. *(fig)* **to be a ~ to** être la honte de; **above ~** irréprochable. **2** *vt* faire des reproches à. **to ~ sb for sth/for having done** reprocher à qn qch/d'avoir fait; **he has nothing to ~ himself with** il n'a rien à se reprocher. ◆ **reproachful** *adj look, tone, person* réprobateur; *words* de reproche. ◆ **reproachfully** *adv* avec reproche.

reprocess [ˌriː'prəʊses] *vt* retraiter. ◆ **reprocessing** *n* retraitement *m*.

reproduce [ˌriːprə'djuːs] **1** *vt* reproduire. **2** *vi* se reproduire. ◆ **reproduction 1** *n (all senses)* reproduction *f* ; **2** *adj*: **reproduction furniture** copies *fpl* de meubles anciens. ◆ **reproductive** *adj* reproducteur.

re-proof ['riː'pruːf] *vt garment* réimperméabiliser.

reproof [rɪ'pruːf] *n* réprimande *f*.

reprove [rɪ'pruːv] *vt person* blâmer (*for* de). ◆ **reproval** *n* blâme *m*. ◆ **reproving** *adj* réprobateur. ◆ **reprovingly** *adv* d'un air *or* ton réprobateur.

reptile ['reptaɪl] *adj, n (also fig pej)* reptile *(m)*.

republic [rɪ'pʌblɪk] *n* république *f*. ◆ **republican** *adj, n* républicain(e) *m(f)*. ◆ **republicanism** *n* républicanisme *m*.

republish ['riː'pʌblɪʃ] *vt book* rééditer.

repudiate [rɪ'pjuːdɪeɪt] *vt friend etc* renier; *secret agent* désavouer; *wife, accusation* répudier; *[government etc] debt, treaty* refuser d'honorer. ◆ **repudiation** *n* reniement *m*; désaveu *m*; répudiation *f*; refus *m* d'honorer *(un traité etc)*.

repugnant [rɪ'pʌgnənt] *adj* répugnant. **to be ~ to sb** répugner à qn; **to find it ~ to do** répugner à faire. ◆ **repugnance** *n* répugnance *f* (*to* pour).

repulse [rɪ'pʌls] *vt* repousser. ◆ **repulsion** *n* répulsion *f*. ◆ **repulsive** *adj* répulsif, repoussant. ◆ **repulsiveness** *n* caractère *m* repoussant.

reputable ['repjʊtəbl] *adj* de bonne réputation.

reputation [ˌrepjʊ'teɪʃ(ə)n] *n* réputation *f* (*as a singer etc* de chanteur *etc*). **to have a ~ for honesty** avoir la réputation d'être honnête.

repute [rɪ'pjuːt] **1** *n* réputation *f*, renom *m*. **by ~** de réputation; **of ~** réputé, en renom. **2** *vt*: **to be ~d to be** être réputé être. ◆ **reputedly** *adv* d'après ce qu'on dit.

request [rɪ'kwest], **1** *n* demande *f*, requête *f*. **at sb's ~** à la demande de qn; **by popular ~** à la demande générale; **on** *or* **by ~** sur demande; **to make a ~ for sth** faire une demande de qch. **2** *vt* demander (*sth from sb* qch à qn; *sb to do* à qn de faire). **'you are ~ed not to smoke'** 'vous êtes priés de ne pas fumer'; *(Rad)* **to play a ~ for sb** faire passer un disque à l'intention de qn. **3** *adj (Rad) programme* des auditeurs; *bus stop* facultatif.

requiem ['rekwɪem] *n* requiem *m*. **~ mass** messe *f* de requiem.

require [rɪ'kwaɪəʳ] *vt* (**a**) *[person]* avoir besoin de; *[thing, action]* demander, nécessiter. **all I ~** tout ce qu'il me faut, tout ce dont j'ai besoin; **it ~s great care** cela demande *or* nécessite beaucoup de soin; **if ~d** au besoin; **when ~d** quand il le faut; **what qualifications are ~d?** quels sont les diplômes nécessaires *or* requis? (**b**) *(order)* exiger (*sb to do* de qn qu'il fasse; *sth of sb* qch de qn). **as ~d by law** comme la loi l'exige.
◆ **required** *adj conditions, qualifications* requis; *amount* voulu; **in the ~d time** dans les délais prescrits. ◆ **requirement** *n* (**a**) *(need)* exigence *f*; **to meet sb's ~ments** satisfaire aux exigences de qn; (**b**) *(condition)* condition *f* requise; **to fit the ~ments** remplir les conditions.

requisite ['rekwɪzɪt] **1** *n* chose *f* nécessaire (*for* pour). *(Comm)* **office ~s** articles *mpl* de bureau; **toilet ~s** accessoires *mpl* de toilette. **2** *adj* requis, nécessaire.

requisition [ˌrekwɪ'zɪʃ(ə)n] **1** *n* réquisition *f*. **2** *vt* réquisitionner.

reredos ['rɪədɒs] *n* retable *m*.

reroute ['riː'ruːt] *vt* dérouter (*through* par).

reschedule [riː'ʃedjuːl], *(US)* [riː'skedjuːl] *vt meeting* changer l'heure (*or* la date) de; *service* changer l'horaire de; *repayments* changer les dates de.

rescind [rɪ'sɪnd] *vt judgment* rescinder; *law* abroger; *contract, decision* annuler.

rescue ['reskjuː] **1** *n (help)* secours *mpl*; *(saving)* sauvetage *m*; *(freeing)* délivrance *f*. **to go/come to sb's ~** aller/venir au secours de qn; **to the ~** à la rescousse. **2** *vt (save)* secourir, sauver; *(free)* délivrer (*from* de). **3** *adj operation, attempt* de sauvetage. **~ party** équipe *f* de sauvetage. ◆ **rescued** *npl*: **the ~d** les rescapés *mpl*. ◆ **rescuer** *n* sauveteur *m*; *(from imprisonment)* libérateur *m*, -trice *f*.

research [rɪ'sɜːtʃ] **1** *n* recherche(s) *f(pl)*. **a piece of ~** un travail de recherche; **to do ~** faire de la recherche (*on* sur); *(Ind)* **R~ and Development** Recherche *f* et Développement *m or* et Réalisation *f*. **2** *vi* faire des recherches (*into, on* sur). **3** *vt article* faire des recherches pour. **4** *adj student* qui fait de la recherche; *laboratory* de recherches. **~ establishment** centre *m* de recherches; *(Univ)* **~ fellow** ≃ chercheur *m*, -euse *f* attaché(e) à l'université. ◆ **researcher** *n* chercheur *m*, -euse *f*.

resemble [rɪ'zembl] *vt* ressembler à. ◆ **resemblance** *n* ressemblance *f*; **to bear a strong/faint**

resemblance to avoir une grande/vague ressemblance avec.

resent [rɪ'zent] *vt* être contrarié de; *(stronger)* être indigné de. **I ~ that!** je proteste!; **I ~ your tone** votre ton me déplaît; **he ~ed having lost his job** il n'a jamais pu admettre d'avoir perdu son emploi. ◆ **resentful** *adj* plein de ressentiment (*about* à cause de). ◆ **resentfully** *adv* avec ressentiment. ◆ **resentment** *n* ressentiment *m.*

reservation [,rezə'veɪʃ(ə)n] *n* (**a**) réserve *f.* **without ~** sans réserve; **with ~s** avec certaines réserves; **mental ~** restriction *f* mentale; **to have ~s about** avoir des doutes sur. (**b**) *(booking)* réservation *f.* **to make a ~ at the hotel** réserver une chambre à l'hôtel; **to have a ~** *(seat/room/table)* avoir une place/chambre/table réservée. (**c**) *(area of land)* réserve *f. [roadway]* **central ~** bande *f* médiane.

reserve [rɪ'zɜːv] **1** *vt (most senses)* réserver. **to ~ one's strength** ménager ses forces, *(Sport)* se réserver; **to ~ judgment** se réserver de prononcer un jugement; **to ~ the right to do** se réserver le droit de faire. **2** *n (most senses)* réserve *f*; *(Sport: substitute)* remplaçant(e) *m(f).* **cash ~** réserve de caisse; **gold ~s** réserves d'or; *(Mil)* **the R~** la réserve; **in ~** en réserve; **without ~** sans réserve ; **he treated me with some ~** il s'est tenu sur la réserve avec moi. **3** *adj fund* de réserve; *price* minimum. *(Aut)* **~ tank** réservoir *m* de secours; **~ team** deuxième équipe *f.* ◆ **reserved** *adj (gen)* réservé; **to be ~d about...** rester sur la réserve quant à... ◆ **reservist** *n* réserviste *m.* ◆ **reservoir** ['rezəvwɑːʳ] *n* réservoir *m.*

resettle [,riː'setl] *vt refugee* établir; *land* repeupler.

reshuffle [,riː'ʃʌfl] **1** *n (Pol)* **Cabinet ~** remaniement *m* ministériel. **2** *vt* remanier.

reside [rɪ'zaɪd] *vi* résider *(fig: in, with* dans). ◆ **residence** ['rezɪd(ə)ns] *n (gen)* résidence *f*; *(hostel)* foyer *m*; **to take up ~nce** s'installer, élire domicile *(Admin)*; **in ~nce** *monarch etc* en résidence; *students etc* rentrés; *doctor* résidant; **~nce permit** permis *m* de séjour. ◆ **residency** *n* résidence *f* officielle. ◆ **resident** **1** *n* habitant(e) *m(f)*; *(in foreign country)* résident(e) *m(f)*; *(in street)* riverain(e) *m(f)*; *(in hostel)* pensionnaire *mf* ; **2** *adj (gen)* résidant; *chaplain, tutor* à demeure; *population* fixe; **they are ~nt in France** ils résident en France. ◆ **residential** *adj area* résidentiel; *work* qui demande résidence; *(US)* **~ntial school** internat *m.*

residue ['rezɪdjuː] *n* reste(s) *m(pl)*; *(Chem)* résidu *m*; *(Math)* reste; *(Jur)* reliquat *m.* ◆ **residual** [re'zɪdjuəl] *adj* restant; *(Chem)* résiduel. ◆ **residuary** *adj* restant; *(Chem)* résiduaire; *(Jur)* **residuary legatee** ≃ légataire *mf* universel(le).

resign [rɪ'zaɪn] **1** *vt one's post* démissionner de; *the leadership etc* céder (*to* à). **to ~ one's commission** démissionner *(se dit d'un officier)*; **to ~ o.s. to (doing) sth** se résigner à (faire) qch. **2** *vi* démissionner (*from* de). ◆ **resignation** [,rezɪg'neɪʃ(ə)n] *n* (**a**) *(from job)* démission *f*; **to tender one's ~ation** donner sa démission; (**b**) *(mental state)* résignation *f.* ◆ **resigned** *adj* résigné; **to become ~ed to (doing) sth** se résigner à (faire) qch. ◆ **resignedly** *adv* avec résignation.

resilient [rɪ'zɪlɪənt] *adj substance* élastique; *character* qui réagit. **he's very ~** *(physically)* il a beaucoup de résistance; *(mentally etc)* il a du ressort. ◆ **resilience** *n* résistance *f*; ressort *m.*

resin ['rezɪn] *n* résine *f.* ◆ **resinous** *adj* résineux.

resist [rɪ'zɪst] **1** *vt (gen)* résister à; *order* refuser d'obéir à; *change* s'opposer à. **I couldn't ~ (eating) another cake** je n'ai pas pu m'empêcher de manger encore un gâteau; **she can't ~ him** elle ne peut rien lui refuser. **2** *vi* résister. ◆ **resistance** **1** *n (gen, Elec, Med, Mil, Phys)* résistance *f*; **he offered no ~ance** il n'a pas résisté (*to* à); *(Med)* **his ~ance was very low** il n'offrait presque plus de résistance (au mal) ; **2** *adj*: **~ance fighter** résistant(e) *m(f)*; **the ~ance movement** la résistance. ◆ **resistant** *adj* résistant; *(of virus, strain)* **~ant to** rebelle à.

resit ['riː'sɪt] *pret, ptp* **resat** **1** *vt* se représenter à. **2** ['riːsɪt] *n* deuxième session *f (d'un examen).*

resolute ['rezəluːt] *adj* résolu. ◆ **resolutely** *adv* résolument. ◆ **resoluteness** *n* résolution *f.*

resolution [,rezə'luːʃ(ə)n] *n (all senses)* résolution *f.* **to make a ~** prendre une résolution.

resolve [rɪ'zɒlv] **1** *vt (gen)* résoudre (*into* en); *problem, difficulty* résoudre. **2** *vi* résoudre, décider (*to do* de faire; *that* que), se décider (*to do* à faire). **it has been ~d that** il a été résolu que. **3** *n* résolution *f.* **to make a ~ to do** prendre la résolution de faire. ◆ **resolved** *adj* résolu (*to do* à faire).

resonant ['rezənənt] *adj* résonant. ◆ **resonance** *n* résonance *f.*

resort [rɪ'zɔːt] **1** *n* (**a**) *(recourse)* recours *m*; *(thing ~ed to)* ressource *f.* **without ~ to violence** sans recourir à la violence; **as a last ~, in the last ~** en dernier ressort; **it was my last ~** c'était mon dernier recours; **it was the only ~ left to them** c'était la seule ressource qui leur restait. (**b**) *(place)* lieu *m* de séjour. **holiday ~** lieu de vacances; **seaside/summer ~** station *f* balnéaire/estivale; **winter sports ~** station de sports d'hiver. **2** *vi* avoir recours (*to sth/sb* à qch/qn), en venir (*to doing* à faire).

resound [rɪ'zaʊnd] *vi* retentir (*with* de); *(fig)* avoir un retentissement. ◆ **resounding** *adj shout, victory, success* retentissant; *defeat* écrasant.

resource [rɪ'sɔːs] *n* ressource *f.* **as a last ~** en dernière ressource; **mineral ~s** ressources en minerais; **left to his own ~s** livré à ses propres ressources; **~ centre** centre *m* de documentation. ◆ **resourceful** *adj person* plein de ressources, débrouillard *; *scheme* ingénieux. ◆ **resourcefully** *adv* d'une manière ingénieuse. ◆ **resourcefulness** *n* ressource *f (qualité).*

respect [rɪs'pekt] **1** *n (gen)* respect *m.* **to have ~ for** respecter; **to treat with ~** traiter avec respect; **out of ~ for** par respect *or* égard pour; **with due ~ I still think...** sans vouloir vous contredire je crois toujours...; **with ~ to** pour *or* en ce qui concerne; **in ~ of** quant à; **in some ~s** à certains égards; **to pay one's ~s to sb** présenter ses respects à qn; **give my ~s to** présentez mes respects à. **2** *vt* respecter. ◆ **respectability** *n* respectabilité *f.* ◆ **respectable** *adj* (**a**) *(decent: gen)* respectable; *clothes, behaviour* convenable; **they are very ~able people** ce sont de très braves gens; **that's not ~able** ça ne se fait pas; (**b**) *(quite big) size, income* considérable, respectable. ◆ **respectably** *adv dress, behave* convenablement; *(quite well)* passablement; **very ~ably** pas mal du tout *. ◆ **respecter** *n*: **he is no ~er of persons** il ne s'en laisse imposer par personne. ◆ **respectful** *adj* respectueux. ◆ **respectfully** *adv* respectueusement. ◆ **respecting** *prep* concernant, touchant. ◆ **respective** *adj* respectif. ◆ **respectively** *adv* respectivement.

respire [rɪs'paɪəʳ] *vti* respirer. ◆ **respiration** [,respɪ'reɪʃ(ə)n] *n* respiration *f.* ◆ **respirator** *n (Med)* respirateur *m*; *(Mil)* masque *m* à gaz. ◆ **respiratory** *adj* respiratoire.

respite ['respaɪt] *n* répit *m.*

resplendent [rɪs'plendənt] *adj* resplendissant.

respond [rɪs'pɒnd] *vi (gen)* répondre (*to* à; *with* par). *[patient]* **to ~ to treatment** bien réagir au traitement; **the illness ~ed to treatment** le traitement a agi sur la maladie.

response [rɪs'pɒns] *n (gen)* réponse *f*; *(to treatment)* réaction *f*; *(Rel)* répons *m.* **in ~ to** en réponse à.

responsible [rɪs'pɒnsəbl] *adj* responsable (*for* de; *to sb for sth* de qch devant qn). **to be directly ~ to sb** relever directement de qn; **he is very ~** il a un grand sens des responsabilités; **it's a ~ job** c'est un poste qui comporte des responsabilités. ◆ **responsibility 1** *n* responsabilité *f*; **to put** *or* **place the responsibility for sth on sb** tenir qn pour responsable de qch; **to take responsibility for sth** prendre la responsabilité de qch; **it's not my responsibility to do that** ce n'est pas à moi de faire ça; **on my own responsibility** sous ma responsabilité ; **2** *adj*: **responsibility payment** prime *f* de fonction. ◆ **responsibly** *adv* avec sérieux.

responsive [rɪs'pɒnsɪv] *adj audience, class, pupil* qui réagit bien; *person* qui n'est pas du tout réservé; *(to affection)* très affectueux.

rest [rest] **1** *n* (**a**) *(gen)* repos *m*; *(Poetry)* césure *f*. **to need ~/a ~** avoir besoin de repos/de se reposer; **to have a ~** se reposer; **to have a good night's ~** passer une bonne nuit; **to be at ~** *(dead)* reposer en paix; **to lay to ~** porter en terre; **to set sb's mind at ~** tranquilliser qn; **to come to ~** *[object]* s'immobiliser; *[bird]* se poser (*on* sur); **it will give him a ~** ça le reposera; **give it a ~! *** laisse tomber! * (**b**) *(support)* support *m*, appui *m*. **arm ~** accoudoir *m*. (**c**) *(remainder)* **the ~** *[substance, money]* le reste, le restant; *[things, people]* les autres *mfpl*; **the ~ of us will wait here** nous (autres), nous attendrons ici; **and all the ~ of it *** et tout ça *. (**d**) *(Mus)* silence *m*.
2 *adj cure, day* de repos. **~ centre** centre *m* d'accueil; **~ home** maison *f* de repos; *(US)* **~ room** toilettes *fpl*.
3 *vi* (**a**) *(repose)* se reposer; *[the dead]* reposer. *(fig)* **he won't ~ till he finds out...** il n'aura de cesse qu'il ne découvre *(subj)*...; *(fig: of actor)* **to be ~ing** se trouver sans engagement; **may he ~ in peace** qu'il repose en paix. (**b**) *(remain)* rester, demeurer. **~ assured that** soyez assuré que; **there the matter ~s** l'affaire en est là; **it ~s with him to decide** il lui appartient de décider; **it doesn't ~ with me** cela ne dépend pas de moi. (**c**) *(lean) [person]* s'appuyer (*on* sur; *against* contre); *[roof, ladder]* appuyer (*on* sur; *against* contre); *[reputation, case]* reposer (*on* sur); *[eyes, gaze]* se poser (*on* sur). **a heavy responsibility ~s on him** il a de lourdes responsabilités.
4 *vt* (**a**) laisser reposer. **I am quite ~ed** je me sens tout à fait reposé; **God ~ his soul!** que Dieu ait son âme! (**b**) *(lean) hand, small object* poser; *ladder, cycle* appuyer (*on* sur, *against* contre).
◆ **restful** *adj* reposant. ◆ **restless** *adj* agité; **to have a ~less night** mal dormir; **to get ~less** s'agiter, s'impatienter. ◆ **restlessly** *adv move* avec agitation; *fidget* nerveusement. ◆ **restlessness** *n* agitation *f*, impatience *f*.

restaurant ['rest(ə)rɔ̃:ŋ] **1** *n* restaurant *m*. **2** *adj (Rail)* **~ car** wagon-restaurant *m*; **~ owner** restaurateur *m*, -trice *f*.

restitution [ˌrestɪ'tju:ʃ(ə)n] *n* restitution *f*. **to make ~ of sth** restituer qch.

restive ['restɪv] *adj horse* rétif; *person* agité, énervé.

restore [rɪs'tɔ:ʳ] *vt* (**a**) *(give back: gen)* rendre (*to* à); *rights, order, calm* rétablir; *confidence* redonner (*to sb* à qn; *in* dans). **~d to health** rétabli; **to ~ sb to life** ramener qn à la vie; **to ~ sth to its former condition** remettre qch en état; **to ~ sb's strength** redonner des forces à qn; **to ~ to the throne** replacer sur le trône; **to ~ to power** ramener au pouvoir. (**b**) *(repair) building etc* restaurer. ◆ **restoration** *n* rétablissement *m*; restauration *f (also Hist)*. ◆ **restorative** *adj, n* reconstituant *(m)*. ◆ **restorer** *n (Art etc)* restaurateur *m*, -trice *f*.

restrain [rɪs'treɪn] *vt (gen)* retenir (*sb from doing* qn de faire); *dangerous person (overcome)* maîtriser; *(control)* contenir; *(imprison)* interner; *anger, feelings* contenir. **~ yourself** dominez-vous. ◆ **restrained** *adj emotions* contenu; *voice, words* mesuré; *person* maître de soi; *style* sobre. ◆ **restraint** *n* (**a**) *(restriction)* contrainte *f*; **wage ~t** contrôle *m* des salaires; (**b**) *(moderation) [person, speech]* retenue *f*; *[style]* sobriété *f*; **to show a lack of ~t** manquer de maîtrise de soi.

restrict [rɪs'trɪkt] *vt authority, freedom* restreindre; *visits, price rise* limiter (*to* à). ◆ **restricted** *adj* restreint, limité; *document* confidentiel; *point of view, horizon* étroit; *(Aut)* **~ed area** zone *f* à vitesse limitée. ◆ **restriction** *n (gen)* restriction *f*, limitation *f*; *[prices etc]* contrôle *m*; **to place ~ions on** apporter des restrictions à; *(Aut)* **speed ~ion** limitation de vitesse. ◆ **restrictive** *adj* restrictif; *(Ind)* **~ive practices** pratiques *fpl* restrictives de production.

restyle ['ri:'staɪl] *vt product* redessiner. **to have one's hair ~d** changer de coiffure.

result [rɪ'zʌlt] **1** *n (gen)* résultat *m*. **as a ~ he...** en conséquence il...; **to be the ~ of** être dû à; **as a ~ of** *(gen)* à la suite de; **he died as a ~ of his injuries** il est mort des suites de ses blessures; **to get ~s *** *[person]* obtenir *or [action]* donner de bons résultats. **2** *vi* résulter (*from* de). **to ~ in** aboutir à, se terminer par; *failure* se solder par. ◆ **resultant** *adj* résultant.

resume [rɪ'zju:m] **1** *vt* (**a**) *(restart: gen)* reprendre; *relations* renouer. **to ~ one's seat** se rasseoir. (**b**) *(sum up)* résumer. **2** *vi [classes etc]* reprendre. ◆ **resumption** *n* reprise *f*.

resurrect [ˌrezə'rekt] *vt* ressusciter; *(fig) fashion, ideas* faire revivre; *memories* réveiller. ◆ **resurrection** *n (Rel, fig)* résurrection *f*.

resuscitate [rɪ'sʌsɪteɪt] *vt (Med)* réanimer. ◆ **resuscitation** *n* réanimation *f*.

retail ['ri:teɪl] **1** *n* vente *f* au détail. **2** *vt* vendre au détail; *(fig) gossip* colporter. **3** *vi* se vendre au détail (*at* à). **4** *adv* au détail. **5** *adj business, price* de détail. **~ price index** ≃ indice *m* des prix de l'INSEE. ◆ **retailer** *n* détaillant(e) *m(f)*.

retain [rɪ'teɪn] *vt (keep)* conserver, garder; *heat* conserver; *(hold)* retenir, maintenir; *lawyer* retenir, engager; *(remember)* garder en mémoire. ◆ **retainer** *n (fee)* provision *f*.

retaliate [rɪ'tælɪeɪt] *vi* se venger (*against sb/sth* de qn/qch; *by doing* en faisant), user de représailles (*against sb* envers qn). ◆ **retaliation** *n* vengeance *f*, représailles *fpl*; **in retaliation** par représailles; **in retaliation for** pour venger. ◆ **retaliatory** *adj*: **retaliatory measures** représailles *fpl*.

retarded [rɪ'tɑ:dɪd] *adj (Med)* retardé, arriéré. **mentally ~** arriéré.

retch [retʃ] *vi* avoir des haut-le-cœur.

retention [rɪ'tenʃ(ə)n] *n* conservation *f*, maintien *m*; *(memory)* mémoire *f*; *(Med)* rétention *f*.

retentive [rɪ'tentɪv] *adj memory* fidèle; *person* qui a bonne mémoire.

rethink ['ri:ˌθɪŋk] *vt* reconsidérer.

reticent ['retɪs(ə)nt] *adj* réticent, réservé. **to be ~ about** ne pas parler beaucoup de. ◆ **reticence** *n* réticence *f*.

retina ['retɪnə] *n* rétine *f*.

retinue ['retɪnju:] *n* suite *f*, escorte *f*.

retire [rɪ'taɪəʳ] **1** *vi* (**a**) *(withdraw)* se retirer (*from* de; *to* à); *(Mil)* reculer; *(Sport)* abandonner. (**b**) *(go to bed)* (aller) se coucher; *(give up work)* prendre sa retraite. **to ~ from business** se retirer des affaires. **2** *vt employee* mettre à la retraite. ◆ **retired** *adj* (**a**) *(no longer working)* retraité, à la retraite; **a ~d person** un(e) retraité(e); (**b**) *(secluded) life* retiré. ◆ **retirement** *n (stopping work)* retraite *f*. ◆ **retiring** *adj* (**a**) *(shy)* réservé; (**b**) *(departing) chairman etc* sortant; (**c**) *age* de la retraite.

retool [ri:'tu:l] *vt* rééquiper; *(US)* réorganiser.

retort¹ [rɪ'tɔ:t] **1** *n (reply)* riposte *f.* **2** *vt* riposter.

retort² [rɪ'tɔ:t] *n (Chem)* cornue *f.*

retrace [rɪ'treɪs] *vt developments etc (research into)* reconstituer; *(give account of)* retracer. **to ~ one's steps** revenir sur ses pas.

retract [rɪ'trækt] **1** *vt (gen)* rétracter; *(Aviat) undercarriage* rentrer. **2** *vi* se rétracter.

retrain ['ri:'treɪn] **1** *vt* recycler *(personne)*. **2** *vi* se recycler. ◆ **retraining** *n* recyclage *m.*

retread ['ri:tred] *n (tyre)* pneu *m* rechapé.

retreat [rɪ'tri:t] **1** *n* (**a**) *(esp Mil)* retraite *f*, recul *m. (Mil)* **to be in ~** battre en retraite; *(fig)* **to beat a hasty ~** partir en vitesse. (**b**) *(place: also Rel)* retraite *f.* **a country ~** une maison tranquille à la campagne. **2** *vi (Mil)* battre en retraite; *(withdraw)* se retirer (*from* de); *[flood, glacier]* reculer; *[chin, forehead]* être fuyant.

retrench [rɪ'tren(t)ʃ] **1** *vt* réduire. **2** *vi* faire des économies.

retrial ['ri:'traɪ(ə)l] *n (Jur)* nouveau procès *m.*

retribution [ˌretrɪ'bju:ʃ(ə)n] *n* châtiment *m.*

retrieve [rɪ'tri:v] *vt (recover) object* récupérer (*from* de); *[dog]* rapporter; *money* recouvrer; *information* extraire; *fortune, honour, position* rétablir; *(set to rights) error* réparer; *situation* redresser; *(rescue)* sauver (*from* de).
◆ **retrievable** *adj object, material* récupérable; *money* recouvrable; *error, loss* réparable. ◆ **retrieval** *n* récupération *f*; recouvrement *m*; réparation *f*; **beyond** *or* **past retrieval** irréparable. ◆ **retriever** *n* chien *m* d'arrêt.

retrograde ['retrəʊ'greɪd] *adj* rétrograde.

retrospect ['retrəʊ'spekt] *n*: **in ~** rétrospectivement. ◆ **retrospective** **1** *adj pay rise* rétroactif ; **2** *n (Art)* rétrospective *f.* ◆ **retrospectively** *adv* rétroactivement.

retune [ri:'tju:n] *vi*: **to ~ to a station** se mettre à l'écoute d'une station.

return [rɪ'tɜ:n] **1** *vi (come back)* revenir; *(go back)* retourner; *[symptoms, doubts]* réapparaître. **to ~ home** rentrer; **have they ~ed?** sont-ils revenus *or* rentrés?; **to ~ to** *work, habit* reprendre; *subject, idea* revenir à; **to ~ to school** rentrer (en classe).
2 *vt* (**a**) *(give back) (gen)* rendre; *money* rembourser (*to sb* à qn); *(bring back)* rapporter; *(put back)* remettre; *(send back)* renvoyer; *compliment, salute, blow, visit, book* rendre; *sb's love* répondre à. *(on letter)* '**~ to sender**' 'retour à l'envoyeur'; **to ~ sb's favour** rendre service à qn en retour. (**b**) *(reply)* répliquer. (**c**) *(declare) income, details* déclarer; *(Jur) verdict* rendre. *(Jur)* **to ~ a verdict of guilty on sb** déclarer qn coupable; **to ~ a verdict of murder** conclure au meurtre. (**d**) *(Parl) candidate* élire.
3 *n* (**a**) *(coming, going, giving back)* retour *m*; *(sending back)* renvoi *m*; *[sth lost etc]* restitution *f*; *[money]* remboursement *m.* **on my ~** dès mon retour; **~ home** retour; **by ~ of post** par retour du courrier; **many happy ~s (of the day)!** bon anniversaire! (**b**) *(~ ticket)* aller et retour *m.* (**c**) *(recompense)* récompense *f* (*for* de); *(from land, business, mine)* rapport *m* (*on* de). **~s** *(profits)* bénéfice *m*; *(receipts)* recettes *fpl*; **small profits and quick ~s** de bas prix et un gros chiffre d'affaires; **in ~** en revanche; **in ~ for** en échange de. (**d**) **official ~s** statistiques *fpl* officielles; **the population ~s** le recensement; **the election ~s** les résultats *mpl* de l'élection; **tax ~** déclaration *f* de revenus *or* d'impôts. (**e**) *(Parl) [candidate]* élection *f.*
4 *adj*: **~ fare, ~ ticket** aller et retour *m*; **~ flight** vol *m* de retour; *[ticket]* **~ half** coupon *m* de retour; *(Pol)* **~ing officer** président *m* du bureau de vote; **~ journey** retour *m*; **~ match** match *m* retour; *(Tech)* **~ stroke** course *f* retour.
◆ **returnable** *adj* qu'on doit rendre; *bottle etc* consigné.

reunification ['ri:ˌju:nɪfɪ'keɪʃ(ə)n] *n* réunification *f.*

reunion [rɪ'ju:njən] *n* réunion *f.*

reunite ['ri:ju:'naɪt] *vt* réunir.

re-use ['ri:ju:z] *vt* réutiliser. ◆ **re-usable** *adj* réutilisable.

rev * [rev] **1** *n (Aut)* tour *m.* **~ counter** compte-tours *m inv*; **4,000 ~s per minute** 4 000 tours minute. **2** *vt engine* emballer. **3** *vi* (**~ up**) *[engine]* s'emballer; *[driver]* emballer le moteur.

reveal [rɪ'vi:l] *vt* révéler (*that* que); *(uncover) hidden object etc* découvrir. ◆ **revealing** *adj* révélateur; *dress* décolleté. ◆ **revelation** [ˌrevə'leɪʃ(ə)n] *n* révélation *f*; **(the Book of the) Revelation** l'Apocalypse *f.*

reveille [rɪ'vælɪ] *n (Mil)* réveil *m.*

revel ['revl] **1** *vi* se délecter (*in sth* de qch; *in doing* à faire). **2** *npl*: **~s** festivités *fpl.* ◆ **reveller** *n*: **the ~lers** les gens *mpl* de la fête. ◆ **revelry** *n* festivités *fpl.*

revenge [rɪ'ven(d)ʒ] **1** *n* vengeance *f*; *(Sport etc)* revanche *f.* **to take ~ on sb for sth** se venger de qch sur qn; *(Sport etc)* prendre sa revanche sur qn de qch; **to get one's ~** se venger; **in ~ he...** pour se venger il... **2** *vt* venger. **to be ~d** se venger (*on sb* de qn; *on sb for sth* de qch sur qn).

revenue ['revənju:] *n* revenu *m.*

reverberate [rɪ'vɜ:b(ə)reɪt] *vi* se répercuter; *(fig)* se propager. ◆ **reverberation** *n* répercussion *f.*

revere [rɪ'vɪə^r] *vt* révérer, vénérer. ◆ **reverence** ['rev(ə)r(ə)ns] **1** *n* vénération *f* ; **2** *vt* révérer.
◆ **reverend** *adj*: **the R~nd Robert Martin** *(Anglican)* le révérend Robert Martin; *(Roman Catholic)* l'abbé (Robert) Martin; *(Nonconformist)* le pasteur (Robert) Martin; **R~nd Mother** révérende mère *f.* ◆ **reverent** *adj* respectueux. ◆ **reverently** *adv* avec vénération.

reverse [rɪ'vɜ:s] **1** *adj (gen)* contraire; *direction* contraire, opposé; *movement, image* inverse. **~ side** *V* **2 b** *below*; **in ~ order** en ordre inverse; *(Aut)* **~ gear** marche *f* arrière; *(US)* **~ discrimination** racisme *m* à l'envers.
2 *n* (**a**) *(opposite)* **the ~** le contraire, l'opposé; **quite the ~!** bien au contraire!; *(Aut)* **in ~** en marche arrière. (**b**) *(~ side) [coin]* revers *m*; *[sheet of paper]* verso *m*; *[cloth]* envers *m*; *[painting]* dos *m.* (**c**) *(setback)* revers *m*; *(defeat)* défaite *f.*
3 *vt* (**a**) *(turn the other way round) object, garment* retourner; *trend, policy, situation* renverser ; *2 objects, order, result* inverser. **to ~ one's policy** faire volte-face *(fig)*; **to ~ a procedure** procéder par ordre inverse; *(Brit Telec)* **to ~ the charges** téléphoner en P.C.V.; **~d charge call** communication *f* en P.C.V. (**b**) *(move backwards) moving belt* renverser la direction de; *typewriter ribbon* changer de sens. **to ~ one's car** = **to reverse** *(V* **4**). (**c**) *(Jur: annul) verdict, judgment* réformer.
4 *vi (Aut)* faire marche arrière. **to ~ into the garage** rentrer dans le garage en marche arrière; **to ~ into a tree** heurter un arbre en faisant une marche arrière; **to ~ across the road** faire une marche arrière en travers de la route; **reversing lights** feux *mpl* de marche arrière.
◆ **reversal** *n (turning upside down)* renversement *m*; *(switching over of 2 objects)* interversion *f*; *[opinion, view etc]* revirement *m*; *(Jur)* réforme *f.*
◆ **reversible** *adj* réversible.

revert [rɪ'vɜ:t] *vi (gen)* retourner (*to* à); *(to subject)* revenir (*to* à). *(Bio)* **to ~ to type** retourner au type primitif; *(fig)* **he has ~ed to type** le naturel a repris le dessus. ◆ **reversion** *n* retour *m* (*to* à); *(Bio)* réversion *f.*

review [rɪ'vju:] **1** *n* (**a**) *[situation, development, the past]* revue *f*, examen *m*; *[wages etc]* révision *f*; *(report)* rapport *m* d'enquête; *(Mil etc)* revue;

[book, film, play etc] critique *f.* **to come up for** ~ *or* **come under** ~ être révisé; **to keep sth under** ~ suivre qch de très près; **to give a** ~ **of sth** passer qch en revue. (**b**) *(magazine)* revue *f.* (**c**) *(US Scol: revision)* révision *f.* **2** *adj [book]* ~ **copy** exemplaire *m* de service de presse. **3** *vt* (**a**) *one's life, the past, troops* passer en revue; *the situation* réexaminer; *book, play, film* faire la critique de. (**b**) *(US Scol etc)* réviser. ◆ **reviewer** *n* critique *m*; **book/film** ~**er** critique littéraire/de cinéma.

revile [rɪ'vaɪl] *vt* insulter.

revise [rɪ'vaɪz] **1** *vt* (**a**) *(change) opinion, estimate* réviser, modifier; *proof* corriger; *text* réviser. ~**d edition** édition *f* revue et corrigée; *(Brit) [Bible]* **R~d Version** traduction (anglaise) de la Bible de 1884. (**b**) *(learn up)* réviser. **2** *vi* réviser (*for* pour). ◆ **revision** *n* révision *f.*

revive [rɪ'vaɪv] **1** *vt person (from fainting)* ranimer; *(from exhaustion)* remonter; *(from near death, esp Med)* réanimer; *fashion* remettre en vogue; *conversation, fire* ranimer; *trade* relancer; *hope, interest* faire renaître; *law* remettre en vigueur; *custom, usage* rétablir; *play* reprendre. **to** ~ **sb's courage** redonner du courage à qn.
2 *vi [person]* reprendre connaissance; *[hope, feelings]* renaître; *[business, trade]* reprendre.
◆ **revival** *n [custom, ceremony]* reprise *f*; *[faith]* renouveau *m*; **revival meeting** réunion *f* pour le renouveau de la foi.

revoke [rɪ'vəʊk] **1** *vt law* abroger; *order, edict* révoquer; *promise* revenir sur; *decision* annuler; *licence* retirer. **2** *vi (Cards)* faire une fausse renonce. ◆ **revocation** *n* abrogation *f*; révocation *f*; annulation *f*; retrait *m.*

revolt [rɪ'vəʊlt] **1** *n* révolte *f.* **to rise** *or* **be in** ~ se révolter (*against* contre). **2** *vi* se révolter (*against* contre). **3** *vt* révolter. ◆ **revolting** *adj* révoltant; *(less strong)* dégoûtant; *(*: unpleasant) weather, colour* épouvantable.

revolution [ˌrevə'luːʃ(ə)n] *n (all senses)* révolution *f.* ◆ **revolutionary** *adj, n* révolutionnaire *(mf).* ◆ **revolutionize** *vt* révolutionner.

revolve [rɪ'vɒlv] **1** *vt (lit)* faire tourner. *(fig)* **to** ~ **a problem in one's mind** retourner un problème dans son esprit. **2** *vi* tourner. **to** ~ **on an axis/around the sun** tourner sur un axe/autour du soleil; *(fig)* **everything** ~**s around him** tout dépend de lui. ◆ **revolving** *adj light, stage* tournant; *chair, bookcase* pivotant; *(Tech)* rotatif; **revolving credit** crédit *m* documentaire renouvelable; **revolving door** tambour *m.*

revolver [rɪ'vɒlvəʳ] *n* revolver *m.*

revue [rɪ'vjuː] *n (Theat)* revue *f.*

revulsion [rɪ'vʌlʃ(ə)n] *n* dégoût *m.*

reward [rɪ'wɔːd] **1** *n* récompense *f.* **as a** ~ **for sth** en récompense de qch; **as a** ~ **for doing** pour vous (*or* le *etc*) récompenser d'avoir fait. **2** *vt* récompenser (*for* de). **to** ~ **sb with a smile** remercier qn d'un sourire. ◆ **rewarding** *adj (financially)* rémunérateur; *(fig) book/film* qui vaut la peine d'être lu/vu; *activity* qui a sa récompense.

rewire ['riː'waɪəʳ] *vt house* refaire l'installation électrique de.

Reykjavik ['reɪkjəviːk] *n* Reykjavik.

rhapsody ['ræpsədɪ] *n (Mus)* rhapsodie *f*; *(fig)* dithyrambe *m.* ◆ **rhapsodize** *vi* s'extasier (*over, about* sur).

rheostat ['riːəʊ'stæt] *n* rhéostat *m.*

rhesus ['riːsəs] **1** *n* rhésus *m.* **2** *adj factor* rhésus *inv.* ~ **monkey** rhésus *m.*

rhetoric ['retərɪk] *n* rhétorique *f.* ◆ **rhetorical** *adj style* ampoulé *(pej)*; ~**al question** question *f* pour la forme. ◆ **rhetorically** *adv declaim* en orateur; *ask* pour la forme.

rheumatism ['ruːmətɪz(ə)m] *n* rhumatisme *m.* ◆ **rheumatic fever** *n* rhumatisme *m* articulaire aigu. ◆ **rheumatics** * *npl* rhumatismes *mpl.* ◆ **rheumatoid arthritis** *n* rhumatisme *m* chronique polyarticulaire.

Rhine [raɪn] *n* Rhin *m.*

rhinoceros [raɪ'nɒs(ə)r(ə)s] *n* rhinocéros *m.*

Rhodesia [rə(ʊ)'dɪːʒə] *n* Rhodésie *f.*

rhododendron [ˌrəʊdə'dendr(ə)n] *n* rhododendron *m.*

Rhone [rəʊn] *n* Rhône *m.*

rhubarb ['ruːbɑːb] **1** *n* rhubarbe *f.* **2** *adj jam* de rhubarbe; *pie* à la rhubarbe.

rhyme [raɪm] **1** *n* rime *f*; *(poetry)* vers *mpl*; *(poem)* poème *m.* *(fig)* **without** ~ **or reason** sans rime ni raison. **2** *vt* faire rimer (*with* avec). **3** *vi* rimer (*with* avec).

rhythm ['rɪð(ə)m] *n* rythme *m.* *(Med)* ~ **method** méthode *f* des températures; *(Mus)* ~ **and blues** rythm and blues *m.* ◆ **rhythmic(al)** *adj movement* rythmique; *music* rythmé. ◆ **rhythmically** *adv* de façon rythmée.

rib [rɪb] *n (Anat, Culin)* côte *f*; *[leaf, ceiling]* nervure *f*; *[umbrella]* baleine *f*; *[knitting]* côte. **to dig** *or* **poke sb in the** ~**s** pousser qn du coude; ~ **cage** cage *f* thoracique.

ribald ['rɪb(ə)ld] *adj* paillard. ◆ **ribaldry** *n* paillardises *fpl.*

ribbon ['rɪb(ə)n] **1** *n* ruban *m.* **in** ~**s** *(tatters)* en lambeaux. **2** *adj*: ~ **development** extension *f* urbaine linéaire en bordure de route.

rice [raɪs] **1** *n* riz *m.* **2** *adj*: ~ **pudding** riz *m* au lait. ◆ **ricefield** *n* rizière *f.* ◆ **rice-growing** **1** *n* riziculture *f* ; **2** *adj* producteur de riz.

rich [rɪtʃ] *adj (gen)* riche (*in* en); *profit* gros; *furniture, gift, clothes* somptueux; *voice* ample; *district of town* très chic. **to grow** *or* **get** ~**(er)** s'enrichir; **to make** ~ enrichir; *(iro)* **that's** ~**!** * ça c'est pas mal! * *(iro).* ◆ **riches** *npl* richesse(s) *f(pl).* ◆ **richly** *adv* richement; somptueusement; *deserve* largement. ◆ **richness** *n* richesse *f* (*in* en); somptuosité *f*; ampleur *f*; *[colour]* éclat *m.*

rickets ['rɪkɪts] *n* rachitisme *m.* **to have** ~ être rachitique. ◆ **rickety** *adj (Med)* rachitique; *furniture, stairs* branlant; *bicycle* délabré.

ricochet ['rɪkəʃeɪ] **1** *n* ricochet *m.* **2** *vi* ricocher.

rid [rɪd] *pret, ptp* **rid** *or* **ridded** *vt (of pests, disease)* débarrasser (*of* de); *(of bandits etc)* délivrer (*of* de). **to get** ~ **of, to** ~ **o.s. of** *fleas, spots, cold, person, rubbish* se débarrasser de; *habit, desire, fears* perdre; *debts* liquider; **to be** ~ **of** être débarrassé de; **the body gets** ~ **of waste** l'organisme élimine les déchets. ◆ **riddance** *n* débarras *m*; **good** ~**dance!** * bon débarras! *

ridden ['rɪdn] *(ptp of* **ride**) *adj ending*: **fear-**~ hanté par la peur; **remorse-** ~ tourmenté par le remords.

riddle[1] ['rɪdl] **1** *n* crible *m.* **2** *vt coal, soil etc* passer au crible; *stove* agiter la grille de; *(fig)* cribler (*with bullets etc* de balles *etc*).

riddle[2] ['rɪdl] *n (mystery)* énigme *f.* **to ask sb a** ~ poser une devinette à qn.

ride [raɪd] *(vb: pret* **rode**, *ptp* **ridden**) **1** *n* (**a**) promenade *f (à cheval, à bicyclette etc)*, tour *m*; *(distance covered)* trajet *m.* **horse** ~ , ~ **on horseback** *(for pleasure)* promenade *or* tour à cheval; *(long journey)* chevauchée *f*; **he gave the child a** ~ **on his back** il a promené l'enfant sur son dos; **coach** ~ tour *or* excursion *f* en car; **it's a short taxi** ~ ce n'est pas loin en taxi (*to* jusqu'à); **he has a long (car/bus)** ~ **to work** il a un long trajet (en voiture/en autobus) jusqu'à son travail; **to go for a** ~ **in a car** faire un tour *or* une promenade en voiture; **to take sb for a** ~ *(in car etc)* emmener

qn en promenade; *(fig: make fool of)* mener qn en bateau *; *(swindle)* rouler qn *; **I've never had a ~ in a train** je n'ai jamais pris le train; **can I have a ~ on your bike?** est-ce que je peux monter sur ton vélo?; **a ~ on the merry-go-round** un tour sur le manège. **(b)** *(forest path)* allée *f* cavalière.
2 *vi* **(a)** *(~ a horse)* monter à cheval, faire du cheval. **can you ~?** savez-vous monter à cheval?; **he ~s well** il monte bien, il est bon cavalier. **(b)** *(go on horseback/by bicycle/by motorcycle)* aller à cheval/à bicyclette/en moto. **to ~ down/away** *etc* descendre/s'éloigner *etc* à cheval (*or* à bicyclette *etc*); **the witch was riding on a broomstick** la sorcière était à cheval sur un balai; **they were riding on a bus/in a car/in a train** ils étaient en autobus/en voiture/en train; **they rode in a bus to...** ils sont allés en autobus à...; *(fig)* **to be riding for a fall** courir à un échec; **to ~ at anchor** être à l'ancre; **to let things ~** laisser courir *.
3 *vt*: **to ~ a horse/donkey/camel** monter à cheval/à dos d'âne/à dos de chameau; **he was riding Malfi** il montait Malfi; **I have never ridden Flash** je n'ai jamais monté Flash; **he rode Cass at Newmarket** il montait Cass à Newmarket; **he rode Buster into town** il a pris Buster pour aller en ville; **Jason will be ridden by J. Bean** Jason sera monté par J. Bean; **he ~s his pony to school** il va à l'école à dos de poney; **he rode his motorbike/cycle to the station** il est allé à la gare en moto/à bicyclette; **I have never ridden a bicycle/a motorbike** je ne suis jamais monté à bicyclette/à moto; **can I ~ your bike?** est-ce que je peux monter sur ton vélo?; **he was riding a bicycle** il était à bicyclette; **he always ~s a bicycle** il va partout à bicyclette; **they had ridden 10 km** ils avaient fait 10 km à cheval (*or* à bicyclette *etc*).
◆ **ride out** *vt sep (fig) difficult period* surmonter, survivre à. **to ~ out the storm** *(Naut)* étaler la tempête; *(fig)* surmonter la crise. ◆ **ride up** *vi [skirt etc]* remonter.
◆ **rider** *n* **(a)** *[horse]* cavalier *m*, -ière *f*; *[racehorse]* jockey *m*; *[circus horse]* écuyer *m*, -ère *f*; **a good ~r** un bon cavalier, une bonne cavalière; **(b)** *(addition: to document)* annexe *f*; *(to insurance policy, jury's verdict)* avenant *m*. ◆ **riding** **1** *n (horse-riding)* équitation *f*; *(horsemanship)* monte *f* ; **2** *adj boots, breeches* de cheval; *teacher* d'équitation; **riding crop** *or* **whip** cravache *f*; **riding habit** tenue *f* d'amazone; **riding school** *or* **stables** manège *m*.

ridge [rɪdʒ] **1** *n [roof, nose, line of hills]* arête *f*; *(ledge on hillside)* corniche *f*; *(chain of mountains)* chaîne *f*; *(on sand)* ride *f*; *(in ploughed land)* billon *m*; *(on cliff, rockface)* strie *f*. *(Met)* **a ~ of high pressure** une ligne de hautes pressions. **2** *adj*: **~ tent** tente *f* (à toit en arête).

ridicule ['rɪdɪkju:l] **1** *n* raillerie *f*, ridicule *m*. **to hold sb/sth up to ~** tourner qn/qch en ridicule. **2** *vt* ridiculiser. ◆ **ridiculous** [rɪ'dɪkjʊləs] *adj* ridicule; **to make o.s. (look) ridiculous** se rendre ridicule. ◆ **ridiculously** *adv* ridiculement. ◆ **ridiculousness** *n* ridicule *m (état)*.

rife [raɪf] *adj [disease, corruption]* **to be ~** sévir; **rumour is ~** des bruits courent.

riffraff ['rɪfræf] *n* racaille *f*.

rifle¹ ['raɪfl] *vt town* piller; **to ~ sb's pockets** *(steal from)* puiser dans les poches de qn; *(go through)* faire les poches à qn; *drawer, till, house* dévaliser.

rifle² ['raɪfl] **1** *n (gun)* fusil *m* (rayé); *(for hunting)* carabine *f* de chasse. **2** *adj*: **~ range** *(outdoor)* champ *m* de tir; *(indoor)* stand *m* de tir.

rift [rɪft] *n (gen)* fissure *f*; *(in clouds)* trouée *f*; *(fig: disagreement)* désaccord *m*; *(Pol: in party)* division *f*.

rig [rɪg] **1** *n* **(a)** *(oil ~)* *(land)* derrick *m*; *(sea)* plateforme *f* pétrolière. **(b)** *(US Aut)* semi-remorque *m*. **2** *vt election* truquer; *prices* fixer illégalement. **it was ~ged** c'était un coup monté. ◆ **rig out** *vt sep* habiller (*with* de; *as* en). ◆ **rig up** *vt sep boat* gréer; *(with mast)* mâter; *(set up) equipment* monter; *(make hastily)* faire avec des moyens de fortune; *(arrange)* arranger. ◆ **rigging** *n (Naut)* gréement *m*. ◆ **rigout** * *n* tenue *f (vestimentaire)*.

right [raɪt] **1** *adj* **(a)** *(just)* juste, équitable; *(morally good)* bien *inv*. **it isn't ~ to lie** ce n'est pas bien de mentir; **to do what is ~** faire ce qui est conforme au devoir *or* à la morale, se conduire bien; **he thought it ~ to warn me** il a cru *or* jugé bon de m'avertir; **it seemed only ~ to do it** il ne semblait que juste de le faire; **it is only ~ that she should go** il n'est que juste qu'elle y aille; **it is only ~ to point out that...** en toute justice il faut signaler que...; **would it be ~ to tell him?** ferait-on bien de le lui dire?; **to do the ~ thing by sb** agir honorablement envers qn.
(b) *(correct)* juste, exact. **to be ~** *[person]* avoir raison (*to do* de faire); *[answer]* être juste, être exact; *[clock]* être à l'heure; **that's ~** c'est juste, c'est exact; **the ~ answer/road/table** la bonne réponse/route/table; **the ~ time** l'heure exacte *or* juste; **at the ~ time** au bon moment; **on the ~ road** sur le bon chemin; *(fig)* sur la bonne voie; **to get one's sums ~** réussir ses additions; **to get one's facts ~** être sûr de ce qu'on avance; **let's get it ~ this time!** essayons d'y arriver cette fois-ci!; **to put** *or* **set ~** *error* corriger; *mistaken person* détromper; *sick person* guérir; *situation* redresser; *clock* remettre à l'heure; **to put things ~** arranger les choses; **put me ~ if I'm wrong** dites-moi si je me trompe; **the ~ clothes** les vêtements appropriés; **what's the ~ thing to do?** qu'est-ce qu'il vaut mieux faire?; **to do sth the ~ way** s'y prendre bien; **that is the ~ way of looking at it** c'est bien ainsi qu'il faut l'envisager; **the ~ word** le mot juste; **the ~ man for the job** l'homme qu'il faut; **the ~ size** la taille qu'il faut; **what is ~ for the country** ce qui est dans l'intérêt du pays; **she is on the ~ side of 40** elle n'a pas encore 40 ans; **to get on the ~ side of sb** * s'insinuer dans les bonnes grâces de qn; **the ~ side of the material** l'endroit *m* du tissu; **to know the ~ people** avoir des relations utiles; **more than is ~** plus que de raison; **~!, ~-oh! *, ~ you are! *** d'accord!; **that's ~!** mais oui!, c'est ça!; **he's the ~ sort *** c'est un type bien *; **all ~** *V* **all 3 b**.
(c) *(well)* **I don't feel quite ~** je ne me sens pas très bien; **to be as ~ as rain *** *(after illness)* se porter comme un charme; *(after fall)* être indemne; **the car's not ~ *** il y a qch qui cloche * dans la voiture; **he put the engine ~** il a remis le moteur en état; **to be in one's ~ mind** avoir toute sa raison; **not ~ in the head** ‡ un peu dingue ‡.
(d) *(Math)* droit. **at ~ angles** à angle droit (*to* avec).
(e) *(opposite of left)* droit, de droite. **~ hand** main droite; **I'd give my ~ hand to know...** je donnerais cher * pour savoir...
2 *adv* **(a)** *(straight)* tout droit, directement; *(exactly, completely)* tout, tout à fait. **~ in front of you** (tout) droit devant vous; **~ behind you** juste derrière vous; **go ~ on** continuez tout droit; **~ away, ~ off *** *(immediately)* tout de suite; *(at the first attempt)* du premier coup; **~ now** en ce moment; *(at once)* tout de suite; **~ here** ici même; **~ in the middle** en plein milieu; **~ at the start** dès le tout début; **~ round the house** tout autour de la maison; **rotten ~ through** complètement pourri; **to turn ~ round** se retourner; **~ at the top of the mountain** tout en haut de la montagne; **~ at the back, ~ at the bottom** tout au fond; **push it ~ in** enfoncez-le complètement *or* jusqu'au bout.
(b) *(correctly) do, remember* bien; *guess, calculate* juste; *answer* correctement; *(well)* bien. **If I remember ~** si je me souviens bien; **you did ~ to refuse**

vous avez eu raison de refuser; **if everything goes** ~ si tout va bien; **if I get you** ~ * si je comprends bien; **I'll see you** ~ ‡ je veillerai à ce que vous n'y perdiez *(subj)* pas.
(**c**) *(opposite of left)* à droite. ~ **and left** *look etc* à droite et à gauche; *(fig)* ~, **left and centre** * de tous les côtés.
3 *n* (**a**) ~ **and wrong** le bien et le mal; **to be in the** ~ avoir raison, être dans le vrai; **I want to know the** ~**s and wrongs of it** je veux savoir qui a tort et qui a raison là-dedans; **to put** *or* **set sth to** ~**s** mettre qch en ordre. (**b**) droit *m*. **to have a** ~ **to sth** avoir droit à qch; **to have a** *or* **the** ~ **to do** avoir le droit de faire; **what** ~ **have you to say that?** de quel droit dites-vous cela?; **within his** ~**s** dans son droit; **by** ~**s** en toute justice; *(Jur)* **in his own** ~ de son propre chef; **she's a good actress in her own** ~ elle est elle-même une bonne actrice; **women's** ~**s movement** mouvement *m* pour les droits de la femme. (**c**) *(not left)* droite *f*. **on** *or* **to the** ~ à droite (*of* de); **to keep to the** ~ *(gen)* garder la droite; *(Aut)* tenir sa droite; **on my** ~ à ma droite; *(Pol)* **the R**~ la droite.
4 *vt vehicle, wrong etc* redresser; *injustice* réparer. **to** ~ **itself** *[vehicle]* se redresser; *[problem]* s'arranger.
◆ **right-angled** *adj* à angle droit; *triangle* rectangle. ◆ **righteous** *adj person* vertueux; *anger, indignation* justifié. ◆ **righteousness** *n* droiture *f*, vertu *f*. ◆ **rightful** *adj* légitime. ◆ **rightfully** *adv* à juste titre. ◆ **right-hand** *adj side* droit; ~**-hand drive car** voiture *f* avec la conduite à droite; **his** ~**-hand man** son bras droit *(personne)*. ◆ **right-handed** *adj person* droitier; *punch, throw* du droit; *screw* fileté à droite. ◆ **rightly** *adv* (**a**) *(correctly)* bien, correctement; **I don't** ~**ly know** * je ne sais pas au juste; (**b**) *(justifiably)* à juste titre; ~**ly or wrongly** à tort ou à raison. ◆ **right-minded** *or* ◆ **right-thinking** *adj* sensé. ◆ **right-of-way** *n* *(across property)* droit *m* de passage; *(Aut: priority)* priorité *f*. ◆ **right-wing** **1** *n (Sport: also* ~**-winger***)* ailier *m* droit; *(Pol)* droite *f* ; **2** *adj (Pol)* de droite. ◆ **right-winger** *n (Pol)* membre *m* de la droite.

rigid ['rɪdʒɪd] *adj material* rigide; *person* rigide, inflexible; *specifications, interpretation* strict; *system* qui manque de flexibilité. **he's quite** ~ **about it** il est inflexible là-dessus. ◆ **rigidity** *n* rigidité *f*; inflexibilité *f* ◆ **rigidly** *adv stand etc* avec raideur; *(fig) behave, treat* inflexiblement; *oppose* absolument.

rigmarole ['rɪgm(ə)rəʊl] *n (speech)* galimatias *m*; *(complicated procedure)* comédie * *f*, histoire * *f*.

rigour, *(US)* **rigor** ['rɪgəʳ] *n* rigueur *f*. ◆ **rigor mortis** *n* rigidité *f* cadavérique. ◆ **rigorous** *adj* rigoureux. ◆ **rigorously** *adv* rigoureusement.

rim [rɪm] *n [cup, bowl]* bord *m*; *[wheel]* jante *f*; *[spectacles]* monture *f*. ◆ **rimless** *adj spectacles* à verres non cerclés.

rind [raɪnd] *n [orange, lemon]* peau *f*; *(cut off)* pelure *f*; *(Culin)* zeste *m*; *[cheese]* croûte *f*; *[bacon]* couenne *f*.

ring¹ [rɪŋ] **1** *n* (**a**) *(gen)* anneau *m*; *(on finger)* anneau; *(with stone)* bague *f*; *(for napkin)* rond *m*; *(for swimmer)* bouée *f* de natation; *(for invalid to sit on)* rond *(pour malade)*. **wedding** ~ alliance *f*. (**b**) *(circle) (of people; in tree trunk)* cercle *m*; *(of smoke, in water etc)* rond *m*. **the** ~**s of Saturn** les anneaux *mpl* de Saturne; **to have** ~**s round the eyes** avoir les yeux cernés; **to stand in a** ~ se tenir en cercle; *(fig)* **to run** ~**s round sb** * battre qn à plate couture. (**c**) *(group) (gen)* coterie *f*; *[dealers]* cartel *m*; *[spies]* réseau *m*. (**d**) *(enclosure) (at circus)* piste *f*; *(at exhibition)* arène *f*; *(Horse-racing)* enceinte *f* des bookmakers; *(Boxing)* ring *m*. **2** *vt (surround)* entourer, encercler; *(put* ~ *on) item on list etc* entourer d'un cercle; *bird, tree* baguer. **3** *adj*: ~ **binder** classeur *m* à anneaux; ~ **finger** annulaire *m*; ~ **road** route *f* de ceinture; *(motorway-type)* périphérique *m*. ◆ **ringleader** *n* meneur *m*. ◆ **ringlet** *n* frisette *f*; *(long)* anglaise *f*. ◆ **ringmaster** *n* ≃ 'Monsieur Loyal'. ◆ **ring-pull** *n* anneau *m*. ◆ **ringworm** *n* teigne *f*.

ring² [rɪŋ] *(vb: pret* **rang,** *ptp* **rung***)* **1** *n* (**a**) *[bell]* sonnerie *f*; *(lighter)* tintement *m*; *[electric bell]* retentissement *m*; *[telephone]* sonnerie. **there was a** ~ **at the door** on a sonné à la porte; **his voice had an angry** ~ il y avait un accent de colère dans sa voix; **that has the** ~ **of truth** ça sonne juste. (**b**) *(*: phone call)* coup *m* de téléphone *or* de fil *. **to give sb a** ~ donner *or* passer un coup de téléphone *or* de fil * à qn.
2 *vi* (**a**) *[bell]* sonner, retentir; *(lightly)* tinter; *[alarm clock, telephone]* sonner. **to** ~ **for sb/sth** sonner qn/pour demander qch; **to** ~ **for the lift** appeler l'ascenseur. (**b**) *(telephone)* téléphoner. (**c**) *[words]* retentir (*through the room* dans la salle; *in his ears* à ses oreilles); *[voice]* vibrer (*with* de); *[coin]* sonner, tinter; *(resound)* résonner, retentir (*with* de); *[ears]* tinter, bourdonner. **to** ~ **false/true** *[coin]* sonner faux/clair; *(fig)* sonner faux/juste.
3 *vt* (**a**) *bell* faire sonner; *coin* faire tinter. **to** ~ **the doorbell** sonner (à la porte); **to** ~ **the bell** sonner, donner un coup de sonnette; *(fig)* **his name** ~**s a bell** * son nom me dit qch; *[bells]* **to** ~ **the changes** carillonner; *(fig)* **to** ~ **the changes on** varier. (**b**) *(Telec:* ~ **up***)* téléphoner à, passer un coup de fil * à.
◆ **ring back** *vi, vt sep (Telec)* rappeler. ◆ **ring off** *vi (Telec)* raccrocher. ◆ **ring out** *vi [bell]* sonner; *[voice]* résonner; *[shot]* retentir. ◆ **ring up** *vt sep (Telec)* = **ring 3 b.**
◆ **ringing** **1** *adj voice, tone* retentissant; *(Telec)* ~**ing tone** sonnerie *f* ; **2** *n [bell, telephone]* sonnerie *f*; *(lighter)* tintement *m*; *[electric bell]* retentissement *m*; *(in ears)* bourdonnement *m*.

rink [rɪŋk] *n [ice-skating]* patinoire *f*; *[rollerskating]* skating *m*.

rinse [rɪns] **1** *n* rinçage *m*. **to give sth a** ~ rincer qch. **2** *vt clothes etc* rincer. **to** ~ **(the soap off) one's hands** se rincer les mains; *(colour)* **to** ~ **one's hair** se faire un rinçage. ◆ **rinse out** *vt sep colour, dirt* faire partir à l'eau; *cup* rincer. **to** ~ **out one's mouth** se rincer la bouche.

Rio (de Janeiro) ['ri:əʊ(dədʒə'nɪərəʊ)] *n* Rio de Janeiro.

riot ['raɪət] **1** *n* émeute *f*, violentes bagarres *fpl*; *[flowers, colours]* profusion *f*. **2** *adj*: ~ **police** forces *fpl* d'intervention (de police); **in** ~ **gear** casqué et portant un bouclier; *(fig)* **to read sb the** ~ **act** tancer qn vertement. **3** *vi* manifester avec violence; *(stronger)* faire une émeute. ◆ **rioter** *n* émeutier *m*, -ière *f*. ◆ **riotous** *adj scene* tapageur; *(*: hilarious)* tordant *; ~**ous living** vie *f* de débauche ; **a** ~**ous success** un succès fou * *or* monstre *. ◆ **riotously** *adv behave* de façon tapageuse; ~**ously funny** * vachement rigolo ‡.

rip [rɪp] **1** *n* déchirure *f*. **2** *vt* déchirer, fendre. **to** ~ **open** ouvrir en hâte. **3** *vi* (**a**) *[cloth]* se déchirer. (**b**) *(Aut)* **let her** ~! fonce! *; **he let** ~ * **a string of oaths** il a lâché un chapelet de jurons ; **he let** ~ * **at me** il m'a passé un bon savon *. ◆ **rip off** *vt sep* (**a**) arracher (*from* de). (**b**) (*‡: steal)* voler; *customer* arnaquer *; *employee* exploiter. ◆ **rip-off** ‡ *n*: **it's a** ~**-off!** c'est de l'arnaque *. ◆ **rip-roaring** * *adj* exubérant; *success* monstre *.

ripe [raɪp] *adj (gen)* mûr (*for* pour); *cheese* fait. **to a** ~ **old age** jusqu'à un bel âge. ◆ **ripen** **1** *vt* (faire) mûrir ; **2** *vi* mûrir. ◆ **ripeness** *n* maturité *f*.

ripple ['rɪpl] **1** *n (movement: on water, corn)* ondulation *f*; *(noise) [waves]* clapotis *m*; *[voices]* murmures *mpl*; *[laughter]* cascade *f*. **2** *vi* onduler.

rise [raɪz] *(vb: pret* **rose,** *ptp* **risen)** **1** *n* **(a)** *[theatre curtain, sun]* lever *m*; *(Mus)* hausse *f*; *(increase)* hausse; *(in wages)* augmentation *f*; *(fig) [person, party]* ascension *f*; *[town, industry, empire]* essor *m*. *[employee]* **to ask for a ~** demander une augmentation (de salaire); *(fig)* **his ~ to power** sa montée au pouvoir; *(fig)* **to get a ~ out of sb *** faire marcher qn *. **(b)** *(small hill)* élévation *f*; *(slope)* côte *f*, pente *f*. **(c)** *(origin)* source *f (also fig)*. *(fig)* **to give ~ to** *trouble, bitterness* causer; *rumour* donner lieu à; *fear, interest* susciter; *impression* donner.

2 *vi* **(a)** *(get up: gen)* se lever; *(after falling)* se relever. **to ~ to one's feet** se mettre debout, se lever; **to ~ from the dead** ressusciter (des morts). **(b)** *(go higher: gen)* monter; *[balloon]* s'élever; *[curtain, sun, wind]* se lever; *[dough]* lever; *[hair]* se dresser; *[barometer]* remonter; *[fish]* mordre; *[hopes, anger]* croître; *(in society, rank)* s'élever; *[cost of living]* augmenter; *[stocks, shares]* être en hausse; *(fig) [mountain, tower]* se dresser (*before sb* devant qn). **to ~ to the surface** remonter à la surface; *(fig)* **he rose to the bait** il a mordu à l'hameçon; **he won't ~ to that** il ne réagira pas à ça; **his eyebrows rose** il a levé les sourcils; **the mountain ~s to 3,000 metres** la montagne a une altitude de 3 000 mètres; **to ~ to the occasion** se montrer à la hauteur de la situation; **I can't ~ to £10** je ne peux pas aller jusqu'à 10 livres; **to ~ in price** augmenter (de prix); *temperature, level* **to ~ above sth** dépasser qch; **her spirits rose** son moral a remonté; **to ~ in the world** réussir; **to ~ from nothing** partir de rien; *(Mil)* **to ~ from the ranks** sortir du rang; **he rose to be President/a captain** il s'est élevé jusqu'à devenir Président/jusqu'au grade de capitaine. **(c)** *(adjourn) [assembly]* clore la session; *[meeting]* lever la séance. *(Parl)* **the House rose** l'Assemblée a levé la séance. **(d)** *(start) [river]* prendre sa source (*in* dans). **(e)** *(rebel:* **~ up***)* se soulever (*against* contre).

◆ **rise up** *vi [person]* se lever; *V also* **rise 2 e**.

◆ **risen** ['rɪzn] *adj (Rel)* **the ~n Lord** le Christ ressuscité. ◆ **riser** *n*: **to be an early/a late ~r** (aimer) se lever tôt/tard. ◆ **rising** **1** *n (rebellion)* soulèvement *m* ; **2** *adj sun* levant; *prices, temperature* en hausse; *tide* montant; *wind* qui se lève; *tone* qui monte; *anger, fury* croissant; *ground* qui monte en pente; *(fig) generation* nouveau; **rising damp** humidité *f* (par capillarité); **rising young doctor** jeune médecin d'avenir; **she's rising six *** elle va sur ses six ans.

risk [rɪsk] **1** *n* risque *m*. **to take** *or* **run ~s** courir des risques; **to run the ~ of doing** courir le risque de faire; **it's not worth the ~** ça ne vaut pas la peine de courir un tel risque; **there is no ~ that he will come** il ne risque pas de venir; **at your own ~** à vos risques et périls; **at the ~ of seeming stupid** au risque de paraître stupide; **at the ~ of his life** au péril de sa vie; **at ~** *child* en danger; *job* menacé; **fire ~** risque d'incendie. **2** *vt life, future, savings* risquer; *battle, defeat, quarrel* s'exposer aux risques de; *accident* risquer d'avoir; *(venture) criticism, remark* risquer. **you ~ falling** vous risquez de tomber; **she won't ~ coming** elle ne se risquera pas à venir; **I'll ~ it** je vais risquer le coup *; **to ~ one's neck** risquer sa peau *. ◆ **riskiness** *n* risques *mpl*. ◆ **risky** *adj* risqué.

rissole ['rɪsəʊl] *n* rissole *f*.

rite [raɪt] *n (gen)* rite *m*. **last ~s** derniers sacrements *mpl*. ◆ **ritual** ['rɪtjʊəl] *adj, n* rituel *(m)*. ◆ **ritually** *adv* rituellement.

rival ['raɪv(ə)l] **1** *n* rival(e) *m(f)*. **2** *adj firm* rival; *attraction, claim* opposé. **3** *vt*: **to ~ sb in sth** *(gen)* rivaliser de qch avec qn; *(equal)* égaler qn en qch. ◆ **rivalry** *n* rivalité *f*.

river ['rɪvəʳ] **1** *n* rivière *f*; *(major)* fleuve *m (also fig)*. **down ~** en aval; **up ~** en amont; **the R~ Seine** la Seine. **2** *adj police, system, fishing* fluvial; *fish* de rivière. ◆ **riverbank** *n* rive *f*, berge *f*. ◆ **riverbed** *n* lit *m* de rivière *or* de fleuve. ◆ **riverside** **1** *n* bord *m* de la rivière *or* du fleuve; **by the ~ side** au bord de l'eau; **along the ~ side** le long de la rivière *etc* ; **2** *adj* au bord de la rivière.

rivet ['rɪvɪt] **1** *n* rivet *m*. **2** *vt* river. **3** *adj*: **~ joint** assemblage *m* par rivets. ◆ **riveter** *n (person)* riveur *m*; *(machine)* riveuse *f*. ◆ **rivet(t)ing** **1** *n* rivetage *m* ; **2** *adj* (*: *fig)* fascinant.

Riviera [ˌrɪvɪ'ɛərə] *n*: **the French ~** la Côte d'Azur; **the Italian ~** la Riviera (italienne).

Riyadh [rɪ'jad] *n* Riyad.

road [rəʊd] **1** *n (gen)* route *f*; *(minor)* chemin *m*; *(in town)* rue *f*; *(fig)* chemin, voie *f*. **trunk ~** grande route, nationale *f*; **country ~** petite route, route de campagne; **'~ up'** 'attention travaux'; **just across the ~** juste en face (*from* de; *from us* de chez nous); **my car is off the ~** ma voiture est *(laid up)* sur cales *or (being repaired)* en réparation; **this vehicle shouldn't be on the ~** on ne devrait pas laisser circuler un véhicule dans cet état; **he is a danger on the ~** au volant c'est un danger public; **to take the ~** se mettre en route; *[salesman, theatre company]* **to be on the ~** être en tournée; **we were on the ~ at 6 o'clock** nous étions sur la route à 6 heures; **we were on the ~ to Paris** nous étions en route pour Paris; **the ~ to London** la route de Londres; *(in towns)* **London R~** rue de Londres; *(fig)* **on the ~ to success** sur le chemin du succès; *(fig)* **somewhere along the ~** à un moment donné; **you're in my ~ *** vous m'empêchez de passer; **(get) out of the ~! *** dégagez!; **to have one for the ~ *** prendre un dernier verre avant de partir.

2 *adj bridge, map, safety, traffic* routier. **~ accident** accident *m* de la route; **~ book** guide *m* routier; **~ haulage** *or* **transport** transports *mpl* routiers; **~ haulier** entrepreneur *m* de transports routiers; *(Cycling)* **~ racer** routier *m*, -ière *f*; **~ racing** compétition *f* automobile (*or* cycliste) sur route; *[driver]* **~ sense** sens *m* de la conduite (sur route); *(Theat)* **~ show** spectacle *m* de tournée; **~ sign** panneau *m* indicateur; **international ~ signs** signalisation *f* routière internationale.

◆ **roadbed** *n (US) [railroad]* ballast *m; [road]* empierrement *m*. ◆ **roadblock** *n* barrage *m* routier. ◆ **roadhog** *n* chauffard *m*. ◆ **roadhouse** *n* relais *m*. ◆ **roadmaking** *n* construction *f* de route. ◆ **roadman** *or* ◆ **roadmender** *n* cantonnier *m*. ◆ **roadroller** *n* rouleau *m* compresseur. ◆ **roadside** **1** *n* bord *m* de la route; **along** *or* **by the ~ side** au bord de la route ; **2** *adj* au bord de la route. ◆ **roadsweeper** *n (person)* balayeur *m*, -euse *f*; *(vehicle)* balayeuse *f*. ◆ **road-test** **1** *n* essais *mpl* sur route ; **2** *vt*: **to ~-test a car** faire les essais sur route. ◆ **road-user** *n* usager *m* de la route. ◆ **roadway** *n* chaussée *f*. ◆ **roadworks** *npl* travaux *mpl* (d'entretien des routes); *(site)* chantier *m*. ◆ **roadworthy** *adj* en état de marche.

roam [rəʊm] **1** *vt streets etc (gen)* parcourir; *[child, dog]* traîner dans. **2** *vi* errer, rôder; *[thoughts]* vagabonder. ◆ **roaming** **1** *adj* errant, vagabond ; **2** *n* vagabondage *m*.

roan [rəʊn] *adj, n (horse)* rouan *(m)*.

roar [rɔːʳ] **1** *vi [person, crowd]* hurler (*with* de); *[lion]* rugir; *[bull, wind, sea]* mugir; *[thunder, gun, waterfall, vehicle]* gronder; *(Aut: rev)* vrombir; *[fire in hearth]* ronfler. **to ~ with laughter** rire à gorge déployée; **to ~ past** *[trucks]* passer bruyamment à toute allure; *[car]* passer en vrombissant. **2** *vt* (**~ out**) *order* vociférer; *song* chanter à tue-tête; *one's disapproval* hurler. **3** *n* hurlement(s) *m(pl)*; rugissement *m*; mugissement *m*; grondement *m*; vrombissement *m*; ronflement *m*. **~s of laughter** de gros éclats *mpl* de rire. ◆ **roaring** *adj* hurlant; rugissant; mugissant; grondant; vrombissant; ronflant; *(in hearth)* **a ~ing fire** une belle flambée; **~ing success** succès *m* fou; **to do a ~ing trade** faire des affaires d'or *.

roast [rəʊst] **1** *n* rôti *m.* **2** *adj (gen)* rôti. **~ beef** rôti *m* de bœuf. **3** *vt (gen)* rôtir; *coffee beans* torréfier. **4** *vi [meat]* rôtir. **I'm ~ing!** * je crève * de chaleur! ◆ **roasting 1** *n* rôtissage *m* ; **2** *adj* (**a**) *(*: hot) day* torride; (**b**) *chicken etc* à rôtir.

rob [rɒb] *vt person, shop* dévaliser; *orchard* piller. **to ~ sb of sth** *(purse etc)* voler *or* dérober qch à qn; *(rights etc)* priver qn de qch; **to ~ the till** voler de l'argent dans la caisse; **he's been ~bed of his watch** on lui a volé sa montre; **I've been ~bed!** j'ai été volé! ◆ **robber** *n* voleur *m.* ◆ **robbery** *n* vol *m*; **highway ~bery** *(lit)* vol de grand chemin; *(* fig)* vol manifeste.

robe [rəʊb] *n* (**a**) *(garment)* robe *f* (de cérémonie); *(for house wear)* peignoir *m.* **his ~ of office** la robe de sa charge. (**b**) *(US: rug)* couverture *f.*

robin ['rɒbɪn] *n (European)* rouge-gorge *m; (US)* merle *m* américain.

robot ['rəʊbɒt] **1** *n* robot *m.* **2** *adj* automatique. ◆ **robotics** *n* robotique *f.*

robust [rə(ʊ)'bʌst] *adj person, humour* robuste ; *defence* vigoureux; *material, appetite* solide. ◆ **robustness** *n* robustesse *f*; solidité *f.*

rock[1] [rɒk] **1** *vt* (**a**) *child* bercer; *cradle, rocking chair* balancer; *boat (gently)* balancer; *(roughly)* ballotter; *[explosion etc]* ébranler. (**b**) *(shake; also fig *: startle)* secouer. *(fig)* **to ~ the boat** * semer le trouble, compromettre la situation. **2** *vi (gently)* se balancer; *(violently)* être ébranlé. **to ~ with laughter** * se tordre de rire. **3** *n (music)* rock *m.* **4** *adj (Mus)* rock *inv.* ◆ **rock-and-roll** *n* rock (and roll) *m.* ◆ **rocker** *n* (**a**) *(chair)* fauteuil *m* à bascule; (**b**) **off one's ~er** ⁑ cinglé *. ◆ **rocking chair** *n* fauteuil *m* à bascule. ◆ **rocking horse** *n* cheval *m* à bascule. ◆ **rocky**[1] *adj table, government* branlant; *health, situation, finances* chancelant.

rock[2] [rɒk] **1** *n* (**a**) *(gen)* roche *f*; *(hard)* roc *m*; *(~ face)* rocher *m*; *(large mass, huge boulder)* rocher; *(smaller)* roche. **a huge ~ blocked their way** un énorme rocher leur bouchait le chemin; **a pile of fallen ~s** des éboulis *mpl* de roches; **the R~ of Gibraltar** le rocher de Gibraltar; *(fig)* **as solid as a ~** solide comme le roc; **the ship went on the ~s** le bateau est allé donner sur les écueils *mpl*; **on the ~ s** *drink* avec des glaçons; (*) *person* qui n'a pas le sou; (*) *marriage* en train de craquer *. (**b**) *(sweet)* **stick of ~** ≃ bâton *m* de sucre d'orge. **2** *adj*: **~ crystal** cristal *m* de roche; **~ face** paroi *f* rocheuse; **~ fall** chute *f* de rochers; **~ garden** rocaille *f*; **~ painting** peinture *f* rupestre; **~ plant** plante *f* de rocaille; **~ salmon** roussette *f*; **~ salt** sel *m* gemme. ◆ **rock-bottom** *n (fig)* **to have reached ~-bottom** * *[person]* ne pas pouvoir tomber plus bas; *(in spirits)* avoir le moral à zéro *; *[prices]* être tombé au niveau le plus bas. ◆ **rock-bun** *or* ◆ **rock-cake** *n* rocher *m (Culin).* ◆ **rock-climber** *n* varappeur *m*, -euse *f.* ◆ **rock-climbing** *n* varappe *f.* ◆ **rockery** *n* rocaille *f.* ◆ **rocky**[2] *adj hill* rocheux; *path* rocailleux; **the R~y Mountains** les montagnes *fpl* Rocheuses.

rocket ['rɒkɪt] **1** *n* fusée *f.* **to fire** *or* **send up a ~** lancer une fusée; *(fig)* **to give sb a ~** * passer un savon * à qn. **2** *vi [prices]* monter en flèche. **3** *adj*: **~ attack** attaque *f* à la roquette; **~ base, ~ range** base *f* de lancement de missiles; **~ launcher** lance-fusées *m inv.* ◆ **rocketry** *n (rockets collectively)* fusées *fpl.*

rod [rɒd] *n (wooden)* baguette *f*; *(metallic)* tringle *f*; *[machinery]* tige *f*; *(fishing ~)* canne *f* à pêche; *(symbol of authority)* verge *f.* **curtain/stair ~** tringle à rideaux/d'escalier; *(fig)* **to make a ~ for one's own back** se préparer des ennuis; **to rule with a ~ of iron** *country* gouverner d'une main de fer; *family* mener à la baguette.

rode [rəʊd] *pret of* **ride.**

rodent ['rəʊd(ə)nt] *adj, n* rongeur *(m).*

roe[1] [rəʊ] *n [fish]* **hard ~** œufs *mpl* (de poisson); **soft ~** laitance *f.*

roe[2]**(-deer)** ['rəʊ(dɪəʳ)] *n (species)* chevreuil *m*; *(female deer)* chevreuil *m* femelle. ◆ **roebuck** *n* chevreuil *m* mâle.

rogue [rəʊg] **1** *n (scoundrel)* gredin *m*; *(scamp)* coquin(e) *m(f). (Police)* **~s' gallery** photographies *fpl* de repris de justice. **2** *adj elephant* solitaire; *(US fig)* dévoyé. ◆ **roguish** *adj* espiègle, coquin. ◆ **roguishly** *adv speak* avec espièglerie; *look* d'un œil coquin.

role [rəʊl] *n* rôle *m.* **~ model** modèle *m* (à imiter).

roll [rəʊl] **1** *n* (**a**) *(gen)* rouleau *m*; *[banknotes]* liasse *f*; *[flesh, fat]* bourrelet *m.* (**b**) *(bread ~)* petit pain *m.* (**c**) *(movement) [ship]* roulis *m*; *(Aviat)* vol *m* en tonneau. (**d**) *[thunder, drums]* roulement *m*; *[organ]* ronflement *m.* (**e**) *(list)* liste *f*, tableau *m*; *(for court, ship's crew etc)* rôle *m.* **we have 60 pupils on our ~** nous avons 60 élèves inscrits; **to call the ~** faire l'appel; **~ of honour** *(Mil)* liste des combattants morts pour la patrie; *(Scol)* tableau d'honneur; *(Jur)* **to strike sb off the ~s** radier qn des listes. **2** *vi* (**a**) *[ball, ship, eyes]* rouler; *[horse, dog]* se rouler. **to ~ over and over** *[object]* rouler sur soi-même; *[person]* se rouler; **it ~ed under the table** ça a roulé sous la table; **to ~ down a slope** *(falling)* dégringoler une pente; *(playing)* rouler le long d'une pente; **tears were ~ing down her cheeks** les larmes roulaient sur ses joues; **the waves were ~ing on to the beach** les vagues déferlaient sur la plage; **the newspapers were ~ing off the presses** les journaux tombaient des rotatives; *(Aut)* **to ~ along** rouler; *(fig)* **to keep the ball** *or* **things ~ing** veiller à ce que tout marche bien; *(fig)* **he's ~ing in money** * il roule sur l'or; **they were ~ing in the aisles** * *(laughing)* ils se tordaient de rire. (**b**) *[thunder, drums, words]* rouler; *[voice]* retentir.

3 *vt ball* faire rouler; *umbrella, cigarette, lawn* rouler; *pastry, dough* étendre au rouleau; *metal* laminer; *road* cylindrer. **to ~ sth in/out** *etc* faire entrer/sortir *etc* qch en le roulant; **to ~ one's eyes** rouler les yeux; **to ~ one's r's** rouler les r; **to ~ string into a ball** enrouler de la ficelle en pelote.

◆ **roll about** *vi [coins, marbles]* rouler çà et là; *[ship]* rouler; *[person, dog]* se rouler par terre. ◆ **roll away** *vi [clouds, vehicle]* s'éloigner; *[ball]* rouler au loin. ◆ **roll back** *vt sep* (**a**) *carpet* rouler; *sheet* enlever (en roulant). *(fig)* **to ~ back the years** ramener le temps passé. (**b**) *(fig: bring back)* ramener. (**c**) *(US fig: reduce)* réduire. ◆ **roll by** *vi [vehicle, years]* passer. ◆ **roll in** *vi [letters, contributions]* affluer; (*) *[person]* arriver, s'amener *. ◆ **roll on** *vi [time]* s'écouler. **~ on Tuesday!** * vivement qu'on soit mardi! ◆ **roll out** *vt sep* (**a**) *sentence, verse* débiter. (**b**) *pastry* étendre au rouleau; *metal* laminer. ◆ **roll over 1** *vi [object]* rouler; *[person, animal] (once)* se retourner (sur soi-même); *(several, times)* se rouler. **2** *vt sep* retourner. ◆ **roll up 1** *vi* (**a**) *[animal]* se rouler (*into* en). (**b**) *(*: arrive)* arriver, s'amener *. *(fairground)* **~ up!** approchez! **2** *vt sep cloth, paper, map* rouler; *one's sleeves* retrousser.

◆ **roll bar** *n* arceau *m* de sécurité. ◆ **roll-call** *n* appel *m.* ◆ **rolled gold 1** *n* plaqué *m* or ; **2** *adj* plaqué or *inv.* ◆ **roller** *n* (**a**) *(gen)* rouleau *m*; *(Papermaking, Tex)* calandre *f*; *[decorator]* rouleau *m* (à peinture); *(in metallurgy)* laminoir *m*; *[blind]* enrouleur *m*; *(little wheel)* roulette *f*; **table on ~ers** table *f* à roulettes; **road ~er** rouleau compresseur; (**b**) *(wave)* lame *f* de houle. ◆ **roller-blind** *n* store *m.* ◆ **roller-coaster** *n* montagnes *fpl* russes. ◆ **roller-skate** **1** *n* patin *m* à roulettes ; **2** *vi* faire du patin à roulettes. ◆ **roller-skating** *n* patinage *m* à roulettes. ◆ **roller-towel** *n* essuie-mains *m* à rouleau. ◆ **rolling** *adj ship* qui roule; *sea* houleux; *countryside, ground* onduleux; *(fig)* **he's a ~ing stone** il a l'âme d'un nomade; **~ing pin** rouleau *m* (à pâtisserie); *(Rail)* **~ing stock** matériel *m* roulant. ◆ **roll-neck(ed)** *adj* à col roulé. ◆ **roll-top desk** *n* bureau *m* à cylindre.

rollicking ['rɒlɪkɪŋ] *adj* joyeux (et bruyant).

Roman ['rəʊmən] **1** *adj* romain. ~ **Catholic** *(adj, n)* catholique *(mf)*; *(Typ)* **r~ letters** caractères *mpl* romains; ~ **nose** nez *m* aquilin; ~ **numerals** chiffres *mpl* romains. **2** *n* Romain(e) *m(f)*.

romance [rə(ʊ)'mæns] **1** *n (tale of chivalry)* roman *m*; *(love story/film)* roman/film *m* à l'eau de rose; *(Mus)* romance *f*; *(love affair)* idylle *f*; *(attraction)* charme *m*. **it's quite a** ~ c'est un vrai roman; *(fig: lies)* **it's pure** ~ c'est du roman. **2** *adj (Ling)* **R~** roman. **3** *vi* enjoliver (à plaisir). ◆ **romantic** **1** *adj (gen)* romantique; *adventure, setting* romanesque ; **2** *n* romantique *mf*. ◆ **romantically** *adv write, describe* d'une façon romanesque; *sing, woo* en romantique. ◆ **romanticism** *n* romantisme *m*. ◆ **romanticize** *vti* romancer.

Romanesque [ˌrəʊmə'nesk] *adj* roman *(Archit)*.

Romania [rə(ʊ)'meɪnɪə] *n* Roumanie *f*. ◆ **Romanian** **1** *adj* roumain ; **2** *n (person)* Roumain(e) *m(f)*; *(language)* roumain *m*.

Rome [rəʊm] *n* Rome. **when in ~ do as the Romans do** à Rome il faut vivre comme les Romains; **the Church of** ~ l'Église *f* (catholique) romaine.

romp [rɒmp] **1** *n* jeux *mpl* bruyants. **2** *vi [children, puppies]* jouer bruyamment. **the horse ~ed home** le cheval est arrivé dans un fauteuil *; *(fig)* **to ~ through an exam** passer un examen haut la main. ◆ **rompers** *npl* barboteuse *f (pour enfant)*.

roof [ru:f] **1** *n (gen)* toit *m*; *[cave, tunnel]* plafond *m*. **the ~ of the mouth** la voûte du palais; **without a ~ over one's head** sans abri; **red-~ed** à toit rouge; **under her** ~ chez elle; **to live under the same ~ as sb** vivre sous le même toit que qn; *(fig)* **to go through the ~** * *[person]* piquer une crise *; *[price, claim]* devenir excessif; *(fig)* **to raise the** ~ faire un boucan terrible *. **2** *adj*: ~ **garden** jardin *m* sur le toit; ~ **light** plafonnier *m*; *(Aut)* ~ **rack** galerie *f*. **3** *vt*: **to ~ sth over** recouvrir qch d'un toit. ◆ **rooftop** *n* toit *m*.

rook¹ [rʊk] **1** *n (bird)* corneille *f*. **2** *vt* (⁑: *swindle)* rouler *. ◆ **rookery** *n* colonie *f* de corneilles.

rook² [rʊk] *n (Chess)* tour *f*.

rookie ⁑ ['rʊkɪ] *n (esp Mil)* bleu * *m*.

room [rʊm] **1** *n* (**a**) *(in house, building)* pièce *f*; *(large)* salle *f*; *(bed~)* chambre *f*; *(office, study)* bureau *m*. **~s to let** chambres à louer; ~ **and board** pension *f*; **his ~s** son appartement *m*; **they live in ~s** ils habitent un meublé; **a 6-~ed house** une maison de 6 pièces. (**b**) *(space)* place *f* (*for* pour). **is there ~?** y a-t-il de la place?; **there's no** ~ il n'y a pas de place; **to make ~ for sb/sth** faire une place pour qn/de la place pour qch; **there is ~ for improvement** cela laisse à désirer. **2** *vi* partager une chambre (*with* avec). **3** *adj*: ~ **divider** meuble *m* de séparation; **ring for ~ service** appelez le garçon d'étage; **wine at ~ temperature** vin *m* chambré. ◆ **roomful** *n* pleine salle *f*. ◆ **rooming-house** *n (US)* meublé *m (immeuble)*. ◆ **roommate** *n* camarade *mf* de chambre; *(US)* colocataire *mf*. ◆ **roomy** *adj flat, handbag* spacieux; *garment* ample.

roost [ru:st] **1** *n* juchoir *m*. **to rule the** ~ faire la loi. **2** *vi* jucher. *(fig)* **to come home to** ~ retomber sur son auteur. ◆ **rooster** *n* coq *m*.

root [ru:t] **1** *n (gen, Ling, Math)* racine *f*; *(fig: of trouble etc)* cause *f*. **to pull up by the ~s** déraciner; **to take** ~ prendre racine; **she has no ~s** c'est une déracinée; **to put down ~s in a country** s'enraciner dans un pays; *(fig)* ~ **and branch** radicalement; **that is at the ~ of...** c'est à l'origine de... **2** *adj*: *(US)* ~ **beer** *sorte de limonade à base d'extraits végétaux;* ~ **cause** cause *f* première; ~ **crops** racines *fpl* alimentaires; ~ **word** mot *m* racine *inv*. **3** *vt* enraciner. *(fig)* **~ed to the spot** cloué sur place. **4** *vi [plant etc]* s'enraciner.
◆ **root about, root around** *vi* fouiller (*for sth* pour trouver qch). ◆ **root for** *vt fus* (*: *esp US)* encourager. ◆ **root out** *vt sep (find)* dénicher; *(remove)* extirper.

rope [rəʊp] **1** *n* corde *f*; *(Naut)* cordage *m*; *[bell]* cordon *m*. *(fig)* **to give sb more** ~ lâcher la bride à qn; *(fig)* **to know/learn the ~s** * être/se mettre au courant; **to show sb the ~s** * mettre qn au courant; **a ~ of pearls** un collier de perles. **2** *adj*: ~ **ladder** échelle *f* de corde; **Indian ~ trick** tour *m* de la corde *(prestidigitation)*. **3** *vt case* corder; *climbers* encorder.
◆ **rope in** * *vt sep helper* enrôler, embringuer *. **to get ~d in for sth** se laisser embringuer * pour faire qch. ◆ **rope off** *vt sep part of area* réserver par une corde; *(block off)* interdire l'accès de. ◆ **rop(e)y** * *adj (bad)* pas fameux *.

rosary ['rəʊzərɪ] *n* chapelet *m*.

rose¹ [rəʊz] *pret of* **rise**.

rose² [rəʊz] **1** *n* (**a**) *(flower)* rose *f*; *(~***bush**, ~ **tree***)* rosier *m*. **wild** ~ églantine *f*; *(fig)* **my life isn't all ~s** * tout n'est pas rose dans ma vie. (**b**) *[watering can]* pomme *f*; *(on ceiling)* rosace *f* (de plafond). (**c**) *(colour)* rose *m*. **2** *adj (colour)* rose; *leaf, petal* de rose. ~ **garden** roseraie *f*; ~ **window** rosace *f*. ◆ **rosé** *n* rosé *m (vin)*. ◆ **rosebed** *n* massif *m* de rosiers. ◆ **rosebud** *n* bouton *m* de rose. ◆ **rose-coloured** *adj (fig)* **to see sth through ~-coloured spectacles** voir qch en rose. ◆ **rose-grower** *n* rosiériste *mf*. ◆ **rose-hip** *n* gratte-cul *m*. ◆ **rosemary** *n* romarin *m*. ◆ **rose-red** *adj* vermeil. ◆ **rosette** *n* rosette *f*; *(Sport: as prize)* cocarde *f*. ◆ **rosewood** *n* bois *m* de rose. ◆ **rosy** *adj* rose; *(fig) future, situation* qui se présente bien; **to paint a rosy picture of sth** dépeindre qch en rose.

rostrum ['rɒstrəm] *n* tribune *f*.

rot [rɒt] **1** *n* pourriture *f*; *(Bot, Med)* carie *f*; (**fig: nonsense)* bêtises *fpl*. *(fig)* **but the ~ set in** * mais les problèmes ont commencé; *(fig)* **to stop the** ~ redresser la situation; **that's a lot of** ~ * ça, c'est de la blague *. **2** *vi* pourrir. **to ~ away** tomber en pourriture. **3** *vt* (faire) pourrir.

rota ['rəʊtə] *n* tableau *m* (de service).

rotate [rə(ʊ)'teɪt] **1** *vt (revolve)* faire tourner ; *(change round) crops* alterner; *[two people] jobs* faire à tour de rôle. **2** *vi* tourner; être alterné. ◆ **rotary** *adj* rotatif. ◆ **rotating** *adj* tournant; alternant. ◆ **rotation** *n* rotation *f*; **in** *or* **by rotation** à tour de rôle. ◆ **rotor** *n* rotor *m*.

rotten ['rɒtn] *adj* (**a**) *(gen)* pourri; *tooth* gâté; *(fig: corrupt)* corrompu. ~ **to the core** complètement pourri. (**b**) (*: *bad)* mauvais. **to feel** ~ se sentir mal fichu *; **what ~ luck!** quelle poisse! *; **what a ~ trick!** quel sale tour! *

rotund [rə(ʊ)'tʌnd] *adj person* rondelet; *object* rond, arrondi.

rouble, *(US)* **ruble** ['ru:bl] *n* rouble *m*.

rouge [ru:ʒ] *n* rouge *m* (à joues).

rough [rʌf] **1** *adj* (**a**) *(uneven) ground* accidenté; *skin, cloth, surface* rugueux; *path, road* rocailleux. ~ **hands** *[peasant]* mains *fpl* rugueuses; *[housewife]* mains rêches. (**b**) *(fig) sound, voice* rude; *taste* âpre; *(coarse, unrefined) person, manners, life* rude; *(harsh etc) person, play, game* brutal; *neighbourhood, weather, sea crossing, tongue* mauvais; *waves, sea* gros. ~

handling of sth manque *m* de soin envers qch; ~ **stuff** * brutalité *f*; **these boys are very** ~ ces garçons sont très durs; **a ~ customer** * un dur *; **to have a ~ time (of it)** en voir de dures *; **to give sb a ~ time (of it)** malmener qn; *(fig)* en faire voir de toutes les couleurs à qn *; *(fig)* **to make things ~ for sb** * mener la vie dure à qn; **it is ~ on him** * ce n'est pas marrant * pour lui; **to feel ~** * *(ill)* être mal fichu *. (**c**) *(approximate) plan* ébauché; *calculation, translation* approximatif. ~ **copy,** ~ **draft,** ~ **work** brouillon *m*; ~ **sketch** ébauche *f*; ~ **paper** papier *m* de brouillon; ~ **justice** justice *f* sommaire; ~ **estimate** approximation *f*; **at a ~ estimate** *or* **guess** approximativement; **in its ~ state** à l'état brut; *(fig)* **he's a ~ diamond** sous ses dehors frustes c'est un brave garçon. **2** *adv live, sleep* à la dure; *play* brutalement. *(fig)* **to cut up ~** * *(angry)* se mettre en rogne *; *(violent)* devenir violent. **3** *n* (**a**) **to take the ~ with the smooth** prendre les choses comme elles viennent. (**b**) *(*: person)* voyou *m*, dur * *m*. **4** *vt*: **to ~ it** * vivre à la dure.
◆ **rough out** *vt sep plan etc* ébaucher.
◆ **roughage** *n* aliments *mpl* de lest *or* de volume.
◆ **rough-and-ready** *adj method, equipment* rudimentaire; *work* fait à la hâte; *person* sans façons.
◆ **rough-and-tumble** *n* mêlée *f*, bagarre *f*.
◆ **roughen** *vt* rendre rude *or* rugueux *or* rêche.
◆ **rough-house** * *n* bagarre *f*. ◆ **roughly** *adv* (**a**) *(not gently) push, play* brutalement; *answer, order* avec brusquerie; **to treat sth/sb ~ly** malmener qch/qn; (**b**) *(not finely) make, sew* grossièrement; **~ly made** grossier; **to sketch sth ~ly** faire un croquis de qch; (**c**) *(approximately)* en gros, à peu près; **~ly speaking** en gros; **she is ~ly 40** elle a à peu près 40 ans. ◆ **roughneck** * *n* voyou *m*, dur *m* à cuire *. ◆ **roughness** *n [hands, surface]* rugosité *f*; *[person]* rudesse *f*; brusquerie *f*; *(stronger)* brutalité *f*; *[sea]* agitation *f*; *[road]* inégalités *fpl*. ◆ **roughshod** *adv*: **to ride ~shod over** *person* passer sur le corps de; *objection* passer outre à.
◆ **rough-spoken** *adj* au langage grossier.

roulette [ruːˈlet] *n* roulette *f (jeu)*.

Roumania [ruːˈmeɪnɪə] *n* = **Rumania.**

round [raʊnd] **1** *adv*: **right ~ , all ~** tout autour; **he went ~ by the bridge** il a fait le détour par le pont; **the long way ~** le chemin le plus long; **it's a long way ~** ça fait un grand détour; **come ~ and see me** venez me voir; **I asked him ~ for a drink** je l'ai invité à passer prendre un verre (chez moi); **I'll be ~ at 8 o'clock** je serai là à 8 heures; **all the year ~** pendant toute l'année; **drinks all ~!** * je paie une tournée! *; *(fig)* **taking things all ~** tout compte fait; ~ **about** *V* **2 b** *below*.
2 *prep* (**a**) *(of place etc)* autour de. ~ **the table/house** *etc* autour de la table/maison *etc*; **sitting ~ the fire** assis au coin du feu; **the villages ~ Lewes** les villages des environs de Lewes; **if you're ~ this way** si tu passes par ici; *(Aut)* **to go ~ a corner** prendre un virage; **to go ~ an obstacle** contourner un obstacle; **to look ~ a house** visiter une maison; **to show sb ~ a town** faire visiter une ville à qn; **they went ~ the cafés looking for...** ils ont fait le tour des cafés à la recherche de...; **put a blanket ~ him** enveloppez-le d'une couverture. (**b**) *(approximately: also ~* **about***)* environ.
3 *adj* rond. **to have ~ shoulders** avoir le dos rond; *(fig)* **a ~ dozen** une douzaine tout rond; **in ~ figures** en chiffres ronds; ~ **robin** pétition *f*; **the ~ trip** le voyage aller et retour; *(US)* ~ **trip ticket** billet *m* aller retour.
4 *n* (**a**) *(circle etc)* rond *m*, cercle *m*; *(slice: of bread, meat)* tranche *f*. (**b**) **to do** *or* **make one's ~(s)** *[watchman, policeman]* faire sa ronde; *[postman, milkman]* faire sa tournée; *[doctor]* faire ses visites; **he has got a paper ~** il distribue des journaux; *[infection, a cold etc]* **to go the ~s** faire des ravages; **the story is going the ~s that...** le bruit court que...; *(fig)* **the daily ~** la routine quotidienne; **one long ~ of pleasures** une longue suite de plaisirs. (**c**) *[cards, golf]* partie *f*; *(Boxing)* round *m*; *(Horse-riding)* parcours *m*; *[competition, tournament]* manche *f*; *[election]* tour *m*; *[talks, discussions]* série *f*. **a ~ of drinks** une tournée *; ~ **of ammunition** cartouche *f*; **a ~ of applause** une salve d'applaudissements. (**d**) *(Mus)* canon *m*. (**e**) **in the ~** *(Theat)* en rond; *(fig)* en détail.
5 *vt* (**a**) *(make ~) edges etc* arrondir. (**b**) *(go ~) corner* tourner; *bend* prendre; *(Naut) cape* doubler; *obstacle* contourner. (**c**) *(Math etc) figure* arrondir.
◆ **round off** *vt sep speech, list, series, meal* terminer; *sentence* parachever; *meeting* mettre fin à. ◆ **round up** *vt sep* (**a**) *(bring together) people, cattle* rassembler; *criminals* effectuer une rafle de. (**b**) *prices etc* arrondir (au chiffre supérieur). ◆ **round (up)on** *vt fus* attaquer.
◆ **roundabout 1** *adj route* détourné; *means* contourné; **~about phrase** circonlocution *f* ; **2** *n (Brit: merry-go-~)* manège *m (de fête foraine)*; *(at road junction)* rond-point *m* (à sens giratoire).
◆ **rounded** *adj (gen)* arrondi; *sentences* élégant.
◆ **rounders** *n (Brit) sorte de baseball.* ◆ **round-eyed** *adj* aux yeux ronds. ◆ **round-faced** *adj* au visage rond. ◆ **roundly** *adv say, tell* carrément.
◆ **round-necked** *adj pullover* ras du cou *inv*.
◆ **roundness** *n* rondeur *f*. ◆ **round-shouldered** *adj* voûté. ◆ **roundsman,** *pl* **roundsmen** *(Brit)* livreur *m*; **milk ~sman** laitier *m*. ◆ **round-up** *n [cattle, people]* rassemblement *m*; *[criminals, suspects]* rafle *f*.

rouse [raʊz] *vt (gen)* éveiller; *(fig) admiration, interest* susciter; *indignation* soulever; *suspicions* éveiller. **to ~ sb to action** pousser qn à agir; **to ~ sb (to anger)** mettre qn en colère. ◆ **rousing** *adj speech, sermon* vibrant; *cheers, applause* frénétique; *music* entraînant.

rout[1] [raʊt] **1** *n (defeat)* déroute *f*. **2** *vt* mettre en déroute.

rout[2] [raʊt] *vi (search: ~* **about***)* fouiller. ◆ **rout out** *vt sep (find)* dénicher; *(force out)* déloger; *(from bed)* tirer.

route [ruːt] **1** *n* (**a**) *(gen, also of train, plane, ship etc)* itinéraire *m*. **shipping/air ~s** routes *fpl* maritimes/aériennes; **we're on a bus ~** nous sommes sur une ligne d'autobus; **a good ~ to London** un bon itinéraire pour aller à Londres; **en ~** en route *(for* pour). (**b**) *(US: often* [raʊt]: *round)* tournée *f*. **2** *adj (Mil)* ~ **march** marche *f* d'entraînement. **3** *vt train etc* faire passer *(through* par); *luggage etc* expédier *(through* par).

routine [ruːˈtiːn] **1** *n* (**a**) routine *f*. **daily ~** train-train *m* de la vie quotidienne; **office ~** travail *m* courant du bureau; **as a matter of ~** automatiquement. (**b**) *(Theat)* numéro *m*. **dance ~** numéro de danse. **2** *adj procedure, inquiry* d'usage; *work etc* habituel; *(pej)* de routine. **it was quite ~** ça n'avait rien de spécial.

roving [ˈrəʊvɪŋ] *adj* vagabond. **he has a ~ eye** il aime reluquer * les filles; ~ **ambassador** ambassadeur *m* itinérant; ~ **reporter** reporter *m* volant.

row[1] [rəʊ] *n [objects, people]* rang *m*; *(behind one another)* file *f*, ligne *f*; *[houses, trees, figures]* rangée *f*; *[cars]* file; *(Knitting)* rang. **in the front ~** au premier rang; **sitting in a ~** assis en rang; **4 failures in a ~** 4 échecs de suite.

row[2] [rəʊ] **1** *vt boat* faire aller à la rame *or* à l'aviron. **to ~ sb across** faire traverser qn en canot. **2** *vi* ramer. **to ~ away/back** s'éloigner/revenir à la rame; **to go ~ing** *(for pleasure)* faire du canotage; *(Sport)* faire de l'aviron. ◆ **rowboat** *or* ◆ **rowing boat** *n* canot *m* (à rames). ◆ **rower** *n* rameur *m*, -euse *f*. ◆ **rowing 1** *n* canotage *m*; *(Sport)* aviron *m*; **2** *adj*: **~ing club** club *m* d'aviron.
◆ **rowlock** [ˈrɒlək] *n* dame *f* de nage.

row³ * [raʊ] **1** *n (noise)* tapage *m*, vacarme *m*; *(quarrel)* querelle *f*, dispute *f*; *(scolding)* réprimande *f*, savon * *m*. **to make a** ~ faire du tapage; **to have a** ~ se disputer (*with* avec); **to give sb a** ~ passer un savon à qn *; **to get (into) a** ~ se faire passer un savon *. **2** *vi* se disputer (*with* avec).

rowan ['raʊən] *n* sorbier *m*.

rowdy ['raʊdɪ] **1** *adj (noisy)* chahuteur; *(rough)* bagarreur *. **2** *n* (*) voyou *m*. ◆ **rowdyism** *n* chahut *m*; bagarre * *f*; *(at football match etc)* violence *f*.

royal ['rɔɪ(ə)l] **1** *adj (gen)* royal. ~ **blue** bleu roi *inv*; *(Brit)* **R**~ **Commission** Commission *f* extraparlementaire; **the** ~ **household** la maison du roi *or* de la reine; *(fig)* **the** ~ **road to** la voie royale de; **they gave him a** ~ **welcome** ils l'ont reçu de façon royale. **2** *n*: **the** ~**s** * la famille royale. ◆ **royalist** *adj, n* royaliste *(mf)*. ◆ **royally** *adv* royalement. ◆ **royalty** *n* (**a**) *(persons)* (membres *mpl* de) la famille royale; (**b**) ~**ties** *(from book)* droits *mpl* d'auteur; *(from oil well, patent)* royalties *fpl*.

rub [rʌb] **1** *n*: **to give sth a** ~ *(furniture, shoes, silver)* donner un coup de chiffon à qch; *(sore place, one's arms)* frotter qch; *(fig)* **there's the** ~! c'est là la difficulté! **2** *vt* frotter; *(Art) brass, inscription* prendre un frottis de. **to** ~ **one's nose** se frotter le nez; **to** ~ **one's hands together** se frotter les mains; **to** ~ **sth dry** sécher qch en le frottant; **to** ~ **a hole in sth** faire un trou dans qch à force de frotter; **to** ~ **sth through a sieve** passer qch au tamis; **to** ~ **lotion into the skin** faire pénétrer de la lotion dans la peau; *(fig)* **to** ~ **shoulders with** coudoyer; *(fig)* **to** ~ **sb's nose in sth** ne jamais laisser oublier qch à qn. **3** *vi [thing]* frotter (*against* contre); *[person, cat]* se frotter (*against* contre). ◆ **rub along** * *vi [two people]* s'accorder tant bien que mal. ◆ **rub away** *vt sep* faire disparaître (en frottant), effacer. ◆ **rub down** *vt sep horse* bouchonner; *person* frictionner (*with* avec); *wall, paintwork (clean)* nettoyer (du haut en bas); *(sandpaper)* poncer. ◆ **rub in** *vt sep liniment* faire pénétrer en frottant; *(fig) idea* insister sur; *lesson* faire entrer (*to* à). *(fig)* **don't** ~ **it in!** * pas besoin de me le rappeler! ◆ **rub off 1** *vi*: **the blue will** ~ **off on to your hands** tu vas avoir les mains toutes bleues; *(fig)* **it might** ~ **off on to her brother** * elle en passera peut-être à son frère. **2** *vt sep writing* effacer; *dirt* enlever en frottant. ◆ **rub out 1** *vi* s'effacer. **2** *vt sep* effacer. ◆ **rub up 1** *vi (fig)* **to** ~ **up against all sorts of people** côtoyer toutes sortes de gens. **2** *vt sep vase, table* frotter, astiquer. *(fig)* **to** ~ **sb up the right/wrong way** savoir/ne pas savoir s'y prendre avec qn.
◆ **rubbing** *n* frottement *m*; *(Art)* frottis *m; (US)* ~**bing alcohol** alcool *m* à 90 degrés.

rubber¹ ['rʌbəʳ] **1** *n (material)* caoutchouc *m*; *(eraser)* gomme *f*. *(shoes)* ~**s** caoutchoucs. **2** *adj goods, boots etc* de *or* en caoutchouc. ~ **band** élastique *m*; ~ **bullet** balle *f* en caoutchouc; *(US fig)* ~ **check** * chèque *m* en bois; ~ **plant** caoutchouc *m* *(plante verte)*; ~ **plantation** plantation *f* d'hévéas; ~ **ring** *(for swimming)* bouée *f* de natation; ~ **solution** dissolution *f*; ~ **stamp** tampon *m*; ~**tree** hévéa *m*. ◆ **rubberized** *adj* caoutchouté. ◆ **rubber-stamp** *vt (pej)* entériner (sans discuter). ◆ **rubbery** *adj* caoutchouteux.

rubber² ['rʌbəʳ] *n (Bridge)* robre *m*.

rubbish ['rʌbɪʃ] **1** *n (waste material)* détritus *mpl*; *(household* ~*)* ordures *fpl*, immondices *fpl*; *[garden]* détritus; *[factory]* déchets *mpl*; *[building site]* décombres *mpl*; *(nonsense)* bêtises *fpl*, absurdités *fpl*. **this shop sells a lot of** ~ ce magasin ne vend que de la camelote *; **it's just** ~ *(nonsense)* ça ne veut rien dire; **to talk** ~ débiter des bêtises *or* des absurdités; ~! * quelle blague! *; **it is** ~ **to say that...** c'est idiot de dire que... **2** *adj (Brit)* ~ **bin** poubelle *f*, boîte *f* à ordures; ~ **cart** voiture *f* d'éboueurs; ~ **collection** ramassage *m* d'ordures; ~ **dump** décharge *f* publique. **3** *vt (fig *: denigrate)* débiner *. ◆ **rubbishy** *adj goods, ideas, book* sans valeur; *shoes etc* de mauvaise qualité.

rubble ['rʌbl] *n (ruins)* décombres *mpl*; *(in road-building)* blocaille *f*. **it was reduced to a heap of** ~ il n'en restait qu'un tas de décombres.

rubicund ['ru:bɪkənd] *adj* rougeaud.

ruby ['ru:bɪ] **1** *n* rubis *m*. **2** *adj (colour)* rubis *inv*; *(made of rubies) necklace, ring* de rubis.

rucksack ['rʌksæk] *n* sac *m* à dos.

ructions * ['rʌkʃ(ə)nz] *npl (rows)* disputes *fpl*, grabuge * *m*; *(riots)* bagarres *fpl*. **there'll be** ~ **if...** il va y avoir du grabuge * si...

rudder ['rʌdəʳ] *n* gouvernail *m*.

ruddy ['rʌdɪ] *adj* (**a**) *complexion (gen)* rubicond *(pej)*, coloré; *(glowing)* rouge de santé; *sky, glow* rougeoyant. (**b**) *(* Brit)* fichu *, sacré * *(before n)*.

rude [ru:d] *adj* (**a**) *(impolite)* impoli, mal élevé; *(stronger)* insolent; *(coarse)* grossier; *(improper)* indécent. **to be** ~ **to sb** être grossier envers qn; **it's** ~ **to stare** c'est très mal élevé de dévisager les gens; ~ **word** gros mot *m*. (**b**) *shock* brusque, rude. *(fig)* **to have a** ~ **awakening** être rappelé brusquement à la réalité. (**c**) *(primitive)* primitif. (**d**) *(vigorous) health* robuste. ◆ **rudely** *adv* impoliment; insolemment; grossièrement; brusque ment. ◆ **rudeness** *n* impolitesse *f*; insolence *f*; grossièreté *f*; brusquerie *f*.

rudiment ['ru:dɪmənt] *n* rudiment *m*. ◆ **rudimentary** *adj* rudimentaire.

rueful ['ru:fʊl] *adj look, person* triste; *situation* attristant. ◆ **ruefully** *adv* avec regret.

ruffian ['rʌfɪən] *n* voyou *m*, brute *f*.

ruffle ['rʌfl] *vt hair, feathers* ébouriffer; *surface, water* agiter; *clothes* déranger, froisser; *person (upset)* froisser; *(annoy)* contrarier. **to grow** ~**d** perdre son calme.

rug [rʌg] *n* petit tapis *m*; *(bedside etc)* carpette *f*; *(travelling* ~*)* couverture *f*; *(in tartan)* plaid *m*.

rugby ['rʌgbɪ] **1** *n (abbr* **rugger** **)* rugby *m*. **2** *adj*: ~ **league** le rugby à treize; ~ **player** rugbyman *m*.

rugged ['rʌgɪd] *adj country, ground, road* accidenté; *cliff, coast, mountains* aux contours déchiquetés; *bark* rugueux; *features* irrégulier; *character, person* bourru; *resolve* farouche; *(*: solid) machine* robuste.

ruin ['ru:ɪn] **1** *n* ruine *f*. **to fall into** ~ tomber en ruine; **in** ~**s** en ruine. **2** *vt (gen)* ruiner; *clothes* abîmer; *event, enjoyment* gâter. ◆ **ruined** *adj building* en ruine; *person* ruiné. ◆ **ruinous** *adj* ruineux. ◆ **ruinously** *adv*: ~**ously expensive** ruineux.

rule [ru:l] **1** *n* (**a**) *(gen)* règle *f*; *(regulation)* règlement *m*. **the** ~**s of the game** la règle du jeu; **against the** ~**s** contraire à la règle *or* au règlement; ~**s and regulations** statuts *mpl*; *(Ind)* **work(ing) to** ~ grève *f* du zèle; **it's a** ~ **that...** il est de règle que... + *subj*; ~ **of the road** règle générale de la circulation; **by** ~ **of thumb** à vue de nez; **golden** ~ règle d'or; *(fig: usual)* **it's the** ~ c'est normal; **he makes it a** ~ **to get up early** il a pour règle de se lever tôt; **as a** ~ en règle générale, normalement. (**b**) *(authority)* **under British** ~ sous l'autorité *f* britannique; *(Pol etc)* **majority** ~ le gouvernement par la majorité; **the** ~ **of law** l'autorité de la loi. (**c**) *(for measuring)* règle *f* (graduée). **folding** ~ mètre *m* pliant.
2 *adj*: ~ **book** règlement *m*.
3 *vt* (**a**) *country* gouverner; *business firm etc* diriger. ~**d by his wife** mené par sa femme. (**b**) *[umpire, judge]* décider, déclarer (*that* que). (**c**) *(draw lines on) paper* régler; *line* tirer à la règle.

4 *vi* (**a**) *[monarch]* régner (*over* sur). *(fig)* **the prices ruling in Paris** les cours pratiqués à Paris. (**b**) *(Jur)* statuer (*against* contre; *in favour of* en faveur de; *on* sur).

◆ **rule out** *vt sep* exclure, écarter. **the age limit ~s him out** il est exclu du fait de la limite d'âge; **murder can't be ~d out** il est impossible d'exclure l'hypothèse d'un meurtre.

◆ **ruler** *n* (**a**) *(sovereign)* souverain(e) *m(f)*; *(political leader)* chef *m* (d'État); **the country's ~rs** les dirigeants *mpl* du pays; (**b**) *(for measuring)* règle *f*.

◆ **ruling** **1** *adj principle* souverain; *factor, passion* dominant; *price* actuel; **the ruling class** la classe dirigeante; *(Pol)* **the ruling party** le parti au pouvoir ; **2** *n (Admin, Jur)* décision *f*; **to get/give a ruling** obtenir/rendre un jugement.

rum [rʌm] *n* rhum *m*.

Rumania [ruːˈmeɪnɪə] *n* = **Romania.**

rumble [ˈrʌmbl] **1** *vi (gen)* gronder; *[stomach, pipes]* gargouiller. *[vehicle]* **to ~ past** passer avec fracas. **2** *n* grondement *m*; gargouillement *m*. ◆ **rumbling** *n* grondement *m*; gargouillement *m*; **tummy rumblings** * borborygmes *mpl*.

ruminate [ˈruːmɪneɪt] *vti* ruminer. ◆ **ruminant** *adj, n* ruminant *(m)*. ◆ **ruminative** *adj* pensif.

rummage [ˈrʌmɪdʒ] **1** *vi* (**~ about, ~ around**) fouiller (*among, in* dans; *for* pour trouver). **2** *adj*: **~ sale** vente *f* de charité *(de bric-à-brac)*.

rumour, *(US)* **rumor** [ˈruːməʳ] **1** *n* rumeur *f*, bruit *m*. **~ has it that there will be war, there is a ~ of war** le bruit court *or* on dit qu'il va y avoir la guerre. **2** *vt*: **it is ~ed that...** on dit que..., le bruit court que...

rump [rʌmp] *n [animal]* croupe *f*; *(Culin)* culotte *f* (de bœuf); *[person]* derrière *m*. ◆ **rumpsteak** *n* culotte *f* (de bœuf); *(single steak)* romsteck *m*.

rumple [ˈrʌmpl] *vt (gen)* chiffonner; *hair* ébouriffer.

rumpus * [ˈrʌmpəs] **1** *n* chahut *m*. **to make a ~** faire du chahut. **2** *adj*: **~ room** salle *f* de jeux.

run [rʌn] *(vb: pret* **ran,** *ptp* **run***)* **1** *n* (**a**) **to go for a ~** faire un peu de course à pied; **to go for a 2-km ~** faire 2 km de course à pied; **at a ~** au pas de course, en courant; **to break into a ~** se mettre à courir; **to make a ~ for it** prendre la fuite; **to have the ~ of a place** avoir un endroit à son entière disposition; **to be on the ~** être en cavale *; **to be on the ~ from the police** être recherché par la police; **to have the enemy on the ~** avoir mis l'ennemi en fuite; **to keep the enemy on the ~** harceler l'ennemi; **we've given him** *(etc)* **a good ~ for his money** on ne s'est pas avoué vaincu d'avance; *(on retirement, death)* **he's had a good ~** il a bien profité de l'existence.
(**b**) *(outing)* tour *m*, excursion *f*. **to go for a ~ in the car** faire un tour *or* une promenade en voiture; **I'll give you a ~ up to town** je vais vous conduire en ville. (**c**) *[bus, tram, boat, plane] (distance)* trajet *m*; *(route)* parcours *m*. **it's a 30-minute bus ~** il y a une demi-heure de trajet en autobus; **the boat no longer does that ~** le bateau ne fait plus cette traversée; **the ships on the China ~** les paquebots qui font la Chine. (**d**) *(series)* série *f*, suite *f*; *(Cards)* séquence *f*; *(Roulette)* série *f* (*on* à). *(Theat)* **the London ~** la saison à Londres; *(Theat)* **the play had a long ~** la pièce a tenu longtemps l'affiche; *(gen)* **it's had a long ~** ça a duré longtemps; **in the long ~** finalement; **to have a ~ of luck** être en veine *; **a ~ of bad luck** une période de malchance. (**e**) *(great demand)* ruée *f* (*on* sur). **there has been a ~ on** on s'est rué sur. (**f**) *[tide]* flux *m*; *(fig: trend)* tendance *f*. **the common ~ of mankind** le commun des mortels; **the ordinary ~ of things** le train-train habituel. (**g**) *(track for sledging, skiing etc)* piste *f*; *(animal enclosure)* enclos *m*. (**h**) *(Typ)* **a ~ of 5,000 copies** un tirage de 5 000 exemplaires. (**i**) *(Cricket, Baseball)* point *m*.

2 *vi* (**a**) courir. **to ~ in/off** *etc* entrer/partir *etc* en courant; **she came ~ning out** elle est sortie en courant; **to ~ for the bus** courir pour attraper l'autobus; **she ran to meet him/to help him** elle a couru à sa rencontre/à son secours; **the car ran into a tree** la voiture a heurté un arbre; *(fig)* **the news ran like wildfire** la nouvelle s'est répandue comme une traînée de poudre; **a ripple of fear ran through the town** la peur a gagné toute la ville; **how does the last sentence ~?** comment la dernière phrase est-elle rédigée?; **so the story ~s** c'est ainsi que l'histoire est racontée; *(Pol etc)* **to ~ for President, to ~ for the Presidency** être candidat à la présidence.
(**b**) *(flee)* fuir, se sauver. **to ~ for one's life** se sauver à toutes jambes; **~ for it!** sauvez-vous!
(**c**) *(become etc) [river]* **to ~ dry** se tarir; **my pen's ~ dry** je n'ai plus d'encre; *[resources etc]* **to ~ dry** *or* **short** *or* **low** s'épuiser; **to ~ short of sth** se trouver à court de qch; **to ~ riot** *[people, imagination]* être déchaîné; *[vegetation]* pousser follement; **to ~ wild** *[person, children]* être déchaîné; *[animals]* courir en liberté; *[plants, garden]* retourner à l'état sauvage.
(**d**) *(move)* filer; *[drawer, curtains]* glisser; *(flow)* couler; *[river, tears, tap, eyes, nose]* couler; *[pen]* fuir; *[sore, abscess]* suppurer; *(melt)* fondre; *[cheese]* couler; *[colour, ink]* baver; *(in washing)* déteindre. **the rope ran through his fingers** la corde lui a filé entre les doigts; **rivers ~ into the sea** les fleuves se jettent dans la mer; **the street ~s into the square** la rue débouche sur la place; **to ~ high** *[river]* être haut; *[sea]* être gros; *[feelings]* être exacerbé; *[prices]* être très haut; **to leave a tap ~ning** laisser un robinet ouvert; **to ~ with blood/sweat/moisture** ruisseler, de sang/de sueur/d'humidité; *(fig)* **his blood ran cold** son sang s'est glacé dans ses veines.
(**e**) *(continue) [play]* tenir l'affiche, se jouer; *[film]* passer; *[contract]* être valide. *(Rad, TV)* **the programme ran for 50 minutes** le programme a duré 50 minutes; **the expenditure ~s into millions** les dépenses s'élèvent à des millions; **I can't ~ to a new car** je ne peux pas me payer * une nouvelle voiture; **the funds won't ~ to...** les fonds ne permettent pas d'acheter...
(**f**) *(Naut)* **to ~ before the wind** courir vent arrière; **to ~ ashore** *or* **aground** s'échouer; *(fig)* **to ~ foul of sb** indisposer qn contre soi.
(**g**) **this train ~s between** ce train fait le service entre; **the buses ~ once an hour** les autobus passent toutes les heures.
(**h**) *(function) [machine, factory]* marcher; *[wheel]* tourner. **the car is ~ning smoothly** la voiture marche bien; **to leave the engine ~ning** laisser tourner le moteur; **to ~ on diesel/on electricity/off batteries** marcher au gas-oil/à l'électricité/sur piles.
(**i**) *(pass) [road, river etc]* passer (*through* à travers; *past* devant); *[mountain range]* s'étendre. **the road ~s north and south** la route va du nord au sud; **he has a scar ~ning across his chest** il a une cicatrice en travers de la poitrine; *(fig)* **this theme ~s through** ce thème se retrouve dans; **it ~s in the family** c'est de famille.
(**j**) *[stockings]* filer; *[knitting]* se démailler.

3 *vt* (**a**) courir. **he ~s 3 km every day** il fait 3 km de course à pied tous les jours; **to ~ a race** courir dans une épreuve; **to ~ errands** faire des commissions; **to ~ a blockade** forcer un blocus; *(US)* **to ~ a stoplight** griller un feu rouge; *(fig)* **to ~ sb close** serrer qn de près; **you're ~ning things a bit close!** * ça va être juste!; **to ~ its course** suivre son cours; **to ~ a temperature** avoir de la fièvre; **to ~ the car into a tree** heurter un arbre.
(**b**) **to ~ to earth** finir par trouver; **to ~ a horse in the Derby** faire courir un cheval dans le Derby;

to ~ sb out of town chasser qn de la ville; **she is ~ off her feet** * elle ne sait plus où donner de la tête.

(**c**) *(transport) person* conduire; *thing* transporter; *(smuggle) guns* passer en contrebande. **he ran her home** il l'a ramenée chez elle (en voiture).

(**d**) *(operate etc) machine* faire marcher; *(Comput) program* exécuter. **he ~s a Rolls** il a une Rolls; **this car is very cheap to ~** cette voiture est très économique; **to ~ into the ground** *car* garder jusqu'à ce qu'elle soit bonne pour la ferraille; *business* laisser péricliter.

(**e**) *(organize etc) business, school, mine, hotel* diriger; *course, competition* organiser. **they ~ trains to London every hour** il y a un train pour Londres toutes les heures; **to ~ extra buses** mettre en service des autobus supplémentaires; **to ~ a house** tenir une maison; **I want to ~ my own life** je veux être maître de ma vie; **she ~s everything** c'est elle qui dirige tout; *(fig)* **I'm ~ning this show!** * c'est moi qui commande ici!

(**f**) *(move) hand, fingers, comb* passer (*over* sur; *through* dans). **to ~ one's finger down a list** suivre une liste du doigt; **to ~ one's eye over** jeter un coup d'œil sur; **he ran the vacuum cleaner over the carpet** il a passé rapidement le tapis à l'aspirateur; **she ran her pencil through the word** elle a barré le mot d'un coup de crayon; **to ~ a rope through** faire passer une corde dans; **to ~ water into a bath** faire couler de l'eau dans une baignoire; **I'll ~ you a bath** je vais te faire couler un bain.

(**g**) *(issue) article* publier; *film* présenter.

◆ **run about, run around** *vi* courir çà et là. ◆ **run across 1** *vi* traverser en courant. **2** *vt fus (meet, find) person, thing, fact* tomber sur. ◆ **run along** *vi* courir; *(go away)* s'en aller. ◆ **run away 1** *vi* (**a**) partir en courant; *(flee) [person]* s'enfuir; *[horse]* s'emballer. **to ~ away from home** s'enfuir (de chez soi); *(fig)* **don't ~ away with the idea that...** n'allez pas vous mettre dans la tête que... (**b**) *[water]* s'écouler. **2** *vt sep water* laisser s'écouler. ◆ **run away with** *vt fus money etc* épuiser. ◆ **run down 1** *vi [watch etc]* s'arrêter; *[battery]* se décharger. **2** *vt sep* (**a**) *(Aut) (knock over)* renverser; *(run over)* écraser; *ship* heurter par l'avant; *(in battle)* éperonner. (**b**) *(reduce) production* restreindre de plus en plus; *factory* restreindre la production de; *shop* réduire peu à peu l'ampleur de. *(Med)* **to be ~ down** être fatigué. (**c**) *(*: disparage)* dénigrer. ◆ **run in** *vt sep* (**a**) *car* roder. '**~ning in**' 'en rodage'. (**b**) *(*: arrest)* emmener au poste. ◆ **run into** *vt fus (meet) person* rencontrer par hasard, tomber sur; *difficulties, trouble* se heurter à; *danger* se trouver exposé à. **to ~ into debt** s'endetter. ◆ **run off 1** *vi* = **run away 1 a. 2** *vt sep (Typ)* tirer. ◆ **run on 1** *vi* (**a**) *(* fig: in talking etc)* parler sans arrêt. **it ran on for 4 hours** ça a duré 4 bonnes heures. (**b**) *(Typ)* suivre sans alinéa. **2** *vt sep letters, words* faire suivre sans laisser d'espace. ◆ **run out 1** *vi* (**a**) *[rope, chain]* se dérouler; *[liquid]* couler. (**b**) *(end) [lease, contract]* expirer; *[supplies]* s'épuiser; *[period of time]* s'écouler. **when the money ~s out** quand il n'y aura plus d'argent. **2** *vt sep rope, chain* laisser filer. ◆ **run out of** *vt fus money, time* manquer de. ◆ **run over 1** *vi* (**a**) *(overflow)* déborder. (**b**) *(go briefly)* passer, faire un saut (*to sb's house* chez qn). **2** *vt fus (reread)* revoir; *(recapitulate)* reprendre. **3** *vt sep (Aut)* écraser. ◆ **run through 1** *vt fus* (**a**) *(use up) fortune* gaspiller. (**b**) *(read quickly) notes, text* jeter un coup d'œil sur. (**c**) *(rehearse) play* répéter; *(recapitulate)* reprendre. **let's ~ through it again** reprenons cela encore une fois. **2** *vt sep (Comput) data* passer (en revue). ◆ **run up** *vt sep* (**a**) *flag* hisser. (**b**) *bill* laisser accumuler. (**c**) *(*: sew quickly)* fabriquer *. ◆ **run up against** * *vt fus person* tomber sur; *difficulties* se heurter à.

◆ **runabout 1** *n (car)* petite voiture *f*; *(boat)* runabout *m* ; **2** *adj (Rail)* **~about ticket** billet *m* circulaire. ◆ **runaway 1** *n* fugitif *m*, -ive *f*; *(teenager etc)* fugueur *m*, -euse *f*. **2** *adj person* fugitif; *horse* emballé; *car* fou; *wedding, couple* clandestin; *inflation* galopant. ◆ **rundown** *n* (**a**) réduction *f* (*in, of* de); *[industry]* réductions *fpl* délibérées; (**b**) **to give sb a ~down * on** mettre qn au courant de. ◆ **runner** *n* (**a**) *(athlete)* coureur *m*; *(horse)* partant *m*; *(messenger)* messager *m*; (**b**) *(sliding part) [sledge]* patin *m*; *[skate]* lame *f*; *[drawer]* coulisseau *m*; *[door]* glissière *f*; *[curtain]* anneau *m*; (**c**) (*table-runner*) chemin *m* de table; *(hall/stair carpet)* chemin de couloir/d'escalier. ◆ **runner-bean** *n* haricot *m* à rames. ◆ **runner-up** *n* second(e) *m(f)*. ◆ **running 1** *n (fig)* **to make the ~ning** mener la course; **to be in the ~ning** avoir des chances de réussir; **in the ~ning for the job** sur les rangs pour avoir le poste ; **2** *adj tap* qui coule; *sore* qui suppure; **a ~ning stream** un cours d'eau; **~ning water (in every room)** eau courante (dans toutes les chambres); **to keep up a ~ning battle** être en lutte continuelle (*with* avec); **~ning commentary** *(Rad, TV)* commentaire *m* suivi; *(fig)* commentaire détaillé (*on* sur); **4 days ~ning** 4 jours de suite; **~ning board** marchepied *m* ; **~ning costs** frais *mpl* d'exploitation; **the ~ning costs of the car are high** la voiture revient cher; *(US Pol)* **~ning mate** candidat *m* à la vice-présidence; **in ~ning order** en état de marche; **~ning shoe** chaussure *f* de course. ◆ **runny** *adj substance* qui coule; *omelette* baveux. ◆ **run-of-the-mill** *adj* banal. ◆ **run-through** *n* essai *m*. ◆ **run- up** *n* période *f* préparatoire (*to* à); *(US: increase)* augmentation *f*. ◆ **runway** *n (Aviat)* piste *f* (d'envol *or* d'atterrissage).

rung¹ [rʌŋ] *ptp of* **ring²**.

rung² [rʌŋ] *n [ladder, chair]* barreau *m*.

rupture ['rʌptʃəʳ] **1** *n* rupture *f*; (*Med* *: *hernia*) hernie *f*. **2** *vt* rompre. *(Med)* **to ~ o.s.** * se donner une hernie. **3** *vi* se rompre.

rural ['rʊər(ə)l] *adj* rural.

ruse [ru:z] *n* ruse *f*.

rush¹ [rʌʃ] **1** *n* (**a**) ruée *f* (*for* vers; *on* sur); *(Mil: attack)* assaut *m*. **gold ~** ruée vers l'or; **we have a ~ on in the office** c'est le coup de feu au bureau; **the Christmas ~** la bousculadc des fêtes de fin d'année; **we've had a ~ of orders** on nous a submergés de commandes; **a ~ of warm air** une bouffée d'air tiède. (**b**) *(hurry)* **to be in a ~** être extrêmement pressé; **I had a ~ to get here in time** j'ai dû me dépêcher pour arriver à l'heure; **I did it in a ~** je l'ai fait à toute vitesse; **what's all the ~?** pourquoi est-ce que c'est si pressé? (**c**) *(Cine)* projection *f* d'essai.

2 *adj*: **~ hours** heures *fpl* de pointe; **~ job** travail *m* d'urgence; *(botched)* travail bâclé.

3 *vi [person]* se précipiter; *[car]* foncer. **to ~ up/down** *etc* monter/descendre *etc* précipitamment; **to ~ at sth** se jeter *or* se ruer sur qch; *(fig)* **don't ~ at it, take it slowly** ne fais pas ça trop vite, prends ton temps; **the train ~ed into the tunnel** le train est entré à toute vitesse dans le tunnel; **I'm ~ing to finish it** je me dépêche pour en avoir fini; **to ~ through** *book* lire à la hâte; *meal* prendre sur le pouce *; *town* traverser à toute vitesse; *work* expédier; **the blood ~ed to his face** le sang lui est monté au visage.

4 *vt* (**a**) *(do hurriedly) job, task* dépêcher; *order* exécuter d'urgence. **to ~ sb to hospital** transporter qn d'urgence à l'hôpital; **they ~ed him out of the room** ils l'ont fait sortir en toute hâte de la pièce ; **I don't want to ~ you** je ne voudrais pas vous bousculer; **to be ~ed off one's feet** être débordé; **to ~ sb into a decision** forcer qn à prendre une décision à la hâte. (**b**) *(take by storm) town* prendre d'assaut; *fence* franchir sur son élan; *[crowd] police* s'élancer contre.

◆ **rush about, rush around** *vi* courir çà et là. ◆ **rush through** *vt sep (Comm) order* exécuter d'urgence; *goods, supplies* envoyer de toute urgence. ◆ **rush up 1** *vi (arrive)* accourir. **2** *vt sep help, reinforcements* faire parvenir d'urgence (*to* à).

rush[2] [rʌʃ] *n (Bot)* jonc *m*. ~ **matting** tapis *m* tressé.

rusk [rʌsk] *n* ≃ biscotte *f*.

russet ['rʌsɪt] **1** *n (apple)* reinette *f* grise. **2** *adj* feuille-morte *inv*.

Russia ['rʌʃə] *n* Russie *f*. ◆ **Russian 1** *adj* russe ; **2** *n* russe *m*; *(person)* Russe *mf*.

rust [rʌst] **1** *n* rouille *f*. **2** *vt* rouiller. **3** *vi* se rouiller. ◆ **rust-coloured** *adj* rouille *inv*. ◆ **rustproof 1** *(also* ~**-resistant***) adj metal* inoxydable; *paint, treatment* antirouille; *bodywork* traité contre la rouille ; **2** *vt* traiter contre la rouille. ◆ **rusty** *adj (lit, fig)* rouillé; *(lit)* **to get** *or* **go** ~**y** se rouiller; *(fig)* **my English is** ~**y** mon anglais est un peu rouillé.

rustic ['rʌstɪk] *adj* rustique.

rustle ['rʌsl] **1** *n* bruissement *m*. **2** *vi* bruire. **3** *vt* (**a**) *papers* faire bruire. (**b**) *(steal) cattle* voler. ◆ **rustle up** * *vt sep (find)* se débrouiller * pour trouver; *(make)* préparer en vitesse.

◆ **rustler** *n* voleur *m* de bétail. ◆ **rustling** *n* vol *m* de bétail.

rut [rʌt] *n* ornière *f (also fig)*. *[person]* **to be in** *or* **get into a** ~ suivre l'ornière.

ruthless ['ru:θlɪs] *adj* impitoyable. ◆ **ruthlessly** *adv* impitoyablement. ◆ **ruthlessness** *n* caractère *m* impitoyable.

rye [raɪ] **1** *n* seigle *m*; *(US: whisky)* whisky *m* (américain). **2** *adj*: ~ **bread** pain *m* de seigle.

S

S, s [es] *n (letter)* S, s *m.*
Sabbath ['sæbəθ] *n (Jewish)* sabbat *m*; *(†: Sunday)* dimanche *m.* ◆ **sabbatical** *adj* sabbatique.
sable ['seɪbl] **1** *n* zibeline *f.* **2** *adj fur* de zibeline, de martre; *brush* en poil de martre.
sabotage ['sæbətɑːʒ] **1** *n* sabotage *m.* **an act of ~** un sabotage. **2** *vt* saboter. ◆ **saboteur** *n* saboteur *m*, -euse *f.*
sabre, *(US)* **saber** ['seɪbəʳ] *n* sabre *m.*
saccharin(e) ['sækərɪn, iːn] *n* saccharine *f.*
sachet ['sæʃeɪ] *n* sachet *m.*
sack[1] [sæk] **1** *n (bag)* sac *m.* **coal ~** sac à charbon; **~ of coal** sac de charbon; *(fig)* **to give sb the ~ *** renvoyer qn, mettre qn à la porte; **to get the ~ *** être renvoyé, être mis à la porte. **2** *adj*: **~ race** course *f* en sac. **3** *vt (*) employee* renvoyer, mettre à la porte. ◆ **sackcloth** *n (Rel)* **~cloth and ashes** le sac et la cendre. ◆ **sackful** *n* plein sac *m.* ◆ **sacking** *n* (**a**) *(cloth)* toile *f* à sac; (**b**) *(*: dismissal)* renvoi *m.*
sack[2] [sæk] **1** *n (plundering: also* **~ing***)* sac *m.* **2** *vt* mettre à sac.
sacrament ['sækrəmənt] *n* sacrement *m.* **to receive the ~s** communier.
sacred ['seɪkrɪd] *adj* sacré *(after n).* **the S~ Heart** le Sacré-Cœur; **~ writings** livres *mpl* sacrés; **~ to the memory of** consacré à la mémoire de; **is nothing ~?** vous ne respectez donc rien?; *(fig)* **~ cow *** chose *f* sacro-sainte.
sacrifice ['sækrɪfaɪs] **1** *n* sacrifice *m.* **to make great ~s** faire de grands sacrifices (*for sb* pour qn; *to do* pour faire). **2** *vt* sacrifier (*to* à; *for sb* pour qn; *for sth* pour avoir qch). ◆ **sacrificial** *adj (Rel)* sacrificiel; *price* extrêmement bas.
sacrilege ['sækrɪlɪdʒ] *n* sacrilège *m.* ◆ **sacrilegious** *adj* sacrilège.
sacristy ['sækrɪstɪ] *n* sacristie *f.* ◆ **sacristan** *n* sacristain(e) *m(f).*
sacrosanct ['sækrəʊ'sæŋ(k)t] *adj* sacro-saint.
sad [sæd] *adj person, smile* triste; *news, duty, condition* triste *(before n)*; *loss* douloureux; *mistake* fâcheux. **to make sb ~** attrister qn; **to grow ~** devenir triste; **a ~ business** une triste affaire; *(US fig)* **~ sack** *(gen)* empoté *m; (Mil)* pauvre troufion *m.* ◆ **sadden** *vt* attrister. ◆ **sad-eyed** *adj* aux yeux tristes. ◆ **sadly** *adv (unhappily)* tristement; *(regrettably)* fâcheusement; **~ly incompetent** fort incompétent; **~ly lacking in...** qui manque fort de... ◆ **sadness** *n* tristesse *f.*
saddle ['sædl] **1** *n* selle *f.* **in(to) the ~** en selle; *(fig)* **when he was in the ~** quand c'était lui qui tenait les rênes; **~ of lamb** selle d'agneau. **2** *vt* (**~ up**) *horse* seller. *(fig)* **to ~ sb with (doing) sth *** imposer qch à qn, coller qch à qn *; **we're ~d with it** nous voilà avec ça sur les bras. ◆ **saddlebag** *n* sacoche *f.* ◆ **saddler** *n* sellier *m.* ◆ **saddlery** *n* sellerie *f.*
sadism ['seɪdɪz(ə)m] *n* sadisme *m.* ◆ **sadist** *adj, n* sadique *(mf).* ◆ **sadistic** *adj* sadique.
safari [sə'fɑːrɪ] *n* safari *m.* **to go** *or* **be on ~** faire un safari; **~ jacket** saharienne *f;* **~ park** réserve *f.*
safe [seɪf] **1** *adj* (**a**) *(not in danger) person* en sécurité, hors de danger. **~ and sound** sain et sauf; **to be ~ from** être à l'abri de; **no girl is ~ with him** les filles courent toujours un risque avec lui; **you'll be quite ~ here** vous êtes en sécurité ici; **his life was not ~** sa vie était en danger; **I don't feel very ~ on this ladder** je ne me sens pas très en sécurité sur cette échelle; *[jewel, secret]* **it's quite ~** ça ne risque rien. (**b**) *(not dangerous) toy, animal, action* sans danger; *method, vehicle* sûr; *ice, ladder, bridge* solide; *beach, bathing* qui n'est pas dangereux; *(secure) hiding place, harbour, investment* sûr; *(prudent) choice, guess, estimate* prudent. **is it ~ to come out?** est-ce qu'on peut sortir sans danger?; **it's not ~ to go alone** il est dangereux d'y aller tout seul; **is that dog ~?** ce chien n'est pas méchant?; **that dog isn't ~ with children** il ne faut pas laisser les enfants s'approcher du chien; **~ journey!** bon voyage!; **I'll keep it ~** *or* **in a ~ place for you** je vais vous le garder en lieu sûr; **in ~ hands** en mains sûres; *(for spy etc)* **~ house** lieu *m* sûr; **it's ~ as houses** *(runs no risk)* cela ne court aucun risque; *(offers no risk)* cela ne présente aucun risque; *(Med)* **the ~ period *** la période sans danger; **~ sex** l'amour *m* sans risques; **the ~st thing to do would be to wait** le plus sûr serait d'attendre; **just to be on the ~ side** pour être plus sûr; **better ~ than sorry!** mieux vaut être trop prudent!; **it's a ~ bet he'll win** il gagnera à coup sûr; *(Pol)* **a ~ seat** un siège assuré; **it is ~ to predict...** on peut prédire sans risque d'erreur...
2 *n (for money, valuables)* coffre-fort *m*; *(for food)* garde-manger *m inv.*
◆ **safe-breaker** *n* perceur *m* de coffre-fort. ◆ **safe-conduct** *n* sauf-conduit *m.* ◆ **safe-deposit** *n (vault)* dépôt *m* de coffres-forts; *(also* **~-deposit box***)* coffre(-fort) *m.* ◆ **safeguard** **1** *vt* sauvegarder (*against* contre) ; **2** *n* sauvegarde *f* (*against* contre). ◆ **safekeeping** *n*: **in ~keeping** en sécurité; **I gave it to him for ~keeping** je le lui ai donné à garder. ◆ **safely** *adv (without mishap)* sans accident; *arrive* bien; *(without risk)* sans danger; *say* sans risque d'erreur; *(securely)* en sûreté; *store* en lieu sûr. ◆ **safeness** *n [construction, equipment]* solidité *f.*
safety ['seɪftɪ] **1** *n [person, valuables]* sécurité *f*; *[construction, equipment]* solidité *f.* **in a place of ~** en lieu sûr; **he reached ~ at last** il était enfin en sûreté *or* en sécurité; **to play for ~** ne pas prendre de risques; **there is ~ in numbers** plus on est nombreux moins il y a de danger; **for ~'s sake** pour plus de sûreté, par mesure de sécurité; **~ on the roads** la sécurité sur les routes; **~ first!** la sécurité d'abord!; *(Aut)* soyez prudents!; **~-first campaign** campagne *f* de sécurité. **2** *adj belt, device, margin, measure, regulations, screen* de sécurité; *bolt, lock, razor, blade, chain, match* de sûreté. **~ catch** cran *m* de sécurité; *(Theat)* **~ curtain** rideau *m* de fer; **~ glass** verre *m* Sécurit ®; **~ net** *(lit)* filet *m* (de protection); *(fig)* filet *m* de sécurité; **~ pin** épingle *f* de sûreté; **~ valve** soupape *f* de sûreté. ◆ **safety-deposit box** *n (US)* coffre(-fort) *m.*
saffron ['sæfrən] **1** *n* safran *m.* **2** *adj colour* safran *inv.*
sag [sæg] *vi [roof, chair]* s'affaisser; *[beam, prices]* fléchir; *[breasts, hemline]* pendre; *[rope]* pendre au milieu, être détendu; *[gate]* être affaissé. ◆ **sagging** *adj* affaissé; fléchi; pendant; détendu.

saga ['sɑːgə] *n* saga *f*; *(novel)* roman-fleuve *m*; *(fig)* aventure *f* épique.

sagacious [sə'geɪʃəs] *adj person* sagace; *comment* perspicace. ◆ **sagaciously** *adv* avec sagacité. ◆ **sagacity** *n* sagacité *f*.

sage[1] [seɪdʒ] *n* sauge *f*. ~ **and onion stuffing** farce *f* à l'oignon et à la sauge; ~ **green** vert cendré *inv*.

sage[2] [seɪdʒ] *adj, n (wise)* sage *(m)*. ◆ **sagely** *adv say, act* avec sagesse; *nod* d'un air solennel.

Sagittarius [,sædʒɪ'tɛərɪəs] *n* le Sagittaire.

sago ['seɪgəʊ] *n* sagou *m*. ~ **pudding** sagou au lait.

Sahara [sə'hɑːrə] *n* Sahara *m*.

said [sed] *pret, ptp of* **say.**

Saigon [saɪ'gɒn] *n* Saigon.

sail [seɪl] **1** *n [boat]* voile *f*; *[windmill]* aile *f*. **under** ~ à la voile; *[boat]* **to set** ~ prendre la mer; **to set** ~ **for** *[boat]* partir à destination de; *[person]* partir pour; **to go for a** ~ faire un tour en bateau. **2** *vi* (**a**) *[boat]* **to** ~ **into harbour** entrer au port; **the ship** ~**ed into Cadiz** le bateau est arrivé à Cadix; **to** ~ **round the cape** doubler le cap; **the boat** ~**s at 6 o'clock** le bateau part à 6 heures. (**b**) *[person]* **to** ~ **away/back** *etc* partir/revenir *etc* en bateau; **to** ~ **round the world** faire le tour du monde en bateau; **he goes** ~**ing** il fait de la voile; *(fig)* **he was** ~**ing close to the wind** il jouait un jeu dangereux. (**c**) *(fig) [swan, clouds etc]* glisser. **the book** ~**ed out of the window** le livre est allé voler par la fenêtre; **she** ~**ed into the room *** elle est entrée dans la pièce toutes voiles dehors. **3** *vt* (**a**) **to** ~ **the seas** parcourir les mers; **to** ~ **the Atlantic** traverser l'Atlantique (en bateau). (**b**) *boat* piloter.
◆ **sail through *** **1** *vi (succeed)* réussir haut la main. **2** *vt fus exam, driving test* avoir haut la main.
◆ **sailboard 1** *n* planche *f* à voile ; **2** *vi:* **to go** ~**boarding** faire de la planche à voile. ◆ **sailboarder** *n* véliplanchiste *mf*. ◆ **sailboat** *n (US)* voilier *m*. ◆ **sailcloth** *n* toile *f* à voile. ◆ **sailing** *n (act)* navigation *f* à voile; *(pastime)* la voile; *(departure)* départ *m*. ◆ **sailing boat** *n* voilier *m*. ◆ **sailing dinghy** *n* dériveur *m*. ◆ **sailing ship** *n* voilier *m*. ◆ **sailmaker** *n* voilier *m (personne)*. ◆ **sailor** *n (gen)* marin *m*; *(before the mast)* matelot *m*; **to be a good/bad** ~**or** avoir/ne pas avoir le pied marin. ◆ **sailplane** *n* planeur *m*.

saint [seɪnt] *n* saint(e) *m(f)*. ~**'s day** fête *f* (de saint); **All S~s' Day** la Toussaint; **S~ Peter** saint Pierre; **S~ Patrick's Day** la Saint-Patrick; **S~ Peter's Church** (l'église *f*) Saint-Pierre; **he's no** ~ ***** ce n'est pas un petit saint. ◆ **saint-like** *or* ◆ **saintly** *adj quality* de saint; *smile* plein de bonté; *person* saint *(before n)*. ◆ **saintliness** *n* sainteté *f*.

sake [seɪk] *n*: **for sb's** ~ pour (l'amour de) qn; **for God's** ~ pour l'amour de Dieu; **for my** ~ pour moi; **for your own** ~ pour ton bien; **to eat for the** ~ **of eating** manger pour le plaisir de manger; **for old times'** ~ en souvenir du passé; **for argument's** ~ à titre d'exemple; **art for art's** ~ l'art pour l'art; **for the** ~ **of peace** pour avoir la paix.

salad ['sæləd] **1** *n* salade *f*. **tomato** ~ salade de tomates; **ham** ~ jambon accompagné de salade. **2** *adj*: ~ **bowl** saladier *m*; ~ **cream** ≃ mayonnaise *f (en bouteille etc)*; *(fig)* ~ **days** années *fpl* de jeunesse et d'inexpérience; ~ **dressing** ≃ mayonnaise *f*; *(oil and vinegar)* vinaigrette *f*; ~ **oil** huile *f* de table; ~ **servers** couvert *m* à salade.

salary ['sælərɪ] **1** *n (professional etc)* traitement *m*, appointements *mpl*; *(pay in general)* salaire *m*. **2** *adj*: ~ **earner** personne *f* qui touche un traitement; ~ **range/scale** éventail *m*/échelle *f* des traitements. ◆ **salaried** *adj (Ind)* **salaried staff** employés *mpl* touchant un traitement (*or* des appointements).

sale [seɪl] **1** *n* (**a**) *(act)* vente *f*. **to put up for** ~ mettre en vente; **(up) for** ~ à vendre; **on** ~ en vente; **sold on a** ~ **or return basis** vendu avec possibilité de reprise des invendus; ~**s are up/down** les ventes ont augmenté/baissé; **auction** ~ vente aux enchères; ~ **in aid of the blind** vente de charité en faveur des aveugles. (**b**) *(Comm: also* ~**s)** soldes *mpl*. **the** ~**s are on** c'est la saison des soldes; **in the** *or* **a** ~ en solde. **2** *adj*: ~ **price** prix *m* de solde; ~**s department** service *m* des ventes; ~**s force** ensemble *m* des représentants; ~**s manager** directeur *m* commercial; ~**s pitch ***, ~**s talk *** baratin ***** *m* publicitaire, boniment *m*. ◆ **saleable** *adj* vendable. ◆ **sale-of-work** *n* vente *f* de charité. ◆ **saleroom** *n* salle *f* des ventes. ◆ **salesman** *n (in shop)* vendeur *m*; *(representative)* représentant *m* de commerce. ◆ **salesmanship** *n* art *m* de la vente. ◆ **saleswoman** *n* vendeuse *f*.

salient ['seɪlɪənt] *adj, n* saillant *(m)*.

saliva [sə'laɪvə] *n* salive *f*.

sallow ['sæləʊ] *adj* jaunâtre. ◆ **sallowness** *n* teint *m* jaunâtre.

sally ['sælɪ] *n (wit)* saillie *f*. ◆ **sally forth, sally out** *vi* sortir gaiement.

salmon ['sæmən] **1** *n* saumon *m*. **2** *adj*: ~ **fishing** pêche *f* au saumon; ~ **pink** saumon *inv*; ~ **steak** darne *f* de saumon; ~ **trout** truite *f* saumonée.

salmonella [,sælmə'nelə] *n* salmonellose *f*.

salon ['sælɔ̃ːŋ] *n* salon *m*.

saloon [sə'luːn] *n* (**a**) *(public room)* salle *f*; *(Brit:* ~ **bar)** bar *m*; *(US: bar)* bar *m*, saloon *m*. (**b**) *(Brit: car)* conduite *f* intérieure.

salsify ['sælsɪfɪ] *n* salsifis *m*.

salt [sɔːlt] **1** *n* sel *m*. **there's too much** ~ **in the potatoes** les pommes de terre sont trop salées; *(fig)* **to rub** ~ **in the wound** retourner le couteau dans la plaie; **he's not worth his** ~ il ne vaut pas grand-chose; **to take sth with a pinch of** ~ ne pas prendre qch au pied de la lettre; *(sailor)* **an old** ~ un vieux loup de mer. **2** *adj water, butter, beef, taste* salé; *mine* de sel; *spoon* à sel. ~ **flat** salant *m*; ~ **lick** *(block)* pierre à lécher; *(place)* salant *m*; ~ **pork** petit salé *m*. **3** *vt meat, one's food* saler.
◆ **salt away** *vt sep meat* saler; *(fig) money* mettre à gauche *****.
◆ **saltcellar** *n* salière *f*. ◆ **salt-free** *adj* sans sel. ◆ **saltiness** *n [water]* salinité *f*; *[food]* goût *m* salé. ◆ **saltpetre,** *(US)* **saltpeter** *n* salpêtre *m*. ◆ **saltwater** *adj fish* de mer. ◆ **salty** *adj taste* salé.

salubrious [sə'luːbrɪəs] *adj* salubre.

salutary ['sæljʊt(ə)rɪ] *adj* salutaire.

salute [sə'luːt] **1** *n (with hand)* salut *m*; *(with guns)* salve *f*. **to take the** ~ passer les troupes en revue. **2** *vt (Mil etc)* saluer; *(fig: acclaim)* saluer (*as* comme). **to** ~ **the flag** saluer le drapeau. **3** *vi* faire un salut.

salvage ['sælvɪdʒ] **1** *n* (**a**) *(saving) [ship etc]* sauvetage *m*; *(for re-use)* récupération *f*. (**b**) *(things saved from fire, wreck)* objets *mpl or* biens *mpl* sauvés; *(for re-use)* objets récupérables. **to collect newspapers for** ~ récupérer les vieux journaux. (**c**) *(payment)* prime *f* de sauvetage. **2** *adj operation, vessel* de sauvetage. **3** *vt* sauver (*from* de); *(for re-use)* récupérer.

salvation [sæl'veɪʃ(ə)n] *n (gen, Rel)* salut *m*. ◆ **Salvation Army** *n* Armée *f* du Salut. ◆ **salvationist** *n* salutiste *mf*.

salve [sælv] **1** *n* baume *m*. **2** *vt*: **to** ~ **his conscience** pour être en règle avec sa conscience.

salver ['sælvəʳ] *n* plateau *m (de métal)*.

salvo ['sælvəʊ] *n (Mil)* salve *f*.

Samaritan [sə'mærɪt(ə)n] *n*: **the Good** ~ le bon Samaritain; *(organization)* **the** ~ **s** ≃ S.O.S. Amitié.

same [seɪm] **1** *adj* même. **the ~ book as** le même livre que; **the ~ day** le même jour; **the very ~ day** le jour même; **that ~ day** ce même jour; **in the ~ way...** de même...; **the ~ table as usual** la table habituelle; **it was just the ~ as usual** c'était comme d'habitude; **one and the ~ person** une seule et même personne; **always the ~ old thing** toujours la même chose; **it comes to the ~ thing** cela revient au même; **at the ~ time** en même temps; **at the very ~ time as...** au moment même où...; *(fig)* **to go the ~ way as sb** suivre les traces de qn; *(in health)* **she's much about the ~** son état est inchangé. **2** *pron*: **the ~** *(gen)* le même, la même; *(the ~ thing)* la même chose; *(Jur: aforementioned)* le susdit, la susdite. **the film is the ~ as before** le film est le même qu'avant; **it's always the ~ in politics** c'est toujours la même chose en politique; **the price is the ~ as last year** c'est le même prix que l'année dernière; **do the ~ as your brother** fais comme ton frère; **he left and I did the ~** il est parti et j'en ai fait autant; **I would do the ~ again** je recommencerais; **I'll do the ~ for you** je te rendrai ça; *(in bar etc)* **the ~ again please** la même chose s'il vous plaît; **I don't feel the ~ about it as I did** maintenant je vois la chose différemment; **I still feel the ~ about you** mes sentiments à ton égard n'ont pas changé; **it's all the ~ to me** cela m'est égal; **all** *or* **just the ~** tout de même, quand même; **it's not the ~ as before** ce n'est plus pareil; **it's the ~ everywhere** c'est partout pareil; **and the ~ to you!** à toi aussi; *(as retort: in quarrel etc)* et je te souhaite la pareille!; **~ here!** * moi aussi! ◆ **same-day** *adj delivery* dans la journée. ◆ **sameness** *n (monotony)* monotonie *f.*

sample ['sɑːmpl] **1** *n (gen)* échantillon *m*; *(Med) [urine]* échantillon; *[blood, tissue]* prélèvement *m.* **as a ~** à titre d'échantillon. **2** *adj*: **~ bottle** *(or* **cigarette** *or* **selection** *etc)* échantillon *m*; **~ line** *(or* **verse** *etc)* exemple *m*; **a ~ section of** une section représentative de. **3** *vt food, wine* goûter.

sanatorium, *pl* **-ia** [ˌsænə'tɔːrɪəm, ɪə] *n* sanatorium *m*; *(Scol)* infirmerie *f.*

sanctify ['sæŋ(k)tɪfaɪ] *vt* sanctifier. ◆ **sanctity** *n [person]* sainteté *f*; *[oath, place]* caractère *m* sacré; *[marriage]* inviolabilité *f.*

sanctimonious [ˌsæŋ(k)tɪ'məʊnɪəs] *adj* moralisateur. ◆ **sanctimoniously** *adv say* d'un ton moralisateur.

sanction ['sæŋ(k)ʃ(ə)n] **1** *n (all senses)* sanction *f.* **to impose economic ~s on** prendre des sanctions économiques contre. **2** *vt (gen)* sanctionner. **~ed by usage** consacré par l'usage.

sanctuary ['sæŋ(k)tjʊərɪ] *n (holy place)* sanctuaire *m*; *(refuge)* asile *m*; *(for wild life)* réserve *f.* **to seek ~** chercher asile.

sand [sænd] **1** *n* sable *m.* *(beach)* **~s** plage *f*; **miles and miles of golden ~s** des kilomètres de plages de sable doré. **2** *adj*: **~ dune** dune *f* (de sable); **~ flea** puce *f* de mer; *(US Golf)* **~ trap** bunker *m*; **~ yacht** char *m* à voile. **3** *vt* (**a**) *road* sabler. (**b**) (**~ down**) *wood etc* poncer au papier de verre. ◆ **sandbag** **1** *n* sac *m* de sable ; **2** *vt stun* assommer; *(reinforce)* renforcer avec des sacs de sable. ◆ **sandbank** *n* banc *m* de sable. ◆ **sandblind** *adj (US)* mal voyant. ◆ **sandbox** *n* tas *m* de sable. ◆ **sandcastle** *n* château *m* de sable. ◆ **sander** *n (tool)* ponceuse. ◆ **sandlot** *n (US)* terrain *m* vague. ◆ **sandpaper** **1** *n* papier *m* de verre ; **2** *vt* poncer au papier de verre. ◆ **sandpit** *n* carrière *f* de sable; *(for children)* tas *m* de sable. ◆ **sandshoes** *npl (rubber-soled)* tennis *fpl*; *(rope-soled)* espadrilles *fpl.* ◆ **sandstone** *n* grès *m.* ◆ **sandstorm** *n* tempête *f* de sable. ◆ **sandy** *adj soil, path* sablonneux; *water, deposit* sableux; *beach* de sable; *(colour)* sable *inv*; *hair* blond roux *inv.*

sandal ['sændl] *n* sandale *f*; *(rope-soled)* espadrille *f.*

sandwich ['sænwɪdʒ] **1** *n* sandwich *m.* **cheese ~** sandwich au fromage; **open ~** canapé *m.* **2** *adj*: **~ bar** sandwich bar *m*; **~ loaf** pain *m* de mie; *(Ind)* **~ course** ≃ cours *mpl* de formation professionnelle; **~ man** homme-sandwich *m.* **3** *vt* (**~ in**) *person, appointment* intercaler. **~ed between** pris en sandwich entre *.

sane [seɪn] *adj person* sain d'esprit; *judgment* sain. **he isn't quite ~** il n'a pas toute sa raison. ◆ **sanely** *adv* sainement. ◆ **sanity** *n [person]* santé *f* mentale, raison *f*; **sanity prevailed** le bon sens l'a emporté.

sang [sæŋ] *pret of* **sing.**

sanguinary ['sæŋgwɪn(ə)rɪ] *adj* sanglant.

sanguine ['sæŋgwɪn] *adj* (**a**) *person* optimiste. (**b**) *complexion* sanguin.

sanitarium [ˌsænɪ'tɛərɪəm] *n* = **sanatorium.**

sanitary ['sænɪt(ə)rɪ] *adj* (**a**) *(clean)* hygiénique. (**b**) *system, equipment* sanitaire. **~ engineer** ingénieur *m* sanitaire; **~ inspector** inspecteur *m*, -trice *f* de la Santé publique; *(US)* **~ man** éboueur *m*; **~ towel,** *(US)* **~ napkin** serviette *f* hygiénique. ◆ **sanitation** *n (in house)* installations *fpl* sanitaires; *(in town)* système *m* sanitaire. ◆ **sanitize** *vt* assainir. ◆ **sanitized** *adj account* édulcoré, expurgé.

sank [sæŋk] *pret of* **sink**[1]**.**

Santa Claus [ˌsæntə'klɔːz] *n* le père Noël.

Santiago [sæntɪ'ɑːgəʊ] *n* Santiago.

sap[1] [sæp] *n (Bot)* sève *f.*

sap[2] [sæp] *vt strength, confidence* saper.

sapling ['sæplɪŋ] *n* jeune arbre *m.*

sapper ['sæpəʳ] *n (Mil)* sapeur *m.* *(Brit)* **the S~s** * le génie.

sapphire ['sæfaɪəʳ] **1** *n* saphir *m.* **2** *adj ring* de saphir(s). **~ blue** saphir *inv.*

Saranwrap [sə'rænræp] *n* ® *(US)* Scellofrais ® *m.*

sarcasm ['sɑːkæz(ə)m] *n* sarcasme *m.* ◆ **sarcastic** *adj* sarcastique; **sarcastic remarks** sarcasmes *mpl.* ◆ **sarcastically** *adv* sarcastiquement.

sardine [sɑː'diːn] *n* sardine *f.* **tinned** *or (US)* **canned ~s** ≃ sardines à l'huile.

Sardinia [sɑː'dɪnɪə] *n* Sardaigne *f.* ◆ **Sardinian** **1** *adj* sarde ; **2** *n* (**a**) Sarde *mf*; (**b**) *(Ling)* sarde *m.*

sardonic [sɑː'dɒnɪk] *adj* sardonique. ◆ **sardonically** *adv* sardoniquement.

Sark [sɑːk] *n* Sercq *m.*

sartorial [sɑː'tɔːrɪəl] *adj* vestimentaire.

sash[1] [sæʃ] *n (on uniform)* écharpe *f*; *(on dress etc)* large ceinture *f* à nœud.

sash[2] [sæʃ] *adj*: **~ window** fenêtre *f* à guillotine.

sat [sæt] *pret, ptp of* **sit.**

Satan ['seɪtn] *n* Satan *m.* ◆ **satanic** *adj* satanique.

satchel ['sætʃ(ə)l] *n* cartable *m.*

satellite ['sætəlaɪt] **1** *n (Space)* satellite *m*; *(US: town)* ville-satellite *f.* **2** *adj (gen)* satellite; *television* par satellite; **~ dish** antenne *f* parabolique.

satiated ['seɪʃɪeɪtɪd] *adj (with food)* repu; *(with pleasures)* comblé, blasé *(pej).* ◆ **satiation** *n* assouvissement *m*; **to satiation point** (jusqu')à satiété. ◆ **satiety** *n* satiété *f.*

satin ['sætɪn] **1** *n* satin *m.* **2** *adj dress* en *or* de satin; *paper, finish* satiné.

satire ['sætaɪəʳ] *n* satire *f (on* contre). ◆ **satirical** *adj* satirique. ◆ **satirically** *adv* d'une manière satirique. ◆ **satirist** *n (writer etc)* écrivain *m etc* satirique; *(cartoonist)* caricaturiste *mf*; *(in cabaret* *etc)* ≃ chansonnier *m.* ◆ **satirize** *vt* faire la satire de.

satisfaction [ˌsætɪsˈfækʃ(ə)n] *n* satisfaction *f* (*at* de). **it was a great ~ to us to hear that...** nous avons appris avec beaucoup de satisfaction que...; **it has not been proved to my ~** cela n'a pas été prouvé de façon à me convaincre; **has it been done to your ~?** est-ce que vous en êtes satisfait?

satisfactory [ˌsætɪsˈfækt(ə)rɪ] *adj (gen)* satisfaisant. **to bring sth to a ~ conclusion** mener qch à bien. ◆ **satisfactorily** *adv* d'une manière satisfaisante.

satisfy [ˈsætɪsfaɪ] *vt* (**a**) *person* satisfaire, contenter. (**b**) *hunger, need, condition, creditor* satisfaire; *(Comm) demand* satisfaire à. (**c**) *(convince)* convaincre, assurer (*sb that* qn que; *of* de). **to ~ o.s. of sth** s'assurer de qch. ◆ **satisfied** *adj person, voice* satisfait, content; **he was satisfied to remain...** il a accepté de rester...; **I am not satisfied with that** cela ne me satisfait pas; **to be satisfied that...** être convaincu *or* persuadé que... ◆ **satisfying** *adj* satisfaisant; *food* substantiel.

saturate [ˈsætʃəreɪt] *vt* saturer (*with* de). ◆ **saturated** *adj (soaked)* trempé. ◆ **saturation 1** *n* saturation *f* ; **2** *adj*: **saturation bombing** tactique *f* de saturation (par bombardement); **to reach saturation point** arriver à saturation.

Saturday [ˈsætədɪ] *n* samedi *m*. **on ~** samedi; **on ~s** le samedi; **next ~ , ~ next** samedi prochain; **last ~** samedi dernier; **every ~** tous les samedis, chaque samedi; **every other ~, every second ~** un samedi sur deux; **it is ~ today** nous sommes aujourd'hui samedi; **on ~ January 23rd** le samedi 23 janvier; **the ~ after next, a week on ~ , ~ week** samedi en huit; **a fortnight on ~, ~ fortnight** samedi en quinze; **a week/fortnight past on ~** il y a huit/quinze jours samedi dernier; **the following ~** le samedi suivant; **the ~ before last** l'autre samedi; **~ morning** samedi matin; **~ afternoon** samedi après-midi; **~ evening** samedi soir; **~ night** samedi soir; *(overnight)* la nuit de samedi; *(TV)* **~ evening viewing** émissions *fpl* du samedi soir; *(Comm)* **~ closing** fermeture *f* le samedi; *(Press)* **the ~ edition** l'édition de *or* du samedi.

Saturn [ˈsætən] *n (Myth)* Saturne *m*; *(Astron)* Saturne *f*.

sauce [sɔːs] *n* (**a**) *(Culin)* sauce *f*. **mint ~** sauce à la menthe. (**b**) *(*: impudence)* toupet * *m*. ◆ **sauceboat** *n* saucière *f*. ◆ **saucepan** *n* casserole *f*. ◆ **saucily** *adv say* avec impertinence; *look* d'un air coquin. ◆ **sauciness** *n (cheekiness)* toupet * *m*. ◆ **saucy** *adj (cheeky)* impertinent; *look* coquin; *hat* coquet.

saucer [ˈsɔːsəʳ] *n* soucoupe *f*.

Saudi Arabia [ˈsaʊdɪəˈreɪbɪə] *n* Arabie *f* Saoudite. ◆ **Saudi (Arabian) 1** *adj* saoudien ; **2** *n* Saoudien(ne) *m(f)*.

sauerkraut [ˈsaʊəkraʊt] *n* choucroute *f*.

sauna [ˈsɔːnə] *n* sauna *m*.

saunter [ˈsɔːntəʳ] *vi*: **to ~ in/out** *etc* entrer/sortir *etc* d'un pas nonchalant.

sausage [ˈsɒsɪdʒ] **1** *n* saucisse *f*; *(pre-cooked)* saucisson *m*. **2** *adj*: **~ meat** chair *f* à saucisse ; **~ roll** ≃ friand *m*.

sauté [ˈsəʊteɪ] **1** *vt* faire sauter *(Culin)*. **2** *adj* sauté.

savage [ˈsævɪdʒ] **1** *adj* (**a**) *(fierce) (gen)* féroce; *person* brutal. (**b**) *(primitive) tribe, customs* sauvage. **2** *n* sauvage *mf*. **3** *vt [dog etc]* attaquer férocement; *[critics etc]* attaquer violemment. ◆ **savagely** *adv* férocement; brutalement. ◆ **savagery** *n (cruelty)* férocité *f*; brutalité *f*.

save¹ [seɪv] **1** *vt* (**a**) *(rescue)* sauver (*from* de). **to ~ sb from death/drowning** *etc* sauver qn de la mort/de la noyade *etc*; **to ~ sb from falling** empêcher qn de tomber; **to ~ sb's life** sauver la vie à *or* de qn; **I couldn't do it to ~ my life** je ne le ferais pour rien au monde; *(fig)* **to ~ one's bacon *** se tirer du pétrin; **to ~ one's skin *** *or* **neck *** *or* **hide *** sauver sa peau *; **to ~ face** sauver la face; **God ~ the Queen!** vive la reine!; *(Sport)* **to ~ a goal** sauver un but; **they ~d the palace for posterity** on a préservé le palais pour la postérité. (**b**) *(store away: ~* **up***) money* mettre de côté; *food, newspapers* garder; *(collect) stamps etc* collectionner. **I've ~d you a piece of cake** je t'ai gardé un morceau de gâteau; **I ~d your letter till the last** j'ai gardé ta lettre pour la bonne bouche. (**c**) *(not spend, not use) money, labour, petrol* économiser; *time* gagner; *(avoid) difficulty* éviter (*sb sth* qch à qn). **you have ~d me a lot of trouble** vous m'avez évité bien des ennuis; **to ~ time let's assume that...** pour gagner du temps admettons que... + *subj*; **it will ~ you 10 minutes** cela vous fera gagner 10 minutes; **to ~ one's strength for** se ménager pour. (**d**) *(Comput)* sauvegarder. **2** *vi* (**a**) (**~ up**) faire des économies. **to ~ up for sth** mettre de l'argent de côté pour qch. (**b**) **to ~ on sth** économiser sur qch. (**c**) *(Comput)* sauvegarder. **3** *n (Sport)* arrêt *m (du ballon)*.
◆ **saving 1** *n [time, money etc]* économie *f*; **to make savings** économiser, faire des économies; **to live on one's savings** vivre de ses économies; *(Econ)* **to encourage saving(s)** encourager l'épargne; **small savings** la petite épargne ; **2** *adj*: **generosity is his saving grace** il se rachète par sa générosité. ◆ **savings account** *n (Brit)* compte *m* d'épargne; *(US)* compte *n* de dépôt. ◆ **savings bank** *n* caisse *f* d'épargne.

save² [seɪv] *prep (except)* sauf.

saveloy [ˈsævəlɔɪ] *n* cervelas *m*.

saviour, *(US)* **savior** [ˈseɪvjəʳ] *n* sauveur *m*.

savory [ˈseɪv(ə)rɪ] *n (herb)* sarriette *f*.

savour, *(US)* **savor** [ˈseɪvəʳ] **1** *n* saveur *f*. **2** *vt* savourer. **3** *vi*: **to ~ of sth** sentir qch. ◆ **savo(u)ry 1** *adj (appetizing)* savoureux; *(not sweet)* salé *(par opposition à sucré)*; *(fig)* **not very ~y** *subject* peu appétissant; *district* peu recommandable ; **2** *n* mets *m* non sucré; *(on toast)* canapé *m* chaud.

saw¹ [sɔː] *(vb: pret* **sawed,** *ptp* **sawed** *or* **sawn)** **1** *n* scie *f*. **2** *vt* scier. **to ~ sth off/up** enlever/débiter qch à la scie. **3** *vi*: **to ~ through sth** scier qch. ◆ **sawdust** *n* sciure *f* (de bois). ◆ **saw-edged knife** *n* couteau-scie *m*. ◆ **sawmill** *n* scierie *f*. ◆ **sawn-off** *or (US)* **sawed-off shotgun** *n* carabine *f* à canon scié.

saw² [sɔː] *pret of* **see¹**.

saxophone [ˈsæksəfəʊn] *n (abbr* **sax ****)* saxophone *m*, saxo * *m*. ◆ **saxophonist** *n* saxophoniste *mf*.

say [seɪ] *pret, ptp* **said 1** *vti* (**a**) *(gen)* dire (*sth to sb* qch à qn; *that* que); *lesson, poem* réciter; *[dial, gauge, clock]* marquer. *(Rel)* **to ~ mass/a prayer** dire la messe/une prière; *(fig)* **to ~ yes/no to an invitation** accepter/refuser une invitation; **~ after me...** répétez après moi...; **to ~ sth again** répéter qch; **I shall have more to ~ about that** je reviendrai là-dessus plus tard; **let's ~ no more about it** n'en parlons plus; **I've got nothing more to ~** je n'ai rien à ajouter; **all of that can be said in 2 sentences** tout cela tient en 2 phrases; **something was said about it** on en a parlé, il en a été question; **I should like to ask Mr Smith to ~ a few words** je voudrais prier M. Smith de prendre la parole; **he said I was to give you this** il m'a dit de vous donner ceci; **to ~ one's say** dire ce qu'on a à dire; **it ~s in the rules** il est dit dans le règlement; **he is said to have...** on dit qu'il a...; **I ~ he should take it** je suis d'avis qu'il le prenne; **I should ~ she's intelligent** je pense qu'elle est intelligente; **what would you ~ is the population of Paris?** quelle est à votre avis *or* d'après vous la population de Paris?; **~ someone left you a fortune** si vous hévitiez d'une fortune.

(**b**) *(in phrases)* dire. **'10 o'clock' he said to himself** '10 heures' se dit-il; **and so ~ all of us** nous sommes tous d'accord là-dessus; **to ~ nothing of her sister/of her breaking it** sans parler de sa sœur/ du fait qu'elle l'a cassé; **that's ~ing a lot** * ce n'est pas peu dire; **that isn't ~ing much** * ça ne veut pas dire grand-chose; **that doesn't ~ much for him** cela en dit long sur lui *(iro)*; **it ~s a lot for his courage that he stayed** il a bien prouvé son courage en restant; **she has nothing to ~ for herself** *(no explanation)* elle se trouve sans excuse; *(no conversation)* elle n'a pas de conversation; **he always has a lot to ~ for himself** il a toujours son mot à dire; **you might as well ~ the earth is flat!** autant dire que la terre est plate!; **you can ~ THAT again!** * c'est le cas de le dire!; *(emphatic)* **you've said it!** * tu l'as dit! *; **enough said!** * en voilà assez!; **to ~ the least** c'est le moins qu'on puisse dire; **it goes without ~ing that...** il va sans dire que...; **just ~ the word and I'll go** vous n'avez qu'un mot à dire pour que je parte; **he hadn't a good word to ~ for her** il n'a rien trouvé à dire en sa faveur; **there's sth to be said for it** cela a du bon; **there's sth to be said for waiting** il y a peut-être intérêt à attendre; **it's easier** *or* **sooner said than done!** c'est plus facile à dire qu'à faire!; **when all is said and done** tout compte fait; **what do you ~ to a cup of tea?** que diriez-vous d'une tasse de thé?; **there's no ~ing what he'll do** il est impossible de dire ce qu'il fera; **so to ~** pour ainsi dire; **that is to ~** c'est-à-dire; **I ~!** * dites donc!; **you don't ~!** * pas possible!; **if there were, ~, 500** s'il y avait, disons, 500; **that's not for me to ~** ce n'est pas à moi de dire ça.
2 *n*: **to have one's ~** dire son mot, dire ce qu'on a à dire; **to have a ~ /no ~ in the matter** avoir/ ne pas avoir voix au chapitre.
◆ **saying** *n* dicton *m*; **as the ~ing goes** comme on dit. ◆ **say-so** * *n*: **on your ~-so** parce que vous le dites.

scab [skæb] *n* (**a**) croûte *f (Med)*. (**b**) *(‡ pej: blackleg)* jaune *m*.

scaffold ['skæf(ə)ld] *n* (**a**) *(gallows)* échafaud *m*. (**b**) *(Constr: also ~ing)* échafaudage *m*.

scald [skɔ:ld] *vt* ébouillanter; *(sterilize)* stériliser. ◆ **scalding (hot)** *adj* brûlant.

scale[1] [skeɪl] **1** *n* (**a**) *(gen)* échelle *f*; *[numbers]* série *f*. **~ of charges** barème *m*; **(drawn) to ~** à l'échelle; **on a ~ of 1 cm to 5 km** à une échelle de 1 cm pour 5 km. (**b**) *(fig) scope* échelle *f*; *(size etc)* importance *f*. **on a large/small ~** sur une grande/petite échelle; **on a national ~** à l'échelle nationale. (**c**) *(Mus)* gamme *f*. **2** *adj*: **~ drawing** dessin *m* à l'échelle; **~ model** modèle *m* réduit. **3** *vt wall, mountain* escalader. ◆ **scale down** *vt sep (gen)* réduire; *salary* réduire proportionnellement; *drawing* réduire l'échelle de; *production* réduire.

scale[2] [skeɪl] **1** *n [fish, rust etc]* écaille *f*; *(on skin)* squame *f*. **2** *vt teeth, kettle* détartrer.

scales [skeɪlz] *npl*: **(pair** *or* **set of) ~** *(in kitchen, shop)* balance *f*; *(in bathroom)* pèse-personne *m inv*; *(for luggage, heavy goods)* bascule *f*. *(Astron)* **the S~** la Balance; **to turn the ~ at 80 kilos** peser 80 kilos; *(fig)* **to tip the ~** faire pencher la balance (*in sb's favour* du côté de qn; *against sb* contre qn).

scallop ['skɒləp] *n* coquille *f* Saint-Jacques. **~ shell** coquille.

scalp [skælp] **1** *n* cuir *m* chevelu; *(trophy)* scalp *m*. **2** *vt* scalper.

scalpel ['skælp(ə)l] *n* scalpel *m*.

scamp[1] * [skæmp] *n (child)* polisson(ne) *m(f)*.

scamp[2] [skæmp] *vt one's work etc* bâcler *.

scamper ['skæmpəʳ] *vi [children]* **to ~ in/out** *etc* entrer/sortir *etc* en gambadant; **to ~ about** gambader.

scampi ['skæmpɪ] *npl* langoustines *fpl* (frites).

scan [skæn] **1** *vt* (**a**) *(examine closely) horizon, sb's face* scruter; *crowd* fouiller du regard; *newspaper* lire attentivement. (**b**) *(glance at) horizon* promener son regard sur; *crowd* parcourir des yeux; *newspaper* parcourir rapidement. (**c**) *(Radar, TV)* balayer; *(Comput)* scruter; *(Med) [machine]* balayer; *[person]* faire une scanographie de. **2** *vi (Poetry)* se scander. **3** *n (Rad, TV)* balayage *m*; *(Med)* scanographie *f*. **(ultra-sound) ~** échographie *f*. ◆ **scanner** *n* scanner *m*; *(optical ~)* lecteur *m* optique. ◆ **scansion** *n* scansion *f*.

scandal ['skændl] *n* (**a**) *(disgrace)* scandale *m*. **it's a ~** c'est scandaleux; **it's a ~ that...** c'est un scandale que... + *subj*. (**b**) *(gossip)* ragots * *mpl*. **there's a lot of ~ going around about him** il y a beaucoup de ragots * qui circulent sur son compte. ◆ **scandalize** *vt* scandaliser; **to be ~ized by** se scandaliser de. ◆ **scandalous** *adj* scandaleux. ◆ **scandalously** *adv* scandaleusement.

Scandinavia [ˌskændɪ'neɪvɪə] *n* Scandinavie *f*. ◆ **Scandinavian 1** *adj* scandinave ; **2** *n* Scandinave *mf*.

scant [skænt] *adj*: **with ~ courtesy** avec bien peu de politesse; **to pay ~ attention** faire à peine attention; **~ praise** éloge *m* des plus brefs. ◆ **scantily** *adv* insuffisamment; **~ily clad** vêtu du strict minimum. ◆ **scanty** *adj meal, harvest* peu abondant; *income, swimsuit* minuscule.

scapegoat ['skeɪpgəʊt] *n* bouc *m* émissaire.

scar [skɑ:ʳ] **1** *n (gen)* cicatrice *f*; *(esp on face)* balafre *f*. *(fig)* **it left a deep ~ on his mind** il en est resté profondément marqué *(fig)*. **2** *vt* marquer d'une cicatrice; *(on face)* balafrer. **~red by smallpox** grêlé par la petite vérole; **war-~red town** ville *f* qui porte des cicatrices de la guerre.

scarce [skɛəs] *adj food, money* peu abondant; *edition* rare. **corn is getting ~** le blé se fait rare; **such people are ~** de telles gens sont rares; **to make o.s. ~** * se sauver *. ◆ **scarcely** *adv see, touch* à peine; **~ly anybody knows** il y a très peu de gens qui savent; **he ~ly ever goes there** il n'y va presque jamais; **I can ~ly believe it** j'ai du mal à le croire. ◆ **scarceness** *or* ◆ **scarcity** *n* pénurie *f*.

scare [skɛəʳ] **1** *n*: **to give sb a ~** effrayer qn, faire peur à qn; **to raise a ~** semer la panique; **the war ~** les rumeurs *fpl* de guerre; **bomb ~** alerte *f* à la bombe. **2** *adj headlines, tactics* alarmiste. **3** *vt* effrayer, faire peur à. **to ~ sb stiff** * faire une peur bleue à qn; **to be ~d** avoir peur (*of* de); **to be ~d stiff** *, **to be ~d to death** *, **to be ~d out of one's wits** * avoir une peur bleue *or* une frousse * terrible (*of* de). ◆ **scare away, scare off** *vt sep [dog etc]* faire fuir; *[price]* faire peur à. ◆ **scare up** *vt sep (US)* arriver à trouver. ◆ **scarecrow** *n* épouvantail *m*. ◆ **scared** *adj* effrayé, affolé (*of* par); *V also* **scare 2** *above*. ◆ **scaremonger** *n* alarmiste *mf*. ◆ **scary** * *adj* qui donne la frousse *.

scarf [skɑ:f] *n* écharpe *f*; *(square)* foulard *m*.

scarlatina [ˌskɑ:lə'ti:nə] *n* scarlatine *f*.

scarlet ['skɑ:lɪt] *adj* écarlate. **~ fever** scarlatine *f*.

scarper ‡ ['skɑ:pəʳ] *vi (Brit)* ficher le camp *.

scathing ['skeɪðɪŋ] *adj remark* cinglant. **to be ~ about sth** critiquer qch de façon cinglante. ◆ **scathingly** *adv* d'une manière cinglante; **to look ~ly at sb** foudroyer qn du regard.

scatter ['skætəʳ] **1** *vt* (**a**) *crumbs, papers* éparpiller; *seeds* semer à la volée; *sand, salt, sawdust* répandre; *coins* jeter à la volée; *cushions* jeter çà et là. (**b**) *clouds, crowd* disperser; *enemy* mettre en déroute. **~ed showers** averses *fpl* intermittentes; **his paintings are ~ed all over the country** ses tableaux sont dispersés aux quatre coins du pays. **2** *vi* *[clouds, crowd]* se disperser. ◆ **scatterbrain** *n* écervelé(e) *m(f)*. ◆ **scatterbrained** *adj* écervelé.

scavenge ['skævɪn(d)ʒ] *vi* fouiller (*for* pour trouver). ◆ **scavenger** *n (insect, animal)* charognard *m; (street cleaner)* éboueur *m*; *(person on dump etc)* pilleur *m* de poubelles.

scenario [sɪ'nɑːrɪəʊ] *n* scénario *m*; *(plan of action)* plan *m* d'action.

scene [siːn] **1** *n* (**a**) *(gen, Theat)* scène *f*. *(Cine, TV)* **outdoor** ~ extérieur *m*; **the** ~ **is set in Paris** la scène se passe à Paris; *(fig)* **the** ~ **was set for** toutes les conditions étaient réunies pour; **this set the** ~ **for** ceci a préparé le terrain pour; *(Theat, fig)* **behind the** ~**s** dans les coulisses; ~**s of violence** scènes de violence; **there were angry** ~**s** des incidents violents ont eu lieu; *(fuss)* **to make a** ~ faire toute une scène *or* toute une histoire *. (**b**) *(place)* lieu *m*, endroit *m*. **the** ~ **of the crime/accident** le lieu du crime/de l'accident; **he needs a change of** ~ il a besoin de changer de cadre; **to come on the** ~ arriver; **it's not my** ~ ‡ ça n'est pas mon genre *. (**c**) *(sight)* spectacle *m*; *(view)* vue *f*. **the** ~ **from the top** la vue *or* le panorama du sommet; **a** ~ **of utter destruction** un spectacle de destruction totale. **2** *adj (Theat)* ~ **change** changement *m* de décors; ~ **painter** peintre *m* de décors; ~ **shifter** machiniste *m*. ◆ **scenery** *n (countryside)* paysage *m*; *(Theat)* décors *mpl*; *(fig)* **a change of** ~**ry** un changement de cadre. ◆ **scenic** *adj* scénique; *(Rail)* **scenic car** voiture *f* panoramique; **scenic railway** *(panoramic)* petit train *m* d'agrément; *(Brit: switchback)* montagnes *fpl* russes; **scenic road** route *f* touristique.

scent [sent] **1** *n* (**a**) *(perfume)* parfum *m*. (**b**) *(animal's track)* fumet *m*; *(fig)* piste *f*. **to lose the** ~ perdre la piste; **to put sb off the** ~ déjouer qn. **2** *adj*: ~ **bottle** flacon *m* à parfum; ~ **spray** vaporisateur *m*; *(aerosol)* atomiseur *m*. **3** *vt* (**a**) *(make ~ed)* parfumer (*with* de). (**b**) *(smell) game, danger* flairer.

sceptic, *(US)* **skeptic** ['skeptɪk] *adj*, *n* sceptique *(mf)*. ◆ **sceptical** *adj* sceptique (*of, about* sur). ◆ **sceptically** *adv* avec scepticisme. ◆ **scepticism** *n* scepticisme *m*.

sceptre, *(US)* **scepter** ['septəʳ] *n* sceptre *m*.

schedule ['ʃedjuːl], *(US)* ['skedjuːl] *n* (**a**) *[work, duties, visits]* programme *m*; *[trains etc]* horaire *m*; *[events]* calendrier *m*. **to go according to** ~ se passer comme prévu; **on** *or* **up to** ~ *train* à l'heure; *work* à jour; **to be behind** ~ avoir du retard; **to be ahead of** ~ *(in work)* avoir de l'avance sur son programme; **to work to a very tight** ~ avoir un programme de travail très serré. (**b**) *(list) [goods, contents]* liste *f*, inventaire *m*; *[prices]* barème *m*; *(Customs, Tax etc)* tarif *m*. ◆ **scheduled** *adj time, date, activity* prévu; *price* tarifé; *flight, train or bus service* régulier; *stop* indiqué dans l'horaire; **he is** ~**d to leave at midday** il doit partir à midi.

scheme [skiːm] **1** *n* (**a**) *(plan)* plan *m*, projet *m* (*of doing* de faire; *to do, for doing* pour faire; *for sth* pour qch). **a** ~ **of work** un plan de travail; **profit-sharing** ~ système *m* de participation (aux bénéfices); **it's not a bad** ~ * ça n'est pas une mauvaise idée. (**b**) *(plot)* complot *m* (*to do* pour faire). **2** *vi* comploter (*to do* pour faire). ◆ **schemer** *n (small-scale)* intrigant(e) *m(f)*; *(large-scale)* comploteur *m*, -euse *f*. ◆ **scheming** **1** *adj* intrigant ; **2** *n* intrigues *fpl*.

schism ['sɪz(ə)m] *n* schisme *m*.

schizophrenia [ˌskɪtsə(ʊ)'friːnɪə] *n* schizophrénie *f*. ◆ **schizophrenic** *adj*, *n* schizophrène *(mf)*.

schmaltzy * [ʃmɔːltsɪ] *adj* à la guimauve.

scholar ['skɒləʳ] *n* lettré(e) *m(f)*, érudit(e) *m(f)*. **a Dickens** ~ un(e) spécialiste de Dickens. ◆ **scholarly** *adj* érudit, savant. ◆ **scholarship** **1** *n (knowledge)* érudition *f*; *(award)* bourse *f* (d'études) *(obtenue sur concours)* ; **2** *adj*: ~**ship holder** boursier *m*, -ière *f*. ◆ **scholastic** *adj* scolaire.

school[1] [skuːl] **1** *n* (**a**) *(gen)* école *f*; *(primary ~)* école; *(secondary ~)* collège *m*; *(grammar ~)* lycée *m*; *(lessons)* cours *mpl*; *(in primary ~)* classes *fpl*. ~ **of motoring** auto-école *f*; **to** *or* **at** *or* **in** ~ à l'école (*or* au collège *etc*); **to leave** ~ quitter l'école *etc*; *(Art)* **the Dutch** ~ l'école hollandaise; **a** ~ **of thought** une école de pensée; *(fig)* **of the old** ~ de la vieille école. (**b**) *(Univ)* faculté *f*. **he's at law/medical** ~ il fait son droit/sa médecine; **S**~ **of Linguistics** *etc* Institut *m or* Département *m* de Linguistique *etc*; *(US)* ~ **of education** école *f* normale (primaire).

2 *adj doctor, holidays, life, report etc* scolaire. ~ **attendance** scolarisation *f*; ~ **attendance officer** fonctionnaire *mf* chargé(e) de faire respecter les règlements de la scolarisation; ~ **bus** car *m* de ramassage scolaire; ~ **bus service** service *m* de ramassage scolaire; ~ **fees** frais *mpl* de scolarité; **during** ~ **hours, in** ~ **time** pendant les heures de classe; ~ **record** dossier *m* d'élève.

3 *vt animal* dresser; *feelings, reactions* contrôler; *voice etc* discipliner. **to** ~ **o.s. to do** s'astreindre à faire.

◆ **school-age** *adj* d'âge scolaire. ◆ **schoolbag** *n* cartable *m*. ◆ **schoolbook** *n* livre *m* de classe. ◆ **schoolboy** **1** *n* élève *m*, écolier *m* ; **2** *adj*: ~**boy slang** argot *m* scolaire. ◆ **schoolchild** *n* écolier *m*, -ière *f*, lycéen(ne) *m(f)*, collégien(ne) *m(f)*. ◆ **schooldays** *npl* années *fpl* d'école. ◆ **schoolgirl** *n* élève *f*, écolière *f*. ◆ **schooling** *n (gen)* études *fpl*; **compulsory** ~**ing** scolarité *f* obligatoire. ◆ **school-leaver** *n* jeune *mf* qui a terminé ses études secondaires. ◆ **school-leaving age** *n* âge *m* de fin de scolarité. ◆ **schoolmarm** * *n (pej)* institutrice *f*. ◆ **schoolmaster** *n (primary)* instituteur *m*; *(secondary)* professeur *m*. ◆ **schoolmate** *n* camarade *mf* de classe. ◆ **schoolmistress** *n (primary)* institutrice *f*; *(secondary)* professeur *m*. ◆ **schoolroom** *n* salle *f* de classe. ◆ **schoolteacher** *n (primary)* instituteur *m*, -trice *f*; *(secondary)* professeur *m*. ◆ **schoolteaching** *n* enseignement *m*.

school[2] [skuːl] *n [fish]* banc *m*.

schooner ['skuːnəʳ] *n (Naut)* goélette *f*.

sciatica [saɪ'ætɪkə] *n* sciatique *f*.

science ['saɪəns] **1** *n* science *f*; *(subject for study)* sciences. **it's a real** ~ c'est une véritable science; **the S**~ **Faculty** la faculté des Sciences. **2** *adj equipment, subject* scientifique; *exam, teacher* de sciences. ~ **fiction** science-fiction *f*; ~ **park** parc *m* scientifique. ◆ **scientific** *adj (gen)* scientifique; *instrument* de précision. ◆ **scientifically** *adv* scientifiquement. ◆ **scientist** *n* scientifique *mf*; **one of our leading scientists** l'un de nos grands savants.

Scilly Isles ['sɪlɪaɪlz] *npl* Sorlingues *fpl*.

scintillate ['sɪntɪleɪt] *vi [star, jewel]* scintiller; *[person]* pétiller d'esprit. ◆ **scintillating** *adj* scintillant; *conversation etc* pétillant.

scissors ['sɪzəz] *npl* ciseaux *mpl*.

scoff [skɒf] *vi* se moquer (*at* de). ◆ **scoffer** *n* moqueur *m*, -euse *f*.

scold [skəʊld] *vt* réprimander (*for doing* pour avoir fait); *child* gronder, attraper (*for doing* pour avoir fait). ◆ **scolding** *n* réprimande *f*, gronderie *f*; **to get a** ~**ing from sb** se faire réprimander *or* gronder par qn.

scone [skɒn] *n* scone *m (petit pain au lait)*.

scoop [skuːp] **1** *n* (**a**) *(for flour, sugar)* pelle *f (à main)*; *(for water)* écope *f*; *(for ice cream/potatoes)* cuiller *f* à glace/à purée. (**b**) **to make a** ~ *(Comm)* faire un gros bénéfice; *(Press)* faire un scoop. **2** *vt (Comm) market* s'emparer de; *competitor* devancer; *profit* ramasser; *(Press) story* publier en exclusivité.

◆ **scoop out** *vt sep water* vider; *hole* creuser. ◆ **scoop up** *vt sep* ramasser.

scooter ['sku:tər] *n* scooter *m*; *[child]* trottinette *f*.

scope [skəʊp] *n (opportunity: for activity, action etc)* possibilités *fpl*; *(range) [law, regulation]* étendue *f*, portée *f*; *(capacity) [person]* compétence *f*, capacité(s) *f(pl)*. **a programme of considerable** ~ un programme d'une envergure considérable; **to extend the** ~ **of one's activities** élargir le champ de ses activités; **it is within/beyond his** ~ cela entre dans/dépasse ses compétences; **it is within/beyond the** ~ **of this book** cela entre dans/dépasse les limites *fpl* de ce livre.

scorch [skɔ:tʃ] **1** *n* (~ **mark**) brûlure *f* légère. **2** *vt linen* roussir; *grass [fire etc]* brûler; *[sun]* dessécher. ~**ed earth policy** tactique *f* de la terre brûlée. **3** *vi [car]* **to** ~ **along** rouler à toute vitesse. ◆ **scorcher** * *n* journée *f* torride. ◆ **scorching** *adj heat* torride; *sand* brûlant; *sun* de plomb; *weather* très chaud.

score [skɔ:r] **1** *n* (**a**) *(Sport)* score *m*; *(Cards)* marque *f*; *(US Scol)* note *f*. **to keep (the)** ~ *(gen)* compter les points; *(Cards)* tenir la marque; *(Tennis)* tenir le score; *(Ftbl)* **there's no** ~ **yet** on n'a pas encore marqué (de but); **there was no** ~ **in the match** ils ont fait match nul; **what's the** ~**?** *(Sport)* où en est le jeu *or* le match?; *(* fig)* où en sommes-nous?; *(fig)* **to know the** ~ * connaître le topo *; *(fig)* **he's got an old** ~ **to settle with him** il a un compte à régler avec lui. (**b**) *(account)* titre *m*. **on that** ~ à ce titre. (**c**) *(mark: on wood etc)* rayure *f*; *(on leather etc)* incision *f*. (**d**) *(Mus)* partition *f*. **piano** ~ partition de piano; **the film** ~ la musique du film. (**e**) *(twenty)* **a** ~ vingt; **a** ~ **of people** une vingtaine de personnes; *(fig)* ~**s of** un grand nombre de, des tas * de.

2 *vt* (**a**) *goal, point* marquer. **to** ~ **70% in an exam** avoir 70 sur 100 à un examen; **to** ~ **a hit** *(Fencing)* toucher; *(Shooting)* viser juste; *(fig)* remporter un grand succès. (**b**) *(cut) rock* strier; *wood, metal* rayer; *leather, skin* inciser. (**c**) *music* écrire *(for violin etc* pour violon *etc)*; *film etc* composer la musique de.

3 *vi [player]* marquer un *or* des point(s); *[footballer etc]* marquer un but; *[scorer]* marquer les points; *(fig)* avoir l'avantage. *(fig)* **to** ~ **over** *or* **off sb** marquer un point aux dépens de qn. ◆ **score off, score out** *vt sep* rayer, barrer. ◆ **scoreboard** *n* tableau *m*. ◆ **scorecard** *n (Shooting)* carton *m*; *(Golf)* carte *f* du parcours; *(Cards)* feuille *f* de marque. ◆ **scorer** *n (keeping ~)* marqueur *m*; *(goal ~r)* marqueur (de but).

scorn [skɔ:n] **1** *n* mépris *m*. **2** *vt person, action* mépriser; *advice, danger* faire fi de; *suggestion* rejeter. **I** ~ **to tell a lie** je ne m'abaisserais pas à mentir. ◆ **scornful** *adj* méprisant; **to be** ~**ful about sth** manifester son mépris pour qch. ◆ **scornfully** *adv* avec mépris.

Scorpio ['skɔ:pɪəʊ] *n* le Scorpion *(Astron)*.

scorpion ['skɔ:pɪən] *n* scorpion *m*.

Scot [skɒt] *n* Écossais(e) *m(f)*.

Scotch [skɒtʃ] **1** *n* (**a**) whisky *m*, scotch *m*. (**b**) *(abusivement pour* **Scottish** *ou* **Scots***)* **the** ~ les Écossais *mpl*. **2** *adj (abusivement)* écossais. ~ **egg** *œuf dur enrobé de chair à saucisse*; ~ **mist** bruine *f*; ~ **tape** Ⓡ scotch *m* Ⓡ, ruban adhésif.

scotch [skɒtʃ] *vt rumour* étouffer; *plan, attempt* faire échouer; *revolt, uprising* réprimer; *claim* démentir.

scot-free ['skɒt'fri:] *adj (unpunished)* sans être puni; *(not paying)* sans payer; *(unhurt)* indemne.

Scotland ['skɒtlənd] *n* Écosse *f*.

Scots [skɒts] *adj, n* écossais *(m)*. ◆ **Scotsman** *n* Écossais *m*. ◆ **Scotswoman** *n* Écossaise *f*.

Scottish ['skɒtɪʃ] *adj* écossais. **the** ~ **Office** le ministère des Affaires écossaises.

scoundrel ['skaʊndr(ə)l] *n* vaurien *m*; *(child)* coquin(e) *m(f)*.

scour ['skaʊər] *vt* (**a**) *pan, sink* récurer; *table, floor* frotter; *(with water)* nettoyer à grande eau; *metal* décaper. (**b**) *(search)* parcourir (*for* à la recherche de). ◆ **scourer** *n (powder)* poudre *f* à récurer; *(pad)* tampon *m* abrasif.

scourge [skɜ:dʒ] *n* fléau *m*.

scout [skaʊt] **1** *n* (**a**) *(Mil)* éclaireur *m*; *(boy)* scout *m (gen Catholic)*; éclaireur *(gen non-Catholic)*. (**b**) **to have a** ~ **round** * reconnaître le terrain. **2** *adj camp, movement* scout; *uniform* de scout. **3** *vi (Mil)* aller en reconnaissance. *(gen)* **to** ~ **about for** chercher. ◆ **scouting** *n* scoutisme *m*. ◆ **scoutmaster** *n* chef *m* scout.

scowl [skaʊl] **1** *n* mine *f* renfrognée. **he said with a** ~ dit-il en se renfrognant. **2** *vi* se renfrogner, froncer les sourcils. **to** ~ **at** jeter un regard mauvais à.

scrabble ['skræbl] **1** *vi:* **to** ~ **about** *or* **around for sth** chercher qch à tâtons. **2** *n (game)* **S**~ Ⓡ Scrabble *m* Ⓡ.

scraggy ['skrægɪ] *adj person, animal* efflanqué; *neck, limb* décharné.

scram * [skræm] *vi* ficher le camp *.

scramble ['skræmbl] **1** *vi* (**a**) **to** ~ **up/ down/along** grimper/descendre/avancer tant bien que mal (et à toute vitesse); **to** ~ **for** *coins, seats* se bousculer pour (avoir); *jobs etc* faire des pieds et des mains pour (avoir). (**b**) *(Sport)* **to go scrambling** faire du moto-cross. **2** *vt (Culin, Telec)* brouiller. ~**d eggs** œufs brouillés. **3** *n* (**a**) *(rush)* ruée *f* (*for* pour). (**b**) *(motorcycle)* (réunion *f* de) moto-cross *m*. ◆ **scrambler** *n (Telec)* brouilleur *m*. ◆ **scrambling** *n (Sport)* trial *m*.

scrap[1] [skræp] **1** *n* (**a**) *(piece: gen)* (petit) bout *m*; *[writing]* quelques lignes *fpl*; *[conversation]* bribe *f*; *[news]* fragment *m*. ~**s** *(broken pieces)* débris *mpl*; *[food]* restes *mpl*; **not a** ~ **of evidence/use** pas la moindre preuve/utilité; **not a** ~ pas du tout. (**b**) (~ **metal**) ferraille *f*. **to sell for** ~ vendre à la casse; **what is it worth as** ~**?** qu'est-ce que cela vaudrait à la casse? **2** *adj car* mis à la ferraille. ~ **dealer** *or* **merchant** marchand *m* de ferraille; *(fig)* **to throw sth on the** ~ **heap** mettre qch au rebut; ~ **iron** ferraille *f*; ~ **paper** *(for scribbling on)* papier *m* de brouillon; *(newspapers etc)* vieux papiers; ~ **yard** chantier *m* de ferraille; *(for cars)* cimetière *m* de voitures. **3** *vt* jeter; *car, ship* envoyer à la ferraille; *equipment* mettre au rebut; *project* laisser tomber. ◆ **scrapbook** *n* album *m (de coupures de journaux etc)*. ◆ **scrappy** *adj conversation, essay* décousu; *education* incomplet; *meal* sur le pouce *.

scrap[2] * [skræp] **1** *n (fight)* bagarre *f*. **2** *vi* se bagarrer * (*with* avec).

scrape [skreɪp] **1** *n* (**a**) *(action)* coup *m* de racloir; *(sound)* raclement *m*; *(mark)* éraflure *f*. (**b**) *(*: trouble)* **to get into/out of a** ~ se mettre dans un/se sortir d'un mauvais pas. **2** *vt (clean)* racler; *vegetables* gratter; *(scratch)* érafler; *(just touch)* frôler. **to** ~ **one's plate clean** tout manger; **to** ~ **sth off sth** enlever qch de qch en raclant; **to** ~ **a living** vivoter; *(Naut)* **to** ~ **the bottom** talonner; *(fig)* **to** ~ **the bottom of the barrel** en être réduit aux raclures; **to** ~ **(up) an acquaintance with sb** réussir à faire la connaissance de qn. **3** *vi (make sound)* racler, gratter; *(rub)* frotter (*against* contre). **to** ~ **along the wall** frôler le mur; **to** ~ **through the doorway** réussir de justesse à passer par la porte; **to** ~ **through an exam** réussir un examen de justesse. ◆ **scrape along** *vi (manage)* se débrouiller; *(live)* vivoter. ◆ **scrape away, scrape off** *vt sep* enlever en raclant. ◆ **scrape through** *vi (succeed)* réussir de justesse. ◆ **scrape together, scrape up** *vt sep objects* rassembler; *money* réunir à grand-peine. ◆ **scraper** *n* racloir *m*; *(at doorstep)* grattoir *m*.

scratch [skrætʃ] **1** *n* (**a**) *(mark) (on skin)* égratignure *f*; *(on paint)* éraflure *f*; *(on glass, record)* rayure *f*. *(unharmed)* **without a** ~ indemne. (**b**) *(action, noise)* grattement *m*; *(by claw/nail)* coup *m* de griffe/d'ongle. (**c**) *(Sport)* scratch *m*. *(fig)* **to start from** ~ partir de zéro *; **to come up to** ~ se montrer à la hauteur; **to bring/keep sb up to** ~ amener/maintenir qn au niveau voulu. **2** *adj crew, team* de fortune; *race, golfer* scratch *inv*; *(Comput)* ~ **file** fichier de travail. **3** *vt* (**a**) *(with nail, claw)* griffer; *varnish* érafler; *record, glass* rayer; *one's name* graver. **to** ~ **a hole in sth** creuser un trou en grattant qch; **he** ~**ed his hand on a nail** il s'est éraflé la main sur un clou. (**b**) *(to relieve itch)* gratter. **to** ~ **one's head** se gratter la tête; *(fig)* **you** ~ **my back and I'll** ~ **yours** un petit service en vaut un autre. (**c**) *(cancel) meeting, game* annuler; *competitor, horse* scratcher; *(US Pol) candidate* rayer de la liste. **4** *vi [person, dog etc]* se gratter; *[hens]* gratter le sol; *[pen]* gratter. **the dog was** ~**ing at the door** le chien grattait à la porte. ◆ **scratch out** *vt sep (from list)* rayer. **to** ~ **sb's eyes out** arracher les yeux à qn. ◆ **scratchy** *adj material* rêche; *pen* qui gratte; *record* rayé.

scrawl [skrɔːl] **1** *n* gribouillage *m*, griffonnage *m*; *(brief letter)* mot *m* griffonné. **2** *vt* gribouiller, griffonner; *letter* griffonner.

scrawny ['skrɔːnɪ] *adj person, animal* efflanqué; *neck, limb* décharné.

scream [skriːm] **1** *n [pain, fear]* cri *m* perçant, hurlement *m*; *[laughter]* éclat *m*. **to give a** ~ pousser un cri; *(fig)* **it was a** ~ * c'était à se tordre (de rire); **he's a** ~ * il est impayable *. **2** *vi* (~ **out**) crier (*at sb* après qn; *for help* à l'aide), hurler (*with pain/rage* de douleur/de colère). **to** ~ **with laughter** rire aux éclats. **3** *vt* (~ **out**) *[person]* hurler (*at* à); *[headlines, posters]* annoncer en toutes lettres. ◆ **screamingly** * *adv*: ~**ingly funny** tordant *.

scree [skriː] *n* éboulis *m (en montagne)*.

screech [skriːtʃ] **1** *n [person, siren]* hurlement *m*; *[brakes]* grincement *m*; *[tyres]* crissement *m*; *[owl]* cri *m* (rauque et perçant). **she gave a** ~ **of laughter** elle est partie d'un rire perçant. **2** *vi* hurler; grincer; crisser; crier. **3** *vt* crier à tue-tête. ◆ **screech-owl** *n* effraie *f*.

screeds * [skriːdz] *npl*: **to write** ~ écrire des volumes.

screen [skriːn] **1** *n* (**a**) *(in room)* paravent *m*; *(for fire)* écran *m* de cheminée; *(fig: of troops, trees)* rideau *m*. (**b**) *(Cine, TV etc)* écran *m*. *(Cine)* **the** ~ l'écran, le cinéma; *(Cine/TV)* **the large/small** ~ le grand/petit écran; **to write for the** ~ écrire des scénarios. **2** *adj actor* de cinéma. ~ **test** bout *m* d'essai; ~ **washer** lave-glace(s) *m*; ~ **writer** scénariste *mf*. **3** *vt* (**a**) *(hide)* masquer (*from sight* aux regards), cacher; *(protect)* protéger (*from* de). **he** ~**ed the book with his hand** il a caché le livre de sa main. (**b**) *film* projeter. (**c**) *(sieve) coal* cribler; *(fig) candidates* passer au crible. *(fig)* **to** ~ **sb (for a job)** passer un candidat au crible; *(Med)* **to** ~ **sb for cancer** faire subir à qn un test de dépistage du cancer. ◆ **screening** *n* (**a**) *[film]* projection *f*; (**b**) *(Med)* test *m* de dépistage. ◆ **screenplay** *n* scénario *m*.

screw [skruː] **1** *n* (**a**) vis *f*; *(action)* tour *m* de vis. *(Brit)* **a** ~ **of sweets** *etc* un cornet de bonbons *etc*; *(fig)* **he's got a** ~ **loose** * il lui manque une case *; **to put the** ~**(s) on sb** * forcer la main à qn. (**b**) *(propeller)* hélice *f*. (**c**) *(Brit* ‡*: income)* salaire *m*. (**d**) *(*‡*: prison officer)* maton(ne) *m(f)*. **2** *vt* (**a**) (~ **down,** ~ **on)** visser (*on* sur; *to* à). **to** ~ **sth tight** visser qch à bloc; *(fig)* **he's got his head** ~**ed on all right** * il a la tête sur les épaules. (**b**) *(extort)* soutirer (*out of* à). **3** *vi* (~ **down,** ~ **on)** se visser. ◆ **screw off 1** *vi* se dévisser. **2** *vt sep* dévisser. ◆ **screw round** *vt sep* tourner, visser. **to** ~ **one's head round** se dévisser la tête. ◆ **screw together** *vt sep two parts* fixer avec une vis; *object* assembler avec des vis. ◆ **screw up** *vt sep paper* froisser; *handkerchief* rouler; *one's eyes* plisser; *(*‡*: spoil)* bousiller *. **to** ~ **up one's face** faire la grimace; *(fig)* **to** ~ **up one's courage** prendre son courage à deux mains (*to do* pour faire). ◆ **screwball** ‡ *adj, n* cinglé(e) *m(f)*. ◆ **screwdriver** *n* tournevis *m*. ◆ **screw-top(ped)** *adj* avec couvercle à pas de vis. ◆ **screwy** ‡ *adj (mad)* cinglé *.

scribble ['skrɪbl] **1** *vti* gribouiller, griffonner. **2** *n* griffonnage *m*. ◆ **scribble down** *vt sep notes* griffonner. ◆ **scribbler** *n (bad author)* plumitif *m*. ◆ **scribbling** *n* gribouillage *m*. ◆ **scribbling pad** *n* bloc-notes *m*.

scribe [skraɪb] *n* scribe *m*.

scrimmage ['skrɪmɪdʒ] *n (gen, Sport)* mêlée *f*.

script [skrɪpt] **1** *n* (**a**) *(Cine)* scénario *m*; *(Rad, Theat, TV)* texte *m*; *(in exam)* copie *f*. (**b**) *(handwriting)* script *m*. **2** *vt film* écrire le scénario de. ◆ **scripted** *adj (Rad, TV) talk* préparé d'avance. ◆ **script-girl** *n* script(-girl) *f*. ◆ **scriptwriter** *n* scénariste *mf*.

Scripture ['skrɪptʃəʳ] *n* Écriture *f* sainte.

scroll [skrəʊl] **1** *n [parchment]* rouleau *m*; *(ancient book)* manuscrit *m*; *(Archit)* volute *f*. **2** *vt (Comput)* défiler. **3** *vi (Comput)* **to** ~ **up/down** faire défiler vers le haut/vers le bas.

scrounge * [skraʊn(d)ʒ] **1** *vt meal, clothes etc* se faire payer (*from, off sb* par qn). **to** ~ **money from sb** taper qn ‡; **he** ~**d £5 off him** il l'a tapé de 5 livres ‡. **2** *vi*: **to** ~ **on sb** vivre aux crochets de qn. ◆ **scrounger** * *n* parasite *m*; *(for meals)* pique-assiette *mf inv*.

scrub¹ [skrʌb] **1** *n*: **to give sth a good** ~ bien nettoyer qch (à la brosse); **give your face a** ~! lave-toi bien la figure! **2** *vt* (**a**) *floor* nettoyer *or* laver à la brosse; *pan* récurer. **to** ~ **one's hands** se brosser les mains. (**b**) *(*: cancel) match etc* annuler. ◆ **scrub down** *vt sep room* nettoyer à fond. **to** ~ **o.s. down** faire une toilette en règle. ◆ **scrub off** *vt sep mark, stain* enlever en frottant. ◆ **scrubber** *n (pan-scrubber)* tampon *m* à récurer. ◆ **scrubbing-brush** *n* brosse *f* dure. ◆ **scrub-woman** *n (US)* femme *f* de ménage.

scrub² [skrʌb] *n (brushwood)* broussailles *fpl*.

scruff [skrʌf] *n* (**a**) **by the** ~ **of the neck** par la peau du cou. (**b**) *(*: untidy person)* personne *f* débraillée. ◆ **scruffiness** *n [person]* débraillé *m*; *[building, clothes]* miteux *m*. ◆ **scruffy** *adj person* débraillé; *child* crasseux; *building, clothes* miteux; *hair* sale et mal peigné.

scrum [skrʌm] *n (Rugby)* mêlée *f*; *(*: in crowd)* bousculade *f*. *(Rugby)* ~ **half** demi *m* de mêlée.

scrumptious * ['skrʌm(p)ʃəs] *adj* succulent.

scruple ['skruːpl] *n* scrupule *m* (*about* au sujet de). **he had no** ~**s about doing it** il ne se faisait pas scrupule de le faire. ◆ **scrupulous** *adj* scrupuleux. ◆ **scrupulously** *adv pay, do* scrupuleusement; **scrupulously honest/clean** d'une honnêteté scrupuleuse/d'une propreté irréprochable. ◆ **scrupulousness** *n* scrupules *mpl*.

scrutinize ['skruːtɪnaɪz] *vt (gen)* scruter; *votes* pointer. ◆ **scrutiny** *n (gen)* regard *m* scrutateur; *[document, conduct]* examen *m* minutieux; *[votes]* pointage *m*.

scuba ['skuːbə] *n* scaphandre *m* autonome. ~ **diver** plongeur *m*, -euse *f*; ~ **diving** plongée *f* sous-marine (autonome).

scuff [skʌf] *vt shoes* érafler; *feet* traîner. ◆ **scuff marks** *npl* éraflures *fpl*.

scuffle ['skʌfl] **1** *n* bagarre *f.* **2** *vi* se bagarrer * (*with* avec).

scull [skʌl] *vi*: **to go ~ing** faire de l'aviron.

scullery ['skʌlərɪ] *n* arrière-cuisine *f.*

sculpt [skʌlpt] *vti* sculpter (*out of* dans). ◆ **sculptor** *n* sculpteur *m.* ◆ **sculptress** *n* femme *f* sculpteur. ◆ **sculpture 1** *n* sculpture *f* ; **2** *vti* sculpter.

scum [skʌm] *n (gen)* écume *f*; *(dirt)* couche *f* de saleté. **to remove the ~ (from)** écumer; nettoyer. *(fig)* **the ~ of the earth** le rebut du genre humain.

scupper *['skʌpə^r] *vt* saboter. **to be ~ed** être fichu.

scurf [skɜːf] *n* pellicules *fpl (du cuir chevelu).*

scurrilous ['skʌrɪləs] *adj* calomnieux.

scurry ['skʌrɪ] *vi*: **to ~ along/away** *etc* avancer/ partir *etc* à toute vitesse.

scuttle[1] ['skʌtl] *vi*: **to ~ in/through** *etc* entrer/ traverser *etc* précipitamment.

scuttle[2] ['skʌtl] *vt ship* saborder; *plans* faire échouer.

scythe [saɪð] **1** *n* faux *f.* **2** *vt* faucher.

sea [siː] **1** *n* mer *f.* **on the ~** *boat* en mer; *town* au bord de la mer; **by** *or* **beside the ~** au bord de la mer; **over** *or* **beyond the ~(s)** *(adj) lands etc* d'outre-mer; *(adv) lie etc* outre-mer; **to go to ~** *[boat]* prendre la mer; *[person]* devenir *or* se faire marin; **to put to ~** prendre la mer; **by ~** par mer, en bateau; **look out to ~** regardez au large; **(out) at ~** en mer; *(fig)* **I'm all at ~** je nage * complètement; *(fig)* **the call of the ~** l'appel *m* du large; **what's the ~ like?** *(for sailing)* quel est l'état de la mer?; *(for bathing)* est-ce que l'eau est bonne?; **the ~ was very rough** la mer était très mauvaise; *(fig)* **a ~ of faces** une multitude de visages.
2 *adj air* de la mer, marin; *bird, breeze, fish, water* de mer; *god, scout* marin; *battle, power* naval; *route, transport* maritime. **~ anemone** anémone *f* de mer; **~ bathing** bains *mpl* de mer; **~ bed** fond *m* de la mer; **~ captain** capitaine *m* (de marine marchande); **~ change** profond changement *m;* **~ coast** côte *f*; **~ front** front *m* de mer; **to find one's ~ legs** s'habituer à la mer; **~ level** niveau *m* de la mer; **~ loch** bras *m* de mer; **~ wall** digue *f.* ◆ **seaboard** *n* littoral *m.* ◆ **seafarer** *n* marin *m.* ◆ **seafaring** *n* vie *f* de marin. ◆ **seafood** *n* fruits *mpl* de mer. ◆ **sea-green** *adj* vert glauque *inv.* ◆ **seagull** *n* mouette *f.* ◆ **sea-lion** *n* otarie *f.* ◆ **seaman,** *pl* **seamen** *n* marin *m.* ◆ **seamanship** *n* qualités *fpl* de marin. ◆ **seaplane** *n* hydravion *m.* ◆ **seaport** *n* port *m* de mer. ◆ **seascape** *n (Art)* marine *f.* ◆ **seashell** *n* coquillage *m.* ◆ **seashore** *n* rivage *m*, plage *f*; **by the ~shore** au bord de la mer; **on the ~shore** sur la plage, sur le rivage. ◆ **seasick** *adj*: **to be ~sick** avoir le mal de mer. ◆ **seasickness** *n* mal *m* de mer. ◆ **seaside 1** *n* bord *m* de la mer; **at** *or* **beside** *or* **by the ~side** au bord de la mer ; **2** *adj holiday, town* au bord de la mer; *hotel* sur le bord de la mer; **~side resort** station *f* balnéaire. ◆ **sea-urchin** *n* oursin *m.* ◆ **seawards** *adv* vers le large. ◆ **seaway** *n* route *f* maritime. ◆ **seaweed** *n* algue(s) *f(pl).* ◆ **seaworthiness** *n* bon état *m* de navigabilité. ◆ **seaworthy** *adj* en état de naviguer.

seal[1] [siːl] *n* phoque *m.* ◆ **sealer** *n (ship)* navire *m* équipé pour la chasse au phoque. ◆ **sealskin** *n* peau *f* de phoque.

seal[2] [siːl] **1** *n (gen)* sceau *m*; *(on letter)* cachet *m*; *(on package)* plomb *m*; *(Aut etc)* joint *m* (d'étanchéité). *(fig)* **to set one's ~ to sth, to give sth the ~ of approval** donner son approbation à qch; *(fig)* **to set the ~ on sth** sceller qch. **2** *vt* (**a**) *(put ~ on) document* sceller; *(close) envelope* coller; *jar* fermer hermétiquement; *tin* souder; *(Culin) meat* saisir. **~ed orders** instructions *fpl* secrètes; **my lips are ~ed** mes lèvres sont scellées. (**b**) *(decide) fate* régler; *bargain* conclure. ◆ **seal off** *vt sep (close up) door, room* condamner; *(forbid entry to)* interdire l'accès de; *(with police etc) district* mettre un cordon autour de. ◆ **seal up** *vt sep jar, door* fermer hermétiquement. ◆ **sealant** *n (device)* joint *m; (substance)* enduit *m* étanche. ◆ **sealing wax** *n* cire *f* à cacheter.

seam [siːm] *n* (**a**) *(in fabric, rubber)* couture *f*; *(in plastic, metal)* joint *m*; *(in welding)* soudure *f.* **to come apart at the ~s** *[garment]* se découdre; *(fig)* se désagréger; *(fig)* **bursting at the ~s *** plein à craquer. (**b**) *(Min)* veine *f*; *(Geol)* couche *f.* ◆ **seamstress** *n* couturière *f.* ◆ **seamy** *adj district* louche; **the ~y side of life** le côté peu reluisant de la vie.

séance ['seɪɑ̃ːns] *n* séance *f* de spiritisme.

search [sɜːtʃ] **1** *n* (**a**) *(for sth lost)* recherches *fpl.* **in ~ of** à la recherche de; **to make a ~ for sb/sth** entreprendre des recherches pour retrouver qn/ qch; **to begin a ~ for** *person* partir à la recherche de; *thing* se mettre à la recherche de. (**b**) *[person, building, drawer, pocket, district]* fouille *f*; *(Admin) [luggage etc]* visite *f.* (**c**) *(Comput)* recherche *f.* **2** *vt* (**a**) *(hunt through) house, woods, district* fouiller *(for sb/sth* à la recherche de qn/qch). (**b**) *(examine) (gen)* fouiller (*for* pour essayer de retrouver); *(Admin) luggage* visiter. **they ~ed him for a weapon** ils l'ont fouillé pour s'assurer qu'il n'avait pas d'arme. (**c**) *(scan) documents, records, photograph* examiner (en détail) (*for* pour trouver); *one's conscience* sonder; *memory* chercher dans. *(fig)* **he ~ed her face for some sign of affection** il a cherché sur son visage un signe d'affection. (**d**) *(Comput) file* consulter. **to ~ a file for sth** rechercher qch dans un fichier. **3** *vi* chercher. **to ~ after** *or* **for sth** chercher qch; **to ~ through sth** fouiller qch. ◆ **searcher** *n* chercheur *m*, -euse *f* (*for, after* en quête de). ◆ **searching** *adj look* pénétrant; *examination* minutieux. ◆ **searchlight** *n* projecteur *m (pour éclairer).* ◆ **search-party** *n* équipe *f or* expédition *f* de secours. ◆ **search-warrant** *n* mandat *m* de perquisition.

season ['siːzn] **1** *n* saison *f.* **to be in/out of ~** être/ ne pas être de saison; **a word in ~** un mot dit à propos; *(fig)* **in ~ and out of ~** à tout bout de champ; **the Christmas ~** la période de Noël *or* des fêtes; **the busy ~** *(for shops etc)* la période de pointe; *(for hotels etc)* la pleine saison; **the fishing/ football** *etc* **~** la saison de la pêche/de football *etc*; **'S~'s greetings'** 'Joyeux Noël et Bonne Année'; **the off-~** la morte-saison; **during the off-~** hors saison; *(Theat)* **he did a ~ at the Old Vic** il a joué à l'Old Vic pendant une saison; **the film is here for a short ~** le film sera projeté quelques semaines; *(Vet)* **in ~** en chaleur. **2** *adj*: **~ ticket** carte *f* d'abonnement; **~ ticket holder** personne *f* qui possède une carte d'abonnement. **3** *vt* (**a**) *wood* faire sécher. (**b**) *(Culin)* assaisonner; *(spice)* épicer, relever. **a highly ~ed dish** un plat relevé. ◆ **seasonable** *adj weather* de saison. ◆ **seasonal** *adj* saisonnier. ◆ **seasoned** *adj wood* séché; *(fig) worker, actor etc* expérimenté; *troops* aguerri; **a ~ed campaigner for** un vétéran des campagnes pour. ◆ **seasoning** *n* assaisonnement *m*; **to add ~ing** assaisonner.

seat [siːt] **1** *n* (**a**) *(gen: chair etc)* siège *m*; *(in theatre etc)* fauteuil *m*; *(in bus, train, car etc) (individual)* siège; *(for several people)* banquette *f*; *(on cycle)* selle *f*; *(place: on train, in theatre)* place *f.* **to take a ~** s'asseoir; **to take one's ~** prendre place; **there were 4 ~s in the room** il y avait 4 sièges dans la pièce; *(Theat)* **2 ~s for...** 2 places pour...; **keep a ~ for me** gardez-moi une place; **there are ~s for 70 people** il y a 70 places assises; **a two-~er car** une (voiture à) deux places. (**b**) *(part of chair)* siège *m*; *[trousers]* fond *m*; (*: *buttocks)* postérieur * *m.* (**c**) *(Parl)* siège *m.* **to keep/lose one's ~** être/

ne pas être réélu; **to take one's ~ in the Commons** prendre son siège aux Communes; **a majority of 50 ~s** une majorité de 50 (députés *etc*). (**d**) *(centre) [government, learning]* siège *m*; *[commerce]* centre *m*; *[infection]* foyer *m*. **country ~** château *m*. **2** *adj*: **~ belt** ceinture *f* de sécurité. **3** *vt child* (faire) asseoir; *(at table) guest* placer. **to ~ o.s., to be ~ed** s'asseoir; **to be ~ed** *(sitting)* être assis; **to remain ~ed** rester assis; *(find room for)* **we cannot ~ them all** nous n'avons pas assez de sièges pour tout le monde; **how many does the hall ~?** combien y a-t-il de places assises dans la salle?; **this table/this car ~s 8** on peut tenir à 8 à cette table/dans cette voiture. ◆ **seating 1** *n* sièges *mpl*; *(as opp to standing room)* places *fpl* assises ; **2** *adj*: **~ing capacity** nombre *m* de places assises.

secateurs [ˌsekəˈtɜːz] *npl* sécateur *m*.

secede [sɪˈsiːd] *vi* faire sécession (*from* de). ◆ **secession** *n* sécession *f*.

secluded [sɪˈkluːdɪd] *adj house* à l'écart; *garden* isolé; *life, place* retiré. ◆ **seclusion** *n* solitude *f*; **to live in seclusion** vivre retiré du monde.

second[1] [ˈsek(ə)nd] **1** *adj (esp one of many)* deuxième; *(gen one of two)* second. **to be ~ in the queue** être le (*or* la) deuxième dans la queue; **to be ~ in command** *(Mil)* commander en second; *(gen)* être deuxième dans la hiérarchie; *(Scol)* **he was ~ in French** il a été deuxième en français; *(fig)* **he's a ~ Beethoven** c'est un autre Beethoven; **give him a ~ chance** donnez-lui encore une chance; **you won't get a ~ chance to do it** vous ne retrouverez pas l'occasion de le faire; **every ~ day** un jour sur deux; *(Aut)* **~ gear** seconde *f*; *(Med)* **to ask for a ~ opinion** demander l'avis d'un autre médecin; **~ cousin** petit(e) cousin(e) *m(f) (issu(e) de germains)*; *(Gram)* **~ person** deuxième personne *f*; **in the ~ place** deuxièmement; **Charles the S~** Charles Deux, Charles II; **to play ~ fiddle to sb** jouer un rôle secondaire auprès de qn; **it's ~ nature to him** c'est une seconde nature chez lui; **~ to none** sans pareil; **my ~ self** un(e) autre moi-même; **to have ~ sight** avoir le don de seconde vue; **to have ~ thoughts** changer d'avis (*about* en ce qui concerne); **on ~ thoughts...** réflexion faite...; *for other phrases V* **sixth.**

2 *adv* (**a**) *(in race, exam, competition)* en seconde place. **he came ~** *(in race, exam)* il s'est classé deuxième *or* second; *(at meeting etc)* il est arrivé le deuxième; **the ~ largest book** le plus grand livre sauf un. (**b**) = **secondly.** (**c**) *(Rail etc)* **to travel ~** voyager en seconde.

3 *n* (**a**) deuxième *mf*, second(e) *m(f)*. **he came a good ~** il s'est fait battre de justesse; **he came a poor ~** il a été largement battu (en deuxième place); *(Comm)* **~s** articles *mpl* de second choix. (**b**) *(Boxing)* soigneur *m*; *(in duel)* second *m*. (**c**) *(Aut: ~ gear)* seconde *f*. **in ~** en seconde.

4 *vt* (**a**) *motion* appuyer; *speaker* appuyer la motion de. *(fig)* **I'll ~ that** je suis d'accord. (**b**) [sɪˈkɒnd] *employee* détacher (*to* à).

◆ **secondary** *adj* secondaire (*V* **school**); **~ary picketing** piquets *mpl* de grève de solidarité. ◆ **second-best 1** *n*: **as a ~-best** faute de mieux ; **2** *adv*: **to come off ~-best** perdre. ◆ **second-class** *adj (Rail)* de seconde (classe); *(pej) food, goods etc* de qualité inférieure; **~-class citizen** déshérité(e) *m(f)* dans la société. **~-class mail** *(Brit)* courrier *m* à tarif réduit; *(US)* imprimés *mpl* périodiques. ◆ **second-guess** *vt (US)* comprendre après coup. ◆ **secondhand 1** *adj clothes, car* d'occasion; *information* de seconde main; **~hand bookseller/bookshop** libraire *m*/librairie *f* d'occasion; **~hand dealer** marchand(e) *m(f)* d'occasion ; **2** *adv buy* d'occasion; *hear sth* de qn d'autre. ◆ **second-in-command** *n (Mil)* commandant *m* en second; *(Naut)* second *m*; *(gen)* adjoint *m*. ◆ **secondly** *adv* deuxièmement; *(more formally)* en second lieu. ◆ **secondment** [sɪˈkɒndmənt] *n* détachement *m*; **on ~ment** en détachement (*to* à). ◆ **second-rate** *adj* médiocre, de deuxième ordre.

second[2] [ˈsek(ə)nd] **1** *n* seconde *f (also Geog, Math etc)*. **at that very ~** à cet instant précis; **just a ~!, half a ~!** * une (petite) seconde! **2** *adj*: **~(s) hand** trotteuse *f*.

secret [ˈsiːkrɪt] **1** *n* secret *m*. **to keep a ~** garder un secret; **to let sb into the ~** mettre qn dans le secret; **to let sb into a ~** révéler un secret à qn; **to be in the ~** être au courant; **there's no ~ about it** cela n'a rien de secret; **to have no ~s from sb** ne pas avoir de secrets pour qn; **he makes no ~ of the fact that** il ne cache pas que; **in ~** en secret. **2** *adj (gen)* secret (*f* -ète); *(secluded)* retiré. **to keep sth ~** ne pas révéler qch (*from sb* à qn); **~ agent** agent *m* secret; **~ admirer** admirateur *m*, -trice *f* inconnu(e); **~ ballot** vote *m* à bulletin secret; **~ police** police *f* secrète; **the S~ Service** *(Brit)* les services *mpl* secrets; *(US)* les services chargés de la protection du président; **~ society** société *f* secrète. ◆ **secrecy** *n* secret *m*; **in secrecy** en secret; **there's no secrecy about it** on n'en fait pas un mystère; **an air of secrecy** un air mystérieux. ◆ **secretive** *adj (by nature)* secret, dissimulé *(pej)*; **to be ~ive about sth** se montrer très réservé à propos de qch. ◆ **secretly** *adv* secrètement, en secret.

secretary [ˈsekrətrɪ] *n* secrétaire *mf*; *(company ~)* secrétaire général *(d'une société)*. **S~ of State** *(Brit)* ministre *m* (*for* de); *(US)* ≃ ministre des Affaires étrangères. ◆ **secretarial** *adj work, college* de secrétariat; **secretarial course** études *fpl* de secrétaire. ◆ **secretariat** *n* secrétariat *m*. ◆ **secretary-general** *n* secrétaire *m* général.

secrete [sɪˈkriːt] *vt* (**a**) *(Anat, Bio, Med)* sécréter. (**b**) *(hide)* cacher. ◆ **secretion** *n* sécrétion *f*.

sect [sekt] *n* secte *f*. ◆ **sectarian** *adj* sectaire.

section [ˈsekʃ(ə)n] **1** *n* (**a**) *(gen)* section *f*, partie *f*; *[country]* partie; *[town]* quartier *m*; *[machine, furniture]* élément *m*; *(Mil)* groupe *m* (de combat). *(Mus)* **the brass** *etc* **~** les cuivres *mpl etc; (Press)* **the financial ~** les pages *fpl* financières; *(Admin)* **~ 2 of the by-laws** l'article *m* 2 des arrêtés. (**b**) *(department)* section *f*. (**c**) *(cut)* coupe *f*. **2** *vt* sectionner. **to ~ off** séparer. ◆ **sectional** *adj bookcase etc* à éléments, démontable; *interests* d'un groupe; *drawing* en coupe.

sector [ˈsektəʳ] *n* secteur *m*.

secular [ˈsekjʊləʳ] *adj authority* séculier; *school* laïque; *writer, music* profane.

secure [sɪˈkjʊəʳ] **1** *adj* (**a**) *(solid, firm) padlock, nail, knot* solide; *rope* bien attaché; *door* bien fermé; *ladder* qui ne bouge pas; *hold* bon. **to make ~** *rope* bien attacher; *door, window* bien fermer; *tile* bien fixer. (**b**) *(in safe place)* en sûreté; *place* sûr; *(certain) career, fame* assuré. **~ from** *or* **against** à l'abri de. (**c**) *(unworried)* tranquille, sans inquiétude. **to feel ~ about** ne pas avoir d'inquiétudes au sujet de; **~ in the knowledge that** ayant la certitude que. **2** *vt* (**a**) *(get) object* obtenir (*for sb* pour qn); *staff, performer* engager. (**b**) *(fix) rope* attacher; *door, window* bien fermer; *tile* fixer; *(tie up) person, animal* attacher. (**c**) *(make safe)* préserver (*against, from* de); *career, future* assurer. ◆ **securely** *adv (firmly)* solidement, bien; *(safely)* en sécurité.

security [sɪˈkjʊərɪtɪ] **1** *n* (**a**) *(safety)* sécurité *f*. **in ~** en sécurité; *(Admin, Ind)* **job ~** sécurité de l'emploi; **~ of tenure** *(in job)* sécurité *f* totale de l'emploi; *(in house)* bail *m* assuré. (**b**) *(against spying)* sécurité *f*. **~ was very lax** les mesures *fpl* de sécurité étaient très relâchées. (**c**) *(Fin: for loan)* caution *f*, garantie *f*. **loans without ~** crédit *m* à découvert; **to stand ~ for sb** se porter garant pour *or* de qn. (**d**) *(St Ex)* **securities** valeurs *fpl*, titres *mpl*; **government securities** fonds *mpl* d'État. **2** *adj council, forces* de sécurité; *officer, inspector* chargé de la sécurité. ~ **blanket** *morceau de tissu que le jeune enfant garde pour se sécuriser;* ~ **guard** garde *m* chargé de la sécurité; *(transporting money)* convoyeur *m* de fonds; ~ **leak** fuite *f (de secrets etc)*; ~ **police** services *mpl* de la sûreté; **he is a** ~ **risk** il n'est pas sûr.

sedan [sɪ'dæn] *n (US: car)* conduite *f* intérieure.

sedate [sɪ'deɪt] **1** *adj* posé, calme. **2** *vt (Med)* mettre sous sédation. ◆ **sedately** *adv* posément, calmement. ◆ **sedation** *n* sédation *f*. ◆ **sedative** ['sedətɪv] *adj*, *n* sédatif *(m)*.

sedentary ['sedntrɪ] *adj* sédentaire.

sediment ['sedɪmənt] *n (Geol, Med)* sédiment *m*; *(in boiler, liquids)* dépôt *m*.

sedition [sə'dɪʃ(ə)n] *n* sédition *f*. ◆ **seditious** *adj* séditieux.

seduce [sɪ'dju:s] *vt* séduire. ◆ **seducer** *n* séducteur *m*, -trice *f*. ◆ **seduction** *n* séduction *f*. ◆ **seductive** *adj person, charms* séduisant; *smile, perfume* séducteur; *offer* alléchant. ◆ **seductively** *adv* d'une manière séduisante.

see[1] [si:] *pret* **saw**, *ptp* **seen** *vti* (**a**) *(gen)* voir. **I can** ~ **him** je le vois; **I saw him read/reading the letter** je l'ai vu lire/qui lisait la lettre; **he was** ~**n to read the letter** on l'a vu lire la lettre; **there was no one to be** ~ **n** il n'y avait pas âme qui vive; **there was not a house to be** ~**n** il n'y avait pas une seule maison en vue; **you can** ~ **for miles** on y voit à des kilomètres; **I'll go and** ~ je vais aller voir; **let me** ~ *(show me)* montre-moi, fais voir; *(let me think)* voyons (un peu); ~ **for yourself** voyez vous-même; **as you can** ~ comme vous pouvez le constater; **so I** ~ c'est bien ce que je vois; *(in anger)* ~ **here!** non, mais dites donc! *; **can I go out? — we'll** ~ est-ce que je peux sortir? — on verra; ~ **page 10** voir page 10; **to** ~ **sth with one's own eyes** voir qch de ses propres yeux; **I must be** ~**ing things** * je dois avoir des visions *; **he couldn't** ~ **to read** il n'y voyait pas assez clair pour lire; **to** ~ **in the dark** voir clair la nuit; **can you** ~ **your way?** est-ce que vous pouvez trouver votre chemin?; *(fig)* **to** ~ **one's way to doing sth** trouver le moyen de faire qch; **to** ~ **the world** voyager; **I saw in the paper that** j'ai vu *or* lu dans le journal que; **I** ~ **nothing wrong in it** je n'y trouve rien à redire; **I don't know what she** ~**s in him** je ne sais pas ce qu'elle lui trouve (de bien); ~ **who's at the door** allez voir qui est à la porte; **to go and** ~ **sb, to go to** ~ **sb** aller voir qn; **they** ~ **a lot of him** ils le voient souvent; ~ **you soon!** *, **I'll be** ~**ing you!** * à bientôt!, salut! *; ~ **you later!** * à tout à l'heure!; ~ **you on Sunday** à dimanche; **this hat has** ~**n better days** ce chapeau a connu des jours meilleurs; **I never thought we'd** ~ **the day when...** je n'aurais jamais cru qu'un jour...; **I couldn't** ~ **her left alone** je ne pouvais pas supporter qu'on la laisse *(subj)* toute seule; **I've** ~**n some things in my time * but...** j'en ai vu des choses dans ma vie * mais...
(**b**) *(understand)* voir, comprendre; *joke* comprendre. **do you** ~ **what I mean?** vous voyez ce que je veux dire?; **I don't** *or* **can't** ~ **how...** je ne vois pas du tout comment...; **the way I** ~ **it, as I** ~ **it** à mon avis; **as far as I can** ~ pour autant que je puisse en juger.
(**c**) *(accompany)* accompagner, conduire. **to** ~ **sb to the station** accompagner *or* conduire qn à la gare; **to** ~ **sb home** raccompagner qn jusque chez lui; **to** ~ **the children to bed** coucher les enfants.
(**d**) *(ensure)* s'assurer. ~ **that he has all he needs** *(make sure)* faites en sorte qu'il ait tout ce dont il a besoin; *(check)* assurez-vous qu'il ne manque de rien; **I'll** ~ **he gets the letter** je me charge de lui faire parvenir la lettre.
(**e**) *(imagine)* imaginer, voir. **I can't** ~ **him as Prime Minister** je ne le vois *or* ne l'imagine pas du tout en Premier ministre; **I can't** ~ **myself doing that** je me vois mal *or* je m'imagine mal faisant cela; **I can't** ~ **myself being elected** je ne vois pas très bien comment je pourrais être élu.
◆ **see about** *vt fus* (**a**) *(deal with)* s'occuper de. (**b**) *(consider)* **to** ~ **about sth** voir si qch est possible; **we'll** ~ **about it** on verra. ◆ **see in** *vt sep:* **to** ~ **the New Year in** fêter la Nouvelle Année. ◆ **see off** *vt sep:* **I saw him off at the station** je l'ai accompagné à la gare; **we'll come and** ~ **you off** on viendra vous dire au revoir à la gare *(etc)*. ◆ **see out** *vt sep person* raccompagner à la porte. **I'll** ~ **myself out** * ne vous dérangez pas, je trouverai le chemin; **he won't** ~ **the week out** il ne passera pas la semaine. ◆ **see over** *vt fus (visit)* visiter. ◆ **see through 1** *vt fus person* ne pas se laisser tromper par; *behaviour, promises* voir clair dans. **I saw through him at once** j'ai tout de suite compris où il voulait en venir. **2** *vt sep project, deal* mener à bonne fin. **£10 should** ~ **you through** 10 livres devraient vous suffire; **I'll** ~ **you through** vous pouvez compter sur moi. ◆ **see to** *vt fus (deal with)* s'occuper de; *(mend)* réparer. **please** ~ **to it that...** veillez s'il vous plaît à ce que... + *subj*.
◆ **seeing** *conj*: ~**ing (that)** vu que, étant donné que. ◆ **see-through** *adj* transparent.

see[2] [si:] *n [bishop]* siège *m* épiscopal.

seed [si:d] **1** *n* (**a**) *(Agr, Bot etc)* graine *f*; *(in apple, grape etc)* pépin *m*. *(for sowing)* **the** ~ les graines *fpl*, la semence; **to go to** ~ *[plant etc]* monter en graine; *[person]* se laisser aller. (**b**) *(Tennis:* ~**ed player**) tête *f* de série. **2** *adj potato etc* de semence. ~ **pearls** semence *f* de perles. **3** *vt* (**a**) *lawn, clouds* ensemencer; *raisin, grape* épépiner. (**b**) *(Tennis)* **he was** ~**ed third** il était classé troisième tête de série. **4** *vi* monter en graine. ◆ **seedless** *adj grapes etc* sans pépins. ◆ **seedling** *n* semis *m*. ◆ **seed-merchant** *or* ◆ **seedsman** *n* grainetier *m*. ◆ **seedy** *adj (shabby)* miteux; *(*: ill)* mal fichu *.

seek [si:k] *pret, ptp* **sought 1** *vt (gen)* chercher (*to do* à faire); *solution, person, thing* chercher; *fame, honours* rechercher; *advice, help* demander (*from sb* à qn). **to** ~ **one's fortune** chercher fortune. **2** *vi*: **to** ~ **for** *or* **after** rechercher; **sought after** recherché, demandé. ◆ **seek out** *vt sep person* aller voir. ◆ **seeker** *n* chercheur *m*, -euse *f* (*after* en quête de).

seem [si:m] *vi* sembler, paraître, avoir l'air; *(impersonal vb)* paraître, sembler. **he** ~**s honest** il semble (être) honnête, il paraît honnête, il a l'air honnête; **she** ~**s to know you** elle semble vous connaître; **she** ~**s not to want to leave** on dirait qu'elle ne veut pas partir; **we** ~ **to have met before** il me semble que nous nous sommes déjà rencontrés; **I** ~ **to have heard that before** il me semble avoir déjà entendu cela; **I can't** ~ **to do it** je n'arrive pas à le faire; **I** ~**ed to be floating** j'avais l'impression de planer; **how did she** ~ **to you?** comment l'as-tu trouvée?; **how does it** ~ **to you?** qu'en penses-tu?; **it** ~**s that the government is going to fall** *(looks as if)* il semble bien que le gouvernement va tomber; *(people say)* il paraît que le gouvernement va tomber; **it** ~**s she's right** il semble qu'elle a raison; **it doesn't** ~ **she's right, it** ~**s she's not right** il ne semble pas qu'elle ait raison; **does it** ~ **that she is right?** est-ce qu'il semble qu'elle ait raison?; **it** ~**s to me that...** il me semble que...; **does it** ~ **to you as though...?** est-ce que tu crois que...?; **so it** ~**s** il paraît; **it** ~**s not** il paraît que non; **he died yesterday, it** ~**s** il est mort hier, paraît-il; **I did what** ~**ed best** j'ai fait ce que j'ai jugé bon; **it** ~**s ages since we last met** il y a des siècles * que nous ne nous sommes vus; **there ~s to be a mistake** il semble y avoir une erreur. ◆ **seeming** *adj* apparent. ◆ **seemingly** *adv* à ce qu'il paraît, apparemment. ◆ **seemly** *adj behaviour* convenable; *dress* correct.

seen [siːn] *ptp of* **see**[1].

seep [siːp] *vi* filtrer (*through* à travers). ◆ **seep away** *vi* s'écouler peu à peu. ◆ **seep in** *vi* s'infiltrer peu à peu. ◆ **seep out** *vi* suinter. ◆ **seepage** *n* déperdition *f.*

seersucker ['sɪəˌsʌkəʳ] *n* crépon *m* de coton.

seesaw ['siːsɔː] **1** *n* (jeu *m* de) bascule *f.* **2** *adj motion* de bascule. **3** *vi (fig)* osciller.

seethe [siːð] *vi [liquid]* bouillonner; *[crowd]* s'agiter. *(fig)* **to ~ (with anger)** bouillir de colère; **the streets were seething with people** les rues grouillaient de monde.

segment ['segmənt] *n (gen)* segment *m*; *[orange etc]* quartier *m.*

segregate ['segrɪgeɪt] *vt (gen, also Pol)* séparer (*from* de); *contagious patient etc* isoler (*from* de). ◆ **segregated** *adj (Pol) school, club* où la ségrégation (raciale) est appliquée. ◆ **segregation** *n (Pol)* ségrégation *f*; *(gen)* séparation *f*, isolement *m* (*from* de). ◆ **segregationist** *adj, n* ségrégationniste *(mf).*

Seine [seɪn] *n* Seine *f.*

seismic ['saɪzmɪk] *adj* sismique. ◆ **seismograph** *n* sismographe *m.* ◆ **seismology** *n* sismologie *f.*

seize [siːz] *vt (gen)* saisir; *(Mil, Police)* s'emparer de. **she ~d (hold of) his hand, she ~d him by the hand** elle lui a saisi la main; **to be ~d with rage** avoir un accès de rage; **she was ~d with fear/with this desire** la peur/ce désir l'a saisie; **he was ~d with a bout of coughing** il a eu un accès de toux. ◆ **seize up** *vi (Tech)* se gripper; *(Med)* s'ankyloser. ◆ **seize (up)on** *vt fus idea, chance* saisir. ◆ **seizure** *n* (**a**) *[goods, gun, property]* saisie *f*; *[city, ship]* capture *f*; *[power, territory]* prise *f*; (**b**) *(Med)* crise *f*, attaque *f.*

seldom ['seldəm] *adv* rarement, peu souvent.

select [sɪ'lekt] **1** *vt team, candidate* sélectionner (*from, among* parmi); *gift, book, colour* choisir (*from, among* parmi). **~ed works** œuvres *fpl* choisies. **2** *adj audience, group* choisi; *club* fermé; *restaurant* chic *inv*, sélect. **a ~ few** quelques privilégiés *mpl.* ◆ **selection 1** *n* sélection *f*, choix *m*; *(Literat, Mus)* **~ions from** morceaux *mpl* choisis de ; **2** *adj committee* de sélection. ◆ **selective** *adj (gen)* sélectif; *school* à recrutement sélectif; **to be ~ive** savoir faire un choix. ◆ **selectivity** *n (gen)* sélectivité *f*; *(Scol)* sélection *f.* ◆ **selector** *n (person)* sélectionneur *m*, -euse *f*; *(Tech)* sélecteur *m.*

self [self] **1** *n, pl* **selves**: **the ~** le moi *inv*; **his better ~** le meilleur de lui-même; **her real ~** son vrai moi; **she's her old ~ again** elle est redevenue complètement elle-même.
2 *pref*: **~-adjusting** *etc* à réglage *etc* automatique; **~-cleaning** autonettoyant; **~-correcting** auto-correctif; **~-adhesive** auto-adhésif, autocollant; **~-criticism** critique *f* de soi; **~-imposed/-inflicted** que l'on s'impose/s'inflige à soi-même.
◆ **self-addressed envelope** *n* enveloppe *f* à mon (*or* son *etc*) nom et adresse. ◆ **self-assurance** *n* assurance *f.* ◆ **self-assured** *adj* plein d'assurance. ◆ **self-awareness** *n* (prise *f* de) conscience *f* de soi-même. ◆ **self-catering** *adj*: **~-catering flat** appartement *m* indépendant (avec cuisine). ◆ **self-centred** *adj* égocentrique. ◆ **self-confessed** *adj*: **he is a ~-confessed thief** *etc* il est voleur *etc* de son propre aveu. ◆ **self-confidence** *n* confiance *f* en soi. ◆ **self-confident** *adj* sûr de soi. ◆ **self-conscious** *adj* embarrassé, gêné (*about* de). ◆ **self-consciousness** *n* gêne *f.* ◆ **self-contained** *adj* indépendant. ◆ **self-control** *n* maîtrise *f* de soi. ◆ **self-controlled** *adj* maître (*f* maîtresse) de soi. ◆ **self-defeating** *adj* qui va à l'encontre du but recherché. ◆ **self-defence** *n* légitime défense *f.* ◆ **self-delusion** *n* aveuglement *m.* ◆ **self-denial** *n* abnégation *f.* ◆ **self-deprecating** *adj*: **to be ~-deprecating** se dénigrer soi-même. ◆ **selfdetermination** *n* autodétermination *f.* ◆ **selfdiscipline** *n* discipline *f* (personnelle). ◆ **selfdiscovery** *n* découverte *f* de soi. ◆ **self-drive** *adj (Aut)* sans chauffeur. ◆ **self-educated** *adj* autodidacte. ◆ **self-employed** *adj* qui travaille à son compte. ◆ **self-esteem** *n* amour-propre *m.* ◆ **self-evident** *adj* évident. ◆ **self-explanatory** *adj* qui se passe d'explication. ◆ **self-expression** *n* expression *f* libre. ◆ **self-governing** *adj* autonome. ◆ **self-government** *n* autonomie *f.* ◆ **self-help** *n* débrouillardise * *f.* ◆ **self-image** *n* image *f* de soi-même. ◆ **self-importance** *n* suffisance *f.* ◆ **self-important** *adj* suffisant, m'as-tu-vu * *inv.* ◆ **self-improvement** *n* progrès *mpl* personnels. ◆ **self-indulgence** *n* sybaritisme *m.* ◆ **self-indulgent** *adj* qui ne se refuse rien, sybarite. ◆ **self-interest** *n* intérêt *m* (personnel). ◆ **selfish** *adj person, behaviour* égoïste; *motive* intéressé. ◆ **selfishly** *adv* égoïstement. ◆ **selfishness** *n* égoïsme *m.* ◆ **selfless** *adj* désintéressé. ◆ **selflessly** *adv* d'une façon désintéressée. ◆ **selflessness** *n* désintéressement *m.* ◆ **self-made man** *n* self-made man *m.* ◆ **self-obsessed** *adj* obsédé par soi-même. ◆ **selfopinionated** *adj* entêté, opiniâtre. ◆ **self-pity** *n* apitoiement *m* sur soi-même. ◆ **self-portrait** *n* autoportrait *m.* ◆ **self-possessed** *adj* qui garde son sang-froid. ◆ **self-possession** *n* sang-froid *m.* ◆ **self-preservation** *n* instinct *m* de conservation. ◆ **self-raising flour** *or (US)* ◆ **self-rising flour** *n* farine *f* à levure. ◆ **self-reliant** *adj* indépendant. ◆ **self-respect** *n* respect *m* de soi. ◆ **self-respecting** *adj* qui se respecte. ◆ **self-righteous** *adj* satisfait de soi. ◆ **self-righteousness** *n* satisfaction *f* de soi. ◆ **selfsacrifice** *n* abnégation *f.* ◆ **selfsame** *adj* même. ◆ **self-satisfied** *adj* suffisant. ◆ **self-service** *n* libreservice *m inv.* ◆ **self-serving** *adj* égoïste, intéressé. ◆ **self-starter** *n* démarreur *m.* ◆ **self-sufficiency** *n* indépendance *f*; *(economic)* indépendance économique. ◆ **self-sufficient** *adj* indépendant; économiquement indépendant. ◆ **self-supporting** *adj* qui subvient à ses propres besoins. ◆ **self-taught** *adj* autodidacte.

sell [sel] *pret, ptp* **sold 1** *vt* vendre. **to ~ sth for 2 francs** vendre qch 2 F; **he sold it (to) me for 10 francs** il me l'a vendu 10 F; **are stamps sold here?** est-ce qu'on vend des timbres ici?; **I was sold this in Grenoble** on m'a vendu cela à Grenoble; *(fig)* **to ~ the pass** trahir la cause; **to ~ one's life dearly** vendre chèrement sa vie; **to ~ sb down the river** lâcher qn *; **to ~ sb a pup** ‡ rouler qn *; **to ~ sb an idea** faire accepter une idée à qn; **he doesn't ~ himself very well** il n'arrive pas à se mettre en valeur; **to be sold on * sb/sth** être emballé * par qn/qch.
2 *vi* se vendre. **these books ~ at** *or* **for 10 francs each** ces livres se vendent 10 F pièce.
◆ **sell off** *vt sep stock, shares* liquider; *goods* solder. ◆ **sell out 1** *vi (Comm)* vendre son affaire. *(fig)* **to ~ out to the enemy** passer à l'ennemi. **2** *vt sep (Comm)* **this item is sold out** cet article est épuisé; **we are sold out** on n'en a plus; **we are sold out of milk** on n'a plus de lait; *(Theat)* **the house was sold out** toutes les places étaient louées. ◆ **sell up** *(esp Brit Comm)* **1** *vi* vendre son affaire. **2** *vt sep business* liquider.
◆ **sell-by date** *n* date *f* limite de vente. ◆ **seller** *n* vendeur *m*, -euse *f*; **~er's market** marché *m* vendeur; **onion-~er** marchand(e) *m(f)* d'oignons. ◆ **selling price** *n* prix *m* de vente. ◆ **sellout** *n* (**a**) *(Theat etc)* **it was a ~out** on a joué à guichets

fermés; (**b**) *(betrayal)* trahison *f* (*of* de); capitulation *f* (*to* devant).

sellotape ['selə(ʊ')teɪp] ® **1** *n* scotch *m* ®, ruban *m* adhésif. **2** *vt* coller avec du ruban adhésif.

seltzer ['seltsəʳ] *n* eau *f* de Seltz.

selvage, selvedge ['selvɪdʒ] *n* lisière *f (d'un tissu)*.

semantic [sɪ'mæntɪk] *adj* sémantique. ◆ **semantically** *adv* du point de vue de la sémantique. ◆ **semantics** *nsg* sémantique *f*.

semaphore ['seməfɔːʳ] *n* (**a**) signaux *mpl* à bras. (**b**) *(Rail)* sémaphore *m*.

semblance ['sembləns] *n* semblant *m*.

semen ['siːmən] *n* sperme *m*.

semester [sɪ'mestəʳ] *n* semestre *m*.

semi ['semɪ] *pref* semi-, demi-, à demi, à moitié. ◆ **semiautomatic** *adj* semi-automatique. ◆ **semicircle** *n* demi-cercle *m*. ◆ **semicircular** *adj* en demi-cercle. ◆ **semicolon** *n* point-virgule *m*. ◆ **semiconductor** *n* semi-conducteur *m*. ◆ **semiconscious** *adj* à demi conscient. ◆ **semidarkness** *n* pénombre *f*. ◆ **semidetached house** *n* maison *f* jumelée. ◆ **semifinal** *n* demi-finale *f*. ◆ **semifinalist** *n* joueur *m*, -euse *f* de demi-finale. ◆ **semiofficial** *adj* semi-officiel. ◆ **semiprecious** *adj* semi-précieux. ◆ **semiprofessional** *adj* semi-professionnel. ◆ **semiskilled** *adj worker* spécialisé; *work* d'ouvrier spécialisé. ◆ **semi-skimmed** *adj* demi-écrémé. ◆ **semitrailer** *n* semi-remorque *f*.

seminal ['semɪnl] *adj (fig)* qui fait école.

seminar ['semɪnɑːʳ] *n* séminaire *m (discussion)* ; *(Univ)* séance *f* de travaux pratiques. ◆ **seminarist** *n* séminariste *m*. ◆ **seminary** *n* séminaire *m (Rel)*.

semiology [ˌsemɪ'ɒlədʒɪ] *n* sémiologie *f*.

semolina [ˌsemə'liːnə] *n* semoule *f*. ~ **pudding** semoule au lait.

senate ['senɪt] *n (Pol)* sénat *m*; *(Univ)* conseil *m* de l'université. ◆ **senator** *n* sénateur *m*.

send [send] *pret, ptp* **sent** *vt* (**a**) *(gen)* envoyer (*to sb* à qn); *letter, parcel* envoyer, expédier; *ball, rocket, arrow* lancer. **I'll ~ a car for you** j'enverrai une voiture vous chercher; **to ~ sb for sth** envoyer qn chercher qch; **to ~ sb to do sth** envoyer qn faire qch; ~ **him along to see me** envoie-le-moi; **to ~ sb to bed** envoyer qn se coucher; **to ~ sb home** renvoyer qn chez lui; *(from abroad)* rapatrier qn; **to ~ sb to sleep** endormir qn; **he was sent to prison** on l'a envoyé en prison; **the rain sent us indoors** la pluie nous a fait rentrer; *(fig)* **to ~ sb packing** * *or* **about his business** * envoyer promener qn *; *(fig)* **to ~ sb to Coventry** mettre qn en quarantaine; **the explosion sent a cloud of smoke into the air** l'explosion a projeté un nuage de fumée en l'air; **to ~ a shiver down sb's spine** faire passer un frisson dans le dos de qn; **the sight of the dog sent her running to her mother** en voyant le chien elle s'est précipitée vers sa mère; **the blow sent him sprawling** le coup l'a envoyé par terre; **he sent the plate flying** il a envoyé voler l'assiette; **to ~ sb flying** envoyer qn rouler à terre. (**b**) *(cause to become)* rendre. **to ~ sb mad** rendre qn fou. (**c**) (⁑) emballer *. **this music ~s me** cette musique m'emballe *.

◆ **send away** **1** *vi*: **to ~ away for sth** commander qch par correspondance. **2** *vt sep person* envoyer (*to* à); *parcel, letter, goods* envoyer, expédier; *(post)* mettre à la poste; *(dismiss)* renvoyer. ◆ **send back** *vt sep* renvoyer. ◆ **send down** *vt sep person* faire descendre; *(expel)* renvoyer; *prices* faire baisser. ◆ **send for** *vt fus* (**a**) *doctor, police etc* faire venir; *help* envoyer chercher. (**b**) *(order by post)* commander par correspondance. ◆ **send in** *vt sep person* faire entrer; *troops, request, names, resignation* envoyer; *report* envoyer, soumettre. **to ~ in an application** faire une demande; *(for job)* poser sa candidature. ◆ **send off** **1** *vi* = **send away 1**. **2** *vt sep person* envoyer (*to do* faire); *letter, parcel, goods* envoyer, expédier; *(post)* mettre à la poste; *(Ftbl etc) player* renvoyer du terrain. ◆ **send on** *vt sep letter* faire suivre; *luggage (in advance)* expédier à l'avance; *(afterwards)* faire suivre; *object left behind* renvoyer. ◆ **send out** **1** *vi*: **to ~ out for sth** envoyer chercher qch. **2** *vt sep* (**a**) *person, dog etc* faire sortir. **she sent the children out to play** elle a envoyé les enfants jouer dehors. (**b**) *(post) correspondence, leaflets* envoyer (par la poste). (**c**) *scouts, messengers* envoyer. (**d**) *(emit) smell, smoke, heat* émettre, répandre; *light* diffuser. ◆ **send round** *vt sep document, bottle etc* faire circuler; *person* envoyer (*to sb's* chez qn). **I'll ~ it round to you as soon as it's ready** je vous le ferai parvenir dès que cela sera prêt. ◆ **send up** *vt sep* (**a**) *person, luggage* faire monter; *smoke* répandre; *aeroplane* envoyer; *spacecraft, flare* lancer; *prices* faire monter en flèche. (**b**) *(*: make fun of) person* mettre en boîte *; *book* parodier. (**c**) *entry form* envoyer. (**d**) *(blow up)* faire sauter *. ◆ **sender** *n* expéditeur *m*, -trice *f*, envoyeur *m*, -euse *f*. ◆ **send-off** * *n*: **to give sb a ~-off** faire des adieux chaleureux à qn. ◆ **send-up** * *n* parodie *f*.

Senegal [senɪ'gɔːl] *n* Sénégal *m*. ◆ **Senegalese** **1** *adj* sénégalais ; **2** *n* Sénégalais(e) *m(f)*.

senile ['siːnaɪl] *adj* sénile. ◆ **senility** *n* sénilité *f*.

senior ['siːnɪəʳ] **1** *adj* (**a**) *(older)* aîné, plus âgé. **he is 3 years ~ to me** il est mon aîné de 3 ans, il est plus âgé que moi de 3 ans; **Smith S~** Smith père; ~ **citizen** personne *f* âgée *or* du troisième âge; **the problems of ~ citizens** les problèmes du troisième âge; *(US)* ~ **high school** ≃ lycée *m*; *(US: Scol, Univ)* ~ **year** dernière année *f* d'études. (**b**) *(of higher rank) employee* de grade supérieur; *officer, executive, position* supérieur. **he is ~ to me in the firm** il est au-dessus de moi dans l'entreprise; **the ~ partner** l'associé *m* principal.

2 *n* (**a**) *(in age)* aîné(e) *m(f)*. (**b**) *(US Univ)* étudiant(e) *m(f)* de licence; *(US Scol)* élève *mf* de terminale.

◆ **seniority** *n (in age)* priorité *f* d'âge; *(in rank)* supériorité *f*; *(in years of service)* ancienneté *f*; **promotion by ~ity** avancement *m* à l'ancienneté.

sensation [sen'seɪʃ(ə)n] *n* (**a**) *(physical feeling; impression)* sensation *f* (*of doing* de faire). (**b**) *(excitement)* sensation *f*. **to be** *or* **cause a ~** faire sensation. ◆ **sensational** *adj* (**a**) *event, fashion* qui fait sensation; (**b**) *film, novel, newspaper* à sensation; *account, description* dramatique; (**c**) *(*: marvellous)* sensationnel *, formidable *. ◆ **sensationally** *adv report, describe* en recherchant le sensationnel ; **~ally successful** qui a connu un succès extraordinaire.

sense [sens] **1** *n* (**a**) *(faculty etc)* sens *m*. ~ **of hearing/smell** *etc* ouïe *f*/odorat *m etc*; **to come to one's ~s** *(regain consciousness)* reprendre connaissance *(V also* **1c**); ~ **of colour/direction** sens de la couleur/de l'orientation; ~ **of duty/humour** sens du devoir/de l'humour; **to lose all ~ of time** perdre toute notion de l'heure; **to have no ~ of shame** ne pas savoir ce que c'est que la honte. (**b**) *(sensation, impression) (physical)* sensation *f*; *(mental)* sentiment *m*. **a ~ of warmth** une sensation de chaleur; **a ~ of guilt** un sentiment de culpabilité. (**c**) *(sanity)* **~s** raison *f*; **to take leave of one's ~s** perdre la raison; **to come to one's ~s** *(become reasonable)* revenir à la raison; **to bring sb to his ~s** ramener qn à la raison; **no one in his ~s would do that** il faudrait être fou pour faire ça. (**d**) *(common ~)* bon sens, intelligence *f*. **you should have had more ~ than to do it** vous auriez dû avoir assez de bon sens pour ne pas le faire; **to see ~** entendre raison; **there's no ~ in doing that, what's**

the ~ of *or* **in doing that?** à quoi bon faire cela? ; *[words, speech]* **to make ~** avoir du sens; **what she did makes ~** ce qu'elle a fait est logique; **to make ~ of sth** arriver à comprendre qch. (**e**) *(meaning)* sens *m*. **in the literal/figurative ~** au sens propre/figuré; **in every ~ of the word** dans toute l'acception du terme; **in a ~** dans un certain sens; **to get the ~ of what sb says** saisir l'essentiel de ce que dit qn.
2 *vt (gen) sb's presence, interest* sentir (intuitivement) (*that* que); *danger* pressentir.
◆ **senseless** *adj* (**a**) *(stupid)* insensé; (**b**) *(unconscious)* sans connaissance. ◆ **senselessly** *adv* d'une façon insensée. ◆ **senselessness** *n [person]* manque *m* de bon sens; *[action, idea]* absurdité *f*. ◆ **sensor** *n* détecteur *m*.

sensible ['sensəbl] *adj* (**a**) *(wise etc) person* raisonnable, sensé; *act, decision, choice* raisonnable; *clothes* pratique. (**b**) *(perceptible) change, difference* sensible, appréciable. ◆ **sensibility** *n* sensibilité *f*; **sensibilities** susceptibilité *f*. ◆ **sensibleness** *n* bon sens *m*. ◆ **sensibly** *adv* (**a**) *(reasonably)* raisonnablement; (**b**) *(perceptibly)* sensiblement.

sensitive ['sensɪtɪv] *adj person, tooth, film* sensible (*to* à); *(delicate) skin* délicat; *(easily offended)* susceptible; *(fig) subject, situation* délicat. **she is ~ about her nose** elle n'aime pas qu'on lui parle *(subj)* de son nez. ◆ **sensitively** *adv* avec sensibilité. ◆ **sensitiveness** *or* ◆ **sensitivity** *n* sensibilité *f*; délicatesse *f*; susceptibilité *f*. ◆ **sensitize** *vt* sensibiliser.

sensual ['sensjʊəl] *adj* sensuel. ◆ **sensuality** *n* sensualité *f*. ◆ **sensually** *adv* sensuellement.

sensuous ['sensjʊəs] *adj* voluptueux. ◆ **sensuously** *adv* voluptueusement. ◆ **sensuousness** *n* volupté *f*.

sent [sent] *pret, ptp of* **send**.

sentence ['sentəns] **1** *n* (**a**) *(Gram)* phrase *f*. (**b**) *(Jur) (judgment)* condamnation *f*, sentence *f*; *(punishment)* peine *f*. *(lit, fig)* **to pass ~ on sb** prononcer une condamnation contre qn; **~ of death** condamnation à mort; **under ~ of death** condamné à mort; **he got a 5-year ~** il a été condamné à 5 ans de prison; **a long ~** une longue peine. **2** *vt*: **to ~ sb to death/to 5 years** condamner qn à mort/à 5 ans de prison.

sententious [sen'tenʃəs] *adj* sentencieux. ◆ **sententiously** *adv* sentencieusement.

sentiment ['sentɪmənt] *n* (**a**) *(feeling)* sentiment *m*; *(opinion)* opinion *f*. (**b**) *(sentimentality)* sentimentalité *f*. ◆ **sentimental** *adj* sentimental. ◆ **sentimentalist** *n* sentimental(e) *m(f)*. ◆ **sentimentality** *n* sentimentalité *f*. ◆ **sentimentally** *adv* sentimentalement.

sentinel ['sentɪnl] *n* sentinelle *f*.

sentry ['sentrɪ] **1** *n* sentinelle *f*. **2** *adj*: **~ box** guérite *f*; **on ~ duty** en *or* de faction.

Seoul [səʊl] *n* Seoul.

sepal ['sepəl] *n* sépale *m*.

separate ['seprɪt] **1** *adj (gen)* séparé; *career, existence, organization* indépendant; *department* spécial; *entrance* particulier; *occasion, day, issue* différent, autre. **they have ~ rooms** ils ont chacun leur propre chambre; **Paul and his wife sleep in ~ beds/rooms** Paul et sa femme font lit/chambre à part; *(in restaurant etc)* **we want ~ bills** nous voudrions des additions séparées; **there will be ~ discussions on this question** cette question sera discutée séparément; **keep the novels ~ from the textbooks** ne mélangez pas les romans et les livres de classe. **2** *n (clothes)* **~s** coordonnés *mpl*. **3** ['sepəreɪt] *vt* séparer (*from* de); *(sort out)* séparer, trier; *(divide up)* diviser; *strands* dédoubler; *milk* écrémer. **they are ~d but not divorced** ils sont séparés mais ils n'ont pas divorcé. **4** ['sepəreɪt] *vi [liquids, people]* se séparer (*from* de); *[fighters]* rompre; *[married couple]* se séparer; *[non-married couple]* rompre. ◆ **separable** *adj* séparable. ◆ **separately** *adv* séparément. ◆ **separation** *n (all senses)* séparation *f (from sth* de qch; *from sb* d'avec qn). ◆ **separatist** *adj, n* séparatiste *(mf)*.

sepia ['si:pjə] *n* sépia *f*.

September [sep'tembəʳ] *n* septembre *m*, mois *m* de septembre. **the first of ~** le premier septembre; **(on) the tenth of ~** le dix septembre; **in ~** en septembre; **in the month of ~** au mois de septembre; **each** *or* **every ~** chaque année en septembre; **at the beginning/in the middle/at the end of ~** au début/au milieu/à la fin (du mois) de septembre; **during ~** pendant le mois de septembre; **there are 30 days in ~** il y a 30 jours au mois de septembre; **~ was cold** septembre a été froid, il a fait froid en septembre.

septic ['septɪk] *adj* septique; *wound* infecté. **to go** *or* **become ~** s'infecter; **~ tank** fosse *f* septique. ◆ **septicaemia**, *(US)* **septicemia** *n* septicémie *f*.

sepulchre, *(US)* **sepulcher** ['sep(ə)lkəʳ] *n* sépulcre *m*. ◆ **sepulchral** [sɪ'pʌlkr(ə)l] *adj* sépulcral.

sequel ['si:kw(ə)l] *n [book, film etc]* suite *f*; *[event etc]* suites *fpl*.

sequence ['si:kwəns] *n* (**a**) *(order)* ordre *m*. **in ~** par ordre; *(Gram)* **~ of tenses** concordance *f* des temps. (**b**) *(series)* suite *f* (*of* de); *(Mus, Cards, Comput)* séquence *f*. **film ~** séquence; **dance ~** numéro *m* (de danse).

sequin ['si:kwɪn] *n* paillette *f*.

Serbo-Croat ['sɜ:bəʊ'krəʊæt] *n (Ling)* serbo-croate *m*.

serenade [ˌserə'neɪd] **1** *n* sérénade *f*. **2** *vt* donner une sérénade à.

serene [sə'ri:n] *adj person, sky* serein; *sea* calme. ◆ **serenely** *adv smile, say* avec sérénité; **~ly indifferent to** suprêmement indifférent à. ◆ **serenity** [sɪ'renɪtɪ] *n* sérénité *f*.

serge [sɜ:dʒ] *n* serge *f*.

sergeant ['sɑ:dʒ(ə)nt] *n (gen)* sergent *m*; *(US Air Force)* caporal-chef *m*; *(Police)* brigadier *m*. ◆ **sergeant-major** *n (Brit)* sergent-major *m*; *(US Mil)* adjudant-chef.

serial ['sɪərɪəl] **1** *n* feuilleton *m*. **television ~** feuilleton télévisé; **3-part ~** feuilleton en 3 épisodes. **2** *adj* (**a**) **~ number** *[goods, car engine]* numéro *m* de série; *[soldier]* matricule *m*; *[cheque, banknote]* numéro. (**b**) *(Comput) (gen)* série *inv*; *access* séquentiel. ◆ **serialize** *vt (Press)* publier en feuilleton; *(Rad, TV)* adapter en feuilleton.

series ['sɪərɪz] *n, pl inv (gen)* série *f*; *(Rad, TV)* série (d'émissions); *(set of books)* collection *f*; *(set of stamps)* série.

serious ['sɪərɪəs] *adj* (**a**) *(in earnest) (gen)* sérieux; *attitude, voice, smile* plein de sérieux, grave; *tone, look* sérieux, grave. **I'm quite ~** je parle sérieusement, je ne plaisante pas; **to give ~ thought to sth** *(ponder)* bien réfléchir à qch; *(intend)* songer sérieusement à (faire) qch; **to be ~ about one's work** être sérieux dans son travail; **the ~ student of jazz** qn qui s'intéresse sérieusement au jazz. (**b**) *(causing concern) illness, mistake, situation, threat* grave, sérieux; *damage* important; *loss, doubt* grave *(before n)*. **the patient's condition is ~** le patient est dans un état grave. ◆ **seriously** *adv* (**a**) *(in earnest)* sérieusement; **to take sth/sb ~ly** prendre qch/qn au sérieux; (**b**) *(dangerously) ill* gravement; *wounded* grièvement; *worried* sérieusement. ◆ **seriousness** *n (gen)* sérieux *m*; *[report, information]* caractère *m* sérieux; *[situation, illness, mistake, injury]* gravité *f*; *[damage]* importance *f*; **in all ~ness** sérieusement.

sermon ['sɜ:mən] *n* sermon *m* (*on* sur).

serpent ['sɜ:p(ə)nt] *n* serpent *m*.

serrated [se'reɪtɪd] *adj edge* en dents de scie; *knife* à dents de scie. ◆ **serration** *n* dentelure *f*.

serum ['sɪərəm] *n* sérum *m*.

serve [sɜːv] **1** *vt* (**a**) *(work for) master, employer, God, one's country, a cause* servir. (**b**) *(be used as etc)* **it ~s her as a table** ça lui sert de table; **it ~s its** (*or* **my** *or* **his** *etc*) **purpose** cela fait l'affaire; **it ~s a variety of purposes** cela sert à divers usages; **it ~s no useful purpose** cela ne sert à rien; **his knowledge ~d him well** ses connaissances lui ont bien servi *or* été très utiles; **it ~s him right** c'est bien fait pour lui; **it ~s you right for being so stupid** cela t'apprendra à être si stupide. (**c**) *food, meal* servir (*to sb* à qn); *(Tennis)* servir. *(in shop, restaurant)* **to ~ sb (with) sth** servir qch à qn; **are you being ~d?** est-ce qu'on vous sert?; **the bus ~s 6 villages** le car dessert 6 villages; **the power station ~s a large district** la centrale alimente une zone étendue. (**d**) *(work out)* **to ~ one's time** *[apprentice]* faire son apprentissage (*as* de); *(Mil)* faire son temps de service; *(Prison)* faire son temps de prison; *(in prison)* **to ~ time** faire de la prison; **to ~ a prison sentence** purger une peine (de prison). (**e**) *(Jur) summons* remettre (*on* à); *warrant* délivrer (*on* à). **to ~ notice on sb to the effect that** notifier à qn que; **to ~ a writ on sb** assigner qn.
2 *vi* (**a**) *[servant, waiter, soldier]* servir *(also Rel, Tennis)*. **to ~ on a committee** être membre d'un comité; **he has ~d for 2 years as chairman** cela fait 2 ans qu'il exerce la fonction de président. (**b**) *(be useful)* servir (*for, as sth* de qch) **it ~s to explain** cela sert à expliquer.
3 *n (Tennis etc)* service *m*.
◆ **serve out** *vt sep meal, soup* servir; *rations, provisions* distribuer. ◆ **serve up** *vt sep* servir, mettre sur la table.
◆ **servant** *n* domestique *mf*; *(maid)* bonne *f*; *(fig)* serviteur *m*. ◆ **server** *n* (**a**) *(Rel)* servant *m*; *(Tennis etc)* serveur *m*, -euse *f*; (**b**) *(tray)* plateau *m*; *(piece of cutlery)* couvert *m* à servir. ◆ **serving** *n (action)* service *m; (portion)* portion *f*, part *f*.

service ['sɜːvɪs] **1** *n* (**a**) *(gen; also Mil etc)* service *m*. *(Mil)* **to see ~** servir (*as* comme); **on Her Majesty's ~** au service de Sa Majesté; *[domestic servant]* **in ~** en service; **at your ~** à votre service; **to be of ~ to sb** être utile à qn, rendre service à qn; **to bring/come into ~** mettre/entrer en service; *(in shop, hotel etc)* **the ~ is very poor** le service est très mauvais; *(on bill)* **15% ~ included** service 15% compris. (**b**) *(department; system)* service *m*. **medical/social** *etc* **~s** services médicaux/sociaux *etc*; **customs ~** douane *f*; *(Mil)* **the S~s** l'armée *f* (*or* la marine *or* l'aviation *f*), les forces *fpl* armées; **the train ~ to London** les trains *mpl* pour Londres; **the number 4 bus ~** la ligne du numéro 4. (**c**) *(help etc rendered)* service *m*. **to do sb a ~** rendre service à qn. (**d**) *(Rel)* service *m*. **to hold a ~** célébrer un service. (**e**) *(maintenance work) [car]* révision *f*; *[washing machine]* entretien *m*. **to put one's car in for ~** donner sa voiture à réviser. (**f**) *(set of crockery)* service *m*. **coffee ~** service à café. (**g**) *(Tennis etc)* service *m*.
2 *adj [motorway]* **~ area** aire *f* de services; **~ charge** service *m*; *(Mil)* **~ families** familles *fpl* de militaires; *(Brit)* **~ flat** appartement *m* avec service; **~ hatch** passe-plat *m*; **~ industries** industries *fpl* de service; *(Aut)* **~ road** voie *f* de service; **~ station** station-service *f*.
3 *vt car* réviser; *washing machine etc* entretenir.
◆ **serviceable** *adj building, clothes (practical)* commode; *(durable)* solide; *(usable, working)* utilisable. ◆ **serviceman** *n* militaire *m*. ◆ **servicing** *n [car etc]* révision *f*.

serviette [ˌsɜːvɪ'et] *n (esp Brit)* serviette *f* (de table). **~ ring** rond *m* de serviette.

servile ['sɜːvaɪl] *adj* servile. ◆ **servility** [sɜː'vɪlɪtɪ] *n* servilité *f*.

servitude ['sɜːvɪtjuːd] *n* servitude *f*.

servo- ['sɜːvəʊ] *pref* servo... **~assisted** servocommandé.

session ['seʃ(ə)n] *n* (**a**) *(sitting, meeting)* séance *f*. **to be in ~** *(gen)* siéger; *[court]* être en séance; **I had a ~ with him** *(work)* nous avons travaillé ensemble; *(discussion)* nous avons eu une longue discussion. (**b**) *(Scol, Univ) (year)* année *f* universitaire *or* scolaire; *(US: term)* trimestre *m* universitaire.

set [set] *(vb: pret, ptp* **set***)* **1** *n* (**a**) *(gen)* jeu *m*, série *f*; *(kit)* trousse *f*; *[keys, golf clubs, knives, spanners]* jeu; *[chairs, rugs, saucepans, numbers, stamps etc]* série; *[books, toy cars, bracelets, magazines]* collection *f*; *[dishes etc]* service *m*; *[tyres]* train *m*. **a ~ of rooms** un appartement; **~ of teeth** dentition *f*; **~ of false teeth** dentier *m*; **a ~ of dining-room furniture** un mobilier de salle à manger; **a whole ~ of telephones on his desk** toute une collection de téléphones sur son bureau; **in ~s** en jeux complets, en séries complètes; **sewing ~** trousse de couture; **painting ~** boîte *f* de peinture; **chess/draughts ~** jeu d'échecs/de dames *(objet)*. (**b**) *(Tennis)* set *m*; *(Math, Philos)* ensemble *m*. (**c**) *(Elec)* appareil *m*; *(Rad, TV)* poste *m*. (**d**) *(group)* bande *f (also pej)*; *(larger)* monde *m*. **a ~ of thieves** une bande de voleurs; **the golfing ~** le monde du golf. (**e**) *(stage) (Cine)* plateau *m*; *(Theat etc)* scène *f*; *(scenery)* décor *m*. **on the ~** sur le plateau, en scène. (**f**) *(Brit Scol)* groupe *m* de niveau. (**g**) *(Hairdressing)* mise *f* en plis. **to have a ~** se faire faire une mise en plis.
2 *adj* (**a**) *(unchanging: gen)* fixe; *smile etc* figé; *purpose, dogma* déterminé; *opinion, idea* arrêté; *lunch* à prix fixe; *(prearranged) time, date* fixe, décidé d'avance; *(Scol etc) book, subject* au programme; *speech, talk* préparé d'avance; *prayer* liturgique. **~ in one's ways** qui tient à ses habitudes; **~ in one's opinions** immuable dans ses convictions; *(Met)* **~ fair** au beau fixe; **~ phrase** expression *f* consacrée. (**b**) *(determined)* résolu; *(ready)* prêt. **to be ~ on (doing) sth** vouloir à tout prix (faire) qch; **to be dead ~ against** s'opposer absolument à; **to be all ~ to do** être prêt pour faire; *(fig)* **the scene is ~ for** tout est prêt pour. (**c**) *(Math)* **~ theory** théorie *f* des ensembles.
3 *vt* (**a**) *(gen)* mettre; *(place)* placer; *(put down)* poser; *signature etc* apposer; *guard* poster. **house ~ on a hill** maison située sur une colline; **his stories, ~ in Paris** ses histoires, situées à Paris; **we must ~ the advantages against the disadvantages** il faut mettre en balance les avantages et les inconvénients; **to ~ fire to sth** mettre le feu à qch; *V also* **foot, store** *etc*. (**b**) *(arrange, adjust) clock, mechanism* régler; *alarm clock* mettre; *(on display) specimen, butterfly etc* monter; *type, page* composer; *(Med) arm, leg (in plaster)* plâtrer; *(with splint)* mettre une attelle à; *fracture* réduire. **he ~ the needle to zero** il a mis l'aiguille à zéro; **to have one's hair ~** se faire faire une mise en plis; *V also* **sail, table** *etc*. (**c**) *(fix, establish) date, limit* fixer; *record* établir; *V also* **course, fashion** *etc*. (**d**) *(assign) task, subject* donner; *exam, test* choisir les questions de; *texts, books* mettre au programme. **to ~ sb a problem** poser un problème à qn; **I ~ him the job of clearing up** je l'ai chargé de ranger; *V also* **example** *etc*. (**e**) *(cause to do, begin etc)* **to ~ a dog on sb** lancer un chien contre qn; **she ~ my brother against me** elle a monté mon frère contre moi; **to ~ sth going** mettre qch en marche; **to ~ sb thinking** faire réfléchir qn; **to ~ sb to do sth** faire faire qch à qn; **to ~ o.s. to do** entreprendre de faire. (**f**) *gem* monter (*in* sur); *ring* orner (*with* de). (**g**) *jelly, concrete* faire prendre; *dye, colour* fixer.
4 *vi* (**a**) *[sun, moon etc]* se coucher. (**b**) *[broken bone, limb]* se ressouder; *[jelly, jam]* prendre; *[glue, concrete]* durcir; *[character]* se former. **his face ~ in a hostile expression** son visage s'est figé dans une

expression hostile. (**c**) *(begin: gen)* se mettre, commencer (*to doing* à faire). **to ~ to work** se mettre au travail.

◆ **set about** *vt fus* (**a**) *(begin) task, essay* se mettre à. **to ~ about doing** se mettre à faire; **I don't know how to ~ about it** je ne sais pas comment m'y prendre. (**b**) *(attack)* attaquer. ◆ **set apart** *vt sep object etc* mettre à part; *(fig) person* distinguer (*from* de). ◆ **set aside** *vt sep* (**a**) *(keep, save)* mettre de côté. (**b**) *(lay aside) book etc* poser. (**c**) *(reject) objection* rejeter; *will* annuler; *judgment* casser. ◆ **set back** *vt sep* (**a**) *(replace)* remettre. (**b**) **the house was ~ back from the road** la maison était en retrait de la route. (**c**) *(retard) progress, clock* retarder (*by* de). (**d**) *(*: cost)* coûter. ◆ **set down** *vt sep* (**a**) *(put down) object, passenger* déposer; *plane* poser. (**b**) *(record)* noter, inscrire. **to ~ sth down in writing** *or* **on paper** mettre qch par écrit. (**c**) *(attribute)* attribuer (*sth to sth* qch à qch). ◆ **set in 1** *vi [complications, difficulties]* surgir; *[disease]* se déclarer; *[reaction]* s'amorcer. **the rain has ~ in for the night** il va pleuvoir toute la nuit. **2** *vt sep (Sewing) sleeve* rapporter. ◆ **set off 1** *vi (leave)* se mettre en route. **to ~ off on a journey/an expedition** partir en voyage/ en expédition. **2** *vt sep* (**a**) *bomb* faire exploser; *firework* faire partir; *mechanism* déclencher. (**b**) *(enhance) hair, furnishings etc* mettre en valeur. (**c**) *(balance etc)* **to ~ off profits against losses** balancer les pertes et les profits. ◆ **set out 1** *vi* partir (*for* pour; *from* de; *in search of* à la recherche de). **to ~ out to do** *(intend)* chercher à faire; *(attempt)* entreprendre de faire; **the book ~s out to show...** ce livre a pour objet de montrer... **2** *vt sep books, goods* exposer; *chessmen etc on board* disposer; *reasons, ideas* présenter, exposer. ◆ **set to** *vi (start)* se mettre (*to do* à faire); *(start work)* s'y mettre *. ◆ **set up 1** *vi (Comm etc)* **to ~ up (in business) as a grocer** s'établir épicier. **2** *vt sep* (**a**) *(place in position) chairs, stall* installer; *tent, statue* dresser; *type* assembler; *camp* établir. (**b**) *(fig: start) school, institution* fonder; *business, company, fund* créer, lancer; *tribunal, government* constituer; *fashion* lancer; *irritation, quarrel* provoquer; *record* établir; *theory* avancer; *inquiry* ouvrir. **to ~ up house** s'installer; **they ~ up house together** ils se sont mis en ménage; *(Comm, also fig)* **to ~ up shop** s'établir; **to ~ sb up in business** lancer qn dans les affaires; **I've ~ it all up for you** je vous ai tout installé *or* préparé; **I've never ~ myself up as a scholar** je n'ai jamais prétendu être savant. (**c**) *(after illness)* remettre sur pied. (**d**) *(equip)* munir (*with* de). ◆ **set upon** *vt fus (attack)* attaquer.

◆ **setback** *n (hitch)* contretemps *m*; *(more serious)* revers *m*; *(in health)* rechute *f*. ◆ **setting 1** *n* (**a**) *[jewel]* monture *f*; *(fig: framework, background)* cadre *m*; (**b**) *(Mus: of poem etc)* mise *f* en musique; **~ting for piano** arrangement *m* pour piano; (**c**) *(Brit Scol)* répartition *f* par groupes de niveau ; **2** *adj*: **~ting lotion** lotion *f* pour mise en plis. ◆ **setting-up** *n [institution etc]* création *f*. ◆ **set-to** * *n (fight)* bagarre *f*; *(quarrel)* prise *f* de bec *. ◆ **setup** * *n (situation)* situation *f*; *(business, firm etc)* affaire *f*; (*: *US)* coup *m* monté.

sett [set] *n (in roadway etc)* pavé *m*.

settee [se'ti:] *n* canapé *m*. **~ bed** canapé-lit *m*.

setter ['setəʳ] *n* (**a**) *(dog)* setter *m*, chien *m* d'arrêt. (**b**) *(person)* *V* **typesetter** *etc*.

settle¹ ['setl] *n* banc *m* à haut dossier.

settle² ['setl] **1** *vt* (**a**) *(place carefully)* placer *or* poser délicatement; *(stop wobbling)* stabiliser; *(adjust)* ajuster; *person* installer. **to ~ o.s., to get ~d** s'installer. (**b**) *(arrange, solve etc) question, details, conditions, bill, account* régler; *date* fixer; *difficulty, problem* résoudre; *debt* rembourser; *(decide)* décider. **that ~s it** *(no more problem)* comme ça, le problème est réglé; *(that's made my mind up)* ça me décide; **that's ~d then?** alors, c'est convenu?; **nothing is ~d** rien n'est décidé; *(Jur)* **to ~ a case out of court** régler une affaire à l'amiable. (**c**) *(calm; stabilize) nerves* calmer; *doubts* dissiper. **to ~ one's digestion** calmer les douleurs d'estomac; **the weather is ~d** le temps est au beau fixe. (**d**) *(Jur)* **to ~ sth on sb** constituer qch à qn. (**e**) *(colonize) land* coloniser.

2 *vi* (**a**) *[bird, insect]* se poser (*on* sur); *[dust etc]* retomber; *[sediment, coffee grounds etc]* se déposer; *[building]* se tasser; *[emotions]* s'apaiser; *[conditions, situation]* s'arranger. *[dust, snow]* **to ~ on sth** couvrir qch; *(fig)* **when the dust has ~d** quand les choses se seront arrangées; **to ~ into** *armchair* s'installer confortablement dans; *new job* se faire à; *routine* adopter; *habit* prendre; **I can't ~ to anything** je suis incapable de me concentrer. (**b**) *(go to live)* s'installer, se fixer; *(as colonist)* s'établir. (**c**) **to ~ with sb for the cost of the meal** régler le prix du repas à qn; *(Jur)* **to ~ out of court** arriver à un règlement à l'amiable; **he ~d for £200** il a accepté 200 livres; **they ~d on £200** ils se sont mis d'accord sur 200 livres; **to ~ on sth** *(choose it)* fixer son choix sur qch.

◆ **settle down** *vi [person] (in armchair, house etc)* s'installer (*in* dans); *(become calmer)* se calmer; *(after wild youth etc)* se ranger; *[situation]* s'arranger. **to ~ down to work** se mettre au travail; **he has ~d down in his new job** il s'est fait à son nouvel emploi; **to get married and ~ down** se marier et mener une vie stable; **when things have ~d down again** quand les choses seront redevenues normales. ◆ **settle in** *vi (get things straight)* s'installer; *(get used to things)* s'adapter. ◆ **settle up** *vi* régler (la note). **to ~ up with sb** *(pay)* régler qn; *(fig)* régler son compte à qn *.

◆ **settlement** *n* (**a**) *[question, bill, debt]* règlement *m*; (**b**) *(agreement)* accord *m*; (**c**) *(dowry)* dot *f*; (**d**) *(colony)* colonie *f*; *(village)* village *m*. ◆ **settler** *n* colon *m*.

seven ['sevn] *adj, n* sept *(m) inv*; *for phrases V* **six**. ◆ **seventeen** *adj, n* dix-sept *(m) inv*. ◆ **seventeenth** *adj, n* dix-septième *(mf)*; *(fraction)* dix-septième *m*. ◆ **seventh** *adj, n* septième *(mf)*; *(fraction, Mus)* septième *m*. ◆ **seventieth** *adj, n* soixante-dixième *(mf)*; *(fraction)* soixante-dixième *m*. ◆ **seventy** *adj, n* soixante-dix *(m) inv*; **he's in his ~ties** il a plus de soixante-dix ans.

sever ['sevəʳ] *vt rope etc* couper; *(fig) relations* rompre; *communications* interrompre. ◆ **severance** *n* séparation *f* (*from* de); *(Ind)* **~ance pay** indemnité *f* de licenciement.

several ['sevr(ə)l] **1** *adj* plusieurs. **~ times** plusieurs fois. **2** *pron* plusieurs *mfpl*. **~ of us** plusieurs d'entre nous. ◆ **severally** *adv* séparément, individuellement.

severe [sɪ'vɪəʳ] *adj (gen)* sévère (*with, on, towards* pour, envers); *examination* dur, difficile; *competition* acharné; *climate, winter* rigoureux; *cold, frost* intense; *pain* violent; *wound, defeat, illness* grave. *(Med)* **a ~ cold** un gros rhume. ◆ **severely** *adv (gen)* sévèrement; *injure* grièvement; *ill* gravement; **to leave ~ly alone** *object* ne jamais toucher à; *politics, deal* ne pas du tout se mêler de; *person* ignorer complètement. ◆ **severity** [sɪ'verɪtɪ] *n* sévérité *f*; difficulté *f*; rigueur *f*; intensité *f*; violence *f*; gravité *f*.

sew [səʊ] *pret* **sewed**, *ptp* **sewn** *or* **sewed** *vti* coudre. **to ~ a button on sth** coudre un bouton à qch. ◆ **sew on** *vt sep button etc* coudre; *(~ back on)* recoudre. ◆ **sew up** *vt sep tear, wound* recoudre; *seam* faire; *sack* fermer par une couture. **to ~ sth up in a sack** coudre qch dans un sac; *(fig)* **it's all ~n up** * c'est dans la poche *. ◆ **sewing 1** *n (skill)* couture *f*; *(work)* ouvrage *m*. **2** *adj*: **~ing basket** boîte *f* à couture; **~ing cotton** fil *m* de coton; **~ing machine** machine *f* à coudre.

sewage ['sju:ɪdʒ] **1** *n* vidanges *fpl*. **2** *adj*: ~ **disposal** évacuation *f* des vidanges; ~ **works** champ *m* d'épandage. ◆ **sewer** *n* égout *m*.

sex [seks] **1** *n* sexe *m*. **to have ~ with sb** coucher avec qn *. **2** *adj discrimination, education, instinct* sexuel. ~ **act** acte *m* sexuel; ~ **appeal** sex-appeal *m*; ~ **maniac** obsédé(e) *m(f)* sexuel(le); ~ **object** objet *m* sexuel; ~ **offender** délinquant(e) *m(f)* sexuel(le); ~ **shop** sex-shop *m*; ~ **symbol** sex-symbol *m;* ~ **therapy** sexothérapie *f;* ~ **urge** pulsion *f* sexuelle. ◆ **sexism** *n* sexisme *m*. ◆ **sexist** *adj* sexiste. ◆ **sexual** *adj* sexuel; **~ual harassment** harcèlement *m* sexuel; **~ual intercourse** rapports *mpl* sexuels. ◆ **sexuality** *n* sexualité *f*. ◆ **sexually** *adv* sexuellement. ◆ **sexy** * *adj* sexy * *inv*.

sextet [seks'tet] *n* sextuor *m*.

sexton ['sekst(ə)n] *n* sacristain *m*.

shabby ['ʃæbɪ] *adj garment* usé; *furniture* minable; *house, district* miteux; *person* pauvrement vêtu, miteux; *behaviour* mesquin. **a ~ trick** un vilain tour. ◆ **shabbily** *adv* pauvrement; mesquinement. ◆ **shabbiness** *n [dress]* aspect *m* usé; *[person]* mise *f* pauvre; *[behaviour]* mesquinerie *f*.

shack [ʃæk] **1** *n* cabane *f*, hutte *f*. **2** *vi*: **to ~ up with sb** ⁑ se coller avec qn ⁑.

shade [ʃeɪd] **1** *n* (**a**) ombre *f*. **in the ~** à l'ombre; *(Art)* **light and ~** les clairs *mpl* et les ombres; *(fig)* **to put sth in the ~** éclipser qch. (**b**) *[colour]* nuance *f*, ton *m*; *[opinion]* nuance. **several ~s darker** plus sombre de plusieurs tons; **a new ~ of lipstick** un nouveau ton de rouge à lèvres; **~ of meaning** nuance; **not a ~ of difference** pas la moindre différence; **a ~ bigger** un tout petit peu plus grand. (**c**) *(lamp ~)* abat-jour *m inv*; *(eye ~)* visière *f*; *(US: blind)* store *m*. *(US: sunglasses)* **~s** lunettes *fpl* de soleil. **2** *vt* (**a**) *(from sun)* abriter du soleil; *(from light)* abriter de la lumière; *eyes* abriter; *light, lamp* voiler. **~d place** endroit *m* ombragé. (**b**) (**~ in**) *outline, drawing* hachurer.
◆ **shade off** **1** *vi [colours]* se fondre (*into* en). **2** *vt sep colours etc* estomper.
◆ **shady** *adj* ombragé; *(dishonest)* louche.

shadow ['ʃædəʊ] **1** *n* ombre *f*. **in the ~** dans l'ombre (*of* de); **to cast a ~ over sth** projeter une ombre sur qch; *(fig)* assombrir qch; **without a ~ of doubt** sans l'ombre d'un doute; **he's only a ~ of his former self** il n'est plus que l'ombre de lui-même; **to have ~s under one's eyes** avoir les yeux cernés; *(on chin)* **five o'clock ~** la barbe du soir. **2** *adj*: ~ **boxing** boxe *f* à vide; *(Parl)* ~ **cabinet** cabinet *m* fantôme *(de l'opposition)*; *(Parl)* **the ~ Foreign Secretary** le porte-parole de l'opposition pour les Affaires étrangères. **3** *vt (follow)* filer *(un suspect etc)*. ◆ **shadowy** *adj form, plan* vague.

shaft [ʃɑ:ft] *n* (**a**) *(stem etc) [arrow, spear]* hampe *f*; *[tool, golf club]* manche *m*; *[feather]* tuyau *m*; *[column]* fût *m*; *(on cart, carriage, plough etc)* brancard *m*; *(Aut, Tech)* arbre *m*. (**b**) *(liter: arrow)* flèche *f*; *[light]* rayon *m*; *[sarcasm]* trait *m*. **~ of lightning** éclair *m*. (**c**) *[mine]* puits *m*; *[lift, elevator]* cage *f*; *(for ventilation)* cheminée *f*.

shaggy ['ʃægɪ] *adj hair, mane* broussailleux; *animal* à longs poils rudes. *(fig)* **~ dog story** histoire *f* sans queue ni tête.

shake [ʃeɪk] *(vb: pret* **shook**, *ptp* **shaken***)* **1** *n*: **to give sth a ~** secouer qch; **with a ~ of his head** avec un hochement de tête; **he's got the ~s** * il a la tremblote *; *(from drink)* il tremble; **I'll be there in a ~** * j'arrive dans un instant; **it is no great ~s** * ça ne casse rien *; **he's no great ~s * at swimming** il ne casse rien * comme nageur.
2 *vt* (**a**) *(gen) object, person* secouer; *dice, bottle* agiter; *house, windows etc* ébranler; *(brandish) stick etc* brandir. **to ~ one's head** *(in refusal etc)* faire non de la tête; *(at bad news etc)* secouer la tête; **he shook his finger at me** il m'a fait signe du doigt; **to ~ one's fist at sb** menacer qn du poing; **to ~ hands with sb** serrer la main à qn; **they shook hands** ils se sont serré la main; **they shook hands on it** ils se sont serré la main en signe d'accord; **to ~ o.s.** se secouer; **he shook the sand out of his shoes** il a secoué ses chaussures pour en vider le sable; **he shook himself free** il s'est libéré d'une secousse. (**b**) *(harm) confidence, belief, health* ébranler; *opinion* affecter; *reputation* nuire à; *(amaze)* stupéfier; *(disturb)* secouer. **even torture could not ~ him** même la torture ne l'a pas ébranlé; **to feel ~n** être bouleversé *or* très secoué; **this will ~ you!** tu vas en être soufflé! *; **4 days which shook the world** 4 jours qui ébranlèrent le monde.
3 *vi* (**a**) *[person, hand, table]* trembler; *[building, windows, walls]* trembler, être ébranlé; *[leaves, grasses]* trembler, être agité. **to ~ with cold/fear** trembler de froid/de peur; **he was shaking with laughter** il se tordait de rire. (**b**) *(~ hands)* **they shook on the deal** ils ont scellé leur accord d'une poignée de main; **(let's) ~ on it!** topez là!
◆ **shake down** *vt sep*: **to ~ down apples from a tree** faire tomber des pommes en secouant l'arbre. ◆ **shake off** *vt sep dust, sand, water* secouer (*from* de); *cold, cough* se débarrasser de; *yoke* se libérer de; *habit* se défaire de, perdre; *pursuer* semer *. ◆ **shake out** *vt sep flag, sail* déployer; *blanket* bien secouer; *bag* vider en secouant. **she shook some money out of her bag** elle a secoué son sac et en a fait tomber de l'argent. ◆ **shake up** *vt sep* (**a**) *pillow* secouer; *bottle* agiter. (**b**) *(disturb)* bouleverser, secouer. (**c**) *(rouse, stir) person* secouer, stimuler; *firm, organization* réorganiser de fond en comble.
◆ **shake-out** *n (US Econ)* tassement *m*. ◆ **shake-up** *n (fig)* grande réorganisation *f*. ◆ **shakily** *adv (gen)* en tremblant; *walk* d'un pas mal assuré; *write* d'une main tremblante; *say, reply* d'une voix tremblante. ◆ **shaky** *adj (trembling)* tremblant; *(nervous)* mal assuré; *writing* tremblé; *table, building* branlant; *(fig) health, memory, knowledge* assez mauvais; *firm, deal* à l'avenir incertain; **I feel a bit shaky** je me sens faible.

shale [ʃeɪl] *n* schiste *m* argileux.

shall [ʃæl] *modal aux vb* (**a**) *(1st person future tense and questions)* **I ~** *or* **I'll arrive on Monday** j'arriverai lundi, je vais arriver lundi; **~ I open the door?** voulez-vous que j'ouvre *(subj)* la porte?; **I'll buy 3, ~ I?** je vais en acheter 3, n'est-ce pas *or* d'accord *?; **let's go in, ~ we?** entrons, voulez-vous?; **~ we ask him to come with us?** si on lui demandait de venir avec nous? (**b**) *(command etc)* **it ~ be done this way** cela doit être fait de cette façon; **thou shalt not kill** tu ne tueras point.

shallot [ʃə'lɒt] *n* échalote *f*.

shallow ['ʃæləʊ] *adj water, dish* peu profond; *breathing, person, conversation* superficiel. ◆ **shallowness** *n* manque *m* de profondeur; esprit *m* superficiel. ◆ **shallows** *npl* hauts-fonds *mpl*.

sham [ʃæm] **1** *n*: **to be a ~** *[person]* être un imposteur; *[jewellery, furniture]* être du toc *; *[election, organization]* être de la frime *. **2** *adj jewellery* faux, en toc *; *piety* feint; *title* faux; *illness, fight* simulé. **3** *vt sickness, emotion* feindre, simuler. **to ~ ill** faire semblant d'être malade; **he is only ~ming** il fait seulement semblant.

shamble ['ʃæmbl] *vi*: **to ~ in/out** *etc* entrer/sortir *etc* en traînant les pieds. ◆ **shambles** *n, no pl (after fire, bombing)* scène *f* de dévastation; *(muddle)* pagaille * *f*; **his room was (in) a ~s** sa chambre était sens dessus dessous; **the match degenerated into a ~s** le match s'est terminé dans la pagaille *.
◆ **shambolic** * *adj* bordélique ⁑.

shame [ʃeɪm] **1** *n* (**a**) *(feeling)* honte *f*. **he hung his head in ~** il a baissé la tête de honte *or* de confusion; **to bring ~ on sb** déshonorer qn; **to put sb/**

sth to ~ faire honte à qn/qch. (**b**) **it is a ~** c'est dommage (*that* que + *subj; to do* de faire); **what a ~ he isn't here** quel dommage qu'il ne soit pas ici. **2** *vt (bring disgrace on)* déshonorer; *(make ashamed)* faire honte à. **to ~ sb into doing sth** obliger qn à faire qch en lui faisant honte; **to be ~d into doing sth** faire qch par amour-propre.

◆ **shamefaced** *adj (ashamed)* honteux; *(confused)* confus. ◆ **shamefacedly** *adv* d'un air honteux; avec confusion. ◆ **shamefacedness** *n* air *m* honteux; confusion *f*. ◆ **shameful** *adj* honteux; **it's ~ful to do that** c'est une honte de faire cela. ◆ **shamefully** *adv behave* honteusement; *bad, late* scandaleusement, abominablement; **he is ~fully ignorant** il est si ignorant que c'en est une honte. ◆ **shameless** *adj person* éhonté; *behaviour* effronté; **he is quite ~less about it** il n'en a pas du tout honte. ◆ **shamelessly** *adv* effrontément, sans honte. ◆ **shamelessness** *n* effronterie *f*. ◆ **shaming** *adj* humiliant.

shammy * ['ʃæmɪ] *n* (**~ leather**) peau *f* de chamois.

shampoo [ʃæm'pu:] **1** *n (product, process)* shampooing *m*. **~ and set** shampooing et mise *f* en plis. **2** *vt hair* faire un shampooing à; *carpet* shampooiner. **to have one's hair ~ed and set** se faire faire un shampooing et mise en plis.

shamrock ['ʃæmrɒk] *n* trèfle *m (de l'Irlande)*.

shandy ['ʃændɪ] *n (Brit)* panaché *m (bière)*.

shan't [ʃɑ:nt] = **shall not.**

shanty[1] ['ʃæntɪ] *n (hut)* baraque *f*. **~ town** bidonville *m*.

shanty[2] ['ʃæntɪ] *n* (**sea ~**) chanson *f* de marins.

shape [ʃeɪp] **1** *n* forme *f*. **what ~ is the room?** quelle est la forme de la pièce?; **of all ~s and sizes** de toutes les formes et de toutes les tailles; **his nose is a funny ~** son nez a une drôle de forme; **in the ~ of a cross** en forme de croix; **I can't stand racism in any ~ or form** je ne peux pas tolérer le racisme sous quelque forme que ce soit; **to take the ~ of sth** prendre la forme de qch; **the news reached him in the ~ of a telegram** c'est par un télégramme qu'il a appris la nouvelle; **that's the ~ of things to come** cela donne une idée de ce qui nous attend; **to take ~** prendre tournure; **to be in good ~** *[person]* être en forme; *[business etc]* marcher bien; **in poor ~** *person, business* mal en point; **to carve** (*or* **hammer** *etc*) **sth into ~** façonner qch; *(fig)* **to knock** *or* **lick * into ~** *assistant, soldier* dresser *; *team, plan* mettre au point; **to get o.s. into ~** retrouver la forme; **to get one's ideas into ~** préciser ses idées; **a ~ loomed up out of the darkness** une forme imprécise a surgi de l'obscurité.

2 *vt clay, stone* façonner (*into* en); *(fig) ideas, character* former; *(influence) course of events, sb's fate* influencer. **oddly ~d** d'une forme bizarre; **heart-~d** en forme de cœur.

3 *vi: (fig)* **things are shaping (up) well** tout marche bien; **how is he shaping?** comment s'en sort-il? *; **he is shaping (up) nicely** il fait des progrès.

◆ **shapeless** *adj* informe. ◆ **shapelessness** *n* manque *m* de forme. ◆ **shapeliness** *n* belles proportions *fpl*, beauté *f*. ◆ **shapely** *adj object* bien proportionné; *woman, legs* bien fait.

share [ʃɛəʳ] **1** *n* (**a**) part *f* (*of, in* de). **to get a ~ of** *or* **in sth** avoir part à qch; **he has a ~ in the business** il est l'un des associés dans cette affaire; **he has a half-~ in the firm** il possède la moitié de l'entreprise; *(fig)* **he had a ~ in it** il y était pour qch; **to go ~s in sth** partager qch; **to take a ~ in sth** participer à qch; **he isn't doing his ~** il ne fournit pas sa part d'efforts; **more than his fair ~ of misfortune** plus que sa part de malheurs; **he does his full ~ of work** il fournit toute sa part de travail. (**b**) *(Fin etc)* action *f* (*in a company* d'une compagnie). **2** *adj (St Ex) prices* des actions. **~ index** indice *m* de la Bourse. **3** *vt* (**a**) *(gen)* partager (*with sb* avec qn); *(get one's ~ of) profits etc* avoir part à. **they ~d the money between them** ils se sont partagé l'argent; *(Telec)* **~d line** ligne *f* partagée; **they ~ certain characteristics** ils ont certaines caractéristiques en commun; **I ~ your hope that...** j'espère comme vous que... (**b**) (**~ out**) partager, répartir (*among, between* entre). **4** *vi* partager. **~ and ~ alike** à chacun sa part; **to ~ in** *(get one's ~ in) profits etc* avoir part à; *(have etc with other people) expenses, work, blame, joy* partager.

◆ **sharecropper** *n (US)* métayer *m*, -ère *f*. ◆ **sharecropping** *n (US)* métayage *m*. ◆ **shareholder** *n* actionnaire *mf*. ◆ **share-out** *n* partage *m*.

shark [ʃɑ:k] *n (fish)* requin *m*; *(fig: businessman)* requin *m*; *(swindler)* escroc *m*. ◆ **sharkskin** *n (Tex)* peau *f* d'ange.

sharp [ʃɑ:p] **1** *adj* (**a**) *razor, knife* tranchant, bien aiguisé; *point, needle* aigu (*f* -guë), acéré; *teeth* acéré; *pencil, nose, chin* pointu; *features* anguleux; *corner, angle* aigu; *bend in road* brusque. (**b**) *(abrupt) descent* raide; *fall in price, change* soudain. (**c**) *(well-defined) outline, (TV) picture* net; *difference* marqué. (**d**) *(Mus)* **C ~** do *m* dièse; **the note was ~** la note était trop haute. (**e**) *(harsh) cry, voice* perçant; *wind, cold* pénétrant, âpre; *frost* fort; *pain* vif; *smell, taste* piquant, âpre *(pej)*; *words, retort, tone* cinglant; *rebuke* sévère. *(fig)* **to have a ~ tongue** avoir la langue acérée. (**f**) *(brisk etc) pace, quarrel* vif. **look ~ about it!** dépêche-toi! (**g**) *(acute) eyesight* perçant; *hearing, smell* fin; *intelligence, mind* pénétrant; *person* vif, dégourdi *. *(pej)* **~ practice** procédés *mpl* malhonnêtes.

2 *adv* (**a**) *(Mus) sing, play* trop haut. (**b**) *(abruptly) stop* brusquement. **take ~ left** tournez tout à fait à gauche. (**c**) *(punctually)* **at 3 o'clock ~** à 3 heures pile.

3 *n (Mus)* dièse *m*.

◆ **sharpen** *vt* (**a**) *blade, tool* aiguiser; *pencil* tailler; (**b**) *outline, (TV) picture* rendre plus net; *difference* rendre plus marqué; *appetite* aiguiser; *desire* exciter; *pain, feeling* aviver; *intelligence* affiner; **to ~en one's wits** se dégourdir. ◆ **sharpener** *n (for knives)* aiguisoir *m*; *(for pencils)* taille-crayons *m inv*. ◆ **sharp-faced** *or* ◆ **sharp-featured** *adj* aux traits anguleux. ◆ **sharply** *adv* (**a**) *(abruptly) change, rise, stop* brusquement; (**b**) *(harshly) criticize* sévèrement; *observe, retort* sèchement; (**c**) *(distinctly) show up, stand out, differ* nettement; (**d**) *(alertly) say, ask, look* avec intérêt. ◆ **sharpness** *n* (**a**) *[razor, knife]* tranchant *m*; *[pencil etc]* pointe *f* aiguë; (**b**) *[turn, bend]* angle *m* brusque; *[outline etc]* netteté *f*; *[pain]* violence *f*; *[criticism, reproach, rebuke]* sévérité *f*; *[tone, voice]* brusquerie *f*; *[taste, smell]* piquant *m*, âpreté *f (pej)*; *[wind, cold]* âpreté. ◆ **sharpshooter** *n* tireur *m* d'élite. ◆ **sharp-sighted** *adj* à qui rien n'échappe. ◆ **sharp-tempered** *adj* coléreux. ◆ **sharp-witted** *adj* à l'esprit vif.

shatter ['ʃætəʳ] **1** *vt window, door* fracasser (*against* contre); *glasses, health, self-confidence, career* briser; *faith* détruire; *hopes, chances* ruiner; *sb's nerves* démolir. **2** *vi [glass, windscreen, cup]* voler en éclats; *[box etc]* se fracasser (*against* contre). ◆ **shattered** *adj (grief-stricken)* anéanti; *(*: aghast)* bouleversé; *(*: exhausted)* éreinté. ◆ **shattering** *adj (fig) attack* destructeur; *defeat* écrasant; *news, experience, disappointment* bouleversant; **this was a ~ing blow to our hopes** nos espoirs ont été gravement compromis.

shave [ʃeɪv] **1** *n*: **to have a ~** se raser; *(fig)* **to have a close** *or* **narrow ~** l'échapper belle. **2** *vt person* raser; *wood* raboter; *(fig: graze)* frôler. **3** *vi* se raser. ◆ **shave off** *vt sep* (**a**) **to ~ off one's beard** se raser la barbe. (**b**) *piece of wood* enlever au rabot. ◆ **shaver** *n* rasoir *m* électrique. ◆ **shaving** *n (wood etc)* copeau *m*. ◆ **shaving brush** *n* blaireau *m*. ◆ **shaving cream** *n* crème *f* à raser. ◆ **shaving soap** *n* savon *m* à barbe. ◆ **shaving stick** *n* bâton *m* de savon à barbe.

shawl [ʃɔːl] *n* châle *m*.

she [ʃiː] *pers pron* (**a**) *(stressed, unstressed)* elle. ~ **has come** elle est venue; **here ~ is** la voici; ~ **is a doctor** elle est médecin, c'est un médecin; **she didn't do it** ce n'est pas elle qui l'a fait; **younger than ~** plus jeune qu'elle. (**b**) *(+ rel pron)* celle. ~ **who** celle qui. (**c**) **it's a ~** *(animal)* c'est une femelle; *(baby)* c'est une fille. ◆ **she-bear** *n* ourse *f*.

sheaf [ʃiːf] *n [corn]* gerbe *f*; *[papers]* liasse *f*.

shear [ʃɪəʳ] *pret* **sheared**, *ptp* **sheared** *or* **shorn** *vt sheep* tondre. *(fig)* **shorn of** dépouillé de. ◆ **shear off** *vt sep wool* tondre; *projecting part, nail* arracher; *car wing etc* emporter. ◆ **shear through** *vt fus cloth* trancher; *wood, metal* fendre. ◆ **shearer** *n (person)* tondeur *m*, -euse *f*; *(machine)* tondeuse *f*. ◆ **shearing** *n (process)* tonte *f*. ◆ **shears** *npl (Gardening)* cisaille *f*; *(gen)* grands ciseaux *mpl*.

sheath [ʃiːθ] *n [sword]* fourreau *m*; *[scissors etc]* étui *m*; *[dagger, electric cable, flex]* gaine *f*; *(Bio, Bot)* enveloppe *f*; *(contraceptive)* préservatif *m*. ◆ **sheath-knife** *n* couteau *m* à gaine.

shed¹ [ʃed] *n (gen)* abri *m; (for tools, cycles etc)* remise *f*; *(smaller)* cabane *f*; *(huge, open-sided: Rail, Agr etc)* hangar *m*; *(lean-to)* appentis *m; (Ind: part of factory)* atelier *m*.

shed² [ʃed] *pret, ptp* **shed** *vt* (**a**) *(get rid of) leaves, fur, horns, weight* perdre; *[truck] load* déverser; *coat etc* enlever; *unwanted thing* se débarrasser de; *employees* se défaire de. **the snake ~s its skin** le serpent mue. (**b**) *blood, tears* verser. (**c**) *(send out) light, warmth, happiness* répandre. **to ~ light on** *(lit)* éclairer; *(fig) sb's motives etc* jeter de la lumière sur; *problem* éclaircir; *subject* éclairer.

sheen [ʃiːn] *n* lustre *m*.

sheep [ʃiːp] **1** *n, pl inv* mouton *m (animal)*; *(ewe)* brebis *f*. *(fig)* **to make ~'s eyes at** faire les yeux doux à; **we must divide the ~ from the goats** il ne faut pas mélanger les torchons et les serviettes * *(fig)*. **2** *adj*: ~ **farm** ferme *f* d'élevage de moutons; ~ **farmer** éleveur *m* de moutons; ~ **farming** élevage *m* de moutons. ◆ **sheepdog** *n* chien *m* de berger. ◆ **sheepish** *adj* penaud. ◆ **sheepishly** *adv* d'un air penaud. ◆ **sheepishness** *n* air *m* penaud. ◆ **sheepskin** *n* peau *f* de mouton; *(US Univ *)* peau *f* d'âne, diplôme *m*; **~skin jacket** canadienne *f*.

sheer¹ [ʃɪəʳ] *adj* (**a**) *(utter) chance, kindness, madness* pur; *impossibility, necessity* absolu; *waste* véritable *(before n)*. **it was ~ mud** ce n'était que de la boue; **by a ~ accident** tout à fait par hasard; **by ~ hard work** uniquement grâce au travail; ~ **robbery** du vol manifeste. (**b**) *stockings, material* extra-fin. (**c**) *rock, cliff* à pic. **a ~ drop** *or* **fall** un à-pic.

sheer² [ʃɪəʳ] *vi (swerve)* **to ~ off** *[ship]* faire une embardée; *(gen)* changer de direction.

sheet [ʃiːt] **1** *n* (**a**) *(on bed)* drap *m*; *(dust ~)* housse *f*; *(tarpaulin)* bâche *f*. (**b**) *(piece etc) [plastic, rubber]* morceau *m*; *[paper, notepaper]* feuille *f*; *[iron, steel]* tôle *f*; *[glass, metal, ice etc]* plaque *f*; *[water, snow]* étendue *f*; *[flames]* rideau *m*. *[paper]* **an odd** *or* **a loose ~** une feuille volante; *(Comm)* **order ~** bulletin *m* de commande. **2** *adj*: ~ **lightning** éclair *m* en nappes; ~ **metal** tôle *f*; *(US Aut)* carosserie *f*; ~ **music** partitions *fpl*.

sheik(h) [ʃeɪk] *n* cheik *m*; *(US fig)* séducteur *m*.

shelf [ʃelf] **1** *n, pl* **shelves** (**a**) étagère *f*, rayon *m*; *(in shop)* rayon; *(in oven)* plaque *f*. **a set of shelves** un rayonnage; **to buy sth off the ~** acheter qch tout fait; **on the ~** *woman* laissée pour compte. (**b**) *(edge) (in rock)* rebord *m*; *(underwater)* écueil *m*. **2** *adj (Comm)* ~ **life** durée *f* de conservation avant vente; *(Libraries)* ~ **mark** cote *f*.

shell [ʃel] **1** *n* (**a**) *[egg, nut, oyster, snail etc]* coquille *f*; *[tortoise, lobster]* carapace *f*; *(seashell)* coquillage *m*; *[peas]* cosse *f*. *(lit, fig)* **to come out of one's ~** sortir de sa coquille. (**b**) *[building]* carcasse *f*; *[ship]* coque *f*. *(Culin)* **pastry ~** fond *m* de tarte. (**c**) *(Mil)* obus *m*. **2** *adj necklace etc* de *or* en coquillages. **3** *vt* (**a**) *peas* écosser; *nut, crab, shrimp* décortiquer; *lobster* retirer de sa carapace. (**b**) *(Mil)* bombarder (d'obus).

◆ **shell out** * **1** *vi* casquer ‡ *(for* pour), payer. **2** *vt sep* cracher ‡, payer.

◆ **shellfish** *n, pl inv (lobster, crab)* crustacé *m*; *(mollusc)* coquillage *m*; *(pl: Culin)* fruits *mpl* de mer. ◆ **shelling** *n (Mil)* bombardement *m (par obus)*. ◆ **shellproof** *adj* blindé.

shelter [ˈʃeltəʳ] **1** *n* (**a**) abri *m*. **under the ~ of** sous l'abri de; **to take ~ , to get under ~** se mettre à l'abri *or* à couvert; **to take ~ from/under** s'abriter de/sous; **to seek ~** chercher un abri *(from* contre). (**b**) *(on mountain)* abri *m*, refuge *m*; *(for sentry)* guérite *f*; *(bus ~)* abribus *m*; *(air-raid ~)* abri. **2** *vt* (**a**) *(protect) (from wind, shells etc)* abriter, protéger *(from* de); *(from blame etc)* protéger *(from* de); *criminal etc* protéger; *(hide)* cacher. **~ed from the wind** à l'abri du vent. (**b**) *(give lodging to)* recueillir. **3** *vi* s'abriter *(from* de; *under* sous). ◆ **sheltered** *adj place* abrité; *(fig) life* bien protégé; *childhood* sans soucis; *conditions, environment, workshop* protégé; **~ed housing** foyers-logements *mpl*.

shelve [ʃelv] **1** *vt* (**a**) *(fig: postpone)* mettre en sommeil. (**b**) *(lit) cupboard, wall* garnir de rayons. **2** *vi (slope:* ~ **down***)* descendre en pente douce. ◆ **shelving** *n* rayonnages *mpl*.

shepherd [ˈʃepəd] **1** *n* berger *m*; *(Rel)* pasteur *m*. *(Culin)* **~'s pie** ≃ hachis *m* Parmentier. **2** *vt (fig)* **to ~ sb in** faire entrer qn; **to ~ sb out** escorter qn jusqu'à la porte; **he ~ed us round Paris** il nous a servi de guide dans Paris. ◆ **shepherdess** *n* bergère *f*.

sherbet [ˈʃɜːbət] *n (Brit: powder)* poudre *f* acidulée; *(US: water ice)* sorbet *m*.

sheriff [ˈʃerɪf] *n* shérif *m*.

sherry [ˈʃerɪ] *n* xérès *m*, sherry *m*.

Shetland [ˈʃetlənd] **1** *n (also* **the ~ Isles, the ~s***)* les îles *fpl* Shetland. **2** *adj* des Shetland. ~ **pony** poney *m* des Shetland; ~ **wool** shetland *m*.

shield [ʃiːld] **1** *n (gen)* bouclier *m*; *(not round)* écu *m*; *(on machine, against radiation etc)* écran *m* (de protection). **2** *vt* protéger *(from* de, contre). **to ~ sb with one's body** faire à qn un rempart de son corps.

shift [ʃɪft] **1** *n* (**a**) *(change)* changement *m (in* de); *(Ling)* mutation *f*; *(movement: of cargo, load etc)* déplacement *m (in* de). **a sudden ~ in policy** un retournement de la politique; **a sudden ~ in the wind** une saute de vent. (**b**) *(period of work)* poste *m*. **to be on day/night ~** être (au poste) de jour/de nuit; **he works ~s** il travaille par roulement; **I work an 8-hour ~** je fais un poste de 8 heures; **they worked in ~s to save him** ils se sont relayés pour le sauver. (**c**) *(expedient)* expédient *m*, truc * *m*. **to make ~** se débrouiller *(with* avec; *without* sans; *to do* pour faire). (**d**) *(US Aut: gear ~)* changement *m* de vitesse. (**e**) *(Comput)* décalage *m*. **2** *adj [typewriter]* ~ **key** touche *f* de majuscule; *(Ind)* ~ **work** travail *m* posté.

3 *vt object, furniture* déplacer, changer de place; *one's head, arm etc* bouger, remuer; *(Theat) scenery* changer; *screw, lid* débloquer; *employee (to another town)* muter *(to* à); *(to another job, department)* affecter *(to* à); *(fig) blame, responsibility* rejeter *(on to* sur). **to ~ sth in/out/nearer** *etc* rentrer/sortir/approcher *etc* qch; **to ~ position** changer de position; *(US Aut)* **to ~ gears** changer de vitesse.

4 *vi* (**a**) *(go)* aller; *(move house)* déménager; *(change position, stir) [person, limb]* bouger; *[wind]* tourner; *[cargo, load]* se déplacer; *[opinions]* changer; *(change one's mind)* changer d'avis. **he ~ed over to the window** il s'est approché de la fenêtre; **~ off the rug** va-t'en du tapis; **to ~ over** *or* **along** *or* **up** se pousser; *(Aut)* **to ~ into second gear** passer la deuxième; **he won't ~** il ne bougera pas; *(fig)* **to ~ from one's position** modifier sa position; **come on, ~!** * allez, remue-toi! * (**b**) **to ~ for o.s.** se débrouiller * tout seul.

◆ **shiftily** *adv behave* sournoisement; *answer* de façon évasive. ◆ **shiftiness** *n* sournoiserie *f*; caractère *m* évasif. ◆ **shiftless** *adj* manquant de ressource. ◆ **shiftlessness** *n* manque *m* de ressource. ◆ **shifty** *adj person, behaviour* louche, sournois; *answer* évasif; *look* fuyant.

Shiite ['ʃiːaɪt] *n, adj* chi'ite *(mf)*.

shilly-shally ['ʃɪlɪˌʃælɪ] *vi* hésiter. **stop ~ing!** décide-toi enfin! ◆ **shilly-shallying** *n* hésitations *fpl*.

shimmer ['ʃɪmə^r] *vi [satin, jewels]* chatoyer; *[water, heat haze]* miroiter. ◆ **shimmering** *adj* chatoyant; miroitant.

shimmy ['ʃɪmɪ] **1** *n* (**a**) *(US Aut)* shimmy *m*. (**b**) *(dance)* shimmy *m*. **2** *vi (US Aut)* avoir du shimmy.

shin [ʃɪn] **1** *n (Anat)* tibia *m*; *(Culin)* jarret *m*. **2** *vi*: **to ~ up a tree** grimper à un arbre; **to ~ down a tree** dégringoler lestement d'un arbre; **to ~ over a wall** escalader un mur. ◆ **shinbone** *n* tibia *m*.

shindy * ['ʃɪndɪ] *n (brawl)* bagarre *f*; *(commotion)* boucan * *m*. **to kick up a ~** faire du boucan *.

shine [ʃaɪn] *(vb: pret, ptp* **shone***)* **1** *n [sun, metal]* éclat *m*; *[shoes]* brillant *m*. **to give sth a ~** faire briller qch; **to take the ~ off** *brass, shoes* ternir; *(* fig) success, news* diminuer l'effet de. **2** *vi* briller. **the sun is shining** il y a du soleil, le soleil brille; **the moon is shining** il y a clair de lune; **to ~ on sth** éclairer qch; **the light was shining in my eyes** j'avais la lumière dans les yeux; **the light shone through the curtains** la lumière passait à travers les rideaux; **her face shone with happiness** son visage rayonnait de bonheur; *(fig)* **to ~ at football** briller au football. **3** *vt* (**a**) **~ your torch** *or* **~ the light over here** éclairez par ici. (**b**) *(polish: pret, ptp* **shone** *or* **shined***)* faire briller. ◆ **shining** *adj furniture etc* reluisant; *(happy) face* rayonnant; *eyes, hair* brillant; *example* resplendissant. ◆ **shiny** *adj (gen)* brillant; *(pej) clothes* lustré.

shingle ['ʃɪŋgl] *n (on beach etc)* galets *mpl*; *(on roof)* bardeaux *mpl*; *(US*: signboard)* petite enseigne *f*. ◆ **shingly** *adj beach* de galets.

shingles ['ʃɪŋglz] *nsg (Med)* zona *m*.

ship [ʃɪp] **1** *n (gen)* bateau *m*; *(large)* navire *m*; *(vessel)* vaisseau *m*, bâtiment *m*. **His** *or* **Her Majesty's S~** *(abbr* **HMS***)* **Maria/Falcon** la Maria/le Falcon; **~'s boat** chaloupe *f*; **~'s company** équipage *m*; **~'s papers** papiers *mpl* de bord. **2** *vt* (**a**) *(transport)* transporter; *(send:* **~ off***)* expédier. (**b**) *(put or take on board) cargo, water* embarquer; *oars* rentrer. ◆ **shipbuilder** *n* constructeur *m* de navires. ◆ **shipbuilding** *n* construction *f* navale. ◆ **shipload** *n (lit)* charge *f*; *(fig)* grande quantité *f*. ◆ **shipmate** *n* camarade *m* de bord. ◆ **shipment** *n (load)* cargaison *f*; *(dispatch)* expédition *f*. ◆ **shipowner** *n* armateur *m*. ◆ **shipper** *n* expéditeur *m*. ◆ **shipping** **1** *n (ships collectively)* navires *mpl*; *(traffic)* navigation *f*; *(Rad)* **attention all ~ping!** avis à la navigation!; **a danger to ~ping** un danger pour la navigation; **canal closed to British ~ping** canal fermé aux navires britanniques ; **2** *adj*: **~ping agent** agent *m* maritime; **~ping company, ~ping line** compagnie *f* de navigation; **~ping lane** voie *f* de navigation. ◆ **shipshape** *adj* en ordre. ◆ **ship-to-shore radio** *n* liaison *f* radio avec la côte. ◆ **shipwreck** **1** *n (event)* naufrage *m*; *(wrecked ship)* épave *f* ; **2** *vt*: **to be ~wrecked** faire naufrage; **~wrecked on a desert island** *ship* échoué sur une île déserte; *person* naufragé sur une île déserte. ◆ **shipwrecked** *adj* naufragé. ◆ **shipwright** *n* constructeur *m* de navires. ◆ **shipyard** *n* chantier *m* naval.

shire ['ʃaɪə^r] *n (Brit)* comté *m*. **~ horse** cheval *m* de gros trait.

shirk [ʃɜːk] **1** *vt task, work* ne pas faire; *duty, difficulty, issue* esquiver. **to ~ doing** s'arranger pour ne pas faire. **2** *vi* tirer au flanc *. ◆ **shirker** *n* tire-au-flanc * *m inv*.

shirt [ʃɜːt] *n (man's)* chemise *f*; *(woman's)* chemisier *m*; *(Sport)* maillot *m*. **in (one's) ~ sleeves** en bras *or* manches de chemise; *(Betting)* **to put one's ~ on sth** jouer tout ce qu'on a sur qch. ◆ **shirty** * *adj (esp Brit)* en rogne *.

shiver[1] ['ʃɪvə^r] **1** *vi* frissonner (*with* de). **2** *n* frisson *m*. **it sent ~s down his spine** cela lui a donné froid dans le dos; **to give sb the ~s** donner le frisson à qn. ◆ **shivery** *adj (from cold)* qui a des frissons; *(from fever)* fiévreux; *(from fear/emotion etc)* frissonnant (de peur/d'émotion *etc*).

shiver[2] ['ʃɪvə^r] **1** *n [glass]* éclat *m*. **2** *vi* voler en éclats. **3** *vt* fracasser.

shoal [ʃəʊl] *n* banc *m (de poissons)*.

shock [ʃɒk] **1** *n* (**a**) *(gen)* choc *m*; *[earthquake, explosion]* secousse *f*; *(Elec)* décharge *f* (électrique). *(Elec)* **to get a ~** recevoir une décharge (électrique) (*from sth* en touchant qch), prendre le jus *; **he got such a ~ when he heard that...** cela lui a donné un tel choc *or* un tel coup d'apprendre que...; **the ~ of the election results** les résultats *mpl* stupéfiants de l'élection; **it came as a ~ to me** ça m'a stupéfié; **it comes as a ~ to hear that...** il est stupéfiant d'apprendre que...; **you gave me a ~!** vous m'avez fait peur!; **I got such a ~!** j'ai eu une de ces émotions! *; **the ~ killed him** il est mort d'émotion; **pale with ~** pâle de saisissement; *(Med)* **in a state of ~** en état de choc. (**b**) *(US Aut)* **~s** * amortisseurs *mpl*. **2** *adj* (**a**) *(Mil etc) tactics, troops* de choc. *(Aut)* **~ absorber** amortisseur *m*; **~ wave** onde *f* de choc. (**b**) (*) *result, reaction* stupéfiant. **3** *vt (take aback)* secouer; *(stronger)* bouleverser; *(scandalize)* choquer. **easily ~ed** qui se choque facilement; **a ~ed silence** un silence accablé. ◆ **shocking** *adj (appalling) crime, news, sight* atroce; *(scandalizing) book, behaviour* choquant; *decision, waste, price* scandaleux; *(very bad) weather, results, handwriting* épouvantable. ◆ **shockingly** *adv unfair, expensive* terriblement; *(very badly)* très mal.

shoddy ['ʃɒdɪ] *adj* de mauvaise qualité. ◆ **shoddily** *adv made* mal. ◆ **shoddiness** *n* mauvaise qualité *f*.

shoe [ʃuː] *(vb: pret, ptp* **shod***)* **1** *n* chaussure *f*, soulier *m*; *(horse ~)* fer *m* (à cheval); *(brake ~)* sabot *m* (de frein). **to shake** *or* **shiver in one's ~s** avoir une peur bleue; *(fig)* **I wouldn't like to be in his ~s** je n'aimerais pas être à sa place. **2** *adj*: **~ polish** cirage *m*; **~ repair** réparation *f* de chaussures. **3** *vt horse* ferrer. *[person]* **well/badly shod** bien/mal chaussé. ◆ **shoebrush** *n* brosse *f* à chaussures. ◆ **shoehorn** *n* chausse-pied *m*. ◆ **shoelace** *n* lacet *m* de soulier. ◆ **shoemaker** *or* ◆ **shoe-repairer** *n* cordonnier *m*; **~maker's shop** cordonnerie *f*. ◆ **shoeshop** *n* magasin *m* de chaussures. ◆ **shoestring** *n* lacet *m*; *(fig)* **on a ~string** à peu de frais. ◆ **shoetree** *n* embauchoir *m*.

shone [ʃɒn] *pret, ptp of* **shine.**

shoo [ʃuː] *vt* (**~ away, ~ off**) chasser.

shook [ʃʊk] *pret of* **shake.**

shoot [ʃu:t] *(vb: pret, ptp* **shot***)* **1** *n* (**a**) *[plant]* pousse *f.* (**b**) *(chute)* glissière *f*, déversoir *m.* (**c**) *(fig)* **the whole** ~ ⁑ tout le tremblement *.

2 *vt* (**a**) *(hit)* atteindre d'un coup de fusil *etc*; *(hunt)* chasser; *(kill)* abattre; *(execute)* fusiller. **shot in the head** *(hit)* atteint *or (killed)* tué d'une balle dans la tête; *(fig)* **you'll get shot for that!** * tu vas te faire incendier * pour ça. (**b**) *(fire) gun* tirer *or* lâcher un coup de (*at* sur); *arrow, rocket, missile* lancer (*at* sur); *bullet* tirer (*at* sur). **to** ~ **a goal** marquer un but; **he shot the bolt** *(fastened)* il a mis le verrou; *(opened)* il a tiré le verrou; *(fig)* **he has shot his bolt** il a joué sa dernière carte; *(fig)* **to** ~ **a line about sth** ⁑ raconter des histoires à propos de qch; **to** ~ **dice** jeter les dés. (**c**) *(direct) look* lancer (*at* à); *smile* jeter (*at* à); *[searchlight etc] beam of light* braquer (*at* sur). **to** ~ **questions at sb** bombarder qn de questions. (**d**) *(Cine etc) film, scene* tourner; *person, subject* prendre (en photo). (**e**) *rapids* descendre.

3 *vi* (**a**) *(with gun, bow)* tirer (*at* sur). **to go** ~**ing** chasser; **to** ~ **to kill** tirer pour abattre; **to** ~ **on sight** tirer à vue. (**b**) *(rush)* **to** ~ **in/past** *etc* entrer/passer *etc* à toute vitesse; **the bullet shot past his ears** la balle lui a sifflé aux oreilles; *[flames, water]* **to** ~ **out** *or* **up** *etc* jaillir; **the pain went** ~**ing up his arm** la douleur au bras le lancinait. (**c**) *(Ftbl etc)* shooter, tirer. **to** ~ **at goal** shooter. (**d**) *(Bot)* bourgeonner, pousser.

◆ **shoot down** *vt sep plane, person* abattre. ◆ **shoot up** *vi* (**a**) *[flame, water]* jaillir; *[rocket, price etc]* monter en flèche. (**b**) *(grow quickly)* pousser vite.

◆ **shooting 1** *n* (**a**) *(shots)* coups *mpl* de feu; *(continuous)* fusillade *f*; (**b**) *(murder)* meurtre *m* (avec une arme à feu); *(execution)* exécution *f*; (**c**) *(Hunting)* chasse *f* ; **2** *adj pain* lancinant; ~**ing brake** break *m*; ~**ing gallery** stand *m* de tir; ~**ing incidents** échanges *mpl* de coups de feu; *(fig)* **the whole** ~**ing match** * tout le tremblement *; ~**ing star** étoile *f* filante; ~**ing stick** canne-siège *f*. ◆ **shooting-down** *n:* **the** ~**ing-down of the diplomat** l'attentat *m* contre le diplomate; **the** ~**ing-down of the plane** la destruction de l'avion.

shop [ʃɒp] **1** *n* (**a**) magasin *m*; *(small)* boutique *f*. **wine** ~ marchand *m* de vins; **at the butcher's** ~ à la boucherie, chez le boucher; *(lit, fig)* **to shut up** ~ fermer boutique; *(fig)* **you've come to the wrong** ~ * tu te trompes d'adresse *; *(fig)* **to talk** ~ parler boutique; *(fig)* **all over the** ~ * *(everywhere)* partout; *(in confusion)* en pagaille *. (**b**) *(Ind: work~)* atelier *m*.

2 *adj (Brit)* ~ **assistant** vendeur *m*, -euse *f*; *(Ind)* ~ **steward** délégué(e) syndical(e) *m(f)*; ~ **window** vitrine *f*.

3 *vi* faire ses courses (*at* chez). **to go** ~**ping** *(locally etc)* faire les courses; *(on shopping expedition)* faire des courses; **I was** ~**ping for a coat** je cherchais un manteau.

4 *vt* (⁑*: betray)* vendre, donner *.

◆ **shop around** *vi* comparer les prix. **to** ~ **around for sth** comparer les prix avant d'acheter qch. ◆ **shopfitter** *n* décorateur *m* de magasin. ◆ **shop-floor** *n (Ind)* **he works on the** ~**-floor** c'est un ouvrier; **the** ~**-floor (workers)** les ouvriers. ◆ **shopgirl** *n (Brit)* vendeuse *f*. ◆ **shopkeeper** *n* commerçant(e) *m(f)*. ◆ **shoplift** *vi* voler à l'étalage. ◆ **shoplifter** *n* voleur *m*, -euse *f* à l'étalage. ◆ **shoplifting** *n* vol *m* à l'étalage. ◆ **shopper** *n* (**a**) *(person)* personne *f* qui fait ses courses; *(customer)* client(e) *m(f)*; (**b**) *(*: bag)* cabas *m*. ◆ **shopping 1** *n (goods)* achats *mpl* ; **2** *adj street, district* commerçant; ~**ping bag** cabas *m*; ~**ping basket** panier *m* (à provisions); ~**ping centre** centre *m* commercial ; ~**ping trolley** caddie *m*. ◆ **shop-soiled** *adj* qui a fait la vitrine.

shore¹ [ʃɔ:ʳ] **1** *n [sea]* rivage *m*; *[lake]* rive *f*; *(coast)* côte *f*; *(beach)* plage *f*. **on** ~ à terre; **to go on** ~ débarquer. **2** *adj (Naut)* ~ **leave** permission *f* à terre.

shore² [ʃɔ:ʳ] *vt:* **to** ~ **up** étayer; *(fig)* consolider.

shorn [ʃɔ:n] *ptp of* **shear.**

short [ʃɔ:t] **1** *adj* (**a**) *(gen)* court; *person* petit, de petite taille; *step, walk* petit; *visit, vowel, syllable* bref. **a** ~ **distance away** à peu de distance; **to take a** ~ **holiday** prendre quelques jours de vacances; **a** ~ **time** *or* **while** peu de temps; **time is getting** ~ il ne reste plus beaucoup de temps; **the days are getting** ~**er** les jours raccourcissent; **make the skirt** ~**er** raccourcis la jupe; **that was** ~ **and sweet** ça n'a pas traîné; **to take a** ~ **cut** prendre un raccourci; **a** ~ **drink** un petit verre d'apéritif (*or* d'alcool); *(Ski)* ~ **ski method** ski *m* évolutif; **to win by a** ~ **head** *(Racing)* gagner d'une courte tête; *(fig)* gagner de justesse; ~ **list** liste *f* des candidats sélectionnés; ~ **story** nouvelle *f*; ~**-story writer** nouvelliste *mf*; **they want a** ~**er working week** on veut réduire la semaine de travail; **to have a** ~ **temper** être coléreux; *(Ind)* **to work** ~ **time** être en chômage partiel; *(fig)* **to make** ~ **work of** *job etc* ne pas mettre beaucoup de temps à faire; (*) *person* envoyer promener *. (**b**) *(phrases)* **in** ~ bref; **'TV' is** ~ **for 'television'** 'TV' est l'abréviation de 'télévision'; **he's called Fred for** ~ son diminutif est Fred; **to be** ~ **of sugar** être à court de sucre; **I'm £2** ~ il me manque 2 livres; **not far** ~ **of £100** pas loin de 100 livres; **it's little** ~ **of suicide** c'est presque un suicide; **it's nothing** ~ **of robbery** c'est du vol ni plus ni moins; ~ **of asking him yourself** à moins de lui demander vous-même; **everything** ~ **of (doing) sth** tout sauf (faire) qch; **to go** ~ **of sth** manquer de qch; **they never went** ~ ils n'ont jamais manqué du nécessaire; *(fig)* **to be taken** ~ * être pris d'un besoin pressant; **petrol is** ~ *or* **in** ~ **supply** on manque d'essence; **to give** ~ **weight** *or* ~ **measure** ne pas donner le poids juste; *(deliberately)* tricher sur le poids. (**c**) *(curt) reply, manner* brusque, sec. **to be rather** ~ **with sb** se montrer assez sec *or* brusque à l'égard de qn.

2 *vti (Elec)* = **short-circuit** ; *V below.*

3 *n* (**a**) (*) *(Cine)* court métrage *m*; *(Elec)* court-circuit *m*. ~**s** des apéritifs *mpl*, de l'alcool *m*. (**b**) *(garment)* **(a pair of)** ~**s** *(gen)* un short; *(Sport)* une culotte; *(US: men's underwear)* un caleçon.

◆ **shortage** *n (gen)* manque *m*, pénurie *f*; **there was no** ~**age of water** on ne manquait pas d'eau; **the food** ~**age** la disette; **the housing** ~**age** la crise du logement. ◆ **shortbread** *or* ◆ **shortcake** *n* sablé *m*. ◆ **short-change** *vt customer* ne pas rendre assez à; *(fig)* rouler *. ◆ **short-circuit 1** *n* court-circuit *m* ; **2** *vt* court-circuiter ; **3** *vi* se mettre en court-circuit. ◆ **shortcoming** *n* défaut *m*. ◆ **short(crust) pastry** *n* pâte *f* brisée. ◆ **shorten 1** *vt skirt, rope* raccourcir; *holiday, journey* écourter; *life, book, programme* abréger; *distance, time* réduire ; **2** *vi [days etc]* raccourcir. ◆ **shortening** *n (Culin)* matière *f* grasse. ◆ **shortfall** *n (money)* montant *m* insuffisant (*in* de); *(in numbers)* nombre *m* insuffisant (*in* de); **there is a** ~**fall of £5,000** il manque 5 000 livres. ◆ **shorthand 1** *n* sténo(graphie) *f*; **in** ~**hand** en sténo ; **2** *adj notes* en sténo; *notebook* de sténo. ◆ **shorthand-typing** *n* sténodactylo *f*. ◆ **shorthand-typist** *n* sténodactylo *mf*. ◆ **shorthand-writer** *n* sténo(graphe) *mf*. ◆ **short-list 1** *n* liste *f* des candidats sélectionnés ; **2** *vt* mettre sur la liste des candidats sélectionnés. ◆ **short-lived** *adj (fig)* de courte durée. ◆ **shortly** *adv* (**a**) *(soon)* bientôt, dans peu de temps; ~**ly before twelve** peu avant midi; (**b**) *(curtly)* sèchement, brusquement. ◆ **shortness** *n* peu *m* de longueur; petite taille *f*; brièveté *f*; *[vowel, syllable]* brévité *f*; *(curtness)* sécheresse *f*. ◆ **short-order cook** *n (US)* cuisinier *m*, -ière *f* préparant des plats rapides. ◆ **short-range** *adj weather forecast* à court terme. ◆ **shorts** *npl*: **(a pair of) ~s** un short. ◆ **short-sighted** *adj person* myope; *policy, measure* qui manque de vision. ◆ **short-sightedness** *n* myopie *f*; manque *m* de vision. ◆ **short-staffed** *adj*: **to be ~-staffed** manquer de personnel. ◆ **short-tempered** *adj (in general)* coléreux; *(in a bad temper)* d'humeur irritable. ◆ **short-term** *adj loan, plan* à court terme; *car park* de courte durée. ◆ **short-wave** *(Rad)* **1** *n* ondes *fpl* courtes ; **2** *adj radio* à ondes courtes; *transmission* sur ondes courtes.

shot [ʃɒt] **1** *n* (**a**) *(act of firing)* coup *m*; *(sound)* coup de feu (*or* de fusil *etc*); *(bullet)* balle *f*; *(pellets:* **lead ~***)* plomb *m*. *(fig)* **a ~ across the bows, a warning ~** un avertissement; **the first ~ killed him** la première balle l'a tué; **he is a good/bad ~** il est bon/ mauvais tireur; *(fig)* **big ~** * personnage *m* important, gros bonnet * *m*; **Parthian ~** flèche *f* du Parthe; *(fig)* **that was a ~ in the dark** c'était dit à tout hasard; **like a ~** *leave, go* comme une flèche; *agree* sans hésiter. (**b**) *(Space)* **moon ~** tir *m* lunaire. (**c**) *(Ftbl, Golf, Tennis etc)* coup *m*; *(Hockey)* tir *m; (throw)* lancer *m*. **good ~**! bien joué!; *(Shooting)* bien visé!; **to put the ~** lancer le poids; **~ put** lancer du poids; **a ~ at goal** un tir au but. (**d**) *(attempt)* essai *m*, coup *m*; *(turn to play)* tour *m*. **to have a ~ at (doing) sth** essayer (de faire) qch; **have a ~ at it!** *(try it)* tentez le coup!; *(guess)* dites voir! * (**e**) *(Phot)* photo *f*; *(Cine)* prise *f* de vues. (**f**) *(injection)* piqûre *f* (*against* contre); *(of alcohol)* coup *m*. *(fig)* **a ~ in the arm** un coup de fouet. **2** *pret, ptp of* **shoot. to get ~ of** ⁑ se débarrasser de. **3** *adj*: **~ with yellow** strié de jaune; **~ silk** soie *f* gorge-de-pigeon.
◆ **shotgun 1** *n* fusil *m* de chasse ; **2** *adj*: **~gun wedding** mariage *m* forcé.

should [ʃʊd] *modal aux vb* (**a**) *(obligation, advisability)* **I ~ go and see her** je devrais aller la voir, il faudrait que j'aille la voir; **he thought he ~ tell you** il a pensé qu'il ferait bien de vous le dire; **you ~ have been a teacher** vous auriez dû être professeur; **everything is as it ~ be** tout est en ordre; **how ~ I know?** comment voulez-vous que je le sache? (**b**) *(probability)* **he ~ win the race** il devrait gagner la course, il va probablement gagner la course; **he ~ have got there by now** il a dû arriver à l'heure qu'il est; **why ~ he suspect me?** pourquoi me soupçonnerait-il? (**c**) *(conditional tense)* **I ~ go, I'd go** j'irais; **we ~ have come** nous serions venus; **I ~ like to** j'aimerais bien; **who ~ come in but Paul!** et devinez qui est entré? Paul!

shoulder [ˈʃəʊldəʳ] **1** *n* (**a**) épaule *f*. **to have broad ~s** être large d'épaules; **put it round your ~s** mets-le sur tes épaules; **to weep on sb's ~** pleurer sur l'épaule de qn; **over one ~** à l'épaule; **to look over sb's ~** regarder par-dessus l'épaule de qn; *(fig)* surveiller qn constamment; **~ to ~** coude à coude; *(fig)* **to put one's ~ to the wheel** s'atteler à la tâche. (**b**) *[road]* accotement *m*, bas-côté *m*; *[hill]* contrefort; *m*. **hard/soft ~** accotement stabilisé/non stabilisé. **2** *adj*: **~ bag** sac *m* à bandoulière; **~ blade** omoplate *f*; **between the ~ blades** en plein entre les épaules; *[garment]* **~ strap** bretelle *f*. **3** *vt load* charger sur son épaule; *responsibility* endosser; *task* se charger de. *(Mil)* **to ~ arms** porter l'arme; **to ~ sb aside** écarter qn d'un coup d'épaule. ◆ **shoulder-high** *adv*: **to carry sb ~-high** porter qn en triomphe.

shout [ʃaʊt] **1** *n* cri *m* (*of joy etc* de joie *etc*). **there were ~s of applause/protest/laughter** des acclamations/des protestations bruyantes/des éclats de rire ont retenti; **to give sb a ~** appeler qn. **2** *vt* crier. **3** *vi* crier (*to sb to do* à qn de faire; *at sb* après qn; *for help* au secours), pousser des cris (*for joy etc* de joie *etc*). **to ~ with laughter** éclater de rire; **she ~ed for someone to help her** elle a appelé pour qu'on l'aide *(subj)*.
◆ **shout down** *vt sep speaker* huer. ◆ **shout out 1** *vi* pousser un cri. **2** *vt sep* crier.
◆ **shouting** *n* cris *mpl*; *(noise of quarrelling)* éclats *mpl* de voix; *(fig)* **it's all over bar the ~ing** c'est dans le sac *.

shove [ʃʌv] **1** *n* poussée *f*. **to give sb/sth a ~** pousser qn/qch. **2** *vt (push)* pousser; *(with effort)* pousser avec peine; *(thrust) stick, finger etc* enfoncer (*into* dans; *between* entre); *rag* fourrer (*into* dans); *(jostle)* bousculer; *(put)* mettre. **to ~ sth in/out** *etc* faire entrer/sortir *etc* qch en poussant; **to ~ sth into a drawer/one's pocket** fourrer qch dans un tiroir/sa poche. **3** *vi* pousser. **he ~d (his way) past me** il m'a dépassé en me bousculant; **he ~d (his way) through the crowd** il s'est frayé un chemin à travers la foule. ◆ **shove off** * *vi (leave)* ficher le camp *. ◆ **shove over** * *vi (move over)* se pousser.

shovel [ˈʃʌvl] **1** *n* pelle *f*; *(mechanical)* pelleteuse *f*. **2** *vt coal, grain* pelleter; **(~ out)** *mud etc* enlever à la pelle; **(~ up)** *sth spilt etc* ramasser avec une pelle; *snow* enlever à la pelle. ◆ **shovelful** *n* pelletée *f*.

show [ʃəʊ] *(vb: pret* **showed,** *ptp* **shown** *or* **showed***)* **1** *n* (**a**) *[hatred, affection etc]* démonstration *f*; *(semblance)* semblant *m*; *(ostentation)* parade *f*. **some fine pieces on ~** quelques beaux objets exposés; **~ of power** étalage *m* de force; **a ~ of hands** un vote à main levée; **the dahlias make a splendid ~** les dahlias sont splendides à voir; **they make a great ~ of their wealth** ils font parade de leur richesse; **with a ~ of emotion** en affectant l'émotion; **to make a ~ of doing** faire semblant de faire; **just for ~** pour l'effet. (**b**) *(exhibition: Agr, Art, Tech etc)* exposition *f*; *(Comm)* foire *f*; *(Agr: contest)* concours *m*. **the Boat S~** le Salon de la Navigation. (**c**) *(Theat etc)* spectacle *m*; *(variety ~)* show *m*. **I often go to a ~** je vais souvent au spectacle; **the last ~ starts at 9** *(Theat)* la dernière représentation *or (Cine)* la dernière séance commence à 21 heures; **on with the ~!** que la représentation commence (*or* continue)! (**d**) *(phrases)* **good ~**! * bravo!; **to put up a good ~** bien se défendre *; **to make a poor ~** faire piètre figure; **it's a poor ~** * il n'y a pas de quoi être fier; **this is Paul's ~** * c'est Paul qui commande ici; **to run the ~** * faire marcher l'affaire; **to give the ~ away** * vendre la mèche *.
2 *adj house, flat* témoin (*f inv*). **~ trial** grand procès *m (souvent idéologique)*.
3 *vt* (**a**) *(gen)* montrer; *film, slides* passer; *(exhibit) goods for sale, picture, dog* exposer; *(express) interest, surprise* montrer, manifester; *gratitude, respect* témoigner; *(indicate) [clock, dial etc]* indiquer, marquer. **~ it me!** faites voir!, montrez-le-moi!; **what is ~ing at the Odeon?** qu'est-ce qu'on donne à l'Odéon?; **it has been ~n on television** c'est passé à la télévision; *(fig)* **there's nothing to ~ for it** on ne le dirait pas; **he has nothing to ~ for it** ça ne lui a rien donné; **he daren't ~ his face there again** il n'ose plus s'y montrer; *(fig)* **to ~ one's hand** *or* **cards** abattre son jeu; *(fig)* **to ~ sb the door** mettre qn à la porte; *(fig)* **to ~ the flag** faire acte de présence; **to ~ a loss/profit** indiquer une perte/ un bénéfice; **roads are ~n in red** les routes sont marquées en rouge; **to ~ loyalty** se montrer loyal (*to sb* envers qn); **this skirt ~s the dirt** cette jupe est salissante; **it ~ed signs of having been used** il était visible qu'on s'en était servi; **to ~ fight** faire montre de combativité; **that ~s his good taste** cela témoigne de son bon goût; **to ~ one's age** faire son âge; **this ~s great intelligence** cela révèle *or* dénote beaucoup d'intelligence; **he ~ed himself (to be) a coward** il s'est montré *or* révélé lâche; **it all goes to ~ that...** tout cela montre bien

que...; **it only goes to ~!** * c'est bien ça la vie!; **I ~ed him that it was impossible** je lui ai prouvé que c'était impossible; *(fig)* **I'll ~ him!** * je lui apprendrai! (**b**) *(conduct)* **to ~ sb in/up** *etc* faire entrer/monter *etc* qn; **to ~ sb to his seat** placer qn; **to ~ sb out, to ~ sb to the door** reconduire qn jusqu'à la porte; **to ~ sb over** *or* **round a house** faire visiter une maison à qn.
4 *vi [emotion]* être visible; *[stain, scar]* se voir; *[underskirt etc]* dépasser. **it doesn't ~** cela ne se voit pas.
◆ **show off 1** *vi (gen)* crâner *; *[child]* faire l'intéressant; *(show one's knowledge)* étaler sa science. **she's always ~ing off** c'est une crâneuse *; **he's ~ing off again** il essaie encore d'en fiche plein la vue *. **2** *vt sep* (**a**) *sb's beauty, complexion etc* mettre en valeur. (**b**) *(pej) one's wealth, knowledge* faire étalage de; *car* faire admirer. ◆ **show through** *vi* se voir au travers. ◆ **show up 1** *vi* (**a**) *(stand out) [feature]* ressortir; *[mistake]* être visible; *[stain]* se voir. **it ~ed up clearly against the sky** cela se détachait nettement sur le ciel. (**b**) *(*: appear)* arriver, se pointer *. **2** *vt sep* (**a**) *fraud, impostor* démasquer; *flaw, defect* faire ressortir. (**b**) *(embarrass)* faire honte à (en public).
◆ **show business** *or* ◆ **show biz** ‡ *n* le monde du spectacle, l'industrie *f* du spectacle. ◆ **showcase** *n* vitrine *f*. ◆ **showdown** *n* épreuve *f* de force. ◆ **showgirl** *n* girl *f*. ◆ **showground** *n* champ *m* de foire. ◆ **showing** *n [film]* projection *f*; *(cinema session)* séance *f*. ◆ **showing-off** *n* pose *f (affectation)*. ◆ **showjumping** *n* concours *m* hippique. ◆ **showman** *n (in fair etc)* forain *m*. ◆ **showmanship** *n (fig)* sens *m* de la mise en scène. ◆ **show-off** *n* m'as-tu-vu(e) * *m(f) (pl inv)*. ◆ **showpiece** *n (of exhibition etc)* trésor *m*; *(new school etc)* modèle *m* du genre. ◆ **showplace** *n (tourist attraction)* lieu *m* de grand intérêt touristique. ◆ **showroom** *n* salle *f* d'exposition. ◆ **showy** *adj colour* éclatant, voyant *(pej)*.

shower ['ʃaʊəʳ] **1** *n* (**a**) *[rain]* averse *f*; *(fig) [blows]* grêle *f*; *[sparks, stones, arrows]* pluie *f*. (**b**) (**~ bath**) douche *f*. **to have** *or* **take a ~** prendre une douche. **2** *adj*: **~ cap** bonnet *m* de douche; **~ unit** bloc-douche *m*. **3** *vt (fig)* **to ~ sb with gifts/praise, to ~ gifts/praise on sb** combler qn de cadeaux/de louanges; **to ~ blows on sb** faire pleuvoir des coups sur qn; **to ~ abuse** *or* **insults on sb** accabler qn d'injures. ◆ **showerproof** *adj* imperméable. ◆ **showery** *adj day* pluvieux; **it will be ~y** il y aura des averses.

shrank [ʃræŋk] *pret of* **shrink.**

shrapnel ['ʃræpnl] *n* éclats *mpl* d'obus.

shred [ʃred] **1** *n [cloth, paper etc]* lambeau *m*; *(fig) [truth, commonsense]* grain *m*. **not a ~ of evidence** pas la moindre preuve; **in ~s** en lambeaux; **to tear to ~s** mettre en lambeaux; *(fig) argument etc* démolir entièrement. **2** *vt paper etc* mettre en lambeaux; *(in shredder)* détruire, déchiqueter; *carrots etc* râper; *cabbage* couper en lanières. ◆ **shredder** *n (for documents)* destructeur *m*; *[food processor]* (disque-)râpeur *m*.

shrew [ʃru:] *n (Zool)* musaraigne *f*; *(woman)* mégère *f*.

shrewd [ʃru:d] *adj person, assessment* perspicace; *businessman, lawyer* habile; *reasoning* judicieux; *plan* astucieux. **I have a ~ idea that...** je soupçonne fortement que... ◆ **shrewdly** *adv suspect* avec perspicacité; *reason* judicieusement; *guess* astucieusement. ◆ **shrewdness** *n* perspicacité *f*; habileté *f*; astuce *f*.

shriek [ʃri:k] **1** *n* hurlement *m*. **~s of laughter** grands éclats *mpl* de rire. **2** *vti* hurler (*with* de). **to ~ with laughter** rire à gorge déployée.

shrill [ʃrɪl] *adj voice, cry* perçant; *whistle, laugh* strident. ◆ **shrillness** *n* ton *m* perçant. ◆ **shrilly** *adv* d'un ton perçant.

shrimp [ʃrɪmp] **1** *n* crevette *f*. **2** *adj*: **~ cocktail** hors-d'œuvre *m* de crevettes. **3** *vi*: **to go ~ing** aller pêcher la crevette.

shrine [ʃraɪn] *n (place)* lieu *m* saint; *(tomb)* tombeau *m* de saint; *(reliquary)* châsse *f*.

shrink [ʃrɪŋk] *pret* **shrank,** *ptp* **shrunk 1** *vi* (**a**) *[clothes]* rétrécir; *[area]* se réduire; *[boundaries]* se resserrer; *[piece of meat]* réduire; *[body, person]* se ratatiner; *[wood]* se contracter; *[quantity, amount]* diminuer. (**b**) (**~ away, ~ back**) reculer (*from sth* devant qch; *from doing* devant l'idée de faire). **she shrank (away** *or* **back) from him** elle a eu un mouvement de recul; **he did not ~ from saying** il n'a pas craint de dire. **2** *vt wool* faire rétrécir; *metal* contracter. ◆ **shrinkage** *n* rétrécissement *m*; contraction *f*; diminution *f*. ◆ **shrink-wrap** *vt* emballer sous film plastique.

shrivel ['ʃrɪvl] (**~ up**) **1** *vi [apple, body]* se ratatiner; *[skin]* se rider; *[leaf, steak]* se racornir. **2** *vt* ratatiner; rider; racornir.

shroud [ʃraʊd] **1** *n* (**a**) *[corpse]* linceul *m*. (**b**) *(Naut)* hauban *m*. **2** *vt (fig)* **~ed in** *mist, snow* sous un linceul de; *mystery* enveloppé de.

Shrove Tuesday [,ʃrəʊv'tju:zdɪ] *n* Mardi *m* gras.

shrub [ʃrʌb] *n* arbrisseau *m*; *(small)* arbuste *m*. ◆ **shrubbery** *n* massif *m* d'arbustes.

shrug [ʃrʌg] **1** *n* haussement *m* d'épaules. **to give a ~ of contempt** hausser les épaules en signe de mépris; **...he said with a ~** ...dit-il en haussant les épaules. **2** *vti*: **to ~ (one's shoulders)** hausser les épaules. ◆ **shrug off** *vt sep suggestion, warning* dédaigner; *remark* ne pas relever; *infection, a cold* se débarrasser de.

shrunk [ʃrʌŋk] *ptp of* **shrink.** ◆ **shrunken** *adj person, body* ratatiné.

shudder ['ʃʌdəʳ] **1** *n [person]* frisson *m*; *[vehicle, ship, engine]* vibration *f*. **to give a ~** *[person]* frissonner, frémir; *[vehicle, ship]* être ébranlé; **it gives me the ~s** * ça me donne des frissons; **he realized with a ~ that...** il a frissonné *or* frémi, comprenant que... **2** *vi [person]* frissonner; *[thing]* vibrer. **I ~ to think what might have happened** je frémis rien qu'à la pensée de ce qui aurait pu se produire; **I ~ to think!** j'en frémis d'avance!

shuffle ['ʃʌfl] **1** *n (fig)* **a cabinet (re)~** un remaniement ministériel. **2** *vt* (**a**) **to ~ one's feet** traîner les pieds. (**b**) *cards* battre; *dominoes* mêler; *papers* remuer. **3** *vi* (**a**) traîner les pieds. **to ~ in/out** *etc* entrer/sortir *etc* d'un pas traînant. (**b**) *(Cards)* battre (les cartes).

shun [ʃʌn] *vt place, temptation, person, publicity* fuir; *work, obligation* esquiver.

shunt [ʃʌnt] **1** *vt (Rail) (direct)* aiguiller; *(divert)* détourner; *(move about)* manœuvrer; *(position)* garer. **2** *n (Rail)* aiguillage *m*; *(fig *)* collision *f*. ◆ **shunting 1** *n* manœuvres *fpl* d'aiguillage; **2** *adj*: **~ing yard** voies *fpl* de garage et de triage.

shush [ʃʊʃ] **1** *excl* chut! **2** *vt* (*) faire chut à; *(silence)* faire taire.

shut [ʃʌt] *pret, ptp* **shut 1** *vt (gen)* fermer. **to ~ one's finger in a drawer** se pincer le doigt dans un tiroir; **to ~ sb in a room** enfermer qn dans une pièce; **~ your mouth!** ‡ la ferme! ‡ **2** *vi [door, box, lid]* se fermer, fermer; *[museum, theatre, shop]* fermer. **the door ~** la porte s'est (re)fermée; **the door ~s badly** la porte ferme mal.
◆ **shut away** *vt sep person, animal* enfermer; *valuables* mettre sous clef. ◆ **shut down 1** *vi [business, theatre]* fermer (définitivement). **2** *vt sep lid* fermer, rabattre; *business, theatre* fermer (définitivement); *machine* arrêter. ◆ **shut in** *vt sep* enfermer. ◆ **shut off** *vt sep* (**a**) *(stop) electricity,*

engine, supplies couper. (**b**) *(isolate) person* isoler (*from* de). ◆ **shut out** *vt sep* (**a**) **he found himself ~ out** il s'est aperçu qu'il ne pouvait pas entrer; **I ~ the cat out** j'ai mis le chat dehors; **close the door and ~ out the noise** ferme la porte pour qu'on n'entende pas le bruit. (**b**) *(block) view* boucher; *memory* chasser de son esprit. (**c**) *(US Sport) opponent* bloquer. ◆ **shut up** **1** *vi (*: be quiet)* se taire. **2** *vt sep* (**a**) *factory, business, theatre, house* fermer. (**b**) *person, animal* enfermer; *valuables* mettre sous clef. **to ~ sb up in prison** mettre qn en prison. (**c**) *(*: silence)* faire taire.
◆ **shutdown** *n* fermeture *f*. ◆ **shut-in** *adj* enfermé.

shutter ['ʃʌtəʳ] **1** *n* volet *m*; *(Phot)* obturateur *m*. **2** *adj*: **~ speed** vitesse *f* d'obturation. ◆ **shuttered** *adj house* aux volets fermés.

shuttle ['ʃʌtl] **1** *n [loom, sewing machine]* navette *f*; *(plane etc)* navette *f*. **space ~** navette spatiale. **2** *adj (Aviat, Rail etc)* **~ service** service *m* de navette; **~ diplomacy** navettes *fpl* diplomatiques. **3** *vi [person, vehicle, boat]* faire la navette (*between* entre). **4** *vt*: **to ~ sb to and fro** envoyer qn à droite et à gauche; **to ~ sb back and forth** faire faire la navette à qn; **the papers were ~d from one department to another** les documents ont été renvoyés d'un service à l'autre. ◆ **shuttlecock** *n* volant *m (Badminton)*.

shy¹ [ʃaɪ] **1** *adj (gen)* timide; *(unsociable)* sauvage. **to make sb feel ~** intimider qn; **don't be ~** ne fais pas le (*or* la) timide; **don't be ~ of saying** n'ayez pas peur de dire, n'hésitez pas à dire. **2** *vi [horse]* broncher (*at* devant). ◆ **shyly** *adv* timidement. ◆ **shyness** *n* timidité *f*.

shy² [ʃaɪ] *vt (throw)* lancer, jeter.

Siamese [ˌsaɪə'mi:z] *adj* siamois. **~ twins** (frères) siamois *mpl*, (sœurs) siamoises *fpl*.

Siberia [saɪ'bɪərɪə] *n* Sibérie *f*.

sibilant ['sɪbɪlənt] **1** *adj* sifflant. **2** *n* sifflante *f*.

sibling ['sɪblɪŋ] *n*: **one of his ~s** l'un de ses frères et sœurs; **Paul and Lucy are ~s** Paul et Lucie sont frère et sœur.

Sicily ['sɪsɪlɪ] *n* Sicile *f*. ◆ **Sicilian** **1** *adj* sicilien ; **2** *n* Sicilien(ne) *m(f)*.

sick [sɪk] **1** *adj* (**a**) *(ill) person* malade; *pallor* maladif. **he's a ~ man** c'est un malade; **he's off ~** il n'est pas là, il est malade; **to go ~** se faire porter malade; **to fall** *or* **take ~** tomber malade; *(vomiting)* **to be ~** vomir; **to feel ~** avoir mal au cœur; **a ~ feeling** un malaise; **I get ~ in planes** je suis malade en avion; **~ headache** migraine *f*. (**b**) *(fig) mind, imagination, joke* malsain; *humour* noir. **to be ~ at heart** avoir la mort dans l'âme; **to be ~ of sth/sb** * en avoir marre * de qch/qn; **to be ~ and tired of, to be ~ to death of** * en avoir par-dessus la tête de; **to be ~ of the sight of sth/sb** * en avoir marre * de voir qch/qn; **it makes me ~ to think that...** ça me dégoûte de penser que... . (**c**) **~ benefit** assurance *f* maladie; **on ~ leave** en congé *m* de maladie; **on the ~ list** *(Admin)* porté malade; *(*: ill)* malade; **~ pay** indemnité *f* de maladie *(versée par l'employeur)*.
2 *npl*: **the ~** les malades *mpl*.
◆ **sick up** * *vt sep* vomir.
◆ **sickbay** *n* infirmerie *f*. ◆ **sickbed** *n* lit *m* de malade. ◆ **sicken** **1** *vt* dégoûter ; **2** *vi* tomber malade; **to ~en for sth** couver qch; **to ~en of** se lasser de. ◆ **sickening** *adj sight, smell* écœurant; *(fig) cruelty, crime* ignoble; *waste* dégoûtant; *(*: annoying) person, behaviour* exaspérant. ◆ **sickeningly** *adv*: **~eningly polite** * d'une politesse écœurante. ◆ **sickliness** *n [person]* état *m* maladif; *[cake]* goût *m* écœurant. ◆ **sickly** *adj person* maladif; *complexion* blafard; *climate* malsain; *plant* étiolé; *smile* faible; *colour, smell, cake* écœurant; **~ly sweet** douceâtre. ◆ **sickness** **1** *n* maladie *f*; **there's a lot of ~ness in the village** il y a beaucoup de malades dans le village; *(vomiting)* **bouts of ~ness** vomissements *mpl*; **mountain ~ness** mal *m* des montagnes ; **2** *adj*: **~ness benefit** (prestations *fpl* de l')assurance *f* maladie. ◆ **sickroom** *n* chambre *f* de malade.

sickle ['sɪkl] *n* faucille *f*.

side [saɪd] **1** *n* (**a**) *[person]* côté *m*; *[animal]* flanc *m*. **he had the phone by his ~** il avait le téléphone à côté de lui; **she was at** *or* **by his ~** elle était à ses côtés; **~ by ~** *(people)* côte à côte; *(things)* à côté l'un de l'autre; **~ of bacon** flèche *f* de lard; **~ of beef/mutton** quartier *m* de bœuf/ mouton.
(**b**) *(as opp to top, bottom etc) [box, house, triangle etc]* côté *m*; *(inside) [cave, ditch, box]* paroi *f*; *(of mountain: gen)* versant *m*; *(flank)* flanc *m*. **by the ~ of the church** à côté de *or* tout près de l'église; **go round the ~ of the house** contournez la maison.
(**c**) *(outer surface) (gen)* côté *m*; *[cube, record, coin]* côté, face *f*; *(fig) [matter, problem etc]* aspect *m*. *[garment, cloth]* **the right ~** l'endroit *m*; **the wrong ~** l'envers *m*; **right/wrong ~ out** à l'endroit/l'envers; **right/wrong ~ up** dans le bon/ mauvais sens; *(on box etc)* **'this ~ up'** 'haut'; **write on both ~s of the paper** écrivez des deux côtés de la feuille; **three-~d** à trois côtés; **many-~d** multilatéral; **I've written 6 ~s** j'ai écrit 6 pages; *(fig)* **the other ~ of the coin** le revers de la médaille; **there are two ~s to every quarrel** dans toute querelle il y a deux points de vue; **he's got a nasty ~ * to him** il a un côté très déplaisant.
(**d**) *(edge)* bord *m*. **by the ~ of** au bord de.
(**e**) *(lateral part) [street, town, face]* côté *m*. **on the other ~ of** de l'autre côté de; *(fig)* **the science ~ of the college** la section sciences du collège; **from all ~s, from every ~** de tous côtés, de toutes parts; **from ~ to ~** d'un côté à l'autre; **he moved to one ~** il s'est écarté; **to take sb on one ~** prendre qn à part; **to put sth to** *or* **on one ~** mettre qch de côté; **on this ~ of London** entre ici et Londres; **he's on the wrong ~ of 50** il a passé la cinquantaine; **he's on the right ~ of 50** il n'a pas encore 50 ans; **he makes a bit of money on the ~ *** il se fait un peu d'argent en plus; **a cousin on his mother's ~** un cousin du côté de sa mère; *(fig)* **on the heavy/cold ~ *** plutôt lourd/froid.
(**f**) *(team) (gen)* camp *m*, côté *m*; *(Sport)* équipe *f*; *(Pol etc)* parti *m*. **he's on our ~** il est avec nous; **we have time on our ~** nous avons le temps pour nous; **whose ~ are you on?** qui soutenez-vous?; **there are faults on both ~s** les deux côtés ont des torts; **to take ~s** prendre parti (*with sb* pour qn); **to pick** *or* **choose ~s** former les camps; **he let the ~ down** il ne leur *(etc)* a pas fait honneur.
(**g**) *(conceit)* **he's got no ~ *** ce n'est pas un crâneur *; **to put on ~ *** crâner *.
2 *adj entrance, chapel, seat* latéral; *(fig) effect, issue* secondaire. **~ dish** plat *m* d'accompagnement; **~ drum** tambour *m* plat; **~ effects** effets *mpl* secondaires; *(Phot)* **~ face** de profil; **~ glance** regard *m* de côté; **~ plate** petite assiette *f*; **~ road** route *f* transversale; **~ street** rue *f* transversale; **~ view** vue *f* de côté.
3 *vi*: **to ~ with sb** prendre parti pour qn.
◆ **sideboard** *n* buffet *m*. ◆ **sideboards** *or (US)* ◆ **sideburns** *npl* rouflaquettes * *fpl*. ◆ **sidecar** *n* side-car *m*. ◆ **sidekick** * *n (assistant)* sous-fifre * *m*; *(friend)* copain * *m*, copine * *f*. ◆ **sidelight** *n (Aut)* feu *m* de position; *(fig)* **it gives us a ~light on...** cela nous donne un aperçu de... ◆ **sideline** *n* (**a**) *(Sport, fig)* **on the ~lines** sur la touche; (**b**) activité *f* (*or* travail *m*) secondaire; **he sells wood as a ~line** il a aussi un petit commerce de bois; *(Comm)* **it's just a ~line** ce n'est pas notre spécialité. ◆ **sidelong** *adj* oblique, de côté. ◆ **sidesaddle** *adv* en amazone. ◆ **sideshows** *npl* attractions *fpl*. ◆ **sidesplitting** * *adj* tordant *. ◆ **side-**

step 1 *vt* éviter; *rules* ne pas tenir compte de ; **2** *vi (lit)* faire un pas de côté; *(fig)* rester évasif; *(Boxing)* esquiver. ◆ **sidetrack** *vt (fig)* faire dévier de son sujet; **to get~tracked** s'écarter de son sujet. ◆ **sidewalk** *n (US)* trottoir *m*. ◆ **sideways 1** *adj* oblique, de côté ; **2** *adv look, fit in* de côté; *walk* en crabe; *stand* de profil. ◆ **side-whiskers** *npl* favoris *mpl*. ◆ **siding** *n (Rail)* voie *f* de garage.

sidle ['saɪdl] *vi*: **to ~ in/out** *etc* entrer/sortir *etc (sideways)* de côté *or (furtively)* furtivement; **he ~d up to me** il s'est glissé vers moi.

siege [siːdʒ] *n* siège *m*. **in a state of ~** en état de siège.

sienna [sɪ'enə] *n* terre *f* de Sienne.

Sierra Leone [sɪ'erəlɪ'əʊn] *n* Sierra Leone *f*.

siesta [sɪ'estə] *n* sieste *f*. **to have a ~** faire une sieste.

sieve [sɪv] **1** *n (for coal, stones)* crible *m*; *(for sugar, flour, soil)* tamis *m*; *(for liquids)* passoire *f*. *(Culin)* **to rub through a ~** passer au tamis; **he's got a memory like a ~ *** sa mémoire est une vraie passoire. **2** *vt* passer au crible; tamiser; passer.

sift [sɪft] **1** *vt* (**a**) *flour, sugar, sand* tamiser; *coal, stones, evidence* passer au crible. **to ~ flour on to sth** saupoudrer qch de farine. (**b**) **(~ out)** *facts, truth* dégager. **2** *vi (fig)* **to ~ through sth** examiner qch. ◆ **sifter** *n* saupoudreuse *f*.

sigh [saɪ] **1** *n* soupir *m*. **to heave a ~** pousser un soupir. **2** *vt* soupirer. **3** *vi* soupirer; *[wind]* gémir. **to ~ with relief** pousser un soupir de soulagement; **to ~ for sth** soupirer après qch; *(for sth lost: also* **~ over sth***)* regretter qch. ◆ **sighing** *n* soupirs *mpl*; *[wind]* gémissements *mpl*.

sight [saɪt] **1** *n* (**a**) *(act of seeing etc)* vue *f*. **to have good/poor ~** avoir une bonne/mauvaise vue; **to lose one's ~** perdre la vue; **to know by ~** connaître de vue; **to shoot on** *or* **at ~** tirer à vue; **at first ~** à première vue; **love at first ~** le coup de foudre; **it was my first ~ of Paris** c'était la première fois que je voyais Paris; **at the ~ of** à la vue de, en voyant; **the train was still in ~** on voyait encore le train; **the end/a solution is in ~** on entrevoit la fin/une solution; **we live within ~ of the sea** de chez nous on voit la mer; **to come into ~** apparaître; **keep the luggage in ~, don't let the luggage out of your ~** ne perdez pas les bagages de vue; **out of ~** hors de vue; **to keep out of ~** *(vi)* ne pas se montrer; *(vt)* cacher; **it is out of ~** on ne le voit pas; **keep out of his ~!** qu'il ne te voie pas!; **to catch ~ of** apercevoir; **to lose ~ of sb/sth** perdre qn/qch de vue; **the ~ of the cathedral/of blood** *etc* la vue de la cathédrale/du sang *etc*; **I can't bear** *or* **stand the ~ of him** je ne peux pas le voir *or* le sentir *; **in the ~ of the law** devant la loi. (**b**) *(spectacle)* spectacle *m (also pej)*. **it is a ~ to be seen** cela vaut la peine d'être vu; **to see the ~s** faire du tourisme, visiter la ville; **it's one of the ~s of Paris** c'est l'une des choses à voir à Paris; **it's not a pretty ~** ça n'est guère joli à voir; **it was a ~ for sore eyes** *(welcome)* c'était un spectacle à réjouir le cœur; *(* pej)* c'était à en pleurer; **I must look a ~!** je dois avoir une de ces allures! * (**c**) *(on gun)* mire *f*. **to take ~** viser; **in one's ~s** dans sa ligne de tir; *(fig)* **to set one's ~s** viser (*on sth* qch). (**d**) *(phrases)* **not by a long ~** loin de là; **a far** *or* **long ~ better** infiniment mieux; **a ~ too clever *** bien trop malin.
2 *vt* apercevoir.
◆ **sighted 1** *adj* qui voit, doué de vision; **to be partially ~ed** avoir un certain degré de vision ; **2** *npl*: **the ~ed** les voyants *mpl (lit)*. ◆ **sighting** *n*: **numerous ~ings have been reported** de nombreuses personnes ont déclaré l'avoir vu. ◆ **sightly** *adj* beau à voir. ◆ **sightread** *vt* déchiffrer *(Mus)*. ◆ **sightreading** *n* déchiffrage *m*. ◆ **sightseeing** *n* tourisme *m*; **to do some ~seeing, to go ~seeing** *(gen)* faire du tourisme ; *(in town)* visiter la ville. ◆ **sightseer** *n* touriste *mf*.

sign [saɪn] **1** *n* (**a**) signe *m*. **they communicated by ~s** ils se parlaient par signes; **to make a ~ to sb** faire signe à qn (*to do* de faire); **to make the ~ of the Cross** faire le signe de la croix (*over* sur); *(cross o.s.)* se signer; *(Astrol)* **born under the ~ of Leo** né sous le signe du Lion; **as a ~ of** en signe de; **it's a good/bad ~** c'est bon/mauvais signe; **a ~ of the times** un signe des temps; **a sure ~** un signe infaillible; **at the slightest ~ of** au moindre signe de; **there is no ~ of his agreeing** rien ne laisse à penser qu'il va accepter; **no ~ of life** aucun signe de vie; **there's no ~ of him anywhere** on n'arrive pas à le retrouver. (**b**) *(notice) (gen and for traffic)* panneau *m*; *(on inn, shop)* enseigne *f*. **2** *adj*: **~ language** langage *m* par signes; **in ~ language** par signes. **3** *vt* (**a**) *letter etc* signer. **to ~ one's name** signer; **he ~s himself John Smith** il signe 'John Smith'. (**b**) *(Ftbl etc) player* engager. **4** *vi* (**a**) signer. **you have to ~ for the key** vous devez signer pour obtenir la clef; **he ~ed for the parcel** il a signé le reçu de livraison du paquet; *(Ftbl)* **Smith has ~ed for Celtic** Smith a signé un contrat d'engagement avec le Celtic. (**b**) **to ~ to sb to do sth** faire signe à qn de faire qch.
◆ **sign away** *vt sep* signer l'abandon de son droit sur. ◆ **sign in** *vi (in factory etc)* pointer (à l'arrivée); *(in hotel)* signer le registre. ◆ **sign off** *vi (in factory etc)* pointer (au départ); *(Rad, TV)* terminer l'émission. ◆ **sign on 1** *vi (Mil)* s'engager (*as* comme); *(Ind etc)* se faire embaucher (*as* comme); *(on arrival at work)* pointer (à l'arrivée); *(enrol)* s'inscrire. **I've ~ed on for German conversation** je me suis inscrit au cours de conversation allemande. **2** *vt sep employee* embaucher; *(Mil)* engager. ◆ **sign over** *vt sep* céder par écrit (*to* à). ◆ **sign up** *vi, vt sep* = **sign on.**
◆ **signpost 1** *n* poteau *m* indicateur ; **2** *vt place* indiquer. ◆ **signposting** *n* signalisation *f*.

signal ['sɪgnl] **1** *n (gen)* signal *m* (*for* de). **at a prearranged ~** à un signal convenu; *(Naut)* **flag ~s** signaux par pavillons; **traffic ~s** feux *mpl* de circulation; *(Rad)* **station ~** indicatif *m* (de l'émetteur); *(Telec)* **I'm getting the engaged ~** ça sonne occupé; *(TV)* **the ~ is very weak** *(sound)* le son *or (picture)* l'image *f* est très faible; *(Mil)* **the S~s** les Transmissions *fpl*. **2** *adj (avant n) success* remarquable; *importance* capital. *(Rail)* **~ box** poste *m* d'aiguillage. **3** *vt message* communiquer par signaux. **to ~ sb on/through** *etc* faire signe à qn d'avancer/de passer *etc*; *(Aut)* **to ~ a turn** indiquer un changement de direction. **4** *vi (gen)* faire des signaux; *(Aut)* indiquer. **to ~ to sb** faire signe à qn (*to do* de faire). ◆ **signally** *adv (gen)* singulièrement; *fail* totalement. ◆ **signalman** *n (Rail)* aiguilleur *m*.

signature ['sɪgnətʃəʳ] **1** *n* (**a**) signature *f*. **to put one's ~ to sth** apposer sa signature à qch. (**b**) *(Mus: key ~)* armature *f*. **2** *adj*: **~ tune** indicatif *m* musical. ◆ **signatory** *n* signataire *mf* (*to* de).

signet ['sɪgnɪt] *n* sceau *m*. **~ ring** chevalière *f*.

signify ['sɪgnɪfaɪ] **1** *vt (mean)* signifier (*that* que); *(indicate)* indiquer; *(make known)* indiquer, faire comprendre (*that* que); *one's approval* signifier. **2** *vi* avoir de l'importance. ◆ **significance** *n (meaning)* signification *f*; *[event, speech]* importance *f*, portée *f*; **that is of no significance** cela importe peu. ◆ **significant** *adj achievement, increase, amount* considérable; *event* important; *look* significatif; **it is significant that...** il est significatif *or* révélateur que... + *subj*. ◆ **significantly** *adv smile etc* d'une façon significative; *improve, change* considérablement; **significantly, he refused** fait révélateur, il a refusé. ◆ **signification** *n* signification *f*.

Sikh [siːk] **1** *n* Sikh *mf*. **2** *adj* sikh *(f inv)*.

silence ['saɪləns] **1** *n* silence *m*. *(lit, fig)* **there was ~** on a gardé le silence (*about* en ce qui concernait); **in ~** en silence; *(fig)* **to pass sth over in ~** passer qch sous silence. **2** *vt person, opposition* réduire au silence; *noise* étouffer; *conscience* faire taire. ◆ **silencer** *n* silencieux *m (dispositif)*. ◆ **silent** *adj (gen)* silencieux; *film, reproach* muet; **it was as silent as the grave** il y avait un silence de mort; **to be** *or* **fall** *or* **remain silent** se taire; **silent 'h'** 'h' muet. ◆ **silently** *adv* silencieusement.

silhouette [ˌsɪluː'et] **1** *n* silhouette *f*. **2** *vt*: **to be ~d against** se découper contre.

silicon ['sɪlɪkən] *n* silicium *m*. **~ chip** puce *f* électronique, pastille *f* de silicium. ◆ **silicone** *n* silicone *f*. ◆ **silicosis** *n* silicose *f*.

silk [sɪlk] **1** *n* soie *f*. **2** *adj blouse etc* de *or* en soie. **~ factory** soierie *f (fabrique)*; **~ industry** soierie *(industrie)*; **~ manufacturer** fabricant *m* en soierie. ◆ **silkscreen printing** *n* sérigraphie *f*. ◆ **silkworm** *n* ver *m* à soie. ◆ **silky** *adj* soyeux; *voice* doucereux.

sill [sɪl] *n* rebord *m*; *(Aut)* bas *m* de marche.

silly ['sɪlɪ] *adj (stupid)* bête, idiot, stupide; *(ridiculous)* ridicule. **you ~ fool!** espèce d'idiot(e)!; **don't be ~** ne fais pas l'idiot(e); **to do sth ~** faire une bêtise. ◆ **silliness** *n* bêtise *f*, stupidité *f*.

silo ['saɪləʊ] *n* silo *m*.

silt [sɪlt] *n (gen)* limon *m*; *(mud)* vase *f*. ◆ **silt up** **1** *vi (with mud)* s'envaser; *(with sand)* s'ensabler. **2** *vt sep* envaser; ensabler.

silver ['sɪlvəʳ] **1** *n (metal)* argent *m*; *(~ ware, cutlery etc)* argenterie *f*. *(money)* **have you got any ~?** est-ce que vous avez de la monnaie?; **£2 in ~** 2 livres en pièces d'argent. **2** *adj (made of ~) cutlery, jewellery etc* d'argent, en argent; *(~-coloured)* argenté. **~ birch** bouleau *m* argenté; **~ coin** pièce *f* d'argent; **~ fir** sapin *m*; **~ foil**, **~ paper** papier *m* d'argent; **~ gilt** plaqué *m* argent; **~ jubilee** vingt-cinquième anniversaire *m (d'un événement)*; *(fig)* **to be born with a ~ spoon in one's mouth** naître avec une cuiller d'argent dans la bouche; **~ wedding** noces *fpl* d'argent. ◆ **silver-grey** *adj* argenté. ◆ **silverhaired** *adj* aux cheveux argentés. ◆ **silver-plate** *n (solid silver)* argenterie *f*; *(electroplate)* plaqué *m* argent. ◆ **silver-plated** *adj* argenté. ◆ **silver-plating** *n* argenture *f*. ◆ **silverside** *n* tranche *f* (grasse) *(viande)*. ◆ **silversmith** *n* orfèvre *mf*. ◆ **silverware** *n* argenterie *f*. ◆ **silvery** *adj colour, scales* argenté; *sound* argentin.

similar ['sɪmɪləʳ] *adj* semblable (*to* à); *(less strongly)* comparable (*to* à). **a ~ house** une maison presque pareille; **~ in size** de dimensions comparables; **the houses are so ~ that...** les maisons sont si semblables que...; **and ~ products** et produits similaires; **vehicles ~ to the bicycle** véhicules apparentés à la bicyclette. ◆ **similarity** [ˌsɪmɪ'lærɪtɪ] *n* ressemblance *f* (*to* avec; *between* entre), similarité *f* (*between* entre). ◆ **similarly** *adv* de la même façon; **and ~ly,...** et de même...

simile ['sɪmɪlɪ] *n* comparaison *f (Literat)*.

simmer ['sɪməʳ] **1** *vi [water]* frémir; *[vegetables, soup]* cuire à feu doux; *(fig) (with excitement)* être en ébullition; *(with rage/discontent)* bouillir de rage/de mécontentement; *[revolt, anger]* couver. **2** *vt* laisser frémir; faire cuire à feu doux. ◆ **simmer down** * *vi (fig)* se calmer.

simper ['sɪmpəʳ] **1** *n* sourire *m* affecté. **2** *vi* minauder. ◆ **simpering** **1** *n* minauderies *fpl* ; **2** *adj* minaudier.

simple ['sɪmpl] *adj (gen)* simple. **as ~ as ABC** simple comme bonjour; **he's a ~ labourer** c'est un simple ouvrier; **they're ~ people** ce sont des gens simples; **to make ~(r)** simplifier; **in ~ terms** *or* **language** pour parler simplement *or* clairement; **in ~ English** ≃ en bon français; **the ~ fact that...** le simple fait que...; **the ~ truth** la vérité pure et simple; **for the ~ reason that...** pour la seule *or* simple raison que...; **~ equation** équation *f* du premier degré; *(Fin)* **~ interest** intérêts *mpl* simples; *(Mus)* **~ time** mesure *f* simple; **a ~ Simon** un nigaud; **he's a bit ~** il est un peu simple d'esprit. ◆ **simple-minded** *adj* simple d'esprit. ◆ **simple-mindedness** *n* simplicité *f* d'esprit. ◆ **simpleton** *n* nigaud(e) *m(f)*. ◆ **simplicity** *n* simplicité *f*. ◆ **simplification** *n* simplification *f*. ◆ **simplify** *vt* simplifier. ◆ **simplistic** *adj* simpliste. ◆ **simply** *adv talk, live* simplement, avec simplicité; *(only)* (tout) simplement; *(absolutely)* **you simply MUST come!** il faut absolument que vous veniez! *(subj)*.

simulate ['sɪmjʊleɪt] *vt* simuler *(also Tech)*. ◆ **simulation** *n* simulation *f*. ◆ **simulator** *n* simulateur *m*.

simultaneous [ˌsɪm(ə)l'teɪnɪəs] *adj (gen)* simultané. *(Math)* **~ equations** équations *fpl* équivalentes. ◆ **simultaneity** *n* simultanéité *f*. ◆ **simultaneously** *adv* simultanément; **~ly with** en même temps que.

sin [sɪn] **1** *n* péché *m*. **~s of omission/commission** péchés par omission/par action; **a ~ against God** un manquement à la loi de Dieu; **it's a ~ to do that** *(Rel)* c'est un péché que de faire cela; *(* fig)* c'est un crime de faire cela. **2** *vi* pécher (*against* contre). ◆ **sinful** *adj (gen)* coupable; *act, waste* scandaleux. ◆ **sinfully** *adv* d'une façon coupable; scandaleusement. ◆ **sinfulness** *n [person]* péchés *mpl*; *[deed]* caractère *m* coupable *or* scandaleux. ◆ **sinner** *n* pécheur *m*, -eresse *f*.

since [sɪns] **1** *conj* (**a**) *(in time)* depuis que. **~ I have been here** depuis que je suis ici; **ever ~ I met him** depuis que je l'ai rencontré; **it's a week ~ I saw him** cela fait une semaine que je ne l'ai pas vu. (**b**) *(because)* puisque, comme. **2** *adv* depuis. **he has not been here ~** il n'est pas venu depuis; **he has been my friend ever ~** il est resté mon ami depuis ce moment-là; **not long ~** il y a peu de temps. **3** *prep* depuis. **~ arriving** *or* **his arrival** depuis son arrivée, depuis qu'il est arrivé; **I have been waiting ~ 10 o'clock** j'attends depuis 10 heures; **~ then** depuis; **ever ~ that we...** depuis ce temps-là nous...; **how long is it ~ the accident?** il s'est passé combien de temps depuis l'accident?

sincere [sɪn'sɪəʳ] *adj* sincère. **are they ~ in their desire to help us?** est-ce que leur désir de nous aider est vraiment sincère? ◆ **sincerely** *adv* sincèrement; *(letter-ending)* **Yours ~ly** ≃ Je vous prie d'agréer, Monsieur (*or* Madame *etc*), l'expression de mes sentiments les meilleurs; *(less formally)* cordialement à vous, bien à vous. ◆ **sincerity** [sɪn'serɪtɪ] *n* sincérité *f*.

sine [saɪn] *n* sinus *m (Math)*.

sinecure ['saɪnɪkjʊəʳ] *n* sinécure *f*.

sinew ['sɪnjuː] *n (Anat)* tendon *m*. **~s** *(muscles)* muscles *mpl*; *(strength)* force *f*. ◆ **sinewy** *adj* nerveux.

sing [sɪŋ] *pret* **sang**, *ptp* **sung** **1** *vt* chanter. **2** *vi [person, bird, kettle]* chanter; *[ears]* bourdonner; *[wind]* siffler. **to ~ like a lark** chanter comme un rossignol; **to ~ soprano** chanter soprano. ◆ **sing out** * *vi (call)* appeler (bien fort). ◆ **singer** *n* chanteur *m*, -euse *f*. ◆ **singing** **1** *n [person, bird]* chant *m*; *[kettle, wind]* sifflement *m*; *(in ears)* bourdonnement *m* ; **2** *adj lessons, teacher* de chant. ◆ **singsong** *n*: **to have a ~song** chanter en chœur; **to repeat sth in a ~song (voice)** répéter qch sur deux tons.

Singapore [ˌsɪŋgə'pɔːʳ] *n* Singapour *m*.

singe [sɪn(d)ʒ] **1** *vt* brûler légèrement; *cloth, clothes* roussir; *poultry* flamber. **2** *n* légère brûlure.

single ['sɪŋgl] **1** *adj* (**a**) *(only one)* seul *(before n)*. **a ~ rose in the garden** une seule rose dans le jardin; **he gave her a ~ rose** il lui a donné une rose; **if there is a ~ objection** s'il y a une seule *or* la moindre objection; **the ~ survivor** le seul *or* l'unique survivant; *(Rail)* **~ track** voie *f* unique; **every ~ day** tous les jours sans exception; **not a ~ person spoke** pas une seule personne n'a parlé; **I didn't see a ~ soul** je n'ai vu personne; **I haven't a ~ moment to lose** je n'ai pas une minute à perdre; **a** *or* **one ~ department should deal with it all** un service unique devrait traiter tout cela. (**b**) *(not double etc) knot, flower* simple. **a ~ ticket** un aller simple (*to* pour); **~ fare** prix *m* d'un aller simple; **~ bed** lit *m* d'une personne; **~ cream** crème *f* fraîche liquide; **~ room** chambre *f* pour une personne; *(Typ)* **in ~ spacing** à simple interligne. (**c**) *(unmarried)* célibataire. **~ people** célibataires *mpl*; **~ parent** parent *m* isolé.
2 *n* (**a**) *(Tennis)* **~s** simple *m*; **ladies' ~s** simple dames. (**b**) *(Rail etc: ticket)* aller *m* simple. (**c**) *(record)* **a ~** un 45 tours. (**d**) *(*: unmarried people)* **~s** célibataires *mfpl;* **~s bar/club** bar *m* /club *m* pour célibataires.
◆ **single out** *vt sep (distinguish)* distinguer; *(choose)* choisir.
◆ **single-breasted** *adj (Dress)* droit. ◆ **single-decker** *n* autobus *m* sans impériale. ◆ **single-engined** *adj* monomoteur. ◆ **single-handed 1** *adv* tout seul, sans aucune aide ; **2** *adj achievement* fait sans aide; *sailing, voyage* en solitaire. ◆ **single-minded** *adj person, attempt* résolu; *determination* tenace; **to be ~-minded about sth** concentrer tous ses efforts sur qch. ◆ **singleness** *n*: **~ness of purpose** ténacité *f*. ◆ **single-parent family** *n* famille *f* monoparentale. ◆ **single-party** *adj (Pol)* à parti unique. ◆ **single-seater aeroplane** *n* (avion *m*) monoplace *m*. ◆ **single-sex school** *n* établissement *m* scolaire non mixte. ◆ **singleton** *n* singleton *m*. ◆ **singly** *adv* séparément, un(e) à un(e).

singlet ['sɪŋglɪt] *n* maillot *m* de corps.

singular ['sɪŋgjʊləʳ] **1** *adj* (**a**) *(Gram) noun, verb* au singulier; *form, ending* du singulier. **the masculine ~** le masculin singulier. (**b**) *(outstanding, strange)* singulier. **2** *n (Gram)* singulier *m*. **in the ~** au singulier. ◆ **singularity** *n* singularité *f*. ◆ **singularly** *adv* singulièrement.

sinister ['sɪnɪstəʳ] *adj* sinistre; *(Heraldry)* sénestre. ◆ **sinisterly** *adv* sinistrement.

sink¹ [sɪŋk] *pret* **sank,** *ptp* **sunk 1** *vi (in water)* couler; *(fig: into despair, sleep)* sombrer (*into* dans); *[ground]* s'affaisser; *[sun]* se coucher; *[foundation, building]* se tasser; *[level, river]* baisser; *[prices, sales, temperature]* baisser (beaucoup); *[shares, the dollar]* tomber (*to* à). **to ~ to the bottom** couler au fond; **to ~ like a stone** couler à pic; *(fig)* **it was ~ or swim** il fallait bien s'en sortir * tout seul; **to ~ out of sight** disparaître; **to ~ to one's knees** tomber à genoux; **to ~ to the ground** s'affaisser; **he sank into a chair** il s'est laissé tomber dans un fauteuil; **he sank into the mud** il s'est enfoncé dans la boue; **the water slowly sank into the ground** l'eau a pénétré lentement dans le sol; *(dying)* **he is ~ing fast** il baisse rapidement; **he has sunk in my estimation** il a baissé dans mon estime; **his voice sank** sa voix s'est faite plus basse; **his heart sank at the thought** il a été pris de découragement à cette idée; **it's enough to make your heart ~** c'est à vous démoraliser *or* à vous donner le cafard *. **2** *vt* (**a**) *ship* couler; *object* faire couler au fond; *(fig) project, book, person* couler. *(fig)* **they sank their differences** ils ont enterré leurs querelles; **sunk in thought/despair** plongé dans ses pensées/le désespoir; **I'm sunk *** je suis fichu *. (**b**) *mine, well, foundations* creuser; *pipe etc* noyer; *stake* enfoncer (*into* dans). *(Golf)* **to ~ the ball** faire entrer la balle dans le trou; *(fig)* **to ~ a lot of money in a project** placer beaucoup d'argent dans une entreprise.
◆ **sink back** *vi [object in water]* retomber; *[person in chair etc]* se laisser retomber. ◆ **sink down** *vi*: **to ~ down into a chair** se laisser tomber dans un fauteuil; **to ~ down on one's knees** tomber à genoux; **to ~ down out of sight** disparaître. ◆ **sink in** *vi [person, post etc]* s'enfoncer; *[water, ointment etc]* pénétrer; *(fig) [explanation]* rentrer; *[remark]* faire son effet. **it hasn't really sunk in yet** il *etc* ne réalise * pas encore; **it took a long time to ~ in** il *etc* a mis longtemps à comprendre.
◆ **sinking 1** *adj*: **to have a ~ing feeling** avoir un serrement de cœur; *(stronger)* avoir la mort dans l'âme; **to have a ~ing feeling that...** avoir le pénible pressentiment que... ; **2** *n (shipwreck)* naufrage *m*; *(in attack)* torpillage *m*.

sink² [sɪŋk] **1** *n (in kitchen)* évier *m*; *(US also in bathroom)* lavabo *m*. **2** *adj*: **~ tidy** coin *m* d'évier *(ustensile ménager)*; **~ unit** bloc-évier *m*.

Sino- ['saɪnəʊ] *pref* sino-.

sinuous ['sɪnjʊəs] *adj* sinueux.

sinus ['saɪnəs] *n* sinus *m inv (Med)*. ◆ **sinusitis** *n* sinusite *f*.

sip [sɪp] **1** *n* petite gorgée *f*. **a ~ of rum** une goutte de rhum. **2** *vt* boire à petites gorgées.

siphon ['saɪf(ə)n] **1** *n* siphon *m*. **2** *vt* siphonner. ◆ **siphon off** *vt sep liquid* siphonner; *(fig) people etc* mettre à part; *profits, funds* canaliser; *(illegally)* détourner.

sir [sɜːʳ] *n* monsieur *m*. **yes, ~** oui, Monsieur; *(to army officer)* oui, mon commandant (*or* mon lieutenant *etc*); *(to surgeon)* oui, docteur; *(in letter)* **(Dear) S~** Monsieur; **S~ John Smith** sir John Smith.

siren ['saɪər(ə)n] *n* sirène *f*.

sirloin ['sɜːlɔɪn] *n* aloyau *m*. **a ~ steak** un bifteck dans l'aloyau.

sisal ['saɪs(ə)l] *n* sisal *m*.

sissy * ['sɪsɪ] *n (coward)* poule *f* mouillée. *(effeminate)* **he's a bit of a ~** il est un peu efféminé.

sister ['sɪstəʳ] **1** *n* (**a**) sœur *f*. (**b**) *(Rel)* (bonne) sœur *f*. **yes, ~** oui, ma sœur; **S~ Mary** sœur Marie. (**c**) *(Brit Med)* infirmière *f* en chef. **yes, ~** oui, Madame (*or* Mademoiselle). **2** *adj*: **~ nations/organizations** nations *fpl*/organisations *fpl* sœurs; **~ peoples/countries** peuples *mpl*/pays *mpl* frères; **~ ship** sister-ship *m*. ◆ **sisterhood** *n (solidarity)* solidarité *f* féminine. ◆ **sister-in-law** *n* belle-sœur *f*. ◆ **sisterly** *adj* de sœur, fraternel.

sit [sɪt] *pret, ptp* **sat 1** *vi* (**a**) **to ~ (down)** s'asseoir; **to be ~ting (down)** être assis; *(to dog)* **~!** assis!; **~ by me** assieds-toi près de moi; **she just ~s at home** elle reste chez elle à ne rien faire; **he was ~ting over his books all evening** il a passé toute la soirée dans ses livres; **to ~ through a play** *etc* assister à une pièce *etc* jusqu'au bout; **don't just ~ there, DO something!** ne reste pas là à ne rien faire!; **to ~ still/straight** se tenir tranquille/droit; **to ~ tight** ne pas bouger; *(fig)* **to be ~ting pretty *** tenir le bon bout *; **to ~ for one's portrait/for an artist** poser pour son portrait/pour un artiste; **to ~ on a committee** être membre d'un comité; **to ~ for an exam** passer un examen, se présenter à un examen; *(Parl)* **he ~s for Moordown** il est (le) député de Moordown. (**b**) *[bird, insect]* se poser, se percher. **to be ~ting** être perché; *(on eggs)* couver; **to ~ on eggs** couver des œufs. (**c**) *[committee, assembly etc]* être en séance, siéger. **the committee is ~ting now** le comité est en séance; **it ~s from November to June** il siège de novembre à juin. (**d**) *[dress, coat etc]* tomber (*on sb* sur qn). **2** *vt* (**a**) (*~ down*) *child, invalid* asseoir, installer; *guest* faire asseoir. (**b**) *exam* passer, se présenter à. ◆ **sit about, sit around** *vi* rester assis (à ne rien faire), traîner. ◆ **sit back** *vi (in an armchair)* se caler. **to ~ back and do nothing about it** s'abstenir de faire quoi que ce soit. ◆ **sit down 1** *vi* s'asseoir; *(at table)* s'attabler. **to be ~ting down** être assis; *(fig)* **to ~ down under an insult** encaisser * une insulte. **2** *vt sep* asseoir. ◆ **sit in** *vi* (**a**) **to ~ in on a discussion** assister à une discussion (sans y prendre part). (**b**) *[demonstrators]* **to ~ in in an office** occuper un bureau. ◆ **sit on** * *vt fus (fig)* (**a**) *(keep secret) news, facts, report* garder secret; *(not pass on) file, document* garder pour soi. (**b**) *person (silence)* faire taire; *(snub)* remettre à sa place. ◆ **sit out** *vt sep lecture, play* rester jusqu'à la fin de. ◆ **sit up 1** *vi* (**a**) *(~ upright)* se redresser. **to be ~ting up** être assis bien droit; **he was ~ting up in bed** il était assis dans son lit; **you can ~ up now** vous pouvez vous asseoir maintenant; *(fig)* **to make sb ~ up** secouer *or* étonner qn; *(fig)* **to ~ up and take notice** se secouer; *(after illness)* reprendre intérêt à la vie. (**b**) *(stay up)* ne pas se coucher. **to ~ up late** se coucher tard; **to ~ up all night** ne pas se coucher de la nuit; **to ~ up with an invalid** veiller un malade. **2** *vt sep doll, child* asseoir.

◆ **sit-down** *adj*: **to have a ~-down lunch** déjeuner à table; **~-down strike** grève *f* sur le tas. ◆ **sit-in** *n [demonstrators]* sit-in *m inv*; *[workers]* grève *f* sur le tas; **to hold a ~-in** *(gen)* occuper les lieux; *[workers]* faire une grève sur le tas. ◆ **sitter** *n (Art)* modèle *m*; *(baby-~ter)* baby-sitter *mf*. ◆ **sitting 1** *n [committee etc]* séance *f*; *(for portrait)* séance de pose; *(in canteen etc)* service *m* ; **2** *adj tenant* en possession des lieux; *(fig)* **~ting duck** * victime *f* facile; *(Parl)* **~ting member** député *m* en exercice; **~ting room** salon *m*. ◆ **sit-up** *n* redressement *m* assis.

sitar ['sɪtɑːʳ] *n* sitar *m*.

sitcom * ['sɪtkɒm] *n (Rad, TV etc)* comédie *f* de situation.

site [saɪt] **1** *n [town, building]* emplacement *m*; *(Archeol)* site *m*; *(Constr)* chantier *m*; *(camp ~)* camping *m*. **the ~ of the battle** le champ de bataille. **2** *vt* placer, situer.

situate ['sɪtjʊeɪt] *vt (locate) building, town* placer; *(put into perspective) problem, event* situer. **the house is ~d in the country** la maison se trouve *or* est située à la campagne; **we are rather badly ~d as there is no bus** nous sommes assez mal situés car il n'y a pas d'autobus; *(fig)* **he is rather badly ~d** il est en assez mauvaise posture; **I am well ~d to do that** je suis bien placé pour faire cela; **how are you ~d for money?** est-ce que tu as besoin d'argent? ◆ **situation 1** *n (all senses)* situation *f*; **in a very difficult situation** dans une situation très difficile; **in an exam situation** dans des conditions d'examen; **to save the situation** sauver la situation; **'situations vacant/wanted'** 'offres *fpl*/demandes *fpl* d'emploi' ; **2** *adj*: **situation comedy** comédie *f* de situation.

six [sɪks] **1** *adj* six *inv*. **he is ~ (years old)** il a six ans; **he lives in number ~** il habite au (numéro) six. **2** *n* six *m inv*. **there were about ~** il y en avait six environ; **~ of the girls came** six des filles sont venues; **there are ~ of us** nous sommes six; **all ~ of us left** nous sommes partis tous les six; **it is ~ o'clock** il est six heures; **come at ~** venez à six heures; **it struck ~** six heures ont sonné; **they are sold in ~es** cela se vend par (lots *or* paquets de) six; **the children arrived in ~es** les enfants sont arrivés par groupes de six; **he lives at ~ Churchill Street** il habite (au) six rue Churchill; *(fig)* **to be at ~es and sevens** *[books, houses etc]* être sens dessus dessous; *[person]* être tout retourné *; *(fig)* **it's ~ of one and half a dozen of the other** c'est du pareil au même *.

◆ **sixfold 1** *adj* sextuple ; **2** *adv* au sextuple. ◆ **six-footer** * *n* ≃ grand *m* d'un mètre quatre-vingts. ◆ **sixish** *adj*: **he is ~ish** il a dans les six ans; **he came at ~ish** il est venu vers six heures. ◆ **six-pack** *n* pack *m* de six. ◆ **six-shooter** *n* pistolet *m* automatique. ◆ **six-sided** *adj* hexagonal. ◆ **sixteen** *adj, n* seize *(m) inv*. ◆ **sixteenth** *adj, n* seizième *(mf)*; *(fraction)* seizième *m*. ◆ **sixth 1** *adj* sixième; **to be ~th in a competition/in German** être sixième à un concours/en allemand; **she was the ~th to arrive** elle est arrivée la sixième; **Charles the S~th** Charles Six; **the ~th of November, November the ~th** le six novembre; *(Brit Scol)* **~th form** classes *fpl* de première et de terminale; *(fig)* **~th sense** sixième sens *m* ; **2** *n* sixième *mf*; *(fraction)* sixième *m*; *(Mus)* sixte *f*; **he wrote on the ~th** il a écrit le six; *(Scol)* **the lower ~th** ≃ la classe de première; **the upper ~th** ≃ la classe terminale ; **3** *adv* (**a**) *(in race, exam, competition)* en sixième place; **he came** *or* **was placed ~th** il s'est classé sixième; (**b**) *(sixthly)* sixièmement. ◆ **sixthly** *adv* sixièmement, en sixième lieu. ◆ **sixtieth** *adj, n* soixantième *(mf)*; *(fraction)* soixantième *m*. ◆ **sixty** *adj, n* soixante *(m) inv*; **about ~ty** une soixantaine, environ soixante; **about ~ty books** une soixantaine de livres; **he is about ~ty** il a une soixantaine d'années; **to be in one's ~ties** avoir la soixantaine, être sexagénaire; *(1960s etc)* **in the ~ties** dans les années soixante; **the temperature was in the ~ties** ≃ il faisait entre quinze et vingt degrés; *(Aut)* **to do ~ty** * ≃ faire du cent (à l'heure). ◆ **sixty-first** *adj, n* soixante et unième *(mf)*; *(fraction)* soixante et unième *m*. ◆ **sixty-four** *adj (fig)* **that's the ~ty-four (thousand) dollar question** * c'est toute la question. ◆ **sixty-odd** * *adj, n*: **there were ~ty-odd** il y en avait soixante et quelques *. ◆ **sixty-one** *adj, n* soixante et un *(m) inv*. ◆ **sixty-second** *adj, n* soixante-deuxième *(mf)*. ◆ **sixty-two** *adj, n* soixante-deux *(m) inv*. ◆ **six-year-old 1** *adj child, horse* de six ans; *house, car* vieux de six ans ; **2** *n (child/horse)* enfant *mf*/cheval *m* de six ans.

size[1] [saɪz] **1** *n (for plaster etc)* colle *f*. **2** *vt* encoller.

size[2] [saɪz] *n* (**a**) *[person, animal, sb's head, hands]* taille *f*; *[room, building, car, chair, parcel]* dimensions *fpl*; *[egg, fruit, jewel]* grosseur *f*; *[book, photograph, sheet of paper, envelope]* taille, dimensions; *(format)* format *m*; *[sum]* montant *m*; *[estate, country, difficulty]* étendue *f*; *[operation, campaign]* envergure *f*. **medium-~d** de taille (*or* grosseur *etc*) moyenne; *[packet, tube etc]* **the small/large ~** le petit/grand modèle; **the ~ of the town** l'importance *f* de la ville; **building of vast ~** bâtiment de belles dimensions; **it's the ~ of a brick** c'est de la taille d'une brique; **it's the ~ of a walnut** c'est de la grosseur d'une noix; **it's the ~ of a house/an elephant** c'est grand comme une maison/un éléphant; **he's about your ~** il est à peu près de la même taille que vous; *(fig)* **that's about the ~ of it!** c'est à peu près ça!; **he cut the wood to ~** il a coupé le bois à la dimension voulue. (**b**) *[garment]* taille *f*; *[shoes, gloves]* pointure *f*; *[shirt]* encolure *f*. **what ~ are you?, what ~ do you take?** *(in dress etc)* quelle taille faites-vous?; *(in shoes, gloves)* quelle pointure faites-vous?; *(in hats)* quel est votre tour de tête?; **what ~ of collar** *or* **shirt?** quelle encolure?; **I take ~ 12** je prends du 12; **hip ~** tour *m* de hanches; **I take ~ 5 shoes** ≃ je fais du 38.

◆ **size up** *vt sep person* juger; *situation* mesurer; *problem* mesurer l'étendue de.

◆ **siz(e)able** *adj dog, building, estate* assez grand; *egg, fruit, jewel* assez gros; *operation* assez important; *sum, problem* assez considérable.

sizzle ['sɪzl] **1** *vi* grésiller. **2** *n* grésillement *m*.

skate[1] [skeɪt] *n (fish)* raie *f*.

skate[2] [skeɪt] **1** *n* patin *m*. *(fig)* **get your ~s on!** * dépêche-toi! **2** *vi* patiner. **to ~ across/down** *etc* traverser/descendre *etc* en patinant; **to go skating** *(ice)* faire du patin *or* du patinage; *(roller)* faire du patin à roulettes; *(fig)* **it went skating across the room** cela a glissé à travers la pièce.

◆ **skate over, skate round** *vt fus problem, objection* glisser sur.

◆ **skateboard** *n* planche *f* à roulettes. ◆ **skater** *n (ice)* patineur *m*, -euse *f*; *(roller)* personne *f* qui fait du skating. ◆ **skating** **1** *n (ice)* patinage *m*; *(roller)* patinage à roulettes ; **2** *adj*: **skating rink** *(ice)* patinoire *f*; *(roller)* skating *m*.

skein [skeɪn] *n [wool etc]* écheveau *m*.

skeleton ['skelɪtn] **1** *n [person, building, ship, model etc]* squelette *m*; *[plan, novel etc]* schéma *m*. **a walking ~** un cadavre ambulant; **staff reduced to a ~** personnel réduit au strict minimum; *(fig)* **the ~ at the feast** le *or* la trouble-fête *inv*; *(fig)* **the ~ in the cupboard** la honte cachée de la famille. **2** *adj army, staff* squelettique *(fig)*; *map* schématique. **~ key** passe(-partout) *m inv*; *[proposals etc]* **~ outline** résumé *m*. ◆ **skeletal** *adj* squelettique.

skeptic(al) ['skeptɪk(əl)] *(US)* = **sceptic(al).**

sketch [sketʃ] **1** *n* (**a**) *(drawing)* croquis *m*, esquisse *f*; *(fig) [ideas, proposals etc]* aperçu *m*, ébauche *f*. **a rough ~** *(drawing)* une ébauche; *(fig: of one's plans etc)* un aperçu. (**b**) *(Theat)* sketch *m*, saynète *f*. **2** *adj*: **~(ing) book/pad** carnet *m*/bloc *m* à dessins; **~ map** carte faite à main levée. **3** *vi* faire des croquis. **4** *vt view, castle, figure* faire un croquis *or* une esquisse de; *map* faire à main levée; *(fig: ~* **out***) ideas, novel, plan* ébaucher, esquisser.

◆ **sketch in** *vt sep detail* ajouter.

◆ **sketchily** *adv answer* incomplètement; *know* superficiellement. ◆ **sketchy** *adj (gen)* incomplet; *knowledge* superficiel.

skewer ['skjʊəʳ] **1** *n (for roast etc)* broche *f*; *(for kebabs)* brochette *f*. **2** *vt* embrocher.

ski [ski:] **1** *n* ski *m (équipement)*; *(Aviat)* patin *m*. **2** *adj school, clothes* de ski. **~ binding** fixation *f*; **~ boot** chaussure *f* de ski; **~(ing) instructor** moniteur *m*, -trice *f* de ski; **~ lift** remonte-pente *m inv*; **~(ing) pants** *or* **trousers** fuseau *m* (de ski); **~ resort** station *f* de ski; **~ run** piste *f* de ski; **~ stick** bâton *m* de ski; **~ tow** téléski *m*. **3** *vi* faire du ski, skier. **to go ~ing** faire du ski; *(as holiday)* partir aux sports d'hiver; **to ~ down a slope** descendre une pente à skis. ◆ **skibob** *n* ski-bob *m*. ◆ **skier** *n* skieur *m*, -euse *f*. ◆ **skiing** **1** *n* ski *m (sport)* ; **2** *adj clothes, school* de ski; *holiday* aux sports d'hiver; **to go on a ~ing holiday** partir aux sports d'hiver. ◆ **skijump** *n (place)* tremplin *m* de ski. ◆ **skijumping** *n* saut *m* à skis. ◆ **ski-pass** *n* forfait-skieur(s) *m*. ◆ **ski-suit** *n* combinaison *f* (de ski).

skid [skɪd] **1** *n (Aut)* dérapage *m*. **to get** *or* **go into a ~** déraper; **to get out of a ~, to correct a ~** redresser un dérapage. **2** *adj (US)* **~ row** quartier *m* de clochards. **3** *vi* déraper. **to ~ to a halt** s'arrêter en dérapant; **to ~ into a tree** déraper et percuter un arbre; **the toy ~ded across the room** le jouet a glissé jusqu'à l'autre bout de la pièce. ◆ **skidlid** * *n* casque *m* (de moto). ◆ **skidmark** *n* trace *f* de dérapage. ◆ **skidpan** *n* piste savonnée.

skiff [skɪf] *n* skiff *m*, yole *f*.

skill [skɪl] *n* (**a**) *(ability)* habileté *f*, adresse *f* (*at* à); *(gen manual)* dextérité *f*; *(talent)* savoir-faire *m*, talent *m* (*at* en matière de). **his ~ in persuading them** l'habileté dont il a fait preuve en les persuadant; **lack of ~** maladresse *f*. (**b**) *(in craft etc)* technique *f*. **it's a ~ that has to be acquired** c'est une technique qui s'apprend; **we could make good use of his ~s** ses capacités *or* ses compétences nous seraient bien utiles. ◆ **skilful,** *(US)* **skillful** *adj* habile, adroit (*at doing* à faire). ◆ **skil(l)fully** *adv* habilement, adroitement. ◆ **skil(l)fulness** *n* habileté *f*, adresse *f*. ◆ **skilled** *adj* (**a**) *person* habile, adroit (*in, at doing* pour faire; *in, at sth* en qch); *movement, stroke* adroit; **~ed in diplomacy** qui a beaucoup d'expérience en diplomatie; **~ed in the art of** versé dans l'art de; (**b**) *(Ind) worker, engineer etc* qualifié; *work* de spécialiste; **it's a ~ed job** *(gen)* ça demande beaucoup d'adresse; *(Ind)* c'est un travail de spécialiste.

skillet ['skɪlɪt] *n* poêlon *m*.

skim [skɪm] **1** *vt* (**a**) *milk* écrémer; *soup* écumer. **to ~ the cream/scum/grease from sth** écrémer/écumer/dégraisser qch; **~(med) milk** lait *m* écrémé. (**b**) *stone* faire ricocher (*across* sur). *[bird etc]* **to ~ the ground/water** raser le sol/ l'eau. **2** *vi* (**a**) **to ~ across the water/along the ground** raser l'eau/ le sol; *(fig)* **to ~ through a book** parcourir un livre. (**b**) *(US * fig: cheat on taxes)* frauder (le fisc).

◆ **skim off** *vt sep cream, grease* enlever; *(fig) best pupils etc* mettre à part.

skimp [skɪmp] *vti (also ~* **on***) butter, cloth etc* lésiner sur; *praise, thanks* être chiche de; *piece of work* faire à la va-vite. ◆ **skimpily** *adv serve, provide* avec parcimonie; *live* chichement. ◆ **skimpiness** *n (gen)* insuffisance *f*; *[dress etc]* ampleur *f* insuffisante. ◆ **skimpy** *adj (gen)* insuffisant; *dress* étriqué.

skin [skɪn] **1** *n (gen)* peau *f*; *[boat, aircraft]* revêtement *m*; *(for duplicating)* stencil *m*; *(for wine)* outre *f*. **fair -~ned** à la peau claire; **next to the ~** à même la peau; **wet** *or* **soaked to the ~** trempé jusqu'aux os; **the snake casts its ~** le serpent mue; **rabbit ~** peau de lapin; **potatoes in their ~s** pommes de terre *fpl* en robe des champs; **banana ~** peau de banane; *(fig)* **to be ~ and bone** n'avoir que la peau sur les os; **to escape by the ~ of one's teeth** l'échapper belle; **we caught the train by the ~ of our teeth** nous avons attrapé le train de justesse; *(fig)* **to have a thick/thin ~** être insensible/ susceptible; *(fig)* **to get under sb's ~** * taper sur les nerfs à qn *; *(fig)* **I've got you under my ~** * je t'ai dans la peau ‡; *(fig)* **it's no ~ off my nose** ‡ *(does not hurt me)* pour ce que ça me coûte!; *(does not concern me)* ce n'est pas mon problème. **2** *adj disease, colour* de (la) peau. **3** *vt animal* écorcher; *fruit, vegetable* éplucher. *(fig)* **I'll ~ him alive!** * je vais l'écorcher tout vif!; **to ~ one's knee** s'écorcher le genou. ◆ **skin-deep** *adj* superficiel; **it's only ~-deep** ça n'est pas bien sérieux. ◆ **skin diver** *n* plongeur *m*, -euse *f* sous-marin(e). ◆ **skin diving** *n* plongée sous-marine. ◆ **skinflick** ‡ *n* film *m* porno * *inv*. ◆ **skinflint** *n* radin(e) * *m(f)*. ◆ **skinful** ‡ *n*: **to have (had) a ~ful** être soûl *. ◆ **skinhead** *n* jeune homme *m* aux cheveux tondus ras; *(thug)* jeune voyou *m*. ◆ **skinny** *adj* maigrichon; *sweater* moulant; *(Fashion)* **the ~ny look** la mode ultra-mince. ◆ **skinnydip** *vi* se baigner à poil. ◆ **skintight** *adj* très ajusté.

skip[1] [skɪp] **1** *n* petit bond, petit saut. **2** *vi* sautiller; *(with rope)* sauter à la corde. **to ~ in/out** *etc* entrer/ sortir *etc* en sautillant; *(fig)* **he ~ped off without paying** il a décampé sans payer; **he ~ped over that point** il a glissé sur ce point; **to ~ from one subject to another** sauter d'un sujet à un autre. **3** *vt (omit) page, class, meal* sauter. **~ it!** * laisse tomber! *; **to ~ school** sécher les cours. ◆ **skipping** *n* saut *m* à la corde. ◆ **skipping rope,** *(US)* **skip rope** *n* corde *f* à sauter.

skip[2] [skɪp] *n (container)* benne *f*.

skipper ['skɪpəʳ] *n (Naut)* capitaine *m*, patron *m*; *(Sport *)* capitaine; *(in race)* skipper *m*.

skirmish ['skɜ:mɪʃ] *n* escarmouche *f*.

skirt [skɜ:t] **1** *n* (**a**) jupe *f*. (**b**) *(Culin)* flanchet *m*. **2** *vti* (**~ round**) *town, obstacle* contourner; *difficulty* esquiver. ◆ **skirting (board)** *n* plinthe *f*.

skit [skɪt] *n* parodie *f* (*on* de); *(Theat)* sketch *m* satirique.

skittle ['skɪtl] *n* quille *f*. **~s** (jeu *m* de) quilles.

skive * [skaɪv] *vi* tirer au flanc *. **to ~ off** se défiler *. ◆ **skiver** * *n* tire-au-flanc * *m inv.*

skivvy * ['skɪvɪ] *n* boniche *f (pej).*

skulduggery * [skʌl'dʌgərɪ] *n* maquignonnage *m.*

skulk [skʌlk] *vi* (**~ about**) rôder furtivement. **to ~ in/out** *etc* entrer/sortir *etc* furtivement.

skull [skʌl] *n* crâne *m.* **~ and crossbones** tête *f* de mort; *(flag)* pavillon *m* à tête de mort. ◆ **skullcap** *n* calotte *f.*

skunk [skʌŋk] *n* mouffette *f*; *(fur)* sconse *m*; *(* pej: person)* mufle * *m.*

sky [skaɪ] *n* ciel *m.* **in the ~** dans le ciel; **under the open ~** à la belle étoile; **the skies of England** le ciel *or* les ciels d'Angleterre; **under warmer skies** sous des cieux plus cléments; **to praise sb to the skies** porter qn aux nues; *(fig)* **the ~'s the limit** * tout est possible. ◆ **sky-blue** *adj* bleu ciel *inv.* ◆ **skydiving** *n* parachutisme *m* (en chute libre). ◆ **sky-high** **1** *adv throw* très haut (dans le ciel); **to blow ~-high** *bridge* faire sauter; *theory* démolir ; **2** *adj prices, temperature* extrêmement haut. ◆ **Skylab** *n* Skylab *m.* ◆ **skylark** **1** *n (bird)* alouette *f* (des champs) ; **2** *vi (* fig)* chahuter. ◆ **skylarking** * *n* chahut *m.* ◆ **skylight** *n* lucarne *f.* ◆ **skyline** *n* ligne *f* d'horizon; *[city]* ligne des toits. ◆ **skyscraper** *n* gratte-ciel *m inv.* ◆ **skyway** *n (US Aut)* route *f* surélevée. ◆ **skywriting** *n* publicité *f* tracée par un avion.

slab [slæb] *n [stone, wood]* bloc *m*; *(paving ~)* dalle *f*; *(flat)* plaque *f*; *[meat]* pièce *f*, *(smaller)* pavé *m* ; *[cake]* pavé; *(smaller)* grosse tranche *f*; *[chocolate]* plaque; *(smaller)* tablette *f.*

slack [slæk] **1** *adj* (**a**) *(loose) rope* lâche; *joint, knot* desserré; *grip* faible. **to be ~** *[screw etc]* avoir du jeu; *[rope etc]* avoir du mou. (**b**) *(inactive) demand, market, trade* faible. **~ periods** périodes *fpl* creuses; *(in the day)* heures *fpl* creuses; **the ~ season** la morte-saison. (**c**) *(lacking energy)* mou; *(lax)* négligent; *student, worker* peu consciencieux. **to be ~ about one's work** négliger son travail; **to grow ~** se laisser aller. **2** *n* (**a**) **to take up the ~ in a rope** tendre un cordage. (**b**) *(coal)* poussier *m.* **3** *vi* (*) ne pas travailler comme il le faudrait. ◆ **slack off** * *vi (stop working etc)* se relâcher; *[trade, demand]* ralentir.

◆ **slacken (off)** **1** *vt rope* donner du mou à; *cable* donner du ballant à; *reins* relâcher; *screw* desserrer; *pressure etc* diminuer; **to ~en speed** *or* **one's pace** ralentir ; **2** *vi* prendre du mou *or* du ballant; se desserrer; *[gale, speed, effort, pressure]* diminuer; *[activity, trade]* ralentir. ◆ **slacker** * *n* flemmard(e) * *m(f).* ◆ **slackness** *n [rope etc]* manque *m* de tension; (*) *[person]* laisser-aller *m*; *[trade]* ralentissement *m.* ◆ **slacks** *npl* pantalon *m.*

slag [slæg] *n (Metal)* scories *fpl*; *(Min)* crasses *fpl.* **~ heap** *(Metal)* crassier *m*; *(Min)* terril *m.*

slain [sleɪn] *(ptp of* **slay***)* *npl*: **the ~** les morts *mpl* (tombés au champ d'honneur).

slake [sleɪk] *vt one's thirst* étancher.

slam [slæm] **1** *vt door, lid* (faire) claquer. **to ~ on the brakes** freiner à mort *; **she ~med the books on the table** elle a flanqué * les livres sur la table; **he ~med the ball into the net** d'un coup violent il a envoyé le ballon dans le filet. **2** *vi [door, lid]* claquer. **3** *n (Bridge)* chelem *m.* ◆ **slammer** *n (Prison sl)* la taule *f.*

slander ['slɑːndəʳ] **1** *n* calomnie *f*; *(Jur)* diffamation *f.* **2** *vt* calomnier; *(Jur)* diffamer. ◆ **slanderous** *adj* calomnieux; diffamatoire. ◆ **slanderously** *adv* calomnieusement; de façon diffamatoire.

slang [slæŋ] **1** *n* argot *m.* **in ~** en argot; **army/school ~** argot militaire/d'écolier; **that word is ~** c'est un mot d'argot; **to talk ~** parler argot. **2** *adj word* d'argot. ◆ **slanging match** * *n* échange *m* d'insultes. ◆ **slangy** * *adj* argotique.

slant [slɑːnt] **1** *n* inclinaison *f*; *(fig: point of view)* angle *m* (*on* sur). **to give/get a new ~ * on sth** présenter/voir qch sous un angle nouveau. **2** *vi* pencher. **3** *vt line* faire pencher; *(fig) account, news* présenter avec parti-pris. ◆ **slant-eyed** *adj* aux yeux bridés. ◆ **slanting** *adj roof, surface* incliné; *handwriting, line* penché; *rain* oblique. ◆ **slantwise** *adv* de biais.

slap [slæp] **1** *n (gen)* claque *f.* **a ~ on the bottom** une fessée; *(lit, fig)* **a ~ in the face** une gifle; *(fig)* **to get a ~ on the wrist** se faire taper sur les doigts; **a ~ on the back** une grande tape dans le dos. **2** *adv* (*) en plein (*into* dans). **~ in the middle** en plein milieu. **3** *vt* (**a**) *(hit) person* donner une tape *or (stronger)* claque à (*on the back* dans le dos). **to ~ a child's bottom** donner une fessée à un enfant; **to ~ sb's face** *or* **sb in the face** gifler qn. (**b**) *(put)* flanquer *. **he ~ped a coat of paint on the wall** il a flanqué * un coup de peinture sur le mur; *(fig)* **to ~ sb down** * rembarrer * qn. ◆ **slapbang** * *adv* en plein (*into* dans). ◆ **slapdash** *adj person* insouciant; *work* fait à la va-vite. ◆ **slapstick (comedy)** *n* grosse farce *f.* ◆ **slap-up** * *adj meal* fameux *.

slash [slæʃ] **1** *n* entaille *f*; (**~mark**) (barre *f*) oblique. **2** *vt* (**a**) entailler; *(several cuts)* taillader; *rope* trancher; *face* balafrer; *(with whip, stick)* cingler. **to ~ sb** taillader qn; **~ed sleeves** manches *fpl* à crevés. (**b**) *prices* casser *; *costs, expenses* réduire radicalement; *speech, text* couper radicalement. (**c**) *(*: condemn) book, play* éreinter.

slat [slæt] *n* lame *f*; *[blind]* lamelle *f.*

slate [sleɪt] **1** *n* ardoise *f.* *(fig)* **put it on the ~** * mettez-le sur mon compte. **2** *adj deposits, industry* ardoisier; *roof* en ardoise. **~ blue/grey** bleu/gris ardoise *inv*; **~ quarry** ardoisière *f.* **3** *vt* (**a**) *roof* ardoiser. (**b**) (*) *book, play, actor* éreinter; *(scold)* attraper *. ◆ **slate-coloured** *adj* ardoise *inv.*

slaughter ['slɔːtəʳ] **1** *n [animals]* abattage *m*; *[people]* carnage *m.* **the ~ on the roads** les hécatombes *fpl* sur la route. **2** *vt animal* abattre; *person* tuer sauvagement; *people* massacrer. ◆ **slaughterhouse** *n* abattoir *m.*

Slav [slɑːv] **1** *adj* slave. **2** *n* Slave *mf.*

slave [sleɪv] **1** *n* esclave *mf* (*fig: to sth* de qch). **2** *adj (fig)* **~ driver** négrier *m*, -ière *f*; *(fig)* **~ labour** travail *m* de forçat; **~ labour camp** camp *m* de travaux forcés; **~ trade** commerce *m* des esclaves. **3** *vi* (**~ away**) travailler comme un nègre. **to ~ away at sth/at doing** s'escrimer sur qch/à faire. ◆ **slavery** *n* esclavage *m.* ◆ **slavey** * *n* boniche * *f.* ◆ **slavish** *adj subjection* d'esclave; *imitation, devotion* servile. ◆ **slavishly** *adv* servilement.

slaver ['slævəʳ] *vi (dribble)* baver.

slay [sleɪ] *pret* **slew**, *ptp* **slain** *vt (liter)* tuer.

sleazy * ['sliːzɪ] *adj* minable, miteux.

sledge [sledʒ] **1** *n (also* **sled***)* traîneau *m*; *(child's)* luge *f.* **2** *vi*: **to go sledging** faire de la luge; **to ~ down** descendre en luge *or* en traîneau.

sledgehammer ['sledʒˌhæməʳ] **1** *n* marteau *m* de forgeron. **2** *adj blow* violent, magistral.

sleek [sliːk] *adj hair, fur* lisse et brillant; *cat* au poil soyeux; *person* (trop) soigné; *(in manner)* onctueux. ◆ **sleekly** *adv reply* doucereusement.

sleep [sliːp] *(vb: pret, ptp* **slept***)* **1** *n* sommeil *m.* **to be in a deep** *or* **sound ~** dormir profondément; **to talk/walk in one's ~** parler/marcher en dormant; **she sang the child to ~** elle a chanté jusqu'à ce que l'enfant s'endorme; **to have a ~ , to get some ~** dormir; *(short while)* faire un somme; **to get** *or* **go to ~** s'endormir; **my leg has gone to ~** j'ai la jambe engourdie; **to put to ~** endormir; *(put down) cat* faire piquer; **a 3-hour ~** 3 heures de sommeil; **to have a good night's ~** passer une bonne nuit; **he didn't lose any ~ over it** il n'en a pas perdu le sommeil pour autant. **2** *vi* (**a**) dormir. **to ~ like a log** *or* **a top** dormir comme une souche; **~ tight!** dors bien!; **to ~ deeply** *or* **soundly** dormir profondément; *(without fear)* **to ~ soundly** dormir sur ses deux oreilles; **to ~ lightly** *(regularly)* avoir le sommeil léger; *(on one occasion)* dormir d'un sommeil léger; **I didn't ~ a wink all night** je n'ai pas fermé l'œil de la nuit; **to ~ on a problem/a letter/a decision** attendre le lendemain pour résoudre un problème/répondre à une lettre/prendre une décision; **I'll have to ~ on it** il faut que j'attende demain pour décider; **he slept through the storm** l'orage ne l'a pas réveillé; **he slept through the alarm clock** il n'a pas entendu son réveil. (**b**) *(spend night)* coucher. **he slept at his aunt's** il a couché chez sa tante; *(have sex)* **to ~ with sb** coucher * avec qn. **3** *vt*: **the house ~s 8** on peut coucher 8 personnes dans cette maison.

◆ **sleep around** * *vi* coucher * avec n'importe qui. ◆ **sleep in** *vi (lie late)* faire la grasse matinée; *(oversleep)* ne pas se réveiller à temps. ◆ **sleep off** *vt sep*: **to ~ sth off** dormir pour faire passer qch.

◆ **sleeper** *n* (**a**) **to be a light/heavy ~er** avoir le sommeil léger/lourd; (**b**) *(Rail) (track)* traverse *f*; *(berth)* couchette *f*; *(train)* train-couchettes *m*; *(rail car)* voiture-lits *m*; (**c**) *(earring)* clou *m*; *(US fig: sudden success)* révélation *f*. ◆ **sleepily** *adv* d'un air *or* ton endormi. ◆ **sleepiness** *n [person]* envie *f* de dormir. ◆ **sleeping** *adj person* qui dort, endormi; **~ing bag** sac *m* de couchage; **the S~ing Beauty** la Belle au bois dormant; *(Rail)* **~ing car** wagon-couchettes *m*; **~ing draught** soporifique *m*; *(Comm)* **~ing partner** commanditaire *m*; **~ing pill** *or* **tablet** somnifère *m*; **~ing policeman** cassevitesse *m*; **~ing sickness** maladie *f* du sommeil. ◆ **sleepless** *adj person* qui ne dort pas, éveillé; *hours* sans sommeil; **to have a ~less night** ne pas dormir de la nuit. ◆ **sleeplessly** *adv* sans dormir. ◆ **sleep-lessness** *n* insomnie *f*. ◆ **sleepwalk** *vi* marcher en dormant, être somnambule. ◆ **sleepwalker** *n* somnambule *mf*. ◆ **sleepwalking** *n* somnambulisme *m*. ◆ **sleepwear** *n* vêtements *mpl* de nuit. ◆ **sleepy** *adj person* qui a envie de dormir; *voice, look, village* endormi; **to be** *or* **feel ~y** avoir sommeil. ◆ **sleepyhead** * *n* endormi(e) *m(f)*.

sleet [sli:t] **1** *n* neige *f* fondue. **2** *vi*: **it is ~ing** il tombe de la neige fondue.

sleeve [sli:v] *n [garment]* manche *f*; *[record]* pochette *f*; *[cylinder etc]* chemise *f*. **long-~d** à manches longues; *(fig)* **he's always got sth up his ~** il a plus d'un tour dans son sac; **he's got sth up his ~** il a qch en réserve. ◆ **sleeveboard** *n* jeannette *f*. ◆ **sleevenote** *n* texte *(sur pochette de disque)*.

sleigh [sleɪ] *n* traîneau *m*.

sleight [slaɪt] *n*: **~ of hand** tour *m* de passe-passe.

slender [ˈslendəʳ] *adj person* mince; *stem, hand, neck, waist* fin; *(fig) hope, chance, majority* faible; *income, means, knowledge* maigre. *[person]* **tall and ~** élancé; **small and ~** menu. ◆ **slenderness** *n* minceur *f*; finesse *f*.

slept [slept] *pret, ptp of* **sleep.**

sleuth [slu:θ] *n* limier *m*.

slew[1] [slu:] *pret of* **slay.**

slew[2] [slu:] *n (US)* **a ~ of...** un tas * de...

slice [slaɪs] **1** *n* (**a**) *(gen)* tranche *f*; *[lemon, cucumber, sausage]* rondelle *f*, tranche. **~ of bread and butter** tartine *f* (beurrée); *(fig)* **a ~ of the profits** une bonne partie des bénéfices; **~ of life** tranche de vie; **~ of luck** coup *m* de chance. (**b**) *(utensil)* truelle *f*.

2 *vt* couper (en tranches *or* en rondelles); *rope etc* couper net; *(Sport) ball* couper. **to ~ sth thin** couper qch en tranches *or* rondelles fines; **a ~d loaf** un pain en tranches.

◆ **slice off** *vt sep meat* couper; *piece of rope etc* couper net. ◆ **slice through** *vt fus rope* couper net; *(fig) the air, the waves* fendre. ◆ **slice up** *vt sep* couper en tranches *or* en rondelles.

◆ **slicer** *n* coupe-jambon *m inv*.

slick [slɪk] **1** *adj explanation* trop prompt; *excuse, answer* facile; *person (glib)* qui a la parole facile; *(cunning)* rusé. **a ~ customer** * une fine mouche. **2** *n (oil ~)* nappe *f* de pétrole. **3** *vt*: **to ~ (down) one's hair** *(with comb)* se lisser les cheveux; *(with haircream)* se brillantiner les cheveux. ◆ **slickly** *adv answer* habilement.

slide [slaɪd] *(vb: pret, ptp* **slid***)* **1** *n (action)* glissade *f*; *(land ~)* glissement *m* (de terrain); *(fig: in prices etc)* baisse *f* (*in* de); *(in playground, pool etc)* toboggan *m*; *[microscope]* porte-objet *m*; *(Phot)* diapositive *f*; *(Mus: between notes)* coulé *m*; *(hair ~)* barrette *f*. **2** *adj (Phot)* **~ box** classeur *m* pour diapositives; **~ projector** projecteur *m* de diapositives; **~ rule** règle *f* à calcul. **3** *vi (gen)* glisser; *(move silently)* se glisser. **to ~ down the bannisters** descendre en glissant sur la rampe; **to ~ down a slope** descendre une pente en glissant ; **he slid into the room** il s'est glissé dans la pièce; **to let things ~** laisser les choses aller à la dérive. **4** *vt box, case, small object* glisser (*into* dans; *across* à travers); *chair, larger object* faire glisser. **to ~ the top back onto a box** remettre le couvercle sur une boîte; **he slid the gun out of the holster** il a sorti le revolver de l'étui. ◆ **sliding** *adj part* qui glisse; *panel, door, seat* coulissant; *(Aut) roof* ouvrant; *(US)* **sliding time** horaire *m* variable; *(Admin etc)* **sliding scale** échelle *f* mobile.

slight [slaɪt] **1** *adj* (**a**) *person (slim)* menu; *(frail)* frêle. (**b**) *(small: gen)* petit, léger *(before n)*; *(negligible: gen)* faible, insignifiant; *error* petit. **some ~ optimism** un peu d'optimisme; **not the ~est danger** pas le moindre danger; **not in the ~est** pas le moins du monde; **he takes offence at the ~est thing** il se pique pour un rien. **2** *vt* manquer d'égards envers; *(stronger)* offenser. **3** *n* manque *m* d'égards; *(stronger)* affront *m*. ◆ **slighting** *adj* offensant. ◆ **slightingly** *adv* d'une manière offensante. ◆ **slightly** *adv* (**a**) *sick, better* légèrement, un peu; *know etc* un peu; (**b**) **~ly built** menu.

slim [slɪm] **1** *adj person, ankle, book* mince; *(fig) hope, excuse* faible; *evidence, resources* insuffisant. **2** *vi* maigrir; *(diet)* être au régime (pour maigrir). **3** *vt* faire maigrir. ◆ **slimmer** *n* personne *f* suivant un régime amaigrissant. ◆ **slimming** *adj diet, pills* amaigrissant, pour maigrir; *food* qui ne fait pas grossir; *dress etc* amincissant. ◆ **slimness** *n* minceur *f*.

slime [slaɪm] *n (mud)* vase *f*; *(sticky substance)* dépôt *m* visqueux; *(from snail)* bave *f*. ◆ **sliminess** *n* nature *f* vaseuse; viscosité *f*. ◆ **slimy** *adj (gen)* visqueux; *walls* suintant; (*muddy*) *stone, hands* couvert de vase; *(fig)* servile.

sling [slɪŋ] *(vb: pret, ptp* **slung***)* **1** *n (catapult)* fronde *f*; *(child's)* lance-pierre *m inv*; *(Med)* écharpe *f*. **in a ~** en écharpe. **2** *vt* (**a**) *(throw)* lancer (*at sb* à *or* contre qn; *at sth* sur qch). (**b**) *(hang) hammock* suspendre; *load etc* hisser. **to ~ across one's shoulder** *rifle, satchel* mettre en bandoulière; *load, coat* rejeter par-dessus l'épaule. ◆ **sling out** * *vt sep person* flanquer * à la porte; *object* jeter.

slink [slɪŋk] *pret, ptp* **slunk** *vi*: **to ~ away/out** *etc* s'en aller/sortir *etc* furtivement. ◆ **slinkily** * *adv walk* d'une démarche ondulante. ◆ **slinking** *adj* furtif.

◆ **slinky** * *adj woman* aguichant; *body* sinueux; *walk* ondulant; *dress* moulant.

slip [slɪp] **1** *n* (**a**) *(slide)* dérapage *m*; *(trip)* faux pas *m*; *(mistake)* erreur *f*, bévue *f*; *(oversight)* oubli *m*; *(moral)* écart *m*. **~ of the tongue, ~ of the pen**

lapsus *m*; **earth ~** éboulement *m* (de terre); **to give sb the ~** fausser compagnie à qn. (**b**) *(pillow ~)* taie *f* (d'oreiller); *(underskirt)* combinaison *f*. (**c**) **in the ~s** *(Naut)* sur cale *f*; *(Theat)* dans les coulisses *fpl*. (**d**) *(paper: in filing system etc)* fiche *f*. **a ~ of paper** *(small sheet)* un bout de papier; *(strip)* une bande de papier; *(fig)* **a mere ~ of a boy/girl** un gamin/une gamine.
2 *vi* (**a**) *(slide) [person, food, hand, object]* glisser (*on* sur; *out of* de); *(Aut) [clutch]* patiner. *(fig)* **money ~s through her fingers** l'argent lui file entre les doigts; **several errors had ~ped into the report** plusieurs erreurs s'étaient glissées dans le rapport; **to let ~ an opportunity** laisser échapper une occasion; **he let (it) ~ that...** il a laissé échapper que...; **he's ~ping** * *(getting old, less efficient)* il baisse; *(making more mistakes)* il ne fait plus assez attention. (**b**) *(move quickly)* **to ~ into/out of** *[person]* se glisser dans/hors de; *[vehicle]* se faufiler dans/hors de; **to ~ away** *[vehicle, boat]* s'éloigner doucement; *[person]* s'esquiver; **to ~ back** *[vehicle, boat]* revenir doucement; *[guest]* revenir discrètement; *[thief, spy]* revenir furtivement; **I'll just ~ through the garden** je vais passer par le jardin; **I must just ~ out for some cigarettes** il faut que je sorte un instant chercher des cigarettes; **she ~ped out to the shops** elle a fait un saut jusqu'aux magasins; **the secret ~ped out** le secret a été révélé par mégarde; **the words ~ped out before he realized it** les mots lui ont échappé avant même qu'il ne s'en rende compte; **the years ~ped past** les années passèrent; **to ~ into/out of a dress** enfiler/enlever (rapidement) une robe; *(fig)* **to ~ into bad habits** prendre insensiblement de mauvaises habitudes.
3 *vt* (**a**) *(slide) coin, small object* glisser (*to sb* à qn; *into* dans). **he ~ped the gun out of its holster** il a sorti le revolver de son étui; **the question was ~ped into the exam** l'épreuve a comporté cette question inattendue; *(Aut)* **to ~ the clutch** faire patiner l'embrayage. *(Med)* **a ~ped disc** une hernie discale. (**b**) *(escape)* échapper à; *anchor, moorings* filer; *[dog] collar* se dégager de; *(Knitting) stitch* glisser. **to ~ sb's attention** *or* **notice** échapper à qn (*that* que); **it ~ped my memory** cela m'était complètement sorti de la tête.
◆ **slip up** * *vi (make mistake)* gaffer *, cafouiller *. ◆ **slipcovers** *npl* housses *fpl*. ◆ **slipknot** *n* nœud *m* coulant. ◆ **slip-on** *adj* facile à mettre. ◆ **slippery** *adj* glissant; *(fig pej) person* fuyant; **it's ~pery underfoot** le sol est glissant; *(fig pej)* **he's as ~pery as an eel** il glisse comme une anguille. ◆ **slippy** * *adj* glissant. ◆ **slip-road** *n [motorway]* bretelle *f* d'accès. ◆ **slipshod** *adj person, work* négligé; *dress* débraillé; *worker* négligent. ◆ **slipstream** *n (Aviat)* sillage *m*. ◆ **slip-up** * *n* gaffe * *f*, bévue *f*; *(in communications)* cafouillage * *m*. ◆ **slipway** *n (Naut)* cale *f*.

slipper ['slɪpəʳ] *n* pantoufle *f*; *(warmer)* chausson *m*.

slit [slɪt] *(vb: pret, ptp* **slit***)* **1** *n (opening)* fente *f*; *(cut)* incision *f*; *(tear)* déchirure *f*. **2** *vt* fendre; inciser; déchirer; *sb's throat* trancher. **to ~ open** *letter* ouvrir; *sack* éventrer; **a ~ skirt** une jupe fendue. ◆ **slit-eyed** *adj* aux yeux bridés.

slither ['slɪðəʳ] *vi [person, animal]* glisser; *[snake]* onduler. **to ~ about** déraper.

sliver ['slɪvəʳ] *n [glass, wood]* éclat *m*; *[cheese etc]* lamelle *f*.

slob * [slɒb] *n* rustaud(e) *m(f)*.

slobber ['slɒbəʳ] *vi* baver.

sloe [sləʊ] *n* prunelle *f*. **~ gin** eau-de-vie *f* de prunelle.

slog [slɒg] **1** *n (work)* long travail *m* pénible, travail de Romain *; *(effort)* gros effort *m*; *(task)* corvée *f*. **2** *vt ball, opponent* donner un grand coup à. **3** *vi* (**a**) *(work etc)* travailler très dur. **he ~ged through the book** il s'est forcé à lire le livre; **to ~ away** travailler comme un nègre *; **to ~ away at sth** trimer * sur qch. (**b**) *(walk)* **to ~ along** avancer avec effort; **he ~ged up the hill** il a gravi la colline avec effort. ◆ **slogger** * *n (hard worker)* bosseur ⁑ *m*, -euse ⁑ *f*.

slogan ['sləʊgən] *n* slogan *m*.

slop [slɒp] **1** *n*: **~s** *(for invalids)* bouillon *m*; *(dirty water)* eaux *fpl* sales; *(in teacup)* fond *m* de tasse. **2** *vt* répandre *(par mégarde)* (*onto* sur; *into* dans). **3** *vi* (**~ over**) déborder. ◆ **sloppily** *adv (carelessly)* sans soin; *(sentimentally)* avec sensiblerie. ◆ **sloppiness** *n (carelessness)* manque *m* de soin; *(sentimentality)* sensiblerie *f*. ◆ **sloppy** *adj food* (trop) liquide; *work* peu soigné, bâclé *; *appearance, language* négligé; *garment* trop grand; *(*: sentimental)* débordant de sensiblerie; *(sweater)* **~py joe** * gros pull *m* vague.

slope [sləʊp] **1** *n* pente *f*. **~ up** montée *f*; **~ down** descente *f*; **on the ~s of Mount Etna** sur les flancs *mpl* de l'Etna; **the southern ~s of the Himalayas** le versant sud de l'Himalaya; **on the (ski) ~s** sur les pistes (de ski). **2** *vi [ground, roof]* être en pente; *[handwriting]* pencher. **to ~ up** monter; **to ~ down** descendre. **3** *vt* pencher, incliner.
◆ **sloping** *adj ground, roof* en pente; *handwriting* penché; *shoulders* tombant.

slosh * [slɒʃ] **1** *vt water, paint* répandre, flanquer * (*onto, over* sur; *into* dans). **2** *vi*: **to ~ about in water/mud** patauger dans l'eau/la boue. ◆ **sloshed** ⁑ *adj (drunk)* bourré ⁑, soûl *.

slot [slɒt] **1** *n (slit: in machine, box etc)* fente *f*; *(groove)* rainure *f*; *(fig: in timetable etc)* heure *f*; *(Rad, TV)* créneau *m*. **2** *adj*: **~ machine** *(selling things)* distributeur *m* (automatique); *(for amusement)* machine *f* à sous; **~ meter** compteur *m* à paiement préalable. **3** *vt object* emboîter (*into* dans); *(fig)* insérer (*into a programme* dans une grille de programmes). **4** *vi* s'emboîter (*into* dans); *(fig)* s'insérer (*into* dans).

sloth [sləʊθ] *n* (**a**) paresse *f*. (**b**) *(animal)* paresseux *m*. ◆ **slothful** *adj* paresseux.

slouch [slaʊtʃ] *vi*: **to ~ in/out** *etc* entrer/sortir *etc* en se traînant; **he was ~ing in a chair** il était affalé dans un fauteuil; **she always ~es** elle ne se tient jamais droite; **stop ~ing!** tiens-toi droit!

slovenly ['slʌvnlɪ] *adj person* débraillé; *work* qui manque de soin. ◆ **slovenliness** *n* débraillé *m*; manque *m* de soin.

slow [sləʊ] **1** *adj (gen)* lent; *(fig) track, surface* lourd; *(boring) party, novel, play* ennuyeux; *person (phlegmatic)* flegmatique; *(stupid)* lent; *(Med) child* retardé. **~ but sure** lent mais sûr; **a ~ train** un omnibus; **at a ~ speed** à petite vitesse; *(lit, fig)* **it's ~ going** on n'avance pas vite; **it's ~ work** c'est un travail qui avance lentement; **he's a ~ worker** il travaille lentement; **~ to anger** lent à se mettre en colère; *(brain working ~ly)* **~ to understand/notice** *etc*, **~ in understanding/noticing** *etc* lent à comprendre/remarquer *etc*; *(taking one's time)* **~ to act/decide** *etc*, **~ in acting/deciding** *etc* long à agir/décider *etc*; **my watch is (10 minutes) ~** ma montre retarde (de 10 minutes); **in a ~ oven** à four doux; *(Culin)* **~ cooker** mijoteuse *f* électrique; **business is ~** les affaires stagnent; *(Cine etc)* **in ~ motion** au ralenti. **2** *adv* lentement. **to go ~** *[walker, vehicle]* aller lentement; *(be cautious)* y aller doucement; *(be less active)* ralentir ses activités; *(Ind)* faire la grève perlée; *[watch etc]* prendre du retard; **to go ~er** ralentir; **~-acting/-burning** *etc* à action/combustion *etc* lente; **it is ~-acting** *etc* cela agit *etc* lentement. **3** *vt* (**~ down, ~ up**) *(gen)* retarder; *walker* faire ralentir; *vehicle, machine, traffic* ralentir; *horse* ralentir le pas de; *progress, production, negotiations, reaction* ralentir, retarder. **these interruptions have ~ed us down** ces interruptions nous ont retardés. **4** *vi* (~ **down,** ~ **off,** ~ **up)** ralentir. ◆ **slowcoach** *or (US)* ◆ **slowpoke** * *n (dawdler)* lambin(e) * *m(f)*; *(dullard)* esprit lent. ◆ **slowdown** *n* ralentissement *m*. ◆ **slowly** *adv* lentement; *(little by little)* peu à peu; ~**ly but surely** lentement mais sûrement; **to go** (*or* **work** *etc*) **more** ~**ly** ralentir. ◆ **slow-moving** *adj* lent. ◆ **slowness** *n* lenteur *f*. ◆ **slow-witted** *adj* qui a l'esprit lent. ◆ **slow-worm** *n* orvet *m*.

sludge [slʌdʒ] *n (mud, sediment)* boue *f*; *(sewage)* vidanges *fpl*.

slug [slʌg] **1** *n (Zool)* limace *f*; *(bullet)* balle *f*; *(blow)* coup *m*. **a** ~ * **of whisky** un coup * de whisky sec. **2** *vt (*: hit)* frapper comme une brute.

sluggish ['slʌgɪʃ] *adj (gen)* lent; *(lazy)* paresseux; *engine* peu nerveux; *market, business* stagnant; *sales* difficile; *liver* paresseux. **to feel** ~ se sentir mou. ◆ **sluggishly** *adv* lentement.

sluice [slu:s] **1** *n* écluse *f*; *(* ~ *gate,* ~ *valve)* vanne *f*; (~ *way)* canal *m* (à vannes). **2** *vt* (~ **down)** laver à grande eau.

slum [slʌm] **1** *n (house)* taudis *m*. **the** ~**s** les quartiers *mpl* pauvres, les bas quartiers. **2** *adj*: ~ **area** quartier *m* pauvre; ~ **clearance** aménagement *m* des quartiers insalubres; ~ **clearance campaign** campagne *f* pour la démolition des taudis. ◆ **slum-dweller** *n* habitant(e) *m(f)* des taudis. ◆ **slumlord** *n (US)* marchand de sommeil. ◆ **slummy** *adj* misérable, sordide.

slumber ['slʌmbəʳ] **1** *n (liter: also* ~**s)** sommeil *m*. **2** *adj (Comm)* ~ **wear** lingerie *f* de nuit. **3** *vi* dormir paisiblement.

slump [slʌmp] **1** *n (gen)* baisse *f* soudaine (*in* de); *(Econ)* crise *f* économique; *(St Ex)* effondrement *m* des cours; *(in prices)* effondrement (*in* de). **the 1929** ~ la crise de 1929. **2** *vi* (**a**) *(gen)* baisser brutalement; *[prices]* s'effondrer. (**b**) (~ **down)** s'effondrer, s'affaisser (*into* dans; *onto* sur). ~**ed on the floor** effondré par terre; ~**ed over the wheel** affaissé sur le volant.

slung [slʌŋ] *pret, ptp of* **sling**.

slunk [slʌŋk] *pret, ptp of* **slink**.

slur [slɜ:ʳ] **1** *n (stigma)* atteinte *f* (*on* à); *(insult)* affront *m*. **it's no** ~ **on him to say...** ce n'est pas le calomnier que de dire... **2** *vt (join) sounds, words* lier à tort; *(Mus)* lier; *(indistinctly) word etc* mal articuler. **his speech was** ~**red** il n'arrivait pas à articuler. **3** *vi (fig)* **to** ~ **over sth** glisser sur qch.

slurp [slɜ:p] *vti* boire à grand bruit.

slush [slʌʃ] **1** *n (snow)* neige *f* fondante; *(mud)* gadoue *f*; *(sentiment)* sentimentalité *f*. **2** *adj*: ~ **fund** fonds *mpl* secrets, caisse *f* noire. ◆ **slushy** *adj* fondant; *(fig)* fadement sentimental.

slut [slʌt] *n (dirty)* souillon *f*; *(immoral)* salope ‡ *f*. ◆ **sluttish** *adj appearance* de souillon; *behaviour* de salope ‡.

sly [slaɪ] **1** *adj (wily)* rusé; *(secretive)* dissimulé; *(underhand)* sournois; *(mischievous)* espiègle. **2** *n*: **on the** ~ en cachette, en douce *. ◆ **slyly** *adv* de façon rusée *or* dissimulée; sournoisement; avec espièglerie; *(in secret)* en cachette, en douce *. ◆ **slyness** *n* ruse *f*; dissimulation *f*; sournoiserie *f*; espièglerie *f*.

smack¹ [smæk] *vi*: **to** ~ **of sth** sentir qch.

smack² [smæk] **1** *n (slap)* tape *f*; *(stronger)* claque *f*; *(on face)* gifle *f*; *(sound)* bruit *m* sec. **it was a** ~ **in the eye for them** * *(snub)* c'était une gifle pour eux; *(setback)* c'était un revers pour eux; *(fig)* **to have a** ~ **at doing sth** * essayer de faire qch. **2** *vt person* donner une tape *or* une claque à. **to** ~ **sb's face** gifler qn; **to** ~ **sb's bottom** donner la fessée à qn; **to** ~ **one's lips** se lécher les babines. **3** *adv* (*) en plein. ~ **in the middle** en plein milieu. ◆ **smacking** *n* fessée *f*; **to give sb a** ~**ing** donner une *or* la fessée à qn.

smack³ [smæk] *n* **(fishing** ~**)** bateau *m* de pêche.

small [smɔ:l] **1** *adj* (**a**) *(gen)* petit; *audience, population* peu nombreux; *income, sum* modeste; *meal* léger; *waist* mince; *(morally mean) person, mind* mesquin, petit. **the** ~**est details** les moindres détails; **the** ~**est possible number of books** le moins de livres possible; **a** ~ **proportion of** un pourcentage limité *or* restreint de; **to grow** *or* **get** ~**er** *(gen)* diminuer; *[town, organization]* décroître; **to make** ~**er** *income, amount* diminuer; *organization* réduire; *garden, object, garment* rapetisser; *(Typ)* **in** ~ **letters** en minuscules *fpl*; *(euph)* **the** ~**est room** le petit coin; **he is a** ~ **eater** il ne mange pas beaucoup; ~ **shopkeeper/farmer** petit commerçant/cultivateur; **to feel** ~ se sentir tout honteux; **to make sb feel** ~ humilier qn; ~ **ads** petites annonces *fpl*; *(TV)* **the** ~ **screen** le petit écran; ~ **talk** papotage *m*; **he's got plenty of** ~ **talk** il a de la conversation; *V also* **print, way** *etc*. (**b**) *(little or no)* **to have** ~ **cause** *or* **reason to do** n'avoir guère de raisons de faire; **a matter of no** ~ **consequence** une affaire d'une grande importance.
2 *adv*: **to cut up** ~ *paper* couper en tout petits morceaux; *meat* hacher menu.
3 *n*: **the** ~ **of the back** le creux des reins; *(Dress: esp Brit)* ~**s** * dessous *mpl*, sous-vêtements *mpl*.
◆ **small-arms** *npl (Mil)* armes *fpl* portatives. ◆ **smallholder** *n (Agr)* ≃ petit cultivateur *m*. ◆ **smallholding** *n* ≃ petite ferme *f (de moins de deux hectares)*. ◆ **small-minded** *adj* mesquin. ◆ **small-mindedness** *n* mesquinerie *f*. ◆ **smallness** *n [person]* petite taille *f*; *[hand, foot, object]* petitesse *f*; *[income, sum, contribution etc]* modicité *f*. ◆ **smallpox** *n* variole *f*. ◆ **small-scale** *adj* peu important; *undertaking* de peu d'importance. ◆ **small-time** *adj* peu important; **a** ~**-time crook** un escroc à la petite semaine. ◆ **small-town** *adj (pej)* provincial.

smarm * [smɑ:m] *vi (Brit)* **to** ~ **over sb** flagorner qn. ◆ **smarmy** * *adj* flagorneur.

smart [smɑ:t] **1** *adj* (**a**) *(not shabby) (gen)* chic *inv*, élégant; *hotel, shop, car, house* élégant; *(fashionable)* à la mode. **she was looking very** ~ elle était très élégante *or* très chic; **the** ~ **set** le grand monde. (**b**) *(clever)* intelligent, dégourdi *; *(shrewd)* malin; *(pej)* retors. ~ **card** * carte *f* à mémoire; **a** ~ **lad** *, *(US)* **a** ~ **guy** * un malin; **he's trying to be** ~ il fait le malin; **he's too** ~ **for me** il est beaucoup trop futé pour moi. (**c**) *(quick) pace* vif, rapide; *action* prompt. **that was** ~ **work!** tu n'as pas (*or* il n'a pas *etc*) mis longtemps!; **look** ~ **about it!** remue-toi! * **2** *vi [cut, graze]* brûler; *[iodine etc]* piquer; *(fig: feel offended)* être piqué au vif. **my eyes were** ~**ing** j'avais les yeux qui me brûlaient *or* piquaient; **to** ~ **under an insult** ressentir vivement une insulte.
◆ **smart-alec(k)** * *n* bêcheur * *m*. ◆ **smarten (up) 1** *vt (beautify) house, town* (bien) arranger; *child* pomponner; *(speed up)* accélérer ; **2** *vi [person]* se faire beau. ◆ **smartly** *adv (elegantly)* avec beaucoup de chic *or* d'élégance; *(cleverly)* astucieusement; *(quickly) move* vivement; *answer* du tac au tac. ◆ **smartness** *n (in appearance etc)* chic *m*, élégance *f*; *(cleverness)* intelligence *f*, astuce *f*; *(quickness)* promptitude *f*. ◆ **smarty** * *n* bêcheur * *m*, -euse * *f*.

smash [smæʃ] **1** *n* (**a**) *(sound)* fracas *m*; *(blow)* coup *m* violent; *(Tennis etc)* smash *m*. (**b**) *(also* ~**-up** *)* accident *m*. **car/rail** ~ accident de voiture/de chemin de fer. (**c**) *(Econ, Fin: collapse)* effondrement *m* (financier); *(St Ex)* krach *m*. **2** *adj*: **it was a** ~ **hit** * cela a eu un succès foudroyant; **the** ~ **hit** * **of the year** le succès de l'année. **3** *adv* (*) en plein. ~ **into a wall** en plein dans un mur. **4** *vt (break)* casser, briser; *(shatter)* fracasser; *(fig) spy ring etc* détruire; *hopes* ruiner; *enemy* écraser; *opponent, sports record* pulvériser. **to** ~ **sth to pieces** *or* **to bits**

briser qch en mille morceaux; *(Tennis)* **he ~ed the ball into the net** il a envoyé son smash dans le filet. **5** *vi [cup etc]* se briser (en mille morceaux), se fracasser. **the car ~ed into the tree** la voiture s'est écrasée contre l'arbre.

◆**smash down** *vt sep door, fence* fracasser. ◆**smash in** *vt sep door* enfoncer. **to ~ sb's face in** * casser la figure à qn *. ◆**smash up** *vt sep room etc* tout casser dans; *car* accidenter, bousiller *.

◆**smash-and-grab (raid)** *n* cambriolage *m* (commis en brisant une devanture). ◆**smasher** ⁑ *n*: **to be a ~er** *(in appearance)* être vachement ⁑ beau; *(in character etc)* être vachement chouette ⁑; **it's a ~er** c'est sensationnel *. ◆**smashing** * *adj* formidable *, terrible *.

smattering ['smæt(ə)rɪŋ] *n*: **a ~ of** quelques connaissances *fpl* vagues en.

smear [smɪəʳ] **1** *n* trace *f*; *(longer)* traînée *f*; *(dirty mark)* tache *f*; *(slander)* diffamation *f* (*on, against* de) ; **this ~ on his reputation** cette atteinte à sa réputation; *(Med)* frottis *m*. **2** *adj tactics* diffamatoire. **~ campaign** campagne *f* de diffamation. **3** *vt* (**a**) *butter etc* étaler (*on* sur). **to ~ cream on one's hands** s'enduire les mains de crème; **he ~ed his face with mud** il s'est barbouillé le visage de boue; **hands ~ed with ink** mains barbouillées d'encre. (**b**) *page of print* maculer; *wet paint* faire une marque sur; *lettering* étaler (accidentellement). *(fig)* **to ~ sb** porter atteinte à la réputation de qn. **4** *vi [ink, paint]* se salir.

smell [smel] *(vb: pret, ptp* **smelled** *or* **smelt**¹*)* **1** *n (sense of ~)* odorat *m*; *(odour)* odeur *f*; *(stench)* mauvaise odeur. **he has no sense of ~** il n'a pas d'odorat; **it has a nice/nasty ~** cela sent bon/ mauvais; **what a ~ in here!** que ça sent mauvais ici!; **a ~ of burning** une odeur de brûlé.

2 *vt* sentir; *(fig) danger* pressentir; *(sniff at)* sentir, renifler; *[animal]* flairer. **he could ~** *or* **he smelt sth burning** il sentait que qch brûlait; **he smelt the meat to see if it were bad** il a senti *or* reniflé la viande pour voir si elle était encore bonne; **the dog could ~ the bone** le chien a flairé l'os; *(fig)* **to ~ a rat** soupçonner qch.

3 *vi* (**a**) **to ~ at sth** renifler qch. (**b**) **it doesn't ~ at all** *[mixture etc]* ça ne sent rien, ça n'a pas d'odeur; *[gas]* c'est inodore; **these socks ~** ces chaussettes sentent mauvais; **his breath ~s** il a mauvaise haleine; **that ~s like chocolate** ça sent le chocolat; **to ~ of onions** sentir l'oignon; **to ~ good** *or* **sweet** sentir bon; **to ~ bad** sentir mauvais; **it ~s delicious!** ça embaume!; **it ~s dreadful!** ça pue!; *(fig)* **that deal ~s a bit** * cette affaire semble plutôt louche; **that idea ~s!** ⁑ cette idée ne vaut rien!; **he ~s!** ⁑ c'est un sale type! *

◆**smell out** *vt sep* (**a**) *[dog etc]* découvrir en flairant; *[person] criminal, treachery* découvrir. (**b**) **it's ~ing the room out** ça empeste la pièce.

◆**smelling salts** *npl* sels *mpl*. ◆**smelly** *adj* qui sent mauvais; **to be ~y** sentir mauvais; *(stronger)* puer.

smelt² [smelt] *vt ore* fondre; *metal* extraire par fusion. ◆**smelting** *n* fonte *f*; extraction *f* par fusion; **~ing works** fonderie *f*.

smidgen ['smɪdʒən] *n*: **a ~ of** un tout petit peu de.

smile [smaɪl] **1** *n* sourire *m*. **he said with a ~** dit-il en souriant; **he had a happy ~ on his face** il avait un sourire heureux; **to give sb a ~** faire un sourire à qn; **she gave a little ~** elle a eu un petit sourire; **to be all ~s** être tout souriant *or* tout sourire; **take that ~ off your face!** arrête donc de sourire comme ça! **2** *vi* sourire (*at, to sb* à qn; *at sth* de qch). **to keep smiling** garder le sourire. ◆**smiling** *adj* souriant. ◆**smilingly** *adv* en souriant.

smirk [smɜːk] **1** *n* petit sourire *m (self-satisfied)* satisfait *or (knowing)* narquois *or (affected)* affecté. **2** *vi* sourire d'un air satisfait *etc.*

smith [smɪθ] *n (shoes horses)* maréchal-ferrant *m*; *(forges iron)* forgeron *m*. ◆**smithy** *n* forge *f*.

smithereens [ˌsmɪðə'riːnz] *npl*: **to smash sth to ~** briser qch en mille morceaux; **in ~** brisé en mille morceaux.

smitten ['smɪtn] *adj*: **to be ~ with** *remorse, desire* être pris de; *terror, deafness* être frappé de; (*) *sb's beauty* être enchanté par; *idea* s'enthousiasmer pour; *(in love) person* être toqué * de.

smock [smɒk] *n (dress, overall, maternity top)* blouse *f*; *(maternity dress)* robe *f* de grossesse. ◆**smocking** *n* smocks *mpl*.

smog [smɒg] *n* smog *m*.

smoke [sməʊk] **1** *n* (**a**) fumée *f*. **there's no ~ without fire** il n'y a pas de fumée sans feu; **to go up in ~** *[house etc]* brûler; *[plans, hopes etc]* partir en fumée. (**b**) **to have a ~** fumer une cigarette (*or* une pipe *etc*). **2** *adj*: **~ bomb** obus *m* fumigène; **~ detector** détecteur *m* de fumée; **~ pollution** *(Ind)* pollution *f* par les fumées; *(tobacco)* pollution par la fumée de tabac; **~ screen** *(Mil)* rideau *m* de fumée; *(fig)* paravent *m (fig)*; **~ signal** signal *m* de fumée. **3** *vi (all senses)* fumer. **4** *vt (all senses)* fumer. **he ~s cigarettes/a pipe** il fume la cigarette/ la pipe; **~d salmon** saumon *m* fumé.

◆**smoke out** *vt sep insects, snake etc* enfumer.

◆**smokeless** *adj*: **~less fuel** combustible *m* non polluant; **~less zone** zone *f* où l'usage de combustibles solides est réglementé. ◆**smoker** *n* (**a**) fumeur *m*, -euse *f*; **~r's cough** toux *f* de fumeur; **heavy ~r** grand fumeur; (**b**) *(Rail)* wagon *m* fumeurs. ◆**smokestack** *n* cheminée *f (extérieure)*; **~stack industries** industries *fpl* traditionnelles. ◆**smoking** *n* tabagisme *m;* **'no smoking'** 'défense de fumer'; **smoking can damage your health** le tabac est nuisible à la santé; **to give up smoking** arrêter de fumer. ◆**smoky** *adj atmosphere, room* enfumé; *fire* qui fume; *glass* fumé.

smolder ['sməʊldəʳ] *vi (US)* = **smoulder.**

smooth [smuːð] **1** *adj* (**a**) *(gen)* lisse; *surface* lisse, égal; *road* à la surface égale; *(hairless) chin* glabre; *paste, sauce* onctueux; *flavour, wine* moelleux; *voice, sound* doux. (**b**) *movement etc* régulier, sans à-coups; *takeoff* en douceur; *flight* confortable; *sea crossing, trip* par mer calme; *breathing, pulse* régulier; *day, life* calme. **~ running** *[machinery etc]* bon fonctionnement; *[organization]* bonne marche; *(fig)* **the way is now ~** il n'y a plus d'obstacles maintenant. (**c**) *(suave)* doucereux, mielleux. **he's a ~ operator** * il sait s'y prendre; **a ~ talker** un beau parleur.

2 *vt* (**a**) (**~ down**) *sheets, pillow, hair* lisser; *wood* rendre lisse. *(fig)* **to ~ the way for sb** aplanir le terrain pour qn. (**b**) **to ~ cream into one's skin** faire pénétrer la crème dans la peau.

◆**smooth out** *vt sep dress* défroisser; *wrinkles, creases* faire disparaître; *difficulties* aplanir.

◆**smooth over** *vt sep (fig)* **to ~ things over** arranger les choses.

◆**smoothie** ⁑ *n (pej)* beau parleur. ◆**smoothly** *adv (easily)* facilement; *(gently)* doucement; *move* sans à-coups; *talk, say* doucereusement; **everything is going ~ly** tout marche comme sur des roulettes; **it went off ~ly** cela s'est bien passé. ◆**smoothness** *n* qualité *f or* aspect *m* lisse *or* égal(e); moelleux *m*; douceur *f*; *[sea]* calme *m*; rythme *m* régulier; régularité *f*; caractère *or* ton doucereux. ◆**smooth-running** *adj engine, machinery* qui n'a pas d'à-coups; *business, scheme* qui marche bien. ◆**smooth-spoken** *or* ◆**smooth-tongued** *adj* enjôleur.

smother ['smʌðəʳ] **1** *vt* (**a**) *(stifle)* étouffer. (**b**) *(cover)* couvrir (*with, in* de). **2** *vi* mourir étouffé.

smoulder ['sməʊldəʳ] *vi* couver.

smudge [smʌdʒ] **1** *n* (légère) tache *f*. **2** *vt face* salir; *print* maculer; *paint* faire une marque sur; *writing* étaler accidentellement. **3** *vi* se salir; se maculer; s'étaler.

smug [smʌg] *adj person* suffisant; *optimism, satisfaction* béat. ◆ **smugly** *adv* avec suffisance. ◆ **smugness** *n [person]* suffisance *f*; *[voice, reply]* ton *m* suffisant.

smuggle ['smʌgl] **1** *vt tobacco, drugs* passer en contrebande. **to ~ in** *etc goods* faire entrer *etc* en contrebande; *(fig) letters, person, animal* faire entrer *etc* clandestinement; **to ~ sth past** *or* **through the customs** passer qch en contrebande. **2** *vi* faire de la contrebande. ◆ **smuggler** *n* contrebandier *m*, -ière *f*. ◆ **smuggling** *n [goods]* contrebande *f (action)*; *[drugs]* trafic *m*.

smut [smʌt] *n (dirt)* petite saleté *f*; *(soot)* flocon *m* de suie; *(mark)* tache *f* de suie; *(in conversation etc)* cochonneries * *fpl*. ◆ **smutty** *adj object* noirci; *joke, film* cochon *.

snack [snæk] *n* casse-croûte *m inv*; *(party ~)* amuse-gueule *m*. **to have a ~** manger un petit quelque chose. ◆ **snack-bar** *n* snack *m*.

snag [snæg] *n (drawback)* inconvénient *m*; *(tear: in cloth)* accroc *m*; *(in stocking)* fil *m* tiré. **there's a ~ in it** il y a un inconvénient *or* une difficulté là-dedans; **to hit a ~** tomber sur un os *; **that's the ~!** voilà la difficulté!; **the ~ is that...** l'embêtant *, c'est que...

snail [sneɪl] *n* escargot *m*. **at a ~'s pace** à un pas de tortue.

snake [sneɪk] *n* serpent *m*. *(fig)* **~ in the grass** traître(sse) *m(f)*; *(US)* **~ oil** *(quack remedy)* remède *m* de charlatan; *(nonsense)* inepties *fpl*. ◆ **snakebite** *n* morsure *f* de serpent. ◆ **snake-charmer** *n* charmeur *m* de serpent. ◆ **snakes-and-ladders** *n* jeu *m* de l'oie. ◆ **snakeskin** *n* peau *f* de serpent.

snap [snæp] **1** *n* (**a**) *(noise)* bruit *m* sec. **with a ~ of his fingers he...** faisant claquer ses doigts il...; *(Met)* **a cold ~** une brève vague de froid. (**b**) *(~shot)* photo *f* (d'amateur). (**c**) *(Cards)* (jeu *m* de) bataille *f*. (**d**) *(US: easy)* **it's a ~** * c'est facile comme tout. **2** *adj* (**a**) *vote, strike* subit; *judgment, answer* irréfléchi. (**b**) *(US *: easy)* facile comme tout. **to make a ~ decision** (se) décider tout d'un coup. **3** *vi* (**a**) *(break)* se casser net *or* avec un bruit sec. (**b**) *[whip, elastic]* claquer. **to ~ open** s'ouvrir avec un bruit sec; **to ~ back into place** revenir à sa place avec un claquement. (**c**) **to ~ at sb** *[dog]* essayer de mordre qn; *[person]* parler à qn d'un ton brusque. **4** *vt* (**a**) *(break)* casser net *or* avec un bruit sec. (**b**) **to ~ one's fingers** faire claquer ses doigts; *(fig)* **to ~ one's fingers at sb** faire la nique à qn; **to ~ sth open/shut** ouvrir/fermer qch d'un coup sec. (**c**) **'shut up!' he ~ped** 'silence!' fit-il avec brusquerie. ◆ **snap off** *vt sep* casser net. *(fig)* **to ~ sb's head off** rabrouer qn, rembarrer * qn. ◆ **snap out 1** *vi*: **to ~ out of** * se sortir de, se tirer de; **~ out of it!** * secoue-toi! * **2** *vt sep question/order* poser/lancer d'un ton brusque. ◆ **snap up** *vt sep [dog etc]* happer; *(fig) bargain* sauter sur. ◆ **snapdragon** *n* gueule-de-loup *f*. ◆ **snap-fastener** *n (on clothes)* pression *f*; *(on handbag etc)* fermoir *m*. ◆ **snapshot** *n* photo *f* (d'amateur). ◆ **snappish** *adj* hargneux, cassant. ◆ **snappy** * *adj reply* bien envoyé; *phrase, slogan* qui a du punch * ; **look ~py!** grouille-toi! *

snare [snɛəʳ] **1** *n* piège *m*. **~ drum** tambour *m* à timbre. **2** *vt* prendre au piège.

snarl[1] [snɑ:l] **1** *vi [dog]* gronder en montrant les dents; *[person]* lancer un grondement (*at sb* à qn). **2** *vt*: **'no' he ~ed** 'non' dit-il avec hargne. **3** *n* grondement *m* féroce.

snarl[2] [snɑ:l] **1** *n (in wool etc)* nœud *m*; *(in traffic: ~-up)* embouteillage *m*. **2** *vt*: **to get ~ed up** *[wool etc]* s'emmêler; *[traffic]* se bloquer.

snatch [snætʃ] **1** *n* (**a**) *[jewellery, wages etc]* vol *m* (à l'arraché); *[child etc]* enlèvement *m*. **there was a wages ~** des voleurs se sont emparés des salaires. (**b**) *(small piece)* fragment *m*. **a ~ of music/poetry** quelques mesures *fpl*/vers *mpl*; **a ~ of conversation** des bribes *fpl* de conversation; **to work in ~es** travailler par à-coups. (**c**) *(Weight-lifting)* arraché *m*. **2** *vt (grab) object* saisir, s'emparer (brusquement) de; *few minutes' peace, short holiday* réussir à avoir; *opportunity* sauter sur; *kiss* voler (*from sb* à qn); *sandwich, drink* avaler à la hâte; *(steal)* voler (*from sb* à qn); *(kidnap)* enlever. **to ~ sth from sb** arracher qch à qn; **to ~ some sleep** réussir à dormir un peu; **to ~ a meal** déjeuner (*or* dîner) à la hâte. **3** *vi*: **to ~ at** *object* essayer de saisir; *opportunity* sauter sur. ◆ **snatch away** *vt sep* enlever d'un geste brusque. ◆ **snatch up** *vt sep* ramasser vivement.

sneak [sni:k] **1** *n* (*) rapporteur * *m*, -euse * *f*. **2** *adj attack, visit* subreptice. **~ thief** chapardeur * *m*, -euse * *f*. **3** *vi* (**a**) **to ~ in/out** *etc* entrer/sortir *etc* à la dérobée; **to ~ into the house** se faufiler dans la maison. (**b**) (*) moucharder * (*on sb* qn). **4** *vt*: **to ~ a look at sth** lancer un coup d'œil furtif à qch; **he was ~ing a cigarette** il était en train de fumer en cachette. ◆ **sneaker** * *n* (chaussure *f* de) tennis *f*. ◆ **sneaking** *adj dislike, preference* inavoué, secret; **I had a ~ing feeling that** je ne pouvais m'empêcher de penser que; **to have a ~ing suspicion that** soupçonner secrètement que. ◆ **sneaky** * *adj* sournois.

sneer [snɪəʳ] **1** *vi* ricaner. **to ~ at sb** se moquer de qn d'un air méprisant; **to ~ at sth** tourner qch en ridicule. **2** *n (act)* ricanement *m*; *(remark)* sarcasme *m*. ◆ **sneering 1** *adj* ricaneur, sarcastique ; **2** *n* ricanements *mpl*, sarcasmes *mpl*. ◆ **sneeringly** *adv* de façon sarcastique.

sneeze [sni:z] **1** *n* éternuement *m*. **2** *vi* éternuer. *(fig)* **it is not to be ~d at** ce n'est pas à dédaigner.

snide [snaɪd] *adj* narquois.

sniff [snɪf] **1** *n* reniflement *m*. **one ~ of that is enough to kill you** il suffit de respirer cela une fois pour en mourir. **2** *vi* renifler; *(disdainfully)* faire la grimace. **to ~ at sth** *[dog, person]* renifler qch; *(fig)* faire la grimace à qch; **it's not to be ~ed at** ce n'est pas à dédaigner. **3** *vt [dog]* renifler, flairer; *[person] food, bottle* renifler; *(suspiciously)* flairer; *air, perfume* humer; *smelling salts, glue etc* respirer; *drug, inhalant etc* aspirer. ◆ **sniffle 1** *n (slight cold)* petit rhume *m* (de cerveau) ; **2** *vi* renifler. ◆ **sniffy** * *adj* (**a**) *(disdainful)* dédaigneux; **to be ~y about sth** faire le (*or* la) dégoûté(e) devant qch; (**b**) *(smelly)* qui a une drôle d'odeur.

snigger ['snɪgəʳ] **1** *n* rire *m* en dessous. **2** *vi* pouffer de rire. **to ~ at** *remark, question* pouffer de rire en entendant; *sb's appearance etc* se moquer de. ◆ **sniggering** *n* rires *mpl* en dessous.

snip [snɪp] **1** *n* (**a**) *(cut)* petit coup *m*; *(small piece)* petit bout *m*; (**b**) *(*: bargain)* bonne affaire *f*; *(Racing)* gagnant *m* sûr. **2** *vt* couper.

snipe [snaɪp] **1** *n (pl inv: bird)* bécassine *f*. **2** *vi*: **to ~ at sb/sth** *(shoot)* canarder * qn/qch; *(fig: verbally)* critiquer qn/qch par en dessous. ◆ **sniper** *n* tireur *m* isolé.

snippet ['snɪpɪt] *n [cloth, paper]* petit bout *m*; *[conversation, news]* bribes *fpl*.

snivel ['snɪvl] *vi* pleurnicher. ◆ **sniveller** *n* pleurnicheur *m*, -euse *f*. ◆ **snivelling 1** *adj* pleurnicheur ; **2** *n* pleurnicheries *fpl*.

snob [snɒb] *n* snob *mf*. **he's a terrible** ~ il est terriblement snob. ◆ **snobbery** *n* snobisme *m*. ◆ **snobbish** *adj (gen)* snob *inv*; *lowly placed person* très impressionné par les gens importants (*or* riches *etc*). ◆ **snobbishness** *n* snobisme *m*. ◆ **snobby** * *adj* snob *inv*.

snog ‡ [snɒg] *vi (Brit)* se peloter *.

snooker ['snu:kəʳ] *n* ≃ jeu *m* de billard.

snoop [snu:p] *vi* se mêler des *or* fourrer son nez * dans les affaires des autres. **he's been ~ing around here again** il est revenu fourrer son nez * par ici; **to ~ on sb** espionner qn. ◆ **snooper** *n* personne *f* qui fourre son nez * partout.

snooze * [snu:z] **1** *n* petit somme *m*. **2** *vi* sommeiller.

snore [snɔ:ʳ] **1** *vi* ronfler *(en dormant)*. **2** *n (also* **snoring***)* ronflement *m*.

snorkel ['snɔ:kl] *n (Sport)* tuba *m*.

snort [snɔ:t] **1** *vi [horse etc]* s'ébrouer; *[person]* grogner; *(laughing)* s'étrangler de rire. **2** *n* ébrouement *m*; grognement *m*. ◆ **snorter** * *n* (**a**) **a ~er of a question/problem** une question/un problème vache ‡; **a ~er of a game** un match formidable *; (**b**) *(drink)* petit verre *m*.

snot * [snɒt] *n* morve *f*. ◆ **snotty** * *adj nose* qui coule; *face, child* morveux.

snout [snaʊt] *n* museau *m*.

snow [snəʊ] **1** *n* neige *f*; *(on TV screen)* neige; *(Drugs sl)* neige ‡, cocaïne *f*. **hard/soft** ~ neige dure/molle; ~ **blower** chasse-neige *m inv* à soufflerie; *(Met)* ~ **report** bulletin *m* d'enneigement; ~ **tyre** *or (US)* **tire** pneu-neige *m*, pneu clouté. **2** *vi* neiger. **3** *vt*: **to be ~ed in** *or* **up** être bloqué par la neige; *(fig)* **to be ~ed under** être submergé (*with* de).

◆ **snowball** **1** *n* boule *f* de neige; **~ball fight** bataille *f* de boules de neige ; **2** *vi* se lancer des boules de neige; *(fig) [project etc]* faire boule de neige. ◆ **snow-blindness** *n* cécité *f* des neiges. ◆ **snowbound** *adj road, country* complètement enneigé; *village, person* bloqué par la neige. ◆ **snow-capped** *adj* couronné de neige. ◆ **snowcat** *or (US)* ◆ **snowmobile** *n* autoneige *f*. ◆ **snow-covered** *adj* enfoui sous la neige. ◆ **snowdrift** *n* congère *f*. ◆ **snowdrop** *n* perce-neige *m inv*. ◆ **snowfall** *n* chute *f* de neige. ◆ **snowflake** *n* flocon *m* de neige. ◆ **snowline** *n* limite *f* des neiges (éternelles). ◆ **snowman** *n* bonhomme *m* de neige; **the abominable ~man** l'abominable homme *m* des neiges. ◆ **snowplough** *or (US)* ◆ **snowplow** *n* chasse-neige *m inv*. ◆ **snowshoe** *n* raquette *f*. ◆ **snowslide** *n* avalanche *f*. ◆ **snowstorm** *n* tempête *f* de neige. ◆ **snow-white** *adj* blanc comme neige. ◆ **Snow White** *n* Blanche-Neige *f*. ◆ **snowy** *adj weather, region* neigeux; *hills, roof* enneigé; *day etc* de neige; *(fig) linen* neigeux; *hair* de neige; **it was very ~y yesterday** il a beaucoup neigé hier.

snub¹ [snʌb] **1** *n* rebuffade *f*. **2** *vt person* snober; *offer* repousser. **to be ~bed** essuyer une rebuffade.

snub² [snʌb] *adj nose* retroussé. ◆ **snub-nosed** *adj* au nez retroussé.

snuff [snʌf] *n* tabac *m* à priser. **pinch of** ~ prise *f*; **to take** ~ priser. ◆ **snuffbox** *n* tabatière *f*.

snug [snʌg] *adj (cosy)* douillet, confortable; *(safe) harbour* bien abrité; *hideout* très sûr. **it's nice and ~ here** il fait bon ici; ~ **in bed** bien au chaud dans son lit. ◆ **snuggle** *vi* (**~gle down, ~gle up**) se blottir (*into sth* dans qch; *beside sb* contre qn). ◆ **snugly** *adv* douillettement, confortablement; **to fit ~ly** *[garment]* être bien ajusté; *[object in box etc]* rentrer juste bien.

so [səʊ] **1** *adv* (**a**) *(to such an extent)* si, tellement, aussi. ~ **tiring** si *or* tellement fatigant; **he was ~ clumsy that he...** il était si *or* tellement maladroit qu'il...; **the body was ~ burnt that it...** le cadavre était brûlé à un point tel qu'il...; **he ~ loves her that he...** il l'aime tant *or* tellement qu'il...; **~... as to** + *infin* assez... pour + *infin*; **he was ~ stupid as to tell her** il a été assez stupide pour le lui dire; **he was not ~ stupid as to say that to her** il n'a pas été bête au point de lui dire cela; **he is not ~ clever as his brother** il n'est pas aussi *or* si intelligent que son frère; **it's not ~ big as all that!** ce n'est pas si grand que ça!
(**b**) *(~ as to, ~ that)* ~ **as to do** pour faire; ~ **as not to be late** pour ne pas être en retard; ~ **that** *(purpose)* pour + *infin*, pour que + *subj*; *(result)* si bien que + *indic*; **I'm going early ~ that I'll get a ticket** j'y vais tôt pour obtenir un billet; **I brought it ~ that you could read it** je l'ai apporté pour que vous le lisiez; **he refused to move, ~ that the police had to carry him away** il a refusé de bouger, si bien que les agents ont dû l'emporter de force.
(**c**) *(very)* si, tellement. **I'm ~ tired!** je suis si *or* tellement fatigué!; ~ **very tired** vraiment si fatigué; ~ **much to do** tellement *or* tant de choses à faire.
(**d**) *(thus, in this way)* ainsi, comme ceci *or* cela. **you should stand just** ~ vous devriez vous tenir ainsi *or* comme ceci; **he likes everything to be just** ~ il aime que tout soit fait comme ça et pas autrement *; **as A is to B ~ C is to D** C est à D ce que A est à B; ~ **it was that...** c'est ainsi que...; *(frm)* ~ **be it** soit; **it ~ happened that** il s'est trouvé que.
(**e**) *(phrases)* ~ **saying...** sur ces mots...; ~ **I believe** c'est ce qu'il me semble; **is that ~?** vraiment?; **that is** ~ c'est exact; **if that is ~...** s'il en est ainsi...; **if** ~ si oui; **perhaps** ~ peut-être bien que oui; **just ~!, quite ~!** exactement!; **I told you ~ yesterday** je vous l'ai dit hier; **I told you ~!** je vous l'avais bien dit!; **he certainly said** ~ il l'a bien dit; **do** ~ faites-le; **I think** ~ je (le) crois, je (le) pense; **I hope** ~ *(answering)* j'espère que oui; *(agreeing)* je l'espère bien; **... only more ~** ... mais encore plus; **how ~?** comment?; **he said they would be there and ~ they were** il a dit qu'ils seraient là, et en effet ils y étaient; ~ **do I!, ~ have I!, ~ am I!** *etc* moi aussi!; ~ **he did!** (*or* ~ **it is!** *etc*) en effet!; **I didn't say that! — you did ~!** * je n'ai pas dit ça! — mais si tu l'as dit!; **20 or ~** à peu près 20, environ 20, une vingtaine; **and ~ on (and ~ forth)** et ainsi de suite; ~ **long!** * à bientôt!
2 *conj* donc, par conséquent; alors. **he was late, ~ he missed the train** il est arrivé en retard, donc *or* par conséquent il a manqué le train; ~ **there he is!** le voilà donc!; **the roads are busy, ~ be careful** il y a beaucoup de circulation, alors fais bien attention; ~ **you're selling it?** alors vous le vendez?; **and ~ you see...** alors comme vous voyez...; ~ **what?** * et alors?
◆ **so-and-so** *n*: **Mr S~-and-~** * Monsieur un tel; **Mrs S~-and-~** * Madame une telle; **he's an old ~-and-~** * c'est un vieil imbécile; **if you ask me to do ~-and-~** si vous me demandez de faire ci et ça. ◆ **so-called** *adj* soi-disant *inv*, prétendu. ◆ **so-so** * *adj* comme ci comme ça.

soak [səʊk] **1** *vt* (**a**) faire tremper (*in* dans). **to be ~ed through** être trempé; **to be/get ~ed to the skin** être trempé/se faire tremper jusqu'aux os; **bread ~ed in milk** pain *m* imbibé de lait. (**b**) (*‡: take money from) (by overcharging)* estamper ‡. *(by taxation)* **to ~ the rich** faire casquer * les riches. **2** *vi* tremper (*in* dans). **3** *n* (*‡: drunkard*) soûlard * *m*. ◆ **soak in** *vi [liquid]* pénétrer. *(fig)* **I told him what I thought and left it to ~ in** * je lui ai donné mon opinion et je l'ai laissé méditer dessus.

◆ **soak up** *vt sep (lit, fig)* absorber. ◆ **soaking (wet)** *adj* trempé.

soap [səʊp] **1** *n* (**a**) savon *m*. (**b**) *(TV)* feuilleton *m* mélo. **2** *vt* (~ **down**) savonner. ◆ **soapbox** *n* (**a**) *(lit)* caisse *f* à savon; *(fig: for speaker)* tribune *f* improvisée; ~**box orator** orateur *m* de carrefour; (**b**) *(go-cart)* auto *f* sans moteur. ◆ **soapdish** *n* porte-savon *m*. ◆ **soapflakes** *npl* paillettes *fpl* de savon. ◆ **soap-opera** *n* feuilleton *m* mélo. ◆ **soap-powder** *n* lessive *f*. ◆ **soapsuds** *npl (lather)* mousse *f* de savon; *(~y water)* eau *f* savonneuse. ◆ **soapy** *adj water* savonneux; *taste* de savon; *(* fig pej) person* doucereux.

soar [sɔːʳ] *vi (often ~* **up**) *[bird, aircraft, prices etc]* monter en flèche; *[ball etc]* voler (*over* par-dessus); *[tower]* s'élancer vers le ciel; *[ambitions, hopes]* grandir démesurément; *[spirits, morale]* remonter en flèche. ◆ **soaring** *adj* qui monte en flèche; élancé.

sob [sɒb] **1** *vi* sangloter. **2** *vt* dire en sanglotant. **3** *n* sanglot *m*. **4** *adj*: ~ **story** * histoire *f* à (vous) fendre le cœur; ~ **stuff** * mélo * *m*, sensiblerie *f*. ◆ **sobbing 1** *n* sanglots *mpl* ; **2** *adj* sanglotant.

sober ['səʊbəʳ] **1** *adj* (**a**) *(moderate) person* sérieux; *estimate, statement* modéré; *occasion* solennel; *suit, colour* sobre. **the ~ truth** la vérité toute simple; **the ~ fact of the matter** les faits tels qu'ils sont; **in a ~ mood** plein de gravité. (**b**) *(not drunk)* **I'm perfectly ~** je n'ai vraiment pas trop bu; **he's never ~** il est toujours ivre; **he is ~ now** il est désenivré maintenant; **to be as ~ as a judge, to be stone-cold ~** n'être absolument pas ivre. **2** *vt* (~ **up**) (**a**) *(calm)* calmer; *(deflate)* dégriser. (**b**) *(stop being drunk)* désenivrer. **3** *vi* (~**up**) *(calm down)* se calmer; *(grow sadder)* être dégrisé; *(stop being drunk)* désenivrer. *(fig)* **it had a ~ing effect on him** ça lui a donné à réfléchir. ◆ **soberly** *adv speak, say* avec modération; *behave, act* de façon posée; *furnish, dress* sobrement. ◆ **soberness** *or* ◆ **sobriety** *n* sérieux *m*; modération *f*; sobriété *f*.

soccer ['sɒkəʳ] **1** *n* football *m*, foot * *m*. **2** *adj match, pitch, team* de football, de foot *; *season* du football. ~ **player** footballeur *m*.

sociable ['səʊʃəbl] *adj person, animal* sociable; *evening, gathering* amical. **I'll have a drink just to be ~** je prendrai un verre rien que pour vous faire plaisir; **I'm not feeling very ~** je n'ai pas envie de voir des gens. ◆ **sociability** *n* sociabilité *f*. ◆ **sociably** *adv invite, say* amicalement.

social ['səʊʃ(ə)l] **1** *adj* (**a**) *behaviour, class, problems, customs, reforms* social. **a ~ outcast** un paria; ~ **administration** administration *f* sociale; ~ **anthropology** anthropologie *f* sociale; ~ **benefits** prestations *fpl* sociales; **S~ Democracy** social-démocratie *f*; **S~ Democrat** social-démocrate *mf*; *(US)* ~ **insurance** sécurité *f* sociale; ~ **science** sciences *fpl* humaines; ~ **scientist** spécialiste *mf* des sciences humaines; ~ **security** *(n)* aide *f* sociale; *(adj) benefits etc* de la sécurité sociale; **to be on ~ security** * recevoir l'aide sociale; **the ~ services** les services *mpl* sociaux; **Department of S~ Services** ministère *m* des Affaires sociales; ~ **studies** sciences sociales; ~ **welfare** sécurité sociale; ~ **work** assistance *f* sociale; ~ **worker** assistant(e) *m(f)* de service social, assistant(e) social(e). (**b**) *(in society) engagements, life* mondain. ~ **climber** *(still climbing)* arriviste *mf*; *(arrived)* parvenu(e) *m(f)*; *(Press)* ~ **column** carnet *m* mondain; **to be a ~ drinker** boire seulement en société; **a gay ~ life** une vie très mondaine; **we've got no ~ life** nous ne sortons jamais; **how's your ~ life?** * est-ce que tu sors beaucoup? (**c**) *(gregarious) person* sociable; *evening* agréable. ~ **club** association *f* amicale; ~ **mobility** mobilité sociale *f*; *(US)* **the ~ register** ≃ le bottin mondain. **2** *n* fête *f*.

◆ **socialism** *n* socialisme *m*. ◆ **socialist** *adj, n* socialiste *(mf)*. ◆ **socialite** *n* personnalité *f* en vue dans la haute société. ◆ **socialize 1** *vt (Pol, Psych)* socialiser ; **2** *vi (be with people)* fréquenter des gens; *(make friends)* se faire des amis; *(chat)* bavarder (*with sb* avec qn). ◆ **socially** *adv interact, be valid* socialement; *acceptable* en société; **I know him ~ly** nous nous rencontrons en société.

society [sə'saɪətɪ] **1** *n* (**a**) *(community)* société *f*. **to live in ~** vivre en société; **it is a danger to ~** cela met la société en danger. (**b**) *(high ~)* haute société *f*. **polite ~** la bonne société. (**c**) *(companionship)* compagnie *f*. **in the ~ of** en compagnie de; **I enjoy his ~** je me plais en sa compagnie. (**d**) *(association, group)* société *f*, association *f*; *(Scol, Univ etc)* club *m*, association. **dramatic ~** club théâtral, association théâtrale; **learned ~** société savante. **2** *adj photographer, wedding* mondain.

socio... ['səʊsɪəʊ] *pref* socio... ~ **economic** socio-économique.

sociology [ˌsəʊsɪ'ɒlədʒɪ] *n* sociologie *f*. ◆ **sociological** *adj* sociologique. ◆ **sociologist** *n* sociologue *mf*.

sock^{1} [sɒk] *n* chaussette *f*; *(shorter)* socquette *f*. *(fig)* **to pull up one's ~s** * se secouer *.

sock^{2} ⁑ [sɒk] *n*: **to give sb a ~ on the jaw** flanquer un coup sur la gueule ⁑ à qn.

socket ['sɒkɪt] *n (gen)* cavité *f (où qch s'emboîte)*; *[bone]* cavité articulaire; *[eye]* orbite *f*; *[tooth]* alvéole *f*; *(Elec: for light bulb)* douille *f*; *(Elec: also* **wall** *~)* prise *f* de courant *(femelle)*.

soda ['səʊdə] **1** *n* (**a**) *(Chem)* soude *f*; *(washing ~)* cristaux *mpl* de soude. (**b**) (~ **water**) eau *f* de Seltz. **whisky and ~** whisky *m* soda. (**c**) *(US: ~* **pop**) soda *m*. **2** *adj*: *(US)* ~ **cracker** biscuit *m* sec à la levure chimique; ~ **fountain** *(siphon)* siphon *m* d'eau de Seltz; *(place)* buvette; *(US)* ~ **jerk(er)** marchand(e) *m(f)* de soda et de glace; ~ **siphon** siphon *m* (d'eau de Seltz).

sodden ['sɒdn] *adj ground* détrempé; *clothes* trempé.

sodium ['səʊdɪəm] **1** *n* sodium *m*. **2** *adj*: ~ **bicarbonate** bicarbonate *m* de soude; ~ **light** lampe *f* à vapeur de sodium.

sofa ['səʊfə] *n* sofa *m*; canapé *m*.

Sofia ['səʊfɪə] *n* Sofia.

soft [sɒft] **1** *adj* (**a**) *(not hard etc) mattress, pillow* doux (*f* douce); *(unpleasantly so)* mou (*f* molle) ; *mud, snow, ground, collar, cheese* mou; *substance* malléable; *wood, stone, pencil* tendre; *butter, leather, brush, contact lenses* souple; *fabric, hand, skin* doux; *hair* soyeux; *toy* de peluche; *(pej: flabby) person, muscle* avachi. ~ **fruit** ≃ fruits *mpl* rouges; *(Comm)* ~ **furnishings** tissus *mpl* d'ameublement *(rideaux etc)*; *(Comm)* ~ **goods** textiles *mpl*; *(Anat)* ~ **palate** voile *m* du palais; **to grow** *or* **become ~(er) = soften 2**; **to make ~(er) = soften 1**; **this sort of life makes you ~** ce genre de vie vous ramollit; ~ **currency** devise *f* faible; ~ **drinks** boissons *fpl* non alcoolisées; ~ **drugs** drogues *fpl* douces; *(fig)* ~ **soap** * flagornerie *f*; **to be a ~ touch** * se faire avoir (facilement); ~ **toy** (jouet *m* en) peluche *f*; *(Aut)* ~ **verges** accotements *mpl* non stabilisés; ~ **water** eau *f* qui n'est pas calcaire. (**b**) *(not rough) tap, pressure* doux, léger; *breeze, rain, weather* doux; *(Aviat) landing* en douceur. (**c**) *(not harsh) look, smile* doux, gentil; *answer* aimable, gentil; *heart* tendre; *life, job, option* facile; *person* indulgent (*with or on sb* envers qn). **he has a ~ time of it** * il se la coule douce *, **to have a ~ spot for** avoir un faible pour; ~ **sell** promotion *f* de vente discrète. (**d**) *(not loud) sound, laugh* doux, léger; *tone, music, voice* doux; *steps* feutré. **in a ~ voice** d'une voix douce; **the radio is too ~** la radio ne joue pas assez fort; **the music is too ~** la musique n'est pas assez forte; ~ **pedal** pédale *f* douce. (**e**) *light, colour,*

(*Ling*) consonant doux. (*Phot*) ~ **focus** flou *m* artistique. (**f**) (**: stupid*) stupide. (**g**) (**: no stamina*) **he's** ~ il n'a pas de nerf. **2** *adv* doucement.
◆ **softback** *n (US)* = **softcover.** ◆ **soft-boiled egg** *n* œuf *m* à la coque. ◆ **softcover** *n* livre *m* broché. ◆ **soften (up) 1** *vt* (**a**) *(gen)* adoucir; *butter, clay, ground* ramollir; *collar, leather* assouplir; *outline* estomper; *resistance* amoindrir; *(fig)* **to ~en the blow** amortir le choc; (**b**) *person* attendrir; (**: by cajoling) customer etc* baratiner *; (**: by bullying)* intimider ; **2** *vi* s'adoucir; se ramollir; s'assouplir; s'estomper; **his heart ~ened** il s'est attendri; **his eyes ~ened** son regard s'est adouci. ◆ **softener** *n (water softener)* adoucisseur *m*; *(fabric softener)* produit *m* assouplissant. ◆ **soft-hearted** *adj* au cœur tendre. ◆ **softie** * *n (tender-hearted)* tendre *mf*; *(no stamina)* mauviette *f*; *(coward)* poule *f* mouillée. ◆ **softly** *adv (quietly) say, sing* doucement; *walk* à pas feutrés; *(gently) tap* légèrement; *(tenderly) smile, look* tendrement, gentiment. ◆ **softness** *n (gen)* douceur *f*; *[bed, mattress, pillow]* douceur, mollesse *f (pej)*; *[snow, ground, butter]* mollesse; *[substance]* malléabilité *f*; *[leather, brush, collar]* souplesse *f*; *[person, muscle]* avachissement *m*; *[outline, photograph]* flou *m*; *[words, glance]* douceur, gentillesse *f*; *[answer]* amabilité *f*, gentillesse; *(indulgence)* manque *m* de sévérité (*towards* envers). ◆ **softspoken** *adj* à la voix douce. ◆ **software** *n (Computers)* software *m*, logiciel *m*; **~ware package** progiciel *m*. ◆ **softwood** *n* bois *m* tendre.

soggy ['sɒgɪ] *adj ground* détrempé; *clothes* trempé; *bread* mal cuit; *heat, pudding* lourd.

soh [səʊ] *n (Mus)* sol *m*.

soil [sɔɪl] **1** *n* sol *m*, terre *f*. **rich/chalky** ~ sol *or* terre riche/calcaire; **cover it over with** ~ recouvre-le de terre; **on French** ~ sur le sol français. **2** *vt (dirty)* salir. **~ed linen** linge *m* sale. **3** *vi [material, garment]* se salir.

solar ['səʊləʳ] *adj (gen)* solaire; *heating* (à l'énergie) solaire. ~ **panel** panneau *m* solaire; ~ **plexus** plexus *m* solaire.

sold [səʊld] *pret, ptp of* **sell.**

solder ['səʊldəʳ] **1** *n* soudure *f*. **2** *vt* souder. **~ing iron** fer *m* à souder.

soldier ['səʊldʒəʳ] **1** *n* soldat *m*, militaire *m*. **woman** ~ femme *f* soldat; **to play at ~s** *(pej)* jouer à la guerre; *[children]* jouer aux soldats; **old** ~ vétéran *m*. **2** *vi* servir dans l'armée. *(fig)* **to ~ on** persévérer (malgré tout). ◆ **soldierly** *adj* typiquement militaire.

sole¹ [səʊl] *n, pl inv (fish)* sole *f*.

sole² [səʊl] **1** *n [shoe]* semelle *f*; *[foot]* plante *f*. **2** *vt* ressemeler.

sole³ [səʊl] *adj* (**a**) *(only)* seul, unique. **the ~ reason** la seule *or* l'unique raison. (**b**) *(exclusive) right* exclusif. *(Comm)* ~ **agent** concessionnaire *mf* (*for* de). ◆ **solely** *adv (only)* seulement, uniquement; *(entirely)* entièrement.

solecism ['sɒləsɪz(ə)m] *n (Ling)* solécisme *m*; *(social offence)* faute *f* de goût.

solemn ['sɒləm] *adj (gen)* solennel; *duty* sacré; *warning* plein de gravité. ◆ **solemnity** [sə'lemnɪtɪ] *n* solennité *f*; caractère *m* sacré; gravité *f*.
◆ **solemnization** *n [marriage]* célébration *f*.
◆ **solemnize** *vt* célébrer. ◆ **solemnly** *adv promise, utter* solennellement; *say, smile* gravement, d'un air solennel.

sol-fa ['sɒl'fɑː] *n* solfège *m*.

solicit [sə'lɪsɪt] **1** *vt* solliciter (*from* de). **2** *vi [prostitute]* racoler. ◆ **soliciting** *n* racolage *m*.

solicitor [sə'lɪsɪtəʳ] *n (Brit) (for wills etc)* ≃ notaire; *(in court cases)* ≃ avocat *m*; *(US)* ≃ juriste *m* conseil.

solicitous [sə'lɪsɪtəs] *adj (anxious)* préoccupé (*for, about* de); *(eager)* désireux (*of* de; *to do* de faire). ◆ **solicitude** *n* sollicitude *f*.

solid ['sɒlɪd] **1** *adj* (**a**) *(gen) substance, structure, reasons, character* solide; *ball, block, tyre* plein; *crowd* dense; *row, line* continu; *vote* unanime. **frozen** ~ complètement gelé; **to become** ~ se solidifier; ~ **geometry** géométrie *f* dans l'espace; **cut out of** ~ **rock** taillé à même la pierre; **in ~ gold/oak** en or/chêne massif; ~ **fuel** combustible *m* solide; **a ~ stretch of yellow** une étendue de jaune uni; **he was 6 ft 2 of ~ muscle** c'était un homme de 2 mètres de haut et tout en muscles; **on ~ ground** sur la terre ferme; *(in discussion etc)* en terrain sûr; ~ **common sense** solide bon sens *m*; **a good ~ worker** un travailleur sérieux; **he's a good ~ bloke** * c'est qn sur qui on peut compter; **the square was ~ with cars** * la place était complètement embouteillée; **packed** ~ *case* plein à craquer; *train* bondé; **Moordown is ~ for Labour** Moordown vote massivement pour les travaillistes; **a ~ hour** une heure entière; **2 ~ days** 2 jours d'affilée; **a ~ day's work** une journée entière de travail. (**b**) *(US: excellent)* au poil *.
2 *n (gen)* solide *m*. *(food)* **~s** aliments *mpl* solides.
◆ **solidarity** *n* solidarité *f*. ◆ **solidification** *n* solidification *f*. ◆ **solidify 1** *vt* solidifier ; **2** *vi* se solidifier. ◆ **solidity** *n* solidité *f*. ◆ **solidly** *adv build etc* solidement; *vote* massivement; **they are ~ly behind him** ils le soutiennent à l'unanimité.
◆ **solid-state** *adj (Phys)* des solides; *electronic device* à circuits intégrés.

soliloquy [sə'lɪləkwɪ] *n* soliloque *m*.

solitary ['sɒlɪt(ə)rɪ] *adj* (**a**) *(alone: gen)* solitaire; *hour* de solitude; *(lonely)* seul. *(Jur)* **in ~ confinement** au régime cellulaire; **to take a ~ walk** se promener tout seul. (**b**) *(only one)* seul, unique *(before n)*. **a ~ example** un seul *or* unique exemple; **not a ~ one** pas un seul. ◆ **solitude** *n* solitude *f*.

solo ['səʊləʊ] **1** *n (Mus)* solo *m*. **piano** ~ solo de piano. **2** *adv play, sing* en solo; *fly* en solitaire. **3** *adj violin etc* solo *inv*; *flight etc* en solitaire.
◆ **soloist** *n* soliste *mf*.

solstice ['sɒlstɪs] *n* solstice *m*.

soluble ['sɒljʊbl] *adj (all senses)* soluble. ◆ **solubility** *n* solubilité *f*.

solution [sə'luːʃ(ə)n] *n (all senses)* solution *f* (*to* de).

solve [sɒlv] *vt equation, problem* résoudre; *crossword puzzle* réussir; *mystery* éclaircir; *murder* élucider; *riddle* trouver la solution de.

solvent ['sɒlv(ə)nt] **1** *adj (Fin)* solvable; *(Chem)* dissolvant. **2** *n (Chem)* solvant *m*. ◆ **solvency** *n* solvabilité *f*.

Somalia [sə(ʊ)'mɑːlɪə] *n* Somalie *f*. ◆ **Somali 1** *adj* somali, somalien ; **2** *n* Somali(e) *m(f)*, Somalien(ne) *m(f)*.

sombre, *(US)* **somber** ['sɒmbəʳ] *adj* sombre.

some [sʌm] **1** *adj* (**a**) *(a certain amount or number of)* ~ **tea/ice/water/cakes** du thé/de la glace/de l'eau/des gâteaux; **there are ~ children outside** il y a des enfants *or* quelques enfants dehors; ~ **old shoes** de vieilles chaussures; ~ **dirty shoes** des chaussures sales; **will you have ~ more meat?** voulez-vous encore de la viande?
(**b**) *(unspecified)* ~ **woman was asking for her** il y avait une dame qui la demandait; **in ~ book or other** quelque part dans un livre; **at ~ place in Africa** quelque part en Afrique; ~ **day** un de ces jours, un jour ou l'autre; ~ **day next week** dans le courant de la semaine prochaine; ~ **other day** un autre jour; ~ **other time!** pas maintenant!; ~ **time last week** un jour la semaine dernière; ~ **more talented person** quelqu'un de plus doué; **there must be ~ solution** il doit bien y avoir une solution quelconque.

(**c**) *(contrasted with others)* ~ **children like school** certains enfants aiment l'école, il y a des enfants qui aiment l'école; ~ **people say that...** il y a des gens qui disent que...; **in ~ ways, he's right** dans un (certain) sens, il a raison; **in ~ way or (an)other** d'une façon ou d'une autre.
(**d**) *(a considerable amount of)* **it took ~ courage to refuse** il a fallu un certain courage *or* pas mal de * courage pour refuser; **at ~ length** assez longuement; ~ **distance away** à quelque distance ; **I haven't seen him for ~ years** cela fait quelques années que je ne l'ai pas vu; *V* **time.**
(**e**) *(emphatic: a little)* **we still have SOME money left** il nous reste quand même un peu d'argent; **that's SOME consolation** c'est quand même une petite consolation.
(**f**) *(intensive)* **that's ~ fish!** * quel poisson!; **that was ~ film!** * c'était un film formidable; *(iro)* **you're ~ help!** * tu parles * d'une aide!
2 *pron* (**a**) *(a certain number)* quelques-un(e)s *m(f)pl*, certain(e)s *m(f)pl*. ~ **went this way and others went that** il y en a qui sont partis par ici et d'autres par là; ~ **(of them) have been sold** certains (d'entre eux) ont été vendus, on en a vendu un certain nombre; **I've still got ~ of them** j'en ai encore quelques-uns; ~ **of my friends** certains *or* quelques-uns de mes amis; **I've got ~** j'en ai quelques-uns. (**b**) *(a certain amount)* **I've got ~** j'en ai; **have ~!** prenez-en!; **have ~ more** reprenez-en; **if you find ~** si vous en trouvez; **have ~ of this cake** prenez un peu de ce gâteau; ~ **(of it) has been eaten** on en a mangé (un morceau); ~ **of this work** une partie de ce travail; ~ **of what you said** certaines choses que vous avez dites.
3 *adv (about)* quelque, environ. ~ **twenty houses** quelque vingt maisons, une vingtaine de maisons.

somebody ['sʌmbədɪ] *pron* quelqu'un. **there is ~ at the door** il y a quelqu'un à la porte; **there is ~ knocking at the door** on frappe à la porte; ~ **else** quelqu'un d'autre; ~ **strong** quelqu'un de fort; ~ **French** un Français, quelqu'un de français; ~ **or other** quelqu'un, je ne sais qui; **Mr S~-or-other** Monsieur Machin *; **she thinks she's ~** elle se prend pour quelqu'un (d'important).

somehow ['sʌmhaʊ] *adv* (**a**) *(in some way)* **it must be done ~ (or other)** il faut que ce soit fait d'une façon ou d'une autre; **he managed it ~** il y est arrivé tant bien que mal; **we'll manage ~** on se débrouillera *; **we saved him ~ or other** nous l'avons sauvé je ne sais comment. (**b**) *(for some reason)* ~ **he's never succeeded** pour une raison ou pour une autre il n'a jamais réussi; **it seems odd ~** je ne sais pas pourquoi, mais ça semble bizarre.

someone ['sʌmwʌn] *pron* = **somebody.**

someplace ['sʌmpleɪs] *adv (US)* = **somewhere.**

somersault ['sʌməsɔ:lt] **1** *n (on ground; also accidental)* culbute *f*; *(by child)* galipette *f*; *(in air)* saut *m* périlleux; *(by car)* tonneau *m*. **2** *vi (also* **turn a ~***)* faire la culbute *or* un saut périlleux *or* un tonneau.

something ['sʌmθɪŋ] **1** *pron* quelque chose. ~ **moved** il y a quelque chose qui a bougé; ~ **has happened** quelque chose est arrivé; ~ **unusual** quelque chose d'inhabituel; **there must be ~ wrong** il doit y avoir quelque chose qui ne va pas; **did you say ~?** pardon?, comment?; **I want ~ to read** je veux quelque chose à lire; **would you like ~ to drink?** voulez-vous boire quelque chose?; **give him ~ to drink** donnez-lui quelque chose à boire; ~ **to live for** une raison de vivre; **I have ~ else to do** j'ai quelque chose d'autre à faire; ~ **or other** quelque chose; ~ **of the kind** quelque chose dans ce genre-là; **there's ~ about her I don't like** il y a chez elle quelque chose que je n'aime pas; **there's ~ in what you say** il y a du vrai dans ce que vous dites; **here's ~ for your trouble** voici pour votre peine; **give him ~ for himself** donnez-lui un petit quelque chose; **you've got ~ there!** * c'est vrai ce que tu dis là!; **that really is ~!** * c'est pas rien! *; **that certain ~** * **which makes all the difference** ce petit je ne sais quoi qui fait toute la différence; **he's called Paul ~** il s'appelle Paul quelque chose; **the 4-~ train** le train de 4 heures et quelques; **I hope to see ~ of you** j'espère vous voir un peu; **it is really ~** * **to find good coffee** ça n'est pas rien * de trouver du bon café; **that's ~!** * ça n'est pas rien! *; **that's always ~** c'est toujours ça; **or ~** ou quelque chose dans ce genre-là; **he is ~ of a miser** il est plutôt avare; **he is ~ of a pianist** il est assez bon pianiste.
2 *adv*: ~ **like 200** quelque chose comme 200; ~ **over £5,000** plus de 5 000 livres; ~ **under £10** un peu moins de 10 livres; ~ **like his father** un peu comme son père; **that's ~ like a claret!** ça au moins, c'est du bordeaux!; **that's ~ like it!** * ça au moins, c'est bien!; **it was ~ dreadful** * c'était vraiment épouvantable.

sometime ['sʌmtaɪm] **1** *adv*: ~ **last month** le mois dernier, au cours du mois dernier; **it was ~ last winter** c'était pendant l'hiver dernier (je ne sais plus exactement quand); **I'll do it ~** je le ferai un de ces jours; ~ **soon** bientôt; ~ **before January** d'ici janvier; ~ **next year** (dans le courant de) l'année prochaine; ~ **after my birthday** après mon anniversaire; ~ **or (an)other it will have to be done** il faudra bien le faire tôt ou tard. **2** *adj (former)* ancien *(before n)*; *(US: occasional)* intermittent.

sometimes ['sʌmtaɪmz] *adv* (**a**) quelquefois, parfois, de temps en temps. (**b**) ~ **happy,** ~ **sad** tantôt gai, tantôt triste.

somewhat ['sʌmwɒt] *adv* quelque peu.

somewhere ['sʌmwɛəʳ] *adv* (**a**) *(in space)* quelque part. ~ **else** autre part, ailleurs; **he's ~ about** il est quelque part par ici; ~ **near Paris** quelque part pas bien loin de Paris; ~ **or other** je ne sais où, quelque part; ~ **or other in France** quelque part en France. (**b**) *(approximately)* environ. ~ **about 10 o'clock** vers 10 heures, à 10 heures environ; ~ **about £12** environ 12 livres, dans les 12 livres.

somnambulism [sɒm'næmbjʊlɪz(ə)m] *n* somnambulisme *m*. ◆ **somnambulist** *n* somnambule *mf*.

somnolence ['sɒmnələns] *n* somnolence *f*. ◆ **somnolent** *adj* somnolent.

son [sʌn] *n* fils *m*. **come here, ~** * viens ici, mon gars *. ◆ **son-in-law** *n* gendre *m*, beau-fils *m*.

sonar ['səʊnɑ:ʳ] *n* sonar *m*.

sonata [sə'nɑ:tə] *n* sonate *f*.

song [sɒŋ] *n (gen)* chanson *f*; *(more formal)* chant *m*; *[birds]* chant. **to burst into ~** se mettre à chanter; **give us a ~** chante-nous qch; ~ **without words** romance *f* sans paroles; *(fig)* **it was going for a ~** c'était à vendre pour une bouchée de pain; **to make a ~ and dance** * faire toute une histoire * *(about* à propos de). ◆ **songbird** *n* oiseau *m* chanteur. ◆ **songbook** *n* recueil *m* de chansons. ◆ **song hit** *n* chanson *f* à succès, tube * *m*. ◆ **song-writer** *n* compositeur *m*, -trice *f* de chansons.

sonic ['sɒnɪk] *adj (gen)* sonique. ~ **depth-finder** sonde *f* à ultra-sons.

sonnet ['sɒnɪt] *n* sonnet *m*.

sonorous ['sɒnərəs] *adj* sonore. ◆ **sonority** *n* sonorité *f*. ◆ **sonorously** *adv* d'un ton sonore.

soon [su:n] *adv* (**a**) *(before long)* bientôt; *(quickly)* vite. **we shall ~ be in Paris** nous serons bientôt à Paris; **you would ~ get lost** vous seriez vite perdu; **he ~ changed his mind** il a vite changé d'avis; **see you ~!** à bientôt!; **very ~** très vite, très bientôt; **quite ~** dans assez peu de temps, assez vite; ~ **afterwards** peu après; **all too ~ it was over** ce ne fut que trop vite fini. (**b**) *(early)* tôt. **why have you come so ~?** pourquoi êtes-vous venu si tôt?; **much ~er than this** bien plus tôt que cela, bien avant; **how ~ can you get here?** dans combien de temps au plus tôt peux-tu être ici?; **how ~ will it be ready?** dans combien de temps est-ce que ce sera prêt? (**c**) *(in phrases)* **as ~ as possible** dès que possible, aussitôt que possible. **I'll do it as ~ as I can** je le ferai aussitôt que je le pourrai *or* aussitôt que possible; **let me know as ~ as you've finished** prévenez-moi dès que *or* aussitôt que vous aurez fini; **as ~ as 7 o'clock** dès 7 heures; **the ~er we get started the ~er we'll be done** plus tôt nous commencerons plus tôt nous aurons fini; **the ~er the better** le plus tôt sera le mieux; **~er or later** tôt ou tard; **no ~er had he finished than...** à peine avait-il fini que... (**d**) *(expressing preference)* **I'd as ~ do that** j'aimerais autant faire ça; **I'd ~er you didn't tell him** je préférerais que vous ne le lui disiez *(subj)* pas; **I would ~er stay here than go** je préférerais *or* j'aimerais mieux rester ici plutôt que d'y aller; **I'd ~er not, I'd as ~ not** je n'y tiens pas; **I'd ~er die!** plutôt mourir!; **~er you than me!** * je n'aimerais pas être à ta place.

soot [sʊt] *n* suie *f*. ◆ **sooty** *adj surface, hands* noir de suie.

soothe [su:ð] *vt person, nerves, pain* calmer; *anger, anxieties* apaiser. ◆ **soothing** *adj medicine, ointment* lénitif; *tone, voice, words* apaisant; *sb's presence* rassurant; *hot bath* relaxant. ◆ **soothingly** *adv* d'une manière apaisante; *say* d'un ton apaisant.

sop [sɒp] *n* (**a**) *(Culin)* **~s** aliments *mpl* semi-liquides; *(fig)* **as a ~ to his pride** pour flatter son amour-propre; **he said that as a ~ to the unions** il a dit cela pour amadouer les syndicats. (**b**) *(*: sissy)* poule *f* mouillée. ◆ **sop up** *vt sep [sponge, rag]* absorber; *[person]* éponger (*with* avec). ◆ **sopping (wet)** *adj* trempé. ◆ **soppy** * *adj* sentimental; *(sissy)* mollasson.

sophisticated [sə'fɪstɪkeɪtɪd] *adj person, mind, tastes* raffiné; *clothes, room* d'une élégance raffinée; *film, book, discussion* subtil; *song* plein de recherche; *machine, method* sophistiqué, hautement perfectionné. **he's not very ~** il est très simple. ◆ **sophistication** *n* raffinement *m*; élégance *f*; subtilité *f*; recherche *f*; sophistication *f*.

sophomore ['sɒfəmɔ:ʳ] *n (US)* étudiant(e) *m(f)* de seconde année.

soporific [ˌsɒpə'rɪfɪk] *adj* soporifique.

soprano [sə'prɑ:nəʊ] **1** *n* soprano *mf*. **2** *adj voice* de soprano.

sorbet ['sɔ:beɪ, 'sɔ:bɪt] *n* sorbet *m*.

sorcery ['sɔ:s(ə)rɪ] *n* sorcellerie *f*. ◆ **sorcerer** *n* sorcier *m*.

sordid ['sɔ:dɪd] *adj (gen)* sordide; *agreement, deal, film, book* ignoble.

sore [sɔ:ʳ] **1** *adj* (**a**) *(painful)* douloureux; *(inflamed)* irrité, enflammé. **that's ~!** ça me fait mal!; **where is it ~?** où est-ce que vous avez mal?; **I'm ~ all over** j'ai mal partout; **I have a ~ finger** j'ai mal au doigt; *(fig)* **a ~ point** un point délicat. (**b**) *(*: offended)* en rogne * (*about* à cause de; *with sb* contre qn). **he was feeling very ~ about it** il en était vraiment ulcéré; **to get ~** râler *, être en rogne *. **2** *n (Med)* plaie *f*. *(fig)* **to open up an old ~** rouvrir une ancienne blessure. ◆ **sorely** *adv wounded* grièvement; *missed, regretted* amèrement; *tempted* fortement; **it is ~ly needed** on en a grandement besoin. ◆ **soreness** *n (painfulness)* endolorissement *m*; *(irritation)* irritation *f*; *(*: anger)* colère *f*, rogne * *f*.

sorrel ['sɒr(ə)l] *n (Bot)* oseille *f*; *(horse)* alezan *m* clair.

sorrow ['sɒrəʊ] **1** *n* peine *f*, chagrin *m*, tristesse *f*; *(stronger)* douleur *f*. **his ~ at the loss of his son** la douleur qu'il a éprouvée à la mort de son fils; **this was a great ~ to me** j'en ai eu beaucoup de peine *or* de chagrin; **more in ~ than in anger** avec plus de peine que de colère. **2** *vi*: **to ~ over sth** pleurer qch. ◆ **sorrowful** *adj person* triste; *(stronger)* affligé. ◆ **sorrowfully** *adv* tristement. ◆ **sorrowing** *adj* affligé.

sorry ['sɒrɪ] *adj* (**a**) *(regretful)* désolé. **I was ~ to hear of your accident** j'étais désolé d'apprendre que vous avez eu un accident; **I am ~ I cannot come/ she cannot come** je regrette *or* je suis désolé de ne pas pouvoir venir/qu'elle ne puisse pas venir; **I am ~ to tell you that...** je regrette de vous dire que...; **he didn't pass, I'm ~ to say** il a échoué, malheureusement; **I am ~ I am late** excusez-moi d'être en retard; **say you're ~** demande pardon; **~!, ~ about that!** * pardon!, excusez-moi!; **I'm very** *or* **terribly ~** je suis vraiment désolé *or* navré; **I'm ~, but you're wrong** je regrette, mais vous avez tort; **~ about that vase** excusez-moi pour ce vase; **you'll be ~ for this** vous le regretterez. (**b**) *(pitying)* **to be** *or* **feel ~ for sb** plaindre qn, être désolé pour qn; **I feel so ~ for her** elle me fait pitié; **to be** *or* **feel ~ for o.s.** s'apitoyer sur son propre sort; **he looked very ~ for himself** il faisait piteuse mine. (**c**) *(woeful) condition, tale* triste, lamentable; *excuse* piètre *(before n)*, lamentable; *sight* désolant, affligeant. **in a ~ state** en piteux état.

sort [sɔ:t] **1** *n (gen)* genre *m*, espèce *f*, sorte *f*; *(make) [car, machine, coffee etc]* marque *f*. **this ~ of thing** ce genre de chose; **what ~ do you want?** vous en voulez de quelle sorte?; **what ~ of man is he?** quel genre d'homme est-ce?; **what ~ of dog is he?** qu'est-ce que c'est comme chien?; **he is not the ~ of man to refuse** ce n'est pas le genre d'homme à refuser; **he's the ~ that will cheat** il est du genre à tricher; **he's not that ~ of person** ce n'est pas son genre; **that's the ~ of person I am** c'est comme ça que je suis; **what ~ of an answer do you call that?** vous appelez ça une réponse?; **and all that ~ of thing** et tout ça *; **you know the ~ of thing I mean** vous voyez ce que je veux dire; **that ~ of behaviour** ce genre de conduite; **they're not our ~** * ce ne sont pas des gens comme nous; **it's my ~ * of film** c'est le genre de film que j'aime; **sth of the ~** qch de ce genre (-là); **nothing of the ~!** pas le moins du monde!; *(pej)* **beef of a ~** qch qui peut passer pour du bœuf; **a painter of ~s** un peintre si l'on peut dire; **after a ~, in some ~** en quelque sorte; **to be out of ~s** ne pas être dans son assiette; *(fig)* **a good ~** * un brave type *, une brave fille; **there was a ~ of box** il y avait une sorte *or* une espèce de boîte, il y avait qch qui ressemblait à une boîte; **I was ~ of * frightened that...** j'avais un peu peur que... + ne + *subj*; **it's ~ of * blue** c'est plutôt bleu.

2 *vt* (**a**) **(~ out)** *(classify) documents, stamps* classer ; *(select those to keep) documents, clothes etc* trier (*according to* selon); *(separate)* séparer (*from* de). (**b**) *(Post: letters etc; Comput: data, files)* trier. ◆ **sort out** *vt sep* (**a**) = **sort 2.** (**b**) *(tidy) papers, clothes* ranger; *ideas* mettre de l'ordre dans; *(solve) problem* régler; *difficulties* venir à bout de; *(fix, arrange)* arranger. **can you ~ this out?** est-ce que vous pourriez régler *or* arranger ça?; **we've got it all ~ed out now** nous avons réglé *or* résolu la question; **things will ~ themselves out** les choses vont s'arranger d'elles-mêmes; **I couldn't ~ out what had happened** je n'ai pas pu comprendre ce qui s'était passé; **did you ~ out with him when you had to be there?** est-ce que tu as décidé *or* fixé avec lui l'heure à laquelle tu dois y être?; **to ~ sb out** * *(by threatening etc)* régler son compte à qn *; *(get* *him out of difficulty etc)* tirer qn d'affaire. ◆ **sort code** *n* numéro *m* d'agence. ◆ **sorter** *n (person)* trieur *m*, -euse *f*; *(machine)* trieur *m*. ◆ **sorting-office** *n* bureau *m* de tri.

sortie ['sɔːtɪ] *n (Aviat, Mil)* sortie *f*.

S.O.S. [ˌesəʊ'es] *n (signal)* S.O.S. *m; (fig)* S.O.S. appel *m* au secours.

soufflé ['suːfleɪ] *n* soufflé *m*. **cheese ~** soufflé au fromage; **~ dish** moule *m* à soufflé.

sought [sɔːt] *pret, ptp of* **seek.**

soul [səʊl] **1** *n* (**a**) âme *f*. **with all one's ~** de toute son âme; **All S~s' Day** le jour des Morts ; **he cannot call his ~ his own** il est complètement dominé; **the ~ of discretion** la discrétion même. (**b**) *(person)* âme *f*, personne *f*. **the ship sank with all ~s** le bateau a péri corps et biens; **I didn't see a (single** *or* **living) ~** je n'ai pas vu âme qui vive ; **you poor ~!** mon (*or* ma) pauvre!; **he's a good ~** c'est une excellente personne. **2** *adj* (**a**) **~ mate** âme *f* sœur. (**b**) *(US: of black Americans) (gen)* noir, des Noirs; *hotel etc* où l'on ne pratique pas la discrimination; *radio* émettant pour un public noir. **~ brother/ sister** frère *m*/sœur *f* de race *(termes employés par les Noirs entre eux)*; **~ music** soul music *f*. ◆ **soul-destroying** *adj (boring)* abrutissant; *(depressing)* démoralisant. ◆ **soulful** *adj expression, music* attendrissant; *eyes, glance* expressif. ◆ **soulfully** *adv* de façon attendrissante; d'un air expressif. ◆ **soulless** *adj person* sans cœur; *task* abrutissant. ◆ **soul-searching** *n*: **after a lot of ~-searching he...** après avoir bien fait son examen de conscience il...

sound[1] [saʊnd] **1** *n (gen)* son *m*; *[sea, breaking glass, car brakes etc]* bruit *m*. **the speed of ~** la vitesse du son; **within ~ of** à portée du son de; **to the ~ of the national anthem** au son de l'hymne national; **there was not a ~ to be heard** on n'entendait pas le moindre bruit; **without a ~** sans bruit; **we heard the ~ of voices** nous avons entendu un bruit de voix; **the Glenn Miller ~** la musique de Glenn Miller; *(fig)* **I don't like the ~ of it** *(it doesn't attract me)* ça ne me dit rien; *(it's worrying)* ça m'inquiète. **2** *adj film, recording* sonore. **~ archives** phonothèque *f*; **~ barrier** mur *m* du son; *(Rad etc)* **~ effects** bruitage *m*; *(Cine, Rad etc)* **~ engineer** ingénieur *m* du son; *(Cine etc)* **~ stage** salle *f* de tournage; *(Cine)* **~ track** bande *f* sonore; **~ wave** onde *f* sonore.
3 *vi* (**a**) *[bell, trumpet, voice]* sonner, retentir; *[car horn, siren, signal, order]* retentir. **footsteps/a gun ~ed a long way off** on entendit un bruit de pas/ un coup de canon dans le lointain; **it ~s better if you read it slowly** ça sonne mieux si vous le lisez lentement. (**b**) **that ~s like a flute** on dirait le son de la flûte; **it ~s empty** on dirait que c'est vide; **a language which ~ed like Dutch** une langue qui semblait être du hollandais; **he ~s like an Australian** à l'entendre parler on dirait un Australien; **it ~ed as if sb were coming in** on aurait dit que qn entrait; **that ~s like Paul arriving** ça doit être Paul qui arrive; **she ~s tired** elle semble fatiguée; **you ~ like your mother** tu me rappelles ta mère. (**c**) *(seem)* **how does it ~ to you?** qu'en penses-tu?; **it ~s like a good idea** ça a l'air d'être une bonne idée, ça semble être une bonne idée; **it doesn't ~ too good** ce n'est pas très prometteur; **it ~s as if she'll come** il semble qu'elle viendra; **it ~s as if she isn't coming** j'ai l'impression qu'elle ne viendra pas.
4 *vt* (**a**) *bell, alarm, (Mil) retreat* sonner; *trumpet, bugle* sonner de. *(Aut)* **to ~ one's horn** klaxonner; *(fig)* **to ~ a note of warning** lancer un avertissement. (**b**) *(Ling) a letter* prononcer. (**c**) *(Med)* **to ~ sb's chest** ausculter qn.
◆ **sound off** ‡ *vi (proclaim one's opinions)* faire de grands discours (*about* sur); *(boast)* se vanter (*about* de); *(grumble)* râler * (*about* à propos de).
◆ **soundless** *adj* silencieux. ◆ **soundlessly** *adv* sans bruit, en silence. ◆ **soundproof** **1** *vt* insonoriser ; **2** *adj* insonorisé. ◆ **soundproofing** *n* insonorisation *f*.

sound[2] [saʊnd] **1** *adj (gen)* sain; *heart, bank, organization* solide; *structure, bridge* en bon état; *alliance, investment* sûr, sans danger; *sleep* profond; *(sensible) reasoning, judgment* juste; *doctrine, argument, case, training* solide; *decision, opinion, policy, behaviour* sensé, valable; *claim* valable; *statesman, player, worker etc* compétent. **of ~ mind** sain d'esprit; **to be ~ in wind and limb** avoir bon pied bon œil; **as ~ as a bell** en parfait état; **he is a ~ socialist** c'est un bon socialiste; **he is ~ enough on theory** il connaît très bien la théorie; **he is a ~ chap** il est très sérieux; **~ sense** bon sens *m*; **that was a ~ move** c'était une action judicieuse *or* sensée; **a ~ thrashing** une bonne correction; **he is a ~ sleeper** il dort bien. **2** *adv*: **to be ~ asleep** être profondément endormi. ◆ **soundly** *adv sleep* profondément; *advise, reason, argue* de façon sensée, avec justesse; *organize, manage, invest* bien; *(Sport) play* de façon compétente; **he was ~ly beaten** *(defeated)* il a été battu à plates coutures; *(thrashed)* il a reçu une bonne correction. ◆ **soundness** *n [body, mind]* santé *f*; *[business, argument]* solidité *f*; *(solvency)* solvabilité *f*; *[judgment]* justesse *f*.

sound[3] [saʊnd] *vt (gen, Med, Naut etc)* sonder; *(fig:* **~ out***) person* sonder (*on, about* sur). ◆ **sounding** *n (Naut etc)* sondage *m*. ◆ **sounding line** *n* ligne *f* de sonde.

soup [suːp] **1** *n* soupe *f*; *(thinner or sieved)* potage *m*; *(very smooth)* velouté *m*. *(fig)* **to be in the ~** * être dans le pétrin *. **2** *adj*: **~ cube** potage *m* en cube; *(stock cube)* cube *m* de bouillon; **~ plate/ spoon** assiette *f*/cuiller *f* à soupe; **~ tureen** soupière *f*. ◆ **souped-up** * *adj* au moteur gonflé *. ◆ **soupy** *adj liquid, fog* épais.

sour ['saʊəʳ] **1** *adj (gen)* aigre; *fruit, juice* acide; *milk* tourné; *(fig) person, voice, remark* acerbe, aigre; *face* revêche. **whisky ~** cocktail *m* de whisky au citron; **~(ed) cream** ≃ crème *f* aigre; **to turn ~** *[milk]* tourner; *[relationship]* tourner au vinaigre; *[plans]* mal tourner; **in a ~ mood** d'humeur revêche; *(fig)* **it was clearly ~ grapes on his part** il l'a manifestement fait (*or* dit *etc*) par dépit. **2** *vt* aigrir.
◆ **sourdough** *n (US)* levain *m*. ◆ **sour-faced** *adj* à la mine revêche. ◆ **sourly** *adv* avec aigreur. ◆ **sourness** *n* aigreur *f*; acidité *f*; humeur *f* *or* ton *m* revêche.

source [sɔːs] *n (gen)* source *f*. *(Med)* **a ~ of infection** un foyer d'infection; **what is the ~ of this information?** quelle est la provenance de cette nouvelle?; **I have it from a reliable ~ that...** je tiens de source sûre que...; **at ~** à la source.

souse [saʊs] *vt (immerse)* tremper (*in* dans); *(soak)* faire tremper (*in* dans); *(Culin)* mariner. **to ~ sth with water** inonder qch d'eau.

south [saʊθ] **1** *n* sud *m*. **to the ~ of** au sud de; **in the ~ of Scotland** dans le sud de l'Écosse; **the wind is in the ~/from the ~** le vent est au sud/ vient du sud; **the S~ of France** le Sud de la France, le Midi.
2 *adj (gen)* sud *inv*; *coast, door* sud, méridional; *wind* du sud. **the ~ Atlantic** l'Atlantique *m* Sud; **S~ Africa** Afrique *f* du Sud; **S~ African** *(adj)* sud-africain; *(n)* Sud-Africain(e) *m(f)*; **S~ America** Amérique *f* du Sud; **S~ American** *(adj)* sud-américain; *(n)* Sud-Américain(e) *m(f)*; **S~ Sea Islands** Océanie *f*; **the S~ Seas** les Mers *fpl* du Sud.
3 *adv go* au sud, vers le sud; *be, lie* au sud, dans le sud. **~ of the border** au sud de la frontière; **to go ~** aller en direction du sud *or* du midi; **to sail due ~** aller droit vers le sud; *(Naut)* avoir le cap au sud.

◆ **southbound** *adj traffic* en direction du sud; *carriageway* sud *inv*. ◆ **south-east** **1** *adj, n* sud-est *(m) inv*; **S~-East Asia** le Sud-Est asiatique ; **2** *adv* vers le sud-est. ◆ **south-eastern** *adj* sud-est *inv*. ◆ **southerly** ['sʌðəlɪ] *adj wind* du sud; *situation, aspect* au sud, au midi; **in a ~erly direction** vers le sud *or* le midi. ◆ **southern** ['sʌðən] *adj region* sud *inv*, du sud; *wall, side* exposé au sud; *coast* sud, méridional; **S~ern Africa** Afrique *f* australe; **~ern France** le Sud de la France, le Midi; **in ~ern Spain** dans le Sud de l'Espagne. ◆ **southerner** ['sʌðənəʳ] *n* homme *m or* femme *f* du Sud; *(in France)* Méridional(e) *m(f)*. ◆ **southernmost** ['sʌðənməʊst] *adj* le plus au sud. ◆ **south-south-east** **1** *adj, n* sud-sud-est *(m) inv* ; **2** *adv* vers le sud-sud-est. ◆ **southward** **1** *adj* au sud ; **2** *adv (also* **~wards***)* vers le sud. ◆ **south-west** **1** *adj, n* sud-ouest *(m) inv* ; **2** *adv* vers le sud-ouest. ◆ **south-western** *adj* sud-ouest *inv*.

souvenir [ˌsuːv(ə)ˈnɪəʳ] *n* souvenir *m (objet)*.

sovereign ['sɒvrɪn] **1** *n* souverain(e) *m(f)*. **2** *adj power, state, remedy* souverain *(after n)*; *rights* de souveraineté; *(fig) contempt* souverain *(before n)*. ◆ **sovereignty** *n* souveraineté *f*.

soviet ['səʊvɪət] **1** *n* soviet *m*. **2** *adj* soviétique. **S~ Russia** Russie *f* soviétique; **the S~ Union** l'Union *f* soviétique.

sow¹ [saʊ] *n (pig)* truie *f*.

sow² [səʊ] *pret* **sowed**, *ptp* **sown** *or* **sowed** *vt seed, grass, (fig) doubt* semer; *field* ensemencer (*with* en). ◆ **sower** *n (person)* semeur *m*, -euse *f*; *(machine)* semoir *m*. ◆ **sowing** *n* semailles *fpl*.

soy [sɔɪ] *or* **soya** ['sɔɪə] *n* **(~ bean)** graine *f* de soja. **~ flour** farine *f* de soja.

spa [spɑː] *n* station *f* thermale. *(US)* **(health)** ~ établissement *m* de cure de rajeunissement.

space [speɪs] **1** *n* (**a**) *(gen, Phys etc)* espace *m*. **the rocket vanished into ~** la fusée a disparu dans l'espace; **to stare into ~** regarder dans le vide. (**b**) *(room)* espace *m*, place *f*. **to clear a ~ for sth** faire de la place pour qch; **to take up a lot of ~** *[car, books, piece of furniture]* prendre beaucoup de place; *[building]* occuper un grand espace; **there isn't enough ~ for it** il n'y a pas assez de place pour ça; **to buy ~ in a newspaper** acheter de l'espace dans un journal. (**c**) *(gap between objects, words etc)* espace *m*; *(Mus)* interligne *m*. **leave a ~ for the name** laissez de la place *or* un espace pour le nom; **in the ~ provided** dans la partie réservée à cet effet; **in an enclosed ~** dans un espace clos; **I'm looking for a ~ to park the car** je cherche une place pour me garer. (**d**) *(interval)* **after a ~ of 10 minutes** après un intervalle de 10 minutes; **for the ~ of a month** pendant une période d'un mois; **a ~ of 5 years** une période de 5 ans; **in the ~ of 3 generations/one hour** en l'espace de 3 générations/d'une heure; **a short ~ of time** un court laps de temps; **for a ~** pendant un certain temps.
2 *adj research, age, capsule, laboratory* spatial. *[typewriter]* **~ bar** barre *f* d'espacement; **~ fiction** science-fiction *f*; **~ flight** *(act of flying in space)* voyages *mpl* spatiaux; *(journey)* voyage spatial *or* dans l'espace; **~ heater** radiateur *m*; **~ station** station *f* spatiale.
3 *vt* **(~ out)** *(gen)* espacer; *payments* échelonner (*over* sur).
◆ **space-age** *adj* de l'ère spatiale. ◆ **spacecraft** *or* ◆ **spaceship** *n* engin spatial. ◆ **spaceman** *n* astronaute *m*, cosmonaute *m*. ◆ **space-saving** *adj* qui gagne de la place. ◆ **spacesuit** *n* scaphandre *m* de cosmonaute. ◆ **spacing** *n* espacement *m (also Typ)*; échelonnement *m*; *(Typ)* **in single/double spacing** avec un interligne simple/double. ◆ **spacious** *adj room, car* spacieux, grand; *garden* grand; *garment* ample. ◆ **spaciousness** *n* grandes dimensions *fpl*.

spade [speɪd] *n* (**a**) bêche *f*, pelle *f*; *(child's)* pelle. *(fig)* **to call a ~ a ~** appeler un chat un chat, ne pas avoir peur des mots. (**b**) *(Cards)* pique *m*. **to play ~s** jouer pique; **one ~** un pique; **he played a ~** il a joué pique; **the six of ~s** le six de pique; *(US fig)* **in ~** * par excellence. ◆ **spadeful** *n* pelletée *f*. ◆ **spadework** *n (fig)* gros *m* du travail.

spaghetti [spəˈgetɪ] **1** *n* spaghetti *mpl*. **2** *adj (Aut)* **~ junction** échangeur *m* à niveaux multiples.

Spain [speɪn] *n* Espagne *f*.

span [spæn] **1** *n [hands, arms]* envergure *f*; *[bridge]* travée *f*; *[arch, roof]* portée *f*; *[plane, bird]* **(wing ~)** envergure. **the average ~ of life** la durée moyenne de vie; **for a brief ~ of time** pendant un court espace de temps. **2** *vt [bridge etc]* enjamber, franchir. *(fig)* **it ~s almost two thousand years** cela embrasse presque deux mille ans.

Spaniard ['spænjəd] *n* Espagnol(e) *m(f)*.

spaniel ['spænjəl] *n* épagneul *m*.

Spanish ['spænɪʃ] **1** *adj (gen)* espagnol; *king, embassy, onion* d'Espagne; *teacher* d'espagnol; *(Culin) omelette, rice* à l'espagnole. **~ America** les pays *mpl* d'Amérique du Sud de langue espagnole. **2** *n* espagnol *m*. *(people)* **the ~** les Espagnols *mpl*.

spank [spæŋk] *vt* donner une fessée à. ◆ **spanking** *n* fessée *f*.

spanner ['spænəʳ] *n* clef *f* (à écrous). *(fig)* **to put a ~ in the works** mettre des bâtons dans les roues.

spar¹ [spɑːʳ] *n (Naut)* espar *m*.

spar² [spɑːʳ] *vi (Boxing)* s'entraîner (*with* avec); *(argue)* se disputer (*with* avec). ◆ **sparring partner** *n* sparring-partner *m*.

spare [spɛəʳ] **1** *adj (reserve)* de réserve, de rechange; *(surplus)* en trop, dont on n'a pas besoin. **take a ~ pen** prends un stylo de réserve *or* de rechange; **there are 2 going ~** il y en a 2 en trop *or* dont on n'a pas besoin; **2 ~ seats for the film** 2 places disponibles pour le film; **~ bed/room** lit *m*/chambre *f* d'ami; **~ cash** *(small amount)* argent *m* en trop; *(larger)* argent disponible; **I have very little ~ time** j'ai très peu de temps libre; **in my ~ time** pendant mes moments de loisir; **~-time activities** loisirs *mpl*; *(Tech)* **~ part** pièce *f* de rechange *or* détachée; *(Aut)* **~ tyre** pneu *m* de rechange; **~ wheel** roue *f* de secours.
2 *vt* (**a**) *(do without)* se passer de. **can you ~ it?** pouvez-vous vous en passer?, vous n'en avez pas besoin?; **can you ~ £10?** est-ce que tu as 10 livres en trop?, **can you ~ me £5?** est-ce que tu peux me passer 5 livres?; **I've only a few minutes to ~** je ne dispose que de quelques minutes; **I can ~ you 5 minutes** je peux vous accorder 5 minutes; **I can't ~ the time to do it** je n'ai pas le temps de le faire; **he had time to ~** il avait du temps devant lui; **to ~ a thought for** penser à; **I've got none to ~** j'en ai juste ce qu'il me faut; **I've enough and to ~** j'en ai plus qu'il ne m'en faut; **with 2 minutes to ~** avec 2 minutes d'avance; **we did it with £5 to ~** nous l'avons fait et il nous reste encore 5 livres. (**b**) *(show mercy to) person, life, tree etc* épargner. **if I'm ~d** * si Dieu me prête vie; **to ~ sb's feelings** ménager les sentiments de qn; **he doesn't ~ himself** il ne se ménage pas. (**c**) *suffering, embarrassment* épargner (*to sb* à qn). **you could have ~d yourself the trouble, you could have ~d your pains** vous vous êtes donné du mal pour rien, vous auriez pu vous épargner tout ce mal; **I'll ~ you the details** je vous fais grâce des détails. (**d**) *(refrain from using etc) one's strength, efforts* ménager. **he ~d no expense to do it** il a dépensé sans compter pour le faire; **'no expense ~d'** 'sans considération de frais'.
◆ **sparerib** *n* travers *m* de porc. ◆ **sparing** *adj amount, use* modéré; **sparing of praise** avare de compliments. ◆ **sparingly** *adv eat, live* frugalement; *spend, drink, praise, use* avec modération.

spark [spɑːk] **1** *n (gen)* étincelle *f (also Elec)*; *[common sense, interest]* lueur *f*. *(fig)* **to make the ~s fly** mettre le feu aux poudres. **2** *vi* jeter des étincelles. **3** *vt* **(~ off)** *rebellion, complaints, quarrel* déclencher; *interest, enthusiasm* susciter (*in sb* chez qn). ◆ **spark(ing) plug** *n (Aut)* bougie *f*.

sparkle [ˈspɑːkl] **1** *vi (gen)* étinceler; *[surface of water, lake, diamond etc]* scintiller; *[wine]* pétiller; *[person]* briller; *[conversation, play, eyes]* pétiller (*with* de), être étincelant. **2** *n* étincellement *m*; scintillement *m*; *(fig)* éclat *m*. ◆ **sparkling** *adj* étincelant (*with* de); scintillant; pétillant (*with* de); brillant.

sparrow [ˈspærəʊ] *n* moineau *m*. ◆ **sparrowhawk** *n* épervier *m*.

sparse [spɑːs] *adj* clairsemé. ◆ **sparsely** *adv wooded, furnished, populated* peu.

spartan [ˈspɑːt(ə)n] *adj* spartiate.

spasm [ˈspæz(ə)m] *n* spasme *m*; *[coughing, activity etc]* accès *m* (*of* de). ◆ **spasmodic** *adj work, attempt* intermittent. ◆ **spasmodically** *adv work, try* par à-coups.

spastic [ˈspæstɪk] **1** *adj movement, colon, paralysis* spasmodique; *child etc* handicapé moteur. **2** *n (Med)* handicapé(e) *m(f)* moteur.

spat [spæt] *pret, ptp of* **spit¹**.

spate [speɪt] *n (fig) [letters, orders etc]* avalanche *f*; *[words, abuse]* torrent *m; [bombings]* série *f*. *[river]* **in ~** en crue; **to have a ~ of work** être débordé de travail; **a fresh ~ of attacks** une recrudescence d'attaques.

spatial [ˈspeɪʃ(ə)l] *adj* spatial.

spatter [ˈspætəʳ] *vt*: **to ~ mud on sth, to ~ sth with mud** *(accidentally)* éclabousser *or (deliberately)* asperger qch de boue.

spatula [ˈspætjʊlə] *n (Culin)* spatule *f; (Med)* abaisse-langue *m inv*.

spawn [spɔːn] **1** *n [fish, frog]* frai *m*, œufs *mpl*; *[mushroom]* blanc *m*. **2** *vt (fig pej)* engendrer. **3** *vi [fish]* frayer.

spay [speɪ] *vt* châtrer.

speak [spiːk] *pret* **spoke,** *ptp* **spoken** **1** *vi* parler (*to* à; *of, about, on* de; *with* avec). **to ~ in a whisper** chuchoter; **to ~ to o.s.** parler tout seul; **I don't know him to ~ to** je ne le connais pas assez bien pour lui parler; **I'll never ~ to him again** je ne lui adresserai plus jamais la parole; **you have only to ~** tu n'as qu'un mot à dire; **so to ~** pour ainsi dire; **biologically ~ing** biologiquement parlant; **~ing personally** personnellement; **~ing as a member of the society I...** en tant que membre de la société je...; *(Telec)* **who's ~ing?** qui est à l'appareil?; *(passing on call)* c'est de la part de qui? ; **this is Paul ~ing** c'est Paul à l'appareil; **~ing!** lui- *or* elle-même!; *(Parl)* **to ~ in the House** faire un discours à l'Assemblée; **to ~ in a debate** *[proposer, seconder]* prendre la parole au cours d'un débat; *(from floor of house)* participer à un débat; **~ for yourself!** * parle pour toi! *; **let him ~ for himself** laisse-le dire lui-même ce qu'il a à dire; **it ~s for itself** c'est évident; **the facts ~ for themselves** les faits parlent d'eux-mêmes; **that is already spoken for** c'est déjà retenu; **he is very well spoken of** on dit beaucoup de bien de lui; **~ing of holidays** à propos de vacances; **he has no money to ~ of** il n'a pour ainsi dire pas d'argent; **it's nothing to ~ of** ce n'est pas grand-chose.
2 *vt language* parler; *a poem, one's lines, the truth* dire. **'English spoken'** 'ici on parle anglais'; **French is spoken everywhere** le français se parle partout; **to ~ one's mind** dire ce que l'on pense; **I didn't ~ a word** je n'ai rien dit.
3 *n ending in cpds, e.g.* **computer speak** langage *or* jargon de l'informatique.
◆ **speak out, speak up** *vi (fig)* **he's not afraid to ~ out** il n'a pas peur de dire ce qu'il pense; **to ~ out for sb** parler en faveur de qn; **to ~ out against sth** s'élever contre qch.
◆ **speaker** *n* **(a)** *(gen)* celui (*or* celle) qui parle; *(in dialogue)* interlocuteur *m*, -trice *f*; *(in public)* orateur *m*, -trice *f*; *(lecturer)* conférencier *m*, -ière *f*; **he's a good/poor ~er** il parle bien/mal; **the previous ~er** la personne qui a parlé la dernière; *(Parl)* **the S~er** le Speaker *(Président de la Chambre des Communes en G.B. ou de la Chambre des Représentants aux E.-U.)*. **(b)** **French ~er** personne *f* qui parle français; *(as native or official language)* francophone *mf*; **he is not a Welsh ~er** il ne parle pas gallois; **(c)** *(loudspeaker)* haut-parleur *m*. ◆ **speaking** **1** *adj doll etc* parlant; **German-~ing** parlant allemand; **to be on ~ing terms with sb** adresser la parole à qn; **~ing tube** tuyau *m* acoustique ; **2** *n (skill)* art *m* de parler.

spear [spɪəʳ] *n* lance *f*. ◆ **spearhead** **1** *n (fig, Mil)* fer *m* de lance. **2** *vt attack etc* être le fer de lance de. ◆ **spearmint** *n* menthe *f* verte; *(chewing gum)* chewing-gum *m* à la menthe.

spec * [spek] *n*: **on ~** à tout hasard.

special [ˈspeʃ(ə)l] **1** *adj* **(a)** *(specific: gen) notebook, box, room* spécial, réservé à cet usage. **are you thinking of any ~ date?** est-ce que tu penses à une date particulière?; **I've no ~ person in mind** je ne pense à personne en particulier. **(b)** *(exceptional) attention, pleasure, effort* tout particulier; *favour, price, study, skill, care* spécial; *occasion, situation, case, circumstances* exceptionnel; *(Pol etc) powers, legislation* extraordinaire. **take ~ care of it** fais-y particulièrement attention; *(Cine etc)* **~ effects** effets *mpl* spéciaux. *(Comm)* **~ offer** réclame *f*; **her ~ friend** l'amie qui lui est particulièrement chère; **you're extra ~!** * tu es quelqu'un à part!; **this is a ~ day for me** c'est une journée importante pour moi; **to ask for ~ treatment** demander à être considéré comme un cas à part; **a ~ feature of the village** une caractéristique du village; *(Press)* **~ feature** article *m* spécial; **my ~ chair** mon fauteuil préféré; *(Univ etc)* **~ subject** option *f*; **nothing ~** rien de spécial *or* de particulier; *(when thanked)* **it's nothing ~** c'est bien normal; **what's so ~ about her?** qu'est-ce qu'elle a d'extraordinaire?; **~ agent** *(Comm etc)* concessionnaire *mf*; *(spy)* agent *m* secret; *(Brit)* **~ constable** auxiliaire *m* de police; *(Press, Rad, TV)* **~ correspondent** envoyé(e) *m(f)* spécial(e); *(Post)* **by ~ delivery** en exprès; *(Jur)* **~ licence** dispense *f*; **by ~ messenger** par messager spécial; **~ school** établissement *m* scolaire spécialisé.
2 *n (train)* train *m* supplémentaire; *(newspaper)* édition *f* spéciale. **the chef's ~** la spécialité du chef; **this week's ~** l'affaire de la semaine.
◆ **specialist** **1** *n (gen, also Med)* spécialiste *mf* (*in* de); *(Med)* **an eye/a heart ~ist** un(e) ophtalmologiste/cardiologue ; **2** *adj knowledge, dictionary* spécial. ◆ **speciality** [ˌspeʃɪˈælɪtɪ] *n* spécialité *f*; **to make a ~ity of sth** se spécialiser dans qch. ◆ **specialization** *n* spécialisation *f* (*in* dans). ◆ **specialize** *vi* se spécialiser (*in* dans). ◆ **specialized** *adj training* spécialisé; *tools* à usage spécial. ◆ **specially** *adv (specifically)* spécialement; *(particularly)* particulièrement, surtout; *(on purpose)* tout spécialement, exprès.

species [ˈspiːʃiːz] *n, pl inv* espèce *f*.

specify [ˈspesɪfaɪ] *vt* spécifier, préciser. **unless otherwise specified** sauf indication contraire. ◆ **specific** [spəˈsɪfɪk] *adj statement, instruction* précis, explicite; *purpose, meaning, case* précis, particulier; *example* précis; *(Bio, Phys etc)* spécifique; **he was very specific on that point** il s'est montré très explicite sur ce point; *(Phys)* **specific gravity** densité *f*. ◆ **specifically** [spəˈsɪfɪk(ə)lɪ] *adv (explicitly) warn, state etc* explicitement, de façon précise; *(especially) design, intend* particulièrement; **I told you quite specifically** je vous l'avais bien précisé *or* spécifié. ◆ **specification** *n (gen)* spécification *f*; *(item in contract etc)* stipulation *f*.

specimen ['spesɪmɪn] **1** *n [rock, species, style]* spécimen *m*; *[blood, tissue]* prélèvement *m*; *[urine]* échantillon *m*; *(fig: example)* exemple *m* (*of* de). *(fig: person)* **an odd** ~ * un drôle de type *, une drôle de bonne femme *. **2** *adj*: ~ **copy** spécimen *m*; ~ **page** page *f* spécimen; ~ **signature** spécimen *m* de signature.

specious ['spi:ʃəs] *adj* spécieux.

speck [spek] *n [dust, soot, truth etc]* grain *m*; *[dirt, ink]* petite tache *f*. **I've got a** ~ **in my eye** j'ai une poussière dans l'œil; **a** ~ **on the horizon** un point noir à l'horizon. ◆ **speckled** *adj* tacheté.

spectacle ['spektəkl] **1** *n* spectacle *m*. **2** *adj*: ~ **case** étui *m* à lunettes.
◆ **spectacles** *npl (abbr* **specs** *)* lunettes *fpl*.
◆ **spectacular** [spek'tækjʊlə^r] **1** *adj (gen)* spectaculaire; *success* fou; *view* splendide ; **2** *n (Cine, Theat)* superproduction *f*.

spectator [spek'teɪtə^r] **1** *n* spectateur *m*, -trice *f*. **2** *adj sport* qui attire un très grand nombre de spectateurs.

spectre, *(US)* **specter** ['spektə^r] *n* spectre *m*, fantôme *m*.

spectrum ['spektrəm] **1** *n, pl* **-tra** *(Phys)* spectre *m*; *(fig)* gamme *f (fig)*. **the political** ~ l'éventail *m* politique. **2** *adj colours* spectral.

speculate ['spekjʊleɪt] *vi (wonder)* s'interroger (*about, on* sur; *whether* pour savoir si); *(Philos, Fin)* spéculer. ◆ **speculation** *n (guessing)* conjectures *fpl* (*about* sur); *(Fin, Philos etc)* spéculation *f*.
◆ **speculative** *adj* spéculatif. ◆ **speculator** *n* spéculateur *m*, -trice *f*.

sped [sped] *pret, ptp of* **speed**.

speech [spi:tʃ] **1** *n* (**a**) *(faculty)* parole *f*; *(enunciation)* élocution *f*; *(manner of speaking)* façon *f* de parler, langage *m*; *(as opp to writing)* parole; *(language: of district or group)* parler *m*; *(Ling) utterances* parole *f*; *(spoken language)* langage *m* parlé. **to lose the power of** ~ perdre l'usage de la parole; **better in** ~ **than in writing** mieux oralement que par écrit; **free** ~**, freedom of** ~ liberté *f* d'expression; *(Gram)* **direct/indirect** ~ discours direct/indirect. (**b**) *(formal talk)* discours *m* (*on* sur). **2** *adj*: ~ **day** distribution *f* des prix; ~ **impediment** défaut *m* d'élocution; *(Anat)* ~ **organ** organe *m* de la parole; ~ **therapist** orthophoniste *mf*; ~ **therapy** orthophonie *f*; ~ **training** leçons *fpl* d'élocution.
◆ **speechless** *adj* muet (*with* de); **it left him** ~**less** il en est resté sans voix. ◆ **speechmaking** *n (slightly pej)* beaux discours *mpl*.

speed [spi:d] *(vb: pret, ptp* **sped** *or* **speeded***)* **1** *n* (**a**) *(rate of movement)* vitesse *f*; *(rapidity)* rapidité *f*; *(promptness)* promptitude *f*. **shorthand/typing** ~**s** nombre *m* de mots-minute en sténo/en dactylo; *(Aut)* **what** ~ **were you doing?** quelle vitesse faisiez-vous?; **at a** ~ **of 80 km/h** à une vitesse de 80 km/h; **at a great** ~ à toute vitesse; **at top** ~ *go, run* à toute vitesse; *do sth* très vite; **with such** ~ si vite; **to pick up** *or* **get up** *or* **gather** ~ prendre de la vitesse. (**b**) *(Tech: gear)* vitesse *f*. **a 3-**~ **gear** une boîte à 3 vitesses. (**c**) *(Phot) [film]* rapidité *f*; *(width of aperture)* degré *m* d'obturation; *(length of exposure)* durée *f* d'exposition.
2 *adj*: *(US: in road)* ~ **bump** casse-vitesse *m*; ~ **cop** ≃ motard *m*; *(Brit)* **there's no** ~ **limit** il n'y a pas de limitation *f* de vitesse; **the** ~ **limit is 80 km/h** la vitesse maximale permise est 80 km/h; ~ **merchant** * mordu(e) * *m(f)* de la vitesse; *(Aut)* ~ **restriction** limitation *f* de vitesse; *(Aut)* ~ **trap** piège *m* de police pour contrôle de vitesse; *(US)* ~ **zone** zone *f* à vitesse limitée.
3 *vi* (**a**) *pret, ptp* **sped**: **to** ~ **along/across** *etc* aller/traverser *etc* à toute vitesse. (**b**) *pret, ptp* **speeded** *(Aut: go too fast)* conduire trop vite.
◆ **speed up** *pret, ptp* **speeded up** **1** *vi (gen)* aller plus vite; *[walker/worker/train etc]* marcher/travailler/rouler *etc* plus vite; *(Aut)* accélérer; *[engine, machine etc]* tourner plus vite; *[production]* s'accélérer. **2** *vt sep (gen)* accélérer; *machine* faire tourner plus vite; *person* faire aller (*or* faire travailler) plus vite. **to** ~ **things up** activer les choses.
◆ **speedboat** *n* vedette *f (Naut)*. ◆ **speedily** *adv (quickly) move, work* vite; *(promptly) reply, return* promptement; *(soon)* bientôt. ◆ **speeding** *n (Aut)* excès *m* de vitesse. ◆ **speedometer** *n* indicateur *m* de vitesse. ◆ **speed-up** *n* accélération *f*; *(Ind)* ~**-up of production** amélioration *f* de rendement.
◆ **speedway racing** *n* courses *fpl* de moto.
◆ **speedy** *adj* rapide.

speleology [ˌspi:lɪ'ɒlədʒɪ] *n* spéléologie *f*. ◆ **speleologist** *n* spéléologue *mf*.

spell[1] [spel] *n* charme *m*; *(words)* formule *f* magique. **an evil** ~ un maléfice; **to put** *or* **cast a** ~ **on sb** jeter un sort à qn; *(fig)* ensorceler qn; *(fig)* **under the** ~ **of** ensorcelé par; **to break the** ~ rompre le charme. ◆ **spellbinding** *adj* ensorcelant. ◆ **spellbound** *adj (fig)* envoûté; *(fig)* **to hold sb** ~**bound** tenir qn sous le charme.

spell[2] [spel] *n* (**a**) *(turn)* tour *m*. ~ **of duty** tour de service. (**b**) *(brief period)* période *f*. *(Met)* **cold/sunny** ~**s** périodes de froid/ensoleillées; **after a** ~ après un certain temps; **for a short** ~ pendant un petit moment.

spell[3] [spel] *pret, ptp* **spelt** *or* **spelled** **1** *vt (in writing)* écrire; *(aloud)* épeler. **how do you** ~ **it?** comment est-ce que cela s'écrit?; **d-o-g** ~**s 'dog'** d-o-g forment le mot 'dog'; *(fig)* **that would** ~ **ruin for him** cela signifierait la ruine pour lui. **2** *vi*: **to learn to** ~ apprendre l'orthographe; **he can't** ~ il fait des fautes d'orthographe. ◆ **spell out** *vt sep (fig) consequences, alternatives* expliquer bien clairement (*for sb* à qn). **do I have to** ~ **it out for you?** faut-il que je mette les points sur les i? ◆ **spelling** **1** *n* orthographe *f* ; **2** *adj*: ~**ing mistake** faute *f* d'orthographe.

spelunker [spɪ'lʌŋkə^r] *n (US)* spéléologue *mf*.

spend [spend] *pret, ptp* **spent** *vt* (**a**) *money* dépenser (*on sth bought: on* en; *on person, car etc bought for: on* pour; *on doing* pour faire). **without** ~**ing a penny** sans dépenser un sou; *(Brit fig)* **to** ~ **a penny** * aller au petit coin *. (**b**) *(pass) holiday, time, one's life* passer (*on sth* sur qch; *in doing* à faire); *(devote) labour, care* consacrer (*on sth* à qch; *doing, in doing* à faire). **I spent 2 hours on that letter** j'ai passé 2 heures sur cette lettre. ◆ **spender** *n*: **to be a big** ~**er** dépenser beaucoup. ◆ **spending** **1** *n* dépenses *fpl*; **government** ~**ing** dépenses publiques ; **2** *adj*: ~**ing money** argent *m* de poche; ~**ing power** pouvoir *m* d'achat. ◆ **spendthrift** *n, adj* dépensier *m*, -ière *f*. ◆ **spent** *adj match, cartridge etc* utilisé; *supplies* épuisé; **spent (nuclear) fuel** combustible *m* irradié.

sperm [spɜ:m] *n* sperme *m*. ~ **bank** banque *f* de sperme; ~ **oil** huile *f* de baleine; ~ **whale** cachalot *m*.

spermicide [ˌspɜ:mɪ'saɪd] *n* spermicide *m*.

sphere [sfɪə^r] *n (gen)* sphère *f*. ~ **of influence** sphère d'influence; **the** ~ **of poetry** le domaine de la poésie; **in the social** ~ dans le domaine social; **in many** ~**s** dans de nombreux domaines; **within a limited** ~ dans un cadre restreint; **that is outside my** ~ cela n'entre pas dans mes compétences.
◆ **spherical** ['sferɪk(ə)l] *adj* sphérique.

sphinx [sfɪŋks] *n* sphinx *m*.

spice [spaɪs] **1** *n (Culin)* épice *f*. **mixed** ~**(s)** épices mélangées; *(fig)* **a story with a bit of** ~ **to it** une histoire qui a du piquant; **the** ~ **of adventure** le piment de l'aventure. **2** *vt (Culin)* épicer (*with* de); *(fig)* relever (*with* de). ◆ **spicy** *adj food* épicé, relevé; *(fig)* piquant.

spick-and-span ['spɪkən'spæn] *adj* propre comme un sou neuf.

spider ['spaɪdəʳ] *n* (**a**) *(Zool)* araignée *f*. **~'s web** toile *f* d'araignée. (**b**) *(Aut: for luggage)* araignée *f* (à bagages). (**c**) *(US Culin)* poêle *f* (à trépied). ◆ **spidery** *adj writing* tremblé.

spiel * [spi:l] *n* baratin * *m* (*about* sur).

spike [spaɪk] **1** *n (gen)* pointe *f*; *(for letters, bills etc)* pique-notes *m inv*; *(Bot)* épi *m*. *(shoes)* **~s** * chaussures *fpl* à pointes; **~ heels** talons *mpl* aiguilles. **2** *vt (fig)* **to ~ sb's guns** mettre des bâtons dans les roues à qn. ◆ **spiky** *adj branch, wall* hérissé de pointes; *hair* en épi.

spill [spɪl] *pret, ptp* **spilt** *or* **spilled** **1** *vt* renverser. **to ~ blood** verser le sang; *(fig)* **to ~ the beans** * vendre la mèche *; *(Naut)* **to ~ (wind from) a sail** étouffer une voile. **2** *vi [liquid, salt etc]* se répandre.

◆ **spill out** **1** *vi* se répandre; *[people etc]* sortir avec précipitation. **they ~ed out into the streets** ils se sont précipités dans la rue. **2** *vt sep contents etc* répandre; *(fig) story, details* révéler. ◆ **spill over** *vi* déborder (*into* dans).

spin [spɪn] *(vb: pret, ptp* **spun***)* **1** *n (turn)* tournoiement *m*; *(Aviat)* vrille *f*. **to give a wheel a ~** faire tourner une roue; *(on washing machine)* **long/short ~** essorage *m* complet/léger; *(Sport)* **to put a ~ on a ball** donner de l'effet à une balle; *(Aviat)* **to go into a ~** tomber en vrille; *(fig) [person]* **to get into a ~** * paniquer *; **everything was in a ~** * c'était la pagaille * complète; *(fig: try out)* **to give sth a ~** * essayer qch; *(ride)* **to go for a ~** * faire un petit tour en voiture (*or* en vélo *etc*). **2** *vt* (**a**) *wool, glass etc* filer (*into* en, pour en faire); *thread etc* fabriquer; *[spider etc]* tisser. *(fig)* **to ~ a yarn** *(make up)* inventer *or (tell)* débiter une longue histoire (*about sth* sur qch). (**b**) *wheel etc* (**~ round**) faire tourner; *top* lancer; *clothes* essorer; *(Sport) ball* donner de l'effet à. **to ~ a coin** jouer à pile ou face. **3** *vi* (**a**) *[spinner etc]* filer; *[spider]* tisser sa toile. (**b**) *(often* **~ round***: gen)* tourner; *[person]* se retourner vivement; *[car wheel]* patiner; *[ball]* tournoyer. **to ~ round and round** tournoyer; **to send sth/sb ~ning** envoyer rouler qch/qn; *(fig)* **my head is ~ning** j'ai la tête qui tourne; *(fig)* **the room was ~ning** la chambre tournait. (**c**) *(Fishing)* **to ~ for trout** pêcher la truite à la cuiller. ◆ **spin out** *vt sep story, visit, money* faire durer.

◆ **spindrift** *n* embruns *mpl*. ◆ **spin-dry** *vt* essorer (à la machine). ◆ **spin-dryer** *n* essoreuse *f*. ◆ **spinner** *n (person)* fileur *m*, -euse *f*; *(Fishing)* cuiller *f*; *(spin-dryer)* essoreuse *f*; *(Baseball, Cricket)* **he sent down a ~ner** * il a donné de l'effet à la balle. ◆ **spinning** **1** *n (by hand)* filage *m*; *(by machine)* filature *f*; *(Fishing)* pêche *f* à la cuiller ; **2** *adj*: **~ning mill** filature *f*; **~ning top** toupie *f*; **~ning wheel** rouet *m*. ◆ **spin-off** *n (gen)* avantage *m* inattendu; *(Ind, Tech etc)* application *f* secondaire.

spina bifida ['spaɪnə'bɪfɪdə] *n* spina-bifida *m*.

spinach ['spɪnɪdʒ] *n (Culin)* épinards *mpl*.

spindle ['spɪndl] *n (Spinning)* fuseau *m*; *(on machine)* broche *f*; *(Tech) [pump]* axe *m*; *[lathe]* arbre *m*; *[valve]* tige *f*. ◆ **spindly** *adj legs, person* grêle; *plant* étiolé.

spine [spaɪn] *n (Anat)* colonne *f* vertébrale; *[fish]* épine *f*; *[hedgehog]* piquant *m*; *(Bot)* épine; *[book]* dos *m*; *[hill etc]* crête *f*. ◆ **spinal** *adj nerve, muscle* spinal; *column, disc* vertébral; *injury* à la colonne vertébrale; **spinal anaesthetic** péridurale *f*; **spinal cord** moelle *f* épinière. ◆ **spine-chilling** *adj* à vous glacer le sang. ◆ **spineless** *adj (fig)* mou, sans caractère. ◆ **spiny** *adj* épineux.

spinney ['spɪnɪ] *n* bosquet *m*.

spinster ['spɪnstəʳ] *n* célibataire *f (also Admin)*, vieille fille *f (pej)*.

spiral ['spaɪər(ə)l] **1** *adj movement, decoration, spring* en spirale; *nebula, galaxy* spiral; *(Aviat)* en vrille. **~ staircase** escalier *m* en colimaçon. **2** *n* spirale *f*. **in a ~** en spirale; **the wage-price ~** la montée inexorable des salaires et des prix; **the inflationary ~** la spirale inflationniste. **3** *vi [smoke]* monter en spirale; *[prices]* monter en flèche; *[prices and wages]* former une spirale; *[plane]* **to ~ down** descendre en vrille; *[rocket etc]* **to ~ up** monter en spirale.

spire ['spaɪəʳ] *n (Archit)* flèche *f*.

spirit ['spɪrɪt] **1** *n* (**a**) *(soul)* esprit *m*. **he was there in ~** il était présent en esprit; **one of the greatest ~s of his day** un des plus grands esprits de son temps; **the leading ~ in the party** l'âme *f* du parti. (**b**) *(supernatural being, ghost etc)* esprit *m*. **evil ~** esprit malin. (**c**) *(attitude etc)* esprit *m*. **in a ~ of forgiveness** dans un esprit de pardon; **he's got the right ~** il a la disposition *or* l'attitude qu'il faut; **you must take it in the ~ in which it was meant** prenez-le dans l'esprit où c'était voulu; **to take sth in the right/wrong ~** prendre qch en bonne/mauvaise part; **you must enter into the ~ of the thing** il faut y participer de bon cœur; **the ~, not the letter of the law** l'esprit et non la lettre de la loi; **that's the ~!** voilà comment il faut réagir!; **community ~** civisme *m*. (**d**) **in good ~s** de bonne humeur; **in poor** *or* **low ~s** qui n'a pas le moral; **to keep one's ~s up** garder le moral; **my ~s rose** j'ai repris courage; **to raise sb's ~s** remonter le moral à qn. (**e**) *(courage)* courage *m*, cran * *m*; *(energy)* énergie *f*; *(vitality)* entrain *m*. (**f**) *(Chem)* alcool *m*. *(drink)* **~s** spiritueux *mpl*, alcool; **raw ~s** alcool pur.

2 *adj* (**a**) *lamp etc* à alcool. (**b**) *(Spiritualism) help, world* des esprits.

◆ **spirit away, spirit off** *vt sep person* faire disparaître comme par enchantement; *object, document etc* subtiliser.

◆ **spirited** *adj person, horse, reply, speech* fougueux; *conversation* animé; *music* plein d'allant; *undertaking, defence* courageux; *(Mus)* **he gave a ~ed performance** il a joué avec fougue *or* avec brio. ◆ **spirit-level** *n* niveau *m* à bulle. ◆ **spiritual** **1** *adj* spirituel *(par opp à matériel)*; **2** *n* chant *m* religieux ; *(also* **Negro ~ual***)* negro-spiritual *m*. ◆ **spiritualism** *n (Rel)* spiritisme *m*. ◆ **spiritualist** *adj, n* spirite *(mf)*. ◆ **spirituality** *n* spiritualité *f*. ◆ **spiritually** *adv* spirituellement.

spit¹ [spɪt] *(vb: pret, ptp* **spat***)* **1** *n (spittle)* crachat *m*; *(saliva)* salive *f*; *(Bot)* crachat de coucou. **~ and polish** astiquage *m*; *(fig)* **he's the dead ~** * **of his uncle** c'est le portrait craché * de son oncle. **2** *vt* cracher. **3** *vi* cracher (*at sb* sur qn); *[fire, fat]* crépiter. **it was ~ting with rain** il tombait quelques gouttes de pluie. ◆ **spit out** *vt sep* cracher. *(fig: say it)* **~ it out!** * allons, dis-le! ◆ **spitfire** *n*: **to be a ~fire** s'emporter pour un rien. ◆ **spitting** **1** *n*: **'~ting prohibited'** 'défense de cracher' ; **2** *adj*: **to be the ~ting image of sb** * être le portrait craché * de qn. ◆ **spittle** *n (ejected)* crachat *m*; *(dribbled)* salive *f*; *[animal]* bave *f*. ◆ **spittoon** *n* crachoir *m*.

spit² [spɪt] *n (Culin)* broche *f*; *(Geog)* langue *f* de terre. ◆ **spitroast** *vt* faire rôtir à la broche.

spite [spaɪt] **1** *n* (**a**) *(ill-feeling)* rancune *f*, dépit *m*. **out of pure ~** par pure rancune *or* malveillance; **to have a ~ against sb** * avoir une dent contre qn. (**b**) **in ~ of** malgré, en dépit de; **in ~ of the fact that** bien que + *subj*; **in ~ of everyone** envers et contre tous. **2** *vt* vexer. ◆ **spiteful** *adj person, remark, comment* malveillant; *tongue* venimeux. ◆ **spitefully** *adv* par dépit.

splash [splæʃ] **1** *n (sound)* plouf *m*; *(series of sounds)* clapotement *m*; *(mark)* éclaboussure *f*; *(fig) [colour]* tache *f*; *[publicity]* étalage *m*. **a ~ of** *(milk etc)* un petit peu de; *(soda water)* une giclée de; *(fig)* **to make a ~ *** faire sensation. **2** *vt* éclabousser (*sth over sb/sth* qch sur qn/qch; *sb/sth with sth* qn/qch de qch). **to ~ milk on the floor** renverser du lait par terre; **he ~ed paint on the floor** il a fait des éclaboussures de peinture par terre; **to ~ cold water on one's face** s'asperger la figure d'eau froide; **the news was ~ed across the front page** la nouvelle a fait cinq colonnes à la une. **3** *vi* (**a**) *[liquid, mud etc]* faire des éclaboussures. **to ~ over sth** éclabousser qch. (**b**) *[person, animal]* barboter, patauger (*in* dans). **to ~ across a stream** traverser un ruisseau en pataugeant; *[stone]* **to ~ into the water** tomber dans l'eau avec un gros plouf. ◆ **splash down** *vi [spacecraft]* amerrir. ◆ **splash out *** *vi (in spending)* faire une folie *(achat)*. ◆ **splash up** *vi* gicler (*on sb* sur qn). ◆ **splashback** *n* revêtement *m (au-dessus d'un évier etc)*. ◆ **splashboard** *n (Aut etc)* garde-boue *m inv*. ◆ **splashdown** *n (Space)* amerrissage *m*.

spleen [spliːn] *n (Anat)* rate *f*; *(bad temper)* mauvaise humeur *f*.

splendid ['splendɪd] *adj (imposing etc) ceremony, beauty* splendide; *(excellent) holiday, idea, teacher etc* excellent, formidable *. **that's ~!** c'est formidable! * ◆ **splendidly** *adv* splendidement; de façon excellente, formidablement *; **it all went ~ly** tout a très bien marché. ◆ **splendour,** *(US)* **splendor** *n* splendeur *f*.

splice [splaɪs] *vt rope* épisser; *film* coller.

splint [splɪnt] *n (Med)* éclisse *f*. **to put in ~s** éclisser; **leg in ~s** jambe éclissée.

splinter ['splɪntəʳ] **1** *n [glass, wood]* éclat *m* ; *[bone]* esquille *f*; *(in finger etc)* écharde *f*. **2** *adj*: **~ group** groupe *m* dissident. **3** *vt wood* fendre en éclats; *glass, bone* briser en éclats; *(fig) party etc* fragmenter. **4** *vi* se fendre *or* se briser en éclats; se fragmenter.

split [splɪt] *(vb: pret, ptp* **split***)* **1** *n* (**a**) *(in garment, fabric)* fente *f*; *(tear)* déchirure *f*; *(in wood, earth's surface)* crevasse *f*; *(fig: quarrel)* rupture *f*; *(Pol)* scission *f*. **there was a 3-way ~ in the committee** le comité s'est trouvé divisé en 3 clans; **to do the ~s** faire le grand écart. (**b**) *(cake etc)* **jam ~** brioche *f* fourrée à la confiture; **banana ~** banana split *m*.

2 *adj (Gram)* **~ infinitive** *infinitif où un adverbe est intercalé entre 'to' et le verbe*; **~ peas** pois *mpl* cassés; **~ personality** double personnalité *f*; **a ~ second** une fraction de seconde; **in a ~ second** en un rien de temps; **~-second timing** *[military operation etc]* précision *f* à la seconde près; *[actor, comedian]* sens *m* du moment.

3 *vt* (**a**) *(gen)* fendre; *slate* cliver; *(tear)* déchirer; *(fig) party etc* diviser. **to ~ the atom** fissionner l'atome; **to ~ sth open** ouvrir qch en le fendant; **he ~ his head open** il s'est fendu le crâne; **to ~ sth in two** *(cut)* couper *or (break)* briser qch en deux; *(fig)* **to ~ hairs** couper les cheveux en quatre; *(fig)* **to ~ one's sides (laughing)** se tordre de rire; **it ~ the party down the middle** cela a divisé le parti en deux. (**b**) *(divide)* partager (*between* entre); *(share)* se partager. **let's ~ a bottle of wine** si on prenait une bouteille de vin à deux (*or* trois *etc*)?; **to ~ the difference** partager la différence; **they ~ the work** ils se sont partagé le travail.

4 *vi* (**a**) *(gen)* se fendre; *(tear)* se déchirer; *(fig) [party etc]* se diviser. **to ~ open** se fendre; *(fig)* **my head is ~ting** j'ai atrocement mal à la tête. (**b**) *(divide) [group]* se diviser, se séparer. (**c**) **to ~ on sb *** dénoncer qn.

◆ **split off** **1** *vi [piece of wood]* se détacher (*from* de); *[group]* se séparer (*from* de). **2** *vt sep piece* enlever (*from* de); *group* séparer (*from* de). ◆ **split up** **1** *vi [ship]* se briser; *[boulder, etc]* se fendre; *[meeting, crowd]* se disperser; *[party, movement]* se diviser; *[married couple]* se séparer; *[friends, engaged couple]* rompre. **2** *vt sep wood, stones* fendre (*into* en); *money, work* partager; *compound, party, organization* diviser (*into* en); *meeting* mettre fin à ; *crowd* disperser; *friends* séparer. **we must ~ the work up amongst us** nous devons nous partager le travail.

◆ **split-cane** *adj* en osier. ◆ **split-level** *adj cooker* à plaques de cuisson et four indépendants; *house* à deux niveaux. ◆ **split-off** *n* séparation *f* (*from* de). ◆ **split-site** *adj* sur plusieurs emplacements. ◆ **splitting** **1** *n (V* **split 3a** *above)* fendage *m*; clivage *m*; déchirement *m*; division *f*; *[atom]* fission *f* ; **2** *adj*: **I have a ~ting headache** j'ai atrocement mal à la tête. ◆ **split-up** *n [engaged couple, friends]* rupture *f*; *[married couple]* séparation *f*; *[political party]* scission *f*.

splodge [splɒdʒ], **splotch** [splɒtʃ] *n [ink, colour, dirt etc]* tache *f*; *[cream]* monceau *m*.

splutter ['splʌtəʳ] **1** *vi [person] (spit)* crachoter; *(stutter)* bafouiller *; *[fire, fat]* crépiter; *[engine]* bafouiller *. **2** *vt* (**~ out**) **bafouiller ***. **3** *n* crachotement *m*; bafouillage * *m*; crépitement *m*.

spoil [spɔɪl] *pret, ptp* **spoiled** *or* **spoilt** **1** *vt* (**a**) *(damage) paint, dress etc* abîmer; *ballot paper* rendre nul. **to ~ one's eyes** s'abîmer la vue. (**b**) *(detract from) view, style, effect, food* gâter; *holiday, occasion, pleasure, one's life* gâcher; *garden etc* enlaidir; *sb's peace of mind* empoisonner. **to ~ sb's fun** gâcher l'amusement de qn; **to ~ one's appetite** se couper l'appétit; **if you tell me the ending you'll ~ the film for me** si vous me racontez la fin vous me gâcherez tout l'intérêt du film. (**c**) *(pamper) child etc* gâter. **2** *vi* (**a**) *[food]* s'abîmer; *(in warehouse etc)* s'avarier. (**b**) **to be ~ing for a fight** brûler de se battre. **3** *n (gen pl)* **~(s)** *(booty)* butin *m*. ◆ **spoiler** *n (Aut)* spoiler *m*, becquet *m*. ◆ **spoilt** *adj ballot paper* nul; *child* gâté.

spoke¹ [spəʊk] *n* rayon *m*. *(fig)* **to put a ~ in sb's wheel** mettre des bâtons dans les roues à qn.

spoke², spoken ['spəʊk(ən)] *pret, ptp of* **speak**. ◆ **spokesman, spokesperson** *n* porte-parole *m inv* (*of, for* de).

sponge [spʌn(d)ʒ] **1** *n* (**a**) éponge *f*. *(fig)* **to throw in the ~ *** s'avouer vaincu. (**b**) (**~ cake**) gâteau *m* de Savoie. **2** *adj*: **~ bag** sac *m* de toilette; **~ mop** balai *m* éponge. **3** *vt* éponger. **4** *vi (*: cadge)* **to ~ on sb** vivre aux crochets de qn.

◆ **sponge down** *vt sep person, walls* laver à l'éponge; *horse* éponger.

◆ **sponger *** *n (pej)* parasite *m*. ◆ **spongy** *adj* spongieux.

sponsor ['spɒnsəʳ] **1** *n (gen: of appeal etc)* personne *f* qui accorde son patronage; *(for loan etc)* répondant(e) *m(f)*; *(for baptism, club membership)* parrain *m*, marraine *f*; *(Rad, TV, Advertising)* personne (*or* organisme *m*) qui assure le patronage; *(of concert)* sponsor *m*, parrain *m*; *(of sports event)* sponsor *m*, commanditaire *m*; *(for fund-raising event)* donateur *m*, -trice *f*; *(US: of club)* animateur *m*, -trice *f*. **2** *vt appeal, proposal, announcement, programme* patronner; *(Fin) borrower* se porter caution pour; *(Rel)* être le parrain (*or* la marraine) de; *club member, concert* parrainer; *sports event* sponsoriser ; *fund-raising walker etc* s'engager à rémunérer (en fonction de sa performance); **government~ed** à l'initiative du gouvernement. ◆ **sponsorship** *n* patronage *m*; cautionnement *m*; parrainage *m*; *(Rad, TV)* commande *f* publicitaire; *(Sport)* sponsoring *m*.

spontaneous [spɒn'teɪnɪəs] *adj (gen)* spontané. **~ combustion** combustion *f* vive. ◆ **spontaneity** *n* spontanéité *f*. ◆ **spontaneously** *adv* spontanément.

spook [spu:k] **1** *n* (**: ghost*) revenant *m*; (*US* ‡: *spy*) barbouze * *f*. **2** *vt* (*US: frighten*) effrayer. ◆ **spooky** * *adj* qui donne le frisson.

spool [spu:l] *n* (*gen*) bobine *f*; [*fishing reel*] tambour *m*; [*sewing machine*] canette *f*; [*wire*] rouleau *m*.

spoon [spu:n] **1** *n* cuiller *f or* cuillère *f*. **2** *vt*: **to ~ sth into a plate** verser qch dans une assiette avec une cuiller. ◆ **spoonfeed** *vt* nourrir à la cuiller; (*fig*) mâcher le travail à. ◆ **spoonful** *n* cuillerée *f*.

spoonerism ['spu:nərɪz(ə)m] *n* contrepèterie *f*.

spoor [spʊəʳ] *n* foulées *fpl*, trace *f*, piste *f*.

sporadic [spəˈrædɪk] *adj* sporadique. ~ **fighting** échauffourées *fpl*. ◆ **sporadically** *adv* sporadiquement.

sport [spɔ:t] **1** *n* (**a**) sport *m*. **he is good at ~** il est très sportif; **outdoor/indoor ~s** sports de plein air/d'intérieur. (**b**) (*amusement*) divertissement *m*. **to have good ~** (*Hunting/Fishing*) faire bonne chasse/bonne pêche; (*gen*) bien se divertir. (**c**) (**: person*) chic type * *m*, chic fille * *f*. **be a ~!** sois chic! * **2** *vt* arborer. ◆ **sporting** *adj* sportif, chic * *inv*; **there's a ~ing chance that** il est possible que + *subj*. ◆ **sportingly** *adv* (*fig*) très sportivement. ◆ **sports 1** *npl* (*meeting*) réunion *f* sportive ; **2** *adj* (*gen*) de sport; *clothes* sport *inv*; **~s car** voiture *f* de sport; **~s ground** terrain *m* de sport; **~s jacket** veston *m* sport *inv*. ◆ **sportsman** *n* sportif *m*; (*fig*) **he's a real ~sman** il est très sportif. ◆ **sportsmanlike** *adj* sportif, chic * *inv*. ◆ **sportsmanship** *n* esprit *m* sportif. ◆ **sportswear** *n* vêtements *mpl* de sport. ◆ **sportswoman** *n* sportive *f*. ◆ **sportswriter** *n* rédacteur *m* sportif. ◆ **sporty** * *adj* sportif.

spot [spɒt] **1** *n* (**a**) (*gen*) tache *f* (*on* sur); (*polka dot*) pois *m*; (*on dice, domino*) point *m*; (*pimple*) bouton *m*. **a ~ of dirt** une tache; **a dress with red ~s** une robe à pois rouges; **a ~ of rain** quelques gouttes *fpl* de pluie; **to have ~s before the eyes** voir des mouches volantes devant les yeux; **to come out in ~s** avoir une éruption de boutons. (**b**) (*small amount*) **a ~ of** un peu de ; *whisky, coffee etc* une goutte de; *truth, common sense* un grain de; **a ~ of sleep** un petit somme; **he did a ~ of work** il a travaillé un peu; **there's been a ~ of trouble** il y a eu un petit incident; **how about a ~ of lunch?** * et si on mangeait un morceau? (**c**) (*place*) endroit *m*. **a good ~ for a picnic** un bon endroit *or* coin pour un pique-nique; **a tender ~ on the arm** un point sensible au bras; **the police were on the ~ in 2 minutes** la police est arrivée sur les lieux en 2 minutes; **it's easy if you're on the ~** c'est facile si vous êtes sur place; **the man on the ~** la personne qui est sur place; (*Press etc*) l'envoyé spécial; **an on-the-~ report** un reportage sur place; **he decided on the ~** il s'est décidé sur le champ *or* tout de suite; (*fig*) **to be in a (bad** *or* **tight) ~** * être dans le pétrin. (**d**) (**: Rad, Theat, TV: in show*) numéro *m*; (*Rad, TV: advertisement*) spot *m*. (**e**) = **spotlight**.

2 *adj*: ~ **cash** argent *m* comptant; ~ **remover** détachant *m*.

3 *vt* (**a**) (*speckle*) tacher (*with* de). (**b**) (*notice*) *person, vehicle* apercevoir, repérer *; *mistake* relever; (*recognize*) *bargain, winner, sb's ability* découvrir.

◆ **spotless** *adj* (*lit*: **~lessly clean**) reluisant de propreté; (*fig*) sans tache. ◆ **spotlight 1** *n* (*Theat: beam*) rayon *m* de projecteur; (*Theat: lamp*) projecteur *m*, spot *m*; (*in home*) spot *m*; (*Aut*) phare *m* auxiliaire; (*Theat*) **in the ~light** sous le feu des projecteurs; (*fig*) **the ~light was on him** il était en vedette ; **2** *vt success* mettre en vedette; *changes* mettre en lumière. ◆ **spotted** *adj animal* tacheté; *fabric* à pois. ◆ **spotter** *n* (**a**) (*as hobby*) **train ~ter** passionné(e) *m(f)* de trains; (**b**) (*Mil etc*) (*for enemy aircraft*) guetteur *m*; (*during firing*) observateur *m*. ◆ **spotty** *adj face* boutonneux. ◆ **spot-weld** *vt* souder par points.

spouse [spaʊz] *n* époux *m*, épouse *f*; (*Jur*) conjoint(e) *m(f)*.

spout [spaʊt] **1** *n* (*gen*) bec *m*; (*for tap*) brise-jet *m inv*; [*gutter, pump etc*] dégorgeoir *m*; [*fountain*] jet *m*. (*Brit fig*) **to be up the ~** ‡ être fichu *. **2** *vt liquid* faire jaillir; *smoke, lava* vomir; (** fig*) *poem etc* débiter.

sprain [spreɪn] **1** *n* entorse *f*; (*less serious*) foulure *f*. **2** *vt muscle etc* fouler. **to ~ one's ankle** se donner une entorse à la cheville; (*less serious*) se fouler la cheville.

sprang [spræŋ] *pret of* **spring**.

sprawl [sprɔ:l] **1** *vi* (*fall*) tomber, s'étaler *; (*lie*) être affalé; [*plant*] ramper (*over* sur); [*handwriting, town*] s'étaler (*over* dans). **2** *n*: **an ugly ~ of buildings down the valley** d'affreux bâtiments qui s'étalent dans la vallée; **London's suburban ~** l'étalement *m* de la banlieue londonienne. ◆ **sprawling** *adj person* affalé; *handwriting* étalé; *city* tentaculaire.

spray¹ [spreɪ] **1** *n* (**a**) (*gen*) nuage *m* de gouttelettes *fpl*; (*from sea*) embruns *mpl*; (*from hose pipe*) pluie *f*; (*from atomizer*) spray *m*; (*from aerosol*) pulvérisation *f*; (*from fountain*) jet *m*. (**b**) (*container*) (*aerosol*) bombe *f*, aérosol *m*; (*for scent etc*) atomiseur *m*; (*refillable*) vaporisateur *m*; (*larger: for garden etc*) pulvérisateur *m*. **insecticide ~** (*aerosol*) bombe (d')insecticide; (*contents*) insecticide *m* (*en bombe*). (**c**) (**~ attachment, ~ nozzle**) pomme *f*. **2** *adj deodorant, insecticide* (présenté) en bombe *etc*. ~ **can** bombe *f etc* (*V* **1b**); ~ **gun** pistolet *m* (*à peinture etc*); ~ **paint** peinture *f* en bombe. **3** *vt* (**a**) *roses, garden, crops* faire des pulvérisations sur; *room* faire des pulvérisations dans; *hair* vaporiser (*with* de). **they ~ed the oil slick with detergent** ils ont répandu du détergent sur la nappe de pétrole; (*fig*) **to ~ sth/sb with bullets** arroser qch/qn de balles. (**b**) *water, insecticide, paint* pulvériser (*on* sur); *scent* vaporiser. **they ~ed foam on the flames** ils ont projeté de la neige carbonique sur les flammes. ◆ **sprayer** *n* (**a**) = **spray¹ 1b**; (**b**) (*aircraft*: **crop-~er**) avion-pulvérisateur *m*. ◆ **spraying machine** *n* (*Agr*) pulvérisateur *m*.

spray² [spreɪ] *n* [*flowers*] gerbe *f*; [*greenery*] branche *f*; (*brooch*) aigrette *f*.

spread [spred] (*vb: pret, ptp* **spread**) **1** *n* (**a**) [*fire, disease, infection*] propagation *f*; [*nuclear weapons*] prolifération *f*; [*idea, knowledge*] diffusion *f*; [*education*] progrès *m*. (**b**) (*extent*) [*wings*] envergure *f*; [*arch*] ouverture *f*; [*bridge*] travée *f*; [*marks, prices, ages etc*] échelle *f*. **he's got a middle-age ~** il a pris de l'embonpoint avec l'âge. (**c**) (*cover*) (*for table*) dessus *m* de table; (*bed ~*) dessusde-lit *m inv*. (**d**) (*Culin*) pâte *f* (à tartiner). **cheese ~** fromage *m* à tartiner; **anchovy ~** ≈ pâte d'anchois. (**e**) (** fig: meal*) festin *m*. (**f**) (*Press, Typ*) (*two pages*) double page *f*; (*across columns*) deux (*or* trois *etc*) colonnes *fpl*.

2 *vt* (**a**) (**~ out**) (*gen*) étendre (*on sth* sur qch); *wings, sails* déployer; *fingers, toes, arms, legs* écarter. (*fig*) **to ~ one's wings** élargir ses horizons. (**b**) *bread etc* tartiner (*with* de); *butter, glue* étaler (*on* sur). (**c**) (*distribute*) *sand etc* répandre (*on, over* sur); *fertilizer* épandre (*over, on* sur); (**~ out**) *objects, cards, goods* étaler (*on* sur); *soldiers etc* disposer (*along* le long de). **policemen ~ out all over the hillside** des agents de police dispersés sur toute la colline. (**d**) *disease, infection* propager; *germs* disséminer; *wealth* distribuer; *rumours* faire courir; *news, knowledge, panic, indignation* répandre; (*in time*: **~ out**) *payment, studies etc* échelonner (*over* sur). **our resources are ~ very thinly** nous n'avons plus aucune marge dans l'emploi de nos ressources.

3 *vi (gen)* se répandre; *[river, stain]* s'étaler; *[flood, weeds, fire, disease, pain]* s'étendre. **to ~ into** *or* **over sth** *(gen)* se répandre dans *or* sur qch; *[fire, pain, disease]* atteindre qch; *[weeds, panic]* envahir qch; **the desert ~s (out) over 500 square miles** le désert s'étend sur 500 milles carrés.

◆ **spread out** **1** *vi [people, animals]* se disperser; *[valley]* s'élargir. **2** *vt sep*: **the valley lay ~ out before him** la vallée s'étendait à ses pieds; **he was ~ out on the floor** il était étendu de tout son long par terre.

◆ **spread-eagled** *adj* étendu bras et jambes écartés. ◆ **spreadsheet** *n (Comput) (chart)* tableau *m*; *(software)* tableur *m*.

spree [spriː] *n* fête *f*. **to go on** *or* **have a ~** faire la fête; **to go on a spending ~** faire des folies *(achats)*.

sprig [sprɪg] *n* rameau *m*, brin *m*.

sprightly ['spraɪtlɪ] *adj* alerte, actif.

spring [sprɪŋ] *(vb: pret* **sprang**, *ptp* **sprung***)* **1** *n* (**a**) *(leap)* bond *m*, saut *m*. **in** *or* **with** *or* **at one ~** d'un bond, d'un saut. (**b**) *(for mattress, watch etc; also Tech)* ressort *m*. *(Aut)* **the ~s** la suspension. (**c**) *(resilience) [mattress]* élasticité *f*. (**d**) *[water]* source *f*. **hot ~** source chaude. (**e**) *(season)* printemps *m*. **in (the) ~** au printemps; **~ is in the air** il fait un temps de printemps.

2 *adj* (**a**) *weather, day, flowers* printanier, de printemps. *(Brit)* **~ greens** chou *m* précoce; *(Brit)* **~ onion** ciboule *f*. (**b**) *mattress* à ressorts. *(file)* **~ binder** classeur *m* à ressort.

3 *vi* (**a**) *(leap)* bondir, sauter (*at* sur). **to ~ in/across** *etc* entrer/traverser *etc* d'un bond; *(fig)* **to ~ to sb's help** bondir à l'aide de qn; **to ~ to the rescue** se précipiter pour porter secours; **he sprang into action** il est passé à l'action; **to ~ into existence/into view** apparaître du jour au lendemain/soudain; **to ~ to mind** venir à l'esprit; **the door sprang open** la porte s'est brusquement ouverte; **hope ~s eternal** l'espoir fait vivre. (**b**) *(originate)* provenir, découler (*from* de).

4 *vt trap, lock* faire jouer. *(fig)* **to ~ a surprise on sb** surprendre qn; **to ~ a question/a piece of news on sb** poser une question/annoncer une nouvelle à qn de but en blanc; **he sprang it on me** il m'a pris de court *or* au dépourvu.

◆ **spring up** *vi [person]* se lever d'un bond; *[flowers, buildings]* surgir de terre; *[corn]* lever brusquement; *[wind, storm]* se lever brusquement; *[rumour, doubt, fear, friendship, alliance]* naître; *[problem, obstacle]* surgir.

◆ **springboard** *n* tremplin *m*. ◆ **spring-clean** *vt* nettoyer de fond en comble. ◆ **spring-cleaning** *n* grand nettoyage *m*. ◆ **spring-like** *adj* printanier. ◆ **springtime** *n* printemps *m*. ◆ **springy** *adj (gen)* souple; *rubber, mattress* élastique; *carpet* moelleux; *plank* flexible.

sprinkle ['sprɪŋkl] *vt (with water)* asperger (*with* de); *(with sugar)* saupoudrer (*with* de). **to ~ sand on** *or* **over sth** répandre une légère couche de sable sur qch; **to ~ sand/grit on the roadway** sabler/cendrer la route. ◆ **sprinkler** *n (for lawn etc)* arroseur *m*; *(for sugar etc)* saupoudreuse *f*; *(for fire-fighting)* diffuseur *m* (d'extincteur automatique d'incendie).

◆ **sprinkling** *n [water]* quelques gouttes *fpl*; *[sand]* légère couche *f*; *(fig)* **there was a sprinkling of young people** il y avait quelques jeunes çà et là.

sprint [sprɪnt] **1** *n (Sport)* sprint *m*. **2** *vi (Sport)* sprinter; *(gen)* foncer (*for the bus* pour attraper l'autobus). **to ~ down the street** descendre la rue à toutes jambes. ◆ **sprinter** *n (Sport)* sprinteur *m*, -euse *f*.

sprout [spraʊt] **1** *n (from bulbs, seeds)* germe *m*. **(Brussels) ~s** choux *mpl* de Bruxelles. **2** *vi [bulbs, onions etc]* germer; *(grow quickly) [plants]* bien pousser; *[child]* pousser vite *; *(appear)* surgir. **3** *vt leaves* produire; (*) *moustache* se laisser pousser. *[potatoes, bulbs]* **to ~ shoots** germer.

spruce¹ [spruːs] *n (tree)* épicéa *m*.

spruce² [spruːs] *adj* pimpant, net. ◆ **spruce up** *vt sep child* faire beau; *house* bien astiquer. **all ~d up** *person* tiré à quatre épingles.

sprung [sprʌŋ] *(ptp of* **spring***)* *adj seat, mattress* à ressorts. *(Aut)* **well-~** bien suspendu.

spry [spraɪ] *adj* alerte, vif.

spud * [spʌd] *n* patate * *f*, pomme *f* de terre.

spun [spʌn] *pret, ptp of* **spin.**

spur [spɜːʳ] **1** *n* (**a**) *(gen)* éperon *m*; *(fig)* aiguillon *m*. *(fig)* **to win one's ~s** faire ses preuves; **on the ~ of the moment** sous l'impulsion du moment. (**b**) *(motorway)* embranchement *m*. **2** *adj*: **~ road** route *f* d'accès. **3** *vt* (**~ on**) *horse* éperonner; *[ambition etc]* éperonner, aiguillonner. **to ~ sb (on) to do sth** pousser qn à faire qch.

spurious ['spjʊərɪəs] *adj (gen)* faux; *claim* fallacieux; *interest, affection* simulé.

spurn [spɜːn] *vt* repousser (avec mépris).

spurt [spɜːt] **1** *n [water, flame]* jaillissement *m*; *[anger, enthusiasm, energy]* sursaut *m*. **to put on a ~** *(Sport)* sprinter; *(in running for bus etc)* foncer; *(fig: in work etc)* donner un coup de collier; **in ~s** par à-coups. **2** *vi* (**~ out, ~ up**) jaillir (*from* de).

spy [spaɪ] **1** *n (gen)* espion(ne) *m(f)*. **police ~** indicateur *m*, -trice *f* de police. **2** *adj film, story etc* d'espionnage. **~ ring** réseau *m* d'espions. **3** *vi (gen)* espionner; *(Ind, Pol)* faire de l'espionnage (*for a country* au service d'un pays). **to ~ on sb/sth** espionner qn/épier qch. **4** *vt (catch sight of)* apercevoir. ◆ **spy out** *vt sep*: **to ~ out the land** reconnaître le terrain. ◆ **spyglass** *n* lunette *f* d'approche. ◆ **spyhole** *n* petit trou *m*. ◆ **spying** *n* espionnage *m*.

squabble ['skwɒbl] **1** *n* chamaillerie * *f*. **2** *vi* se chamailler * (*over sth* à propos de qch). ◆ **squabbling** *n* chamailleries * *fpl*.

squad [skwɒd] **1** *n [policemen, workmen, prisoners]* escouade *f*; *[soldiers]* groupe *m*; *(US Sport)* équipe *f*. *(Ftbl)* **the England ~** le contingent anglais. **2** *adj (Police)* **~ car** voiture *f* de police.

squadron ['skwɒdr(ə)n] *n (Mil)* escadron *m*; *(Aviat, Naut)* escadrille *f*.

squalid ['skwɒlɪd] *adj (gen)* sordide; *motive* vil. ◆ **squalor** *n* conditions *fpl* sordides.

squall [skwɔːl] **1** *n (Met)* rafale *f or* bourrasque *f* de pluie; *(at sea)* grain *m*. **2** *vi [baby]* hurler, brailler. ◆ **squalling** *adj* criard, braillard *.

squander ['skwɒndəʳ] *vt time, money, talents* gaspiller; *inheritance* dilapider; *opportunity* perdre.

square [skwɛəʳ] **1** *n* (**a**) *(gen)* carré *m*; *[chessboard, crossword, graph paper]* case *f*; *(in pattern, on fabric)* carreau *m*; *(head ~)* carré, foulard *m*. **to fold into a ~** plier en carré; *(fig)* **now we're back to ~ one *** nous repartons à zéro *; **~ dance** quadrille *m*. (**b**) *(in town)* place *f*; *(with gardens)* square *m*; *(US: block of houses)* pâté *m* de maisons; *(Mil:* **barrack ~***)* cour *f* (de caserne). **the town ~** la grand-place. (**c**) *(Math)* carré *m*. **4 is the ~ of 2** 4 est le carré de 2. (**d**) *(pej)* **he's a real ~ *** il est vraiment vieux jeu.

2 *adj* (**a**) *(in shape)* carré. **to cut sth ~** couper qch au carré; *(Typ)* **~ bracket** crochet *m*; *(fig)* **he is a ~ peg in a round hole** il n'est pas à son affaire; *(fig)* **a ~ meal** un bon repas. (**b**) *(even, balanced) books, accounts, figures* en ordre. **to get one's accounts ~** mettre ses comptes en ordre; **to get ~ with sb** *(financially)* régler ses comptes avec qn; *(get even with)* régler son compte à qn; *(fig)* **to be all ~** être quitte; *(Sport)* être à égalité. (**c**) *(honest) dealings* honnête, régulier *. **he is absolutely ~** il est l'honnêteté même; **to get** *or* **have a ~ deal** être traité équitablement; **to give sb a ~ deal** agir hon-

nêtement avec qn. (**d**) *(Math etc) number* carré. **6 ~ metres** 6 mètres carrés; **6 metres** ~ de 6 mètres sur 6; ~ **root** racine *f* carrée. (**e**) *(* pej: conventional)* vieux jeu *inv*, rétro * *inv*.
3 *adv*: ~ **in the middle** en plein milieu; **to look sb ~ in the face** regarder qn bien en face.
4 *vt* (**a**) *(make ~) figure, shape* rendre carré; *stone, timber* équarrir; *shoulders* redresser. (**b**) *(settle etc) books, accounts* mettre en ordre; *debts, creditors* régler; *(reconcile)* faire cadrer (*A with B* A avec B). **I can't ~ that with what he told me** ça ne cadre pas avec ce qu'il m'a dit; **he managed to ~ it with his conscience/the boss** il s'est arrangé avec sa conscience/le patron; **I can ~ * him** je m'occupe de lui. (**c**) *(Math) number* élever au carré. **four ~d is sixteen** quatre au carré fait seize.
5 *vi* cadrer, s'accorder (*with* avec).
◆ **square off** **1** *vi (US) [opponents]* se faire face. **2** *vt sep paper* quadriller; *wood, edges* équarrir.
◆ **square up** *vi* (**a**) *[boxers, fighters]* se mettre en garde (*to sb* devant qn). (**b**) *(pay debts)* régler ses comptes (*with sb* avec qn).
◆ **square-bashing** *n (Brit Mil sl)* exercice *m*.
◆ **square-built** *adj* trapu. ◆ **square-cut** *adj* coupé à angle droit. ◆ **square-faced** *adj* au visage carré. ◆ **squarely** *adv* (**a**) *(completely)* carrément; **we must face this ~ly** nous devons carrément y faire face; **~ly in the middle** en plein milieu; (**b**) *(honestly) treat etc* honnêtement.

squash [skwɒʃ] **1** *n* (**a**) *(crowd, crush)* cohue *f*. (**b**) **lemon/orange** ~ citronnade *f*/orangeade *f* (concentrée). (**c**) *(Sport: ~* **rackets***)* squash *m*. ~ **court/racket** court *m*/raquette *f* de squash.
2 *vt (gen)* écraser; *(fig) argument* réfuter; *(snub) person* remettre à sa place. **to ~ flat** *fruit, beetle* écraser; *hat, box* aplatir.
3 *vi* (**a**) *[people]* **they ~ed into the elevator** ils se sont entassés dans l'ascenseur; **they ~ed out of the gate** ils sont sortis en se bousculant près du portail. (**b**) *[fruit, parcel etc]* s'écraser.
◆ **squash in** **1** *vi [people]* s'entasser. **2** *vt sep (into box, suitcase etc)* réussir à faire rentrer. ◆ **squash together** **1** *vi [people]* se serrer (les uns contre les autres). **2** *vt sep objects* serrer. ◆ **squash up** **1** *vi [people]* se serrer. **2** *vt sep object* écraser; *paper* chiffonner en boule.
◆ **squashy** *adj fruit* mou.

squat [skwɒt] **1** *adj person* ramassé; *building* lourd; *armchair etc* bas et ramassé ; **2** *vi* (**a**) (**~ down**) *[person]* s'accroupir; *[animal]* se tapir. **to be ~ting (down)** *[person]* être accroupi; *[animal]* être tapi. (**b**) *[squatters]* faire du squattage *. **to ~ in a house** squatteriser * une maison. **3** *n (act of squatting)* squat *m*, squattage *m*; *(place)* squat. ◆ **squatter** *n* squatter *m*.

squawk [skwɔːk] **1** *vi [hen, parrot]* pousser un gloussement; *[baby]* brailler; *[person]* pousser un cri rauque; *(*: complain)* râler *. **2** *n* gloussement *m*; braillement *m*; cri *m* rauque.

squeak [skwiːk] **1** *vi [hinge, wheel, pen, chalk]* grincer; *[shoe]* craquer; *[mouse, doll]* vagir; *[person]* glapir. **2** *vt*: **'no' she ~ed** 'non' glapit-elle. **3** *n* grincement *m*; craquement *m*; vagissement *m*; glapissement *m*. **to give a ~ of surprise** pousser un petit cri de surprise; **not a ~ *!** pas un murmure, hein!; **I don't want another ~ out of you** je ne veux plus t'entendre. ◆ **squeaky** *adj hinge, wheel* grinçant; *shoes* qui craquent.

squeal [skwiːl] **1** *vi* (**a**) *[animal, person]* pousser un cri aigu; *[brakes]* hurler; *[tyres]* crisser. (**b**) *(⁑: inform)* vendre la mèche *. **to ~ on sb** dénoncer qn, donner * qn. **2** *vt*: **'help' he ~ed** 'au secours' cria-t-il d'une voix perçante. **3** *n* cri *m* aigu ; hurlement *m*; crissement *m*. **to give a ~ of pain** pousser un cri de douleur; **with a ~ of laughter** avec un rire aigu.

squeamish ['skwiːmɪʃ] *adj (easily nauseated; fastidious)* facilement dégoûté; *(queasy)* qui a mal au cœur; *(easily shocked)* qui s'effarouche facilement. **I'm too ~ to do that** je n'ose pas faire cela.
◆ **squeamishness** *n (queasiness)* nausée *f*; *(prudishness)* pruderie *f*.

squeeze [skwiːz] **1** *n (act, pressure)* pression *f*, compression *f*; *(in crowd)* cohue *f*. **a ~ of lemon** quelques gouttes *fpl* de citron; **a ~ of toothpaste** un peu de dentifrice; **it was a tight ~ to get through** il y avait à peine la place de passer; *(fig)* **to put the ~ on sb** ⁑ harceler qn; *(Econ)* **credit ~** restrictions *fpl* de crédit. **2** *vt* (**a**) *(press) (gen)* presser; *doll, teddy bear* appuyer sur; *sb's hand, arm* serrer. **she ~d it into the case** elle a réussi à le faire rentrer dans la valise; *(fig)* **he ~d his victim dry** * il a saigné sa victime à blanc. (**b**) *(extract: ~* **out***) water, toothpaste* exprimer (*from, out of* de); *names, information, money* soutirer, arracher (*out of* à). **3** *vi* se glisser (*under* sous; *into* dans). **he ~d past me** il s'est glissé devant moi en me poussant un peu; **they all ~d into the car** ils se sont entassés dans la voiture; **he ~d through the crowd** il a réussi à se faufiler à travers la foule; **the car ~d into the empty space** il y avait juste assez de place pour la voiture.
◆ **squeeze in** **1** *vi [person]* trouver une petite place; *[car etc]* rentrer tout juste. **can I ~ in?** est-ce qu'il y a une petite place pour moi? **2** *vt sep object into box, (* fig) item on programme etc* réussir à faire rentrer.
◆ **squeeze-box** * *n (accordion)* accordéon *m*; *(concertina)* concertina *m*. ◆ **squeezer** *n* presse-fruits *m inv*; **lemon ~r** presse-citron *m inv*.

squelch [skwel(t)ʃ] *vi*: **to ~ in/out** *etc* entrer/sortir *etc* en pataugeant.

squib [skwɪb] *n* pétard *m*.

squid [skwɪd] *n* calmar *m*.

squiggle ['skwɪgl] **1** *n* gribouillis *m*. **2** *vi* gribouiller.

squint [skwɪnt] **1** *n (Med)* strabisme *m*; *(quick glance)* coup *m* d'œil. *(Med)* **to have a ~** loucher. **2** *vi (Med)* loucher. **to ~ at sth** *(obliquely)* regarder qch du coin de l'œil; *(quickly)* jeter un coup d'œil à qch.

squire ['skwaɪəʳ] *n* ≃ châtelain *m*; *(Hist)* écuyer *m*.

squirm [skwɜːm] *vi [worm etc]* se tortiller; *[person] (from embarrassment)* ne pas savoir où se mettre; *(from distaste)* avoir un haut-le-corps.

squirrel ['skwɪr(ə)l] **1** *n* écureuil *m*. **2** *adj coat etc* en petit-gris.

squirt [skwɜːt] **1** *vt water* faire jaillir (*at, on, onto* sur; *into* dans); *oil* injecter; *detergent* verser une giclée de; *(from aerosol) insecticide etc* pulvériser (*on* sur). *(scent etc)* **to ~ sb with sth** asperger qn de qch. **2** *vi [liquid]* jaillir (*from* de). **the water ~ed into my eye** j'ai reçu une giclée d'eau dans l'œil. **3** *n [water]* jet *m*; *[detergent]* giclée *f*; *[scent]* quelques gouttes *fpl*.

Sri Lanka [srɪ'læŋkə] *n* Sri Lanka *m or f*.

stab [stæb] **1** *n (with dagger/knife etc)* coup *m* (de poignard/de couteau *etc*). *(fig)* **a ~ in the back** un coup déloyal; **a ~ of pain** un élancement; **a ~ of remorse/grief** un remords/une douleur lancinant(e); *(fig)* **to have a ~ at (doing) sth** * s'essayer à (faire) qch. **2** *adj*: **~ wound** coup *m* de poignard (*or* couteau *etc*). **3** *vt (kill or wound with knife)* tuer *or* blesser d'un coup de *or* à coups de couteau; *(with dagger)* poignarder. **to ~ sb to death** tuer qn d'un coup de couteau *etc*; **he was ~bed through the heart** il a reçu un coup de couteau *etc* dans le cœur; *(lit, fig)* **to ~ sb in the back** poignarder qn dans le dos.
◆ **stabbing** **1** *n* agression *f* (à coups de couteau *etc*) ; **2** *adj pain* lancinant.

stable¹ ['steɪbl] *adj (gen)* stable; *prices* stable; *(St Ex)* ferme; *relationship, marriage* solide; *person* équilibré. ◆ **stability** *n* stabilité *f*; fermeté *f*; solidité *f*; équilibre *m*. ◆ **stabilize** *vt* stabiliser. ◆ **stabilizer** *n (Aut, Aviat, Naut)* stabilisateur *m*.

stable² ['steɪbl] **1** *n (gen, fig)* écurie *f*. **racing** ~ écurie de courses; **riding** ~**s** manège *m*. **2** *vt horse* mettre à l'écurie. ◆ **stableboy** *or* ◆ **stablelad** *n* lad *m*.

stack [stæk] **1** *n* (**a**) *(gen)* tas *m*; *(hay ~)* meule *f*. ~**s * of** un tas * de; **to have** ~**s * of money** rouler sur l'or; **we've got** ~**s * of time** on a tout le temps. (**b**) *(chimney)* cheminée *f*. (**c**) *(Comput)* pile *f*. **2** *vt* (**a**) (~ **up**) *objects* empiler; *aircraft* faire attendre (sur niveaux différents); *calls* mettre en attente; *(fig pej) jury, committee* sélectionner avec partialité (*in favour of* pour favoriser; *against* pour défavoriser). (**b**) *shelves* remplir.
◆ **stack up** *vi* se comparer.

stadium ['steɪdɪəm] *n* stade *m (sportif)*.

staff [stɑ:f] **1** *n* (**a**) *(work force: gen)* personnel *m*; *(Scol, Univ)* professeurs *mpl*; *(servants)* domestiques *mpl*; *(Mil)* état-major *m*. **a large** ~ un personnel nombreux; **to be on the** ~ faire partie du personnel; **he joined our** ~ **in 1974** il est entré chez nous en 1974. (**b**) *(liter: pole)* bâton *m*; *(flag ~)* mât *m*. **2** *adj*: ~ **canteen** restaurant *m* d'entreprise; *(Mil)* ~ **college** école *f* supérieure de guerre; *(Scol, Univ)* ~ **meeting** conseil *m* des professeurs. **3** *vt school etc* pourvoir en personnel. **it is** ~**ed mainly by immigrants** le personnel se compose surtout d'immigrants; **well-**~**ed** pourvu d'un personnel nombreux. ◆ **staffroom** *n (Scol etc)* salle *f* des professeurs.

stag [stæg] **1** *n* cerf *m*. **2** *adj*: ~ **party *** réunion *f* entre hommes; *(US *)* ~ **show** spectacle *m* porno. ◆ **stag beetle** *n* cerf-volant *m (Zool)*.

stage [steɪdʒ] **1** *n* (**a**) *(platform: in theatre)* scène *f*; *(in hall)* estrade *f*. *(profession etc)* **the** ~ le théâtre; **on** ~ sur scène; **to come on** ~ entrer en scène; **to go on the** ~ monter sur la scène; *(fig: as career)* monter sur les planches; **to write for the** ~ écrire des pièces de théâtre; *(fig)* **to hold the** ~ occuper le devant de la scène. (**b**) *(point, part) [journey]* étape *f*; *[road, pipeline]* section *f*; *[rocket]* étage *m*; *[operation, process, disease]* stade *m*; *[career]* échelon *m*. *[bus]* **fare** ~ section; **in** ~**s** *travel* par étapes; *study* par degrés; **in** *or* **by easy** ~**s** par petites étapes, par degrés; **in the early** ~**s** au début; **at an early** ~ **in** vers le début de; **at this** ~ **in the negotiations** à ce stade des négociations; **it has reached the** ~ **of being translated** c'en est au stade de la traduction; **we have reached a** ~ **where...** nous en sommes arrivés à un stade où...; **he's going through a difficult** ~ il passe par une période difficile. **2** *adj*: ~ **designer** décorateur *m*, -trice *f* de théâtre; ~ **director** metteur *m* en scène; ~ **door** entrée *f* des artistes; ~ **fright** trac * *m*; ~ **manager** régisseur *m*; ~ **name** nom *m* de théâtre; *(fig)* **in a** ~ **whisper** en aparté. **3** *vt (Theat)* monter, mettre en scène; *(fig) accident etc (organize)* organiser; *(feign)* monter. **to** ~ **a demonstration** *(organize)* organiser une manifestation; *(carry out)* manifester; **to** ~ **a strike** *(organize)* organiser une grève; *(go on strike)* faire la grève; **that was** ~**d** c'était un coup monté. ◆ **stagecraft** *n* technique *f* de la scène. ◆ **stagehand** *n* machiniste *m*. ◆ **stage-manage** *vt play, production* être régisseur pour; *(fig) event, confrontation* orchestrer. ◆ **stage-struck** *adj*: **to be** ~**-struck** brûler d'envie de faire du théâtre. ◆ **staging** *n (Theat)* mise *f* en scène. ◆ **staging post** *n* relais *m*.

stagger ['stægəʳ] **1** *vi* chanceler, tituber. **to** ~ **along/in** *etc* avancer/entrer *etc* en chancelant *or* titubant. **2** *vt* (**a**) *(amaze)* renverser, stupéfier; *(upset)* bouleverser. (**b**) *(space out) objects* espacer; *visits, payments* échelonner; *working hours, holidays* étaler. ◆ **staggering** *adj* renversant, bouleversant; *(lit, fig)* ~**ing blow** coup *m* de massue.

stagnant ['stægnənt] *adj* stagnant. ◆ **stagnate** *vi [water]* être stagnant; *(fig)* stagner. ◆ **stagnation** *n* stagnation *f*.

staid [steɪd] *adj* (trop) sérieux, (trop) posé. ◆ **staidness** *n* caractère *m* trop sérieux *or* posé.

stain [steɪn] **1** *n* (**a**) *(mark)* tache *f* (*on* sur). **grease** ~ tache de graisse; **without a** ~ **on his character** sans une tache à sa réputation. (**b**) *(colouring)* colorant *m*. **wood** ~ couleur *f* pour bois. **2** *adj*: ~ **remover** détachant *m*. **3** *vt* (**a**) tacher (*with* de). (**b**) *(colour) wood* teinter; *glass* colorer. ~**ed glass** *(substance)* verre *m* coloré; *(windows collectively)* vitraux *mpl*; ~**ed-glass window** vitrail *m*. ◆ **stainless steel** *n* acier *m* inoxydable, inox *m*.

stair [stɛəʳ] **1** *n (step)* marche *f*; *(also* ~ **s***)* escalier *m*. **on the** ~**s** dans l'escalier; **below** ~**s** à l'office. **2** *adj carpet* d'escalier. ~ **rod** tringle *f* d'escalier. ◆ **staircase** *or* ◆ **stairway** *n* escalier *m*.

stake [steɪk] **1** *n* (**a**) *(gen)* pieu *m*, poteau *m*; *(for plant)* tuteur *m*. *(Hist)* **to be burnt at the** ~ mourir sur le bûcher. (**b**) *(Betting)* enjeu *m*; *(share)* intérêt *m*. *(horse-race)* ~**s** course *f* de chevaux; *(lit, fig)* **to play for high** ~**s** jouer gros jeu; **to be at** ~ être en jeu; **there is a lot at** ~ l'enjeu est considérable; **he has got a lot at** ~ il joue gros jeu, il a gros à perdre; **to have a** ~ **in sth** avoir des intérêts dans qch; *(on large scale)* avoir de gros investissements dans qch. **2** *vt* (**a**) (~ **out**) *area* marquer avec des piquets. **to** ~ **one's claim to** établir son droit à. (**b**) (~ **up**) *plant* mettre un tuteur à. (**c**) *(bet)* jouer (*on* sur). **I'd** ~ **my life on it** j'en mettrais ma tête à couper. ◆ **stake out** *vt sep* (**a**) = **stake 2a.** (**b**) *(Police)* surveiller.
◆ **stake-out** *n* surveillance *f*.

stalactite ['stæləktaɪt] *n* stalactite *f*.

stalagmite ['stæləgmaɪt] *n* stalagmite *f*.

stale [steɪl] *adj meat, eggs etc* qui n'est plus frais; *bread* rassis; *(stronger)* dur; *air* confiné; *news* déjà vieux; *joke* rebattu; *athlete* surentraîné. **the room smells** ~ cette pièce sent le renfermé; **I'm getting** ~ je perds mon enthousiasme. ◆ **stalemate** *n (Chess)* mat *m*; *(fig)* impasse *f*; **to have reached** ~**mate** être dans l'impasse; **to break the** ~**mate** sortir de l'impasse. ◆ **staleness** *n (gen)* manque *m* de fraîcheur.

stalk¹ [stɔ:k] *n [plant]* tige *f*; *[fruit]* queue *f*; *[cabbage]* trognon *m*.

stalk² [stɔ:k] **1** *vt game, prey* traquer; *suspect* filer. **2** *vi*: **to** ~ **in/off** *etc* entrer/partir *etc* avec raideur; **he** ~**ed in angrily** il est entré d'un air furieux.

stall [stɔ:l] **1** *n (in market, at fair)* éventaire *m*; *(in exhibition)* stand *m*; *(in stable, cowshed)* stalle *f*. *(Theat)* **the** ~**s** l'orchestre *m*; **newspaper/flower** ~ kiosque *m* à journaux/de fleuriste; **station book** ~ librairie *f* de gare; **coffee** ~ buvette *f*. **2** *vi [car, engine]* caler; *[aircraft]* être en perte de vitesse. *(fig)* **to** ~ **for time** essayer de gagner du temps. **3** *vt (Aut)* caler; *(Aviat)* causer une perte de vitesse à. *(fig)* **I managed to** ~ **him** j'ai réussi à le tenir à distance; **to be** ~**ed** *(Aut)* avoir calé; *(fig)* être grippé. ◆ **stallholder** *n* marchand(e) *m(f) (en plein air)*.

stallion ['stæljən] *n* étalon *m (cheval)*.

stalwart ['stɔ:lwət] *adj (in build)* vigoureux; *(in spirit)* résolu. **to be a** ~ **supporter of sb/sth** soutenir qn/qch de façon inconditionnelle.

stamen ['steɪmen] *n (Bot)* étamine *f*.

stamina ['stæmɪnə] *n* résistance *f*, endurance *f*. **he's got** ~ il est résistant.

stammer ['stæməʳ] **1** *n* bégaiement *m*. **2** *vti* bégayer. ◆ **stammerer** *n* bègue *mf*. ◆ **stam-**

mering *n* bégaiement *m*. ◆**stammeringly** *adv* en bégayant.

stamp [stæmp] **1** *n* (**a**) timbre *m*. **postage** ~ timbre-poste *m*; **savings** ~ timbre-épargne *m*; **trading** ~ timbre-prime *m*; **National Insurance** ~ cotisation *f* à la Sécurité sociale. (**b**) *(rubber ~)* timbre *m*. **date** ~ timbre dateur. (**c**) *(mark)* **look at the date** ~ regardez la date sur le cachet; *(fig)* **the** ~ **of genius/truth** le sceau du génie/de la vérité. **2** *adj*: ~ **album** album *m* de timbres-poste; ~ **collecting** philatélie *f*; ~ **collection** collection *f* de timbres (-poste); ~ **collector** philatéliste *mf*; ~ **dealer** marchand(e) *m(f)* de timbres(-poste); ~ **duty** droit *m* de timbre; ~ **machine** distributeur *m* automatique de timbres(-poste). **3** *vt* (**a**) **to** ~ **one's foot** taper du pied; **to** ~ **one's feet** *(in rage)* trépigner; *(in dance)* frapper du pied; *(to keep warm)* battre la semelle. (**b**) *(stick a ~ on) letter, insurance card* timbrer. ~**ed addressed envelope** enveloppe timbrée pour la réponse. (**c**) *(mark with ~)* timbrer; *passport, document* viser; *visa, date* apposer (*on* sur); *metal* poinçonner. **4** *vi* taper du pied; *[horse]* piaffer. **to** ~ **on sth** piétiner qch; *(angrily)* **to** ~ **in/out** *etc* entrer/sortir *etc* en tapant du pied. ◆**stamp out** *vt sep fire* éteindre en piétinant; *rebellion* enrayer; *custom, tendency* détruire.

stampede [stæm'piːd] **1** *n [animals, people]* débandade *f*, sauve-qui-peut *m inv*; *(fig: rush)* ruée *f* (*for sth* pour obtenir qch; *for the door* vers la porte). **2** *vi* s'enfuir à la débandade (*from* de), fuir à la débandade (*towards* vers); *(fig: rush)* se ruer (*for sth* pour obtenir qch; *for the door* vers la porte). **3** *vt animals, people* jeter la panique parmi. *(fig)* **we mustn't let ourselves be** ~**d** il faut que nous prenions le temps de réfléchir.

stance [stæns] *n* position *f*.

stand [stænd] *(vb: pret, ptp* **stood***)* **1** *n* (**a**) *(position: lit, fig)* position *f*; *(resistance: Mil, fig)* résistance *f*, opposition *f*. *(lit, fig)* **to take (up) one's** ~ prendre position (*against* contre); **he took (up) his** ~ **beside me** *(lit)* il s'est placé à côté de moi; *(fig)* il m'a soutenu; *(fig)* **to make a** ~ résister (*against* à), prendre position (*against* contre). (**b**) *(taxi ~)* station *f* (de taxis). (**c**) *(for plant, bust etc)* guéridon *m*; *(for displaying goods)* étalage *m*; *(at exhibition, trade fair)* stand *m*; *(at fair)* baraque *f*; *(market stall)* éventaire *m*; *(US: witness ~)* barre *f*; *(in sports stadium, along procession route etc)* tribune *f*. **lamp** ~ support *m or* pied *m* de lampe; **hat** ~ porte-chapeaux *m inv*; **coat** ~ portemanteau *m*; **music** ~ pupitre *m* à musique; **newspaper** ~ kiosque *m* à journaux; **band** ~ kiosque (à musique).

2 *vt* (**a**) *(place: ~ up) object* mettre, poser (*on* sur; *against* contre). **to** ~ **sth on its end** faire tenir qch debout. (**b**) *(tolerate, withstand)* supporter. **I can't** ~ **it any longer** *(pain etc)* je ne peux plus le supporter; *(boredom etc)* j'en ai assez, j'en ai pardessus la tête *; **I can't** ~ **(the sight of) her** je ne peux pas la supporter *or* la voir *; **she can't** ~ **being laughed at** elle ne supporte pas qu'on se moque *(subj)* d'elle; **I can't** ~ **gin/Giraudoux** je déteste le gin/Giraudoux; **to** ~ **the strain** *[rope, beam etc]* supporter la tension; *[person]* tenir le coup; **it won't** ~ **close examination** cela ne résiste pas à un examen serré; **the town stood constant bombardment** la ville a résisté à un bombardement continuel. (**c**) *(pay for)* payer, offrir. **to** ~ **sb a drink** payer *or* offrir à boire à qn; **to** ~ **the cost of sth** payer le coût de qch. (**d**) *(phrases)* **to** ~ **a chance** avoir une bonne chance (*of doing* de faire); **to** ~ **no chance** ne pas avoir la moindre chance (*of doing* de faire); **to** ~ **one's ground** tenir bon; **to** ~ **trial** passer en jugement (*for* pour).

3 *vi* (**a**) *(be ~ing: ~ up)* être debout; *(stay ~ing)* rester debout. **too weak to** ~ trop faible pour se tenir debout; **to** ~ **erect** *(stay upright)* rester debout; *(straighten up)* se redresser; ~ **up straight!** tiens-toi droit!; *(fig)* **to** ~ **on one's own feet** se débrouiller tout seul; **he** ~**s over 6 feet** il fait plus de 1 mètre 80; **the house is still** ~**ing** la maison existe toujours; **not much still** ~**s of the walls** il ne reste plus grand-chose des murs; **they didn't leave a stone** ~**ing** ils n'ont rien laissé debout. (**b**) *(rise: ~ up)* se lever, se mettre debout. (**c**) *(~ still)* rester (debout), être (debout). **we stood talking for an hour** nous sommes restés là à parler pendant une heure; **he stood in the doorway** il se tenait dans l'embrasure de la porte; **don't** ~ **there, do something!** ne reste pas là à ne rien faire!; *(fig)* **he left the others** ~**ing** il dépassait les autres d'une tête; **the man** ~**ing over there** cet homme là-bas; ~ **over there till...** mets-toi là-bas jusqu'à ce que...; **they stood in a circle** ils se tenaient en cercle; **to** ~ **in line** faire la queue; ~ **still!** ne bougez pas!; *(fig)* **time seemed to** ~ **still** le temps semblait s'être arrêté; *(lit, fig)* **to** ~ **fast** *or* **firm** tenir bon; *(lit)* **to** ~ **in sb's way** barrer le passage à qn; *(fig)* **I won't** ~ **in your way** je ne vous ferai pas obstacle; **nothing** ~**s in our way** la voie est libre; **his age** ~**s in his way** son âge constitue un sérieux handicap; **that was all that stood between him and...** c'était tout ce qui le séparait de...; **to** ~ **clear** s'écarter; **you're** ~**ing on my foot** tu me marches sur le pied; *(Aut)* **to** ~ **on the brakes** freiner à mort; *(fig)* **to** ~ **on ceremony** faire des manières; **to** ~ **on one's dignity** garder ses distances; **it** ~**s to reason that...** il va sans dire que...; **where do you** ~ **on this question?** quelle est votre position sur cette question?; **I like to know where I** ~ j'aime savoir où j'en suis. (**d**) *(be situated)* se trouver. **the village** ~**s in the valley** le village se trouve dans la vallée; *[statue, argument etc]* **to** ~ **on** reposer sur. (**e**) *(be)* être. **to** ~ **accused/convicted of** être accusé/déclaré coupable de; *(Parl)* **to** ~ **(as a candidate** *or* **for election)** être candidat (*for* à); **he stood for the council** il était candidat au poste de conseiller; **to** ~ **for re-election** se représenter; *(have reached)* **to** ~ **at** *[thermometer, clock]* indiquer; *[offer, price, bid]* être à; *[score]* être de; **accept the offer as it** ~**s** acceptez l'offre telle quelle; *(Sport etc)* **the record stood at...** le record est resté à...; **as things** ~ les choses étant ce qu'elles sont; **how do things** ~**?** où en sont les choses? (**f**) *(remain undisturbed) [liquid, dough etc]* reposer; *[tea, coffee]* infuser; *[offer]* demeurer valable. **let the matter** ~ **as it is** laissez les choses comme elles sont; **they let the regulation** ~ ils n'ont rien changé au règlement; *[project, results]* **to** ~ **or fall by sth** reposer sur qch. (**g**) *(be likely)* **to** ~ **to lose** risquer de perdre; **to** ~ **to win** avoir des chances de gagner; **he** ~**s to make a fortune** il pourrait bien faire fortune. (**h**) *(Naut)* **to** ~ **out to sea** *(move)* mettre le cap sur le large; *(stay)* être *or* rester au large.

◆**stand about, stand around** *vi* rester là, traîner *(pej)*. **to keep sb** ~**ing about** faire faire le pied de grue à qn. ◆**stand aside** *vi* s'écarter, se pousser. *(fig)* **to** ~ **aside in favour of sb** laisser la voie libre à qn. ◆**stand back** *vi (move back)* reculer, s'écarter. **the farm** ~**s back from the motorway** la ferme est à l'écart de l'autoroute. ◆**stand by** **1** *vi* (**a**) *(be onlooker)* rester là (à ne rien faire). (**b**) *[troops]* être en état d'alerte; *[person, ship, vehicle] (be ready)* se tenir prêt; *(be at hand)* attendre sur place. ~ **by for takeoff** paré pour le décollage; ~ **by to drop anchor** paré à mouiller l'ancre; ~ **by for further news** tenez-vous prêt à recevoir d'autres nouvelles. **2** *vt fus promise* tenir; *sb else's decision* accepter; *one's own decision* s'en tenir à; *friend* ne pas abandonner; *colleague etc* soutenir. ◆**stand down** *vi [troops]* être déconsigné (en fin d'alerte); *(fig: withdraw) [candidate]* se désister. ◆**stand for** *vt fus* (**a**) *(represent) [initials, political* *party]* représenter. (**b**) *(tolerate)* supporter, tolérer. ◆ **stand in** *vi*: **to ~ in for sb** remplacer qn. ◆ **stand out** *vi (project) [ledge, buttress]* avancer (*from* sur); *[vein etc]* ressortir (*on* sur); *(be conspicuous)* ressortir, se détacher (*against* sur). *(fig)* **he ~s out above all the rest** il surpasse tout le monde; *(fig)* **that ~s out a mile!** * cela saute aux yeux!; **to ~ out for sth** revendiquer qch; **to ~ out against** *attack* résister à; *demand* s'opposer fermement à. ◆ **stand over** **1** *vi [items for discussion]* rester en suspens. **2** *vt fus person* surveiller, être sur le dos de. ◆ **stand to** *vi (Mil)* se mettre en état d'alerte. ◆ **stand up** **1** *vi (rise)* se lever, se mettre debout; *(be ~ing)* être debout; *(fig) [argument, case]* être valable. *(fig)* **to ~ up for sb/sth** défendre qn/qch; **to ~ up to** *opponent* affronter; *(in argument)* tenir tête à; *rough treatment, cold etc* résister à; *V also* **stand 3a, 3b.** **2** *vt sep box etc* mettre debout. *(fig)* **she stood me up** * elle m'a fait faux bond; *V also* **stand 2a.**

◆ **stand-alone** *adj (Comput) system* autonome. ◆ **stand-by** **1** *n* (**a**) **it's a useful ~-by** ça peut toujours être utile; **to be on ~-by** *[troops]* être sur pied d'intervention; *[plane]* se tenir prêt à décoller; *[doctor]* être de garde; (**b**) *(US Theat)* doublure *f*; **2** *adj car, battery etc* de réserve; *generator* de secours; *(Aviat) ticket, passenger* sans garantie. ◆ **stand-in** *n* remplaçant(e) *m(f)*; *(Cine)* doublure *f*. ◆ **stand-off** *n (pause)* temps d'arrêt; *(stalemate)* impasse *f*; *(counterbalancing situation)* contrepartie *f*. ◆ **stand-offish** *adj (pej)* distant, froid. ◆ **stand-offishly** *adv* avec froideur. ◆ **standpoint** *n* point *m* de vue. ◆ **standstill** *n* arrêt *m*; **to come to a ~still** s'arrêter; **to bring to a ~still** arrêter; **to be at a ~still** *[person, car]* être immobile; *[production]* être paralysé; *[discussion]* être au point mort; *[trade]* être dans le marasme complet. ◆ **stand-to** *n (Mil)* alerte *f*. ◆ **stand-up** *adj collar* droit; *meal etc* (pris) debout; *fight, quarrel* en règle; **~-up comic** comique *m* (qui se produit en solo).

standard ['stændəd] **1** *n* (**a**) *(flag)* étendard *m*; *(Naut)* pavillon *m*. (**b**) *(norm)* norme *f*; *(criterion)* critère *m*; *(for weights and measures)* étalon *m*; *(intellectual etc)* niveau *m* (voulu). **monetary ~** titre *m* de monnaie; **the gold ~** l'étalon or; *(fig)* **to be** *or* **come up to ~** *[person]* être à la hauteur; *[thing]* être de la qualité voulue; **you are applying a double ~** vous appliquez deux mesures; **his ~s are high** il cherche l'excellence; *(morally, artistically)* **he has set us a high ~** il a établi un modèle difficile à surpasser; **first-year university ~** du niveau de première année d'université; **high/low ~ of living** niveau de vie élevé/bas; **to have high moral ~s** avoir un sens moral très développé; **I couldn't accept their ~s** je ne pouvais pas accepter leur échelle de valeurs. (**c**) *(street light)* pylône *m* d'éclairage; *(base: for lamp, street light)* pied *m*. **2** *adj size, height, procedure* ordinaire, normal; *metre, weight etc* étalon *inv*; *(Comm: regular) design, model, size* standard *inv*; *(Statistics) deviation etc* type; *reference book* classique, de base; *pronunciation, usage* correct. **it is now ~ practice to do so** c'est maintenant courant de faire ainsi; **a ~ model car** une voiture de série; **~ time** l'heure légale.

◆ **standard-bearer** *n* porte-étendard *m inv*. ◆ **standardization** *n* standardisation *f*; normalisation *f*. ◆ **standardize** *vt (gen)* standardiser; *product, terminology* normaliser. ◆ **standard-lamp** *n* lampadaire *m*.

standing ['stændɪŋ] **1** *adj* (**a**) *passenger* debout *inv*; *crop* sur pied. *(in bus etc)* **~ room** places *fpl* debout; **~ stone** pierre *f* levée. (**b**) *(permanent) army, committee, invitation* permanent; *rule* fixe; *grievance, reproach* constant. **~ expenses** frais *mpl* généraux; **a ~ joke** un sujet de plaisanterie continuel; **~ order** *(Banking)* prélèvement *m* bancaire; *(Comm)* commande *f* permanente (*for* pour); *(Mil, Parl)* **~ orders** règlement *m*. **2** *n* (**a**) *(importance etc) [person, newspaper]* importance *f*; *[restaurant, business]* réputation *f*, standing *m*. **social ~** position *f* sociale, standing; **professional ~** rang *m or* standing professionnel; **firms of that ~** des compagnies aussi réputées; **he has no ~ in this matter** il n'a aucune autorité dans cette affaire. (**b**) *(duration)* **of 10 years' ~** *friendship* qui dure depuis 10 ans; *agreement, contract* qui existe depuis 10 ans; *doctor, teacher* qui a 10 ans de métier; **of long ~** de longue date. (**c**) *(US Sport)* **the ~** le classement.

stank [stæŋk] *pret of* **stink.**

stanza ['stænzə] *n [poem]* strophe *f*; *[song]* couplet *m*.

staple¹ ['steɪpl] *adj crop, industry* principal; *products, foods* de base. **~ diet** nourriture *f* de base.

staple² ['steɪpl] **1** *n (for papers)* agrafe *f*; *(Tech)* crampon *m*. **2** *vt* (**~ together**) agrafer (*on to* à); cramponner. ◆ **stapler** *n* agrafeuse *f*.

star [stɑːʳ] **1** *n* (**a**) étoile *f*; *(Typ etc)* astérisque *m*. **the S~s and Stripes** la Bannière étoilée; **3-~ hotel** hôtel *m* 3 étoiles; **4-~ petrol** super * *m*; *(US)* **four-~ general** général *m* à quatre étoiles; **born under a lucky ~** né sous une bonne étoile; **you can thank your (lucky) ~s * that...** tu peux remercier le ciel de ce que...; *(fig)* **to see ~s *** voir trente-six chandelles; *(horoscope)* **the ~s** l'horoscope *m*; **it was written in his ~s that...** il était écrit que... (**b**) *(Cine, Sport etc)* vedette *f*; *(actress only)* star *f*. **2** *adj (Theat etc)* **~ part** premier rôle; **a ~(ring) role** l'un des principaux rôles; *(Theat, fig)* **the ~ turn** la vedette. **3** *vt*: **the film ~s John Wayne** John Wayne est la vedette du film; **~ring Greta Garbo as...** avec Greta Garbo dans le rôle de... **4** *vi* être la vedette (*in a film* d'un film); *(fig)* briller. **he ~red as Hamlet** c'est lui qui a joué le rôle de Hamlet. ◆ **stardom** *n (Cine, Sport etc)* célébrité *f*. ◆ **starfish** *n* étoile *f* de mer. ◆ **stargaze** *vi*: **to be ~gazing** être dans la lune. ◆ **starlet** *n (Cine)* starlette *f*. ◆ **starlight** *n*: **by ~light** à la lumière des étoiles. ◆ **starlit** *adj* étoilé. ◆ **starry** *adj sky, night* étoilé. ◆ **starry-eyed** *adj (idealistic)* idéaliste; *(innocent)* innocent; *(from wonder)* éberlué; *(from love)* éperdument amoureux. ◆ **star-studded** *adj sky* parsemé d'étoiles; *(fig) cast etc* à vedettes.

starboard ['stɑːbəd] *(Naut)* **1** *n* tribord *m*. **2** *adj* de tribord.

starch [stɑːtʃ] **1** *n (gen)* amidon *m*. *(food)* **~es** féculents *mpl*. **2** *vt collar* amidonner, empeser. ◆ **starch-reduced** *adj bread* de régime. ◆ **starchy** *adj*: **~y food** féculents *mpl*.

stare [stɛəʳ] **1** *n* regard *m* (fixe). **curious/vacant ~** long regard curieux/vague. **2** *vi*: **to ~ at sb/sth** regarder qn/qch fixement, fixer qn/qch du regard; **to ~ at sb/sth in surprise** regarder qn/qch avec surprise; **what are you staring at?** qu'est-ce que tu regardes comme ça?; **to ~ into space** avoir le regard perdu dans le vague. **3** *vt*: **to ~ sb in the face** fixer qn du regard, dévisager qn; *(fig)* **they're staring you in the face!** ils sont là devant ton nez; **that ~s you in the face** cela crève les yeux. ◆ **stare out** *vt sep* faire baisser les yeux à.

stark [stɑːk] **1** *adj countryside* morne; *décor* austère. *(fig)* **the ~ truth** la vérité telle qu'elle est. **2** *adv*: **~ raving** *or* **staring mad** * complètement fou *or* dingue *; **~ naked** complètement nu.

starling ['stɑːlɪŋ] *n* étourneau *m (oiseau)*.

start [stɑːt] **1** *n* (**a**) *(beginning: gen)* commencement *m*, début *m*; *[negotiations]* ouverture *f*; *[race etc]* départ *m*; *(~ing line)* point *m* de départ. **the ~ of the academic year** la rentrée universitaire et scolaire; **that was the ~ of all the trouble** c'est là que tous les ennuis ont commencé; **from the ~** dès le début, dès le commencement; **for a ~** d'abord; **from ~ to finish** du début jusqu'à la fin;

to get off to a good ~ bien commencer, prendre un bon départ; **to get a good** ~ **in life** bien débuter dans la vie; **a good** ~ **to his career** un bon début pour sa carrière; **to make a** ~ commencer; **to make an early** ~ commencer de bonne heure; *(in journey)* partir de bonne heure; **to make a fresh** ~ recommencer. (**b**) *(advantage) (Sport)* avance *f*; *(fig)* avantage *m* (*over* sur). **to give sb 10 metres'** ~ *or* **a 10-metre** ~ donner 10 mètres d'avance à qn; *(fig)* **that gave him a** ~ **over the others** cela lui a donné un avantage sur les autres. (**c**) *(sudden movement) [person]* sursaut *m*; *[animal]* tressaillement *m*. **to wake with a** ~ se réveiller en sursaut; **to give a** ~ sursauter; **to give sb a** ~ faire sursauter qn; **you gave me such a** ~! ce que vous m'avez fait peur!

2 *vt* (**a**) *(begin) (gen)* commencer (*to do, doing* à faire, de faire); *work* commencer, se mettre à; *task* entreprendre; *bottle, cheese etc* entamer. **to** ~ **a journey** partir en voyage; **to** ~ **life as** débuter dans la vie comme; **to** ~ **again** *or* **afresh** recommencer (*to do* à faire). (**b**) (~ **off,** ~ **up**) *discussion* commencer, ouvrir; *conversation* engager; *quarrel, rumour* faire naître; *reform, series of events* déclencher; *fashion, policy* lancer; *phenomenon, institution* donner naissance à; *war* causer. **to** ~ **a fire** *(in grate etc)* faire du feu; *(accidentally)* provoquer un incendie; **she has ~ed a baby** * elle est enceinte. (**c**) *(also* ~ **up, get ~ed**) *engine, vehicle* mettre en marche, démarrer; *clock* mettre en marche; (~ **off**) *race* donner le signal du départ. **to** ~ **sb (off** *or* **out) on a career** lancer qn dans une carrière; **if you** ~ **him (off) on that subject...** si tu le lances sur ce sujet...; **that ~ed him remembering** alors il s'est mis à se souvenir; *(fig)* **now you've ~ed sth!** quelle histoire!; **to get ~ed on (doing) sth** commencer (à faire) qch; **let's get ~ed** allons-y; **to get sb ~ed on (doing) sth** faire commencer qch à qn; **once I get ~ed I work very quickly** une fois lancé, je travaille très vite.

3 *vi* (**a**) *(also* ~ **off,** ~ **up**: *gen)* commencer (*with* par; *by doing* par faire); *[road]* partir (*at* de). **to** ~ **on** *book, study* commencer; *new bottle* entamer; **we must** ~ **at once** il faut commencer *or* nous y mettre immédiatement; **it's ~ing (off) rather well/badly** cela s'annonce plutôt bien/mal; **to** ~ **in business** se lancer dans les affaires; **before October ~s** avant le début d'octobre; **to** ~ **again** *or* **afresh** recommencer; **~ing from Monday** à partir de lundi; **to** ~ **with, there were only 3** d'abord, ils n'étaient que 3; ~ **on a new page** prenez une nouvelle page; **he ~ed (out) to say that...** son intention était de dire que... (**b**) *(leave:* ~ **off,** ~ **out**) partir (*from* de; *for* pour; *on a journey* en voyage). **he ~ed (off** *or* **out) down the street** il a commencé à descendre la rue; *(fig)* **to** ~ **(off) as a clerk** débuter comme employé; **to** ~ **(off** *or* **out) as a Marxist** commencer par être marxiste. (**c**) (~ **up**) *[car, machine]* démarrer; *[clock]* se mettre à marcher. (**d**) *(jump nervously) [person]* sursauter; *[animal]* tressaillir.

◆ **starter** *n* (**a**) *(Sport) (official)* starter *m*; *(horse, runner)* partant *m*; *(Scol etc)* **the child was a late ~er** cet enfant a mis du temps à se développer; *(fig)* **it's a non-~er** * ça ne vaut rien; (**b**) *(Aut)* démarreur *m*; *(on machine etc)* bouton *m* de démarrage; (**c**) **for ~ers** * *(Culin)* comme hors-d'œuvre *m inv*; *(for a start)* pour commencer. ◆ **starting** *adj*: **~ing point** point *m* de départ; **~ing price** *(St Ex)* prix *m* initial; *(Racing)* cote *f* de départ; **~ing salary** salaire *m* d'embauche. ◆ **start-up costs** *npl* capital *m* de lancement.

startle ['stɑ:tl] *vt [sound, sb's arrival]* faire sursauter *or* tressaillir; *[news, telegram]* alarmer. **to** ~ **sb out of his wits** donner un choc à qn; **you ~d me!** vous m'avez fait peur! ◆ **startled** *adj animal* effarouché; *person, voice* très surpris. ◆ **startling** *adj (surprising)* surprenant; *(alarming)* alarmant.

starve [stɑ:v] **1** *vt* (**a**) *(deliberately)* affamer. **to** ~ **sb to death** laisser qn mourir de faim; **she ~d herself to feed him** elle s'est privée de nourriture pour lui donner à manger; **to** ~ **sb into submission** soumettre qn par la faim. (**b**) *(deprive)* priver (*sb of sth* qn de qch). **2** *vi* manquer de nourriture, être affamé. **to** ~ **(to death)** mourir de faim. ◆ **starvation 1** *n* inanition *f* ; **2** *adj rations, wages* de famine. ◆ **starving** *adj* affamé; *(fig)* **I'm starving** * je meurs de faim.

stash * [stæʃ] *vt* (~ **away**) *(hide)* cacher; *(store away)* mettre de côté. **£500 ~ed away** 500 livres *(stored away)* en réserve *or (safe)* en lieu sûr.

state [steɪt] **1** *n* (**a**) état *m*. ~ **of alert/war** état d'alerte/de guerre; **the** ~ **of the art** l'état actuel de la technique; **in your** ~ **of health/mind** dans votre état de santé/d'esprit; **in an odd** ~ **of mind** d'une humeur étrange; **you're in no** ~ **to reply** vous n'êtes pas en état de répondre; **to lie in** ~ être exposé solennellement; **to live in** ~ mener grand train; *(fig)* **what's the** ~ **of play?** où en est-on?; **in a good/bad** ~ **of repair** bien/mal entretenu; **to be in a good/bad** ~ *[chair, car, house]* être en bon/mauvais état; *[person, marriage]* aller bien/mal; **the** ~ **the car was in** l'état de la voiture; **he's not in a fit** ~ **to drive** il est hors d'état de conduire; **what a** ~ **you're in!** vous êtes dans un bel état!; **he got into a terrible** ~ **about it** * ça l'a mis dans tous ses états; **don't get into such a** ~! * ne vous affolez pas! (**b**) *(Pol)* **the S**~ l'État *m*; *(US)* **the S~s** les États-Unis *mpl*; **affairs of** ~ affaires *fpl* de l'État.

2 *adj business, secret* d'État; *security, control* de l'État; *medicine* étatisé; *(US: often* **S**~) *law, prison* d'État. ~ **apartments** appartements *mpl* officiels; ~ **banquet** banquet *m* de gala; *(US)* **S~ Department** Département *m* d'État, ≃ ministère *m* des Affaires étrangères; *(Brit)* ~ **education** enseignement *m* public; *(US)* **the S~ line** la frontière entre les États; *(US)* **S~'s attorney** procureur *m*; *(Brit)* ~ **school** école publique; ~ **sector** secteur *m* public; *(US)* ~ **trooper** ≃ CRS *m*; **to make a** ~ **visit to a country** se rendre en visite officielle dans un pays.

3 *vt* déclarer (*that* que); *one's views, the facts, problem* exposer; *time, place* fixer, spécifier; *conditions, theory, restrictions* formuler. **it is ~d in the records that...** il est écrit dans les archives que...; **as ~d above** ainsi qu'il est dit plus haut; ~ **your name and address** déclinez vos nom, prénoms et adresse; **cheques must** ~ **the sum clearly** les chèques doivent indiquer la somme clairement; **to** ~ **one's case** présenter ses arguments.

◆ **state-controlled** *adj* étatisé. ◆ **stated** *adj date, sum* fixé; *interval* fixe; *limit* prescrit; **on ~d days** à jours fixes; **at the time ~d** à l'heure dite. ◆ **state-enrolled nurse** *n (Brit)* infirmier *m*, -ière *f* auxiliaire, aide-soignante *f*. ◆ **statehouse** *n* siège *m* de la législature d'un État. ◆ **stateless** *adj* apatride ; **~less person** apatride *mf*. ◆ **stateliness** *n* majesté *f*. ◆ **stately** *adj* majestueux; *(Brit)* **~ly home** château *m (de l'aristocratie)*. ◆ **statement** *n* (**a**) *[views]* exposition *f*; *[conditions]* formulation *f*; *(written, verbal)* déclaration *f*; *(Jur)* déposition *f*; **official ~ment** communiqué *m* officiel; **to make a ~ment** faire une déclaration; (**b**) *(Comm: bill)* facture *f*; **bank ~ment** relevé *m* de compte. ◆ **state-of-the-art** *adj* dernier cri *inv*. ◆ **state-owned** *adj* étatisé. ◆ **state-registered nurse** *n (Brit)* infirmier *m*, -ière *f* diplômé(e) d'État. ◆ **stateroom** *n [palace]* grande salle *f* de réception; *[ship, train]* cabine *f* de luxe. ◆ **statesman** *n* homme *m* d'État; *(fig)* **he is a real ~sman** il est extrêmement diplomate. ◆ **statesmanlike** *adj* diplomatique. ◆ **statesmanship** *n* habileté *f* politique. ◆ **state-subsidized** *adj* subventionné par l'État. ◆ **state-wide** *adj, adv* d'un bout à l'autre de l'État.

static ['stætɪk] **1** *adj* statique. **2** *n* (**a**) ~**s** statique *f.* (**b**) *(Elec, Rad etc)* parasites *mpl.*

station ['steɪʃ(ə)n] **1** *n* (**a**) *(place)* poste *m*, station *f*; *(Mil)* poste. **fire** ~ caserne *f* de pompiers; **lifeboat** ~ centre *m* de secours en mer; **police** ~ commissariat *m* (de police), gendarmerie *f*; **radio** ~ station de radio; **one's** ~ **in life** sa situation sociale; *(Rel)* **the S~s of the Cross** le Chemin de Croix. (**b**) *(Rail)* gare *f*; *[underground]* station *f.* **bus** *or* **coach** ~ gare routière; **the train came into the** ~ le train est entré en gare; *(in underground)* la rame est entrée dans la station. (**c**) *(US Telec)* poste *m.* **2** *adj (Rail) staff, bookstall etc* de (la) gare. *(US Rad)* ~ **break** page *f* de publicité; *(Rail)* ~ **master** chef *m* de gare; *(Aut)* ~ **wag(g)on** break *m.* **3** *vt (gen)* placer; *look-out, troops* poster. **to** ~ **o.s.** se placer; **to be** ~**ed at** *[troops]* être en garnison à; *[sailors]* être en station à. ◆ **stationary** *adj* stationnaire. ◆ **stationer** *n* papetier *m*, -ière *f*; ~**er's (shop)** papeterie *f (magasin).* ◆ **stationery** **1** *n* papeterie *f (articles)*; *(writing paper)* papier *m* à lettres ; **2** *adj (Brit)* **the S~ery Office** ≃ l'Imprimerie nationale.

statistics [stə'tɪstɪks] *npl* statistique *f*; *(measurements)* statistiques; *(hum: woman's)* mensurations *fpl.* **a set of** ~ une statistique. ◆ **statistical** *adj error* de statistiques; *probability, table* statistique; *expert* en statistiques. ◆ **statistically** *adv* statistiquement. ◆ **statistician** [ˌstætɪs'tɪʃ(ə)n] *n* statisticien(ne) *m(f).*

statue ['stætju:] *n* statue *f.* ◆ **statuesque** *adj* sculptural. ◆ **statuette** *n* statuette *f.*

stature ['stætʃəʳ] *n* stature *f*, taille *f*; *(fig)* envergure *f.* *(fig)* **his** ~ **increased when...** il a pris de l'envergure quand...; **moral/intellectual** ~ envergure sur le plan moral/intellectuel.

status ['steɪtəs] **1** *n* (**a**) *(economic etc position)* situation *f*, position *f*; *(Admin, Jur)* statut *m.* **social** ~ standing *m*; **civil** ~ état *m* civil; **what is his official** ~**?** quelle est sa position officielle?; **economic** ~ situation économique; **the** ~ **of the black population** la condition sociale *or (Admin)* le statut de la population noire; **his** ~ **as an assistant director** son standing de directeur-adjoint. (**b**) *(prestige) [person, job]* prestige *m.* **2** *adj*: ~ **symbol** signe *m* extérieur de richesse. ◆ **status quo** *n* statu quo *m.*

statute ['stætju:t] **1** *n (Jur etc)* loi *f.* **by** ~ selon la loi. **2** *adj*: ~ **book** code *m.* ◆ **statutory** *adj duty, right, control* statutaire; *holiday* légal; *offence* défini par un article de loi; *(US)* ~ **rape** relations *fpl* sexuelles avec mineur(s); *(fig)* **the** ~ * **woman** la femme de rigueur.

staunch¹ [stɔ:n(t)ʃ] *vt flow* arrêter; *blood* étancher.

staunch² [stɔ:n(t)ʃ] *adj support* loyal; *friend, ally* à toute épreuve. ◆ **staunchly** *adv* loyalement.

stave [steɪv] *(vb: pret, ptp* **stove** *or* **staved***) n [barrel etc]* douve *f*; *(Mus)* portée *f*; *(Poetry)* stance *f*, strophe *f.* ◆ **stave in** *vt sep* enfoncer. ◆ **stave off** *vt sep danger, threat* écarter; *disaster, defeat* éviter; *hunger* tromper; *attack* parer.

stay [steɪ] **1** *n* (**a**) séjour *m.* **he is in Rome for a short** ~ il est à Rome pour une courte visite *or* un bref séjour; **a** ~ **in hospital** un séjour à l'hôpital. (**b**) *(Jur)* ~ **of execution** sursis *m* à l'exécution (d'un jugement).

2 *vt* (**a**) *(check)* arrêter; *disease, epidemic* enrayer; *(delay)* retarder; *(Jur) judgment* surseoir à; *proceedings* suspendre; *decision* remettre. (**b**) **to** ~ **the course** *(Sport)* aller jusqu'au bout; *(fig)* tenir bon.

3 *vi (remain)* rester. ~ **there!** restez là!; **to** ~ **still, to** ~ **put** * ne pas bouger; **to** ~ **to dinner** rester dîner; *(Rad)* ~ **tuned!** restez à l'écoute!; ~ **with it** * tenez bon; **it is here to** ~ c'est bien établi; **he's here to** ~ il est là pour de bon; **if the weather** ~**s fine** si le temps se maintient au beau; **has she come to** ~**?** est-ce qu'elle est venue avec l'intention de rester?; **she came to** ~ **for a few weeks** elle est venue passer quelques semaines; **I'm** ~**ing with my aunt** je loge chez ma tante; **to** ~ **in a hotel** descendre à l'hôtel; **he was** ~**ing in Paris** il séjournait à Paris.

◆ **stay away** *vi*: **he** ~**ed away for 3 years** il n'est pas rentré avant 3 ans; **he** ~**ed away from the meeting/from school** il n'est pas allé à la réunion/à l'école. ◆ **stay behind** *vi* rester (en arrière *or* à la fin). ◆ **stay down** *vi* rester en bas; *(bending)* rester baissé; *(lying down)* rester couché; *(under water)* rester sous l'eau. ◆ **stay in** *vi (at home)* rester à la maison, ne pas sortir; *(Scol)* être en retenue; *[screw etc]* tenir. ◆ **stay out** *vi (away from home)* ne pas rentrer; *(outside)* rester dehors; *(on strike)* rester en grève. **get out and** ~ **out!** sortez et ne revenez pas!; **to** ~ **out late** rentrer tard; **to** ~ **out all night** ne pas rentrer de la nuit; *(fig)* **to** ~ **out of** *argument etc* ne pas se mêler de; *prison* éviter; **to** ~ **out of trouble** se tenir tranquille. ◆ **stay over** *vi* s'arrêter (un *or* plusieurs jour(s)), faire une halte. **can you** ~ **over till Thursday?** est-ce que vous pouvez rester jusqu'à jeudi? ◆ **stay up** *vi [person]* rester debout, ne pas se coucher; *[trousers, fence etc]* tenir. **to** ~ **up late** se coucher tard.

◆ **stay-at-home** *n, adj* casanier *(m)*, -ière *(f).* ◆ **stayer** *n (horse)* cheval *m or (runner)* coureur *m* qui a du fond; *(fig)* **he's a** ~**er** il n'abandonne pas facilement. ◆ **staying power** *n* endurance *f.*

stead [sted] *n*: **in my/his** *etc* ~ à ma/sa *etc* place; **to stand sb in good** ~ être très utile à qn.

steadfast ['stedfəst] *adj (unshakeable)* ferme; *(constant)* constant. ◆ **steadfastly** *adv* fermement. ◆ **steadfastness** *n* fermeté *f.*

steady ['stedɪ] **1** *adj* (**a**) *(firm) table, pole, boat* stable; *hand* sûr; *gaze* franc; *nerves* solide; *person* sérieux; *(not nervous)* calme. **he isn't very** ~ **on his feet** il n'est pas très solide sur ses jambes; **he plays a very** ~ **game** il a un jeu très régulier; ~ **on!** * doucement! (**b**) *(regular: gen) temperature, demand, speed* constant; *improvement, income, progress* régulier; *job, prices, sales, market* stable. **to keep prices** ~ stabiliser les prix; **we were doing a** ~ **60 km/h** nous roulions à une vitesse constante de 60 km/h; **her** ~ **boyfriend** son petit ami. **2** *adv*: **to go** ~ **with sb** * sortir avec qn; **they're going** ~ ils sortent ensemble. **3** *vt wobbling object* assujettir; *chair, table (with hand)* maintenir; *(wedge)* caler; *nervous person, horse* calmer. **to** ~ **o.s.** reprendre son aplomb; **to** ~ **one's nerves** se calmer; **to have a** ~**ing effect on sb** *(make less nervous)* calmer qn; *(make less wild)* assagir qn. ◆ **steadily** *adv* (**a**) *walk* d'un pas ferme; *hold, grasp* d'une main ferme; *gaze, look* longuement; *stay, reply, insist* avec fermeté; (**b**) *improve, decrease, rise* régulièrement; *rain, work, continue* sans arrêt. ◆ **steadiness** *n* (**a**) *(V* **steady 1a***)* stabilité *f*; sûreté *f*; sérieux *m*; calme *m*; (**b**) *(V* **steady 1b***)* constance *f*; régularité *f*; stabilité *f.*

steak [steɪk] **1** *n [beef]* bifteck *m*, steak *m*; *[other meat, fish]* tranche *f.* **frying** ~ bifteck; **stewing** ~ bœuf *m* à braiser; ~ **and kidney pie** tourte *f* à la viande de bœuf et aux rognons. **2** *adj*: ~ **knife** couteau *m* à steak. ◆ **steakhouse** *n* ≃ grill-room *m.*

steal [sti:l] *pret* **stole,** *ptp* **stolen** **1** *vt (gen)* voler *(from sb* à qn). **he stole money from the drawer** *etc* il a volé de l'argent dans le tiroir *etc*; **to** ~ **the credit for sth** s'attribuer tout le mérite de qch; **to** ~ **a glance at** jeter un coup d'œil furtif à; **to** ~ **a march on sb** * prendre qn de vitesse; *(fig)* **he**

stole the show on n'a eu d'yeux que pour lui. **2** *vi*: **to ~ up/out** *etc* monter/sortir *etc* à pas de loup; **he stole into the room** il s'est glissé dans la pièce. **3** *n (US: theft)* vol *m*. *(fig)* **it's a ~ *** c'est une bonne affaire. ◆ **stealing** *n* vol *m*.

stealth [stelθ] *n*: **by ~** furtivement. ◆ **stealthily** *adv* furtivement. ◆ **stealthy** *adj* furtif.

steam [sti:m] **1** *n* vapeur *f*. **it works by ~** ça marche à la vapeur; *(Naut)* **full ~ ahead!** en avant toute!; *(fig)* **it's going full ~ ahead** ça va de l'avant à plein régime; **to get up ~** *[train, ship]* prendre de la vitesse; *[worker, project]* démarrer vraiment *; *(fig)* **to run out of ~** *[speaker, worker]* s'essouffler *(fig)*; *[programme, project]* tourner court; **under one's own ~** par ses propres moyens; **to let off ~ *** *(energy)* se défouler *; *(anger)* épancher sa bile. **2** *adj boiler, iron, engine* à vapeur. **3** *vt (Culin)* cuire à la vapeur. **~ed pudding** pudding *m* cuit à la vapeur; **to ~ open an envelope** décacheter une enveloppe à la vapeur. **4** *vi* (**a**) *[liquid, wet clothes]* fumer. (**b**) **to ~ along/away** *etc [ship, train]* avancer/partir *etc*; *(* fig) [person, car]* avancer/partir *etc* à toute vapeur *; **the ship ~ed up the river** le vapeur remontait la rivière.

◆ **steam up** **1** *vi [glass]* se couvrir de buée. **2** *vt sep* embuer. *(fig)* **to get ~ed up *** se mettre dans tous ses états (*about* à propos de).

◆ **steamboat** *n* vapeur *m*. ◆ **steam-driven** *adj* à vapeur. ◆ **steamer** *n* (**a**) *(boat)* vapeur *m*; *(liner)* paquebot *m*; (**b**) *(Culin)* ≃ couscoussier *m*. ◆ **steamroller** **1** *n* rouleau *m* compresseur ; **2** *adj tactics* dictatorial. ◆ **steamship** *n* paquebot *m*. ◆ **steamy** *adj atmosphere, heat* humide; *room, window* embué; *(fig *: erotic)* érotique.

steel [sti:l] **1** *n* acier *m*. *(fig)* **to be made of ~** avoir une volonté de fer ; **nerves of ~** nerfs *mpl* d'acier. **2** *adj knife, tool* d'acier; *engraving* sur acier; *industry* sidérurgique; *(St Ex) shares, prices* de l'acier. **~ band** steel band *m*; **~ guitar** guitare *f* aux cordes d'acier; **~ helmet** casque *m*; **~ wool** paille *f* de fer. **3** *vt (fig)* **to ~ o.s. to do** s'armer de courage pour faire; **to ~ o.s. against** se cuirasser contre. ◆ **steel-plated** *adj* revêtu d'acier. ◆ **steelworker** *n* sidérurgiste *m*. ◆ **steelworks** *n* aciérie *f*. ◆ **steely** *adj substance* dur comme l'acier; *colour* acier *inv*; *(fig) person, eyes, expression* dur; *refusal, attitude* inflexible; **~y blue/grey** bleu/gris acier *inv*.

steep[1] [sti:p] *adj slope, stairs, climb* raide; *cliff* à pic; *hill, path, road* escarpé; *(* fig) price* (trop) élevé. *(fig)* **it's rather ~ if...** c'est un peu fort * que... + *subj*. ◆ **steeply** *adv*: **to rise** *or* **climb ~ly** *[road etc]* monter en pente raide; *[prices etc]* monter en flèche. ◆ **steepness** *n [road etc]* pente *f* (raide); *[slope]* abrupt *m*.

steep[2] [sti:p] **1** *vt (in water, dye etc)* tremper (*in* dans); *washing* faire tremper; *(Culin)* macérer (*in* dans). *(fig)* **~ed in** *ignorance, vice* croupissant dans; *prejudice* imbu de; *history, the classics* imprégné de. **2** *vi [clothes etc]* tremper; *(Culin)* macérer.

steeple ['sti:pl] *n* clocher *m*, flèche *f*. ◆ **steeplechase** *n* steeple-chase *m (course)*. ◆ **steeplechasing** *n* steeple-chase *m (sport)*. ◆ **steeplejack** *n* réparateur *m* de hautes cheminées *etc*.

steer[1] [stɪəʳ] *n (ox)* bœuf *m*; *(esp US: castrated)* bouvillon *m*.

steer[2] [stɪəʳ] **1** *vt* (**a**) *(handle controls of) ship* gouverner; *boat* barrer. (**b**) *(move) ship, boat, conversation* diriger (*towards* vers); *car* conduire; *(fig) person* guider. **2** *vi (Naut)* tenir le gouvernail (*or* la barre); *(Aut)* conduire. **to ~ by the stars** se guider sur les étoiles; **to ~ for sth** faire route vers qch; *(fig)* **to ~ clear of** éviter. **3** *n (US *: tip)* tuyau * *m*. ◆ **steering** **1** *n (Aut, Naut)* conduite *f*; **2** *adj* (**a**) *(Aut)* **~ing arm/column** bras *m*/colonne *f* de direction; **~ing gear** *(Aut)* boîte *f* de direction; *(Aviat)* direction *f*; *(Aut)* **~ing lock** *(when driving)* rayon *m* de braquage; *(anti-theft)* antivol *m* de direction; **~ing wheel** volant *m*; (**b**) *committee* d'organisation.

stem[1] [stem] *vt (stop) flow* contenir; *river* endiguer; *disease, attack* juguler. *(fig)* **to ~ the course of events** endiguer la marche des événements; *(fig)* **to ~ the tide** *or* **flow of** endiguer.

stem[2] [stem] **1** *n* (**a**) *[flower, plant]* tige *f*; *[fruit, leaf]* queue *f*; *[glass]* pied *m*; *[word]* radical *m*. (**b**) *(Naut)* **from ~ to stern** de bout en bout. **2** *vi*: **to ~ from** provenir de.

stench [sten(t)ʃ] *n* puanteur *f*.

stencil ['stensl] **1** *n (gen)* pochoir *m*; *(of paper)* poncif *m*; *(in typing etc)* stencil *m*; *(decoration)* décoration *f* au pochoir. *(Typing)* **to cut a ~** préparer un stencil. **2** *vt lettering* marquer au pochoir; *document* polycopier.

stenographer [ste'nɒgrəfəʳ] *n* sténographe *mf*. ◆ **stenography** *n* sténographie *f*.

step [step] **1** *n* (**a**) *(gen)* pas *m*. **to take a ~ back/forward** faire un pas en arrière/en avant; **with slow ~s** à pas lents; *(lit, fig)* **at every ~** à chaque pas; **~ by ~** pas à pas; *(fig)* petit à petit; **he didn't move a ~** il n'a pas bougé d'un pas; **a waltz ~** un pas de valse; *(fig)* **it is a great ~ for them to take** c'est pour eux un grand pas à faire; **a ~ in the right direction** un pas dans la bonne voie; **a ~ up in his career** une promotion pour lui; **to take ~s** prendre des dispositions *or* des mesures (*to do* pour faire); **what's the next ~?** qu'est-ce qu'il faut faire maintenant?; **the first ~ is to decide...** la première chose à faire est de décider...; **to keep (in) ~** *(in marching)* marcher au pas; *(in dance)* danser en mesure; *(lit, fig)* **to keep ~ with sb** ne pas se laisser distancer par qn; **to fall into ~** se mettre au pas; **to get out of ~** rompre le pas. (**b**) *(stair)* marche *f*; *(door ~)* seuil *m*; *(on bus etc)* marchepied *m*. **(flight of) ~s** *(indoors)* escalier *m*; *(outdoors)* perron *m*; **(pair of) ~s** escabeau *m*; **mind the ~** attention à la marche.
2 *vi* faire un (*or* des) pas, aller. **~ this way** venez par ici; **to ~ off sth** descendre de qch; **to ~ aside/back** *etc* s'écarter/reculer *etc*; **he ~ped into the car** il est monté dans la voiture; **to ~ on sth** marcher sur qch; **to ~ on the brakes** donner un coup de frein; *(Aut)* **to ~ on the gas *** appuyer sur le champignon *; *(fig)* **~ on it! *** dépêche-toi!; *(fig)* **to ~ out of line** s'écarter du droit chemin *(iro)*; **to ~ over sth** enjamber qch.

◆ **step down** *vi* descendre (*from* de); *(fig)* se désister (*in favour of sb* en faveur de qn). ◆ **step forward** *vi* faire un pas en avant; *(show o.s.)* se faire connaître; *(volunteer)* se présenter. ◆ **step in** *vi* entrer; *(fig)* intervenir. ◆ **step up** *vt sep production, sales* augmenter; *campaign, efforts* intensifier; *attempts* multiplier; *(Elec) current* augmenter.

◆ **stepbrother** *n* demi-frère *m*. ◆ **step-by-step** *adj instructions* point par point. ◆ **stepchild** *n* beau-fils *m*, belle-fille *f (remariage)*. ◆ **stepdaughter** *n* belle-fille *f*. ◆ **stepfather** *n* beau-père *m*. ◆ **stepladder** *n* escabeau *m*. ◆ **stepmother** *n* belle-mère *f*. ◆ **stepping-stone** *n (lit)* pierre *f* de gué; *(fig)* tremplin *m* (*to* pour obtenir). ◆ **stepsister** *n* demi-sœur *f*. ◆ **stepson** *n* beau-fils *m*.

stereo ['stɪərɪəʊ] **1** *n (system)* stéréo *f*; *(record player/radio etc)* chaîne *f*/radio *f etc* stéréo *inv*. **in ~** en stéréo. **2** *adj record player, tape etc* stéréo *inv*; *broadcast, recording* en stéréo. ◆ **stereophonic** *adj* stéréophonique. ◆ **stereoscope** *n* stéréoscope *m*. ◆ **stereoscopic** *adj* stéréoscopique. ◆ **stereotype** **1** *n (Psych etc)* stéréotype *m* ; **2** *vt* stéréotyper.

sterile ['steraɪl] *adj* stérile. ◆ **sterility** *n* stérilité *f*. ◆ **sterilization** *n* stérilisation *f*. ◆ **sterilize** *vt* stériliser.

sterling ['stɜ:lɪŋ] **1** *n (Econ)* livre *f* sterling *inv.* **2** *adj gold, silver* fin; *(Econ) pound, area* sterling *inv*; *(fig) qualities, worth* à toute épreuve; *person* de confiance.

stern¹ [stɜ:n] *n (Naut)* arrière *m*, poupe *f.*

stern² [stɜ:n] *adj (gen)* sévère; *discipline* strict. **he was made of ~er stuff** il était d'une autre trempe. ◆ **sternly** *adv* sévèrement. ◆ **sternness** *n* sévérité *f.*

steroid ['stɪərɔɪd] *n* stéroïde *m.*

stet [stet] *impers vb (Typ)* à maintenir.

stethoscope ['steθəskəʊp] *n* stéthoscope *m.*

stevedore ['sti:vɪdɔ:ʳ] *n* docker *m.*

stew [stju:] **1** *n [meat]* ragoût *m*; *[rabbit, hare]* civet *m. (fig)* **in a ~** * *(in trouble)* dans le pétrin; *(worried)* dans tous ses états. **2** *vt meat* cuire en ragoût; *rabbit, hare* cuire en civet; *fruit* faire cuire. **3** *vi [food]* cuire; *[tea]* devenir trop infusé. *(fig)* **to let sb ~ in his own juice** laisser qn mijoter dans son jus. ◆ **stewed** *adj meat* en ragoût; *fruit* en compote; *(pej) tea* trop infusé; *(‡: drunk)* soûl *. ◆ **stewpan** *or* ◆ **stewpot** *n* cocotte *f.*

steward ['stju:əd] *n (on estate, in club, etc)* intendant *m*; *(on ship, plane)* steward *m*; *(at meeting)* membre *m* du service d'ordre; *(at dance)* organisateur *m.* **shop ~** délégué(e) *m(f)* syndical(e). ◆ **stewardess** *n* hôtesse *f.* ◆ **stewardship** *n (duties)* intendance *f*, économat *m.*

stick [stɪk] *(vb: pret, ptp* **stuck***)* **1** *n (gen)* bâton *m*; *(twig)* brindille *f*; *(walking ~)* canne *f*; *(support for plants)* tuteur *m*; *(Mil, Mus)* baguette *f*; *(Hockey, Lacrosse)* crosse *f*; *(Ice Hockey)* stick *m*; *(piece: of chalk etc: gen)* bâton; *[chewing gum]* tablette *f*; *[celery]* branche *f*; *[rhubarb]* tige *f*; *[bombs]* chapelet *m. (for fire)* **~s** du petit bois; **a few ~s of furniture** quelques pauvres meubles *mpl*; *(pej: backwoods)* **in the ~s** * dans l'arrière-pays, en pleine cambrousse *; *(fig)* **to wield the big ~** manier la trique *(fig)*; *(Pol)* faire de l'autoritarisme; **the policy of the big ~** la politique du bâton; *(fig)* **to give sb/get a lot of ~ * for sth** éreinter qn/se faire éreinter à propos de qch; *(fig)* **to get hold of the wrong end of the ~** mal comprendre; **he is a dull old ~** * il est rasoir *.
2 *vt* (**a**) *(thrust: gen)* enfoncer, planter *(into* dans); *pin, needle* piquer, enfoncer *(into* dans). **to ~ a pin through sth** transpercer qch avec une épingle; **I stuck the needle into my finger** je me suis piqué le doigt avec l'aiguille. (**b**) *(put: gen)* mettre *(on* sur; *under* sous; *into* dans); *(put down)* mettre, poser *(on* sur); *(into drawer, pocket, hole)* mettre, fourrer *(into* dans). **he stuck his head through the window** il a passé la tête par la fenêtre. (**c**) *(glue)* coller *(on sth* sur qch; *on the wall* au mur; *with* avec). (**d**) *(tolerate) thing* supporter; *person,* souffrir, sentir *. (**e**) **to be stuck** *(gen)* être coincé *(between* entre); *(in mud)* être embourbé; *(in sand)* être enlisé; *(broken down) [vehicle, machine, lift]* être en panne; **stuck fast** bien coincé ; **it got stuck in my throat** ça s'est mis en travers de ma gorge; *(fig)* **he was stuck here all summer/for the night** il a été obligé de rester ici tout l'été/de passer la nuit ici; **I'm stuck at home all day** je suis cloué à la maison toute la journée; **I was stuck * with him all evening** je l'ai eu sur le dos toute la soirée; **to be stuck for an answer** ne pas savoir que répondre; *(in puzzle, essay etc)* **I'm stuck** * je sèche *; **I'll help you if you're stuck** * je t'aiderai si tu as un problème; **I was stuck * with organizing it all** on m'a collé * le boulot de tout organiser.
3 *vi* (**a**) *[needle, spear etc]* se planter, s'enfoncer *(into* dans). **a knife ~ing into it** un couteau planté là-dedans; **the nail was ~ing through the plank** le clou dépassait de la planche. (**b**) *[glue, paste]* tenir *(to* à); *[stamp, label]* être collé *(to* à); *(Culin) [sauce etc]* attacher *(to* à); *(fig) [habit, name etc]* rester *(to sb* à qn). **it stuck to the table** c'est resté collé à la table. (**c**) *(stay)* rester. **to ~ close to sb** rester aux côtés de qn; *(fig)* **to ~ by sb** rester fidèle à qn, ne pas abandonner qn; *(fig)* **to ~ to sb like a limpet** se cramponner à qn; **to ~ to** *promise* tenir; *principles* rester fidèle à; *one's post* rester à; *the facts* s'en tenir à; *the subject* ne pas s'éloigner de; **to ~ at a job** rester dans un emploi; **~ at it!** persévère!; **to ~ to one's guns** * ne pas en démordre; **he stuck to his story** il a maintenu ce qu'il avait dit; **decide what you're going to say then ~ to it** décidez ce que vous allez dire et tenez-vous-y; **to ~ with sb** * *(stay beside)* rester avec qn; *(stay loyal)* rester fidèle à qn. (**d**) *(get jammed) (gen)* se coincer; *(in mud)* être embourbé; *(in sand)* être enlisé; *(break down) [vehicle, machine, lift]* tomber en panne. **to ~ fast** être bien coincé; **it stuck in my throat** ça s'est mis en travers de ma gorge; *(fig)* je ne suis pas arrivé à digérer * ça; *(balk)* **he will ~ at nothing to get what he wants** il ne recule devant rien pour obtenir ce qu'il veut; **he wouldn't ~ at murder** il irait jusqu'au meurtre. ◆ **stick around** * *vi (stay near)* rester dans les parages; *(hang about)* traîner (à attendre). ◆ **stick down** *vt sep envelope etc* coller. ◆ **stick in 1** *vi* (*) persévérer. **2** *vt sep (put in) (gen)* enfoncer, planter; *needle, pin* piquer, enfoncer; *photo in album etc* coller. *(fig)* **he stuck in a few quotations** il a collé * quelques citations par-ci par-là; *(fig)* **to get stuck in** * s'y mettre sérieusement. ◆ **stick on** *vt sep label, stamp* coller. ◆ **stick out 1** *vi* (**a**) *(protrude) (gen)* sortir *(from* de); *[teeth]* avancer; *[rod etc]* dépasser; *[balcony etc]* faire saillie. **his ears ~ out** il a les oreilles décollées; *(fig)* **it ~s out a mile** * ça crève les yeux *(that* que). (**b**) *(persevere etc)* **to ~ out for more money** tenir bon dans ses revendications pour une augmentation de salaire. **2** *vt sep* (**a**) *one's arm, head* sortir *(of* de); *one's chest* bomber. **to ~ one's tongue out** tirer la langue. (**b**) *(*: endure)* supporter. **to ~ it out** tenir le coup. ◆ **stick together 1** *vi [labels, pages, objects]* rester collés ensemble; *(stay together) [people]* rester ensemble; *(fig)* se serrer les coudes. **2** *vt sep* coller (ensemble). ◆ **stick up 1** *vi* (**a**) **to ~ up out of the water** sortir de l'eau. (**b**) **to ~ up for sb/sth** * défendre qn/qch. **2** *vt sep* (**a**) *notice etc* afficher. (**b**) *one's hand* lever la main. **~'em up!** * haut les mains! (**c**) *(rob) person, bank* dévaliser.
◆ **sticker** *n* (**a**) *(label)* autocollant *m*; (**b**) *(fig)* **he's a ~er** * il n'abandonne pas facilement. ◆ **stickiness** *n (V* **sticky***)* caractère poisseux *or* collant *or* gluant; moiteur *f.* ◆ **sticking-plaster** *n* sparadrap *m.* ◆ **sticking point** *n* point *m* de friction. ◆ **stick insect** *n* phasme *m.* ◆ **stick-in-the-mud** * *adj, n* encroûté(e) * *m(f).* ◆ **stick-on** *adj* adhésif. ◆ **stickup** * *n* hold-up *m.* ◆ **sticky** *adj* (**a**) *paste* poisseux, collant; *label* adhésif; *paint, toffee, road, surface, pitch* gluant; *hands (sweaty)* moite; *(with jam etc)* poisseux; *climate* chaud et humide; **~y tape** scotch *m* ®, ruban *m* adhésif; (**b**) *(* fig) problem, situation* délicat; *person* peu accommodant; *(fig)* **to be on a ~y wicket** être dans une situation délicate; **to come to a ~y end** mal finir; **to have a ~y time** * passer un mauvais quart d'heure; **he's very ~y about lending his car** * il répugne à prêter sa voiture. ◆ **sticky-fingered** * *adj* porté sur la fauche ‡.

stickleback ['stɪklbæk] *n* épinoche *f.*

stickler ['stɪkləʳ] *n:* **to be a ~ for** être pointilleux sur le chapitre de, insister sur.

stiff [stɪf] *adj* (**a**) *(gen)* raide, rigide; *arm, joint* ankylosé; *door, lock, brush* dur; *dough, paste* ferme; *(starched) shirt etc* empesé. **as ~ as a poker** *or* **a ramrod** raide comme un piquet; **you'll feel ~ tomorrow** vous aurez des courbatures demain; **he's getting ~ as he grows older** il se raidit avec l'âge; **to have a ~ back** avoir mal au dos; **to have a ~ neck** avoir le torticolis; **~ with cold** engourdi par le froid; *(fig)* **to keep a ~ upper lip** rester impassible. (**b**) *(fig) smile, reception, person* froid, distant; *resistance* opiniâtre; *exam, course, task* difficile; *climb* raide; *wind, breeze* fort; *price, bill* (trop) élevé. **that's a bit ~!** * c'est un peu fort! *; **I could do with a ~ drink** je boirais bien qch de fort; **a ~ whisky** un grand verre de whisky. ◆ **stiffen (up) 1** *vt (gen)* raidir ; *joint* ankyloser; *(fig) morale, resistance etc* affermir; **2** *vi (gen)* devenir raide *or* rigide ; *[limb, joint]* s'ankyloser; *[door, lock]* devenir dur; *[resistance]* devenir opiniâtre; *[morale]* s'affermir; **he ~ened when...** il s'est raidi quand... ◆ **stiffener** *n (in collar)* baleine *f.* ◆ **stiffly** *adv move, bend* avec raideur; *stand to attention* sans bouger un muscle; *(fig) smile, greet, say* froidement. ◆ **stiffness** *n* (**a**) raideur *f*, rigidité *f*; ankylose *f*; dureté *f*; fermeté *f*; (**b**) froideur *f*; difficulté *f*.

stifle ['staɪfl] **1** *vt person, fire, sobs* étouffer; *anger, smile, desire* réprimer. **to ~ a yawn** réprimer une envie de bâiller. **2** *vi* étouffer. ◆ **stifling** *adj fumes* suffocant; *heat* étouffant; **it's stifling** * on étouffe.

stigma, *pl (gen)* **-s**, *(Bot, Rel)* **-mata** ['stɪgmə, mɑ:tə] *n* stigmate *m* (*on* sur). ◆ **stigmatize** *vt* stigmatiser.

stile [staɪl] *n* échalier *m*; *(turn ~)* tourniquet *m*.

stiletto [stɪ'letəʊ] *n* stylet *m*. **~ heel** talon *m* aiguille.

still¹ [stɪl] **1** *adv* (**a**) *(up to now)* encore, toujours. **he is ~ in bed** il est encore *or* toujours au lit; **he ~ hasn't arrived** il n'est pas encore arrivé, il n'est toujours pas arrivé; **you ~ don't believe me** vous ne me croyez toujours pas. (**b**) *(+ comp: even)* encore. **~ better, better ~** encore mieux. (**c**) *(nonetheless)* quand même, tout de même. **you'll ~ come?** vous viendrez quand même *or* tout de même?; **he's ~ your brother** il n'en est pas moins votre frère; *(US)* **~ and all** * tout compte fait. **2** *conj (nevertheless)* néanmoins, quand même.

still² [stɪl] **1** *adj (motionless)* immobile; *(peaceful)* calme, tranquille; *(quiet)* silencieux; *(not fizzy) lemonade* non gazeux. **keep ~!** reste tranquille!, ne bouge pas!; *(Art)* **~ life** nature *f* morte. **2** *adv sit, stand, hold* sans bouger. **3** *n* (**a**) **in the ~ of the night** dans le silence de la nuit. (**b**) *(Cine)* photo *f*. ◆ **stillbirth** *n* enfant *m(f)* mort-né(e). ◆ **stillborn** *adj* mort-né. ◆ **stillness** *n* calme *m*, tranquillité *f*; silence *m*.

still³ [stɪl] *n (object)* alambic *m*; *(place)* distillerie *f*.

stilts [stɪlts] *npl* échasses *fpl*. ◆ **stilted** *adj* guindé, qui manque de naturel.

stimulate ['stɪmjʊleɪt] *vt (Physiol, gen)* stimuler. **to ~ sb to do** inciter qn à faire. ◆ **stimulant** *adj, n* stimulant *(m)*. ◆ **stimulating** *adj* stimulant. ◆ **stimulation** *n* stimulation *f*. ◆ **stimulus,** *pl* **-li** *n (Physiol)* stimulus *m*; *(fig)* stimulant *m*; **it gave trade a new stimulus** cela a donné une nouvelle impulsion au commerce; **under the stimulus of** stimulé par.

sting [stɪŋ] *(vb: pret, ptp* **stung***)* **1** *n [insect]* dard *m*; *(pain, mark) [insect, nettle etc]* piqûre *f*; *[iodine etc]* brûlure *f*; *[attack, criticism, remark]* mordant *m*; *(US* ‡*: confidence trick)* arnaque * *m*. *(fig)* **a ~ in the tail** une mauvaise surprise à la fin. **2** *vt [insect, nettle]* piquer; *[iodine]* brûler; *[rain, hail, whip]* cingler; *[remark, criticism]* piquer au vif. **stung by remorse** bourrelé de remords; **to ~ sb into action** pousser qn à agir; *(fig: robbed)* **I've been stung!** * je me suis fait avoir! * **3** *vi* (**a**) piquer; brûler; *[blow, whip]* provoquer une sensation cuisante; *[remark, criticism]* être cuisant. (**b**) *[eyes]* piquer; *[cut, skin]* brûler. **the fumes made his eyes ~** les fumées picotaient ses yeux. ◆ **stinging** *adj cut, remark* cuisant; **~ing nettle** ortie *f* brûlante.

stingy ['stɪn(d)ʒɪ] *adj person* avare, ladre; *portion* misérable. **to be ~ with** *food* lésiner sur; *praise* être chiche de. ◆ **stingily** *adv spend* avec avarice; *serve* en lésinant. ◆ **stinginess** *n* avarice *f*.

stink [stɪŋk] *(vb: pret* **stank,** *ptp* **stunk***)* **1** *n* (**a**) puanteur *f*. **what a ~!** ce que ça pue! (**b**) *(fig: trouble)* **to make** *or* **kick up a ~** ‡ faire toute une scène (*about* à propos de). **2** *vi* puer *(also fig)*, empester (*of sth* qch); (‡*: fig) [person, thing]* être dégueulasse ‡. *(lit, fig)* **it ~s to high heaven** * cela sent à plein nez. **3** *vt* (**~ out**) *room etc* empester. ◆ **stinker** ‡ *n (person)* salaud ‡ *m*, salope ‡ *f*; *(question, essay etc)* vacherie ‡ *f*; *(angry letter)* lettre *f* d'engueulade ‡; **to be a ~er** être affreux. ◆ **stinking 1** *adj substance* puant; (‡ *fig)* infect; **to have a ~ing ‡ cold** avoir un rhume épouvantable ; **2** *adv*: **~ing rich** ‡ bourré de fric ‡.

stint [stɪnt] **1** *n*: **to do one's ~** *(daily work)* faire son travail (quotidien); *(do one's share)* faire sa part de travail; **he does a ~ in the gym every day** il passe un certain temps chaque jour au gymnase; **I've done my ~ at the wheel** j'ai pris mon tour au volant. **2** *vt (also* **~ on***) food* lésiner sur; *compliments* être chiche de. **to ~ sb of sth** mesurer qch à qn; **to ~ o.s.** se priver (*of* de).

stipend ['staɪpend] *n (Rel)* traitement *m*.

stipulate ['stɪpjʊleɪt] *vt (gen)* stipuler (*that* que); *quantity* prescrire. ◆ **stipulation** *n* stipulation *f*; **on the stipulation that...** à la condition expresse que... *(+ fut or subj)*.

stir [stɜ:ʳ] **1** *n*: **to give sth a ~** remuer qch; *(fig)* **there was a great ~ about...** il y a eu beaucoup d'agitation à propos de...; **to cause a ~** faire sensation. **2** *vt* (**a**) *tea, soup* remuer; *mixture* tourner; *fire* tisonner. **to ~ sth into sth** ajouter qch à qch (en tournant). (**b**) *(move etc) papers, leaves* agiter; *curiosity, passions, imagination* exciter; *emotions* éveiller; *person* émouvoir. *(fig)* **to ~ o.s.** * se secouer; **to ~ sb to do sth** inciter qn à faire qch; **to ~ sb's blood** réveiller l'enthousiasme de qn. **3** *vi [person]* bouger (*from* de); *[leaves, curtains etc]* remuer. **nobody is ~ring yet** personne n'est encore levé. ◆ **stir up** *vt sep (fig) (gen)* exciter; *memories* réveiller; *revolt, hatred* susciter; *mob* ameuter; *trouble* provoquer; *person* secouer *(fig)*. **to ~ sb up to (do) sth** pousser qn à (faire) qch. ◆ **stir-fry** *vt* faire sauter à feu vif (en remuant). ◆ **stirring** *adj speech, music* enthousiasmant; *years* passionnant.

stirrup ['stɪrəp] *n* étrier *m*.

stitch [stɪtʃ] **1** *n (Sewing)* point *m*; *(Knitting)* maille *f*; *(Surgery)* point de suture; *(pain in side)* point de côté. **she put a few ~es in the tear** elle a fait un point à la déchirure; **to put ~es in a wound** suturer une plaie; *(Med)* **to get one's ~es out** se faire retirer ses fils de suture; *(fig)* **he hadn't a ~ (of clothing) on** * il était tout nu; *(fig)* **to be in ~es** * se tenir les côtes (de rire); **it had us in ~es** * on se tordait de rire. **2** *vt (by hand)* coudre; *(on machine)* piquer; *(Med)* suturer. **3** *vi* coudre. ◆ **stitch down** *vt sep* rabattre. ◆ **stitch on** *vt sep button* coudre; *button that's come off* recoudre. ◆ **stitch up** *vt sep* coudre; *(mend)* recoudre; *(Med)* suturer.

stoat [stəʊt] *n* hermine *f (d'été)*.

stock [stɒk] **1** *n* (**a**) *[goods]* réserve *f*, *(Comm)* stock *m*; *[money]* réserve; *[learning]* fonds *m*. *(Comm)* **in ~** en stock; **out of ~** épuisé; **to lay in a ~ of** s'approvisionner en; **to take ~** *(Comm)* faire l'inventaire; *(fig)* faire le point; *(fig)* **to take ~ of** *situation, prospects etc* faire le point de; *person* évaluer les mérites de. (**b**) *(Agr: animals and equipment)* cheptel *m* (vif et mort). **live ~** bétail *m*; *(Rail)* **rolling ~** matériel *m* roulant. (**c**) *(Cards)* talon *m*. (**d**) *(Culin)* bouillon *m*. (**e**) *(Fin)* valeurs *fpl*, titres *mpl*; *(government ~s)* fonds *mpl* d'État; *(company shares)* actions

fpl. **~s and shares** valeurs (mobilières), titres. (**f**) *(flower)* giroflée *f.* (**g**) **to be on the ~s** *[ship]* être sur cale; *(fig) [piece of work, scheme]* être en chantier; *(Hist)* **the ~s** le pilori. (**h**) *(lineage)* souche *f*, lignée *f.*
2 *adj (Comm) goods, size* courant; *(stereotyped) argument, excuse* classique. *(Aut, Sport)* ~ **car** stock-car *m*; *(Culin)* ~ **cube** bouillon-cube *m*; ~ **market** Bourse *f*, marché *m* financier; *(fig)* ~ **phrase** expression *f* toute faite.
3 *vt* (**a**) *(supply) shop, larder* approvisionner (*with* en); *library/farm* monter en livres/en bétail; *river, lake* peupler (*with* de). **well-~ed** *shop etc* bien approvisionné; *library, farm, garden* bien fourni. (**b**) *(Comm: hold in ~)* avoir, vendre.
◆ **stock up** **1** *vi* s'approvisionner (*with, on* en; *for* pour). **2** *vt sep shop, cupboard* garnir; *library* accroître le stock de livres de; *river, lake* empoissonner.
◆ **stockbreeder** *n* éleveur *m*, -euse *f.* ◆ **stockbroker** *n* agent *m* de change; *(Brit)* **the ~broker belt** la banlieue résidentielle. ◆ **stock exchange** *n* Bourse *f* (des valeurs); **on the ~ exchange** à la Bourse. ◆ **stockholder** *n* actionnaire *mf.* ◆ **stock-in-trade** *n (goods)* marchandises *fpl* en stock; *(tools, materials etc: also fig)* outils *mpl* du métier. ◆ **stockist** *n* stockiste *mf.* ◆ **stockpile** *vt* stocker. ◆ **stockpiling** *n* stockage *m.* ◆ **stockpot** *n (Culin)* marmite *f* de bouillon. ◆ **stockroom** *n* réserve *f*, magasin *m.* ◆ **stock-still** *adv*: **to stand ~-still** rester planté comme une borne; *(in fear, amazement)* rester cloué sur place. ◆ **stocktaking** **1** *n* inventaire *m* ; **2** *vi*: **to be ~taking** *(Comm)* faire l'inventaire; *(fig)* faire le point. ◆ **stocky** *adj* trapu, râblé.

stockade [stɒ'keɪd] *n (fencing)* palissade *f*; *(US Mil)* salle *f* de police.

Stockholm ['stɒkhəʊm] *n* Stockholm.

stocking ['stɒkɪŋ] **1** *n* bas *m.* **2** *adj*: **in one's ~ feet** sans chaussures; ~ **mask** bas *m (d'un bandit masqué)*; *(Knitting)* ~ **stitch** point *m* de jersey. ◆ **stockinet(te)** *n* jersey *m.*

stodge * [stɒdʒ] *n (food)* aliment *m* bourratif. ◆ **stodgy** *adj food* bourratif; *(heavy) cake* lourd; *book* indigeste; *(*: dull) person* sans imagination.

stoic(al) ['stəʊɪk(əl)] *adj* stoïque. ◆ **stoically** *adv* stoïquement. ◆ **stoicism** *n* stoïcisme *m.*

stoke [stəʊk] *vt* (~ **up**) *fire* garnir; *furnace* alimenter; *engine, boiler* chauffer. ◆ **stoker** *n* chauffeur *m (Naut etc).*

stole[1] [stəʊl] *n* étole *f.*

stole[2] [stəʊl], **stolen** ['stəʊl(ə)n] *pret, ptp of* **steal.**

stolid ['stɒlɪd] *adj* impassible. ◆ **stolidly** *adv* avec impassibilité.

stomach ['stʌmək] **1** *n (gen)* ventre *m*; *(Anat)* estomac *m.* **lying on his ~** couché sur le ventre; **to have a pain in one's ~** avoir mal au ventre. **2** *adj ulcer* à l'estomac. ~ **ache** mal *m* de ventre; ~ **pump** pompe *f* stomacale; ~ **trouble** ennuis *mpl* gastriques. **3** *vt (fig)* encaisser *.

stone [stəʊn] **1** *n* (**a**) *(gen)* pierre *f*; *(pebble)* caillou *m*; *(on beach etc)* galet *m*; *(gravestone)* pierre tombale; *(in fruit)* noyau *m*; *(Med)* calcul *m.* **(made) of ~** de pierre; *(fig)* **within a ~'s throw of** à deux pas de; *(fig)* **to leave no ~ unturned** remuer ciel et terre (*to do* pour faire); **to turn to ~** *(vt)* pétrifier; *(vi)* se pétrifier. (**b**) *(Brit: weight: pl gen inv)* = *6,348 kg.* **2** *adj building* de *or* en pierre. **S~ Age** l'âge *m* de la pierre. **3** *vt* (**a**) *person, object* lancer *or* jeter des pierres sur. **to ~ sb to death** lapider qn. (**b**) *date, olive* dénoyauter. ◆ **stone-blind** *adj* complètement aveugle. ◆ **stone-cold** *adj* complètement froid; **~-cold sober** * pas du tout ivre. ◆ **stoned** ‡ *adj (drunk)* soûl *; *(Drugs)* défoncé ‡. ◆ **stone-deaf** *adj* sourd comme un pot *. ◆ **stonemason** *n* tailleur *m* de pierre(s). ◆ **stonewall** *vi (fig)* donner des réponses évasives. ◆ **stoneware** *n* poterie *f* de grès. ◆ **stonework** *n* maçonnerie *f.* ◆ **stonily** *adv* avec froideur. ◆ **stony** *adj road, soil* pierreux; *beach* de galets; *(fig) person, heart* de pierre, dur; *look, welcome* froid. ◆ **stony-broke** * *adj* fauché comme les blés *. ◆ **stony-faced** *adj* au visage impassible.

stood [stʊd] *pret, ptp of* **stand.**

stooge [stu:dʒ] *n (Theat)* comparse *mf*; *(gen pej)* laquais *m.*

stool [stu:l] *n* (**a**) tabouret *m*; *(folding)* pliant *m.* *(fig)* **to fall between two ~s** se retrouver le bec dans l'eau *. (**b**) *(Med)* selle *f.* ◆ **stool-pigeon** * *n* indicateur *m*, -trice *f (de police).*

stoop [stu:p] **1** *n*: **to have a ~** avoir le dos voûté. **2** *vi (have a ~)* avoir le dos voûté; (**~ down**) se courber; *(fig)* s'abaisser (*to sth* jusqu'à qch; *to do, to doing* jusqu'à faire). *(fig)* **he would ~ to anything** il est prêt à toutes les bassesses. ◆ **stooping** *adj* voûté, courbé.

stop [stɒp] **1** *n* (**a**) *(halt)* arrêt *m*; *(short stay)* halte *f.* **a ~ for coffee** une pause-café; **6 hours without a ~** 6 heures *fpl* d'affilée; **a 5-minute ~** 5 minutes d'arrêt; **to be at a ~** *[traffic, vehicle]* être à l'arrêt; *[work, production]* avoir cessé; **to come to a ~** *[traffic etc]* s'arrêter; *[work etc]* cesser; **to bring to a ~** *traffic etc* arrêter; *work etc* faire cesser; **to make a ~** *[bus, train]* s'arrêter; *[plane, ship]* faire escale; **to put a ~ to sth** mettre fin *or* un terme à qch. (**b**) *(place) [bus, train]* arrêt *m*; *[plane, ship]* escale *f.* (**c**) *[organ]* jeu *m.* *(fig)* **to pull out all the ~s** faire un suprême effort (*to do* pour faire). (**d**) *(Punctuation)* point *m*; *(in telegrams)* stop *m.*
2 *adj button, lever, signal* d'arrêt. *(Aut)* ~ **sign** stop *m (panneau).*
3 *vt* (**a**) (**~ up**) *hole, pipe, leak, jar* boucher; *tooth* plomber. **to ~ one's ears** se boucher les oreilles; **to ~ a gap** boucher un trou; *(fig)* combler une lacune. (**b**) *(halt, block: gen)* arrêter; *noise* étouffer; *activity, progress* interrompre; *(suspend)* suspendre; *(Boxing) fight* suspendre; *allowance, leave* supprimer; *part of wages* retenir (*out of* sur); *gas, electricity, water supply* couper; *subscription* résilier; *cheque* faire opposition à; *light* empêcher de passer; *pain, worry, enjoyment* mettre fin à. **to ~ sb short** *or* **in his tracks** *(lit)* arrêter qn net; *(fig)* couper qn dans son élan; *(silence)* couper la parole à qn; **he ~ped a bullet** * il a reçu une balle; **rain ~ped play** la pluie a interrompu la partie; *[bank]* **to ~ payment** suspendre ses paiements; **he ~ped the milk for a week** il a fait interrompre la livraison du lait pendant une semaine. (**c**) *(cease)* arrêter, cesser (*doing* de faire). **~ it!** ça suffit!; **~ that noise!** assez de bruit!; **to ~ work** arrêter *or* cesser de travailler. (**d**) *(prevent)* empêcher (*sb's doing, sb from doing* qn de faire; *sth happening, sth from happening* que qch n'arrive *(subj)*). **there's nothing to ~ you** rien ne vous en empêche.
4 *vi* (**a**) *(halt: gen)* s'arrêter; *(end: gen)* cesser, se terminer; *[allowance, privileges]* être supprimé; *[play, programme, concert]* finir, se terminer. ~ **thief!** au voleur!; **you can ~ now** vous pouvez (vous) arrêter maintenant; **he ~ped (dead) in his tracks** il s'est arrêté net *or* pile *; **I'd ~ short of murder** je n'irais pas jusqu'au meurtre; **he never knows where to ~** il ne sait pas s'arrêter; **he will ~ at nothing** il ne recule devant rien (*to do* pour faire). (**b**) (*) *(remain)* rester; *(live temporarily)* loger (*with sb* chez qn).
◆ **stop by** * *vi* s'arrêter en passant. ◆ **stop off, stop over** *vi* s'arrêter, faire une halte. ◆ **stop up** *vt sep hole, pipe, jar* boucher. **my nose is ~ped up** j'ai le nez bouché.
◆ **stopcock** *n* robinet *m* d'arrêt. ◆ **stopgap** **1** *n* bouche-trou *m* ; **2** *adj measure* intérimaire. ◆ **stoplight** *n (traffic light)* feu *m* rouge; *(brake*

light) feu *m* de stop. ◆ **stop-off** *n* arrêt *m.* ◆ **stopover** *n* halte *f.* ◆ **stoppage** *n (gen)* arrêt *m*; *(interruption)* interruption *f*; *(Ftbl)* arrêt *m* de jeu; *(strike)* grève *f*; *[leave, wages, payment]* suspension *f*; *(amount deducted)* retenue *f.* ◆ **stopper** *n* bouchon *m*; **to put the ~per in/take the ~per out of sth** boucher/ déboucher qch; *(fig)* **to put a ~per on sth** * mettre un terme à qch; *V* **conversation. 2** *vt* boucher. ◆ **stopping 1** *n (gen)* arrêt *m*; *(in tooth)* plombage *m* ; **2** *adj (Aut)* **we were looking for a ~ping place** nous cherchions un coin où nous arrêter; **~ping train** omnibus *m.* ◆ **stop-press** *n* nouvelles *fpl* de dernière heure. ◆ **stopwatch** *n* chronomètre *m.*

storage ['stɔːrɪdʒ] **1** *n [goods, fuel, furniture]* entreposage *m*; *[food]* rangement *m*, conservation *f*; *[radioactive waste]* stockage *m*; *[heat, electricity]* accumulation *f*; *[documents]* conservation *f*; *(Comput)* mémoire *f.* **to put in(to)** ~ entreposer. **2** *adj capacity, problems* d'entreposage; *charges* de magasinage. ~ **battery** accumulateur *m*; ~ **heater** radiateur *m* électrique par accumulation; ~ **space** espace *m* de rangement; *[oil etc]* ~ **tank** réservoir *m* d'emmagasinage; ~ **unit** meuble *m* de rangement.

store [stɔːʳ] **1** *n* (**a**) *(supply)* provision *f*, réserve *f*; *[learning, information]* fonds *m.* **~s** provisions *fpl*; **to lay in ~s** s'approvisionner, faire des provisions; **to get in** *or* **lay in a ~ of sth** faire provision de qch; *(fig)* **to set great ~/little ~ by sth** faire grand cas/peu de cas de qch. (**b**) *(depot, warehouse)* entrepôt *m*; *(furniture ~)* garde-meuble *m*; *[ammunition etc]* dépôt *m*; *(in office, factory etc: also* **~s***)* réserve *f*; *(larger)* service *m* des approvisionnements. **to put in(to)** ~ *goods etc* entreposer; *furniture* mettre au garde-meuble; **to keep sth in** ~ garder qch en réserve; *(fig)* **to have sth in ~ for sb** réserver qch à qn. (**c**) *(shop)* magasin *m* ; *(large)* grand magasin; *(small)* boutique *f.* **book** ~ librairie *f.*
2 *vt* (**a**) *(keep, collect:* ~ **up***) food, fuel, goods* mettre en réserve; *documents* conserver; *electricity, heat* accumuler, emmagasiner; *(fig: in one's mind) facts etc* enregistrer dans sa mémoire. (**b**) *(place in* ~ *:* ~ **away***) food, fuel, goods* entreposer; *one's furniture* mettre au garde-meuble; *crops* engranger; *(Comput)* mémoriser; *information (in filing system etc)* classer; *(in mind)* enregistrer. **I've got them ~d (away)** je les ai mis de côté.
3 *vi [food]* **to ~ well** bien se conserver.
◆ **store-house** *n* entrepôt *m*; *(fig: of information etc)* mine *f.* ◆ **storekeeper** *n* magasinier *m*; *(shopkeeper)* commerçant(e) *m(f).* ◆ **storeroom** *n* réserve *f.*

storey ['stɔːrɪ] *n* étage *m.* **on the 3rd** *or (US)* **4th** ~ au 3ᵉ (étage); **4-~(ed) building** bâtiment de 4 étages.

stork [stɔːk] *n* cigogne *f.*

storm [stɔːm] **1** *n* tempête *f*; *(thunder ~)* orage *m*; *(fig) [arrows, missiles]* grêle *f*; *[abuse]* torrent *m*; *[cheers, protests, applause]* tempête. *(fig)* **a ~ in a teacup** une tempête dans un verre d'eau; *(fig)* **it caused quite a ~** cela a provoqué une véritable tempête; **to take by ~** *(Mil)* prendre d'assaut; *(fig) audience etc* conquérir. **2** *adj signal, warning* de tempête; *window, door* double. *(US)* ~ **cellar** abri *m* tempête; *(fig)* ~ **centre** centre *m* de l'agitation; ~ **cloud** nuage *m* orageux; *(fig)* nuage noir; *(Mil)* ~ **troops** troupes *fpl* d'assaut. **3** *vt (Mil, also fig)* prendre d'assaut. **4** *vi [wind, rain]* faire rage; *(fig) [person]* fulminer *(with rage* de colère; *at sb* contre *qn).* **to ~ in/out** *etc* entrer/sortir *etc* comme un ouragan. ◆ **stormy** *adj weather, sky* orageux; *sea* démonté; *(fig) meeting* houleux; *person* violent.

story¹ ['stɔːrɪ] *n* (**a**) *(gen)* histoire *f*; *[play, film]* action *f.* **short ~** nouvelle *f*; **do you know the ~ about...?** connaissez-vous l'histoire de...?; **it's a long ~** c'est toute une histoire; **that's not the whole ~** mais ce n'est pas tout; **according to your ~** d'après ce que vous dites, d'après votre version des faits; **or so the ~ goes** ou du moins c'est ce qu'on raconte; **quite another ~** une tout autre histoire; **it's the same old ~** c'est toujours la même histoire; *(fig)* **it tells its own ~** cela en dit long; **to tell stories** * *(fibs)* raconter des histoires. (**b**) *(Press) (event)* affaire; *(article)* article *m.* **he was sent to cover the ~ of the refugees** on l'a envoyé faire un reportage sur les réfugiés; **they daren't print that ~** ils n'osent pas publier cette nouvelle. ◆ **storybook** *n* livre *m* de contes *or* d'histoires. ◆ **storyteller** *n* conteur *m*, -euse *f*; *(*: fibber)* menteur *m*, -euse *f.*

story² ['stɔːrɪ] *n (US)* = **storey.**

stout [staʊt] **1** *adj* (**a**) *(fat)* gros, corpulent. **to grow ~** prendre de l'embonpoint. (**b**) *(strong) (gen)* solide; *horse* vigoureux; *resistance, soldier* vaillant; *supporter* fidèle. **with ~ hearts** vaillamment; **a ~ fellow** * un brave type *. **2** *n (beer)* bière *f* brune *(forte).* ◆ **stout-hearted** *adj* vaillant. ◆ **stoutly** *adv defend* vaillamment; *deny* catégoriquement; *maintain* dur comme fer. ◆ **stoutness** *n (fatness)* embonpoint *m.*

stove [stəʊv] *n* (**a**) *(heater)* poêle *m.* (**b**) *(cooker) (solid fuel)* fourneau *m*; *(gas, electricity)* cuisinière *f*; *(small)* réchaud *m.* (**c**) *(Ind, Tech)* four *m.*

stow [stəʊ] *vt (put away)* ranger; *(hide)* cacher. ◆ **stow away 1** *vi* s'embarquer clandestinement. **2** *vt sep (put away)* ranger; *(hide)* cacher. ◆ **stowaway** *n* passager *m*, -ère *f* clandestin(e).

straddle ['strædl] *vt* être à cheval sur.

straggle ['strægl] *vi*: **to ~ in/out** *etc* entrer/sortir *etc* par petits groupes détachés. ◆ **straggler** *n (person)* traînard(e) *m(f).* ◆ **straggling** *or* ◆ **straggly** *adj plant, village* tout en longueur; *hair* en désordre; *objects in row* disséminés; *line* irrégulier.

straight [streɪt] **1** *adj* (**a**) *(not curved, not askew: gen) line, edge, picture* droit; *route* direct; *hair* raide; *posture, back* bien droit; *(Geom) angle* plat; *(in order) room, books* en ordre. **to put** *or* **set ~** *picture* remettre d'aplomb; *hat, tie* ajuster; *house, books, accounts* mettre de l'ordre dans; **the picture isn't ~** le tableau est de travers; *(fig)* **to keep a ~ face** garder son sérieux; *(US)* ~ **razor** rasoir *m* à main; *(Theat)* **a ~ man** un faire-valoir; **let's get this ~** entendons-nous bien sur ce point; **to put** *or* **set sb ~ about sth** éclairer qn sur qch; **to keep sb ~ about sth** empêcher qn de se tromper sur qch; *(don't owe anything)* **now we're ~** maintenant on est quitte. (**b**) *(frank)* franc; *(honest)* honnête; *dealing* régulier; *denial, refusal* catégorique. ~ **speaking,** ~ **talking** franc-parler *m*; **to play a ~ game** agir loyalement; **he's ~** il est très honnête; *(*: not homosexual)* c'est un hétéro *; *(*: not criminal)* il est régulier. (**c**) *(plain etc) whisky etc* sans eau; *(Theat) part, actor* sérieux; *(fig *: dishonesty etc)* pur et simple. **a ~ play** une pièce de théâtre proprement dite; *(Pol)* **a ~ fight** une campagne électorale à deux candidats.
2 *n* (**a**) *[racecourse etc]* **the ~** la ligne droite; *(fig)* **we're in the ~** nous sommes dans la dernière ligne droite. (**b**) **to cut sth on the ~** couper qch droit fil; *(fig)* **to keep to the ~ and narrow** rester dans le droit chemin.
3 *adv* (**a**) *(in a ~ line) walk, grow, stand* droit; *sit* correctement. **he came ~ at me** il est venu tout droit vers moi; **to shoot ~** tirer juste; **I can't see ~** * j'y vois trouble; ~ **up in the air** droit en l'air, ~ **above/across** juste au-dessus/en face; ~ **ahead** *go* tout droit; *look* droit devant soi; **to look sb ~ in the face/the eye** regarder qn bien en face/droit dans les yeux; *[criminal]* **to go ~** rester dans le droit chemin. (**b**) *(directly)* tout droit, directement; *(immediately)* tout de suite, aussitôt. ~ **away,** ~ **off** tout de suite, sur-le-champ; ~ **out,**

~ **off** *(without hesitation)* sans hésiter; *(without beating about the bush)* sans mâcher ses mots; *(fig)* ~ **from the horse's mouth** de source sûre; **I'm telling you** ~ je vous le dis tout net.

◆ **straightedge** *n (tool)* limande *f (Menuiserie)*.

◆ **straighten 1** *vt* (**~en out**) *wire, nail* redresser; *road* refaire en éliminant les tournants; *hair* défriser; (**~en up**) *tie, hat* ajuster; *picture* remettre d'aplomb; *room* mettre de l'ordre dans; *papers* ranger; **to ~en one's shoulders** se redresser ; **2** *vi* (**~en up**) *[person]* se redresser. ◆ **straighten out** *vt sep situation* débrouiller; *problem* résoudre; *ideas* mettre de l'ordre dans; **to ~en things out** * arranger les choses; **to ~en sb out** * remettre qn dans la bonne voie. ◆ **straight-faced** *adv* en gardant son sérieux. ◆ **straightforward** *adj (frank)* franc; *(uncomplicated)* simple. ◆ **straightforwardly** *adv answer* franchement; *behave* honnêtement; *(without a hitch)* sans anicroche *. ◆ **straightforwardness** *n* franchise *f*; simplicité *f*.

strain[1] [streɪn] **1** *n* (**a**) *(Tech: on rope etc)* tension *f (on* de); *(on beam)* pression *f (on* sur); *(on person) (physical)* effort *m* (physique); *(mental)* tension nerveuse; *(overwork)* surmenage *m; (tiredness)* fatigue *f*. **under the** ~ sous la tension *or* la pression; **to take the** ~ **off sth** diminuer la tension de qch *or* la pression sur qch; *(fig)* **to put a great** ~ **on** *friendship* mettre à rude épreuve; *the economy, savings, budget* grever; *person* épuiser nerveusement; **the ~(s) of city life** la tension de la vie urbaine; **listening for 3 hours is a** ~ écouter pendant 3 heures demande un grand effort; **the** ~ **of climbing the stairs** l'effort requis pour monter l'escalier; **he has been under a great deal of** ~ ses nerfs ont été mis à rude épreuve. (**b**) *(Med: sprain)* entorse *f*, foulure *f*. (**c**) *(Mus)* **to the ~s of** aux accents *mpl* de.

2 *vt* (**a**) *rope, beam* tendre excessivement; *(Med) muscle* froisser; *arm, ankle* fouler; *(fig) friendship, marriage, sb's patience* mettre à rude épreuve; *resources, savings, budget, the economy* grever; *meaning* forcer. **to** ~ **one's back** se donner un tour de reins; **to** ~ **one's heart** se fatiguer le cœur; **to** ~ **one's shoulder** se froisser un muscle dans l'épaule; **to** ~ **one's voice** forcer sa voix; **to** ~ **one's eyes** s'abîmer les yeux; **to** ~ **one's ears to hear sth** tendre l'oreille pour entendre qch; **to** ~ **every nerve to do** fournir un effort intense pour faire; **to** ~ **o.s.** *(damage muscle)* se froisser un muscle; *(overtire o.s.)* se surmener; *(iro)* **don't** ~ **yourself!** surtout ne te fatigue pas! (**b**) *(filter) liquid, soup* passer; *vegetables* égoutter.

3 *vi*: **to** ~ **to do** *(physically)* peiner pour faire; *(mentally)* s'efforcer de faire; **to** ~ **at sth** *(pushing/pulling)* pousser/tirer qch de toutes ses forces.

◆ **strain off** *vt sep liquid* vider.

◆ **strained** *adj* (**a**) *arm, ankle* foulé; *muscle* froissé; *eyes* fatigué; *voice, smile, cough* forcé; *look* contraint; *person, relations, atmosphere, nerves* tendu; *style* affecté; **he has a ~ed shoulder/back** il s'est froissé un muscle dans l'épaule/le dos; (**b**) *baby food* en purée. ◆ **strainer** *n (Culin)* passoire *f*.

strain[2] [streɪn] *n (breed, lineage)* race *f*; *[virus]* souche *f*. **a** ~ **of madness** des tendances *fpl* à la folie; *(fig)* **a lot more in the same** ~ encore beaucoup du même genre; **he continued in this** ~ il a continué dans ce sens.

strait [streɪt] *n (Geog: also* **~s**: *gen)* détroit *m*. **the S~s of Dover** le Pas de Calais; *(fig)* **in dire ~s** dans une situation difficile. ◆ **straitened** *adj*: **in ~ened circumstances** dans la gêne. ◆ **straitjacket** *n* camisole *f* de force. ◆ **strait-laced** *adj* collet monté *inv*.

strand [strænd] *n [thread, wire]* brin *m*; *[pearls]* rang *m*; *(in narrative etc)* fil *m*. **a** ~ **of hair** une mèche.

stranded ['strændɪd] *adj ship* échoué; *(fig) person* en rade *. **to leave sb** ~ laisser qn en rade *.

strange [streɪndʒ] *adj* (**a**) *(unfamiliar) language, country* inconnu; *work, activity* inaccoutumé. **you'll feel rather** ~ vous vous sentirez un peu dépaysé; **several** ~ **people** plusieurs personnes que je ne connaissais pas, plusieurs inconnus; **I never sleep well in a** ~ **bed** je ne dors jamais bien dans un lit autre que le mien. (**b**) *(odd, unusual)* étrange, bizarre. **it is** ~ **that** il est étrange *or* bizarre que + *subj;* ~ **as it may seem** aussi étrange que cela puisse paraître. ◆ **strangely** *adv* étrangement, curieusement; **~ly enough,...** chose curieuse,... ◆ **strangeness** *n* étrangeté *f*, bizarrerie *f*. ◆ **stranger** *n (unknown)* inconnu(e) *m(f)*; *(from another place)* étranger *m*, -ère *f*; **he's a ~r to me** il m'est inconnu; **I'm a ~r here** je ne suis pas d'ici; **I am a ~r to Paris** je ne connais pas Paris; **a ~r to politics** un novice en matière de politique.

strangle ['stræŋgl] *vt* étrangler *(also fig)*. ◆ **stranglehold** *n*: **to have a ~hold on** tenir à la gorge; *(fig)* **a ~hold on the market** une domination du marché. ◆ **strangler** *n* étrangleur *m*, -euse *f*. ◆ **strangulation** *n* strangulation *f*.

strap [stræp] **1** *n (of leather, cloth)* courroie *f*, sangle *f*; *(on shoe)* lanière *f*; *(ankle ~)* bride *f*; *(on garment)* bretelle *f*; *(on shoulder bag)* bandoulière *f*; *(watch ~)* bracelet *m*; *(in bus, tube)* poignée *f* de cuir; *(Tech)* lien *m*. **2** *vt (tie*: ~ **down**, ~ **in**, ~ **on**, ~ **up***)* attacher (*sth to sth* qch à qch). ◆ **straphanger** *n (standing)* voyageur *m*, -euse *f* debout *inv (dans le métro etc)*; *(US)* usager *m* des transports en commun. ◆ **strapless** *adj dress, bra* sans bretelles. ◆ **strapping** *adj* costaud * *(f inv)*.

Strasbourg ['stræzbɜ:g] *n* Strasbourg.

strategy ['strætɪdʒɪ] *n* stratégie *f*. ◆ **stratagem** *n* stratagème *m*. ◆ **strategic(al)** *adj* stratégique. ◆ **strategist** *n* stratège *m*.

stratosphere ['strætəʊsfɪəʳ] *n* stratosphère *f*.

stratum, *pl* **-ta** ['strɑ:təm, tə] *n (Geol, fig)* couche *f*.

straw [strɔ:] **1** *n (all senses)* paille *f*. **to drink sth through a** ~ boire qch avec une paille; *(fig)* **to clutch at a** ~ se raccrocher désespérément à un semblant d'espoir; *(fig)* **a** ~ **in the wind** une indication des choses à venir; *(fig)* **the last** ~ *or* **the** ~ **that breaks the camel's back** la goutte d'eau qui fait déborder le vase. **2** *adj (made of ~)* de paille. ~ **hat** chapeau *m* de paille; *(fig)* ~ **poll** *or* **vote** sondage *m* d'opinion. ◆ **strawberry 1** *n (fruit)* fraise *f*; *(plant)* fraisier *m*; **wild ~berry** fraise des bois ; **2** *adj jam* de fraises; *ice cream* à la fraise; *tart* aux fraises; *(Anat)* **~berry mark** tache *f* de vin, envie *f*. ◆ **straw-coloured** *adj* paille *inv*.

stray [streɪ] **1** *adj dog, child, bullet* perdu; *sheep, cow* égaré; *taxi, shot etc* isolé. **a few** ~ **cars** quelques rares voitures; **a** ~ **motorist** un des rares automobilistes. **2** *n (child/dog)* enfant *mf*/chien *m* perdu(e). **3** *vi [person, animal]* s'égarer; *[thoughts]* vagabonder. **to** ~ **from** s'écarter de; **to** ~ **into enemy territory** s'égarer et se retrouver en territoire ennemi.

streak [stri:k] **1** *n (line, band)* raie *f*; *[ore, mineral]* veine *f*; *[light, blood, paint]* filet *m*. **his hair had ~s of grey in it** ses cheveux commençaient à grisonner; *(deliberate)* **blond ~s** mèches blondes; **like a** ~ **of lightning** comme un éclair; **a** ~ **of jealousy** des tendances *fpl* à la jalousie; **a** ~ **of luck** une période de chance. **2** *vt* zébrer, strier (*with* de). **~ed with** *[sky]* strié de; *[mirror]* zébré de; *[clothes]* maculé de; **hair ~ed with grey** cheveux qui commencent à grisonner. **3** *vi* (**a**) **to** ~ **in/past** *etc* entrer/passer *etc* comme un éclair. (**b**) (**: naked)* courir tout nu en public. ◆ **streaker** * *n* streaker *m*, -euse *f*. ◆ **streaky** *adj colour* marbré; *window, mirror, sky* zébré; *bacon* pas trop maigre.

stream [stri:m] **1** *n* (**a**) *(brook)* ruisseau *m*. *(current)* **against the** ~ contre le courant. (**b**) *(flow) [water, blood, light, excuses, cars etc]* flot *m*; *[cold air]* courant *m*. *[oil]* **to be/come on** ~ être/être mis en service; **~s of people** des flots de gens; *(Brit Scol)* **divided into 5 ~s** répartis en 5 classes de niveau; *(Brit Scol)* **the B** ~ le groupe B. **2** *vi [liquid, walls]* ruisseler (*with* de). **his eyes were ~ing** il pleurait à chaudes larmes; *[cold air, sunlight]* **to** ~ **into** entrer à flots dans; *[people, cars etc]* **to** ~ **in/past** *etc* entrer/passer *etc* à flots. **3** *vt (Scol) pupils* répartir par niveau. **to** ~ **French** répartir les élèves par niveau en français.
◆ **streamer** *n* serpentin *m*. ◆ **streaming 1** *n (Scol)* répartition *f* des élèves par niveau ; **2** *adj*: **a ~ing cold** un gros rhume. ◆ **streamline** *vt (Aut, Aviat)* donner un profil aérodynamique à; *(fig)* rationaliser. ◆ **streamlined** *adj (Aviat)* fuselé; *(Aut)* aérodynamique; *(fig)* rationalisé.

street [stri:t] **1** *n* rue *f*. **in the** ~ dans la rue; *(fig)* **the man in the** ~ l'homme de la rue; **she is on the ~s** elle fait le trottoir *; *(fig)* **that is right up my** ~ * c'est tout à fait dans mes cordes; **he is not in the same** ~ **as you** * il ne vous vient pas à la cheville; **to be ~s ahead of sb** * dépasser qn de loin; *(fig)* **~s better** * beaucoup mieux. **2** *adj noises* de la rue; *accident* de la circulation. ~ **directory** *or* **guide** répertoire *m* des rues; ~ **door** porte *f* sur la rue; ~ **fighting** combats *mpl* de rue; ~ **lamp** réverbère *m*; **at** ~ **level** au rez-de-chaussée; ~ **lighting** éclairage *m* des rues; ~ **map** plan *m* des rues; ~ **market** marché *m* à ciel ouvert; ~ **musician** musicien *m* des rues; ~ **sweeper** *(person)* balayeur *m*; *(machine)* balayeuse *f*; ~ **urchin** gamin *m* des rues; *[drugs]* ~ **value** valeur *f* au niveau du revendeur. ◆ **streetcar** *n (US)* tramway *m*. ◆ **streetwise** *adj child* dégourdi *; *worker* futé, réaliste.

strength [streŋθ] *n* (**a**) *(gen)* force *f*; *[building, wood, shoes, claim, case]* solidité *f*; *[current]* intensité *f*; *[drink]* teneur *f* en alcool; *[solution]* titre *m*. **he hadn't the** ~ **to lift it** il n'avait pas la force de le soulever; **his** ~ **failed him** ses forces l'ont abandonné; **to get one's** ~ **back** reprendre des forces; ~ **of character** force de caractère; ~ **of purpose** résolution *f*; ~ **of will** volonté *f*; *(Fin)* **the** ~ **of the pound** la solidité de la livre; *(fig)* **on the** ~ **of** en vertu de. (**b**) *(Mil, Naut)* effectif *m*. **fighting** ~ effectif mobilisable; **they are below** *or* **under** ~ leur effectif n'est pas au complet; *(fig)* **they were there in** ~ ils étaient là en grand nombre; *(gen)* **to be on the** ~ faire partie du personnel.
◆ **strengthen 1** *vt (gen)* renforcer; *person, muscle* fortifier; *eyesight* améliorer; *(Fin) the pound* consolider ; **2** *vi [muscle, limb]* se fortifier; *[wind, influence, characteristic]* augmenter. ◆ **strengthening** *n* renforcement *m*; amélioration *f*; consolidation *f*.

strenuous ['strenjʊəs] *adj exercise, work* ardu; *game, march, day* fatigant; *life, holiday* très actif; *effort, resistance* acharné; *protest* vigoureux, énergique. *(Med)* **he must not do anything too** ~ il ne doit pas se fatiguer. ◆ **strenuously** *adv work, protest* énergiquement; *exercise, pull* vigoureusement; *resist, try* avec acharnement.

stress [stres] **1** *n* (**a**) *(load: on bridge, beam etc)* charge *f* (*of* de); *(on metal)* travail *m*; *(pressure: psychological, moral etc)* pression *f*; *(mental, nervous)* tension *f* nerveuse, stress *m*. **in times of** ~ à des moments de grande tension; **the ~es and strains of modern life** les agressions *fpl* de la vie moderne; **to be under** ~ *[person]* être stressé; *[relationship]* être tendu. (**b**) *(emphasis)* insistance *f*; *(Ling, Mus, Poetry) (gen)* accentuation *f*; *(on syllable)* accent *m*. **2** *adj (Ling)* ~ **mark** accent *m*. **3** *vt (gen)* insister sur; *(Ling, Mus, Poetry)* accentuer. ◆ **stressful** *adj* difficile, stressant.

stretch [stretʃ] **1** *n* (**a**) **there's a lot of** ~ **in this material** ce tissu prête bien; **by a** ~ **of the imagination** en faisant un effort d'imagination; **vast ~es of sand/snow** de vastes étendues de sable/de neige; **there's a straight** ~ **(of road)** la route est toute droite; **a magnificent** ~ **of country** une campagne magnifique; **in that** ~ **of the river** dans cette partie de la rivière; *(distance)* **for a long** ~ sur des kilomètres; **not by a long ~!** loin de là! (**b**) *(time)* période *f*. **a long** ~ **of time** longtemps; **for hours at a** ~ pendant des heures d'affilée; *(Prison)* **he's done a 10-year** ~ ‡ il a fait 10 ans de prison. **2** *adj fabric, garment* extensible; *(elasticated)* élastique. ~ **mark** vergeture *f*. **3** *vt* (**a**) *rope, spring* tendre; *elastic* étirer; *shoe, glove, hat* élargir; *muscle* distendre; *(fig) law, rules* tourner; *meaning, truth* forcer; *one's principles* adapter; *one's authority* outrepasser. *(fig)* **to** ~ **a point** faire une concession. (**b**) *(often* ~ **out**) *neck* tendre; *arm, leg* tendre; *(extend)* allonger; *wing* déployer; *net, rope* tendre (*between* entre; *above* au-dessus de); *rug, linen* étendre; *(fig) athlete, student* pousser. *(fig: go for walk)* **I'm just going to** ~ **my legs** je vais me dégourdir les jambes; *(after sleep)* **to** ~ **o.s.** s'étirer; **to be fully ~ed** *[rope etc]* être complètement tendu; *[engine, factory]* tourner à plein; *[person]* travailler à la limite de ses possibilités; **the work he is doing does not** ~ **him enough** le travail qu'il fait n'exige pas assez de lui. **4** *vi* (**a**) *[person, animal]* s'étirer. **he ~ed across and touched her cheek** il a tendu la main et touché sa joue. (**b**) *(lengthen)* s'allonger; *(widen) [shoes]* s'élargir; *[elastic]* s'étirer; *[fabric, jersey]* prêter. (**c**) *[forest, procession, influence]* s'étendre (*over* sur); *(in time) [meeting etc]* se prolonger (*into* jusqu'à). **the rope won't** ~ **to that post** la corde ne va pas jusqu'à ce poteau; **how far will it ~?** jusqu'où ça va?; *(fig)* **my money won't** ~ * **to a new car** mon budget ne me permet pas d'acheter une nouvelle voiture.
◆ **stretch out 1** *vi* s'étendre. **2** *vt sep (reach) arm, hand, foot* tendre; *(extend) leg etc* allonger, étendre; *wing* déployer; *net, rope* tendre; *rug, linen* étendre; *(lengthen) meeting, discussion* prolonger; *story, explanation* allonger.
◆ **stretcher 1** *n (Med)* brancard *m*, civière *f* ; **2** *adj*: **~er case** malade *mf* or blessé(e) *m(f)* qui ne peut pas marcher. ◆ **stretcher-bearer** *n* brancardier *m*. ◆ **stretchy** *adj* extensible.

strew [stru:] *pret* **strewed,** *ptp* **strewed** *or* **strewn** *vt straw, sand* répandre (*on, over* sur); *flowers, objects, wreckage* éparpiller (*over* sur); *ground, room* joncher (*with* de).

stricken ['strɪk(ə)n] *adj (wounded)* grièvement blessé; *(grief-~)* affligé; *(damaged) city* dévasté; *ship* très endommagé. ~ **with remorse/fear** pris de remords/peur.

strict [strɪkt] *adj* (**a**) *(severe: gen) person, principle, views* strict, sévère (*with sb* avec qn); *ban, rule* strict; *order* formel; *etiquette* rigide. (**b**) *(precise) meaning* strict *(after n)*; *translation, time limit* précis; *(absolute) accuracy, secrecy, truth* strict *(before n)*. **in the** ~ **sense of the word** au sens strict du mot.
◆ **strictly** *adv (gen)* strictement; **~ly between ourselves** strictement entre nous; **~ly speaking** à strictement parler; **~ly prohibited** formellement interdit. ◆ **strictness** *n [person etc]* sévérité *f*.
◆ **stricture** *n* critique *f* (*on* de).

stride [straɪd] *(vb: pret* **strode,** *ptp* **stridden***)* **1** *n* grand pas *m*; *[runner]* foulée *f*. **with giant ~s** à pas de géant; **in a few ~s** en quelques enjambées; *(fig)* **to make great ~s** faire de grands progrès (*in French* en français; *in one's studies* dans ses études; *in doing* pour ce qui est de faire); **to get into one's** ~, *(US)* **hit one's** ~ trouver son rythme; **to take in one's** ~ *changes etc* accepter sans sourciller; *exam/interrogation etc* passer/subir *etc* comme si de rien n'était. **2** *vi*: **to** ~ **along/away** *etc* avancer/

s'éloigner *etc* à grands pas; **he was striding up and down the room** il arpentait la pièce.

strident ['straɪd(ə)nt] *adj* strident.

strife [straɪf] *n* conflits *mpl*, dissensions *fpl*. **internal** ~ dissensions intestines; **industrial** ~ conflits sociaux.

strike [straɪk] *(vb: pret, ptp* **struck***)* **1** *n* (**a**) *(Ind)* grève *f* (*of, by* de). **electricity/rail** ~ grève des employés de l'électricité/du chemin de fer; **to be on** ~ être en grève (*for* pour obtenir; *against* pour protester contre); **to go on** ~, **to come out on** ~ se mettre en grève; **to call a** ~ lancer un ordre de grève. (**b**) *(Aviat, Mil)* raid *m* (aérien). (**c**) *(Fishing)* touche *f*; *(Baseball, Bowling)* strike *m*; *(of oil etc)* découverte *f*. *(Miner etc)* **to make a** ~ découvrir un gisement; *(fig)* **a lucky** ~ un coup de chance. **2** *adj* (**a**) *(Ind) committee, fund* de grève; *leader* des grévistes; *pay* de gréviste. (**b**) ~ **force** *(gen: of police etc)* brigade *f* spéciale; *(Aviat, Mil)* détachement *m* d'avions.

3 *vt* (**a**) *(hit) person, ball* frapper; *nail, table* frapper sur; *(knock against)* heurter; *(Mus) string* toucher; *[snake]* mordre. **to** ~ **sth with one's fist** frapper du poing sur qch; *(fig)* **to** ~ **a man when he is down** frapper un homme à terre; **to** ~ **the first blow** donner le premier coup; *(fig)* **to** ~ **a blow for freedom** rompre une lance pour la liberté; **to** ~ **sth from sb's hand** faire tomber qch de la main de qn; **to** ~ **fear into sb** remplir qn d'effroi; **to** ~ **terror into sb** terroriser qn; **he struck his head against the table** sa tête a heurté la table, il s'est cogné la tête contre la table; **the stone struck him on the head** la pierre l'a frappé à la tête; **he was struck by a bullet** il a reçu une balle; **to be struck by lightning** être frappé par la foudre; **to** ~ **sb dumb** rendre qn muet; *(fig)* **I was struck by his intelligence** j'ai été frappé par son intelligence; **I wasn't very struck * with him** il ne m'a pas fait très bonne impression; **the funny side of it struck me** le côté drôle de la chose m'a frappé; **that ~s me as a good idea** cela me semble une bonne idée; **an idea struck him** il a eu une idée; **it ~s me that...** j'ai l'impression que...; **how did the film** ~ **you?** qu'avez-vous pensé du film? (**b**) *(find, discover) gold* trouver; *(fig) hotel, road* tomber sur; *(fig) difficulty, obstacle* rencontrer. **to** ~ **oil** *(Miner)* trouver du pétrole; *(fig)* trouver le filon *; *(fig)* **to** ~ **it rich** faire fortune. (**c**) *(make, produce etc) coin, medal* frapper; *sparks, fire* faire jaillir (*from* de); *match* gratter. **to** ~ **a light** allumer une allumette (*or* un briquet *etc*); **to** ~ **an average** établir une moyenne; **to** ~ **a balance** trouver le juste milieu; **to** ~ **a bargain** conclure un marché; **to** ~ **an attitude** poser; **to** ~ **an attitude of surprise** faire l'étonné(e). (**d**) *chord, note* sonner; *[clock]* sonner (*3 o'clock* 3 heures). *(fig)* **that ~s a chord** cela me dit qch; *(fig)* **to** ~ **a false note** sonner faux; **it has just struck six** six heures viennent juste de sonner. (**e**) *(take down) tent* plier; *camp* lever; *flag* baisser. (**f**) *(delete: from list, record) name* rayer (*from* de); *(from professional register)* radier (*from* de).

4 *vi* (**a**) *(hit)* frapper; *(Mil)* attaquer; *[snake]* mordre; *[tiger]* sauter sur sa proie; *[disease etc]* frapper; *[panic]* s'emparer des esprits. *(lit, fig)* **to** ~ **home** faire mouche; **to** ~ **at** *person* porter un coup à; *(fig) root of sth* porter atteinte à; *evil etc* attaquer; **his foot struck against a rock** son pied a heurté un rocher. (**b**) *[clock]* sonner. (**c**) *(Ind: go on ~)* faire grève (*for* pour obtenir; *against* pour protester contre). (**d**) *(turn, go)* aller, prendre. ~ **left** prenez à gauche; **to** ~ **uphill** se mettre à grimper la côte; **he struck (out** *or* **off) across the fields** il s'en est allé à travers champs.

◆ **strike back** *vi (Mil)* user de représailles (*at sb* à l'égard de qn); *(gen)* se venger (*at sb* de qn). ◆ **strike down** *vt sep* terrasser. ◆ **strike off** *vt sep* (**a**) *sb's head* trancher; *branch* couper. (**b**) *(from list)* rayer; *doctor etc* radier. ◆ **strike out 1** *vi (hit out)* se débattre. **he struck out at his attackers** il a lancé des coups dans la direction de ses attaquants; *(in business)* **to** ~ **out on one's own** se mettre à son propre compte. **2** *vt sep (delete) word, question* rayer. ◆ **strike up 1** *vi [band etc]* commencer à jouer; *[music]* commencer. **2** *vt sep [band]* se mettre à jouer; *[singers]* se mettre à chanter. ~ **up the band!** faites jouer l'orchestre!; **to** ~ **up an acquaintance/a friendship** lier connaissance/amitié (*with sb* avec qn).

◆ **strikebound** *adj* immobilisé par une grève. ◆ **strikebreaker** *n* briseur *m* de grève. ◆ **strikebreaking** *n*: **he was accused of ~breaking** on l'a accusé d'être un briseur de grève. ◆ **striker** *n (Ind)* gréviste *mf*; *(Ftbl)* buteur *m*. ◆ **striking** *adj* (**a**) *change, sight* frappant, saisissant; (**b**) *(Mil) power* de frappe ; *(Mil, fig)* **within striking distance of** à portée de ; (**c**) *(Ind) workers* en grève. ◆ **strikingly** *adv change, improve* d'une manière frappante; *beautiful etc* remarquablement.

string [strɪŋ] *(vb: pret, ptp* **strung***)* **1** *n* (**a**) *(gen)* ficelle *f*; *[violin, bow, racket etc]* corde *f*; *[apron, bonnet]* cordon *m*. **a piece of** ~ un bout de ficelle; **to pull ~s for sb** pistonner qn; *(fig)* **there are no ~s attached** cela ne vous *etc* engage à rien; **to have more than one** ~ **to one's bow** avoir plus d'une corde à son arc; **his first/second** ~ sa première/deuxième ressource; *(Mus)* **the ~s** les (instruments *mpl* à) cordes. (**b**) *[beads, pearls]* rang *m*; *[onions, garlic, lies, excuses]* chapelet *m*; *[people, vehicles]* file *f*; *[racehorses]* écurie *f*. (**c**) *(Ling)* séquence *f; (Comput)* chaîne *f*. **2** *adj* (**a**) *instrument, orchestra, quartet* à cordes; *serenade, piece* pour cordes. (**b**) ~ **bag** filet *m* à provisions; ~ **bean** haricot *m* vert; *(US Press)* ~ **correspondent** correspondant(e) *m(f)* local(e) à temps partiel; ~ **vest** tricot *m* de corps à grosses mailles. **3** *vt racket* corder; *violin etc* monter; *bow* garnir d'une corde; *beads, pearls* enfiler; *rope* tendre (*across* en travers de; *between* entre); *lights, decorations* suspendre, attacher (*on* sur; *between* entre); *beans* enlever les fils de.

◆ **string along * 1** *vi* suivre. **to** ~ **along with sb** accompagner qn. **2** *vt sep (pej)* faire marcher *(fig)*. ◆ **string out 1** *vi [people, things]* s'échelonner (*along a road* le long d'une route). **2** *vt sep lanterns, washing etc* suspendre; *guards, posts* échelonner. ◆ **string up** *vt sep lantern, onions* suspendre; *(*: lynch)* pendre. *(fig)* **to be strung up** être très tendu (*about* à la pensée de).

◆ **stringed** *adj (Mus)* à cordes. ◆ **stringer** *n* correspondant(e) *m(f)* local(e) à temps partiel. ◆ **stringpulling** *n (fig)* piston * *m (fig)*. ◆ **stringy** *adj celery, meat* filandreux; *cooked cheese* filant; *plant* tout en longueur.

stringent ['strɪn(d)ʒ(ə)nt] *adj (gen)* rigoureux; *reasons, arguments* irrésistible; *necessity* impérieux. ◆ **stringency** *n* rigueur *f*; **economic stringency** austérité *f*.

strip [strɪp] **1** *n* (**a**) *(piece: gen)* bande *f*; *[water, sea]* bras *m*. **a** ~ **of garden** un petit jardin tout en longueur; **comic** ~, ~ **cartoon** bande dessinée; *(fig)* **to tear a** ~ **off sb** ‡ bien sonner les cloches à qn *. (**b**) *(Aviat: landing ~)* piste *f* d'atterrissage. (**c**) *(Sport: clothes)* tenue *f*. **2** *adj*: ~ **lighting** éclairage *m* au néon; ~ **poker** strip-poker *m*; ~ **show** strip-tease *m*. **3** *vt person* déshabiller; *(often* ~ **down***) room, house* vider; *car, engine, gun* démonter complètement; *screw, gears* arracher le filet de; *branches, bushes* dépouiller; *bed* défaire complètement; *(remove) wallpaper, decorations etc* enlever (*from sth* de qch; *from sb* à qn); *paint, furniture* décaper; *(deprive) person, object* dépouiller (*of* de). **~ped pine** pin *m* décapé; **to** ~ **the walls** enlever le papier peint; **to** ~ **a room of all its pictures** enlever tous les tableaux dans une pièce; *(Fin)* **to** ~

a company of its assets cannibaliser * une compagnie. **4** *vi (undress)* se déshabiller; *[striptease artist]* faire du strip-tease. **to ~ naked** se mettre nu; **to ~ to the waist** se déshabiller jusqu'à la ceinture; **~ped to the waist** nu jusqu'à la ceinture.
◆ **strip off** **1** *vi* se déshabiller complètement. **2** *vt sep (gen)* enlever (*from sth* de qch); *leaves* faire tomber (*from* de); *berries* prendre (*from* de).
◆ **stripper** *n* (**a**) *(paint-stripper)* décapant *m*; (**b**) *(*: striptease)* strip-teaseuse *f*; **male ~per** strip-teaseur *m*. ◆ **striptease** *n* strip-tease *m*.

stripe [straɪp] *n* (**a**) rayure *f*, raie *f*. *(pattern)* **~s** rayures; **yellow with a white ~** jaune rayé de blanc. (**b**) *(Mil)* galon *m*. ◆ **striped** *adj* rayé (*with* de).

stripling ['strɪplɪŋ] *n* tout jeune homme *m*.

strive [straɪv] *pret* **strove,** *ptp* **striven** *vi* s'efforcer (*to do* de faire; *for sth* d'obtenir qch).

strobe [strəʊb] **1** *adj* stroboscopique. **2** *n (also ~* **light***)* lumière *f* stroboscopique.

strode [strəʊd] *pret of* **stride.**

stroke [strəʊk] **1** *n* (**a**) *(movement; blow: gen)* coup *m*; *(Swimming: style)* nage *f*. *(lit, fig)* **at a ~, at one ~** d'un seul coup; **with a ~ of his axe** d'un coup de hache; **to put sb off his ~** *(Sport)* faire perdre son rythme à qn; *(fig)* faire perdre tous ses moyens à qn; **he hasn't done a ~ (of work)** il n'a rien fait du tout; **~ of diplomacy** chef-d'œuvre *m* de diplomatie; **~ of genius** trait *m* de génie; **~ of luck** coup de chance; **master ~** coup de maître. (**b**) *(mark) [pen, pencil]* trait *m*; *[brush]* touche *f*; *(Typ: oblique)* barre *f*. **with a ~ of the pen** d'un trait de plume. (**c**) *[bell, clock]* coup *m*. **on the ~ of 10** sur le coup de 10 heures; **in the ~ of time** juste à temps. (**d**) *(Med)* **to have a ~** avoir une attaque. (**e**) *(Tech: of piston)* course *f*. **a two-/four-~ engine** un moteur à deux/quatre temps. (**f**) *(Rowing: person)* chef *m* de nage. **2** *vt* caresser.

stroll [strəʊl] **1** *n* petite promenade *f*. **to take a ~, to go for a ~** aller faire un tour. **2** *vi*: **to ~ in/away** *etc* entrer/s'éloigner *etc* nonchalamment.
◆ **stroller** *n (person)* flâneur *m*, -euse *f*; *(US: push-chair)* poussette *f*.

strong [strɒŋ] **1** *adj (gen)* fort; *(solid, robust) wall, table, shoes, bolt, reasons, evidence, stomach, heart, nerves* solide; *eyesight* très bon; *candidate, contender* sérieux; *magnet* puissant; *(Elec) current* intense; *characteristic* marqué; *emotion, desire, interest* vif; *(St Ex) market* ferme; *(Econ) the pound, dollar* solide; *letter, protest, measures* énergique; *(Mus) beat* fort; *solution* concentré. **to be as ~ as a horse** *or* **an ox** *(powerful)* être fort comme un bœuf; *(healthy)* avoir une santé de fer; *(in circus etc)* **~ man** hercule *m*; **do you feel ~?** est-ce que vous avez des forces?; *(in health)* **when you are ~ again** quand vous aurez repris des forces; **she has never been very ~** elle a toujours eu une petite santé; *(in courage etc)* **you must be ~** soyez courageux; *(mentally etc)* **he's a very ~ person** c'est un homme qui a du ressort; **an army 500 ~** une armée de 500 hommes; **they were 100 ~** ils étaient au nombre de 100; **in a ~ position** bien placé (*to do* pour faire); **his ~ suit** *(Cards)* sa couleur forte; *(fig: also* **his ~ point***)* son fort; **to be ~ in maths** être fort en maths; **in ~ terms** en termes non équivoques; **there are ~ indications that...** tout semble indiquer que...; **a ~ effect** beaucoup d'effet; *(fig: too much)* **that's a bit ~!** * ça c'est un peu fort! *; **I had a ~ sense of...** je ressentais vivement...; **I've a ~ feeling that...** j'ai bien l'impression que...; **he's got ~ feelings on this matter** cette affaire lui tient à cœur; **it is my ~ opinion that** je suis fermement convaincu que; **a ~ socialist** un socialiste fervent; **~ supporters of** d'ardents partisans de; **I am a ~ believer in** je crois fermement à; **~ verb** verbe *m* fort; **~ drink** alcool *m*; **it has a ~ smell** ça sent fort.
2 *adv*: **to be going ~** *[person]* être toujours solide; *[car etc]* marcher toujours bien; *[firm, business]* être florissant; *[relationship]* aller bien.
◆ **strong-arm** *adj* brutal. ◆ **strongbox** *n* coffre-fort *m*. ◆ **stronghold** *n (Mil)* forteresse *f*; *(fig)* bastion *m*. ◆ **strongly** *adv fight, attack, protest* énergiquement; *attract, influence, desire* vivement; *accentuate, remind, indicate* fortement; *believe* fermement; *feel, sense* profondément; *constructed, made* solidement; **~ly-worded letter** lettre *f* bien sentie; **it smells very ~ly** cela sent très fort; **it smells ~ly of onions** cela a une forte odeur d'oignons.
◆ **strong-minded** *adj* qui sait ce qu'il veut.
◆ **strong-mindedly** *adv* avec ténacité. ◆ **strong-room** *n* chambre *f* forte. ◆ **strong-willed** *adj*: **to be ~-willed** avoir de la volonté.

strove [strəʊv] *pret of* **strive.**

struck [strʌk] *pret, ptp of* **strike.**

structure ['strʌktʃəʳ] **1** *n* (**a**) *(gen, Chem etc)* structure *f*; **social/administrative ~** structure sociale/administrative. (**b**) *(Constr: of building etc)* ossature *f*; *(the building, bridge etc itself)* édifice *m*. **2** *vt* structurer. ◆ **structural** *adj* (**a**) *(gen, Chem etc)* structural; *(relating to structuralism)* structural; (**b**) *(Constr) fault etc* de construction; *alterations* des parties portantes; **structural engineering** ponts et chaussées *mpl*. ◆ **structurally** *adv (gen, Chem etc)* du point de vue de la structure; *(Constr)* du point de vue de la construction.

struggle ['strʌgl] **1** *n (lit, fig)* lutte *f* (*for* pour; *against* contre; *with* avec; *to do* pour faire). **to put up a ~** résister; **he lost his glasses in the ~** il a perdu ses lunettes dans la bagarre; **without a ~** *surrender etc* sans résistance; *(without difficulty)* sans beaucoup de difficulté; **the ~ to find somewhere to live** les difficultés qu'on a à trouver un logement; **I had a ~ to persuade him** j'ai eu beaucoup de mal à le persuader; **it was a ~** cela a demandé beaucoup d'efforts.
2 *vi* (**a**) *(gen)* lutter; *(fight)* se battre, lutter (*against sth* contre qch; *with sb* avec qn); *(resist)* résister (*against sth* à qch); *(thrash around)* se débattre; *(fig: try hard)* se démener (*to do* pour faire). **they were struggling for power** ils se disputaient le pouvoir; *(fig)* **he was struggling to make ends meet** il avait beaucoup de mal à joindre les deux bouts. (**b**) **to ~ in/out** *etc* entrer/sortir *etc* avec peine; **to ~ through the crowd** se frayer péniblement un chemin à travers la foule; **he ~d to his feet** *(from armchair etc)* il s'est levé non sans peine; *(during fight etc)* il s'est relevé péniblement; **he ~d into a jersey** il a enfilé non sans peine un pullover.
◆ **struggle through** *vi (fig)* s'en sortir.
◆ **struggling** *adj artist etc* qui tire le diable par la queue.

strum [strʌm] *vti* (**~ on**) *piano* tapoter de; *guitar etc* racler.

strung [strʌŋ] *pret, ptp of* **string.**

strut¹ [strʌt] *vi*: **to ~ about** *or* **around** se pavaner; **to ~ in/along** *etc* entrer/avancer *etc* d'un air important.

strut² [strʌt] *n (support)* étai *m*, support *m*.

strychnine ['strɪkni:n] *n* strychnine *f*.

stub [stʌb] **1** *n [tree, plant]* souche *f*; *[pencil]* bout *m*; *[cigarette, cigar]* mégot * *m*; *[cheque, ticket]* talon *m*. **2** *vt* (**a**) **to ~ one's toe** se cogner le doigt de pied (*against* contre). (**b**) (**~ out**) *cigar, cigarette* écraser. ◆ **stubby** *adj person* trapu; *finger* boudiné; *pencil* gros et court.

stubble ['stʌbl] *n (Agr)* chaume *m*; *(on chin)* barbe *f* de plusieurs jours.

stubborn ['stʌbən] *adj (gen)* opiniâtre; *person* têtu, obstiné; *animal* rétif; *fever, disease* rebelle. ◆ **stub-**

bornly *adv* obstinément. ◆ **stubbornness** *n* opiniâtreté *f*; entêtement *m*; obstination *f*.

stucco ['stʌkəʊ] *n* stuc *m*.

stuck [stʌk] *pret, ptp of* **stick.** ◆ **stuck-up** * *adj* prétentieux.

stud¹ [stʌd] **1** *n (gen, also on roadway)* clou *m* (à grosse tête); *(on football boots)* crampon *m*. **collar ~** bouton *m* de col. **2** *vt* clouter. **~ded tyre** pneu *m* clouté. *(fig)* **~ded with** parsemé de.

stud² [stʌd] **1** *n (racing ~)* écurie *f* (de courses); *(~ farm)* haras *m*. **to be at ~** étalonner. **2** *adj*: **~ book** stud-book *m*; **~ horse** étalon *m*; **~ mare** poulinière *f*.

student ['stjuːd(ə)nt] **1** *n (gen)* étudiant(e) *m(f)*; *(at school)* élève *mf*. **medical ~** étudiant(e) en médecine; **he is a ~ of bird life** il étudie la vie des oiseaux; **he is a keen ~** il est très studieux. **2** *adj life, power, unrest* étudiant; *residence, restaurant* universitaire; *attitudes, opinions (Univ)* des étudiants; *(Scol)* des élèves. **the ~ community** les étudiants *mpl*; *(US)* **~ driver** conducteur *m*, -trice *f* débutant(e); **~ nurse** élève *mf* infirmier (-ière); **~ teacher** professeur *m* stagiaire. ◆ **studentship** *n* bourse *f* d'études.

studio ['stjuːdɪəʊ] **1** *n* studio *m (de TV, d'artiste etc)*. **2** *adj*: **~ (appartment** *or* **flat)** studio *m*; **~ couch** divan *m*; *(Phot)* **~ portrait** portrait *m* photographique.

studious ['stjuːdɪəs] *adj person* studieux; *piece of work* soigné; *effort* assidu; *politeness* étudié; *avoidance* délibéré. ◆ **studiously** *adv* studieusement; soigneusement; délibérément; **~ly polite** d'une politesse étudiée. ◆ **studiousness** *n* application *f* (à l'étude).

study ['stʌdɪ] **1** *n* (**a**) étude *f* (*of* sur). *(fig)* **his face was a ~** il fallait voir son visage. (**b**) *(room)* bureau *m (particulier)*. **2** *adj visit, hour* d'étude; *group* de travail. **3** *vt (gen)* étudier; *sb's face, reactions, stars* observer. **4** *vi* étudier. **to ~ hard** travailler dur; **to ~ under sb** *(Univ)* travailler sous la direction de qn; *[painter, composer]* être l'élève de qn; **to ~ for an exam** préparer un examen; **he is ~ing to be a doctor/teacher** il fait des études de médecine/pour devenir professeur. ◆ **studied** *adj calm, politeness* étudié; *insult, avoidance* délibéré; *(pej) style* affecté.

stuff [stʌf] **1** *n* (**a**) *(substance)* **what's this ~ in this jar?** qu'est-ce que c'est que ça dans ce pot?; **it's good ~** c'est bien *or* bon; **there's some good ~ in it** il y a de bonnes choses là-dedans; **it's poor ~** ça ne vaut pas grand-chose; **it's dangerous ~** c'est dangereux; **I can't listen to his ~ at all** je ne peux pas souffrir sa musique (*or* sa poésie *etc*); *(pej)* **all that ~ about how he...** tous ces grands discours comme quoi il...; **that's the ~!** * bravo, c'est ça!; **~ and nonsense!** * balivernes!; **he is the ~ that heroes are made of** il a l'étoffe d'un héros; **he knows his ~** * il s'y connaît; **do your ~!** * vas-y!, c'est à toi!; **he did his ~ very well** * il s'en est bien sorti; **put your ~ away** range tes affaires; **he brought back a lot of ~** il a rapporté des tas de choses. (**b**) *(cloth)* étoffe *f*.
2 *vt (fill) cushion etc* rembourrer (*with* avec); *(Taxidermy) animal* empailler; *box, pockets* bourrer (*with* de); *(Culin)* farcir (*with* avec); *hole* boucher (*with* avec); *(cram) objects* fourrer (*in, into* dans). **to ~ one's fingers into one's ears** fourrer ses doigts dans ses oreilles; **he ~ed some money into my hand** il m'a fourré de l'argent dans la main; *(fig)* **he is a ~ed shirt** * il est pompeux; **~ed toy** jouet *m* de peluche; **to ~ o.s. with food** se gaver de nourriture.
3 *vi* (‡: *guzzle)* se gaver.
◆ **stuffed-up** *adj*: **my nose is ~ed-up** j'ai le nez bouché. ◆ **stuffily** *adv say etc* d'un ton désapprobateur. ◆ **stuffiness** *n (in room)* manque *m* d'air; *[person]* esprit *m* vieux jeu. ◆ **stuffing** *n (gen)* rembourrage *m*; *(Culin)* farce *f*; *(fig)* **he's got no ~ing** c'est une chiffe molle; **to knock the ~ing out of sb** *[boxer, blow]* dégonfler qn; *[illness, news]* mettre qn à plat. ◆ **stuffy** *adj* (**a**) *room* mal aéré; **it's ~y in here** on manque d'air ici; **it smells ~y** ça sent le renfermé; (**b**) *person* vieux jeu *inv*.

stumble ['stʌmbl] *vi* trébucher (*over* sur, contre); *[horse]* broncher. **to ~ in/along** *etc* entrer/avancer *etc* en trébuchant; *(fig)* **to ~ across** *or* **on sth** tomber sur qch; **he ~d through the first verse** il a récité la première strophe d'une voix hésitante. ◆ **stumbling block** *n* pierre *f* d'achoppement.

stump [stʌmp] **1** *n [tree]* souche *f*; *[limb, tail]* moignon *m*; *[tooth]* chicot *m*; *[cigar, pencil, chalk etc]* bout *m*; *(Cricket)* piquet *m*. *(US)* **to go on the ~** faire campagne. **2** *vt* (**a**) (*: *puzzle)* faire sécher *. **to be ~ed by sth** être incapable de répondre à qch, sécher * sur qch. (**b**) *(Cricket)* mettre hors jeu. **3** *vi*: **to ~ in/along** *etc* entrer/avancer *etc (heavily)* à pas lourds *or (limping)* clopin-clopant *.
◆ **stump up** * *(Brit)* **1** *vi* casquer ‡, payer. **2** *vt sep* cracher *, y aller de.
◆ **stumpy** *adj person* ramassé; *object* épais et court.

stun [stʌn] *vt* étourdir; *(fig: amaze)* stupéfier. ◆ **stun grenade** *n* grenade *f* incapacitante. ◆ **stunned** *adj (lit)* étourdi; *(fig)* stupéfait (*by* de). ◆ **stunning** *adj* étourdissant; stupéfiant; (*: *lovely) girl, dress, car* sensationnel *.

stung [stʌŋ] *pret, ptp of* **sting.**

stunk [stʌŋk] *ptp of* **stink.**

stunt¹ [stʌnt] *n (feat)* tour *m* de force; *[stuntman]* cascade *f; (Aviat)* acrobatie *f*; *(trick)* truc * *m*, coup *m* monté; *(publicity ~)* truc * publicitaire. ◆ **stuntman** *n (Cine etc)* cascadeur *m*.

stunt² [stʌnt] *vt growth* retarder; *person, plant* retarder la croissance de. ◆ **stunted** *adj* rabougri.

stupefy ['stjuːpɪfaɪ] *vt [blow]* étourdir; *[drink, drugs]* abrutir; *(fig: astound)* stupéfier. ◆ **stupefaction** *n* stupéfaction *f*. ◆ **stupefying** *adj (fig)* stupéfiant.

stupendous [stju(ː)'pendəs] *adj ceremony, beauty* prodigieux; (*) *film, holiday* fantastique. ◆ **stupendously** *adv* formidablement *.

stupid ['stjuːpɪd] *adj* stupide, idiot; *(from sleep, drink etc)* abruti. **I've done a ~ thing** j'ai fait une bêtise; **you ~ idiot!** * espèce d'idiot(e)!; **he drank himself ~** il s'est abruti d'alcool. ◆ **stupidity** *or* ◆ **stupidness** *n* stupidité *f*, bêtise *f*. ◆ **stupidly** *adv look, smile* stupidement; **I ~ly told him your name** j'ai été assez bête pour lui dire votre nom.

stupor ['stjuːpəʳ] *n* stupeur *f*.

sturdy ['stɜːdɪ] *adj person, chair* robuste; *(fig) resistance, refusal* énergique. ◆ **sturdily** *adv* robustement; énergiquement. ◆ **sturdiness** *n* robustesse *f*.

sturgeon ['stɜːdʒ(ə)n] *n* esturgeon *m*.

stutter ['stʌtəʳ] **1** *n* bégaiement *m*. **2** *vti* bégayer. ◆ **stutterer** *n* bègue *mf*. ◆ **stuttering** *n* bégaiement *m*.

sty [staɪ] *n [pigs]* porcherie *f*.

sty(e) [staɪ] *n (Med)* orgelet *m*.

style [staɪl] **1** *n* (**a**) *(gen)* style *m*; *(sort, type)* genre *m*. **in the Renaissance ~** de style Renaissance; **~ of life** *or* **living** style de vie; **he won in fine ~** il l'a emporté haut la main; **just the ~ of book I like** justement le genre de livre que j'aime; *(fig)* **it's not my ~** * ce n'est pas mon genre; **that's the ~!** * bravo! (**b**) *(Dress etc)* modèle *m*; *(Hairdressing)* coiffure *f*. **in the latest ~** *(adv)* à la dernière mode; *(adj)* du dernier cri; **sth in that ~** qch dans ce genre-là *or* dans ce goût-là. (**c**) *(distinction) [person]* allure *f*, chic *m*; *[building, car, film, book]* style *m*, cachet *m*. **to live in ~** vivre sur un grand pied; **he does things in ~** il fait bien les choses; **they**

got married in ~ ils se sont mariés en grande pompe; **he certainly travels in** ~ quand il voyage il fait bien les choses. **2** *vt* (**a**) *(call, designate)* appeler. (**b**) **to** ~ **sb's hair** créer une nouvelle coiffure pour qn. ◆ **styling** *n (Hairdressing)* coupe *f*. ◆ **stylish** *adj person* qui a du chic; *garment, hotel, district* chic *inv*; *film, book, car* qui a une certaine élégance. ◆ **stylishly** *adv live, dress* élégamment; *travel* dans les règles de l'art. ◆ **stylishness** *n* élégance *f*, chic *m*. ◆ **stylist** *n (Literat)* styliste *mf*; *(Hairdressing)* coiffeur *m*, -euse *f*. ◆ **stylistic 1** *adj (Literat etc)* stylistique; **2** *n*: **stylistics** stylistique *f*. ◆ **stylize** *vt* styliser.

stylus ['staɪləs] *n (tool)* style *m*; *[record player]* pointe *f* de lecture.

suave [swɑːv] *adj* doucereux. ◆ **suavely** *adv* doucereusement. ◆ **suavity** *n* manières *fpl* doucereuses.

sub... [sʌb] **1** *pref* sub..., sous-. **2** (*) *abbr of* **subaltern, submarine, subscription, substitute.** ◆ **subcommittee** *n* sous-comité *m*; *(in local government)* sous-commission *f*; **the Housing S~committee** la sous-commission du logement. ◆ **subcontinent** *n* sous-continent *m*. ◆ **subcontract 1** *n* sous-traité *m* ; **2** *vt* sous-traiter. ◆ **subcontractor** *n* sous-traitant *m*. ◆ **subdivide 1** *vt* subdiviser (*into* en) ; **2** *vi* se subdiviser. ◆ **subdivision** *n* subdivision *f*. ◆ **sub-edit** *vt* préparer pour l'impression. ◆ **sub-editor** *n* secrétaire *mf* de rédaction. ◆ **subhead(ing)** *n* sous-titre *m*. ◆ **subhuman** *adj* moins qu'humain. ◆ **sublet** *(pret, ptp* ~**let***)* **1** *n* sous-location *f* ; **2** *vti* sous-louer. ◆ **sub-librarian** *n* bibliothécaire *mf* adjoint(e). ◆ **sub-lieutenant** *n (Naut)* enseigne *m* de vaisseau. ◆ **submachine gun** *n* mitraillette *f*. ◆ **subnormal** *adj temperature* au-dessous de la normale; *person* arriéré. ◆ **sub-post office** *n* petit bureau *m* de poste *(de quartier etc)*. ◆ **subsoil** *n (Agr)* sous-sol *m*. ◆ **subsonic** *adj* subsonique. ◆ **substandard** *adj (gen)* inférieur; *goods* de qualité inférieure; *housing* inférieur aux normes exigées. ◆ **substratum,** *pl* ~**strata** *n* substrat *m*. ◆ **subtenant** *n* sous-locataire *mf*. ◆ **subtitle 1** *n* sous-titre *m* ; **2** *vt* sous-titrer. ◆ **subtitling** *n* sous-titrage *m*. ◆ **subtotal** *n* total *m* partiel. ◆ **sub-zero** *adj* au-dessous de zéro.

subaltern ['sʌblt(ə)n] *n (Brit Mil) officier d'un rang inférieur à celui de capitaine.*

subconscious ['sʌb'kɒnʃəs] *adj, n* inconscient *(m)*. ◆ **subconsciously** *adv* inconsciemment.

subdue [səb'djuː] *vt people, country* soumettre; *feelings* maîtriser. ◆ **subdued** *adj emotion* contenu; *reaction, response* faible; *voice, tone* bas; *conversation, discussion* à voix basse; *light* voilé; **she was very ~d** elle avait perdu son entrain.

subject ['sʌbdʒɪkt] **1** *n (gen: most senses)* sujet *m* (*of, for* de); *(Scol etc)* matière *f*; *(citizen)* sujet(te) *m(f)*. **he is a French** ~ *(in France)* c'est un sujet français, il est de nationalité française; *(elsewhere)* c'est un ressortissant français; **to get off the** ~ sortir du sujet; **let's get back to the** ~ revenons à nos moutons; **on the** ~ **of** au sujet de; **while we're on the** ~ **of...** à propos de...; *(Scol, Univ)* **his best** ~ sa matière forte.
2 *adj* (**a**) *people, tribes, state* soumis. ~ **to** *(liable to) disease etc* sujet à; *flooding, subsidence etc* exposé à; *the law, taxation* soumis à; *(conditional upon)* sous réserve de; **our prices are** ~ **to alteration** nos prix sont donnés sous réserve de modifications; ~ **to doing that** à condition de faire cela. (**b**) ~ **heading** rubrique *f*; ~ **index** *(in book)* index *m* des matières; *(in library)* fichier *m* par matières; ~ **matter** *(theme)* sujet *m*; *(content)* contenu *m*.
3 [səb'dʒekt] *vt*: **to** ~ **sb to sth** soumettre qn à qch; **to** ~ **sth to heat** exposer qch à la chaleur; **he was ~ed to much criticism** il a été très critiqué. ◆ **subjection** *n* sujétion *f*, soumission *f*. ◆ **subjective** *adj* subjectif. ◆ **subjectively** *adv* subjectivement.

subjugate ['sʌbdʒʊgeɪt] *vt* subjuguer.

subjunctive [səb'dʒʌŋ(k)tɪv] *adj, n* subjonctif *(m)*. **in the** ~ au subjonctif.

sublime [sə'blaɪm] *adj (gen)* sublime; *contempt, indifference* suprême *(before n)*; *(*: excellent) dinner, person* divin, fantastique. ◆ **sublimate** *vt* sublimer. ◆ **sublimation** *n* sublimation *f*. ◆ **sublimely** *adv* (**a**) ~**ly beautiful** d'une beauté sublime; (**b**) *contemptuous etc* suprêmement; ~**ly unaware of** dans une ignorance absolue de. ◆ **subliminal** *adj* subliminal. ◆ **subliminally** *adv* au-dessous du niveau de la conscience.

submarine [ˌsʌbmə'riːn] **1** *n* (**a**) sous-marin *(m)*. (**b**) *(US *: sandwich)* grand sandwich *m* mixte. **2** *adj* sous-marin. ~ **pen** abri *m* pour sous-marins.

submerge [səb'mɜːdʒ] **1** *vt* submerger. **to** ~ **sth in sth** immerger qch dans qch. **2** *vi [submarine]* s'immerger.

submit [səb'mɪt] **1** *vt* soumettre (*to* à). **to** ~ **that** suggérer que. **2** *vi (Mil, also fig)* se soumettre (*to* à). ◆ **submission** *n (all senses)* soumission *f* (*to* à); **starved/beaten into submission** réduit par la faim/les coups. ◆ **submissive** *adj* soumis, docile. ◆ **submissively** *adv* avec soumission, docilement. ◆ **submissiveness** *n* soumission *f*, docilité *f*.

subordinate [sə'bɔːdnɪt] **1** *adj (gen)* subalterne; *(Gram)* subordonné. **2** *n* subordonné(e) *m(f)*. **3** [sə'bɔːdɪneɪt] *vt* subordonner (*to* à). ◆ **subordination** *n* subordination *f*.

subpoena [səb'piːnə] *(Jur)* **1** *n* citation *f*, assignation *f*. **2** *vt* citer *or* assigner (à comparaître).

subscribe [səb'skraɪb] **1** *vt money* donner (*to* à). **2** *vi* verser une somme d'argent. **to** ~ **to** *new publication, fund* souscrire à; *newspaper* être abonné à; *idea, project* être partisan de. ◆ **subscriber** *n* souscripteur *m*, -trice *f* (*to* de); abonné(e) *m(f)* (*to* de) *(also Telec)*; partisan *m* (*to* de); ~**r trunk dialling** automatique *m*. ◆ **subscription** *n* souscription *f*; abonnement *m*; *(to club)* cotisation *f*; **to pay one's subscription** payer sa cotisation *or* son abonnement; *(Press)* **to take out a subscription to** s'abonner à.

subsequent ['sʌbsɪkwənt] *adj* ultérieur, suivant. **a** ~ **visit** une visite ultérieure; **his** ~ **visit** sa visite suivante; ~ **to** à la suite de. ◆ **subsequently** *adv* par la suite.

subservient [səb'sɜːvɪənt] *adj* obséquieux. ◆ **subservience** *n* obséquiosité *f*.

subside [səb'saɪd] *vi [land, building]* s'affaisser; *[flood, river]* baisser; *[wind, emotion]* tomber; *[threat]* s'éloigner; *[person] (fall)* s'affaisser (*into* dans; *on to* sur); *(*: be quiet)* se taire. ◆ **subsidence** *n [land etc]* affaissement *m (de terrain)*.

subsidiary [səb'sɪdɪərɪ] **1** *adj* subsidiaire. **2** *n (~ company)* filiale *f*.

subsidize ['sʌbsɪdaɪz] *vt* subventionner. ◆ **subsidy** *n* subvention *f*; **government** *or* **state subsidy** subvention de l'État.

subsist [səb'sɪst] *vi* subsister. **to** ~ **on sth** vivre de qch. ◆ **subsistence 1** *n* existence *f*, subsistance *f*; *(allowance)* frais *mpl* de subsistance ; **2** *adj wage* tout juste suffisant pour vivre; **to live at ~ence level** avoir tout juste de quoi vivre.

substance ['sʌbst(ə)ns] *n (gen)* substance *f*. **the** ~ **of his speech** la substance *or* l'essentiel de son discours; **a man of** ~ un homme riche; **to lack** ~ *[film, book]* manquer d'étoffe; *[argument]* être plutôt mince; *[accusation, claim]* être sans grand fondement. ◆ **substantial** *adj* (**a**) *(large) (gen)* important, considérable; *meal* substantiel; *firm* solide; *landowner, businessman* riche; *house etc* grand; (**b**) *(real)* substantiel, réel. ◆ **substantially** *adv* (**a**) *(considerably) improve etc* considérablement; **substantially bigger** beaucoup plus grand; **substantially different** très différent; (**b**) *(to a large extent)* en grande partie; (**c**) *built, constructed* solidement. ◆ **substantiate** *vt* justifier.

substantive ['sʌbst(ə)ntɪv] *n, adj (Gram)* substantif *(m)*.

substitute ['sʌbstɪtju:t] **1** *n (person)* remplaçant(e) *m(f)* (*for* de); *(thing)* produit *m* de remplacement, succédané *m (gen pej)* (*for* de). *(Comm)* **'beware of ~ s'** 'se méfier des contrefaçons'; **there is no ~ for wool** rien ne peut remplacer la laine. **2** *adj player etc* remplaçant. **~ coffee** succédané *m* de café; **~ teacher** suppléant(e) *m(f)*. **3** *vt* substituer (*A for B* A à B), remplacer (*A for B* B par A). **4** *vi*: **to ~ for sb** remplacer qn. ◆ **substitution** *n* substitution *f*, remplacement *m*.

subteen [ˌsʌb'ti:n] *n (US)* préadolescent(e) *m(f)*.

subterfuge ['sʌbtəfju:dʒ] *n* subterfuge *m*.

subterranean [ˌsʌbtə'reɪnɪən] *adj* souterrain.

subtle ['sʌtl] *adj (gen)* subtil; *person* subtil, qui a beaucoup de finesse; *mind, intelligence* subtil, pénétrant. ◆ **subtleness** *or* ◆ **subtlety** *n* subtilité *f* ; finesse *f*. ◆ **subtly** *adv* subtilement.

subtract [səb'trækt] *vt* soustraire (*from* de). ◆ **subtraction** *n* soustraction *f*.

suburb ['sʌbɜ:b] *n* faubourg *m*. **the ~s** la banlieue; **in the ~s** en banlieue; **the outer ~s** la grande banlieue. ◆ **suburban** *adj (gen)* de banlieue, suburbain; *(pej) person, accent* banlieusard. ◆ **suburbanite** *n* banlieusard(e) *m(f)*. ◆ **suburbia** *n* la banlieue.

subvention [səb'venʃ(ə)n] *n* subvention *f*.

subvert [səb'vɜ:t] *vt the law, tradition* bouleverser; *(corrupt) person* corrompre. ◆ **subversion** *n* subversion *f*. ◆ **subversive** *adj* subversif.

subway ['sʌbweɪ] *n (underpass)* passage *m* souterrain; *(railway: esp US)* métro *m*.

succeed [sək'si:d] **1** *vi* (**a**) *(be successful: gen)* réussir (*in sth* dans qch; *in doing* à faire). **he ~s in all he does** il réussit tout ce qu'il entreprend; **to ~ in business/as a politician** réussir en affaires/en tant qu'homme politique. (**b**) *(follow)* succéder (*to sth* à qch). **2** *vt* succéder à. **he was ~ed by his son** son fils lui a succédé. ◆ **succeeding** *adj (in past)* suivant; *(in future)* à venir, futur; **each ~ing year brought...** chaque année qui passait apportait...; **each ~ing year will bring...** chacune des années à venir apportera...; **on 3 ~ing Saturdays** 3 samedis consécutifs *or* de suite.

success [sək'ses] **1** *n [plan, venture, attempt, person]* succès *m*, réussite *f* (*in an exam* à un examen; *in maths* en maths; *in one's aim* dans son but; *in business* en affaires; *in one's career* dans sa carrière). **his ~ in doing sth** le fait qu'il ait réussi à faire qch; **his ~ in his attempts** la réussite qui a couronné ses efforts; **without ~** sans succès, en vain; **to make a ~ of** *project, enterprise* mener à bien; *job, meal* réussir; **he was a ~ at last** il avait enfin réussi; **he was a great ~ at the dinner/as Hamlet/as a writer** il a eu beaucoup de succès au dîner/dans le rôle de Hamlet/en tant qu'écrivain; **it was a ~** *(gen)* c'était une réussite; *[play, book, attempt]* ça a été couronné de succès; *[hotel etc]* on en a été très content. **2** *adj*: **~ story** (histoire *f* d'une) réussite *f*. ◆ **successful** *adj plan, venture, application, deal* couronné de succès; *writer, painter, book* à succès; *candidate (in exam)* reçu; *(in election)* élu; *marriage, outcome* heureux; *career, businessman* prospère; *[performer, play etc]* **to be ~ful** avoir un succès fou; **to be ~ful in doing** réussir à faire. ◆ **successfully** *adv* avec succès.

succession [sək'seʃ(ə)n] *n (gen)* succession *f*. **in ~** successivement; **4 times in ~** 4 fois de suite; **in close ~** coup sur coup; **in ~ to his father** à la suite de son père. ◆ **successive** *adj generations, discoveries* successif; *days, months* consécutif; **on 4 successive days** pendant 4 jours consécutifs *or* de suite; **each successive failure** chaque nouvel échec. ◆ **successively** *adv* successivement. ◆ **successor** *n* successeur *m* (*to, of* de); *(to throne)* héritier *m*, -ière *f* (*to* de).

succinct [sək'sɪŋkt] *adj* succinct. ◆ **succinctly** *adv* succinctement.

succulent ['sʌkjʊlənt] **1** *adj* succulent. **2** *n (Bot)* **~s** plantes *fpl* grasses. ◆ **succulence** *n* succulence *f*.

succumb [sə'kʌm] *vi* succomber (*to* à).

such [sʌtʃ] **1** *adj* tel, pareil. **~ a book** un tel livre, un livre pareil; **~ books** de tels livres, des livres pareils; **we had ~ a case last year** nous avons eu un cas semblable l'année dernière; **in ~ cases** en pareil cas; **did you ever hear of ~ a thing?** avez-vous jamais entendu une chose pareille?; **there's no ~ thing!** ça n'existe pas!; **there are no ~ things as unicorns** les licornes n'existent pas; **there is no ~ thing in France** il n'y a rien de tel en France; **I said no ~ thing!** je n'ai jamais dit cela!; **or some ~ thing** ou une chose de ce genre; **no ~ book exists** un tel livre n'existe pas; **~ was my reply** telle a été ma réponse; **~ is life!** c'est la vie!; **it was SUCH weather!** il a fait un de ces temps!; **I had ~ a fright!** j'ai eu une de ces peurs!; **a friend ~ as Paul, ~ a friend as Paul** un ami tel que *or* comme Paul; **~ writers as Molière** des écrivains tels que Molière; **he's not ~ a fool as you think** il n'est pas aussi bête que vous croyez; **I'm not ~ a fool as to believe that!** je ne suis pas assez bête pour croire ça!; **have you ~ a thing as a penknife?** auriez-vous un canif par hasard?; **~ as?** comme quoi, par exemple?; **~ books as I have** les quelques livres que je possède; **you can take my car, ~ as it is** vous pouvez prendre ma voiture pour ce qu'elle vaut; *(so much)* **~ a noise** tellement de bruit.

2 *adv* (**a**) *(so very)* si, tellement. **~ good coffee** un si bon café; **~ big boxes** de si grandes boîtes, des boîtes si grandes; **it was SUCH a long time ago!** il y a si *or* tellement longtemps de ça!; **~ an expensive car that...** une voiture si *or* tellement chère que... (**b**) *(in comparisons)* aussi. **I haven't had ~ good coffee for years** ça fait des années que je n'ai pas bu un aussi bon café; **~ lovely children as his** des enfants aussi gentils que les siens.

3 *pron*: **~ as wish to go** ceux qui veulent partir; **~ as I have** ceux que j'ai; **teachers as ~ are...** les professeurs en tant que tels sont...; **the work as ~ is boring but...** le travail en soi est ennuyeux mais...; **there are no houses as ~** il n'y a pas de maisons à proprement parler; **he was not recognized as ~** il n'était pas considéré comme tel; **teachers and doctors and ~(like)** * les professeurs, les docteurs et autres gens de la sorte.

◆ **such-and-such** **1** *n*: **Mr S~-and-~** * Monsieur Untel ; **2** *adj*: **in ~-and-~ a street** dans telle rue. ◆ **suchlike** * *adj* de la sorte; *V also* **such 3**.

suck [sʌk] **1** *vt (gen)* sucer; *(through straw) drink* aspirer (*through* avec); *[baby]* téter; *[pump, machine]* aspirer (*from* de). **to ~ one's thumb** sucer son pouce; **to ~ dry** *orange etc* sucer tout le jus de; *(fig) person (of money)* sucer jusqu'au dernier sou; *(of energy)* sucer jusqu'à la moelle. **2** *vi [baby]* téter. **to ~ at sth** sucer qch.

◆ **suck down** *vt sep [sea, mud]* engloutir. ◆ **suck in** *vt sep [sea, mud]* engloutir; *[pump, machine]* aspirer. ◆ **suck out** *vt sep [person]* sucer (*of, from* de); *[machine]* refouler à l'extérieur (*of, from* de). ◆ **suck up** **1** *vi* (‡) **to ~ up to sb** lécher les bottes * de qn. **2** *vt sep* aspirer.

◆ **sucker** *n* (**a**) *(on machine, octopus etc)* ventouse *f*; *(plunger)* piston *m*; *(Bot)* surgeon *m*; (**b**) *(‡: person)* poire * *f*, imbécile *mf*; **to be a ~er for sth *** ne pas pouvoir résister à qch. ◆ **suckle** **1** *vt* allaiter ; **2** *vi* téter. ◆ **suction** **1** *n* succion *f* ; **2** *adj device* de succion; *pump* aspirant.

Sudan [suːˈdæn] *n* Soudan. ◆ **Sudanese** **1** *adj* soudanais ; **2** *n* Soudanais(e) *m(f)*.

sudden [ˈsʌdn] *adj (gen)* soudain, brusque; *death, inspiration* subit; *bend in road, marriage, appointment* imprévu. **all of a ~** soudain, tout à coup; **it's all so ~!** c'est arrivé tellement vite! ◆ **suddenly** *adv (gen)* brusquement, tout à coup, soudain; *die* subitement. ◆ **suddenness** *n* soudaineté *f*; caractère *m* imprévu.

suds [sʌdz] *npl* **(soap~)** *(lather)* mousse *f* de savon; *(soapy water)* eau *f* savonneuse.

sue [suː] **1** *vt (gen)* poursuivre en justice (*for sth* pour obtenir qch; *over, about* au sujet de). **to ~ sb for damages** poursuivre qn en dommages-intérêts; **to ~ sb for libel** intenter un procès en diffamation à qn; **to ~ sb for divorce** entamer une procédure de divorce contre qn. **2** *vi* intenter un procès. **to ~ for divorce** entamer une procédure de divorce.

suede [sweɪd] **1** *n* daim *m (cuir)*. **2** *adj (gen)* de daim; *gloves* de suède.

suet [ˈsʊɪt] *n* graisse *f* de rognon.

Suez [ˈsuːɪz] *n*: **the ~ Canal** le canal de Suez.

suffer [ˈsʌfəʳ] **1** *vt* (**a**) *(undergo) (gen)* subir; *martyrdom, hardship* souffrir; *punishment, change, pain* éprouver; *hunger, headaches* souffrir de. **he ~ed a lot of pain** il a beaucoup souffert. (**b**) *(bear) pain* endurer, tolérer; *(allow) opposition, sb's rudeness, refusal etc* tolérer. **he doesn't ~ fools gladly** il n'a aucune patience pour les imbéciles.
2 *vi (gen)* souffrir. **he ~ed for it** il en a souffert les conséquences; **you'll ~ for this** vous le paierez *(fig)*; **to ~ from** *rheumatism, heart trouble, the cold, hunger* souffrir de; *deafness* être atteint de; *a cold, influenza, frostbite, pimples, bad memory* avoir; **he ~s from a limp/stammer** il boite/bégaie; **he was ~ing from shock** il était commotionné; **to ~ from the effects of** *fall, illness* se ressentir de; *alcohol, drug* subir le contrecoup de; **she ~s from lack of friends** son problème, c'est qu'elle n'a pas d'amis; **the house is ~ing from neglect** la maison se ressent du manque d'entretien; **your health will ~** votre santé en souffrira; **the regiment ~ed badly** le régiment a essuyé de grosses pertes.
◆ **sufferance** *n*: **on ~ance** par tolérance. ◆ **sufferer** *n (from illness)* malade *mf*; **diabetes ~ers** diabétiques *mfpl*. ◆ **suffering** **1** *n* souffrances *fpl* ; **2** *adj* qui souffre.

suffice [səˈfaɪs] **1** *vi* suffire. **~ it to say** qu'il suffise de dire. **2** *vt* suffire à.

sufficient [səˈfɪʃ(ə)nt] *adj (enough) money, food, people* assez de, suffisamment de; *(big enough) number, quantity* suffisant. **to be ~** être suffisant *or* assez (*for* pour), suffire (*for* à); **I've got ~** j'en ai assez *or* suffisamment; **~ to eat** assez à manger; **he earns ~ to live on** il gagne de quoi vivre; **that's quite ~** cela suffit. ◆ **sufficiency** *n* quantité *f* suffisante. ◆ **sufficiently** *adv* suffisamment, assez ; **~ly clever to do** suffisamment *or* assez intelligent pour faire; **~ly large** *amount, number* suffisant.

suffix [ˈsʌfɪks] *n* suffixe *m*.

suffocate [ˈsʌfəkeɪt] *vti* suffoquer (*with* de). ◆ **suffocating** *adj* suffocant; *(fig)* étouffant; **it's suffocating in here** on étouffe ici. ◆ **suffocation** *n* suffocation *f*; *(Med)* asphyxie *f*; **to die from suffocation** mourir asphyxié.

suffrage [ˈsʌfrɪdʒ] *n* suffrage *m*. **universal ~** suffrage universel. ◆ **suffragette** *n* suffragette *f*.

sugar [ˈʃʊgəʳ] **1** *n* sucre *m*. **2** *vt* sucrer. *(fig)* **to ~ the pill** dorer la pilule. **3** *adj*: **~(ed) almond** dragée *f*; **~ basin** *or* **bowl** sucrier *m*; **~ beet** betterave *f* à sucre; **~ cane** canne *f* à sucre; *(fig)* **~ daddy *** vieux protecteur *m*; **~ lump** morceau *m* de sucre; **~ maple** érable *m* à sucre; **~ plantation** plantation *f* de canne à sucre; **~ refinery** raffinerie *f* de sucre; **~ tongs** pince *f* à sucre. ◆ **sugar-free** *or* ◆ **sugarless** *adj* sans sucre. ◆ **sugary** *adj food, drink, taste* sucré; *(fig pej) person, voice* mielleux.

suggest [səˈdʒest] *vt* suggérer (*sth to sb* qch à qn; *that* que). **I ~ that we go there** je suggère qu'on y aille; **he ~ed that they should go there** il leur a suggéré d'y aller; **what are you trying to ~?** que voulez-vous dire par là?; **the facts ~ that he did it** les faits semblent indiquer qu'il l'a fait. ◆ **suggestible** *adj* influençable. ◆ **suggestion** *n (gen)* suggestion *f*; *(insinuation)* allusion *f*; **have you any ~ions?** avez-vous qch à suggérer?; **there is no ~ion of** il ne saurait être question de; *(trace)* **a ~ion of** un soupçon de. ◆ **suggestive** *adj* suggestif *(also pej)*.

suicide [ˈsʊɪsaɪd] **1** *n* suicide *m*. **it was political ~** cela représentait un véritable suicide politique. **2** *adj attack* suicide. **~ attempt, ~ bid** tentative *f* de suicide. ◆ **suicidal** *adj* suicidaire; *(fig)* **that would be suicidal!** ce serait un véritable suicide!

suit [suːt] **1** *n* (**a**) *(man's)* costume *m*, complet *m*; *(woman's)* tailleur *m*; *(non-tailored, also for children)* ensemble *m*; *(diver's, astronaut's etc)* combinaison *f*. **~ of clothes** tenue *f*; **~ of armour** armure *f* complète. (**b**) *(Jur)* procès *m*. **to bring a ~** intenter un procès (*against sb* à qn). (**c**) *(Cards)* couleur *f*. **long** *or* **strong ~** couleur longue; *(fig)* fort *m*. **2** *vt (gen)* convenir à; *[garment, colour, hairstyle]* aller à. **it doesn't ~ me to leave now** cela ne me convient pas *or* ne m'arrange pas de partir maintenant; **it ~ed him perfectly, it just ~ed his book *** cela lui convenait *or* l'arrangeait parfaitement; **~ yourself! *** c'est comme vous voudrez!; **~s me! *** ça me va!; **the part ~ed him perfectly** le rôle lui allait comme un gant *or* était fait pour lui; **to be ~ed to sth** être fait pour qch; **they are well ~ed** ils sont faits l'un pour l'autre; **to ~ the action to the word** joindre le geste à la parole.
◆ **suitability** *n* fait *m* de convenir *etc (V* **2** *above)*; *[action, reply, example, choice]* à-propos *m*; **his ~ability for the post** son aptitude *f* au poste. ◆ **suitable** *adj (gen)* approprié (*to, for* à); *climate, food* qui convient (*for* à); *colour, size* qui va (*for* à); *place, time* propice (*for* à); *clothes* approprié (*for* à); *(socially)* convenable; **the most ~able man for the job** l'homme le plus apte à ce poste; **I can't find anything ~able** je ne trouve rien qui me convienne; *(clothes)* je ne trouve rien qui m'aille; **the 25th is the most ~able for me** c'est le 25 qui m'arrange le mieux; **he is not at all a ~able person** ce n'est pas du tout l'homme qu'il faut; **the film isn't ~able for children** ce n'est pas un film pour les enfants. ◆ **suitably** *adv reply* à propos; *explain* de manière adéquate; *thank, apologize* comme il convient (*or* convenait *etc*); *behave* convenablement; **~ably impressed** favorablement impressionné. ◆ **suitcase** *n* valise *f*. ◆ **suiting** *n (Tex)* tissu *m* pour complet. ◆ **suitor** *n* soupirant *m*.

suite [swiːt] *n (gen)* suite *f*; *(furniture)* mobilier *m*. **a dining-room ~** une salle à manger.

sulk [sʌlk] **1** *npl*: **to be in the ~s, to have the ~s** bouder, faire la tête. **2** *vi* bouder. ◆ **sulkily** *adv* en boudant. ◆ **sulkiness** *n (state)* bouderie *f*; *(temperament)* caractère *m* boudeur. ◆ **sulky** *adj* boudeur; **to be** *or* **look ~y** faire la tête.

sullen [ˈsʌlən] *adj (gen)* maussade; *comment, silence* renfrogné. ◆ **sullenly** *adv say etc* d'un ton maussade; *promise, agree* de mauvaise grâce. ◆ **sullenness** *n* humeur *f or* aspect *m* maussade.

sulphur, *(US)* **sulfur** ['sʌlfəʳ] *n* soufre *m.* ◆ **sulphate** *n* sulfate *m.* ◆ **sulphide** *n* sulfure *m.* ◆ **sulphonamide** *n* sulfamide *m.* ◆ **sulphuric** *adj* sulfurique. ◆ **sulphurous** *adj* sulfureux.

sultan ['sʌlt(ə)n] *n* sultan *m.*

sultana [sʌl'tɑ:nə] *n* raisin *m* sec (de Smyrne).

sultry ['sʌltrɪ] *adj heat, atmosphere* étouffant ; *weather, air* lourd; *(fig) voice, look, smile* sensuel ; *person* passionné.

sum [sʌm] **1** *n (amount, total)* somme *f (of* de). *(Scol: arithmetic)* **~s** le calcul; **~ of money** somme d'argent. **2** *adj*: **~ total** *(amount)* somme *f* totale; *(money)* montant *m* global; *(fig: result)* résultat *m.* ◆ **sum up 1** *vi (gen)* résumer *(also Jur).* **to ~ up, let me say that...** en résumé, je voudrais dire que... **2** *vt sep* (**a**) *(summarize)* résumer; *facts, arguments* récapituler. (**b**) *(assess) person* jauger; *situation* apprécier d'un coup d'œil.
◆ **summarily** *adv* sommairement. ◆ **summarize** *vt (gen)* résumer; *facts, arguments* récapituler. ◆ **summary 1** *n* résumé *m*; **a ~mary of the news** les nouvelles *fpl* en bref ; **2** *adj (all senses)* sommaire. ◆ **summing-up** *n* résumé *m (also Jur).*

Sumatra [su:'mɑ:trə] *n* Sumatra.

summer ['sʌməʳ] **1** *n* été *m.* **in ~** en été; **in the ~ of 1987** au cours de l'été 1987. **2** *adj weather, day, activities* d'été, estival. **~ camp** colonie *f* de vacances; **~ holidays** grandes vacances *fpl*; **~ lightning** éclair *m* de chaleur; **~ school** université *f* d'été; *(by clock)* **~ time** heure *f* d'été; **~ visitor** estivant(e) *m(f).* ◆ **summerhouse** *n* pavillon *m* (dans un jardin). ◆ **summertime** *n (season)* été *m.* ◆ **summery** *adj* d'été.

summit ['sʌmɪt] **1** *n (gen, also Pol)* sommet *m*; *(fig) [power, honours, glory]* apogée *m*; *[ambition]* summum *m.* **2** *adj (Pol) meeting* au sommet.

summon ['sʌmən] *vt (gen)* appeler, faire venir; *(to meeting)* convoquer *(to* à); *(Jur)* citer, assigner (*as* comme); *help, reinforcements* requérir. **to ~ sb to do** sommer qn de faire; *(Jur)* **to ~ sb to appear** citer *or* assigner qn; **to ~ sb in** *(gen)* appeler qn. ◆ **summon up** *vt sep one's energy, strength, courage* rassembler (*to do* pour faire); *interest, enthusiasm* faire appel à.
◆ **summons 1** *n* sommation *f (also Mil)*; *(Jur)* assignation *f*; *(Jur)* **to take out a ~s against sb** faire assigner qn ; **2** *vt (Jur)* citer, assigner *(à comparaître).*

sump [sʌmp] *n (Tech)* puisard *m*; *(Aut)* carter *m.* **~ oil** huile *f* de carter.

sumptuous ['sʌm(p)tjʊəs] *adj* somptueux. ◆ **sumptuously** *adv* somptueusement. ◆ **sumptuousness** *n* somptuosité *f.*

sun [sʌn] **1** *n* soleil *m.* **the ~ is shining** il fait du soleil, le soleil brille; **in the ~** au soleil; **right in the ~** en plein soleil; **a place in the ~** *(lit)* un endroit ensoleillé; *(fig)* une place au soleil; **the ~ is in my eyes** j'ai le soleil dans les yeux; **everything under the ~** tout ce qu'il est possible d'imaginer; **nothing under the ~** rien au monde; **there's no prettier place under the ~** il n'est pas de plus joli coin au monde; **no reason under the ~** pas la moindre raison; **there is nothing new under the ~** il n'y a rien de nouveau sous le soleil. **2** *vt*: **to ~ o.s.** *[lizard, cat]* se chauffer au soleil; *[person]* prendre un bain de soleil.
3 *adj oil, lotion* solaire. **~ dress** robe *f* bain de soleil; **~ umbrella** parasol *m.*
◆ **sunbathe** *vi* prendre un bain *or* des bains de soleil. ◆ **sunbather** *n* personne *f* qui prend un bain de soleil. ◆ **sunbathing** *n* bains *mpl* de soleil. ◆ **sunbeam** *n* rayon *m* de soleil. ◆ **sunbed** *n (in garden etc)* lit *m* pliant; *(for tanning)* lit à ultra-violets. ◆ **sunblind** *n* store *m.* ◆ **sunburn** *n* coup *m* de soleil. ◆ **sunburned** *or* ◆ **sunburnt** *adj (tanned)* bronzé; *(painfully)* brûlé par le soleil; **to get ~burnt** bronzer; prendre un coup de soleil. ◆ **sundial** *n* cadran *m* solaire. ◆ **sundown** *n* coucher *m* du soleil. ◆ **sun-drenched** *adj* inondé de soleil. ◆ **sun-dried** *adj* séché au soleil. ◆ **sunflower 1** *n* tournesol *m* ; **2** *adj oil, seeds* de tournesol. ◆ **sunglasses** *npl* lunettes *fpl* de soleil. ◆ **sun-lamp** *n* lampe *f* à rayons ultraviolets. ◆ **sunlight** *n* (lumière *f* du) soleil *m*; **in the ~light** au soleil, à la lumière du soleil. ◆ **sunlit** *adj* ensoleillé. ◆ **sunlounger** *n* fauteuil *m* bain de soleil. ◆ **sunny** *adj* ensoleillé; *(fig) smile, person* épanoui; **it is ~ny** il fait du soleil; *(Met)* **~ny intervals** éclaircies *fpl*; *(Met)* **the outlook is ~ny** on prévoit du soleil; *(fig)* **he always sees the ~ny side of things** il voit tout du bon côté; *(US Culin)* **eggs ~ny side up** œufs sur le plat. ◆ **sunrise** *n* lever *m* du soleil; **~rise industry** industrie *f* en expansion. ◆ **sunroof** *n* toit *m* ouvrant. ◆ **sunset** *n* coucher *m* du soleil. ◆ **sunshade** *n (lady's parasol)* ombrelle *f*; *(for eyes)* visière *f*; *(for table, on pram)* parasol *m*; *(in car)* pare-soleil *m inv.* ◆ **sunshine 1** *n* (lumière *f* du) soleil *m*; **in the ~shine** au soleil; *(Met)* **5 hours of ~shine** 5 heures *fpl* d'ensoleillement; *(iro)* **he's a real ray of ~shine** il est gracieux comme une porte de prison ; **2** *adj (Aut)* **~shine roof** toit *m* ouvrant. ◆ **sunspecs** * *npl* lunettes *fpl* de soleil. ◆ **sunspot** *n* tache *f* solaire. ◆ **sunstroke** *n* insolation *f.* ◆ **sunsuit** *n* costume *m* bain de soleil. ◆ **suntan 1** *n* bronzage *m*; **to get a ~tan** bronzer ; **2** *adj*: **~tan lotion/oil** lotion *f*/huile *f* solaire. ◆ **suntanned** *adj* bronzé. ◆ **suntrap** *n* coin *m* très ensoleillé. ◆ **sunup** * *n* lever *m* du soleil.

sundae ['sʌndeɪ] *n* sundae *m*, coupe *f* glacée Chantilly.

Sunday ['sʌndɪ] **1** *n* dimanche *m*; *for phrases V* **Saturday. 2** *adj clothes, paper* du dimanche; *walk, rest, peace* dominical. **in one's ~ best** en habits du dimanche; **~ school** ≃ catéchisme *m.*

sundry ['sʌndrɪ] **1** *adj* divers, différent. **all and ~** tout le monde. **2** *npl*: **sundries** articles *mpl* divers.

sung [sʌŋ] *ptp of* **sing.**

sunk [sʌŋk] *ptp of* **sink¹.** ◆ **sunken** *adj ship, rock* submergé; *eyes, cheeks* creux; *garden* en contrebas; *bath* encastré *(au ras du sol).*

super ['su:pəʳ] **1** *adj (*)* formidable *, sensationnel *. **2** *n (US)* super(carburant) *m.*

super... ['su:pəʳ] *pref* super..., sur..., hyper... **~salesman** super-vendeur *m*; *(Pol)* **~power** superpuissance *f*; **~fine** surfin; **~sensitive** hypersensible. ◆ **superabundant** *adj* surabondant. ◆ **supercharged** *adj* surcomprimé. ◆ **supercharger** *n* compresseur *m.* ◆ **superego** *n* surmoi *m.* ◆ **superette** *n (US)* supérette *f.* ◆ **supergrass** *n* super-indicateur *m* de police. ◆ **superhighway** *n (US)* voie f express *(à plusieurs files).* ◆ **superhuman** *adj* surhumain. ◆ **superman**, *pl* **~men** *n* surhomme *m.* ◆ **supermarket** *n* supermarché *m.* ◆ **supernatural** *adj, n* surnaturel *(m).* ◆ **superpower** *n* superpuissance *f.* ◆ **supersonic** *adj* supersonique. ◆ **supersonically** *adv* en supersonique. ◆ **superstar** *n (Cine, Theat)* superstar *f*; *(Sport)* superchampion(ne) *m(f).* ◆ **superstore** *n* hypermarché *m.* ◆ **superstructure** *n* superstructure *f.* ◆ **super-tanker** *n* pétrolier *m* géant.

superannuate [ˌsu:pə'rænjʊeɪt] *vt* mettre à la retraite. *(fig)* **~d** suranné. ◆ **superannuation** *n (pension)* pension *f* de retraite; *(contribution)* cotisations *fpl* pour la pension.

superb [su:'pɜ:b] *adj* superbe. ◆ **superbly** *adv* superbement; **he is ~ly fit** il est dans une forme éblouissante.

supercilious [ˌsu:pə'sɪlɪəs] *adj* hautain. ◆ **superciliously** *adv* d'un air *or* d'un ton hautain. ◆ **superciliousness** *n* hauteur *f.*

superficial [ˌsuːpəˈfɪʃ(ə)l] *adj* superficiel. ◆ **superficiality** *n* caractère superficiel, manque *m* de profondeur. ◆ **superficially** *adv* superficiellement.

superfluous [sʊˈpɜːflʊəs] *adj (gen)* superflu. **it is ~ to say that...** inutile de dire que...; **he felt rather ~*** il se sentait de trop. ◆ **superfluity** *n* surabondance *f* (*of* de). ◆ **superfluously** *adv* d'une manière superflue.

superimpose [ˌsuːp(ə)rɪmˈpəʊz] *vt* superposer (*on* à). *(Cine, Phot)* **~d** en surimpression.

superintend [ˌsuːp(ə)rɪnˈtend] *vt work, shop, department* diriger; *exam* surveiller; *production* contrôler; *vote-counting* présider à. ◆ **superintendence** *n* direction *f*; surveillance *f*; contrôle *m*. ◆ **superintendent** *n [institution, orphanage]* directeur *m*, -trice *f*; *[department]* chef *m*; *(Police)* ≃ commissaire *m* (de police).

superior [sʊˈpɪərɪəʳ] **1** *adj* supérieur (*to* à); *product, goods* de qualité supérieure; *(pej: smug) person* suffisant; *air, smile* de supériorité, suffisant. **he felt rather ~** il a éprouvé un certain sentiment de supériorité. **2** *n* supérieur(e) *m(f)*. ◆ **superiority** **1** *n* supériorité *f* (*to, over* par rapport à) ; **2** *adj*: **~ity complex** complexe *m* de supériorité.

superlative [sʊˈpɜːlətɪv] **1** *adj quality, achievement* sans pareil; *happiness, indifference* suprême; *(Gram)* superlatif. **2** *n (Gram)* superlatif *m*. **in the ~** au superlatif. ◆ **superlatively** *adv* extrêmement.

supernumerary [ˌsuːpəˈnjuːm(ə)rərɪ] *adj, n* surnuméraire *(mf)*.

supersede [ˌsuːpəˈsiːd] *vt belief, object, order* remplacer; *person* supplanter. **~d method** méthode périmée.

superstition [ˌsuːpəˈstɪʃ(ə)n] *n* superstition *f*. ◆ **superstitious** *adj* superstitieux. ◆ **superstitiously** *adv* superstitieusement.

supervise [ˈsuːpəvaɪz] *vt (gen)* surveiller; *(Univ) research* diriger. ◆ **supervision** *n* surveillance *f*. ◆ **supervisor** *n (gen)* surveillant(e) *m(f)*; *(Comm)* chef *m* de rayon; *(Univ: for studies)* directeur *m*, -trice *f* de thèse. ◆ **supervisory** *adj duty* de surveillance.

supine [ˈsuːpaɪn] *adj* étendu sur le dos.

supper [ˈsʌpəʳ] *n (main meal)* dîner *m*; *(after theatre etc)* souper *m*; *(snack)* collation *f*. **to have ~** dîner (*or* souper); *(Rel)* **the Last S~** la Cène. ◆ **suppertime** *n* l'heure *f* du dîner; **at ~time** au dîner.

supplant [səˈplɑːnt] *vt* supplanter.

supple [ˈsʌpl] *adj* souple. **to become ~(r)** s'assouplir. ◆ **suppleness** *n* souplesse *f*. ◆ **supply¹** [ˈsʌplɪ] *adv* avec souplesse.

supplement [ˈsʌplɪmənt] **1** *n* supplément *m* (*to* à). **2** [ˌsʌplɪˈment] *vt income* augmenter (*by doing* en faisant); *book, information* ajouter à, compléter. ◆ **supplementary** *adj* supplémentaire; *(Admin)* **~ary benefit** allocation *f* supplémentaire.

supplication [ˌsʌplɪˈkeɪʃ(ə)n] *n* supplication *f*.

supply² [səˈplaɪ] **1** *n* (**a**) *(amount, stock)* provision *f*, réserve *f*, stock *m (also Comm)*. **to get** *or* **lay in a ~ of** faire des provisions de; **to get in a fresh ~ of sth** se réapprovisionner en qch; **supplies** *(gen)* provisions, réserves; *(food)* vivres *mpl*; *(Mil)* approvisionnements *mpl*; **electrical supplies** matériel *m* électrique; **office supplies** fournitures *fpl* de bureau. (**b**) alimentation *f*. **the ~ of fuel to the engine** l'alimentation du moteur en combustible; **the electricity/gas ~** l'alimentation en électricité/gaz; *(Econ)* **~ and demand** l'offre et la demande.
2 *adj train, truck, ship* ravitailleur; *pharmacist etc* intérimaire. **~ teacher** remplaçant(e) *m(f)*.
3 *vt* (**a**) *(gen)* fournir (*sth to sb* qch à qn; *sb with goods* qn en marchandises; *sb with help/information* de l'aide/des renseignements à qn); *(Comm)* fournir, approvisionner (*with* en, de). **to ~ electricity/gas/water to the town** alimenter la ville en électricité/gaz/eau; **they kept us supplied with milk** grâce à eux nous n'avons jamais manqué de lait; **to ~ from stock** livrer sur stock; **a battery is not supplied with the torch** une pile n'est pas livrée avec la torche. (**b**) *(make good) need, deficiency* suppléer à; *sb's needs* subvenir à; *loss* compenser. ◆ **supplier** *n* fournisseur *m*.

support [səˈpɔːt] **1** *n* (**a**) appui *m*, soutien *m*. **he leaned on me for ~** il s'est appuyé sur moi; *(fig)* il a cherché mon appui; **to give ~ to sb/sth** soutenir qn/qch; *(fig)* **the proposal got no ~** personne n'a parlé en faveur de la proposition; **in ~ of the motion** en faveur de la motion; **in ~ of his theory/claim** à l'appui de sa théorie/ revendication; **to give** *or* **lend one's ~ to** prêter son appui à; **that lends ~ to it** ceci le corrobore; **a collection in ~ of** une collecte au profit de; **they stopped work in ~** ils ont cessé le travail par solidarité; **he has no visible means of ~** il n'a pas de moyens d'existence connus. (**b**) *(object) (gen)* appui *m*; *(Constr, Tech)* support *m*, soutien *m*; *(fig: moral, financial etc)* soutien; *(US Econ: subsidy)* subvention *f*. **the sole ~ of his family** le seul soutien de sa famille; **he has been a great ~ to me** il a été pour moi un soutien précieux.
2 *adj (Mil etc) troops, vessel* de soutien. *(Econ)* **~ price** prix *m* de soutien; **~ hose** bas *mpl* anti-fatigue.
3 *vt* (**a**) *(hold up) [pillar, beam]* soutenir, supporter; *[bridge]* porter; *[person]* soutenir. **the elements necessary to ~ life** les éléments nécessaires à l'entretien de la vie. (**b**) *(uphold) (gen)* être en faveur de, être partisan de; *candidate, action, protest* soutenir; *team* être supporter de. **the socialists will ~ it** les socialistes seront *or* voteront pour; **I cannot ~ what you are doing** je ne peux pas approuver ce que vous faites; **a subsidy to ~ the price of beef** une subvention pour maintenir le prix du bœuf; *(Ftbl)* **he ~s Celtic** c'est un supporter du Celtic. (**c**) *(financially)* subvenir aux besoins de. **he has a wife and 3 children to ~** il doit subvenir aux besoins de sa femme et de ses 3 enfants; **to ~ o.s.** subvenir à ses propres besoins; **the school is ~ed by money from...** l'école reçoit une aide financière de... (**d**) *(endure)* supporter, tolérer.
◆ **supportable** *adj* supportable, tolérable. ◆ **supporter** *n [party]* partisan *m*; *[cause, opinion]* adepte *mf*, partisan; *(Sport)* supporter *m*. ◆ **supporting** *adj wall* de soutènement; *film* qui passe en premier; *(Theat) role* secondaire; *actor* qui a un rôle secondaire; **~ing cast** partenaires *mpl*. ◆ **supportive** *adj* qui est d'un grand soutien. ◆ **supportively** *adv* de façon très positive.

suppose [səˈpəʊz] *vt* (**a**) *(imagine)* supposer (*that* que + *subj*); *(assume)* supposer (*that* que + *indic*). **~ he doesn't come?** et s'il ne vient pas?; **you'll come, I ~?** vous viendrez, je suppose?; *(as suggestion)* **~** *or* **supposing we go for a walk?** et si nous allions nous promener?; **even supposing that** à supposer même que + *subj*; **always supposing that** en supposant que + *subj*. (**b**) *(believe)* supposer, penser, imaginer (*that* que). **what do you ~ he wants?** à votre avis, que peut-il bien vouloir?; **he is generally ~d to be rich** on dit qu'il est riche; **I don't ~ he'll agree** je suppose qu'il ne sera pas d'accord, je ne pense pas qu'il soit d'accord ; **I ~ so** probablement; **I ~ not** je ne (le) pense pas, probablement pas. (**c**) *(ought)* **to be ~d to do sth** être censé faire qch, devoir faire qch; **he isn't ~d to know** il n'est pas censé le savoir; **you're not ~d to do that** il ne vous est pas permis de faire cela. ◆ **supposed** *adj (presumed)* présumé, supposé; *(so-called)* prétendu. ◆ **supposedly** *adv* soi-disant, à ce que l'on suppose (*or* supposait *etc*). ◆ **supposition** *n* supposition *f*; **on the supposition that...** à supposer que... + *subj.*

suppository [sə'pɒzɪt(ə)rɪ] *n* suppositoire *m*.

suppress [sə'pres] *vt (gen)* supprimer; *revolt, one's feelings* réprimer; *yawn, scandal* étouffer; *facts, truth* dissimuler; *publication* interdire; *(Psych)* refouler; *(Elec, Rad etc)* anti-parasiter; *(*: silence) heckler etc* faire taire. **to ~ a cough/sneeze** *etc* se retenir de tousser/d'éternuer *etc.* ◆ **suppression** *n* suppression *f*; répression *f*; étouffement *m*; dissimulation *f*; interdiction *f*; refoulement *m*; antiparasitage *m.* ◆ **suppressor** *n* dispositif *m* antiparasite.

suppurate ['sʌpjʊ(ə)reɪt] *vi* suppurer. ◆ **suppuration** *n* suppuration *f.*

supra... ['suːprə] *pref* supra... **~national** supranational.

supreme [sʊ'priːm] *adj (all senses)* suprême. **to make the ~ sacrifice** faire le sacrifice de sa vie. ◆ **supremacy** *n* suprématie *f* (*over* sur). ◆ **supremo** * *n* grand patron * *m.*

surcharge ['sɜːtʃɑːdʒ] **1** *n (gen)* surcharge *f*; *(tax)* surtaxe *f.* **2** [sɜː'tʃɑːdʒ] *vt* surcharger; surtaxer.

sure [ʃʊəʳ] **1** *adj (gen)* sûr (*of* de). **it is ~ that she will come, she is ~ to come** il est sûr *or* certain qu'elle viendra; **it is not ~ that she will come, she is not ~ to come** il n'est pas sûr *or* certain qu'elle vienne; **it's ~ to rain** il va pleuvoir à coup sûr; **be ~ to tell me** ne manquez pas de me le dire; **you're ~ of a good meal** un bon repas vous est assuré; **he's ~ of success** *or* **of succeeding** *or* **to succeed** il est sûr *or* certain de réussir; **to be ~ of sb** être sûr de qn; **to make ~ of sth** s'assurer de qch; **get a ticket and make ~** prenez un billet pour plus de sûreté; **I've made ~ of having enough coffee** j'ai veillé à ce qu'il y ait assez de café; **~ thing!** * oui, bien sûr!; *(excl)* **well, to be ~!** * bien ça alors!; **he'll leave for ~** il partira sans aucun doute; **I'll find out for ~** je me renseignerai pour savoir exactement ce qu'il en est; **do you know for ~?** êtes-vous absolument certain?; **I'll do it for ~** je le ferai sans faute; **I'm ~ I've seen him** je suis sûr de l'avoir vu; **I'm ~ he'll help us** je suis sûr qu'il nous aidera; **I'm not ~** je ne suis pas sûr (*that* que + *subj*); **I'm not ~ how/why** *etc* je ne sais pas très bien comment/pourquoi *etc*; **I'm not ~ (if) he can** je ne suis pas sûr qu'il puisse; **I'm ~ I didn't mean to** je ne l'ai vraiment pas fait exprès; **~ of o.s.** sûr de soi.
2 *adv*: **and ~ enough he did arrive** et effectivement *or* en effet il est arrivé; **~ enough!** assurément!; **as ~ as my name's Smith** aussi sûr que je m'appelle Smith; **as ~ as fate, as ~ as anything, as ~ as eggs is eggs** * aussi sûr que deux et deux font quatre; *(*: esp US)* **he can ~ play the piano** il sait drôlement * bien jouer du piano.
◆ **sure-fire** * *adj* certain, infaillible. ◆ **surefooted** *adj* au pied sûr. ◆ **surely** *adv* (**a**) *(expressing confidence: assuredly)* sûrement, certainement; *(expressing incredulity)* tout de même; **~ly he didn't say that!** il n'a pas pu dire ça, tout de même!; **there is ~ly some mistake** il doit sûrement *or* certainement y avoir quelque erreur; **that's ~ly not true** ça ne peut pas être vrai; **~ly not!** pas possible!; *(US: with pleasure)* **~ly!** bien volontiers!; (**b**) **slowly but ~ly** lentement mais sûrement. ◆ **sureness** *n (certainty)* certitude *f*; *[judgment, method, footing]* sûreté *f*; *[aim, shot]* justesse *f.* ◆ **surety** *n (Jur)* caution *f*; **to stand ~ty for sb** se porter caution pour qn.

surf [sɜːf] **1** *n (waves)* vague *f* déferlante; *(foam)* écume *f.* **2** *vi*: **to go ~ing** surfer. ◆ **surfboard 1** *n* planche *f* de surf ; **2** *vi* surfer. ◆ **surfboarder** *or* ◆ **surfrider** *n* surfeur *m*, -euse *f.* ◆ **surfboarding** *or* ◆ **surfriding** *n* surf *m.* ◆ **surf-boat** *n* surf-boat *m.* ◆ **surfing** *n* surf *m.*

surface ['sɜːfɪs] **1** *n (gen)* surface *f*; *(side: of solid)* côté *m*, face *f. [sea, lake etc]* **under the ~** sous l'eau; **he rose to the ~** il est remonté à la surface; **on the ~** *(Naut)* en surface; *(Min: also* **at the ~***)* à la surface; *(fig)* à première vue; **on the ~ of the table** sur la surface de la table; **his faults are all on the ~** il a des défauts, mais il a bon fond; **the road ~** la chaussée. **2** *adj tension* superficiel *(also fig)*; *(Naut) vessel etc* de surface; *(Min) work* à la surface. **by ~ mail** par voie de terre; *(by sea)* par voie maritime; **~ reaction** réaction superficielle. **3** *vt road* revêtir (*with* de). **4** *vi [diver, whale]* remonter à la surface; *[submarine]* faire surface; *(* fig) (after absence)* réapparaître; *(after hard work)* faire surface. ◆ **surface-to-air** *adj (Mil)* sol-air *inv.*

surfeit ['sɜːfɪt] *n* excès *m* (*of* de). **to have a ~ of** avoir une indigestion de *(fig).*

surge [sɜːdʒ] **1** *n [rage, enthusiasm]* vague *f*; *(fig: in sales etc)* afflux *m.* **the ~ of the sea** la houle; **he felt a ~ of anger** il a senti la colère monter en lui. **2** *vi* (**a**) *[waves]* s'enfler; *[anger]* monter (*within sb* en qn). **the sea ~d against the rocks** la houle battait les rochers; *(Elec)* **the power ~d suddenly** il y a eu une brusque surtension de courant; **the blood ~d to his cheeks** le sang lui est monté au visage. (**b**) *[crowd, vehicles etc]* déferler. **to ~ in/out** *etc* entrer/sortir *etc* à flots; **they ~d round the car** ils se pressaient autour de la voiture; **they ~d forward** ils se sont lancés en avant. ◆ **surging** *adj sea* houleux; *crowd* déferlant.

surgeon ['sɜːdʒ(ə)n] *n* chirurgien *m. (US Admin)* **S~ General** ministre *m* de la Santé. ◆ **surgery 1** *n (gen)* chirurgie *f*; *(consulting room)* cabinet *m* (de consultation); *(interview)* consultation *f*; **come to the surgery** venez à la consultation; **when is his surgery?** à quelle heure sont ses consultations?; **during his surgery** pendant ses heures de consultation; **to have surgery** se faire opérer ; **2** *adj*: **surgery hours** heures *fpl* de consultation. ◆ **surgical** *adj* chirurgical; **surgical appliance** appareil *m* orthopédique; **surgical cotton** coton *m* hydrophile; **surgical dressing** pansement *m*; **surgical spirit** alcool *m* à 90 (degrés).

surly ['sɜːlɪ] *adj* revêche, maussade. ◆ **surliness** *n* caractère *m or* air *m* revêche.

surmise ['sɜːmaɪz] **1** *n* conjecture *f.* **2** [sɜː'maɪz] *vt* conjecturer (*from sth*, d'après qch; *that* que).

surmount [sɜː'maʊnt] *vt* surmonter.

surname ['sɜːneɪm] *n* nom *m* de famille.

surpass [sɜː'pɑːs] *vt person* surpasser (*in* en); *hopes* dépasser.

surplice ['sɜːplɪs] *n* surplis *m.*

surplus ['sɜːpləs] **1** *n (gen)* surplus *m*; *(Fin)* boni *m*, excédent *m.* **2** *adj (gen)* en surplus; *(Fin)* de boni, excédentaire. **it is ~ to requirements** cela excède nos besoins; *[book, document etc]* **~ copies** exemplaires *mpl* de passe; **~ stock** surplus *mpl*; **~ wheat** surplus *or* excédent *m* de blé; **his ~ energy** son surcroît d'énergie; **~ store** magasin *m* de surplus.

surprise [sə'praɪz] **1** *n (gen)* surprise *f*, étonnement *m*; *(event etc)* surprise. **much to my ~** à ma grande surprise, à mon grand étonnement; **to take by ~** *person* prendre au dépourvu; *(Mil) fort, town* prendre par surprise; **a look of ~** un regard surpris; **to give sb a ~** faire une surprise à qn; **nasty ~** mauvaise surprise; **it came as a ~ to me to learn that...** j'ai eu la surprise d'apprendre que...
2 *adj (gen)* inattendu; *attack* par surprise.
3 *vt* (**a**) *(astonish)* surprendre, étonner. **he was ~d to hear that...** il a été surpris *or* étonné d'apprendre que...; **I shouldn't be ~d if it snowed** cela ne m'étonnerait pas qu'il neige *(subj)*; **don't be ~d if he refuses** ne soyez pas étonné *or* surpris s'il refuse; **I'm ~d at his ignorance** son ignorance me surprend; **I'm ~d at you!** cela me surprend

de votre part!; **I'm ~d he agreed** j'ai été étonné *or* surpris qu'il accepte *(subj); (iro)* **go on, ~ me!** allez, étonne-moi!; **he ~d me into agreeing to do it** j'ai été tellement surpris que j'ai accepté de le faire. (**b**) *(catch unawares)* surprendre.
◆ **surprised** *adj* surpris, étonné. ◆ **surprising** *adj* surprenant, étonnant; **it is surprising that** il est surprenant *or* étonnant que + *subj.* ◆ **surprisingly** *adv big, sad etc* étonnamment; **you look surprisingly cheerful for sb who...** vous m'avez l'air de bien bonne humeur pour qn qui...; **surprisingly enough,...** chose étonnante,...; **not surprisingly he didn't come** comme on pouvait s'y attendre, il n'est pas venu.

surrealism [sə'rɪəlɪz(ə)m] *n* surréalisme *m.* ◆ **surreal** *adj* surréaliste *(fig).* ◆ **surrealist** *adj, n* surréaliste *(mf).* ◆ **surrealistic** *adj* surréaliste.

surrender [sə'rendəʳ] **1** *vi* se rendre (*to* à). **to ~ to the police** se livrer à la police. **2** *vt (Mil) town, hill* livrer (*to* à); *firearms* rendre (*to* à); *stolen property, documents* remettre (*to* à); *lease* céder; *one's rights, claims, liberty* renoncer à; *hopes* abandonner. **3** *n (Mil etc)* reddition *f* (*to* à). **no ~!** on ne se rend pas!

surreptitious [ˌsʌrəp'tɪʃəs] *adj entry, removal* subreptice; *movement, gesture* furtif. ◆ **surreptitiously** *adv* subrepticement; furtivement.

surrogate ['sʌrəgɪt] **1** *n (gen)* substitut *m.* **2** *adj pleasure etc* de remplacement. **~ mother** mère-porteuse *f.*

surround [sə'raʊnd] **1** *vt* entourer; *(totally)* encercler. **~ed by** entouré de; *(Police etc)* **you are ~ed** vous êtes encerclé. **2** *n* bordure *f.* ◆ **surrounding** **1** *adj* environnant; **the ~ing countryside** les environs *mpl* ; **2** *npl*: **~ings** *[town]* environs *mpl*; *(setting)* cadre *m*; **in their natural ~ings** dans leur cadre naturel.

surtax ['sɜːtæks] *n* tranche *f* supérieure de l'impôt sur le revenu.

surveillance [sɜː'veɪləns] *n* surveillance *f.* **to keep sb under ~** garder qn à vue.

survey ['sɜːveɪ] **1** *n* (**a**) *(comprehensive view) [prospects, development etc]* vue *f* d'ensemble (*of* de). **he gave a general ~ of the situation** il a fait un tour d'horizon de la situation. (**b**) *(study)* enquête *f* (*of* sur). **to carry out a ~ of** enquêter sur; **~ of public opinion** sondage *m* d'opinion. (**c**) *(Surveying: of land, coast etc)* levé *m*; *(in housebuying)* visite *f* d'expert; *(report)* expertise *f.* **2** *adj*: **~ ship** bateau *m* hydrographique. **3** [sɜː'veɪ] *vt* (**a**) *(look at) (gen)* regarder; *view, crowd* embrasser du regard; *prospects, trends* passer en revue. (**b**) *(study) ground etc* inspecter; *needs, prospects* enquêter sur. (**c**) *site, land* faire le levé de; *house, building* inspecter; *country, coast* faire le levé topographique de; *seas* faire le levé hydrographique de.
◆ **surveying** *n* arpentage *m.* ◆ **surveyor** *n [property, buildings etc]* expert *m*; *[land, site]* arpenteur *m* géomètre; *[country, coastline]* topographe *mf*; *[seas]* hydrographe *mf.*

survive [sə'vaɪv] **1** *vi (gen)* survivre. **only three volumes ~** il ne reste *or* il ne subsiste plus que trois tomes; *(iro)* **you'll ~!** vous n'en mourrez pas! **2** *vt (gen)* survivre à; *injury, disease* réchapper de. ◆ **survival** **1** *n (gen)* survie *f*; **the survival of the fittest** la persistance du plus apte; **it's the survival of an old law** c'est la survivance d'une vieille loi ; **2** *adj*: **survival course/kit** cours *m*/kit *m* de survie. ◆ **surviving** *adj* survivant. ◆ **survivor** *n* survivant(e) *m(f).*

sus [sʌs] *adj*: **~ law** garde *f* à vue préventive.

susceptible [sə'septəbl] *adj (sensitive)* sensible; *(touchy)* susceptible. **to be ~ to** *(gen)* être sensible à; *suggestion, sb's influence* être ouvert à; *(Med) disease* être prédisposé à; *treatment* répondre à; **~ of** susceptible de. ◆ **susceptibility** *n* vive sensibilité *f*; susceptibilité *f*; *(Med)* prédisposition *f* (*to* à).

suspect ['sʌspekt] **1** *n* suspect(e) *m(f).* **2** *adj evidence, act* suspect. **3** [səs'pekt] *vt (gen)* soupçonner (*that* que; *of a crime* d'un crime; *of doing* de faire *or* d'avoir fait); *ambush, swindle* flairer, soupçonner; *(have doubts about) sb's motives etc* suspecter, douter de. **he ~s nothing** il ne se doute de rien; **I ~ed as much** je m'en doutais; **he'll come, I ~** il viendra, j'imagine.

suspend [səs'pend] *vt* (**a**) *(hang)* suspendre (*from* à). (**b**) *(stop: gen)* suspendre; *licence, permission* retirer provisoirement; *bus service* interrompre provisoirement; *employee* suspendre (*from* de); *student, pupil* renvoyer temporairement. *(Jur)* **he received a ~ed sentence of 6 months** il a été condamné à 6 mois de prison avec sursis; *(fig)* **to be in a state of ~ed animation** ne donner aucun signe de vie. ◆ **suspender** **1** *n*: **~ers** *(Brit) (for stockings)* jarretelles *fpl*; *(for socks)* fixe-chaussettes *mpl*; *(US)* bretelles *fpl* ; **2** *adj (Brit)* **~er belt** porte-jarretelles *m inv.* ◆ **suspense** *n* incertitude *f*; *(in book, film etc)* suspense *m*; **we waited in great suspense** nous avons attendu haletants; **to keep sb in suspense** tenir qn en suspens; **to put sb out of his suspense** mettre fin à l'incertitude de qn; **novel of suspense** roman *m* à suspense; **the suspense is killing me!** * ce suspense me tue! *(also iro).* ◆ **suspension** **1** *n* suspension *f (also Aut)*; retrait *m* provisoire; interruption *f* provisoire ; **2** *adj bridge* suspendu.

suspicion [səs'pɪʃ(ə)n] *n* soupçon *m.* **laden with ~** chargé de soupçons; **above ~** au-dessus de tout soupçon; **under ~** considéré comme suspect; **he was regarded with ~** on s'est montré soupçonneux à son égard; *(Jur)* **to arrest on ~** arrêter sur des présomptions; **on ~ of murder** sur présomption de meurtre; **I had a ~ that...** je soupçonnais que...; **I had no ~ that...** je ne me doutais pas du tout que...; **I had (my) ~s about that** j'avais mes doutes là-dessus. ◆ **suspicious** *adj* (**a**) *(feeling ~)* soupçonneux, méfiant; **to be suspicious about sb/sth** avoir des soupçons à l'égard de qn/quant à qch; **to be suspicious of** se méfier de; (**b**) *(causing ~*: **suspicious-looking***) person, vehicle* suspect; *move, action* louche. ◆ **suspiciously** *adv examine, glance, ask etc* avec méfiance; *behave, run away etc* d'une manière suspecte *or* louche; **it looks suspiciously like measles** ça m'a tout l'air d'être la rougeole; **it sounds suspiciously as though...** ça m'a tout l'air de signifier que...; **he arrived suspiciously early** il me paraît suspect qu'il soit arrivé si tôt. ◆ **suspiciousness** *n* caractère *m* soupçonneux *or* suspect.

suss * [sʌs] *vt (Brit)* **to ~ out** découvrir.

sustain [səs'teɪn] *vt* (**a**) *weight, beam etc* supporter; *body* donner des forces à; *life* maintenir; *(Mus) note* tenir; *effort, role, theory* soutenir; *pretence* poursuivre. *(Jur)* **objection ~ed** ≃ objection accordée. (**b**) *(suffer) attack, damage* subir; *loss* éprouver; *injury* recevoir. ◆ **sustained** *adj effort, applause* prolongé; **~ed growth** expansion *f* soutenue. ◆ **sustaining** *adj food* nourrissant. ◆ **sustenance** *n (food)* nourriture *f*; *(means of livelihood)* moyens *mpl* de subsistance; **there's not much sustenance in it** cela n'est pas très nourrissant.

swab [swɒb] **1** *n (mop, cloth)* serpillière *f*; *(Med: cotton wool etc)* tampon *m*; *(Med: specimen)* prélèvement *m* (*of* dans). **2** *vt* (**~ down**) *floor etc* nettoyer, essuyer; (**~ out**) *wound* tamponner.

swagger ['swægəʳ] **1** *n*: **to walk with a ~** marcher d'un air fanfaron. **2** *vi*: **to ~ about/in** *etc* se promener/entrer *etc* d'un air fanfaron. ◆ **swaggering** **1** *adj gait* assuré; *person, look, gesture* fanfaron ; **2** *n* air *m* fanfaron.

swallow[1] ['swɒləʊ] **1** *n (bird)* hirondelle *f*. **2** *adj*: ~ **dive** saut *m* de l'ange. ◆ **swallowtail butterfly** *n* machaon *m*.

swallow[2] ['swɒləʊ] **1** *n (act)* avalement *m*; *(amount)* gorgée *f*. **at one** ~ d'un seul coup. **2** *vi* avaler. *(emotionally)* **he ~ed hard** sa gorge s'est serrée. **3** *vt food, story, insult* avaler; *anger, pride* ravaler. *(fig)* **to ~ the bait** se laisser prendre à l'appât; **that's hard to** ~ c'est dur à avaler; **they ~ed it whole** ils ont tout avalé. ◆ **swallow up** *vt sep (fig)* engloutir. **he was ~ed up in the crowd** il a disparu dans la foule.

swam [swæm] *pret of* **swim**.

swamp [swɒmp] **1** *n* marais *m*, marécage *m*. **2** *adj*: ~ **fever** paludisme *m*. **3** *vt (flood)* inonder; *boat* emplir d'eau; *(fig)* submerger (*with* de). *(fig)* **~ed with requests/letters** submergé de requêtes/lettres; **~ed * with work** débordé de travail; *(Ftbl etc)* **towards the end of the game they ~ed us** vers la fin de la partie ils ont fait le jeu. ◆ **swampland** *n* marécages *mpl*. ◆ **swampy** *adj* marécageux.

swan [swɒn] **1** *n* cygne *m*. **2** *adj (US)* ~ **dive** saut *m* de l'ange; *(fig)* ~ **song** chant *m* du cygne. **3** *vi* (*) **he ~ned off to London** il est parti à Londres sans s'en faire *; **he's ~ning around in Paris** il se balade dans Paris sans s'en faire *. ◆ **swansdown** *n* duvet *m* de cygne.

swank * [swæŋk] **1** *n* (**a**) esbroufe * *f*. **out of** ~ pour faire de l'esbroufe *. (**b**) *(person)* esbroufeur * *m*, -euse * *f*. **2** *vi* chercher à en mettre plein la vue *. **to ~ about sth** se vanter de qch. ◆ **swanky** * *adj* qui en met plein la vue *.

swap * [swɒp] **1** *n* troc *m*, échange *m*. **it's a fair** ~ ça se vaut; *(stamps etc)* **~s** doubles *mpl*. **2** *vt* échanger (*A for B* A contre B; *with sb* avec qn). **let's ~ places** changeons de place (l'un avec l'autre); **I'll ~ you!** tu veux échanger avec moi? **3** *vi* échanger.

swarm[1] [swɔ:m] **1** *n [bees, flying insects]* essaim *m*; *[ants, crawling insects]* grouillement *m*; *[people]* nuée *f*. *(fig)* **in ~s** en masse. **2** *vi [bees]* essaimer. *[crawling insects]* **to ~ about** grouiller; *[people]* **to ~ in/out** *etc* entrer/sortir *etc* en masse; *[ground, town]* **to ~ with** grouiller de.

swarm[2] [swɔ:m] *vt* (**~ up**) *tree* grimper à toute vitesse à.

swarthy ['swɔ:ðɪ] *adj* basané. ◆ **swarthiness** *n* teint *m* basané.

swastika ['swɒstɪkə] *n* swastika *m*; *(Nazi)* croix *f* gammée.

swat [swɒt] **1** *vt* écraser. **2** *n* (**fly ~**, *also* **~ter**) tapette *f*.

swathe [sweɪð] *vt* emmailloter (*in bandages* de bandages), envelopper (*in blankets* dans des couvertures).

sway [sweɪ] **1** *n* (**a**) *(motion) (gen)* oscillation *f*; *[boat]* balancement *m*. (**b**) *(liter)* emprise *f* (*over* sur). **under his** ~ sous son emprise. **2** *vi (gen)* osciller, se balancer; *[tower block, bridge]* osciller; *[train]* tanguer; *[person]* tanguer, osciller; *(fig: vacillate)* balancer (*between* entre). **3** *vt* (**a**) *hanging object* balancer, faire osciller; *hips* rouler; *[wind, waves]* balancer. (**b**) *(influence)* influencer.

Swaziland ['swɑ:zɪlænd] *n* Swaziland *m*.

swear [swɛəʳ] *pret* **swore**, *ptp* **sworn** **1** *vt* jurer (*on sth* sur qch; *that* que; *to do* de faire). **to ~ an oath** *(solemnly)* prêter serment; *(curse)* lâcher un juron; **I could have sworn he touched it** j'aurais juré qu'il l'avait touché; **to ~ sb to secrecy** faire jurer le secret à qn. **2** *vi* (**a**) jurer. **to ~ to the truth of sth** jurer que qch est vrai; **I wouldn't ~ to it** je n'en jurerais pas; *(fig)* **he ~s by vitamin C tablets** il ne jure que par la vitamine C. (**b**) *(curse)* jurer (*at* contre, après). **to ~ like a trooper** jurer comme un charretier. ◆ **swear in** *vt sep jury etc* faire prêter serment à. ◆ **swearword** *n* juron *m*, gros mot.

sweat [swet] **1** *n* sueur *f*. **by the ~ of his brow** à la sueur de son front; **to be dripping with** ~ ruisseler de sueur; *(fig)* **to be in a cold ~** * avoir des sueurs froides; **it was an awful ~** * on en a eu du mal!; **no ~!** ‡ pas de problème! **2** *vi [person, animal, cheese]* suer (*with, from* de); *[walls]* suinter. **to ~ like a bull** suer comme un bœuf; **he was ~ing profusely/over his essay** * il suait à grosses gouttes/sur sa dissertation. **3** *vt* (**a**) *(fig) workers* exploiter. **~ed labour** main-d'œuvre *f* exploitée. (**b**) **to ~ blood** * *(work hard)* suer sang et eau (*over sth* sur qch); *(be anxious)* avoir des sueurs froides. ◆ **sweat out** * *vt sep (fig)* **you'll have to ~ it out** il faudra t'armer de patience; **they left him to ~ it out** ils n'ont rien fait pour l'aider. ◆ **sweatband** *n (Sport)* bandeau *m*. ◆ **sweater** *n* pullover *m*, pull * *m*. ◆ **sweating** *n* transpiration *f*; *(Med)* sudation *f*; *[wall]* suintement *m*. ◆ **sweatshirt** *n* sweat-shirt *m*. ◆ **sweat-shop** *n* atelier *m* où les ouvriers sont exploités. ◆ **sweat suit** *n* survêtement *m*. ◆ **sweaty** *adj body* en sueur; *feet* qui suent; *hand* moite; *smell* de sueur; *sock* mouillé de sueur.

swede [swi:d] *n* rutabaga *m*.

Sweden ['swi:dn] *n* Suède *f*. ◆ **Swede** *n* Suédois(e) *m(f)*. ◆ **Swedish** **1** *adj* suédois ; **2** *n* suédois *m*; **the Swedish** les Suédois *mpl*.

sweep [swi:p] *(vb: pret, ptp* **swept***)* **1** *n* (**a**) (**chimney ~**) ramoneur *m*. (**b**) *(movement) [arm]* grand geste *m*; *[sword, net]* grand coup *m*; *[scythe]* mouvement *m* circulaire; *[lighthouse etc beam]* trajectoire *f*; *(fig) [progress, events]* marche *f*. **with one** ~ d'un seul coup; **with a ~ of his arm** d'un geste large; **the police made a ~ of the district** la police a ratissé le quartier; **a wide ~ of meadowland** une vaste étendue de prairie.

2 *vt room, street, snow etc* balayer; *chimney* ramoner; *channel, mines* draguer. *(Naut)* **to ~ sth clean of mines** déminer qch; **to ~ the horizon** *(with binoculars)* parcourir l'horizon; *[lighthouse beam]* balayer l'horizon; **his glance swept the room** il a parcouru la pièce du regard; **a wave of indignation swept the city** une vague d'indignation a déferlé sur la ville; **he swept the rubbish off the pavement** il a enlevé les ordures du trottoir d'un coup de balai; *(fig)* **to ~ sth under the carpet** tirer le rideau sur qch; **to ~ sth on to the floor** faire tomber qch par terre d'un geste large; *(fig)* **to ~ everything before one, to ~ the board** remporter un succès complet; **they swept the board at the election** ils ont remporté l'élection haut la main; **the crowd swept him into the square** la foule l'a emporté sur la place; **the wave swept him overboard** la vague l'a jeté par-dessus bord; **the current swept the boat downstream** le courant a emporté le bateau; **the water swept him off his feet** le courant lui a fait perdre pied; *(fig)* **to be swept off one's feet** être enthousiasmé (*by* par); *(fig)* **he swept her off her feet** elle a eu le coup de foudre pour lui.

3 *vi*: **to ~ in/out/along** *etc* entrer/sortir/avancer *etc (swiftly)* rapidement *or (impressively)* majestueusement *or (angrily)* avec furie; **the car swept round the corner** la voiture a pris le virage comme un bolide; **the rain swept across the plain** la pluie a balayé la plaine; **panic swept through the city** la panique s'est emparée de la ville; *(fig: Pol)* **to ~ into office** être porté au pouvoir; **the Alps ~ down to the coast** les Alpes descendent majestueusement vers la côte.

◆ **sweep along** *vt sep [crowd, flood]* emporter. ◆ **sweep aside** *vt sep object, person, suggestion* repousser; *difficulty, obstacle* écarter. ◆ **sweep away** *vt sep dust, snow, rubbish* balayer; *[crowd, current, gale]* entraîner. ◆ **sweep out** *vt sep* balayer. ◆ **sweep up 1** *vi* balayer. **2** *vt sep leaves, dust etc* balayer; *(pick up) books etc* ramasser d'un geste brusque.

◆ **sweeper** *n* (**a**) *(worker)* balayeur *m*; *(machine)* balayeuse *f*; *(carpet ~er)* balai *m* mécanique; *(vacuum cleaner)* aspirateur *m*. (**b**) *(Ftbl)* arrière *m* volant. ◆ **sweeping** *adj movement, gesture* large; *bow, curtsy* profond; *glance* circulaire; *change, reorganization* radical; *reduction* considérable; *price cut* imbattable; *(at election)* **~ing gains/losses** progression *f* /recul *m* très net(te); **~ing statement** *or* **generalization** généralisation *f* hâtive; **that's pretty ~ing!** c'est beaucoup dire! ◆ **sweepstake** *n* sweepstake *m*.

sweet [swi:t] **1** *adj* (**a**) *(not sour) apple, cider, wine* doux (*f* douce); *tea, biscuit, taste* sucré. **to have a ~ tooth** être friand de sucreries; **I love ~ things** j'aime les sucreries *fpl*; *(Culin)* **~ and sour** aigre-doux; **a sickly ~ smell** une odeur fétide. (**b**) *(pleasant etc) air, breath* frais; *water* pur; *soil* sain; *scent* agréable; *sound, voice* mélodieux; *running of engine* sans à-coups; *person* gentil, charmant; *revenge, success, character, smile* doux; *child, dog, house, dress* mignon. *(fig)* **the ~ smell of success** la douceur exquise du succès; **it was ~ to his ear** c'était doux à son oreille; *(pej)* **~ words** *or* **talk** flagorneries *fpl*; **~ herbs** fines herbes *fpl*; **~ potato** patate *f* douce; **he carried on in his own ~ way** il a continué comme il l'entendait; **to be ~ on sb** * avoir le béguin * pour qn; **~ Fanny Adams** ‡ rien de rien *; **a ~ old lady** une adorable vieille dame; **~ little baby** mignon petit bébé *m*.

2 *adv*: **to smell ~** sentir bon; **to taste ~** avoir un goût sucré.

3 *n (toffee etc)* bonbon *m*; *(dessert)* dessert *m*.

◆ **sweetbread** *n* ris *m* de veau *or* d'agneau. ◆ **sweetcorn** *n* maïs *m* doux. ◆ **sweeten** *vt food etc* sucrer; *air* purifier; *(fig) person, temper, task* adoucir; *(*: bribe)* graisser la patte à *. ◆ **sweetener** *n (for coffee, food)* édulcorant *m; (* fig: bribe)* pot-de-vin *m*. ◆ **sweetening** *n (substance)* édulcorant *m*. ◆ **sweetheart** *n* petit(e) ami(e) *m(f)*; **yes ~heart** oui mon ange. ◆ **sweetie** * *n (toffee etc)* bonbon *m*; **she's a ~ie** c'est un ange; **yes ~ie** oui mon ange. ◆ **sweetly** *adv sing, play* mélodieusement; *smile, answer* gentiment; *[engine] run* sans à-coups. ◆ **sweet-natured** *or* ◆ **sweet-tempered** *adj* d'un naturel doux. ◆ **sweetness** *n (gen)* douceur *f*; *(to taste)* goût sucré; *(in smell)* odeur *f* suave. ◆ **sweetpea** *n* pois *m* de senteur. ◆ **sweet-scented** *or* ◆ **sweet-smelling** *adj* parfumé, odorant. ◆ **sweetshop** *n* confiserie *f*. ◆ **sweet-william** *n* œillet *m* de poète.

swell [swel] *(vb: pret* **swelled**, *ptp* **swollen** *or* **swelled**) **1** *n [sea]* houle *f*; *(Mus)* crescendo *m inv*. **2** *adj (*: esp US: excellent)* sensationnel *, formidable *. **3** *vi* (**~ up**) *[tyre, airbed, sails]* se gonfler; *[part of body]* enfler; *[wood]* gonfler; *[river]* grossir; *[sound, music, voice]* s'enfler; *[numbers, membership]* augmenter. **4** *vt sail* gonfler; *sound* enfler; *river, population* grossir; *number* augmenter, grossir. **swollen with pride** gonflé d'orgueil. ◆ **swellheaded** * *adj* bêcheur. ◆ **swelling** *n (Med)* enflure *f*; *(lump)* grosseur *f*; *(on tyre etc)* hernie *f*.

swelter ['sweltə^r] *vi* étouffer de chaleur. ◆ **sweltering** *adj* oppressant; **it's ~ing in here** on étouffe de chaleur ici.

swept [swept] *pret, ptp of* **sweep.**

swerve [sw3:v] **1** *vi [boxer, fighter]* faire un écart; *[ball]* dévier; *[vehicle, ship]* faire une embardée; *[driver]* donner un coup de volant; *(fig)* dévier (*from* de). **2** *n* écart *m*; embardée *f*.

swift [swɪft] **1** *adj (gen)* prompt (*to do* à faire), rapide; *vehicle, journey* rapide; *movement* vif. **2** *n (Orn)* martinet *m*. ◆ **swiftly** *adv* rapidement, vite. ◆ **swiftness** *n* promptitude *f*; rapidité *f*.

swig * [swɪg] **1** *n* lampée * *f*; *(larger)* coup *m*. **to take a ~ at a bottle** boire un coup à même la bouteille. **2** *vt* lamper *.

swill [swɪl] **1** *n (for pigs etc)* pâtée *f*; *(garbage)* eaux *fpl* grasses. **2** *vt* (**a**) (**~ out**) *floor* laver à grande eau; *glass* rincer. (**b**) *(*: drink)* boire à grands traits.

swim [swɪm] *(vb: pret* **swam**, *ptp* **swum**) **1** *n*: **to go for a ~, to have a ~ = to go ~ming** *(V* **2**); **after a 2-km ~** après avoir fait 2 km à la nage; **I had a lovely ~** ça m'a fait du bien de nager comme ça; *(fig)* **to be in the ~** être dans le mouvement. **2** *vi (gen)* nager; *(as sport)* faire de la natation. **to go ~ming** *(in sea etc)* aller nager, aller se baigner; *(in ~ming baths)* aller à la piscine; **to ~ away/back** *etc [person]* s'éloigner/revenir *etc* à la nage; *[fish]* s'éloigner/revenir *etc*; **he swam under the boat** il est passé sous le bateau; *(fig)* **to ~ with the tide** suivre le courant; *(fig)* **the meat was ~ming in gravy** la viande baignait dans la sauce; **eyes ~ming with tears** yeux baignés de larmes; **the bathroom was ~ming** * la salle de bains était inondée; **the room swam before his eyes** la pièce semblait tourner autour de lui; **his head was ~ming** la tête lui tournait.

3 *vt* traverser à la nage. **it was first swum in 1900** la première traversée à la nage a eu lieu en 1900; **to ~ 10 km** faire 10 km à la nage; **I can't ~ a stroke** je suis incapable de faire une brasse. ◆ **swimmer** *n* nageur *m*, -euse *f*. ◆ **swimming 1** *n* nage *f (as sport)* natation *f* ; **2** *adj*: **~ming bath(s)** *or* **pool** piscine *f*; **~ming cap** bonnet *m* de bain; **~ming costume** *or* **suit** maillot *m* (de bain) une pièce ; **~ming gala** fête *f* de natation; **~ming trunks** caleçon *m* de bain. ◆ **swimmingly** *adv*: **to go ~mingly** aller à merveille. ◆ **swimsuit** *n* maillot *m* (de bain).

swindle ['swɪndl] **1** *n* escroquerie *f*. **it's a ~** c'est du vol. **2** *vt* escroquer, rouler *. **to ~ sb out of sth, to ~ sth out of sb** escroquer qch à qn. ◆ **swindler** *n* escroc *m*.

swine [swaɪn] *n, pl inv* pourceau *m*; *(‡ fig: person)* salaud ‡ *m*.

swing [swɪŋ] *(vb: pret, ptp* **swung**) **1** *n* (**a**) *(movement)* balancement *m*; *[pendulum, needle, pointer]* oscillations *fpl*; *(distance)* arc *m*; *(Boxing, Golf)* swing *m*. **to take a ~ at sb** décocher un coup de poing à qn; *(fig)* **the ~ of the pendulum** le mouvement du pendule; *(Pol)* **a ~ of 5% to the left** un revirement de 5% en faveur de la gauche; **to walk with a ~ (in one's step)** marcher d'un pas rythmé; **music that goes with a ~** musique *f* entraînante; *(fig)* **to go with a ~** *[evening, party]* marcher du tonnerre *; *[business, shop]* très bien marcher; **to be in full ~** battre son plein; **to get into the ~ of things** se mettre dans le bain. (**b**) *(play equipment)* balançoire *f*. **to have a ~** se balancer; *(fig)* **what you gain on the ~s you lose on the roundabouts** ce qu'on gagne d'un côté on le perd de l'autre. (**c**) (**~ music**) swing *m*.

2 *adj* (**a**) *(Mus) band* de swing. (**b**) *bridge* tournant; *door* battant.

3 *vi (gen)* se balancer; *[pendulum]* osciller; *(pivot: ~* **round**) tourner, pivoter; *[person]* se retourner. **~ing by his hands** suspendu par les mains; **to ~ to and fro** se balancer; **it swung round through the air** cela a décrit une courbe dans l'air; **he swung across on the rope** agrippé à la corde il s'est élancé et est passé de l'autre côté; **the door swung open/shut** la porte s'est ouverte/refermée; **he swung round on his heels** il a virevolté; **to ~ along/away** *etc* avancer/s'éloigner *etc* d'un pas rythmé; *(fig)* **to ~ into action** passer à l'action; **music that really ~s** musique *f* au rythme entraînant; **the river ~s north** la rivière décrit une courbe vers le nord; *(fig Pol)* **to ~ to the right** virer à droite; *(be hanged)* **he'll ~ for it *** on lui mettra la corde au cou pour cela.

4 *vt* (**a**) *(gen)* balancer; *child on swing* pousser; *(brandish)* brandir. **he swung the case (up) on to his shoulders** il a balancé la valise sur ses épaules; **he swung himself over the wall** il a sauté par-dessus le mur; **to ~ o.s. up into the saddle** sauter en selle; **to ~ one's hips** rouler *or* balancer les hanches. (**b**) (**~ round**) *propeller* lancer ; *starting handle* tourner. **to ~ a door open/shut** ouvrir/fermer une porte. (**c**) *(influence) election, decision* influencer. **to ~ a deal *** emporter une affaire. (**d**) *(Mus) the classics etc* jouer de manière rythmée.

◆ **swing round 1** *vi [person]* se retourner; *[crane etc]* pivoter; *[vehicle]* virer; *(after collision)* faire un tête-à-queue; *(fig) [voters]* virer de bord; *[opinions etc]* connaître un revirement. **2** *vt sep object on rope etc* faire tourner.

◆ **swinging** *adj step* rythmé; *music, rhythm* entraînant; *(* fig) (lively)* dynamique; *(fashionable etc)* dans le vent *; *party* du tonnerre *. ◆ **swing-wing** *adj (Aviat)* à géométrie variable.

swingeing ['swɪn(d)ʒɪŋ] *adj blow, attack* violent; *defeat, majority* écrasant; *damages, taxation, price* énorme.

swipe [swaɪp] **1** *n* (*) *(at ball etc)* grand coup *m*; *(slap)* gifle *f*. **2** *vt* (**a**) *(*: hit) ball* frapper à toute volée; *person* gifler à toute volée. (**b**) *(‡: steal)* piquer *, voler *(sth from sb* qch à qn).

swirl [swɜːl] **1** *n (gen)* tourbillon *m*; *[cream etc]* volute *f*. **2** *vi* tourbillonner.

swish [swɪʃ] **1** *vi [cane, whip]* siffler, cingler l'air; *[water, long grass, skirts]* bruire. **2** *vt whip, cane* faire siffler. **3** *n* sifflement *m*; bruissement *m*. **4** *adj (‡: smart: also* **swishy ***) rupin ‡.

Swiss [swɪs] **1** *adj* suisse. ~ **French/German** suisse romand/allemand; *(Culin)* ~ **roll** gâteau *m* roulé. **2** *n, pl inv* Suisse(sse) *m(f)*.

switch [swɪtʃ] **1** *n* (**a**) *(Elec)* interrupteur *m*, commutateur *m*; *(Aut:* **ignition ~**) contact *m*. *(Elec)* **the ~ was on/off** c'était allumé/éteint. (**b**) *(Rail: points)* aiguille *f*. (**c**) *[opinion, allegiance]* revirement *m*; *[funds]* transfert *m* (*from* de; *to* en faveur de). *(Bridge)* **the ~ to hearts** le passage à cœur.

2 *vt* (**a**) *(transfer) one's support, allegiance, attention* reporter (*from* de; *to* sur). **to ~ production to another factory** transférer la production dans une autre usine; **to ~ the conversation to another subject** changer de sujet de conversation. (**b**) *(exchange)* échanger (*A for B* A contre B; *sth with sb* qch avec qn); (**~ over, ~ round**) *two objects, letters in word* intervertir; *(rearrange:* ~ **round**) *books, objects* changer de place. **to ~ plans** changer de projet. (**c**) *(Rail)* aiguiller (*to another track* sur une autre voie). (**d**) *(Elec etc)* **to ~ the heater to 'low'** mettre le radiateur sur 'doux'; **to ~ the radio/TV to another programme** changer de station/de chaîne. **3** *vi* (**~ over**) **he ~ed (over) to Conservative** il a voté conservateur cette fois; **we ~ed (over) to gas** (nous avons changé et) nous avons maintenant fait installer le gaz; **many have ~ed (over) to teaching** beaucoup se sont recyclés dans l'enseignement.

◆ **switch back 1** *vi (gen)* revenir (*to* à). *(Rad, TV)* **to ~ back to the other programme** remettre l'autre émission. **2** *vt sep*: **to ~ the heater back to 'low'** remettre le radiateur sur 'doux'; *(Elec)* **to ~ back on** rallumer. ◆ **switch off 1** *vi* (**a**) *(Elec)* éteindre; *(Rad, TV)* éteindre le poste; *(fig: lose interest)* décrocher *. (**b**) *[heater, oven etc]* s'éteindre; *alarm clock* arrêter. **2** *vt sep* éteindre. *(Rad, TV)* **he ~ed the programme off** il a fermé le poste; *(Aut)* **to ~ off the engine** arrêter le moteur.

◆ **switch on 1** *vi* (**a**) *(Elec)* allumer; *(Rad, TV)* allumer le poste. (**b**) *[heater, oven etc]* s'allumer. **2** *vt sep (gen)* allumer; *water supply* ouvrir; *engine, machine* mettre en marche; *(‡ fig: excite)* exciter. **to ~ on the light** allumer; *(fig)* **to be ~ed on ‡** *(up-to-date)* être dans le vent *; *(by drugs)* planer *; *(sexually)* être tout excité (*by* par).

◆ **switch over** *vi (TV/Rad)* changer de chaîne/de station. *(Rad, TV)* **to ~ over to sth** mettre qch.

◆ **switchback 1** *n* montagnes *fpl* russes *(also fig)* ; **2** *adj (up and down)* tout en montées et descentes. ◆ **switchblade (knife)** *n (US)* couteau *m* à cran d'arrêt. ◆ **switchboard 1** *n (Elec)* tableau *m* de distribution; *(Telec)* standard *m* ; **2** *adj (Telec)* **~board operator** standardiste *mf*. ◆ **switchover** *n* passage *m* (*from* de; *to* à).

Switzerland ['swɪts(ə)lənd] *n* Suisse *f*. **French-/German-/Italian-speaking** ~ la Suisse romande/allemande/italienne.

swivel ['swɪvl] **1** *n* pivot *m*. **2** *adj seat etc* pivotant. **3** *vt* (**~ round**) faire pivoter. **4** *vi* (**~ round**) pivoter.

swollen ['swəʊl(ə)n] *(ptp of* **swell**) *adj arm, face* enflé; *eyes, stomach* gonflé (*with* de); *river, lake* en crue; *population* accru. **to have ~ glands** avoir une inflammation des ganglions. ◆ **swollen-headed *** *adj* bêcheur.

swoon [swuːn] *vi* se pâmer; *(fig)* se pâmer d'admiration (*over sb/sth* devant qn/qch).

swoop [swuːp] **1** *n (attack)* attaque *f* en piqué (*on* sur); *[police etc]* descente *f* (*on* dans). **at one fell ~** d'un seul coup. **2** *vi* (**~ down**) *[bird]* fondre; *[aircraft]* descendre en piqué; *[police etc]* faire une descente.

swop [swɒp] = **swap.**

sword [sɔːd] **1** *n* épée *f*. **to wear a ~** porter l'épée. **2** *adj wound* d'épée. ~ **arm** bras *m* droit; ~ **dance** danse *f* du sabre. ◆ **swordfish** *n* espadon *m*. ◆ **swordsman** *n*: **to be a good ~sman** être une fine lame. ◆ **swordsmanship** *n* habileté *f* dans le maniement de l'épée. ◆ **swordstick** *n* canne *f* à épée. ◆ **sword-swallower** *n* avaleur *m* de sabres.

swore [swɔːʳ] *pret of* **swear.**

sworn [swɔːn] *(ptp of* **swear**) *adj evidence, statement* donné sous serment; *enemy* juré; *ally, friend* à la vie et à la mort.

swot * [swɒt] **1** *n* bûcheur * *m*, -euse * *f*. **2** *vti* bûcher *. **to ~ for an exam** bachoter; **to ~ up (on) sth** potasser * qch. ◆ **swotting *** *n* bachotage *m*.

swum [swʌm] *ptp of* **swim.**

swung [swʌŋ] *(pret, ptp of* **swing**) *adj (Typ)* ~ **dash** tilde *m*.

sycamore ['sɪkəmɔːʳ] *n* sycomore *m*.

sycophant ['sɪkəfənt] *n* flagorneur *m*, -euse *f*.

Sydney ['sɪdnɪ] *n* Sydney.

syllable ['sɪləbl] *n* syllabe *f*. ◆ **syllabic** *adj* syllabique.

syllabus ['sɪləbəs] *n (Scol, Univ)* programme *m*. **on the ~** au programme.

syllogism ['sɪlədʒɪz(ə)m] *n* syllogisme *m*.

sylph [sɪlf] *n* sylphe *m*. ◆ **sylphlike** *adj woman* gracile; *figure* de sylphide.

symbiosis [ˌsɪmbɪ'əʊsɪs] *n (also fig)* symbiose *f*. ◆ **symbiotic** *adj* symbiotique.

symbol ['sɪmb(ə)l] *n* symbole *m*. ◆ **symbolic(al)** *adj* symbolique. ◆ **symbolically** *adv* symboliquement. ◆ **symbolism** *n* symbolisme *m*. ◆ **symbolist** *adj, n* symboliste *(mf)*. ◆ **symbolization** *n* symbolisation *f*. ◆ **symbolize** *vt* symboliser.

symmetry ['sɪmɪtrɪ] *n* symétrie *f*. ◆ **symmetric(al)** *adj* symétrique. ◆ **symmetrically** *adv* symétriquement.

sympathy ['sɪmpəθɪ] *n* (**a**) *(pity)* compassion *f*. **please accept my deepest ~** veuillez agréer mes condoléances; **to feel ~ for** éprouver de la compassion pour; **to show one's ~ for sb** témoigner sa sympathie à qn. (**b**) *(fellow feeling)* solidarité *f* (*for* avec). **I have no ~ with lazy people** je n'ai aucune indulgence pour les paresseux; **he is in ~ with the workers** il est du côté des ouvriers; **I am in ~ with your proposals** je suis en accord avec vos propositions; **to strike in ~ with sb** faire grève en solidarité avec qn. ◆ **sympathetic** *adj (showing pity)* compatissant (*to, towards* envers); *(kind)* bien disposé (*to* envers), compréhensif; **you will find him very sympathetic** vous le trouverez bien disposé à votre égard. ◆ **sympathetically** *adv (showing pity)* avec compassion; *(kindly)* avec bienveillance. ◆ **sympathize** *vi*: **her cousin called to sympathize** sa cousine est venue témoigner sa sympathie; **I sympathize with you in your grief** je m'associe à votre douleur; **I sympathize with you** *(pity)* je vous plains; *(understand)* je comprends votre point de vue. ◆ **sympathizer** *n (in adversity)* personne *f* qui compatit; *(fig: esp Pol)* sympathisant(e) *m(f)* (*with* de).

symphony ['sɪmfənɪ] **1** *n* symphonie *f.* **2** *adj concert, orchestra* symphonique. ◆ **symphonic** *adj* symphonique.

symposium, *pl* **-ia** [sɪm'pəʊzɪəm, ɪə] *n* symposium *m.*

symptom ['sɪmptəm] *n* symptôme *m.* ◆ **symptomatic** *adj* symptomatique (*of* de).

synagogue ['sɪnəgɒg] *n* synagogue *f.*

synchronize ['sɪŋkrənaɪz] **1** *vt* synchroniser. **~d swimming** natation *f* synchronisée. **2** *vi [events]* se passer en même temps (*with* que). ◆ **sync** * *n:* **in/out of sync** bien/mal synchronisé. ◆ **synchronization** *n* synchronisation *f.*

syncopate ['sɪŋkəpeɪt] *vt* syncoper. ◆ **syncopation** *n* syncope *f (Mus).*

syndicate ['sɪndɪkɪt] **1** *n (Comm etc)* syndicat *m*, coopérative *f.* **2** ['sɪndɪkeɪt] *vt* (**a**) *(US Press) article etc* vendre *or* publier par l'intermédiaire d'un syndicat de distribution. (**b**) *workers* syndiquer. ◆ **syndicalism** *n* syndicalisme *m.* ◆ **syndicalist** *n* syndicaliste *mf.*

syndrome ['sɪndrəʊm] *n (also fig)* syndrome *m.*

synod ['sɪnəd] *n* synode *m.*

synonym ['sɪnənɪm] *n* synonyme *m.* ◆ **synonymous** *adj* synonyme (*with* de). ◆ **synonymy** *n* synonymie *f.*

synopsis, *pl* **-ses** [sɪ'nɒpsɪs, sɪ:z] *n* résumé *m.*

syntax ['sɪntæks] *n* syntaxe *f.* ◆ **syntactic(al)** *adj* syntaxique.

synthesis, *pl* **-ses** ['sɪnθəsɪs, sɪ:z] *n* synthèse *f.* ◆ **synthesize** *vt (combine)* synthétiser; *(produce)* produire synthétiquement. ◆ **synthesizer** *n* synthétiseur *m.* ◆ **synthetic** **1** *adj* synthétique ; **2** *n* produit *m* synthétique; *(Tex)* **synthetics** fibres *fpl* synthétiques.

syphilis ['sɪfɪlɪs] *n* syphilis *f.* ◆ **syphilitic** *adj, n* syphilitique *(mf).*

syphon ['saɪf(ə)n] = **siphon**.

Syria ['sɪrɪə] *n* Syrie *f.*

syringe [sɪ'rɪn(d)ʒ] **1** *n* seringue *f.* **2** *vt* seringuer.

syrup ['sɪrəp] *n* sirop *m*; *(Culin:* **golden ~***)* mélasse *f* raffinée. ◆ **syrupy** *adj* sirupeux.

system ['sɪstəm] **1** *n* (**a**) *(structured whole)* système *m.* **a political/social ~** un système politique/social; **solar ~** système solaire; **nervous ~** système nerveux; **digestive ~** appareil *m* digestif; **the railway ~** le réseau de chemin de fer; **the Social Security ~** le régime de la Sécurité sociale. (**b**) *(method, process)* système *m.* (**c**) *(the body)* organisme *m. (fig)* **let him get it out of his ~** * *anger* laisse-le décharger sa bile; *passion* laisse-le faire — ça lui passera. (**d**) *(established order)* **the ~** le système. (**e**) *(Comput)* système *m.* (**f**) *(order)* **to lack ~** manquer de méthode. **2** *adj (Comput)* **~ disk** disque *m* système. ◆ **systematic** *adj* systématique. ◆ **systematically** *adv* systématiquement. ◆ **systematization** *n* systématisation *f.* ◆ **systematize** *vt* systématiser. ◆ **systemic** *adj (gen)* du système ; *insecticide* systémique. ◆ **systems analyst** *n* analyste *mf* fonctionnel(le).

T

T, t [tiː] *n (letter)* T, t *m*. *(fig)* **that's it to a T** * c'est exactement ça; **it fits him to a T** * ça lui va comme un gant. ◆ **T-bone (steak)** *n* steak *m* avec un os en T. ◆ **T-junction** *n* intersection *f* en T. ◆ **T-shirt** *n* T-shirt *m*. ◆ **T-square** *n* équerre *f* en T.

ta ⁑ [tɑː] *excl* merci!

tab [tæb] *n (part of garment)* patte *f*; *(loop on garment etc)* attache *f*; *(label)* étiquette *f*; *(on shoelace)* ferret *m*; *(marker: on file etc)* onglet *m*; *(US *: café check)* addition *f*. **to keep ~s on** * *person* avoir à l'œil *; *thing* avoir l'œil sur *; *(lit, fig)* **to pick up the ~** * payer l'addition.

tabby ['tæbɪ] *n (~* **cat***)* chat(te) *m(f)* tigré(e).

tabernacle ['tæbənækl] *n* tabernacle *m*.

table ['teɪbl] **1** *n* (**a**) table *f*. **ironing/garden** ~ table à repasser/de jardin; **at** ~ à table; **to sit down to** ~ se mettre à table; **to lay** *or* **set the** ~ mettre la table *or* le couvert; *(fig: drunk)* **he was nearly under the** ~ un peu plus et il roulait sous la table *. (**b**) *[facts, statistics]* table *f (also Math)*; *[prices, names]* liste *f*; *(Sport:* **league** *~)* classement *m*. ~ **of contents** table des matières; *(Math)* **the two-times** ~ la table de deux.
2 *vt bill, motion etc (Brit: submit)* présenter; *(US: postpone)* ajourner.
3 *adj wine, knife, lamp* de table. *(US)* ~ **cream** crème *f* fraîche liquide. **he has good** ~ **manners** il sait se tenir à table; ~ **napkin** serviette *f* (de table); ~ **salt** sel *m* fin.
◆ **tablecloth** *n* nappe *f*. ◆ **table-cover** *n* tapis *m* de table. ◆ **table d'hôte** **1** *adj* à prix fixe ; **2** *n* repas *m* à prix fixe. ◆ **tableland** *n (Geog)* (haut) plateau *m*. ◆ **tablemat** *n (of linen)* napperon *m*; *(heat-resistant)* dessous-de-plat *m inv*. ◆ **table-runner** *n* chemin *m* de table. ◆ **tablespoon** *n* cuiller *f* de service; *(measurement: ~* **spoonful***)* cuillerée *f* à soupe *(US Culin = 29,5 ml)*. ◆ **table-tennis** **1** *n* ping-pong *m* ; **2** *adj* de ping-pong; **~-tennis player** joueur *m*, -euse *f* de ping-pong. ◆ **tabletop** *n* dessus *m* de table. ◆ **table-turning** *n* spiritisme *m* par les tables tournantes. ◆ **tableware** *n* vaisselle *f*.

tableau, *pl* **-x** ['tæbləʊ,əʊz] *n*, *(Theat)* tableau *m* vivant; *(fig)* tableau.

tablet ['tæblɪt] *n (stone: inscribed)* plaque *f* commémorative; *(of wax, slate etc)* tablette *f*; *(Pharm)* comprimé *m*; *(for sucking)* pastille *f*; *[chocolate]* tablette. ~ **of soap** savonnette *f*.

tabloid ['tæblɔɪd] *n (newspaper)* tabloïd *m*.

taboo, tabu [tə'buː] *adj*, *n* tabou *(m)*.

tabular ['tæbjʊləʳ] *adj* tabulaire. ◆ **tabulate** *vt (gen)* mettre sous forme de table; *results etc* classifier; *(Typing)* mettre en colonnes. ◆ **tabulator** *n [typewriter]* tabulateur *m*.

tachograph ['tækəgrɑːf] *n* tachygraphe *m*.

tacit ['tæsɪt] *adj* tacite. ◆ **tacitly** *adv* tacitement.

taciturn ['tæsɪtɜːn] *adj* taciturne. ◆ **taciturnity** *n* taciturnité *f*.

tack [tæk] **1** *n* (**a**) *(for wood, lino, carpets etc)* broquette *f*; *(for upholstery)* semence *f*; *(US:* **thumb** *~)* punaise *f*. (**b**) *(Sewing)* point *m* de bâti. (**c**) *(Naut)* bord *m*. **to make a** ~ tirer un bord; **on a starboard** ~ tribord amures; *(fig)* **on the wrong** ~ sur la mauvaise voie; *(fig)* **to try another** ~ essayer une autre tactique. (**d**) *(for horse)* sellerie *f (articles)*. **2** *vt (Sewing)* bâtir. **3** *vi (make a ~)* tirer un bord. **to** ~ **along** avancer en tirant des bords.
◆ **tack on** *vt sep wood, lino* clouer; *(Sewing)* bâtir; *(fig)* ajouter après coup *(to* à).
◆ **tacking** *n (~***ing stitches***)* points *mpl* de bâti.
◆ **tackroom** *n* sellerie *f (endroit)*.

tackle ['tækl] **1** *n* (**a**) *(esp Naut: ropes, pulleys)* appareil *m* de levage; *(gen: gear)* équipement *m*. **fishing** ~ matériel *m* de pêche. (**b**) *(Ftbl etc)* tac(k)le *m*; *(US Ftbl: player)* plaqueur *m*. **2** *vt (Ftbl etc)* tac(k)ler; *thief, intruder* saisir (à bras le corps); *task, problem* s'attaquer à; *question, subject* aborder; (*) *meal, food* attaquer *. **I'll** ~ **him about it** je vais lui en parler; **I ~d him about what he had done** je l'ai questionné sur ce qu'il avait fait.

tacky ['tækɪ] *adj glue* qui commence à prendre; *paint* pas tout à fait sec; *surface* poisseux.

taco, *pl* **-os** ['tɑːkəʊ] *n (US) crêpe de maïs farcie servie chaude.*

tact [tækt] *n* tact *m*. ◆ **tactful** *adj person, answer* plein de tact; *hint, inquiry, reference* discret (*f* -ète); **to be ~ful with sb** agir envers qn avec tact; **you could have been a bit more ~ful** tu aurais pu avoir un peu plus de tact. ◆ **tactfully** *adv* avec tact. ◆ **tactless** *adj person, answer* qui manque de tact; *hint* grossier; *inquiry, reference* indiscret. ◆ **tactlessly** *adv* sans tact.

tactic ['tæktɪk] *n* tactique *f*. **~s** la tactique. ◆ **tactical** *adj (gen)* tactique; *error etc* de tactique. ◆ **tactically** *adv* du point de vue tactique. ◆ **tactician** *n* tacticien *m*, -ienne *f*.

tadpole ['tædpəʊl] *n* têtard *m*.

taffeta ['tæfɪtə] *n* taffetas *m*.

tag [tæg] **1** *n* (**a**) *[shoelace, cord etc]* ferret *m*; *(on garment etc: loop)* attache *f*; *(label)* étiquette *f*; *(marker: on file etc)* onglet *m*. (**b**) *(quotation)* citation *f*; *(cliché)* cliché *m*; *(catchword)* slogan *m*. **question** ~ queue *f* de phrase interrogative; ~ **(question)** question-tag *f*. (**c**) *(game)* (jeu *m* du) chat *m*. **2** *vt* (**a**) *(label)* étiqueter. (**b**) *(*: follow)* suivre; *[detective]* filer. ◆ **tag along** *vi* suivre le mouvement *. **to** ~ **along behind sb** traîner derrière qn; **to** ~ **along with sb** venir (*or* aller) avec qn.

tail [teɪl] **1** *n (gen)* queue *f*; *[shirt]* pan *m*; *[coin]* pile *f*. *(Dress)* **~s** * queue de pie; **heads or ~s** pile ou face; **long-~ed** à la queue longue; *(fig)* **with his** ~ **between his legs** la queue entre les jambes; **he was right on my** ~ il me suivait de très près; *(fig: have followed)* **to put a** ~ **on sb** * faire filer qn. **2** *adj*: ~ **coat** habit *m*; ~ **end** *(gen)* bout *m*; *[procession etc]* queue *f*; *[storm, debate]* toutes dernières minutes *fpl*; *(Aut, Rail etc)* ~ **lamp** *or* **light** feu *m* arrière *inv*. **3** *vt* (*) *suspect etc* suivre, filer. ◆ **tail away, tail off** *vi [sounds]* se taire peu à peu; *[interest, numbers]* diminuer petit à petit. ◆ **tailback** *n (Aut)* bouchon *m*. ◆ **tailboard** *or* ◆ **tailgate** *n (Aut)* hayon *m* arrière. ◆ **tailspin** *n (Aviat)* vrille *f*. ◆ **tailwind** *n* vent *m* arrière *inv*.

tailor ['teɪləʳ] **1** *n* tailleur *m*. **~'s chalk** craie *f* de tailleur; **~'s dummy** mannequin *m*. **2** *vt garment* façonner; *(fig) speech, book* adapter *(to, to suit* à; *for* pour). **a ~ed skirt** une jupe ajustée. ◆ **tailor-made** *adj garment* fait sur mesure; *(fig) building* fonctionnalisé *(for* pour); *lesson* préparé spécialement (*for* pour); **the job was ~-made for him** le poste était fait pour lui.

taint [teɪnt] *vt (gen)* polluer; *meat, food* gâter; *(fig) reputation* porter tache à. ◆ **tainted** *adj* pollué; gâté; entaché; *action* impur; *money* mal acquis.

Taiwan ['taɪ'wɑːn] *n* Taiwan *(no article)*.

take [teɪk] *(vb: pret* **took,** *ptp* **taken)** **1** *n (Cine, Phot)* prise *f* de vues; *(Sound recording)* enregistrement *m; (US Comm: takings)* recette *f.*

2 *vt* (**a**) *(gen)* prendre (*from sth* dans qch; *from sb* à qn); *prize, degree* avoir, obtenir; *a bet* accepter. **to ~ sb's hand** prendre la main de qn; **to ~ sb by the throat** saisir qn à la gorge; **to ~ sth from one's pocket** prendre qch dans *or* tirer qch de sa poche; **I took these statistics from...** j'ai tiré ces statistiques de...; *(Math)* **~ 6 from 9** 9 moins 6; **he took 10 francs off the price** il a rabattu 10 F sur le prix; **he must be ~n alive** il faut le prendre *or* le capturer vivant; *(Cards)* **to ~ a trick** faire une levée; **my ace took his king** j'ai pris son roi avec mon as; **the grocer ~s about £500 per day** l'épicier se fait à peu près 500 livres de recette par jour; **you'll have to ~ your** *or* **a chance** il va falloir que tu prennes le risque; **to ~ sth upon o.s.** prendre qch sur soi; **to ~ it upon o.s. to do** prendre sur soi de faire; *(Med)* **to ~ cold** prendre froid; **to be ~n ill** tomber malade; **to ~ fright** prendre peur; **he took no food for 4 days** il n'a rien mangé *or* pris pendant 4 jours; **how much alcohol has he ~n?** combien d'alcool a-t-il bu?; **I can't ~ alcohol** je ne supporte pas l'alcool; **to ~ one's seat** s'asseoir; **is this seat ~n?** cette place est-elle prise *or* occupée?; **to ~ the train** prendre le train; **~ the first on the left** prenez la première à gauche; **the bus ~s 60 passengers** l'autobus a une capacité de 60 places; **the hall will ~ 200 people** la salle contient jusqu'à 200 personnes; **he won't ~ less than £50 for it** il en demande au moins 50 livres; **~ it from me!** croyez-moi!; **~ it or leave it** c'est à prendre ou à laisser; **I can ~ it or leave it *** j'aime ça mais sans plus; **how did he ~ the news?** comment a-t-il réagi en apprenant la nouvelle?; **she took his death quite well/very badly** elle s'est montrée très calme/a été très affectée en apprenant sa mort; **you must ~ us as you find us** vous devez nous prendre comme nous sommes; **to ~ things as they come/are** prendre les choses comme elles viennent/sont; *(handing over task etc)* **will you ~ it from here?** pouvez-vous prendre la suite?

(**b**) *(require)* prendre, demander; *(Gram)* être suivi de. **the journey ~s 5 days** le voyage prend *or* demande 5 jours; **it took me 2 hours to do it, I took 2 hours to do it** j'ai mis 2 heures à le faire; **~ your time!** prenez votre temps!; **that ~s courage** cela demande du courage; **it ~s a brave man to do that** il faut être courageux pour faire cela; **it ~s some doing *** cela n'est pas facile (à faire); **it ~s some believing *** c'est à peine croyable; **it took 3 policemen to hold him down** il a fallu 3 gendarmes pour le tenir; **he has got what it ~s to do the job** il est à la hauteur.

(**c**) *(carry) child, object* porter, apporter, emporter; *one's gloves, umbrella* prendre; *(lead)* emmener, conduire; *(accompany)* accompagner. **he took her some flowers** il lui a apporté des fleurs; **~ his suitcase upstairs** montez sa valise; **he took her to the cinema** il l'a emmenée au cinéma; **they took him over the factory** ils lui ont fait visiter l'usine; **to ~ sb to hospital** transporter qn à l'hôpital; **he took me home in his car** il m'a ramené dans sa voiture; **this road/bus will ~ you to...** cette route/cet autobus vous mènera à...; *(fig)* **what took you to Lille?** qu'est-ce qui vous a fait aller à Lille?

(**d**) *(negotiate) bend* prendre; *hill* grimper; *fence* sauter; *exam, test* se présenter à; *(study) subject* prendre, faire.

(**e**) *(tolerate)* accepter. **he won't ~ no for an answer** il n'acceptera pas un refus; **I can't ~ it any more** je n'en peux plus; **we can ~ it!** on ne se laissera pas abattre!

(**f**) *(assume)* supposer, imaginer. **I ~ it that...** je suppose *or* j'imagine que...; **how old do you ~ him to be?** quel âge lui donnez-vous?; **what do you ~ me for?** pour qui me prenez-vous?; **I took him to be foreign** je le croyais étranger, je l'ai pris pour un étranger; **now ~ Ireland** prenons par exemple l'Irlande; **taking one thing with another...** tout bien considéré...

(**g**) *(refer)* **to ~ a matter to sb** soumettre une affaire à qn.

3 *vi [fire, vaccination, plant etc]* prendre.

◆ **take after** *vt fus* ressembler à, tenir de. ◆ **take along** *vt sep person* emmener; *camera etc* prendre. ◆ **take apart** *vt sep machine, toy* démonter; *(*fig: criticize harshly)* démolir *. ◆ **take aside** *vt sep* prendre à part. ◆ **take away** **1** *vi*: **it ~s away from its value** cela diminue sa valeur. **2** *vt sep* (**a**) *(carry, lead away) object* emporter; *person* emmener. (**b**) *(remove) object* prendre, enlever (*from sb* à qn; *from sth* de qch); *sb's child, wife* enlever (*from sb* à qn). **she took her children away from the school** elle a retiré ses enfants de l'école. (**c**) *(Math)* soustraire, ôter (*from* de). ◆ **take back** *vt sep* (**a**) *gift, promise, one's wife etc* reprendre. **to ~ back a** *or* **one's promise** reprendre sa parole. (**b**) *(return) book, goods* rapporter (*to* à); *(accompany) person* raccompagner (*to* à). *(fig)* **it ~s me back to my childhood** cela me rappelle mon enfance; **that ~s me back!** ça me rappelle de vieux souvenirs! ◆ **take down** *vt sep* (**a**) *vase from shelf etc* descendre (*from, off* de); *trousers* baisser; *picture, poster* enlever. (**b**) *(dismantle) scaffolding* démonter; *building* démolir. (**c**) *(write etc) notes, letter, address* prendre. ◆ **take in** *vt sep* (**a**) *chairs, harvest* rentrer; *person* faire entrer; *lodgers* prendre; *friend* recevoir; *orphan, stray dog* recueillir; *newspaper etc* prendre; *sewing, washing* prendre à domicile. (**b**) *skirt, dress, waistband* reprendre; *knitting* diminuer. (**c**) *(include, cover)* couvrir, inclure. **we cannot ~ in all the cases** nous ne pouvons pas couvrir *or* inclure tous les cas; *(fig)* **we took in Venice on the way home** nous avons visité Venise sur le chemin du retour. (**d**) *(grasp, understand)* saisir, comprendre. **the children were taking it all in** les enfants étaient tout oreilles; **he hadn't fully ~n in that she was dead** il n'avait pas vraiment réalisé * qu'elle était morte; **he took in the situation at a glance** il a apprécié la situation en un clin d'œil. (**e**) *(*: cheat, deceive)* avoir *, rouler *. **he's easily ~n in** il se fait facilement avoir *; **to be ~n in by appearances/a disguise** se laisser prendre aux apparences/à un déguisement. ◆ **take off** **1** *vi [person]* partir (*for* pour); *[aircraft]* décoller; *(head for)* s'envoler (*for* pour); *[high jumper etc]* s'élancer. **2** *vt sep* (**a**) *(remove) garment, price tag, lid* enlever; *telephone receiver* décrocher; *item on menu, train* supprimer. *(Med)* **they had to ~ his leg off** on a dû l'amputer d'une jambe; *(Comm)* **he took £5 off** il a fait un rabais de 5 livres. (**b**) *(lead etc away) person* emmener; *object* emporter. **he took her off to lunch** il l'a emmenée déjeuner; **to ~ sb off to jail** emmener qn en prison; **he was ~n off to hospital** on l'a transporté à l'hôpital; **to ~ o.s. off** s'en aller. (**c**) *(imitate)* imiter. ◆ **take on** **1** *vi* (**a**) *[song, fashion etc]* prendre, marcher *. (**b**) *(*: be upset)* s'en faire *. **2** *vt sep* (**a**) *work, responsibility, bet* accepter; *challenger (for game/fight)* accepter de jouer/de se battre contre; *enemy* s'attaquer à. **I'll ~ you on** *(Betting)* je parie avec vous; *(Sport)* je joue contre vous; **he has ~n on more than he bargained for** il n'avait pas compté prendre une si lourde responsabilité. (**b**) *employee*

prendre; *cargo, passenger* embarquer; *form, qualities* revêtir.

◆**take out** *vt sep* (**a**) *(lead, carry outside) prisoner* faire sortir; *chair, dog, children etc* sortir. **he took her out to lunch/the theatre** il l'a emmenée déjeuner/au théâtre; **he has often ~n her out** il l'a souvent sortie. (**b**) *(from pocket, drawer)* prendre (*from, of* dans); *(remove)* sortir, enlever (*from, of* de); *tooth* arracher; *appendix, tonsils* enlever; *stain* ôter, enlever (*from* de). *(fig)* **that will ~ you out of yourself** cela vous changera les idées; *(fig)* **that ~s it out of you** * ces choses-là fatiguent beaucoup; **to ~ it out on sb** s'en prendre à qn. (**c**) *insurance policy, patent* prendre; *licence* se procurer. ◆**take over 1** *vi [dictator, political party etc]* prendre le pouvoir. **to ~ over from sb** prendre la relève de qn; **let him ~ over** cédez-lui la place. **2** *vt sep* (**a**) *(assume responsibility for) business, goods etc* reprendre; *new car* prendre livraison de; *sb's debts* prendre à sa charge. **to ~ a job over from sb** remplacer qn à un poste. (**b**) *(Fin) another company* absorber. *(fig)* **the tourists have ~n over Venice** les touristes ont envahi Venise. ◆**take to** *vt fus* (**a**) *(conceive liking for) person* se prendre d'amitié pour, sympathiser avec; *game, action, study* prendre goût à. **I didn't ~ to the idea** l'idée me disait rien. (**b**) *(start, adopt) habit* prendre; *hobby* se mettre à. **to ~ to drink/drugs** se mettre à boire/à se droguer; **she took to saying...** elle s'est mise à dire... (**c**) **to ~ to one's bed** s'aliter; **to ~ to the woods** *[walker]* passer par les bois; *[hunted man]* s'enfuir à travers bois; **to ~ to the boats** abandonner le navire. ◆**take up 1** *vi*: **to ~ up with sb** se lier avec qn. **2** *vt sep* (**a**) *(lead, carry upstairs, uphill etc) person* faire monter; *object* monter. (**b**) *(lift) object from ground etc* ramasser; *carpet* enlever; *roadway, pavement* dépaver; *hem, skirt* raccourcir; *passenger* prendre; *(fig: after interruption) one's work, conversation, book etc* reprendre. (**c**) *(occupy) space, attention* occuper; *time* prendre. **he's very ~n up** il est très pris; **he's quite ~n up with her/with his plan** il ne pense plus qu'à elle/qu'à son projet. (**d**) *(absorb) liquids* absorber. (**e**) *(raise question of) subject* aborder. **I'll ~ that up with him** je lui en parlerai. (**f**) *(start doing etc) hobby, sport etc* se mettre à; *career* embrasser; *method* adopter; *challenge* relever; *shares* souscrire à; *person* adopter. *(fig)* **I'll ~ you up on your promise** je me souviendrai de votre promesse. (**g**) *(understand)* comprendre. **you've ~n me up wrongly** vous m'avez mal compris.

◆**takeaway 1** *n* café *m* qui fait des plats à emporter ; **2** *adj food, meal* à emporter. ◆**take-home pay** *n* salaire *m* net. ◆**taken** *adj seat* pris, occupé; *(fig)* **to be very ~n with sb/sth** être très impressionné par qn/qch; **I'm not very ~n** *with him* il ne m'a pas fait une grosse impression; **I'm quite ~n with** *or* **by that idea** cette idée me plaît énormément. ◆**takeoff** *n* (**a**) *(Aviat)* décollage *m*; *(fig)* démarrage *m*; (**b**) *(imitation)* pastiche *m*. ◆**take-over 1** *n (Pol)* prise *f* de pouvoir; *(Fin)* rachat *m* ; **2** *adj*: **~over bid** offre *f* publique d'achat. ◆**taker** *n*: **drug- ~rs** les drogués *mpl*; **at £5 he found no ~rs** il n'a pas trouvé de preneurs pour 5 livres. ◆**taking 1** *adj person, manners* engageant, attirant ; **2** *n (Mil: capture)* prise *f*. ◆**takings** *npl (Comm)* recette *f*.

talc [tælk], **talcum (powder)** ['tælkəm(,paʊdə^r)] *n* talc *m*.

tale [teɪl] *n (gen)* histoire *f*; *(story)* conte *m*; *(legend)* légende *f*; *(account)* récit *m*. **'T~s of King Arthur'** 'La Légende du Roi Arthur'; **he told us the ~ of his adventures** il nous a fait le récit de ses aventures; **I've been hearing ~s about you** on m'a raconté des choses sur vous; **to tell ~s** rapporter, cafarder *; *(fig)* **to tell ~s out of school** raconter ce qu'on devait taire. ◆**talebearer** *n* rapporteur *m*, -euse *f*. ◆**talebearing** *or* ◆**taletelling** *n* rapportage *m*.

talent ['tælənt] **1** *n* talent *m*. **to have a ~ for drawing** être doué pour le dessin; **he is looking for ~ amongst the schoolboy players** il cherche de futurs grands joueurs parmi les lycéens. **2** *adj*: **~ scout** *or* **spotter** *(Theat/Sport)* dénicheur *m*, -euse *f* de vedettes/de futurs grands joueurs. ◆**talented** *adj person* doué; *book, painting etc* plein de talent.

talisman ['tælɪzmən] *n* talisman *m*.

talk [tɔ:k] **1** *n* (**a**) conversation *f*, discussion *f*; *(more formal)* entretien *m*; *(chat)* causerie *f*. **we've had several ~s about this** nous en avons parlé *or* discuté plusieurs fois; **I must have a ~ with him** il faut que je lui parle. (**b**) *(informal lecture)* exposé *m* (*on* sur); *(less academic)* causerie *f* (*on* sur). **to give a ~** faire un exposé, donner une causerie; **he will give us a ~ on...** il va nous parler de...; **to give a ~ on the radio** parler à la radio. (**c**) propos *mpl*; *(gossip)* bavardages *mpl*; *(pej)* racontars *mpl*. **the ~ was all about the wedding** les propos tournaient autour du mariage; **there is some ~ of his returning** *(being discussed)* il est question qu'il revienne; *(being rumoured)* on dit qu'il va peut-être revenir; **it's common ~ that...** on dit partout que...; **it's just ~** ce ne sont que des racontars; **there has been a lot of ~ about her** il a beaucoup été question d'elle, on a raconté beaucoup d'histoires sur elle *(pej)*; **I've heard a lot of ~ about the factory** j'ai beaucoup entendu parler de l'usine; **all that ~ about what he was going to do!** tous ces beaux discours sur ce qu'il allait faire!; *(pej)* **he's all ~** c'est un hâbleur; **she's the ~ of the town** on ne parle que d'elle.

2 *adj (Rad/TV)* **~ show** entretien *m* (radiodiffusé/télévisé).

3 *vi* (**a**) *(speak)* parler (*to sb* à qn; *with sb* avec qn; *about, of sth* de qch); *(chatter)* bavarder (*with* avec); *(converse)* discuter (*to, with* avec); *(more formally)* s'entretenir (*to, with* avec). **to ~ to o.s.** se parler tout seul; **the Foreign Ministers ~ed about...** les ministres des Affaires étrangères se sont entretenus de...; **try to keep him ~ing** essaie de le faire parler aussi longtemps que possible; **to get o.s. ~ed about** faire parler de soi; **now you're ~ing!** * voilà qui devient intéressant!; **it's all right for him to ~** il peut parler; **look who's ~ing!** * tu peux toujours parler, toi! *; **he ~s too much** il parle trop, *(indiscreet)* il ne sait pas se taire; **don't ~ to me like that!** ne me parle pas sur ce ton!; **he knows what he's ~ing about when he's on the subject of cars** il s'y connaît quand il parle de voitures; **he doesn't know what he's ~ing about** il ne sait pas ce qu'il dit; **he was ~ing of going to Greece** il parlait d'aller en Grèce; *(fig)* **it's not as if we're talking about...** ce n'est pas comme s'il s'agissait de...; **I'm not ~ing to him any more** je ne lui adresse plus la parole; **~ing of films, have you seen...?** à propos de films, avez-vous vu...?; **~ about a stroke of luck!** * tu parles d'une aubaine! *; **who were you ~ing to?** à qui parlais-tu?; **I saw them ~ing (to each other)** je les ai vus en conversation l'un avec l'autre.

4 *vt a language, slang* parler. **to ~ business/politics** parler affaires/politique; **to ~ sb into doing sth** persuader qn de faire qch *(à force de paroles)*; **to ~ sb out of doing** dissuader qn de faire (en lui parlant).

◆**talk down 1** *vi*: **to ~ down to sb** parler à qn comme à un enfant. **2** *vt sep (Aviat) pilot, aircraft* aider à atterrir par radio-contrôle. ◆**talk over** *vt sep* discuter de. **I must ~ it over with my wife** je dois en parler à ma femme. ◆**talk up** *(US)* **1** *vi (speak frankly)* ne pas mâcher ses mots. **2** *vt fus project* pousser, vanter.

◆**talkative** *adj* bavard, volubile. ◆**talkativeness** *n* volubilité *f*. ◆**talker** *n* causeur *m*, -euse *f*; *(pej)* bavard(e) *m(f)*. ◆ **talkie** * *n (Cine)* film *m* parlant; **the ~ies** le cinéma parlant. ◆ **talking 1** *n* bavardage *m*; **he did all the ~ing** il a fait tous les frais de la conversation; **'no ~ ing'** 'silence s'il vous plaît' ; **2** *adj doll, parrot, film* parlant; **~ing book** livre *m* enregistré; **~ing point** sujet *m* de conversation; **~ing shop** * parlot(t)e *f*. ◆ **talking-to** * *n*: **to give sb a good ~ing-to** passer un bon savon à qn *.

tall [tɔːl] *adj person* grand, de haute taille; *building etc* haut, élevé. **how ~ is that mast?** quelle est la hauteur de ce mât?; **how ~ are you?** combien mesurez-vous?; **he is 6 feet ~** ≃ il mesure 1 mètre 80; *(fig)* **a ~ story** une histoire à dormir debout; **that's a ~ order!** c'est demander un peu trop! ◆ **tallboy** *n* commode *f*. ◆ **tallness** *n* grande taille *f*; hauteur *f*.

tally ['tælɪ] **1** *n* compte *m*. **to keep a ~ of** *(count)* tenir le compte de; *(mark off on list)* pointer. **2** *vi* correspondre (*with* à).

talon ['tælən] *n [bird]* serre *f*; *[tiger etc]* griffe *f*.

tamarisk ['tæmərɪsk] *n* tamaris *m*.

tambourine [ˌtæmbə'riːn] *n* tambourin *m*.

tame [teɪm] **1** *adj bird, animal* apprivoisé; *(fig) story, match* insipide. **to become** *or* **grow ~(r)** s'apprivoiser; *(hum)* **our ~ American** notre Américain de service. **2** *vt bird, wild animal* apprivoiser; *esp lion, tiger* dompter; *(fig) passion* maîtriser; *person* mater. ◆ **tamely** *adv agree* docilement. ◆ **tamer** *n* dresseur *m*, -euse *f*; **lion-~r** dompteur *m*, -euse *f* (de lions).

tamper ['tæmpəʳ] *vi*: **to ~ with** *(gen)* toucher à *(sans permission)*; *lock* essayer de crocheter; *document, text, (Jur) evidence* falsifier; *(US) jury* soudoyer.

tampon ['tæmpən] *n (Med)* tampon *m*.

tan [tæn] **1** *n* **(sun~)** bronzage *m*. **she's got a lovely ~** elle est bien bronzée. **2** *adj* brun roux *inv*. **3** *vt* (**a**) *hides* tanner. *(fig)* **to ~ sb's hide** * rosser qn *. (**b**) *[sun] sunbather* bronzer; *sailor, farmer etc* basaner. **to get ~ned = to tan** *(V* **4***)*. **4** *vi* bronzer. ◆ **tanned** *adj* **(sun ~ned)** bronzé; basané. ◆ **tanner** *n* tanneur *m*. ◆ **tannery** *n* tannerie *f (établissement)*. ◆ **tanning** *n [hides]* tannage *m*; *(* ⁑ *fig: beating)* tannée ⁑ *f*; *(suntanning)* bronzage *m*.

tang [tæŋ] *n (taste)* saveur *f* forte et piquante; *(smell)* odeur *f* forte et piquante.

tangent ['tæn(d)ʒ(ə)nt] *n (Math)* tangente *f*. *(fig)* **to fly off at a ~** partir dans une digression.

tangerine [ˌtæn(d)ʒə'riːn] **1** *n* mandarine *f*. **2** *adj (colour)* mandarine *inv*.

tangible ['tæn(d)ʒəbl] *adj (gen)* tangible; *assets* matériel, réel. ◆ **tangibly** *adv* tangiblement.

tangle ['tæŋgl] **1** *n [wool, rope, bushes]* enchevêtrement *m*; *(fig: muddle)* confusion *f*. **to get into a ~** *(gen)* s'enchevêtrer; *[hair]* s'emmêler; *(fig) [accounts etc]* s'embrouiller; *[traffic]* se bloquer; *[person]* s'embrouiller; **the whole affair was a hopeless ~** toute cette histoire était affreusement embrouillée. **2** *vt (~* **up**: *lit, fig)* enchevêtrer, embrouiller. **~d** *string, rope, wool* embrouillé, enchevêtré; *hair* emmêlé, enchevêtré; **to get ~d (up) = to get into a tangle** *(V* **1***)*. **3** *vi (* fig)* **to ~ with sb** se colleter avec qn *.

tank [tæŋk] *n* (**a**) *(container) (for storage: for gas, petrol etc)* réservoir *m*; *(esp for rainwater)* citerne *f*; *(for transporting)* réservoir, cuve *f*; *(esp oil)* tank *m*; *(for fermenting, processing etc)* cuve *(also Phot)*; *(for fish)* aquarium *m*. **fuel ~** réservoir à carburant. (**b**) *(Mil)* char *m* (de combat), tank *m*. ◆ **tank up** * *vi (Aut)* faire le plein. ◆ **tanker** *n (truck)* camion-citerne *m*; *(ship)* pétrolier *m*; *(aircraft)* avion-ravitailleur *m*; *(Rail)* wagon-citerne *m*. ◆ **tankful** *n*: **a ~ful of petrol** un réservoir (plein) d'essence; **a ~ful of water** une citerne (pleine) d'eau. ◆ **tank top** *n* débardeur *m (vêtement)*.

tankard ['tæŋkəd] *n* chope *f* (à bière).

tannoy ['tænɔɪ] *n* ®: **over the ~** par les haut-parleurs.

tantalize ['tæntəlaɪz] *vt* tourmenter *(par de faux espoirs)*. ◆ **tantalizing** *adj (gen)* terriblement tentant; *smell* terriblement appétissant; *slowness etc* désespérant. ◆ **tantalizingly** *adv* d'une façon cruellement tentante; **tantalizingly slowly** avec une lenteur désespérante.

tantamount ['tæntəmaʊnt] *adj*: **~ to** équivalent à.

tantrum ['tæntrəm] *n* **(temper ~)** crise *f* de colère. **to have** *or* **throw a ~** piquer une colère.

Tanzania [tænzə'nɪə] *n* Tanzanie *f*. ◆ **Tanzanian 1** *adj* tanzanien ; **2** *n* Tanzanien(ne) *m(f)*.

Taoism ['tɑːəʊɪz(ə)m] *n* taoïsme *n*. ◆ **Taoist** *adj, n* taoïste *(mf)*.

tap¹ [tæp] **1** *n (Brit)* robinet *m*. **beer on ~** bière *f* en fût; *(fig)* **funds/resources on ~** fonds *mpl*/ressources *fpl* disponibles. **2** *adj*: *(Brit)* **~ water** eau *f* du robinet. **3** *vt cask, barrel* mettre en perce; *pine* gemmer; *other tree* inciser; *(Elec) current* capter; *wire* brancher; *telephone* mettre sur écoute; *(fig) resources, supplies* exploiter. **my phone is being ~ped** mon téléphone est sur écoute; **they ~ped her for a loan** * ils lui ont demandé un prêt; **to ~ sb for information** soutirer des renseignements à qn. ◆ **taproom** *n* salle *f* de bistrot. ◆ **taproot** *n (Bot)* racine *f* pivotante.

tap² [tæp] **1** *n* petit coup *m*. **there was a ~ at the door** on a frappé doucement à la porte. **2** *vi* frapper doucement. **3** *vt (knock)* frapper doucement; *(pat)* tapoter. **he ~ped me on the shoulder** il m'a tapé sur l'épaule; **to ~ out a message in Morse** transmettre un message en morse. ◆ **tap-dance 1** *n* claquettes *fpl* ; **2** *vi* faire des claquettes. ◆ **tapdancer** *n* danseur *m*, -euse *f* de claquettes.

tape [teɪp] **1** *n (gen)* ruban *m*, bande *f*; *(Sewing: decoration)* ruban, ganse *f*; *(Sewing: for binding)* extra-fort *m*; *(for parcels)* bolduc *m*; *(sticky ~)* ruban *m* adhésif; *(Med)* sparadrap *m*; *(for recording)* bande magnétique; *(cassette ~, video ~)* cassette *f*; *(Sport)* fil *m* d'arrivée; *(at opening ceremonies)* ruban. **the message was coming through on the ~** le message nous parvenait sur bande (perforée). **2** *adj*: **~ deck** platine *f* de magnétophone; *(Brit)* **~ machine** téléscripteur *m*; **~ measure** mètre *m* ruban. **3** *vt* (**a**) **(~ up)** *parcel etc* attacher avec du ruban *or* du bolduc; *(with sticky ~)* coller avec du scotch; **(~ up, ~ together)** *broken vase etc* recoller avec du scotch *etc*. *(Brit fig)* **I've got him/it all ~d** * je sais parfaitement ce qu'il vaut/de quoi il retourne *; **they had the game/situation ~d** * ils avaient le jeu/la situation bien en main. (**b**) *(record) song, message, video material* enregistrer. ◆ **tape-record** *vt* enregistrer. ◆ **tape-recorder** *n* magnétophone *m*. ◆ **tape-recording** *n* enregistrement *m* (au magnétophone). ◆ **tapeworm** *n* ténia *m*, ver *m* solitaire.

taper ['teɪpəʳ] **1** *n (for lighting)* bougie *f* fine; *(Rel: narrow candle)* cierge *m*. **2** *vt table leg, trouser leg* fuseler; *hair* effiler; *structure, shape* terminer en pointe. ◆ **taper off** *vi [sound, storm]* aller en diminuant; *[speech, conversation]* s'effilocher. ◆ **tapered** *or* ◆ **tapering** *adj column, fingers* fuselé; *structure etc* en pointe.

tapestry ['tæpɪstrɪ] *n* tapisserie *f*.

tapioca [ˌtæpɪ'əʊkə] *n* tapioca *m*.

tar [tɑːʳ] **1** *n* goudron *m*. **2** *vt* goudronner. ◆ **tarring** *n* goudronnage *m*. ◆ **tarry** *adj substance* goudronneux; *(tarstained)* plein de goudron.

tarantula [tə'ræntjʊlə] *n* tarentule *f*.

tardy ['tɑːdɪ] *adj* tardif.

target ['tɑːgɪt] **1** *n (gen; also fig: of criticism etc)* cible *f*; *(Mil: in attack; fig: objective)* objectif *m*. **to be on**

~ *[missile etc]* suivre la trajectoire prévue; *[remark, criticism]* mettre en plein dans le mille; *(in timing etc)* ne pas avoir de retard; **dead on** ~! pile!; **to set o.s. a** ~ **of £100** se fixer comme objectif de réunir 100 livres. **2** *adj date, amount etc* fixé, prévu. ~ **group** groupe *m* cible; ~ **practice** exercices *mpl* de tir. **3** *vt* (**a**) *(Mil etc) enemy* viser; *missile* pointer. (**b**) *(Advertising)* cibler.

tariff ['tærɪf] *n (tax)* tarif *m* douanier; *(price list)* tarif. ~ **barrier** barrière *f* douanière.

tarmac ['tɑːmæk]® **1** *n (substance)* macadam *m* goudronné; *(runway)* piste *f*; *(airport apron)* aire *f* d'envol. **2** *vt* goudronner.

tarnish ['tɑːnɪʃ] **1** *vt (gen)* ternir; *mirror* désargenter. **2** *vi* se ternir; se désargenter.

tarot ['tærəʊ] *n* : **the** ~ le(s) tarot(s). ~ **card** tarot.

tarpaulin [tɑː'pɔːlɪn] *n (material)* toile *f* goudronnée; *(sheet)* bâche *f* (goudronnée).

tarragon ['tærəgən] *n* estragon *m*.

tart[1] [tɑːt] *adj (gen)* âpre; *answer etc* acerbe. ◆ **tartly** *adv* d'une manière acerbe. ◆ **tartness** *n* aigreur *f*.

tart[2] [tɑːt] *n* (**a**) *(Culin)* tarte *f*; *(small)* tartelette *f*. **apple** ~ tarte(lette) aux pommes. (**b**) (*‡: prostitute)* poule ‡ *f*, putain ‡ *f*. ◆ **tart up** ‡ *vt sep* retaper *.

tartan ['tɑːtən] **1** *n* tartan *m*. **2** *adj garment* écossais. ~ **rug** plaid *m*.

tartar[1] ['tɑːtər] *n (Chem etc)* tartre *m*. ◆ **tartaric** *adj* tartrique.

tartar[2] ['tɑːtər] **1** *n* homme *m* intraitable; *(woman)* mégère *f*. **2** *adj (Culin)* tartare.

task [tɑːsk] **1** *n* tâche *f*. **a hard** ~ une lourde tâche; **to take sb to** ~ prendre qn à partie *(for, about* pour). **2** *vt brain, patience* mettre à l'épreuve. **it didn't** ~ **him too much** cela ne lui a pas demandé trop d'effort. **3** *adj* ~ **force** *(Mil)* corps *m* expéditionnaire; *(Police)* détachement *m* spécial. ◆ **taskmaster** *n*: **a hard** ~**master** un véritable tyran.

Tasmania [tæz'meɪnɪə] *n* Tasmanie *f*. ◆ **Tasmanian** **1** *adj* tasmanien ; **2** *n* Tasmanien(ne) *m(f)*.

tassel ['tæs(ə)l] *n* gland *m (de tapisserie)*.

taste [teɪst] **1** *n* goût *m*. **it has no** ~ cela n'a aucun goût; **it left a bad** ~ cela m'a laissé un goût déplaisant; *(fig)* j'en ai gardé une amertume; *(fig)* **to have (good)** ~ avoir du goût; **he has no** ~ il a très mauvais goût; **in good/bad** ~ de bon/mauvais goût; **would you like a** ~? voulez-vous y goûter?; **I gave him a** ~ **of the wine** je lui ai fait goûter le vin; *(fig)* **it gave him a** ~ **of the work** cela lui a donné un aperçu du travail; **a** ~ **of happiness** une idée du bonheur; *(small amount)* **a** ~ **of** un tout petit peu de; **to be to sb's** ~ plaire à qn; **to have a** ~ **for** avoir du goût *or* un penchant pour; **to acquire a** ~ **for** prendre goût à; *(Culin)* **sweeten to** ~ sucrer à volonté; **there's no accounting for** ~ des goûts et des couleurs on ne discute pas; **each to his own** ~, ~**s differ** chacun son goût; **one's** ~**(s) in music** ses goûts musicaux; **he has expensive** ~**s in cars** il a le goût des voitures de luxe.
2 *vt* (**a**) *(perceive flavour of)* sentir (le goût de). **I can't** ~ **the garlic** je ne sens pas l'ail; **you won't** ~ **it** tu n'en sentiras pas le goût. (**b**) *(sample) food, drink, power, freedom* goûter à; *(esp for first time)* goûter de; *(to test quality) food, drink* goûter; *wine (at table)* goûter; *(at wine-tasting etc)* déguster. ~ **this!** goûtez à ça!; **I have never** ~**d snails** je n'ai jamais mangé d'escargots; **he had not** ~**d food for a week** il n'avait rien mangé depuis une semaine.
3 *vi*: **it doesn't** ~ **at all** cela n'a aucun goût; **to** ~ **bitter** avoir un goût amer; **to** ~ **good/bad** avoir bon/mauvais goût; **to** ~ **of** *or* **like sth** avoir un goût de qch; **it** ~**s all right to me** d'après moi cela a un goût normal.
◆ **tasteful** *adj* de bon goût. ◆ **tastefully** *adv* avec goût. ◆ **tastefulness** *n* bon goût *m*. ◆ **tasteless** *adj food* fade; *medicine* qui n'a aucun goût; *remark, decoration* de mauvais goût. ◆ **tastelessly** *adv* sans goût. ◆ **tastelessness** *n* fadeur *f*; mauvais goût *m*. ◆ **taster** *n* dégustateur *m*, -trice *f*. ◆ **tastiness** *n* saveur *f* agréable. ◆ **tasty** *adj food* savoureux; *titbit* succulent.

ta-ta * [tæ'tɑː] *excl (Brit)* salut! *

tatters ['tætəz] *npl* lambeaux *mpl*. ◆ **tattered** *adj object* en lambeaux; *person* déguenillé.

tattle ['tætl] **1** *vi* cancaner. **2** *n* cancans *mpl*. ◆ **tattler** *n* commère *f (pej)*. ◆ **tattletale** *(US)* **1** *n* commère *f* ; **2** *adj mark etc* révélateur.

tattoo[1] [tə'tuː] **1** *vt* tatouer. **2** *n* tatouage *m*.

tattoo[2] [tə'tuː] *n (Mil: show)* parade *f* militaire.

tatty * ['tætɪ] *adj (gen)* défraîchi; *paint* écaillé; *poster, book* écorné.

taught [tɔːt] *pret, ptp of* **teach.**

taunt [tɔːnt] **1** *n* raillerie *f*. **2** *vt* railler. **to** ~ **sb with cowardice** taxer qn de lâcheté. ◆ **taunting** **1** *adj* railleur ; **2** *n* railleries *fpl*.

Taurus ['tɔːrəs] *n (Astron)* le Taureau.

taut [tɔːt] *adj (lit, fig)* tendu.

tautology [tɔː'tɒlədʒɪ] *n* tautologie *f*. ◆ **tautological** *adj* tautologique.

tavern † ['tævən] *n* taverne † *f*.

tawdry ['tɔːdrɪ] *adj goods* de camelote *, médiocre; *clothes* tapageur; *(fig) motive etc* indigne. ◆ **tawdriness** *n* qualité *f* médiocre.

tawny ['tɔːnɪ] *adj* fauve *(couleur)*.

tax [tæks] **1** *n (on goods, services)* taxe *f*, impôt *m (on* sur); *(income* ~*)* impôts. **before/after** ~ avant/après l'impôt; **half of it goes in** ~ on en perd la moitié en impôts; **how much** ~ **do you pay?** combien d'impôts payez-vous?; **I paid £1,000 in** ~ j'ai payé 1 000 livres d'impôts *or* de contributions; **free of** ~ exempt d'impôt; **to put a** ~ **on sth** taxer *or* imposer qch; **petrol** ~ taxe sur l'essence. **2** *adj incentive, system etc* fiscal. *(Brit Aut)* ~ **disc** vignette *f* automobile; ~ **evasion** fraude *f* fiscale; ~ **exile** personne *f* fuyant le fisc; ~ **form** feuille *f* d'impôts; **for** ~ **purposes** pour des raisons fiscales; ~ **relief** dégrèvement *m or* allègement *m* fiscal; ~ **year** année *f* fiscale. **3** *vt* (**a**) *goods etc* taxer, imposer; *income, profits, person* imposer; *(fig) patience etc* mettre à l'épreuve. (**b**) taxer *(sb with sth* qn de qch). **to** ~ **sb with doing** accuser qn de faire *(or* d'avoir fait). ◆ **taxable** *adj* imposable. ◆ **taxation** **1** *n (act)* taxation *f*; *(taxes)* impôts *mpl*; **2** *adj authority, system* fiscal. ◆ **tax-collector** *n* percepteur *m*. ◆ **tax-deductible** *adj* sujet à dégrèvements (d'impôts). ◆ **tax-free** *adj* exempt d'impôts. ◆ **taxing** *adj* éprouvant. ◆ **taxman** * *n*: **the** ~**man** le percepteur. ◆ **taxpayer** *n* contribuable *mf*.

taxi ['tæksɪ] **1** *n* taxi *m*. **by** ~ en taxi. **2** *adj charges etc* de taxi. **3** *vi* (**a**) *[aircraft]* **to** ~ **along the runway** rouler lentement le long de la piste. (**b**) *(go by* ~*)* aller en taxi. ◆ **taxicab** *n* taxi *m*. ◆ **taxi-driver** *n* chauffeur *m* de taxi. ◆ **taximeter** *n* taximètre *m*. ◆ **taxi-rank** *n* station *f* de taxis.

taxidermy ['tæksɪdɜːmɪ] *n* empaillage *m*, taxidermie *f*. ◆ **taxidermist** *n* empailleur *m*, -euse *f*.

tea [tiː] *n* (**a**) thé *m*. **she made a pot of** ~ elle a fait du thé; **mint** *etc* ~ tisane *f* de menthe *etc*; **beef** ~ bouillon *m* de viande; *(fig)* **not for all the** ~ **in China** pour rien au monde. (**b**) *(meal)* thé *m*; *(for children)* ≃ goûter *m*. **to have** ~ prendre le thé; *[children]* goûter. ◆ **tea-bag** *n* sachet *m* de thé. ◆ **tea-break** *n* pause-thé *f*; **to have a** ~**-break** faire la pause-thé. ◆ **tea-caddy** *n* boîte *f* à thé. ◆ **tea-cake** *n* petit pain *m* brioché. ◆ **tea-chest** *n* caisse *f* (à thé). ◆ **teacloth** *n (for dishes)* torchon *m*; *(for table)* nappe *f*; *(for trolley, tray)* napperon *m*. ◆ **tea-**

cosy *n* couvre-théière *m*. ◆ **teacup** *n* tasse *f* à thé. ◆ **tea-leaf** *n* feuille *f* de thé; **to read the ~-leaves** ≃ lire dans le marc de café. ◆ **tea party** *n* thé *m (réception)*. ◆ **tea-plate** *n* petite assiette. ◆ **teapot** *n* théière *f*. ◆ **tearoom** *n* salon *m* de thé. ◆ **tea-service** *or* ◆ **tea-set** *n* service *m* à thé. ◆ **teashop** *n* pâtisserie-salon de thé *f*. ◆ **teaspoon** *n* petite cuiller *f*. ◆ **teaspoonful** *n* cuillerée *f* à café. ◆ **tea-things** *npl* service *m* à thé; *(dirty dishes)* vaisselle *f* après le thé. ◆ **teatime** *n* l'heure *f* du thé. ◆ **tea-towel** *n* torchon *m* (à vaisselle).

teach [ti:tʃ] *pret, ptp* **taught** **1** *vt (gen)* apprendre (*sb sth, sth to sb* qch à qn); *(Scol, Univ etc)* enseigner (*sb sth, sth to sb* qch à qn). **to ~ sb (how) to do** apprendre à qn à faire; **I'll ~ you what to do** je t'apprendrai ce qu'il faut faire; **he ~es French** il enseigne le français; *(US)* **to ~ school** être professeur (*or* instituteur *etc*); **to ~ o.s. (to do) sth** apprendre (à faire) qch tout seul; *(fig)* **that will ~ him a lesson!** ça lui apprendra!; **that will ~ you to mind your own business!** ça t'apprendra à te mêler de tes affaires!
2 *vi (gen)* enseigner. **he wanted to ~** il voulait enseigner; **he had been ~ing all morning** il avait fait cours toute la matinée.
◆ **teachable** *adj subject* enseignable. ◆ **teacher** *n (gen)* professeur *m*; *(primary school)* instituteur *m*, -trice *f*; *(in special school, prison)* éducateur *m*, -trice *f*; **she is a maths ~er** elle est professeur de maths; **the ~ers accepted the government's offer** les enseignants *mpl* ont accepté l'offre du gouvernement; **~er's handbook** livre *m* du maître; **~er(s') training college** ≃ école *f* normale; **~er training** *or (US)* **education** formation *f* pédagogique; **to get one's ~er training certificate** *(primary)* ≃ sortir de l'école normale; *(secondary)* ≃ avoir son C.A.P.E.S. *etc*. ◆ **teach-in** *n* séance *f* d'études. ◆ **teaching** **1** *n (gen)* enseignement *m* (*on, about* sur); **to go into ~ing** entrer dans l'enseignement ; **2** *adj staff* enseignant; *material* pédagogique; *machine* à enseigner; **~ing hospital** centre *m* hospitalo-universitaire; *(US)* **~ing assistant** étudiant(e) *m(f)* chargé(e) de travaux dirigés; **~ing practice** stage *m* de formation des maîtres; **the ~ing profession** *(teachers collectively)* les enseignants *mpl*.

teak [ti:k] *n* teck *m*.

team [ti:m] **1** *n (gen)* équipe *f*; *[horses, oxen]* attelage *m*. **football/research ~** équipe de football/de chercheurs. **2** *adj*: **~ games/spirit** jeux *mpl*/esprit *m* d'équipe; **~ teaching** enseignement *m* coordonné pour groupes. **3** *vt* **(~ up)** *person* mettre en collaboration (*with* avec); *thing* associer (*with* avec).
◆ **team up** *vi [people]* faire équipe (*with* avec; *to do* pour faire).
◆ **team-mate** *n* coéquipier *m*, -ière *f*. ◆ **team-member** *n* équipier *m*, -ière *f*. ◆ **teamster** *n (US)* camionneur *m* syndiqué. ◆ **teamwork** *n* collaboration *f* (d'équipe).

tear¹ [tɛəʳ] *(vb: pret* **tore**, *ptp* **torn***)* **1** *n* déchirure *f*, accroc *m*. **to make a ~ in sth** déchirer qch; **it has a ~ in it** c'est déchiré. **2** *vt* (**a**) *(gen)* déchirer. **to ~ a hole in** faire une déchirure *or* un accroc à; **to ~ to pieces** *or* **to bits** * *paper* déchirer en menus morceaux; *garment* mettre en lambeaux; *prey* mettre en pièces; *(fig) play etc* éreinter; *argument* démolir; **to ~ open** *envelope* déchirer; *letter* déchirer l'enveloppe de; *parcel* ouvrir en déchirant l'emballage de; **to ~ one's hair** s'arracher les cheveux; *(Méd)* **to ~ a muscle** se déchirer un muscle; *(fig)* **that's torn it!** * voilà qui flanque tout par terre! *; *(fig)* **torn by war/remorse** *etc* déchiré par la guerre/le remords *etc*; **to be torn between...** balancer entre... (**b**) *(snatch)* arracher (*from sb* à qn; *out of, off, from sth* de qch). **3** *vi* (**a**) *[cloth etc]* se déchirer. (**b**) *(rush)* **to ~ out/down** *etc* sortir/descendre *etc* à toute allure.
◆ **tear away** *vt sep (lit, fig)* arracher (*from sb* à qn; *from sth* de qch). *(fig)* **I couldn't ~ myself away** je n'arrivais pas à m'en arracher. ◆ **tear down** *vt sep poster, flag* arracher (*from* de); *building* démolir. ◆ **tear off** *vt sep wrapping* arracher (*from* de); *sth perforated* détacher (*from* de). ◆ **tear out** *vt sep* arracher (*from* de); *cheque, ticket* détacher (*from* de). ◆ **tear up** *vt sep* (**a**) *paper, (fig) contract* déchirer; *offer* reprendre. (**b**) *stake, shrub* arracher.
◆ **tearing** **1** *n* déchirement *m* ; **2** *adj*: **in a ~ing hurry** * terriblement pressé.

tear² [tɪəʳ] *n* larme *f*. **in ~s** en larmes; **there were ~s in her eyes** elle avait les larmes aux yeux; **near** *or* **close to ~s** au bord des larmes; **to burst into ~s** fondre en larmes; **it brought ~s to his eyes** cela lui a fait venir les larmes aux yeux. ◆ **teardrop** *n* larme *f*. ◆ **tearful** *adj (gen)* larmoyant; **she was very ~ful** elle a beaucoup pleuré. ◆ **tearfully** *adv* les larmes aux yeux. ◆ **teargas** *n* gaz *m* lacrymogène. ◆ **tear-stained** *adj* barbouillé de larmes.

tease [ti:z] **1** *vt (playfully)* taquiner; *(cruelly)* tourmenter. **2** *n (person)* taquin(e) *m(f)*. ◆ **teasel** *n (Bot)* cardère *f*. ◆ **teaser** *n* problème *m* (difficile). ◆ **teasing** **1** *n* taquineries *fpl* ; **2** *adj* taquin.

teat [ti:t] *n [animal, bottle etc]* tétine *f*; *[woman]* bout *m* de sein.

technical ['teknɪk(ə)l] *adj (gen)* technique. **~ college** collège *m* (d'enseignement) technique; **~ hitch** incident *m* technique; *(US)* **~ institute** ≃ I.U.T. *m*, institut *m* universitaire de technologie; *(Jur)* **~ offence** contravention *f*; **a ~ point** un point de détail. ◆ **technicality** *n (detail/difficulty/fault)* détail *m*/difficulté *f*/ennui *m* technique; **the ~ities** les détails techniques. ◆ **technically** *adv* techniquement; *(fig)* **~ly we shouldn't be here** en principe on ne devrait pas être là. ◆ **technician** *n* technicien(ne) *m(f)*. ◆ **technique** [tek'ni:k] *n* technique *f*.

technology [tek'nɒlədʒɪ] *n* technologie *f*. **Ministry of T~** ministère *m* des Affaires technologiques; **the new ~** les nouvelles technologies. ◆ **technological** *adj* technologique. ◆ **technologist** *n* technologue *mf*.

teddy ['tedɪ] *n* **(~ bear)** nounours *m (baby talk)*, ours *m* en peluche.

tedious ['ti:dɪəs] *adj* ennuyeux, assommant *. ◆ **tediously** *adv* d'une façon ennuyeuse. ◆ **tediousness** *or* ◆ **tedium** *n* ennui *m*.

tee [ti:] *(Golf)* *n* tee *m*.

teem [ti:m] *vi* (**a**) *[crowds, river, street]* grouiller (*with* de). (**b**) **it was ~ing (with rain), the rain was ~ing down** il pleuvait à verse. ◆ **teeming** *adj* (**a**) *crowd* grouillant; *street* grouillant de monde; *river* grouillant de poissons; (**b**) *rain* battant.

teenage ['ti:neɪdʒ] *adj* adolescent *(de 13 à 19 ans)*; *behaviour* d'adolescent, de jeune; *fashions* pour jeunes. ◆ **teenager** *n* jeune *mf*, adolescent(e) *m(f)*. ◆ **teens** *npl* jeunesse *f*, adolescence *f*; **still in his teens** encore adolescent; **he is in his early teens** il a un peu plus de treize ans.

teeny * ['ti:nɪ] *adj* tout petit.

tee-shirt ['ti:ʃɜ:t] *n* T-shirt *m*.

teeter ['ti:təʳ] *vi [person]* chanceler; *[pile]* vaciller. **to ~ on the edge of** être prêt à tomber dans. ◆ **teeter totter** *n jeu de bascule*.

teeth [ti:θ] *npl of* **tooth**. ◆ **teethe** [ti:ð] *vi* faire ses dents. ◆ **teething** **1** *n* poussée *f* des dents ; **2** *adj*: **~ing ring** anneau *m (de bébé qui fait ses dents)*; *(fig)* **~ing troubles** difficultés *fpl* initiales.

teetotal ['ti:'təʊtl] *adj* qui ne boit jamais d'alcool. ◆ **teetotaller**, *(US)* **teetotaler** *n* personne *f* qui ne boit jamais d'alcool.

Teheran [teə'rɑːn] *n* Téhéran.

Tel Aviv ['telə'viːv] *n* Tel Aviv.

tele... ['telɪ] *pref* télé... ◆ **telecamera** *n* caméra de télévision *f.* ◆ **telecommunications** *npl* télécommunications *fpl.* ◆ **teletext** *n* télétexte *m.*

telegram ['telɪgræm] *n* télégramme *m*; *(Diplomacy, Press)* dépêche *f.*

telegraph ['telɪgrɑːf] **1** *n* télégraphe *m.* ~ **pole** poteau *m* télégraphique. **2** *vti* télégraphier. ◆ **telegraphic** *adj* télégraphique. ◆ **telegraphist** [tə'legrəfɪst] *n* télégraphiste *mf.* ◆ **telegraphy** [tə'legrəfɪ] *n* télégraphie *f.*

telepathy [tɪ'lepəθɪ] *n* télépathie *f.* ◆ **telepathic** [ˌtelɪ'pæθɪk] *adj* télépathique; *(iro)* **I'm not telepathic!** * je ne suis pas devin!

telephone ['telɪfəʊn] **1** *n* téléphone *m.* **on the** ~ au téléphone. **2** *vt person* téléphoner à; *message* téléphoner (*to* à). **3** *vi* téléphoner. **4** *adj*: ~ **book** *or* **directory** annuaire *m*; ~ **booth** *or* **box** *or* **kiosk** cabine *f* téléphonique; ~ **call** coup *m* de téléphone *, appel *m* téléphonique; ~ **exchange** central *m* téléphonique; ~ **line** ligne *f* téléphonique; ~ **message** message *m* téléphonique; ~ **number** numéro *m* de téléphone; ~ **operator** standardiste *mf*, téléphoniste *mf*; ~ **subscriber** abonné(e) *m(f)* au téléphone; ~ **tapping** écoutes *fpl* téléphoniques. ◆ **telephonic** [ˌtelɪ'fɒnɪk] *adj* téléphonique. ◆ **telephonist** [tɪ'lefənɪst] *n* téléphoniste *mf.*

telephoto ['telɪ'fəʊtəʊ] *adj*: ~ **lens** téléobjectif *m.*

teleprint ['telɪˌprɪnt] *vt* transmettre par téléscripteur. ◆ **teleprinter** *n* téléscripteur *m.*

telescope ['telɪskəʊp] **1** *n (reflecting, also Astron)* télescope *m*; *(refracting)* lunette *f* d'approche. **2** *vi [railway carriages etc]* se télescoper; *[umbrella]* se plier. ◆ **telescopic** [ˌtelɪs'kɒpɪk] *adj* télescopique; *umbrella* pliant; **telescopic lens** téléobjectif *m.*

telethon ['teləθɒn] *n (TV)* téléthon *m.*

teletype ['telɪtaɪp] ® **1** *vt* transmettre par télétype ®. **2** *n* télétype *m* ®.

televiewer ['telɪˌvjuːəʳ] *n* téléspectateur *m*, -trice *f.* ◆ **televiewing** *n (watching TV)* la télévision; **this evening's televiewing contains...** le programme de la télévision pour ce soir comprend...

television ['telɪˌvɪʒ(ə)n] **1** *n* télévision *f*; **(~ set)** télévision, téléviseur *m.* **on** ~ à la télévision, à la télé *; **colour** ~ télévision (en) couleur. **2** *adj actor, camera, studio* de télévision; *play, report, serial* télévisé. ~ **programme** émission *f* de télévision. ◆ **televise** *vt* téléviser.

telex ['teleks] **1** *n* télex *m.* ~ **operator** télexiste *mf.* **2** *vt* envoyer par télex.

tell [tel] *pret, ptp* **told** **1** *vt* (**a**) *(gen)* dire (*sb sth* qch à qn; *sb to do* à qn de faire; *that* que); *story, adventure* raconter (*to* à); *a lie, the truth* dire; *secret, sb's age* révéler (*to* à); *the future* prédire. **I told him where/why** je lui ai dit où/pourquoi; **I told him the way to London** je lui ai expliqué comment aller à Londres; **to ~ sb sth again** répéter *or* redire qch à qn; **he's mad, I can ~ you!** il est fou, c'est moi qui te le dis! *; **don't ~ me you've lost it!** tu ne vas pas me dire que tu l'as perdu!; **I told you so!** je te l'avais bien dit!; **...or so I've been told** ...ou du moins c'est ce qu'on m'a dit; **do as you're told** fais ce qu'on te dit; **I ~ you what *, let's go...** tiens, si on allait... *; **you're ~ing me!** * à qui le dis-tu!; ~ **me another!** * à d'autres! *; **to ~ sb's fortune** dire la bonne aventure à qn; **to ~ fortunes** dire la bonne aventure; **can you ~ the time?**, *(US)* **can you ~ time?** sais-tu lire l'heure?; **can you ~ me the time?** peux-tu me dire l'heure qu'il est?; **that ~s me all I need to know** maintenant je sais tout ce qu'il me faut savoir; **that ~s us a lot about...** cela nous en dit long sur...; **she was ~ing him about it** elle lui en parlait; **I told him about what had happened** je lui ai dit ce qui était arrivé. (**b**) *(distinguish)* distinguer (*sth from sth* qch de qch); *(know)* savoir. **I can't ~ them apart** je ne peux pas les distinguer l'un de l'autre; **how can I ~ what he will do?** comment puis-je savoir ce qu'il va faire?; **there's no ~ing what...** impossible de dire ce que...; **no one can ~ what...** personne ne peut savoir ce que...; **you can ~ he's clever** on voit bien qu'il est intelligent; **I can't ~ the difference** je ne vois pas la différence (*between* entre); **you can't ~ much from his letter** sa lettre n'en dit pas très long.
(**c**) **30 all told** 30 en tout.
2 *vi* (**a**) parler (*of, about* de). **more than words can** ~ plus qu'on ne peut dire; **I won't ~!** je ne le répéterai à personne!; **to ~ on sb** * rapporter *or* cafarder * sur qn. (**b**) *(know)* savoir. **how can I ~?** comment le saurais-je?; **I can't ~** je n'en sais rien; **who can ~?** qui sait?; **you never can ~** on ne sait jamais; **you can't ~ from his letter** on ne peut pas savoir d'après sa lettre. (**c**) *(have effect)* se faire sentir (*on sb/sth* sur qn/qch). **his age told against him** il était handicapé par son âge. ◆ **tell off** * *vt sep* gronder, attraper * (*sb for sth* qn pour qch; *for doing* pour avoir fait). **to be told off** * se faire attraper *.
◆ **teller** *n (Banking)* caissier *m*, -ière *f*; *[votes]* scrutateur *m*, -trice *f.* ◆ **telling** *adj figures, point* révélateur; *argument, style* efficace; *blow* bien assené. ◆ **telling-off** * *n* attrapade * *f*; **to get/give a good ~ing-off** * recevoir/passer un bon savon * (*from* de; *to* à). ◆ **telltale** **1** *n* rapporteur *m*, -euse *f*, cafard * *m* ; **2** *adj mark etc* révélateur.

telly * ['telɪ] *n (abbr of* **television***)* télé * *f.* **on the** ~ à la télé.

temerity [tɪ'merɪtɪ] *n* audace *f*, témérité *f.*

temp * [temp] *(abbr of* **temporary***)* **1** *n* intérimaire *mf.* **2** *vi* travailler comme intérimaire.

temper ['tempəʳ] **1** *n (nature, disposition)* tempérament *m*, caractère *m*; *(mood)* humeur *f*; *(fit of bad ~)* (accès *m* de) colère *f.* **to have an even ~, to be even-~ed** être d'un caractère *or* tempérament égal; **to have a hot** *or* **quick** ~ être soupe au lait ; **to have a nasty** ~ avoir un sale caractère; **in a foul** ~ d'une humeur massacrante; **in a good/bad** ~ de bonne/mauvaise humeur; **to keep one's** ~ garder son calme; **to lose one's** ~ se mettre en colère; **to be in a** ~ être en colère (*with sb* contre qn; *over, about sth* à propos de qch); **to put sb into a** ~ mettre qn en colère; **in a fit of ~ he...** dans un accès de colère il...; **he flew into a ~** il a explosé. **2** *vt (fig) effects etc* tempérer (*with* par). ◆ **temperament** *n (nature)* tempérament *m* ; *(moodiness)* humeur *f.* ◆ **temperamental** *adj* (**a**) *(capricious)* capricieux; (**b**) *(innate)* inné.

temperance ['temp(ə)r(ə)ns] **1** *n* modération *f*; *(in drinking)* tempérance *f.* **2** *adj movement* antialcoolique; *hotel* où l'on ne sert pas de boissons alcoolisées. ◆ **temperate** *adj climate* tempéré.

temperature ['temprɪtʃəʳ] *n* température *f.* **at a high** ~ à une forte température; **to have** *or* **run a** ~ avoir de la température *or* de la fièvre; **to take sb's** ~ prendre la température de qn.

tempest ['tempɪst] *n* tempête *f.* ◆ **tempestuous** *adj (fig) meeting, relationship* orageux; *person* passionné.

template ['templɪt] *n (pattern)* gabarit *m*; *(beam)* traverse *f.*

temple[1] ['templ] *n (Rel)* temple *m.*

temple[2] ['templ] *n (Anat)* tempe *f.*

tempo, *pl* **-pi** ['tempəʊ, pɪ] tempo *m.*

temporal ['temp(ə)r(ə)l] *adj* temporel.

temporary ['temp(ə)rərɪ] *adj job, worker* temporaire; *secretary* intérimaire; *teacher* suppléant; *tick-*

et, licence valide à titre temporaire; *building, decision, method, powers* provisoire; *relief, improvement* passager. ◆ **temporarily** *adv agree, appoint etc* provisoirement, temporairement; *lame, disappointed etc* pendant un certain temps. ◆ **temporize** *vi* chercher à gagner du temps.

tempt [tem(p)t] *vt* tenter. **to ~ sb to do** donner à qn l'envie *or* la tentation de faire; **try and ~ her to eat** tâchez de la persuader de manger; **I am very ~ed to accept** je suis très tenté d'accepter; **I'm very ~ed** c'est très tentant; **to ~ Providence** *or* **fate** tenter la Providence. ◆ **temptation** *n* tentation *f*; **there is no ~ation to do so** on n'est nullement tenté de le faire. ◆ **tempter** *n* tentateur *m*. ◆ **tempting** *adj* tentant; *food* appétissant. ◆ **temptingly** *adv* d'une manière tentante. ◆ **temptress** *n* tentatrice *f*.

ten [ten] *adj, n* dix *(m) inv*. **there were about ~** il y en avait une dizaine; **about ~ books** une dizaine de livres; **~s of thousands of...** des milliers de...; **to count in ~s** compter par dizaines; *(fig)* **~ to one he won't come** je parie qu'il ne viendra pas; *(fig)* **they're ~ a penny** il y en a tant qu'on en veut; *for other phrases V* **six**. ◆ **ten-cent store** *n (US)* bazar *m*. ◆ **tenth** *adj, n* dixième *(mf)*; *(fraction)* dixième *m*; **nine-~ths of** les neuf dixièmes de; *(fig)* la majeure partie de.

tenable ['tenəbl] *adj* défendable.

tenacious [tɪ'neɪʃəs] *adj* tenace. ◆ **tenaciously** *adv* avec ténacité. ◆ **tenacity** *n* ténacité *f*.

tenant ['tenənt] *n* locataire *mf*. ◆ **tenancy** *n* location *f*.

tench [tentʃ] *n* tanche *f*.

tend[1] [tend] *vt sheep, shop* garder; *invalid* soigner; *machine* surveiller.

tend[2] [tend] *vi* avoir tendance (*to do* à faire). **to ~ towards** incliner à *or* vers; **I ~ to think that...** j'incline *or* j'ai tendance à penser que...; **that ~s to be the case with...** c'est en général le cas avec...; **grey ~ing to blue** gris tirant sur le bleu. ◆ **tendency** *n* tendance *f*; **to have a ~ency to do** avoir tendance à faire; **the ~ency towards socialism** les tendances socialistes.

tender[1] ['tendə'] *n (boat)* embarcation *f*.

tender[2] ['tendə'] **1** *vt (proffer) object, money, apologies* offrir; *resignation* donner. **2** *vi (Comm)* faire une soumission (*for sth* pour qch). **3** *n* (**a**) *(Comm)* soumission *f* (*for sth* pour qch). **to invite ~s for sth, to put sth out to ~** mettre qch en adjudication. (**b**) *(Fin)* **that is no longer legal ~** cela n'a plus cours.

tender[3] ['tendə'] *adj (gen)* tendre; *flower* délicat, fragile; *spot, bruise* sensible; *conscience, subject* délicat. ◆ **tender-hearted** *adj* sensible. ◆ **tenderloin** *n* filet *m*. ◆ **tenderly** *adv* tendrement. ◆ **tenderness** *n* tendresse *f* (*towards* envers); *[meat etc]* tendreté *f*; délicatesse *f*; fragilité *f*; sensibilité *f*.

tendon ['tendən] *n* tendon *m*.

tendril ['tendrɪl] *n (Bot)* vrille *f*.

tenement ['tenɪmənt] *n* (**~ house**) immeuble *m*.

tenet ['tenət] *n* principe *m*.

tennis ['tenɪs] **1** *n* tennis *m*. **a game of ~** une partie de tennis. **2** *adj player, racket, club, shoe* de tennis. **~ ball** balle *f* de tennis; **~ court** (court *m* de) tennis *m*; *(Med)* **~ elbow** synovite *f* du coude.

tenor ['tenə'] **1** *n* (**a**) *[speech etc]* sens *m*, substance *f*; *[life, events]* cours *m*. (**b**) *(Mus)* ténor *m*. **2** *adj (Mus) voice, part* de ténor; *aria* pour ténor; *recorder, saxophone etc* ténor *inv*.

tense[1] [tens] *n (Gram)* temps *m*. **in the present ~** au temps présent.

tense[2] [tens] **1** *adj muscles, person, voice* tendu; *period* de tension; *smile* crispé. **they were ~ with fear** ils étaient crispés de peur; **things were getting ~** l'atmosphère devenait tendue. **2** *vt muscles* tendre. ◆ **tensely** *adv say* d'une voix tendue; *wait* dans l'anxiété. ◆ **tenseness** *or* ◆ **tension** *n* tension *f*.

tent [tent] **1** *n* tente *f*. **2** *adj*: **~ peg/pole** piquet *m*/montant *m* de tente; **~ trailer** caravane *f* pliante. **3** *vi* camper.

tentacle ['tentəkl] *n* tentacule *m*.

tentative ['tentətɪv] *adj suggestion, gesture, smile* timide; *offer, voice* hésitant; *scheme* expérimental; *conclusion, solution, plan* provisoire. **everything is very ~** rien n'est encore décidé. ◆ **tentatively** *adv* timidement; avec hésitation; expérimentalement; provisoirement.

tenterhooks ['tentəhʊks] *npl*: **on ~** sur des charbons ardents.

tenuous ['tenjʊəs] *adj link* ténu; *evidence* mince.

tenure ['tenjʊə'] *n (Univ)* fait *m* d'être titulaire; *[property]* bail *m*.

tepid ['tepɪd] *adj (lit, fig)* tiède. ◆ **tepidly** *adv (fig)* sans enthousiasme.

term [tɜːm] **1** *n* (**a**) *(limit)* terme *m*; *(period)* période *f*. **in the long ~** à long terme; **in the short ~** dans l'immédiat; **long-/short-~** *loan* à long/ court terme; *view* à longue/brève échéance; **his ~ of office** la période où il exerçait ses fonctions; **~ of imprisonment** peine *f* de prison.
(**b**) *(Scol, Univ)* trimestre *m*; *(Jur)* session *f*. **the autumn/spring/summer ~** le premier/deuxième/ troisième trimestre.
(**c**) *(Math, Philos)* terme *m*. **A expressed in ~s of B** A exprimé en fonction de B; *(fig)* **in ~s of production** sur le plan de la production.
(**d**) *(conditions)* **~s** *(gen)* conditions *fpl*; *[contract etc]* termes *mpl*; *(Comm etc)* prix *mpl*, tarif *m*; **you can name your own ~s** vous êtes libre de stipuler vos conditions; **not on any ~s** à aucune condition; **on his own ~s** sans concessions de sa part; **to come to ~s with** *person* arriver à un accord avec; *problem, situation* accepter; *(Jur)* **~s and conditions** modalités *fpl*; **~s of surrender/of payment** conditions de la reddition/de paiement; **it is not within our ~s of reference** cela n'entre pas dans les termes de notre mandat; **credit ~s** conditions de crédit; *(Comm)* **we offer it on easy ~s** nous offrons des facilités *fpl* de paiement; **our ~s for full board** notre tarif pension complète; **'inclusive ~s: £20'** '20 livres tout compris'.
(**e**) *(relationship)* **to be on good/bad ~s with sb** être en bons/mauvais termes *or* rapports avec qn; **they're on fairly friendly ~s** ils ont des rapports assez amicaux.
(**f**) *(expression)* terme *m*, expression *f*. **technical/ colloquial ~** terme technique/familier; **in plain** *or* **simple ~s** en termes clairs.
2 *adj exams etc* trimestriel. *(US)* **~ paper** dissertation *f* trimestrielle.
3 *vt* appeler, nommer.
◆ **termtime** *n*: **in ~time** pendant le trimestre.

terminal ['tɜːmɪnl] **1** *adj stage* terminal; *illness* dans sa phase terminale; *patient* en phase terminale. **2** *n* (**a**) *(Rail, Coach)* terminus *m inv*. **air ~** aérogare *f*; **container ~** terminus de containers; **oil ~** terminal *m* de conduites pétrolières. (**b**) *(Elec)* borne *f*. (**c**) *(Comput)* terminal *m*. ◆ **terminate 1** *vt (gen)* terminer; *contract* résilier ; **2** *vi* se terminer (*in* en, par). ◆ **termination** *n* fin *f*; *[contract]* résiliation *f*; *(Med)* **termination of pregnancy** interruption *f* de grossesse. ◆ **terminus,** *pl* **-ni** *n* terminus *m inv*.

terminology [ˌtɜːmɪ'nɒlədʒɪ] *n* terminologie *f*. ◆ **terminological** *adj* terminologique.

termite ['tɜːmaɪt] *n* termite *m*.

tern [tɜːn] *n* hirondelle *f* de mer.

terrace ['terəs] **1** *n (gen)* terrasse *f*; *(houses)* rangée *f* de maisons *(attenantes les unes aux autres)*. *(Sport)*

the ~s les gradins *mpl.* **2** *vt hillside* arranger en terrasses. ◆ **terraced** *adj garden, hillside* en terrasses; *house* attenant aux maisons voisines.

terracotta ['terə'kɒtə] *n* terre *f* cuite.

terrain [te'reɪn] *n* terrain *m (sol).*

terrestrial [tɪ'restrɪəl] *adj* terrestre.

terrible ['terəbl] *adj (gen)* terrible, effroyable; *heat, pain* atroce, terrible; *(less strong) holiday, disappointment, report* épouvantable. ◆ **terribly** *adv (very)* terriblement; *(very badly) play, sing* affreusement mal.

terrier ['terɪəʳ] *n* terrier *m.*

terrific [tə'rɪfɪk] *adj* (**a**) *(terrifying)* terrifiant, épouvantable. (**b**) *(*: extreme etc) amount, height* énorme, fantastique; *speed* fou; *noise* épouvantable; *hill, climb* terriblement raide; *heat, cold, anxiety* terrible; *pleasure* formidable *, terrible *. (**c**) *(*: excellent) result, news* formidable *. ◆ **terrifically** * *adv* (**a**) *(extremely)* terriblement; *(pej)* épouvantablement. (**b**) *(very well) sing, play* formidablement bien *.

terrify ['terɪfaɪ] *vt* terrifier. **to be terrified of** avoir une terreur folle de. ◆ **terrifying** *adj* terrifiant, épouvantable. ◆ **terrifyingly** *adv loud, near* épouvantablement; *bellow etc* de façon terrifiante.

territory ['terɪt(ə)rɪ] *n* territoire *m.* ◆ **territorial** **1** *adj* territorial ; **2** *n (Mil)* **Territorial** territorial *m*; **the Territorials** l'armée territoriale.

terror ['terəʳ] **1** *n* terreur *f.* **to go in ~ of** avoir très peur de; **he went in ~ of his life** il craignait fort pour sa vie; **I have a ~ of flying** j'ai la terreur de monter en avion; **he's a ~ on the roads** * c'est un danger public sur les routes; **that child is a ~** * cet enfant est une vraie terreur *. **2** *adj attack, group* terroriste; *act* de terrorisme. ◆ **terrorism** *n* terrorisme *m.* ◆ **terrorist** *adj, n* terroriste *(mf).* ◆ **terrorize** *vt* terroriser. ◆ **terror-stricken** *adj* épouvanté.

terry ['terɪ] *n* (**~ towelling**) tissu *m* éponge.

terse [tɜːs] *adj* laconique. ◆ **tersely** *adv* laconiquement. ◆ **terseness** *n* laconisme *m.*

tertiary ['tɜːʃərɪ] *adj (gen)* tertiaire. **~ education** enseignement *m* post-scolaire.

terylene ['terəliːn] *n* ® tergal *m* ®.

test [test] **1** *n (of product)* essai *m*; *(of strength etc)* épreuve *f*; *(Med: of blood, urine)* analyse *f*; *(Med: of organ)* examen *m*; *(Pharm, Chem)* analyse; *(Physiol, Psych etc)* test *m*; *(Scol)* interrogation *f* écrite (*or* orale); *(criterion)* critère *m. (Pharm etc)* **to do a ~ for sugar** faire une analyse pour déterminer le taux de glucose; **they did a ~ for diphtheria** ils ont fait une analyse pour voir s'il s'agissait de la diphthérie; **they did ~s on the water** ils ont analysé l'eau; **driving ~** (examen du) permis *m* de conduire; **hearing ~** examen de l'ouïe; **it wasn't a fair ~ of her abilities** cela n'a pas permis d'évaluer correctement ses aptitudes; **to put to the ~** mettre à l'essai *or* à l'épreuve; **to stand the ~** *[person]* se montrer à la hauteur *; *[machine, vehicle]* résister aux épreuves; **to stand the ~ of time** résister au passage du temps.

2 *adj pilot, flight, shot etc* d'essai; *district, experiment, year* test *inv.* **~ ban treaty** traité *m* d'interdiction d'essais nucléaires; *[oil]* **~ bore** sondage *m* de prospection; *(TV)* **~ card** *or (US)* **pattern** mire *f*; *(Jur)* **~ case** affaire-test *f (destinée à faire jurisprudence)*; **the strike is a ~ case** c'est une grève-test; *(Comput)* **~ data** données *fpl* d'essai; *(Cricket, Rugby)* **~ match** ≃ match international; **~ run** *(lit)* essai; *(fig)* période *f* d'essai; **~ tube** éprouvette *f* ; **~-tube baby** bébé-éprouvette *m.*

3 *vt object, product, machine* essayer, mettre à l'essai; *(Comm) goods* vérifier; *(Chem) metal, water* analyser; *(Pharm) blood* faire des analyses de; *new drug etc* expérimenter; *(Psych) person, animal* tester; *(gen) person, intelligence, nerves* mettre à l'épreuve; *sight, hearing* examiner; *sb's reactions* mesurer. **they ~ed the material for resistance to...** ils ont soumis le matériau à des essais destinés à vérifier sa résistance à...; **these conditions ~ a car's tyres/strength** ces conditions mettent à l'épreuve les pneus/la résistance d'une voiture; **they ~ed him for hearing difficulties** ils lui ont fait passer un examen de l'ouïe; **they ~ed the children in geography** ils ont fait subir aux enfants une interrogation de contrôle en géographie; **they ~ed him for the job** ils lui ont fait passer des tests d'aptitude pour le poste.

4 *vi*: **to ~ for sugar** faire une recherche de sucre; **to ~ for a gas leak** faire des essais pour découvrir une fuite de gaz; *(Telec etc)* **'~ing, ~ing'** ≃ 'un, deux, trois'.

◆ **test-drive** *(Aut)* **1** *n* essai *m* de route ; **2** *vt* faire faire un essai de route à. ◆ **testing** *adj*: **~ing bench** banc *m* d'essai; **~ing ground** terrain *m* d'essai; *(fig)* **a ~ing time** une période éprouvante (*for sb* pour qn). ◆ **test-market** *vt* commercialiser à titre expérimental.

testament ['testəmənt] *n* testament *m.* **the Old/New T~** l'Ancien/le Nouveau Testament.

testicle ['testɪkl] *n* testicule *m.*

testify ['testɪfaɪ] **1** *vt* témoigner (*that* que). **2** *vi* porter témoignage. **to ~ against/in favour of sb** déposer contre/en faveur de qn; **to ~ to sth** *(Jur)* attester qch; *(gen)* témoigner de qch. ◆ **testimonial** *n (reference)* recommandation *f*; *(gift)* témoignage *m* d'estime *(offert à qn par ses collègues etc).* ◆ **testimony** *n (Jur)* témoignage *m*, déposition *f*; *(statement)* déclaration *f.*

testy ['testɪ] *adj* grincheux. ◆ **testily** *adv* d'un ton *or* d'un air irrité.

tetanus ['tetənəs] *n* tétanos *m.*

tetchy ['tetʃɪ] *adj* irritable.

tête-à-tête ['teɪtɑː'teɪt] *n* tête à tête *m inv.*

tether ['teðəʳ] **1** *n* longe *f. (fig)* **at the end of one's ~** à bout de forces *or* de nerfs. **2** *vt* attacher (*to* à).

text [tekst] *n* texte *m. (Comput)* **~ editor** éditeur *m* de texte(s). ◆ **textbook** *n* manuel *m* scolaire. ◆ **textual** *adj error* de texte.

textile ['tekstaɪl] *adj, n* textile *(m).*

texture ['tekstʃəʳ] *n (gen)* texture *f*; *[cloth]* contexture *f*; *[skin, wood etc]* grain *m.*

thalidomide [θə'lɪdəʊ'maɪd] *n* ® thalidomide *f* ®. **~ baby** victime *f* de la thalidomide.

Thames [temz] *n* Tamise *f. (fig)* **he'll never set the ~ on fire** il n'a pas inventé la poudre.

than [ðæn], *forme faible* [ðən] *conj* (**a**) que. **more ~** plus que; **taller ~** plus grand que; **I'd do anything rather ~ admit it** je ferais tout plutôt que d'avouer cela; **no sooner did he arrive ~...** il était à peine arrivé que...; **it was a better play ~ we expected** la pièce était meilleure que nous ne l'avions prévu. (**b**) *(with numerals)* de. **more/less ~ 20** plus/moins de 20; **less ~ half** moins de la moitié; **more ~ once** plus d'une fois.

thank [θæŋk] **1** *vt* remercier, dire merci à (*sb for sth* qn de qch; *for doing* de faire, d'avoir fait). **~ you** merci (*for sth* pour qch; *for doing* d'avoir fait); **~ you very much** merci bien *(also iro)*, merci beaucoup; **no ~ you** (non) merci; **~ goodness *, ~ heaven(s) *, ~ God *** Dieu merci; *(fig)* **you've got him to ~ for that** c'est à lui que tu dois cela; **he's only got himself to ~** il ne peut s'en prendre qu'à lui-même. **2** *npl*: **~s** remerciements *mpl*; *(excl)* **~s! *** merci!; **many ~s** merci mille fois; **with my best ~s** avec mes remerciements les plus sincères; **give him my ~s** remerciez-le de ma part; **to give ~s to God** rendre grâces à Dieu; **~s to you** grâce à toi. ◆ **thankful** *adj* reconnaissant (*for* de); **let us be ~ful that** estimons-nous heureux que + *subj*; **I was ~ful that** j'ai été bien content que + *subj*. ◆ **thankfully** *adv (gratefully)* avec reconnaissance; *(with relief)* avec soulagement. ◆ **thankless** *adj* ingrat. ◆ **thanksgiving** *n* action *f* de grâces; *(Can, US)* **T~sgiving Day** fête *f* nationale.

that [ðæt], *forme faible* [ðət] **1** *dem adj, pl* **those** (**a**) *(unstressed)* ce *(before vowel or mute 'h'* cet), cette *f*, ces *mfpl*. ~ **book** ce livre; ~ **man** cet homme; ~ **car** cette voiture; **those books** ces livres; **those cars** ces voitures; **I love ~ house of yours!** votre maison, je l'adore!; ~ **awful car of theirs** leur fichue * voiture; **what about ~ £5?** et ces 5 livres? (**b**) *(stressed; or as opposed to* **this, these***)* ce...-là, cet...-là, cette...-là, ces...-là. **I mean THAT book** c'est de ce livre-là que je parle; **I like ~ photo better than this one** je préfère cette photo-là à celle-ci; ~ **hill over there** cette colline là-bas.
2 *dem pron, pl* **those** (**a**) cela, ça; ce. **what's ~?** qu'est-ce que c'est que ça?; **who's ~?** qui est-ce?; **is ~ you, Paul?** c'est toi, Paul?; **~'s what they've been told** c'est *or* voilà ce qu'on leur a dit; **those are my children** ce sont mes enfants; *(pointing out)* voilà mes enfants; **do you like ~?** vous aimez ça *or* cela?; **~'s fine!** c'est parfait!; **~'s enough!** ça suffit!; **she's not as stupid as (all) ~** elle n'est pas si bête que ça; **you're not going and ~'s ~!** tu n'y vas pas, un point c'est tout!; **well, ~'s ~!** eh bien voilà!; ~ **was ~** les choses se sont arrêtées là; **if it comes to ~...** en fait...; **before ~** avant cela; **with** *or* **at ~ she...** là-dessus *or* sur ce, elle...; **there were 6 at ~!** en plus il y en avait 6!; ~ **is (to say)...** c'est-à-dire...; **like ~** comme ça; **friendship and all ~** * l'amitié et tout ça. (**b**) *(~ one)* celui-là *m*, celle-là *f*, ceux-là *mpl*, celles-là *fpl*. **I prefer this to ~** je préfère celui-ci à celui-là (*or* celle-ci à celle-là); **those over there** ceux-là (*or* celles-là) là-bas. (**c**) *(before rel pron)* **those who** ceux (*or* celles) qui.
3 *adv (so)* si, aussi. **it's ~ high** c'est haut comme ça; **it's not ~ cold!** il ne fait pas si froid que ça!; **he was ~ ill!** * il était vraiment malade.
4 *rel pron* (**a**) *(nominative)* qui; *(accusative)* que; *(with prep)* lequel *m*, laquelle *f*, lesquels *mpl*, lesquelles *fpl*. **the man ~ came to see you** l'homme qui est venu vous voir; **the letter ~ I sent** la lettre que j'ai envoyée; **fool ~ I am!** imbécile que je suis!; **the men ~ I was speaking to** les hommes auxquels je parlais; **the girl ~ I told you about** la jeune fille dont je vous ai parlé. (**b**) *(in expressions of time)* où. **the evening/summer** *etc* **~...** le soir/l'été *etc* où...
5 *conj* que. **he said ~ he had seen her** il a dit qu'il l'avait vue, il a dit l'avoir vue; **so big ~...** si grand que...; **not ~ I want to do it** non pas que je veuille le faire; **so ~, in order ~** pour que + *subj*, afin que + *subj*.

thatch [θætʃ] **1** *n* chaume *m*. **2** *vi* faire un toit de chaume. ◆ **thatched** *adj roof* de chaume; **~ed cottage** chaumière *f*.

thaw [θɔː] **1** *n (Met)* dégel *m*; *(fig: Pol etc)* détente *f*. **2** *vt* (**~ out**) *(gen; also fig)* dégeler; *ice, snow* faire fondre. **3** *vi* (**~ out**) *(gen, Met; also fig)* dégeler; *[ice, snow]* fondre.

the [ðiː], *forme faible* [ð(ə)] **1** *def art* (**a**) le, la, *(before vowel or mute 'h')* l', les. **of ~, from ~** du, de la, de l', des; **to ~, at ~** au, à la, à l', aux. (**b**) *(with sg n denoting whole class)* ~ **aeroplane is an invention of our century** l'avion est une invention de notre siècle. (**c**) *(distributive use)* **50p ~ pound** 50 pence la livre; **2 dollars to ~ pound** 2 dollars la livre; **paid by ~ hour** payé à l'heure; **30 miles to ~ gallon** ≃ 9 litres au 100 (km). (**d**) *(with names etc)* **Charles ~ First/Second/Third** Charles premier/deux/trois; ~ **Browns** les Brown. (**e**) *(stressed)* **THE Professor Smith** le célèbre professeur Smith; **it's THE restaurant in this part of town** c'est le meilleur restaurant du quartier; **it's THE book just now** c'est le livre à lire en ce moment. (**f**) *(with demonstrative force)* ~ **summer we went to France** l'été où nous sommes allés en France; ~ **shop over there** le magasin là-bas; **he hasn't ~ sense to refuse** il n'a pas assez de bon sens pour refuser; **how's ~ leg?** * et cette jambe? * **2** *adv*: ~ **more he works ~ more he earns** plus il travaille plus il gagne d'argent; ~ **sooner ~ better** le plus tôt sera le mieux; **all ~ more difficult** d'autant plus difficile.

theatre, *(US)* **theater** ['θɪətəʳ] **1** *n* (**a**) théâtre *m*. **to go to the ~** aller au théâtre; **it makes good ~** c'est du bon théâtre. (**b**) *(large room)* salle *f* de conférences. **lecture ~** amphithéâtre *m*; **operating ~** salle *f* d'opération. (**c**) *(Mil etc)* théâtre *m*. ~ **of war** théâtre des hostilités. **2** *adj ticket* de théâtre; *visit* au théâtre; *management* du théâtre; *(Med) staff* de la salle d'opération. ~ **company** troupe *f* de théâtre. ◆ **theatregoer** *n* habitué(e) *m(f)* du théâtre. ◆ **theatreland** *n*: **London's ~land** le Londres des théâtres. ◆ **theatrical** **1** *adj* théâtral *(also fig pej)* ; **2** *npl*: **amateur theatricals** théâtre *m* d'amateurs; *(fig pej)* **all those theatricals** toute cette comédie. ◆ **theatrically** *adv* théâtralement.

thee [ðiː] *pron (†, liter)* te; *(before vowel)* t' ; *(stressed; after prep)* toi.

theft [θeft] *n* vol *m*.

their [ðɛəʳ] *poss adj* leur *(f inv)*. ◆ **theirs** *poss pron* le leur, la leur, les leurs; **this car is ~s** cette voiture est à eux (*or* à elles); **a friend of ~s** un de leurs amis (à eux *or* à elles); *(pej)* **that car of ~s** leur fichue * voiture.

them [ðem], *forme faible* [ð(ə)m] *pers pron pl* (**a**) *(direct) (unstressed)* les; *(stressed)* eux *mpl*, elles *fpl*. **I have seen ~** je les ai vu(e)s; **I don't know THEM** eux (*or* elles), je ne les connais pas; **if I were ~** si j'étais à leur place; **it's ~!** ce sont eux!, les voilà! (**b**) *(indirect)* leur. **I gave ~ the book** je leur ai donné le livre; **I'm speaking to ~** je leur parle. (**c**) *(after prep etc)* eux *mpl*, elles *fpl*. **I'm thinking of ~** je pense à eux; **as for ~** quant à eux; **younger than ~** plus jeune qu'eux; **both of ~** tous (*or* toutes) les deux; **several of ~** plusieurs d'entre eux; **give me a few of ~** donnez-m'en quelques-un(e)s; **I don't like either of ~** je ne les aime ni l'un(e) ni l'autre; **none of ~ would do it** aucun d'entre eux (*or* aucune d'entre elles) n'a voulu le faire; **it was very good of ~** c'était très gentil de leur part. ◆ **themselves** *pers pron pl (reflexive)* se; *(emphatic)* eux-mêmes *mpl*, elles-mêmes *fpl*; *(after prep)* eux, elles; **they've hurt ~selves** ils se sont blessés, elles se sont blessées; **they said to ~selves** ils (*or* elles) se sont dit; **they saw it ~selves** ils l'ont vu eux-mêmes; **they were talking amongst ~selves** ils discutaient entre eux; **all by ~selves** tout seuls, toutes seules.

theme [θiːm] **1** *n* thème *m*, sujet *m*; *(Mus)* thème, motif *m*. **2** *adj*: ~ **song** chanson principale *(d'un film etc)*; *(signature tune)* indicatif *m*; *(fig)* refrain *m* habituel.

then [ðen] **1** *adv* (**a**) *(at that time)* alors, à cette époque-là, à ce moment-là. **we had 2 dogs ~** nous avions alors 2 chiens, nous avions 2 chiens à cette époque-là; **I'll see him ~** je le verrai à ce moment-là; **(every) now and ~** de temps en temps; ~ **and there** sur-le-champ; **from ~ on** dès lors, dès cette époque-là *or* ce moment-là; **before ~** avant cela, avant ce moment-là; **I'll have it finished by ~** je l'aurai fini d'ici là; **between now and ~** d'ici là; **until ~** jusque-là, jusqu'alors. (**b**) *(afterwards)* ensuite, puis, alors. **first to London, ~ to Paris** d'abord à Londres, puis *or* et ensuite à Paris; **and ~ what?** et puis après? (**c**) *(in that case)* alors, donc. ~ **it must be in the sitting room** alors ça doit être au salon; **someone had warned you ~?** on vous avait donc prévenu?; **now ~...** alors...

(**d**) *(and also)* et puis, d'ailleurs. ~ **there's my aunt** et puis il y a ma tante; **...and ~ it's none of my business** ...et d'ailleurs cela ne me regarde pas; **and ~ again...** remarquez... **2** *adj*: **the ~ Prime Minister** le Premier ministre de l'époque.

thence [ðens] *adv († , liter)* de là.

theodolite [θɪ'ɒdəlaɪt] *n* théodolite *m*.

theology [θɪ'ɒlədʒɪ] *n* théologie *f*. ◆ **theologian** *n* théologien(ne) *m(f)*. ◆ **theological** *adj* théologique; **theological college** séminaire *m*.

theorem ['θɪərəm] *n* théorème *m*.

theory ['θɪərɪ] *n* théorie *f*. **in ~** en théorie. ◆ **theoretic(al)** *adj* théorique. ◆ **theoretically** *adv* théoriquement. ◆ **theoretician** *or* ◆ **theorist** *n* théoricien(ne) *m(f)*. ◆ **theorize** *vi [scientist etc]* élaborer des théories (*about* sur); *(fig)* se lancer dans de grandes théories (*about* sur).

therapy ['θerəpɪ] *n* thérapie *f*. ◆ **therapeutic(al)** *adj* thérapeutique. ◆ **therapeutics** *nsg* thérapeutique *f*. ◆ **therapist** *n* thérapeute *mf*.

there [ðɛə^r] **1** *adv* (**a**) *(place)* y, là. **we shall be ~** nous y serons, nous serons là; **put it ~** posez-le là; **we left ~** nous en sommes partis, nous sommes partis de là; **on ~** là-dessus; **in ~** là-dedans; **back** *or* **down** *or* **over ~** là-bas; **he lives round ~** il habite par là; *(further away)* il habite par là-bas; **here and ~** çà et là, par-ci par-là; **from ~** de là; **they went ~ and back** ils ont fait l'aller et retour; **~ and then** sur-le-champ; **he's all ~ *** c'est un malin; **he's not all ~ *** il est un peu demeuré. (**b**) **~ is, ~ are** il y a; **once upon a time ~ was...** il était une fois...; **~ will be dancing** on dansera; **~ are 3 apples left** il reste 3 pommes; **~ comes a time when...** il vient un moment où...; **~'s no denying it** c'est indéniable. (**c**) *(pointing out etc)* **~'s my brother!** voilà mon frère!; **~ are the others!** voilà les autres!; **~ he is!** le voilà!; **that man ~** cet homme-là; **hey you ~!** hé toi, là-bas!; **hurry up ~!** dépêchez-vous, là-bas!; **~'s my mother calling me** voilà ma mère qui m'appelle; **I disagree with you ~** là je ne suis pas d'accord avec vous; **you press this switch and ~ you are!** tu appuies sur ce bouton et ça y est!; **~ you are, I told you that would happen** voilà *or* tiens, je t'avais dit que ça allait arriver; **~ you go again *...** ça y est, tu recommences à... **2** *excl*: **~, what did I tell you?** alors, qu'est-ce que je t'avais dit?; **~, ~!** allons, allons!; **but ~, what's the use?** mais enfin, à quoi bon?

◆ **thereabouts** *adv (place)* par là, près de là; **£5 or ~abouts** environ 5 livres. ◆ **thereafter** *adv* par la suite. ◆ **thereby** *adv* de cette façon; **~by hangs a tale!** c'est toute une histoire! ◆ **therefore** *adv* donc, par conséquent. ◆ **thereupon** *adv (then)* sur ce; *(on that subject)* à ce sujet.

therm [θɜ:m] *n* = 1,055 × 10^8 joules; *(formerly)* thermie *f*. ◆ **thermal** *adj* thermal; *(Elec, Phys)* thermique; *paper, printer* thermosensible, à sensibilité thermique; *underwear* en thermolactyl ®; **~al baths** thermes *mpl*.

thermo... ['θɜ:məʊ'] *pref* therm(o)... ◆ **thermodynamic** *adj* thermodynamique. ◆ **thermonuclear** *adj* thermonucléaire.

thermometer [θə'mɒmɪtə^r] *n* thermomètre *m*.

Thermos ['θɜ:məs] *n* ®: **~ (flask)** (bouteille *f*) thermos *f*.

thermostat ['θɜ:məstæt] *n* thermostat *m*.

thesaurus [θɪ'sɔ:rəs] *n [words]* dictionnaire *m* synonymique.

these [ði:z] *pl of* **this**.

thesis, *pl* **-ses** ['θi:sɪs] thèse *f*.

they [ðeɪ] *pers pron pl* (**a**) ils *mpl*, elles *fpl* ; *(stressed)* eux *mpl*, elles *fpl*. **~ have gone** ils sont partis, elles sont parties; **there ~ are!** les voilà!; **~ are teachers** ce sont des professeurs; **THEY know nothing about it** eux, ils n'en savent rien. (**b**) *(people in general)* on. **~ say that...** on dit que...

thick [θɪk] **1** *adj (gen)* épais (*f* -aisse); *book, lips, nose, wool* épais, gros (*f* grosse); *print* gras (*f* grasse); *honey, vegetation* épais, touffu; *(stupid)* bête, borné. **to grow ~(er)** (s')épaissir; **to make ~(er)** épaissir; **wall 50 cm ~** mur de 50 cm d'épaisseur; *(fig)* **to give sb a ~ ear *** frotter les oreilles à qn *; *(fig)* **that's a bit ~! *** ça, c'est un peu fort! *; **the air is very ~ in here** on manque d'air ici; **furniture ~ with dust** meubles couverts de poussière; **road ~ with cars** rue encombrée de voitures; **town ~ with tourists** ville envahie de touristes; *(fig)* **they are as ~ as thieves** ils s'entendent comme larrons en foire; **Paul and he are very ~ *** Paul et lui sont comme les deux doigts de la main.

2 *adv spread, lie etc* en couche épaisse; *cut* en tranches épaisses. **the snow fell ~** la neige tombait dru; *(fig)* **he lays it on a bit ~ *** il exagère un peu.

3 *n*: **in the ~ of** *crowd* au plus fort de; *fight* en plein cœur de; **they were in the ~ of it** ils étaient en plein dedans; **through ~ and thin** à travers toutes les épreuves.

◆ **thicken 1** *vt sauce* épaissir ; **2** *vi (gen; also fig)* s'épaissir; *[crowd]* grossir. ◆ **thickheaded *** *adj* bête, borné. ◆ **thick-knit** *adj* en grosse laine. ◆ **thick-lipped** *adj* aux lèvres charnues. ◆ **thickly** *adv spread* en une couche épaisse; *cut* en tranches épaisses; *speak, say (from head cold, fear)* d'une voix voilée; *(from drink)* d'une voix pâteuse; *wooded, populated* très; **~ly spread** (*or* **covered** *etc*) **with** couvert d'une épaisse couche de; **the snow fell ~ly** la neige tombait dru. ◆ **thickness** *n* (**a**) *(gen)* épaisseur *f*; *[lips etc]* grosseur *f*; *[fog, forest]* densité *f*; *[hair]* abondance *f*; (**b**) *(layer)* épaisseur *f*. ◆ **thickset** *adj (and small)* râblé; *(and tall)* bien bâti. ◆ **thickskinned** *adj orange* à la peau épaisse; *(fig) person* peu sensible.

thicket ['θɪkɪt] *n* fourré *m*, hallier *m*.

thief, *pl* **thieves** [θi:f, θi:vz] *n* voleur *m*, -euse *f*. **set a ~ to catch a ~** à voleur voleur et demi; **stop ~!** au voleur! ◆ **thieve** *vti* voler. ◆ **thieving 1** *adj* voleur ; **2** *n* vol *m*.

thigh [θaɪ] *n* cuisse *f*. **~ boots** cuissardes *fpl*. ◆ **thighbone** *n* fémur *m*.

thimble ['θɪmbl] *n* dé *m* (à coudre).

thin [θɪn] **1** *adj* (**a**) *(gen)* mince; *glass* fin; *paper, waist, nose* mince, fin; *leg, person* mince, maigre *(slightly pej)*; *string* petit. *[person]* **to get ~(ner)** maigrir; **as ~ as a rake** maigre comme un clou. (**b**) *soup, gravy, oil* peu épais (*f* -aisse); *cream, honey, mud* liquide; *hair, eyebrows, hedge* clairsemé; *fog, smoke* léger; *crowd* épars; *voice* grêle; *blood* anémié. **he's rather ~ on top *** il perd ses cheveux; **the air is ~** l'air est raréfié; *(fig)* **to vanish into ~ air** se volatiliser. (**c**) *profits* maigre; *excuse, story* peu convaincant; *disguise* facilement percé à jour. **to have a ~ time of it *** passer par une période plutôt pénible. **2** *adv spread* en une couche mince; *cut* en tranches minces. **3** *vt* (**~ down**) *paint, sauce* délayer; (**~ out**) *trees, hair* éclaircir. **4** *vi* (**~ out**) *[fog, crowd]* se disperser. **his hair is ~ning** il perd ses cheveux. ◆ **thin-lipped** *adj* aux lèvres minces; *(with rage etc)* les lèvres pincées. ◆ **thinly** *adv cut* en tranches minces; *spread* en couche mince; *wooded etc* peu; *clad* insuffisamment; **~ly disguised as** à peine déguisé en. ◆ **thinner** *n* diluant *m*. ◆ **thinness** *n* minceur *f*; maigreur *f*. ◆ **thinskinned** *adj orange etc* à la peau mince; *(fig) person* susceptible.

thine [ðaɪn] *(†, liter)* **1** *poss pron* le tien, la tienne, les tiens, les tiennes. **2** *poss adj* ton, ta, tes.

thing [θɪŋ] *n* (**a**) *(gen)* chose *f*. **~ of beauty** bel objet, belle chose; **such ~s as** des choses comme; **the ~ he loves most is...** ce qu'il aime le plus au

monde c'est...; what's that ~? qu'est-ce que c'est que cette chose-là *or* ce machin-là * *or* ce truc-là? *; **what sort of ~ is that to say?** ça n'est pas une chose à dire; **the good ~s in life** les plaisirs *mpl* de la vie; **he thinks the right ~s** il pense comme il faut; **the ~ is this** voilà de quoi il s'agit; **as ~s are** dans l'état actuel des choses; **the next ~ to do is...** ce qu'il y a à faire maintenant c'est...; **the best ~ would be to refuse** le mieux serait de refuser; **the last ~ on the agenda** le dernier point à l'ordre du jour; **you worry about ~s too much** tu te fais trop de soucis; **I must think ~s over** il faut que j'y réfléchisse; **how are ~s with you?** et vous, comment ça va?; **to expect great ~s of** attendre beaucoup de; **they were talking of one ~ and another** ils parlaient de choses et d'autres; **taking one ~ with another** somme toute; **the ~ is to know...** la question est de savoir...; **the ~ is, she'd already seen him** ce qu'il y a, c'est qu'elle l'avait déjà vu; **it's a strange ~, but...** c'est drôle, mais...; **for one ~, it doesn't make sense** d'abord, ça n'a pas de sens; **and for another ~...** et en plus...; **it's the usual ~** c'est le coup * classique; **it's just one of those ~s** ce sont des choses qui arrivent; **it's just one ~ after another** les embêtements se succèdent ; **I hadn't done a ~ about it** je n'avais strictement rien fait.
(**b**) *(belongings etc)* **~s** affaires *fpl*; **to take off one's ~s** se débarrasser de son manteau *etc*; **do take your ~s off!** débarrassez-vous!; **your swimming ~s** tes affaires de bain; **the first-aid ~s** la trousse de secours.
(**c**) **he's doing his own ~** * il fait ce qui lui plaît; **she has got a ~ about spiders** * elle a horreur des araignées; **he has got a ~ about blondes** * il est obsédé par les blondes; **he made a great ~ of it** il en a fait tout un plat *; **Mr T~ * rang up** Monsieur Machin * a téléphoné; **poor little ~!** pauvre petit(e)!; **poor ~, he's very ill** le pauvre, il est très malade; **she's a spiteful ~** c'est une rosse *; **that's just the ~ for me** voilà justement ce qu'il me faut; **yoga is the ~ nowadays** le yoga c'est le truc * à la mode aujourd'hui; **it's quite the ~** ça se fait beaucoup; **the latest ~ in hats** un chapeau dernier cri.
◆ **thingumabob** * *or* ◆ **thingumajig** * *or* ◆ **thingummy** * *n* machin * *m*, truc * *m*.

think [θɪŋk] *(vb: pret, ptp* **thought***)* **1** *vi* (**a**) *(gen)* penser (*of, about* à; *of, about doing* à faire); *(more carefully)* réfléchir (*of, about* à). **you can't ~ of everything** on ne peut pas penser à tout; **I've too many things to ~ of** j'ai trop de choses en tête; **he ~s about nothing but money** il ne pense qu'à l'argent; **what else is there to ~ about?** c'est ce qu'il y a de plus important; **~ carefully** réfléchissez bien; **~ twice before speaking** réfléchissez-y à deux fois avant de parler; **~ again!** *(reflect on it)* repensez-y!; *(have another guess)* ce n'est pas ça, recommencez!; **to ~ ahead** tout prévoir; **let me ~** que je réfléchisse *, laissez-moi réfléchir; **to ~ aloud** penser tout haut; **to ~ big** * avoir de grandes idées; *(iro)* **I don't ~!** * ça m'étonnerait!; **I'll ~ about it** j'y penserai, je vais y réfléchir; **it's not worth ~ing about** ça ne vaut pas la peine d'y penser; **there's so much to ~ about** il y a tant de choses à prendre en considération; **what are you ~ing about?** à quoi pensez-vous?; **what were you ~ing about!** où avais-tu la tête?; **I wouldn't ~ of such a thing!** ça ne me viendrait jamais à l'idée!; **would** YOU **~ of letting him go alone?** vous le laisseriez partir seul?; **I didn't ~ to ask** *or* **of asking** je n'ai pas eu l'idée de demander.
(**b**) *(remember, consider)* penser (*of, about* à). **he ~s of nobody but himself** il ne pense qu'à lui; **he's got his children to ~ of** *or* **about** il faut qu'il pense à ses enfants; **I can't ~ of her name** je n'arrive pas à me rappeler son nom; **I couldn't ~ of the right word** le mot juste ne me venait pas.
(**c**) *(imagine)* **to ~ of** imaginer; **~ of what might have happened** imagine ce qui aurait pu arriver; **just ~!** imagine un peu!
(**d**) *(devise etc)* **to ~ of** *(gen)* avoir l'idée de (*doing* faire); *plan* inventer; *solution* trouver; **what will he ~ of next?** qu'est-ce qu'il va encore inventer?
(**e**) *(have as opinion)* penser (*of* de). **to ~ well** *or* **highly** *or* **a lot of sb/sth** avoir une haute opinion de qn/qch; **very well thought of** très respecté ; **I don't ~ much of that** cela ne me semble pas très bon; **to ~ better of doing sth** décider à la réflexion de ne pas faire qch; **he thought better of it** il a changé d'avis; **~ nothing of it!** n'y attachez aucune importance!; **he thought nothing of walking there** il trouvait tout naturel d'y aller à pied; **to my way of ~ing** à mon avis.
2 *vt* (**a**) *(believe)* penser, croire (*that* que). **I ~ so/not** je pense *or* crois que oui/non; **I rather ~ so** j'ai plutôt l'impression que oui; **I thought as much!, I thought so!** je m'en doutais!; **she's pretty, don't you ~?** elle est jolie, tu ne trouves pas?; **I don't know what to ~** je ne sais pas qu'en penser; **I ~ that** je pense *or* crois que + *indic*; **I don't ~ that** je ne pense *or* crois pas que + *subj;* **do you ~ that** croyez-vous que + *subj;* **what do you ~?** qu'est-ce que tu en penses?; *(iro)* **what do** YOU **~?** qu'est-ce que tu crois, toi?; **what do you ~ of him?** comment le trouves-tu?; **who do you ~ you are?** pour qui te prends-tu?; **you must ~ me very rude** vous devez me trouver très impoli; **he ~s he is intelligent** il se croit intelligent; **they are thought to be rich** ils passent pour être riches ; **I didn't ~ to see you here** je ne m'attendais pas à vous voir ici.
(**b**) *(imagine)* imaginer. **~ what we could do** imagine ce que nous pourrions faire; **I can't ~ what he means** je ne vois vraiment pas ce qu'il veut dire; **who would have thought it!** qui l'aurait dit!; **to ~ that she's only 10!** quand on pense qu'elle n'a que 10 ans!; **to ~ evil thoughts** avoir de mauvaises pensées.
(**c**) *(reflect)* penser à. **~ what you're doing** pense à ce que tu fais; **we must ~ how to do it** il faut nous demander comment le faire; **I was ~ing (to myself) how ill he looked** je me disais qu'il avait l'air bien malade; **I didn't ~ to let him know** il ne m'est pas venu à l'idée de le mettre au courant; **did you ~ to bring it?** est-ce que tu as pensé à l'apporter?
3 *n*: **to have a ~ * about sth** penser à qch; **to have a good long ~ * about sth** bien réfléchir à qch; **he's got another ~ coming** * il se fait des illusions.
4 *adj*: **~ tank** groupe *m* de réflexion.
◆ **think back** *vi* essayer de se souvenir (*to* de). ◆ **think out** *vt sep problem, proposition* étudier; *plan, answer* préparer. ◆ **think over** *vt sep offer, suggestion* bien réfléchir à. **I'll have to ~ it over** il va falloir que j'y réfléchisse. ◆ **think up** *vt sep plan, improvement* avoir l'idée de; *idea* avoir; *answer* trouver; *excuse* inventer. **what will he ~ up next?** qu'est-ce qu'il va encore bien pouvoir inventer? ◆ **thinkable** *adj*: **it's not ~able that** il n'est pas pensable que + *subj.* ◆ **thinker** *n* penseur *m*, -euse *f*. ◆ **thinking** **1** *adj creature* rationnel; **to any ~ing person** pour toute personne qui réfléchit; **to put on one's ~ing cap** réfléchir ; **2** *n (act)* pensée *f*, réflexion *f*; *(thoughts)* opinions *fpl* (*on, about* sur); **I'll have to do some ~ing about it** il va falloir que j'y réfléchisse.

third [θɜ:d] **1** *adj* troisième. **~ person**, *(Jur)* **~ party** tiers *m*; **~ party insurance** (assurance *f*) responsabilité *f* civile; **~ time lucky!** la troisième fois sera la bonne; **the ~ finger** le majeur; **the T~**

World le Tiers-Monde. **2** *n* troisième *mf*; *(fraction)* tiers *m*; *(Mus)* tierce *f*; *(Aut:* ~ *gear)* troisième vitesse *f*. **in** ~ en troisième; *for phrases V* **sixth. 3** *adv* (**a**) *(in race, exam)* **to come** *or* **be placed** ~ se classer troisième. (**b**) *(thirdly)* troisièmement. ◆ **third-class 1** *adj (gen, Rail etc)* de troisième classe; *hotel* de troisième catégorie; *(fig pej) meal, goods* de qualité très inférieure; *(Univ)* **~-class degree** ≃ licence *f* sans mention ; **2** *adv (Rail) travel* en troisième. ◆ **thirdly** *adv* troisièmement. ◆ **third-rate** *adj* de qualité très inférieure.

thirst [θɜːst] **1** *n* soif *f* (*for* de). **2** *vi (liter)* avoir soif (*for* de). *(fig)* **~ing for** assoiffé de. ◆ **thirsty** *adj* qui a soif; *(stronger)* assoiffé; *(fig) land* desséché; **to be ~y** avoir soif (*for* de); **it makes you ~y, it's ~y work** ça donne soif.

thirteen [θɜːˈtiːn] *adj, n* treize *(m) inv*; *for phrases V* **six.** ◆ **thirteenth** *adj, n* treizième *(mf)*; *(fraction)* treizième *m*.

thirty [ˈθɜːtɪ] *adj, n* trente *(m) inv*. **about** ~ une trentaine; **about** ~ **books** une trentaine de livres; *for other phrases V* **sixty.** ◆ **thirtieth** *adj, n* trentième *(mf)*; *(fraction)* trentième *m*.

this [ðɪs] **1** *dem adj, pl* **these** (**a**) ce (*before vowel and mute 'h'* cet), cette *f*, ces *mfpl*. ~ **book** ce livre; ~ **man** cet homme; ~ **woman** cette femme; **these books** ces livres; **these women** ces femmes; ~ **week** cette semaine; ~ **time last week** la semaine dernière à pareille heure; ~ **time next year** l'année prochaine à la même époque; ~ **coming week** la semaine prochaine. (**b**) *(stressed; or as opposed to* **that, those***)* ce...-ci, cet...-ci, cette...-ci, ces... -ci. **I like** ~ **photo better than that one** je préfère cette photo-ci à celle-là; ~ **chair over here** cette chaise-ci.
2 *dem pron, pl* **these** (**a**) ceci, ce. **what is** ~**?** qu'est-ce que c'est?; **who's** ~**?** qui est-ce?; ~ **is my son** *(in introduction)* je vous présente mon fils; *(in photo etc)* c'est mon fils; ~ **is the boy I told you about** c'est *or* voici le garçon dont je t'ai parlé; *(on phone)* ~ **is Joe Brown** Joe Brown à l'appareil; ~ **is Tuesday/May** nous sommes mardi/en mai; ~ **is what he showed me** voici ce qu'il m'a montré; ~ **is where we live** c'est ici que nous habitons; **it was like** ~... voici comment les choses se sont passées...; **do it like** ~ faites-le comme ceci; **after** ~ après ceci; **before** ~ **I'd never noticed him** je ne l'avais jamais remarqué auparavant; **it ought to have been done before** ~ cela devrait être déjà fait; **we were talking of** ~ **and that** nous parlions de choses et d'autres; **so it has come to** ~**!** nous en sommes donc là!; **at** ~ sur ce; **with** ~ **he left us** sur ces mots il nous a quittés; **what's all** ~ **I hear about your new job?** qu'est-ce que j'apprends, vous avez un nouvel emploi? (**b**) *(~ one)* celui-ci *m*, celle-ci *f*, ceux-ci *mpl*, celles-ci *fpl*. **I prefer that to** ~ je préfère celui-là à celui-ci (*or* celle-là à celle-ci).
3 *adv*: ~ **long** aussi long que ça; ~ **far** jusqu'ici.

thistle [ˈθɪsl] *n* chardon *m*. ◆ **thistledown** *n* duvet *m* de chardon.

thither [ˈðɪðəʳ] *adv (†, liter)* là, y.

tho' [ðəʊ] *abbr of* **though.**

thong [θɒŋ] *n* lanière *f (de cuir)*.

thorax [ˈθɔːræks] *n* thorax *m*.

thorn [θɔːn] *n* épine *f*; *(haw~)* aubépine *f*. *(fig)* **a ~ in sb's flesh** une source d'irritation constante pour qn. ◆ **thorny** *adj (lit, fig)* épineux.

thorough [ˈθʌrə] *adj work, worker* consciencieux; *search, research* minutieux; *knowledge, examination* approfondi; *(fig) hooligan, idiot* véritable *(before n)*; *scoundrel, rogue* fieffé. **to give sth a ~ clean** nettoyer qch à fond. ◆ **thoroughbred 1** *adj horse* pur-sang *inv*; *other animal* de race ; **2** *n* pur-sang *m inv*; bête *f* de race. ◆ **thoroughfare** *n (street)* rue *f*; *(public highway)* voie *f* publique; **'no ~fare'** 'passage interdit'. ◆ **thoroughgoing** *adj examination, revision* complet; *hooligan* véritable *(before n)*; *rogue, scoundrel* fieffé. ◆ **thoroughly** *adv (gen)* à fond; *understand* parfaitement; *agree* tout à fait; *(very) clean, nasty* tout à fait, tout ce qu'il y a de *; **to search ~ly** *house* fouiller de fond en comble; *drawer* fouiller à fond. ◆ **thoroughness** *n [worker etc]* minutie *f*.

those [ðəʊz] *pl of* **that.**

thou [ðaʊ] *pers pron (†, liter)* tu; *(stressed)* toi.

though [ðəʊ] **1** *conj* (**a**) *(despite the fact that)* bien que + *subj*, quoique + *subj*. ~ **it's raining** bien qu'il pleuve, malgré la pluie. (**b**) *(even if)* **strange ~ it may seem** si *or* pour étrange que cela puisse paraître; **even ~ I shan't be there I'll think of you** je ne serai pas là, mais je n'en penserai pas moins à toi. (**c**) *(gen)* **as** ~ comme si; **it looks as** ~ il semble que + *subj*. **2** *adv* pourtant, cependant. **it's not easy** ~ ce n'est pourtant pas facile.

thought [θɔːt] *(pret, ptp of* **think***)* *n* (**a**) *(gen)* pensée *f*; *(daydreaming)* rêverie *f*. **lost** *or* **deep in** ~ plongé dans ses pensées *or* dans une rêverie; **after much** ~ après mûre réflexion; **without** ~ sans réfléchir; **without** ~ **for** *or* **of himself** sans considérer son propre intérêt; **to take ~ for, to give a ~ to** penser à; **to give ~ to** bien réfléchir à; **don't give it another** ~ n'y pensez plus. (**b**) *(idea)* pensée *f*, idée *f*. **it's a happy** ~ voilà une idée qui fait plaisir; **what a ~! *** imagine un peu!; **what a horrifying ~! *** quel cauchemar!; **what a lovely ~! *** comme ça serait bien!; **what a brilliant ~! *** quelle idée de génie!; **that's a ~! *** tiens, mais c'est une idée!; **the mere ~ of it** rien que d'y penser; **my ~s were elsewhere** j'avais l'esprit ailleurs; **the T~s of Chairman Mao** les pensées du Président Mao; **scientific ~ on the subject** les opinions *fpl* des scientifiques sur la question ; **I had ~s of going to Paris** j'avais vaguement l'intention d'aller à Paris; **he gave up all ~ of marrying her** il a renoncé à toute idée de l'épouser; **it's the ~ that counts** c'est l'intention *f* qui compte; *(fig)* **it is a ~ too large** c'est un tout petit peu trop grand. ◆ **thoughtful** *adj* (**a**) *(pensive)* pensif; *(serious) person, book, remark* sérieux; (**b**) *(considerate) person* prévenant; *act, remark, invitation* gentil; **how ~ful of you!** comme c'est gentil à vous! ◆ **thoughtfully** *adv* pensivement; avec prévenance; **he ~fully offered...** il a eu la prévenance d'offrir... ◆ **thoughtfulness** *n* air *m* pensif; prévenance *f*. ◆ **thoughtless** *adj behaviour, words* irréfléchi; *person* étourdi; **he's very ~less** il se soucie fort peu des autres. ◆ **thoughtlessly** *adv (carelessly)* étourdiment; *(inconsiderately)* avec insouciance. ◆ **thoughtlessness** *n (carelessness)* étourderie *f*; *(lack of consideration)* manque *m* de prévenance. ◆ **thought-provoking** *adj* qui pousse à la réflexion. ◆ **thought-read** *vi* lire dans la pensée de qn. ◆ **thought-reader** *n* liseur *m*, -euse *f* de pensées.

thousand [ˈθaʊz(ə)nd] *adj, n* mille *(m) inv*. **a ~, one** ~ mille; **five** ~ cinq mille; **a ~ thanks!** mille fois merci!; **about a** ~ un millier; **about a ~ men** un millier d'hommes; **~s of** des milliers de; **they came in their ~s** ils sont venus par milliers. ◆ **thousandth** *adj, n* millième *(mf)*; *(fraction)* millième *m*.

thrash [θræʃ] *vt (beat)* rouer de coups; *(as punishment)* donner une bonne correction à; *(*: Sport etc)* battre à plates coutures.
◆ **thrash about** *vi* se débattre. ◆ **thrash out** *vt sep problem, difficulty (discuss)* débattre de; *(solve)* démêler; *plan* mettre au point avec difficulté.
◆ **thrashing** *n* correction *f*; **to give sb a good ~ing** = **to ~ sb.**

thread [θred] **1** *n* (**a**) fil *m*. *(fig)* **to hang by a ~** ne tenir qu'à un fil; *(fig)* **to lose the ~ (of what one is saying)** perdre le fil de son discours; *(fig)* to pick up the ~ again retrouver le fil. (**b**) *[screw]* pas *m*, filetage *m*. **2** *vt needle, beads* enfiler; *wire, cotton* faire passer (*through* à travers); *film* monter (*on to* sur). **to ~ one's way through** se faufiler à travers. ◆**threadbare** *adj rug, clothes* usé, râpé; *room* défraîchi; *(fig) excuse* rebattu.

threat [θret] *n* menace *f* (*to sb/sth* pour qn/qch). **to make a ~ against sb** proférer une menace à l'égard de qn; **under the ~ of** menacé de. ◆**threaten** *vti* menacer (*sb with sth* qn de qch; *to do* de faire); **to ~en** *violence etc* proférer des menaces de; **~ened species** espèce *f* menacée; **~ened with** menacé de. ◆**threatening** *adj (gen)* menaçant; *letter* de menaces; *(fig)* **to find sb ~ening** se sentir menacé par qn. ◆**threateningly** *adv* d'un ton *or* d'une manière menaçant(e).

three [θri:] *adj, n* trois *(m) inv*. *(Pol)* **the Big T~** les trois Grands; *(Sport)* **the best of ~** deux jeux et la belle; *for other phrases V* **six**. ◆**three-cornered** *adj* triangulaire. ◆**three-day eventing** *n (Equitation)* concours *m* complet. ◆**three-dimensional** *adj object* à trois dimensions; *film* en relief. ◆**three-legged** *adj table* à trois pieds; *race* à pieds liés. ◆**three-piece suite** *n* salon *m* comprenant canapé et deux fauteuils. ◆**three-ply** *adj wool* trois fils *inv*. ◆**three-quarter** *n (Rugby)* trois-quarts *m inv*. ◆**three-quarters** *npl (fraction)* trois quarts *mpl*. ◆**three-ring circus** * *n (US: fig)* véritable cirque *m*. ◆**threesome** *n (people)* groupe *m* de trois; **in a ~some** à trois. ◆**three-way** *adj division* en trois; *discussion* à trois. ◆**three-wheeler** *n (car)* voiture *f* à trois roues; *(tricycle)* tricycle *m*.

thresh [θreʃ] *vt (Agr)* battre. ◆**thresher** *n (machine)* batteuse *f*. ◆**threshing** *n* battage *m*.

threshold ['θreʃ(h)əʊld] *n (lit, fig)* seuil *m*. **to cross the ~** franchir le seuil; *(fig)* **on the ~ of** au seuil de.

threw [θru:] *pret of* **throw**.

thrice [θraɪs] *adv* trois fois.

thrift [θrɪft] *n* économie *f*. ◆**thriftless** *adj* imprévoyant. ◆**thrifty** *adj* économe.

thrill [θrɪl] **1** *n (gen)* frisson *m*. **what a ~!** quelle émotion!; **it gave me a big ~** ça m'a vraiment fait qch! *; **to get a ~ out of doing sth** se procurer des sensations fortes en faisant qch; **film packed with ~s** film *m* à sensations. **2** *vt (gen) person, crowd* électriser. **his glance ~ed her** son regard l'a enivrée; **I was ~ed!** j'étais aux anges!; **I was ~ed to meet him** ça m'a vraiment fait qch * de le rencontrer. **3** *vi* frissonner (de joie). ◆**thriller** *n (novel/film)* roman *m*/film *m* à suspense. ◆**thrilling** *adj play, journey* palpitant; *news* saisissant.

thrive [θraɪv] *pret* **throve, thrived,** *ptp* **thriven, thrived** *vi [person, animal]* être florissant de santé; *[plant]* pousser bien; *[industry, businessman]* prospérer. **children ~ on milk** le lait est excellent pour les enfants; **he ~s on hard work** le travail lui réussit. ◆**thriving** *adj person etc* florissant de santé; *plant* robuste; *industry etc* prospère.

throat [θrəʊt] *n* gorge *f*. **to take sb by the ~** prendre qn à la gorge; **I have a sore ~** j'ai mal à la gorge, j'ai une angine; **he had a bone stuck in his ~** il avait une arête dans le gosier; *(fig)* **that sticks in my ~** je n'arrive pas à accepter ça; *(fig)* **to thrust** *or* **shove * sth down sb's ~** rebattre les oreilles de qn avec qch. ◆**throaty** *adj* guttural.

throb [θrɒb] **1** *vi [heart]* palpiter, battre fort; *[voice, engine]* vibrer; *[drums]* battre (en rythme); *[pain]* lanciner. **town ~bing with life** ville vibrante d'animation; **my head is ~bing** j'ai des élancements dans la tête. **2** *n [heart]* battement *m*; *[engine]* vibration *f*; *[music]* rythme *m* (fort); *[pain]* élancement *m*.

throes [θrəʊz] *npl*: **in the ~ of death** à l'agonie; **in the ~ of** *war, disease, crisis etc* en proie à; *quarrel, debate* au cœur de; **in the ~ of writing a book** aux prises avec la rédaction d'un livre.

thrombosis [θrɒm'bəʊsɪs] *n* thrombose *f*.

throne [θrəʊn] *n* trône *m*. **to come to the ~** monter sur le trône; **on the ~** sur le trône.

throng [θrɒŋ] **1** *n* foule *f*. **2** *vi* se presser (*round* autour de; *to see* pour voir). **3** *vt streets* se presser dans. **~ed with people** plein de monde.

throttle ['θrɒtl] **1** *n (Aut, Tech)* papillon *m* des gaz. **to open the ~** mettre les gaz; **to close the ~** réduire l'arrivée des gaz. **2** *vt (strangle)* étrangler. ◆**throttle back, throttle down** *vt sep engine* mettre au ralenti.

through [θru:] **1** *adv* (**a**) *(gen)* **the nail went right ~** le clou est passé à travers; **just go ~** passez donc; **to let sb ~** laisser passer qn; **to get a train ~ to London** attraper un train direct pour Londres; *(in exam)* **did you get ~?** as-tu été reçu?; **all night ~** toute la nuit; **I knew all ~ that...** je savais depuis le début que...; **wet ~** trempé; **wet ~ and ~** complètement trempé; **he's a liar ~ and ~** il ment comme il respire; **he's a Scot ~ and ~** il est écossais jusqu'au bout des ongles; **read it right ~** lis-le jusqu'au bout; **I read it ~ quickly** je l'ai lu rapidement; *(Telec)* **to put sb ~ to sb** passer qn à qn; **I'll put you ~ to her** je vous la passe; **you're ~ now** vous avez votre correspondant; **you're ~ to him** il est en ligne. (**b**) *(finished)* **I'm ~ *** ça y est, j'ai fini; **I'm not ~ with you yet *** je n'en ai pas encore fini avec vous; **are you ~ with that book? *** tu n'as plus besoin de ce livre?; **he told me we were ~ *** il m'a dit que c'était fini entre nous.

2 *prep* (**a**) *(place)* à travers. **a stream flows ~ the garden** un ruisseau traverse le jardin *or* coule à travers le jardin; **to go ~** *forest, garden, building* traverser; *hedge* passer au travers de; *(Aut) red light* griller; *(fig) sb's pockets, luggage* fouiller; **to hammer a nail ~ a plank** enfoncer un clou dans une planche; **he was shot ~ the head** on lui a tiré une balle dans la tête; **to look ~ a window/telescope** regarder par une fenêtre/dans un télescope; **he has really been ~ it *** il en a vu de dures *; **to get ~ an exam** réussir à un examen; **I'm half-way ~ the book** j'en suis à la moitié du livre; **to speak ~ one's nose** parler du nez.
(**b**) *(time)* pendant, durant. **all** *or* **right ~ his life** pendant *or* durant toute sa vie; **he won't live ~ the night** il ne passera pas la nuit; *(US)* **Monday ~ Friday** de lundi à vendredi; **~ the week** pendant la semaine.
(**c**) *(by, from)* par; *(thanks to)* grâce à; *(because of)* à cause de. **~ the post** par la poste; **it was all ~ him that...** c'est à cause de lui que...; **I heard it ~ my sister** je l'ai appris par ma sœur; **~ his own efforts** par ses propres efforts; **absent ~ illness** absent pour cause de maladie; **~ fear** par peur; **~ not knowing the way he...** parce qu'il ne connaissait pas le chemin il...
3 *adj train, ticket* direct. **'no ~ way'** 'impasse'; **the ~ traffic** la circulation *f* de passage.
◆**throughout** **1** *prep* (**a**) *(place)* partout dans ; **~out the world** partout dans le monde; (**b**) *(time)* pendant; **~out his life** pendant toute sa vie ; **~out his career** tout au long de sa carrière ; **2** *adv (everywhere)* partout; *(the whole time)* tout le temps. ◆**throughway** *n (US)* autoroute *f* à péage.

throve [θrəʊv] *pret of* **thrive**.

throw [θrəʊ] *(vb: pret* **threw,** *ptp* **thrown***)* **1** *n [ball, javelin etc]* **a good ~** un bon jet; **with one ~ of the ball he...** d'un seul coup il...; *(in table games)* **you lose a ~** vous perdez un tour.
2 *vt* (**a**) *(gen)* jeter (*to, at* à; *over* sur; *into* dans; *into jail* en prison); *object, stone* lancer, jeter (*to, at* à); *ball, javelin etc* lancer; *dice* jeter; *[fighter etc] opponent* envoyer au sol; *[explosion, car crash etc]*

projeter; *pottery* tourner; *(fig) responsibility etc* rejeter (*on* sur); (*) *party* organiser (*for sb* en l'honneur de qn); *(*: fig: disconcert)* déconcerter, décontenancer. *(dice)* **to ~ a six** avoir un six; **the horse threw him** le cheval l'a désarçonné; **he was ~n clear of the car** il a été projeté hors de la voiture; **to ~ o.s. to the ground/into sb's arms** se jeter à terre/dans les bras de qn; **to ~ o.s. on sb's mercy** s'en remettre à la merci de qn; *(fig)* **to ~ o.s. into a job** se mettre au travail avec enthousiasme; **to ~ open** *door, window* ouvrir tout grand; *(fig) house, gardens* ouvrir au public; *race, competition etc* ouvrir à tout le monde; **to ~ a switch** actionner l'interrupteur; **to ~ a question at sb** poser une question à qn à brûle-pourpoint; **to ~ sth/sb into confusion** jeter la confusion dans qch/dans l'esprit de qn; **to ~ sb off the trail** dépister qn; *(fig: disconcert)* **I was quite ~n * when...** je n'en revenais pas quand...
(**b**) *(direct) light, shadow, glance* jeter; *slides* projeter; *kiss* envoyer (*to* à); *punch* lancer (*at* à).
◆ **throw about, throw around** *vt sep litter, confetti* éparpiller. **to be ~n about** être ballotté; *(fig)* **to ~ one's weight about** faire l'important. ◆ **throw away** *vt sep rubbish etc* jeter; *(fig) one's life, talents* gâcher; *money, sb's affection, chance* perdre; *line, remark (say casually)* laisser tomber; *(lose effect of)* perdre tout l'effet de. **to ~ o.s. away** gaspiller ses dons. ◆ **throw back** *vt sep* (**a**) *(return) ball etc* renvoyer (*to* à); *fish* rejeter; *(fig) image* renvoyer. (**b**) *head, hair* rejeter en arrière; *shoulders* redresser. *(fig)* **to be ~n back upon sth** être obligé de se rabattre sur qch. ◆ **throw down** *vt sep object* jeter; *weapons* déposer; *challenge* lancer. **to ~ o.s. down** se jeter à terre. ◆ **throw in 1** *vi (US)* **to ~ in with sb** rallier qn. **2** *vt sep object into box etc* jeter; *(Ftbl) ball* remettre en jeu; *(fig) one's cards* jeter sur la table; *(fig) remark, question* interposer; *reference* mentionner en passant. *(fig)* **to ~ in one's hand** *or* **the towel** abandonner la partie; *(as extra)* **with £5 ~n in** avec 5 livres en plus; *(included)* **with meals ~n in** repas compris. ◆ **throw off** *vt sep (get rid of) (gen)* se débarrasser de; *disguise* jeter; *pursuers, dogs* perdre, semer *. ◆ **throw on** *vt sep coal, sticks* ajouter; *clothes* enfiler à la hâte. ◆ **throw out** *vt sep* (**a**) *(lit)* jeter dehors; *rubbish etc* jeter; *person* expulser; *suggestion, (Parl) bill* repousser. *(fig)* **to ~ out one's chest** bomber la poitrine. (**b**) *(offer) suggestion, idea* laisser tomber; *challenge* lancer. (**c**) *(make wrong) calculation, prediction* fausser. ◆ **throw over** *vt sep* abandonner, laisser tomber * (*for sth else* pour autre chose; *for sb else* pour qn d'autre). ◆ **throw together** *vt sep* (**a**) *(pack) belongings etc* rassembler; *(make hastily) object* faire à la six-quatre-deux *; (*) *essay* torcher. (**b**) *(fig: by chance) people* réunir (par hasard). **they were ~n together** le hasard les avait réunis. ◆ **throw up 1** *vi (vomit)* vomir. **2** *vt sep* (**a**) *(into air) ball etc* lancer en l'air; *arms* lever. *(fig)* **it threw up several good ideas** quelques bonnes idées en sont sorties. (**b**) *(vomit)* vomir. (**c**) *(*: abandon etc) job, studies* abandonner; *opportunity* laisser passer.
◆ **throwaway** *adj packaging* à jeter; *remark* qui n'a l'air de rien. ◆ **throwback** *n (fig)* **it's a ~back to** ça remonte à. ◆ **thrower** *n* lanceur *m*, -euse *f*. ◆ **throw-in** *n (Ftbl)* rentrée *f* en touche.

thru [θruː] *(US)* = **through.** ◆ **thruway** *n (US)* voie *f* express.

thrush[1] [θrʌʃ] *n (bird)* grive *f*.

thrush[2] [θrʌʃ] *n (Med)* muguet *m*.

thrust [θrʌst] *(vb: pret, ptp* **thrust***)* **1** *n* (**a**) *(push)* poussée *f (also Mil)*; *(stab: with knife, stick etc)* coup *m*; *(fig: remark)* pointe *f* (*at sb* contre qn). (**b**) *[propeller, jet engine etc]* poussée *f*; *(* fig: energy)* dynamisme *m*; **the main ~ of his speech** l'idée maîtresse de son discours. **2** *vt (push: gen)* pousser brusquement; *finger, stick, dagger* enfoncer (*into* dans; *between* entre); *sth into drawer, pocket, hole* fourrer * (*into* dans); *(fig) job, responsibility* imposer (*upon sb* à qn). **he ~ it into my hand** il me l'a fourré * dans la main; **he ~ it at me** il me l'a brusquement mis sous le nez; **to ~ one's hands into one's pockets** enfoncer les mains dans ses poches; **he ~ his head through the window** il a passé la tête par la fenêtre; *(fig)* **some have greatness ~ upon them** certains ont de la grandeur sans la rechercher; **to ~ o.s. upon sb** imposer sa présence à qn; **to ~ one's way in/out** *etc* entrer/sortir *etc* en se frayant un passage; **to ~ aside** *object, person* écarter brusquement; *suggestion* rejeter violemment.

thud [θʌd] **1** *n* bruit *m* sourd. **2** *vi* faire un bruit sourd (*on, against* en heurtant); *[guns]* gronder sourdement; *(fall)* tomber avec un bruit sourd.

thug [θʌg] *n* voyou *m*.

thumb [θʌm] **1** *n* pouce *m*. *(fig)* **to be under sb's ~** être sous la coupe de qn; **she's got him under her ~** elle le mène par le bout du nez; *(fig)* **to be all ~s** être très maladroit; **he gave me the ~s up sign *** *(all well)* il m'a fait signe que tout allait bien; *(for luck)* il m'a fait signe pour me souhaiter bonne chance. **2** *adj nail, print* du pouce. **~ index** répertoire *m* à onglets. **3** *vt book, magazine* feuilleter. **well ~ed** tout écorné (par l'usage); **to ~ one's nose** faire un pied de nez (*at sb* à qn); **he ~ed a lift to Paris** il est allé à Paris en stop *; **I managed to ~ a lift** je suis arrivé à arrêter une voiture. ◆ **thumb through** *vt fus book* feuilleter; *card index* consulter rapidement.
◆ **thumbnail** *adj*: **~nail sketch** croquis *m* sur le vif. ◆ **thumbscrew** *n (Tech)* vis *f* à papillon.
◆ **thumbtack** *n (US)* punaise *f*.

thump [θʌmp] **1** *n (blow: with fist/stick etc)* grand coup *m* de poing/de canne *etc*; *(sound)* bruit *m* lourd et sourd. **to fall with a ~** tomber lourdement. **2** *vt (gen)* taper sur; *door* cogner à. **3** *vi* cogner, taper (*on* sur; *at* à); *[heart]* battre fort; *(with fear)* battre la chamade. ◆ **thumping *** *adj* (**~ing great**) monumental *.

thunder [ˈθʌndəʳ] **1** *n* tonnerre *m*; *[applause]* tonnerre; *[hooves, vehicles, trains]* fracas *m*. **there's ~ in the air** il y a de l'orage dans l'air. **2** *vi (Met)* tonner; *[guns]* tonner; *[hooves]* retentir. **the train ~ed past** le train est passé dans un grondement de tonnerre. **3** *vt* (**~ out**) *threat, order* proférer d'une voix tonitruante.
◆ **thunderbolt** *n* coup *m* de foudre; *(fig)* coup de tonnerre. ◆ **thunderclap** *n* coup *m* de tonnerre. ◆ **thundercloud** *n* nuage orageux; *(fig)* nuage noir. ◆ **thundering** *adj* (**a**) *rage* fou; *temper* massacrant; (**b**) (*: **~ing great**) monumental *; *success* monstre. ◆ **thunderous** *adj welcome, shouts, noise* étourdissant; *applause* frénétique.
◆ **thunderstorm** *n* orage *m*. ◆ **thunderstruck** *adj* abasourdi. ◆ **thundery** *adj* orageux.

Thursday [ˈθɜːzdɪ] *n* jeudi *m*; *for phrases V* **Saturday.**

thus [ðʌs] *adv* ainsi. **~ far** *(up to here/now)* jusqu'ici; *(up to there/then)* jusque-là.

thwart [θwɔːt] *vt plan* contrecarrer; *person* contrecarrer les projets de. **to be ~ed** essuyer un échec.

thy [ðaɪ] *poss adj (†, liter)* ton, ta, tes.

thyme [taɪm] *n* thym *m*.

thyroid [ˈθaɪrɔɪd] *adj, n* (**~ gland**) thyroïde *(f)*.

ti [tiː] *n (Mus)* si *m*.

tiara [tɪˈɑːrə] *n* diadème *m*.

Tibet [tɪˈbet] *n* Tibet *m*. ◆ **Tibetan 1** *adj* tibétain ; **2** *n (person)* Tibétain(e) *m(f)*; *(Ling)* tibétain.

tibia [ˈtɪbɪə] *n* tibia *m*.

tic [tɪk] *n* tic *m* (nerveux). ◆ **tic-tac-toc** *n (US)* (jeu *m* de) morpion *m*.

tichy ‡ [ˈtɪtʃɪ] *adj* (**~ little**) minuscule.

tick[1] [tɪk] **1** *n* (**a**) *[clock]* tic-tac *m*; *(* fig)* instant *m*. **just a ~! *, half a ~! *** un instant!; **in a ~ *,**

in a couple of ~s * en un rien de temps; **I shan't be a ~** * j'en ai pour une seconde. (**b**) *(mark)* coche *f*. **to put a ~ against sth** cocher qch. **2** *vt name, item* cocher; *(mark right) answer etc* marquer juste. **3** *vi [clock, bomb etc]* faire tic-tac. *(fig)* **I don't understand what makes him ~** * il est un mystère pour moi.

◆ **tick off** *vt sep* (**a**) *name, item* cocher. (**b**) (*: *reprimand)* passer un savon à *. ◆ **tick over** *vi [engine]* tourner au ralenti; *[taximeter]* tourner; *[business etc]* aller doucettement.

◆ **ticker** ‡ *n (heart)* cœur *m*, palpitant ‡ *m*. ◆ **ticker-tape** *n (US: at parades etc)* ≃ serpentin *m*; **to get a ~er-tape welcome** être accueilli par une pluie de serpentins. ◆ **ticking¹** *n [clock]* tic-tac *m*. ◆ **ticking-off** * *n* attrapade * *f*; **to give sb a ~ing-off** passer un savon à qn *; **to get a ~ing-off** se faire attraper. ◆ **tick-tack-toe** *n (US)* ≃ jeu *m* de morpion. ◆ **tick-tock** *n [clock]* tic-tac *m*.

tick² [tɪk] *n (Zool)* tique *f*.

tick³ [tɪk] *n*: **on ~** * à crédit.

ticket ['tɪkɪt] **1** *n* (**a**) *(gen)* billet *m*; *(for bus, tube, cloakroom)* ticket *m*; *(Comm: label)* étiquette *f*; *(from cash register)* ticket, reçu *m*; *(for left-luggage)* bulletin *m*; *(for library)* carte *f*. **to buy a ~** prendre un billet; **coach ~** billet de car; *(fig)* **that's the ~!** * voilà ce qu'il nous faut!; *(US Pol)* **he is running on the Democratic ~** il se présente sur la liste des démocrates. (**b**) *(Aut: for fine)* P.-V. *m*, papillon *m*. **a ~ on the windscreen** un papillon sur le pare-brise; **to give sb/get a ~ for parking** mettre à qn/attraper un P.-V. pour stationnement illégal. **2** *adj*: *(Theat)* **~ agency** agence *f* de spectacles; **~ collector** contrôleur *m*; **~ holder** personne *f* munie d'un billet; **~ office** guichet *m*. **3** *vt goods* étiqueter.

ticking² ['tɪkɪŋ] *n (Tex)* toile *f* (à matelas).

tickle ['tɪkl] **1** *vt person, sb's vanity, palate etc* chatouiller; (*: *delight)* faire plaisir à; (*: *amuse)* faire rire. **to be ~d to death** ‡ *or* **~d pink** ‡ *(pleased)* être heureux comme tout; *(amused)* rire aux larmes. **2** *vi* chatouiller. **3** *n* chatouillement *m*. ◆ **tickler** * *n (problem)* colle * *f*; *(situation)* situation *f* délicate. ◆ **tickling 1** *n* chatouillement *m* ; **2** *adj sensation* de chatouillement; *cough* d'irritation. ◆ **ticklish** *or* ◆ **tickly** * *adj* (**a**) *sensation* de chatouillement; *blanket* qui chatouille; *cough* d'irritation; *person* chatouilleux; (**b**) *(touchy) person* chatouilleux; *(difficult) situation* délicat.

tiddler * ['tɪdləʳ] *n (stickleback)* épinoche *f*; *(tiny fish)* petit poisson *m*; *(child)* petit(e) mioche * *m(f)*.

tiddly * ['tɪdlɪ] *adj* pompette *, ivre. ◆ **tiddly-winks** *n* jeu *m* de puce.

tide [taɪd] **1** *n* marée *f*; *(fig: of events)* cours *m*. **at high/low ~** à marée haute/basse; **the ~ turns at...** la marée commence à monter (*or* à descendre) à...; *(fig)* **the ~ has turned** la chance a tourné; *(fig)* **to go with the ~** suivre le courant; **to go against the ~** aller à contre-courant. **2** *vt*: **to ~ sb over (a difficulty)** dépanner * qn (*till* en attendant); **that should ~ me over until...** avec ça je devrais m'en sortir jusqu'à... ◆ **tidal** *adj river* qui a des marées; **tidal wave** raz-de-marée *m inv*; *(of enthusiasm etc)* immense vague *f*. ◆ **tidemark** *n* laisse *f* de haute mer; *(on neck, bath)* ligne *f* de crasse. ◆ **tideway** *n (channel)* chenal *m* de marée; *(current)* flux *m*.

tidy ['taɪdɪ] **1** *adj* (**a**) *room, drawer, objects* bien rangé; *dress, hair, schoolwork* net; *habits* d'ordre; *person (in appearance)* soigné; *(in character)* ordonné. **to make ~** *or* **tidier** = **to ~** *(V* **3**); **to have a ~ mind** avoir l'esprit méthodique. (**b**) (*) *amount, income* rondelet; *speed* bon. **it cost him a ~ bit** ça lui a coûté une jolie somme; **a ~ bit of his salary** une bonne partie de son salaire. **2** *n (in car, cupboard etc)* vide-poches *m inv*. **sink ~** coin *m* d'évier *(ustensile)*. **3** *vti* (**~ away**, **~ out**, **~ up**) ranger. **to ~ o.s. (up)** s'arranger; **to ~ (up) one's hair** arranger sa coiffure. ◆ **tidily** *adv arrange, fold* soigneusement; *write* proprement; *dress* avec soin. ◆ **tidiness** *n [room, drawer, books]* ordre *m*; *[handwriting, schoolwork]* propreté *f*; *[person]* sens *m* de l'ordre. ◆ **tidy-out** * *or* ◆ **tidy-up** * *n*: **to have a ~-out** *or* **~-up** faire du rangement; **to give sth a (good) ~-out** *or* **~-up** ranger qch à fond.

tie [taɪ] **1** *n* (**a**) *(neck ~)* cravate *f*; *(on garment, curtain)* attache *f*; *(on shoe)* lacet *m*; *(Mus)* liaison *f*. *(on invitation)* **black ~** smoking *m*; **white ~** habit *m*; **family ~s** *(links)* liens *mpl* de famille; *(responsibilities)* attaches *fpl* familiales; **children are a great ~** avec les enfants on n'est pas libre. (**b**) *(Sport) (draw)* égalité *f* (de points); *(drawn match)* match *m* nul; *(drawn race/ competition)* course *f*/concours *m* dont les vainqueurs sont ex æquo. **the match ended in a ~** les deux équipes ont fait match nul; **the election ended in a ~** les candidats ont terminé à égalité de voix; **to play off a ~** rejouer un match nul; **there was a ~ for second place** il y avait deux ex æquo en seconde position; **cup ~** match de coupe.

2 *vt (fasten)* attacher (*to* à); *(knot)* nouer (*to* à); *ribbon* faire un nœud à; *shoes* lacer; *(link: also Mus)* lier (*to* à); *(restrict)* restreindre. *(fig)* **his hands are ~d** il a les mains liées; **to be ~d hand and foot** avoir pieds et poings liés; **to ~ a bow in sth** faire un nœud avec qch; **to ~ a knot in sth** faire un nœud à qch; **to get ~d in knots** *[rope etc]* faire des nœuds; *(fig) [person]* s'embrouiller; **house ~d to the job** maison liée au travail; **I'm ~d to the house** je suis retenu à la maison; **are we ~d to this plan?** sommes-nous obligés de nous en tenir à ce projet?; **we are very ~d in the evenings** nous sommes rarement libres le soir.

3 *vi (draw) (Sport etc)* faire match nul; *(in competition)* être ex æquo; *(in election)* obtenir le même nombre de voix. **they ~d for first place** ils ont été premiers ex æquo.

◆ **tie back** *vt sep curtains* attacher sur les côtés; *hair* retenir (en arrière). ◆ **tie down** *vt sep* attacher. *(fig)* **to be ~d down** ne pas avoir assez de temps libre; **to ~ sb down to a promise/a price/a time** obliger qn à tenir sa promesse/à fixer un prix/à venir à une certaine heure; **to ~ o.s. down to doing sth** se trouver contraint de faire qch. ◆ **tie in 1** *vi (be linked)* être lié (*with* à); *(be consistent)* correspondre (*with* à). **2** *vt sep meeting, visit, work* combiner (*with* avec). ◆ **tie on** *vt sep* attacher. ◆ **tie together** *vt sep* attacher (ensemble). ◆ **tie up 1** *vi (Naut)* accoster. **2** *vt sep parcel* ficeler; *prisoner, boat, horse* attacher (*to* à); *(fig) money* immobiliser; *(conclude) deal etc* conclure; *details* régler. **it's all ~d up** tout est réglé; *(fig)* **to be ~d up** *(linked)* être lié (*with* avec); *(busy)* être très pris; *(muddled)* être embrouillé; *(obstructed) [traffic]* être bloqué; *[production, sales]* être arrêté; *[project]* être suspendu.

◆ **tie-break(er)** *n (Tennis)* tie-break *m*; *(in quiz)* question *f* subsidiaire. ◆ **tie-in** *n (link)* lien *m*, rapport *m* (*with* avec). ◆ **tie-on** *adj label* à œillet. ◆ **tiepin** *n* épingle *f* de cravate. ◆ **tie-up** *n (connection)* lien *m* (*with* avec; *between* entre).

tier [tɪəʳ] *n (in stadium etc)* gradin *m*; *(of cake)* étage *m*. **in ~s** *(gen)* par étages; *seating* en gradins; **to rise in ~s** s'étager; **three-~ed cake** ≃ pièce montée *f* à trois étages; **a three-~ system** un système à trois niveaux.

tiff [tɪf] *n* prise *f* de bec *.

tiger ['taɪgəʳ] **1** *n* tigre *m*. **2** *adj*: **~ lily** lis *m* tigré; **~ moth** écaille *f (papillon)*. ◆ **tigress** *n* tigresse *f*.

tight [taɪt] **1** *adj* (**a**) *(not loose) rope* raide, tendu; *garment* ajusté; *(too ~)* trop étroit; *belt, shoes* qui serre; *tap, lid, drawer* dur; *bend in road* raide; *knot,* *weave, knitting* serré; *restrictions, control* sévère, strict; *programme, schedule* très chargé. **my shoes are too ~** mes chaussures me serrent; **it's a ~ fit** c'est juste; **to keep a ~ hold on sth** bien tenir qch; *(fig)* avoir qch en main; **it will be ~ but we'll make it in time** ce sera juste, mais nous y arriverons; *(fig)* **in a ~ corner** dans une situation difficile. (**b**) *credit* serré; *business* difficile; *budget* juste; *transaction* qui laisse peu de marge. **money is very ~** *(Econ)* l'argent est rare; *(at home)* les finances sont très justes; **to be ~** *(miserly)* être avare *or* radin *. (**c**) *(*: drunk)* rond *, ivre. **to get ~** se cuiter ‡. **2** *adv grasp* bien, solidement; *close* bien, hermétiquement; *squeeze* très fort. **screw the nut up ~** serrez l'écrou à bloc; **don't fasten** *or* **tie it too ~** ne le serrez pas trop (fort); **to pack sth ~** bien empaqueter qch; *V* **hold, sit, sleep** *etc.*

◆ **tighten** **1** *vt* (**~en up**) *rope* tendre; *garment* ajuster; *screw, wheel, grasp* resserrer; *legislation, restrictions* renforcer; *(lit, fig)* **to ~en one's belt** se serrer la ceinture ; **2** *vi* (**~en up**) se tendre; se resserrer; être renforcé; *(fig)* **to ~en up on sth** devenir plus strict en matière de qch. ◆ **tight-fisted** *adj* avare, radin *. ◆ **tight-fitting** *adj garment* ajusté; *lid, stopper* qui ferme bien. ◆ **tight-knit** *adj (fig) family* uni; *programme, schedule* très chargé. ◆ **tightly** *adv* = **tight 2.** ◆ **tightness** *n [garment]* étroitesse *f*; *[screw, lid]* dureté *f*; *[restrictions, control]* sévérité *f*; **he felt a ~ness in his chest** il avait la poitrine oppressée. ◆ **tightrope** **1** *n* corde *f* raide ; **2** *adj*: **~rope walker** funambule *mf*. ◆ **tights** *npl* collant *m*.

tile [taɪl] **1** *n (on roof)* tuile *f*; *(on floor, wall)* carreau *m*. *(fig)* **to be out on the ~s *** faire la noce *. **2** *vt* couvrir de tuiles; carreler. ◆ **tiled** *adj roof* en tuiles; *floor, room etc* carrelé. ◆ **tiling** *n (tiles) [roof]* tuiles *fpl*; *[floor, wall]* carrelage *m*.

till[1] [tɪl] = **until.**

till[2] [tɪl] *n* caisse *f*. *(fig)* **caught with one's hand in the ~** pris sur le fait.

till[3] [tɪl] *vt (Agr)* labourer.

tiller ['tɪləʳ] *n (Naut)* barre *f (du gouvernail)*.

tilt [tɪlt] **1** *n* (**a**) *(slope)* inclinaison *f*. (**b**) **(at) full ~** à toute vitesse. **2** *vt object, one's head* pencher, incliner; *backrest* incliner; *hat* rabattre (*over* sur). **to ~ one's chair back** se balancer sur sa chaise. **3** *vi* (**~ over**) pencher, être incliné.

timber ['tɪmbəʳ] **1** *n (wood)* bois *m* de construction; *(trees collectively)* arbres *mpl*. **2** *adj fence etc* en bois. ◆ **timbered** *adj house* en bois; *land* boisé. ◆ **timber-merchant** *n* négociant *m* en bois. ◆ **timberyard** *n* chantier *m* de bois.

time [taɪm] **1** *n* (**a**) *(gen)* temps *m*. **~ and space** le temps et l'espace; **~ flies** le temps passe vite; **only ~ will tell** ≃ qui vivra, verra; **~ will show if...** le temps dira si...; **with ~, in (the course of) ~, as ~ goes by** avec le temps; **it takes ~** ça prend du temps; **from ~ out of mind** de toute éternité; **I've no ~ for that sort of thing** *(lit)* je n'ai pas le temps de faire ce genre de chose; *(fig)* ce genre de chose m'agace; **I've enough ~** *or* **I have the ~ to go there** j'ai le temps d'y aller; **we've got plenty of ~, we've all the ~ in the world** nous avons tout notre temps; **you've got plenty of ~ to wait for me** vous avez bien le temps de m'attendre; **I can't find ~ to do** *or* **for (doing) that** je n'arrive pas à trouver le temps de faire ça; **to make up for lost ~** rattraper le temps perdu; **in no ~ at all, in less than no ~** en un rien de temps; **he had ~ on his hands** *or* **~ to spare** il avait du temps devant lui; **I spent a lot of ~ preparing this, it took me a lot of ~ to prepare this** il m'a fallu pas mal de temps pour le préparer; **to spend one's ~ doing** passer son temps à faire; **for part** *or* **some of the ~** pendant une partie du temps; **some of the ~ he looks cheerful** quelquefois *or* par moments il a l'air gai; **most of the ~** la plupart du temps; **all the ~** *(the whole ~)* tout le temps; *(from the start)* dès le début; **take your ~ (over it)** prenez votre temps (pour le faire); *(fig)* **it took me all my ~ to finish it** j'ai eu du mal à le finir; **to take ~ out to do sth** *(gen)* trouver le temps de faire qch; **your ~ is up** *(in exam, visit etc)* c'est l'heure; **free ~, ~ off** temps libre; **in his own good ~** quand bon lui semblera; **in good ~** à temps; **in good ~ for** en avance pour; **all in good ~!** chaque chose en son temps!; **a race against ~** une course contre la montre; **he was working against ~** il travaillait d'arrache-pied (*to finish* pour terminer); **for the ~ being** pour le moment.

(**b**) *(period, length of ~)* **for a ~** pendant un certain temps; **a long ~** longtemps; **he hasn't been seen for a long ~** on ne l'a pas vu depuis longtemps; **it's a long ~ since...** il y a bien longtemps que...; **what a (long) ~ you've been!** il vous en a fallu du temps!; **it took a very long ~ for that to happen** il a fallu attendre longtemps pour que cela arrive *(subj)*; **for a long ~ (to come** *or* **past)** longtemps; **a short ~** peu de temps; **for a short ~** (pendant) un moment; **in a short ~ they were all gone** quelques moments plus tard ils avaient tous disparu; **I waited for some ~** j'ai attendu assez longtemps; **some considerable ~** un temps considérable; **some little ~** un certain temps; **some ~ ago** il y a quelque temps *or* un certain temps; **it won't be ready for some ~** ce ne sera pas prêt avant un certain temps; **in half the ~** deux fois plus vite; **in 2 weeks' ~** dans 2 semaines; **what ~ did he do it in?** il a mis combien de temps?; **cooking ~** temps de cuisson; *[prisoner]* **to do ~ *** faire de la prison; *(US: hurry)* **to make ~** se dépêcher; **we made good ~** nous avons bien marché; **to be on** *or* **to work full ~** travailler à plein temps; **to be on ~ and a half** faire des heures supplémentaires payées à 150%; **it is paid at double ~** c'est payé double; **in the firm's ~** pendant les heures de service; **in one's own ~** après les heures de service.

(**c**) *(era: often pl)* époque *f*. **the ~s we live in** l'époque où nous vivons; **in medieval ~s** à l'époque médiévale; **in Gladstone's ~** du temps de Gladstone; **in ~s past, in former ~s** dans le temps, jadis; **in my ~ it was different** de mon temps c'était différent; **I've seen some queer things in my ~** j'ai vu des choses étranges dans ma vie; **before my ~** *(before I was born)* avant que je ne sois né; *(before I came here)* avant que je ne vienne ici; **in ~(s) of peace** en temps de paix; **peace in our ~** la paix de notre vivant; *(fig)* **he is ahead of his ~, he was born before his ~** il est en avance sur son époque; **to keep up with the ~s** être de son époque; **to be behind the ~s** être vieux jeu *inv*; **at the best of ~s** déjà quand tout va bien; **~s are hard** les temps sont durs; **to have a rough** *or* **bad** *or* **tough * ~ (of it)** en voir de dures *; **to give sb a bad ~** en faire voir de dures * à qn; **what great ~s we've had!** c'était le bon temps!; **to have a good ~ (of it)** bien s'amuser; **to have the ~ of one's life** s'amuser comme un fou; **a tense ~** une période très tendue (*for* pour).

(**d**) *(by clock)* heure *f*. **what is the ~?, what ~ is it?** quelle heure est-il?; **what ~ do you make it?** quelle heure avez-vous?; **have you got the right ~?** est-ce que vous avez l'heure exacte?; **the ~ is 10.30** il est 10 h 30; **what ~ is he arriving at?** à quelle heure est-ce qu'il arrive?; **he looked at the ~** il a regardé l'heure; **it keeps good ~** c'est toujours à l'heure; **there's a ~ and a place for everything** il y a un temps pour tout; *(fig)* **to pass the ~ of day** échanger quelques mots (*with sb* avec qn); **at this ~ of (the) night** à cette heure de la nuit; **at any ~ of the day or night** à n'importe quelle heure du jour ou de la nuit; **open at all**

~**s** ouvert à toute heure; *(US)* **midnight, by Eastern** ~ minuit, heure de la côte est; **ahead of/behind** ~ en avance/retard; **just in** ~ juste à temps (*for sth* pour qch; *to do* pour faire); **on** ~ à l'heure; **it's** ~ **for tea, it's tea** ~ c'est l'heure du thé; **it's** ~ **to go** c'est l'heure de partir, il est temps de partir; **it's** ~ **I was going, it's** ~ **for me to go** il est temps que je m'en aille; **it's about** ~ **he was here** il serait temps qu'il arrive *(subj)*; **it's (high)** ~ **that** il est grand temps que + *subj;* **and about** ~ **too!** et ce n'est pas trop tôt!
(**e**) *(point of* ~*)* moment *m.* **at the** *or* **that** ~ à ce moment-là; **at this** ~ en ce moment; **at the present** ~ en ce moment, actuellement; **at one** ~ à un moment donné; **sometimes... at other** ~**s...** quelquefois... d'autres fois...; **at all** ~**s** à tous moments; **I have at no** ~ **said that** je n'ai jamais dit cela; **at** ~**s** par moments; **there are** ~**s when** il y a des moments où; **at his** ~ **of life** à son âge; **at an inconvenient** ~ à un moment inopportun; **he may come (at) any** ~ il peut arriver d'un moment à l'autre; **come (at) any** ~ venez n'importe quand; **at this** ~ **of year** à cette époque de l'année; **two things at the same** ~ deux choses à la fois; **at the same** ~ **as** en même temps que; **but at the same** ~**, you must admit...** cependant, il faut avouer...; **by the** ~ **I had finished** le temps que je termine *(subj)*; **by this** *or* **that** ~ **they had drunk it all** à ce moment-là ils avaient déjà tout bu; **you must be cold by this** ~ vous devez avoir froid maintenant; **by this** ~ **next year** dans un an; **this** ~ **tomorrow** demain à cette heure-ci; **this** ~ **last year** l'année dernière à cette époque-ci; **this** ~ **last week** il y a exactement huit jours; **in between** ~**s** entre temps; **from** ~ **to** ~ de temps en temps; **from that** ~ *or* **this** ~ **on** *(+ past)* à partir de ce moment; *(+ future)* désormais; **until such** ~ **as** jusqu'à ce que + *subj*; **this is no** ~ **for quarrelling** ce n'est pas le moment de se disputer; **to choose one's** ~ choisir son moment; **now's the** ~ **to do it** c'est maintenant qu'il faut le faire; **to die before one's** ~ mourir avant l'âge; **his** ~ **has come** son heure a sonné; **when the** ~ **comes** quand le moment viendra; **the** ~ **has come to do...** il est temps de faire...; **the** ~ **has come for us to leave** il est temps que nous partions *(subj)*; **it's** ~ **to get up** c'est l'heure de nous *etc* lever.
(**f**) *(occasion)* fois *f.* **this** ~ cette fois; **(the) next** ~ **you come** la prochaine fois que vous viendrez; **every** *or* **each** ~ chaque fois; **several** ~**s** plusieurs fois; **at other** ~**s** d'autres fois; **at odd** ~**s** parfois; **many a** ~**, many** ~**s** bien des fois; ~ **after** ~**,** ~ **and (**~**) again** maintes et maintes fois; **hundreds of** ~**s** * cent fois; **(the) last** ~ la dernière fois; **the previous** ~**, the** ~ **before** la dernière fois; **some other** ~ une autre fois; **some** ~ **or other** un jour ou l'autre; **I remember the** ~ **when** je me rappelle le jour où; **2 at a** ~ 2 par 2; *(stairs, steps)* 2 à 2; **for weeks at a** ~ pendant des semaines entières; **10 francs a** ~ 10 F chaque fois.
(**g**) *(multiplying)* fois *f.* **2** ~**s 3 is 6** 2 fois 3 (font) 6; **10** ~**s as big** 10 fois plus grand (*as* que).
(**h**) *(Mus etc)* mesure *f.* **in** ~ en mesure (*to, with* avec); **three-four** ~ mesure à trois temps; **to keep** ~ rester en mesure.
2 *adj* (**a**) *bomb, fuse* à retardement; *(US) loan etc* à terme. (**b**) *(Phot)* ~ **exposure** pose *f*; ~ **frame** délais *mpl;* **to set a** ~ **limit** fixer une limite de temps *or* un délai (*on, for* pour); **without a** ~ **limit** sans limitation de temps; ~ **lock** fermeture *f* à mouvement d'horlogerie; ~ **share** *(vt) (Comput)* exploiter en temps partagé; *holiday home* avoir en multipropriété; *(n)* maison *f* (*or* appartement *m*) en multipropriété; *(Ind etc)* ~ **sheet** feuille *f* de présence; *(Rad)* ~ **signal** signal *m* horaire; ~ **switch** *(on apparatus)* minuteur *m*; *(for lighting)* minuterie *f*; ~ **trial** course *f* contre la montre; ~ **zone** fuseau *m* horaire.
3 *vt* (**a**) *(choose* ~ *of) invasion, visit* fixer (*for* à); *remark, interruption* choisir le moment de. **it was** ~**d to begin at...** le commencement était fixé *or* prévu pour...; **you** ~**d that perfectly** vous ne pouviez pas mieux choisir votre moment. (**b**) *(count* ~ *of) race, worker etc* chronométrer (*over* sur); *programme, piece of work* minuter; *egg* minuter la cuisson de. ~ **how long it takes you** notez le temps qu'il vous faut pour le faire. ◆**time (and motion) study** *n (Ind etc)* étude *f* des cadences. ◆**timeclock** *n (Ind) (machine)* enregistreur *m* de temps; *(place)* pointage *m.* ◆**time-consuming** *adj* qui prend du temps. ◆**time-honoured** *adj* consacré (par l'usage). ◆**timekeeper** *n (person: at race etc)* chronométreur *m*; **to be a good** ~**keeper** être toujours à l'heure. ◆**time-lag** *n* décalage *m.* ◆**timeless** *adj* éternel. ◆**timeliness** *n* à-propos *m.* ◆**timely** *adj* à propos. ◆**timeout** *n (US)* temps *m* mort. ◆**timepiece** *n (gen)* mécanisme *m* d'horlogerie; *(watch)* montre *f*; *(clock)* horloge *f.* ◆**timer** *n (Culin etc)* compte-minutes *m inv*; *(with sand)* sablier *m*; *(on machine etc)* minuteur *m*; *(Aut)* distributeur *m* d'allumage. ◆**time-saver** *n*: **it is a great** ~**-saver** ça fait gagner beaucoup de temps. ◆**time-saving** **1** *adj* qui fait gagner du temps ; **2** *n* gain *m* de temps. ◆**time-server** *n (pej)* opportuniste *mf.* ◆**time-sharing** *n* multipropriété *f.* ◆**timetable** *n (Rail etc)* horaire *m*; *(Scol)* emploi *m* du temps. ◆**time-warp** *n* distorsion *f* du temps. ◆**time-wasting** **1** *adj* qui fait perdre du temps ; **2** *n* perte *f* de temps. ◆**timing** **1** *n (Aut)* réglage *m* de l'allumage; *(Ind, Sport)* chronométrage *m*; *[musician etc]* sens *m* du rythme; *[actor]* minutage *m*; *(in formation flying etc)* synchronisation *f*; **the timing of this demonstration** *(date/hour)* la date/l'heure *f* de cette manifestation; *(programme of various stages)* le minutage de cette manifestation ; **2** *adj*: **timing mechanism** *[bomb etc]* mouvement *m* d'horlogerie; *[electrical apparatus]* minuteur *m.*

timid ['tɪmɪd] *adj (shy)* timide; *(unadventurous)* timoré, craintif. ◆**timidity** *n* timidité *f*; caractère timoré. ◆**timidly** *adv* timidement; craintivement.

timorous ['tɪm(ə)rəs] *adj* timoré, craintif.

timpani ['tɪmpənɪ] *npl* timbales *fpl.*

tin [tɪn] **1** *n* (**a**) étain *m*; *(*~*plate)* fer-blanc *m.* (**b**) *(can)* boîte *f* (en fer-blanc); *(mould)* moule *m*; *(dish)* plat *m.* ~ **of salmon** boîte de saumon; **cake** ~ *(for storing)* boîte à gâteaux; *(for baking)* moule à gâteau; **roasting** ~ plat à rôtir. **2** *vt food etc* mettre en conserve. **3** *adj (made of* ~*)* en étain (*or* fer-blanc); *mine* d'étain; *soldier* de plomb. ~ **can** boîte *f* (en fer-blanc); ~ **hat** casque *m*; ~ **whistle** flûteau *m.* ◆**tinfoil** *n* papier *m* d'aluminium. ◆**tinned** *adj fruit, salmon* en boîte, en conserve ; ~**ned food** conserves *fpl.* ◆**tinny** *adj sound, taste* métallique; (**pej*) *car, machine* de camelote. ◆**tin-opener** *n* ouvre-boîtes *m.* ◆**tin-plate** *n* fer-blanc *m.* ◆**tinpot** * *adj* qui ne vaut pas grand-chose. ◆**tintack** *n* semence *f (de tapissier)*.

tinder ['tɪndəʳ] *n*: **as dry as** ~ sec comme de l'amadou.

tinge [tɪn(d)ʒ] **1** *n* teinte *f.* **2** *vt* teinter (*with* de).

tingle ['tɪŋgl] **1** *vi* picoter; *(with excitement)* frissonner. **her face was tingling** le visage lui picotait; **her cheeks were tingling with cold** le froid lui piquait les joues. **2** *n* picotement *m*; frisson *m.* *(sound)* **to have a** ~ **in one's ears** avoir les oreilles qui tintent. ◆**tingling** **1** *n* = **tingle 2** ; **2** *adj sensation* de picotement.

tinker ['tɪŋkəʳ] **1** *n (gen: often pej)* romanichel(le) *m(f)*; *(mending etc)* rétameur *m* ambulant. **2** *vi* (**a**) (~ **about)** bricoler (*with sth* qch). (**b**) *(fig)* **to** ~ **with**

(change) faire des retouches à; *(dishonestly)* tripatouiller.

tinkle ['tɪŋkl] **1** *vi* tinter. **2** *vt* faire tinter. **3** *n* tintement *m*. *(Telec)* **to give sb a ~ *** passer un coup de fil à qn *. ◆**tinkling** *n* tintement *m*.

tinnitus [tɪ'naɪtəs] *n* acouphène *m*.

tinsel ['tɪns(ə)l] *n* guirlandes *fpl* de Noël (argentées); *(fig pej)* clinquant *m*.

tint [tɪnt] **1** *n* teinte *f*. **2** *vt* teinter (*with* de). **to ~ one's hair** se faire un shampooing colorant.

tiny ['taɪnɪ] *adj* tout petit, minuscule.

tip[1] [tɪp] *n (gen)* bout *m*; *(pointed)* pointe *f*; *(metalled: of cane etc)* embout *m*; *[billiard cue]* procédé *m*. *(fig)* **it's on the ~ of my tongue** je l'ai sur le bout de la langue; *(fig)* **the ~ of the iceberg** la partie émergée de l'iceberg. ◆**tipped** *adj cigarettes* filtre *inv*; **steel-~ped** qui a un embout de fer. ◆**tiptoe 1** *n*: **on ~toe** sur la pointe des pieds ; **2** *vi*: **to ~toe in/out** *etc* entrer/sortir *etc* sur la pointe des pieds. ◆**tiptop** * *adj* excellent.

tip[2] [tɪp] **1** *n* **(a)** *(gratuity)* pourboire *m*. **the ~ is included** le service est compris. **(b)** *(hint)* suggestion *f*; *(advice)* conseil *m*; *(information; also Racing)* tuyau * *m*. **take my ~** suivez mon conseil. **2** *vt* **(a)** donner un pourboire à. **to ~ sb 5 francs** donner 5 F de pourboire à qn. **(b)** *winner* pronostiquer; *horse* pronostiquer la victoire de (*for the race* dans la course). *(fig)* **he was ~ped for the job** on avait pronostiqué qu'il serait nommé. ◆**tip off** *vt sep (gen)* donner un tuyau * à (*about sth* sur qch); *police* prévenir. ◆**tip-off** *n* tuyau * *m;* **to give sb a ~-off** prévenir qn. ◆**tipster** *n* pronostiqueur *m*.

tip[3] [tɪp] **1** *n (for rubbish)* décharge *f*. **2** *vt* **(~ over)** incliner; *(overturn)* renverser; **(~ out)** *liquid* verser; *load, rubbish, books etc* déverser (*into* dans; *out of* de). **to ~ sth back** incliner qch en arrière; **to ~ sb into/out of sth** faire tomber qn dans/de qch. **3** *vi* pencher. **to ~ back(wards)** *[chair]* se rabattre en arrière; *[person]* se pencher en arrière. ◆**tip up 1** *vi [table etc] (tilt)* pencher; *(overturn)* basculer; *[box, jug]* se renverser; *[seat]* se rabattre; *[truck]* basculer. **2** *vt sep* incliner. ◆**tipper** *n (truck)* camion *m* à benne (basculante). ◆**tipping** *n*: **'no ~ ping'** 'défense de déposer des ordures'.

Tippex ['tɪpeks] ® **1** *n* Tippex *m* ®. **2** *vt (also* **~ out***)* blanchir au Tippex ®.

tipple ['tɪpl] **1** *vi* picoler *. **2** *n*: **gin is his ~** ce qu'il préfère boire c'est du gin. ◆**tippler** *n* picoleur * *m*, -euse * *f*.

tipsy ['tɪpsɪ] *adj* éméché, parti *. **to get ~** devenir gai.

tirade [taɪ'reɪd] *n* diatribe *f*.

tire[1] ['taɪəʳ] *n (US)* = **tyre.**

tire[2] ['taɪəʳ] **1** *vt* fatiguer; *(weary)* fatiguer, lasser. **2** *vi* se fatiguer; se lasser. **he ~s easily** il se fatigue vite; **he never ~s of saying...** il ne se lasse jamais de dire... ◆**tire out** *vt sep* épuiser, crever *. ◆**tired** *adj person* fatigué; *(weary)* las; *movement, voice* las; *(fig) cliché etc* rebattu; **to be ~d of sth/sb** en avoir assez de qch/qn; **to be ~d of doing** en avoir assez de faire; **to get ~d of** commencer à en avoir assez de; **you make me ~ d!** * tu me fatigues! ◆**tiredness** *n* fatigue *f*; lassitude *f*. ◆**tireless** *adj* infatigable; inlassable. ◆**tirelessly** *adv* infatigablement; inlassablement. ◆**tiresome** *adj* ennuyeux. ◆**tiring** *adj* fatigant.

tissue ['tɪʃuː] **1** *n (Anat, Tex)* tissu *m*; *(paper handkerchief)* mouchoir *m* en papier, kleenex *m* ®. *(fig)* **~ of lies** tissu de mensonges. **2** *adj*: **~ paper** papier *m* de soie.

tit[1] [tɪt] *n (bird*: **~ mouse***)* mésange *f*.

tit[2] [tɪt] *n*: **~ for tat** un prêté pour un rendu.

tit[3] ‡ [tɪt] *n (breast)* sein *m*, nichon ‡ *m*.

titanic [taɪ'tænɪk] *adj* titanesque.

titbit ['tɪtbɪt] *n [food]* friandise *f*; *[news]* détail *m* croustillant. **~s** *(with drinks)* amuse-gueule *mpl*.

titillate ['tɪtɪleɪt] *vt* titiller.

titivate ['tɪtɪveɪt] **1** *vi* se pomponner. **2** *vt* pomponner.

title ['taɪtl] **1** *n (gen)* titre *m*; *(Jur)* titres *mpl* (*to* à). *(Cine, TV)* **(credit) ~s** générique *m*. **2** *adj*: **~ deed** titre *m* de propriété; *(Sport)* **~ holder** détenteur *m*, -trice *f* du titre; **~ page** page *f* de titre; *(Theat)* **~ role** ≃ rôle principal. ◆**titled** *adj person* titré.

titter ['tɪtəʳ] **1** *vi* rire sottement (*at* de). **2** *n* petit rire *m* sot.

tittle-tattle ['tɪtl,tætl] *n* cancans *mpl*.

tizzy * ['tɪzɪ] *n*: **to be in/get into a ~** être/se mettre dans tous ses états.

to [tuː], *forme faible* [tə] **1** *prep* **(a)** *(gen)* à; *(direction)* à, vers, en, chez. **to give sth ~ sb** donner qch à qn; **he went ~ the door** il est allé à la porte; **he was walking ~ the door** il marchait vers la porte; **to go ~ school/town** aller à l'école/en ville ; **boats ~ and from Cherbourg** les bateaux à destination ou en provenance de Cherbourg; **to go ~ the doctor('s)** aller chez le docteur; **~ the left** à gauche; **the road ~ London** la route de Londres; **to count ~ 20** compter jusqu'à 20; **it comes ~ £20** ça fait 20 livres (en tout); **it is 90 km ~ Paris** nous sommes à 90 km de Paris; **8 years ago ~ the day** il y a 8 ans jour pour jour; **from morning ~ night** du matin au soir; **from town ~ town** de ville en ville; **50 ~ 60 people** de 50 à 60 personnes; **back ~ back** dos à dos; **bumper ~ bumper** pare-chocs contre pare-chocs; **what's it ~ you?** qu'est-ce que ça peut vous faire?; **be nice ~ her** sois gentil avec elle; **it's a great help ~ him** cela lui est très utile; **known ~ the Ancients** connu des anciens; **assistant ~ the manager** adjoint(e) *m(f)* du directeur; **ambassador ~ France/~ the king** ambassadeur en France/auprès du roi; **he has been a good friend ~ us** il a été pour nous un ami fidèle.
(b) *(in geog names) (countries: gen)* en; *(countries: all plurals, and masc sing with initial consonant)* au *or* aux; *(towns: gen)* à. **to go ~ England/France** *etc* en Angleterre/France *etc;* **~ Japan/the United States** *etc* au Japon/aux États-Unis *etc;* **~ London/Paris** *etc* à Londres/Paris *etc.*
(c) *(in time phrases)* **20 (minutes) ~ 2** 2 heures moins 20; **at (a) quarter ~ 4** à 4 heures moins le quart; **it was 10 ~** il était moins 10.
(d) *(in proportions etc)* **A is ~ B as C is ~ D** A est à B ce que C est à D; **to bet 10 ~ 1** parier 10 contre 1; **by a majority of 10 ~ 7** avec une majorité de 10 contre 7; **they won by 4 goals ~ 2** ils ont gagné 4 (buts) à 2; **one person ~ a room** une personne par chambre; **200 people ~ the square km** 200 personnes au km carré; **how many miles ~ the gallon?** ≃ combien de litres au cent?; **that's nothing ~ what is to come** ce n'est rien à côté de ce qui va venir.
(e) *(phrases)* **here's ~ you!** à la vôtre!; **~ absent friends!** à la santé des absents!; **what would you say ~ a beer?** que diriez-vous d'une bière?; **that's all there is ~ it** *(it's easy)* ça n'est pas plus difficile que ça; *(no ulterior motive etc)* c'est aussi simple que ça; *(Comm)* **'~ repairing cooker: 100 francs'** 'remise en état d'une cuisinière: 100 F'; **~ the best of my recollection** pour autant que je m'en souvienne; **~ my delight** à ma grande joie; *(Math)* **3 ~ the 4th** 3 à la puissance 4.
2 *particle (forming infin: shown in French by vb ending)* **~ be** être; **~ eat** manger; **I'll try ~** j'essaierai; **I forgot ~** j'ai oublié.
3 *adv*: **to push the door ~** fermer la porte; **the door is ~** la porte est fermée; **to go ~ and fro** *[person]* aller et venir; *(stride up and down)* faire les cent pas; *[machine part etc]* avoir un mouve-

ment de va-et-vient; *[train, bus etc]* faire la navette (*between* entre). ◆ **to-do** * *n*: **to make a ~-do** faire toute une histoire * (*about* à propos de). ◆ **to-ing and fro-ing** *n* allées et venues *fpl*.

toad [təʊd] *n* crapaud *m*. ◆ **toad-in-the-hole** *n (Culin) saucisses cuites dans de la pâte à crêpes*. ◆ **toadstool** *n* champignon *m*; *(poisonous)* champignon vénéneux. ◆ **toady** **1** *n* flagorneur *m*, -euse *f*; **2** *vi* flagorner; **to ~y to sb** flatter qn bassement. ◆ **toadying** *n* flagornerie *f*.

toast [təʊst] **1** *n* (**a**) pain *m* grillé, toast *m*. **you've burnt the** ~ tu as laissé brûler le pain *or* les toasts; **a piece** *or* **slice of** ~ une tartine grillée, un toast; **sardines on** ~ sardines *fpl* sur canapé. (**b**) toast *m*. **to drink a ~ to sb** porter un toast à qn (*in champagne* au champagne); **the ~ of the town** la vedette de la ville. **2** *vt* (**a**) *bread etc* faire griller. **~ed cheese** toast *m* au fromage. (**b**) *(drink ~ to)* porter un toast à; *event, victory* arroser (*in champagne* au champagne). ◆ **toaster** *n* grille-pain *m inv (électrique)*. ◆ **toast-rack** *n* porte-toast *m inv*.

tobacco [tə'bækəʊ] **1** *n* tabac *m*. **2** *adj plantation, company* de tabac; *pouch* à tabac; *industry* du tabac. ◆ **tobacconist** *n* marchand(e) *m(f)* de tabac; **~nist's (shop)** (bureau *m* de) tabac *m*.

toboggan [tə'bɒg(ə)n] **1** *n* toboggan *m*; *(on runners)* luge *f*. **2** *vi*: **to go ~ing** faire de la luge.

today [tə'deɪ] *adv, n* aujourd'hui. **all** ~ toute la journée aujourd'hui; **a week (past)** ~ il y a huit jours aujourd'hui; ~ **week, a week (from)** ~ aujourd'hui en huit; **what day is (it) ~?** quel jour est-on *or* est-ce aujourd'hui?; **what date is (it) ~?** quelle est la date aujourd'hui?; ~ **is Friday/the 4th** aujourd'hui c'est vendredi/le 4; ~ **is wet** il pleut aujourd'hui; ~ **was a bad day** aujourd'hui ça s'est mal passé; **~'s paper** le journal d'aujourd'hui; *(fig)* **here ~ and gone tomorrow** ça va, ça vient; **the writers of** ~ les écrivains d'aujourd'hui.

toddle ['tɒdl] *vi [child]* **to ~ in/out** *etc* entrer/ sortir *etc* à pas hésitants; *[adult]* **to ~ along** * se balader *. ◆ **toddler** *n* tout(e) petit(e) *m(f)* (qui commence à marcher), bambin * *m*.

toddy ['tɒdɪ] *n* ≃ grog *m*.

toe [təʊ] **1** *n* orteil *m*, doigt *m* de pied; *[sock, shoe]* bout *m*. **big/little** ~ gros/petit orteil; **three- ~d** à trois orteils; *(lit, fig)* **to tread on sb's ~s** marcher sur les pieds de qn; *(fig)* **to keep sb on his ~s** forcer qn à rester alerte. **2** *vt (fig)* **to ~ the line** *or (US)* **mark** obéir. ◆ **toecap** *n* bout *m* renforcé *(de soulier)*. ◆ **toeclip** *n [cyclist]* cale-pied *m inv*. ◆ **toenail** *n* ongle *m* du pied.

toffee ['tɒfɪ] *n* caramel *m (au beurre)*. ~ **apple** pomme *f* caramélisée; *(fig)* **he can't do it for ~** * il n'est pas fichu * de le faire.

together [tə'geðə^r] *adv* (**a**) *(gen)* ensemble. **I've seen them** ~ je les ai vus ensemble; *(fig)* **we're in this** ~ *(in same situation)* nous sommes logés à la même enseigne; *(must act ~)* il faut que nous fassions front commun; *(pej)* **they were both in it** ~ ils avaient partie liée tous les deux; **tie the ropes** ~ nouez les cordes; **all ~ now!** *(shouting, singing)* tous en chœur maintenant!; *(pulling)* (oh!) hisse!; ~ **with** avec; **if you look at the reports** ~ si vous considérez les rapports conjointement; **for weeks** ~ pendant des semaines entières; **for 5 weeks** ~ pendant 5 semaines de suite; *(*: fig)* **to get it** *or* **one's act** ~ s'organiser.
(**b**) *(simultaneously)* en même temps; *(Mus etc)* à l'unisson. ◆ **togetherness** *n* camaraderie *f*.

toggle ['tɒgl] *n (Dress)* bouton *m* de duffel-coat.

toil [tɔɪl] **1** *n* labeur *m*. **2** *vi* (**~ away**) peiner (*at, over* sur; *to do* pour faire). **to ~ along/up** *etc* avancer/monter *etc* péniblement.

toilet ['tɔɪlɪt] **1** *n* (**a**) *(dressing etc)* toilette *f*. (**b**) *(lavatory)* toilettes *fpl*, waters * *mpl*. **to go to the** ~ aller aux toilettes *or* aux waters *; **to put sth down the** ~ jeter qch dans la cuvette des cabinets. **2** *adj soap, water* de toilette. ~ **bag** sac *m* de toilette; ~ **case** trousse *f* de toilette; ~ **paper** papier *m* hygiénique; ~ **roll** rouleau *m* de papier hygiénique. ◆ **toiletries** *npl* articles *mpl* de toilette.

token ['təʊk(ə)n] **1** *n (symbol)* témoignage *m*, marque *f*; *(metal disc: for telephone etc)* jeton *m*; *(voucher)* bon *m*. **gift** ~ bon-cadeau *m*; **book** ~ chèque-livre *m*; **record** ~ chèque-disque *m*; **milk** ~ bon de lait; **as a ~ of, in ~ of** en témoignage de; *(fig)* **by the same** ~ de même. **2** *adj payment, strike* symbolique. **a ~ resistance** un semblant de résistance pour la forme; *(pej)* **the ~ woman** la femme-alibi.

Tokyo ['təʊkjəʊ] *n* Tokyo.

told [təʊld] *pret, ptp of* **tell**.

tolerate ['tɒləreɪt] *vt (gen, Med, Tech)* tolérer; *heat, pain* supporter. ◆ **tolerable** *adj (bearable)* tolérable; *(fairly good)* passable. ◆ **tolerably** *adv work etc* passablement; *certain, competent* à peu près. ◆ **tolerance** *n* tolérance *f*. ◆ **tolerant** *adj* tolérant (*of sth* de qch, *(Med)* à qch; *of sb* à l'égard de qn). ◆ **tolerantly** *adv* d'une manière tolérante. ◆ **toleration** *n* tolérance *f*.

toll[1] [təʊl] **1** *n (gen, also Aut)* péage *m*. *(fig)* **to take a heavy ~ of** *soldiers etc* faire beaucoup de victimes parmi; *sb's strength* ébranler sérieusement; *savings* manger une grande partie de; **the accident ~ on the roads** le nombre des victimes de la route; **the ~ of dead** le nombre des morts. **2** *adj bridge, road* à péage. ◆ **tollbooth** *n* poste *m* de péage. ◆ **toll-free** *adv (US Telec)* en service libre appel.

toll[2] [təʊl] **1** *vi [bell]* sonner. **2** *vt bell* sonner; *sb's death* sonner le glas pour.

Tom [tɒm] *n (fig)* **any ~, Dick or Harry** n'importe qui. ◆ **tom(cat)** *n* matou *m*.

tomato [tə'mɑːtəʊ], *(US)* [tə'meɪtəʊ] **1** *n, pl* **-es** tomate *f*. **2** *adj*: ~ **juice** jus *m* de tomates; ~ **ketchup** ketchup *m*; ~ **sauce** sauce *f* tomate.

tomb [tuːm] *n* tombeau *m*, tombe *f*. ◆ **tombstone** *n* pierre *f* tombale.

tomboy ['tɒmbɔɪ] *n* garçon *m* manqué.

tome [təʊm] *n* tome *m*, gros volume *m*.

tomfool ['tɒm'fuːl] *adj* absurde, idiot. ◆ **tomfoolery** *n* âneries *fpl*.

tommy gun ['tɒmɪgʌn] *n* mitraillette *f*.

tomorrow [tə'mɒrəʊ] *adv, n* demain. **all** ~ toute la journée demain; **a week (past)** ~ il y aura huit jours demain; ~ **week, a week from** ~ demain en huit; **he'll have been here a week** ~ cela fera huit jours demain qu'il est là; **see you ~!** à demain!; **the day after** ~ après-demain; **what day will ~ be** *or* **will it be ~?** quel jour sera-t-on demain?; **what date will it be ~?** quelle sera la date demain?; ~ **will be Saturday/the 5th** demain ce sera samedi/le 5; ~ **will be dry** il ne pleuvra pas demain; ~ **never comes** demain n'arrive jamais; ~ **is another day!** ça ira peut-être mieux demain!; *(fig)* **the writers of** ~ les écrivains de demain; ~ **morning/evening** demain matin/soir.

tomtom ['tɒmtɒm] *n* tam-tam *m*.

ton [tʌn] *n* (**a**) *(weight)* tonne *f (Brit = 1016,06 kg; Can, US etc = 907,20 kg)*. **metric** ~ tonne *(= 1000 kg)*; **a 7-~ truck, a 7-~ner** un camion de 7 tonnes; *(fig)* **~s of** * des tas de *. (**b**) *(Naut) (register ~)* tonneau *m*; *(displacement ~)* tonne *f*. **a 60,000-~ steamer** un paquebot de 60 000 tonnes. ◆ **tonnage** *n* tonnage *m*.

tone [təʊn] **1** *n* (**a**) *(sound: gen)* ton *m*; *[musical instrument]* sonorité *f*; *(Telec: also of radio, record player etc)* tonalité *f*. **in low ~s** à voix basse; **in angry**

~s sur le ton de la colère; **don't speak to me in that ~ of voice!** ne me parlez sur ce ton!; *(fig)* **the ~ of his letter** le ton de sa lettre; **the whole ~ of the school** la tenue générale de l'école; *(Fin)* **the ~ of the market** la tenue du marché; **to raise/ lower the ~ of sth** rehausser/rabaisser le ton de qch. (**b**) *(colour)* ton *m*. **two-~ car** voiture *f* de deux tons. (**c**) *[muscles etc]* tonus *m*. **2** *adj*: **~ control** bouton *m* de tonalité. **3** *vi* (**~ in**) s'harmoniser (*with* avec). ◆ **tone down** *vt sep colour* adoucir; *sound, radio etc* baisser; *(fig) criticism, effect* atténuer; *language, policy* modérer. ◆ **tone up** *vt sep (Med)* tonifier. ◆ **tonal** *adj* tonal. ◆ **tone-deaf** *adj*: **to be ~-deaf** ne pas avoir d'oreille. ◆ **tonelessly** *adv speak* d'une voix blanche.

tongs [tɒŋz] *npl* **(pair of ~)** pinces *fpl*; *(for coal)* pincettes *fpl*; *(for sugar)* pince *f* à sucre; *(curling ~)* fer *m* (à friser).

tongue [tʌŋ] *n* (**a**) *(gen)* langue *f*; *[shoe]* languette *f*; *[bell]* battant *m*. **to put out one's ~** tirer la langue (*at sb* à qn); **his ~ was hanging out** il tirait la langue; *(fig)* **he's lost his ~** il a perdu sa langue; **~ in cheek** ironiquement; **keep a civil ~ in your head!** tâchez d'être plus poli!; **I can't get my ~ round it** je n'arrive pas à le prononcer correctement. (**b**) *(language)* langue *f*. ◆ **tongue-tied** *adj* muet *(fig)*. ◆ **tongue-twister** *n* phrase *f* très difficile à prononcer.

tonic ['tɒnɪk] **1** *adj (gen)* tonique. *(Mus)* **~ solfa** solfège *m*. **2** *n* (**a**) *(Med; fig)* tonique *m*. *(lit, fig)* **you need a ~** il vous faut un bon tonique; *(fig)* **it was a real ~** cela m'a vraiment remonté le moral. (**b**) **~ (water)** ≃ Schweppes *m* ®; **gin and ~** gin-tonic *m*. (**c**) *(Mus)* tonique *f*.

tonight [tə'naɪt] *adv, n (before bed)* ce soir; *(during sleep)* cette nuit.

tonsil ['tɒnsl] *n* amygdale *f*. **to have one's ~s out** être opéré des amygdales. ◆ **tonsillectomy** *n* amygdalectomie *f*. ◆ **tonsillitis** *n* amygdalite *f*; **to have ~litis** avoir une angine *or (more formally)* une amygdalite.

too [tu:] *adv* (**a**) *(excessively)* trop. **it's ~ hard for me** c'est trop difficile pour moi; **it's ~ hard for me to explain** c'est trop difficile pour que je puisse vous l'expliquer; **~ heavy to carry** trop lourd à porter; **it's ~ heavy for me to carry** c'est trop lourd à porter pour moi; **he's ~ mean to pay for it** il est trop pingre pour le payer; **that's ~ kind of you!** vous êtes vraiment trop aimable!; **I'm not ~ sure about that** je n'en suis pas très certain. (**b**) *(also)* aussi; *(moreover)* en plus, en outre. **I went ~** moi aussi j'y suis allé; **they asked for a discount ~!** et en plus ils ont demandé un rabais!; **and then, ~, there's...** et puis, il y a également...

took [tʊk] *pret of* **take**.

tool [tu:l] *n (gen, Tech)* outil *m*; *(fig)* instrument *m* (*of* de). **set of ~s** panoplie *f* d'outils; **garden ~s** outils *or* ustensiles *mpl* de jardinage; **the ~s of my trade** les outils de mon métier. ◆ **toolbag** *or* ◆ **toolcase** *or* ◆ **toolkit** *n* trousse *f* à outils. ◆ **toolbox** *or* ◆ **toolcase** *or* ◆ **toolchest** *n* boîte *f* à outils. ◆ **tooled** *adj silver* ciselé; *leather* repoussé; *book-cover* en cuir repoussé. ◆ **toolhouse** *or* ◆ **toolshed** *n* cabane *f* à outils. ◆ **toolmaker** *n* outilleur *m*.

toot [tu:t] *vti* klaxonner.

tooth, *pl* **teeth** [tu:θ, ti:θ] *n* dent *f*. **front ~** dent de devant; **back ~** molaire *f*; **(set of) false teeth** dentier *m*; **to have a ~ out** se faire arracher une dent; *(fig)* **he's a bit long in the ~** il n'est plus tout jeune; *(fig)* **in the teeth of** *wind* contre; *opposition* en dépit de; **~ and nail** avec acharnement; *(fig)* **to get one's teeth into sth** se mettre à fond à qch; **there's nothing you can get your teeth into** ce n'est pas très substantiel; **the legislation has no teeth** la législation est impuissante; *(fig)* **to throw sth in sb's teeth** jeter qch à la tête de qn; **to be sick to the (back) teeth of sth** ‡ en avoir ras le bol * de qch. ◆ **toothache** *n* mal *m* de dents; **to have ~ache** avoir mal aux dents. ◆ **toothbrush** *n* brosse *f* à dents. ◆ **toothcomb** *n* peigne *m* fin; *(fig)* **to go through sth with a (fine) ~comb** passer qch au peigne fin. ◆ **toothless** *adj* édenté. ◆ **toothpaste** *n* pâte *f* dentifrice. ◆ **toothpick** *n* cure-dent *m*. ◆ **tooth-powder** *n* poudre *f* dentifrice. ◆ **toothy** *adj*: **to be ~y** avoir des dents de cheval.

top[1] [tɒp] **1** *n* (**a**) *[ladder, page, wall, pile, street etc]* haut *m*; *[mountain, tree, hill, head]* sommet *m*; *[box, container]* dessus *m*; *[plant, vegetable]* fane *f*; *[list, table, classification, queue]* tête *f*; *[profession etc]* faîte *m*; *(surface)* surface *f*; *(roof: of car etc)* toit *m*. **at the ~ of** en haut de, au sommet de, en tête de, au faîte de; **at/near the ~ of the pile** en haut de/ vers le haut de la pile; *(Scol)* **to be at the ~ of the class** être premier de la classe; **~ of the milk** crème *f* du lait; **it's ~ of the pops** c'est en tête du hit-parade; **the men at the ~** ceux qui sont au pouvoir; **the ~ of the table** *(solid piece)* le plateau de la table; *(surface)* le dessus de la table; **to sit at the ~ of the table** être assis à la place d'honneur; *(Mil)* **to go over the ~** monter à l'assaut; *(fig)* **to get to the ~** *(gen)* réussir; *(in hierarchy etc)* arriver en haut de l'échelle; **on (the) ~ of** sur; **the one on (the) ~** celui qui est en dessus; *(fig)* **to come out on ~** avoir le dessus; *(in career etc)* **he'll get to the ~** il réussira; *(fig)* **he's on ~ of things** * il s'en sort très bien; **things are getting on ~ of her** * elle est dépassée; **on ~ of the one he's got already** en plus de celui qu'il a déjà; **on ~ of all that he...** et puis par-dessus le marché il...; **from ~ to toe** de la tête aux pieds; **from ~ to bottom** *search etc* de fond en comble; *paint etc* complètement; *(whole) system etc* tout entier; **he's saying that off the ~ of his head** * il dit ça comme ça (mais il n'en est pas certain); **in ~ (gear)** en quatrième; **he's the ~s** * il est champion *; *(on bus)* **seats on ~** places *fpl* à l'étage supérieur; **let's go up on ~** on va en haut. (**b**) *(lid etc) [box]* couvercle *m*; *[bottle] (screw-on)* bouchon *m*; *(snap-on)* capsule *f*; *[pen]* capuchon *m*. (**c**) *(Dress: blouse etc)* haut *m*; *[pyjamas]* haut *m*.

2 *adj (highest) shelf, drawer* du haut; *(Mus) note* le plus haut; *storey, step* dernier; *(in rank etc)* premier; *(best) score, mark etc* (le) meilleur. *[paint]* **the ~ coat** la dernière couche; **~ copy** original *m*; **the ~ right-hand corner** le coin en haut à droite; **~ price** *(highest)* prix *m* maximum; *(best)* le meilleur prix; **at ~ speed** à toute vitesse; *(Scol)* **~ in maths** premier en maths; *(fig)* **~ marks** vingt sur vingt (*for* pour); **in the ~ class** *(secondary school)* ≃ en terminale; *(primary)* ≃ au cours moyen 2; *(~ stream)* dans le premier groupe; *(Mus)* **the ~ 20** les 20 premiers du hit-parade; **one of the ~ pianists** un des plus grands pianistes; **a ~ job** un poste prestigieux; **~ people** l'élite *f*; *(fig)* **the ~ brass** * les huiles * *fpl*; *(fig)* **he's ~ dog * around here** c'est lui qui commande ici; *(US)* **to pay ~ dollar for sth** payer qch au prix fort.

3 *vt* (**a**) *radish, carrot etc* couper les fanes de. **to ~ and tail fruit** ≃ préparer des fruits. (**b**) **~ped by a dome** surmonté d'un dôme. (**c**) *(exceed) previous figures etc* dépasser. *(fig)* **and to ~ it all...** et pour couronner le tout... (**d**) *list, queue* être en tête de. *(Theat)* **to ~ the bill** être en tête d'affiche. ◆ **top off** *vt sep (finish)* terminer (*with* par). ◆ **top up** *vt sep (Aut) battery* remettre de l'eau dans. **to ~ up a car with oil** remettre de l'huile dans une voiture; **can I ~ up your glass?** je vous en remets? ◆ **topcoat** *n* pardessus *m*. ◆ **topflight** * *adj* de premier ordre. ◆ **top hat** *n* (chapeau *m*) haut-de-forme *m*. ◆ **top-heavy** *adj structure etc* trop lourd du haut; *(fig) organization* mal équilibré.

◆ **topless** *adj costume* sans haut; *girl* aux seins nus; **~less swimsuit** monokini * *m*. ◆ **top-level** *adj meeting, discussion* au plus haut niveau; *decision* pris au sommet. ◆ **topmost** *adj* le plus haut. ◆ **topping** *n (Culin)* **with chocolate ~ping** nappé d'une crème au chocolat. ◆ **top-ranking** *adj* (très) haut placé. ◆ **top-secret** *adj* ultra-secret. ◆ **top-security wing** *n [prison]* quartier *m* de haute surveillance. ◆ **topside** *n (Culin)* gîte *m* (à la noix). ◆ **topsoil** *n* terre *f*; *(Agric)* couche *f* arable.

top² [tɒp] *n (toy)* toupie *f*.

topaz ['təʊpæz] *n* topaze *f*.

topic ['tɒpɪk] *n [essay, speech]* sujet *m*; *(for discussion)* sujet de discussion. ◆ **topical** *adj* d'actualité. ◆ **topicality** *n* actualité *f*.

topography [tə'pɒgrəfɪ] *n* topographie *f*.

topple ['tɒpl] **1** *vi (wobble)* basculer; **(~ over, ~ down)** tomber. **2** *vt* faire tomber.

topsy-turvy ['tɒpsɪ'tɜːvɪ] *adj, adv* sens dessus dessous.

torch [tɔːtʃ] *n* lampe *f* de poche, torche *f* électrique; *(flaming)* flambeau *m*. ◆ **torchlight procession** *n* retraite *f* aux flambeaux.

tore [tɔːʳ], **torn** [tɔːn] *pret, ptp of* **tear¹**.

torment ['tɔːment] **1** *n* supplice *m*. **to be in ~** être au supplice; **to suffer ~s** souffrir le martyre. **2** [tɔː'ment] *vt (gen)* tourmenter. **~ed by** torturé par. ◆ **tormentor** *n* persécuteur *m*, -trice *f*.

tornado, *pl* **-es** [tɔː'neɪdəʊ] *n* tornade *f*.

torpedo [tɔː'piːdəʊ] **1** *n, pl* **-es** torpille *f*. **2** *adj*: **~ boat** torpilleur *m*. **3** *vt* torpiller *(also fig)*.

torpid ['tɔːpɪd] *adj* engourdi. ◆ **torpor** *n* torpeur *f*.

torrent ['tɒr(ə)nt] *n* torrent *m (also fig)*. **the rain was coming down in ~s** il pleuvait à torrents. ◆ **torrential** *adj* torrentiel.

torrid ['tɒrɪd] *adj* torride; *(fig)* ardent.

torso ['tɔːsəʊ] *n (Anat)* torse *m*; *(Sculp)* buste *m*.

tortilla [tɔː'tiːə] *n* crêpe *f* mexicaine.

tortoise ['tɔːtəs] *n* tortue *f*. ◆ **tortoiseshell** *n* écaille *f* (de tortue).

tortuous ['tɔːtjʊəs] *adj* tortueux.

torture ['tɔːtʃəʳ] **1** *n* torture *f*, supplice *m*. *(fig)* **it was sheer ~!** c'était un vrai supplice! **2** *vt person* torturer; *language* écorcher; *tune* massacrer.

Tory ['tɔːrɪ] *n (Pol)* tory *mf*, conservateur *m*, -trice *f*.

toss [tɒs] **1** *n (throw)* lancement *m*; *(by bull)* coup *m* de cornes. *(from horse)* **to take a ~** faire une chute; **with a ~ of his head** d'un mouvement brusque de la tête; **by the ~ of a coin** à pile ou face; **to win/lose the ~** gagner/perdre à pile ou face; *(Sport: before match)* gagner/perdre le tirage au sort. **2** *vt ball etc* lancer *(to* à); *pancake* faire sauter; *salad* remuer; *head, mane* rejeter en arrière; *[bull]* projeter en l'air; *[horse]* désarçonner. **to ~ sb in a blanket** faire sauter qn dans une couverture; **to ~ a coin** jouer à pile ou face (*to decide* pour décider); *(Sport: before match)* tirer au sort; **I'll ~ you for it** on le joue à pile ou face; **boat ~ed by the waves** bateau ballotté par les vagues. **3** *vi* **(a)** **(~ about, ~ around)** *[person]* s'agiter; *[trees]* se balancer; *[boat]* tanguer. **to ~ and turn** se tourner et se retourner. **(b)** **(~ up)** jouer à pile ou face (*to decide* pour décider); *(Sport: before match)* tirer au sort. **let's ~ for it** on le joue à pile ou face; **I'll ~ you for the drinks** on joue à pile ou face et le perdant paie à boire. ◆ **toss off** *vt sep drink* avaler d'un coup; *letter etc* écrire au pied levé. ◆ **toss-up** *n [coin]* coup *m* de pile ou face; *(fig)* **it was a ~-up between the theatre and the cinema** le théâtre ou le cinéma, ça nous était égal.

tot¹ [tɒt] *n* **(a)** *(child)* **(tiny) ~** tout(e) petit(e) enfant *m(f)*. **(b)** **a ~ of whisky** un petit verre de whisky; **just a ~** juste une goutte.

tot² [tɒt] **1** *vt* **(~ up)** faire le total de. **2** *vi*: **to ~ up** faire le total.

total ['təʊtl] **1** *adj (gen)* total; *sum* total, global; *ignorance, disagreement* complet. **the ~ losses/sales** le total des pertes/ventes; **it was a ~ loss** on a tout perdu; *(memory)* **~ recall** remémoration *f* totale. **2** *n* **(a)** total *m*. **grand ~** somme *f* globale. **(b)** **in ~** au total. **3** *vt* **(a)** *(add: ~ up) figures* faire le total de. **(b)** *(amount to)* s'élever à. ◆ **totalitarian** *adj, n* totalitaire *(mf)*. ◆ **totalitarianism** *n* totalitarisme *m*. ◆ **totality** *n* totalité *f*. ◆ **totalizator** *or* ◆ **totalizer** *n (abbr* **tote¹** *: *Betting)* pari *m* mutuel. ◆ **totally** *adv* totalement.

tote² * [təʊt] *vt (gen)* trimballer *; *gun* porter.

totem ['təʊtəm] *n* totem *m*. **~ pole** mât *m* totémique.

totter ['tɒtəʳ] *vi [person]* chanceler; *[object]* vaciller; *[government etc]* chanceler. **to ~ in/out** *etc* entrer/sortir *etc* d'un pas chancelant.

touch [tʌtʃ] **1** *n* **(a)** *(sense of ~)* toucher *m*; *(act of ~ing)* contact *m*; *(light brushing)* frôlement *m*; *[pianist, typist]* toucher; *[artist]* touche *f*. **soft to the ~** doux au toucher; **the slightest ~** le moindre contact; **at the ~ of her hand** au contact de sa main; **with the ~ of a finger** à la simple pression d'un doigt; **to put the final** *or* **finishing ~(es) to sth** mettre la dernière main à qch; **the personal ~** *(gen)* la chaleur humaine; *(in business, décor etc)* la note personnelle; **you've got the right ~ with him** vous savez vous y prendre avec lui; *(fig: borrowing)* **he's a soft** *or* **an easy ~** * il est toujours prêt à se laisser taper *.
(b) *(small amount)* **a ~ of** *(gen)* un tout petit peu de; *colour, gaiety* une touche de; *sadness, humour* une pointe de; *paint* une petite couche de; **a ~ of the sun** un petit coup de soleil; **to have a ~ of flu** être un peu grippé; **to have a ~ of rheumatism** faire un peu de rhumatisme.
(c) *(contact)* **to be in/get in/keep in ~ with sb** être/se mettre/rester en contact *or* en rapport avec qn; **I'll be in ~** je t'écrirai (*or* je te téléphonerai); **keep in ~** ne nous (*or* m')oubliez pas!; **to be out of ~ with, to have lost ~ with** *person* ne plus être en contact *or* en rapport avec; *developments etc* ne plus être au courant de; **he's out of ~** il n'est plus dans le coup *; **to lose ~ with reality** ne plus avoir le sens des réalités; **you can get in ~ with me at this number** vous pouvez me contacter à ce numéro; **I'll put you in ~ with him** je vous mettrai en rapport avec lui.
(d) *(Ftbl, Rugby)* touche *f*. **the ball went into ~** le ballon est sorti en touche; **it is in ~** il y a touche.
2 *vt* **(a)** *(gen)* toucher (*with* de); *(brush lightly)* frôler. **he ~ed her arm** il lui a touché le bras; **the ship ~ed the bottom** le bateau a touché; **to ~ the ground** toucher terre. **(b)** *(tamper with)* toucher à. **don't ~ that!** n'y touchez pas!; **I didn't ~ him!** je ne lui ai rien fait; **~ nothing** ne touchez à rien. **(c)** *(fig)* toucher à; *topic, problem* effleurer; *(concern, move)* toucher. **their land ~es ours** leur terre touche à la nôtre; **Switzerland ~es Italy** la Suisse et l'Italie se touchent; **the fire didn't ~ the paintings** l'incendie a épargné les tableaux; **they can't ~ you if...** ils ne peuvent rien contre vous si...; **he won't ~ anything illegal** si c'est illégal il n'y touchera pas; **he didn't ~ his meal** il n'a pas touché à son repas; **I never ~ onions** je ne mange jamais d'oignons; **her cooking can't ~ yours** sa cuisine est loin de valoir la tienne; **there's no pianist to ~ him** personne ne peut l'égaler comme pianiste; **it ~es us all closely** cela nous touche *or* nous concerne tous de très près; **we were very ~ed by your letter** nous avons été très touchés

de votre lettre; **to ~ sb for a loan *** taper * qn; **I ~ed him for £10 *** je l'ai tapé * de 10 livres.
3 *vi* (**a**) *[hands, ends, lands etc]* se toucher. *(fig)* **to ~ (up)on a subject** effleurer un sujet. (**b**) *(meddle)* **don't ~!** n'y touchez pas!; **'do not ~'** 'défense de toucher'.

◆**touch down** *vi* (**a**) *(on land)* atterrir; *(on sea)* amerrir; *(on moon)* alunir. (**b**) *(Rugby etc)* marquer un essai. ◆**touch off** *vt sep fuse, firework* faire partir; *mine etc* faire exploser; *explosion, crisis, riot, reaction, argument* déclencher. ◆**touch up** *vt sep painting* retoucher.

◆**touch-and-go** *adj*: **it's ~-and-go with the sick man** le malade est entre la vie et la mort; **it was ~-and-go whether she did it** elle a failli ne pas le faire; **it was ~-and-go until the last minute** c'est resté incertain jusqu'au bout. ◆**touch-down** *n (on land)* atterrissage *m*; *(on sea)* amerrissage *m*; *(on moon)* alunissage *m*; *(US Ftbl)* but *m*. ◆**touched** *adj (moved)* touché *(by* de); (*: *mad)* toqué *. ◆**touchiness** *n* susceptibilité *f*. ◆**touching 1** *adj* touchant ; **2** *prep* concernant. ◆**touchingly** *adv* d'une manière touchante. ◆**touchline** *n (Ftbl etc)* ligne *f* de touche. ◆**touch-type** *vi* taper au toucher. ◆**touchy** *adj person* susceptible (*about* sur la question de); *business, situation* délicat; **he's very ~y** il se vexe *or* s'offense pour un rien.

tough [tʌf] **1** *adj* (**a**) *substance, fabric etc* solide, résistant; *(pej) meat* dur; *(fig) resistance, struggle* acharné; *task, journey* fatigant, pénible; *obstacle, sport* rude; *problem* épineux; *regulations* sévère; *conditions* dur. **it's ~ work** c'est un travail dur *or* pénible. (**b**) *(of person) (physically hard) mountaineer, athlete etc* robuste, résistant; *(mentally strong)* solide, endurant; *(hard: in character) negotiator etc* dur, impitoyable; *(rough) criminal, gangster* dur, brutal. **he is a ~ man to deal with** il ne fait pas souvent de concessions; **a ~ guy** un dur *; *(pej)* **they're a ~ lot** ce sont des durs à cuire *; **to get ~ with sb *** se montrer dur envers qn. (**c**) *(unfortunate)* **that's ~ *** c'est vache * (*on sb* pour qn); **that's ~ luck on him *** *(pity)* il n'a pas de veine; *(he'll have to put up with it)* tant pis pour lui; **to have a ~ time of it *** en voir de dures *. **2** *n* (*) dur * *m*. **3** *adv*: **to talk** *or* **act ~** jouer au dur. **4** *vt (fig)* **to ~ it out** tenir bon. ◆**toughen** *vt substance* renforcer; *person* endurcir; *conditions* rendre plus sévère ; **~ened glass** verre *m* trempé. ◆**toughly** *adv fight* avec acharnement; *answer* durement. ◆**toughness** *n* (**a**) solidité *f*, résistance *f*; dureté *f*; acharnement *m*; caractère *m* fatigant *or* pénible (*or* rude *or* épineux); sévérité *f*; (**b**) résistance *f*; endurance *f*; dureté *f*.

tour [tʊəʳ] **1** *n (journey)* voyage *m*; *(by team, actors, musicians etc)* tournée *f*; *(of town, factory, museum etc)* visite *f*, tour *m*; *(day ~)* excursion *f*; *(package ~)* voyage organisé. **to go on a ~ of** *region, country* faire un voyage dans (*or* en *etc*); *(guided ~)* faire un voyage organisé dans (*or* en *etc*); *museums, castles* visiter; **to go on a ~ round the world** faire le tour du monde; **to go on a walking/cycling ~** faire une randonnée à pied/en bicyclette; *(Sport, Theat etc)* **to go on/be on ~** faire une/être en tournée; **~ of inspection** tournée d'inspection; *(Mil etc)* **~ of duty** période *f* de service. **2** *adj*: **~ operator** tour-opérateur *m*, voyagiste *m*. **3** *vt [tourist, visitor]* visiter; *[team, actors, play]* être en tournée en (*or* dans *etc*). **4** *vi*: **to go ~ing** faire du tourisme. ◆**touring 1** *n* tourisme *m* ; **2** *adj team, theatre company* en tournée. ◆**tourism** *n* tourisme *m*. ◆**tourist 1** *n* touriste *mf* ; **2** *adj class, ticket* touriste *inv*; *attraction, guidebook, season* touristique; *industry* du tourisme; **~ist agency** agence *f* de tourisme ; **~ist bureau** *or* **office** syndicat *m* d'initiative; **the ~ist trade** le tourisme; **~ist trap** attrape-touriste *m* ; **3** *adv travel* en classe touriste. ◆**touristy *** *adj (pej)* trop touristique.

tournament ['tʊənəmənt] *n* tournoi *m*.

tourniquet ['tʊənɪkeɪ] *n (Med)* garrot *m*.

tousled ['taʊzld] *adj hair, person* ébouriffé; *clothes* chiffonné; *bedclothes* en désordre.

tout [taʊt] **1** *n (seller)* vendeur ambulant; *(for custom)* racoleur *m*; *(for hotels)* rabatteur *m*; *(Racing)* pronostiqueur *m*. **ticket ~** revendeur *m* de billets *(au marché noir)*. **2** *vt wares* vendre (avec insistance); *tickets* revendre. **3** *vi*: **to ~ for custom** racoler les clients.

tow¹ [təʊ] **1** *n*: **on ~** en remorque; **to give sb a ~** remorquer qn; *(Aut)* **to give sb a ~ to start him** faire démarrer qn en remorque; *(fig)* **he had a couple of girls in ~ *** il remorquait deux filles. **2** *vt boat, vehicle* remorquer (*to, into* jusqu'à); *caravan, trailer* tirer; *barge* haler. *[police]* **to ~ a car away** emmener une voiture en fourrière. ◆**tow bar** *n* barre *f* de remorquage. ◆**towboat** *n* remorqueur *m*. ◆**towline** *or* ◆**towrope** *n* câble *m* de remorquage. ◆**towpath** *n* chemin *m* de halage. ◆**towing-truck** *or (US)* ◆**tow-truck** *n* dépanneuse *f*.

tow² [təʊ] *n (Tex)* filasse *f*. ◆**tow-headed** *adj* aux cheveux filasse.

toward(s) [t(ə)'wɔːd(z)] *prep (gen)* vers; *(of attitude)* envers, à l'égard de. **he came ~ me** il est venu vers moi; **we are moving ~ a solution/war** *etc* nous nous acheminons vers une solution/la guerre *etc*; **to save ~ sth** faire des économies pour acheter qch; **~ 10 o'clock/the end of the century** vers 10 heures/la fin du siècle; **my feelings ~ him** mes sentiments à son égard *or* envers lui.

towel ['taʊəl] **1** *n* serviette *f* (de toilette); *(dish ~, tea ~)* torchon *m*; *(for hands)* essuie-mains *m inv*; *(for glasses)* essuie-verres *m inv*; *(sanitary ~)* serviette hygiénique. **2** *adj*: **~ rail** porte-serviettes *m inv*. **3** *vt*: **to ~ o.s. (dry)** se sécher avec une serviette. ◆**towelling** *n (Tex)* tissu *m* éponge.

tower ['taʊəʳ] **1** *n (gen)* tour *f*; *[church]* clocher *m*. *(fig)* **a ~ of strength** un grand soutien (*to sb* pour qn). **2** *adj*: **~ block** tour *f* (d'habitation). **3** *vi [building etc]* s'élever très haut. *(lit, fig)* **to ~ over sth/sb** dominer qch/qn. ◆**towering** *adj building* très haut, imposant; *figure* imposant; *(fig)* **in a ~ing rage** dans une colère noire.

town [taʊn] **1** *n* ville *f*. **in (a)~, into ~** en ville; **in the ~** dans la ville; **in a little ~** dans une petite ville; **he's out of ~** il est en déplacement, il n'est pas là; **a country ~** une ville de province; *(fig)* **to have a night on** *or* **to go out on the ~ *** faire la bombe *; *(fig)* **he really went to ~ on that essay *** il a mis le paquet * quand il a écrit cette dissertation. **2** *adj centre* de la ville; *house* en ville; *life* urbain. **~ clerk** ≃ secrétaire *m* de mairie; **~ council** conseil *m* municipal; **~ hall** ≃ mairie *f*, hôtel *m* de ville; *(US)* **~ meeting** assemblée *f* générale *(des habitants d'une localité)*. ◆**town-and-country planning** *n* ≃ aménagement *m* du territoire. ◆**town-dweller** *n* citadin(e) *m(f)*. ◆**town-planner** *n* urbaniste *mf*. ◆**town-planning** *n* urbanisme *m*. ◆**township** *n* bourgade *f*. ◆**townspeople** *npl* citadins *mpl*.

toxic ['tɒksɪk] *adj* toxique. ◆**tox(a)emia** *n* toxémie *f*. ◆**toxin** *n* toxine *f*.

toy [tɔɪ] **1** *n* jouet *m*. **2** *adj train, car, soldier* petit; *house, railway* miniature; *trumpet* d'enfant; *(fig) dog* d'appartement. **3** *vi*: **to ~ with** *object, sb's affections* jouer avec; *idea* caresser; **to ~ with one's food** manger du bout des dents. ◆**toybox** *n* coffre *m* à jouets. ◆**toyshop** *n* magasin *m* de jouets.

trace¹ [treɪs] **1** *n* (**a**) *(gen)* trace *f* (*of* de). **to vanish** *etc* **without ~** disparaître *etc* sans laisser de traces; **there is no ~ of it** il n'en reste plus trace; **we have**

lost all ~ of them nous avons complètement perdu leur trace; **without a ~ of ill-feeling** sans la moindre rancune. (**b**) *(US: trail)* piste *f.* **2** *vt* (**a**) *(draw)* tracer; *(with tracing paper etc)* décalquer. (**b**) *(locate) person, object* retrouver. **to ~ sb** suivre la trace de qn (*as far as* jusqu'à), retrouver la trace de qn (*to* à); **this may be ~d back to...** ceci peut être attribué à...; **they ~d the weapon (back) to here** ils ont établi que l'arme provenait d'ici; **to ~ back one's family to** faire remonter sa famille à. ◆ **tracer** *n (instrument)* traçoir *m*; *(Biochemistry)* traceur *m*; *(bullet)* balle *f* traçante. ◆ **tracery** *n (on window)* réseau *m (de fenêtre ajourée)*; *[frost etc]* dentelles *fpl.* ◆ **tracing** *n (process)* calquage *m*; *(result)* calque *m.* ◆ **tracing-paper** *n* papier-calque *m inv.*

trace² [treɪs] *n [harness]* trait *m.*

track [træk] **1** *n* (**a**) *(mark, trail)* trace *f*; *[animal, person]* trace, piste *f*; *(route: on radar screen; also of bullet, comet, rocket etc)* trajectoire *f.* **to destroy everything in its ~** tout détruire sur son passage; **to follow in sb's ~s** suivre la trace de qn; *(fig)* marcher sur les traces de qn; **to be on sb's ~** être sur la piste de qn; *(fig)* **to be on the right ~** être sur la bonne voie; **to be on the wrong ~** faire fausse route; **to put** *or* **throw sb off the ~** désorienter qn; **to keep ~ of** *spacecraft, events, developments* suivre; *person* suivre la trace de; *(fig: keep in touch with)* rester en contact avec; **to lose ~ of** *spacecraft etc* perdre; *(fig) developments etc* ne plus être au courant de; *person* perdre la trace de; *(fig)* perdre tout contact avec; **I've lost ~ of what he is saying** j'ai perdu le fil de ce qu'il dit; *(fig)* **to make ~s** * filer (*for* à). (**b**) *(path)* chemin *m*, piste *f*; *(Sport)* piste. **sheep ~** piste à moutons; **mule ~** chemin muletier; **race ~** piste; **motor-racing ~** autodrome *m*; **dog-racing ~** cynodrome *m.* (**c**) *(Rail)* voie *f*, rails *mpl.* **to leave the ~(s)** dérailler; **to cross the ~** traverser la voie. (**d**) *[tape, disk]* piste *f*; *[record]* plage *f.* **4-~ tape** bande *f* à 4 pistes. (**e**) *[tractor]* chenille *f.* (**f**) *(US Scol)* classe *f* de niveau; **the B ~** le groupe B.

2 *adj (Sport) racing, event, athletics* sur piste. *(also fig)* **to have a good ~ record** avoir eu de bons résultats; *(Elec)* **~ lighting** rampe *f* de spots.

3 *vt animal, person, vehicle* suivre la trace de; *game, prey, wanted man* traquer; *rocket, comet* suivre la trajectoire de.

◆ **track down** *vt sep animal, wanted man* traquer et capturer; *sth or sb wanted* (finir par) retrouver. ◆ **tracked** *adj vehicle* à chenille. ◆ **tracker 1** *n (Hunting)* traqueur *m*; *(gen)* poursuivant(e) *m(f)* ; **2** *adj*: **~er dog** chien *m* policier. ◆ **tracking** *adj (Space)* **~ing station** station *f* d'observation. ◆ **tracksuit** *n* survêtement *m.*

tract¹ [trækt] *n* (**a**) *[land, water]* étendue *f*; *(US: housing estate)* résidence *f.* (**b**) *(Anat)* **digestive ~** appareil *m* digestif.

tract² [trækt] *n (pamphlet)* tract *m.*

tractable ['træktəbl] *adj person* accommodant; *animal* docile; *material* malléable; *problem* résoluble.

traction ['trækʃ(ə)n] **1** *n* traction *f.* **2** *adj*: **~ engine** locomobile *f.*

tractor ['træktəʳ] *n* tracteur *m.*

trade [treɪd] **1** *n* (**a**) *(Econ etc)* commerce *m.* **overseas ~** commerce extérieur; **the wool ~** le commerce de la laine; **he's in the wool ~** il est négociant en laine; **to do a lot of ~ with** faire beaucoup de commerce *or* d'affaires avec; **to do a brisk** *or* **roaring ~** vendre beaucoup (*in* de); *(Brit)* **Board of T~** , *(US)* **Department of T~** ministère *m* du Commerce. (**b**) *(job)* métier *m.* **he is a butcher by ~** il est boucher de son métier; **to learn a ~** apprendre un métier; *(lit, fig)* **he's in the ~** il est du métier; **known in the ~ as...** que les gens du métier appellent...

2 *adj association, fair, route, school* commercial; *barriers* douanier; *price* de gros; *journal* professionnel. **~ deficit** balance *f* commerciale déficitaire; **the T~ Descriptions Act** la loi de protection du consommateur; **~ discount** remise *f* au détaillant; **~ figures** *or* **returns** résultats *mpl* financiers; **~ name** nom *m* de marque; *(lit, fig)* **~ secret** secret *m* de fabrication; **~ wind** alizé *m.*

3 *vi* (**a**) *(gen)* faire le commerce (*in* de; *with* avec). *(fig)* **to ~ on sb's kindness** abuser de la gentillesse de qn. (**b**) *(US: shop)* faire ses achats (*with* chez, à).

4 *vt (exchange)* échanger (*sth for sth* qch contre qch; *sth with sb* qch avec qn).

◆ **trade in** *vt sep car, television etc* faire reprendre. **I've ~d it in for a new one** je l'ai fait reprendre quand j'en ai acheté un nouveau. ◆ **trade off** *vt sep*: **to ~ off A against B** accepter que A compense B.

◆ **trade-in 1** *n (Comm)* reprise *f*; **he took it as a ~-in** il me l'a repris ; **2** *adj price, value* à la reprise. ◆ **trademark** *n* marque *f* de fabrique; **registered ~mark** marque déposée. ◆ **trade-off** *n (exchange)* échange *m; (balancing)* compromis *m.* ◆ **trader** *n* commerçant(e) *m(f)*; *(bigger)* négociant(e) *m(f)* (*in* en); *(street ~)* vendeur *m*, -euse *f* de rue. ◆ **tradesman** *n* commerçant *m.* ◆ **trade(s) union** *n* syndicat *m.* ◆ **trade(s) unionism** *n* syndicalisme *m.* ◆ **trade(s) unionist** *n* syndicaliste *mf.* ◆ **trading 1** *n* commerce *m* ; **2** *adj nation* commerçant; *port, centre* de commerce; *(Brit)* **trading estate** zone *f* artisanale et commerciale; **trading stamp** timbre-prime *m.*

tradition [trə'dɪʃ(ə)n] *n* tradition *f.* **according to ~** selon la tradition; *(fig)* **it's in the best ~** c'est dans la plus pure tradition (*of* de). ◆ **traditional** *adj* traditionnel (*to do* de faire). ◆ **traditionally** *adv* traditionnellement.

traffic ['træfɪk] *(vb: pret, ptp* **trafficked***)* **1** *n* (**a**) *(Aut)* circulation *f*; *(Aviat, Naut, Rail, Telec)* trafic *m.* **road ~** circulation routière; **rail ~** trafic ferroviaire; *(Aut)* **holiday ~** circulation des grands départs (*or* des grandes rentrées); **the ~ is heavy** *(Aut)* il y a beaucoup de circulation; *(Aviat etc)* le trafic est intense; *(Aut)* **closed to heavy ~** interdit aux poids lourds; *(Aut)* **build-up** *or* **backlog of ~** bouchon *m*; **~ coming into Paris** la circulation dans le sens province-Paris; **~ in and out of the airport** le trafic à destination et en provenance de l'aéroport. (**b**) *(trade)* commerce *m* (*in* de); *(pej)* trafic *m* (*in* de). **the drug ~** le trafic de la drogue. **2** *vi* faire le commerce *or* le trafic *(pej)* (*in* de). **3** *adj (Aut) regulations, policeman* de la circulation; *police* de la route; *offence* au code de la route; *sign* de signalisation. *(Aviat)* **~ controller** aiguilleur *m* du ciel; **~ island** refuge *m*; **~ jam** embouteillage *m*; **~ light** *or* **signal** feu *m* (de signalisation); **the ~ lights were at green** le feu était au vert; **~ warden** contractuel(le) *m(f).* ◆ **traficker** *n* trafiquant(e) *m(f)* (*in* en).

tragedy ['trædʒɪdɪ] *n (gen, Theat)* tragédie *f.* **the ~ of it is that..., it is a ~ that...** il est tragique que... + *subj.* ◆ **tragic** *adj* tragique; **tragic actor** tragédien *m.* ◆ **tragically** *adv* tragiquement.

trail [treɪl] **1** *n* (**a**) *(of blood, smoke; from plane, comet etc)* traînée *f*; *(tracks: gen)* trace *f*; *(Hunting)* piste *f*, trace. **a long ~ of refugees** une longue colonne de réfugiés; **to leave a ~ of destruction** tout détruire sur son passage; *(lit, fig)* **on the ~ of** sur la piste de. (**b**) *(path)* sentier *m*, chemin *m.* **2** *vt* (**a**) *(follow)* suivre la piste de; *(fig: lag behind)* être dépassé par. (**b**) *(tow) object on rope etc* traîner; *(Aut) caravan etc* tirer. **they ~ed dirt all over the carpet** ils ont couvert le tapis de traces sales; **to ~ one's fingers through the water** laisser traîner ses doigts dans l'eau. **3** *vi* (**a**) *[object]* traîner (*in* dans; *from* de); *[plant]* ramper. *(Sport)* **to ~ by 13**

points être en retard de 13 points. (**b**) **to ~ along/in** *etc (in straggling line)* passer/entrer *etc* à la queue leu leu; *(wearily)* passer/entrer *etc* en traînant les pieds.

◆**trail away, trail off** *vi [sound]* s'estomper. ◆**trail bike** * *n* moto *f* de cross. ◆**trailblazer** *n* pionnier *m*, -ière *f*. ◆**trailer** **1** *n* (**a**) *(Aut)* remorque *f*; *(caravan)* caravane *f*; (**b**) *(Cine, TV)* bande-annonce *m* ; **2** *adj (US)* **~er park** camp *m* de caravaning; **~er tent** tente *f* remorque. ◆**trailing** *adj hair, blanket etc* traînant; *plant* rampant.

train [treɪn] **1** *n* (**a**) *(Rail)* train *m*; *(in underground)* rame *f*. **fast ~** rapide *m*; **slow ~** omnibus *m*; **to go by ~** prendre le train; **to go to London by ~** aller à Londres en train *or* par le train; **on** *or* **in the ~** dans le train; **to transport by ~** transporter par voie ferroviaire. (**b**) *(line: of vehicles, camels etc)* file *f*; *(entourage)* suite *f*. *(fig)* **it brought famine in its ~** cela a amené la famine dans son sillage. (**c**) *(series: of events etc)* suite *f*; *[gunpowder]* traînée *f*. **in an unbroken ~** en succession ininterrompue; **his ~ of thought** le fil de ses pensées. (**d**) *[robe etc]* traîne *f*.
2 *adj workers, strike* des chemins de fer; *crash* de chemin de fer. **~ ferry** ferry-boat *m*; **the ~ service to London** les trains pour Londres; **~ set** train *m* électrique *(jouet)*.
3 *vt* (**a**) *(instruct etc) teacher, craftsman, employee, soldier etc* former; *(Sport)* entraîner; *animal* dresser (*to do* à faire); *voice* travailler; *ear, mind, memory* exercer. *(house ~)* **to ~ a puppy/child** apprendre à un chiot/à un enfant à être propre; **to ~ sb to do** apprendre à qn à faire; *(professionally)* former qn à faire; **to ~ o.s. to do** s'entraîner à faire; **to ~ sb in a craft** préparer qn à un métier; **he was ~ed in weaving** *or* **as a weaver** il a reçu une formation de tisserand; **where were you ~ed?** où avez-vous reçu votre formation? (**b**) *(direct etc) gun, telescope etc* braquer (*on* sur); *plant* faire grimper (*along* le long de).
4 *vi* recevoir une (*or* sa) formation; *(Sport)* s'entraîner (*for* pour). **to ~ as** *or* **to be a teacher** *etc* recevoir une formation de professeur *etc*.
◆**trained** *adj person (gen)* compétent (*for* pour); *(professionally)* qualifié (*for* pour); *engineer, nurse* diplômé; *teacher* habilité à enseigner; *animal* dressé; *eye, ear* exercé; **she has a ~ed voice** elle a pris des leçons de chant; **he is not ~ed** il n'a reçu aucune formation professionnelle; **well-~ed** *child* bien élevé; *animal, (iro) husband etc* bien dressé. ◆**trainee** *adj, n* stagiaire *(mf)*; **management ~ee** stagiaire de direction; **~ee typist** dactylo *f* stagiaire. ◆**trainer** *n* (**a**) *(Sport)* entraîneur *m*; *(Cycling etc)* soigneur *m*; *(in circus)* dresseur *m*, -euse *f*; (**b**) *(shoe)* chaussure *f* de sport. ◆**training** **1** *n (for job)* formation *f*; *(Sport)* entraînement *m*; *[animal]* dressage *m*; *(Sport)* **to be in ~ing** *(preparing o.s.)* être en cours d'entraînement; *(on form)* être en forme; **she has had secretarial ~ing** elle a suivi des cours de secrétariat ; **2** *adj scheme, centre (for job)* de formation; *(Sport)* d'entraînement; **~ing college** *(gen)* école *f* professionnelle; *(for teachers)* ≃ école normale; **~ing course** cours *mpl* professionnels; **~ing plane/ship** avion-/navire-école *m*. ◆**train-spotter** *n* passionné(e) *m(f)* de trains. ◆**train-spotting** *n*: **to go ~-spotting** observer les trains.

traipse * [treɪps] *vi*: **to ~ in/out** *etc* entrer/sortir *etc* d'un pas traînant; **to ~ around** se balader *.

trait [treɪt] *n* trait *m (de caractère)*.

traitor ['treɪtəʳ] *n* traître *m*. **to be a ~ to sth** trahir qch; **to turn ~** passer à l'ennemi. ◆**traitress** *n* traîtresse *f*.

trajectory [trəˈdʒekt(ə)rɪ] *n* trajectoire *f*.

tram(car) ['træm(kɑːʳ)] *n* tram(way) *m*.

tramp [træmp] **1** *n* (**a**) *[footsteps]* bruit *m* (de pas). (**b**) *(hike)* randonnée *f* (à pied). (**c**) *(vagabond)* vagabond(e) *m(f)*, clochard(e) *m(f)*. *(pej)* **she's a ~** * elle est coureuse *. (**d**) **~ (steamer)** tramp *m*. **2** *vi*: **to ~ along** *(hike)* poursuivre son chemin à pied; *(walk heavily)* marcher d'un pas lourd; *[soldiers etc]* marteler le pavé. **3** *vt*: **to ~ the streets** battre le pavé; **I ~ed the town looking for...** j'ai parcouru la ville à pied pour trouver...

trample ['træmpl] *vti (lit, fig)* **to ~ on sth/sb, to ~ sth/sb underfoot** piétiner qch/qn, fouler qch/qn aux pieds; **to ~ on sb's feelings** bafouer les sentiments de qn; **to ~ sth into the ground** enfoncer qch dans le sol.

trampoline ['træmpəlɪn] *n* trampolino *m*.

trance [trɑːns] *n* transe *f*. **to go** *or* **fall into a ~** entrer en transe.

tranquil ['træŋkwɪl] *adj* tranquille. ◆**tranquillity,** *(US)* **tranquility** *n* tranquillité *f*. ◆**tranquil(l)ize** *vt (Med)* mettre sous tranquillisants. ◆**tranquil(l)izer** *n* tranquillisant *m*.

trans... [trænz] *pref* trans... ◆**transatlantic** *adj* transatlantique.

transact [trænˈzækt] *vt* traiter, régler. ◆**transaction** *n (Econ, Fin, St Ex)* transaction *f*; *(in bank, shop)* opération *f*; **cash ~ion** opération au comptant.

transcend [trænˈsend] *vt (gen)* transcender; *(excel over)* surpasser. ◆**transcendent** *adj* transcendant. ◆**transcendental** *adj* transcendantal; **~ental meditation** méditation *f* transcendantale.

transcribe [trænˈskraɪb] *vt* transcrire. ◆**transcript** *or* ◆**transcription** *n* transcription *f*.

transect [trænˈsekt] *vt* sectionner (transversalement).

transept ['trænsept] *n* transept *m*.

transfer [trænsˈfɜːʳ] **1** *vt (gen)* transférer (*to* à); *power* faire passer (*from* de; *to* à); *money* virer; *design, drawing, one's affections* reporter (*to* sur). *(Telec)* **to ~ the charges** téléphoner en P.C.V. ; **~red charge call** communication *f* en P.C.V. **2** *vi (gen)* être transféré (*to* à; *from* de). *(Univ etc)* **he's ~red from Science to Geography** il ne fait plus de science, il s'est réorienté en géographie. **3** ['trænsfɜːʳ] *n* (**a**) *(gen)* transfert *m* (*to* à; *from* de); *(Pol: of power)* passation *f*. **by bank ~** par virement *m* bancaire. (**b**) *(design etc) (rub-on type)* décalcomanie *f*; *(stick-on)* auto-collant *m*. **4** *adj (Aviat)* **~ lounge** salle *f* de transit. ◆**transferable** *adj* transmissible; **not ~able** personnel.

transfigure [trænsˈfɪgəʳ] *vt* transfigurer. ◆**transfiguration** *n* transfiguration *f*.

transfix [trænsˈfɪks] *vt (lit)* transpercer. *(fig)* **~ed** cloué sur place (*with* de).

transform [trænsˈfɔːm] *vt* transformer (*into* en). **to be ~ed into** se transformer en. ◆**transformation** *n* transformation *f*. ◆**transformational** *adj* transformationnel. ◆**transformer** *n (Elec)* transformateur *m*.

transfuse [trænsˈfjuːz] *vt* transfuser. ◆**transfusion** *n (Med, fig)* transfusion *f*; **to give sb a transfusion** faire une transfusion à qn.

transgress [trænsˈgres] *vi* pécher. ◆**transgressor** *n* pécheur *m*, -eresse *f*.

transient ['trænzɪənt] *adj* transitoire, éphémère.

transistor [trænˈzɪstəʳ] *n (Elec, Rad)* transistor *m*. ◆**transistorize** *vt* transistoriser.

transit ['trænzɪt] **1** *n*: **in ~** en transit *m*. **2** *adj goods, passengers* en transit; *documents, visa, (Aviat) lounge* de transit; *(Mil etc) camp* volant. ◆**transition** *n* transition *f* (*from* de; *to* à). ◆**transitional** *adj period, government* de transition; *measures* transitoire.

transitive ['trænzɪtɪv] *adj* transitif.

transitory ['trænzɪt(ə)rɪ] *adj* transitoire, éphémère.

translate [trænz'leɪt] **1** *vt* traduire (*from* de; *into* en). **the word is ~d as...** le mot se traduit par...; (*fig*) **to ~ ideas into actions** passer des idées aux actes. **2** *vi [person]* traduire. **it won't ~** c'est intraduisible. ◆ **translatable** *adj* traduisible. ◆ **translation** *n* traduction *f* (*from* de; *into* en); *(Scol etc)* version *f*. ◆ **translator** *n* traducteur *m*, -trice *f*.

transliterate [trænz'lɪtəreɪt] *vt* translittérer.

translucence [trænz'lu:sns] *n* translucidité *f*. ◆ **translucent** *adj* translucide.

transmit [trænz'mɪt] **1** *vt (gen, Aut, Med etc)* transmettre; *(Rad, Telec, TV)* émettre. **2** *vi (Rad etc)* émettre. ◆ **transmissible** *adj* transmissible. ◆ **transmission** **1** *n (gen)* transmission *f*; *(US: gearbox)* boîte *f* de vitesses ; **2** *adj (Aut)* **transmission shaft** arbre *m* de transmission. ◆ **transmitter** *n (transmitting device)* transmetteur *m*; *(microphone)* capsule *f* microphonique; *(Rad, TV)* émetteur *m*. ◆ **transmitting** *adj (Telec) set, station* émetteur.

transmute [trænz'mju:t] *vt* transmuer (*into* en).

transom ['trænsəm] *n* traverse *f*; *(US: in window)* vasistas *m*.

transparent [træns'pεər(ə)nt] *adj* transparent. ◆ **transparency** *n* transparence *f*; *(Phot)* diapositive *f*; *(for overhead projector)* transparent *m*.

transpire [træns'paɪər] *vi* (**a**) *(happen)* se passer. **it ~d that...** on a appris par la suite que... (**b**) *(Bot, Physiol)* transpirer.

transplant [træns'plɑ:nt] **1** *vt (gen)* transplanter; *(Med)* greffer; *seedlings etc* repiquer. **2** ['trænsplɑ:nt] *n (Med)* transplantation *f*. **he's had a heart ~** on lui a fait une greffe du cœur *or* une transplantation cardiaque.

transport ['trænspɔ:t] **1** *n* (**a**) transport *m*. **road/rail ~** transport par route/par chemin de fer; **Ministry of T~** ministère *m* des Transports; **have you got any ~? *** tu as une voiture? (**b**) *[delight etc]* transport *m*; *[fury etc]* accès *m*. **2** *adj costs, ship etc* de transport; *strike, system* des transports. **~ café** ≈ restaurant *m* de routiers. **3** [træns'pɔ:t] *vt (lit, fig)* transporter. ◆ **transportation** *n* transport *m*; *[criminals]* transportation *f*. ◆ **transporter** *n (Mil: vehicle, ship)* transport *m*; *(plane)* avion *m* de transport; *(car transporter) (Aut)* camion *m* *or (Rail)* wagon *m* pour transport d'automobiles.

transpose [træns'pəʊz] *vt* transposer. ◆ **transposition** *n* transposition *f*.

transsexual [trænz'seksjʊəl] *n* transsexuel(le) *m(f)*.

transship [træns'ʃɪp] *vt* transborder. ◆ **transshipment** *n* transbordement *m*.

transubstantiation ['trænsəbˌstænʃɪ'eɪʃ(ə)n] *n* transsubstantiation *f*.

transverse ['trænzvɜ:s] *adj* transversal. ◆ **transversely** *adv* transversalement.

transvestite [trænz'vestaɪt] *n* travesti(e) *m(f)* *(Psych)*.

trap [træp] **1** *n* (**a**) *(gen)* piège *m*; *(gin-~)* collet *m*; *(covered hole)* trappe *f*; *(mouse ~)* souricière *f*. *(lit, fig)* **to set** *or* **lay a ~** tendre un piège (*for sb* à qn); **to catch in a ~** prendre au piège; **caught like a rat in a ~** fait comme un rat. (**b**) **~ (door)** trappe *f*; **keep your ~ shut ‡** ferme ta gueule ‡. **2** *vt* (**a**) *(snare) animal, person* prendre au piège. (**b**) *(catch, cut off) miner, climber, vehicle, ship* bloquer; *gas, liquid* retenir; *object, one's finger* coincer (*in sth* dans qch). ◆ **trapper** *n* trappeur *m*. ◆ **trapshooting** *n* ball-trap *m*.

trapeze [trə'pi:z] **1** *n* trapèze *m*. **2** *adj*: **~ artist** trapéziste *mf*.

trappings ['træpɪŋz] *npl [kingship etc]* cérémonial *m*; *[success]* signes *mpl* extérieurs.

Trappist ['træpɪst] **1** *n* trappiste *m*. **2** *adj* de la Trappe.

trash [træʃ] **1** *n (refuse)* ordures *fpl*; *(cheap goods)* camelote * *f*; *(nonsense)* bêtises *fpl*, blagues * *fpl*. **this is ~** ça ne vaut rien, *(message, letter etc)* c'est de la blague *; *[people]* **they're just ~ ‡** ce sont des moins que rien. **2** *adj*: **~ can** poubelle *f*, boîte *f* à ordures; **~ heap** tas *m* d'ordures. **3** *vt (US *) (vandalize)* saccager; *(criticize)* débiner *. ◆ **trasher** *n (US)* vandale *m*. ◆ **trashy** *adj (gen)* qui ne vaut rien; *goods* de camelote *.

trauma ['trɔ:mə] *n (Med, Psych)* trauma *m*; *(fig)* traumatisme *m*. ◆ **traumatic** *adj (Med)* traumatique; *(Psych, fig)* traumatisant. ◆ **traumatize** *vt* traumatiser.

travel ['trævl] **1** *vi* (**a**) *(journey)* voyager; *(Comm)* être représentant (*for* de; *in* en). **they have ~led a long way** ils sont venus de loin; *(fig)* ils ont fait beaucoup de chemin; **he is ~ling in Spain** il est en voyage en Espagne; **as he was ~ling across France** pendant qu'il voyageait à travers la France; **to ~ through a region** parcourir une région; **to ~ round the world** faire le tour du monde; **to ~ light** voyager avec peu de bagages; *[food, wine]* **it ~s well** ça supporte bien le voyage. (**b**) *(move, go)* aller; *[machine part etc]* se déplacer. **you were ~ling too fast** vous alliez trop vite; **to ~ at 80 km/h** faire du 80 km/h; **light ~s at a speed of...** la vitesse de la lumière est de...; **news ~s fast** les nouvelles circulent vite. **2** *vt country, district, distance* parcourir. **much-~led road** route très fréquentée. **3** *n* les voyages *mpl*. **his ~s** ses voyages; **he's off on his ~s again** il repart en voyage; **on your ~s** au cours de vos voyages; *(fig hum)* au cours de vos allées et venues. **4** *adj allowance, expenses* de déplacement; *story, film* de voyages; *organization* de tourisme. **~ agency** agence *f* de voyages; **~ agent** agent *m* de voyages; **~ brochure** dépliant *m* touristique; **~ insurance** assurance *f* voyage. ◆ **travelator** *n* tapis roulant. ◆ **traveller,** *(US)* **traveler** *n* voyageur *m*, -euse *f*; *(Comm)* représentant *m* (de commerce) (*in* en); **~ler's cheque**, *(US)* **~er's check** chèque *m* de voyage. ◆ **travel(l)ing** **1** *n* voyages *mpl* ; **2** *adj* (**a**) *circus, troupe* ambulant; *crane* mobile; *(Comm)* **~(l)ing salesman** représentant *m* de commerce; (**b**) *bag, rug, clock, scholarship* de voyage; *expenses, allowance* de déplacement. ◆ **travelogue** *n (talk/film/book)* compte rendu *m*/film *m*/récit *m* de voyages. ◆ **travel-sick** *adj (in car/plane/boat)* **to be ~-sick** avoir le mal de la route/de l'air/de mer. ◆ **travel-sickness** **1** *n* mal *m* de la route *etc* ; **2** *adj pills* contre le mal de la route *etc*.

traverse ['trævəs] *vt* traverser.

travesty ['trævɪstɪ] *n (Art, Literat etc)* pastiche *m*; *(pej) [freedom, justice]* simulacre *m*.

trawl [trɔ:l] **1** *n (net)* chalut *m*. **2** *vi*: **to ~ (for sth)** pêcher (qch) au chalut. ◆ **trawler** *n* chalutier *m*. ◆ **trawling** *n* pêche *f* au chalut.

tray [treɪ] *n (for carrying)* plateau *m*; *(for storing) (box)* boîte *f*; *(basket)* corbeille *f*; *(drawer)* tiroir *m*. ◆ **traycloth** *n* napperon *m*.

treacherous ['tretʃ(ə)rəs] *adj person, action, answer (gen; also fig)* traître (*f* traîtresse). **road conditions are ~** il faut se méfier de l'état des routes. ◆ **treacherously** *adv* traîtreusement; *say* perfidement. ◆ **treachery** *n* traîtrise *f*.

treacle ['tri:kl] *n* mélasse *f*.

tread [tred] *(vb: pret* **trod,** *ptp* **trodden)** **1** *n* (**a**) *(footsteps)* pas *mpl*; *(sound)* bruit *m* de pas. (**b**) *[tyre]* bande *f* de roulement; *[stair]* marche *f*. **2** *vi* marcher. **to ~ on sth** *(accidentally)* marcher sur qch; *(deliberately)* écraser qch; **to ~ carefully** *or* **warily** avancer avec précaution. **3** *vt path, road* parcourir. **to ~ sth underfoot** fouler qch aux pieds; **to ~ grapes** fouler du raisin; **to ~ water** nager en chien. ◆**treadle** **1** *n* pédale *f (de tour etc)* ; **2** *adj machine* à pédale. ◆**treadmill** *n (fig)* routine *f* mortellement ennuyeuse.

treason ['tri:zn] *n* trahison *f.* ◆**treasonable** *adj* qui constitue une trahison.

treasure ['treʒəʳ] **1** *n* trésor *m. (fig)* **she's a real ~** elle est adorable; *(of servant etc)* c'est une perle. **2** *adj*: **~ house** trésor *m (lieu)*; **~ hunt** chasse *f* au trésor. **3** *vt (value)* attacher une grande valeur à; *(keep:* **~ up***) money, valuables* garder précieusement; *memory, thought* chérir. ◆**treasurer** *n* trésorier *m*, -ière *f.* ◆**treasure-trove** *n* trésor *m (dont le propriétaire est inconnu).* ◆**treasury** **1** *n* trésorerie *f*; *(Brit)* **the Treasury,** *(US)* **the Department of the Treasury** ≃ le ministère des Finances ; **2** *adj*: **treasury bill** ≃ bon *m* du Trésor.

treat [tri:t] **1** *vt* (**a**) traiter (*sb like a child* qn comme un enfant; *(Chem etc) sth with sth* qch à qch; *(Med) sb for sth* qn pour qch). **to ~ sb well** bien traiter qn, bien se conduire envers qn; **to ~ sb badly** mal se conduire envers qn, traiter qn fort mal; **to ~ sb with respect** montrer du respect envers qn; **to ~ sth with care** faire attention à qch; **it ~s the problems of...** cela traite les problèmes de...; **he ~ed the whole thing as a joke** il a pris tout cela à la plaisanterie; *(Med)* **to ~ sb/sth with penicillin** soigner qn/qch à la pénicilline. (**b**) **to ~ sb to sth** offrir *or* payer * qch à qn; **to ~ o.s. to sth** se payer * qch.
2 *vi*: **to ~ with sb** traiter avec qn (*for sth* pour qch); *[article etc]* **to ~ of** traiter de.
3 *n (pleasure)* plaisir *m*; *(outing)* sortie *f*; *(present)* cadeau *m.* **a ~ in store** un plaisir à venir; **it was a great ~ (for us) to see them** ça nous a vraiment fait plaisir de les voir; **it is a ~ for her to go out to a meal** c'est tout un événement * pour elle de dîner en ville; **to give sb a ~** faire plaisir à qn; **to stand ~** inviter; **this is my ~** c'est moi qui paie *. ◆**treatise** *n* traité *m* (*on* de). ◆**treatment** *n (gen)* traitement *m*; **his ~ment of his parents/this subject** la façon dont il traite ses parents/ce sujet; **he got good ~ment** *(gen)* on l'a bien traité; *(Med)* il a été bien traité *or* soigné; **to give sb preferential ~ment** accorder à qn un régime de faveur; **medical ~ment** soins *mpl* médicaux, traitement; *(Med)* **to have ~ment for sth** suivre un traitement pour qch. ◆**treaty** *n (Pol)* traité *m* (*with* avec; *between* entre); **to make a ~y** signer un traité.

treble ['trebl] **1** *adj* (**a**) *(triple)* triple. (**b**) *(Mus) voice* de soprano *(voix d'enfant).* **the ~ clef** la clef de sol. **2** *adv (thrice)* trois fois plus que. **3** *vti* tripler.

tree [tri:] *n* arbre *m.* **cherry ~** cerisier *m*; **the ~ line** la limite des arbres; *(fig)* **to be at the top of the ~** être arrivé au haut de l'échelle. ◆**tree-covered** *adj* boisé. ◆**tree-house** *n* cabane *f* construite dans un arbre. ◆**tree-lined** *adj* bordé d'arbres. ◆**treetop** *n* cime *f* d'un arbre. ◆**tree-trunk** *n* tronc *m* d'arbre.

trefoil ['trefɔɪl] *n (Bot)* trèfle *m.*

trek [trek] **1** *vi* voyager à la dure. *(fig)* **I had to ~ * over to the library** il a fallu que je me traîne jusqu'à la bibliothèque. **2** *n* voyage *m* difficile. **it was quite a ~ * to the hotel** il y avait un bon bout de chemin à faire jusqu'à l'hôtel. ◆**trekking** *n* voyage-randonnée *m.*

trellis ['trelɪs] *n* treillis *m*; *(tougher)* treillage *m.*

tremble ['trembl] **1** *vi (gen)* trembler (*with, from* de); *(from fear, passion)* frémir, trembler; *[engine, ship]* vibrer. **2** *n* tremblement *m.* **to be all of a ~ *** trembler de la tête aux pieds. ◆**trembling** **1** *adj* tremblant; frémissant ; **2** *n* tremblement *m.*

tremendous [trə'mendəs] *adj (huge) difference, number, pleasure* énorme; *(dreadful) storm, blow* terrible; *victory* foudroyant; *speed, success* fou; *(*: excellent)* formidable *. **we had a ~ time *** on s'est drôlement bien amusé *. ◆**tremendously** *adv* extrêmement, terriblement.

tremor ['treməʳ] *n* tremblement *m.*

tremulous ['tremjʊləs] *adj (timid)* timide; *(trembling)* tremblant. ◆**tremulously** *adv* timidement; en tremblant.

trench [trenʃ] *n* tranchée *f (also Mil)*; *(wider)* fossé *m.* ◆**trenchcoat** *n* trench-coat *m.*

trenchant ['tren(t)ʃ(ə)nt] *adj* incisif, mordant.

trend [trend] *n (tendency)* tendance *f* (*towards* à); *[river, road]* direction *f*; *[events]* cours *m*; *(fashion: in clothes etc)* mode *f.* **there is a ~ towards doing/away from doing** on a tendance à faire/à ne plus faire; **~s in popular music** les tendances de la musique populaire; **to set a ~** donner le ton; *(fashion)* lancer une mode. ◆**trendsetter** *n* personne *f* qui donne le ton. ◆**trendy** * *adj clothes* dernier cri *inv*; *opinions, person* dans le vent *.

trepidation [ˌtrepɪ'deɪʃ(ə)n] *n* vive inquiétude *f.*

trespass ['trespəs] *vi* s'introduire sans permission (*on sb's land* dans la propriété de qn). **'no ~ing'** 'entrée interdite'; **you're ~ing** vous êtes dans une propriété privée. ◆**trespasser** *n* intrus(e) *m(f)* ; **'~ers will be prosecuted'** 'défense d'entrer sous peine de poursuites'.

trestle ['tresl] *adj*: **~ table** table *f* à tréteaux.

trial ['traɪ(ə)l] **1** *n* (**a**) *(Jur: proceedings)* procès *m*; *(gen)* jugement *m.* **at** *or* **during the ~** au cours du procès; **~ by jury** jugement par jury; **to be** *or* **go on ~** passer en jugement; **on ~ for theft** jugé pour vol; **he was on ~ for his life** il encourait la peine de mort; **to put sb on ~, to bring sb to ~** faire passer qn en jugement. (**b**) *(test) [machine, vehicle, drug etc]* essai *m.* **~s** *(Ftbl etc)* match *m* de sélection; *(Athletics etc)* épreuve *f* de sélection; *[sheepdogs, horses]* concours *m*; **~ of strength** épreuve *f* de force; **by ~ and error** par tâtonnements; **to be/take on ~** être/prendre à l'essai; **to give sb a ~** mettre qn à l'essai. (**c**) *(hardship)* épreuve *f.* **it was a great ~** cela a été une véritable épreuve (*for* pour); **the ~s of old age** les afflictions *fpl* de la vieillesse; **~s and tribulations** tribulations *fpl*; **he is a ~ to his mother** il donne beaucoup de souci à sa mère. **2** *adj flight, period etc* d'essai; *offer, marriage* à l'essai. *(US)* **~ balloon** *(lit, fig)* ballon *m* d'essai; **on a ~ basis** à titre d'essai; **~ run** essai *m*; *(fig)* période *f* d'essai.

triangle ['traɪæŋgl] *n* triangle *m.* ◆**triangular** *adj* triangulaire.

tribe [traɪb] *n* tribu *f.* ◆**tribal** *adj (gen)* tribal; *warfare* entre tribus. ◆**tribesman** *n* membre *m* de la tribu.

tribunal [traɪ'bju:nl] *n (gen, Jur)* tribunal *m.* **~ of inquiry** commission *f* d'enquête.

tribute ['trɪbju:t] *n* tribut *m.* **to pay ~ to** payer tribut à, rendre hommage à; **that is a ~ to his generosity** cela témoigne de sa générosité. ◆**tributary** *n (river)* affluent *m.*

trice [traɪs] *n*: **in a ~** en un clin d'œil.

trick [trɪk] **1** *n* (**a**) *(ruse)* ruse *f*, truc * *m*; *(joke, hoax)* tour *m*, blague * *f*; *[conjurer, dog etc]* tour; *(special skill)* truc * (*for doing* pour faire). **it's a ~ to make you believe...** c'est une ruse *or* un truc * pour vous faire croire...; **to play a ~ on sb** jouer un tour à qn; **a dirty** *or* **low** *or* **shabby** *or* **nasty ~** un sale tour; **a ~ of the trade** une ficelle du métier; **a ~ of the light** une illusion d'optique; **he's up to his old ~s again *** il fait de nouveau des siennes *; *(fig)* **he knows a ~ or two *** c'est un petit malin; **to do the ~ *** faire l'affaire; **I'll soon get the ~ of it** je vais bientôt prendre le pli. (**b**) *(habit)* manie *f* (*of doing* de faire); *(mannerism)* tic *m.* **he has a ~ of scratching his ear** il a le tic de se gratter l'oreille; **he has a ~ of arriving just when...** il a le don d'arriver au moment où... (**c**) *(Cards)* levée *f.* **to take a ~** faire une levée; *(fig)* **he never misses a ~** rien ne lui échappe. **2** *adj photograph* truqué. **~ question** question-piège *f.* **3** *vt (deceive)* attraper, avoir *; *(swindle)* escroquer. **I've been ~ed!** on m'a eu! *; **to ~ sb into doing** amener qn à faire par la ruse; **to ~ sb out of sth** obtenir qch de qn par la ruse. ◆ **trickery** *n* ruse *f.* ◆ **trickster** *n* filou *m.* ◆ **tricky** *adj problem, situation, task* difficile, délicat; *(pej) person* rusé; **he's a ~y man to deal with** *(scheming)* avec lui il faut se méfier; *(touchy)* il n'est pas commode.

trickle ['trɪkl] **1** *n [water, blood etc]* filet *m.* *(fig)* **a ~ of people** quelques rares personnes; **there was a steady ~ of letters** les lettres arrivaient en petit nombre mais régulièrement. **2** *adj (Elec)* **~ charger** chargeur *m* à régime lent. **3** *vi (drop slowly)* couler goutte à goutte; *(flow slowly)* couler en un filet. **tears ~d down her cheeks** les larmes coulaient *or* dégoulinaient le long de ses joues; **to ~ in** *[water]* couler goutte à goutte; *[people]* entrer les uns après les autres; *[money, letters]* arriver peu à peu; **the ball ~d into the net** le ballon a roulé doucement dans le filet.

tricolo(u)r ['trɪkələʳ] *n* drapeau *m* tricolore.

tricycle ['traɪsɪkl] *n* tricycle *m.*

trier ['traɪəʳ] *n*: **to be a ~** être persévérant.

trifle ['traɪfl] **1** *n* (**a**) *(object, sum of money)* bagatelle *f.* **it's only a ~** ce n'est rien; **he worries over ~s** il se fait du mauvais sang pour un rien; **a ~ difficult** un peu difficile. (**b**) *(Culin)* ≃ diplomate *m.* **2** *vi*: **to ~ with** traiter à la légère. ◆ **trifling** *adj* insignifiant.

trigger ['trɪgəʳ] **1** *n [gun]* détente *f*, gâchette *f*; *[tool]* déclic *m.* **to press** *or* **pull the ~** appuyer sur la détente. **2** *vt* (**~ off**) *explosion, revolt* déclencher; *reaction, protest* provoquer. ◆ **trigger-happy** * *adj person* qui a la gâchette facile; *(fig) nation etc* prêt à déclencher la guerre pour un rien.

trigonometry [ˌtrɪgə'nɒmɪtrɪ] *n* trigonométrie *f.*

trill [trɪl] **1** *n (Mus)* trille *m*; *(Ling)* consonne roulée. **2** *vi* triller. **3** *vt (gen)* triller; *(Ling) one's rs* rouler.

trilogy ['trɪlədʒɪ] *n* trilogie *f.*

trim [trɪm] **1** *adj person, clothes* net, soigné; *boat, garden, house* coquet, net. **~ figure** taille *f* svelte. **2** *n* (**a**) **in (good) ~** *garden, house etc* en bon état; *person, athlete* en forme; *[athlete etc]* **to get into ~** se remettre en forme; *(Naut)* **the ~ of the sails** l'orientation *f* des voiles. (**b**) *(cut)* **to give sth a ~ = to trim sth** *(V* **3a***)*; *(at hairdresser's)* **to have a ~** se faire rafraîchir les cheveux. (**c**) *(decoration: Archit)* moulures *fpl*; *(Aut: outside)* finitions *fpl* extérieures; *(on garment)* garniture *f.* **car with blue interior ~** voiture à habillage intérieur bleu. **3** *vt* (**a**) *(cut) hair* rafraîchir; *wick, lamp* tailler; *beard, hedge, roses* tailler légèrement; *edges* couper; *wood, paper* couper les bords de, rogner. **to ~ one's nails** se rogner les ongles; **to ~ costs** réduire les dépenses. (**b**) *(decorate) garment* garnir, orner (*with* de); *Christmas tree, shop window* décorer (*with* de). ◆ **trimming** *n (on garment)* garniture *f*; *(edging)* bordure *f*; **~mings** *(cuttings)* chutes *fpl*; **it costs £100 without the ~mings** cela coûte 100 livres sans les extra; *(Culin)* **and all the ~mings** avec la garniture habituelle.

trimaran ['traɪməræn] *n* trimaran *m.*

Trinidad ['trɪnɪdæd] *n* (l'île *f* de) la Trinité. **~ and Tobago** Trinité-et-Tobago.

trinity ['trɪnɪtɪ] *n* trinité *f.* **T~ (Sunday)** la fête de la Trinité.

trinket ['trɪŋkɪt] *n (knick-knack)* bibelot *m*; *[jewellery]* colifichet *m.*

trio ['trɪəʊ] *n* trio *m.*

trip [trɪp] **1** *n* (**a**) voyage *m*; *(excursion)* excursion *f.* **away on a ~** en voyage; **to take a ~** *(go on journey)* partir en voyage; *(go)* aller (*to* à); **cheap ~s to Spain** des voyages à prix réduit en Espagne; **he does 3 ~s to Scotland a week** il va en Écosse 3 fois par semaine; **I don't want another ~ to the shops** je ne veux pas retourner dans les magasins. (**b**) *(Drugs sl)* **to be on a ~** faire un trip; **a bad ~** un trip qui tourne mal. **2** *vi* (**a**) (**~ over, ~ up**) trébucher (*on, over* contre, sur), faire un faux pas; *(make mistake:* **~ up***)* gaffer *. (**b**) **to ~ along/in** *etc* marcher/entrer *etc* d'un pas sautillant. **3** *vt* (**~ up**) faire trébucher; *(deliberately)* faire un croche-pied à; *(in questioning etc)* prendre en défaut. ◆ **tripper** *n* touriste *mf*; *(day ~)* excursionniste *mf.* ◆ **tripwire** *n* fil *m* de détente.

tripe [traɪp] *n (Culin)* tripes *fpl*; *(*: nonsense)* bêtises *fpl*, foutaises ‡ *fpl.*

triphthong ['trɪfθɒŋ] *n* triphtongue *f.*

triple ['trɪpl] **1** *adj, n* triple *(m).* **2** *adv* trois fois plus que. **3** *vti* tripler. ◆ **triplets** *npl* triplé(e)s *m(f)pl.* ◆ **triplicate** *n*: **in triplicate** en trois exemplaires.

tripod ['traɪpɒd] *n* trépied *m.*

triptych ['trɪptɪk] *n* triptyque *m.*

trite [traɪt] *adj* banal. ◆ **tritely** *adv* banalement.

triumph ['traɪʌmf] **1** *n (victory)* triomphe *m* (*for* pour; *of* de; *over* sur); *(sense of ~)* sentiment *m* de triomphe. **in ~** en triomphe. **2** *vi* triompher (*over* de). ◆ **triumphal** *adj* triomphal. ◆ **triumphant** *adj (gen)* triomphant; *homecoming* triomphal. ◆ **triumphantly** *adv* triomphalement.

trivia ['trɪvɪə] *npl* futilités *fpl.* ◆ **trivial** *adj amount, reason* insignifiant; *remark, mistake, matter* sans importance; *film, book* banal. ◆ **triviality** *n* caractère *m* insignifiant; manque *m* d'importance; banalité *f*; **~lities** futilités *fpl.* ◆ **trivialize** *vt* banaliser.

trod [trɒd], **trodden** ['trɒdn] *pret, ptp of* **tread.**

trolley ['trɒlɪ] **1** *n (in station, supermarket)* chariot *m*; *(two-wheeled)* diable *m*; *(tea ~)* table roulante; *(in office)* chariot à boissons. **2** *adj*: **~ bus** trolleybus *m.*

trombone [trɒm'bəʊn] *n* trombone *m (Mus).*

troop [tru:p] **1** *n (gen)* groupe *m*, troupe *f*; *[scouts]* troupe. *(Mil)* **~s** troupes. **2** *adj movements etc* de troupes; *train* militaire. **~ carrier** *(Aut)* transport *m* de troupes; *(Naut: also* **~ ship***)* transport *(navire)*; *(Aviat)* avion *m* de transport militaire. **3** *vi*: **to ~ in/past** *etc* entrer/passer *etc* en groupe. ◆ **trooper** *n (Mil)* soldat *m* de cavalerie; *(US: state trooper)* ≃ C.R.S. *m.* ◆ **trooping** *n*: **~ing the colour** le salut au drapeau.

trophy ['trəʊfɪ] *n* trophée *m.*

tropic ['trɒpɪk] *n* tropique *m.* **T~ of Cancer/ Capricorn** tropique du cancer/du capricorne; **in the ~s** sous les tropiques. ◆ **tropical** *adj* tropical.

trot [trɒt] **1** *n (pace)* trot *m.* **at a ~** au trot; *(fig)* **5 days on the ~** * 5 jours de suite; **to keep sb on the ~** * ne pas accorder une minute de tranquillité à qn. **2** *vi* trotter, courir. *[person]* **to ~ in/past** *etc* entrer/passer *etc* au trot; **she ~ted round to the grocer's** elle a fait un saut chez l'épicier. ◆ **trot out** *vt sep excuses, reasons* débiter; *names, facts etc* réciter d'affilée. ◆ **trotter** *n (Culin)* **pig's ~ters** pieds *mpl* de porc. ◆ **trotting** *n (Sport)* trot *m*; **~ting race** course *f* de trot.

trouble ['trʌbl] **1** *n* (**a**) *(difficulties)* ennuis *mpl.* **to be in ~** avoir des ennuis (*with sb* avec qn; *for doing* pour avoir fait), être en difficulté; **to get into ~** s'attirer des ennuis (*for sth* pour qch; *for doing* pour avoir fait); **to get into ~ with sb** s'attirer la colère de qn; **to get sb into ~** causer des ennuis à qn; **to get sb/get o.s out of ~** tirer qn/se tirer d'affaire; **to make ~** causer des ennuis (*for sb* à qn); **it's asking for ~** c'est se chercher des ennuis; **there's ~ brewing** il y a de l'orage dans l'air.

(**b**) *(bother, effort)* mal *m*. **it's no** ~ cela ne me dérange pas (*to do* de faire); **it's not worth the** ~ ça ne vaut pas la peine; **nothing is too much** ~ **for her** elle se dépense sans compter; **I had all that** ~ **for nothing** je me suis donné tout ce mal pour rien; **he went to enormous** ~ il s'est donné un mal fou (*to help* pour aider); **to go to the** ~ **of doing, to take the** ~ **to do** se donner le mal de faire; **he took a lot of** ~ **over it** il s'est donné beaucoup de mal pour cela; **to put sb to a lot of** ~ donner beaucoup de mal à qn.
(**c**) *(problem, nuisance)* ennui *m*, problème *m*; *(worry)* souci *m*, ennui; *(Pol etc)* troubles *mpl*. **what's the** ~**?** qu'est-ce qu'il y a?; **that's the** ~**!** c'est ça l'ennui!; **the** ~ **is that...** l'ennui *or* le problème, c'est que...; **the carburettor is giving us** ~ nous avons des problèmes de carburateur; **he is trying to locate the** ~ il essaie de localiser le problème; **there is** ~ **between them** ils s'entendent mal; **to cause** ~ **between** causer des désaccords entre; **I'm having** ~ **with him** il me donne des soucis, il me cause des ennuis; **he is a** ~ **to his parents** il est un souci pour ses parents; **to have** ~ **in doing** avoir du mal à faire; **your** ~**s are over** vous voilà au bout de vos peines; *(Med)* **I have back** ~ mon dos me fait souffrir; **kidney** ~ ennuis rénaux; *(Aut)* **engine** ~ ennuis de moteur; **there is a lot of** ~ **in Africa** la situation est très tendue en Afrique; **labour** ~**s** troubles sociaux; **there's** ~ **at the factory** ça chauffe * à l'usine.
2 *adj*: ~ **spot** point *m* chaud *or* névralgique.
3 *vt (worry)* inquiéter; *(upset)* troubler; *(bother)* déranger; *(inconvenience)* gêner. **his eyes** ~ **him** ses yeux lui posent des problèmes; **the heat** ~**d us** la chaleur nous a gênés; **nothing** ~**s him** rien ne le trouble; **I am sorry to** ~ **you** je suis désolé de vous déranger; **does it** ~ **you if...** est-ce que cela vous dérange si... + *indic or* que... + *subj;* **don't** ~ **yourself!** ne vous dérangez pas!; **to** ~ **o.s. to do** se donner la peine de faire; **may I** ~ **you for a light?** puis-je vous demander du feu?; **I shan't** ~ **you with the details** je vous ferai grâce des détails.
4 *vi* se déranger. **please don't** ~ ne vous dérangez pas; **to** ~ **to do** se donner la peine de faire.
◆ **troubled** *adj (gen)* inquiet; *life, sleep* agité; *water* trouble; **to be** ~**d about sth** s'inquiéter de qch; **in** ~**d times** à une époque agitée. ◆ **trouble-free** *adj (gen)* sans ennuis *or* problèmes; *car* qui ne tombe jamais en panne. ◆ **troublemaker** *n* provocateur *m*, -trice *f*. ◆ **troubleshooter** *n (Tech)* expert *m* (appelé en cas de crise); *(Ind, Pol)* conciliateur *m*. ◆ **troublesome** *adj person* pénible; *request, cough* gênant; *task* ennuyeux; **his back is** ~**some** son dos le fait souffrir.

trough [trɒf] *n* (**a**) *(dip)* creux *m*; *(fig)* point *m* bas. *(Met)* ~ **of low pressure** zone *f* dépressionnaire. (**b**) *(drinking* ~*)* abreuvoir *m*; *(feeding* ~*)* auge *f*.

trounce [traʊns] *vt* battre à plates coutures.

troupe [tru:p] *n* troupe *f (Theat)*.

trousers ['traʊzəz] *npl*: **(pair of)** ~ pantalon *m*; **long** ~ pantalon long; **short** ~ culottes *fpl* courtes; *(fig)* **she wears the** ~ * c'est elle qui porte la culotte *or* qui commande. ◆ **trouser-suit** *n* tailleur-pantalon *m*.

trousseau ['tru:səʊ] *n* trousseau *m (de mariée)*.

trout [traʊt] **1** *n, pl inv* truite *f*. **2** *adj stream* à truites; *fishing* à la truite.

trowel ['traʊəl] *n (Constr)* truelle *f*; *(gardening)* déplantoir *m*. *(fig)* **to lay it on with a** ~ * y aller un peu fort.

truant ['trʊənt] *n* élève *mf* absent(e) sans autorisation. **to play** ~ *(Scol etc)* manquer les cours; *(fig: from office etc)* faire l'école buissonnière. ◆ **truancy** *n* absentéisme *m* (scolaire).

truce [tru:s] *n* trêve *f*. **to call a** ~ faire trêve (*to* à).

truck[1] [trʌk] *n* (**a**) *(fig)* **to have no** ~ **with** refuser d'avoir affaire à. (**b**) *(US: vegetables)* produits *mpl* maraîchers. ~ **farmer** maraîcher *m*.

truck[2] [trʌk] **1** *n (lorry)* camion *m*; *(Rail)* truck *m*; *(luggage handcart)* chariot *m* à bagages, *(twowheeled)* diable *m*. **2** *vt (esp US)* camionner. ◆ **truckdriver** *or* ◆ **trucker** *n* camionneur *m*. ◆ **trucking** *n* camionnage *m*. ◆ **truckload** *n* plein camion. ◆ **truck stop** *n* routier *m (restaurant)*.

truculent ['trʌkjʊlənt] *adj* brutal, agressif. ◆ **truculence** *n* brutalité *f*. ◆ **truculently** *adv* brutalement, agressivement.

trudge [trʌdʒ] *vi*: **to** ~ **in/along** *etc* entrer/ marcher *etc* péniblement; **to** ~ **round the town** se traîner dans la ville.

true [tru:] **1** *adj* (**a**) *(accurate: gen)* vrai; *description, account* exact, véridique; *copy* conforme; *statistics, measure* exact. **it's all** ~ tout est vrai; **too** ~**!** * ah oui alors!; **can it be** ~ **that** est-il possible que + *subj;* **it is** ~ **that** il est vrai que + *indic*; **is it** ~ **that** est-il vrai que + *indic or subj;* **it's not** ~ **that** il n'est pas vrai que + *indic or subj;* **if it is** ~ **that** s'il est vrai que + *indic;* **to come** ~ se réaliser; **the same holds** ~ **for** il en est de même pour. (**b**) *(genuine) repentance, friendship* vrai *(before n)*, véritable; *friend, scholar etc* vrai, véritable *(both before n)*. **what is the** ~ **situation?** quelle est la situation réelle?; **it is not a** ~ **reptile** ce n'est pas vraiment un reptile. (**c**) *(faithful)* fidèle (*to sb/sth* à qn/qch). ~ **to life/to type** conforme à la réalité/au type. (**d**) *wall, upright* d'aplomb; *beam* droit; *machine part* juste; *wheel* dans l'axe; *(Mus) voice etc* juste. **2** *n*: **out of** ~ *upright, wall* pas d'aplomb; *beam* tordu; *wheel* voilé. **3** *adv aim, sing* juste. ◆ **true-blue** * *adj* loyal. ◆ **truism** *n* truisme *m*. ◆ **truly** *adv (genuinely) love, believe* vraiment; *(faithfully) reflect, show* fidèlement; *(truthfully) answer, tell* franchement; *(without doubt) great, terrible* vraiment, véritablement; **well and truly** bel et bien; *(letter ending)* **yours truly** je vous prie d'agréer l'expression de mes sentiments respectueux.

truffle ['trʌfl] *n* truffe *f*.

trump [trʌmp] **1** *n* atout *m*. **spades are** ~**(s)** atout pique; **what's** ~**(s)?** quel est l'atout?; **no** ~**(s)** sans atout; *(fig)* **he was holding all the** ~**s** il avait tous les atouts dans son jeu; *(fig)* **to turn up** ~**s** * faire des merveilles. **2** *adj (lit, fig)* ~ **card** atout *m*. **3** *vt (Cards)* prendre avec l'atout. *(fig)* **to** ~ **sb's ace** faire encore mieux que qn. ◆ **trump up** *vt sep charge etc* inventer de toutes pièces.

trumpet ['trʌmpɪt] **1** *n (Mus)* trompette *f*. **2** *vi [elephant]* barrir. ◆ **trumpeter** *n (Mil)* trompette *m*. ◆ **trumpet-player** *n (Mus)* trompettiste *mf*.

truncheon ['trʌn(t)ʃ(ə)n] *n* matraque *f*; *(directing traffic)* bâton *m (d'agent de police)*.

trundle ['trʌndl] **1** *vt (push etc)* pousser *etc* bruyamment. **2** *vi*: **to** ~ **along/down** rouler/ descendre bruyamment.

trunk [trʌŋk] **1** *n (Anat, Bot)* tronc *m*; *[elephant]* trompe *f*; *(luggage)* malle *f*; *(US Aut)* coffre *m*. ~**s** *(swimming)* slip *m* de bain; *(underwear)* slip (d'homme). **2** *adj (Telec)* ~ **call** communication *f* interurbaine; *(Rail)* ~ **line** grande ligne *f*; ~ **road** route *f* nationale.

truss [trʌs] **1** *n [hay etc]* botte *f*; *[flowers, fruit]* grappe *f*; *(Constr)* ferme *f*; *(Med)* bandage *m* herniaire. **2** *vt chicken* trousser; **(**~ **up)** *prisoner* ligoter.

trust [trʌst] **1** *n* (**a**) confiance *f* (*in* en). **breach of** ~ abus *m* de confiance; **to have** ~ **in** avoir confiance en; **to put one's** ~ **in** faire confiance à; **you'll have to take it on** ~ il vous faudra me (*or* le *etc*) croire sur parole. (**b**) *(Jur)* **to leave money in** ~ faire administrer un legs par fidéicommis (*for* à l'intention de). (**c**) *(Fin)* trust *m*. **2** *adj fund, account* en fidéicommis.

3 *vt* (**a**) *person, object* avoir confiance en; *method, promise* se fier à. **he is not to be ~ed** on ne peut pas lui faire confiance; **to ~ sb with sth** confier qch à qn; **to ~ sb to do sth** compter sur qn pour faire qch; **he is too young to be ~ed on the roads** il est trop petit pour qu'on le laisse aller dans la rue tout seul; **I can't ~ him out of my sight** je n'ose pas le quitter des yeux; *(iro)* **~ you!** * pour ça on peut te faire confiance! (**b**) *(entrust)* confier (*sth to sb* qch à qn). (**c**) *(hope)* espérer (*that* que). **4** *vi*: **to ~ in sb** se fier à qn; **to ~ to luck** s'en remettre à la chance.
◆ **trusted** *adj person* en qui l'on a toute confiance; *method* éprouvé. ◆ **trustee** *n (Jur)* fidéicommissaire *m*; *[institution, school]* administrateur *m*, -trice *f*; **the ~ees** le conseil d'administration. ◆ **trustful** *or* ◆ **trusting** *adj* confiant. ◆ **trustfully** *or* ◆ **trustingly** *adv* avec confiance. ◆ **trustworthiness** *n [person]* loyauté *f*; *[statement]* véracité *f*. ◆ **trustworthy** *adj person* digne de confiance; *report, account* exact. ◆ **trusty** *adj (hum)* fidèle.

truth [tru:θ] *n* vérité *f*. **to tell the ~** dire la vérité; **to tell (you) the ~, ~ to tell** à vrai dire; **there's some/no ~ in what he says** il y a du vrai/il n'y a pas un mot de vrai dans ce qu'il dit; **~ will out** la vérité finira toujours par se savoir; **the ~, the whole ~ and nothing but the ~** la vérité, toute la vérité et rien que la vérité; **the plain unvarnished ~** la vérité toute nue; **in ~** en vérité. ◆ **truthful** *adj person* qui dit la vérité; *statement* véridique; *portrait* fidèle. ◆ **truthfully** *adv answer* sans mentir; **I don't mind, ~fully** sincèrement, ça m'est égal. ◆ **truthfulness** *n* véracité *f*.

try [traɪ] **1** *n* (**a**) *(attempt)* essai *m*, tentative *f*. **to have a ~** essayer (*at doing* de faire); **to give sth a ~** essayer qch; **it was a good ~** il a (*or* tu as *etc*) vraiment essayé; **it's worth a ~** cela vaut le coup d'essayer; **at the first ~** du premier coup; **after 3 tries** après avoir essayé 3 fois. (**b**) *(Rugby)* essai *m*. **to score a ~** marquer un essai.
2 *vt* (**a**) *(attempt)* essayer, tâcher (*to do* de faire). **~ to eat it, ~ and eat it** essaie *or* tâche de le manger; **I'll ~ anything once** je suis toujours prêt à faire un essai; *(warning)* **just you ~ it!** essaie un peu pour voir! *; **he tried 3 questions** il a essayé de répondre à 3 questions; **to ~ one's best** *or* **one's hardest** faire de son mieux (*to do* pour faire); **to ~ one's hand at sth/at doing** s'essayer à qch/à faire; **it's ~ing to rain** * il a l'air de vouloir pleuvoir *. (**b**) *(sample) food, method, car etc* essayer. **won't you ~ me for the job?** vous ne voulez pas me faire faire un essai?; **~ pushing that button** essayez de presser ce bouton; *(also *fig)* **~ this for size** essaie ça pour voir. (**c**) *(test etc) person, sb's patience, strength* mettre à l'épreuve; *eyes* fatiguer; *vehicle, plane, machine* tester. **to ~ one's strength against sb** se mesurer à qn; **to ~ one's luck** tenter sa chance; **well-tried** qui a fait ses preuves; **sorely tried** durement éprouvé. (**d**) *(Jur) person, case* juger (*for* pour).
3 *vi* essayer (*for sth* d'obtenir qch). **~ again!** essaie encore une fois!
◆ **try on** *vt sep* (**a**) *garment, shoe* essayer. (**b**) *(fig)* **to ~ it on** essayer de voir jusqu'où on peut aller (*with sb* avec qn); **don't ~ anything on!** ne fais pas le malin! ◆ **try out** *vt sep thing, method* essayer; *employee etc* mettre à l'essai. **~ it out on the cat first** essaie d'abord de voir quelle est la réaction du chat. ◆ **trying** *adj person, experience* pénible; *work* ennuyeux; **to have a ~ing time** passer des moments difficiles. ◆ **try-on** * *n*: **it's a ~-on** c'est du bluff. ◆ **tryout** *n* essai *m*.

tsar [zɑ:ʳ] *n* tsar *m*. ◆ **tsarina** *n* tsarine *f*.

tsetse fly ['tsetsɪflaɪ] *n* mouche *f* tsé-tsé *inv*.

tub [tʌb] *n (gen, also in washing machine)* cuve *f*; *(for washing clothes)* baquet *m*; *(for flowers)* bac *m*; *(for cream etc)* petit pot *m*; *(bath ~)* tub *m*; *(in bathroom)* baignoire *f*. ◆ **tubby** * *adj* replet.

tuba ['tju:bə] *n* tuba *m*.

tube [tju:b] **1** *n (gen)* tube *m*; *[tyre]* chambre *f* à air. *(Brit: underground)* **the ~** le métro; **to go by ~** prendre le métro; *(TV)* **the ~** * la télé *. **2** *adj*: **~ station** station *f* de métro. ◆ **tubeless** *adj tyre* sans chambre à air. ◆ **tubing** *n* tubes *mpl*; **rubber tubing** tube *m or* tuyau *m* en caoutchouc. ◆ **tubular** *adj* tubulaire.

tuber ['tju:bəʳ] *n (Bot)* tubercule *m*. ◆ **tubercle** *n (Med)* tubercule *m*. ◆ **tubercular** *adj* tuberculeux. ◆ **tuberculin** *n* tuberculine *f*. ◆ **tuberculin-tested** *adj milk* ≃ certifié. ◆ **tuberculosis** *(abbr* **TB** *)* *n* tuberculose *f*; **he's got TB** * il est tuberculeux.

tuck [tʌk] **1** *n (Sewing etc)* rempli *m*. **to take a ~ in** faire un rempli dans. **2** *vt*: **to ~ sth under one's arm** mettre qch sous son bras; **~ it away out of sight** cache-le; **~ed away among the trees** caché parmi les arbres; **to ~ one's shirt into one's trousers** rentrer sa chemise dans son pantalon; **he was sitting with his feet ~ed under him** il avait les pieds repliés sous lui. **3** *vi*: **to ~ into a meal** * attaquer * un repas. ◆ **tuck in 1** *vi (*: eat)* bien boulotter *. **~ in!** allez-y! **2** *vt sep shirt, flap* rentrer; *sheets, child* border. ◆ **tuck up** *vt sep skirt, sleeves* remonter; *legs* replier; *(in bed)* border. ◆ **tuckbox** *n (Scol)* boîte *f* à provisions. ◆ **tuck-in** * *n*: **they had a good ~-in** ils ont vraiment bien boulotté *. ◆ **tuck-shop** *n (Scol)* boutique *f* à provisions.

Tuesday ['tju:zdɪ] *n* mardi *m*; *for phrases V* **Saturday**.

tuft [tʌft] *n* touffe *f*. ◆ **tufted** *adj bird* huppé.

tug [tʌg] **1** *n* (**a**) *(pull)* petite saccade *f*. **to give sth a ~** tirer sur qch; **I felt a ~ at my sleeve/on the rope** j'ai senti qu'on me tirait par la manche/qu'on tirait sur la corde. (**b**) (**~ boat**) remorqueur *m*. **2** *vt rope, sleeve etc* tirer sur; *(drag)* tirer, traîner; *(Naut)* remorquer. **3** *vi* tirer fort (*at, on* sur). ◆ **tug-of-war** *n (Sport)* lutte *f* à la corde; *(fig)* lutte acharnée.

tuition [tjʊ'ɪʃ(ə)n] *n* cours *mpl*. **private ~** cours particuliers (*in* de); **~ fee** frais *mpl* de scolarité.

tulip ['tju:lɪp] *n* tulipe *f*.

tulle [tju:l] *n* tulle *m*.

tumble ['tʌmbl] **1** *n* (**a**) *(fall)* chute *f*; *[acrobat etc]* culbute *f*. **to have** *or* **take a ~** faire une chute. (**b**) *(confused heap)* amas *m*. **in a ~** en désordre. **2** *vi* (**a**) *(fall)* tomber; *(trip)* trébucher (*over* sur); *[acrobat etc]* faire des culbutes. **to ~ head over heels** faire la culbute; **to ~ downstairs** dégringoler dans l'escalier. (**b**) *(rush)* **he ~d into bed** il s'est jeté au lit; **he ~d out of bed** il a bondi hors du lit; **they ~d out of the car** ils ont déboulé * de la voiture. (**c**) *(realize)* **to ~ to sth** * réaliser * qch. **3** *vt pile* renverser; *[washing machine]* faire tourner. ◆ **tumble about, tumble around** *vi [puppies, children]* gambader; *[acrobat]* cabrioler. ◆ **tumble down** *vi: [building etc]* **to be tumbling down** tomber en ruine. ◆ **tumbledown** *adj* délabré. ◆ **tumbledryer** *n* sèche-linge *m*. ◆ **tumbler** *n (glass)* verre *m* (droit); *(of plastic, metal)* gobelet *m*; *(tumbledryer)* séchoir *m* à linge (à air chaud).

tummy * ['tʌmɪ] *n* ventre *m*. ◆ **tummy-ache** *n* mal *m* de ventre.

tumour, *(US)* **tumor** ['tju:məʳ] *n* tumeur *f*.

tumult ['tju:mʌlt] *n* tumulte *m*. **in a ~** dans le tumulte; *(emotionally)* en émoi. ◆ **tumultuous** *adj (gen)* tumultueux; *applause* frénétique. ◆ **tumultuously** *adv* tumultueusement.

tumulus, *pl* **-li** ['tju:mjʊləs, lɪ] *n* tumulus *m*.

tuna ['tju:nə] *n* (**~ fish**) thon *m*.

tundra ['tʌndrə] *n* toundra *f*.

tune [tju:n] **1** *n* (**a**) air *m*. **he gave us a ~** il nous a joué un air; **to the ~ of** *sing* sur l'air de; *march, process* aux accents de; *(fig)* **repairs** *etc* **to the ~**

of £30 réparations *etc* s'élevant à la coquette somme de 30 livres; *(fig)* **to change one's ~** changer de ton; *(fig)* **to call the ~** commander. (**b**) **to be in ~ /out of ~** *[instrument]* être accordé/désaccordé; *[singer]* chanter juste/faux; **to sing/play in ~** chanter/jouer juste; **to sing/play out of ~** chanter/jouer faux; *(fig)* **in ~ with** en accord avec. **2** *vt (Mus)* accorder; *(Rad, TV)* régler (*to* sur); *(Aut)* régler. *(Rad)* **to be ~d (in) to...** être à l'écoute de...
◆**tune in** *(Rad, TV)* **1** *vi* se mettre à l'écoute (*to* de). **2** *vt sep* régler (*to* sur). ◆**tune out** * *(US fig)* **1** *vi* faire la sourde oreille. **2** *vt sep* faire la sourde oreille à. ◆**tune up** *vi [orchestra]* accorder ses instruments.
◆**tuneful** *adj (gen)* mélodieux; *singer* à la voix mélodieuse. ◆**tunefully** *adv* mélodieusement. ◆**tuneless** *adj* peu mélodieux. ◆**tunelessly** *adv sing* faux. ◆**tuner** **1** *n* (**a**) **piano-~r** accordeur *m* de pianos; (**b**) *(Rad: knob)* bouton *m* de réglage ; **2** *adj*: **~r amplifier** radio-ampli *m*. ◆**tuning** *n (Mus)* accord *m*; *(Aut, Rad, TV)* réglage *m*. ◆**tuning-fork** *n* diapason *m*. ◆**tuning-knob** *n (Rad etc)* bouton *m* de réglage.

tungsten ['tʌŋstən] *n* tungstène *m*.

tunic ['tju:nɪk] *n* tunique *f*.

Tunisia [tju:'nɪzɪə] *n* Tunisie *f*.

tunnel ['tʌnl] **1** *n (gen)* tunnel *m*; *(Min)* galerie *f*. **to make a ~ = to tunnel** *(V* **2**). **2** *vi* percer un tunnel (*into* dans; *under* sous). **to ~ in/out** *etc* entrer/sortir *etc* en creusant un tunnel.

tunny ['tʌnɪ] *n* thon *m*.

turban ['tɜ:bən] *n* turban *m*.

turbid ['tɜ:bɪd] *adj* trouble; épais; turbide.

turbine ['tɜ:baɪn] *n* turbine *f*.

turbo... ['tɜ:bəʊ] *pref* turbo... **~(charged) engine** moteur *m* turbo. ◆**turbojet** *n (engine)* turboréacteur *m*; *(aircraft)* avion *m* à turboréacteur. ◆**turboprop** *n* turbopropulseur *m*.

turbot ['tɜ:bət] *n* turbot *m*.

turbulent ['tɜ:bjʊlənt] *adj* turbulent. ◆**turbulence** *n* turbulence *f*.

tureen [tə'rɪ:n] *n* soupière *f*.

turf [tɜ:f] **1** *n (grass)* gazon *m*; *(one piece)* motte *f* de gazon; *(peat)* tourbe *f*. *(Sport)* **the ~** le turf. **2** *adj*: **~ accountant** bookmaker *m*. **3** *vt* (**a**) (**~ over**) *land* gazonner. (**b**) (*) *(throw)* balancer *, jeter; *(put)* flanquer *. **to ~ sb out** flanquer * qn à la porte.

Turkey ['tɜ:kɪ] *n* Turquie *f*. ◆**Turkish** **1** *adj* turc (*f* turque); **Turkish bath** bain *m* turc; **Turkish delight** loukoum *m* ; **2** *n (Ling)* turc *m*.

turkey ['tɜ:kɪ] *n* dindon *m*, dinde *f*; *(Culin)* dinde. ◆**turkey-cock** *n* dindon *m*.

turmeric ['tɜ:mərɪk] *n* safran *m* des Indes.

turmoil ['tɜ:mɔɪl] *n* agitation *f*; *(emotional)* émoi *m*. **everything was in a ~** c'était le bouleversement le plus complet.

turn [tɜ:n] **1** *n* (**a**) *[wheel, handle etc]* tour *m*. **to give sth a ~** tourner qch (une fois); *(Culin)* **done to a ~** à point.
(**b**) *(bend: in road etc)* tournant *m*. **'no left ~'** 'défense de tourner à gauche'; **take the next left ~** prenez la prochaine route à gauche; *(walk)* **to take a ~ in the park** aller faire un tour dans le parc; **at the ~ of the year/century** en fin d'année/de siècle; *(fig)* **at every ~** à tout instant; **things took a new ~** les choses ont pris une nouvelle tournure; **to take a ~ for the worse** s'aggraver; **to take a ~ for the better** s'améliorer; **a scientific ~ of mind** une tournure d'esprit scientifique; **~ of phrase** tournure *f*.
(**c**) *(Med)* crise *f*. **he had one of his ~s** il a eu une nouvelle crise; **she has giddy ~s** elle a des vertiges; **it gave me quite a ~** * ça m'a fait un coup *.
(**d**) *(action etc)* **to do sb a good ~** rendre un service à qn; **to do sb a bad ~** jouer un mauvais tour à qn; **his good ~ for the day** sa bonne action pour la journée; **one good ~ deserves another** un prêté pour un rendu; **it has served its ~** ça a fait son temps.
(**e**) *(Theat etc)* numéro *m*. **to do a ~** faire un numéro.
(**f**) *(in game, queue etc)* tour *m*. **it's your ~** c'est à vous (*to play* de jouer); **whose ~ is it?** c'est à qui le tour?; **wait your ~** attendez votre tour; **they answered in ~, they answered ~ and ~ about** ils ont répondu à tour de rôle; **and he, in ~, said...** et lui, à son tour, a dit...; **hot and cold by ~s** tour à tour chaud et froid; **to take ~s at doing sth, to take it in ~(s) to do sth** faire qch à tour de rôle; **take it in ~s!** chacun son tour!; **to take ~s at the wheel** se relayer au volant; **to take a ~ at the wheel** faire un bout de conduite *; *(fig)* **to speak out of ~** commettre une indiscrétion.
2 *vt* (**a**) *(gen) handle, key, wheel etc* tourner; *(mechanically etc)* faire tourner. **~ the key in the lock** ferme la porte à clef.
(**b**) *page* tourner; *mattress, steak, record* retourner. **to ~ one's ankle** se tordre la cheville; **it ~s my stomach** cela me soulève le cœur.
(**c**) *(direct) car, object, thoughts* tourner, diriger (*towards* vers); *gun, telescope etc* braquer (*on* sur); *eyes* tourner (*to* vers); *steps* diriger (*to* vers); *conversation* détourner (*to* sur). **to ~ a picture to the wall** tourner un tableau face au mur; **they ~ed hoses on them** ils les ont aspergés avec des lances d'incendie; **he ~ed his back on us** il nous a tourné le dos; *(fig)* il s'est mis à nous battre froid; **he ~ed his back on the past** il a tourné la page; **as soon as his back is ~ed** dès qu'il a le dos tourné; **without ~ing a hair** sans sourciller; *(fig)* **to ~ the other cheek** tendre l'autre joue; **he ~ed his hand to writing** il s'est mis à écrire; **he can ~ his hand to anything** il sait tout faire; *(fig)* **to ~ the tables** renverser les rôles (*on sb* aux dépens de qn); **they ~ed him against his father** ils l'ont monté contre son père.
(**d**) *(deflect) blow* détourner. **to ~ sb from doing** dissuader qn de faire.
(**e**) *(shape) wood, metal* tourner. **well-~ed phrase** expression *f* bien tournée.
(**f**) *(go past)* **to ~ the corner** tourner le coin de la rue; *(fig)* passer le moment critique; **he has ~ed 40** il a 40 ans passés; **it's ~ed 3 o'clock** il est 3 heures passées.
(**g**) *(change)* transformer (*sth into sth* qch en qch), changer (*sb into sth* qn en qch); *(translate)* traduire (*into* en); *milk* faire tourner. *(fig)* **it ~ed him into an old man** cela a fait de lui un vieillard; **actor ~ed writer** acteur devenu écrivain; **to ~ a book into a play/film** adapter un livre pour la scène/l'écran; **to ~ sth black** noircir qch; **to ~ a boat adrift** faire partir un bateau à la dérive.
3 *vi* (**a**) *[handle, wheel, key]* tourner; *[person]* (**~ round, ~ over**) se tourner (*to, towards* vers); (*~ right round*) se retourner; *[person, vehicle] (change course:* **~ off***)* tourner (*into* dans; *towards* vers), *(reverse direction:* **~ round***)* faire demi-tour; *[ship]* virer; *[road, river]* faire un coude; *[wind, milk]* tourner; *[tide]* changer de direction; *[weather]* changer; *[leaves]* jaunir. **he ~ed to look at me** il s'est retourné pour me regarder; **~ to face me** tourne-toi vers moi; *(Mil)* **right ~!** à droite, droite!; **to ~ (to the) left** tourner à gauche; **they ~ed and came back** ils ont fait demi-tour et ils sont revenus; *(Aut)* **there's nowhere to ~** il n'y a pas d'endroit où faire demi-tour; **the car ~ed into a side street** la voiture a tourné dans une rue transversale; **it ~s on its axis** cela tourne autour de son axe; *(fig)* **my head is ~ing** j'ai la tête qui tourne; **it all ~s on whether...** tout dépend si...;

to ~ tail (and run) prendre ses jambes à son cou; **he would ~ in his grave if he knew...** il se retournerait dans sa tombe s'il savait...; **our luck has ~ed** la chance a tourné pour nous; **the conversation ~ed on...** la conversation en est venue à...; **to ~ on sb** attaquer qn; **to ~ against sb** se retourner contre qn; *(fig)* **he didn't know which way to ~** il ne savait plus où donner de la tête; **he ~ed to me for advice** il s'est tourné vers moi pour me demander conseil; **he ~ed to politics** il s'est tourné vers la politique; **he ~ed to drink** il s'est mis à boire.

(**b**) *(become)* **to ~ into** devenir; *(fig)* **he ~ed into an old man overnight** il est devenu vieux en l'espace d'une nuit; **his admiration ~ed to scorn** son admiration s'est changée en mépris; **to ~ black** noircir; **to ~ angry** se mettre en colère; **to ~ communist/professional** devenir communiste/professionnel.

◆ **turn aside** **1** *vi* se détourner (*from* de). **2** *vt sep* détourner. ◆ **turn away** **1** *vi* se détourner (*from* de). **2** *vt sep* (**a**) *object* détourner. (**b**) *(reject) person (gen)* renvoyer; *(stronger)* chasser; *offer, business, customers* refuser. ◆ **turn back** **1** *vi (in journey etc)* faire demi-tour; *(to page)* revenir (*to* à). **2** *vt sep* (**a**) *bedclothes, collar* rabattre. (**b**) *(send back) person, vehicle* faire faire demi-tour à. (**c**) *clock, hands of clock* reculer (*to* jusqu'à). *(fig)* **to ~ the clock back 50 years** revenir en arrière de 50 ans. ◆ **turn down** *vt sep* (**a**) *bedclothes, collar* rabattre. **to ~ down the corner of the page** corner la page. (**b**) *(reduce) gas, heat, music* baisser. (**c**) *(refuse) offer, suitor* rejeter; *candidate, volunteer* refuser. ◆ **turn in** **1** *vi* (**a**) *[car, person]* tourner (*to* dans). (**b**) *(*: go to bed)* aller se coucher. **2** *vt sep (*: hand over) object* rendre (*to* à); *wanted man* livrer (à la police); *stolen goods* apporter à la police. ◆ **turn off** **1** *vi* (**a**) *[person, vehicle]* tourner. (**b**) *[automatic heater etc]* s'éteindre. **2** *vt sep water, electricity, gas, radio, tap* fermer; *light* éteindre; *(at main) all services* couper; *engine* arrêter. *(fig)* **it ~ed me off** ‡ ça m'a totalement rebuté. ◆ **turn on** **1** *vi [automatic heater etc]* s'allumer. **2** *vt sep* (**a**) *tap* ouvrir; *water* faire couler; *gas, electricity, light, radio, heater* allumer; *(at main) all services* brancher; *engine, machine* mettre en marche. (**b**) *(*: gen excite)* exciter. **that really ~s me on** ‡ ça me fait vraiment qch *. ◆ **turn out** **1** *vi* (**a**) *(go out)* sortir; *[troops etc]* aller au rassemblement. **they ~ed out to see her** ils sont venus la voir. (**b**) *(prove to be)* s'avérer; *[person]* se révéler. **it ~ed out that...** il s'est avéré que...; **it ~ed out to be true** cela s'est avéré juste; **he ~ed out to be a good student** il s'est révélé bon étudiant; **as it ~ed out** en l'occurrence; **everything will ~ out all right** tout finira bien. **2** *vt sep* (**a**) *light, gas* éteindre. (**b**) *(empty out) pockets, contents* vider (*of* de); *room, cupboard* nettoyer à fond; *cake etc* démouler (*on to* sur; *of* de); *(expel) person* mettre à la porte; *tenant* expulser; *employee* renvoyer. (**c**) *troops, police* envoyer. (**d**) *(produce) goods* produire; *(fig) teachers, salesmen etc* former. *(fig)* **well ~ed out** élégant. ◆ **turn over** **1** *vi* (**a**) *[person, car etc]* se retourner; *[car engine]* tourner au ralenti. **to ~ over and over** faire des tours sur soi-même; **my stomach ~ed over** *(nausea)* j'ai eu l'estomac retourné; *(fright etc)* mon sang n'a fait qu'un tour. (**b**) *(in reading)* tourner la page. *(in letter etc)* **please ~ over** *(abbr* **PTO***)* tournez s'il vous plaît *(abbr* T.S.V.P.*)*. **2** *vt sep* (**a**) *page* tourner; *mattress, patient, card* retourner. *(fig)* **to ~ over an idea in one's mind** retourner une idée dans sa tête. (**b**) *(hand over) object* rendre (*to* à); *person* livrer (*to* à). ◆ **turn round** **1** *vi [person]* se retourner; *(change direction) [person, vehicle]* faire demi-tour; *(rotate) [object]* tourner. **to ~ round and round** tournoyer sur soi-même. **2** *vt sep* (**a**) *(gen)* tourner; *vehicle, ship etc* faire faire demi-tour à. **to ~ the car round** faire demi-tour; *(fig)* **to ~ sb round** faire changer d'avis à qn. ◆ **turn up** **1** *vi* (**a**) *(arrive)* arriver; *(be found)* être retrouvé; *[playing card]* sortir. **sth will ~ up** on va bien trouver qch; **to ~ up again** refaire surface. (**b**) *(point upwards)* remonter. **his nose ~s up** il a le nez retroussé. **2** *vt sep* (**a**) *collar, sleeve* remonter. **~ed-up nose** nez *m* retroussé; *(fig: stop)* **~ it up!** ‡ la ferme! ‡ (**b**) *buried object* déterrer; *(find) lost object etc* dénicher. (**c**) *heat, gas, television etc* mettre plus fort; *(Rad, TV) volume* augmenter.

◆ **turncoat** *n* renégat(e) *m(f)*. ◆ **turning** **1** *n (side road)* route *f* (*or* rue *f*) latérale; *(fork)* embranchement *m*; *(bend)* coude *m*; **the second ~ing on the left** la deuxième à gauche ; **2** *adj (fig)* **~ing point** moment *m* décisif (*in* de). ◆ **turn-off** *n* (**a**) *(in road)* embranchement *m;* (**b**) **it's a real ~-off!** ‡ c'est vraiment à vous rebuter! ◆ **turn-on** ‡ *n:* **it's a real ~-on!** c'est excitant! ◆ **turnout** *n* (**a**) *(attendance)* **there was a good/bad ~out** beaucoup de gens/peu de gens sont venus; *(Brit)* **~out at the polls,** *(US)* **voter ~out** (taux *m* de) participation *f* électorale; (**b**) *(clean)* **to have a good ~out of a room** *etc* nettoyer une pièce à fond. ◆ **turnover** *n* (**a**) *(Comm etc) [stock, goods]* roulement *m*; *(total business)* chiffre *m* d'affaires; **he sold them cheaply hoping for a quick ~over** il les a vendus bon marché pour les écouler rapidement; **a high ~over of staff** de fréquents changements de personnel; (**b**) *(Culin)* **apple** *etc* **~over** chausson *m* aux pommes *etc.* ◆ **turnpike** *n (US)* autoroute *f* à péage. ◆ **turn signal** *m (US Aut)* clignotant *m.* ◆ **turnstile** *n* tourniquet *m (barrière)*. ◆ **turntable** *n [record player]* platine *f*; *(for trains, cars etc)* plaque *f* tournante. ◆ **turn-up** *n [trousers]* revers *m.*

turnip ['tɜːnɪp] *n* navet *m.*

turpentine ['tɜːpəntaɪn] *n (abbr* **turps** **)* térébenthine *f.* **~ substitute** white-spirit *m.*

turquoise ['tɜːkwɔɪz] **1** *n (stone)* turquoise *f*; *(colour)* turquoise *m.* **2** *adj ring* de turquoise; *(colour)* turquoise *inv.*

turret ['tʌrɪt] *n* tourelle *f.*

turtle ['tɜːtl] *n* tortue *f* marine. **~ soup** consommé *m* à la tortue; *(fig)* **to turn ~** chavirer. ◆ **turtledove** *n* tourterelle *f.* ◆ **turtlenecked** *adj (Brit)* à encolure montante; *(US)* à col roulé.

Tuscany ['tʌskənɪ] *n* Toscane *f.*

tusk [tʌsk] *n* défense *f (d'éléphant etc)*.

tussle ['tʌsl] **1** *n (struggle)* lutte *f* (*for* pour). **to have a ~ with sb** se bagarrer * avec qn. **2** *vi* se battre (*with sb* avec qn; *for sth* pour qch). **to ~ over sth** se disputer qch.

tussock ['tʌsək] *n* touffe *f* d'herbe.

tutor ['tjuːtəʳ] **1** *n (private teacher)* précepteur *m*, -trice *f* (*in* de); *(Brit Univ)* ≃ directeur *m*, -trice *f* d'études; *(US Univ)* ≃ assistant(e) *m(f) (en faculté)*. **2** *vt:* **to ~ sb in Latin** donner des cours particuliers de latin à qn. ◆ **tutorial** *n (Univ)* travaux *mpl* pratiques (*in* de).

tuxedo [tʌk'siːdəʊ] *n (US)* smoking *m.*

TV * [ˌtiː'viː] *n (abbr of* **television***)* télé * *f.* **~ dinner** repas *m* congelé (sur un plateau).

twaddle ['twɒdl] *n* balivernes *fpl*, fadaises *fpl.*

twang [twæŋ] **1** *n [wire etc]* son *m* (de corde pincée); *(in voice)* nasillement *m.* **to speak with a ~** parler du nez. **2** *vt guitar etc* pincer les cordes de. **3** *vi [wire]* vibrer.

tweak [twiːk] *vt ear, nose* tordre; *rope, hair* tirer.

twee * [twiː] *adj: (pej)* **it's rather ~** ça fait un peu maniéré.

tweed [twiːd] *n* tweed *m. (suit)* **~s** costume *m* de tweed.

tweet [twiːt] **1** *n (also* **~-~***)* gazouillis *m.* **2** *vi* gazouiller.

tweezers ['twi:zəz] *npl* pince *f* à épiler.

twelve [twelv] *adj, n* douze *(m) inv*; *for phrases V* **six.** ◆ **twelfth** *adj, n* douzième *(mf)*; *(fraction)* douzième *m*; **Twelfth Night** la fête des Rois.

twenty ['twentɪ] *adj, n* vingt *(m).* **about** ~ une vingtaine; **about** ~ **books** une vingtaine de livres; *for phrases V* **sixty.** ◆ **twentieth** *adj, n* vingtième *(mf)*; *(fraction)* vingtième *m*.

twerp ‡ [twɜ:p] *n* andouille ‡ *f*, idiot(e) *m(f)*.

twice [twaɪs] *adv* deux fois. ~ **as long as** deux fois plus long que; **she is** ~ **your age** elle a deux fois votre âge; ~ **a week** deux fois par semaine.

twiddle ['twɪdl] *vti (also* ~ **with**: *gen)* tripoter. *(fig)* **to** ~ **one's thumbs** se tourner les pouces.

twig[1] [twɪg] *n* brindille *f*.

twig[2] * [twɪg] *vti (understand)* piger *, saisir.

twilight ['twaɪlaɪt] *n (evening)* crépuscule *m (also fig)*; *(morning)* aube *f* naissante. **at** ~ au crépuscule, à l'aube naissante; *(half light)* **in the** ~ dans la pénombre.

twill [twɪl] *n (Tex)* sergé *m*.

twin [twɪn] **1** *n* jumeau *m*, -elle *f*. **2** *adj son, brother* jumeau; *daughter, sister* jumelle; *town* jumelé. ~ **beds** lits *mpl* jumeaux. **3** *vt town etc* jumeler (*with* avec). ◆ **twin-engined** *adj* bimoteur. ◆ **twinning** *n* jumelage *m*.

twine [twaɪn] **1** *n* ficelle *f*. **2** *vt* enrouler (*round* autour de). **3** *vi* s'enrouler.

twinge [twɪn(d)ʒ] *n*: ~ **(of pain)** élancement *m*; **to feel a** ~ **of sadness** *or* **regret** avoir un pincement au cœur; **a** ~ **of conscience** *or* **remorse** un petit remords.

twinkle ['twɪŋkl] **1** *vi [star, lights]* scintiller; *[eyes]* pétiller. **2** *n* scintillement *m*; pétillement *m*. **...he said with a** ~ **in his eye** ...dit-il avec un pétillement dans les yeux. ◆ **twinkling 1** *adj* scintillant; pétillant ; **2** *n*: **in the twinkling of an eye** en un clin d'œil.

twirl [twɜ:l] **1** *n [body]* tournoiement *m*; *[dancer]* pirouette *f*; *(in writing)* fioriture *f*. **2** *vi* **(~ round)** *[dancer etc]* tournoyer. **3** *vt* **(~ round)** *cane, lasso* faire tournoyer; *handle* faire pivoter; *moustache* tortiller.

twirp ‡ [twɜ:p] *n* = **twerp** ‡.

twist [twɪst] **1** *n* **(a)** *(Med)* foulure *f*. **to give sth a** ~ *(handle)* faire tourner qch; *(wire)* tordre qch; **with a quick** ~ **of the wrist** d'un rapide tour de poignet. **(b)** *(in wire etc)* tortillon *m*; *[events]* tournure *f*. **a** ~ **of** *yarn* une torsade de; *tobacco* un rouleau de; *paper* un tortillon de; *lemon* un zeste de; **road full of** ~**s and turns** route qui fait des zigzags; *(fig)* **to give a new** ~ **to sth** donner un tour nouveau à qch; *(fig)* **to go round the** ~ ‡ devenir dingue *. **2** *vt (gen)* tordre; **(~ together)** *strands etc* entortiller (*into sth* pour en faire qch); *(coil)* enrouler (*round* autour de); *(turn) knob, handle, top* tourner; *(fig) meaning, facts, truth* déformer. *[rope etc]* **to get** ~**ed** s'entortiller; **to** ~ **one's ankle** se fouler la cheville; **to** ~ **one's neck** attraper le torticolis; **to** ~ **sb's arm** tordre le bras à qn; *(fig)* forcer la main à qn. **3** *vi [rope etc]* s'enrouler (*round* autour de). *[road, motorcycle etc]* **to** ~ **and turn** zigzaguer.

◆ **twist off** *vt sep branch* enlever en tordant; *bottle-top* enlever en dévissant. ◆ **twist round** *vi [person]* se retourner.

◆ **twisted** *adj (gen)* tordu; *rope, cord* entortillé; *wrist, ankle* foulé; *socks* tirebouchonnant; *(fig) logic* faux; *mind* tordu. ◆ **twister** * *n* escroc *m*. ◆ **twist grip** *n* poignée *f* d'accélération *or (gear change)* de changement de vitesses. ◆ **twisting 1** *n (gen)* torsion *f*; *[meaning]* déformation *f* ; **2** *adj path* sinueux.

twit[1] [twɪt] *vt (tease)* taquiner (*about* à propos de).

twit[2] ‡ [twɪt] *n* idiot(e) *m(f)*, crétin(e) *m(f)*.

twitch [twɪtʃ] **1** *n (nervous)* tic *m* (*in sth* à qch); *(pull on rope etc)* saccade *f*. **to give sth a** ~ tirer d'un coup sec sur qch. **2** *vi* **(a)** *[person, animal, hands]* avoir un mouvement convulsif, *(permanent condition)* avoir un tic; *[face, muscle]* se convulser; *[nose, tail, ears]* remuer. **(b)** *(be nervous)* s'agiter. **3** *vt rope etc* tirer d'un coup sec. **it** ~**ed its ears** ses oreilles ont remué.

twitter ['twɪtəʳ] **1** *vi [bird]* gazouiller; *[person]* parler avec agitation (*about* de). **2** *n [birds]* gazouillis *m*. *(fig)* **to be in a** ~ * être tout sens dessus dessous * (*about* à cause de).

two [tu:] *adj, n* deux *(m) inv*. **to cut in** ~ couper en deux; ~ **by** ~ *take, do* deux par deux; *climb steps* deux à deux; **in** ~**s** par deux; **in** ~**s and threes** *sell* deux ou trois à la fois; *arrive* par petits groupes; **they're** ~ **of a kind** ils se ressemblent; *(fig)* **to put** ~ **and** ~ **together** faire le rapport; ~**'s company** on est mieux à deux; *V* **one**, *and for other phrases V* **six.** ◆ **two-bits** *npl (US)* 25 cents *mpl*. ◆ **two-bit** * *adj (US pej)* de pacotille. ◆ **two-by-four** * *adj (small)* exigu; *(unimportant)* minable. ◆ **two-edged** *adj (lit, fig)* à double tranchant. ◆ **two-faced** *adj (fig)* hypocrite. ◆ **twofold 1** *adj* double ; **2** *adv* au double. ◆ **two-legged** *adj* bipède. ◆ **two-party** *adj (Pol)* bipartite. ◆ **two-piece suit** *n (man's)* costume *m* deux-pièces; *(woman's)* tailleur *m*. ◆ **two-ply** *adj wool* à deux fils. ◆ **two-seater** *n (car)* voiture *f or (plane)* avion *m* à deux places. ◆ **twosome** *n*: **in a** ~**some** à deux. ◆ **two-star** *n (Brit)* (essence *f*) ordinaire *f*. ◆ **two-stroke** *n (engine)* deux-temps *m inv*; *(mixture/fuel)* mélange *m*/carburant *m* pour deux-temps. ◆ **two-time** ‡ *vt* doubler *, tromper. ◆ **two-way** *adj switch* à deux départs; *street* à double sens; *traffic* dans les deux sens; ~**-way mirror** miroir *m* sans tain; **a** ~**-way radio** un émetteur-récepteur. ◆ **two-wheeler** *n* deux-roues *m inv*.

tycoon [taɪ'ku:n] *n* gros homme *m* d'affaires. **oil** ~ magnat *m* du pétrole.

type [taɪp] **1** *n* **(a)** *(gen, Bio, Soc etc)* type *m*; *(sort)* genre *m*, espèce *f*, sorte *f*; *(make: of machine, coffee etc)* marque *f*; *[aircraft, car]* modèle *m*. **true to** ~ conforme au type; **gruyère-**~ **cheese** fromage genre gruyère *; **what** ~ **do you want?** vous en (*or* le *etc*) voulez de quelle sorte?; **what** ~ **of man is he?** quel genre d'homme est-ce?; **you know the** ~ **of thing I mean** vous voyez ce que je veux dire; **he's not my** ~ * il n'est pas mon genre *; **it's my** ~ **of film** c'est le genre de film que j'aime; *(person)* **an odd** ~ * un drôle de numéro *. **(b)** *(Typ) (one letter)* caractère *m*; *(letters collectively: print)* caractères, type *m*. **to set** ~ composer; **in large/small** ~ en gros/petits caractères; **in italic** ~ en italiques.

2 *vt* **(a)** *blood sample etc* classifier. *(Theat etc)* **he is** ~**d as...** on ne lui donne plus que les rôles de... **(b)** **(~ out)** *letter etc* taper (à la machine); **(~ out, ~ up)** *notes* taper.

3 *vi* taper à la machine.

◆ **type-cast** *adj (Theat etc)* **to be** ~**-cast as** être enfermé dans le rôle de. ◆ **typeface** *n* œil *m* de caractère. ◆ **typescript** *n* manuscrit *m* dactylographié. ◆ **typeset** *vt* composer. ◆ **typesetter** *n* compositeur *m*, -trice *f*. ◆ **typesetting** *n* composition *f*. ◆ **typewriter** *n* machine *f* à écrire. ◆ **typewriting** *n* dactylographie *f*. ◆ **typewritten** *adj* tapé à la machine, dactylographié. ◆ **typing 1** *n (skill)* dactylo *f*; **pages of typing** pages *fpl* dactylographiées ; **2** *adj lesson, teacher* de dactylo; *paper* machine *inv*; **typing error** faute *f* de frappe; **typing pool** bureau *m* des dactylos *f*. ◆ **typist** *n* dactylo *mf*. ◆ **typography** *n* typographie *f*. ◆ **typology** *n* typologie *f*.

typhoid ['taɪfɔɪd] *n* typhoïde *f*.

typhoon [taɪ'fu:n] *n* typhon *m*.

typhus ['taɪfəs] *n* typhus *m*.

typical ['tɪpɪk(ə)l] *adj (gen)* typique, caractéristique (*of* de); *case, example* typique, type *inv*. **a ~ day in spring** un jour de printemps comme il y en a tant; **the ~ Frenchman** le Français type *or* typique; **with ~ modesty he said...** avec sa modestie habituelle il a dit...; **that's ~ of him!** c'est bien lui!; *(iro)* ~! ça ne m'étonne pas! ◆ **typically** *adv* typiquement; **he was ~ly rude** il s'est conduit avec sa grossièreté habituelle. ◆ **typify** *vt [thing]* être caractéristique de; *[person]* avoir le type même de.

tyrant ['taɪər(ə)nt] *n* tyran *m*. ◆ **tyrannic(al)** *adj* tyrannique. ◆ **tyrannize** *vi*: **to tyrannize over sb** tyranniser qn. ◆ **tyranny** *n* tyrannie *f*.

tyre ['taɪəʳ] **1** *n* pneu *m*. **2** *adj*: ~ **gauge** manomètre *m* (pour pneus); ~ **lever** démonte-pneu *m*; ~ **pressure** pression *f* de gonflage.

tyro ['taɪərəʊ] *n* novice *mf*.

tzar [zɑːʳ] *n* = **tsar**.

U

U, u [juː] **1** *n (letter)* U, u *m.* **2** *adj (*: upper-class)* **U** distingué; **non-U** vulgaire. ◆ **U-bend** *n* coude *m (angle).* ◆ **U-turn** *n (Aut)* demi-tour *m*; *(fig, Pol)* volte-face *f inv.*

ubiquitous [juːˈbɪkwɪtəs] *adj* doué d'ubiquité. ◆ **ubiquity** *n* ubiquité *f.*

udder [ˈʌdəʳ] *n* pis *m*, mamelle *f.*

Uganda [juːˈgændə] *n* Ouganda *m.* ◆ **Ugandan** **1** *adj* ougandais ; **2** *n* Ougandais(e) *m(f).*

ugh [ɜːh] *excl* pouah!

ugly [ˈʌglɪ] *adj (gen)* laid; *custom, vice etc* répugnant; *situation* moche *; *war* brutal; *expression, look* menaçant; *wound, rumour, word* vilain *(before n).* **it is an ~ sight** ce n'est pas beau à voir; **~ customer** * sale individu *m*; *(fig)* **~ duckling** vilain petit canard *m.* ◆ **ugliness** *n* laideur *f.*

Ukraine [juːˈkreɪn] *n* Ukraine *f.*

ulcer [ˈʌlsəʳ] *n* ulcère *m.* ◆ **ulcerated** *or* ◆ **ulcerous** *adj* ulcéreux.

Ulster [ˈʌlstəʳ] *n* Ulster *m.*

ulterior [ʌlˈtɪərɪəʳ] *adj* ultérieur. **~ motive** motif *m* secret.

ultimate [ˈʌltɪmɪt] *adj aim, destination, outcome* final; *victory* final, ultime; *authority* suprême; *principle, cause* fondamental. *(Mil)* **the ~ deterrent** l'ultime moyen de dissuasion; *(fig)* **the ~ (in) luxury** le summum du luxe; **the ~ (in) selfishness** le comble de l'égoïsme. ◆ **ultimately** *adv (at last)* finalement; *(eventually)* par la suite; *(in the last analysis)* en dernière analyse. ◆ **ultimatum,** *pl* **-ta** *n* ultimatum *m*; **to issue an ultimatum** adresser un ultimatum (*to* à). ◆ **ultimo** *adv (Comm)* du mois dernier.

ultra... [ˈʌltrə] *pref* ultra..., hyper... ◆ **ultrafashionable** *adj* du tout dernier cri. ◆ **ultrahigh** *adj*: **~ high frequency** très haute fréquence *f.* ◆ **ultralight** *n (Aviat)* U.L.M. *m*, ultra-léger motorisé *m.* ◆ **ultramarine** *adj, n* bleu outremer *(m) inv.* ◆ **ultramodern** *adj* ultramoderne. ◆ **ultrasensitive** *adj* hypersensible. ◆ **ultrashort** *adj* ultracourt. ◆ **ultrasonic** *adj* ultrasonique. ◆ **ultrasound** *n* ultrasons *mpl;* **~sound scan** échographie *f.* ◆ **ultraviolet** *adj* ultra-violet.

umber [ˈʌmbəʳ] *adj, n* terre *(f)* d'ombre.

umbilical [ˌʌmbɪˈlaɪk(ə)l] *adj* ombilical. **~ cord** cordon *m* ombilical.

umbrage [ˈʌmbrɪdʒ] *n*: **to take ~** prendre ombrage (*at* de).

umbrella [ʌmˈbrelə] **1** *n* parapluie *m; (against sun)* parasol *m.* **beach ~** parasol; *(Mil)* **air ~** écran *m* de protection aérienne; *(fig)* **under the ~ of** sous les auspices *mpl* de. **2** *adj*: **~ pine** pin *m* parasol; **~ stand** porte-parapluies *m inv;* **~ term** terme général.

umlaut [ˈʊmlaʊt] *n* tréma *m.*

umpire [ˈʌmpaɪəʳ] *(Sport)* **1** *n* arbitre *m.* **2** *vt* arbitrer. **3** *vi* être l'arbitre.

umpteen * [ˈʌm(p)tiːn] *adj* je ne sais combien de. ◆ **umpteenth** * *adj* énième.

unabashed [ˈʌnəˈbæʃt] *adj* nullement décontenancé.

unabated [ˈʌnəˈbeɪtɪd] *adj:* **to remain ~** *(gen)* rester inchangé.

unable [ˈʌnˈeɪbl] *adj*: **to be ~ to do** *(gen)* ne (pas) pouvoir faire; *(be incapable of)* être incapable de faire, ne pas pouvoir faire; *(not know how to)* ne pas savoir faire.

unabridged [ˈʌnəˈbrɪdʒd] *adj edition* intégral.

unacceptable [ˈʌnəkˈseptəbl] *adj suggestion* inacceptable; *amount, extent* inadmissible.

unaccompanied [ˈʌnəˈkʌmp(ə)nɪd] *adj child, luggage* non accompagné; *singing* sans accompagnement; *instrument* seul.

unaccountable [ˈʌnəˈkaʊntəbl] *adj* inexplicable. ◆ **unaccountably** *adv* inexplicablement. ◆ **unaccounted** *adj*: **they are still unaccounted for** ils n'ont toujours pas été retrouvés.

unaccustomed [ˈʌnəˈkʌstəmd] *adj slowness etc* inhabituel, inaccoutumé. **to be ~ to sth/to doing** ne pas avoir l'habitude de qch/de faire.

unacquainted [ˈʌnəˈkweɪntɪd] *adj*: **to be ~ with** ignorer.

unadorned [ˈʌnəˈdɔːnd] *adj* tout simple; *(fig) facts* tout nu.

unadulterated [ˈʌnəˈdʌltəreɪtɪd] *adj (gen)* pur; *wine* non frelaté; *(fig) bliss, nonsense* pur et simple.

unadventurous [ˈʌnədˈventʃ(ə)rəs] *adj* conventionnel, qui manque d'audace.

unaffected [ˈʌnəˈfektɪd] *adj* (**a**) *(sincere) person* naturel, simple; *behaviour* non affecté; *style* sans recherche, simple. (**b**) non affecté (*by* par); *(emotionally)* non touché (*by* par). ◆ **unaffectedly** *adv* sans affectation.

unafraid [ˈʌnəˈfreɪd] *adj* qui n'a pas peur (*of* de).

unaided [ˈʌnˈeɪdɪd] *adj:* **his own ~ efforts** ses propres efforts.

unalloyed [ˈʌnəˈlɔɪd] *adj (fig)* sans mélange.

unalterable [ʌnˈɒlt(ə)rəbl] *adj rule* invariable; *fact* certain; *friendship* inaltérable. ◆ **unaltered** *adj* inchangé.

unambiguous [ˈʌnæmˈbɪgjʊəs] *adj* non ambigu. ◆ **unambiguously** *adv* sans ambiguïté.

unambitious [ˈʌnæmˈbɪʃəs] *adj person* peu ambitieux; *plan* modeste.

un-American [ˈʌnəˈmerɪkən] *adj* antiaméricain.

unanimous [juːˈnænɪməs] *adj group, decision* unanime (*in sth* pour qch; *in doing* à faire); *vote* à l'unanimité. ◆ **unanimity** *n* unanimité *f.* ◆ **unanimously** *adv* à l'unanimité.

unannounced [ˈʌnəˈnaʊnst] *adj* sans se faire annoncer.

unanswerable [ʌnˈɑːns(ə)rəbl] *adj question* à laquelle il est impossible de répondre; *argument* irréfutable. ◆ **unanswered** *adj letter, question* sans réponse; *criticism* non réfuté.

unappetizing [ˈʌnˈæpɪtaɪzɪŋ] *adj* peu appétissant.

unappreciated [ˈʌnəˈpriːʃɪeɪtɪd] *adj person* méconnu; *offer, help* non apprécié. ◆ **unappreciative** *adj* indifférent (*of* à).

unapproachable [ˈʌnəˈprəʊtʃəbl] *adj* d'un abord difficile.

unarmed [ˈʌnˈɑːmd] *adj person* non armé; *combat* sans armes.

unashamed [ˈʌnəˈʃeɪmd] *adj pleasure, greed* effronté. **he was quite ~ about it** il n'en avait absolument pas honte.

unasked ['ʌn'ɑ:skt] *adj do* spontanément; *arrive* sans y avoir été invité.

unassisted ['ʌnə'sɪstɪd] *adj* sans aide.

unassuming ['ʌnə'sju:mɪŋ] *adj* modeste.

unattached ['ʌnə'tætʃt] *adj part etc* non attaché; *(fig) person, group* indépendant; *(not married etc)* sans attaches.

unattainable ['ʌnə'teɪnəbl] *adj* inaccessible.

unattended ['ʌnə'tendɪd] *adj (not looked after) luggage* abandonné; *shop, person* laissé sans surveillance.

unattractive ['ʌnə'træktɪv] *adj thing* peu attrayant; *person* déplaisant.

unauthorized ['ʌn'ɔ:θəraɪzd] *adj* non autorisé.

unavailable ['ʌnə'veɪləbl] *adj (Comm) article* épuisé; *person* qui n'est pas disponible.

unavailing ['ʌnə'veɪlɪŋ] *adj effort* vain, inutile.

unavoidable [ˌʌnə'vɔɪdəbl] *adj* inévitable (*that* que + *subj*). ◆ **unavoidably** *adv slow, large* inévitablement; *prevented, delayed* malencontreusement.

unaware ['ʌnə'wɛəʳ] *adj*: **to be ~ of sth/that...** ignorer qch/que... ◆ **unawares** *adv do sth* inconsciemment; **to catch** *or* **take sb ~s** prendre qn au dépourvu.

unbalanced ['ʌn'bælənst] *adj* déséquilibré.

unbandage ['ʌn'bændɪdʒ] *vt* débander.

unbearable [ʌn'bɛərəbl] *adj* insupportable. ◆ **unbearably** *adv* insupportablement.

unbeatable ['ʌn'bi:təbl] *adj* imbattable. ◆ **unbeaten** *adj army, player* invaincu; *record, price* non battu.

unbecoming ['ʌnbɪ'kʌmɪŋ] *adj garment* peu seyant; *behaviour* malséant.

unbeknown(st) ['ʌnbɪ'nəʊn(st)] *adv*: **~ to** à l'insu de.

unbelievable [ˌʌnbɪ'li:vəbl] *adj* incroyable (*that* que + *subj*). ◆ **unbelievably** *adv* incroyablement. ◆ **unbeliever** *n* incrédule *mf*. ◆ **unbelieving** *adj* incrédule. ◆ **unbelievingly** *adv* d'un air incrédule.

unbend ['ʌn'bend] *pret, ptp* **unbent** **1** *vt pipe etc* redresser. **2** *vi (fig) [person]* se détendre. ◆ **unbending** *adj (fig)* inflexible.

unbias(s)ed ['ʌn'baɪəst] *adj* impartial.

unbidden ['ʌn'bɪdn] *adj* sans y avoir été invité.

unbleached ['ʌn'bli:tʃt] *adj linen* écru.

unblemished [ʌn'blemɪʃt] *adj* sans tache.

unblock ['ʌn'blɒk] *vt pipe* déboucher; *road, harbour* dégager.

unblushing [ʌn'blʌʃɪŋ] *adj* effronté. ◆ **unblushingly** *adv* sans rougir.

unbolt ['ʌn'bəʊlt] *vt door* déverrouiller.

unborn ['ʌn'bɔ:n] *adj child* qui n'est pas encore né; *generation* à venir, futur.

unbounded [ʌn'baʊndɪd] *adj* sans borne.

unbreakable ['ʌn'breɪkəbl] *adj* incassable.

unbridled [ʌn'braɪdld] *adj (fig)* débridé.

unbroken ['ʌn'brəʊk(ə)n] *adj (gen)* intact; *line* continu; *(Genealogy)* direct; *(fig) promise* tenu; *series, silence, sleep* ininterrompu; *record* non battu; *horse* indompté. **his spirit remained ~** il ne s'est pas découragé.

unburden [ʌn'bɜ:dn] *vt*: **to ~ o.s.** s'épancher (*to sb* avec qn).

unbusinesslike [ʌn'bɪznɪslaɪk] *adj trader* qui n'a pas le sens des affaires; *transaction* irrégulier; *(fig) person* qui manque d'organisation; *report* peu méthodique.

unbutton ['ʌn'bʌtn] *vt* déboutonner.

uncalled-for [ʌn'kɔ:ldfɔ:ʳ] *adj criticism* injustifié; *remark* déplacé. **that was quite ~** vous n'aviez nullement besoin de faire (*or* dire) ça.

uncanny [ʌn'kænɪ] *adj sound, atmosphere* étrange, inquiétant; *resemblance, knack* troublant. ◆ **uncannily** *adv silent, cold* sinistrement; *alike* étrangement.

uncared-for ['ʌn'kɛədfɔ:ʳ] *adj garden, building, child* laissé à l'abandon; *appearance* négligé.

unceasing [ʌn'si:sɪŋ] *adj* incessant. ◆ **unceasingly** *adv* sans cesse.

unceremonious ['ʌnˌserɪ'məʊnɪəs] *adj* brusque. ◆ **unceremoniously** *adv* sans cérémonie.

uncertain [ʌn'sɜ:tn] *adj (gen)* incertain (*of, about* de); *temper* inégal. **it is ~ whether** on ne sait pas exactement si; **he is ~ whether** il ne sait pas au juste si; **in no ~ terms** en des termes on ne peut plus clairs. ◆ **uncertainly** *adv* d'une manière hésitante. ◆ **uncertainty** *n* incertitude *f*; *(doubts)* doutes *mpl*.

uncertificated ['ʌnsə'tɪfɪkeɪtɪd] *adj* non diplômé.

unchallengeable ['ʌn'tʃælɪn(d)ʒəbl] *adj* incontestable. ◆ **unchallenged** *adj leader, rights* incontesté; *statement, figures* non contesté; *(Jur) witness* non récusé; **to let sth go unchallenged** laisser passer qch sans protester.

unchangeable [ʌn'tʃeɪn(d)ʒəbl] *adj* invariable. ◆ **unchanged** *adj* inchangé. ◆ **unchanging** *adj* invariable.

uncharitable [ʌn'tʃærɪtəbl] *adj* peu charitable.

uncharted ['ʌn'tʃɑ:tɪd] *adj region* inexploré.

unchecked ['ʌn'tʃekt] *adj* (**a**) *(unrestrained) anger* non maîtrisé. **to advance ~** avancer sans rencontrer d'opposition; **to continue ~** continuer sans la moindre opposition. (**b**) *(not verified) figures, statement* non vérifié; *typescript* non relu.

unchristian ['ʌn'krɪstjən] *adj* peu chrétien.

uncivilized ['ʌn'sɪvɪlaɪzd] *adj (gen)* barbare; *amount, time etc* impossible *.

unclaimed ['ʌn'kleɪmd] *adj* non réclamé.

uncle ['ʌŋkl] *n* oncle *m*. **yes, ~** oui, mon oncle; *(US)* **to cry ~** * s'avouer vaincu.

unclean ['ʌn'kli:n] *adj* malpropre; *(fig)* impur.

unclear [ˌʌn'klɪəʳ] *adj* qui n'est pas clair. **it is ~ whether...** on ne sait pas encore très bien si...

unclouded ['ʌn'klaʊdɪd] *adj (lit, fig)* sans nuages.

uncoil ['ʌn'kɔɪl] **1** *vt* dérouler. **2** *vi* se dérouler.

uncollected ['ʌnkə'lektɪd] *adj tax* non perçu; *bus fare* non encaissé; *luggage, lost property* non réclamé; *refuse* non ramassé.

uncoloured ['ʌn'kʌləd] *adj* non coloré; *(fig) description* objectif. *(fig)* **~ by** non déformé par.

uncombed ['ʌn'kəʊmd] *adj* non peigné.

uncomfortable [ʌn'kʌmf(ə)təbl] *adj thing* inconfortable; *afternoon* désagréable. *[person]* **to be** *or* **feel ~** ne pas être à l'aise; *(uneasy)* être mal à l'aise (*about sth* au sujet de qch); **this chair is very ~** ce fauteuil n'est pas du tout confortable; **I had an ~ feeling that** je ne pouvais pas m'empêcher de penser que; **to make things ~ for sb** créer des ennuis à qn; **to have an ~ time** passer un moment pénible. ◆ **uncomfortably** *adv hot* désagréablement; *seated, dressed* inconfortablement; *(uneasily) think* avec une certaine inquiétude; *say* avec gêne; *near, similar etc* un peu trop.

uncommitted ['ʌnkə'mɪtɪd] *adj (gen)* non engagé; *attitude, country* neutraliste.

uncommon [ʌn'kɒmən] *adj (unusual)* rare, peu commun; *(outstanding)* rare, extraordinaire. **it is not ~ that** il n'est pas rare que + *subj*. ◆ **uncommonly** *adv (extremely)* extraordinairement; **not ~ly** assez souvent.

uncommunicative ['ʌnkə'mju:nɪkətɪv] *adj* peu communicatif.

uncomplaining ['ʌnkəm'pleɪnɪŋ] *adj* patient, résigné. ◆ **uncomplainingly** *adv* sans se plaindre.

uncomplicated [ʌn'kɒmplɪkeɪtɪd] *adj* peu compliqué, simple.

uncomplimentary ['ʌn,kɒmplɪ'ment(ə)rɪ] *adj* peu flatteur.

uncompromising [ʌn'kɒmprəmaɪzɪŋ] *adj person* intransigeant; *honesty* absolu.

unconcealed ['ʌnkən'si:ld] *adj* non dissimulé.

unconcern ['ʌnkən'sɜ:n] *n* sang-froid *m*; *(lack of interest)* indifférence *f*. ◆ **unconcerned** *adj (unworried)* imperturbable (*by* devant); *(unaffected)* indifférent (*by* à). ◆ **unconcernedly** *adv* sans s'inquiéter; avec indifférence.

unconditional ['ʌnkən'dɪʃənl] *adj (gen)* inconditionnel; *surrender* sans condition. ◆ **unconditionally** *adv* inconditionnellement; sans condition.

unconfirmed ['ʌnkən'fɜ:md] *adj* non confirmé.

uncongenial ['ʌnkən'dʒi:nɪəl] *adj person* peu sympathique; *work, place* peu agréable.

unconnected ['ʌnkə'nektɪd] *adj events, facts* sans rapport; *languages* sans connexion; *ideas* décousu; *(Elec)* débranché.

unconscious [ʌn'kɒnʃəs] **1** *adj* (**a**) *(Med)* sans connaissance. **to be ~ for 3 hours** rester sans connaissance pendant 3 heures; **to become ~** perdre connaissance; **knocked ~** assommé. (**b**) *(unaware) person, humour, desire* inconscient (*of* de). **2** *n (Psych)* inconscient *m*. ◆ **unconsciously** *adv* inconsciemment, sans s'en rendre compte.

unconstitutional ['ʌn,kɒnstɪ'tju:ʃənl] *adj* anticonstitutionnel.

uncontested ['ʌnkən'testɪd] *adj* incontesté; *(Parl) seat* non disputé.

uncontrollable ['ʌnkən'trəʊləbl] *adj child, animal* indiscipliné; *desire, emotion* irrésistible; *epidemic, inflation* qui ne peut être enrayé. **to have an ~ temper** ne pas savoir se contrôler. ◆ **uncontrollably** *adv (gen)* irrésistiblement; **to laugh uncontrollably** avoir le fou rire; **the car skidded uncontrollably** le conducteur a dérapé et a perdu le contrôle de sa voiture. ◆ **uncontrolled** *adj emotion* non contenu; *price rises* effréné; *inflation* incontrôlé.

unconventional ['ʌnkən'venʃənl] *adj* peu conventionnel.

unconvinced ['ʌnkən'vɪnst] *adj*: **to be** *or* **remain ~** ne pas être convaincu (*of* de). ◆ **unconvincing** *adj* peu convaincant. ◆ **unconvincingly** *adv* d'une manière peu convaincante.

uncooked ['ʌn'kʊkt] *adj* cru.

uncooperative ['ʌnkəʊ'ɒp(ə)rətɪv] *adj* peu coopératif.

uncork ['ʌn'kɔ:k] *vt* déboucher.

uncountable ['ʌn'kaʊntəbl] *adj* (**a**) *(many)* incalculable. *(Ling)* **~ noun** nom *m* non dénombrable.

uncouple ['ʌn'kʌpl] *vt train* découpler; *trailer* détacher.

uncouth [ʌn'ku:θ] *adj* fruste.

uncover [ʌn'kʌvə^r] *vt* découvrir.

uncritical ['ʌn'krɪtɪk(ə)l] *adj* qui manque d'esprit critique (*of* à l'égard de); *attitude, report* non critique.

uncrossed ['ʌn'krɒst] *adj cheque* non barré.

uncrushable ['ʌn'krʌʃəbl] *adj* infroissable.

unction ['ʌŋkʃ(ə)n] *n*: **extreme ~** extrême-onction *f*.

uncultivated ['ʌn'kʌltɪveɪtɪd] *adj* inculte.

uncurl ['ʌn'kɜ:l] *vt (gen)* dérouler; *legs* déplier.

uncut ['ʌn'kʌt] *adj (gen)* non coupé; *diamond* brut; *gem, stone* non taillé; *edition etc* intégral.

undamaged [ʌn'dæmɪdʒd] *adj goods* non endommagé; *reputation* intact.

undated ['ʌn'deɪtɪd] *adj* non daté.

undaunted ['ʌn'dɔ:ntɪd] *adj* non intimidé (*by* par). **to carry on ~** continuer sans se laisser intimider.

undecided ['ʌndɪ'saɪdɪd] *adj* indécis. **that is still ~** cela n'a pas encore été décidé; **I am ~ whether...** je n'ai pas décidé si...

undefeated ['ʌndɪ'fi:tɪd] *adj* invaincu.

undefined [,ʌndɪ'faɪnd] *adj word* non défini; *sensation etc* vague.

undelivered ['ʌndɪ'lɪvəd] *adj* non distribué. **if ~ return to sender** ≃ en cas d'absence, prière de retourner à l'expéditeur.

undemonstrative ['ʌndɪ'mɒnstrətɪv] *adj* peu démonstratif.

undeniable [,ʌndɪ'naɪəbl] *adj* incontestable. ◆ **undeniably** *adv* incontestablement.

under ['ʌndə^r] **1** *adv* (**a**) *(below)* au-dessous, en dessous. **to stay ~** *(~ water)* rester sous l'eau; *(~ anaesthetic)* rester sous l'effet de l'anesthésie; *(Comm etc)* **as ~** comme ci-dessous. (**b**) *(less)* au-dessous. **children of 15 and ~** les enfants de 15 ans et moins.
2 *prep* (**a**) *(beneath)* sous. **~ the table** sous la table; **from ~ the bed** de dessous le lit; **it's ~ there** c'est là-dessous; **he went and sat ~ it** il est allé s'asseoir dessous; **to stay ~ water** rester sous l'eau; **~ the microscope** au microscope. (**b**) *(less than)* moins de; *(in series, rank, scale etc)* au-dessous de. **to be ~ age** être mineur; **children ~ 15** enfants de moins de *or* enfants au-dessous de 15 ans; **~ £10** moins de 10 livres; **any number ~ 10** un chiffre au-dessous de 10. (**c**) *(fig)* sous. **~ the Tudors** sous les Tudors; **~ the circumstances** dans les circonstances; **~ an assumed name** sous un faux nom; **you'll find him ~ 'plumbers' in the book** vous le trouverez sous 'plombiers' dans l'annuaire; *(Mil etc)* **to serve ~ sb** servir sous les ordres de qn; **to study ~ sb** *[undergraduate]* suivre les cours de qn; *[postgraduate]* travailler sous la direction de qn; *[painter etc]* être l'élève de qn. (**d**) *(according to)* selon, conformément à. **~ this law** selon *or* conformément à cette loi.
3 *(in compounds) (insufficiently)* sous-; *(junior)* aide-, sous-. **~capitalized** sous-financé; **~populated** sous-peuplé; **~cooked** pas assez cuit; **~used/~appreciated** *etc* qui n'est pas assez utilisé/apprécié *etc;* **~gardener** aide-jardinier *m*; *(in age)* **the ~-10's** les moins *mpl* de 10 ans.
◆ **underachieve** *vi* être sous-performant. ◆ **underarm** **1** *adv* par en-dessous ; **2** *adj deodorant* pour les aisselles. ◆ **underbelly** *n (fig)* point *m* vulnérable. ◆ **undercarriage** *n* train *m* d'atterrissage. ◆ **undercharge** *vt* ne pas faire payer assez à. ◆ **underclothes** *npl or* ◆ **underclothing** *n* sous-vêtements *mpl*. ◆ **undercoat** *n [paint]* couche *f* de fond. ◆ **undercover** *adj* secret. ◆ **undercurrent** *n* courant *m* (sous-marin); *(fig)* courant sous-jacent. ◆ **undercut** *pret, ptp* **undercut** *vt (Comm)* vendre moins cher que. ◆ **underdeveloped** *adj (Anat, Phot)* insuffisamment développé; *(Econ)* sous-développé. ◆ **underdog** *n (fig)* **the ~dog** *(in fight)* celui qui perd; *(socially)* l'opprimé *m*. ◆ **underdone** *adj (Culin)* saignant; *(pej)* pas assez cuit. ◆ **underemployed** *adj* sous-employé. ◆ **underestimate** *vt* sous-estimer. ◆ **underexpose** *vt (Phot)* sous-exposer. ◆ **underexposure** *n* sous-exposition *f*. ◆ **underfeed** *pret, ptp* **underfed** *vt* sous-alimenter. ◆ **underfelt** *n* thibaude *f*. ◆ **under-floor heating** *n* chauffage *m* par le sol. ◆ **underfoot** *adv* sous les pieds; **it is wet ~foot** le sol est humide; **to trample sth ~foot** fouler qch aux pieds. ◆ **underfunded** *adj project* pas doté de fonds suffisants. ◆ **undergarment** *n* sous-vêtement *m*. ◆ **undergo** *pret* **underwent** *ptp* **undergone** *vt (gen)* subir; *medical treatment* suivre. ◆ **undergraduate** **1** *n* étudiant(e) *m(f)* ; **2** *adj circles* étudiant; *opinion*

des étudiants; *attitude* d'étudiant. ◆ **underground 1** *adj (gen)* souterrain; *(fig) organization* secret; *press* clandestin; *(Art, Cine)* underground *inv* ; **2** *adv* sous (la) terre; **to go ~ground** *[wanted man]* entrer dans la clandestinité; *[guerrilla]* prendre le maquis ; **3** *n*: **the ~ground** *(railway)* le métro; *(Mil, Pol etc)* la résistance; *(Art, etc)* le mouvement underground; **by ~ground** en métro. ◆ **undergrowth** *n* sous-bois *m inv*. ◆ **underhand 1** *adv (Sport)* par en-dessous ; **2** *adj (also* **~handed***)* sournois, en sous-main. ◆ **underlay** *n* thibaude *f*. ◆ **underlie** *pret* **underlay** *ptp* **underlain** *vt* être à la base de. ◆ **underline** *vt (lit, fig)* souligner. ◆ **underling** *n (pej)* subalterne *m*. ◆ **underlining** *n* soulignement *m*. ◆ **underlying** *adj rock, cause* sous-jacent; *principle* fondamental. ◆ **undermentioned** *adj* (cité) ci-dessous. ◆ **undermine** *vt (gen)* saper; *health* miner; *effect* amoindrir. ◆ **underneath 1** *prep* sous, au-dessous de ; **2** *adv* (en) dessous ; **3** *adj* d'en dessous ; **4** *n* dessous *m*. ◆ **undernourish** *vt* sous-alimenter. ◆ **undernourishment** *n* sous-alimentation *f*. ◆ **underpaid** *adj* sous-payé. ◆ **underpants** *npl* slip *m (pour homme)*. ◆ **underpass** *n (for cars)* passage *m* inférieur *(de l'autoroute)*; *(for pedestrians)* passage souterrain. ◆ **underpay** *vt* sous-payer. ◆ **underpin** *vt (lit, fig)* étayer. ◆ **underplay** *vt* minimiser. ◆ **underpriced** *adj* dont le prix est trop bas. ◆ **underprivileged** *adj (gen)* défavorisé; *(Econ)* économiquement faible; **the ~privileged** les économiquement faibles *mpl*. ◆ **underrate** *vt* sous-estimer. ◆ **undersea** *adj* sous-marin. ◆ **underseal** *vt* traiter contre la rouille. ◆ **undersecretary** *n* sous-secrétaire *m*. ◆ **undersell** *vt* vendre moins cher que; *(fig)* **to ~sell o.s.** ne pas se mettre en valeur. ◆ **undersexed** *adj* de faible libido. ◆ **undershirt** *n (US)* tricot *m* de corps. ◆ **underside** *n* dessous *m*. ◆ **undersigned** *adj, n* soussigné(e) *m(f)*; **I the ~signed...** je soussigné(e)... ◆ **undersized** *adj* trop petit. ◆ **underskirt** *n* jupon *m*. ◆ **understaffed** *adj* à court de personnel. ◆ **understand** *V below*. ◆ **understate** *vt* minimiser. ◆ **understated** *adj* discret. ◆ **understatement** *n* affirmation *f* en dessous de la vérité; *(Ling)* litote *f*; **that's an ~statement** c'est peu dire. ◆ **understudy 1** *n* doublure *f* ; **2** *vt* doubler. ◆ **undertake** *pret* **undertook** *ptp* **undertaken** *vt task* entreprendre; *duty* se charger de; *responsibility* assumer; *obligation* contracter; **to ~take to do** s'engager à faire. ◆ **undertaker** *n* entrepreneur *m* des pompes funèbres; **the ~taker's** les pompes funèbres *fpl*. ◆ **undertaking** *n* (**a**) *(operation)* entreprise *f*; **it is quite an ~taking** c'est toute une entreprise; (**b**) *(promise)* engagement *m*; **to give an ~taking** promettre (*that* que; *to do* de faire). ◆ **under-the-counter** *adj, adv* en douce. ◆ **undertone** *n*: **in an ~tone** à mi-voix. ◆ **undervalue** *vt (fig)* sous-estimer. ◆ **undervalued** *adj (lit)* qui vaut plus que son prix. ◆ **undervest** *n* tricot *m* de corps. ◆ **underwater** *adj* sous-marin. ◆ **underwear** *n* sous-vêtements *mpl*. ◆ **underworld 1** *n (hell)* enfers *mpl*; *(criminals)* milieu *m*, pègre *f* ; **2** *adj organization* du milieu; *connections etc* avec le milieu. ◆ **underwrite** *vt (Insurance, St Ex) risk, amount, issue* garantir; *policy* réassurer; *(Fin) project* soutenir; *(fig) decision* soutenir. ◆ **underwriter** *n (insurance)* assureur *m*; *(St Ex)* syndicataire *m*.

understand [ˌʌndəˈstænd] *pret, ptp* **understood 1** *vt (gen)* comprendre (*that* que; *why etc* pourquoi *etc*). **to make o.s. understood** se faire comprendre; **I can't ~ a word of it** je n'y comprends rien; **I understood we were to be paid** j'ai cru comprendre que nous devions être payés; **I ~ you are leaving** si je comprends bien vous partez; **she is understood to have left** on croit qu'elle est partie; **to let it be understood that** donner à entendre que; **to be understood** *[price, date]* ne pas être spécifié; *[word]* être sous-entendu; **it's understood that** il est entendu que; **that's quite understood** c'est entendu. **2** *vi* comprendre. **now I ~!** je comprends *or* j'y suis maintenant!; **he was, I ~...** il était, si j'ai bien compris... ◆ **understandable** *adj* compréhensible; **it is ~able that** on comprend que + *subj*; **that's ~able** ça se comprend. ◆ **understandably** *adv*: **he's ~ably angry** il est en colère et ça se comprend, naturellement il est en colère. ◆ **understanding 1** *adj person* compréhensif (*about* à propos de); *smile, look* bienveillant ; **2** *n* (**a**) compréhension *f* (*of* de); **to have a good ~ing of sth** bien comprendre qch; **the age of ~ing** l'âge *m* de discernement; (**b**) *(agreement)* accord *m*; *(arrangement)* arrangement *m*; **to come to an ~ing with sb** s'entendre *or* s'arranger avec qn; **on the ~ing that** à condition que + *subj*; **this will encourage ~ing between...** ceci favorisera l'entente *f* entre... ◆ **understandingly** *adv* avec bienveillance.

undeserved [ˈʌndɪˈzɜːvd] *adj* immérité. ◆ **undeservedly** [ˈʌndɪˈzɜːvɪdlɪ] *adv* indûment.

undesirable [ˈʌndɪˈzaɪərəbl] **1** *adj* peu souhaitable (*that* que + *subj*); *(stronger)* indésirable. **2** *n* indésirable *mf*.

undetected [ˈʌndɪˈtektɪd] *adj*: **to go ~** passer inaperçu.

undeveloped [ˈʌndɪˈveləpt] *adj (gen)* qui ne s'est pas développé; *film* non développé; *land, resources* non exploité.

undies * [ˈʌndɪz] *npl* dessous *mpl*, lingerie *f*.

undignified [ʌnˈdɪgnɪfaɪd] *adj* qui manque de dignité.

undiluted [ˈʌndaɪˈluːtɪd] *adj concentrate* non dilué; *pleasure* sans mélange; *nonsense* pur.

undiplomatic [ˈʌnˌdɪpləˈmætɪk] *adj person* peu diplomate; *action, answer* peu diplomatique.

undipped [ˈʌnˈdɪpt] *adj: (Aut)* **his headlights were ~** il était en phares.

undischarged [ˈʌndɪsˈtʃɑːdʒd] *adj bankrupt* non réhabilité; *debt* non acquitté.

undisciplined [ʌnˈdɪsɪplɪnd] *adj* indiscipliné.

undiscovered [ˈʌndɪsˈkʌvəd] *adj (unknown)* inconnu. **it remained ~ for 700 years** cela n'a été découvert que 700 ans après.

undiscriminating [ˈʌndɪsˈkrɪmɪneɪtɪŋ] *adj* qui manque de discernement.

undisguised [ˈʌndɪsˈgaɪzd] *adj* non déguisé.

undisputed [ˈʌndɪsˈpjuːtɪd] *adj* incontesté.

undistinguished [ˈʌndɪsˈtɪŋgwɪʃt] *adj* médiocre, quelconque.

undisturbed [ˈʌndɪsˈtɜːbd] *adj* (**a**) *papers, clues* non dérangé; *sleep* paisible. **to work ~** travailler sans être dérangé. (**b**) *(unworried)* non inquiet, calme. **he was ~ by the news** la nouvelle ne l'a pas inquiété.

undivided [ˈʌndɪˈvaɪdɪd] *adj* entier. **your ~ attention** toute votre attention.

undo [ˈʌnˈduː] *pret* **undid** *ptp* **undone** *vt (gen: unfasten etc)* défaire; *good effect* annuler; *mischief, wrong* réparer. ◆ **undoing** *n* perte *f*; **that was his ~ing** c'est ce qui l'a perdu. ◆ **undone** *adj (unfastened etc)* défait; **to come undone** se défaire; **to leave sth undone** ne pas faire qch.

undoubted [ʌnˈdaʊtɪd] *adj* indubitable. ◆ **undoubtedly** *adv* indubitablement, sans aucun doute.

undreamed-of [ʌnˈdriːmdɒv] *adj (unhoped-for)* inespéré; *(unsuspected)* insoupçonné.

undress [ˈʌnˈdres] **1** *vt* déshabiller. **2** *vi* se déshabiller.

undrinkable [ˈʌnˈdrɪŋkəbl] *adj (unpalatable)* imbuvable; *(poisonous)* non potable.

undue ['ʌn'dju:] *adj* excessif. ◆ **unduly** *adv* trop, excessivement.

undulate ['ʌndjʊleɪt] *vi* onduler. ◆ **undulating** *adj (gen)* onduleux; *countryside* vallonné.

undying [ʌn'daɪɪŋ] *adj (fig)* éternel.

unearned ['ʌn'ɜ:nd] *adj reward* immérité. ~ **income** rentes *fpl*.

unearth ['ʌn'ɜ:θ] *vt (lit, fig)* déterrer.

unearthly [ʌn'ɜ:θlɪ] *adj* surnaturel; *(* fig) noise etc* impossible *. ~ **hour** * heure indue.

uneasy [ʌn'i:zɪ] *adj peace, truce* difficile; *silence* gêné; *sleep, night* agité; *conscience* non tranquille; *person (ill-at-ease)* gêné; *(worried)* inquiet. ◆ **uneasily** *adv (ill-at-ease)* avec gêne; *(worriedly)* avec inquiétude; *sleep* d'un sommeil agité. ◆ **uneasiness** *or* ◆ **unease** *n* inquiétude *f*.

uneatable ['ʌn'i:təbl] *adj* immangeable. ◆ **uneaten** *adj* non mangé.

uneconomic(al) ['ʌn,i:kə'nɒmɪk(əl)] *adj machine, car* peu économique; *work, method* peu rentable.

uneducated ['ʌn'edjʊkeɪtɪd] *adj person* sans instruction; *handwriting* d'illettré; *speech* populaire *(pej)*.

unemotional ['ʌnɪ'məʊʃənl] *adj* impassible. ◆ **unemotionally** *adv* avec impassibilité.

unemployed ['ʌnɪm'plɔɪd] **1** *adj* sans travail, en chômage. **2** *npl* **the** ~ les chômeurs *mpl*; *(esp Admin)* les demandeurs d'emploi. ◆ **unemployable** *adj* incapable de travailler. ◆ **unemployment** **1** *n* chômage *m* ; **2** *adj*: **unemployment benefit** allocation *f* de chômage.

unending [ʌn'endɪŋ] *adj* interminable.

unendurable ['ʌnɪn'djʊərəbl] *adj* insupportable.

unenforceable ['ʌnɪn'fɔ:səbl] *adj law* inapplicable.

unenterprising ['ʌn'entəpraɪzɪŋ] *adj person* qui manque d'initiative; *act* qui manque de hardiesse.

unenthusiastic ['ʌnɪn,θu:zɪ'æstɪk] *adj* peu enthousiaste. ◆ **unenthusiastically** *adv* sans enthousiasme.

unenviable ['ʌn'envɪəbl] *adj* peu enviable.

unequal ['ʌn'i:kw(ə)l] *adj (gen)* inégal. **to be** ~ **to a task** ne pas être à la hauteur d'une tâche. ◆ **unequalled** *adj* inégalé. ◆ **unequally** *adv* inégalement.

unequivocal ['ʌnɪ'kwɪvək(ə)l] *adj* sans équivoque. ◆ **unequivocally** *adv* sans équivoque.

unerring ['ʌn'ɜ:rɪŋ] *adj judgment, accuracy* infaillible; *aim, skill, blow* sûr.

unethical ['ʌn'eθɪk(ə)l] *adj* immoral.

uneven ['ʌn'i:v(ə)n] *adj* inégal. ◆ **unevenly** *adv* inégalement. ◆ **unevenness** *n* inégalité *f*.

uneventful ['ʌnɪ'ventfʊ'l] *adj* peu mouvementé.

unexceptionable [,ʌnɪk'sepʃnəbl] *adj* irréprochable. ◆ **unexceptional** *adj* qui n'a rien d'exceptionnel.

unexciting ['ʌnɪk'saɪtɪŋ] *adj* peu intéressant.

unexpected ['ʌnɪks'pektɪd] *adj* inattendu. **it was all very** ~ on ne s'y attendait pas du tout. ◆ **unexpectedly** *adv (gen)* subitement; *arrive* inopinément.

unexplained ['ʌnɪks'pleɪnd] *adj* inexpliqué.

unexposed ['ʌnɪks'pəʊzd] *adj film* vierge.

unexpurgated ['ʌn'ekspɜ:geɪtɪd] *adj* non expurgé.

unfailing [ʌn'feɪlɪŋ] *adj supply, zeal* inépuisable; *optimism* inébranlable; *remedy* infaillible. ◆ **unfailingly** *adv* infailliblement.

unfair ['ʌn'fɛəʳ] *adj person, decision, deal* injuste (*to sb* envers qn; *that* que + *subj*); *competition, play, tactics* déloyal. ◆ **unfairly** *adv decide* injustement; *play* déloyalement. ◆ **unfairness** *n* injustice *f*; déloyauté *f*.

unfaithful ['ʌn'feɪθfʊ'l] *adj* infidèle (*to* à).

unfamiliar ['ʌnfə'mɪljəʳ] *adj* peu familier, inconnu. **to be** ~ **with sth** mal connaître qch.

unfashionable ['ʌn'fæʃnəbl] *adj dress, subject* démodé; *district, shop* peu chic *inv*. **it is** ~ **to say** ça ne se fait plus de dire.

unfasten ['ʌn'fɑ:sn] *vt (gen)* défaire; *door* déverrouiller.

unfavourable, *(US)* **unfavorable** ['ʌn'feɪv(ə)rəbl] *adj (gen)* défavorable; *terms* désavantageux; *moment* peu propice. ◆ **unfavo(u)rably** *adv* défavorablement.

unfazed ⁑ ['ʌn'feɪzd] *adj (US)* imperturbable.

unfeeling [ʌn'fi:lɪŋ] *adj* insensible. ◆ **unfeelingly** *adv* sans pitié.

unfeminine [ʌn'femɪnɪn] *adj* peu féminin.

unfinished ['ʌn'fɪnɪʃt] *adj (gen)* inachevé. **3** ~ **letters** 3 lettres à finir; **some** ~ **business** une affaire à régler; **it looks rather** ~ c'est mal fini.

unfit ['ʌn'fɪt] *adj (incompetent)* inapte (*for* à; *to do* à faire); *(unworthy)* indigne (*to do* de faire). *[footballer etc]* **he's** ~ il n'est pas en état de jouer; **he is** ~ **to be a teacher** il ne devrait pas enseigner; **he was** ~ **to drive/for work** il n'était pas en état de conduire/de reprendre le travail; ~ **for military service** inapte au service militaire; ~ **for habitation** inhabitable; ~ **for consumption/publication** impropre à la consommation/publication; **road** ~ **for lorries** route *f* impraticable aux camions.

unflattering ['ʌn'flæt(ə)rɪŋ] *adj* peu flatteur.

unfold [ʌn'fəʊld] **1** *vt (gen)* déplier; *wings* déployer; *arms* décroiser; *(fig) plans* exposer; *secret* dévoiler. **2** *vi [view, plot]* se dérouler.

unforeseeable ['ʌnfɔ:'si:əbl] *adj* imprévisible. ◆ **unforeseen** *adj* imprévu.

unforgettable ['ʌnfə'getəbl] *adj* inoubliable. ◆ **unforgotten** *adj* inoublié.

unforgivable ['ʌnfə'gɪvəbl] *adj* impardonnable. ◆ **unforgivably** *adv* impardonnablement. ◆ **unforgiving** *adj* implacable.

unformed ['ʌn'fɔ:md] *adj* informe.

unforthcoming ['ʌnfɔ:θ'kʌmɪŋ] *adj* réticent.

unfortunate [ʌn'fɔ:tʃnɪt] **1** *adj (gen)* malheureux (*that* que + *subj*); *circumstances* triste; *event* fâcheux. **how** ~! quel dommage!; **he has been** ~ il n'a pas eu de chance. **2** *n* malheureux *m*, -euse *f*. ◆ **unfortunately** *adv* malheureusement.

unfounded ['ʌn'faʊndɪd] *adj* sans fondement.

unframed ['ʌn'freɪmd] *adj picture* sans cadre.

unfreeze ['ʌn'fri:z] *pret* **unfroze** *ptp* **unfrozen** *vt* dégeler; *(Econ, Fin)* débloquer.

unfriendly ['ʌn'frendlɪ] *adj person, reception* froid; *attitude, behaviour, remark* inamical. **to be** ~ **towards sb** manifester de la froideur à qn. ◆ **unfriendliness** *n* froideur *f* (*towards* envers).

unfulfilled ['ʌnfʊl'fɪld] *adj promise* non tenu; *ambition, prophecy* non réalisé; *desire* insatisfait; *condition* non rempli. *[person]* **to feel** ~ se sentir frustré.

unfurl [ʌn'fɜ:l] *vt* déployer.

unfurnished ['ʌn'fɜ:nɪʃt] *adj* non meublé.

ungainly [ʌn'geɪnlɪ] *adj* gauche, disgracieux.

un-get-at-able * ['ʌnget'ætəbl] *adj* inaccessible.

ungodly [ʌn'gɒdlɪ] *adj* impie. *(fig)* ~ **hour** * heure *f* indue.

ungovernable [ʌn'gʌv(ə)nəbl] *adj country* ingouvernable; *passion* irrépressible.

ungracious ['ʌn'greɪʃəs] *adj* peu gracieux. ◆ **ungraciously** *adv* avec mauvaise grâce.

ungrammatical ['ʌngrə'mætɪk(ə)l] *adj* incorrect, non grammatical. ◆ **ungrammatically** *adv* incorrectement.

ungrateful [ʌn'greɪtfʊ'l] *adj* ingrat (*towards* envers). ◆ **ungratefully** *adv* avec ingratitude.

ungrudging ['ʌn'grʌdʒɪŋ] *adj help* donné sans compter; *praise* très sincère. ◆ **ungrudgingly** *adv give* généreusement; *help* de bon cœur.

unguarded ['ʌn'gɑːdɪd] *adj (Mil etc)* sans surveillance; *(fig) remark* irréfléchi. **in an ~ moment** dans un moment d'inattention.

unhappy [ʌn'hæpɪ] *adj person (sad)* malheureux, triste; *(ill-pleased)* mécontent; *(worried)* inquiet; *(unfortunate)* malchanceux; *childhood, remark, coincidence* malheureux; *situation* regrettable; *circumstances* triste. **I feel ~ about it** cela m'inquiète. ◆ **unhappily** *adv (miserably)* d'un air malheureux; *(unfortunately)* malheureusement. ◆ **unhappiness** *n* tristesse *f*.

unharmed ['ʌn'hɑːmd] *adj person* indemne; *thing* intact.

unhealthy [ʌn'helθɪ] *adj person* maladif; *place, habit, curiosity* malsain.

unheard-of ['ʌn'hɜːdɒv] *adj* inouï.

unhedged ['ʌn'hedʒd] *adj (esp US)* hasardeux.

unheeded ['ʌn'hiːdɪd] *adj (ignored)* négligé; *(unnoticed)* inaperçu. **it went ~** on n'y a pas prêté attention.

unhelpful ['ʌn'helpfʊ'l] *adj person* peu obligeant; *thing* qui n'aide guère. **I found that very ~** ça ne m'a pas aidé du tout.

unhesitating [ʌn'hezɪteɪtɪŋ] *adj reply, reaction* immédiat; *person* qui n'hésite pas. ◆ **unhesitatingly** *adv* sans hésitation.

unhindered ['ʌn'hɪndəd] *adj* sans encombre.

unhinged ['ʌnhɪndʒd] *adj* déséquilibré, dingue *.

unholy [ʌn'həʊlɪ] *adj* impie; *(* fig)* impossible *. **~ hour** * heure indue.

unhook ['ʌn'hʊk] *vt* décrocher (*from* de).

unhoped-for [ʌn'həʊptfɔːʳ] *adj* inespéré.

unhurried ['ʌn'hʌrɪd] *adj movement* lent; *reflection* mûr *(before n)*; *journey/meal etc* fait/pris *etc* sans se presser. ◆ **unhurriedly** *adv* sans se presser.

unhurt ['ʌn'hɜːt] *adj* indemne, sain et sauf.

unhygienic ['ʌnhaɪ'dʒiːnɪk] *adj* non hygiénique.

unicorn ['juːnɪkɔːn] *n* licorne *f*.

unidentified ['ʌnaɪ'dentɪfaɪd] *adj (gen)* non identifié. **~ flying object** *(abbr* **UFO***)* objet *m* volant non identifié *(abbr* O.V.N.I. *m)*.

uniform ['juːnɪfɔːm] **1** *n* uniforme *m*. **in ~** en uniforme; **in full ~** en grand uniforme; **out of ~** en civil. **2** *adj length* uniforme; *colour* uni; *temperature* constant. ◆ **uniformed** *adj policeman etc* en tenue; *organization* qui porte un uniforme. ◆ **uniformity** *n* uniformité *f*. ◆ **uniformly** *adv* uniformément.

unify ['juːnɪfaɪ] *vt* unifier. ◆ **unification** *n* unification *f*.

unilateral ['juːnɪ'læt(ə)r(ə)l] *adj* unilatéral. ◆ **unilaterally** *adv* unilatéralement.

unimaginable [ˌʌnɪ'mædʒ(ɪ)nəbl] *adj* inimaginable. ◆ **unimaginative** *adj* qui manque d'imagination. ◆ **unimaginatively** *adv* sans imagination.

unimpaired ['ʌnɪm'pɛəd] *adj (gen)* aussi bon qu'auparavant; *quality* non diminué.

unimportant ['ʌnɪm'pɔːtənt] *adj* sans importance.

unimpressed ['ʌnɪm'prest] *adj (gen)* peu impressionné (*by* par); *(unconvinced)* peu convaincu (*by* par). **I was ~** ça ne m'a pas impressionné.

uninformative ['ʌnɪn'fɔːmətɪv] *adj report* qui n'apprend rien.

uninhabitable ['ʌnɪn'hæbɪtəbl] *adj* inhabitable. ◆ **uninhabited** *adj* inhabité.

uninhibited ['ʌnɪn'hɪbɪtɪd] *adj person* sans inhibitions; *emotion* non refréné; *dance* sans retenue.

uninitiated ['ʌnɪ'nɪʃɪeɪtɪd] *npl (fig)* **the ~** les non-initiés *mpl*.

uninjured ['ʌn'ɪn(d)ʒəd] *adj* indemne, sain et sauf.

uninspired ['ʌnɪn'spaɪəd] *adj* qui manque d'inspiration. ◆ **uninspiring** *adj* qui n'est guère inspirant.

unintelligent ['ʌnɪn'telɪdʒənt] *adj* inintelligent.

unintelligible ['ʌnɪn'telɪdʒɪbl] *adj* inintelligible. ◆ **unintelligibly** *adv* inintelligiblement.

unintentional ['ʌnɪn'tenʃənl] *adj* involontaire. **it was quite ~** ce n'était pas fait exprès. ◆ **unintentionally** *adv* involontairement, sans le faire exprès.

uninterested [ʌn'ɪntrɪstɪd] *adj* indifférent (*in* à). ◆ **uninteresting** *adj book, activity* inintéressant; *person* ennuyeux; *offer* non intéressant.

uninterrupted ['ʌnˌɪntə'rʌptɪd] *adj* ininterrompu. ◆ **uninterruptedly** *adv* sans interruption.

uninvited ['ʌnɪn'vaɪtɪd] *adj*: **to arrive ~** arriver sans invitation; **to do sth ~** faire qch sans y avoir été invité.

union ['juːnjən] **1** *n (gen)* union *f*; *(also* **trade ~**, *(US)* **labor ~***)* syndicat *m*. *(US)* **the U~** les États-Unis *mpl*; **U~ of Soviet Socialist Republics** *(abbr* **USSR***)* Union des républiques socialistes soviétiques *(abbr* U.R.S.S. *f)*. **2** *adj* (**a**) *(Ind) card, leader, movement* syndical; *headquarters* du syndicat; *(US) factory* syndiqué. **~ member** membre *m* du syndicat; *(US)* **~ shop** atelier *m* d'ouvriers syndiqués. (**b**) **U~ Jack** *drapeau du Royaume-Uni.* ◆ **unionism** *n (trade unionism)* syndicalisme *m*. ◆ **unionist** *n* (**a**) *(trade unionist)* syndicaliste *mf*; **the militant ~ists** les militants *mpl* syndicaux; (**b**) *(Pol: Ir etc)* unioniste *mf*. ◆ **unionize** *vt (Ind)* syndiquer.

unique [juː'niːk] *adj* unique. ◆ **uniquely** *adv* exceptionnellement. ◆ **uniqueness** *n* caractère *m* unique.

unisex ['juːnɪseks] *adj* unisexe.

unison ['juːnɪzn] *n*: **in ~** *(Mus)* à l'unisson *m*; *(gen)* en chœur.

unit ['juːnɪt] **1** *n* (**a**) *(gen, Elec, Math, Mil etc)* unité *f*. **administrative/linguistic/monetary ~** unité administrative/linguistique/monétaire; **~ of length** unité de longueur. (**b**) *(section)* groupe *m*; *[furniture]* élément *m*. **compressor ~** groupe compresseur; **kitchen ~** élément de cuisine; **sink ~** bloc-évier *m*. (**c**) *(building(s))* locaux *mpl; (offices)* bureaux *mpl; (for engineering)* bloc *m; (for activity)* centre *m; (looking after public)* service *m*. **assembly ~** bloc de montage. (**d**) *(people)* unité; *(in firm)* service. **research ~** unité de recherches. **2** *adj* (**a**) *price* unitaire. **~ trust** ≃ fond *m* commun de placement. (**b**) **~ furniture** mobilier *m* par éléments.

unite [juː'naɪt] **1** *vt (join) countries etc* unir (*A with B* A à B); *(unify) one country etc* unifier. **2** *vi (join together)* s'unir (*with sth* à qch; *with sb* à *or* avec qn; *against* contre; *in doing, to do* pour faire); *[companies]* fusionner; *(become united) [party]* s'unifier. ◆ **united** *adj (gen)* uni; *(unified)* unifié; *front* uni; *efforts* conjugué; **U~d Arab Emirates** Émirats *mpl* arabes unis; **U~d Kingdom** Royaume-Uni *m*; **U~d Nations Organization** *(abbr* **UN** *or* **UNO***)* Organisation *f* des Nations unies *(abbr* O.N.U. *f)*; **U~d States of America** *(abbr* **US** *or* **USA***)* États-Unis *mpl*. ◆ **unity** ['juːnɪtɪ] *n* unité *f*; *(fig)* **in unity** en harmonie *f* (*with* avec).

universe ['juːnɪvɜːs] *n* univers *m*. ◆ **universal** *adj* universel; **she's a universal favourite** tout le monde l'aime; **to make sth universal** universaliser qch; **universal joint** joint *m* de cardan. ◆ **universally** *adv* universellement.

university [ˌjuːnɪ'vɜːsɪtɪ] **1** *n* université *f*. **to be at/go to ~** être/aller à l'université; **to study at ~** faire des études universitaires. **2** *adj degree, town, library* universitaire; *professor, student* d'université. **he has a ~ education** il a fait des études universitaires.

unjust ['ʌn'dʒʌst] *adj* injuste (*to* envers). ◆ **unjustly** *adv* injustement.

unjustifiable [ʌn'dʒʌstɪfaɪəbl] *adj* injustifiable. ◆ **unjustifiably** *adv* sans justification. ◆ **unjustified** *adj* injustifié.

unkempt ['ʌn'kem(p)t] *adj (gen)* débraillé; *hair* mal peigné.

unkind [ʌn'kaɪnd] *adj person, behaviour* peu aimable, pas gentil (*to sb* avec qn); *(stronger)* méchant (*to sb* avec qn); *fate* cruel. ◆ **unkindly** *adv (gen)* méchamment; **don't take it ~ly if...** ne soyez pas offensé si... ◆ **unkindness** *n* manque *m* de gentillesse; méchanceté *f*; **an ~ness** une méchanceté.

unknown ['ʌn'nəʊn] **1** *adj* inconnu. **it was ~ to him** cela lui était inconnu, il l'ignorait; **~ to him, the plane had crashed** l'avion s'était écrasé, ce qu'il ignorait; **she did it quite ~ to him** elle l'a fait à son insu; **substance ~ to science** substance inconnue de la science; *(Math, fig)* **~ quantity** inconnue *f*; **the U~ Soldier** *or* **Warrior** le Soldat inconnu. **2** *n* (**a**) *(gen)* **the ~** l'inconnu *m*; *(Math, fig)* **many ~s** de nombreuses inconnues *fpl*. (**b**) *(person)* inconnu(e) *m(f)*. ◆ **unknowable** *adj* inconnaissable. ◆ **unknowing** *adj* inconscient. ◆ **unknowingly** *adv* inconsciemment.

unladen ['ʌn'leɪdn] *adj weight* à vide.

unladylike ['ʌn'leɪdɪlaɪk] *adj girl* mal élevée. **it's ~ to yawn** une jeune fille bien élevée ne bâille pas.

unlawful ['ʌn'lɔːfʊ'l] *adj* illégal, illicite. ◆ **unlawfully** *adv* illégalement.

unleaded ['ʌn'ledɪd] *adj* sans plomb.

unleavened ['ʌn'levnd] *adj* azyme *(Rel)*.

unless [ən'les] *conj* à moins que... (ne) + *subj*, à moins de + *infin*. **take it, ~ you can find another** prenez-le, à moins que vous (n')en trouviez un autre *or* à moins d'en trouver un autre; **~ I am mistaken** si je ne me trompe; **~ I hear to the contrary** sauf contrordre; **~ otherwise stated** sauf indication contraire.

unlicensed ['ʌn'laɪs(ə)nst] *adj activity* illicite; *vehicle* sans vignette; *hotel etc* qui n'a pas de licence de débit de boissons.

unlike ['ʌn'laɪk] **1** *adj* dissemblable, différent. **they are quite ~** ils ne se ressemblent pas du tout. **2** *prep* à la différence de. **~ his brother, he...** à la différence de son frère, il...; **it's quite ~ him to do that** ça ne lui ressemble pas de faire cela; **how ~ him!** on ne s'attendait pas à ça de sa part; **it is quite ~ mine** ça n'est pas du tout comme le mien.

unlikeable ['ʌn'laɪkəbl] *adj person* peu sympathique; *thing* peu agréable.

unlikely [ʌn'laɪklɪ] *adj happening, outcome* peu probable; *explanation* peu plausible. **it is ~ that she will come, she is ~ to come** il est peu probable qu'elle vienne, il y a peu de chances pour qu'elle vienne; **she is ~ to succeed** elle a peu de chances de réussir; **that is ~ to happen** cela ne risque guère d'arriver; **in the ~ event of his accepting** dans le cas fort improbable où il accepterait. ◆ **unlikelihood** *n* improbabilité *f*.

unlimited [ʌn'lɪmɪtɪd] *adj* illimité.

unlined ['ʌn'laɪnd] *adj garment* sans doublure; *face* sans rides; *paper* non réglé.

unlisted ['ʌn'lɪstɪd] *adj (US Telec)* qui est sur la liste rouge.

unlit ['ʌn'lɪt] *adj lamp* non allumé; *road* non éclairé; *vehicle* sans feux.

unload ['ʌn'ləʊd] **1** *vt (gen)* décharger; *(get rid of)* se débarrasser de; *shares* se défaire de. **to ~ sth onto sb** se décharger de qch sur qn. **2** *vi* être déchargé. ◆ **unloaded** *adj gun* qui n'est pas chargé. ◆ **unloading** *n* déchargement *m*.

unlock ['ʌn'lɒk] *vt* ouvrir. **it is ~ed** ce n'est pas fermé à clef.

unlooked-for [ʌn'lʊktfɔːʳ] *adj* inattendu.

unlovable ['ʌn'lʌvəbl] *adj* peu attachant.

unlucky [ʌn'lʌkɪ] *adj person* malchanceux; *coincidence, event* malencontreux; *choice, decision* malheureux; *day* de malchance; *omen* néfaste; *colour, number* qui porte malheur. **he's ~** il n'a pas de chance; **he tried to get a seat but he was ~** il a essayé d'avoir une place mais il n'y est pas arrivé; **he was ~ enough to meet her** il a eu la malchance de la rencontrer; **it is ~ to do that** ça porte malheur de faire ça. ◆ **unluckily** *adv* malheureusement (*for sb* pour qn). ◆ **unluckiness** *n* manque *m* de chance.

unmade ['ʌn'meɪd] *adj bed* défait.

unmanageable [ʌn'mænɪdʒəbl] *adj vehicle, parcel, size* peu maniable; *animal* indocile; *person* impossible; *hair* rebelle.

unmanned ['ʌn'mænd] *adj spacecraft, flight* non habité. **it was left ~** il n'y avait personne là.

unmarked ['ʌn'mɑːkt] *adj (unscratched etc)* sans marque; *(unnamed)* non marqué; *(uncorrected) essay* non corrigé; *police car* banalisé.

unmarried ['ʌn'mærɪd] *adj* célibataire, qui n'est pas marié. **~ mother** mère *f* célibataire.

unmask ['ʌn'mɑːsk] *vt (lit, fig)* démasquer.

unmentionable [ʌn'menʃnəbl] *adj* dont il ne faut pas parler.

unmerciful [ʌn'mɜːsɪf(ʊ)l] *adj* impitoyable (*towards* pour). ◆ **unmercifully** *adv* impitoyablement.

unmistakable ['ʌnmɪs'teɪkəbl] *adj evidence, sympathy* indubitable; *voice, walk* qu'on ne peut pas ne pas reconnaître. **it is quite ~** on ne peut pas se tromper. ◆ **unmistakably** *adv* manifestement, sans aucun doute.

unmitigated [ʌn'mɪtɪgeɪtɪd] *adj terror, admiration* absolu; *folly* pur; *disaster* total; *scoundrel, liar* fieffé *(before n)*.

unmixed ['ʌn'mɪkst] *adj* pur, sans mélange.

unmounted ['ʌn'maʊntɪd] *adj gem, picture* non monté.

unmoved ['ʌn'muːvd] *adj* indifférent (*by* à). **he was ~** ça ne l'a pas ému, ça l'a laissé indifférent.

unmusical ['ʌn'mjuːzɪk(ə)l] *adj sound* peu mélodieux; *person* peu musicien.

unnamed ['ʌn'neɪmd] *adj person* anonyme; *thing* innommé; *(unlabelled)* non marqué.

unnatural [ʌn'nætʃr(ə)l] *adj* anormal; *habit, vice, love* contre nature; *(affected)* qui manque de naturel. **it is ~ for her to do that** il n'est pas normal *or* naturel qu'elle fasse cela. ◆ **unnaturally** *adv* anormalement; *(affectedly)* d'une manière affectée; **not ~ly** naturellement.

unnecessary [ʌn'nesɪs(ə)rɪ] *adj (useless)* inutile (*to do* de faire); *(superfluous)* superflu. **it is ~ for you to come** il n'est pas nécessaire *or* il est inutile que vous veniez *(subj)*. ◆ **unnecessarily** *adv do, say* inutilement; *strict* sans nécessité.

unnerve ['ʌn'nɜːv] *vt* démoraliser; *(less strong)* déconcerter. ◆ **unnerving** *adj* démoralisant; déconcertant.

unnoticed ['ʌn'nəʊtɪst] *adj* inaperçu. **to go ~** passer inaperçu.

unnumbered ['ʌn'nʌmbəd] *adj (lit)* sans numéro.

unobjectionable ['ʌnəb'dʒekʃnəbl] *adj thing* acceptable; *person* à qui l'on ne peut rien reprocher.

unobserved *adj*: **to escape ~** s'échapper sans être vu; **to go ~** passer inaperçu.

unobstructed ['ʌnəb'strʌktɪd] *adj pipe* non bouché; *road* dégagé. **the driver has an ~ view** le conducteur a une excellente visibilité.

unobtainable ['ʌnəb'teɪnəbl] *adj* impossible à obtenir.

unobtrusive ['ʌnəb'truːsɪv] *adj* discret. ◆ **unobtrusively** *adv* discrètement.

unoccupied ['ʌn'ɒkjʊpaɪd] *adj person* inoccupé, qui n'a rien à faire; *house* inoccupé; *seat, (Mil) zone* libre; *post* vacant.

unofficial ['ʌnə'fɪʃ(ə)l] *adj report etc* officieux; *visit* privé. **in an ~ capacity** à titre privé; *(Ind)* **~ strike** grève *f* sauvage. ◆ **unofficially** *adv* officieusement.

unopened ['ʌn'əʊp(ə)nd] *adj* qui n'a pas été ouvert. **to remain ~** rester fermé.

unopposed ['ʌnə'pəʊzd] *adj* sans opposition.

unorganized ['ʌn'ɔ:gənaɪzd] *adj* inorganisé; *(badly organized)* mal organisé; *person* qui ne sait pas s'organiser.

unoriginal ['ʌnə'rɪdʒɪn(ə)l] *adj* qui manque d'originalité.

unorthodox ['ʌn'ɔ:θədɒks] *adj* peu orthodoxe.

unostentatious ['ʌn,ɒstən'teɪʃəs] *adj* sans ostentation, simple. ◆ **unostentatiously** *adv* sans ostentation.

unpack ['ʌn'pæk] **1** *vt suitcase* défaire; *belongings* déballer. **2** *vi* déballer ses affaires. ◆ **unpacking** *n* déballage *m*; **to do one's ~ing** déballer ses affaires.

unpaid ['ʌn'peɪd] *adj bill* impayé; *debt* non acquitté; *work, helper* non rétribué; *leave* non payé. **to work ~** travailler gratuitement.

unpalatable [ʌn'pælɪtəbl] *adj food* qui n'a pas bon goût; *fact, truth* désagréable.

unparalleled [ʌn'pærəleld] *adj* sans égal.

unpardonable [ʌn'pɑ:dnəbl] *adj* impardonnable.

unpatriotic ['ʌn,pætrɪ'ɒtɪk] *adj person* peu patriote; *thing* antipatriotique.

unperturbed ['ʌnpə'tɜ:bd] *adj (gen)* imperturbable. **~ by** non déconcerté par.

unpick ['ʌn'pɪk] *vt seam* défaire.

unpin ['ʌn'pɪn] *vt* détacher (*from* de).

unplaced ['ʌn'pleɪst] *adj horse* non placé; *athlete* non classé.

unplanned ['ʌn'plænd] *adj occurrence* imprévu; *baby* non prévu.

unpleasant [ʌn'pleznt] *adj (gen)* désagréable; *person, remark* désagréable (*to sb* avec qn), déplaisant; *house, town* déplaisant. **he had an ~ time** il a passé de mauvais moments. ◆ **unpleasantly** *adv reply* désagréablement; *behave, smile* de façon déplaisante; **~ly close** un peu trop près. ◆ **unpleasantness** *n* caractère *m* désagréable *or* déplaisant; *(quarrelling)* **a lot of ~ness** beaucoup de frictions *fpl*.

unplug ['ʌn'plʌg] *vt (Elec)* débrancher.

unpolished ['ʌn'pɒlɪʃt] *adj furniture, floor, shoes* non ciré; *diamond* non poli; *(fig) person* fruste; *manners* peu raffiné; *style* qui manque de poli.

unpolluted ['ʌnpə'lu:tɪd] *adj* non pollué.

unpopular ['ʌn'pɒpjʊlə^r] *adj (gen)* impopulaire. **to be ~ with sb** *[person]* être impopulaire auprès de qn; *[decision etc]* être impopulaire chez qn; **to make o.s. ~** se rendre impopulaire. ◆ **unpopularity** *n* impopularité *f*.

unpractical ['ʌn'præktɪk(ə)l] *adj thing* peu pratique; *suggestion* qui n'est pas pratique; *person* qui manque de sens pratique.

unprecedented [ʌn'presɪd(ə)ntɪd] *adj* sans précédent.

unpredictable ['ʌnprɪ'dɪktəbl] *adj (gen)* imprévisible; *weather* incertain. **he is quite ~** on ne sait jamais ce qu'il va faire.

unprejudiced [ʌn'predʒʊdɪst] *adj* impartial.

unprepared ['ʌnprɪ'pɛəd] *adj speech etc* improvisé. **I was ~ for the exam** je n'avais pas suffisamment préparé l'examen; *(fig)* **he was quite ~ for it** cela l'a pris au dépourvu; **he began it quite ~** il l'a commencé sans y être préparé.

unprepossessing ['ʌn,pri:pə'zesɪŋ] *adj* qui fait mauvaise impression.

unpretentious ['ʌnprɪ'tenʃəs] *adj* sans prétention.

unprincipled [ʌn'prɪnsɪpld] *adj* sans scrupules.

unprintable ['ʌn'prɪntəbl] *adj (lit)* impubliable; *(fig)* que l'on n'oserait pas répéter.

unproductive ['ʌnprə'dʌktɪv] *adj* improductif.

unprofessional ['ʌnprə'feʃənl] *adj* contraire au code professionnel.

unprofitable [,ʌn'prɒfɪtəbl] *adj* peu rentable; *job* peu lucratif. ◆ **unprofitably** *adv* sans profit.

unpromising [,ʌn'prɒmɪsɪŋ] *adj* peu prometteur.

unpronounceable [,ʌnprə'naʊnsəbl] *adj* imprononçable.

unprotected [,ʌnprə'tektɪd] *adj person, town* sans défense; *(exposed to elements)* découvert.

unprovided-for [,ʌnprə'vaɪdɪdfɔ:^r] *adj person* sans ressources.

unprovoked [,ʌnprə'vəʊkt] *adj* sans provocation.

unpublished [,ʌn'pʌblɪʃt] *adj* inédit. ◆ **unpublishable** *adj* impubliable.

unpunctual ['ʌn'pʌŋ(k)tjʊəl] *adj* peu ponctuel.

unpunished ['ʌn'pʌnɪʃt] *adj* impuni. **to go ~** rester impuni.

unqualified ['ʌn'kwɒlɪfaɪd] *adj* (**a**) *(gen)* non qualifié (*to do* pour faire); *(in professions)* non diplômé. **no ~ person will be considered** les candidats n'ayant pas les diplômes requis ne seront pas considérés. (**b**) *statement, promise, approval etc* inconditionnel; *praise* sans réserve; *success* fou; (*) *idiot* fini; *rogue, liar* fieffé *(before n)*.

unquestionable [ʌn'kwestʃənəbl] *adj fact* incontestable; *honesty* certain. ◆ **unquestionably** *adv* incontestablement. ◆ **unquestioned** *adj* incontesté. ◆ **unquestioning** *adj acceptance* inconditionnel; *belief, obedience* aveugle.

unravel [ʌn'ræv(ə)l] **1** *vt material* effilocher; *knitting* défaire; *threads* démêler; *(fig) mystery* débrouiller; *plot* dénouer. **2** *vi* s'effilocher.

unreadable ['ʌn'ri:dəbl] *adj* illisible.

unready ['ʌn'redɪ] *adj* mal préparé (*for sth* pour qch). ◆ **unreadiness** *n* impréparation *f*.

unreal ['ʌn'rɪəl] *adj* irréel. ◆ **unrealistic** *adj* peu réaliste. ◆ **unreality** *n* irréalité *f*.

unreasonable [ʌn'ri:znəbl] *adj (gen)* qui n'est pas raisonnable, déraisonnable; *demand, length* excessif; *price* exagéré. **~ hour** heure *f* indue; **it is ~ to do** on ne peut pas raisonnablement faire. ◆ **unreasonableness** *n [person]* attitude *f* déraisonnable. ◆ **unreasonably** *adv* déraisonnablement; excessivement; exagérément. ◆ **unreasoning** *adj* irraisonné.

unrecognizable ['ʌn'rekəgnaɪzəbl] *adj* méconnaissable, qui n'est pas reconnaissable. ◆ **unrecognized** *adj talent etc* méconnu; *(Pol) régime etc* non reconnu; **to do sth unrecognized** faire qch sans être reconnu.

unrecorded ['ʌnrɪ'kɔ:dɪd] *adj event etc* non mentionné.

unrefined ['ʌnrɪ'faɪnd] *adj substance* non raffiné; *person* fruste.

unreformed ['ʌnrɪ'fɔ:md] *adj person* non amendé; *institution* non réformé.

unrehearsed ['ʌnrɪ'hɜ:st] *adj speech etc* improvisé; *incident* inattendu.

unrelated ['ʌnrɪ'leɪtɪd] *adj*: **to be ~ to** *[facts, events]* n'avoir aucun rapport avec; *[person]* n'avoir aucun lien de parenté avec.

unrelenting ['ʌnrɪ'lentɪŋ] *adj person* implacable; *persecution* acharné.

unreliable ['ʌnrɪ'laɪəbl] *adj person* sur qui on ne peut pas compter; *firm* qui n'est pas sérieux; *car, machine, map* peu fiable; *news* sujet à caution;

source of information douteux. **my watch is** ~ je ne peux pas me fier à ma montre. ◆ **unreliability** *n [person etc]* manque *m* de sérieux; *[machine]* manque de fiabilité.

unrelieved [ˈʌnrɪˈliːvd] *adj pain, gloom* constant; *boredom* mortel; *grey, black etc* uniforme.

unremarkable [ˈʌnrɪˈmɑːkəbl] *adj* médiocre.

unremitting [ˈʌnrɪˈmɪtɪŋ] *adj kindness* inlassable; *hatred* opiniâtre.

unremunerative [ˈʌnrɪˈmjuːn(ə)rətɪv] *adj* peu rémunérateur, mal payé.

unrepeatable [ˈʌnrɪˈpiːtəbl] *adj offer, bargain* exceptionnel; *comment* que l'on n'ose pas répéter.

unrepentant [ˈʌnrɪˈpentənt] *adj* impénitent.

unrepresentative [ˈʌnˌreprɪˈzentətɪv] *adj* peu représentatif (*of* de).

unrequited [ˈʌnrɪˈkwaɪtɪd] *adj* non partagé.

unreserved [ˈʌnrɪˈzɜːvd] *adj seat* non réservé; *admiration* sans réserve. ◆ **unreservedly** *adv* sans réserve.

unresponsive [ˈʌnrɪsˈpɒnsɪv] *adj* qui ne réagit pas. ~ **to** insensible à.

unrest [ʌnˈrest] *n* agitation *f*; *(stronger)* troubles *mpl*.

unrestricted [ˈʌnrɪˈstrɪktɪd] *adj time, power* illimité; *access* libre.

unrewarded [ˈʌnrɪˈwɔːdɪd] *adj [efforts etc]* **to go** ~ rester sans récompense. ◆ **unrewarding** *adj* ingrat; *(financially)* peu rémunérateur.

unripe [ˈʌnˈraɪp] *adj* vert, qui n'est pas mûr.

unrivalled, *(US)* **unrivaled** [ʌnˈraɪv(ə)ld] *adj* sans égal.

unroll [ˈʌnˈrəʊl] **1** *vt* dérouler. **2** *vi* se dérouler.

unromantic [ˈʌnrəˈmæntɪk] *adj* peu romantique.

unruffled [ˈʌnˈrʌfld] *adj hair, water* lisse; *person* calme.

unruled [ˈʌnˈruːld] *adj paper* uni, non réglé.

unruly [ʌnˈruːlɪ] *adj* indiscipliné.

unsaddle [ˈʌnˈsædl] *vt* desseller.

unsafe [ˈʌnˈseɪf] *adj* (**a**) *(dangerous) machine, bridge, toy* dangereux; *journey* périlleux; *method* peu sûr. ~ **to eat** *or* **drink** *(gen)* impropre à la consommation; *water* non potable. (**b**) *(in danger)* en danger. **to feel** ~ ne pas se sentir en sécurité.

unsaid [ˈʌnˈsed] *adj*: **to leave sth** ~ passer qch sous silence.

unsaleable [ˈʌnˈseɪləbl] *adj* invendable.

unsatisfactory [ˈʌnˌsætɪsˈfækt(ə)rɪ] *adj* peu satisfaisant, qui laisse à désirer. ◆ **unsatisfied** *adj person, desire* insatisfait (*with* de); *need, demand, appetite* non satisfait; *(unconvinced)* non convaincu. ◆ **unsatisfying** *adj result* peu satisfaisant; *work* ingrat; *food* peu nourrissant.

unsaturated [ˈʌnˈsætʃəreɪtɪd] *adj (Chem)* non saturé.

unsavoury, *(US)* **unsavory** [ˈʌnˈseɪv(ə)rɪ] *adj food* mauvais au goût; *(fig) person, district* peu recommandable; *reputation* équivoque; *subject* plutôt répugnant. **an** ~ **business** une sale affaire.

unsay [ˈʌnˈse(ɪ)] *pret, ptp* **unsaid** *vt* se dédire de.

unscathed [ˈʌnˈskeɪðd] *adj* indemne.

unscientific [ˈʌnˌsaɪənˈtɪfɪk] *adj* peu scientifique.

unscratched [ˈʌnˈskrætʃt] *adj surface* intact; *person* indemne.

unscrew [ˈʌnˈskruː] **1** *vt* dévisser. **2** *vi* se dévisser.

unscripted [ˈʌnˈskrɪptɪd] *adj (Rad, TV)* improvisé.

unscrupulous [ʌnˈskruːpjʊləs] *adj person* dénué de scrupules; *act* malhonnête. ◆ **unscrupulously** *adv* sans scrupules. ◆ **unscrupulousness** *n* manque *m* de scrupules; malhonnêteté *f*.

unseasonable [ʌnˈsiːznəbl] *adj fruit etc* hors de saison; *weather* qui n'est pas de saison. ◆ **unseasonably** *adv*: **unseasonably warm** chaud pour la saison.

unseasoned [ˈʌnˈsiːznd] *adj timber* vert; *food* non assaisonné.

unseat [ˈʌnˈsiːt] *vt rider* désarçonner.

unseemly [ʌnˈsiːmlɪ] *adj* inconvenant.

unseen [ˈʌnˈsiːn] *adj* inaperçu. **to escape** ~ s'échapper sans être vu; ~ **translation** version *f (sans préparation)*.

unselfconscious [ˈʌnˌselfˈkɒnʃəs] *adj* naturel. ◆ **unselfconsciously** *adv* sans la moindre gêne.

unselfish [ˈʌnˈselfɪʃ] *adj person* généreux; *act* désintéressé. ◆ **unselfishly** *adv* sans penser à soi. ◆ **unselfishness** *n* générosité *f*.

unserviceable [ˈʌnˈsɜːvɪsəbl] *adj* inutilisable.

unsettle [ˈʌnˈsetl] *vt* perturber. ◆ **unsettled** *adj person* perturbé; *weather, future* incertain; *stomach* dérangé; **he feels** ~**d** il n'est pas bien dans sa peau. ◆ **unsettling** *adj news* inquiétant; *effect* perturbateur.

unshakeable [ˈʌnˈʃeɪkəbl] *adj* inébranlable. ◆ **unshaken** *adj resolve* inébranlable; *person* non déconcerté.

unshaven [ˈʌnˈʃeɪvn] *adj* non rasé.

unshrinkable [ˈʌnˈʃrɪŋkəbl] *adj* irrétrécissable.

unsightly [ʌnˈsaɪtlɪ] *adj* disgracieux, laid.

unsinkable [ˈʌnˈsɪŋkəbl] *adj* insubmersible.

unskilful, *(US)* **unskillful** [ˈʌnˈskɪlfʊˈl] *adj (clumsy)* maladroit; *(inexpert)* malhabile. ◆ **unskil(l)fully** *adv* avec maladresse; malhabilement. ◆ **unskilled** *adj (gen)* inexpérimenté; *(Ind) work* de manœuvre; **unskilled worker** manœuvre *m*.

unsociable [ʌnˈsəʊʃəbl] *adj* insociable. **I'm feeling** ~ je n'ai guère envie de voir des gens.

unsocial [ʌnˈsəʊʃ(ə)l] *adj (Ind)* **to work** ~ **hours** travailler en dehors des heures normales.

unsold [ˈʌnˈsəʊld] *adj* invendu.

unsolved [ˈʌnˈsɒlvd] *adj mystery* non résolu; *crossword* non terminé.

unsophisticated [ˈʌnsəˈfɪstɪkeɪtɪd] *adj person* simple, naturel; *thing* simple.

unsound [ˈʌnˈsaʊnd] *adj timber* pourri; *structure, floor, bridge* en mauvais état; *organization, business* peu solide; *investment* peu sûr; *judgment, argument* peu valable; *policy, decision, advice* peu judicieux; *statesman, player* incompétent. *(Jur)* **of** ~ **mind** qui ne jouit pas de toutes ses facultés mentales.

unsparing [ʌnˈspɛərɪŋ] *adj* prodigue (*of* de). ◆ **unsparingly** *adv give* généreusement; *work* inlassablement.

unspeakable [ʌnˈspiːkəbl] *adj* indescriptible. ◆ **unspeakably** *adv (bad etc)* affreusement.

unspoiled [ˈʌnˈspɔɪld] *adj countryside, beauty* qui n'est pas défiguré; *style* naturel; *person* qui reste simple.

unspoken [ˈʌnˈspəʊk(ə)n] *adj thought* inexprimé; *approval* tacite.

unsporting [ˈʌnˈspɔːtɪŋ] *adj* déloyal. **that's very** ~ **of you** ce n'est pas très chic de votre part.

unstable [ˈʌnˈsteɪbl] *adj* instable.

unstamped [ˈʌnˈstæm(p)t] *adj letter* non affranchi.

unsteady [ˈʌnˈstedɪ] *adj ladder, structure* instable, branlant; *hand* tremblant; *voice* mal assuré; *step* chancelant; *rhythm* irrégulier. **to be** ~ **on one's feet** ne pas très bien tenir sur ses jambes; *(from drink)* tituber. ◆ **unsteadily** *adv walk* d'un pas chancelant; *say* d'une voix mal assurée.

unstick [ˈʌnˈstɪk] *pret, ptp* **unstuck** *vt* décoller. **to come unstuck** *[stamp etc]* se décoller; (*) *[plan]* tomber à l'eau *; *[person]* tomber sur un bec *.

unstinting [ʌnˈstɪntɪŋ] *adj praise* sans réserve; *generosity* sans bornes; *efforts* illimité.

unstressed [ˈʌnˈstrest] *adj* inaccentué.

unsubstantiated ['ʌnsəb'stænʃɪeɪtɪd] *adj accusation* non prouvé; *rumour* non confirmé.

unsuccessful ['ʌnsək'sesf(ʊ)l] *adj negotiation, attempt, visit* infructueux, qui est un échec; *candidate, marriage, outcome* malheureux; *application* non retenu; *writer, painter, book* qui n'a pas de succès; *firm* qui ne prospère pas. **to be ~** *(gen)* ne pas réussir (*in doing* à faire); *(Scol etc)* échouer (*in an exam* à un examen; *in maths* en maths); **I tried but I was ~** j'ai essayé mais sans succès; **after 3 ~ attempts** après avoir échoué 3 fois. ◆ **unsuccessfully** *adv* en vain, sans succès.

unsuitable ['ʌn'su:təbl] *adj (gen)* qui ne convient pas; *moment* inopportun; *colour, size* qui ne va pas; *action, example, device* peu approprié. **to be ~ for sth** *(gen)* ne pas convenir à qch; *[film, book]* ne pas être conseillé pour qch; **he is ~ for the post** ce n'est pas l'homme qu'il faut pour le poste. ◆ **unsuited** *adj person* inapte (*to* à); *thing* impropre (*to* à); **they are quite unsuited** ils ne sont pas compatibles.

unsupported ['ʌnsə'pɔ:tɪd] *adj structure, hypothesis* non soutenu; *statement* non confirmé; *mother, family* sans soutien financier.

unsure ['ʌn'ʃʊəʳ] *adj* incertain (*of, about* de). **to be ~ of o.s.** manquer d'assurance.

unsuspected ['ʌnsəs'pektɪd] *adj* insoupçonné. ◆ **unsuspecting** *adj* qui ne se doute de rien.

unsweetened ['ʌn'swi:tnd] *adj* sans sucre.

unswerving [ʌn'swɜ:vɪŋ] *adj (fig)* inébranlable.

unsympathetic ['ʌn,sɪmpə'θetɪk] *adj* indifférent (*to* à). ◆ **unsympathetically** *adv* froidement.

unsystematic ['ʌn,sɪstɪ'mætɪk] *adj* peu systématique. ◆ **unsystematically** *adv* sans système.

untangle ['ʌn'tæŋgl] *vt wool etc* démêler.

untapped ['ʌn'tæpt] *adj resources* inexploité.

untaxed ['ʌn'tækst] *adj goods* exempt de taxes; *income* non imposable.

unteachable ['ʌn'ti:tʃəbl] *adj person* à qui on ne peut rien apprendre.

untenable ['ʌn'tenəbl] *adj position* intenable.

untested ['ʌn'testɪd] *adj person, theory, method* qui n'a pas été mis à l'épreuve; *product, invention* qui n'a pas été essayé; *new drug* non encore expérimenté.

unthinkable [ʌn'θɪŋkəbl] *adj* impensable (*that* que + *subj*). ◆ **unthinking** *adj* irréfléchi. ◆ **unthinkingly** *adv* sans réfléchir.

untidy [ʌn'taɪdɪ] *adj person (in appearance)* dont les vêtements sont en désordre; *(habitually)* débraillé; *(in character)* désordonné; *appearance* négligé; *clothes* débraillé; *hair* mal peigné; *writing, work* brouillon; *room, desk* en désordre. ◆ **untidily** *adv work, live* sans ordre; *write, dress* sans soin. ◆ **untidiness** *n (in appearance)* débraillé *m*; *(in habits)* manque *m* d'ordre; *[room]* désordre *m*.

untie ['ʌn'taɪ] *vt knot, string, parcel* défaire; *prisoner, hands, bonds* détacher.

until [ən'tɪl] **1** *prep* jusqu'à. **~ such time as** *(in future)* jusqu'à ce que + *subj*; *(in past)* avant que + ne + *subj*; **from morning ~ night** du matin jusqu'au soir; **~ now** jusqu'ici; **~ then** jusque-là; **it won't be ready ~ tomorrow** ce ne sera pas prêt avant demain; **he didn't leave ~ the following day** il n'est parti que le lendemain; **I had heard nothing of it ~ 5 minutes ago** j'en ai seulement entendu parler il y a 5 minutes. **2** *conj (in future)* jusqu'à ce que + *subj*; *(in past)* avant que + ne + *subj*. **wait ~ I come** attendez que je vienne; **~ they built the new road** avant qu'ils ne fassent la nouvelle route; **~ they build the new road** en attendant qu'ils fassent la nouvelle route; **he won't come ~ you invite him** il ne viendra pas avant que vous ne l'invitiez *or* avant d'être invité; **do nothing ~ you get my letter/~ I come** ne faites rien avant d'avoir reçu ma lettre/avant que je n'arrive *(subj)*.

untimely [ʌn'taɪmlɪ] *adj spring, death* prématuré; *moment, arrival, remark* inopportun. **to come to an ~ end** *[person]* mourir prématurément; *[project]* être enterré prématurément.

untiring [ʌn'taɪərɪŋ] *adj* infatigable. ◆ **untiringly** *adv* infatigablement.

untold ['ʌn'təʊld] *adj amount, wealth* incalculable; *agony, delight* indescriptible.

untouchable [ʌn'tʌtʃəbl] *adj, n* intouchable *(mf)*. ◆ **untouched** *adj* (**a**) *(Comm)* **untouched by hand** sans manipulation directe; **he left his meal untouched** il n'a pas touché à son repas; (**b**) *(safe) person* indemne; *thing* intact; *(unaffected)* insensible (*by* à).

untoward [,ʌntə'wɔ:d] *adj* fâcheux.

untrained ['ʌn'treɪnd] *adj worker* qui n'a pas reçu de formation professionnelle; *animal* non dressé; *ear* inexercé.

untranslatable ['ʌntrænz'leɪtəbl] *adj* intraduisible.

untried ['ʌn'traɪd] *adj product, invention* qui n'a pas été essayé; *person, method* qui n'a pas été mis à l'épreuve.

untroubled ['ʌn'trʌbld] *adj* calme.

untrue ['ʌn'tru:] *adj (gen)* faux (*f* fausse); *lover etc* infidèle (*to* à). **it is ~ that** il est faux *or* il n'est pas vrai que + *subj*. ◆ **untruth** *n* contre-vérité *f*. ◆ **untruthful** *adj statement* mensonger; *person* menteur. ◆ **untruthfully** *adv* mensongèrement.

untrustworthy [,ʌn'trʌst,wɜ:ðɪ] *adj person* indigne de confiance; *source of information* douteux; *witness* récusable.

untwist ['ʌn'twɪst] *vt wire* détordre.

untypical ['ʌn'tɪpɪk(ə)l] peu typique (*of* de).

unusable ['ʌn'ju:zəbl] *adj* inutilisable. ◆ **unused** *adj* (**a**) ['ʌn'ju:zd] *(new)* neuf; *(not in use)* inutilisé; (**b**) ['ʌn'ju:st] **to be unused to (doing) sth** ne pas avoir l'habitude de (faire) qch.

unusual [ʌn'ju:ʒʊəl] *adj (rare)* peu commun, inhabituel; *(strange)* étrange, insolite; *talents, size* exceptionnel. **it is ~ for him to be early** il est rare qu'il arrive *(subj)* de bonne heure; **that's ~ for him!** ce n'est pas dans ses habitudes!; **that's ~!** ça n'arrive pas souvent! ◆ **unusually** *adv (more than normally for this person) happy, warm* exceptionnellement, anormalement; *(more than one normally finds) tall, gifted* exceptionnellement, extraordinairement; **~ly early** plus tôt que d'habitude.

unutterable [ʌn'ʌt(ə)rəbl] *adj joy, boredom* indescriptible; (*) *idiot, fool* fini.

unvarnished ['ʌn'vɑ:nɪʃt] *adj wood* non verni; *account, truth* pur et simple.

unvarying [ʌn'vɛərɪɪŋ] *adj* invariable, constant.

unveil [ʌn'veɪl] *vt* dévoiler. ◆ **unveiling** *n (ceremony)* inauguration *f*.

unventilated ['ʌn'ventɪleɪtɪd] *adj* sans ventilation.

unvoiced ['ʌn'vɔɪst] *adj opinion* inexprimé; *consonant* sourd.

unwaged ['ʌn'weɪdʒd] *npl (Admin)* **the ~** les sans-emploi, étudiants et retraités *mpl*.

unwanted ['ʌn'wɒntɪd] *adj clothing etc* superflu, dont on n'a pas besoin; *child* non désiré; *effect* non recherché.

unwarranted [ʌn'wɒr(ə)ntɪd] *adj* injustifié. ◆ **unwarrantable** *adj* injustifiable.

unwary [ʌn'wɛərɪ] *adj* imprudent.

unwearying [ʌn'wɪərɪɪŋ] *adj* inlassable.

unwelcome [ʌn'welkəm] *adj visitor, gift* importun; *news, delay, change* fâcheux. **they made us feel ~** ils nous ont mal accueillis.

unwell ['ʌn'wel] *adj* souffrant. **to feel ~** ne pas se sentir très bien.

unwholesome ['ʌn'həʊlsəm] *adj* malsain.

unwieldy [ʌn'wiːldɪ] *adj* difficile à manier.

unwilling ['ʌn'wɪlɪŋ] *adj*: **to be ~ to do** *(reluctant)* être peu disposé à faire; *(refuse)* ne pas vouloir faire. ◆ **unwillingly** *adv* à contrecœur.

unwind ['ʌn'waɪnd] *pret, ptp* **unwound 1** *vt* dérouler. **2** *vi* se dérouler; *(*: relax)* se détendre.

unwise ['ʌn'waɪz] *adj person* malavisé; *move, decision* imprudent. ◆ **unwisely** *adv* imprudemment.

unwitting [ʌn'wɪtɪŋ] *adj* involontaire. ◆ **unwittingly** *adv* involontairement.

unwonted [ʌn'wəʊntɪd] *adj* inaccoutumé.

unworkable ['ʌn'wɜːkəbl] *adj scheme etc* impraticable.

unworldly ['ʌn'wɜːldlɪ] *adj* détaché de ce monde.

unworthy [ʌn'wɜːðɪ] *adj* indigne (*of* de; *to do* de faire).

unwrap ['ʌn'ræp] *vt* défaire, ouvrir.

unwritten ['ʌn'rɪtn] *adj agreement* verbal. **it is an ~ law that...** il est tacitement admis que...

unyielding [ʌn'jiːldɪŋ] *adj person* inflexible.

unzip ['ʌn'zɪp] *vt* ouvrir la fermeture éclair ® de.

up [ʌp] **1** *adv* (**a**) *(gen)* en haut, en l'air; *throw etc* en l'air. **hold it ~ higher** tiens-le plus haut; **~ there** là-haut; **~ in the air** en l'air; **~ in the sky/mountains** dans le ciel/les montagnes; **~ on the hill** sur la colline; **~ on top of** sur; **~ at the top of** en haut de; **~ above** au-dessus; **~ above sth** au-dessus de qch; **he lives 5 floors ~** il habite au 5ᵉ étage; **all the way ~** jusqu'en haut; **I met him on my way ~** je l'ai rencontré en montant; **farther ~** *(on wall etc)* plus haut; *(along bench etc)* plus loin; **close ~ to** tout près de; **with his head ~ (high)** la tête haute; **the blinds were ~** les stores étaient levés; **~ against the wall** appuyé contre le mur; **~ on end** debout; **'this side ~'** 'haut'; **you've been ~ and down all evening** tu n'as pas arrêté toute la soirée; *[invalid]* **he's been rather ~ and down** il a eu des hauts et des bas; **to jump ~ and down** sauter; **to walk ~ and down** faire les cent pas.

(**b**) *(out of bed)* **to be ~** être levé, être debout *inv*; **get ~!** debout!, levez-vous!; **I was ~ late last night** je me suis couché tard hier soir; **he was ~ all night** il ne s'est pas couché de la nuit; **~ and about, ~ and doing *** à l'ouvrage; **to be ~ and about again** être de nouveau sur pied.

(**c**) *(fig)* **when the sun was ~** quand le soleil était levé; **the tide is ~** la marée est haute; **the river is ~** la rivière a monté; **the road is ~** la route est en travaux; *(Parl)* **the House is ~** la Chambre ne siège pas; **~ with Joe Bloggs!** vive Joe Bloggs!; **~ with** *or* **~ among the leaders** dans les premiers; **he's well ~ in Latin** *(place in class)* il a une bonne place en latin; *(knows a lot)* il est fort en latin; **I'm ~ with him in maths** nous sommes au même niveau en maths; **I'm not very well ~ on what's been going on** je ne suis pas vraiment au fait de ce qui s'est passé; **~ in London** à Londres; **~ in Scotland** en Écosse; **he's ~ from Birmingham** il arrive de Birmingham; **to come ~ to town** venir en ville; **~ north** dans le nord; **I'll play you 100 ~** je vous fais une partie en 100; **Chelsea were 3 goals ~** Chelsea menait par 3 buts; **we were 20 points ~ on them** nous avions 20 points d'avance sur eux; **to be one ~ on sb *** faire mieux que qn; **what's ~? *** *(what's happening)* qu'est-ce qu'il y a?; *(what's wrong)* qu'est-ce qui ne va pas?; **what's ~ with him? *** qu'est-ce qu'il a?; **there's sth ~ *** *(happening)* il se passe qch; *(wrong)* il y a qch qui ne va pas (*with sb* chez qn).

(**d**) *(higher etc)* **to be ~** *[prices, salaries, goods]* avoir augmenté (*by* de); *[temperature, level]* avoir monté (*by* de); *[standard]* être plus élevé; **it is ~ on last year** cela a augmenté par rapport à l'an dernier.

(**e**) *(upwards)* **from £2 ~** à partir de 2 livres.

(**f**) *(installed, built etc)* **to be ~** *[curtains, shutters]* être posé; *[pictures]* être accroché; *[building]* être construit; *[tent]* être planté; *[flag]* être hissé; *[notice]* être affiché.

(**g**) *(finished)* **his leave is ~** sa permission est terminée; **it is ~ on the 20th** ça se termine le 20; **when 3 days were ~** au bout de 3 jours; **time's ~!** c'est l'heure!; **it's all ~ with him *** il est fichu *.

(**h**) **to be ~ against** *difficulties* se heurter à; *competitors, competition* avoir affaire à; **you don't know what you're ~ against!** tu n'as pas idée des difficultés qui t'attendent!; **he's ~ against a very powerful man** il a contre lui un homme très puissant; **we're really ~ against it** nous allons avoir du mal à nous en sortir.

(**i**) *(as far as)* **~ to** jusqu'à; **~ to now** jusqu'à maintenant, jusqu'ici; **~ to here** jusqu'ici; **~ to there** jusque-là; **what page are you ~ to?** à quelle page en êtes-vous?; **~ to and including chapter 5** jusqu'au chapitre 5 inclus.

(**j**) *(depending on)* **it's ~ to you to decide** c'est à vous de décider; **it's ~ to you (whether you go or not)** c'est à vous de décider (si vous y allez ou non); **it's ~ to us to help him** c'est à nous de l'aider.

(**k**) *(busy doing etc)* **what is he ~ to?** qu'est-ce qu'il peut bien faire?; **he's ~ to sth** il manigance qch; **what have you been ~ to recently?** qu'est-ce que vous devenez ces temps-ci?; **what have you been ~ to?** qu'est-ce que tu as manigancé?; **he's ~ to no good** il prépare une bêtise; *[adult]* il prépare un mauvais coup.

(**l**) *(equal to)* **to be ~ to a task** être à la hauteur d'une tâche; **is he ~ to advanced work?** est-il capable de faire des études supérieures?; **it isn't ~ to his usual standard** d'habitude il fait mieux que ça; **are you feeling ~ to going?** est-ce que tu te sens assez d'attaque * pour y aller?; **I just don't feel ~ to it** je ne m'en sens pas le courage; **he really isn't ~ to going back to work** il n'est vraiment pas en état de reprendre le travail; **it's not ~ to much** ça ne vaut pas grand-chose.

2 *prep*: **to be ~ a tree/~ a ladder** être dans un arbre/sur une échelle; **to go ~** *stairs, street* monter; *river* remonter; **he pointed ~ the hill** il a indiqué du doigt le haut de la colline; **the house is ~ that road** la maison est dans cette rue; **they live just ~ the road** ils habitent un peu plus haut dans la rue; **~ and down the country** un peu partout dans le pays; **he went ~ and down the country** il parcourait le pays; **I've been ~ and down the stairs all evening** je n'ai pas arrêté de monter et descendre les escaliers de toute la soirée; **further ~ the page** plus haut sur la même page; **halfway ~ the hill** à mi-côte.

3 *n*: **~s and downs** *(in road)* accidents *mpl*; *(in career, health)* hauts *mpl* et bas *mpl*; **he is on the ~ and ~ *** *(Brit)* tout va de mieux en mieux pour lui, il est tout à fait honnête, on peut compter sur lui.

4 *adj (Brit) train* qui va à Londres.

5 *vi*: **I ~ped ‡ and told him** sans plus attendre je lui ai dit.

◆ **up-and-coming** *adj* plein d'avenir. ◆ **up-and-down** *adj movement* de va-et-vient; *(fig) career, business* qui a des hauts et des bas. ◆ **upbringing** *n* éducation *f*. ◆ **upcoming** *adj (US)* imminent, prochain. ◆ **upcountry** *adv go* vers l'intérieur *(d'un pays)*; *be* à l'intérieur. ◆ **update 1** *vt* mettre à jour ; **2** *n* mise *f* à jour. ◆ **upend** *vt box etc* mettre debout; *(* fig) system etc* renverser. ◆ **up-front * 1** *adj* (**a**) *(esp US) (frank)* franc, ouvert; *(important)* important; (**b**) *(paid in advance)* payé d'avance ; **2** *adv* (**a**) *(in advance)* d'avance; (**b**) *(esp US: openly)* ouvertement. ◆ **upgrade** *vt (improve)* améliorer; *(modernize)* moderniser; *(promote) employee* promouvoir; *job, post* revaloriser. ◆ **upheaval** *n (gen)* bouleversement *m*; *(esp Pol)* perturbations *fpl*; *(esp in home, family)* remue-ménage *m*; **it caused a lot of ~heaval** cela a tout perturbé. ◆ **uphill 1** *adv*: **to go ~hill** monter ; **2** *adj road* qui monte; *(fig) task* pénible; **it's ~hill all the way** ça monte tout le long; *(fig)* c'est une lutte continuelle. ◆ **uphold** *pret, ptp* **upheld** *vt institution, person* soutenir; *law* faire respecter; *(Jur) verdict* confirmer. ◆ **upholder** *n* défenseur *m*. ◆ **upholster** *vt* recouvrir. ◆ **upholsterer** *n* tapissier *m*. ◆ **upholstery** *n (in car)* garniture *f*. ◆ **upkeep** *n* entretien *m*. ◆ **uplands** *npl* hautes terres *fpl*. ◆ **uplifted** *adj* grandi, exalté. ◆ **upmarket** *adj product* haut de gamme *inv; newspaper* sérieux. ◆ **upon** *prep* = **on 1**. ◆ **upper 1** *adj (gen)* supérieur; *part, floor* supérieur, du dessus; *(in place names)* haut; **the ~per classes** les couches *fpl* supérieures de la société; **the ~per middle class** la haute bourgeoisie; *(fig)* **the ~per crust** le gratin *; **the ~per income bracket** la tranche des revenus élevés; **the ~per school** les grandes classes ; **2** *n [shoe]* empeigne *f*. ◆ **upper-class** *adj* aristocratique. ◆ **uppermost** *adj (highest)* le plus haut, le plus élevé; *(on top)* en dessus; **it was ~permost in my mind** j'y pensais avant tout autre chose. ◆ **uppish** * *adj* prétentieux. ◆ **upright 1** *adj, adv* droit ; **2** *n* (**a**) *[door, window]* montant *m*; *[goal-post]* montant de but; (**b**) *(piano)* piano *m* droit. ◆ **uprising** *n* soulèvement *m*, insurrection *f* (*against* contre). ◆ **uproar** *n (shouts)* tumulte *m*; *(protesting)* tempête *f* de protestations; **the hall was in (an) ~roar** le tumulte régnait dans la salle. ◆ **uproarious** *adj meeting, evening, discussion* tordant *, désopilant; *joke, mistake* hilarant; *laughter* éclatant; **~roarious success** grand succès comique. ◆ **uproariously** *adv laugh* aux éclats; *greet etc* avec de grands éclats de rire; **~roariously funny** désopilant. ◆ **uproot** *vt* déraciner. ◆ **upset** *etc V below*. ◆ **upshot** *n* résultat *m*. ◆ **upside down 1** *adv hold etc* à l'envers; **to turn ~side down** *object* retourner; *(fig) cupboard etc* mettre sens dessus dessous; (*) *plans* flanquer à l'eau * ; **2** *adj (gen)* à l'envers; *(upturned)* retourné; *(in disorder)* sens dessus dessous. ◆ **upstairs 1** *adv* en haut *(d'un escalier)*; **he's ~stairs** il est en haut; **to go ~stairs** monter; **to take ~stairs** *person* faire monter; *luggage etc* monter; **the people ~stairs** les gens du dessus; **the room ~stairs** la pièce d'en haut ; **2** *n* étage *m (du dessus)* ; **3** *adj*: **an ~stairs room** une chambre à l'étage. ◆ **upstanding** *adj (well-built)* bien bâti; *(honest)* droit; **a fine ~standing young man** un jeune homme très bien. ◆ **upstart** *n* parvenu(e) *m(f)*. ◆ **upstate** *(US)* **1** *adv go* vers l'intérieur *(d'un État)*; *be* à l'intérieur ; **2** *adj* de l'intérieur. ◆ **upstream** *adv be* en amont (*from* de); *sail* vers l'amont; *swim* contre le courant. ◆ **upsurge** *n [feeling]* vague *f*; *[interest]* regain *m*. ◆ **upswept** *adj (Aut, Aviat)* profilé. ◆ **uptake** *n*: **to be quick/slow on the ~take** avoir l'esprit vif/lent. ◆ **uptight** * *adj (tense)* crispé; *(touchy)* susceptible; *(conventional)* collet monté *inv*; **to get ~tight** *(tense)* se crisper (*about* à propos de); *(upset)* se froisser (*about* à propos de). ◆ **up-to-date** *adj report, information* très récent; *(updated)* à jour; *building, person, ideas* moderne. ◆ **up-to-the-minute** *adj* de dernière heure. ◆ **uptown** *(US)* **1** *adv* dans le centre (-ville); **2** *adj* du centre(-ville). ◆ **upturned** *adj nose* retroussé. ◆ **upward 1** *adj movement* ascendant; *pull, thrust* vers le haut; *trend* à la hausse; *glance* levé ; **2** *adv (also* **~wards***)* vers le haut; *(fig)* **from 10 francs ~wards** à partir de 10 F; **from childhood ~wards** dès sa jeunesse; **~wards of 300** 300 et plus. ◆ **upwardly** *adv:* **~wardly mobile** à mobilité sociale ascendante.

upset [ʌp'set] *pret, ptp* **upset 1** *vt container, contents* renverser; *boat* faire chavirer; *(fig) plan, timetable, system, stomach* déranger; *calculation* fausser; *person (offend)* vexer; *(grieve)* faire de la peine à; *(annoy)* contrarier; *(make ill)* rendre malade. **don't ~ yourself** ne vous en faites pas *. **2** *adj stomach, digestion* dérangé; *person (offended)* vexé; *(grieved)* peiné, triste; *(annoyed)* fâché, contrarié; *(ill)* souffrant. **to get ~** se vexer, devenir triste, se fâcher; **what are you so ~ about?** qu'est-ce qui ne va pas? **3** ['ʌpset] *n (upheaval)* désordre *m*; *(in plans etc)* bouleversement *m* (*in* de); *(emotional)* chagrin *m*. **to have a stomach ~** avoir l'estomac dérangé. ◆ **upsetting** *adj (offending)* vexant; *(saddening)* triste; *(stronger)* affligeant; *(annoying)* contrariant.

uranium [jʊə'reɪnɪəm] *n* uranium *m*.

Uranus [jʊə'reɪnəs] *n (Astron)* Uranus *f*.

urban ['ɜ:bən] *adj* urbain. **~ blight** dégradation *f* urbaine. ◆ **urbanization** *n* urbanisation *f*.

urbane [ɜ:'beɪn] *adj* urbain, courtois. ◆ **urbanity** *n* urbanité *f*.

urchin ['ɜ:tʃɪn] *n* polisson(ne) *m(f)*.

urge [ɜ:dʒ] **1** *n* forte envie *f* (*to do* de faire). **to have the ~ to do** éprouver une forte envie de faire. **2** *vt person* pousser (*to do* à faire), conseiller vivement (*sb to do* à qn de faire); *caution, measure* préconiser, conseiller vivement; *(emphasize)* insister sur. **he needed no urging** il ne s'est pas fait prier; **to ~ that** recommander vivement que + *subj*; **'now!' he ~d** 'tout de suite!' insista-t-il; **to ~ sb in** *etc* presser qn d'entrer *etc*. ◆ **urge on** *vt sep horse* presser; *person, troops* faire avancer; *(fig) worker* presser; *work* activer; *(Sport) team* encourager. **to ~ sb on to (do) sth** inciter qn à (faire) qch.

urgent ['ɜ:dʒ(ə)nt] *adj need, case, attention* urgent; *tone* insistant; *entreaty, request* pressant. ◆ **urgency** *n [case etc]* urgence *f*; *[tone, entreaty]* insistance *f*; **a matter of urgency** une affaire urgente. ◆ **urgently** *adv need, request* d'urgence; *plead* instamment.

urine ['jʊərɪn] *n* urine *f*. ◆ **urinal** *n* urinoir *m*. ◆ **urinary** *adj* urinaire. ◆ **urinate** *vi* uriner.

urn [ɜ:n] *n (gen)* urne *f*. **tea ~** fontaine *f* à thé.

Uruguay ['jʊərəgwaɪ] *n* Uruguay *m*. ◆ **Uruguayan 1** *adj* uruguayen ; **2** *n* Uruguayen(ne) *m(f)*.

us [ʌs] *pers pron* nous. **he hit ~** il nous a frappés; **give it to ~** donnez-le-nous; **in front of ~** devant nous; **let ~** *or* **let's go!** allons-y!; **younger than ~** plus jeune que nous; **both of ~** nous deux, tous les deux; **he is one of ~** il est des nôtres; **~ English** nous autres Anglais; *(me)* **give ~ it!** ‡ donne-le-moi!

USA [ju:es'e(ɪ)] *n* États-Unis d'Amérique *mpl*, É.-U.(A.). *mpl*.

use [ju:s] **1** *n* (**a**) *(gen)* usage *m*, emploi *m*; *(way of using)* emploi, utilisation *f*. **the ~ of steel** l'emploi de l'acier; **to learn the ~ of** apprendre à se servir de; **directions for ~** mode *m* d'emploi; **'for the ~ of teachers only'** *book, equipment* 'à l'usage des professeurs seulement'; *room* 'réservé aux professeurs'; **for one's own ~** à son usage personnel; **for ~ in emergency** à utiliser en cas d'urgence; **fit for ~** en état de servir; **ready for ~** prêt à l'emploi; **to improve with ~** s'améliorer à l'usage; **in ~** *machine, word* en usage; **no longer in ~** *machine* hors d'usage; *word* qui ne s'emploie plus; *(notice)* **'out of ~'** 'en dérangement'; **in general ~** d'usage courant; **it is in daily ~** on s'en sert tous les jours; **it's gone out of ~** on ne l'emploie plus; **to make ~ of** se servir de, utiliser; **to make good ~ of, to put to good ~** *time, money* faire un bon emploi de; *opportunity, facilities* tirer parti de; **a new ~ for** un nouvel emploi de, une nouvelle utilisation de; **I'll find a ~ for it** je trouverai un moyen de m'en servir; **I've no further ~ for it** je n'en ai plus besoin; *(fig)* **I've no ~ for that sort of thing!** * je n'ai rien à en faire!

(**b**) *(usefulness)* **to be of** ~ servir, être utile (*for, to* à); **to be (of) no** ~ ne servir à rien; **he gave me the** ~ **of his car** il m'a permis de me servir de sa voiture; **to have lost the** ~ **of one's arm** avoir perdu l'usage de son bras; **what's the** ~ **of doing...?** à quoi bon faire...?; **is this (of) any** ~ **to you?** est-ce que cela peut vous être utile?; **he's no** ~ il est nul (*as* comme); **it's no** ~ **protesting** il ne sert à rien de protester; **it's no** ~ rien à faire, ça ne sert à rien.

2 [ju:z] *vt* (**a**) *(gen)* se servir de, utiliser, employer (*to do, for doing* pour faire); *a language* utiliser, se servir de; *money* utiliser (*to do* pour faire); *car* prendre, se servir de; *force, discretion* user de; *opportunity* profiter de; *method, means* employer; *sb's name* faire usage de. **are you using this?** vous servez-vous de ceci?; **he** ~**d it as a hammer** il s'en est servi comme marteau; **I** ~ **that as a table** ça me sert de table; **'to be** ~**d regularly'** 'à utiliser régulièrement'; **no longer** ~**d** *machine, room* qui ne sert plus; *word* qui ne s'emploie plus; ~ **your head** *or* **brains!** réfléchis un peu!; ~ **your eyes!** ouvre l'œil!; **I could** ~ **a drink!** * je prendrais bien un verre!; **it could** ~ **a bit of paint** * une couche de peinture ne ferait pas de mal. (**b**) *petrol etc* user, consommer; **(~ up)** *(finish)* finir; *left-overs* utiliser. **have you** ~**d all the paint?** avez-vous utilisé toute la peinture?; (**c**) *(treat) person* traiter, agir envers. **he was badly** ~**d** on a mal agi envers lui.

3 *aux vb (translated by imperfect tense)* **I** ~**d to see him every day** je le voyais *or* j'avais l'habitude de le voir tous les jours.

◆ **use up** *vt sep supplies, strength* épuiser; *food, paper* finir; *scraps* utiliser; *money* dépenser. **it is all** ~**d up** c'est épuisé, il n'en reste plus. ◆ **usable** *adj* utilisable. ◆ **usage** *n* (**a**) *(custom; also Ling)* usage *m*; (**b**) *(treatment) [object]* manipulation *f*; *[person]* traitement *m*; **it's had some rough usage** on s'en est mal servi. ◆ **used** [ju:zd] *adj* (**a**) *stamp* oblitéré; *car* d'occasion; (**b**) [ju:st] *(accustomed)* **to be** ~**d to (doing) sth** être habitué à *or* avoir l'habitude de (faire) qch; **to get** ~**d to** s'habituer à; **you'll get** ~**d to it** vous vous y ferez. ◆ **useful** *adj (gen)* utile; *discussion, time* utile, profitable; *(fig) player etc* compétent; **it is** ~**ful for him to be able to...** il est très utile qu'il puisse...; **to make o.s.** ~**ful** se rendre utile; **to come in** ~**ful** être utile; **to be** ~**ful to** rendre service à; **he's a** ~**ful man to know** c'est un homme utile à connaître; **it's a** ~**ful thing to know** c'est bon à savoir; **he's** ~**ful with a gun** il sait bien manier un fusil. ◆ **usefully** *adv* utilement. ◆ **usefulness** *n* utilité *f*. ◆ **useless** *adj (no good)* qui ne vaut rien; *(unusable)* inutilisable; *remedy* inefficace; *person* incompétent; *volunteer* incapable; **shouting is** ~**less** il est inutile de crier, il ne sert à rien de crier; **he's** ~**less** il est nul (*as* comme). ◆ **uselessly** *adv* inutilement. ◆ **user** *n* (**a**) *[machine, tool, computer]* utilisateur *m*, -trice *f*; *[public service, telephone, dictionary, road, train]* usager *m*; **car** ~**rs** automobilistes *mpl*. (**b**) *(Drugs)* usager *m*, consommateur *m*. ◆ **user-friendly** *adj* facile à utiliser, convivial.

usher ['ʌʃəʳ] **1** *n (in law courts etc)* huissier *m (audiencier)*; *(in theatre, church)* placeur *m*. **2** *vt*: **to** ~ **sb through/along** *etc* faire traverser/ avancer *etc* qn; **to** ~ **sb to the door** reconduire qn à la porte; **to** ~ **in** *person* faire entrer; *(fig) period* inaugurer. ◆ **usherette** *n* ouvreuse *f*.

usual ['ju:ʒʊəl] **1** *adj (gen)* habituel; *word* usuel; *remarks, conditions* d'usage. **his** ~ **drink is beer** d'habitude il boit de la bière; **the** ~ **practice** ce qui se fait d'habitude; **his** ~ **practice** son habitude *f*; **as is** ~ **with such machines it...** comme toutes les machines de ce genre elle...; **as is** ~ **on these occasions** comme le veut la coutume en ces occasions; **he'll soon be his** ~ **self again** il retrouvera bientôt sa santé (*or* sa gaieté *etc*); **as** ~ comme d'habitude, comme à l'ordinaire; **more than** ~ plus que d'habitude *or* d'ordinaire; **it's not** ~ **for him to be late** il est rare qu'il soit en retard; **it was the** ~ **kind of party** c'était une soirée typique. **2** *n (drink)* **the** ~**!** * comme d'habitude! ◆ **usually** *adv* d'habitude, d'ordinaire; **more than** ~**ly careful** encore plus prudent que d'habitude.

usurp [ju:'zɜ:p] *vt* usurper. ◆ **usurper** *n* usurpateur *m*, -trice *f*.

usury ['ju:ʒʊrɪ] *n* usure *f (prêt)*.

utensil [ju:'tensl] *n* ustensile *m*.

uterus ['ju:tərəs] *n* utérus *m*.

utility [ju:'tɪlɪtɪ] **1** *n (use)* utilité *f*; *(public ~)* service *m* public. **2** *adj (gen)* utilitaire. ~ **room** ≃ buanderie *f*. ◆ **utilitarian** *adj* utilitaire. ◆ **utilizable** *adj* utilisable. ◆ **utilization** *n* utilisation *f*. ◆ **utilize** *vt* utiliser.

utmost ['ʌtməʊst] **1** *adj* (**a**) *(greatest) simplicity, care etc* le plus grand; *skill* suprême; *danger* extrême. **with the** ~ **speed** à toute vitesse; **it is of the** ~ **importance that...** il est extrêmement important que... + *subj*; **a matter of the** ~ **importance** une affaire de la plus haute importance. (**b**) *(furthest) place, part* le plus éloigné, extrême. **2** *n*: **to do one's** ~ faire tout son possible (*to do* pour faire); **to the** ~ **of one's ability** à la limite de ses capacités; **to the** ~ au plus haut degré; **at the** ~ tout au plus.

Utopia [ju:'təʊpɪə] *n* utopie *f*. ◆ **Utopian** *adj* utopique.

utter[1] ['ʌtəʳ] *adj sincerity, disaster* complet, total; *madness* pur; *idiot, fool* fini; *rogue, liar* fieffé *(before n)*. **it was** ~ **nonsense!** c'était complètement absurde; **he's an** ~ **stranger** il m'est complètement inconnu. ◆ **utterly** *adv* complètement, tout à fait. ◆ **uttermost** = **utmost**.

utter[2] ['ʌtəʳ] *vt word* prononcer; *cry* pousser; *threat, insult* proférer; *libel* publier; *counterfeit money* émettre. **he didn't** ~ **a word** il n'a pas soufflé mot.

V, v [viː] *n (letter)* V, v *m.* ◆ **V-neck** *n* décolleté *m* en V *or* en pointe.

vacant [ˈveɪk(ə)nt] *adj job* vacant, à remplir; *room, house, seat* libre; *hours* de loisir; *mind* vide; *stare* vague; *person (stupid)* stupide; *(dreamy)* sans expression. **'situations ~'** 'offres d'emploi'. ◆ **vacancy** *n (in boarding house)* chambre *f* à louer; *(job)* poste *m* vacant; **vacancy for a typist** poste de dactylo à suppléer; *(notice)* 'on cherche dactylo'; **'no vacancies'** *(of jobs)* 'pas d'embauche'; *(in hotel)* 'complet'. ◆ **vacantly** *adv*: **to gaze ~ly into space** avoir le regard perdu dans le vide. ◆ **vacate** *vt room, seat, job, house* quitter; **to vacate the premises** vider les lieux.

vacation [vəˈkeɪʃ(ə)n] **1** *n* vacances *fpl.* **on ~** en vacances; **to take a ~** prendre des vacances; *(Scol etc)* **long ~** grandes vacances. **2** *adj*: **~ course** cours *mpl* de vacances. ◆ **vacationer** *n (US)* vacancier *m*, -ière *f.*

vaccinate [ˈvæksɪneɪt] *vt* vacciner (*against* contre). **to get ~d** se faire vacciner; **have you been ~d against...?** est-ce que vous êtes vacciné contre...? ◆ **vaccination** *n* vaccination *f.* ◆ **vaccine** *n* vaccin *m*; **polio vaccine** vaccin contre la polio.

vacillate [ˈvæsɪleɪt] *vi* hésiter (*between* entre).

vacuum [ˈvækjʊm] **1** *n* vide *m*; *(Phys,)* vacuum *m.* **2** *adj brake, pump* à vide. **~ cleaner** aspirateur *m*; **~ flask** *or (US)* **bottle** bouteille *f* thermos ®. **3** *vt carpet* passer à l'aspirateur. ◆ **vacuity** *n* vacuité *f.* ◆ **vacuous** *adj eyes, stare* vide; *remark* bête. ◆ **vacuum-packed** *adj* emballé sous vide.

vagabond [ˈvægəbɒnd] *n* vagabond(e) *m(f).*

vagary [ˈveɪgərɪ] *n* caprice *m.*

vagina [vəˈdʒaɪnə] *n* vagin *m.* ◆ **vaginal** *adj* vaginal; **~l discharge** pertes *fpl* blanches.

vagrant [ˈveɪgr(ə)nt] *n, adj* vagabond(e) *m(f).* ◆ **vagrancy** *n* vagabondage *m.*

vague [veɪg] *adj (not clear: gen)* vague, imprécis; *outline, photograph, memory* flou; *feeling, expression, idea* vague, confus; *(absent-minded) person* distrait. **I haven't the ~st idea** je n'en ai pas la moindre idée; **I had a ~ idea that** je pensais vaguement que; **he was ~ about it** *(didn't, say exactly)* il ne l'a pas bien précisé; *(didn't know exactly)* il n'en était pas sûr; **I'm still very ~ about all this** je n'ai pas encore compris tout ça; **to look ~, to have a ~ look in one's eyes** avoir l'air vague. ◆ **vaguely** *adv* vaguement. ◆ **vagueness** *n [person]* distraction *f*, étourderie *f.*

vain [veɪn] *adj* (**a**) *(useless, empty) attempt, hope* vain *(before n)*; *promise* vide; *words* creux. **in ~** en vain, vainement; **she tried in ~ to open the door** elle a essayé en vain d'ouvrir la porte; **I looked for him in ~, he had left** j'ai eu beau le chercher, il était parti. (**b**) *(conceited)* vaniteux. ◆ **vainly** *adv* (**a**) *(to no effect)* en vain, vainement; (**b**) *(conceitedly)* vaniteusement.

valentine [ˈvæləntaɪn] *n* (**~ card**) carte *f* de la Saint-Valentin *(gage d'amour).*

valet [ˈvæleɪ] *n* valet *m* de chambre.

valiant [ˈvæljənt] *adj (gen)* courageux, vaillant. **to make a ~ effort to do** essayer vaillamment de faire. ◆ **valiantly** *adv* vaillamment.

valid [ˈvælɪd] *adj claim, contract, document, ticket* valable, valide (*for* pour); *excuse, argument* valable. ◆ **validate** *vt document etc* valider; *argument* prouver la justesse de. ◆ **validity** *n [document etc]* validité *f*; *[argument]* justesse *f.*

valise [vəˈliːz] *n* sac *m* de voyage.

valley [ˈvælɪ] *n* vallée *f*; *(small)* vallon *m.* **the Seine/Rhône** *etc* **~** la vallée de la Seine/du Rhône *etc*; **the Loire V~** *(between Orléans and Tours)* le Val de Loire.

valour, *(US)* **valor** [ˈvæləʳ] *n* bravoure *f.* ◆ **valorous** *adj* valeureux.

value [ˈvæljuː] **1** *n* valeur *f.* **to gain (in) ~** prendre de la valeur; **to lose (in) ~** se déprécier; *(Tax etc)* **increase/decrease in ~** plus-/moins-value *f*; **he paid the ~ of the cup he broke** il a remboursé la tasse qu'il a cassée; **of no ~** sans valeur; **it has been of no ~ to her** ça ne lui a servi à rien; **to be of great ~** valoir cher; **to get good ~ for money** en avoir pour son argent; **it's the best ~** c'est le plus avantageux; **to put too high/too low a ~ on sth** surestimer/sous-estimer qch; **to the ~ of £100** d'une valeur de 100 livres; **at his (***or* **its** *etc***) proper ~** à sa juste valeur; *(moral standards)* **~s** valeurs. **2** *adj*: **~ added tax** *(abbr* **V.A.T.***)* taxe *f* sur la valeur ajoutée *(abbr* T.V.A.*)*; *(fig)* **~ judgment** jugement *m* de valeur. **3** *vt* (**a**) *house, painting* évaluer (*at* à); *(Comm, Jur)* expertiser (*at* à). (**b**) *friendship, comforts* apprécier; *independence* tenir à. ◆ **valuable 1** *adj object* de valeur; *advice, time* précieux ; **2** *npl*: **valuables** objets *mpl* de valeur. ◆ **valuation** *n (Comm, Jur)* expertise *f*; *(value decided upon)* appréciation *f*; **to have a valuation made of sth** faire expertiser qch; **the valuation is too high** l'appréciation est trop élevée; *(fig)* **to take sb at his own valuation** prendre qn pour celui qu'il croit être. ◆ **valued** *adj friend* précieux; *colleague* estimé. ◆ **valueless** *adj* sans valeur.

valve [vælv] *n (Anat)* valvule *f*; *(Bot, Zool)* valve *f*; *(Tech) [machine]* soupape *f*; *[tyre etc]* valve; *(Electronics, Rad)* lampe *f*; *[musical instrument]* piston *m.*

vampire [ˈvæmpaɪəʳ] *n* vampire *m.* **~ bat** vampire *(chauve-souris).*

van¹ [væn] *n* (**a**) *(Aut: large)* camion *m*, fourgon *m*; *(smaller)* camionnette *f.* (**b**) *(Rail)* fourgon *m.* (**c**) *(*: abbr of* **caravan***)* caravane *f.* ◆ **van-boy** *or* ◆ **van-man** *n* livreur *m.*

van² [væn] *n abbr of* **vanguard.**

vandal [ˈvænd(ə)l] *n* vandale *mf.* ◆ **vandalism** *n* vandalisme *m.* ◆ **vandalize** *vt* saccager.

vane [veɪn] *n* (**weather ~**) girouette *f.*

vanguard [ˈvængɑːd] *n* avant-garde *f.* **in the ~** *(Mil etc)* en tête (*of* de); *(fig)* à l'avant-garde (*of* de).

vanilla [vəˈnɪlə] **1** *n* vanille *f.* **2** *adj cream, ice* à la vanille.

vanish [ˈvænɪʃ] *vi* disparaître. **to ~ into thin air** se volatiliser. ◆ **vanished** *adj* disparu. ◆ **vanishing** *adj*: **~ing cream** crème *f* de jour; **~ing point** point *m* de fuite; **~ing trick** tour *m* de passe-passe.

vanity [ˈvænɪtɪ] **1** *n* vanité *f.* **2** *adj*: **~ case** mallette *f* pour affaires de toilette; **~ mirror** miroir *m* de courtoisie; **~ unit** élément *m* de salle de bains à lavabo encastré.

vanquish [ˈvæŋkwɪʃ] *vt* vaincre.

vantage ['vɑːntɪdʒ] **1** *n* avantage *m.* **2** *adj:* ~ **point,** *(Mil)* ~ **ground** position *f* avantageuse.

vapid ['væpɪd] *adj* sans intérêt.

vapour, *(US)* **vapor** ['veɪpəʳ] **1** *n* vapeur *f*; *(on glass)* buée *f.* **2** *adj (Aviat)* ~ **trail** traînée *f* de condensation. ◆ **vaporize** **1** *vt* vaporiser ; **2** *vi* se vaporiser. ◆ **vaporizer** *n (Med)* inhalateur *m.*

varicose ['værɪkəʊs] *adj:* ~ **vein** varice *f.*

varnish ['vɑːnɪʃ] **1** *n* vernis *m.* **nail** ~ vernis à ongles. **2** *vt* vernir. ◆ **varnishing** *n (Art)* vernissage *m.*

vary ['vɛərɪ] **1** *vi (gen)* varier (*with* selon). **to** ~ **from sth** différer de qch. **2** *vt (gen)* varier; *temperature, results* faire varier. ◆ **variability** *n* variabilité *f.* ◆ **variable** *adj, n* variable *(f).* ◆ **variance** *n [people]* **to be at variance** être en désaccord (*with sb* avec qn; *about, over sth* à propos de qch); *[facts, statements]* ne pas s'accorder (*with* avec). ◆ **variant** *n* variante *f.* ◆ **variation** *n* variation *f.* ◆ **varied** *adj* varié. ◆ **variegated** *adj* bigarré; *(Bot)* panaché. ◆ **variety** [və'raɪətɪ] **1** *n* (**a**) *(gen)* variété *f*; **for a variety of reasons** pour diverses raisons; **a large variety of** un grand mombre de; (**b**) *(type, kind)* type *m*, espèce *f;* (**c**) *(Theat)* variétés *fpl* ; **2** *adj (Theat) artiste* de variétés; **variety show** *(Theat, TV)* spectacle *m* de variétés; *(Rad, TV)* émission *f* de variétés. *(US Culin)* **variety meats** abats *mpl (de boucherie).* ◆ **various** ['vɛərɪəs] *adj (different)* divers *(before n)*, différent; *(several)* divers *(before n)*, plusieurs; **at various times** *(different)* en diverses occasions; *(several)* à plusieurs reprises; **various people** plusieurs *or* diverses personnes. ◆ **variously** *adv* diversement. ◆ **varying** *adj* qui varie, variable; **with** ~**ing degrees of success** avec plus ou moins de succès.

vase [vɑːz] *n* vase *m.* **flower** ~ vase à fleurs.

vasectomy [væ'sektəmɪ] *n* vasectomie *f.*

vaseline ['væsɪliːn] *n* vaseline *f.*

vast [vɑːst] *adj (gen)* vaste *(usually before n)*; *success* énorme. **a** ~ **amount of** énormément de; **to a** ~ **extent** dans une très large mesure; **at** ~ **expense** à grands frais; ~ **sums** des sommes folles. ◆ **vastly** *adv grateful, amused* infiniment; *rich* extrêmement; **to be** ~**ly mistaken** se tromper du tout au tout; ~**ly improved** infiniment meilleur. ◆ **vastness** *n* immensité *f.*

vat [væt] *n* cuve *f*, bac *m.*

Vatican ['vætɪkən] *n* Vatican *m.* **the** ~ **Council** le Concile du Vatican.

vaudeville ['vəʊdəvɪl] *n* spectacle *m* de music-hall.

vault[1] [vɔːlt] *n* (**a**) *(cellar)* cave *f*; *(tomb)* caveau *m*; *(in bank) (strongroom)* chambre *f* forte; *(for safe deposit boxes)* salle *f* des coffres. (**b**) *(Archit)* voûte *f.* ◆ **vaulting** *n (Archit)* voûtes *fpl.*

vault[2] [vɔːlt] *vti:* **to** ~ **(over) sth** sauter qch (d'un bond).

vaunt [vɔːnt] *vt:* **much** ~**ed** dont on (*or* il *etc*) fait tant l'éloge.

veal [viːl] *n* veau *m (Culin).* ~ **cutlet** escalope *f* de veau.

veer [vɪəʳ] *vi* **(**~ **round)** *[wind]* tourner (*to* vers, à); *[ship, car, road]* virer. *(fig: change one's mind)* **to** ~ **round** changer d'opinion; **to** ~ **off the subject** s'éloigner du sujet.

vegan ['viːgən] *n, adj* végétalien(ne) *m(f).*

vegetable ['vedʒ(ɪ)təbl] **1** *n* (**a**) légume *m.* **early** ~**s** primeurs *fpl.* (**b**) *(generic term: plant)* végétal *m.* (**c**) *(fig: brain damaged etc person)* épave *f.* **2** *adj oil, matter* végétal; *soup* de légumes. ~ **dish** légumier *m*; ~ **garden** potager *m*; ~ **kingdom** règne *m* végétal; ~ **knife** couteau *m* à éplucher ; ~ **salad** macédoine *f* de légumes. ◆ **vegetarian** [ˌvedʒɪ'tɛərɪən] *adj, n* végétarien(ne) *m(f).* ◆ **vegetarianism** *n* végétarisme *m.* ◆ **vegetate** *vi* végéter. ◆ **vegetation** *n* végétation *f.*

vehement ['viːɪmənt] *adj (gen)* véhément; *attack* violent. ◆ **vehemence** *n [feelings, speech]* véhémence *f*; *[actions]* fougue *f.* ◆ **vehemently** *adv speak etc* avec véhémence; *attack* avec violence.

vehicle ['viːɪkl] *n* véhicule *m.* ◆ **vehicular traffic** [vɪ'hɪkjʊlə'træfɪk] *n* circulation *f.*

veil [veɪl] **1** *n (gen)* voile *m*; *(on hat)* voilette *f*; *(fig)* voile. *(Rel)* **to take the** ~ prendre le voile; *(fig)* **to draw a** ~ **over** mettre un voile sur. **2** *vt* voiler. ◆ **veiled** *adj (lit, fig)* voilé.

vein [veɪn] *n (gen)* veine *f*; *(in leaf)* nervure *f. (fig)* **a** ~ **of truth/cruelty** un fond de vérité/de cruauté; **in humorous** ~ dans un esprit humoristique ; **in the same** ~ dans le même esprit. ◆ **veined** *adj hand, stone* veiné; *leaf* nervuré.

Velcro ['velkrəʊ] *n* ® velcro *m* ®.

veld(t) [velt] *n* veld(t) *m.*

vellum ['veləm] *n* vélin *m.*

velocity [vɪ'lɒsɪtɪ] *n* vélocité *f*, vitesse *f.*

velour(s) [və'lʊəʳ] *n (for clothes)* velours *m* rasé; *(for upholstery)* velours épais.

velvet ['velvɪt] **1** *n* velours *m.* *(fig)* **to be on** ~ * jouer sur du velours *. **2** *adj dress* de velours. ◆ **velveteen** *n* velvet *m.* ◆ **velvety** *adj* velouté.

venal ['viːnl] *adj* vénal. ◆ **venality** *n* vénalité *f.*

vendetta [ven'detə] *n* vendetta *f.*

vending ['vendɪŋ] *n* vente *f.* ~ **machine** distributeur *m* automatique. ◆ **vendor** *n (gen)* marchand(e) *m(f); (Jur)* vendeur *m.*

veneer [və'nɪəʳ] **1** *n* placage *m*; *(fig)* apparence *f.* **2** *vt* plaquer.

venerate ['venəreɪt] *vt* vénérer. ◆ **venerable** *adj* vénérable. ◆ **veneration** *n* vénération *f.*

venereal [vɪ'nɪərɪəl] *adj:* ~ **disease** *(abbr* **V.D.***)* maladie *f* vénérienne.

Venetian [vɪ'niːʃ(ə)n] *adj* vénitien. ~ **glass** cristal *m* de Venise; ~ **blind** store *m* vénitien.

vengeance ['ven(d)ʒ(ə)ns] *n* vengeance *f.* **to take** ~ **on** se venger de *or* sur; *(fig)* **with a** ~ pour de bon *.

venial ['viːnɪəl] *adj* véniel.

Venice ['venɪs] *n* Venise.

venison ['venɪs(ə)n] *n* venaison *f.*

venom ['venəm] *n* venin *m.* ◆ **venomous** *adj (lit, fig)* venimeux; *tongue* de vipère. ◆ **venomously** *adv* d'une manière venimeuse.

vent [vent] **1** *n (hole)* orifice *m*; *(pipe)* conduit *m*; *[chimney]* tuyau *m. (fig)* **to give** ~ **to** donner libre cours à. **2** *vt (fig) anger etc* décharger (*on* sur).

ventilate ['ventɪleɪt] *vt room, tunnel* ventiler; *(fig) question* livrer à la discussion; *grievance* étaler au grand jour. ◆ **ventilation** *n* ventilation *f*; **ventilation shaft** conduit *m* d'aération. ◆ **ventilator** *n* ventilateur *m*; *(Aut)* déflecteur *m.*

ventricle ['ventrɪkl] *n* ventricule *m.*

ventriloquist [ven'trɪləkwɪst] *n* ventriloque *mf.* ◆ **ventriloquism** *n* ventriloquie *f.*

venture ['ventʃəʳ] **1** *n* entreprise *f.* **at a** ~ au hasard; **my first artistic** ~ ma première entreprise artistique; **business** ~**s** tentatives *fpl* commerciales; **a new** ~ **in publishing** qch de nouveau en matière d'édition. **2** *adj:* ~ **capital** capital-risques *m.* **3** *vt life, fortune, reputation* risquer; *explanation, opinion* hasarder. **to** ~ **a guess** hasarder une réponse; **he did not** ~ **to speak** il n'a pas osé parler. **3** *vi* se risquer (*on doing* à faire). **to** ~ **in/through** *etc* se risquer à entrer/traverser *etc*; **to** ~ **out of doors** se risquer à sortir; **to** ~ **into town** s'aventurer dans la ville; **when we** ~**d on this** quand nous avons entrepris cela.

venue ['venjuː] *n* lieu *m* (de rendez-vous). **the** ~ **of the meeting is...** la réunion aura lieu à...

Venus ['viːnəs] *n (Astron, Myth)* Vénus *f.*

veracious [və'reɪʃəs] *adj* véridique. ◆ **veracity** [və'ræsɪtɪ] *n* véracité *f.*

veranda(h) [və'rændə] *n* véranda *f.*

verb [vɜ:b] *n* verbe *m.* ◆ **verbal** *adj (gen)* verbal; *memory* auditif. ◆ **verbalize** *vt* exprimer. ◆ **verbally** *adv* verbalement. ◆ **verbatim** *adj, adv* mot pour mot.

verbena [vɜ:'bi:nə] *n* verveine *f.*

verbiage ['vɜ:bɪɪdʒ] *n* verbiage *m.* ◆ **verbose** *adj* verbeux. ◆ **verbosely** *adv* avec verbosité. ◆ **verbosity** *n* verbosité *f.*

verdict ['vɜ:dɪkt] *n (Jur, also gen)* verdict *m.* ~ **of guilty/not guilty** verdict de culpabilité/de non-culpabilité; *(gen)* **to give one's ~ on** se prononcer sur.

verge [vɜ:dʒ] **1** *n (gen)* bord *m; [road]* accotement *m*; *[forest]* orée *f.* **to be on the ~ of** *ruin, death, tears* être au bord de; *a discovery* être à la veille de; **on the ~ of doing** sur le point de faire. **2** *vi* incliner, tendre (*towards* vers). **to ~ on sth** *[ideas, actions]* approcher de qch; *[person]* frôler qch.

verger ['vɜ:dʒə^r] *n* bedeau *m.*

verify ['verɪfaɪ] *vt (gen)* vérifier; *documents* contrôler. ◆ **verifiable** *adj* vérifiable. ◆ **verification** *n* vérification *f.*

veritable ['verɪtəbl] *adj* véritable, vrai *(both before n).*

vermicelli [,vɜ:mɪ'selɪ] *n* vermicelle *m.*

vermilion [və'mɪljən] *adj, n* vermillon *(m) inv.*

vermin ['vɜ:mɪn] *collective n (animals)* animaux *mpl* nuisibles; *(insects, also people)* vermine *f.* ◆ **verminous** *adj* couvert de vermine.

vermouth ['vɜ:məθ] *n* vermouth *m.*

vernacular [və'nækjʊlə^r] *n* langue *f* vernaculaire.

veronica [və'rɒnɪkə] *n* véronique *f.*

verruca [və'ru:kə] *n* verrue *f (plantaire).*

versatile ['vɜ:sətaɪl] *adj person* aux talents variés; *mind* souple; *genius* universel. ◆ **versatility** *n [person]* variété *f* de talents.

verse [vɜ:s] *n* (**a**) *(poetry)* poésie *f*, vers *mpl.* **in ~** en vers. (**b**) *(stanza) [poem]* strophe *f*; *[song]* couplet *m*; *[Bible]* verset *m.* ◆ **versed** *adj* (**well-~d**) versé (*in* dans). ◆ **versification** *n* versification *f.* ◆ **versify** *vi* faire des vers.

version ['vɜ:ʃ(ə)n] *n (most senses)* version *f*; *[car]* modèle *m.*

versus ['vɜ:səs] *prep (Jur, Sport, gen)* contre. **public ~ private ownership** la propriété publique par opposition à la propriété privée.

vertebra, *pl* **-ae** ['vɜ:tɪbrə, i:] *n* vertèbre *f.* ◆ **vertebrate** *adj, n* vertébré *(m).*

vertex, *pl* **-tices** ['vɜ:teks, tɪsi:z] *n (gen, Math)* sommet *m*; *(Anat)* vertex *m.*

vertical ['vɜ:tɪk(ə)l] **1** *adj (gen)* vertical; *cliff* à pic. **2** *n* verticale *f.* ◆ **vertically** *adv* verticalement.

vertigo ['vɜ:tɪgəʊ] *n* vertige *m.* **to suffer from ~** avoir des vertiges.

verve [vɜ:v] *n* verve *f*, brio *m.*

very ['verɪ] **1** *adv* (**a**) *(extremely)* très, bien. **~ amusing** très *or* fort amusant; **I am ~ cold** j'ai très froid; **~ well** très bien; **~ little** très peu (de); **~ much** beaucoup, bien; **~ much bigger** beaucoup *or* bien plus grand; **he doesn't work ~ much** il ne travaille pas beaucoup; **~ high frequency** *(Rad)* ondes *fpl* ultra-courtes; *(Electronics)* très haute fréquence. (**b**) *(absolutely)* tout, de loin. **~ best quality** toute première qualité; **~ last/first** tout dernier/premier; **the ~ cleverest** de loin le plus intelligent; **at the ~ latest** au plus tard; **at the ~ most/least** tout au plus/moins; **in the ~ best of health** en excellente santé; **the ~ best of friends** les meilleurs amis du monde; **it's my ~ own** c'est à moi tout seul; **the ~ next shop** le magasin tout de suite après; **the ~ same day** le jour même; **the ~ same hat** exactement le même chapeau; **the ~ next day** le lendemain même.
2 *adj* (**a**) *(precise)* même. **that ~ day** ce jour même; **his ~ words** ses propos mêmes; **the ~ thing!** *(of object)* voilà justement ce qu'il me faut; *(of idea etc)* c'est idéal; **the ~ man I need** tout à fait l'homme qu'il me faut. (**b**) *(extreme)* tout. **at the ~ end** *[year]* tout à la fin; *[road]* tout au bout; **to the ~ end** jusqu'au bout; **in the ~ depths of** au plus profond de. (**c**) *(mere)* seul. **the ~ word** le mot seul, rien que le mot; **the ~ thought of it** rien que d'y penser; **the ~ idea!** quelle idée alors!

vespers ['vespəz] *npl* vêpres *fpl.*

vessel ['vesl] *n (all senses)* vaisseau *m.*

vest[1] [vest] **1** *n* (**a**) *(Brit) [man]* tricot *m* de corps; *[woman]* chemise *f* américaine. (**b**) *(US)* gilet *m.* **2** *adj*: *(US)* **~ pocket** poche *f* de gilet. ◆ **vest-pocket** *adj (US) calculator* de poche; *(fig)* minuscule.

vest[2] [vest] *vt*: **to ~ sb with sth, to ~ sth in sb** investir qn de qch; **the authority ~ed in me** l'autorité dont je suis investi; *(Fin)* **~ed interests** droits *mpl* acquis; *(fig)* **he has a ~ed interest in it** il est directement intéressé là-dedans.

vestibule ['vestɪbju:l] *n* vestibule *m.*

vestige ['vestɪdʒ] *n (gen)* vestige *m. (fig)* **not a ~ of truth/common sense** pas une trace de vérité/de bon sens.

vestment ['vestmənt] *n* vêtement *m* sacerdotal.

vestry ['vestrɪ] *n* sacristie *f.*

vet [vet] **1** *n (abbr of* **veterinary surgeon***)* vétérinaire *mf.* **2** *vt text* revoir; *application* examiner minutieusement; *figures* vérifier; *report (check)* vérifier le contenu de; *(approve)* approuver. **it was ~ted by him** c'est lui qui l'a approuvé; **to ~ sb for a job** se renseigner de façon approfondie au sujet de qn avant de lui offrir un poste.

vetch [vetʃ] *n* vesce *f.*

veteran ['vet(ə)r(ə)n] **1** *n* vétéran *m.* **war ~** ancien combattant *m. (US)* **V~s Day** le onze novembre *(anniversaire de l'armistice).* **2** *adj traveller, writer* chevronné. **she is a ~ campaigner for...** elle fait campagne depuis toujours pour...; **a ~ teacher/golfer** un vétéran de l'enseignement/du golf; **~ car** voiture *f* d'époque *(avant 1916).*

veterinary ['vet(ə)rɪn(ə)rɪ] *adj* vétérinaire. **~ surgeon** vétérinaire *mf.*

veto ['vi:təʊ] **1** *n, pl* **-es** veto *m.* **to have a/use one's ~** avoir un/exercer son droit de veto. **2** *vt (also* **put a ~ on***)* opposer son veto à.

vex [veks] *vt* contrarier, fâcher. ◆ **vexation** *n* ennui *m.* ◆ **vexatious** *or* ◆ **vexing** *adj* contrariant. ◆ **vexed** *adj* fâché (*with sb* contre qn); *question* controversé; **to get ~ed** se fâcher.

via ['vaɪə] *prep* par, via. **to go ~ Paris** passer par Paris; **to send a message ~ the computer** envoyer un message par l'ordinateur; **detected ~ a satellite** détecté au moyen d'un satellite.

viable ['vaɪəbl] *adj* viable. ◆ **viability** *n* viabilité *f.*

viaduct ['vaɪədʌkt] *n* viaduc *m.*

vibes ⁑ [vaɪbz] *npl (abbr of* **vibrations***)* atmosphère *f.* **the ~ are wrong** ça ne gaze pas *.

vibrate [vaɪ'breɪt] *vi* vibrer (*with* de). ◆ **vibrant** *adj* vibrant. ◆ **vibration** *n* vibration *f.*

viburnum [vaɪ'bɜ:nəm] *n* viorne *f.*

vicar ['vɪkə^r] *n (C of E)* pasteur *m*; *(RC)* vicaire *m.* ◆ **vicarage** *n* presbytère *m (anglican).*

vicarious [vɪ'kɛərɪəs] *adj suffering etc* à la place d'un autre. **to get ~ pleasure from** retirer indirectement du plaisir de. ◆ **vicariously** *adv* indirectement.

vice[1] [vaɪs] **1** *n* vice *m*; *(less strong)* défaut *m*. *[animal]* **he has no ~s** il n'est pas vicieux. **2** *adj (Police)* **V~ Squad** brigade *f* des mœurs.

vice[2] [vaɪs] *n (tool)* étau *m*.

vice[3] ['vaɪsɪ] *prep* à la place de.

vice- [vaɪs] *pref* vice-. **~admiral** vice-amiral *m* d'escadre; **~chairman** vice-président(e) *m(f)* ; **~chancellor** *(Univ)* vice-président(e) *m(f)* d'université; *(Jur)* vice-chancelier *m*; **~president** vice-président(e) *m(f)*; **~presidential** vice-présidentiel. ◆ **viceroy** *n* vice-roi *m*.

vice versa ['vaɪsɪ'vɜːsə] *adv* vice versa.

vicinity [vɪ'sɪnɪtɪ] *n (nearby area)* environs *mpl*, alentours *mpl*; *(closeness)* proximité *f*. **in the ~** dans les environs; **in the ~ of** aux alentours de.

vicious ['vɪʃəs] *adj remark, look* méchant; *kick, attack* brutal; *tongue* de vipère; *habit, animal, circle* vicieux. ◆ **viciously** *adv* méchamment; brutalement. ◆ **viciousness** *n* méchanceté *f*; brutalité *f*.

vicissitude [vɪ'sɪsɪtjuːd] *n* vicissitude *f*.

victim ['vɪktɪm] *n* victime *f*. **to be the ~ of** être victime de; **to fall (a) ~ to** devenir la victime de; *(fig: to sb's charms etc)* succomber à. ◆ **victimization** *n* représailles *fpl (subies par un ou plusieurs des responsables)*; **he alleged ~ization** il a prétendu être victime de représailles. ◆ **victimize** *vt* prendre pour victime; *(after strike etc)* exercer des représailles sur; **to be ~ized** être victime de représailles.

Victorian [vɪk'tɔːrɪən] **1** *n* Victorien(ne) *m(f)*. **2** *adj* victorien. ◆ **Victoriana** *n* antiquités *fpl* victoriennes.

victory ['vɪkt(ə)rɪ] *n* victoire *f*. **to win a ~ over** remporter une victoire sur. ◆ **victor** *n* vainqueur *m*. ◆ **victorious** [vɪk'tɔːrɪəs] *adj (gen)* victorieux; *shout* de victoire; **to be victorious** sortir victorieux (*in* de). ◆ **victoriously** *adv* victorieusement.

victuals ['vɪtlz] *npl* victuailles *fpl*.

video ['vɪdɪəʊ] **1** *n* (**a**) *(medium)* vidéo *f*; *(machine)* magnétoscope *m*; *(cassette)* vidéocassette *f*. (**b**) *(US: television)* télévision *f*, télé * *f*. (**c**) *(for song)* clip *m*. **2** *adj (on ~) film* en vidéo; *facilities, game* vidéo *inv*; *(US: on television) film* télévisé. **~ camera** caméra *f* vidéo; **~ cassette** vidéocassette *f*; **~ frequency** vidéofréquence *f*; **~ game** jeu *m* vidéo; **~ nasty** * vidéocassette à caractère violent; **~ recorder** magnétoscope *m*; **~ recording** enregistrement *m* en vidéo; **~ tape** bande *f* vidéo; *(cassette)* vidéocassette *f*. **3** *vt programe* enregistrer sur magnétoscope; *wedding* filmer en vidéo. ◆ **videotex** ® *n* vidéotex *m* ®.

vie [vaɪ] *vi* rivaliser (*with sb in doing* avec qn pour faire), lutter (*with sb for sth* avec qn pour (avoir) qch; *with sb for doing* avec qn pour faire).

Vietnam ['vjet'næm] Viet-Nam *m*. ◆ **Vietnamese** **1** *adj* vietnamien ; **2** *n* (**a**) *(pl inv)* Vietnamien(ne) *m(f)*; (**b**) *(Ling)* vietnamien *m*.

view [vjuː] **1** *n* (**a**) *(gen)* vue *f*. **in full ~ of** en plein devant; **to come into ~** apparaître; **to come into ~ of** arriver en vue de; **the house is within ~ of the sea** de la maison on voit la mer; **hidden from ~** caché; *(lit, fig)* **to keep sth in ~** ne pas perdre qch de vue; *[exhibit]* **on ~** exposé; **the house is on ~** on peut visiter la maison; **back/front ~ of the house** la maison vue de derrière/de devant; **you'll get a better ~ from here** vous verrez mieux d'ici; **there is a splendid ~** la vue est splendide; **a ~ over...** une vue sur...; **50 ~s of Paris** 50 vues de Paris; **a room with a ~** une chambre avec une belle vue. (**b**) *(opinion)* avis *m*, opinion *f*. **in my ~** à mon avis; **to hold ~s on** avoir des opinions sur; **to take the ~ that** penser que; **to take a dim *** *or* **a poor ~ of sth** apprécier médiocrement qch; **to fall in with sb's ~s** tomber d'accord avec qn; **point of ~** point *m* de vue. (**c**) *(survey)* vue *f*, aperçu *m*. **a general** *or* **an overall ~ of a problem** une vue d'ensemble d'un problème; **to take the long ~** prévoir les choses de loin; **in ~ of** étant donné, vu; **in ~ of the fact that** étant donné que, vu que. (**d**) *(intention)* but *m*. **to have in ~** envisager (*sth* qch; *doing* de faire); **with this in ~** dans ce but; **with a ~ to doing** dans l'intention de faire.
2 *vt* (**a**) *(look at, see)* voir; *(TV programme)* regarder. **London ~ed from the air** Londres vu d'avion. (**b**) *(examine)* examiner, inspecter; *slides* visionner; *house* visiter. (**c**) *(think of, understand)* considérer, envisager. **to ~ sb/sth as...** considérer qn/qch comme...; **he ~s it very objectively** il se montre très objectif; **they ~ed the scheme favorably** ils ont été favorables au projet.
3 *vi (TV)* regarder la télévision.
◆ **viewer** *n* (**a**) *(TV)* téléspectateur *m*, -trice *f*; (**b**) *(for slides)* visionneuse *f*. ◆ **viewfinder** *n* viseur *m*. ◆ **viewing** **1** *n*: **it makes good ~ing** c'est un excellent spectacle de télévision ; **2** *adj*: **~ing figures** taux *m* d'écoute; **~ing public** téléspectateurs *mpl*. ◆ **viewpoint** *n* point *m* de vue.

vigil ['vɪdʒɪl] *n (gen)* veille *f*; *(by sickbed etc)* veillée *f*; *(Rel)* vigile *f*; *(Pol)* manifestation *f* silencieuse. ◆ **vigilance** *n* vigilance *f*. ◆ **vigilant** *adj* vigilant. ◆ **vigilante** *n* membre *m* d'un groupe d'autodéfense. ◆ **vigilantly** *adv* avec vigilance.

vigour, *(US)* **vigor** ['vɪgəʳ] *n* vigueur *f*. ◆ **vigorous** *adj* vigoureux; *defense* énergique. ◆ **vigorously** *adv* vigoureusement; énergiquement.

vile [vaɪl] *adj (base, evil)* vil, ignoble; *(extremely bad)* exécrable. **in a ~ temper** d'une humeur massacrante. ◆ **vilely** *adv* vilement. ◆ **vileness** *n* vilenie *f*. ◆ **vilification** [ˌvɪlɪfɪ'keɪʃ(ə)n] *n* calomnie *f*. ◆ **vilify** *vt* calomnier.

villa ['vɪlə] *n (in town)* pavillon *m (de banlieue)*; *(in country)* maison *f* de campagne; *(by sea)* villa *f*.

village ['vɪlɪdʒ] **1** *n* village *m*, bourgade *f*, patelin * *m*. **2** *adj school etc, idiot* du village. **~ green** pré *m* communal; **the ~ inn** l'auberge *f* du village; **a ~ inn** une auberge de campagne. ◆ **villager** *n* villageois(e) *m(f)*.

villain ['vɪlən] *n* scélérat *m*; *(in drama, novel)* traître(sse) *m(f)*; *(*: rascal)* coquin(e) *m(f)*; *(Police etc sl: criminal)* bandit *m*. ◆ **villainous** *adj (gen) deed etc* infâme; *(*: bad) coffee, weather* abominable. ◆ **villainy** *n* infamie *f*.

vim * [vɪm] *n* entrain *m*.

vinaigrette [ˌvɪneɪ'gret] *n (Culin)* vinaigrette *f*.

vindicate ['vɪndɪkeɪt] *vt (gen)* justifier; *rights* faire valoir. ◆ **vindication** *n* justification *f*; **in vindication of** pour justifier.

vindictive [vɪn'dɪktɪv] *adj* vindicatif. ◆ **vindictively** *adv* vindicativement.

vine [vaɪn] *n* vigne *f*. ◆ **vine-grower** *n* viticulteur *m*, vigneron *m*. ◆ **vine-growing** *adj district* viticole. ◆ **vineyard** ['vɪnjəd] *n* vignoble *m*.

vinegar ['vɪnɪgəʳ] *n* vinaigre *m*.

vintage ['vɪntɪdʒ] **1** *n (harvesting; season)* vendanges *fpl*; *(year)* année *f*. **what ~ is it?** c'est de quelle année?; **the 1972 ~** le vin de 1972. **2** *adj* (**a**) *wine* de grand cru. **a ~ year** une bonne année (*for* pour); **~ car** voiture *f* d'époque *(1917-1930)*. (**b**) *(typical)* typique.

vinyl ['vaɪnɪl] **1** *n* vinyle *m*. **2** *adj* de vinyle.

viola[1] [vɪ'əʊlə] *n (Mus)* alto *m*. **~ player** altiste *mf*.

viola[2] ['vaɪ'əʊlə] *n (Bot)* pensée *f*.

violate ['vaɪəleɪt] *vt rule* violer; *rights* bafouer; *frontier* ne pas respecter. ◆ **violation** *n* (**a**) violation *f*; **it's a violation of his privacy** c'est s'ingérer dans sa vie privée; (**b**) *(US: offence)* contravention *f*.

violence ['vaɪələns] *n* violence *f*. **to use ~ against** employer la violence contre; **there was an outbreak of ~** de violents incidents *mpl* ont éclaté;

racial ~ violents incidents raciaux; **terrorist** ~ actes *mpl* de violence terroristes; **crime of** ~ voie *f* de fait; *(Jur)* **robbery with** ~ vol *m* avec coups et blessures; *(fig)* **to do** ~ **to** faire violence à. ◆ **violent** *adj (gen)* violent; *halt, braking* brutal; *colour* criard; **violent scenes** scènes *fpl* de violence; **to die a violent death** mourir de mort violente; **to have a violent temper** avoir un tempérament violent; **to be in a violent temper** être dans une rage folle; **by violent means** par la violence; **a violent dislike** une vive aversion (*for* envers). ◆ **violently** *adv struggle, react* violemment; *(severely) ill, angry* terriblement; **to behave violently** se montrer violent; **to fall violently in love with** tomber follement amoureux de.

violet ['vaɪəlɪt] **1** *n (Bot)* violette *f*; *(colour)* violet *m*. **2** *adj* violet.

violin [ˌvaɪə'lɪn] **1** *n* violon *m*. **2** *adj sonata* pour violon. ◆ **violinist** *n* violoniste *mf*.

viper ['vaɪpəʳ] *n* vipère *f*.

virgin ['vɜːdʒɪn] **1** *n* vierge *f*; garçon *m* vierge. **she/he is a** ~ elle/il est vierge; **the Blessed V**~ la Sainte Vierge. **2** *adj (fig) forest* vierge; *snow* frais. ◆ **virginity** *n* virginité *f*.

Virginia creeper [və'dʒɪnjə'kriːpəʳ] *n* vigne *f* vierge.

Virgo ['vɜːgəʊ] *n (Astron)* la Vierge.

virile ['vɪraɪl] *adj* viril. ◆ **virility** *n* virilité *f*.

virtual ['vɜːtjʊəl] *adj*: **he is the** ~ **leader** en fait c'est lui le chef; **a** ~ **impossibility** une quasi-impossibilité; **it was a** ~ **failure** ce fut pratiquement un échec. ◆ **virtually** *adv (in reality)* en fait; *(almost)* pratiquement; **he is** ~**ly the leader** en fait c'est lui le chef; **it** ~**ly failed** ça a pratiquement échoué; ~**ly certain** pratiquement certain.

virtue ['vɜːtjuː] *n* vertu *f*. **to make a** ~ **of necessity** faire de nécessité vertu; **by** ~ **of** en vertu de; **to have the** ~ **of being** *[thing]* avoir l'avantage d'être; *[person]* avoir le mérite d'être; **there is no** ~ **in doing that** il n'y a aucun mérite à faire cela. ◆ **virtuous** *adj* vertueux. ◆ **virtuously** *adv* vertueusement.

virtuoso [ˌvɜːtjʊ'əʊzəʊ] **1** *n* virtuose *mf*. **violin** ~ virtuose du violon. **2** *adj performance* de virtuose. ◆ **virtuosity** *n* virtuosité *f*.

virulence ['vɪrʊləns] *n* virulence *f*. ◆ **virulent** *adj* virulent.

virus ['vaɪərəs] *n* virus *m*. **rabies** ~ virus de la rage; ~ **disease** maladie *f* virale.

visa ['viːzə] *n* visa *m (de passeport)*.

vis-à-vis ['viːzəviː] *prep (+ person)* vis-à-vis de; *(+ thing)* par rapport à.

viscera ['vɪsərə] *npl* viscères *mpl*.

viscount ['vaɪkaʊnt] *n* vicomte *m*.

viscous ['vɪskəs] *adj* visqueux.

vise [vaɪs] *n (US)* = **vice²**.

visible ['vɪzəbl] *adj* (**a**) visible. ~ **to the naked eye** visible à l'œil nu; **to become** ~ apparaître. (**b**) *(obvious)* manifeste. **with** ~ **impatience** avec une impatience manifeste. ◆ **visibility** *n* visibilité *f*. ◆ **visibly** *adv* visiblement; *(obviously)* manifestement.

vision ['vɪʒ(ə)n] *n (gen)* vision *f*; *(eyesight)* vue *f*. **a man of** ~ un homme qui voit loin; **his** ~ **of the future** la façon dont il voit l'avenir; **to see** ~**s** avoir des visions; **to have** ~**s of wealth** avoir des visions de richesses; **she had** ~**s of being drowned** elle s'est vue noyée. ◆ **visionary** *adj, n* visionnaire *(mf)*. ◆ **vision-mixing** *n* mixage *m* d'images.

visit ['vɪzɪt] **1** *n (call, tour)* visite *f*; *(stay)* séjour *m*. **to pay a** ~ **to** *person* rendre visite à; *place* aller à; **to be on a** ~ **to** *person* être en visite chez; *place* faire un séjour à; **on a private/an official** ~ en visite privée/officielle; *(fig)* **to pay a** ~ * aller au petit coin *. **2** *vt* (**a**) *(go and see) person* aller voir; *(more formally)* rendre visite à; *town, museum, zoo, theatre* aller à. (**b**) *(stay with or in) person* faire un séjour chez; *town, country* faire un séjour à (*or* en). (**c**) *(inspect) place* inspecter; *troops* passer en revue. ◆ **visitation** *n [official]* visite *f* d'inspection; *[bishop]* visite pastorale. ◆ **visiting** *adj friends* de passage; *lecturer* invité; *professor etc* associé; ~**ing card** carte *f* de visite; *(US)* ~**ing fireman** * visiteur *m* de marque; ~**ing hours** *or* **time** heures *fpl* de visite; *(US)* ~**ing teacher** ≃ visiteuse *f* scolaire; *(Sport)* **the** ~**ing team** les visiteurs *mpl*; **I'm not on** ~**ing terms with him** nous ne nous rendons pas visite. ◆ **visitor** *n (guest)* invité(e) *m(f)*; *(in hotel)* client(e) *m(f)*; *(tourist; also at exhibition etc)* visiteur *m*, -euse *f*; ~**ors' book** livre *m* d'or; *(in hotel)* registre *m*; ~**ors to Paris** les visiteurs de passage à Paris; ~**ors to the exhibition** les personnes *fpl* visitant l'exposition.

visor ['vaɪzəʳ] *n* visière *f*.

vista ['vɪstə] *n (view)* panorama *m*; *(fig)* perspective *f*.

visual ['vɪzjʊəl] *adj* visuel. ~ **aid** support *m* visuel; **to teach with** ~ **aids** enseigner par des méthodes visuelles; ~ **arts** arts *mpl* plastiques; *(Comput)* ~ **display unit** *(abbr* **V.D.U.***)* console *f* de visualisation, visuel *m*. ◆ **visualize** *vt (imagine)* se représenter (*sth* qch; *sb doing* qn faisant); *(foresee)* envisager. ◆ **visually** *adv* visuellement.

vital ['vaɪtl] *adj* (**a**) *(gen)* vital; *importance* capital; *error* fatal. ~ **statistics** *[population]* statistiques *fpl* démographiques; *(*: woman's)* mensurations *fpl*; ~ **to sb/sth** indispensable à qn/pour qch; **it is** ~ **that...** il est indispensable *or* vital que... + *subj*. (**b**) *(lively)* plein d'entrain. ◆ **vitality** *n* vitalité *f*. ◆ **vitally** *adv necessary* absolument; *urgent* extrêmement; **it is** ~**ly important** c'est d'une importance capitale; **it is** ~**ly important that** il est absolument indispensable que + *subj*.

vitamin ['vɪtəmɪn] **1** *n* vitamine *f*. ~ **A/B** *etc* vitamine A/B *etc*; **with added** ~ **s**, ~**-enriched** vitaminé. **2** *adj content* en vitamines; *tablets* de vitamines. ~ **deficiency** carence *f* en vitamines.

vitiate ['vɪʃɪeɪt] *vt* vicier.

vitreous ['vɪtrɪəs] *adj (gen)* vitreux; *enamel* vitrifié. ◆ **vitrify** *vt* vitrifier.

vitriol ['vɪtrɪəl] *n (Chem, fig)* vitriol *m*. ◆ **vitriolic** *adj (fig)* venimeux.

vitro ['viːtrəʊ]: *(Med)* **in** ~ **fertilization** fécondation *f* in vitro.

vituperation [vɪˌtjuːpə'reɪʃ(ə)n] *n* vitupérations *fpl*.

viva ['vaɪvə] *n* oral *m*. ◆ **viva voce** ['vaɪvə'vəʊsɪ] *adv* de vive voix.

vivacious [vɪ'veɪʃəs] *adj* vif, enjoué. ◆ **vivaciously** *adv* avec vivacité. ◆ **vivacity** [vɪ'væsɪtɪ] *n* vivacité *f*.

vivid ['vɪvɪd] *adj colour* vif, éclatant; *tie etc* voyant; *imagination* vif; *memory* net; *description* vivant; *dream* impressionnant. ◆ **vividly** *adv describe* d'une manière vivante; *imagine* de façon précise; *remember* très nettement. ◆ **vividness** *n [colour, light]* éclat *m*; *[style]* vigueur *f*.

vivisection [ˌvɪvɪ'sekʃ(ə)n] *n* vivisection *f*.

vixen ['vɪksn] *n* renarde *f*; *(woman)* mégère *f*.

viz [vɪz] *adv* c'est-à-dire.

vizier [vɪ'zɪəʳ] *n* vizir *m*.

vocabulary [və(ʊ)'kæbjʊlərɪ] *n (gen)* vocabulaire *m*; *(in textbook)* lexique *m*.

vocal ['vəʊk(ə)l] *adj* (**a**) *(gen)* vocal. ~ **cords** cordes *fpl* vocales. (**b**) *(voicing opinion) group, person* qui se fait entendre. ◆ **vocalic** *adj* vocalique. ◆ **vocalist** *n* chanteur *m*, -euse *f (dans un groupe)*.

◆ **vocalize** *vt (Ling)* vocaliser; *opinions etc* exprimer. ◆ **vocally** *adv* vocalement.

vocation [və(ʊ)'keɪʃ(ə)n] *n (Rel etc)*, vocation *f*. **to have a ~ for teaching** avoir la vocation de l'enseignement. ◆ **vocational** *adj training etc* professionnel; **~al guidance/training** orientation *f*/formation *f* professionnelle.

vocative ['vɒkətɪv] *adj, n* vocatif *(m)*.

vociferate [və(ʊ)'sɪfəreɪt] *vi* vociférer, brailler *. ◆ **vociferous** *adj* bruyant. ◆ **vociferously** *adv* en vociférant.

vodka ['vɒdkə] *n* vodka *f*.

vogue [vəʊg] *n* vogue *f*. **to be the ~** *or* **in ~** être en vogue; **to have a great ~** être très en vogue.

voice [vɔɪs] **1** *n (gen, Gram etc)* voix *f*. **to lose one's ~** avoir une extinction de voix; **in good ~** en voix; **in a soft ~** d'une voix douce; **soft-~d** à voix douce; **at the top of his ~** à tue-tête; *(fig)* **to have a ~ in the matter** avoir voix au chapitre; **with one ~** à l'unanimité. **2** *vt feelings etc* exprimer; *(Ling) consonant* voiser. ◆ **voiceless** *adj* sans voix; *consonant* sourd. ◆ **voice-over** *n* commentaire *m* (voix hors champ).

void [vɔɪd] **1** *n* vide *m*. **to fill the ~** combler le vide. **2** *adj (gen)* vide; *(Jur)* nul. **~ of** dépourvu de.

volatile ['vɒlətaɪl] *adj (Chem)* volatil; *(fig) situation* explosif; *person* versatile.

volcano [vɒl'keɪnəʊ] *n* volcan *m*. ◆ **volcanic** [vɒl'kænɪk] *adj* volcanique.

vole [vəʊl] *n (Zool)* campagnol *m*.

volition [vɒ'lɪʃ(ə)n] *n*: **of one's own ~** de son propre gré.

volley ['vɒlɪ] **1** *n* (**a**) *(Mil)* volée *f*; *[stones]* grêle *f*; *[insults]* bordée *f*; *[questions]* feu *m* roulant; *[applause]* salve *f*. (**b**) *(Sport)* volée *f*. **2** *vt ball* reprendre de volée. ◆ **volleyball** *n* volley(-ball) *m*.

volt [vəʊlt] *n* volt *m*. ◆ **voltage** *n* voltage *m*, tension *f*; **high/low ~age** haute/basse tension.

volte-face ['vɒlt'fɑːs] *n* volte-face *f inv*.

voluble ['vɒljʊbl] *adj* volubile. ◆ **volubility** *n* volubilité *f*. ◆ **volubly** *adv* avec volubilité.

volume ['vɒljuːm] *n* (**a**) *(book)* volume *m*. **in 6 ~s** en 6 volumes; **~ one** tome *m* premier; **~ two/three** *etc* tome deux/trois *etc*. (**b**) *(size; sound)* volume *m*; *[tank]* capacité *f*. **~ of water/production** volume d'eau/de la production; *(Rad, TV)* **to turn the ~ up/down** augmenter/diminuer le volume; **~s of smoke** nuages *mpl* de fumée; **~s of tears** flots *mpl* de larmes; **to write ~s** écrire des volumes; **it speaks ~s for...** cela en dit long sur... ◆ **voluminous** *adj* volumineux.

volunteer [ˌvɒlən'tɪəʳ] **1** *n (Mil, gen)* volontaire *mf*; *(helper)* bénévole. **2** *adj army, group* de volontaires; *helper* bénévole; *driver* qui se porte volontaire. **3** *vt help etc* offrir de son plein gré; *information, suggestion, facts* fournir spontanément. **'seven' he ~ed** 'sept' dit-il spontanément. **4** *vi* s'offrir, se proposer (*for sth* pour qch; *to do* pour faire); *(Mil)* s'engager comme volontaire (*for* dans). ◆ **voluntarily** *adv (willingly)* volontairement; *(without payment)* bénévolement. ◆ **voluntary** *adj confession, contribution* volontaire; *(unpaid) help, work, worker* bénévole; *(US)* **voluntary hospital** hôpital *m* de l'assistance publique; *(Brit)* **Voluntary Service Overseas** ≃ coopération *f* technique à l'étranger.

voluptuous [və'lʌptjʊəs] *adj* voluptueux. ◆ **voluptuously** *adv* voluptueusement. ◆ **voluptuousness** *n* volupté *f*.

vomit ['vɒmɪt] **1** *vti* vomir. **2** *n* vomi *m*. ◆ **vomiting** *n* vomissements *mpl*.

voracious [və'reɪʃəs] *adj (gen)* vorace; *reader* avide. ◆ **voraciously** *adv eat* avec voracité. ◆ **voracity** [vɒ'ræsɪtɪ] *n* voracité *f*.

vortex ['vɔːteks] *n* vortex *m*; *(fig)* tourbillon *m*.

votary ['vəʊtərɪ] *n* fervent(e) *m(f)* (*of* de).

vote [vəʊt] **1** *n (gen)* vote *m*; *(~ cast)* vote, voix *f* (*for* pour; *against* contre). **to give the ~ to sb** accorder le droit de vote à qn; **~s for women!** droit de vote pour les femmes!; **to put sth to the ~** mettre qch au vote; **to take a ~** *(gen)* voter; *(on motion)* procéder au vote (*on* sur); **~ of censure** *or* **no confidence** motion *f* de censure; **to pass a ~ of censure** voter la censure; **to pass a ~ of confidence in** passer un vote de confiance à l'égard de; **~ of thanks** discours *m* de remerciement; **to win ~s** gagner des voix; **to count the ~s** compter les voix *or* les votes; *(Pol)* dépouiller le scrutin; **the Labour ~** les voix travaillistes. **2** *vt* (**a**) (**~ through**) *bill, sum of money etc* voter. **the committee ~d to request a subsidy** le comité a voté une demande de subvention. (**b**) *(elect*: **~ in**) élire. **he was ~d chairman** il a été élu président; *(fig)* **they ~d her the best cook** ils l'ont proclamée la meilleure cuisinière; **I ~ * we go** je propose qu'on y aille. **3** *vi* voter (*for sb/sth* pour qn/qch; *against* contre). **~ for Robert!** votez Robert!; **to ~ Socialist** voter socialiste; **to ~ on sth** mettre qch au vote. ◆ **voter** *n* électeur *m*, -trice *f*; *(US Pol)* **~r registration** inscription *f* sur les listes électorales. ◆ **voting** **1** *n (process of voting)* scrutin *m*; *(result)* vote *m* ; **2** *adj*: **voting booth** isoloir *m*; **voting paper** bulletin *m* de vote.

votive ['vəʊtɪv] *adj* votif.

vouch [vaʊtʃ] *vi*: **to ~ for** *(gen)* répondre de; *truth of sth* garantir. ◆ **voucher** *n (gen)* bon *m*; *(receipt)* reçu *m*.

vow [vaʊ] **1** *n* vœu *m*. **to take** *or* **make a ~** faire vœu (*to do* de faire); *(Rel)* **to take one's ~s** prononcer ses vœux. **2** *vt* jurer (*to do* de faire; *that* que); *obedience etc* vouer. **to ~ (to o.s.) to do** se jurer de faire.

vowel ['vaʊ(ə)l] **1** *n* voyelle *f*. **2** *adj* vocalique.

voyage ['vɔɪɪdʒ] **1** *n* voyage *m* par mer, traversée *f*. **to go on a ~** partir en voyage (par mer); **the ~ out/home** le voyage d'aller/de retour; **~ of discovery** voyage d'exploration. **2** *vi* voyager (par mer). ◆ **voyager** *n* voyageur *m*, -euse *f*.

vulcanize ['vʌlkənaɪz] *vt* vulcaniser. ◆ **vulcanite** *n* ébonite *f*. ◆ **vulcanization** *n* vulcanisation *f*.

vulgar ['vʌlgəʳ] *adj (gen)* vulgaire; *(pej)* vulgaire, grossier. **~ Latin** latin *m* vulgaire; **~ word** gros mot *m*; **~ fraction** fraction *f* ordinaire. ◆ **vulgarity** *n* vulgarité *f*. ◆ **vulgarly** *adv (all senses)* vulgairement. ◆ **Vulgate** *n* Vulgate *f*.

vulnerable ['vʌln(ə)rəbl] *adj* vulnérable. **his ~ spot** son point faible. ◆ **vulnerability** *n* vulnérabilité *f*.

vulture ['vʌltʃəʳ] *n* vautour *m*.

W, w ['dʌblju:] *n (letter)* W, w *m.*

wad [wɒd] **1** *n [cloth, paper, cotton wool]* tampon *m*; *[putty, chewing gum]* boulette *f*; *[straw]* bouchon *m*; *[tobacco]* carotte *f*; *(chewing)* chique *f*; *[documents, banknotes]* liasse *f*. **2** *vt garment* ouater; *quilt* rembourrer. ◆ **wadding** *n (gen)* bourre *f*; *(for lining)* rembourrage *m*; *(for garments)* ouate *f*.

waddle ['wɒdl] *vi* se dandiner. **to ~ in/out** *etc* entrer/sortir *etc* en se dandinant.

wade [weɪd] **1** *vi (for fun)* barboter. **to ~ through** *water, mud* patauger dans; *long grass* avancer avec difficulté dans; *(* fig) book, work etc* venir péniblement à bout de; **to ~ ashore** regagner la rive à pied; *(fig)* **to ~ into sb** * *(attack)* tomber sur qn; *(scold)* engueuler ‡ qn; **to ~ into a meal** * attaquer * un repas. **2** *vt stream* traverser à gué. ◆ **wader** *n (boot)* botte *f* de pêcheur; *(bird)* échassier *m*. **wading pool** *n (US)* petit bassin *m*.

wafer ['weɪfəʳ] *n (Culin)* gaufrette *f*; *(Rel)* hostie *f*; *(Comput)* galette *f*. ◆ **wafer-thin** *adj* mince comme une pelure d'oignon.

waffle¹ ['wɒfl] *n (Culin)* gaufre *f*. **~ iron** gaufrier *m*.

waffle² * ['wɒfl] **1** *n (words)* verbiage *m*. **2** *vi* parler interminablement (*about* de), parler pour ne rien dire.

wag [wæg] **1** *vt (gen)* agiter, remuer (*sth at sb/sth* qch dans la direction de qn/qch). **the dog ~ged its tail at me** le chien a remué la queue en me voyant. **2** *vi [tail]* remuer. *(fig)* **his tongue never stops ~ging** il a la langue bien pendue; **it set tongues ~ging** cela a fait jaser. **3** *n*: **with a ~ of its tail** en remuant la queue. ◆ **wagtail** *n* hoche-queue *m*.

wage [weɪdʒ] **1** *n (also* **~s***)* salaire *m*, paye *f*; *[servant]* gages *mpl*. **hourly/weekly ~** salaire horaire/hebdomadaire; **2 days' ~s** 2 jours de salaire *or* de paye; **his ~s are £75 per week** il touche 75 livres par semaine; **he gets a good ~** il est bien payé. **2** *adj rise* de salaire; *scale, freeze* des salaires. **~ bill** masse *f* salariale; **~ demand** *or* **claim** revendication *f* salariale; **~ earner** salarié(e) *m(f)*; **the family ~ earner** le soutien de la famille; **~ packet** paye *f*; **~s clerk** ≃ aide-comptable *mf*; **~ restraint** limitation *f* des salaires; **~s slip** fiche *f* de paye. **3** *vt*: **to ~ war** faire la guerre (*against* à, contre); **to ~ a campaign** mener une campagne (*for* pour).

wager ['weɪdʒəʳ] **1** *vt* parier (*sth on* qch sur; *that* que). **2** *n* pari *m*.

waggle ['wægl] **1** *vt pencil, tail etc* agiter; *loose screw etc* faire jouer; *hips* tortiller de. **2** *vi [tail]* frétiller; *[tooth]* branler.

waggon, *(esp US)* **wagon** ['wægən] *n (horse-drawn)* chariot *m*; *(truck)* camion *m*; *(Rail)* wagon *m* (de marchandises); *(*: car)* auto *f*, bagnole * *f*; *(US: also* **station ~***)* break *m*; *(tea trolley)* table *f* roulante; *(larger: for tea urn)* chariot. *(fig)* **to go on the ~** * ne plus boire (d'alcool). ◆ **wag(g)oner** *n* roulier *m*. ◆ **wag(g)onload** *n (Agr)* charretée *f*; *(Rail)* wagon *m*.

waif [weɪf] *n* enfant *mf* misérable. **~s and strays** enfants *mpl* abandonnés.

wail [weɪl] **1** *vi (gen)* gémir; *(cry)* pleurer; *(whine)* pleurnicher; *[baby]* vagir; *[siren]* hurler. **2** *n* gémissement *m*; pleurs *mpl*; pleurnichements *mpl*; vagissement *m*; hurlement *m*. ◆ **wailing** **1** *n* gémissements *mpl*; vagissements *mpl*; hurlements *mpl* ; **2** *adj child* gémissant; *sound* plaintif.

wainscot(t)ing ['weɪnskətɪŋ] *n* lambrissage *m (en bois)*.

waist [weɪst] **1** *n (gen)* taille *f*, ceinture *f*. **to put one's arm round sb's ~** prendre qn par la taille; **stripped to the ~** torse nu; **he was up to the ~ in water** l'eau lui arrivait à la ceinture; **high-/low-~ed dress** robe *f* à taille haute/basse. **2** *adj*: **~ measurement** *or* **size** tour *m* de taille. ◆ **waistband** *n* ceinture *f (de jupe etc)*. ◆ **waistcoat** *n* gilet *m*. ◆ **waistline** *n* taille *f*; **to watch one's ~line** faire attention à sa ligne.

wait [weɪt] **1** *n* (**a**) *(gen)* attente *f*. **a 3-hour ~** 3 heures d'attente; *(between trains)* 3 heures de battement *m*; **to lie in ~** être à l'affût; **to lie in ~ for sb** *[huntsman, lion, reporter]* guetter qn; *[bandits, guerrillas]* dresser un guet-apens à qn. (**b**) *(Brit)* **the ~s** les chanteurs *mpl* de Noël.
2 *vi* (**a**) attendre (*for sb/sth* qn/qch; *for sb to do, until sb does* que qn fasse). **~ a moment!** un instant!; **~ till you're old enough** attends d'être assez grand; **just you ~!** tu vas voir ce que tu vas voir!; **just ~ till your father finds out!** attends un peu que ton père apprenne ça!; **~ and see!** attends voir!; **we'll just have to ~ and see** il va falloir attendre; **to keep sb ~ing** faire attendre qn; **they'll do it while you ~** on va le faire pendant que vous attendez; **'repairs while you ~'** 'réparations à la minute'; **he didn't ~ to be told twice** il ne se l'est pas fait dire deux fois; **that was worth ~ing for** cela valait la peine d'attendre; **I can't ~ to see him again** je meurs d'envie de le revoir; **they can't ~ to reverse this policy** ils brûlent de révoquer cette politique; **parcel ~ing to be collected** colis *m* en souffrance. (**b**) **to ~ at table** servir à table.
3 *vt* (**a**) attendre. **we'll ~ lunch for you** nous vous attendrons pour nous mettre à table. (**b**) *(US)* **to ~ table** servir à table.
◆ **wait about, wait around** *vi* attendre (*for sb/sth* qn/qch); *(loiter)* traîner. ◆ **wait behind** *vi* rester (*for sb* pour attendre qn). ◆ **wait on** *vt fus [servant]* servir. **she ~s on him hand and foot** elle est aux petits soins pour lui. ◆ **wait up** *vi* ne pas se coucher (*till 2 o'clock* avant 2 heures; *for sb* avant que qn ne revienne). **don't ~ up for me** couchez-vous sans m'attendre; **you can ~ up to see the programme** tu peux voir le programme avant de te coucher. ◆ **wait upon** *vt fus [ambassador etc]* présenter ses respects à.
◆ **waiter** *n* garçon *m* (de café); **~er!** garçon!, monsieur! ◆ **waiting** **1** *n* attente *f*; *(Aut)* **'no ~ing'** 'stationnement strictement interdit'; **2** *adj crowd etc* qui attend; *(fig)* **to play a ~ing game** *(gen)* attendre son heure; *(in negotiations etc)* mener une politique d'attente; **~ing list** liste *f* d'attente; **~ing room** salon *m* d'attente; *(in station etc)* salle *f* d'attente. ◆ **wait-list** *vt:* **to be ~-listed on a flight** être sur la liste d'attente d'un vol. ◆ **waitress** *n* serveuse *f*.

waive [weɪv] *vt claim* renoncer à; *condition* abandonner. ◆ **waiver** *n* renonciation *f* (*of* à).

wake¹ [weɪk] *n [ship]* sillage *m*. *(fig)* **in the ~ of** à la suite de; **to bring sth in its ~** amener qch dans son sillage; **to follow in sb's ~** marcher sur les traces de qn.

wake² [weɪk] *pret* **woke, waked,** *ptp* **waked, woken** **1** *vi* **(~ up)** se réveiller (*from* de); *(fig: start to work etc)* se secouer. **~ up!** réveille-toi!; **she woke (up) to find them gone** à son réveil elle s'est aperçue qu'ils étaient partis; *(fig)* **to ~ (up) to sth** prendre conscience de qch. **2** *vt* **(~ up)** *person* réveiller (*from* de); *(fig) memories, desires* éveiller. **a noise that would ~ the dead** un bruit à réveiller les morts; *(fig)* **he needs sth to ~ him up** il a besoin d'être secoué. **3** *n* (**a**) *(over corpse)* veillée *f* mortuaire. (**b**) *(N Engl)* **W~s (Week)** *semaine de congé annuel.* ◆**wakeful** *adj (awake)* éveillé; *(alert)* vigilant; *hours etc* sans sommeil. ◆**waken** *vti* = **wake²**. ◆**wakey-wakey** ⁑ *excl* réveillez-vous! ◆**waking** **1** *adj (not sleeping)* éveillé; **in one's waking hours** pendant les heures de veille; **all his waking hours** chaque heure de sa journée ; **2** *n*: **between waking and sleeping** entre la veille et le sommeil.

Wales [weɪlz] *n* pays *m* de Galles. **North/South ~** le Nord/le Sud du pays de Galles; **Secretary of State for ~** ministre *m* chargé du pays de Galles.

walk [wɔːk] **1** *n* (**a**) promenade *f*; *(~ing race)* épreuve *f* de marche. **to go for a ~** se promener, faire une promenade; *(shorter)* faire un tour; *(hike)* faire une randonnée; **a long ~** une grande promenade; **to take sb for a ~** emmener qn se promener; **to take the dog for a ~** promener le chien; **it is 10 minutes' ~ from here** c'est à 10 minutes à pied d'ici; **it's only a short ~ to the shops** il n'y a pas loin à marcher jusqu'aux magasins; *(US)* **in a ~** *win* dans un fauteuil; *do sth* les doigts dans le nez *. (**b**) *(gait)* démarche *f*. **I knew him by his ~** je l'ai reconnu à sa démarche. (**c**) **to slow down to a ~** ralentir pour aller au pas; **at a ~** sans courir. (**d**) *(avenue)* avenue *f*; *(path: in garden)* allée *f*; *(in country)* chemin *m*. *(fig)* **from all ~s of life** de toutes conditions sociales.

2 *vi (gen)* marcher (*on* sur); *(not run)* aller au pas; *(not ride or drive)* aller à pied; *(go for a ~)* se promener; *[ghost]* apparaître. **to ~ back/down** *etc* rentrer/descendre *etc* (à pied *or* sans courir); *(fig)* **you must ~ before you can run** on apprend petit à petit; **he ~s in his sleep** il est somnambule; **he's ~ing in his sleep** il marche en dormant; **to ~ up and down** marcher de long en large; *(fig)* **my pen seems to have ~ed** * mon stylo a fichu le camp *; **to ~ all the way to London** faire tout le chemin à pied jusqu'à Londres; **to ~ home** rentrer à pied; **to ~ into** *trap, ambush* tomber dans; *(bump into) table, person* se cogner à.

3 *vt* (**a**) *distance* faire à pied. **you can ~ it in a couple of minutes** à pied cela vous prendra deux minutes; *(fig: easy)* **he ~ed it** * cela a été un jeu d'enfant pour lui. (**b**) *town, road* parcourir. **to ~ the streets** se promener dans les rues; *(from poverty)* errer dans les rues; *[prostitute]* faire le trottoir; **to ~ the plank** subir le supplice de la planche. (**c**) *(cause to ~) invalid, prisoner* faire se promener; *dog* promener; *horse* conduire à pied; *cycle* pousser. **I ~ed him round Paris** je l'ai promené dans Paris; **to ~ sb in** *etc* faire entrer *etc* qn; **I'll ~ you home/to the station** je vais vous raccompagner/vous accompagner à la gare; **they ~ed him off his feet** ils l'ont tellement fait marcher qu'il ne tenait plus debout.

◆**walk about, walk around** *vi* aller et venir. ◆**walk across** *vi (over bridge etc)* traverser. **to ~ across to sb** s'approcher de qn. ◆**walk away** *vi* s'éloigner (*from* de), partir. *(fig: unharmed)* **to ~ away from an accident** sortir indemne d'un accident; **to ~ away with sth** *(steal)* emporter qch en partant; *(win easily)* gagner qch haut la main. ◆**walk in** *vi* entrer. **who should ~ in but Paul!** et voilà que Paul est entré à ce moment-là!; **he just ~ed in and gave me the sack** il est entré sans crier gare et m'a annoncé qu'il me mettait à la porte. ◆**walk off** **1** *vi* (**a**) = **walk away.** (**b**) *(steal)* **to ~ off with sth** barboter * *or* piquer * qch. **2** *vt sep excess weight* perdre en marchant. **to ~ off a headache** faire une promenade pour se débarrasser d'un mal de tête. ◆**walk on** *vi (Theat)* être figurant(e). ◆**walk out** *vi (go out)* sortir; *(go away)* partir; *(as protest)* partir en signe de protestation; *(strike)* se mettre en grève. **they ~ed out of the discussion** ils ont quitté la séance de discussion (en signe de protestation); **to ~ out on sb** * laisser tomber qn *. ◆**walk up** *vi (approach)* s'approcher (*to sb* de qn). *(at fair etc)* **~ up, ~ up!** approchez, approchez!

◆**walkabout** * *n [celebrity]* bain *m* de foule; **to go on a ~about** prendre un bain de foule. ◆**walker** *n* (**a**) *(esp Sport)* marcheur *m*, -euse *f*; *(for pleasure)* promeneur *m*, -euse *f*; **he's a good ~er** il est bon marcheur; **he's a fast ~er** il marche vite; (**b**) *(support: for convalescents etc)* déambulateur *m*; *(for babies)* trotte-bébé *m*. ◆**walkie-talkie** *n* talkie-walkie *m*. ◆**walk-in** *adj cupboard* de plain-pied. ◆**walking** **1** *n* (**a**) marche *f* à pied, promenade *f*; (**b**) *(Sport)* marche *f* athlétique ; **2** *adj shoes* de marche; *miracle* ambulant; *(Mil)* **the ~ing wounded** les blessés *mpl* capables de marcher; **a ~ing encyclopedia** une encyclopédie vivante; **it is within ~ing distance** on peut facilement y aller à pied (*of* de); **we had a ~ing holiday in the Tyrol** pour nos vacances nous avons fait de la marche dans le Tyrol; **~ing race** épreuve *f* de marche; **~ing stick** canne *f*; **to be on a ~ing tour** faire une longue randonnée à pied. ◆**walk(ing)-on part** *n (Theat)* rôle *m* de figurant(e). ◆**walkman** ® *n* walkman ® *m*, baladeur *m*. ◆**walkout** *n (strike)* grève *f* surprise; *(from meeting etc)* départ *m* en signe de protestation; **to stage a ~out** faire une grève surprise, partir en signe de protestation. ◆**walkover** *n (Racing)* walk-over *m*; *(fig) (game etc)* victoire *f* facile; *(exam etc)* jeu *m* d'enfant. ◆**walk-up** *n (US) (house)* immeuble *m* sans ascenseur; *(apartment)* appartement *m* dans un immeuble sans ascenseur. ◆**walkway** *n* passage *m* pour piétons.

wall [wɔːl] **1** *n (gen)* mur *m*; *(as defence)* rempart *m*, muraille *f*; *(interior; also of tunnel, stomach etc)* paroi *f*; *[tyre]* flanc *m*; *(fig: of smoke etc)* muraille. **within the (city) ~s** dans les murs; **the Great W~ of China** la grande muraille de Chine; **the Berlin W~** le mur de Berlin; **they left only the bare ~s standing** ils n'en ont laissé que les murs; *(Econ)* **tariff ~** barrière *f* douanière; **~s have ears** les murs ont des oreilles; *[prisoner]* **to go over the ~** s'évader; *(fig)* **to go to the ~** *[person]* perdre la partie; *(go bankrupt)* faire faillite; *[plan, activity]* être sacrifié; **it's the weakest to the ~** les plus faibles doivent céder le pas; *(fig)* **he had his back to the ~, he was up against the ~** il était acculé; *(fig)* **to bang one's head against a brick ~** se taper la tête contre les murs; *(fig)* **to come up against a blank ~** se heurter à un mur; **to drive sb up the ~** * rendre qn dingue * *or* fou; *(US)* **off the ~** * dingue *. **2** *adj cupboard, clock, map, socket* mural. **~ chart** planche *f* murale *(gravure)*; **~ lamp** *or* **light** applique *f (lampe)*. **3** *vt* **(~ in)** *garden* entourer d'un mur; *city* fortifier. **to ~ sb/sth up** murer qn/qch. ◆**walled** *adj garden* clos; *city* fortifié. ◆**wall-eyed** *adj* qui louche. ◆**wallflower** *n* giroflée *f*; *(fig)* **to be a ~flower** faire tapisserie. ◆**wallpaper** **1** *n* papier *m* peint ; **2** *vt* tapisser (de papier peint). ◆**wall-to-wall carpeting** *n* moquette *f*.

wallaby ['wɒləbɪ] *n* wallaby *m*.

wallet ['wɒlɪt] *n* portefeuille *m*.

Walloon [wɒ'luːn] **1** *adj* wallon. **2** *n* Wallon(ne) *m(f)*; *(Ling)* wallon *m*.

wallop * ['wɒləp] **1** *n* (grand) coup *m*; *(sound)* fracas *m*. **it hit the floor with a ~** vlan! c'est tombé par terre. **2** *vt person* flanquer une raclée à; *object* taper sur. ◆ **walloping** ‡ **1** *adj (big etc)* sacré * *(before n)*, formidable * ; **2** *n (beating)* rossée * *f*.

wallow ['wɒləʊ] *vi (gen: also in vice etc)* se vautrer (*in* dans); *(in self-pity etc)* se complaire (*in* à); *[ship]* être ballotté.

wally ‡ ['wɒlɪ] *n* idiot *m*.

walnut ['wɔːlnʌt] **1** *n* noix *f*; *(tree, wood)* noyer *m*. **2** *adj table etc* en noyer; *cake* aux noix; *oil* de noix.

walrus ['wɔːlrəs] *n* morse *m (Zool)*. *(hum)* **~ moustache** moustache *f* à la gauloise.

waltz [wɔːlts] **1** *n* valse *f*. **2** *vi* valser. *(fig)* **to ~ in/out** *etc* entrer/sortir *etc (gaily)* d'un pas joyeux *or (brazenly)* avec désinvolture.

wan [wɒn] *adj (gen)* pâle; *person, look* triste. ◆ **wanly** *adv smile, say* tristement.

wand [wɒnd] *n* baguette *f* (magique); *[usher etc]* verge *f*, bâton *m*.

wander ['wɒndəʳ] **1** *n*: **to go for a ~ around the town/the shops** aller faire un tour en ville/dans les magasins. **2** *vi* (**~ about, ~ around)** *(gen)* errer; *(idly)* flâner; *[river, road]* serpenter; *(stray)* s'écarter (*from* de), s'égarer. **to ~ in/away** *etc* entrer/partir *etc* sans se presser; **they ~ed round the shop** ils ont flâné dans le magasin; **he ~ed off the path** il s'est écarté du chemin, il s'est égaré; **his thoughts ~ed back to...** ses pensées se sont distraitement reportées à...; **my mind was ~ing** j'étais distrait; *(pej)* **his mind is ~ing** il divague. **3** *vt streets, hills* errer dans. **to ~ the world** courir le monde. ◆ **wanderer** *n* vagabond(e) *m(f)*; *(on seeing sb)* **the ~er's returned!** tiens, un revenant! ◆ **wandering 1** *adj way of life, person* errant, vagabond; *river, road* qui serpente; *tribe* nomade; *minstrel* ambulant; *glance* distrait; *thoughts* vagabond; *speech* diffus; **the W~ing Jew** le Juif errant ; **2** *npl*: **~ings** vagabondages *mpl*. ◆ **wanderlust** *n* envie *f* de voir le monde.

wane [weɪn] *vi, n (also* **be on the ~***) [moon]* décroître; *[interest, emotion]* diminuer; *[strength, reputation]* décliner. ◆ **waning** *adj* décroissant; diminuant; déclinant.

wangle * ['wæŋgl] **1** *n* combine *f*. **2** *vt (get)* se débrouiller pour obtenir (*sth from sb* qch de qn; *sth for sb* qch pour qn); *(without paying)* carotter * (*sth for sb* qch pour qn; *sth from sb* qch à qn). **I'll ~ it somehow** je me débrouillerai pour arranger ça. ◆ **wangler** * *n* débrouillard(e) * *m(f)*. ◆ **wangling** * *n* système D * *m*.

want [wɒnt] **1** *vt* (**a**) *(gen)* vouloir (*to do* faire); *(wish, desire)* avoir envie de, désirer (*to do* faire). **what do you ~?** que voulez-vous?, que désirez-vous?; **what do you ~ with** *or* **of him?** qu'est-ce que vous lui voulez?; **what does he ~ for that picture?** combien veut-il pour ce tableau?; **I don't ~ to!** je n'en ai pas envie!; *(more definite)* je ne veux pas!; **all I ~ is...** tout ce que je veux, c'est...; **I ~ your opinion on this** je voudrais votre avis là-dessus; **I ~ you to tell me...** je veux que tu me dises...; **I ~ it done** je veux qu'on le fasse; **I was ~ing to leave** j'avais envie de partir; **to ~ out** * vouloir sortir; *(fig: from project etc)* vouloir laisser tomber *; **you're not ~ed here** on n'a pas besoin de vous ici; **I know when I'm not ~ed!** * je me rends compte que je suis de trop; *(fig)* **you've got him where you ~ him** vous le tenez à votre merci; *(iro)* **you don't ~ much** il n'en faut pas beaucoup pour vous faire plaisir; **he ~s you in his office** il veut vous voir dans son bureau; **you're ~ed on the phone** on vous demande au téléphone; **to be ~ed by the police** être recherché par la police (*for sth* pour qch); **the ~ed man** l'homme que la police recherche; **'good cook ~ed'** 'on demande une bonne cuisinière'; *(Press)* **'articles ~ed'** 'articles demandés'; *(sexually)* **to ~ sb** désirer qn. (**b**) *(need) [person]* avoir besoin de; *[task etc] care, skill* exiger; (*: *ought)* devoir (*to do* faire). **we have all we ~** nous avons tout ce qu'il nous faut; **you ~ a hammer if...** tu as besoin d'un marteau si...; **the car ~s cleaning** la voiture a besoin d'être lavée; **you ~ to see his boat!** * tu devrais voir son bateau!; *(lack)* **it ~ed only his agreement** il ne manquait que son accord.
2 *vi (lack)* **to ~ for sth** manquer de qch, avoir besoin de qch.
3 *n* (**a**) *(lack)* manque *m*. **for ~ of** faute de; **for ~ of anything better** faute de mieux; **for ~ of anything better to do** faute d'avoir quelque chose de mieux à faire; **for ~ of sth to do** par désœuvrement; **it wasn't for ~ of trying that he...** ce n'était pas faute d'avoir essayé qu'il...; **there was no ~ of enthusiasm** ce n'était pas l'enthousiasme qui manquait. (**b**) *(poverty)* besoin *m*, misère *f*. **to live in ~** être dans le besoin. (**c**) *(requirement)* **his ~s are few** il a peu de besoins *mpl*; **it meets a long-felt ~** cela comble enfin cette lacune.
◆ **want ad** * *n (Press)* demande *f* (*for* de). ◆ **wanting 1** *adj*: **to be ~ing** manquer; **~ing in** qui manque de; **to be tried and found ~ing** *[person]* être jugé insuffisant; *[thing]* ne pas être suffisamment bien; *(pej)* **he is a bit ~ing** * il est simplet ; **2** *prep (without)* sans; *(minus)* moins.

wanton ['wɒntən] *adj cruelty, destruction* gratuit, injustifié; *woman* dévergondé. ◆ **wantonly** *adv destroy etc* de façon injustifiée.

war [wɔːʳ] **1** *n* guerre *f*. **to be at ~** être en guerre (*with* avec); *[country]* **to go to ~** entrer en guerre (*against* contre; *over* à propos de); *[soldier]* **to go off to ~** partir pour la guerre; *(also fig)* **to make ~ on** faire la guerre à; **~ of attrition** guerre d'usure; **the Great W~** la guerre de 14-18; **the period between the ~s** *(1918-39)* l'entre-deux-guerres *m inv*; *(Brit)* **the W~ Office**, *(US)* **the W~ Department** le ministère de la Guerre; **to carry the ~ into the enemy's camp** prendre l'offensive; *(fig)* **it was ~ to the knife** *or* **the death** c'était une lutte à couteaux tirés (*between* entre); *(fig)* **~ of words** guerre de paroles; *(fig)* **you've been in the ~s again** * tu t'es encore fait estropier. **2** *adj (gen) crime, widow, wound, zone* de guerre. **~ bride** mariée *f* de la guerre; *(fig)* **~ clouds** nuages *mpl* avant-coureurs de la guerre; **~ cry** cri *m* de guerre; **~ dance** danse *f* guerrière; **on a ~ footing** sur le pied de guerre; **~ games** *(Mil: for training)* kriegspiel *m*; *(practice manoeuvres)* manœuvres *fpl* militaires; *(board games)* jeux *mpl* de stratégie militaire; **~ memorial** monument *m* aux morts. **3** *vi* faire la guerre (*against* à).
◆ **war-disabled** *npl* invalides *mfpl* de guerre. ◆ **warfare** *n* guerre *f (activité)*; **class ~fare** lutte *f* des classes. ◆ **warhead** *n* ogive *f*. ◆ **warhorse** *n (fig)* **an old ~horse** *(Mil)* un vieux militaire; *(Pol etc)* un vétéran. ◆ **warlike** *adj* guerrier. ◆ **warmonger** *n* belliciste *mf*. ◆ **warmongering 1** *adj* belliciste ; **2** *n* propagande *f* belliciste. ◆ **warpath** *n (fig)* **to be on the ~path** * chercher la bagarre *. ◆ **warring** *adj nations* en guerre; *(fig) interests* contradictoires; *ideologies* en conflit. ◆ **warship** *n* navire *m* de guerre. ◆ **wartime 1** *n* temps *m* de guerre; **in ~time** en temps de guerre ; **2** *adj* de guerre. ◆ **war-weary** *adj* las de la guerre.

warble ['wɔːbl] *vi [bird]* gazouiller; *[person]* roucouler. ◆ **warbler** *n* fauvette *f*. ◆ **warbling** *n* gazouillis *m*.

ward [wɔːd] **1** *n* (**a**) *[hospital]* salle *f*. **~ round** visite *f (de médecin hospitalier)*. (**b**) *(Local Government)* section *f* électorale. (**c**) *(Jur)* pupille *mf*. **~ of court** pupille sous tutelle judiciaire. **2** *vt*: **to ~ sth off**

éviter qch. ◆ **warden** *n [city, castle]* gouverneur *m*; *[park, game reserve]* gardien *m*, -ienne *f*; *[institution, student hostel etc]* directeur *m*, -trice *f*; *[youth hostel]* père *m or* mère *f* aubergiste; *(traffic warden)* contractuel(le) *m(f)*. ◆ **warder** *n* (**a**) *(Brit)* gardien *m* (de prison); (**b**) *(US) (in building)* concierge *m; (in museum)* gardien *m* (de musée). ◆ **wardress** *n* gardienne *f* (de prison). ◆ **wardroom** *n (Naut)* carré *m*.

wardrobe ['wɔːdrəʊb] *n (cupboard)* armoire *f*; *(clothes)* garde-robe *f*; *(Theat)* costumes *mpl*. *(Theat)* ~ **mistress** costumière *f*.

warehouse ['wɛəhaʊs] *n* entrepôt *m*, magasin *m*. ◆ **warehouseman** *n* magasinier *m*.

wares [wɛəz] *npl* marchandises *fpl*.

warm [wɔːm] **1** *adj* (**a**) *(gen)* (assez) chaud; *iron, oven* moyen. **I am** ~ j'ai (assez) chaud; **this room is quite** ~ il fait (assez) chaud dans cette pièce; **as** ~ **as toast** chaud comme une caille; **it's** ~**, the weather is** ~ il fait chaud; **it's nice and** ~ **in here** il fait bon ici; **in** ~ **weather** par temps chaud; *(Met)* ~ **front** front *m* chaud; **the water is just** ~ l'eau est juste chaude; **this coffee's only** ~ ce café est tiède; **to get sth** ~ chauffer qch; **to get** *or* **grow** ~ *[person]* se réchauffer; *[water, object]* chauffer; *(in guessing etc games)* **you're getting** ~**(er)!** tu chauffes!; **to keep sth** ~ tenir qch au chaud; **it keeps me** ~ ça me tient chaud; **keep him** ~ ne le laissez pas prendre froid; **keep (yourself)** ~ ne prenez pas froid; **it's** ~ **work** c'est du travail qui donne chaud. (**b**) *(fig) colour, discussion* chaud; *voice, feelings, welcome, congratulations* chaleureux; *apologies, thanks* vif; *supporter* ardent. **she is a very** ~ **person** elle est très chaleureuse de nature; *(in letter)* **with** ~**est wishes** avec tous mes vœux les plus amicaux.

2 *n*: **to give sth a** ~ * chauffer qch; **to have a** ~ * **by the fire** se chauffer près du feu; **come and sit in the** ~ * venez vous asseoir au chaud.

3 *vt* (~ **up**) *person, room* réchauffer; *water, food, coat* chauffer, réchauffer. **to** ~ **one's hands** se (ré)chauffer les mains; *(fig)* **it** ~**ed my heart** ça m'a réchauffé le cœur.

4 *vi* (**a**) (~ **up**) *[person etc]* se réchauffer; *[water etc]* chauffer. (**b**) *(fig)* **to** ~ **to sth** s'enthousiasmer peu à peu pour qch; **to** ~ **to sb** se prendre de sympathie pour qn.

◆ **warm up 1** *vi* (**a**) = **warm 4 a.** (**b**) *[engine, car]* se réchauffer; *[athlete, dancer]* s'échauffer; *[discussion, audience]* devenir animé; *[party]* commencer à être plein d'entrain; *[game]* devenir excitant. **things are** ~**ing up** ça commence à chauffer *. **2** *vt sep person, room* réchauffer; *water, food, coat* chauffer; *engine, car* faire chauffer; *discussion* animer; *(Theat etc) audience* mettre en train.

◆ **warm-blooded** *adj* à sang chaud. ◆ **warm-hearted** *adj* chaleureux. ◆ **warming** *adj drink* qui réchauffe; *(heartwarming)* qui réchauffe le cœur. ◆ **warm(ing)-up exercises** *npl* exercices *mpl* d'échauffement. ◆ **warmly** *adv clothe, wrap up* chaudement; *(fig) welcome, applaud* chaleureusement; *thank, recommend* vivement; **tucked up** ~**ly in bed** bordé bien au chaud dans son lit. ◆ **warmth** *n* chaleur *f*. ◆ **warm-up** * *n (Sport)* période *f* d'échauffement; *(Theat, TV etc)* mise *f* en train.

warn [wɔːn] *vt (gen)* prévenir, avertir (*of* de, *that* que); *authorities, police* alerter. **you have been** ~**ed!** vous êtes averti!; **to** ~ **sb against doing** *or* **not to do** conseiller à qn de ne pas faire; **to** ~ **sb off** *or* **against sth** mettre qn en garde contre qch.

◆ **warning 1** *n (gen; also informal note)* avertissement *m*; *(formal letter)* avis *m*; *(signal)* alerte *f*; **without** ~**ing** *fall, happen* inopinément; *arrive, leave* à l'improviste, sans prévenir; **thank you for the** ~**ing** merci de m'avoir prévenu; **a note of** ~**ing in his voice** une mise en garde dans le ton qu'il a pris; **I gave you due** ~**ing** je vous avais bien prévenu (*that* que); *(Met)* **gale** ~**ing** avis de grand vent ; **2** *adj glance, cry* d'avertissement; *sign* avertisseur; ~**ing device** dispositif *m* d'alarme; ~**ing light** voyant *m* avertisseur; ~**ing shot** *(gen, Mil)* coup *m* tiré en guise d'avertissement; *(Naut)* coup de semonce; *(fig)* avertissement *m*; **...he said in a** ~**ing tone** ...dit-il pour mettre en garde; *(Aut)* ~**ing triangle** triangle *m* de présignalisation.

warp [wɔːp] **1** *n* (**a**) *(Tex)* chaîne *f*; *(fig: essence)* fibre *f*. (**b**) *(distortion: in wood etc)* voilure *f; (on record)* voile *m*. **2** *vt object* voiler; *(fig) judgment* fausser; *character* corrompre. **3** *vi* se voiler. ◆ **warped** *adj mind* tordu; *sense of humour* morbide; *account* tendancieux.

warrant ['wɒr(ə)nt] **1** *n (for travel, payment)* bon *m*; *(guarantee)* garantie *f*; *(Mil)* brevet *m*; *(Jur, Police)* mandat *m*. *(Jur)* **there is a** ~ **out for his arrest** on a émis un mandat d'arrêt contre lui; *(gen)* **he has no** ~ **for saying so** il ne s'appuie sur rien pour justifier cela. **2** *adj*: ~ **officer** adjudant *m (auxiliaire de l'officier)*. **3** *vt* (**a**) *(justify)* justifier. **the facts do not** ~ **it** les faits ne le justifient pas. (**b**) *(guarantee)* garantir. **I'll** ~ **(you) he won't do it again!** je vous assure qu'il ne recommencera pas! ◆ **warranted** *adj goods* garanti; *remark* justifié. ◆ **warranty** *n* autorisation *f*; *(Comm, Jur)* garantie *f*.

warren ['wɒr(ə)n] *n [rabbits]* garenne *f*; *(overcrowded house)* taupinière *f (fig)*. **a** ~ **of little streets** un dédale de petites rues.

warrior ['wɒrɪəʳ] *n* guerrier *m*, -ière *f*.

Warsaw ['wɔːsɔː] *n* Varsovie. ~ **Pact** pacte *m* de Varsovie.

wart [wɔːt] *n* verrue *f*. *(fig)* ~**s and all** sans aucun embellissement. ◆ **wart-hog** *n* phacochère *m*.

wary ['wɛərɪ] *adj (gen)* prudent; *manner* précautionneux. **to be** ~ **about sb/sth** se méfier de qn/qch; **to be** ~ **of doing** hésiter beaucoup à faire; **to keep a** ~ **eye on sb/sth** surveiller qn/qch de près. ◆ **warily** *adv (gen)* avec prudence; *say* avec précaution. ◆ **wariness** *n* prudence *f*.

wash [wɒʃ] **1** *n* (**a**) **to give sth a** ~ laver qch; **to have a** ~ se laver; **to have a quick** ~ se débarbouiller; **it needs a** ~ cela a besoin d'être lavé; **to send sth to the** ~ envoyer qch au blanchissage; **put your jeans in the** ~ mets tes jeans au sale; **your shirt is in the** ~ ta chemise est à la lessive; **the colours ran in the** ~ cela a déteint à la lessive; *(fig)* **it will all come out in the** ~ * *(be known)* on finira bien par savoir ce qu'il en est; *(be all right)* ça finira par se tasser *. (**b**) = **washing 1b.** (**c**) *[ship]* sillage *m*; *(sound: of waves etc)* clapotis *m*. (**d**) *(Art)* lavis *m*. *(with paint)* **to give sth a blue** ~ badigeonner qch en bleu.

2 *vt* (**a**) *(gen)* laver. **to** ~ **o.s.** *[person]* se laver, faire sa toilette; *[cat]* faire sa toilette; *(fig)* **to** ~ **one's hands of** *sth* se laver les mains de; *sb* se désintéresser de; **he** ~**ed the dirt off his hands** il s'est lavé les mains (pour en enlever la saleté); **to** ~ **the dishes/clothes** faire la vaisselle/la lessive; *(fig)* **to** ~ **one's dirty linen in public** laver son linge sale en public; **to** ~ **sth clean** bien nettoyer qch; *(fig)* ~**ed clean of sin** lavé de tout péché. (**b**) *[river etc] (carry away)* emporter; *(to shore)* rejeter; *(flow over) coast etc* baigner. ~**ed out to sea** entraîné vers le large.

3 *vi* (**a**) *(have a* ~*)* se laver (*in hot water* à l'eau chaude), faire sa toilette; *(do the washing)* faire la lessive. **this fabric won't** ~ ce tissu n'est pas lavable; *(fig)* **that just won't** ~ * ça ne prend pas (*with* avec). (**b**) *[waves etc]* **to** ~ **over sth** balayer qch.

◆ **wash away** *vt sep* (**a**) *stain* faire partir au lavage; *mud etc* enlever à l'eau; *[rain]* faire partir; *(fig) sins* laver. (**b**) *[river etc] boat* emporter; *river bank* éroder; *footprints* effacer. ◆ **wash down** *vt* *sep* (**a**) *deck, car* laver à grande eau; *wall* lessiver. (**b**) *pill* faire descendre (*with* avec); *food* arroser (*with* de). ◆ **wash off 1** *vi (with soap)* partir au lavage; *(with water)* partir à l'eau; *(from walls)* partir au lessivage. **it won't ~ off** ça ne s'en va pas. **2** *vt sep* faire partir au lavage *or* à l'eau; *(from wall)* faire partir en lessivant. ◆ **wash out 1** *vi* = **wash off 1. 2** *vt sep* (**a**) = **wash off 2.** (**b**) *(clean) bottle, pan* laver. *(fig)* **the match was ~ed out** le match n'a pas eu lieu à cause de la pluie; **that has ~ed out any chance of...** ça a anéanti toute possibilité de...; *(tired etc)* **to be/look ~ed out** * être/avoir l'air complètement lessivé *. ◆ **wash through** *vt sep* laver rapidement. ◆ **wash up 1** *vi* (**a**) *(Brit: dishes)* faire la vaisselle. (**b**) *(US: have a ~)* se débarbouiller. **2** *vt sep* (**a**) *(Brit) plates, cups* laver. (**b**) *[sea, tide]* rejeter (sur le rivage). (**c**) *(fig)* **to be all ~ed up** * *[scheme]* être fichu *; *[marriage, relationship]* être en ruines.

◆ **washable** *adj* lavable. ◆ **wash-and-wear** *adj shirt* sans entretien. ◆ **washbasin** *or* ◆ **washbowl** *or* ◆ **wash-hand basin** *n* lavabo *m*. ◆ **washcloth** *n* gant *m* de toilette. ◆ **washday** *n* jour *m* de lessive. ◆ **washdown** *n*: **to give sth a ~down** laver qch à grande eau. ◆ **washer** *n* (**a**) *(in tap etc)* rondelle *f*; (**b**) *(~ing machine)* machine *f* à laver; *(for windscreen)* lave-glace *m inv*. ◆ **wash-house** *n* lavoir *m*. ◆ **washing 1** *n* (**a**) *(act) [car]* lavage *m*; *[clothes]* lessive *f*; *[walls]* lessivage *m*; (**b**) *(clothes themselves)* linge *m*, lessive *f*; **to do the ~ing** faire la lessive ; **2** *adj*: **~ing day** jour *m* de lessive; **~ing line** corde *f* à linge; **~ing machine** machine *f* à laver; **~ing powder** lessive *f* (en poudre); **~ing soda** cristaux *mpl* de soude. ◆ **washing-up 1** *n (Brit)* vaisselle *f (à laver etc)*; **to do the ~ing-up** faire la vaisselle ; **2** *adj*: **~ing-up bowl** bassine *f*; **~ing-up liquid** lave-vaisselle *m inv (produit)*; **~ing-up water** eau *f* de vaisselle. ◆ **wash-leather** *n* peau *f* de chamois. ◆ **wash-out** * *n (event, play)* fiasco *m*; *(person)* nullité *f*. ◆ **washroom** *n* toilettes *fpl*. ◆ **washstand** *n* lavabo *m*. ◆ **washtub** *n (bath)* tub *m*; *(for clothes)* bassine *f*.

Washington [ˈwɒʃɪŋtən] *n* Washington.

wasp [wɒsp] *n* guêpe *f*. **~'s nest** guêpier *m*. ◆ **waspish** *adj* hargneux. ◆ **waspishly** *adv* avec hargne.

waste [weɪst] **1** *n* (**a**) *(gen)* gaspillage *m*; *[time]* perte *f*. **to go** *or* **run to ~** *(gen)* être gaspillé; *[land]* être à l'abandon; **the ~ in the kitchens** le gaspillage *or* le gâchis dans les cuisines; **it's a ~ of money to do that** on gaspille de l'argent en faisant cela; **that machine was a ~ of money** cela ne valait vraiment pas la peine d'acheter cette machine; **a ~ of effort** un effort inutile; **it's a ~ of time doing that** on perd son temps à faire *or* en faisant cela; **it's a ~ of time and energy** c'est peine perdue; **it's a ~ of breath** c'est dépenser sa salive pour rien. (**b**) *(~* **material:** *also (US) ~***s***)* déchets *mpl*; *(household ~)* ordures *fpl*; *(water)* eaux *fpl* sales. **nuclear ~** déchets nucléaires. (**c**) *(expanse: of snow etc)* désert *m* (immense); *(in town)* terrain *m* vague. **2** *adj material* de rebut; *energy, heat* perdu; *food* inutilisé; *water* sale; *ground, district* à l'abandon. **~ products** *(Ind)* déchets *mpl* de fabrication; *(Physiol)* déchets de l'organisme; **to lay ~** dévaster.

3 *vt (gen)* gaspiller (*on sth* pour qch; *on doing* pour faire); *time, an evening* perdre; *opportunity* laisser passer. **nothing is ~d** il n'y a aucun gaspillage; **to ~ one's breath** dépenser sa salive pour rien; **the sarcasm was ~d on him** il n'a pas compris le sarcasme; **caviar is ~d on him** ça ne vaut pas la peine de lui donner du caviar.

4 *vi [food, goods, resources]* se perdre, être gaspillé. **you mustn't let it ~** il ne faut pas le laisser perdre; **~ not want not** l'économie protège du besoin. ◆ **waste away** *vi* dépérir.

◆ **wastage** *n (gen)* gaspillage *m*; *[time]* perte *f*; *(amount lost from container)* pertes; *(rejects)* déchets *mpl*; *(as part of industrial process etc)* déperdition *f*; *(Comm: through pilfering etc)* coulage *m*; **there is a huge wastage of** on gaspille énormément de. ◆ **wastebasket** *n* corbeille *f* (à papier). ◆ **wastebin** *n (basket)* corbeille *f* (à papier); *(in kitchen)* poubelle *f*. ◆ **wasted** *adj* (**a**) *limb (from disease, starvation)* décharné; *(withered)* atrophié. (**b**) *food, resources* gaspillé; *effort* inutile, vain; *life* gâché; *time* perdu. ◆ **waste-disposal unit** *n* broyeur *m* d'ordures. ◆ **wasteful** *adj person* gaspilleur; *process* peu rentable; *expenditure* inutile. ◆ **wastefully** *adv spend, throw away* bêtement; **to use sth ~fully** ne pas utiliser qch au mieux. ◆ **wastefulness** *n [person]* manque *m* d'économie; *[process]* manque de rentabilité. ◆ **wasteland** *n* terres *fpl* à l'abandon; *(in town)* terrain *m* vague; *(after war)* désert *m*. ◆ **wastepaper** *n* vieux papiers *mpl*; **~paper basket** corbeille *f* (à papier). ◆ **waste-pipe** *n* (tuyau *m* de) vidange *f*. ◆ **wasting** *adj disease* qui ronge. ◆ **wastrel** *n (good-for-nothing)* propre *mf* à rien; *(spendthrift)* dépensier *m*, -ière *f*.

watch [wɒtʃ] **1** *n* (**a**) montre *f*. **by my ~** à ma montre. (**b**) **to keep ~** faire le guet; **to keep (a) close ~ on** *or* **over sth/sb** surveiller qch/qn de près; **to be on the ~ for** *person, enemy, animal, vehicle* guetter; *danger* être sur ses gardes à cause de; *bargains* être à l'affût de. (**c**) *(Naut)* quart *m*. **to be on ~** être de quart; **officer of the ~** officier *m* de quart.

2 *vt* (**a**) *(gen)* regarder (*sb doing sth* qn faire qch), observer; *(keep an eye on) suspect, house, dish cooking, luggage, child, shop* surveiller; *expression, birds etc* observer; *notice board, small ads etc* consulter régulièrement; *political situation, developments* suivre de près. **~ what I do** regarde-moi faire; **he ~ed his chance and slipped out** il a guetté le moment propice et s'est esquivé; **have you ever ~ed an operation?** avez-vous déjà assisté à une opération?; **we are being ~ed** on nous surveille; **~ tomorrow's paper** ne manquez pas de lire le journal de demain. (**b**) *(be careful of) money, expenses, dangerous thing* faire attention à. **~ that knife!** fais attention avec ce couteau!; **~ your head!** attention *or* gare à votre tête!; **~ it!** * attention!; **~ your step!, ~ how you go!** (fais) attention!; **to ~ one's step** se surveiller; **I must ~ the time** il faut que je surveille l'heure; **he does tend to ~ the clock** il a tendance à surveiller la pendule; **to ~ sb's interests** veiller aux intérêts de qn; **~ your language** surveille ton langage; **~ you don't burn yourself** attention, ne vous brûlez pas!; **~ that he does his homework** veillez à ce qu'il fasse ses devoirs.

3 *vi (gen)* regarder; *(pay attention)* faire attention. **to ~ by sb's bedside** veiller au chevet de qn; **to ~ over sb/sth** surveiller qn/qch; **to ~ for sth/sb** guetter qch/qn; **he's ~ing to see what you're going to do** il attend pour voir ce que vous allez faire. ◆ **watch out** *vi (keep a look-out)* guetter (*for sb/sth* qn/qch); *(take care)* faire attention, prendre garde. **~ out!** attention!; **~ out for cars** faites attention *or* prenez garde aux voitures; **to ~ out for thieves** être sur ses gardes contre les voleurs; **~ out for trouble if...** préparez-vous à des ennuis si...

◆ **watchdog** *n* chien *m* de garde; *(fig)* gardien *m*, -ienne *f*; **~dog committee** comité *m* de vigilance. ◆ **watcher** *n (observer)* observateur *m*, -trice *f*; *(hidden or hostile)* guetteur *m*; *(spectator)* spectateur *m*, -trice *f*; *(Pol)* **China ~er** spécialiste *mf* des questions chinoises. ◆ **watchful** *adj* vigilant; **to keep a ~ful eye on sth/sb** garder qch/qn à l'œil; **under the ~ful eye of...** sous l'œil vigilant de... ◆ **watchmaker** *n* horloger *m*, -ère *f*. ◆ **watchmaking** *n* horlogerie *f*. ◆ **watchman** *n* gardien *m*. ◆ **watch-**

night service *n* messe *f* de minuit de la Saint-Sylvestre. ◆ **watchstrap** *n* bracelet *m* de montre. ◆ **watchtower** *n* tour *f* de guet. ◆ **watchword** *n (password)* mot *m* de passe; *(fig: motto)* mot d'ordre.

water ['wɔːtəʳ] **1** *n* eau *f*. **hot and cold ~ in all rooms** eau courante chaude et froide dans toutes les chambres; **drinking ~** eau potable; **I want a drink of ~** je voudrais un verre d'eau; **to turn on the ~** *(at main)* ouvrir l'eau; *(from tap)* ouvrir le robinet; **the road is under ~** la route est inondée; **to swim under ~** nager sous l'eau; *(tide)* **at high/low ~** à marée haute/basse; **to make ~** *[ship]* faire eau; *(urinate: also* **to pass ~***)* uriner; **it won't hold ~** *[container]* ça n'est pas étanche; *[plan, excuse]* ça ne tient pas debout; *(fig)* **a lot of ~ has passed under the bridge** il est passé beaucoup d'eau sous les ponts; **he spends money like ~** l'argent lui fond entre les mains; *(fig)* **to pour** *or* **throw cold ~ on sth** se montrer peu enthousiaste pour qch; *(fig)* **it's like ~ off a duck's back *** c'est comme si on chantait *; **lavender/rose ~** eau de lavande/de rose; *(at spa)* **to take the ~s** faire une cure thermale; **in French ~s** dans les eaux territoriales françaises; **the ~s of the Rhine** les eaux du Rhin; *(in pregnancy)* **the ~s** les eaux; *(Med)* **~ on the knee** épanchement *m* de synovie; **~ on the brain** hydrocéphalie *f*.
2 *adj level, pressure, pipe, snake, rat* d'eau; *pump, mill, clock, pistol* à eau; *plant, bird* aquatique. **~ bed** matelas *m* d'eau; **~ biscuit** craquelin *m*; *[soldier etc]* **~ bottle** bidon *m*; **~ cannon** canon *m* à eau; *(in streets)* **~ cart** arroseuse *f* (municipale); *(Culin)* **~ ice** sorbet *m*; **~ level** *(gen)* niveau *m* de l'eau; *(Aut: in radiator)* niveau *m* d'eau; **~ main** conduite *f* principale d'eau; **~ polo** water-polo *m*; **~ power** énergie *f* hydraulique; **~ purifier** *(device)* épurateur *m* d'eau; *(tablet)* cachet *m* pour purifier l'eau; **~ rate** taxe *f* sur l'eau; **~ softener** adoucisseur *m* d'eau; **~ supply** *(for town)* approvisionnement *m* en eau; *(for house etc)* alimentation *f* en eau; *(for traveller)* provision *f* d'eau; **to cut off the ~ supply** couper l'eau; *(Geog)* **~ table** niveau *m* hydrostatique; **~ tank** réservoir *m* d'eau, citerne *f*; **~ tower** château *m* d'eau.
3 *vi [eyes]* pleurer. **his mouth ~ed** il a eu l'eau à la bouche; **it made his mouth ~** cela lui a fait venir l'eau à la bouche.
4 *vt [gardener, river]* arroser; *animal* donner à boire à; *wine etc* couper (d'eau).
◆ **water down** *vt sep milk, wine* couper (d'eau); *(fig) story, version* édulcorer; *effect* atténuer.
◆ **watercolour** **1** *n (painting)* aquarelle *f*; *(paints)* **~colours** couleurs *fpl* pour aquarelle; **in ~colours** à l'aquarelle ; **2** *adj* à l'aquarelle. ◆ **watercourse** *n* cours *m* d'eau. ◆ **watercress** *n* cresson *m* (de fontaine). ◆ **watered** *adj silk* moiré. ◆ **watered-down** *adj (fig) version* édulcoré. ◆ **waterfall** *n* chute *f* d'eau. ◆ **waterfowl** *npl* gibier *m* d'eau. ◆ **waterfront** *n (at docks etc)* quais *mpl*; *(sea front)* front *m* de mer. ◆ **water-heater** *n* chauffe-eau *m inv*. ◆ **water-hole** *n* mare *f*. ◆ **watering** *n* arrosage *m*; **~ing hole** *[animal]* point *m* d'eau; *(* fig)* bar *m*. ◆ **watering-can** *n* arrosoir *m*. ◆ **waterlily** *n* nénuphar *m*. ◆ **waterline** *n (Naut)* ligne *f* de flottaison. ◆ **waterlogged** *adj wood* imprégné d'eau; *shoes* imbibé d'eau; *land, pitch* détrempé. ◆ **watermark** *n (in paper)* filigrane *m*; *(left by tide)* laisse *f* de haute mer. ◆ **water-meadow** *n* prairie *f* souvent inondée. ◆ **watermelon** *n* pastèque *f*. ◆ **waterproof** **1** *adj material* imperméable; *watch* étanche; **~proof sheet** *(for bed)* alaise *f*; *(tarpaulin)* bâche *f* ; **2** *n* imperméable *m*; **3** *vt* imperméabiliser. ◆ **waterproofing** *n* imperméabilisation *f*. ◆ **water-repellent** *adj, n* hydrofuge *(m)*. ◆ **watershed** *n (Geog)* ligne *f* de partage des eaux; *(fig)* grand tournant *m*. ◆ **waterside** *n* bord *m* de l'eau; **at** *or* **on** *or* **by the ~side** au bord de l'eau; **along the ~side** le long de la rive. ◆ **water-ski** *vi* faire du ski nautique. ◆ **water-skiing** *n* ski *m* nautique. ◆ **water-soluble** *adj* soluble dans l'eau. ◆ **waterspout** *n (on roof etc)* tuyau *m* de descente; *(Met)* trombe *f*. ◆ **watertight** *adj container* étanche; *(fig) excuse, plan* inattaquable; *(fig)* **in ~tight compartments** séparé par des cloisons étanches. ◆ **waterway** *n* voie *f* navigable. ◆ **water-wings** *npl* bouée *f*, flotteurs *mpl* de natation. ◆ **waterworks** *n (sg: place)* station *f* hydraulique; *(fig: cry)* **to turn on the ~works *** se mettre à pleurer comme une Madeleine *; **to have sth wrong with one's ~works *** avoir des ennuis de vessie. ◆ **watery** *adj substance* aqueux; *eyes* larmoyant; *(pej) tea, coffee* trop faible; *soup* trop liquide; *taste* fade; *colour* délavé.

Waterloo [ˌwɔːtə'luː] *n* Waterloo. *(fig)* **to meet one's ~** essuyer un revers irrémédiable.

watt [wɒt] *n (Elec)* watt *m*. ◆ **wattage** *n* puissance *f* en watts.

wave [weɪv] **1** *n* (**a**) *(at sea, on lake)* vague *f*; *(on beach)* rouleau *m*; *(on river, pond)* vaguelette *f*; *(in hair, on surface)* ondulation *f*; *(fig: of attack, enthusiasm, strikes etc)* vague. *(liter)* **the ~s** les flots *mpl*; **her hair has a natural ~ in it** ses cheveux ondulent naturellement; **to come in ~s** *[people]* arriver par vagues; *[explosions etc]* se produire par vagues; *(Cine etc)* **the new ~** la nouvelle vague; *(fig)* **to make ~s** faire des vagues; **~ power** énergie *f* des vagues. (**b**) *(Phys, Rad, Telec etc)* onde *f*. **long ~** grandes ondes; **medium/short ~** ondes moyennes/courtes. (**c**) *(gesture)* **to give sb a ~** faire un signe de la main à qn; **with a ~ of his hand** d'un signe de la main.
2 *vi* (**a**) *[person]* faire signe de la main; *[flag]* flotter au vent; *[branch, tree]* être agité; *[grass, corn]* onduler. **to ~ to sb** *(in greeting)* saluer qn de la main; *(as signal)* faire signe à qn (*to do* de faire). (**b**) *[hair]* onduler.
3 *vt* (**a**) *flag, handkerchief etc* agiter; *(threateningly) stick, sword* brandir. **he ~d the ticket at me furiously** il a agité vivement le ticket sous mon nez; **to ~ goodbye to sb** dire au revoir de la main à qn; **to ~ sb back/on** *etc* faire signe à qn de reculer/d'avancer *etc*. (**b**) *hair* onduler.
◆ **wave about, wave around** *vt sep object, one's arms* agiter dans tous les sens. ◆ **wave aside, wave away** *vt sep person, object* écarter d'un geste; *offer, help* refuser d'un geste.
◆ **waveband** *n* bande *f* de fréquences. ◆ **wavelength** *n* longueur *f* d'ondes; *(fig)* **we're not on the same ~length** nous ne sommes pas sur la même longueur d'ondes. ◆ **wavy** *adj hair, surface* ondulé; *line* onduleux. ◆ **wavy-haired** *adj* aux cheveux ondulés.

waver ['weɪvəʳ] *vi [flame, courage]* vaciller; *[voice]* trembler; *[person] (weaken)* lâcher pied; *(hesitate)* hésiter (*between* entre). ◆ **waverer** *n* indécis(e) *m(f)*. ◆ **wavering** **1** *adj* vacillant; tremblant; hésitant ; **2** *n* vacillation *f*; tremblement *m*; hésitations *fpl*.

wax¹ [wæks] **1** *n (gen)* cire *f*; *(for skis)* fart *m*; *(in ear)* bouchon *m* de cire. **2** *adj candle etc* de *or* en cire. **~(ed) paper** papier *m* sulfurisé. **3** *vt floor, furniture, shoes* cirer; *car* lustrer. ◆ **waxen** *adj colour* cireux. ◆ **waxworks** *n (pl: figures)* personnages *mpl* en cire; *(sg: wax museum)* musée *m* de cire. ◆ **waxy** *adj substance, complexion, colour* cireux; *potato* qui ne s'émiette pas.

wax² [wæks] *vi [moon]* croître. **to ~ poetic** *etc* devenir d'humeur poétique *etc*; **to ~ eloquent** déployer toute son éloquence (*about, over* à propos de); **to ~ enthusiastic** s'enthousiasmer (*about* pour).

way [weɪ] **1** *n* (**a**) *(road etc)* chemin *m*, voie *f*. **the ~ across the fields** le chemin qui traverse les champs; **they drove a ~ through the hills** ils ont ouvert un passage à travers les collines; **the**

Appian W~ la voie Appienne; *(Rel)* **the W~ of the Cross** le chemin de la Croix; **private/public ~** voie privée/publique; **across the ~** de l'autre côté de la rue (*from* par rapport à), en face; *(fig)* **the middle ~** le juste milieu.

(**b**) *(route)* chemin *m* (*to* de, vers). **which is the ~ to...?** pouvez-vous m'indiquer le chemin de...?; **he talked/it rained** *etc* **all the ~** il a parlé/il a plu *etc* pendant tout le chemin (*to* jusqu'à); **there are houses all the ~** il y a des maisons tout le long du chemin; *(fig)* **I'm with you all the ~ *** je suis entièrement d'accord avec vous; **the ~ to success** le chemin du succès; **the shortest** *or* **quickest ~ to Leeds** le chemin le plus court pour aller à Leeds; **I went the long ~ round** j'ai pris le chemin le plus long; **on the ~ to London we...** en allant à Londres nous...; **it's on the ~ to the station** c'est sur le chemin de la gare; **we met him on the ~** nous l'avons rencontré en route; **on the ~ here I saw...** en venant ici j'ai vu...; **on your ~ home** en rentrant chez vous; **I must be on my ~** il faut que je parte; **to start on one's ~** se mettre en route; **to go on one's ~** reprendre son chemin; **he went by ~ of Glasgow** il est passé par Glasgow; **they met him by the ~** ils l'ont rencontré en chemin; *(fig)* **by the ~, what did he say?** à propos, qu'est-ce qu'il a dit?; *(fig)* **that is by the ~** tout ceci est secondaire; **the village is quite out of the ~** le village est vraiment à l'écart; *(fig)* **it's nothing out of the ~** cela n'a rien de spécial; **an out-of-the-~ subject** un sujet peu commun; **if it's not out of my ~** si c'est sur mon chemin; *(fig)* **to go out of one's ~ to do sth** se donner du mal pour faire qch; **don't go out of your ~ to do it** ne vous dérangez pas pour le faire; **to lose the** *or* **one's ~** perdre son chemin (*to* en allant à); **to ask the** *or* **one's ~** demander son chemin (*to* pour aller à); **I know the** *or* **my ~ to the station** je sais comment aller à la gare; *(fig)* **she knows her ~ about** elle sait se débrouiller; **they went their separate ~s** *(lit)* ils sont partis chacun de leur côté; *(fig)* chacun a suivi son chemin; *(fig)* **he went his own ~** il a fait à son idée; *(fig)* **he has gone the ~ of...** il a fait comme...; **to make one's ~ towards...** se diriger vers...; **to make one's ~ through sth** traverser qch; **to make one's ~ back to sth** retourner *or* revenir vers qch; *(fig)* **he had to make his own ~** il a dû faire son chemin tout seul; **the ~ back** le chemin du retour; **the ~ back to the station** le chemin pour retourner à la gare; **the ~ down/up** le chemin pour descendre/monter; **the ~ forward is dangerous** le chemin devient dangereux plus loin; **the ~ in** l'entrée *f*; **I'm looking for a ~ in/out** je cherche un moyen d'entrer/de sortir; **do you know the ~ into/out of...?** savez-vous par où on entre dans/sort de...?; *[fashion etc]* **it's on the ~ in/out** c'est la nouvelle mode/passé de mode; **the ~ out** la sortie; **on the** *or* **your ~ out** en sortant; *(fig)* **there is no ~ out of it** *or* **no ~ round it** il n'y a pas moyen de s'en sortir; **the ~ through the forest** le chemin à travers la forêt; **'no ~ through'** 'sans issue'.

(**c**) *(path)* **to be in sb's ~** barrer le passage à qn; *(fig)* **am I in the** *or* **your ~?** est-ce que je vous gêne?; **it's out of the ~ over there** ça ne gêne pas là-bas; **to get out of the ~** s'écarter; **to get out of sb's ~** laisser passer qn; **to get out of the ~ of the car** s'écarter de la voiture; **get it out of the ~!** poussez-le!, écartez-le!; **as soon as I've got the exam out of the ~** dès que je serai débarrassé de l'examen; **keep matches out of children's ~** ne laissez pas les allumettes à la portée des enfants; **to keep out of sb's ~** éviter qn; **he kept well out of the ~** il a pris soin de rester à l'écart; **to put sth out of the ~** ranger qch; **to want sb/sth out of the ~ *** vouloir se débarrasser de qn/qch; **to put difficulties in sb's ~** créer des difficultés à qn; **he put me in the ~ of one or two good bargains** il m'a indiqué quelques bonnes affaires; **to make ~ for sb** s'écarter pour laisser passer qn; *(fig)* laisser la voie libre à qn; **make ~!** écartez-vous!; *(fig)* **this made ~ for a reform of...** ceci a préparé le terrain pour une réforme de...; **to push** *or* **thrust** *or* **elbow one's ~ through a crowd** se frayer un chemin à travers une foule; **to hack** *or* **cut one's ~ through sth** s'ouvrir un chemin à la hache *etc* dans qch; **to crawl/limp** *etc* **one's ~ to the door** ramper/boiter *etc* jusqu'à la porte; **he talked his ~ out of it** il s'en est sorti avec de belles paroles; **to give ~** *V* **give 1d.**

(**d**) *(distance)* distance *f*. **a long ~ off** *or* **away** loin; **a little ~ away** *or* **off** pas très loin; **it's a long ~** c'est loin (*from* de); **it's a long** *or* **good ~ to London** ça fait loin pour aller à Londres *; **it's a long ~ from here to...** cela fait loin d'ici à...; *(fig)* **they've come a long ~** ils ont fait du chemin; **we've a long ~ to go** *(lit)* nous avons encore un grand bout de chemin à faire; *(fig)* nous ne sommes pas au bout de nos peines; **your work has still a long ~ to go** vous avez encore de grands efforts à faire dans votre travail; *(fig)* **it should go a long ~ towards improving it/paying the bill** cela devrait l'améliorer considérablement/cela devrait couvrir une grande partie de la facture; **he makes a little go a long ~** il tire le meilleur parti de ce qu'il a; **a little kindness goes a long ~** un peu de gentillesse facilite bien des choses.

(**e**) *(direction)* direction *f*, sens *m*. **this ~** par ici; **'this ~ for** *or* **to the cathedral'** 'vers la cathédrale'; **this ~ and that** par-ci par-là, en tous sens; **which ~ did he go?** par où est-il passé?; **which ~ do we go from here?** *(lit)* par où passons-nous maintenant?; *(fig)* quelle voie devons-nous choisir maintenant?; **are you going my ~?** est-ce que vous allez dans la même direction que moi?; *(fig)* **everything's going his ~ *** tout lui sourit; **he went that ~** il est parti par là; **she didn't know which ~ to look** elle ne savait pas où regarder; **he looked the other ~** il a détourné les yeux; **he never looks my ~** il ne regarde jamais dans ma direction; **I'll be down** *or* **round your ~** je serai près de chez vous; **if the chance comes your ~** si jamais vous en avez l'occasion; **over Oxford ~** du côté d'Oxford; *(fig)* **he's in a fair ~ to succeed** il est en passe de réussir; **the right ~ round** *or* **out** à l'endroit; **the wrong ~ round** *or* **out** à l'envers, dans le mauvais sens; **'this ~ up'** 'haut'; **the right ~ up** dans le bon sens; **the wrong ~ up** sens dessus dessous; **the other ~ round** dans l'autre sens; **it's the other ~ round** c'est juste le contraire; **a one-~ street** une rue à sens unique; **a three-~ discussion** une discussion à trois participants.

(**f**) *(manner, method)* façon *f*, moyen *m* (*to do, of doing* de faire). **there are ~s and means** il y a différents moyens (*of doing* de faire); **we haven't the ~s and means to do it** nous n'avons pas les ressources suffisantes pour le faire; *(Admin)* **W~s and Means Committee** Commission *f* des Finances; **the French ~ of life** la manière de vivre des Français; **these shortages are a ~ of life** ces pénuries sont entrées dans les mœurs; **(in) this ~** comme ceci, de cette façon; **that's the ~ to do it** voilà comment il faut s'y prendre; *(encouraging)* **that's the ~!** voilà, c'est bien!; *(refusing)* **no ~! *** pas question! *; **do it either ~** fais-le de l'une ou l'autre façon; **either ~ * I can't help you** de toute façon je ne peux pas vous aider; **do it your own ~** fais-le à ta façon; **to get one's own ~** obtenir ce que l'on désire; **to want one's own ~** ne vouloir en faire qu'à sa tête; **Arsenal had it all their own ~** Arsenal a complètement dominé le match; **I won't let him have things all his own ~** je ne vais pas lui passer tous ses caprices; **to my ~ of thinking** à mon avis; **her ~ of looking at it** son point de vue sur la question; **that's the ~ the money goes** c'est à ça que l'argent passe; **whatever ~ you like to look at it** de quelque façon que vous envisagiez *(subj)* la chose; **it's the ~ things are** c'est la vie; **it's just the ~ I'm made** c'est comme ça que je suis; **leave it all the ~ it is** laisse les choses comme elles sont; **the ~ things are going we shall have nothing left** du train où vont les choses il ne nous restera rien; **that's always the ~** c'est toujours comme ça; **it was this ~...** voici comment cela s'est passé...; **to do sth the right/wrong ~** faire qch bien/mal; **in a general ~** en général; **once in a ~** de temps en temps; **by ~ of being a joke** en guise de plaisanterie.

(**g**) *(state; degree)* état *m*. **to be in a bad ~** *[person, situation]* aller mal; *[car etc]* être en piteux état; **there are no two ~s about it** c'est absolument clair; **one ~ or (an)other** d'une façon ou d'une autre; *(Racing)* **each ~** gagnant ou placé; **you can't have it both ~s** il faut choisir; *(fig)* **in a small ~** d'une façon limitée; **in his own small ~** dans la limite de ses moyens; **he is a bookseller in a big ~** c'est un gros libraire; **we lost in a really big ~** nous avons vraiment beaucoup perdu; **in the ordinary ~ of things** normalement.

(**h**) *(custom)* coutume *f*; *(manner)* façon *f* (*of doing* de faire). **the ~s of the Spaniards** les coutumes espagnoles; **the ~s of God and men** les voies *fpl* de Dieu et de l'homme; **his foreign ~s** ses habitudes *fpl* d'étranger; **he is very slow in his ~s** il fait tout très lentement; **he is amusing in his (own) ~** il est amusant à sa façon; **it's not my ~** ce n'est pas mon genre (*to do* de faire); **she has a ~ with her** elle sait persuader; **he has a ~ with people/cars** il sait s'y prendre avec les gens/les voitures; **to mend one's ~s** s'amender; **to get into/out of the ~ of doing** prendre/perdre l'habitude de faire.

(**i**) *(respect, detail)* égard *m*, point *m*. **in some ~s** à certains égards; **in many ~s** à bien des égards; **can I help you in any ~?** puis-je vous aider en quoi que ce soit?; **does that in any ~ explain it?** est-ce là une explication satisfaisante?; **he's in no ~ to blame** ce n'est vraiment pas sa faute; **without in any ~ wishing to do so** sans vouloir le moins du monde le faire; **he's right in a** *or* **one ~** il a raison dans un certain sens; **what is there in the ~ of books?** qu'est-ce qu'il y a comme livres?

(**j**) *[ship]* **to gather/lose ~** prendre/perdre de la vitesse; **to have ~ on** avoir de l'erre; **to be under ~** *[ship]* faire route; *[meeting, discussion]* être en cours; *[plans]* être en voie de réalisation; **to get under ~** *[ship]* appareiller; *[person]* se mettre en route; *[vehicle, meeting, discussion]* démarrer; **to get sth under ~** faire démarrer qch.

2 *adv*: **~ back** *etc* = **away back** *etc* (*V* **away 1a**); **you're ~ out * in your calculations** tu es très loin du compte dans tes calculs.

◆ **wayfarer** *n* voyageur *m*, -euse *f*. ◆ **wayfaring** *n* voyages *mpl*. ◆ **waylay** *pret, ptp* **waylaid** *vt (attack)* attaquer; *(speak to)* arrêter au passage. ◆ **way-out** * *adj (odd)* excentrique; *(great)* super * *inv*. ◆ **wayside 1** *n* bord *m or* côté *m* de la route; **along the ~side** le long de la route; **by the ~side** au bord de la route; *(fig)* **to fall by the ~side** *(not persevere)* abandonner en route; *(be stopped)* tomber à l'eau ; **2** *adj café etc* au bord de la route. ◆ **wayward** *adj* qui n'en fait qu'à sa tête.

W.C. ['dʌblju(:)'si:] *n* W.-C. *mpl*, waters *mpl*.

we [wi:] *pers pron pl* nous. **~ know** nous savons; *(stressed)* nous, nous savons; **~ went to the pictures** nous sommes allés *or* on est allé * au cinéma; **~ French** nous autres Français; **as ~ do in Scotland** comme on fait en Écosse; **~ all make mistakes** tout le monde peut se tromper.

weak [wi:k] *adj (gen)* faible; *structure, material* qui manque de solidité; *coffee, tea* léger; *(fig) chin* fuyant; *(Med) health, lungs, stomach* fragile. **~ from** *or* **with hunger** affaibli par la faim; **to grow ~(er)** = **to weaken 1**; **to have a ~ heart** avoir le cœur malade; **to have ~ eyes** *or* **eyesight** avoir une mauvaise vue; **~ in the head *** faible d'esprit, débile *; **he went ~ at the knees** il avait les jambes comme du coton; **~ in maths** faible en maths; **~ spot** point *m* faible; *(fig)* **the ~ link in the chain** le point faible; *(US)* **the ~ sister *** le faiblard *, la faiblarde * (dans un groupe); **~ verb** verbe *m* faible. ◆ **weaken 1** *vi (gen)* faiblir; *(in health)* s'affaiblir; *(relent)* se laisser fléchir; *[influence, power]* baisser; *[prices]* fléchir ; **2** *vt (gen)* affaiblir; *join, structure, material* enlever de la solidité à; *heart* fatiguer; *coffee, solution, mixture* diluer. ◆ **weakening 1** *n (gen)* affaiblissement *m*; *[structure, material]* fléchissement *m* ; **2** *adj (gen)* affaiblissant; *disease* débilitant. ◆ **weak-kneed** *adj* mou, faible. ◆ **weakling** *n (physically)* mauviette *f*; *(morally etc)* faible *mf*. ◆ **weakly 1** *adj* faible, chétif ; **2** *adv* faiblement. ◆ **weak-minded** *adj* faible d'esprit. ◆ **weakness** *n* faiblesse *f*; manque *m* de solidité; fragilité *f*; **one of his ~nesses** un de ses points faibles; **to have a ~ness for** avoir un faible pour. ◆ **weak-willed** *adj* faible.

weal [wi:l] *n (on skin)* marque *f* d'un coup de fouet.

wealth [welθ] *n (fact of being rich)* richesse *f*; *(money, possessions, resources)* richesses, fortune *f*. **a man of great ~** un homme richissime; **mineral ~** richesses minières; *(fig)* **a ~ of ideas** une profusion d'idées. ◆ **wealthy** *adj* (très) riche.

wean [wi:n] *vt baby* sevrer; *(fig: from bad habits etc)* détourner (*from, off* de). **I've managed to ~ him off gin** je l'ai habitué à se passer de gin.

weapon ['wepən] *n* arme *f*.

wear [wɛəʳ] *(vb: pret* **wore**, *ptp* **worn**) **1** *n*: **clothes for everyday ~** vêtements *mpl* pour tous les jours; **evening/town ~** tenue *f* de soirée/de ville; *(Comm)* **children's/summer ~** vêtements pour enfants/d'été; **what is the correct ~?** quelle est la tenue convenable (*for* pour)?; **this carpet has had some hard ~** ce tapis a beaucoup servi; **it will stand up to a lot of ~** cela fera beaucoup d'usage; **there is still some ~ left in it** *(garment)* c'est encore mettable; *(carpet, tyre)* cela fera encore de l'usage; **he got 4 years' ~ out of it** cela lui a fait 4 ans; **it has had a lot of ~ and tear** c'est très usagé; **fair ~ and tear** usure *f* normale; **the ~ and tear on the engine** l'usure du moteur; **to show signs of ~, to look the worse for ~** commencer à être fatigué.

2 *vt* (**a**) *(gen)* porter; *(fig) smile, look* avoir. **he was ~ing a hat** il portait un chapeau, il avait (mis) un chapeau; **I never ~ a hat** je ne mets *or* porte jamais de chapeau; **what shall I ~?** qu'est-ce que je vais mettre?; **I've nothing to ~** je n'ai rien à me mettre; **she was ~ing blue** elle était en bleu; **she ~s her hair long** elle a les cheveux longs; **I never ~ scent** je ne me mets jamais de parfum; **she was ~ing make-up** elle était maquillée; **she was ~ing lipstick** elle s'était mis du rouge à lèvres; **she wore a frown** elle fronçait les sourcils; *(fig: agree to)* **he won't ~ that *** il ne marchera pas *.

(**b**) *(rub etc) clothes, stone etc* user; *groove, path* creuser peu à peu; *hole* faire peu à peu (*in sth* dans *or* à qch). **worn thin** *blade* aminci à l'usage; *rug* complètement râpé; *(fig)* **worn with care** usé par les soucis.

3 *vi* (**a**) *(last)* faire de l'usage. **these shoes will ~ for years** ces chaussures feront des années; **to ~ well** *[garment, carpet]* faire beaucoup d'usage; *[theory, friendship]* résister au temps; **she has worn well *** elle est bien conservée.

(**b**) *(rub etc thin)* s'user. **worn at the knees** usé aux genoux; **to ~ into holes** se trouer; **the rock has worn smooth** la roche a été polie par le temps; **to ~ thin** *[cloth]* être râpé; *[patience]* s'épuiser; *(fig)* **that excuse has worn thin!** cette excuse ne prend plus!

◆ **wear away** **1** *vi [substance]* s'user; *[inscription]* s'effacer. **2** *vt sep* user; effacer. ◆ **wear down** **1** *vi [heels, pencil etc]* s'user. **2** *vt sep materials* user; *patience, strength, person* épuiser; *courage, resistance* miner. ◆ **wear off** *vi [colour, inscription]* s'effacer; *[pain, anger, excitement]* passer; *[effects, anaesthetic]* se dissiper. **the novelty has worn off** cela n'a plus l'attrait de la nouveauté. ◆ **wear on** *vi [day, winter etc]* avancer; *[war, discussions etc]* se poursuivre. **as the years wore on** avec le temps. ◆ **wear out** **1** *vi (gen)* s'user; *[patience etc]* s'épuiser. **2** *vt sep shoes, clothes* user; *strength, patience, person, horse* épuiser. **to ~ o.s. out** s'épuiser (*doing* à faire); **to be worn out** être exténué.

◆ **wearable** *adj garment* mettable. ◆ **wearer** *n*: **they will delight the ~er** ils feront la joie de la personne qui les portera; **uniform ~ers** ceux qui portent l'uniforme; **from maker to ~er** du fabricant au client. ◆ **wearing** *adj* épuisant.

weary ['wɪərɪ] **1** *adj person, smile, look* las (*f* lasse) (*of sth* de qch; *of doing* de faire); *sigh* de lassitude; *journey (tiring)* fatigant; *(irksome)* lassant. **to grow ~ of sth/of doing** se lasser de qch/de faire; **4 ~ hours** 4 heures mortelles. **2** *vi* se lasser (*of sth* de qch; *of doing* de faire). **3** *vt (tire)* fatiguer; *(try patience of)* lasser (*with* à force de). ◆ **wearied** *adj* las. ◆ **wearily** *adv say, sigh, look* avec lassitude; *move* péniblement. ◆ **weariness** *n* lassitude *f*; fatigue *f*. ◆ **wearisome** *adj (tiring)* épuisant; *(boring)* lassant, ennuyeux.

weasel ['wi:zl] *n* belette *f*. *(pej)* **~ words** paroles *fpl* équivoques.

weather ['weðə^r] **1** *n* temps *m*. **~ permitting** si le temps le permet; **what's the ~ like?** quel temps fait-il?; **it's fine/bad ~** il fait beau/mauvais; **in hot ~** par temps chaud; **in all ~s** par tous les temps; *(fig)* **to be under the ~** * être mal fichu *. **2** *vt* (**a**) *(survive) tempest, crisis* réchapper à. (**b**) *wood etc* faire mûrir. **~ed rocks** rochers *mpl* patinés par la pluie *etc*. **3** *adj knowledge, map, station* météorologique; *conditions, variations* atmosphérique; *(Naut) side, sheet* du vent. *(Brit)* **W~ Centre,** *(US)* **W~ Bureau** Office *m* national de la météorologie; **~ chart** carte *f* du temps; *(fig)* **to keep a ~ eye on sth** surveiller qch; **~ forecast** prévisions *fpl* météorologiques, météo * *f*; **~ report** bulletin *m* météorologique, météo *; **~ ship** navire *m* météo *inv*; **the ~ situation** le temps. ◆ **weather-beaten** *adj person* tanné; *building* dégradé par les intempéries. ◆ **weather-boarding** *n* planches *fpl* de recouvrement. ◆ **weathercock** *or* ◆ **weathervane** *n* girouette *f*. ◆ **weatherman** * *n* météorologiste *m*. ◆ **weatherproof** *adj clothing* imperméable; *house* étanche.

weave [wi:v] *(vb: pret* **wove,** *ptp* **woven***)* **1** *n* tissage *m*. **2** *vt (gen)* tisser; *strands* entrelacer; *basket, garland* tresser; *(fig) story* inventer. **3** *vi* (**a**) (**~ along**) *[road, river]* serpenter. (**b**) **to ~ (one's way) through sth** se faufiler à travers qch; *(fig)* **let's get weaving!** * allons, remuons-nous! ◆ **weaver** *n* tisserand(e) *m(f)*.

web [web] *n (fabric; also of lies etc)* tissu *m*; *[spider]* toile *f*. ◆ **webbed** *adj* palmé. ◆ **webbing** *n (on chair)* sangles *fpl*. ◆ **webfooted** *adj*: **to be ~footed** avoir les pieds palmés.

wed [wed] **1** *vt* épouser. *(fig) [person]* **she is ~ded to her work** elle ne vit que pour son travail; **cunning ~ded to ambition** la ruse alliée à l'ambition. **2** *vi* se marier. **3** *npl*: **the newly- ~s** les jeunes mariés *mpl*. ◆ **wedding** **1** *n (ceremony)* mariage *m*; **silver/golden ~ding** noces *fpl* d'argent/d'or; **to have a quiet/a church ~ding** se marier dans l'intimité/à l'église ; **2** *adj cake, night* de noces; *present, invitation, anniversary* de mariage; *dress* de mariée; *ceremony, march* nuptial; **~ding breakfast** lunch *m* de mariage; **their ~ding day** le jour de leur mariage; **~ding ring** alliance *f*.

wedge [wedʒ] **1** *n (under wheel etc)* cale *f*; *(for splitting sth)* coin *m*; *(piece: of cake etc)* part *f*. *(fig)* **it's the thin end of the ~** c'est le commencement de la fin. **2** *vt (fix) table, wheels* caler; *(push)* enfoncer (*into* dans; *between* entre). **to ~ a door open** maintenir une porte ouverte à l'aide d'une cale; **car ~d between two trucks** voiture coincée entre deux camions; **to ~ sth in** faire rentrer qch; **to be ~d in** être coincé. ◆ **wedge-heeled** *adj* à semelles compensées.

Wednesday ['wenzdeɪ] *n* mercredi *m*; *for phrases V* **Saturday.**

wee [wi:] *adj (Scot)* tout petit.

weed [wi:d] **1** *n* mauvaise herbe *f*; (* *pej: person)* mauviette *f*. **2** *vt* désherber. ◆ **weed out** *vt sep (fig) person* éliminer (*from* de); *old books, clothes* trier et jeter. ◆ **weeding** *n* désherbage *m*; **I've done some ~ing** j'ai un peu désherbé. ◆ **weedkiller** *n* désherbant *m*. ◆ **weedy** *adj (fig) person* qui a l'air d'une mauviette.

week [wi:k] *n* semaine *f*. **in a ~** dans une semaine, dans huit jours; **what day of the ~ is it?** quel jour de la semaine sommes-nous?; **~ in ~ out, ~ after ~** semaine après semaine; **this ~** cette semaine; **next/last ~** la semaine prochaine/dernière; **in the middle of the ~** vers le milieu *or* dans le courant de la semaine; **a ~ today** aujourd'hui en huit; **a ~ past yesterday** il y a eu une semaine hier; **every two ~s** toutes les deux semaines, tous les quinze jours; **two ~s ago** il y a deux semaines, il y a quinze jours; **in 3 ~s' time** dans 3 semaines; **the ~ ending May 6th** la semaine qui se termine le 6 mai; **the working ~** la semaine de travail; **a 36-hour ~** une semaine de 36 heures.

◆ **weekday** **1** *n* jour *m* de semaine; **on ~days** en semaine; *(Comm)* les jours ouvrables ; **2** *adj activities, timetable* de la semaine. ◆ **weekend** **1** *n* week-end *m*, fin *f* de semaine; **at ~ends** pendant les week-ends; **at the ~end** pendant le week-end; **we're going away for the ~end** nous partons en week-end; **a long ~end** un week-end prolongé ; **2** *adj visit, programme* de *or* du weekend; **~end case** sac *m* de voyage; **~end cottage** maison *f* de campagne. ◆ **weekly** **1** *adj* hebdomadaire ; **2** *adv* une fois par semaine; **twice ~ly** deux fois par semaine ; **3** *n (magazine)* hebdomadaire *m*.

weep [wi:p] *pret, ptp* **wept** **1** *vi* pleurer (*for joy* de joie; *for sb* qn; *over sth* sur qch; *to see* de voir); *[wound etc]* suinter. **to ~ bitterly** pleurer à chaudes larmes; **I could have wept!** j'en aurais pleuré! **2** *n*: **to have a good/a little ~** pleurer un bon coup/un peu. ◆ **weeping** **1** *n* larmes *fpl* ; **2** *adj person* qui pleure; **~ing willow** saule *m* pleureur. ◆ **weepy** **1** *adj voice* larmoyant; **to be ~y** avoir envie de pleurer ; **2** *n (Brit)* mélo * *m*.

weevil ['wi:vl] *n* charançon *m*.

weewee * ['wi:wi:] **1** *n* pipi * *m*. **2** *vi* faire pipi *.

weft [weft] *n (Tex)* trame *f*.

weigh [weɪ] **1** *vt* (**a**) peser. **it ~s 9 kilos** ça pèse 9 kilos; **what do you ~?** combien est-ce que vous pesez?; *(fig)* **it ~s a ton** c'est du plomb; **to ~ one's words** peser ses mots; **to ~ sth in one's hand** soupeser qch; **to ~ (up) A against B** mettre en balance A et B; **to ~ (up) the pros and cons** peser le pour et le contre. (**b**) **to ~ anchor** lever l'ancre. **2** *vi [object, responsibilities]* peser (*on* sur). **to ~ heavy/light** peser lourd/peu; *(fig)* **it was ~ing on her mind** cela la tracassait; *(stronger)* cela la tourmentait.

◆ **weigh down** **1** *vi* peser de tout son poids (*on sth* sur qch). **2** *vt sep branch etc* faire plier. **to be ~ed down by** *load, parcels etc* plier sous le poids de; *responsibilities etc* être accablé de. ◆ **weigh in** *vi [boxer, jockey etc]* se faire peser. **to ~ in at 70 kilos** peser 70 kilos avant le match (*or* la course). ◆ **weigh out** *vt sep sugar etc* peser. ◆ **weigh up** *vt sep (consider)* examiner; *(compare)* mettre en balance (*A with B, A against B* A et B). ◆ **weighbridge** *n* pont-bascule *m*. ◆ **weigh-in** *n (Sport)* pesage *m*. ◆ **weighing-machine** *n* balance *f*. ◆ **weight 1** *n* (**a**) poids *m (also fig)*; **atomic ~t** poids atomique; **to be sold by ~t** se vendre au poids; **what is your ~t?** combien pesez-vous?; **what a ~t it is!** que c'est lourd!; **they are the same ~t** ils font le même poids; *(fig)* **it is worth its ~t in gold** cela vaut son pesant d'or; **under-/ over~t** trop maigre/gros; **to put on/lose ~t** grossir/maigrir; **he put his full ~t on...** il a pesé de tout son poids sur...; **feel the ~t of this box!** soupesez-moi cette boîte!; *(fig)* **it's a ~t off my mind** c'est un gros souci de moins; *(fig)* **to give ~t to sth** donner du poids à qch; **to carry ~t** *[argument, factor]* avoir du poids (*with* pour); *[person]* avoir de l'influence; (**b**) *(for scales etc)* poids *m*; **~ts and measures** poids et mesures ; **2** *vt* (**~t down)** *(sink)* lester *or (hold down)* maintenir avec un poids (*or* une pierre *etc*). ◆ **weighting** *n (on salary)* indemnité *f*; *(Scol)* coefficient *m;* **London ~ting** indemnité de résidence pour Londres. ◆ **weightless** *adj* en état d'apesanteur. ◆ **weightlessness** *n* apesanteur *f*. ◆ **weightlifter** *n* haltérophile *m*. ◆ **weightlifting** *n* haltérophilie *f*. ◆ **weighty** *adj load, responsibility* lourd; *argument, matter* de poids; *reason* probant; *consideration, deliberation* mûr; *problem* grave.

weir [wɪəʳ] *n* barrage *m (de rivière)*.

weird [wɪəd] *adj (eerie)* surnaturel, mystérieux; *(odd)* bizarre, étrange. ◆ **weirdly** *adv* mystérieusement; bizarrement, étrangement. ◆ **weirdness** *n* étrangeté *f*. ◆ **weirdo** ⁑ *or* ◆ **weirdy** ⁑ *n* drôle d'oiseau * *m (pej)*.

welcome ['welkəm] **1** *adj* (**a**) *reminder, interruption* opportun. *[person, thing]* **to be ~** être le (*or* la) bienvenu(e); **~!** soyez le bienvenu *etc*; **~ to our house/to England** bienvenue chez nous/en Angleterre; **to make sb ~** faire bon accueil à qn; **I didn't feel very ~** je me suis senti de trop; **it was ~ news/ a ~ sight** nous avons été (*or* il a été *etc*) heureux de l'apprendre/de le voir; **it is a ~ change** c'est un changement agréable; **it was a ~ relief** j'ai été vraiment soulagé. (**b**) **thank you — you're ~** merci — il n'y a pas de quoi; **you're ~ to try** libre à vous d'essayer; **you're ~ to use my car** n'hésitez pas à prendre ma voiture; **you're ~ to any help I can give you** si je peux vous être utile, ce sera avec plaisir; *(iro)* **you're ~ to it** je vous souhaite bien du plaisir. **2** *n* accueil *m*. **to bid sb ~** souhaiter la bienvenue à qn; **to give sb a warm ~** faire un accueil chaleureux à qn; **I got a fairly cold ~** j'ai été reçu plutôt froidement. **3** *vt (greet formally)* accueillir; *(greet warmly)* accueillir chaleureusement; *(bid ~)* souhaiter la bienvenue à; *news, suggestion, change* se réjouir de. **I'd ~ a cup of coffee** je prendrais volontiers une tasse de café. ◆ **welcoming** *adj smile, handshake* accueillant; *speech* d'accueil.

weld [weld] **1** *n* soudure *f*. **2** *vt* souder (*on to* à). ◆ **welder** *n (person)* soudeur *m*; *(machine)* soudeuse *f*. ◆ **welding 1** *n* soudure *f* ; **2** *adj*: **~ing torch** chalumeau *m*.

welfare ['welfɛəʳ] **1** *n* (**a**) *(gen)* bien *m*; *(comfort)* bien-être *m*. **the nation's ~, the ~ of all** le bien public; **the physical/spiritual ~ of** la santé physique/morale de; **child/animal ~** protection *f* de l'enfance/des animaux; **to look after sb's ~** avoir la responsabilité de qn. (**b**) **(social) ~** assistance *f* sociale. **to be on ~** recevoir l'aide sociale. **2** *adj milk, meals* gratuit. **~ centre** centre *m* d'assistance sociale; *(US)* **~ hotel** foyer *m* d'hébergement *(réservé aux bénéficiaires de l'aide sociale)*; **~ payments** prestations *fpl* sociales; *(gen)* **the W~ State** l'État-providence *m*; **thanks to the W~ State** grâce à la Sécurité sociale; **~ work** travail social; **~ worker** ≃ travailleur *m*, -euse *f* social(e).

well¹ [wel] **1** *n (for water etc; also between buildings)* puits *m*; *[staircase, lift]* cage *f*. **2** *vi* (**a**) (**~ up)** *[tears, emotion]* monter. (**b**) (**~ out)** *[spring]* sourdre; *[blood]* couler (*from* de).

well² [wel] **1** *adv, comp* **better**, *superl* **best** (**a**) *(gen)* bien. **very ~** très bien; **he sings as ~ as he plays** il chante aussi bien qu'il joue; **he sings as ~ as she does** il chante aussi bien qu'elle; **~ done!** bravo!; **~ played!** bien joué!; **to do ~** *(succeed: in work etc)* bien réussir; *(manage sth)* bien se débrouiller; **the patient is doing ~** le malade est en bonne voie; **you did ~ to come** vous avez bien fait de venir; **to do as ~ as one can** faire de son mieux; **he did himself ~** il ne s'est privé de rien; **to do ~ by sb** bien agir envers qn; **you're ~ out of it** c'est une chance que tu n'aies plus rien à voir avec cela (*or* lui *etc*); **how ~ I understand!** comme je vous (*or* le *etc*) comprends!; **~ I know it!** je le sais bien!

(**b**) *(intensifying etc)* bien. **~ over 100** bien plus de 100; **he is ~ past fifty** il a largement dépassé la cinquantaine; **~ and truly** bel et bien; **he could ~ afford to pay for it** il avait largement les moyens de le payer; **you would be ~ advised to leave** vous feriez bien de partir; **you may ~ be surprised to learn** vous serez sans aucun doute surpris d'apprendre; **one might ~ ask why** on pourrait à juste titre demander pourquoi; **you might ~ ask!** belle question!; **he couldn't very ~ refuse** il ne pouvait guère refuser; **you might as ~ say** autant dire que; **you may as ~ tell me** autant me le dire, tu ferais aussi bien de me le dire; **we might (just) as ~ have stayed** autant valait rester, nous aurions aussi bien fait de rester; **as ~ she might** comme il se devait; **~ she might!** c'était la moindre des choses!

(**c**) **as ~** *(also)* aussi; *(on top of it all)* par-dessus le marché; **by night as ~ as by day** aussi bien de jour que de nuit, de jour comme de nuit; **as ~ as his dog he has...** en plus de son chien il a...

2 *excl (gen)* eh bien!; *(resignation)* enfin!; *(after interruption)* **~, as I was saying...** donc, comme je disais...; *(hesitation)* **~...** c'est que...; *(surprise)* **well, well, well!** tiens, tiens, tiens!; **~ I never!** ça par exemple!; **very ~ then** bon, d'accord.

3 *adj, comp* **better**, *superl* **best** (**a**) bien; bon. **all's ~ that ends well** tout est bien qui finit bien; **all's ~** tout va bien; **all is not ~** il y a qch qui ne va pas; **it's all very ~ to say...** c'est bien joli de dire...; **if you want to do it, ~ and good** si vous voulez le faire, d'accord; **it would be ~ to leave** on ferait bien de partir; **it is as ~ to remember** on ferait bien de se rappeler; **it would be just as ~ for you to stay** vous feriez tout aussi bien de rester; **it's as ~ for you that...** heureusement pour vous que... (**b**) *(healthy)* **how are you? — very ~** comment allez-vous? — très bien; **I hope you're ~** j'espère que vous allez bien; **to feel ~** se sentir bien; **to get ~** se remettre; **get ~ soon!** remets-toi vite!

4 *n*: **to think/speak ~ of** penser/dire du bien de; **I wish you ~!** je vous souhaite de réussir!; **sb who wishes you ~** qn qui vous veut du bien; **to let** *or* **leave ~ alone** s'arrêter là; **leave ~ alone** *(gen)* il faut savoir s'arrêter là; *(Prov)* le mieux est l'ennemi du bien.

5 *pref*: **well-** bien; **~-chosen/-dressed** *etc* bien choisi/habillé *etc*.

◆ **well-behaved** *adj child* sage; *animal* obéissant. ◆ **well-being** *n* bien-être *m*. ◆ **well-bred** *adj (good family)* de bonne famille; *(courteous)* bien élevé; *animal* de bonne race. ◆ **well-built** *adj* solide. ◆ **well-educated** *adj* qui a reçu une bonne éducation. ◆ **well-fed** *adj* bien nourri. ◆ **well-fixed** * *adj (US)* nanti. ◆ **well-heeled** * *adj* nanti. ◆ **well-informed** *adj* bien informé (*about* sur); *(knowledgeable) person* instruit; *(Press etc)* **~-informed circles** milieux *mpl* bien informés.

◆ **well-judged** *adj remark* judicieux; *shot* bien visé; *estimate* juste. ◆ **well-kept** *adj house, garden* bien tenu; *hands* soigné; *hair* bien entretenu; *secret* bien gardé. ◆ **well-known** *adj* bien connu, célèbre. ◆ **well-made** *adj* bien fait. ◆ **well-mannered** *adj* bien élevé. ◆ **well-meaning** *adj person* bien intentionné; *(also* **~-meant***) remark, action* fait avec les meilleures intentions. ◆ **well-nigh** *adv* presque. ◆ **well-off** *adj* (**a**) *(rich)* riche; (**b**) *(fortunate)* **you don't know when you're ~-off** tu ne connais pas ton bonheur; **she's ~-off without him** c'est un bon débarras pour elle. ◆ **well-spent** *adj time* bien employé; *money* utilement dépensé. ◆ **well-thought-of** *adj* bien considéré. ◆ **well-thought-out** *adj* bien conçu. ◆ **well-timed** *adj remark* tout à fait opportun; *blow* bien calculé. ◆ **well-to-do** *adj* aisé. ◆ **well-wishers** *npl* amis *mpl*; *(unknown)* amis *or* admirateurs *mpl* inconnus; *(supporters)* sympathisants *mpl*. ◆ **well-worn** *adj path* battu; *carpet, clothes* usagé; *(fig) expression* rebattu.

wellington ['welɪŋtən] *n (~* **boot**: *also* **wellie** **)* botte *f* de caoutchouc.

Welsh [welʃ] **1** *adj* gallois. ~ **dresser** vaisselier *m*; *(Pol)* **the ~ Office** le ministère des Affaires galloises; ~ **rarebit** toast *m* au fromage. **2** *n* gallois *m*. *(people)* **the ~** les Gallois *mpl*. ◆ **Welshman** *n* Gallois *m*. ◆ **Welshwoman** *n* Galloise *f*.

welsh * [welʃ] *vi*: **to ~ on sb** lever le pied * en emportant l'argent de qn.

welterweight ['weltəweɪt] *n (Boxing)* poids *m* welter.

wend [wend] *vt*: **to ~ one's way** aller son chemin (*to, towards* vers).

Wendy house ['wendɪˌhaʊs] *n (Brit)* modèle *m* réduit de maison *(jouet d'enfant)*.

went [went] *pret of* **go**.

wept [wept] *pret, ptp of* **weep**.

were [wɜːʳ] *pret of* **be**.

werewolf, *pl* **-wolves** ['wɪəwʊlf, wʊlvz] *n* loup-garou *m*.

west [west] **1** *n* ouest *m*. **(to the) ~ of** à l'ouest de; **in the ~ of** dans l'ouest de; **the wind is in the ~** le vent est à l'ouest; **the wind is from the ~** le vent vient de l'ouest; **to live in the ~** habiter dans l'ouest; *(Pol)* **the W~** l'Occident *m*, l'Ouest *m*. **2** *adj side* ouest *inv*; *wind* d'ouest; *coast, door* ouest, occidental. **W~ Africa** Afrique *f* occidentale; **the W~ Bank (of the Jordan)** la Cisjordanie; **W~ Indies** Antilles *fpl*; **W~ Indian** *(adj)* antillais; *(n)* Antillais(e) *m(f)*; *(London)* **the W~ End** *le quartier élégant de Londres*; **the W~ Country** le sud-ouest (de l'Angleterre). **3** *adv drive, travel etc* en direction de l'ouest, vers l'ouest. ~ **of the border** à l'ouest de la frontière; **to go due ~** aller droit vers l'ouest; *(fig)* **to go ~** * *[thing]* être fichu *; *[person]* passer l'arme à gauche *. ◆ **westbound** *adj traffic, vehicles* en direction de l'ouest; *carriageway* ouest *inv*. ◆ **westerly** *adj wind* de l'ouest; *situation, aspect* à l'ouest; **in a ~erly direction** en direction de l'ouest. ◆ **western** **1** *adj region* ouest *inv*, de l'ouest; *coast* ouest, occidental; *wall, side* exposé à l'ouest; **in ~ern France** dans la France de l'ouest; **~ern France** l'Ouest *m* de la France; **W~ern Europe** Europe *f* occidentale; *(Pol)* **W~ern countries** pays *mpl* de l'Ouest *or* occidentaux ; **2** *n (film)* western *m*; *(novel)* roman-western *m*. ◆ **westerner** *n* homme *m or* femme *f* de l'Ouest; *(Pol)* Occidental(e) *m(f)*. ◆ **westernization** *n* occidentalisation *f*. ◆ **westernize** *vt* occidentaliser; **to become ~ernized** s'occidentaliser. ◆ **westward** **1** *adj* à l'ouest ; **2** *adv (also* **~wards***)* vers l'ouest.

wet [wet] **1** *adj (gen)* (tout) mouillé; *(damp)* humide; *(soaking ~)* trempé; *paint* frais; *ink, watercolours* pas encore sec; *weather* pluvieux; *climate* humide; *day* de pluie; *season* des pluies. **it grows in ~ places** ça pousse dans les endroits humides; **~ to the skin, ~ through** trempé jusqu'aux os; **to get ~** se mouiller; **to get one's feet ~** se mouiller les pieds; *(fig)* **he's still ~ behind the ears** * il manque d'expérience; *(weather)* **it's going to be ~** il va pleuvoir; *(fig)* **a ~ blanket** * un rabat-joie; **he's really ~** ‡ c'est une vraie lavette *; *(US)* **you're all ~** *! tu te fiches complètement dedans *! **2** *n* (**a**) **the ~** *(rain)* la pluie; *(damp)* l'humidité *f*; **it got left out in the ~** c'est resté dehors sous la pluie. (**b**) *(‡ pej: person)* lavette * *f*. **3** *vt* mouiller. **to ~ one's lips** se mouiller les lèvres; **to ~ o.s.** *or* **one's pants** mouiller sa culotte; **to ~ the bed** mouiller le lit. ◆ **wetness** *n* humidité *f*. ◆ **wetsuit** *n* combinaison *f* de plongée.

whack [wæk] **1** *n* (**a**) *(blow)* grand coup *m*; *(sound)* claquement *m*. *(attempt)* **to have a ~ at doing** * essayer de faire; **I'll have a ~ at it** * je vais tenter le coup *. (**b**) *(*: share)* part *f*. **2** *vt thing, person* donner un grand coup à; *(spank)* fesser; *(*: defeat)* donner une raclée * à. ◆ **whacked** ‡ *adj (exhausted)* crevé *. ◆ **whacker** ‡ *n (fish etc)* poisson *m etc* énorme; *(lie)* mensonge *m* énorme. ◆ **whacking** **1** *n (spanking)* fessée *f*; *(beating: lit, fig)* raclée * *f* ; **2** *adj (also* **~ing big** **)* énorme.

whale [weɪl] **1** *n* baleine *f*. *(fig)* **we had a ~ of a time** * on s'est drôlement * bien amusé; **a ~ of a difference** * une sacrée * différence. **2** *adj*: ~ **oil** huile *f* de baleine. **3** *vi* : **to go whaling** pêcher la baleine. ◆ **whalebone** *n* fanon *m* de baleine; *(in corset etc)* baleine *f*. ◆ **whaler** *n (man)* pêcheur *m* de baleine; *(ship)* baleinier *m*. ◆ **whaling** **1** *n* pêche *f* à la baleine ; **2** *adj industry* baleinier.

whammy ['wæmɪ] *n* mauvais sort *m*, poisse * *f*.

wharf [wɔːf] *n* quai *m*. ◆ **wharfage** *n* droits *mpl* de quai.

what [wɒt] **1** *adj* (**a**) quel. **~ play did you see?** quelle pièce avez-vous vue?; **~ news?** quelles nouvelles?; **she showed me ~ book it was** elle m'a montré quel livre c'était; **~ a man!** quel homme!; **~ a nuisance!** que c'est ennuyeux!; **~ fools we are!** que nous sommes bêtes!; **~ a huge house!** quelle maison immense! (**b**) **I gave him ~ money I had** je lui ai donné tout l'argent que j'avais; **~ little I said** le peu que j'ai dit.

2 *pron* (**a**) *(in questions: subject)* qu'est-ce qui; *(object)* que, qu'est-ce que; *(after prep)* quoi. **~'s happening?** qu'est-ce qui se passe?; **~ did you do?** qu'est-ce que vous avez fait?, qu'avez-vous fait?; **~ were you talking about?** de quoi parliez-vous?; **~'s that?** *(gen)* qu'est-ce que c'est que ça?; *(pardon?)* comment?; **~'s that book?** qu'est-ce que c'est que ce livre?; **~ is his address?** quelle est son adresse?; **~ is this called?** comment ça s'appelle?; **~'s the French for 'pen'?** comment dit-on 'pen' en français?; **~ can we do?** qu'est-ce que nous pouvons faire?, que pouvons-nous faire?; **~ will it cost?** combien est-ce que ça coûtera?; **it's WHAT?** c'est quoi?

(**b**) *(that which: subject)* ce qui; *(object)* ce que. **I wonder ~ will happen** je me demande ce qui va arriver; **tell us ~ you're thinking about** dites-nous ce à quoi vous pensez; **he asked me ~ she'd told me** il m'a demandé ce qu'elle m'avait dit; **I don't know ~ that book is** je ne sais pas ce que c'est que ce livre; **he just doesn't know ~'s ~** il est complètement dépassé *; **I'll show them ~'s ~** je vais leur montrer de quoi il retourne; **~ is done is done** ce qui est fait est fait; **say ~ you like** vous pouvez dire ce que vous voulez; **~ I need is...** ce dont j'ai besoin c'est...; **I don't know who is doing ~** je ne sais pas qui fait quoi; **I know ~, I'll tell you ~** tu sais quoi; **he's not ~ he was** il n'est plus ce qu'il était; **I've no clothes except ~ I'm wearing** je n'ai d'autres vêtements que ceux que je porte.

(c) ~ **about Robert?** et Robert?; ~ **about writing that letter?** et si vous écriviez cette lettre?; ~ **about the money you owe me?** et l'argent que vous me devez?; ~ **about it?** *(so ~?)* et alors?; *(~ do you think?)* alors, qu'est-ce que tu en penses?; ~ **about a coffee?** si on prenait un café?; ~ **for?** pourquoi?; ~ **did you do that for?** pourquoi avez-vous fait ça?; ... **and** ~ **have you *, ... and** ~ **not *** et je ne sais quoi encore; **and** ~ **is more** et qui plus est; **and** ~ **is worse** et ce qui est pire; **and,** ~ **is less common** et, ce qui est plus inhabituel; ~ **with X and Y** avec X et Y en plus; ~ **with one thing and another** avec ceci et cela; *(after listing things)* avec tout ça.
3 *excl*: ~ **, no tea!** quoi *or* comment, pas de thé! ◆ **whatever 1** *adj, adv (any)* **~ever (the) book you choose** quel que soit le livre que vous choisissiez *(subj); (all)* **~ever money you've got** tout ce que tu as comme argent; **nothing ~ever** absolument rien ; **2** *pron* (**a**) *(no matter what)* quoi que + *subj*; **~ever happens** quoi qu'il arrive *(subj);* **~ever you (may) find** quoi que vous trouviez; **~ever it may be** quoi que ce soit; **I'll pay ~ever it costs** je paierai ce que ça coûtera; **~ever it costs, get it** achète-le quel qu'en soit le prix; (**b**) *(anything that)* tout ce que; **do ~ever you please** faites ce que vous voulez; (**c**) *(emphatic)* **~ever did you do? *** qu'est-ce que vous êtes allé faire? (**d**) **the books and ~ever** les livres et ainsi de suite. ◆ **what's-it *** *or* ◆ **what's-his-name *** *or* ◆ **what-d'ye-call-him *** *etc n* machin * *m*. ◆ **whatsoever** = **whatever.**

wheat [wi:t] **1** *n* blé *m*, froment *m*. **2** *adj flour, field* de blé. ◆ **wheatgerm** *n* germes *mpl* de blé. ◆ **wheatmeal** *n* farine *f* brute *(à 80%)*.

wheedle ['wi:dl] *vt* cajoler. **to** ~ **sth out of sb** obtenir qch de qn par des cajoleries; **to** ~ **sb into doing** cajoler qn pour qu'il fasse. ◆ **wheedling 1** *adj* enjôleur ; **2** *n* cajoleries *fpl*.

wheel [wi:l] **1** *n (gen)* roue *f*; *(Naut)* roue de gouvernail; *(Aut: steering ~)* volant *m*; *(spinning ~)* rouet *m*; *(potter's ~)* tour *m*. ~ **of fortune** roue de la fortune; **at the** ~ *(Naut)* au gouvernail; *(Aut)* au volant; **to take the** ~ *(Naut)* prendre le gouvernail; *(Aut)* se mettre au volant; *(fig)* **the ~s of government** les rouages *mpl* du gouvernement; **to oil** *or* **grease the ~s** huiler les rouages; **there are ~s within ~s** il y a toutes sortes de forces en jeu; **the** ~ **has come full circle** la boucle est bouclée.
2 *vt barrow, pushchair, bed* pousser, rouler; *cycle* pousser; *person* pousser (dans un landau *or* un fauteuil roulant *etc*). *(fig)* ~ **him in!** ‡ amenez-le!
3 *vi* **(~ round)** *[birds]* tournoyer; *[person]* se retourner (brusquement); *(Mil)* effectuer une conversion; *[procession]* tourner. *(Mil)* **right ~!** à droite!; *(fig)* **to be ~ing and dealing *** chercher des combines *fpl*; **there has been a lot of ~ing and dealing * over that** cela a donné lieu à toutes sortes de combines.
◆ **wheelbarrow** *n* brouette *f*. ◆ **wheelbase** *n* empattement *m*. ◆ **wheelchair** *n* fauteuil *m* roulant. ◆ **wheel clamp** *n* sabot *m* de Denver. ◆ **wheeled** *adj* à roues; **three-~ed** à trois roues. ◆ **-wheeler** *n ending*: **four-~er** voiture *f* à quatre roues. ◆ **wheeler-dealer** *n (pej)* affairiste *m*. ◆ **wheeling** *n: (pej)* **~ing and dealing** combines * *fpl*. ◆ **wheelspin** *n (Aut)* patinage. ◆ **wheelwright** *n* charron *m*.

wheeze [wi:z] **1** *n* respiration *f* bruyante. **2** *vi [person]* avoir du mal à respirer.

whelk [welk] *n* buccin *m*.

whelp [welp] **1** *n* petit(e) *m(f) (d'un animal)*. **2** *vi* mettre bas.

when [wen] **1** *adv* quand. ~ **does the train leave?** quand *or* à quelle heure part le train?; ~ **is your birthday?** c'est quand, votre anniversaire?; ~ **did Columbus...?** quand *or* en quelle année Christophe Colomb a-t-il...?; **I don't know** ~ **we'll see him again** je ne sais pas quand nous le reverrons; **~'s the wedding?** à quand le mariage?; ~ **is the best time** quel est le meilleur moment (*to do* pour faire); **till ~?** jusqu'à quand?; **he's got to go by ~?** il faut qu'il soit parti quand?; *(iro)* **since ~? *** depuis quand? *
2 *conj* (**a**) *(at the time that)* quand, lorsque. ~ **I heard his voice I smiled** quand *or* lorsque j'ai entendu sa voix j'ai souri; ~ **I was a child there was...** quand *or* lorsque j'étais enfant il y avait...; **let me know** ~ **she comes** faites-moi savoir quand elle arrivera; ~ **writing to her, remember to say...** quand vous lui écrirez n'oubliez pas de dire...; ~ **you like** quand vous voulez *or* voudrez; **hardly had I got back** ~... je venais à peine de rentrer quand... (**b**) *(on, at etc which)* où; que. **on the day** ~ le jour où; **at the time** ~ au moment *or* à l'heure où; **in spring,** ~... au printemps, au moment où...; **on Saturday(s),** ~... le samedi, quand...; *(each Saturday that)* **on Saturday(s)** ~... les samedis où...; *(last etc Saturday ~)* **on Saturday,** ~... samedi, quand...; **at 8 o'clock,** ~... à 8 heures, heure à laquelle...; **at the very moment** ~ juste au moment où; **one day** ~ **the sun was shining** un jour où le soleil brillait; **this is a time** ~ **we must speak** c'est dans un moment comme celui-ci qu'il faut parler; **there are times** ~... il y a des moments où...; *(drinks etc)* **say ~! *** vous me direz..., vous m'arrêterez...
(**c**) *(the time that)* **he told me about** ~ **you...** il m'a raconté le jour où vous...; **she spoke of** ~ **they had visited London** elle a parlé de la semaine (*or* du jour *etc*) où ils avaient visité Londres; **now is** ~ **I need you** c'est maintenant que j'ai besoin de vous; **that's** ~ **the train leaves** c'est l'heure à laquelle le train part; **that's** ~ **Napoleon was born** c'est l'année (*or* le jour) où Napoléon est né; **that's** ~ **you ought to try...** c'est le moment d'essayer...; **that was** ~ **the trouble started** c'est alors que les ennuis ont commencé.
(**d**) *(after)* quand, une fois que. ~ **you've read the book you'll know why** quand vous aurez lu le livre vous saurez pourquoi; ~ **it is finished the bridge will measure...** une fois terminé, le pont mesurera...; ~ **they had left he...** après leur départ *or* après qu'ils furent partis, il...; ~ **he'd been to Greece he...** après être allé en Grèce, il...; **do it** ~ **he's finished** faites-le quand il aura fini.
(**e**) *(whereas)* alors que. **he walked** ~ **he could have taken the bus** il est allé à pied alors qu'il aurait pu prendre le bus.
◆ **whenever 1** *conj* (**a**) *(at whatever time)* quand; **~ever you wish** quand vous voulez; **leave ~ever you're ready** partez quand vous serez prêt; (**b**) *(every time that)* chaque fois que; **~ever I see her I think of Jenny** chaque fois que je la vois je pense à Jenny ; **2** *adv*: **last Monday, or ~ever** lundi dernier, ou je ne sais quand.

whence [wens] *adv, conj (liter)* d'où.

where [wɛəʳ] **1** *adv* où. ~ **do you live?** où habitez-vous?; ~ **are you going (to)?** où allez-vous?; **I wonder** ~... je me demande où...; **~'s the theatre?** où est le théâtre?; ~ **do you come from?** d'où venez-vous?; **near ~?** près d'où?
2 *conj* (**a**) *(gen)* (là) où. **stay** ~ **you are** restez où vous êtes; **there is a school** ~ **our house once stood** il y a une école là où se dressait autrefois notre maison; **go** ~ **you like** allez où vous voulez; **it's not** ~ **I left it** ce n'est plus là où je l'avais laissé; **it's not** ~ **I expected to see it** je ne m'attendais pas à le voir là.
(**b**) *(in etc which)* où. **the house** ~... la maison où...; **in the place** ~ à l'endroit où; **England is** ~ **you'll**

find... c'est en Angleterre que vous trouverez...; **this is ~ it was found** c'est là qu'on l'a retrouvé. (**c**) *(the place that)* là que. **so that's ~ my gloves have got to!** voilà où sont passés mes gants!; *(fig)* **that's ~ things started to go wrong** c'est là que les choses se sont gâtées; **this is ~ you've got to decide** là il faut que tu décides; **I walked past ~ he was standing** j'ai dépassé l'endroit où il se tenait; **from ~ I am** d'où *or* de là où je suis. (**d**) *(whereas)* alors que. **he walked ~ he could have taken the bus** il est allé à pied alors qu'il aurait pu prendre le bus.

◆ **whereabouts 1** *adv* où (donc) ; **2** *npl*: **to know sb's ~abouts** savoir où est qn. ◆ **whereas** *conj* *(while)* alors que, tandis que; *(although)* bien que + *subj*, quoique + *subj; (Jur: since)* attendu que. ◆ **whereby** *(conj: frm)* par quoi, par lequel (*or* laquelle *etc*). ◆ **wherefore** *n V* **why.** ◆ **whereupon** *conj* sur quoi, et sur ce. ◆ **wherever 1** *conj* (**a**) *(no matter where)* où que + *subj*; **~ver I am I'll always remember** où que je sois, je n'oublierai jamais; (**b**) *(anywhere)* (là) où; **sit ~ver you like** asseyez-vous (là) où vous voulez; **Barcombe, ~ver that is** un endroit qui s'appellerait Barcombe; (**c**) *(everywhere)* partout où; **~ver you go, I'll go too** partout où tu iras, j'irai; **~ver you see it, you know that...** partout où vous le voyez, vous savez que... ; **2** *adv*: **in London or Liverpool or ~ver *** à Londres, Liverpool ou Dieu sait où.

◆ **wherewithal** *n*: **the ~withal** les moyens *mpl* (*to do* de faire).

whet [wet] *vt (lit, fig)* aiguiser. ◆ **whetstone** *n* pierre *f* à aiguiser.

whether ['weðəʳ] *conj* (**a**) si. **I don't know ~ it's true or not** je ne sais pas si c'est vrai ou non; **I don't know ~ to go** je ne sais pas si je dois y aller; **it is doubtful ~** il est peu probable que + *subj*; **I doubt ~** je doute que + *subj*; **I'm not sure ~** je ne suis pas sûr que + *subj*. (**b**) que + *subj*. **~ it rains or snows** qu'il pleuve ou qu'il neige; **~ you go or not, he...** que tu y ailles ou non, il... (**c**) soit. **~ before or after** soit avant, soit après.

whew [hwu:] *excl* ouf!

whey [weɪ] *n* petit-lait *m*.

which [wɪtʃ] **1** *adj* (**a**) *(in questions etc)* quel. **~ card?** quelle carte?, laquelle des cartes?; **I don't know ~ books** je ne sais pas quels livres; **~ one?** lequel (*or* laquelle)?; **~ one of you?** lequel (*or* laquelle) d'entre vous?
(**b**) **in ~ case** auquel cas; **a week, during ~ time...** une semaine au cours de laquelle...
2 *pron* (**a**) *(in questions etc)* lequel *m*, laquelle *f*. **~ have you taken?** lequel avez-vous pris?; **~ of your sisters?** laquelle de vos sœurs?; **~ of you?** *(two people)* lequel de vous deux?; *(more than two)* lequel d'entre vous?; **~ are the ripest apples?** quelles sont les pommes les plus mûres?
(**b**) *(the one or ones that: subject)* celui *(or* celle *etc)* qui; *(object)* celui *etc* que. **show me ~ is the cheapest** montrez-moi celui qui est le moins cher; **I know ~ I'd rather have** je sais celui que je préférerais; **I don't know ~ is ~** je ne peux pas les distinguer; **I don't mind ~** ça m'est égal.
(**c**) *(that: subject)* qui; *(object)* que; *(after prep)* lequel *etc*. **the book ~ is on the table** le livre qui est sur la table; **the apple ~ you ate** la pomme que vous avez mangée; **the box ~ you put it in** la boîte dans laquelle vous l'avez mis; **the book ~ I told you about** le livre dont je vous ai parlé.
(**d**) *(and that: subject)* ce qui; *(object)* ce que; *(after prep)* quoi. **you're late, ~ reminds me...** vous êtes en retard, ce qui me fait penser...; **she said she was 40, ~ I don't believe** elle a dit qu'elle avait 40 ans, ce que je ne crois pas; **after ~ she left** après quoi elle est partie; **of ~ more later** ce dont je reparlerai plus tard; **from ~ we deduce** d'où nous déduisons.

◆ **whichever 1** *adj* (**a**) *(that one which)* **I'll have ~ever apple you don't want** je prendrai la pomme dont vous ne voulez pas; **keep ~ever one you prefer** gardez celui que vous préférez (peu importe lequel); (**b**) *(no matter which: subject)* quel que soit... qui + *subj*; *(object)* quel que soit... que + *subj*; **~ever book is left** quel que soit le livre qui reste *(subj)*; **~ever dress you wear** quelle que soit la robe que tu portes *(subj)*; **~ever way you look at it** de quelque manière que vous le considériez *(subj)* ; **2** *pron* (**a**) *(the one which: subject)* celui *m* (*or* celle *f etc*) qui; *(object)* celui *etc* que; **~ever is best for him** celui qui lui convient le mieux; **~ever you like** celui que vous voulez; **choose ~ever is easiest** choisissez le plus facile; (**b**) *(no matter which one: subject)* quel que soit celui qui + *subj*; *(object)* quel que soit celui que + *subj*; **~ever of the two books he chooses** quel que soit le livre qu'il choisisse; **~ever of the apples is left** quelle que soit la pomme qui reste *(subj)*.

whiff [wɪf] *n (puff: of chloroform, sea air etc)* bouffée *f*; *(smell)* odeur *f*. **one ~ of this is enough to kill you** il suffit de respirer ça une fois pour mourir; **I caught a ~ of gas** j'ai senti l'odeur du gaz.

while [waɪl] **1** *conj* (**a**) *(during the time that)* pendant que. **~ I was out of the room** pendant que j'étais hors de la pièce; **she fell asleep ~ reading** elle s'est endormie en lisant; **~ you're away I'll write some letters** pendant ton absence *or* pendant que tu seras absent j'écrirai quelques lettres; **and ~ you're about it** et pendant que vous y êtes. (**b**) *(as long as)* tant que. **it won't happen ~ I'm here** cela n'arrivera pas tant que je serai là. (**c**) *(although)* bien que + *subj*, quoique + *subj*. **~ there are a few people who like that** bien qu'il *or* quoiqu'il y ait un petit nombre de gens qui aiment cela. (**d**) *(whereas)* alors que, tandis que. **she sings quite well, ~ her sister can't sing a note** elle ne chante pas mal alors que *or* tandis que sa sœur ne sait pas chanter du tout.
2 *n*: **a ~** quelque temps; **a short ~, a little ~** un moment; **a long ~, a good ~** (assez) longtemps ; **after a ~** au bout de quelque temps; **for a ~ I thought...** j'ai pensé un moment...; *(longer)* pendant quelque temps j'ai pensé...; **once in a ~** une fois de temps en temps; **in between ~s** entretemps; **all the ~** pendant tout ce temps-là.

◆ **while away** *vt sep* (faire) passer.

◆ **while-you-wait heel repairs** *npl* ≃ talon minute. ◆ **whilst** *conj* = **while 1.**

whim [wɪm] *n* caprice *m*, fantaisie *f*. **he gives in to her every ~** il lui passe tous ses caprices; **as the ~ takes him** comme l'idée lui vient. ◆ **whimsical** *adj person* fantasque; *smile, book* étrange; *idea* saugrenu. ◆ **whimsically** *adv say, suggest* de façon saugrenue; *smile, look* étrangement.

whimper ['wɪmpəʳ] **1** *vi [person, baby]* gémir faiblement; *(whine)* pleurnicher; *[dog]* pousser de petits cris plaintifs. **2** *n* gémissement *m*. ◆ **whimpering 1** *n* gémissements *mpl* ; **2** *adj voice* larmoyant; *(whining)* pleurnicheur; *person, animal* qui gémit faiblement.

whimwhams * ['wɪmwæmz] *npl (US)* trouille ***** *f*, frousse ***** *f*.

whin [wɪn] *n (Bot)* ajonc *m*.

whine [waɪn] **1** *vi [person, dog]* gémir; *(fig: complain)* se lamenter (*about* sur), se plaindre (*about* de); *[siren]* gémir. **2** *vt*: **'no', he ~d** 'non', dit-il d'une voix geignarde. **3** *n* gémissement *m* prolongé; *(fig)* plainte *f*; *[bullet, machine]* plainte stridente. ◆ **whining 1** *n [person, child]* gémissements *mpl* continus, pleurnicheries *fpl*; *[dog]* gémissements; *(fig: complaining)* plaintes *fpl* continuelles ; **2** *adj voice, child* geignard; *dog* qui gémit.

whinny ['wɪnɪ] **1** *vi* hennir. **2** *n* hennissement *m*.

whip [wɪp] **1** *n* (**a**) fouet *m*; *(riding ~)* cravache *f*. (**b**) *(Parl) (person)* chef *m* de file *(d'un groupe parlementaire)*. *(summons)* **three-line** ~ convocation *f* impérative *(pour voter)*. (**c**) *(Culin)* **strawberry** *etc* ~ mousse *f* instantanée à la fraise *etc*.
2 *adj (fig)* **to have the** ~ **hand** avoir l'avantage (*over* sur).
3 *vt* (**a**) fouetter; *(Culin)* battre au fouet. **~ped cream** crème *f* fouettée. (**b**) *(*: defeat)* battre à plates coutures. (**c**) *(seize etc)* **to** ~ **sth out of sb's hands** enlever brusquement qch des mains de qn; **he ~ped a gun out of his pocket** il a brusquement sorti un revolver de sa poche; **to** ~ **sth away** *etc* enlever *etc* qch brusquement. (**c**) *(‡: steal)* faucher *, voler. (**d**) *rope* surlier; *(Sewing)* surfiler.
4 *vi*: **to** ~ **along/away** *etc* filer/partir *etc* à toute allure; **the car ~ped round the corner** la voiture a pris le tournant à toute allure; **to** ~ **round** *[person]* se retourner vivement; *[object]* pivoter brusquement.
◆ **whip up** *vt sep cream etc* battre au fouet; *(fig) indignation, interest* stimuler; *(*: prepare) meal* préparer en vitesse. **can you** ~ **us up sth to eat?** * est-ce que vous pourriez nous faire à manger * en vitesse?
◆ **whiplash** *n (blow from whip)* coup *m* de fouet; *(fig: in car accident)* coup du lapin *. ◆ **whippersnapper** *n* freluquet *m*. ◆ **whipping 1** *n (punishment)* correction *f*; **to give sb a ~ping** fouetter qn ; **2** *adj*: **~ping cream** crème fraîche *(à fouetter)*; *(fig)* **~ping boy** bouc *m* émissaire. ◆ **whip-round** * *n*: **to have a ~-round** faire une collecte (*for* pour).

whippet ['wɪpɪt] *n* whippet *m*.

whirl [wɜːl] **1** *vi* (**a**) (**~ round**) *[leaves, dancers, water]* tourbillonner; *[wheel, merry-go-round]* tourner. **the leaves ~ed down** les feuilles tombaient en tourbillonnant. (**b**) *(move rapidly)* **to** ~ **along/away** *etc* aller/partir *etc* à toute vitesse. **2** *vt* (**~ round**) *leaves etc* faire tourbillonner; *sword, object on rope* faire tournoyer. *(fig)* **they ~ed us round the Louvre** ils nous ont fait visiter le Louvre à toute vitesse; **the train ~ed us along** le train nous emportait à toute allure. **3** *n* tourbillon *m*. *(fig)* **the social** ~ la vie mondaine; **her thoughts/emotions were in a** ~ tout tourbillonnait dans sa tête/son cœur; **my head is in a** ~ la tête me tourne; *(fig: try)* **to give sth a** ~ * essayer qch. ◆ **whirlpool** tourbillon *m*; *(US)* **~pool bath** bain *m* à remous. ◆ **whirlwind 1** *n* tornade *f*, trombe *f* ; **2** *adj* éclair * *inv*.

whirr [wɜːʳ] **1** *vi [bird's wings, insect's wings]* bruire; *[cameras, machinery]* ronronner; *(louder)* vrombir. **to go ~ing off** partir en vrombissant. **2** *n* bruissement *m*; ronronnement *m*; vrombissement *m*.

whisk [wɪsk] **1** *n (Culin)* fouet *m*; *(rotary)* batteur *m* à œufs. **with a** ~ **of his tail** d'un coup de queue; *(Culin)* **to give sth a good** ~ bien battre qch. **2** *vt* (**a**) *(Culin)* battre au fouet; *egg whites* battre en neige. ~ **the eggs into it** incorporez-y les œufs avec un fouet. (**b**) **to** ~ **sth out of sb's hands** enlever brusquement qch des mains de qn; **she ~ed the letter off the table** elle a prestement fait disparaître la lettre de la table; **to** ~ **sth away/off** *etc* emporter/enlever *etc* qch brusquement; **the lift ~ed us up to the top floor** l'ascenseur nous a emportés jusqu'au dernier étage à toute allure.

whiskers ['wɪskəz] *npl (side ~)* favoris *mpl*; *(beard)* barbe *f*; *(moustache)* moustache *f*; *[animal]* moustaches.

whisky, *(US, Ir)* **whiskey** ['wɪskɪ] *n* whisky *m*. **a** ~ **and soda** un whisky soda.

whisper ['wɪspəʳ] **1** *vi (gen)* chuchoter (*to sb* à l'oreille de qn). **you'll have to** ~ il faudra que vous parliez bas. **2** *vt* chuchoter, dire à voix basse (*sth to sb* qch à qn; *that* que). **he ~ed a word in my ear** il m'a dit qch à l'oreille; *(fig)* **it is ~ed that...** le bruit court que... **3** *n (gen)* chuchotement *m*; *[wind etc]* murmure *m*; *(fig: rumour)* bruit *m*. **in a** ~ à voix basse. ◆ **whispering 1** *n* chuchotement *m*; *(fig)* **there has been a lot of ~ing about them** toutes sortes de rumeurs ont couru sur leur compte ; **2** *adj (fig)* **~ing campaign** campagne *f* (diffamatoire) insidieuse; **~ing gallery** galerie *f* à écho.

whist [wɪst] *n* whist *m*. ~ **drive** tournoi *m* de whist.

whistle ['wɪsl] **1** *n* (**a**) *(sound: gen)* sifflement *m*; *(made with a ~)* coup *m* de sifflet; *[audience] (cheering)* sifflements d'admiration; *(booing)* sifflets *mpl*. (**b**) *(thing blown)* sifflet *m*. **penny** ~ flûteau *m*; **he blew his** ~ il a donné un coup de sifflet; **the referee blew his** ~ **for half-time** l'arbitre a sifflé la mi-temps; **it broke off as clean as a** ~ ça a cassé net; *(fig)* **he blew the** ~ **on it** ‡ *(informed on it)* il a dévoilé le pot aux roses; *(stopped it)* il y a mis le holà.
2 *vi (gen)* siffler; *(casually, light-heartedly)* siffloter. **to** ~ **at** *or* **for** *or* **to sb/sth** siffler qn/qch; *(fig)* **he's whistling in the dark** il fait (*or* dit) ça pour se rassurer; *(fig)* **he can** ~ **for it!** * il peut toujours courir! *; **an arrow ~d past his ear** une flèche a sifflé à son oreille; **the cars ~d past** les voitures passaient à toute allure.
3 *vt tune* siffler; *(casually)* siffloter.
◆ **whistle up** *vt sep dog, taxi* siffler; *(* fig) helpers, more food etc* dégoter *, trouver.
◆ **whistle-stop** *adj (Pol etc)* **he made a ~-stop tour of...** il a fait à toute allure le tour de...

Whit [wɪt] **1** *n (also* **~sun***)* la Pentecôte. **2** *adj week, holiday etc* de Pentecôte. ~ **Sunday/Monday** le dimanche/lundi de Pentecôte.

whit [wɪt] *n*: **not a** ~ **of truth** pas un brin de vérité; **it wasn't a** ~ **better** ce n'était pas mieux du tout.

white [waɪt] **1** *adj* (**a**) *(gen)* blanc (*f* blanche). **as** ~ **as a sheet/a ghost** pâle comme un linge/la mort; **as** ~ **as snow** blanc comme neige; ~ **with fear** blême de peur; **to go** *or* **turn** ~ *(with fear, anger)* blêmir; *[hair]* blanchir; **it gets the clothes ~r than** ~ ça lave encore plus blanc; ~ **coffee** café au lait; **a** ~ **Christmas** un Noël sous la neige; *(fig)* **it's a** ~ **elephant** c'est tout à fait superflu; **the** ~ **flag** le drapeau blanc; ~ **frost** gelée *f* blanche; *(fig)* **the** ~ **hope of** le grand espoir de; *(at sea)* ~ **horses,** *(US)* ~ **caps** moutons *mpl*; *(US)* **the W~ House** la Maison-Blanche; *(fig)* **a** ~ **lie** un pieux mensonge; *(Acoustics)* ~ **noise** son *m* blanc; *(Parl)* ~ **paper** livre *m* blanc *(du gouvernement)* (*on* sur); *(Comm)* ~ **sale** vente *f* de blanc; *(Culin)* ~ **sauce** béchamel *f*; ~ **wedding** mariage *m* en blanc; ~ **whale** baleine *f* blanche. (**b**) *(racially) person, skin* blanc; *supremacy* de la race blanche. **a** ~ **man** un Blanc; **a** ~ **woman** une Blanche; **the** ~ **South Africans** les Blancs d'Afrique du Sud.
2 *n* (**a**) *(colour)* blanc *m*; *(whiteness)* blancheur *f*; *[egg, eye]* blanc. **dressed in** ~ vêtu de blanc; *(linen etc)* **the ~s** le linge blanc; **his face was a deathly** ~ son visage était d'une pâleur mortelle; **to be a dazzling** ~ être d'une blancheur éclatante. (**b**) *(person)* Blanc *m*, Blanche *f*.
◆ **whitebait** *n (Culin)* petite friture *f*. ◆ **white-collar** *adj*: **a ~-collar job** un emploi dans un bureau; **~-collar worker** employé(e) *m(f)* de bureau, col *m* blanc. ◆ **white-faced** *adj* blême. ◆ **white-haired** *adj person* aux cheveux blancs. ◆ **white-hot** *adj* chauffé à blanc. ◆ **whiten** *vt* blanchir. ◆ **whitener** *n (for coffee)* ersatz *m* de lait en poudre; *(for clothes)* agent *m* blanchissant. ◆ **whiteness** *n* blancheur *f*. ◆ **whitening** *n (substance)* blanc *m*. ◆ **white spirit** *n* white-spirit *m*. ◆ **whitethorn** *n* aubépine *f*. ◆ **whitewash 1** *n* lait *m* de chaux; *(fig)* **it was a ~wash of his character** ça visait à blanchir sa réputation ; **2** *vt wall etc* blanchir à la chaux; *(fig) person, sb's reputation,*

motives blanchir; *sb's faults* justifier (par des arguments fallacieux); *event, episode* peindre sous des traits anodins. ◆ **whitewall (tire)** *n (US)* pneu *m* à flanc blanc. ◆ **whitewood** *n* bois *m* blanc. ◆ **whitish** *adj* blanchâtre.

whiting ['waɪtɪŋ] *n (fish)* merlan *m.*

whitlow ['wɪtləʊ] *n* panaris *m.*

whittle ['wɪtl] *vt* tailler au couteau (*out of* dans). **to ~ down** *wood* tailler; *(fig) costs* amenuiser.

whiz(z) [wɪz] **1** *n (sound)* sifflement *m.* **2** *adj*: **~ kid** * petit prodige *m.* **3** *vi*: **to ~** *or* **go ~ing through the air** fendre l'air (en sifflant); **to ~ past** *etc* passer *etc* à toute vitesse.

who [hu:] *pron* (**a**) *(in questions: remplace aussi 'whom' dans le langage parlé)* (qui est-ce) qui; *(after prep)* qui. **~'s there?** qui est là?; **~ are you?** qui êtes-vous?; **~ has the book?** (qui est-ce) qui a le livre?; **~ should it be but Robert!** qui vois-je? Robert!; **I don't know ~'s ~ in the office** je ne connais pas très bien les gens au bureau; **'W~'s W~'** ≃ 'Bottin *m* Mondain'; **~(m) did you see?** qui avez-vous vu?; **~'s the book by?** le livre est de qui?; **you-know-~ * said...** qui vous savez a dit... (**b**) *(that)* qui. **my aunt ~ lives in London** ma tante qui habite à Londres; **those ~ can swim** ceux qui savent nager. ◆ **whodunit** * *n* roman *m* policier. ◆ **whoever** *pron* (**a**) *(anyone that)* quiconque; **~ever wishes may...** quiconque le désire peut...; **~ever finds it can keep it** celui qui le trouvera pourra le garder; **~ever said that was...** celui qui a dit ça était...; **ask ~ever you like** demandez à qui vous voulez; (**b**) *(no matter who: subject)* qui que ce soit qui + *subj*; *(object)* qui que ce soit que + *subj*; **~ever you are** qui que vous soyez; **~ever he marries** qui que ce soit qu'il épouse *(subj)*; (**c**) **~ever told you that?** qui donc vous a dit ça?

whoa [wəʊ] *excl* (**~ there**) ho!, holà!

whole [həʊl] **1** *adj* (**a**) *(entire)* (+ *sing n*) entier, tout; (+ *pl n*) entier. **the ~ book** le livre entier, tout le livre; **a ~ hour** toute une heure, une heure entière; **3 ~ days** 3 jours entiers; **the ~ world** le monde entier; **~ villages** des villages entiers; **the ~ road** toute la route; **~ milk** lait *m* entier; **to swallow sth ~** avaler qch tout entier; **roasted ~** rôti tout entier; **the ~ truth** toute la vérité; **the ~ point of it** tout l'intérêt de la chose; **with my ~ heart** de tout mon cœur; **the ~ lot** le tout; **the ~ lot of you** vous tous; **a ~ lot better** * vraiment beaucoup mieux; **a ~ lot of things** tout un tas de choses; **to go the ~ hog** * aller jusqu'au bout, s'engager à fond. (**b**) *(unbroken) glass, seal, egg* intact; *series, set* complet; *(unhurt)* sain et sauf. *(Math)* **~ number** nombre *m* entier.

2 *n* (**a**) *(all)* **the ~ of the book** tout le livre, le livre entier; **the ~ of the sum** la somme tout entière, la totalité de la somme; **the ~ of the time** tout le temps; **the ~ of France** la France tout entière; **the ~ of Paris was talking about it** dans tout Paris on parlait de ça; **as a ~** dans son ensemble; **on the ~** dans l'ensemble. (**b**) *(complete unit)* tout *m.* **they make a ~** ils font un tout; **estate sold as a ~** propriété vendue en bloc.

◆ **wholefood(s)** *n(pl)* aliments *mpl* complets; **a ~food restaurant** un restaurant qui n'utilise que des aliments complets. ◆ **wholegrain** *adj* complet. ◆ **wholehearted** *adj approval, admiration* sans réserve; **to make a ~hearted attempt** essayer de tout cœur. ◆ **wholeheartedly** *adv* de tout cœur. ◆ **wholemeal** *adj flour* brut; *bread* ≃ complet. ◆ **wholesale** **1** *n* (vente *f* en) gros *m* ; **2** *adj price, firm, trade etc* de gros; *(fig) slaughter, destruction, dismissals* en masse; *criticism, acceptance* en bloc; *campaign, movement* généralisé; **there was a ~sale attempt to do it** on a essayé par tous les moyens de le faire ; **3** *adv buy, sell* en gros; *get, obtain* au prix de gros; *(fig) dismiss, imprison, destroy* en masse; *reject, accept* en bloc. ◆ **wholesaler** *n* grossiste *mf.* ◆ **wholesome** *adj (gen)* sain; *air, climate* sain, salubre. ◆ **wholewheat** = **wholemeal.** ◆ **wholly** *adv* complètement, entièrement.

whom [hu:m] *pron* (**a**) *(souvent remplacé par 'who' dans le langage parlé) (in questions)* qui. **~ did you see?** qui avez-vous vu?; **with ~?** avec qui? (**b**) *(that)* que; *(after prep)* qui. **my aunt, ~ I love** ma tante, que j'aime; **those ~ he had seen** ceux qu'il avait vus; **the man to ~** l'homme à qui, l'homme auquel; **the man of ~** l'homme dont.

whoop [hu:p] **1** *n* cri *m (de triomphe etc).* **2** *vi* pousser des cris; *(Med)* avoir des quintes de toux coquelucheuse. **3** *vt*: **to ~ it up** ‡ bien se marrer ‡. ◆ **whoopee** **1** *excl* youpi! ; **2** *n*: **to make ~ee** ‡ bien se marrer ‡. ◆ **whoopee cushion** * *n* coussin(-péteur) *m* de farces et attrapes. ◆ **whooping cough** *n* coqueluche *f.* ◆ **whoops** *excl* houp-là!

whopper * ['wɒpəʳ] *n (car/parcel etc)* voiture *f*/colis *m etc* énorme; *(lie)* mensonge *m* énorme. ◆ **whopping** * *adj* énorme.

whore ‡ [hɔ:ʳ] *n* putain ‡ *f.*

whose [hu:z] **1** *poss pron* à qui. **~ is this?** à qui est ceci?; **I know ~ it is** je sais à qui c'est; **let's see ~ lasts longest** voyons celui de qui durera le plus longtemps. **2** *poss adj* (**a**) *(in questions: gen)* de qui; *(ownership)* à qui. **~ hat is this?** à qui est ce chapeau?; **~ son are you?** de qui êtes-vous le fils?; **~ fault is it?** à qui la faute? (**b**) dont, de qui. **the man ~ hat I took** l'homme dont j'ai pris le chapeau; **the boy ~ sister I was talking to** le garçon à la sœur duquel *or* à la sœur de qui je parlais; **those ~ passports are here** ceux dont les passeports sont ici.

why [waɪ] **1** *adv, conj* pourquoi. **~ did you do it?** pourquoi l'avez-vous fait?; **I wonder ~** je me demande pourquoi; **he told me ~ he did it** il m'a dit pourquoi il l'a fait *or* la raison pour laquelle il l'a fait; **that's (the reason) ~** voilà pourquoi; **~ not?** pourquoi pas?; **the reasons ~ he did it** les raisons pour lesquelles il l'a fait; **there's no reason ~ you shouldn't try again** il n'y a pas de raison pour que tu n'essayes *(subj)* pas de nouveau; **~ not phone her?** pourquoi ne pas lui téléphoner? **2** *excl (surprise)* tiens!; *(remonstrating)* mais voyons donc!; *(explaining)* eh bien! **3** *n*: **the ~(s) and the wherefore(s)** les causes *fpl* et les raisons *fpl*; **the ~ and the how** le pourquoi et le comment.

wick [wɪk] *n* mèche *f.*

wicked ['wɪkɪd] *adj (iniquitous) person* méchant; *act* mauvais; *system, policy* inique; *(unpleasant) blow, wound* vilain *(before n)*; *pain* violent; *satire, criticism* méchant; *waste* scandaleux; *(mischievous etc) person, smile, remark* malicieux. **that was a ~ thing to do** c'était vraiment méchant!; **he has a ~ temper** il a un caractère épouvantable; *(fig: admiringly)* **a ~ * shot/game** *etc* un coup/un jeu *etc* du tonnerre *. ◆ **wickedly** *adv (evilly) behave* très mal; *destroy, kill* par un raffinement de méchanceté; *(mischievously)* malicieusement; *(*: skilfully) play, manage etc* formidablement bien *. ◆ **wickedness** *n* méchanceté *f*; scandale *m*; malice *f*; *[murder]* atrocité *f.*

wicker ['wɪkəʳ] **1** *n* osier *m.* **2** *adj basket etc* d'osier. ◆ **wickerwork** *n* vannerie *f.*

wicket ['wɪkɪt] *n* (**a**) *(door)* portillon *m.* (**b**) *(Cricket)* guichet *m.* ◆ **wicket-keeper** *n* gardien *m* de guichet.

wide [waɪd] **1** *adj (gen)* large; *margin, variety* grand; *ocean, desert* immense; *(fig) knowledge* vaste, grand; *selection* grand, considérable; *survey, study* de grande envergure. **how ~ is the room?** quelle est la largeur de la pièce?; **it is 5 metres ~** cela fait 5 mètres de large; *(Cine)* **~ screen** écran *m* panoramique; *(fig)* ~ **boy** * filou *m*; **the shot was** ~ le coup est passé à côté; ~ **of the target** loin de la cible. **2** *adv aim, shoot, fall* loin du but. **the bullet went** ~ la balle est passée à côté; **(set)** ~ **apart** *trees, houses* largement espacés; *eyes, legs* très écartés; ~ **awake** bien éveillé; ~ **open** grand ouvert. ◆ **wide-bodied** *adj aircraft* à fuselage élargi. ◆ **wide-eyed** *adj* aux yeux écarquillés (*from fear etc* de peur *etc*). ◆ **widely** *adv scatter, spread* sur une grande étendue; *travel* beaucoup; *differ, different* radicalement; *spaced* largement; *believed, understood etc* généralement; **~ly-held opinions** des opinions *fpl* très répandues; **~ly known for** connu partout pour; **to be ~ly read** *[author, book]* être très lu; *[reader]* avoir beaucoup lu (*in sth* qch). ◆ **widen** **1** *vt (gen)* élargir; *margin* augmenter; *knowledge* accroître; *survey, study* accroître la portée de ; **2** *vi* (*~n out)* s'élargir; s'accroître. ◆ **wide-ranging** *adj report* de grande envergure; *interests* divers, variés. ◆ **widespread** *adj arms* en croix; *wings* déployés; *belief* très répandu.

widget * ['wɪdʒɪt] *n (US) (device)* gadget *m; (thingummy)* truc *m.*

widow ['wɪdəʊ] **1** *n* veuve *f. (fig)* **she's a golf** ~ son mari la délaisse pour aller jouer au golf; **~'s peak** pousse *f* de cheveux en V sur le front. **2** *vt*: **to be ~ed** devenir veuf (*f* veuve); **his ~ed mother** sa mère qui est veuve. ◆ **widower** *n* veuf *m.* ◆ **widowhood** *n* veuvage *m.*

width [wɪdθ] *n (gen)* largeur *f*; *[garment]* ampleur *f.* **it is 5 metres in** ~ cela fait 5 mètres de large; **a** ~ **of cloth** une largeur d'étoffe. ◆ **widthwise** *adv* en largeur.

wield [wi:ld] *vt tool, weapon etc* manier; *(brandish)* brandir; *power etc* exercer.

wife, *pl* **wives** [waɪf,waɪvz] *n (gen)* femme *f*; *(Admin etc)* épouse *f.* **the farmer's/butcher's** *etc* ~ la fermière/bouchère *etc*; **the** ~ ⁑ la patronne ⁑; *(Admin etc)* **wives who have...** les femmes mariées qui ont...; **old wives' tale** conte *m* de bonne femme; *(woman)* **a poor old** ~ * une pauvre vieille. ◆ **wifely** *adj duties* conjugal; *feelings* d'une bonne épouse. ◆ **wife-swapping** *n* échange *m* de partenaires *(par deux couples).*

wig [wɪg] *n* perruque *f*; *(hair-piece)* postiche *m.*

wiggle ['wɪgl] **1** *vt pencil, stick, toes* agiter, remuer; *loose screw, tooth* faire jouer. **to** ~ **one's hips** tortiller des hanches. **2** *vi [sth loose]* branler; *[tail]* remuer. ◆ **wiggly** *adj line* ondulé.

wigwam ['wɪgwæm] *n* wigwam *m.*

wild [waɪld] **1** *adj* (**a**) *animal, plant, tribe, countryside* sauvage; *rabbit* de garenne. ~ **beast** *(gen)* bête *f* sauvage; *(dangerous)* bête féroce; **it was growing** ~ ça poussait à l'état sauvage; *(fig)* ~ **horses wouldn't make me tell** je ne le dirais pour rien au monde; *(fig)* **to sow one's** ~ **oats** jeter sa gourme; *(US)* **the W~ West** le Far West. (**b**) *wind* furieux; *sea* en furie; *weather* gros; *night* de tempête. (**c**) *(excited etc) person, youth, scheme, laughter* fou (*f* folle); *eyes* égaré; *appearance, look* farouche; *imagination, enthusiasm* débordant; *life, evening* mouvementé; *(*: angry)* furieux. **a gang of** ~ **kids** une bande de casse-cou; **we had some** ~ **times** nous avons fait bien des folies; **there was a lot of** ~ **talk about...** on a agité des tas d'idées folles au sujet de...; **to make a** ~ **guess** risquer à tout hasard une hypothèse (*at sth* sur qch); *(excited)* **to go** ~ *[dog etc]* devenir comme fou; *[person]* ne plus se tenir (*with joy* de joie); *[audience]* entrer en délire; ~ **with indignation** fou d'indignation; *(enthusiastic)* **to be,** ~ **about sb/sth** être dingue * *or* fou de qn/qch; **I'm not** ~ **about it** * ça ne m'emballe * pas beaucoup; **it's enough to drive you** ~**!** * c'est à vous rendre dingue *! *or* fou!

2 *n*: **the call of the** ~ l'appel *m* de la nature; **into the ~s** dans les régions *fpl* sauvages; **in the ~s of Alaska** au fin fond de l'Alaska. ◆ **wildcat** **1** *n* chat *m* sauvage ; **2** *adj (fig) scheme* insensé; *strike* sauvage. ◆ **wilderness** ['wɪldənɪs] *n (gen)* région *f* sauvage; *(Bible; also fig: of streets, snow etc)* désert *m*; *(overgrown garden)* jungle *f.* ◆ **wild-eyed** *adj (mad)* au regard fou; *(grief-stricken)* au regard égaré. ◆ **wildfire** *n*: **to spread like ~fire** se répandre comme une traînée de poudre. ◆ **wildfowl** *npl (collective)* oiseaux *mpl* sauvages; *(Hunting)* gibier *m* à plume. ◆ **wild-goose** *n:* **he sent me off on a ~-goose chase** il m'a fait courir partout pour rien. ◆ **wildlife** **1** *n* la nature; *(more formally)* la flore et la faune ; **2** *adj*: **~life sanctuary** réserve *f* naturelle. ◆ **wildly** *adv blow, rage* furieusement; *behave* de façon extravagante; *gesticulate, talk* comme un fou; *applaud* frénétiquement; *protest* violemment; *shoot, hit out, guess* au hasard; *rush around* dans tous les sens; *(*: very) happy, enthusiastic* follement; **her heart was beating ~ly** son cœur battait à se rompre; **he looked at them ~ly** il leur a jeté un regard fou. ◆ **wildness** *n [countryside, scenery]* aspect *m* sauvage; *[tribe]* sauvagerie *f*; *[wind, sea]* fureur *f*; *[appearance]* désordre *m*; *[imagination]* extravagance *f*; *[enthusiasm]* ferveur *f*; **the ~ness of the weather** le sale temps qu'il fait (*or* faisait *etc*).

wildebeest ['wɪldɪbi:st] *n* gnou *m.*

wiles [waɪlz] *npl* artifices *mpl*; *(stronger)* ruses *fpl.*

wilful, *(US)* **willful** ['wɪlf(ʊ)l] *adj person, character* têtu, obstiné; *action* délibéré; *murder* prémédité; *damage* commis avec préméditation. ◆ **wil(l)fully** *adv (obstinately)* obstinément; *(deliberately)* délibérément.

will [wɪl] **1** *modal aux vb* (**a**) *(making future tense)* **he** ~ *or* **he'll speak** il parlera; *(near future)* il va parler; **you won't lose it** tu ne le perdras pas; **you** ~ **come to see us, won't you?** vous viendrez nous voir, n'est-ce pas?; ~ **he come? — yes he** ~ est-ce qu'il viendra? — oui; **no you won't!** non, certainement pas!; **they'll arrive tomorrow —** ~ **they?** ils arriveront demain — ah bon?; *(in requests)* ~ **you please sit down!** voulez-vous vous asseoir, s'il vous plaît!; *(in commands)* **you** ~ **speak to no one** vous ne parlerez à personne; ~ **you be quiet!** veux-tu bien te taire!

(**b**) *(conjecture)* **that** ~ **be the postman** ça doit être le facteur; **that** ~ **have been last year** c'était l'année dernière, sans doute.

(**c**) *(willingness)* **I** ~ **help you** je vous aiderai, je veux bien vous aider; ~ **you help me? — yes I** ~**/ no I won't** tu veux m'aider? — oui je veux bien/ non je ne veux pas; **if you'll help me** si vous voulez bien m'aider; **won't you come with us?** tu ne veux pas venir avec nous?; ~ **you have a cup of coffee?** voulez-vous un petit café?; **won't you have a drink?** vous prendrez bien un verre?; **just a moment,** ~ **you?** un instant, s'il vous plaît; *(in marriage service)* **I** ~ oui; **I WILL see him!** on ne m'empêchera pas de le voir!; **I won't have it!** je n'admets pas ça!; **it won't open** ça ne s'ouvre pas; **do what you** ~ faites ce que vous voulez.

(**d**) *(habit, characteristic: usually present tense in French)* **he** ~ **sit for hours doing nothing** il reste assis pendant des heures à ne rien faire; **the car** ~ **do 150 km/h** cette voiture fait 150 km/h; **he WILL talk all the time!** il ne peut pas s'empêcher de parler!; **if you WILL tell her everything** si tu insistes pour lui raconter tout; *(ruefully)* **I WILL call him Richard** il faut toujours que je l'appelle *(subj)* Richard; **accidents** ~ **happen** il y aura toujours des accidents.

2 *pret, ptp* **willed** *vt* (**a**) *(wish, intend)* vouloir (*sth* qch; *that* que + *subj*). **it is as God ~s** c'est la volonté de Dieu; **you must** ~ **it really hard** il faut le vouloir très fort; **to** ~ **sb to do** prier inté-

rieurement pour que qn fasse; **to ~ o.s. to do sth** faire un suprême effort pour faire qch.
(**b**) *(Jur: leave in one's ~)* léguer (*sth to sb* qch à qn).
3 *n* (**a**) volonté *f.* **he has a ~ of his own** il est très volontaire; **an iron ~** une volonté de fer; **the ~ to live** la volonté de survivre; **where there's a ~ there's a way** vouloir, c'est pouvoir; **it is his ~ that** sa volonté est que + *subj*; **to take the ~ for the deed** juger la chose sur l'intention; **Thy ~ be done** que Ta volonté soit faite; **at ~** *(as much as you like) borrow etc* à volonté; *(whenever you like) join, leave etc* quand vous le voulez *etc*; **to do sth against one's ~** faire qch à contre-cœur; **with the best ~ in the world** avec la meilleure volonté du monde; **to work with a ~** travailler avec détermination.
(**b**) *(Jur)* testament *m.* **the last ~ and testament of...** les dernières volontés *fpl* de...; **in his ~** dans son testament.
◆ **willing 1** *adj* (**a**) **I'm quite ~ing to do it** je veux bien le faire, je suis prêt à le faire; **he wasn't very ~ing to help** il n'était pas tellement prêt à aider; **they are ~ing and able to go** ils veulent et ils peuvent y aller; **God ~ing** si Dieu le veut; (**b**) *obedience, help* spontané; *helper, worker* de bonne volonté; **he's very ~ing** il est plein de bonne volonté; **~ing hands** des mains *fpl* empressées; *(fig)* **the ~ing horse** la bonne âme (qui se sacrifie toujours) ; **2** *n*: **to show ~ing** faire preuve de bonne volonté. ◆ **willingly** *adv (with pleasure)* volontiers; *(voluntarily)* volontairement, spontanément; *(agreeing)* **~ingly!** volontiers!; **did he do it ~ingly?** l'a-t-il fait de lui-même *or* volontairement? ◆ **willingness** *n*: **I don't doubt his ~ingness** ce n'est pas sa bonne volonté que je mets en doute; **his ~ingness to help me** son empressement *m* à m'aider. ◆ **willpower** *n* volonté *f*, vouloir *m.*

will-o'-the-wisp ['wɪləðə'wɪsp] *n (lit, fig)* feu *m* follet.

willow ['wɪləʊ] *n* saule *m.* ◆ **willowherb** *n* épilobe *m.* ◆ **willow-pattern 1** *n* motif *m* chinois (bleu); **2** *adj china* à motif chinois (bleu). ◆ **willowy** *adj person* élancé; *object* mince.

willy-nilly ['wɪlɪ'nɪlɪ] *adv* bon gré mal gré.

wilt [wɪlt] *vi [flower]* se faner; *[plant]* se dessécher; *[person]* commencer à flancher *; *[effort, enthusiasm etc]* diminuer.

wily ['waɪlɪ] *adj* rusé, malin. **a ~ old devil *** *or* **bird *** un vieux renard.

wimp [wɪmp] *n (pej)* mauviette *f.*

wimple ['wɪmpl] *n* guimpe *f.*

win [wɪn] *(vb: pret, ptp* **won***)* **1** *n (Sport etc)* victoire *f (for* pour). **to have a ~** gagner; **to back a horse for a ~** jouer un cheval gagnant.
2 *vi* (**a**) gagner, l'emporter (*by a length etc* d'une longueur *etc*). (**b**) **to ~ free** se dégager (*from sth* de qch).
3 *vt* (**a**) *(gen)* gagner; *prize, victory* remporter; *scholarship* obtenir; *fame, fortune* trouver; *sb's attention* captiver; *sb's friendship, esteem, sympathy, admirers* s'attirer; *friends, reputation* se faire (*as* en tant que). **he won it for growing radishes** il l'a eu pour sa culture de radis; **he won £5 from her** il lui a gagné 5 livres; **to ~ the day** *(Mil)* remporter la victoire; *(gen)* l'emporter; **this won him attention/the prize** *etc* ceci lui a valu l'attention/le prix *etc*; **to ~ sb's love/respect** se faire aimer/respecter de qn. (**b**) *(reach) shore, goal* parvenir à.
◆ **win back** *vt sep land, trophy* reprendre (*from* à); *gaming loss etc* recouvrer; *sb's support, girlfriend etc* reconquérir. ◆ **win out, win through** *vi* y parvenir. ◆ **win over, win round** *vt sep* convaincre. **I won him over to my point of view** je l'ai gagné à ma façon de voir.
◆ **winnable** *adj* gagnable. ◆ **winner** *n (in fight, argument)* vainqueur *m*; *(in game, competition)* gagnant(e) *m(f)*; **to be the ~ner** gagner; *(fig)* **it's a ~ner** c'est sensationnel *; **to pick a ~ner** *(Racing)* choisir un gagneur; *(gen)* tirer le bon numéro. ◆ **winning 1** *adj* (**a**) *person, car etc* gagnant; *goal, shot etc* décisif; (**b**) *(captivating) person* charmant; *smile, manner* charmeur ; **2** *npl (Betting etc)* **~nings** gains *mpl.* ◆ **winning-post** *n* poteau *m* d'arrivée.

wince [wɪns] *vi* tressaillir; *(grimace)* grimacer (de douleur *or* dégoût *etc*). **he ~d at the thought** cette pensée l'a fait tressaillir; **without wincing** sans broncher.

winch [wɪn(t)ʃ] **1** *n* treuil *m.* **2** *vt*: **to ~ sth up/down** *etc* monter/descendre *etc* qch au treuil.

wind[1] [wɪnd] **1** *n* (**a**) vent *m.* **high ~** grand vent, vent violent; **the ~ was in the east** le vent venait de l'est; **to go/run like the ~** aller/filer comme le vent; *(Naut)* **to run before the ~** avoir vent arrière; *(fig)* **to sail close to the ~** *(gen)* y aller un peu fort; *(almost illegal)* friser l'illégalité; *(blue joke etc)* friser la vulgarité; *(fig)* **to take the ~ out of sb's sails** couper l'herbe sous le pied de qn; *(fig)* **to see how the ~ blows** voir la tournure que prennent les choses; *(fig)* **the ~ of change is blowing** un grand courant d'air frais souffle; *(fig)* **there's sth in the ~** il y a qch dans l'air; *(fig)* **to get ~ of sth** avoir vent de qch; **he threw caution to the ~s** il a fait fi de toute prudence. (**b**) *(breath)* souffle *m.* **he has still plenty of ~** il a encore du souffle; **he had lost his ~** il avait perdu le souffle; **to get one's ~ back** *or* **one's second ~** reprendre son souffle; *(fig pej)* **it's all ~** ce n'est que du vent; *(fig)* **to put the ~ up sb *** flanquer la frousse * à qn; **to get/have the ~ up *** attraper/avoir la frousse * (*about* à propos de). (**c**) *(Med)* vents *mpl.* **to break ~** lâcher un vent, avoir des gaz; **to bring up ~** avoir un renvoi. (**d**) *(Mus)* **the ~(s)** les instruments *mpl* à vent.
2 *adj erosion, power etc* éolien; *instrument* à vent.
3 *vt*: **to ~ sb** *[blow, boxer]* couper le souffle à qn; *[fall, exertion]* essouffler qn; **I'm only ~ed** j'ai la respiration coupée, c'est tout.
◆ **windbag *** *n* moulin *m* à paroles. ◆ **windbreak** *n (tree, fence etc)* abat-vent *m inv*; *(for camping etc)* pare-vent *m inv.* ◆ **windcheater** *n* anorak *m* léger. ◆ **windfall** *n (fruit)* fruit *m* abattu par le vent; *(fig)* aubaine *f.* ◆ **wind-gauge** *n* anémomètre *m.* ◆ **windmill** *n* moulin *m* à vent. ◆ **windpipe** *n (Anat)* trachée *f.* ◆ **windproof** *adj* qui ne laisse pas passer le vent. ◆ **windscreen** *or (US)* ◆ **windshield 1** *n* pare-brise *m inv* ; **2** *adj*: **~screen washer** lave-glace *m inv*; **~screen wiper** essuie-glace *m inv.* ◆ **windsleeve** *or* ◆ **windsock** *n* manche *f* à air. ◆ **windsurf** *vi* faire de la planche à voile. ◆ **windsurfer** *n (board)* planche *f* à voile; *(person)* véliplanchiste *mf.* ◆ **windsurfing** *n* planche *f* à voile *(sport).* ◆ **windswept** *adj* battu par les vents. ◆ **windward 1** *adj, adv* du côté du vent ; **2** *n*: **to ~ward of sth** contre le vent par rapport à qch. ◆ **windy** *adj* (**a**) *place* battu par les vents, exposé au vent; *day, weather* de grand vent; **it's ~y** il y a du vent; (**b**) *(scared)* **to be** *or* **get ~y * about sth** paniquer * à cause de qch; (**c**) *(US: wordy)* verbeux.

wind[2] [waɪnd] *(vb: pret, ptp* **wound***)* **1** *n*: **to give sth a ~ = to ~ sth** *(V* **2***).*
2 *vt* (**a**) *(roll)* enrouler (*on* sur; *round* autour de). **to ~ wool (into a ball)** enrouler de la laine (en pelote); **he wound his way home** il a pris lentement le chemin du retour. (**b**) *clock, watch, toy* remonter; *handle* donner des tours de. *(with winch etc)* **to ~ sth up/down** monter/descendre qch (avec un treuil *etc*).
3 *vi (also* **~ its way***)* *[river, path, procession]* serpenter (*through* à travers). **to ~ up/down** *[path etc]*

monter/descendre en serpentant; *[stairs]* monter/descendre en tournant.

◆ **wind down** **1** *vi* (* *relax*) se détendre. **2** *vt sep car window* baisser; *(fig) department* réduire progressivement. ◆ **wind up** **1** *vi [meeting, discussion]* se terminer (*with* par). **they wound up * in Cannes/in jail** ils se sont retrouvés à Cannes/en prison; **he wound up * as a doctor** il a fini par devenir médecin; *(fig)* **to ~ up with sth** se retrouver avec qch. **2** *vt sep* (**a**) *(end) meeting, speech* clore, terminer (*with* par); *(Comm) business* liquider; *account* clore. (**b**) *watch etc* remonter; *car window* monter. *(fig: tense)* **to be all wound up *** être crispé (*about* à propos de).

◆ **winding** *adj road, river* sinueux, qui serpente; *staircase* tournant.

windlass ['wɪndləs] *n* treuil *m*.

window ['wɪndəʊ] *n* (**a**) *(gen)* fenêtre *f*; *(in car, train)* vitre *f*; *(~ pane)* vitre, carreau *m*; *(stained-glass ~)* vitrail *m*; *(larger)* verrière *f*; *[shop, café etc]* vitrine *f*; *(in post office, ticket office etc)* guichet *m*; *(in envelope)* fenêtre. **at the ~** à la fenêtre (*or* vitre); **don't lean out of the ~** ne te penche pas par la fenêtre; *(in train, car etc)* ne te penche pas au dehors; **to look** *etc* **out of the ~** regarder *etc* par la fenêtre; *(in train etc)* regarder *etc* dehors; **to break a ~** casser une vitre; **to clean the ~s** nettoyer les carreaux; *[shop]* **in the ~** en vitrine. (**b**) *(space: also* **launch** *~)* fenêtre *f* de lancement.

◆ **window-box** *n* jardinière *f (à plantes)*.

◆ **window-cleaner** *n (person)* laveur *m*, -euse *f* de carreaux. ◆ **window-dresser** *n (Comm)* étalagiste *mf*. ◆ **window-dressing** *n (Comm)* composition *f* d'étalage; *(fig pej)* **it's only ~-dressing** ce n'est qu'une façade. ◆ **window envelope** *n* enveloppe *f* à fenêtre. ◆ **window-ledge** *n* rebord *m* de fenêtre. ◆ **window-pane** *n* vitre *f*. ◆ **window-seat** *n (in room)* banquette *f* (située sous la fenêtre); *(in vehicle: gen)* place *f* côté fenêtre *inv*; *(in train)* coin *m* fenêtre. ◆ **window-shopping** **1** *n* lèche-vitrines *m* ; **2** *vi*: **to go ~-shopping** faire du lèche-vitrines. ◆ **windowsill** *n (inside)* appui *m* de fenêtre; *(outside)* rebord *m* de fenêtre.

wine [waɪn] **1** *n* vin *m*. **2** *vt*: **to ~ and dine sb** emmener qn faire un très bon dîner. **3** *adj bottle, cellar* à vin; *(colour)* lie-de-vin *inv*. **~ list** carte *f* des vins; **~ merchant** marchand(e) *m(f)* de vin; *(larger scale)* négociant(e) *m(f)* en vins; **~ vinegar** vinaigre *m* de vin; **~ waiter** sommelier *m*. ◆ **wine-glass** *n* verre *m* à vin. ◆ **wine-grower** *n* viticulteur *m*, -trice *f*, vigneron(ne) *m(f)*. ◆ **wine-growing** **1** *n* viticulture *f* ; **2** *adj district, industry* viticole. ◆ **wine-tasting** *n* dégustation *f* (de vins).

wing [wɪŋ] **1** *n (gen)* aile *f*; *[armchair]* oreillette *f*; *(Sport: player)* ailier *m*. *(fig)* **to take sb under one's ~** prendre qn sous son aile; *(Theat)* **the ~s** les coulisses *fpl*; *(Theat; fig)* **in the ~s** dans les coulisses; *(Pol)* **on the left ~ of the party** sur l'aile gauche du parti. **2** *adj (Aut)* **~ mirror** rétroviseur *m* de côté; **~ tip** bout *m* de l'aile. ◆ **winged** *adj* ailé. ◆ **winger** *n (Sport)* ailier *m*. ◆ **wingspan** *n* envergure *f*.

wink [wɪŋk] **1** *n* clin *m* d'œil; *(blink)* clignement *m*. **with a ~** en clignant de l'œil; **in a ~, as quick as a ~** en un clin d'œil. **2** *vi* faire un clin d'œil (*to, at* à); *(blink)* cligner des yeux; *[star]* clignoter.

◆ **winking** **1** *adj light* clignotant. **2** *n*: **as easy as ~ing** simple comme bonjour.

winkle ['wɪŋkl] **1** *n* bigorneau *m*. **2** *vt* (*) extirper (*sth/sb out of* qch/qn de).

winter ['wɪntəʳ] **1** *n* hiver *m*. **in ~** en hiver; **in the ~ of 1977** pendant l'hiver de 1977. **2** *adj weather, day, activities, clothes* d'hiver. **~ sports** sports *mpl* d'hiver. ◆ **wintertime** *n* hiver *m*. ◆ **wintry** *adj* d'hiver; *(fig) smile* glacial.

wipe [waɪp] **1** *n*: **to give sth a ~** donner un coup de torchon (*or* d'éponge *etc*) à qch. **2** *vt (gen)* essuyer (*with* avec); *blackboard* effacer; *tape, computer disk* effacer. **to ~ one's feet** s'essuyer les pieds (*on* sur; *with* avec); **to ~ one's nose** se moucher; **to ~ one's bottom** s'essuyer; **to ~ sth dry** essuyer soigneusement qch; *(fig)* **to ~ the floor with sb *** réduire qn en miettes *.

◆ **wipe away** *vt sep tears* essuyer; *marks* effacer. ◆ **wipe off** *vt sep* effacer. ◆ **wipe out** *vt sep* (**a**) *container* bien essuyer; *writing, insult, memory* effacer; *debt* régler. (**b**) *(annihilate) town, people, opposing team* anéantir. ◆ **wipe up** **1** *vi (dry dishes)* essuyer la vaisselle. **2** *vt sep* essuyer.

◆ **wipe-out** *n (destruction)* destruction *f*; *(US: windsurfing)* chute *f*. ◆ **wiper** *n (Aut)* essuie-glace *m inv*.

wire ['waɪəʳ] **1** *n* (**a**) fil *m* de fer; *(Elec)* fil (électrique); *(~ fence)* grillage *m*. **telephone ~s** fils téléphoniques; *(fig)* **to pull ~s for sb** pistonner qn; *(fig)* **we've got our ~s crossed *** nous ne sommes pas sur la même longueur d'ondes. (**b**) *(telegram)* télégramme *m*. **2** *adj* (**a**) *object* en fil de fer; *brush* métallique. **~ cutters** cisaille *f*. (**b**) *(US Press)* **~ service** agence *f* de presse *(utilisant les téléscripteurs)*. **3** *vt* (**a**) *(Elec) house* faire l'installation électrique de; *circuit* installer. **to ~ sth to sth** *(tie)* rattacher qch à qch (avec du fil de fer); *(Elec)* brancher qch sur qch; **to ~ a room for sound** sonoriser une pièce; *(for cable TV)* **to be ~d** être raccordé. (**b**) *(telegraph)* télégraphier (*to* à). **4** *vi* télégraphier.

◆ **wireless** **1** *n* T.S.F. *f*; **by ~less** par sans-fil; **on the ~less** à la T.S.F. ; **2** *adj station, programme* radiophonique; **~less message** radio *m*, sans-fil *m* ; **~less operator** radiotélégraphiste *mf*; **~less set** poste *m* de T.S.F. ◆ **wire-netting** *n* treillis *m* métallique. ◆ **wirepulling** * *n* le piston *. ◆ **wiretapping** *n* mise *f* sur écoute d'une ligne téléphonique. ◆ **wiring** *n (Elec)* installation *f* électrique. ◆ **wiry** *adj hair* dru; *animal* nerveux, vigoureux; *person* maigre et nerveux.

wisdom ['wɪzd(ə)m] **1** *n [person]* sagesse *f*; *[action, remark]* prudence *f*. **2** *adj*: **~ tooth** dent *f* de sagesse.

wise[1] [waɪz] *adj person* sage; *(learned)* savant; *look, nod* averti; *action, remark, advice* judicieux; *(prudent)* prudent. **a ~ man** un sage; **the Three W~ Men** les trois Rois mages; **to grow ~r** s'assagir; **how ~ of you!** vous avez (eu) bien raison; **the ~st thing to do is to wait** le plus sage est d'attendre; **I'm none the ~r** ça ne m'avance pas beaucoup; **nobody will be any the ~r if...** personne n'en saura rien si...; **~ guy *** gros malin * *m*; **to put sb/be ~ to sth *** mettre qn/être au courant de qch; **to get ~ to sb *** piger * le petit jeu de qn. ◆ **wisecrack** * *n* vanne ‡ *f*, remarque désobligeante.

◆ **wisely** *adv* sagement; judicieusement; prudemment.

wise[2] [waɪz] **1** *n*: **in no ~** en aucune façon; **in this ~** ainsi. **2** *adv ending, e.g.* **health ~** du point de vue santé.

wish [wɪʃ] **1** *vt* (**a**) *(desire)* souhaiter, désirer (*sth* qch; *to do* faire; *that* que + *subj*). **what do you ~ him to do?** que voudrais-tu *or* souhaites-tu *or* désires-tu qu'il fasse?; **I ~ I'd gone with you** j'aurais bien voulu vous accompagner, je regrette de ne pas vous avoir accompagné; **I ~ I hadn't said that** je regrette d'avoir dit cela; **I ~ you'd stop talking!** tu ne peux donc pas te taire!; **I ~ I could!** si seulement je pouvais!; **I ~ to heaven *** *or* **to goodness * he hadn't done it** si seulement il n'avait pas fait ça!; **he doesn't ~ her any harm** il ne lui veut aucun mal; *(fig)* **it was ~ed on to me *** je n'ai pas pu faire autrement que de l'accepter. (**b**) *(bid)* souhaiter. **I ~ you well** je vous souhaite de réussir; *(iro)* **I ~ you luck of it!** je te souhaite bien du plaisir!; **he ~ed us good luck** il nous a souhaité

bonne chance; **to ~ sb good-bye** dire au revoir à qn; **to ~ sb a happy birthday** souhaiter bon anniversaire à qn.
2 *vi* faire un vœu. **to ~ for sth/for sth to happen** souhaiter qch/que qch se produise; **everything he could ~ for** tout ce qu'il pourrait désirer; **what more could you ~ for?** que pourrais-tu souhaiter de plus?
3 *n* (**a**) désir *m* (*to do* de faire). **he had no ~ to go** il n'avait pas envie d'y aller; **against my ~(es)** contre mon gré. (**b**) souhait *m*, vœu *m*. **to make a ~** faire un vœu; **3 ~es** 3 souhaits; **his ~ came true, he got his ~** son souhait s'est réalisé. (**c**) **give him my good** *or* **best ~es** *(in conversation)* faites-lui mes amitiés; *(in letter)* transmettez-lui mes meilleures pensées; **he sends his best ~es** *(in conversation)* il vous fait ses amitiés; *(in letter)* il vous envoie ses meilleures pensées; **best ~es for a happy birthday** tous mes meilleurs vœux pour votre anniversaire; *(in letter)* **with best ~es from Paul** bien amicalement, Paul.
◆ **wishbone** *n* (**a**) *[bird]* fourchette *f*; (**b**) *(Sport)* wishbone *m*. ◆ **wishful** *adj*: **it's ~ful thinking** c'est prendre ses désirs pour la réalité.

wishy-washy * ['wɪʃɪˌwɒʃɪ] *adj (gen)* fadasse *; *colour* délavé.

wisp [wɪsp] *n [straw]* brin *m*; *[hair]* fine mèche *f*; *[smoke]* mince volute *f*. ◆ **wispy** *adj* (trop) fin.

wisteria [wɪs'tɪərɪə] *n* glycine *f*.

wistful ['wɪstf(ʊ)'l] *adj* nostalgique. ◆ **wistfully** *adv* avec regret.

wit [wɪt] *n* (**a**) *(intelligence)* **~(s)** esprit *m*, intelligence *f*; **quick-~ted** à l'esprit vif; **native ~** bon sens; **you'll need all your ~s about you** il va te falloir toute ta présence d'esprit; **keep your ~s about you!** restez attentif!; **use your ~s!** sers-toi de ton intelligence!; **it was a battle of ~s** ils jouaient au plus fin; **he lives by his ~s** il vit d'expédients; **to collect one's ~s** rassembler ses esprits; **he was at his ~s' end** il ne savait plus que faire; *(fig)* **out of one's ~s** fou (*f* folle). (**b**) *(wittiness)* esprit *m*; *(witty person)* homme *m* *or* femme *f* d'esprit. **flash of ~** trait *m* d'esprit. ◆ **witticism** *n* mot *m* d'esprit. ◆ **wittily** *adv* avec beaucoup d'esprit. ◆ **witty** *adj* plein d'esprit.

witch [wɪtʃ] *n* sorcière *f*. ◆ **witchcraft** *n* sorcellerie *f*. ◆ **witch-doctor** *n* sorcier *m (de tribu)*. ◆ **witch-hunt** *n (fig)* chasse *f* aux sorcières.

with [wɪð, wɪθ] *prep* (**a**) *(gen)* avec. **I was ~ her** j'étais avec elle; **she was staying ~ friends** elle était chez des amis; **he's with IBM** il travaille chez IBM; **I'll be ~ you in a minute** je suis à vous dans un instant; **I have no money ~ me** je n'ai pas d'argent sur moi; **she had her umbrella ~ her** elle avait pris son parapluie; **that problem is always ~ us** ce problème ne nous lâche pas; **the hat doesn't go ~ the dress** le chapeau ne va pas avec la robe; *(fig)* **I'm ~ you** *(agree ~ you)* je suis d'accord avec vous; *(support you)* je suis avec vous; **he just wasn't ~ us** * *(didn't understand)* il ne voyait * pas du tout; *(wasn't paying attention)* il était tout à fait ailleurs; *(up-to-date)* **to be ~ it** ⁑ être dans le vent *.
(**b**) *(having etc)* à, qui a. **the boy ~ brown eyes** le garçon aux yeux marron; **a coat ~ a fur collar** un manteau à col de fourrure; **a room ~ a view of the sea** une chambre qui a vue sur la mer.
(**c**) *(manner, means, cause)* avec, de. **~ my whole heart** de tout mon cœur; **~ pleasure** avec plaisir; **~ all speed** à toute vitesse; **~ no trouble at all** sans la moindre difficulté; **...he said ~ a smile** ...dit-il en souriant *or* avec un sourire; **she left ~ tears in her eyes** elle est partie, les larmes aux yeux; **cut it ~ a knife** coupe-le avec un couteau; **take it ~ both hands** prenez-le à deux mains; **trembling ~ fear** tremblant de peur; **white ~ snow** blanc de neige; **in bed ~ flu** retenu au lit par la grippe; **to go down ~ measles** attraper la rougeole; **~ the price of food these days you can't...** au prix où est la nourriture de nos jours on ne peut pas...
(**d**) *(as regards)* **the trouble ~ Paul is that** ce qu'il y a avec Paul, c'est que; **it's a habit ~ him** c'est une habitude chez lui; **she's good ~ children** elle sait bien s'occuper des enfants; **what do you want ~ that book?** qu'est-ce que tu veux faire de ce livre?; **pleased ~** satisfait de.
(**e**) *(indicating time)* avec. **he rose ~ the sun** il se levait avec le jour; **~ the approach of winter** à l'approche de l'hiver; **~ time** avec le temps; **~ these words** *or* **~ that he left us** là-dessus *or* sur ce il nous a quittés.
(**f**) *(despite)* malgré. **~ all his faults I still like him** malgré tous ses défauts je l'aime bien quand même; **~ all that, he is still better than...** malgré tout ça il est encore meilleur que...
◆ **with-it** ⁑ *adj* dans le vent *.

withdraw [wɪθ'drɔː] *pret*, **withdrew**, *ptp* **withdrawn** **1** *vt (gen)* retirer (*from* de); *ambassador* rappeler; *opinion, statement* rétracter; *claim* renoncer à; *order* annuler; *(Comm) faulty goods etc* retirer de la vente; *banknotes* retirer de la circulation. **2** *vi (gen)* se retirer (*from* de); *[person] (move away)* se retirer; *(move back)* reculer (*from* de; *a few paces* de quelques pas); *(retract offer etc)* se rétracter; *[candidate]* se désister (*from* de; *in favour of* en faveur de). *(Mil)* **to ~ to a new position** se replier; *(fig)* **to ~ into o.s.** se replier sur soi-même.
◆ **withdrawal** **1** *n (gen)* retrait *m* (*of* de); *(Mil: retreat)* repli *m* (*to* sur); *(of candidate)* désistement *m; (Med, Psych)* repli *m* sur soi-même; *(with symptoms)* état *m* de manque ; **2** *adj (Med, Psych)* **to have ~al symptoms** être en état de manque. ◆ **withdrawn** *adj person* renfermé.

wither ['wɪðəʳ] **1** *vi (gen)* se flétrir; *[hope, love etc]* s'évanouir; *[beauty]* se faner. **2** *vt plant* flétrir. **to ~ sb with a look** foudroyer qn du regard. ◆ **withered** *adj* flétri; *(gen) limb* atrophié; *old person* tout desséché. ◆ **withering** *adj tone, look* profondément méprisant; *remark, criticism* cinglant.

withhold [wɪθ'həʊld] *pret, ptp* **withheld** *vt money from pay etc* retenir (*from sth* de qch); *payment, decision* remettre; *one's taxes* refuser de payer; *one's consent, help, support* refuser (*from sb* à qn); *truth, news* cacher (*from sb* à qn).

within [wɪð'ɪn] *prep* (**a**) *(inside)* à l'intérieur de. **~ the box/park** à l'intérieur de la boîte/du parc; **a voice ~ him** une voix en lui; **to be ~ the law** être dans les limites de la légalité; **to live ~ one's income** vivre selon ses moyens. (**b**) *(less than)* **~ a kilometre of** à moins d'un kilomètre de; **correct to ~ a centimetre** correct à un centimètre près; **~ a week of her visit** moins d'une semaine après (*or* avant) sa visite; **~ an hour (from now)** d'ici une heure; **he returned ~ the week** il est revenu avant la fin de la semaine.

without [wɪð'aʊt] *prep* sans. **~ a coat** sans manteau; **~ a coat or hat** sans manteau ni chapeau; **~ any money** sans argent; **he is ~ friends** il n'a pas d'amis; **not ~ difficulty** non sans difficulté; **he was quite ~ shame** il n'avait aucune honte; **~ speaking** sans parler; **~ anybody knowing** sans que personne le sache; **to go** *or* **do ~ sth** se passer de qch.

withstand [wɪθ'stænd] *pret, ptp* **withstood** *vt* résister à.

witness ['wɪtnɪs] **1** *n* (**a**) *(person)* témoin *m* (*to or of an incident* d'un incident; *to sb's signature* certifiant la signature de qn; *to a document* attestant l'authenticité d'un document). *(Jur)* **~ for the defence/prosecution** témoin à décharge/à charge; *(Jur)* **to call sb as ~** citer qn comme témoin. (**b**) *(evidence)* témoignage *m*. **in ~ whereof** en témoignage de quoi; **to bear ~ to sth** *[thing, result etc]* témoigner de qch; *[person]* attester qch; **~ the case of** témoin le cas de. **2** *adj*: **~ box** *or (US)* **stand** barre *f* des témoins; **in the ~ box** à la barre. **3** *vt* (**a**) *(see) event, crime* être témoin de; *(notice) change, improvement* remarquer. (**b**) *(esp Jur) document* attester l'authenticité de. **to ~ sb's signature** être témoin. **4** *vi (Jur)* témoigner (*to sth* de qch; *to having done* avoir fait).

witter ['wɪtəʳ] *vi* **to ~ on about sth** parler interminablement de qch.

wizard ['wɪzəd] *n* enchanteur *m*, sorcier *m*. *(fig)* **a financial ~** un génie en matière financière; **a ~ with a paintbrush** un champion * du pinceau.

wizened ['wɪznd] *adj* ratatiné.

wobble ['wɒbl] **1** *vi (gen)* trembler; *[object about to fall, compass needle, cyclist etc]* osciller; *[acrobat, dancer]* chanceler; *[wheel]* avoir du jeu. **the table was wobbling** la table tremblait; **this table ~s** cette table est branlante. **2** *n (Aut)* **wheel ~** shimmy *m*.
◆ **wobbly** *adj hand, voice* tremblant; *jelly* qui tremble; *table, chair* branlant, bancal; *object about to fall* qui oscille dangereusement; *wheel* qui a du jeu; *(feel weak)* **to be wobbly** se sentir faible.

woe [wəʊ] *n* malheur *m*. **~ is me!** pauvre de moi!; **~ betide him who...** malheur à celui qui...; **a tale of ~** une litanie de malheurs. ◆ **woebegone** *adj* désolé, abattu. ◆ **woeful** *adj (gen)* malheureux; *news, story, sight* affligeant. ◆ **woefully** *adv (sadly) say, look* très tristement; *(regrettably) small etc* regrettablement.

wok [wɒk] *n* wok *m*.

woke(n) ['wəʊk(n)] *pret (ptp) of* **wake²**.

wold [wəʊld] *n* haute plaine *f*, plateau *m*.

wolf [wʊlf] **1** *n, pl* **wolves** loup *m*; (**fig: Don Juan type)* tombeur *m* de femmes. **she-~** louve *f*; *(fig)* **a ~ in sheep's clothing** un loup déguisé en brebis; **that will keep the ~ from the door** cela nous *etc* mettra à l'abri du besoin. **2** *adj (fig)* **he gave a ~ whistle** il a sifflé la fille. **3** *vt* (**~ down**) engloutir. ◆ **wolfhound** *n* chien-loup *m*. ◆ **wolfish** *adj* vorace.

woman, *pl* **women** ['wʊmən, 'wɪmɪn] **1** *n* femme *f*. **young ~** jeune femme; **come along, young ~!** allez mademoiselle, venez!; *(hum: wife)* **the little ~** ⁑ ma *etc* petite femme *; **~ of the world** femme d'expérience; **Paul and all his women** Paul et toutes les femmes de sa vie; **I've got a ~ who comes in 3 times a week** j'ai une femme de ménage qui vient 3 fois par semaine; **Women's Liberation Movement, Women's Lib** * mouvement *m* de libération de la femme, M.L.F. *m*; **a women's group** un groupe de féministes; *(Press)* **the women's page** la page des lectrices; **women's team** équipe *f* féminine. **2** *adj*: **a ~ music teacher** un professeur de musique femme; **~ worker** ouvrière *f*; **women doctors** les femmes *fpl* médecins; **he's got a ~ driver** son chauffeur est une femme; **women drivers are...** les femmes au volant sont...; **~ friend** amie *f*; *(Brit)* **~ police constable** femme *f* agent de police. ◆ **woman-hater** *n* misogyne *mf*. ◆ **womanhood** *n* féminité *f*; **to reach ~hood** devenir une femme. ◆ **womanizer** *n* coureur *m* de jupons. ◆ **womankind** *n* les femmes *fpl (en général)*. ◆ **womanlike 1** *adj* féminin ; **2** *adv* d'une manière très féminine. ◆ **womanliness** *n* féminité *f*. ◆ **womanly** *adj figure, bearing* féminin; *behaviour* digne d'une femme; *gentleness etc* tout féminin. ◆ **womenfolk** *npl* les femmes *fpl*.

womb [wu:m] *n* utérus *m*; *(fig: of nature etc)* sein *m*.

won [wʌn] *pret, ptp of* **win**.

wonder ['wʌndəʳ] **1** *n* (**a**) émerveillement *m*, étonnement *m*. **(lost) in ~** émerveillé. (**b**) *(sth wonderful)* merveille *f*, miracle *m*. **the ~s of science** les miracles de la science; **the Seven W~s of the World** les Sept Merveilles du monde; **the ~ of it all is that...** le plus étonnant dans tout cela c'est que...; **it's a ~ that...** c'est extraordinaire que... + *subj*; **it's a ~ to me that...** je n'en reviens pas que... + *subj*; **no ~ he...** ce n'est pas étonnant qu'il... + *subj or* s'il... + *indic*; **no ~!** cela n'a rien d'étonnant!; **it's small ~ that...** il n'est guère étonnant que... + *subj*.
2 *vi* (**a**) *(marvel)* s'étonner, s'émerveiller (*at sth* de qch). **I ~ that...** cela m'étonne que... + *subj*; **he'll be back, I shouldn't ~** cela ne m'étonnerait pas qu'il revienne. (**b**) *(reflect)* penser, songer (*about sth* à qch). **it makes you ~** cela donne à penser; **I'm ~ing about going to the pictures** j'ai à moitié envie d'aller au cinéma.
3 *vt* se demander (*where/who etc* où/qui *etc*; *whether, if* si). **I ~ what to do** je ne sais pas quoi faire.
◆ **wonderful** *adj* merveilleux; **~ful to relate, he...** chose étonnante, il... ◆ **wonderfully** *adv hot, quiet etc* merveilleusement; *manage, work etc* à merveille; **he looks ~fully well** il a très bonne mine. ◆ **wondering** *adj (astonished)* étonné; *(thoughtful)* songeur. ◆ **wonderland** *n* pays *m* merveilleux. ◆ **wonderment** *n* émerveillement *m*.

wonky * ['wɒŋkɪ] *adj chair, table* bancal; *machine* détraqué; *person (not well)* patraque *. **it's a bit ~** il y a quelque chose qui cloche; **to go ~** *[machine]* se détraquer; *[TV picture etc]* se dérégler; *[handicraft, drawing]* aller de travers.

won't [wəʊnt] = **will not** ; *V* **will**.

woo [wu:] *vt woman* faire la cour à, courtiser; *(fig) audience, influential person* chercher à plaire à; *fame, success* rechercher.

wood [wʊd] **1** *n* (**a**) bois *m*. **touch ~!**, *(US)* **knock on ~!** touchons du bois!; **aged in the ~** vieilli au tonneau. (**b**) *(forest)* bois *m*. **~s** bois *mpl*; **a pine ~** un bois de pins; *(fig)* **he can't see the ~ for the trees** les arbres lui cachent la forêt; *(fig)* **we're out of the ~** nous sommes tirés d'affaire. (**c**) *(Golf)* bois *m*; *(Bowls)* boule *f*.
2 *adj* (**a**) *floor, object* de bois, en bois; *fire* de bois; *stove* à bois. **~ carving** sculpture *f* en bois; **~ engraving** gravure *f* sur bois; **~ pulp** pâte *f* à papier; **~ shavings** copeaux *mpl* (de bois); *(US)* **~ trim** boiseries *fpl*; **~ wool** copeaux *mpl* de bois. (**b**) *nymph etc* des bois. **~ anemone** anémone *f* des bois.
◆ **woodbine** *n* chèvrefeuille *m*. ◆ **woodchuck** *n* marmotte *f* d'Amérique. ◆ **wood-burning stove** *n* poêle *m* à bois. ◆ **woodcock** *n* bécasse *f*. ◆ **woodcraft** *n* connaissance *f* des forêts. ◆ **woodcut** *n* gravure *f* sur bois. ◆ **woodcutter** *n* bûcheron *m*. ◆ **wooded** *adj* boisé; **thickly/sparsely ~ed** très/peu boisé. ◆ **wooden** *adj object* de bois, en bois; *leg* de bois; *(fig) movement* raide; *look, acting* sans expression; *personality, response* gauche; **to try to sell sb ~en nickels** * essayer de rouler qn. ◆ **wooden-headed** *adj* idiot. ◆ **woodland 1** *n* région *f* boisée ; **2** *adj flower etc* des bois. ◆ **woodlouse,** *pl* **-lice** *n* cloporte *m*. ◆ **woodman** *n* forestier *m*. ◆ **woodpecker** *n* pic *m*. ◆ **woodpigeon** *n* ramier *m*. ◆ **woodpile** *n* tas *m* de bois. ◆ **woodshed** *n* bûcher *m*. ◆ **woodwind** *npl (Mus)* bois *mpl*. ◆ **woodwork** *n (craft, subject)* menuiserie *f*; *(cabinet-making)* ébénisterie *f*; *(in house) (beams etc)* charpente *f*; *(doors etc)* boiseries *fpl*. ◆ **woodworm** *n* ver *m* du bois; **it's got ~worm** c'est vermoulu. ◆ **woody** *adj stem etc* ligneux.

woof¹ [wʊf] *n (Tex)* trame *f*.

woof² [wʊf] *vi [dog]* aboyer. **woof, woof!** oua, oua!

wool [wʊl] **1** *n* laine *f*. **a ball of** ~ une pelote de laine; **knitting/darning** ~ laine à tricoter/repriser; *(fig)* **to pull the** ~ **over sb's eyes** en faire accroire à qn; **it's pure** ~ c'est pure laine. **2** *adj cloth, trade* de laine; *dress* en *or* de laine; *shop* de laines. ◆ **wool-gathering** *n (fig)* **to be** ~**-gathering** être dans les nuages. ◆ **woollen,** *(US)* **woolen 1** *adj cloth* de laine; *garment* en *or* de laine; *industry* lainier; *manufacturer* de lainages ; **2** *npl*: ~**lens** lainages *mpl*. ◆ **woolly,** *(US)* **wooly 1** *adj (gen)* laineux; *(fig) clouds* cotonneux; *ideas* confus; *essay, book* verbeux ; **2** *n* tricot *m*; *(collectively)* ~**lies** lainages *mpl*. ◆ **wool-merchant** *n* négociant *m* en laines.

word [wɜːd] **1** *n* (**a**) *(gen)* mot *m*; *(spoken)* mot, parole *f*. *[song etc]* ~**s** paroles; **the written/spoken** ~ ce qui est écrit/dit; **by** ~ **of mouth** de vive voix; **man of few** ~**s** homme peu loquace; ~ **for** ~ *repeat, copy out* mot pour mot, textuellement; *translate* mot à mot; *analyze, go over* mot par mot; **in other** ~**s** autrement dit; **in a** ~ en un mot; **what's the** ~ **for 'table' in German?** comment dit-on 'table' en allemand?; **in the** ~**s of Racine** comme dit Racine; **to put sth into** ~**s** exprimer qch; ~**s fail me!** je ne sais plus que dire!; **without a** ~ sans dire un mot; **with these** ~ **s, he...** sur ces mots, il...; **too stupid for** ~**s** vraiment trop stupide; **that's not the** ~ **for it!** c'est trop peu dire!; **that's a better** ~ **for it** ce serait plus près de la vérité; **those were his very** ~**s** c'est ce qu'il a dit mot pour mot; **a flood of** ~**s** un flot de paroles; **in so many** ~**s** explicitement; **to have the last** ~ avoir le dernier mot; *(fig)* **the last** ~ **in** ce qu'on fait de mieux en matière de; **I'll give you a** ~ **of warning** je voudrais juste vous mettre en garde; **he won't hear a** ~ **against her** il n'admet absolument pas qu'on la critique *(subj)*; **nobody had a good** ~ **to say about him** personne n'a trouvé la moindre chose à dire en sa faveur; **to put in a (good)** ~ **for** glisser un mot en faveur de; **I want a** ~ **with you** j'ai à vous parler; **I'll have a** ~ **with him about it** je vais lui en parler; **I never said a** ~ je n'ai rien dit du tout; **he didn't say a** ~ **about it** il n'en a absolument pas parlé; **I can't get a** ~ **out of him** je ne peux rien en tirer; **you took the** ~**s right out of my mouth** c'est exactement ce que j'allais dire; **you put** ~**s into my mouth!** vous me faites dire ce que je n'ai pas dit!; *(quarrel)* **to have** ~**s with sb** se disputer avec qn.
(**b**) *(fig: no pl) (message)* mot *m*; *(news)* nouvelles *fpl* (*of, about* de). **to leave** ~ laisser un mot (*with sb for sb* à qn pour qn; *that* que); ~ **came from H.Q. that...** le Q.G. nous *etc* a fait savoir que...; **there's no** ~ **from John yet** on est toujours sans nouvelles de Jean; ~ **of command** mot d'ordre; **his** ~ **is law** c'est lui qui fait la loi; **to give the** ~ **to advance** donner l'ordre d'avancer; *(Rel)* **the W**~ le Verbe; **the W**~ **of God** la parole de Dieu.
(**c**) *(promise)* parole *f*. ~ **of honour** parole d'honneur; **a man of his** ~ un homme de parole; **he was as good as his** ~ il a tenu parole; **to give one's** ~ donner sa parole (*to sb* à qn; *that* que); **to break/go back on/keep one's** ~ manquer à/retirer/tenir sa parole; **to take sb at his** ~ prendre qn au mot; **his** ~ **against mine** sa parole contre la mienne; **I've only got her** ~ **for it** c'est elle qui le dit, je n'ai aucune preuve; **to take sb's** ~ **for it** croire qn sur parole; **(upon) my** ~**!** * ma parole!
2 *adj*: ~ **game** jeu *m* avec des mots; ~ **list** nomenclature *f*; ~ **order** ordre *m* des mots.
3 *vt document, protest* formuler.
◆ **word-blind** *adj* dyslexique. ◆ **word-blindness** *n* dyslexie *f*. ◆ **wordbook** *n* lexique *m*. ◆ **word-for-word** *adj analysis* mot par mot; *translation* mot à mot. ◆ **wordiness** *n* verbosité *f*. ◆ **wording** *n [letter, statement]* termes *mpl*; **the** ~**ing is clumsy** c'est maladroitement exprimé; **the** ~**ing is important** le choix des termes est important; **change the** ~**ing slightly** changez quelques mots. ◆ **word-perfect** *adj*: **to be** ~**-perfect in sth** savoir qch sur le bout du doigt. ◆ **wordplay** *n* jeu *m* de mots. ◆ **word-processing** *n* traitement *m* de textes. ◆ **word-processor** *n* système *m* de traitement de textes. ◆ **wordy** *adj* verbeux.

wore [wɔːʳ] *pret of* **wear.**

work [wɜːk] **1** *n* (**a**) *(gen)* travail *m*. **to be at** ~ travailler (*on* sur), être à l'œuvre *or* au travail; *(fig)* **other forces are at** ~ d'autres forces sont en jeu; **to start** ~**, to set to** ~ se mettre au travail *or* à l'œuvre; **to set to** ~ **doing** se mettre à faire; **to set sb to** ~ **doing** donner pour tâche à qn de faire; **good** ~**!** bravo!; **a good piece of** ~ du bon travail; **she put a lot of** ~ **into it** elle a passé beaucoup de temps dessus; **there's a lot of** ~ **to be done on it** il reste beaucoup à faire; **I'm trying to get some** ~ **done** j'essaie de travailler un peu; ~ **has begun on the bridge** les travaux du pont ont commencé; **it's women's** ~ c'est un travail de femme; **it's quite easy** ~ ce n'est pas difficile à faire; **it's hot** ~ ça donne chaud; **to make short** ~ **of** *sth* faire très rapidement; *(fig) sb* envoyer promener *; **it's the** ~ **of a professional** c'est un travail de professionnel.
(**b**) *(as, employment)* travail *m*. **to go to** ~ aller travailler, aller à l'usine (*or* au bureau *etc*); **to look for** ~ chercher du travail *or* un emploi; **he's at** ~ il est au bureau (*or* à l'usine *etc*); **he is in** ~ il a un emploi; **out of** ~ en chômage, sans emploi; **to put** *or* **throw sb out of** ~ réduire qn au chômage; **he's off** ~ il n'est pas allé (*or* venu) travailler; *(longer-term)* il est absent; **a day off** ~ un jour de congé; **I've got time off** ~ j'ai du temps libre; **domestic** ~ travaux *mpl* domestiques; **office** ~ travail de bureau; **I've done a full day's** ~ *(lit)* j'ai fait ma journée; *(fig)* j'ai eu une journée bien remplie; *(fig)* **it's all in the day's** ~ ça n'a rien d'extraordinaire.
(**c**) *[writer, musician, politician, scholar etc]* œuvre *f*; *(writing)* ouvrage *m* (*on sb/sth* sur qn/qch; *of fiction etc* de fiction *etc*); *(piece of sewing)* ouvrage. **the** ~**s of God** les œuvres de Dieu; **good** ~**s** bonnes œuvres; **his life's** ~ l'œuvre de sa vie; **his** ~ **will be remembered** son œuvre restera dans la mémoire des hommes; ~ **of art** œuvre d'art; **the complete** ~**s of** les œuvres complètes de; **he sells a lot of his** ~ il vend beaucoup de tableaux (*or* de livres *etc*); *(fig)* **he's a nasty piece of** ~ * c'est un sale type *.
(**d**) *(pl)* ~**s** *(gen, Admin, Mil)* travaux *mpl*; *[clock, machine etc]* mécanisme *m*. **Ministry of W**~**s** ministère *m* des Travaux publics; **building/road** ~**s** travaux de construction/d'entretien de la route; *(fig)* **they gave him the** ~**s** ‡ ils lui en ont fait voir de dures *; *(fig)* **the whole** ~**s** * tout le tralala *.
(**e**) *(pl inv: factory)* ~**s** usine *f*; *(processing plant etc)* installations *fpl*; **gas** ~**s** usine à gaz.
2 *adj* (**a**) **the** ~ **ethic** l'attitude moraliste envers le travail; ~ **experience** stage *m*; *(Comput)* ~ **file** fichier *m* de travail; ~ **force** main-d'œuvre *f*; ~ **load** part *f* du travail; **his** ~ **load is too heavy** il a trop de travail; ~ **permit** permis *m* de travail; *(Comput)* ~ **sheet** feuille *f* de programmation; ~ **station** poste *m* de travail; *(US)* ~ **week of 38 hours** semaine *f* de 38 heures.
(**b**) ~**s car park/entrance** parking *m*/entrée *f* de l'usine; ~**s committee** *or* **council** comité *m* d'entreprise; ~**s manager** chef *m* d'exploitation.
3 *vi* (**a**) *(gen)* travailler (*at sth* à qch; *on sth* sur qch; *in wood etc* avec le bois *etc*). **to** ~ **hard** travailler dur; **to** ~ **like a horse** *or* **a Trojan** travailler comme un forçat *or* un bœuf; *(Ind)* **to** ~ **to rule** faire la grève du zèle; *(fig)* **I've been** ~**ing on him** j'ai bien essayé de le convaincre; **the police are** ~**ing on**

the case la police enquête sur l'affaire; *(gen)* **we're ~ing on it** on y travaille; **they are ~ing on the principle that...** ils partent du principe que...; **there are not many facts to ~ on** on manque de faits sur lesquels on puisse se baser; **to ~ for/against sth** lutter pour/contre qch; *(fig)* **to ~ towards sth** se diriger petit à petit vers qch.
(**b**) *[machine, car, scheme]* marcher; *[drug, medicine, spell]* agir; *[brain]* fonctionner. **the lift isn't ~ing** l'ascenseur ne marche pas *or* est en panne; **it ~s on electricity** ça marche à l'électricité; *(fig)* **that ~s both ways** c'est à double tranchant.
(**c**) *(move) [mouth]* se contracter. *[person]* **to ~ (one's way) along/up** *etc* arriver petit à petit à avancer/à monter *etc.*
4 *vt* (**a**) *(cause to ~) person, staff* faire travailler; *mechanism, machine* faire marcher, actionner. **to ~ sb too hard** exiger trop de qn; **he ~s himself too hard** il se surmène; **can you ~ the machine?** sais-tu te servir de la machine?; **it's ~ed by electricity** ça marche à l'électricité.
(**b**) *miracle* faire, accomplir; *change* apporter. **to ~ wonders** *[person]* faire des merveilles; *[thing]* faire merveille; **to ~ one's passage** payer son passage en travaillant; **to ~ one's way through college** travailler pour payer ses études; *(fig)* **he has managed to ~ his promotion *** il s'est débrouillé pour obtenir de l'avancement; **can you ~ it * so that...** pouvez-vous faire en sorte que... + *subj*; **I'll ~ it *** je le ferai; **to ~ o.s. into a rage** se mettre dans une colère noire; **he ~ed the rope through the hole** il est petit à petit arrivé à faire passer la corde dans le trou; **to ~ sth free/loose** arriver à délier/desserrer qch; **he ~ed it into his speech** il s'est arrangé pour l'introduire dans son discours; **to ~ one's way along** arriver petit à petit à avancer; **the roots have ~ed their way into the foundations** les racines ont pénétré dans les fondations; *(fig)* **to ~ one's way into a firm** arriver à se faire une place dans une compagnie.
(**c**) *mine, land* exploiter; *metal, leather, dough* travailler; *object* façonner (*out of* dans); *(sew)* coudre; *(embroider) design etc* broder.
◆ **work in** *vi [arrangement etc]* cadrer (*with sb's plans* avec les projets de qn). ◆ **work off** *vt sep* (**a**) *debt, obligation* acquitter en travaillant. (**b**) *surplus fat* se débarrasser de; *weight* éliminer; *annoyance* passer (*on sb* sur qn); *energy* dépenser son surplus de. ◆ **work out 1** *vi [plan, arrangement]* réussir, marcher; *[problem, sum]* se résoudre exactement. *[total]* **to ~ out at** s'élever à; **it ~s out at 5 apples per child** ça fait 5 pommes par enfant; **it's all ~ing out as planned** tout se déroule comme prévu; **things didn't ~ out for her** les choses ont plutôt mal tourné pour elle; **it will ~ out right in the end** tout finira par s'arranger; **how did it ~ out?** comment ça a marché? * **2** *vt sep calculation, problem* résoudre; *answer, total* trouver; *code* déchiffrer; *scheme, idea, settlement* mettre au point. **I'll have to ~ it out** *(gen)* il faut que je réfléchisse; *(counting)* il faut que je calcule; **to ~ out where/why** *etc* finir par découvrir où/pourquoi *etc*; *(of behaviour etc)* **I can't ~ it out** ça me dépasse *. ◆ **work over *** *vt sep (beat up)* tabasser *. ◆ **work round** *vi*: **to ~ round to a subject** aborder un sujet (avec tact); **what are you ~ing round to?** où voulez-vous en venir? ◆ **work up 1** *vi*: **to ~ up to sth/to doing** préparer le terrain pour qch/pour faire; **what is he ~ing up to?** où veut-il bien en venir? **2** *vt sep trade* développer. **he ~ed it up from almost nothing into...** en partant de rien il a réussi à en faire...; **to ~ one's way up** s'élever à la force du poignet (*from* de; *to be* jusqu'à être); **to ~ one's way up to the top** gravir un à un tous les échelons de la hiérarchie; **to ~ sb up into a fury** déchaîner la fureur de qn; **to ~ up an appetite** s'ouvrir l'appétit; **to ~ up enthusiasm for** s'enthousiasmer pour; **to get ~ed up** se mettre dans tous ses états.
◆ **workable** *adj arrangement etc* possible, réalisable. ◆ **workaday** *adj clothes* de tous les jours; *event* banal. ◆ **workaholic** *n* drogué(e) de travail. ◆ **workbag** *n* sac *m* à ouvrage. ◆ **workbasket** *n* corbeille *f* à ouvrage. ◆ **workbench** *n* établi *m*. ◆ **workbook** *n (exercise book)* cahier *m* d'exercices; *(manual)* manuel *m*. ◆ **workbox** *n* boîte *f* à ouvrage. ◆ **workcamp** *n (prison)* camp *m* de travail forcé; *(voluntary)* chantier *m* de travail bénévole. ◆ **workdesk** *n* bureau *m* de travail. ◆ **worker 1** *n (gen)* ouvrier *m*, -ière *f*; *(esp Pol)* travailleur *m*, -euse *f*; **he's a good ~er** il travaille bien; **all the ~ers in this industry** tous ceux qui travaillent dans cette industrie; *(Ind)* **management and ~ers** patronat *m* et travailleurs; **office ~er** employé(e) *m(f)* de bureau ; **2** *adj participation etc* des travailleurs; **~er priest** prêtre-ouvrier *m*. ◆ **work-in** *n* ≃ occupation *f* du lieu de travail. ◆ **working** *adj clothes, lunch, week etc* de travail; *population, wife* qui travaille; *model* qui marche; *partner* actif; **the ~ing class** la classe ouvrière *(V also* **working-class***)*; **8-hour ~ing day** journée *f* de travail de 8 heures; **~ing hypothesis** hypothèse *f* de travail; *(Pol etc)* **~ing majority** majorité *f* suffisante; **an ordinary ~ing man** un simple ouvrier; **the ~ing woman** la femme active; **~ing party** *(gen)* groupe *m* de travail; *(committee)* commission *f* d'enquête; *(squad: of soldiers etc)* escouade *f*. ◆ **working-class** *adj background, suburb* ouvrier; *person* qui appartient à la classe ouvrière. ◆ **workings** *npl (mechanism)* mécanisme *m*; *[government, organization]* rouages *mpl*; *(Min)* chantier *m* d'exploitation; **the ~ings of her mind** ce qui se passe dans sa tête. ◆ **workman,** *pl* **workmen** *n (gen, Comm, Ind etc)* ouvrier *m*; **he's a good ~man** il travaille bien. ◆ **workmanlike** *adj method, person* professionnel; *tool, product, essay* bien fait; *attempt* honnête. ◆ **workmanship** *n [craftsman]* habileté *f* professionnelle; **a superb piece of ~manship** un travail superbe. ◆ **workmate** *n* camarade *mf* de travail. ◆ **workout** *n (Sport)* séance *f* d'entraînement. ◆ **workroom** *n* salle *f* de travail. ◆ **workshop** *n* atelier *m*. ◆ **workshy** *adj* fainéant. ◆ **work-to-rule,** *(US)* **work-rule** *n* grève *f* du zèle.

world [wɜːld] **1** *n* (**a**) *(gen)* monde *m*. **all over the ~** dans le monde entier; **to go round the ~** faire le tour du monde; **to see the ~** voir du pays; **known throughout the ~** connu dans le monde entier; **alone in the ~** seul au monde; **it's a small ~!** le monde est petit!; **the New W~** le Nouveau Monde; **the ancient ~** l'antiquité *f*; **the ~ we live in** le monde où nous vivons; **since the beginning of the ~** depuis que le monde est monde; **~ without end** dans les siècles des siècles; *(Rel)* **in the ~** dans le siècle; **in this ~** ici-bas, en ce monde; **the next ~, the ~ to come** l'au-delà; **he's not long for this ~** il n'en a plus pour longtemps à vivre; **to bring a child into the ~** mettre un enfant au monde; **the ~ of nature** le monde de la nature; **the business ~** le monde *or* le milieu des affaires.
(**b**) *(phrases)* **he lives in a ~ of his own** il vit dans un monde à lui; **it's out of this ~** c'est extraordinaire; **to be dead to the ~** *(asleep)* dormir profondément; *(drunk)* être ivre mort; **to be on top of the ~ *** être aux anges; **to think the ~ of sb** mettre qn sur un piédestal; **it did him a ~ of good** ça lui a fait énormément de bien; **there's a ~ of difference between...** il y a un monde entre...; **~s apart** diamétralement opposés; **it's not the end of the ~** ce n'est pas la fin du monde; **it was for all the ~ as if...** c'était exactement comme si...; **the ~'s worst cook** la pire cuisinière qui soit; **I'd give the ~ to know...** je donnerais tout au monde pour savoir...; **a man of the ~** un homme d'expérience; **to go up in the ~** faire du chemin *(fig)*;

he has come down in the ~ il a connu des jours meilleurs; **the** ~ **and his wife** absolument tout le monde; **it's what he wants most in (all) the** ~ c'est ce qu'il veut plus que tout au monde; **nowhere in the (whole wide)** ~ nulle part au monde; **not for anything in the** ~ pour rien au monde; **where/ why in the** ~ **has he...?** où/pourquoi donc a-t-il...? **2** *adj power, scale* mondial; *record, champion, tour* du monde; *language* universel. *(Ftbl)* **the W~ Cup** la Coupe du monde; *(Comm)* **W~ Fair** Exposition *f* Internationale; **W~ Health Organization** *(abbr* **WHO***)* Organisation *f* mondiale de la santé *(abbr* O.M.S.); *(Sport)* **the** ~ **title** le titre de champion du monde; **W~ War One/Two** la Première/ Seconde guerre mondiale.
◆ **world-famous** *adj* de renommée mondiale. ◆ **worldly** *adj matters, pleasures* de ce monde; *attitude, person* matérialiste; *(Rel)* temporel; **all his ~ly goods** tout ce qu'il possède. ◆ **worldly-wise** *adj* qui a l'expérience du monde. ◆ **world-wide** *adj* mondial, universel.

worm [wɜːm] **1** *n (gen)* ver *m*. **earth** ~ ver de terre; *(Med)* **to have ~s** avoir des vers; *(fig)* **the** ~ **has turned** il *etc* en a eu assez de se faire marcher sur les pieds; *(US fig)* **a can of ~s** * un véritable guêpier; **you ~!** * misérable! **2** *vt* **(a) to** ~ **(one's way) into sth** se glisser dans qch; *(fig: into group, sb's confidence etc)* s'insinuer dans qch. **(b)** *(extract)* **to** ~ **it** *or* **information out of sb** tirer les vers du nez à qn *(about* à propos de; *why etc* pour savoir pourquoi *etc)*. ◆ **worm-eaten** *adj fruit* véreux; *furniture* vermoulu. ◆ **worm's eye view** *n (Phot, Cine)* contre-plongée *f*; *(fig)* point *m* de vue des humbles. ◆ **wormwood** *n* armoise *f*.

worn [wɔːn] *(ptp of* **wear***) adj object* usé; *person* las. ◆ **worn-out** *adj object* complètement usé; *person* épuisé.

worry ['wʌrɪ] **1** *n* souci *m* (*of doing* de faire; *to sb* pour qn). **the least of my worries** le cadet de mes soucis; **it's causing us a lot of** ~ cela nous donne beaucoup de souci. **2** *vi* **(a)** se faire du souci, s'inquiéter (*about, over* au sujet de, pour). **don't** ~ **about me** ne vous inquiétez pas *or* ne vous en faites pas * pour moi. **(b) to** ~ **at sth = to** ~ **sth** ; *V* **3b**. **3** *vt* **(a)** inquiéter, tracasser. **it worries me that** cela m'inquiète que + *subj*; **don't** ~ **yourself** *or* **your head * about it** ne te fais pas de mauvais sang pour ça; **to** ~ **o.s. sick** se rendre malade d'inquiétude (*about* au sujet de); **what's ~ing you?** qu'est-ce qui ne va pas? **(b)** *[dog] bone etc* jouer avec; *sheep* harceler. ◆ **worried** *adj* inquiet (*about* au sujet de); **worried to death *** fou d'inquiétude. ◆ **worrier** *n* anxieux *m*, -euse *f*. ◆ **worrisome** *adj* inquiétant. ◆ **worrying** *adj* inquiétant; **to have a ~ing time** passer un mauvais quart d'heure; *(longer)* en voir de dures *.

worse [wɜːs] **1** *adj (comp of* **bad** *and* **ill***)* pire, plus mauvais (*than* que). **you're** ~ **than he is!** tu es pire que lui!; **and, what's ~...** le pire, c'est que...; ~ **than ever** pire que jamais; **it could have been** ~ ç'aurait pu être pire; **things couldn't be** ~ ça ne pourrait pas aller plus mal; ~ **things have happened** on a vu pire; **to make matters** *or* **things** ~ aggraver la situation (*by doing* en faisant); **and, to make matters** *or* **things** ~ **, he...** et, pour comble de malheur, il...; **it gets** ~ **and** ~ ça ne fait qu'empirer; **he is getting** ~ *(in behaviour, memory)* il ne s'arrange pas; *(in health)* il va de plus en plus mal; **to get** ~ *(gen)* se détériorer; *[rheumatism, smell etc]* empirer; **I feel** ~ je me sens plus mal; **so much the** ~ **for him!** tant pis pour lui!; ~ **luck!** * hélas!; **none the** ~; *V* **none 2**.
2 *adv (comp of* **badly** *and* **ill***) sing, play etc* plus mal (*than* que); *(more) rain, hate etc* plus (*than* que). **you might** *or* **could do** ~ vous pourriez faire pire (*than to do* que de faire); **he is** ~ **off than before** *(gen)* il se retrouve dans une situation pire qu'avant; *(less money)* il y a perdu; **I shan't think any the** ~ **of you** je n'en aurai pas une moins bonne opinion de toi (*for having done* pour avoir fait).
3 *n* pire *m*. **there's** ~ **to come** on n'a pas vu le pire; ~ **followed** ensuite cela a été pire; **a change for the** ~ *(gen)* une détérioration très nette de la situation; *(Med)* une aggravation très nette.
◆ **worsen** *vi (gen)* se détériorer, empirer; *[health etc]* empirer; *[chances of success]* diminuer.

worship ['wɜːʃɪp] **1** *n* **(a)** *(gen)* culte *m*. *(Rel)* **place of** ~ lieu *m* de culte; **hours of** ~ heures *fpl* des offices. **(b) His** *or* **Your W~** *(Mayor)* Monsieur le Maire; *(magistrate)* Monsieur le Juge. **2** *vt (Rel)* adorer; *(gen) person* adorer, vénérer; *money, success etc* avoir le culte de. **he ~ped the ground she trod on** il vénérait jusqu'au sol qu'elle foulait. **3** *vi (Rel)* faire ses dévotions. ◆ **worshipper** *n* adorateur *m*, -trice *f*; *(in church)* **~pers** fidèles *mpl*.

worst [wɜːst] **1** *adj (superl of* **bad** *and* **ill***)* le (*or* la) plus mauvais(e), le (*or* la) pire. **the** ~ **student in the class** le plus mauvais élève de la classe; **his** ~ **mistake** son erreur la plus grave; **the** ~ **thing he ever did** la pire chose qu'il ait jamais faite; **the** ~ **winter for 20 years** l'hiver le plus rude depuis 20 ans; **at the** ~ **possible time** au plus mauvais moment; **the** ~ **possible job for him** l'emploi le plus contre-indiqué pour lui.
2 *adv (superl of* **badly** *and* **ill***)* le plus mal. **he sings** ~ **of all** c'est lui qui chante le plus mal de tous; **the ~-dressed man in England** l'homme le plus mal habillé d'Angleterre; **he came off** ~ c'est lui qui s'en est le plus mal sorti; **they are the** ~ **off** ce sont ces gens-là qui sont le plus affectés *or (poorest)* sont le plus dans la gêne; **my leg hurts** ~ **of all** c'est ma jambe qui me fait le plus mal.
3 *n* pire *m*. **the** ~ **that can happen** le pire *or* la pire chose qui puisse arriver; **at (the)** ~ au pis aller; **to be at its** *etc* ~ *[crisis, storm, epidemic]* être à son *etc* point culminant; *[situation, conditions, relationships]* n'avoir jamais été aussi mauvais; **at the** ~ **of the storm** au plus fort de l'orage; **matters were at their** ~ les choses ne pouvaient pas aller plus mal; **the** ~ **is yet to come** on n'a pas encore vu le pire; **the** ~ **of it is that...** le pire c'est que...; **that's the** ~ **of...** ça c'est l'inconvénient de...; **if the** ~ **comes to the** ~ en mettant les choses au pis; **to get the** ~ **of it** être le perdant; **do your ~!** vous pouvez toujours essayer!; **it brings out the** ~ **in me** ça réveille en moi les pires instincts.
◆ **worst-case** *adj projection* qui envisage le pire.

worsted ['wʊstɪd] *n* worsted *m*.

worth [wɜːθ] **1** *n* **(a)** *(value)* valeur *f* (*in gold etc* en or *etc*). **I know his** ~ je sais ce qu'il vaut; **he showed his true** ~ il a montré sa vraie valeur. **(b)** *(quantity)* **he bought 20 pence** ~ **of sweets** il a acheté pour 20 pence de bonbons; **he bought 20 pence** ~ il en a acheté pour 20 pence.
2 *adj*: **to be** ~ **£10** valoir 10 livres; **what** *or* **how much is it ~?** ça vaut combien?; **how much is he ~?** à combien s'élève sa fortune?; *(lit, fig)* **it's** ~ **a great deal** ça a beaucoup de valeur (*to me* pour moi); **it's more than my life (***or* **job** *etc***) is** ~ **to do that** je ne peux pas risquer de faire ça; **to be** ~ **one's weight in gold** valoir son pesant d'or; **it's not** ~ **the paper it's written on** ça ne vaut pas le papier sur lequel c'est écrit; **this pen is** ~ **10 others** ce stylo en vaut 10 autres; *(fig)* **what's it** ~ **to you? *** vous donneriez combien pour le savoir (*or* l'avoir *etc*)?; **take it for what it's** ~ prenez-le pour ce que ça vaut; **it's well** ~ **the trouble (***or* **effort** *or* **time)** ça vaut la peine; **it's** ~ **reading/ having** *etc* ça vaut la peine d'être lu/d'en avoir un *etc*; **it's well** ~ **it** ça vaut la peine *or* le coup *; **life isn't** ~ **living** la vie ne vaut pas la peine d'être vécue; **it's** ~ **a visit** ça vaut la visite; **it is** ~ **while to do that** on gagne à faire ça; **it's not** ~ **(my) while waiting** je perdrais mon temps à attendre;

it wasn't ~ his while to take the job ça ne valait pas le coup * qu'il accepte *(subj)* l'emploi; **I'll make it ~ your while** * je vous récompenserai de votre peine.

◆ **worthless** *adj (gen)* qui ne vaut rien; *effort* vain; *person* qui ne vaut pas cher. ◆ **worthwhile** *adj visit* qui en vaut la peine; *book/film etc* qui mérite d'être lu/vu *etc*; *work, life* utile; *contribution* très valable; *cause* louable. ◆ **worthy** ['wɜːðɪ] *adj (gen)* digne (*of* de; *to do* de faire); *citizen etc* digne *(before n)*; *aim, effort* louable; **he found a ~y opponent** il a trouvé un adversaire digne de lui; **it is ~y of note that...** il est bon de remarquer que...; **nothing ~y of mention** rien de notable.

would [wʊd] *modal aux vb (cond of* **will**) (**a**) *(cond tense)* **he ~ do it if you asked him** il le ferait si vous le lui demandiez; **he ~ have done it if you had asked him** il l'aurait fait si vous le lui aviez demandé; **I wondered if you'd come** je me demandais si vous viendriez *or* si vous alliez venir; **you ~ think she had enough to do** on pourrait penser qu'elle a assez à faire. (**b**) *(conjecture)* **it ~ have been about 8 o'clock** il devait être 8 heures à peu près. (**c**) *(willingness)* **I said I ~ do it** je lui ai dit que je le ferais *or* que je voulais bien le faire; **he ~n't help me** il ne voulait pas m'aider, il n'a pas voulu m'aider; **the car ~n't start** la voiture n'a pas démarré; **~ you like some tea?** voulez-vous *or* voudriez-vous du thé?; **~ you like to go?** voulez-vous y aller?, est-ce que vous aimeriez y aller?; **~ you please help me?** pourriez-vous m'aider, s'il vous plaît? (**d**) *(habit, characteristic)* **he ~ always read in bed** il lisait toujours *or* il avait l'habitude de lire au lit; **50 years ago the streets ~ be empty on Sundays** il y a 50 ans, les rues étaient vides le dimanche; **you WOULD (do that)!** c'est bien de toi (de faire ça)!; **it WOULD rain!** il pleut, naturellement! (**e**) *(liter)* **~ to God that...** plût à Dieu que... + *subj*; **~ I were younger!** si seulement j'étais plus jeune! ◆ **would-be** *adj*: **a ~-be poet** *etc* une personne qui veut être poète *etc*; *(pej)* un prétendu poète *etc.*

wound[1] [wuːnd] **1** *n (lit, fig)* blessure *f; (esp Med)* plaie *f.* **chest/bullet ~** blessure à la poitrine/par balle. **2** *vt (lit, fig)* blesser (*in the leg etc* à la jambe *etc*). ◆ **wounded 1** *adj (lit, fig)* blessé; **a ~ed man** un blessé ; **2** *npl*: **the ~ed** les blessés *mpl.* ◆ **wounding** *adj* blessant.

wound[2] [waʊnd] *pret, ptp of* **wind**[2].

wove(n) ['wəʊvə(n)] *pret (ptp) of* **weave.**

wraith [reɪθ] *n* apparition *f*, spectre *m.*

wrangle ['ræŋgl] **1** *n (also* **wrangling***)* dispute *f.* **2** *vi* se disputer (*about, over* à propos de).

wrap [ræp] **1** *n (shawl)* châle *m*; *(housecoat etc)* peignoir *m*; *(rug, blanket)* couverture *f. (on parcel etc)* **~s** emballage *m*; *(fig)* **to keep a scheme under ~s** * ne pas dévoiler un projet.

2 *vt (cover: gen)* envelopper (*in* dans); *(pack) parcel* emballer (*in* dans); *(wind) tape etc* enrouler (*round* autour de). *(fig)* **~ped in mist/mystery** enveloppé de brume/de mystère.

◆ **wrap up 1** *vi (dress warmly)* s'habiller chaudement. **~ up well!** couvrez-vous bien! **2** *vt sep* (**a**) *(gen)* envelopper (*in* dans); *parcel* emballer (*in* dans). *(fig)* **he ~ped it up a bit *, but what he meant was...** il ne l'a pas dit franchement, mais ce qu'il voulait dire c'est...; *(fig: engrossed)* **~ped up in one's work** absorbé par son travail; **he is ~ped up in himself** il ne pense qu'à lui-même. (**b**) *(*: conclude) deal* conclure. **he had everything ~ped up** il avait tout arrangé.

◆ **wrapover** *adj skirt* portefeuille *inv.* ◆ **wrapped** *adj bread etc* pré-emballé. ◆ **wrapper** *n [chocolate, parcel]* papier *m* (d'emballage); *[newspaper for post]* bande *f*; *[book]* jaquette *f.* ◆ **wrapping 1** *n [parcel]* papier *m* (d'emballage); *[sweet]* papier ; **2** *adj*: **~ping paper** *(brown paper)* papier *m* d'emballage; *(decorated)* papier cadeau. ◆ **wrap-up** *n (US) (summary)* résumé; *(concluding event)* conclusion *f.*

wrath [rɒθ] *n (liter)* courroux *m.*

wreak [riːk] *vt*: **to ~ vengeance on sb** assouvir une vengeance sur qn; **to ~ havoc** faire des ravages; **it ~ed havoc with their plans** cela a bouleversé tous leurs projets.

wreath [riːθ] *n* couronne *f (de fleurs)*; *[smoke]* volute *f.* **laurel ~** couronne de laurier. ◆ **wreathed** *adj*: **~ed in mist** enveloppé de brume; **face ~ed in smiles** visage rayonnant.

wreck [rek] **1** *n (of ship, plans etc)* naufrage *m*; *(~ed ship)* épave *f*; *(~ed plane/car etc)* avion *m*/voiture *f etc* accidenté(e), épave *f; (building)* ruines *fpl.* **the car was a ~** la voiture était bonne à mettre à la ferraille; **he looks a ~** il a une mine de déterré. **2** *vt train* faire dérailler; *plane, car [accident, bomb]* détruire; *[pilot, driver]* démolir; *building, furniture* démolir; *mechanism* détraquer; *(fig) marriage, friendship, life, career* briser; *plans, health* ruiner; *negotiations* faire échouer; *chances* anéantir. *[ship, sailor]* **to be ~ed** faire naufrage; **the plane was ~ed** il n'est resté que des débris de l'avion; **he ~ed the whole house** il a tout démoli dans la maison. ◆ **wreckage** *n (pieces)* débris *mpl*; *[building]* décombres *mpl*; *(~ed ship)* épave *f.* ◆ **wrecked** *adj ship* naufragé; *train, car* accidenté; *plans* anéanti. ◆ **wrecker** *n (unlawful)* vandale *m*; *(lawful)* démolisseur *m*; *[cars]* marchand *m* de ferraille.

wren [ren] *n* roitelet *m.*

wrench [rentʃ] **1** *n* (**a**) **to give sth a ~** tirer de toutes ses forces sur qch; *(fig: emotional)* **it was a ~** cela a été un déchirement. (**b**) *(tool)* clé *f* (à écrous); *(Aut: for wheels)* clé en croix. *(US fig)* **to throw a ~ into the works** mettre des bâtons dans les roues. **2** *vt handle etc* tirer violemment sur. **to ~ sth off** *or* **out** *or* **away** arracher qch (*of, from sth* de qch; *from sb* des mains de qn); **he ~ed himself free** il s'est dégagé avec un mouvement violent; *(Med)* **to ~ one's ankle** se tordre la cheville.

wrestle ['resl] *vi* lutter (*with sb* contre qn); *(Sport)* pratiquer la lutte libre; *(as staged fight)* catcher (*with sb* contre qn). *(fig)* **to ~ with** *conscience, sums, device* se débattre avec; *temptation* lutter contre. ◆ **wrestler** *n* lutteur *m*, -euse *f*; catcheur *m*, -euse *f.* ◆ **wrestling 1** *n* lutte *f*; **all-in wrestling** catch *m* ; **2** *adj*: **wrestling match** rencontre *f* de catch *or* de lutte.

wretch [retʃ] *n* misérable *mf. (hum)* **you ~!** misérable!; **little ~!** petit polisson! ◆ **wretched** ['retʃɪd] *adj (very poor) person, conditions, house* misérable; *(unhappy)* malheureux; *(depressed)* déprimé; *(ill)* malade; *(too small) wage* de misère; *sum, amount* dérisoire; *(pej) behaviour, remark* mesquin; *weather, holiday, results* lamentable; *(conscience-stricken etc)* **I feel ~ed about it** je me sens vraiment coupable; **what ~ed luck!** quelle déveine! *; **they played a ~ed game** ils ont très mal joué; **that ~ed dog** * ce maudit chien. ◆ **wretchedly** *adv live* misérablement; *say, weep, apologize* pitoyablement; *treat, behave, pay, perform, play* très mal. ◆ **wretchedness** *n (poverty)* misère *f* ; *(unhappiness)* extrême tristesse *f.*

wrick [rɪk] **1** *vt*: **to ~ one's ankle** se tordre la cheville; **to ~ one's neck** attraper un torticolis. **2** *n* entorse *f*; torticolis *m.*

wriggle ['rɪgl] **1** *vi* (**~ about**) *[worm, snake, eel]* se tortiller; *[fish]* frétiller; *[person] (restlessly)* remuer; *(in embarrassment)* se tortiller; *(excitedly)* frétiller. **to ~ along** *[worm etc]* avancer en se tortillant; *[person]* avancer en rampant; **to ~ free** se dégager en se contorsionnant; **to ~ through sth** se glisser dans qch; *(fig)* **to ~ out of sth** esquiver qch; **he'll**

manage to ~ out of it il trouvera un moyen de s'esquiver. **2** *vt toes* remuer. ◆ **wriggly** *or* ◆ **wriggling** *adj worm* qui se tortille; *fish* frétillant; *child* remuant.

wring [rɪŋ] *pret, ptp* **wrung** *vt* (**a**) *(twist) handkerchief etc* tordre. **to ~ a chicken's neck** tordre le cou à un poulet; **I'll ~ your neck!** * je te tordrai le cou! *; **to ~ one's hands** se tordre les mains de désespoir; **to ~ sb's hand** serrer longuement la main à qn; *(fig)* **a story to ~ one's heart** une histoire à vous fendre le cœur. (**b**) (**~ out**) *wet clothes etc* essorer; *water* exprimer *(from sth* de qch); *(fig) confession etc* arracher *(from sb* à qn); *money* soutirer *(from sb* à qn). ◆ **wringer** *n* essoreuse *f* (à rouleaux). ◆ **wringing (wet)** *adj garment* trempé; *person* trempé jusqu'aux os.

wrinkle ['rɪŋkl] **1** *n (on skin, fruit)* ride *f*; *(in socks, cloth etc)* pli *m*. **2** *vt* (**~ up**) *skin* rider; *forehead* plisser; *nose* froncer; *rug, sheet* faire des plis dans. **3** *vi* se plisser; se froncer; faire des plis. ◆ **wrinkled** *adj skin, apple* ridé; *brow* plissé; *nose* froncé; *sheet, sweater* qui fait des plis.

wrist [rɪst] *n* poignet *m*. ◆ **wristband** *n [shirt etc]* poignet *m*; *[watch etc]* bracelet *m*. ◆ **wrist-watch** *n* montre-bracelet *f*.

writ [rɪt] *n (Jur)* acte *m* judiciaire. **to issue a ~ against sb, to serve a ~ on sb** assigner qn en justice *(for libel etc* pour diffamation *etc)*; **~ of habeas corpus** ordre *m* (écrit) d'habeas corpus.

write [raɪt] *pret* **wrote,** *ptp* **written** **1** *vt (gen)* écrire; *computer program* écrire; *cheque, list, bill* faire; *prescription, certificate* rédiger. **how is it written?** comment est-ce que ça s'écrit?; *(fig)* **it was written all over his face** cela se lisait sur son visage; *(fig)* **he had 'policeman' written all over him** * cela sautait aux yeux qu'il était policier. **2** *vi* écrire *(to sb* à qn; *on, about sth* sur qch). **he can read and ~** il sait lire et écrire; **~ on both sides of the paper** écrivez des deux côtés de la feuille; **he had always wanted to ~** il avait toujours voulu écrire *or* être écrivain; **what shall I ~ about?** sur quoi est-ce que je vais écrire?; *(Comm)* **~ for our brochure** demandez notre brochure.

◆ **write away** *vi (Comm etc)* **to ~ away for** *form, details* écrire pour demander; *goods* commander par lettre. ◆ **write back** *vi* répondre (par lettre). ◆ **write down** *vt sep* écrire; *(note)* noter; *(put in writing)* mettre par écrit. ◆ **write in** **1** *vi*: **a lot of people have written in** beaucoup de gens nous ont écrit; **to ~ in for sth** écrire pour demander qch. **2** *vt sep word, item on list etc* ajouter. ◆ **write off** **1** *vi* = **write away.** **2** *vt sep debt* passer aux profits et pertes; *operation, scheme* mettre un terme à; *(smash up) car, machine* détruire, bousiller *. *(fig)* **I've written off the whole thing** j'ai fait une croix dessus *, je le considère comme perdu; *(fig)* **he had been written off as a failure** on avait décidé qu'il ne ferait jamais rien de bon. ◆ **write out** *vt sep (gen)* écrire; *cheque, list, bill* faire; *prescription, bill* rédiger; *(copy) essay etc* recopier. ◆ **write up** *vt sep notes, diary* mettre à jour; *(write report on) developments etc* faire un compte rendu de; *(record) (Chem etc) experiment* rédiger; *(Archeol etc) one's findings* consigner. **to ~ sth up in a notebook** consigner qch dans un agenda.

◆ **write-off** *n (Comm)* perte *f* sèche; *(Fin: tax)* déduction *f* fiscale; *(fig)* **to be a ~-off** *[car]* être bon pour la casse; *[project]* se révéler une perte de temps. ◆ **writer** *n (of letter, book etc)* auteur *m*; *(as profession)* écrivain *m*; *(of computer program)* auteur *m;* **a thriller ~r** un auteur de romans policiers; **he is a ~r** il est écrivain, c'est un écrivain; **to be a good/bad ~r** écrire bien/mal; **~r's block** hantise *f* de la page blanche; **~r's cramp** crampe *f* des écrivains. ◆ **write-up** *n (gen, also Comput)* description *f; (review etc)* compte rendu *m*. ◆ **writing** *n (handwriting)* écriture *f*; *(sth written)* qch d'écrit; **in his own writing** écrit de sa main; *(fig)* **he saw the writing on the wall** il a vu le signe sur le mur; **to put sth in writing** mettre qch par écrit; **he devoted his life to writing** il a consacré sa vie à son œuvre d'écrivain; **writing is his hobby** écrire est son passe-temps favori; **in this author's writing(s)** dans les écrits *mpl* de cet auteur. ◆ **writing-case** *n* nécessaire *m* de correspondance. ◆ **writing-desk** *n* secrétaire *m (bureau)*. ◆ **writing-pad** *n* bloc *m* de papier à lettres, bloc-notes *m*. ◆ **writing-paper** *n* papier *m* à lettres. ◆ **writing-table** *n* bureau *m*. ◆ **written** *adj (gen)* écrit, par écrit; *evidence* par écrit; **written exam** écrit *m*.

wrong [rɒŋ] **1** *adj* (**a**) *(bad)* mal *inv*; *(unfair)* injuste. **it is ~ to lie, lying is ~** c'est mal de mentir; **it is ~ that she should do that** il est injuste qu'elle fasse cela; **what's ~ with going to the pictures?** quel mal y a-t-il à aller au cinéma?; **there's nothing ~ in that** il n'y a rien à redire à ça; **there's nothing ~ in** *or* **with doing that** il n'y a aucun mal à faire cela.

(**b**) *(incorrect) belief, guess* erroné; *answer, calculation* faux, inexact; *(Mus) note* faux. **to be ~** se tromper *(about* sur, à propos de), avoir tort *(to do, in doing* de faire); **you were ~ to hit him** tu as eu tort de le frapper; **my watch is ~** ma montre n'est pas à l'heure; **to get sth ~** se tromper dans qch; **they got it ~ again** ils se sont encore trompés; **he told me the ~ time** *(gen)* il ne m'a pas donné l'heure exacte; *(for appointment etc)* il ne m'a pas donné la bonne heure; **at the ~ time** à un moment inopportun; **the letter has the ~ date on it** ils se sont trompés de date sur la lettre; *(Telec)* **to get a ~ number** se tromper de numéro; **that's the ~ number** ce n'est pas le bon numéro; **he got on the ~ train** il s'est trompé de train, il n'a pas pris le bon train; *(fig)* **you're on the ~ road** vous faites fausse route; **I'm in the ~ job** ce n'est pas le travail qu'il me faut; **he's got the ~ kind of friends** il a de mauvaises fréquentations; **that's the ~ kind of plug** ce n'est pas la prise qu'il faut; **to say the ~ thing** dire ce qu'il ne fallait pas dire; **that's the ~ way to go about it** ce n'est pas comme ça qu'il faut s'y prendre; **the bread went down the ~ way** j'ai avalé le pain de travers; **on the ~ side** du mauvais côté; *(fig)* **he got out of bed on the ~ side, he got out of the ~ side of the bed** il s'est levé du pied gauche; **the ~ side of the cloth** le mauvais côté *or* l'envers *m* du tissu; **he's on the ~ side of forty** il a dépassé la quarantaine; *(fig)* **to get on the ~ side of sb** se faire mal voir de qn; **it's in the ~ place** ce n'est pas à sa place.

(**c**) *(amiss)* **sth's ~** *or* **there's sth ~ (with it** *or* **him** *etc)* il y a qch qui ne va pas; **sth's ~ with my leg** j'ai qch à la jambe; **sth's ~ with my watch** ma montre ne marche pas comme il faut; **what's ~?** qu'est-ce qui ne va pas?; **there's sth ~** il y a qch qui cloche *; **what's ~ with you?** qu'est-ce que vous avez?; **what's ~ with your arm?** qu'est-ce que vous avez au bras?; **what's ~ with the car?** qu'est-ce qu'elle a, la voiture?; **there's nothing ~** tout va bien; **nothing ~, I hope?** tout va bien, j'espère?; **there's nothing ~ with it** *(theory, translation)* c'est tout à fait correct; *(method, plan)* c'est tout à fait valable; *(machine, car)* ça marche très bien; **there's nothing ~ with him** il va très bien.

2 *adv answer, guess* mal, incorrectement. **you've spelt it ~** vous l'avez mal écrit; **you're doing it all ~** tu t'y prends mal; **you did ~ to refuse** vous avez eu tort de refuser; **you've got it ~** vous avez fait une erreur; *(misunderstood)* vous avez mal compris; **don't get me ~** * comprends-moi bien; **to go ~** *(gen)* se tromper; *(on road)* se tromper de route; *[plan]* mal tourner; *[business deal etc]* tomber à l'eau; *[machine, car]* tomber en panne;

[clock, watch etc] se détraquer; **you can't go ~** c'est très simple; **you won't go far ~ if...** vous ne pouvez guère vous tromper si...; **sth went ~** il est arrivé qch; **sth went ~ with the gears** qch s'est détraqué dans l'embrayage; **nothing can go ~ now** tout doit marcher comme sur des roulettes maintenant; **everything went ~** tout est allé de travers.

3 *n* (**a**) *(evil)* mal *m.* **to do ~** mal agir; *(fig)* **he can do no ~ in her eyes** il lui semble parfait. (**b**) *(injustice)* injustice *f.* **he suffered great ~** il a été la victime de graves injustices; **to right a ~** réparer une injustice. (**c**) **to be/put sb in the ~** être/mettre qn dans son tort.

4 *vt* faire tort à.

◆ **wrongdoer** *n* malfaiteur *m*, -trice *f.* ◆ **wrongdoing** *n* méfaits *mpl.* ◆ **wrongful** *adj arrest* arbitraire ; *accusation, dismissal* injustifié. ◆ **wrongfully** *adv* à tort. ◆ **wrong-headed** *adj* buté. ◆ **wrongly** *adv* (**a**) *answer, do, count, state* incorrectement; *treat* injustement; *accuse, dismiss* à tort ; (**b**) *(by mistake)* par erreur.

wrote [rəʊt] *pret of* **write.**

wrought [rɔːt] *adj iron* forgé; *silver* ouvré. ◆ **wrought-iron** *adj* en fer forgé. ◆ **wrought-up** *adj* très tendu.

wrung [rʌŋ] *pret, ptp of* **wring.**

wry [raɪ] *adj* désabusé. **to make a ~ face** faire la grimace. ◆ **wryly** *adv* avec une ironie désabusée.

X, x [eks] *n (letter)* X, x *m*; *(Math)* x *m*. **for x years** pendant x années; **X marks the spot** l'endroit est marqué d'une croix. ◆ **X-certificate** *adj film* interdit aux moins de 18 ans. ◆ **X-ray** **1** *n (ray)* rayon *m* X; *(photo)* radiographie *f*, radio * *f*; **to have an X-ray** se faire radiographier, se faire faire une radio * ; **2** *vt* radiographier ; **3** *adj examination* radioscopique; **X-ray photo** radio * *f*; **X-ray treatment** radiothérapie *f*.

Xerox ['zɪərɒks] *vt* ® photocopier.

Xmas ['krɪsməs, 'eksməs] *n abbr of* **Christmas.**

xylophone ['zaɪləfəʊn] *n* xylophone *m*.

Y, y [waɪ] *n (letter)* Y, y *m*. **Y-fronts** ® slip *m* (d'homme); **Y-shaped** en forme d'Y.

yacht [jɒt] **1** *n* yacht *m*. **2** *vi*: **to go ~ing** faire de la navigation de plaisance. **3** *adj*: **~ club** cercle *m* nautique.
◆ **yachting** **1** *n* yachting *m*, navigation *f* de plaisance ; **2** *adj cap* de marin; *magazine etc* de la voile.
◆ **yachtsman** *n* plaisancier *m*.

yak¹ [jæk] *n (Zool)* yak *m*.

yak² * [jæk] *vi (also* **yackety-yak***)* caqueter.

yam [jæm] *n* igname *f*; *(sweet potato)* patate *f*.

yang [jæŋ] *n (Philos)* yang *m*.

yank [jæŋk] **1** *n* coup sec. **2** *vt* tirer d'un coup sec. **to ~ sth off** *or* **out** arracher qch.

Yank * [jæŋk] **1** *adj* amerloque ‡ *(pej)*. **2** *n* Amerloque ‡ *mf (pej)*. ◆ **Yankee** * *n* Yankee *mf*.

yap [jæp] **1** *vi [dog]* japper; (*) *[person]* jacasser. **2** *n* jappement *m*.
◆ **yapping** **1** *adj dog* jappeur ; **2** *n* jappements *mpl*.

yard¹ [jɑːd] *n* (**a**) yard *m (91,44 cm)* ≃ mètre *m*. **about a ~ long** long d'un mètre; **by the ~** au mètre; *(fig)* **~s of** * des kilomètres de *. (**b**) *(Naut)* vergue *f*. ◆ **yardage** *n* ≃ métrage *m*. ◆ **yardarm** *n* bout *m* de vergue. ◆ **yardstick** *n (fig)* mesure *f*.

yard² [jɑːd] *n (gen)* cour *f*; *(US: garden)* jardin *m*; *(work-site)* chantier *m*; *(for storage)* dépôt *m*. **back ~** cour de derrière; **builder's/shipbuilding ~** chantier de construction/de construction navale; **timber/coal ~** dépôt de bois/de charbon; *(Brit)* **the Y~** , **Scotland Y~** Scotland Yard *m (≃ le Quai des Orfèvres)*; *(US)* **~ sale** vente *f* d'objets usagés (chez un particulier).

yarn [jɑːn] *n* (**a**) fil *m*; *(Tech: for weaving)* filé *m*. **nylon** *etc* **~** fil de nylon *etc*. (**b**) *(tale)* longue histoire *f*.

yawn [jɔːn] **1** *vi [person]* bâiller (*with boredom* d'ennui); *[chasm etc]* s'ouvrir. **2** *vt*: **to ~ one's head off** bâiller à se décrocher la mâchoire; **'no' he ~ed** 'non' dit-il en bâillant. **3** *n* bâillement *m*. **to give a ~** bâiller. ◆ **yawning** *adj chasm* béant.

yeah * [jɛə] *particle* oui, ouais *.

year [jɪəʳ] *n* (**a**) an *m*, année *f*. **this ~** cette année; **next ~** l'an prochain, l'année prochaine; **3 times a ~** 3 fois l'an *or* par an; **in the ~ of grace/of Our Lord** en l'an de grâce/de Notre Seigneur; **in the ~ 1969** en 1969; **~ by ~ , from ~ to ~** d'année en année; **from one ~ to the other** d'une année à l'autre; **~ in, ~ out** année après année; **all the ~ round** d'un bout de l'année à l'autre; **over the ~s, as the ~s go by** au fil des années; **taking the good ~s with the bad** bon an mal an; **~s and ~s ago** il y a bien des années; **for ~s together** plusieurs années de suite; **to pay by the ~** payer à l'année; **valid one ~** valide un an; **a ~ last January** il y a eu un an au mois de janvier; **they have not met for ~s** ils ne se sont pas vus depuis des années; *(fig)* **I've been waiting for ~s** * ça fait une éternité que j'attends; **15 ~s' imprisonment** 15 ans de prison; **he is 6 ~s old** il a 6 ans; **in his fortieth ~** dans sa quarantième année; **£10 a ~** 10 livres par an; **that new hat takes ~s off her** ce nouveau chapeau la rajeunit. (**b**) *(age)* **young for his ~s** jeune pour son âge; **to get on in ~s** prendre de l'âge; **~s of discretion** l'âge adulte *(fig)*. (**c**) *(Scol, Univ)* année *f*. **she was in my ~ at school** elle était de mon année au lycée; **in the second ~** *(Univ)* en deuxième année; *(school)* ≃ en cinquième. (**d**) *[coin, stamp, wine]* année *f*. ◆ **yearbook** *n* annuaire *m (d'un organisme etc)*. ◆ **yearling** *n* animal *m* d'un an; *(racehorse)* yearling *m*.
◆ **yearly** **1** *adj* annuel ; **2** *adv* annuellement; **twice ~ly** deux fois par an.

yearn [jɜːn] *vi* languir (*for sb* après qn), aspirer (*for sth* à qch; *to do* à faire). **to ~ for home** avoir la nostalgie de chez soi. ◆ **yearning** *n* désir *m* ardent (*for* de; *to do* de faire).

yeast [jiːst] *n*, levure *f*. **dried ~** levure déshydratée.

yell [jel] **1** *n (gen)* hurlement *m*, cri *m* (*of* de). **to give a ~** pousser un hurlement *or* un cri; **a ~ of laughter** un grand éclat de rire. **2** *vti* (**~ out**) hurler (*with* de). ◆ **yelling** **1** *n* hurlements *mpl* ; **2** *adj* hurlant.

yellow ['jeləʊ] **1** *adj object etc* jaune; *hair, curls* blond; *(fig: cowardly)* lâche. **to go** *or* **turn ~** jaunir; *(Ftbl)* **~ card** carton *m* jaune; *(Med)* **~ fever** fièvre *f* jaune; *(Telec)* **the ~ pages** ≃ l'annuaire *m* des professions. **2** *n (colour: also of egg)* jaune *m*. **3** *vti* jaunir. **~ed with age** jauni par le temps.
◆ **yellowhammer** *n (bird)* bruant *m* jaune.

yelp [jelp] **1** *n [dog]* jappement *m*; *[fox]* glapissement *m*. **2** *vi* japper; glapir. ◆ **yelping** **1** *n* jappements *mpl*; glapissements *mpl* ; **2** *adj* jappeur; glapissant.

Yemen ['jemən] *n* Yémen. ◆ **Yemeni** **1** *adj* yéménite ; **2** *n* Yéménite *mf*.

yen * [jen] *n*: **to have a ~ for sth/to do** avoir grande envie de qch/de faire.

yep ‡ [jep] *particle* ouais *, oui.

yes [jes] **1** *particle* oui; *(answering neg question or contradicting)* si. **to say ~** dire oui; **~ certainly** mais oui. **2** *n* oui *m inv*. ◆ **yes-man** *n* béni-oui-oui * *m inv (pej)*; **he's a ~-man** il dit amen à tout.

yesterday ['jestədeɪ] **1** *adv, n* hier *(m)*. **all (day) ~** toute la journée d'hier; **a week (from) ~** d'hier en huit; **a week (past) ~, ~ week** il y a eu hier huit jours; **late ~** hier dans la soirée; **~ was the second** c'était hier le deux; **~ was Friday** c'était hier vendredi; **~ was very wet** il a beaucoup plu hier; **~ was a bad day for him** la journée d'hier s'est mal passée pour lui; **the day before** ~ avant-hier *(m)*; *(fig)* **the great men of** ~ tous les grands hommes du passé *or* d'hier; **all our ~s** tout notre passé. **2** *adj*: ~ **evening/morning** hier soir/matin.

yet [jet] **1** *adv* (**a**) *(as ~, still)* encore; *(till now)* jusqu'ici; *(till then)* jusqu'alors. **they haven't ~ returned** ils ne sont pas encore *or* ne sont toujours pas revenus; **no one has come** ~ jusqu'ici, personne n'est venu; **no one had come** ~ jusqu'alors, personne n'était venu; **places we have ~ to see** des endroits qu'il nous reste encore à voir, des endroits que nous n'avons pas encore vus; ~ **more difficult** encore plus difficile; ~ **once more** encore une fois, une fois de plus; **and ~ another** et encore un autre; **he may ~ come** il peut encore *or* toujours venir; **I'll do it ~** je finirai bien par le faire. (**b**) *(so far)* **has he arrived ~?** est-il déjà arrivé?; **I wonder if he's come ~** je me demande s'il est arrivé maintenant; **not (just) ~** pas encore; **don't come in (just) ~** n'entrez pas encore; **must you go just ~?** faut-il que vous partiez *(subj)* déjà?; **I needn't go just ~** je n'ai pas besoin de partir tout de suite. (**c**) **nor ~** ni, et... non plus; **I do not like him nor ~ his sister** je ne les aime ni lui ni sa sœur, je ne l'aime pas et sa sœur non plus. **2** *conj* pourtant, néanmoins, quand même. **and ~ everyone liked her** et pourtant *or* néanmoins tout le monde l'aimait, mais tout le monde l'aimait quand même; **strange ~ true** étrange mais pourtant vrai.

yew [ju:] *n* if *m*.

Yiddish [ˈjɪdɪʃ] *n* yiddish *m*.

yield [ji:ld] **1** *vt* (**a**) *(produce etc: gen)* rendre; *[mine, oil well]* débiter; *[an industry]* produire; *[business, tax, shares] amount, profit* rapporter; *opportunity* fournir; *results* produire. (**b**) *(surrender: gen, Mil)* céder (*to* à). **2** *vi (give way: gen, Mil)* céder (*to* devant), se rendre (*to* à); *[ice, door etc]* céder. **they begged him but he would not ~** ils l'ont supplié mais il n'a pas cédé; *(Mil etc)* **they ~ed to us** ils se rendirent à nous; *(US Aut)* **'yield'** céder le passage'; **to ~ to temptation** succomber à la tentation. **3** *n (V* **1a***)* rendement *m*; débit *m*; production *f*; rapport *m*.

yin [jɪn] *n (Philos)* yin *m*.

yippee ‡ [jɪˈpi:] *excl* hourra!

yob(bo) ‡ [ˈjɒb(əʊ)] *n (pej)* loubard *m (pej)*.

yod [jɒd] *n (Ling)* yod *m*.

yodel [ˈjəʊdl] *vi* faire des tyroliennes.

yoga [ˈjəʊgə] *n* yoga *m*. ◆ **yogi** *n* yogi *m*.

yoghourt, yog(h)urt [ˈjəʊgət] *n* yaourt *m*.

yoke [jəʊk] **1** *n* (**a**) *(lit, fig)* joug *m*. **under the ~ of** sous le joug de. (**b**) *[dress, blouse]* empiècement *m*. **2** *vt* accoupler.

yokel [ˈjəʊk(ə)l] *n* rustre *m*.

yolk [jəʊk] *n* jaune *m* (d'œuf).

yonder [ˈjɒndəʳ] *adv* (**over ~**) là-bas.

you [ju:] *pers pron* (**a**) *(subject)* tu, vous; *(object)* te, vous; *(stressed and after prep)* toi, vous. ~ **are very kind** tu es très gentil, vous êtes très gentil(s); **I shall see ~ soon** je te *or* je vous verrai bientôt; **for ~** pour toi *or* vous; **younger than ~** plus jeune que toi *or* vous; ~ **and yours** toi et les tiens, vous et les vôtres; ~ **French** vous autres Français; ~ **and I will go together** toi et moi *or* vous et moi, nous irons ensemble; ~ **fool!** espèce d'imbécile!; ~ **darling!** tu es un amour!; **it's ~** c'est toi *or* vous; **there's a fine house for ~!** en voilà une belle maison! (**b**) *(one, anyone) (nominative)* on; *(accusative, dative)* vous, te. ~ **never know your luck** on ne connaît jamais son bonheur; **fresh air does ~ good** l'air frais (vous *or* te) fait du bien. ◆ **you-know-who** * *pron* qui vous savez. ◆ **your** [jʊəʳ] *poss adj* (**a**) ton, ta, tes; votre, vos; **~r book** ton *or* votre livre; **YOUR book** ton livre à toi, votre livre à vous; **~r table** ta *or* votre table; **~r friend** ton ami(e), votre ami(e); **~r clothes** tes *or* vos vêtements; **give me ~r hand** donne-moi la main; (**b**) *(one's)* son, sa, ses; ton *etc*, votre *etc*; **you give him ~r form and he gives you ~r pass** on lui donne son formulaire et il vous remet votre laissez-passer; **it's good for ~r health** c'est bon pour la santé; **~r ordinary Englishman** l'Anglais moyen. ◆ **you're** = **you are.** ◆ **yours** *poss pron* le tien, la tienne, les tiens, les tiennes; le vôtre, la vôtre, les vôtres; **this book is ~rs** ce livre est à toi *or* à vous, ce livre est le tien *or* le vôtre; **a cousin of ~rs** un de tes *or* de vos cousins; **it's no fault of ~rs** ce n'est pas de votre faute (à vous); *(pej)* **that dog of ~rs** ton *or* votre sacré * *or* fichu * chien; *(in pub etc)* **what's ~rs?** qu'est-ce que tu prends *or* vous prenez?; *V* **sincerely, faithfully.** ◆ **yourself** *pers pron, pl* **-selves** *(reflexive)* te, vous; *(after prep)* toi, vous; *(emphatic)* toi-même, vous-même; **have you hurt ~rself?** tu t'es fait mal?, vous vous êtes fait mal?; **you never speak of ~rself** tu ne parles jamais de toi, vous ne parlez jamais de vous; **you told me ~rself** tu me l'as dit toi-même, vous me l'avez dit vous-même; **all by ~rself** tout seul.

young [jʌŋ] **1** *adj (gen)* jeune. ~ **people** jeunes *mpl*, jeunes gens *mpl*; ~ **lady** *(unmarried)* jeune fille *f*; *(married)* jeune femme *f*; **listen to me, ~ man** écoutez-moi, jeune homme; ~ **at heart** jeune de cœur; ~ **for his age** jeune pour son âge; **to marry ~** se marier jeune; **3 years ~er than you** plus jeune que vous de 3 ans; **my ~er brother** mon frère cadet; **my ~er sister** ma sœur cadette; **the ~er son** le cadet; **I'm not so ~ as I was** je n'ai plus mes vingt ans; **in my ~ days** quand j'étais jeune; **to grow** *or* **get ~er** rajeunir; **if I were ~er** si j'étais plus jeune; **if I were 10 years ~er** si j'avais 10 ans de moins; **you're only ~ once** jeunesse n'a qu'un temps; ~ **Mr Brown, Mr Brown the ~er** le jeune M. Brown; *(as opposed to his father)* M. Brown fils; **the ~er generation** la jeune génération; **the ~ idea** ce que pensent les jeunes; *(fig)* la jeune génération; ~ **wine** vin *m* vert; ~ **nation** nouvelle nation *f*; *(fig)* ~ **blood** sang *m* nouveau *or* jeune. **2** *npl* (**a**) **the ~** les jeunes *mpl*, les jeunes gens *mpl*; ~ **and old** les jeunes comme les vieux; **books for the ~** livres pour les jeunes *or* la jeunesse. (**b**) *[animal]* petits *mpl*. ◆ **youngster** *n* jeune *mf*.

youth [ju:θ] **1** *n* (**a**) jeunesse *f*. **in my ~** dans ma jeunesse, lorsque j'étais jeune; **in early ~** dans la première jeunesse. (**b**) *(young man)* jeune homme *m*. **~s** jeunes gens *mpl*. (**c**) *(collective: young people)* jeunesse *f*, jeunes *mpl*. **the ~ of a country** la jeunesse d'un pays; **the ~ of today** les jeunes *or* la jeunesse d'aujourd'hui. **2** *adj orchestra etc* de jeunes, de jeunesse. ~ **club** foyer *m or* centre *m* de jeunes; ~ **hostel** *V* **hostel**; ~ **leader** animateur *m*, -trice *f* de groupes de jeunes; ~ **movement** mouvement *m* de la jeunesse; **Y~ Training Scheme** *(abbr* **Y.T.S.** ≃ pacte *m* national pour l'emploi des jeunes. ◆ **youthful** *adj (gen)* jeune; *air, mistake* de jeunesse; *quality, freshness* juvénile. ◆ **youthfulness** *n* jeunesse *f*.

yowl [jaʊl] *vi [person, dog]* hurler; *[cat]* miauler.

yucky ‡, **yukky** ‡ [ˈjʌkɪ] *adj* dégoûtant.

Yugoslavia [ˈju:gə(ʊ)ˈslɑ:vɪə] *n* Yougoslavie *f*. ◆ **Yugoslav** **1** *adj (also* **Yugoslavian***)* yougoslave ; **2** *n* Yougoslave *mf*.

Yule [ju:l] *n* (†) Noël *m*. ~ **log** bûche *f* de Noël. ◆ **Yuletide** † *n* époque *f* de Noël.

yummy ‡ [ˈjʌmɪ] **1** *adj food* délicieux. **2** *excl* miam, miam! *

yuppie [ˈjʌpɪ] *n* jeune cadre urbain.

Z

Z, z *(US)* [zed, zi:] *n (letter)* Z, z *m*.

Zaire [zɑ:'i:ər] *n* Zaïre *m*. ◆ **Zairean 1** *n* Zaïrois(e) *m(f)* ; **2** *ad* zaïrois.

Zambia ['zæmbɪə] *n* Zambie *f*. ◆ **Zambian 1** *n* Zambien(ne) *m(f)* ; **2** *adj* zambien.

zap * [zæp] **1** *excl* vlan! **2** *vt* (**a**) *(destroy) town* bombarder; *person* supprimer. (**b**) *(delete)* supprimer. (**c**) *(astonish)* épater *. **3** *vi* (**a**) *(move quickly)* foncer. (**b**) *(TV)* zapper *.

zany ['zeɪnɪ] *adj* dingue *, fou.

zeal [zi:l] *n* zèle *m* (*for* pour). ◆ **zealot** ['zelət] *n* fanatique *mf*. ◆ **zealous** ['zeləs] *adj (fervent)* zélé; *(devoted)* dévoué; ~**ous for** plein de zèle pour. ◆ **zealously** *adv* avec zèle.

zebra ['zi:brə] **1** *n* zèbre *m*. **2** *adj (Brit)* ~ **crossing** passage *m* pour piétons.

zed [zed], *(US)* **zee** [zi:] *n* (la lettre) z *m*.

zenith ['zenɪθ] *n* zénith *m*.

zephyr ['zefə'] *n* zéphyr *m*.

zero ['zɪərəʊ] **1** *n, pl* **-s** *or* **-es** zéro *m*. **2** *adj tension, voltage* nul; *altitude, growth* zéro *inv*. ~ **hour** *(Mil)* l'heure H; *(fig)* le moment décisif. **3** *vi:* **to** ~ **in on sth** piquer droit sur qch; *(fig) (identify)* mettre le doigt sur qch; *(concentrate on)* se concentrer sur qch.

zest [zest] *n* (**a**) *(gusto)* entrain *m; (fig: spice)* piquant *m*. **with** ~ *(gen)* avec entrain; *eat* avec grand appétit; ~ **for living** appétit *m* de vivre; **it adds** ~ **to the episode** cela donne du piquant à l'histoire. (**b**) *(Culin: of orange etc)* zeste *m*. ◆ **zestful** *adj* plein d'entrain.

zigzag ['zɪgzæg] **1** *n* zigzag *m*. **2** *adj path, course, line* en zizgaz; *road* en lacets; *pattern, design* à zigzags. **3** *adv* en zigzag. **4** *vi* zigzaguer. **to** ~ **out/through** *etc* sortir/traverser *etc* en zigzaguant.

Zimbabwe [zɪm'bɑ:bwɪ] *n* Zimbabwe *m*. ◆ **Zimbabwean 1** *adj* zimbabwéen ; **2** *n* Zimbabwéen(ne) *m(f)*.

zinc [zɪŋk] **1** *n* zinc *m*. **2** *adj plate, alloy* de zinc; *roof* zingué.

Zionism ['zaɪənɪz(ə)m] *n* sionisme *m*.

zip [zɪp] **1** *n* (**a**) *(also* ~ **fastener, zipper**) fermeture *f* éclair ®. **pocket with a** ~ poche *f* à fermeture éclair, poche zippée *. (**b**) (*: *energy etc)* entrain *m*. **put a bit of** ~ **into it** * activez-vous! **2** *adj (US Post)* ~ **code** code *m* postal. **3** *vt* (~ **up**) *dress, bag* fermer avec une fermeture éclair ® **to** ~ **sth on** attacher qch avec une fermeture éclair; **she** ~**ped open her bag** elle a ouvert la fermeture éclair de son sac. **4** *vi* (**a**) *[garment etc]* **to** ~ **up/on** *etc* se fermer/s'attacher *etc* avec une fermeture éclair. (**b**) (*) *[car, person]* **to** ~ **in/past** *etc* entrer/passer *etc* comme une flèche. ◆ **zip-on** *adj* à fermeture éclair ®.

zircon ['zɜ:kən] *n* zircon *m*.

zither ['zɪðə'] *n* cithare *f*.

zodiac ['zəʊdɪæk]*n* zodiaque *m*.

zombie * ['zɒmbɪ] *n (fig pej)* automate *m*.

zone [zəʊn] **1** *n (gen)* zone *f; (esp Mil) (area)* zone ; *(subdivision of town)* secteur *m*. **danger** ~ zone dangereuse. **2** *vt (divide into* ~*s) area* diviser en zones. **district** ~**d for industry** zone réservée à l'implantation industrielle. ◆ **zonal** *adj* zonal. ◆ **zoning** *n* répartition *f* en zones.

zoo [zu:] *n* zoo *m*. ~ **keeper** gardien(ne) *m(f)* de zoo.

zoology [zəʊ'ɒlədʒɪ] *n* zoologie *f*. ◆ **zoological** *adj* zoologique; **zoological gardens** jardin *m* zoologique. ◆ **zoologist** *n* zoologiste *mf*.

zoom [zu:m] *1 n* vrombissement *m*. **2** *vi* vrombir. **to** ~ **away/through** *etc* démarrer/traverser *etc* en trombe; *(Cine)* **to** ~ **in** faire un zoom (*on* sur). ◆ **zoom lens** *n (Phot)* zoom *m*.

zucchini [zu:'ki:nɪ] *n (US)* courgette *f*.

Zurich ['zjʊərɪk] *n* Zurich.

		Present	Imperfect	Future	Past Historic	Past Participle	Subjunctive
(1)	**arriver** (regular: see table at the end of the list)						
(2)	**finir** (regular: see table)						
(3)	**placer**	je place nous plaçons	je plaçais	je placerai	je plaçai	placé	que je place
	bouger	je bouge nous bougeons	je bougeais	je bougerai	je bougeai	bougé	que je bouge
(4)	**appeler**	j'appelle nous appelons	j'appelais	j'appellerai	j'appelai	appelé	que j'appelle
	jeter	je jette nous jetons	je jetais	je jetterai	je jetai	jeté	que je jette
(5)	**geler**	je gèle nous gelons	je gelais	je gèlerai	je gelai	gelé	que je gèle
(6)	**céder**	je cède nous cédons	je cédais	je céderai	je cédai	cédé	que je cède
(7)	**épier**	j'épie nous épions	j'épiais	j'épierai	j'épiai	épié	que j'épie
(8)	**noyer**	je noie nous noyons	je noyais	je noierai	je noyai	noyé	que je noie
	envoyer			j'enverrai			
	payer	je paie *ou* paye		je paierai *ou* payerai			que je paie *ou* paye
(9)	**aller** (see table)						
(10)	**haïr**	je hais il hait nous haïssons ils haïssent	je haïssais	je haïrai	je haïs	haï	que je haïsse
(11)	**courir**	je cours il court nous courons	je courais	je courrai	je courus	couru	que je coure
(12)	**cueillir**	je cueille nous cueillons	je cueillais	je cueillerai	je cueillis	cueilli	que je cueille
(13)	**assaillir**	j'assaille nous assaillons	j'assaillais	j'assaillirai	j'assaillis	assailli	que j'assaille
(14)	**servir**	je sers il sert nous servons	je servais	je servirai	je servis	servi	que je serve
(15)	**bouillir**	je bous il bout nous bouillons	je bouillais	je bouillirai	je bouillis	bouilli	que je bouille
(16)	**partir**	je pars il part nous partons	je partais	je partirai	je partis	parti	que je parte
(17)	**fuir**	je fuis il fuit nous fuyons ils fuient	je fuyais	je fuirai	je fuis	fui	que je fuie

	Present	*Imperfect*	*Future*	*Past Historic*	*Past Participle*	*Subjunctive*
(18) couvrir	je couvre nous couvrons	je couvrais	je couvrirai	je couvris	couvert	que je couvre
(19) mourir	je meurs il meurt nous mourons ils meurent	je mourais	je mourrai	je mourus	mort	que je meure
(20) vêtir	je vêts il vêt nous vêtons	je vêtais	je vêtirai	je vêtis	vêtu	que je vête
(21) acquérir	j'acquiers il acquiert nous acquérons ils acquièrent	j'acquérais	j'acquerrai	j'acquis	acquis	que j'acquière
(22) venir	je viens il vient nous venons ils viennent	je venais	je viendrai	je vins	venu	que je vienne
(23) pleuvoir	il pleut	il pleuvait	il pleuvra	il plut	plu	qu'il pleuve
(24) prévoir	je prévois il prévoit nous prévoyons ils prévoient	je prévoyais	je prévoirai	je prévis	prévu	que je prévoie
(25) pourvoir	je pourvois il pourvoit nous pourvoyons ils pourvoient	je pourvoyais	je pourvoirai	je pourvus	pourvu	que je pourvoie
(26) asseoir	j'assois il assoit nous assoyons ils assoient *ou* j'assieds il assied noús asseyons ils asseyent	j'assoyais *ou* j'asseyais	j'assoirai *ou* j'asseyerai *ou* j'assiérai	j'assis	assis	que j'assoie *ou* que j'asseye
(27) mouvoir	je meus il meut nous mouvons il meuvent	je mouvais nous mouvions	je mouvrai	je mus	mû	que je meuve
	N.B. *émouvoir* and *promouvoir* have the past participle *ému* and *promu* respectively.					
(28) recevoir	je reçois il reçoit nous recevons ils reçoivent	je recevais nous recevions	je recevrai	je reçus	reçu	que je reçoive
devoir					dû	
(29) valoir	je vaux il vaut nous valons	je valais nous valions	je vaudrai	je valus	valu	que je vaille
falloir	il faut	il fallait	il faudra	il fallut	fallu	qu'il faille
(30) voir	je vois il voit nous voyons ils voient	je voyais nous voyions	je verrai	je vis	vu	que je voie
(31) vouloir	je veux il veut nous voulons ils veulent	je voulais nous voulions	je voudrai	je voulus	voulu	que je veuille

	Present	*Imperfect*	*Future*	*Past Historic*	*Past Participle*	*Subjunctive*
(32) savoir	je sais il sait nous savons	je savais nous savions	je saurai	je sus	su	que je sache
(33) pouvoir	je peux *ou* puis il peut nous pouvons ils peuvent	je pouvais nous pouvions	je pourrai	je pus	pu	que je puisse
(34) avoir (see table)						
(35) conclure	je conclus il conclut nous concluons	je concluais	je conclurai	je conclus	conclu	que je conclue
inclure					inclus	
(36) rire	je ris il rit nous rions ils rient	je riais	je rirai	je ris	ri	que je rie
(37) dire	je dis il dit nous disons vous dites ils disent	je disais	je dirai	je dis	dit	que je dise
suffire	vous suffisez					
médire	vous médisez					
etc	*etc*					
(38) nuire	je nuis il nuit nous nuisons	je nuisais	je nuirai	je nuisis	nui	que je nuise
(39) écrire	j'écris il écrit nous écrivons	j'écrivais	j'écrirai	j'écrivis	écrit	que j'écrive
(40) suivre	je suis il suit nous suivons	je suivais	je suivrai	je suivis	suivi	que je suive
(41) rendre	je rends il rend nous rendons	je rendais	je rendrai	je rendis	rendu	que je rende
rompre	il rompt					
battre	je bats il bat nous battons	je battais	je battrai	je battis	battu	que je batte
(42) vaincre	je vaincs il vainc nous vainquons	je vainquais	je vaincrai	je vainquis	vaincu	que je vainque
(43) lire	je lis il lit nous lisons	je lisais	je lirai	je lus	lu	que je lise
(44) croire	je crois il croit nous croyons ils croient	je croyais	je croirai	je crus	cru	que je croie
(45) clore	je clos il clôt *ou* clot ils closent	je closais	je clorai	not applicable	clos	que je close
(46) vivre	je vis il vit nous vivons	je vivais	je vivrai	je vécus	vécu	que je vive

	Present	Imperfect	Future	Past Historic	Past Participle	Subjunctive
(47) moudre	je mouds il moud nous moulons	je moulais	je moudrai	je moulus	moulu	que je moule
(48) coudre	je couds il coud nous cousons	je cousais	je coudrai	je cousis	cousu	que je couse
(49) joindre	je joins il joint nous joignons	je joignais	je joindrai	je joignis	joint	que je joigne
(50) traire	je trais il trait nous trayons ils traient	je trayais	je trairai	not applicable	trait	que je traie
(51) absoudre	j'absous il absout nous absolvons	j'absolvais	j'absoudrai	j'absolus	absous	que j'absolve
résoudre					résolu	
(52) craindre	je crains il craint nous craignons	je craignais	je craindrai	je craignis	craint	que je craigne
peindre	je peins il peint nous peignons	je peignais	je peindrai	je peignis	peint	que je peigne
(53) boire	je bois il boit nous buvons il boivent	je buvais	je boirai	je bus	bu	que je boive
(54) plaire	je plais il plaît nous plaisons	je plaisais	je plairai	je plus	plu	que je plaise
taire	il tait					
(55) croître	je croîs il croît nous croissons	je croissais	je croîtrai	je crûs	crû	que je croisse
	N.B. *accroître* and *décroître*: the vowel only takes a circumflex when it precedes the letter *t*.					
(56) mettre	je mets il met nous mettons	je mettais	je mettrai	je mis	mis	que je mette
(57) connaître	je connais il connaît nous connaissons	je connaissais	je connaîtrai	je connus	connu	que je connaisse
(58) prendre	je prends il prend nous prenons ils prennent	je prenais	je prendrai	je pris	pris	que je prenne
(59) naître	je nais il naît nous naissons	je naissais	je naîtrai	je naquis	né	que je naisse
(60) faire (see table)						
(61) être (see table)						

(1) **arriver** (regular verb)

INDICATIVE

Present
j'arrive
tu arrives
il arrive
nous arrivons
vous arrivez
ils arrivent

Imperfect
j'arrivais
tu arrivais
il arrivait
nous arrivions
vous arriviez
ils arrivaient

Past Historic
j'arrivai
tu arrivas
il arriva
nous arrivâmes
vous arrivâtes
ils arrivèrent

Future
j'arriverai
tu arriveras
il arrivera
nous arriverons
vous arriverez
ils arriveront

Perfect
je suis arrivé
nous sommes arrivés

Pluperfect
j'étais arrivé

Past Anterior
je fus arrivé

Future Perfect
je serai arrivé

Present Participle
arrivant

Past Participle
arrivé

CONDITIONAL

Present
j'arriverais
tu arriverais
il arriverait
nous arriverions
vous arriveriez
ils arriveraient

Past I
je serais arrivé

Past II
je fusse arrivé

IMPERATIVE

Present
arrive
arrivons
arrivez

Past
sois arrivé
soyons arrivés
soyez arrivés

SUBJUNCTIVE

Present
que j'arrive
que tu arrives
qu'il arrive
que nous arrivions
que vous arriviez
qu'ils arrivent

Imperfect
que j'arrivasse
que tu arrivasses
qu'il arrivât
que nous arrivassions
que vous arrivassiez
qu'ils arrivassent

Past
que je sois arrivé

Pluperfect
que je fusse arrivé

(2) **finir** (regular verb)

INDICATIVE

Present
je finis
tu finis
il finit
nous finissons
vous finissez
ils finissent

Imperfect
je finissais
tu finissais
il finissait
nous finissions
vous finissiez
ils finissaient

Past Historic
je finis
tu finis
il finit
nous finîmes
vous finîtes
ils finirent

Future
je finirai
tu finiras
il finira
nous finirons
vous finirez
ils finiront

Perfect
j'ai fini
nous avons fini

Pluperfect
j'avais fini

Past Anterior
j'eus fini

Future Perfect
j'aurai fini

Present Participle
finissant

Past Participle
fini

CONDITIONAL

Present
je finirais
tu finirais
il finirait
nous finirions
vous finiriez
ils finiraient

Past I
j'aurais fini

Past II
j'eusse fini

IMPERATIVE

Present
finis
finissons
finissez

Past
aie fini
ayons fini
ayez fini

SUBJUNCTIVE

Present
que je finisse
que tu finisses
qu'il finisse
que nous finissions
que vous finissiez
qu'ils finissent

Imperfect
que je finisse
que tu finisses
qu'il finît
que nous finissions
que vous finissiez
qu'ils finissent

Past
que j'aie fini

Pluperfect
que j'eusse fini

(9) aller

INDICATIVE

Present
je vais
tu vas
il va
nous allons
vous allez
ils vont

Imperfect
j'allais
tu allais
il allait
nous allions
vous alliez
ils allaient

Past Historic
j'allai
tu allas
il alla
nous allâmes
vous allâtes
ils allèrent

Future
j'irai
tu iras
il ira
nous irons
vous irez
ils iront

Present Participle
allant

Past Participle
allé

Past Infinitive
être allé

CONDITIONAL

Present
j'irais
tu irais
il irait
nous irions
vous iriez
ils iraient

IMPERATIVE

Present
va
allons
allez

Past
sois allé
soyons allés
soyez allés

SUBJUNCTIVE

Present
que j'aille
que tu ailles
qu'il aille
que nous allions
que vous alliez
qu'ils aillent

Imperfect
que j'allasse
que tu allasses
qu'il allât
que nous allassions
que vous allassiez
qu'ils allassent

(34) avoir

INDICATIVE

Present
j'ai
tu as
il a
nous avons
vous avez
ils ont

Imperfect
j'avais
tu avais
il avait
nous avions
vous aviez
ils avaient

Past Historic
j'eus
tu eus
il eut
nous eûmes
vous eûtes
ils eurent

Future
j'aurai
tu auras
il aura
nous aurons
vous aurez
ils auront

Present Participle
ayant

Past Participle
eu

Past Infinitive
avoir eu

CONDITIONAL

Present
j'aurais
tu aurais
il aurait
nous aurions
vous auriez
ils auraient

IMPERATIVE

Present
aie
ayons
ayez

SUBJUNCTIVE

Present
que j'aie
que tu aies
qu'il ait
que nous ayons
que vous ayez
qu'ils aient

Imperfect
que j'eusse
que tu eusses
qu'il eût
que nous eussions
que vous eussiez
qu'ils eussent

(60) faire

INDICATIVE

Present
je fais
tu fais
il fait
nous faisons
vous faites
ils font

Imperfect
je faisais
tu faisais
il faisait
nous faisions
vous faisiez
ils faisaient

Past Historic
je fis
tu fis
il fit
nous fîmes
vous fîtes
ils firent

Future
je ferai
tu feras
il fera
nous ferons
vous ferez
ils feront

Present Participle
faisant

Past Participle
fait

Past Infinitive
avoir fait

CONDITIONAL

Present
je ferais
tu ferais
il ferait
nous ferions
vous feriez
ils feraient

IMPERATIVE

Present
fais
faisons
faites

Past
aie fait
ayons fait
ayez fait

SUBJUNCTIVE

Present
que je fasse
que tu fasses
qu'il fasse
que nous fassions
que vous fassiez
qu'ils fassent

Imperfect
que je fisse
que tu fisses
qu'il fît
que nous fissions
que vous fissiez
qu'ils fissent

(61) être

INDICATIVE

Present
je suis
tu es
il est
nous sommes
vous êtes
ils sont

Imperfect
j'étais
tu étais
il était
nous étions
vous étiez
ils étaient

Past Historic
je fus
tu fus
il fut
nous fûmes
vous fûtes
ils furent

Future
je serai
tu seras
il sera
nous serons
vous serez
ils seront

Present Participle
étant

Past Participle
été

Past Infinitive
avoir été

CONDITIONAL

Present
je serais
tu serais
il serait
nous serions
vous seriez
il seraient

IMPERATIVE

Present
sois
soyons
soyez

SUBJUNCTIVE

Present
que je sois
que tu sois
qu'il soit
que nous soyons
que vous soyez
qu'ils soient

Imperfect
que je fusse
que tu fusses
qu'il fût
que nous fussions
que vous fussiez
qu'ils fussent

FRENCH ABBREVIATIONS AND ACRONYMS

A2 † Antenne 2 ; aujourd'hui France 2 (2e chaîne de télévision française)
ADN Acide désoxyribonucléique
AF 1. Air France
2. Anciens francs
3. Allocations familiales
AFNOR Association française de normalisation
AFP Agence France-Presse
AG Assemblée générale
ANPE Agence nationale pour l'emploi
AOC Appellation d'origine contrôlée
AP Assistance publique
ap. J.-C. après Jésus-Christ
AR Altesse royale
arrt arrondissement
ARN Acide ribonucléique
AS 1. Association sportive
2. Assurances sociales
ASSEDIC Associations pour l'emploi dans l'industrie et le commerce
ASSU Association du sport scolaire et universitaire
Av. Avenue
av. J.-C. avant Jésus-Christ
BA bonne action
BAFA Brevet d'aptitude aux fonctions d'animateur
Bat. Bâtiment
BCBG bon chic, bon genre
BCG Bacille Calmette-Guérin
BD bande dessinée
Bd boulevard
Benelux Union douanière de la Belgique, du Luxembourg et des Pays-Bas
BEP Brevet d'études professionnelles
BEPC Brevet d'études du premier cycle
BIC Bénéfices industriels et commerciaux
BIT Bureau international du travail
BK Bacille de Koch (tuberculose)
BN Bibliothèque nationale
BO Bulletin officiel
BP boîte postale
BPF bon pour francs
BT Brevet de technicien
BTn Baccalauréat de technicien
BTS Brevet de technicien supérieur
C. Celsius, centigrade
CA 1. Chiffre d'affaires
2. Conseil d'administration
c.-à-d. c'est-à-dire
CAO conception assistée par ordinateur
CAP Certificat d'aptitude professionnelle
CAPES Certificat d'aptitude au professorat de l'enseignement du second degré
CAPET Certificat d'aptitude au professorat de l'enseignement technique
CB 1. Carte Bleue
2. Citizen band
CBI Carte Bleue Internationale
CC 1. Corps consulaire
2. Compte courant
cc centimètre cube

CCP	1. Centre de chèques postaux
	2. Compte chèque postal
	3. Compte courant postal
CD	Corps diplomatique
CDD	Contrat à durée déterminée
CDI	1. Centre des impôts
	2. Centre de documentation et d'information
CE	Cours élémentaire
CEA	Commissariat à l'énergie atomique
CEDEX	Courrier d'entreprise à distribution exceptionnelle
CEE	Communauté économique européenne
CEEA	Communauté européenne de l'énergie atomique
CÉI	Communauté des États indépendants
CERN	Conseil européen pour la recherche nucléaire
CES	Collège d'enseignement secondaire
CET	Collège d'enseignement technique
Cf.	Confer (reportez-vous à)
CFA	Communauté financière africaine
CFDT	Confédération française et démocratique du travail
CFTC	Confédération française des travailleurs chrétiens
cg	centigramme
CGC	Confédération générale des cadres
CGT	Confédération générale du travail
CHU	Centre hospitalier universitaire
Cial	commercial
CIDJ	Centre d'information et de documentation de la jeunesse
Cie	Compagnie
CIO	1. Centre d'information et d'orientation
	2. Comité international olympique
cl	centilitre
CM	Cours moyen
cm	centimètre
CNAM	Conservatoire national des arts et métiers
CNC	1. Comité national de la consommation
	2. Centre national de cinématographie
CNEC	Centre national d'enseignement par correspondance
CNPF	Conseil national du patronat français
CNRS	Centre national de la recherche scientifique
CNTE	Centre national de télé-enseignement
CODEVI	Compte pour le développement industriel
CP	Cours préparatoire
CPA	Classe préparatoire à l'apprentissage
CPPN	Classe pré-professionnelle de niveau
CQFD	ce qu'il fallait démontrer
CREPS	Centres régionaux d'éducation physique et sportive
CROUS	Centre régional des œuvres universitaires et scolaires
CRS	membre des Compagnies républicaines de sécurité
CV	curriculum vitæ
DASS	Direction de l'action sanitaire et sociale
DCA	Défense contre avions
DDT	Dichloro-diphényl-trichloréthane
DEA	Diplôme d'études approfondies
dép.	département
DES	Diplôme d'études supérieures
DESS	Diplôme d'études supérieures spécialisées
DEST	Diplôme d'enseignement supérieur technique
DEUG	Diplôme d'études universitaires générales
DEUST	Diplôme d'études universitaires de sciences et de techniques
dg	décigramme
DG	1. Directeur général
	2. Direction générale
DGRST	Délégation générale à la recherche scientifique et technique
Dir.	Direction
dl	décilitre
dm	décimètre
DOM	Département d'outre-mer
DOM-TOM	Départements et territoires d'outre-mer
Dr	docteur

DST Direction de la surveillance du territoire
DT diphtérie, tétanos
DTTAB vaccin antityphoïdique et antiparathyphoïdique A et B, antidiphtérique et tétanique
DUT Diplôme universitaire de technologie
EAO Enseignement assisté par ordinateur
ECU *nm inv* European currency unit
EDF Électricité de France
ENA École nationale d'administration
ENS École normale supérieure
ENS... École nationale supérieure...
ESEU Examen spécial d'entrée à l'université
etc. et cætera (et le reste)
E.-U. États-Unis
ex. 1. exemple
2. exercice
F 1. Franc
2. Fahrenheit
FAO Fabrication assistée par ordinateur
FB Franc belge
FEN Fédération de l'éducation nationale
FF 1. Franc français
2. frères
FFI Forces françaises de l'intérieur
FFL Forces françaises libres
FLN Front de libération nationale
FM Fréquence modulée
FMI Fonds monétaire international
FNSEA Fédération nationale des syndicats d'exploitants agricoles
FO Force ouvrière
FR3 † France Régions 3 ; aujourd'hui France 3 (3e chaîne de télévision française)
FS Franc suisse
g gramme
GB Grande-Bretagne
GDF Gaz de France
GIC Grand infirme civil
GIG Grand invalide de guerre
GIGN Groupe d'intervention de la gendarmerie nationale
Go gigaoctet
G.O. Grandes ondes
GPL Gaz de pétrole liquéfié
GQG Grand Quartier Général
GR (Sentier de) grande randonnée
Ha hectare
HEC École des hautes études commerciales
HF Haute fréquence
HLM Habitation à loyer modéré
HS 1. Hors service
2. heure supplémentaire
HT 1. Haute tension
2. hors taxe(s)
Hz Hertz
i.e. id est (c'est-à-dire)
IFOP Institut français d'opinion publique
IGF Impôt sur les grandes fortunes
IGN Institut géographique national
IGS Inspection générale des services
ILM Immeuble à loyer moyen ou modéré
IMP Institut médico-pédagogique
IN... Institut national...
INC Institut national de la consommation
INSEE Institut national de la statistique et des études économiques
INSERM Institut national de la santé et de la recherche médicale
ISF Impôt de solidarité sur la fortune
IUT Institut universitaire de technologie
IVG Interruption volontaire de grossesse
J.-C. Jésus-Christ

JO	1. Journal officiel
	2. Jeux olympiques
kg	kilogramme
km	kilomètre
kW	kilowatt
kWh	kilowatt(s)-heure
Ko	kilo-octet
l	litre
LEP	1. Lycée d'enseignement
	2. Livret d'épargne populaire
LP	Lycée professionnel
m	mètre
M.	Monsieur
M^{o}	Métro
M^{e}	Maître
Mlle	Mademoiselle
Mlles	Mesdemoiselles
MF	Modulation de fréquence
mg	milligramme
Mgr	Monseigneur
MIDEM	Marché international du disque et des éditions musicales
MJC	Maison des jeunes et de la culture
ml	millilitre
MLF	Mouvement de libération de la femme
mm	millimètre
MM.	Messieurs
Mme	Madame
Mmes	Mesdames
mn	minute
Mo	mégaoctet
MST	Maladies sexuellement transmissibles
N.B.	nota bene (notez bien)
N.-D.	Notre-Dame
N.D.L.R.	Note de la rédaction
NF	1. Norme française
	2. Nouveau(x) franc(s)
N^{o}	numéro
N.-S. J.-C.	Notre-Seigneur Jésus-Christ
O.A.S.	Organisation de l'armée secrète
O.C.	Ondes courtes
OCDE	Organisation de coopération et de développement économiques
OIT	Organisation internationale du travail
O.L.	Ondes longues
OLP	Organisation de libération de la Palestine
O.M.	Ondes moyennes
OMS	Organisation mondiale de la santé
OMT	Organisation mondiale du tourisme
ONISEP	Office national d'information sur les enseignements et les professions
ONU	Organisation des nations unies
OPA	Offre publique d'achat
OPEP	Organisation des pays exportateurs de pétrole
ORL	oto-rhino-laryngologie
	oto-rhino-laryngologiste
ORSEC	Organisation de secours
ORTF	Office de radiodiffusion-télévision française
OS	Ouvrier spécialisé
OTAN	Organisation du traité de l'Atlantique Nord
OUA	Organisation de l'unité africaine
OVNI	Objet volant non identifié
PAL	Procédé - Phase Alternative Line
PAP	1. Programme d'action prioritaire
	2. Prêt pour l'accession à la propriété
PC	1. Parti communiste
	2. Poste de commandement
	3. autobus desservant la Petite Ceinture parisienne
PCC	Pour copie conforme
PCF	Parti communiste français

PCV (Per-Ce-Voir) communication téléphonique payable par le destinataire
PDG Président-directeur général
PEGC Professeur d'enseignement général des collèges
PEL Plan d'épargne logement
P et T Postes et Télécommunications
p. ex. par exemple
PIB Produit intérieur brut
PJ Police judiciaire
PME Petites et moyennes entreprises
PMI Petites et moyennes industries
PMU Pari mutuel urbain
PNB Produit national brut
P.O. Petites ondes
PS Parti socialiste
P.-S. Post-scriptum
PTT Postes télégraphes téléphones; Postes, télécommunications et télédiffusion
P.-V. Procès-verbal
qcm Questionnaire à choix multiple
QF Quotient familial
QG Quartier général
QI Quotient intellectuel
R.A.S. Rien à signaler
RATP Régie autonome des transports parisiens
RDA République démocratique allemande
rdc rez-de-chaussée
réf référence
RER Réseau express régional
RF République française
RFA République fédérale allemande
RIB Relevé d'identité bancaire
RIP Relevé d'identité postal
RMI Revenu minimum d'insertion
RN Route nationale
RPR Rassemblement pour la République
RSVP Répondez s'il vous plaît
r.v. rendez-vous
SA Société anonyme
SACEM Société des auteurs, compositeurs et éditeurs de musique
SAMU Service d'assistance médicale d'urgence
SARL Société à responsabilité limitée
SAV Service après-vente
SC Service compris
SDN Société des nations
SECAM Séquentiel à mémoire
SEITA Service d'exploitation industrielle des tabacs et allumettes
SERNAM Service national de messagerie
SFP Société française de production
SGDG Sans garantie du gouvernement
SICAV Société d'investissement à capital variable
SICOB Salon des industries, du commerce et de l'organisation du bureau
SIDA Syndrome immuno-déficitaire acquis
SMIC Salaire minimum interprofessionnel de croissance
SMIG Salaire minimum interprofessionnel garanti
SNC Service non compris
SNCF Société nationale des chemins de fer français
SNECMA Société nationale d'études et de construction de moteurs d'avions
SOFRES Société française d'enquêtes pour sondage
SPA Société protectrice des animaux
SRPJ Service régional de la police judiciaire
S.S. Sécurité sociale
Sté société
SVP s'il vous plaît
TD Travaux dirigés
TEE Trans-Europe Express

tél. téléphone
TF1 Télévision française un (1re chaîne de télévision française)
TGV Train à grande vitesse
TIR Transports internationaux routiers
TNT Trinitrotoluène
TOM Territoire d'outre-mer
TP 1. Trésor public
2. Travaux pratiques
3. Travaux publics
TSVP Tournez s'il vous plaît
TT(A) Transit temporaire (autorisé)
TTC toutes taxes comprises
TUC Travaux d'utilité collective
TUP Titre universel de paiement
TV télévision
TVA Taxe sur la valeur ajoutée
UDF Union pour la démocratie française
UE Unité d'enseignement
UER Unité d'enseignement et de recherche
UFR Unité de formation et de recherches
UHT Ultra-haute température
ULM ultra-léger motorisé
UNESCO United Nations Educational Scientific and Cultural Organization
UNICEF United Nations Children's Fund
URSS † Union des républiques socialistes soviétiques
U.S. ... Union sportive de...
USA United States of America
UV 1. Unité de valeur
2. Ultra-violet
VDQS Vin délimité de qualité supérieure
VF version française
VO version originale
VRP Voyageur représentant placier
VVF Village-vacances-famille
W.-C. Water-closet
X École polytechnique
ZAC Zone d'aménagement concerté
ZAD Zone d'aménagement différé
ZEP 1. Zone d'environnement protégé
2. Zone d'éducation prioritaire
ZI Zone industrielle
ZUP Zone à urbaniser en priorité

SIGLES ET ABRÉVIATIONS ANGLAIS

AA	1. Automobile Association
	2. Alcoholics Anonymous
AAA	1. Amateur Athletics Association
	2. American Automobile Association
A.B.C.	American Broadcasting Corporation
ABM	anti-ballistic missile
a/c	account
AC	alternating current
A.C.L.U.	American Civil Liberties Union
A.D.	Anno domini, in the year of our Lord
ADC	aide-de-camp
ADP	automatic data processing
A.D.T.	*(US)* Atlantic Daylight Time
AEA	Atomic Energy Authority
A.E.C.	*(US)* Atomic Energy Commission
AGM	annual general meeting
AI	artificial intelligence
AIDS	acquired-immune deficiency syndrome
a.k.a.	also known as
a.m.	ante meridiem, before noon
AM	amplitude modulation
A.M.A.	American Medical Association
ANSI	American National Standards Institute
AOB	any other business
APEX	advance purchase excursion
APR	annual percentage rate
A.S.A.	American Standards Association
a.s.a.p.	as soon as possible
A.S.P.C.A.	American Society for the Prevention of Cruelty to Animals
AV	Authorized Version
Ave	avenue
A.Y.H.	American Youth Hostels
BA	Bachelor of Arts
BBC	British Broadcasting Corporation
B.C.	before Christ
Benelux	Belgium, Netherlands, Luxembourg
b/f	brought forward
BMA	British Medical Association
BR	British Rail
Bros.	Brothers
BSc	Bachelor of Science
BSI	British Standards Institution
BST	British Summer Time
BT	British Telecom
c.	1. *(US Fin)* cent; *(Fin: France)* centime
	2. century
	3. circa, about
	4. cubic
CAA	1. *(Brit)* Civil Aviation Authority
	2. *(US)* Civil Aeronautics Authority
CAB	Citizens' Advice Bureau
CAD	computer-aided design
CAP	common agricultural policy
CB	Citizens' Band (Radio)
CBI	Confederation of British Industry
cc	cubic centimetres
C.B.S.	Columbia Broadcasting System

CD	1. compact disc
	2. *(Brit)* Civil Defence (Corps)
	3. *(US)* Civil Defense
CDV	compact disc video
CET	Central European Time
cf	confer, compare
cfc	chlorofluorocarbon
C.I.A.	*(US)* Central Intelligence Agency
CID	Criminal Investigation Department
CIS	Commonwealth of Independent States
cm	centimetre(s)
C.N.N.	*(US)* Cable News Network
CNAA	Council for National Academic Awards
CND	Campaign for Nuclear Disarmament
c/o	care of
CO	Commanding officer
COD	cash on delivery
C of E	Church of England
C of S	Church of Scotland
COI	Central Office of Information
CORE	*(US)* Congress of Racial Equality
C.P.I.	*(US)* Consumer Price Index
CPU	central processing unit
CRE	Commission for Racial Equality
C.S.T.	*(US)* Central Standard Time
cwt	hundredweight
D.A.	*(US)* District Attorney
dB	decibel
DC	direct current
dec.	deceased
Dem.	*(US)* Democrat
DIY	do-it-yourself
DNA	deoxyribonucleic acid
do.	ditto
DOA	dead on arrival
d.o.b.	date of birth
DOS	disk operating system
DPP	Director of Public Prosecutions
Dr	doctor
DSS	Department of Social Security
D.S.T.	*(US)* Daylight Saving Time
DTP	desktop publishing
EC	European community
ECG	electrocardiogram
ECU	European Currency Unit
EDP	electronic data processing
E.D.T.	*(US)* Eastern Daylight Time
EEC	European Economic Community
EFL	English as a Foreign Language
e.g.	exempli gratia, for example
ELT	English Language Teaching
EMS	European Monetary System
ENT	Ear, Nose and Throat
E.P.A.	*(US)* Environmental Protection Agency
ESP	extramemory perception
Esq.	Esquire
E.S.T.	*(US)* Eastern Standard Time
ETA	estimated time of arrival
ETD	estimated time of departure
ext.	extension
FA	Football Association
F.A.A.	*(US)* Federal Aviation Administration
F.B.I.	*(US)* Federal Bureau of Investigation
F.D.A.	*(US)* Food and Drug Administration
FM	frequency modulation
FO	Foreign Office
FRG	Federal Republic of Germany
F.R.S.	Fellow of the Royal Society

ft. foot, feet
g gram(s)
GB Great Britain
GCE General Certificate of Education
GCSE General Certificate of Secondary Education
GDR German Democratic Republic
GHQ General Headquarters
GMT Greenwich Mean Time
GNP gross national product
GP general practitioner
GPO General Post Office
h. & c. hot and cold (water)
HF high frequency
HGV heavy goods vehicle
HM His (Her) Majesty
HMG His (Her) Majesty's Government
HMS His (Her) Majesty's Ship
HND Higher National Diploma
H.P., h.p. 1. *(Comm)* hire purchase
2. *(Tech)* horsepower
HQ headquarters
hr, hrs hour(s)
H.R. *(US)* House of Representatives
HRH His (Her) Royal Highness
Hz hertz
ib(id). ibidem, from the same source
i/c in charge
i.e. id est, that is, namely
IMF International Monetary Fund
in., ins. inch(es)
Inc. *(US)* Incorporated
I/O input/output
IOU I owe you
IQ intelligence quotient
IRA Irish Republican Army
I.R.S. *(US)* Internal Revenue Service
ISBN International Standard Book Number
IT information technology
ITV Independent Television
IUD intra-uterine device
IVF in vitro fertilization
J.C. Jesus Christ
JP Justice of the Peace
Jr junior
K 1. kilobyte
2. one thousand
KC King's Counsel
kg kilogram(s)
KGB *Russian Secret Police*
km kilometre(s)
km/h kilometres per hour
KO knockout
kW kilowatt
l litre(s)
L large
L.A. *(US)* Los Angeles
lb libra, pound
LCD liquid crystal display
LEA local education authority
LLB Bachelor of Laws
LP long-playing (record)
L.P.N. *(US)* Licensed Practical Nurse
l.s.d. Librae, solidi, denarii; pounds, shillings and pence
LSD lysergic acid diethylomide
Ltd Limited
LW long wave

m	1. metre(s)
	2. mile(s)
	3. million(s)
M	medium
MA	Master of Arts
MBA	Master of Business Administration
MC	1. Master of Ceremonies
	2. *(US)* Member of Congress
	3. *(Mil)* Military Cross
MD	1. Managing Director
	2. Doctor of Medicine
M.D.T.	*(US)* Mountain Daylight Time
MEP	Member of the European Parliament
mg	milligram(s)
Mgr	manager
MHz	megahertz
MI5	Military Intelligence (5)
min.	1. minimum
	2. minute
MLR	minimum lending rate
mm	millimetre(s)
MP	Member of Parliament
mpg	miles per gallon
mph	miles per hour
MS.	1. manuscript
	2. multiple sclerosis
MSc	Master of Science
M.S.T.	*(US)* Mountain Standard Time
MW	medium wave
n/a	not applicable
NASA	*(US)* National Astronautics and Space Administration
NATO	North Atlantic Treaty Organization
N.B.	nota bene, note well
N.B.C.	*(US)* National Broadcasting Company
NCCL	National Council for Civil Liberties
NCO	non-commissioned officer
NEB	New English Bible
N.F.L.	*(US)* National Football
N.G.	*(US)* National Guard
NHS	National Health Service
NI	1. National Insurance
	2. Northern Ireland
NMR	nuclear magnetic resonance
no.	number
N.S.C.	*(US)* National Security Council
NSPCC	National Society for the Prevention of Cruelty to Children
NT	New Testament
N.Y.	New York
NZ	New Zealand
OAP	old age pensioner
O.A.S.	Organization of American States
OAU	Organization of African Unity
OCR	1. optical character reader
	2. optical character recognition
OECD	Organization for European Cooperation and Development
OHMS	On His (Her) Majesty's Service
O & M	organization and method
o.n.o.	or near(est) offer
OPEC	Organization of Petroleum-Exporting Countries
OS	1. Ordinary Seaman
	2. Ordnance Survey
OT	Old Testament
OU	Open University
oz	ounces
p.	1. page
	2. penny, pence
p.a.	per annum, yearly

PA	1. personal assistant 2. public address system
PAYE	pay as you earn
P.B.S.	*(US)* Public Broadcasting Service
PBX	private branch exchange
pc	per cent
PC	1. personal computer 2. police constable 3. Privy Councillor
pd	paid
P.D.T.	*(US)* Pacific Daylight Time
PG	*(Brit Cine)* parental guidance
p & h	*(US)* postage and handling
PhD	Doctor of Philosophy
PLO	Palestine Liberation Organization
p.m.	post meridiem, after noon
PM	Prime Minister
PMT	premenstrual tension
p.o.	postal order
POB	post office box
POW	prisoner of war
p & p	postage and packing
pp	per procurationem, by proxy
PPS	Parliamentary Private Secretary
PR	public relations
PS	postscript
psi	pounds per square inch
P.S.T.	*(US)* Pacific Standard Time
PSV	public service vehicle
pt.	1. pint(s) 2. point(s)
PTA	Parent-Teacher Association
PTO	please turn over
PVC	polyvinyl chloride
QC	Queen's Counsel
qty	quantity
RAC	Royal Automobile Club
RAF	Royal Air Force
RAM	random access memory
RC	Roman Catholic
Rd	road
R & D	research and development
Rep.	1. *(US)* Representative 2. *(US)* Republican
RIP	requiescat in pace, rest in peace
RL	Rugby League
RN	1. Royal Navy 2. *(US)* registered nurse
ROM	read-only memory
RPI	Retail Price Index
rpm	revolutions per minute
RSM	regimental sergeant major
RSPCA	Royal Society for the Prevention of Cruelty to Animals
RSV	Revised Standard Version
RSVP	répondez s'il vous plaît
RU	Rugby Union
RV	Revised Version
S	small
SA	South Africa
s.a.e.	stamped addressed envelope
SAS	*(Brit Mil)* Special Air Service
SDLP	Social Democratic and Labour Party
SDP	Social Democratic Party
Sen.	1. Senator 2. Senior
SEN	State Enrolled Nurse
S.G.	*(US)* Surgeon General
SHAPE	Supreme Headquarters Allied Powers, Europe

SLD Social and Liberal Democrats
SNP Scottish National Party
SOP standard operating procedure
Sr Senior
SRN State Registered Nurse
St 1. saint
2. street
STD 1. sexually transmitted disease
2. subscriber trunk dialling
stg sterling
SW short wave
TA Territorial Army
TB tuberculosis
TM 1. trademark
2. transcendental meditation
TNT trinitrotoluene
TT 1. teetotal, teetotaller
2. *(Agr)* tuberculin-tested
TUC Trades Union Congress
U *(Brit Cine)* universal
UEFA Union of European Football Associations
UFO unidentified flying object
UHF ultra-high frequency
UHT ultra-heat treated
U.K. United Kingdom
UN United Nations
UNCTAD United Nations Conference on Trade and Development
UNESCO United Nations Educational, Scientific and Cultural Organization
UNICEF United Nations International Children's Emergency Fund
UNO United Nations Organization
USA 1. United States of America
2. United States Army
U.S.A.F. United States Air Force
USN United States Navy
USSR † Union of Soviet Socialist Republics
v volt
VAT value-added tax
VCR video cassette recorder
VD venereal disease
VDU visual display unit
VHF very high frequency
VIP very important person
VISTA Volunteers in Service to America
V.O.A. Voice of America
VP, V. Pres. Vice-President
VSO Voluntary Service Overseas
VSOP Very superior old pale
WASP White Anglo-Saxon Protestant
WCC World Council of Churches
WHO World Health Organization
WI 1. West Indies
2. Women's Institute
wk week
WP 1. word processor
2. weather permitting
WPC Woman Police Constable
WRVS Women's Royal Voluntary Service
wt. weight
WWF World Wildlife Fund
X *(Brit Cine)* adults only
XL extra large
Xmas Christmas
yd. yard
YHA Youth Hostels Association
YMCA Young Men's Christian Association
yr year
YTS Youth Training Scheme
YWCA Young Women's Christian Association